AN INTERNATIONAL REFERENCE BOOK

NINTH EDITION 1995
VOLUME V

Indexes

Division of EBSCO Industries Inc., Birmingham, Alabama

Published by EBSCO Publishing
division of EBSCO Industries, Inc.
P.O. Box 1943, Birmingham, AL 35201-1943   USA

Copyright © 1995 by EBSCO Industries, Inc.
Printed and bound in the United States of America.

All rights reserved. Reproduction of this Directory, in whole or in part, by any method, without prior written permission of the publisher is prohibited.

Direct all editorial inquiries to EBSCO Publishing, P.O. Box 1943, Birmingham, AL 35201-1943.

Direct all other inquiries to EBSCO Publishing, 83 Pine Street, PO Box 2250, Peabody, MA 01960-7250

International Standard Book Number (5-Volume Set) 0-913956-86-4
International Standard Book Number (Volume-1) 0-913956-81-3
International Standard Book Number (Volume-2) 0-913956-82-1
International Standard Book Number (Volume-3) 0-913956-83-X
International Standard Book Number (Volume-4) 0-913956-84-8
International Standard Book Number (Volume-5) 0-913956-85-6

International Standard Serial Number 0886-4179

Every effort has been made to ensure the accuracy of information in *The Serials Directory* and since no payment has been made for the inclusion of any entries, the publisher cannot accept liability for errors or omissions, regardless of the cause.

THE SERIALS DIRECTORY

AN INTERNATIONAL REFERENCE BOOK

Editorial Advisory Board

Susan A. Cady
Associate Director
of Technical Services
Linderman Library
Lehigh University Libraries

Mary Elizabeth Clack
Serial Records Librarian
Harvard College Library

Genevieve Clay
Head, Central Serials
Eastern Kentucky University
Crabbe Library

Claude Daris
Head of Serials Department
Universite Libre de Bruxelles
Belgium

Kenneth E. Dowlin
Director, San Francisco Public Library
City Librarian
Main Library Civic Center

Ludo Holans
Librarian
Campus Bibliotheekdienst
Katholieke Universiteit Leuven
Belgium

Sul H. Lee
Dean, University Libraries
University of Oklahoma

Lois N. Upham
Uncle Remus Regional Library
Madison, Georgia

The 9th Edition of *The Serials Directory: An International Reference Book* was compiled and published by EBSCO Publishing, division of EBSCO Industries, Inc.

J.T. Stephens, President-EBSCO Industries, Inc.
Tim Collins, Vice President, Division General Manager-EBSCO Publishing
Mary Beth Vanderpoorten, M.S.L.S., Vice President-EBSCO Subscription Services, General Manager-Title Information

EDITORIAL / PRODUCTION

Leanne Wofford, Editorial Manager
Jill Hinds, Special Projects Editor
Stefanie Letanosky, Titles Editor

Jean Bowick, Editorial Assistant
Joe B. Crowe, Editorial Assistant
Kathy Entrekin, Editorial Assistant

Loyd McIntosh, Editorial Assistant
Mona Powell, Editorial Assistant
Kelly Rogers, Editorial Assistant

Database and publishing software
provided by Syscomp, Inc., Atlanta, Georgia, using Advanced Revelation®

Typesetting software provided by
Laser Solutions, Inc., Atlanta, Georgia using FrameMaker®

CONTENTS

Preface vii
User's Guide ix
Filing Rules... xvi
Subject Headings.. xvii
Subject Cross References xxi
Tables xxxvii
   Frequency.. xxxviii
   Document Delivery xxxviii
   Wire Services... xxxix
   Country of Publication by Code..................................... xl
   Country of Publication by Country xli
   Unit of Currency xlii
   Indexes/Abstracts... xliii

Volume 1
   Serial Listings (A–Em) 3

Volume 2
   Serial Listings (En-L)... 1923

Volume 3
   Serial Listings (M-Z).. 3475

Volume 4
   Newspapers
      US Newspapers... 5625
      International Newspapers 5777
   Alphabetical Title Index... 5815

Volume 5
   ISSN Index... 7607
   Peer Reviewed Index 7987
   Serials on CD-ROM Index.. 8051
   Serials Online Index... 8075
   Book Review Index 8113
   Advertising Accepted Index...................................... 8275
   Controlled Circulation Index 8465
   Copyright Clearance Center Index................................ 8601
   New Title Index 8675

PREFACE

At EBSCO Publishing it is our goal to produce the primary serial reference source available. We have directed our energies toward obtaining the most up-to-date and accurate information on every title -- from the most familiar to the most obscure. In working toward this goal, several additions and changes have been made to the newest edition of *The Serials Directory: An International Reference Book*.

Eight new bibliographic elements are included in this edition to provide information professionals with a means for quick and easy serial research. In the newspaper section, Full and Half-page ad rates are now listed along with Publication Size, Wire Service Affiliations, and a notation for the inclusion of Photographs. Also included is data on document delivery availability/vendors, "Acid Free" notations and both Internet and E-mail addresses when provided by the publisher.

This edition of *The Serials Directory* contains approximately 151,000 serial titles with up to 60 bibliographic elements available for each one. Included in Volumes I, II and III are over 6,500 new titles, 2,800 titles available on CD-ROM or an online database, 10,600 titles registered with the Copyright Clearance Center, 24,000 serials publishing book reviews, and over 27,000 serials accepting advertising. This Edition contains verified information for over 100,000 serial titles representing approximately 65,000 publishers worldwide.

EBSCO Publishing is a sister division to EBSCO Subscription Services; therefore, gaining access to serial information on an ongoing basis is more simplified. EBSCO remains in constant contact with publishers throughout the world ensuring the accuracy of title and publisher information as well as providing the latest pricing and subscription data.

Information found in *The Serials Directory* is maintained through four sources. First, through the internal EBSCO Subscription Services database, updated daily as a result of continuous contact with publishers worldwide. The second source is The Library of Congress' CONSER file of which EBSCO is an affiliate member. The CONSER file is maintained by the National Serials Data Program, National Library of Canada, National Library of Medicine, Chemical Abstracts Service, and the National Agricultural Library. The third source is The ISSN Register (formerly ISDS) which provides extensive coverage of international serials. The fourth source for data is direct correspondence with thousands of publishers throughout the world.

With this edition, you will receive two cumulative Updates throughout 1995 to keep you abreast of changes in title status, publisher and subscription addresses, format changes or additions, price and frequency changes, as well as information on new titles. With a subscription to *The Serials Directory: EBSCO CD-ROM*, you will receive four quarterly updated discs containing all historical serial data that may not be included in the print version.

Our other international offering is *The Index and Abstract Directory: An International Guide to Services and Serials Coverage*. This valuable reference tool, which is now contained in two volumes, consists of information on over 950 "active" Indexing/Abstracting services and includes bibliographic information on the more than 56,000 serials that are monitored by each.

You will also find that we go beyond just providing reference products alone. As always, we will continue to offer free serials research to any of our customers needing assistance in locating the more ambiguous serial publications. We receive thousands of calls each year and have proven very successful in pinpointing the answers to a variety of serials questions.

At EBSCO Publishing, we continue to grow -- to change -- to improve. *The Serials Directory* and the *Index and Abstract Directory* reflect this growth and, combined with EBSCO's valued reputation within the library community, provide the highest standard of quality available in serials reference.

Leanne Wofford
Editorial Manager

EBSCO Publishing, PO Box 1943, Birmingham, AL 35201-1943 USA
(800)826-3024 / (205)980-2773 / FAX (205)995-1582

AN INTERNATIONAL
REFERENCE BOOK

USER'S GUIDE

USER'S GUIDE

How to Use The Serials Directory.
Twelve sections comprise The Serials Directory. Each of these sections allows the user to access information easily. The following is a brief explanation of each section.

- **Serial Listings (Subjects A-Z)**
  (Volumes I, II and III)
- **Newspaper Listings**
  (Volume IV)
- **Alphabetical Title Index**
  (Volume IV)
- **ISSN Index**
  (Volume V)
- **Peer Reviewed Index**
  (Volume V)
- **Serials Available on CD-ROM Index**
  (Volume V)
- **Serials Available Online Index**
  (Volume V)
- **Book Review Index**
  (Volume V)
- **Advertising Accepted Index**
  (Volume V)
- **Controlled Circulation Index**
  (Volume V)
- **Copyright Clearance Center Index**
  (Volume V)
- **New Title Index**
  (Volume V)

● Serial Listings—
The Serial Listings are arranged alphabetically by subject category. Titles given under each subject heading are in alphabetical order (See Filing Rules—page xvi). The Serial Listing arrangement enables the user to quickly locate the relevant subject area and to review all serial titles relating to that subject. There are over 18,000 "see notes" throughout the 146 major subject headings and 330 subheadings in the Serial Listings. These notes refer the user from related subject areas to the primary subject heading under which the full title listing appears. See pages xvii-xxxvi for a list of subject headings and subject cross references.

● Newspaper Listings—
This section lists all US and international newspapers included in our database. US newspapers will be listed alphabetically by state. International titles will follow and are arranged alphabetically, by country. Newspaper listings can be found in the Alphabetical Title Index as well as the ISSN Index along with the regular listings in Volume IV.

● Alphabetical Title Index—
Arranged alphabetically by title, this index lists the primary title, along with Country of Publication/ISSN, and MARC control number, when available.

The following notations are made in the Alphabetical Title Index:

1. New Titles— Titles are denoted with a bullet "●". Bullets will appear in both the Serial Listing, as well as the Alphabetical Title Index. This edition includes over 6,500 new titles which began publication after 1992 and were active at the time data was secured for publication.

2. Ceased Titles— Titles that have ceased publication and do not have a "succeeding entry." Ceased titles are denoted with "*CEASED*" in bold italics, following the primary title in the Serial Listing, as well as the Alphabetical Title Index. Ceased titles are included in the Directory for two consecutive editions after EBSCO is notified of the status change. This edition contains over 4,700 cessations.

3. Title Changes— Titles which have a succeeding entry, MARC field 785. These entries are included in the Alphabetical Title Index with a reference to the current title(s). Title changes are included in the Directory for two consecutive editions based on the "ending date of publication," MARC field 008/11-14. This edition contains over 4,840 title changes. See the User's Guide/Sample Listing for more information.

4. Suspended Titles— Titles for which EBSCO has received notification of suspension. Suspended titles are denoted in both the Serial Listing and the index with "*SUSPENDED*" in bold italics, following the primary title. These titles will remain suspended until EBSCO is notified otherwise.

5. Preceding Entries— Preceding entries print with a "see" note to the primary title provided the primary title has a MARC publication start date (008/7-10) later than 1992. Preceding entries will remain in the Directory for two consecutive editions with a reference to the newer title(s).

6. Main Entry - Corporate Name— A corporate name used as a main entry, this element prints in the Alphabetical Title Index as another access point to the publication in question. To further aid the user, the Main Entry-Corporate Name is listed with a "see" note to the primary title in the Serial Listings. Over 24,000 Main Entry-Corporate Names are included in the Directory.

USER'S GUIDE

● **ISSN Index—**
The ISSN Index contains current as well as preceding ISSN's, arranged in numerical order. The ISSN will be followed by a "see" note giving the title under which the ISSN will appear. The preceding ISSN is included with a "see" note to the primary title provided the MARC publication start date (field 008/7-10) is later than 1992. Preceding ISSN will appear in italicized typeface in order to distinguish it from the current ISSN. The page number for which the Serial Listing appears prints in boldface. There are over 100,400 titles included in the ISSN Index.

● **Peer Reviewed Index—**
Arranged alphabetically by title, the Peer Reviewed Index lists all active serials found in Volumes I, II and III which contain peer reviewed articles. Country of Publication/ISSN and MARC control number are provided, when available. The page number for which the Serial Listing appears prints in boldface. There are over 8,800 titles included in the Peer Reviewed Index.

● **Serials Available on CD-ROM Index—**
Arranged alphabetically by title, this index lists all active serial titles in Volumes I, II and III that are available on CD-ROM, either as the primary format, or as an "additional" available format. Included in this index are the Country of Publication/ISSN and publisher address/telephone number(s) when available. The page number for which the Serial Listing appears prints in boldface. There are over 1,300 titles included in the Serials Available on CD-ROM Index.

● **Serials Available Online Index—**
Arranged alphabetically by title, this index lists all active serials found in Volumes I, II and III that are available online, either as the primary format, or as an "additional" available format. Included in this index are the Country of Publication/ISSN and publisher address/telephone number(s) when available. The page number for which the Serial Listing appears prints in boldface. There are over 2,500 titles included in the Serials Available Online Index.

● **Book Review Index—**
Arranged alphabetically by title, this index lists all active serials found in Volumes I, II and III that contain book reviews. Included in this index are Country of Publication/ISSN and the quantity of book reviews published "per year" (unless otherwise specified). The page number for which the Serial Listing appears prints in boldface. There are over 24,000 titles included in the Book Review Index.

● **Advertising Accepted Index—**
Arranged alphabetically by title, this index contains all active serials found in Volumes I, II and III that accept advertising. The Country of Publication/ISSN and advertising manager/telephone number(s) are also provided, when supplied by the publisher. The page number for which the Serial Listing appears prints in boldface. There are over 27,000 titles included in the Advertising Accepted Index.

● **Controlled Circulation Index—**
Arranged alphabetically by title, this index lists all active titles in the Directory that have a controlled circulation. The Country of Publication/ISSN and circulation figures [printing in brackets] are provided when available. The page number for which the Serial Listing appears prints in boldface. There are over 19,000 titles included in the Controlled Circulation Index.

● **Copyright Clearance Center Index—**
Arranged alphabetically by title, this index lists all active serials found in Volumes I, II and III that are registered with the Copyright Clearance Center (CCC). The Country of Publication/ISSN are provided when available. The page number for which the Serial Listing appears prints in boldface. There are over 10,600 titles included in the Copyright Clearance Center Index.

● **New Title Index—**
Arranged by subject, then alphabetically by title, this index consists of all active titles that have a MARC "beginning date" of "1992" or greater, as well as, "non-MARC" titles where the start date has been verified by the publisher. Country of Publication/ISSN follow the title, with the page number on which the Serial Listing appears. There are over 6,500 titles included in the New Title Index.

USER'S GUIDE/SAMPLE LISTING

SAMPLE LISTING

Country of Publication/ISSN
● **KEY TITLE.** *CEASED/SUSPENDED.* (TITLE STATEMENT). [Abbreviated Title]. **Main/Conf** Main Entry—Meeting. **Main/Corp** Main Entry—Corporate Name. **Added/Corp** Added Entry—Corporate Name. **Series/Conf** Series Statement—Meeting Name. **VFOAT** Varying Form of a Title. **VAT** Variant Access Title. Date of Publication. Type of Serial. Language(s). Frequency. Price. Publisher Name & Address. **Tel** Telephone/Telex Number/Fax/Internet Address/Email Address. (subscription address:) **ED** Editor. **LC** Library of Congress Classification. **DD** Dewey Decimal Classification. **UDC** Universal Decimal Classification. **NLM** National Library of Medicine Classification. **CODEN** CODEN Designation. **[CCC]** Copyright Clearance Center. Index Availability. cum. index (Cumulative Index Availability). **Bk Rev** (Book reviews published), (Qty: Quantity Published). **Photos** [Photographs published]. **Ad Acc** (Advertising accepted), **Adv. Mgr**: Advertising Manager. **Tel** Telephone. Full Page (B&W) - Full page black and white ad rates. Half Page (B&W) - Half page black and white ad rates. Full Page (Color) - Full page color ad rates. Half Page (Color) - Half page color ad rates. **Pub. Size** [Publication trim size]. **Wire Svcs** [Newspaper wire services]. **Pr Rev.** (Peer Reviewed or Refereed). **Acid Free** [Acid free paper]. Circulation. (ctrl) - Controlled circulation. Document Delivery Available. Additional Physical Forms Available. *Preceding Entry-Title, Preceding Entry-ISSN. Succeeding Entry-Title, Succeeding Entry-ISSN.*
   Desc: Descriptive listing.
      Ind/Abst Indexes/Abstracts. Dates of Coverage. Full Text. Full/Selective Coverage

SERIAL LISTING CONTENTS

For the purpose of defining a serial, the definition as given in the USMARC Bibliographic Format is used: a bibliographic item issued in successive parts bearing numerical or chronological designations and intended to be continued indefinitely. Serials include periodicals; newspapers; annuals (reports, yearbooks, etc.); the journals, memoirs, proceedings, transactions, etc., of societies; and numbered monographic series, etc.

The following data elements (when available) are shown in order of appearance within a listing. Some definitions are taken in part from USMARC Formats Bibliographic Data.

Country of Publication. A two letter code indicating the place of publication, production, or execution. See Country of Publication Table, Page xxxvi for additions/changes.

ISSN. International Standard Serial Number, a unique identification number assigned to a serial title by national centers under the auspices of the ISSN Register (formerly ISDS).

●Denotes new titles beginning after 1992, that were active at the time data was secured for publication.

Key Title. Key Title is assigned by various national centers under the auspices of the ISSN Register (formerly International Serials Data System /ISDS). It is formed from title information transcribed from a piece of the serial and is constructed with qualifiers to make it unique when necessary. Since serial titles are taken from both the CONSER and ISSN Register databases, the primary title has not been altered to differentiate the alternative format from the original. In cases where CONSER or the ISSN Register has included a notation for the alternative format within the primary title, the primary title will reflect that notation. Serials in an alternative format (microfiche, microfilm, CD-ROM, etc.) are included in the Directory. Also in cases where multiple language entries appear, the user must refer to the primary language of the publication to ensure that the correct title is located. These titles may appear to be identical with the primary language being the only unique qualifier.

Ceased. This element is present only when a title has ceased publication. This does not include titles that have a succeeding entry or have had a title change. The word "*CEASED*" in bold italics, follows the primary title in the Serial Listing. Ceased titles are included in the Directory for two consecutive editions after the actual date of cessation. This edition contains over 4,700 cessations.

Suspended. Denotes temporary suspension of a title. The word "*SUSPENDED*" in bold italics, follows the primary title in the Serial Listing to denote suspended titles. These titles remain suspended in the database until the publisher notifies EBSCO otherwise.

Title Statement. Title Statement is present only when it differs from Key Title in any way, other than initial articles and prepositions. It consists of the title proper (including short title and alternative title, the numerical designation of a part/section and the name of a part/section) and may also contain the medium, remainder of title, other title information, and the statement of responsibility/remainder of title page transcription. Title Statement will follow Key Title in uppercase and will be enclosed in parentheses.

Abbreviated Title. Assigned by the ISSN Register (formerly ISDS), in accordance with ISO 4-1984, Documentation - Rules for the Abbreviation of Title Words and Titles of Publications and List of Serial Title Word Abbreviations. The Abbreviated Title is based on the Key Title and files in [brackets].

USER'S GUIDE/SAMPLE LISTING

Main Entry-Meeting. A meeting or conference name used as a main entry. Main entry under a meeting name is assigned to works that contain proceedings, reports, etc. Main Entry-Meeting will be preceded by the prefix "**Main/Conf**" in boldface.

Main Entry-Corporate Name. A corporate name used as a main entry. Main entry under corporate name is assigned to works that represent the collective thought of a body, including conference and meeting names that are entered subordinately to a corporate body. Main Entry-Corporate Name is preceded by the prefix "**Main/Corp**" in boldface.

Added Entry-Corporate Name. Contains a corporate heading used as main entry. A corporate body is identified by a name that acts or may act as an entity. Included in this definition are: associations, institutions, business firms, governments and their agencies, ships, churches and programs. The Added Entry-Corporate Name will be preceded by a prefix of "**Added/Corp**" in boldface.

Series Statement-Meeting Name. Series statement entered under a named conference or meeting. Series Statement-Meeting is preceded by "**Series/Conf**" in boldface.

Varying Form of a Title. Titles which may appear on different parts of a serial, or consisting of portions of the title proper or alternative forms of titles. Varying Form of a Title differs substantially from Key Title/Title Statement and contributes to the further identification of the serial. It is preceded by the prefix "**VFOAT**" in boldface. Additional titles are separated by commas.

Variant Access Title. A variant form of the title that does not appear on the serial. It is used when the title contains an initialism, non-roman alphabet character, etc. It provides additional access for searching purposes when access is not provided by any other title. Variant Access Title is preceded by the prefix of "**VAT**" in boldface. Additional titles are separated by commas.

Dates of Publication and Volume Information. Beginning (and ending) dates of publication and volume designation. The date may consist of the year, month, or day; month or season and year; or year alone, depending upon the frequency of publication and the usage of the publisher. Dates may appear in the vernacular and/or may be abbreviated.

Type of Serial. Indicates if the serial is a periodical, monographic series, or newspaper. When available, more specific types will be used such as bibliography, catalog, bulletin, directory, government publication, newsletter, proceedings, trade publication, consumer publication, corporate report, academic scholarly publication and abstracting/indexing publication.

Language(s). If the serial is published in more than one language, the predominant language will appear first and any additional languages will follow in parentheses (including languages for translations, summaries, tables of contents, etc.) with appropriate explanation if necessary.

Frequency. Indicated by a two letter code - see Frequency Table, page xxxviii. Exceptions to frequency are noted and in parentheses following code.

Price. The current annual subscription price at the time information was secured for publication. Prices are usually given in US dollars and currency of Country of Publication, if other than US. Exceptions are noted and explained.

Publisher Name and Address/Telecommunications Numbers. The complete name and address of the publisher when available. Telephone, telex and/or facsimile number as well as Internet and E-mail addresses are given for serials. Preceded by a prefix of "**Tel**" in boldface.

Subscription Address. The complete name and subscription/fulfillment address. Telecommunication numbers are listed when available.

Editor(s). Name, address and telephone number(s), when available. Preceded by a prefix of "**ED**" in boldface.

Library of Congress Classification. Contains an LC class/call number, shelf number, or pseudo-call-number assigned by The Library of Congress or one of its authorized agencies. Preceded by a prefix of "**LC**" in boldface.

Dewey Decimal Classification. Assigned according to the Dewey Decimal schedules maintained by The Library of Congress. Preceded by a prefix of "**DD**" in boldface.

Universal Decimal Classification. Derived from the Dewey Decimal Classification, the UDC differs in arrangement and philosophy. The UDC is distinguished from the DDC by its extensive expansions. Preceded by a prefix of "**UDC**" in boldface.

National Library of Medicine Classification. Contains either a complete NLM call number or an NLM classification number. Preceded by a prefix of "**NLM**" in boldface.

CODEN Designation. Abbreviation for periodical titles, which is assigned by the CODEN section of Chemical Abstracts Service. It is a unique identifier for scientific and technical publications. Preceded by a prefix of "**CODEN**" in boldface.

Copyright Clearance Center. [CCC] indicates titles registered with the Copyright Clearance Center. The Copyright Clearance Center has been authorized to give photocopy permission and to collect any pre-set royalty fees set by the publisher.

Index Availability. Shows the existence of an index, or a table of contents issued as an index, and the method of acquisition.

Cumulative Index Availability. Specifies if a cumulative index, or a table of contents issued as a cumulative index, is published.

USER'S GUIDE/SAMPLE LISTING

Appears in abbreviated form as "cum. index."

Book Reviews. If book reviews are published, "**Bk Rev**" will appear in the Serial Listing.

Book Review Quantity. Quantity of book reviews published "per year," unless otherwise specified. Quantity is preceded by "Qty:" and prints in parentheses.

Photos. If photographs are included within the serial, "**Photos**" will appear in the listing.

Advertising. If advertising is accepted in a serial, the abbreviation "**Ad Acc**" will appear in boldface.

Advertising Manager/Telephone. Lists the name and telephone number of the Advertising Manager, when available. Advertising Manager name is preceded by "**Adv Mgr:**" in boldface. Telephone is preceded by the prefix "**Tel**" in boldface.

Advertising Rates. Advertising rates for full and half-page ads. (B&W) designates rates for ads in black and white. (Color) designates ads printed in color.

Publication Size. The trim size of the serial or newspaper. Preceded by the abbreviation **Pub. Size**. Common publication sizes include Tabloid, Standard and Broadsheet.

Wire Services. Lists the news and photograph wire services affiliated with any given newspaper. These are preceded by a prefix of "**Wire Svcs**" in boldface. A chart of abbreviations used can be found on page xxxix.

Peer Reviewed. If a journal is peer reviewed or refereed, the abbreviation "**Pr Rev**" will appear.

Acid Free. If a publication is available on acid free paper, "**Acid Free**" will be seen in boldface.

Circulation. Annual circulation of publication, unless noted otherwise. Multiple circulation figures are separated by a comma.

Controlled Circulation. If circulation of a serial is controlled by the publisher, the abbreviation "ctrl" in parentheses follows the circulation figures. If no circulation figures are given, but the publisher has notified us that circulation is controlled, "ctrl circ" will appear.

Document Delivery. Indicates the availability of that serial for document delivery through the specified service(s). Refer to the chart on page xxxviii.

Additional Physical Forms Available. Additional media in which a serial is published, other than its original or conventional form.

Preceding Entry - Title/Preceding Entry - ISSN. The immediate predecessor(s) for the title, along with ISSN, appears in italics. Depending on indicators taken from the CONSER 780 field, a title's preceding entry will be preceded by one of the following: Continues, Continues in part, Supersedes, Supersedes in part, Formed by the union of... and..., Absorbed, Absorbed in part, or Separated from. If the title Continues in part, another title which is current, both titles will then be listed. Additional titles and ISSN are separated by semicolons and are preceded by one of the above, in boldface.

Succeeding Entry Title/Succeeding Entry - ISSN. The immediate successor(s) for the serial title (along with corresponding ISSN) will be listed. Multiple titles and ISSN are separated by semicolons, and preceded by a prefix of one of the following: Continued by, Continued in part by, Superseded by, Superseded in part by, Absorbed by, Absorbed in part by, Split into... and..., Merged with... to form..., Merged into, or Changed back to. In cases where CONSER did not give an ending date or a title was only continued "in part" both titles will be listed.

Descriptive Listing. Description of content submitted by publisher or by CONSER. Descriptions may have been edited for clarity. Description is preceded by "**Desc:**" in boldface.

Indexes/Abstracts. Specifies the publication(s) in which a serial has been indexed and/or abstracted. These are preceded by a prefix of "**Ind/Abst**" in boldface. Over 920 "active" Indexing/Abstracting services are used for the purposes of this Directory and can be found within the Serial Listings. See Indexes/Abstracts Abbreviations Table on page xliii.

Dates of Coverage. Dates of coverage are included for each index or abstract, when available. Dates are enclosed in parentheses and follow the abbreviation as used in the Serial Listing for each Indexing/Abstracting service. If no dates are provided by the Indexing/Abstracting service publisher, and we have been notified that a serial is no longer covered by a particular service, question marks will be used to notify the user that coverage of the particular serial by the service has been discontinued.

Full Text. Specifies if a journal is covered by an Indexing/Abstracting service in "Full Text." Full Text coverage indicates that all articles in the journal are indexed/abstracted completely, with any pertinent graphics, charts etc. For the purposes of this Directory, "Full Text" and "Full Image" are treated as if they were the same. These will be coded in the Serial Listing as [Full Txt.]. This notation will follow the dates of coverage in the Serial Listing.

Full/Selective Coverage — Full coverage indicates that journals are indexed/abstracted cover to cover. Selective coverage specifies serials in which the Indexing / Abstracting service selects only articles relevant to their publication. These will be coded in the Serial Listing as [Full Cov.] or [Select. Cov.]. This notation will follow the dates of coverage, when available, or will precede the Index or Abstract abbreviation when no dates of coverage are noted in the Serial Listing.

FILING RULES

A. General Rules— Filing is word for word with exceptions noted below. The order of characters applies the principle "nothing files before something," with numerals before letters, file A to Z.

1. Spaces, hyphens, diagonal slashes, and periods are filed as blanks:

> AAG-AAG
> AAG Directory / Association of American Geographers
> AAG Newsletter
> AAHA Directory of Membership

2. Variant spellings are filed as written:

> Ageing and Society
> Aging and Aging Disorders

B. Special Rules and Exceptions.

1. Modified letters and diacritics— Modified letters are written as their plain English alphabet equivalents.

2. Punctuation— Punctuation and non-alphabetic symbols (except those noted in A above) are ignored for filing purposes:

> "A" Magazine
> A Magyar Talalkozo Kronikaja
> A.N.A. Audiologia Protesica

3. Abbreviations— Filed exactly as written.

> Dr. McBirnie's Newsletter
> St. Louis Review
> U.N. Observer & International Report
> U.S. Census Report

4. Numerals— Filed character by character according to the numeric value of each string of characters.
Numerals precede letters:

> 33 Metal Producing
> 35/70; Journal of the Feature Film Industry
> 35MM Photography London England : 1983)
> 36 Cities : Real Estate Forecast and Review

5. Initials, initialisms, acronyms— Those in which each letter is separated by a space, dash, hyphen, period, or diagonal slash are regarded as a series of separate words. Those in which characters are separated by other marks or symbols, or which are not separated in any way, are regarded as single words:

> A. C. C. L. Union List of Serials
> A C E Q-A C G R Information
> A/C Flyer, The
> A.C.G.C.-Information : Bulletin d'Information de l'Association des Cadres et Gerants des Colleges du Quebec
> ACIS
> A. C. L. : Agence Cambodge Laos

6. Initial Articles— The following words are ignored when they appear at the beginning of an entry.

A	Eine	Hio	'n
al	Eit	Hin	Na
An	el-	Hinar	Nje
As	El	Hinir	Nji
Az	Els	Hinn	O
Bir	En	Ho	Os
Das	Et	Hoi	't
De	Ett	I	Ta
Dei	Gl'	Il	The
Den	Gli	Ka	To
Der	ha-	Ke	Um
Di	Hai	L'	Uma
Die	He	La	Un
Dos	he-	Las	Un'
Een	Heis	Le	Una
Eene	Hen	Les	Une
Egy	Hena	Lo	Uno
Ei	Henas	Los	Y
Ein	Het	Mia	Yr

Exceptions— Titles composed entirely of words on the list above are filed as written, as well as place names.
Hence:

> A Tavola
> A to Z of Who is Who in Australia's History, The
> A Traverso

7. Names and prefixes— A prefix that is part of the name of a person or place is treated as a separate word unless it is joined to the rest of the name:

> De Paul Law Review
> McCall's Book for Brides
> Van Buren Register

SUBJECT HEADINGS

The following section lists the subject headings used throughout the Directory. The list is arranged alphabetically, by subject, with the major subject (printing in boldface) followed by specific subheadings within the same category.

CROSS REFERENCES

This section combines all subject headings into one alphabetical list, regardless of whether it is a general, main subject or specific, subordinate subject. Cross references from a subject or topic not used in the Directory are made to that which is used. "See also" notes from one subject to a similar subject are included as well.

SUBJECT HEADINGS

Aeronautics, Astronautics 3	Communication 1103	Emigration and Immigration....... 1918
Agriculture 42	Broadcasting 1125	Encyclopedias and General
Agricultural Equipment 158	Postal Communications 1144	Reference Books 1923
Crop Production and Soil 161	Telecommunications............ 1148	Energy 1930
Dairy Industry 191	Computers 1169	Engineering 1963
Feed Grain and Milling 199	Artificial Intelligence 1210	Chemical Engineering 2007
Livestock and Poultry 204	Automation................... 1217	Civil Engineering 2018
Animal Welfare.................. 225	Computer Assisted Instruction 1222	Electricity, Electrical
Anthropology.................... 227	Computer Crimes and Security ... 1225	Engineering, Electronics......... 2034
Antiques 248	Computer Engineering 1227	Hydraulic Engineering 2087
Archaeology 253	Computer Games 1230	Industrial Engineering
Architecture 286	Computer Graphics and Design.... 1231	and Design 2096
Arts, The 311	Computer Industry and Industry	Materials Engineering and
Art........................... 335	Directories................... 1235	Mechanics................. 2100
Crafts and Decorative Arts 369	Computer Music 1240	Mechanical Engineering and
Graphic Arts 376	Computer Networks 1240	Machinery 2108
Performing Arts................. 383	Computer Sales, Service	Mines and Mining Engineering..... 2132
Astrology 389	and Supply................. 1244	Nuclear Engineering............ 2153
Astronomy 391	Computer Systems............. 1246	Environmental Issues............ 2159
Beauty and Cosmetics 402	Cybernetics 1250	Conservation and Natural
Bibliographies 406	Data Base Management.......... 1252	Resources................. 2185
Bicycles and Bicycling 427	Data Processing................ 1255	Ecology 2210
Biographies 429	Desktop Publishing.............. 1263	Pollution and Waste
Biology 439	Hardware 1264	Management................ 2222
Biochemistry.................. 479	Microcomputers, Personal	Ethics 2248
Biophysics.................... 494	Computers................. 1265	Ethnic Interests 2253
Botany....................... 496	Minicomputers 1273	Family and Marriage 2276
Cytology and Histology........... 531	Online Computing and	Fire Prevention 2287
Embryology................... 541	Information................. 1274	Fish and Fisheries............... 2293
Genetics 541	Optical Storage, CD-ROM	Folklore 2318
Marine Biology 552	Applications................ 1276	Food and Food Industry 2325
Microbiology 558	Programs and Programming 1277	Beverage Industry 2363
Microscopy 572	Simulation.................... 1282	Forestry 2373
Mycology..................... 574	Software 1283	Lumber and Wood 2399
Physiology 577	Word Processing 1292	Funeral Service 2406
Birth Control.................... 587	Consumer Interests.............. 1293	Gardening and Horticulture 2407
Boats and Boating............... 591	Copyright, Intellectual Property.... 1300	Florist Trade.................. 2434
Building and Construction 597	Dance 1310	Genealogy and Heraldry.......... 2436
Carpentry and Woodwork.......... 633	Dentistry...................... 1314	Archives 2478
Business....................... 636	Drug Abuse and Alcoholism....... 1338	General Interest................. 2484
Accounting 735	Earth Sciences.................. 1351	General Interest-Africa........... 2497
Advertising and Public Relations 753	Geology 1364	General Interest-Asia............ 2501
Banking and Finance 768	Geophysics................... 1402	General Interest-Australia
Chamber of Commerce 817	Hydrology.................... 1412	and Oceania................ 2510
Commerce 821	Meteorology 1419	General Interest-Central
General Management............ 858	Mineralogy 1437	America................... 2511
Investments 890	Oceanography 1445	General Interest-Europe.......... 2513
Marketing 920	Petrology 1458	General Interest-Middle East.........
Personnel Management........... 938	Economics 1459	General Interest-North America.... 2526
Purchasing 948	Cooperatives 1541	General Interest-South America.... 2551
Retail........................ 952	Economic History, Conditions...... 1544	Geography..................... 2553
Chemistry...................... 958	Economic Theory 1589	Cartography 2580
Analytical Chemistry............. 1012	Industry and Production 1596	Gifts, Toys 2583
Chemical Technology 1020	International Economics.......... 1632	Glass and Ceramics 2585
Crystallography................. 1031	Labor 1642	Health and Personal Fitness 2595
Electrochemistry................ 1033	Education 1720	Heating, Plumbing, and
Inorganic Chemistry 1035	Adult and Continuing Education.... 1799	Refrigeration................ 2602
Organic Chemistry 1038	Early Childhood and	History(General) 2609
Physical and Theoretical Chemistry. 1049	Primary Education 1802	History of Africa 2636
Children and Youth Interests 1059	Higher Education 1806	History of Asia 2644
Civil Defense 1072	Physical Education and	History of Australia and
Classical Studies................ 1073	Training 1854	Oceania................... 2668
Clothing Industry and Fashion..... 1081	School Organization and	History of Europe 2671
College and School Publications... 1088	Administration............... 1859	History of North, South, and
Alumni....................... 1096	Special Education and	Central America 2717
	Rehabilitation................ 1874	History of the Middle East 2767
	Teaching and Curriculum 1887	
	Vocational Education 1909	

SUBJECT HEADINGS

Hobbies. 2770
   Numismatics. 2779
   Philately 2784
Home Economics. 2788
Homosexuality 2793
Horses and Horsemanship. 2796
Hotels/Motels 2803
Household Hardware
   and Appliances 2810
Housing and Urban Development . . 2812
Humanities 2841
Hypnosis. 2857
Industrial Health and Safety 2858
Insurance 2872
Interior Design 2898
   Home Furnishings 2904
International Assistance and
   Development. 2907
Jewelry 2913
   Clocks and Watches. 2916
Journalism 2917
Law 2926
   Banking Law. 3084
   Civil Law 3088
   Constitutional Law 3091
   Corporate Law 3094
   Criminal Law. 3104
   Environmental Law. 3109
   Estate Planning 3117
   Family Law. 3119
   International Law 3122
   Judicial Systems. 3138
   Labor Law. 3143
   Law Enforcement and
      Criminology. 3156
   Legal Aid. 3179
   Maritime Law 3180
   Military Law. 3182
Leather and Fur Industry 3183
Library and Information Sciences . . 3186
Linguistics 3260
Literary and Political Reviews 3337
Literature 3357
   Poetry. 3459
Manufacturing 3475
Mathematics 3490
Medical Science and Technology. . . 3543
   Allergy and Immunology. 3662
   Anatomy 3678
   Anesthesiology. 3680
   Biotechnology. 3685
   Cardiology 3697
   Communicable Diseases 3711
   Dermatology. 3717
   Emergency Medicine 3723
   Endocrinology. 3726
   Epidemiology. 3733
   Family Practice. 3736
   Forensic Medicine, Medical
      Jurisprudence 3739
   Gastroenterology 3743
   Geriatrics 3748
   Gynecology and Obstetrics 3755
   Hematology 3769
   Homeopathy. 3774

   Hospital Administration and
      Medical Centers. 3775
   Internal Medicine 3794
   Musculoskeletal System. 3802
   Neoplasma, Neoplastic 3808
   Neurology. 3825
   Nuclear Medicine 3847
   Nursing. 3849
   Ophthalmology. 3871
   Orthopedics 3880
   Otorhinolaryngology. 3885
   Pathology. 3891
   Pediatrics 3899
   Physicians and Medical
      Personnel 3912
   Podiatry 3917
   Psychiatry. 3918
   Radiology 3938
   Respiratory System 3947
   Sports Medicine 3953
   Surgery. 3957
   Toxicology 3978
   Tropical Medicine 3985
   Urology and Nephrology 3987
Men's Interests 3994
Metals and Metallurgy. 3996
   Welding 4026
Metrology and Standardization 4029
Military and Defense 4033
Motion Picture 4062
Motorcycles 4080
Museums and Galleries 4083
Music 4098
Natural History. 4161
Naval Science, Navigation 4174
New Age Publications. 4185
Newspapers 5625
Nutrition and Dietetics 4186
Occupations and Careers. 4201
Office Equipment and Services 4210
Optometry 4214
Packaging 4217
Paints and Painting. 4222
Paleontology 4226
Paper and Pulp Industry 4232
Parapsychology and
   Occultism. 4240
Pest Control 4243
Petroleum and Natural Gas 4248
Pets. 4285
Pharmacy and Pharmacology 4288
Philanthropy. 4334
Philosophy 4339
Photography and Video 4366
Physical Therapy 4378
Physically Impaired 4382
Physics. 4395
   Analytic and Experimental
      Mechanics 4427
   Heat 4430
   Light, Optics, Radiation 4432
   Magnetism 4443
   Nuclear Physics 4445
   Sound. 4451

Plastics. 4453
Political Science 4461
   Civil Rights. 4503
   International Relations. 4514
   Socialism, Communism,
      Anarchism, Utopianism 4539
Population Studies 4549
Printing Industry 4563
Psychology 4570
Public Administration 4623
   Civil Service. 4701
   Parks and Recreation 4705
   Public Finance and Taxation 4708
   Public Utilities. 4759
Public Health and Safety 4763
Publishing 4811
   Books and Bookmaking. 4822
Real Estate. 4833
Recreation, Leisure. 4848
   Games and Amusements 4856
   Outdoor Life 4868
   Sports. 4881
Religion and Theology 4931
   Bible. 5013
   Buddhism. 5020
   Catholicism 5022
   Eastern Christian Churches. 5039
   Hinduism 5040
   Islam, Bahaism, Theosophy. 5041
   Judaism 5045
   Protestantism. 5054
Restaurants 5070
Romance and Adventure 5073
Rubber 5075
Science and Technology 5078
Security Systems and Alarms 5176
Senior Citizens 5177
Sewing and Needlework. 5182
Sexual Life. 5186
Social Sciences. 5189
Societies and Clubs 5228
Sociology. 5237
   Manners and Customs. 5267
   Social Services and Welfare 5269
Sound Recordings and
   Systems 5315
Statistics 5320
Textiles. 5347
Theater. 5361
Tobacco 5372
Transportation 5375
   Automobiles. 5403
   Railroads 5429
   Roads and Traffic. 5438
   Ships and Shipping 5447
Travel and Tourism 5458
Veterinary Sciences 5501
Water Resources. 5528
Women's Interests 5550
Zoology 5572
   Entomology 5604
   Ornithology. 5614

SUBJECT HEADINGS

The 117 subject headings listed below all contain a sub-heading for "Abstracting, Bibliographies, and Statistics." This sub-heading, which follows the major heading in the Serial Listing, contains serials which abstract and/or index publications in the applicable subject area. Bibliographies and statistical publications pertaining to each subject are also included.

Aeronautics, Astronautics	3
Agriculture	42
Anthropology	227
Antiques	248
Archaeology	253
Architecture	286
Arts, The	311
Astronomy	391
Bicycles and Bicycling	427
Biographies	429
Biology	439
Birth Control	587
Boats and Boating	591
Building and Construction	597
Business	636
Chemistry	958
Children and Youth Interests	1059
Classical Studies	1073
Clothing Industry and Fashion	1081
Communication	1103
Computers	1169
Consumer Interests	1293
Copyright, Intellectual Property	1300
Dance	1310
Dentistry	1314
Drug Abuse and Alcoholism	1338
Earth Sciences	1351
Economics	1459
Education	1720
Encyclopedias and General Reference Books	1923
Energy	1930
Engineering	1963
Environmental Issues	2159
Ethnic Interests	2253
Family and Marriage	2276
Fire Prevention	2287
Fish and Fisheries	2293
Folklore	2318
Food and Food Industry	2325
Forestry	2373
Gardening and Horticulture	2407
Genealogy and Heraldry	2436
General Interest	2484
Geography	2553
Glass and Ceramics	2585
Health and Personal Fitness	2595
History (General)	2609
Hobbies	2770
Homosexuality	2793
Horses and Horsemanship	2796
Hotels/Motels	2803
Household Hardware and Appliances	2810
Housing and Urban Development	2812
Humanities	2841
Industrial Health and Safety	2858
Insurance	2872
International Assistance and Development	2907
Journalism	2917
Law	2926
Library and Information Sciences	3186
Linguistics	3260
Literary and Political Reviews	3337
Literature	3357
Manufacturing	3475
Mathematics	3490
Medical Science and Technology	3543
Metals and Metallurgy	3996
Metrology and Standardization	4029
Military and Defense	4033
Motion Picture	4062
Motorcycles	4080
Museums and Galleries	4083
Music	4098
Natural History	4161
Naval Science, Navigation	4174
New Age Publications	4185
Newspapers	5625
Nutrition and Dietetics	4186
Occupations and Careers	4201
Packaging	4217
Paints and Painting	4222
Paleontology	4226
Paper and Pulp Industry	4232
Parapsychology and Occultism	4240
Pest Control	4243
Petroleum and Natural Gas	4248
Pharmacy and Pharmacology	4288
Philosophy	4339
Photography and Video	4366
Physically Impaired	4382
Physics	4395
Plastics	4453
Political Science	4461
Population Studies	4549
Printing Industry	4563
Psychology	4570
Public Administration	4623
Public Health and Safety	4763
Publishing	4811
Real Estate	4833
Recreation, Leisure	4848
Religion and Theology	4931
Restaurants	5070
Rubber	5075
Science and Technology	5078
Social Sciences	5189
Sociology	5237
Sound Recordings and Systems	5315
Textiles	5347
Theater	5361
Tobacco	5372
Transportation	5375
Travel and Tourism	5458
Veterinary Sciences	5501
Water Resources	5528
Women's Interests	5550
Zoology	5572

SUBJECT CROSS REFERENCES

Abortion –See **Medical Science and Technology -- Gynecology and Obstetrics** pg 3755

Abrasives –See **Metals and Metallurgy** pg 3996

Accessories –See **Clothing Industry and Fashion** pg 1081

Accident Prevention –See **Industrial Health and Safety** pg 2858; **Public Health and Safety** pg 4763; **Transportation -- Roads and Traffic** pg 5438

Accounting –pg 735; see also Law pg 2926; Public Administration -- Public Finance and Taxation pg 4708

Acoustics –See **Physics -- Sound** pg 4451

Acquired Immune Deficiency Syndrome (AIDS) –See **Medical Science and Technology -- Allergy and Immunology** pg 3662; see also Medical Science and Technology -- Communicable Diseases pg 3711; Public Health and Safety pg 4763

Acting –See **Motion Picture** pg 4062; **The Arts -- Performing Arts** pg 383; **Theater** pg 5361

Actuarial Science –See **Insurance** pg 2872

Acupuncture –See **Medical Science and Technology** pg 3543

Addictions –See **Drug Abuse and Alcoholism** pg 1338; see also Psychology pg 4570

Adhesives –See **Chemistry -- Physical and Theoretical Chemistry** pg 1049; see also Chemistry -- Chemical Technology pg 1020; Engineering -- Chemical Engineering pg 2007; Engineering -- Materials Engineering and Mechanics pg 2100; Metals and Metallurgy -- Welding pg 4026; Paints and Painting pg 4222; Plastics pg 4453

Administrative Law –See **Law -- Constitutional Law** pg 3091

Adoption –See **Sociology -- Social Services and Welfare** pg 5269

Adult and Continuing Education –pg 1799

Adventure –See **Romance and Adventure** pg 5073

Advertising –See **Business -- Advertising and Public Relations** pg 753

Advertising and Public Relations –pg 753

Aerobics –See **Health and Personal Fitness** pg 2595

Aerodynamics –See **Aeronautics, Astronautics** pg 3

Aeronautics, Astronautics –pg 3; see also Military and Defense pg 4033; Transportation pg 5375

Aerospace Medicine –See **Aeronautics, Astronautics** pg 3; **Medical Science and Technology** pg 3543

Aesthetics –See **The Arts -- Art** pg 335; see also Philosophy pg 4339

Africa –See **General Interest -- General Interest-Africa** pg 2497; **History(General) -- History of Africa** pg 2636

African Studies –See **History(General) -- History of Africa** pg 2636; **Literature** pg 3357

Aging –See **Medical Science and Technology -- Geriatrics** pg 3748; **Sociology -- Social Services and Welfare** pg 5269; see also Senior Citizens pg 5177

Agricultural Aviation –See **Aeronautics, Astronautics** pg 3; see also Agriculture pg 42

Agricultural Chemistry –See **Agriculture** pg 42; see also Chemistry pg 958

Agricultural Economics –See **Agriculture** pg 42; see also Economics pg 1459

Agricultural Engineering –See **Agriculture** pg 42; see also Engineering pg 1963

Agricultural Equipment –pg 157

Agricultural Marketing –See **Agriculture** pg 42; see also Business -- Marketing pg 920

Agricultural Meteorology –See **Earth Sciences -- Meteorology** pg 1419; see also Agriculture pg 42

Agriculture –pg 42; see also Food and Food Industry pg 2325; Gardening and Horticulture pg 2407

Agronomy –See **Agriculture** pg 42; see also Agriculture -- Crop Production and Soil pg 161

AIDS –See **Medical Science and Technology -- Allergy and Immunology** pg 3662; see also Medical Science and Technology -- Communicable Diseases pg 3711; Public Health and Safety pg 4763

Air Cargo –See **Transportation** pg 5375; see also Aeronautics, Astronautics pg 3

Air Conditioning –See **Heating, Plumbing, and Refrigeration** pg 2810

Air Force –See **Aeronautics, Astronautics** pg 3; **Military and Defense** pg 4033

Air Pollution –See **Environmental Issues -- Pollution and Waste Management** pg 2222

Air Travel –See **Aeronautics, Astronautics** pg 3; **Travel and Tourism** pg 5458

Airplanes –See **Aeronautics, Astronautics** pg 3

Airports –See **Aeronautics, Astronautics** pg 3

Alarm/Security Systems –See **Engineering -- Electricity, Electrical Engineering, Electronics** pg 2034

Alcoholic Beverages –See **Food and Food Industry -- Beverage Industry** pg 2363

Alcoholism –See **Drug Abuse and Alcoholism** pg 1338

Alimony –See **Law -- Family Law** pg 3119

Allergy and Immunology –pg 3662

Almanacs –See **Encyclopedias and General Reference Books** pg 1923

Alumni –pg 1096

Amateur Radio –See **Communication -- Broadcasting** pg 1125; see also Communication pg 1103

American Studies –See **History(General) -- History of North, South, and Central America** pg 2717

Amusements –See **Recreation, Leisure -- Games and Amusements** pg 4856

Analytic and Experimental Mechanics –pg 4427

Analytical Chemistry –pg 1012

Anarchism –See **Political Science -- Socialism, Communism, Anarchism, Utopianism** pg 4539

Anatomy –See **Medical Science and Technology -- Anatomy** pg 3543; see also Biology -- Embryology pg 541; Medical Science and Technology -- Pathology pg 3891

Anesthesia –See **Medical Science and Technology -- Anesthesiology** pg 3680; see also Medical Science and Technology -- Surgery pg 3957; Pharmacy and Pharmacology pg 4288

Anesthesiology –pg 3680; see also Medical Science and Technology -- Surgery pg 3957

Angiology –See **Medical Science and Technology -- Cardiology** pg 3697

Anglo-Saxon Studies –See **History(General) -- History of Europe** pg 2671; **Literature** pg 3357

Animal Husbandry –See **Agriculture** pg 42; **Veterinary Sciences** pg 5501

Animal Science –See **Veterinary Sciences** pg 5501; see also Zoology pg 5572

SUBJECT CROSS REFERENCES

Animal Welfare –pg 225; see also Ethics pg 2248

Animals –See **Horses and Horsemanship** pg 2796; **Pets** pg 4285; see also Veterinary Sciences pg 5501; Zoology pg 5572

Anthropology –pg 227; see also Archaeology pg 253; Paleontology pg 4226; Sociology pg 5237

Antibiotics –See **Medical Science and Technology** pg 3543; **Pharmacy and Pharmacology** pg 4288; see also Chemistry pg 958

Antiques –pg 248; see also Hobbies pg 2770; Museums and Galleries pg 4083

Antitrust Law –See **Law -- Corporate Law** pg 3094

Anxiety –See **Medical Science and Technology -- Psychiatry** pg 3918; see also Psychology pg 4570

Apartments –See **Housing and Urban Development** pg 2812

Apparel –See **Clothing Industry and Fashion** pg 1081; see also Business -- Retail pg 952; Textiles pg 5347

Appliances –See **Household Hardware and Appliances** pg 2810

Applied Mechanics –See **Engineering -- Materials Engineering and Mechanics** pg 2100; **Physics -- Analytic and Experimental Mechanics** pg 4427; see also Engineering -- Mechanical Engineering and Machinery pg 2108

Apprenticeship –See **Economics -- Labor** pg 1642

Aquaculture –See **Fish and Fisheries** pg 2293; see also Biology pg 439; Biology -- Marine Biology pg 552

Archaeology –pg 253; see also Anthropology pg 227; History(General) pg 2609; Paleontology pg 4226

Archery –See **Recreation, Leisure -- Sports** pg 4881

Architecture –pg 286; see also Building and Construction pg 597; Engineering pg 1963; Interior Design pg 2898

Archives –pg 2478; see also History(General) pg 2609; Library and Information Sciences pg 3186

Army –See **Military and Defense** pg 4033

Aromatherapy –See **Beauty and Cosmetics** pg 402

Art –pg 335; see also Humanities pg 2841

Art Galleries –See **Museums and Galleries** pg 4083; see also The Arts -- Art pg 335

Art History –See **The Arts -- Art** pg 335; see also Humanities pg 2841; Museums and Galleries pg 4083; The Arts pg 311

Arthritis –See **Medical Science and Technology -- Musculoskeletal System** pg 3802

Artificial Intelligence –pg 1210; see also Computers -- Automation pg 1217; Science and Technology pg 5078

Arts and Sciences –See **The Arts** pg 311; see also Humanities pg 2841; Social Sciences pg

Asbestos –See **Building and Construction** pg 597; **Engineering -- Mines and Mining Engineering** pg 2132; see also Public Health and Safety pg 4763

Asia –See **General Interest -- General Interest-Asia** pg 2501; **History(General) -- History of Asia** pg 2644

Asian Studies –See **History(General) -- History of Asia** pg 2644; **Literature** pg 3357

Associations –See **Societies and Clubs** pg 5228

Asthma –See **Medical Science and Technology -- Respiratory System** pg 3947

Astrology –pg 389

Astronautics –See **Aeronautics, Astronautics** pg 3

Astronomy –pg 391

Atheism –See **Philosophy** pg 4339

Athletic Clubs –See **Health and Personal Fitness** pg 2595; see also Recreation, Leisure -- Sports pg 4881

Athletics –See **Recreation, Leisure -- Sports** pg 4881; see also Health and Personal Fitness pg 2595

Atlas –See **Geography** pg 2553

Atmospheric Science –See **Earth Sciences -- Meteorology** pg 1419; see also Science and Technology pg 5078

Atomic Energy –See **Energy** pg 1930; **Engineering -- Nuclear Engineering** pg 2153

Attorney General –See **Law -- Judicial Systems** pg 3138

Audio-Visual Education –See **Education -- Teaching and Curriculum** pg 1887

Audiology –See **Medical Science and Technology -- Otorhinolaryngology** pg 3885

Auditing –See **Business -- Accounting** pg 735; see also Public Administration -- Public Finance and Taxation** pg 4708

Audubon Society –See **Environmental Issues -- Conservation and Natural Resources** pg 2185; see also Natural History pg 4161

Australia –See **General Interest -- General Interest-Australia and Oceania** pg 2510; **History(General) -- History of Australia and Oceania** pg 2668

Authors –See **Biographies** pg 429; **Literature** pg 3357; see also Literature -- Poetry pg 3459; Publishing pg 4811

Automation –pg 1217

Automobile Racing –See **Recreation, Leisure -- Sports** pg 4881

Automobiles –pg 5403

Aviation –See **Aeronautics, Astronautics** pg 3

Bacteriology –See **Biology** pg 439; **Biology -- Microbiology** pg 558

Badminton –See **Recreation, Leisure -- Sports** pg 4881

Bahaism –See **Religion and Theology -- Islam, Bahaism, Theosophy** pg 5041

Bakers and Bakeries –See **Food and Food Industry** pg 2325

Balkan Studies –See **History(General) -- History of Europe** pg 2671

Banking –See **Business -- Banking and Finance** pg 768

Banking and Finance –pg 768; see also Business -- Cooperatives pg 1541; Business -- Investments pg 890; Economics pg 1459; Public Administration -- Public Finance pg 4708

Banking Law –pg 3084; see also Business -- Banking and Finance pg 768; Law -- Corporate Law pg 3094

Bankruptcy –See **Law -- Banking Law** pg 3084; see also Business -- Banking and Finance pg 768

Baptist –See **Religion and Theology -- Protestantism** pg 5054

Baseball –See **Recreation, Leisure -- Sports** pg 4881

Baseball Cards –See **Hobbies** pg 2770; **Recreation, Leisure -- Sports** pg 4881

Beauty and Cosmetics –pg 402

Beekeeping –See **Agriculture** pg 42

Behavior Therapy –See **Psychology** pg 4570

Behavioral Science –See **Medical Science and Technology -- Psychiatry** pg 3918; **Psychology** pg 4570; see also Sociology pg 5237

SUBJECT CROSS REFERENCES

Belizean Studies –See **History(General) -- History of North, South, and Central America** pg 2717

Beverage Industry –pg 2363

Bible –pg 5013

Bibliographies –pg 406; see also Library and Information Sciences pg 3186

Bicycles and Bicycling –pg 427

Bilingual –See **Education -- Special Education and Rehabilitation** pg 1874; **Linguistics** pg 3260; see also Education pg 1720

Biochemistry –pg 479

Bioengineering –See **Medical Science and Technology -- Biotechnology** pg 3685

Biofeedback –See **Psychology** pg 4570; see also Biology -- Physiology pg 577; Medical Science and Technology pg 3543

Biographies –pg 429

Biology –pg 439; see also Medical Science and Technology pg 3543; Zoology pg 5572

Biomechanics –See **Medical Science and Technology -- Biotechnology** pg 3685

Biomedical Engineering –See **Medical Science and Technology -- Biotechnology** pg 3685

Biomedicine –See **Medical Science and Technology -- Biotechnology** pg 3685

Biophysics –pg 494

Biotechnology –pg 3685

Birds –See **Zoology -- Ornithology** pg 5614; see also Environmental Issues -- Conservation and Natural Resources pg 2185; Natural History pg 4161

Birth Control –pg 587; see also Population Studies pg 4549

Blind –See **Physically Impaired** pg 4382; see also Education -- Special Education and Rehabilitation pg 1874; Medical Science and Technology -- Ophthalmology pg 3871; Sociology -- Social Services and Welfare pg 5269

Blood –See **Medical Science and Technology -- Hematology** pg 3769

Blood Groups –See **Medical Science and Technology -- Hematology** pg 3769

Blood Preservation –See **Medical Science and Technology -- Hematology** pg 3769

Blood Transfusions –See **Medical Science and Technology -- Hematology** pg 3769; see also Medical Science and Technology pg 3543; Medical Science and Technology -- Internal Medicine pg 3794; Medical Science and Technology -- Surgery pg 3957

Boats and Boating –pg 591

Bodybuilding –See **Health and Personal Fitness** pg 2595; see also Recreation, Leisure -- Sports pg 4881

Books and Bookmaking –pg 4822

Booksellers –See **Publishing -- Books and Bookmaking** pg 4822; see also Publishing pg 4811

Botany –pg 496; see also Agriculture -- Crop Production and Soil pg 161; Gardening and Horticulture pg 2407

Bowling –See **Recreation, Leisure -- Sports** pg 4881

Boxing –See **Recreation, Leisure -- Sports** pg 4881

Brahmanism –See **Hinduism** pg 5040

Braille –See **Physically Impaired** pg 4382; see also Education -- Special Education and Rehabilitation pg 1874

Breast-feeding –See **Medical Science and Technology -- Gynecology and Obstetrics** pg 3755; see also Medical Science and Technology -- Pediatrics pg 3899

Breweries –See **Food and Food Industry -- Beverage Industry** pg 2363

Bricks –See **Building and Construction** pg 597

Bride –See **Family and Marriage** pg 2276

Bridges –See **Transportation** pg 5375; see also Engineering -- Civil Engineering pg 2018; Transportation -- Roads and Traffic pg 5438

British Studies –See **History(General) -- History of Europe** pg 2671; **Literature** pg 3357

Broadcasting –pg 1125

Buddhism –pg 5020

Budget –See **Public Administration -- Public Finance and Taxation** pg 4708; see also Business -- Banking and Finance pg 768

Building and Construction –pg 597; see also Engineering -- Civil Engineering pg 2018; Housing and Urban Development pg 2812

Burns –See **Medical Science and Technology** pg 3543

Buses –See **Transportation** pg 5375

Business –pg 636

Business Education –See **Business** pg 636; see also Education pg 1720

Business Law –See **Business** pg 636; **Law -- Corporate Law** pg 3094; see also Law -- International Law pg 3122

Buying –See **Business -- Purchasing** pg 948

Cable Television –See **Communication -- Broadcasting** pg 1125

CAD/CAM –See **Computers -- Computer Graphics and Design** pg 1231; see also Computers -- Computer Engineering pg 1227

Calligraphy –See **The Arts -- Graphic Arts** pg 376

Cameras –See **Photography and Video** pg 4366; see also Hobbies pg 2770; Motion Picture pg 4062

Camping –See **Recreation, Leisure -- Outdoor Life** pg 4868

Canadian Studies –See **History(General) -- History of North, South, and Central America** pg 2717

Cancer –See **Medical Science and Technology -- Neoplasma, Neoplastic** pg 3808

Candy –See **Food and Food Industry** pg 2325

Canning and Preserving –See **Food and Food Industry** pg 2325; see also Gardening and Horticulture pg 2407

Canoeing –See **Boats and Boating** pg 591

Canon Law –See **Religion and Theology** pg 4931

Cardiology –pg 3697; see also Medical Science and Technology -- Hematology pg 3769

Careers –See **Occupations and Careers** pg 4201

Cargo –See **Transportation** pg 5375

Caribbean Studies –See **History(General) -- History of North, South, and Central America** pg 2717

Carpentry and Woodwork –pg 633; see also Hobbies pg 2770; Interior Design -- Home Furnishings pg 2904

Carpet, Rugs –See **Interior Design -- Home Furnishings** pg 2904

Cartography –pg 2580

Cartoons –See **The Arts -- Graphic Arts** pg 376; see also Recreation, Leisure -- Games and Amusements pg 4856

Catalogues –See **Bibliographies** pg 406

Catalysis –See **Chemistry -- Physical and Theoretical Chemistry** pg 1049

SUBJECT CROSS REFERENCES

Catalysts –See **Chemistry -- Physical and Theoretical Chemistry** pg 1049

Catering –See **Food and Food Industry** pg 2325; **Hotels/Motels** pg 2803; **Restaurants** pg 5070

Catholicism –pg 5022

Cattle –See **Agriculture -- Livestock and Poultry** pg 204; see also Agriculture pg 42; Agriculture -- Dairy Industry pg 191; Veterinary Sciences pg 5501

Caves –See **Earth Sciences -- Geophysics** pg 1402; see also Earth Sciences -- Geology pg 1364

CD-ROM –See **Computers -- Optical Storage, CD-ROM Applications** pg 1276

Celebrity Interests –See **General Interest** pg 2484; see also Motion Picture pg 4062

Celtic Studies –See **History(General) -- History of Europe** pg 2671; **Literature** pg 3357

Cement –See **Building and Construction** pg 597; **Chemistry -- Chemical Technology** pg 1020; see also Engineering -- Civil Engineering pg 2018; Industry and Production pg 1596

Cemeteries –See **Funeral Service** pg 2406

Central America –See **General Interest -- General Interest-Central America** pg 2511; **History(General) -- History of North, South, and Central America** pg 2717

Ceramics –See **Glass and Ceramics** pg 2585

Cereals –See **Agriculture -- Feed Grain and Milling** pg 199; see also Food and Food Industry pg 2325

Cerebral Palsy –See **Medical Science and Technology -- Neurology** pg 3825

Chamber of Commerce –pg 817

Charities –See **Philanthropy** pg 4334; see also Sociology -- Social Services and Welfare pg 5269

Chemical Engineering –pg 2007; see also Chemistry pg 958; Chemistry -- Chemical Technology pg 1020

Chemical Technology –pg 1020; see also Chemistry pg 958; Engineering -- Chemical Engineering pg 2007; Medical Science and Technology -- Biotechnology pg 3685

Chemistry –pg 958; see also Engineering -- Chemical Engineering pg 2007

Chemotherapy –See **Medical Science and Technology -- Neoplasma, Neoplastic** pg 3808; see also Pharmacy and Pharmacology pg 4288

Chess –See **Recreation, Leisure -- Games and Amusements** pg 4856

Child Development –See **Education -- Early Childhood and Primary Education** pg 1802

Child Psychology –See **Psychology** pg 4570

Child Welfare –See **Sociology -- Social Services and Welfare** pg 5269

Children and Youth Interests –pg 1059

China, Tableware –See **Glass and Ceramics** pg 2585; see also Gifts, Toys pg 2583

Chinese Studies –See **History(General) -- History of Asia** pg 2644; **Literature** pg 3357

Chiropractor –See **Medical Science and Technology -- Musculoskeletal System** pg 3802; **Physical Therapy** pg 4378

Christianity –See **Religion and Theology** pg 4931

Chromatography –See **Chemistry -- Analytical Chemistry** pg 1012; see also Chemistry pg 958

Churches –See **Religion and Theology** pg 4931; see also Religion and Theology -- Eastern Christian Churches pg 5039; Religion and Theology -- Protestantism pg 5054

Cinema –See **Motion Picture** pg 4062

Cinematography –See **Photography and Video** pg 4366; see also Motion Picture pg 4062

Citrus Industry –See **Agriculture -- Crop Production and Soil** pg 161; **Food and Food Industry** pg 2325; **Gardening and Horticulture** pg 2407

City Directory –See **Geography** pg 2553

City Planning –See **Housing and Urban Development** pg 2812

Civil Defense –pg 1072

Civil Engineering –pg 2018

Civil Law –pg 3088

Civil Rights –pg 4503

Civil Service –pg 4701; see also Public Administration pg 4623

Classical Studies –pg 1073; see also Archaeology pg 253; History(General) pg 2609; Linguistics pg 3260; Literature pg 3357

Climatology –See **Earth Sciences -- Meteorology** pg 1419

Clinical Medicine –See **Medical Science and Technology** pg 3543; **Medical Science and Technology** pg 3543

Clocks –See **Jewelry -- Clocks and Watches** pg 2916

Clocks and Watches –pg 2916

Clothing Industry and Fashion –pg 1081; see also Leather and Fur Industry pg 3183; Textiles pg 5347

Clubs –See **Societies and Clubs** pg 5228

Coaching –See **Recreation, Leisure -- Sports** pg 4881

Coal –See **Earth Science -- Mineralogy** pg 1437; see also Energy pg 1930; Engineering -- Mines and Mining Engineering pg 2132

Coast Guard –See **Naval Science, Navigation** pg 4174

Coins –See **Hobbies -- Numismatics** pg 2779

Collectors and Collecting –See **Antiques** pg 248; see also Hobbies pg 2770

College and School Publications –pg 1088; see also Education -- Higher Education pg 1806

Colleges and Universities –See **Education -- Higher Education** pg 1806; see also College and School Publications pg 1088

Combustion –See **Chemistry -- Physical and Theoretical Chemistry** pg 1049; **Energy** pg 1930; **Engineering** pg 1963

Comics –See **Recreation, Leisure -- Games and Amusements** pg 4856

Commerce –pg 821

Commercial Art –See **The Arts -- Graphic Arts** pg 376

Commercial Law –See **Law -- Corporate Law** pg 3094

Commodities –See **Business -- Commerce** pg 821

Common Law –See **Law -- Civil Law** pg 3088

Communicable Diseases –pg 3711; See also **Medical Science and Technology -- Epidemiology** pg 3733; Public Health and Safety pg 248

Communication –pg 1103

Communism –See **Political Science -- Socialism, Communism, Anarchism, Utopianism** pg 4539

Community Affairs –See **Public Administration** pg 4623

SUBJECT CROSS REFERENCES

Community Development –See **Housing and Urban Development** pg 2812

Compact Disc –See **Computers -- Optical Storage, CD-ROM Applications** pg 1276

Company Law –See **Law -- Corporate Law** pg 3094

Comparative Law –See **Law -- International Law** pg 3122

Composite Materials –See **Engineering -- Materials Engineering and Mechanics** pg 2100

Computer Architecture –See **Computers -- Computer Graphics and Design** pg 1231

Computer Assisted Instruction –pg 1222; see also Education -- Teaching and Curriculum pg 1887

Computer Crimes –See **Computers -- Computer Crimes and Security** pg 1225

Computer Crimes and Security –pg 1225

Computer Directories –See **Computers -- Computer Industry and Industry Directories** pg 1235

Computer Engineering –pg 1227

Computer Games – pg 1230; see also Recreation, Leisure -- Games and Amusements pg 4856

Computer Graphics and Design –pg 1231

Computer Industry –See **Computers -- Computer Industry and Industry Directories** pg 1235

Computer Industry and Industry Directories –pg 1235; see also Computers -- Computer Sales, Service and Supply pg 1244

Computer Music –pg 1240; see also Music pg 4098

Computer Networks –pg 1240

Computer Products –See **Computers -- Computer Sales, Service and Supply** pg 1244

Computer Sales, Service and Supply –pg 1244

Computer Science –See **Computers** pg 1169

Computer Simulation –See **Computers -- Simulation** pg 1282

Computer Systems –pg 1246

Computers –pg 1169

Confectioners –See **Food and Food Industry** pg 2325

Congress –See **Public Administration** pg 4623

Conservation and Natural Resources –pg 2185; see also Environmental Issues -- Ecology pg 2210; Natural History pg 4161; Public Administration -- Parks and Recreation pg 4705; Water Resources pg 5528

Constitutional Law –pg 3091

Construction –See **Building and Construction** pg 597; see also Engineering -- Civil Engineering pg 2018

Consumer Interests –pg 1293; see also Economics pg 1459

Consumer Protection –See **Consumer Interests** pg 1293; see also Law -- Corporate Law pg 3094

Contact Lenses –See **Medical Science and Technology -- Ophthalmology** pg 3871; **Optometry** pg 4214

Continuing Education –See **Education -- Adult and Continuing Education** pg 1799

Contraception –See **Birth Control** pg 587

Contractors –See **Building and Construction** pg 597; **Engineering -- Civil Engineering** pg 2018; see also Architecture pg 286

Conventions –See **Business -- Advertising and Public Relations** pg 753; **Science and Technology** pg 5078

Cookbooks, Cooking –See **Home Economics** pg 2788

Cooperatives –pg 1541; see also Agriculture pg 42; Business -- Banking and Finance pg 768

Copyright, Intellectual Property –pg 1300

Corporate Law –pg 3094

Corporation Law –See **Law -- Corporate Law** pg 3094

Corrosion –See **Engineering -- Chemical Engineering** pg 2007; see also Metals and Metallurgy pg 3996

Cosmetic Surgery –See **Medical Science and Technology -- Surgery** pg 3957

Cosmetics –See **Beauty and Cosmetics** pg 402

Cotton –See **Agriculture -- Crop Production and Soil** pg 161; see also Textiles pg 5347

Counseling –See **Psychology** pg 4570; see also Family and Marriage pg 2276; Religion and Theology pg 4931; Sociology -- Social Services and Welfare pg 5269

Court Rules –See **Law -- Judicial Systems** pg 3138

Courts –See **Law -- Judicial Systems** pg 3138

Crafts and Decorative Arts –pg 369; see also Gifts, Toys pg 2583; Glass and Ceramics pg 2585; Hobbies pg 2770; Sewing and Needlework pg 5182

Credit Unions –See **Business -- Banking and Finance** pg 768

Crime Prevention –See **Law -- Law Enforcement and Criminology** pg 3156

Crime Statistics –See **Law -- Law Enforcement and Criminology** pg 3156; see also Statistics pg 5320

Criminal Justice –See **Law -- Law Enforcement and Criminology** pg 3156; see also Law -- Criminal Law pg 3104

Criminal Law –pg 3104; see also Law -- Law Enforcement and Criminology pg 3156

Criminal Procedure –See **Law -- Judicial Systems** pg 3138; **Law -- Law Enforcement and Criminology** pg 3156; see also Law -- Criminal Law pg 3104

Criminology –See **Law -- Law Enforcement and Criminology** pg 3156

Croatian Studies –See **History(General) -- History of Europe** pg 2671

Crop Production and Soil –pg 161

Crystallography –pg 1031

Currency –See **Business -- Banking and Finance** pg 768; **Business -- Investments** pg 890; see also Economics -- International Economics pg 1632

Curriculum –See **Education -- Teaching and Curriculum** pg 1887

Customs –See **Sociology -- Manners and Customs** pg 5267

Customs and Excise –See **Public Administration -- Public Finance and Taxation** pg 4708; see also Law pg 2926

Cybernetics –pg 1250

Cystic Fibrosis –See **Medical Science and Technology -- Musculoskeletal System** pg 3802

Cytology –See **Biology -- Cytology and Histology** pg 531

Cytology and Histology –pg 531

Dairy Industry –pg 191

Dance –pg 1310; see also The Arts -- Performing Arts pg 383

Data Base Management –pg 1252

Data Processing –pg 1255

Data Protection –See **Computers -- Computer Crimes and Security** pg 1225

Daycare –See **Sociology -- Social Services and Welfare** pg 5269

SUBJECT CROSS REFERENCES

Deaf –See **Physically Impaired** pg 4382; see also Medical Science and Technology -- Otorhinolaryngology pg 3885

Decorative Arts –See **The Arts -- Crafts and Decorative Arts** pg 369

Defense –See **Military and Defense** pg 4033; see also Civil Defense pg 1072

Demography –See **Population Studies** pg 4549; see also Statistics pg 5320

Dentistry –pg 1314

Department Stores –See **Business -- Retail** pg 952; see also Business -- Marketing pg 920

Dermatology –pg 3717

Desktop Publishing –pg 1263; see also Publishing pg 4811

Diabetes –See **Endocrinology** pg 3726

Diagnostic Imaging –See **Medical Science and Technology -- Radiology** pg 3938

Dialysis –See **Medical Science and Technology -- Urology and Nephrology** pg 3987; see also Medical Science and Technology pg 3543; Medical Science and Technology -- Internal Medicine pg 3794

Dictionaries –See **Encyclopedias and General Reference Books** pg 1923

Dietetics –See **Nutrition and Dietetics** pg 4186

Directories –See **Encyclopedias and General Reference Books** pg 1923

Disarmament –See **Military and Defense** pg 4033; see also Law -- International Law pg 3122

Divorce –See **Family and Marriage** pg 2276; **Law -- Family Law** pg 3119

Doctrinal Theology –See **Religion and Theology** pg 4931

Dog Racing –See **Recreation, Leisure -- Sports** pg 4881

Domestic Relations –See **Law -- Family Law** pg 3119

Drama –See **Theater** pg 5361; see also The Arts -- Performing Arts pg 383

Drink –See **Food and Food Industry -- Beverage Industry** pg 2363

Drug Abuse and Alcoholism –pg 1338

Dyes and Dyeing –See **Chemistry -- Chemical Technology** pg 1020; **Textiles** pg 5347; see also The Arts -- Crafts and Decorative Arts pg 369

Early Childhood and Primary Education –pg 1802

Early Childhood Education –See **Education -- Early Childhood and Primary Education** pg 1802

Earth Sciences –pg 1351

Eastern Christian Churches –pg 5039

Ecology –pg 2210; see also Natural History pg 4161

Economic Conditions –See **Economics -- Economic History, Conditions** pg 1544

Economic History –See **Economics -- Economic History, Conditions** pg 1544

Economic History, Conditions –pg 1544

Economic Theory –pg 1589

Economics –pg 1459

Editing –See **Publishing** pg 4811; see also Journalism pg 2917; Literature pg 3357

Education –pg 1720

Educational Psychology –See **Education -- Teaching and Curriculum** pg 1887; **Psychology** pg 4570; see also Education pg 1720; Education -- Special Education and Rehabilitation pg 1874

Elections –See **Political Science** pg 4461; see also Public Administration pg 4623

Electric Power –See **Engineering -- Electricity, Electrical Engineering and Electronic** pg 2034

Electricity, Electrical Engineering, Electronics –pg 2034; see also Energy pg 1930; Heating, Plumbing and Refrigeration pg 2602; Public Administration -- Public Utilities pg 4759; Sound Recordings and Systems pg 5315

Electrochemistry –pg 1033; see also Chemistry -- Analytical Chemistry pg 1012; Chemistry -- Physical and Theoretical Chemistry pg 1049

Electronic Publishing –See **Desktop Publishing** pg 1263

Electronics –See **Engineering -- Electricity, Electrical Engineering, Electronics** pg 2034

Embroidery –See **Sewing and Needlework** pg 5182

Embryology –pg 541; see also Medical Science and Technology -- Anatomy pg 3678

Emergencies –See **Medical Science and Technology -- Emergency Medicine** pg 3723

Emergency Health Services –See **Medical Science and Technology -- Emergency Medicine** pg 3723

Emergency Medicine –pg 3723

Emigration and Immigration –pg 1918

Employment Law –See **Law -- Labor Law** pg 3143

Encyclopedias and General Reference Books –pg 1923

Endocrinology –pg 3726

Energy –pg 1930; see also Engineering -- Electricity, Electrical Engineering, Electronics pg 2034; Engineering -- Nuclear Engineering pg 2153; Petroleum and Natural Gas pg 4248; Physics -- Nuclear Physics pg 4445; Public Administration -- Public Utilities pg 4759

Engineering –pg 1963; see also Computers -- Artificial Intelligence pg 1210

Entomology –pg 5604

Environmental Health –See **Environmental Issues** pg 2159; see also Public Health and Safety pg 4763

Environmental Issues –pg 2159

Environmental Law –pg 3109; see also Environmental Issues pg 2159

Environmental Protection –See **Environmental Issues** pg 2159; see also Environmental Issues -- Pollution and Waste Management pg 2222

Environmental Studies –See **Environmental Issues** pg 2159; see also Environmental Issues -- Conservation and Natural Resources pg 2185; Environmental Issues -- Ecology pg 2210; Environmental Issues -- Pollution and Waste Management pg 2222

Environmental Technology –See **Environmental Issues** pg 2159; see also Science and Technology pg 5078

Environmental Waste Management –See **Environmental Issues** pg 2159

Enzymes –See **Biology -- Biochemistry** pg 479

Epidemiology –pg 3733; see also Medical Science and Technology -- Epidemiology pg 3711; Public Health and Safety pg 4763

Epilepsy –See **Medical Science and Technology -- Neurology** pg 3825

Episcopal –See **Religion and Theology -- Protestantism** pg 5054

Ergonomics –See **Engineering -- Mechanical Engineering and Machinery** pg 2108; see also Computers -- Cybernetics pg 1250

Esperanto –See **Linguistics** pg 3260; see also Education -- Teaching and Curriculum pg 1887

SUBJECT CROSS REFERENCES

Estate Planning —pg 3117; see also Business -- Banking and Finance pg 768; Business -- Investments pg 890

Ethics —pg 2248

Ethnic Interests —pg 2253

Ethnology —See **Anthropology** pg 227

Europe —See **General Interest-Europe** pg 2513; **History(General) -- History of Europe** pg 2671

European Studies —See **History(General) -- History of Europe** pg 2671; **Literature** pg 3357

Evangelism —See **Religion and Theology** pg 4931

Exceptional Children —See **Education -- Special Education and Rehabilitation** pg 1874

Exercise —See **Health and Personal Fitness** pg 2595

Exhibits/Exhibitions —See **Business -- Advertising and Public Relations** pg 753; **Science and Technology** pg 5078

Experimental Mechanics —See **Physics -- Analytic and Experimental Mechanics** pg 4427

Expert Systems —See **Computers -- Artificial Intelligence** pg 1210

Expositions —See **Business -- Advertising and Public Relations** pg 753; **Recreation, Leisure -- Games and Amusements** pg 4856; **Science and Technology** pg 5078

Fabric —See **Textiles** pg 5347; see also Clothing Industry and Fashion pg 1081; Sewing and Needlework pg 5182

Fairs —See **Recreation, Leisure -- Games and Amusements** pg 4856

Family and Marriage —pg 2276; see also Home Economics pg 2788

Family Law —pg 3119

Family Medicine —See **Medical Science and Technology -- Family Practice** pg 3736

Family Physicians —See **Medical Science and Technology -- Family Practice** pg 3736; see also Medical Science and Technology -- Physicians and Medical Personnel pg 3912

Family Planning —See **Birth Control** pg 587; **Family and Marriage** pg 2276

Family Practice —pg 3736

Fashion —See **Clothing Industry and Fashion** pg 1081

Federal Aid to Education —See **Education -- Higher Education** pg 1806; see also Education -- School Organization and Administration pg 1859

Federal Employees —See **Public Administration -- Civil Service** pg 4701

Federal Government —See **Public Administration** pg 4623; see also Political Science pg 4461

Feed Grain and Milling —pg 199

Feminism —See **Women's Interests** pg 5550

Fencing —See **Recreation, Leisure -- Sports** pg 4881

Fertility —See **Birth Control** pg 587; **Population Studies** pg 4549; see also Biology -- Physiology pg 577; Medical Science and Technology -- Gynecology and Obstetrics pg 3755

Fertilizers —See **Agriculture -- Crop Production and Soil** pg 161; **Chemistry -- Chemical Technology** pg 1020

Fiber Optics —See **Communication -- Telecommunications** pg 1148; **Physics -- Light, Optics, Radiation** pg 4432

Fiction —See **Literature** pg 3357; see also Literary and Political Reviews pg 3337

Films and Filmmaking —See **Motion Picture** pg 4062; see also Photography and Video pg 4366

Finance —See **Business -- Banking and Finance** pg 768; **Public Administration -- Public Finance and Taxation** pg 4708

Fire Prevention —pg 2287

Fish and Fisheries —pg 2293

Fishing —See **Fish and Fisheries** pg 2293

Floor Coverings —See **Building and Construction** pg 597; **Interior Design -- Home Furnishings** pg 2904

Florist Trade —pg 2434

Flowers —See **Gardening and Horticulture -- Florist Trade** pg 2434

Fluid Mechanics —See **Engineering -- Hydraulic Engineering** pg 2087; **Physics -- Analytic and Experimental Mechanics** pg 4427

Folk Music —See **Folklore** pg 2318; **Music** pg 4098

Folklore —pg 2318; see also History(General) pg 2609; Literature pg 3357; Sociology -- Manners and Customs pg 5267

Food and Food Industry —pg 2325; see also Agriculture pg 42; Home Economics pg 2788; Restaurants pg 5070

Food Production —See **Agriculture -- Crop Production and Soil** pg 3475; see also Food and Food Industry pg 2325

Football —See **Recreation, Leisure -- Sports** pg 4881

Footwear —See **Clothing Industry and Fashion** pg 1081; see also Leather and Fur Industry pg 3183

Foreign Affairs —See **International Relations** pg 4514; see also Law -- International Law pg 3122

Foreign Trade —See **Business -- Commerce** pg 821; see also Economics -- International Economics pg 1632

Forensic Medicine —See **Medical Science and Technology -- Forensic Medicine, Medical Jurisprudence** pg 3739

Forensic Medicine, Medical Jurisprudence —pg 3739

Forestry —pg 2373; see also Environmental Issues -- Conservation and Natural Resources pg 2185; Gardening and Horticulture pg 2407; Paper and Pulp Industry pg 4232

Franchises —See **Business** pg 636

Fraternities —See **Societies and Clubs** pg 5228

Freight —See **Transportation** pg 5375; see also Aeronautics, Astronautics pg 3; Business -- Commerce pg 821; Transportation - Ships and Shipping pg 5447; Transportation -- Railroads pg 5429

French Studies —See **History(General) History of Europe** pg 2671; **Literature** pg 3357

Frozen Foods —See **Food and Food Industry** pg 2325

Fruit —See **Agriculture -- Crop Production and Soil** pg 161; **Food and Food Industry** pg 2325; **Gardening and Horticulture** pg 2407

Fuel —See **Petroleum and Natural Gas** pg 4248; see also Energy pg 1930; Engineering -- Electricity, Electrical Engineering, Electronics pg 2034

Fund Raising —See **Philanthropy** pg 4334; see also Sociology -- Social Services and Welfare pg 5269

Funeral Service —pg 2406

Fungi —See **Biology -- Mycology** pg 574

Fur —See **Leather and Fur Industry** pg 3183

Furniture —See **Interior Design -- Home Furnishings** pg 2904; see also Antiques pg 248; Building and Construction -- Carpentry and Woodwork pg 633; Interior Design pg 2898

Galleries —See **Museums and Galleries** pg 4083

SUBJECT CROSS REFERENCES

Gambling –See **Recreation, Leisure -- Games and Amusements** pg 4856; see also Psychology pg 4570; Public Administration pg 4623

Games and Amusements –pg 4856; see also Children and Youth Interests pg 1059

Gardening and Horticulture –pg 2407

Gastroenterology –pg 3743

Gay/Lesbian –See **Homosexuality** pg 2793

Genealogy and Heraldry –pg 2436; see also History(General) pg 2609

General Interest –pg 2484

General Interest-Africa –pg 2497

General Interest-Asia –pg 2501

General Interest-Australia and Oceania –pg 2510

General Interest-Central America –pg 2511

General Interest-Europe –pg 2513

General Interest-Middle East –pg 2525

General Interest-North America –pg 2526

General Interest-South America –pg 2551

General Management –pg 858

General Management and Administration –See **Business -- General Management** pg 858

General Practice –See **Medical Science and Technology -- Family Practice** pg 3736

General Reference Books –See **Encyclopedias and General Reference Books** pg 1923

Genetic Engineering –See **Medical Science and Technology -- Biotechnology** pg 3685; see also Biology -- Genetics pg 541

Genetics –pg 541

Geochemistry –See **Chemistry** pg 958

Geodesy –See **Earth Sciences -- Geophysics** pg 1402; **Geography** pg 2553

Geography –pg 2553; see also Travel and Tourism pg 5458

Geology –pg 1364

Geophysics –pg 1402

Geriatrics –pg 3748; see also Senior Citizens pg 5177

Germanic Studies –See **History(General) -- History of Europe** pg 2671; **Literature** pg 3357

Gifted Children –See **Education -- Special Education and Rehabilitation** pg 1874

Gifts, Toys –pg 2583; see also Glass and Ceramics pg 2585; Recreation, Leisure -- Games and Amusements pg 4856; The Arts -- Crafts and Decorative Arts pg 369

Glass and Ceramics –pg 2585; see also The Arts -- Crafts and Decorative Arts pg 369

Golf –See **Recreation, Leisure -- Sports** pg 4881

Government –See **Public Administration** pg 4623; see also Political Science pg 4461

Government Employees –See **Public Administration -- Civil Service** pg 4701

Graphic Arts –pg 376; see also Printing Industry pg 4563

Grocery Trade –See **Food and Food Industry** pg 2325

Guns –See **Recreation, Leisure -- Sports** pg 4881; see also Military and Defense pg 4033

Gymnastics –See **Recreation, Leisure -- Sports** pg 4881

Gynecology and Obstetrics –pg 3755

Handicrafts –See **The Arts -- Crafts and Decorative Arts** pg 369

Hardware –pg 1264; **Household Hardware and Appliances** pg 2810; see also Building and Construction pg 597

Hazardous Waste –See **Environmental Issues -- Pollution and Waste Management** pg 2222; see also Environmental Issues pg 2159

Health and Personal Fitness –pg 2595; see also Physical Education and Training pg 1854; Recreation, Leisure -- Sports pg 4881

Hearing Disorders –See **Medical Science and Technology -- Otorhinolaryngology** pg 3885; **Physically Impaired** pg 4382

Heat –pg 4430

Heating, Plumbing, and Refrigeration –pg 2602; see also Electricity, Electrical Engineering, Electronics pg 2034; Household Hardware and Appliances pg 2810

Helicopters –See **Aeronautics, Astronautics** pg 3

Helminthology –See **Zoology** pg 5572

Hematologic Diseases –See **Medical Science and Technology -- Hematology** pg 3769

Hematology –pg 3769; see also Biology -- Physiology pg 577; Medical Science and Technology -- Cardiology pg 3697; Medical Science and Technology -- Internal Medicine pg 3794

Hemodialysis –See **Medical Science and Technology -- Hematology** pg 3769

Heraldry –See **Genealogy and Heraldry** pg 2436

Herbs and Spices –See **Food and Food Industry** pg 2325; see also Gardening and Horticulture pg 2407

Heredity –See **Biology -- Genetics** pg 541

Higher Education –pg 1806

Hinduism –pg 5040

Histology –See **Biology -- Cytology and Histology** pg 531

History of Africa –pg 2636

History of Asia –pg 2644

History of Australia and Oceania –pg 2668

History of Europe –pg 2671

History of North, South, and Central America –pg 2717

History of the Middle East –pg 2767

History(General) –pg 2609

Hobbies –pg 2770; see also Recreation, Leisure -- Sports pg 4881; Sewing and Needlework pg 5182; The Arts -- Crafts and Decorative Arts pg 369

Hockey –See **Recreation, Leisure -- Sports** pg 4881

Home and Gardening Publications –See **Gardening and Horticulture** pg 2407

Home Computing –See **Computers -- Microcomputers, Personal Computers** pg 1265

Home Economics –pg 2788; see also Family and Marriage pg 2276

Home Furnishings –pg 2904; see also Building and Construction -- Carpentry and Woodwork pg 633; Interior Design pg 2898

Homeopathy –pg 3774

Homosexuality –pg 2793

Hormones –See **Endocrinology** pg 3726; see also Biology -- Biochemistry pg 479; Biology -- Physiology pg 577

Horse Racing –See **Horses and Horsemanship** pg 2796; see also Recreation, Leisure -- Sports pg 4881

Horses and Horsemanship –pg 2796; see also Recreation, Leisure -- Sports pg 4881

Horticulture –See **Gardening and Horticulture** pg 2407; see also Agriculture -- Crop Production and Soil pg 161; Biology -- Botany pg 496; Forestry pg 2373

SUBJECT CROSS REFERENCES

Hospital Administration –See **Medical Science and Technology -- Hospital Administration and Medical Centers** pg 3775

Hospital Administration and Medical Centers –pg 3775

Hospitals –See **Medical Science and Technology -- Hospital Administration and Medical Centers** pg 3775

Hotels/Motels –pg 2803; see also Travel and Tourism pg 5458; see also Restaurants pg 5070

Household Hardware and Appliances –pg 2810; see also Electricity, Electrical Engineering, Electronics pg 2034; Heating, Plumbing, and Refrigeration pg 2602

Housing and Urban Development –pg 2812; see also Building and Construction pg 597; Real Estate pg 4833

Human Sexuality –See **Sexual Life** pg 5186

Humane Society –See **Animal Welfare** pg 225

Humanities –pg 2841; see also Social Sciences pg 5189; The Arts pg 311

Hunting –See **Recreation, Leisure -- Outdoor Life** pg 4868

Hydraulic Engineering –pg 2087; see also Earth Sciences -- Hydrology pg 1412; Energy pg 1930; Water Resources pg 5528

Hydrobiology –See **Biology -- Marine Biology** pg 552; see also Earth Sciences -- Oceanography pg 1445

Hydrology –pg 1412; see also Engineering -- Hydraulic Engineering pg 2087; Water Resources pg 5528

Hygiene –See **Industrial Health and Safety** pg 2858; **Public Health and Safety** pg 4763

Hypertension –See **Medical Science and Technology -- Cardiology** pg 3697; see also Medical Science and Technology -- Internal Medicine pg 3794

Hypnosis –pg 2857

Immigration –See **Emigration and Immigration** pg 1918

Immunology –See **Medical Science and Technology -- Allergy and Immunology** pg 3662

Imports/Exports –See **Business -- Commerce** pg 821

Income Tax –See **Public Administration -- Public Finance and Taxation** pg 4708; see also Business -- Accounting pg 735

Industrial Arts –See **Education -- Vocational Education** pg 1909; see also Science and Technology pg 5078

Industrial Design –See **Engineering -- Industrial Engineering and Design** pg 2096; see also Manufacturing pg 3475

Industrial Engineering and Design –pg 2096

Industrial Health and Safety –pg 2858

Industrial Medicine –See **Industrial Health and Safety** pg 2858

Industry –See **Economics -- Industry and Production** pg 1596

Industry and Production –pg 1596

Infectious Diseases –See **Medical Science and Technology -- Communicable Diseases** pg 3711; see also Medical Science and Technology -- Epidemiology pg 3733; Public Health and Safety pg 4763

Information Retrieval –See **Library and Information Sciences** pg 3186

Information Science –See **Library and Information Sciences** pg 3186

Inheritance –See **Law -- Estate Planning** pg 3117

Inorganic Chemistry –pg 1035

Insecticide –See **Pest Control** pg 4243

Insects –See **Zoology -- Entomology** pg 5604; see also Pest Control pg 4243

Insulation –See **Building and Construction** pg 597; see also Engineering -- Electricity, Electrical Engineering, Electronics pg 2034

Insurance –pg 2872

Insurance Law –See **Insurance** pg 2872; **Law -- Corporate Law** pg 3094

Integrated Circuits –See **Engineering -- Electricity, Electrical Engineering, Electronics** pg 2034

Intellectual Property –See **Copyright, Intellectual Property** pg 1300

Intensive Care –See **Medical Science and Technology** pg 3543; see also Medical Science and Technology -- Nursing pg 3849

Interior Design –pg 2898; see also Architecture pg 286

Internal Medicine –pg 3794

International Assistance and Development –pg 2907; see also Economics -- International Economics pg 1632; Sociology -- Social Services and Welfare pg 5269

International Economics –pg 1632

International Law –pg 3122; see also Political Science -- International Relations pg 4514

International Relations –pg 4514; see also History(General) pg 2609; Law -- International Law pg 3122; Military and Defense pg 4033

Invertebrates/Vertebrates –See **Zoology** pg 5572

Investing –See **Business -- Investments** pg 890

Investments –pg 890; see also Business -- Banking and Finance pg 768

Irish Slavonic Studies –See **History(General) -- History of Europe** pg 2671; **Literature** pg 3357

Irish Studies –See **History(General) -- History of Europe** pg 2671; **Literature** pg 3357

Irrigation –See **Engineering -- Hydraulic Engineering** pg 2087; see also Agriculture -- Crop Production and Soil pg 161

Islam –See **Religion and Theology -- Islam, Bahaism, Theosophy** pg 5041

Islam, Bahaism, Theosophy –pg 5041

Jails –See **Law -- Law Enforcement and Criminology** pg 3156

Jewelry –pg 2913

Journalism –pg 2917; see also Communication -- Broadcasting pg 1125; Publishing pg 4811

Judaism –pg 5045; see also Ethnic Interests pg 2253

Judges –See **Law -- Judicial Systems** pg 3138

Judicial Ethics –See **Law -- Judicial Systems** pg 3138

Judicial Statistics –See **Law -- Judicial Systems** pg 3138

Judicial Systems –pg 3138

Judo/Karate –See **Recreation, Leisure -- Sports** pg 4881; see also Health and Personal Fitness pg 2595

Juvenile Delinquency –See **Law -- Law Enforcement and Criminology** pg 3156; see also Sociology -- Social Services and Welfare pg 5269

Kidneys –See **Medical Science and Technology -- Urology and Nephrology** pg 3987

Kindergarten –See **Education -- Early Childhood and Primary Education** pg 1802

Knitting –See **Sewing and Needlework** pg 5182; see also Textiles pg 5347

SUBJECT CROSS REFERENCES

Korean Studies –See **History(General) -- History of Asia** pg 2644; see also Literature pg 3357

Labels/Labelling –See **Packaging** pg 4217

Labor –pg 1642; see also Business -- Personnel Management pg 938; Industrial Health and Safety pg 2858

Labor Law –pg 3143; see also Law pg 2926; see also Economics -- Labor pg 1642

Labor Unions –See **Economics -- Labor** pg 1642

LAN (Local Area Networks) –See **Computers -- Computer Networks** pg 1240

Land –See **Economics** pg 1459; **Environmental Issues -- Conservation and Natural Resources** pg 2185; **Public Administration** pg 4623; **Real Estate** pg 4833; see also Geography pg 2553

Landscape Architecture –See **Gardening and Horticulture** pg 2407

Language –See **Linguistics** pg 3260

Lasers –See **Physics -- Light, Optics, Radiation** pg 4432; see also Chemistry pg 958; Engineering pg 1963; Medical Science and Technology -- Surgery pg 3957; Physics pg 4395

Latin American Studies –See **History(General) -- History of North, South, and Central America** pg 2717; see also Literature pg 3357

Laundry –See **Chemistry -- Chemical Technology** pg 1020; see also Textiles pg 5347

Law –pg 2926; see also Public Administration pg 4623

Law Enforcement –See **Law -- Law Enforcement and Criminology** pg 2926

Law Enforcement and Criminology –pg 3156

Law Offices –See **Law** pg 2926; see also Business -- General Management pg 858

Learning Disabilities –See **Education -- Special Education and Rehabilitation** pg 1874

Leather and Fur Industry –pg 3183; see also Clothing Industry and Fashion pg 1081

Legal Aid –pg 3179

Legislation –See **Law** pg 2926; see also Public Administration pg 4623

Leisure –See **Recreation, Leisure** pg 4848

Leukemia –See **Medical Science and Technology -- Neoplasma, Neoplastic** pg 3808; see also Medical Science and Technology -- Internal Medicine pg 3794

Library and Information Sciences –pg 3186; see also Archives pg 2478; Bibliographies pg 406

Life/Death –See **Philosophy** pg 4339

Light, Optics, Radiation –pg 4432

Linguistics –pg 3260; see also Literature pg 3357

Liquor –See **Food and Food Industry -- Beverage Industry** pg 2363

Literacy –See **Education -- Special Education and Rehabilitation** pg 1874

Literary and Political Reviews –pg 3337; see also Literature pg 3357

Literary Criticism –See **Literary and Political Reviews** pg 3337

Literary Theory –See **Literary and Political Reviews** pg 3337

Literature –pg 3357; see also Linguistics pg 3260; Literary and Political Reviews pg 3337; Romance and Adventure pg 5073

Livestock and Poultry –pg 204

Local Area Networks –See **Computers -- Computer Networks** pg 1240

Local Government –See **Political Science** pg 4461; **Public Administration** pg 4623; **Public Administration** pg 4708

Lotteries –See **Public Administration** pg 4623

Lumber and Wood –pg 2399; see also Paper and Pulp Industry pg 4232

Lutheran –See **Religion and Theology -- Protestantism** pg 5054

Machinery –See **Engineering -- Mechanical Engineering and Machinery** pg 2108

Macroeconomics –See **Economics -- Economic Theory** pg 1589; see also Economics pg 1459; Economics -- International Economics pg 1632

Magic –See **Recreation, Leisure -- Games and Amusements** pg 4856; see also Parapsychology and Occultism pg 4240

Magnetic Resonance Imaging –See **Medical Science and Technology -- Radiology** pg 3938

Magnetism –pg 4443

Mainframe Computing –See **Computers -- Data Processing** pg 1255

Manners and Customs –pg 5267

Manufacturing –pg 3475; see also Industry and Production pg 1596

Maps and Mapmaking –See **Geography -- Cartography** pg 2580

Marine Biology –pg 552; see also Earth Sciences -- Oceanography pg 1445; Zoology pg 5572

Marine Engineering –See **Engineering** pg 1963

Marine Pollution –See **Environmental Issues -- Pollution and Waste Management** pg 2222

Marine Toxins –See **Biology -- Marine Biology** pg 552

Marines –See **Naval Science, Navigation** pg 4174

Maritime Law –pg 3180

Marketing –pg 920

Marriage –See **Family and Marriage** pg 2276

Marriage Law –See **Law -- Family Law** pg 3119

Martial Arts –See **Health and Personal Fitness** pg 2595

Marxism –See **Political Science -- Socialism, Communism, Anarchism, Utopianism** pg 4539; see also Sociology pg 5237

Masonry –See **Building and Construction** pg 597

Materials Engineering and Mechanics –pg 2100

Mathematical Geography –See **Geography** pg 2553

Mathematics –pg 3490

Matrimonial Actions –See **Law -- Family Law** pg 3119

Meat –See **Food and Food Industry** pg 2325; see also Agriculture -- Livestock and Poultry pg 204

Mechanical Engineering and Machinery –pg 2108

Media –See **Communication** pg 1103; see also Journalism pg 2917

Medical Centers –See **Medical Science and Technology -- Hospital Administration and Medical Centers** pg 3775

Medical Jurisprudence –See **Medical Science and Technology -- Forensic Medicine, Medical Jurisprudence** pg 3739

Medical Malpractice –See **Law** pg 2926; see also Medical Science and Technology pg 3543

Medical Personnel –See **Medical Science and Technology -- Physicians and Medical Personnel** pg 3912

Medical Science and Technology –pg 3543; see also Public Health and Safety pg 4763

SUBJECT CROSS REFERENCES

Medieval Studies –See **History(General) -- History of Europe** pg 2671; see also Classical Studies pg 1073

Meetings –See **Business** pg 636

Memory –See **Psychology** pg 4570

Men's Interests –pg 3994

Mental Health –See **Medical Science and Technology -- Psychiatry** pg 3918; **Psychology** pg 4570; **Public Health and Safety** pg 4763; **Sociology -- Social Services and Welfare** pg 5269

Mentally Disabled –See **Education -- Special Education and Rehabilitation** pg 1874; see also Medical Science and Technology -- Psychiatry pg 3918; Psychology pg 4570

Mergers/Acquisitions –See **Business** pg 636

Metabolic Diseases –See **Medical Science and Technology -- Allergy and Immunology** pg 3662

Metallurgy –See **Metals and Metallurgy** pg 3996

Metals and Metallurgy –pg 3996; see also Mines and Mining Engineering pg 2132

Meteorology –pg 1419

Methodist –See **Religion and Theology -- Protestantism** pg 5054

Metrology and Standardization –pg 4029

Microbiology –pg 558

Microcomputers –See **Computers -- Microcomputers, Personal Computers** pg 1265

Microcomputers, Personal Computers –pg 1265

Microscopy –pg 572

Midwifery –See **Medical Science and Technology -- Gynecology and Obstetrics** pg 3755

Migration –See **Emigration and Immigration** pg 1918; **Population Studies** pg 4549; see also Economics -- Labor pg 1642; Zoology pg 5572

Military Administration –See **Military and Defense** pg 4033

Military and Defense –pg 4033; see also Political Science -- International Relations pg 4514

Military History –See **Military and Defense** pg 4033

Military Law –pg 3182

Military Medicine –See **Medical Science and Technology** pg 3543; see also Military and Defense pg 4033

Milling –See **Agriculture -- Feed Grain and Milling** pg 199

Mineralogy –pg 1437

Mines and Mining Engineering –pg 2132; see also Earth Sciences -- Mineralogy pg 1437; Metals and Metallurgy pg 4026; Petroleum and Natural Gas pg 4248

Minicomputers –pg 1273; see also Computers -- Microcomputers, Personal Computers pg 1265

Mobile Homes –See **Building and Construction** pg 597; **Housing and Urban Development** pg 2812; **Transportation** pg 5375

Money –See **Business -- Banking and Finance** pg 768; **Economics** pg 1459

Monuments –See **History(General)** pg 2609; see also Architecture pg 286; The Arts -- Art pg 335

Mormons –See **Religion and Theology** pg 4931

Morphology –See **Biology -- Botany** pg 496

Motels –See **Hotels/Motels** pg 2803

Motion Picture –pg 4062

Motorcycles –pg 4080

Mountain Climbing –See **Recreation, Leisure -- Outdoor Life** pg 4868; see also Recreation, Leisure -- Sports pg 4881

Movies –See **Motion Picture** pg 4062

Multiple Sclerosis –See **Medical Science and Technology -- Neurology** pg 3825

Muscular Dystrophy –See **Medical Science and Technology -- Musculoskeletal System** pg 3802; see also Medical Science and Technology -- Neurology pg 3825

Musculoskeletal System –pg 3802

Museums and Galleries –pg 4083; see also Natural History pg 4161; The Arts -- Art pg 335

Music –pg 4098; see also Computers -- Computer Music pg 1240; Sound Recordings and Systems pg 5315; The Arts -- Performing Arts pg 383

Music Therapy –See **Medical Science and Technology** pg 3543; **Music** pg 4098; see also Psychology pg 4570

Mutual Funds –See **Business -- Investments** pg 890; see also Business -- Banking and Finance pg 768

Mycology –pg 574; see also Biology -- Botany pg 496

Mysticism –See **Parapsychology and Occultism** pg 4240; see also Literature pg 3357; Religion and Theology pg 4931

Mythology –See **Folklore** pg 2318

Narcotics –See **Drug Abuse and Alcoholism** pg 1338; see also Law -- Law Enforcement and Criminology pg 3156; Pharmacy and Pharmacology pg 4288

Natural Gas –See **Petroleum and Natural Gas** pg 4248

Natural History –pg 4161; see also Biology pg 4570; Environmental Issues -- Conservation and Natural Resources pg 2185; Environmental Issues -- Ecology pg 2185

Natural Resources –See **Environmental Issues -- Conservation and Natural Resources** pg 2185

Naturalist –See **Natural History** pg 4161; see also Environmental Issues -- Ecology pg 2210

Naval Architecture –See **Architecture** pg 286; **Naval Science and Navigation** pg 4174

Naval Science, Navigation –pg 4174; see also Transportation -- Ships and Shipping pg 5447

Navigation –See **Naval Science, Navigation** pg 4174

Navy –See **Naval Science, Navigation** pg 4174

Needlework –See **Sewing and Needlework** pg 5182

Neoplasma –See **Medical Science and Technology -- Neoplasma, Neoplastic** pg 3808

Neoplasma, Neoplastic –pg 3808; see also Medical Science and Technology -- Radiology pg 3938

Neoplastic –See **Medical Science and Technology -- Neoplasma, Neoplastic** pg 3808

Nephrology –See **Medical Science and Technology -- Urology and Nephrology** pg 3987

Neural Networks –See **Computers -- Artificial Intelligence** pg 1210

Neurology –pg 3825; see also Medical Science and Technology -- Psychiatry pg 3918; Psychology pg 4570

New Age Publications –pg 4185

Newspapers –pg 5625

Noise Control –See **Environmental Issues** pg 2159

North America –See **General Interest -- General Interest-North America** pg 2526; **History(General) -- History of North, South, and Central America** pg 2717

Nuclear Engineering –pg 2153

Nuclear Medicine –See **Medical Science and Technology -- Internal Medicine** pg 3794; Medical Science and Technology -- Radiology pg 3938

SUBJECT CROSS REFERENCES

Nuclear Physics –pg 4445

Nuclear Waste –See **Environmental Issues -- Pollution and Waste Management** pg 2222

Numismatics –pg 2779

Nursing –pg 3849; see also Medical Science and Technology -- Surgery pg 3849

Nursing Homes –See **Medical Science and Technology -- Hospital Administration and Medical Centers** pg 3775; see also Sociology -- Social Services and Welfare pg 5269

Nutrition and Dietetics –pg 4186; see also Food and Food Industry pg 2325

Nutritional Disorders –See **Nutrition and Dietetics** pg 4186

Obstetrics –See **Medical Science and Technology -- Gynecology and Obstetrics** pg 3755

Occultism –See **Parapsychology and Occultism** pg 4240

Occupational Health –See **Industrial Health and Safety** pg 2858

Occupational Therapy –See **Industrial Health and Safety** pg 2858; see also Education -- Special Education and Rehabilitation pg 1874; Medical Science and Technology -- Psychiatry pg 3918

Occupations and Careers –pg 4201; see also Economics -- Labor pg 1642; Education -- Special Aspects of Education pg 1874

Ocean Engineering –See **Engineering -- Hydraulic Engineering** pg 2087; see also Earth Sciences -- Oceanography pg 1445

Oceania –See **General Interest -- General Interest-Australia and Oceania** pg 2510; see also History(General) -- History of Australia and Oceania pg 2668

Oceanography –pg 1445

Office Equipment and Services –pg 4210; see also Computers pg 1169

Oil –See **Petroleum and Natural Gas** pg 4248

Oncology –See **Medical Science and Technology -- Neoplasma, Neoplastic** pg 3808

Online Computing and Information –pg 1274

Opera –See **The Arts -- Performing Arts** pg 383; see also Music pg 4098

Ophthalmology –pg 3871

Optical Storage, CD-ROM Applications –pg 1276

Optics –See **Physics -- Light, Optics, Radiation** pg 4432

Optometry –pg 4214

Oral Surgery –See **Medical Science and Technology -- Surgery** pg 3957; see also Dentistry pg 1314

Organic Chemistry –pg 1038

Oriental Studies –See **History(General) -- History of Asia** pg 2644; see also Literature pg 3357

Ornithology –pg 5614; see also Natural History pg 4161

Orthodontics –See **Dentistry** pg 1314

Orthopedics –pg 3880

Otorhinolaryngology –pg 3885

Outdoor Life –pg 4868; see also Environmental Issues -- Conservation and Natural Resources pg 2185; Fish and Fisheries pg 2293; Recreation, Leisure -- Sports pg 4881

Pacific Studies –See **History(General) -- History of Australia and Oceania** pg 2671; see also Literature pg 3357

Packaging –pg 4217

Pain –See **Medical Science and Technology -- Neurology** pg 3825

Paints and Painting –pg 4222

Paleontology –pg 4226

Paper and Pulp Industry –pg 4232

Parachuting –See **Recreation, Leisure -- Sports** pg 4881

Paramedics –See **Medical Science and Technology -- Emergency Medicine** pg 3723

Parapsychology and Occultism –pg 4240

Parenting –See **Family and Marriage** pg 2276

Parks –See **Environmental Issues -- Conservation and Natural Resources** pg 2185; Recreation, Leisure pg 4848

Parks and Recreation –pg 4705; see also Environmental Issues -- Conservation and Natural Resources pg 2185

Parliament/House of Commons –See **Public Administration** pg 4623; see also Political Science pg 4461

Patents –See **Copyright, Intellectual Property** pg 1300

Pathology –pg 3891; see also Medical Science and Technology -- Anatomy pg 3678

Pediatric Surgery –See **Medical Science and Technology -- Pediatrics** pg 3899; see also Medical Science and Technology -- Surgery pg 3957

Pediatrics –pg 3899

Penology –See **Law -- Law Enforcement and Criminology** pg 3156

Pensions –See **Business -- Investments** pg 890; see also Economics -- Labor pg 1642; Insurance pg 2872

Performing Arts –pg 383; see also Motion Picture pg 4062; Music pg 4098; The Arts -- Dance pg 1310; Theater pg 5361

Perfumes –See **Beauty and Cosmetics** pg 402; see also Chemistry -- Chemical Technology pg 1020

Perinatology –See **Medical Science and Technology -- Gynecology and Obstetrics** pg 3755; see also Medical Science and Technology -- Pediatrics pg 3899

Personal Computers –See **Computers -- Microcomputers, Personal Computers** pg 1265

Personal Hygiene –See **Health and Personal Fitness** pg 2595

Personnel Management –pg 938; see also Economics -- Labor pg 1642

Pest Control –pg 4243

Petroleum and Natural Gas –pg 4248; see also Energy pg 1930; Engineering -- Mines and Mining Engineering pg 2132

Petrology –pg 1458

Pets –pg 4285

Pharmaceutical Industry –See **Pharmacy and Pharmacology** pg 4288

Pharmacy and Pharmacology –pg 4288; see also Medical Science and Technology -- Toxicology pg 3978

Philanthropy –pg 4334; see also Sociology -- Social Services and Welfare pg 5269

Philately –pg 2784

Philology –See **Linguistics** pg 3260; see also Classical Studies pg 1073

Philosophy –pg 4339

Phonetics –See **Linguistics** pg 3260

Photography and Video –pg 4366

Physical and Theoretical Chemistry –pg 1049

Physical Education –See **Education -- Physical Education and Training** pg 2595; **Education -- Physical Education and Training** pg 1854; see also Health and Personal Fitness pg 2595

Physical Education and Training –pg 1854

Physical Fitness –See **Health and Personal Fitness** pg 2595

Physical Therapy –pg 4378

Physical Training –See **Education -- Physical Education and Training** pg 1854

SUBJECT CROSS REFERENCES

Physically Impaired –pg 4382; see also Education -- Special Education and Rehabilitation pg 1874; Sociology -- Social Services and Welfare pg 5269

Physician's Assistants –See **Medical Science and Technology -- Physicians and Medical Personnel** pg 3912

Physicians –See **Medical Science and Technology -- Physicians and Medical Personnel** pg 3912; see also Medical Science and Technology -- Family Practice pg 3736

Physicians and Medical Personnel –pg 3912

Physics –pg 4395

Physiology –pg 577

Phytopathology –See **Biology -- Botany** pg 496; **Gardening and Horticulture** pg 2407

Planned Parenthood –See **Birth Control** pg 587; see also Family and Marriage pg 2276

Plant Breeding –See **Biology -- Botany** pg 496; see also Agriculture -- Crop Production and Soil pg 161; Gardening and Horticulture pg 2407

Plant Culture –See **Gardening and Horticulture** pg 2407

Plastic Surgery –See **Medical Science and Technology -- Surgery** pg 3957

Plastics –pg 4453; see also Engineering -- Materials Engineering and Mechanics pg 2100

Plays –See **Literature** pg 3357; **The Arts -- Performing Arts** pg 383; **Theater** pg 5361

Plumbing –See **Heating, Plumbing, and Refrigeration** pg 2602

Podiatry –pg 3917

Poetry –pg 3459; see also Literary and Political Reviews pg 3337

Political Reviews –See **Literary and Political Reviews** pg 3337

Political Science –pg 4461; see also Military and Defense pg 4033; Public Administration pg 4623

Polling –See **Public Administration** pg 4623; see also Sociology pg 5237; Statistics pg 5320

Pollution and Waste Management –pg 2222; see also Earth Sciences -- Ecology pg 2210; Environmental Issues -- Ecology pg 2210

Polymers –See **Chemistry -- Organic Chemistry** pg 1038; see also Paints and Painting pg 4222; Plastics pg 4453

Population Studies –pg 4549; see also Birth Control pg 587; Statistics pg 5320

Portable Computers –See **Computers -- Microcomputers, Personal Computers** pg 1265

Postage Stamps –See **Hobbies -- Philately** pg 2784

Postal Communications –pg 1144; see also Public Administration -- Civil Service pg 4701

Pottery –See **Glass and Ceramics** pg 2585

Poultry –See **Agriculture -- Livestock and Poultry** pg 204

Poverty –See **Sociology -- Social Services and Welfare** pg 5269; see also International Assistance and Development pg 2907

Power –See **Engineering -- Electricity, Electrical Engineering, Electronics** pg 2034

Powerlifting –See **Health and Personal Fitness** pg 2595; see also Recreation, Leisure -- Sports pg 4881

Practical Theology –See **Religion and Theology** pg 4931

Presbyterian –See **Religion and Theology -- Protestantism** pg 5054

Preschool Education –See **Education -- Early Childhood and Primary Education** pg 1802

Preventive Medicine –See **Medical Science and Technology** pg 3543; see also Public Health and Safety pg 4763

Primary Care –See **Medical Science and Technology -- Family Practice** pg 3736

Primary Education –See **Education -- Early Childhood and Primary Education** pg 1802

Printing Industry –pg 4563; see also The Arts -- Graphic Arts pg 376

Prisons –See **Law -- Law Enforcement and Criminology** pg 3156

Private Schools –See **Education** pg 1720

Probation –See **Law -- Law Enforcement and Criminology** pg 3156

Production –See **Economics -- Industry and Production** pg 1596

Programs and Programming –pg 1277; see also Computers -- Software pg 1283

Protestantism –pg 5054

Psychiatry –pg 3918; see also Medical Science and Technology -- Neurology pg 3825; Psychology pg 4570

Psychoanalysis –See **Medical Science and Technology -- Psychiatry** pg 3918; **Psychology** pg 4570

Psychology –pg 4570; see also Medical Science and Technology -- Psychiatry pg 3918; Sociology pg 5237

Psychopathology –See **Medical Science and Technology -- Psychiatry** pg 3918

Psychosomatic Medicine –See **Medical Science and Technology** pg 3543; **Psychology** pg 4570

Psychotherapy –See **Medical Science and Technology -- Psychiatry** pg 3918; see also Family and Marriage pg 2276; Psychology pg 4570

PTA –See **Education -- School Organization and Administration** pg 1859

Public Administration –pg 4623; see also Political Science pg 4461

Public Affairs –See **Public Administration** pg 4623

Public Finance and Taxation –pg 4708; see also Law pg 2926

Public Health and Safety –pg 4763; see also Environmental Issues -- Pollution and Waste Management pg 2222; Medical Science and Technology -- Communicable Diseases pg 3711; Medical Science and Technology -- Epidemiology pg 3733

Public Opinion –See **Sociology** pg 5237

Public Relations –See **Business -- Advertising and Public Relations** pg 753

Public Transportation –See **Transportation** pg 5375; see also Public Administration pg 4623

Public Utilities –pg 4759

Publishing –See **Computers -- Desktop Publishing** pg 1263; Journalism pg 2917

Pulp Industry –See **Paper and Pulp Industry** pg 4232

Puppetry –See **The Arts -- Performing Arts** pg 383

Purchasing –pg 948

Puzzles –See **Recreation, Leisure -- Games and Amusements** pg 4856

Quarries –See **Engineering -- Mines and Mining Engineering** pg 2132; see also Industrial Health and Safety pg 2858

Race Relations –See **Sociology** pg 5237; see also Ethnic Interests pg 2253

Radiation –See **Physics -- Light, Optics, Radiation** pg 4432

Radio –See **Communication -- Broadcasting** pg 1125

xxxiii

SUBJECT CROSS REFERENCES

Radiology –pg 3938; see also Medical Science and Technology -- Neoplasma, Neoplastic pg 3808; Medical Science and Technology -- Nuclear Medicine pg 3847

Railroads –pg 5429

Rationalism –See **Philosophy** pg 4339

Real Estate –pg 4833; see also Housing and Urban Development pg 2812

Record Industry –See **Music** pg 4098; see also Communication -- Broadcasting pg 1125; Sound Recordings and Systems pg 5315

Recreation, Leisure –pg 4848; see also Hobbies pg 2770; Travel and Tourism pg 5458

Recreational Vehicles –See **Transportation** pg 5375; see also Recreation, Leisure pg 4848

Recycling –See **Environmental Issues -- Pollution and Waste Management** pg 2222

Red Cross –See **Sociology -- Social Services and Welfare** pg 5269; see also Medical Science and Technology pg 3543

Reformed Church –See **Religion and Theology -- Protestantism** pg 5054

Refrigeration –See **Heating, Plumbing, and Refrigeration** pg 2602

Regional Planning –See **Housing and Urban Development** pg 2812

Rehabilitation –See **Education -- Special Education and Rehabilitation** pg 1874; **Physically Impaired** pg 4382; see also Drug Abuse and Alcoholism pg 1338; Physical Therapy pg 4378; Sociology -- Social Services and Welfare pg 5269

Religion and Theology –pg 4931

Religious Education –See **Religion and Theology** pg 4931

Religious Music –See **Music** pg 4098

Research –See **Science and Technology** pg 5078; see also Education -- Higher Education pg 1806

Residential Homes –See **Housing and Urban Development** pg 2812

Resorts –See **Hotels/Motels** pg 2803; **Travel and Tourism** pg 5458

Respiratory System –pg 3947

Restaurants –pg 5070; see also Food and Food Industry pg 2325; Hotels/Motels pg 2803

Retail –pg 952

Rheumatology –See **Medical Science and Technology -- Musculoskeletal System** pg 3802; see also Pharmacy and Pharmacology pg 4288

Roads and Traffic –pg 5438

Robotics –See **Computers -- Artificial Intelligence** pg 1210; see also Computers -- Automation pg 1217

Roman Catholic Church –See **Religion and Theology -- Catholicism** pg 5022

Romance and Adventure –pg 5073; see also Literature pg 3357

Rubber –pg 5075

Rugby –See **Recreation, Leisure -- Sports** pg 4881

Running –See **Health and Personal Fitness** pg 2595

Safety –See **Industrial Health and Safety** pg 2858; see also Public Health and Safety pg 4763

Safety Engineering –See **Engineering -- Industrial Engineering and Design** pg 2096

Sailing –See **Boats and Boating** pg 591

Salary/Wages –See **Economics** pg 1459; **Economics -- Labor** pg 1642

Sanitation/Municipal Engineering –See **Environmental Issues -- Pollution and Waste Management** pg 2222; **Public Health and Safety** pg 4763; see also Environmental Issues -- Conservation and Natural Resources pg 2185; Environmental Issues -- Ecology pg 2210

Scholarships –See **Education -- Higher Education** pg 1806

School Counseling –See **Education -- Special Education and Rehabilitation** pg 1874

School Law/Legislation –See **Education -- School Organization and Administration** pg 1859

School Organization and Administration –pg 1859

Science –See **Science and Technology** pg 5078

Science and Technology –pg 5078; see also Chemistry -- Chemical Technology pg 1020; Engineering pg 1963

Science Fiction –See **Literature** pg 3357; see also Literary and Political Reviews pg 3337

Scuba Diving –See **Recreation, Leisure -- Sports** pg 4881

Sculpture –See **The Arts -- Art** pg 335; see also Architecture pg 286

Secondary Education –See **Education** pg 1720

Securities Law –See **Law -- Corporate Law** pg 3094

Security –See **Computers -- Computer Crimes and Security** pg 1225

Security Systems and Alarms –pg 5176; see also Engineering -- Electricity, Electrical Engineering, Electronics pg 2034

Sedimentology –See **Earth Sciences -- Geology** pg 1364; see also Earth Sciences -- Geophysics pg 1402

Seismology –See **Earth Sciences -- Geophysics** pg 1402

Semantics –See **Linguistics** pg 3260

Senior Citizens –pg 5177; see also Medical Science and Technology -- Geriatrics pg 3748; Sociology -- Social Services and Welfare pg 5269

Sewage –See **Environmental Issues -- Pollution and Waste Management** pg 2222; see also Water Resources pg 5528

Sewing and Needlework –pg 5182; see also Hobbies pg 2770; The Arts -- Crafts and Decorative Arts pg 369

Sexual Life –pg 5186

Sexually Transmitted Diseases –See **Medical Science and Technology -- Communicable Diseases** pg 3711; **Public Health and Safety** pg 4763

Ship Design –See **Engineering** pg 1459; **Naval Science, Navigation** pg 4174; see also Transportation -- Ships and Shipping pg 5447

Shipbuilding –See **Naval Science, Navigation** pg 4174; **Transportation -- Ships and Shipping** pg 5447

Ships and Shipping –pg 5447; see also Business -- Commerce pg 821; Naval Science, Navigation pg 4174

Shoes –See **Clothing Industry and Fashion** pg 1081

Simulation –pg 1282

Skiing –See **Recreation, Leisure -- Sports** pg 4881

Slavery –See **Civil Rights** pg 4503

Slavic Studies –See **History(General) -- History of Europe** pg 2671; **Literature** pg 3357

Small Business –See **Business** pg 636; see also Economics pg 1459

Smoking –See **Public Health and Safety** pg 4763; **Tobacco** pg 5372

Soap Operas –See **General Interest** pg 2484

Soccer –See **Recreation, Leisure -- Sports** pg 4881

Social Sciences –pg 5189; see also Humanities pg 2841

SUBJECT CROSS REFERENCES

Social Security —See **Sociology -- Social Services and Welfare** pg 5269; see also Economics -- Labor pg 1642; Insurance pg 2872

Social Services —See **Sociology -- Social Services and Welfare** pg 5269

Social Services and Welfare —pg 5269

Socialism —See **Political Science -- Socialism, Communism, Anarchism, Utopianism** pg 1589

Socialism, Communism, Anarchism, Utopianism —pg 4539

Societies and Clubs —pg 5228

Sociology —pg 5237

Software —pg 1283; see also Computer Industry and Industry Directories pg 1235; Programs and Programming pg 1277

Soil —See **Agriculture -- Crop Production and Soil** pg 161

Solar Energy —See **Energy** pg 1930; see also Engineering -- Mechanical Engineering and Machinery pg 2108

Sound —pg 4451

Sound Recordings and Systems —pg 5315; see also Engineering -- Electricity, Electrical Engineering, Electronics pg 2034; Music pg 4098

South America —See **General Interest -- General Interest-South America** pg 2551; **History(General) -- History of North, South, and Central America** pg 2717

Special Education —See **Education -- Special Education and Rehabilitation** pg 1874

Special Education and Rehabilitation —pg 1874

Spectroscopy —See **Physics -- Light, Optics, Radiation** pg 4432

Speech Disorders —See **Medical Science and Technology -- Otorhinolaryngology** pg 3885; see also Education -- Special Education and Rehabilitation pg 1874; Physically Impaired pg 4382

Speech Pathology —See **Physically Impaired** pg 4382; see also Education -- Special Education and Rehabilitation pg 1874

Speleology —See **Earth Sciences -- Geophysics** pg 1402

Sports —pg 4881; see also Recreation, Leisure -- Games and Amusements pg 4856; Recreation, Leisure -- Health and Personal Fitness pg 2595; Recreation, Leisure -- Outdoor Life pg 4868

Sports Medicine —pg 3953

Stained Glass —See **Glass and Ceramics** pg 2585

Standardization —See **Metrology and Standardization** pg 4029

State Government —See **Public Administration** pg 4623; see also Public Administration -- Public Finance and Taxation pg 4708

Statistics —pg 5320

Stomatology —See **Dentistry** pg 1314

Stress —See **Medical Science and Technology** pg 3543; **Psychology** pg 4570

Sugar —See **Agriculture -- Crop Production and Soil** pg 161; see also Food and Food Industry pg 2325

Surface Chemistry —See **Chemistry -- Physical and Theoretical Chemistry** pg 1049

Surgeons —See **Medical Science and Technology -- Physicians and Medical Personnel** pg 3912

Surgery —pg 3957

Surveying —See **Engineering -- Civil Engineering** pg 2018; **Geography** pg 2553

Swimming —See **Recreation, Leisure -- Sports** pg 4881

Tax Planning —See **Law -- Estate Planning** pg 3117

Taxation —See **Public Administration -- Public Finance and Taxation** pg 4708; see also Business -- Accounting pg 735; Law -- Estate Planning pg 3117

Taxidermy —See **Hobbies** pg 2770

Tea —See **Food and Food Industry -- Beverage Industry** pg 2363; see also Agriculture pg 42

Teaching and Curriculum —pg 1887

Teaching Materials —See **Education -- Teaching and Curriculum** pg 1887

Technical Education —See **Education -- Vocational Education** pg 1909

Technology —See **Science and Technology** pg 5078

Telecommunications —pg 1148

Telegraph —See **Communication -- Telecommunications** pg 1148

Telephone —See **Communication -- Telecommunications** pg 1148

Telephone Directories —See **Communication -- Telecommunications** pg 1148

Television —See **Communication -- Broadcasting** pg 1125

Tennis —See **Recreation, Leisure -- Sports** pg 4881

Textbooks —See **Education** pg 1720

Textiles —pg 5347; see also Clothing Industry and Fashion pg 1081

The Arts —pg 311

Theater —pg 5361; see also The Arts -- Performing Arts pg 383

Theology —See **Religion and Theology** pg 4931

Theoretical Chemistry —See **Chemistry -- Physical and Theoretical Chemistry** pg 1049

Theosophy —See **Religion and Theology -- Islam, Bahaism, Theosophy** pg 5041

Thrombosis —See **Medical Science and Technology -- Internal Medicine** pg 3794; see also Medical Science and Technology -- Cardiology pg 3697; Medical Science and Technology -- Hematology pg 3769; Medical Science and Technology -- Pathology pg 3891

Tobacco —pg 5372

Total Quality Management —See **Business -- General Management** pg 858; **Business -- Personnel Management** pg 938

Tourism —See **Travel and Tourism** pg 5458

Toxicology —pg 3978; see also Pharmacy and Pharmacology pg 4288

Toys —See **Gifts, Toys** pg 2583

Track and Field —See **Recreation, Leisure -- Sports** pg 4881

Trade —See **Business -- Commerce** pg 821

Trade Regulation —See **Business -- Commerce** pg 821; see also Law -- Corporate Law pg 3094

Trade Schools —See **Education -- Vocational Education** pg 1909

Trade Shows —See **Business -- Advertising and Public Relations** pg 753

Trade Unions —See **Economics -- Labor** pg 1642

Trademarks —See **Copyright, Intellectual Property** pg 1300

Traffic —See **Transportation -- Roads and Traffic** pg 5438

Transportation —pg 5375; see also Business -- Commerce pg 821

Travel and Tourism —pg 5458; see also Geography pg 2553; Recreation, Leisure pg 4848

Trees —See **Gardening and Horticulture** pg 2407; see also Forestry pg 2373

Tropical Diseases —See **Medical Science and Technology -- Tropical Medicine** pg 3985

Tropical Medicine —pg 3985

Trucks and Trucking —See **Transportation** pg 5375

Trustees —See **Law -- Estate Planning** pg 3117

SUBJECT CROSS REFERENCES

Trusts —See **Law -- Estate Planning** pg 3117

Ukrainian Studies —See **History(General) -- History of Europe** pg 2671; see also Literature pg 3357

Ultrafication —See **Medical Science and Technology -- Hematology** pg 3769

Ultrasonic Therapy —See **Medical Science and Technology -- Radiology** pg 3938

Ultrasound —See **Medical Science and Technology -- Radiology** pg 3938

Unemployment —See **Economics -- Labor** pg 1642; see also Law pg 2926

Unions —See **Economics -- Labor** pg 1642

Universities and Colleges —See **Education -- Higher Education** pg 1806; see also College and School Publications pg 1088

Urban Development —See **Housing and Urban Development** pg 2812

Urinary Tract —See **Medical Science and Technology -- Urology and Nephrology** pg 3987

Urology —See **Medical Science and Technology -- Urology and Nephrology** pg 3987

Urology and Nephrology —pg 3987

Utopianism —See **Political Science -- Socialism, Communism, Anarchism, Utopianism** pg 4539

Vacations —See **Travel and Tourism** pg 5458; see also Recreation,Leisure pg 4848

Veterans —See **Military and Defense** pg 4033; see also Naval Science, Navigation pg 4174

Veterinary Sciences —pg 5501; see also Zoology pg 5572

Video —See **Communication -- Broadcasting** pg 1125; **Photography and Video** pg 4366; see also Motion Picture pg 4062

Video Games/Arcades —See **Recreation, Leisure -- Games and Amusements** pg 4856

Virology —See **Biology -- Microbiology** pg 558

Virtual Reality —See **Computers -- Artificial Intelligence** pg 1210; see also Computers -- Automation pg 1217

Visual Arts —See **The Arts -- Art** pg 335

Vitamins —See **Nutrition and Dietetics** pg 4186

Vocational Education —pg 1909

Vocational Guidance —See **Education -- Vocational Education** pg 1909; see also Occupations and Careers pg 4201

Volcanoes —See **Earth Sciences -- Geophysics** pg 1402

Volunteer Work —See **Philanthropy** pg 4334

Voting —See **Political Science** pg 4461; see also Public Administration pg 4623

WAN (Wide Area Networks) —See **Computer** pg 1240

War —See **History(General)** pg 2609; see also Political Science pg 4461

Waste Management —See **Environmental Issues -- Pollution and Waste Management** pg 2222

Watches —See **Jewelry -- Clocks and Watches** pg 2916

Water Pollution —See **Environmental Issues -- Pollution and Waste Management** pg 2222; see also Water Resources pg 5528

Water Resources —pg 5528; see also Earth Sciences -- Hydrology pg 1412; Engineering -- Hydraulic Engineering pg 2087; Environmental Issues -- Conservation and Natural Resources pg 2185

Water Utilities —See **Public Administration -- Public Utilities** pg 4759; see also Water Resources pg 5528

Weaponry —See **Military and Defense** pg 4033

Weather —See **Earth Sciences -- Meteorology** pg 1419

Weightlifting —See **Health and Personal Fitness** pg 2595; see also Recreation, Leisure -- Sports pg 4881

Weights and Measures —See **Metrology and Standardization** pg 4029

Welding —pg 4026

Welfare —See **Sociology -- Social Services and Welfare** pg 5269

Western Australian Studies —See **History(General) -- History of Australia and Oceania** pg 2668

Who's Who —See **Biographies** pg 429

Wide Area Networks —See **Computers -- Computer Networks** pg 1240

Wildlife —See **Environmental Issues -- Conservation and Natural Resources** pg 2185; see also Environmental Issues -- Ecology pg 2210; Recreation, Leisure -- Outdoor Life pg 4868

Wills —See **Law -- Estate Planning** pg 3117

Wine —See **Food and Food Industry -- Beverage Industry** pg 2363

Women's Interests —pg 5550

Wood —See **Forestry -- Lumber and Wood** pg 2399

Woodwork —See **Building and Construction -- Carpentry and Woodwork** pg 633

Word Processing —pg 1292

Workmen's Compensation —See **Economics -- Labor** pg 1642; see also Insurance pg 2872

World Politics —See **Political Science** pg 4461

Wrestling —See **Recreation, Leisure -- Sports** pg 4881

Writing —See **Journalism** pg 2917; see also Literature pg 3357

Yachts and Yachting —See **Boats and Boating** pg 591; see also Travel and Tourism pg 5458

Yearbooks —See **Encyclopedias and General Reference Books** pg 1923

Youth —See **Children and Youth Interests** pg 1059

Zoning —See **Housing and Urban Development** pg 2812; **Law** pg 2926; see also Real Estate pg 4833

Zoology —pg 5572; see also Veterinary Sciences pg 5501

TABLES

Frequency
Document Delivery
Wire Services
Country of Publication
Unit of Currency
Indexes/Abstracts

FREQUENCY TABLE

an	Annual		sa	Semiannual
be	Biennial		sm	Semimonthly
bm	Bimonthly		sw	Semiweekly
bw	Biweekly		te	Triennial
da	Daily		tm	Three times a month
ir	Irregular		tq	Tri-quarterly
mo	Monthly		tw	Three times a week
qt	Quarterly		wk	Weekly

Additional frequencies may appear in the Serial Listing when provided by the publisher.

DOCUMENT DELIVERY

The following document supplier notations, when noted in a Serial Listing, indicate the availability of that serial for document delivery through the specified service. Permission has been granted by the copyright owner and is subject to change without notice. Only the portion in boldface will appear in the listing.

ADONIS™
ADONIS B.V.
Spuistraat 112D
1012VA Amsterdam, The Netherlands

Article Express International
Engineering Information Inc.
469 Union Avenue
Westbury, New York 11590

Ask*IEEE
(in cooperation with EBSCOdoc™)
1722 Gilbreth Road
Burlingame, CA 94010

BIOSIS Document Express™
(in cooperation with EBSCOdoc™)
1722 Gilbreth Road
Burlingame, CA 94010

BLDSC
British Library Document Supply Centre - Customer Services
Boston Spa, Wetherby
LS23 7BQ, United Kingdom

CASDDS ®
Chemical Abstracts Service Document Delivery Service
PO Box 3012
Columbus, Ohio 43210-0012

Documents on Demand
Congressional Information Service
4520 East-West Highway
Bethesda, MD 20814-3389

FAXON Xpress
FAXON Research Services, Inc.
15 Southwest Park
Westwood, MA 02090

Haworth Document Delivery Service
The Haworth Press, Inc.
10 Alice Street
Binghamton, New York 13904-1580

Magazine Collection™
Information Access Company
362 Lakeside Drive
Foster City, CA 94404

Petroleum Abstracts Document Delivery Service
University of Tulsa
600 South College
Tulsa, OK 74104-3189

Quick Copies
Williams and Wilkins Company
428 East Preston Street
Baltimore, MD 21202-3993

SWETSCAN-SWETDOC
Swets & Zeitlinger bv
Hereweg 347, PO Box 830
2160 SZ Lisse, The Netherlands

The Genuine Article®
Institute for Scientific Information
3501 Market Street
Philadelphia, PA 19104

The Uncover Company
3801 East Florida Avenue
Suite 200
Denver, CO 80210

UMI Article Clearinghouse
300 North Zeeb Road
PO Box 1346
Ann Arbor, MI 48106-1346

WIRE SERVICES

The following abbreviations represent the news and photograph wire services found in the Directory. Each code is followed by the complete name of the service.

CODE:	SERVICE:
AF	Agence France Presse
AN	Alternet
AP	Associated Press
API	Associated Press International
BU	British United Press
CA	Canadian Press
CH	Chicago Tribune - New York
CN	Capital News
CM	Christian Science Monitor
CO	Copley News Service
CP	Colorado Press
CQ	Congressional Quarterly
CS	Catholic News Service
CT	Chicago Sun Times
CP	China and Taiwan News Age
CU	Canadian United Press
DJ	Dow Jones
EI	Empire Information Service
ER	Editorial Research Service
FN	Federation News Service
GN	Gannett News Service
GP	Georgia Press Association
HH	Hearst Headline Service
HN	Harris News Service
IT	Independent Television Network
IM	Iowa Medialink
JT	Jewish Telegraphic Agency
KF	King Features
KN	Knight News Service
KR	Knight-Ridder
LA	Los Angeles Times
LO	London Daily News
LT	Times of London
MG	Manchester Guardian
ML	MediaLink
MN	Morris News Service
MP	Montana Press Association
NC	NEWSCOM
NE	Newspaper Enterprises Association
NF	Newsfinder
NM	Notimex
NN	Newhouse News Service
NP	NNAP
NU	News USA
NW	National Weather Service
NY	New York Times
ON	Ottawa News Service
PN	Pacific News Service
RN	Reuters News Service
SH	Scripps-Howard Newspaper Alliance-Scripps Howard News Service
SS	SportsStats
WN	World News
WP	Washington Post Writer's Guild
WS	Women's News Service
WW	Women's Wear Daily

COUNTRY OF PUBLICATION TABLE

The following lists of country codes have been taken directly from the USMARC Bibliographic Format, with the exception being that the United States and Canada state and province codes have been grouped under their respective countries, rather than being listed individually.

COUNTRY OF PUBLICATION BY CODE

Code	Country	Code	Country	Code	Country
AA	Albania	GS	Georgia (Republic)	PY	Paraguay
AE	Algeria	GT	Guatemala	QA	Qatar
AF	Afghanistan	GU	Guam	RE	Reunion
AG	Argentina	GV	Guinea	RH	Zimbabwe
AI	Armenia	GW	Germany	RM	Romania
AJ	Azerbaijan	GY	Guyana	RW	Rwanda
AM	Anguilla	GZ	Gaza Strip	RU	Russia (Republic)
AN	Andorra	HK	Hong Kong	SA	South Africa
AO	Angola	HM	Heard and McDonald Islands	SE	Seychelles
AQ	Antigua and Barbuda	HO	Honduras	SF	Sao Tome and Principe
AS	American Samoa	HT	Haiti	SG	Senegal
AT	Australia	HU	Hungary	SH	Spanish North Africa
AU	Austria	IC	Iceland	SI	Singapore
AW	Aruba	IE	Ireland	SJ	Sudan
AY	Antarctica	II	India	SL	Sierra Leone
BA	Bahrain	IO	Indonesia	SM	San Marino
BB	Barbados	IQ	Iraq	SO	Somalia
BD	Burundi	IR	Iran	SP	Spain
BE	Belgium	IS	Israel	SQ	Swaziland
BF	Bahamas	IT	Italy	SR	Surinam
BG	Bangladesh	IV	Ivory Coast	SS	Western Sahara
BH	Belize	IY	Iraq-Saudi Arabia Neutral Zone	SU	Saudi Arabia
BI	British Indian Ocean Territory			SW	Sweden
BL	Brazil	JA	Japan	SX	Namibia
BM	Bermuda Islands	JI	Johnson Atoll	SY	Syria
BN	Bosnia Hercegovina	JM	Jamaica	SZ	Switzerland
BO	Bolivia	JO	Jordan	TA	Tajikstan
BP	Solomon Islands	KE	Kenya	TC	Turks and Caicos Islands
BR	Burma	KG	Kyrgyzstan	TG	Togo
BS	Botswana	KN	Korea (North)	TH	Thailand
BT	Bhutan	KO	Korea (South)	TI	Tunisia
BU	Bulgaria	KU	Kuwait	TK	Turkmenistan
BV	Bouvet Island	KZ	Kazakhstan	TL	Tokelau Islands
BW	Byelarus	LB	Liberia	TO	Tonga
BX	Brunei	LE	Lebanon	TR	Trinidad and Tobago
CB	Cambodia	LH	Liechtenstein	TS	Trucial States (United Arab Emirates)
CC	China	LI	Lithuania		
CD	Chad	LO	Lesotho	TU	Turkey
CE	Sri Lanka	LS	Laos	TZ	Tanzania
CF	Congo (Brazzaville)	LU	Luxembourg	UA	Egypt
CG	Zaire	LV	Latvia	UC	United States Misc. Caribbean Islands
CH	China (Republic: 1949)	LY	Libya		
CI	Croatia	MC	Monaco	UG	Uganda
CJ	Cayman Islands	MF	Mauritius	UK	United Kingdom (Including Scotland)
CK	Colombia	MG	Madagascar		
CL	Chile	MH	Macao	UN	Ukraine
CM	Cameroon	MJ	Montserrat	UP	United States Misc. Pacific Islands
CN	Canada	MK	Oman		
CP	Canton and Enderbury Islands	ML	Mali	UR	USSR
CQ	Comorus	MM	Malta	US	United States
CR	Costa Rica	MP	Mongolia	UV	Burkina Faso
CS	Czechoslovakia	MQ	Martinique	UY	Uruguay
CU	Cuba	MR	Morocco	UZ	Uzbekistan
CV	Cape Verde	MU	Mauritania	VB	Virgin Islands (British V.I.)
CW	Cook Islands	MV	Moldova	VC	Vatican City
CX	Central African Republic	MW	Malawi	VE	Venezuela
CY	Cyprus	MX	Mexico	VI	Virgin Islands (U.S.)
DK	Denmark	MY	Malaysia	VM	Vietnam
DM	Benin	MZ	Mozambique	WF	Wallis and Futuna
DQ	Dominica	NA	Netherlands Antilles	WJ	West Bank of the Jordan River
DR	Dominican Republic	NE	Netherlands	WK	Wake Island
EC	Ecuador	NG	Niger	WS	Western Samoa
EG	Equatorial Guinea	NL	New Caledonia	XA	Christmas Island (Indian Ocean)
ER	Estonia	NN	Vanuatu		
ES	El Salvador	NO	Norway	XB	Cocos (Keeling) Islands
ET	Ethiopia	NP	Nepal	XC	Maldives
FA	Faroe Islands	NQ	Nicaragua	XD	Saint Kitts-Nevis
FG	French Guiana	NR	Nigeria	XE	Marshall Islands
FI	Finland	NU	Nauru	XF	Midway Island
FJ	Fiji	NW	Northern Mariana Islands	XH	Niue
FM	Micronesia (Federated States)	NX	Norfolk Island	XJ	Saint Helena
FP	French Polynesia	NZ	New Zealand	XK	Saint Lucia
FR	France	OT	Mayotte	XL	Saint Pierre and Miquelon
FS	Terres Australes et Antarctiques Francaises	PC	Pitcairn Island	XM	Saint Vincent and the Grenadines
		PE	Peru		
FT	Djibouti	PF	Paracel Islands	XN	Macedonia
GB	Kiribati	PG	Guinea-Bissau	XO	Slovakia
GD	Grenada	PH	Philippines	XP	Spratly Islands
GH	Ghana	PK	Pakistan	XR	Czech Republic
GI	Gibralter	PL	Poland	XS	Falkland Islands
GL	Greenland	PN	Panama	XV	Slovenia
GM	Gambia	PO	Portugal	YE	Yemen
GO	Gabon	PP	Papua New Guinea	YU	Yugoslavia
GP	Guadeloupe	PR	Puerto Rico	ZA	Zambia
GR	Greece	PW	Palau		

COUNTRY OF PUBLICATION TABLE

COUNTRY OF PUBLICATION BY COUNTRY

Country	Code	Country	Code	Country	Code
Afghanistan	AF	Greenland	GL	Paracel Islands	PF
Albania	AA	Grenada	GD	Paraguay	PY
Algeria	AE	Guadeloupe	GP	Peru	PE
American Samoa	AS	Guam	GU	Philippines	PH
Andorra	AN	Guatemala	GT	Pitcairn Island	PC
Angola	AO	Guinea	GV	Poland	PL
Anguilla	AM	Guinea-Bissau	PG	Portugal	PO
Antarctica	AY	Guyana	GY	Puerto Rico	PR
Antigua and Barbuda	AQ	Haiti	HT	Qatar	QA
Argentina	AG	Heard and McDonald Islands	HM	Reunion	RE
Armenia	AI	Honduras	HO	Romania	RM
Aruba	AW	Hong Kong	HK	Russia (Republic)	RU
Australia	AT	Hungary	HU	Rwanda	RW
Austria	AU	Iceland	IC	Saint Helena	XJ
Azerbaijan	AJ	India	II	Saint Kitts-Nevis	XD
Bahamas	BF	Indonesia	IO	Saint Lucia	XK
Bahrain	BA	Iran	IR	Saint Pierre and Miquelon	XL
Bangladesh	BG	Iraq	IQ	Saint Vincent and the Grenadines	XM
Barbados	BB	Iraq-Saudi Arabia Neutral Zone	IY	San Marino	SM
Belgium	BE	Ireland	IE	Sao Tome and Principe	SF
Belize	BH	Israel	IS	Saudi Arabia	SU
Benin	DM	Italy	IT	Senegal	SG
Bermuda Islands	BM	Ivory Coast	IV	Seychelles	SE
Bhutan	BT	Jamaica	JM	Sierra Leone	SL
Bolivia	BO	Japan	JA	Singapore	SI
Bosnia Hercegovina	BN	Johnson Atoll	JI	Slovakia	XO
Botswana	BS	Jordan	JO	Slovenia	XV
Bouvet Island	BV	Kazakhstan	KZ	Solomon Islands	BP
Brazil	BL	Kenya	KE	Somalia	SO
British Indian Ocean Territory	BI	Kiribati	GB	South Africa	SA
Brunei	BX	Korea (North)	KN	Spain	SP
Bulgaria	BU	Korea (South)	KO	Spanish North Africa	SH
Burkina Faso	UV	Kuwait	KU	Spratly Island	XP
Burma	BR	Kyrgyzstan	KG	Sri Lanka	CE
Burundi	BD	Laos	LS	Sudan	SJ
Byelarus	BW	Latvia	LV	Surinam	SR
Cambodia	CB	Lebanon	LE	Swaziland	SQ
Cameroon	CM	Lesotho	LO	Sweden	SW
Canada	CN	Liberia	LB	Switzerland	SZ
Canton and Enderbury Islands	CP	Libya	LY	Syria	SY
Cape Verde	CV	Liechtenstein	LH	Tajikstan	TA
Cayman Islands	CJ	Lithuania	LI	Tanzania	TZ
Central African Republic	CX	Luxembourg	LU	Terres Australes et Antarctiques Francaises	FS
Chad	CD	Macao	MH	Thailand	TH
Chile	CL	Macedonia	XN	Togo	TG
China	CC	Madagascar	MG	Tokelau Islands	TL
China (Republic: 1949)	CH	Malawi	MW	Tonga	TO
Christmas Island (Indian Ocean)	XA	Malaysia	MY	Trinidad and Tobago	TR
Cocos (Keeling) Islands	XB	Maldives	XC	Trucial States (United Arab Emirates)	TS
Colombia	CK	Mali	ML	Tunisia	TI
Comoros	CQ	Malta	MM	Turkey	TU
Congo (Brazzaville)	CF	Marshall Islands	XE	Turkmenistan	TK
Cook Islands	CW	Martinique	MQ	Turks and Caicos Islands	TC
Costa Rica	CR	Mauritania	MU	Uganda	UG
Croatia	CI	Mauritius	MF	Ukraine	UN
Cuba	CU	Mayotte	OT	United Kingdom (Including Scotland)	UK
Cyprus	CY	Mexico	MX	United States	US
Czech Republic	XR	Micronesia (Federated States)	FM	United States (Misc. Caribbean Islands)	UC
Czechoslovakia	CS	Midway Island	XF	United States (Misc. Pacific Islands)	UP
Denmark	DK	Moldova	MV	Uruguay	UY
Djibouti	FT	Monaco	MC	USSR	UR
Dominica	DQ	Mongolia	MP	Uzbekistan	UZ
Dominican Republic	DR	Montserrat	MJ	Vanuatu	NN
Ecuador	EC	Morocco	MR	Vatican City	VC
Egypt	UA	Mozambique	MZ	Venezuela	VE
El Salvador	ES	Namibia	SX	Vietnam	VM
Equatorial Guinea	EG	Nauru	NU	Virgin Islands (British V.I.)	VB
Estonia	ER	Nepal	NP	Virgin Islands (U.S.)	VI
Ethiopia	ET	Netherlands	NE	Wake Island	WK
Falkland Islands	XS	Netherlands Antilles	NA	Wallis and Futuna	WF
Faroe Islands	FA	New Caledonia	NL	West Bank of the Jordan River	WJ
Fiji	FJ	New Zealand	NZ	Western Sahara	SS
Finland	FI	Nicaragua	NQ	Western Samoa	WS
France	FR	Niger	NG	Yemen	YE
French Guiana	FG	Nigeria	NR	Yugoslavia	YU
French Polynesia	FP	Niue	XH	Zaire	CG
Gabon	GO	Norfolk Island	NX	Zambia	ZA
Gambia	GM	Northern Mariana Islands	NW	Zimbabwe	RH
Gaza Strip	GZ	Norway	NO		
Georgia (Republic)	GS	Oman	MK		
Germany	GW	Pakistan	PK		
Ghana	GH	Palau	PW		
Gibraltar	GI	Panama	PN		
Greece	GR	Papua New Guinea	PP		

UNIT OF CURRENCY TABLE

In the Serial Listing, prices are given in country of publication currency and are one-year library subscription rates, unless designated otherwise.

Country	Currency	Country	Currency	Country	Currency
Afghanistan	afghanin	Greece	Greek drachma	Papua New Guinea	kina
Albania	lek	Guadeloupe	French franc	Paraguay	guarani
Algeria	Algerian dinar	Guatemala	quetzal	Peru	sole
Angola	kwanza	Guyana	Guyana dollar	Philippines	peso
Antigua and Barbuda	East Caribbean dollar	Haiti	gourde	Papua New Guinea	kina
Argentina	peso argentino	Honduras	lempira	Paraguay	guarani
Australia	Australian dollar	Hong Kong	Hong Kong dollar	Peru	sole
Austria	schilling	Hungary	forint	Philippines	peso
Bahamas	Bahamian dollar	Iceland	krona	Poland	zloty
Bangladesh	taka	India	rupee	Portugal	escudo
Barbados	Barbados dollar	Indonesia	rupiah	Qatar	Qatar riyal
Belgium	Belgian franc	Iran	rial	Reunion	French franc
Bermuda Islands	Bermuda dollar	Iraq	Iraqi dinar	Romania	lei
Bolivia	peso	Ireland	Irish pound	Rwanda	Rwanda franc
Botswana	pula	Israel	shekel	San Marino	Italian lira
Brazil	cruzeiro	Italy	lira	Saudi Arabia	Saudi riyal
Belize	Belize dollar	Ivory Coast	CFA franc	Senegal	CFA franc
Benin	CFA franc	Jamaica	Jamaican dollar	Sierra Leone	leone
Bulgaria	lev	Japan	yen	Singapore	Singapore dollar
Burkina Faso	CFA franc	Jordan	Jordanian dinar	Somalia	Somali shilling
Burma	kyat	Kenya	Kenya shilling	South Africa	South African rand
Cameroon	CFA franc	Korea (North)	won	Southern Yemen	dinar
Canada	Canadian dollar	Korea (South)	won	Spain	pesata
Cayman Islands	cordoba/dollar	Kuwait	Kuwaiti dinar	Sri Lanka	rupee
Central African Republic	CFA franc	Lebanon	Lebanese pound	Sudan	Sudanese pound
		Liberia	U.S. dollar	Surinam	Surinam guilder
		Libya	Libyan dinar	Swaziland	emalangeni
Chad	CFA franc	Liechtenstein	Swiss franc	Sweden	krona
Chile	peso	Luxembourg	Luxembourg franc	Switzerland	franc
China	renminbi yuan	Madagascar	Malagasy franc	Syria	Syrian pound
China (Republic: 1949)	New Taiwan dollar	Malawi	Malawi kwacha	Tanzania	Tanzanian shilling
		Malaysia	ringgit	Thailand	baht
Colombia	peso	Mali	CFA franc	Togo	CFA franc
Cook Islands	New Zealand dollar	Malta	Maltese pound	Trinidad and Tobago	Trinidad and Tobago dollar
Costa Rica	colon	Martinique	French franc		
Cuba	peso	Mauritius	Mauritian rupee	Tunisia	Tunisian dinar
Cyprus	Cyprus pound	Mexico	peso	Turkey	Turkish lira
Czechoslovakia	korona	Monaco	French franc	Uganda	Uganda shilling
Benin	CFA franc	Morocco	dirham	United Kingdom	pound sterling
Denmark	krone	Mozambique	meticais	United States	U.S. dollar
Djibouti	Djibouti franc	Nauru	Australian dollar	Uruguay	new peso
Dominican Republic	peso	Nepal	Nepalese rupee	USSR	ruble
Ecuador	sucre	Netherlands	guilder	Vatican City	lira
Egypt	Egyptian pound	New Caledonia	CFP franc	Venezuela	bolivare
El Salvador	colon	New Zealand	New Zealand dollar	Vietnam	dong
Ethiopia	Ethiopian birr	Nicaragua	cordoba	Yemen (Yemen (Sana))	riyal
Fiji	Fiji dollar	Niger	CFA franc		
Finland	fim (finnmark)	Nigeria	naira	Yugoslavia	dinar
France	French franc	Norway	krone	Zaire	CFA franc
Gambia	dalasi	Oman	rial	Zambia	Zambian kwacha
Germany	mark	Pakistan	rupee	Zimbabwe	Zimbabwean dollar
Ghana	cedi	Panama	balboa		

INDEXES/ABSTRACTS TABLE

The following is a list of all publications which may index, or contain an abstract of, titles in the Directory. The Abbreviated Title in boldface is the abbreviation of the index or abstract as used in the Serial Listing. The complete title of the index or abstract follows. Succeeding information or a Ceased/Suspended indicator will follow the complete title for those serials where it applies. For services that share the same journal source list, a reference will be made to that service which will appear in the Serial Listing. This table includes over 1,300 Indexing/Abstracting services, 921 of which are active.

A.I.D. RES. DEV. ABSTR.
[US/0096-1507]
A.I.D. RESEARCH AND DEVELOPMENT ABSTRACTS.
(**Continues** A.I.D. Reference Center. A.I.D. Research Abstracts.)

ABC POL SCI
[US/0001-0456]
ABC POL SCI. ADVANCE BIBLIOGRAPHY OF CONTENTS: POLITICAL SCIENCE & GOVERNMENT.

ABI/INFORM ONDISC
[US/1062-5127]
ABI/INFORM ONDISC.

ABI/INFORM ONDISC: EXPR. ED.
[US]
ABI/INFORM ONDISC: EXPRESS EDITION [COMPUTER FILE].

ABI/INFORM GLOB. ED.
[US]
ABI/INFORM GLOBAL EDITION [COMPUTER FILE].

ABR. CATHOL. PERIOD. LIT. INDEX
[US/0737-3457]
ABRIDGED CATHOLIC PERIODICAL AND LITERATURE INDEX, THE.

ABR. INDEX MED.
[US/0001-3331]
ABRIDGED INDEX MEDICUS.
(**Continues** American Medical Association. Abridged Index Medicus.)

ABR. READ. GUIDE PERIOD. LIT.
[US/0001-334X]
ABRIDGED READERS' GUIDE TO PERIODICAL LITERATURE.

ABS INT. GUIDE CLASSICAL STUD.
[US]
ABS INTERNATIONAL GUIDE TO CLASSICAL STUDIES.
(**Continued by** International Guide to Classical Studies (1966).)

ABSTR. ABSTR. BOOK REV. CUR. LEG. PERIOD.
[US]
ABSTRACTS : ABSTRACTS OF BOOK REVIEWS IN CURRENT LEGAL PERIODICALS.
(**Continues** Abstracts of Book Reviews in Current Legal Periodicals.)

ABSTR. AIT REP. PUBL. ENERGY
[TH/0857-6181]
ABSTRACTS OF AIT REPORTS AND PUBLICATIONS ON ENERGY.
(**Continues** Abstracts of AIT Reports and Publications on Renewable Energy Resources.)

ABSTR. ANTHROPOL.
[US/0001-3455]
ABSTRACTS IN ANTHROPOLOGY.

ABSTR. BIOCOMMER.
[UK/0263-6778]
ABSTRACTS IN BIOCOMMERCE.

ABSTR. BOOK REV. CURR. LEG. PERIOD.
[US/0362-1065]
ABSTRACTS OF BOOK REVIEWS IN CURRENT LEGAL PERIODICALS.
(**Continued by** Abstracts : Abstracts of Book Reviews in Current Legal Periodicals.)

ABSTR. BULL. INST. PAP. SCI. TECH.
[US/1047-2088]
ABSTRACT BULLETIN OF THE INSTITUTE OF PAPER SCIENCE AND TECHNOLOGY.
(**Continues** Institute of Paper Chemistry (Appleton, Wis.) Abstract Bulletin of the Institute of Paper Chemistry.)

ABSTR. BULL. INST. PAPER CHEM.
[US]
ABSTRACT BULLETIN OF THE INSTITUTE OF PAPER CHEMISTRY.
(**Continued by** Abstract Bulletin of the Institute of Paper Science and Technology.)

ABSTR. CLIN. CARE GUIDEL.
[US/1042-4423]
ABSTRACTS OF CLINICAL CARE GUIDELINES.

ABSTR. CRIMINOL. PENOL.
[NE/0001-3684]
ABSTRACTS ON CRIMINOLOGY AND PENOLOGY.
(**Continued by** Criminology & Penology Abstracts.)

ABSTR. ENGL. STUD.
[US/0001-3560]
ABSTRACTS OF ENGLISH STUDIES.
(Suspended)

ABSTR. ENTOMOL.
[US/0001-3579]
ABSTRACTS OF ENTOMOLOGY.
***Refer to Biological Abstracts for complete source list.

ABSTR. FOLK. STUD.
[US/0001-3587]
ABSTRACTS OF FOLKLORE STUDIES.
(Ceased)

ABSTR. GRAPHIC ARTS TECH. FOUND.
[US]
ABSTRACTS (GRAPHIC ARTS TECHNICAL FOUNDATION).
(**Continues** Graphic Arts Abstracts (Pittsburgh, PA. : 1968).)

ABSTR. HEALTH CARE MANAGE. STUD.
[US/0194-4908]
ABSTRACTS OF HEALTH CARE MANAGEMENT STUDIES.
(**Continues** Abstracts of Hospital Management Studies.)

ABSTR. HEALTH ENVIRON. POLLUTANTS
[US/0044-5819]
ABSTRACTS ON HEALTH EFFECTS OF ENVIRONMENTAL POLLUTANTS.
(Ceased)

ABSTR. HOSPIT. MANAGE. STUD.
[US/0001-3595]
ABSTRACTS OF HOSPITAL MANAGEMENT STUDIES.
(**Continued by** Abstracts of Health Care Management Studies.)

ABSTR. HUM. COMPUT. INTERACT.
[US/1042-0193]
ABSTRACTS IN HUMAN-COMPUTER INTERACTION.
(Suspended)

ABSTR. HYG.
[UK/0001-3692]
ABSTRACTS ON HYGIENE.
(**Continued by** Abstracts on Hygiene and Communicable Diseases.)

ABSTR. HYG. COMMUN. DIS.
[UK/0260-5511]
ABSTRACTS ON HYGIENE AND COMMUNICABLE DISEASES.
(**Continues** Abstracts on Hygiene.)
***Refer to Tropical Diseases Bulletin for complete source list.

ABSTR. J. EARTHQ. ENG.
[US/0363-5732]
ABSTRACT JOURNAL IN EARTHQUAKE ENGINEERING.

ABSTR. MIL. BIBLIOGR.
[AG]
ABSTRACTS OF MILITARY BIBLIOGRAPHY.
(**Continues** Resumenes Analiticos Sobre Defensa y Seguridad Nacional.)

ABSTR. NEW WORLD ARCHAEOL.
[US]
ABSTRACTS OF NEW WORLD ARCHAEOLOGY.
(Ceased)

ABSTR. NORTH AM. GEOL.
[US/0001-3625]
ABSTRACTS OF NORTH AMERICAN GEOLOGY.
(Ceased)

ABSTR. OF MYCOL.
[US/0001-3617]
ABSTRACTS OF MYCOLOGY.
***Refer to Biological Abstracts for complete source list.

ABSTR. PHOTOGR. SCI. ENG. LIT.
[US/0001-3633]
ABSTRACTS OF PHOTOGRAPHIC SCIENCE & ENGINEERING LITERATURE.
(**Continues** Monthly Abstract Bulletin from the Kodak Research Laboratories; ANSCO Abstracts.)

ABSTR. POP. CULT.
[US/0147-2615]
ABSTRACTS OF POPULAR CULTURE.
(Ceased)

ABSTR. RES. PASTOR. CARE COUNS.
[US/0733-2599]
ABSTRACTS OF RESEARCH IN PASTORAL CARE AND COUNSELING.
(**Continues** Pastoral Care and Counseling Abstracts.)

INDEXES/ABSTRACTS TABLE

ABSTR. SOC. GERONTOL.
[US/1047-4862]
ABSTRACTS IN SOCIAL GERONTOLOGY.
(*Continues* Current Literature on Aging.)

ABSTR. SOC. WORK.
[US/0001-3412]
ABSTRACTS FOR SOCIAL WORKERS.
(*Continued by* Social Work Research & Abstracts.)

ABSTR. TROP. AGRIC.
[NE/0304-5951]
ABSTRACTS ON TROPICAL AGRICULTURE.
(*Supersedes* Tropical Abstracts.)

ABSTR. WORLD MED.
[UK]
ABSTRACTS OF WORLD MEDICINE.
(*Absorbed* Abstracts of World Surgery, Obstetrics and Gynaecology.)

ACAD. ABSTR.
[US/1056-7496]
ACADEMIC ABSTRACTS.

ACAD. ABSTR. FULL TEXT ELITE
[US/1060-6750]
ACADEMIC ABSTRACTS FULL TEXT ELITE.

ACAD. IND. [COMPUTER FILE]
[US]
ACADEMIC INDEX. [COMPUTER FILE].

ACAD. SEARCH
[US/1071-2720]
ACADEMIC SEARCH.

ACCESS
[US/0095-5698]
ACCESS (SYRACUSE).
(*Absorbed* Monthly Periodical Index.)

ACCESS INDEX LITTLE MAG.
[US/0363-065X]
ACCESS INDEX TO LITTLE MAGAZINES.
(Ceased)

ACCOUNT. ART.
[US]
ACCOUNTING ARTICLES.

ACCOUNT. DATA PROCESS. ABSTR.
[UK/0001-4796]
ACCOUNTING + DATA PROCESSING ABSTRACTS.
(*Continued by* Accounting + Finance Abstracts.)

ACCOUNT. INDEX
[US]
ACCOUNTANTS INDEX.
(*Continued by* Accounting & Tax Index.)

ACCOUNT. INDEX SUPPL.
[US/0748-7975]
ACCOUNTANTS' INDEX. SUPPLEMENT.
(*Continued by* Accounting & Tax Index.)

ACCOUNT. TAX DATAB.
[US]
ACCOUNTING AND TAX DATABASE [ONLINE DATABASE].

ACCOUNT. TAX INDEX
[US/1063-0287]
ACCOUNTING AND TAX INDEX.
(*Continues* Accountants' Index. Supplement.)
***Refer to Accounting and Tax Database for complete source list.

ACCUMU. VET. INDEX
[US/0567-7033]
ACCUMULATIVE VETERINARY INDEX.
(Ceased)

ACID RAIN ABSTR.
[US/0882-1402]
ACID RAIN ABSTRACTS.
(*Absorbed by* Environment Abstracts.)

ACM GUIDE COMPUT. LIT.
[US/0149-1199]
ACM GUIDE TO COMPUTING LITERATURE.
(*Continues* Computing Reviews. Bibliography and Subject Index of Current Computing Literature.)

ACOUST. ABSTR.
[UK/0001-4974]
ACOUSTICS ABSTRACTS.

ADOLESC. MENT. HEALTH ABSTR.
[US]
ADOLESCENT MENTAL HEALTH ABSTRACTS.
(Ceased)

ADONIS
[NE]
ADONIS CD-ROM.

AERO. DEF. MARK. TECHNOL.
[US/0885-2286]
AEROSPACE/DEFENSE MARKETS & TECHNOLOGY.
(*Continues* Defense Markets & Technology.)

AESIS Q.
[AT/0313-704x]
AESIS QUARTERLY.

AFR. ABSTR.
[UK/0568-1200]
AFRICAN ABSTRACTS.
(Ceased)

AGBIOTECH NEWS INF.
[UK/0954-9897]
AGBIOTECH NEWS AND INFORMATION.

AGRIC. ENG. ABSTR.
[UK/0308-8863]
AGRICULTURAL ENGINEERING ABSTRACTS.

AGRIC. ENVIRON. BIOTECHNOL. ABSTR.
[US/1063-1151]
AGRICULTURAL & ENVIRONMENTAL BIOTECHNOLOGY ABSTRACTS.
(*Continues in part* Biotechnology Research Abstracts.)
***Refer to Biotechnology Research Abstracts for complete source list.

AGRIC. INDEX
[US/0196-5883]
AGRICULTURAL INDEX.
(*Continued by* Biological & Agricultural Index.)

AGRICOLA
[US/1050-6810]
AGRICOLA.

AGRINDEX
[IT/0254-8801]
AGRINDEX.

AGROFOR. ABSTR.
[UK/0952-1453]
AGROFORESTRY ABSTRACTS.

AIDS ABSTR.
[US/1066-1107]
AIDS ABSTRACTS (ATLANTA, GA.).

AIR POLLUT. TITLES
[US/0002-2497]
AIR POLLUTION TITLES.
(Ceased)

AIR UNIV. LIBR. INDEX MIL. PERIOD.
[US/0002-2586]
AIR UNIVERSITY LIBRARY INDEX TO MILITARY PERIODICALS.
(*Continues* Air University Periodical Index.)

AIR UNIV. PERIOD. INDEX
[US]
AIR UNIVERSITY PERIODICAL INDEX.
(*Continued by* Air University Library Index to Military Periodicals.)

ALCOHOL CLIN. UPDATE
[US/0740-1035]
ALCOHOL CLINICAL UPDATE.
(Ceased)

ALCOHOL. DIG.
[US/0093-7010]
ALCOHOLISM DIGEST.
(Ceased)

ALTERN. PRESS INDEX
[US/0002-662X]
ALTERNATIVE PRESS INDEX.

ALUM. IND. ABSTR.
[US/1066-0623]
ALUMINIUM INDUSTRY ABSTRACTS.
(*Continues* World Aluminum Abstracts.)

AM. BIBLIOGR. SLAVIC EAST EUROP. STUD.
[US/0094-3770]
AMERICAN BIBLIOGRAPHY OF SLAVIC AND EAST EUROPEAN STUDIES.
(*Continues* American Bibliography of Russian and East European Studies.)

AM. HIST. LIFE
[US/0002-7065]
AMERICA, HISTORY AND LIFE (SANTA BARBARA, CALIF. : 1989).
(*Formed by the union of* America, History and Life. Part A, Article Abstracts and Citations *and* America, History and Life. Part B, Index to Book Reviews America, History and Life. Part C, American History Bibliography, Books, Articles and Dissertations America, History and Life. Part D, Annual Index.)

AM. HIST. LIFE PART B
[US/0002-7065]
AMERICA: HISTORY AND LIFE. PART B: INDEX TO BOOK REVIEWS.
(*Merged with* America, History and Life. Part A, Article Abstracts and Citations; America, History and Life. Part C, American History Bibliography, Books, Articles and Dissertations *and* America, History and Life. Part D, Annual Index *to form* America, History and Life.)

AM. HUMANIT. INDEX
[US/0361-0144]
AMERICAN HUMANITIES INDEX, THE.

AM. INDIAN INDEX
[US/0569-5244]
AMERICAN INDIAN INDEX.
(Ceased)

AM. STAT. INDEX
[US/0091-1658]
AMERICAN STATISTICS INDEX.

ANAL. ABSTR.
[UK/0003-2689]
ANALYTICAL ABSTRACTS.
(*Continues* British Abstracts. Section C, Analysis and Apparatus.)

INDEXES/ABSTRACTS TABLE

ANBAR ACCOUNT. FINAN. ABSTR.
[UK/0961-2742]
ANBAR ACCOUNTING & FINANCE ABSTRACTS.
(*Continues* Accounting + Data Processing Abstracts.)

ANBAR MANAG. SERV. ABSTR.
[UK]
ANBAR MANAGEMENT SERVICES ABSTRACTS.
(*Superseded in part by* Accounting + Data Processing Abstracts; Marketing + Distribution Abstracts; Personnel + Training Abstracts *and* Top Management Abstracts.)

ANBAR MARK. DISTR. ABSTR.
[UK/0305-0661]
ANBAR MARKETING & DISTRIBUTION ABSTRACTS.
(*Continues* Marketing + Distribution Abstracts.)

ANBAR TOP MANAG. ABSTR.
[UK]
ANBAR TOP MANAGEMENT ABSTRACTS.
(*Continues* Top Management Abstracts.)

ANIM. BEHAV. ABSTR.
[US/0301-8695]
ANIMAL BEHAVIOR ABSTRACTS.
(*Continues* Animal Behaviour Abstracts.)

ANIM. BREED. ABSTR.
[UK/0003-3499]
ANIMAL BREEDING ABSTRACTS.
(*Formed by the union of* Imperial Bureau of Animal Breeding and Genetics. Quarterly Bulletin *and* Imperial Bureau of Animal References to Literature Contained in Periodicals Received.)

ANIM. DISEASE OCCURR.
[UK/0144-3879]
ANIMAL DISEASE OCCURRENCE.
(Ceased)

ANNALS BEHAV. MED.
[US/0883-6612]
ANNALS OF BEHAVIORAL MEDICINE.
(*Continues* Behavioral Medicine Update; **Absorbed** Behavioral Medicine Abstracts.)

ANNOT. BIBLIOGR. ECON. GEOL.
[US/0003-5076]
ANNOTATED BIBLIOGRAPHY OF ECONOMIC GEOLOGY.
(Ceased)

ANNU. BIBLIOGR. ENGL. LANG. LIT.
[UK/0066-3786]
ANNUAL BIBLIOGRAPHY OF ENGLISH LANGUAGE AND LITERATURE.
(*Continues* Bibliography of English Language and Literature.)

ANNU. INDEX POP. MUSIC REC. REV.
[US/0092-3486]
ANNUAL INDEX TO POPULAR MUSIC RECORD REVIEWS.
(*Continues* Annual Index to Popular Music Record Reviews.)

ANNU. LEG. BIBLIOGR.
[US/0073-0793]
ANNUAL LEGAL BIBLIOGRAPHY.
(Ceased)

ANTHROPOL. INDEX
[UK/0003-5467]
ANTHROPOLOGICAL INDEX TO CURRENT PERIODICALS IN THE LIBRARY OF THE ROYAL ANTHROPOLOGICAL INSTITUTE.
(*Continues* Anthropological Index to Current Periodicals in the Museum of Mankind (Library Incorporating the Royal Anthropological Institute Library).)

ANTHROPOL. LIT.
[US/0190-3373]
ANTHROPOLOGICAL LITERATURE.
(*Continues* Anthropological Literature (Cambridge, Mass. : 1984).)

ANTHROPOL. LIT. MICRO.
[US/0190-3373]
ANTHROPOLOGICAL LITERATURE.
(*Continued by* Anthropological Literature (Cambridge, Mass. : 1989).)

APAIS, AUST. PUBLIC AFF. INF. SER.
[AT/0727-8926]
APAIS. AUSTRALIAN PUBLIC AFFAIRS INFORMATION SERVICE.

API ABSTR. HEALTH ENVIRON.
[US]
API ABSTRACTS. HEALTH & ENVIRONMENT.
(*Continued by* Literature Abstracts. Health & Environment.)

API ABSTR. OIL. CHEM.
[US]
API ABSTRACTS : OILFIELD CHEMICALS.
(*Continued by* Literature & Patent Abstracts. Oilfield Chemicals.)

APIBIZ
[US]
APIBIZ [ONLINE DATABASE].
***Refer to Petroleum/Energy Business News Index for complete source list.

APIC. ABSTR.
[UK/0003-648X]
APICULTURAL ABSTRACTS.

APILIT
[US]
APILIT [ONLINE DATABASE].
***Refer to Literature & Patent Abstracts Oilfield Chemicals for a complete source list.

APPL. ECOL. ABSTR.
[UK/0305-3040]
APPLIED ECOLOGY ABSTRACTS.
(*Continued by* Ecology Abstracts.)

APPL. MECH. REV.
[US/0003-6900]
APPLIED MECHANICS REVIEWS.

APPL. SCI. TECHNOL. INDEX
[US/0003-6986]
APPLIED SCIENCE & TECHNOLOGY INDEX.
(*Continues in part* Industrial Arts Index.)

APPL. SOC. SCI. INDEX ABSTR.
[UK/0950-2238]
ASSIA. APPLIED SOCIAL SCIENCES INDEX & ABSTRACTS.

AQUALINE ABSTR.
[UK/0263-5534]
AQUALINE ABSTRACTS.
(*Continues* Water Research Centre (Great Britain). WRC Information.)

AQUAREF
[CN]
AQUAREF.
(*Continues* Canadian Environment; Environnement.)

AQUAT. SCI. FISH. ABSTR.
[UK/0044-8516]
AQUATIC SCIENCES & FISHERIES ABSTRACTS.
(*Split into* Aquatic Sciences and Fisheries Abstracts. Part 1, Biological Sciences and Living Resources **and** Aquatic Sciences and Fisheries Abstracts. Part 2, Ocean Technology, Policy and Non-Living Resources.)

AQUAT. SCI. FISH. ABSTR. (COMPUTER FILE)
[US/1064-0460]
AQUATIC SCIENCES & FISHERIES ABSTRACTS (CD-ROM ED.).

AQUAT. SCI. FISH. ABSTR. PART 1
[US/0140-5373]
AQUATIC SCIENCES AND FISHERIES ABSTRACTS. PART 1 : BIOLOGICAL SCIENCES AND LIVING RESOURCES.
(*Continued in part by* Aquatic Sciences and Fisheries Abstracts. Part 3, Aquatic Pollution and Environmental Quality.)
***Refer to Aquatic Science & Fisheries Abstracts [Computer File]: ASFA / Cambridge Scientific Abstracts for complete source list.

AQUAT. SCI. FISH. ABSTR. 2, OCEAN TECHNOL. POLICY NON-LIVING RESOUR.
[US/0140-5381]
AQUATIC SCIENCES AND FISHERIES ABSTRACTS. PART 2 : OCEAN TECHNOLOGY, POLICY AND NON-LIVING RESOURCES.
(*Continued in part by* Aquatic Sciences and Fisheries Abstracts. Part 3, Aquatic Pollution and Environmental Quality.)
***Refer to Aquatic Sciences & Fisheries Abstracts [Computer File] : ASFA / Cambridge Scientific Abstracts for complete source list.

AQUAT. SCI. FISHER. ABSTR. 3, AQUAT. POLLUT. ENVIRO. QUAL.
[US/1045-6031]
AQUATIC SCIENCES AND FISHERIES ABSTRACTS. PART 3 : AQUATIC POLLUTION AND ENVIRONMENTAL QUALITY.
(*Continues in part* Aquatic Sciences and Fisheries Abstracts. Part 1, Biological Sciences & Living Resources **and** Aquatic Sciences and Fisheries Abstracts. Part 2, Ocean Technology, Policy and Non-Living Resources.)
***Refer to Aquatic Sciences & Fisheries Abstracts [Computer File] : ASFA / Cambridge Scientific Abstracts for complete source list.

ARCHIT. PERIOD. INDEX
[UK/0266-4380]
API. ARCHITECTURAL PERIODICALS INDEX.
(*Supersedes* Royal Institute of British Architects. RIBA Library Bulletin; Royal Institute of British Architects. RIBA Annual Review of Periodical Articles.)

ARCT. BIBLIOGR.
[CN/0066-6947]
ARCTIC BIBLIOGRAPHY.
(Ceased)

ARECO Q. INDEX PERIOD. LIT. AGING
[US/0734-5569]
ARECO'S QUARTERLY INDEX TO PERIODICAL LITERATURE ON AGING.
(*Continued by* Index to Periodical Literature on Aging.)

ART ARCHAEOL. TECH. ABSTR.
[US/0004-2994]
ART AND ARCHAEOLOGY TECHNICAL ABSTRACTS.
(*Continues* I.I.C. Abstracts.)

ART DES. PHOTO
[UK/0306-817X]
ART, DESIGN, PHOTO.
(Ceased)

ART INDEX
[US/0004-3222]
ART INDEX.

INDEXES/ABSTRACTS TABLE

ART INTELL. ABSTR.
[US/0882-1410]
ARTIFICIAL INTELLIGENCE ABSTRACTS.
(Ceased)

ARTBIBLIOGR. CURR. TITLES
[UK/0307-9961]
ARTBIBLIOGRAPHIES. CURRENT TITLES.

ARTBIBLIOGR. MOD.
[UK/0300-466X]
ARTBIBLIOGRAPHIES MODERN.
(**Continues** LOMA; Literature on Modern Art.)

ARTS HUMANIT. CITATION INDEX
[US/0162-8445]
ARTS & HUMANITIES CITATION INDEX (PRINT ED.).

ASCATOPICS
[US/0730-8574]
ASCATOPICS.
(**Continued by** Research Alert.)

ASCE
[US/0730-3149]
ASCE.
(**Continued by** ASCE Annual Combined Index.)

ASCE ANNU. COMB. INDEX
[US/0742-1753]
ASCE ANNUAL COMBINED INDEX.
(**Continues** American Society of Civil Engineers. ASCE.)

ASCE PUBL. INF.
[US/0734-1962]
ASCE PUBLICATIONS INFORMATION.
(**Continues** ASCE Publications Abstracts.)

ASIA.-PAC. ECON. LIT.
[UK/0818-9935]
ASIAN-PACIFIC ECONOMIC LITERATURE.

ASSIA PLUS
[UK]
ASSIA PLUS [COMPUTER FILE].
***Refer to Applied Social Sciences Index & Abstracts for complete source list.

ASTIS BIBLIOGR.
[CN/0226-1685]
ASTIS BIBLIOGRAPHY.

ASTIS CURR. AWARE. BULL.
[CN/0705-8454]
A S T I S CURRENT AWARENESS BULLETIN.
(**Continues** Arctic Institute of North America. Library Accessions.)

ASTRON. ASTROPHYS. ABSTR.
[GW/0067-0022]
ASTRONOMY AND ASTROPHYSICS ABSTRACTS.
(**Continues** Astronomischer Jahresbericht.)

AUST. EDUC. INDEX
[AT/0004-9026]
AUSTRALIAN EDUCATION INDEX.

AUST. LEG. MON. DIG.
[AT/0004-9646]
AUSTRALIAN LEGAL MONTHLY DIGEST.

AUST. LIBR. INF. SCI. ABSTR.
[AT/0810-9265]
ALISA. AUSTRALIAN LIBRARY AND INFORMATION SCIENCE ABSTRACTS.

AUST. SCI. INDEX
[AT/0005-0229]
AUSTRALIAN SCIENCE INDEX.
(**Continues** C.S.I.R.O. Science Abstracts.)

AUTOM. SUBJ. CITATION ALERT
[US]
AUTOMATIC SUBJECT CITATION ALERT.
(**Continued by** Research Alert.)

AVERY INDEX ARCHIT. PERIOD. SUPPL.
[US/0588-540X]
AVERY INDEX TO ARCHITECTURAL PERIODICALS. SUPPLEMENT.
(**Continued by** Avery Index to Architectural Periodicals. Supplement / Columbia University.)

AVERY INDEX ARCHIT. PERIOD. SUPPL. COLUM. UNIV.
[US/0196-0008]
AVERY INDEX TO ARCHITECTURAL PERIODICALS. SECOND EDITION. REVISED AND ENLARGED. SUPPLEMENT.
(**Continues** Avery Library. Avery Index to Architectural Periodicals. Supplement.)

AVIAT. TRADESCAN
[US/0899-1928]
AVIATION TRADESCAN.

BEHAV. ABSTR.
[UK/0262-236X]
BEHAVIOURAL ABSTRACTS.
(Ceased)

BEHAV. MED. ABSTR.
[US/0197-7717]
BEHAVIORAL MEDICINE ABSTRACTS.
(**Absorbed by** Annals of Behavioral Medicine.)

BER. BIOCHEM. BIOL.
[GW/0005-9013]
BERICHTE BIOCHEMIE UND BIOLOGIE.
(**Continues** Berichte uber die Wissenschaftliche Biologie.)

BHA : BIBLIO. HIST. ART
[FR/1150-1588]
BIBLIOGRAPHY OF THE HISTORY OF ART : BHA.
(**Formed by the union of** Repertoire International de la Litterature de l'Art **and** Repertoire d'Art et d'Archeologie.)

BHI PLUS
[UK/0966-8772]
BHI PLUS [COMPUTER FILE].
***Refer to British Humanities Index for complete source list.

BIBLIOGR. AGRIC.
[US/0006-1530]
BIBLIOGRAPHY OF AGRICULTURE.
(**Continues** Bibliography of Agriculture with Subject Index.)
***Refer to AGRICOLA for complete source list.

BIBLIOGR. BRAS. CIEN. INF.
[BL/0102-2865]
BIBLIOGRAFIA BRASILEIRA DE CIENCIA DA INFORMACAO.
(Ceased)

BIBLIOGR. BRAS. MED.
[BL/0067-6675]
BIBLIOGRAFIA BRASILEIRA DE MEDICINA.
(**Continues** Indice-Catalogo Medico Brasileiro.)

BIBLIOGR. CARTO.
[GW/0340-0409]
BIBLIOGRAPHIA CARTOGRAPHICA.
(**Supersedes** Bibliotheca Cartographica.)

BIBLIOGR. ENGL. LIT.
[UK]
BIBLIOGRAPHY OF ENGLISH LANGUAGE AND LITERATURE.
(**Continued by** Annual Bibliography of English Language and Literature.)

BIBLIOGR. HIST. MED.
[US/0067-7280]
BIBLIOGRAPHY OF THE HISTORY OF MEDICINE.
***Refer to Index Medicus for complete source list.

BIBLIOGR. INDEX GEOL.
[US/0098-2784]
BIBLIOGRAPHY AND INDEX OF GEOLOGY.
(**Continues** Bibliography and Index of Geology Exclusive of North America; **Absorbed** Bibliography of North American Geology.)
***Refer to GeoRef [Computer File] for complete source list.

BIBLIOGR. INDEX GEOL. EXCLUS. NORTH AM.
[US/0376-1673]
BIBLIOGRAPHY AND INDEX OF GEOLOGY EXCLUSIVE OF NORTH AMERICA.
(**Continued by** Bibliography and Index of Geology.)

BIBLIOGR. INDEX HEALTH EDUC. PERIOD.
[US/0278-2340]
BIBLIOGRAPHIC INDEX OF HEALTH EDUCATION PERIODICALS : BIHEP.
(Ceased)

BIBLIOGR. INDEX MICROPALEONTOLOGY
[US/0300-7227]
BIBLIOGRAPHY AND INDEX OF MICROPALEONTOLOGY.
***Refer to GeoRef [Computer File] for complete source list.

BIBLIOGR. MISSION.
[IT]
BIBLIOGRAFIA MISSIONARIA.
(**Continued by** Bibliographia Missionaria.)

BIBLIOGR. MISSION.
[VC/0394-9869]
BIBLIOGRAPHIA MISSIONARIA / PONTIFICAL MISSIONARY LIBRARY OF THE CONGREGATION FOR THE EVANGELIZATION OF PEOPLES.
(**Continues** Bibliografia Missionaria.)

BIBLIOGR. NORTH AM. GEOL.
[US/0740-6347]
BIBLIOGRAPHY OF NORTH AMERICAN GEOLOGY.
(**Absorbed by** Bibliography and Index of Geology.)

BIOBUSINESS
[US]
BIOBUSINESS.

BIOCONT. NEWS INF.
[UK/0143-1404]
BIOCONTROL NEWS AND INFORMATION.

BIODETER. ABSTR.
[UK/0951-0621]
BIODETERIORATION ABSTRACTS.
(**Separated from** International Biodeterioration.)

BIOENG. ABSTR.
[US/0093-8378]
BIOENGINEERING ABSTRACTS.
(**Continued by** Engineering Index Bioengineering Abstracts.)

INDEXES/ABSTRACTS TABLE

BIOENG. ABSTR.
[US/1068-5693]
BIOENGINEERING ABSTRACTS (1993).
(*Continues* Engineering Index Bioengineering and Biotechnology Abstracts.)

BIOGR. INDEX
[US/0006-3053]
BIOGRAPHY INDEX.

BIOL. ABSTR. RRM
[US/0192-6985]
BIOLOGICAL ABSTRACTS / RRM.
(*Continues* Bioresearch Index.)
***Refer to Biological Abstracts for complete source list.

BIOL. ABSTR.
[US/0006-3169]
BIOLOGICAL ABSTRACTS.
(*Formed by the union of* Abstracts of Bacteriology *and* Botanical Abstracts.)

BIOL. ABSTR. ON COMPACT DISC
[US/1058-4129]
BIOLOGICAL ABSTRACTS ON COMPACT DISC.
***Refer to Biological Abstracts for complete source list.

BIOL. AGRIC. INDEX
[US/0006-3177]
BIOLOGICAL & AGRICULTURAL INDEX.
(*Continues* Agricultural Index.)

BIOL. DIG.
[US/0095-2958]
BIOLOGY DIGEST.

BIOSTATISTICA
[US/1041-7648]
BIOSTATISTICA (DAVENPORT, IOWA).

BIOTECHNOL. ABSTR.
[UK/0262-5318]
DERWENT BIOTECHNOLOGY ABSTRACTS.
(*Continued by* Biotechnology Abstracts.)

BIOTECHNOL. ABSTR.
[UK]
BIOTECHNOLOGY ABSTRACTS.
(*Continues* Derwent Biotechnology Abstracts.)
***Refer to PESTDOC for complete source list.

BIOTECHNOL. RES. ABSTR.
[US/0733-5709]
BIOTECHNOLOGY RESEARCH ABSTRACTS.
(*Continued in part by* Medical & Pharmaceutical Biotechnology Abstracts *and* Agricultural & Environmental Biotechnology Abstracts.)

BLACK INF. INDEX
[US/0045-2173]
BLACK INFORMATION INDEX.
(Ceased)

BMT ABSTR.
[UK/0268-9650]
BMT ABSTRACTS : BRITISH MARITIME TECHNOLOGY ABSTRACTS.
(*Continues* Journal of Abstracts of the British Ship Research Association.)

BOOK REV. DIGEST
[US/0006-7326]
BOOK REVIEW DIGEST.
(*Continues* Cumulative Book Review Digest.)

BOOK REV. INDEX
[US/0524-0581]
BOOK REVIEW INDEX.

BOOK REV. MON.
[US/0006-7342]
BOOK REVIEWS OF THE MONTH.
(Ceased)

BOSTON GLOBE INDEX
[US/0893-2727]
BOSTON GLOBE INDEX (1987), THE.
(*Continues* Bell & Howell Newspaper Index to the Boston Globe.)

BOWNE DIG. CORP. SEC. LAWYERS
[US/0896-906X]
BOWNE DIGEST FOR CORPORATE & SECURITIES LAWYERS.
(*Continues* Abstracts of Legal Periodicals (Corporate & Securities Ed.).)

BR. ARCHAEOL. ABSTR.
[UK/0007-0270]
BRITISH ARCHAEOLOGICAL ABSTRACTS.
(*Continued by* British Archaeological Bibliography.)

BR. ARCHAEOL. BIBLIOGR.
[UK/0964-7104]
BRITISH ARCHAEOLOGICAL BIBLIOGRAPHY.
(*Continues* British Archaeological Abstracts.)

BR. CERAM. ABSTR.
[UK/0300-4570]
BRITISH CERAMIC ABSTRACTS.
(*Continued by* World Ceramics Abstracts.)

BR. EDUC. INDEX
[UK/0007-0637]
BRITISH EDUCATION INDEX.

BR. HUMANIT. INDEX
[UK/0007-0815]
BRITISH HUMANITIES INDEX.
(*Supersedes in part* Subject Index to Periodicals.)

BR. TECHNOL. INDEX
[UK/0007-1889]
BRITISH TECHNOLOGY INDEX.
(*Continued by* Current Technology Index.)

BULL. ANAL. ENTOMOL. MED. VET.
[FR/0007-4098]
BULLETIN ANALYTIQUE D'ENTOMOLOGIE MEDICALE ET VETERINAIRE.
(Ceased)

BULL. SIGNAL.
[FR]
BULLETIN SIGNALETIQUE.
(Ceased)

BUS. ASAP
[US]
BUSINESS ASAP [COMPUTER FILE].

BUS. DATELINE
[US]
BUSINESS DATELINE.

BUS. EDUC. INDEX
[US/0068-4414]
BUSINESS EDUCATION INDEX.

BUS. INDEX
[US/0273-3684]
BUSINESS INDEX.

BUS. PERIOD. INDEX
[US/0007-6961]
BUSINESS PERIODICALS INDEX.
(*Continues in part* Industrial Arts Index.)

BUS. SOURCE
[US]
BUSINESS SOURCE. [COMPUTER FILE].

CA QUICK SEARCH
[US]
CA QUICK SEARCH [COMPUTER FILE].
***Refer to Concrete Abstracts for complete source list.

CA SEL., ACID RAIN ACID AIR
[US/0885-0097]
CA SELECTS: ACID RAIN & ACID AIR.
***Refer to Chemical Abstracts for complete source list.

CA SEL., ADHESIVES
[US/0162-7686]
CA SELECTS: ADHESIVES.
***Refer to Chemical Abstracts for complete source list.

CA SEL., AIDS RELAT. IMMUNODEFIC.
[US/1040-7111]
CA SELECTS: AIDS & RELATED IMMUNODEFICIENCIES.
***Refer to Chemical Abstracts for complete source list.

CA SEL., AIR POLLUT. BOOKS REV.
[US/0895-5980]
CA SELECTS: AIR POLLUTION (BOOKS & REVIEWS).
***Refer to Chemical Abstracts for complete source list.

CA SEL., ALKYL. CATAL.
[US/0895-5964]
CA SELECTS: ALKYLATION & CATALYSTS.
***Refer to Chemical Abstracts for complete source list.

CA SEL., ALUMIN. LITH. ALUMIN. CER. ALLOYS
[US/1066-1166]
CA SELECTS: ALUMINUM-LITHIUM & ALUMINUM-CERIUM ALLOYS.
***Refer to Chemical Abstracts for complete source list.

CA SEL., ALZHEIMER'S DIS. RELAT. MEM. DYSFUNC.
[US/1047-8183]
CA SELECTS: ALZHEIMER'S DISEASE & RELATED MEMORY DYSFUNCTIONS.
***Refer to Chemical Abstracts for complete source list.

CA SEL., AMINO ACIDS PEP. PROT.
[US/0275-701X]
CA SELECTS: AMINO ACIDS, PEPTIDES & PROTEINS.
***Refer to Chemical Abstracts for complete source list.

CA SEL., ANALYT. ELECTROCHEM.
[US/0160-8959]
CA SELECTS: ANALYTICAL ELECTROCHEMISTRY.
***Refer to Chemical Abstracts for complete source list.

CA SEL., ANIMAL LONG. AGING
[US/0162-7694]
CA SELECTS: ANIMAL LONGEVITY & AGING.
***Refer to Chemical Abstracts for complete source list.

CA SEL., ANTI INFLAM. AGENTS ARTHRIT.
[US/0148-2394]
CA SELECTS: ANTI-INFLAMMATORY AGENTS & ARTHRITIS.
***Refer to Chemical Abstracts for complete source list.

CA SEL., ANTIBAC. AGENTS
[US/1045-8522]
CA SELECTS: ANTIBACTERIAL AGENTS.
(*Continues* CA Selects. Bactericides, Disinfectants & Antiseptics.)
***Refer to Chemical Abstracts for complete source list.

CA SEL., ANTIOXID.
[US/0275-7028]
CA SELECTS: ANTIOXIDANTS.
***Refer to Chemical Abstracts for complete source list.

INDEXES/ABSTRACTS TABLE

CA SEL., ANTITUMOR AGENTS
[US/0148-2386]
CA SELECTS: ANTITUMOR AGENTS.
***Refer to Chemical Abstracts for complete source list.

CA SEL., ARTIF. SWEETEN.
[US/0890-1813]
CA SELECTS: ARTIFICIAL SWEETENERS.
***Refer to Chemical Abstracts for complete source list.

CA SEL., ASYMMET. SYNTH. INDUC.
[US/0890-183X]
CA SELECTS: ASYMMETRIC SYNTHESIS & INDUCTION.
***Refer to Chemical Abstracts for complete source list.

CA SEL., AT. SPECTROSC.
[US/0195-4911]
CA SELECTS: ATOMIC SPECTROSCOPY.
***Refer to Chemical Abstracts for complete source list.

CA SEL., ATHEROSCL. HEART DIS.
[US/0148-2378]
CA SELECTS: ATHEROSCLEROSIS & HEART DISEASE.
***Refer to Chemical Abstracts for complete source list.

CA SEL., AUTOM. CHEM. ANAL.
[US/0740-0683]
CA SELECTS: AUTOMATED CHEMICAL ANALYSIS.
***Refer to Chemical Abstracts for complete source list.

CA SEL., B-LACTAM ANTIB.
[US/0148-2459]
CA SELECTS: B-LACTAM ANTIBIOTICS.
***Refer to Chemical Abstracts for complete source list.

CA SEL., BACTER. DISINFECT. ANTISEP.
[US/0890-1848]
CA SELECTS: BACTERICIDES, DISINFECTANTS & ANTISEPTICS.
(*Continued by* CA Selects: Antibacterial Agents.)

CA SEL., BATTER. FUEL CELLS
[US/0162-7708]
CA SELECTS: BATTERIES & FUEL CELLS.
***Refer to Chemical Abstracts for complete source list.

CA SEL., BIOGEN. AMINES NERV. SYST.
[US/0162-7716]
CA SELECTS: BIOGENIC AMINES & THE NERVOUS SYSTEM.
***Refer to Chemical Abstracts for complete source list.

CA SEL., BIOL. INFO. TRANSF.
[US/0162-7724]
CA SELECTS: BIOLOGICAL INFORMATION TRANSFER.
(Ceased)

CA SEL., BISMUTH CHEM.
[US/1061-5342]
CA SELECTS: BISMUTH CHEMISTRY.
***Refer to Chemical Abstracts for complete source list.

CA SEL., BLOCK GRAFT POLYM.
[US/0734-8851]
CA SELECTS: BLOCK & GRAFT POLYMERS.
***Refer to Chemical Abstracts for complete source list.

CA SEL., BLOOD COAG.
[US/0162-7732]
CA SELECTS: BLOOD COAGULATION.
***Refer to Chemical Abstracts for complete source list.

CA SEL., CARBOHYDR. (CHEM. ASP.)
[US/0740-0756]
CA SELECTS: CARBOHYDRATES (CHEMICAL ASPECTS).
***Refer to Chemical Abstracts for complete source list.

CA SEL., CARBON FIBER COMPOS.
[US/0895-5956]
CA SELECTS: CARBON FIBER COMPOSITES.
***Refer to Chemical Abstracts for complete source list.

CA SEL., CARBON GRAPH. FIB.
[US/0890-1856]
CA SELECTS: CARBON & GRAPHITE FIBERS.
***Refer to Chemical Abstracts for complete source list.

CA SEL., CARBON HETERO. NMR
[US/0190-9401]
CA SELECTS: CARBON & HETEROATOM NMR.
(*Continues in part* CA Selects. Nuclear Magnetic Resonance, Chemical Aspects.)
***Refer to Chemical Abstracts for complete source list.

CA SEL., CARCIN. MUT. TERATO.
[US/0148-2408]
CA SELECTS: CARCINOGENS, MUTAGENS & TERATOGENS.
***Refer to Chemical Abstracts for complete source list.

CA SEL., CATAL. (APPL. PHYS. ASP.)
[US/0146-440X]
CA SELECTS: CATALYSIS (APPLIED AND PHYSICAL ASPECTS).
***Refer to Chemical Abstracts for complete source list.

CA SEL., CATAL. (ORG. REACT.)
[US/0146-4396]
CA SELECTS: CATALYSIS (ORGANIC REACTIONS).
***Refer to Chemical Abstracts for complete source list.

CA SEL., CATAL. KINET. ANAL.
[US/0890-1864]
CA SELECTS: CATALYTIC & KINETIC ANALYSIS.
***Refer to Chemical Abstracts for complete source list.

CA SEL., CATAL. REGEN.
[US/0734-8800]
CA SELECTS: CATALYST REGENERATION.
***Refer to Chemical Abstracts for complete source list.

CA SEL., CERAM. MATER. J.
[US/0895-5948]
CA SELECTS: CERAMIC MATERIALS (JOURNALS).
***Refer to Chemical Abstracts for complete source list.

CA SEL., CERAM. METER. PAT.
[US/0885-0100]
CA SELECTS: CERAMIC MATERIALS (PATENTS).
***Refer to Chemical Abstracts for complete source list.

CA SEL., CHELATING AGENTS
[US/0734-8797]
CA SELECTS: CHELATING AGENTS.
***Refer to Chemical Abstracts for complete source list.

CA SEL., CHEM. ENG. OPER.
[US/1040-712X]
CA SELECTS: CHEMICAL ENGINEERING OPERATIONS.
***Refer to Chemical Abstracts for complete source list.

CA SEL., CHEM. HAZ. HEALTH SAFETY
[US/0190-9398]
CA SELECTS: CHEMICAL HAZARDS, HEALTH, & SAFETY.
(*Continues* CA Selects. Chemical Hazards.)
***Refer to Chemical Abstracts for complete source list.

CA SEL., CHEM. INSTRUM.
[US/0195-4938]
CA SELECTS: CHEMICAL INSTRUMENTATION.
***Refer to Chemical Abstracts for complete source list.

CA SEL., CHEM. IR OS RH RU
[US/1040-7146]
CA SELECTS: CHEMISTRY OF IR, OS, RH, & RU.
***Refer to Chemical Abstracts for complete source list.

CA SEL., CHEM. PROCESS. APPAR.
[US/0195-4946]
CA SELECTS: CHEMICAL PROCESSING APPARATUS.
***Refer to Chemical Abstracts for complete source list.

CA SEL., CHEM. VAPOR DEPOS.
[US/0885-0119]
CA SELECTS. CHEMICAL VAPOR DEPOSITION.
***Refer to Chemical Abstracts for complete source list.

CA SEL., CHEMILUMIN.
[US/1040-7138]
CA SELECTS: CHEMILUMINESCENCE.
***Refer to Chemical Abstracts for complete source list.

CA SEL., COAL SCI. PROC. CHEM.
[US/0146-4426]
CA SELECTS: COAL SCIENCE & PROCESS CHEMISTRY.
***Refer to Chemical Abstracts for complete source list.

CA SEL., COAT. INKS REALT. PROD.
[US/0275-7036]
CA SELECTS: COATINGS, INKS, & RELATED PRODUCTS.
***Refer to Chemical Abstracts for complete source list.

CA SEL., COLLOIDS (APPL. ASP.)
[US/0160-8967]
CA SELECTS: COLLOIDS (APPLIED ASPECTS).
(*Continued by* CA Selects. Colloids (Macromolecular Aspects).)

CA SEL., COLLOIDS (MACROMOL. ASP.)
[US/0190-9444]
CA SELECTS: COLLOIDS (MACROMOLECULAR ASPECTS).
(*Supersedes in part* CA Selects. Colloids (Applied Aspects).)
***Refer to Chemical Abstracts for complete source list.

CA SEL., COLLOIDS (PHYSICO. ASP.)
[US/0160-8975]
CA SELECTS: COLLOIDS (PHYSICOCHEMICAL ASPECTS).
***Refer to Chemical Abstracts for complete source list.

CA SEL., COLOR SCI.
[US/0885-0127]
CA SELECTS: COLOR SCIENCE.
***Refer to Chemical Abstracts for complete source list.

CA SEL., COLOR. DYES
[US/0734-8789]
CA SELECTS: COLORANTS & DYES.
***Refer to Chemical Abstracts for complete source list.

CA SEL., COMPOS. MATER. (CERAM.)
[US/1066-1158]
CA SELECTS: COMPOSITE MATERIALS (CERAMIC).
***Refer to Chemical Abstracts for complete source list.

CA SEL., COMPOS. MATER. (MET.)
[US/1066-114X]
CA SELECTS: COMPOSITE MATERIALS (METALLIC).
***Refer to Chemical Abstracts for complete source list.

CA SEL., COMPOS. MATER. (POLYM.)
[US/1040-7154]
CA SELECTS: COMPOSITE MATERIALS (POLYMERIC).
***Refer to Chemical Abstracts for complete source list.

CA SEL., COMPUT. CHEM.
[US/0160-9025]
CA SELECTS: COMPUTERS IN CHEMISTRY.
***Refer to Chemical Abstracts for complete source list.

INDEXES/ABSTRACTS TABLE

CA SEL., CONDUCT. POLYM.
[US/0885-0135]
CA SELECTS: CONDUCTIVE POLYMERS.
***Refer to Chemical Abstracts for complete source list.

CA SEL., CONTROL. RELEASE TECHNOL.
[US/0740-0748]
CA SELECTS: CONTROLLED RELEASE TECHNOLOGY.
***Refer to Chemical Abstracts for complete source list.

CA SEL., CORROS.
[US/0146-4434]
CA SELECTS: CORROSION.
***Refer to Chemical Abstracts for complete source list.

CA SEL., CORROS.-INHIB. COAT.
[US/0749-7296]
CA SELECTS: CORROSION-INHIBITING COATINGS.
***Refer to Chemical Abstracts for complete source list.

CA SEL., COSMET. CHEM.
[US/0275-7044]
CA SELECTS: COSMETIC CHEMICALS.
***Refer to Chemical Abstracts for complete source list.

CA SEL., COSMOCHEM.
[US/0195-4954]
CA SELECTS: COSMOCHEMISTRY.
(Ceased)

CA SEL., CROSSLINK. REACT.
[US/0740-0721]
CA SELECTS: CROSSLINKING REACTIONS.
***Refer to Chemical Abstracts for complete source list.

CA SEL., CRYS. GROWTH
[US/0162-7740]
CA SELECTS: CRYSTAL GROWTH.
***Refer to Chemical Abstracts for complete source list.

CA SEL., DETER. SOAPS, SURFAC.
[US/0162-7767]
CA SELECTS: DETERGENTS, SOAPS, & SURFACTANTS.
***Refer to Chemical Abstracts for complete source list.

CA SEL., DISTILL. TECHNOL.
[US/0275-7052]
CA SELECTS: DISTILLATION TECHNOLOGY.
***Refer to Chemical Abstracts for complete source list.

CA SEL., DRILL. MUDS
[US/0749-730X]
CA SELECTS: DRILLING MUDS.
***Refer to Chemical Abstracts for complete source list.

CA SEL., DRUG COSMET. TOXIC.
[US/0162-7775]
CA SELECTS: DRUG & COSMETIC TOXICITY.
***Refer to Chemical Abstracts for complete source list.

CA SEL., DRUG DELIV. SYST. DOS. FORMS
[US/1040-7162]
CA SELECTS: DRUG DELIVERY SYSTEMS & DOSAGE FORMS.
***Refer to Chemical Abstracts for complete source list.

CA SEL., ELECT. AUG. SPECTRO.
[US/0146-4450]
CA SELECTS: ELECTRON & AUGER SPECTROSCOPY.
***Refer to Chemical Abstracts for complete source list.

CA SEL., ELECT. SPIN RESON. (CHEM. ASP.)
[US/0146-4469]
CA SELECTS: ELECTRON SPIN RESONANCE (CHEMICAL ASPECTS).
***Refer to Chemical Abstracts for complete source list.

CA SEL., ELECTR. CONDUCT. ORG.
[US/0885-0143]
CA SELECTS: ELECTRICALLY CONDUCTIVE ORGANICS.
***Refer to Chemical Abstracts for complete source list.

CA SEL., ELECTROCHEM. ORG. SYNTH.
[US/0734-8770]
CA SELECTS: ELECTROCHEMICAL ORGANIC SYNTHESIS.
***Refer to Chemical Abstracts for complete source list.

CA SEL., ELECTROCHEM. REAC.
[US/0146-4442]
CA SELECTS: ELECTROCHEMICAL REACTIONS.
***Refer to Chemical Abstracts for complete source list.

CA SEL., ELECTRODEPOSIT.
[US/0162-7783]
CA SELECTS: ELECTRODEPOSITION.
***Refer to Chemical Abstracts for complete source list.

CA SEL., ELECTRON. CHEM. MATER.
[US/0885-0151]
CA SELECTS: ELECTRONIC CHEMICALS & MATERIALS.
***Refer to Chemical Abstracts for complete source list.

CA SEL., ELECTROPHOR.
[US/0195-4962]
CA SELECTS: ELECTROPHORESIS.
***Refer to Chemical Abstracts for complete source list.

CA SEL., EMULS. POLYM.
[US/0195-4970]
CA SELECTS: EMULSION POLYMERIZATION.
***Refer to Chemical Abstracts for complete source list.

CA SEL., EMULSIF. & DEMULSIF.
[US/0734-8754]
CA SELECTS: EMULSIFIERS & DEMULSIFIERS.
***Refer to Chemical Abstracts for complete source list.

CA SEL., ENERGY REV. BOOKS
[US/0162-7791]
CA SELECTS: ENERGY REVIEWS & BOOKS.
***Refer to Chemical Abstracts for complete source list.

CA SEL., ENGINE EXH.
[US/0160-9033]
CA SELECTS: ENGINE EXHAUST.
(Ceased)

CA SEL., ENHANC. PETRO. RECOV.
[US/0734-8746]
CA SELECTS: ENHANCED PETROLEUM RECOVERY.
***Refer to Chemical Abstracts for complete source list.

CA SEL., ENVIRON. POLLUT.
[US/0160-9041]
CA SELECTS: ENVIRONMENTAL POLLUTION.
***Refer to Chemical Abstracts for complete source list.

CA SEL., ENZYM. APPL.
[US/0895-593X]
CA SELECTS: ENZYME APPLICATIONS.
***Refer to Chemical Abstracts for complete source list.

CA SEL., ENZYM. ASSAYS
[US/0895-5808]
CA SELECTS: ENZYME ASSAYS.
***Refer to Chemical Abstracts for complete source list.

CA SEL., EPOXY RESINS
[US/0275-7060]
CA SELECTS: EPOXY RESINS.
***Refer to Chemical Abstracts for complete source list.

CA SEL., FATS OILS
[US/0275-7079]
CA SELECTS: FATS & OILS.
***Refer to Chemical Abstracts for complete source list.

CA SEL., FERMENT. CHEM.
[US/0740-0713]
CA SELECTS: FERMENTATION CHEMICALS.
***Refer to Chemical Abstracts for complete source list.

CA SEL., FIBER OPT. OPT. COMMUN.
[US/0890-1872]
CA SELECTS: FIBER OPTICS & OPTICAL COMMUNICATION.
***Refer to Chemical Abstracts for complete source list.

CA SEL., FIBER-REINFOR. PLAST.
[US/0734-869X]
CA SELECTS: FIBER-REINFORCED PLASTICS.
***Refer to Chemical Abstracts for complete source list.

CA SEL., FLAMMABIL.
[US/0162-7805]
CA SELECTS: FLAMMABILITY.
***Refer to Chemical Abstracts for complete source list.

CA SEL., FLAV. FRAGR.
[US/0148-2327]
CA SELECTS: FLAVORS & FRAGRANCES.
***Refer to Chemical Abstracts for complete source list.

CA SEL., FLUID. SOLIDS TECHNOL.
[US/0195-4989]
CA SELECTS: FLUIDIZED SOLIDS TECHNOLOGY.
***Refer to Chemical Abstracts for complete source list.

CA SEL., FLUOROPOLY.
[US/0895-5921]
CA SELECTS: FLUOROPOLYMERS.
***Refer to Chemical Abstracts for complete source list.

CA SEL., FOOD DRUGS COSMET.
[US/1051-3914]
CA SELECTS: FOOD, DRUGS, & COSMETICS.
***Refer to Chemical Abstracts for complete source list.

CA SEL., FOOD FEED ANAL.
[US/0895-5913]
CA SELECTS: FOOD & FEED ANALYSIS.
***Refer to Chemical Abstracts for complete source list.

CA SEL., FOOD TOXIC.
[US/0162-7813]
CA SELECTS: FOOD TOXICITY.
***Refer to Chemical Abstracts for complete source list.

CA SEL., FORENS. CHEM.
[US/0362-9880]
CA SELECTS: FORENSIC CHEMISTRY.
***Refer to Chemical Abstracts for complete source list.

CA SEL., FORMUL. CHEM.
[US/0890-1880]
CA SELECTS: FORMULATION CHEMISTRY.
***Refer to Chemical Abstracts for complete source list.

CA SEL., FREE RADIC.
[US/0885-016X]
CA SELECTS: FREE RADICALS.
(**Continued by** CA Selects: Free Radicals (Organic Aspects).)

CA SEL., FREE RADIC. (BIOCHEM. ASP.)
[US/0895-5905]
CA SELECTS: FREE RADICALS (BIOCHEMICAL ASPECTS).
***Refer to Chemical Abstracts for complete source list.

INDEXES/ABSTRACTS TABLE

CA SEL., FREE RADIC. (ORG. ASP.)
[US/0895-5972]
CA SELECTS: FREE RADICALS (ORGANIC ASPECTS).
(*Continues* CA Selects. Free Radicals.)
***Refer to Chemical Abstracts for complete source list.

CA SEL., FUEL LUBR. ADDIT.
[US/0195-4997]
CA SELECTS: FUEL & LUBRICANT ADDITIVES.
***Refer to Chemical Abstracts for complete source list.

CA SEL., FUNGICID.
[US/0160-9068]
CA SELECTS: FUNGICIDES.
***Refer to Chemical Abstracts for complete source list.

CA SEL., GAS CHROMAT.
[US/0146-4477]
CA SELECTS: GAS CHROMATOGRAPHY.
***Refer to Chemical Abstracts for complete source list.

CA SEL., GAS. WASTE TREAT.
[US/0160-9076]
CA SELECTS: GASEOUS WASTE TREATMENT.
***Refer to Chemical Abstracts for complete source list.

CA SEL., GEL PERM. CHROMAT.
[US/0146-4485]
CA SELECTS: GEL PERMEATION CHROMATOGRAPHY.
***Refer to Chemical Abstracts for complete source list.

CA SEL., GEOCHEM.
[US/1066-5730]
CA SELECTS: GEOCHEMISTRY.
***Refer to Chemical Abstracts for complete source list.

CA SEL., HEAT-RESIST. ABLAT. POLYM.
[US/0162-7821]
CA SELECTS: HEAT-RESISTANT & ABLATIVE POLYMERS.
***Refer to Chemical Abstracts for complete source list.

CA SEL., HERBIC.
[US/0160-9084]
CA SELECTS: HERBICIDES.
***Refer to Chemical Abstracts for complete source list.

CA SEL., HIGH PERFORM. LIQ. CHROMATOGR.
[US/0195-5217]
CA SELECTS: HIGH PERFORMANCE LIQUID CHROMATOGRAPHY.
(*Continues* CA Selects. High Speed Liquid Chromatography.)
***Refer to Chemical Abstracts for complete source list.

CA SEL., HOT-MELT ADHES.
[US/0895-5891]
CA SELECTS: HOT-MELT ADHESIVES.
***Refer to Chemical Abstracts for complete source list.

CA SEL., HYPERTENS. ANTIHYPERTENS.
[US/1051-3922]
CA SELECTS: HYPERTENSION & ANTIHYPERTENSIVES.
***Refer to Chemical Abstracts for complete source list.

CA SEL., INFR. SPECTRO. (ORG. ASP.)
[US/0190-9428]
CA SELECTS: INFRARED SPECTROSCOPY (ORGANIC ASPECTS).
(*Continues in part* CA Selects. Infrared Spectroscopy.)
***Refer to Chemical Abstracts for complete source list.

CA SEL., INFR. SPECTRO. (PHYSICOCHEM. ASP.)
[US/0190-9436]
CA SELECTS: INFRARED SPECTROSCOPY (PHYSICOCHEMICAL ASPECTS).
(*Continues in part* CA Selects. Infrared Spectroscopy.)
***Refer to Chemical Abstracts for complete source list.

CA SEL., INIT. POLYMER.
[US/0734-8843]
CA SELECTS: INITIATION OF POLYMERIZATION.
***Refer to Chemical Abstracts for complete source list.

CA SEL., INORG. ANAL. CHEM.
[US/0275-7087]
CA SELECTS: INORGANIC ANALYTICAL CHEMISTRY.
***Refer to Chemical Abstracts for complete source list.

CA SEL., INORG. CHEM. REACT.
[US/0275-7095]
CA SELECTS: INORGANIC CHEMICALS & REACTIONS.
***Refer to Chemical Abstracts for complete source list.

CA SEL., INORG. FLOUR. CHEM.
[US/0195-5004]
CA SELECTS: INORGANIC FLOURINE CHEMISTRY.
(Ceased)

CA SEL., INORG. ORGANOMET. REACT. MECHAN.
[US/0195-5012]
CA SELECTS: INORGANIC & ORGANOMETALLIC REACTION MECHANISMS.
***Refer to Chemical Abstracts for complete source list.

CA SEL., INSECTIC.
[US/0160-9092]
CA SELECTS: INSECTICIDES.
***Refer to Chemical Abstracts for complete source list.

CA SEL., ION CHROMATOGR.
[US/0890-1899]
CA SELECTS: ION CHROMATOGRAPHY.
***Refer to Chemical Abstracts for complete source list.

CA SEL., ION EXCHANGE
[US/0146-4493]
CA SELECTS: ION EXCHANGE.
***Refer to Chemical Abstracts for complete source list.

CA SEL., ION-CONTAIN. POLYM.
[US/0195-5020]
CA SELECTS: ION-CONTAINING POLYMERS.
***Refer to Chemical Abstracts for complete source list.

CA SEL., ISOMERI. CATAL.
[US/0895-5883]
CA SELECTS: ISOMERIZATION & CATALYSTS.
***Refer to Chemical Abstracts for complete source list.

CA SEL., LASER APPL.
[US/0195-5039]
CA SELECTS: LASER APPLICATIONS.
***Refer to Chemical Abstracts for complete source list.

CA SEL., LASER-INDUC. CHEM REACT.
[US/0885-0178]
CA SELECTS: LASER-INDUCED CHEMICAL REACTIONS.
***Refer to Chemical Abstracts for complete source list.

CA SEL., LASERS MASERS
[US/0195-5047]
CA SELECTS: LASERS & MASERS.
(Ceased)

CA SEL., LIQ. CRYST.
[US/0148-2351]
CA SELECTS: LIQUID CRYSTALS.
***Refer to Chemical Abstracts for complete source list.

CA SEL., LIQ. WASTE TREAT.
[US/0160-9106]
CA SELECTS: LIQUID WASTE TREATMENT.
***Refer to Chemical Abstracts for complete source list.

CA SEL., LUBR. GREAS. LUBRICAT.
[US/0734-8738]
CA SELECTS: LUBRICANTS, GREASES & LUBRICATION.
***Refer to Chemical Abstracts for complete source list.

CA SEL., MACROCYCL. ANTIBIOT.
[US/0195-5055]
CA SELECTS: MACROCYCLIC ANTIBIOTICS.
(Ceased)

CA SEL., MASS SPECTRO.
[US/0362-9872]
CA SELECTS: MASS SPECTROMETRY.
***Refer to Chemical Abstracts for complete source list.

CA SEL., MEM. REC. DEVICES MATER.
[US/0890-1821]
CA SELECTS: MEMORY & RECORDING DEVICES & MATERIALS.
***Refer to Chemical Abstracts for complete source list.

CA SEL., MEMBR. SEP.
[US/1040-7197]
CA SELECTS: MEMBRANE SEPARATION.
***Refer to Chemical Abstracts for complete source list.

CA SEL., METAL. GLASS.
[US/1062-8681]
CA SELECTS: METALLIC GLASSES.
***Refer to Chemical Abstracts for complete source list.

CA SEL., METALLO ENZ. METALLO COENZ.
[US/0160-9114]
CA SELECTS: METALLO ENZYMES & METALLO COENZYMES.
***Refer to Chemical Abstracts for complete source list.

CA SEL., MOLEC. MODEL. (BIOCHEM. ASP.)
[US/1059-2784]
CA SELECTS: MOLECULAR MODELING (BIOCHEMICAL ASPECTS).
***Refer to Chemical Abstracts for complete source list.

CA SEL., NAT. PROD. SYNTH.
[US/0740-0691]
CA SELECTS: NATURAL PRODUCT SYNTHESIS.
***Refer to Chemical Abstracts for complete source list.

CA SEL., NEW ANTIBIOT.
[US/0895-5875]
CA SELECTS: NEW ANTIBIOTICS.
***Refer to Chemical Abstracts for complete source list.

CA SEL., NEW BOOKS CHEM.
[US/0148-2416]
CA SELECTS: NEW BOOKS IN CHEMISTRY.
***Refer to Chemical Abstracts for complete source list.

CA SEL., NEW PLAST.
[US/0734-8673]
CA SELECTS: NEW PLASTICS.
***Refer to Chemical Abstracts for complete source list.

CA SEL., NITROGEN FIXAT.
[US/1047-8108]
CA SELECTS: NITROGEN FIXATION.
***Refer to Chemical Abstracts for complete source list.

CA SEL., NONLINEAR OPT. MATER.
[US/0895-5867]
CA SELECTS: NONLINEAR OPTICAL MATERIALS.
***Refer to Chemical Abstracts for complete source list.

INDEXES/ABSTRACTS TABLE

CA SEL., NOV. PESTIC. HERBIC.
[US/0749-7318]
CA SELECTS: NOVEL PESTICIDES & HERBICIDES.
***Refer to Chemical Abstracts for complete source list.

CA SEL., NOVEL NAT. PROD.
[US/0734-872X]
CA SELECTS: NOVEL NATURAL PRODUCTS.
***Refer to Chemical Abstracts for complete source list.

CA SEL., NOVEL POLYM. PAT.
[US/0734-8819]
CA SELECTS: NOVEL POLYMERS FROM PATENTS.
***Refer to Chemical Abstracts for complete source list.

CA SEL., NOVEL SULFUR HETEROCYCL.
[US/0275-7109]
CA SELECTS: NOVEL SULFUR HETEROCYCLES.
***Refer to Chemical Abstracts for complete source list.

CA SEL., OMEGA THREE FAT. ACID. FISH OIL
[US/1052-1984]
CA SELECTS: OMEGA THREE FATTY ACIDS & FISH OIL.
***Refer to Chemical Abstracts for complete source list.

CA SEL., OPT. PHOTOSENSIT. MATER.
[US/0195-5063]
CA SELECTS: OPTICAL & PHOTOSENSITIVE MATERIALS.
***Refer to Chemical Abstracts for complete source list.

CA SEL., OPTIMIZ. ORG. REACT.
[US/0195-5071]
CA SELECTS: OPTIMIZATION OF ORGANIC REACTIONS.
***Refer to Chemical Abstracts for complete source list.

CA SEL., ORAGNOPHOS. CHEM.
[US/0162-783X]
CA SELECTS: ORGANOPHOSPHORUS CHEMISTRY.
***Refer to Chemical Abstracts for complete source list.

CA SEL., ORG. ANAL. CHEM.
[US/0275-7117]
CA SELECTS: ORGANIC ANALYTICAL CHEMISTRY.
***Refer to Chemical Abstracts for complete source list.

CA SEL., ORG. OPT. MATER.
[US/0885-0186]
CA SELECTS: ORGANIC OPTICAL MATERIALS.
***Refer to Chemical Abstracts for complete source list.

CA SEL., ORG. REACT. MECHAN.
[US/0162-7848]
CA SELECTS: ORGANIC REACTION MECHANISMS.
***Refer to Chemical Abstracts for complete source list.

CA SEL., ORG. STEREOCHEM.
[US/0195-508X]
CA SELECTS: ORGANIC STEREOCHEMISTRY.
***Refer to Chemical Abstracts for complete source list.

CA SEL., ORG.-TRANS. MET. COMPL.
[US/0160-9130]
CA SELECTS: ORGANO-TRANSITION METAL COMPLEXES.
***Refer to Chemical Abstracts for complete source list.

CA SEL., ORGANOBOR. CHEM. BORAN.
[US/0195-5098]
CA SELECTS: ORGANOBORON CHEMISTRY & BORANES.
(Ceased)

CA SEL., ORGANOFLOUR. CHEM.
[US/0160-905X]
CA SELECTS: ORGANOFLUORINE CHEMISTRY.
***Refer to Chemical Abstracts for complete source list.

CA SEL., ORGANOMET. ORG. SYNTH.
[US/0895-5859]
CA SELECTS: ORGANOMETALLICS IN ORGANIC SYNTHESIS.
***Refer to Chemical Abstracts for complete source list.

CA SEL., ORGANOSIL. CHEM.
[US/0362-9899]
CA SELECTS: ORGANOSILICON CHEMISTRY.
***Refer to Chemical Abstracts for complete source list.

CA SEL., ORGANOSUL. CHEM. J.
[US/1040-7189]
CA SELECTS: ORGANOSULFUR CHEMISTRY (JOURNALS).
***Refer to Chemical Abstracts for complete source list.

CA SEL., ORGANOTIN CHEM.
[US/0195-5101]
CA SELECTS: ORGANOTIN CHEMISTRY.
***Refer to Chemical Abstracts for complete source list.

CA SEL., OXID. CATAL.
[US/1040-7170]
CA SELECTS: OXIDATION CATALYSTS.
***Refer to Chemical Abstracts for complete source list.

CA SEL., OXIDE SUPERCOND.
[US/1040-7219]
CA SELECTS: OXIDE SUPERCONDUCTORS.
***Refer to Chemical Abstracts for complete source list.

CA SEL., PAINT ADDIT.
[US/0734-8762]
CA SELECTS: PAINT ADDITIVES.
***Refer to Chemical Abstracts for complete source list.

CA SEL., PAP. CHEM.
[US/1040-7200]
CA SELECTS: PAPER CHEMISTRY.
***Refer to Chemical Abstracts for complete source list.

CA SEL., PAP. THIN-LAY. CHROMATOGR.
[US/0146-4515]
CA SELECTS: PAPER & THIN-LAYER CHROMATOGRAPHY.
***Refer to Chemical Abstracts for complete source list.

CA SEL., PAPER ADDIT.
[US/0734-8711]
CA SELECTS: PAPER ADDITIVES.
***Refer to Chemical Abstracts for complete source list.

CA SEL., PHARM. ANAL.
[US/0890-1902]
CA SELECTS: PHARMACEUTICAL ANALYSIS.
***Refer to Chemical Abstracts for complete source list.

CA SEL., PHARM. CHEM. (PAT.)
[US/0890-1929]
CA SELECTS: PHARMACEUTICAL CHEMISTRY (PATENTS).
***Refer to Chemical Abstracts for complete source list.

CA SEL., PHARM. CHEM. J.
[US/0890-1910]
CA SELECTS: PHARMACEUTICAL CHEMISTRY (JOURNALS).
***Refer to Chemical Abstracts for complete source list.

CA SEL., PHASE TRANSF. CATAL.
[US/0885-0194]
CA SELECTS: PHASE TRANSFER CATALYSIS.
***Refer to Chemical Abstracts for complete source list.

CA SEL., PHOTOBIOCHEM.
[US/0148-2335]
CA SELECTS: PHOTOBIOCHEMISTRY.
***Refer to Chemical Abstracts for complete source list.

CA SEL., PHOTOCHEM.
[US/0362-9856]
CA SELECTS: PHOTOCHEMISTRY.
***Refer to Chemical Abstracts for complete source list.

CA SEL., PHOTOCHEM. ORG. SYNTH.
[US/0885-0208]
CA SELECTS: PHOTOCHEMICAL ORGANIC SYNTHESIS.
***Refer to Chemical Abstracts for complete source list.

CA SEL., PHOTORESIS.
[US/0885-0216]
CA SELECTS: PHOTORESISTS.
***Refer to Chemical Abstracts for complete source list.

CA SEL., PHOTOSENSIT. POLYM.
[US/0749-7326]
CA SELECTS: PHOTOSENSITIVE POLYMERS.
***Refer to Chemical Abstracts for complete source list.

CA SEL., PLAS. REACT. ION ETCHING
[US/0749-7334]
CA SELECTS: PLASMA & REACTIVE ION ETCHING.
***Refer to Chemical Abstracts for complete source list.

CA SEL., PLAST. ADDIT.
[US/0734-8681]
CA SELECTS: PLASTICS ADDITIVES.
***Refer to Chemical Abstracts for complete source list.

CA SEL., PLAST. FABR. USES
[US/0275-7125]
CA SELECTS: PLASTICS FABRICATION & USES.
***Refer to Chemical Abstracts for complete source list.

CA SEL., PLAST. FILMS
[US/0195-511X]
CA SELECTS: PLASTIC FILMS.
***Refer to Chemical Abstracts for complete source list.

CA SEL., PLAST. MANUF. PROCESS.
[US/0275-7133]
CA SELECTS: PLASTICS MANUFACTURING & PROCESSING.
***Refer to Chemical Abstracts for complete source list.

CA SEL., PLAT. PALLAD. CHEM.
[US/0890-1937]
CA SELECTS: PLATINUM & PALLADIUM CHEMISTRY.
***Refer to Chemical Abstracts for complete source list.

CA SEL., POLLUT. MONIT.
[US/0160-9149]
CA SELECTS: POLLUTION MONITORING.
***Refer to Chemical Abstracts for complete source list.

CA SEL., POLYACRYL. J.
[US/0890-1945]
CA SELECTS: POLYACRYLATES (JOURNALS).
***Refer to Chemical Abstracts for complete source list.

CA SEL., POLYEST.
[US/0734-8703]
CA SELECTS: POLYESTERS.
***Refer to Chemical Abstracts for complete source list.

CA SEL., POLYIMIDES
[US/0895-5840]
CA SELECTS: POLYIMIDES.
***Refer to Chemical Abstracts for complete source list.

CA SEL., POLYM. BLENDS
[US/0734-8827]
CA SELECTS: POLYMER BLENDS.
***Refer to Chemical Abstracts for complete source list.

CA SEL., POLYM. DEGRAD.
[US/0734-8835]
CA SELECTS: POLYMER DEGRADATION.
***Refer to Chemical Abstracts for complete source list.

INDEXES/ABSTRACTS TABLE

CA SEL., POLYM. KINET. PROCESS CONTROL
[US/0885-0224]
CA SELECTS: POLYMERIZATION KINETICS & PROCESS CONTROL.
***Refer to Chemical Abstracts for complete source list.

CA SEL., POLYM. MORPHOL.
[US/0195-5128]
CA SELECTS: POLYMER MORPHOLOGY.
***Refer to Chemical Abstracts for complete source list.

CA SEL., POLYURETH.
[US/0740-0705]
CA SELECTS: POLYURETHANES.
***Refer to Chemical Abstracts for complete source list.

CA SEL., PORPHYR.
[US/0195-5136]
CA SELECTS: PORPHYRINS.
***Refer to Chemical Abstracts for complete source list.

CA SEL., PROSTAGLAND.
[US/0148-2343]
CA SELECTS: PROSTAGLANDINS.
***Refer to Chemical Abstracts for complete source list.

CA SEL., PROT. MAG. RESON.
[US/0190-941X]
CA SELECTS: PROTON MAGNETIC RESONANCE.
(*Continues in part* CA Selects. Nuclear Magnetic Resonance, Chemical Aspects.)
***Refer to Chemical Abstracts for complete source list.

CA SEL., PSYCHOBIOCHEM.
[US/0362-9848]
CA SELECTS: PSYCHOBIOCHEMISTRY.
***Refer to Chemical Abstracts for complete source list.

CA SEL., QUAT. AMMON. COMP.
[US/0890-1953]
CA SELECTS: QUATERNARY AMMONIUM COMPOUNDS.
***Refer to Chemical Abstracts for complete source list.

CA SEL., RADIAT. CHEM.
[US/0146-4523]
CA SELECTS: RADIATION CHEMISTRY.
***Refer to Chemical Abstracts for complete source list.

CA SEL., RADIAT. CURING
[US/0749-7342]
CA SELECTS: RADIATION CURING.
***Refer to Chemical Abstracts for complete source list.

CA SEL., RAMAN SPECTROS.
[US/0148-2432]
CA SELECTS: RAMAN SPECTROSCOPY.
***Refer to Chemical Abstracts for complete source list.

CA SEL., RECOV. RECYCL. WASTES
[US/0160-9157]
CA SELECTS: RECOVERY & RECYCLING OF WASTES.
***Refer to Chemical Abstracts for complete source list.

CA SEL., SELEN. TELLUR. CHEM.
[US/0749-7350]
CA SELECTS: SELENIUM & TELLURIUM CHEMISTRY.
***Refer to Chemical Abstracts for complete source list.

CA SEL., SHAPE MEM. ALLOYS
[US/1062-869X]
CA SELECTS: SHAPE MEMORY ALLOYS.
***Refer to Chemical Abstracts for complete source list.

CA SEL., SILICAS SILICAT.
[US/0890-1961]
CA SELECTS: SILICAS & SILICATES.
***Refer to Chemical Abstracts for complete source list.

CA SEL., SILOX. SILIC.
[US/0895-5832]
CA SELECTS: SILOXANES & SILICONES.
***Refer to Chemical Abstracts for complete source list.

CA SEL., SILVER CHEM.
[US/0148-2440]
CA SELECTS: SILVER CHEMISTRY.
***Refer to Chemical Abstracts for complete source list.

CA SEL., SOL. ENERGY
[US/0148-236X]
CA SELECTS: SOLAR ENERGY.
***Refer to Chemical Abstracts for complete source list.

CA SEL., SOLID RADIOACT. WASTE TREAT.
[US/0160-9165]
CA SELECTS: SOLID & RADIOACTIVE WASTE TREATMENT.
***Refer to Chemical Abstracts for complete source list.

CA SEL., SOLID STATE NMR
[US/0895-5824]
CA SELECTS: SOLID STATE NMR.
***Refer to Chemical Abstracts for complete source list.

CA SEL., SOLV. EXTRACT.
[US/0146-4531]
CA SELECTS: SOLVENT EXTRACTION.
***Refer to Chemical Abstracts for complete source list.

CA SEL., SPECTROCHEM. ANAL.
[US/0885-0232]
CA SELECTS: SPECTROCHEMICAL ANALYSIS.
***Refer to Chemical Abstracts for complete source list.

CA SEL., STEROIDS (BIOCHEM. ASP.)
[US/0160-9173]
CA SELECTS: STEROIDS (BIOCHEMICAL ASPECTS).
***Refer to Chemical Abstracts for complete source list.

CA SEL., STEROIDS (CHEM. ASP.)
[US/0160-9181]
CA SELECTS: STEROIDS (CHEMICAL ASPECTS).
***Refer to Chemical Abstracts for complete source list.

CA SEL., STRESS CORROS.-MET.
[US/1066-1174]
CA SELECTS: STRESS CORROSION - METALS.
***Refer to Chemical Abstracts for complete source list.

CA SEL., STRUCT.-ACT. RELAT.
[US/0895-5816]
CA SELECTS: STRUCTURE-ACTIVITY RELATIONSHIPS.
***Refer to Chemical Abstracts for complete source list.

CA SEL., SUBSTIT. EFFECTS LIN. FREE ENERGY RELAT.
[US/0162-7856]
CA SELECTS: SUBSTITUENT EFFECTS & LINEAR FREE ENERGY RELATIONSHIPS.
(Ceased)

CA SEL., SURF. ANAL.
[US/0195-5152]
CA SELECTS: SURFACE ANALYSIS.
***Refer to Chemical Abstracts for complete source list.

CA SEL., SURF. CHEM. (PHYSICOCHEM. ASP.)
[US/0146-454X]
CA SELECTS: SURFACE CHEMISTRY (PHYSICOCHEMICAL ASPECTS).
***Refer to Chemical Abstracts for complete source list.

CA SEL., SYNFUELS
[US/0195-5160]
CA SELECTS: SYNFUELS.
***Refer to Chemical Abstracts for complete source list.

CA SEL., SYNTH. HIGH POLYM.
[US/0275-7168]
CA SELECTS: SYNTHETIC HIGH POLYMERS.
***Refer to Chemical Abstracts for complete source list.

CA SEL., SYNTH. MACROCY. COMP.
[US/0195-5179]
CA SELECTS: SYNTHETIC MACROCYCLIC COMPOUNDS.
***Refer to Chemical Abstracts for complete source list.

CA SEL., TECH. CERAM.
[US/1062-8703]
CA SELECTS: TECHNICAL CERAMICS.
***Refer to Chemical Abstracts for complete source list.

CA SEL., THERM. ANAL.
[US/0195-5187]
CA SELECTS: THERMAL ANALYSIS.
***Refer to Chemical Abstracts for complete source list.

CA SEL., THERMOCHEM.
[US/0162-7864]
CA SELECTS: THERMOCHEMISTRY.
***Refer to Chemical Abstracts for complete source list.

CA SEL., TRACE ELEM. ANAL.
[US/0160-919X]
CA SELECTS: TRACE ELEMENT ANALYSIS.
***Refer to Chemical Abstracts for complete source list.

CA SEL., ULTRAFILTR.
[US/0195-5195]
CA SELECTS: ULTRAFILTRATION.
***Refer to Chemical Abstracts for complete source list.

CA SEL., ULTRAVIOL. VISI. SPECTRO.
[US/0195-5209]
CA SELECTS: ULTRAVIOLET & VISIBLE SPECTROSCOPY.
***Refer to Chemical Abstracts for complete source list.

CA SEL., WATER TREAT.
[US/0740-073X]
CA SELECTS: WATER TREATMENT.
***Refer to Chemical Abstracts for complete source list.

CA SEL., WATER-BASED COAT.
[US/0749-7369]
CA SELECTS: WATER-BASED COATINGS.
***Refer to Chemical Abstracts for complete source list.

CA SEL., X-RAY ANAL. SPECTRO.
[US/0162-7872]
CA SELECTS: X-RAY ANALYSIS & SPECTROSCOPY.
***Refer to Chemical Abstracts for complete source list.

CA SEL., ZEOLITES
[US/0190-4949]
CA SELECTS: ZEOLITES.
***Refer to Chemical Abstracts for complete source list.

CALCIUM CALCIF. TISSUE ABSTR.
[US/1069-5540]
CALCIUM AND CALCIFIED TISSUE ABSTRACTS.
(*Continues* Calcified Tissue Abstracts.)

CALIF. PERIOD. INDEX
[US/0730-1367]
CALIFORNIA PERIODICALS INDEX.
(Ceased)

CALIF. PERIOD. MICROFI.
[US]
CALIFORNIA PERIODICALS ON MICROFILM.
(Ceased)

INDEXES/ABSTRACTS TABLE

CAN. BUS. INDEX
[CN/0227-8669]
CANADIAN BUSINESS INDEX.
(*Merged with* Canadian News Index *and* Canadian Magazine Index (Toronto, Ont.) *to form* Canadian Index (Toronto, Ont.).)

CAN. BUS. PERIOD. INDEX
[CN/0318-6717]
CANADIAN BUSINESS PERIODICALS INDEX.
(*Continued by* Canadian Business Index.)

CAN. CURR. LAW
[CN/0835-9768]
CANADIAN CURRENT LAW.
(*Split into* Jurisprudence (Scarborough, Ont.); Legislation (Scarborough, Ont.) *and* Canadian Legal Literature.)

CAN. EDUC. INDEX
[CN/0008-3453]
CANADIAN EDUCATION INDEX.
(*Absorbed* Directory of Education Studies in Canada.)

CAN. ENVIRON.
[CN]
CANADIAN ENVIRONMENT.
(*Continued by* AQUAREF.)

CAN. ESSAY LIT. INDEX
[CN/0316-0696]
CANADIAN ESSAY AND LITERATURE INDEX.
(Ceased)

CAN. INDEX
[CN/1192-4160]
CANADIAN INDEX (TORONTO).
(*Formed by the union of* Canadian Business Index *and* Canadian News Index Canadian Magazine Index (Toronto, Ont.).)

CAN. LEGAL LIT.
[CN/0832-9257]
CANADIAN LEGAL LITERATURE.
(*Continues in part* Canadian Current Law (1988).)

CAN. LIT. INDEX
[CN/0838-6021]
CANADIAN LITERATURE INDEX.
(Ceased)

CAN. MAG. INDEX
[CN/0829-8777]
CANADIAN MAGAZINE INDEX.
(*Merged with* Canadian Business Index *and* Canadian News Index *to form* Canadian Index (Toronto, Ont.).)

CAN. NEWS INDEX
[CN/0225-7459]
CANADIAN NEWS INDEX TORONTO.
(*Merged with* Canadian Business Index *and* Canadian Magazine Index (Toronto, Ont.) *to form* Canadian Index (Toronto, Ont.).)

CAN. PERIOD. INDEX
[CN/0008-4719]
CANADIAN PERIODICAL INDEX (1964).
(*Continues* Canadian Index to Periodicals and Documentary Films.)

CAN., MICROFICHE
[CN/0225-3216]
CANADIANA. MICROFICHE.
(Ceased)

CANON LAW ABSTR.
[UK/0008-5650]
CANON LAW ABSTRACTS.

CATCH. TRADE NAME INDEX : CATNI
[UK]
CATCHWORD AND TRADE NAME INDEX : CATNI.
***Refer to Current Technology Index for complete source list.

CATHOL. PERIOD. INDEX
[US/0363-6895]
CATHOLIC PERIODICAL INDEX.
(*Continued by* Catholic Periodical and Literature Index.)

CATHOL. PERIOD. LIT. INDEX
[US/0008-8285]
CATHOLIC PERIODICAL AND LITERATURE INDEX, THE.
(*Continues* Catholic Periodical Index; *Absorbed* Guide to Catholic Literature.)

CCLP CONTENTS CURR. LEG. PERIOD.
[US/0300-7391]
CCLP. CONTENTS OF CURRENT LEGAL PERIODICALS.
(*Continued by* Legal Contents.)

CERAM. ABSTR.
[US/0095-9960]
CERAMIC ABSTRACTS.
(*Continues in part* American Ceramic Society. Journal of the American Ceramic Society.)

CHEM INFORM
[GW/0931-7597]
CHEM INFORM.
(*Continues* Chemischer Informationsdienst.)

CHEM. ABSTR.
[US/0009-2258]
CHEMICAL ABSTRACTS.
(*Supersedes* Review of American Chemical Research.)

CHEM. BUS. BULL.
[UK]
CHEMICAL BUSINESS BULLETINS.

CHEM. BUS. NEWSBASE
[UK]
CHEMICAL BUSINESS NEWSBASE [ONLINE DATABASE].

CHEM. BUS. UPDATE
[UK/0950-6144]
CHEMICAL BUSINESS UPDATE.

CHEM. ENG. ABSTR.
[UK/0262-6438]
CHEMICAL ENGINEERING ABSTRACTS.
(*Continued by* Process & Chemical Engineering.)

CHEM. HAZARDS IND.
[UK/0265-5721]
CHEMICAL HAZARDS IN INDUSTRY.

CHEM. IND. NOTES
[US/0045-639X]
CHEMICAL INDUSTRY NOTES.
(*Supersedes* Plastics Industry Notes.)

CHEM. INF. DIENST.
[GW/0009-2975]
CHEMISCHER INFORMATIONSDIENST.
(*Continued by* Chem Inform.)

CHEM. TITLES
[US/0009-2711]
CHEMICAL TITLES.

CHEMORECEPT. ABSTR.
[US/0300-1261]
CHEMORECEPTION ABSTRACTS.

CHICAGO PSYCHOANAL. LIT. INDEX.
[US/0009-3661]
CHICAGO PSYCHOANALYTIC LITERATURE INDEX.
(Ceased)

CHICANO INDEX
[US/1044-3487]
CHICANO INDEX, THE.
(*Continues* Chicano Periodical Index.)

CHICOREL INDEX MENT. HEALTH BOOK REV.
[US/0149-4090]
CHICOREL INDEX TO MENTAL HEALTH BOOK REVIEWS.
(*Continues* Mental Health Book Review Index.)

CHILD DEV. ABSTR. BIBLIOGR.
[US/0009-3939]
CHILD DEVELOPMENT ABSTRACTS AND BIBLIOGRAPHY.
(*Continues* Selected Child Development Abstracts Currently Published in the Journal of Nervous and Mental Disease, the Wistar Institute Bibliographic Service, American Journal of Diseases of Children, Archives of Neurology and Psychiatry, Psychological Abstracts, Physiological Abstracts, Biological Abstracts, Chemical Abstracts, Endocrinology.)

CHILD. LIT. ABSTR.
[UK/0306-2015]
CHILDREN'S LITERATURE ABSTRACTS.

CHILD. MAG. GUIDE
[US/0743-9873]
CHILDREN'S MAGAZINE GUIDE.
(*Continues* Subject Index to Children's Magazines.)

CHRIST. PERIOD. INDEX
[US/0069-3871]
CHRISTIAN PERIODICAL INDEX.

CIS ABSTR.
[US/0302-7651]
CIS ABSTRACTS.
(*Continued by* Safety and Health at Work.)

CIS INDEX PUBL. U.S. CONGR.
[US/0007-8514]
CIS INDEX TO PUBLICATIONS OF THE UNITED STATES CONGRESS.

CIV. STRUCT. ENG. ABSTR.
[US/1063-7338]
CIVIL AND STRUCTURAL ENGINEERING ABSTRACTS.
(Ceased)

CLARK'S DIG.-ANNOT.
[US]
CLARK'S DIGEST-ANNOTATOR.
(*Continued by* New York Law Journal Digest-Annotator.)

CLASSIFIED ABSTR. ARCH. ALCOHOL LIT.
[US]
CLASSIFIED ABSTRACT ARCHIVE OF THE ALCOHOL LITERATURE.
(Ceased)

CLIN. BEHAV. THERAPY REV.
[US/0162-2269]
CLINICAL BEHAVIOR THERAPY REVIEW.
(Ceased)

COAL ABSTR.
[UK/0309-4979]
COAL ABSTRACTS.
(Ceased)

INDEXES/ABSTRACTS TABLE

COLL. STUD. PERS. ABSTR.
[US/0010-1168]
COLLEGE STUDENT PERSONNEL ABSTRACTS.
(*Continued by* Higher Education Abstracts.)

COMB. CUMUL. INDEX CARDIOL.
[US/0747-5330]
COMBINED CUMULATIVE INDEX TO CARDIOLOGY.
(**Ceased**)

COMB. CUMUL. INDEX OB. GYN.
[US/0884-8092]
COMBINED CUMULATIVE INDEX TO OBSTETRICS AND GYNECOLOGY.

COMB. CUMUL. INDEX PEDIATR.
[US/0190-4981]
COMBINED CUMULATIVE INDEX TO PEDIATRICS.

COMM. FISH. ABSTR.
[US/0010-2970]
COMMERCIAL FISHERIES ABSTRACTS.
(*Continued by* Marine Fisheries Abstracts.)

COMMUN. ABSTR.
[US/0162-2811]
COMMUNICATION ABSTRACTS.

COMMUNITY DEV. ABSTR.
[US]
COMMUNITY DEVELOPMENT ABSTRACTS.
(**Ceased**)

COMMUNITY MENT. HEALTH REV.
[US/0363-1605]
COMMUNITY MENTAL HEALTH REVIEW.
(*Continued by* Prevention in Human Services.)

COMPEND. PLUS
[US/1063-8709]
COMPENDEX PLUS.
***Refer to Engineering Index for complete source list.

COMPUMATH CIT. INDEX
[US/0730-6199]
COMPUMATH CITATION INDEX : CMCI.

COMPUT-A-CAL
[US/0742-5686]
COMPUT-A-CAL.
(**Ceased**)

COMPUT. ABSTR.
[UK/0010-4469]
COMPUTER ABSTRACTS.
(*Continues* Computer Bibliography.)

COMPUT. ASAP
[US]
COMPUTER ASAP [ONLINE DATABASE].

COMPUT. BUS.
[US/0732-8346]
COMPUTER BUSINESS (LOS ANGELES, CALIF.).

COMPUT. CONTENTS
[US/0747-0193]
COMPUTER CONTENTS.
(**Ceased**)

COMPUT. CONTROL ABSTR.
[UK/0036-8113]
COMPUTER & CONTROL ABSTRACTS.
(*Continues* Control Abstracts.)
***Refer to INSPEC [Online Database] for a complete source list.

COMPUT. DATABASE
[US]
COMPUTER DATABASE [ONLINE DATABASE].

COMPUT. IND. UPDATE
[US/0744-0081]
COMPUTER INDUSTRY UPDATE.

COMPUT. INF. SYST.
[US/0010-4507]
COMPUTER & INFORMATION SYSTEMS.
(*Continued by* Computer and Information Systems Abstracts Journal.)

COMPUT. INF. SYST. ABSTR. J.
[US/0191-9776]
COMPUTER AND INFORMATION SYSTEMS ABSTRACTS JOURNAL.
(*Continued by* Computer and Information Systems Abstracts.)

COMPUT. LIT. INDEX
[US/0270-4846]
COMPUTER LITERATURE INDEX.
(*Continues* Quarterly Bibliography of Computers and Data Processing.)

COMPUT. REV.
[US/0010-4884]
COMPUTING REVIEWS.

COMPUT. REV. INDEX
[US/1040-5003]
COMPUTER REVIEW INDEX.

COMPUT. REV., BIBLIOGR. SUBJ. INDEX CURR. COMPUT. LIT.
[US/0149-1202]
COMPUTING REVIEWS. BIBLIOGRAPHY AND SUBJECT INDEX OF CURRENT COMPUTING LITERATURE.
(*Continued by* ACM Guide to Computing Literature.)

CONCR. ABSTR.
[US/0045-8007]
CONCRETE ABSTRACTS.

CONSTR. INDEX
[US/0892-2047]
CONSTRUCTION INDEX.

CONSUM. HEALTH NUTR. INDEX
[US/0883-1963]
CONSUMER HEALTH & NUTRITION INDEX.

CONSUM. INDEX PROD. EVAL. INF. SOURCE
[US/0094-0534]
CONSUMERS INDEX TO PRODUCT EVALUATIONS AND INFORMATION SOURCES.

CONTENTS CONTEMP. MATH. J.
[US/0010-759X]
CONTENTS OF CONTEMPORARY MATHEMATICAL JOURNALS.
(**Merged with** New Publications - American Mathematical Society **to form** Contents of Contemporary Mathematical Journals and New Publications.)

CONTENTS CONTEMP. MATH. J. NEW PUBL.
[US]
CONTENTS OF CONTEMPORARY MATHEMATICAL JOURNALS AND NEW PUBLICATIONS.
(*Continued by* Current Mathematical Publications.)

CONTENTS CURR. LEG. PERIOD.
[US/0300-7391]
CONTENTS OF CURRENT LEGAL PERIODICALS.
(*Continued by* CCLP. Contents of Current Legal Periodicals.)

CONTENTS PAGES EDUC.
[UK/0265-9220]
CONTENTS PAGES IN EDUCATION.

CONTENTS RECENT ECON. J.
[UK]
CONTENTS OF RECENT ECONOMICS JOURNALS.
(**Ceased**)

CORROS. ABSTR.
[US/0010-9339]
CORROSION ABSTRACTS.
(**Supersedes in part** Corrosion.)

COT. TROP. FIBR. ABSTR. BIBLIOGR.
[UK]
COTTON AND TROPICAL FIBRES ABSTRACTS BIBLIOGRAPHY.
(*Continues* Cotton and Tropical Fibres Abstracts.)

CRIM. JUSTICE ABSTR.
[US/0146-9177]
CRIMINAL JUSTICE ABSTRACTS.
(*Continues* Crime and Delinquency Literature.)

CRIM. JUSTICE PERIOD. INDEX
[US/0145-5818]
CRIMINAL JUSTICE PERIODICAL INDEX.

CRIM. PENOL. POLICE SCI. ABSTR.
[NE/0928-8759]
CRIMINOLOGY, PENOLOGY AND POLICE SCIENCE ABSTRACTS.
(**Formed by the union of** Criminology & Penology Abstracts **and** Police Science Abstracts.)

CRIME DELINQ. ABSTR.
[US/0045-902X]
CRIME AND DELINQUENCY ABSTRACTS.
(*Continues* International Bibliography on Crime and Delinquency.)

CRIME DELINQ. LIT.
[US/0037-1327]
CRIME AND DELINQUENCY LITERATURE.
(*Continued by* Criminal Justice Abstracts.)

CRIMINOL. PENOL. ABSTR.
[NE/0166-6231]
CRIMINOLOGY & PENOLOGY ABSTRACTS.
(**Merged with** Police Science Abstracts **to form** Criminology, Penology, and Police Science Abstracts.)

CROP PHYSIOL. ABSTR.
[UK/0306-7556]
CROP PHYSIOLOGY ABSTRACTS.

CSA NEURO. ABSTR.
[US/0141-7711]
CSA NEUROSCIENCES ABSTRACTS.

CTI PLUS
[UK]
CTI PLUS [COMPUTER FILE].
***Refer to Current Technology Index for complete source list.

CUMUL. INDEX MED.
[US/0090-1423]
CUMULATED INDEX MEDICUS.
(*Continues* Quarterly Cumulative Index Medicus.)
***Refer to Index Medicus for complete source list.

CUMUL. INDEX NURS. ALLIED HEALTH LIT.
[US/0146-5554]
CUMULATIVE INDEX TO NURSING & ALLIED HEALTH LITERATURE.
(*Continued in part by* Nursing and Allied Health Index.)

CUMUL. INDEX NURS. LIT.
[US/0011-3018]
CUMULATIVE INDEX TO NURSING LITERATURE.
(*Continued by* Cumulative Index to Nursing & Allied Health Literature.)

INDEXES/ABSTRACTS TABLE

CURR. ABSTR. CHEM. INDEX CHEM.
[US/0161-455X]
CURRENT ABSTRACTS OF CHEMISTRY AND INDEX CHEMICUS.
(*Continued by* Index Chemicus : IC.)

CURR. ADV. APPL. MICROBIOL. BIOTECHNOL.
[UK/0964-8712]
CURRENT ADVANCES IN APPLIED MICROBIOLOGY & BIOTECHNOLOGY.
(*Continues* Current Advances in Microbiology.)
***Refer to Current Awareness in Biological Sciences : CABS for complete source list.

CURR. ADV. BIOCHEM.
[UK/0741-1618]
CURRENT ADVANCES IN BIOCHEMISTRY.
(*Continued by* Current Advances in Protein Biochemistry.)

CURR. ADV. CANCER RES.
[UK/0895-9803]
CURRENT ADVANCES IN CANCER RESEARCH.
***Refer to Current Awareness in Biological Sciences : CABS for complete source list.

CURR. ADV. CELL DEV. BIOL.
[UK/0741-1626]
CURRENT ADVANCES IN CELL AND DEVELOPMENTAL BIOLOGY.
(*Continues in part* Current Awareness in Biological Sciences.)
***Refer to Current Awareness in Biological Sciences : CABS for complete source list.

CURR. ADV. CLIN. CHEM.
[UK/0885-1980]
CURRENT ADVANCES IN CLINICAL CHEMISTRY.
(*Continues* Current Clinical Chemistry.)
***Refer to Current Awareness in Biological Sciences : CABS for complete source list.

CURR. ADV. ECOL. ENVIRON. SCI.
[UK/0955-6648]
CURRENT ADVANCES IN ECOLOGICAL & ENVIRONMENTAL SCIENCES.
(*Continues* Current Advances in Ecological Sciences.)
***Refer to Current Awareness in Biological Sciences : CABS for complete source list.

CURR. ADV. ECOL. SCI.
[UK/0306-3291]
CURRENT ADVANCES IN ECOLOGICAL SCIENCES.
(*Continued by* Current Advances in Ecological & Environmental Sciences.)

CURR. ADV. ENDOCRIN.
[UK/0741-1634]
CURRENT ADVANCES IN ENDOCRINOLOGY.
(*Continues in part* Current Awareness in Biological Sciences.)

CURR. ADV. ENDOCRIN. METAB.
[UK/0964-8720]
CURRENT ADVANCES IN ENDOCRINOLOGY AND METABOLISM.
(*Continues* Current Advances in Physiology.)
***Refer to Current Awareness in Biological Sciences : CABS for complete source list.

CURR. ADV. GENET. MOL. BIOL.
[UK/0741-1642]
CURRENT ADVANCES IN GENETICS & MOLECULAR BIOLOGY.
(*Continues* Current Advances in Genetics.)
***Refer to Current Awareness in Biological Sciences : CABS for complete source list.

CURR. ADV. IMMUNOL.
[UK/0741-1650]
CURRENT ADVANCES IN IMMUNOLOGY.
(*Continued by* Current Advances in Immunology & Infectious Diseases.)

CURR. ADV. IMMUNOL. INFECT. DISEAS.
[UK/0964-8747]
CURRENT ADVANCES IN IMMUNOLOGY & INFECTIOUS DISEASES.
(*Continues* Current Advances in Immunology.)
***Refer to Current Awareness in Biological Sciences : CABS for complete source list.

CURR. ADV. MICROBIOL.
[UK/0741-1669]
CURRENT ADVANCES IN MICROBIOLOGY.
(*Continued by* Current Advances in Applied Microbiology & Biotechnology.)

CURR. ADV. NEUROSCI.
[UK/0741-1677]
CURRENT ADVANCES IN NEUROSCIENCE.
(*Continues in part* Current Awareness in Biological Sciences.)
***Refer to Current Awareness in Biological Sciences : CABS for complete source list.

CURR. ADV. PHARMACOL. TOXICOL.
[UK/0741-1685]
CURRENT ADVANCES IN PHARMACOLOGY & TOXICOLOGY.
(*Continued by* Current Advances in Toxicology.)

CURR. ADV. PHYSIOL.
[UK/0741-1693]
CURRENT ADVANCES IN PHYSIOLOGY.
(*Continued by* Current Advances in Endocrinology & Metabolism.)

CURR. ADV. PLANT SCI.
[UK/0306-4484]
CURRENT ADVANCES IN PLANT SCIENCE.
***Refer to Current Awareness in Biological Sciences : CABS for complete source list.

CURR. ADV. PROT. BIOCHEM.
[UK/0965-0504]
CURRENT ADVANCES IN PROTEIN BIOCHEMISTRY.
(*Continues* Current Advances in Biochemistry.)
***Refer to Current Awareness in Biological Sciences : CABS for complete source list.

CURR. ADV. PROT. CHEM.
[UK/0965-0504]
CURRENT ADVANCES IN PROTEIN CHEMISTRY.
(*Continues* Current Advances in Biochemistry.)
***Refer to Current Awareness in Biological Sciences : CABS for complete source list.

CURR. ADV. TOXICOL.
[UK/0965-0512]
CURRENT ADVANCES IN TOXICOLOGY.
(*Continues* Current Advances in Pharmacology & Toxicology.)
***Refer to Current Awareness in Biological Sciences : CABS for complete source list.

CURR. AUST. NEW Z. LEG. LIT. INDEX
[AT]
CURRENT AUSTRALIAN AND NEW ZEALAND LEGAL LITERATURE INDEX.
(Ceased)

CURR. AWARE. BIOL. SCI., CABS
[UK/0733-4443]
CURRENT AWARENESS IN BIOLOGICAL SCIENCES.
(*Continued in part by* Current Advances in Neuroscience; Current Advances in Cell & Developmental Biology.)

CURR. AWARENESS LIBR. LIT., CALL
[US/0091-5270]
CURRENT AWARENESS-LIBRARY LITERATURE : CALL.
(Ceased)

CURR. BIOTECHNOL.
[UK/0960-5037]
CURRENT BIOTECHNOLOGY.
(*Continues* Current Biotechnology Abstracts.)

CURR. BIOTECHNOL. ABSTR.
[UK/0264-3391]
CURRENT BIOTECHNOLOGY ABSTRACTS.
(*Continued by* Current Biotechnology.)

CURR. BOOK REV. CITATIONS
[US/0360-1250]
CURRENT BOOK REVIEW CITATIONS.
(Ceased)

CURR. CHEM. REACT.
[US/0163-6278]
CURRENT CHEMICAL REACTIONS.

CURR. CONTENTS
[US/0272-1430]
CURRENT CONTENTS.
(*Continued by* Current Contents of Pharmaceutical Publications.)

CURR. CONTENTS AFR.
[UK/0721-5207]
CURRENT CONTENTS AFRICA.
(*Continues* CCA, Current Contents Afrika.)

CURR. CONTENTS AGRIC. BIOL. ENVIRON. SCI.
[US/0090-0508]
CURRENT CONTENTS. AGRICULTURE, BIOLOGY, & ENVIRONMENTAL SCIENCES.
(*Continues* Current Contents. Agricultural, Food & Veterinary Sciences.)

CURR. CONTENTS AGRIC. FOOD VET. SCI.
[US/0011-3379]
CURRENT CONTENTS : AGRICULTURAL, FOOD AND VETERINARY SCIENCES.
(*Continued by* Current Contents. Agriculture, Biology & Environmental Sciences.)

CURR. CONTENTS ARTS HUMANIT.
[US/0163-3155]
CURRENT CONTENTS. ARTS & HUMANITIES.

CURR. CONTENTS BEHAV. SOC. EDUC. SCI.
[US/0011-3387]
CURRENT CONTENTS: BEHAVIORAL, SOCIAL & EDUCATIONAL SCIENCES.
(*Continued by* Current Contents. Social & Behavioral Sciences.)

CURR. CONTENTS BEHAV. SOC. MANAGE. SCI.
[US/0590-384X]
CURRENT CONTENTS: BEHAVIORAL, SOCIAL & MANAGEMENT SCIENCES.
(*Continued by* Current Contents. Behavioral, Social & Educational Sciences.)

CURR. CONTENTS CLIN. MED.
[US/0891-3358]
CURRENT CONTENTS. CLINICAL MEDICINE.
(*Continues* Current Contents. Clinical Practice.)

CURR. CONTENTS CLIN. PRACT.
[US/0091-1704]
CURRENT CONTENTS. CLINICAL PRACTICE.
(*Continued by* Current Contents. Clinical Medicine.)

INDEXES/ABSTRACTS TABLE

CURR. CONTENTS EDUC.
[US/0590-3866]
CURRENT CONTENTS. EDUCATION.
(*Absorbed by* Current Contents: Behavioral, Social & Management Sciences.)

CURR. CONTENTS ENG. TECH. APPL. SCI.
[US/0095-7917]
CURRENT CONTENTS. ENGINEERING, TECHNOLOGY & APPLIED SCIENCES.
(*Continues* Current Contents: Engineering & Technology.)

CURR. CONTENTS ENG. TECH.
[US/0011-3395]
CURRENT CONTENTS: ENGINEERING & TECHNOLOGY.
(*Continued by* Current Contents. Engineering, Technology & Applied Sciences.)

CURR. CONTENTS LIFE SCI.
[US/0011-3409]
CURRENT CONTENTS. LIFE SCIENCES.
(*Continues* Current Contents. Your Weekly Guide to the Chemical, Pharmaco-Medical & Life Sciences.)

CURR. CONTENTS PHARM. PUBL.
[US/0272-1422]
CURRENT CONTENTS OF PHARMACEUTICAL PUBLICATIONS.
(*Superseded by* Current Contents of Pharmaco-Medical Publications.)

CURR. CONTENTS PHARM.-MED. PUBL.
[US/0272-1414]
CURRENT CONTENTS OF PHARMACO-MEDICAL PUBLICATIONS.
(*Continued by* Current Contents: Your Weekly Survey of Chemical, Pharmacological & Clinical Publications.)

CURR. CONTENTS PHYS. CHEM. EARTH SCI.
[US/0163-2574]
CURRENT CONTENTS. PHYSICAL, CHEMICAL & EARTH SCIENCES.
(*Continues* Current Contents. Physical and Chemical Sciences.)

CURR. CONTENTS PHYS. CHEM. SCI.
[US/0011-3417]
CURRENT CONTENTS. PHYSICAL & CHEMICAL SCIENCES.
(*Continued by* Current Contents. Physical, Chemical & Earth Sciences.)

CURR. CONTENTS SOC. BEHAV. SCI.
[US/0092-6361]
CURRENT CONTENTS. SOCIAL & BEHAVIORAL SCIENCES.
(*Continues* Current Contents. Behavioral, Social & Educational Sciences.)

CURR. CONTENTS YOUR WKLY. GUIDE CHEM. PHARM.-MED. LIFE SCI.
[US/0272-1503]
CURRENT CONTENTS: YOUR WEEKLY GUIDE OF THE CHEMICAL, PHARMACO-MEDICAL & LIFE SCIENCES.
(*Continued by* Current Contents. Life Sciences.)

CURR. CONTENTS YOUR WKLY. SURV. CHEM. PHARMACOL. CLIN. PUBL.
[US/0272-1449]
CURRENT CONTENTS: YOUR WEEKLY SURVEY OF CHEMICAL, PHARMACOLOGICAL & CLINICAL PUBLICATIONS.
(*Continued by* Current Contents. Your Weekly Guide to the Chemical, Pharmaco-Medical & Life Sciences.)

CURR. DIG. POST SOV. PRESS
[US/1067-7542]
CURRENT DIGEST OF THE POST-SOVIET PRESS, THE.
(*Continues* Current Digest of the Soviet Press.)

CURR. GEOGR. PUBL.
[US/0011-3514]
CURRENT GEOGRAPHICAL PUBLICATIONS.

CURR. INDEX J. EDUC.
[US/0011-3565]
CURRENT INDEX TO JOURNALS IN EDUCATION.

CURR. INDEX STAT.
[US/0364-1228]
CURRENT INDEX TO STATISTICS.

CURR. LAW INDEX
[US/0196-1780]
CURRENT LAW INDEX.

CURR. LIT. AGING
[US/0011-3662]
CURRENT LITERATURE ON AGING.
(*Continued by* Abstracts in Social Gerontology.)

CURR. LIT. BLOOD
[US/0001-7108]
CURRENT LITERATURE OF BLOOD.
(Ceased)

CURR. LIT. FAM. PLAN.
[US/0092-6000]
CURRENT LITERATURE IN FAMILY PLANNING.
(*Continues* Acquisitions List - Katharine Dexter McCormick Library.)

CURR. LIT. SCI. SCI.
[II]
CURRENT LITERATURE ON SCIENCE OF SCIENCE.
(*Supersedes* Index to Literature on Science of Science.)

CURR. MATH. PUBL.
[US/0361-4794]
CURRENT MATHEMATICAL PUBLICATIONS.
(*Continues* Contents of Contemporary Mathematical Journals and New Publications.)
***Refer to Mathematical Reviews for complete source list.

CURR. MIL. POL. LIT.
[UK/0954-3589]
CURRENT MILITARY & POLITICAL LITERATURE.
(*Continues* Current Military Literature.)

CURR. PAP. COMPUT. CONTROL
[UK/0011-3794]
CURRENT PAPERS ON COMPUTERS & CONTROL.
(*Continues* Current Papers on Control.)
***Refer to INSPEC [Online Database] for complete source list.

CURR. PAP. ELECTR. ELECTRON. ENG.
[UK/0011-3778]
CURRENT PAPERS IN ELECTRICAL & ELECTRONICS ENGINEERING.
(*Continues* Current Papers in Eletrotechnology.)
***Refer to INSPEC [Online Database] for complete source list.

CURR. PAP. PHYS.
[UK/0011-3786]
CURRENT PAPERS IN PHYSICS.
***Refer to INSPEC [Online Database] for complete source list.

CURR. PHYS. INDEX
[US/0098-9819]
CURRENT PHYSICS INDEX.

CURR. PRIMATE REF.
[US/0590-4102]
CURRENT PRIMATE REFERENCES.
(*Supersedes* Unverified Primate References.)

CURR. REF. FISH RES.
[US/0739-540X]
CURRENT REFERENCES IN FISH RESEARCH.

CURR. TECHNOL. INDEX
[UK/0260-6593]
CURRENT TECHNOLOGY INDEX : CTI.
(*Continues* British Technology Index.)

CURR. THOUGHTS TRENDS
[US/1054-8688]
CURRENT THOUGHTS AND TRENDS.
(*Continues* Current Christian Abstracts.)

CURR. TITL. DENT.
[DK/0903-3483]
CURRENT TITLES IN DENTISTRY.

CURR. TITLES ELECTROCHEM.
[II/0300-4376]
CURRENT TITLES IN ELECTROCHEMISTRY.
(*Absorbed* Electrochemical News.)

DAIRY SCI. ABSTR.
[UK/0011-5681]
DAIRY SCIENCE ABSTRACTS.

DATA PROCESS. DIG.
[US/0011-6858]
DATA PROCESSING DIGEST.

DEEP-SEA OCEANOGR. ABSTR.
[UK/0011-7471]
DEEP-SEA RESEARCH AND OCEANOGRAPHIC ABSTRACTS.
(*Continued by* Deep-Sea Research.)

DEEP-SEA RES.
[UK/0146-6291]
DEEP-SEA RESEARCH.
(*Continued by* Deep-Sea Research. Part A. Oceanographic Research Papers.)

DEEP-SEA RES., B, OCEANOGR. LIT. REV.
[UK/0198-0254]
DEEP-SEA RESEARCH. PART B. OCEANOGRAPHIC LITERATURE REVIEW.
(*Continued by* Oceanographic Literature Review.)

DENT. ABSTR.
[US/0011-8486]
DENTAL ABSTRACTS (CHICAGO).

DESALIN. ABSTR.
[IS/0011-9202]
DESALINATION ABSTRACTS.
(*Continued by* Desalination and Recycling Abstracts.)

DESALIN. RECYC. ABSTR.
[IS/0011-9172]
DESALINATION AND RECYCLING ABSTRACTS.
(*Continues* Desalination Abstracts.)

DEV. DISABIL. ABSTR.
[US/0191-1600]
DEVELOPMENTAL DISABILITIES ABSTRACTS.
(*Continues* Mental Retardation & Developmental Disabilities Abstracts.)

DEV. MED. CHILD NEUROL.
[UK/0012-1622]
DEVELOPMENTAL MEDICINE & CHILD NEUROLOGY.
(*Continued in part by* American Academy For Cerebral Palsy & Developmental Medicine. Meeting. Abstracts.)

INDEXES/ABSTRACTS TABLE

DIABETES LIT. INDEX
[US/0012-1819]
DIABETES LITERATURE INDEX.
(*Supersedes* Diabetes-Related Literature Index.)

DOANE INF. CENT. INDEX. SYST. SUBJ. INDEX
[US]
DICIS, DOANE INFORMATION CENTER INDEXING SYSTEM : SUBJECT INDEX.
(Ceased)

DOK. GEFAHRDUNG ALKOHOL, RAUCH., DROGEN, ARZNEIMITTEL
[GW/0341-8022]
DOKUMENTATION GEFAHRDUNG DURCH ALKOHOL, RAUCHEN, DROGEN, ARZNEIMITTEL.
(*Continues* Dokumentation Drogengefahrdung und Alkoholmissbrauch.)

DOK. RAUMENTWICKL.
[GW]
DOKUMENTATION ZUR RAUMENTWICKLUNG.
(*Continues* Documentatio Geographica.)

DSH ABSTR.
[US/0011-5150]
DSH ABSTRACTS.
(Ceased)

ECOL. ABSTR.
[UK/0305-196X]
ECOLOGICAL ABSTRACTS.

ECOLOGY ABSTR.
[US/0143-3296]
ECOLOGY ABSTRACTS.
(*Continues* Applied Ecology Abstracts.)

ECON. LIT. INDEX
[US]
ECONOMIC LITERATURE INDEX.

ECONLIT
[US]
ECONLIT [COMPUTER FILE].
***Refer to Economic Literature Index for a complete source list.

EDUC. ADM. ABSTR.
[US/0013-1601]
EDUCATIONAL ADMINISTRATION ABSTRACTS.

EDUC. INDEX
[US/0013-1385]
EDUCATION INDEX.

EDUC. TECHNOL. ABSTR.
[UK/0266-3368]
EDUCATIONAL TECHNOLOGY ABSTRACTS.

EI PAGE ONE
[US]
EI PAGE ONE [COMPUTER FILE].

ELECT. COMM. ABSTR.
[US/1069-5303]
ELECTRONICS AND COMMUNICATIONS ABSTRACTS.
(*Continues* Electronics & Communications Abstracts Journal.)

ELECTR. ELECTRON. ABSTR.
[UK/0036-8105]
ELECTRICAL & ELECTRONICS ABSTRACTS.
(*Continues* Science Abstracts. Electrical & Electronics Abstracts.)
***Refer to INSPEC [Online Database] for a complete source list.

ELECTROANAL. ABSTR.
[SZ/0013-4775]
ELECTROANALYTICAL ABSTRACTS.
(*Continues* Journal of Electroanalytical Chemistry. Abstracts Section.)

ELECTRON. COMMUN. ABSTR. J.
[US/0361-3313]
ELECTRONICS AND COMMUNICATIONS ABSTRACTS JOURNAL (RIVERDALE, MD.).
(*Continued by* Electronics and Communications Abstracts.)

ELECTRON. PUB. ABSTR.
[UK/0739-2907]
ELECTRONIC PUBLISHING ABSTRACTS.
(*Continued by* World Publishing Monitor.)

EMBASE LIST J. INDEXED
[NE]
EMBASE LIST OF JOURNALS INDEXED.
(*Continues* List of Journals Abstracted (1983).)
***Refer to EMBASE [Online Database] for complete source list.

EMBASE
[NE]
EMBASE [ONLINE DATABASE].

EMPLOY. RELAT. ABSTR.
[US]
EMPLOYMENT RELATIONS ABSTRACTS.
(*Continued by* Work Related Abstracts.)

ENERGY INDEX
[US/0094-6281]
ENERGY INDEX.
(*Absorbed by* Energy Information Abstracts Annual.)

ENERGY INF. ABSTR.
[US/0147-6521]
ENERGY INFORMATION ABSTRACTS.
(Ceased)

ENERGY INF. ABSTR. ANNU.
[US/0739-3679]
ENERGY INFORMATION ABSTRACTS ANNUAL.
(*Absorbed* Energy Index.)
***Refer to Energy Information Abstracts for complete source list.

ENERGY RES. ABSTR.
[US/0160-3604]
ENERGY RESEARCH ABSTRACTS.
(*Continues* ERDA Energy Research Abstracts.)

ENG. INDEX
[US/0739-4624]
ENGINEERING INDEX (1919), THE.
(*Continued by* Engineering Index Annual.)

ENG. INDEX ANNU.
[US/0360-8557]
ENGINEERING INDEX ANNUAL.
(*Continues* Engineering Index (New York, N.Y. : 1919).)

ENG. INDEX BIOENG. ABSTR.
[US/0736-6213]
ENGINEERING INDEX BIOENGINEERING ABSTRACTS.
(*Continued by* Engineering Index Bioengineering and Biotechnology Abstracts.)

ENG. INDEX ENERGY ABSTR.
[US/0093-8408]
ENGINEERING INDEX ENERGY ABSTRACTS.
***Refer to Engineering Index Annual for a complete source list.

ENG. INDEX MON.
[US/0742-1974]
ENGINEERING INDEX MONTHLY.
(*Continues* Engineering Index Monthly and Author Index.)
***Refer to Engineering Index Annual for a complete source list.

ENG. INDEX MON. AUTHOR INDEX
[US/0162-3036]
ENGINEERING INDEX MONTHLY AND AUTHOR INDEX.
(*Continued by* Engineering Index Monthly (1984).)

ENG. MATER. ABSTR.
[US/0951-9998]
ENGINEERED MATERIALS ABSTRACTS.

ENTOMOL. ABSTR.
[US/0013-8924]
ENTOMOLOGY ABSTRACTS.

ENVIRO ENERGYLINE PLUS
[US/1076-6464]
ENVIRO/ENERGYLINE ABSTRACTS PLUS.
(*Continued by* Environment Abstracts.)
***Refer to Environment Abstracts and Energy Infomation Abstracts for complete source list.

ENVIRON.
[CN/0709-8847]
ENVIRONNEMENT (MONTREAL).
(*Continues* Journal l'Environnement.)

ENVIRON. ABSTR.
[US/0093-3287]
ENVIRONMENT ABSTRACTS.
(*Continues* Environment Information Access; *Absorbed* Acid Rain Abstracts.)

ENVIRON. ABSTR.
[US]
ENVIRONMENT ABSTRACTS [COMPUTER FILE].
(*Continues* Enviro/Energyline Abstracts Plus.)
***Refer to Environment Abstracts and Energy Infomation Abstracts for complete source list.

ENVIRON. ABSTR. ANNU.
[US/0000-1198]
ENVIRONMENT ABSTRACTS ANNUAL.
(*Absorbed* Environment Index and Acid Raid Abstracts Annual.)
***Refer to Environment Abstracts for complete source list.

ENVIRON. ENG. ABSTR.
[US/1063-7346]
ENVIRONMENTAL ENGINEERING ABSTRACTS.
(Ceased)

ENVIRON. INDEX
[US/0090-791X]
ENVIRONMENT INDEX.
(*Absorbed by* Environment Abstracts Annual.)

ENVIRON. PERIOD. BIBLIOGR.
[US/0145-3815]
ENVIRONMENTAL PERIODICALS BIBLIOGRAPHY.
(*Continues* Environmental Periodicals.)

ERGON. ABSTR.
[UK/0046-2446]
ERGONOMICS ABSTRACTS.
(*Continues* Ergonomics Abstracts (1959).)

ETHNIC STUD. BIBLIOGR.
[US/0149-1555]
ETHNIC STUDIES BIBLIOGRAPHY.
(Ceased)

INDEXES/ABSTRACTS TABLE

ETHNOARTS INDEX
[US/0893-0120]
ETHNOARTS INDEX.
(*Continues* Tribal Arts Review.)

EUR. RES.
[NE/0304-4297]
EUROPEAN RESEARCH.
(*Continued by* Marketing and Research Today.)

EXCEPT. CHILD EDUC. RESOUR.
[US/0160-4309]
EXCEPTIONAL CHILD EDUCATION RESOURCES.
(*Continues* Exceptional Child Education Abstracts.)

EXCEPT. CHILD EDUC. ABSTR.
[US/0014-4010]
EXCEPTIONAL CHILD EDUCATION ABSTRACTS.
(*Continued by* Exceptional Child Education Resources.)

EXCEPT. HUM. EXP.
[US/1053-4768]
EXCEPTIONAL HUMAN EXPERIENCE.
(*Continues* Parapsychology Abstracts International.)

EXCERPTA MED. LIST J. ABSTR.
[US]
EXCERPTA MEDICA : LIST OF JOURNALS ABSTRACTED.
(*Continued by* List of Journals Abstracted.)

EXCERPTA MED., SECT. 06B, ARTHR. RHEUM.
[NE]
EXCERPTA MEDICA. SECTION 06B. ARTHRITIS AND RHEUMATISM.
(Ceased)

EXCERPTA MEDICA., SECT. 1, ANATOM. ANTHROPOL. EMBRYOL. HISTOL.
[NE/0014-4053]
EXCERPTA MEDICA. SECTION 1. ANATOMY, ANTHROPOLOGY, EMBRYOLOGY AND HISTOLOGY.
***Refer to EMBASE [Online Database] for complete source list.

EXCERPTA MED., SECT. 2, PHYSIOL.
[NE/0367-1089]
EXCERPTA MEDICA. SECTION 2A. PHYSIOLOGY.
(*Continues* Excerpta Medica. Section 2A. Physiology.)
***Refer to EMBASE [Online Database] for complete source list.

EXCERPTA MED., SECT. 2A, PHYSIOL.
[NE/0367-1089]
EXCERPTA MEDICA. SECTION 2A. PHYSIOLOGY.
(*Continued by* Excerpta Medica. Section 2. Physiology.)

EXCERPTA MED., SECT. 3, ENDOCRINOL.
[NE/0014-407X]
EXCERPTA MEDICA. SECTION 3. ENDOCRINOLOGY.
(*Continues* Excerpta Medica. Section 3. Endocrinology, Experimental and Clinical.)
***Refer to EMBASE [Online Database] for complete source list.

EXCERPTA MED., SECT. 4, MICROBIOL.
[NE/0167-4285]
EXCERPTA MEDICA. SECTION 4. MICROBIOLOGY.
(*Continued by* Excerpta Medica. Section 4, Microbiology, Bacteriology, Mycology, and Virology.)

EXCERPTA MED., SECT. 4, MICROBIOL. BACTERIOL. MYCOL. PARASITOL. VIROL.
[NE]
EXCERPTA MEDICA. SECTION 4. MICROBIOLOGY, BACTERIOLOGY, MYCOLOGY, PARASITOLOGY, AND VIROLOGY.
(*Continues* Excerpta Medica. Section 4, Microbiology; *Absorbed* Virology.)
***Refer to EMBASE [Online Database] for complete source list.

EXCERPTA MED., SECT. 5, GEN. PATHOL. PATHOLOGIC. ANAT.
[NE/0014-4096]
EXCERPTA MEDICA. SECTION 5. GENERAL PATHOLOGY AND PATHOLOGICAL ANATOMY.
***Refer to EMBASE [Online Database] for complete source list.

EXCERPTA MED., SECT. 6, INTERN. MED.
[NE/0014-410X]
EXCERPTA MEDICA. SECTION 6. INTERNAL MEDICINE.
***Refer to EMBASE [Online Database] for complete source list.

EXCERPTA MED., SECT. 7, PEDIATR. PEDIATR. SUR.
[NE/0373-6512]
EXCERPTA MEDICA. SECTION 7. PEDIATRICS AND PEDIATRIC SURGERY.
(*Continues* Excerpta Medica. Section 7. Pediatrics.)
***Refer to EMBASE [Online Database] for complete source list.

EXCERPTA MED., SECT. 8, NEUROL. NEUROSURG.
[NE/0014-4126]
EXCERPTA MEDICA. SECTION 8. NEUROLOGY AND NEUROSURGERY.
(*Continues* Excerpta Medica. Section 8A. Neurology and Neurosurgery.)
***Refer to EMBASE [Online Database] for complete source list.

EXCERPTA MED., SECT. 8A, NEUROL. NEUROSURG.
[NE/0014-4126]
EXCERPTA MEDICA. SECTION 8A. NEUROLOGY AND NEUROSURGERY.
(*Continued by* Excerpta Medica. Section 8. Neurology and Neurosurgery.)

EXCERPTA MED., SECT. 9, SURG.
[NE/0014-4134]
EXCERPTA MEDICA. SECTION 9. SURGERY.
(*Continued by* Excerpta Medica. Section 28, Urology.)

EXCERPTA MED., SECT. 9B, ORTHO. TRAUMATOL.
[NE]
EXCERPTA MEDICA. SECTION 9B. ORTHOPAEDICS AND TRAUMATOLOGY.
(*Continued by* Orthopedic Surgery.)

EXCERPTA MED., SECT. 10, OBSTETR. GYNECOL.
[NE/0014-4142]
EXCERPTA MEDICA. SECTION 10. OBSTETRICS AND GYNECOLOGY.
***Refer to EMBASE [Online Database] for complete source list.

EXCERPTA MED., SECT. 12, OPHTHALMOL.
[NE/0014-4169]
EXCERPTA MEDICA. SECTION 12. OPHTHALMOLOGY.
***Refer to EMBASE [Online Database] for complete source list.

EXCERPTA MED., SECT. 13, DERMATOL.
[NE/0014-4177]
EXCERPTA MEDICA. SECTION 13. DERMATOLOGY AND VENEREOLOGY.
***Refer to EMBASE [Online Database] for complete source list.

EXCERPTA MED., SECT. 14, RADIOL.
[NE/0014-4185]
EXCERPTA MEDICA. SECTION 14. RADIOLOGY.
***Refer to EMBASE [Online Database] for complete source list.

EXCERPTA MED., SECT. 16, CANCER
[NE/0014-4207]
EXCERPTA MEDICA. SECTION 16. CANCER.
(*Continues* Cancer, Experimental and Clinical.)
***Refer to EMBASE [Online Database] for complete source list.

EXCERPTA MED., SECT. 17, PUBL. HEALTH SOC. MED EPIDEM.
[NE]
EXCERPTA MEDICA. SECTION 17. PUBLIC HEALTH, SOCIAL MEDICINE AND EPIDEMIOLOGY.
(*Continues* Excerpta Medica. Section 17, Public Health, Social Medicine and Hygiene.)
***Refer to EMBASE [Online Database] for complete source list.

EXCERPTA MED., SECT. 17, PUBL. HEALTH SOC. MED. HYG.
[NE/0014-4215]
EXCERPTA MEDICA. SECTION 17. PUBLIC HEALTH, SOCIAL MEDICINE AND HYGIENE.
(*Continued by* Excerpta Medica. Section 17, Public Health, Social Medicine and Epidemiology.)

EXCERPTA MED., SECT. 18, CARDIOVASC. DISEAS. CARDIOVASC. SURG.
[NE/0014-4223]
EXCERPTA MEDICA. SECTION 18. CARDIOVASCULAR DISEASES AND CARDIOVASCULAR SURGERY.
(*Continues* Excerpta Medica. Section 18. Cardiovascular Diseases.)
***Refer to EMBASE [Online Database] for complete source list.

EXCERPTA MED., SECT. 19, REHABIL. PHYS. MED.
[NE/0014-4231]
EXCERPTA MEDICA. SECTION 19. REHABILITATION AND PHYSICAL MEDICINE.
(*Continues* Excerpta Medica. Section 19. Rehabilitation.)
***Refer to EMBASE [Online Database] for complete source list.

EXCERPTA MED., SECT. 20, GERONTOL. GERIATR.
[NE/0014-424X]
EXCERPTA MEDICA. SECTION 20. GERONTOLOGY AND GERIATRICS.
***Refer to EMBASE [Online Database] for complete source list.

INDEXES/ABSTRACTS TABLE

EXCERPTA MED., SECT. 21, DEVELOP. BIOL. TERATOL.
[NE/0014-4258]
EXCERPTA MEDICA. SECTION 21. DEVELOPMENTAL BIOLOGY AND TERATOLOGY.
(*Continues* Excerpta Medica. Section 21. Human Developmental Biology.)
***Refer to EMBASE [Online Database] for complete source list.

EXCERPTA MED., SECT. 22, HUMAN GENET.
[NE/0014-4266]
EXCERPTA MEDICA. SECTION 22. HUMAN GENETICS.
(*Continues* Human Genetics Abstracts.)
***Refer to EMBASE [Online Database] for complete source list.

EXCERPTA MED., SECT. 23, NUCL. MED.
[NE/0014-4274]
EXCERPTA MEDICA. SECTION 23. NUCLEAR MEDICINE.
***Refer to EMBASE [Online Database] for complete source list.

EXCERPTA MED., SECT. 24, ANESTHESIOL.
[NE/0014-4282]
EXCERPTA MEDICA. SECTION 24. ANESTHESIOLOGY.
***Refer to EMBASE [Online Database] for complete source list.

EXCERPTA MED., SECT. 25, HEMATOL.
[NE/0014-4290]
EXCERPTA MEDICA. SECTION 25. HEMATOLOGY.
***Refer to EMBASE [Online Database] for complete source list.

EXCERPTA MED., SECT. 26, IMMUNOL. SEROL. TRANSPLANT.
[NE/0014-4304]
EXCERPTA MEDICA. SECTION 26. IMMUNOLOGY, SEROLOGY AND TRANSPLANTATION.
(*Supersedes in part* Excerpta Medica. Section 4, Medical Microbiology, Immunology and Serology.)
***Refer to EMBASE [Online Database] for complete source list.

EXCERPTA MED., SECT. 27, BIOPHYS. BIOENG. MED. INSTRUMEN.
[NE/0014-4312]
EXCERPTA MEDICA. SECTION 27. BIOPHYSICS, BIOENGINEERING AND MEDICAL INSTRUMENTATION.
(*Continues* Excerpta Medica. Section 27. Medical Instrumentation.)
***Refer to EMBASE [Online Database] for complete source list.

EXCERPTA MED., SECT. 28, UROL.
[NE]
EXCERPTA MEDICA. SECTION 28. UROLOGY.
(*Continued by* Excerpta Medica. Section 28, Urology and Nephrology.)

EXCERPTA MED., SECT. 28, UROL. NEPHROL.
[NE/0014-4320]
EXCERPTA MEDICA. SECTION 28. UROLOGY AND NEPHROLOGY.
(*Continues* Excerpta Medica. Section 28, Urology.)
***Refer to EMBASE [Online Database] for complete source list.

EXCERPTA MED., SECT. 29, CLIN. BIOCHEM.
[NE/0300-5372]
EXCERPTA MEDICA. SECTION 29. CLINICAL BIOCHEMISTRY.
(*Continues* Excerpta Medica. Section 29. Biochemistry.)
***Refer to EMBASE [Online Database] for complete source list.

EXCERPTA MED., SECT. 30, CLIN. EXPER. PHARMACOL.
[NE]
EXCERPTA MEDICA. SECTION 30. CLINICAL AND EXPERIMENTAL PHARMACOLOGY.
(*Formed by the union of* Excerpta Medica. Section 30, Pharmacology *and* Excerpta Medica. Section 130, Clinical Pharmacology.)
***Refer to EMBASE [Online Database] for complete source list.

EXCERPTA MED., SECT. 30, PHARMACOL.
[IE/0167-9643]
EXCERPTA MEDICA. SECTION 30. PHARMACOLOGY.
(*Continued in part by* Excerpta Medica. Section 130, Clinical Pharmacology; *Merged into* Excerpta Medica. Section 30. Clinical and Experimental Pharmacology.)
***Refer to EMBASE [Online Database] for complete source list.

EXCERPTA MED., SECT. 32, PSYCH.
[NE/0014-4363]
EXCERPTA MEDICA. SECTION 32. PSYCHIATRY.
(*Continues* Excerpta Medica. Section 8B, Psychiatry.)
***Refer to EMBASE [Online Database] for complete source list.

EXCERPTA MED., SECT. 35, OCCUPAT. HEALTH INDUSTR. MED.
[NE/0014-4398]
EXCERPTA MEDICA. SECTION 35. OCCUPATIONAL HEALTH AND INDUSTRIAL MEDICINE.
***Refer to EMBASE [Online Database] for complete source list.

EXCERPTA MED., SECT. 36, HEALTH POLICY ECON. MANAG.
[NE]
EXCERPTA MEDICA. SECTION 36. HEALTH POLICY, ECONOMICS, AND MANAGEMENT.
(*Continues* Health Economics and Hospital Management.)
***Refer to EMBASE [Online Database] for complete source list.

EXCERPTA MED., SECT. 37, DRUG LIT. INDEX
[NE/0167-9171]
EXCERPTA MEDICA. SECTION 37. DRUG LITERATURE INDEX.
(*Continues* Drug Literature Index.)

EXCERPTA MED., SECT. 38, ADVERSE REACT. TITLES
[NE/0167-9090]
EXCERPTA MEDICA. SECTION 38. ADVERSE REACTIONS TITLES.
(*Continues* Adverse Reactions Titles.)
***Refer to EMBASE [Online Database] for complete source list.

EXCERPTA MED., SECT. 40, DRUG DEPEND. ALCOHOL ABUSE ALCOHOL.
[NE/0304-4041]
EXCERPTA MEDICA. SECTION 40. DRUG DEPENDENCE, ALCOHOL ABUSE, AND ALCOHOLISM.
(*Continues* Excerpta Medica. Section 40, Drug Dependence.)
***Refer to EMBASE [Online Database] for complete source list.

EXCERPTA MED., SECT. 46, ENVIRON. HEALTH POLLUT. CONT.
[NE/0300-5194]
EXCERPTA MEDICA. SECTION 46. ENVIRONMENTAL HEALTH AND POLLUTION CONTROL.
(*Continues* Environmental Health and Pollution Control.)
***Refer to EMBASE [Online Database] for complete source list.

EXCERPTA MED., SECT. 50, EPILEP. ABSTR.
[NE/0303-8459]
EXCERPTA MEDICA. SECTION 50. EPILEPSY ABSTRACTS.
(*Continues* Epilepsy Abstracts.)
***Refer to EMBASE [Online Database] for complete source list.

EXCERPTA MED., SECT. 52, TOXICOL.
[NE/0167-8353]
EXCERPTA MEDICA. SECTION 52. TOXICOLOGY.
(*Continues in part* Excerpta Medica. Section 30, Pharmacology and Toxicology.)
***Refer to EMBASE [Online Database] for complete source list.

EXCERPTA MED., SECT. 54, AIDS
[NE/0922-6532]
EXCERPTA MEDICA. SECTION 54. AIDS (ACQUIRED IMMUNE DEFICIENCY SYNDROME).
(Ceased)

EXCERPTA MED., SECT. 65, CANCER IMMUNOL. LIT. INDEX
[NE/0304-3789]
EXCERPTA MEDICA. SECTION 65. CANCER IMMUNOLOGY. LITERATURE INDEX.
***Refer to EMBASE [Online Database] for complete source list.

EXCERPTA MED., SECT. 130, CLINIC. PHARMACOL.
[NE/0921-4496]
EXCERPTA MEDICA. SECTION 130. CLINICAL PHARMACOLOGY.
(*Separated from* Excerpta Medica. Section 30, Pharmacology.)

EXCERPTA MED., SECT. 151, MYCOBACTER. DISEAS. LEPROSY TUBERCUL. RELATED SUBJ.
[NE/0168-8944]
EXCERPTA MEDICA. SECTION 151. MYCOBACTERIAL DISEASES--LEPROSY, TUBERCULOSIS, AND RELATED SUBJECTS.
(*Continues* Excerpta Medica. Section 51, Mycobacterial Diseases--Leprosy, Tuberculosis, and Related Subjects.)

EXPAND. ACAD. INDEX
[US]
EXPANDED ACADEMIC INDEX [COMPUTER FILE].

INDEXES/ABSTRACTS TABLE

F & S INDEX CORP. IND.
[US/0014-567X]
F & S INDEX OF CORPORATIONS AND INDUSTRIES.
(*Continued by* Predicasts F & S Index United States (Annual Edition).)

F & S INDEX PLUS TEXT, INT.
[US/1065-5956]
F & S INDEX PLUS TEXT. INTERNATIONAL.

F & S INDEX PLUS TEXT, U.S.
[US/1065-5964]
F & S INDEX PLUS TEXT. UNITED STATES.
***Refer to F&S Index Plus Text International for complete source list.

FABA BEAN ABSTR.
[UK/0260-8456]
FABA BEAN ABSTRACTS.
(Ceased)

FAMLI, FAM. MED. LIT. INDEX
[CN/0227-2393]
FAMLI : FAMILY MEDICINE LITERATURE INDEX.
(Ceased)

FARM GARD. INDEX
[US/0736-9980]
FARM & GARDEN INDEX.
(Ceased)

FDA CLIN. EXP. ABSTR.
[US/0429-9442]
FDA CLINICAL EXPERIENCE ABSTRACTS.
(Ceased)

FED. PRINT
[US/0891-2769]
FED IN PRINT.
(*Continued by* Fed in Print: Economics and Banking Topics.)

FED. PRINT ECON. BANK. TOP.
[US]
FED IN PRINT: ECONOMICS AND BANKING TOPICS.
(*Continues* Fed in Print: Business and Banking Topics.)

FED. TAX ARTIC.
[US]
FEDERAL TAX ARTICLES: INCOME, ESTATE, GIFT, EXCISE, EMPLOYMENT TAXES.

FERT. ABSTR.
[US/0015-0290]
FERTILIZER ABSTRACTS.
(Ceased)

FIELD CROP ABSTR.
[UK/0015-069X]
FIELD CROP ABSTRACTS.

FILM LIT. INDEX
[US/0093-6758]
FILM LITERATURE INDEX.

FISH REV.
[US/1042-6299]
FISHERIES REVIEW (FORT COLLINS, COLO.).
(*Continues* Sport Fishery Abstracts; **Absorbed** Fish Health News.)

FLUID ABSTR. CIVIL ENG.
[UK/0962-7170]
FLUID ABSTRACTS. CIVIL ENGINEERING.
(*Formed by the union of* Civil Engineering Hydraulics Abstracts; Industrial Aerodynamics Abstracts; Offshore Engineering Abstracts and World Ports & Harbours Abstracts (Incorporating International Dredging Abstracts).)

FLUID ABSTR. PROC. ENG.
[UK/0962-7162]
FLUID ABSTRACTS. PROCESS ENGINEERING.
(*Formed by the union of* Fluid Flow Measurements Abstracts; Fluid Power Abstracts; Fluid Sealing Abstracts; Pipelines Abstracts; Pumps and Other Fluids Machinery Abstracts; Solid-Liquid Flow Abstracts; Computer-Aided Process Control Abstracts **and** Mixing and Separation Technology Abstracts.)

FLUIDEX
[UK]
FLUIDEX [ONLINE DATABASE].

FOOD SCI. TECHNOL. ABSTR.
[UK/0015-6574]
FOOD SCIENCE AND TECHNOLOGY ABSTRACTS.

FOODS ADLIBRA
[US/0146-9304]
FOODS ADLIBRA (1975).

FOR. ABSTR.
[UK/0015-7538]
FORESTRY ABSTRACTS.

FOR. PROD. ABSTR.
[UK/0140-4784]
FOREST PRODUCTS ABSTRACTS.

FOREIGN LANG. INDEX
[US/0048-5810]
FOREIGN LANGUAGE INDEX.
(*Continued by* PAIS Foreign Language Index.)

FRESH. AQUA. CONTENTS TABLES
[IT]
FRESHWATER AND AQUACULTURE CONTENTS TABLES. ACTUALITES DES EAUX DOUCES ET DE L'AQUACULTURE.

FUNK & SCOTT ANNU. INDEX CORP. LIB.
[US]
FUNK & SCOTT ANNUAL INDEX OF CORPORATIONS & INDUSTRIES, THE.
(*Continued by* F & S Index of Corporations and Industries.)

FUNK & SCOTT INDEX CORP. IND.
[US/0532-8705]
FUNK & SCOTT INDEX OF CORPORATIONS AND INDUSTRIES.
(*Continued by* Funk & Scott Annual Index of Corporations & Industries.)

FUT. SURV.
[US/0190-3241]
FUTURE SURVEY.
(*Continues* Public Policy Book Forecast.)

GARDEN LIT.
[US/1061-3722]
GARDEN LITERATURE.

GAS ABSTR.
[US/0016-4844]
GAS ABSTRACTS.

GASTROENTEROL. ABSTR. CITATIONS
[US/0016-5093]
GASTROENTEROLOGY: ABSTRACTS & CITATIONS.
(Ceased)

GEN. BUSINESSFILE
[US]
GENERAL BUSINESSFILE [COMPUTER FILE].

GEN. PERIOD. INDEX
[US]
GENERAL PERIODICALS INDEX [COMPUTER FILE].

GEN. PERIOD. ONDISC
[US/1064-8380]
GENERAL PERIODICALS ONDISC (RESEARCH 1 ED.).
***Refer to Newspaper and Periodical Abstracts for complete source list.

GEN. SCI. INDEX
[US/0162-1963]
GENERAL SCIENCE INDEX.

GEN. SCI. SOURCE
[US/1073-1954]
GENERAL SCIENCE SOURCE.

GENEALOGICAL PERIOD. ANNU. INDEX
[US/0072-0593]
GENEALOGICAL PERIODICAL ANNUAL INDEX.

GENET. ABSTR.
[US/0016-674X]
GENETICS ABSTRACTS.

GEO ABSTR.
[UK]
GEO ABSTRACTS.
(*Continued by* Geographical Abstracts : Physical Geography; Geographical Abstracts. Human Geography.)

GEOGR. ABSTR.
[UK]
GEOGRAPHICAL ABSTRACTS.
(*Continued by* Geo Abstracts.)

GEOGR. ABSTR. HUMAN GEOGR.
[UK/0953-9611]
GEOGRAPHICAL ABSTRACTS. HUMAN GEOGRAPHY.
(*Formed by the union of* Geographical Abstracts. C, Economic Geography (1986); Geographical Abstracts. D, Social and Historical Geography **and** Geographical Abstracts. F, Regional and Community Planning.)

GEOGR. ABSTR. PHYS. GEOGR.
[UK/0954-0504]
GEOGRAPHICAL ABSTRACTS : PHYSICAL GEOGRAPHY.
(*Formed by the union of* Geographical Abstracts. A, Landforms and the Quaternary; Geographical Abstracts. B, Climatology and Hydrology; Geographical Abstracts. E, Sedimentology **and** Geographical Abstracts. G, Remote Sensing, Photogrammetry, and Cartography.)

GEOL. ABSTR.
[UK/0954-0512]
GEOLOGICAL ABSTRACTS.
(*Formed by the union of* Geological Abstracts. Economic Geology; Geological Abstracts. Geophysics & Tectonics Abstracts; Geological Abstracts. Palaeontology & Stratigraphy **and** Geological Abstracts. Sedimentary Geology.)

GEOL. ABSTR. ECON. GEOL.
[UK]
GEOLOGICAL ABSTRACTS. ECONOMIC GEOLOGY.
(**Merged with** Geological Abstracts. Geophysics & Tectonics Abstracts; Geological Abstracts. Palaeontology & Stratigraphy **and** Geological Abstracts. Sedimentary Abstracts **to form** Geological Abstracts.)

GEOL. ABSTR. GEOPHYS. TECTON.
[UK/0262-0847]
GEOLOGICAL ABSTRACTS. GEOPHYSICS & TECTONICS.
(**Merged with** Geological Abstracts. Economic Geology; Geological Abstracts. Palaeontology & Stratigraphy **and** Geological Abstracts. Sedimentary Geology **to form** Geological Abstracts.)

INDEXES/ABSTRACTS TABLE

GEOL. ABSTR. PALAEON. STRAT.
[UK/0268-8018]
GEOLOGICAL ABSTRACTS. PALAEONTOLOGY & STRATIGRAPHY.
(*Merged with* Geological Abstracts. Economic Geology; Geological Abstracts. Geophysics & Tectonics Abstracts *and* Geological Abstracts. Sedimentary Geology *to form* Geological Abstracts.)

GEOL. ABSTR. SEDIMEN. GEOL.
[UK/0268-8026]
GEOLOGICAL ABSTRACTS. SEDIMENTARY GEOLOGY.
(*Merged with* Geological Abstracts. Economic Geology; Geological Abstracts. Geophysics & Tectonics Abstracts *and* Geological Abstracts. Palaeontology & Stratigraphy *to form* Geological Abstracts.)

GEOPHYS. ABSTR.
[UK/0309-4332]
GEOPHYSICAL ABSTRACTS.
(*Continued by* Geological Abstracts. Geophysics & Tectonics Abstracts.)

GEOREF
[US/0197-7482]
GEOREF (CD-ROM).

GEOSCI. ABSTR.
[US/0435-5628]
GEOSCIENCE ABSTRACTS.
(*Supersedes* Geological Abstracts.)

GEOSCI. DOC.
[UK/0016-8483]
GEOSCIENCE DOCUMENTATION.

GEOTECH. ABSTR.
[US/0016-8491]
GEOTECHNICAL ABSTRACTS.
(Ceased)

GERONTOL. ABSTR.
[US/0736-4342]
GERONTOLOGICAL ABSTRACTS.
(Ceased)

GRAPH. ARTS ABSTR.
[US/0017-3282]
GRAPHIC ARTS ABSTRACTS.
(*Continued by* Abstracts (Graphic Arts Technical Foundation).)

GRAPH. ARTS BULL. INST. PAP. SCI. TECHNOL.
[US/1064-9638]
GRAPHIC ARTS BULLETIN OF THE INSTITUTE OF PAPER SCIENCE AND TECHNOLOGY.
(*Continues* Graphic Arts Literature Abstracts.)

GRAPH. ARTS LIT. ABSTR.
[US/0090-8207]
GRAPHIC ARTS LITERATURE ABSTRACTS.
(*Continued by* Graphic Arts Bulletin of the Institute of Paper Science and Technology.)

GUIDE PERFORM. ARTS
[US/0072-873X]
GUIDE TO THE PERFORMING ARTS.
(*Absorbed* Guide to Dance Periodicals.)

GUIDE REV. BOOKS HISP. AM.
[US/0716-0348]
GUIDE TO REVIEWS OF BOOKS FROM AND ABOUT HISPANIC AMERICA.
(Ceased)

GUIDE SOC. SCI. RELIG.
[US/1054-0946]
GUIDE TO SOCIAL SCIENCE AND RELIGION.
(*Continues* Guide to Social Science and Religion in Periodical Literature.)

GUIDE SOC. SCI. RELIG. PERIOD. LIT.
[US/0017-5307]
GUIDE TO SOCIAL SCIENCE AND RELIGION IN PERIODICAL LITERATURE.
(*Continued by* Guide to Social Science and Religion.)

HEALTH DEVICES ALERTS
[US/0163-0458]
HEALTH DEVICES ALERTS.

HEALTH INDEX
[US]
HEALTH INDEX [COMPUTER FILE].

HEALTH PERIOD. DATABASE
[US]
HEALTH PERIODICALS DATABASE [ONLINE DATABASE].

HEALTH PLAN. ADMINIS.
[US/1065-0679]
HEALTH PLANNING AND ADMINISTRATION.

HEALTH SAF. SCI. ABSTR.
[US/0892-9351]
HEALTH AND SAFETY SCIENCE ABSTRACTS.
(*Continues* Safety Science Abstracts Journal.)

HEALTH SERV. ABSTR.
[UK/0268-0459]
HEALTH SERVICE ABSTRACTS.
(*Formed by the union of* Current Literature on Health Services; Current Literature on General Medical Practice *and* Hospital Abstracts.)

HEALTH SOURCE
[US/1063-9810]
HEALTH SOURCE (PEABODY, MASS.).

HELMINTHOL. ABSTR.
[UK/0957-6789]
HELMINTHOLOGICAL ABSTRACTS.
(*Continues* Helminthological Abstracts. Series A, Animal and Human Helminthology.)

HELMINTHOL. ABSTR. SER. A, ANIM. HUM. HELMINTHOL.
[UK/0300-8339]
HELMINTHOLOGICAL ABSTRACTS. SERIES A, ANIMAL AND HUMAN HELMINTHOLOGY.
(*Continued by* Helminthological Abstracts.)

HELMINTHOL. ABSTR. SER. B, PLANT NEMATOLOGY
[UK/0300-8320]
HELMINTHOLOGICAL ABSTRACTS. SERIES B, PLANT NEMATOLOGY.
(*Continued by* Nematological Abstracts.)

HERB. ABSTR.
[UK/0018-0602]
HERBAGE ABSTRACTS.
(*Continued by* Grasslands and Forage Abstracts.)

HIGH. EDUC. ABSTR.
[US/0748-4364]
HIGHER EDUCATION ABSTRACTS.
(*Continues* College Student Personnel Abstracts.)

HIGHW. RES. ABSTR.
[US/0018-1730]
HIGHWAY RESEARCH ABSTRACTS.
(*Continued by* Transportation Research Abstracts.)

HIGHW. RES. ABSTR.
[US/1050-0804]
HIGHWAY RESEARCH ABSTRACTS (1990).
(*Continues* HRIS Abstracts.)

HILITES
[US]
HILITES DATABASE [ONLINE DATABASE].

HISP. AM. PERIOD. INDEX
[US/0270-8558]
HISPANIC AMERICAN PERIODICALS INDEX (LOS ANGELES, CALIF.).

HIST. ABSTR.
[US/0018-2435]
HISTORICAL ABSTRACTS.
(*Split into* Historical Abstracts. Part A, Modern History Abstracts *and* Historical Abstracts. Part B, Twentieth Century Abstracts.)

HIST. ABSTR., PART A, MOD. HIST. ABSTR.
[US/0363-2717]
HISTORICAL ABSTRACTS. PART A, MODERN HISTORY ABSTRACTS.
(*Continues in part* Historical Abstracts.)
***Refer to America: History and Life for complete source list.

HIST. ABSTR., PART B, TWENT. CENTURY ABSTR.
[US/0363-2725]
HISTORICAL ABSTRACTS. PART B, TWENTIETH CENTURY ABSTRACTS.
(*Continues in part* Historical Abstracts.)
***Refer to America: History and Life for complete source list.

HIST. SOURCE
[US/1063-9799]
HISTORY SOURCE.
(*Merged into* Humanities Source CD-ROM.)

HORTIC. ABSTR.
[UK/0018-5280]
HORTICULTURAL ABSTRACTS.

HOSPIT. ABSTR.
[UK/0018-5507]
HOSPITAL ABSTRACTS.
(*Merged with* Current Literature on Health Services *and* Current Literature on General Medical Practice *to form* Health Service Abstracts.)

HOSPIT. HEALTH ADMIN. INDEX
[US/1077-1719]
HOSPITAL AND HEALTH ADMINISTRATION INDEX.
(*Continues* Hospital Literature Index.)

HOSPIT. LIT. INDEX
[US/0018-5736]
HOSPITAL LITERATURE INDEX.
(*Continued by* Hospital and Health Administration Index.)

HOSPIT. MANAGE. REV.
[US/0737-903X]
HOSPITAL MANAGEMENT REVIEW.

HRIS ABSTR.
[US/0017-6222]
HRIS ABSTRACTS.
(*Continued by* Highway Research Abstracts (Washington, D.C. : 1990).)

HTFS DIG.
[UK/0952-2654]
HTFS DIGEST (1987).
(*Continues* Heat Transfer & Fluid Flow Digest; *Absorbed* Fouling Prevention Research Digest.)

INDEXES/ABSTRACTS TABLE

HUM. GENOME ABSTR.
[US/1045-4470]
HUMAN GENOME ABSTRACTS.

HUM. RESOUR. ABSTR.
[US/0099-2453]
HUMAN RESOURCES ABSTRACTS.
(*Continues* Poverty and Human Resources Abstracts.)

HUM. RIGHTS INTERN. REP.
[US/0275-049X]
HUMAN RIGHTS INTERNET REPORTER.
(*Continues* Human Rights Internet Newsletter.)

HUMANIT. INDEX
[US/0095-5981]
HUMANITIES INDEX.
(*Supersedes in part* Social Sciences & Humanities Index.)

HUMANIT. SOURCE
[US/1073-1962]
HUMANITIES SOURCE.
(*Absorbed* History Source CD-ROM.)

HUNGAR. LIBR. INFO. SCI. ABSTR.
[HU/0046-8304]
HUNGARIAN LIBRARY AND INFORMATION SCIENCE ABSTRACTS.

IAG, LIT. AUTO.
[NE/0376-9666]
IAG - LITERATURE ON AUTOMATION.
(*Continued by* New Literature on Automation.)

IMAGING ABSTR.
[US/0896-100X]
IMAGING ABSTRACTS.
(*Continues* Photographic Abstracts.)

IMMUNOL. ABSTR.
[US/0307-112X]
IMMUNOLOGY ABSTRACTS.

IND. ARTS INDEX
[US/0275-1682]
INDUSTRIAL ARTS INDEX.
(*Split into* Business Periodicals Index *and* Applied Science & Technology Index.)

IND. HYG. DIG.
[US/0019-8382]
INDUSTRIAL HYGIENE DIGEST.

INDEX AM. PERIOD. VERSE
[US/0090-9130]
INDEX OF AMERICAN PERIODICAL VERSE.

INDEX BLACK PERIOD.
[US/0899-6253]
INDEX TO BLACK PERIODICALS.
(*Continues* Index to Periodical Articles by and About Blacks.)

INDEX BOOK REV. HUMANIT.
[US/0073-5892]
INDEX TO BOOK REVIEWS IN THE HUMANITIES.
(Ceased)

INDEX BOOK REV. RELIG.
[US/0887-1574]
INDEX TO BOOK REVIEWS IN RELIGION.
(*Continues in part* Religion Index One. Periodicals.)

INDEX BUS. REPORTS
[UK]
INDEX TO BUSINESS REPORTS.
(*Continues* Index to Special Reports in UK Newspapers and Selected Periodicals.)

INDEX CAN. LEG. PERIOD. LIT.
[CN/0316-8891]
INDEX TO CANADIAN LEGAL PERIODICAL LITERATURE.

INDEX CHEM.
[US/0891-6055]
INDEX CHEMICUS (1987).
(*Continues* Current Abstracts of Chemistry and Index Chemicus (Philadelphia, Pa. : 1978).)

INDEX DENT. LIT.
[US/0019-3992]
INDEX TO DENTAL LITERATURE.
(*Continues* Index to Dental Literature in the English Language.)

INDEX ECON. ARTIC. J. COLLECT. VOL.
[US/0536-647X]
INDEX OF ECONOMIC ARTICLES IN JOURNALS AND COLLECTIVE VOLUMES.
(*Formed by the union of* Index of Economic Journals *and* Index of Economic Articles in Collective Volumes.)
***Refer to Journal of Economic Literature for complete source list.

INDEX ECON. J.
[US/0893-9527]
INDEX OF ECONOMIC JOURNALS.
(*Merged with* Index of Economic Articles in Collective Volumes *to form* Index of Economic Articles in Journals and Collective Volumes.)

INDEX FOREIGN LEG. PER.
[UK/0019-400X]
INDEX TO FOREIGN LEGAL PERIODICALS.

INDEX FREE PERIOD.
[US/0147-5630]
INDEX TO FREE PERIODICALS.
(*Merged into* Matter of Fact.)

INDEX IEEE PUBL.
[US/0099-1368]
INDEX TO IEEE PUBLICATIONS.
(*Supersedes* Institute of Electrical and Electronics Engineers. Index to IEEE Periodicals.)

INDEX INF.
[US/0073-5930]
INDEX TO HOW TO DO IT INFORMATION.

INDEX ISLAM.
[UK]
INDEX ISLAMICUS.
(*Continues* Index Islamicus. Supplement.)

INDEX ISLAM. LIT.
[UK]
INDEX OF ISLAMIC LITERATURE.

INDEX JEW. PERIOD.
[US/0019-4050]
INDEX TO JEWISH PERIODICALS.

INDEX LEG. PERIOD.
[US/0019-4077]
INDEX TO LEGAL PERIODICALS.

INDEX LIT. AM. INDIAN
[US/0091-7346]
INDEX TO LITERATURE ON THE AMERICAN INDIAN.
(Ceased)

INDEX MATH. PAP.
[US/0019-3917]
INDEX OF MATHEMATICAL PAPERS.
(Ceased)

INDEX MED.
[US/0019-3879]
INDEX MEDICUS (1960).
(*Continues* Current List of Medical Literature; *Absorbed* Monthly Bibliography of Medical Reviews.)

INDEX NEW Z. PERIOD.
[NZ]
INDEX TO NEW ZEALAND PERIODICALS.
(Ceased)

INDEX PERIOD. ARTIC. BLACKS
[US/0161-8245]
INDEX TO PERIODICAL ARTICLES BY AND ABOUT BLACKS.
(*Continued by* Index to Black Periodicals.)

INDEX PERIOD. ARTIC. NEGROES
[US/0073-5973]
INDEX TO PERIODICAL ARTICLES BY AND ABOUT NEGROES.
(*Continued by* Index to Periodical Articles by and About Blacks.)

INDEX PERIOD. ARTIC. RELAT. LAW
[US/0019-4093]
INDEX TO PERIODICAL ARTICLES RELATED TO LAW.

INDEX PERIOD. LIT. AGING
[US/0882-3405]
INDEX TO PERIODICAL LITERATURE ON AGING.
(*Continues* ARECO's Quarterly Index to Periodical Literature on Aging.)

INDEX PHILIP. PERIOD.
[PH/0073-599X]
INDEX TO PHILIPPINE PERIODICALS.

INDEX RELIG. PERIOD. LIT.
[US/0019-4107]
INDEX TO RELIGIOUS PERIODICAL LITERATURE.
(*Continued by* Religion Index One. Periodicals.)

INDEX SCI. REV.
[US/0360-0661]
INDEX TO SCIENTIFIC REVIEWS.

INDEX U.S. GOV. PERIOD.
[US/0098-4604]
INDEX TO U.S. GOVERNMENT PERIODICALS.
(Ceased)

INDEX VET.
[UK/0019-4123]
INDEX VETERINARIUS.

INDIAN GEOSCI. ABSTR.
[II]
INDIAN GEOSCIENCE ABSTRACTS.

INDIAN LIBR. SCI. ABSTR.
[II/0019-5790]
INDIAN LIBRARY SCIENCE ABSTRACTS.

INDIAN SCI. ABSTR.
[II/0019-6339]
INDIAN SCIENCE ABSTRACTS.
(*Continues* Bibliography of Scientific Publications of South and South East Asia.)

INDICE AGRICOLA AM. LAT. CARIBE
[CR/0304-0119]
INDICE AGRICOLA DE AMERICA LATINA Y EL CARIBE.
(*Continues* Bibliografia Agricola Latinoamericana y del Caribe.)

INDICE HIST. ESP.
[SP/0537-3522]
INDICE HISTORICO ESPANOL.

INDEXES/ABSTRACTS TABLE

INDICE MED. ESP.
[SP]
INDICE MEDICO ESPANOL.

INF. INSTRUC. TECHNOL.
[US]
INFORMATION & INSTRUCTION TECHNOLOGIES.

INF. MANAGE. TECHNOL.
[UK]
INFORMATION MANAGEMENT & TECHNOLOGY.
(*Continues* Information Media & Technology.)

INF. SCI. ABSTR.
[US/0020-0239]
INFORMATION SCIENCE ABSTRACTS.
(*Continues* Documentation Abstracts and Information Science Abstracts.)

INFO-SOUTH ABSTR.
[US/1059-5910]
INFO-SOUTH ABSTRACTS.

INFOBANK
[IO]
INFOBANK.

INFOMAT INT. BUS.
[US]
INFOMAT INTERNATIONAL BUSINESS [ONLINE DATABASE].

INIS ATOMINDEX
[AU/0004-7139]
INIS ATOMINDEX.
(*Continued by* INIS Atomindex.)

INIS ATOMINDEX [MICRO.]
[AU]
INIS ATOMINDEX [MICROFORM].
(*Continues* INIS Atomindex.)

INS. PERIOD. INDEX
[US/0074-073X]
INSURANCE PERIODICALS INDEX.

INSPEC
[UK]
INSPEC [ONLINE DATABASE].

INT. ABSTR. BIOL. SCI.
[UK/0020-5818]
INTERNATIONAL ABSTRACTS OF BIOLOGICAL SCIENCES.
(*Continued by* Current Awareness in Biological Sciences : CABS.)

INT. ABSTR. OPER. RES.
[UK/0020-580X]
INTERNATIONAL ABSTRACTS IN OPERATIONS RESEARCH.

INT. AEROSP. ABSTR.
[US/0020-5842]
INTERNATIONAL AEROSPACE ABSTRACTS.
(*Supersedes in part* Aerospace Engineering.)

INT. BIBLIOGR. BOOK REV.
[GW]
INTERNATIONAL BIBLIOGRAPHY OF BOOK REVIEWS.
(*Continued by* Internationale Bibliographie der Rezensionen Wissenschaftlicher Literatur (Osnabruck, Germany : 1984).)

INT. BIBLIOGR. HIST. RELIG.
[NE/0538-5105]
INTERNATIONAL BIBLIOGRAPHY OF THE HISTORY OF RELIGIONS.
(Ceased)

INT. BIBLIOGR. PERIOD. LIT.
[GW]
INTERNATIONAL BIBLIOGRAPHY OF PERIODICAL LITERATURE.
(*Continued by* Internationale Bibliographie der Zeitschriftenliteratur aus Allen Gebieten des Wissens (Osnabruck, Germany : 1984).)

INT. BIBLIOGR. REZEN. WISSEN. LIT.
[GW/0020-918X]
INTERNATIONALE BIBLIOGRAPHIE DER REZENSIONEN WISSENSCHAFTLICHER LITERATUR.
(*Continues* Internationale Bibliographie der Rezensionen.)

INT. BIBLIOGR. SOCIOL.
[UK/0085-2066]
INTERNATIONAL BIBLIOGRAPHY OF SOCIOLOGY.
(*Continues in part* Current Sociology (Paris, France).)

INT. BIBLIOGR. ZEITSCHRIFTENLITERATUR ALLEN GEBIETEN WISSENS
[GW]
INTERNATIONALE BIBLIOGRAPHIE DER ZEITSCHRIFTENLITERATUR AUS ALLEN GEBIETEN DES WISSENS.
(*Continues* Internationale Bibliographie der Zeitschriftenliteratur.)

INT. BUILD. SERV. ABSTR.
[UK/0140-4237]
INTERNATIONAL BUILDING SERVICES ABSTRACTS.
(*Continues* Thermal Abstracts.)

INT. CIVIL ENG. ABSTR.
[IE/0332-4095]
INTERNATIONAL CIVIL ENGINEERING ABSTRACTS.
(*Continues* Institution of Civil Engineers (Great Britain). I.C.E. Abstracts.)

INT. COPPER INF. BULL.
[UK/0309-2216]
INTERNATIONAL COPPER INFORMATION BULLETIN.
(*Formed by the union of* Selected Abstracts of Recent Literature on Copper and Copper Alloys **and** Kupfer-Mitteilungen.)

INT. DEV. ABSTR.
[UK/0262-0855]
INTERNATIONAL DEVELOPMENT ABSTRACTS.
(*Absorbed* International Development Index.)

INT. EXEC.
[US/0020-6652]
INTERNATIONAL EXECUTIVE.

INT. GUIDE CLASSICAL STUD.
[US/0020-6849]
INTERNATIONAL GUIDE TO CLASSICAL STUDIES.
(*Continues* ABS International Guide to Classical Studies.)

INT. INDEX
[US/0363-0382]
INTERNATIONAL INDEX.
(*Continued by* Social Sciences & Humanities Index.)

INT. INDEX FILM PERIOD.
[US/0000-0388]
INTERNATIONAL INDEX TO FILM PERIODICALS.

INT. INDEX MULTI MEDIA INF.
[US/0094-6818]
INTERNATIONAL INDEX TO MULTI-MEDIA INFORMATION.
(*Continues* Film Review Index.)

INT. INDEX PERIOD.
[US]
INTERNATIONAL INDEX TO PERIODICALS.
(*Continued by* International Index.)

INT. LABOUR DOC.
[SZ/0020-7756]
INTERNATIONAL LABOUR DOCUMENTATION.
(*Continues* International Labour Office. Library. International Labour Documentation.)

INT. NURS. INDEX
[US/0020-8124]
INTERNATIONAL NURSING INDEX.

INT. PACKAG. ABSTR.
[UK/0260-7409]
INTERNATIONAL PACKAGING ABSTRACTS.
(*Continues* PIRA Packaging Abstract.)

INT. PET. ABSTR.
[UK/0309-4944]
INTERNATIONAL PETROLEUM ABSTRACTS.
(*Continued by* International Petroleum Abstracts Incorporating Offshore Abstracts.)

INT. PHARM. ABSTR.
[US/0020-8264]
INTERNATIONAL PHARMACEUTICAL ABSTRACTS.

INT. POLIT. SCI. ABSTR.
[FR/0020-8345]
INTERNATIONAL POLITICAL SCIENCE ABSTRACTS.

INT. POLYM. SCI. TECH.
[UK/0307-174X]
INTERNATIONAL POLYMER SCIENCE AND TECHNOLOGY.
(*Formed by the union of* Soviet Plastics **and** Soviet Rubber Technology.)

INT. RISK CONTROL REV.
[US/0739-389X]
INTERNATIONAL RISK CONTROL REVIEW.
(*Continued by* International Loss Control Review.)

INT. ZEITSCHRIFTENSCHAU BIBELWISS. GRENZGEB.
[GW/0074-9745]
INTERNATIONALE ZEITSCHRIFTENSCHAU FUER BIBELWISSENSCHAFT UND GRENZGEBIETE.

IOWA DRUG INF. SERV.
[US]
IOWA DRUG INFORMATION SERVICE.

IRR. DRAIN. ABSTR.
[UK/0306-7327]
IRRIGATION AND DRAINAGE ABSTRACTS / COMMONWEALTH AGRICULTURAL BUREAUX.

ISMEC BULL.
[US/0306-0039]
ISMEC BULLETIN.
(*Continued by* ISMEC, Mechanical Engineering Abstracts.)

ISMEC MECH. ENG. ABSTR.
[US/0896-7113]
ISMEC, MECHANICAL ENGINEERING ABSTRACTS.
(*Continued by* Mechanical Engineering Abstracts.)

J. ABSTR. ARTIC. INT. EDUC.
[US/1064-0746]
JOURNAL OF ABSTRACTS (AND ARTICLES) IN INTERNATIONAL EDUCATION.
(*Continues* Journal of Abstracts in International Education.)

INDEXES/ABSTRACTS TABLE

J. ABSTR. BR. SHIP RES. ASSOC.
[UK/0141-903X]
JOURNAL OF ABSTRACTS OF THE BRITISH SHIP RESEARCH ASSOCIATION.
(*Continued by* BMT Abstracts.)

J. ABSTR. INT. EDUC.
[US/0094-2383]
JOURNAL OF ABSTRACTS IN INTERNATIONAL EDUCATION.
(*Continued by* Journal of Abstract (and Articles) in International Education.)

J. CONTENTS QUAN. METHODS
[UK/0142-5951]
JOURNAL CONTENTS IN QUANTITATIVE METHODS.

J. ECON. ABSTR.
[US/0364-281X]
JOURNAL OF ECONOMIC ABSTRACTS.
(*Continued by* Journal of Economic Literature.)

J. ECON. LIT.
[US/0022-0515]
JOURNAL OF ECONOMIC LITERATURE.
(*Continues* Journal of Economic Abstracts.)

J. FERROCEMENT
[TH/0125-1759]
JOURNAL OF FERROCEMENT.

J. PLAN. LIT.
[US/0885-4122]
JOURNAL OF PLANNING LITERATURE.

J. WATCH
[US/0896-7210]
JOURNAL WATCH.

JAZZ INDEX
[GW/0344-5399]
JAZZ INDEX.
(Ceased)

JMR ABSTR.
[US/1066-2375]
JMR ABSTRACTS.
(*Absorbed by* MRS Bulletin.)

JR. HIGH MAG. ABSTR.
[US/1045-5493]
JUNIOR HIGH MAGAZINE ABSTRACTS.
(Ceased)

KEY ABSTR., ADV. MATER.
[UK/0950-4753]
KEY ABSTRACTS. ADVANCED MATERIALS.
***Refer to INSPEC [Online Database] for complete source list.

KEY ABSTR., ANTENNAS PROPAG.
[UK/0950-4761]
KEY ABSTRACTS. ANTENNAS & PROPAGATION.
(*Continues in part* Key Abstracts. Communication Technology.)
***Refer to INSPEC [Online Database] for complete source list.

KEY ABSTR., ARTIF. INTELL.
[UK/0950-477X]
KEY ABSTRACTS. ARTIFICIAL INTELLIGENCE.
(*Continues* Key Abstracts. Systems Theory.)
***Refer to INSPEC [Online Database] for complete source list.

KEY ABSTR., BUS. AUTOMAT.
[UK/0954-9153]
KEY ABSTRACTS. BUSINESS AUTOMATION.
(*Continues* IT Focus.)
***Refer to INSPEC [Online Database] for complete source list.

KEY ABSTR., COMPUT. COMMUN. STOR.
[UK/0950-4788]
KEY ABSTRACTS. COMPUTER COMMUNICATIONS & STORAGE.
***Refer to INSPEC [Online Database] for complete source list.

KEY ABSTR., COMPUT. ELECTRON. POWER
[UK/0950-4796]
KEY ABSTRACTS. COMPUTING IN ELECTRONICS AND POWER.
***Refer to INSPEC [Online Database] for complete source list.

KEY ABSTR., ELECTR. MEAS. INSTRUM.
[UK/0307-7977]
KEY ABSTRACTS : ELECTRICAL MEASUREMENTS AND INSTRUMENTATION.
(*Continued by* Key Abstracts. Electronic Instrumentation.)

KEY ABSTR., ELECTRON. CIRC.
[UK/0306-557X]
KEY ABSTRACTS. ELECTRONIC CIRCUITS.
***Refer to INSPEC [Online Database] for complete source list.

KEY ABSTR., ELECTRON. INSTRUM.
[UK/0950-480X]
KEY ABSTRACTS. ELECTRONIC INSTRUMENTATION.
(*Continues* Key Abstracts. Electrical Measurements and Instrumentation.)
***Refer to INSPEC [Online Database] for complete source list.

KEY ABSTR., FACTORY AUTOMAT.
[UK]
KEY ABSTRACTS. FACTORY AUTOMATION.
***Refer to INSPEC [Online Database] for complete source list.

KEY ABSTR., HIGH-TEMP. SUPERCONDUC.
[UK/0953-1262]
KEY ABSTRACTS. HIGH-TEMPERATURE SUPERCONDUCTORS.
***Refer to INSPEC [Online Database] for complete source list.

KEY ABSTR., HUMAN-COMPUT. INTERACT.
[UK]
KEY ABSTRACTS. HUMAN-COMPUTER INTERACTION.
***Refer to INSPEC [Online Database] for complete source list.

KEY ABSTR., MACH. VISION
[UK/0952-7052]
KEY ABSTRACTS. MACHINE VISION.
***Refer to INSPEC [Online Database] for complete source list.

KEY ABSTR., MEAS. PHYS.
[UK/0950-4818]
KEY ABSTRACTS. MEASUREMENTS IN PHYSICS.
(*Continues* Key Abstracts. Physical Measurements and Instrumentation.)
***Refer to INSPEC [Online Database] for complete source list.

KEY ABSTR., MICROELECTRON. PRINT. CIRC.
[UK/0952-7060]
KEY ABSTRACTS. MICROELECTRONICS AND PRINTED CIRCUITS.
***Refer to INSPEC [Online Database] for complete source list.

KEY ABSTR., MICROWAVE TECHNOL.
[UK/0952-7079]
KEY ABSTRACTS. MICROWAVE TECHNOLOGY.
***Refer to INSPEC [Online Database] for complete source list.

KEY ABSTR., NEUR. NETWORKS
[UK]
KEY ABSTRACTS. NEURAL NETWORKS.
***Refer to INSPEC [Online Database] for complete source list.

KEY ABSTR., OPTOELECTRON.
[UK/0950-4826]
KEY ABSTRACTS. OPTOELECTRONICS.
(*Continues in part* Key Abstracts. Solid State Devices.)
***Refer to INSPEC [Online Database] for complete source list.

KEY ABSTR., PHYS. MEAS. INSTRUM.
[UK/0307-7969]
KEY ABSTRACTS : PHYSICAL MEASUREMENTS AND INSTRUMENTATION.
(*Continued by* Key Abstracts. Measurements in Physics.)

KEY ABSTR., POWER SYST. APPL.
[UK/0950-4834]
KEY ABSTRACTS. POWER SYSTEMS AND APPLICATIONS.
(*Continues* Key Abstracts. Power Transmission and Distribution.)
***Refer to INSPEC [Online Database] for complete source list.

KEY ABSTR., ROBOT. CONTROL
[UK/0950-4842]
KEY ABSTRACTS. ROBOTICS & CONTROL.
(*Continues* Key Abstracts. Industrial Power and Control Systems.)
***Refer to INSPEC [Online Database] for complete source list.

KEY ABSTR., SEMICOND. DEVICES
[UK/0950-4850]
KEY ABSTRACTS. SEMICONDUCTOR DEVICES.
(*Continues in part* Key Abstracts. Solid State Devices.)
***Refer to INSPEC [Online Database] for complete source list.

KEY ABSTR., SOFTW. ENG.
[UK/0950-4869]
KEY ABSTRACTS. SOFTWARE ENGINEERING.
***Refer to INSPEC [Online Database] for complete source list.

KEY ABSTR., TELECOM.
[UK/0950-4877]
KEY ABSTRACTS. TELECOMMUNICATIONS.
(*Continues* Key Abstracts. Communication Technology.)
***Refer to INSPEC [Online Database] for complete source list.

KEY ECON. SCI.
[NE]
KEY TO ECONOMIC SCIENCE.
(*Continued by* Key to Economic Science and Managerial Sciences.)

KEY ECON. SCI. MANAGE. SCI.
[NE/0165-4748]
KEY TO ECONOMIC SCIENCE AND MANAGERIAL SCIENCES.
(*Continues* Key to Economic Science.)

KEY WORD INDEX WILDL. RES.
[SZ]
KEY-WORD-INDEX OF WILDLIFE RESEARCH.

INDEXES/ABSTRACTS TABLE

KEY WORD INDEX MED. LIT.
[US/0145-9716]
KEY-WORD INDEX FOR THE MEDICAL LITERATURE.
(*Continues* Keyword Index in Internal Medicine.)

KEYWORD INDEX INTERN. MED.
[US/0097-0220]
KEYWORD INDEX IN INTERNAL MEDICINE.
(*Continued by* Key-Word Index for the Medical Literature.)

LAB. HAZARDS BULL.
[UK/0261-2917]
LABORATORY HAZARDS BULLETIN.

LABORDOC
[SZ]
LABORDOC [ONLINE DATABASE].

LANG. LANG. BEHAV. ABSTR.
[US/0023-8295]
LANGUAGE AND LANGUAGE BEHAVIOR ABSTRACTS : LLBA.
(*Continued by* Linguistics and Language Behavior Abstracts.)

LANG. TEACH.
[UK/0261-4448]
LANGUAGE TEACHING.
(*Continues* Language Teaching & Linguistics. Abstracts.)

LANG. TEACH. LINGUIST. ABSTR.
[UK/0306-6304]
LANGUAGE TEACHING & LINGUISTICS ABSTRACTS.
(*Continued by* Language Teaching.)

LAW OFFICE INF. SERV.
[US/0164-5390]
LAW OFFICE INFORMATION SERVICE.
(Ceased)

LEAD ABSTR.
[US/0023-9569]
LEAD ABSTRACTS.
(*Continued by* Leadscan.)

LEADSCAN
[UK/0950-1584]
LEADSCAN.
(*Continues* Lead Abstracts (London, England : 1962).)

LEFT INDEX
[US/0733-2998]
LEFT INDEX.

LEG. CONTENTS, LC
[US/0279-5787]
LEGAL CONTENTS : LC.
(*Continues* CCLP, Contents of Current Legal Periodicals.)

LEG. INF. MANAGE. INDEX
[US/0747-9298]
LEGAL INFORMATION MANAGEMENT INDEX.

LEG. RESOUR. INDEX
[US/0272-9296]
LEGAL RESOURCE INDEX.

LEGALTRAC
[US]
LEGALTRAC [COMPUTER FILE].

LEIS. RECREAT. TOUR. ABSTR.
[UK/0261-1392]
LEISURE, RECREATION, AND TOURISM ABSTRACTS.
(*Continues* Rural Recreation and Tourism Abstracts.)

LEUKEMIA ABSTR.
[US/0024-1466]
LEUKEMIA ABSTRACTS.
(Ceased)

LIBR. INF. SCI. ABSTR.
[UK/0024-2179]
LIBRARY & INFORMATION SCIENCE ABSTRACTS.
(*Supersedes* Library Science Abstracts.)

LIBR. LIT.
[US/0024-2373]
LIBRARY LITERATURE.

LIBR. SCI. ABSTR.
[UK/0459-262X]
LIBRARY SCIENCE ABSTRACTS.
(*Continued by* Library & Information Science Abstracts.)

LIFE SCI. COLLECT.
[US/0891-3889]
PERIODICALS SCANNED AND ABSTRACTED. LIFE SCIENCES COLLECTION.

LINGUIST. LANG. BEHAV. ABSTR.
[US/0888-8027]
LINGUISTICS AND LANGUAGE BEHAVIOR ABSTRACTS.
(*Continues* Language and Language Behavior Abstracts; *Absorbed* Reading Abstracts.)

LISA PLUS
[UK/0966-8799]
LISA PLUS [COMPUTER FILE].
***Refer to Library and Information Science Abstracts for complete source list.

LIST J. ABSTR.
[NE/0923-5582]
LIST OF JOURNALS ABSTRACTED.
(*Continued by* EMBASE List of Journals Indexed.)

LIT. ABSTR., CATAL. CATAL.
[US/1065-0539]
LITERATURE ABSTRACTS. CATALYSTS & CATALYSIS.
(*Continued by* Literature Abstracts. Catalysts/Zeolites.)

LIT. ABSTR., HEALTH ENVIRON.
[US/1065-0490]
LITERATURE ABSTRACTS. HEALTH & ENVIRONMENT.
(*Continues* API Abstracts. Health & Environment.)

LIT. ABSTR., PET. REFIN. PETROCHEM.
[US/1065-0512]
LITERATURE ABSTRACTS. PETROLEUM REFINING & PETROCHEMICALS.
(*Continues* Petroleum Refining and Petrochemicals.)

LIT. ABSTR., PET. SUBSTIT.
[US/1065-0504]
LITERATURE ABSTRACTS. PETROLEUM SUBSTITUTES.
(*Continues* Petroleum Substitutes.)

LIT. ABSTR., TRANSP. STORAGE
[US/1065-0520]
LITERATURE ABSTRACTS. TRANSPORTATION & STORAGE.
(*Continues* Transportation and Storage.)

LIT. ANALY. MICROCOMPUT. PUBL.
[US/0735-9721]
LITERATURE ANALYSIS OF MICROCOMPUTER PUBLICATIONS : LAMP.
(Ceased)

LIT. CRIT. REGIST.
[US/0733-2165]
LITERARY CRITICISM REGISTER.

LIT. PAT. ABSTR., OILFIELD CHEM.
[US/1065-0547]
LITERATURE & PATENT ABSTRACTS. OILFIELD CHEMICALS.
(*Continued in part by* Literature Abstracts. Oilfield Chemicals *and* Patent Abstracts. Oilfield Chemicals.)

LOMA LIT. MOD. ART
[US/0090-7235]
LOMA; LITERATURE ON MODERN ART.
(*Continued by* ARTbibliographies Modern.)

MAG. ARTIC. SUMMAR.
[US/0895-3376]
MAGAZINE ARTICLE SUMMARIES (PRINT ED.).
(*Continues* Popular Magazine Review.)

MAG. ARTIC. SUMMAR. CD-ROM
[US/1041-1151]
MAGAZINE ARTICLE SUMMARIES (CD-ROM ED.).

MAG. ARTIC. SUMMAR. ELITE
[US/1060-6769]
MAGAZINE ARTICLE SUMMARIES FULL TEXT ELITE.

MAG. ARTIC. SUMMAR. SELECT
[US/1058-0255]
MAGAZINE ARTICLE SUMMARIES FULL TEXT SELECT.

MAG. ASAP PLUS
[US]
MAGAZINE ASAP PLUS [COMPUTER FILE].

MAG. ASAP SEL.
[US]
MAGAZINE ASAP SELECT [COMPUTER FILE].

MAG. EXPRESS
[US]
MAGAZINE EXPRESS [COMPUTER FILE].

MAG. INDEX
[US]
MAGAZINE INDEX, THE.

MAG. INDEX PLUS
[US]
MAGAZINE INDEX PLUS [COMPUTER FILE].

MAG. INDEX SEL. MICROFICHE
[US]
MAGAZINE INDEX SELECT MICROFICHE.

MAG. INDEX. SEL.
[US]
MAGAZINE INDEX SELECT [COMPUTER FILE].

MAG. SEARCH
[US/1071-2739]
MAGAZINE SEARCH.

MAGYAR KONYV. SZAK. BIBLIO.
[HU/0133-736X]
MAGYAR KONYVTARI SZAKIRODALOM BIBLIOGRAFIAJA, A.

MAIZE ABSTR.
[UK/0267-2987]
MAIZE ABSTRACTS.
(*Continues* Maize Quality Protein Abstracts.)

MANAGE. BIBLIOGR. REV.
[UK/0309-0582]
MANAGEMENT BIBLIOGRAPHIES & REVIEWS.
(*Continues* Business Education.)

MANAGE. CONTENTS
[US/0360-2400]
MANAGEMENT CONTENTS.
(Ceased)

INDEXES/ABSTRACTS TABLE

MANAGE. CONTENTS
[US]
MANAGEMENT CONTENTS [ONLINE DATABASE].

MANAGE. INDEX
[US]
MANAGEMENT INDEX.
(Ceased)

MANAGE. MARKET. ABSTR.
[UK/0308-2172]
MANAGEMENT AND MARKETING ABSTRACTS.

MANAGE. RES.
[US/0099-2224]
MANAGEMENT RESEARCH.
(**Continues** Bi-Monthly Review of Management Research.)

MANUF. PROCESS ENG. ABSTR.
[US/1063-7354]
MANUFACTURING AND PROCESS ENGINEERING ABSTRACTS.
(Ceased)

MAR. FISH. ABSTR.
[US/0735-3782]
MARINE FISHERIES ABSTRACTS.
(**Continues** Commercial Fisheries Abstracts.)

MAR. SCI. CONTENTS TABLES
[IT/0025-3308]
MARINE SCIENCE CONTENTS TABLES. ACTUALITES DES SCIENCES DE LA MER. INDICES DE REVISTAS SOBRE CIENCIAS MARINAS.
(**Continues** Current Contents in Marine Sciences; **Continues in part** International Marine Science.)

MARK. ADVERT. REF. SERV.
[US]
MARKETING AND ADVERTISING REFERENCE SERVICE [ONLINE DATABASE].

MARK. DISTR. ABSTR.
[UK]
MARKETING + DISTRIBUTION ABSTRACTS.
(**Continued by** Anbar Marketing & Distribution Abstracts.)

MARK. INF. GUIDE
[US/0025-374X]
MARKETING INFORMATION GUIDE.
(**Continues** Marketing Information Guide (Washington : 1961).)

MARK. RES. ABSTR.
[UK/0025-3596]
MARKET RESEARCH ABSTRACTS.

MARK. RES. TODAY
[NE/0923-5957]
MARKETING AND RESEARCH TODAY : THE JOURNAL OF THE EUROPEAN SOCIETY FOR OPINION AND MARKETING RESEARCH.
(**Continues** European Research.)

MASS SPECT. BULL.
[UK/0025-4738]
MASS SPECTROMETRY BULLETIN.

MATER. SCI. ENG. ABSTR.
[US/1063-732X]
MATERIALS SCIENCE AND ENGINEERING ABSTRACTS.
(Ceased)

MATH. REV.
[US/0025-5629]
MATHEMATICAL REVIEWS.

MECH. ENG. ABSTR.
[US/1063-7311]
MECHANICAL ENGINEERING ABSTRACTS.
(**Continues** ISMEC, Mechanical Engineering Abstracts.)

MED. ABSTR. NEWSL.
[US/0730-7810]
MEDICAL ABSTRACTS NEWSLETTER.

MED. ELECTRON. COMMUN. ABSTR.
[UK/0025-7222]
MEDICAL ELECTRONICS AND COMMUNICATIONS ABSTRACTS.
(Ceased)

MED. PHARM. BIOTECHNOL. ABSTR.
[US/1063-1178]
MEDICAL & PHARMACEUTICAL BIOTECHNOLOGY ABSTRACTS.
(**Continues in part** Biotechnology Research Abstracts.)
***Refer to Biotechnology Research Abstracts for complete source list.

MED. REV. DIG.
[US/0363-7778]
MEDIA REVIEW DIGEST.
(**Continues** Multi Media Reviews Index.)

MED. SOCIOECON. RES. SOURCE.
[US/0025-7540]
MEDICAL SOCIOECONOMIC RESEARCH SOURCES.
(**Supersedes** Weekly Bulletin **and** Index to Medical Socioeconomic Literature.)

MEDOC
[US/0097-9732]
MEDOC.
(Ceased)

MENT. HEALTH BOOK REV. INDEX
[US/0076-6445]
MENTAL HEALTH BOOK REVIEW INDEX.
(**Continued by** Chicorel Index to Mental Health Book Reviews.)

MENT. RETARD. ABSTR.
[US/0025-9691]
MENTAL RETARDATION ABSTRACTS.
(**Continued by** Mental Retardation & Developmental Disabilities Abstracts.)

MENT. RETARD. DEV. DISABIL. ABSTR.
[US/0361-3798]
MENTAL RETARDATION & DEVELOPMENTAL DISABILITIES ABSTRACTS.
(**Continued by** Developmental Disabilities Abstracts.)

MET. ABSTR.
[UK/0026-0924]
METALS ABSTRACTS.
(**Formed by the union of** Metallurgical Abstracts **and** Review of Metal Literature.)

MET. ABSTR. INDEX
[UK/0026-0932]
METALS ABSTRACTS INDEX.
(**Formed by the union of** Metallurgical Abstracts **and** Review of Metal Literature.)
***Refer to Metals Abstracts for complete source list.

MET. FINISHING ABSTR.
[UK/0026-0584]
METAL FINISHING ABSTRACTS.
(**Continued by** Surface Treatment Technology Abstracts.)

METEOROL. GEOASTROPHYS. ABSTR.
[US/0026-1130]
METEOROLOGICAL AND GEOASTROPHYSICAL ABSTRACTS.
(**Continues** Meteorological Abstracts and Bibliography.)

METEOROL. GEOASTROPHYS. ABSTR. [CD-ROM]
[US/1066-2707]
METEOROLOGICAL & GEOASTROPHYSICAL ABSTRACTS.
***Refer to Meteorological and Geoastrophysical Abstracts for a complete source list.

METHODIST PERIOD. INDEX
[US]
METHODIST PERIODICAL INDEX.
(**Continued by** United Methodist Periodical Index.)

METHODS ORGAN. SYNTH.
[UK/0265-4245]
METHODS IN ORGANIC SYNTHESIS.

MICROBIOL. ABSTR. SECT. A
[US/0300-838X]
MICROBIOLOGY ABSTRACTS. SECTION A : INDUSTRIAL & APPLIED MICROBIOLOGY.
(**Continues** Microbiology Abstracts. Section A. Industrial Microbiology.)

MICROBIOL. ABSTR. SECT. B
[US/0300-8398]
MICROBIOLOGY ABSTRACTS. SECTION B, BACTERIOLOGY.
(**Continues** Microbiology Abstracts. Section B: General Microbiology and Bacteriology.)

MICROBIOL. ABSTR. SECT. C
[US/0301-2328]
MICROBIOLOGY ABSTRACTS. SECTION C, ALGOLOGY, MYCOLOGY & PROTOZOOLOGY.

MICROCOMPUT. IND. UPDATE
[US/0741-6016]
MICROCOMPUTER INDUSTRY UPDATE.

MICROCOMPUT. INDEX
[US/8756-7040]
MICROCOMPUTER INDEX.
(**Continued by** Microcomputer Abstracts.)

MID. SEARCH
[US/1071-2755]
MIDDLE SEARCH.
(**Continues** Junior Search.)

MIDDLE EAST ABSTR. INDEX
[US/0162-766X]
MIDDLE EAST, ABSTRACTS AND INDEX.

MIDDLE EAST J.
[US/0026-3141]
MIDDLE EAST JOURNAL, THE.

MINERAL. ABSTR.
[UK/0026-4601]
MINERALOGICAL ABSTRACTS.

MINPROC
[CN/0828-8461]
MINPROC : MINERAL PROCESSING ABSTRACTS.
(Ceased)

MINTEC, MIN. TECHNOL. ABSTR.
[CN/0823-0773]
MINTEC : MINING TECHNOLOGY ABSTRACTS.
(Ceased)

INDEXES/ABSTRACTS TABLE

MISSIONALIA
[SA/0256-9507]
MISSIONALIA.
(*Formed by the union of* Lux Mundi (Pretoria, South Africa) *and* Missionaria.)

MLA INT. BIBL. BOOKS ARTIC. MOD. LANG. LIT.
[US/0024-8215]
MLA INTERNATIONAL BIBLIOGRAPHY OF BOOKS AND ARTICLES ON THE MODERN LANGUAGES AND LITERATURES (COMPLETE ED.).
(*Continues* MLA International Bibliography of Books and Articles on the Modern Languages and Literatures.)

MOD. MED.
[US/0026-8070]
MODERN MEDICINE (MINNEAPOLIS).

MON. PERIOD. INDEX
[US/0197-6567]
MONTHLY PERIODICAL INDEX.
(*Absorbed by* Access.)

MOSHER PERIOD. INDEX
[US/0194-0716]
MOSHER PERIODICAL INDEX.
(*Continues* Subject Index to Select Periodical Literature.)

MRS BULL.
[US/0883-7694]
MRS BULLETIN.
(*Absorbed* JMR Abstracts.)

MULTI MEDIA REV. INDEX
[US/0091-5858]
MULTI MEDIA REVIEWS INDEX.
(*Continued by* Media Review Digest.)

MULTICULT. EDUC. ABSTR.
[UK/0260-9770]
MULTICULTURAL EDUCATION ABSTRACTS.

MUSCULAR DYSTROPHY ABSTR.
[US/0027-3732]
MUSCULAR DYSTROPHY ABSTRACTS.
(Ceased)

MUSEUM ABSTR.
[UK/0267-8594]
MUSEUM ABSTRACTS.

MUSIC ARTIC. GUIDE
[US/0027-4240]
MUSIC ARTICLE GUIDE.

MUSIC INDEX
[US/0027-4348]
MUSIC INDEX, THE.

N. Y. LAW J. DIG.-ANNOT.
[US/0745-4406]
NEW YORK LAW JOURNAL DIGEST-ANNOTATOR.
(*Continues* Clark's Digest-Annotator.)

NAPRALERT
[US]
NAPRALERT [ONLINE DATABASE].

NAT. PROD. UPDATES
[UK/0950-1711]
NATURAL PRODUCT UPDATES.

NATL. NEWSP. INDEX
[US/0273-3676]
NATIONAL NEWSPAPER INDEX.

NEMATOL. ABSTR.
[UK/0957-6797]
NEMATOLOGICAL ABSTRACTS.
(*Continues* Helminthological Abstracts. Series B, Plant Nematology.)

NEW LIT. AUTOMAT.
[NE]
NEW LITERATURE ON AUTOMATION.
(*Continues* IAG-Literature on Automation.)

NEW PERIOD. INDEX
[US/0146-5716]
NEW PERIODICALS INDEX.
(Ceased)

NEW TESTAM. ABSTR.
[US/0028-6877]
NEW TESTAMENT ABSTRACTS.

NEWSP. ABSTR.
[US/1064-993X]
NEWSPAPER ABSTRACTS ONDISC.

NEWSP. ABSTR.
[US]
NEWSPAPER ABSTRACTS.

NEWSP. PERIOD. ABSTR.
[US]
NEWSPAPER & PERIODICAL ABSTRACTS [ONLINE DATABASE].

NEXIS
[US]
NEXIS.

NONWOVENS ABSTR.
[UK/9036-1234]
NONWOVENS ABSTRACTS.

NUCL. ACIDS ABSTR.
[US/1070-2466]
NUCLEIC ACIDS ABSTRACTS (1994).
(*Continues* Cambridge Scientific Biochemistry Abstracts, Part 2: Nucleic Acids.)

NUCL. SCI. ABSTR.
[US/0029-5612]
NUCLEAR SCIENCE ABSTRACTS.
(*Continues* Abstracts of Declassified Documents; Guide to Published Research on Atomic Energy.)

NUMIS. LIT.
[US/0029-6031]
NUMISMATIC LITERATURE.

NURS. ABSTR.
[US/0195-3354]
NURSING ABSTRACTS.

NURS. ALLIED HEALTH INDEX
[US/0744-8732]
NURSING AND ALLIED HEALTH INDEX.
(*Absorbed by* Cumulative Index to Nursing & Allied Health Literature.)

NURS. DIG.
[US/0091-4215]
NURSING DIGEST.
(*Continued by* Nursing Dimensions.)

NURS. DIMEN.
[US/0164-0232]
NURSING DIMENSIONS.
(*Continues* Nursing Digest.)

NUTR. ABSTR. REV.
[UK/0029-6619]
NUTRITION ABSTRACTS AND REVIEWS.
(*Split into* Nutrition Abstracts and Reviews. Series A. Human and Experimental *and* Nutrition Abstracts and Reviews. Series B, Livestock Feeds and Feeding.)

NUTR. ABSTR. REV., SER. A, HUM. EXP.
[UK/0309-1295]
NUTRITION ABSTRACTS AND REVIEWS. SERIES A: HUMAN & EXPERIMENTAL.
(*Continues in part* Nutrition Abstracts and Reviews.)

NUTR. ABSTR. REV., SER. B, LIVE FEEDS AND FEED.
[UK/0309-135X]
NUTRITION ABSTRACTS AND REVIEWS. SERIES B. LIVESTOCK FEEDS AND FEEDING.
(*Continues in part* Nutrition Abstracts and Reviews.)

NUTR. RES. NEWSL.
[US/0736-0037]
NUTRITION RESEARCH NEWSLETTER.

OCCUP. MENT. HEALTH
[US/0090-1679]
OCCUPATIONAL MENTAL HEALTH.
(*Supersedes* Occupational Mental Health News.)

OCCUP. MENT. HEALTH NOTES
[US/0029-795X]
OCCUPATIONAL MENTAL HEALTH NOTES.
(*Superseded by* Occupational Mental Health.)

OCEAN. ABSTR.
[US/0748-1489]
OCEANIC ABSTRACTS (BETHESDA, MD.).
(*Continues* Oceanic Abstracts with Indexes.)

OCEAN. ABSTR. INDEXES
[US/0093-6901]
OCEANIC ABSTRACTS WITH INDEXES.
(*Continued by* Oceanic Abstracts (Bethesda, Md.).)

OCEANIC CIT. J. ABSTR.
[US]
OCEANIC CITATION JOURNAL WITH ABSTRACTS / OCEANIC RESEARCH INSTITUTE.
(*Merged with* Oceanic Index *to form* Oceanic Abstracts with Indexes.)

OCEANIC INDEX CIT. J. ABSTR.
[US]
OCEANIC INDEX CITATION JOURNAL WITH ABSTRACTS.
(*Continued by* Oceanic Citation Journal with Abstracts.)

OCEANOGR. LIT. REV.
[UK/0967-0653]
OCEANOGRAPHIC LITERATURE REVIEW.
(*Continues* Deep-Sea Research. Part B, Oceanographic Literature Review.)

OLD TESTAM. ABSTR.
[US/0364-8591]
OLD TESTAMENT ABSTRACTS.

ONCOG. GROWTH FACTORS ABSTR.
[US/1043-8963]
ONCOGENES AND GROWTH FACTORS ABSTRACTS.

OPER. PROD. MANAGE. ABSTR.
[UK]
OPERATIONS & PRODUCTION MANAGEMENT ABSTRACTS.
(*Continues* Management Services and Production Abstracts.)

OPER. RES. MANAG. SCI.
[US/0030-3658]
OPERATIONS RESEARCH/MANAGEMENT SCIENCE.

ORAL RES. ABSTR.
[US/0030-4212]
ORAL RESEARCH ABSTRACTS.
(Ceased)

ORNAMENTAL HORT.
[UK/0305-4934]
ORNAMENTAL HORTICULTURE.

INDEXES/ABSTRACTS TABLE

ORTHO. SUR.
[NE/0014-4371]
ORTHOPEDIC SURGERY.
(*Continues* Orthopedics and Traumatology.)
***Refer to EMBASE [Online Database] for complete source list.

OZARK PERIOD. INDEX
[US/0275-9713]
OZARK PERIODICAL INDEX.

PAIS BULL.
[US/0898-2201]
PAIS BULLETIN.
(*Merged with* PAIS Foreign Language Index *to form* PAIS International in Print.)

PAIS FOREIGN LANG. INDEX
[US/0896-792X]
PAIS FOREIGN LANGUAGE INDEX.
(*Merged with* PAIS Bulletin *to form* PAIS International in Print.)

PAIS INT. PRINT
[US/1051-4015]
PAIS INTERNATIONAL IN PRINT.
(*Formed by the union of* PAIS Bulletin *and* PAIS Foreign Language Index.)

PAP. BOARD ABSTR.
[UK/0307-0778]
PAPER & BOARD ABSTRACTS.
(*Continues in part* Kenley Abstracts.)

PARAPSYCHOL. ABSTR. INT.
[US/0740-7629]
PARAPSYCHOLOGY ABSTRACTS INTERNATIONAL.
(*Continued by* Exceptional Human Experience.)

PASTOR. CARE COUNS. ABSTR.
[US]
PASTORAL CARE AND COUNSELING ABSTRACTS.
(*Continued by* Abstracts of Research in Pastoral Care and Counseling.)

PEACE RES. ABSTR. J.
[US/0031-3599]
PEACE RESEARCH ABSTRACTS JOURNAL.

PERIODEX
[CN]
PERIODEX: INDEX ANALYTIQUE DE PERIODIQUES DE LANGUE FRANCAISE.
(*Merged with* Radar *to form* Point de Repere.)

PERSON. MANAGE. ABSTR.
[US/0031-577X]
PERSONNEL MANAGEMENT ABSTRACTS.

PERSON. TRAIN. ABSTR.
[UK/0305-067X]
PERSONNEL + TRAINING ABSTRACTS.
(*Continues in part* Anbar Management Services Abstracts.)

PESTDOC
[UK]
PESTDOC.

PET. ABSTR.
[US/0031-6423]
PETROLEUM ABSTRACTS (TULSA, OKLA.).

PET. ENERGY BUS. NEWS INDEX
[US/0098-7743]
PETROLEUM/ENERGY BUSINESS NEWS INDEX.

PET. REFIN. PETROCHEM.
[US]
PETROLEUM REFINING AND PETROCHEMICALS.
(*Continued by* Literature Abstracts. Petroleum Refining & Petrochemicals.)

PET. SUBS.
[US]
PETROLEUM SUBSTITUTES.
(*Continued by* Literature Abstracts. Petroleum Substitutes.)

PHARM. NEWS INDEX
[US/0362-4439]
PHARMACEUTICAL NEWS INDEX.

PHILIP. ABSTR.
[PH/0031-7438]
PHILIPPINE ABSTRACTS.
(*Continued by* Philippine Science & Technology Abstracts.)

PHILIP. SCI. TECHNOL. ABSTR.
[PH/0115-8724]
PHILIPPINE SCIENCE & TECHNOLOGY ABSTRACTS.
(*Continues* Philippine Science and Technology Abstract Bibliography.)

PHILOS. INDEX
[US/0031-7993]
PHILOSOPHER'S INDEX.

PHOTOGR. ABSTR.
[UK/0031-8701]
PHOTOGRAPHIC ABSTRACTS.
(*Continued by* Imaging Abstracts.)

PHYS. ABSTR.
[UK/0036-8091]
PHYSICS ABSTRACTS.
(*Continues* Science Abstracts. Physics Abstracts.)
***Refer to INSPEC [Online Database] for a complete source list.

PHYS. BRIEFS
[UK/0170-7434]
PHYSICS BRIEFS.
(*Supersedes* Physikalische Berichte.)

PHYS. EDUC. INDEX
[US/0191-9202]
PHYSICAL EDUCATION INDEX (CAPE GIRARDEAU).

PHYS. MED. BIOL.
[UK/0031-9155]
PHYSICS IN MEDICINE & BIOLOGY.

PHYSIC. MEDLINE PLUS
[US/1065-6545]
PHYSICIAN'S MEDLINE PLUS.

PIG NEWS INF.
[UK/0143-9014]
PIG NEWS AND INFORMATION.

PINPOINTER
[AT/0031-9910]
PINPOINTER.
(Ceased)

PLANT BREED. ABSTR.
[UK/0032-0803]
PLANT BREEDING ABSTRACTS.

PLANT GROW. REG. ABSTR.
[UK/0305-9154]
PLANT GROWTH REGULATOR ABSTRACTS.

POINT REPERE
[CN/0822-8833]
POINT DE REPERE (MONTREAL).
(*Continued by* Repere.)

POLICE SCI. ABSTR.
[NE/0166-6282]
POLICE SCIENCE ABSTRACTS.
(*Merged with* Criminology & Penology Abstracts *to form* Criminology, Penology, and Police Science Abstracts.)

POLLUT. ABSTR. INDEXES
[US/0032-3624]
POLLUTION ABSTRACTS WITH INDEXES.

POLYMER CONTENTS
[UK/0883-153X]
POLYMER CONTENTS.
(*Continues* PRA Report: Polymer Contents.)

POP. MAG. REV.
[US/0740-3763]
POPULAR MAGAZINE REVIEW : PMR.
(*Continued by* Magazine Article Summaries.)

POP. PERIOD. INDEX
[US/0092-9727]
POPULAR PERIODICAL INDEX.
(Ceased)

POPUL. INDEX
[US/0032-4701]
POPULATION INDEX.
(*Continues* Population Literature.)

POTATO ABSTR.
[UK/0308-7344]
POTATO ABSTRACTS.

POULT. ABSTR.
[UK/0306-1582]
POULTRY ABSTRACTS.

POVER. HUM. RESOUR.
[US/0032-5864]
POVERTY & HUMAN RESOURCES.
(*Continued by* Poverty and Human Resources Abstracts.)

POVER. HUM. RESOUR. ABSTR.
[US/0094-4394]
POVERTY & HUMAN RESOURCES ABSTRACTS.
(*Continued by* Human Resources Abstracts.)

PREDICASTS
[US/0032-7166]
PREDICASTS.
(*Continued by* Predicasts Forecasts.)

PREDICASTS F & S INDEX INT.
[US/0270-4528]
PREDICASTS F & S INDEX INTERNATIONAL.
(*Continued by* F&S Index International (Foster City, Calif.).)
***Refer to Predicasts Forecasts for a complete source list.

PREDICASTS F&S INDEX, U. S. ANNU. ED.
[US/0277-9676]
PREDICASTS F&S INDEX. UNITED STATES ANNUAL EDITION.
(*Continued by* F&S Index United States Annual.)

PREDICASTS FORECASTS
[US/0278-0135]
PREDICASTS FORECASTS.
(*Continues* Predicasts.)

PREV. HUM. SERV.
[US/0270-3114]
PREVENTION IN HUMAN SERVICES.
(*Continues* Community Mental Health Review.)

PRIM. SEARCH
[US/1065-2485]
PRIMARY SEARCH.

PRINT. ABSTR.
[UK/0031-109X]
PRINTING ABSTRACTS.

INDEXES/ABSTRACTS TABLE

PROC. CHEM. ENG.
[UK/0960-5045]
PROCESS AND CHEMICAL ENGINEERING.
(*Continues* Chemical Engineering Abstracts.)

PROMT
[US/0161-8032]
PROMT / PREDICASTS OVERVIEW OF MARKETS AND TECHNOLOGY.
(*Formed by the union of* Chemical Market Abstracts and EMA, Equipment Market Abstracts.)

PROTOZOOLOG. ABSTR.
[UK/0309-1287]
PROTOZOOLOGICAL ABSTRACTS.

PSYCHEDELIC REV.
[US/0033-2631]
PSYCHEDELIC REVIEW.
(Ceased)

PSYCHOANAL. ABSTR.
[US/1066-9884]
PSYCHOANALYTIC ABSTRACTS.
(*Continues* Psycscan. Psychoanalysis.)

PSYCHOL. ABSTR.
[US/0033-2887]
PSYCHOLOGICAL ABSTRACTS.

PSYCHOL. READ. GUIDE
[SZ/0300-0443]
PSYCHOLOGICAL READER'S GUIDE.
(Ceased)

PSYCHOPHARMACOLOGY ABSTR.
[US/0033-3166]
PSYCHOPHARMACOLOGY ABSTRACTS.
(Ceased)

PSYCINFO
[US]
PSYCINFO.

PSYCLIT
[US]
PSYCLIT DATABASE.

PSYCSCAN PSYCHOANAL.
[US/0889-5236]
PSYCSCAN: PSYCHOANALYSIS.
(*Continued by* Psychoanalytic Abstracts.)

PSYCSCAN: APPL. EXP. ENG. PSYCH.
[US/0891-0685]
PSYCSCAN: APPLIED EXPERIMENTAL AND ENGINEERING PSYCHOLOGY.

PSYCSCAN: APPL. PSYCH.
[US/0271-7506]
PSYCSCAN. APPLIED PSYCHOLOGY.

PSYCSCAN: CLIN. PSYCH.
[US/0197-1484]
PSYCSCAN. CLINICAL PSYCHOLOGY.

PSYCSCAN: DEVELOP. PSYCH.
[US/0197-1492]
PSYCSCAN. DEVELOPMENTAL PSYCHOLOGY.

PSYCSCAN: LD/MR
[US/0730-1928]
PSYCSCAN. LD/MR.

PSYCSCAN: NEUROPSYCH.
[US/1058-6660]
PSYCSCAN. NEUROPSYCHOLOGY.

PTS NEWSL. DATABASE
[US]
PTS NEWSLETTER DATABASE [ONLINE DATABASE].

PUBLIC ADM. ABSTR. INDEX ARTIC. INDIA
[II/0033-331X]
PUBLIC ADMINISTRATION ABSTRACTS AND INDEX OF ARTICLES (INDIA).
(Ceased)

PUBLIC AFF. INF. SERV. BULL.
[US/0033-3409]
PUBLIC AFFAIRS INFORMATION SERVICE BULLETIN.
(*Continued by* PAIS Bulletin (Annual).)

Q. BIBLIOGR. COMPUT. DATA PROCESS.
[US/0048-6132]
QUARTERLY BIBLIOGRAPHY OF COMPUTERS AND DATA PROCESSING.
(*Continued by* Computer Literature Index.)

Q. INDEX ISLAM.
[UK/0308-7395]
QUARTERLY INDEX ISLAMICUS.
***Refer to Index Islamicus for complete source list.

QUAL. CONTROL APPL. STAT.
[US/0033-5207]
QUALITY CONTROL AND APPLIED STATISTICS.

RAPRA ABSTR.
[UK/0033-6750]
RAPRA ABSTRACTS.
(*Formed by the union of* Plastics. RAPRA Abstracts and Rubbers. RAPRA Abstracts.)

READ. ABSTR.
[US/0361-6118]
READING ABSTRACTS.
(*Continued by* Linguistics and Language Behavior Abstracts.)

READ. GUIDE ABSTR.
[US/0899-1553]
READERS' GUIDE ABSTRACTS (PRINT EDITION).
(*Continued by* Readers' Guide Abstracts (School and Public Library Ed. : Monthly).)

READ. GUIDE ABSTR.
[US/1058-1219]
READERS' GUIDE ABSTRACTS (SCHOOL AND PUBLIC LIBRARY ED.).
(*Continued by* Readers' Guide Abstracts Select Edition.)

READ. GUIDE ABSTR. SELECT ED.
[US]
READERS' GUIDE ABSTRACTS SELECT EDITION.
(*Continues* Readers' Guide Abstracts School and Public Library Edition.)

READ. GUIDE PERIOD. LIT.
[US/0034-0464]
READERS' GUIDE TO PERIODICAL LITERATURE.
(*Continues* Monthly Cumulative Index to ... Important Periodicals; *Absorbed* Cumulative Index to a Selected List of Periodicals (Annual).)

RECENT. PUBL. ARTIC.
[US/0145-5311]
RECENTLY PUBLISHED ARTICLES - AMERICAN HISTORICAL ASSOCIATION.
(Ceased)

RECIPE PERIOD. INDEX
[US/0743-3484]
RECIPE PERIODICAL INDEX.
(Ceased)

REF. BOOK REV. INDEX
[US]
REFERENCE BOOK REVIEW INDEX.
(Ceased)

REF. SOURCES
[US/0163-3546]
REFERENCE SOURCES.
(Ceased)

REF. UPD. BASIC ED.
[US]
REFERENCE UPDATE BASIC EDITION [COMPUTER FILE].

REF. UPD. CLINICAL ED.
[US]
REFERENCE UPDATE CLINICAL EDITION [COMPUTER FILE].

REF. UPD. DELUXE ED.
[US]
REFERENCE UPDATE DELUXE EDITION [COMPUTER FILE].

REFER. Z.
[RU]
REFERATIVNYI ZHURNAL: ORGANIZATSIIA I BEZOPASNOST DOROZHNOGO DVIZHENIIA.

REHABIL. LIT.
[US/0034-3579]
REHABILITATION LITERATURE.
(Ceased)

RELIG. INDEX ONE PERIOD.
[US/0149-8428]
RELIGION INDEX ONE. PERIODICALS.
(*Continued in part by* Index to Book Reviews in Religion.)

RELIG. PERIOD. INDEX
[US/0034-4117]
RELIGIOUS PERIODICALS INDEX.
(Ceased)

RELIG. THEOL. ABSTR.
[US/0034-4044]
RELIGIOUS AND THEOLOGICAL ABSTRACTS.

REPERT. ANAL. ARTIC. REV. QUE.
[CN/0315-2316]
RADAR: REPERTOIRE ANALYTIQUE D'ARTICLES DE REVUES DU QUEBEC.
(*Merged with* Periodex *to form* Point de Repere.)

RES. ALERT
[US]
RESEARCH ALERT.
(*Continues* Ascatopics.)

RES. HIGH. EDUC. ABSTR.
[UK/0034-5326]
RESEARCH INTO HIGHER EDUCATION ABSTRACTS.

RESOURCE/ONE ONDISC
[US]
RESOURCE/ONE ONDISC [COMPUTER FILE].

REV. AGRIC. ENTOMOL.
[UK/0957-6762]
REVIEW OF AGRICULTURAL ENTOMOLOGY.
(*Continues* Review of Applied Entomology. Series A, Agricultural.)

REV. APPL. ENTOMOL. SER. A, AGRIC.
[UK/0305-0076]
REVIEW OF APPLIED ENTOMOLOGY. SERIES A: AGRICULTURAL.
(*Continued by* Review of Agricultural Entomology.)

INDEXES/ABSTRACTS TABLE

REV. APPL. ENTOMOL. SER. B, MED. VET.
[UK/0305-0084]
REVIEW OF APPLIED ENTOMOLOGY. SERIES B, MEDICAL AND VETERINARY.
(*Continued by* Review of Medical and Veterinary Entomology.)

REV. MED. VET. ENTOMOL.
[UK/0957-6770]
REVIEW OF MEDICAL AND VETERINARY ENTOMOLOGY.
(*Continues* Review of Applied Entomology. Series B, Medical and Veterinary.)

REV. MED. VET. MYCOLOGY
[UK/0034-6624]
REVIEW OF MEDICAL AND VETERINARY MYCOLOGY.
(*Continues* Annotated Bibliography of Medical Mycology.)

REV. PLANT PATHOL.
[UK/0034-6438]
REVIEW OF PLANT PATHOLOGY.
(*Continues* Review of Applied Mycology.)

RIBA LIB. BULL.
[UK]
RIBA LIBRARY BULLETIN.
(*Superseded by* Architectural Periodicals Index.)

RILA, INT. REP. LIT. ART
[US/0145-5982]
RILA : INTERNATIONAL REPERTORY OF THE LITERATURE OF ART.
(*Merged with* Repertoire d'Art et d'Archeologie *to form* Bibliography of the History of Art.)

RILM ABSTR.
[US/0033-6955]
RILM ABSTRACTS.

RINGDOC
[UK]
RINGDOC.
***Refer to PESTDOC for complete source list.

RISK ABSTR.
[CN/0824-3336]
RISK ABSTRACTS.

ROBOMATIX REPORT.
[US/0748-1624]
ROBOMATIX REPORTER.
(*Continued by* Robotics Abstracts.)

ROBOTICS ABSTR.
[US/0000-1139]
ROBOTICS ABSTRACTS.
(*Continues* Robomatix Reporter.)

ROMANT. MOVE.
[US/0557-2738]
ROMANTIC MOVEMENT.

ROTHS AM. POETRY ANNUAL
[US/1040-5461]
ROTH'S AMERICAN POETRY ANNUAL.
(*Formed by the union of* Annual Survey of American Poetry; Annual Index to Poetry in Periodicals *and* American Poetry Index.)

RURAL EXT. EDUC. TRAIN. ABSTR.
[UK/0140-4776]
RURAL EXTENSION, EDUCATION AND TRAINING ABSTRACTS.
(Ceased)

RURAL RECREAT. TOUR. ABSTR.
[UK/0308-0137]
RURAL RECREATION AND TOURISM ABSTRACTS.
(*Continued by* Leisure, Recreation and Tourism Abstracts.)

SAF. HEALTH WORK
[SZ/1010-7053]
SAFETY AND HEALTH AT WORK : ILO-CIS BULLETIN.
(*Continues* International Occupational Safety and Health Information Centre. CIS Abstracts.)

SAF. SCI. ABSTR.
[US/0092-542X]
SAFETY SCIENCE ABSTRACTS.
(*Continued by* Safety Science Abstracts Journal.)

SAF. SCI. ABSTR. J.
[US/0160-1342]
SAFETY SCIENCE ABSTRACTS JOURNAL.
(*Continued by* Health and Safety Science Abstracts.)

SAGE FAM. STUD. ABSTR.
[US/0164-0283]
SAGE FAMILY STUDIES ABSTRACTS.

SAGE PUBLIC ADM. ABSTR.
[US/0094-6958]
SAGE PUBLIC ADMINISTRATION ABSTRACTS.

SAGE RACE RELAT. ABSTR.
[UK/0307-9201]
SAGE RACE RELATIONS ABSTRACTS.
(*Continues* Race Relations Abstracts.)

SAGE URBAN STUD. ABSTR
[US/0090-5747]
SAGE URBAN STUDIES ABSTRACTS.

SCHOOL ORGAN. MANAGE. ABSTR.
[UK/0261-2755]
SCHOOL ORGANISATION & MANAGEMENT ABSTRACTS.

SCI. ABSTR. PHYS. ABSTR.
[UK]
SCIENCE ABSTRACTS. PHYSICS ABSTRACTS.
(*Continued by* Science Abstracts. Series A, Physics Abstracts.)

SCI. ABSTR. SECT. A. PHYS. ABSTR.
[UK]
SCIENCE ABSTRACTS. SECTION A, PHYSICS ABSTRACTS / EDITED AND ISSUED MONTHLY BY THE INSTITUTION OF ELECTRICAL ENGINEERS, IN ASSOCIATION WITH THE PHYSICAL SOCIETY, THE AMERICAN PHYSICAL SOCIETY, THE AMERICAN INSTITUTE OF ELECTRICAL ENGINEERS.
(*Continued by* Science Abstracts. Physics Abstracts.)

SCI. ABSTR. SER. A, PHYS. ABSTR.
[UK]
SCIENCE ABSTRACTS. SERIES A, PHYSICS ABSTRACTS.
(*Continued by* Physics Abstracts.)

SCI. CIT. INDEX
[US/0036-827X]
SCIENCE CITATION INDEX (PRINT ED.).

SCI. CIT. INDEX ABSTR.
[US/1061-1290]
SCIENCE CITATION INDEX WITH ABSTRACTS.
***Refer to Science Citation Index (US/0036-827X) for a complete source list.

SCI. CIT. INDEX [CD-ROM]
[US/1044-6052]
SCIENCE CITATION INDEX (COMPACT DISC ED.).
***Refer to Science Citation Index (US/0036-827X) for a complete source list.

SCI. CIT. INDEX, ABR. ED.
[US/0737-2108]
SCIENCE CITATION INDEX. ABRIDGED EDITION.
(Ceased)

SCI. FICT. FANTASY BOOK REV. INDEX
[US/1046-1922]
SCIENCE FICTION AND FANTASY BOOK REVIEW INDEX.
(*Continues* Science Fiction Book Review Index.)

SCI. RES. ABSTR. J.
[US/0731-0943]
SCIENCE RESEARCH ABSTRACTS JOURNAL.
(*Absorbed by* Solid State Abstracts Journal.)

SCI. RES. ABSTR. J. PART A.
[US/0194-7486]
SCIENCE RESEARCH ABSTRACTS JOURNAL. PART A: SUPERCONDUCTIVITY, MAGNETOHYDRODYNAMICS AND PLASMAS, THEORETICAL PHYSICS.
(*Merged with* Science Research Abstracts Journal. Part B: Laser and Electro-Opticreviews, Quantum Electronics and Unconventional Energy Sources *to form* Science Research Abstracts Journal.)

SCISEARCH
[US]
SCISEARCH [ONLINE DATABASE].

SEA ABSTR.
[PH]
SEA ABSTRACTS.

SEED ABSTR.
[UK/0141-0180]
SEED ABSTRACTS.

SEL. PHILIP. PERIOD. INDEX
[PH/0037-1335]
SELECTED PHILIPPINE PERIODICAL INDEX.
(Ceased)

SEL. WATER RESOUR. ABSTR.
[US/0037-136X]
SELECTED WATER RESOURCES ABSTRACTS (WASHINGTON, D.C.).
(Ceased)

SELEC. COOP. INDEX MANAGE. PERIOD.
[FI/0782-2979]
SCIMP SELECTIVE CO-OPERATIVE INDEX OF MANAGEMENT PERIODICALS.
(Ceased)

SEVENTH-DAY ADVENTIST PERIOD. INDEX
[US/0270-3599]
SEVENTH-DAY ADVENTIST PERIODICAL INDEX.

SHIP ABSTR.
[NO/0346-1025]
SHIP ABSTRACTS.
(*Absorbed by* Journal of Abstracts of the British Ship Research Association.)

SHOCK VIBR. DIG.
[US/0583-1024]
SHOCK AND VIBRATION DIGEST, THE.

SMALL ANIM. ABSTR. BIBLIOGR.
[UK]
SMALL ANIMAL ABSTRACTS BIBLIOGRAPHY.
(*Continues* Small Animal Abstracts.)

SOC. PLANN. POLICY DEV. ABSTR.
[US/1042-8380]
SOCIAL PLANNING, POLICY & DEVELOPMENT ABSTRACTS.
(*Continues* Social Welfare, Social Planning/Policy & Social Development.)

INDEXES/ABSTRACTS TABLE

SOC. RES. METHODOL. ABSTR.
[NE/0167-8477]
SOCIAL RESEARCH METHODOLOGY ABSTRACTS.
(*Continues in part* SRM Abstract Bulletin.)

SOC. SCI. CIT. INDEX
[US/0091-3707]
SOCIAL SCIENCES CITATION INDEX (PRINT ED.).

SOC. SCI. HUMANIT. INDEX
[US/0037-7899]
SOCIAL SCIENCES & HUMANITIES INDEX.
(*Split into* Social Sciences Index *and* Humanities Index.)

SOC. SCI. INDEX
[US/0094-4920]
SOCIAL SCIENCES INDEX.
(*Supersedes in part* Social Sciences & Humanities Index.)

SOC. SCI. INDEX FULLTEXT
[US]
SOCIAL SCIENCES INDEX / FULLTEXT.

SOC. SCI. SOURCE
[US/1063-9802]
SOCIAL SCIENCE SOURCE.

SOC. WELF. SOC. PLAN./POLICY SOC. DEV.
[US/0195-7988]
SOCIAL WELFARE, SOCIAL PLANNING/POLICY & SOCIAL DEVELOPMENT.
(*Continued by* Social Planning, Policy & Development Abstracts.)

SOC. WORK ABSTR.
[US/1070-5317]
SOCIAL WORK ABSTRACTS.
(*Continues in part* Social Work Research and Abstracts.)

SOC. WORK RES.
[US/1070-5309]
SOCIAL WORK RESEARCH.
(*Continues in part* Social Work Research and Abstracts.)
***Refer to Social Work Abstracts for a complete source list.

SOC. WORK RES. ABSTR.
[US/0148-0847]
SOCIAL WORK RESEARCH & ABSTRACTS.
(*Split into* Social Work Abstracts *and* Social Work Research.)

SOCIOL. ABSTR.
[US/0038-0202]
SOCIOLOGICAL ABSTRACTS.

SOCIOL. EDUC. ABSTR.
[UK/0038-0415]
SOCIOLOGY OF EDUCATION ABSTRACTS.

SOFT. ABSTR. ENG.
[IE/0790-150X]
SOFTWARE ABSTRACTS FOR ENGINEERS : SAFE.

SOILS FERT.
[UK/0038-0792]
SOILS AND FERTILIZERS.
(*Supersedes* Imperial Bureau of Soil Science. Monthly Letter.)

SOLID STATE ABSTR. J.
[US/0038-108X]
SOLID STATE ABSTRACTS JOURNAL.
(*Continued by* Solid State and Superconductivity Abstracts.)

SOLID STATE SUPERCOND. ABSTR.
[US/0896-5900]
SOLID STATE AND SUPERCONDUCTIVITY ABSTRACTS.
(*Continues* Solid State Abstracts Journal.)

SORGHUM MILL. ABSTR.
[UK/03082970]
SORGHUM AND MILLETS ABSTRACTS.
(Ceased)

SOUTH. BAPTIST PERIOD. INDEX
[US/0081-3028]
SOUTHERN BAPTIST PERIODICAL INDEX.

SOYABEAN ABSTR.
[UK/0141-0172]
SOYABEAN ABSTRACTS.

SPEC. EDUC. NEEDS ABSTR.
[UK/0954-0822]
SPECIAL EDUCATIONAL NEEDS ABSTRACTS.

SPIN
[US]
SPIN.

SPORT DISCUS
[US]
SPORT DISCUS [COMPUTER FILE].

SPORT FISH. ABSTR.
[US/0038-786X]
SPORT FISHERY ABSTRACTS.
(*Continued by* Fisheries Review.)

SPORTSEARCH
[US/0882-553X]
SPORTSEARCH.

STAT. REF. INDEX
[US/0885-6834]
STATISTICAL REFERENCE INDEX.

STAT. THEORY METHOD ABSTR.
[UK/0039-0518]
STATISTICAL THEORY AND METHOD ABSTRACTS.
(*Continues* International Journal of Abstracts: Statistical Theory and Method.)

STUD. WOMEN ABSTR.
[UK/0262-5644]
STUDIES ON WOMEN ABSTRACTS.

SUBJ. INDEX CHILD. MAG.
[US/0039-4351]
SUBJECT INDEX TO CHILDREN'S MAGAZINES.
(*Continued by* Children's Magazine Guide.)

SUBJ. INDEX PERIOD.
[UK]
SUBJECT INDEX TO PERIODICALS.
(*Split into* British Humanities Index *and* British Technology Index.)

SUBJ. INDEX SEL. PERIOD. LIT.
[US/0194-0708]
SUBJECT INDEX TO SELECT PERIODICAL LITERATURE.
(*Continued by* Mosher Periodical Index.)

SUG. INDUS. ABSTR.
[UK/0957-5022]
SUGAR INDUSTRY ABSTRACTS / [CAB INTERNATIONAL, BUREAU OF HORTICULTURE AND PLANTATION CROPS IN ASSOCIATION WITH TATE & LYLE PLC].
(*Continues* Tate & Lyle's Sugar Industry Abstracts.)

SURF. TREAT. TECHNOL. ABSTR.
[UK]
SURFACE TREATMENT TECHNOLOGY ABSTRACTS.
(*Continues* Metal Finishing Abstracts.)

TECH. DATA DIG.
[US]
TECHNICAL DATA DIGEST.
(Ceased)

TECH. EDUC. ABSTR.
[UK/0040-0920]
TECHNICAL EDUCATION ABSTRACTS.
(*Continued by* Technical Education & Training Abstracts.)

TECH. EDUC. TRAIN. ABSTR.
[UK]
TECHNICAL EDUCATION & TRAINING ABSTRACTS.
(*Continues* Technical Education Abstracts.)

TELEGEN ABSTR.
[US/0000-118X]
TELEGEN ABSTRACTS.
(*Continues* Telegen Reporter.)

TELEGEN REPORT.
[US/0743-8443]
TELEGEN REPORTER.
(*Continued by* Telegen Abstracts.)

TERMITE ABSTR.
[UK/0144-5995]
TERMITE ABSTRACTS.
(Ceased)

TEXT. TECHNOL. DIG.
[US/0040-5191]
TEXTILE TECHNOLOGY DIGEST.

THEOL. RELIG. INDEX
[UK]
THEOLOGICAL AND RELIGIOUS INDEX.
(Ceased)

THEOR. CHEM. ENG.
[UK/0960-5053]
THEORETICAL CHEMICAL ENGINEERING.
(*Continues* Theoretical Chemical Engineering Abstracts.)

THEOR. CHEM. ENG. ABSTR.
[UK/0040-5787]
THEORETICAL CHEMICAL ENGINEERING ABSTRACTS.
(*Continued by* Theoretical Chemical Engineering.)

TOM GEN. INDEX
[US]
TOM GENERAL INDEX.

TOP MANAGE. ABSTR.
[UK/0049-4100]
TOP MANAGEMENT ABSTRACTS.
(*Continued by* Anbar Top Management Abstracts.)

TOPICATOR
[US/0040-9340]
TOPICATOR.

TOXICOL. ABSTR.
[US/0140-5365]
TOXICOLOGY ABSTRACTS.

TRADE IND. ASAP
[US]
TRADE & INDUSTRY ASAP [ONLINE DATABASE].

TRADE IND. INDEX
[US]
TRADE & INDUSTRY INDEX [ONLINE DATABASE].

INDEXES/ABSTRACTS TABLE

TRANS. AM. SOC. CIV. ENG.
[US/0066-0604]
TRANSACTIONS OF THE AMERICAN SOCIETY OF CIVIL ENGINEERS.

TRANSP. RES. ABSTR.
[US/0095-2648]
TRANSPORTATION RESEARCH ABSTRACTS.
(*Absorbed in part by* HRIS Abstracts.)

TRANSP. STORAGE
[US]
TRANSPORTATION AND STORAGE.
(*Continued by* Literature Abstracts. Transportation & Storage.)

TROP. ABSTR.
[NE/0041-3208]
TROPICAL ABSTRACTS.
(*Superseded by* Abstracts on Tropical Agriculture.)

TROP. DIS. BULL.
[UK/0041-3240]
TROPICAL DISEASES BULLETIN.
(*Supersedes* Bulletin of the Sleeping Sickness Bureau and the Kala Azar Bulletin.)

U.S. POLIT. SCI. DOC.
[US/0148-6063]
UNITED STATES POLITICAL SCIENCE DOCUMENTS.
(*Absorbed* Asian Studies Indexed Journal Reference Guide.)

UMI ABI/INFORM--BUS. PERIOD. ONDISC
[US/1064-5381]
UMI ABI/INFORM--BUSINESS PERIODICALS ONDISC.

UNITED METHODIST PERIOD. INDEX
[US/0041-7319]
UNITED METHODIST PERIODICAL INDEX.
(*Continues* Methodist Periodical Index.)

URBAN AFF. ABSTR.
[US/0300-6859]
URBAN AFFAIRS ABSTRACTS.

VET. BULL.
[UK/0042-4854]
VETERINARY BULLETIN (LONDON).
(*Supersedes* Tropical Veterinary Bulletin; *Absorbed* Veterinary Reviews.)

VETDOC
[UK]
VETDOC.
***Refer to PESTDOC for complete source list.

VIROL. ABSTR.
[US/0042-6830]
VIROLOGY ABSTRACTS.
(*Continued by* Virology and AIDS Abstracts.)

VIROL. AIDS ABSTR.
[US/0896-5919]
VIROLOGY & AIDS ABSTRACTS.
(*Continues* Virology Abstracts.)

VIS. INDEX
[US/0049-6510]
VISION INDEX.
(Ceased)

VITIS VITIC. ENOL. ABSTR.
[GW/0175-8292]
VITIS, VITICULTURE AND ENOLOGY ABSTRACTS.
(*Separated from* Vitis.)

VOCAT. SEARCH
[US/1071-2747]
VOCATIONAL SEARCH.

WALL STREET J. INDEX
[US/0083-7075]
WALL STREET JOURNAL INDEX.
(Ceased)

WATER POLLUT. ABSTR.
[UK/0043-1281]
WATER POLLUTION ABSTRACTS.
(*Merged with* Water Research Association Library List *to form* WRC Information.)

WEED ABSTR.
[UK/0043-1729]
WEED ABSTRACTS.

WEST. HIST. Q.
[US/0043-3810]
WESTERN HISTORICAL QUARTERLY.

WHEAT BARLEY TRIT. ABSTR.
[UK/0265-7880]
WHEAT, BARLEY AND TRITICALE ABSTRACTS.
(*Continues* Triticale Abstracts.)

WILDL. REV.
[US/0043-5511]
WILDLIFE REVIEW (FORT COLLINS).

WILSON BUS. ABSTR.
[US/1057-6533]
WILSON BUSINESS ABSTRACTS.

WOMEN MANAG. REV. ABSTR.
[UK/0955-8357]
WOMEN IN MANAGEMENT REVIEW & ABSTRACTS.
(*Continued by* Women in Management Review.)

WOMEN MANAGE. REV.
[UK/0964-9425]
WOMEN IN MANAGEMENT REVIEW.
(*Continues* Women in Management Review & Abstracts.)

WOMEN STUD. ABSTR.
[US/0049-7835]
WOMEN STUDIES ABSTRACTS.

WORK RELAT. ABSTR.
[US/0273-3234]
WORK RELATED ABSTRACTS.
(*Continues* Employment Relations Abstracts.)

WORLD AGRIC. ECON. RURAL SOCIOL. ABSTR.
[UK/0043-8219]
WORLD AGRICULTURAL ECONOMICS AND RURAL SOCIOLOGY ABSTRACTS.

WORLD ALUM. ABSTR.
[US/0002-6697]
WORLD ALUMINUM ABSTRACTS.
(*Continued by* Aluminium Industry Abstracts.)

WORLD CERAM. ABSTR.
[UK/0957-8897]
WORLD CERAMICS ABSTRACTS.
(*Continues* British Ceramic Abstracts.)

WORLD FISH. ABSTR.
[IT/0043-8472]
WORLD FISHERIES ABSTRACTS.
(Ceased)

WORLD PUBL. MONIT.
[UK/0960-653X]
WORLD PUBLISHING MONITOR.
(*Continues* Electronic Publishing Abstracts.)

WORLD SURF. COAT. ABSTR.
[UK/0043-9088]
WORLD SURFACE COATINGS ABSTRACTS.
(*Continues* Review of Current Literature Relating to the Paint, Colour, Varnish and Allied Industries.)

WORLD TEXT. ABSTR.
[UK/0043-9118]
WORLD TEXTILE ABSTRACTS.
(*Supersedes* Textile Abstracts.)

WRC INF.
[UK/0306-6649]
WRC INFORMATION.
(*Continued by* Aqualine Abstracts.)

WRIT. AM. HIST.
[US/0364-2887]
WRITINGS ON AMERICAN HISTORY.
(Ceased)

ZENTRALBL. MATH. IHRE GRENZGEB.
[GW/0044-4235]
ZENTRALBLATT FUER MATHEMATIK UND IHRE GRENZGEBIETE.
(*Superseded in part by* Zentralblatt fuer Mechanik.)

ZOOL. REC.
[UK/0144-3607]
ZOOLOGICAL RECORD (LONDON).
(*Continues* Record of Zoological Literature.)

ISSN Index

The following index lists every ISSN in the Directory, with a "see" note to the primary title under which it appears. The page number printed in bold is the page upon which the serial listing/ISSN is shown. The preceding ISSN on serial titles are included with a "see" note to the serial if the serial title publication start date (CONSER field 008/7-10) is later than 1992. Preceding ISSN are in italicized typeface.

0000-0019 *See* PUBLISHERS WEEKLY. **4831**

0000-006X *See* SOFTWARE ENCYCLOPEDIA, THE. **1210**

0000-0140 *See* SUBJECT COLLECTIONS. **3260**

0000-0159 *See* SUBJECT GUIDE TO BOOKS IN PRINT. **3459**

0000-0175 *See* ULRICH'S INTERNATIONAL PERIODICALS DIRECTORY. **3254**

0000-0191 *See* WHO'S WHO IN AMERICAN ART. **335**

0000-0205 *See* WHO'S WHO IN AMERICAN POLITICS. **436**

0000-0213 *See* WILLING'S PRESS GUIDE. **767**

0000-0221 *See* WORLD GUIDE TO LIBRARIES. **3256**

0000-0310 *See* BOOKS IN PRINT SUPPLEMENT. **411**

0000-0345 *See* CANADIAN SERIALS DIRECTORY. **3200**

0000-0388 *See* INTERNATIONAL INDEX TO FILM PERIODICALS. **4080**

0000-0485 *See* SMALL PRESS. **4569**

0000-054X *See* SCIENTIFIC AND TECHNICAL BOOKS AND SERIALS IN PRINT. **5176**

0000-0604 *See* WORLD DICTIONARIES IN PRINT. **1930**

0000-0671 *See* PUBLISHERS, DISTRIBUTORS, & WHOLESALERS OF THE UNITED STATES. **4822**

0000-0698 *See* WORLD MUSEUM PUBLICATIONS. **4097**

0000-0736 *See* BOOKS OUT-OF-PRINT. **4826**

0000-0752 *See* BOWKER'S LAW BOOKS AND SERIALS IN PRINT. **3079**

0000-0825 *See* EL-HI TEXTBOOKS AND SERIALS IN PRINT. **1794**

0000-0833 *See* RETAILERS' MICROCOMPUTER MARKET PLACE. **1272**

0000-085X *See* MEDICAL AND HEALTH CARE BOOKS AND SERIALS IN PRINT. **3660**

0000-0876 *See* BOWKER'S COMPLETE SOURCEBOOK OF PERSONAL COMPUTING. **1265**

0000-0906 *See* BOOKS IN SERIES. **4826**

0000-0914 *See* MAGAZINES FOR LIBRARIES. **3229**

0000-0957 See MAGAZINES FOR YOUNG PEOPLE. **1066**

0000-0965 *See* FORTHCOMING BOOKS FOR CHILDREN. **3388**

0000-0973 *See* EDUCATIONAL FILM & VIDEO LOCATOR OF THE CONSORTIUM OF COLLEGE AND UNIVERSITY MEDIA CENTERS AND R. R. BOWKER. **4068**

0000-0981 *See* ULRICH'S ON MICROFICHE. **3254**

0000-1023 *See* TRADESHOW WEEK DATA BOOK, THE. **734**

0000-1058 *See* CODE OF FEDERAL REGULATIONS INDEX. **3079**

0000-1074 *See* ULRICH'S UPDATE. **3254**

0000-1120 *See* COMPLETE DIRECTORY OF LARGE PRINT BOOKS & SERIALS, THE. **4828**

0000-1139 *See* ROBOTICS ABSTRACTS. **1209**

0000-1155 *See* LITERARY MARKET PLACE (1988). **4821**

0000-1163 *See* ULRICH'S NEWS. **3254**

0000-1198 *See* ENVIRONMENT ABSTRACTS ANNUAL. **2184**

0000-1287 *See* AMERICAN MEN & WOMEN OF SCIENCE. **5173**

0000-1325 *See* VOLUNTEERISM (NEW YORK, N.Y.). **5267**

0000-1333 *See* LEGAL PUBLISHING PREVIEW. **3000**

0000-135X *See* EDUCATIONAL FILM & VIDEO LOCATOR OF THE CONSORTIUM OF COLLEGE AND UNIVERSITY MEDIA CENTERS AND R. R. BOWKER. **4068**

0000-1368 *See* MAGAZINES FOR YOUNG PEOPLE. **1066**

0000-1376 See OF CABBAGES AND KINGS. **1067**

0000-1384 See BROADCASTING & CABLE MARKET PLACE. **1128**

0000-1392 *See* CORNERSTONE (NEW PROVIDENCE, N.J.), THE. **3204**

0000-1406 *See* OFFICIAL AMERICAN BOARD OF MEDICAL SPECIALTIES (ABMS) DIRECTORY OF BOARD CERTIFIED MEDICAL SPECIALISTS, THE. **3623**

0000-1406 *See* OFFICIAL AMERICAN BOARD OF MEDICAL SPECIALTIES (ABMS) DIRECTORY OF BOARD CERTIFIED MEDICAL SPECIALISTS, THE. **3623**

0000-1457 *See* OFFICIAL AMERICAN BOARD OF MEDICAL SPECIALTIES (ABMS) DIRECTORY OF BOARD CERTIFIED NUCLEAR MEDICINE SPECIALISTS, THE. **3849**

0000-1481 *See* OFFICIAL AMERICAN BOARD OF MEDICAL SPECIALTIES (ABMS) DIRECTORY OF BOARD CERTIFIED THORACIC SURGEONS, THE. **3971**

0000-1511 *See* BROADCASTING & CABLE YEARBOOK. **1124**

0000-1546 *See* OFFICIAL AMERICAN BOARD OF MEDICAL SPECIALTIES (ABMS) DIRECTORY OF BOARD CERTIFIED ANESTHESIOLOGISTS, THE. **3683**

0000-1597 *See* OFFICIAL AMERICAN BOARD OF MEDICAL SPECIALTIES (ABMS) DIRECTORY OF BOARD CERTIFIED ORTHOPAEDIC SURGEONS, THE. **3883**

0000-1600 *See* OFFICIAL AMERICAN BOARD OF MEDICAL SPECIALTIES (ABMS) DIRECTORY OF BOARD CERTIFIED OTOLARYNGOLOGISTS, THE. **3890**

0000-1627 *See* OFFICIAL AMERICAN BOARD OF MEDICAL SPECIALTIES (ABMS) DIRECTORY OF BOARD CERTIFIED PEDIATRICIANS, THE. **3907**

0000-1678 *See* OFFICIAL AMERICAN BOARD OF MEDICAL SPECIALTIES (ABMS) DIRECTORY OF BOARD CERTIFIED SURGEONS, THE. **3971**

0001-009X *See* AALC REPORTER. **1642**

0001-0154 *See* AAMVA BULLETIN / AMERICAN ASSOCIATION OF MOTOR VEHICLE ADMINISTRATORS. **5399**

0001-0197 *See* A A R N NEWSLETTER. **3849**

0001-0340 *See* AB BOOKMAN'S WEEKLY. **4822**

0001-0413 *See* ABC FILM REVIEW. **4062**

0001-0456 *See* ABC POL SCI. ADVANCE BIBLIOGRAPHY OF CONTENTS: POLITICAL SCIENCE & GOVERNMENT. **4501**

0001-0472 *See* ABC RAIL GUIDE. **5460**

0001-0480 *See* ABC PASSENGER SHIPPING GUIDE. **5447**

0001-0502 *See* ABD. **3**

0001-0545 *See* ABN CORRESPONDENCE. **4514**

0001-0634 *See* CHEMICAL ABSTRACTS SERVICE SOURCE INDEX. **1011**

0001-0669 *See* ACEC REVIEW. **2034**

0001-0782 *See* COMMUNICATIONS OF THE ACM. **1175**

0001-0898 *See* ADE BULLETIN. **3261**

0001-0936 See ADL ON THE FRONTLINE. **2254**

0001-0944 *See* REVISTA ADM. **1334**

0001-1096 *See* AEU. ARCHIV. FUER ELEKTRONIK UND UBERTRAGUNGSTECHNIK. **1148**

0001-1185 *See* AFL-CIO NEWS. **1642**

0001-1258 *See* AFZ. ALLGEMEINE FISCHWIRTSCHAFTSZEITUNG. **2293**

0001-1452 *See* AIAA JOURNAL. **6**

0001-1460 *See* AIAA STUDENT JOURNAL. **6**

0001-1487 *See* MEMO - AMERICAN INSTITUTE OF ARCHITECTS (1971). **303**

0001-1541 See AICHE JOURNAL. 2007
0001-1673 See AIZ. ALLGEMEINE IMMOBILIEN-ZEITUNG. 4833
0001-1746 See ALA WASHINGTON NEWSLETTER. 3188
0001-1754 See A.L.B.A. BOWLS. 4881
0001-1800 See ATUALIDADES MEDICAS. 3553
0001-1843 See AMERICAN MEDICAL NEWS. 3549
0001-1932 See AM NEWS. 1126
0001-2068 See ANU HISTORICAL JOURNAL. 2610
0001-2084 See AOPA PILOT, THE. 12
0001-2092 See AORN JOURNAL. 3851
0001-2092 See AORN JOURNAL. 3851
0001-2114 See APA MONITOR. 4574
0001-2122 See APAVE. 2035
0001-2165 See APCO BULLETIN, THE. 4767
0001-2181 See APEC, ANALISE E PERSPECTIVA ECONOMICA. 1546
0001-2203 See APLA BULLETIN. 3191
0001-2343 See ARCHIV FUER RECHTS- UND SOZIALPHILOSOPHIE. 2936
0001-2351 See TRANSACTIONS OF THE ASAE. 1999
0001-2386 See ASB BULLETIN, THE. 443
0001-2408 See ASBSD BULLETIN. 1860
0001-2475 See ASHA (ROCKVILLE, MD.). 1875
0001-2483 See ASHP NEWSLETTER. 4293
0001-2491 See ASHRAE JOURNAL. 2603
0001-2505 See ASHRAE TRANSACTIONS. 2603
0001-253X See ASLIB PROCEEDINGS. 3192
0001-2610 See PLANNING (CHICAGO, ILL. 1969). 2831
0001-267X See A T A NEWS. 1887
0001-2696 See ATB METALLURGIE (BRUSSELS, BELGIUM). 3998
0001-2718 See ATE NEWS LETTER. 1888
0001-2777 See ATR; AUSTRALIAN TELECOMMUNICATION RESEARCH. 1149
0001-2785 See ATZ. AUTOMOBILTECHNISCHE ZEITSCHRIFT. 5404
0001-2793 See A.U.M.L.A. 3260
0001-2815 See TISSUE ANTIGENS. 3802
0001-2947 See A.W.R. BULLETIN. 5269
0001-2998 See SEMINARS IN NUCLEAR MEDICINE. 3849
0001-3048 See CHRONICLE OF THE AARON BURR ASSOCIATION, THE. 2728
0001-3072 See ABACUS (SYDNEY). 735
0001-3102 See ABBIA. 5267
0001-3196 See BULLETIN OF THE ABERDEEN UNIVERSITY AFRICAN STUDIES GROUP. 2638
0001-320X See ABERDEEN UNIVERSITY REVIEW. 1088
0001-3218 See ABITARE. 287
0001-3242 See ABOUT THE HOUSE. 4098
0001-3331 See ABRIDGED INDEX MEDICUS. 3654
0001-334X See ABRIDGED READERS' GUIDE TO PERIODICAL LITERATURE. 2496
0001-3374 See ABSATZWIRTSCHAFT DUSSELDORF. 1969. 920
0001-3455 See ABSTRACTS IN ANTHROPOLOGY. 248
0001-3536 See ABSTRACTS OF BULGARIAN SCIENTIFIC MEDICAL LITERATURE. 3543
0001-3560 See ABSTRACTS OF ENGLISH STUDIES. 3356
0001-3579 See ABSTRACTS OF ENTOMOLOGY. 5604
0001-3617 See ABSTRACTS OF MYCOLOGY. 476
0001-3714 See REVISTA DE MICROBIOLOGIA. 569
0001-3757 See BOLETIN DE LA ACADEMIA ARGENTINA DE LETRAS. 3368
0001-3765 See ANAIS DA ACADEMIA BRASILEIRA DE CIENCIAS. 5082
0001-3773 See BOLETIN DE LA ACADEMIA COLOMBIANA. 2513
0001-3838 See BOLETIM DA ACADEMIA NACIONAL DE MEDICINA. 3558

0001-3846 See REVISTA DA ACADEMIA PAULISTA DE LETRAS. 2853
0001-3935 See MINZUXUE YANJIUSUO JIKAN, ZHONGYANG YANJIUYUAN. 241
0001-3943 See CHUNG YANG YEN CHIU YUAN TUNG WU YEN CHUI SO CHI KAN. 5580
0001-3994 See ACADEMIE D'ARCHITECTURE. 287
0001-4001 See CHIRURGIE (PARIS). 3962
0001-4001 See CHIRURGIE. 3962
0001-4079 See BULLETIN DE L'ACADEMIE NATIONALE DE MEDICINE. 3559
0001-4141 See BULLETIN DE LA CLASSE DES SCIENCES. ACADEMIE ROYALE DE BELGIQUE. 5090
0001-4176 See BULLETIN DES SEANCES - ACADEMIE ROYALE DES SCIENCES D'OUTRE-MER. 5091
0001-4176 See MEDEDELINGEN DER ZITTINGEN - KONINKLIJKE ACADEMIE VOOR OVERZEESE WETTENSCHAPEN. 5127
0001-4192 See BULLETIN DE L'ACADEMIE VETERINAIRE DE FRANCE. 5506
0001-4214 See REVUE ROUMAINE DE BIOCHIMIE. 493
0001-4249 See ACADEMY BOOKMAN, THE. 3654
0001-4273 See ACADEMY OF MANAGEMENT JOURNAL. 858
0001-4311 See BULLETIN OF THE ACADEMY OF MEDICINE, TORONTO. 3560
0001-432X See BULLETIN OF THE RUSSIAN ACADEMY OF SCIENCES. PHYSICS. 4399
0001-4338 See IZVESTIYA. ATMOSPHERIC AND OCEANIC PHYSICS. 1407
0001-4338 See IZVESTIYA. ATMOSPHERIC AND OCEANIC PHYSICS. 1407
0001-4346 See MATHEMATICAL NOTES (ROSSIISKAIA AKADEMIIA NAUK). 3519
0001-4354 See IZVESTIYA, ACADEMY OF SCIENCES, USSR. PHYSICS OF THE SOLID EARTH. 1407
0001-4370 See OCEANOLOGY (WASHINGTON. 1965). 1454
0001-4397 See ACADIANA PROFILE. 2254
0001-4419 See ATTI DELLA ACCADEMIA DELLE SCIENZE DI TORINO. CLASSE DI SCIENZE FISICHE, MATEMATICHE E NATURALI. 5086
0001-4427 See ATTI DELLA ACCADEMIA MEDICA LOMBARDA. 3553
0001-4451 See ACCADEMIE E BIBLIOTECHE D'ITALIA. 3186
0001-4532 See CHUGOKUGO CHOSENGO TOSHO SOKUHO. 413
0001-4575 See ACCIDENT ANALYSIS AND PREVENTION. 4763
0001-4664 See ACCOUNTANCY (LONDON). 735
0001-4672 See ACCOUNTANCY AGE. 735
0001-4699 See ACCOUNTANCY IRELAND. 735
0001-4710 See ACCOUNTANT (LONDON). 735
0001-4729 See ACCOUNTANT (AMSTERDAM). 735
0001-4745 See ACCOUNTANTS' JOURNAL (WELLINGTON). 735
0001-4753 See ACCOUNTANTS' JOURNAL. 735
0001-4761 See ACCOUNTANT'S MAGAZINE, THE. 736
0001-4788 See ACCOUNTING AND BUSINESS RESEARCH. 736
0001-4796 See ACCOUNTING + DATA PROCESSING ABSTRACTS. 725
0001-4826 See ACCOUNTING REVIEW, THE. 737
0001-4842 See ACCOUNTS OF CHEMICAL RESEARCH. 958
0001-4850 See ACERO Y ENERGIA. 3996
0001-4893 See ACHATS ET ENTREPRISE PARIS. 948
0001-4907 See ACHIEVEMENT (LONDON. 1969). 1596
0001-494X See ACME. 2841
0001-4958 See ACONCAGUA (VADUZ). 4288
0001-4966 See JOURNAL OF THE ACOUSTICAL SOCIETY OF AMERICA, THE. 4452
0001-4974 See ACOUSTICS ABSTRACTS. 4426

0001-4982 See INQUINAMENTO. 2233
0001-5083 See ACT (WHITING). 4931
0001-5105 See ACTA ACADEMIAE ABOENSIS. SERIES: B, MATHEMATICA ET PHYSICA. 3490
0001-5113 See ACTA ADRIATICA. 552
0001-5121 See ACTA AGRICULTUR SCANDINAVICA. SECTION B, SOIL AND PLANT SCIENCE. 43
0001-5121 See ACTA AGRICULTUR SCANDINAVICA. SECTION A, ANIMAL SCIENCE. 43
0001-5164 See ACTA ANAESTHESIOLOGICA BELGICA. 3680
0001-5172 See ACTA ANAESTHESIOLOGICA SCANDINAVICA. 3680
0001-5180 See ACTA ANATOMICA. 3678
0001-5199 See ACTA APOSTOLICA SEDIS, COMMENTARIUM OFFICIALE. 5022
0001-5202 See ACTA ARACHNOLOGICA. 5573
0001-5210 See ACTA ARCHAEOLOGICA ACADEMIAE SCIENTIARUM HUNGARICAE. 253
0001-5229 See ACTA ARCHAEOLOGICA CARPATHICA. 253
0001-5237 See ACTA ASTRONOMICA. 391
0001-5245 See TIEN WEN HSUEH PAO. 401
0001-527X See ACTA BIOCHIMICA POLONICA. 479
0001-5296 See ACTA BIOLOGICA CRACOVIENSIA. SERIES: BOTANICA. 496
0001-530X See ACTA BIOLOGICA CRACOVIENSIA. SERIES: ZOOLOGIA. 5573
0001-5326 See ACTA BIOLOGICA VENEZUELICA. 440
0001-5334 See SHIH YEN SHENG WU HSUEH PAO. 473
0001-5342 See ACTA BIOTHEORETICA. 440
0001-5369 See ACTA BOTANICA FENNICA. 496
0001-5385 See ACTA CARDIOLOGICA. 3697
0001-5415 See ACTA CHIRURGIAE ORTHOPAEDICAE ET TRAUMATOLOGIAE CECHOSLOVACA. 3880
0001-544X See ACTA CHIRURGICA AUSTRIACA. 3957
0001-5458 See ACTA CHIRURGICA BELGICA. 3957
0001-5466 See ACTA CHIRURGICA ITALICA. 3957
0001-5474 See ACTA CHIRURGICA IUGOSLAVICA. 3957
0001-5482 See EUROPEAN JOURNAL OF SURGERY, THE. 3964
0001-5504 See ACTA CIENTIFICA VENEZOLANA. 5080
0001-5512 See ACTA CLINICA BELGICA. 3544
0001-5547 See ACTA CYTOLOGICA. 531
0001-5555 See ACTA DERMATO-VENEREOLOGICA. 3717
0001-5563 See ACTA DIABETOLOGICA. 3726
0001-5598 See ACTA ENDOCRINOLOGICA (COPENHAGEN). 3726
0001-5601 See ACTA ENTOMOLOGICA BOHEMOSLOVACA. 5604
0001-5628 See ACTA ETHNOGRAPHICA HUNGARICA. 227
0001-5636 See ACTA FORESTALIA FENNICA. 2373
0001-5644 See ACTA GASTRO-ENTEROLOGICA BELGICA. 3743
0001-5652 See HUMAN HEREDITY. 547
0001-5660 See ACTA GENETICAE MEDICAE ET GEMELLOLOGIAE. 541
0001-5687 See ACTA GEOGRAPHICA (PARIS). 2553
0001-5709 See ACTA GEOLOGICA POLONICA. 1364
0001-5717 See DIZHIXUE BAO. 1373
0001-5725 See ACTA GEOPHYSICA POLONICA. 1402
0001-5733 See DIQIU WULIXUE BAO. 1404
0001-5768 See ACTA GERONTOLOGICA JAPONICA. 3748
0001-5776 See ACTA GINECOLOGICA. 3756
0001-5792 See ACTA HAEMATOLOGICA. 3769

0001-5806 See INTERNATIONAL JOURNAL OF HEMATOLOGY. 3772

0001-5814 See ACTA HAEMATOLOGICA POLONICA. 3794

0001-5830 See ACTA HISTORIAE ARTIUM ACADEMIAE SCIENTARIUM HUNGARICAE. 335

0001-5849 See ACTA HISTORICA ACADEMIAE SCIENTIARUM HUNGARICAE. 2672

0001-5857 See ACTA HISTORICA LEOPOLDINA. 5080

0001-5903 See ACTA INFORMATICA. 1255

0001-5938 See ACTA LEPROLOGICA. 3544

0001-5962 See ACTA MATHEMATICA. 3490

0001-5970 See ACTA MECHANICA. 2109

0001-5997 See ACTA MEDICA (MEXICO). 3544

0001-6004 See ACTA MEDICA AUXOLOGICA. 3544

0001-6012 See ACTA MEDICA COSTARRICENSE. 3544

0001-6055 See ACTA MEDICA NAGASAKIENSIA. 3544

0001-6071 See ACTA MEDICA PHILIPPINA. 3544

0001-608X See ACTA MEDICA POLONA. 3545

0001-6098 See ACTA MEDICA ROMANA. 3545

0001-6136 See ACTA MEDICA VETERINARIA. 5501

0001-6195 See ACTA MICROBIOLOGICA POLONICA. 558

0001-6209 See WEI SHENG WU HSUEH PAO. 571

0001-6233 See ACTA MOZARTIANA. 4098

0001-6241 See ACTA MUSICOLOGICA. 4098

0001-625X See ACTA MYCOLOGICA. 574

0001-6268 See ACTA NEUROCHIRURGICA. 3957

0001-6276 See ACTA NEUROLOGICA. 3825

0001-6314 See ACTA NEUROLOGICA SCANDINAVICA. 3825

0001-6322 See ACTA NEUROPATHOLOGICA. 3892

0001-6349 See ACTA OBSTETRICIA ET GYNECOLOGICA SCANDINAVICA. 3756

0001-6357 See ACTA ODONTOLOGICA SCANDINAVICA. 1315

0001-6373 See ACTA OECONOMICA. 1460

0001-6381 See ACTA ONCOLOGICA. 3808

0001-639X See ACTA OPHTHALMOLOGICA. 3545

0001-6411 See ACTA ORDINIS FRATRUM MINORUM. 5022

0001-6438 See ACTA ORIENTALIA (KBENHAVN). 3261

0001-6446 See ACTA ORIENTALIA ACADEMIAE SCIENTIARUM HUNGARICAE. 2644

0001-6454 See ACTA ORNITHOLOGICA. 5614

0001-6462 See ACTA ORTHOPAEDICA BELGICA. 3880

0001-6470 See ACTA ORTHOPAEDICA SCANDINAVICA. 3880

0001-6497 See ACTA OTO-RHINO-LARYNGOLOGICA BELGICA. 3885

0001-6519 See ACTA OTORRINOLARINGOLOGICA ESPANOLA. 3885

0001-6543 See NIHON SHONIKA GAKKAI ZASSHI. 3907

0001-656X See ACTA PAEDIATRICA (OSLO). 3899

0001-6578 See ZHONGHUA MINGUO XIAOERKE YIXUEHUI ZAZHI. 3912

0001-6586 See ACTA PAEDOPSYCHIATRICA. 3918

0001-6594 See ACTA PALAEOBOTANICA. 497

0001-6616 See GUSHENG WUXUE BAO. 4227

0001-6632 See ACTA PATHOLOGICA JAPONICA. 3892

0001-6659 See ACTA PHARMACEUTICA HUNGARICA (BUDAPEST. 1953). 4288

0001-6772 See ACTA PHYSIOLOGICA SCANDINAVICA. 577

0001-6799 See ACTA PHYTOTAXONOMICA ET GEOBOTANICA. SHOKUBUTSU BUNRUI CHIRI. 497

0001-6810 See ACTA POLITICA. 4461

0001-6829 See ACTA POLONIAE HISTORICA. 2672

0001-6837 See ACTA POLONIAE PHARMACEUTICA. 4289

0001-6845 See ACTA POLYTECHNICA SCANDINAVICA. ELECTRICAL ENGINEERING SERIES. 2034

0001-6853 See ACTA POLYTECHNICA SCANDINAVICA. CHEMICAL TECHNOLOGY AND METALLURGY SERIES. 1963

0001-687X See ACTA POLYTECHNICA SCANDINAVICA. MECHANICAL ENGINEERING SERIES. 2109

0001-6896 See ACTA PSIQUIATRICA Y PSICOLOGICA DE AMERICA LATINA. 3918

0001-690X See ACTA PSYCHIATRICA SCANDINAVICA. 3919

0001-6918 See ACTA PSYCHOLOGICA. 4570

0001-6942 See ACTA SAGITTARIANA. 4098

0001-6969 See ACTA SCIENTIARUM MATHEMATICARUM. 3490

0001-6977 See ACTA SOCIETATIS BOTANICORUM POLONIAE. 497

0001-6993 See ACTA SOCIOLOGICA. 5237

0001-7000 See ACTA STOMATOLOGICA BELGICA. 1315

0001-7019 See ACTA STOMATOLOGICA CROATICA. 3545

0001-7035 See ACTA TECHNICA / ACADEMIAE SCIENTIARUM HUNGARICAE. 5080

0001-7043 See ACTA TECHNICA CSAV. 5080

0001-7051 See ACTA THERIOLOGICA. 204

0001-706X See ACTA TROPICA. 3985

0001-7094 See DRUG THERAPY (NEW YORK, N.Y.). 3573

0001-7116 See ACTA UNIVERSITATIS CAROLINAE. MEDICA. 3545

0001-7124 See ACTA UNIVERSITATIS CAROLINAE. BIOLOGICA. 440

0001-7132 See ACTA UNIVERSITATIS CAROLINAE. GEOLOGICA. 1364

0001-7140 See ACTA UNIVERSITATIS CAROLINAE. MATHEMATICA ET PHYSICA. 3491

0001-7183 See ACTA UROLOGICA BELGICA. 3987

0001-7213 See ACTA VETERINARIA (BRNO, CZECHOSLOVAKIA). 1020

0001-7221 See ACTA VETERINARIA JAPONICA. 5501

0001-723X See ACTA VIROLOGICA (ANGLICKA VERZE). 3545

0001-7272 See ACTA ZOOLOGICA (STOCKHOLM). 5574

0001-7280 See ACTA ZOOLOGICA ET PATHOLOGICA ANTVERPIENSIA. 5573

0001-7299 See ACTA ZOOLOGICA FENNICA. 5573

0001-7302 See TUNG WU HSUEH PAO. 5599

0001-7310 See ACTAS DERMO-SIFILOGRAFICAS. 3717

0001-7396 See ACTION (ALBANY). 1338

0001-7418 See ACTION AUTOMOBILE ET TOURISTIQUE, L'. 5403

0001-7442 See ACTION LINE (BALTIMORE). 1722

0001-7469 See ACTION NATIONALE. 2526

0001-7523 See ACTION VETERINAIRE, L'. 5501

0001-7604 See HOMEOSTASIS IN HEALTH AND DISEASE : INTERNATIONAL JOURNAL DEVOTED TO INTEGRATIVE BRAIN FUNCTIONS AND HOMEOSTATIC SYSTEMS. 3833

0001-7655 See ACTUALIDAD ECONOMICA. 1544

0001-7701 See GENERAL RELATIVITY AND GRAVITATION. 4403

0001-771X See ACTUALITE ECONOMIQUE. 1589

0001-7736 See ACTUALITE JURIDIQUE. PROPRIETE IMMOBILIERE, L'. 2927

0001-7779 See ACTUALITE TERMINOLOGIQUE. 3261

0001-7817 See ACTUALITES ODONTO-STOMATOLOGIQUES. 1315

0001-7825 See ACTUARY. 2872

0001-785X See AKTUELLE CHIRURGIE. 3958

0001-7868 See AKTUELLE UROLOGIE. 3988

0001-7884 See ACUSTICA. 4452

0001-799X See VIERTELJAHRESSCHRIFT. 3451

0001-8015 See ADAM INTERNATIONAL REVIEW. 3187

0001-8066 See AC. THE ADCRAFTER. 753

0001-8171 See ADEM. 4098

0001-8198 See ADHAESION. 1049

0001-821X See ADHESIVES AGE. 2007

0001-8236 See ADIRONDAC. 4868

0001-8244 See BEHAVIOR GENETICS. 543

0001-8252 See ADIRONDACK LIFE. 2526

0001-8260 See ADLER (WIEN). 2436

0001-8325 See ADMINISTRATION (DUBLIN). 4624

0001-8333 See QUARTERLY JOURNAL OF ADMINISTRATION, THE. 1869

0001-8368 See ADMINISTRATIVE LAW REVIEW. 3092

0001-8392 See ADMINISTRATIVE SCIENCE QUARTERLY. 4624

0001-8406 See ADMINISTRATIVE SCIENCE REVIEW. 4624

0001-8430 See ADMINISTRATOR'S NOTEBOOK. 1859

0001-8449 See ADOLESCENCE. 1059

0001-8473 See ADULT AND CONTINUING EDUCATION TODAY. 1799

0001-8503 See ADULT EDUCATION IN FINLAND. 1799

0001-8589 See ADVANCE (SPRINGFIELD). 5054

0001-8627 See ADVANCED BATTERY TECHNOLOGY. 2034

0001-8678 See ADVANCES IN APPLIED PROBABILITY. 3491

0001-8686 See ADVANCES IN COLLOID AND INTERFACE SCIENCE. 1049

0001-8708 See ADVANCES IN MATHEMATICS (NEW YORK. 1965). 3491

0001-8724 See SHINKEI KENKYU NO SHIMPO. 3641

0001-8732 See ADVANCES IN PHYSICS. 4396

0001-8783 See ADVENTURE (NASHVILLE). 4932

0001-8791 See JOURNAL OF VOCATIONAL BEHAVIOR. 4602

0001-8899 See ADVERTISING AGE. 754

0001-8996 See ADVOCATE (LOS ANGELES, CALIF.), THE. 2793

0001-9003 See ADVOCATE (NEW YORK, N.Y.), THE. 2254

0001-902X See ADYAR LIBRARY BULLETIN, THE. 5041

0001-9046 See AEGYPTUS. 253

0001-9054 See AEQUATIONES MATHEMATICAE. 3491

0001-9186 See AERO REVUE. 4

0001-9232 See AERO MODELLER, THE. 4

0001-9240 See AERONAUTICAL JOURNAL, THE. 4

0001-9267 See JOURNAL OF THE AERONAUTICAL SOCIETY OF INDIA, THE. 26

0001-9275 See AERONAUTIQUE ET L'ASTRONAUTIQUE, L'. 4

0001-9291 See SPRAY TECHNOLOGY & MARKETING. 4222

0001-9313 See AEROSOL SPRAY REPORT : INTERNATIONAL PERIODICAL FOR THE AEROSOL AND SPRAY INDUSTRY. 1020

0001-9410 See AEROSPACE MEDICINE AND BIOLOGY. 3547

0001-947X See ARZTEBLATT BADEN-WURTTEMBERG. 3553

0001-9518 See ARZTLICHE JUGENDKUNDE. 3553

0001-9534 See ARZTLICHE PRAXIS. 3553

0001-9593 See AEVUM. 3262

0001-9615 See AFFAIRES, LES. 1544

0001-964x See AFFARI ESTERI. 4514

0001-9674 See AFFIRMATION (RICHMOND, VA.). 4932

0001-9682 See AFGHANISTAN (KABUL). 2644

0001-9704 See AFINIDAD. 960

0001-9720 See AFRICA (LONDON. 1928). 3262

0001-9747 See AFRICA. 2254
0001-9747 See AFRICA (ROME, ITALY). 2636
0001-9828 See AFRICA QUARTERLY. 2636
0001-9836 See AFRICA REPORT. 2636
0001-9844 See AFRICA RESEARCH BULLETIN. POLITICAL, SOCIAL, AND CULTURAL SERIES. 5238
0001-9852 See AFRICA RESEARCH BULLETIN : ECONOMIC, FINANCIAL AND TECHNICAL SERIES. 1632
0001-9887 See AFRICA TODAY. 4462
0001-9909 See AFRICAN AFFAIRS (LONDON). 4462
0001-9933 See AFRICAN ARTS. 312
0001-9968 See AFRICAN CHALLENGE. 4933
0001-9976 See AFRICAN COMMUNIST. 4539
0002-0052 See AFRICAN LAW DIGEST. 2928
0002-0087 See AFRICAN NOTES. 2254
0002-0117 See AFRICAN REVIEW (DAR ES SALAAM, TANZANIA). 5189
0002-0125 See AFRICAN RECORDER. 2497
0002-0168 See AFRICAN SOCIAL RESEARCH. 5189
0002-0184 See AFRICAN STUDIES (JOHANNESBURG). 227
0002-0206 See AFRICAN STUDIES REVIEW. 2498
0002-0265 See AFRICAN VIOLET MAGAZINE. 2408
0002-0273 See AFRICAN WILDLIFE. 2185
0002-0281 See AFRICANA. 5574
0002-029X See AFRICANA BULLETIN. 2637
0002-0311 See AFRICANA MARBURGENSIA. 2637
0002-032X See AFRICANA NOTES AND NEWS. 2498
0002-0362 See 3. WELT MAGAZIN. 4514
0002-0389 See AFRIKA-POST. 4515
0002-0397 See AFRIKASPECTRUM. 5189
0002-0427 See AFRIKA UND UBERSEE. 3262
0002-0443 See JOURNAL OF NURSING ADMINISTRATION, THE. 3859
0002-0478 See AFRIQUE CONTEMPORAINE. 4515
0002-0516 See AFRIQUE MEDICALE. 3892
0002-0532 See AFRIQUE NOUVELLE. 2498
0002-0591 See AFRO-ASIA. 2637
0002-0664 See LOTUS (CAIRO). 3408
0002-0710 See AGRARISCHE RUNDSCHAU. 46
0002-0729 See AGE AND AGEING. 3748
0002-0796 See AGENDA (LONDON). 3459
0002-080X See AGENOR. 4515
0002-0915 See AGGIORNAMENTI DI TERAPIA OFTALMOLOGICA. 3871
0002-094X See AGGIORNAMENTI SOCIALI. 4933
0002-0958 See AGGIORNAMENTO PEDIATRICO. 3899
0002-0966 See AGING. 3749
0002-1016 See AGORA (POTSDAM). 2841
0002-1024 See AGRA EUROPE (BRITISH EDITION). 46
0002-1032 See AGRA UNIVERSITY JOURNAL OF RESEARCH. SCIENCE. 5081
0002-1075 See AGRARISCH WEEKOVERZICHT. 46
0002-1121 See AGRARWIRTSCHAFT. 637
0002-1148 See AGRESSOLOGIE. 4572
0002-1164 See AGRI FINANCE. 768
0002-1172 See AGRI HORTIQUE GENETICA. 2408
0002-1180 See AGRI MARKETING. 47
0002-1334 See AGRICULTURA (MADRID, SPAIN). 49
0002-1350 See AGRICULTURA DE LAS AMERICAS (OVERLAND PARK, KANS.). 48
0002-1369 See BIOSCIENCE, BIOTECHNOLOGY, AND BIOCHEMISTRY. 3687
0002-1407 See NIPPON NOGEI KAGAKU KAISHI. 113
0002-1458 See AGRICULTURAL ENGINEERING. 1964

0002-1466 See AGRICULTURAL FINANCE REVIEW. 769
0002-1482 See AGRICULTURAL HISTORY. 50
0002-1490 See AGRICULTURAL HISTORY REVIEW, THE. 50
0002-1555 See AGRICULTURAL MARKETING. 161
0002-1601 See AGRICULTURAL PRICES (WASHINGTON, D.C.). 51
0002-161X See AGRICULTURAL RESEARCH (WASHINGTON). 51
0002-1628 See AGRICULTURAL RESEARCH JOURNAL OF KERALA. 51
0002-1636 See SELSKOSTOPANSKA NAUKA : ORGAN NA PREZIDIUMA NA ASN. 133
0002-1679 See AGRICULTURAL SITUATION IN INDIA. 52
0002-1687 See AGRICULTURE (MONTREAL). 54
0002-1709 See AGRICULTURE PARIS. 54
0002-1725 See AGRICULTURE AND AGRO-INDUSTRIES JOURNAL. 53
0002-1741 See AGRICULTURE DECISIONS. 53
0002-1822 See AGROBOREALIS. 55
0002-1830 See AGROCHEMIA (BRATISLAVA). 55
0002-1849 See AGROCHEMIA. 55
0002-1857 See AGROCHIMICA. 55
0002-1865 See AGROHEMIJA. 56
0002-1873 See AGROKEMIA ES TALAJTAN. 56
0002-1881 See AGROHIMIJA. 56
0002-1911 See AGRONOMIA LUSITANA. 56
0002-192X See AGRONOMIA TROPICAL. 56
0002-1946 See AGRONOMIE TROPICALE, L'. 162
0002-1962 See AGRONOMY JOURNAL. 162
0002-2152 See AIR ACTUALITES PARIS. 4033
0002-2241 See AIR CLASSICS. 7
0002-2276 See AIR CONDITIONING, HEATING & REFRIGERATION NEWS. 2602
0002-2322 See AIR FACTS. 7
0002-2365 See AIR FORCE COMPTROLLER, THE. 4033
0002-2403 See AIR FORCE TIMES. 4034
0002-2411 See AIR LINE EMPLOYEE, THE. 1643
0002-242X See AIR LINE PILOT. 7
0002-2462 See AIR PICTORIAL. 8
0002-2497 See AIR POLLUTION TITLES. 2183
0002-2500 See AIR PROGRESS. 8
0002-2543 See AIR TRANSPORT WORLD. 8
0002-2586 See AIR UNIVERSITY LIBRARY INDEX TO MILITARY PERIODICALS. 4061
0002-2608 See AIR/WATER POLLUTION REPORT. 2159
0002-2675 See AIRCRAFT ILLUSTRATED. 9
0002-2756 See AIRMAN, THE. 4034
0002-2802 See AIRPORT FORUM. 10
0002-2853 See AIRPORTS INTERNATIONAL. 11
0002-2918 See AJASTAN KENSABANAKAN ANDES. 441
0002-2942 See AJIA KEIZAI. 1461
0002-2969 See BIOLOGICHESKII ZHURNAL ARMENII. 446
0002-2977 See ABHANDLUNGEN DER GEISTES- UND SOZIALWISSENSCHAFTLICHEN KLASSE / AKADEMIE DER WISSENSCHAFTEN UND DER LITERATUR. 5189
0002-2985 See ABHANDLUNGEN DER KLASSE DER LITERATUR / AKADEMIE DER WISSENSCHAFTEN UND DER LITERATUR. 3357
0002-2993 See ABHANDLUNGEN DER MATHEMATISCH-NATURWISSENSCHAFTLICHEN KLASSE - AKADEMIE DER WISSENSCHAFTEN UND DER LITERATUR. 5079
0002-3027 See VESTNIK AKADEMII MEDITSINSKIKH NAUK SSSR. 3649
0002-3035 See IZVESTIJA AKADEMII NAUK ARMJANSKOJ SSR. FIZIKA. 4407
0002-3051 See IZVESTIJA AKADEMII NAUK ARMJANSKOJ SSR. MEHANIKA. 2117
0002-3078 See DOKLADY / AKADEMIIA NAUK AZERBAIDZHANSKOI SSR. 5101

0002-3108 See IZVESTIJA AKADEMII NAUK AZERBAJDZANSKOJ SSR. SERIJA FIZIKO-TEHNICESKIH I MATEMATICESKIH NAUK. 4407
0002-3124 See IZVESTIJA AKADEMII NAUK AZERBAJDZANSKOJ SSR. SERIJA NAUK O ZEMLE. 1384
0002-3124 See IZVESTIJA AKADEMII NAUK AZERBAIDZANSKOI SSR. SERIJA NAUK O ZEMLE. 1384
0002-3175 See QAZAQ SSR GHYLYM AKADEMIIASYNYNG KHABARLARY. 1392
0002-3183 See IZVESTIJA AKADEMII NAUK KAZAKHSKOI SSR. SERIIA BIOLOGICHESKAIA. 459
0002-3191 See IZVESTIIA AKADEMII NAUK KAZAKHSKOI SSR. SERIIA FIZIKO-MATEMATICHESKAIA. 5117
0002-3205 See IZVESTIIA AKADEMII NAUK KAZAKHSKOI SSR. SERIIA KHIMICHESKAIA. 979
0002-3248 See LATVIJAS KIMIJAS ZURNALS. 984
0002-3264 See DOKLADY AKADEMII NAUK SSSR. 1354
0002-3329 See IZVESTIIA AKADEMII NAUK SSSR. SERIIA BIOLOGICHESKAIA. 459
0002-3329 See IZVESTIIA AKADEMII NAUK SSSR. SERIIA BIOLOGICHESKAIA. 459
0002-3337 See IZVESTIIA AKADEMII NAUK SSSR. FIZIKA ZEMLI. 4407
0002-3353 See IZVESTIA AKADEMII NAUK SSSR. SERIA HIMICESKAA. 979
0002-3353 See IZVESTIIA. SERIIA KHIMICHESKAIA. 979
0002-337X See IZVESTIJA. AKADEMIJA NAUK SSSR. NEORGANICESKIE MATERIALY. 1036
0002-3442 See VESTNIK AKADEMII NAUK SSSR. 5168
0002-3469 See DOKLADHOI AKADEMIAI FANHOI RSS TOCIKISTON. 3504
0002-3477 See IZVESTIJA AKADEMII NAUK TADZIKSKOJ SSR. OTDELENIE BIOLOGICESKIH NAUK. 460
0002-3485 See AKHBOROTI AKADEMIAI FANHOI RSS TOJIKISTON. SHUBAI FANHOI FIZIKAIU MATEMATIKA, KHIMIIA VA GEOLOGIIA. 5081
0002-371X See AKRON LAW REVIEW. 2929
0002-3728 See AKROS. 3459
0002-3752 See AKTIENGESELLSCHAFT, DIE. 1596
0002-3787 See AKTUALNE PROBLEMY INFORMACJI I DOKUMENTACJI. 1923
0002-3906 See AKUSERSTVO I GINEKOLOGIJA (MOSKVA). 3756
0002-3949 See AKWESASNE NOTES. 5268
0002-3957 See AKZENTE (MUNCHEN). 3358
0002-3973 See AL-ABHATH. 2841
0002-399X See AL-DIRASAT AL-ISLAMIYAH. 5041
0002-4112 See JOURNAL OF THE ALABAMA ACADEMY OF SCIENCE, THE. 5120
0002-4147 See ALABAMA BAPTIST HISTORIAN, THE. 5054
0002-4171 See ALABAMA CONSERVATION. 2185
0002-4198 See JOURNAL OF THE ALABAMA DENTAL ASSOCIATION, THE. 1328
0002-4279 See ALABAMA LAW REVIEW. 2929
0002-4287 See ALABAMA LAWYER, THE. 2929
0002-4295 See ALABAMA LIBRARIAN, THE. 3188
0002-4309 See ALABAMA MUNICIPAL JOURNAL, THE. 4625
0002-4317 See ALABAMA NURSE, THE. 3850
0002-4325 See ALABAMA PURCHASOR. 948
0002-4341 See ALABAMA REVIEW, THE. 2718
0002-435X See ALABAMA SCHOOL JOURNAL. 1860
0002-4384 See ALABAMA TRUCKER. 5375
0002-4406 See ALAMBRE. 3475
0002-4503 See ALASKA JOURNAL (JUNEAU, ALASKA : 1971). 2527
0002-4538 See ALASKA MEDICINE. 3547
0002-4546 See ALASKA NURSE, THE. 3850
0002-4562 See ALASKA (ANCHORAGE, ALASKA). 4868

0002-4619 See ALAUDA. 5614
0002-4651 See ALBANIA REPORT. 4462
0002-4678 See ALBANY LAW REVIEW. 2929
0002-4775 See ALBERTA GAZETTE. 4625
0002-4805 See ALBERTA JOURNAL OF EDUCATIONAL RESEARCH. 1723
0002-4821 See ALBERTA LAW REVIEW. 2929
0002-497X See TEXAS ALCALDE. 1103
0002-502X See ALCOHOLISM (ZAGREB). 1340
0002-5054 See ALCOOL OU SANTE PARIS. 1340
0002-5100 See ALDRICHIMICA ACTA. 960
0002-5151 See ALERGIA (MEXICO). 3665
0002-5208 See ALEXANOR. 5574
0002-5216 See ALFA. 3359
0002-5224 See ALFRED HITCHCOCK'S MYSTERY MAGAZINE. 5074
0002-5232 See ALGEBRA AND LOGIC. 3491
0002-5240 See ALGEBRA UNIVERSALIS. 3491
0002-5275 See ALGEMEEN NEDERLANDS TIJDSCHRIFT VOOR WIJSBEGEERTE. 4340
0002-5402 See ALIMENTA. 2326
0002-5577 See ALL HANDS (ALEXANDRIA, VA.). 4174
0002-5593 See ALL INDIA REPORTER. 2501
0002-5623 See ALL THE WORLD. [A QUARTERLY REVIEW OF THE WORLD-WIDE WORK OF THE SALVATION ARMY]. 5271
0002-564X See ALLAM- ES JOGTUDOMANY. 2931
0002-5658 See ALLATTANI KOEZLEMENYEK. 5574
0002-5674 See ALLE HENS. 4174
0002-5704 See ALLEGRO (NEW YORK, N.Y.). 4099
0002-5712 See ALLEMAGNE D'AUJOURD'HUI. 2513
0002-5852 See ALLGEMEINE FORST UND JAGDZEITUNG. 2374
0002-5895 See ALLGEMEINE HOTEL- UND GASTSTATTEN-ZEITUNG. 2803
0002-5917 See APR. ALLGEMEINE PAPIER-RUNDSCHAU (1966). 4232
0002-5968 See AVN. ALLGEMEINE VERMESSUNGS-NACHRICHTEN. 2019
0002-6018 See ALLGEMEINES STATISTISCHES ARCHIV. 5320
0002-6107 See ALLIED INDUSTRIAL WORKER. 1643
0002-614X See ALLOY DIGEST. 3997
0002-6387 See ALPHA DELTA KAPPAN. 5228
0002-6417 See ALPHA OMEGAN. 1315
0002-6476 See QUARTERLY BULLETIN OF THE ALPINE GARDEN SOCIETY. 2429
0002-6530 See MICROFORM REVIEW. 3231
0002-6549 See ALTA DIRECCION. 1596
0002-662X See ALTERNATIVE PRESS INDEX. 4186
0002-6638 See ALTERNATIVES (PETERBOROUGH). 2159
0002-6646 See ALTERTUM, DAS. 2673
0002-6670 See ALTSPRACHLICHE UNTERRICHT, DER. 3263
0002-6689 See ALUMINIUM (DUSSELDORF). 3997
0002-6697 See ALUMINIUM INDUSTRY ABSTRACTS. 4025
0002-6816 See AMATEUR BASEBALL NEWS. 4882
0002-6824 See AMATEUR D'ART, L'. 335
0002-6840 See AMATEUR PHOTOGRAPHER. 4366
0002-6883 See AMATEUR WINE MAKER. 2363
0002-6972 See AMBIT. 3459
0002-6980 See AMBIX. 960
0002-7014 See AMEGHINIANA. 4226
0002-7049 See AMERICA (NEW YORK, N.Y. 1909). 5023
0002-7065 See AMERICA, HISTORY AND LIFE (SANTA BARBARA, CALIF. : 1989). 2634
0002-7065 See AMERICA, HISTORY AND LIFE ON DISC. COMPUTER FILE. 2718

0002-712X See BULLETIN - AMERICAN ACADEMY OF ARTS AND SCIENCES. 316
0002-7162 See ANNALS OF THE AMERICAN ACADEMY OF POLITICAL AND SOCIAL SCIENCE. 5190
0002-7189 See JOURNAL OF THE AMERICAN ACADEMY OF RELIGION. 4970
0002-7197 See INDEPENDENT AGENT. 2882
0002-7200 See AMERICAN AGENT & BROKER. 2873
0002-7243 See JOURNAL OF THE AMERICAN ANALGESIA SOCIETY. 3597
0002-726X See AMERICAN ANNALS OF THE DEAF (WASHINGTON, D.C. 1886). 4383
0002-7294 See AMERICAN ANTHROPOLOGIST. 227
0002-7294 See AMERICAN ANTHROPOLOGIST [MICROFORM]. 227
0002-7316 See AMERICAN ANTIQUITY; A QUARTERLY REVIEW OF AMERICAN ARCHAEOLOGY. 253
0002-7359 See AMERICAN ART JOURNAL, THE. 336
0002-7375 See AMERICAN ARTIST. 336
0002-7499 See QUARTERLY BULLETIN OF THE AMERICAN ASSOCIATION OF TEACHERS OF ESPERANTO. 3313
0002-7529 See AMERICAN ASTROLOGY. 389
0002-7537 See BULLETIN - AMERICAN ASTRONOMICAL SOCIETY. 402
0002-7545 See AUTOMATIC MERCHANDISER. 2328
0002-7561 See AMERICAN BANKER. 769
0002-757X See AMERICAN BAPTIST, THE. 5055
0002-7626 See AMERICAN BEE JOURNAL. 58
0002-7642 See AMERICAN BEHAVIORAL SCIENTIST (BEVERLY HILLS). 5190
0002-7650 See AMERICAN BENEDICTINE REVIEW, THE. 5023
0002-7677 See AMERICAN BICYCLIST AND MOTORCYCLIST. 427
0002-7685 See AMERICAN BIOLOGY TEACHER, THE. 441
0002-7707 See AMERICAN BOOK PUBLISHING RECORD. 4812
0002-7707 See AMERICAN BOOK PUBLISHING RECORD. 4812
0002-7731 See AMERICAN BUILDING SUPPLIES. 598
0002-774X See AMERICAN BULLMASTIFF, THE. 4285
0002-7766 See AMERICAN BUSINESS LAW JOURNAL. 3095
0002-7782 See AMERICAN CAGE-BIRD MAGAZINE. 4285
0002-7790 See RECORDS OF THE AMERICAN CATHOLIC HISTORICAL SOCIETY OF PHILADELPHIA. 5035
0002-7804 See AMERICAN CEMETERY, THE. 2406
0002-7812 See AMERICAN CERAMIC SOCIETY BULLETIN. 2586
0002-7820 See JOURNAL OF THE AMERICAN CERAMIC SOCIETY. 2591
0002-7847 See JOURNAL OF THE AMERICAN CHAMBER OF COMMERCE IN JAPAN / ACCJ, THE. 820
0002-7855 See THAI-AMERICAN BUSINESS. 853
0002-7863 See JOURNAL OF THE AMERICAN CHEMICAL SOCIETY. 982
0002-7928 See AMERICAN CINEMATOGRAPHER. 4063
0002-7979 See JOURNAL OF THE AMERICAN COLLEGE OF DENTISTS, THE. 1328
0002-8045 See BULLETIN OF THE AMERICAN COLLEGE OF SURGEONS. 3961
0002-807X See AMERICAN COONER. 4882
0002-8150 See BULLETIN OF THE AMERICAN DAHLIA SOCIETY, INC. 2411
0002-8177 See JOURNAL OF THE AMERICAN DENTAL ASSOCIATION (USA ED.), THE. 1328
0002-8193 See NEWSLETTER OF THE AMERICAN DIALECT SOCIETY. 3306

0002-8207 See PUBLICATION OF THE AMERICAN DIALECT SOCIETY. 3312
0002-8223 See JOURNAL OF THE AMERICAN DIETETIC ASSOCIATION. 4194
0002-8231 See JOURNAL OF THE AMERICAN SOCIETY FOR INFORMATION SCIENCE. 3220
0002-8258 See AMERICAN DRYCLEANER. 5347
0002-8258 See AMERICAN DRY CLEANER. 1596
0002-8266 See AMERICAN DYESTUFF REPORTER. 5347
0002-8282 See AMERICAN ECONOMIC REVIEW, THE. 1461
0002-8312 See AMERICAN EDUCATIONAL RESEARCH JOURNAL. 1723
0002-8320 See TRANSACTIONS OF THE AMERICAN ENTOMOLOGICAL SOCIETY (1890). 5614
0002-838X See AMERICAN FAMILY PHYSICIAN (1970). 3736
0002-8436 See AMERICAN FENCING. 4882
0002-8444 See AMERICAN FERN JOURNAL. 498
0002-8452 See AMERICAN FIELD. 4868
0002-8487 See TRANSACTIONS OF THE AMERICAN FISHERIES SOCIETY (1900). 2315
0002-8525 See AMERICAN FLINT. 1643
0002-8541 See AMERICAN FORESTS. 2374
0002-8568 See AMERICAN FRUIT GROWER (WILLOUGHBY, OHIO : 1931). 2408
0002-8576 See AMERICAN FUNERAL DIRECTOR. 2406
0002-8592 See AMERICAN GENEALOGIST (DES MOINES). 2437
0002-8606 See PROCEEDINGS OF THE WESTERN SNOW CONFERENCE. 1359
0002-8614 See JOURNAL OF THE AMERICAN GERIATRICS SOCIETY. 3753
0002-8649 See AMERICAN GLASS REVIEW. 2586
0002-869X See AMERICAN HARP JOURNAL, THE. 4099
0002-8703 See AMERICAN HEART JOURNAL, THE. 3698
0002-8711 See JOURNAL OF THE AMERICAN HELICOPTER SOCIETY. 26
0002-872X See AMERICAN HEREFORD JOURNAL. 205
0002-8738 See AMERICAN HERITAGE. 2718
0002-8762 See AMERICAN HISTORICAL REVIEW. 2609
0002-8770 See AMERICAN HISTORY ILLUSTRATED. 2719
0002-8789 See REDBOOK. 5565
0002-8886 See AMERICAN INDIAN LAW NEWSLETTER. 2932
0002-8894 See AMERICAN INDUSTRIAL HYGIENE ASSOCIATION JOURNAL. 2858
0002-8908 See AMERICAN INDUSTRY. 859
0002-8916 See AMERICAN INKMAKER. 4563
0002-8940 See FOOD INSTITUTE REPORT, THE. 2337
0002-8959 See FOOD INSTITUTE REPORT, THE. 2337
0002-8967 See JOURNAL OF THE AMERICAN INSTITUTE OF HOMEOPATHY. 3775
0002-905X See AMERICAN JEWISH ARCHIVES. 2255
0002-905X See MONOGRAPHS OF THE AMERICAN JEWISH ARCHIVES. 2268
0002-9084 See AMERICAN JEWISH WORLD, THE. 5045
0002-9092 See AMERICAN JOURNAL OF AGRICULTURAL ECONOMICS. 58
0002-9106 See DEVELOPMENTAL DYNAMICS. 3679
0002-9114 See AMERICAN JOURNAL OF ARCHAEOLOGY. 254
0002-9122 See AMERICAN JOURNAL OF BOTANY. 498
0002-9149 See AMERICAN JOURNAL OF CARDIOLOGY, THE. 3698
0002-9157 See AMERICAN JOURNAL OF CLINICAL HYPNOSIS, THE. 2857
0002-9165 See AMERICAN JOURNAL OF CLINICAL NUTRITION, THE. 4187

0002-9173 See AMERICAN JOURNAL OF CLINICAL PATHOLOGY. **3892**

0002-919X See AMERICAN JOURNAL OF COMPARATIVE LAW, THE. **3123**

0002-922X See AMERICAN JOURNAL OF DISEASES OF CHILDREN (1960). **3899**

0002-9238 See AMERICAN JOURNAL OF EEG TECHNOLOGY, THE. **3827**

0002-9246 See AMERICAN JOURNAL OF ECONOMICS AND SOCIOLOGY, THE. **5190**

0002-9254 See AMERICAN JOURNAL OF ENOLOGY AND VITICULTURE. **2363**

0002-9262 See AMERICAN JOURNAL OF EPIDEMIOLOGY. **3734**

0002-9270 See AMERICAN JOURNAL OF GASTROENTEROLOGY, THE. **3743**

0002-9289 See AMERICAN JOURNAL OF HOSPITAL PHARMACY. **4290**

0002-9297 See AMERICAN JOURNAL OF HUMAN GENETICS. **542**

0002-9300 See AMERICAN JOURNAL OF INTERNATIONAL LAW, THE. **3123**

0002-9319 See AMERICAN JOURNAL OF LEGAL HISTORY, THE. **2932**

0002-9327 See AMERICAN JOURNAL OF MATHEMATICS. **3492**

0002-9343 See AMERICAN JOURNAL OF MEDICINE, THE. **3548**

0002-936X See AMERICAN JOURNAL OF NURSING, THE. **3850**

0002-9378 See AMERICAN JOURNAL OF OBSTETRICS AND GYNECOLOGY. **3756**

0002-9394 See AMERICAN JOURNAL OF OPHTHALMOLOGY. **3871**

0002-9432 See AMERICAN JOURNAL OF ORTHOPSYCHIATRY. **3919**

0002-9440 See AMERICAN JOURNAL OF PATHOLOGY, THE. **3892**

0002-9459 See AMERICAN JOURNAL OF PHARMACEUTICAL EDUCATION. **4290**

0002-9475 See AMERICAN JOURNAL OF PHILOLOGY. **1073**

0002-9483 See AMERICAN JOURNAL OF PHYSICAL ANTHROPOLOGY. **228**

0002-9505 See AMERICAN JOURNAL OF PHYSICS. **4396**

0002-9513 See AMERICAN JOURNAL OF PHYSIOLOGY. **577**

0002-953X See AMERICAN JOURNAL OF PSYCHIATRY, THE. **3920**

0002-9548 See AMERICAN JOURNAL OF PSYCHOANALYSIS. **3920**

0002-9556 See AMERICAN JOURNAL OF PSYCHOLOGY, THE. **4573**

0002-9564 See AMERICAN JOURNAL OF PSYCHOTHERAPY. **3920**

0002-9599 See AMERICAN JOURNAL OF SCIENCE (1880). **5082**

0002-9602 See AMERICAN JOURNAL OF SOCIOLOGY. **5238**

0002-9610 See AMERICAN JOURNAL OF SURGERY, THE. **3958**

0002-9629 See AMERICAN JOURNAL OF THE MEDICAL SCIENCES, THE. **3549**

0002-9637 See AMERICAN JOURNAL OF TROPICAL MEDICINE AND HYGIENE, THE. **3985**

0002-9645 See AMERICAN JOURNAL OF VETERINARY RESEARCH. **5502**

0002-967X See JOURNAL OF THE AMERICAN KILLIFISH ASSOCIATION, THE. **2307**

0002-9718 See AMERICAN LAUNDRY DIGEST. **5347**

0002-9726 See JOURNAL OF THE AMERICAN LEATHER CHEMISTS ASSOCIATION, THE. **3184**

0002-9769 See AMERICAN LIBRARIES (CHICAGO, ILL.). **3189**

0002-9823 See AMERICAN LITERARY REALISM, 1870-1910. **3337**

0002-9831 See AMERICAN LITERATURE. **3360**

0002-9866 See AMERICAN MARINE ENGINEER, THE. **4174**

0002-9890 See AMERICAN MATHEMATICAL MONTHLY, THE. **3492**

0002-9920 See NOTICES OF THE AMERICAN MATHEMATICAL SOCIETY. **3525**

0002-9939 See PROCEEDINGS OF THE AMERICAN MATHEMATICAL SOCIETY. **3528**

0002-9947 See TRANSACTIONS OF THE AMERICAN MATHEMATICAL SOCIETY. **3539**

0002-998X See AMERICAN MERCURY (1951), THE. **2527**

0003-0007 See BULLETIN OF THE AMERICAN METEOROLOGICAL SOCIETY. **1421**

0003-0031 See AMERICAN MIDLAND NATURALIST, THE. **4161**

0003-004X See AMERICAN MINERALOGIST, THE. **1437**

0003-0066 See AMERICAN MOTOR CARRIER. **5375**

0003-0082 See AMERICAN MUSEUM NOVITATES. **5574**

0003-0090 See BULLETIN OF THE AMERICAN MUSEUM OF NATURAL HISTORY. **4164**

0003-0112 See AMERICAN MUSIC TEACHER, THE. **4099**

0003-0139 See JOURNAL OF THE AMERICAN MUSICOLOGICAL SOCIETY. **4126**

0003-0147 See AMERICAN NATURALIST, THE. **4161**

0003-0155 See AMERICAN NEPTUNE, THE. **4174**

0003-018X See TRANSACTIONS OF THE AMERICAN NUCLEAR SOCIETY. **2159**

0003-0198 See AMERICAN NURSERYMAN. **2408**

0003-021X See JOURNAL OF THE AMERICAN OIL CHEMISTS' SOCIETY. **1043**

0003-0228 See AMERICAN OLD TIME FIDDLERS' NEWS. **4099**

0003-0244 See JOURNAL OF THE AMERICAN OPTOMETRIC ASSOCIATION. **4216**

0003-0252 See AMERICAN ORCHID SOCIETY BULLETIN. **2408**

0003-0279 See JOURNAL OF THE AMERICAN ORIENTAL SOCIETY. **3292**

0003-0295 See AMERICAN OXONIAN, THE. **1808**

0003-0325 See AMERICAN PAINTING CONTRACTOR. **4222**

0003-0376 See AMERICAN PEN, THE. **3360**

0003-0422 See ABSTRACTS OF REFINING LITERATURE. **4283**

0003-0473 See AMERICAN PHILATELIST, THE. **2784**

0003-0481 See AMERICAN PHILOSOPHICAL QUARTERLY (OXFORD). **4340**

0003-049X See PROCEEDINGS OF THE AMERICAN PHILOSOPHICAL SOCIETY. **4357**

0003-0503 See BULLETIN OF THE AMERICAN PHYSICAL SOCIETY. **4399**

0003-0511 See AMERICAN PIGEON JOURNAL. **5574**

0003-0554 See AMERICAN POLITICAL SCIENCE REVIEW, THE. **4463**

0003-0589 See AMERICAN POTATO JOURNAL. **162**

0003-0627 See PHARMACY TIMES. **4323**

0003-0651 See JOURNAL OF THE AMERICAN PSYCHOANALYTIC ASSOCIATION. **4601**

0003-066X See AMERICAN PSYCHOLOGIST, THE. **4573**

0003-0678 See AMERICAN QUARTERLY. **2719**

0003-0686 See AMERICAN RACING PIGEON NEWS, THE. **58**

0003-0686 See AMERICAN RACING PIGEON NEWS, THE. **225**

0003-0694 See BULLETIN - AMERICAN RAILWAY ENGINEERING ASSOCIATION. **5430**

0003-0708 See AMERICAN RATIONALIST, THE. **4340**

0003-0716 See AMERICAN RECORD GUIDE. **5315**

0003-0724 See AMERICAN RECORDER, THE. **4099**

0003-0805 See AMERICAN REVIEW OF RESPIRATORY DISEASE, THE. **3948**

0003-083X See AMERICAN RIFLEMAN. **4883**

0003-0864 See BULLETIN OF THE AMERICAN ROCK GARDEN SOCIETY. **2411**

0003-0902 See AMERICAN SALESMAN, THE. **859**

0003-0937 See AMERICAN SCHOLAR, THE. **2484**

0003-0945 See AMERICAN SCHOOL & UNIVERSITY. **1860**

0003-0953 See AMERICAN SCHOOL BOARD JOURNAL, THE. **1860**

0003-097X See BULLETIN OF THE AMERICAN SCHOOLS OF ORIENTAL RESEARCH. **264**

0003-0996 See AMERICAN SCIENTIST. **5082**

0003-1003 See AMERICAN SECONDARY EDUCATION. **1724**

0003-102X See AMERICAN SEPHARDI, THE. **5045**

0003-1038 See AMERICAN SHOEMAKING. **3183**

0003-1062 See JOURNAL OF THE AMERICAN SOCIETY FOR HORTICULTURAL SCIENCE. **2421**

0003-1070 See JOURNAL OF THE AMERICAN SOCIETY FOR PSYCHICAL RESEARCH (1932). **4242**

0003-116X See JOURNAL OF THE AMERICAN SOCIETY OF FARM MANAGERS AND RURAL APPRAISERS. **101**

0003-1178 See BULLETIN OF THE AMERICAN SOCIETY OF NEWSPAPER EDITORS, THE. **2917**

0003-1186 See BULLETIN OF THE AMERICAN SOCIETY OF PAPYROLOGISTS, THE. **264**

0003-1224 See AMERICAN SOCIOLOGICAL REVIEW. **5238**

0003-1232 See AMERICAN SOCIOLOGIST, THE. **5239**

0003-1283 See AMERICAN SPEECH. **3263**

0003-1305 See AMERICAN STATISTICIAN, THE. **5320**

0003-1313 See AMERICAN STRING TEACHER. **4100**

0003-1348 See AMERICAN SURGEON, THE. **3958**

0003-1380 See AMERICAN TEACHER. **1888**

0003-1399 See NEWSLETTER - AMERICAN THEOLOGICAL LIBRARY ASSOCIATION. **3235**

0003-1402 See AMERICAN THEOSOPHIST, THE. **4934**

0003-1445 See AMERICAN TURF MONTHLY. **2796**

0003-1453 See AMERICAN UNIVERSITY LAW REVIEW, THE. **2933**

0003-1488 See JOURNAL OF THE AMERICAN VETERINARY MEDICAL ASSOCIATION. **5513**

0003-150X See JOURNAL / AMERICAN WATER WORKS ASSOCIATION. **5535**

0003-1518 See AMERICAN WAY (DALLAS, TEX.). **11**

0003-1542 See AMERICAN YOUTH. **1060**

0003-1550 See AMERICAN ZIONIST, THE. **2645**

0003-1569 See AMERICAN ZOOLOGIST. **5574**

0003-1593 See AMERICA'S FUTURE (NEW ROCHELLE, N.Y.). **4463**

0003-1615 See AMERICAS (WASHINGTON. 1944), THE. **2720**

0003-1771 See AMI COOP LIMOGES, L'. **1081**

0003-1844 See AMIS DES ROSES, LES. **2408**

0003-200X See AMPHORA. **4823**

0003-2018 See AMPLEFORTH JOURNAL, THE. **5023**

0003-2344 See AMUSEMENT BUSINESS. **4856**

0003-2409 See ANAESTHESIA. **3680**

0003-2417 See ANAESTHESIST, DER. **3681**

0003-2425 See ANAIS AZEVEDOS. **4290**

0003-2441 See ANAIS DE FARMACIA E QUIMICA DE SAO PAULO. **4290**

0003-2468 See ANALECTA BOLLANDIANA. **4934**

0003-2476 See ANALECTA CISTERCIENSIA. **5023**

0003-2476 See ANALECTA CISTERCIENSIA. **4934**

0003-2492 See ANALES DE BROMATOLOGIA. **4187**

0003-2506 See ANALES DE MECANICA Y ELECTRICIDAD. **2035**

0003-2573 See ANALISE SOCIAL. **5239**

0003-2638 See ANALYSIS (NEW YORK (N.Y.). **4340**

0003-2654 See ANALYST (LONDON). **1012**

0003-2670 See ANALYTICA CHIMICA ACTA. **1012**

0003-2689 See ANALYTICAL ABSTRACTS. **996**

0003-2697 See ANALYTICAL BIOCHEMISTRY. 479

0003-2700 See ANALYTICAL CHEMISTRY (WASHINGTON). 1013

0003-2719 See ANALYTICAL LETTERS. 1013

0003-2751 See ANARCHY. 4539

0003-276X See ANATOMICAL RECORD, THE. 3678

0003-2778 See JOURNAL OF THE ANATOMICAL SOCIETY OF INDIA. 3679

0003-2786 See ANATOMISCHER ANZEIGER. 3678

0003-2956 See ANDHRA AGRICULTURAL JOURNAL, THE. 58

0003-2980 See ANDREWS UNIVERSITY SEMINARY STUDIES. 4934

0003-2999 See ANESTHESIA AND ANALGESIA. 3681

0003-3006 See ANESTHESIA PROGRESS. 1316

0003-3022 See ANESTHESIOLOGY (PHILADELPHIA). 3681

0003-3049 See ANGEIOLOGIE. 3549

0003-3081 See ANGELICUM. 4340

0003-3146 See ANGEWANDTE MAKROMOLEKULARE CHEMIE. 4454

0003-3162 See ANGEWANDTE PARASITOLOGIE. 5575

0003-3170 See ANGIOLOGIA. 3698

0003-3197 See ANGIOLOGY. 3794

0003-3219 See ANGLE ORTHODONTIST, THE. 1316

0003-3278 See ANGLICAN DIGEST, THE. 5055

0003-3286 See ANGLICAN THEOLOGICAL REVIEW. 4934

0003-343X See RELATORIOS E COMUNICOES - INSTITUTO DE INVESTIGACAO CIENTIFICA DE ANGOLA. 5145

0003-3464 See ANGORABOT & SYBOTHAAR -BLAD. 205

0003-3472 See ANIMAL BEHAVIOUR. 5575

0003-3499 See ANIMAL BREEDING ABSTRACTS. 151

0003-3561 See ANIMAL PRODUCTION. 205

0003-3588 See BANGLADESH JOURNAL OF ANIMAL SCIENCE. 5505

0003-3685 See VETERINER FAKULTESI DERGISI. 5527

0003-3790 See ANNALS OF SCIENCE. 5083

0003-3804 See ANNALEN DER PHYSIK. 4396

0003-3847 See ANNALES BOTANICI FENNICI. 499

0003-3898 See ANNALES DE BIOLOGIE CLINIQUE (PARIS). 3892

0003-3901 See ANNALES DE BOURGOGNE. 2674

0003-3928 See ANNALES DE CARDIOLOGIE ET D'ANGEIOLOGIE. 3698

0003-3944 See ANNALES DE CHIRURGIE. 3958

0003-3960 See ANNALES DE CHIRURGIE PLASTIQUE ET ESTHETIQUE. 3959

0003-3995 See ANNALES DE GENETIQUE. 542

0003-4010 See ANNALES DE GEOGRAPHIE. 2553

0003-4088 See ANNALES DE LIMNOLOGIE. 1412

0003-410X See ANNALES DE MEDECINE INTERNE. 3794

0003-4118 See ANNALES DE MEDECINE VETERINAIRE. 5503

0003-4134 See ANNALES DE NORMANDIE. 2674

0003-4150 See ANNALES DE PARASITOLOGIE HUMAINE ET COMPAREE. 441

0003-4169 See ANNALES DE PHYSIQUE (PARIS). 4397

0003-4185 See ANNALES DE RADIOLOGIE. 3938

0003-4193 See ANNALES DE RECHERCHES VETERINAIRES. 5503

0003-4215 See ANNALES DE SPELEOLOGIE. 1402

0003-424X See ANNALES DE ZOOTECHNIE. 5575

0003-4266 See ANNALES D'ENDOCRINOLOGIE. 3726

0003-4290 See ANNALES DES MINES DE BELGIQUE. 2133

0003-4312 See ANNALES DES SCIENCES FORESTIERES. 2374

0003-4320 See ANNALES DES SCIENCES NATURELLES. 499

0003-4339 See ANNALES DES SCIENCES NATURELLES. ZOOLOGIE ET BIOLOGIE ANIMALE. 5575

0003-4347 See ANNALES DES TELECOMMUNICATIONS. 1148

0003-438X See ANNALES D'OTO-LARYNGOLOGIE ET DE CHIRURGIE CERVICO FACIALE : BULLETIN DE LA SOCIETE D'OTO-LARYNGOLOGIE DES HOPITAUX DE PARIS. 3886

0003-4398 See ANNALES DU MIDI. 255

0003-4401 See ANNALES D'UROLOGIE. 3988

0003-4436 See ANNALES HISTORIQUES DE LA REVOLUTION FRANCAISE. 2674

0003-4452 See ANNALES INTERNATIONALES DE CRIMINOLOGIE. 3156

0003-4487 See ANNALES MEDICO PSYCHOLOGIQUES. 4573

0003-4495 See SHONIKA KIYO. 3911

0003-4509 See ANNALES PHARMACEUTIQUES FRANCAISES. 4291

0003-4541 See ANNALES ZOOLOGICI. 5575

0003-4592 See ANNALI DI CHIMICA. 961

0003-4630 See ANNALI DI MEDICINA NAVALE. 3550

0003-4649 See ANNALI DI MICROBIOLOGIA ED ENZIMOLOGIA. 558

0003-4665 See ANNALI DI OTTALMOLOGIA E CLINICA OCULISTICA. 3872

0003-469X See ANNALI ITALIANI DI CHIRURGIA. 3959

0003-472X See ANNALI SCLAVO. 558

0003-472X See ANNALI SCLAVO. COLLANA MONOGRAFICA. 3666

0003-4738 See ANNALS OF ALLERGY. 3666

0003-4746 See ANNALS OF APPLIED BIOLOGY. 442

0003-4770 See ANNALS OF DENTISTRY. 1316

0003-4800 See ANNALS OF HUMAN GENETICS. 542

0003-4819 See ANNALS OF INTERNAL MEDICINE. 3794

0003-4827 See ANNALS OF IOWA. 2720

0003-4835 See ANNALS OF LIBRARY SCIENCE AND DOCUMENTATION. 3190

0003-486X See ANNALS OF MATHEMATICS. 3494

0003-4878 See ANNALS OF OCCUPATIONAL HYGIENE, THE. 2858

0003-4886 See ANNALS OF OPHTHALMOLOGY (BIRMINGHAM). 3872

0003-4894 See ANNALS OF OTOLOGY, RHINOLOGY & LARYNGOLOGY, THE. 3886

0003-4916 See ANNALS OF PHYSICS. 4397

0003-4932 See ANNALS OF SURGERY. 3959

0003-4967 See ANNALS OF THE RHEUMATIC DISEASES. 3802

0003-4975 See ANNALS OF THORACIC SURGERY, THE. 3959

0003-4983 See ANNALS OF TROPICAL MEDICINE AND PARASITOLOGY. 3985

0003-4991 See ANNALS OF WYOMING. 2720

0003-5017 See ANNEE BIOLOGIQUE, L'. 442

0003-5033 See ANNEE PSYCHOLOGIQUE, L'. 4574

0003-5130 See DOBUTSU SHINRIGAKU NENPO. 4585

0003-5149 See ANNUARIO DI DIRITTO COMPARATO E DI STUDI LEGISLATIVI. 3123

0003-5157 See ANNUARIUM HISTORIAE CONCILIORUM. 2610

0003-5238 See ANSCHNITT, DER. 2134

0003-5246 See ANSEARCHIN' NEWS. 2437

0003-5319 See ANTUS. 3362

0003-5327 See ANTARCTIC. 1351

0003-5335 See ANTARCTIC JOURNAL OF THE UNITED STATES. 2554

0003-5424 See ANTHOS; GARTEN- UND LANDSCHAFTSGESTALTUNG. 2409

0003-5459 See ANTHROPOLOGICA (OTTAWA). 228

0003-5467 See ANTHROPOLOGICAL INDEX TO CURRENT PERIODICALS IN THE LIBRARY OF THE ROYAL ANTHROPOLOGICAL INSTITUTE. 248

0003-5483 See ANTHROPOLOGICAL LINGUISTICS. 229

0003-5491 See ANTHROPOLOGICAL QUARTERLY. 229

0003-5505 See JINRUIGAKU ZASSHI. JOURNAL OF THE ANTHROPOLOGICAL SOCIETY OF NIPPON. 238

0003-5521 See ANTHROPOLOGIE (PARIS). 229

0003-553X See ANTHROPOLOGIE : INTERNATIONAL JOURNAL FOR THE SCIENCE OF MAN. 229

0003-5548 See ANTHROPOLOGISCHER ANZEIGER. 229

0003-5564 See ANTHROPOLOGY UCLA. 230

0003-5599 See ANTI-CORROSION METHODS AND MATERIALS. 2008

0003-5629 See ANTIBIOTICA. 559

0003-5645 See ANTICHITA VIVA. 337

0003-5653 See ANTIEK. 337

0003-5661 See ANTIGONISH REVIEW, THE. 3337

0003-5688 See ANTIKE KUNST. 255

0003-5696 See ANTIKE UND ABENDLAND. 1074

0003-570X See ANTIKE WELT. 2610

0003-5769 See ANTIOCH REVIEW, THE. 3337

0003-5785 See ANTIQUARIAN HOROLOGY AND THE PROCEEDINGS OF THE ANTIQUARIAN HOROLOGICAL SOCIETY. 2916

0003-5815 See ANTIQUARIES JOURNAL. 255

0003-5831 See ANTIQUE AUTOMOBILE, THE. 5404

0003-5858 See ANTIQUE COLLECTOR, THE. 249

0003-5866 See ANTIQUE DEALER AND COLLECTORS' GUIDE. 249

0003-598X See ANTIQUITY. 255

0003-5998 See ANTISEPTIC, THE. 3551

0003-6021 See ANTITRUST & TRADE REGULATION REPORT. 3095

0003-603X See ANTITRUST BULLETIN. 3095

0003-6048 See ANTITRUST LAW & ECONOMICS REVIEW. 3095

0003-6056 See ANTITRUST LAW JOURNAL. 3096

0003-6064 See ANTONIANUM. 4935

0003-6072 See ANTONIE VAN LEEUWENHOEK. 559

0003-6102 See ANTROPOLOGIA E HISTORIA DE GUATEMALA. 2721

0003-6110 See ANTROPOLOGICA. 231

0003-6277 See BUCH. 4827

0003-6293 See ANZEIGER FUER DIE ALTERTUMSWISSENSCHAFT. 256

0003-6390 See APEIRON (CLAYTON). 1074

0003-6420 See APERTURE (MILLERTON, N.Y.). 4366

0003-6439 See APEX. 1316

0003-6455 See APIACTA. 62

0003-648X See APICULTURAL ABSTRACTS. 5604

0003-6536 See APOLLO (LONDON. 1925). 337

0003-6560 See APOTHECARY (BOSTON), THE. 4292

0003-6579 See APOTHEKERSBLAD, HET. 4292

0003-6587 See APPALACHIA (BOSTON). 4869

0003-6595 See APPALACHIA (WASHINGTON). 1463

0003-6609 See APPALACHIA MEDICINE. 3551

0003-6625 See APPALACHIAN OUTLOOK. 407

0003-6641 See APPALACHIAN TRAILWAY NEWS. 4869

0003-6765 See APPLE (SPRINGFIELD). 3460

0003-6781 See APPLIANCE. 2810

0003-679X See APPLIANCE MANUFACTURER. 2810

0003-6803 See APPLIANCE SERVICE NEWS. 2810

0003-6811 See APPLICABLE ANALYSIS. 3494

0003-682X See APPLIED ACOUSTICS. 2097

0003-6838 See APPLIED BIOCHEMISTRY AND MICROBIOLOGY. 480
0003-6846 See APPLIED ECONOMICS. 1463
0003-6862 See APPLIED ENTOMOLOGY AND ZOOLOGY. 5605
0003-6870 See APPLIED ERGONOMICS. 1965
0003-6900 See APPLIED MECHANICS REVIEWS. 2002
0003-6935 See APPLIED OPTICS. 4433
0003-6951 See APPLIED PHYSICS LETTERS. 4397
0003-6986 See APPLIED SCIENCE & TECHNOLOGY INDEX. 5173
0003-6994 See APPLIED SCIENTIFIC RESEARCH. 2109
0003-701X See APPLIED SOLAR ENERGY. 1932
0003-7028 See APPLIED SPECTROSCOPY. 4433
0003-7052 See APPRAISAL. 5085
0003-7060 See APPRAISAL DIGEST. 4834
0003-7087 See APPRAISAL JOURNAL, THE. 4834
0003-7095 See APPRAISER NEWS. 4834
0003-7117 See APUROCHI. APPROACH. 599
0003-7176 See APRES-DEMAIN. 4464
0003-7214 See AQUA (LONDON). 5530
0003-7214 See JOURNAL OF WATER SUPPLY RESEARCH AND TECHNOLOGY - AQUA. 5535
0003-7273 See AQUARIST AND PONDKEEPER. 2296
0003-7303 See AQUARIUS. 3460
0003-7362 See AQUINAS. 4341
0003-7494 See ARABIAN HORSE WORLD. 2797
0003-7583 See ARARAT (NEW YORK). 3363
0003-7648 See ARBEIT UND RECHT. 3144
0003-7761 See ARBEITSRECHT IN STICHWORTEN. 1651
0003-780X See AV. DIE ARBEITSVORBEREITUNG. 5087
0003-7877 See ARBITRATION (LONDON, ENGLAND). 2936
0003-7885 See ARBITRATION IN THE SCHOOLS. 1726
0003-7893 See ARBITRATION JOURNAL, THE. 2936
0003-794X See ARBORICULTURE FRUITIERE, L'. 163
0003-7982 See ARCADIA. 3363
0003-8008 See ARCHAEOLOGIA AUSTRIACA. 256
0003-8032 See ARCHOLOGIAI ERTESITO. 259
0003-8067 See BULLETIN OF THE ARCHAEOLOGICAL SOCIETY OF DELAWARE. 264
0003-8075 See KOKOGAKU ZASSHI. 272
0003-8105 See ARCHAOLOGISCHER ANZEIGER. 258
0003-8113 See ARCHAEOLOGY. 257
0003-813X See ARCHAEOMETRY. 257
0003-8164 See ARCHEOLOGIA (ROMA). 258
0003-8180 See ARCHEOLOGIA POLSKI. 258
0003-8202 See QUARTERLY BULLETIN - ARCHEOLOGICAL SOCIETY OF VIRGINIA. 280
0003-8210 See ARCHEOLOGIE BRUXELLES. 259
0003-8237 See ARCHER (CAMAS VALLEY, OR.), THE. 4884
0003-8326 See TRAJECTA. 5037
0003-8369 See ARCHIMEDE. 3495
0003-8393 See ARCHITECT, W.A. : THE OFFICIAL JOURNAL OF THE ROYAL AUSTRALIAN INSTITUTE OF ARCHITECTS, W.A. CHAPTER, THE. 288
0003-8407 See ARCHITECT AND BUILDER. 288
0003-8423 See ARCHITECT AND CONTRACTOR. 288
0003-8466 See ARCHITECTS' JOURNAL (LONDON). 288
0003-8490 See KENCHIKU BUNKA. 302
0003-8504 See ARCHITECTURAL DESIGN. 288
0003-8520 See ARCHITECTURAL DIGEST (LOS ANGELES, CALIF.). 289
0003-858X See ARCHITECTURAL RECORD. 289

0003-861X See ARCHITECTURAL REVIEW (LONDON). 289
0003-8628 See ARCHITECTURAL SCIENCE REVIEW. 289
0003-8687 See ARCHITECTURE CONCEPT. 290
0003-8695 See ARCHITECTURE D'AUJOURD'HUI, L'. 290
0003-8725 See ARCHITECTURE AUSTRALIA. 289
0003-8733 See ARCHITECTURE NEW JERSEY. 290
0003-875X See ARCHITEKT (STUTTGART), DER. 290
0003-8822 See ARCHITETTO, L'. 291
0003-8830 See ARCHITETTURA, L'. 291
0003-889X See ARCHIV DER MATHEMATIK. 3495
0003-8911 See ARCHIV DES OFFENTLICHEN RECHTS. 3092
0003-892X See ARCHIV DES VOLKERRECHTS. 3124
0003-8946 See ARCHIV FUER BEGRIFFSGESCHICHTE. 4341
0003-8970 See ARCHIV FUR DAS STUDIUM DER NEUEREN SPRACHEN UND LITERATUREN (1961). 3266
0003-8989 See ARCHIV FUER DEUTSCHE POSTGESCHICHTE. 1144
0003-8997 See ARCHIV FUER DIE CIVILISTISCHE PRAXIS. 3088
0003-9039 See ARCHIV FUER ELEKTROTECHNIK (BERLIN). 2036
0003-9055 See ARCHIV FUER EXPERIMENTELLE VETERINAERMEDIZIN. 5504
0003-9063 See ARCHIV FUER FISCHEREIWISSENSCHAFT. 2296
0003-9098 See ARCHIV FUER GEFLUGELKUNDE. 206
0003-9101 See ARCHIV FUER GESCHICHTE DER PHILOSOPHIE. 4341
0003-9101 See ARCHIV FUER GESCHICHTE DER PHILOSOPHIE. 4341
0003-9136 See ARCHIV FUER HYDROBIOLOGIE. 5530
0003-9152 See ARCHIV FUER JAPANISCHE CHIRURGIE. NIPPON GEKA HOKAN. 3959
0003-9160 See ARCHIV FUER KATHOLISCHES KIRCHENRECHT. 2936
0003-9209 See ARCHIV FUER KOMMUNALWISSENSCHAFTEN. 4630
0003-9225 See ARCHIV FUER KRIMINOLOGIE. 3158
0003-9233 See ARCHIV FUER KULTURGESCHICHTE. 2610
0003-925X See ARCHIV FUER LEBENSMITTELHYGIENE. 2327
0003-9284 See ARCHIV FUER MOLLUSKENKUNDE DER SENCKENBERGISCHE NATURFORSCHENDE GESELLSCHAFT. 5576
0003-9292 See ARCHIV FUER MUSIKWISSENSCHAFT. 4100
0003-9306 See ARCHIV FUER NATURSCHUTZ UND LANDSCHAFTSFORSCHUNG. 2187
0003-9322 See ARCHIV FUER OSTERREICHISCHE GESCHICHTE. 2676
0003-9357 See ZEITSCHRIFT FUER PHYSIOTHERAPIE. 4382
0003-9365 See ARCHIV FUER PROTISTENKUNDE. 5576
0003-9381 See ARCHIV FUER REFORMATIONSGESCHICHTE. 2676
0003-9403 See ARCHIV FUR SIPPENFORSCHUNG UND ALLE VERWANDTEN GEBIETE. 2437
0003-942X See ARCHIV FUER TIERERNAHRUNG. 5504
0003-9438 See ARCHIV FUER TIERZUCHT. 206
0003-9462 See ARCHIV FUER VATERLANDISCHE GESCHICHTE UND TOPOGRAPHIE. HRSG. VON DEM GESCHICHTVEREINE FUER KARNTEN. UNTER VERANTWORTLICHER REDACTION DES VEREINS-AUSSCHUSSES. 2676
0003-9497 See ARCHIVALISCHE ZEITSCHRIFT. 2479

0003-9500 See ARCHIVAR, DER. 2479
0003-9519 See ARCHIVE FOR HISTORY OF EXACT SCIENCES. 5085
0003-9527 See ARCHIVE FOR RATIONAL MECHANICS AND ANALYSIS. 4427
0003-9535 See ARCHIVES (LONDON). 2479
0003-9578 See ARCHIVES BELGES DE MEDECINE SOCIALE HYGIENE, MEDECINE DU TRAVAIL ET MEDECINE LEGALE. 3552
0003-9632 See ARCHIVES DE PHILOSOPHIE. 4341
0003-9640 See ARCHIVES DE PSYCHOLOGIE. 4575
0003-9675 See ARCHIVES DES LETTRES MODERNES. 3363
0003-9683 See ARCHIVES DES MALADIES DU COEUR ET DES VAISSEAUX. 3699
0003-9691 See ARCHIVES DES MALADIES PROFESSIONNELLES DE MEDECINE DU TRAVAIL ET SECURITE SOCIALE. 3552
0003-9748 See ARCHIVES ET BIBLIOTHEQUES DE BELGIQUE. 2479
0003-9756 See ARCHIVES EUROPEENNES DE SOCIOLOGIE. 5240
0003-9764 See ARCHIVES FRANCAISES DE PEDIATRIE. 3900
0003-9780 See ARCHIVES INTERNATIONALES DE PHARMACODYNAMIE ET DE THERAPIE. 4292
0003-9799 See ARCHIVES INTERNATIONALES DE PHYSIOLOGIE, DE BIOCHIMIE ET DE BIOPHYSIQUE. 578
0003-9810 See ARCHIVES INTERNATIONALES D'HISTOIRE DES SCIENCES. 5085
0003-9829 See ARCHIVES ITALIENNES DE BIOLOGIE. 442
0003-9853 See JOURNAL - ARCHIVES OF AMERICAN ART. 354
0003-9861 See ARCHIVES OF BIOCHEMISTRY AND BIOPHYSICS. 480
0003-987X See ARCHIVES OF DERMATOLOGY. 3718
0003-9888 See ARCHIVES OF DISEASE IN CHILDHOOD. 3900
0003-9896 See ARCHIVES OF ENVIRONMENTAL HEALTH. 4767
0003-990X See ARCHIVES OF GENERAL PSYCHIATRY. 3921
0003-9926 See ARCHIVES OF INTERNAL MEDICINE (1960). 3795
0003-9942 See ARCHIVES OF NEUROLOGY (CHICAGO). 3827
0003-9950 See ARCHIVES OF OPHTHALMOLOGY. 3872
0003-9969 See ARCHIVES OF ORAL BIOLOGY. 1316
0003-9985 See ARCHIVES OF PATHOLOGY & LABORATORY MEDICINE. 3893
0003-9993 See ARCHIVES OF PHYSICAL MEDICINE AND REHABILITATION. 4379
0004-0002 See ARCHIVES OF SEXUAL BEHAVIOR. 5186
0004-0010 See ARCHIVES OF SURGERY (CHICAGO. 1960). 3959
0004-0037 See ROUMANIAN ARCHIVES OF MICROBIOLOGY AND IMMUNOLOGY. 3676
0004-007X See ARCHIVIO DI CHIRURGIA TORACICA E CARDIOVASCOLARE. 3960
0004-0088 See ARCHIVIO DI FILOSOFIA. 4341
0004-0096 See ARCHIVIO DI FISIOLOGIA. 578
0004-010X See ARCHIVIO DI MEDICINA INTERNA PARMA. 3795
0004-0126 See ARCHIVIO DI OSTETRICIA E GINECOLOGIA. 3757
0004-0150 See ARCHIVIO DI PSICOLOGIA, NEUROLOGIA E PSICHIATRIA. 4575
0004-0177 See ARCHIVIO DI STUDI URBANI E REGIONALI. 2815
0004-0207 See ARCHIVIO GLOTTOLOGICO ITALIANO. 3266
0004-0223 See ARCHIVIO ITALIANO DI ANATOMIA E DI EMBRIOLOGIA. 3678
0004-0266 See ARCHIVIO ITALIANO DI PATOLOGIA E CLINICA DEI TUMORI. 3809

0004-0282 See ARCHIVIO ITALIANO DI SCIENZE MEDICHE TROPICALI E DI PARASSITOLOGIA. 3552

0004-0304 See ARCHIVIO PENALE. 2936

0004-0320 See ARCHIVIO STOMATOLOGICO. 1316

0004-0347 See ARCHIVIO STORICO LODIGIANO. 2611

0004-0355 See ARCHIVIO STORICO PER LA CALABRIA E LA LUCANIA. 2676

0004-0363 See ARCHIVIO STORICO PER LA SICILIA ORIENTALE. 2676

0004-038X See ARCHIVMITTEILUNGEN. 2480

0004-0398 See ARCHIVNI CASOPIS. 2480

0004-0428 See ARCHIVO ESPANOL DE ARTE. 337

0004-0452 See ARCHIVO IBERO-AMERICANO. 2721

0004-0479 See ARCHIVIO VETERINARIO ITALIANO. 5504

0004-0533 See ARCHIVOS DE BIOLOGIA Y MEDICINA EXPERIMENTALES. 442

0004-0576 See ARCHIVOS DE NEUROBIOLOGIA. 3827

0004-0592 See ARCHIVOS DE ZOOTECNIA. 206

0004-0606 See ARCHIVOS DOMINICANOS DE PEDIATRIA. 3900

0004-0614 See ARCHIVOS ESPANOLES DE UROLOGIA. 3988

0004-0622 See ARCHIVOS LATINOAMERICANOS DE NUTRICION. 4187

0004-0630 See ARCHIVOS LEONESES. 2480

0004-0665 See ARCHIVUM FRANCISCANUM HISTORICUM. 5024

0004-0738 See ARCHIWUM BUDOWY MASZYN. 2110

0004-0746 See ARCHIWUM ELEKTROTECHNIKI. 2036

0004-0754 See ARCHIWUM GORNICTWA. 2134

0004-0770 See ARCHIWUM HUTNICTWA. 3998

0004-0789 See ARCHIWUM HYDROTECHNIKI. 2087

0004-0843 See ARCTIC. 2555

0004-0851 See ARCTIC AND ALPINE RESEARCH. 2555

0004-0894 See AREA (LONDON 1969). 2555

0004-0916 See AREA TRENDS IN EMPLOYMENT AND UNEMPLOYMENT. 1652

0004-0932 See ARENA. 4464

0004-0975 See ARETHUSA. 1074

0004-1157 See ARGUMENT, DAS. 4341

0004-1238 See ARHITEKTURA, URBANIZAM. 291

0004-1254 See ARHIV ZA HIGIJENU RADA I TOKSIKOLOGIJU. 2859

0004-1262 See ARHIV ZA POLJOPRIVREDNE NAUKE. 62

0004-1289 See ARHIV ZA ZASTITU MAJKE I DJETETA. 3757

0004-1327 See ARIEL. 3363

0004-1343 See ARIEL (ENGLISH EDITION). 3363

0004-136X See ARITHMETIC TEACHER, THE. 3496

0004-1386 See ARIZONA ADVOCATE. 2936

0004-1416 See ARIZONA ARCHITECT. 291

0004-1459 See ARIZONA DENTAL JOURNAL. 1316

0004-1483 See ARIZONA ENGLISH BULLETIN. 3267

0004-1505 See ARIZONA GROCER. 2327

0004-1521 See ARIZONA HIGHWAYS. 5461

0004-153X See ARIZONA LAW REVIEW. 2937

0004-1564 See ARIZONA MOBILE CITIZEN. 2815

0004-1599 See ARIZONA NURSE. 3851

0004-1602 See ARIZONA PHARMACIST, THE. 4292

0004-1610 See ARIZONA QUARTERLY, THE. 3363

0004-1629 See ARIZONA REVIEW. 639

0004-1718 See ARKANSAS ARCHAEOLOGIST, THE. 259

0004-1726 See ARKANSAS BANKER, THE. 773

0004-1742 See ARKANSAS BUSINESS AND ECONOMIC REVIEW. 639

0004-1750 See ARKANSAS CATTLE BUSINESS. 206

0004-1769 See ARKANSAS DENTISTRY. 1316

0004-1785 See ARKANSAS FARM RESEARCH. 62

0004-1807 See ARKANSAS WILDLIFE. 2187

0004-1815 See ARKANSAS GROCER. 2327

0004-1823 See ARKANSAS HISTORICAL QUARTERLY, THE. 2721

0004-1831 See ARKANSAS LAW REVIEW. 2937

0004-184X See ARKANSAS LIBRARIES. 3191

0004-1858 See JOURNAL OF THE ARKANSAS MEDICAL SOCIETY, THE. 3598

0004-1882 See ARKA TECH. 1089

0004-1890 See ARKANSAS VALLEY JOURNAL. 63

0004-1920 See ARKHIMEDES. 3496

0004-1947 See ARKHIV ANATOMII, GISTOLOGII I EMBRIOLOGII. 3679

0004-1955 See ARHIV PATOLOGIJ. 3893

0004-1963 See ARHIV ZA FARMACIJU. 4292

0004-198X See ARKITEKTEN. 291

0004-1998 See ARKITEKTNYTT. 292

0004-2013 See ARKITEKTUR DK. 292

0004-2021 See ARKITEKTUR (STOCKHOLM, SWEDEN : 1959). 292

0004-203X See ARKIV. 2480

0004-2056 See CHEMICA SCRIPTA. 967

0004-2072 See ARKIV FOR LUFTRETT. 2937

0004-2080 See ARKIV FUER MATEMATIK. 3496

0004-2129 See ARKKITEHTI. 292

0004-217X See ARMCHAIR DETECTIVE, THE. 3363

0004-2188 See ARMED FORCES COMPTROLLER, THE. 4035

0004-2242 See ARMEE ET DEFENSE. 4036

0004-2293 See ARMENIA TODAY. 2255

0004-234X See ARMENIAN MIRROR-SPECTATOR, THE. 5687

0004-2366 See ARMENIAN REVIEW, THE. 2501

0004-2374 See ARMENIAN WEEKLY, THE. 5687

0004-2420 See ARMOR. 4036

0004-2439 See JOURNAL OF THE ARMS & ARMOUR SOCIETY, THE. 4048

0004-2455 See ARMY (WASHINGTON. 1956). 4037

0004-2463 See ARMY, AIR FORCE AND NAVAL AIR STATISTICAL RECORD. 4036

0004-248X See ARMY AVIATION. 12

0004-2528 See ARMY LOGISTICIAN. 4036

0004-2552 See ARMY QUARTERLY AND DEFENCE JOURNAL, THE. 4036

0004-2579 See ARMY RESERVE MAGAZINE. 4036

0004-2595 See ARMY TIMES. 4037

0004-2633 See ARNOLDIA (JAMAICA PLAIN). 2409

0004-2676 See ARQUITECTO PERUANO, EL. 292

0004-2684 See ARQUITECTURA/MEXICO. 292

0004-2706 See ARQUITECTURA (MADRID, 1959). 292

0004-2714 See ARQUIVIO DE PATOLOGIA. 3893

0004-2730 See ARQUIVOS BRASILEIROS DE ENDOCRINOLOGIA E METABOLOGIA. 3726

0004-2749 See ARQUIVOS BRASILEIROS DE OFTALMOLOGIA. 3872

0004-2773 See ARQUIVOS CATARINENSES DE MEDICINA. 3552

0004-2781 See ARQUIVOS DE ANGOLA. 2638

0004-2803 See ARQUIVOS DE GASTROENTEROLOGIA. 3743

0004-282X See ARQUIVOS DE NEURO-PSIQUIATRIA. 3827

0004-2838 See ARQUIVOS DO CENTRO DE ESTUDOS DO CURSO DE ODONTOLOGIA. UNIVERSIDADE FEDERAL DE MINAS GERAIS. 1316

0004-2870 See ARS AEQUI. 2937

0004-2889 See BUKKYO GEIJUTSU. 345

0004-2897 See ARS MEDICI, MONATSSCHRIFT FUER ALLGEMEINMEDIZIN. 3552

0004-2919 See ARS ORGANI. 4101

0004-2927 See ARS PHARMACEUTICA. 4292

0004-2994 See ART AND ARCHAEOLOGY TECHNICAL ABSTRACTS. 333

0004-301X See ART AND AUSTRALIA. 338

0004-3052 See SCHOLASTIC ART. 364

0004-3079 See ART BULLETIN (NEW YORK, N.Y.), THE. 338

0004-3109 See ART DIRECTION. 338

0004-3125 See ART EDUCATION (RESTON). 338

0004-3168 See ART & DECORATION. 338

0004-3184 See ART GALLERY, THE. 339

0004-3214 See ART IN AMERICA (1939). 339

0004-3222 See ART INDEX. CD-ROM. 334

0004-3222 See ART INDEX. 334

0004-3249 See ART JOURNAL (NEW YORK. 1960). 339

0004-3265 See ART MATERIAL TRADE NEWS. 339

0004-3273 See ARTNEWS. 314

0004-329X See ART OF THE AMERICAS BULLETIN. 340

0004-3354 See ARTA (BUCURESTI). 340

0004-3400 See ARTE CRISTIANA. 340

0004-3443 See ARTE LOMBARDA. 313

0004-3559 See ARTHA VIJNANA. 1546

0004-3567 See ARTHA-VIKAS. 1546

0004-3575 See ARTHANITI. 1590

0004-3591 See ARTHRITIS AND RHEUMATISM. 3803

0004-3648 See ARTIBUS ASIAE. 341

0004-3680 See ARTIFACT, THE. 260

0004-3702 See ARTIFICIAL INTELLIGENCE. 1211

0004-3788 See ARTILLERI-TIDSKRIFT. 4061

0004-3842 See ARTIS (KONSTANZ). 341

0004-3842 See ARTIS. 370

0004-3877 See ARTIST (LONDON. 1931). 341

0004-3931 See ARTS AND ACTIVITIES. 314

0004-3958 See ARTS ASIATIQUES (PARIS). 342

0004-4008 See ARTS & METIERS. 5086

0004-4032 See ARTS IN VIRGINIA. 315

0004-4059 See ARTS MAGAZINE (NEW YORK). 342

0004-4067 See ARTS MANAGEMENT. 315

0004-4091 See ARTS REVIEW. 315

0004-4121 See ARTWEEK (CASTRO VALLEY, CALIF.). 342

0004-4172 See ARZNEIMITTEL FORSCHUNG. 4292

0004-4210 See ASAHI GARASU KENKYU HOKOKU. 1021

0004-4229 See ASPAREZ. 5633

0004-4237 See ASBESTOS. 599

0004-4377 See ASHTREE ECHO. 2438

0004-4431 See ASIA CALLING. 2646

0004-4466 See ASIA LETTER, THE. 1463

0004-4474 See ASIA MAGAZINE, THE. 2501

0004-4482 See ASIA MAJOR. 2646

0004-4520 See ASIAN ALMANAC. 2646

0004-4547 See ASIAN BOOKS NEWSLETTER. 4823

0004-4555 See ASIAN ECONOMIC REVIEW, THE. 1547

0004-461X See ASIAN MEDICAL JOURNAL. 3553

0004-4644 See ASIAN RECORDER. 2646

0004-4679 See ASIAN STUDIES. 2501

0004-4687 See ASIAN SURVEY. 5192

0004-4717 See ASIATISCHE STUDIEN. 2646

0004-4768 See REVISTA DE LA ASOCIACION BIOQUIMICA ARGENTINA. 493

0004-4849 See BOLETIN DE LA ASOCIACION MEDICA DE PUERTO RICO. 3558

0004-4881 See REVISTA DE LA ASOCIACION ODONTOLOGICA ARGENTINA. 1334

0004-4903 See ASOMANTE. 3364

0004-4938 See ASPEN : THE MAGAZINE IN A BOX. 2528

0004-5098 See ASSICURAZIONE; QUINDICINALE DI TECNICA, CRONACA E GIURISPRUDENZA ASSICURATIVA. 2874

0004-5136 See SUPERVISOR'S NEWSLETTER, THE. 947

0004-5152 See ASSISTANT LIBRARIAN. 3192

0004-5292 See ASSOCIATION & SOCIETY MANAGER. 860

0004-5322 See BULLETIN DE L'ASSOCIATION DE GEOGRAPHES FRANCAIS. 2556

0004-5365 See BULLETIN D'INFORMATIONS DE L'ASSOCIATION DES BIBLIOTHECAIRES FRANCAIS. 3198

0004-5411 See JOURNAL OF THE ASSOCIATION FOR COMPUTING MACHINERY. 1192

0004-542X See BULLETIN - ASSOCIATION FOR PSYCHOANALYTIC MEDICINE. 3922

0004-5551 See BULLETIN - ASSOCIATION INTERNATIONALE D'ETUDES DU SUD-EST EUROPEEN. 2680

0004-5578 See ASSOCIATION MANAGEMENT. 640

0004-5608 See ANNALS OF THE ASSOCIATION OF AMERICAN GEOGRAPHERS. 2554

0004-5632 See ANNALS OF CLINICAL BIOCHEMISTRY. 480

0004-5659 See BULLETIN OF THE ASSOCIATION OF COLLEGE UNIONS-INTERNATIONAL, THE. 1861

0004-5691 See BULLETIN - ASSOCIATION OF ENGINEERING GEOLOGISTS. 1368

0004-5756 See JOURNAL OF AOAC INTERNATIONAL. 1016

0004-5764 See NEWSLETTER OF THE ASSOCIATION OF OFFICIAL SEED ANALYSTS, THE. 112

0004-5780 See JOURNAL OF THE ASSOCIATION OF PUBLIC ANALYSTS. 4787

0004-5837 See RECORD OF THE ASSOCIATION OF THE BAR OF THE CITY OF NEW YORK, THE. 3036

0004-587X See BULLETIN DE L'ASSOCIATION SUISSE DES ELECTRICIENS. 2037

0004-5934 See BOLLETTINO AIB. 3196

0004-5977 See BOLLETTINO - ASSOCIAZIONE ITALIANA VETERINARI PER PICCOLI ANIMALI. 5506

0004-6019 See ASSURANCE FRANCAISE. 2874

0004-6027 See ASSURANCES. 2874

0004-6116 See ASTRADO, L'. 3364

0004-6140 See ASTROLOGICAL MAGAZINE, THE. 390

0004-6191 See ASTROLOGY GUIDE. 390

0004-6221 See ASTRONAUTIK. 12

0004-623X See ASTRONAUTYKA. 12

0004-6256 See ASTRONOMICAL JOURNAL (NEW YORK), THE. 392

0004-6264 See PUBLICATIONS OF THE ASTRONOMICAL SOCIETY OF JAPAN. 398

0004-6280 See PUBLICATIONS OF THE ASTRONOMICAL SOCIETY OF THE PACIFIC. 398

0004-6299 See ASTRONOMICHESKII ZHURNAL. 392

0004-6337 See ASTRONOMISCHE NACHRICHTEN. 392

0004-6345 See ASTRONOMISK TIDSSKRIFT. 392

0004-6361 See ASTRONOMY AND ASTROPHYSICS (BERLIN). 392

0004-637X See ASTROPHYSICAL JOURNAL, THE. 393

0004-640X See ASTROPHYSICS AND SPACE SCIENCE. 393

0004-6493 See ATENE E ROMA. 1074

0004-6507 See ATENEA (CONCEPCION, CHILE: 1972). 2611

0004-6558 See ATENEO VENETO : REVISTA DI SCIENZE, LETTERE ED ARTI. 315

0004-6574 See ATHENAEUM (PAVIA, ITALY). 1074

0004-6604 See ARCHAIOLOGIKA ANALEKTA EX ATHENON. ATHENS ANNALS OF ARCHAEOLOGY. 258

0004-6639 See ATHLETES IN ACTION. 4884

0004-6671 See ATHLETICS WEEKLY. 4884

0004-6701 See ATLANTA (ATLANTA). 823

0004-6736 See ATLANTE. 2555

0004-6744 See ATLANTIC ADVOCATE, THE. 2722

0004-6752 See ATLANTIC BAPTIST, THE. 5055

0004-6809 See ATLANTIC NATURALIST. 2187

0004-6841 See ATLANTIC REPORT (HALIFAX, N.S.). 1547

0004-7015 See ATOM (LONDON, ENGLAND). 4446

0004-7090 See ATOMIC ENERGY IN AUSTRALIA. 1933

0004-7104 See ATOMIC ENERGY LAW JOURNAL. 2937

0004-7120 See NIHON GENSHIRYOKU GAKKAISHI. 1951

0004-7139 See INIS ATOMINDEX. 4426

0004-7163 See ATOMNAIA ENERGIIA. 1933

0004-7171 See ATOMO E INDUSTRIA. 2154

0004-7473 See AUDECIBEL. 4384

0004-7481 See AUDENSHAW PAPERS. 4937

0004-752X See AUDIO (PHILADELPHIA, PA.). 5315

0004-7546 See AUDIO AMATEUR. 5315

0004-7627 See AUDIOVISIVI. 4064

0004-7686 See AMERICAN BIRDS. 5614

0004-7708 See AUERBACH GUIDE TO COMPUTING EQUIPMENT SPECIFICATIONS. 1256

0004-7813 See AUFBAU (NEW YORK, N.Y.). 5713

0004-783X See AUFBEREITUNGS-TECHNIK. 2134

0004-7856 See AUFSCHLUSS. 1366

0004-7880 See AUFTRAG (BASEL. 1967). 4937

0004-7910 See AUGENOPTIK. 4215

0004-7929 See AUGENOPTIKER, DER. 3872

0004-8003 See AUGUSTINIANA. 2611

0004-8011 See AUGUSTINIANUM. 4342

0004-802X See AUGUSTINUS. 4937

0004-8038 See AUK, THE. 5615

0004-8062 See AUREA PARMA. 2842

0004-8127 See AUSGRABUNGEN UND FUNDE. 260

0004-8143 See AUSONIA. 2513

0004-8194 See AUSSENPOLITIK. 4516

0004-8216 See AUSSENWIRTSCHAFT: ZEITSCHRIFT FUER INTERNATIONALE WIRTSCHAFTSBEZIEHUNGEN. 4516

0004-8216 See AUSSENWIRTSCHAFT. 824

0004-8259 See HAUSTEX. 5351

0004-8283 See AUSTRALIAN CITRUS NEWS. 2328

0004-8291 See AUSTRALIAN AND NEW ZEALAND JOURNAL OF MEDICINE. 3795

0004-8313 See AUSTRALASIAN BEEKEEPER, THE. 63

0004-833X See AUSTRALASIAN CORROSION ENGINEERING. 2008

0004-8380 See AUSTRALASIAN JOURNAL OF DERMATOLOGY, THE. 3718

0004-8402 See AUSTRALASIAN JOURNAL OF PHILOSOPHY. 4342

0004-8437 See AUSTRALASIAN POST. 5777

0004-8461 See AUSTRALASIAN RADIOLOGY. 3939

0004-8623 See AUSTRALIAN ACADEMIC AND RESEARCH LIBRARIES. 3193

0004-8631 See AUSTRALIAN ACCOUNTANT, THE. 739

0004-8658 See AUSTRALIAN & NEW ZEALAND JOURNAL OF CRIMINOLOGY, THE. 3158

0004-8666 See AUSTRALIAN AND NEW ZEALAND JOURNAL OF OBSTETRICS AND GYNAECOLOGY. 3757

0004-8674 See AUSTRALIAN AND NEW ZEALAND JOURNAL OF PSYCHIATRY. 3921

0004-8682 See AUSTRALIAN AND NEW ZEALAND JOURNAL OF SURGERY. 3960

0004-8690 See AUSTRALIAN AND NEW ZEALAND JOURNAL OF SOCIOLOGY, THE. 5240

0004-8828 See AUSTRALIAN CHEMICAL ENGINEERING. 2008

0004-8852 See AUSTRALIAN CHRISTIAN. 4937

0004-8887 See AUSTRALIAN COIN REVIEW. 2779

0004-8917 See AUSTRALIAN COMPUTER JOURNAL, THE. 1256

0004-895X See AUSTRALIAN CRICKET. 4885

0004-8992 See AUSTRALIAN ECONOMIC HISTORY REVIEW. 1547

0004-900X See AUSTRALIAN ECONOMIC PAPERS. 1590

0004-9018 See AUSTRALIAN ECONOMIC REVIEW. 1464

0004-9026 See AUSTRALIAN EDUCATION INDEX. 1793

0004-9042 See AUSTRALIAN ELECTRONICS ENGINEERING. 2036

0004-9050 See JOURNAL OF THE AUSTRALIAN ENTOMOLOGICAL SOCIETY. 5588

0004-9115 See AUSTRALIAN FISHERIES. 2297

0004-9123 See AUSTRALIAN FLYING. 12

0004-914X See AUSTRALIAN FOREST RESEARCH. 2375

0004-9158 See AUSTRALIAN FORESTRY. 2375

0004-9166 See AUSTRALIAN GAS JOURNAL, THE. 4251

0004-9174 See AUSTRALIAN GEMMOLOGIST. 2913

0004-9182 See AUSTRALIAN GEOGRAPHER. 2555

0004-9190 See AUSTRALIAN GEOGRAPHICAL STUDIES. 2555

0004-9328 See AUSTRALIAN HUMANIST, THE. 2842

0004-9395 See AUSTRALIAN JOURNAL OF AGRICULTURAL ECONOMICS, THE. 64

0004-9409 See AUSTRALIAN JOURNAL OF AGRICULTURAL RESEARCH. 64

0004-9425 See AUSTRALIAN JOURNAL OF CHEMISTRY. 961

0004-9433 See AUSTRALIAN JOURNAL OF DAIRY TECHNOLOGY, THE. 192

0004-9441 See AUSTRALIAN JOURNAL OF EDUCATION, THE. 1726

0004-9468 See AUSTRALIAN JOURNAL OF FRENCH STUDIES. 3364

0004-9484 See AUSTRALIAN JOURNAL OF MUSIC EDUCATION. 4101

0004-9506 See AUSTRALIAN JOURNAL OF PHYSICS. 4398

0004-9514 See AUSTRALIAN JOURNAL OF PHYSIOTHERAPY, THE. 4379

0004-9522 See AUSTRALIAN JOURNAL OF POLITICS AND HISTORY, THE. 4464

0004-9530 See AUSTRALIAN JOURNAL OF PSYCHOLOGY. 4575

0004-9549 See SEARCH (SYDNEY). 5156

0004-9573 See AUSTRALIAN JOURNAL OF SOIL RESEARCH. 164

0004-9581 See AUSTRALIAN JOURNAL OF STATISTICS. 5322

0004-959X See AUSTRALIAN JOURNAL OF ZOOLOGY. 5577

0004-9611 See AUSTRALIAN LAW JOURNAL, THE. 2938

0004-9638 See AUSTRALIAN LEFT REVIEW. 4465

0004-9646 See AUSTRALIAN LEGAL MONTHLY DIGEST. 3078

0004-9670 See AUSTRALIAN LIBRARY JOURNAL, THE. 3193

0004-9697 See AUSTRALIAN LITERARY STUDIES. 3338

0004-9709 See JOURNAL OF THE ASIATIC SOCIETY OF BOMBAY. 5232

0004-9719 See AUSTRALIAN MACHINERY AND PRODUCTION ENGINEERING. 2110

0004-9727 See BULLETIN OF THE AUSTRALIAN MATHEMATICAL SOCIETY. 3498

0004-9743 See AUSTRALIAN METEOROLOGICAL MAGAZINE. 1420

0004-976X See AUSTRALIAN MINING. 2134

0004-9808 See AUSTRALIAN MUNICIPAL JOURNAL, THE. 4631

ISSN Index

0004-9816 See AUSTRALIAN NATIONAL BIBLIOGRAPHY. 2496

0004-9840 See AUSTRALIAN NATURAL HISTORY. 4162

0004-9875 See AUSTRALIAN NUMISMATIC JOURNAL. 2771

0004-9875 See AUSTRALIAN NUMISMATIC JOURNAL. 2780

0004-9921 See AUSTRALIAN PACKAGING. 4218

0004-9964 See AUSTRALIAN PHOTOGRAPHY. 4367

0004-9972 See AUSTRALIAN & NEW ZEALAND PHYSICIST : A PUBLICATION OF THE AUSTRALIAN INSTITUTE OF PHYSICS & THE NEW ZEALAND INSTITUTE OF PHYSICS, THE. 4398

0005-0008 See AUSTRALIAN PLANTS. 2410

0005-0024 See AUSTRALIAN POLICE JOURNAL. 3158

0005-0067 See AUSTRALIAN PSYCHOLOGIST. 4575

0005-0091 See AUSTRALIAN QUARTERLY. 2668

0005-0164 See ROAD & TRANSPORT RESEARCH : [A JOURNAL OF AUSTRALIAN AND NEW ZEALAND RESEARCH AND PRACTICE]. 5443

0005-0180 See AUSTRALIAN SAFETY NEWS. 2859

0005-0245 See AUSTRALIAN SHOOTERS JOURNAL. 4885

0005-0326 See AUSTRALIAN SURVEYOR. 2019

0005-0334 See AUSTRALIAN TEACHER OF THE DEAF. 1875

0005-0385 See AUSTRALIAN TRANSPORT. 5377

0005-0423 See AUSTRALIAN VETERINARY JOURNAL. 5505

0005-0431 See AUSTRALIAN WELDING JOURNAL. 4026

0005-0458 See AUSTRALIAN WOMEN'S WEEKLY, THE. 5551

0005-0571 See AUSZUGE AUS DEN GEBRAUCHSMUSTERN. AUSGABE A. 1301

0005-0601 See AUT AUT. 4342

0005-0628 See AUTHOR (LONDON. 1949). 3364

0005-0717 See AUTO AND FLAT GLASS JOURNAL. 2586

0005-0725 See AUTO CLUB NEWS (LOS, ANGELES CALIF.). 5404

0005-0768 See AUTO-JOURNAL (PARIS), L'. 5404

0005-0776 See AUTO LAUNDRY NEWS. 5404

0005-0806 See AUTO, MOTOR UND SPORT. 5405

0005-1055 See AUTOMATIC DOCUMENTATION AND MATHEMATICAL LINGUISTICS. 3193

0005-1071 See AUTOMATIC MACHINING. 2110

0005-1098 See AUTOMATICA (OXFORD). 1217

0005-111X See AVTOMATICESKAJA SVARKA (KIEV). 2036

0005-1128 See AUTOMATIE. 1217

0005-1152 See AUTOMATION (LONDON). 1218

0005-1179 See AUTOMATION AND REMOTE CONTROL. 1218

0005-125X See AUTOMATIZACE. 1218

0005-1306 See AUTOMOBIL-INDUSTRIE. 5405

0005-1330 See AUTOMOBILE (DON MILLS). 5405

0005-1349 See AUTOMOBILE. 4885

0005-1438 See AUTOMOBILE QUARTERLY. 5406

0005-1497 See AUTOMOTIVE COOLING JOURNAL : ACJ. 5406

0005-1519 See AUTOMOTIVE FLEET. 5406

0005-1551 See AUTOMOTIVE NEWS. 5406

0005-1578 See AUTOMOTIVE RETAILER (VANCOUVER). 5407

0005-1748 See AUTOSPRINT. 5407

0005-1861 See VOLUNTEER LEADER, THE. 3793

0005-1926 See AVANT GARDENER, THE. 2410

0005-1961 See AUTOREVISTA. 5407

0005-1969 See AVENIRS. 1911

0005-1993 See AVES. 5615

0005-2086 See AVIAN DISEASES. 5505

0005-2094 See AVIASPORT. 4885

0005-2116 See NATIONAL AERONAUTICS. 30

0005-2132 See AVIATION MAGAZINE INTERNATIONAL. 13

0005-2140 See AVIATION MECHANICS BULLETIN. 13

0005-2159 See AVIATION REPORTS. CIVIL AND/OR MILITARY. 14

0005-2175 See AVIATION WEEK & SPACE TECHNOLOGY. 14

0005-2256 See AVICULTURAL MAGAZINE, THE. 5615

0005-2299 See AVODAH U-VITUAH LEUMI. 1654

0005-2310 See AVTOMATIKA I TELEMEHANIKA. 2110

0005-2329 See AVTOMATIKA, TELEMEHANIKA I SVJAZ. 5429

0005-2337 See AVTOMOBILNAJA PROMYSLENNOST. 5407

0005-2353 See AVTOMOBILNYE DOROGI. 5439

0005-2361 See AVVENIRE AGRICOLE, L'. 64

0005-237X See AWAKE (BROOKLYN). 4937

0005-2442 See AYRSHIRE CATTLE SOCIETY'S JOURNAL, THE. 207

0005-2450 See AYRSHIRE DIGEST. 192

0005-2469 See AYU. 3554

0005-2523 See AZERBAIDZANSKIJ MEDICINSKIJ ZURNAL. 3554

0005-2531 See AZERBAIDZHANSKII KHIMICHESKII ZHURNAL / AKADEMIIA NAUK AZERBAIDZHANSKOI SSR. 962

0005-2574 See AZIIA I AFRIKA SEGODNIA. 2502

0005-2604 See AZTLAN. 2256

0005-2728 See BIOCHIMICA ET BIOPHYSICA ACTA. BIOENERGETICS. 962

0005-2736 See BIOCHIMICA ET BIOPHYSICA ACTA. BIOMEMBRANES. 482

0005-2760 See BIOCHIMICA ET BIOPHYSICA ACTA. LIPIDS AND LIPID METABOLISM. 962

0005-2787 See NUCLEIC ACIDS AND PROTEIN SYNTHESIS. 491

0005-2825 See BBC NACHRICHTEN. 2036

0005-2833 See BOKREVY. 3457

0005-2841 See BCA NEWS (NEW YORK, N.Y.). 642

0005-2876 See BCLA REPORTER. 3193

0005-2949 See BC STUDIES. 2722

0005-3120 See BTJ. BIBLIOTHEQUE DE TRAVAIL JUNIOR. 1728

0005-3155 See BIOS (MADISON, N.J.). 477

0005-3198 See BLM. BONNIERS LITTERARA MAGASIN. 3367

0005-321X See BMG; BANJO, MANDOLIN, GUITAR. 4104

0005-3228 See BNA POLICY AND PRACTICE SERIES. 939

0005-3309 See B.S.I. NEWS. 4029

0005-3309 See BSI NEWS. 4029

0005-3392 See B.T.O. NEWS. 5615

0005-3414 See BT 2 CANNES. 1728

0005-3503 See BABEL. 3267

0005-3554 See B & J. BABY & JUNIOR. 1081

0005-3600 See BACH. 4101

0005-3635 See BACK STAGE. 4064

0005-3643 See BACK TO GODHEAD. 4342

0005-366X See BACKSTRETCH, THE. 2797

0005-3775 See BADGER SPORTSMAN. 4869

0005-383X See BACKER UND KONDITOR. 2328

0005-3848 See BANDER BLECHE ROHRE. 3475

0005-3856 See DET BASTA UR READER'S DIGEST. 2515

0005-397X See BAHAMIAN REVIEW. 2528

0005-3988 See BAHANA. 3267

0005-4003 See BAILEYA. 501

0005-4070 See BAKER STREET JOURNAL, THE. 3365

0005-4097 See BAKERS JOURNAL. 2328

0005-4100 See BAKERS' REVIEW (WATFORD). 2328

0005-4127 See BAKERY PRODUCTION AND MARKETING. 2328

0005-4216 See BALANCE LONDON. 3555

0005-4232 See BALANCE SHEET (CINCINNATI, OHIO), THE. 641

0005-4259 See BALANS (DEN HAAG). 641

0005-4283 See BULGARSKI JAZIK. 3270

0005-4313 See BALKAN STUDIES. 2677

0005-4453 See BALTIMORE MAGAZINE. 2528

0005-4496 See BALTIMORE ENGINEER, THE. 1966

0005-450X See BALTIMORE JEWISH TIMES. 5046

0005-4585 See BANAS. 773

0005-4607 See BANCA NAZIONALE DEL LAVORO QUARTERLY REVIEW. 1590

0005-4615 See BANCA Y COMERCIO. 773

0005-4623 See BANCARIA. 774

0005-4631 See BANCNI VESTNIK. 774

0005-481X See BOLETIN ESTADISTICO - BANCO DE GUATEMALA. 779

0005-4828 See REVISTA DEL BANCO DE LA REPUBLICA. 810

0005-4968 See BANDWAGON (COLUMBUS, OHIO : 1957). 4857

0005-5026 See BANK AND QUOTATION RECORD. 774

0005-5123 See BANK NEWS. 775

0005-5166 See BANK OF ENGLAND QUARTERLY BULLETIN. 775

0005-5255 See MONTHLY ECONOMIC REVIEW. 799

0005-5298 See BANK OF LONDON & SOUTH AMERICA REVIEW. 775

0005-531X See BUSINESS REVIEW (MONTREAL). 652

0005-5395 See BANKER (LONDON). 776

0005-5409 See BANKER & TRADESMAN. 4834

0005-5425 See BANKERS DIGEST (DALLAS, TEX.). 776

0005-5433 See BANKERS LETTER OF THE LAW, THE. 3084

0005-545X See BANKERS MAGAZINE (BOSTON), THE. 776

0005-5476 See BANKERS MONTHLY. 776

0005-5506 See BANKING LAW JOURNAL, THE. 3085

0005-5557 See BANNER (GRAND RAPIDS), THE. 4937

0005-5581 See BANQUE (PARIS. 1926). 778

0005-559X See NOTES D'INFORMATION ET STATISTIQUES. 5335

0005-5611 See BULLETIN DE LA BANQUE NATIONALE DE BELGIQUE. 780

0005-5670 See BANYASZATI ES KOHASZATI LAPOK. KOHASZAT. 1654

0005-5689 See BAPTIST BULLETIN, THE. 5056

0005-5700 See BAPTIST HERALD, THE. 4938

0005-5719 See BAPTIST HISTORY AND HERITAGE. 5056

0005-5727 See BAPTIST LEADER (PHILADELPHIA). 4938

0005-5743 See BAPTIST PROGRAM, THE. 5056

0005-5751 See BAPTIST PROGRESS. 5056

0005-576X See BAPTIST QUARTERLY (LONDON). 5056

0005-5778 See BAPTIST RECORD (JACKSON, MISS.), THE. 5056

0005-5786 See BAPTIST TIMES. 5056

0005-5808 See BAPTIST WORLD (WASHINGTON, D.C.). 5056

0005-5824 See BAR EXAMINER, THE. 2940

0005-5891 See JOURNAL OF THE BARBADOS MUSEUM AND HISTORICAL SOCIETY, THE. 4090

0005-6014 See BARNARD BULLETIN. 1089

0005-6073 See BARRON'S NATIONAL BUSINESS AND FINANCIAL WEEKLY. 642

0005-609X See BASEBALL DIGEST. 4886

0005-6138 See BASIS. 2647

0005-6170 See BASKETBALL WEEKLY. 4887

0005-6219 See BASTERIA. 5577

0005-6227 See BAT RESEARCH NEWS. 5577

0005-6359 See BATTERY MAN. 1933

0005-6529 See WERK, BAUEN + WOHNEN (GERMAN ED.). 310

0005-6545 See BAUEN MIT HOLZ. 600

0005-6650 See BAUINGENIEUR, DER. 2019

0005-6693 See BMT : BAUMASCHINENTECHNIK. 601

0005-674X See BAUMEISTER. 293

0005-6758 See BAUPLANUNG-BAUTECHNIK. 293

0005-6847 See BAUVERWALTUNG. 4632

0005-6855 See BAUWELT (BERLIN, GERMANY : WEST : 1952). 293

0005-6871 See BAUZEITUNG. 600

0005-6944 See BAY STATE LIBRARIAN. 3193

0005-7215 See BAYERN IN ZAHLEN. 4550

0005-7266 See BAYLOR GEOLOGICAL STUDIES. 1366

0005-7274 See BAYLOR LAW REVIEW. 2940

0005-7339 See BEACON (LONDON, ENGLAND). 4342

0005-738X See BEAKEN. 1089

0005-7460 See BEAUTIFUL BRITISH COLUMBIA. 5462

0005-7487 See BEAUTY FASHION. 1081

0005-7517 See BEAVER, THE. 2722

0005-7533 See BEBIDAS. 2364

0005-755X See BECKMAN REPORT. 4029

0005-7592 See BEDFORDSHIRE MAGAZINE, THE. 2678

0005-7622 See MAANDBLAD VOOR BEDRIJFSADMINISTRATIE EN-ORGANISATIE. 4212

0005-772X See BEE WORLD. 5577

0005-7738 See BEEF (ST. PAUL, MINN.). 207

0005-7770 See BEER WHOLESALER. 2364

0005-7894 See BEHAVIOR THERAPY. 4576

0005-7916 See JOURNAL OF BEHAVIOR THERAPY AND EXPERIMENTAL PSYCHIATRY. 3928

0005-7940 See BEHAVIORAL SCIENCE. 4576

0005-7959 See BEHAVIOUR. 443

0005-7967 See BEHAVIOUR RESEARCH AND THERAPY. 3921

0005-8017 See GEOLOGISCHES JAHRBUCH, REIHE C : HYDROGEOLOGIE, INGENIEURGEOLOGIE. 1413

0005-8041 See BEITRAEGE ZUR BIOLOGIE DER PFLANZEN. 501

0005-805X See BEITRAEGE ZUR ENTOMOLOGIE. 5605

0005-8068 See BEITRAEGE ZUR GESCHICHTE DER ARBEITERBEWEGUNG (BERLIN, DDR). 2678

0005-8076 See BEITRAEGE ZUR GESCHICHTE DER DEUTSCHEN SPRACHE UND LITERATUR (TUEBINGEN). 3268

0005-8106 See BEITRAEGE ZUR MUSIKWISSENSCHAFT. 4102

0005-8114 See BEITRAEGE ZUR NAMENFORSCHUNG. 2438

0005-8149 See BEITRAEGE ZUR ORTHOPADIE UND TRAUMATOLOGIE. 3555

0005-8211 See BEITRAEGE ZUR VOGELKUNDE. 5615

0005-8335 See MBB : BELASTINGBESCHOUWINGEN. 4737

0005-8343 See BELEGGERS BELANGEN. 778

0005-8351 See BELFAGOR. 3338

0005-8467 See BELGISCHE FRUITREVUE. 2328

0005-8483 See BELGISCHE TUINBOUW. INTERNATIONALE EDITIE, DE. 2410

0005-8521 See LISTE MENSUELLE. 1535

0005-8629 See BELLEZA Y MODA. 5551

0005-8645 See BELLONA. KWARTALNIK WOJSKOWO-HISTORYCZNY. 4037

0005-8661 See BELOIT POETRY JOURNAL, THE. 3460

0005-8726 See BENEDICTINES. 5024

0005-8807 See BENGAL PAST AND PRESENT. 2647

0005-884X See BENT OF TAU BETA PI, THE. 1966

0005-8874 See BEREA ALUMNUS, THE. 1101

0005-8912 See BHM. BERG- UND HUTTENMANNISCHE MONATSHEFTE. 1966

0005-8955 See BERGAMUM. 2678

0005-9021 See BERICHTE DER BUNSENGESELLSCHAFT FUER PHYSIKALISCHE CHEMIE. 1050

0005-9048 See BERICHTE PHYSIOLOGIE, PHYSIOLOGISCHE CHEMIE UND PHARMAKOLOGIE. 578

0005-9080 See BERICHTE UBER LANDWIRTSCHAFT. 65

0005-9099 See BERICHTE ZUR DEUTSCHEN LANDESKUNDE. 2678

0005-9102 See BERICHTE ZUR RAUMFORSCHUNG UND RAUMPLANUNG. 2816

0005-9145 See BERITA SELULOSA. 4232

0005-9285 See HAUSTEX. 5351

0005-9366 See BERLINER UND MUNCHENER TIERARZTLICHE WOCHENSCHRIFT. 5505

0005-951X See BERUFSBILDENDE SCHULE, DIE. 1599

0005-9668 See BESTE AUS READER'S DIGEST, DAS. 2485

0005-9692 See BESTE UIT READER'S DIGEST, HET. 2513

0005-9706 See BEST'S REVIEW. (LIFE-HEALTH INSURANCE EDITION). 2876

0005-979X See BETH MIKRA : KETAV-ET SHEL HA-HEVRAH LE-HEKER HA-MIKRA BE-YISRAEL. 5046

0005-982X See BETHEL COLLEGE BULLETIN. 1089

0005-9846 See BETON. 600

0005-9889 See BETON I ZHELEZOBETON. 600

0005-9900 See BETON- UND STAHLBETONBAU. 601

0005-9935 See BETRIEB, DER. 2941

0006-0089 See BETTER CROPS WITH PLANT FOOD. 164

0006-0151 See BETTER HOMES AND GARDENS. 2788

0006-016X See BETTER INVESTING. 892

0006-0208 See BETTER ROADS. 5439

0006-0267 See BETTY AND ME. 4857

0006-0348 See BAR: BEVERAGE ALCOHOL REPORTER. 2364

0006-0372 See BEVERAGE MEDIA. 2364

0006-0410 See BEVERLY REVIEW, THE. 5658

0006-0461 See BHAGIRATH. 2087

0006-0518 See BHAVAN'S JOURNAL. 4342

0006-0585 See BIBBIA E ORIENTE. 5014

0006-0615 See BIBEL UND GEMEINDE. 5014

0006-0623 See BIBEL UND KIRCHE. 5014

0006-064X See BIBEL UND LITURGIE. 5014

0006-0763 See BIBLE LANDS. 5014

0006-0798 See BIBLE SEARCHERS : TEACHER. 5015

0006-0801 See AMERICAN BIBLE SOCIETY RECORD. 5014

0006-081X See BIBLE STANDARD AND HERALD OF CHRIST'S KINGDOM, THE. 4938

0006-0836 See BIBLE TODAY, THE. 5015

0006-0879 See BIBLIA REVUO. 5015

0006-0887 See BIBLICA. 5015

0006-0895 See BIBLICAL ARCHAEOLOGIST, THE. 261

0006-0909 See BIBLICAL MISSIONS. 5057

0006-0925 See BIBLICAL VIEWPOINT. 5015

0006-0941 See BIBLIOFILIA (FLORENCE, ITALY). 4824

0006-1042 See BIBLIOGRAFIA ITALIANA DI IDRAULICA. 2087

0006-1069 See BIBLIOGRAFIA MEXICANA (BIBLIOTECA NACIONAL DE MEXICO). 409

0006-1077 See BIBLIOGRAFIA NAZIONALE ITALIANA. PUBBLICAZIONE MENSILE. 409

0006-1093 See BIBLIOGRAFIA ZAWARTOSCI CZASOPISM / BIBLIOTEKA NARODOWA, INSTYTUT BIBLIOGRAFICZNY. 3257

0006-1255 See BIBLIOGRAPHIC INDEX. 3457

0006-128X See PAPERS OF THE BIBLIOGRAPHICAL SOCIETY OF AMERICA, THE. 422

0006-1336 See BIBLIOGRAPHIE DE BELGIQUE. 409

0006-1352 See BIBLIOGRAPHIE DE LA PHILOSOPHIE. 4365

0006-1387 See BIBLIOGRAPHIE DER PFLANZENSCHUTZLITERATUR. 2434

0006-1409 See BIBLIOGRAPHIE DER UBERSETZUNGEN DEUTSCHSPRACHIGER WERKE. 3457

0006-1417 See BIBLIOGRAPHIE DER WIRTSCHAFTSPRESSE. 1530

0006-1441 See BIBLIOGRAPHIE DU QUEBEC. 410

0006-1468 See BIBLIOGRAPHIE : STAAT UND RECHTDER DEUTSCHEN DEMOKRATISCHEN REPUBLIK. 3079

0006-1530 See BIBLIOGRAPHY OF AGRICULTURE. 151

0006-1565 See BIBLIOGRAPHY OF REPRODUCTION. 477

0006-1573 See BIBLIOGRAPHY OF SYSTEMATIC MYCOLOGY. 574

0006-1646 See BOLETIN DE LA BIBLIOTECA DE MENENDEZ PELAYO / SOCIEDAD DE MENENDEZ PELAYO. 411

0006-1727 See REVISTA DE LA BIBLIOTECA NACIONAL JOSE MARTI. 423

0006-1778 See BIBLIOTECONOMIA. 1464

0006-1786 See BIBLIOTEK FOR LAGER. 3555

0006-1808 See BIBLIOTEKA. 3194

0006-1816 See BIBLIOTEKAR (BEOGRAD). 3194

0006-1867 See BBL. BIBLIOTEKSBLADET. 3193

0006-1883 See PERFORMANCE. 387

0006-1913 See BIBLIOTHECA ORIENTALIS. 2647

0006-1921 See BIBLIOTHECA SACRA (1864). 4939

0006-193X See BIBLIOTHECK. 410

0006-1964 See BIBLIOTHEKAR. 3195

0006-1972 See BIBLIOTHEKSDIENST. 3195

0006-1999 See BIBLIOTHEQUE D'HUMANISME ET RENAISSANCE. 2611

0006-2006 See BULLETIN DES BIBLIOTHEQUES DE FRANCE. 3198

0006-2014 See BIBLISCHE ZEITSCHRIFT. 5015

0006-2022 See BIBLOS; OSTERREICHISCHE ZEITSCHRIFT FUER BUCH- UND BIBLIOTEKSWESEN, DOKUMENTATION, BIBLIOGRAPHIE, UND BIBLIOPHILIE. 3195

0006-2030 See BIBUROSU. 3195

0006-2073 See BICYCLING. 428

0006-2146 See BIENENVATER. 66

0006-2294 See BIJDRAGEN TOT DE TAAL-, LAND- EN VOLKENKUNDE. 232

0006-2375 See BILD DER WISSENSCHAFT. 5088

0006-2383 See BILD UND TON (BERLIN, DDR). 4064

0006-2391 See BILDENDE KUNST (DRESDEN). 344

0006-2456 See BILDUNG UND ERZIEHUNG. 1728

0006-2499 See BILL OF RIGHTS JOURNAL, THE. 2941

0006-2510 See BILLBOARD [MICROFORM]. 5362

0006-2510 See BILLBOARD (CINCINNATI, OHIO. 1963). 4103

0006-2537 See BILLED BLADET. 2485

0006-2766 See BIM (CHRIST CHURCH). 3367

0006-2863 See BIO-DYNAMICS. 66

0006-291X See BIOCHEMICAL AND BIOPHYSICAL RESEARCH COMMUNICATIONS. 481

0006-2928 See BIOCHEMICAL GENETICS. 543

0006-2952 See BIOCHEMICAL PHARMACOLOGY. 4293

0006-2960 See BIOCHEMISTRY (EASTON). 482

0006-2979 See BIOCHEMISTRY (NEW YORK). 482
0006-3002 See BIOCHIMICA ET BIOPHYSICA ACTA. 482
0006-3029 See BIOFIZIKA. 494
0006-3053 See BIOGRAPHY INDEX. 439
0006-3088 See BIOLOGIA. 444
0006-3096 See BIOLOGIA (LAHORE). 444
0006-3126 See BIOLOGY OF THE NEONATE. 3900
0006-3134 See BIOLOGIA PLANTARUM. 502
0006-3169 See BIOLOGICAL ABSTRACTS. 477
0006-3177 See BIOLOGICAL & AGRICULTURAL INDEX. 477
0006-3185 See BIOLOGICAL BULLETIN (LANCASTER), THE. 444
0006-3193 See SHENG WU HSUEH TUNG PAO. 473
0006-3207 See BIOLOGICAL CONSERVATION. 2188
0006-3223 See BIOLOGICAL PSYCHIATRY (1969). 3921
0006-3231 See BIOLOGICAL REVIEWS OF THE CAMBRIDGE PHILOSOPHICAL SOCIETY. 445
0006-324X See PROCEEDINGS OF THE BIOLOGICAL SOCIETY OF WASHINGTON. 469
0006-3274 See BIOLOGIEUNTERRICHT, DER. 446
0006-3282 See BIOLOGISCHE ABHANDLUNGEN. 446
0006-3304 See BIOLOGISCHES ZENTRALBLATT. 446
0006-3347 See BIOLOGIST (LONDON). 446
0006-3363 See BIOLOGY OF REPRODUCTION. 578
0006-3398 See BIOMEDICAL ENGINEERING. 3686
0006-341X See BIOMETRICS. 5323
0006-3436 See BIOMETRIE-PRAXIMETRIE. 477
0006-3444 See BIOMETRIKA. 447
0006-3495 See BIOPHYSICAL JOURNAL. 494
0006-3509 See BIOPHYSICS (OXFORD). 494
0006-3525 See BIOPOLYMERS. 483
0006-355X See BIORHEOLOGY (OXFORD). 447
0006-3568 See BIOSCIENCE. 448
0006-3592 See BIOTECHNOLOGY AND BIOENGINEERING. 3688
0006-3606 See BIOTROPICA. 448
0006-3657 See BIRD STUDY. 5615
0006-3665 See BIRDS : MAGAZINE FOR MEMBERS OF THE ROYAL SOCIETY FOR THE PROTECTION OF BIRDS. 5616
0006-369X See BIRMINGHAM. 2529
0006-3835 See BIT (NORDISK TIDSKRIFT FOR INFORMATIONSBEHANDLING). 1172
0006-3894 See BITS AND PIECES (NEWCASTLE). 861
0006-3908 See BITTERROOT. 3460
0006-3916 See BITUMEN. 2019
0006-3932 See BITZARON. 5046
0006-3967 See BIULETYN HISTORII SZTUKI. 344
0006-4025 See BIULETYN STATYSTYCZNY. 5323
0006-4033 See BIULETYN ZYDOWSKIEGO INSTYTUTU HISTORYCZNEGO W POLSCE. 5046
0006-4149 See BLACK DIAMOND, THE. 2135
0006-4165 See BLACK ENTERPRISE. 643
0006-4246 See BLACK SCHOLAR, THE. 2257
0006-4335 See BLACKCOUNTRYMAN. 2678
0006-4408 See BLATTER FUER DEUTSCHE LANDESGESCHICHTE. 2611
0006-4416 See BLATTER FUER DEUTSCHE UND INTERNATIONALE POLITIK. 2611
0006-4424 See BLAETTER FUER FRAENKISCHE FAMILIENKUNDE. 2439
0006-4459 See BLATTER FUER HEIMATKUNDE 2611
0006-4688 See BLECH, ROHRE, PROFILE. 3999
0006-4696 See BLESSINGS OF LIBERTY, THE. 5193
0006-470X See BLETER FAR GESHIKHTE. 2257
0006-4971 See BLOOD. 3770
0006-4998 See BLOOD-HORSE, THE. 2797

0006-5005 See BLOOD THERAPY JOURNAL INTERNATIONAL. 3770
0006-5099 See BLUE JAY. 4163
0006-5129 See BLUEGRASS MUSIC NEWS. 4104
0006-5137 See BLUEGRASS UNLIMITED. 4104
0006-5153 See BLUES UNLIMITED. 4104
0006-5188 See BLUESTONE; THE LITERARY QUARTERLY. 3367
0006-5196 See BLUMEA. 502
0006-5242 See ANNALS OF HEMATOLOGY. 3770
0006-5250 See BLUTALKOHL. 3740
0006-5269 See BLYTTIA. 502
0006-5285 See BO BEDRE. 2816
0006-5366 See BOAT AND MOTOR DEALER. 591
0006-5374 See BOATING (NEW YORK, N.Y.). 592
0006-5404 See BOATING INDUSTRY, THE. 592
0006-5471 See BODENKULTUR (1964). 67
0006-5501 See BODY LEEDS. 5407
0006-5579 See BOEKENGIDS. 410
0006-5692 See BOGENS VERDEN. 3196
0006-5722 See BOGOSLOVNI VESTNIK. 4939
0006-579X See BOIS ET FORETS DES TROPIQUES. 2376
0006-5811 See BOK OG BIBLIOTEK. 3257
0006-5838 See BIRDING IN SOUTHERN AFRICA. 5616
0006-5846 See BOKVAENNEN. 3368
0006-5935 See BOLETIM DE MINAS. 2135
0006-6079 See BOLETIM PAULISTA DE GEOGRAFIA. 2556
0006-6117 See BOLETIM TECNICO DA PETROBRAS. 4252
0006-6176 See BOLETIN CHILENO DE PARASITOLOGIA. 449
0006-6249 See BOLETIN DE ESTUDIOS ECONOMICOS. 1465
0006-6281 See BOLETIN DE GEOLOGIA (CARACAS). 1367
0006-6303 See BOLETIN DE HISTORIA Y ANTIGUEDADES. 2723
0006-6575 See BOLLETTINO DI PESCA, PISCICOLTURA E IDROBIOLOGIA. 2297
0006-6583 See BOLLETTINO DI STUDI LATINI. 3270
0006-6591 See BOLLETTINO STORICO PIACENTINO. 2679
0006-6648 See BOLLETTINO CHIMICO FARMACEUTICA. 4294
0006-6710 See BOLLETTINO DI GEODESIA E SCIENZE AFFINI. 1352
0006-6729 See BOLLETTINO DI GEOFISICA TEORICA ED APPLICATA. 1403
0006-6761 See BOLLETTINO DI PSICOLOGIA APPLICATA. 4577
0006-677X See BOLLETTINO DI OCULISTICA. 3872
0006-6893 See BOLLETTINO TRIBUTARIO D'INFORMAZIONI. 2942
0006-6966 See YELMO. 3334
0006-6982 See JOURNAL OF THE BOMBAY NATURAL HISTORY SOCIETY. 4166
0006-6990 See BON APPETIT. 2788
0006-7121 See BONJOUR (NEW YORK). 3270
0006-713X See BONNE CUISINE. 2329
0006-7156 See BONNER METEOROLOGISCHE ABHANDLUNGEN. 1421
0006-7172 See BONNER ZOOLOGISCHE BEITRAEGE. 5578
0006-7202 See QUARTERLY NEWS-LETTER - BOOK CLUB OF CALIFORNIA. 4831
0006-7237 See BOOK COLLECTOR, THE. 4824
0006-7296 See BOOK NEWSLETTER (MINNEAPOLIS, MINN.). 3338
0006-7326 See BOOK REVIEW DIGEST. CD-ROM. 4821
0006-7326 See BOOK REVIEW DIGEST. 3356
0006-7369 See BOOK WORLD (WASHINGTON). 4825
0006-7377 See BOOKBIRD. 3368

0006-7385 See BOOKLIST (CHICAGO, ILL. 1969). 3196
0006-7407 See BOOKMARK, THE. 3197
0006-7474 See BOOKS AT IOWA. 3197
0006-7482 See BOOKS FOR YOUR CHILDREN. 3338
0006-7490 See BOOKS FROM FINLAND. 4821
0006-7520 See BOOKS OF THE SOUTHWEST. 3457
0006-7539 See BOOKSELLER (LONDON). 4821
0006-7563 See BOOKSTORE JOURNAL. 4939
0006-7598 See NEWSLETTER - BOOSEY AND HAWKES INC. 4140
0006-7741 See BORGAZDASAG. 68
0006-775X See BORGHESE, IL. 2514
0006-7768 See BORGYOGYASZATI ES VENEROLOGIAI SZEMLE. 3718
0006-7792 See BORN & BOGER. 3197
0006-7806 See BORNEO RESEARCH BULLETIN. 2647
0006-7903 See TRANSACTIONS OF THE BOSE RESEARCH INSTITUTE, CALCUTTA. 475
0006-8020 See BOSTON SYMPHONY ORCHESTRA. 4104
0006-8047 See BOSTON UNIVERSITY LAW REVIEW. 2943
0006-8055 See BOTANICA MARINA. 503
0006-8063 See BOTANICAL BULLETIN OF ACADEMIA SINICA. 503
0006-8071 See INTERNATIONAL JOURNAL OF PLANT SCIENCES. 514
0006-8071 See INTERNATIONAL JOURNAL OF PLANT SCIENCES. MICROFORM. 514
0006-808X See SHOKUBUTSUGAKU ZASSHI. 527
0006-8101 See BOTANICAL REVIEW, THE. 503
0006-8128 See BULLETIN OF THE BOTANICAL SURVEY OF INDIA. 505
0006-8136 See BOTANICESKIJ ZURNAL. 503
0006-8144 See BOTANIKAI KOZLEMENYEK. 503
0006-8152 See BOTANISCHE JAHRBUCHER FUER SYSTEMATIK, PFLANZENGESCHICHTE UND PFLANZENGEOGRAPHIE. 503
0006-8179 See MITTEILUNGEN DER BOTANISCHEN STAATSSAMMLUNG MUNCHEN. 518
0006-8241 See BOTHALIA. 504
0006-825X See BOTICARIO, EL. 4294
0006-8314 See BOUNDARY-LAYER METEOROLOGY. 1421
0006-8330 See BOUWBELANGEN. 601
0006-8446 See BOWLING PROPRIETOR. 4858
0006-8497 See BOXBOARD CONTAINERS. 4218
0006-8500 See BOXING ILLUSTRATED. 4888
0006-8519 See BOXING NEWS. 4888
0006-8527 See BOXOFFICE. 4064
0006-8535 See BOXWOOD BULLETIN, THE. 5229
0006-8608 See BOYS' LIFE. 1060
0006-8705 See BRAGANTIA : BOLETIM TECNICO DO INSTITUTO AGRONOMICO DO ESTADO DE SAO PAULO. 165
0006-873X See BRAILLE BOOK REVIEW. 4384
0006-8829 See BRAILLE MONITOR, THE. 4384
0006-8918 See BRAILLE STAR THEOSOPHIST, THE. 4384
0006-8950 See BRAIN. 3828
0006-8969 See NO TO SHINKEI. 3844
0006-8977 See BRAIN, BEHAVIOR AND EVOLUTION. 3828
0006-8993 See BRAIN RESEARCH. 3829
0006-906X See BRANDHILFE. 2288
0006-9078 See BRANDING IRON, THE. 2724
0006-9116 See BRANDWACHT. 2288
0006-9132 See BRANGUS JOURNAL. 207
0006-9248 See BRATISLAVSKE LEKARSKE LISTY. 3558
0006-9256 See FRATERNAL HERALD. 5231
0006-9264 See BRATSTVO (TORONTO). 5229
0006-9566 See BREF RHONE ALPES. 1549
0006-9612 See BRENNSTOFF-WAERME-KRAFT. 1934

0006-9663 See BRETHREN LIFE AND THOUGHT. 4940
0006-9698 See BREVIORA. 5578
0006-9701 See BREWERS BULLETIN, THE. 2365
0006-971X See BREWER'S DIGEST, THE. 2365
0006-9728 See BREWERS' GUARDIAN. 2365
0006-9736 See BREWER (LONDON). 2365
0006-9787 See BRIDES AND SETTING UP HOME. 2277
0006-9809 See BRIDGE (LAFAYETTE, IND.). 1089
0006-9876 See BRIDGE WORLD, THE. 4858
0007-0025 See BRIEFING PAPERS (WASHINGTON, D.C.). 1549
0007-0106 See BRIGHAM YOUNG UNIVERSITY STUDIES (1984). 4940
0007-0165 See BRINKMAN'S CUMULATIEVE CATALOGUS VAN BOEKEN. 411
0007-0173 See BRIO (UNITED KINGDOM BRANCH, INTERNATIONAL ASSOCIATION OF MUSIC LIBRARIES). 4105
0007-0270 See BRITISH ARCHAEOLOGICAL BIBLIOGRAPHY. 286
0007-0289 See BRITISH ARCHER, THE. 4888
0007-0297 See JOURNAL OF THE BRITISH ASTRONOMICAL ASSOCIATION. 396
0007-0300 See BRITISH BAKER. 2329
0007-0327 See BRITISH BEE JOURNAL. 5578
0007-0335 See BRITISH BIRDS. 5616
0007-0343 See BRITISH BOOK NEWS. 4827
0007-0440 See BRITISH CHESS MAGAZINE, THE. 4858
0007-0483 See B. C. CATHOLIC, THE. 5024
0007-0491 See DIOCESAN POST. 5059
0007-0505 See BRITISH COLUMBIA GAZETTE MICROFORM, THE. 4634
0007-0556 See BRITISH COLUMBIA MEDICAL JOURNAL. 3558
0007-0599 See BRITISH CORROSION JOURNAL. 2008
0007-0602 See BRITISH DEAF NEWS. 4385
0007-0610 See BRITISH DENTAL JOURNAL. 1317
0007-0629 See BRITISH DENTAL SURGERY ASSISTANT. 1317
0007-0637 See BRITISH EDUCATION INDEX. 1793
0007-070X See BRITISH FOOD JOURNAL (1966). 2329
0007-0718 See FOUNDRYMAN, THE. 4002
0007-0769 See BRITISH HEART JOURNAL. 3699
0007-0785 See BRITISH HOMEOPATHIC JOURNAL, THE. 3558
0007-0815 See BRITISH HUMANITIES INDEX. 2857
0007-084X See JBIS. JOURNAL OF THE BRITISH INTERPLANETARY SOCIETY. 25
0007-0874 See BRITISH JOURNAL FOR THE HISTORY OF SCIENCE, THE. 5089
0007-0882 See BRITISH JOURNAL FOR THE PHILOSOPHY OF SCIENCE, THE. 5089
0007-0904 See BRITISH JOURNAL OF AESTHETICS. 344
0007-0912 See BRITISH JOURNAL OF ANAESTHESIA. 3682
0007-0920 See BRITISH JOURNAL OF CANCER. 3809
0007-0947 See BRITISH JOURNAL OF CLINICAL PRACTICE, THE. 3558
0007-0955 See BRITISH JOURNAL OF CRIMINOLOGY, DELINQUENCY AND DEVIANT SOCIAL BEHAVIOR, THE. 3158
0007-0963 See BRITISH JOURNAL OF DERMATOLOGY (1951). 3718
0007-0998 See BRITISH JOURNAL OF EDUCATIONAL PSYCHOLOGY, THE. 4578
0007-1005 See BRITISH JOURNAL OF EDUCATIONAL STUDIES. 1728
0007-1013 See BRITISH JOURNAL OF EDUCATIONAL TECHNOLOGY. 1889
0007-1048 See BRITISH JOURNAL OF HAEMATOLOGY. 3771
0007-1064 See BRITISH JOURNAL OF HOSPITAL MEDICINE. 3559

0007-1072 See BRITISH JOURNAL OF INDUSTRIAL MEDICINE. 2859
0007-1080 See BRITISH JOURNAL OF INDUSTRIAL RELATIONS. 1656
0007-1102 See BRITISH JOURNAL OF MATHEMATICAL & STATISTICAL PSYCHOLOGY, THE. 4622
0007-1129 See BRITISH JOURNAL OF MEDICAL PSYCHOLOGY. 4578
0007-1137 See BRITISH JOURNAL OF NON-DESTRUCTIVE TESTING. 2101
0007-1145 See BRITISH JOURNAL OF NUTRITION, THE. 4188
0007-1161 See BRITISH JOURNAL OF OPHTHALMOLOGY. 3872
0007-1188 See BRITISH JOURNAL OF PHARMACOLOGY. 4294
0007-1196 See BRITISH JOURNAL OF PHOTOGRAPHY. 4367
0007-1226 See BRITISH JOURNAL OF PLASTIC SURGERY. 3961
0007-1234 See BRITISH JOURNAL OF POLITICAL SCIENCE. 4466
0007-1250 See BRITISH JOURNAL OF PSYCHIATRY, THE. 3922
0007-1269 See BRITISH JOURNAL OF PSYCHOLOGY (1955). 4578
0007-1285 See BRITISH JOURNAL OF RADIOLOGY, THE. 3939
0007-1315 See BRITISH JOURNAL OF SOCIOLOGY, THE. 5240
0007-1323 See BRITISH JOURNAL OF SURGERY. 3961
0007-1331 See BRITISH JOURNAL OF UROLOGY. 3988
0007-1420 See BRITISH MEDICAL BULLETIN. 3559
0007-1498 See BULLETIN OF THE BRITISH MUSEUM (NATURAL HISTORY). ZOOLOGY SERIES. 5579
0007-1544 See BRITISH NATIONAL BIBLIOGRAPHY. 3257
0007-1595 See BULLETIN OF THE BRITISH ORNITHOLOGIST'S CLUB. 5616
0007-1617 See BRITISH PHYCOLOGICAL JOURNAL. 504
0007-1668 See BRITISH POULTRY SCIENCE. 207
0007-1684 See BRITISH PRINTER, THE. 4564
0007-1773 See JBSP. JOURNAL OF THE BRITISH SOCIETY FOR PHENOMENOLOGY. 4350
0007-182X See BRITISH STEEL. 1600
0007-1854 See BRITISH SUGAR BEET REVIEW. 165
0007-1870 See BRITISH TAX REVIEW. 4714
0007-1935 See BRITISH VETERINARY JOURNAL, THE. 5506
0007-196X See BRITTONIA. 504
0007-1994 See BROADCAST ENGINEERING (OVERLAND PARK). 1127
0007-2028 See BROADCASTING (WASHINGTON, D.C. 1957). 1128
0007-2176 See BROILER INDUSTRY. 207
0007-2249 See BRONX COUNTY HISTORICAL SOCIETY JOURNAL, THE. 2724
0007-2303 See BROOKINGS PAPERS ON ECONOMIC ACTIVITY. 1465
0007-232X See BROOKLYN BARRISTER. 2944
0007-2346 See BROOKLYN HEIGHTS PRESS & COBBLE HILL NEWS. 5714
0007-2362 See BROOKLYN LAW REVIEW. 2944
0007-2494 See BROWN GOLD. 4940
0007-2516 See BROWN SWISS BULLETIN, THE. 207
0007-2621 See BRUEL & KJAER TECHNICAL REVIEW. 1967
0007-2710 See BRUSHWARE (WASHINGTON, D.C.). 2810
0007-2737 See BRYGMESTEREN. 2365
0007-2745 See BRYOLOGIST, THE. 504
0007-2761 See BUCH DER ZEIT. 4812
0007-2826 See OHIO BEVERAGE JOURNAL. 2370
0007-2834 See BUCKEYE FARM NEWS. 68

0007-2869 See BUCKNELL REVIEW. 3338
0007-2907 See BUDAVOX TELECOMMUNICATION REVIEW. 1150
0007-3059 See BUECHERSCHIFF; DIE DEUTSCHE BUECHERZEITUNG. 4827
0007-3075 See BUHNE (VIENNA, AUSTRIA : 1958). 5362
0007-3075 See BUEHNE. 4105
0007-3091 See BUEHNENTECHNISCHE RUNDSCHAU. 5362
0007-3229 See BUILD; JOURNAL OF THE INDUSTRY. 602
0007-3318 See BUILDING (LONDON. ENGLAND). 603
0007-3407 See BUILDING DESIGN & CONSTRUCTION. 294
0007-3423 See BUILDING DESIGN. 294
0007-3431 See BUILDING ECONOMIST, THE. 603
0007-3490 See BUILDING OPERATING MANAGEMENT. 603
0007-3547 See BUILDING OFFICIAL AND CODE ADMINISTRATOR, THE. 603
0007-3555 See BUILDING-PERMIT ACTIVITY IN FLORIDA (MONTHLY). 603
0007-3636 See BUILDING SCIENCE ABSTRACTS. 604
0007-3644 See BUILDING SERVICES CONTRACTOR. 604
0007-3717 See BUILDING TRADESMAN, THE. 605
0007-3725 See BUILDINGS (CEDAR RAPIDS. 1947). 605
0007-3776 See BUKHGALTERSKII UCHET. 740
0007-389X See BULETIN VURH VODNANY. 2297
0007-392X See BULGARIAN FOREIGN TRADE. 825
0007-3938 See SPISANIE NA BALGARSKOTO GEOLOGICESKO DRUZESTVO. 1398
0007-3989 See SPISANIE NA BULGARSKATA AKADEMIIA NA NAUKITE. 5159
0007-4039 See BULLETIN (SYDNEY). 2510
0007-4071 See BULLETIN ANALYTIQUE DE DOCUMENTATION POLITIQUE, ECONOMIQUE ET SOCIALE CONTEMPORAINE / FONDATION NATIONAL DES SCIENCES POLITIQUES. 5193
0007-4101 See BULLETIN ANALYTIQUE PETROLIER. 4252
0007-4128 See BULLETIN BAUDELAIRIEN. 3460
0007-4160 See BULLETIN BIBLIOGRAPHIQUE INTERNATIONAL DU MACHINISME AGRICOLE. 152
0007-4209 See BULLETIN CRITIQUE DU LIVRE FRANCAIS. 3338
0007-4217 See BULLETIN DE CORRESPONDANCE HELLENIQUE. 4343
0007-4314 See BULLETIN DE L'A.I.M. 4940
0007-4322 See BULLETIN DE LITTERATURE ECCLESIASTIQUE. 5025
0007-4403 See BULLETIN DE PSYCHOLOGIE. 4578
0007-4411 See BULLETIN DE PSYCHOLOGIE SCOLAIRE ET D'ORIENTATION. 4578
0007-442X See BULLETIN DE THEOLOGIE ANCIENNE ET MEDIEVALE. 4941
0007-4446 See BULLETIN DES AGRICULTEURS. 69
0007-4497 See BULLETIN DES SCIENCES MATHEMATIQUES. 3498
0007-4519 See BULLETIN DES TRANSPORTS ET DE LA LOGISTIQUE PARIS. 5378
0007-4551 See BULLETIN DU CANCER. 3810
0007-4624 See BULLETIN FOR INTERNATIONAL FISCAL DOCUMENTATION. 4715
0007-4632 See BULLETIN GEODESIQUE. 1403
0007-4640 See BULLETIN HISPANIQUE. 3370
0007-4713 See BULLETIN MENSUEL DE STATISTIQUE. 5324
0007-473X See BULLETIN MONUMENTAL. 345
0007-4764 See AMERICAN JOURNAL OF ART THERAPY. 336
0007-4802 See BULLETIN OF CANADIAN PETROLEUM GEOLOGY. 4252
0007-4810 See BULLETIN OF CONCERNED ASIAN SCHOLARS. 2647

0007-4837 *See* BULLETIN OF DENTAL EDUCATION. **1318**

0007-4845 *See* BULLETIN OF ENDEMIC DISEASES. **4769**

0007-4853 *See* BULLETIN OF ENTOMOLOGICAL RESEARCH. **5606**

0007-4861 *See* BULLETIN OF ENVIRONMENTAL CONTAMINATION AND TOXICOLOGY. **3979**

0007-4888 *See* BULLETIN OF EXPERIMENTAL BIOLOGY AND MEDICINE. **3560**

0007-4896 *See* BULLETIN OF GRAIN TECHNOLOGY. **200**

0007-490X *See* BULLETIN OF HISPANIC STUDIES. **3271**

0007-4918 *See* BULLETIN OF INDONESIAN ECONOMIC STUDIES. **1466**

0007-4950 *See* BULLETIN OF LABOUR STATISTICS. **1530**

0007-4969 *See* BULLETIN OF LEGAL DEVELOPMENTS. **3125**

0007-4977 *See* BULLETIN OF MARINE SCIENCE. **1447**

0007-5027 *See* LABORATORY MEDICINE. **3603**

0007-5035 *See* BULLETIN OF PEACE PROPOSALS. **4466**

0007-5108 *See* BULLETIN OF THE COMEDIANTES. **3370**

0007-5124 *See* JIKKEN DOBUTSU. **3592**

0007-5132 *See* BULLETIN OF THE HISTORY OF DENTISTRY. **1318**

0007-5140 *See* BULLETIN OF THE HISTORY OF MEDICINE. **3560**

0007-5167 *See* BULLETIN OF ZOOLOGICAL NOMENCLATURE, THE. **5580**

0007-523X *See* BULLETIN ON NARCOTICS. **1342**

0007-5248 *See* BULLETIN ON THE RHEUMATIC DISEASES. **3804**

0007-5256 *See* BULLETIN ORNITHOLOGIQUE (ORSAINVILLE). **5616**

0007-5264 *See* BULLETIN QUOTIDIEN D'AFRIQUE. **2498**

0007-5302 *See* BULLETIN SIGNALETIQUE DES TELECOMMUNICATIONS. **1150**

0007-5434 *See* BULLETIN SIGNALETIQUE 320: BIOCHEMIE. BIOPHYSIQUE. CHEMIE ANALYTIQUE BIOLOGIQUE. BIOPHYSIQUE. GENIE BIOLOGIQUE ET MEDICAL. **450**

0007-554X See FRANCIS BULLETIN SIGNALETIQUE. 519, PHILOSOPHIE. **4347**

0007-5558 See FRANCIS BULLETIN SIGNALETIQUE. 520, SCIENCES DE L'EDUCATION. **1747**

0007-5574 See FRANCIS BULLETIN SIGNALETIQUE. 522, HISTOIRE DES SCIENCES ET DES TECHNIQUES. **5106**

0007-5590 See FRANCIS BULLETIN SIGNALETIQUE. 524, SCIENCES DU LANGAGE. **3282**

0007-5612 See FRANCIS BULLETIN SIGNALETIQUE. 526, ART ET ARCHEOLOGIE. **268**

0007-5655 *See* BULLETIN SIGNALETIQUE. 740, METAUX, METALLURGIE. **3999**

0007-5663 *See* BULLETIN SIGNALETIQUE. [SECTION] 761. MICROSCOPIE ELECTRONIQUE, DIFFRACTION ELECTRONIQUE. **572**

0007-568X *See* BULLETIN SIGNALETIQUE. 800 : GENIE CHEMIQUE, INDUSTRIES CHEMIQUE ET PARACHIMIQUE. **1021**

0007-5752 *See* BULLETIN TECHNIQUE DU BUREAU VERITAS. **4175**

0007-5779 *See* BULLETINS OF AMERICAN PALEONTOLOGY. **4226**

0007-5795 *See* BULLETTINO STORICO EMPOLESE. **2682**

0007-5809 *See* BULLETTINO STORICO PISTOIESE. **2682**

0007-585X *See* AMTLICHE NACHRICHTEN DER BUNDESANSTALT FUER ARBEIT. **1799**

0007-5868 *See* BUNDESARBEITSBLATT. **1657**

0007-5876 *See* BUNDESBAHN, DIE. **5430**

0007-5884 *See* BUNDESBAUBLATT. **2816**

0007-5914 *See* BUNDESGESUNDHEITSBLATT. **4770**

0007-5922 *See* MITTEILUNGEN KLOSTERNEUBURG : REBE UND WEIN, OBSTBAU UND FRUCHTEVERWERTUNG. **2369**

0007-6007 *See* BUR (CHICAGO, ILL.), THE. **1318**

0007-6031 *See* BURDA-MODEN (1964). **1082**

0007-6201 *See* BURGEN UND SCHLOSSER. **2682**

0007-6260 *See* BURIED HISTORY. **265**

0007-6287 *See* BURLINGTON MAGAZINE. **346**

0007-6309 *See* BURNING BUSH. **5057**

0007-6392 *See* BUSES SHEPPERTON. **5378**

0007-6465 *See* BUSINESS AND ECONOMIC REVIEW (COLUMBIA). **862**

0007-6473 *See* BUSINESS AND FINANCE. **781**

0007-6503 *See* BUSINESS AND SOCIETY. **645**

0007-6538 *See* BUSINESS ARCHIVES. **3199**

0007-6570 *See* BUSINESS COMMERCIAL AVIATION. **15**

0007-666X *See* BUSINESS ECONOMICS (CLEVELAND, OHIO). **1466**

0007-6678 *See* BUSINESS EDUCATION FORUM. **647**

0007-6708 *See* BUSINESS EQUIPMENT DIGEST. **4210**

0007-6724 *See* BUSINESS EUROPE. **648**

0007-6791 *See* BUSINESS HISTORY. **648**

0007-6805 *See* BUSINESS HISTORY REVIEW. **648**

0007-6805 *See* BUSINESS HISTORY REVIEW. **648**

0007-683X *See* BUSINESS IN NEBRASKA. **649**

0007-6856 *See* BUSINESS INQUIRY. **649**

0007-6864 *See* BUSINESS INSURANCE. **2877**

0007-6872 *See* BUSINESS INTERNATIONAL. **649**

0007-6880 *See* BUSINESS LATIN AMERICA. **650**

0007-6899 *See* BUSINESS LAWYER, THE. **3097**

0007-6945 *See* BUSINESS MEMO FROM BELGIUM. **893**

0007-6961 *See* BUSINESS PERIODICALS INDEX. CD-ROM. **727**

0007-6961 *See* BUSINESS PERIODICALS INDEX. **727**

0007-6996 *See* BUSINESS QUARTERLY, THE. **652**

0007-7011 *See* BUSINESS REVIEW (PHILADELPHIA). **1467**

0007-7097 *See* BUSINESS SYSTEMS AND EQUIPMENT (LONDON, 1972). **4211**

0007-7100 *See* BUSINESS TODAY. **653**

0007-7135 *See* BUSINESS WEEK. **653**

0007-7194 *See* BUSKAP OG AVDRATT. **208**

0007-7356 *See* BUVAR. **450**

0007-7518 *See* BYGGEKUNST. **294**

0007-7550 *See* BYGGMASTAREN. **294**

0007-7658 *See* BYPLAN. **2816**

0007-7682 *See* BULLETEN' MOSKOVSKOGO OBSESTVA ISPYTATELEJ PRIRODY. NOVAA SERIA. OTDEL BIOLOGICESKIJ. **449**

0007-7704 *See* BYZANTINISCHE ZEITSCHRIFT. **2682**

0007-7712 *See* BYZANTINOSLAVICA. **3457**

0007-7720 *See* CANADIAN REVIEW OF AMERICAN STUDIES. **2530**

0007-7771 *See* CAHS JOURNAL, THE. **15**

0007-7798 *See* CALF NEWS. **208**

0007-8034 *See* CEA FORUM. **3273**

0007-8050 *See* CEA ADVISOR. **1731**

0007-8069 *See* CEA CRITIC, THE. **3273**

0007-8069 *See* CEA CRITIC. **3373**

0007-8204 *See* ENGLISH EDUCATION. **1894**

0007-8506 *See* CIRP ANNALS. **2111**

0007-8514 *See* CIS INDEX TO PUBLICATIONS OF THE UNITED STATES CONGRESS. **4697**

0007-8549 *See* CLA JOURNAL. **3273**

0007-8638 *See* CMEA NEWS. **4110**

0007-8654 *See* CMM, CONFECTIONERY MANUFACTURE AND MARKETING. **3477**

0007-8816 *See* COPNIP LIST. **4298**

0007-8867 See CPA LETTER, THE. **742**

0007-8883 *See* CPCU NEWS. **2878**

0007-8905 *See* CPH COMMENTATOR. **4813**

0007-893X *See* CQ. **1130**

0007-8972 *See* FOODSERVICE & HOSPITALITY. **5071**

0007-912X *See* CSIRO ABSTRACTS. **5097**

0007-9219 *See* CTVD, CINEMA, TV DIGEST. **1109**

0007-9227 *See* CWA NEWS. **1662**

0007-9235 *See* CA. **3810**

0007-9243 *See* CA VA. **1890**

0007-928X *See* AUSTRALIAN HOME BEAUTIFUL. **2898**

0007-9367 *See* CACTUS AND SUCCULENT JOURNAL (SANTA BARBARA). **2411**

0007-9405 *See* CADENZA (LOLO, MONT.). **4106**

0007-9502 *See* CAESARAUGUSTA. **265**

0007-9510 *See* CAFE, CACAO, THE. **165**

0007-9537 *See* CAFE SOLO. **3461**

0007-9553 *See* CAFFE; SATIRICO DI LETTERATURA E ATTUALITA, IL. **3370**

0007-9588 *See* AFRICAN ADMINISTRATIVE STUDIES. **4625**

0007-9588 *See* CAHIERS AFRICAINS D'ADMINISTRATION PUBLIQUE. **4635**

0007-9626 *See* CAHIERS BRUXELLOIS. **2682**

0007-9685 *See* CAHIERS D'ANESTHESIOLOGIE. **3682**

0007-9693 *See* CAHIERS D'ARCHEOLOGIE ET D'HISTORIE DU BERRY. **265**

0007-9723 *See* CAHIERS DE BIOLOGIE MARINE. **553**

0007-9731 *See* CAHIERS DE CIVILISATION MEDIEVALE. **2682**

0007-974X *See* CAHIERS DE DROIT (QUEBEC). **2946**

0007-9758 *See* CAHIERS DE DROIT EUROPEEN. **2946**

0007-9766 *See* CAHIERS DE GEOGRAPHIE DU QUEBEC. **2557**

0007-9782 *See* CAHIERS DE KINESITHERAPIE. **3953**

0007-9804 *See* CAHIERS DE LA DOCUMENTATION. **3199**

0007-9820 *See* CAHIERS DE LA PUERICULTRICE. **3852**

0007-9871 *See* CAHIERS DE LEXICOLOGIE. **3271**

0007-988X *See* CAHIERS DE LINGUISTIQUE THEORIQUE ET APPLIQUEE. **3271**

0007-9936 *See* CAHIERS DE MEDECINE INTERPROFESSIONNELLE. **3561**

0007-9952 *See* CAHIERS DE NOTES DOCUMENTAIRES. **4770**

0007-9960 *See* CAHIERS DE NUTRITION ET DE DIETETIQUE. **4188**

0007-9995 *See* CAHIERS DE SOCIOLOGIE ET DE DEMOGRAPHIE MEDICALES. **4770**

0008-0012 *See* CAHIERS DE TUNISIE. **2638**

0008-0039 *See* CAHIERS DES NATURALISTES. **5194**

0008-0047 *See* CAHIERS DES RELIGIONS AFRICAINES. **4942**

0008-0055 *See* CAHIERS D'ETUDES AFRICAINES. **2638**

0008-0063 *See* CAHIERS D'ETUDES CATHARES. **4942**

0008-008X *See* CAHIERS D'HISTOIRE. **2612**

0008-011X *See* CAHIERS DU CINEMA. **4064**

0008-0136 *See* CAHIERS DU COMMUNISME. **4540**

0008-0152 *See* CAHIERS DU MONDE HISPANIQUE ET LUSO-BRESILIEN. **3371**

0008-0152 *See* CAHIERS DU MONDE HISPANIQUE ET LUSO-BRESILIEN. **2725**

0008-0160 *See* CAHIERS DU MONDE RUSSE ET SOVIETIQUE. **2682**

0008-0195 *See* CAHIERS ECONOMIQUES DE BRUXELLES. **1467**

0008-0209 *See* CAHIERS ECONOMIQUES ET SOCIAUX (KINSHASA). **1550**

0008-0217 *See* CAHIERS FRANCAIS, LES. **2682**

0008-0241 *See* CAHIERS GEOLOGIQUES. **1371**

0008-025X *See* CAHIERS HAUT-MARNAIS, LES. **2613**

0008-0276 *See* CAHIERS INTERNATIONAUX DE SOCIOLOGIE. **5241**

0008-0284 See CAHIERS INTERNATIONAUX DE SYMBOLISME. 4579
0008-0365 See CAHIERS NATURALISTES, LES. 3371
0008-0381 See CAHIERS O.R.S.T.O.M: SERIE HYDROBIOLOGIE. 450
0008-0497 See CAHIERS VILFREDO PARETO. 5194
0008-0543 See CAL-TAX NEWS. 4716
0008-0578 See CALAVO NEWSLETTER. 165
0008-0586 See CALCIFIED TISSUE ABSTRACTS. 3655
0008-0624 See CALCOLO. 3499
0008-0659 See BULLETIN OF THE CALCUTTA MATHEMATICAL SOCIETY. 3498
0008-0667 See CALCUTTA MEDICAL JOURNAL. 3561
0008-0683 See BULLETIN - CALCUTTA STATISTICAL ASSOCIATION. 5324
0008-0802 See CALIFORNIA AFL-CIO NEWS. 1657
0008-0845 See CALIFORNIA AGRICULTURE (BERKELEY, CALIF.). 71
0008-087X See CALIFORNIA AIR QUALITY DATA. 2226
0008-0896 See CALIFORNIA APPAREL NEWS. 1082
0008-090X See CALIFORNIA-ARIZONA COTTON. 166
0008-0918 See CALIFORNIA BOWLING NEWS. 4889
0008-0926 See CALIFORNIA BUSINESS. 654
0008-0942 See CALIFORNIA CATTLEMAN. 208
0008-1000 See BULLETIN / CALIFORNIA DIVISION OF MINES AND GEOLOGY. 2135
0008-1027 See CALIFORNIA ENGINEER. 1967
0008-1051 See CALIFORNIA FARMER. 71
0008-106X See WESTERN FINANCIAL JOURNAL. 4758
0008-1078 See CALIFORNIA FISH AND GAME. 2189
0008-1108 See CALIFORNIA FUTURE FARMER. 71
0008-1116 See CALIFORNIA GARDEN. 2411
0008-1124 See CALIFORNIA GRANGE NEWS. 5633
0008-1140 See CALIFORNIA HIGHWAY PATROLMAN, THE. 3159
0008-1205 See CALIFORNIA JOURNAL. 4466
0008-1221 See CALIFORNIA LAW REVIEW. 2946
0008-1256 See CALIFORNIA MANAGEMENT REVIEW. 862
0008-1299 See CALIFORNIA MINING JOURNAL. 2136
0008-1302 See CALIFORNIA MONTHLY. 1090
0008-1310 See CALIFORNIA NURSE. 3852
0008-1329 See PACIFIC OIL WORLD. 4271
0008-1418 See CALIFORNIA PROFESSOR. 1813
0008-1434 See CALIFORNIA PUBLISHER. 4813
0008-1450 See CALIFORNIA REAL ESTATE (1975). 4835
0008-1515 See CALIFORNIA SCHOOL EMPLOYEE, THE. 1861
0008-1558 See CALIFORNIA SOUTHERN BAPTIST, THE. 5057
0008-1566 See CALIFORNIA STATE EMPLOYEE, THE. 1658
0008-1582 See CALIFORNIA TECH, THE. 1090
0008-1612 See CALIFORNIA VETERINARIAN, THE. 5507
0008-1620 See BULLETIN - CALIFORNIA WATER POLLUTION CONTROL ASSOCIATION. 2225
0008-1639 See CALIFORNIA WESTERN LAW REVIEW. 2947
0008-1663 See CALIFORNIA WOMAN, THE. 5552
0008-1795 See CALVIN THEOLOGICAL JOURNAL. 4942
0008-1973 See CAMBRIDGE LAW JOURNAL, THE. 2947
0008-199X See CAMBRIDGE QUARTERLY. 3339
0008-2007 See CAMBRIDGE REVIEW, THE. 1090

0008-2015 See CAMBRIDGE UNIVERSITY REPORTER. 1090
0008-204X See CAMELLIA JOURNAL, THE. 2411
0008-2082 See CAMERART. 4368
0008-2090 See CAMERA CANADA. 4368
0008-2287 See CAMP FIRE LEADERSHIP. 5229
0008-2309 See CAMPAIGN (LONDON. 1968). 757
0008-2473 See CAMPO; REVISTA MENSUAL AGRICOLA Y GANADERA. 72
0008-2538 See CAMPUS LIFE (WHEATON, ILL.). 1061
0008-2570 See AIR CARRIER OPERATIONS IN CANADA. 7
0008-2627 See RESTAURANT, CATERER AND TAVERN STATISTICS. 5073
0008-2732 See CANADA POULTRYMAN. 208
0008-2775 See CANADAN UUTISET. 5781
0008-2791 See CANADA'S MENTAL HEALTH. 4770
0008-2813 See CANADIAN ADMINISTRATOR, THE. 1861
0008-2821 See CANADIAN AERONAUTICS AND SPACE JOURNAL. 15
0008-2848 See CANADIAN AIRCRAFT OPERATOR, THE. 15
0008-2872 See CANADIAN ARCHITECT, THE. 294
0008-2937 See CANADIAN AUTHOR & BOOKMAN. 3372
0008-2961 See CANADIAN AYRSHIRE REVIEW. 72
0008-2988 See CANADIAN BAPTIST, THE. 4942
0008-3003 See CANADIAN BAR REVIEW, THE. 3125
0008-3003 See CANADIAN BAR REVIEW. REVUE DU BARREAU CANADIEN, THE. 2947
0008-302X See BULLETIN OF THE CANADIAN BIOCHEMICAL SOCIETY. 484
0008-3038 See BROADCASTER (TORONTO). 1128
0008-3046 See BULLETIN - CANADIAN BOTANICAL ASSOCIATION. 504
0008-3097 See CANADIAN BUILDING DIGEST. 606
0008-3100 See CANADIAN BUSINESS (1977). 654
0008-3143 See CATTLEMEN. 209
0008-3194 See JOURNAL OF THE CANADIAN CHIROPRACTIC ASSOCIATION, THE. 3805
0008-3208 See JOURNAL OF THE CANADIAN CHURCH HISTORICAL SOCIETY. 4970
0008-3224 See CANADIAN CLEANER & LAUNDERER. 1600
0008-3232 See CANADIAN CLOTHING JOURNAL. 1082
0008-3259 See COMPOSITEUR CANADIEN. 4111
0008-3259 See CANADIAN COMPOSER, THE. 4107
0008-3259 See CANADIAN COMPOSER. 4107
0008-3267 See CANADIAN CONSULTING ENGINEER. 1967
0008-3275 See CANADIAN CONSUMER (1963). 1294
0008-3291 See CANADIAN COPPER. 3999
0008-3348 See CANADIAN CRIMINAL CASES (BOUND CUMULATION). 3105
0008-3364 See CANADIAN DATASYSTEMS. 1256
0008-3402 See CANADIAN DIMENSION. 4467
0008-3410 See CANADIAN DISCIPLE. 4942
0008-3445 See NEWSLETTER - CANADIAN EDUCATION ASSOCIATION. 1867
0008-3453 See CANADIAN EDUCATION INDEX. 1793
0008-347X See CANADIAN ENTOMOLOGIST, THE. 5606
0008-3496 See CANADIAN ETHNIC STUDIES. 2257
0008-350X See CANADIAN FAMILY PHYSICIAN. 3737
0008-3577 See CANADIAN FLIGHT. 16
0008-3585 See CANADIAN FLORIST, GREENHOUSE AND NURSERY. 2435
0008-3631 See CANADIAN FORUM. 3339

0008-3658 See CANADIAN GEOGRAPHER. 2558
0008-3674 See CANADIAN GEOTECHNICAL JOURNAL. 1352
0008-3704 See CANADIAN GROCER. 2330
0008-3712 See CANADIAN GUIDE. 2530
0008-3720 See CANADIAN HAIRDRESSER. 402
0008-3739 See CANADIAN HEREFORD DIGEST. 208
0008-3755 See CANADIAN HISTORICAL REVIEW. 2726
0008-3763 See CANADIAN HOME ECONOMICS JOURNAL. 2789
0008-3828 See CANADIAN INDEPENDENT ADJUSTER, THE. 2877
0008-3879 See CANADIAN INSURANCE. 2877
0008-3887 See CANADIAN INTERIORS. 2899
0008-3909 See CANADIAN JERSEY BREEDER. 208
0008-3917 See CANADIAN JEWELLER. 2913
0008-3941 See CANADIAN JEWISH NEWS (TORONTO). 2257
0008-3968 See CANADIAN JOURNAL OF AFRICAN STUDIES. 2638
0008-3976 See CANADIAN JOURNAL OF AGRICULTURAL ECONOMICS. 72
0008-3984 See CANADIAN JOURNAL OF ANIMAL SCIENCE. 208
0008-400X See CANADIAN JOURNAL OF BEHAVIOURAL SCIENCE. 4579
0008-4026 See CANADIAN JOURNAL OF BOTANY. 505
0008-4034 See CANADIAN JOURNAL OF CHEMICAL ENGINEERING, THE. 2008
0008-4042 See CANADIAN JOURNAL OF CHEMISTRY. 966
0008-4077 See CANADIAN JOURNAL OF EARTH SCIENCES. 1353
0008-4085 See CANADIAN JOURNAL OF ECONOMICS, THE. 1468
0008-4107 See CANADIAN JOURNAL OF HISTORY. 2613
0008-4123 See CANADIAN JOURNAL OF HOSPITAL PHARMACY. 4295
0008-4131 See CANADIAN JOURNAL OF LINGUISTICS. 3272
0008-414X See CANADIAN JOURNAL OF MATHEMATICS. 3499
0008-4158 See CANADIAN JOURNAL OF MEDICAL TECHNOLOGY. 3562
0008-4166 See CANADIAN JOURNAL OF MICROBIOLOGY. 560
0008-4174 See CANADIAN JOURNAL OF OCCUPATIONAL THERAPY (1939). 3922
0008-4182 See CANADIAN JOURNAL OF OPHTHALMOLOGY. 3873
0008-4204 See CANADIAN JOURNAL OF PHYSICS. 4399
0008-4212 See CANADIAN JOURNAL OF PHYSIOLOGY AND PHARMACOLOGY. 579
0008-4220 See CANADIAN JOURNAL OF PLANT SCIENCE. 505
0008-4239 See CANADIAN JOURNAL OF POLITICAL SCIENCE. 4467
0008-4255 See CANADIAN JOURNAL OF PSYCHOLOGY. 4579
0008-4263 See CANADIAN JOURNAL OF PUBLIC HEALTH. 4770
0008-4263 See CANADIAN JOURNAL OF PUBLIC HEALTH. 4770
0008-4271 See CANADIAN JOURNAL OF SOIL SCIENCE. 1371
0008-4271 See CANADIAN JOURNAL OF SOIL SCIENCE. 166
0008-428X See CANADIAN JOURNAL OF SURGERY. 3961
0008-4298 See STUDIES IN RELIGION. 5001
0008-4301 See CANADIAN JOURNAL OF ZOOLOGY. 5580
0008-4352 See CANADIAN LIBRARY JOURNAL. 3200
0008-4360 See CANADIAN LITERATURE. 3372
0008-4379 See CANADIAN MACHINERY AND METALWORKING. 2111

0008-4395 See CANADIAN MATHEMATICAL BULLETIN. 3499
0008-4433 See CANADIAN METALLURGICAL QUARTERLY. 3999
0008-4433 See CANADIAN METALLURGICAL QUARTERLY. 3999
0008-4468 See CANADIAN MILITARY JOURNAL. 4038
0008-4476 See CANADIAN MINERALOGIST, THE. 1438
0008-4492 See CANADIAN MINING JOURNAL. 2136
0008-4506 See CANADIAN MODERN LANGUAGE REVIEW, THE. 3272
0008-4549 See CANADIAN MUSIC EDUCATOR, THE. 4107
0008-4557 See BULLETIN - CANADIAN COMMISSION FOR UNESCO. 5193
0008-4565 See CANADIAN NEWS FACTS. 2530
0008-4573 See CANADIAN NUMISMATIC JOURNAL, THE. 2780
0008-4581 See CANADIAN NURSE (1924). 3852
0008-4611 See CANADIAN OCCUPATIONAL SAFETY. 2860
0008-4654 See CANADIAN PACKAGING. 4218
0008-4670 See PATENT OFFICE RECORD, THE. 1307
0008-4689 See CANADIAN PATENT REPORTER. 1302
0008-4697 See PEACE RESEARCH. 4531
0008-4719 See CANADIAN PERIODICAL INDEX (1964). 412
0008-476X See CANADIAN PLANT DISEASE SURVEY. 72
0008-4778 See CANADIAN PLASTICS. 4454
0008-4840 See CANADIAN PUBLIC ADMINISTRATION. 4636
0008-4859 See CANADIAN PUBLISHERS' DIRECTORY. 4813
0008-4875 See CANADIAN RAIL. 5430
0008-4948 See CANADIAN REVIEW OF SOCIOLOGY AND ANTHROPOLOGY, THE. 233
0008-4972 See CANADIAN SAILOR. 5448
0008-5006 See CANADIAN SLAVONIC PAPERS. 3272
0008-5030 See CANADIAN SOCIETY OF FORENSIC SCIENCE JOURNAL. 3740
0008-5073 See CANADIAN SPORTSMAN, THE. 2798
0008-5111 See CANADIAN TAX JOURNAL. 4716
0008-512X See CANADIAN TAX PAPERS. 4716
0008-5170 See CANADIAN TEXTILE JOURNAL. 5348
0008-5189 See CANADIAN TOBACCO GROWER, THE. 5372
0008-5219 See CANADIAN TRAVEL COURIER. 5465
0008-5251 See CANADIAN UNDERWRITER. 2877
0008-5286 See CANADIAN VETERINARY JOURNAL. 5507
0008-5391 See CANADIANA. 412
0008-5405 See CANARD ENCHAINE, LE. 4467
0008-543X See CANCER. 3810
0008-5464 See CANCER NEWS (NEW YORK, N.Y.). 3812
0008-5472 See CANCER RESEARCH (BALTIMORE). 3812
0008-5650 See CANON LAW ABSTRACTS. 5012
0008-5677 See CANTERAS Y EXPLOTACIONES. 2111
0008-5774 See CAPAHA ARROW, THE. 1090
0008-5790 See CAPE LIBRARIAN, THE. 3200
0008-5847 See CAPITAL (HAMBURG). 1550
0008-5898 See CAPITAL VOICE. 4942
0008-5952 See CCCO NEWS NOTES. 4039
0008-5987 See CAR. 5408
0008-6002 See CAR AND DRIVER. 5408
0008-6010 See CAR CRAFT. 5409
0008-6029 See CAR-DEL SCRIBE. 2441
0008-6037 See CAR MECHANICS. 5409
0008-6126 See CARACTERE. 4564

0008-6207 See CARAVEL MAGAZINE. 2530
0008-6215 See CARBOHYDRATE RESEARCH. 1040
0008-6223 See CARBON (NEW YORK). 1035
0008-6312 See CARDIOLOGY. 3700
0008-6347 See CARDIOLOGY DIGEST (1979). 3701
0008-6355 See CARDIO-VASCULAR NURSING. 3853
0008-6363 See CARDIOVASCULAR RESEARCH. 3702
0008-6436 See CARIBBEAN CHALLENGE. 5015
0008-6452 See CARIBBEAN JOURNAL OF SCIENCE. 5092
0008-6460 See CARIBBEAN JOURNAL OF SCIENCE AND MATHEMATICS, THE. 5092
0008-6525 See CARIBBEAN REVIEW. 4467
0008-6533 See CARIBBEAN STUDIES (RIO PIEDRAS, SAN JUAN, P.R.). 2727
0008-6568 See CARIES RESEARCH. 1318
0008-6606 See CARINTHIA I. 2683
0008-6614 See CARITAS (FREIBURG IM BREISGAU). 4334
0008-6622 See CARITAS-KORRESPONDENZ. 5276
0008-6673 See CARMELUS. 5025
0008-6681 See CARNEGIE MAGAZINE. 2844
0008-672X See CAROLINA CHRISTIAN. 4942
0008-6746 See CAROLINA COUNTRY. 1541
0008-6797 See CAROLINA QUARTERLY. 3373
0008-6843 See CARPENTER. 633
0008-6878 See CARRE BLEU, LE. 294
0008-6894 See CARRELL, THE. 3373
0008-6916 See CARRIAGE JOURNAL, THE. 2772
0008-6975 See CARS & PARTS. 5409
0008-7009 See CARTACTUAL. 2558
0008-7041 See CARTOGRAPHIC JOURNAL, THE. 2581
0008-7068 See CARTOONIST PROFILES. 377
0008-7114 See CARYOLOGIA. 450
0008-7157 See REVISTA CASA DE LAS AMERICAS, LA. 3430
0008-7157 See CASA DE LAS AMERICAS. 3373
0008-7173 See CASA VOGUE. 2899
0008-7181 See CASABELLA (MILAN, ITALY, 1965). 294
0008-7211 See CASCADE CAVER, THE. 1403
0008-7254 See CASE WESTERN RESERVE JOURNAL OF INTERNATIONAL LAW. 3125
0008-7262 See CASE WESTERN RESERVE LAW REVIEW. 2949
0008-7289 See CASH BOX, THE. 5316
0008-7297 See ONTARIO CORN PRODUCER. 117
0008-7327 See CASKET & SUNNYSIDE. 2406
0008-7335 See CASOPIS LEKARU CESKYCH. 3562
0008-7378 See CASOPIS PRO MINERALOGII A GEOLOGII. 1371
0008-7378 See JOURNAL OF THE CZECH GEOLOGICAL SOCIETY. 1385
0008-7424 See CASSAZIONE PENALE : RIVISTA MENSILE DI GIURISPRUDENZA. 3092
0008-7475 See CASTANEA. 506
0008-7505 See CASTILLOS DE ESPANA. 294
0008-7521 See CASTINGS. 3999
0008-7556 See CASTRUM PEREGRINI. 3373
0008-7629 See CATALOGUE & INDEX. 3200
0008-7661 See CATALYST (PETERBOROUGH). 5241
0008-767X See CATALYST (PHILADELPHIA), THE. 967
0008-7726 See CATECHIST. 5025
0008-7750 See ANALES DE LA CATEDRA FRANCISCO SUAREZ. 4340
0008-7777 See CATERER & HOTELKEEPER. 2330
0008-7815 See CATERING INDUSTRY EMPLOYEE. 1658
0008-7874 See CATHEDRAL AGE. 294

0008-7882 See MACHLETT CATHODE PRESS. 2071
0008-7904 See CATHOLIC ADVANCE, THE. 5025
0008-7971 See CATHOLIC CHRONICLE, THE. 5025
0008-7998 See CATHOLIC DIGEST (SAINT PAUL, MINN.). 5025
0008-8056 See CATHOLIC FREE PRESS, THE. 5026
0008-8064 See CATHOLIC GAZETTE. 5026
0008-8072 See CATHOLIC HERALD. 5026
0008-8080 See CATHOLIC HISTORICAL REVIEW, THE. 5026
0008-8129 See CATHOLIC JOURNALIST. 2918
0008-8137 See CATHOLIC LAWYER, THE. 2949
0008-820X See CATHOLIC LIBRARY WORLD, THE. 3201
0008-8226 See CATHOLIC MEDICAL QUARTERLY : JOURNAL OF THE GUILD OF CATHOLIC DOCTORS. 3562
0008-8234 See CATHOLIC MESSENGER. 5026
0008-8285 See CATHOLIC PERIODICAL AND LITERATURE INDEX, THE. 5012
0008-8307 See CATHOLIC PRESS DIRECTORY. 5012
0008-8315 See CATHOLIC REVIEW (BALTIMORE, MD.), THE. 5026
0008-8390 See CATHOLIC UNIVERSITY LAW REVIEW (1975). 2949
0008-8404 See CATHOLIC VIRGINIAN. 5027
0008-8463 See CATHOLIC WORKER, THE. 5027
0008-8501 See CATHOLICA (MUNSTER). 5027
0008-8544 See CATS MAGAZINE. 4286
0008-8552 See CATTLEMAN. 209
0008-8625 See CAVES AND KARST. 1404
0008-8668 See CEBU Y DERIVADOS. 209
0008-8692 See CEIBA. 72
0008-8730 See CELL PROLIFERATION. 534
0008-8749 See CELLULAR IMMUNOLOGY. 3667
0008-8757 See CELLULE, LA. 534
0008-8765 See CELLULOSA E CARTA. 4233
0008-8781 See CELULOIDE. 4065
0008-8803 See CEMENT (BOMBAY). 606
0008-8811 See CEMENT AMSTERDAM. 606
0008-882X See CEMENT. ZAGREB. 607
0008-8838 See CEMENT & CONCRETE. 606
0008-8846 See CEMENT AND CONCRETE RESEARCH. 2020
0008-8897 See CEMENT, WAPNO, GIPS. 607
0008-8919 See CEMENTO HORMIGON. 607
0008-896X See CENOBIO. 5074
0008-8994 See CENTAURUS. 5093
0008-9036 See BULLETIN OF THE CENTER FOR CHILDREN'S BOOKS. 3370
0008-9176 See CENTRAL AFRICAN JOURNAL OF MEDICINE. 3562
0008-9192 See CENTRAL ASIATIC JOURNAL. 2648
0008-9362 See CENTRAL EUROPE JOURNAL. 2514
0008-9389 See CENTRAL EUROPEAN HISTORY. 2683
0008-9427 See BULLETIN - CENTRAL INLAND FISHERIES RESEARCH INSTITUTE BARRACKPORE. 2297
0008-9532 See CENTRAL RAILWAY CHRONICLE. 5430
0008-9559 See CENTRAL STATES ARCHAEOLOGICAL JOURNAL. 265
0008-9583 See CENTRALBLATT FUER DAS GESAMTE FORSTWESEN. 2377
0008-9680 See TRAVAUX DU CENTRE DE RECHERCHES ET D'ETUDES OCEANOGRAPHIQUES. 1457
0008-9737 See CAHIERS - CENTRE D'ETUDES DE RECHERCHE OPERATIONNELLE. 1173
0008-9826 See CENTRE MEDICAL (MOULINS). 3562
0008-9850 See CAHIERS DU CENTRE SCIENTIFIQUE ET TECHNIQUE DU BATIMENT. 5092

0008-9958 *See* CEMLA BOLETIN MENSUEL. **1469**

0009-0131 *See* BOLETIN DEL CENTRO PANAMERICANO DE FIEBRE AFTOSA. **3558**

0009-0190 *See* CERAMIC ARTS & CRAFTS. **2587**

0009-0220 *See* CERAMIC INDUSTRY. **2587**

0009-0247 *See* CERAMIC SCOPE. **2587**

0009-0271 *See* CERAMICA INFORMAZIONE. **2587**

0009-031X *See* SERAMIKKUSU. **2594**

0009-0328 *See* COPPER ENAMELING. **2588**

0009-0328 *See* CERAMIC PROJECTS. **2587**

0009-0328 *See* BRUSH DECORATION. **2586**

0009-0328 *See* CERAMICS MONTHLY. **2588**

0009-0328 *See* UNDERGLAZE DECORATION. **2595**

0009-0336 *See* CERAMIQUE MODERNE, LA. **2588**

0009-0344 *See* BULLETIN TRIMESTRIEL - CERCLE D'ETUDES NUMISMATIQUES. **2780**

0009-0352 *See* CEREAL CHEMISTRY. **1021**

0009-0379 *See* CERES (ROME, ENGLISH EDITION). **73**

0009-0409 *See* CERTIFICATED ENGINEER. **1968**

0009-0468 *See* CESKA LITERATURA. **3373**

0009-0476 *See* CESKA MYKOLOGIE. **506**

0009-0492 *See* VESTNIK CESKOSLOVENSKE AKADEMIE VED. **3649**

0009-0514 *See* CESKOSLOVENSKA DERMATOLOGIE. **3718**

0009-0522 *See* CESKOSLOVENSKA EPIDEMIOLOGIE, MIKROBIOLOGIE, IMUNOLOGIE. **3734**

0009-0530 *See* CESKOSLOVENSKA FARMACIE. **4296**

0009-0549 *See* FOTOGRAFIE. **4369**

0009-0557 *See* CESKOSLOVENSKA FYSIOLOGIE. **579**

0009-0565 *See* CESKOSLOVENSKA GASTROENTEROLOGIA A VYZIVA. **3795**

0009-0573 *See* CESKOSLOVENSKA HYGIENA. **561**

0009-059X *See* CESKOSLOVENSKA OFTALMOLOGIE. **3873**

0009-0603 *See* CESKOSLOVENSKA OTOLARYNGOLOGIE. **3887**

0009-0611 *See* CESKOSLOVENSKA PATOLOGIE. **3893**

0009-062X *See* CESKOSLOVENSKA PSYCHOLOGIE. **4580**

0009-0654 *See* CESKOSLOVENSKA STOMATOLOGIE. **1318**

0009-0689 *See* CESKOSLOVENSKE ZDRAVOTNICTVI. **4771**

0009-0697 *See* CESKOSLOVENSKY ARCHITEKT. **295**

0009-0700 *See* CESKOSLOVENSKY CASOPIS PRO FYSIKU. **4399**

0009-0743 *See* CESKOSLOVENSKY SACH. **4858**

0009-0751 *See* VECKO : B.V. **4060**

0009-0786 *See* CESKY JAZYK A LITERATURA. **3373**

0009-0794 *See* CESKY LID. **2683**

0009-0875 *See* CEYLON MEDICAL JOURNAL. **3562**

0009-0891 *See* CEYLON VETERINARY JOURNAL. **5507**

0009-0921 *See* CHAIN MERCHANDISER. **952**

0009-1049 *See* CHALLENGE (NEW YORK, N.Y.). **5714**

0009-1162 *See* CHAMBER OF MINES JOURNAL. **2136**

0009-1308 *See* CHAMPIGNON. **166**

0009-1316 *See* CHAMPIGNONCULTUUR, DE. **166**

0009-1383 *See* CHANGE (NEW ROCHELLE, N.Y.). **1814**

0009-143X *See* KIPLINGER'S PERSONAL FINANCE MAGAZINE. **795**

0009-143X *See* KIPLINGER'S PERSONAL FINANCE MAGAZINE [MICROFORM]. **795**

0009-1723 *See* CHARITY AND CHILDREN. **5277**

0009-1774 *See* TRANSACTIONS OF THE CHARLES S. PIERCE SOCIETY. **4364**

0009-188X *See* CHARTERED ACCOUNTANT, THE. **740**

0009-1987 *See* CHAT (TRYON), THE. **5580**

0009-1995 *See* CHATELAINE (TORONTO, ONT.: 1928). **5553**

0009-2002 *See* CHAUCER REVIEW, THE. **3339**

0009-2029 *See* CHAUFFAGE, VENTILATION, CONDITIONNEMENT. **2604**

0009-2142 *See* CHEESE REPORTER. **192**

0009-2185 *See* CHELSEA (NEW YORK, N.Y.). **3374**

0009-2223 *See* CHEMIA ANALITYCZNA. **1014**

0009-2258 *See* CHEMICAL ABSTRACTS. **1011**

0009-2258 *See* CHEMICAL ABSTRACTS. **967**

0009-2274 *See* CHEMICAL ABSTRACTS. MACROMOLECULAR SECTION. **967**

0009-2282 *See* CHEMICAL ABSTRACTS. ORGANIC CHEMISTRY SECTIONS. **1040**

0009-2304 *See* CHEMICAL ABSTRACTS. BIOCHEMISTRY SECTIONS. **485**

0009-2320 *See* CHEMICAL AGE OF INDIA. **968**

0009-2347 *See* CHEMICAL & ENGINEERING NEWS. **1022**

0009-2355 *See* CHEMICAL AND PETROLEUM ENGINEERING. **2009**

0009-2363 *See* CHEMICAL & PHARMACEUTICAL BULLETIN. **4296**

0009-2401 *See* CHEMICAL BULLETIN, THE. **968**

0009-2460 *See* CHEMICAL ENGINEERING (NEW YORK). **1034**

0009-2479 *See* CHEMICAL ENGINEERING EDUCATION. **2009**

0009-2509 *See* CHEMICAL ENGINEERING SCIENCE. **2010**

0009-2517 *See* CEW, CHEMICAL ENGINEERING WORLD. **2009**

0009-2525 *See* CHEMICAL EQUIPMENT. **968**

0009-2533 *See* CHEMICAL ERA. **1022**

0009-2541 *See* CHEMICAL GEOLOGY. **1040**

0009-255X *See* CHEMICAL HIGHLIGHTS. **1040**

0009-2614 *See* CHEMICAL PHYSICS LETTERS. **1050**

0009-2630 *See* CHEMICAL PROCESSING (CHICAGO, ILL.). **969**

0009-2665 *See* CHEMICAL REVIEWS. **969**

0009-2673 *See* BULLETIN OF THE CHEMICAL SOCIETY OF JAPAN. **963**

0009-2703 *See* CHEMTECH. **1022**

0009-2711 *See* CHEMICAL TITLES. **1011**

0009-272X *See* CHEMICAL WEEK. **1022**

0009-2770 *See* CHEMICKE LISTY. **969**

0009-2789 *See* CHEMICKY PRUMYSL. **1022**

0009-2797 *See* CHEMICO-BIOLOGICAL INTERACTIONS. **485**

0009-2800 *See* CHEMIE-ANLAGEN + VERFAHREN. **2010**

0009-2819 *See* CHEMIE DER ERDE. **1438**

0009-2851 *See* CHEMIE IN UNSERER ZEIT. **969**

0009-286X *See* CHEMIEINGENIEURTECHNIK. **2010**

0009-2886 *See* CHEMIK. **1022**

0009-2894 *See* JOURNAL FUER PRAKTISCHE CHEMIE, CHEMIKER-ZEITUNG. **979**

0009-2924 *See* CHEMINS DE FER : BULLETIN OFFICIEL. **5430**

0009-2940 *See* CHEMISCHE BERICHTE. **970**

0009-2959 *See* CHEMISCHE INDUSTRIE (DUSSELDORF). **970**

0009-2967 *See* CHEMISCHE INDUSTRIE INTERNATIONAL. **1022**

0009-2983 *See* CHEMISCHE RUNDSCHAU ORGAN FUER FORSCHUNG, TECHNIK, FABRIKATION, HANDEL, IMPORT AND EXPORT CHEMISCHER, PHARMAZEUTISCHER UND VERWANDTER ERZEUGNISSE. **970**

0009-2983 *See* CHEMISCHE RUNDSCHAU. **970**

0009-3025 *See* CHEMIST (NEW YORK), THE. **970**

0009-3033 *See* CHEMIST & DRUGGIST. **4296**

0009-3068 *See* CHEMISTRY AND INDUSTRY (LONDON). **970**

0009-3084 *See* CHEMISTRY AND PHYSICS OF LIPIDS. **485**

0009-3092 *See* CHEMISTRY AND TECHNOLOGY OF FUELS AND OILS. **970**

0009-3106 *See* CHEMISTRY IN BRITAIN. **970**

0009-3122 *See* CHEMISTRY OF HETEROCYCLIC COMPOUNDS (NEW YORK. 1965). **971**

0009-3130 *See* CHEMISTRY OF NATURAL COMPOUNDS. **1040**

0009-3157 *See* CHEMOTHERAPY (BASEL). **3814**

0009-3165 *See* CHEMOTHERAPY (TOKYO). **3815**

0009-3173 *See* CHEMPRESS. **971**

0009-3238 *See* CAA MAGAZINE. **4889**

0009-3300 *See* CHESOPIEAN, THE. **265**

0009-3319 *See* CHESS. **4858**

0009-3327 *See* CHESS CORRESPONDENT, THE. **4858**

0009-3335 *See* CHESS DIGEST MAGAZINE. **4858**

0009-3378 *See* KYOTO DAIGAKU KEKKAKU KYOBU SHIKKAN KENKYUJO KIYO. **3799**

0009-3386 *See* CHESTER WHITE JOURNAL. **209**

0009-3394 *See* CHESTNUT HILL LOCAL, THE. **5735**

0009-3424 *See* CHEZ NOUS (NEW YORK). **3273**

0009-3491 *See* BULLETIN OF THE CHICAGO ACADEMY OF SCIENCES. **5091**

0009-3505 *See* CHICAGO BAR RECORD. **2949**

0009-3513 *See* CHICAGO BOWLER. **4890**

0009-3548 *See* LOCAL 2 NEWS. **2291**

0009-3556 *See* CHICAGO GENEALOGIST. **2443**

0009-3599 *See* CHICAGO-KENT LAW REVIEW. **2949**

0009-3637 *See* CHICAGO MEDICINE. **3563**

0009-367X *See* CHICAGO PURCHASOR, THE. **949**

0009-3696 *See* CHICAGO REVIEW. **3374**

0009-370X *See* CHICAGO SHIMPO, THE. **2258**

0009-3718 *See* CHICAGO STUDIES. **5027**

0009-3823 *See* JIEFANGJUN HUABAO. **2505**

0009-3831 *See* CHIGAKU KYOIKU. **1353**

0009-3882 *See* CHILD AND FAMILY. **2277**

0009-3890 *See* CHILD AND MAN. **1731**

0009-3920 *See* CHILD DEVELOPMENT. **4580**

0009-3939 *See* CHILD DEVELOPMENT ABSTRACTS AND BIBLIOGRAPHY. **3655**

0009-3947 *See* CHILD EDUCATION. **1890**

0009-3971 *See* CHILD LIFE (INDIANAPOLIS, IND. 1922). **1061**

0009-398X *See* CHILD PSYCHIATRY AND HUMAN DEVELOPMENT. **3923**

0009-3998 *See* CHILD PSYCHIATRY QUARTERLY. **3901**

0009-4005 *See* CHILD STUDY JOURNAL. **4580**

0009-4021 *See* CHILD WELFARE. **5278**

0009-4056 *See* CHILDHOOD EDUCATION. **1803**

0009-4102 *See* FRIEND (SALT LAKE CITY), THE. **4960**

0009-4161 *See* CHILDREN'S PLAYMATE MAGAZINE. **1062**

0009-4293 *See* CHIMIA. **1023**

0009-4315 *See* CHIMICA E L'INDUSTRIA, LA. **971**

0009-4323 *See* CHIMIE ACTUALITES. **971**

0009-4382 *See* CHINA GLASS & TABLEWARE. **2588**

0009-4404 *See* CHINA NEWS ANALYSIS. **2502**

0009-4412 *See* CHINA NOTES. **4943**

0009-4420 *See* CHINA PICTORIAL. **2502**

0009-4455 *See* CHINA REPORT (NEW DELHI). **5242**

0009-4455 *See* CHINA REPORT (NEW DELHI). **2648**

0009-448X *See* CHINA TRADE REPORT. **827**

0009-4498 *See* CHUNG-KUO TUI WAI MAO I. **827**

0009-4501 *See* CHINATOWN NEWS. **2486**

0009-4536 *See* JOURNAL OF THE CHINESE CHEMICAL SOCIETY (TAIPEI). **982**

0009-4544 *See* CHINESE CULTURE. **3374**

0009-4552 *See* CHINESE ECONOMIC STUDIES. **1469**

0009-4560 See CHINESE EDUCATION. 1731

0009-4595 See JOURNAL OF THE CHINESE LANGUAGE TEACHERS ASSOCIATION. 3292

0009-4609 See CHINESE LAW AND GOVERNMENT. 2950

0009-4617 See CHINESE LITERATURE (BEIJING). 3375

0009-4625 See CHINESE SOCIOLOGY AND ANTHROPOLOGY. 5242

0009-4633 See CHINESE STUDIES IN HISTORY. 2649

0009-4668 See CHING FENG (ENGLISH EDITION). 4943

0009-4706 See JOURNAL OF BRITISH PODIATRIC MEDICINE LONDON 1991. 3918

0009-4714 See CHIROPODY REVIEW. 3917

0009-4722 See CHIRURG. 3961

0009-4749 See CHIRURGIA DEGLI ORGANI DI MOVIMENTO. 3961

0009-4765 See CHIRURGIA GASTROENTEROLOGICA. 3743

0009-4773 See CHIRURGIA ITALIANA. 3962

0009-479X See CHIRURGIA NARZADOW RUCHY I ORTOPEDIA POLSKA. 3881

0009-4811 See CHIRURGIA TRIVENETA. 3962

0009-4838 See CHIRURGIEN - DENTISTE DE FRANCE, LE. 1319

0009-4846 See CHIRURGISCHE PRAXIS. 3962

0009-4897 See CHIZU. MAP. 2558

0009-4919 See CHODNICTWO. 73

0009-4943 See CHOCOLATERIE, CONFISERIE DE FRANCE. 2331

0009-4978 See CHOICE. 3201

0009-5028 See CHORAL JOURNAL, THE. 4109

0009-5176 See CHRISTELIJKE MUZIEKBODE, DE. 4109

0009-5192 See CHRISTENLEHRE, DIE. 4944

0009-5265 See CHRISTIAN BEACON. 4944

0009-5281 See CHRISTIAN CENTURY (1902), THE. 4944

0009-5303 See CHRISTIAN COMMUNICATIONS. 4944

0009-5338 See CHRISTIAN ENDEAVOR WORLD, THE. 4945

0009-5354 See CHRISTIAN HERALD (CHAPPAQUA). 4945

0009-5354 See CHRISTIAN HERALD. 431

0009-5419 See CHRISTIAN LEADER (HILLSBORO). 5058

0009-5478 See CHRISTIAN MESSENGER. 4945

0009-5494 See CHRISTIAN MONTHLY. 4945

0009-5516 See CHRISTIAN NEWS (NEW HAVEN, MO.). 4945

0009-5532 See CHRISTIAN NEWS FROM ISRAEL. 4945

0009-5559 See CHRISTIAN ORDER. 4945

0009-5613 See CHRISTIAN SCIENCE JOURNAL, THE. 4946

0009-5621 See CHRISTIAN SCIENCE QUARTERLY. 4946

0009-5648 See CHRISTIAN SOCIALIST, THE. 4540

0009-5656 See CHRISTIAN STANDARD. 4946

0009-5664 See CHRISTIAN STATESMAN. 4946

0009-5702 See CHRISTIAN WOMAN. 4946

0009-5729 See CHRISTIANISME AU VINGTIEME SIECLE, LE. 4946

0009-5745 See CHRISTIANITY AND CRISIS. 4946

0009-5753 See CHRISTIANITY TODAY (WASHINGTON). 4946

0009-5834 See CHRISTUS. 5027

0009-5893 See CHROMATOGRAPHIA. 1014

0009-5915 See CHROMOSOMA. 534

0009-5931 See CHRONICA (DAVIS). 3375

0009-5982 See CHRONICLE OF HIGHER EDUCATION, THE. 1815

0009-5990 See CHRONICLE OF THE HORSE, THE. 2798

0009-6008 See CHRONICLE OF THE U.S. CLASSIC POSTAL ISSUES, THE. 2784

0009-6024 See CHRONICLES OF OKLAHOMA. 2728

0009-6067 See CHRONIQUE D'EGYPTE. 265

0009-6083 See TRANSPORT ECHO ED. BILINGUE. 5395

0009-6172 See CHROMNY PRZYRODE OJCZYSTA. 2189

0009-6245 See CHULPAN MUNHWA. 4828

0009-6296 See HOGAKU SHINPO. 2978

0009-630X See CHURCH ADVOCATE (FINDLAY, OHIO), THE. 4947

0009-6334 See CHURCH AND STATE. 4468

0009-6342 See CHURCH & SYNAGOGUE LIBRARIES. 3202

0009-6393 See CHURCH HERALD, THE. 4947

0009-6407 See CHURCH HISTORY. 4947

0009-6431 See CHURCH MANAGEMENT. 4947

0009-6466 See CHURCH MUSICIAN, THE. 4109

0009-6482 See CHURCH OBSERVER. 4947

0009-6504 See CHURCH OF GOD MISSIONS. 4947

0009-6563 See CHURCH SCENE (MELBOURNE, AUSTRALIA). 4948

0009-6598 See CHURCH WOMAN, THE. 4948

0009-6601 See CHURCH WORLD. 5027

0009-661X See CHURCHMAN (LONDON. 1879). 4948

0009-6709 See CIEL ET TERRE. 394

0009-6725 See CIENCIA E CULTURA (SAO PAULO). 5094

0009-6733 See CIENCIA E INVESTIGACION. 5094

0009-675X See CIENCIA INTERAMERICANA. 5094

0009-6768 See CIENCIA Y NATURALEZA. 5094

0009-6776 See CIENCIAS (MADRID), LAS. 5095

0009-6784 See CIENCIAS ADMINISTRATIVAS. 4638

0009-6830 See CIMAISE. 347

0009-6849 See CIMARRON REVIEW. 3461

0009-6881 See UNIVERSITY OF CINCINNATI LAW REVIEW. 3068

0009-689X See CINCINNATI. 2530

0009-6903 See CINCINNATI PURCHASOR. 949

0009-692X See CINE AL DIA. 4065

0009-6946 See CINE CUBANO. 4065

0009-7004 See CINEASTE (NEW YORK, N.Y.). 4066

0009-7039 See CINEFORUM. 4066

0009-7101 See CINEMA JOURNAL. 4066

0009-711X See CINEMA NUOVO. 4066

0009-7128 See CINEMA PRATIQUE. 4066

0009-7152 See CINEMA SOCIETA. 4066

0009-7209 See CINESIOLOGIE. 3804

0009-725X See RENDICONTI DEL CIRCOLO MATEMATICO DI PALERMO. 3531

0009-7322 See CIRCULATION (NEW YORK, N.Y.). 3702

0009-7330 See CIRCULATION RESEARCH. 3702

0009-7330 See CIRCULATION RESEARCH. 3702

0009-7349 See CIRCULO - CIRCULO DE CULTURA PANAMERICANO. 3376

0009-7365 See CIRCUS (NEW YORK, N.Y. 1979). 4110

0009-7381 See CIRUGIA DEL URUGUAY. 3962

0009-739X See CIRUGIA ESPANOLA. 3962

0009-7411 See CIRUGIA Y CIRUJANOS. 3962

0009-7446 See CITATION (CHICAGO, ILL.). 2950

0009-7489 See CITE LIBRE (1991). 5466

0009-7527 See CITHARA. 4948

0009-7535 See CITIES & VILLAGES. 4638

0009-7543 See CITIZEN (DENVER), THE. 4702

0009-7578 See CITROGRAPH (FRESNO, CALIF.). 167

0009-7632 See CITTA DI VITA. 4948

0009-7640 See CITTA E SOCIETA. 2817

0009-7691 See BULLETIN - THE ST. LOUIS ART MUSEUM. 4086

0009-7756 See CIUDAD DE DIOS, LA. 4948

0009-7772 See CIVIC AFFAIRS. 4638

0009-7810 See CIVIL AIR PATROL NEWS. 16

0009-7845 See CIVIL ENGINEER IN SOUTH AFRICA, THE. 2020

0009-7888 See CIVIL ENGINEERING CONTRACTOR. 2020

0009-790X See CIVIL LIBERTIES (NEW YORK, N.Y.). 4506

0009-8078 See CIVIL WAR HISTORY. 2728

0009-8086 See CIVIL WAR ROUND TABLE DIGEST. 2728

0009-8094 See CIVIL WAR TIMES ILLUSTRATED. 2728

0009-8140 See CIVILISATIONS. 5242

0009-8167 See CIVILTA CATTOLICA, LA. 5027

0009-8191 See CIVITAS. 4468

0009-8310 See CLASSIC CAR. 5411

0009-8337 See CLASSICAL BULLETIN (ST. LOUIS, MO.), THE. 1075

0009-8353 See CLASSICAL JOURNAL (CLASSICAL ASSOCIATION OF THE MIDDLE WEST AND SOUTH), THE. 1075

0009-8361 See CLASSICAL OUTLOOK, THE. 1075

0009-837X See CLASSICAL PHILOLOGY. 1075

0009-8388 See CLASSICAL QUARTERLY. 1075

0009-840X See CLASSICAL REVIEW. 1076

0009-8418 See CLASSICAL WORLD, THE. 1076

0009-8515 See CLAUDIA. 2531

0009-8523 See CLAUSTHALER GEOLOGISCHE ABHANDLUNGEN. 1372

0009-854X See CLAVIER. 4110

0009-8558 See CLAY MINERALS. 1438

0009-8574 See CLAY SCIENCE. 1353

0009-8604 See CLAYS AND CLAY MINERALS. 1438

0009-8620 See CLEAN WATER REPORT. 5532

0009-8647 See CLEAN AIR (HEIDELBERG). 2226

0009-8655 See CLEARING HOUSE (MENASHA, WIS.). 1732

0009-868X See CLEARINGHOUSE REVIEW. 3179

0009-8701 See CLEFT PALATE-CRANIOFACIAL JOURNAL. 3564

0009-871X See SEMESTER REVIEW, THE. 1847

0009-8809 See CLEVELAND ENGINEERING. 1968

0009-8825 See CLEVELAND JEWISH NEWS, THE. 5727

0009-8841 See BULLETIN OF THE CLEVELAND MUSEUM OF ART, THE. 345

0009-8876 See CLEVELAND STATE LAW REVIEW. 2951

0009-8914 See CCI. CLIMA COMMERCE INTERNATIONAL. 2604

0009-8930 See CLIMATE CONTROL. 2604

0009-8981 See CLINICA CHIMICA ACTA. 972

0009-9007 See CLINICA EUROPEA. 3565

0009-9058 See CLINICA PEDIATRICA. 3902

0009-9074 See CLINICA TERAPEUTICA, LA. 3565

0009-9082 See CLINICA VETERINARIA; RASSEGNA DI POLIZIA SANITARIA E DI IGIENE. 5508

0009-9104 See CLINICAL AND EXPERIMENTAL IMMUNOLOGY. 3667

0009-9120 See CLINICAL BIOCHEMISTRY (NEW YORK, N.Y.). 485

0009-9147 See CLINICAL CHEMISTRY (REFERENCE EDITION). 972

0009-9147 See CLINICAL CHEMISTRY (BALTIMORE, MD.). 972

0009-9155 See CLINICAL EEG ELECTROENCEPHALOGRAPHY. 3830

0009-9163 See CLINICAL GENETICS. 543

0009-918X See RINSHO SHINKEIGAKU. 3845

0009-9201 See CLINICAL OBSTETRICS AND GYNECOLOGY. 3759

0009-921X See CLINICAL ORTHOPAEDICS AND RELATED RESEARCH. 3881

0009-9228 See CLINICAL PEDIATRICS. 3902

0009-9236 See CLINICAL PHARMACOLOGY AND THERAPEUTICS. 4297

0009-9252 See RINSHO HOSHASEN. JAPANESE JOURNAL OF CLINICAL RADIOLOGY. 3946

0009-9260 See CLINICAL RADIOLOGY. 3940

0009-9279 See CLINICAL RESEARCH. 3566
0009-9295 See CLINICAL SYMPOSIA (1957). 3566
0009-9325 See CLINICAL TRIALS AND META-ANALYSIS. 4297
0009-9368 See CLINIQUE OPHTALMOLOGIQUE PARIS, LA. 3873
0009-9376 See CLIO (SANTO DOMINGO). 2844
0009-9589 See CLUB MANAGEMENT. 5230
0009-9716 See IMI DESCRIPTIONS OF FUNGI AND BACTERIA / C.A.B. INTERNATIONAL. 458
0009-9880 See COACHING CLINIC, THE. 4890
0010-003X See COAT OF ARMS, THE. 2443
0010-0064 See COBOUW. 607
0010-0161 See COCUK SAGLIGI VE HASTALIKLARI DERGISI. 4771
0010-0277 See COGNITION. 4581
0010-0285 See COGNITIVE PSYCHOLOGY. 4581
0010-0412 See COIN PRICES. 2780
0010-0447 See COIN WORLD. 2780
0010-0455 See COINAGE. 2780
0010-0471 See COINS (IOLA, WIS.). 2780
0010-0544 See COLADA. 4000
0010-065X See COLEOPTERISTS' BULLETIN, THE. 5580
0010-0730 See COLLECTANEA BOTANICA. 507
0010-0749 See COLLECTANEA FRANCISCANA. 5027
0010-0757 See COLLECTANEA MATHEMATICA (BARCELONA). 3500
0010-0765 See COLLECTION OF CZECHOSLOVAK CHEMICAL COMMUNICATIONS. 973
0010-079X See COLLECTIVE BARGAINING NEGOTIATIONS AND CONTRACTS. 3145
0010-0803 See COLLECTIVE BARGAINING REVIEW. 1660
0010-0811 See COLLECTIVITES EXPRESS. 5279
0010-082X See COLLECTOR (MINNEAPOLIS, MINN.). 783
0010-0838 See COLLECTORS CLUB PHILATELIST, THE. 2785
0010-0870 See COLLEGE & RESEARCH LIBRARIES. 3203
0010-0889 See COLLEGE AND UNIVERSITY. 1816
0010-0951 See COLLEGE BOARD REVIEW, THE. 1816
0010-096X See COLLEGE COMPOSITION AND COMMUNICATION. 1816
0010-0994 See COLLEGE ENGLISH. 3274
0010-101X See COLLEGE LAW BULLETIN. 2952
0010-1087 See TRANSACTIONS & STUDIES OF THE COLLEGE OF PHYSICIANS OF PHILADELPHIA. 3647
0010-1125 See COLLEGE PRESS SERVICE. 5659
0010-1141 See COLLEGE STORE EXECUTIVE. 922
0010-115X See COLLEGE STORE JOURNAL, THE. 1817
0010-1281 See COLLIERY GUARDIAN. 2137
0010-1303 See COLLOID JOURNAL OF THE RUSSIAN ACADEMY OF SCIENCES. 5095
0010-1338 See COLLOQUIA GERMANICA. 3274
0010-1354 See COLLOQUIUM MATHEMATICUM. 3500
0010-1443 See COLONIAL NEWSLETTER (HUNTSVILLE), THE. 2781
0010-1451 See COLOQUIO : LETRAS. 3376
0010-1516 See COLORADO BEVERAGE ANALYST. 2366
0010-1559 See JOURNAL - COLORADO DENTAL ASSOCIATION. 1326
0010-1575 See COLORADO EDUCATION REVIEW. 1732
0010-1583 See COLORADO ENGINEER, THE. 1968
0010-1613 See COLORADO GENEALOGIST, THE. 2443
0010-163X See COLORADO JOURNAL OF PHARMACY, THE. 4297
0010-1664 See COLORADO MUNICIPALITIES. 4639

0010-1672 See COLORADO MUSIC EDUCATOR. 4111
0010-1699 See COLORADO OUTDOORS. 2190
0010-1702 See COLORADO PROSPECTOR. 2729
0010-1729 See COLORADO RANCHER AND FARMER. 75
0010-180X See SHIKIZAI KYOKAISHI. 1030
0010-1826 See COLOURAGE. 5349
0010-1869 See COLUMBIA (NEW HAVEN). 5028
0010-1923 See COLUMBIA JOURNAL OF LAW AND SOCIAL PROBLEMS. 2953
0010-1931 See COLUMBIA JOURNAL OF TRANSNATIONAL LAW. 3126
0010-1958 See COLUMBIA LAW REVIEW. 2953
0010-1966 See COLUMBIA LIBRARY COLUMNS. 2844
0010-1982 See COLUMBIA REVIEW. 3340
0010-2091 See COLUMNS (FAIRMONT), THE. 1090
0010-213X See COMBAT CREW / STRATEGIC AIR COMMAND. 4039
0010-2164 See INTERNATIONAL LABORATORY. EUROPEAN ED. 1016
0010-2180 See COMBUSTION AND FLAME. 1051
0010-2202 See COMBUSTION SCIENCE AND TECHNOLOGY. 1051
0010-244X See CAHIERS DES COMITES DE PREVENTION DU BATIMENT ET DES TRAVAUX PUBLICS. 2860
0010-2474 See COMMAND (DENVER, COLO.). 4039
0010-2571 See COMMENTARII MATHEMATICI HELVETICI. 3500
0010-258X See COMMENTARII MATHEMATICI UNIVERSITATIS SANCTI PAULI. 3500
0010-2601 See COMMENTARY (NEW YORK). 5047
0010-2628 See COMMENTATIONES MATHEMATICAE UNIVERSITATIS CAROLINAE. 3500
0010-2687 See COMMENTS ON ATOMIC AND MOLECULAR PHYSICS. 4446
0010-2709 See COMMENTS ON NUCLEAR AND PARTICLE PHYSICS. 4446
0010-2733 See COMMERCE INTERNATIONAL. 828
0010-275X See COMMERCE. 828
0010-2776 See COMMERCE (MANILA, PHILIPPINES). 828
0010-2849 See COMMERCE IN FRANCE. 828
0010-3055 See COMMERCIAL LAW JOURNAL. 3098
0010-3063 See COMMERCIAL MOTOR, THE. 5412
0010-3098 See COMMERCIAL RECORD (SOUTH WINDSOR, CT.), THE. 4836
0010-3101 See COMMERCIAL REVIEW (PORTLAND, OR.). 75
0010-3179 See COMMISSION, THE. 4949
0010-3233 See STATISTICAL PAPERS - UNITED NATIONS. SERIES D. COMMODITY TRADE STATISTICS. 733
0010-325X See COMMON GROUND. 4949
0010-3330 See COMMONWEAL. 2531
0010-3349 See COMMONWEALTH (SAN FRANCISCO), THE. 2531
0010-3381 See COMMONWEALTH FORESTRY REVIEW, THE. 2399
0010-3454 See COMMUNAUTE CHRETIENNE. 4949
0010-3497 See COMMUNICATIO SOCIALIS. 1106
0010-3519 See COMMUNICATION ARTS. 377
0010-3551 See ORVOSTORTENETI KOZLEMENYEK. 2625
0010-356X See COMMUNICATIONS (ENGLEWOOD. 1964). 1152
0010-3616 See COMMUNICATIONS IN MATHEMATICAL PHYSICS. 4400
0010-3624 See COMMUNICATIONS IN SOIL SCIENCE AND PLANT ANALYSIS. 167
0010-3632 See COMMUNICATIONS NEWS (GENEVA, ILL.). 1108
0010-3640 See COMMUNICATIONS ON PURE AND APPLIED MATHEMATICS. 3501

0010-3705 See COMMUNIO (SEVILLA). 4949
0010-3802 See COMMUNITY DEVELOPMENT JOURNAL. 5242
0010-3829 See JOURNAL OF THE COMMUNITY DEVELOPMENT SOCIETY. 5250
0010-3853 See COMMUNITY MENTAL HEALTH JOURNAL. 5280
0010-3926 See COMMUTATION & ELECTRONIQUE. 1108
0010-3985 See COMPANION (TORONTO). 5028
0010-4027 See COMPANY NEWS AND NOTES. 3098
0010-4043 See C I E S NEWSLETTER. 1729
0010-4051 See COMPARATIVE AND INTERNATIONAL LAW JOURNAL OF SOUTHERN AFRICA, THE. 3126
0010-4078 See COMPARATIVE DRAMA. 5363
0010-4086 See COMPARATIVE EDUCATION REVIEW. 1733
0010-4124 See COMPARATIVE LITERATURE. 3377
0010-4132 See COMPARATIVE LITERATURE STUDIES (URBANA). 3377
0010-4140 See COMPARATIVE POLITICAL STUDIES. 4469
0010-4159 See COMPARATIVE POLITICS. 4469
0010-4167 See COMPARATIVE ROMANCE LINGUISTICS NEWSLETTER. 3274
0010-4175 See COMPARATIVE STUDIES IN SOCIETY AND HISTORY. 5196
0010-4272 See COMPETITIVE BRAND CUMULATIVE. 757
0010-4361 See COMPOSITES. 2101
0010-437X See COMPOSITIO MATHEMATICA. 3501
0010-440X See COMPREHENSIVE PSYCHIATRY. 3923
0010-4418 See COMPRENDRE. 5242
0010-4426 See COMPRESSED AIR (1965). 1602
0010-4469 See COMPUTER ABSTRACTS. 1208
0010-4485 See COMPUTER AIDED DESIGN. 1231
0010-4531 See COMPUTER BULLETIN. 1256
0010-4566 See COMPUTER DESIGN (WINCHESTER). 1176
0010-4582 See COMPUTER DISPLAY REVIEW, THE. 1264
0010-4590 See COMPUTER EDUCATION. 1222
0010-4620 See COMPUTER JOURNAL. 1176
0010-4639 See COMPUTER MANAGEMENT. 1253
0010-4655 See COMPUTER PHYSICS COMMUNICATIONS. 4400
0010-4760 See COMPUTER SURVEY. 1236
0010-4787 See COMPUTER WEEKLY. 1178
0010-4809 See COMPUTERS AND BIOMEDICAL RESEARCH. 3691
0010-4817 See COMPUTERS AND THE HUMANITIES. 2844
0010-4825 See COMPUTERS IN BIOLOGY AND MEDICINE. 3691
0010-4841 See COMPUTERWORLD. 1236
0010-485X See COMPUTING. 1257
0010-4876 See COMPUTING REPORT IN SCIENCE AND ENGINEERING. 5096
0010-4884 See COMPUTING REVIEWS. 1208
0010-4973 See COMUNI D'EUROPA. 4640
0010-504X See COMUNITA. 3340
0010-5066 See COMUNITA INTERNAZIONALE. 4518
0010-5082 See COMBUSTION, EXPLOSION, AND SHOCK WAVES. 1051
0010-5155 See CONCEPTUS. 4344
0010-5236 See CONCILIUM (ENGLISH LANGUAGE EDITION). 4949
0010-5260 See CONCORDIA HISTORICAL INSTITUTE QUARTERLY. 5058
0010-5309 See CONCOURS MEDICAL. 3568
0010-5317 See CONCRETE (LONDON). 2021
0010-535X See CONCRETE INDUSTRY BULLETIN. 608
0010-5368 See CONCRETE PRODUCTS (1975). 608

0010-5376 See CONCRETE QUARTERLY. 608
0010-5422 See CONDOR (LOS ANGELES, CALIF.), THE. 5617
0010-5449 See CONFECTIE. 1602
0010-5473 See CONFECTIONERY PRODUCTION. 2332
0010-5716 See CONFRONTATION (SOUTHAMPTON, N.Y.). 3377
0010-5759 See CONGIUNTURA ITALIANA. 1552
0010-5821 See BULLETIN OF THE CONGREGATIONAL LIBRARY. 3198
0010-5856 See CONGREGATIONALIST (BELOIT), THE. 4950
0010-5899 See CONGRESSIONAL DIGEST, THE. 4469
0010-5910 See CONGRESSIONAL QUARTERLY WEEKLY REPORT. 4469
0010-5929 See CONIGLICOLTURA. 209
0010-5945 See CONJUNTURA ECONOMICA. 1471
0010-597X 175
0010-6038 See CONNCHORD. 4111
0010-6054 See CONNECTICUT ANTIQUARIAN, THE. 2729
0010-6070 See CONNECTICUT BAR JOURNAL. 2955
0010-6151 See CONNECTICUT LAW REVIEW. 2955
0010-616X See CONNECTICUT LIBRARIES (1954-). 3204
0010-6178 See CONNECTICUT MEDICINE. 3568
0010-6216 See CONNECTICUT REVIEW (NEW BRITAIN). 2729
0010-6232 See JOURNAL - CONNECTICUT STATE DENTAL ASSOCIATION, THE. 1326
0010-6259 See CONNECTICUT WOODLANDS. 2163
0010-6275 See CONNOISSEUR, THE. 348
0010-6348 See CONQUISTE DEL LAVORO. 1661
0010-6356 See CONRADIANA. 431
0010-650X See CONSERVATIONIST, THE. 2190
0010-6542 See CONSERVATIVE JUDAISM. 5047
0010-6569 See CONSIGLIO DI STATO. 4640
0010-6623 See CONSTITUTIONAL AND PARLIAMENTARY INFORMATION. 3092
0010-6658 See CONSTRUCTEUR. 2112
0010-6704 See CONSTRUCTION (ARLINGTON). 608
0010-6720 See CONSTRUCTION BULLETIN. 609
0010-6755 See CONSTRUCTION EQUIPMENT DISTRIBUTION. 609
0010-6771 See CONSTRUCTION EQUIPMENT, OPERATION AND MAINTENANCE. 609
0010-6836 See CONSTRUCTION LABOR REPORT. 1661
0010-6860 See CONSTRUCTION NEWS. 610
0010-6917 See CONSTRUCTION REVIEW. 610
0010-6925 See CONSTRUCTION SPECIFIER, THE. 610
0010-695X See CONSTRUCTIONAL REVIEW. 611
0010-6968 See CONSTRUCTIONEER. 611
0010-7050 See CONSULENTE IMMOBILIARE. 2819
0010-7069 See CONSULTANT (HACKENSACK). 3568
0010-7085 See CONSULTANT - ASSOCIATION OF CONSULTING FORESTERS OF AMERICA, THE. 2378
0010-7174 See CONSUMER REPORTS. 1295
0010-7182 See CONSUMERS DIGEST (CHICAGO, ILL.). 1296
0010-7204 See CONSUMPTION. 3378
0010-7344 See SPOTLIGHT CONTACTS. 388
0010-7360 See CONTAINER NEWS. 5380
0010-7379 See CONTAINERISATION INTERNATIONAL. 864
0010-7468 See CONTEMPORARY AUTHORS. 431
0010-7476 See CONTEMPORARY EDUCATION. 1891
0010-7484 See CONTEMPORARY LITERATURE. 3378
0010-7514 See CONTEMPORARY PHYSICS. 4401

0010-7530 See CONTEMPORARY PSYCHOANALYSIS. 3923
0010-7549 See CONTEMPORARY PSYCHOLOGY. 4582
0010-7565 See CONTEMPORARY REVIEW (LONDON, ENGLAND). 2486
0010-7581 See CONTENIDO. 2531
0010-762X See CONTENUTI. 3378
0010-7646 See JAYBEES. 2774
0010-7824 See CONTRACEPTION (STONEHAM). 588
0010-7840 See CONTRACT BRIDGE BULLETIN, THE. 4859
0010-7859 See CONTRACT JOURNAL (SUTTON). 611
0010-793X See CONTRARY INVESTOR, THE. 895
0010-7980 See CONTRIBUTIONS TO GEOLOGY (LARAMIE). 1372
0010-7999 See CONTRIBUTIONS TO MINERALOGY AND PETROLOGY. 1439
0010-8022 See CONTROL & INSTRUMENTATION. 1219
0010-8049 See CONTROL ENGINEERING. 1219
0010-8073 See CONTROLLER. 17
0010-8146 See CONVERGENCE (TORONTO). 1800
0010-8154 See CONVERGENCE (FRIBOURG). 5028
0010-8189 See CONVERTER. 4233
0010-8200 See CONVEYANCER AND PROPERTY LAWYER, THE. 2956
0010-826X See COOKBOOK DIGEST. 2789
0010-8367 See COOPERATION AND CONFLICT. 4470
0010-8391 See COOPERATIVE ACCOUNTANT, THE. 742
0010-8448 See COOPERATIVE FARMER. 76
0010-8545 See COORDINATION CHEMISTRY REVIEWS. 1051
0010-8626 See COPYRIGHT (GENEVA). 1303
0010-8634 See COPYRIGHT BULLETIN : QUARTERLY REVIEW / UNESCO. 1303
0010-8650 See COR ET VASA (ENGLISH ED.). 3703
0010-8669 See CORANTO (LOS ANGELES, CALIF.). 4828
0010-8685 See CORD (ST. BONAVENTURE, N.Y.), THE. 5028
0010-8731 See JOURNAL OF THE CORK HISTORICAL AND ARCHAEOLOGICAL SOCIETY. 2695
0010-8782 See CORNELL COUNTRYMAN. 77
0010-8790 See CORNELL ENGINEER, THE. 1969
0010-8804 See CORNELL HOTEL AND RESTAURANT ADMINISTRATION QUARTERLY, THE. 2804
0010-8812 See CORNELL INTERNATIONAL LAW JOURNAL. 3126
0010-8839 See CORNELL LAW FORUM (ITHACA, N.Y. : 1974). 2956
0010-8847 See CORNELL LAW REVIEW. 2956
0010-8863 See CORNELL PLANTATIONS, THE. 1818
0010-8901 See CORNELL VETERINARIAN, THE. 5508
0010-8995 See CORPORATE PRACTICE COMMENTATOR. 3099
0010-9312 See CORROSION (HOUSTON, TEX.). 2011
0010-9339 See CORROSION ABSTRACTS. 2003
0010-9355 See ZAIRYO TO KANKYO. 2002
0010-9371 See CORROSION PREVENTION AND CONTROL. 2011
0010-938X See CORROSION SCIENCE. 2011
0010-938X See CORROSION SCIENCE [MICROFORM]. 2011
0010-9452 See CORTEX. 3830
0010-9525 See COSMIC RESEARCH. 1404
0010-9541 See COSMOPOLITAN (1952). 5554
0010-955X See COSMOPOLITAN CONTACT. 4541
0010-9568 See CHUNG WAI HUA PAO. 2502
0010-9606 See COST ENGINEER. 864

0010-9665 See COSTRUZIONI. 611
0010-9673 See COSTRUZIONI METALLICHE. 611
0010-9711 See COTON ET FIBRES TROPICALES. 2413
0010-9754 See COTTON, REVIEW OF THE WORLD SITUATION. 1603
0010-9800 See COTTON GIN AND OIL MILL PRESS, THE. 5349
0010-9827 See COTTON PRICE STATISTICS. 152
0010-9894 See BULLETIN - COUNCIL FOR RESEARCH IN MUSIC EDUCATION. 4105
0010-9975 See ACCI NEWSLETTER / AMERICAN COUNCIL ON CONSUMER INTERESTS. 1293
0011-0000 See COUNSELING PSYCHOLOGIST, THE. 4583
0011-0027 See COUNSELOR. 758
0011-0035 See COUNSELOR EDUCATION AND SUPERVISION. 1877
0011-0140 See COUNTRY GUIDE. 77
0011-0183 See COUNTRY LIFE IN BRITISH COLUMBIA. 77
0011-023X See COUNTRY-SIDE. 2213
0011-0248 See COUNTRY SONG ROUNDUP. 4112
0011-0256 See COUNTRY STANDARD. 77
0011-0272 See COUNTRYMAN, THE. 2514
0011-0353 See COUNTY PROGRESS. 4641
0011-0418 See COURIER (SYRACUSE). 3204
0011-0442 See COURRIER AUSTRALIEN. 2486
0011-0450 See COURRIER AVICOLE, LE. 77
0011-0647 See COURT REVIEW. 3140
0011-0671 See COVENANT COMPANION. 5058
0011-0728 See CIP. COVJEK I PROSTOR. 295
0011-0787 See CRANBERRIES (PORTLAND). 168
0011-0841 See CRAZYHORSE (LITTLE ROCK, ARK.). 3462
0011-0876 See CREATIVE CAMERA. 4368
0011-1066 See CREDIT UNION MAGAZINE. 786
0011-1074 See CREDIT WORLD, THE. 786
0011-1147 See CREEM (NEW YORK, N.Y.). 4113
0011-1155 See CREIGHTON LAW REVIEW. 2957
0011-118X See CRESCENDO & JAZZ MUSIC. 4113
0011-1198 See CRESSET (VALPARAISO), THE. 3340
0011-1287 See CRIME AND DELINQUENCY. 3161
0011-1295 See CRIME CONTROL DIGEST. 3161
0011-1317 See CRIMINAL LAW BULLETIN. 3106
0011-1325 See CRIMINAL LAW JOURNAL. 3106
0011-1333 See CRIMINAL LAW QUARTERLY (TORONTO). 3106
0011-1341 See CRIMINAL LAW REPORTER, THE. 3106
0011-135X See CRIMINAL LAW REVIEW (LONDON, ENGLAND). 3106
0011-1376 See CRIMINOLOGIST, THE. 3163
0011-1384 See CRIMINOLOGY (BEVERLY HILLS). 3163
0011-1422 See CRISIS (NEW YORK, N.Y.), THE. 2259
0011-1449 See CRISTALLO / CENTRO DI CULTURA DELL'ALTO ADIGE, IL. 3340
0011-1465 See CHRIST TO THE WORLD. 4943
0011-1473 See CRITERIO. 5028
0011-149X See CRITIC; A CATHOLIC REVIEW OF BOOKS AND THE ARTS, THE. 5028
0011-149X See CRITIC, THE. 3340
0011-1503 See CRITICA; REVISTA HISPANOAMERICANA DE FILOSOFIA. 4344
0011-1511 See CRITICA D'ARTE. 348
0011-152X See CRITICA MARXISTA. 4541
0011-1538 See CRITICA SOCIALE. 4541
0011-1546 See CRITICA SOCIOLOGICA, LA. 5243
0011-1562 See CRITICAL QUARTERLY, THE. 3379
0011-1570 See CRITICAL SURVEY. 3379
0011-1589 See CRITICISM (DETROIT). 2845
0011-1600 See CRITIQUE. 3341

0011-1619 See CRITIQUE - BOLINGBROKE SOCIETY. 3341
0011-1643 See CROATICA CHEMICA ACTA. 973
0011-1775 See CRONACHE ECONOMICHE. 1478
0011-1783 See CRONACHE FARMACEUTICHE. 4298
0011-183X See CROP SCIENCE. 169
0011-1848 See NIHON SAKUMOTSU GAKKAI KIJI. 179
0011-1953 See CROSS CURRENTS. 4951
0011-2100 See CRUCIBLE. 4951
0011-2151 See CRUSADER (MEMPHIS). 5058
0011-216X See CRUSTACEANA. 5581
0011-2186 See CRUX. 4951
0011-2232 See CEYLON JOURNAL OF MEDICAL SCIENCE. 3562
0011-2240 See CRYOBIOLOGY. 452
0011-2275 See CRYOGENICS (GUILFORD). 4401
0011-2356 See CUADERNOS AMERICANOS. 2730
0011-250X See CUADERNOS HISPANOAMERICANOS. 2514
0011-2593 See CUBA INTERNACIONAL. 2486
0011-2771 See CULTURA E SCUOLA. 1734
0011-2798 See CULTURA NEL MONDO, LA. 2486
0011-2968 See CUMBERLAND FLAG, THE. 4952
0011-2976 See CUMBERLAND PRESBYTERIAN, THE. 5058
0011-300X See CUMULATIVE BOOK INDEX, THE. 3458
0011-300X See CUMULATIVE BOOK INDEX. CD-ROM. 3458
0011-3034 See CUOIO, PELLI, MATERIE CONCIANTI. 3183
0011-3069 See CURATOR (NEW YORK, N.Y.). 4087
0011-3093 See CURLEW, THE. 4165
0011-3123 See CURRENT, THE. 2503
0011-3131 See CURRENT (NEW YORK). 2487
0011-3182 See CURRENT AFFAIRS BULLETIN. 4470
0011-3204 See CURRENT ANTHROPOLOGY. 234
0011-3212 See CURRENT ARCHAEOLOGY. 266
0011-3255 See CURRENT BIBLIOGRAPHY ON AFRICAN AFFAIRS, A. 2635
0011-3271 See KAGAKU GIJUTSU BUNKEN SOKUHO. KAGAKU. KAGAKU KOGYO HEN : KOKUNAI-HEN. 2005
0011-3336 See KAGAKU GIJUTSU BUNKEN SOKUHO. BUTSURI, OYO BUTSURI-HEN. 4426
0011-3344 See CURRENT BIOGRAPHY. 431
0011-3409 See CURRENT CONTENTS. LIFE SCIENCES. 5174
0011-3425 See CURRENT DIGEST OF THE SOVIET PRESS, THE. 4470
0011-3492 See CURRENT EVENTS (MIDDLETOWN). 1734
0011-3514 See CURRENT GEOGRAPHICAL PUBLICATIONS. 2580
0011-3530 See CURRENT HISTORY (1941). 2614
0011-3565 See CURRENT INDEX TO JOURNALS IN EDUCATION. 1794
0011-3654 See CURRENT LITERATURE IN TRAFFIC AND TRANSPORTATION. 5380
0011-3700 See CURRENT MEDICAL PRACTICE. 3963
0011-3735 See CURRENT MUSICOLOGY. 4113
0011-3778 See CURRENT PAPERS IN ELECTRICAL & ELECTRONICS ENGINEERING. 2003
0011-3786 See CURRENT PAPERS IN PHYSICS. 4426
0011-3794 See CURRENT PAPERS ON COMPUTERS & CONTROL. 1208
0011-3840 See CURRENT PROBLEMS IN SURGERY. 3963
0011-3859 See CURRENT PUBLICATIONS IN LEGAL AND RELATED FIELDS. 3080
0011-3891 See CURRENT SCIENCE. 5098
0011-3905 See CURRENT SCIENCE (MIDDLETOWN). 5098

0011-3921 See CURRENT SOCIOLOGY (PARIS, FRANCE). 5244
0011-393X See CURRENT THERAPEUTIC RESEARCH. 4298
0011-3999 See CURRENT WORK IN THE HISTORY OF MEDICINE. 3570
0011-4049 See CURRICULUM THEORY NETWORK. 1892
0011-4111 See CUSTOM APPLICATOR. 170
0011-4146 See CUSTOMS BULLETIN AND DECISIONS. 2958
0011-4162 See CUTIS (NEW YORK, N.Y.). 3719
0011-4189 See CUTTING TOOL ENGINEERING. 4000
0011-4227 See CYBERNETICA. 1250
0011-4235 See CYBERNETICS AND SYSTEMS ANALYSIS. 1251
0011-4243 See CYBERNETICS ABSTRACTS / SCIENTIFIC INFORMATION CONSULTANTS LIMITED, LONDON, ENGLAND. 1250
0011-4286 See CYCLE WORLD. 4081
0011-4294 See CYCLES (PITTSBURGH). 5098
0011-4359 See CYCLO-FLAME. 3379
0011-4421 See CYLCHGRAWN LLYFRGELL GENEDLAETHOL CYMRU. 3205
0011-4529 See CYTOBIOS. 535
0011-4545 See CYTOLOGIA. 535
0011-4553 See CZASOPISMO STOMATOLOGICZNE. 1319
0011-4588 See CZECHOSLOVAK FILM, THE. 4067
0011-460X See CZECHOSLOVAK FOREIGN TRADE. 830
0011-4626 See CZECHOSLOVAK JOURNAL OF PHYSICS. 4401
0011-4634 See CZECHOSLOVAK LIFE. 2514
0011-4642 See CZECHOSLOVAK MATHEMATICAL JOURNAL. 3503
0011-4650 See CZECHOSLOVAK MOTOR REVIEW. 5380
0011-4707 See D.A.C. NEWS. 4892
0011-4782 See DBZ-DEUTSCHE BAUZEITSCHRIFT. 296
0011-4820 See DDR VERKEHR. 5380
0011-4936 See D.H. LAWRENCE REVIEW, THE. 3341
0011-5010 See LANDTECHNISCHE ZEITSCHRIFT. 104
0011-5029 See DISEASE-A-MONTH. 3572
0011-507X See DNZ INTERNATIONAL. 5350
0011-5088 See DO, THE. 3573
0011-5134 See DRP BULLETIN. 4472
0011-5223 See DACCA UNIVERSITY STUDIES, THE. 1819
0011-5258 See DADOS (RIO DE JANEIRO). 5197
0011-5266 See DAEDALUS (CAMBRIDGE). 5098
0011-5290 See DAFFODIL JOURNAL, THE. 2413
0011-5347 See DAI DAMU / LARGE DAMS. 2088
0011-5401 See DAILY CONSTRUCTION SERVICE. 612
0011-5487 See DAILY REPORTER (COLUMBUS, OHIO). 5728
0011-5509 See DAILY VARIETY. 4067
0011-5525 See DAILY WORD. 4952
0011-5568 See DAIRY COUNCIL DIGEST. 193
0011-5576 See DAIRY FARMER (IPSWICH, SUFFOLK). 193
0011-5592 See DAIRY GOAT JOURNAL. 193
0011-5614 See DAIRY HERD MANAGEMENT. 193
0011-5681 See DAIRY SCIENCE ABSTRACTS. 153
0011-572X See DAIRYMAN (CORONA), THE. 194
0011-5738 See DAIRYNEWS (PEARL RIVER, N.Y.). 194
0011-5762 See DAK TAR. 1144
0011-5819 See DALHOUSIE GAZETTE, THE. 1091
0011-5827 See DALHOUSIE REVIEW, THE. 3380
0011-586X See DALLAS MEDICAL JOURNAL. 3570
0011-5983 See DANCE AND DANCERS. 1311
0011-6009 See DANCE MAGAZINE. 1312

0011-605X See DANCING TIMES. 1312
0011-6084 See DANISH JOURNAL. 2685
0011-6092 See DANISH MEDICAL BULLETIN. 3570
0011-6297 See BULLETIN OF THE GEOLOGICAL SOCIETY OF DENMARK. 1370
0011-6335 See DANSK KEMI. 974
0011-6394 See DANSK ORNITHOLOGISK FORENINGS TIDSSKRIFT. 5617
0011-6408 See DANSK PAEDAGOGISK TIDSSKRIFT. 1734
0011-6424 See DANSK PELSDYRAVL. 3183
0011-6637 See DARBININKAS. 2259
0011-6734 See DARSHANA INTERNATIONAL. 4344
0011-6750 See DARTMOUTH COLLEGE LIBRARY BULLETIN. 3205
0011-6793 See DARWINIANA. 508
0011-6807 See DASEIN. 318
0011-684X See DATA PROCESSING. 1257
0011-6858 See DATA PROCESSING DIGEST. 1209
0011-6963 See DATAMATION. 1258
0011-6963 See DATAMATION [MICROFORM]. 2097
0011-7013 See DAUGHTERS OF THE AMERICAN REVOLUTION MAGAZINE. 2730
0011-7048 See DAVKA. 2650
0011-7110 See DAYIG U-MIDGEH BE-YISRAEL. 2300
0011-7129 See DAYTIME TV. 1131
0011-7137 See DAYTON. 2730
0011-7153 See D.C. GAZETTE. 2532
0011-7188 See DE PAUL LAW REVIEW. 2959
0011-7269 See DECCAN GEOGRAPHER. 2559
0011-7307 See DECISION (NORTH AMERICA ED.). 4952
0011-7315 See DECISION SCIENCES. 664
0011-7331 See DECISIONS OF THE DEPARTMENT OF THE INTERIOR (MONTHLY). 4642
0011-7358 See DECOR (ST. LOUIS). 349
0011-7404 See DECORATING RETAILER. 2899
0011-748X See DEFENSE SCIENCE JOURNAL. 4042
0011-751X See DEFENDER NEWSLETTER. 2959
0011-7587 See DEFENSE LAW JOURNAL. 2959
0011-7625 See DEFENSE TRANSPORTATION JOURNAL. 4042
0011-7633 See DEFENSOR CHIEFTAIN. 5712
0011-7749 See REPORT OF INVESTIGATIONS - DELAWARE GEOLOGICAL SURVEY. 1394
0011-7765 See DELAWARE HISTORY. 2730
0011-7781 See DELAWARE MEDICAL JOURNAL. 3571
0011-7862 See DELI NEWS. 2333
0011-7935 See DELO (BEOGRAD). 3380
0011-7951 See DELOS. 3462
0011-8036 See DELTA FARM PRESS. 78
0011-8044 See DELTA KAPPA GAMMA BULLETIN, THE. 1734
0011-8052 See DELTA PI EPSILON JOURNAL. 665
0011-8214 See DEMOCRATIC JOURNALIST, THE. 2918
0011-8249 See DEMOGRAFIA. 4551
0011-8265 See DEMOGRAFIE. 4551
0011-8389 See DENKI-SEIKO. 4001
0011-8427 See DENMARK QUARTERLY REVIEW. 1555
0011-8486 See DENTAL ABSTRACTS (CHICAGO). 1338
0011-8516 See TYDSKRIF VAN DIE TANDHEELKUNDIGE VERENIGING VAN SUID AFRIKA. 1337
0011-8524 See DENTAL CADMOS. 1320
0011-8532 See DENTAL CLINICS OF NORTH AMERICA. 1320
0011-8575 See DENTAL-ECHO. 1320
0011-8583 See DENTAL ECONOMICS (PITTSBURGH. 1968). 1320

0011-8605 See DENTAL HEALTH (LONDON, ENGLAND). 1320
0011-8656 See DENTAL-LABOR, DAS. 1321
0011-8710 See DENTAL PRACTICE (EWELL). 1321
0011-8737 See DENTAL PRODUCTS REPORT. 1321
0011-8796 See DENTAL TECHNICIAN. 1321
0011-8869 See DENVER QUARTERLY. 3380
0011-8915 See LOCAL 1-S NEWS. 1688
0011-9008 See DEREVOOBRABATYVAJUSCAJA PROMYSLENNOST. 634
0011-9059 See INTERNATIONAL JOURNAL OF DERMATOLOGY. 3721
0011-9075 See DERMATOLOGY (BASEL). 3719
0011-9083 See DERMATOLOGISCHE MONATSSCHRIFT. 3719
0011-9164 See DESALINATION. 5532
0011-9172 See DESALINATION AND RECYCLING ABSTRACTS. 2184
0011-9210 See DESCANT (FORT WORTH, TEX.). 1091
0011-9229 See DESERT CALL / SPIRITUAL LIFE INSTITUTE. 4953
0011-9245 See DESIGN (LONDON). 2097
0011-9261 See DESIGN. 296
0011-9342 See DESIGN ENGINEERING (TORONTO). 1970
0011-9407 See DESIGN NEWS. 2097
0011-9415 See DESIGN QUARTERLY (MINNEAPOLIS, MINN.). 297
0011-9474 See DESMOS OF DELTA SIGMA DELTA. 1819
0011-9571 See DETAIL (MUNCHEN). 297
0011-9601 See DETROIT DENTAL BULLETIN. 1322
0011-9636 See BULLETIN OF THE DETROIT INSTITUTE OF ARTS. 345
0011-9652 See DETROIT LAWYER, THE. 2960
0011-9709 See DETROITER, THE. 819
0011-9741 See DEUTSCH ALS FREMDSPRACHE. 3276
0011-9822 See MITTEILUNGEN - DEUTSCHE AKADEMIE FUER STADTEBAU UND LANDESPLANUNG. 2828
0011-9857 See DEUTSCHE APOTHEKER-ZEITUNG. 4299
0011-9865 See DEUTSCHE ARCHITEKTUR. 311
0011-9881 See DEUTSCHE AUSSENPOLITIK. 4519
0011-992X See DEUTSCHE BAUMSCHULE. 2413
0012-0073 See DEUTSCHE ENTOMOLOGISCHE ZEITSCHRIFT. 5607
0012-009X See DEFAZET. DEUTSCHE FARBEN-ZEITSCHRIFT. 4223
0012-0189 See ZEITSCHRIFT DER DEUTSCHEN GEOLOGISCHEN GESELLSCHAFT. 1401
0012-0235 See DEUTSCHE GEWAESSERKUNDLICHE MITTEILUNGEN. 5532
0012-0278 See DEUTSCHE HEBE- UND FORDERTECHNIK. 5099
0012-0294 See DEUTSCHE HUGENOTT, DER. 5059
0012-0308 See DEUTSCHE HYDROGRAPHISCHE ZEITSCHRIFT. 1354
0012-0332 See DEUTSCHE JUGEND. 5282
0012-0375 See DEUTSCHE KUNST UND DENKMALPFLEGE. 297
0012-0413 See DEUTSCHE LEBENSMITTEL-RUNDSCHAU. 2333
0012-043X See DEUTSCHE LITERATURZEITUNG. 3380
0012-0448 See DEUTSCHE MALERBLATT, DAS. 4223
0012-0456 See JAHRESBERICHT DER DEUTSCHEN MATHEMATIKER-VEREINIGUNG. 3511
0012-0472 See DEUTSCHE MEDIZINISCHE WOCHENSCHRIFT. 3571
0012-0480 See DEUTSCHE MILCHWIRTSCHAFT (HILDESHEIM). 194

0012-0502 See DEUTSCHE MUSIKBIBLIOGRAPHIE. 4114
0012-0553 See DEUTSCHE PELZTIERZUCHTER, DER. 5581
0012-057X See DEUTSCHE POLIZEI. 3163
0012-0618 See DEUTSCHE RENTENVERSICHERUNG. 2878
0012-0669 See DEUTSCHE SCHACHZEITUNG / ORGAN FUR DAS GESAMMTE SCHACHLEBEN. 4860
0012-0731 See DEUTSCHE SCHULE, DIE. 1735
0012-074X See DEUTSCHE KRANKENPFLEGEZEITSCHRIFT. 3855
0012-0812 See DEUTSCHE STUDIEN (SCHLOSS BLECKEDE). 2515
0012-088X See DEUTSCHE UNIVERSITATSZEITUNG VEREINIGT MIT HOCHSCHUL-DIENST BONN, DIE. 5801
0012-0936 See DEUTSCHE VIERTELJAHRSSCHRIFT FUER LITERATURWISSENSCHAFT UND GEISTESGESCHICHTE. 3380
0012-0979 See DEUTSCHE WEINBAU. 2366
0012-1029 See DEUTSCHE ZAHNAERZTLICHE ZEITSCHRIFT. 1322
0012-1045 See DEUTSCHE ZEITSCHRIFT FUER PHILOSOPHIE. 4344
0012-1096 See DEUTSCHER DRUCKER STUTTGART. 4233
0012-1169 See ZEITSCHRIFT DES DEUTSCHEN PALASTINA-VEREINS (1953). 2634
0012-1185 See NACHRICHTENDIENST. 5297
0012-1193 See DEUTSCHES ADELSBLATT. 2445
0012-1207 See DEUTSCHES ARZTEBLATT. 3571
0012-1215 See DEUTSCHES ARCHITEKTENBLATT. AUSGABE BADEN-WURTTEMBERG. 297
0012-1223 See DEUTSCHES ARCHIV FUER ERFORSCHUNG DES MITTELALTERS. 2685
0012-124X See DACHDECKER-HANDWERK, DAS. 612
0012-1258 See ELEKTROMEISTER + DEUTSCHES ELEKTROHANDWERK. 2051
0012-1304 See WOCHENBERICHT - DEUTSCHES INSTITUT FUER WIRTSCHAFTSFORSCHUNG. 1589
0012-1347 See DEUTSCHES STEUERRECHT. 4720
0012-1363 See DEUTSCHES VERWALTUNGSBLATT. 2960
0012-1428 See DEUTSCHLAND ARCHIV. 4471
0012-1460 See DEUTSCHUNTERRICHT. 3381
0012-1533 See DEVELOPING ECONOMIES, THE. 5198
0012-155X See DEVELOPMENT AND CHANGE. 5198
0012-1592 See DEVELOPMENT, GROWTH & DIFFERENTIATION. 541
0012-1606 See DEVELOPMENTAL BIOLOGY. 453
0012-1622 See DEVELOPMENTAL MEDICINE & CHILD NEUROLOGY. 3657
0012-1630 See DEVELOPMENTAL PSYCHOBIOLOGY. 453
0012-1649 See DEVELOPMENTAL PSYCHOLOGY. 4584
0012-1681 See DEVON & CORNWALL NOTES & QUERIES. 2685
0012-1762 See DIA MEDICO, EL. 3571
0012-1789 See DIABETE ET NUTRITION. 3727
0012-1797 See DIABETES (NEW YORK, N.Y.). 3728
0012-186X See DIABETOLOGIA. 3728
0012-1924 See DIAGNOSTICA (GOTTINGEN). 4585
0012-1932 See DIAGNOSTYKJA LABORATORYJNA. 3571
0012-1959 See DIAKONIA (BRONX, N.Y.). 5039
0012-2009 See D.A.I.R.S. AND SYSTEMS FOR INSTRUCTION. 1892
0012-2017 See DIALECTICA. 4345
0012-2033 See DIALOG (ST. PAUL). 4953
0012-2041 See DIALOG (WARSAW, POLAND). 3381

0012-2122 See DIALOGOS. 4345
0012-2157 See DIALOGUE (LOS ANGELES). 5059
0012-2173 See DIALOGUE - CANADIAN PHILOSOPHICAL ASSOCIATION. 4345
0012-2181 See DIALOGUE (COLOMBO, SRI LANKA). 5021
0012-2246 See DIALOGUE (MILWAUKEE, WIS.). 4345
0012-2378 See DIAPASON (CHICAGO), THE. 4114
0012-2440 See DICKENSIAN, THE. 3381
0012-2459 See DICKINSON LAW REVIEW. 2960
0012-253X See DIE CASTING ENGINEER. 2102
0012-2645 See DWB. 3383
0012-2645 See DIETSCHE WARANDE EN BELFORT. 3381
0012-2653 See DIFESA SOCIALE. 4773
0012-2661 See DIFFERENTIAL EQUATIONS. 3503
0012-2742 See DIGEST OF INVESTMENT ADVICES, THE. 896
0012-2769 See DIGEST OF NEUROLOGY AND PSYCHIATRY. 3831
0012-2777 See DIGEST OF OPINIONS OF THE ATTORNEY GENERAL. 3140
0012-2785 See DIGEST OF PUBLIC GENERAL BILLS AND RESOLUTIONS. 4642
0012-2823 See DIGESTION. 3744
0012-2858 See DILIMAN REVIEW, THE. 5198
0012-2874 See DIME NOVEL ROUND-UP (1953). 3381
0012-2882 See DIMENSION; CONTEMPORARY GERMAN ARTS AND LETTERS. 3381
0012-3013 See DINTERIA. 508
0012-3099 See DIPLOMATIC LIST (WASHINGTON). 3127
0012-3188 See DIRECT MARKETING. 923
0012-320X See DIRECTION ET GESTION DES ENTREPRISES. 665
0012-3242 See DIRECTOR (LONDON. 1935). 666
0012-3250 See DIRECTOR, THE. 665
0012-3277 See DIRECTORY OF CHEMICAL PRODUCERS : UNITED STATES OF AMERICA. 1023
0012-3293 See DIRECTORY OF PUBLISHED PROCEEDINGS. SERIES MLS, MEDICAL/LIFE SCIENCES. 3572
0012-3307 See DIRECTORY OF PUBLISHED PROCEEDINGS. SERIES SSH: SOCIAL SCIENCES/HUMANITIES. 5227
0012-3323 See DIRETTORE COMMERCIALE, IL. 759
0012-3366 See DIRIGENTE INDUSTRIAL. 866
0012-3374 See DIRIGENTE RURAL, O. 79
0012-3390 See DIRITTO AEREO. 2962
0012-3404 See DIRITTO DEL LAVORO. 3146
0012-3420 See DIRITTO DI AUTORE, IL. 1304
0012-3447 See DIRITTO E PRATICA TRIBUTARIA. 2963
0012-3455 See DIRITTO ECCLESIASTICO E RASSEGNA DI DIRITTO MATRIMONIALE, IL. 2963
0012-348X See DIRITTO MARITTIMO. 3180
0012-351X See DISCIPLINE AND GRIEVANCES. WHITE COLLAR EDITION. 940
0012-3579 See DISCOUNT MERCHANDISER, THE. 954
0012-3587 See DISCOUNT STORE NEWS. 954
0012-3625 See DISCOVERY (NEW HAVEN, CONN.). 4087
0012-3641 See DISCOVERY (SKOKIE, ILL.). 5468
0012-365X See DISCRETE MATHEMATICS. 3504
0012-3692 See CHEST. 3702
0012-3706 See DISEASES OF THE COLON & RECTUM. 3744
0012-3765 See DISPATCHER, THE. 1663
0012-3811 See DISPOSABLES AND NONWOVENS. 5350
0012-3846 See DISSENT (NEW YORK). 4541
0012-3889 See DISTAFF, A CRITICAL-LITERARY QUARTERLY, THE. 1091
0012-3935 See DISTRIBUTION D'AUJOURD'HUI. 3478

0012-396X See DISTRIBUTION MAPS OF PLANT DISEASES. 508
0012-3986 See DISTRIBUTIVE WORKER, THE. 1663
0012-4222 See DIVINITAS. 4954
0012-4257 See DIVUS THOMAS; COMMENTARIUM DE PHILOSOPHIA ET THEOLOGIA. 4954
0012-4273 See DIX-SEPTIEME SIECLE. 2685
0012-4281 See DIXIE CONTRACTOR, THE. 2022
0012-4370 See DO IT YOURSELF. 613
0012-4419 See DOCK AND HARBOUR AUTHORITY. 5449
0012-4443 See DOCTOR COMMUNIS. 5028
0012-446X See DOCTRINE AND LIFE. 4954
0012-4486 See DOCUMENTA OPHTHALMOLOGICA. 3874
0012-4494 See DOCUMENTACION ADMINISTRATIVA. 4645
0012-4508 See DOCUMENTALISTE (PARIS). 3208
0012-4613 See DOCUMENTATION CATHOLIQUE, LA. 5028
0012-4664 See AFRICA : A DOCUMENTATION LIST. 407
0012-4893 See DOG WORLD. 4286
0012-4915 See DOGS IN CANADA. 4286
0012-4958 See DOKLADY. BIOCHEMISTRY. 486
0012-4966 See DOKLADY. BIOLOGICAL SCIENCES. 454
0012-4974 See DOKLADY. BIOPHYSICS. 495
0012-4982 See DOKLADY. BOTANICAL SCIENCES. 508
0012-5008 See DOKLADY. CHEMISTRY. 974
0012-5016 See DOKLADY. PHYSICAL CHEMISTRY. 1051
0012-5016 See DOKLADY. PHYSICAL CHEMISTRY. 1051
0012-5032 See DOKUMENTACJA GEOGRAFICZNA. 2560
0012-5148 See DOKUMENTATION STRASSE. 2003
0012-5156 See DW DOKUMENTATION WASSER. 5533
0012-5172 See DOKUMENTE (KOLN). 5198
0012-5229 See DOLL TALK FOR COLLECTORS. 2773
0012-5245 See DOLLARS & SENSE (SOMERVILLE, MASS.). 1480
0012-5350 See DOMINION LAW REPORTS. 3089
0012-5377 See DOMUS. 2900
0012-5385 See BOLLETTINO DELLA DOMUS MAZZINIANA. 2679
0012-5563 See DORNIER-POST. 18
0012-561X See DOSHKOLNOE VOSPITANIE. 1737
0012-5709 See DOUBLE LIAISON-CHIMIE DES PEINTURES. 4223
0012-5709 See DOUBLE LIAISON. 4223
0012-5768 See DOWN BEAT. 4115
0012-5776 See DOWN EAST. 5468
0012-5792 See DOWN TO EARTH. 80
0012-5806 See DOWNSIDE REVIEW, THE. 3382
0012-5822 See DOWNTOWN IDEA EXCHANGE. 669
0012-5865 See DRAFT HORSE JOURNAL, THE. 2798
0012-5881 See DRAGOCO REPORT (FLAVORS EDITION. ENGLISH). 4299
0012-5911 See DRAHT. 4001
0012-592X See DRAHT-WELT. 4001
0012-5938 See DRAKE LAW REVIEW. 2964
0012-5946 See DRAMA. 5363
0012-5989 See DRAMATICS. 384
0012-6004 See DRAMATISTS GUILD QUARTERLY, THE. 5364
0012-6063 See DREI (STUTTGART, GERMANY : 1948). 2846
0012-611X See DRESSMAKING. 1083
0012-6136 See DREVARSKY VYSKUM. 2400
0012-6144 See DREVO. 634

0012-6152 See DREW GATEWAY, THE. 4954
0012-6179 See DREXEL TECHNICAL JOURNAL. 5102
0012-6330 See NIEUWE DROGIST. 4318
0012-6411 See DROIT & LIBERTE : ORGANE MENSUEL DE MOUVEMENT CONTER LE RACISME, L'ANTISEMITISME, ET POUR LA PAIX. 4507
0012-642X See DROIT MARITIME FRANCAIS, LE. 3180
0012-6438 See DROIT SOCIAL. 3146
0012-6454 See DROVER'S JOURNAL (SHAWNEE MISSION, KAN.). 210
0012-6462 See DRUCK PRINT. 4564
0012-6500 See DRUCKSPIEGEL, DER. 4564
0012-6519 See DRUCKWELT. 4564
0012-6527 See DRUG & COSMETIC INDUSTRY. 4299
0012-6535 See 1199 NEWS. 1642
0012-6543 See DRUG AND THERAPEUTICS BULLETIN. 4299
0012-6586 See DRUG MERCHANDISING. 4300
0012-6616 See DRUG TOPICS. 4301
0012-6667 See DRUGS (NEW YORK, N.Y.). 4302
0012-6683 See DRUGS MADE IN GERMANY. 4302
0012-6748 See DRUM CORPS NEWS. 4115
0012-6756 See DRUZBA NARODOV. 3341
0012-6772 See DRVNA INDUSTRIJA. 2400
0012-6802 See DRYCLEANER NEWS. 5350
0012-6837 See DU. 2515
0012-6861 See DUBLIN HISTORICAL RECORD. 2685
0012-6918 See DUBUQUE LEADER, THE. 5670
0012-6950 See DUCKS UNLIMITED. 2191
0012-6969 See DUDE RANCHER. 2532
0012-7086 See DUKE LAW JOURNAL. 2964
0012-7094 See DUKE MATHEMATICAL JOURNAL. 3504
0012-7116 See DULUTHIAN, THE. 832
0012-7132 See DUNE BUGGIES AND HOT VWS. 5413
0012-7183 See DUODECIM. 3573
0012-723X See DURBAN MUSEUM NOVITATES. 4165
0012-7280 See DURHAM UNIVERSITY JOURNAL, THE. 1822
0012-7299 See DUROC NEWS. 210
0012-7337 See DVM. 5509
0012-7396 See DYNAMIC SUPERVISION. 670
0012-740X See DYNAMISCHE PSYCHIATRIE. 3924
0012-7477 See ETHNOGRAPHISCH-ARCHAOLOGISCHE ZEITSCHRIFT : EAZ. 267
0012-7515 See EDN; ELECTRONIC ENGINEER'S DESIGN MAGAZINE. 2042
0012-7515 See EDN. 2042
0012-7655 See EFTA BULLETIN. 832
0012-7825 See EOS. 3279
0012-8023 See ETV NEWSLETTER. 1745
0012-8147 See CHRONICLE OF THE EARLY AMERICAN INDUSTRIES ASSOCIATION, INC, THE. 5094
0012-8155 See EARLY AMERICAN LIFE. 2731
0012-8163 See EARLY AMERICAN LITERATURE. 3341
0012-8171 See EARLY CHILDHOOD EDUCATION. 1737
0012-821X See EARTH AND PLANETARY SCIENCE LETTERS. 1374
0012-8236 See EARTH SCIENCE BULLETIN. 1354
0012-8252 See EARTH-SCIENCE REVIEWS. 1374
0012-8295 See EAST (TOKYO, JAPAN). 2650
0012-8317 See JOURNAL OF THE EAST AFRICA NATURAL HISTORY SOCIETY AND NATIONAL MUSEUM. 4166
0012-8325 See EAST AFRICAN AGRICULTURAL AND FORESTRY JOURNAL. 80
0012-835X See EAST AFRICAN MEDICAL JOURNAL, THE. 3573

0012-8376 See EAST AND WEST (ROME, ITALY). 349
0012-8406 See EAST ASIA MILLIONS (ROBESONIA). 4954
0012-8430 See EAST EUROPE. 2686
0012-8449 See EAST EUROPEAN QUARTERLY. 2686
0012-8481 See EAST MIDLAND GEOGRAPHER. 2560
0012-852X See EAST RIDING ARCHAEOLOGIST : A JOURNAL OF THE EAST RIDING ARCHAEOLOGICAL SOCIETY. 267
0012-8570 See EAST WEST FORTNIGHTLY BULLETIN. 1634
0012-8678 See EASTERN AFRICA LAW REVIEW. 2965
0012-8686 See EASTERN ANTHROPOLOGIST, THE. 235
0012-8708 See EASTERN BUDDHIST, THE. 5021
0012-8775 See EASTERN EUROPEAN ECONOMICS. 1481
0012-8856 See EASTERN METALS REVIEW, THE. 4001
0012-8872 See EASTERN PHARMACIST. 4302
0012-8953 See EASTERN WORKER. 1664
0012-8961 See EASTERN WORLD. 2650
0012-9003 See INFORMATION EAUX. 5534
0012-9011 See EBONY. 2259
0012-9038 See ECCLESIA MADRID. 5029
0012-9143 See ECHO. 1893
0012-9283 See ECHO DES RECHERCHES, L'. 1154
0012-933X See ECHOES (COLUMBUS). 2732
0012-9356 See ECHOS DU MONDE CLASSIQUE. 267
0012-9402 See ECLOGAE GEOLOGICAE HELVETIAE. 1374
0012-9410 See ECO. 3383
0012-9585 See ECOLE MATERNELLE FRANCAISE, L'. 1737
0012-9593 See ANNALES SCIENTIFIQUES DE L'ECOLE NORMALE SUPERIEURE. 3493
0012-9615 See ECOLOGICAL MONOGRAPHS. 2214
0012-9623 See BULLETIN OF THE ECOLOGICAL SOCIETY OF AMERICA. 2212
0012-9658 See ECOLOGY (TEMPE). 2214
0012-9682 See ECONOMETRICA. 1481
0012-9704 See ECONOMIA (QUITO). 1481
0012-9755 See EM; ECONOMIA DE MOCAMBIQUE. 1488
0012-9771 See ECONOMIA E CREDITO. 1481
0012-978X See ECONOMIA & LAVORO (1967). 1481
0012-981X See ECONOMIA INTERNAZIONALE. 1634
0012-9836 See ECONOMIA MONTANA ROMA. 2214
0012-9895 See ECONOMIA Y CIENCIAS SOCIALES. 5199
0012-9976 See ECONOMIC AND POLITICAL WEEKLY. 1556
0012-9984 See ECONOMIC AND SOCIAL REVIEW, THE. 5199
0013-0001 See ECONOMIC BOTANY. 508
0013-0079 See ECONOMIC DEVELOPMENT AND CULTURAL CHANGE. 1482
0013-0095 See ECONOMIC GEOGRAPHY. 1483
0013-0117 See ECONOMIC HISTORY REVIEW, THE. 1557
0013-0125 See ECONOMIC INDICATORS (WASHINGTON, D.C.). 1557
0013-0133 See ECONOMIC JOURNAL (LONDON). 1483
0013-0141 See ECONOMIC LEAFLETS. 1483
0013-0206 See ECONOMIC OPPORTUNITY REPORT. 5284
0013-0222 See ECONOMIC PLANNING IN FREE SOCIETIES. 81
0013-0249 See ECONOMIC RECORD, THE. 1484
0013-0281 See ECONOMIC REVIEW (CLEVELAND). 1484

0013-029X See ECONOMIC REVIEW (TAIPEI, TAIWAN). 1485
0013-032X See ECONOMIC REVIEW OF THE ARAB WORLD. 1485
0013-0362 See ECONOMIC STUDIES (CALCUTTA, INDIA). 1558
0013-0400 See ECONOMIC TRENDS (LONDON). 1485
0013-0419 See ECONOMICA. 1486
0013-0427 See ECONOMICA (LONDON). 1486
0013-0451 See ECONOMICS OF PLANNING. 1558
0013-0478 See ECONOMIE, L'. 1558
0013-0486 See MAANDSCHRIFT ECONOMIE. 1503
0013-0494 See ECONOMIE APPLIQUEE. 1591
0013-0508 See ECONOMIE ELECTRIQUE, L'. 2042
0013-0559 See ECONOMIE RURALE. 1487
0013-0567 See ECONOMIES ET SOCIETES. 1487
0013-0575 See ECONOMISCH EN SOCIAAL TIJDSCHRIFT. 671
0013-0583 See ECONOMISCH-STATISTISCHE BERICHTEN. 1559
0013-0613 See ECONOMIST (LONDON). 1559
0013-0621 See EKONOMISUTO TOKYO. 1946. 1488
0013-063X See ECONOMIST, DE. 1559
0013-0656 See ECONOMISTA MADRID. 1886, EL. 1487
0013-0710 See ECRITS DE PARIS. 2515
0013-0710 See ECRITS DE PARIS. 4472
0013-0729 See ECRITS DU CANADA FRANCAIS. 3383
0013-0796 See ECUMENICAL REVIEW, THE. 4955
0013-0818 See EDDA. 3341
0013-0842 See EDESIPAR. 2334
0013-0907 See EDINBURGH DENTAL HOSPITAL GAZETTE. 1322
0013-0915 See PROCEEDINGS OF THE EDINBURGH MATHEMATICAL SOCIETY. 3528
0013-094X See EDITOR & PUBLISHER. 4814
0013-0966 See EDITORIALS ON FILE. 4472
0013-1059 See EDUCACION, LA. 1737
0013-1067 See EDUCACION. 1737
0013-1091 See EDUCACION MEDICA Y SALUD. 3573
0013-1164 See EDUCATION (EDINBURGH). 1863
0013-1172 See EDUCATION (CHULA VISTA). 1738
0013-1245 See EDUCATION AND URBAN SOCIETY. 1738
0013-1253 See EDUCATION CANADA. 1738
0013-1261 See EDUCATION DAILY. 1739
0013-127X See EDUCATION DIGEST, THE. 1739
0013-1288 See EDUCATION ENFANTINE, L'. 1739
0013-1350 See EDUCATION IN CHEMISTRY. 974
0013-1377 See EDUCATION IN SCIENCE. 5102
0013-1385 See EDUCATION INDEX. 1794
0013-1385 See EDUCATION INDEX. CD-ROM. 1794
0013-1415 See EDUCATION MUSICALE, L'. 4116
0013-1423 See EDUCATION, L'. 1738
0013-144X See EDUCATION NEWSLETTER. 4955
0013-1482 See EDUCATION QUARTERLY, THE. 1740
0013-1547 See EDUCATION TODAY. 1740
0013-1571 See EDUCATION U.S.A. 1741
0013-1601 See EDUCATIONAL ADMINISTRATION ABSTRACTS. 1794
0013-161X See EDUCATIONAL ADMINISTRATION QUARTERLY. 1863
0013-1725 See EDUCATIONAL FORUM (WEST LAFAYETTE, IND.), THE. 1741
0013-1741 See EDUCATIONAL FREEDOM. 2965
0013-175X See EDUCATIONAL HORIZONS. 1741
0013-1768 See EDUCATIONAL INDIA. 1742
0013-1784 See EDUCATIONAL LEADERSHIP : JOURNAL OF THE ASSOCIATION FOR SUPERVISION AND CURRICULUM DEVELOPMENT. 1742
0013-1806 See EDUCATIONAL MARKETER. 1742

0013-1849 See EDUCATIONAL PERSPECTIVES. 1742
0013-1857 See EDUCATIONAL PHILOSOPHY AND THEORY. 1893
0013-1873 See EDUCATIONAL RECORD, THE. 1822
0013-1881 See EDUCATIONAL RESEARCH (WINDSOR). 1742
0013-189X See EDUCATIONAL RESEARCHER (WASHINGTON, D.C. : 1972). 1742
0013-1911 See EDUCATIONAL REVIEW (BIRMINGHAM). 1742
0013-1946 See EDUCATIONAL STUDIES (AMES). 1743
0013-1954 See EDUCATIONAL STUDIES IN MATHEMATICS. 1743
0013-1962 See EDUCATIONAL TECHNOLOGY. 1893
0013-1997 See EDUCATIONAL THEATRE NEWS. 5364
0013-2004 See EDUCATIONAL THEORY. 1743
0013-2047 See EDUCATORS' ADVOCATE. 1743
0013-2322 See EGLISE CANADIENNE, L'. 4955
0013-2349 See EGLISE ET THEOLOGIE. 4955
0013-2357 See EGLISE QUI CHANTE. 4116
0013-2373 See EGRETTA : VOGELKUNDLICHE NACHRICHTEN AUS OSTERREICH. 4165
0013-239X See EGYPTE CONTEMPORAINE, L'. 1488
0013-2411 See JOURNAL OF THE EGYPTIAN MEDICAL ASSOCIATION. 3598
0013-242X See EGYPTIAN ORTHOPEDIC JOURNAL. 3881
0013-2438 See AL-NASRA AS-SAYDALIYYA AL-MISRIYYA. 4290
0013-2446 See JOURNAL OF THE EGYPTIAN PUBLIC HEALTH ASSOCIATION, THE. 4787
0013-2586 See EIGHTEENTH-CENTURY STUDIES. 319
0013-2586 See EIGHTEENTH CENTURY STUDIES NEWS CIRCULAR. 2615
0013-2608 See EIGSE. 3278
0013-2683 See EIRE-IRELAND (ST. PAUL). 3341
0013-273X See EISEI KAGAKU. 975
0013-2810 See EISENBAHNINGENIEUR, DER. 5431
0013-2845 See ETR. 5431
0013-2918 See EJERCITO MADRID. 4043
0013-2942 See EKISTICS. 2821
0013-2969 See WIADOMOSCI EKOLOGICZNE. 2222
0013-3027 See EKONOMICKO-MATEMATICKY OBZOR. 1591
0013-3035 See EKONOMICKY CASOPIS. 1488
0013-3051 See EKONOMIKA I ZHIZN. 5813
0013-3116 See EKONOMIKA STROITELSTVA. 613
0013-3183 See EKONOMISKA SAMFUNDETS TIDSKRIFT. 1488
0013-3191 See EKONOMIST : ORGAN DRUSTVA EKONOMISTA SRBIJE. 1488
0013-3248 See EKONOMSKA POLITIKA. 671
0013-4023 See EL PASO ARCHAEOLOGY. 267
0013-4074 See ELDER STATESMAN, THE. 5179
0013-4120 See ELECTRIC LIGHT & POWER. 2043
0013-4155 See ELECTRICAL TECHNOLOGY. 2045
0013-4244 See ELECTRICAL BUSINESS. 2044
0013-4252 See ELECTRICAL COMMUNICATION. 1154
0013-4260 See ELECTRICAL CONSTRUCTION AND MAINTENANCE. 2044
0013-4317 See ELECTRICAL EQUIPMENT LONDON. 2045
0013-4333 See ELECTRICAL EQUIPMENT NEWS. 2045
0013-435X See ELECTRICAL INDIA. 2045
0013-4414 See ELECTRICAL TIMES. 2045
0013-4422 See ELECTRICAL WHOLESALER. 2045
0013-4430 See ELECTRICAL WHOLESALING. 2045
0013-4457 See ELECTRICAL WORLD. 2045
0013-4481 See ELECTRICITE. 2045

0013-449X See BULLETIN DE LA DIRECTION DES ETUDES ET RECHERCHES. SERIE A. NUCLEAIRE, HYDRAULIQUE, THERMIQUE. 2087
0013-4503 See BULLETIN DE LA DIRECTION DES ETUDES ET RECHERCHES. SERIE B. RESEAUX ELECTRIQUES, MATERIELS ELECTRIQUES. 2037
0013-4511 See BULLETIN DE LA DIRECTION DES ETUDES ET RECHERCHES, ELECTRICITE DE FRANCE - SERIE C. MATHEMATIQUES, INFORMATIQUE. 3497
0013-4589 See ELECTRO OPTICS. 4434
0013-4651 See JOURNAL OF THE ELECTROCHEMICAL SOCIETY. 1034
0013-466X See JOURNAL OF THE ELECTROCHEMICAL SOCIETY OF INDIA. 1026
0013-4686 See ELECTROCHIMICA ACTA. 1034
0013-4694 See ELECTROENCEPHALOGRAPHY AND CLINICAL NEUROPHYSIOLOGY. 3831
0013-4724 See ELECTROMEDICA. 3941
0013-4813 See ELECTRONIC APPLICATION NEWS. 2046
0013-4872 See ELECTRONIC DESIGN. 2047
0013-4902 See ELECTRONIC ENGINEERING. 2047
0013-4945 See ELECTRONIC PACKAGING AND PRODUCTION. 2048
0013-4953 See ELECTRONIC PRODUCTS (1981). 2048
0013-5011 See ELECTRONIC TRENDS INTERNATIONAL. 2048
0013-5119 See ELECTRONICS & COMMUNICATIONS ABSTRACTS. 2049
0013-5194 See ELECTRONICS LETTERS. 2049
0013-5224 See ELECTRONICS WEEKLY. 2050
0013-5380 See ELEKTRICESTVO. 2051
0013-5399 See ELEKTRIE. 2051
0013-5437 See ELEKTRISCHE BAHNEN. 5431
0013-5445 See EMA. ELEKTRISCHE MASCHINEN. 2053
0013-5496 See ELEKTRIZITATSWIRTSCHAFT. 2051
0013-550X See ELEKTRO. 2051
0013-5518 See ELEKTRO-ANZEIGER. 2051
0013-5542 See ELEKTROHANDEL HEIDELBERG. 2051
0013-5585 See BIOMEDIZINISCHE TECHNIK. 3687
0013-5658 See ELEKTRONIK (MUNCHEN). 2051
0013-5674 See ELEKTRONIKJOURNAL. 2052
0013-5739 See ELEKTRONNAJA OBRABOTKA MATERIALOV. 2052
0013-5771 See ELEKTROSVIAZ (MOSKVA. 1934). 1154
0013-578X See ELEKTROTECHNICKY CASOPIS. 2052
0013-5798 See ELEKTROTECHNICKY OBZOR. 2052
0013-581X See ELEKTROTECHNIK. 2052
0013-5844 See ELEKTROTEHNIKA (ZAGREB). 2052
0013-5852 See ELEKTROTEHNISKI VESTNIK. 2052
0013-5860 See ELEKTROTEKHNIKA (MOSKVA, 1963). 2052
0013-5895 See ELEKTUUR. 2052
0013-5933 See ELEMENTA. 4345
0013-5976 See ELEMENTARY SCHOOL GUIDANCE AND COUNSELING. 1878
0013-5984 See ELEMENTARY SCHOOL JOURNAL. MICROFORM, THE. 1743
0013-6018 See ELEMENTE DER MATHEMATIK. 3504
0013-6069 See ELEPAIO. 2192
0013-6093 See ELETTRIFICAZIONE. 2052
0013-6123 See ELETTRONICA E TELECOMUNICAZIONI. 2052
0013-6131 See ELETTROTECNICA, L'. 2053
0013-6158 See ELEVATOR WORLD. 2113
0013-6220 See JOURNAL OF THE ELISHA MITCHELL SCIENTIFIC SOCIETY. 5120

0013-6263 See ELKS MAGAZINE, THE. 5231
0013-6298 See ELLE (NEUILLY-SUR-SEINE, FRANCE). 5555
0013-6336 See ELLENIKA (THESSALONIKE). 3278
0013-6395 See ELSEVIERS MAGAZINE. MICROFORM. 2487
0013-6484 See ELVIS MONTHLY. 4116
0013-6506 See EMAJL-KERAMIKA-STAKLO. 2588
0013-6530 See EMBALAGEM (RIO DE JANEIRO). 4218
0013-6557 See EMBALLAGE DIGEST. 4218
0013-6573 See EMBALLAGES. 4218
0013-6611 See EMBROIDERY. 5184
0013-6654 See EMERGENCY MEDICINE. 3724
0013-6662 See EMERITA. 1076
0013-6719 See EMMANUEL (NEW YORK, N.Y.). 4955
0013-6727 See EMORY MAGAZINE. 1822
0013-6751 See EMPIRE STATE ARCHITECT. 298
0013-676X See EMPIRE STATE GEOGRAM. 1375
0013-6794 See EMPIRE STATE MASON. 5231
0013-6808 See EMPLOYEE BENEFIT PLAN REVIEW. 2879
0013-6824 See EMPLOYEE RELATIONS IN ACTION. 1665
0013-6840 See EMPLOYMENT AND EARNINGS (1969). 1666
0013-6883 See EMPLOYMENT REVIEW. 1667
0013-6980 See ENACT. 5364
0013-7006 See ENCEPHALE. 3832
0013-7081 See ENCOUNTER (INDIANAPOLIS). 4956
0013-7154 See TRENDS IN END-USE MARKETS FOR PLASTICS. 4460
0013-7219 See ENDOCRINOLOGIA JAPONICA. 3729
0013-7227 See ENDOCRINOLOGY (PHILADELPHIA). 3730
0013-726X See ENDOSCOPY. 3744
0013-7278 See ENERGETIK (MOSKVA). 2053
0013-7294 See ENERGETYKA. 1938
0013-7308 See ENERGIA ELETTRICA. 2053
0013-7316 See ENERGIA ES ATOMTECHNIKA. 1938
0013-7324 See ENERGIA NUCLEAR (MADRID). 2155
0013-7332 See ENERGIA NUCLEARE (MILANO). 2155
0013-7359 See ENERGIE (MUNCHEN). 2113
0013-7405 See ENERGIEANWENDUNG. 1938
0013-7421 See ENERGIETECHNIK. 1938
0013-7472 See ENERGY AND CHARACTER. 4586
0013-7502 See ENERGY DEVELOPMENTS (NEW YORK, N.Y. 1957). 1940
0013-7545 See ENFANCE. 4586
0013-7561 See ENFANT EN MILIEU TROPICAL, L'. 3903
0013-7626 See ENGEI GAKKAI ZASSHI. 2413
0013-7758 See ENGINEER (LONDON). 1972
0013-7782 See ENGINEERING (LONDON). 1973
0013-7812 See ENGINEERING & SCIENCE. 1972
0013-7898 See ENGINEERING DESIGNER. 2098
0013-7901 See ENGINEERING DIGEST (TORONTO). 1972
0013-791X See ENGINEERING ECONOMIST, THE. 1973
0013-7944 See ENGINEERING FRACTURE MECHANICS. 2102
0013-7952 See ENGINEERING GEOLOGY. 1973
0013-8029 See ENGINEERING JOURNAL (NEW YORK). 614
0013-8037 See ENGINEERING MANPOWER BULLETIN. 1973
0013-8088 See ENGINEERING OUTLOOK. 1973
0013-8142 See ENGINEERS AND ENGINES MAGAZINE. 158

0013-8150 See JOURNAL OF THE ENGINEERS' CLUB OF ST. LOUIS. A MONTHLY PERIODICAL DEVOTED TO THE INTERESTS OF THE ENGINEERING PROFESSION IN ST. LOUIS. 1983
0013-8185 See ENGLISCH. 3278
0013-8215 See ENGLISH (LONDON). 3384
0013-8231 See ENGLISH DANCE AND SONG. 384
0013-8266 See ENGLISH HISTORICAL REVIEW, THE. 2615
0013-8274 See ENGLISH JOURNAL. 1894
0013-8282 See ENGLISH LANGUAGE NOTES. 3342
0013-8304 See ELH. 3342
0013-8312 See ENGLISH LITERARY RENAISSANCE. 3342
0013-8339 See ENGLISH LITERATURE IN TRANSITION, 1880-1920. 3342
0013-8355 See ENGLISH QUARTERLY, THE. 1894
0013-8363 See ENGLISH RECORD, THE. 1744
0013-838X See ENGLISH STUDIES. 3384
0013-8398 See ENGLISH STUDIES IN AFRICA. 3384
0013-841X See ENGLISH WESTERNERS' TALLY SHEET. 2732
0013-8495 See STAFF REPORTER. 3251
0013-8584 See ENSEIGNEMENT MATHEMATIQUE. 3505
0013-8657 See ENTERPRISE. 2533
0013-8703 See ENTOMOLOGIA EXPERIMENTALIS ET APPLICATA. 5607
0013-8711 See ENTOMOLOGICA SCANDINAVICA. 5607
0013-872X See ENTOMOLOGICAL NEWS. 5607
0013-8738 See ENTOMOLOGICAL REVIEW. 5607
0013-8746 See ANNALS OF THE ENTOMOLOGICAL SOCIETY OF AMERICA. 5605
0013-8762 See BULLETIN OF ENTOMOLOGY. 5606
0013-8770 See KONCHU. 5611
0013-8789 See JOURNAL OF THE ENTOMOLOGICAL SOCIETY OF SOUTHERN AFRICA. 5589
0013-8797 See PROCEEDINGS OF THE ENTOMOLOGICAL SOCIETY OF WASHINGTON. 5595
0013-8800 See ENTOMOLOGIE ET PHYTOPATHOLOGIE APPLIQUEES. 5582
0013-8827 See ENTOMOLOGISCHE BERICHTEN. 5582
0013-8835 See ENTOMOLOGISCHE BLATTER FUER BIOLOGIE UND SYSTEMATIK DER KAFER. 5582
0013-8851 See ENTOMOLOGISKE MEDDELELSER. 5608
0013-886X See ENTOMOLOGISK TIDSKRIFT / ENTOMOLOGISKA FORENINGEN I STOCKHOLM. 5608
0013-8878 See ENTOMOLOGIST, THE. 5608
0013-8886 See ENTOMOLOGISTE, L'. 5608
0013-8894 See ENTOMOLOGIST'S GAZETTE. 5608
0013-8908 See ENTOMOLOGIST'S MONTHLY MAGAZINE, THE. 5608
0013-8916 See ENTOMOLOGIST'S RECORD AND JOURNAL OF VARIATION, THE. 5582
0013-8924 See ENTOMOLOGY ABSTRACTS. 5604
0013-8932 See ENTOMOLOGY CIRCULAR. 5583
0013-8959 See ENTOMOPHAGA. 4244
0013-9017 See ENTRELINEAS. 298
0013-9084 See ENTROPIE. 1975
0013-9106 See ENTSCHEIDUNGEN DES BUNDESVERWALTUNGSGERICHT. 2966
0013-9157 See ENVIRONMENT (ST. LOUIS). 2228
0013-9157 See ENVIRONMENT (ST. LOUIS). 2215
0013-9165 See ENVIRONMENT AND BEHAVIOR. 2215
0013-919X See ENVIRONMENT MONTHLY, THE. 2166
0013-9211 See ENVIRONMENT REPORTER. 3111

0013-922X See ENVIRONMENTAL ACTION (WASHINGTON, D.C.). 2166
0013-9238 See ENVIRONMENTAL CONTROL NEWS FOR SOUTHERN INDUSTRY. 2167
0013-9270 See ENVIRONMENTAL HEALTH (LONDON). 2822
0013-9351 See ENVIRONMENTAL RESEARCH (NEW YORK, N.Y.). 2169
0013-936X See ENVIRONMENTAL SCIENCE & TECHNOLOGY MICROFORM. 2169
0013-936X See ENVIRONMENTAL SCIENCE & TECHNOLOGY. 2169
0013-9386 See ENVIRONMENTAL SPECTRUM. 2170
0013-9394 See ENVOI. 3462
0013-9408 See ENVOY (PITTSBURGH). 4956
0013-9432 See ENZYME. 486
0013-9440 See EOS (MADRID). 5608
0013-9483 See EPHEMERE, L'. 3342
0013-9491 See EPHEMERIDES IURIS CANONICI. 5029
0013-9505 See EPHEMERIDES LITURGICAE. 4956
0013-9513 See EPHEMERIDES THEOLOGICAE LOVANIENSES. 4956
0013-9521 See EPICIER (MONTREAL). 2334
0013-9572 See EPIGRAPHICA (FAENZA). 267
0013-9580 See EPILEPSIA (COPENHAGEN). 3832
0013-9610 See EPISCOPAL RECORDER. 5059
0013-9645 See EPISTEMOLOGIE SOCIOLOGIQUE. 235
0013-9696 See EPITHEORESIS KOINONIKON EREUNON. 5199
0013-970X See EPITOANYAG. 614
0013-9718 See EPOCA (MILANO). 2515
0013-9831 See EQUESTRIAN TRAILS. 2798
0013-9947 See ERANOS. 1076
0013-9955 See ERASMUS. 4821
0013-9963 See ERBE UND AUFTRAG (BEURON). 5029
0013-9971 See ERCILLA. 2551
0013-9998 See ERDE. 2560
0014-0015 See ERDKUNDE. 1375
0014-0031 See ERDO, AZ. 2379
0014-0058 See ERDOL & KOHLE, ERDGAS, PETROCHEMIE. 4255
0014-0066 See ERDOGAZDASAG ES FAIPAR. 2400
0014-0082 See ERFAHRUNGSHEILKUNDE. 3575
0014-0120 See ERGONOMIA. 82
0014-0139 See ERGONOMICS. 1251
0014-0171 See ERICSSON REVIEW (ENGLISH EDITION). 1154
0014-021X See ERNAHRUNGS- UMSCHAU. 4190
0014-0309 See ERWERBSOBSTBAU. 170
0014-0325 See ERZIEHUNG UND UNTERRICHT. 1745
0014-0325 See ERZIEHUNG UND UNTERRICHT. 1745
0014-0376 See ESCRIBANO, EL. 2732
0014-0481 See ESPACES ET SOCIETES. 298
0014-0635 See ESPERANTO. 3279
0014-0708 See ESPIRAL. 349
0014-0716 See ESPIRITU. 4346
0014-0759 See ESPRIT (PARIS, 1932-). 2515
0014-0767 See ESPRIT CREATEUR, L'. 3342
0014-0775 See ESPRIT ET VIE. 4956
0014-083X See ESSAY AND GENERAL LITERATURE INDEX. 3458
0014-083X See ESSAY AND GENERAL LITERATURE INDEX. CD-ROM. 3458
0014-0848 See ESSAY PROOF JOURNAL, THE. 1144
0014-0856 See ESSAYS IN CRITICISM. 3385
0014-0880 See ESSENCE. 5555
0014-0902 See ESSENZE E DERIVATI AGRUMARI. 1024
0014-0910 See ESSEX COUNTRYSIDE. 2515

0014-0937 *See* BULLETIN OF THE ESSEX COUNTY MEDICAL SOCIETY, THE. **3560**

0014-0953 See PEABODY ESSEX MUSEUM COLLECTIONS. **2753**

0014-0961 *See* ESSEX JOURNAL. **2686**

0014-1011 *See* ESSO MAGAZINE. **4255**

0014-1097 *See* EST EUROPEEN, L'. **2686**

0014-1135 *See* ESTADISTICA. **5327**

0014-1151 *See* ESTADISTICA ESPANOLA. **5327**

0014-1216 *See* ESTATE PLANNING (ENGLEWOOD CLIFFS, N.J.). **3118**

0014-1224 *See* ESTATE PLANNING CHECKLISTS AND FORMS. **3118**

0014-1240 *See* ESTATES GAZETTE. **4837**

0014-1259 *See* ESTATES TIMES. **4837**

0014-1267 *See* EST & OUEST. **4541**

0014-1267 *See* EST & OUEST : BULLETIN DE L'ASSOCIATION D'ETUDES ET D'INFORMATIONS POLITIQUES INTERNATIONALES. **4520**

0014-1291 *See* ESTETIKA. **320**

0014-1445 *See* ECA. **5198**

0014-1453 *See* ESTUDIOS CLASICOS (MADRID). **1076**

0014-1461 *See* ESTUDIOS DE DERECHO. **2967**

0014-1496 *See* ESTUDIOS GEOGRAFICOS. **2560**

0014-164X *See* ETC. **3280**

0014-1704 *See* ETHICS. **2250**

0014-1755 *See* ETHIOPIAN MEDICAL JOURNAL. **3575**

0014-1763 *See* ETHIOPIAN TRADE JOURNAL. **833**

0014-178X *See* ETHNIE FRANCAISE : REVUE TRIMESTRIELLE DE LA FONDATION CHARLES PLISNIER, L'. **2260**

0014-1798 *See* ETHNOGRAPHIA (BUDAPEST. 1949). **235**

0014-1801 *See* ETHNOHISTORY. **2261**

0014-1828 *See* ETHNOLOGY. **235**

0014-1836 *See* ETHNOMUSICOLOGY. **4117**

0014-1844 *See* ETHNOS. **236**

0014-1941 *See* ETUDES (PARIS. 1897). **2846**

0014-195X *See* ETUDES ANGLAISES. **3342**

0014-1992 *See* ETUDES CINEMATOGRAPHIQUES. **4068**

0014-200X *See* ETUDES CLASSIQUES (NAMUR, BELGIUM). **1076**

0014-2026 *See* ETUDES DE LETTRES. **3385**

0014-2069 *See* ETUDES ET STATISTIQUES - BANQUE DES ETATS DE L'AFRIQUE CENTRALE. **728**

0014-2085 *See* ETUDES FRANCAISES (MONTREAL). **3385**

0014-2115 *See* ETUDES GERMANIQUES. **3280**

0014-2123 *See* ETUDES INTERNATIONALES (QUEBEC). **4521**

0014-2123 *See* ETUDES INTERNATIONALES (QUEBEC). **4473**

0014-214X *See* ETUDES LITTERAIRES (UNIVERSITE LAVAL). **3386**

0014-2158 *See* ETUDES NORMANDES. **2687**

0014-2182 *See* ETUDES RURALES. **5245**

0014-2239 *See* ETUDES THEOLOGIQUES ET RELIGIEUSES. **4956**

0014-2247 *See* ETUDES TSIGANES. **4553**

0014-2255 *See* WORLD STUDENT NEWS. **1792**

0014-2263 *See* ETYKA. **2250**

0014-2328 *See* EUPHORION (HEIDELBERG, GERMANY). **3386**

0014-2328 *See* EUPHORION. **3386**

0014-2336 *See* EUPHYTICA. **509**

0014-2476 *See* EUROPA-ARCHIV. **4521**

0014-2484 *See* EUROPA CHEMIE. **2012**

0014-2492 *See* EUROPA ETHNICA. **2261**

0014-2573 *See* EUROPA MEDICOPHYSICA. **3575**

0014-2603 *See* EUROPA STAR. **2916**

0014-2751 *See* EUROPE. **3342**

0014-2794 *See* EUROPE ECHECS. **4860**

0014-2808 *See* EUROPE EN FORMATION, L'. **4521**

0014-2816 *See* OUTREMER (PARIS, FRANCE : 1982). **2500**

0014-2824 *See* EUROPE OIL-TELEGRAM. **4256**

0014-2875 *See* ECN. EUROPEAN CHEMICAL NEWS. **974**

0014-2921 *See* EUROPEAN ECONOMIC REVIEW. **1489**

0014-2956 *See* EUROPEAN JOURNAL OF BIOCHEMISTRY. **487**

0014-2972 *See* EUROPEAN JOURNAL OF CLINICAL INVESTIGATION. **3575**

0014-2980 *See* EUROPEAN JOURNAL OF IMMUNOLOGY. **3669**

0014-2999 *See* EUROPEAN JOURNAL OF PHARMACOLOGY. **4303**

0014-3006 *See* EUROPEAN JUDAISM. **5047**

0014-3022 *See* EUROPEAN NEUROLOGY. **3832**

0014-3057 *See* EUROPEAN POLYMER JOURNAL. **1041**

0014-3065 *See* POTATO RESEARCH. **182**

0014-312X *See* EUROPEAN SURGICAL RESEARCH. **3964**

0014-3138 *See* EUROPEAN TAXATION. **4722**

0014-3154 *See* EUROPEAN TRANSPORT LAW. **2967**

0014-3162 *See* EUROPEAN TRENDS. **1635**

0014-3189 *See* EUROPEO MILANO, L'. **2516**

0014-3324 *See* EVANGELICAL BAPTIST. **5059**

0014-3332 *See* EVANGELICAL BEACON, THE. **4957**

0014-3340 *See* EVANGELICAL FRIEND. **4957**

0014-3359 *See* EVANGELICAL MISSIONS QUARTERLY. **4957**

0014-3367 *See* EVANGELICAL QUARTERLY. **4957**

0014-3413 *See* EVANGELISCHE ERZIEHER, DER. **4957**

0014-3502 *See* EVANGELISCHE THEOLOGIE. **4957**

0014-3650 *See* EVANS-NOVAK POLITICAL REPORT. **4473**

0014-3820 *See* EVOLUTION. **544**

0014-3855 *See* EVOLUTION PSYCHIATRIQUE, L'. **3925**

0014-388X *See* EX-CBI ROUNDUP. **2733**

0014-3960 *See* REVIEW OF THE ECONOMIC SITUATION OF MEXICO. **1581**

0014-3995 *See* EXCAVATING CONTRACTOR. **614**

0014-4029 *See* EXCEPTIONAL CHILDREN. **1878**

0014-4037 *See* EXCERPTA BOTANICA. SECTIO A. TAXONOMICA ET CHOROLOGICA. **509**

0014-4045 *See* EXCERPTA BOTANICA. SECTIO B. SOCIOLOGICA. **5245**

0014-4053 *See* EXCERPTA MEDICA. SECTION 1. ANATOMY, ANTHROPOLOGY, EMBRYOLOGY AND HISTOLOGY. **3657**

0014-407X *See* EXCERPTA MEDICA. SECTION 3. ENDOCRINOLOGY. **3657**

0014-4096 *See* EXCERPTA MEDICA. SECTION 5. GENERAL PATHOLOGY AND PATHOLOGICAL ANATOMY. **3657**

0014-410X *See* EXCERPTA MEDICA. SECTION 6. INTERNAL MEDICINE. **3657**

0014-4126 *See* EXCERPTA MEDICA. SECTION 8. NEUROLOGY AND NEUROSURGERY. **3657**

0014-4134 *See* EXCERPTA MEDICA. SECTION 9. SURGERY. **3657**

0014-4142 *See* EXCERPTA MEDICA. SECTION 10. OBSTETRICS AND GYNECOLOGY. **3657**

0014-4150 *See* EXCERPTA MEDICA. SECTION 11. OTO-, RHINO-, LARYNGOLOGY. **3888**

0014-4169 *See* EXCERPTA MEDICA. SECTION 12. OPHTHALMOLOGY. **3658**

0014-4177 *See* EXCERPTA MEDICA. SECTION 13. DERMATOLOGY AND VENEREOLOGY. **3658**

0014-4185 *See* EXCERPTA MEDICA. SECTION 14. RADIOLOGY. **3658**

0014-4193 *See* CHEST DISEASES, THORACIC SURGERY AND TUBERCULOSIS. **3949**

0014-4207 *See* EXCERPTA MEDICA. SECTION 16. CANCER. **3658**

0014-4223 *See* EXCERPTA MEDICA. SECTION 18. CARDIOVASCULAR DISEASES AND CARDIOVASCULAR SURGERY. **3658**

0014-4231 *See* EXCERPTA MEDICA. SECTION 19. REHABILITATION AND PHYSICAL MEDICINE. **3658**

0014-424X *See* EXCERPTA MEDICA. SECTION 20. GERONTOLOGY AND GERIATRICS. **3658**

0014-4258 *See* EXCERPTA MEDICA. SECTION 21. DEVELOPMENTAL BIOLOGY AND TERATOLOGY. **3658**

0014-4266 *See* EXCERPTA MEDICA. SECTION 22. HUMAN GENETICS. **3658**

0014-4274 *See* EXCERPTA MEDICA. SECTION 23. NUCLEAR MEDICINE. **3658**

0014-4282 *See* EXCERPTA MEDICA. SECTION 24. ANESTHESIOLOGY. **3658**

0014-4290 *See* EXCERPTA MEDICA. SECTION 25. HEMATOLOGY. **3658**

0014-4304 *See* EXCERPTA MEDICA. SECTION 26. IMMUNOLOGY, SEROLOGY AND TRANSPLANTATION. **3658**

0014-4312 *See* EXCERPTA MEDICA. SECTION 27. BIOPHYSICS, BIOENGINEERING AND MEDICAL INSTRUMENTATION. **3658**

0014-4320 *See* EXCERPTA MEDICA. SECTION 28. UROLOGY AND NEPHROLOGY. **3658**

0014-4355 *See* ARTHRITIS AND RHEUMATISM. **3803**

0014-4363 *See* EXCERPTA MEDICA. SECTION 32. PSYCHIATRY. **3659**

0014-4371 *See* ORTHOPEDIC SURGERY. **3661**

0014-438X *See* PLASTIC SURGERY. **3972**

0014-4398 *See* EXCERPTA MEDICA. SECTION 35. OCCUPATIONAL HEALTH AND INDUSTRIAL MEDICINE. **2872**

0014-4452 *See* EXCHANGE & COMMISSARY NEWS. **4044**

0014-4487 *See* EXCHANGITE, THE. **5231**

0014-4649 *See* EXHIBITION BULLETIN. **759**

0014-4711 *See* CAHIERS DE L'EXPANSION REGIONALE, LES. **2816**

0014-4738 *See* EXPEDITION. **268**

0014-4754 *See* EXPERIENTIA. **5104**

0014-4770 *See* EXPERIMENT. **3463**

0014-4797 *See* EXPERIMENTAL AGRICULTURE. **82**

0014-4800 *See* EXPERIMENTAL AND MOLECULAR PATHOLOGY. **3894**

0014-4819 *See* EXPERIMENTAL BRAIN RESEARCH. **3832**

0014-4827 *See* EXPERIMENTAL CELL RESEARCH. **536**

0014-4835 *See* EXPERIMENTAL EYE RESEARCH. **3874**

0014-4851 *See* EXPERIMENTAL MECHANICS. **4427**

0014-4886 *See* EXPERIMENTAL NEUROLOGY. **3833**

0014-4894 *See* EXPERIMENTAL PARASITOLOGY. **562**

0014-4924 *See* EXPERIMENTELLE TECHNIK DER PHYSIK. **4402**

0014-4932 *See* EXPERIODICA. **2516**

0014-4940 *See* EXPLICATOR, THE. **3386**

0014-4975 *See* EXPLORATIONS. **3281**

0014-4983 *See* EXPLORATIONS IN ECONOMIC HISTORY. **1561**

0014-5009 *See* EXPLORER, THE. **4165**

0014-5025 *See* EXPLORERS JOURNAL. **5104**

0014-505X *See* EXPLOSIVES AND PYROTECHNICS. **2012**

0014-519X *See* EXPORT (NEW YORK, N.Y.). **2811**

0014-5211 *See* EXPORTMARKTEN, OESO-LANDEN/OOST-EUROPA. **835**

0014-5238 *See* EXPOSITOR BIBLICO. MAESTROS DE ADOLESCENTES-JOVENES-ADULTOS, EL. **4958**

0014-5246 *See* EXPOSITORY TIMES, THE. **5016**

0014-5270 *See* EXPRESS (PARIS), L'. **2516**

0014-5483 *See* EXTRAPOLATION. **3342**

0014-5602 *See* FAO FISHERIES SYNOPSIS. **2300**

0014-5637 *See* FAO PLANT PROTECTION BULLETIN. **2414**

0014-5688 *See* FBI LAW ENFORCEMENT BULLETIN. **3164**

0014-5793 See FEBS LETTERS. 487
0014-5815 See FF COMMUNICATIONS. 2319
0014-5858 See FORUM ITALICUM. 3388
0014-5874 See F.I.D. NEWS BULLETIN. 3210
0014-5904 See FIRA BULLETIN. 2905
0014-5920 See FLACS. 975
0014-6137 See F R I MONTHLY PORTFOLIO. 4335
0014-6242 See FABULA. 2319
0014-6269 See FACE AU RISQUE. 5200
0014-651X See FACT FINDER (CHICAGO, ILL.), THE. 4474
0014-6552 See FEM. FACTORY EQUIPMENT & MATERIALS. 2102
0014-6579 See FACTORY EQUIPMENT NEWS. 3479
0014-6617 See FACTS AND COMPARISONS (MONTHLY ED.). 4304
0014-6641 See FACTS ON FILE. 2616
0014-6722 See REVISTA DE LA FACULTAD DE CIENCIAS MEDICAS DE CORDOBA. 3635
0014-679X See FAENZA. 2589
0014-6897 See FAIPAR. 2379
0014-6919 See FAIR EMPLOYMENT REPORT. 1669
0014-6943 See FAIRCHILD TROPICAL GARDEN BULLETIN. 2414
0014-7001 See FAITH & FORM. 298
0014-701X See FAITH AND FREEDOM OXFORD. 4958
0014-7079 See FALCON (MANSFIELD), THE. 3387
0014-7095 See FAMIGLIA CRISTIANA. 5029
0014-7117 See FAMILIA. 2447
0014-7206 See FAMILY CIRCLE. 2790
0014-7230 See FAMILY HANDYMAN, THE. 2790
0014-7257 See FAMILY HEALTH BULLETIN. 3576
0014-7265 See FAMILY HISTORY. 2447
0014-7281 See FAMILY LAW (CHICHESTER). 3120
0014-729X See FAMILY LAW QUARTERLY. 3120
0014-7303 See FAMILY LIFE. 2279
0014-7311 See FAMILY PERSPECTIVE. 2279
0014-7354 See FAMILY PLANNING PERSPECTIVES. 588
0014-7370 See FAMILY PROCESS. 2279
0014-7508 See FANTASTIC (FLUSHING. 1958). 3387
0014-7508 See FANTASTIC. 3387
0014-7575 See FAR EAST REPORTER. 2487
0014-7591 See FAR EASTERN ECONOMIC REVIEW. 1635
0014-7591 See FAR EASTERN ECONOMIC REVIEW. 1561
0014-7680 See FARBE. 1024
0014-7699 See FARBE + LACK. 4223
0014-7702 See FARBE UND RAUM. 614
0014-7788 See FARHANG-I IRAN ZAMIN. 2651
0014-7826 See FARM AND DAIRY (SALEM, OHIO : 1914). 5728
0014-7958 See FARM EQUIPMENT. 159
0014-8008 See FARM JOURNAL (PHILADELPHIA. 1956). 85
0014-8059 See FARM MANAGEMENT (KENILWORTH). 85
0014-8083 See FARM POND HARVEST. 2301
0014-8121 See FARM STORE. 85
0014-8202 See FARMACEUTSKI GLASNIK. 4304
0014-8210 See FARMACEVTISK REVY. 4304
0014-8229 See FARMACEVTSKI VESTNIK (LJUBLJANA). 4304
0014-8237 See FARMACIA (BUCURESTI). 4304
0014-8261 See FARMACJA POLSKA. 4304
0014-8318 See EKSPERIMENTALNAIA I KLINICHESKAIA FARMAKOLOGIIA. 4303
0014-8326 See FARMAKOTERAPI. 4305
0014-8369 See FARMER AND PARLIAMENT. 85
0014-844X See FARMERS' NEWSLETTER. 86
0014-8474 See FARMER'S WEEKLY. 86
0014-8601 See FARUMASHIA. 4305

0014-8776 See FATE (MARION). 4241
0014-8822 See FATHOM (NORFOLK). 4176
0014-8857 See FATS AND OILS IN CANADA. 1606
0014-8881 See FAUNA (OSLO). 5583
0014-8903 See FAUNA OCH FLORA. 509
0014-8962 See FEDDES REPERTORIUM. 509
0014-9063 See FEDERAL CONTRACTS REPORT. 2969
0014-9071 See FEDERAL EMPLOYEE, THE. 4702
0014-9128 See FEDERAL PROBATION. 3164
0014-9187 See REVIEW / FEDERAL RESERVE BANK OF ST. LOUIS. 809
0014-9225 See NEWSLETTER - FEDERAL STATISTICS USERS' CONFERENCE. 5334
0014-9233 See FEDERAL TIMES. 4703
0014-925X See FEDERALISTE; REVUE DE POLITIQUE, LE. 4474
0014-9306 See FEDERATION BULLETIN (FULTON). 3740
0014-9470 See ECONOMIC TRENDS (NEW DELHI). 1591
0014-9527 See QUAERENDO. 4831
0014-956X See FEED MANAGEMENT. 201
0014-9624 See FEEDSTUFFS. 201
0014-9659 See FEGATO, IL. 3796
0014-9667 See CHUNG KUNG YEN CHIU STUDIES ON CHINESE COMMUNISM. 4540
0014-9756 See FELD WALD WASSER. SCHWEIZERISCHE JAGDZEITUNG. 4871
0014-9772 See FELDSER I AKUSERKA. 3760
0014-9799 See FELDWIRTSCHAFT. 86
0014-9802 See FELICITER. 3210
0014-9810 See FELLOWSHIP (NEW YORK). 4521
0014-9837 See FELLOWSHIP IN PRAYER. 4958
0014-9918 See FEMME-LINES. 1084
0014-9926 See FEMME PRATIQUE. 5556
0015-0002 See FENIX (LIMA). 3258
0015-0010 See FENNIA. 2560
0015-010X See FERNMELDE-INGENIEUR. 1111
0015-0118 See TELEKOM PRAXIS /HERAUSGEGEBEN IM BENEHMEN MIT DEM FERNMELDETECHNISCHEN ZENTRALAMT. 1166
0015-0142 See FERNSEH- UND KINOTECHNIK. 4068
0015-0193 See FERROELECTRICS. 4402
0015-024X See FERTIGUNGSTECHNIK UND BETRIEB. 2114
0015-0266 See FERTILISER NEWS. 87
0015-0282 See FERTILITY AND STERILITY. 3576
0015-0304 See FERTILIZER INTERNATIONAL. 87
0015-0371 See FETES ET SAISONS. 4959
0015-0517 See FIBONACCI QUARTERLY, THE. 3505
0015-0541 See FIBRE CHEMISTRY. 5351
0015-0592 See FICHERO BIBLIOGRAFICO HISPANOAMERICANO. 416
0015-0630 See FIDDLEHEAD, THE. 3387
0015-0657 See FIELD (OBERLIN, OHIO). 3463
0015-0673 See FIELD & STREAM (FAR WEST ED.). 4872
0015-0673 See FIELD & STREAM (WEST ED.). 4872
0015-0673 See FIELD & STREAM (NORTHEAST ED.). 4872
0015-069X See FIELD CROP ABSTRACTS. 153
0015-0711 See FIELD NOTES - ARKANSAS ARCHEOLOGICAL SOCIETY. 268
0015-0746 See FIELDIANA. BOTANY. 510
0015-0754 See FIELDIANA : ZOOLOGY. 5583
0015-0770 See FIELDS WITHIN FIELDS WITHIN FIELDS. 1185
0015-0800 See FIFTH ESTATE. 4541
0015-086X See FIGYELO. 675
0015-0886 See FIJI AGRICULTURAL JOURNAL. 87
0015-1025 See FILM (LONDON, ENGLAND : 1954). 4070
0015-1068 See FILM A DOBA. 5268

0015-1165 See FILM BULLETIN. 4069
0015-119X See FILM COMMENT. 4069
0015-1211 See FILM CULTURE. 4069
0015-1297 See FILM INFORMATION. 3210
0015-1351 See FILM & KINO. 4069
0015-1386 See FILM QUARTERLY. 4070
0015-1580 See FILMKULTURA. 4071
0015-1599 See FILMKUNST. 4071
0015-1661 See FILMRUTAN. 4071
0015-1688 See FILMS IN REVIEW. 4071
0015-1785 See FILOLOGIAI KOZLONY. 3281
0015-1815 See FILOMATA. 1077
0015-1823 See FILOSOFIA. 4346
0015-1831 See FILOZOFICKY CASOPIS (USTAV PRO FILOZOFII A SOCIOLOGII CSAV). 4347
0015-184X See FILOSOFSKA MISUL. 4346
0015-1874 See FILSON CLUB HISTORY QUARTERLY, THE. 2733
0015-1882 See FILTRATION & SEPARATION. 2012
0015-1947 See FINANCE & DEVELOPMENT. 1635
0015-198X See FINANCIAL ANALYSTS JOURNAL, THE. 898
0015-2021 See FINANCIAL POST, THE. 898
0015-203X See FINANCIAL STATISTICS LONDON. 1532
0015-2064 See FINANCIAL WORLD. 898
0015-2102 See FINANCIERO; REVISTA INTERNACIONAL DE ECONOMIA, COMERCIO E INDUSTRIA. 1491
0015-2110 See FINANCING AGRICULTURE. 87
0015-2218 See FINANZARCHIV. 4726
0015-2242 See FINANZIERE. 4044
0015-2358 See FINISHERS' MANAGEMENT. 868
0015-2390 See TILASTOKATSAUKSIA. 5345
0015-2463 See FINNISH TRADE REVIEW. 835
0015-2501 See FINSKA LAKARESALLSKAPETS HANDLINGAR. 3576
0015-2552 See FIRE CHIEF. 2289
0015-2587 See FIRE ENGINEERING. 2289
0015-2595 See FIRE FIGHTING IN CANADA. 2289
0015-2609 See FIRE INTERNATIONAL. 2289
0015-2617 See NFPA JOURNAL. 2292
0015-2625 See FIRE NEWS (BOSTON). 2289
0015-2625 See FIRE NEWS (BOSTON). 2289
0015-2668 See FIRE SERVICE INFORMATION. 2290
0015-2684 See FIRE TECHNOLOGY. 2290
0015-2714 See FIRESIDE CHATS. 2785
0015-2838 See FISCH UND FANG. 4894
0015-2854 See FISCHERBLATT, DAS. 2301
0015-2862 See FISCHERS TARIF-NACHRICHTEN FUER EISENBAHN UND KRAFTWAGEN. 4727
0015-2919 See FISH CULTURIST, THE. 2301
0015-2986 See FISHERMAN, THE. 2302
0015-2994 See FISHERMEN'S NEWS, THE. 2303
0015-3001 See FISHERY TECHNOLOGY. 2303
0015-301X See FISHING & HUNTING NEWS (WESTERN WASHINGTON ED.). 4872
0015-3044 See FISHING NEWS INTERNATIONAL. 2303
0015-3060 See FISHING TACKLE TRADE NEWS. 2303
0015-3079 See FISHING WORLD. 2303
0015-3117 See FISKERIDIREKTORATETS SKRIFTER. SERIE HAVUNDERSKELSER. 2304
0015-3206 See FIZIKA B : A JOURNAL OF EXPERIMENTAL AND THEORETICAL PHYSICS. 4403
0015-3214 See FIZIKA I KHIMIIA OBRABOTKI MATERIALOV. 2114
0015-3222 See FIZIKA I TECHNIKA POLUPROVODNIKOV. 2055
0015-3230 See FIZIKA METALLOV I METALLOVEDENIE. 4002
0015-3257 See FIZIKAI SZEMLE. 4403
0015-3265 See FIZIKO-MATEMATICHESKO SPISANIE. 4403

0015-3273 *See* FIZIKO-TEKHNICHESKIE PROBLEMY RAZRABOTKI POLEZNYKH ISKOPAEMYKH. **2139**

0015-329X *See* FIZIOLOGICESKIJ ZURNAL SSSR IMENI I.M. SECENOVA. **580**

0015-3303 *See* FIZIOLOGIIA RASTENII. **510**

0015-3370 *See* FLAG BULLETIN, THE. **2616**

0015-3486 *See* FLAMMES VIVES. **3343**

0015-3575 *See* FLEISCH. **2335**

0015-3613 *See* FLEISCHEREI. **2335**

0015-363X *See* FLEISCHWIRTSCHAFT, DIE. **211**

0015-3710 *See* FLIGHT INTERNATIONAL. **20**

0015-3761 *See* FLOOR COVERING WEEKLY. **2905**

0015-3796 *See* BIOCHEMIE UND PHYSIOLOGIE DER PFLANZEN. **502**

0015-3818 *See* FLORA OG FAUNA. **5584**

0015-3826 *See* FLORESTA. **2379**

0015-3869 *See* FLORIDAGRICULTURE (GAINESVILLE, FLA.). **87**

0015-3885 *See* FLORIDA SPORTSMAN (MIAMI). **4895**

0015-3893 *See* FLORIDA ANTHROPOLOGIST, THE. **236**

0015-3907 *See* FLORIDA ARCHITECT. **298**

0015-3915 *See* FLORIDA BAR JOURNAL, THE. **2970**

0015-3958 *See* FLORIDA CATTLEMAN AND LIVESTOCK JOURNAL, THE. **211**

0015-3966 *See* FLORIDA CERTIFIED PUBLIC ACCOUNTANT, THE. **744**

0015-4016 *See* FLORIDA EDUCATION. **1747**

0015-4032 *See* JOURNAL / FLORIDA ENGINEERING SOCIETY. **1981**

0015-4040 *See* FLORIDA ENTOMOLOGIST, THE. **5608**

0015-4067 *See* FLORIDA FAMILY PHYSICIAN. **3737**

0015-4091 *See* FLORIDA GROWER & RANCHER. **87**

0015-4113 *See* FLORIDA HISTORICAL QUARTERLY, THE. **2733**

0015-4148 *See* JOURNAL OF THE FLORIDA MEDICAL ASSOCIATION (1974). **3598**

0015-4156 *See* FLORIDA MOTEL JOURNAL. **2805**

0015-4172 *See* FLORIDA NATURALIST, THE. **226**

0015-4199 *See* FLORIDA NURSE, THE. **3856**

0015-4229 *See* FLORIDA POLICE JOURNAL. **3164**

0015-4261 *See* FLORIDA READING QUARTERLY, THE. **1747**

0015-4326 *See* FLORIDA TREND. **1561**

0015-4334 *See* FLORIDA TRUCK NEWS. **5382**

0015-4369 *See* FLORIDA WILDLIFE. **2194**

0015-4385 *See* FLORIST (SOUTHFIELD, MICH.). **2435**

0015-4393 *See* FLORIST (GUNZBURG, GERMANY). **2435**

0015-4415 *See* FLORIST TRADE MAGAZINE. **2435**

0015-4423 *See* FLORISTS' REVIEW. **2435**

0015-4490 *See* FLOWER NEWS : THE FLORAL INDUSTRY'S NATIONAL WEEKLY. **2414**

0015-4504 *See* FLOWERING PLANTS OF AFRICA, THE. **2415**

0015-4512 *See* FLUE CURED TOBACCO FARMER, THE. **5373**

0015-4539 *See* FLUSSIGES OBST. **2335**

0015-4547 *See* FLUG REVUE. **21**

0015-461X *See* FLUID. **2089**

0015-4628 *See* FLUID DYNAMICS. **2023**

0015-4644 *See* FLUID POWER ABSTRACTS. **2089**

0015-4652 *See* FLUID POWER INTERNATIONAL. **2089**

0015-4660 *See* FLUID SEALING ABSTRACTS. **2089**

0015-4725 *See* FLUORIDE. **487**

0015-4741 *See* FLY FISHERMAN. **2304**

0015-4806 *See* FLYING (LOS ANGELES, CALIF.). **21**

0015-4849 *See* FLYING MODELS. **2773**

0015-4881 *See* FLYING SAUCER REVIEW. **21**

0015-489X *See* FLYING SAUCERS. **21**

0015-4997 *See* FOCUS (AMERSFOORT). **5105**

0015-5004 *See* FOCUS (NEW YORK, N.Y. 1950). **2561**

0015-5055 *See* SOUTH AFRICA INTERNATIONAL. **2500**

0015-511X *See* FOCUS ON EXCEPTIONAL CHILDREN. **1879**

0015-5152 *See* FOCUS ON INDIANA LIBRARIES. **3211**

0015-5160 *See* FOCUS ON JAMAICA. **5470**

0015-525X *See* FORDERUNGSDIENST, DER. **88**

0015-5314 *See* FOGORVOSI SZEMLE. **3577**

0015-5322 *See* FOGRA-LITERATURDIENST. **3388**

0015-5357 *See* FOI ET LA VIE, LA. **4959**

0015-5403 *See* FOELDRAJZI ERTESITO. **2561**

0015-5411 *See* FOLDRAJZI KOZLEMENYEK. **2561**

0015-542X *See* FOLDTANI KOZLONY. **1376**

0015-5454 *See* FOLHA MEDICA. **3577**

0015-5497 *See* FOLIA BIOLOGICA (WARSZAWA). **5584**

0015-5500 *See* FOLIA BIOLOGICA. **455**

0015-5543 *See* FOLIA FORESTALIA. **2379**

0015-5551 *See* FOLIA GEOBOTANICA & PHYTOTAXONOMICA. **511**

0015-5578 *See* FOLIA HEREDITARIA ET PATHOLOGICA. **545**

0015-5594 *See* FOLIA HUMANISTICA. **2846**

0015-5616 *See* FOLIA MEDICA CRACOVIENSIA. **3577**

0015-5632 *See* FOLIA MICROBIOLOGICA. **563**

0015-5640 *See* FUNCTIONAL AND DEVELOPMENTAL MORPHOLOGY. **456**

0015-5659 *See* FOLIA MORPHOLOGICA. **5584**

0015-5675 *See* FOLIA ORIENTALIA. **2651**

0015-5676 *See* FIBULA. **2616**

0015-5683 *See* FOLIA PARASITOLOGICA / CZECHOSLOVAK ACADEMY OF SCIENCE. **5584**

0015-5691 *See* NIHON YAKURIGAKU ZASSHI. **4318**

0015-5705 *See* FOLIA PHONIATRICA. **3888**

0015-5713 *See* FOLIA PRIMATOLOGICA. **5584**

0015-573X *See* FOLIA QUATERNARIA. **1376**

0015-5748 *See* FOLIA VETERINARIA. **5510**

0015-5772 *See* FOLIO, THE. **4828**

0015-587X *See* FOLKLORE (LONDON). **2320**

0015-5896 *See* FOLKLORE (CALCUTTA). **2320**

0015-590X *See* FOLKLORE BRABANCON. **2320**

0015-5918 *See* FOLKLORE DE FRANCE. **2320**

0015-5926 *See* FOLKLORE FORUM. **2320**

0015-5950 *See* NEWSLETTER. **4140**

0015-5969 *See* FOLKLORE SUISSE. **2320**

0015-6000 *See* FOLLIA DI NEW YORK. **2846**

0015-6035 *See* FOMENTO DE LA PRODUCCION. **676**

0015-6043 *See* REVISTA DE FOMENTO SOCIAL. **5216**

0015-6078 *See* FONDERIA. **4002**

0015-6140 *See* FONO FORUM. **4118**

0015-6175 *See* FONTANE BLATTER. **3388**

0015-6191 *See* FONTES ARTIS MUSICAE. **4118**

0015-6209 *See* ADB BUSINESS OPPORTUNITIES : PROPOSED PROJECTS, PROCUREMENT NOTICES AND CONTRACT AWARDS / ASIAN DEVELOPMENT BANK. **768**

0015-6221 *See* FOOD AND AGRICULTURAL LEGISLATION. **2336**

0015-6272 *See* FOOD AND DRUG PACKAGING. **4219**

0015-6310 *See* FOOD & NUTRITION NEWS. **4191**

0015-6337 *See* FOOD CHEMICAL NEWS. **1024**

0015-6361 *See* FOOD AND DRUG LAW JOURNAL. **2971**

0015-6426 *See* SHOKUHIN EISEIGAKU ZASSHI. **4803**

0015-6450 *See* FOOD INDUSTRIES OF SOUTH AFRICA. **2337**

0015-6450 *See* FOOD INDUSTRIES OF SOUTH AFRICA. **2337**

0015-6477 *See* FOOD MANUFACTURE. **2338**

0015-6493 *See* FOOD MERCHANTS ADVOCATE. **2338**

0015-6523 *See* FOOD PROCESSING. **2339**

0015-6574 *See* FOOD SCIENCE AND TECHNOLOGY ABSTRACTS. **2362**

0015-6639 *See* FOOD TECHNOLOGY (CHICAGO). **2340**

0015-6655 *See* FOOD TECHNOLOGY IN NEW ZEALAND. **2340**

0015-6663 *See* FOOD TRADE NEWS. **2340**

0015-6671 *See* FOOD TRADE REVIEW. **2340**

0015-6701 *See* FOODPRESS. **2341**

0015-6760 *See* FOOTBALL DIGEST. **4895**

0015-6884 *See* FOR THE DEFENSE (MILWAUKEE, WIS.). **3089**

0015-6892 *See* FOR YOU FROM CZECHOSLOVAKIA. **819**

0015-6914 *See* FORBES. **676**

0015-6957 *See* FORCES (MONTREAL). **2734**

0015-699X *See* FORD FOUNDATION REPORT, THE. **1824**

0015-704X *See* FORDHAM LAW REVIEW. **2971**

0015-7066 *See* FORD'S INTERNATIONAL CRUISE GUIDE. **5449**

0015-7120 *See* FOREIGN AFFAIRS (NEW YORK, N.Y.). **4521**

0015-7155 *See* FOREIGN AFFAIRS REPORTS. **4522**

0015-718X *See* FOREIGN LANGUAGE ANNALS. **3282**

0015-7228 *See* FOREIGN POLICY. **4522**

0015-7317 *See* FOREIGN TRADE BULLETIN. **836**

0015-7325 *See* FOREIGN TRADE REVIEW. **836**

0015-735X *See* FORENSIC OF PI KAPPA DELTA, THE. **1111**

0015-7368 *See* JOURNAL - FORENSIC SCIENCE SOCIETY. **3741**

0015-7392 *See* FOREST AND TIMBER. **2400**

0015-7406 *See* FOREST FARMER. **2379**

0015-7430 *See* FOREST INDUSTRIES (SAN FRANCISCO, CALIF.). **2400**

0015-7449 *See* FOREST LOG (SALEM). **2380**

0015-7457 *See* FOREST NOTES. **2380**

0015-7473 *See* FOREST PRODUCTS JOURNAL. **2380**

0015-749X *See* FOREST SCIENCE. **2381**

0015-752X *See* FORESTRY (LONDON). **2382**

0015-7538 *See* FORESTRY ABSTRACTS. **2399**

0015-7546 *See* FORESTRY CHRONICLE, THE. **2381**

0015-7589 *See* FORESTS AND PEOPLE. **2382**

0015-766X *See* FORM. **2900**

0015-7678 *See* FORM (SEEHEIM-JUGENHEIM, WEST GERMANY). **2098**

0015-7686 *See* FORM & FUNCTION. **615**

0015-7813 *See* FORNVANNEN. **2688**

0015-783X *See* FORO ITALIANO, IL. **2972**

0015-7880 *See* FORSAKRINGSTIDNINGEN (STOCKHOLM, SWEDEN). **2881**

0015-7899 *See* FORSCHUNG IM INGENIEURWESEN. **1975**

0015-7902 *See* FORSCHUNGEN ZUR VOLKS- UND LANDESKUNDE. **2261**

0015-7988 *See* FORSTLICHE UMSCHAU. **2383**

0015-8003 *See* FORSTWISSENSCHAFTLICHES CENTRALBLATT. **2383**

0015-8054 *See* FORT HARE PAPERS. **5106**

0015-8089 *See* FORT WORTH. **2533**

0015-8097 *See* FORT WORTH COMMERCIAL RECORDER. **2972**

0015-8119 *See* FORTHCOMING BOOKS. **416**

0015-816X *See* FORTSCHRITTE DER KIEFERORTHOPAEDIE. **1323**

0015-8178 *See* FORTSCHRITTE DER MEDIZIN. **3577**

0015-8208 *See* FORTSCHRITTE DER PHYSIK (BERLIN : 1953). **4403**

0015-8259 See FORTUNE. 676
0015-8275 See FORTUNE NEWS. 3164
0015-8305 See FORUM (WASHINGTON, D.C.), THE. 2972
0015-8399 See FORUM (SCRANTON, PA.). 2516
0015-8445 See FORUM. 3388
0015-8496 See FORUM DER LETTEREN. 3388
0015-8518 See FORUM FOR MODERN LANGUAGE STUDIES. 3282
0015-8542 See FORUM OF EDUCATION, THE. 1824
0015-8682 See FOTO. 4369
0015-8801 See FOTOGRAFIA (WARSAW, POLAND). 4369
0015-8836 See FOTOGRAFIE. 4369
0015-8933 See FOUNDATION FACTS. 2023
0015-8976 See FOUNDATION NEWS. 4336
0015-9018 See FOUNDATIONS OF PHYSICS. 4403
0015-9026 See FWP JOURNAL. 4027
0015-9042 See FOUNDRY TRADE JOURNAL, THE. 4002
0015-9093 See PEACE AND FREEDOM. 5564
0015-9107 See FOUR QUARTERS. 3388
0015-9123 See FOUR WHEELER. 5382
0015-9158 See FOURNEE, LA. 2341
0015-9182 See FOURSQUARE WORLD ADVANCE. 4959
0015-9204 See FOURTH INTERNATIONAL (LONDON, ENGLAND). 4474
0015-9220 See FOXFIRE. 3388
0015-9247 See FRA FYSIKKENS VERDEN. 4403
0015-9271 See FRACASTORO, IL. 3577
0015-9298 See FRAGMENTA BALCANICA - MUSEI MACEDONICI SCIENTARIUM NATURALIUM. 456
0015-9301 See FRAGMENTA FAUNISTICA. 5584
0015-931X See FRAGMENTA FLORISTICA ET GEOBOTANICA. 511
0015-9344 See FRAGMENTS. 1825
0015-9387 See FRANCAIS AU NIGERIA. 3282
0015-9395 See FRANCAIS DANS LE MONDE, LE. 3282
0015-9409 See FRANCAIS MODERNE, LE. 3282
0015-9565 See FRANCE GRAPHIQUE, LA. 4565
0015-9573 See FRANCE HORLOGERE, LA. 2916
0015-9743 See PROBLEMES POLITIQUES ET SOCIAUX. 5213
0015-9840 See FRANCISCANA. 5029
0016-0032 See JOURNAL OF THE FRANKLIN INSTITUTE. 5120
0016-0067 See FRANZISKANISCHE STUDIEN. 5029
0016-0105 See FRATERNAL MONITOR, THE. 2881
0016-0237 See FRAUENARZT HERNE, DER. 1747
0016-0296 See FREDDO. 2605
0016-030X See FREE CHINA REVIEW. 2651
0016-0326 See FREE CHURCH CHRONICLE. 4960
0016-0369 See FREE LANCE, THE. 3389
0016-0520 See FREEDOM REVIEW. 4508
0016-0652 See FREEMAN (IRVINGTON-ON-HUDSON, N.Y.), THE. 1592
0016-0687 See FREETHINKER, THE. 4347
0016-0725 See FREIBURGER ZEITSCHRIFT FUER PHILOSOPHIE UND THEOLOGIE. 4347
0016-0873 See FREIGHT MANAGEMENT. 5383
0016-089X See FREIGHTER TRAVEL NEWS. 837
0016-0970 See FREMDSPRACHEN. 3282
0016-0989 See FREMDSPRACHENUNTERRICHT. 1879
0016-1071 See FRENCH HISTORICAL STUDIES. 2688
0016-111X See FRENCH REVIEW, THE. 3283
0016-1128 See FRENCH STUDIES. 3343
0016-1136 See FREQUENZ ZEITSCHRIFT FUER SCHWINGUNGS-UND SCHWACHSTROMTECHNIK. 2055
0016-1187 See FREUNDIN MUNCHEN. 2790

0016-1268 See FRIEND (LONDON), THE. 5060
0016-1284 See FRIEND O'WILDLIFE. 2194
0016-1322 See FRIENDS JOURNAL. 4960
0016-1357 See FRIENDS' QUARTERLY, THE. 4960
0016-1365 See FRIENDS WORLD NEWS : NEWS BULLETIN OF THE FRIENDS WORLD COMMITTEE FOR CONSULTATION. 4960
0016-1446 See FRIPOUNET PARIS. 4850
0016-1616 See FROM NINE TO FIVE. 677
0016-1705 See FROM THE STATE CAPITALS. HIGHWAY FINANCING AND CONSTRUCTION. 5440
0016-1748 See FROM THE STATE CAPITALS. INSURANCE REGULATION. 2881
0016-1810 See FROM THE STATE CAPITALS. MOTOR VEHICLE REGULATION. 5415
0016-1888 See FROM THE STATE CAPITALS. PUBLIC UTILITIES. 4650
0016-2043 See FRONT PAGE DETECTIVE. 5074
0016-2116 See FRONTIER NURSING SERVICE QUARTERLY BULLETIN. 3856
0016-2159 See FRONTIERS (PHILADELPHIA). 4165
0016-2167 See FRONTIERS OF PLANT SCIENCE. 172
0016-2191 See FROZEN FOOD AGE. 2341
0016-2213 See CONFRUCTA. 2332
0016-2248 See FRUIT BELGE, LE. 2415
0016-2256 See FRESH PRODUCE JOURNAL. 172
0016-2299 See FRUITS. 2415
0016-2302 See FRUITTEELT, DE. 172
0016-2361 See FUEL (GUILFORD). 4256
0016-237X See FUL-, ORR-, GEGEGYOGYASZAT. 3888
0016-2396 See FUEL OIL NEWS. 4256
0016-2450 See FUER SIE HAMBURG. 2517
0016-2485 See FUERZAS ARMADAS. 4044
0016-2515 See FUJITSU. 1976
0016-2523 See FUJITSU SCIENTIFIC & TECHNICAL JOURNAL. 2055
0016-254X See FUKUOKA IGAKU ZASSHI. 3577
0016-2582 See FUKUSHIMA IGAKU ZASSHI. 3577
0016-2590 See FUKUSHIMA JOURNAL OF MEDICAL SCIENCE. 3577
0016-2612 See FULDAER GESCHICHTSBLATTER. 2689
0016-2620 See FULL CRY (SEDALIA). 4872
0016-2663 See FUNCTIONAL ANALYSIS AND ITS APPLICATIONS. 3506
0016-268X See FUND RAISING MANAGEMENT. 868
0016-2701 See BOLETIN HISTORICO (CARACAS). 2724
0016-2736 See FUNDAMENTA MATHEMATICAE. 3506
0016-2841 See FUNKSCHAU. 2055
0016-2884 See FUR AGE WEEKLY. 3184
0016-2914 See FUR BULLETIN. 3184
0016-2922 See FUR-FISH-GAME. 4872
0016-2965 See FUR TAKER, THE. 3184
0016-3058 See FURNITURE HISTORY. 2905
0016-3090 See FURNITURE WORKERS PRESS. 1675
0016-3120 See FURROW, THE. 5029
0016-3155 See FUSION WILMINGTON, DEL. 2589
0016-3228 See FUSSBALL TRAINER. 4895
0016-3252 See FUTURA. 1084
0016-3287 See FUTURES (LONDON). 1492
0016-3317 See FUTURIST. [MICROFILM], THE. 5107
0016-3317 See FUTURIST, THE. 5107
0016-3392 See FYSISK TIDSSKRIFT. 4403
0016-3406 See GA. GAS + ARCHITEKTUR. 2605
0016-3503 See GEN, GASTROENTEROLOGIA, ENDOCRINOLOGIA I NUTRICION. 3746
0016-3538 See G-I-T. 2589
0016-3570 See GMBH-RUNDSCHAU. 678
0016-3619 See GRA REPORTER. 4652

0016-3651 See GAS- UND WASSERFACH. WASSER, ABWASSER : GWF, DAS. 5533
0016-3724 See GACETA (TAMPA, FLA.), LA. 5649
0016-3805 See GACETA MATEMATICA. 3506
0016-3813 See GACETA MEDICA DE MEXICO. 3578
0016-3929 See GAIRM. 3343
0016-4089 See GALLAUDET TODAY. 1879
0016-4097 See GALLERIA. 3389
0016-4100 See GALLEY SAIL REVIEW, THE. 3343
0016-4119 See GALLIA. 2689
0016-4232 See GALVANOTECHNIK. 2055
0016-4259 See GAM ON YACHTING. 593
0016-4313 See GAMECOCK, THE. 211
0016-4437 See GANDHI MARG (ENGLISH ED.). 4522
0016-4607 See GARDEN PATH, THE. 2415
0016-464X See GARDENER. 2415
0016-4720 See GARTEN UND LANDSCHAFT. 2416
0016-4739 See GARTENAMT, DAS. 2416
0016-478X See GARTENBAUWISSENSCHAFT. 2416
0016-4828 See GAS. 4257
0016-4844 See GAS ABSTRACTS. 4283
0016-4895 See GAS CHROMATOGRAPHY LITERATURE, ABSTRACTS AND INDEX. 1015
0016-4909 See GAS- UND WASSERFACH. GAS, ERDGAS : GWF, DAS. 4258
0016-5018 See GAS, WASSER, WARME. 4258
0016-5085 See GASTROENTEROLOGY (NEW YORK, N.Y. 1943). 3745
0016-5107 See GASTROINTESTINAL ENDOSCOPY. 176
0016-5182 See GASVERWENDUNG. 4259
0016-5301 See GAYANA : BOTANICA. 511
0016-531X See GAYANA : ZOOLOGIA. 5584
0016-5328 See GAZ D'AUJOURD'HUI. 4259
0016-5352 See GAZ, WODA I TECHNIKA SANITARNA. 2230
0016-5360 See GAZDASAG. 1492
0016-5395 See GAZETA CUKROWNICZA. 172
0016-5492 See GAZETTE. 1111
0016-5522 See GAZETTE DES ARCHIVES, LA. 2481
0016-5530 See GAZETTE DES BEAUX-ARTS. 351
0016-5581 See GAZOVAIA PROMYSHLENNOST. 4259
0016-559X See GAZZETTA ANTIQUARIA. 250
0016-5603 See GAZZETTA CHIMICA ITALIANA. 976
0016-5751 See GEBURTSHILFE UND FRAUENHEILKUNDE. 3761
0016-5808 See GEFAEHRLICHE LADUNG. 5383
0016-5816 See GEFIEDERTE WELT, DIE. 5584
0016-5840 See GEGENBAURS MORPHOLOGISCHES JAHRBUCH. 5584
0016-5867 See GEGENWART. 4960
0016-5875 See GEGENWARTSKUNDE. 5200
0016-5921 See GEIST UND LEBEN (WURZBURG). 3390
0016-6006 See GELBEN HEFTE, DIE. 3578
0016-626X See GEMS & GEMOLOGY (GEMOLOGICAL INSTITUTE OF AMERICA : 1967). 1439
0016-6286 See GEMUSE (MUNCHEN). 172
0016-6359 See EVERTON'S GENEALOGICAL HELPER. 2446
0016-6367 See GENEALOGICAL MAGAZINE OF NEW JERSEY, THE. 2450
0016-6383 See GENEALOGIE. 2450
0016-6391 See GENEALOGISTS' MAGAZINE : OFFICIAL ORGAN OF THE SOCIETY OF GENEALOGISTS, THE. 2450
0016-6448 See GENEESKUNDE EN SPORT. 3954
0016-6464 See GENEESKUNDIGE GIDS (1969-). 3578
0016-6480 See GENERAL AND COMPARATIVE ENDOCRINOLOGY. 3730
0016-6553 See GENERAL LINGUISTICS. 3283

0016-6618 *See* UMBRA. **5237**
0016-6669 *See* GENESIS 2. **5047**
0016-6707 *See* GENETICA. **546**
0016-6715 *See* GENETICA POLONICA. **2416**
0016-6723 *See* GENETICAL RESEARCH. **546**
0016-6731 *See* GENETICS (AUSTIN). **546**
0016-674X *See* GENETICS ABSTRACTS. **478**
0016-6758 *See* GENETIKA. **546**
0016-6766 *See* GENETIKA I SELEKTSIYA. **2416**
0016-6774 *See* GENEVE-AFRIQUE. **5246**
0016-6812 *See* GENIE CIVIL, LE. **2023**
0016-6812 *See* GENIE CIVIL. **1976**
0016-6855 *See* GENII. **4862**
0016-6863 *See* GENIO RURALE. **89**
0016-6898 *See* GENOS. **2451**
0016-6928 *See* GENRE (NORMAN, OKLA.). **3343**
0016-6936 *See* GENS NOSTRA. **2451**
0016-6979 *See* GQ. **3995**
0016-6987 *See* GENUS. **4553**
0016-6995 *See* GEOBIOS (LYON, FRANCE). **4227**
0016-7002 *See* GEOCHEMICAL JOURNAL. **1376**
0016-7029 *See* GEOCHEMISTRY INTERNATIONAL. **1376**
0016-7037 *See* GEOCHIMICA ET COSMOCHIMICA ACTA. **1376**
0016-7053 *See* BIBLIOGRAPHY OF ECONOMIC GEOLOGY. **1361**
0016-7061 *See* GEODERMA. **173**
0016-7096 *See* GEODETICKY A KARTOGRAFICKY OBZOR. **2561**
0016-7118 *See* GEODEZIA ES KARTOGRAFIA. **2581**
0016-7126 *See* GEODEZIIA I KARTOGRAFIJA. **2581**
0016-7134 *See* GEODEZJA I KARTOGRAFIA. **2581**
0016-7142 See JOURNAL OF APPLIED GEOPHYSICS. **1407**
0016-7169 *See* GEOFISICA INTERNACIONAL : REVISTA DE LA UNION GEOFISICA MEXICANA AUSPICIADA POR EL INSTITUTO DE GEOFISICA DE LA UNIVERSIDAD NACIONAL AUTONOMA DE MEXICO. **4404**
0016-7185 *See* GEOFORUM. **1355**
0016-7193 *See* GEOGRAFICKY CASOPIS. GEOGRAFICHESKII ZHURNAL. GEOGRAPHICAL REVIEW. GEOGRAPHISCHE ZEITSCHRIFT. REVUE DE GEOGRAPHIE. **2562**
0016-7207 *See* GEOGRAFIIA V SHKOLE / UPRAVLENIE NACHALNOI I SREDNEI SHKOLY NARKOMPROSA RSFSR. **2562**
0016-7215 See GEOGRAFIE. **2562**
0016-7223 *See* GEOGRAFISK TIDSSKRIFT. **2562**
0016-7282 *See* GEOGRAPHIA POLONICA. **2562**
0016-7312 *See* GEOGRAPHICA HELVETICA. **2562**
0016-7363 *See* GEOGRAPHICAL ANALYSIS. **2562**
0016-738X *See* JOURNAL OF THE GEOGRAPHICAL ASSOCIATION OF TANZANIA. **2567**
0016-7398 *See* GEOGRAPHICAL JOURNAL, THE. **2563**
0016-7428 *See* GEOGRAPHICAL REVIEW. **2563**
0016-7444 *See* CHIRIGAKU HYORON. **2558**
0016-7460 *See* GEOGRAPHISCHE RUNDSCHAU. **2564**
0016-7479 *See* GEOGRAPHISCHE ZEITSCHRIFT. **2564**
0016-7487 *See* GEOGRAPHY. **2564**
0016-7525 *See* GEOHIMIJA. **1377**
0016-755X *See* GEOLOGICA BAVARICA. **1377**
0016-7568 *See* GEOLOGICAL MAGAZINE. **1378**
0016-7576 *See* BULLETIN OF THE GEOLOGICAL, MINING AND METALLURGICAL SOCIETY OF INDIA. **1370**
0016-7592 *See* ABSTRACTS WITH PROGRAMS - GEOLOGICAL SOCIETY OF AMERICA. **1364**
0016-7606 *See* GEOLOGICAL SOCIETY OF AMERICA BULLETIN. **1378**
0016-7606 *See* GEOLOGICAL SOCIETY OF AMERICA BULLETIN. **1378**

0016-7622 *See* JOURNAL OF THE GEOLOGICAL SOCIETY OF INDIA. **1385**
0016-7630 *See* JOURNAL - GEOLOGICAL SOCIETY OF JAPAN. **1384**
0016-7649 *See* JOURNAL OF THE GEOLOGICAL SOCIETY. **1385**
0016-7665 *See* CHISHITSU CHOSAJO GEPPO. **1371**
0016-7671 *See* BULLETIN / GEOLOGICAL SURVEY OF SOUTH AUSTRALIA. **1352**
0016-7681 *See* REPORT OF INVESTIGATIONS - GEOLOGICAL SURVEY OF SOUTH AUSTRALIA. **1394**
0016-772X *See* GEOLOGICKY PRUZKUM. **1379**
0016-7738 *See* GEOLOGICKY ZBORNIK / GEOLOGICA CARPATHICA. **1379**
0016-7746 *See* GEOLOGIE EN MIJNBOUW. **1379**
0016-7762 *See* IZVESTIJA VYSSYHUCEBNYH ZAVEDENIJ. GEOLOGIJA I RAZVEDKA. **1384**
0016-7770 *See* GEOLOGIJA RUDNYH MESTOROZDENIJ. **2139**
0016-7835 *See* GEOLOGISCHE RUNDSCHAU. **1379**
0016-7851 See GEOLOGISCHES JAHRBUCH, REIHE C : HYDROGEOLOGIE, INGENIEURGEOLOGIE. **1413**
0016-786X *See* GEOLOGISKA FORENINGENS I STOCKHOLM FORHANDLINGAR. **1380**
0016-7878 *See* PROCEEDINGS OF THE GEOLOGISTS' ASSOCIATION. **1391**
0016-7886 *See* GEOLOGIIA I GEOFIZIKA (NOVOSIBIRSK). **1379**
0016-7894 *See* GEOLOGIJA NEFTI I GAZA. **1379**
0016-7916 *See* GEOLOGUES. **1380**
0016-7924 *See* GEOLOSKI VJESNIK. **1380**
0016-7932 *See* GEOMAGNETISM AND AERONOMY. **22**
0016-7940 *See* GEOMAGNETIZM I AERONOMIJA. **4443**
0016-7967 *See* GEOMETRE. **2023**
0016-8017 *See* GEOPHYSICAL MAGAZINE, THE. **1406**
0016-8025 *See* GEOPHYSICAL PROSPECTING. **1406**
0016-8033 *See* GEOPHYSICS. **1406**
0016-8076 *See* GEORGE WASHINGTON LAW REVIEW, THE. **2973**
0016-8092 *See* GEORGETOWN LAW JOURNAL, THE. **2974**
0016-8106 *See* GEORGETOWN MEDICAL BULLETIN. **3780**
0016-8130 *See* GEORGIA ALUMNI RECORD. **1102**
0016-8149 *See* GEORGIA ANCHORAGE. **5449**
0016-8297 *See* GEORGIA HISTORICAL QUARTERLY, THE. **2734**
0016-8300 *See* GEORGIA LAW REVIEW (ATHENS, GA.: 1966). **2974**
0016-8319 *See* GEORGIA LIBRARIAN, THE. **3212**
0016-8335 *See* GEORGIA NURSING. **3856**
0016-8386 *See* GEORGIA REVIEW, THE. **3390**
0016-8408 *See* GEORGIA SOCIAL SCIENCE JOURNAL. **5200**
0016-8416 *See* GEORGIA STATE BAR JOURNAL. **2974**
0016-8483 *See* GEOSCIENCE DOCUMENTATION. **1363**
0016-8491 *See* GEOTECHNICAL ABSTRACTS. **1363**
0016-8505 *See* GEOTECHNIQUE. **2023**
0016-8505 *See* GEOTECHNIQUE [MICROFORM]. **1976**
0016-8521 *See* GEOTECTONICS. **1381**
0016-853X *See* GEOTEKTONIKA. **1381**
0016-8548 *See* GEOTEKTONISCHE FORSCHUNGEN. **1381**
0016-8556 *See* GEOTIMES. **1381**
0016-8599 *See* GERANIUMS AROUND THE WORLD. **2416**
0016-8610 *See* GEREFORMEERD THEOLOGISCH TIJDSCHRIFT. **4960**
0016-867X *See* GERIATRICS. **3751**
0016-8769 *See* GERMAN INTERNATIONAL. **2488**

0016-8831 *See* GERMAN QUARTERLY, THE. **3390**
0016-8858 *See* GERMAN TRIBUNE, THE. **2517**
0016-8874 *See* GERMANIA (BERLIN). **269**
0016-8890 *See* GERMANIC REVIEW, THE. **3343**
0016-8904 *See* GERMANISCH-ROMANISCHE MONATSSCHRIFT. **3283**
0016-8912 *See* GERMANISTIK (TUEBINGEN). **3336**
0016-9013 *See* GERONTOLOGIST, THE. **3751**
0016-9056 *See* GESCHICHTE IN WISSENSCHAFT UND UNTERRICHT. **2616**
0016-9080 *See* NACHRICHTEN DER GESELLSCHAFT FUER NATUR- UND VOLKERKUNDE OSTASIENS/HAMBURG. **2623**
0016-9099 *See* GESELLSCHAFT UND POLITIK. **5201**
0016-9161 *See* GESNERUS. **3578**
0016-920X *See* GESTA (FORT TRYON PARK, N.Y.). **351**
0016-9218 *See* GESTIONS HOSPITALIERES. **3780**
0016-9307 *See* GESUNDHEITSPOLITISCHE UMSCHAU. **4306**
0016-9447 *See* GEWERKSCHAFTLICHE MONATSHEFTE. **1676**
0016-9536 *See* BULLETIN OF THE GHANA GEOGRAPHICAL ASSOCIATION. **2557**
0016-9544 *See* GHANA JOURNAL OF SCIENCE. **5108**
0016-9560 *See* GHANA MEDICAL JOURNAL. **3578**
0016-9633 *See* GHOST DANCE. **3391**
0016-9706 *See* GIDROLIZNAIA I LESOKHIMICHESKAILA PROMYSHLENNOST. **2401**
0016-9714 *See* GIDROTEHNICESKOE STROITELSTVO (MOSKVA). **5533**
0016-9730 *See* GIDS. **3343**
0016-9765 *See* GIESSEREI. **4003**
0016-979X *See* GIESSEREI RUNDSCHAU. **4003**
0016-9862 *See* GIFTED CHILD QUARTERLY, THE. **1879**
0016-9889 *See* GIFTS & DECORATIVE ACCESSORIES. **2584**
0016-9900 *See* GIGIENA I SANITARIIA (1943). **2597**
0016-9919 *See* GIGIENA TRUDA I PROFESSIONALNYE ZABOLEVANIJA. **2862**
0017-0062 *See* GIOIA. **5557**
0017-0070 *See* GIORNALE BOTANICO ITALIANO (FLORENCE, ITALY : 1962). **512**
0017-0089 *See* GIORNALE CRITICO DELLA FILOSOFIA ITALIANA. **1077**
0017-0097 *See* GIORNALE DEGLI ECONOMISTI E ANNALI DI ECONOMIA. **1492**
0017-016X *See* GIORNALE DEL GENIO CIVILE. **2024**
0017-0224 *See* GIORNALE DELL'ARTERIOSCLEROSI. **3704**
0017-0232 *See* GIORNALE DELLO SPETTACOLO. **385**
0017-0240 *See* GIORNALE DELL' OFFICINA. **2115**
0017-0291 *See* GIORNALE DI GEOLOGIA. **1381**
0017-0305 *See* GIORNALE DI GERONTOLOGIA. **3752**
0017-0321 *See* GIORNALE DI MALATTIE INFETTIVE E PARASSITARIE. **4777**
0017-0364 *See* GIORNALE DI MEDICINA MILITARE. **3578**
0017-0437 *See* GIORNALE ITALIANO DELLE MALATTIE DEL TORACE. **3949**
0017-0445 *See* GIORNALE ITALIANO DI CHEMIOTERAPIA. **3578**
0017-0453 *See* GIORNALE ITALIANO DI CHIRURGIA. **3965**
0017-0461 *See* GIORNALE ITALIANO DI FILOLOGIA. **3284**
0017-0496 *See* GIORNALE STORICO DELLA LETTERATURA ITALIANA. **3391**
0017-050X *See* GIORNALE STORICO DELLA LUNIGIANA. **269**
0017-0577 *See* GIRL SCOUT LEADER. **5231**
0017-0631 *See* GIUSTIZIA CIVILE. **3090**
0017-0658 *See* GIUSTIZIA PENALE. **2975**

0017-0682 See GJUTERIET. 4003
0017-0747 See GLAMOUR. 5557
0017-0771 See GLAS ISTRE. 5799
0017-078X See GLAS OCH PORSLIN. 2589
0017-0852 See GLASFORUM. 2589
0017-0895 See GLASGOW MATHEMATICAL JOURNAL. 3507
0017-095X See GLASNIK MATEMATICKI. SERIJA III. 3507
0017-0984 See GLASS (REDHILL). 2590
0017-0992 See GLASS AGE. 2589
0017-1018 See GLASS DIGEST. 2589
0017-1026 See GLASS INDUSTRY, THE. 2590
0017-1050 See GLASS TECHNOLOGY. 2590
0017-1069 See GLASS WORKERS NEWS. 2590
0017-1085 See GLASTECHNISCHE BERICHTE. 2590
0017-1093 See GLASTEKNISK TIDSKRIFT. 2590
0017-1107 See GLASWELT. 2590
0017-114X See GLEANINGS IN BEE CULTURE. 5585
0017-1190 See GLOBAL DIALOGUE. 4523
0017-1204 See GLOBE AND LAUREL. 4044
0017-1263 See GOS NAUCZYCIELSKI. 1748
0017-1298 See GLOTTA (GOTTINGEN). 3284
0017-1352 See GLOXINIAN, THE. 512
0017-1387 See GLUCKAUF-FORSCHUNGSHEFTE. 2139
0017-1417 See GNOMON (MUNCHEN). 3284
0017-1425 See GNOZIS. 4347
0017-1506 See GOBBLES. 211
0017-1549 See GOTTINGISCHE GELEHRTE ANZEIGEN. 2847
0017-1557 See GOLD BULLETIN & GOLD PATENT DIGEST. 789
0017-1573 See GOLD + SILBER, UHREN + SCHMUCK. 2914
0017-176X See GOLF DIGEST. 4896
0017-1794 See GOLF JOURNAL. 4896
0017-1816 See GOLF MONTHLY. 4896
0017-1824 See GOLFSHOP OPERATIONS. 924
0017-1883 See GOLF WORLD. 4897
0017-1891 See GOLF WORLD. 4897
0017-1956 See GOLTDAMMER'S ARCHIV FUER STRAFRECHT. 2975
0017-2081 See GOOD HOUSEKEEPING (BRITISH EDITION). 2790
0017-209X See GOOD HOUSEKEEPING (U.S. ED.). 2790
0017-2235 See GOPHER MUSIC NOTES. 4119
0017-2243 See GORDIAN (1948). 2342
0017-2251 See CHRISTIAN SCHOLAR'S REVIEW. 4946
0017-2278 See GORNYI ZHURNAL. 1440
0017-2294 See GORTERIA. 512
0017-2308 See GOSHEN COLLEGE BULLETIN. 1825
0017-2367 See GOSPEL STANDARD. 4961
0017-2375 See GOSPEL TIDINGS (AUSTIN, TEX.). 4961
0017-2448 See GOSPODARKA WODNA. 5533
0017-2499 See GOTTESDIENST UND KIRCHENMUSIK. 4119
0017-2553 See GOURMET. 2790
0017-257X See GOVERNMENT AND OPPOSITION (LONDON). 4475
0017-2588 See GOVERNMENT BUSINESS WORLD REPORT. 678
0017-2596 See GOVERNMENT CONTRACTOR, THE. 4651
0017-260X See GOVERNMENT EMPLOYEE RELATIONS REPORT. 4703
0017-2626 See GOVERNMENT EXECUTIVE. 4651
0017-2642 See GOVERNMENT PRODUCT NEWS. 950
0017-2715 See GOYA. 351
0017-2723 See GOZDARSKI VESTNIK. 2384
0017-2774 See GRADBENI VESTNIK. 615
0017-2901 See GRAFICAS. 4565

0017-2936 See GRAFICUS. 4565
0017-3029 See GRAIN AGE. 201
0017-307X See REVUE TECHNIQUE AUTOMOBILE. 5424
0017-310X See GRAMOPHONE INCLUDING COMPACT DISC NEWS AND REVIEWS. 5316
0017-310X See GRAMOPHONE. 4119
0017-3134 See GRANA. 512
0017-3185 See GRANI. 2517
0017-3207 See GRANITE CUTTERS' JOURNAL, THE. 1676
0017-3223 See GRANMA (DAILY EDITION, SPANISH). 5799
0017-3231 See GRANTA. 3343
0017-3436 See GRAPHICUS. 2488
0017-3452 See GRAPHIS. 379
0017-3495 See GRASAS Y ACEITES (SEVILLA). 488
0017-3517 See GRASS ROOTS FORUM. 4475
0017-3541 See GRASSROOTS EDITOR. 2920
0017-3614 See GREAT BASIN NATURALIST, THE. 4165
0017-3622 See MONTHLY DIGEST OF STATISTICS. 5333
0017-3630 See STATISTICAL NEWS (GREAT BRITAIN. CENTRAL STATISTICAL OFFICE). 5340
0017-3673 See GREAT PLAINS JOURNAL. 2735
0017-3835 See GREECE & ROME. 1077
0017-3894 See GREEK ORTHODOX THEOLOGICAL REVIEW, THE. 4961
0017-3916 See GREEK, ROMAN AND BYZANTINE STUDIES. 1077
0017-3932 See GREEN BOOK (LONDON). 159
0017-3983 See GREEN REVOLUTION (YORK, PA.). 4542
0017-4084 See GREENSBORO REVIEW, THE. 3392
0017-4092 See GREENSWARD. 90
0017-4106 See GREETINGS MAGAZINE. 2584
0017-4114 See GREGORIANUM. 4961
0017-4181 See GRIAL. 321
0017-4289 See GRIT (NATIONAL ED.). 5676
0017-4297 See GRIT AND STEEL. 4873
0017-4491 See GROENTEN EN FRUIT : G & F. 2417
0017-4505 See GRONDBOOR EN HAMER. 1381
0017-453X See GRONK. 3343
0017-4556 See GRNLAND (1953). 4553
0017-4629 See GROSSE POINTER, THE. 5478
0017-4645 See GROSSWETTERLAGEN EUROPAS, DIE. 4030
0017-4653 See GROUND ENGINEERING. 2024
0017-467X See GROUND WATER. 1413
0017-4688 See GROUNDS MAINTENANCE. 2417
0017-4696 See GROUNDSMAN. 2418
0017-4742 See GROUP RESEARCH REPORT. 4475
0017-4777 See GROWER (TORONTO). 2418
0017-4785 See GROWER. 2418
0017-4815 See GROWTH AND CHANGE. 2823
0017-4831 See GROWTH FUND GUIDE. 900
0017-4904 See GRUNDFOERBAETTRING. 91
0017-4920 See GRUNDLAGEN DER LANDTECHNIK. 91
0017-4939 See GRUNDLAGENSTUDIEN AUS KYBERNETIK UND GEISTESWISSENSCHAFT. 1251
0017-498x See GUAJANA. 3463
0017-5021 See GUARDIAN (NEW YORK, N.Y.), THE. 2920
0017-5056 See GUATEMALA INDIGENA. 237
0017-5110 See GUERNSEY BREEDERS' JOURNAL. 211
0017-5137 See GUETERVERKEHR, DER. 5383
0017-520X See GUIDANCE EXCHANGE. 1879
0017-5226 See GUIDE (WASHINGTON). 5060
0017-5285 See GUIDE TO INDIAN PERIODICAL LITERATURE. 416

0017-5323 See GUIDEPOST (WASHINGTON, D.C.). 4588
0017-5331 See GUIDEPOSTS (CARMEL). 4961
0017-5404 See GUILD REPORTER, THE. 1676
0017-5447 See GUION LITERARIO. 3392
0017-5471 See GUITAR REVIEW, THE. 4120
0017-5552 See GULF COAST CATTLEMAN. 211
0017-5617 See GUN REPORT. 250
0017-5625 See GUN TALK. 2774
0017-5641 See GUN WORLD. 4897
0017-5668 See GUNMA DAIGAKU KYOIKU GAKUBU KIYO : SHIZEN KAGAKU HEN. 5108
0017-5684 See GUNS & AMMO. 4897
0017-5749 See GUT. 3746
0017-5870 See GUY'S HOSPITAL GAZETTE. 3780
0017-5900 See GYERMEKGYOGYASZAT. 3903
0017-5994 See GYNAKOLOGE (BERLIN). 3761
0017-6001 See GYNAKOLOGISCH-GEBURTSHILFLICHE RUNDSCHAU. 3761
0017-6036 See GYOGYSZERESZET. 4306
0017-6087 See JOURNAL OF THE GYPSY LORE SOCIETY. 2321
0017-6192 See HNO. 3888
0017-6486 See HACIENDA, LA. 91
0017-6516 See HADASSAH MAGAZINE. 5048
0017-6524 See DOAR, HA-. 5047
0017-6540 See HADTORTENELMI KOZLEMENYEK. 2690
0017-6559 See HAEMATOLOGIA. 3797
0017-6834 See HALVE MAEN, DE. 2452
0017-7083 See MIZAH HE-HADASH. 2770
0017-7245 See HANDEL ZAGRANICZNY. 839
0017-7296 See HANDELSBLATT. 839
0017-7393 See HANDLOADER. 4898
0017-7504 See HANSA. 4177
0017-7512 See HANSENIASE: RESUMOS E NOTICIAS. HANSENIASIS: ABSTRACTS AND NEWS. 4777
0017-7547 See HANZAI SHINRIGAKU KENKYU. 4588
0017-7636 See HARBOUR & SHIPPING. 5450
0017-7709 See HARDWARE MERCHANDISER (CHICAGO). 2811
0017-7768 See HAREFUAH. 3580
0017-7849 See HARMONIZER (KENOSHA, WIS.), THE. 4120
0017-7873 See HARPER'S BAZAAR. 1085
0017-789X See HARPER'S (NEW YORK, N.Y.). 3343
0017-7903 See HARPERS WINE AND SPIRIT GAZETTE. 2367
0017-7962 See HARTFORD AGENT. A JOURNAL OF FIRE INSURANCE, THE. 2881
0017-8004 See HARVARD ADVOCATE (CAMBRIDGE, MASS.), THE. 3393
0017-8012 See HARVARD BUSINESS REVIEW. 679
0017-8012 See HARVARD BUSINESS REVIEW. 679
0017-8020 See HARVARD BUSINESS SCHOOL BULLETIN. 679
0017-8039 See HARVARD CIVIL RIGHTS-CIVIL LIBERTIES LAW REVIEW. 4508
0017-8047 See HARVARD DIVINITY BULLETIN. 4962
0017-8055 See HARVARD EDUCATIONAL REVIEW. 1749
0017-8055 See HARVARD EDUCATIONAL REVIEW. 1749
0017-8063 See HARVARD INTERNATIONAL LAW JOURNAL. 3128
0017-808X See HARVARD JOURNAL ON LEGISLATION. 2977
0017-8101 See HARVARD LAW RECORD. 2977
0017-811X See HARVARD LAW REVIEW. 2977
0017-8136 See HARVARD LIBRARY BULLETIN. 3213
0017-8160 See HARVARD THEOLOGICAL REVIEW, THE. 4962

0017-8179 See HARVARD TODAY. 1827
0017-8217 See HARVESTER, THE. 5017
0017-8271 See AWARE. 4937
0017-8314 See HASSADEH. 91
0017-8322 See HASTINGS LAW JOURNAL. 2977
0017-8357 See HATCHET. 1102
0017-842X See HAUSFRAU, MONATSSCHRIFT FUR DIE FRAUENWELT AMERIKAS, DIE. 2517
0017-8438 See HAUSTECHNISCHE RUNDSCHAU. 616
0017-8454 See HAUSWIRTSCHAFT UND WISSENSCHAFT. 2790
0017-8470 See HAUTARZT. 3720
0017-8543 See HAWAII BEVERAGE GUIDE. 2367
0017-8594 See HAWAII MEDICAL JOURNAL (1962). 3581
0017-8624 See HAWAIIAN SHELL NEWS. 1449
0017-8721 See HEAD START NEWSLETTER. 5287
0017-873X See HEAD TEACHERS REVIEW. 1895
0017-8748 See HEADACHE. 3833
0017-8780 See HEADLINE SERIES. 4523
0017-8810 See HEALDSBURG TRIBUNE-ENTERPRISE AND SCIMITAR. 5635
0017-8934 See HEALTH BULLETIN (RALEIGH), THE. 4778
0017-8969 See HEALTH EDUCATION JOURNAL, THE. 2598
0017-9019 See HEALTH INSURANCE UNDERWRITER, THE. 2882
0017-9051 See HEALTH/PAC BULLETIN. 4780
0017-9078 See HEALTH PHYSICS (1958). 4404
0017-9124 See HEALTH SERVICES RESEARCH. 3582
0017-9132 See HEALTH TRENDS. 4781
0017-9140 See HEALTH VISITOR : THE JOURNAL OF THE HEALTH VISITORS' ASSOCIATION. 3856
0017-9167 See HEALTHY LIVING LONDON. 2598
0017-9310 See INTERNATIONAL JOURNAL OF HEAT AND MASS TRANSFER. 4431
0017-9329 See HEAT ENGINEERING (LIVINGSTON). 1946
0017-9337 See HEAT TECHNOLOGY. 4431
0017-9345 See HEAT TREATING. 4003
0017-9396 See HEATING & VENTILATING REVIEW. 2605
0017-940X See HEATING, PIPING, AND AIR CONDITIONING. 2605
0017-9418 See HEATING-PLUMBING, AIR CONDITIONING. 2605
0017-9426 See HEAVY CONSTRUCTION NEWS. 616
0017-9434 See HEAVY DUTY TRUCKING. 5383
0017-9442 See HEBEZEUGE UND FORDERMITTEL. 2115
0017-9515 See HEENSCHUT. 299
0017-9574 See ABHANDLUNGEN DER HEIDELBERGER AKADEMIE DER WISSENSCHAFTEN, PHILOSOPHISCH-HISTORISCHE KLASSE. 4339
0017-9604 See HEILBERUFE, DIE. 3583
0017-9620 See HEILIGER DIENST. 4962
0017-9655 See VIERTELJAHRESSCHRIFT FUER HEILPADAGOGIK UND IHRE NACHBARGEBIETE. 1790
0017-9841 See HEIMEN. 2690
0017-9876 See HEIMTEX. 2900
0017-9884 See HEIRS. 3393
0017-9906 See HLH. 2605
0017-9973 See HELICTITE. 5109
0017-9981 See HELIKON (ROMA). 3285
0017-999X See HELIKON. 3393
0018-0009 See HELINIUM. 2690
0018-0068 See ELLENIKE KTENIATRIKE. 5509
0018-0114 See HELMANTICA. 1077
0018-0181 See HELVETICA CHIRURGICA ACTA. 3903
0018-019X See HELVETICA CHIMICA ACTA. 976

0018-022X See HELVETICA PAEDIATRICA ACTA. 3903
0018-0238 See HELVETICA PHYSICA ACTA. 4404
0018-0424 See HENRY GEORGE NEWS. 1827
0018-0483 See HERALD OF FREEDOM (MANVILLE), THE. 2534
0018-0513 See HERALD OF HOLINESS. 5061
0018-0521 See HERALD OF LIBRARY SCIENCE. 3213
0018-0602 See HERBAGE ABSTRACTS. 154
0018-0637 See HERCYNIA. 5109
0018-0645 See HERDER-KORRESPONDENZ. 5030
0018-0661 See HEREDITAS. 547
0018-067X See HEREDITY. 547
0018-0696 See HERE'S HEALTH (WEST BYFLEET). 4782
0018-0718 See HERITAGE OF VERMILION COUNTY, THE. 2617
0018-0750 See HERMATHENA. 4348
0018-0777 See HERMES (WIESBADEN). 3393
0018-0831 See HERPETOLOGICA. 5585
0018-084X See HERPETOLOGICAL REVIEW. 5585
0018-0971 See HERZOGIA. 512
0018-098X See HESPERIA. 1077
0018-0998 See HESPERIDE, L'. 2690
0018-1005 See HESPERIS TAMUDA. 2639
0018-1137 See HETEROFONIA. 4121
0018-1153 See HEWLETT-PACKARD JOURNAL. 1186
0018-1196 See HEYTHROP JOURNAL. 5030
0018-120X See TEEN LIFE (SPRINGFIELD, MO.). 5002
0018-1285 See HIDALGUIA. 2690
0018-1323 See HIDROLOGIAI KOZLONY. 1414
0018-1390 See HIFU. SKIN RESEARCH. 3720
0018-1420 See HIGH COUNTRY, THE. 2736
0018-1439 See HIGH ENERGY CHEMISTRY. 1052
0018-1447 See HIGH ENERGY PHYSICS INDEX / HOCHENERGIEPHYSIK-INDEX. 4404
0018-1471 See HIGH PLAINS JOURNAL, THE. 5676
0018-1498 See HIGH SCHOOL JOURNAL, THE. 1750
0018-151X See HIGH TEMPERATURE. 4431
0018-1536 See HIGH TEMPERATURE SCIENCE. 1052
0018-1544 See HIGH TEMPERATURES - HIGH PRESSURES. 4431
0018-1560 See HIGHER EDUCATION. 1828
0018-1579 See HIGHER EDUCATION & NATIONAL AFFAIRS. 1828
0018-1609 See HIGHER EDUCATION REVIEW. 1828
0018-165X See HIGHLIGHTS FOR CHILDREN. 1064
0018-1668 See HIGHLIGHTS OF AGRICULTURAL RESEARCH. 92
0018-1811 See HIKAKU KAGAKU. 3184
0018-1846 See HILLANDALE NEWS, THE. 4121
0018-1927 See HINDUISM. 4963
0018-1935 See HINDUSTAN ANTIBIOTICS BULLETIN. 4306
0018-1951 See HINSHITSU KANRI. 1977
0018-1994 See HINYOKIKA KIYO. 3990
0018-2036 See HIRAM POETRY REVIEW, THE. 3464
0018-2044 See HIROSAKI IGAKU. 3583
0018-2052 See HIROSHIMA JOURNAL OF MEDICAL SCIENCES. 3584
0018-2060 See HIROSHIMA DAIGAKU KOGAKUBU KENKYU HOKOKU. 1977
0018-2079 See HIROSHIMA MATHEMATICAL JOURNAL. 3507
0018-2087 See HIROSHIMA DAIGAKU IGAKU ZASSHI. 3584
0018-2125 See HISPALIS MEDICA. 3584
0018-2133 See HISPANIA. 3285
0018-2141 See HISPANIA (MADRID). 2690

0018-215X See HISPANIA SACRA. 5030
0018-2168 See HISPANIC AMERICAN HISTORICAL REVIEW [MICROFORM], THE. 2736
0018-2168 See HISPANIC AMERICAN HISTORICAL REVIEW, THE. 2262
0018-2176 See HISPANIC REVIEW. 3285
0018-2206 See HISPANOFILA. 3394
0018-2214 See HISTOCHEMICAL JOURNAL. 536
0018-2257 See HISTOIRE SOCIALE. 5201
0018-2281 See HISTORIA (PARIS). 2617
0018-229X See HISTORIA (THREE RIVERS). 2640
0018-2311 See HISTORIA (WIESBADEN). 2617
0018-2346 See HISTORIA NATURAL Y PRO NATURA. 4166
0018-2354 See HISTORIA Y VIDA. 2617
0018-2362 See HISTORIALLINEN AIKAKAUSKIRJA. 2617
0018-2370 See HISTORIAN (KINGSTON), THE. 2618
0018-2419 See HISTORIC PRESERVATION (WASHINGTON, D.C.). 2737
0018-246X See HISTORICAL JOURNAL (CAMBRIDGE, CAMBRIDGESHIRE). 2618
0018-2508 See HISTORICAL NEW HAMPSHIRE. 2737
0018-2516 See HISTORICAL REVIEW. 2669
0018-2524 See HISTORICAL REVIEW OF BERKS COUNTY. 2737
0018-2540 See JOURNAL OF THE HISTORICAL SOCIETY OF NIGERIA. 2641
0018-2575 See HISTORICKY CASOPIS. 2691
0018-2583 See HISTORIE A VOJENSTVI. 2691
0018-2605 See HISTORISCH-POLITISCHE BUCH, DAS. 2618
0018-2613 See HISTORISCHE ZEITSCHRIFT. 2619
0018-2621 See HISTORISCHES JAHRBUCH. 2619
0018-263x See HISTORISK TIDSSKRIFT. 2691
0018-2648 See HISTORY (LONDON). 2619
0018-2656 See HISTORY AND THEORY. 2635
0018-2680 See HISTORY OF EDUCATION QUARTERLY. 1750
0018-2699 See HISTORY OF EDUCATION SOCIETY BULLETIN. 1750
0018-2702 See HISTORY OF POLITICAL ECONOMY. 1565
0018-2710 See HISTORY OF RELIGIONS. 4963
0018-2745 See HISTORY TEACHER (LONG BEACH, CALIF.), THE. 1896
0018-2753 See HISTORY TODAY. 2619
0018-277X See HITACHI REVIEW. 5110
0018-277X See HITACHI TECHNOLOGY. 5110
0018-2788 See HITACHI ZOSEN GIHO. 5110
0018-2796 See HITOTSUBASHI JOURNAL OF COMMERCE AND MANAGEMENT. 839
0018-280X See HITOTSUBASHI JOURNAL OF ECONOMICS. 1493
0018-2818 See HITOTSUBASHI RONSO. 5201
0018-2869 See HLAS L'UDU. 5810
0018-2885 See HOARD'S DAIRYMAN. 195
0018-2974 See HOCHSCHULWESEN : WISSENSCHAFTPOLITISCHE RUNDSCHAU, DAS. 1750
0018-3008 See HOCKEY FIELD. 4899
0018-3016 See HOCKEY NEWS, THE. 4899
0018-3040 See HODOWLA ROSLIN AKLIMTYZACJA I NASIENNICTWO. 173
0018-3091 See HOHLE, DIE. 1356
0018-3113 See HOER ZU. 5479
0018-3180 See HOG FARM MANAGEMENT. 212
0018-3229 See EL HOGAR CRISTIANO. 4955
0018-3377 See HOKKAIDO SEIKEI SAIGAI GEKA ZASSHI. 3881
0018-3393 See HOKKAIDO KYOIKU DAIGAKU KIYO. DAI 2-BU. 457
0018-344X See JOURNAL OF THE FACULTY OF AGRICULTURE. HOKKAIDO UNIVERSITY. 101
0018-3458 See HOKKAIDO DAIGAKU SUISANGAKUBU KENKYU IHO. 2305

0018-3466 See MEMOIRS OF THE FACULTY OF FISHERIES, HOKKAIDO UNIVERSITY. 2308
0018-3474 See JOURNAL OF THE FACULTY OF SCIENCE, HOKKAIDO UNIVERSITY. SERIES 4. GEOLOGY AND MINERALOGY. 1357
0018-3644 See HOLLINS CRITIC, THE. 3344
0018-3660 See HOLLYWOOD REPORTER, THE. 4072
0018-3768 See HOLZ ALS ROH- UND WERKSTOFF. 2401
0018-3776 See HOLZ IM HANDWERK. 2906
0018-3792 See HOLZ-ZENTRALBLATT. 2384
0018-3822 See HOB. DIE HOLZBEARBEITUNG. 5110
0018-3830 See HOLZFORSCHUNG. 2401
0018-3849 See HOLZFORSCHUNG UND HOLZVERWERTUNG. 2401
0018-3954 See GREEN BOOK BUYERS' GUIDE FOR GARDEN MERCHANDISE. 2417
0018-4004 See HOME EC NEWS. 2790
0018-4071 See HOME LIFE (NASHVILLE). 5061
0018-4195 See PERSPECTIVES IN LONG-TERM CARE. 3626
0018-4233 See HOMES AND GARDENS INCORPORATING HOME. 2824
0018-4268 See HOMILETIC & PASTORAL REVIEW. 5030
0018-4306 See HOMME ET LA SOCIETE, L'. 5247
0018-4357 See HOMMES ET FONDERIE. 4428
0018-439X See HOMMES ET TERRES DU NORD. 2565
0018-4411 See HOMMES VOLANTS PARIS, LES. 4899
0018-442X See HOMO. 237
0018-4543 See HONEST ULSTERMAN, THE. 3394
0018-4578 See HONG KONG ECONOMIC PAPERS. 1493
0018-4586 See HONG KONG ENTERPRISE. 680
0018-4683 See HOOF BEATS (COLUMBUS, OHIO). 2799
0018-4721 See HOOSHARAR. 2263
0018-473X See HB. HOOSIER BANKER. 790
0018-4748 See HOOSIER FARMER. 93
0018-4780 See HOOSIER OUTDOORS. 4873
0018-4861 See HOPITAL A PARIS, L'. 3783
0018-490X See HOPPLANTER, DE. 173
0018-4942 See HOREN : JUNGER LITERATURKREIS, DIE. 3394
0018-4950 See HORISONT (VASSA, FINLAND). 3394
0018-5027 See HORIZONTES (PONCE, P.R.). 2847
0018-5043 See HORMONE AND METABOLIC RESEARCH. 3730
0018-506X See HORMONES AND BEHAVIOR. 3730
0018-5078 See HORN BOOK MAGAZINE (1945), THE. 1064
0018-5108 See HOROLOGICAL JOURNAL. 2916
0018-5116 See HOROSCOPE (NEW YORK). 390
0018-5159 See HORSE & RIDER. 2799
0018-5183 See HORSE WORLD : PONY EXPRESS. 2800
0018-5191 See HORSE WORLD. 2800
0018-5213 See HORSELESS CARRIAGE GAZETTE. 5416
0018-5221 See HORSEMAN (HOUSTON, TEX.). 2800
0018-5256 See HORSEMEN'S JOURNAL, THE. 2800
0018-5280 See HORTICULTURAL ABSTRACTS. 2434
0018-5329 See HORTICULTURE. 2419
0018-5345 See HORTSCIENCE. 2419
0018-5485 See HOSPITAL, EL. 3783
0018-5531 See HOSPITAL ADMINISTRATION (NEW DELHI). 3783
0018-5574 See NEWS - HOSPITAL ASSOCIATION OF NEW YORK STATE. 3790
0018-5604 See REVISTA MEDICA DEL HOSPITAL COLONIA. 3636

0018-5620 See HOSPITAL EQUIPMENT & SUPPLIES. 3784
0018-5647 See BULLETIN / HOSPITAL FOR JOINT DISEASES. 3804
0018-5728 See HOSPITAL LAW MANUAL. ATTORNEYS VOLUME. 2979
0018-5736 See HOSPITAL LITERATURE INDEX. 3659
0018-5787 See HOSPITAL PHARMACY (PHILADELPHIA). 4306
0018-585X See HOSPITAL SUPERVISOR'S BULLETIN. 941
0018-5868 See HOSPITAL TOPICS. 3785
0018-5973 See HOSPITALS (CHICAGO, ILL. 1936). 3786
0018-599X See HOSPODAR. 2263
0018-6031 See HOT ROD. 5416
0018-6082 See HOTEL & MOTEL MANAGEMENT. 2806
0018-6368 See HOUILLE BLANCHE, LA. 2090
0018-6384 See HOUNDS AND HUNTING. 4286
0018-6406 See HOUSE & GARDEN (NEW YORK). 2901
0018-6422 See HOUSE BEAUTIFUL. 300
0018-6554 See HOUSING AFFAIRS LETTER. 2824
0018-6589 See HOUSING & PLANNING REVIEW. 2824
0018-6651 See HOUSING REVIEW (LONDON). 2825
0018-6686 See BULLETIN OF THE HOUSTON GEOLOGICAL SOCIETY, THE. 1370
0018-6694 See HOUSTON LAW REVIEW. 2979
0018-6813 See HOWARD LAW JOURNAL. 2979
0018-6856 See HOY DIA. 3286
0018-6872 See HRANA I ISHRANA. 2343
0018-6910 See HRVATSKI KATOLICKI GLASNIK. 4963
0018-6996 See HUDEBNI ROZHLEDY. 4121
0018-7003 See HUDEBNI VEDA. 4121
0018-702X See HUDSON REVIEW, THE. 322
0018-7070 See HUISARTS EN WETENSCHAP. 3585
0018-7143 See HUMAN BIOLOGY. 457
0018-716X See HUMAN DEVELOPMENT. 4588
0018-7178 See HUMAN ECOLOGY FORUM. 2216
0018-7194 See HUMAN EVENTS (WASHINGTON). 4476
0018-7208 See HUMAN FACTORS. 1251
0018-7240 See HUMAN MOSAIC. 5247
0018-7259 See HUMAN ORGANIZATION. 237
0018-7267 See HUMAN RELATIONS (NEW YORK). 5202
0018-7399 See HUMANIST (BUFFALO, N.Y.), THE. 4348
0018-7429 See HUMANIST OUTLOOK. 4348
0018-7437 See QUEST. 3350
0018-7445 See HUMANITAS BERLIN, DDR. 2847
0018-7526 See HUMANITIES (WASHINGTON). 2847
0018-7577 See HUMANITIES IN THE SOUTH. 2847
0018-7615 See HUMBOLDT SPANISCHE AUSGABE. 2847
0018-7623 See HUMBOLDT (PORTUGIESISCHE AUSGABE). 2517
0018-7747 See HUNGARIAN FOREIGN TRADE. 1635
0018-781X See STATISZTIKAI HAVI KOZLEMENYEK. 5344
0018-7844 See HUNTERDON COUNTY DEMOCRAT. 5710
0018-7860 See HUNTER'S HORN, THE. 4899
0018-7895 See HUNTINGTON LIBRARY QUARTERLY, THE. 352
0018-8026 See HUSMODERN. 5558
0018-8069 See HUTNICKE LISTY. 4003
0018-8077 See HUTNIK (KATOWICE). 4003
0018-8085 See HUTOIPAR. 2343
0018-8093 See HVEDEKORN. 3464
0018-814X See HYDRAULICS & PNEUMATICS. 2090

0018-8158 See HYDROBIOLOGIA. 457
0018-8166 See HYDROBIOLOGICAL JOURNAL. 457
0018-8190 See HYDROCARBON PROCESSING (INTERNATIONAL ED.). 4260
0018-8220 See HYDROTECHNICAL CONSTRUCTION. 2090
0018-8247 See HIGIENA I ZDRAVEOPAZVANE. 3583
0018-8271 See HYMN, THE. 4121
0018-828X See BULLETIN - HYMN SOCIETY OF GREAT BRITAIN AND IRELAND. 4106
0018-8328 See HYPERION (BERKELEY). 3395
0018-8409 See IAPA NEWS. 2920
0018-8441 See IASLIC BULLETIN. 3214
0018-8611 See INTERNATIONAL BENEFITS INFORMATION SERVICE. 2884
0018-862X See IBLA. 3286
0018-8646 See IBM JOURNAL OF RESEARCH AND DEVELOPMENT. 2056
0018-8662 See IBM NACHRICHTEN. 1186
0018-8670 See IBM SYSTEMS JOURNAL. 1259
0018-8689 See IBM TECHNICAL DISCLOSURE BULLETIN. 1187
0018-8727 See INDIAN BEHAVIOURAL SCIENCES ABSTRACTS. 5203
0018-8778 See ICAO JOURNAL. 23
0018-8808 See ICASALS NEWSLETTER. 174
0018-8999 See I C O M NEWS. 4089
0018-9049 See ICSSR NEWSLETTER. 5202
0018-9073 See IDB NEWSLETTER. 790
0018-9081 See IDIA, INFORMATIVO DE INVESTIGACIONES AGRICOLAS. 93
0018-912X See DISCOVER THE BIBLE. 5016
0018-9138 See IEC BULLETIN. 2057
0018-9146 See I.E.E.-I.E.R.E. PROCEEDINGS INDIA. 2056
0018-9162 See COMPUTER (LONG BEACH, CALIF.). 1266
0018-9189 See IEEE GRID. 2059
0018-9197 See IEEE JOURNAL OF QUANTUM ELECTRONICS. 2060
0018-9200 See IEEE JOURNAL OF SOLID-STATE CIRCUITS. 2060
0018-9219 See PROCEEDINGS OF THE IEEE. 2076
0018-9227 See SCANFAX. 2080
0018-9235 See IEEE SPECTRUM. 2060
0018-9251 See IEEE TRANSACTIONS ON AEROSPACE AND ELECTRONIC SYSTEMS. 2061
0018-926X See IEEE TRANSACTIONS ON ANTENNAS AND PROPAGATION. 2061
0018-9286 See IEEE TRANSACTIONS ON AUTOMATIC CONTROL. 1219
0018-9316 See IEEE TRANSACTIONS ON BROADCASTING. 1133
0018-9340 See IEEE TRANSACTIONS ON COMPUTERS. 1247
0018-9359 See IEEE TRANSACTIONS ON EDUCATION. 2062
0018-9367 See IEEE TRANSACTIONS ON ELECTRICAL INSULATION. 2062
0018-9375 See IEEE TRANSACTIONS ON ELECTROMAGNETIC COMPATIBILITY. 2062
0018-9383 See IEEE TRANSACTIONS ON ELECTRON DEVICES. 2062
0018-9391 See IEEE TRANSACTIONS ON ENGINEERING MANAGEMENT. 2062
0018-9448 See IEEE TRANSACTIONS ON INFORMATION THEORY. 2062
0018-9456 See IEEE TRANSACTIONS ON INSTRUMENTATION AND MEASUREMENT. 2063
0018-9464 See IEEE TRANSACTIONS ON MAGNETICS. 4443
0018-9472 See IEEE TRANSACTIONS ON SYSTEMS, MAN, AND CYBERNETICS. 1251
0018-9480 See IEEE TRANSACTIONS ON MICROWAVE THEORY AND TECHNIQUES. 2063

0018-9499 See IEEE TRANSACTIONS ON NUCLEAR SCIENCE. 2155
0018-9529 See IEEE TRANSACTIONS ON RELIABILITY. 2063
0018-9545 See IEEE TRANSACTIONS ON VEHICULAR TECHNOLOGY. 2064
0018-9634 See BULLETIN DE L'INSTITUT FONDAMENTAL D'AFRIQUE NOIRE. SERIE A: SCIENCES NATURELLES. 449
0018-9731 See IFO-STUDIEN. 1494
0018-974X See IFO SCHNELLDIENST. 681
0018-9766 See IGA GROCERGRAM. 2344
0018-9804 See IGU BULLETIN. 2565
0018-9820 See IHI ENGINEERING REVIEW. 1977
0018-9855 See IIC; INTERNATIONAL REVIEW OF INDUSTRIAL AND COPYRIGHT LAW. 1304
0018-988X See STATUS REPORT - INSURANCE INSTITUTE FOR HIGHWAY SAFETY. 5444
0018-991X See IJA REPORT. 3090
0018-9960 See ILAR NEWS. 3585
0019-0012 See IMC JOURNAL. 4212
0019-0020 See IMM ABSTRACTS. 4003
0019-0144 See INFO JOURNAL / INTERNATIONAL FORTEAN ORGANIZATION. 4241
0019-0217 See INSPEL. 3217
0019-0233 See INFORMATIVO DO INT. 5113
0019-0314 See IPI REPORT. 2921
0019-0357 See IPPF MEDICAL BULLETIN (ENGLISH EDITION). 589
0019-0365 See INTERNATIONAL PHILOSOPHICAL QUARTERLY. 4349
0019-042X See IRAL, INTERNATIONAL REVIEW OF APPLIED LINGUISTICS IN LANGUAGE TEACHING. 3288
0019-0446 See REVISTA DO IRB / INSTITUTO DE RESSEGUROS DO BRASIL. 2892
0019-0578 See ISA TRANSACTIONS. 5116
0019-0624 See ISEA COMMUNIQUE. 1865
0019-073X See IT. 2518
0019-0829 See ITL. INSTITUUT VOOR TOEGEPASTE LINGUISTIK. 3288
0019-0861 See IUE NEWS. 1681
0019-0918 See IVS. INDEX OF VETERINARY SPECIALITIES. 5512
0019-0993 See IBEROROMANIA. 3286
0019-1019 See IBIS (LONDON, ENGLAND). 5617
0019-1027 See ICARUS. 3395
0019-1035 See ICARUS (NEW YORK, N.Y. 1962). 395
0019-1043 See ICE. 1415
0019-1094 See ICELAND REVIEW (REYKJAVIK, ICELAND : 1984). 2692
0019-1205 See IDAHO LAW REVIEW. 2979
0019-1213 See IDAHO LIBRARIAN, THE. 3214
0019-1221 See IDAHO PHARMACIST, THE. 4307
0019-1264 See IDAHO YESTERDAYS. 2738
0019-1272 See IDEA (CONCORD, N.H.). 1304
0019-1280 See IDEA (ROME). 2620
0019-1299 See IDEA. 380
0019-1361 See IDEAL HOME. 616
0019-137X See IDEALS. 5558
0019-1604 See IGAKU TO SEIBUTSUGAKU. 3585
0019-1639 See IGIENE E SANITA PUBBLICA. 4783
0019-1655 See IGIENE MODERNA. 4783
0019-1744 See IKON. 1113
0019-1795 See ILIFF REVIEW, THE. 4964
0019-1809 See ILLIANA GENEALOGIST. 2454
0019-185X See ILLINOIS BANKER. 790
0019-1868 See ILLINOIS BAPTIST. 5061
0019-1876 See ILLINOIS BAR JOURNAL. 2980
0019-1892 See ILLINOIS BEVERAGE JOURNAL. 2367
0019-1922 See ILLINOIS BUSINESS REVIEW. 681
0019-1949 See ILLINOIS COUNTY AND TOWNSHIP OFFICIAL. 4655
0019-1973 See ILLINOIS DENTAL JOURNAL. 1324
0019-2015 See ILLINOIS ENGINEER. 1977
0019-2031 See BULLETIN - ILLINOIS GEOGRAPHICAL SOCIETY. 2557
0019-2058 See ILLINOIS HISTORY. 2738
0019-2082 See ILLINOIS JOURNAL OF MATHEMATICS. 3508
0019-2104 See ILLINOIS LIBRARIES. 3214
0019-2112 See ILLINOIS MASTER PLUMBER. 2606
0019-2139 See ILLINOIS MUNICIPAL REVIEW. 4655
0019-2147 See ILLINOIS MUSIC EDUCATOR, THE. 4122
0019-2155 See ILLINOIS PARKS & RECREATION. 4706
0019-2171 See OFFICIAL JOURNAL - ILLINOIS POLICE ASSOCIATION. 3171
0019-218X See ILLINOIS PRINCIPAL. 1864
0019-2198 See ILLINOIS PSYCHOLOGIST : NEWSLETTER OF THE ILLINOIS PSYCHOLOGICAL ASSOCIATION. 4589
0019-221X See ILLINOIS SCHOOL BOARD JOURNAL. 1864
0019-2236 See ILLINOIS SCHOOLS JOURNAL. 1896
0019-2252 See TRANSACTIONS OF THE ILLINOIS STATE ACADEMY OF SCIENCE. 5166
0019-2279 See WEEKLY NEWS LETTER - ILLINOIS STATE AFL-CIO. 1717
0019-2309 See ILLINOIS TRUCK NEWS. 5384
0019-2317 See ILLINOIS WILDLIFE. 2195
0019-2422 See ILLUSTRATED LONDON NEWS, THE. 2517
0019-2430 See ILLUSTRATED WEEKLY OF INDIA, THE. 5803
0019-2457 See ILLUSTRATION 63. I.E. DREIUNDSECHZIG. 380
0019-2465 See ILLUSTRATOR, THE. 380
0019-2538 See ILOCOS REVIEW, THE. 2653
0019-2635 See REVUE DU CINEMA (PARIS. 1969). 4077
0019-2708 See IMBALLAGGIO : ORGANO UFFICIALE DELL'ISTITUTO ITALIANO IMBALLAGGIO. 5112
0019-2724 See IMFAMA. 4389
0019-2805 See IMMUNOLOGY. 3671
0019-2821 See IMPACT (CONSERVATIVE BAPTIST FOREIGN MISSION SOCIETY). 5061
0019-2872 See IMPACT OF SCIENCE ON SOCIETY. 5112
0019-2880 See IMPACTO (MEXICO). 2535
0019-2953 See IMPLEMENT & TRACTOR. 159
0019-3046 See IMPRINT. 2504
0019-3062 See IMPRINT (NEW YORK, NEW YORK). 3857
0019-3127 See ANIMALAND. 5575
0019-3143 See IN BRITAIN. 5480
0019-3259 See IN REVIEW (TORONTO). 1064
0019-3291 See IN TRANSIT (WASHINGTON). 5384
0019-3348 See INCENTIVE (NEW YORK). 955
0019-3429 See INCOME OPPORTUNITIES (NEW YORK, N.Y.). 681
0019-3451 See INCOMES DATA REPORT. 4731
0019-3453 See INCOME TAX REPORTS, THE. 4731
0019-3577 See INDAGATIONES MATHEMATICAE. 3508
0019-3674 See INDEPENDENT BANKER. 790
0019-3763 See INDEPENDENT SHAVIAN, THE. 3396
0019-3844 See INDEX INDIA. 417
0019-3852 See INDEX INDO-ASIATICUS. 2653
0019-3879 See INDEX MEDICUS (1960). 3660
0019-3895 See INDEX OF FUNGI / COMMONWEALTH MYCOLOGICAL INSTITUTE. 513
0019-3925 See INDEX OF NEW PRODUCTS. 4334
0019-3941 See INDEX OF VETERINARY SPECIALITIES. 5511
0019-3992 See INDEX TO DENTAL LITERATURE. 1338
0019-400X See INDEX TO FOREIGN LEGAL PERIODICALS. 3081
0019-4026 See INDEX TO INDIAN ECONOMIC JOURNALS. 1494
0019-4034 See INDEX TO INDIAN LEGAL PERIODICALS. 2981
0019-4050 See INDEX TO JEWISH PERIODICALS. 5013
0019-4077 See INDEX TO LEGAL PERIODICALS. 3081
0019-4077 See INDEX TO LEGAL PERIODICALS. CD-ROM. 3081
0019-4093 See INDEX TO PERIODICAL ARTICLES RELATED TO LAW. 3081
0019-4123 See INDEX VETERINARIUS. 5528
0019-4131 See INDEXER. 3215
0019-4247 See JOURNAL OF THE INDIAN ACADEMY OF APPLIED PSYCHOLOGY. 4602
0019-4271 See JOURNAL OF THE INDIAN ACADEMY OF PHILOSOPHY, THE. 4351
0019-4301 See INDIAN ADVOCATE. 2981
0019-4336 See INDIAN AGRICULTURIST. 94
0019-4344 See INDOGAKU BUKKYOGAKU KENKYU. 2653
0019-4387 See JOURNAL OF THE INDIAN ANTHROPOLOGICAL SOCIETY. 239
0019-4409 See INDIAN ARCHITECT, THE. 301
0019-4425 See INDIAN BEE JOURNAL. 94
0019-4433 See INDIAN BOOK INDUSTRY. 4829
0019-4468 See JOURNAL OF THE INDIAN BOTANICAL SOCIETY, THE. 516
0019-4484 See INDIAN CASHEW JOURNAL. 2344
0019-4492 See INDIAN CERAMICS. 2591
0019-4506 See INDIAN CHEMICAL ENGINEER. 2013
0019-4522 See JOURNAL OF THE INDIAN CHEMICAL SOCIETY. 982
0019-4530 See INDIAN CHURCH HISTORY REVIEW. 4964
0019-4549 See INDIAN COFFEE. 174
0019-4565 See INDIAN CONCRETE JOURNAL, THE. 617
0019-4581 See INDIAN COOPERATIVE REVIEW. 1542
0019-4603 See INDIAN DAIRYMAN. 195
0019-4611 See JOURNAL OF THE INDIAN DENTAL ASSOCIATION. 1328
0019-462X See INDIAN DRUGS. 4307
0019-4646 See INDIAN ECONOMIC AND SOCIAL HISTORY REVIEW, THE. 1566
0019-4654 See INDIAN ECONOMIC DIARY. 1566
0019-4662 See INDIAN ECONOMIC JOURNAL, THE. 1566
0019-4670 See INDIAN ECONOMIC REVIEW. 1494
0019-4697 See INDIAN EDUCATION ABSTRACTS. 1752
0019-4700 See INDIAN EDUCATIONAL REVIEW. 1752
0019-4735 See INDIAN EXPORT TRADE JOURNAL, THE. 4523
0019-476X See INDIAN FACTORIES JOURNAL, THE. 3481
0019-4786 See INDIAN FARMING. 94
0019-4794 See INDIAN FINANCE. 790
0019-4808 See INDIAN FOOD PACKER. 2344
0019-4816 See INDIAN FORESTER, THE. 2384
0019-4824 See INDIAN GEOGRAPHICAL JOURNAL, THE. 2566
0019-4832 See INDIAN HEART JOURNAL. 3706
0019-4875 See INDIAN HORTICULTURE. 2420
0019-4891 See INDIAN INDUSTRIES (MADRAS). 3481
0019-4913 See JOURNAL OF THE INDIAN INSTITUTE OF ARCHITECTS. 302
0019-4921 See JOURNAL OF THE INDIAN INSTITUTE OF BANKERS. 795
0019-493X See TRANSACTIONS OF THE INDIAN INSTITUTE OF METALS. 4022
0019-4964 See JOURNAL OF THE INDIAN INSTITUTE OF SCIENCE. 5120
0019-4999 See MONTHLY NEWSLETTER - INDIAN INVESTMENT CENTRE. 907
0019-5006 See INDIAN JOURNAL OF ADULT EDUCATION. 1801

0019-5014 See INDIAN JOURNAL OF AGRICULTURAL ECONOMICS, THE. 94
0019-5022 See INDIAN JOURNAL OF AGRICULTURAL SCIENCES, THE. 95
0019-5030 See INDIAN JOURNAL OF AMERICAN STUDIES. 2738
0019-5049 See INDIAN JOURNAL OF ANAESTHESIA. 3683
0019-5057 See INDIAN JOURNAL OF ANIMAL HEALTH. 5511
0019-5065 See INDIAN JOURNAL OF APPLIED CHEMISTRY. 2013
0019-5073 See INDIAN JOURNAL OF APPLIED PSYCHOLOGY. 4589
0019-509X See INDIAN JOURNAL OF CANCER. 3818
0019-512x See INDIAN JOURNAL OF COMMERCE, THE. 840
0019-5138 See JOURNAL OF COMMUNICABLE DISEASES. 4786
0019-5146 See INDIAN JOURNAL OF DAIRY SCIENCE. 195
0019-5154 See INDIAN JOURNAL OF DERMATOLOGY. 3720
0019-5170 See INDIAN JOURNAL OF ECONOMICS. 1494
0019-5189 See INDIAN JOURNAL OF EXPERIMENTAL BIOLOGY. 458
0019-5200 See INDIAN JOURNAL OF GENETICS & PLANT BREEDING, THE. 548
0019-5219 See INDIAN JOURNAL OF GERONTOLOGY. 3752
0019-5227 See INDIAN JOURNAL OF HELMINTHOLOGY / HELMINTHOLOGICAL SOCIETY OF INDIA. 5586
0019-5235 See INDIAN JOURNAL OF HISTORY OF SCIENCE. 5112
0019-5251 See INDIAN JOURNAL OF HORTICULTURE, THE. 2420
0019-526X See INDIAN JOURNAL OF HOSPITAL PHARMACY. 4307
0019-5278 See INDIAN JOURNAL OF INDUSTRIAL MEDICINE. 2863
0019-5286 See INDIAN JOURNAL OF INDUSTRIAL RELATIONS. 681
0019-5294 See INDIAN JOURNAL OF INTERNATIONAL LAW, THE. 3129
0019-5308 See INDIAN JOURNAL OF LABOUR ECONOMICS. 1566
0019-5324 See INDIAN JOURNAL OF MATHEMATICS. 3508
0019-5332 See INDIAN JOURNAL OF MEDICAL EDUCATION. 3586
0019-5359 See INDIAN JOURNAL OF MEDICAL SCIENCES. 3586
0019-5375 See INDIAN JOURNAL OF MENTAL RETARDATION. 1880
0019-5391 See INDIAN JOURNAL OF OCCUPATIONAL HEALTH. 2863
0019-5413 See INDIAN JOURNAL OF ORTHOPAEDICS. 3881
0019-5421 See INDIAN JOURNAL OF OTOLARYNGOLOGY. 3888
0019-5456 See INDIAN JOURNAL OF PEDIATRICS. 3904
0019-5464 See INDIAN JOURNAL OF PHARMACEUTICAL EDUCATION. 4307
0019-5480 See INDIAN JOURNAL OF PHYSICS AND PROCEEDINGS OF THE INDIAN ASSOCIATION FOR THE CULTIVATION OF SCIENCE. 5112
0019-5499 See INDIAN JOURNAL OF PHYSIOLOGY AND PHARMACOLOGY. 581
0019-5502 See INDIAN JOURNAL OF PLANT PHYSIOLOGY. 513
0019-5510 See INDIAN JOURNAL OF POLITICAL SCIENCE, THE. 4476
0019-5529 See INDIAN JOURNAL OF POULTRY SCIENCE. 212
0019-5537 See INDIAN JOURNAL OF POWER AND RIVER VALLEY DEVELOPMENT. 5534
0019-5545 See INDIAN JOURNAL OF PSYCHIATRY. 3926
0019-5553 See INDIAN JOURNAL OF PSYCHOLOGY. 4589
0019-5561 See INDIAN JOURNAL OF PUBLIC ADMINISTRATION, THE. 4656
0019-557X See INDIAN JOURNAL OF PUBLIC HEALTH. 4784
0019-5588 See INDIAN JOURNAL OF PURE AND APPLIED MATHEMATICS. 3508
0019-5596 See INDIAN JOURNAL OF PURE & APPLIED PHYSICS. 4405
0019-5626 See INDIAN JOURNAL OF SOCIAL RESEARCH. 5203
0019-5634 See INDIAN JOURNAL OF SOCIAL WORK, THE. 5289
0019-5650 See INDIAN JOURNAL OF SURGERY. 3966
0019-5669 See INDIAN JOURNAL OF TECHNOLOGY. 5112
0019-5677 See INDIAN JOURNAL OF HISTORY OF MEDICINE. 3586
0019-5685 See INDIAN JOURNAL OF THEOLOGY, THE. 4964
0019-5693 See INDIAN JOURNAL OF THEORETICAL PHYSICS. 4405
0019-5707 See INDIAN JOURNAL OF TUBERCULOSIS. 3949
0019-5723 See INDIAN LABOUR JOURNAL. 1678
0019-574X See INDIAN LEATHER. 3184
0019-5758 See JOURNAL OF THE INDIAN LEATHER TECHNOLOGISTS' ASSOCIATION. 3184
0019-5766 See INDIAN LIBERTARIAN, THE. 1592
0019-5790 See INDIAN LIBRARY SCIENCE ABSTRACTS. 3258
0019-5804 See INDIAN LITERATURE (NEW DELHI). 3396
0019-5812 See INDIAN MANAGEMENT. 870
0019-5839 See JOURNAL OF THE INDIAN MATHEMATICAL SOCIETY, THE. 3515
0019-5847 See JOURNAL OF THE INDIAN MEDICAL ASSOCIATION. 3598
0019-5863 See INDIAN MEDICAL GAZETTE. 3587
0019-5871 See INDIAN MEDICAL JOURNAL. 3587
0019-5901 See JOURNAL OF THE INDIAN MERCHANTS' CHAMBER. 843
0019-5928 See INDIAN MINERALOGIST, THE. 1440
0019-5936 See INDIAN MINERALS. 2140
0019-5944 See INDIAN MINING & ENGINEERING JOURNAL, THE. 2140
0019-5987 See BULLETIN - INDIAN MUSEUM. 4085
0019-5995 See INDIAN MUSIC JOURNAL. 4122
0019-6002 See INDIAN NATIONAL BIBLIOGRAPHY. 417
0019-6010 See CONGRESS BULLETIN - INDIAN NATIONAL CONGRESS. 2649
0019-6061 See INDIAN PEDIATRICS. 3904
0019-607X See INDIAN PERFUMER. 404
0019-6150 See INDIAN POULTRY REVIEW. 213
0019-6169 See INDIAN PRACTITIONER. 3587
0019-6177 See INDIAN PRESS INDEX. 5803
0019-6193 See INDIAN PROGRESS. 2264
0019-6215 See INDIAN PSYCHOLOGICAL REVIEW. 4589
0019-6223 See INDIAN PUBLISHER AND BOOKSELLER, THE. 4815
0019-6266 See INDIAN RAILWAY TECHNICAL BULLETIN. 5432
0019-6274 See INDIAN RAILWAYS. 5432
0019-6304 See INDIAN REVIEW (MADRAS). 2505
0019-6339 See INDIAN SCIENCE ABSTRACTS. 5175
0019-6355 See INDIAN SILK. 5351
0019-6363 See JOURNAL OF THE INDIAN SOCIETY OF AGRICULTURAL STATISTICS. 154
0019-638X See JOURNAL OF THE INDIAN SOCIETY OF SOIL SCIENCE. 177
0019-6398 See INTERNATIONAL JOURNAL OF CONTEMPORARY SOCIOLOGY. 5248
0019-6401 See INDIAN SPICES. 840
0019-6428 See INDIAN SUGAR. 2344
0019-6436 See INDIAN TEXTILE JOURNAL, THE. 5351
0019-6444 See INDIAN TRADE JOURNAL. 840
0019-6479 See INDIAN VETERINARY JOURNAL, THE. 5512
0019-6525 See INDIANA AUDUBON QUARTERLY. 5617
0019-6541 See INDIANA BUSINESS REVIEW. 1495
0019-6568 See JOURNAL OF THE INDIANA DENTAL ASSOCIATION. 1328
0019-6622 See INDIANA FREEMASON, THE. 5232
0019-6649 See INDIANA HISTORY BULLETIN. 2739
0019-6665 See INDIANA LAW JOURNAL (BLOOMINGTON). 2982
0019-6673 See INDIANA MAGAZINE OF HISTORY. 2739
0019-6711 See INDIANA PUBLISHER, THE. 4815
0019-672X See INDIANA READING QUARTERLY. 1896
0019-6754 See INDIANA STATE BOARD OF HEALTH BULLETIN, THE. 4784
0019-686X See INDICA. 2653
0019-6924 See INDICATOR, THE. 978
0019-6940 See BIG PICTURE (ALEXANDRIA, VA.), THE. 892
0019-7084 See INDICE PENALE, L'. 3107
0019-719X See INDO ASIA. 2653
0019-7211 See INDO-BRITISH REVIEW. 2692
0019-7246 See INDO-IRANIAN JOURNAL. 4349
0019-7289 See INDONESIA (ITHACA). 2654
0019-7297 See INDONESIA LETTER, THE. 1495
0019-7467 See INDUSTRIA AVICOLA. 213
0019-7483 See INDUSTRIA CONSERVE. 2344
0019-7491 See INDUSTRIA COTONIERA. 5352
0019-7548 See INDUSTRIA DELLA CARTA. 4234
0019-7556 See INDUSTRIA DELLA GOMMA, L'. 5076
0019-7637 See INDUSTRIA ITALIANA DEL CEMENTO, L'. 1978
0019-7734 See INDUSTRIA SACCARIFERA ITALIANA. 2344
0019-7777 See INDUSTRIA TURISTICA (MIAMI). 5480
0019-7793 See INDUSTRIAL ACCOUNTANT. 745
0019-784X See PROFESSIONAL PHOTOGRAPHER. 4375
0019-7858 See INDUSTRIAL AND COMMERCIAL TRAINING. 942
0019-7971 See INDUSTRIAL ARCHAEOLOGY (TAVISTOCK). 270
0019-8021 See INDUSTRIAL PRODUCT BULLETIN. 3481
0019-8145 See IDR. INDUSTRIAL DIAMOND REVIEW. 2115
0019-8153 See INDUSTRIAL DISTRIBUTION. 926
0019-8234 See INDUSTRIAL ENGINEERING (NORCROSS, GA.). 2098
0019-8277 See IEN. INDUSTRIAL EQUIPMENT NEWS (SUTTON). 1609
0019-8285 See INDUSTRIAL EQUIPMENT NEWS (NEW YORK). 2098
0019-8307 See INDUSTRIAL FABRIC PRODUCTS REVIEW. 5352
0019-8323 See INDUSTRIAL FINISHING (WHEATON). 4224
0019-8366 See INDUSTRIAL HEALTH. 2863
0019-8374 See INDUSTRIAL HEATING. 4431
0019-8382 See INDUSTRIAL HYGIENE DIGEST. 2872
0019-8447 See INDUSTRIAL LABORATORY. 1015
0019-8471 See INDUSTRIAL MANAGEMENT (DES PLAINES). 1610
0019-848X See SLOAN MANAGEMENT REVIEW. 886
0019-8501 See INDUSTRIAL MARKETING MANAGEMENT. 926
0019-8528 See INDUSTRIAL MATHEMATICS. 3509
0019-8544 See INDUSTRIAL MINERALS. 1440
0019-8595 See INDUSTRIAL PHOTOGRAPHY. 4370

0019-8625 See INDUSTRIAL PROPERTY. 1304
0019-8641 See INDUSTRIAL PURCHASING AGENT. 950
0019-8676 See INDUSTRIAL RELATIONS (BERKELEY). 1678
0019-8692 See INDUSTRIAL RELATIONS JOURNAL (LONDON, ENGLAND). 1678
0019-8765 See INDUSTRIAL SAFETY & HEALTH BULLETIN. 2863
0019-8862 See INDUSTRIAL WATER TREATMENT. 5534
0019-901X See INDUSTRIE ALIMENTARI (PINEROLO). 2344
0019-9036 See INDUSTRIE-ANZEIGER. 617
0019-9044 See INDUSTRIE CERAMIQUE, L'. 2591
0019-9079 See INDUSTRIE ELEKTRIK + ELEKTRONIK. 2064
0019-9109 See INDUSTRIE LACKIER BETRIEB. 4224
0019-9176 See INDUSTRIE TEXTILE (PARIS). 5352
0019-9281 See IO, MANAGEMENT-ZEITSCHRIFT INDUSTRIELLE ORGANISATION. 872
0019-9311 See INDUSTRIES ALIMENTAIRES ET AGRICOLES. 95
0019-946X See INDUSTRY OF FREE CHINA. 791
0019-9532 See INFANTRY. 4046
0019-9567 See INFECTION AND IMMUNITY. 563
0019-977X See INFORMACION COMERCIAL ESPANOLA. 1612
0019-9907 See INFORMATIE. 1297
0019-9915 See INFORMATIK. 5113
0019-994X See INFORMATION AGRICOLE, L'. 95
0020-0018 See INFORMATION DENTAIRE, L'. 1325
0020-0034 See INFORMATION DIETETIQUE COLOMBES, L'. 4192
0020-0050 See INFORMATION ECONOMIQUE AFRICAINE. 1495
0020-0093 See INFORMATION GEOGRAPHIQUE, L'. 2566
0020-0115 See INFORMATION LEGISLATIVE SERVICE (1969). 2982
0020-0123 See INFORMATION LITTERAIRE, L'. 3396
0020-0204 See INFORMATION PSYCHIATRIQUE. 3926
0020-0220 See INFORMATION RETRIEVAL & LIBRARY AUTOMATION. 1275
0020-0239 See INFORMATION SCIENCE ABSTRACTS. 3258
0020-0255 See INFORMATION SCIENCES. 3216
0020-0336 See INFORMATIONEN AUS ORTHODONTIE UND KIEFERORTHOPAEDIE. 1325
0020-0344 See INFORMATIONEN FUER DIE FISCHWIRTSCHAFT. 2305
0020-045X See INFORMATIONS CHIMIE (EDITION FRANCAISE). 978
0020-0697 See INFORMATORE BOTANICO ITALIANO. 514
0020-0735 See INFORMATORE FITOPATOLOGICO. 514
0020-0778 See INFORMATORE ZOOTECNICO. 213
0020-0883 See INFORMES DE LA CONSTRUCCION. 617
0020-0891 See INFRARED PHYSICS. 4405
0020-0956 See INGEGNERIA FERROVIARIA. 1978
0020-1022 See INGENIERIA CIVIL (LA HABANA). 2024
0020-1073 See INGENIERIA NAVAL (MADRID). 4177
0020-1146 See INGENIEUR (DEN HAAG). 1978
0020-1154 See ARCHIVE OF APPLIED MECHANICS (1991). 2109
0020-1170 See INGENIEUR FUER POST UND TELEKOMMUNIKATION, DER. 1978
0020-1200 See INGENIEURS DE L'AUTOMOBILE (PARIS). 5417
0020-1235 See INGENIEURSBLAD. 1978
0020-1324 See RESPIRATORY CARE. 3951

0020-1383 See INJURY. 3587
0020-1472 See INLAND ARCHITECT. 301
0020-1537 See INLAND SEAS. 2739
0020-157X See INNES REVIEW, THE. 5030
0020-1669 See INORGANIC CHEMISTRY. 1036
0020-1685 See INORGANIC MATERIALS. 1036
0020-1693 See INORGANICA CHIMICA ACTA : BIOINORGANIC CHEMISTRY ARTICLES AND LETTERS. 1036
0020-1723 See INQUIRER, THE. 4965
0020-174X See INQUIRY (OSLO). 4349
0020-1790 See INSECT BIOCHEMISTRY AND MOLECULAR BIOLOGY. 5609
0020-1804 See INSECTA MATSUMURANA. 5609
0020-1812 See INSECTES SOCIAUX. 5609
0020-1839 See ENTOMOLOGISCHE ZEITSCHRIFT MIT INSEKTENBOERSE. 5582
0020-1847 See INSIDE DETECTIVE. 5074
0020-1871 See INSIEME. 683
0020-1944 See INSIGHT (WASHINGTON). 5061
0020-2029 See INSITE. 1753
0020-2061 See INSPIRATION. 926
0020-2118 See INSTALLATORE ITALIANO. 2606
0020-2142 See INSTANTANES MEDICAUX, LES. 3588
0020-2177 See BULLETIN TRIMESTRIEL DI L'INSTITUT ARCHEOLOGIQUE DU LUXEMBOURG. 265
0020-2185 See ANNALES DE L'INSTITUT BELGE DU PETROLE. 4249
0020-2274 See REVUE DE L'INSTITUT FRANCAIS DU PETROLE. 4277
0020-2398 See BULLETIN BIBLIOGRAPHIQUE - INSTITUT NATIONALE DE LA STATISTIQUE ET DES ETUDES ECONOMIQUES. 1530
0020-2452 See BULLETIN DE L'INSTITUT PASTEUR. 3667
0020-2460 See ARCHIVES DE L'INSTITUT PASTEUR D'ALGERIE. 3552
0020-2495 See ARCHIVES DE L'INSTITUT PASTEUR DE MADAGASCAR. 3666
0020-2509 See ARCHIVES DE L'INSTITUT PASTEUR DE TUNIS. 3552
0020-2568 See ANNALES DE L'INSTITUT TECHNIQUE DU BATIMENT ET DES TRAVAUX PUBLICS. 598
0020-2622 See ISR NEWSLETTER. 5205
0020-2681 See JOURNAL OF THE INSTITUTE OF ACTUARIES. 2886
0020-269X See JOURNAL OF THE INSTITUTE OF ACTUARIES STUDENTS' SOCIETY. 1759
0020-2703 See RESEARCH REVIEW - INSTITUTE OF AFRICAN STUDIES. 2643
0020-2754 See TRANSACTIONS - INSTITUTE OF BRITISH GEOGRAPHERS (1965). 2577
0020-2789 See CLERK OF WORKS. 607
0020-2827 See AJIA KEIZAI SHIRYO GEPPO. 3188
0020-2843 See NEWS LETTER FROM THE INSTITUTE OF EARLY AMERICAN HISTORY & CULTURE, A. 2749
0020-2851 See JOURNAL OF INSTITUTE OF ECONOMIC RESEARCH. 1570
0020-2908 See LANDSCAPE DESIGN. 2423
0020-2940 See MEASUREMENT AND CONTROL. 2121
0020-2967 See TRANSACTIONS OF THE INSTITUTE OF METAL FINISHING. 4022
0020-2983 See JOURNAL OF THE INSTITUTE OF MINE SURVEYORS OF SOUTH AFRICA. 2142
0020-2991 See TECHNICAL BULLETIN - INSTITUTE OF MUNICIPAL ASSESSORS OF ONTARIO. 4690
0020-3076 See PETROLEUM REVIEW (LONDON. 1978). 4273
0020-3084 See RIKA GAKU KENKYUSHO HOKOKU. 4420
0020-3106 See KOSHU EISEI KENKYU. 4788
0020-3122 See TRANSPORT ENGINEER, THE. 1999
0020-3157 See ANNALS OF THE INSTITUTE OF STATISTICAL MATHEMATICS. 3542

0020-3203 See JOURNAL OF THE INSTITUTE OF WOOD SCIENCE. 2402
0020-3254 See JOURNAL OF THE INSTITUTION OF CHEMISTS, CALCUTTA. 983
0020-3270 See PROCEEDINGS OF THE INSTITUTION OF ELECTRICAL ENGINEERS. 2077
0020-3343 See BULLETIN OF THE INSTITUTION OF ENGINEERS (INDIA). 2037
0020-3351 See JOURNAL OF THE INSTITUTION OF ENGINEERS. INDIA. PART CH: CHEMICAL ENGINEERING DIVISION. 2014
0020-3386 See JOURNAL OF THE INSTITUTION OF ENGINEERS (INDIA). COMPUTER ENGINEERING DIVISION. 1230
0020-3386 See JOURNAL OF THE INSTITUTION OF ENGINEERS (INDIA). 2070
0020-3408 See JOURNAL OF THE INSTITUTION OF ENGINEERS (INDIA). MECHANICAL ENGINEERING DIVISION. 2118
0020-3483 See PROCEEDINGS OF THE INSTITUTION OF MECHANICAL ENGINEERS. 2125
0020-3572 See INSTITUTIONAL DISTRIBUTION. 2344
0020-3580 See INSTITUTIONAL INVESTOR (U.S. ED.). 901
0020-3637 See BOLETIN DEL INSTITUTO AMERICANO DE ESTUDIOS VASCOS. 3269
0020-3645 See ANALES DEL INSTITUTO BARRAQUER. 3872
0020-370X See NOTICIAS CULTURALES. 2851
0020-3726 See BOLETIM DO INSTITUTO DE ANGOLA. 2638
0020-3785 See ARCHIVOS DEL INSTITUTO DE CARDIOLOGIA DE MEXICO. 3699
0020-3815 See REVISTA DEL INSTITUTO DE CULTURA PUERTORRIQUENA. 2758
0020-384X See BOLETIN DEL INSTITUTO DE ESTUDIOS ASTURIANOS. 2679
0020-3874 See REVISTA DO INSTITUTO DE ESTUDOS BRASILEIROS. 5216
0020-3939 See BOLETIN / SERVICIO NACIONAL DE GEOLOGIA Y MINERIA, CHILE. 1368
0020-417X See BOLETIN DEL INSTITUTO OCEANOGRAFICO DE LA UNIVERSIDAD DE ORIENTE. 1447
0020-4277 See INSTRUCTIONAL SCIENCE. 1896
0020-4331 See INSTRUMENTALIST, THE. 4122
0020-4366 See INSTRUMENTATION. 2065
0020-4412 See INSTRUMENTS AND EXPERIMENTAL TECHNIQUES (NEW YORK). 4405
0020-4536 See INSULA (MADRID). 417
0020-4587 See INSURANCE ADVOCATE. 2882
0020-4595 See CANADIAN INSURANCE. 2877
0020-4668 See INSURANCE ECONOMICS SURVEYS. 2883
0020-4714 See INSURANCE JOURNAL. 2883
0020-4803 See INSURANCE RECORD (DALLAS, TEX.), THE. 2884
0020-4846 See INSURANCEWEEK. 2884
0020-4900 See INTELLIGENCE DIGEST. 1496
0020-4919 See INTENSIVE AGRICULTURE. 96
0020-4994 See REVISTA INTERAMERICANA DE BIBLIOGRAFIA (1972). 423
0020-5079 See INTER-PARLIAMENTARY BULLETIN. 4524
0020-5168 See INTERAVIA (ENGLISH ED.). 24
0020-5214 See INTERCERAM. 2591
0020-5249 See INTERCOLLEGIATE REVIEW, THE. 1831
0020-5346 See INTER ECONOMICS. 1636
0020-5419 See INTERFACE (BETHESDA). 1189
0020-5508 See INTERIOR DESIGN (NEW YORK, N.Y.). 2901
0020-5613 See INTERMEDIAIRE DES CHERCHEURS ET CURIEUX, L'. 1926
0020-5621 See INTERMEDIAIRE DES GENEALOGISTES. 2454
0020-5656 See INTERMOUNTAIN CONTRACTOR. 617
0020-5745 See INTERNAL AUDITOR, THE. 745

0020-5761 See INTERNAL REVENUE BULLETIN. 4732

0020-577X See INTERNASJONAL POLITIKK (OSLO, NORWAY). 4524

0020-580X See INTERNATIONAL ABSTRACTS IN OPERATIONS RESEARCH. 5175

0020-5826 See INTERNATIONAL ACCOUNTANT, THE. 745

0020-5842 See INTERNATIONAL AEROSPACE ABSTRACTS. 41

0020-5850 See INTERNATIONAL AFFAIRS (LONDON). 4524

0020-5877 See INTERNATIONAL AFRICAN BIBLIOGRAPHY. 417

0020-5885 See OFFICIAL BULLETIN OF THE THEATRICAL STAGE EMPLOYEES AND MOVING PICTURE MACHINE OPERATORS OF THE UNITED STATES AND CANADA. 5367

0020-5893 See INTERNATIONAL AND COMPARATIVE LAW QUARTERLY, THE. 3129

0020-5907 See INTERNATIONAL ANESTHESIOLOGY CLINICS. 3683

0020-5915 See INTERNATIONAL ARCHIVES OF ALLERGY AND IMMUNOLOGY. 3672

0020-5974 See IAEI NEWS. 2290

0020-6008 See NEWS - INTERNATIONAL ASSOCIATION OF PERSONNEL IN EMPLOYMENT SECURITY. 1694

0020-6016 See JOURNAL OF THE INTERNATIONAL ASSOCIATION OF PUPIL PERSONNEL WORKERS, THE. 1759

0020-6059 See TRANSNATIONAL ASSOCIATIONS. 4691

0020-6067 See INTERNATIONAL ATOMIC ENERGY AGENCY BULLETIN. 1947

0020-6091 See AUDIOLOGY. 3886

0020-6113 See INTERNATIONAL BANK CREDIT ANALYST, THE. 901

0020-613X See INTERNATIONAL BEHAVIOURAL SCIENTIST. 5204

0020-6172 See INTERNATIONAL BOAT INDUSTRY. 593

0020-6180 See INTERNATIONAL BOOKBINDER / OFFICIAL JOURNAL OF THE INTERNATIONAL BROTHERHOOD OF BOOKBINDERS OF NORTH AMERICA, THE. 4829

0020-6199 See INTERNATIONAL BOTTLER AND PACKER, THE. 4219

0020-6229 See INTERNATIONAL BROADCAST ENGINEER : IBE. 1133

0020-6274 See OSPEDALI ITALIANI-PEDIATRIA (E SPECIALITA CHIRURGICHE). 3907

0020-6318 See INTERNATIONAL CHEMICAL ENGINEERING. 2013

0020-6393 See REVIEW (INTERNATIONAL COMMISSION OF JURISTS (1952-)). 3134

0020-6415 See INTERNATIONAL CONSTRUCTION. 2024

0020-6466 See ICES JOURNAL OF MARINE SCIENCE. 1449

0020-6490 See INTERNATIONAL CURRENCY REVIEW. 792

0020-6512 See INTERNATIONAL DEFENSE REVIEW. 4046

0020-6539 See INTERNATIONAL DENTAL JOURNAL. 1325

0020-6563 See INTERNATIONAL DIGEST OF HEALTH LEGISLATION. 2983

0020-6571 See INTERNATIONAL DRUG THERAPY NEWSLETTER. 4308

0020-6598 See INTERNATIONAL ECONOMIC REVIEW (PHILADELPHIA). 1496

0020-6652 See INTERNATIONAL EXECUTIVE. 4502

0020-6725 See INTERNATIONAL FINANCIAL STATISTICS. 730

0020-6733 See INTERNATIONAL FIRE FIGHTER. 2291

0020-675X See INTERNATIONAL FLYING FARMER. 96

0020-6814 See INTERNATIONAL GEOLOGY REVIEW. 1383

0020-6938 See INTERNATIONAL HYDROGRAPHIC BULLETIN. BULLETIN HYDROGRAPHIQUE INTERNATIONAL. 5534

0020-6946 See INTERNATIONAL HYDROGRAPHIC REVIEW, THE. 1415

0020-6970 See BULLETIN DE L'INSTITUT INTERNATIONAL DU FROID. 2604

0020-6997 See INTERNATIONAL INSURANCE MONITOR. 2884

0020-7004 See INTERNATIONAL INTERTRADE INDEX. 841

0020-7020 See INTERNATIONAL JOURNAL. 2692

0020-7047 See INTERNATIONAL JOURNAL FOR PHILOSOPHY OF RELIGION. 4965

0020-7071 See INTERNATIONAL JOURNAL OF AMERICAN LINGUISTICS. 3287

0020-7101 See INTERNATIONAL JOURNAL OF BIOMEDICAL COMPUTING. 3589

0020-711X See INTERNATIONAL JOURNAL OF BIOCHEMISTRY, THE. 488

0020-7128 See INTERNATIONAL JOURNAL OF BIOMETEOROLOGY. 1426

0020-7136 See INTERNATIONAL JOURNAL OF CANCER. 3818

0020-7144 See INTERNATIONAL JOURNAL OF CLINICAL AND EXPERIMENTAL HYPNOSIS, THE. 2858

0020-7152 See INTERNATIONAL JOURNAL OF COMPARATIVE SOCIOLOGY. 5248

0020-7160 See INTERNATIONAL JOURNAL OF COMPUTER MATHEMATICS. 3509

0020-7179 See INTERNATIONAL JOURNAL OF CONTROL. 5115

0020-7187 See INTERNATIONAL JOURNAL OF EARLY CHILDHOOD. 1753

0020-7209 See INTERNATIONAL JOURNAL OF ELECTRICAL ENGINEERING EDUCATION. 2066

0020-7217 See INTERNATIONAL JOURNAL OF ELECTRONICS THEORETICAL & EXPERIMENTAL. 2066

0020-7225 See INTERNATIONAL JOURNAL OF ENGINEERING SCIENCE. 1980

0020-7233 See INTERNATIONAL JOURNAL OF ENVIRONMENTAL STUDIES. SECTION A, ENVIRONMENTAL STUDIES, THE. 2195

0020-7233 See INTERNATIONAL JOURNAL OF ENVIRONMENTAL STUDIES. SECTION B, ENVIRONMENTAL SCIENCE AND TECHNOLOGY, THE. 2175

0020-7233 See INTERNATIONAL JOURNAL OF ENVIRONMENTAL STUDIES, THE. 2174

0020-725X See INTERNATIONAL JOURNAL OF FERTILITY. 581

0020-7276 See INTERNATIONAL JOURNAL OF GAME THEORY. 3509

0020-7284 See INTERNATIONAL JOURNAL OF GROUP PSYCHOTHERAPY, THE. 3927

0020-7292 See INTERNATIONAL JOURNAL OF GYNAECOLOGY AND OBSTETRICS. 3762

0020-7314 See INTERNATIONAL JOURNAL OF HEALTH SERVICES. 4785

0020-7322 See INTERNATIONAL JOURNAL OF INSECT MORPHOLOGY & EMBRYOLOGY. 5610

0020-7373 See INTERNATIONAL JOURNAL OF MAN-MACHINE STUDIES. 1251

0020-739X See INTERNATIONAL JOURNAL OF MATHEMATICAL EDUCATION IN SCIENCE AND TECHNOLOGY. 1754

0020-7403 See INTERNATIONAL JOURNAL OF MECHANICAL SCIENCES. 2116

0020-7411 See INTERNATIONAL JOURNAL OF MENTAL HEALTH. 3927

0020-7438 See INTERNATIONAL JOURNAL OF MIDDLE EAST STUDIES. 2768

0020-7446 See INTERNATIONAL JOURNAL OF NEUROLOGY. 3834

0020-7454 See INTERNATIONAL JOURNAL OF NEUROSCIENCE. 3834

0020-7462 See INTERNATIONAL JOURNAL OF NON-LINEAR MECHANICS. 4428

0020-7489 See INTERNATIONAL JOURNAL OF NURSING STUDIES. 3857

0020-7500 See INTERNATIONAL JOURNAL OF ORTHODONTICS. 1325

0020-7543 See INTERNATIONAL JOURNAL OF PRODUCTION RESEARCH. 871

0020-7578 See INTERNATIONAL JOURNAL OF PSYCHO-ANALYSIS, THE. 4591

0020-7594 See INTERNATIONAL JOURNAL OF PSYCHOLOGY. 4591

0020-7608 See INTERNATIONAL JOURNAL OF QUANTUM CHEMISTRY. 978

0020-7640 See INTERNATIONAL JOURNAL OF SOCIAL PSYCHIATRY, THE. 3927

0020-7659 See INTERNATIONAL JOURNAL OF SOCIOLOGY. 5248

0020-7667 See INTERNATIONAL JOURNAL OF SOCIOLOGY OF THE FAMILY. 2281

0020-7683 See INTERNATIONAL JOURNAL OF SOLIDS AND STRUCTURES. 2025

0020-7691 See INTERNATIONAL JOURNAL OF SPELEOLOGY. 1407

0020-7713 See INTERNATIONAL JOURNAL OF SYSTEMATIC BACTERIOLOGY. 564

0020-7721 See INTERNATIONAL JOURNAL OF SYSTEMS SCIENCE. 2116

0020-773X See INTERNATIONAL JOURNAL OF THE ADDICTIONS. 1345

0020-7748 See INTERNATIONAL JOURNAL OF THEORETICAL PHYSICS. 4406

0020-7756 See INTERNATIONAL LABOUR DOCUMENTATION. 1534

0020-7780 See INTERNATIONAL LABOUR REVIEW. 1680

0020-7810 See INTERNATIONAL LAWYER, THE. 3130

0020-7829 See INTERNATIONAL LEGAL MATERIALS. 3130

0020-7837 See INTERNATIONAL INFORMATION & LIBRARY REVIEW, THE. 3218

0020-7853 See INTERNATIONAL LIGHTING REVIEW. 2067

0020-7888 See INTERNATIONAL MANAGEMENT (LAUSANNE, SWITZERLAND). 872

0020-7918 See INTERNATIONAL MARINE SCIENCE NEWSLETTER. 555

0020-7950 See INTERNATIONAL MEDIEVAL BIBLIOGRAPHY. 3458

0020-7985 See INTERNATIONAL MIGRATION (GENEVA, SWITZERLAND). 1919

0020-8027 See STAFF PAPERS - INTERNATIONAL MONETARY FUND. 812

0020-8051 See INTERNATIONAL MUSICIAN. 4123

0020-8124 See INTERNATIONAL NURSING INDEX. 3660

0020-8132 See INTERNATIONAL NURSING REVIEW (LONDON, ENGLAND). 3857

0020-8159 See INTERNATIONAL OPERATING ENGINEER, THE. 1680

0020-8167 See INTERNATIONAL OPHTHALMOLOGY CLINICS. 3875

0020-8183 See INTERNATIONAL ORGANIZATION. 4525

0020-8191 See INTERNATIONAL PAPER BOARD INDUSTRY. 4234

0020-8256 See INTERNATIONAL PEST CONTROL. 4245

0020-8264 See INTERNATIONAL PHARMACEUTICAL ABSTRACTS. 4334

0020-8299 See INTERNATIONAL PHOTOGRAPHER. 4371

0020-8345 See INTERNATIONAL POLITICAL SCIENCE ABSTRACTS. 4502

0020-840X See INTERNATIONAL PROBLEMS. 4525

0020-8442 See RAIL INTERNATIONAL. 5434

0020-8477 See INTERNATIONAL REHABILITATION REVIEW. 4389

0020-8507 See INTERNATIONAL REPORTS. 792

0020-8523 See INTERNATIONAL REVIEW OF ADMINISTRATIVE SCIENCES. 4657

0020-8566 See INTERNATIONAL REVIEW OF EDUCATION. 1754

0020-8574 See INTERNATIONAL REVIEW OF HISTORY AND POLITICAL SCIENCE. 4525

0020-8582 See INTERNATIONAL REVIEW OF MISSIONS. 4966

0020-8590 See INTERNATIONAL REVIEW OF SOCIAL HISTORY. 5248

0020-8604 See INTERNATIONAL REVIEW OF THE RED CROSS. 5290

0020-8671 See BULLETIN OF THE INTERNATIONAL SEISMOLOGICAL CENTRE. 1403

0020-868X See INTERNATIONAL SHIPBUILDING PROGRESS. 4177

0020-8701 See INTERNATIONAL SOCIAL SCIENCE JOURNAL. 5204

0020-871X See INTERNATIONAL SOCIAL SECURITY REVIEW (ENGLISH EDITION). 5290

0020-8728 See INTERNATIONAL SOCIAL WORK. 5290

0020-8736 See INTERNATIONAL SOCIALISM. SERIES 2. 4477

0020-8752 See QUARTERLY / INTERNATIONAL SOCIETY OF BARRISTERS. 3033

0020-8760 See BULLETIN OF THE INTERNATIONAL SOCIETY OF SOIL SCIENCE. BULLETIN DE L'ASSOCIATION INTERNATIONALE DE LA SCIENCE DU SOL. MITTEILUNGEN DER INTERNATIONALEN BODENKUNDLICHEN GESELLSCHAFT. 165

0020-8817 See INTERNATIONAL STUDIES (SAHIBABAD). 3131

0020-8825 See INTERNATIONAL STUDIES OF MANAGEMENT & ORGANIZATION. 872

0020-8833 See INTERNATIONAL STUDIES QUARTERLY. 4525

0020-8841 See INTERNATIONAL SUGAR JOURNAL. 2345

0020-8868 See INTERNATIONAL SURGERY. 3966

0020-8892 See INTERNATIONAL TEAMSTER : OFFICIAL MAGAZINE, INTERNATIONAL BROTHERHOOD, TEAMSTERS, CHAUFFEURS, WAREHOUSEMEN & HELPERS OF AMERICA, THE. 1680

0020-8914 See INTERNATIONAL TEXTILES. 5352

0020-8922 See INTERNATIONAL TEXTILES INTERIOR. 5353

0020-8957 See INTERNATIONAL TRADE FORUM. 926

0020-8981 See INTERNATIONAL TRADE REVIEW. 842

0020-899X See INTERNATIONAL TRADE UNION NEWS. 1680

0020-9007 See ITF JOURNAL. 1681

0020-904X See BULLETIN - INTERNATIONAL TYPOGRAPHICAL UNION, THE. 4564

0020-9058 See IUCN BULLETIN. 2196

0020-9112 See INTERNATIONAL WILDLIFE. 2195

0020-9120 See INTERNATIONAL WOMEN'S NEWS JOURNAL OF THE INTERNATIONAL ALLIANCE OF WOMEN, INCORPORATING LE DROIT DES FEMMES. 5559

0020-9155 See INTERNATIONAL ZOO-NEWS. 5586

0020-918X See INTERNATIONALE BIBLIOGRAPHIE DER REZENSIONEN WISSENSCHAFTLICHER LITERATUR. 3357

0020-9252 See INTERNATIONALE KIRCHLICHE ZEITSCHRIFT. 4966

0020-9309 See INTERNATIONALE REVUE DER GESAMTEN HYDROBIOLOGIE. 555

0020-9317 See INTERNATIONALE SPECTATOR. 4478

0020-9341 See INTERNATIONALE TRANSPORT ZEITSCHRIFT. 5384

0020-9384 See GAS WARME INTERNATIONAL. 4258

0020-9422 See INTERNATIONALER HOLZMARKT. 2402

0020-9430 See INTERNATIONALES AFRIKA-FORUM. 4526

0020-9449 See INTERNATIONALES ASIEN FORUM. 5204

0020-9465 See WELTGESCHEHEN. 4538

0020-9481 See INTENATIONALES GEWERBEARCHIV. 683

0020-9503 See INTERNATIONALES RECHT UND DIPLOMATIE. 4526

0020-9511 See INTERNATIONALES VERKEHRSWESEN. 5384

0020-952X See INTERNATIONELLA STUDIER. 4526

0020-9538 See INTERNI. 2901

0020-9546 See INTERNIST (SAN FRANCISCO, CALIF.), THE. 3590

0020-9554 See INTERNIST (BERLIN), DER. 3798

0020-9570 See INTERNISTISCHE PRAXIS. 3590

0020-9635 See INTERPRETATION (THE HAGUE). 4478

0020-9643 See INTERPRETATION (RICHMOND). 4966

0020-9651 See INTERPRETER (DURHAM, N.C.), THE. 2885

0020-9678 See INTERPRETER (EVANSTON, ILL.), THE. 5061

0020-9864 See INTREPID. 3397

0020-9872 See INUKTITUT (ENGLISH AND INUIT EDITION). 2264

0020-9910 See INVENTIONES MATHEMATICAE. 3510

0020-9996 See INVESTIGATIVE RADIOLOGY. 3942

0021-0013 See INVESTIGATOR. 2669

0021-003X See INVESTING, LICENSING AND TRADING CONDITIONS ABROAD. 684

0021-0080 See INVESTMENT DEALERS' DIGEST, THE. 793

0021-0110 See INVESTMENT QUALITY TRENDS. 903

0021-0250 See INWARD LIGHT. 4966

0021-0285 See INZENERNO-FIZICESKIJ ZURNAL. 1981

0021-0331 See IO. 238

0021-0439 See IOWA ARCHITECT. 301

0021-0455 See IOWA BIRD LIFE. 5617

0021-0463 See BUSINESS & INDUSTRY. 645

0021-0471 See IOWA CONSERVATIONIST. 2195

0021-0498 See IOWA DENTAL JOURNAL, THE. 1325

0021-051X See IOWA FARM BUREAU SPOKESMAN. 97

0021-0552 See IOWA LAW REVIEW. 2984

0021-0595 See IOWA MUNICIPALITIES. 4657

0021-0617 See IOWA PTA BULLETIN. 1865

0021-065X See IOWA REVIEW, THE. 3397

0021-0668 See IOWA SCHOOL BOARD DIALOGUE, THE. 1865

0021-0676 See IOWA SCIENCE TEACHERS' JOURNAL. 5116

0021-0722 See IOWAN, THE. 2536

0021-0757 See ENERGIAGAZDALKODAS. 1938

0021-0773 See IQBAL REVIEW. 3397

0021-0838 See IRANIAN JOURNAL OF PLANT PATHOLOGY. 514

0021-0862 See IRANIAN STUDIES. 2768

0021-0870 See IRANICA ANTIQUA. 270

0021-0889 See IRAQ. 2768

0021-0943 See IRELAND OF THE WELCOMES. 2518

0021-0951 See IRELAND'S OWN. 5803

0021-0978 See IRENIKON. 4966

0021-1052 See IRISH ASTRONOMICAL JOURNAL, THE. 396

0021-1060 See IRISH BANKING REVIEW, THE. 793

0021-1133 See JOURNAL OF THE IRISH DENTAL ASSOCIATION, THE. 1328

0021-1192 See IRISH FORESTRY. 2385

0021-1214 See IRISH HISTORICAL STUDIES. 2692

0578-7483 See IRISH JOURNAL OF AGRICULTURAL AND FOOD RESEARCH. 97

0021-1257 See IRISH JOURNAL OF EDUCATION, THE. 1755

0021-1265 See IRISH JOURNAL OF MEDICAL SCIENCE. 3590

0021-1273 See IRISH JURIST, THE. 2985

0021-1281 See IRISH LAW TIMES AND SOLICITORS' JOURNAL, THE. 2985

0021-1311 See IRISH NATURALISTS' JOURNAL, THE. 4166

0021-1389 See IRISH SWORD, THE. 2693

0021-1400 See IRISH THEOLOGICAL QUARTERLY. 4966

0021-1419 See IRISH TRAVEL TRADE NEWS. 5481

0021-1427 See IRISH UNIVERSITY REVIEW. 3344

0021-1478 See IRODALOMTORTENET (BUDAPEST. 1912). 3397

0021-1486 See IRODALOMTORTENETI KOZLEMENYEK. 3458

0021-1559 See IRON AND STEEL ENGINEER. 4004

0021-1575 See TETSU TO HAGANE. 4021

0021-1583 See TRANSACTIONS OF THE IRON AND STEEL INSTITUTE OF JAPAN. 4022

0021-163X See IRONWORKER, THE. 2025

0021-1680 See IRRIGAZIONE, L'. 97

0021-1699 See IRYO. 3590

0021-1753 See ISIS. 5116

0021-1761 See ISKRA (GRAND FORKS). 4966

0021-177X See ISKUSSTVO. 353

0021-1818 See ISLAM (BERLIN), DER. 5043

0021-1826 See ISLAM AND THE MODERN AGE. 5042

0021-1834 See ISLAMIC CULTURE. 5043

0021-1842 See ISLAMIC QUARTERLY, THE. 4966

0021-1907 See ISOTOPE AND RADIATION RESEARCH. 4435

0021-1915 See ISOTOPENPRAXIS. 4406

0021-1982 See YARHON HA-STATISTI LE-YISRAEL, HA-. 5346

0021-2059 See ISRAEL EXPLORATION JOURNAL. 270

0021-2083 See ISRAEL HORIZONS. 5048

0021-213X See ISRAEL JOURNAL OF BOTANY. 514

0021-2148 See ISRAEL JOURNAL OF CHEMISTRY. 978

0021-2164 See ISRAEL JOURNAL OF EARTH SCIENCES. 1383

0021-2172 See ISRAEL JOURNAL OF MATHEMATICS. 3510

0021-2180 See ISRAEL JOURNAL OF MEDICAL SCIENCES. 3590

0021-2210 See ISRAEL JOURNAL OF ZOOLOGY. 5587

0021-2237 See ISRAEL LAW REVIEW. 2985

0021-2288 See ISRAEL NUMISMATIC JOURNAL. 2781

0021-2423 See ISTINA. 4966

0021-2520 See ATTI UFFICIALI / ISTITUTO NAZIONALE DELLA PREVIDENZA SOCIALE. 2874

0021-2547 See BOLLETTINO DELL'INSTITUTO SIEROTERAPICO MILANESE. 3667

0021-2571 See ANNALI DELL'ISTITUTO SUPERIORE DI SANITA. 4765

0021-261X See ISTMO. 5249

0021-2636 See ISTORICHESKI PREGLED. 2693

0021-2644 See ISTORIJSKI GLASNIK. 2620

0021-275X See ITALIA AGRICOLA, L'. 98

0021-2776 See ITALIA FORESTALE E MONTANA. 1497

0021-2784 See ITALIA GRAFICA, L'. 4566

0021-2849 See ITALIA SCACCHISTICA, L'. 5329

0021-2881 See ITALIAN BOOKS AND PERIODICALS. 3458

0021-2881 See ITALIA CHE SCRIVE, L'. 3397

0021-2911 See ITALIAN ECONOMIC SURVEY. 1568

0021-292X See ITALIAN GENERAL REVIEW OF DERMATOLOGY. 3721

0021-2938 See ITALIAN JOURNAL OF BIOCHEMISTRY. 488

0021-2954 See ITALIAN QUARTERLY. 2693

0021-2997 See ITALIAN TRADE TOPICS. 842

0021-3020 See ITALICA (NEW YORK, N.Y.). 3288

0021-3039 See ITALIMUSE ITALIC NEWS. 380

0021-3063 See ITALY. 2518

0021-3098 See ITALY CANADA TRADE. 1636

0021-3128 See INFORMAZIONI DOC. 5432

0021-3136 See BOLLETTINO MENSILE DI STATISTICA - ISTITUTO CENTRALE DI STATISTICA. 5323
0021-3225 See IUGOSLAVICA PHYSIOLOGICA ET PHARMOCOLOGICA ACTA. 581
0021-3241 See IVRA. 2985
0021-325X See IUS CANONICUM. 2985
0021-3276 See IVY LEAF (CHICAGO). 1102
0021-3292 See IYO DENSHI TO SEITAI KOGAKU. 3693
0021-3306 See YWN. 4365
0021-3314 See OUTDOOR AMERICA (1971). 4170
0021-3381 See IZRAZ. 3398
0021-3411 See IZVESTIIA VYSSHIKH UCHEBNYKH ZAVEDENII. FIZIKA / MINISTERSTVO VYSSHEGO OBRAZOVANIIA SSSR. 4407
0021-342X See IZVESTIIA TIMIRIAZEVSKOI SELSKOKHOZIAISTVENNOI AKADEMII. 98
0021-3438 See IZVESTIJA VYSSIKH UCEBNYH ZAVEDENIJ. CVETNAJA METALLURGIJA. 4005
0021-3446 See IZVESTIJA VYSSIH UCEBNYH ZAVEDENIJ. MATEMATIKA. 3510
0021-3454 See IZVESTIJA VYSSIH UCEBNYH ZAVEDENIJ. PRIBOROSTROENIE. 4124
0021-3462 See IZVESTIJA VYSSIH UCEBNYH ZAVEDENIJ. RADIOFIZIKA. 1114
0021-3470 See IZVESTIJA VYSSIH UCEBNYH ZAVEDENIJ. RADIOELEKTRONIKA. 2067
0021-3489 See IZVESTIJA VYSSIH UCEBNYH ZAVEDENIJ. TEHNOLOGIJA LEGKOJ PROMYSLENNOSTI. 3482
0021-3497 See IZVESTIJA VYSSIH UCEBNYH ZAVEDENIJ. TEHNOLOGIJA TEKSTILNOJ PROMYSLENNOSTI. 5353
0021-3551 See JARQ. JAPAN AGRICULTURAL RESEARCH QUARTERLY. 98
0021-3624 See JEI. JOURNAL OF ECONOMIC ISSUES. 1592
0021-3640 See JETP LETTERS. 4408
0021-3667 See JOURNAL OF GENERAL EDUCATION (UNIVERSITY PARK, PA.), THE. 1757
0021-3721 See JNKVV RESEARCH JOURNAL. 98
0021-3772 See JTA DAILY NEWS BULLETIN. 5050
0021-387X See JACOBSEN'S FATS AND OILS BULLETIN. 2345
0021-3985 See JAHRBUCH DER ABSATZ- UND VERBRAUCHSFORSCHUNG. 1568
0021-3993 See JAHRBUCH FUER INTERNATIONALES RECHT. 3131
0021-4019 See JAHRBUCHER FUER GESCHICHTE OSTEUROPAS. 2694
0021-4027 See JAHRBUCHER FUER NATIONALOKONOMIE UND STATISTIK. 1497
0021-4124 See JAMAICA JOURNAL. 2536
0021-4140 See JAMAICAN NURSE. 3858
0021-4183 See JAMES JOYCE QUARTERLY. 3345
0021-4221 See JANATA. 4478
0021-4264 See JANUS (AMSTERDAM). 3591
0021-4353 See JAPAN CHRISTIAN ACTIVITY NEWS. 4967
0021-437X See TONYOBYO. 3733
0021-4396 See IMONO. 977
0021-440X See JAPAN HARVEST. 4967
0021-4450 See JAPAN INTERPRETER. 5205
0021-4469 See JAPAN LABOR BULLETIN. 1681
0021-4493 See NIPPON ISHIKAI ZASSHI. JOURNAL OF THE JAPAN MEDICAL ASSOCIATION. 3622
0021-4523 See JAPAN METAL BULLETIN. AIR MAIL ED. 4005
0021-4531 See JAPAN MISSIONARY BULLETIN, THE. 4967
0021-4582 See JAPAN PLASTICS AGE. 4455
0021-4590 See JAPAN QUARTERLY. 2654
0021-4620 See NIHON KAIKU SUISAN KENKYUJO KENKYU. 2309
0021-4639 See GESUIDO KYOKAI SHI. 2230
0021-4647 See JAPAN SHIPBUILDING & MARINE ENGINEERING. 4177
0021-4663 See JOURNAL OF THE JAPAN SOCIETY FOR AERONAUTICAL AND SPACE SCIENCES. 26
0021-4671 See NIHON GAN CHIRYO GAKKAI SHI. 3821
0021-468X See DOBOKU GAKKAI SHI. 2022
0021-4736 See JAPAN STOCK JOURNAL, THE. 904
0021-4795 See MOKUZAI GAKKAISHI. 2403
0021-4809 See NAIKA HOKAN. 3800
0021-4825 See SHI - NIHON GANSEKI, KOBUTSU, KOSHOGAKKAI. JOURNAL OF THE JAPANESE ASSOCIATION OF MINERALOGISTS, PETROLOGISTS AND ECONOMIC GEOLOGISTS. 1360
0021-4833 See ECONOMIC SURVEY OF JAPAN. 1558
0021-4841 See JAPANESE ECONOMIC STUDIES. 1569
0021-485X See NIHON RINGAKKAI SHI. 2389
0021-4876 See NIPPON KINZOKU GAKKAISHI. 4013
0021-4884 See ARERUGI. 3666
0021-4892 See MASUI. 3683
0021-4914 See NIHON OYO DOBUTSU KONCHU GAKKAISHI. 5612
0021-4930 See NIHON SAIKINGAKU ZASSHI. 467
0021-4949 See GAN NO RINSHO. 3817
0021-499X See NIPPON HIFUKA GAKKAI ZASSHI. 3722
0021-5007 See NIHON SEITAI GAKKAI SHI. 2219
0021-5015 See KYOIKU SHINRIGAKU KENKYU. 4602
0021-5082 See NIPPON EISEIGAKU ZASSHI. 4794
0021-5090 See GYORUIGAKU ZASSHI. 2304
0021-5104 See RIKUSUIGAKU ZASSHI. 472
0021-5112 See JAPANESE JOURNAL OF MEDICAL SCIENCE & BIOLOGY. 3591
0021-5147 See EIYO-GAKU ZASSHI. 4190
0021-5155 See JAPANESE JOURNAL OF OPHTHALMOLOGY. 3875
0021-5171 See KISEICHUGAKU ZASSHI. 462
0021-5198 See JAPANESE JOURNAL OF PHARMACOLOGY. 4309
0021-521X See JAPANESE JOURNAL OF PHYSIOLOGY, THE. 581
0021-5228 See KEISEI GEKA. 3969
0021-5236 See SHINRIGAKU KENKYU. 4618
0021-5260 See NETTAI NOGYO. 111
0021-5287 See NIPPON HINYOKIKA GAKKAI ZASSHI. 3992
0021-5295 See JOURNAL OF VETERINARY MEDICAL SCIENCE. 5514
0021-5325 See NIPPON SEIKEIGEKAGAKKAI ZASSHI. 3883
0021-5333 See JAPANESE PATENTS ABSTRACTS. 1305
0021-5368 See JAPANESE PSYCHOLOGICAL RESEARCH. 4592
0021-5384 See NIHON NAIKA GAKKAI ZASSHI. 3800
0021-5392 See NIHON SUISAN GAKKAI SHI. 2309
0021-5406 See DENPUN KAGAKU. 2333
0021-5414 See SHAKAIGAKU HYORON. 5258
0021-5457 See JARDIN DES MODES. 1085
0021-5481 See JARDINS DE FRANCE PARIS. 2421
0021-5511 See JARMUVEK, MEZOGAZDASAGI GEPEK. 2117
0021-5597 See JAZYKOVEDNY CASOPIS. 3289
0021-5600 See MAGAZYN MUZYCZNY : MM. 4129
0021-5635 See JAZZ FORUM. 4124
0021-566X See OK AGE TENDRE. 1067
0021-566X See JAZZ MAGAZINE (PARIS). 4125
0021-5686 See JAZZ-PODIUM. 4125
0021-5724 See JAZZFREUND (MENDEN), DER. 4125
0021-5872 See JENGA : MAGAZINE OF THE NATIONAL DEVELOPMENT CORPORATION. 1613
0021-5880 See JEOPARDY (BELLINGHAM, WASH.). 3399
0021-5953 See JERSEY JOURNAL. 213
0021-5961 See JERSEY PUBLISHER. 4816
0021-5996 See JET. 2265
0021-6003 See JET CARGO NEWS. 5385
0021-6089 See JEUNE AFRIQUE (PARIS, FRANCE : 1980). 4526
0021-6127 See QUEBEC SCIENCE. 5143
0021-6208 See JEUNESSE ET ORGUE. 4125
0021-6305 See JEWISH AFFAIRS (NEW YORK, N.Y.). 2654
0021-633X See JEWISH CHRONICLE (LONDON, ENGLAND : 1845). 5048
0021-6380 See JEWISH CURRENT EVENTS (ELMONT, N.Y.). 5048
0021-6399 See JEWISH CURRENTS. 5048
0021-6429 See JEWISH EDUCATION. 5049
0021-6437 See JEWISH EXPONENT, THE. 5049
0021-6453 See JEWISH FRONTIER. 2265
0021-6534 See JEWISH JOURNAL OF SOCIOLOGY, THE. 5249
0021-6550 See JEWISH LEDGER (ROCHESTER NY). 5717
0021-6615 See JEWISH OBSERVER, THE. 5049
0021-6674 See JEWISH PRESS (BROOKLYN), THE. 2265
0021-6682 See JEWISH QUARTERLY REVIEW (PHILADELPHIA, PA.). 5049
0021-6704 See JEWISH SOCIAL STUDIES. 5049
0021-6712 See JEWISH SOCIAL WORK FORUM, THE. 5291
0021-6720 See JEWISH SPECTATOR. 5049
0021-6739 See JEWISH STANDARD (TORONTO). 5049
0021-6747 See JEWISH STANDARD (JERSEY CITY, N.J.). 2265
0021-6763 See JTA WEEKLY NEWS DIGEST. 2266
0021-678X See JEWISH TRANSCRIPT, THE. 2265
0021-681X See JEWISH VEGETARIAN. 2265
0021-6828 See JEWISH VOICE, THE. 5049
0021-6860 See JEWISH WEEKLY NEWS. 2265
0021-6879 See JEWISH WESTERN BULLETIN. 5787
0021-6925 See JEZIK : CASOPIS ZA KULTURU HRVATSKOGA KNJIZEVNOG JEZIKA. 3399
0021-6933 See JEZIK IN SLOVSTVO. 3289
0021-6941 See JEZYK POLSKI (KRAKOW 1919). 3289
0021-695X See JICARILLA CHIEFTAIN. 2265
0021-6968 See JIKEIKAI MEDICAL JOURNAL. 3592
0021-7050 See JOBBER NEWS (TORONTO). 5417
0021-7069 See JOBBER TOPICS. 5417
0021-7204 See JOHN LINER LETTER, THE. 2885
0021-7255 See JOHNS HOPKINS MAGAZINE. 1102
0021-728X See JOHNSONIAN NEWS LETTER. 3399
0021-7298 See JOHO KANRI. 3219
0021-731X See JOINT ACQUISITIONS LIST OF AFRICANA. 418
0021-7441 See JORDBRUKSEKONOMISKA MEDDELANDEN: JEM. 98
0021-7468 See JORDEMODERN. 3763
0021-7557 See JORNAL DE PEDIATRIA. 3904
0021-7603 See JOSEPHITE HARVEST, THE. 4967
0021-762X See JOURNAL ASIATIQUE. 3289
0021-7646 See JOURNAL BELGE DE RADIOLOGIE (1924). 3942
0021-7670 See JOURNAL D' ANALYSE MATHEMATIQUE (JERUSALEM). 3511
0021-7689 See JOURNAL DE CHIMIE PHYSIQUE ET DE PHYSICO-CHIMIE BIOLOGIQUE. 1053
0021-7697 See JOURNAL DE CHIRURGIE. 3966
0021-7794 See JOURNAL DE LA PAIX. 4478
0021-7824 See JOURNAL DE MATHEMATIQUES PURES ET APPLIQUEES. 3511

0021-7883 *See* JOURNAL DE MEDECINE DE LYON. **3592**

0021-7905 *See* JOURNAL DE MEDECINE DE STRASBOURG. **3592**

0021-7948 See JOURNAL OF PHYSIOLOGY, PARIS. **583**

0021-8065 *See* JOURNAL DES INGENIEURS (BRUSSELS, BELGIUM : 1984). **1981**

0021-8073 *See* JOURNAL DES INSTITUTEURS ET DES INSTITUTRICES. **1865**

0021-8103 *See* JOURNAL DES SAVANTS. **4478**

0021-8170 *See* JOURNAL DU DROIT INTERNATIONAL. **3131**

0021-8197 *See* JOURNAL DU TEXTILE 1964. **5353**

0021-8235 *See* JOURNAL FOR ANTHROPOSOPHY. **4967**

0021-8251 *See* JOURNAL FOR RESEARCH IN MATHEMATICS EDUCATION. **3511**

0021-8286 *See* JOURNAL FOR THE HISTORY OF ASTRONOMY. **396**

0021-8294 *See* JOURNAL FOR THE SCIENTIFIC STUDY OF RELIGION. **4967**

0021-8308 *See* JOURNAL FOR THE THEORY OF SOCIAL BEHAVIOUR. **4593**

0021-8359 *See* JOURNAL FUER HIRNFORSCHUNG. **3834**

0021-8375 *See* JOURNAL FUER ORNITHOLOGIE. **5618**

0021-8383 See JOURNAL FUER PRAKTISCHE CHEMIE, CHEMIKER-ZEITUNG. **979**

0021-843X *See* JOURNAL OF ABNORMAL PSYCHOLOGY (1965). **4593**

0021-8448 *See* JOURNAL OF ACCOUNTANCY. **746**

0021-8456 *See* JOURNAL OF ACCOUNTING RESEARCH. **746**

0021-8464 *See* JOURNAL OF ADHESION, THE. **1053**

0021-8480 *See* JOURNAL OF ADVENTIST EDUCATION, THE. **1897**

0021-8499 *See* JOURNAL OF ADVERTISING RESEARCH. **761**

0021-8502 *See* JOURNAL OF AEROSOL SCIENCE. **1053**

0021-8510 *See* JOURNAL OF AESTHETIC EDUCATION, THE. **2848**

0021-8529 *See* JOURNAL OF AESTHETICS AND ART CRITICISM, THE. **354**

0021-8537 *See* JOURNAL OF AFRICAN HISTORY. **2640**

0021-8553 *See* JOURNAL OF AFRICAN LAW. **2986**

0021-8561 *See* JOURNAL OF AGRICULTURAL AND FOOD CHEMISTRY. **99**

0021-857X *See* JOURNAL OF AGRICULTURAL ECONOMICS. **99**

0021-8588 *See* NOGYO KISHO. **1432**

0021-8596 *See* JOURNAL OF AGRICULTURAL SCIENCE, THE. **99**

0021-8618 *See* JOURNAL OF AGRICULTURE (SOUTH PERTH). **100**

0021-8634 *See* JOURNAL OF AGRICULTURAL ENGINEERING RESEARCH. **1981**

0021-8642 *See* JOURNAL OF AIR LAW AND COMMERCE, THE. **2987**

0021-8650 *See* JOURNAL OF AIR TRAFFIC CONTROL, THE. **25**

0021-8669 *See* JOURNAL OF AIRCRAFT. **26**

0021-8693 *See* JOURNAL OF ALGEBRA. **3511**

0021-8715 *See* JOURNAL OF AMERICAN FOLKLORE. **2321**

0021-8723 *See* JOURNAL OF AMERICAN HISTORY, THE. **2740**

0021-8731 *See* JOURNAL OF AMERICAN INDIAN EDUCATION. **1756**

0021-874X *See* JOURNAL OF AMERICAN INSURANCE. **2885**

0021-8758 *See* JOURNAL OF AMERICAN STUDIES. **2740**

0021-8766 See JOURNAL OF ANALYTICAL CHEMISTRY (NEW YORK, N.Y.). **1016**

0021-8774 *See* JOURNAL OF ANALYTICAL PSYCHOLOGY. **4593**

0021-8782 *See* JOURNAL OF ANATOMY. **3679**

0021-8790 *See* JOURNAL OF ANIMAL ECOLOGY, THE. **5587**

0021-8804 *See* JOURNAL OF ANIMAL MORPHOLOGY AND PHYSIOLOGY, THE. **5587**

0021-8812 *See* JOURNAL OF ANIMAL SCIENCE. **5513**

0021-8820 *See* JOURNAL OF ANTIBIOTICS (NIHON KOSEIBUSSHITSU GAKUJUTSU KYOGIKAI : 1968). **4310**

0021-8839 *See* JOURNAL OF APICULTURAL RESEARCH. **5587**

0021-8855 *See* JOURNAL OF APPLIED BEHAVIOR ANALYSIS. **4593**

0021-8863 *See* JOURNAL OF APPLIED BEHAVIORAL SCIENCE, THE. **5205**

0021-888X *See* JOURNAL OF APPLIED CHEMISTRY OF THE USSR. **979**

0021-8898 *See* JOURNAL OF APPLIED CRYSTALLOGRAPHY. **1032**

0021-8901 *See* JOURNAL OF APPLIED ECOLOGY, THE. **2217**

0021-891X *See* JOURNAL OF APPLIED ELECTROCHEMISTRY. **1034**

0021-8928 *See* JOURNAL OF APPLIED MATHEMATICS AND MECHANICS. **4428**

0021-8936 *See* JOURNAL OF APPLIED MECHANICS. **2117**

0021-8944 *See* JOURNAL OF APPLIED MECHANICS AND TECHNICAL PHYSICS. **2117**

0021-8960 *See* JOURNAL OF APPLIED NUTRITION, THE. **4192**

0021-8979 *See* JOURNAL OF APPLIED PHYSICS. **4408**

0021-8995 *See* JOURNAL OF APPLIED POLYMER SCIENCE. **2013**

0021-9002 *See* JOURNAL OF APPLIED PROBABILITY. **3511**

0021-9010 *See* JOURNAL OF APPLIED PSYCHOLOGY. **4593**

0021-9029 *See* JOURNAL OF APPLIED SOCIAL PSYCHOLOGY. **4594**

0021-9037 *See* JOURNAL OF APPLIED SPECTROSCOPY. **1016**

0021-9045 *See* JOURNAL OF APPROXIMATION THEORY. **3512**

0021-9053 *See* JOURNAL OF ARIZONA HISTORY, THE. **2740**

0021-907X *See* BIJUTSU KENKYU. THE JOURNAL OF ART STUDIES. **316**

0021-907X *See* BIJUTSU SHI. **344**

0021-9096 *See* JOURNAL OF ASIAN AND AFRICAN STUDIES (LEIDEN). **2769**

0021-910X *See* JOURNAL OF ASIAN HISTORY. **2655**

0021-9118 *See* JOURNAL OF ASIAN STUDIES, THE. **2655**

0021-9126 *See* ASEA YONGU. **2645**

0021-9142 *See* JOURNAL OF THE ASTRONAUTICAL SCIENCES, THE. **26**

0021-9150 *See* ATHEROSCLEROSIS. **3699**

0021-9169 *See* JOURNAL OF ATMOSPHERIC AND TERRESTRIAL PHYSICS. **1407**

0021-9193 *See* JOURNAL OF BACTERIOLOGY. **564**

0021-9207 *See* JOURNAL OF BAND RESEARCH. **4125**

0021-9231 *See* JOURNAL OF BIBLICAL LITERATURE. **5017**

0021-9231 *See* JOURNAL OF BIBLICAL LITERATURE. **5017**

0021-924X *See* JOURNAL OF BIOCHEMISTRY (TOKYO). **489**

0021-924x *See* JOURNAL OF BIOCHEMISTRY (TOKYO). **489**

0021-9258 *See* JOURNAL OF BIOLOGICAL CHEMISTRY, THE. **489**

0021-9266 *See* JOURNAL OF BIOLOGICAL EDUCATION. **460**

0021-9282 *See* JOURNAL OF BIOLOGICAL SCIENCES, THE. **460**

0021-9290 *See* JOURNAL OF BIOMECHANICS. **582**

0021-9304 *See* JOURNAL OF BIOMEDICAL MATERIALS RESEARCH. **3593**

0021-9320 *See* JOURNAL OF BIOSOCIAL SCIENCE. **5205**

0021-9347 *See* JOURNAL OF BLACK STUDIES. **2266**

0021-9355 *See* JOURNAL OF BONE AND JOINT SURGERY. AMERICAN VOLUME (PRINT ED.). **3882**

0021-9371 *See* JOURNAL OF BRITISH STUDIES, THE. **2694**

0021-9398 *See* JOURNAL OF BUSINESS (CHICAGO, ILL.), THE. **686**

0021-941X *See* JOURNAL OF BUSINESS ADMINISTRATION (VANCOUVER). **686**

0021-9428 *See* JOURNAL OF BUSINESS AND SOCIAL STUDIES, THE. **686**

0021-9436 *See* JOURNAL OF BUSINESS COMMUNICATION (1973). **1114**

0021-9460 *See* JOURNAL OF BUSINESS LAW, THE. **3101**

0021-9487 *See* JOURNAL OF CANADIAN PETROLEUM TECHNOLOGY, THE. **4262**

0021-9495 *See* JOURNAL OF CANADIAN STUDIES. **2740**

0021-9509 *See* JOURNAL OF CARDIOVASCULAR SURGERY. **3966**

0021-9517 *See* JOURNAL OF CATALYSIS. **1053**

0021-9525 *See* JOURNAL OF CELL BIOLOGY, THE. **537**

0021-9533 *See* JOURNAL OF CELL SCIENCE. **537**

0021-9541 *See* JOURNAL OF CELLULAR PHYSIOLOGY. **582**

0021-955X *See* JOURNAL OF CELLULAR PLASTICS. **4455**

0021-9568 *See* JOURNAL OF CHEMICAL AND ENGINEERING DATA. **2014**

0021-9584 *See* JOURNAL OF CHEMICAL EDUCATION. **980**

0021-9592 *See* JOURNAL OF CHEMICAL ENGINEERING OF JAPAN. **2014**

0021-9606 *See* JOURNAL OF CHEMICAL PHYSICS, THE. **4408**

0021-9614 *See* JOURNAL OF CHEMICAL THERMODYNAMICS, THE. **1054**

0021-9630 *See* JOURNAL OF CHILD PSYCHOLOGY AND PSYCHIATRY AND ALLIED DISCIPLINES. **4594**

0021-9649 *See* JOURNAL OF CHRISTIAN CAMPING. **4874**

0021-9657 *See* JOURNAL OF CHRISTIAN EDUCATION. **4968**

0021-9665 *See* JOURNAL OF CHROMATOGRAPHIC SCIENCE. **1016**

0021-9673 *See* JOURNAL OF CHROMATOGRAPHY. **1016**

0021-969X *See* JOURNAL OF CHURCH AND STATE. **4478**

0021-972X *See* JOURNAL OF CLINICAL ENDOCRINOLOGY AND METABOLISM, THE. **3731**

0021-9738 *See* JOURNAL OF CLINICAL INVESTIGATION, THE. **3594**

0021-9746 *See* JOURNAL OF CLINICAL PATHOLOGY. **3895**

0021-9762 *See* JOURNAL OF CLINICAL PSYCHOLOGY. **4595**

0021-9797 *See* JOURNAL OF COLLOID AND INTERFACE SCIENCE. **1054**

0021-986X See JOURNAL OF COMMERCIAL LENDING, THE. **793**

0021-9886 *See* JOURNAL OF COMMON MARKET STUDIES. **1569**

0021-9894 *See* JOURNAL OF COMMONWEALTH LITERATURE. **3399**

0021-9916 *See* JOURNAL OF COMMUNICATION. **1114**

0021-9924 *See* JOURNAL OF COMMUNICATION DISORDERS. **3835**

0021-9967 *See* JOURNAL OF COMPARATIVE NEUROLOGY (1911). **3835**

0021-9975 *See* JOURNAL OF COMPARATIVE PATHOLOGY. **3895**

0021-9983 *See* JOURNAL OF COMPOSITE MATERIALS. **2103**

0021-9991 *See* JOURNAL OF COMPUTATIONAL PHYSICS. **4408**

0022-0000 See JOURNAL OF COMPUTER AND SYSTEM SCIENCES. 1247
0022-0019 See JOURNAL OF CONCHOLOGY. 5587
0022-0027 See JOURNAL OF CONFLICT RESOLUTION, THE. 4527
0022-0043 See JOURNAL OF CONSTITUTIONAL AND PARLIAMENTARY STUDIES. 2987
0022-006X See JOURNAL OF CONSULTING AND CLINICAL PSYCHOLOGY. 4595
0022-0078 See JOURNAL OF CONSUMER AFFAIRS, THE. 1297
0022-0094 See JOURNAL OF CONTEMPORARY HISTORY. 2621
0022-0116 See JOURNAL OF CONTEMPORARY PSYCHOTHERAPY. 4595
0022-0124 See JOURNAL OF CONTINUING EDUCATION IN NURSING, THE. 3858
0022-0132 See JOURNAL OF COOPERATIVE EDUCATION. 1756
0022-0140 See JOURNAL OF EXTENSION. 1914
0022-0167 See JOURNAL OF COUNSELING PSYCHOLOGY. 4595
0022-0175 See JOURNAL OF CREATIVE BEHAVIOR, THE. 4596
0022-0183 See JOURNAL OF CRIMINAL LAW (HERTFORD). 3107
0022-0213 See JOURNAL OF CRITICAL ANALYSIS, THE. 1756
0022-0221 See JOURNAL OF CROSS-CULTURAL PSYCHOLOGY. 4596
0022-023X See OPHTHALMIC SURGERY. 3971
0022-0248 See JOURNAL OF CRYSTAL GROWTH. 1032
0022-0256 See JOURNAL OF CUNEIFORM STUDIES. 3290
0022-0264 See JOURNAL OF CURRENT LASER ABSTRACTS. 4426
0022-0272 See JOURNAL OF CURRICULUM STUDIES. 1898
0022-0299 See JOURNAL OF DAIRY RESEARCH, THE. 195
0022-0302 See JOURNAL OF DAIRY SCIENCE. 195
0022-0337 See JOURNAL OF DENTAL EDUCATION. 1326
0022-0345 See JOURNAL OF DENTAL RESEARCH. 1326
0022-0353 See JOURNAL OF DENTISTRY FOR CHILDREN. 1326
0022-037X See JOURNAL OF DEVELOPING AREAS, THE. 2910
0022-0388 See JOURNAL OF DEVELOPMENT STUDIES, THE. 1569
0022-0396 See JOURNAL OF DIFFERENTIAL EQUATIONS. 3512
0022-040X See JOURNAL OF DIFFERENTIAL GEOMETRY. 3512
0022-0418 See JOURNAL OF DOCUMENTATION. 3219
0022-0426 See JOURNAL OF DRUG ISSUES. 1346
0022-0434 See JOURNAL OF DYNAMIC SYSTEMS, MEASUREMENT, AND CONTROL. 1982
0022-0442 See JOURNAL OF EARTH SCIENCES, NAGOYA UNIVERSITY, THE. 1357
0022-0469 See JOURNAL OF ECCLESIASTICAL HISTORY, THE. 4968
0022-0477 See JOURNAL OF ECOLOGY, THE. 515
0022-0485 See JOURNAL OF ECONOMIC EDUCATION, THE. 1499
0022-0493 See JOURNAL OF ECONOMIC ENTOMOLOGY. 5610
0022-0507 See JOURNAL OF ECONOMIC HISTORY, THE. 1569
0022-0515 See JOURNAL OF ECONOMIC LITERATURE. 1535
0022-0531 See JOURNAL OF ECONOMIC THEORY. 1593
0022-0558 See JOURNAL OF ECUMENICAL STUDIES. 4968

0022-0566 See JOURNAL OF EDUCATION (HALIFAX). 1756
0022-0574 See JOURNAL OF EDUCATION (BOSTON, MASS.). 1756
0022-0590 See JOURNAL OF EDUCATION & PSYCHOLOGY. 4596
0022-0620 See JOURNAL OF EDUCATIONAL ADMINISTRATION AND HISTORY. 1865
0022-0639 See JOURNAL OF EDUCATIONAL ADMINISTRATION, THE. 1865
0022-0655 See JOURNAL OF EDUCATIONAL MEASUREMENT. 1757
0022-0663 See JOURNAL OF EDUCATIONAL PSYCHOLOGY. 4596
0022-0671 See JOURNAL OF EDUCATIONAL RESEARCH (WASHINGTON, D.C.), THE. 1757
0022-068X See JOURNAL OF EDUCATIONAL RESEARCH AND EXTENSION. 1898
0022-0701 See JOURNAL OF EDUCATIONAL THOUGHT. 1757
0022-0728 See JOURNAL OF ELECTROANALYTICAL CHEMISTRY AND INTERFACIAL ELECTROCHEMISTRY. 1034
0022-0736 See JOURNAL OF ELECTROCARDIOLOGY. 3707
0022-0744 See JOURNAL OF ELECTRON MICROSCOPY. 572
0022-0787 See JOURNAL OF EMPLOYMENT COUNSELING. 4206
0022-0795 See JOURNAL OF ENDOCRINOLOGY, THE. 3731
0022-0809 See ASEE PRISM. 1965
0022-0809 See JOURNAL OF ENGINEERING EDUCATION (WASHINGTON, D.C.). 1982
0022-0817 See JOURNAL OF ENGINEERING FOR INDUSTRY. 1982
0022-0833 See JOURNAL OF ENGINEERING MATHEMATICS. 1982
0022-0841 See JOURNAL OF ENGINEERING PHYSICS AND THERMOPHYSICS. 4408
0022-0876 See JOURNAL OF ENGLISH LANGUAGE TEACHING (INDIA), THE. 3290
0022-0892 See JOURNAL OF ENVIRONMENTAL HEALTH. 2175
0022-0914 See JOURNAL OF ETHIOPIAN LAW. 2987
0022-0930 See JOURNAL OF EVOLUTIONARY BIOCHEMISTRY AND PHYSIOLOGY. 582
0022-0949 See JOURNAL OF EXPERIMENTAL BIOLOGY. 582
0022-0957 See JOURNAL OF EXPERIMENTAL BOTANY. 515
0022-0965 See JOURNAL OF EXPERIMENTAL CHILD PSYCHOLOGY. 4596
0022-0973 See JOURNAL OF EXPERIMENTAL EDUCATION, THE. 1898
0022-0981 See JOURNAL OF EXPERIMENTAL MARINE BIOLOGY AND ECOLOGY. 555
0022-1007 See JOURNAL OF EXPERIMENTAL MEDICINE, THE. 3673
0022-1031 See JOURNAL OF EXPERIMENTAL SOCIAL PSYCHOLOGY. 4597
0022-104X See JOURNAL OF EXPERIMENTAL ZOOLOGY, THE. 5587
0022-1058 See JOURNAL OF EXTRA-CORPOREAL TECHNOLOGY, THE. 3772
0022-1066 See JOURNAL OF FAMILY LAW. 3121
0022-1074 See JOURNAL OF FAMILY WELFARE, THE. 589
0022-1082 See JOURNAL OF FINANCE (NEW YORK), THE. 794
0022-1090 See JOURNAL OF FINANCIAL AND QUANTITATIVE ANALYSIS. 794
0022-1112 See JOURNAL OF FISH BIOLOGY. 2306
0022-1120 See JOURNAL OF FLUID MECHANICS. 2091
0022-1139 See JOURNAL OF FLUORINE CHEMISTRY. 981
0022-1147 See JOURNAL OF FOOD SCIENCE. 2346
0022-1155 See JOURNAL OF FOOD SCIENCE AND TECHNOLOGY. 4193

0022-1198 See JOURNAL OF FORENSIC SCIENCES. 3741
0022-1201 See JOURNAL OF FORESTRY. 2385
0022-1236 See JOURNAL OF FUNCTIONAL ANALYSIS. 3513
0022-1244 See JOURNAL OF GEM INDUSTRY. 2915
0022-1252 See JOURNAL OF GEMMOLOGY AND PROCEEDINGS OF THE GEMMOLOGICAL ASSOCIATION OF GREAT BRITAIN. 1440
0022-1260 See JOURNAL OF GENERAL AND APPLIED MICROBIOLOGY, THE. 565
0022-1279 See JOURNAL OF GENERAL CHEMISTRY OF THE USSR. 981
0022-1287 See JOURNAL OF GENERAL MICROBIOLOGY, THE. 565
0022-1295 See JOURNAL OF GENERAL PHYSIOLOGY, THE. 582
0022-1309 See JOURNAL OF GENERAL PSYCHOLOGY, THE. 4597
0022-1317 See JOURNAL OF GENERAL VIROLOGY, THE. 565
0022-1325 See JOURNAL OF GENETIC PSYCHOLOGY, THE. 4597
0022-1333 See JOURNAL OF GENETICS. 548
0022-1341 See JOURNAL OF GEOGRAPHY (HOUSTON). 2567
0022-135X See CHIGAKU ZASSHI. 2558
0022-1368 See JOURNAL OF GEOLOGICAL EDUCATION. 1384
0022-1376 See JOURNAL OF GEOLOGY, THE. 1385
0022-1392 See JOURNAL OF GEOMAGNETISM AND GEOELECTRICITY. 1407
0022-1414 See JOURNAL OF GERIATRIC PSYCHIATRY. 3928
0022-1422 See JOURNAL OF GERONTOLOGY (KIRKWOOD). 3753
0022-1430 See JOURNAL OF GLACIOLOGY, THE. 1416
0022-1465 See JOURNAL OF HEALTH AND SOCIAL BEHAVIOR. 4786
0022-1481 See JOURNAL OF HEAT TRANSFER. 1983
0022-149X See JOURNAL OF HELMINTHOLOGY. 5588
0022-1503 See JOURNAL OF HEREDITY, THE. 548
0022-1511 See JOURNAL OF HERPETOLOGY. 5588
0022-152X See JOURNAL OF HETEROCYCLIC CHEMISTRY. 1042
0022-1546 See JOURNAL OF HIGHER EDUCATION (COLUMBUS), THE. 1833
0022-1554 See JOURNAL OF HISTOCHEMISTRY AND CYTOCHEMISTRY, THE. 537
0022-1562 See JOURNAL OF HISTORICAL RESEARCH. 2655
0022-1570 See JOURNAL OF HOME ECONOMICS (WASHINGTON). 2791
0022-1589 See JOURNAL OF HORTICULTURAL SCIENCE, THE. 2421
0022-1597 See HOSPITAL & COMMUNITY PSYCHIATRY. 3926
0022-1597 See HOSPITAL & COMMUNITY PSYCHIATRY. MICROFILM. 3926
0022-166X See JOURNAL OF HUMAN RESOURCES, THE. 1914
0022-1678 See JOURNAL OF HUMANISTIC PSYCHOLOGY, THE. 4597
0022-1686 See JOURNAL OF HYDRAULIC RESEARCH. 2092
0022-1694 See JOURNAL OF HYDROLOGY (AMSTERDAM). 1416
0022-1708 See JOURNAL OF HYDROLOGY, NEW ZEALAND. 1416
0022-1732 See JOURNAL OF HYGIENE, EPIDEMIOLOGY, MICROBIOLOGY, AND IMMUNOLOGY. 4787
0022-1759 See JOURNAL OF IMMUNOLOGICAL METHODS. 3673
0022-1767 See JOURNAL OF IMMUNOLOGY (1950), THE. 3673

0022-1775 See JOURNAL OF INDIAN HISTORY. 2655

0022-1791 See JOURNAL OF INDIAN PHILOSOPHY. 4350

0022-1805 See JOURNAL OF INDIVIDUAL PSYCHOLOGY. 4597

0022-1821 See JOURNAL OF INDUSTRIAL ECONOMICS, THE. 1614

0022-1856 See JOURNAL OF INDUSTRIAL RELATIONS, THE. 1682

0022-1864 See JOURNAL OF INDUSTRIAL TEACHER EDUCATION. 1914

0022-1872 See JOURNAL OF INDUSTRY, THE. 1614

0022-1899 See JOURNAL OF INFECTIOUS DISEASES, THE. 3714

0022-1910 See JOURNAL OF INSECT PHYSIOLOGY. 5610

0022-1937 See JOURNAL OF INTERAMERICAN STUDIES AND WORLD AFFAIRS. 4527

0022-1945 See JOURNAL OF INTERDISCIPLINARY CYCLE RESEARCH. 461

0022-1953 See JOURNAL OF INTERDISCIPLINARY HISTORY, THE. 2621

0022-1996 See JOURNAL OF INTERNATIONAL ECONOMICS. 1637

0022-2011 See JOURNAL OF INVERTEBRATE PATHOLOGY. 5611

0022-202X See JOURNAL OF INVESTIGATIVE DERMATOLOGY, THE. 3721

0022-2038 See JOURNAL OF IRREPRODUCIBLE RESULTS, THE. 5118

0022-2062 See SHOKUBUTSU KENKYU ZASSHI. 527

0022-2089 See JOURNAL OF JEWISH COMMUNAL SERVICE. 2266

0022-2097 See JOURNAL OF JEWISH STUDIES, THE. 5050

0022-2143 See JOURNAL OF LABORATORY AND CLINICAL MEDICINE, THE. 3595

0022-2151 See JOURNAL OF LARYNGOLOGY AND OTOLOGY. 3889

0022-216X See JOURNAL OF LATIN AMERICAN STUDIES. 2741

0022-2186 See JOURNAL OF LAW & ECONOMICS, THE. 2988

0022-2194 See JOURNAL OF LEARNING DISABILITIES. 1880

0022-2208 See JOURNAL OF LEGAL EDUCATION. 2988

0022-2216 See JOURNAL OF LEISURE RESEARCH. 4851

0022-2224 See VISIBLE LANGUAGE. 4570

0022-2232 See JOURNAL OF LIBRARIANSHIP AND INFORMATION SCIENCE. 3220

0022-2267 See JOURNAL OF LINGUISTICS. 3290

0022-2275 See JOURNAL OF LIPID RESEARCH. 583

0022-2291 See JOURNAL OF LOW TEMPERATURE PHYSICS. 4409

0022-2313 See JOURNAL OF LUMINESCENCE. 4436

0022-2348 See JOURNAL OF MACROMOLECULAR SCIENCE. PHYSICS. 4409

0022-2356 See JOURNAL OF MACROMOLECULAR SCIENCE. REVIEWS IN MACROMOLECULAR CHEMISTRY. 1042

0022-2364 See JOURNAL OF MAGNETIC RESONANCE. 4444

0022-2372 See JOURNAL OF MAMMALOGY. 5588

0022-2380 See JOURNAL OF MANAGEMENT STUDIES, THE. 874

0022-2402 See JOURNAL OF MARINE RESEARCH. 555

0022-2429 See JOURNAL OF MARKETING. 928

0022-2437 See JMR, JOURNAL OF MARKETING RESEARCH. 927

0022-2445 See JOURNAL OF MARRIAGE AND THE FAMILY. 2282

0022-2461 See JOURNAL OF MATERIALS SCIENCE. 4006

0022-247X See JOURNAL OF MATHEMATICAL ANALYSIS AND APPLICATIONS. 3513

0022-2488 See JOURNAL OF MATHEMATICAL PHYSICS. 4409

0022-2496 See JOURNAL OF MATHEMATICAL PSYCHOLOGY. 4598

0022-250X See JOURNAL OF MATHEMATICAL SOCIOLOGY, THE. 5250

0022-2518 See INDIANA UNIVERSITY MATHEMATICS JOURNAL. 3509

0022-2526 See STUDIES IN APPLIED MATHEMATICS (CAMBRIDGE). 3537

0022-2585 See JOURNAL OF MEDICAL ENTOMOLOGY. 5611

0022-2593 See JOURNAL OF MEDICAL GENETICS. 549

0022-2615 See JOURNAL OF MEDICAL MICROBIOLOGY. 565

0022-2623 See JOURNAL OF MEDICINAL CHEMISTRY. 490

0022-2631 See JOURNAL OF MEMBRANE BIOLOGY, THE. 538

0022-264X See JOURNAL OF INTELLECTUAL DISABILITY RESEARCH. 4598

0022-2720 See JOURNAL OF MICROSCOPY (OXFORD). 572

0022-2755 See JOURNAL OF MINES, METALS & FUELS. 2141

0022-2763 See JOURNAL OF MINING AND GEOLOGY. 2141

0022-2771 See JOURNAL OF MISSISSIPPI HISTORY, THE. 2741

0022-278X See JOURNAL OF MODERN AFRICAN STUDIES, THE. 2640

0022-2801 See JOURNAL OF MODERN HISTORY, THE. 2621

0022-281X See JOURNAL OF MODERN LITERATURE. 3345

0022-2828 See JOURNAL OF MOLECULAR AND CELLULAR CARDIOLOGY. 3707

0022-2836 See JOURNAL OF MOLECULAR BIOLOGY. 461

0022-2844 See JOURNAL OF MOLECULAR EVOLUTION. 549

0022-2852 See JOURNAL OF MOLECULAR SPECTROSCOPY. 4436

0022-2860 See JOURNAL OF MOLECULAR STRUCTURE. 1054

0022-2879 See JOURNAL OF MONEY, CREDIT, AND BANKING. 795

0022-2895 See JOURNAL OF MOTOR BEHAVIOR. 583

0022-2909 See JOURNAL OF MUSIC THEORY. 4126

0022-2917 See JOURNAL OF MUSIC THERAPY. 4126

0022-2925 See JOURNAL OF NARRATIVE TECHNIQUE, THE. 3400

0022-2933 See JOURNAL OF NATURAL HISTORY. 4166

0022-2941 See JOURNAL OF NATURAL SCIENCES AND MATHEMATICS. 5119

0022-2968 See JOURNAL OF NEAR EASTERN STUDIES. 3291

0022-2984 See JOURNAL OF NEGRO EDUCATION, THE. 1758

0022-2992 See JOURNAL OF NEGRO HISTORY, THE. 2741

0022-300X See JOURNAL OF NEMATOLOGY. 5588

0022-3018 See JOURNAL OF NERVOUS AND MENTAL DISEASE, THE. 3835

0022-3034 See JOURNAL OF NEUROBIOLOGY. 3835

0022-3042 See JOURNAL OF NEUROCHEMISTRY. 3836

0022-3050 See JOURNAL OF NEUROLOGY, NEUROSURGERY AND PSYCHIATRY. 3836

0022-3069 See JOURNAL OF NEUROPATHOLOGY AND EXPERIMENTAL NEUROLOGY. 3836

0022-3077 See JOURNAL OF NEUROPHYSIOLOGY. 3836

0022-3085 See JOURNAL OF NEUROSURGERY. 3837

0022-3093 See JOURNAL OF NON-CRYSTALLINE SOLIDS. 2591

0022-3115 See JOURNAL OF NUCLEAR MATERIALS. 2156

0022-3131 See JOURNAL OF NUCLEAR SCIENCE AND TECHNOLOGY. 2156

0022-314X See JOURNAL OF NUMBER THEORY. 3514

0022-3166 See JOURNAL OF NUTRITION, THE. 4193

0022-3174 See INDIAN JOURNAL OF NUTRITION AND DIETETICS, THE. 4192

0022-3182 See JOURNAL OF NUTRITION EDUCATION. 4193

0022-3190 See JOURNAL OF OBSTETRICS AND GYNAECOLOGY OF INDIA. 3763

0022-3239 See JOURNAL OF OPTIMIZATION THEORY AND APPLICATIONS. 3514

0022-3263 See JOURNAL OF ORGANIC CHEMISTRY. 1043

0022-3271 See JOURNAL OF ORGANIC CHEMISTRY OF THE USSR. 1043

0022-328X See JOURNAL OF ORGANOMETALLIC CHEMISTRY. 1043

0022-3298 See JOURNAL OF ORGONOMY, THE. 3596

0022-3301 See JOURNAL OF ORIENTAL RESEARCH, MADRAS, THE. 3291

0022-331X See JOURNAL OF ORIENTAL STUDIES (HONG KONG). 2655

0022-3336 See JOURNAL OF OUTDOOR EDUCATION. 1758

0022-3344 See JOURNAL OF PACIFIC HISTORY, THE. 2669

0022-3360 See JOURNAL OF PALEONTOLOGY. 4227

0022-3379 See JOURNAL OF PALYNOLOGY. 515

0022-3387 See JOURNAL OF PARAPSYCHOLOGY, THE. 4241

0022-3395 See JOURNAL OF PARASITOLOGY, THE. 5588

0022-3409 See JOURNAL OF PASTORAL CARE, THE. 4969

0022-3417 See JOURNAL OF PATHOLOGY. 3895

0022-3433 See JOURNAL OF PEACE RESEARCH. 4527

0022-3468 See JOURNAL OF PEDIATRIC SURGERY. 3968

0022-3476 See JOURNAL OF PEDIATRICS, THE. 3905

0022-3484 See JOURNAL OF PERIODONTAL RESEARCH. 1327

0022-3492 See JOURNAL OF PERIODONTOLOGY (1970). 1327

0022-3506 See JOURNAL OF PERSONALITY. 4599

0022-3514 See JOURNAL OF PERSONALITY AND SOCIAL PSYCHOLOGY. 4599

0022-3530 See JOURNAL OF PETROLOGY. 1458

0022-3549 See JOURNAL OF PHARMACEUTICAL SCIENCES. 4312

0022-3565 See JOURNAL OF PHARMACOLOGY AND EXPERIMENTAL THERAPEUTICS, THE. 4312

0022-3573 See JOURNAL OF PHARMACY AND PHARMACOLOGY. 4312

0022-359X See JOURNAL OF PHILIPPINE LIBRARIANSHIP. 3220

0022-3603 See JOURNAL OF PHILIPPINE STATISTICS. 5329

0022-3611 See JOURNAL OF PHILOSOPHICAL LOGIC. 3291

0022-362X See JOURNAL OF PHILOSOPHY, THE. 4350

0022-3638 See JOURNAL OF PHOTOGRAPHIC SCIENCE, THE. 4371

0022-3646 See JOURNAL OF PHYCOLOGY. 515

0022-3654 See JOURNAL OF PHYSICAL CHEMISTRY (1952). 1054

0022-3670 See JOURNAL OF PHYSICAL OCEANOGRAPHY. 1450

0022-3697 See JOURNAL OF PHYSICS AND CHEMISTRY OF SOLIDS, THE. 4409

0022-3727 See JOURNAL OF PHYSICS. D : APPLIED PHYSICS. 4410

0022-3743 See JOURNAL OF PHYSICS OF THE EARTH. 1408
0022-3751 See JOURNAL OF PHYSIOLOGY (LONDON). 583
0022-3778 See JOURNAL OF PLASMA PHYSICS. 4410
0022-3808 See JOURNAL OF POLITICAL ECONOMY, THE. 1500
0022-3816 See JOURNAL OF POLITICS, THE. 4479
0022-3840 See JOURNAL OF POPULAR CULTURE. 2741
0022-3859 See JOURNAL OF POSTGRADUATE MEDICINE (BOMBAY). 3597
0022-3867 See JOURNAL OF PRACTICAL NURSING, THE. 3860
0022-3875 See JOURNAL OF CLINICAL ORTHODONTICS. 1326
0022-3891 See JOURNAL OF PERSONALITY ASSESSMENT. 4599
0022-3905 See JOURNAL OF PROPERTY MANAGEMENT. 4839
0022-3913 See JOURNAL OF PROSTHETIC DENTISTRY, THE. 1327
0022-3921 See JOURNAL OF PROTOZOOLOGY, THE. 5588
0022-3956 See JOURNAL OF PSYCHIATRIC RESEARCH. 3929
0022-3972 See JOURNAL OF PSYCHOLOGICAL RESEARCHES. 4600
0022-3980 See JOURNAL OF PSYCHOLOGY, THE. 4600
0022-3999 See JOURNAL OF PSYCHOSOMATIC RESEARCH. 3597
0022-4006 See JOURNAL OF PUBLIC HEALTH DENTISTRY. 1328
0022-4049 See JOURNAL OF PURE AND APPLIED ALGEBRA. 3514
0022-4057 See JOURNAL OF PURE AND APPLIED SCIENCES (ANKARA). 5119
0022-4065 See JOURNAL OF QUALITY TECHNOLOGY. 5119
0022-4073 See JOURNAL OF QUANTITATIVE SPECTROSCOPY & RADIATIVE TRANSFER. 4436
0022-409X See JOURNAL OF RANGE MANAGEMENT. 100
0022-4103 See JOURNAL OF READING. 1898
0022-4111 See JOURNAL OF READING BEHAVIOR. 1758
0022-412X See JOURNAL OF RECREATIONAL MATHEMATICS. 3514
0022-4146 See JOURNAL OF REGIONAL SCIENCE. 1500
0022-4154 See JOURNAL OF REHABILITATION. 5292
0022-4162 See JOURNAL OF REHABILITATION IN ASIA, THE. 4380
0022-4189 See JOURNAL OF RELIGION, THE. 4969
0022-4197 See JOURNAL OF RELIGION AND HEALTH. 4969
0022-4200 See JOURNAL OF RELIGION IN AFRICA. 4970
0022-4227 See JOURNAL OF RELIGIOUS HISTORY, THE. 4970
0022-4235 See JOURNAL OF RELIGIOUS THOUGHT, THE. 4970
0022-4243 See JOURNAL OF REPRINTS FOR ANTITRUST LAW AND ECONOMICS, THE. 3101
0022-4251 See JOURNAL OF REPRODUCTION & FERTILITY. 3597
0022-426X See JOURNAL OF RESEARCH AND DEVELOPMENT IN EDUCATION. 1758
0022-4278 See JOURNAL OF RESEARCH IN CRIME AND DELINQUENCY, THE. 3167
0022-4278 See JOURNAL OF RESEARCH IN CRIME AND DELINQUENCY, THE. 3167
0022-4294 See JOURNAL OF RESEARCH IN MUSIC EDUCATION. 4126
0022-4308 See JOURNAL OF RESEARCH IN SCIENCE TEACHING. 5119
0022-4324 See JOURNAL OF RESEARCH ON THE LEPIDOPTERA, THE. 5611

0022-4359 See JOURNAL OF RETAILING. 955
0022-4367 See JOURNAL OF RISK AND INSURANCE, THE. 2885
0022-4375 See JOURNAL OF SAFETY RESEARCH. 2864
0022-4383 See JOURNAL OF SAN DIEGO HISTORY, THE. 2742
0022-4391 See JOURNAL OF SCHOOL HEALTH, THE. 4787
0022-4405 See JOURNAL OF SCHOOL PSYCHOLOGY. 4601
0022-4472 See JOURNAL OF SEDIMENTARY PETROLOGY. 1458
0022-4480 See JOURNAL OF SEMITIC STUDIES. 2266
0022-4499 See JOURNAL OF SEX RESEARCH, THE. 5187
0022-4499 See JOURNAL OF SEX RESEARCH, THE. 5187
0022-4502 See JOURNAL OF SHIP RESEARCH. 4177
0022-4510 See JOURNAL OF SMALL ANIMAL PRACTICE, THE. 5513
0022-4529 See JOURNAL OF SOCIAL HISTORY. 5206
0022-4537 See JOURNAL OF SOCIAL ISSUES, THE. 5206
0022-4545 See JOURNAL OF SOCIAL PSYCHOLOGY, THE. 4601
0022-4561 See JOURNAL OF SOIL AND WATER CONSERVATION. 2196
0022-457X See JOURNAL OF SOIL AND WATER CONSERVATION IN INDIA. 2196
0022-4588 See JOURNAL OF SOIL SCIENCE, THE. 176
0022-4596 See JOURNAL OF SOLID STATE CHEMISTRY. 982
0022-460X See JOURNAL OF SOUND AND VIBRATION. 4452
0022-4634 See JOURNAL OF SOUTHEAST ASIAN STUDIES (SINGAPORE). 2655
0022-4642 See JOURNAL OF SOUTHERN HISTORY, THE. 2742
0022-4650 See JOURNAL OF SPACECRAFT AND ROCKETS. 26
0022-4669 See JOURNAL OF SPECIAL EDUCATION, THE. 1881
0022-4685 See JOURNAL OF SPEECH AND HEARING RESEARCH. 4390
0022-4693 See JOURNAL OF SPELEAN HISTORY, THE. 1357
0022-4707 See JOURNAL OF SPORTS MEDICINE AND PHYSICAL FITNESS. 3954
0022-4715 See JOURNAL OF STATISTICAL PHYSICS. 4410
0022-474X See JOURNAL OF STORED PRODUCTS RESEARCH. 2347
0022-4766 See JOURNAL OF STRUCTURAL CHEMISTRY. 1055
0022-4774 See JOURNAL OF STRUCTURAL LEARNING. 1758
0022-4790 See JOURNAL OF SURGICAL ONCOLOGY. 3820
0022-4804 See JOURNAL OF SURGICAL RESEARCH, THE. 3968
0022-4812 See JOURNAL OF SYMBOLIC LOGIC, THE. 3515
0022-4839 See JOURNAL OF SYSTEMS MANAGEMENT. 687
0022-4855 See JOURNAL OF TAMIL STUDIES. 2849
0022-4863 See JOURNAL OF TAXATION, THE. 4735
0022-4871 See JOURNAL OF TEACHER EDUCATION. 1865
0022-4898 See JOURNAL OF TERRAMECHANICS. 2026
0022-4901 See JOURNAL OF TEXTURE STUDIES. 2347
0022-4928 See JOURNAL OF THE ATMOSPHERIC SCIENCES. 1427
0022-4936 See JOURNAL OF THE CHEMICAL SOCIETY, CHEMICAL COMMUNICATIONS. 982

0022-4995 See JOURNAL OF THE ECONOMIC AND SOCIAL HISTORY OF THE ORIENT. 2656
0022-5002 See JOURNAL OF THE EXPERIMENTAL ANALYSIS OF BEHAVIOR. 4601
0022-5010 See JOURNAL OF THE HISTORY OF BIOLOGY. 462
0022-5037 See JOURNAL OF THE HISTORY OF IDEAS. 4351
0022-5045 See JOURNAL OF THE HISTORY OF MEDICINE AND ALLIED SCIENCES. 3598
0022-5053 See JOURNAL OF THE HISTORY OF PHILOSOPHY. 4351
0022-5061 See JOURNAL OF THE HISTORY OF THE BEHAVIORAL SCIENCES. 4601
0022-507X See JOURNAL OF THE INDIAN MEDICAL PROFESSION. 3598
0022-5088 See JOURNAL OF ALLOYS AND COMPOUNDS. 4006
0022-5096 See JOURNAL OF THE MECHANICS AND PHYSICS OF SOLIDS. 2104
0022-510X See JOURNAL OF THE NEUROLOGICAL SCIENCES. 3837
0022-5142 See JOURNAL OF THE SCIENCE OF FOOD AND AGRICULTURE. 2347
0022-5169 See JOURNAL OF THE WEST. 2742
0022-5185 See JOURNAL OF THEOLOGICAL STUDIES. 4971
0022-5193 See JOURNAL OF THEORETICAL BIOLOGY. 462
0022-5223 See JOURNAL OF THORACIC AND CARDIOVASCULAR SURGERY. 3968
0022-5231 See JOURNAL OF THOUGHT. 1759
0022-524X See JOURNAL OF TRANSPERSONAL PSYCHOLOGY, THE. 4602
0022-5258 See JOURNAL OF TRANSPORT ECONOMICS AND POLICY. 5385
0022-5266 See JOURNAL OF TRANSPORT HISTORY, THE. 5385
0022-5274 See KOTSU IGAKU. 3602
0022-5282 See JOURNAL OF TRAUMA, THE. 3969
0022-5304 See JOURNAL OF TROPICAL MEDICINE AND HYGIENE. 3986
0022-5339 See JOURNAL OF UNDERGRADUATE MATHEMATICS. 3516
0022-5347 See JOURNAL OF UROLOGY, THE. 3991
0022-5363 See JOURNAL OF VALUE INQUIRY, THE. 4351
0022-538X See JOURNAL OF VIROLOGY. 566
0022-5401 See JOURNAL OF WEST AFRICAN LANGUAGES, THE. 3292
0022-541X See JOURNAL OF WILDLIFE MANAGEMENT, THE. 2196
0022-5428 See COLUMBIA JOURNAL OF WORLD BUSINESS, THE. 658
0022-5452 See JOURNAL OF THE YUGOSLAV FOREIGN TRADE. 4527
0022-5517 2921
0022-5525 2921
0022-5541 See JOURNALIST. 2921
0022-555X See JOURNALIST, DE. 2921
0022-5711 See JUCUNDA LAUDATIO; RASSEGNA DI MUSICA ANTICA. 4127
0022-572X See JUDAICA. 5050
0022-5738 See JUDAICA BOHEMIAE. 5050
0022-5754 See JUDAICA BOOK NEWS. 5013
0022-5762 See JUDAISM. 5050
0022-5800 See JUDICATURE. 2990
0022-5819 See JUDO. 2599
0022-5975 See JUGENDWOHL. 1065
0022-5991 See JUGHEAD (MAMARONECK, ILL.). 4862
0022-6114 See JUGOSLOVENSKI PREGLED; INFORMATIVNO DOKUMENTARNI PRIRUCNIK O JUGOSLAVIJI. 5207
0022-6157 See JUGUETES Y JUEGOS DE ESPANA. 2584
0022-6319 See JUNGE KIRCHE; EINE ZEITSCHRIFT EUROPAISCHER CHRISTEN. 4971
0022-6505 See JUNIOR BOOKSHELF. 1072

0022-6602 *See* TEXAS HISTORIAN, THE. **2763**
0022-6688 *See* JUNIOR SCHOLASTIC. **1065**
0022-6718 *See* JUNIOR TRAILS. **4971**
0022-6769 *See* JUNTENDO IGAKU. **3601**
0022-6785 *See* JURIDICAL REVIEW, THE. **2990**
0022-6807 *See* JURIS. **2990**
0022-6815 *See* HOGAKU KYOKAI ZASSHI. **2978**
0022-6858 *See* JURIST (WASHINGTON), THE. **5031**
0022-6882 *See* JURISTENZEITUNG. **2991**
0022-6912 *See* JURISTISCHE BLATTER. **2991**
0022-6920 *See* JURISTISCHE RUNDSCHAU. **2991**
0022-6939 *See* JUS. JURISTISCHE SCHULUNG. **2991**
0022-6955 *See* JUS (MILAN, ITALY). **1833**
0022-6963 *See* JUS GENTIUM. **3131**
0022-6971 *See* JUSSENS VENNER. **2991**
0022-7013 *See* JUSTICE (NEW YORK, N.Y. 1919). **1682**
0022-7161 *See* JUVENILE MERCHANDISING. **929**
0022-7226 *See* JUZEN IGAKKAI ZASSHI. **3601**
0022-7269 *See* KAHPER JOURNAL (RICHMOND, KY.). **1856**
0022-7277 *See* K & I.E. EN C. KUNST EN CULTUUR. **323**
0022-7498 *See* KADMOS. **272**
0022-7560 *See* KARNTNER HEIMATLEBEN. **2695**
0022-7587 *See* KARNTNER MUSEUMSSCHRIFTEN. **4090**
0022-7684 *See* KAGAKU TO KOGYO (TOKYO). **983**
0022-7692 *See* KAGAKUSHI KENKYU. **5122**
0022-7722 *See* KAIBOGAKU ZASSHI. **3679**
0022-7757 *See* KAIROS; ZEITSCHRIFT FUER RELIGIONSWISSENSCHAFT UND THEOLOGIE. **4971**
0022-7838 *See* KAKAO + ZUCKER. **2347**
0022-7846 *See* KAKTEEN UND ANDERE SUKKULENTEN. **516**
0022-7854 *See* KAKU IGAKU. **3848**
0022-7951 *See* KALI UND STEINSALZ. **1440**
0022-7994 *See* KALKI (ORADELL). **3345**
0022-8109 *See* KAMERA UND SCHULE. **4371**
0022-815X *See* KAMI PA GIKYOSHI. **4234**
0022-8206 *See* KAMPANA (NEW YORK, N.Y.). **2266**
0022-8338 *See* SCIENCE REPORTS OF THE KANAZAWA UNIVERSITY, THE. **5153**
0022-8400 *See* KANSAI IKA DAIGAKU ZASSHI. **3601**
0022-8419 *See* ECONOMIC REVIEW - KANSALLIS-OSAKE-PANKKI. **1558**
0022-8427 *See* KANSANTALOUDELLINEN AIKAKAUSKIRJA. **1501**
0022-8435 *See* KANSAS. **2536**
0022-8443 *See* TRANSACTIONS OF THE KANSAS ACADEMY OF SCIENCE (1903). **5166**
0022-8478 *See* KANSAS BANKER, THE. **795**
0022-8486 *See* JOURNAL OF THE KANSAS BAR ASSOCIATION, THE. **2989**
0022-8524 *See* KANSAS CITY JEWISH CHRONICLE. **5676**
0022-8567 *See* JOURNAL OF THE KANSAS ENTOMOLOGICAL SOCIETY. **5611**
0022-8583 *See* KANSAS FARMER. **102**
0022-8613 *See* KANSAS GOVERNMENT JOURNAL. **4659**
0022-8702 *See* KANSAS MUSIC REVIEW. **4127**
0022-8710 *See* KANSAS NURSE, THE. **3860**
0022-8729 *See* BULLETIN - KANSAS ORNITHOLOGICAL SOCIETY. **5616**
0022-8737 *See* KANSAS PUBLISHER, THE. **2921**
0022-8745 *See* KANSAS QUARTERLY. **2536**
0022-8753 *See* KANSAS RESTAURANT. **5071**
0022-877X *See* KANSAS SCHOOL NATURALIST. **1899**
0022-8826 *See* KANSAS STOCKMAN, THE. **213**
0022-8850 *See* UNIVERSITY OF KANSAS SCIENCE BULLETIN, THE. **5167**

0022-8877 *See* KANT-STUDIEN. **4351**
0022-8958 *See* KAPPA DELTA PI RECORD. **1759**
0022-8990 *See* KARAMU (CHARLESTON, ILL.). **3401**
0022-9032 *See* KARDIOLOGIA POLSKA (1957). **3708**
0022-9040 *See* KARDIOLOGIJA. **3708**
0022-9113 *See* KARTEI DER PRAKTISCHEN MEDIZIN. **3601**
0022-913X *See* KARTING. **4903**
0022-9148 *See* KARTOFEL I OVOSHCHI. **177**
0022-9156 *See* KARTOFFELBAU. **177**
0022-9164 *See* KARTOGRAPHISCHE NACHRICHTEN. **2582**
0022-9202 *See* KASEKI. **4227**
0022-927X *See* KASVATUS. **1759**
0022-9466 *See* KAUCHUK I REZINA. **5076**
0022-9504 *See* KAUPPAREKISTERILEHTI. **688**
0022-9520 *See* KAUTSCHUK + GUMMI KUNSTSTOFFE. **5076**
0022-9555 *See* KAYAK (SANTA CRUZ). **3465**
0022-9601 *See* KEEL JA KIRJANDUS. **3293**
0022-9709 *See* KEIO ECONOMIC STUDIES. **1570**
0022-9717 *See* KEIO JOURNAL OF MEDICINE. **3601**
0022-9733 *See* KEIZAI KENKYU / HITOTSUBASHI DAIGAKU KEIZAI KENKYUJO HEN. **1501**
0022-9741 *See* KEIZAI SHIRIN. **1501**
0022-9776 *See* KEKKAKU. **3950**
0022-9814 *See* KEMIAI KOEZLEMENYEK. **983**
0022-9830 *See* KEMIJA U INDUSTRIJI. **983**
0023-0014 *See* KENT ARCHAEOLOGICAL REVIEW. **272**
0023-0081 *See* TRANSACTIONS OF THE KENTUCKY ACADEMY OF SCIENCE. **5166**
0023-0103 *See* KENTUCKY ANCESTORS. **2456**
0023-0197 *See* KENTUCKY ENGLISH BULLETIN. **3401**
0023-0200 *See* KENTUCKY FARM BUREAU NEWS. **102**
0023-0219 *See* KENTUCKY FARMER, THE. **102**
0023-0235 *See* KENTUCKY HAPPY HUNTING GROUND. **4874**
0023-0243 *See* REGISTER OF THE KENTUCKY HISTORICAL SOCIETY, THE. **2756**
0023-0251 *See* KENTUCKY LABOR NEWS. **1682**
0023-026X *See* KENTUCKY LAW JOURNAL. **2992**
0023-0294 *See* JOURNAL OF THE KENTUCKY MEDICAL ASSOCIATION, THE. **3598**
0023-0480 *See* KEP ES HANGTECHNIKA. **4437**
0023-0561 *See* KERAMISCHE ZEITSCHRIFT. **2592**
0023-0677 *See* KERTESZET ES SZOLESZET. **2422**
0023-0693 *See* KERYGMA (OTTAWA). **4972**
0023-0707 *See* KERYGMA UND DOGMA. **4972**
0023-0790 *See* KEY OFFICERS OF FOREIGN SERVICE POSTS. **3131**
0023-0804 *See* KEY REPORTER, THE. **1092**
0023-0839 *See* KEY TO CHRISTIAN EDUCATION. **4972**
0023-1029 *See* KHADI GRAMODYOG. **1614**
0023-1088 *See* KHETI. **102**
0023-110X *See* HIMICESKAJ PROMYSLENNOST. **977**
0023-1118 *See* HIMICESKIE VOLOKNA. **4455**
0023-1126 *See* HIMICESKOE I NEFTJANOE MASINOSTROENIE. **1025**
0023-1134 *See* HIMIKO-FARMACEVTICESKIJ ZURNAL. **4306**
0023-1150 *See* KHIMIIA PRIRODNYKH SOEDINENII. **1043**
0023-1169 *See* HIMIJA I TEHNOLOGIJA TOPLIV I MASEL. **4260**
0023-1177 *See* HIMIJA TVERDOVO TOPLIVA. **4260**
0023-1193 *See* HIMIJA VYSOKIH ENERGIJ. **1052**
0023-1207 *See* HIRURGIJA (MOSKVA). **3965**
0023-1304 *See* KIDNEY, THE. **3991**
0023-1312 *See* KIDS. **1065**

0023-1347 *See* KIELER MILCHWIRTSCHAFTLICHE FORSCHUNGSBERICHTE. **196**
0023-1363 *See* KIJK OP HET NOORDEN. **1501**
0023-1371 *See* KIKAIKA NOGYO. **159**
0023-1495 *See* KINDERARZTLICHE PRAXIS. **3906**
0023-1568 *See* KINESIS (CARBONDALE, ILL.). **4351**
0023-1576 *See* KINESITHERAPIE SCIENTIFIQUE. **4381**
0023-1584 *See* KINETICS AND CATALYSIS. **1044**
0023-1592 *See* BULLETIN - KING COUNTY MEDICAL SOCIETY, THE. **3913**
0023-1606 *See* KINGBIRD, THE. **5618**
0023-1673 *See* KINO. **4073**
0023-1703 *See* KINSHIP. **5294**
0023-1738 *See* KIPLING JOURNAL. **3402**
0023-1746 *See* KIPLINGER AGRICULTURE LETTER, THE. **102**
0023-1754 *See* KIPLINGER FLORIDA LETTER, THE. **905**
0023-1762 *See* KIPLINGER TAX LETTER, THE. **4735**
0023-1770 *See* KIPLINGER WASHINGTON LETTER, THE. **4480**
0023-1800 *See* KIRCHENCHOR, DER. **4128**
0023-1819 *See* KIRCHENMUSIKER, DER. **4128**
0023-1843 *See* KIRJASTOLEHTI. **3221**
0023-1851 *See* KIRYAT SEFER. **5050**
0023-186X *See* KIRKE OG KULTUR. **4972**
0023-1878 *See* KISERLETES ORVOSTUDOMANY. **3602**
0023-1908 *See* KITA KANTO IGAKU. **3602**
0023-1924 *See* KITASATO ARCHIVES OF EXPERIMENTAL MEDICINE, THE. **3602**
0023-1940 *See* KIVA (TUSCON, ARIZ.), THE. **272**
0023-1983 *See* KJEMI. **1027**
0023-2076 *See* KLEINTIER-PRAXIS. **5515**
0023-2084 *See* KLEIO. **2641**
0023-2130 *See* KLINICESKAJA HIRURGIJA (KIEV). **3969**
0023-2149 *See* KLINICESKAJA MEDICINA. **3602**
0023-2157 *See* KLINIKA OCZNA. **3876**
0023-2165 *See* KLINISCHE MONATSBLATTER FUER AUGENHEILKUNDE. **3876**
0023-2173 *See* CLINICAL INVESTIGATOR, THE. **3565**
0023-2211 *See* DEUTSCHE MONATSHEFTE (BERG (STARNBERG, GERMANY) : 1982). **2515**
0023-2300 *See* KNITTING TIMES. **5184**
0023-2378 *See* KNIZHNOE OBOZRENIE. **5809**
0023-2416 *See* KNJIZEVNE NOVINE : ORGAN SAVEZA KNJIZEVNIKA JUGOSLAVIJE. **5813**
0023-2424 *See* KNJIZNICA. **3221**
0023-2513 *See* KOBE JOURNAL OF MEDICAL SCIENCES. **3602**
0023-2653 *See* KOLNER ZEITSCHRIFT FUER SOZIOLOGIE UND SOZIALPSYCHOLOGIE. **5251**
0023-270X *See* KOERS. **4351**
0023-2718 *See* KYUSHU DAIGAKU KOGAKU SHUHO. **1985**
0023-2777 *See* KOJO KANRI. **875**
0023-2785 *See* KOKKA. **355**
0023-2793 *See* KOKKA GAKKAI ZASSHI. **4480**
0023-2815 *See* KOKS I HIMIJA. **1044**
0023-2831 *See* KOKU EISEI GAKKAI ZASSHI. **1329**
0023-2866 *See* KOKUSAIHO GAIKO ZASSHI. **3132**
0023-2912 *See* KOLLOIDNYJ ZURNAL. **1055**
0023-3056 *See* KOMMUNAL LITTERATUR. **4698**
0023-3234 *See* KONDITOREI UND CAFE. **2347**
0023-3323 *See* KONGELIGE DANSKE VIDENSKABERNES SELSKAB. MATEMATISK-FYSISKE MEDDELELSER. **3516**
0023-334X *See* KONGETSU NO NOYAKU. **984**
0023-3439 *See* KONJUNKTUR VON MORGEN. **1615**
0023-3498 *See* KONJUNKTURPOLITIK. **1571**
0023-3528 *See* KONKRET. **2518**

0023-3609 See KONSTHISTORISK TIDSKRIFT. 355
0023-3633 See KONSTRUKTIVER IGENIEURBAU. 619
0023-365X See KONTAKT (TORONTO). 2567
0023-369X See KYONGYONG NONJIP (SOUL TAEHAKKYO. KYONGYONG YONGUSO). 1615
0023-3765 See KONTYNENTY. 2567
0023-3773 See KONYVTARI FIGYELO. 3222
0023-3900 See KOREA JOURNAL. 2657
0023-3951 See KOREA WEEK. 2657
0023-4001 See KOREAN JOURNAL OF PARASITOLOGY. 3715
0023-401X See GONJUN BOGEN JABJI. 4777
0023-4028 See TAEHAN UIHAK HYOPHOE CHAPCHI. 3644
0023-4036 See KOREAN NATURE. 2197
0023-4044 See JOURNAL OF SOCIAL SCIENCES AND HUMANITIES (SEOUL). 2849
0023-4052 See KOREAN SCIENTIFIC ABSTRACTS. 5124
0023-4109 See KOROT. 3602
0023-415X See KORTARS. 3402
0023-4206 See KOSMICESKIE ISSLEDOVANIJA. 27
0023-4222 See KOSMORAMA. 4073
0023-4230 See KOSMOS (STUTTGART). 5124
0023-4249 See KOSMOS (WARSAW, POLAND). 462
0023-4311 See KOVOEXPORT. 843
0023-432X See KOVOVE MATERIALY. 4007
0023-4338 See KOZARSTVI. 3184
0023-4346 See KOZGAZDASAGI SZEMLE. 689
0023-4354 See KOZHEVENNO-OBUVNAIA PROMYSHLENNOST. 3184
0023-4362 See KOEZLEKEDESTUDOMANYI SZEMLE. 5385
0023-4419 See KRAFTFAHRZEUGTECHNIK. 5418
0023-4427 See KRAFTFUTTER. 202
0023-4486 See KRANKENDIENST. 3602
0023-4494 See KRANKENGYMNASTIK. 4381
0023-4508 See KRANKENHAUSUMSCHAU. 3787
0023-4567 See KRATYLOS. 3293
0023-4591 See KREDIT UND KAPITAL. 796
0023-4699 See KRIMINALISTIK. 3168
0023-4761 See KRISTALLOGRAFIJA. 1032
0023-4834 See KRITISCHE JUSTIZ. 2993
0023-4850 See KRMIVA. 103
0023-4869 See PAPERS - KROEBER ANTHROPOLOGICAL SOCIETY. 243
0023-4885 See KROLIKOVODSTVO I ZVEROVODSTVO. 3184
0023-4923 See KRONIKA; CASOPIS ZA SLOVENSKO KRAJENO ZGODOVINO. 2696
0023-5032 See KUKI SEIJO. 2235
0023-513X See HORIZONTN FUN KULTUR UN LEBN / WORKMEN'S CIRCLE. 5247
0023-5148 See KULTURA (PARIS). 3403
0023-5164 See KULTURA. 2518
0023-5172 See KULTURA I SPOECZENSTWO. 2849
0023-5199 See KULTURA I ZHIZN. 4528
0023-5202 See KULTURA SLOVA. 3293
0023-5288 See KULTUURLEVEN. 5251
0023-5326 See KUMAMOTO MEDICAL JOURNAL, THE. 3660
0023-5334 See MEMOIRS OF THE FACULTY OF ENGINEERING, KUMAMOTO UNIVERSITY. 1987
0023-5350 See KUNGL. SKOGS- OCH LANTBRUKSAKADEMIENS TIDSKRIFT. 103
0023-5369 See MILITARHISTORISK TIDSKRIFT. 4050
0023-5415 See KUNST OG KULTUR. 373
0023-5423 See KUNST UND DAS SCHONELTEIM, DIE. 356
0023-5431 See KUNST UND KIRCHE. 356
0023-544X See KUNST UND LITERATUR. 356
0023-5466 See KUNST + UNTERRICHT. 4351

0023-5474 See KUNSTCHRONIK. 356
0023-5504 See KUNSTHANDEL, DER. 356
0023-5563 See KUNSTSTOFFE. 4456
0023-5598 See KUNSTSTOFFE-PLASTICS (SOLOTHURN). 4456
0023-5652 See KURSBUCH. 2518
0023-5660 See KURUKSHETRA. 5251
0023-5679 See KURUME MEDICAL JOURNAL. 3603
0023-5733 See KUTLWANO. 2641
0023-5776 See JOURNAL OF THE KUWAIT MEDICAL ASSOCIATION, THE. 3598
0023-5830 See KVASNY PRUMYSL. 2368
0023-5849 See KVETY. 2518
0023-5865 See KWARTALNIK ARCHITEKTURY I URBANISTYKI. 302
0023-5873 See KWARTALNIK GEOLOGICZNY. 1386
0023-5881 See KWARTALNIK HISTORII KULTURY MATERIALNEJ. 2696
0023-589X See KWARTALNIK HISTORII NAUKI I TECHNIKI. 5124
0023-5903 See KWARTALNIK HISTORYCZNY. 2622
0023-5911 See KWARTALNIK NEOFILOLOGICZNY. 3294
0023-592X See KWARTALNIK OPOLSKI. 2696
0023-5938 See KWARTALNIK PEDAGOGICZNY. 1760
0023-5954 See KYBERNETIKA. 1252
0023-5962 See KYKLOS. 5208
0023-6063 See MEMOIRS OF THE FACULTY OF ENGINEERING, KYOTO UNIVERSITY. 1987
0023-6071 See BULLETIN OF THE INSTITUTE FOR CHEMICAL RESEARCH, KYOTO UNIVERSITY. 963
0023-608X See JOURNAL OF MATHEMATICS OF KYOTO UNIVERSITY. 3514
0023-6144 See KYUSHU SHINKEI SEISHIN IGAKU. 3930
0023-6152 See JOURNAL OF THE FACULTY OF AGRICULTURE, KYUSHU UNIVERSITY. 101
0023-6160 See MEMOIRS OF THE FACULTY OF ENGINEERING KYUSHU UNIVERSITY. 1987
0023-6179 See MEMOIRS OF THE FACULTY OF SCIENCE, KYUSHU UNIVERSITY. SERIES D, EARTH AND PLANETARY SCIENCES. 1387
0023-6195 See REPORTS OF RESEARCH INSTITUTE FOR APPLIED MECHANICS, KYUSHU UNIVERSITY. 1994
0023-625X See LBI NEWS (NEW YORK, N.Y.). 2696
0023-6349 See LOGA. LOCAL GOVERNMENT ANNOTATIONS. 4663
0023-6365 See LSA BULLETIN. 3300
0023-639X See LSE MAGAZINE. 1503
0023-6438 See LEBENSMITTEL-WISSENSCHAFT + I.E. UND TECHNOLOGIE. 2348
0023-6462 See LABEO; RASSEGNA DI DIRETTO ROMANO. 2993
0023-6500 See LABOR ARBITRATION AWARDS. 1683
0023-656X See LABOR HISTORY. 1683
0023-6586 See LABOR LAW JOURNAL (CHICAGO). 3150
0023-6659 See LABOR TRENDS (SOUTHFIELD, MICH.). 1685
0023-6667 See LABOR WORLD, THE. 1685
0023-6748 See KLINICHESKAIA LABORATORNAIA DIAGNOSTIKA. 3896
0023-6764 See LABORATORY ANIMAL SCIENCE (CHICAGO). 5515
0023-6772 See LABORATORY ANIMALS (LONDON). 5515
0023-6810 See LABORATORY EQUIPMENT. 950
0023-6829 See LABORATORY EQUIPMENT DIGEST. 5125
0023-6837 See LABORATORY INVESTIGATION. 3896
0023-6853 See LABORATORY PRACTICE. 5125
0023-6861 See LABORATORY PRIMATE NEWSLETTER. 5515

0023-6888 See LABORER (WASHINGTON), THE. 1685
0023-690X See LABOUR ARBITRATION CASES. 3151
0023-6942 See LABOUR HISTORY (CANBERRA). 1686
0023-6977 See LABOUR LAW JOURNAL. 3151
0023-7000 See LABOUR RESEARCH (LONDON). 1686
0023-7051 See LACERTA. 5590
0023-7078 See LACKAWANNA JURIST. 2993
0023-7086 See LACROSSE (LONDON, ENG.). 4903
0023-7124 See LADIES' HOME JOURNAL. 5560
0023-7167 See LADY. 2518
0023-7191 See LADY'S CIRCLE. 5560
0023-7205 See LAKARTIDNINGEN. 3603
0023-7302 See LAIT, LE. 196
0023-7353 See LAKIMIES. 2993
0023-737X See LAKOKRASOCHNYE MATERIALY I IKH PRIMENENIE. 4224
0023-7388 See LAL-BAUGH; JOURNAL OF THE MYSORE HORTICULTURAL SOCIETY, THE. 2422
0023-7396 See LALIT KALA CONTEMPORARY. 356
0023-7418 See LAMP (NEW YORK), THE. 4263
0023-7477 See JOURNAL OF THE LANCASTER COUNTY HISTORICAL SOCIETY. 2742
0023-7485 See LANCASTER FARMING. 103
0023-754X See LANDSCAPE ARCHITECTURE NEWS DIGEST. 2423
0023-7604 See LAND & WATER INTERNATIONAL. 2093
0023-7612 See LAND AND WATER LAW REVIEW. 3113
0023-7639 See LAND ECONOMICS. 103
0023-768X See LAND USE DIGEST. 4840
0023-7795 See LANDBOUWMECHANISATIE. 159
0023-7930 See LANDFALL. 3403
0023-8023 See LANDSCAPE (BERKELEY, CALIF.). 2568
0023-8031 See LANDSCAPE ARCHITECTURE. 2423
0023-8066 See LANDSKAB. 2423
0023-8082 See LANDTECHNIK, DIE. 159
0023-8171 See LANDWIRTSCHAFTLICHES JAHRBUCH DER SCHWEIZ. ANNUAIRE AGRICOLE DE LA SUISSE. 104
0023-821X See LANDWIRTSCHAFTLICHES ZENTRALBLATT. ABTEILUNG IV. VETERINARMEDIZIN. 5515
0023-8236 See LANGENBECKS ARCHIV FUER CHIRURGIE. 3969
0023-8252 See LANGENSCHEIDT'S SPRACH-ILLUSTRIERTE. 3294
0023-8309 See LANGUAGE AND SPEECH. 3295
0023-8317 See LANGUAGE AND STYLE. 3295
0023-8333 See LANGUAGE LEARNING. 3295
0023-8368 See LANGUE FRANCAISE. 3296
0023-8376 See LANGUES MODERNES, LES. 3296
0023-8422 See LANTERN. 2499
0023-8457 See LAPIDARY JOURNAL, THE. 2915
0023-852X See LARYNGOSCOPE, THE. 3889
0023-8600 See LASER REPORT. 4437
0023-8627 See CHINESE STUDIES IN PHILOSOPHY. 4343
0023-8694 See LASTECHNIEK. 4027
0023-8791 See LATIN AMERICAN RESEARCH REVIEW. 2743
0023-8813 See LATIN AMERICAN THEATRE REVIEW. 5365
0023-883X See LATINITAS. 3296
0023-8856 See LATOMUS. 3404
0023-8910 See LATVIJAS PSR PRESES HRONIKA; LATVIJAS PSR VALSTS REGISTRACIJAS UN ANALITISKAS BIBLIOGRAFIJAS ORGANS. 418
0023-8945 See LAUGH (MAMARONECK, N.Y.). 4863
0023-8988 See LAUREL MESSENGER. 2744

0023-9003 *See* LAUREL REVIEW / WEST VIRGINIA WESLEYAN COLLEGE, THE. **3404**
0023-902X *See* LAURENTIANUM. **5031**
0023-9054 *See* LAVAL THEOLOGIQUE ET PHILOSOPHIQUE. **4973**
0023-9054 *See* LAVAL THEOLOGIQUE ET PHILOSOPHIQUE. **4973**
0023-9143 *See* LAVOURA ARROZEIRA. **104**
0023-9186 *See* LAW AND CONTEMPORARY PROBLEMS. **2994**
0023-9194 *See* LAW AND ORDER. **3168**
0023-9208 *See* LAW AND POLICY IN INTERNATIONAL BUSINESS. **3101**
0023-9216 *See* LAW & SOCIETY REVIEW. **2994**
0023-9240 *See* LAW BOOKS PUBLISHED. **2995**
0023-9267 *See* LAW INSTITUTE JOURNAL. **2995**
0023-9275 *See* LAW LIBRARIAN (LONDON). **3222**
0023-9283 *See* LAW LIBRARY JOURNAL. **3222**
0023-933X *See* LAW QUARTERLY REVIEW, THE. **2996**
0023-9356 *See* BUFFALO LAW REVIEW. **2944**
0023-9364 *See* GAZETTE - THE LAW SOCIETY OF UPPER CANADA. **2973**
0023-9542 *See* LEABHARLANN, AN. **3223**
0023-9577 *See* LEAD AND ZINC STATISTICS. **4025**
0023-9631 *See* LEADERS MAGAZINE (LEXINGTON). **2886**
0023-964X *See* LEAFLET, THE. **1761**
0023-9666 *See* LEAGUER, THE. **1761**
0023-9690 *See* LEARNING AND MOTIVATION. **4602**
0023-9739 *See* LEATHER (LONDON). **3185**
0023-9763 *See* LEATHER MANUFACTURER, THE. **3185**
0023-9771 *See* LEATHER SCIENCE (MADRAS). **3185**
0023-981X *See* LEATHERNECK. **4049**
0023-9836 *See* LEAVES OF TWIN OAKS, THE. **5269**
0023-9852 *See* LEBANESE MEDICAL JOURNAL. **3604**
0023-9909 *See* LEBENDE SPRACHEN. **3297**
0024-0001 *See* LEBENSMITTEL-ZEITUNG. **2348**
0024-0028 *See* LEBENSMITTEL-INDUSTRIE, DIE. **2791**
0024-0176 *See* LEDER. **3185**
0024-0192 *See* LSL; LEDER, SCHUKE, LEDERWAREN. **3185**
0024-0257 *See* LEEDS ARTS CALENDAR. **357**
0024-0281 *See* PROCEEDINGS OF THE LEEDS PHILOSOPHICAL AND LITERARY SOCIETY, LITERARY AND HISTORICAL SECTION. **5235**
0024-0362 *See* LEGAL EXECUTIVE, THE. **2999**
0024-0435 *See* LEGION. **4049**
0024-0540 *See* LEGON OBSERVER, THE. **2641**
0024-0621 *See* LEICA-FOTOGRAFIE. **4371**
0024-0672 *See* ZOOLOGISCHE MEDEDELINGEN. **5603**
0024-0745 *See* LEKARZ WOJSKOWY. **3604**
0024-0761 *See* LEMOUZI. **2321**
0024-0788 *See* LENAU-FORUM. **3404**
0024-0796 *See* LENGUAJE Y CIENCIAS. **3297**
0024-094X *See* LEONARDO (OXFORD). **357**
0024-0966 *See* JOURNAL OF THE LEPIDOPTERISTS' SOCIETY. **5589**
0024-1091 *See* LESHONENU. **3297**
0024-1105 *See* LESNICTVI. **2387**
0024-1113 *See* LESNOE KHOZAJSTVO (MOSKVA). **2387**
0024-1148 *See* LESOVEDENIE. **2387**
0024-1156 *See* LETECTVI + I.E. A KOSMONAUTIKA. **27**
0024-1164 *See* LETHAIA. **4227**
0024-1172 *See* LETOPIS' GAZETNYKH STATEI. **5809**
0024-1202 *See* LETOPIS ZHURNALNYKH STATEI. **418**
0024-1253 *See* LET'S DANCE. **1313**
0024-127X *See* JAPAN FORUM. **4526**

0024-1288 *See* LET'S LIVE. **4194**
0024-130X *See* LETTERATO. **3404**
0024-1334 *See* LETTERE ITALIANE. **3405**
0024-1350 *See* LETTORE DI PROVINCIA, IL. **3405**
0024-144X *See* LETTURE. **5365**
0024-1482 *See* LEUVENSE BIJDRAGEN. **3297**
0024-1504 *See* LEVANTE. **2518**
0024-1512 *See* LEVELTARI KOEZLEMENYEK. **2622**
0024-1520 *See* LEVENDE NATUUR, DE. **2197**
0024-1539 *See* LEVENDE TALEN. **3297**
0024-1598 *See* LEX; LEGISLAZIONE ITALIANA. **3002**
0024-1628 *See* LEXINGTON THEOLOGICAL QUARTERLY. **4973**
0024-1652 *See* ZOOLOGISCHE VERHANDELINGEN. **5603**
0024-1679 *See* LEYTE-SAMAR STUDIES. **2658**
0024-1717 *See* LIAISONS PARIS. 1963. **3169**
0024-1792 *See* LIBERAL CATHOLIC. **5031**
0024-1822 *See* LIBERAL EDUCATION (WASHINGTON, D.C.). **1834**
0024-1873 *See* LIBERATION (LONDON). **2622**
0024-1989 *See* LIBERIAN STUDIES JOURNAL. **2641**
0024-2020 *See* LIBERTE (MONTREAL). **3465**
0024-2055 *See* LIBERTY (WASHINGTON. 1906). **5062**
0024-2152 *See* LIBRARIUM. **4830**
0024-2160 *See* LIBRARY. **418**
0024-2179 *See* LIBRARY & INFORMATION SCIENCE ABSTRACTS. **3258**
0024-2217 *See* LIBRARY BOOKSELLER, THE. **3224**
0024-2233 *See* LIBRARY CHRONICLE (PHILADELPHIA, PA.), THE. **418**
0024-2241 *See* LIBRARY CHRONICLE OF THE UNIVERSITY OF TEXAS AT AUSTIN, THE. **2849**
0024-2292 *See* LIBRARY HERALD. **3225**
0024-2306 *See* LIBRARY HISTORY. **3225**
0024-2373 *See* LIBRARY LITERATURE. **3258**
0024-2519 *See* LIBRARY QUARTERLY (CHICAGO), THE. **3226**
0024-2527 *See* LIBRARY RESOURCES & TECHNICAL SERVICES. **3227**
0024-2535 *See* LIBRARY REVIEW (GLASGOW). **3227**
0024-2543 *See* LIBRARY SCIENCE WITH A SLANT TO DOCUMENTATION. **3227**
0024-2586 *See* LIBRARY TECHNOLOGY REPORTS. **3227**
0024-2594 *See* LIBRARY TRENDS. **3227**
0024-2632 *See* LSA. LIBRE SERVICE ACTUALITES. **955**
0024-2667 *See* LIBRI (KBENHAVN). **3228**
0024-2683 *See* LIBRI E RIVISTE D'ITALIA. **3405**
0024-2764 *See* LICENSED BEVERAGE JOURNAL. **2369**
0024-2829 *See* LICHENOLOGIST (LONDON). **517**
0024-2896 *See* LIDE A ZEME. **2568**
0024-2950 *See* LIETUVIU DIENOS. **2267**
0024-2969 *See* LITOVSKIJ FIZICESKIJ SBORNIK. **4411**
0024-3019 *See* LIFE (CHICAGO). **2489**
0024-306X *See* LIFE AND WORK. **5062**
0024-3078 *See* LIFE ASSOCIATION NEWS. **2886**
0024-3116 *See* LIFE INSURANCE IDEAS. **2887**
0024-3132 *See* LIFE INSURANCE PLANNING. **2887**
0024-3140 *See* LIFE INSURANCE SELLING. **2887**
0024-3248 *See* LIFE WITH ARCHIE. **4863**
0024-3299 *See* LIGHT AND LIFE (WINONA LAKE). **5062**
0024-3345 *See* LIGHT METAL AGE. **4007**
0024-3418 *See* LIGHTING EQUIPMENT NEWS. **2071**
0024-3426 *See* LIGHTING RESEARCH & TECHNOLOGY. **2071**
0024-3450 *See* LIGUORIAN. **5031**

0024-3469 *See* LIIKETALOUDELLINEN AIKAKAUSKIRJA. **1503**
0024-3477 *See* LIJECNICKI VJESNIK. **3604**
0024-3523 *See* LIMBA ROMANA. **3298**
0024-3590 *See* LIMNOLOGY AND OCEANOGRAPHY. **1451**
0024-3620 *See* LIMOSA. **5618**
0024-3639 *See* LINACRE QUARTERLY, THE. **2252**
0024-3671 *See* LINCOLN HERALD. **2744**
0024-368X *See* LINCOLN LAW REVIEW (SAN FRANCISCO, CALIF.). **3003**
0024-3728 See BERICHTE AUS TECHNIK UND WISSENSCHAFT / LINDE. **5087**
0024-3744 *See* LINEAGRAFICA. **380**
0024-3795 *See* LINEAR ALGEBRA AND ITS APPLICATIONS. **3517**
0024-3841 *See* LINGUA (AMSTERDAM, NETHERLANDS). **3298**
0024-385X *See* LINGUA E STILE. **3298**
0024-3868 *See* LINGUA NOSTRA. **3298**
0024-3892 *See* LINGUISTIC INQUIRY. **3298**
0024-3922 *See* LINGUISTICA. **3298**
0024-3930 *See* LINGUISTISCHE BERICHTE. **3299**
0024-3949 *See* LINGUISTICS. **3299**
0024-4007 *See* LINK (NEW YORK), THE. **2658**
0024-4023 *See* LINKING RING, THE. **4863**
0024-404X *See* LINKS : SOZIALISTISCHE ZEITUNG. **4543**
0024-4066 *See* BIOLOGICAL JOURNAL OF THE LINNEAN SOCIETY. **445**
0024-4082 *See* ZOOLOGICAL JOURNAL OF THE LINNEAN SOCIETY. **5601**
0024-4090 *See* LINNEANA BELGICA. **463**
0024-4163 *See* LION (UNITED STATES ED.), THE. **5233**
0024-4201 *See* LIPIDS. **583**
0024-435X *See* LISTEN (MOUNTAIN VIEW, CALIF.). **1346**
0024-4414 *See* LISTENING (RIVER FOREST). **4974**
0024-4457 *See* LISTY FILOLOGICKE (PRAGUE, CZECHOSLOVAKIA : 1946). **3300**
0024-449X *See* LITEJNOE PROIZVODSTVO. **4007**
0024-4511 *See* LITERARY CAVALCADE. **3406**
0024-452X *See* LITERARY CRITERION, THE. **3406**
0024-4554 *See* LITERARY HALF-YEARLY, THE. **3406**
0024-4589 *See* LITERARY REVIEW (TEANECK), THE. **3406**
0024-4597 *See* LITERARY SKETCHES. **3406**
0024-4627 *See* LITERAT, DER. **3406**
0024-4643 *See* LITERATUR IN WISSENSCHAFT UND UNTERRICHT : LWU. **3406**
0024-4708 *See* LITERATURA LUDOWA. **2321**
0024-4716 *See* LITERATURA RADZIECKA. **3406**
0024-4724 *See* LITERATURA V SHKOLE. **3406**
0024-4759 *See* LITERATURE AND PSYCHOLOGY. **3407**
0024-4767 *See* LITERATURE EAST & WEST. **3407**
0024-4791 *See* LITERATUREN ZBOR. **3407**
0024-4902 *See* LITHOLOGY AND MINERAL RESOURCES. **2143**
0024-4937 *See* LITHOS. **1441**
0024-497X *See* LITOLOGIA I POLEZNYE ISKOPAEMYE. **2143**
0024-5054 *See* LITTLE REVIEW, THE. **3408**
0024-5089 *See* LITUANUS. **2697**
0024-5100 *See* LITURGISCHES JAHRBUCH. **4974**
0024-5208 *See* LIVESTOCK MARKET DIGEST. **214**
0024-5232 *See* LIVING BLUES. **4129**
0024-5240 *See* LIVING CHURCH (1942), THE. **4974**
0024-5275 *See* LIVING LIGHT, THE. **5031**
0024-5283 *See* LIVING MUSEUM, THE. **4090**
0024-5313 *See* LIVINGSTON COUNTY AGRICULTURAL NEWS. **105**
0024-533X *See* LIVRE ET L'ESTAMPE, LE. **4830**
0024-5372 *See* LIVRUSTKAMMAREN. **4049**

0024-5399 See LIVSMEDELSTEKNIK. 2348
0024-547X See LLOYDS BANK REVIEW. 796
0024-5488 See LLOYD'S LAW REPORTS. 3181
0024-5585 See LOCAL HISTORIAN (LONDON. 1968). 2697
0024-5798 See LOG (HAYES), THE. 28
0024-5801 See LOG (ANNAPOLIS), THE. 4863
0024-581X See LOG ANALYST, THE. 1949
0024-5828 See LOG OF MYSTIC SEAPORT, THE. 2744
0024-5836 See LOGIQUE ET ANALYSE. 3517
0024-5852 See LOGISTICS SPECTRUM. 5126
0024-5887 See LOGOS. 4352
0024-5925 See LOK UDYOG. 690
0024-5984 See LONDON ARCHAEOLOGIST, THE. 273
0024-6085 See LONDON MAGAZINE. 3408
0024-6093 See BULLETIN OF THE LONDON MATHEMATICAL SOCIETY, THE. 3498
0024-6107 See JOURNAL OF THE LONDON MATHEMATICAL SOCIETY. 3515
0024-6115 See PROCEEDINGS OF THE LONDON MATHEMATICAL SOCIETY. 3528
0024-6158 See JOURNAL OF THE LONDON SOCIETY, THE. 354
0024-628X See LONG ISLAND FORUM. 2744
0024-6301 See LONG RANGE PLANNING. 876
0024-631X See LONG ROOM. 3229
0024-6379 See LOOK AT FINLAND. 2519
0024-6425 See LOOKOUT (NEW YORK), THE. 5295
0024-645X See LOON, THE. 5618
0024-6514 See LORIS. 2197
0024-6522 See LOS ANGELES. 2537
0024-6735 See LOUISIANA AGRICULTURE. 105
0024-6778 See LOUISIANA CONSERVATIONIST (1948). 2197
0024-6794 See LOUISIANA ENGINEER. 1985
0024-6816 See LOUISIANA HISTORY. 2745
0024-6832 See LOUISIANA INSUROR. 2887
0024-6859 See LOUISIANA LAW REVIEW. 3004
0024-6891 See LOUISIANA-REVY. 324
0024-6921 See JOURNAL OF THE LOUISIANA STATE MEDICAL SOCIETY, THE. 3599
0024-6948 See LOUISVILLE. 2537
0024-6956 See LOUVAIN MEDICAL. 3605
0024-6964 See LOUVAIN STUDIES. 4974
0024-6980 See LOV OG RETT. 3004
0024-7022 See LOVEJOY'S GUIDANCE DIGEST. 1834
0024-7081 See LOYOLA UNIVERSITY OF CHICAGO LAW JOURNAL. 3005
0024-7103 See LP-GAS. 4263
0024-7146 See LUBRICATION (NEW YORK, N.Y. : 1911). 2120
0024-7154 See LUBRICATION ENGINEERING. 2120
0024-7219 See LUCKNOW LIBRARIAN. 3229
0024-7251 See LUFT- UND KALETECHNIK. 619
0024-7286 See LUISTER. 4129
0024-7294 See LUMBER CO-OPERATOR, THE. 2402
0024-7316 See PHILIPPINE LUMBERMAN, THE. 2403
0024-7324 See LUMEN VITAE. 4975
0024-7359 See LUMIERE ET VIE. 4975
0024-7383 See LUONNON TUTKIJA. 4167
0024-7413 See LUSO-BRAZILIAN REVIEW. 1078
0024-7421 See LUSTRUM. 1078
0024-743X See LUTHERAN (CHICAGO, ILL. : 1988). 5062
0024-7448 See LUTHERAN EDUCATION. 5063
0024-7456 See LUTHERAN FORUM. 5063
0024-7464 See LUTHERAN LAYMAN, THE. 4975
0024-7472 See LUTHERAN LIBRARIES. 3229
0024-7499 See LUTHERAN QUARTERLY (GETTYSBURG. 1949). 4975
0024-7510 See LUTHERAN SENTINEL. 5063

0024-7537 See LUTHERAN SPOKESMAN. 5063
0024-7553 See LUTHERAN THEOLOGICAL JOURNAL. 5063
0024-757X See LUTHERAN WITNESS (ST. LOUIS), THE. 5063
0024-7588 See LUTHERAN WITNESS REPORTER. 5063
0024-7618 See LUTHERISCHE MONATSHEFTE. 4975
0024-7634 See LUTRA. 5590
0024-7669 See LUX; LA REVUE DE L'ECLAIRAGE. 2071
0024-7758 See JOURNAL OF REPRODUCTIVE MEDICINE. 3764
0024-7766 See LYMPHOLOGY. 3773
0024-7782 See LYON CHIRURGICAL. 3969
0024-7804 See LYON PHARMACEUTIQUE. 4314
0024-7820 See LYRIC (CHRISTIANSBURG, VA.), THE. 3465
0024-7928 See NEWSLETTER - MANITOBA ASSOCIATION OF SCHOOL TRUSTEES. 1867
0024-8142 See MFM. MODERNE FOTOTECHNIK. 4371
0024-8215 See MLA INTERNATIONAL BIBLIOGRAPHY OF BOOKS AND ARTICLES ON THE MODERN LANGUAGES AND LITERATURES (COMPLETE ED.). 3336
0024-8266 See MONTHLY NOTES OF THE ASTRONOMICAL SOCIETY OF SOUTHERN AFRICA. 397
0024-8320 See MRAX INFORMATION. 5209
0024-8495 See WEEKLY BULLETIN - HUNGARIAN NEWS AGENCY (BUDAPEST, 1970). 2524
0024-8525 See MTZ. MOTORTECHNISCHE ZEITSCHRIFT. 2123
0024-855X See MALL OG MINNE. 3301
0024-8711 See MAANDSTATISTIEK VAN BEVOLKING EN VOLKSGEZONDHEID. 4789
0024-8746 See MAANDSTATISTIEK VAN DE BUITENLANDSE HANDEL PER LAND. 844
0024-8851 See MAATSTAF. 3300
0024-886X See MABON. 324
0024-8908 See MCCALL'S. 5561
0024-8924 See MCCALL'S NEEDLEWORK & CRAFTS. 5185
0024-8959 See MACCHINE. 2120
0024-8967 See MACCHINE E MOTORI AGRICOLI. 159
0024-9009 See MAKEDONSKA TRIBUNA. 5665
0024-9033 See MCGILL JOURNAL OF EDUCATION. 1763
0024-9041 See MCGILL LAW JOURNAL. 3132
0024-905X See MCGILL MEDICAL JOURNAL. 3606
0024-9068 See MCGILL NEWS, THE. 1093
0024-9114 See MACHINE DESIGN. 2120
0024-9149 See MACHINE OUTIL. 2120
0024-919X See MACHINERY AND PRODUCTION ENGINEERING. 2120
0024-9211 See MACHINERY MARKET. 2121
0024-9262 See MACLEAN'S. 2489
0024-9270 See LIBRARY RESEARCH NEWS / MCMASTER UNIVERSITY. 3227
0024-9289 See MACOMB COUNTY LEGAL NEWS. 3005
0024-9297 See MACROMOLECULES. 1044
0024-9319 See MAD (NEW YORK, N.Y.). 4863
0024-936X See MADAME. 404
0024-9394 See MADEMOISELLE (NEW YORK, N.Y. 1935). 5560
0024-9602 See MADRAS AGRICULTURAL JOURNAL, THE. 106
0024-9637 See MADRONO. 517
0024-9645 See MAELKERITIDENDE. 106
0024-9777 See MAGAZIN KUNST. 357
0024-9793 See MEDIA INDUSTRY NEWSLETTER. 1116
0024-9807 See MAGAZINE LITTERAIRE. 3409
0024-9831 See MAGAZINE OF CONCRETE RESEARCH. 2027

0024-984X See FANTASY & SCIENCE FICTION. 3387
0024-9947 See MAGLIE CALZE INDUSTRIA. 1085
0024-998X See MAGNETOHYDRODYNAMICS (NEW YORK, N.Y. 1965). 4444
0025-0015 See MAGNITNAJA GIDRODINAMIKA. 4444
0025-004X See MAGYAR ALLATORVOSOK LAPJA. 5516
0025-0058 See MAGYAR ALUMINUM. 4008
0025-0066 See MAGYAR BELORVOSI ARCHIVUM (1955). 3605
0025-0082 See MAGYAR EPITOMUVESZET (BUDAPEST, 1952). 303
0025-0120 See MAGYAR GEOFIZIKA. 1408
0025-0147 See MAGYAR JOG (MAGYAR JOGASZ SZOVETSEG : 1982). 3005
0025-0155 See MAGYAR KEMIAI FOLYOIRAT. 985
0025-0163 See MAGYAR KEMIKUSOK LAPJA. 985
0025-0171 See MAGYAR KONYVSZEMLE. 3259
0025-0201 See MAGYAR MUHELY. 3300
0025-021X See MAGYAR NOORVOSOK LAPJA. 3764
0025-0228 See MAGYAR NYELV. 3300
0025-0236 See MAGYAR NYELVOR. 3300
0025-0244 See MAGYAR ONKOLOGIA. 3820
0025-0252 See MAGYAR ORVOSI BIBLIOGRAFIA. 3660
0025-0260 See MAGYAR PEDAGOGIA. 1762
0025-0279 See MAGYAR PSZICHOLOGIAI SZEMLE. 4603
0025-0309 See MAGYAR TEXTILTECHNIKA. 5354
0025-0317 See MAGYAR TRAUMATOLOGIA, ORTHOPAEDIA ES HELYREALLIT SEBESZET. 3969
0025-0325 See MAGYAR TUDOMANY. 5126
0025-0384 See MAGYAR ZENE. 4129
0025-0406 See MAHA BODHI, THE. 5021
0025-0422 See JOURNAL OF THE MAHARAJA SAYAJIRAO UNIVERSITY OF BARODA. 1759
0025-0538 See MAIA. 1078
0025-0570 See MAIN CURRENTS IN MODERN THOUGHT. 2538
0025-0600 See MAIN SHEET. 594
0025-0619 See MAINE BUSINESS INDICATORS. 1573
0025-0651 See MAINE LAW REVIEW (1963). 3005
0025-0767 See MAINE NURSE, THE. 3861
0025-0775 See MAINE TEACHER, THE. 1762
0025-0783 See MAINE TIMES. 5685
0025-0791 See MAINE TOWNSMAN, THE. 4664
0025-0805 See JOURNAL - MAINE WATER UTILITIES ASSOCIATION. 4761
0025-0880 See MAINTENANCE & ENTREPRISE PARIS. 1985
0025-0929 See MAINTENANCE SUPPLIES. 2236
0025-0937 See MAISON-DIEU, LA. 5032
0025-0945 See MAISON & JARDIN. 2902
0025-0953 See MAISON FRANCAISE, LA. 2792
0025-0988 See MAITRE ELECTRICIEN, LE. 2071
0025-0996 See MAITRE IMPRIMEUR, LE. 4566
0025-1003 See JOURNAL OF THE INTERNATIONAL PHONETIC ASSOCIATION. 3292
0025-1089 See MAKEDONSKI JAZIK. 3301
0025-1127 See MATEKON. 1504
0025-116X See MAKROMOLEKULARE CHEMIE (BASEL, SWITZERLAND : 1981). 1044
0025-1216 See MALAHAT REVIEW, THE. 3409
0025-1283 See MALAYAN LAW JOURNAL (BILINGUAL ED.). 3005
0025-1291 See MALAYAN NATURE JOURNAL, THE. 4167
0025-1321 See MALAYSIAN AGRICULTURAL JOURNAL, THE. 106
0025-1348 See MALAYSIAN MANAGEMENT REVIEW. 691
0025-1429 See STUDIA HISTORYCZNE. 2631
0025-1461 See MAMMALIA (PARIS). 5590
0025-1496 See MAN (LONDON). 240

0025-1534 See MAN AND WORLD. 4352
0025-1550 See MAN-ENVIRONMENT SYSTEMS. 303
0025-1569 See MAN IN INDIA. 240
0025-1615 See MANAB MON. 4603
0025-1623 See MANAGE. 876
0025-164X See MANAGEMENT (DUBLIN). 877
0025-1658 See MANAGEMENT AUCKLAND. 876
0025-1674 See MANAGEMENT ACCOUNTANT, THE. 747
0025-1682 See MANAGEMENT ACCOUNTING (LONDON). 747
0025-1690 See MANAGEMENT ACCOUNTING (NEW YORK, N.Y.). 747
0025-1747 See MANAGEMENT DECISION. 877
0025-181X See MANAGEMENT INTERNATIONAL REVIEW. 877
0025-1828 See MANAGEMENT JAPAN. 877
0025-1844 See MANAGEMENT NEWS : THE NEWSPAPER OF THE BRITISH INSTITUTE OF MANAGEMENT. 877
0025-1860 See MANAGEMENT QUARTERLY. 877
0025-1895 See MANAGEMENT REVIEW (SARANAC LAKE). 944
0025-1909 See MANAGEMENT SCIENCE. 878
0025-1925 See MANAGEMENT TODAY. 878
0025-1968 See MANAGER'S MAGAZINE. 2887
0025-1984 See MANAS. 4603
0025-200X See MANCHESTER GUARDIAN WEEKLY. 5812
0025-2034 See MANCHESTER SCHOOL OF ECONOMIC AND SOCIAL STUDIES, THE. 1504
0025-2158 See MANIFESTO. 5804
0025-2239 See MANITOBA CO-OPERATOR. 5789
0025-2255 See MANITOBA MEDICAL REVIEW (MICROFICHE). 3606
0025-2271 See MANITOBA PROFESSIONAL ENGINEER. 1985
0025-228X See MANITOBA TEACHER. 1762
0025-2344 See MANKIND QUARTERLY. 240
0025-2409 See MANPOWER AND APPLIED PSYCHOLOGY. 4603
0025-2492 See MANTEIA. 3410
0025-2514 See MANUELLE MEDIZIN. 3606
0025-2530 See MANUFACTURERS' MONTHLY. 3483
0025-2565 See MANUFACTURING CLOTHIER (LONDON). 1085
0025-2603 See MANUSCRIPTA (ST. LOUIS, MO.). 2850
0025-2611 See MANUSCRIPTA MATHEMATICA. 3517
0025-262X See MANUSCRIPTS (NEW YORK, N.Y.). 2774
0025-2638 See MANUSKRIPTE. 3410
0025-2646 See MANUTENCION Y ALMACENAJE. 5127
0025-2697 See MAPPE, DIE. 2902
0025-2735 See MAR Y PESCA. 2308
0025-2751 See MARATHWADA UNIVERSITY JOURNAL. 1835
0025-2816 See ASAHI EVENING NEWS. 5805
0025-2859 See MARCHES TROPICAUX ET MEDITERRANEENS. 845
0025-2867 See MARCOLIAN, THE. 1093
0025-2913 See MARG. 357
0025-2921 See MARGIN. 1573
0025-2948 See MARGINALIEN. 419
0025-2956 See MARGRIET. 2519
0025-2980 See MARIAGES. 2283
0025-3057 See MARIE-FRANCE. 1086
0025-3103 See MARINA MERCANTILE, LA. 5452
0025-312X See M&R. MARINE AND RECREATION NEWS. 594
0025-3146 See JOURNAL OF THE MARINE BIOLOGICAL ASSOCIATION OF INDIA. 555
0025-3154 See JOURNAL OF THE MARINE BIOLOGICAL ASSOCIATION OF THE UNITED KINGDOM. 555
0025-3162 See MARINE BIOLOGY. 556

0025-3170 See MARINE CORPS GAZETTE. 4049
0025-3227 See MARINE GEOLOGY. 1386
0025-3235 See MARINE GEOPHYSICAL RESEARCHES. 1451
0025-3251 See MARINE OBSERVER, THE. 1430
0025-326X See MARINE POLLUTION BULLETIN. 2236
0025-3308 See MARINE SCIENCE CONTENTS TABLES. ACTUALITES DES SCIENCES DE LA MER. INDICES DE REVISTAS SOBRE CIENCIAS MARINAS. 1363
0025-3324 See MARINE TECHNOLOGY SOCIETY JOURNAL. 1452
0025-3340 See MARINEBLAD. 4179
0025-3359 See MARINER'S MIRROR. 4179
0025-3367 See MARINERS WEATHER LOG. 1430
0025-3375 See MARINNYTT. 4179
0025-3413 See TRIDENT (HALIFAX). 4059
0025-3472 See MARITIMES. 1452
0025-3499 See MARK TWAIN JOURNAL (1954). 433
0025-3596 See MARKET RESEARCH ABSTRACTS. 731
0025-360X See MARKET RESEARCH FACTS AND TRENDS FROM MACLEAN-HUNTER RESEARCH BUREAU. 1504
0025-3618 See JOURNAL OF THE MARKET RESEARCH SOCIETY. 929
0025-3642 See MARKETING (TORONTO). 932
0025-3650 See MARKETING (LONDON). 931
0025-3723 See MARKETING IN EUROPE. 931
0025-3774 See MARKETING-JOURNAL. 762
0025-3782 See MARKETING MIX DIGEST. 931
0025-3790 See MARKETING NEWS. 931
0025-388X See MAROC MEDICAL. 3606
0025-3987 See MARQUETTE LAW REVIEW. 3006
0025-3995 See MARQUETTE TRIBUNE (MILWAUKEE), THE. 5768
0025-4118 See MARXISM TODAY. 2519
0025-4142 See MARYKNOLL. 5032
0025-4150 See MARYLAND AND DELAWARE GENEALOGIST, THE. 2459
0025-4177 See MARYLAND BAR JOURNAL, THE. 3006
0025-4223 See MARYLAND FRUIT GROWER, THE. 178
0025-4231 See BULLETIN OF THE MARYLAND HERPETOLOGICAL SOCIETY. 5579
0025-424X See MARYLAND HISTORIAN, THE. 2622
0025-4258 See MARYLAND HISTORICAL MAGAZINE. 2745
0025-4282 See MARYLAND LAW REVIEW (1936). 3006
0025-4347 See MARYLAND PHARMACIST, THE. 4314
0025-4355 See JOURNAL OF THE MARYLAND STATE DENTAL ASSOCIATION. 1328
0025-4495 See MASCHINENBAUTECHNIK. 2121
0025-4509 See MASCHINENMARKT. 1986
0025-4517 See MASCHINEN SCHADEN, DER. 2121
0025-4517 See MASCHINENSCHADEN, DER. 2121
0025-4533 See MASCHINENWELT ELEKTROTECHNIK. 2121
0025-455X See MASHINOSTROENE. 2121
0025-4606 See MASKE UND KOTHURN. 3410
0025-4673 See WASHINGTON MASONIC TRIBUNE : THE OFFICIAL MAGAZINE OF THE MASONIC GRAND LODGE OF WASHINGTON. 5237
0025-4681 See MASONRY. 620
0025-4738 See MASS SPECTROMETRY BULLETIN. 1011
0025-4770 See MASSACHUSETTS CPA REVIEW. 748
0025-4800 See JOURNAL OF THE MASSACHUSETTS DENTAL SOCIETY. 1328
0025-4878 See MASSACHUSETTS REVIEW, THE. 2850

0025-4924 See MASSACHUSETTS WILDLIFE. 2198
0025-4940 See MASSIMARIO DELLA GIURISPRUDENZA ITALIANA. 3007
0025-5017 See MASTER DETECTIVE. 2538
0025-5025 See MASTER DRAWINGS. 380
0025-5122 See MASTHEAD, THE. 2922
0025-5149 See MATEMAATTISTEN AINEIDEN AIKAKAUSKIRJA. 3517
0025-5165 See MATEMATICKI VESNIK. 3518
0025-519X See MATEMATIKAI LAPOK. 3518
0025-5246 See MATERIA MEDICA POLONA (ENGLISH EDITION). 4314
0025-5262 See MATERIAL HANDLING ENGINEERING. HANDBOOK DIRECTORY. 2104
0025-5262 See MATERIAL HANDLING ENGINEERING. 2104
0025-5270 See MATERIAL UND ORGANISMEN. 1986
0025-5270 See MATERIAL UND ORGANISMEN; BEIHEFT. 1017
0025-5289 See MATERIALE PLASTICE. 4456
0025-5300 See MATERIALPRUFUNG. 2104
0025-5319 See MATERIALS ENGINEERING. 2105
0025-5327 See MATERIALS EVALUATION. 2105
0025-5343 See MATERIALS MANAGEMENT AND DISTRIBUTION. 1618
0025-5351 See MATERIALS HANDLING NEWS. 2121
0025-5408 See MATERIALS RESEARCH BULLETIN. 2105
0025-5459 See MATERIE PLASTICHE ED ELASTOMERI. 4456
0025-5513 See MATHEMATICA JAPONICA. 3518
0025-5521 See MATHEMATICA SCANDINAVICA. 3518
0025-553X See MATHEMATICAE NOTAE. 3518
0025-5556 See BULLETIN OF THE MATHEMATICAL ASSOCIATION OF INDIA. 3499
0025-5564 See MATHEMATICAL BIOSCIENCES. 464
0025-5572 See MATHEMATICAL GAZETTE. 3519
0025-5580 See MATHEMATICAL LOG, THE. 3519
0025-5629 See MATHEMATICAL REVIEWS. 3542
0025-5645 See JOURNAL OF THE MATHEMATICAL SOCIETY OF JAPAN. 3515
0025-5653 See MATHEMATICAL SPECTRUM. 3520
0025-5661 See MATHEMATICAL SYSTEMS THEORY. 3520
0025-567X See MATEMATICHESKIE ZAMETKI. 3517
0025-570X See MATHEMATICS MAGAZINE. 3521
0025-5718 See MATHEMATICS OF COMPUTATION. 3521
0025-5726 See MATHEMATICS OF THE USSR : IZVESTIJA. 3521
0025-5734 See MATHEMATICS OF THE USSR : SBORNIK. 3521
0025-5742 See MATHEMATICS STUDENT (AHMEDABAD), THE. 3521
0025-5769 See MATHEMATICS TEACHER, THE. 3521
0025-5785 See MATHEMATICS TEACHING. 3521
0025-5793 See MATHEMATIKA. 3521
0025-5807 See MATHEMATIKUNTERRICHT. 3521
0025-5831 See MATHEMATISCHE ANNALEN. 3522
0025-584X See MATHEMATISCHE NACHRICHTEN. 3522
0025-5858 See ABHANDLUNGEN AUS DEM MATHEMATISCHEN SEMINAR DER HAMBURGISCHEN UNIVERSITAT. 3490
0025-5866 See MMU, DER MATHEMATISCHE UND NATURWISSENSCHAFTLICHE UNTERRICHT. 3523
0025-5874 See MATHEMATISCHE ZEITSCHRIFT. 3522
0025-5912 See MATI (TEL-AVIV). 2027
0025-5955 See MATILDA ZIEGLER MAGAZINE FOR THE BLIND. 4391

0025-5998 See MATRIX AND TENSOR QUARTERLY, THE. 3522
0025-6021 See MATURE YEARS. 4976
0025-6110 See MAXWELL REVIEW. 5209
0025-6129 See MAY DAY PICTORIAL NEWS. 5452
0025-6153 See MAYDICA. 107
0025-6161 See MAYFAIR LONDON. 3995
0025-6196 See MAYO CLINIC PROCEEDINGS. 3799
0025-6218 See MAZPUTNINS. 1066
0025-6277 See ME NAISET. 5561
0025-6285 See MEANDER. 1078
0025-6390 See MEAT PROCESSING. 2349
0025-6420 See MECANICA POPULAR. 2538
0025-6439 See MECANIQUE, MATERIAUX, ELECTRICITE. 2121
0025-6455 See MECCANICA (MILAN). 4428
0025-6471 See MECH. 4179
0025-6501 See MECHANICAL ENGINEERING (NEW YORK, N.Y. 1919). 2122
0025-651X See MECHANICAL ENGINEERING NEWS (FAYETTEVILLE, ARK.). 2122
0025-6544 See MECHANICS OF SOLIDS. 4412
0025-6552 See MECHANIK. 2122
0025-6633 See MEDAL COLLECTOR, THE. 2774
0025-6692 See MEDECIN DU QUEBEC. 3607
0025-6722 See MEDECINE DU SPORT. 3955
0025-6749 See MEDECINE ET HYGIENE. 3607
0025-6773 See MEDECINE INFANTILE, LA. 3906
0025-682X See MEDECINE TROPICALE. 3986
0025-6897 See MEDIA AND METHODS. 1900
0025-7001 See MEDICAL ASPECTS OF HUMAN SEXUALITY. 5188
0025-7028 See JOURNAL OF THE MEDICAL ASSOCIATION OF GEORGIA. 3599
0025-7036 See JOURNAL OF THE MEDICAL ASSOCIATION OF THAILAND. 3599
0025-7079 See MEDICAL CARE. 3608
0025-7087 See MEDICAL CARE REVIEW. 3608
0025-7109 See TRADITIONAL MEDICAL SYSTEMS. 3647
0025-7125 See MEDICAL CLINICS OF NORTH AMERICA, THE. 3608
0025-7206 See MEDICAL ECONOMICS. 3608
0025-7230 See MEDICAL ELECTRONICS & EQUIPMENT NEWS. 3609
0025-7265 See MEDICAL GROUP NEWS. 3609
0025-7273 See MEDICAL HISTORY. 3609
0025-729X See MEDICAL JOURNAL OF AUSTRALIA. 3610
0025-732X See MEDICAL LETTER ON DRUGS AND THERAPEUTICS (ENGLISH ED.), THE. 4315
0025-732X See MEDICAL LETTER. 3610
0025-7338 See BULLETIN OF THE MEDICAL LIBRARY ASSOCIATION. 3198
0025-7354 See MEDICAL MARKETING & MEDIA. 933
0025-7397 See MEDICAL-MORAL NEWSLETTER, THE. 3610
0025-7435 See MEDICAL POST, THE. 3611
0025-746X See MEDICAL RADIOGRAPHY AND PHOTOGRAPHY. 3943
0025-7591 See MEDICAL TRIAL TECHNIQUE QUARTERLY. 3742
0025-7597 See MC : THE MODERN CHURCHMAN. 4976
0025-763X See MEDICAL WORLD NEWS. 3612
0025-7656 See MEDICAMENTOS DE ACTUALIDAD. 4315
0025-7664 See MEDICAMUNDI. 3612
0025-7680 See MEDICINA (BUENOS AIRES). 3613
0025-7699 See MEDICINA. 3612
0025-7753 See MEDICINA CLINICA. 3613
0025-7818 See MEDICINA DEL LAVORO. 3613
0025-7834 See MEDICINA E MORALE. 3613
0025-7850 See JOURNAL OF MEDICINE (WESTBURY). 3596

0025-7893 See MEDICINA PSICOSOMATICA. 3613
0025-7915 See MEDICINA SOCIALE. 3613
0025-7931 See RESPIRATION. 3951
0025-7974 See MEDICINE (BALTIMORE). 3613
0025-8024 See MEDICINE, SCIENCE, AND THE LAW. 3742
0025-8075 See MEDICINSKAJA TEHNIKA. 3614
0025-8105 See MEDICINSKI PREGLED. 3614
0025-8121 See MEDICINSKI RAZGLEDI. 3614
0025-8172 See MEDICO-LEGAL JOURNAL, THE. 3742
0025-8296 See MEDITERRANEE. 2698
0025-830X See MEDITSINSKII ZHURNAL UZBEKISTANA. 3614
0025-8318 See MEDITSINSKAIA GAZETA. 4790
0025-8326 See MEDICINSKAJA PARAZITOLOGIJA I PARAZITARNYE BOLEZNI. 3986
0025-8334 See MEDICINSKAJA RADIOLOGIJA. 3943
0025-8342 See MEDICINSKAJA SESTRA. 3861
0025-8350 See MEDIUM (FRANKFURT). 1117
0025-8377 See MEDIUM (SASKATOON). 1763
0025-8385 See MEDIUM AEVUM. 3301
0025-8431 See MEDIZINHISTORISCHES JOURNAL. 3615
0025-8474 See MEDIZINISCHE MONATSSCHRIFT (STUTTGART). 3615
0025-8512 See MEDIZINISCHE WELT. 3615
0025-8601 See MEDYCYNA DOSWIADCZALNA I MIKROBIOLOGIA. 3615
0025-8628 See MEDYCYNA WETERYNARYJNA. 5516
0025-8644 See MEERESTECHNIK. 2093
0025-8652 See MEETINGS AND CONVENTIONS. 692
0025-8679 See MEGAMOT / MOSAD SOLD LEMAAN HA-YELED VEHA-NOAR. 5209
0025-8776 See MEIERIPOSTEN. 196
0025-8830 See MEDICAL EQUIPMENT JOURNAL OF JAPAN. 3609
0025-8903 See MEKHANIZATSIIA STROITELSTVA. 2027
0025-8911 See MELANGES DE SCIENCE RELIGIEUSE. 4976
0025-8938 See MELBOURNE UNIVERSITY LAW REVIEW. 3009
0025-9004 See MELODIE UND RHYTHMUS. 4130
0025-9012 See MELODY MAKER (LONDON). 4130
0025-9195 See MEMOIRES C.E.R.E.S. 2027
0025-9233 See MENCKENIANA. 3411
0025-925X See MENDELEEV CHEMISTRY JOURNAL. 985
0025-9284 See BULLETIN OF THE MENNINGER CLINIC. 3922
0025-9292 See MENNINGER PERSPECTIVE. 3930
0025-9330 See MENNONITE (1936), THE. 5063
0025-9349 See MENNONITE BRETHREN HERALD. 5063
0025-9357 See MENNONITE HISTORICAL BULLETIN. 5064
0025-9365 See MENNONITE LIFE. 5064
0025-9373 See MENNONITE QUARTERLY REVIEW, THE. 5064
0025-9454 See MENS EN MAATSCHAPPIJ. 5252
0025-9462 See MENS & MELODIE. 4131
0025-9535 See MEN'S WEAR OF CANADA. 1086
0025-9543 See MENSA BULLETIN. 5233
0025-956X See MENSAJE (SANTIAGO, CHILE). 4976
0025-9756 See MERCADO DE VALORES, EL. 798
0025-987X See MERCER LAW REVIEW. 3009
0025-990X See MERCIAN GEOLOGIST. 1387
0025-9969 See MERCURY (LOS ANGELES, CALIF.). 4904
0025-9993 See MERES ES AUTOMATIKA. 4031
0026-0010 See MERGERS & ACQUISITIONS. 798
0026-0029 See MERIAN (HAMBURG, GERMANY). 2519

0026-0096 See MERKUR. 3347
0026-0231 See MESSAGE (NASHVILLE, TENN.). 5064
0026-0452 See META (MONTREAL). 3302
0026-0452 See META (MONTREAL). 3302
0026-0460 See METAAL & KUNSTSTOF. 4008
0026-0495 See METABOLISM, CLINICAL AND EXPERIMENTAL. 3674
0026-0509 See METABOLISMO. 3799
0026-0533 See METAL BULLETIN, THE. 4009
0026-055X See METAL FABRICATING NEWS. 3484
0026-0568 See METAL FABRICATOR, THE. 4009
0026-0576 See METAL FINISHING. 4009
0026-0657 See METAL POWDER REPORT. 4009
0026-0673 See METALLOVEDENIE I TERMICHESKAYA OBRABOTKA METALLOV. 4010
0026-0746 See METALL (BERLIN). 4009
0026-0797 See METALLOBERFLACHE. 4009
0026-0819 See METALLOVEDENIE I TERMICESKAJA OBRABOTKA (KALININ). 4009
0026-0827 See METALLURG. 4010
0026-0843 See METALLURGIA ITALIANA, LA. 4010
0026-0894 See METALLURGIST (NEW YORK). 4010
0026-0908 See METALLVERARBEITUNG. 4011
0026-0924 See METALS ABSTRACTS. 4026
0026-0932 See METALS ABSTRACTS INDEX. 4026
0026-0959 See METALS AND MINERALS REVIEW. 4011
0026-0975 See METALS WEEK. 4011
0026-0983 See METALURGIA (SAO PAULO). 4011
0026-0991 See METALURGIA Y ELECTRICIDAD. 4011
0026-1009 See METALWORKING DIGEST. 4011
0026-1033 See METALWORKING PRODUCTION. 4012
0026-1068 See METAPHILOSOPHY. 4352
0026-1084 See METAUX, CORROSION - INDUSTRIE. 2015
0026-1084 See METAUX. CORROSION INDUSTRIE. 4012
0026-1114 See METEORITICS. 1387
0026-1130 See METEOROLOGICAL AND GEOASTROPHYSICAL ABSTRACTS. 1363
0026-1149 See METEOROLOGICAL MAGAZINE. 1430
0026-1165 See JOURNAL OF THE METEOROLOGICAL SOCIETY OF JAPAN. 1427
0026-1173 See METEOROLOGICKE ZPRAVY. 1431
0026-1181 See METEOROLOGIE, LA. 1431
0026-1211 See METEOROLOGISCHE ZEITSCHRIFT / HERAUSGEGEBEN VON DER DEUTSCHEN METEOROLOGISCHEN GESELLSCHAFT, OSTERREICHISCHEN GESELLSCHAFT FEUR METEOROLOGIE, SCHWEIZERISCHEN GESELLSCHAFT FUER GEOPHYSIK. 1431
0026-1238 See METHODIST HISTORY. 5064
0026-1270 See METHODS OF INFORMATION IN MEDICINE. 3616
0026-1297 See METLFAX. 4012
0026-1335 See METRIKA. 3523
0026-1386 See METROECONOMICA. 1505
0026-1394 See METROLOGIA. 4031
0026-1394 See RAPPORT BIPM. 1434
0026-1424 See METRON. 5332
0026-1521 See BULLETIN - METROPOLITAN MUSEUM OF ART. 4085
0026-1580 See METROPOLITAN STAR. 2267
0026-1599 See GREATER WASHINGTON BOARD OF TRADE NEWS, THE. 1564
0026-1858 See MEXLETTER. 798
0026-1874 See MEZHDUNARODNAIA ZHIZN. 4528
0026-1947 See MIAMI BUSINESS REVIEW. 693
0026-1998 See MICHIGAN AFL-CIO NEWS. 1690

0026-2005 *See* MICHIGAN ACADEMICIAN. 2850
0026-2021 *See* MICHIGAN BEVERAGE NEWS. 2369
0026-203X *See* MICHIGAN BOTANIST. 518
0026-2048 *See* NEWS BULLETIN / MICHIGAN BUSINESS EDUCATION ASSOCIATION. 699
0026-2064 *See* MICHIGAN CPA, THE. 748
0026-2072 *See* MICHIGAN CHRISTIAN ADVOCATE. 4977
0026-2102 *See* JOURNAL OF THE MICHIGAN DENTAL ASSOCIATION, THE. 1328
0026-2153 *See* MICHIGAN FARMER. 108
0026-217X *See* MICHIGAN FLORIST, THE. 2435
0026-2196 *See* MICHIGAN HISTORY. 2746
0026-220X *See* MICHIGAN HOSPITALS. 3789
0026-2234 *See* MICHIGAN LAW REVIEW. 3009
0026-2285 *See* MICHIGAN MATHEMATICAL JOURNAL, THE. 3523
0026-2293 *See* MICHIGAN MEDICINE. 3616
0026-2315 *See* MICHIGAN MILK MESSENGER. 196
0026-2331 *See* MICHIGAN MUNICIPAL REVIEW. 4665
0026-2366 *See* MICHIGAN NURSE. 3861
0026-2382 *See* MICHIGAN OUT-OF-DOORS. 2198
0026-2420 *See* MICHIGAN QUARTERLY REVIEW. 3347
0026-2617 *See* MICROBIOLOGY (NEW YORK). 567
0026-2633 *See* MICROBIOS. 567
0026-265X *See* MICROCHEMICAL JOURNAL. 986
0026-2692 *See* MICROELECTRONICS. 2072
0026-2714 *See* MICROELECTRONICS AND RELIABILITY. 2072
0026-2773 *See* MICROMEGAS (CEDAR FALLS, IOWA). 3466
0026-279X *See* MICRONESICA. 4167
0026-2803 *See* MICROPALEONTOLOGY. 4228
0026-282X *See* MICROSCOPE (LONDON). 573
0026-2838 *See* MICROSCOPY. 573
0026-2854 *See* MICROTECNIC. 4031
0026-2862 *See* MICROVASCULAR RESEARCH. 3773
0026-2927 *See* MID-AMERICA (CHICAGO). 5032
0026-2935 *See* MID AMERICA INSURANCE. 2888
0026-2978 *See* MID-CONTINENT BOTTLER. 2369
0026-3044 *See* MID-WEST CONTRACTOR. 621
0026-3079 *See* AMERICAN STUDIES (LAWRENCE). 2719
0026-3141 *See* MIDDLE EAST JOURNAL, THE. 2635
0026-315X *See* MIDDLE EAST MONITOR. 4482
0026-3184 *See* MIDDLE EAST STUDIES ASSOCIATION BULLETIN. 2769
0026-3206 *See* MIDDLE EASTERN STUDIES. 2769
0026-332X *See* MIDSTREAM (NEW YORK). 5051
0026-3338 *See* MIDWEST AUTOMOTIVE NEWS. 5419
0026-3370 *See* MIDWEST ENGINEER. 1987
0026-3435 *See* MIDWEST MOTORIST, THE. 5484
0026-3451 *See* MIDWEST QUARTERLY (PITTSBURG), THE. 2538
0026-3478 *See* MIDWESTERN DENTIST. 1330
0026-3524 *See* MIDWIVES CHRONICLE AND NURSING NOTES. 3765
0026-3532 *See* MIE MEDICAL JOURNAL. 3616
0026-3567 *See* MIESIECZNIK LITERACKI. 3411
0026-3575 *See* MIGRANT, THE. 5618
0026-3583 *See* MIGRATION NEWS. 1920
0026-3621 *See* MIKE SHAYNE MYSTERY MAGAZINE. 5074
0026-3648 *See* MIKOLOGIJA I FITOPATOLOGIJA. 575
0026-3656 *See* MIKROBIOLOGIJA (MOSKVA. 1932). 567
0026-3672 *See* MIKROCHIMICA ACTA. 1018
0026-3680 *See* MIKROKOSMOS (STUTTGART). 573
0026-3699 *See* MIKRONIEK. 465

0026-3788 *See* MILCHWISSENSCHAFT. 196
0026-3826 *See* MILITARGESCHICHTLICHE MITTEILUNGEN. 2698
0026-3850 *See* MILITRT TIDSSKRIFT. 4051
0026-3885 *See* MILITANT (NEW YORK, N.Y. 1941), THE. 5718
0026-3958 *See* MILITARY CHAPLAIN, THE. 4050
0026-3966 *See* MILITARY COLLECTOR & HISTORIAN. 4050
0026-3982 *See* MILITARY ENGINEER, THE. 1987
0026-4008 *See* BULLETIN - MILITARY HISTORICAL SOCIETY. 4038
0026-4016 *See* MILITARY HISTORY JOURNAL. 4050
0026-4024 *See* MILITARY INTELLIGENCE. 4050
0026-4040 *See* MILITARY LAW REVIEW. 3183
0026-4067 *See* MILITARY MARKET. 4051
0026-4075 *See* MILITARY MEDICINE. 3617
0026-4083 *See* MILITARY MODELLING. 2774
0026-413X *See* DEFENSE ACQUISITION REPORT. 4040
0026-4148 *See* MILITARY REVIEW. 4051
0026-4172 *See* MILK INDUSTRY. 196
0026-4180 *See* MILK PRODUCER. 197
0026-4202 *See* MILK PRODUCTION (WASHINGTON). 197
0026-4326 *See* MILTON QUARTERLY. 3347
0026-4334 *See* MILWAUKEE. 1574
0026-4350 *See* MILWAUKEE COURIER. 5769
0026-4369 *See* MILWAUKEE PROFESSIONAL NURSE. 3861
0026-4377 *See* MILWAUKEE READER. 4830
0026-4415 *See* MINARET, THE. 5044
0026-4423 *See* MIND. 4353
0026-4474 *See* MINDSZENTY REPORT, THE. 4977
0026-4539 *See* EARTH AND MINERAL SCIENCES. 1354
0026-4555 *See* CALIFORNIA GEOLOGY. 1371
0026-458X *See* MINERALES. 2072
0026-4598 *See* MINERALIUM DEPOSITA. 1441
0026-4601 *See* MINERALOGICAL ABSTRACTS. 1363
0026-461X *See* MINERALOGICAL MAGAZINE. 1441
0026-4628 *See* MINERALOGICAL RECORD, THE. 1441
0026-4644 *See* MINERALS PROCESSING. 1442
0026-4695 *See* MINERVA (LONDON). 5129
0026-4709 *See* MINERVA AEROSPAZIALE. 28
0026-4725 *See* MINERVA CARDIOANGIOLOGICA. 3708
0026-4733 *See* MINERVA CHIRURGICA. 3970
0026-4784 *See* MINERVA GINECOLOGICA. 3765
0026-4806 *See* MINERVA MEDICA. 3799
0026-4849 *See* MINERVA MEDICOLEGALE : ORGANO UFFICIALE DELLA SOCIETA ITALIANA DI MMEDICINA LEGALE E DELLE ASSICURAZIONI. 3742
0026-4903 *See* MINERVA OFTALMOLOGICA. 3876
0026-4946 *See* MINERVA PEDIATRICA. 3906
0026-4954 *See* MINERVE PNEUMOLOGICA. 3950
0026-4970 *See* MINERVA STOMATOLOGICA. 1330
0026-5179 *See* MINING ENGINEER (LONDON). 2145
0026-5187 *See* MINING ENGINEERING. 2145
0026-5225 *See* MINING JOURNAL (LONDON. 1908). 2146
0026-5241 *See* MINING RECORD (1968), THE. 2146
0026-5268 *See* MINING SURVEY (JOHANNESBURG). 2146
0026-5276 *See* MINING TECHNOLOGY (MANCHESTER). 2146
0026-5314 *See* MINISTRY (WASHINGTON, D.C.). 4977
0026-539X *See* JOURNAL OF THE MINNESOTA ACADEMY OF SCIENCE. 5121

0026-5403 *See* MINNESOTA ARCHAEOLOGIST, THE. 275
0026-5411 *See* MINNESOTA CHEMIST, THE. 986
0026-5470 *See* MINNESOTA FIRE CHIEF. 2291
0026-5497 *See* MINNESOTA HISTORY. 2746
0026-5500 *See* MINNESOTA HORTICULTURIST, THE. 2424
0026-5535 *See* MINNESOTA LAW REVIEW. 3010
0026-5543 *See* MINNESOTA LEGAL REGISTER. 3141
0026-556X *See* MINNESOTA MEDICINE. 3617
0026-5586 *See* MNA ACCENT. 3862
0026-5608 *See* MINNESOTA OUT-OF-DOORS. 4874
0026-5616 *See* MINNESOTA PHARMACIST. 4316
0026-5624 *See* MINNESOTA POLICE JOURNAL. 3169
0026-5667 *See* MINNESOTA REVIEW (NEW YORK, N.Y.). 3347
0026-5675 *See* MINNESOTA SCIENCE. 108
0026-5748 *See* LG ARGOMENTI : RIVISTA CENTRO STUDI LETTERATURA GIOVANILE. 3405
0026-5829 *See* MIROVAJA EKONOMIKA I MEZDUNARODNYE OTNOSENIJA. 1574
0026-5888 *See* MISCELLANEA STORICA DELLA VALDELSA. 2699
0026-5934 *See* BAKKERSWERELD. 2328
0026-5942 *See* BOUWWERELD. 602
0026-6051 *See* MISSIONARY NEWS SERVICE. 4978
0026-6094 *See* MONDO E MISSIONE. 5032
0026-6116 *See* MISSIONS ETRANGERES. 4978
0026-6159 *See* MISSISSIPPI BANKER, THE. 799
0026-6205 *See* MISSISSIPPI FARM BUREAU NEWS. 109
0026-6248 *See* MISSISSIPPI FOLKLORE REGISTER. 2322
0026-6280 *See* MISSISSIPPI LAW JOURNAL. 3011
0026-6299 *See* MISSISSIPPI LEGION'AIRE. 5233
0026-6337 *See* MISSISSIPPI MUNICIPALITIES. 4666
0026-637X *See* MISSISSIPPI QUARTERLY, THE. 2850
0026-6388 *See* MISSISSIPPI RN, THE. 3861
0026-6396 *See* JOURNAL OF THE MISSISSIPPI STATE MEDICAL ASSOCIATION. 3599
0026-6442 *See* MISSISSIPPI'S BUSINESS (UNIVERSITY, MISS.). 695
0026-6485 *See* JOURNAL OF THE MISSOURI BAR. 2989
0026-6493 *See* ANNALS OF THE MISSOURI BOTANICAL GARDEN. 499
0026-6507 *See* MISSOURI BOTANICAL GARDEN BULLETIN. 518
0026-6515 *See* MISSOURI CONSERVATIONIST. 2198
0026-6574 *See* MISSOURI FB NEWS. 109
0026-6582 *See* MISSOURI HISTORICAL REVIEW. 2747
0026-6604 *See* MISSOURI LAW REVIEW. 3011
0026-6620 *See* MISSOURI MEDICINE. 3617
0026-6647 *See* MISSOURI MUNICIPAL REVIEW. 4666
0026-6655 *See* MISSOURI NURSE, THE. 3861
0026-6663 *See* MISSOURI PHARMACISTS. 4316
0026-6671 *See* MISSOURI PRESS NEWS. 4817
0026-668X *See* MISSOURI RURALIST. 109
0026-6728 *See* MISSOURI TEAMSTER. 1691
0026-6760 *See* MITA GAKKAI ZASSHI. 1505
0026-6779 *See* MITARBEIT, DIE. 4978
0026-6809 *See* MERI'S MONTHLY CIRCULAR. 1574
0026-6817 *See* TECHNICAL REVIEW - MITSUBISHI HEAVY INDUSTRIES. 1629
0026-6825 *See* MITSUI ZOSEN GIHO. 1988
0026-6841 *See* MITTEILUNGEN AUS DEM GEBIETE DER LEBENSMITTELUNTERSUCHUNG UND HYGIENE. 491

0026-6884 See MITTEILUNGEN DER DEUTSCHEN PATENTANWALTE. 1306
0026-6957 See DOKUMENTATION FUER UMWELTSCHUTZ UND LANDESPFLEGE. 2191
0026-7015 See MIZU SHORI GIJUTSU. 5536
0026-704X See MLJEKARSTVO. 197
0026-7058 See MLYNSKO-PEKARENSKY PRUMYSL A TECHNIKA SKLADOVANI OBILI. 202
0026-7074 See MNEMOSYNE. 3303
0026-7112 See MOBILE MILANO, IL. 2906
0026-7295 See MODEL AIRPLANE NEWS. 28
0026-7325 See MODEL ENGINEER, THE. 2775
0026-7341 See MODEL RAILROADER. 2775
0026-7457 See MODERN AGE (CHICAGO). 2539
0026-749X See MODERN ASIAN STUDIES. 2659
0026-7503 See MODERN AUSTRIAN LITERATURE. 3412
0026-7538 See MODERN BREWERY AGE. 2369
0026-7546 See MODERN BRIDE. 2283
0026-7562 See MODERN CASTING. 4012
0026-7597 See MODERN CHURCHMAN, THE. 4978
0026-7651 See MODERN DAIRY. 197
0026-7694 See MODERN DRAMA. 5366
0026-7724 See MODERN FICTION STUDIES. 3347
0026-7732 See MODERN FISHING. 4905
0026-7775 See MODERN GEOLOGY. 1388
0026-7805 See MODERN GROCER. 2350
0026-7821 See MODERN HAIKU. 3466
0026-7856 See MODERN INTERNATIONAL DRAMA. 3412
0026-7902 See MODERN LANGUAGE JOURNAL (BOULDER, COLO.), THE. 3303
0026-7910 See MLN. 3303
0026-7929 See MODERN LANGUAGE QUARTERLY (SEATTLE). 3347
0026-7937 See MODERN LANGUAGE REVIEW, THE. 3303
0026-7961 See MODERN LAW REVIEW. 3011
0026-8003 See MODERN MACHINE SHOP. 2122
0026-8038 See MODERN MATERIALS HANDLING. 3484
0026-8046 See MODERN MATURITY. 5180
0026-8070 See MODERN MEDICINE (MINNEAPOLIS). 3661
0026-8127 See MODERN METALS. 4013
0026-8232 See MODERN PHILOLOGY. 3303
0026-8275 See MODERN PLASTICS. 4456
0026-8283 See MODERN PLASTICS INTERNATIONAL. 4457
0026-833X See MODERN PURCHASING. 950
0026-8356 See MODERN RAILWAYS. 5433
0026-8380 See MODERN REVIEW (CALCUTTA), THE. 2507
0026-8399 See MODERN ROMANCES. 5074
0026-8402 See MODERN SCHOOLMAN, THE. 4353
0026-8445 See MODERN STEEL CONSTRUCTION. 621
0026-8496 See MODERN TIRE DEALER. 5419
0026-8577 See MODERNA SPRAK. 3303
0026-8666 See MODERNE SPRACHEN. 3303
0026-8739 See MODES ET TRAVAUX. 325
0026-8925 See MOLECULAR & GENERAL GENETICS : MGG. 549
0026-8933 See MOLECULAR BIOLOGY (NEW YORK). 465
0026-895X See MOLECULAR PHARMACOLOGY. 4316
0026-8976 See MOLECULAR PHYSICS. 1056
0026-8984 See MOLEKULJARNAJA BIOLOGIJA (MOSKVA). 568
0026-900X See MOLINERIA Y PANADERIA. 155
0026-9018 See MOLINI D'ITALIA. 202
0026-9034 See MOLOCHNOE I MIASNOE SKOTOVODSTVO. 216
0026-9042 See MOLODA UKRAINA. 2519

0026-9050 See VOENNO-MEDICINSKIJ ZURNAL. 3650
0026-914X See MOMENTUM (WASHINGTON). 4978
0026-9190 See MONASTIC STUDIES. 5032
0026-9247 See MONATSHEFTE FUER CHEMIE. 986
0026-9255 See MONATSHEFTE FUER MATHEMATIK. 3523
0026-9263 See MONATSHEFTE FUER VETERINAERMEDIZIN. 5516
0026-9271 See MONATSHEFTE (MADISON, 1946). 3303
0026-9298 See MONATSSCHRIFT FUER KINDERHEILKUNDE. 3906
0026-9301 See MONATSSCHRIFT FUER KRIMINOLOGIE UND STRAFRECHTSREFORM. 3169
0026-9360 See MONDE. SELECTION HEBDOMADAIRE, LE. 5801
0026-9379 See MONDE DE L'ELECTRICITE, LE. 2073
0026-9395 See MONDE DIPLOMATIQUE, LE. 4529
0026-9425 See MONDE JUIF, LE. 2699
0026-9492 See MONDO APERTO. 1638
0026-9506 See MONDO BANCARIO. 799
0026-9522 See MONDO ECONOMICO. 1574
0026-9565 See MONDO ODONTOSTOMATOLOGICO. 1330
0026-959X See MONEDA Y CREDITO. 1593
0026-9611 See MONETA E CREDITO. 799
0026-9662 See MONIST, THE. 4353
0026-9689 See MONITEUR DES PHARMACIES ET DES LABORATOIRES. 4316
0026-9700 See MONITEUR DES TRAVAUX PUBLICS ET DU BATIMENT, LE. 621
0026-9719 See MOCI; MONITEUR DU COMMERCE INTERNATIONAL, LE. 3011
0026-9832 See MONOGRAPHIEN ZUR GESCHICHTE DES MITTELALTERS. 2699
0026-9891 See MONTANA. 2747
0026-9921 See MONTANA BUSINESS QUARTERLY. 1506
0026-9972 See MONTANA LAW REVIEW. 3012
0027-0016 See MONTANA OUTDOORS. 4875
0027-0024 See MONTANA WOOLGROWER. 216
0027-0113 See COMUNICACIONES ZOOLOGICAS DEL MUSEO DE HISTORIA NATURAL DE MONTEVIDEO. 5581
0027-0172 See MONTH (LONDON. 1882), THE. 4979
0027-0288 See MONTHLY CHECKLIST OF STATE PUBLICATIONS. 420
0027-0296 See MONTHLY CLIMATIC DATA FOR THE WORLD. 1431
0027-030X See MONTHLY COMMENTARY ON INDIAN ECONOMIC CONDITIONS. 1574
0027-0318 See MONTHLY COTTON LINTERS REVIEW. 179
0027-0377 See MONTHLY DIGEST OF STATISTICS. 5333
0027-0385 See MONTHLY DIGEST OF TAX ARTICLES, THE. 4737
0027-0431 See MIMS MEDICAL SPECIALTIES. 4316
0027-0431 See MIMS. 4315
0027-0482 See MONTHLY RADIATION SUMMARY. 1431
0027-0520 See MONTHLY REVIEW (NEW YORK. 1949). 4543
0027-0636 See MONTHLY WEATHER REPORT. 1432
0027-0644 See MONTHLY WEATHER REVIEW. 1432
0027-0741 See MONUMENTA NIPPONICA. 2659
0027-0814 See MOODY'S BANK & FINANCE NEWS REPORTS. 800
0027-0822 See MOODY'S BOND SURVEY. 907
0027-0830 See MOODY'S HANDBOOK OF COMMON STOCKS. 907
0027-0849 See MOODY'S INDUSTRIAL NEWS REPORTS. 907

0027-1004 See MORALITY IN MEDIA INC. NEWSLETTER. 3170
0027-1098 See MORGAN HORSE, THE. 2801
0027-125X See MORTON ARBORETUM QUARTERLY, THE. 518
0027-1268 See MORTUARY MANAGEMENT. 2407
0027-1276 See MOSAIC (WINNIPEG). 3413
0027-1284 See MOSAIC (WASHINGTON). 5129
0027-1306 See MOSCOW NEWS. 5809
0027-1314 See MOSCOW UNIVERSITY CHEMISTRY BULLETIN. 987
0027-1322 See MOSCOW UNIVERSITY MATHEMATICS BULLETIN. 3523
0027-1330 See MOSCOW UNIVERSITY MECHANICS BULLETIN. 4429
0027-1349 See MOSCOW UNIVERSITY PHYSICS BULLETIN. 4412
0027-1403 See BJULLETEN MOSKOVSKOGO OBSCESTVA ISPYTATELEJ PRIRODY. OTDEL BIOLOGICESKIJ. 448
0027-1438 See MOST (LAUSANNE). 3413
0027-1748 See MOTOR (NEW YORK). 5420
0027-1780 See MOTOR BOAT AND YACHTING. 594
0027-1799 See MOTOR BOATING & SAILING. 594
0027-1853 See MOTOR CYCLE NEWS PETERBOROUGH. 5387
0027-190X See MOTOR IN CANADA. 5420
0027-1961 See MOTOCICLISMO. 4082
0027-1977 See MOTOR SERVICE (CHICAGO, ILL. : 1951). 5420
0027-2000 See MOTOR SHIP. 5453
0027-2019 See MOTOR SPORT. 4905
0027-2043 See MOTOR TRADER. 5420
0027-206X See MOTOR TRANSPORT [MICROFORM]. 5387
0027-2094 See MOTOR TREND. 5420
0027-2108 See MOTOR TRUCK. 5387
0027-2205 See MOTORCYCLIST (LOS ANGELES, CALIF. 1912). 4082
0027-2264 See MOTORING NEWS LONDON. 4905
0027-2302 See MOTORISTS GUIDE TO NEW & USED CAR PRICES. 5421
0027-2310 See MOTORLAND. 5421
0027-2396 See MOTRIX. 5421
0027-2507 See MOUNT SINAI JOURNAL OF MEDICINE, NEW YORK, THE. 3618
0027-254X See MOUNTAIN GEOLOGIST, THE. 1388
0027-2590 See BANK NEWS. 775
0027-2604 See MOUNTAIN TROUBADOUR, THE. 3466
0027-2620 See MOUNTAINEER (SEATTLE, WASH.). 4875
0027-2639 See MOUSAION (PRETORIA, SOUTH AFRICA: 1983). 3232
0027-2671 See MOUVEMENT SOCIAL, LE. 2623
0027-268X See MOVIE (LONDON). 4075
0027-271X See MOVIE MIRROR. 4075
0027-2833 See MOVOZNAVSTVO; NAUKOVI ZAPYSKY. 3304
0027-2833 See MOVOZNAVSTVO (KIEV). 3304
0027-2841 See MOYEN-AGE. 3304
0027-2892 See MOZNAYIM. 3413
0027-2892 See MOZNAYIM. 3413
0027-2914 See MUANYAG ES GUMI. 4457
0027-2930 See MUEBLE, EL. 2906
0027-2949 See MUEHLE + MISCHFUTTERTECHNIK, DIE. 203
0027-2957 See MULL UND ABFALL. 4792
0027-299X See MUNSTER (MUNCHEN), DAS. 359
0027-3015 See MUSZAKI EGYETEMI KONYVTAROS. 3232
0027-3112 See MULCH. 3413
0027-3120 See MULINO, IL. 3348
0027-3171 See MULTIVARIATE BEHAVIORAL RESEARCH. 4605
0027-3252 See MUNDO CRISTIANO. 5032

0027-3449 See MUNICIPAL ATTORNEY, THE. 3012

0027-3465 See MUNICIPAL ENGINEERS JOURNAL, THE. 2237

0027-3503 See MUNICIPAL LAW COURT DECISIONS. 3012

0027-352X See MUNICIPAL NEWS (SEATTLE). 4667

0027-3562 See MUNICIPAL REVIEW & AMA NEWS. 4667

0027-3570 See MUNICIPAL SOUTH. 4667

0027-3589 See MUNICIPAL WORLD. 879

0027-3597 See MUNICIPALITY (1916), THE. 4667

0027-3791 See BULLETIN DU MUSEE NATIONAL DE VARSOVIE. 4085

0027-3821 See MUSEES DE GENEVE. 4091

0027-383X See MUSEES ET COLLECTIONS PUBLIQUES DE FRANCE. 4091

0027-3856 See BULLETIN - MUSEES ROYAUX DES BEAUX-ARTS DE BELGIQUE. 345

0027-3996 See MUSEUM (ENGLISH ED.). 4092

0027-4054 See MUSEUM HELVETICUM. 275

0027-4089 See MUSEUM NEWS (WASHINGTON). 4092

0027-4097 See MUSEUM NOTES (PROVIDENCE, R.I.). 359

0027-4100 See BULLETIN OF THE MUSEUM OF COMPARATIVE ZOOLOGY. 5579

0027-4135 See QUARTERLY - MUSEUM OF THE FUR TRADE. 2756

0027-4135 See QUARTERLY - THE MUSEUM OF THE FUR TRADE. 3185

0027-416X See MUSEUMS JOURNAL. 4093

0027-4178 See MUSEUMSKUNDE. 4093

0027-4186 See MUSEUMSNYTT. 4093

0027-4224 See MUSIC & LETTERS. 4132

0027-4240 See MUSIC ARTICLE GUIDE. 4160

0027-4283 See MUSIC CATALOGING BULLETIN. 4133

0027-4291 See MUSIC CITY NEWS. 4133

0027-4321 See MUSIC EDUCATORS JOURNAL. 4133

0027-4348 See MUSIC INDEX, THE. 4160

0027-4372 See MUSIC LEADER, THE. 4134

0027-4380 See NOTES (PHILADELPHIA, PA.). 4142

0027-4410 See MUSIC NEWS FROM PRAGUE. 4134

0027-4437 See MUSIC NOW. 4134

0027-4445 See MUSIC REVIEW, THE. 4134

0027-4461 See MUSIC TEACHER. 4135

0027-447X See MUSIC TEMPO. 4135

0027-4488 See MUSIC TRADES. 4135

0027-4518 See MUSICA. 4135

0027-4542 See MUSICA JAZZ. 4136

0027-4585 See MUSICAL DENMARK. 4160

0027-4615 See MUSICAL MERCHANDISE REVIEW. 4136

0027-4623 See MUSICAL OPINION. 4136

0027-4631 See MUSICAL QUARTERLY, THE. 4136

0027-4666 See MUSICAL TIMES (LONDON, ENGLAND : 1957). 4136

0027-4704 See MUSIK IN DER SCHULE. 4137

0027-4747 See MUSIK UND BILDUNG. 4138

0027-4755 See MUSIK UND GESELLSCHAFT (BERLIN, DDR). 4138

0027-4771 See MUSIK UND KIRCHE. 4138

0027-478X See MUSIKERN. 4138

0027-4798 See MUSIKERZIEHUNG. 4138

0027-4801 See MUSIKFORSCHUNG. 4138

0027-4828 See MUSIKINSTRUMENT, DAS. 4138

0027-4844 See MUSIKREVY. 4138

0027-4909 See MUSLIM WORLD (HARTFORD), THE. 5044

0027-5107 See MUTATION RESEARCH. 549

0027-5123 See MUTISIA. 518

0027-514X See MUTTERSPRACHE (WIESBADEN). 3304

0027-5247 See MUVESZETTORTENETI ERTESITO. 325

0027-5263 See MUZEUM BRATISLAVA. 4093

0027-5336 See MUZSIKA. 4139

0027-5344 See MUZYKA (1956). 4139

0027-5387 See MY DEVOTIONS. 4979

0027-5514 See MYCOLOGIA. 575

0027-5522 See MYCOLOGICAL PAPERS. COMMONWEALTH MYCOLOGICAL INSTITUTE. 575

0027-5697 See NABET NEWS. INTERNATIONAL EDITION. 1135

0027-576X See N.A.C.W.P.I JOURNAL. 4139

0027-5794 See N.A.D.A. OFFICIAL USED CAR GUIDE. 5421

0027-5824 See NEWSLETTER - NAFSA: ASSOCIATION OF INTERNATIONAL EDUCATORS (WASHINGTON, D.C.). 1768

0027-5913 See N.A.M.M. MUSIC RETAILER NEWS. 4139

0027-5972 See NARD JOURNAL. 4317

0027-6014 See NASPA JOURNAL. 1866

0027-6022 See NASW NEWS. 5297

0027-6065 See NATO'S FIFTEEN NATIONS. 4529

0027-6170 See NCAA NEWS, THE. 4907

0027-6189 See NCAE NEWS BULLETIN. 1867

0027-6219 See NCA TODAY. 1837

0027-6383 See PROSECUTOR, THE. 3108

0027-6448 See NEW ENGLAND LIBRARIES. 3233

0027-657X See NHK LABORATORIES NOTE. 5133

0027-6650 See NIH PUBLICATIONS LIST. 4810

0027-6685 See NIN. NEDELJNE INFORMATIVNE NOVINE. 2520

0027-6723 See NIR. NORDISKT IMMATERIELLT RATTSSKYDD. 1306

0027-6758 See NJEA REVIEW. 1769

0027-6782 See NLGI SPOKESMAN. 2123

0027-6839 See NML TECHNICAL JOURNAL. 4013

0027-7010 See NSS NEWS. 1359

0027-7045 See NTDRA DEALER NEWS. 5076

0027-707X See NTZ : NACHRICTENTECHNISCHE ZEITSCHRIFT. 1161

0027-7134 See NYLA BULLETIN. 3238

0027-724X See NEW ZEALAND SHIPPING GAZETTE CHRISTCHURCH. 5453

0027-7436 See NACHRICHTEN FUER DOKUMENTATION. 3232

0027-7452 See NACHRICHTENBLATT DER BAYERISCHEN ENTOMOLOGEN. 5612

0027-7479 See NACHRICHTENBLATT DES DEUTSCHEN PFLANZENSCHUTZDIENSTES. 519

0027-7568 See NAGAOKA KOGYO KOTO SENMON GAKKO KENKYU KIYO. 5130

0027-7584 See NAGARLOK. 4667

0027-7606 See NAGOYA SHIRITSU DAIGAKU IGAKKAI ZASSHI. JOURNAL OF THE NAGOYA CITY UNIVERSITY MEDICAL ASSOCIATION. 3618

0027-7614 See NAGOYA KOGYO GIJUTSU SHIKENJO HOKOKU. 1619

0027-7622 See NAGOYA JOURNAL OF MEDICAL SCIENCE. 3618

0027-7630 See NAGOYA MATHEMATICAL JOURNAL. 3523

0027-7649 See NAGOYA MEDICAL JOURNAL. 3618

0027-7657 See MEMOIRS OF THE FACULTY OF ENGINEERING, NAGOYA UNIVERSITY. 1987

0027-769X See NAHRUNG, DIE. 4194

0027-772X See NAMARI TO AEN / LEAD AND ZINC. NIHON NAMARI AEN JUYO KENKYUKAI. 1443

0027-7738 See NAMES. 2461

0027-7835 See NAPOLI NOBILISSIMA. 325

0027-7878 See SCANDINAVIAN JOURNAL OF NUTRITION NARINGSFORSKNING. 4199

0027-7894 See NAROD POLSKI. 5032

0027-7908 See NARODNA ARMIJA. 4052

0027-8017 See NARODNO STVARALASTVO. FOLKLOR. 2322

0027-8033 See NARODNOE OBRAZOVANIE. 1766

0027-8041 See NARODY AZII I AFRIKI. 2642

0027-8084 See NAS JEZIK. 3305

0027-8203 See NASE REC. 3305

0027-8238 See NAS SOVREMENNIK. 3348

0027-8246 See NASH SVIT. 2747

0027-8378 See NATION (NEW YORK, N.Y.), THE. 3348

0027-8424 See PROCEEDINGS OF THE NATIONAL ACADEMY OF SCIENCE OF THE UNITED STATES OF AMERICA. 5141

0027-8432 See NEWS REPORT (NATIONAL RESEARCH COUNCIL (US)). 5133

0027-8513 See NATIONAL ALLIANCE. 1692

0027-8599 See NATIONAL ACAC JOURNAL. 1836

0027-8637 See NEWSLETTER (NATIONAL ASSOCIATION OF PRIVATE PSYCHIATRIC HOSPITALS). 3790

0027-8645 See BULLETIN NATIONAL ASSOCIATION OF REGULATORY UTILITY COMMISSIONERS. 4634

0027-8777 See NATIONAL BIBLIOGRAPHY OF BOTSWANA, THE. 420

0027-8785 See NATIONAL BOARD EXAMINER, THE. 3618

0027-8807 See NATIONAL BUILDER (LONDON). 621

0027-8815 See JOURNAL OF THE NATIONAL BUILDINGS ORGANISATION. 618

0027-8831 See NATIONAL BUSINESS WOMAN. 5562

0027-884X See NATIONAL BUTTON BULLETIN, THE. 2775

0027-8874 See JOURNAL OF THE NATIONAL CANCER INSTITUTE. 3820

0027-8890 See NATIONAL CAPITAL PHARMACIST, THE. 4317

0027-8920 See NATIONAL CATHOLIC REGISTER. 5032

0027-8939 See NATIONAL CATHOLIC REPORTER. 5033

0027-898X See NATIONAL CHRONICLE (HAYDEN LAKE). 4483

0027-9013 See NATIONAL CIVIC REVIEW. 4668

0027-9048 See AMERICAN BANKRUPTCY LAW JOURNAL, THE. 3084

0027-9153 See KOKURITSU KOKKAI TOSHOKAN GEPPO. 3222

0027-9218 See NATIONAL ENGINEER, THE. 1988

0027-9226 See NATIONAL FARMERS UNION WASHINGTON NEWSLETTER. 110

0027-9250 See NATIONAL FISHERMAN. 2309

0027-9269 See NATIONAL FLUORIDATION NEWS. 3982

0027-9331 See NATIONAL GARDENER, THE. 2424

0027-934X See NATIONAL GENEALOGICAL SOCIETY QUARTERLY. 2462

0027-9358 See NATIONAL GEOGRAPHIC. 2570

0027-9374 See NATIONAL GEOGRAPHICAL JOURNAL OF INDIA, THE. 2570

0027-9447 See NATIONAL HOG FARMER. 216

0027-9455 See NATIONAL HORSEMAN, THE. 2801

0027-9501 See NATIONAL INSTITUTE ECONOMIC REVIEW. 1507

0027-9544 See NATIONAL JEWELER. 2915

0027-9587 See NATIONAL LAMPOON. 2539

0027-9633 See NATIONAL LIBRARY NEWS. 3233

0027-965X See NEWS (NATIONAL LIBRARY OF MEDICINE (US)). 3234

0027-9684 See JOURNAL OF THE NATIONAL MEDICAL ASSOCIATION. 3599

0027-9722 See NMRA BULLETIN. 5433

0027-9846 See NATIONAL PALACE MUSEUM BULLETIN. 4093

0027-9897 See JOURNAL - NATIONAL PHARMACEUTICAL ASSOCIATION. 4310

0027-9943 See NATIONAL PROGRAM LETTER. 1766

0027-996X See NATIONAL PROVISIONER, THE. 2351

0027-9978 See NATIONAL PUBLIC ACCOUNTANT (1957), THE. 748
0027-9994 See NATIONAL REAL ESTATE INVESTOR. 909
0028-0011 See JOURNAL OF THE NATIONAL RESEARCH COUNCIL OF THAILAND. 5121
0028-0038 See NATIONAL REVIEW (NEW YORK). 4483
0028-0089 See NATIONAL RURAL LETTER CARRIER, THE. 1146
0028-016X See SHERIFF (ALEXANDRIA, VA.). 3176
0028-0208 See NATIONAL SPEED SPORT NEWS. 4906
0028-0267 See NATIONAL STOCK DOG MAGAZINE. 4287
0028-0275 See GUOLI TAIWAN DAXUE YIXUEYUAN YANJIU BAOGAO. 3579
0028-0283 See NATIONAL TAX JOURNAL. 4738
0028-0291 See NATIONAL TECHNICAL REPORT. 5130
0028-0372 See NATIONAL VOTER, THE. 4483
0028-0399 See QUARTERLY REVIEW / NATIONAL WESTMINSTER BANK. 1514
0028-0410 See NATIONAL WOOL GROWER. 110
0028-0453 See NATIONALKONOMISK TIDSSKRIFT. 1507
0028-047X See NATION'S BUSINESS. 697
0028-0496 See NATION'S HEALTH (1971), THE. 4792
0028-0518 See NATION'S RESTAURANT NEWS. 5072
0028-0534 See NATIVE NEVADAN, THE. 2539
0028-0542 See NATIVE VOICE. 2539
0028-0593 See NATUR UND HEIMAT. 4168
0028-0607 See NATUR UND LAND. 2178
0028-0615 See NATUR UND LANDSCHAFT (STUTTGART). 4168
0028-0631 See NATURA. 4168
0028-0682 See NATURAL AND APPLIED SCIENCE BULLETIN. 5130
0028-0712 See NATURAL HISTORY. 4168
0028-0739 See NATURAL RESOURCES JOURNAL. 3115
0028-0755 See NATURAL RUBBER NEWS. 5076
0028-0763 See TEACHING SCIENCE. 5161
0028-0771 See NATURALIST (LEEDS). 4168
0028-0798 See NATURALISTE CANADIEN, LE. 2219
0028-0801 See NATURALISTES BELGES. 4168
0028-0836 See NATURE (LONDON). 5131
0028-0844 See NATURE AND RESOURCES. 2199
0028-0860 See NATURE STUDY - AMERICAN NATURE STUDY SOCIETY. 2219
0028-0887 See NATUREN. 5131
0028-0895 See NATURENS VERDEN. 5131
0028-0917 See BERICHTE DER NATURFORSCHENDEN GESELLSCHAFT ZU FREIBURG I. BR. 5088
0028-1042 See NATURWISSENSCHAFTEN, DIE. 5131
0028-1050 See NATURWISSENSCHAFTLICHE RUNDSCHAU. 5131
0028-1093 See NATUUR EN TECHNIEK. 5131
0028-1263 See NAUKA I ZIZN. 5131
0028-1271 See NAUKA POLSKA. 5132
0028-1298 See NAUNYN-SCHMIEDEBERG'S ARCHIVES OF PHARMACOLOGY. 4317
0028-1301 See NATUR UND MUSEUM (FRANKFURT AM MAIN : 1962). 4168
0028-1336 See NAUTICAL MAGAZINE. 4179
0028-1344 See NAUTILUS (PHILADELPHIA), THE. 5592
0028-1409 See NAVAL AFFAIRS. 4179
0028-1417 See NAVAL AVIATION NEWS. 30
0028-1425 See NAVAL ENGINEERS JOURNAL. 4179
0028-145X See NAVAL RESEARCH REVIEWS. 4180
0028-1484 See NAVAL WAR COLLEGE REVIEW. 4180

0028-1492 See NAVALAKATHA. 3414
0028-1522 See NAVIGATION (WASHINGTON). 4180
0028-1530 See NAVIGATION (PARIS). 4180
0028-159X See NAVIRES, PORTS & CHANTIERS. 4180
0028-1662 See NAVY NEWS. 4180
0028-1670 See NAVY NEWS. 5759
0028-1697 See NAVY TIMES. 4180
0028-1735 See NEA ESTIA. 2519
0028-176X See NEAR EAST REPORT. 4529
0028-1778 See NEAR NORTH NEWS. 5661
0028-1808 See NEBRASKA BEVERAGE ANALYST. 2369
0028-1816 See NEBRASKA BIRD REVIEW, THE. 5592
0028-1859 See NEBRASKA HISTORY. 2748
0028-1883 See NEBRASKA LIBRARY ASSOCIATION QUARTERLY. 3233
0028-1891 See NEBRASKA MORTAR & PESTLE. 4317
0028-1905 See NEBRASKA MUNICIPAL REVIEW. 4668
0028-1913 See NEBRASKA NEWSPAPER. 5706
0028-1921 See NEBRASKA NURSE. 3862
0028-1948 See NEBRASKA RETAILER. 955
0028-1964 See NEBRASKALAND. 4852
0028-2030 See NEDERLANDS ARCHIEF VOOR KERKGESCHIEDENIS. 4980
0028-2049 See NEDERLANDSCH ARCHIEVENBLAD. 2482
0028-209X See NEDERLANDS MELK- EN ZUIVELTIJSCHRIFT. 5132
0028-212X See NEDERLANDS THEOLOGISCH TIJDSCHRIFT. 4980
0028-2162 See NEDERLANDS TIJDSCHRIFT VOOR GENEESKUNDE. 3619
0028-2200 See NEDERLANDS TIJDSCHRIFT VOOR TANDHEELKUNDE. 1330
0028-2235 See NEDERLANDS TIJDSCHRIFT VOOR DE PSYCHOLOGIE EN HAAR GRENSGEBIEDEN. 4605
0028-2421 See NEFTEHIMIJA. 4266
0028-243X See NEFTJANIK. 4266
0028-2448 See NEFTJANOE HOZJAJSTVO. 4013
0028-2456 See NEGOCIOS Y BANCOS : REVISTA PARA EL EJECUTIVO. 801
0028-249X See NEW IDEA MELBOURNE. 2792
0028-2529 See NEGRO HISTORY BULLETIN. 2748
0028-2561 See NEJROFIZIOLOGIJA (KIEV, 1969). 3839
0028-2588 See NEMAN. 3348
0028-2596 See NEMATOLOGICA. 466
0028-2677 See NEOPHILOLOGUS. 3305
0028-2685 See NEOPLASMA. 3821
0028-2723 See NEPAL PRESS DIGEST. 2507
0028-2731 See NEPAL PRESS REPORT. 2507
0028-2766 See NEPHRON. 3992
0028-2804 See NERVENARZT. 3839
0028-2812 See NESTOR. 286
0028-2928 See NETHERLANDS JOURNAL OF AGRICULTURAL SCIENCE. 111
0028-2944 See NETHERLANDS JOURNAL OF PLANT PATHOLOGY. 519
0028-2960 See NETHERLANDS JOURNAL OF ZOOLOGY. 5592
0028-3045 See NETWORKS (NEW YORK). 5132
0028-3126 See NEUE BUECHEREI, DIE. 3233
0028-3150 See NEUE DEUTSCHE LITERATUR. 3415
0028-3207 See NEUE HUTTE. 4013
0028-3231 See NEUE JUSTIZ. 3014
0028-3282 See NEUE MUSEUMSKUNDE. 4093
0028-3320 See NEUE POLITISCHE LITERATUR. 5210
0028-3347 See NEUE RUNDSCHAU. 5801
0028-3355 See NEUE SAMMLUNG. 1767
0028-3398 See NEUE TECHNIK. 5132
0028-3401 See NEUE TECHNIK IM BURO. 698

0028-3479 See ZEITSCHRIFT FUER PARAPSYCHOLOGIE UND GRENZGEBIETE DER PSYCHOLOGIE. 4243
0028-3495 See NEUE ZEITSCHRIFT FUER MISSIONSWISSENSCHAFT. NOUVELLE REVUE DE SCIENCE MISSIONAIRE. 4980
0028-3517 See NEUE ZEITSCHRIFT FUER SYSTEMATISCHE THEOLOGIE UND RELIGIONSPHILOSOPHIE. 4980
0028-3630 See NEUES JAHRBUCH FUER GEOLOGIE UND PALAONTOLOGIE. MONATSHEFTE. 1389
0028-3649 See NEUES JAHRBUCH FUER MINERALOGIE. MONATSHEFTE. 1443
0028-3754 See NEUPHILOLOGISCHE MITTEILUNGEN. 3305
0028-3770 See NEURO-CHIRURGIE. 3839
0028-3800 See NEUROBIOLOGIA (RECIFE). 3839
0028-3819 See NEUROCHIRURGIA. 3970
0028-3835 See NEUROENDOCRINOLOGY. 3840
0028-3843 See NEUROLOGIA I NEUROCHIRURGIA POLSKA. 3840
0028-3878 See NEUROLOGY. 3840
0028-3886 See NEUROLOGY, INDIA. 3841
0028-3894 See NEUROPATOLOGIA POLSKA. 3841
0028-3908 See NEUROPHARMACOLOGY. 4317
0028-3916 See NEUROPSICHIATRIA. 3841
0028-3932 See NEUROPSYCHOLOGIA. 3842
0028-3940 See NEURORADIOLOGY. 3842
0028-3983 See NEUSPRACHLICHE MITTEILUNGEN AUS WISSENSCHAFT UND PRAXIS : NM. 1767
0028-4009 See NEVA. 3415
0028-4181 See NEW AMBEROLA GRAPHIC, THE. 5318
0028-4270 See NEW BEACON. 4391
0028-4289 See NEW BLACKFRIARS. 4980
0028-4459 See NEW COIN POETRY. 3466
0028-4467 See NEW COLLAGE MAGAZINE. 3466
0028-453X See NEW DAY (PHILADELPHIA). 4980
0028-4580 See NEW DEPARTURES. 326
0028-470X See NEW ENGLAND CONSTRUCTION. 622
0028-4726 See NEW ENGLAND ECONOMIC REVIEW. 801
0028-4785 See NEW ENGLAND HISTORICAL AND GENEALOGICAL REGISTER, THE. 2462
0028-4793 See NEW ENGLAND JOURNAL OF MEDICINE, THE. 3620
0028-4793 See NEW ENGLAND JOURNAL OF MEDICINE (OVERSEAS ED.). 3620
0028-4793 See NEW ENGLAND JOURNAL OF MEDICINE, THE. 3620
0028-4807 See NEW ENGLAND JOURNAL OF OPTOMETRY. 4216
0028-4823 See NEW ENGLAND LAW REVIEW. 3015
0028-4858 See NEW ENGLAND PURCHASER. 950
0028-4866 See NEW ENGLAND QUARTERLY, THE. 2748
0028-4882 See NEW ENGLAND READING ASSOCIATION JOURNAL. 1901
0028-4890 See NEW ENGLAND REAL ESTATE JOURNAL. 4842
0028-4939 See JOURNAL OF THE NEW ENGLAND WATER WORKS ASSOCIATION. 4761
0028-4947 See NEW ENGLANDER, THE. 2540
0028-4955 See NEW ENTOMOLOGIST. 5612
0028-4963 See NEW EQUIPMENT DIGEST. 2123
0028-4971 See NEW EQUIPMENT NEWS. 3485
0028-5048 See NEW ERA IN EDUCATION. 1767
0028-5056 See NEW ERA LAUNDRY & CLEANING LINES. 698
0028-5137 See NEW GUARD. 4484
0028-5307 See NEW HAMPSHIRE PROFILES. 2748
0028-5315 See NEW HAMPSHIRE QUARTER NOTES. 4140
0028-5412 See LIGHT ON THE WORD. TEACHER. 1900

0028-5455 See BULLETIN - NEW JERSEY ACADEMY OF SCIENCE, THE. **5091**
0028-5552 See NEW JERSEY BEVERAGE JOURNAL. **2369**
0028-5560 See NEW JERSEY BUSINESS. **698**
0028-5757 See NEW JERSEY HISTORY. **2748**
0028-5773 See NEW JERSEY JOURNAL OF PHARMACY, THE. **4317**
0028-5803 See NEW JERSEY LAW JOURNAL, THE. **3015**
0028-5811 See NEW JERSEY LIBRARIES. **3234**
0028-5838 See BULLETIN - NEW JERSEY MOTOR TRUCK ASSOCIATION. **5378**
0028-5846 See NEW JERSEY MUNICIPALITIES. **4669**
0028-5889 See NEW JERSEY OUTDOORS. **2200**
0028-5897 See NEW JERSEY PARENT-TEACHER. **1867**
0028-5919 See NEW JERSEY REALTOR. **4842**
0028-5935 See JOURNAL OF THE NEW JERSEY SPEECH AND HEARING ASSOCIATION. **4390**
0028-6001 See NEW JOURNAL (NEW HAVEN, CONN.), THE. **1093**
0028-6044 See NEW LEADER (NEW YORK, N.Y.), THE. **4543**
0028-6060 See NEW LEFT REVIEW. **4544**
0028-6087 See NEW LITERARY HISTORY. **3348**
0028-6176 See NEW MEXICO DENTAL JOURNAL. **1330**
0028-6192 See NEW MEXICO FARM AND RANCH. **112**
0028-6206 See NEW MEXICO HISTORICAL REVIEW. **2748**
0028-6214 See NEW MEXICO LAW REVIEW. **3015**
0028-6249 See NEW MEXICO MAGAZINE (SANTA FE, N.M. : 1974). **2540**
0028-6257 See MUNICIPAL REPORTER (SANTE FE, N.M.), THE. **4667**
0028-6273 See NEW MEXICO NURSE. **3862**
0028-6338 See NEW MEXICO WILDLIFE. **2200**
0028-6362 See NEW MUSICAL EXPRESS. MICROFORM, THE. **5812**
0028-6400 See NEW ORLEANS REVIEW, THE. **3348**
0028-6427 See NEW OUTLOOK (TEL AVIV). **4529**
0028-6443 See NEW PHILOSOPHY, THE. **4353**
0028-6451 See NEW PHYSICIAN. **3620**
0028-646X See NEW PHYTOLOGIST, THE. **519**
0028-6486 See NEW POLISH PUBLICATIONS. **4817**
0028-6494 See NEW POLITICS. **4544**
0028-6540 See NEW RAMBLER. **3416**
0028-6575 See NEW RENAISSANCE, THE. **326**
0028-6583 See NEW REPUBLIC (NEW YORK, N.Y.). **2851**
0028-6591 See NEW RESEARCH CENTERS. **5132**
0028-6613 See NEW SCHOLAR, THE. **5210**
0028-6680 See NEW SERIAL TITLES. **3234**
0028-6737 See NEW SOLIDARITY. **2540**
0028-677X See NEW SOUTH WALES INDUSTRIAL GAZETTE. **3152**
0028-6869 See NEW TECHNICAL BOOKS. **987**
0028-6877 See NEW TESTAMENT ABSTRACTS. **5013**
0028-6885 See NEW TESTAMENT STUDIES. **5018**
0028-6974 See NEW WOMAN. **5562**
0028-7091 See BULLETIN OF THE NEW YORK ACADEMY OF MEDICINE (1925). **3560**
0028-7164 See NEW YORK CONSTRUCTION NEWS. **622**
0028-7199 See JOURNAL OF THE NEW YORK ENTOMOLOGICAL SOCIETY. **5589**
0028-7237 See NEW YORK GENEALOGICAL AND BIOGRAPHICAL RECORD, THE. **2462**
0028-727X See NEW YORK HOLSTEIN NEWS. **216**
0028-7326 See NEW YORK LAW JOURNAL. **3016**
0028-7342 See N.Y. LETTER CARRIERS' OUTLOOK. **1145**
0028-7369 See NEW YORK (1968). **2540**

0028-7385 See NEW YORK MOTORIST. **5421**
0028-7458 See NEW YORK PROFESSIONAL ENGINEER. **1988**
0028-7482 See NEW YORK QUARTERLY : NYQ, THE. **3467**
0028-7539 See NEW YORK STATE BANKER, THE. **801**
0028-7547 See NEW YORK STATE BAR JOURNAL. **3016**
0028-7571 See NEW YORK STATE DENTAL JOURNAL. **1330**
0028-7628 See NEW YORK STATE JOURNAL OF MEDICINE. **3621**
0028-7636 See NEW YORK STATE LAW DIGEST. **3016**
0028-7644 See JOURNAL OF THE NEW YORK STATE NURSES ASSOCIATION, THE. **3860**
0028-7784 See NEW YORK THEATRE CRITICS' REVIEWS. **5366**
0028-7806 See NEW YORK TIMES BOOK REVIEW, THE. **3349**
0028-7822 See NEW YORK TIMES MAGAZINE, THE. **2540**
0028-7830 See NEW YORK TIMES SCHOOL WEEKLY, THE. **1093**
0028-7873 See NEW YORK UNIVERSITY JOURNAL OF INTERNATIONAL LAW & POLITICS. **3133**
0028-7881 See NEW YORK UNIVERSITY LAW REVIEW (1950). **3016**
0028-792X See NEW YORKER (NEW YORK, N.Y. : 1925). **2490**
0028-8047 See NEW ZEALAND DENTAL JOURNAL. **1330**
0028-808X See NEW ZEALAND ENGINEERING. **1988**
0028-8136 See NEW ZEALAND GARDENER. **2425**
0028-8144 See NEW ZEALAND GEOGRAPHER. **2570**
0028-8233 See NEW ZEALAND JOURNAL OF AGRICULTURAL RESEARCH. **112**
0028-825X See NEW ZEALAND JOURNAL OF BOTANY. **519**
0028-8276 See NEW ZEALAND JOURNAL OF EDUCATIONAL STUDIES. **1768**
0028-8292 See NEW ZEALAND JOURNAL OF GEOGRAPHY. **2570**
0028-8306 See NEW ZEALAND JOURNAL OF GEOLOGY AND GEOPHYSICS. **1389**
0028-8314 See NEW ZEALAND JOURNAL OF HEALTH, PHYSICAL EDUCATION & RECREATION. **1857**
0028-8322 See NEW ZEALAND JOURNAL OF HISTORY, THE. **2670**
0028-8330 See NEW ZEALAND JOURNAL OF MARINE AND FRESHWATER RESEARCH. **556**
0028-8349 See NEW ZEALAND JOURNAL OF MEDICAL LABORATORY SCIENCE. **3621**
0028-8373 See NEW ZEALAND LAW JOURNAL, THE. **3016**
0028-8381 See NEW ZEALAND LIBRARIES. **3234**
0028-8446 See NEW ZEALAND MEDICAL JOURNAL. **3621**
0028-8497 See NEW ZEALAND NATIONAL BIBLIOGRAPHY (WELLINGTON, N.Z. : 1983). **421**
0028-8500 See NEW ZEALAND NEWS UK. **5812**
0028-8535 See NEW ZEALAND NURSING JOURNAL, THE. **3862**
0028-8624 See NEW ZEALAND RAILWAY OBSERVER. **5433**
0028-8667 See NEW ZEALAND SCIENCE REVIEW. **5133**
0028-8802 See NEW ZEALAND WILDLIFE. **4875**
0028-8888 See NEWFOUNDLAND GAZETTE, THE. **3017**
0028-8918 See NEWPORT HISTORY. **2749**
0028-8969 See NEWS & LETTERS. **1508**
0028-9043 See HABITAT (LONDON). **2194**
0028-9108 See NEWS FROM ROHDE & SCHWARZ. **934**
0028-9205 See NEWS IN ENGINEERING. **1989**
0028-923X See NN&Q. NEWS, NOTES, AND QUOTES. **1769**

0028-9256 See NEWS NOTES - NEWARK MUSEUM. **4094**
0028-9264 See NEWS OF NEW YORK. **3621**
0028-9272 See NEWS OF NORWAY. **2700**
0028-9299 See NEWS OF THE WORLD'S CHILDREN (UNITED STATES COMMITTEE FOR UNICEF). **5298**
0028-9396 See NEWSBOY. **3416**
0028-9485 See NEWSLETTER ON INTELLECTUAL FREEDOM. **3236**
0028-9507 See NEWSLETTER ON NEWSLETTERS, THE. **2922**
0028-9604 See NEWSWEEK (U.S. ED.). **2490**
0028-9795 See NIEDERSACHSISCHES ARZTEBLATT. **3622**
0028-9817 See NIEMAN REPORTS. **2923**
0028-9922 See NIEUWE TAALGIDS. **3306**
0028-9930 See NIEUWE WEST-INDISCHE GIDS. **5211**
0029-005X See NIGERIAN CHRISTIAN, THE. **4982**
0029-0076 See NIGERIAN FIELD. **4169**
0029-0092 See NIGERIAN JOURNAL OF ECONOMIC AND SOCIAL STUDIES, THE. **1508**
0029-0114 See NIGERIAN JOURNAL OF SCIENCE. **5134**
0029-0122 See NIGERIAN LIBRARIES. **3236**
0029-0173 See NIGRIZIA. **4982**
0029-0181 See NIPPON BUTSURIGAKKAI SHI. **4413**
0029-0203 See NIPPON GANKA GAKKAI ZASSHI. **3877**
0029-0211 See NIHON GASU KYOKAISHI. **4266**
0029-022X See NIPPON GOMU KYOKAISHI. **5076**
0029-0254 See NIHON KAKIN GAKKAISHI. **216**
0029-0289 See NIPPON KINGAKKAI KAIHO. **520**
0029-0297 See NIPPON KOKUKA GAKKAI ZASSHI. **1331**
0029-0343 See NIPPON ONSEN KIKO BUTSURI IGAKKAI ZASSHI. **3622**
0029-0351 See NIHON PURASUCHIKKUSU SHINPO. **4457**
0029-0386 See NIHON SHINSEIJI GAKKAI ZASSHI. **3765**
0029-0394 See NIHON SHOKUHIN KOGYO GAKKAI SHI. **2351**
0029-0424 See NICHIDAI IGAKU ZASSHI. **3622**
0029-0432 See JOURNAL OF NIHON UNIVERSITY SCHOOL OF DENTISTRY. **1327**
0029-0440 See NIIGATA IGAKKAI ZASSHI. **3622**
0029-0483 See NIKKAKYO GEPPO. **987**
0029-053X See NIMROD (TULSA). **3417**
0029-0610 See NIHON DOJO HIRYOGAKU ZASSHI. **179**
0029-0629 See NIPPON FUNIN GAKKAI ZASSHI. **3765**
0029-0661 See NIHON NAIBUNPI GAKKAI ZASSHI. **467**
0029-0726 See NISHI NIHON HINYOKIKA. **3992**
0029-0777 See NITROGEN. **987**
0029-103X See NON-FOODS MERCHANDISING. **2351**
0029-1064 See PHILANTHROPY MONTHLY, THE. **4338**
0029-1080 See NONCELLO, IL. **326**
0029-1188 See NORD E SUD. **2700**
0029-1277 See NORDIC HYDROLOGY. **1416**
0029-1285 See NORDISK ADMINISTRATIVT TIDSSKRIFT. **4669**
0029-1315 See NORDISK DOMSSAMLING. **3018**
0029-1358 See NORDISK FORSAKRINGSTIDSKRIFT. **2889**
0029-1420 See NORDISK MEDICIN. **3622**
0029-1455 See NORDIC JOURNAL OF PSYCHIATRY. **3931**
0029-1463 See NORDISK PSYKOLOGI. **4606**
0029-1471 See NORDISK TIDSKRIFT FOR DOVUNDERVISNINGEN. **1883**
0029-148X See NORDISK TIDSKRIFT FOR BOK-OCH BIBLIOTEKSVASEN. **3237**
0029-1528 See NORDISK TIDSSKRIFT FOR KRIMINALVIDENSKAB. **3170**

0029-1625 See NORELCO REPORTER. 5134
0029-1668 See NORGES APOTEKERFORENINGS TIDSSKRIFT. 4318
0029-1676 See ECONOMIC BULLETIN. 1482
0029-182X See NOROIS. 2570
0029-1846 See NORSEMAN. 2520
0029-1870 See NORSK BOKFORTEGNELSE. 5807
0029-1935 See NORSK FARMACEUTISK TIDSSKRIFT. 4318
0029-1943 See NORSK FILOSOFISK TIDSSKRIFT. 4353
0029-1951 See NORSK GEOGRAFISK TIDSSKRIFT. 2571
0029-196X See NORSK GEOLOGISK TIDSSKRIFT. 1390
0029-1986 See NORSK HAGETIDEND. 2426
0029-1994 See NORSK IDRETT. 4908
0029-2028 See NORSK MILITRT TIDSSKRIFT. 4053
0029-2044 See NORSK MUSIKERBLAD. 4142
0029-2087 See NORSK SKOGBRUK. 2389
0029-2141 See NORSK SLEKTSHISTORISK TIDSSKRIFT. 2464
0029-2168 See NORSK TEKSTILTIDENDE. 5354
0029-2176 See NORSK TEOLOGISK TIDSSKRIFT. 4982
0029-2206 See NORSK TIDENDE FOR DET INDUSTRIELLE RETTSVERN. DEL I : PATENTER. 1306
0029-2214 See NORSK TIDSSKRIFT FOR MISJON. 4982
0029-2222 See NORSK TIDSSKRIFT FOR SJOVESEN. 4181
0029-2257 See NORSK UKEBLAD. 5807
0029-2281 See TIDSSKRIFT FOR DEN NORSKE LAEGEFORENING; TIDSSKRIFT FOR PRAKTISK MEDISIN. THE JOURNAL OF THE NORWEGIAN MEDICAL ASSOCIATION. 3645
0029-2370 See BULLETIN - NORTH AMERICAN GLADIOLUS COUNCIL. 505
0029-2397 See NORTH AMERICAN REVIEW, THE. 3349
0029-2435 See NORTH CAROLINA CHRISTIAN ADVOCATE. 5724
0029-2451 See NORTH CAROLINA EDUCATION. 1769
0029-2494 See NORTH CAROLINA HISTORICAL REVIEW, THE. 2750
0029-2524 See NORTH CAROLINA LAW REVIEW. 3018
0029-2540 See NORTH CAROLINA LIBRARIES. 3237
0029-2559 See NORTH CAROLINA MEDICAL JOURNAL (WINSTON-SALEM). 3916
0029-2567 See BULLETIN - NORTH CAROLINA MUSEUM OF ART. 4086
0029-2710 See NORTH DAKOTA HISTORY. 2750
0029-2745 See NORTH DAKOTA LAW REVIEW. 3018
0029-2753 See NORTH DAKOTA MUSIC EDUCATOR. 4142
0029-2761 See NORTH DAKOTA OUTDOORS. 4876
0029-277X See NORTH DAKOTA QUARTERLY, THE. 2541
0029-280X See TRANSACTIONS - NORTH EAST COAST INSTITUTION OF ENGINEERS AND SHIPBUILDERS. 1999
0029-2850 See NORTH JERSEY HIGHLANDER, THE. 2750
0029-2885 See EAST MIDLANDS BIBLIOGRAPHY. 415
0029-2915 See NORTHWEST DENTISTRY. 1331
0029-2958 See NORTH WOODS CALL, THE. 4876
0029-3032 See NORTHEASTERN NEWS, THE. 1093
0029-3083 See NORTHERN ENGINEER, THE. 1989
0029-3105 See NORTHERN IRELAND LEGAL QUARTERLY, THE. 3018
0029-3156 See NORTHERN LOGGER AND TIMBER PROCESSOR, THE. 2403
0029-3164 See NORTHERN MINER, THE. 2147

0029-3296 See NORTHWEST ANTHROPOLOGICAL RESEARCH NOTES. 242
0029-3350 See NORTHWEST FARM EQUIPMENT JOURNAL. 160
0029-3369 See NORTHWEST FOLKLORE. 2323
0029-3407 See NORTHWEST OHIO QUARTERLY. 2751
0029-3423 See NORTHWEST REVIEW (EUGENE, OR.). 3349
0029-3431 See SALMON TROUT STEELHEADER. 4854
0029-344X See NORTHWEST SCIENCE. 5134
0029-3474 See NORTHWEST TECHNOCRAT, THE. 1593
0029-3490 See NORTHWESTERN JEWELER, THE. 2915
0029-3512 See NORTHWESTERN LUTHERAN (MILWAUKEE, WIS.), THE. 5065
0029-3571 See NORTHWESTERN UNIVERSITY LAW REVIEW. 3019
0029-3601 See NORVEG. 242
0029-3636 See STATISTISK MANEDSHEFTE. 5344
0029-3652 See NORWEGIAN ARCHAEOLOGICAL REVIEW. 276
0029-3725 See NOS OISEAUX. 4169
0029-3954 See NOTES AFRICAINES. 2642
0029-3962 See NOTES AND ABSTRACTS IN AMERICAN AND INTERNATIONAL EDUCATION. 1796
0029-3970 See NOTES AND QUERIES. 3306
0029-3989 See NOTES & QUERIES FOR SOMERSET AND DORSET. 2700
0029-4004 See NOTES ET ETUDES DOCUMENTAIRES. 2520
0029-4047 See NOTES ON CONTEMPORARY LITERATURE. 3349
0029-4071 See NOTES ON MISSISSIPPI WRITERS. 3418
0029-4128 See NOTICIA GEOMORFOLOGICA. 2571
0029-4292 See SEW BUSINESS. 5186
0029-4306 See NOTITIAE. 5033
0029-4470 See NOTORNIS. 5619
0029-4527 See NOTRE DAME JOURNAL OF FORMAL LOGIC. 4354
0029-4543 See NOTRE DAME TECHNICAL REVIEW, THE. 5134
0029-456X See NOTRE TEMPS PARIS. 1968. 2851
0029-4578 See NOTRES. 5033
0029-4586 See NOTTINGHAM FRENCH STUDIES. 3418
0029-4608 See NOTULAE NATURAE OF THE ACADEMY NATURAL SCIENCES OF PHILADELPHIA. 5134
0029-4624 See NOUS (BLOOMINGTON). 4354
0029-4675 See NOUVEAU JOURNAL DE CHARPENTE MENUISERIE PARQUETS. 623
0029-4713 See NOUVEL OBSERVATEUR (PARIS), LE. 2520
0029-4802 See NOUVELLE REVUE FRANCAISE (PARIS, FRANCE : 1959). 3418
0029-4810 See NOUVELLE REVUE FRANCAISE D'HEMATOLOGIE. 3773
0029-4837 See NOUVELLE REVUE PEDAGOGIQUE. 1769
0029-4845 See NOUVELLE REVUE THEOLOGIQUE. 4982
0029-4853 See NOUVELLES ARCHIVES HOSPITALIERES. 3790
0029-4888 See NOUVELLES DE L'ESTAMPE. 4567
0029-4926 See NOUVELLES GRAPHIQUES. 381
0029-5027 See NOVA ET VETERA (FRIBOURG). 4982
0029-5035 See NOVA HEDWIGIA. 520
0029-5051 See NOVA PROIZVODNJA. 5135
0029-5132 See NOVEL. 3349
0029-5302 See NOVY ORIENT. 2660
0029-5310 See NOVIJ SLAH. 5791
0029-5337 See NOVYJ ZURNAL. 2851
0029-5361 See NOW AND THEN (MUNCY). 2751

0029-5388 See NOWE DROGI. 5211
0029-540X See NOWOTWORY. 3821
0029-5450 See NUCLEAR TECHNOLOGY. 2157
0029-5493 See NUCLEAR ENGINEERING AND DESIGN. 2156
0029-5507 See NUCLEAR ENGINEERING INTERNATIONAL. 2157
0029-5515 See NUCLEAR FUSION. 4448
0029-5523 See NUCLEAR INDIA. 2157
0029-5566 See NUCLEAR MEDICINE. 3848
0029-5574 See NUCLEAR NEWS (HINSDALE). 2157
0029-5604 See NUCLEAR SAFETY. 2157
0029-5620 See NUCLEAR SCIENCE INFORMATION OF JAPAN. 4449
0029-5639 See NUCLEAR SCIENCE AND ENGINEERING. 2157
0029-5647 See HE ZI KE XUE. 4447
0029-5655 See NUCLEAR STANDARDS NEWS. 2157
0029-5671 See RECHERCHE (PARIS. 1970). 5145
0029-568X See NUCLEUS (CALCUTTA). 550
0029-5698 See NUCLEUS (KARACHI). 1952
0029-5701 See NUESTRA ARQUITECTURA. 305
0029-571X See NUESTRA HISTORIA. 2552
0029-5736 See REVISTA TECNOLOGICA. 5148
0029-5795 See NUESTRO TIEMPO. 2851
0029-5922 See NUKLEONIKA. 2158
0029-5973 See NUMEN (INTERNATIONAL ASSOCIATION FOR THE HISTORY OF RELIGIONS). 4982
0029-5981 See INTERNATIONAL JOURNAL FOR NUMERICAL METHODS IN ENGINEERING. 1979
0029-599X See NUMERISCHE MATHEMATIK. 3525
0029-6015 See NUMISMA (MADRID). 2782
0029-6031 See NUMISMATIC LITERATURE. 2779
0029-604X See NUMISMATIC NEWS (KRAUSE PUBLICATIONS : 1977). 2782
0029-6066 See JOURNAL OF THE NUMISMATIC SOCIETY OF INDIA, THE. 2781
0029-6090 See NUMISMATIST: FOR COLLECTORS OF COINS, MEDALS, TOKENS AND PAPER MONEY, THE. 2782
0029-6090 See NUMISMATIST, THE. 2782
0029-6147 See NUOVA ANTOLOGIA. 2491
0029-6155 See NUOVA CORRENTE. 4354
0029-6228 See NUOVA RIVISTA MUSICALE ITALIANA. 4142
0029-6236 See NUOVA RIVISTA STORICA. 2624
0029-6295 See NUOVI ARGOMENTI. 2520
0029-6368 See IP NUOVO DIRITTO. 2985
0029-6376 See NUOVO MEZZOGIORNO. 1509
0029-6422 See NURSERY WORLD. 2284
0029-6430 See N&GC : JOURNAL OF THE HORTICULTURAL TRADES ASSOCIATION. 2424
0029-6465 See NURSING CLINICS OF NORTH AMERICA, THE. 3863
0029-6473 See NURSING FORUM (HILLSDALE). 3864
0029-6503 See NURSING JOURNAL OF INDIA. 3864
0029-6554 See NURSING OUTLOOK. 3865
0029-6562 See NURSING RESEARCH (NEW YORK). 3865
0029-6570 See NURSING STANDARD. 3865
0029-6597 See NUTIDA MUSIK. 4142
0029-6643 See NUTRITION REVIEWS. 4197
0029-6651 See PROCEEDINGS OF THE NUTRITION SOCIETY. 4197
0029-666X See NUTRITION TODAY (ANNAPOLIS). 4197
0029-6759 See NY POLITIK. 2520
0029-6783 See NYE BONYTT. 2520
0029-6791 See NYELVTUDOMANYI KOEZLEMENYEK. 3307
0029-6961 See OCLAE. 1770
0029-7054 See OECD OBSERVER. 1510

0029-7127 See BULLETIN DE L'OIV. 69
0029-7224 See CAHIERS O.R.S.T.O.M. SERIE ENTOMOLOGIE MEDICALE ET PARASITOLOGIE. 5606
0029-7259 See CAHIERS O.R.S.T.O.M. SERIE PEDOLOGIE. 1352
0029-7437 See OB. GYN. NEWS. 3766
0029-7445 See OB-GYN OBSERVER. 3766
0029-7488 See OBERFLACHE. 4014
0029-7526 See OBERLIN REVIEW, THE. 1093
0029-7550 See OBEROSTERREICHISCHE HEIMATBLATTER. 2701
0029-7585 See OBITER DICTA (1963). 3020
0029-7593 See OBJECTIVE : JUSTICE. 4511
0029-7615 See OBJETS ET MONDES. 4169
0029-7682 See BULLETIN MENSUEL. OBSERVATIONS CLIMATOLOGIQUES / INSTITUT ROYAL METEOROLOGIQUE DE BELGIQUE / MAANDBERICHT. KLIMATOLOGISCHE WAARNEMINGEN / KONINKLIJK METEOROLOGISCH INSTITUUT VAN BELGIEE. 4029
0029-7704 See OBSERVATORY, THE. 397
0029-7712 See OBSERVER (LONDON). 5813
0029-7739 See OBSERVER (ROCKFORD), THE. 5033
0029-7798 See OBST UND GARTEN. 2426
0029-7828 See OBSTETRICAL & GYNECOLOGICAL SURVEY. 3766
0029-7836 See OBSTETRICIA Y GINECOLOGIA LATINO-AMERICANAS. 3766
0029-7844 See OBSTETRICS AND GYNECOLOGY (NEW YORK. 1953). 3766
0029-7852 See OBZOR. 3419
0029-7909 See OCCUPATIONAL HAZARDS. 2866
0029-7917 See OCCUPATIONAL HEALTH. 2866
0029-7968 See OOQ, OCCUPATIONAL OUTLOOK QUARTERLY. 4207
0029-7984 See OCCUPATIONAL SAFETY AND HEALTH ABSTRACTS. 2867
0029-8018 See OCEAN ENGINEERING. 2093
0029-8026 See OCEAN INDUSTRY. 4267
0029-8069 See OCEAN SCIENCE NEWS. 1453
0029-8077 See OCEANIA. 2670
0029-8115 See OCEANIC LINGUISTICS. 3307
0029-8131 See JOURNAL OF OCEANOGRAPHY. 1450
0029-814X See HAI YANG YU HU CHAO. 1449
0029-8158 See OCEANOLOGY (WASHINGTON. 1966). 1454
0029-8182 See OCEANUS (WOODS HOLE). 1454
0029-8190 See NATURAL SCIENCE REPORT OF THE OCHANOMIZU UNIVERSITY. 5131
0029-8220 See OCHRONA PRACY. 2867
0029-8239 See OCHRONO ROSLIN. 116
0029-8247 See OCHRONA ZABYTKOW. 2701
0029-845X See SCANDINAVIAN JOURNAL OF DENTAL RESEARCH. 1335
0029-8506 See ODONTOSTOMATOLOGIKE PROODOS. 1331
0029-8514 See ODRODZENIE I REFORMACJA W POLSCE. 2701
0029-8522 See ODU. 2642
0029-8549 See OECOLOGIA. 2219
0029-8573 See GESUNDHEITSWESEN, DAS. 4776
0029-859X See OFFENTLICHE VERWALTUNG, DIE. 3021
0029-862X See OEIL LAUSANNE, L'. 327
0029-8654 See OKUMENISCHE RUNDSCHAU. 4983
0029-8786 See OSTERREICHISCHE ARZTEZEITUNG. 3624
0029-8832 See SITZUNGSBERICHTE / OSTERREICHISCHE AKADEMIE DER WISSENSCHAFTEN, PHILOSOPHISCH-HISTORISCHE KLASSE. 2629
0029-8891 See OSTERREICHISCHE BAUZEITUNG. 623
0029-9162 See OESTERREICHISCHE GLASER-ZEITUNG. 2592

0029-9251 See OSTERREICHISCHE JURISTEN-ZEITUNG. 3024
0029-9308 See OSTERREICHISCHE MONATSHEFTE. 2701
0029-9359 See MITTEILUNGEN DER OSTERREICHICHEN NUMISMATISCHEN GESELLSCHAFT. 2781
0029-9375 See OSTERREICHISCHE OSTHEFTE. 2701
0029-9588 See OESTERREICHISCHE WASSERWIRTSCHAFT. 2094
0029-9618 See OZE. OSTERREICHISCHE ZEITSCHRIFT FUER ELEKTRIZITATSWIRTSCHAFT. 2074
0029-9626 See OESTERREICHISCHE ZEITSCHRIFT OBJER KUNST UND DENKMALPFLEGE. 361
0029-9669 See OESTERREICHISCHE ZEITSCHRIFT FUER VOLKSKUNDE. 2323
0029-9820 See OSTERREICHISCHES ARCHIV FUER KIRCHENRECHT. 4984
0029-9898 See MONATSBERICHTE - OESTERREICHISCHES INSTITUT FUER WIRTSCHAFTSFORSCHUNG. 1505
0029-9960 See STATISTISCHE NACHRICHTEN - OSTERREICHISCHES STATISTISCHES ZENTRALAMT. 5343
0029-9987 See OSTERREICHS FISCHEREI. 2310
0030-0047 See OF CONSUMING INTEREST (ARLINGTON, VA.). 1298
0030-0055 See OF SEA AND SHORE. 5593
0030-0071 See OFF OUR BACKS. 5563
0030-0128 See OFFICE (STAMFORD. 1936), THE. 4213
0030-0187 See OFFICE EQUIPMENT NEWS. 4213
0030-0268 See OFFICER, THE. 4053
0030-0284 See OFFICIAL BOARD MARKETS. 4235
0030-0330 See OFFICIAL JOURNAL (PATENTS). 1307
0030-0373 See OFFICIAL RAILWAY EQUIPMENT REGISTER, THE. 5433
0030-0381 See OFFICIAL STEAMSHIP GUIDE INTERNATIONAL. 5487
0030-0454 See OFFICIEL DE L'AUTOMOBILE, L'. 5422
0030-0594 See OFFSETPRAXIS. 4372
0030-0608 See OFFSHORE (CONROE, TEX.). 4267
0030-0632 See BOLETIN DE LA OFICINA SANITARIA PANAMERICANA. 4769
0030-0675 See OFTALMOLOGICESKIJ ZURNAL (KIEV). 3877
0030-0691 See OGAM. 2701
0030-0705 See OGGI. 2491
0030-0802 See OHIO BANKER, THE. 802
0030-0845 See OHIO CHRISTIAN NEWS. 4983
0030-087X See OHIO DENTAL JOURNAL, THE. 1331
0030-0896 See OHIO FARMER, THE. 116
0030-090X See BULLETIN - OHIO FLORISTS' ASSOCIATION. 2434
0030-0934 See OHIO HISTORY. 2752
0030-0950 See OHIO JOURNAL OF SCIENCE, THE. 5136
0030-0985 See OHIO MOTORIST. 5422
0030-0993 See OHIO NURSES' REVIEW. 3866
0030-1035 See OHIO READING TEACHER. 3308
0030-1086 See OHIO SCHOOLS - OHIO EDUCATION ASSOCIATION. 1868
0030-1132 See JOURNAL - COLLEGE OF MEDICINE, THE OHIO STATE UNIVERSITY. 3592
0030-1183 See OHIO TAVERN NEWS. 5072
0030-1221 See OHIO WESLEYAN MAGAZINE, THE. 1093
0030-1248 See OHIOANA QUARTERLY. 3420
0030-1280 See OIGA. 2552
0030-1299 See OIKOS. 2220
0030-1310 See OIL, LIFESTREAM OF PROGRESS. 4269
0030-1353 See OIL, GAS & PETROCHEM EQUIPMENT. 4269

0030-1388 See OIL & GAS JOURNAL. 4268
0030-1396 See OIL & GAS TAX QUARTERLY. 4269
0030-1434 See OIL DAILY, THE. 4269
0030-1442 See OIL MILL GAZETTEER. 2015
0030-1515 See OILWEEK. 4270
0030-1531 See OISEAU ET LA REVUE FRANCAISE D'ORNITHOLOGIE. 5619
0030-154X See OKAJIMAS FOLIA ANATOMICA JAPONICA. 3679
0030-1566 See MATHEMATICAL JOURNAL OF OKAYAMA UNIVERSITY. 3519
0030-1574 See OKEANOLOGIJA. 1454
0030-1620 See OKLAHOMA UNION FARMER, THE. 117
0030-1647 See OKLAHOMA BANKER. 802
0030-1655 See OKLAHOMA BAR JOURNAL, THE. 3022
0030-1671 See OKLAHOMA BUSINESS BULLETIN. 701
0030-1698 See OKLAHOMA COWMAN. 217
0030-1701 See CURRENT FARM ECONOMICS (1984). 170
0030-171X See OKLAHOMA DAILY, THE. 5732
0030-1736 See OKLAHOMA GEOLOGY NOTES. 1443
0030-1752 See OKLAHOMA LAW REVIEW. 3022
0030-1760 See OKLAHOMA LIBRARIAN. 3239
0030-1787 See OKLAHOMA NURSE, THE. 3866
0030-1795 See OKLAHOMA OBSERVER, THE. 4485
0030-1833 See OKLAHOMA READER, THE. 3308
0030-1841 See OKLAHOMA RETAILER. 956
0030-1876 See JOURNAL - OKLAHOMA STATE MEDICAL ASSOCIATION. 3601
0030-1892 See OKLAHOMA TODAY. 2752
0030-1892 See OKLAHOMA TODAY. 2542
0030-1906 See OKONOMI OG POLITIK. 1577
0030-1965 See OLD BOTTLE MAGAZINE. 252
0030-1973 See OLD ENGLISH NEWSLETTER. 3420
0030-2058 See OLD WEST. 2752
0030-2082 See OLEAGINEUX. 117
0030-2139 See OLAMENU. 1805
0030-2163 See OLYMPIAN (SAN FRANCISCO). 4910
0030-2201 See CHRONICLE (OMAHA, NEB.), THE. 4188
0030-2228 See OMEGA (FARMINGDALE). 4606
0030-2333 See ON DIT. 5777
0030-235X See ON THE DECK. 117
0030-2414 See ONCOLOGY. 3821
0030-2430 See ONDE ELECTRIQUE. 2074
0030-2465 See ONDERSTEPOORT JOURNAL OF VETERINARY RESEARCH, THE. 5517
0030-2503 See ONE CHURCH. 5039
0030-252X See ONE IN CHRIST. 4983
0030-2600 See ONGAKU GEIJUTSU. 4143
0030-2651 See ONS ERFDEEL. 327
0030-283X See JOURNAL - ONTARIO ASSOCIATION OF CHILDREN'S AID SOCIETIES. 5293
0030-2848 See DIALOGUE - ANGLICAN CHURCH OF CANADA. DIOCESE OF ONTARIO. 4953
0030-2937 See ONTARIO GAZETTE, THE. 3022
0030-2945 See FAMILIES. 2447
0030-2953 See ONTARIO HISTORY. 2752
0030-3011 See ONTARIO MATHEMATICS GAZETTE. 3525
0030-302X See ONTARIO MEDICAL REVIEW. 3624
0030-3038 See ONTARIO MILK PRODUCER. 197
0030-3054 See ONTARIO PSYCHOLOGIST, THE. 4606
0030-3062 See OPAL, THE. 5367
0030-3089 See ONTARIO REPORTS (1963). 3023
0030-3283 See CIVIS MUNDI. 4540
0030-3305 See OP CIT. 361
0030-3372 See OPEN. 3239

0030-3399 See OPEN DEUR - MINISTERIE VAN NEDERLANDSE KULTUUR. 327
0030-3410 See OPEN DOOR (RALEIGH). 1839
0030-3461 See OPENBAAR VERVOER. 5389
0030-3518 See OPER UND KONZERT (MUNCHEN). 4143
0030-3526 See OPERA (LONDON). 4143
0030-3577 See OPERA CANADA. 4143
0030-3585 See OPERA JOURNAL, THE. 4143
0030-3607 See OPERA NEWS. 4143
0030-3631 See OPERATIONS FORESTIERES ET DE SCIERIE. 2390
0030-364X See OPERATIONS RESEARCH. 3525
0030-3658 See OPERATIONS RESEARCH/MANAGEMENT SCIENCE. 1209
0030-3690 See OPERNWELT. 4144
0030-3720 See OPHTHALMIC LITERATURE. 3877
0030-3747 See OPHTHALMIC RESEARCH. 3877
0030-3755 See OPHTHALMOLOGICA (BASEL). 3877
0030-3887 See OPSEARCH. 881
0030-3917 See OPTICA PURA Y APLICADA. 4439
0030-3968 See OPTICIAN, THE. 4216
0030-3992 See OPTICS AND LASER TECHNOLOGY. 4439
0030-400X See OPTICS AND SPECTROSCOPY. 4439
0030-4018 See OPTICS COMMUNICATIONS. 4439
0030-4026 See OPTIK (STUTTGART). 4440
0030-4034 See OPTIKA I SPEKTROSKOPIJA. 4440
0030-4069 See OPTIMIST (ABILENE), THE. 1094
0030-4085 See OPTOMETRIC MANAGEMENT. 4216
0030-4107 See OPTOMETRIC WORLD. 4216
0030-4123 See OPTOMETRIE. 4216
0030-414X See OPUSCULA MEDICA. 3624
0030-4204 See ORAL HEALTH. 1332
0030-4220 See ORAL SURGERY, ORAL MEDICINE, ORAL PATHOLOGY. 1332
0030-4263 See QUARTERLY - ORANGE COUNTY CALIFORNIA GENEALOGICAL SOCIETY. 2469
0030-4298 See ORANGE COUNTY JEWISH HERITAGE. 5638
0030-4379 See ORBIS; BULLETIN INTERNATIONAL DE DOCUMENTATION LINGUISTIQUE. 3308
0030-4387 See ORBIS (PHILADELPHIA). 4485
0030-4395 See ORBIS GEOGRAPHICUS. ADRESSAR GEOGRAPHIQUE DU MONDE. WORLD DIRECTORY OF GEOGRAPHY. GEOGRAPHISCHES WELTADRESSBUCH. 2571
0030-4425 See ORBIS (YOULGREAVE, DERBYSHIRE). 3467
0030-4433 See ORBIT (TORONTO). 1902
0030-4468 See ORCHESTER, DAS. 4144
0030-4476 See ORCHID REVIEW. 2436
0030-4492 See ORD & BILD. 3349
0030-4565 See BULLETIN DE L'ORDRE DES MEDECINS. 3560
0030-4611 See OREGON FARM BUREAU NEWS. 117
0030-4670 See JOURNAL OF THE OREGON DENTAL ASSOCIATION, THE. 1329
0030-4689 See OREGON EDUCATION. 1770
0030-4697 See OREGON GRANGE BULLETIN. 117
0030-4727 See OREGON HISTORICAL QUARTERLY. 2752
0030-4735 See OREGON LIBRARY NEWS. 3239
0030-4751 See OREGON NURSE. 3866
0030-4778 See ORNAMENTALS NORTHWEST (1981). 2426
0030-4816 See OREGON STATE BAR BULLETIN, THE. 3023
0030-4883 See ORGAN (BOURNEMOUTH). 4144
0030-493X See ORGANIC MASS SPECTROMETRY. 1018
0030-4948 See ORGANIC PREPARATIONS AND PROCEDURES INTERNATIONAL. 1045

0030-5065 See ESPERANTOUSA. 3280
0030-5138 See ORGANOMETALLIC COMPOUNDS. 1045
0030-5170 See ORGUE (PARIS), L'. 4145
0030-5189 See ORIENS ANTIQUUS. 2661
0030-5197 See ORIENS EXTREMUS. 3420
0030-5227 See ORIENT (DEUTSCHES ORIENT-INSTITUT). 2661
0030-5278 See ORIENTAL ART. 361
0030-5308 See ORIENTAL GEOGRAPHER. 2571
0030-5316 See ORIENTAL INSECTS. 5612
0030-5324 See JOURNAL OF THE ORIENTAL INSTITUTE, M.S. UNIVERSITY OF BARODA. 2505
0030-5340 See JOURNAL OF THE ORIENTAL SOCIETY OF AUSTRALIA, THE. 2656
0030-5367 See ORIENTALIA; COMMENTARI PERIODICI DE REBUS ORIENTIS ANTIQUI. 2661
0030-5375 See ORIENTALIA CHRISTIANA PERIODICA. 5039
0030-5391 See ORIENTAMENTI PEDAGOGICI. 1770
0030-5448 See ORIENTATIONS (HONG KONG). 2661
0030-5472 See ORIENTE MODERNO. 2661
0030-5502 See ORIENTIERUNG (ZURICH). 4984
0030-5553 See ORIOLE (ATLANTA), THE. 5593
0030-557X See ORION. 398
0030-5596 See ORITA. 4984
0030-560X See ORIZONT. 3420
0030-5642 See ORKESTER JOURNALEN. 4145
0030-5685 See ORNIS FENNICA. 5619
0030-5693 See ORNIS SCANDINAVICA. 5619
0030-5707 See ORNITHOLOGISCHE BEOBACHTER. 5619
0030-5715 See ANZEIGER DER ORNITHOLOGISCHE GESELLSCHAFT IN BAYERN. 5614
0030-5723 See ORNITHOLOGISCHE MITTEILUNGEN. 5619
0030-5790 See ORPHEUS : RIVISTA DI UMANITA CLASSICA E CRISTIANA. 1079
0030-5804 See ORPHIC LUTE. 3467
0030-5820 See ORTHODOX LIFE. 5040
0030-5839 See ORTHODOX WORD, THE. 5040
0030-588X See ORTHOPADISCHE PRAXIS. 3883
0030-5898 See ORTHOPEDIC CLINICS OF NORTH AMERICA, THE. 3884
0030-5987 See ORTOPEDIJA, TRAVMATOLOGIJA I PROTEZIROVANIE. 3884
0030-6002 See ORVOSI HETILAP. 3624
0030-6010 See ORVOSI KONYVTAROS, AZ. 3240
0030-6037 See ORVOSKEPZES (BUDAPEST). 3624
0030-6053 See ORYX. 2201
0030-6096 See OSAKA CITY MEDICAL JOURNAL. 3624
0030-6126 See OSAKA JOURNAL OF MATHEMATICS. 3526
0030-6169 See OSAKA DAIGAKU IGAKU ZASSHI. 3624
0030-6177 See TECHNOLOGY REPORTS OF THE OSAKA UNIVERSITY. 1998
0030-6185 See OSGOODE HALL LAW JOURNAL (1960). 3023
0030-6231 See OSPEDALE. 3790
0030-6266 See OSPEDALI D'ITALIA-CHIRURGIA. 3971
0030-6312 See OSSERVATORE ROMANO, L'. 5813
0030-6428 See OSTEUROPA (STUTTGART). 4486
0030-6444 See OSTEUROPA-RECHT. 3024
0030-6460 See OSTEUROPA WIRTSCHAFT. 1511
0030-6487 See OSTKIRCHLICHE STUDIEN. 5040
0030-6517 See OSTOMY QUARTERLY. 3971
0030-6525 See OSTRICH, THE. 5619

0030-6614 See AUSTRALIAN JOURNAL OF OTO-LARYNGOLOGY : THE OFFICIAL JOURNAL OF THE AUSTRALIAN SOCIETY OF OTO-LARYNGOLOGY HEAD AND NECK SURGERY. 3887
0030-6622 See NIPPON JIBI INKOKA GAKKAI KAIHO. 3889
0030-6657 See OTOLARYNGOLOGIA POLSKA. 3890
0030-6665 See OTOLARYNGOLOGIC CLINICS OF NORTH AMERICA, THE. 3890
0030-6703 See OTTAR. 4170
0030-6711 See JOURNAL OF THE OTTO RANK ASSOCIATION. 4602
0030-672X See OUD HOLLAND. 361
0030-6789 See OUR ANIMALS. 2252
0030-6835 See ANIMALS (BOSTON). 225
0030-6843 See OUR FAMILY (BATTLEFORD). 4984
0030-6851 See OUR FOURFOOTED FRIENDS. 4287
0030-686X See OUR GENERATION (MONTREAL). 4544
0030-6886 See OUR LADY'S DIGEST. 4984
0030-6967 See OUR SUNDAY VISITOR. 5034
0030-7025 See OUTDOOR CALIFORNIA. 4876
0030-7068 See OUTDOOR INDIANA. 4707
0030-7076 See OUTDOOR LIFE (NEW YORK, N.Y.). 4877
0030-7106 See OUTDOOR OKLAHOMA. 4877
0030-7157 See WONDERFUL WEST VIRGINIA. 2210
0030-7181 See OUTDOORS UNLIMITED. 3421
0030-7246 See OUTLOOK (NEW YORK, N.Y. 1937), THE. 910
0030-7270 See OUTLOOK ON AGRICULTURE. 118
0030-7319 See OUTRIDER / WYOMING STATE LIBRARY, THE. 3240
0030-7416 See OVERLAND. 2511
0030-7556 See OVERTURE (LOS ANGELES). 4145
0030-7564 See OVERVIEW. 5034
0030-7572 See OVTSEVODSTVO. 217
0030-7580 See OWL OF MINERVA, THE. 4354
0030-7645 See OXFORD. 1094
0030-7653 See OXFORD ECONOMIC PAPERS. 1594
0030-7661 See OXFORD MEDICAL SCHOOL GAZETTE. 3625
0030-770X See OXIDATION OF METALS. 4014
0030-7769 See OZARKS MOUNTAINEER, THE. 2753
0030-7777 See OZONE DATA FOR THE WORLD. 1433
0030-7858 See GRADUATE SCHOOL RESEARCH JOURNAL : A PUBLICATION OF GRADUATE SCHOOL OF BUSINESS ADMINISTRATION AND GRADUATE SCHOOL OF EDUCATION. 1826
0030-7912 See PEGG, THE. 1990
0030-8064 See PORT OF LONDON. 5454
0030-8102 See PMEA NEWS. 4146
0030-8129 See PUBLICATIONS OF THE MODERN LANGUAGE ASSOCIATION OF AMERICA. 3313
0030-8188 See PNLA QUARTERLY. 3241
0030-8196 See PNPA PRESS. 4818
0030-8250 See PRS JOURNAL. 4358
0030-8277 See PSA JOURNAL. 4376
0030-834X See MITTEILUNGEN - PTB. 5129
0030-851X See PACIFIC AFFAIRS. 4486
0030-8544 See PACIFIC BUILDER & ENGINEER. 2028
0030-8552 See PACIFIC BUSINESS NEWS. 5656
0030-8579 See PACIFIC CITIZEN, THE. 5638
0030-8641 See PACIFIC DISCOVERY. 5137
0030-8668 See PACIFIC FRUIT NEWS. 2352
0030-8684 See PACIFIC HISTORICAL REVIEW. 2753
0030-8722 See PACIFIC ISLANDS MONTHLY. 2670

0030-8730 See PACIFIC JOURNAL OF MATHEMATICS. 3526
0030-8757 See PACIFIC LAW JOURNAL. 3024
0030-8803 See PACIFIC NORTHWEST QUARTERLY. 2753
0030-882X See PACIFIC NORTHWESTERNER, THE. 2753
0030-8870 See PACIFIC SCIENCE. 5137
0030-8889 See INFORMATION BULLETIN - PACIFIC SCIENCE ASSOCIATION. 5113
0030-8900 See PACIFIC SHIPPER. 5453
0030-8943 See PACIFIC TRAFFIC. 5442
0030-8978 See PACIFIC VIEWPOINT. 1577
0030-8986 See PACIFIC YACHTING. 595
0030-8994 See PACIFICAN. 1094
0030-901X See PACK-O-FUN. 1067
0030-9060 See PACKAGING. 4220
0030-9109 See PACKAGING DESIGN. 4220
0030-9117 See PACKAGING DIGEST (CHICAGO, ILL.). 4220
0030-9125 See PACKAGING INDIA. 4220
0030-9133 See PACKAGING NEWS (LONDON). 4220
0030-9168 See PACKER, THE. 2352
0030-9222 See PADRES' TRAIL. 4985
0030-9230 See PAEDAGOGICA HISTORICA. 1771
0030-9311 See PAEDIATRICA INDONESIANA. 3907
0030-932X See PADIATRIE UND GRENZGEBIETE. 3907
0030-9338 See PADIATRIE UND PADOLOGIE. 3907
0030-9346 See PADIATRISCHE PRAXIS. 3907
0030-9435 See PAIDEIA. 421
0030-9540 See PAINTINDIA. ANNUAL. 4224
0030-963X See PAKISTAN AFFAIRS. 2661
0030-9680 See PAKISTAN CHEMIST AND DRUGGIST. 4319
0030-9729 See PAKISTAN DEVELOPMENT REVIEW. 1511
0030-977X See PAKISTAN EXPORTS. 848
0030-9796 See JOURNAL OF THE PAKISTAN HISTORICAL SOCIETY. 2656
0030-980X See PAKISTAN HORIZON. 2770
0030-9818 See PAKISTAN JOURNAL OF FORESTRY, THE. 2390
0030-9850 See PAKISTAN JOURNAL OF PHARMACY. 4319
0030-9869 See PAKISTAN JOURNAL OF PSYCHOLOGY. 4606
0030-9877 See PAKISTAN JOURNAL OF SCIENCE. 5137
0030-9885 See PAKISTAN JOURNAL OF SCIENTIFIC AND INDUSTRIAL RESEARCH. 5137
0030-9923 See PAKISTAN JOURNAL OF ZOOLOGY. 5593
0030-9966 See PAKISTAN LIBRARY BULLETIN. 3240
0030-9982 See JOURNAL OF THE PAKISTAN MEDICAL ASSOCIATION. 3599
0031-0131 See PAKKAUS. 702
0031-0158 See PALACIO, EL. 2753
0031-0174 See PALAEOBOTANIST (LUCKNOW). 521
0031-0182 See PALAEOGEOGRAPHY, PALAEOCLIMATOLOGY, PALAEOECOLOGY. 4228
0031-0204 See TRANSACTIONS AND PROCEEDINGS OF THE PALAEONTOLOGICAL SOCIETY OF JAPAN. 4231
0031-0220 See PALAONTOLOGISCHE ZEITSCHRIFT. 4229
0031-0239 See PALAEONTOLOGY. 4229
0031-0247 See PALAEOVERTEBRATA. 4229
0031-0298 See PALEOBIOS. 4229
0031-0301 See PALEONTOLOGICAL JOURNAL. 4229
0031-031X See PALEONTOLOGICESKIJ ZURNAL. 4230

0031-0328 See PALESTINE EXPLORATION QUARTERLY. 278
0031-0336 See PALESTINE REFUGEES TODAY. 5300
0031-0352 See PALETTEN. 361
0031-0360 See PALIMPSEST (IOWA CITY), THE. 2753
0031-0379 See PALLADIO. 305
0031-0387 See PALLAS (TOULOUSE, FRANCE). 3309
0031-0417 See PALM BEACH LIFE. 2542
0031-0425 See PALM SPRINGS LIFE. 2542
0031-045X See PALOMINO HORSES. 2801
0031-0506 See PAMATKY ARCHEOLOGICKE. 278
0031-0514 See PAMIETNIK LITERACKI. 3421
0031-0522 See PAMIETNIK TEATRALNY. 3421
0031-0581 See REVISTA GEOGRAFICA DEL INSTITUTO PANAMERICANO DE GEOGRAFIA E HISTORIA. 2575
0031-0603 See PAN-PACIFIC ENTOMOLOGIST, THE. 5612
0031-062X See PANACHE. 3422
0031-0646 See PANAMA CANAL REVIEW, THE. 5454
0031-0743 See EXCERPTA MEDICA. SECTION 49. FORENSIC SCIENCE ABSTRACTS. 3740
0031-0808 See PANMINERVA MEDICA. 3625
0031-0867 See PANORAMA. 5488
0031-0980 See PANSTWO I PRAWO. 3024
0031-1049 See PAPEIS AVULSOS DE ZOOLOGIA (SAO PAULO). 5594
0031-1057 See PAPEL, O. 4235
0031-1081 See PAPER AGE. 4235
0031-109X See PRINTING ABSTRACTS. 4570
0031-1103 See PAPER & TWINE JOURNAL. 4235
0031-1138 See PAPER, FILM AND FOIL CONVERTER. 4236
0031-1162 See PAPER MONEY. 2783
0031-1227 See PAPERBOARD PACKAGING. 4221
0031-1235 See PAPERBOUND BOOKS IN PRINT. 4822
0031-1243 See PAPERI JA PUU. 4236
0031-126X See PAPERS IN METEOROLOGY AND GEOPHYSICS. 1433
0031-1294 See PAPERS ON LANGUAGE & LITERATURE. 3422
0031-1308 See PAPETERIE, LA. 4236
0031-1340 See PAPIER, DAS. 4236
0031-1367 See PAPIER, CARTON ET CELLULOSE. 4236
0031-1375 See PAPIER UND DRUCK. 4237
0031-1448 See PAPIRIPAR. 4237
0031-1472 See PAPUA NEW GUINEA JOURNAL OF EDUCATION. 1771
0031-1480 See PAPUA NEW GUINEA MEDICAL JOURNAL. 3626
0031-1588 See PARACHUTIST (WASHINGTON). 4911
0031-1650 See PARAGONE. 327
0031-1723 See PARAMETERS (CARLISLE, PA.). 4053
0031-1731 See PARAMETRO. 2830
0031-1758 See PARAPLEGIA. 4392
0031-1766 See PARAPLEGIA NEWS. 4392
0031-1804 See PARAPSYCHOLOGY REVIEW. 4242
0031-1812 See PARASITICA. 521
0031-1820 See PARASITOLOGY. 492
0031-1847 See PARAZITOLOGIJA. 468
0031-1952 See PARFUMERIE UND KOSMETIK. 405
0031-2029 See PARIS-MATCH. 2521
0031-2037 See PARIS REVIEW, THE. 3422
0031-2193 See PARKING (WASHINGTON, D.C.). 5423
0031-2215 See PARKS & RECREATION (ARLINGTON, VA.). 4707
0031-2231 See RECREATION CANADA. 4853
0031-2231 See RECREATION CANADA (FRENCH EDITION). 4853

0031-224X See PARKS & SPORTS GROUNDS. 5488
0031-2282 See PARLIAMENTARIAN. 4672
0031-2290 See PARLIAMENTARY AFFAIRS. 4672
0031-2320 See PARNASSO. 3422
0031-2355 See PAROLA DEL PASSATO, LA. 1079
0031-2460 See PARTICLE ACCELERATORS. 4413
0031-2495 See PARTICULIER, LE. 2285
0031-2525 See PARTISAN REVIEW (1936). 4544
0031-2614 See PASICRISIE BELGE. RECUEIL GENERAL DE LA JURISPRUDENCE DES COURS ET TRIBUNAUX. 3025
0031-2649 See PASQUE PETALS. 3467
0031-2703 See PASSENGER PIGEON, THE. 5619
0031-2711 See PASSERELLE, LA. 3422
0031-272X See PASSPORT (CHICAGO). 5488
0031-2738 See PASSWORD (EL PASO). 2753
0031-2746 See PAST & PRESENT. 2625
0031-2762 See PASTORAL LIFE. 4985
0031-2789 See PASTORAL PSYCHOLOGY. 4607
0031-2827 See PASTORALTHEOLOGIE. 4985
0031-286X See PATENT JOURNAL, INCLUDING TRADE MARKS DESIGNS AND COPYRIGHT IN CINEMATOGRAPH FILMS. 1307
0031-2894 See PATENTBLATT. 1307
0031-2908 See PATENTNI GLASNIK. 1308
0031-2983 See PATHOLOGICA. 3896
0031-2991 See PATOLOGICESKAJA FIZIOLOGIJA I EKSPERIMENTALNAJA TERAPIJA. 584
0031-3025 See PATHOLOGY. 3897
0031-305X See PATIENT CARE. 3738
0031-3114 See PATOLOGIA POLSKA. 3897
0031-3203 See PATTERN RECOGNITION. 1215
0031-322X See PATTERNS OF PREJUDICE. 2270
0031-3262 See PAUNCH. 3422
0031-3297 See PAVO. 5619
0031-3335 See PAX REGIS. 4985
0031-3386 See PAYS BAS-NORMAND, LE. 2702
0031-3394 See PAYS LORRAIN, LE. 2702
0031-3556 See PEACE OFFICER (WARREN, MICH.). 3171
0031-3599 See PEACE RESEARCH ABSTRACTS JOURNAL. 4502
0031-3602 See PEACEMAKER, THE. 4487
0031-3610 See PEACH TIMES. 2427
0031-3637 See BULLETIN OF THE PEAK DISTRICT MINES HISTORICAL SOCIETY. 2135
0031-3653 See PEANUT FARMER, THE. 180
0031-3661 See PEANUT JOURNAL AND NUT WORLD. 2353
0031-3696 See PEBBLE (CRETE). 3423
0031-3718 See PECHE ET LES POISSONS PARIS, LA. 2310
0031-3726 See PECHE MARITIME (PARIS, FRANCE). 5454
0031-3777 See PEDAGOGIA E VITA. 1067
0031-3793 See PEDAGOGIC REPORTER, THE. 1772
0031-3815 See PEDAGOGIKA. 1772
0031-3831 See SCANDINAVIAN JOURNAL OF EDUCATIONAL RESEARCH. 1781
0031-3890 See PEDIATRIA (NAPOLI). 3907
0031-3920 See PEDIATRIA MODERNA. 3907
0031-3939 See PEDIATRIA POLSKA. 3907
0031-3955 See PEDIATRIC CLINICS OF NORTH AMERICA, THE. 3908
0031-3963 See PEDIATRIC CONFERENCES FROM THE CHILDREN'S HOSPITAL OF NEWARK. 3908
0031-398X See PEDIATRIC NEWS. 3909
0031-3998 See PEDIATRIC RESEARCH. 3909
0031-4005 See PEDIATRICS (EVANSTON). 3910
0031-4021 See PEDIATRIE. 3910
0031-403X See PEDIATRIJA. 3910
0031-4056 See PEDOBIOLOGIA. 181
0031-4080 See PEGASUS. 4053
0031-4161 See PELICAN NEWS. 3866
0031-4242 See PEN WOMAN (1944), THE. 5564

0031-4307 See PENINSULA POETS. 3468
0031-4331 See PENN DENTAL JOURNAL, THE. 1332
0031-434X See PENNSYLVANIA ANGLER. 2310
0031-4358 See PENNSYLVANIA ARCHAEOLOGIST. 278
0031-4382 See PENNSYLVANIA BUSINESS SURVEY. 702
0031-4404 See PENNSYLVANIA CHIEFS OF POLICE ASSOCIATION BULLETIN. 3171
0031-4412 See PENNSYLVANIA CONTRACTOR. 2607
0031-4439 See PENNSYLVANIA DENTAL JOURNAL. 1332
0031-4455 See PENNSYLVANIA EDUCATION. 1772
0031-4471 See PENNSYLVANIA FARMER. 119
0031-448X See BULLETIN - PENNSYLVANIA FLOWER GROWERS. 2435
0031-4498 See PENNSYLVANIA FOLKLIFE. 2754
0031-4501 See PENNSYLVANIA FORESTS. 2390
0031-451X See PENNSYLVANIA GAME NEWS. 4877
0031-4528 See PENNSYLVANIA HISTORY. 2754
0031-4587 See PENNSYLVANIA MAGAZINE OF HISTORY AND BIOGRAPHY, THE. 2754
0031-4595 See PENNSYLVANIA MEDICINE. 3626
0031-4609 See PENNSYLVANIA MESSAGE. 4392
0031-4617 See PENNSYLVANIA NURSE, THE. 3866
0031-4633 See PENNSYLVANIA PHARMACIST. 4319
0031-4714 See PENNSYLVANIAN. 4673
0031-4749 See PENSAMIENTO (MADRID). 4354
0031-4773 See PENSEE. 2521
0031-4781 See PENSEE CATHOLIQUE, LA. 5034
0031-4846 See PENSIERO POLITICO, IL. 4487
0031-4897 See PENTECOSTAL EVANGEL. 5066
0031-4919 See PENTECOSTAL MESSENGER, THE. 5066
0031-4927 See PENTECOSTAL TESTIMONY, THE. 4986
0031-5036 See PEOPLE'S KOREA, THE. 5805
0031-5044 See PEOPLE'S WORLD (BERKELEY). 5638
0031-5060 See PEP (MAMARONECK, N.Y.). 4864
0031-5117 See PERCEPTION & PSYCHOPHYSICS. 4607
0031-5125 See PERCEPTUAL AND MOTOR SKILLS. 4607
0031-5222 See PERFORMING ARTS (LOS ANGELES EDITION). 387
0031-5230 See PERFORMING ARTS & ENTERTAINMENT IN CANADA. 387
0031-5303 See PERIODICA MATHEMATICA HUNGARICA. 3526
0031-532X See PERIODICA POLYTECHNICA: ELECTRICAL ENGINEERING. ELEKTROTECHNIK. 2075
0031-5362 See PERIODICUM BIOLOGORUM. 468
0031-5524 See JOURNAL AND REPORT OF PROCEEDINGS - PERMANENT WAY INSTITUTION. 2025
0031-5605 See PERSONAL (MUNCHEN). 945
0031-5613 See PERSONAL ROMANCES. 5074
0031-5656 See PERSONEELSBELEID. 945
0031-5699 See PERSONHISTORISK TIDSKRIFT. 434
0031-5702 See HR FOCUS. 941
0031-5745 See PERSONNEL JOURNAL. 945
0031-5753 See PERSONNEL LITERATURE. 4704
0031-5761 See PERSONNEL MANAGEMENT (LONDON. 1969). 945
0031-577X See PERSONNEL MANAGEMENT ABSTRACTS. 732
0031-5826 See PERSONNEL PSYCHOLOGY. 4607
0031-5842 See PERSOON EN GEMEENSCHAP. 1773
0031-5850 See PERSOONIA. 576
0031-594X See PEACE COURIER. 4531

0031-5982 See PERSPECTIVES IN BIOLOGY AND MEDICINE. 468
0031-5990 See PERSPECTIVES IN PSYCHIATRIC CARE. 3866
0031-6016 See PERSPECTIVES OF NEW MUSIC. 1240
0031-6032 See PERSPECTIVES PSYCHIATRIQUES PARIS. 3932
0031-6059 See PERSPEKTYWY. 2521
0031-6067 See BOLETIN DE LA BIBLIOTECA NACIONAL (LIMA). 3196
0031-6121 See PEST CONTROL. 4246
0031-613X See PESTICIDE SCIENCE. 4246
0031-6229 See PETERMANNS GEOGRAPHISCHE MITTEILUNGEN. 2572
0031-6245 See PETFOOD INDUSTRY. 4287
0031-6253 See PETIT JOURNAL DU BRASSEUR. 2370
0031-630X See PETRA. 5564
0031-6342 See PETROCHEMICAL NEWS. 4271
0031-6369 See ARAB OIL & GAS. 4250
0031-6423 See PETROLEUM ABSTRACTS (TULSA, OKLA.). 4284
0031-6458 See PETROLEUM CHEMISTRY. 4272
0031-6490 See PETROLEUM OUTLOOK. 4273
0031-6555 See PETROLEUM TODAY. 4274
0031-6652 See PEZ Y LA SERPIENTE, EL. 327
0031-6679 See PFALZER HEIMAT. 2702
0031-6733 See PFLANZENARZT, DER. 521
0031-6768 See PFLUGERS ARCHIV. 584
0031-6792 See PERADARSTVO. 119
0031-6849 See PHARMATIMES BOMBAY. 4324
0031-6857 See PHARMACA. 4319
0031-6865 See PHARMACEUTICA ACTA HELVETIAE. 4319
0031-6873 See PHARMACEUTICAL JOURNAL (1933). 4320
0031-6903 See YAKUGAKU ZASSHI. 4333
0031-6911 See PHARMACEUTISCH WEEKBLAD. 4321
0031-692X See PHARMACIEN, LE. 4321
0031-6938 See PHARMACIEN DE FRANCE. 4321
0031-6970 See EUROPEAN JOURNAL OF CLINICAL PHARMACOLOGY. 4303
0031-6997 See PHARMACOLOGICAL REVIEWS. 4322
0031-7004 See PHARMACOLOGIST, THE. 4322
0031-7012 See PHARMACOLOGY. 4322
0031-711X See PHARMAZEUTISCHE INDUSTRIE, DIE. 4324
0031-7128 See PHARMAZEUTISCHE RUNDSCHAU. 4324
0031-7136 See PHARMAZEUTISCHE ZEITUNG. 4324
0031-7144 See PHARMAZIE, DIE. 4324
0031-7152 See PHARMINDEX. 4324
0031-7179 See PHAROS OF ALPHA OMEGA ALPHA-HONOR MEDICAL SOCIETY, THE. 3627
0031-7217 See PHI DELTA KAPPAN. 1773
0031-7233 See PHILADELPHIA MAGAZINE (1967). 2543
0031-7306 See PHILADELPHIA MEDICINE. 3627
0031-7314 See BULLETIN - PHILADELPHIA MUSEUM OF ART. 345
0031-7381 See PHILATELIC EXPORTER, THE. 1146
0031-7438 See PHILIPPINE ABSTRACTS. 422
0031-7454 See PHILIPPINE AGRICULTURIST, THE. 119
0031-7470 See PHILIPPINE ARCHITECTURE, ENGINEERING, & CONSTRUCTION RECORD. 306
0031-7500 See PHILIPPINE ECONOMIC JOURNAL, THE. 1512
0031-7551 See PHILIPPINE GEOGRAPHICAL JOURNAL. 2572
0031-7624 See PHILIPPINE JOURNAL OF EDUCATION, THE. 1773
0031-7640 See PHILIPPINE JOURNAL OF NUTRITION. 4197

0031-7659 See PHILIPPINE JOURNAL OF OPHTHALMOLOGY. 3878
0031-7675 See PHILIPPINE JOURNAL OF PUBLIC ADMINISTRATION. 4673
0031-7683 See PHILIPPINE JOURNAL OF SCIENCE, THE. 5138
0031-7705 See PHILIPPINE JOURNAL OF VETERINARY MEDICINE. 5518
0031-7721 See PHILIPPINE LAW JOURNAL. 3029
0031-7780 See PHILIPPINE REVIEW OF BUSINESS AND ECONOMICS, THE. 703
0031-7810 See PHILIPPINE SOCIOLOGICAL REVIEW. 5253
0031-7829 See PHILIPPINE STATISTICIAN, THE. 5336
0031-7837 See PHILIPPINE STUDIES. 2625
0031-7969 See PHILOBIBLON. 362
0031-7977 See PHILOLOGICAL QUARTERLY. 3310
0031-7985 See PHILOLOGUS. 3310
0031-7993 See PHILOSOPHER'S INDEX. 4365
0031-8019 See PHILOSOPHIA MATHEMATICA. 3526
0031-8027 See PHILOSOPHIA NATURALIS. 4355
0031-8035 See PHILOSOPHIA REFORMATA. 4355
0031-8051 See PHILOSOPHICAL BOOKS. 4355
0031-806X See PHILOSOPHICAL FORUM, THE. 4355
0031-8094 See PHILOSOPHICAL QUARTERLY, THE. 4356
0031-8108 See PHILOSOPHICAL REVIEW, THE. 4356
0031-8116 See PHILOSOPHICAL STUDIES. 4356
0031-8159 See PHILOSOPHISCHE RUNDSCHAU. 4356
0031-8175 See PHILOSOPHISCHER LITERATURANZEIGER. 4356
0031-8183 See PHILOSOPHISCHES JAHRBUCH (FREIBURG). 4356
0031-8191 See PHILOSOPHY (LONDON). 4357
0031-8205 See PHILOSOPHY AND PHENOMENOLOGICAL RESEARCH. 4356
0031-8213 See PHILOSOPHY & RHETORIC. 4357
0031-8221 See PHILOSOPHY EAST & WEST. 4357
0031-8248 See PHILOSOPHY OF SCIENCE (EAST LANSING). 5138
0031-8256 See PHILOSOPHY TODAY (CELINA). 4357
0031-8280 See PHLEBOLOGIE. 3709
0031-8299 See PHOENIX (TORONTO). 1079
0031-8388 See PHONETICA. 3310
0031-8426 See PHOSPHORUS AND POTASSIUM. 988
0031-8523 See PHOTO INTERPRETATION. 4373
0031-8531 See PHOTO MARKETING. 4373
0031-8655 See PHOTOCHEMISTRY AND PHOTOBIOLOGY. 1056
0031-868X See PHOTOGRAMMETRIC RECORD, THE. 2572
0031-8698 See PHOTOGRAPHER, THE. 4374
0031-8736 See PHOTOGRAPHIC JOURNAL (1956). 4374
0031-8744 See PHOTOGRAPHIC PROCESSING. 4374
0031-8868 See PHRONESIS. 4357
0031-8868 See PHRONESIS (HEIDELBERG, GERMANY). 4357
0031-8876 See PHYTIATRIE-PHYTOPHARMACIE. 521
0031-8884 See PHYCOLOGIA (OXFORD). 521
0031-8906 See PHYLON (1960). 5213
0031-8949 See PHYSICA SCRIPTA. 4414
0031-8965 See PHYSICA STATUS SOLIDI. A: APPLIED RESEARCH. 4414
0031-8981 See PHYSICAL EDUCATOR, THE. 1857
0031-9007 See PHYSICAL REVIEW LETTERS. 4415
0031-9015 See JOURNAL OF THE PHYSICAL SOCIETY OF JAPAN. 4410
0031-9023 See PHYSICAL THERAPY. 4381

0031-9066 See PHYSICIAN'S MANAGEMENT. 3627

0031-9082 See SEIBUTSU-BUTSURI-KAGAKU. 493

0031-9090 See PHYSICS AND CHEMISTRY OF GLASSES. 2593

0031-9104 See PHYSICS AND CHEMISTRY OF LIQUIDS. 1056

0031-9120 See PHYSICS EDUCATION. 4415

0031-9147 See PHYSICS IN CANADA. 4415

0031-9155 See PHYSICS IN MEDICINE & BIOLOGY. 479

0031-918X See PHYSICS OF METALS AND METALLOGRAPHY, THE. 4014

0031-9201 See PHYSICS OF THE EARTH AND PLANETARY INTERIORS. 1391

0031-921X See PHYSICS TEACHER, THE. 1902

0031-9228 See PHYSICS TODAY. 4416

0031-9252 See PHYSIK IN UNSERER ZEIT. 4416

0031-9279 See PHYSIKALISCHE BLATTER. 4417

0031-9317 See PHYSIOLOGIA PLANTARUM. 521

0031-9333 See PHYSIOLOGICAL REVIEWS. 585

0031-9341 See NIPPON SEIRIGAKU ZASSHI. 584

0031-935X See PHYSIOLOGICAL ZOOLOGY. 5594

0031-9376 See PHYSIOLOGIST, THE. 585

0031-9384 See PHYSIOLOGY & BEHAVIOR. 585

0031-9406 See PHYSIOTHERAPY. 4382

0031-9414 See PHYSIS (FIRENZE). 5138

0031-9422 See PHYTOCHEMISTRY (OXFORD). 522

0031-9430 See PHYTOLOGIA. 522

0031-9449 See PHYTOMORPHOLOGY. 522

0031-9457 See PHYTON (BUENOS AIRES). 522

0031-9465 See PHYTOPATHOLOGIA MEDITERRANEA. 522

0031-9473 See NIPPON SHOKUBUTSU BYORI GAKKAI. 520

0031-949X See PHYTOPATHOLOGY. 522

0031-9511 See PHYTOPROTECTION. 181

0031-952X See PI MU EPSILON JOURNAL. 3526

0031-9546 See PIANO GUILD NOTES. 4146

0031-9554 See PIANO QUARTERLY, THE. 4146

0031-9562 See PIANO TECHNICIAN'S JOURNAL. 4146

0031-9627 See PSG NEWSLETTER. 4147

0031-9740 See PIG FARMER, THE. 217

0031-9759 See PIG FARMING. 217

0031-9953 See PINTURAS Y ACABADOS INDUSTRIALES. 4225

0032-0145 See PIPE LINE INDUSTRY (HOUSTON, TEX.). 2124

0032-0188 See PIPELINE & GAS JOURNAL. 4274

0032-020X See PIPES & PIPELINES INTERNATIONAL (1965). 4274

0032-0293 See PIT & QUARRY. 2147

0032-0331 See PITTSBURGH LEGAL JOURNAL. 3029

0032-0412 See PLAIN RAPPER, THE. 5301

0032-0420 See PLAIN TRUTH (PASADENA, CALIF.), THE. 4986

0032-0447 See PLAINS ANTHROPOLOGIST. 2271

0032-0528 See PLAMUK. 3424

0032-0536 See PLAN (MONTREAL). 1990

0032-0544 See PLAN CANADA. 2830

0032-0560 See SWEDISH TOWN AND COUNTRY PLANNING REVIEW, THE. 2836

0032-0595 See PLAN AND PRINT. 1234

0032-0609 See PLAN OG ARBEID. 1702

0032-0633 See PLANETARY AND SPACE SCIENCE. 398

0032-0668 See PLANNED SAVINGS. 803

0032-0684 See PLANNING & CHANGING. 1774

0032-0714 See JOURNAL OF ENVIRONMENTAL PLANNING AND MANAGEMENT. 2826

0032-0781 See PLANT AND CELL PHYSIOLOGY. 523

0032-079X See PLANT AND SOIL. 181

0032-0803 See PLANT BREEDING ABSTRACTS. 155

0032-082X See PLANT ENGINEERING. 1990

0032-0862 See PLANT PATHOLOGY. 524

0032-0870 See PLANT PATHOLOGY CIRCULAR. 524

0032-0889 See PLANT PHYSIOLOGY (BETHESDA). 524

0032-0897 See PLANT PROTECTION ABSTRACTS. 4247

0032-0919 See PLANT SCIENCE BULLETIN. 524

0032-0935 See PLANTA. 524

0032-0943 See PLANTA MEDICA. 4325

0032-096X See PLANTER'S BULLETIN (RUBBER RESEARCH INSTITUTE OF MALAYSIA). 5076

0032-0978 See PLANTERS' CHRONICLE, THE. 2353

0032-0986 See PLANTERS JOURNAL AND AGRICULTURIST, THE. 120

0032-0994 See PLANTES MEDICINALES ET PHYTOTHERAPIE. 525

0032-1052 See PLASTIC AND RECONSTRUCTIVE SURGERY (1963). 3972

0032-1168 See PLASTICS & RUBBER WEEKLY. 4457

0032-1206 See PLASTICS INDUSTRY NEWS. 4458

0032-1257 See PLASTICS TECHNOLOGY. 4458

0032-1273 See PLASTICS WORLD. 4458

0032-1303 See PLASTIQUES MODERNES ELASTOMERES. 4459

0032-1338 See PLASTVERARBEITER, DER. 4459

0032-1346 See PLATEAU (FLAGSTAFF, AZ : 1939). 2543

0032-1370 See CO-OPERATORS' PLATFORM. 4468

0032-1400 See PLATINUM METALS REVIEW. 4015

0032-1427 See PLATT'S OILGRAM NEWS. 4274

0032-1494 See PLAYGIRL. 5564

0032-1540 See PLAYS (BOSTON). 5367

0032-1559 See PLAYS AND PLAYERS. 5367

0032-1567 See PLAYTHINGS. 2585

0032-1613 See PLOW, THE. 2625

0032-1656 See PLUMBING. 2607

0032-1680 See WHOLESALER (ELMHURST), THE. 2609

0032-1737 See PLYMOUTH BULLETIN. 5423

0032-1761 See PLYN. 4275

0032-180X See POCHVOVEDENIE. 182

0032-1826 See POCKET LIST OF RAILROAD OFFICIALS, THE. 5434

0032-1885 See POEM. 3468

0032-1893 See POESIA DE VENEZUELA. 3468

0032-194X See POET. 3468

0032-1958 See POET AND CRITIC (AMES, IOWA). 3468

0032-1966 See POET LORE. 3468

0032-2024 See POETIQUE. 3469

0032-2032 See POETRY (CHICAGO). 3469

0032-2040 See POETRY & AUDIENCE. 3469

0032-2059 See POETRY AUSTRALIA. 3469

0032-2105 See POETRY NIPPON. 3469

0032-2113 See POETRY NORTHWEST. 3469

0032-2156 See POETRY REVIEW (LONDON). 3350

0032-2202 See POETRY WALES. 3469

0032-2237 See POEZJA. 3470

0032-2318 See POINT OF VIEW (CLEVELAND). 4674

0032-2350 See POINTER, THE. 1774

0032-2369 See POINTS ET CONTREPOINTS. 3470

0032-2423 See POKROKY MATEMATIKY, FYSIKY A ASTRONOMIE. 5138

0032-2474 See POLAR RECORD, THE. 5138

0032-2482 See POLAR TIMES, THE. 2572

0032-2490 See POLARFORSCHUNG. 5138

0032-2571 See POLICE CHIEF, THE. 3171

0032-258X See POLICE JOURNAL (CHICHESTER). 3172

0032-2636 See POLICLINICO, SEZIONE CHIRURGICA. 3972

0032-2660 See PLASTICS SOUTHERN AFRICA. 2107

0032-2679 See PH, POLICY HOLDER INSURANCE JOURNAL. 2890

0032-2687 See POLICY SCIENCES. 4488

0032-2695 See POLIGRAFIA. 4567

0032-2725 See POLIMERY. 1037

0032-2768 See POLIPLASTI E PLASTICI RINFORZATI. 4459

0032-2806 See POLISH AMERICAN STUDIES (CHICAGO, ILL.). 2754

0032-2830 See POLISH ECOLOGICAL BIBLIOGRAPHY. 2185

0032-2946 See POLISH MUSIC. 4146

0032-2970 See POLISH REVIEW (NEW YORK. 1956), THE. 5213

0032-2997 See POLISH SOCIOLOGICAL BULLETIN, THE. 5253

0032-3004 See POLISH TECHNICAL AND ECONOMIC ABSTRACTS. 1512

0032-3012 See POLISH TECHNICAL REVIEW. 5138

0032-3039 See POLISH WESTERN AFFAIRS. 4488

0032-3063 See POLITICA DEL DIRITTO. 4488

0032-3128 See POLITICAL AFFAIRS. 4488

0032-3179 See POLITICAL QUARTERLY (LONDON. 1930). 4489

0032-3187 See POLITICAL SCIENCE. 4490

0032-3195 See POLITICAL SCIENCE QUARTERLY. 4490

0032-3209 See POLITICAL SCIENTIST. 4490

0032-3217 See POLITICAL STUDIES. 4490

0032-3233 See POLITIKA EKONOMIE. 1512

0032-3241 See POLITICKA MISAO. 4490

0032-325x See POLITICO; RIVISTA ITALIANA DI SCIENZE POLITICHE, IL. 4490

0032-3276 See BIPAC POLITICS. 4465

0032-3292 See POLITICS & SOCIETY. 5213

0032-3365 See POLITIIKKA. 4491

0032-3446 See POLITISCHE MEINUNG, DIE. 5213

0032-3462 See POLITISCHE STUDIEN. 4491

0032-3497 See POLITY. 4491

0032-3500 See POLITYKA. 4491

0032-3624 See POLLUTION ABSTRACTS WITH INDEXES. 2185

0032-3632 See POLLUTION ATMOSPHERIQUE (PARIS, FRANCE). 2238

0032-3640 See POLLUTION ENGINEERING. 2238

0032-3659 See POLLUTION EQUIPMENT NEWS. 2239

0032-3721 See POLSKA SZTUKA LUDOWA. 362

0032-373X See POLSKI PRZEGLAD CHIRURGICZNY. 3972

0032-3756 See POLSKI TYGODNIK LEKARSKI (1960). 3628

0032-3764 See POLSKIE ARCHIWUM HYDROBIOLOGII. 557

0032-3772 See POLSKIE ARCHIWUM MEDYCYNY WEWNETRZNEJ. 3800

0032-3780 See POLSKIE PISMO ENTOMOLOGICZNE. 5612

0032-3802 See BIULETYN POLSKIEGO TOWARZYSTWA JEZYKOZNAWCZEGO. 3269

0032-3845 See POLYGRAPH, DER. 4567

0032-3861 See POLYMER (GUILFORD). 1046

0032-3888 See POLYMER ENGINEERING AND SCIENCE. 988

0032-3896 See POLYMER JOURNAL. 1046

0032-3918 See POLYMER NEWS. 4459

0032-3934 See POLYMER PREPRINTS, AMERICAN CHEMICAL SOCIETY, DIVISION OF POLYMER CHEMISTRY. 989

0032-3950 See POLYMER SCIENCE. 989

0032-3977 See QUARTERLY LITERATURE REPORTS : POLYMERS. 1047

0032-4000 See JOURNAL OF THE POLYNESIAN SOCIETY. 3292

0032-406X See POLYTECHNIC ENGINEER, THE. 1991

0032-4086 See PT. ELEKTROTECHNIEK ELEKTRONICA. 2077
0032-4094 See PT. PROCESTECHNIEK. 1992
0032-4108 See POLYTECHNISCH TIJDSCHRIFT. WERKTUIGBOUW. 2124
0032-4140 See POMIARY, AUTOMATYKA, KONTROLA. 1221
0032-4159 See POMME DE TERRE FRANCAISE, LA. 182
0032-4183 See POMONA COLLEGE TODAY. 1841
0032-423X See PONTE (FIRENZE), IL. 3350
0032-4353 See POPE SPEAKS, THE. 5034
0032-4477 See POPULAR CERAMICS. 2593
0032-4493 See POPULAR FLYING. 31
0032-4515 See POPULAR GOVERNMENT. 4491
0032-4523 See POPULAR HOT RODDING. 5423
0032-4558 See POPULAR MECHANICS (NEW YORK. 1959). 5139
0032-4582 See POPULAR PHOTOGRAPHY (1955). 4375
0032-4655 See POPULAR TALISMAN BULLETIN. 3350
0032-4663 See POPULATION. 4556
0032-468X See POPULATION BULLETIN. 4556
0032-4701 See POPULATION INDEX. 4562
0032-471X See POPULATION REVIEW. 4558
0032-4728 See POPULATION STUDIES. 4558
0032-4752 See PORADNIK BIBLIOTEKARZA. 3241
0032-4795 See POROSKOVAJA METALLURGIJA (KIEV). 4015
0032-4868 See PORT OF TOLEDO NEWS. 4181
0032-4884 See PORTALS OF PRAYER. 5018
0032-5007 See IFW. INTERNATIONAL FREIGHTING WEEKLY. 5383
0032-5147 See PORTUGALIAE ACTA BIOLOGICA. SERIE A. MORFOLOGIA, FISIOLOGIA, GENETICA E BIOLOGIA GERAL. 585
0032-5155 See PORTUGALIAE MATHEMATICA. 3527
0032-5201 See POSEV. 4491
0032-5228 See POSITIONS LUTHERIENNES. 5066
0032-5341 See POSTAL HISTORY JOURNAL. 1146
0032-5368 See POSTAL LIFE. 1146
0032-5376 See POSTAL RECORD, THE. 1146
0032-5384 See POSTAL SUPERVISOR, THE. 1146
0032-5414 See POSTEPY ASTRONOMII. 398
0032-5422 See POSTEPY BIOCHEMII. 492
0032-5430 See POSTEPY FIZYKI. 4417
0032-5449 See POSTEPY HIGIENY I MEDYCYNY DOSWIADCZALNEJ. 4795
0032-5457 See POSTEPY NAUK ROLNICZYCH. 120
0032-5473 See POSTGRADUATE MEDICAL JOURNAL. 3628
0032-5481 See POSTGRADUATE MEDICINE. 3628
0032-5511 See POSTMASTERS' ADVOCATE. 1147
0032-552X See POSTMASTERS GAZETTE. 1147
0032-5546 See POTASH REVIEW. 182
0032-5600 See POTENCIA. 624
0032-5619 See POTENTIALS IN MARKETING. 935
0032-5716 See POULTRY AND EGG MARKETING. 218
0032-5767 See POULTRY INTERNATIONAL. 218
0032-5783 See POULTRY PRESS. 218
0032-5791 See POULTRY SCIENCE. 218
0032-5813 See POULTRY WORLD. 219
0032-5856 See POVERTY. 5301
0032-5899 See POWDER METALLURGY. 4015
0032-5910 See POWDER TECHNOLOGY. 2016
0032-5929 See POWER. 1953
0032-5953 See POWER ENGINEER (BOMBAY). 2124
0032-5961 See POWER ENGINEERING (BARRINGTON, ILL.). 2124
0032-6070 See POWER TRANSMISSION DESIGN. 2124

0032-6089 See POWERBOAT (VAN NUYS, CALIF.). 595
0032-6143 See POZNAJ SWIAT. 2573
0032-6178 See PRABUDDHA BHARATA. 5041
0032-6186 See PRACA I ZABEZPIECZENIE SPOECZNE. 1621
0032-6240 See PRACE INSTYTUT TECHNOLOGII DREWNA. 2403
0032-6291 See PRACOVNI LEKARSTVI. 3628
0032-6313 See JIBI INKOKA RINSHO. 3888
0032-6321 See PRACTICAL ACCOUNTANT, THE. 749
0032-6348 See PRACTICAL BOAT OWNER. 595
0032-6372 See PRACTICAL ELECTRONICS. 2075
0032-6380 See SCHOLASTIC VOICE. 3319
0032-6399 See PRACTICAL GARDENING. 2428
0032-6429 See PRACTICAL LAWYER, THE. 3030
0032-647X See TELEVISION LONDON. 1970. 1141
0032-6488 See PRACTICAL WOOD WORKING. 634
0032-6518 See PRACTITIONER, THE. 3738
0032-6534 See PRAHISTORISCHE FORSCHUNGEN / HERAUSGEGEBEN VON DER ANTHROPOLOGISCHEN GESELLSCHAFT IN WIEN. 243
0032-6542 See PRAPARATOR. 4170
0032-6585 See PRAGUE BULLETIN OF MATHEMATICAL LINGUISTICS, THE. 3311
0032-6615 See PRAIRIE FARMER. 121
0032-6623 See PRAIRIE GLEANER, THE. 2468
0032-6631 See PRAIRIE LORE. 2755
0032-664X See PRAIRIE MESSENGER. 5793
0032-6666 See PRAIRIE ROSE, THE. 3867
0032-6682 See PRAIRIE SCHOONER. 3424
0032-6690 See PRAJNAN. 803
0032-678X See PRAKTISCHE METALLOGRAPHIE. 4015
0032-6801 See PRAKTISCHE SCHADLINGSBEKAMPFER, DER. 182
0032-681X See PRAKTISCHE TIERARZT. 5518
0032-6895 See MATERIAUX ET TECHNIQUES. 2106
0032-6925 See PRATO STORIA E ARTE. 362
0032-6992 See PRAVOSLAVNAJA ZIZN. 5040
0032-7018 See PRAVOSLAVNAIA RUS. 4987
0032-7034 See PRAXIS DER KINDERPSYCHOLOGIE UND KINDERPSYCHIATRIE. 4608
0032-7042 See PM. PRAXIS DER MATHEMATIK. 3527
0032-7255 See PREFABBRICAZIONE, LA. 624
0032-7328 See PREHL'AD LESNICKEJ, DREVARSKEJ, CELULOZOVEJ A PAPIERENSKEJ LITERATURY. 4237
0032-7407 See WORSHIP AND PREACHING. 5010
0032-745X See PRENSA MEDICA ARGENTINA. 3629
0032-7484 See PREPARATIVE BIOCHEMISTRY. 492
0032-7530 See PRESBYTERIAN HERALD : THE RECORD OF THE PRESBYTERIAN CHURCH IN IRELAND, THE. 5066
0032-7565 See PRESBYTERIAN OUTLOOK (RICHMOND, VA.). 5066
0032-7573 See PRESBYTERIAN RECORD (MONTREAL). 5066
0032-759X See PRESBYTERIAN SURVEY. 5066
0032-7611 See PRESCRIBERS' JOURNAL. 4325
0032-7638 See PRESENCE AFRICAINE (PARIS, FRANCE : 1967). 2271
0032-7697 See PRESENT BAMBERG. 375
0032-7700 See PRESENT TRUTH AND HERALD OF CHRIST'S EPIPHANY, THE. 4987
0032-7727 See PRESENZA PASTORALE. 5034
0032-7786 See PRESLIA. 525
0032-7824 See PRESS WOMAN, THE. 2923
0032-7832 See PRESSE, DIE. 5778
0032-7875 See PRESSE THERMALE ET CLIMATIQUE. 1433

0032-7972 See PREUSSENLAND : MITTEILUNGEN DER HISTORISCHEN KOMMISSION FUR OST- UND WESTPREUSSISCHE LANDESFORSCHUNG. 2703
0032-8006 See PREVENTION (EMMAUS). 4796
0032-8138 See PRZEGLAD BIBLIOGRAFICZNY PISMIENNICTWA EKONOMICZNEGO. 1537
0032-8154 See PRIBORY I SISTEMY UPRAVLENIJA. 1248
0032-8162 See PRIBORY I TEHNIKA EKSPERIMENTA. 5139
0032-8200 See PRIEST, THE. 5034
0032-8235 See PRIKLADNAJA MATEMATIKA I MEHANIKA. 2125
0032-8243 See PRIKLADNAJA MEHANIKA (KIEV). 2125
0032-8294 See PRIMARY MATHEMATICS. 3527
0032-8316 See PRIMARY TREASURE. 1068
0032-8324 See PRIMATE NEWS. 5518
0032-8332 See PRIMATES. 5594
0032-8359 See PRIME AREAS. 1902
0032-8367 See PRIMER ACTO. 5367
0032-8413 See PRINCETON SEMINARY BULLETIN, THE. 4987
0032-843X See RECORD OF THE ART MUSEUM, PRINCETON UNIVERSITY. 4095
0032-8447 See PRISMET. 4988
0032-8456 See PRINCETON UNIVERSITY LIBRARY CHRONICLE, THE. 2852
0032-8472 See PRINCIPE DE VIANA. 2703
0032-8480 See PRINCIPES. 525
0032-8510 See PRINT (NEW YORK). 381
0032-8537 See PRINT COLLECTOR'S NEWSLETTER, THE. 381
0032-860X See PRINTING IMPRESSIONS. 4568
0032-8715 See PRINTING WORLD. 4568
0032-8731 See PRIORDA. 5139
0032-8758 See PRIRODOVEDNE PRACE USTAVU CESKOSLOVENSKE AKADEMIE VED V BRNE. 5594
0032-8790 See PRISM INTERNATIONAL. 3425
0032-8855 See PRISON JOURNAL (PHILADELPHIA, PA.), THE. 3173
0032-8871 See PRIVATE CARRIER. 5389
0032-888X See PRIVATE EYE. 3350
0032-8898 See PRIVATE LIBRARY. 3241
0032-8901 See PRIVATE PILOT (NEW YORK, N.Y.). 31
0032-891X See PRIVATE PRACTICE. 3629
0032-9053 See PRO FOOTBALL WEEKLY. 4913
0032-9150 See PROA. 306
0032-9185 See PROBE (LONDON. 1954). 1333
0032-9223 See PROBLEMAS BARCELONA. 4865
0032-924X See PROBLEME DE INFORMARE SI DOCUMENTARE. 3242
0032-9304 See PROBLEMES ECONOMIQUES. 1579
0032-9398 See PROBLEMIST, THE. 4865
0032-941X See PROBLEMS OF COMMUNISM (WASHINGTON, D.C.). 4545
0032-9428 See PROBLEMY OSVOENIIA PUSTYN. 121
0032-9436 See PROBLEMS OF ECONOMICS. 1513
0032-9452 See JOURNAL OF ICHTHYOLOGY. 2307
0032-9460 See PROBLEMS OF INFORMATION TRANSMISSION. 2076
0032-9487 See PROBLEMY. 5140
0032-9495 See PROBLEMY ALKOHOLIZMU 1976. 1348
0032-9533 See PROBLEMY TUBERKULEZA. 3951
0032-9568 See PROCEEDINGS IN PRINT. 41
0032-9622 See PROCHE-ORIENT CHRETIEN. 5040
0032-9649 See PROCHE-ORIENT, ETUDES JURIDIQUES. 3032
0032-9673 See PRODOTTO CHIMICO & AEROSOL SELEZIONE. 989
0032-969X See PRODUCE NEWS. 2354

0032-9762 See PRODUCT FINISHING (LONDON). 4016

0032-9819 See PRODUCTION. 2126

0032-9827 See ALBERTA DRILLING PROGRESS AND PIPELINE RECEIPTS WEEKLY REPORT. 4249

0032-9878 See PRODUCTION JOURNAL. 4818

0032-9940 See PRODUCTS FINISHING. 3486

0032-9991 See PRODUTTIVITA. 5142

0033-0000 See PRODUZIONE ANIMALE. 5519

0033-0124 See PROFESSIONAL GEOGRAPHER, THE. 2573

0033-0140 See PROFESSIONAL MEDICAL ASSISTANT, THE. 3630

0033-0167 See PROFESSIONAL PHOTOGRAPHER (1964), THE. 4375

0033-0205 See PROFESSIONI INFERMIERISTICHE. 3867

0033-0329 See PROFOTO. 4376

0033-0337 See PROGRAM (ASLIB). 3242

0033-0337 See PROGRAM; NEWS OF COMPUTERS IN LIBRARIES. 3242

0033-0620 See PROGRESS IN CARDIOVASCULAR DISEASES. 3709

0033-0663 See PROGRESS OF EDUCATION, THE. 1775

0033-0671 See PROGRESS OF PHYSICS. 4418

0033-068X See PROGRESS OF THEORETICAL PHYSICS. 4429

0033-0701 See PROGRESSI IN PATOLOGIA CARDIOVASCOLARE. 3709

0033-0736 See PROGRESSIVE (MADISON), THE. 4532

0033-0752 See PROGRESSIVE ARCHITECTURE. 306

0033-0760 See PROGRESSIVE FARMER. 123

0033-0779 See PROGRESSIVE FISH-CULTURIST, THE. 2311

0033-0787 See PROGRESSIVE GROCER, THE. 2354

0033-0817 See PROGRESSIVE RAILROADING. 5434

0033-0833 See PROGRESSIVE WOMAN. 5564

0033-0884 See PROJET. 1639

0033-0957 See PROJEKT. 362

0033-1031 See PROLOGUE (WASHINGTON). 2482

0033-1058 See PROMENY (CZECHOSLOVAK SOCIETY OF ARTS AND SCIENCES IN AMERICA). 2852

0033-1155 See PROMYSLENNAJA ENERGETIKA. 2077

0033-1163 See ZVARTNOTS. 5173

0033-1198 See PROMYSLENNOE STROITELSTVO I INZENERNYE SOORUZENIJA. 624

0033-1236 See PROOFS (TULSA). 1333

0033-1260 See PROPANE CANADA. 4275

0033-1287 See PROPERTIES. 4843

0033-1481 See PROSPECT (AFRICAN EXPLOSIVES AND CHEMICAL INDUSTRIES). 3487

0033-1538 See PROSPECTS (PARIS). 1775

0033-1732 See PROTECTION OF METALS. 4017

0033-1767 See PROTESTANTESIMO. 5066

0033-183X See PROTOPLASMA. 540

0033-1856 See PROVENCE HISTORIQUE; REVUE TRIMESTRIELLE. 2703

0033-2003 See PRZEGLAD ANTROPOLOGICZNY. 243

0033-202X See PRZEGLAD BIBLIOTECZNY. 3242

0033-2038 See PRZEGLAD BUDOWLANY. 625

0033-2089 See ELEKTRONIKA. 2052

0033-2097 See PRZEGLAD ELEKTROTECHNICZNY. 2077

0033-2100 See PRZEGLAD EPIDEMIOLOGICZNY. 3736

0033-2135 See PRZEGLAD GEOFIZYCZNY. 1433

0033-2143 See PRZEGLAD GEOGRAFICZNY. 2573

0033-2151 See PRZEGLAD GEOLOGICZNY. 1392

0033-216X See PRZEGLAD GORNICZY. 2149

0033-2178 See PRZELAND HISTORYCZNO-OSIATOWY. 1775

0033-2186 See PRZEGLAD HISTORYCZNY. 2703

0033-2194 See PRZEGLAD HUMANISTYCZNY. 2852

0033-2224 See PRZEGLAD KOLEJOWY MECHANICZNY. 5434

0033-2240 See PRZEGLAD LEKARSKI. 3631

0033-2259 See PRZEGLAD MECHANICZNY. 2127

0033-2275 See PRZEGLAD ODLEWNICTWA. 4017

0033-2283 See PRZEGLAD ORIENTALISTYCZNY. 3426

0033-2291 See PRZEGLAD PAPIERNICZY. 4237

0033-2356 See PRZEGLAD SOCJOLOGICZNY. 5254

0033-2364 See PRZEGLAD SPAWALNICTWA. 5142

0033-2372 See PRZEGLAD STATYSTYCZNY. 5336

0033-2380 See PRZEGLAD TECHNICZNY. 5143

0033-2410 See PRZEGLAD WOKIENNICZY; MIESIECZNIK NAUKOWO-TECHNICZNY. 5355

0033-2437 See PRZEGLAD ZACHODNI. 2703

0033-2461 See PRZEGLAD ZBOZOWO-MYNARSKI. 203

0033-247X See PRZEGLAD ZOOLOGICZNY. 5595

0033-2496 See PRZEMYS CHEMICZNY. 2016

0033-250X See PRZEMYS SPOZYWCZY. 2354

0033-2518 See PRZEWODNIK BIBLIOGRAFICZNY. 422

0033-2526 See PRZEGLAD DERMATOLOGICZNY. 3722

0033-2542 See PSALLITE. 4147

0033-2569 See PSI CHI NEWSLETTER. 4609

0033-2615 See PSYCHE (CAMBRIDGE, MASS.). 5595

0033-2623 See PSYCHE. 4609

0033-2658 See PSYCHIATRIA ET NEUROLOGIA JAPONICA. 3933

0033-2674 See PSYCHIATRIA POLSKA. 3933

0033-2690 See PSYCHIATRIC FORUM, THE. 3933

0033-2704 See PSYCHIATRIC NEWS. 3933

0033-2720 See PSYCHIATRIC QUARTERLY. 3933

0033-2747 See PSYCHIATRY (WASHINGTON, D.C.). 3934

0033-2798 See PSYCHIC (SAN FRANCISCO). 4242

0033-2801 See PSYCHIC NEWS. 4610

0033-2828 See PSYCHOANALYTIC QUARTERLY, THE. 4610

0033-2836 See PSYCHOANALYTIC REVIEW (1963). 4610

0033-2852 See PSYCHOLOGIA. 4610

0033-2860 See PSYCHOLOGIA WYCHOWAWCZA. 1903

0033-2879 See PSYCHOLOGICA BELGICA. 4610

0033-2887 See PSYCHOLOGICAL ABSTRACTS. 4623

0033-2909 See PSYCHOLOGICAL BULLETIN. 4610

0033-2917 See PSYCHOLOGICAL MEDICINE. 4611

0033-2925 See PSYCHOLOGICAL PERSPECTIVES. 4611

0033-2933 See PSYCHOLOGICAL RECORD, THE. 4611

0033-2941 See PSYCHOLOGICAL REPORTS. 4611

0033-295X See PSYCHOLOGICAL REVIEW. 4611

0033-2968 See PSYCHOLOGICAL STUDIES. 4611

0033-2984 See PSYCHOLOGIE FRANCAISE. 4612

0033-300X See PSYCHOLOGIE V EKONOMICKE PRAXI. 705

0033-3018 See PSYCHOLOGISCHE BEITRAEGE. 4612

0033-3042 See PSYCHOLOGISCHE RUNDSCHAU. 4612

0033-3077 See PSYCHOLOGY (SAVANNAH). 4613

0033-3085 See PSYCHOLOGY IN THE SCHOOLS. 4612

0033-3107 See PSYCHOLOGY TODAY. 4613

0033-3107 See PSYCHOLOGY TODAY. 4613

0033-3115 See PSYCHOLOOG. 4613

0033-3123 See PSYCHOMETRIKA. 4613

0033-3158 See PSYCHOPHARMACOLOGIA. 4326

0033-3174 See PSYCHOSOMATIC MEDICINE. 3631

0033-3182 See PSYCHOSOMATICS (WASHINGTON, D.C.). 3631

0033-3190 See PSYCHOTHERAPY AND PSYCHOSOMATICS. 3935

0033-3239 See PTITSEVODSTVO. 219

0033-3298 See PUBLIC ADMINISTRATION (LONDON). 4704

0033-3352 See PAR. PUBLIC ADMINISTRATION REVIEW POPULATION. 4672

0033-3395 See PUBLIC AFFAIRS COMMENT. 4676

0033-3417 See PUBLIC AFFAIRS REPORT. 4676

0033-3441 See PUBLIC CONTRACT LAW JOURNAL. 3033

0033-345X See PUBLIC EMPLOYEE PRESS (NEW YORK). 1704

0033-3476 See PUBLIC FINANCE. 4743

0033-3506 See PUBLIC HEALTH (LONDON). 4797

0033-3549 See PUBLIC HEALTH REPORTS (1974). 4797

0033-3549 See PUBLIC HEALTH REPORTS (1974). 4797

0033-3557 See PUBLIC INTEREST, THE. 5214

0033-3565 See PUBLIC LAW. 3033

0033-362X See PUBLIC OPINION QUARTERLY. 5254

0033-3654 See PUBLIC POWER. 4762

0033-3670 See PUBLIC RELATIONS JOURNAL, THE. 764

0033-3689 See PUBLIC RELATIONS JOURNAL OF INDIA. 764

0033-3700 See PUBLIC RELATIONS QUARTERLY. 765

0033-3735 See PUBLIC ROADS. 5442

0033-376X See PUBLIC SERVANT. DIE STAATSAMPTENAAR, THE. 4677

0033-3808 See PUBLIC UTILITIES FORTNIGHTLY. 4762

0033-3816 See PUBLIC WELFARE (WASHINGTON). 5303

0033-3840 See PUBLIC WORKS. 1992

0033-3883 See PUBLICATIONES MATHEMATICAL (DEBRECEN). 3529

0033-3913 See MEDIA NEWS KEYS. 1117

0033-4006 See PUBLIZISTIK. 2923

0033-4030 See PUERTO RICO LIBRE!. 4492

0033-4049 See PUERTO RICO LIVING. 2544

0033-4081 See PULP & PAPER. 4237

0033-409X See PULP & PAPER INTERNATIONAL. 4238

0033-4138 See CHRISTIAN MINISTRY, THE. 4945

0033-4278 See PUNCH (LONDON). 3426

0033-4324 See PUNJAB HORTICULTURAL JOURNAL, THE. 2429

0033-4340 See PUNJAB MEDICAL JOURNAL. 3631

0033-443X See PUPPETRY JOURNAL, THE. 5367

0033-4448 See PURCHASING (1936). 951

0033-4502 See PURDUE ALUMNUS, THE. 1102

0033-4545 See PURE AND APPLIED CHEMISTRY. 990

0033-4553 See PURE AND APPLIED GEOPHYSICS. 1409

0033-4561 See PURE-BRED DOGS, AMERICAN KENNEL GAZETTE. 4287

0033-4685 See PURSUIT (COLUMBIA). 4243

0033-474X See PYRENEES LOURDES. 1950. 2574

0033-4812 See QST. 1136

0033-4839 See QADMONIOT. 279

0033-488X See QUADERNI DELLA NUTRIZIONE. 4198

0033-4901 See QUADERNI DI AZIONE SOCIALE. 1704

0033-491X See QUADERNI DI CLINICA OSTETRICA E GINECOLOGICA. 3767
0033-4952 See QUADERNI DI SOCIOLOGIA. 5254
0033-4960 See QUADERNI IBERO-AMERICANI. 3350
0033-4987 See QUADERNI URBINATI DI CULTURA CLASSICA. 1079
0033-5002 See QUADRANT. 2511
0033-5010 See QUADRANT (NEW YORK). 4614
0033-5053 See QUAKER HISTORY. 4989
0033-5061 See QUAKER LIFE. 4989
0033-507X See QUAKER MONTHLY. 4989
0033-5088 See QUAKER RELIGIOUS THOUGHT. 5066
0033-510X See QUAKER SERVICE BULLETIN / AMERICAN FRIENDS SERVICE COMMITTEE. 5254
0033-5118 See ELECTRICAL CONTRACTOR (WASHINGTON). 2044
0033-5177 See QUALITY & QUANTITY. 3529
0033-5207 See QUALITY CONTROL AND APPLIED STATISTICS. 5176
0033-524X See QUALITY PROGRESS. 1993
0033-5266 See QUARRY (KINGSTON). 3427
0033-5533 See QUARTERLY JOURNAL OF ECONOMICS, THE. 1514
0033-5568 See QUARTERLY JOURNAL OF FORESTRY. 2391
0033-5606 See QUARTERLY JOURNAL OF MATHEMATICS. 3530
0033-5614 See QUARTERLY JOURNAL OF MECHANICS AND APPLIED MATHEMATICS, THE. 2127
0033-5622 See QUARTERLY JOURNAL OF MEDICINE, THE. 3632
0033-5630 See QUARTERLY JOURNAL OF SPEECH, THE. 1120
0033-5657 See QUARTERLY JOURNAL OF SURGICAL SCIENCES. 3973
0033-569X See QUARTERLY OF APPLIED MATHEMATICS. 3530
0033-5711 See QUARTERLY PREDICTIONS. 1580
0033-5770 See QUARTERLY REVIEW OF BIOLOGY, THE. 471
0033-5789 See QUARTERLY REVIEW OF DRILLING STATISTICS FOR THE UNITED STATES. 4284
0033-5797 See QUARTERLY REVIEW OF ECONOMICS AND FINANCE, THE. 1515
0033-5800 See QUARTERLY REVIEW OF HISTORICAL STUDIES, THE. 2627
0033-5835 See QUARTERLY REVIEWS OF BIOPHYSICS. 496
0033-5894 See QUATERNARY RESEARCH. 1393
0033-5932 See QUE CHOISIR ? PARIS. 1299
0033-5940 See QUE TAL? (NEW YORK, N.Y.). 3313
0033-6041 See QUEEN'S QUARTERLY. 5214
0033-6084 See QUEENSLAND COUNTRY LIFE. 124
0033-6122 See QUEENSLAND FRUIT AND VEGETABLE NEWS. 2429
0033-6149 See QUEENSLAND GOVERNMENT MINING JOURNAL. 2149
0033-6238 See QUEENSLAND TEACHERS JOURNAL. 1903
0033-6246 See QUELLE (KOLN). 1705
0033-6297 See QUEST (NATIONAL ASSOCIATION FOR PHYSICAL EDUCATION IN HIGHER EDUCATION). 3955
0033-6351 See QUESTIONS ACTUELLES DU SOCIALISME. 4545
0033-6416 See QUICK FROZEN FOODS INTERNATIONAL. 2355
0033-6475 See QUILL (CHICAGO), THE. 2923
0033-6505 See QUILL AND SCROLL (IOWA CITY). 2923
0033-6521 See QUIMICA E INDUSTRIA (MADRID). 1029
0033-6556 See QUINCY COLLEGE BULLETIN. 1094
0033-6599 See QUINTESSENZ JOURNAL. 1334
0033-6602 See QUINTO LINGO. 3313

0033-6750 See RAPRA ABSTRACTS. 5078
0033-6769 See RAS; ROHR, ARMATUR, SANITAR, HEIZUNG. 2608
0033-6793 See R & D CONTRACTS MONTHLY. 5144
0033-6807 See R & D MANAGEMENT. 5144
0033-684X See R.C.M. MAGAZINE. 4148
0033-6866 See RC MODELER (1969). 2777
0033-6874 See REFA NACHRICHTEN. 946
0033-6882 See RELC JOURNAL. 3315
0033-6955 See RILM ABSTRACTS. 4160
0033-698X See RLA, REVISTA DE LINGUISTICA TEORICA Y APLICADA. 3317
0033-7021 See RN. 3868
0033-7064 See R P M WEEKLY. 4148
0033-7072 See RQ. 3247
0033-7129 See RSI. ROOFING SIDING INSULATION. 627
0033-7161 See RTTY JOURNAL. 1163
0033-7196 See RWDSU RECORD. 1709
0033-7250 See RABELS ZEITSCHRIFT FUER AUSLANDISCHES UND INTERNATIONALES PRIVATRECHT. 3134
0033-7315 See RACE RELATIONS & INDUSTRY. 946
0033-7390 See RACING PIGEON, THE. 4914
0033-7404 See RACING PIGEON PICTORIAL. 4914
0033-7439 See RACING STAR WEEKLY. 2802
0033-7455 See RAD (NEW YORK), DAS. 3313
0033-7587 See RADIATION RESEARCH. 4441
0033-7617 See RADICAL AMERICA. 4493
0033-765X See RADIO. 1137
0033-7706 See RADIO AMATEUR CALLBOOK MAGAZINE : UNITED STATES LISTINGS. 1137
0033-7749 See ELEKTRONIK VARLDEN. 2052
0033-779X See PROCEEDINGS - THE RADIO CLUB OF AMERICA, INC. 1120
0033-7803 See RADIO COMMUNICATION. 2078
0033-7838 See RADIO CONTROL MODELS & ELECTRONICS. 2777
0033-7862 See RADIO-ELECTRONICS. 2078
0033-7900 See RADIO, FERNSEHEN, ELEKTRONIK. 1137
0033-8060 See RADIO TIMES. 1137
0033-8133 See RADIO Y TELEVISION. 1138
0033-8184 See RADIOBIOLOGIA. RADIOTHERAPIA. 3945
0033-8192 See RADIOBIOLOGIIA. 3945
0033-8222 See RADIOCARBON. 1393
0033-8230 See RADIOCHIMICA ACTA. 1057
0033-8273 See RADIOGRAPHER. 3632
0033-8303 See RADIOISOTOPES. 5144
0033-8311 See RADIOHIMIJA. 3945
0033-832X See RADIOLOGE, DER. 3945
0033-8338 See RADIOLOGIA MADRID. 3945
0033-8354 See RADIOLOGIA DIAGNOSTICA. 3945
0033-8362 See RADIOLOGIA MEDICA. 3945
0033-8389 See RADIOLOGIC CLINICS OF NORTH AMERICA, THE. 3945
0033-8397 See RADIOLOGIC TECHNOLOGY. 3945
0033-8419 See RADIOLOGY. 3945
0033-8443 See RADIOPHYSICS AND QUANTUM ELECTRONICS. 4441
0033-8451 See RADIOPROTECTION. 4798
0033-8486 See RADIOTEHNIKA (MOSKVA). 1138
0033-8494 See RADIOTEKHNIKA I ELEKTRONIKA. 1138
0033-8532 See RADIUS (STUTTGART, GERMANY). 4989
0033-8575 See CROATIAN MEDICAL JOURNAL. 3569
0033-8591 See RADUGA. 3427
0033-8648 See RAGGUAGLIO LIBRARIO, IL. 423
0033-8672 See RAGTIMER, THE. 4148
0033-877X See RAILROAD MODEL CRAFTSMAN. 2777

0033-8826 See RAILWAY AGE (BRISTOL). 5435
0033-8850 See RAILWAY CARMEN'S JOURNAL. 5435
0033-8923 See RAILWAY MAGAZINE (LONDON). 5436
0033-8931 See RAILWAY MODELLER. 2777
0033-9008 See QUARTERLY REPORTS - RAILWAY TECHNICAL RESEARCH INSTITUTE. 5434
0033-9067 See MAGLIERIA. 1085
0033-9075 See RAISON PRESENTE. 4358
0033-9083 See RAJASTHAN BOARD JOURNAL OF EDUCATION. RAJASTHANA BORDA SIKSHANA PATRIKA, THE. 1776
0033-9113 See RAKAM. 5565
0033-913X See RAKENNUSTEKNIIKKA. 625
0033-9156 See BULLETIN OF THE RAMAKRISHNA MISSION INSTITUTE OF CULTURE. 2843
0033-9199 See RANGE. 1162
0033-9202 See RANGEFINDER (SANTA MONICA), THE. 4376
0033-9334 See RASSEGNA CHIMICA. 990
0033-9423 See RASSEGNA DELLA LETTURATURA ITALIANA, LA. 1079
0033-944X See RASSEGNA DELLA LETTERATURA SUI CICLI ECONOMICI / ISTITUTO NAZIONALE PER LO STUDIO DELLA CONGIUNTURA. 1594
0033-9466 See RASSEGNA DELL' ISTRUZIONE SECONDARIA. 1776
0033-9490 See RASSEGNA DI DERMATOLOGIA E SIFILOGRAFIA. 3722
0033-9512 See RASSEGNA DI DIRITTO PUBBLICO. 3034
0033-9555 See RASSEGNA DI MEDICINA SPERIMENTALE. 586
0033-9601 See RASSEGNA DI SERVIZIO SOCIALE. 4798
0033-9601 See RASSEGNA DI SERVIZIO SOCIALE. 5304
0033-961X See RASSEGNA DI STATISTICHE DEL LAVORO. 1537
0033-9636 See RASSEGNA DI STUDI PSICHIATRICI. 3935
0033-9644 See RASSEGNA DI TEOLOGIA. 4989
0033-9695 See RASSEGNA INTERNAZIONALE DI CLINICA E TERAPIA. 3632
0033-9725 See RASSEGNA ITALIANA DI LINGUISTICA APPLICATA. 3314
0033-9776 See RASSEGNA MEDICA SARDA. 3632
0033-9792 See RASSEGNA MENSILE DI ISRAEL, LA. 5052
0033-9806 See RASSEGNA MUSICALE CURCI. 4148
0033-9849 See RASSEGNA SINDACALE. 1705
0033-9857 See RASSAGNA SOVIETICA. 329
0033-9873 See RASSEGNA STORICA DEL RISORGIMENTO. 2704
0033-9881 See RASSEGNA STORICA TOSCANA. 2704
0033-992X See RASSEGNA DI UROLOGIA E NEFROLOGIA. 3992
0033-9938 See RASTER. 3428
0033-9946 See RASTITELNYE RESURSY. 526
0033-9962 See RATEKO. 1120
0034-0006 See RATIO (OXFORD). 4358
0034-0111 See RAUMFORSCHUNG UND RAUMORDNUNG. 33
0034-0146 See RAVEN, THE. 5596
0034-0219 See RAZA, LA. 2271
0034-0235 See RAZON Y FE. 2853
0034-026X See RAZVEDKA I OKHRANA NEDR. 2149
0034-0359 See READ (MIDDLETOWN). 1903
0034-0375 See READER'S DIGEST, THE. 2491
0034-0383 See READER'S DIGEST BASIA ED. 2271
0034-0413 See READER'S DIGEST (CANADIAN EDITION). 2544
0034-0456 See READER'S DIGEST SOUTH AFRICAN ED. 2500

0034-0464 See READERS' GUIDE TO PERIODICAL LITERATURE. 2497

0034-0472 See READING (SUNDERLAND). 1903

0034-0502 See READING HORIZONS. 3314

0034-0510 See READING IMPROVEMENT. 3314

0034-0553 See READING RESEARCH QUARTERLY. 3314

0034-0561 See READING TEACHER, THE. 3314

0034-0596 See REVISTA DE LA REAL ACADEMIA DE CIENCIAS EXACTAS, FISICAS Y NATURALES DE MADRID. 5148

0034-060X See BOLETIN DE LA REAL ACADEMIA DE CORDOBA, DE CIENCIAS, BELLAS LETRAS Y NOBLES ARTES. 2843

0034-0618 See ANALES. 4290

0034-0626 See BOLETIN DE LA REAL ACADEMIA DE LA HISTORIA (MADRID). 2611

0034-0634 See ANALES DE LA REAL ACADEMIA NACIONAL DE MEDICINA, MADRID. 3549

0034-0707 See REAL ESTATE FORUM. 4844

0034-0715 See REAL ESTATE INSIDER. 4844

0034-0758 See REAL ESTATE LAW BRIEF CASE. 4844

0034-0774 See REAL ESTATE RECORD AND BUILDER'S GUIDE (1941). 4845

0034-0790 See REAL ESTATE REVIEW (BOSTON, MASS.). 4845

0034-0804 See REAL ESTATE TODAY. 4845

0034-0855 See REAL PROPERTY, PROBATE AND TRUST JOURNAL. 3118

0034-0863 See BOLETIN ARQUEOLOGICO TARRAGONA. 1943. 262

0034-0898 See REAL WEST. 2756

0034-0960 See REALITY DUBLIN. 5035

0034-1045 See REALTY AND BUILDING. 4846

0034-107X See REAPER; NEW ZEALAND'S EVANGELICAL MONTHLY. 4989

0034-1118 See REBE UND WEIN WEINSBERG. 2370

0034-1150 See RECALL. 1903

0034-1193 See RECENTI PROGRESSI IN MEDICINA. 3801

0034-1223 See RECHERCHE AEROSPATIALE. 33

0034-124X See RECHERCHE SOCIALE. 5255

0034-1258 See RECHERCHES DE SCIENCE RELIGIEUSE. 4989

0034-1266 See RECHERCHES DE THEOLOGIE ANCIENNE ET MEDIEVALE. 4989

0034-1282 See RECHERCHES SOCIOGRAPHIQUES. 5255

0034-1312 See RECHT DER JUGEND UND DES BILDUNGSWESEN. 3035

0034-1398 See RECHTSTHEORIE. 3036

0034-1452 See RECOMMEND FLORIDA. 5490

0034-1479 See RECONCILIATION QUARTERLY (NEW MALDEN, SURREY). 4990

0034-1495 See RECONSTRUCTIONIST. 5052

0034-155X See RECORD COLLECTOR, THE. 4149

0034-1592 See RECORD RESEARCH. 4149

0034-1614 See RECORD STOCKMAN, THE. 220

0034-1622 See RECORD WORLD. 5318

0034-1738 See RECORDS OF HUNTINGDONSHIRE. 2705

0034-1827 See RECRUITING TRENDS. 706

0034-1835 See RECUEIL DALLOZ SIREY DE DOCTRINE, DE JURISPRUDENCE ET DE LEGISLATION. 3036

0034-1843 See RECUEIL DE MEDECINE VETERINAIRE. 5520

0034-1851 See RECUEIL DES BREVETS D'INVENTION. 1308

0034-1932 See RECUSANT HISTORY. 2705

0034-1967 See RED CEDAR REVIEW. 3428

0034-2106 See REDBOOK. 5565

0034-2165 See REDSTART, THE. 5596

0034-222X See REEDUCATION ORTHOPHONIQUE. 3315

0034-2262 See BIBLIOGRAPHIE PHILOSOPHIE. 4365

0034-2300 See REFERATIVNYJ ZURNAL - VSESOJUZNYJ INSTITUT NAUCNOJ I TEHNICESKOJ INFORMACII. BIOLOGIJA. 479

0034-2327 See REFERATIVNYI ZHURNAL: ELEKTROTEKHNIKA I ENERGETIKA. 2079

0034-2343 See REFERATIVNYI ZHURNAL. FIZIKA. 4419

0034-2378 See REFERATIVNYJ ZURNAL - VSESOJUZNYJ INSTITUT NAUCNOJ I TEHNICESKOJ INFORMACII, GEOGRAFIJA. 2574

0034-2483 See REFERATIVNYJ ZURNAL - VSESOUZNYJ INSTITUT NAUCNOJ I TEHNICESKOJ INFORMACII. MEHANIKA. 2127

0034-2491 See REFERATIVNYI ZHURNAL : METALLURGIIA. 4017

0034-2505 See REFERATIVNYI ZHURNAL: METROLOGIIA I IZMERITELNAIA TEKHNIKA. 4032

0034-2599 See REFERATIVNYJ ZURNAL - VSESOJUZNYJ INSTITUT NAUCNOJ I TEHNICESKOJ INFORMACII. TEHNOLOGIJA MASINOSTROENIJA. 2127

0034-2971 See REFLETS ET PERSPECTIVES DE LA VIE ECONOMIQUE. 1639

0034-303X See REFORMATION REVIEW, THE. 5019

0034-3048 See REFORMATION TODAY. 4990

0034-3056 See REFORMED WORLD. 4990

0034-3064 See REFORMED REVIEW (HOLLAND, MICH.). 4990

0034-3072 See REFORMED THEOLOGICAL REVIEW, THE. 4990

0034-3102 See REFRACTORIES (NEW YORK). 4017

0034-3129 See REFRIGERATED TRANSPORTER. 5391

0034-317X See REGAN REPORT ON HOSPITAL LAW, THE. 3037

0034-3188 See REGAN REPORT ON MEDICAL LAW. 3037

0034-3196 See REGAN REPORT ON NURSING LAW, THE. 3868

0034-3269 See REGGEBOGE, DER. 2756

0034-334X See REGIONAL CATALOGUE OF EARTHQUAKES. 1410

0034-3374 See REGIONAL PLAN NEWS. 4679

0034-3404 See REGIONAL STUDIES. 5215

0034-3420 See REGION'S AGENDA, THE. 2833

0034-3498 See REGNO, IL. 5035

0034-3501 See REHABILITASIE IN SUID-AFRIKA. 3633

0034-3536 See REHABILITATION (STUTTGART). 3633

0034-3552 See REHABILITATION COUNSELING BULLETIN. 1884

0034-3617 See REINFORCED PLASTICS (LONDON). 4460

0034-3625 See REINIGER + WASCHER. 5355

0034-3641 See REINSURANCE REPORTER. 2891

0034-365X See REINWARDTIA. 526

0034-3714 See REITO. 2608

0034-3781 See RELATIONS (MONTREAL). 5035

0034-379X See RELATIONS INDUSTRIELLES / INDUSTRIAL RELATIONS. 1706

0034-3811 See RELATIONS PUBLIQUES INFORMATIONS. 765

0034-3846 See RELAZIONI INTERNAZIONALI. 4533

0034-3897 See RELICS. 2757

0034-3951 See RELIGION AND SOCIETY (BANGALORE, INDIA). 4991

0034-3978 See RCDA. RELIGION IN COMMUNIST DOMINATED AREAS. 4546

0034-401X See RELIGION TEACHER'S JOURNAL. 4991

0034-4044 See RELIGIOUS AND THEOLOGICAL ABSTRACTS. 5013

0034-4079 See RELIGIOUS BROADCASTING. 1138

0034-4087 See RELIGIOUS EDUCATION. 4991

0034-4095 See RELIGIOUS HUMANISM. 4992

0034-4249 See REMODELING CONTRACTOR. 626

0034-4257 See REMOTE SENSING OF ENVIRONMENT. 1410

0034-429X See RENAISSANCE AND REFORMATION. 2705

0034-429X See RENAISSANCE AND REFORMATION. 2705

0034-4338 See RENAISSANCE QUARTERLY. 3428

0034-4346 See RENASCENCE. ESSAYS ON VALUES IN LITERATURE. 3429

0034-4400 See RENDEZVOUS (POCATELLO, IDAHO). 3429

0034-4451 See RENFRO VALLEY BUGLE. 2544

0034-4508 See RENSSELAER ENGINEER. 1993

0034-4524 See RENTAL EQUIPMENT REGISTER. 935

0034-4567 See REPERTOIRE BIBLIOGRAPHIQUE DE LA PHILOSOPHIE. 4366

0034-4605 See REPERTORIO BOYACENSE. 2627

0034-4621 See LITERATUURBULLETIN GEESTELIJKE VOLKSGEZONDHEID. 876

0034-4680 See REPORT ON EDUCATION OF THE DISADVANTAGED. 1884

0034-4699 See REPORT ON EDUCATION RESEARCH. 1778

0034-4737 See REPORT ON WORLD AFFAIRS. 4533

0034-477X See REPORTER - NEW JERSEY ASSOCIATION FOR HEALTH, PHYSICAL EDUCATION AND RECREATION, THE. 4799

0034-4796 See REPORTER FOR CONSCIENCE' SAKE, THE. 4055

0034-4877 See REPORTS ON MATHEMATICAL PHYSICS. 4419

0034-4885 See REPORTS ON PROGRESS IN PHYSICS. 4419

0034-4907 See REPRESENTATIVE RESEARCH IN SOCIAL PSYCHOLOGY. 4615

0034-4931 See REPRINTS FROM THE SOVIET PRESS. 1516

0034-4958 See REPRODUCTION. 4569

0034-5016 See NATIONAL CENTRAL LIBRARY NEWSLETTER. 3233

0034-5024 See BULLETIN VAN STATISTIEK / REPUBLIEK VAN SUID-AFRIKA, SENTRALE STATISTIEKDIENS. 4696

0034-5075 See REPUBLICAN JOURNAL (BELFAST, ME.). 5685

0034-513X See RESEARCH AND INDUSTRY. 5146

0034-5164 See RESEARCH COMMUNICATIONS IN CHEMICAL PATHOLOGY AND PHARMACOLOGY. 4327

0034-5210 See RESEARCH IN AFRICAN LITERATURES. 3429

0034-5237 See RESEARCH IN EDUCATION (MANCHESTER). 1779

0034-527X See RESEARCH IN THE TEACHING OF ENGLISH. 1903

0034-5288 See RESEARCH IN VETERINARY SCIENCE. 5520

0034-5296 See RESEARCH INDEX. 707

0034-5318 See PUBLICATIONS OF THE RESEARCH INSTITUTE FOR MATHEMATICAL SCIENCES. SERIES A. 3529

0034-5326 See RESEARCH INTO HIGHER EDUCATION ABSTRACTS. 1797

0034-5407 See RESEARCH REPORTS: AMERICAN INSTITUTE FOR ECONOMIC RESEARCH. 1517

0034-5431 See JOURNAL OF THE RESEARCH SOCIETY OF PAKISTAN. 5207

0034-5466 See RESEARCHES ON POPULATION ECOLOGY. 2220

0034-5512 See RESERVE BANK OF INDIA BULLETIN. 809

0034-5539 See BULLETIN - RESERVE BANK OF NEW ZEALAND. 781

0034-5547 See RESERVE MARINE, THE. 4055

0034-5555 See RESIDENT AND STAFF PHYSICIAN. 3634

0034-5687 See RESPIRATION PHYSIOLOGY. 586

0034-5709 See RESPONSE (NEW YORK. 1967). 5052
0034-5725 See RESPONSE (CINCINNATI). 5067
0034-5806 See RESTAURATOR. 2483
0034-5822 See RESTORATION AND 18TH CENTURY THEATRE RESEARCH. 5368
0034-5830 See RESTORATION HERALD. 4993
0034-5865 See RESUMEN (MIAMI). 329
0034-5970 See RESURGENCE. 4494
0034-6004 See RETAIL & BUSINESS REVIEW. 956
0034-6047 See RETAIL CONTROL. 956
0034-6063 See RETAIL JEWELLER. 2915
0034-6160 See RETIRED OFFICER (ALEXANDRIA, VA.), THE. 4055
0034-6179 See RETIREMENT LIFE. 4683
0034-6233 See REUMATOLOGIA. 3634
0034-6284 See REVEIL MISSIONNAIRE. 4993
0034-6349 See REVIEW, THE. 2892
0034-6373 See REVIEW AND EXPOSITOR (BERNE). 5067
0034-639X See REVIEW FOR RELIGIOUS. 5035
0034-6403 See REVIEW OF AGRICULTURAL ECONOMICS MALAYSIA. 128
0034-6438 See REVIEW OF PLANT PATHOLOGY. 479
0034-6446 See REVIEW OF BLACK POLITICAL ECONOMY, THE. 1517
0034-6454 See REVIEW OF BUSINESS. 708
0034-6500 See REVIEW OF ECONOMIC CONDITIONS. 1581
0034-6527 See REVIEW OF ECONOMIC STUDIES, THE. 1517
0034-6543 See REVIEW OF EDUCATIONAL RESEARCH. 1779
0034-6551 See REVIEW OF ENGLISH STUDIES. 3429
0034-6578 See REVIEW OF GHANA LAW. 3040
0034-6586 See REVIEW OF INCOME AND WEALTH, THE. 1518
0034-6616 See REVIEW OF MARKETING AND AGRICULTURAL ECONOMICS. 128
0034-6624 See REVIEW OF MEDICAL AND VETERINARY MYCOLOGY. 5528
0034-6632 See REVIEW OF METAPHYSICS, THE. 4359
0034-6640 See REVIEW OF NATIONAL LITERATURES. 3351
0034-6659 See NUTRITION & FOOD SCIENCE. 4195
0034-6659 See NUTRITION & FOOD SCIENCE. 4195
0034-6667 See REVIEW OF PALAEOBOTANY AND PALYNOLOGY. 4230
0034-6691 See REVIEW OF POLAROGRAPHY. PORAROGURAFII. 1018
0034-6705 See REVIEW OF POLITICS, THE. 4494
0034-6721 See REVIEW OF RELIGIOUS. 4993
0034-673X See REVIEW OF RELIGIOUS RESEARCH. 4993
0034-6748 See REVIEW OF SCIENTIFIC INSTRUMENTS. 5147
0034-6764 See REVIEW OF SOCIAL ECONOMY. 1581
0034-6799 See REVIEW OF THE ECONOMIC CONDITIONS IN ITALY. 1581
0034-6861 See REVIEWS OF MODERN PHYSICS. 4419
0034-690X See REVIJA ZA KRIMINALISTIKO IN KRIMINOLOGIJO. 3175
0034-6934 See REVISTA AEREA. 33
0034-7000 See REVISTA ARGENTINA DE CARDIOLOGIA. 3710
0034-7043 See REVISTA ARHIVELOR. 2483
0034-7078 See REVISTA BIBLICA. 5019
0034-7094 See REVISTA BRASILEIRA DE ANESTESIOLOGIA. 3684
0034-7108 See REVISTA BRASILEIRA DE BIOLOGIA. 471
0034-7124 See REVISTA BRASILEIRA DE CIRURGIA. 3973

0034-7140 See REVISTA BRASILEIRA DE ECONOMIA. 1518
0034-7175 See REVISTA BRASILEIRA DE ESTATISTICA. 5337
0034-7183 See REVISTA BRASILEIRA DE ESTUDOS PEDAGOGICOS. 1780
0034-7191 See REVISTA BRASILEIRA DE ESTUDOS POLITICOS. 4494
0034-7205 See REVISTA BRASILEIRA DE FILOSOFIA. 4359
0034-723X See REVISTA BRASILEIRA DE GEOGRAFIA. 2574
0034-7256 See REVISTA BRASILEIRA DE MALARIOLOGIA E DOENCAS TROPICAIS. 3634
0034-7264 See REVISTA BRASILEIRA DE MEDICINA. 3634
0034-7280 See REVISTA BRASILEIRA DE OTTALMOLOGIA. 3879
0034-7299 See REVISTA BRASILEIRA DE OTO-RINO-LARINGOLOGIA. 3891
0034-7302 See REVISTA BRASILEIRA DE PATOLOGIA CLINICA. 3897
0034-7329 See REVISTA BRASILEIRA DE POLITICA INTERNACIONAL. 4534
0034-737X See REVISTA CERES. 128
0034-7388 See REVISTA CHILENA DE NEURO-PSIQUIATRIA. 3935
0034-740X See REVISTA CHILENA DE ENTOMOLOGIA. 5613
0034-7418 See REVISTA COLOMBIANA DE CIENCIAS QUIMICO-FARMACEUTICAS. 991
0034-7426 See REVISTA COLOMBIANA DE MATEMATICAS. 3531
0034-7434 See REVISTA COLOMBIANA DE OBSTETRICIA Y GINECOLOGIA. 3768
0034-7450 See REVISTA COLOMBIANA DE PSIQUIATRIA. 3935
0034-7493 See REVISTA CUBANA DE CIRUGIA. 3973
0034-7507 See REVISTA CUBANA DE ESTOMATOLOGIA. 1334
0034-7523 See REVISTA CUBANA DE MEDICINA. 3635
0034-7531 See REVISTA CUBANA DE PEDIATRIA. 3911
0034-7590 See REVISTA DE ADMINISTRACAO DE EMPRESAS. 885
0034-7612 See REVISTA DE ADMINISTRACAO PUBLICA (RIO DE JANEIRO). 4683
0034-7639 See REVISTA DE ADMINISTRACION PUBLICA (MADRID, SPAIN). 4683
0034-7655 See REVISTA DE AGRICULTURA. 129
0034-7701 See REVISTA DE ANTROPOLOGIA (SAO PAULO). 244
0034-771X See REVISTA DE ARCHIVOS BIBLIOTECAS Y MUSEOS (MADRID, SPAIN : 1897). 3246
0034-7736 See REVISTA DE BIOLOGIA (LISBOA). 471
0034-7744 See REVISTA DE BIOLOGIA TROPICAL. 3986
0034-7752 See REVISTA DE CHIMIE. 991
0034-7817 See REVISTA DE CIENCIAS SOCIALES (RIO PIEDRAS, P.R.). 5216
0034-785X See REVISTA DE CULTURA BRASILENA. 329
0034-7930 See REVISTA DE DERECHO PUERTORRIQUENO. 3040
0034-7949 See REVISTA DE DERECHO Y CIENCIAS POLITICAS. 3041
0034-7973 See REVISTA DE DIAGNOSTICO BIOLOGICO. 471
0034-7981 See REVISTA DE DIALECTOLOGIA Y TRADICIONES POPULARES. 2324
0034-7981 See REVISTA DE DIALECTOLOGIA Y TRADICIONES AND POULARES. 2324
0034-8015 See REVISTA DE DIREITO PUBLICO. 3041
0034-8082 See REVISTA DE EDUCACION (SPAIN. MINISTERIO DE EDUCACION NACIONAL). 1780
0034-8147 See REVISTA DE ESPIRITUALIDAD. 5035
0034-818X See REVISTA DE ESTUDIOS HISPANICOS (UNIVERSITY, AL.). 3315

0034-8198 See REVISTA DE ETNOGRAFIE SI FOLCLOR. 244
0034-8252 See REVISTA DE FILOSOFIA DE LA UNIVERSIDAD DE COSTA RICA. 4359
0034-8279 See REVISTA DE GEOFISICA. 1410
0034-8309 See REVISTA DE HISTORIA (SAO PAULO). 2627
0034-8325 See REVISTA DE HISTORIA DE AMERICA. 2758
0034-8341 See REVISTA DE INDIAS. 2758
0034-835X See REVISTA DE INFORMACAO LEGISLATIVA. 3041
0034-8376 See REVISTA DE INVESTIGACION CLINICA. 3801
0034-8392 See REVISTA DE ISTORIE SI TEORIE LITERARA. 3351
0034-849X See REVISTA DE LITERATURA. 3459
0034-8511 See REVISTA DE MARINA. 4055
0034-8570 See REVISTA DE METALURGIA (MADRID). 4018
0034-8597 See REVISTA DE NEURO-PSIQUIATRIA. 3845
0034-8619 See REVISTA DE OBRAS PUBLICAS. 2030
0034-8635 See REVISTA DE OCCIDENTE. 3351
0034-8708 See REVISTA DE PLASTICOS MODERNOS. 4460
0034-8716 See REVISTA DE POLITICA INTERNACIONAL. 4494
0034-8724 See REVISTA DE POLITICA SOCIAL. 5216
0034-8732 See REVISTA DE PREVENCION. 4799
0034-8740 See REVISTA DE PSICOANALYSIS. 4616
0034-8759 See REVISTA DE PSIHOLOGIE. 4616
0034-8899 See REVISTA DE SANIDAD E HIGIENE PUBLICA. 4799
0034-8910 See REVISTA DE SAUDE PUBLICA. 4799
0034-8953 See REVISTA DE TEATRO. 5368
0034-897X See REVISTA DE TRABAJO (MADRID). 1708
0034-9003 See REVISTA DEL ARCHIVO NACIONAL. 2483
0034-9003 See REVISTA DEL ARCHIVO NACIONAL (SAN JOSE). 2758
0034-9089 See REVISTA DEL IDIEM. 1994
0034-9097 See REVISTA DEL MEXICO AGRARIO. 129
0034-916X See RIVISTA DI INGEGNERIA AGRARIA. 1994
0034-9313 See REVISTA ECUATORIANA DE MEDICINA Y CIENCIAS BIOLOGICAS. 3635
0034-9356 See REVISTA ESPANOLA DE ANESTESIOLOGIA Y REANIMACION. 3684
0034-9372 See REVISTA ESPANOLA DE DERECHO CANONICO. 4993
0034-9380 See REVISTA ESPANOLA DE DERECHO INTERNACIONAL. 3135
0034-9402 See REVISTA ESPANOLA DE FISIOLOGIA. 586
0034-9445 See REVISTA ESPANOLA DE OBSTETRICIA Y GINECOLOGIA. 3768
0034-9453 See REVISTA ESPANOLA DE OTO-NEURO-OFTALMOLOGIA Y NEUROCIRUGIA. 3845
0034-9461 See REVISTA ESPANOLA DE PEDAGOGIA. 1780
0034-947X See REVISTA ESPANOLA DE PEDIATRIA. 3911
0034-9585 See REVISTA GOIANA DE MEDICINA. 3636
0034-9593 See REVISTA HISPANICA MODERNA. 3430
0034-9631 See REVISTA IBEROAMERICANA. 3430
0034-9690 See REVISTA INTERAMERICANA DE PSICOLOGIA. 4616
0034-9712 See REVISTA INTERNACIONAL DE SOCIOLOGIA. 5216
0034-9860 See REVISTA MARITIMA BRASILEIRA. 4182
0034-9887 See REVISTA MEDICA DE CHILE. 3801

0034-9909 See REVISTA MEDICA DE COSTA RICA. 3636

0034-995X See REVISTA MEDICALA (TIRGU-MURES). 4328

0034-9984 See REVISTA MEXICANA DE CIRUGIA, GINECOLOGIA Y CANCER. 3768

0034-9992 See REVISTA MEXICANA DE DERECHO PENAL. 3108

0035-001X See REVISTA MEXICANA DE FISICA. 4420

0035-0028 See REVISTA MEXICANA DE INGENIERIA Y ARQUITECTURA : ORGANO DE LA ASSOCIACION DE INGENIEROS Y ARQUITECTOS DE MEXICO. 1994

0035-0052 See REVISTA MEXICANA DE PEDIATRIA. 3911

0035-0079 See REVISTA MEXICANA DE PSICOLOGIA. 4616

0035-0222 See REVISTA NACIONAL DE AGRICULTURA (BOGOTA). 129

0035-0230 See REVISTA NACIONAL DE CULTURA (CARACAS, VENEZUELA). 5216

0035-0354 See REVISTA PARAGUAYA DE SOCIOLOGIA. 5216

0035-0362 See REVISTA PAULISTA DE MEDICINA. 3636

0035-0389 See REVISTA PORTUGUESA DE CIENCIAS VETERINARIAS. 5520

0035-0397 See REVISTA PORTUGUESA DE ESTOMATOLOGIA E CIRURGIA MAXILO-FACIAL. 1334

0035-0419 See REVISTA PORTUGUESA DE QUIMICA. 991

0035-0451 See SIGNOS. 330

0035-0451 See REVISTA SIGNOS. 3316

0035-0478 See SUR (BUENOS AIRES, ARGENTINA). 2552

0035-0516 See REVISTA TELEGRAFICA ELECTRONICA. 2079

0035-0575 See REVISTA VENEZOLANA DE FOLKLORE. 2324

0035-0621 See REVOLUTION AFRICAINE. 4494

0035-0672 See REVUE ADMINISTRATIVE, LA. 4683

0035-0699 See REVUE ALGERIENNE DES SCIENCES JURIDIQUES, ECONOMIQUES ET POLITIQUES. 3042

0035-0737 See REVUE ARCHEOLOGIQUE. 281

0035-0745 See REVUE ARCHEOLOGIQUE DE L'EST ET DU CENTRE-EST. 281

0035-077X See REVUE BELGE D'ARCHEOLOGIE ET D'HISTOIRE DE L'ART. 330

0035-0788 See REVUE BELGE DE DROIT INTERNATIONAL. 3135

0035-0796 See REVUE BELGE DE GEOGRAPHIE. 2575

0035-0818 See REVUE BELGE DE PHILOLOGIE ET D'HISTOIRE. 3316

0035-0877 See REVUE BELGE D'HISTOIRE MILITAIRE. 4056

0035-0885 See REVUE BELGE D'HOMOEOPATHIE. 3775

0035-0893 See REVUE BENEDICTINE. 4993

0035-0907 See REVUE BIBLIQUE. 5019

0035-0958 See REVUE CRITIQUE DE DROIT INTERNATIONAL PRIVE. 3135

0035-0966 See REVUE CRITIQUE DE JURISPRUDENCE BELGE. 3042

0035-0974 See REVUE D'ALLEMAGNE. 2706

0035-1008 See REVUE D'AUVERGNE. 2706

0035-1016 See REVUE DE BELLES-LETTRES. 3430

0035-1040 See REVUE DE CHIRURGIE ORTHOPEDIQUE ET REPARATRICE DE L'APPAREIL MOTEUR. 3973

0035-1059 See REVUE DE COMMINGES. 2706

0035-1091 See REVUE DE DROIT INTERNATIONAL, DE SCIENCES DIPLOMATIQUES ET POLITIQUES. 3135

0035-1121 See REVUE DE GEOGRAPHIE ALPINE. 2575

0035-113X See REVUE DE GEOGRAPHIE DE LYON. 2575

0035-1156 See REVUE DE GEOGRAPHIE DU MAROC. 2575

0035-1237 See REVUE DE LA POLICE NATIONALE. 3175

0035-127X See REVUE DE LA SOUDURE (BRUXELLES). 4027

0035-1296 See REVUE DE L'AGRICULTURE. 129

0035-130X See REVUE DE L'ALCOOLISME, LA. 1348

0035-1326 See REVUE DE L'ART. 363

0035-1334 See REVUE DE LARYNGOLOGIE, D'OTOLOGIE ET DE RHINOLOGIE. 3891

0035-1342 See REVUE DE L'AVRANCHIN ET DU PAYS DE GRANVILLE. 330

0035-1423 See REVUE DE L'HISTOIRE DES RELIGIONS. 4993

0035-1458 See REVUE DE LINGUISTIQUE ROMANE. 3316

0035-1466 See REVUE DE LITTERATURE COMPAREE. 3430

0035-1504 See REVUE DE MATHEMATIQUES SPECIALES. 3531

0035-1555 See REVUE DE MEDECINE VETERINAIRE. 5520

0035-1563 See REVUE DE METALLURGIE (PARIS). 4018

0035-1571 See REVUE DE METAPHYSIQUE ET DE MORALE (PARIS, FRANCE : 1945). 4359

0035-158X See METROLOGIE PRATIQUE ET LEGALE. 4031

0035-1598 See REVUE DE MICROPALEONTOLOGIE. 4230

0035-1601 See REVUE DE MUSICOLOGIE. 4150

0035-161X See REVUE DE NEUROPSYCHIATRIE DE L'OUEST. 3936

0035-1652 See REVUE DE PHILOLOGIE, DE LITTERATURE ET D'HISTOIRE ANCIENNES. 3316

0035-1660 See REVUE DE PHONETIQUE APPLIQUEE. 3316

0035-1687 See JOURNAL DE PHYSIQUE. III (LES ULIS). 4408

0035-1725 See REVUE DE QUMRAN. 5052

0035-1733 See REVUE DE SCIENCE CRIMINELLE ET DE DROIT PENAL COMPARE. 3108

0035-175X See REVUE DE STATISTIQUE APPLIQUEE. 5337

0035-1768 See REVUE DE STOMATOLOGIE ET DE CHIRURGIE MAXILLO-FACIALE. 3973

0035-1776 See REVUE DE SYNTHESE. 2628

0035-1784 See REVUE DE THEOLOGIE ET DE PHILOSOPHIE. 4359

0035-1822 See EUROPEAN JOURNAL OF SOIL BIOLOGY. 171

0035-1849 See REVUE D'EGYPTOLOGIE. 2628

0035-1865 See REVUE D'ELEVAGE ET DE MEDECINE VETERINAIRE DES PAYS TROPICAUX. 5521

0035-2004 See REVUE DES ETUDES ANCIENNES. 1079

0035-2012 See REVUE DES ETUDES AUGUSTINIENNES. 4993

0035-2039 See REVUE DES ETUDES GRECQUES. 3316

0035-2047 See REVUE DES ETUDES ITALIENNES. 3430

0035-2063 See REVUE DES ETUDES SUD-EST EUROPEENNES. 2706

0035-2136 See REVUE DES LETTRES MODERNES. 3430

0035-2160 See REVUE DES QUESTIONS SCIENTIFIQUES. 5148

0035-2195 See REVUE DES SCIENCES HUMAINES. 4359

0035-2209 See REVUE DES SCIENCES PHILOSOPHIQUES ET THEOLOGIQUES (PARIS : 1947). 4359

0035-2217 See REVUE DES SCIENCES RELIGIEUSES. 4993

0035-2284 See REVUE DESJARDINS, LA. 810

0035-2330 See REVUE D'HISTOIRE DE LA MEDECINE HEBRAIQUE. 3636

0035-2357 See REVUE D'HISTOIRE DE L'AMERIQUE FRANCAISE. 2758

0035-2365 See REVUE D'HISTOIRE DIPLOMATIQUE. 4534

0035-2373 See REVUE D'HISTOIRE DU THEATRE. 5368

0035-2381 See REVUE D'HISTOIRE ECCLESIASTIQUE. 5013

0035-2403 See REVUE D'HISTOIRE ET DE PHILOSOPHIE RELIGIEUSES. 4993

0035-2411 See REVUE D'HISTOIRE LITTERAIRE DE LA FRANCE. 3430

0035-2470 See REVUE D'ODONTO-STOMATOLOGIE DU MIDI DE LA FRANCE. 1334

0035-2578 See REVUE DU DROIT PUBLIC ET DE LA SCIENCE POLITIQUE EN FRANCE ET A L'ETRANGER. 3135

0035-2594 See REVUE DU JOUET, LA. 2585

0035-2624 See REVUE DU NORD. 2706

0035-2632 See REVUE DU NOTARIAT, LA. 3043

0035-2640 See REVUE DU PRACTICIEN, LA. 3636

0035-2659 See REVUE DU RHUMATISME ET DES MALADIES OSTEO-ARTICULAIRES. 3806

0035-2659 See REVUE DU RHUMATISME : MALADIES DES OS ET DES ARTICULATIONS. 3806

0035-2667 See REVUE DU ROUERGUE. 2706

0035-2713 See REVUE DU TRESOR, LA. 751

0035-273X See REVUE DU VIN DE FRANCE (ENGLISH EDITION). 2370

0035-2748 See REVUE DU VIVARAIS. 330

0035-2764 See REVUE ECONOMIQUE. 1595

0035-2772 See REVUE ECONOMIQUE ET SOCIALE (LAUSANNE). 1595

0035-2799 See REVUE ECONOMIQUE FRANCO-SUISSE. 821

0035-2829 See REVUE FORESTIERE FRANCAISE. 2394

0035-2853 See REVUE FRANCAISE D'APICULTURE. 130

0035-2888 See REVUE FRANCAISE DE GASTRO-ENTEROLOGIE. 3747

0035-290X See REVUE FRANCAISE DE GYNECOLOGIE ET D'OBSTETRIQUE. 3768

0035-2942 See REVUE FRANCAISE DE PSYCHANALYSE : ORGANE OFFICIEL DE LA SOCIETE PSYCHANALYTIQUE DE PARIS. 4616

0035-2950 See REVUE FRANCAISE DE SCIENCE POLITIQUE. 4495

0035-2969 See REVUE FRANCAISE DE SOCIOLOGIE. 5256

0035-2985 See REVUE FRANCAISE DES AFFAIRES SOCIALES. 5256

0035-3000 See REVUE FRANCAISE DES CORPS GRAS. 1047

0035-3051 See REVUE FRANCAISE DU MARKETING. 936

0035-306X See REVUE GENERALE. PERSPECTIVES EUROPEENES DES SCIENCES HUMAINES. 5217

0035-3086 See REVUE GENERALE DE DROIT. 3043

0035-3116 See REVUE GENERALE DE L'ELECTRICITE. 2079

0035-3132 See REVUE GENERALE DE L'ETANCHEITE ET DE L'ISOLATION. 2628

0035-3159 See REVUE GENERALE DE THERMIQUE. 2128

0035-3175 See REVUE GENERALE DES CAOUTCHOUCS & PLASTIQUES. 5077

0035-3183 See REVUE GENERALE DES CHEMINS DE FER (1924). 5436

0035-3191 See REVUE GENERALE DES ROUTES ET DES AERODROMES. 33

0035-3205 See REVUE GENERALE DU FROID, LA. 2608

0035-3213 See REVUE GEOGRAPHIQUE DE L'EST. 2575

0035-3221 See REVUE GEOGRAPHIQUE DES PYRENEES ET DU SUD-OUEST. 2575

0035-3256 See REVUE HELLENIQUE DE DROIT INTERNATIONAL. 3135

0035-3264 See REVUE HISTORIQUE. 2628

0035-3272 See REVUE HISTORIQUE ARDENNAISE. 2706

0035-3280 See REVUE HISTORIQUE DE DROIT FRANCAIS ET ETRANGER. 3043

0035-3299 See REVUE HISTORIQUE DES ARMEES. 4056

0035-3329 See REVUE INTERNATIONALE DE CRIMINOLOGIE ET DE POLICE TECHNIQUE. 3175

0035-3337 See REVUE INTERNATIONALE DE DROIT COMPARE. 3135

0035-3396 See REVUE INTERNATIONALE DE POLICE CRIMINELLE. 3175

0035-3434 See REVUE INTERNATIONALE DES HAUTES TEMPERATURES ET DES REFRACTAIRES. 1057

0035-3493 See REVUE INTERNATIONALE D'OCEANOGRAPHIE MEDICALE. 3636

0035-3515 See REVUE INTERNATIONALE DU DROIT D'AUTEUR. 1308

0035-354X See REVUE INTERNATIONALE POUR L'ENSEIGNEMENT COMMERCIAL. INTERNATIONAL REVIEW FOR BUSINESS EDUCATION. INTERNATIONAL ZEITSCHRIFT FUR KAUFMANNISCHES BILDUNGSWESEN. RIVISTA INTERNAZIONALE PER LA CULTURA COMMERCIALE. REVISTA INTERNACIONAL PARA LA ENSENANZA COMMERCIAL. 708

0035-3574 See REVUE JURIDIQUE ET POLITIQUE, INDEPENDANCE ET COOPERATION. 3043

0035-3590 See REVUE LAITIERE FRANCAISE. 220

0035-3620 See REVUE MABILLON. 4994

0035-3639 See REVUE MEDICALE DE BRUXELLES. 3636

0035-3655 See REVUE MEDICALE DE LA SUISSE ROMANDE. 3637

0035-3728 See REVUE MUNICIPALE (MONTREAL). 4684

0035-3787 See REVUE NEUROLOGIQUE. 3845

0035-3795 See R N D REVUE NOTRE DAME. 5035

0035-3809 See REVUE NOUVELLE, LA. 2522

0035-3833 See REVUE PHILOSOPHIQUE DE LA FRANCE ET DE L'ETRANGER. 4359

0035-3841 See REVUE PHILOSOPHIQUE DE LOUVAIN. 4360

0035-385X See REVUE POLITIQUE ET PARLEMENTAIRE. 5217

0035-3884 See REVUE REFORMEE, LA. 5067

0035-3906 See REVUE ROMANE. 3317

0035-3930 See REVUE ROUMAINE DE CHIMIE. 991

0035-3957 See REVUE ROUMAINE DE LINGUISTIQUE. 3317

0035-3965 See REVUE ROUMAINE DE MATHEMATIQUES PURES ET APPLIQUEES. 3531

0035-4007 See REVUE ROUMAINE D'EMBRYOLOGIE ET DE CYTOLOGIE. SERIE DE CYTOLOGIE. 540

0035-4023 See REVUE ROUMAINE DES SCIENCES SOCIALES. SERIE DE SCIENCES JURIDIQUES. 5217

0035-4066 See REVUE ROUMAINE DES SCIENCES TECHNIQUES. SERIE ELECTROTECHNIQUE ET ENERGETIQUE. 4420

0035-4074 See REVUE ROUMAINE DES SCIENCES TECHNIQUES. SERIE DE MECANIQUE APPLIQUEE. 2128

0035-4090 See REVUE ROUMAINE DE PHYSIQUE. 4420

0035-4112 See REVUE SENEGALAISE DE DROIT. 3044

0035-4147 See REVUE STOMATO ODONTOLOGIQUE DU NORD DE LA FRANCE. 1335

0035-418X See REVUE SUISSE DE ZOOLOGIE. 5596

0035-421X See REVUE SYNDICALE SUISSE. 1708

0035-4244 See R.I.A. (PARIS, 1977). 2355

0035-4260 See REVUE TECHNIQUE LUXEMBOURGEOISE. 5148

0035-4279 See REVUE TECHNIQUE THOMSON-CSF. 2079

0035-4295 See REVUE THOMISTE. 4994

0035-4317 See REVUE TRIMESTRIELLE DE DROIT EUROPEEN (COURT OF JUSTICE OF THE EUROPEAN COMMUNITIES). 3044

0035-4333 See REVUE TUNISIENNE DE SCIENCES SOCIALES. 5217

0035-4465 See RWI-MITTEILUNGEN. 3637

0035-4473 See RHEINISCHE VIERTELJAHRSBLATTER. 2707

0035-449X See RHEINISCHES MUSEUM FUER PHILOLOGIE. 3317

0035-4511 See RHEOLOGICA ACTA. 4420

0035-452X See RHEOLOGY ABSTRACTS. 4429

0035-4619 See RHODE ISLAND HISTORY. 2759

0035-4635 See RHODE ISLAND RESOURCES. 130

0035-4902 See RHODORA. 526

0035-4961 See RICE JOURNAL (1938), THE. 185

0035-5038 See RICERCHE DI MATEMATICA. 3532

0035-5046 See RICERCHE DIDATTICHE. 1781

0035-5054 See RICERCHE ECONOMICHE. 1518

0035-5119 See RICHMOND COUNTY HISTORY. 2759

0035-5135 See RSG. RICHTING SPORT-GERICHT. 1904

0035-5240 See RDS. 1869

0035-5259 See RIFORMA MEDICA. 3637

0035-5267 See RIG. 2707

0035-5275 See RIGHT OF WAY. 4846

0035-5283 See RIGHTS (NEW YORK, N.Y. 1953). 4512

0035-5356 See RIKKYO KEIZAIGAKU KENKYU. 1519

0035-5372 See RIMBA INDONESIA. 2394

0035-5410 See RING (NEW YORK), THE. 4915

0035-5488 See RINSHO SHIKA. 1335

0035-5526 See RIPON FORUM. 4495

0035-5593 See RISK MANAGEMENT. 2892

0035-5607 See RISORGIMENTO, IL. 2707

0035-5739 See RIVISTA ABRUZZESE. 2853

0035-5798 See RIVISTA BIBLICA. 5019

0035-5836 See RIVISTA DEGLI INFORTUNI E DELLE MALATTIE PROFESSIONALI. 3637

0035-5879 See RIVISTA DEL CINEMATOGRAFO. 4077

0035-5887 See RIVISTA DEL DIRITTO COMMERCIALE E DEL DIRITTO GENERALE DELLE OBBLIGAZIONI. 3103

0035-5917 See RIVISTA DEL NUOVO CIMENTO. 4420

0035-5925 See RIVISTA DEL PORTO DI NAPOLI, LA. 850

0035-595X See RIVISTA DELLA GUARDIA DI FINANZA. 4056

0035-6018 See RIVISTA DELLE SOCIETA. 3103

0035-6026 See RIVISTA DI AGRICOLTURA SUBTROPICALE E TROPICALE. 130

0035-6034 See RIVISTA DI AGRONOMIA. 130

0035-6042 See REVISTI DI ARCHEOLOGIA CRISTIANA. 281

0035-6050 See RIVISTA DI BIOLOGIA. 472

0035-6085 See RIVISTA DI CULTURA CLASSICA E MEDIOEVALE. 3431

0035-6093 See RIVISTA DI DIRITTO CIVILE. 3091

0035-6123 See RIVISTA DI DIRITTO EUROPEO. 3044

0035-614X See RIVISTA DI DIRITTO INDUSTRIALE. 1308

0035-6158 See RIVISTA DI DIRITTO INTERNAZIONALE. 3135

0035-6174 See RIVISTA DI DIRITTO INTERNAZIONALE PRIVATO E PROCESSUALE. 3135

0035-6190 See RIVISTA DI ECONOMIA AGRARIA. 130

0035-6204 See RIVISTA DI EMOTERAPIA ED IMMUNOEMATOLOGIA. 3676

0035-6212 See RIVISTA DI ESTETICA. 4360

0035-6239 See RIVISTA DI FILOSOFIA. 4360

0035-6247 See RIVISTA DI FILOSOFIA NEO-SCOLASTICA. 4360

0035-6255 See RIVISTA DI GASTRO-ENTEROLOGIA. 3747

0035-6263 See INGEGNERIA. 1978

0035-6298 See RIVISTA DI MATEMATICA DELLA UNIVERSITA DI PARMA. 3532

0035-6301 See RIVISTA DI MECCANICA. 2128

0035-6328 See REVISTA DI METEOROLOGIA AERONAUTICA. 1434

0035-6336 See RIVISTA DI NEUROBIOLOGIA. 3845

0035-6352 See RIVISTA DI NEUROPSICHIATRIA E SCIENZE AFFINI. 3845

0035-6387 See RIVISTA DI PARASSITOLOGIA. 569

0035-6395 See RIVISTA DI PASTORALE LITURGICA. 4994

0035-6417 See RIVISTA DI PATOLOGIA E CLINICA. 3898

0035-6433 See RIVISTA DI PATOLOGIA NERVOSA E MENTALE. 3936

0035-6441 See RIVISTA DI PATOLOGIA VEGETALE. 526

0035-645X See RIVISTA DI POLITICA AGRARIA. 130

0035-6484 See RIVISTA DI PSICHIATRIA. 3936

0035-6492 See RIVISTA DI PSICOANALISI. 4617

0035-6514 See RIVISTA DI SCIENZE PREISTORICHE. 281

0035-6522 See RIVISTA DI SERVIZIO SOCIALE, LA. 5306

0035-6549 See RIVISTA DI STATISTICA APPLICATA. 5337

0035-6557 See RIVISTA DI STORIA DELLA CHIESA IN ITALIA. 4994

0035-6573 See RIVISTA DI STORIA E LETTERATURA RELIGIOSA. 4994

0035-6603 See RIVISTA DI STUDI LIGURI. 281

0035-6611 See RIVISTA DI STUDI POLITICI INTERNAZIONALI. 4534

0035-6638 See RIVISTA DI VITA SPIRITUALE. 4994

0035-6689 See RIVISTA GENERALE ITALIANA DI CHIRURGIA. 3974

0035-6697 See RIVISTA GEOGRAFICA ITALIANA. 2575

0035-6727 See RIVISTA INTERNAZIONALE DI FILOSOFIA DEL DIRITTO. 3044

0035-6751 See RIVISTA INTERNAZIONALE DI SCIENZE ECONOMICHE E COMMERCIALI. 1519

0035-676X See RIVISTA INTERNAZIONALE DI SCIENZE SOCIALI. 5217

0035-6794 See RIVISTA ITALIANA DELLA SALDATURA. 4027

0035-6808 See RIVISTA ITALIANA DELLE SOSTANZE GRASSE. 1029

0035-6816 See IMPRESA. 1609

0035-6832 See RIVISTA ITALIANA DI ECONOMIA, DEMOGRAFIA E STATISTICA. 1519

0035-6867 See RIVISTA ITALIANA DI MUSICOLOGIA. 4150

0035-6875 See RIVISTA ITALIANA DI ORNITOLOGIA. 472

0035-6883 See RIVISTA ITALIANA DI PALEONTOLOGIA E STRATIGRAFIA. 4230

0035-6913 See RIVISTA ITALIANA DI STUDI NAPOLENOICI. 2707

0035-6921 See RIVISTA ITALIANA D'IGIENE. 4800

0035-6948 See RIVISTA ITALIANA ESSENZE, PROFUMI, PIANTE OFFICINALI, AROMI, SAPONI, COSMETICI, AEROSOL. 1029

0035-6956 See RIVISTA LITURGICA. 5035

0035-6964 See RIVISTA MARITTIMA. 4182

0035-6980 See RIVISTA MILITARE. 4056

0035-7030 See RIVISTA ROSMINIANA DI FILOSOFIA E DI CULTURA. 586

0035-7073 See RIVISTA STORICA ITALIANA. 2707

0035-7189 See ROAD AND TRACK. 5424

0035-7200 See ROAD APPLE REVIEW. 3352

0035-7243 See ROAD RIDER. 4082

0035-7367 See ROANOKE REVIEW. 3431

0035-7405 See ROCHESTER ENGINEER, THE. 1994

0035-7413 See ROCHESTER HISTORY. 2759
0035-7499 See ROCKET-JET FLYING. 34
0035-7529 See ROCKS AND MINERALS. 1444
0035-7537 See ROCKS AND MINERALS IN CANADA. 1444
0035-7596 See ROCKY MOUNTAIN JOURNAL OF MATHEMATICS, THE. 3532
0035-7650 See ROCKY MOUNTAIN UNION FARMER. 130
0035-7685 See ROCZNIKI FILOSOFICZNE. 4360
0035-7707 See ROCZNIKI HUMANISTYCZNE. 2853
0035-7715 See ROCZNIKI PANSTWOWEGO ZAKADU HIGIENY. 4800
0035-7774 See RODO KAGAKU. 1708
0035-7812 See ROEMISCHE QUARTALSCHRIFT FUER CHRISTLICHE ALTERTUMSKUNDE UND KIRCHENGESCHICHTE. 4994
0035-7820 See RONTGENPRAXIS (STUTTGART). 3946
0035-788X See ROLL CALL (WASHINGTON, D.C.). 4495
0035-791X See ROLLING STONE. 4151
0035-7936 See ROLLINS SANDSPUR. 1094
0035-7995 See ROMANCE NOTES. 3318
0035-8002 See ROMANCE PHILOLOGY. 3318
0035-8029 See ROMANIA. 3318
0035-8053 See ROMANIAN BULLETIN. 2272
0035-8088 See RUMANIAN REVIEW. 3352
0035-8118 See ROMANIC REVIEW. 3431
0035-8126 See ROMANISCHE FORSCHUNGEN. 3318
0035-8169 See ROND DE TAFEL. 4994
0035-8215 See ROOPA-LEKHA. 363
0035-8231 See ROPA A UHLIE. 4277
0035-8339 See ROSICRUCIAN DIGEST. 4243
0035-8355 See ROSS REPORTS TELEVISION. 1138
0035-838X See ROTARIAN, THE. 5236
0035-8495 See ROTUNDA (TORONTO). 4096
0035-8525 See ROUGH NOTES (INDIANAPOLIS). 2893
0035-8533 See ROUND TABLE, THE. 4534
0035-8606 See ROYAL AIR FORCE COLLEGE JOURNAL, THE. 1094
0035-8665 See JOURNAL OF THE ROYAL ARMY MEDICAL CORPS. 3599
0035-869X See JOURNAL OF THE ROYAL ASIATIC SOCIETY OF GREAT BRITAIN & IRELAND. 2769
0035-8711 See MONTHLY NOTICES OF THE ROYAL ASTRONOMICAL SOCIETY. 397
0035-872X See JOURNAL OF THE ROYAL ASTRONOMICAL SOCIETY OF CANADA, THE. 396
0035-8738 See QUARTERLY JOURNAL OF THE ROYAL ASTRONOMICAL SOCIETY, THE. 399
0035-8762 See JOURNAL OF THE ROYAL AUSTRALIAN HISTORICAL SOCIETY. 2670
0035-8800 See ANNALS OF THE ROYAL COLLEGE OF PHYSICIANS AND SURGEONS OF CANADA. 3913
0035-8819 See JOURNAL OF THE ROYAL COLLEGE OF PHYSICIANS OF LONDON. 3599
0035-8835 See JOURNAL OF THE ROYAL COLLEGE OF SURGEONS OF EDINBURGH. 3968
0035-8843 See ANNALS OF THE ROYAL COLLEGE OF SURGEONS OF ENGLAND. 3959
0035-8878 See ROYAL ENGINEERS JOURNAL, THE. 1995
0035-8908 See ROYAL GAZETTE. PRINCE EDWARD ISLAND. 2544
0035-8959 See PROCEEDINGS OF THE ROYAL INSTITUTION OF GREAT BRITAIN. 5141
0035-8967 See TRANSACTIONS OF THE ROYAL INSTITUTION OF NAVAL ARCHITECTS. 310
0035-8975 See PROCEEDINGS OF THE ROYAL IRISH ACADEMY. SECTION A. MATHEMATICAL AND PHYSICAL SCIENCES. 3528
0035-8983 See PROCEEDINGS OF THE ROYAL IRISH ACADEMY. SECTION B. BIOLOGICAL, GEOLOGICAL AND CHEMICAL SCIENCE. 470

0035-8991 See PROCEEDINGS OF THE ROYAL IRISH ACADEMY. SECTION C. ARCHAEOLOGY, CELTIC STUDIES, HISTORY, LINGUISTICS AND LITERATURE. 279
0035-9009 See QUARTERLY JOURNAL OF THE ROYAL METEOROLOGICAL SOCIETY. 1434
0035-9017 See PROCEEDINGS - ROYAL MICROSCOPICAL SOCIETY. 573
0035-9033 See JOURNAL OF THE ROYAL NAVAL MEDICAL SERVICE. 3599
0035-905X See ROYAL NEIGHBOR, THE. 5236
0035-9084 See ROYAL SERVICE. 5067
0035-9106 See JOURNAL OF THE ROYAL SOCIETY OF ANTIQUARIES OF IRELAND, THE. 2695
0035-9122 See TRANSACTIONS OF THE ROYAL SOCIETY OF CANADA. 2855
0035-9149 See NOTES AND RECORDS OF THE ROYAL SOCIETY OF LONDON. 5134
0035-9173 See JOURNAL AND PROCEEDINGS OF THE ROYAL SOCIETY OF NEW SOUTH WALES. 5118
0035-919X See TRANSACTIONS OF THE ROYAL SOCIETY OF SOUTH AFRICA. 5167
0035-9203 See TRANSACTIONS OF THE ROYAL SOCIETY OF TROPICAL MEDICINE AND HYGIENE. 3987
0035-9211 See PROCEEDINGS OF THE ROYAL SOCIETY OF VICTORIA. 5141
0035-922X See JOURNAL OF THE ROYAL SOCIETY OF WESTERN AUSTRALIA. 4166
0035-9238 See JOURNAL OF THE ROYAL STATISTICAL SOCIETY. SERIES A (GENERAL). 5330
0035-9246 See JOURNAL OF THE ROYAL STATISTICAL SOCIETY. SERIES B (METHODOLOGICAL). 5330
0035-9254 See APPLIED STATISTICS. 5322
0035-9351 See ROZHLEDY V CHIRURGII. 3974
0035-9475 See RUBBER CHEMISTRY AND TECHNOLOGY. 5077
0035-9483 See RUBBER DEVELOPMENTS. 5077
0035-9491 See RUBBER INDIA. 5077
0035-9513 See RUBBER NEWS. 5077
0035-9548 See RUBBER STATISTICAL BULLETIN. 5078
0035-9564 See RUBBER TRENDS. 5078
0035-9572 See RUBBER WORLD. 5078
0035-9602 See TUCH LITERACKI (KRAKOW, POLAND). 3448
0035-9610 See RUCH MUZYCZNY (WARSAW, POLAND). 4151
0035-9629 See RUCH PRAWNICZY, EKONOMICZNY I SOCJOLOGICZNY. 5217
0035-9645 See RUDARSKO-METALURSKI ZBORNIK. 4018
0035-9696 See RUDY I METALE NIEZELAZNE. 1444
0035-970X See RUE, LA. 3352
0035-9742 See RUGBY LEAGUE WEEK. 4915
0035-9777 See RUGBY WORLD. 4915
0035-9874 See RUNDFUNK UND FERNSEHEN. 1138
0035-9890 See RUNDFUNKTECHNISCHE MITTEILUNGEN. 1138
0035-998X See RUPERTO CAROLA. 1846
0036-0007 See RURAL COUNCILLOR, THE. 131
0036-0058 See RURAL INDIA. 5256
0036-0066 See KENTUCKY LIVING. 2536
0036-0074 See RURAL LIFE. 5256
0036-0112 See RURAL SOCIOLOGY. 5257
0036-0163 See RUSSELL. 4360
0036-0171 See RUSSELL'S OFFICIAL NATIONAL MOTOR COACH GUIDE. 5392
0036-0171 See RUSSELL'S OFFICIAL NATIONAL MOTOR COACH GUIDE. 5392
0036-021X See RUSSIAN CHEMICAL REVIEWS. 992
0036-0236 See RUSSIAN JOURNAL OF INORGANIC CHEMISTRY. 1037
0036-0244 See RUSSIAN JOURNAL OF PHYSICAL CHEMISTRY. 1057

0036-0252 See RUSSIAN LANGUAGE JOURNAL. 3318
0036-0279 See RUSSIAN MATHEMATICAL SURVEYS. 3532
0036-0295 See RUSSIAN METALLURGY. 4018
0036-0317 See RUSSIAN ORTHODOX JOURNAL, THE. 5040
0036-0325 See RUSSIAN PHARMACOLOGY AND TOXICOLOGY. 4328
0036-0341 See RUSSIAN REVIEW (STANFORD), THE. 2708
0036-0368 See RUSSKAIA RECH. 3318
0036-0384 See RUSSKIJ JAZYK ZA RUBEZOM. 3319
0036-0406 See RUSSKII GOLOS (NEW YORK, N.Y.). 2272
0036-0465 See RUTGERS LAW REVIEW. 3045
0036-0473 See JOURNAL OF THE RUTGERS UNIVERSITY LIBRARY, THE. 3221
0036-052X See RYNKI ZAGRANICZNE. 708
0036-0678 See TRANSACTIONS OF THE SAEST. 1035
0036-0759 See SOUTH AFRICAN HAIRDRESSING AND BEAUTY CULTURE. 405
0036-0767 See SAIPA. 4684
0036-0775 See SAIS REVIEW (JOHNS HOPKINS UNIVERSITY. SCHOOL OF ADVANCED INTERNATIONAL STUDIES: 1981). 4534
0036-0821 See S.A.M.P.E. QUARTERLY. 1995
0036-0848 See SOUTH AFRICAN MACHINE TOOL REVIEW. 2129
0036-0864 See SOUTH AFRICAN NATIONAL BIBLIOGRAPHY. 425
0036-102X See SB. SPORTSTATTENBAU UND BADERANLAGEN. 627
0036-1275 See NEWSLETTER AND PROCEEDINGS OF THE S.E.H.A. 276
0036-1313 See PROCEEDINGS, OF THE SOCIETY FOR EXPERIMENTAL STRESS ANALYSIS. 2126
0036-1321 See BULLETIN DES SCHWEIZERISCHEN ELEKTROTECHNISCHEN VEREINS (ZURICH). 2037
0036-1364 See BULLETIN OF THE SCIENCE FICTION WRITERS OF AMERICA. 3370
0036-1399 See SIAM JOURNAL ON APPLIED MATHEMATICS. 3534
0036-1410 See SIAM JOURNAL ON MATHEMATICAL ANALYSIS. 3534
0036-1429 See SIAM JOURNAL ON NUMERICAL ANALYSIS. 3535
0036-1445 See SIAM REVIEW. 3535
0036-1488 See SIDA, CONTRIBUTIONS TO BOTANY. 527
0036-1607 See BULLETIN - SPECIAL LIBRARIES ASSOCIATION. GEOGRAPHY AND MAP DIVISION. 2557
0036-1682 See SMPTE JOURNAL (1976). 4078
0036-181X See S.P.A. JOURNAL. 2787
0036-1917 See SSRS NEWSLETTER. 5160
0036-2050 See ZPRAVY - SVU. 2857
0036-2115 See SAARBRUCKER HEFTE. 2708
0036-2131 See SABAH SOCIETY JOURNAL. 2663
0036-214X See SABBATH RECORDER, THE. 5067
0036-2158 See SABENA REVUE. 34
0036-2190 See SACRA DOCTRINA. 4995
0036-2204 See SACRAMENTO BUSINESS. 708
0036-2212 See SACRAMENTO OBSERVER, THE. 5639
0036-2247 See SACRAMENTO VALLEY UNION LABOR BULLETIN. 1709
0036-2255 See SACRED MUSIC. 5035
0036-2263 See SACRED ORGAN JOURNAL, THE. 4151
0036-2271 See SADDLE AND BRIDLE. 2802
0036-2344 See SAUGETIERKUNDLICHE MITTEILUNGEN. 472
0036-2670 See SAHKO TELE. 2080
0036-2700 See SAIL. 595
0036-2719 See SAILING. 596
0036-2735 See SAILPLANE & GLIDING. 34

0036-2743 See SAINIK SAMACHAR. 4056
0036-276X See ST. ANTHONY MESSENGER. 5036
0036-2778 See SAINT BARTHOLOMEW'S HOSPITAL JOURNAL. 3638
0036-2905 See ST. JOHN'S LAW REVIEW. 3058
0036-293X See ST. LOUIS COMMERCE. 851
0036-2948 See ST. LOUIS COUNTIAN, THE. 5704
0036-2956 See QUARTERLY - ST. LOUIS GENEALOGICAL SOCIETY. 2469
0036-2972 See ST. LOUIS JOURNALISM REVIEW, THE. 2924
0036-3014 See ST. LOUIS UNIVERSITY RESEARCH JOURNAL. 2855
0036-3022 See ST. LOUIS REVIEW. 5036
0036-3030 See SAINT LOUIS UNIVERSITY LAW JOURNAL. 3045
0036-3065 See GLAS UND RAHMEN. 2589
0036-309X See SEWANEE THEOLOGICAL REVIEW. 4996
0036-3103 See ST. MARK'S REVIEW. 4999
0036-3227 See ST. VLADIMIR'S THEOLOGICAL QUARTERLY. 5040
0036-3251 See SAINTS HERALD. 5067
0036-3375 See SALAMANDRA (FRANKFURT-AM-MAIN). 5597
0036-3421 See SALES MANAGER'S BULLETIN. 885
0036-3480 See SALESIAN. 4995
0036-3502 See SALESIANUM. 5036
0036-3529 See SALMAGUNDI (SARATOGA SPRINGS). 2853
0036-3537 See SALMANTICENSIS. 5036
0036-3545 See SALMON AND TROUT MAGAZINE, THE. 2312
0036-3618 See SALT WATER SPORTSMAN. 4916
0036-3650 See SALUT LES COPAINS. 4495
0036-3774 See SAMFERDSEL TRANSPORT. 5392
0036-3847 See SAMOSTIINA UKRAINA. 2272
0036-3898 See SAMPLE CASE, THE. 709
0036-3928 See SAMTIDEN. 2522
0036-4037 See SAN DIEGO LAW REVIEW, THE. 3046
0036-4045 See SAN DIEGO MAGAZINE (1949). 2544
0036-407X See SAN DIEGO SOUND POST, THE. 4151
0036-4096 See SAN FRANCISCO BAY GUARDIAN, THE. 2545
0036-410X See SAN FRANCISCO BUSINESS. 709
0036-4185 See SAN JOSE POST-RECORD, THE. 5640
0036-4304 See SANEFREEZE NEWS / CAMPAIGN FOR GLOBAL SECURITY. 4056
0036-4339 See SANGEET NATAK. 4152
0036-4401 See SANITAR UND HEIZUNGTECHNIK. 2608
0036-4436 See SANITARY MAINTENANCE. 2242
0036-455X See SANTA GERTRUDIS JOURNAL, THE. 221
0036-4665 See REVISTA DO INSTITUTO DE MEDICINA TROPICAL DE SAO PAULO. 3986
0036-4681 See SAPERE. 5149
0036-469X See SAPEUR-POMPIER, LE. 2292
0036-4703 See SAPIENTIA. 4360
0036-4711 See SAPIENZA. 4360
0036-472X See SAPPORO IGAKU ZASSHI. 3638
0036-4827 See SARSIA. 557
0036-4835 See SARVODAYA. 4832
0036-4843 See SASH. 4512
0036-4886 See SASKATCHEWAN BULLETIN, THE. 1781
0036-4894 See SASKATCHEWAN GAZETTE. 4685
0036-4894 See SASKATCHEWAN GAZETTE, THE. 4685
0036-4908 See SASKATCHEWAN HISTORY. 2759
0036-4916 See SASKATCHEWAN LAW REVIEW. 3046
0036-4975 See SATURDAY NIGHT. 2545

0036-5041 See SAUVEGARDE DE L'ENFANCE. 5307
0036-505X See SAUVEGARDE DES CHANTIERS. 627
0036-5068 See SAVACOU. 364
0036-5106 See SAVING HEALTH. 4995
0036-519X See SAVREMENIK. 3433
0036-5246 See SBORNIK ARCHIVNICH PRACI. 2483
0036-5270 See SBORNIK GEOLOGICKYCH VED. ANTROPOZOIKUM. 1396
0036-5289 See SBORNIK GEOLOGICKYCH VED. HYDROGEOLOGIE INZENYRSKA GEOLOGIE. 1417
0036-5297 See SBORNIK GEOLOGICKYCH VED. PALEONTOLOGIE. 4230
0036-5300 See SBORNIK GEOLOGICKYCH VED. TECHNOLOGIE, GEOCHEMIE. 1444
0036-5327 See SBORNIK LEKARSKY. 3638
0036-5335 See SBORNIK NARODNIHO MUZEA V PRAZE. RADA A, HISTORIE. 2628
0036-5351 See SBORNIK NARODNIHO MUZEA V PRAZE. RADA C, LITERARNI HISTORIE. 3433
0036-5408 See SCABBARD AND BLADE JOURNAL. 4056
0036-5424 See SCALE MODELER. 34
0036-5505 See SCANDINAVIAN JOURNAL OF REHABILITATION MEDICINE. 3639
0036-5513 See SCANDINAVIAN JOURNAL OF CLINICAL & LABORATORY INVESTIGATION. 586
0036-5521 See SCANDINAVIAN JOURNAL OF GASTROENTEROLOGY. 3747
0036-5548 See SCANDINAVIAN JOURNAL OF INFECTIOUS DISEASES. 3716
0036-5564 See SCANDINAVIAN JOURNAL OF PSYCHOLOGY. 4617
0036-5580 See SCANDINAVIAN JOURNAL OF THORACIC AND CARDIOVASCULAR SURGERY. 3974
0036-5599 See SCANDINAVIAN JOURNAL OF UROLOGY AND NEPHROLOGY. 3993
0036-5602 See SCANDINAVIAN PUBLIC LIBRARY QUARTERLY. 3247
0036-5637 See SCANDINAVIAN STUDIES: PUBLICATION OF THE SOCIETY FOR THE ADVANCEMENT OF SCANDINAVIAN STUDY. 3433
0036-5653 See SCANDINAVICA. 3433
0036-5742 See SCENA ILLUSTRATA. 2492
0036-5955 See SCHEDARIO. 4819
0036-6056 See SCHIFFBAUFORSCHUNG. 4183
0036-6145 See SCHLERN, DER. 2708
0036-6153 See SCHLESIEN. 2708
0036-6250 See SCHOFFE, DER. 3046
0036-6277 See SCHOENER WOHNEN. 2903
0036-634X See SCHOLARLY PUBLISHING. 4819
0036-6382 See SCHOLASTIC COACH. 4917
0036-6412 See SCHOLASTIC SCOPE. 1094
0036-6439 See SCHOOL ADMINISTRATOR (WASHINGTON). 1870
0036-6447 See SCHOOL AND COMMUNITY (COLUMBIA). 1782
0036-6463 See SCHOOL ARTS. 364
0036-6501 See SCHOOL BUS FLEET. 5392
0036-651X See SCHOOL BUSINESS AFFAIRS. 1871
0036-6536 See SCHOOL COUNSELOR, THE. 1885
0036-6595 See SCHOOL LIBRARIAN, THE. 3247
0036-6668 See SCHOOL MUSIC NEWS, THE. 4152
0036-679X See SCHOOL SCIENCE. 5149
0036-6803 See SCHOOL SCIENCE AND MATHEMATICS. 5149
0036-6811 See SCHOOL SCIENCE REVIEW. 5149
0036-6854 See SCHOOL TRUSTEE (REGINA). 1872
0036-6978 See NTM. 5135
0036-6986 See SCHRIFTTUM DER AGRARWIRTSCHAFT, DAS. 132
0036-7176 See SCHWEINEZUCHT UND SCHWEINEMAST. 132

0036-7184 See SCHWEISSEN UND SCHNEIDEN. 4027
0036-7230 See SCHWEIZ; LA SUISSE; LA SVIZZERA; SWITZERLAND, DIE. 5490
0036-7257 See SCHWEIZER ALUMINIUM RUNDSCHAU. 4018
0036-7281 See SCHWEIZER ARCHIV FUER TIERHEILKUNDE. 5521
0036-732X See SCHWEIZER BUCH. 424
0036-7362 See SCHWEIZER ILLUSTRIERTE ZEITUNG. 2522
0036-7400 See SCHWEIZER MONATSHEFTE. 2522
0036-7508 See SCHWEIZERISCHE APOTHEKER-ZEITUNG. GIORNALE SVIZZERO DI FARMACIA. 4329
0036-7540 See SCHWEIZERISCHE BIENEN-ZEITUNG. 5597
0036-7575 See MITTEILUNGEN DER SCHWEIZERISCHEN ENTOMOLOGISCHEN GESELLSCHAFT. 5612
0036-763X See SCHWEIZERISCHE LANDWIRTSCHAFTLICHE FORSCHUNG. 132
0036-7672 See SCHWEIZERISCHE MEDIZINISCHE WOCHENSCHRIFT. 3639
0036-7699 See SCHWEIZERISCHE MINERALOGISCHE UND PETROGRAPHISCHE MITTEILUNGEN. 1444
0036-777X See SVA BULLETIN : OFFIZIELLES ORGAN DER SVA UND DESOAF. 4451
0036-7834 See SCHWEIZERISCHE ZEITSCHRIFT FUER GESCHICHTE. 2708
0036-7842 See SCHWEIZERISCHE ZEITSCHRIFT FUER HYDROLOGIE. 1417
0036-7885 See SCHWEIZERISCHE ZEITSCHRIFT FUER SPORTMEDIZIN. 3955
0036-7893 See SCHWEIZERISCHE ZEITSCHRIFT FUER STRAFRECHT. 3176
0036-794X See SCHWEIZERISCHES ARCHIV FUER VOLKSKUNDE. 2324
0036-8032 See SCHWENKFELDIAN, THE. 5067
0036-8059 See SCI-TECH NEWS. 3248
0036-8075 See SCIENCE (WASHINGTON, D.C.). 5154
0036-8091 See PHYSICS ABSTRACTS. 4427
0036-8105 See ELECTRICAL & ELECTRONICS ABSTRACTS. 2003
0036-8113 See COMPUTER & CONTROL ABSTRACTS. 1208
0036-8121 See SCIENCE ACTIVITIES. 5150
0036-8148 See SCIENCE AND CHILDREN. 1904
0036-8156 See SCIENCE & CULTURE. 5150
0036-8164 See SCIENCE & ENGINEERING. 5150
0036-8172 See DOSHISHA DAIGAKU RIKOGAKU KENKYU HOKOKU. 5102
0036-8237 See SCIENCE AND SOCIETY (NEW YORK. 1936). 5218
0036-827X See SCIENCE CITATION INDEX (PRINT ED.). 5176
0036-827X See SCIENCE CITATION INDEX. GUIDE AND LISTS OF SOURCE PUBLICATIONS. 5151
0036-8288 See SCIS NEWSLETTER. 5156
0036-8326 See SCIENCE EDUCATION (SALEM, MASS.). 5151
0036-8369 See SCIENCE ET VIE. MICROFORM. 5151
0036-8369 See SCIENCE ET VIE. 5151
0036-8423 See SCIENCE NEWS (WASHINGTON). 5152
0036-8458 See SCIENCE OF MIND. 4360
0036-8504 See SCIENCE PROGRESS (1916). 5152
0036-8512 See SCIENCE REPORTER. 5153
0036-8555 See SCIENCE TEACHER (WASHINGTON, D.C.), THE. 5153
0036-8598 See SCIENCE TOOLS. 5153
0036-8601 See SCIENCE WORLD. 5154
0036-861X See SCIENCES (NEW YORK), THE. 5154
0036-8636 See SCIENCES ET AVENIR. 5154
0036-8695 See SCIENTIA ELECTRICA. 2080

ISSN Index

0036-8709 See SCIENTIA PHARMACEUTICA. 4329

0036-8717 See SCIENTIAE. 1639

0036-8733 See SCIENTIFIC AMERICAN. 5155

0036-8741 See SCIENTIFIC AND TECHNICAL AEROSPACE REPORTS. 35

0036-8768 See SCIENTIFIC, ENGINEERING, TECHNICAL MANPOWER COMMENTS. 5155

0036-8792 See INDUSTRIAL LUBRICATION AND TRIBOLOGY. 3481

0036-8857 See SCIENTIFIC WORLD. 5156

0036-908X See SCOTS LAW TIMES; NOTES OF RECENT DECISIONS, THE. 3046

0036-908X See SCOTS LAW TIMES; LYON COURT REPORTS, THE. 3046

0036-908X See SCOTS LAW TIMES; SHERIFF COURT REPORTS, THE. 3047

0036-908X See SCOTS LAW TIMES, THE. 3046

0036-908X See SCOTS LAW TIMES; SCOTTISH LAND COURT REPORTS, THE. 3047

0036-908X See SCOTS LAW TIMES; THE LANDS TRIBUNAL FOR SCOTLAND REPORTS, THE. 3047

0036-908X See SCOTS LAW TIMES; REPORTS, THE. 3047

0036-911X See SCOTTISH ART REVIEW. 364

0036-9136 See SCOTTISH BAPTIST MAGAZINE. 5067

0036-9144 See SCOTTISH BIRDS. 5620

0036-9209 See SCOTTISH FIELD (GLASGOW). 2709

0036-9217 See SCOTTISH FORESTRY. 2395

0036-9225 See SCOTTISH GEOGRAPHICAL MAGAZINE. 2576

0036-9241 See SCOTTISH HISTORICAL REVIEW, THE. 2709

0036-9276 See SCOTTISH JOURNAL OF GEOLOGY. 1396

0036-9292 See SCOTTISH JOURNAL OF POLITICAL ECONOMY. 1595

0036-9306 See SCOTTISH JOURNAL OF THEOLOGY. 4995

0036-9314 See SCOTTISH LAW GAZETTE, THE. 3047

0036-9322 See SCOTTISH LICENSED TRADE NEWS. 851

0036-9330 See SCOTTISH MEDICAL JOURNAL. 3639

0036-9411 See SCOTTISH STUDIES (EDINBURGH). 3434

0036-9500 See SCOUTING (NORTH BRUNSWICK). 5236

0036-9543 See SCREEN. 4077

0036-956X See SCREEN ACTOR. 4077

0036-973X See SCRIPTA MERCATURAE. 1583

0036-9764 See SCRIPTA THEOLOGICA. 4996

0036-9772 See SCRIPTORIUM. 3435

0036-9780 See SCRIPTURE BULLETIN. 5019

0036-9810 See SCUOLA CATTOLICA, LA. 5036

0036-9853 See SCUOLA E CITTA. 1783

0036-9861 See SCUOLA E DIDATTICA. 1872

0036-9888 See SCUOLA ITALIANA MODERNA. 1904

0036-9977 See SEA BREEZES. 5455

0037-007X See SEAFARER (LONDON). 4183

0037-010X See SEAFOOD EXPORT JOURNAL. 2313

0037-0142 See SEAMAN, THE. 1710

0037-0150 See SEAPORTS AND THE SHIPPING WORLD. 5455

0037-0193 See SEARCH AND SEIZURE BULLETIN. 3176

0037-0290 See SEARCH MAGAZINE (AMHERST). 35

0037-0479 See SPECTATOR (SEATTLE), THE. 1095

0037-0487 See SEAWAY REVIEW. 5456

0037-0495 See SETCHAKU. 1030

0037-0517 See SECOLUL 20. 3352

0037-0576 See SECOND LINE, THE. 4152

0037-0622 See SECRETARY, THE. 710

0037-0622 See SECRETARY, THE. 4209

0037-0649 See SECRETS (NEW YORK, N.Y.). 2545

0037-0665 See SECURITIES REGULATION & LAW REPORT. 3088

0037-0738 See SEDIMENTARY GEOLOGY. 1396

0037-0746 See SEDIMENTOLOGY. 1410

0037-0789 See SEED TRADE NEWS. 133

0037-0797 See SEED WORLD. 186

0037-0819 See SEEING EYE GUIDE. 4393

0037-0894 See SEFARAD. 5052

0037-1017 See SEIKAGAKU. 493

0037-105X See SEISAN KENKYU. 5156

0037-1106 See BULLETIN OF THE SEISMOLOGICAL SOCIETY OF AMERICA. 1403

0037-1114 See JISIN. 1407

0037-1122 See SEIVA. 133

0037-119X See SELECCIONES DE TEOLOGIA. 4996

0037-1343 See SELECTED RAND ABSTRACTS. 424

0037-1351 See SELECTED REFERENCES - INDUSTRIAL RELATIONS SECTION, PRINCETON UNIVERSITY. 1538

0037-1378 See SELECTION DU READER'S DIGEST (EDITION CANADIENNE). 2492

0037-1386 See SELECTION DU READER'S DIGEST PARIS. 2522

0037-1459 See SELEKTSIIA I SEMENOVODSTVO. 527

0037-1467 See SELENIUM AND TELLURIUM ABSTRACTS. 1037

0037-1483 See SELEZIONE DAL READER'S DIGEST. 2522

0037-1521 See SELEZIONE VETERINARIA. 5521

0037-1564 See SELF-REALIZATION. 4360

0037-1688 See SELSKOKHOZIAISTVENNAIA LITERATURA SSSR. 133

0037-1718 See SELSKOSTOPANSKA TEKHNIKA. 161

0037-1777 See SEMAINE DES HOPITAUX. 3792

0037-1823 See SEMANA MEDICA DE MEXICO. 3640

0037-184X See SEMANA VITIVINICOLA, LE. 2370

0037-1890 See SEMENTI ELETTE. 186

0037-1912 See SEMIGROUP FORUM. 3533

0037-1939 See SEMINAR (TORONTO). 3320

0037-1947 See SEMINAR. 5156

0037-1963 See SEMINARS IN HEMATOLOGY. 3774

0037-1998 See SEMIOTICA. 3320

0037-2072 See SENI SEIHIN SHOHI KAGAKU. 5355

0037-2099 See SENALES. 424

0037-2102 See SENCKENBERGIANA BIOLOGICA. 4172

0037-2110 See SENCKENBERGIANA LETHAEA. 4230

0037-2145 See SENECA REVIEW, THE. 3435

0037-2234 See SENIOR NEWS. 5181

0037-2285 See CONGENITAL ANOMALIES. 543

0037-2307 See SENTINEL (POINTE CLAIRE). 5067

0037-2315 See SENTINEL (OTTAWA. 1973). 4056

0037-2331 See SENTINEL (CHICAGO, ILL.). 5662

0037-2374 See SEPIA (FORT WORTH, TEX.). 2760

0037-2412 See SEQUENCES (MONTREAL). 4077

0037-2420 See SEQUOIA (STANFORD, CALIF.). 3435

0037-2455 See NIPPON SANSHI-GAKU ZASSHI. 5593

0037-2498 See SERPE. 3435

0037-2501 See SERRA D'OR. 3352

0037-2579 See REVUE TECHNIQUE DIESEL. 5424

0037-2633 See SERVICE SOCIALE (QUEBEC). 5307

0037-2641 See SERVICE SOCIAL DANS LE MONDE. 5307

0037-2773 See SERVIZIO DELLA PAROLA. 4996

0037-301X See SEVENTEEN. 1069

0037-3028 See SEVENTEENTH CENTURY NEWS. 3435

0037-3044 See SEWANEE NEWS, THE. 1095

0037-3052 See SEWANEE REVIEW, THE. 3352

0037-3214 See SHAKESPEARE NEWSLETTER, THE. 3352

0037-3222 See SHAKESPEARE QUARTERLY. 3435

0037-3257 See SHALE SHAKER. 1397

0037-329X See SHANTIH. 3436

0037-3338 See SHAVER NEWS. 221

0037-3346 See SHAVIAN (LONDON). 3436

0037-3400 See SHEEP BREEDER AND SHEEPMAN MAGAZINE. 221

0037-3435 See SHEET METAL INDUSTRIES. 4019

0037-3451 See SHEET METAL WORKERS JOURNAL. 4019

0037-3583 See SHENANDOAH. 3436

0037-3621 See SHERLOCK HOLMES JOURNAL, THE. 3436

0037-3656 See SHEVILEY HA-HINNUKH. 5052

0037-3680 See TRANSACTIONS OF THE SHIKOKU ENTOMOLOGICAL SOCIETY. 5598

0037-3699 See SHIKOKU IGAKU ZASSHI. 3641

0037-3702 See SHIKOKU NOGYO SHIKENJO HOKOKU. 134

0037-3710 See SHIKA GAKUHO. 1335

0037-377X See SHINGLE, THE. 3055

0037-3818 See JOURNAL OF THE FACULTY OF ENGINEERING. SHINSHU UNIVERSITY. 1983

0037-3826 See SHINSHU IGAKU ZASSHI. 3641

0037-3826 See SHINSHU MEDICAL JOURNAL. 3641

0037-3834 See SHIP & BOAT INTERNATIONAL. 5456

0037-3893 See SHIPPING DIGEST. 5456

0037-3931 See SHIPPING WORLD & SHIPBUILDER. 5456

0037-394X See SHIPS MONTHLY. 4183

0037-4091 See SHOKUBUTSU BOEKI. 134

0037-4148 See SHOOTING INDUSTRY, THE. 4917

0037-4210 See DIRECTORY OF SHOPPING CENTERS IN THE UNITED STATES. 954

0037-4237 See SHORE AND BEACH. 2205

0037-4261 See SHORT WAVE MAGAZINE. 1139

0037-427X See SHORTHORN NEWS. 221

0037-4326 See SHOW-ME LIBRARIES. 3249

0037-4342 See SHOWA IGAKKAI ZASSHI. 3641

0037-4377 See SHOYAKUGAKU ZASSHI. 4329

0037-4466 See SIBERIAN MATHEMATICAL JOURNAL. 3535

0037-4474 See SIBIRSKIJ MATEMATICESKIH ZURNAL. 3535

0037-4504 See SICHER IST SICHER. 2870

0037-458X See SICULORUM GYMNASIUM. 2854

0037-4806 See SIGHT AND SOUND (LONDON). 4078

0037-4814 See SIGHT & SOUND MARKETING. 936

0037-4830 See SIGHTLINES (NEW YORK, N.Y.). 4078

0037-4911 See SIGNAL (MONTREAL). 4803

0037-4938 See SIGNAL (1950). 1121

0037-4954 See SIGNAL (AMBERLEY). 3437

0037-4997 See SIGNAL UND DRAHT. 5436

0037-5020 See SIGNALMAN'S JOURNAL, THE. 5436

0037-5047 See SIGNS OF THE TIMES (MOUNTAIN VIEW). 5067

0037-5128 See SIKH REVIEW, THE. 4997

0037-5187 See SILENT ADVOCATE, THE. 4393

0037-5209 See SILENT PICTURE, THE. 4078

0037-5225 See SILICATES INDUSTRIELS. 2594

0037-5233 See SILIKATTECHNIK. 1030

0037-5284 See SILLIMAN JOURNAL. 2854

0037-5349 See SILVAE GENETICA. 528

0037-5403 See SIMIENTE. 134

0037-5411 See SIMIOLUS. 364

0037-5454 See SIMON STEVIN. 3535

0037-5497 *See* SIMULATION (SAN DIEGO, CALIF.). **1283**
0037-5624 *See* SING OUT. **4153**
0037-5659 *See* ECONOMIC BULLETIN - SINGAPORE INTERNATIONAL CHAMBER OF COMMERCE. **819**
0037-5675 *See* SINGAPORE MEDICAL JOURNAL. **3641**
0037-5721 *See* SINGENDE KIRCHE. **4153**
0037-5748 *See* SINGLE PARENT, THE. **2286**
0037-5756 *See* SINN UND FORM. **2522**
0037-5837 *See* SIPAPU. **3352**
0037-5888 *See* SISTEMATICA. **4361**
0037-590X *See* SISTERS TODAY. **5036**
0037-5969 *See* SEVENTIES, THE. **3471**
0037-6132 *See* SKATING. **4918**
0037-6140 *See* SKEET SHOOTING REVIEW. **4918**
0037-6159 *See* SKI (NEW YORK, N.Y.). **4918**
0037-6175 *See* SKI AREA MANAGEMENT. **4918**
0037-6191 *See* SKI BUSINESS. **4918**
0037-6213 *See* SKI RACING. **4918**
0037-6264 *See* SKIING (NEW YORK, N.Y.). **4918**
0037-6299 *See* SKIING TRADE NEWS. **4918**
0037-6329 *See* SKILLINGS' MINING REVIEW. **2151**
0037-6337 *See* SKIN & ALLERGY NEWS. **3722**
0037-6345 *See* SKIN DIVER. **4918**
0037-637X *See* SKLAR A KERAMIK. **2594**
0037-6477 *See* BARN OCH KULTUR. **3193**
0037-6493 See PSYKOLOGISK PDAGOGISK RADGIVNING. **4614**
0037-6604 *See* SKY AND TELESCOPE. **399**
0037-6639 *See* SKYLINE (PITTSBURGH, PA.). **35**
0037-668X *See* SLABOPROUDY OBZOR. **5158**
0037-6736 *See* SLAVIA. **3321**
0037-6744 *See* SLAVIA ORIENTALIS. **3321**
0037-6752 *See* SLAVIC AND EAST EUROPEAN JOURNAL. **3321**
0037-6779 *See* SLAVIC REVIEW. **2854**
0037-6787 *See* SLAVICA SLOVACA. **3321**
0037-6795 *See* SLAVONIC AND EAST EUROPEAN REVIEW, THE. **2629**
0037-6825 *See* SLEVARENSTVI. **4019**
0037-6833 *See* SLEZSKY SBORNIK. **5258**
0037-6868 *See* SLOBODA (CHICAGO, ILL.). **3353**
0037-6922 *See* SLOVANSKY PREHLED. **4496**
0037-6930 *See* BIOLOGICKE PRACE (V BRATISLAVA). **446**
0037-6949 *See* SLOVENSKA ARCHEOLOGIA. **282**
0037-6957 *See* SLOVENSKA DRZAVA. **4496**
0037-6973 *See* SLOVENSKA LITERATURA. **3437**
0037-6981 *See* SLOVENSKA REC. **3322**
0037-699X *See* SLOVENSKE DIVADLO. **5368**
0037-7023 *See* SLOVENSKY NARODOPIS. **245**
0037-7031 *See* SLOVO A SLOVESNOST. **3322**
0037-7198 *See* VOICE OF SMALL BUSINESS, THE. **718**
0037-7228 *See* SMALL PRESS REVIEW. **3353**
0037-7260 *See* SMALL WORLD (GUILFORD). **2907**
0037-7317 *See* SMITH COLLEGE STUDIES IN SOCIAL WORK. **5307**
0037-7333 *See* SMITHSONIAN. **4172**
0037-7406 *See* SNACK FOOD. **2358**
0037-7457 *See* SNIPS. **2608**
0037-7473 *See* SNOWY EGRET. **4172**
0037-749X *See* SPC. SOAP, PERFUMERY, AND COSMETICS. **405**
0037-7503 *See* SOARING. **35**
0037-7511 *See* SLASKI KWARTALNIK HISTORYCZNY SOBOTKA / WROCAWSKIE TOWARZYSTWO MIOSNIKOW HISTORII. **2629**
0037-7619 *See* SOCIALNYTT. **4803**
0037-7627 *See* SOCIAL ACTION (NEW DELHI). **5258**
0037-7651 *See* SOCIAL AND ECONOMIC STUDIES. **5219**
0037-766X *See* SOCIAL BIOLOGY. **551**

0037-7686 *See* SOCIAL COMPASS. **5219**
0037-7716 *See* SOCIAL DEFENCE. **3177**
0037-7724 *See* SOCIAL EDUCATION. **5219**
0037-7732 *See* SOCIAL FORCES. **5258**
0037-7767 *See* SOCIAL JUSTICE REVIEW. **5036**
0037-7783 *See* SOCIAL POLICY. **5259**
0037-7791 *See* SOCIAL PROBLEMS. **5220**
0037-7805 *See* CHURCH AND SOCIETY (NEW YORK). **4947**
0037-783X *See* SOCIAL RESEARCH. **5220**
0037-7872 *See* SOCIAL SCIENCE RECORD. **5221**
0037-7910 *See* SOCIAL SECURITY BULLETIN (WASHINGTON, D.C. : 1938). **5308**
0037-7961 *See* SOCIAL SERVICE REVIEW (CHICAGO), THE. **5309**
0037-7996 *See* SOCIAL STUDIES (PHILADELPHIA, PA. : 1953). **5222**
0037-8011 *See* SOCIAL SURVEY. **5259**
0037-802X *See* SOCIAL THEORY AND PRACTICE. **5222**
0037-8038 *See* SOCIAL WELFARE. **5309**
0037-8046 *See* SOCIAL WORK (NEW YORK). **5309**
0037-8054 *See* SOCIAL WORK STELLENBOSCH. **5310**
0037-8062 *See* SOCIAL WORK EDUCATION REPORTER. **5309**
0037-8070 *See* SOCIAL WORK TODAY. **5310**
0037-8089 *See* SOCIAL WORKER. TRAVAILLEUR SOCIAL. **5310**
0037-8127 *See* SOCIALISME (BRUXELLES). **4546**
0037-8259 *See* SOCIALIST STANDARD. **4547**
0037-8364 *See* ARCHIVOS - SOCIEDAD AMERICANA DE OFTALMOLOGIA Y OPTOMETRIA. **3872**
0037-8437 *See* ANALES DE LA SOCIEDAD CIENTIFICA ARGENTINA. **5082**
0037-847X *See* REVISTA DE LA SOCIEDAD CUBANA DE HISTORIA DE LA MEDICINA. **3635**
0037-8542 *See* REVISTA DE LA SOCIEDAD DE OBSTETRICIA Y GINECOLOGIA DE BUENOS AIRES. **3768**
0037-8577 *See* BOLETIN DE LA SOCIEDAD GEOGRAFICA DE COLOMBIA. **2556**
0037-8585 *See* BOLETIN DE LA SOCIEDAD GEOGRAFICA DE LIMA. **2556**
0037-8615 *See* BOLETIN DE LA SOCIEDAD MATEMATICA MEXICANA. **3497**
0037-8623 *See* BOLETIN DE LA SOCIEDAD QUIMICA DEL PERU. **962**
0037-8658 *See* BOLETIN DE LA SOCIEDAD VASCO-NAVARRA DE PEDIATRIA. **3901**
0037-8682 *See* REVISTA DA SOCIEDADE BRASILEIRA DE MEDICINA TROPICAL. **3986**
0037-8720 *See* MEMORIE DELLA SOCIETA ASTRONOMICA ITALIANA. **397**
0037-8739 *See* BOLLETTINO DELLA SOCIETA DI STUDI VALDESI. **4939**
0037-8747 *See* MEMORIE DELLA SOCIETA ENTOMOLOGICA ITALIANA. **5612**
0037-8755 *See* BOLLETTINO DELLA SOCIETA GEOGRAFICA ITALIANA. **2556**
0037-8763 *See* BOLLETTINO DELLA SOCIETA GEOGRAFICA ITALIANA. **2556**
0037-8763 *See* BOLLETTINO DELLA SOCIETA GEOLOGICA ITALIANA. **1368**
0037-8771 *See* BOLLETTINO DELLA SOCIETA ITALIANA DI BIOLOGIA SPERIMENTALE. **449**
0037-8798 *See* BOLLETTINO DELLA SOCIETA ITALIANA DI FARMACIA OSPEDALIERA. **4294**
0037-8844 *See* ATTI DELLA SOCIETA ITALIANA DI SCIENZE NATURALI E DEL MUSEO CIVICO DI STORIA NATURALE DI MILANO. **4162**
0037-8887 *See* ARCHIVUM HISTORICUM SOCIETATIS IESU. **5024**
0037-8895 *See* BULLETIN DE LA SOCIETE ARCHEOLOGIQUE, HISTORIQUE, LITTERAIRE & SCIENTIFIQUE DU GERS. **5193**
0037-8895 *See* BULLETIN DE LA SOCIETE ARCHEOLOGIQUE HISTORIQUE LITTERAIRE & SCIENTIFIQUE DU GERS. **263**
0037-8925 *See* BULLETIN DE LA SOCIETE BELGE D'ETUDES GEOGRAPHIQUES. **2556**

0037-8968 *See* BULLETIN DE LA SOCIETE CHIMIQUE DE FRANCE (PARIS, FRANCE : 1985). **963**
0037-8984 *See* BULLETINS ET MEMOIRES DE LA SOCIETE D'ANTHROPOLOGIE DE PARIS. **233**
0037-9018 *See* COMPTE RENDU DES SEANCES DE LA SOCIETE DE BIOGEOGRAPHIE. **2558**
0037-9026 *See* COMPTES RENDUS DES SEANCES DE LA SOCIETE DE BIOLOGIE ET DES SES FILIALES. **452**
0037-9050 *See* BULLETIN DE LA SOCIETE DE L'HISTOIRE DU PROTESTANTISME FRANCAIS (1981). **5057**
0037-9069 *See* BULLETIN DE LA SOCIETE DE LINGUISTIQUE DE PARIS. **3270**
0037-9093 *See* BULLETIN DE LA SOCIETE DE PHARMACIE DE BORDEAUX. **4294**
0037-9107 *See* BULLETIN DES TRAVAUX DE LA SOCIETE DE PHARMACIE DE LYON. **4294**
0037-914X *See* JOURNAL DE LA SOCIETE DE STATISTIQUE DE PARIS. **5329**
0037-9174 *See* JOURNAL DE LA SOCIETE DES AMERICANISTES. **271**
0037-9190 *See* BULLETIN DE LA SOCIETE DES ANTIQUAIRES DE L'OUEST ET DES MUSEES DE POITIERS. **4085**
0037-9204 *See* BULLETIN TRIMESTRIEL DE LA SOCIETE DES ANTIQUAIRES DE PICARDIE. **2681**
0037-9212 *See* REVUE FRANCAISE D'HISTOIRE DU LIVRE. **3430**
0037-9247 *See* BULLETIN DE LA SOCIETE DES SCIENCES MEDICALES DU GRAND-DUCHE DE LUXEMBOURG. **3559**
0037-9271 *See* ANNALES DE LA SOCIETE ENTOMOLOGIQUE DE FRANCE. **5575**
0037-928X *See* BULLETIN DE LA SOCIETE ENTOMOLOGIQUE DE FRANCE. **5606**
0037-9336 See JOURNAL DE MYCOLOGIE MEDICALE PARIS. **575**
0037-9344 *See* BULLETIN DE LA SOCIETE FRANCAISE DE NUMISMATIQUE. **2780**
0037-9352 *See* BULLETIN DE LA SOCIETE FRANCAISE DE PHILOSOPHIE. **4343**
0037-9360 *See* BULLETIN DE LA SOCIETE FRANCAISE DE PHYSIQUE. **4398**
0037-9387 *See* MEMOIRES DE LA SOCIETE GENEALOGIQUE CANADIENNE-FRANCAISE. **2460**
0037-9395 *See* ANNALES DE LA SOCIETE GEOLOGIQUE DE BELGIQUE. **1365**
0037-9409 *See* BULLETIN DE LA SOCIETE GEOLOGIQUE DE FRANCE. **1368**
0037-9417 *See* COMPTE RENDU SOMMAIRE DES SEANCES DE LA SOCIETE GEOLOGIQUE DE FRANCE. **1372**
0037-9441 *See* BULLETIN DE LA SOCIETE INDUSTRIELLE DE MULHOUSE. **5090**
0037-9468 *See* BULLETIN OFFICIEL DE LA SOCIETE INTERNATIONALE DE PSYCHO-PROPHYLAXIE OBSTETRICALE. **3758**
0037-9484 *See* BULLETIN DE LA SOCIETE MATHEMATIQUE DE FRANCE. **3497**
0037-9506 *See* BULLETIN DE LA SOCIETE PAUL CLAUDEL. **3369**
0037-9530 *See* BULLETIN. **2037**
0037-9565 *See* BULLETIN DE LA SOCIETE ROYALE DES SCIENCES DE LIEGE. **5090**
0037-9581 *See* BULLETIN DE LA SOCIETE SCIENTIFIQUE DE BRETAGNE. **5090**
0037-9603 *See* BULLETIN DE LA SOCIETE VAUDOISE DES SCIENCES NATURELLES. **4163**
0037-9611 *See* MEMOIRES DE LA SOCIETE VAUDOISE DES SCIENCES NATURELLES. **5128**
0037-962X *See* BULLETIN DE LA SOCIETE ZOOLOGIQUE DE FRANCE. **5579**
0037-9646 *See* BULLETIN DES SOCIETES CHIMIQUES BELGES. **963**
0037-9662 *See* SOCIETY AND CULTURE. **5259**
0037-9700 *See* JOURNAL OF THE SOCIETY FOR ARMY HISTORICAL RESEARCH. **4048**
0037-9727 *See* PROCEEDINGS OF THE SOCIETY FOR EXPERIMENTAL BIOLOGY AND MEDICINE. **3630**

0037-9743 See JOURNAL OF THE SOCIETY FOR ITALIC HANDWRITING, THE. 380

0037-9751 See JOURNAL OF THE SOCIETY FOR PSYCHICAL RESEARCH. 4242

0037-976X See MONOGRAPHS OF THE SOCIETY FOR RESEARCH IN CHILD DEVELOPMENT. 4604

0037-9794 See TRANSACTIONS - SOCIETY OF ACTUARIES. 2895

0037-9808 See JOURNAL OF THE SOCIETY OF ARCHITECTURAL HISTORIANS. 302

0037-9816 See JOURNAL OF THE SOCIETY OF ARCHIVISTS. 2482

0037-9832 See JOURNAL OF THE SOCIETY OF COSMETIC CHEMISTS. 1026

0037-9840 See JOURNAL OF THE SOCIETY OF DAIRY TECHNOLOGY. 196

0037-9859 See JOURNAL OF THE SOCIETY OF DYERS AND COLOURISTS. 1026

0037-9875 See SENI GAKKAI SHI. 5355

0037-9921 See JOURNAL OF THE SOCIETY OF LEATHER TECHNOLOGISTS AND CHEMISTS. 3184

0037-993X See SOCIETY OF MALAWI JOURNAL, THE. 2643

0037-9980 See YUKI GOSEI KAGAKU KYOKAISHI. 1049

0038-0024 See SRA JOURNAL. 5159

0038-0075 See SOCIETY PAGE. 2893

0038-0113 See SHAKAI KEIZAI SHIGAKU. 1583

0038-0121 See SOCIO-ECONOMIC PLANNING SCIENCES. 1521

0038-0156 See SOCIOLOGIA. 5260

0038-0164 See SOCIOLOGIA INTERNATIONALIS. 5260

0038-0199 See SOCIOLOGIA RURALIS. 5260

0038-0202 See SOCIOLOGICAL ABSTRACTS. 5267

0038-0210 See SOCIOLOGICAL ANALYSIS. 4998

0038-0229 See SOCIOLOGICAL BULLETIN. 5260

0038-0237 See SOCIOLOGICAL FOCUS (KENT, OHIO). 5260

0038-0245 See SOCIOLOGICAL INQUIRY. 5260

0038-0253 See SOCIOLOGICAL QUARTERLY. 5261

0038-0261 See SOCIOLOGICAL REVIEW, THE. 5261

0038-0288 See SOCIOLOGICKY CASOPIS. 5261

0038-0296 See SOCIOLOGIE DU TRAVAIL (PARIS). 1711

0038-030X See SOCIOLOGIE ET SOCIETES. 5262

0038-0318 See SOCIOLOGIJA. 5262

0038-0326 See SOCIOLOGIJA SELA. 5262

0038-0334 See SOCIOLOGISCHE GIDS. 5262

0038-0342 See SOCIOLOGISK FORSKNING. 5262

0038-0350 See SOCIOLOGISKE MEDDELELSER. 5262

0038-0377 See SOCIOLOGUS; ZEITSCHRIFT FUER EMPIRISCHE ETHNOSOZIOLOGIE UND ETHNOPSYCHOLOGIE. JOURNAL FOR EMPIRICAL ETHNO-SOCIOLOGY AND ETHNO-PSYCHOLOGY. 5262

0038-0385 See SOCIOLOGY (OXFORD). 5262

0038-0393 See SOCIOLOGY AND SOCIAL RESEARCH. 5262

0038-0407 See SOCIOLOGY OF EDUCATION. 1784

0038-0415 See SOCIOLOGY OF EDUCATION ABSTRACTS. 1797

0038-0482 See SODOBNOST. 2523

0038-0644 See SOFTWARE : PRACTICE & EXPERIENCE. 1291

0038-0652 See SOFTWARE WORLD. 1291

0038-0687 See SOIL AND HEALTH. 186

0038-0717 See SOIL BIOLOGY & BIOCHEMISTRY. 186

0038-0741 See SOIL MECHANICS AND FOUNDATION ENGINEERING. 2129

0038-075X See SOIL SCIENCE. 187

0038-0768 See SOIL SCIENCE AND PLANT NUTRITION (TOKYO). 187

0038-0792 See SOILS AND FERTILIZERS. 156

0038-0806 See SOILS AND FOUNDATIONS. 2031

0038-0814 See SOINS PARIS. 3869

0038-0830 See SOKUCHI GAKKAISHI. 2576

0038-0849 See SOL (NEW YORK), EL. 3322

0038-0903 See SOLANUS. 3250

0038-0911 See SOLAR-GEOPHYSICAL DATA. 1411

0038-092X See SOLAR ENERGY (PHOENIX, ARIZ.). 1957

0038-0938 See SOLAR PHYSICS. 400

0038-0946 See SOLAR SYSTEM RESEARCH. 400

0038-0989 See SOLDAT UND TECHNIK. 4057

0038-1039 See SOLIA. 4998

0038-1047 See SOLICITORS' JOURNAL (LONDON, ENGLAND : 1928). 3056

0015-4644 See FLUID ABSTRACTS. PROCESS ENGINEERING. 2004

0038-1098 See SOLID STATE COMMUNICATIONS. 4421

0038-1101 See SOLID-STATE ELECTRONICS. 2081

0038-111X See SOLID STATE TECHNOLOGY. 2081

0038-1128 See SOLID WASTE REPORT. 2243

0038-1152 See WBF IN ACTION. 1717

0038-1160 See SOLIDARITY (MANILA). 4513

0038-1217 See SOLS. 2031

0038-1365 See SONG HITS' HEARTBREAKERS. 4153

0038-1373 See SONGWRITER'S REVIEW. 4153

0038-1462 See SONS OF NORWAY VIKING, THE. 2273

0038-1497 See SOONER, THE. 1095

0038-1527 See SOPHIA. 4998

0038-156X See SORRISI E CANZONI TV. 2493

0038-1578 See SORUI. 528

0038-1586 See SOSEI TO KAKO : NIHON SOSEI KAKO GAKKAI SHI. 4460

0038-1640 See SOSIOLOGIA. 5262

0038-1683 See SOTSIOLOGICHESKI PROBLEMI. 5263

0038-173X See SOUDAGE ET TECHNIQUES CONNEXES. 4027

0038-1810 See SV. SOUND AND VIBRATION. 4453

0038-1845 See SOUND & COMMUNICATIONS. 1122

0038-1853 See SOUNDINGS (SANTA BARBARA). 3250

0038-1861 See SOUNDINGS (KNOXVILLE, TENN.). 4998

0038-187X See SOUNDS OF TRUTH AND TRADITION. 5036

0038-1969 See SOUTH AFRICAN ARCHAEOLOGICAL BULLETIN, THE. 282

0038-2019 See SOUTH AFRICAN BEE JOURNAL. 5597

0038-2167 See SOUTH AFRICAN FORESTRY JOURNAL. 2395

0038-2167 See SUID-AFRIKAANSE BOSBOUTYDSKRIF. 2396

0038-2221 See TRANSACTIONS - THE SOUTH AFRICAN INSTITUTE OF ELECTRICAL ENGINEERS. 2084

0038-223X See JOURNAL OF THE SOUTH AFRICAN INSTITUTE OF MINING & METALLURGY. 2142

0038-2280 See SOUTH AFRICAN JOURNAL OF ECONOMICS, THE. 1521

0038-2353 See SOUTH AFRICAN JOURNAL OF SCIENCE. 5158

0038-2361 See SOUTH AFRICAN JOURNAL OF SURGERY. 3975

0038-2388 See SOUTH AFRICAN LAW JOURNAL. 3056

0038-2418 See QUARTERLY BULLETIN OF THE SOUTH AFRICAN LIBRARY. 3243

0038-2442 See SOUTH AFRICAN MECHANICAL ENGINEER, THE. 2129

0038-2469 See SOUTH AFRICAN MEDICAL JOURNAL. 3642

0038-2493 See SOUTH AFRICAN MUSIC TEACHER. 4154

0038-2523 See SOUTH AFRICAN OUTLOOK. 4998

0038-254X See SOUTH AFRICAN PANORAMA. 4686

0038-2558 See SUID-AFRIKAANSE TYDSKRIF VIR APTEEKWESE. 4330

0038-2620 See QUARTERLY BULLETIN - SOUTH AFRICAN RESERVE BANK. 805

0038-2671 See SOUTH AFRICAN SHIPPING NEWS AND FISHING INDUSTRY REVIEW, THE. 5457

0038-271X See SOUTH AFRICAN STATISTICAL JOURNAL. 3542

0038-2728 See SOUTH AFRICAN SUGAR JOURNAL, THE. 187

0038-2752 See SOUTH AFRICAN TAX CASES, INCLUDING DECISIONS OF THE SUPREME COURT OF SOUTH AFRICA, THE HIGH COURT OF ZIMBABWE AND THE SPECIAL COURTS FOR HEARING INCOME TAX APPEALS. 3056

0038-2779 See SOUTH AFRICAN TREASURER, THE. 4748

0038-2841 See SOUTH ASIAN REVIEW. 2665

0038-285X See SOUTH ASIAN STUDIES (JAIPUR). 2665

0038-2876 See SOUTH ATLANTIC QUARTERLY, THE. 2854

0038-2965 See SOUTH AUSTRALIAN NATURALIST; THE JOURNAL OF THE FIELD NATURALISTS' SECTION OF THE ROYAL SOCIETY OF SOUTH AUSTRALIA. 4172

0038-2973 See SOUTH AUSTRALIAN ORNITHOLOGIST. 5620

0038-304X See SOUTH CAROLINA ECONOMIC INDICATORS. 1584

0038-3082 See SOUTH CAROLINA HISTORICAL MAGAZINE. 2761

0038-3104 See SOUTH CAROLINA LAW REVIEW. 3057

0038-3139 See JOURNAL OF THE SOUTH CAROLINA MEDICAL ASSOCIATION (1975). 3599

0038-3163 See SOUTH CAROLINA REVIEW, THE. 3353

0038-3198 See SOUTH CAROLINA WILDLIFE. 2205

0038-3201 See SOUTH CAROLINA YOUNG FARMER AND FUTURE FARMER MAGAZINE. 136

0038-3236 See SOUTH DAKOTA. 1521

0038-3252 See SOUTH DAKOTA BIRD NOTES. 5620

0038-3260 See SOUTH DAKOTA BUSINESS REVIEW. 4748

0038-3279 See SOUTH DAKOTA CONSERVATION DIGEST. 2205

0038-3295 See SOUTH DAKOTA FARM & HOME RESEARCH. 136

0038-3309 See SOUTH DAKOTA HIGH LINER. 2082

0038-3317 See SOUTH DAKOTA JOURNAL OF MEDICINE. 3642

0038-3325 See SOUTH DAKOTA LAW REVIEW. 3057

0038-3341 See SOUTH DAKOTA MUSICIAN. 4154

0038-335X See SOUTH DAKOTA NURSE, THE. 3869

0038-3368 See SOUTH DAKOTA REVIEW. 3438

0038-3473 See SOUTH INDIAN HORTICULTURE. 2431

0038-352X See SOUTH SHORE RECORD. 2546

0038-3600 See SOUTHEAST ASIA JOURNAL. 2508

0038-3619 See SOUTHEAST ASIAN JOURNAL OF TROPICAL MEDICINE AND PUBLIC HEALTH, THE. 4803

0038-366X See SOUTHEASTERN GEOGRAPHER. 2576

0038-3678 See SOUTHEASTERN GEOLOGY. 1397

0038-3686 See SOUTHEASTERN LIBRARIAN, THE. 3250

0038-3694 See SOUTHEASTERN PEANUT FARMER. 188

0038-3732 See SOUTHERLY. 3438
0038-3813 See PROCEEDINGS - SOUTHERN ASSOCIATION OF COLLEGES AND SCHOOLS; THE SOUTHERN ASSOCIATION NEWSLETTER. 1842
0038-383X See SOUTHERN BANKER, THE. 812
0038-3848 See SOUTHERN BAPTIST EDUCATOR, THE. 5067
0038-3864 See SOUTHERN BUILDING. 628
0038-3872 See BULLETIN / SOUTHERN CALIFORNIA ACADEMY OF SCIENCES. 5092
0038-3880 See SOUTHERN CALIFORNIA BUSINESS. 821
0038-3899 See JOURNAL OF THE SOUTHERN CALIFORNIA DENTAL HYGIENISTS' ASSOCIATION. 1329
0038-3910 See SOUTHERN CALIFORNIA LAW REVIEW. 3057
0038-3929 See SOUTHERN CALIFORNIA QUARTERLY. 2761
0038-3945 See BULLETIN - SOUTHERN CALIFORNIA DENTAL LABORATORY ASSOCIATION. 1318
0038-3953 See SOUTHERN CALIFORNIA TEAMSTER. 1711
0038-4038 See SOUTHERN ECONOMIC JOURNAL. 1521
0038-4046 See SOUTHERN ECONOMIST. 1521
0038-4135 See SOUTHERN FUNERAL DIRECTOR. 2407
0038-4178 See SOUTHERN HOSPITALS. 3792
0038-4186 See SOUTHERN HUMANITIES REVIEW. 2854
0038-4216 See SOUTHERN INSURANCE. 2894
0038-4283 See SOUTHERN JOURNAL OF PHILOSOPHY, THE. 4361
0038-4291 See SOUTHERN LITERARY JOURNAL, THE. 3438
0038-4305 See SOUTHERN LIVING. 2546
0038-4313 See SOUTHERN LUMBERMAN. 2404
0038-4348 See SOUTHERN MEDICAL JOURNAL (BIRMINGHAM). 3975
0038-4372 See SOUTHERN MOTOR CARGO. 5425
0038-4461 See SOUTHERN PLUMBING, HEATING, COOLING. 2608
0038-447X See SOUTHERN POETRY REVIEW. 3471
0038-4496 See SOUTHERN QUARTERLY, THE. 331
0038-4526 See SOUTHERN REVIEW (ADELAIDE). 3353
0038-4534 See SOUTHERN REVIEW (BATON ROUGE), THE. 3438
0038-4577 See SOUTHERN SOCIOLOGIST / THE SOUTHERN SOCIOLOGICAL SOCIETY, THE. 5263
0038-4607 See SOUTHERN TEXTILE NEWS. 5356
0038-4704 See SOUTHWEST NEWS-HERALD. 5662
0038-4712 See SOUTHWEST REVIEW. 3353
0038-4739 See SOUTHWESTERN ART. 365
0038-478X See SOUTHWESTERN HISTORICAL QUARTERLY. 2761
0038-4828 See SOUTHWESTERN JOURNAL OF THEOLOGY. 5067
0038-4836 See SOUTHWESTERN LAW JOURNAL. 3057
0038-4844 See SOUTHWESTERN LORE. 282
0038-4852 See SOUTHWESTERN. 1095
0038-4909 See SOUTHWESTERN NATURALIST, THE. 4172
0038-4917 See SOUTHWESTERN NEWS. 4998
0038-4941 See SOCIAL SCIENCE QUARTERLY. 5220
0038-4968 See SOUVENIRS & NOVELTIES. 2585
0038-4976 See SOU'WESTER (EDWARDSVILLE), THE. 3438
0038-4984 See SOU'WESTER (RAYMOND, WASH.), THE. 2546
0038-5034 See SOVETSKAIA ARKHEOLOGIIA. 283
0038-5069 See SOVETSKAJA GEOLOGIJA. 1397

0038-5077 See ROSSISKII MEDITSINSKII ZHURNAL : ORGAN MINISTERSTVA ZDRAVOOKHRANENIIA RSFSR. 3637
0038-5174 See SOVETSKIE PROFSOIUZY. 1711
0038-5204 See SOVETSKOE GOSUDARSTVO I PRAVO. 3057
0038-5239 See SOVETSKOE ZDRAVOOKHRANENIE. 4803
0038-5263 See SOVIET AND EASTERN EUROPEAN FOREIGN TRADE. 1640
0038-528X See SOVIET ANTHROPOLOGY AND ARCHAEOLOGY. 245
0038-5298 See SOVIET APPLIED MECHANICS. 2129
0038-5301 See SOVIET ASTRONOMY. 400
0038-531X See SOVIET ATOMIC ENERGY. 2158
0038-5344 See SOVIET CHEMICAL INDUSTRY, THE. 1038
0038-5360 See RUSSIAN EDUCATION AND SOCIETY. 1781
0038-5379 See SOVIET ELECTRICAL ENGINEERING. 2082
0038-5387 See SOVIET ELECTROCHEMISTRY. 1035
0038-5409 See SOVIET GENETICS. 551
0038-5417 See POST-SOVIET GEOGRAPHY. 2573
0038-5425 See SOVIET HYDROLOGY. 1418
0038-5484 See TSVETNYE METALLY (ENGLISH TRANSLATION ED.). 4023
0038-5492 See SOVIET JOURNAL OF NONDESTRUCTIVE TESTING, THE. 2031
0038-5506 See SOVIET JOURNAL OF NUCLEAR PHYSICS. 4451
0038-5530 See SOVIET LAW AND GOVERNMENT. 3057
0038-5549 See RUSSIAN LIFE. 2522
0038-5565 See SOVIET MATERIALS SCIENCE. 2108
0038-5581 See SOVIET MINING SCIENCE. 2151
0038-559X See SOVIET NEUROLOGY & PSYCHIATRY. 3846
0038-562X See SOVIET PHYSICS-ACOUSTICS. 4453
0038-5638 See SOVIET PHYSICS-CRYSTALLOGRAPHY. 1033
0038-5646 See SOVIET PHYSICS-JETP. 4421
0038-5654 See SOVIET PHYSICS-SOLID STATE. 4422
0038-5662 See SOVIET PHYSICS-TECHNICAL PHYSICS. 4422
0038-5670 See SOVIET PHYSICS-USPEKHI. 4422
0038-5689 See SOVIET PHYSICS-DOKLADY. 4421
0038-5697 See SOVIET PHYSICS JOURNAL. 4421
0038-5700 See SOVIET PHYSICS-SEMICONDUCTORS. 4422
0038-5719 See SOVIET PLANT PHYSIOLOGY. 528
0038-5735 See SOVIET POWDER METALLURGY AND METAL CERAMICS. 4019
0038-5735 See POROSHKOVAIA METALLURGIIA. 4015
0038-5743 See UKRAINIAN CHEMISTRY JOURNAL. 994
0038-5751 See JOURNAL OF RUSSIAN AND EAST EUROPEAN PSYCHOLOGY. 4601
0038-576X See SOVIET RADIOCHEMISTRY. 992
0038-5786 See SOVIET REVIEW INDIA. 2710
0038-5794 See SOVIET REVIEW (WHITE PLAINS), THE. 2523
0038-5824 See SOCIOLOGICAL RESEARCH. 5261
0038-5832 See SOVIET SOIL SCIENCE. 188
0038-5840 See STATUTES & DECISIONS. 3059
0038-5859 See SOVIET STUDIES. 4547
0038-5867 See SOVIET STUDIES IN HISTORY. 2710
0038-5875 See RUSSIAN STUDIES IN LITERATURE. 3432
0038-5883 See SOVIET STUDIES IN PHILOSOPHY. 4361
0038-5999 See SOWJETSTUDIEN. 2710
0038-6014 See SOYBEAN DIGEST. 188

0038-6065 See SOZIALE SICHERHEIT (WIEN). 5310
0038-6073 See SOZIALE WELT. 5223
0038-609X See SOZIALER FORTSCHRITT (BERLIN). 5223
0038-6308 See SPACE SCIENCE REVIEWS. 400
0038-6561 See SPARKASSE. 812
0038-6596 See SPARTACIST. 4547
0038-6804 See SPECIAL PAPERS IN PALEONTOLOGY. 4231
0038-6944 See SPECTACLE DU MONDE, LE. 3353
0038-6952 See SPECTATOR (LONDON. 1828). 2523
0038-6995 See SPECTROSCOPIA MOLECULAR. 4441
0038-7002 See BUNKO KENKYU. 4434
0038-7010 See SPECTROSCOPY LETTERS. 4442
0038-7061 See SPECTRUM (SANTA BARBARA, CALIF.). 1095
0038-7134 See SPECULUM. 2710
0038-7142 See SPEECH AND DRAMA. 5368
0038-7274 See SPEKTRUM. 3471
0038-7282 See S.P.E.L.D - INFORMATION. 3045
0038-7347 See SPENSER NEWSLETTER. 3471
0038-738X See SPETTACOLO, LO. 331
0038-7452 See SPIEGEL (HAMBURG), DER. 2523
0038-7479 See SPIEGEL DER LETTEREN. 3439
0038-7487 See SPIEGEL HISTORIAEL. 2630
0038-7525 See SPIELZEUG, DAS. 2585
0038-7533 See SPIN. 2324
0038-7584 See SPIRIT (SOUTH ORANGE). 3471
0038-7592 See SPIRIT & LIFE (CLYDE, MO.). 4999
0038-7614 See SPIRITUAL FRONTIERS. 4999
0038-7630 See SPIRITUAL LIFE (WASHINGTON). 5036
0038-7665 See SPIRITUS. 5036
0038-772X See SPOKEN ENGLISH. 3323
0038-7797 See SPORT (NEW YORK). 4920
0038-7835 See SPORT AVIATION. 4920
0038-8017 See SPORTING GOODS DEALER, THE. 4921
0038-805X See SPORTING NEWS, THE. 4921
0038-8084 See SHOOTING TIMES. 4917
0038-8149 See SPORTS AFIELD (1940). 4922
0038-822X See SPORTS ILLUSTRATED. 4922
0038-8432 See SPOTTED NEWS. 222
0038-8440 See SPRAKVARD. 3323
0038-8459 See SPRACHDIENST, DER. 3323
0038-8475 See SPRACHE IM TECHNISCHEN ZEITALTER. 3353
0038-8483 See SPRACHKUNST. 3323
0038-8505 See SPRACHMITTLER, DER. 3323
0038-8513 See SPRACHSPIEGEL. 3323
0038-853X See SPRAWY MIEDZYNARODOWE. 4535
0038-8610 See CONCORDIA THEOLOGICAL QUARTERLY. 4949
0038-8645 See SPROG OG KULTUR. 3323
0038-8661 See SPUDMAN. 137
0038-884X See STAAT, DER. 3094
0038-9048 See STAEDTETAG (1948), DER. 4687
0038-9056 See STARKE, DIE. 993
0038-9056 See STARKE, DIE. 137
0038-9099 See STAGE AND TELEVISION TODAY, THE. 5368
0038-9145 See STAHLBAU, DER. 628
0038-9153 See BIOTECHNIC & HISTOCHEMISTRY. 532
0038-9161 See STAINED GLASS. 2594
0038-920X See STAL. 4020
0038-9218 See STEEL IN TRANSLATION. 4020
0038-9277 See STAMP LOVER, THE. 2787
0038-9315 See STAMP WHOLESALER, THE. 2787
0038-9323 See STAMPA MEDICA. 3642
0038-9358 See STAMPS (NEW YORK, N.Y. 1932). 2787

0038-9382 See STANDARD (EVANSTON, ILL.), THE. 5068
0038-9390 See STANDARD (BOSTON), THE. 2894
0038-9447 See STANDARD BEARER (SACRAMENTO), THE. 4394
0038-948X See BUSINESS PUBLICATION RATES AND DATA. 651
0038-9498 See CANADIAN ADVERTISING RATES & DATA. 757
0038-9544 See NEWSPAPER RATES AND DATA. 763
0038-9552 See SPOT TELEVISION RATES AND DATA. 766
0038-9560 See SPOT RADIO RATES AND DATA. 766
0038-9579 See TARIF MEDIA. 767
0038-9595 See CONSUMER MAGAZINE AND FARM PUBLICATION RATES AND DATA. 758
0038-9633 See STANDARDS ACTION. 4032
0038-9668 See STANDARDS ENGINEERING. 4032
0038-9676 See ANSI REPORTER. 4029
0038-9730 See STANDPUNTE. 3439
0038-9765 See STANFORD LAW REVIEW. 3058
0038-979X See STANFORD OBSERVER, THE. 1095
0038-982X See STANOVNISTVO. 4560
0038-9854 See STAR AND LAMP OF PI KAPPA PHI, THE. 1095
0038-996X See STARTLING DETECTIVE. 5075
0038-9986 See STAT. 3869
0038-9994 See STATE (CHARLOTTE, N.C.), THE. 2762
0039-0011 See BULLETIN - STATE BANK OF PAKISTAN. 781
0039-0089 See STATE GEOLOGIST'S JOURNAL, THE. 1398
0039-0119 See STATE GOVERNMENT NEWS. 4687
0039-0232 See STATEN ISLAND HISTORIAN, THE. 2762
0039-0240 See PROCEEDINGS - STATEN ISLAND INSTITUTE OF ARTS AND SCIENCES. 328
0039-0313 See STATESMAN, THE. 3353
0039-0402 See STATISTICA NEERLANDICA. 5339
0039-0518 See STATISTICAL THEORY AND METHOD ABSTRACTS. 5340
0039-0526 See STATISTICIAN, THE. 5341
0039-0534 See STATISTICKA REVIJA. 5341
0039-0577 See STATISTICS ON SCHEDULED BANKS IN PAKISTAN. 733
0039-0690 See STATISZTIKAI SZEMLE. 1540
0039-0747 See STATSVETENSKAPLIG TIDSKRIFT. 4497
0039-0748 See TJI : TOBACCO JOURNAL INTERNATIONAL. 5373
0039-0771 See STAUB, REINHALTUNG DER LUFT. 2244
0039-078X See STAVEBNICKY CASOPIS. 628
0039-0801 See STAVIVO. 628
0039-0828 See ENERGY & FUEL USERS' JOURNAL. 1939
0039-0844 See STEAMBOAT BILL (1958). 2762
0039-0895 See INDUSTRY WEEK. 4004
0039-0925 See STEEL HORIZONS. 4020
0039-095X See STEEL TIMES. 4020
0039-100X See STEINBECK QUARTERLY. 435
0039-1018 See STEINBRUCH UND SANDGRUBE (1952). 2151
0039-1093 See STEIRISCHE STATISTIKEN / AMT DER STEIERMAERKISCHEN LANDESREGIERUNG, PRAESIDIALABTEILUNG, REFERAT STATISTIK. 5344
0039-1158 See STENDHAL CLUB (GRENOBLE). 3440
0039-1220 See STEREO REVIEW. 5319
0039-1255 See STERNE, DIE. 400
0039-1263 See STERNE UND WELTRAUM. 400
0039-128X See STEROIDS. 473
0039-1298 See STEERING WHEEL (AUSTIN). 5393

0039-1344 See JOURNAL OF THE STEWARD ANTHROPOLOGICAL SOCIETY. 239
0039-1492 See STIMMEN DER ZEIT (FREIBURG). 4999
0039-1522 See STIRPES. 2473
0039-1565 See STOCK & LAND. 138
0039-1638 See STOCK MARKET MAGAZINE, THE. 916
0039-1735 See STOMATOLOGIJA. 1336
0039-1743 See STOMATOLOSKI GLASNIK SRBIJE. 1336
0039-1778 See STONE INDUSTRIES. 1445
0039-1867 See STORES. 958
0039-1875 See STORIA CONTEMPORANEA. 2630
0039-1905 See STORIA E POLITICA. 2630
0039-1972 See STORM DATA. 1435
0039-1999 See STORY ART; A MAGAZINE FOR STORYTELLERS. 3440
0039-2030 See STORYVILLE (CHIGWELL). 4154
0039-2049 See STRAD, THE. 4154
0039-2103 See STRAIN. 2129
0039-2138 See STRANI PRAVNI ZIVOT / INSTITUT ZA UPOREDNO PRAVO. 3060
0039-2162 See STRASSE UND AUTOBAHN. 2031
0039-2197 See STRASSEN- UND TIEFBAU. 2031
0039-2219 See STRASSEN- VERKEHRSTECHNIK. 5444
0039-2235 See TRAVAUX DE L'INSTITUT DE PHONETIQUE DE STRASBOURG REVUE. 3329
0039-2308 See STRENGTH AND HEALTH. 2601
0039-2316 See STRENGTH OF MATERIALS. 2129
0039-2359 See IGAKU NO AYUMI. 3585
0039-2375 See STROITEL. 629
0039-2413 See STROITELSTVO I ARKHITEKTURA LENINGRADA. 309
0039-2421 See STROITELSTVO I ARKHITEKTURA MOSKVY. 629
0039-2448 See STROITELSTVO TRUBOPROVODOV. 4279
0039-2464 See STROJIRENSTVI. 2129
0039-2472 See STROJNICKY CASOPIS. 1997
0039-2480 See STROJNISKI VESTNIK. 5160
0039-2499 See STROKE (1970). 3710
0039-2502 See STROLLING ASTRONOMER, THE. 400
0039-2510 See STROM + SEE. 5393
0039-2618 See STRUMENTI CRITICI. 3440
0039-2685 See STUDENT (NASHVILLE), THE. 5068
0039-274X See STUDENT LAWYER (CHICAGO. 1972). 3060
0039-2804 See STUDENT VOICE. 1095
0039-2901 See STUDI CATTOLICI. 5036
0039-291X See STUDI DI SOCIOLOGIA. 5263
0039-2928 See STUDI ECONOMICI. 1522
0039-2936 See STUDI EMIGRAZIONE. 1921
0039-2944 See STUDI FRANCESI. 3440
0039-2952 See STUDI GERMANICI. 3440
0039-2987 See STUDI ITALIANI DI FILOLOGIA CLASSICA. 1080
0039-2995 See STUDI ROMANI. 2630
0039-3002 See STUDI SALENTINI. 2711
0039-3010 See STUDI SENESI NEL CIRCOLO GIURIDICO DELLA R. UNIVERSITA. 3060
0039-3037 See STUDI STORICI. 2711
0039-3045 See STUDI STORICI DELL'ORDINE DEI SERVI DI MARIA. 5036
0039-310X See STUDIA CANONICA. 5036
0039-3134 See STUDIA DEMOGRAFICZNE. 4560
0039-3142 See STUDIA FILOZOFICZNE. 4361
0039-3150 See STUDIA FORESTALIA SUECICA. 2396
0039-3169 See STUDIA GEOPHYSICA ET GEODAETICA. 1411
0039-3185 See STUDIA LEIBNITIANA. 4361
0039-3193 See STUDIA LINGUISTICA. 3324
0039-3207 See STUDIA LITURGICA. 5000
0039-3215 See STUDIA LOGICA. 4362

0039-3223 See STUDIA MATHEMATICA. 3536
0039-3231 See STUDIA MEDIEWISTYCZNE. 5263
0039-3266 See STUDIA MUSICOLOGICA. ACADEMIAE SCIENTIARUM HUNGARICA. 4155
0039-3274 See STUDIA NEOPHILOLOGICA. 3325
0039-3282 See STUDIA ORIENTALIA. 3325
0039-3304 See STUDIA PATAVINA. 5000
0039-3312 See STUDIA PRAWNICZE. 3060
0039-3320 See STUDIA PSYCHOLOGICA. 4619
0039-3339 See STUDIA ROMANICA ET ANGLICA ZAGRABIENSIA. 3325
0039-3347 See STUDIA ROSENTHALIANA. 2273
0039-3363 See STUDIA SLAVICA ACADEMIAE SCIENTIARUM HUNGARICAE. 3325
0039-3371 See STUDIA SOCJOLOGICZNE. 5223
0039-338X See STUDIA THEOLOGICA. 5000
0039-3398 See STUDIA UNIVERSITATIS BABES-BOLYAI. BIOLOGIA. 474
0039-3401 See STUDIA UNIVERSITATIS BABES-BOLYAI. CHEMIA. 993
0039-3452 See STUDIEKAMRATEN. 365
0039-3495 See STUDIES. 2523
0039-3533 See STUDIES IN AFRICAN LINGUISTICS. 3325
0039-3541 See STUDIES IN ART EDUCATION. 365
0039-3568 See STUDIES IN BIBLIOGRAPHY AND BOOKLORE. 5013
0039-3592 See STUDIES IN COMPARATIVE COMMUNISM. 4548
0039-3606 See STUDIES IN COMPARATIVE INTERNATIONAL DEVELOPMENT. 5223
0039-3622 See STUDIES IN COMPARATIVE RELIGION. 5000
0039-3630 See STUDIES IN CONSERVATION. 366
0039-3657 See STUDIES IN ENGLISH LITERATURE, 1500-1900. 3442
0039-3665 See STUDIES IN FAMILY PLANNING. 591
0039-3681 See STUDIES IN HISTORY AND PHILOSOPHY OF SCIENCE. 5160
0039-3738 See STUDIES IN PHILOLOGY. 3326
0039-3746 See STUDIES IN PHILOSOPHY AND EDUCATION. 4362
0039-3762 See STUDIES IN ROMANTICISM. 3442
0039-3770 See STUDIES IN SCOTTISH LITERATURE. 3354
0039-3789 See STUDIES IN SHORT FICTION. 3354
0039-3797 See STUDIES IN SOVIET THOUGHT. 4362
0039-3819 See STUDIES IN THE LITERARY IMAGINATION. 3442
0039-3827 See STUDIES IN THE NOVEL. 3354
0039-3851 See TOYO ONGAKU KENKYU. 4157
0039-3940 See STUDII SI CERCETARI DE FIZICA. 4423
0039-3941 See JOURNAL OF THE OPTICAL SOCIETY OF AMERICA. 4437
0039-3983 See STUDII SI CERCETARI DE ISTORIA ARTEI. SERIA ARTA PLASTICA. 366
0039-3991 See STUDII SI CERCETARI DE ISTORIA ARTEI. SERIA TEATRU, MUZICA, CINEMATOGRAFIE. 388
0039-4017 See STUDII SI CERCETARI DE MECANICA APLICATA. 4429
0039-4041 See STUDII DE DREPT ROMANESC / ACADEMIA ROMANA, INSTITUTUL DE CERCETARI JURIDICE. 3060
0039-405X See STUDII SI CERCETARI LINGVISTICE. 3326
0039-4068 See STUDII SI CERCETARI MATEMATICE. 3537
0039-4238 See STYLE (FAYETTEVILLE). 3443
0039-4246 See STYLE (TORONTO). 1087
0039-4254 See STYLE AUTO. 5426
0039-4394 See SUBTERRANEAN SOCIOLOGY NEWSLETTER / SUBTERRANEAN SOCIOLOGICAL ASSOCIATION, THE. 5263
0039-4432 See SUCCESSFUL FARMING. 138
0039-4467 See SUCCULENTA. 528

0039-4521 See SUDEBNO-MEDICINSKAJA EKSPERTIZA. 3742
0039-4564 See SUDHOFFS ARCHIV. 3643
0039-4653 See SUSSWAREN. 2359
0039-467X See SUFFOLK COUNTY AGRICULTURAL NEWS. 138
0039-4696 See SUFFOLK UNIVERSITY LAW REVIEW. 3060
0039-470X See SUGAKU (TOKYO. 1947). 3537
0039-4726 See SUGAR BULLETIN, THE. 2358
0039-4734 See SUGAR JOURNAL. 188
0039-4742 See SUGAR Y AZUCAR. 138
0039-4750 See SUGARBEET GROWER, THE. 188
0039-4777 See SUGARLAND. 188
0039-4807 See NUUSBRIEF. 5234
0039-4858 See SUIRI KAGAKU. WATER SCIENCE. 5540
0039-4890 See SULPHUR. 1030
0039-4963 See SUMITOMO KEIKINZOKU GIHO. 4021
0039-5005 See SUMMARY OF LABOR ARBITRATION AWARDS. 1712
0039-5056 See SUMMIT (BIG BEAR LAKE). 4879
0039-5161 See SUNDAY (ATLANTA, GA.). 5001
0039-5218 See SUNDAY INDEPENDENT. 5803
0039-5285 See SUNDAY SCHOOL COUNSELOR. 5068
0039-5404 See SUNSET (MENLO PARK, CALIF.). 2547
0039-5471 See SUO. 138
0039-5501 See SUOMEN ELAINLAAKARILEHTI. 5522
0039-551X See SUOMEN HAMMASLAAKARISEURAN TOIMITUKSIA. 1336
0039-5552 See SUOMEN KUVALEHTI. 2523
0039-5560 See SUOMEN LAAKARILEHTI. FINLANDS LAKARTIDNING. 3643
0039-5692 See SUPER STOCK & DRAG ILLUSTRATED. 4924
0039-5781 See SUPERMARKET. 937
0039-5803 See SUPERMARKET NEWS. 2359
0039-5803 See SUPERMARKET NEWS. 2359
0039-5854 See SUPERVISION (BURLINGTON). 947
0039-5889 See SUPERVISOR'S BULLETIN. 947
0039-5935 See SUPPLY HOUSE TIMES. 2608
0039-5978 See SUPREME COURT PRACTICE, THE. 3143
0039-6028 See SURFACE SCIENCE. 1058
0039-6036 See SURFER. 4924
0039-6060 See SURGERY. 3975
0039-6087 See SURGERY, GYNECOLOGY & OBSTETRICS. 3975
0039-6109 See SURGICAL CLINICS OF NORTH AMERICA, THE. 3975
0039-615X See SURPLUS RECORD, THE. 2129
0039-6168 See SURREALIST TRANSFORMA(C)TION. 366
0039-6206 See SURVEY OF ANESTHESIOLOGY. 3684
0039-6214 See SURVEY OF CURRENT AFFAIRS. 4497
0039-6222 See SURVEY OF CURRENT BUSINESS. 714
0039-6249 See SURVEY OF JAPANESE FINANCE AND INDUSTRY. 813
0039-6257 See SURVEY OF OPHTHALMOLOGY. 3879
0039-6265 See SURVEY REVIEW - DIRECTORATE OF OVERSEAS SURVEYS. 2032
0039-6338 See SURVIVAL (LONDON). 4058
0039-6443 See SVENSK BOKFORTECKNING. 3459
0039-6451 See SVENSK BOKHANDEL. 4832
0039-646X See SVENSK BOTANISK TIDSKRIFT. 528
0039-6524 See SVENSK FARMACEUTISK TIDSKRIFT. 4330
0039-6583 See SVENSK JAKT. 4879

0039-6591 See SVENSK JURISTTIDNING. 3061
0039-6605 See KEMISK TIDSKRIFT. 983
0039-663X See SVENSK LITTERATURTIDSKRIFT. 3443
0039-6680 See SVENSK PAPPERSTIDNING. 4239
0039-6702 See SVENSK SJOFARTSTIDNING. 4184
0039-6761 See SVENSK TEOLOGISK KVARTALSKRIFT. 5001
0039-677X See SVENSK TIDSKRIFT. 3354
0039-6796 See SVENSK TRAVARU- OCH PAPPERSMASSETIDNING. 2405
0039-6834 See GASNYTT. 4258
0039-6842 See SKRIFTER UTGIVNA AV SVENSKA LITTERATURSALLSKAPET I FINLAND. 3437
0039-6907 See SVENSKA TIDNINGSARTIKLAR. 426
0039-6974 See SVERIGES NATUR. 2206
0039-6982 See TANDLAKARTIDNINGEN. 1336
0039-6990 See SVERIGES UTSADESFORENINGS TIDSKRIFT. 189
0039-7075 See SVETOVA LITERATURA. 3443
0039-7091 See SVETSEN. 4028
0039-713X See SVINOVODSTVO (MOSKVA). 222
0039-7253 See ALLMAN MANADSSTATISTIK. 5320
0039-7261 See STATISTISK TIDSKRIFT. 5344
0039-7288 See UTRIKESHANDEL. MANADSSTATISTIK. 1641
0039-7296 See SWEDISH ECONOMY (STOCKHOLM. 1961), THE. 1523
0039-7318 See SWEDISH JOURNAL OF ECONOMICS, THE. 1523
0039-7342 See ALUMNAE MAGAZINE - SWEET BRIAR COLLEGE. 1808
0039-7415 See SWIMMING TECHNIQUE. 4925
0039-7431 See SWIMMING WORLD AND JUNIOR SWIMMER (1965). 4925
0039-7490 See SWISS REVIEW OF WORLD AFFAIRS. 4536
0039-7520 See SWISS WATCH AND JEWELRY JOURNAL. 2916
0039-7547 See SWORD OF THE LORD, THE. 5001
0039-7660 See SYLWAN : CZASOPISMO MIESIECZNE DLA LESNIKOW I WASCICIELI ZIEMSKICH / ORGAN GALIC. TOWARZYSTWA LESNEGO. 2396
0039-7679 See SYMBOLAE OSLOENSES. 3327
0039-7709 See SYMPOSIUM (SYRACUSE). 3327
0039-7717 See SYN OG SEGN. 2523
0039-7857 See SYNTHESE (DORDRECHT). 4363
0039-7873 See WHO PUT THE BOMP!. 4159
0039-7881 See SYNTHESIS (STUTTGART). 1048
0039-7911 See SYNTHETIC COMMUNICATIONS. 1048
0039-792X See SYRACUSE CHEMIST, THE. 994
0039-7938 See SYRACUSE LAW REVIEW. 3062
0039-7946 See SYRIA. 2577
0039-7962 See SYRIE & MONDE ARABE. 1523
0039-7989 See SYSTEMATIC BIOLOGY. 474
0039-8047 See SYSTEMS TECHNOLOGY. 2158
0039-8098 See SZAZADOK. 2631
0039-8136 See SZINHAZ. 5369
0039-8144 See SZKO I CERAMIKA. 2594
0039-8152 See SZPILKI. 3354
0039-8233 See TAMS JOURNAL. 2783
0039-8292 See TEA NEWS (NASHVILLE, TENN.). 1873
0039-8322 See TESOL QUARTERLY. 3328
0039-8403 See TIPRO REPORTER. 4280
0039-8543 See TV GUIDE. 1141
0039-8551 See T V HEBDO (MONTREAL). 1140
0039-8624 See TV TIMES. 1142
0039-8659 See TWU EXPRESS. 1715
0039-8675 See TA-KUNG-PAO. 5802
0039-8691 See TAAL EN TONGVAL. 3327
0039-8780 See TABLE ET CADEAU, L'OBJET POUR LA MAISON. 2907

0039-8837 See TABLET (LONDON), THE. 5002
0039-8845 See TABLET, THE. 5037
0039-8888 See TACHYDROMOS. 2493
0039-8977 See TAIDE. 366
0039-8993 See TAIKABUTSU. 4021
0039-9140 See TALANTA (OXFORD). 1019
0039-9183 See TALKING BOOK TOPICS. 4394
0039-9418 See TANK. 4058
0039-9450 See TANPAKUSHITSU KAKUSAN KOSO. 474
0039-9620 See TAR HEEL NURSE. 3870
0039-9663 See TARHEEL BANKER, THE. 813
0039-968X See TARHEEL WHEELS. 5394
0039-971X See TARSADALMI SZEMLE. 4548
0039-9809 See PAPERS AND PROCEEDINGS - TASMANIAN HISTORICAL RESEARCH ASSOCIATION. 2670
0039-9949 See TAX ADMINISTRATORS NEWS. 4751
0039-9957 See TAX ADVISER, THE. 4751
0039-9965 See TAX AFFAIRS. 3062
0040-0017 See REPORTS - UNITED STATES. TAX COURT. 3039
0040-0025 See TAX EXECUTIVE, THE. 4752
0040-0041 See TAX LAW REVIEW. 3062
0040-005X See TAX LAWYER : BULLETIN OF THE SECTION OF TAXATION, AMERICAN BAR ASSOCIATION, THE. 3062
0040-0076 See TAX NEWS SERVICE. 3062
0040-0092 See TAX PLANNING IDEAS. 4754
0040-0149 See TAXATION. 4754
0040-0165 See TAXATION FOR ACCOUNTANTS. 752
0040-0181 See TAXES (CHICAGO, ILL.). 4755
0040-0203 See TAXES INTERPRETED. 3063
0040-0262 See TAXON. 529
0040-0343 See TEA & COFFEE TRADE JOURNAL, THE. 2371
0040-0599 See TEACHING EXCEPTIONAL CHILDREN. 1886
0040-0602 See TEACHING HISTORY SYDNEY. 1907
0040-0610 See TEACHING HISTORY (LONDON). 1907
0040-0645 See TEACHING PICTURES FOR BIBLE SEARCHERS. 5020
0040-0823 See TEBIWA. 4172
0040-0866 See TECHNICA (BASEL). 2915
0040-0912 See EDUCATION & TRAINING (BRADFORD). 1912
0040-0920 See TECHNICAL EDUCATION ABSTRACTS. 1798
0040-1099 See TECHNIK, DIE. 5162
0040-1145 See TECHNIKA LOTNICZA I ASTRONAUTYCZNA. 37
0040-117X See TECHNIKGESCHICHTE. 5162
0040-1188 See TECHNION. 5162
0040-120X See TECHNIQUE DE L'EAU ET DE L'ASSAINISSEMENT, LA. 5540
0040-1242 See TECHNIQUE LAITIERE. 199
0040-1250 See TECHNIQUE MODERNE, LA. 5162
0040-1366 See ARTS ET TECHNIQUES GRAPHIQUES. 376
0040-1382 See TECHNIQUES NOUVELLES. 2762
0040-1471 See TECHNISCHE MITTEILUNGEN DER SCHWEIZERISCHEN TELEGRAPHEN- UND TELEPHON-VERWALTUNG. 5162
0040-148X See TECHNISCHE RUNDSCHAU. 5163
0040-151X See SCHWEIZERISCHE TECHNISCHE ZEITSCHRIFT. 5150
0040-1528 See WISSENSCHAFTLICHE ZEITSCHRIFT. 2495
0040-1587 See TECHNOCRACY DIGEST. 5224
0040-1625 See TECHNOLOGICAL FORECASTING AND SOCIAL CHANGE. 5163
0040-165X See TECHNOLOGY AND CULTURE. 5163
0040-1676 See TECHNOLOGY IRELAND. 5164
0040-1692 See TECHNOLOGY REVIEW. 5164
0040-1706 See TECHNOMETRICS. 5176

0040-1714 See TECNICA LISBOA. 1998
0040-1838 See TECNICA INDUSTRIAL (MADRID). 3488
0040-1846 See TECNICA ITALIANA. 2032
0040-1862 See TECNICA MOLITORIA. 204
0040-1889 See TECNICA PECUARIA EN MEXICO. 222
0040-1900 See TECNICA TEXTIL INTERNACIONAL. 5356
0040-1927 See TECNICHE DELL AUTOMAZIONE & ROBOTICA. 1221
0040-1951 See TECTONOPHYSICS. 1411
0040-2001 See 'TEEN. 1070
0040-2176 See TEHNIKA (BEOGRAD). 5165
0040-2184 See TEILHARD REVIEW, THE. 246
0040-2206 See TEINTURE ET APPRETS. 5356
0040-2230 See TEHNICESKAJA ESTETIKA (MOSKVA). 1998
0040-2265 See TEKHNIKA V SELSKOM KHOZIAISTE. 161
0040-2303 See TEKNIIKKA. 5165
0040-2397 See TEKSTILNAJA PROMYSLENNOST. 5357
0040-2427 See TELE. 1164
0040-2486 See TELECOMMUNICATION JOURNAL OF AUSTRALIA, THE. 1165
0040-2494 See TELECOMMUNICATIONS (INTERNATIONAL ED.). 1165
0040-2508 See TELECOMMUNICATIONS AND RADIO ENGINEERING. 1165
0040-2621 See TELEMETRY JOURNAL. 2084
0040-263X See TELEPHONE ENGINEER & MANAGEMENT. 1167
0040-263X See TELEPHONE ENGINEER & MANAGEMENT. 2084
0040-2656 See TELEPHONY. 1167
0040-2672 See TP. TELEPROGRAMA. 1141
0040-2699 See TELERAMA ED. PARISIENNE. 1123
0040-2702 See TELESCOPE (DETROIT). 4184
0040-2710 See TELESIS. 1167
0040-2788 See BROADCAST (BORDON). 1127
0040-2796 See TELEVISION QUARTERLY (BEVERLY HILL). 1141
0040-2869 See TEMAS (NEW YORK, N.Y.). 2493
0040-2982 See TEMPO (LONDON). 4156
0040-3016 See TEMPO (ROCKAWAY, N.J.). 4156
0040-3075 See TEMPS MODERNES. 3354
0040-3083 See TENANT. 2836
0040-313X See JOURNAL OF THE TENNESSEE ACADEMY OF SCIENCE. 5121
0040-3148 See BULLETIN / UNIVERSITY OF TENNESSEE, AGRICULTURAL EXPERIMENT STATION. 70
0040-3180 See TENNESSEE ARCHAEOLOGIST. 284
0040-3199 See TENNESSEE BANKER, THE. 813
0040-3202 See TENNESSEE CONSERVATIONIST, THE. 2207
0040-3229 See TENNESSEE FARM AND HOME SCIENCE. 140
0040-3245 See TENNESSEE FARMER (NASHVILLE, TENN.). 140
0040-3253 See TENNESSEE FOLKLORE SOCIETY BULLETIN. 2324
0040-3261 See TENNESSEE HISTORICAL QUARTERLY. 2762
0040-327X See TENNESSEE LAW ENFORCEMENT JOURNAL. 3177
0040-3288 See TENNESSEE LAW REVIEW. 3063
0040-3318 See JOURNAL OF THE TENNESSEE MEDICAL ASSOCIATION. 3600
0040-3334 See TENNESSEE MUSICIAN. 4156
0040-3385 See JOURNAL OF THE TENNESSEE DENTAL ASSOCIATION, THE. 1329
0040-3407 See TENNESSEE TEACHER. 1907
0040-3415 See TENNESSEE TOWN & CITY. 4690
0040-3423 See TENNIS (NORWALK, CONN.). 4926
0040-3474 See TENNIS WORLD. 4926
0040-3482 See TENRIKYO. 5002

0040-3504 See TENSOR. 3538
0040-3555 See TEOLOGINEN AIKAKAUSKIRJA. TEOLOGISK TIDSKRIFT. 5002
0040-3571 See TEORETICESKIE OSNOVY HIMICESKOJ TEHNOLOGII. 994
0040-358X See TEORIE A PRAXE TELESNE VYCHOVY. 2601
0040-3601 See TEORIJA I PRAKTIKA FIZICESKOJ KULTURY. 1859
0040-361X See TEORIIA VEROIATNOSTEI I EE PRIMENENIIA. 3538
0040-3636 See TEPLOENERGETIKA (MOSKVA, 1954). 2130
0040-3644 See TEPLOFIZIKA VYSOKIKH TEMPERATUR. 4423
0040-3660 See TERAPEVTICESKIJ ARHIV. 3645
0040-3709 See TERATOLOGY (PHILADELPHIA). 474
0040-3717 See TERMESZET VILAGA. 5165
0040-3725 See TERMOTECNICA. 1998
0040-3733 See TERRA (LOS ANGELES, CALIF.). 4173
0040-3741 See TERRA. 2577
0040-375X See TERRA AMERIGA. 2763
0040-3768 See TERRA E SOLE. 161
0040-3776 See TERRA E VITA. 141
0040-3830 See TERRE DE CHEZ NOUS (MONTREAL). 141
0040-3865 See TERRE ET LA VIE, LA. 2221
0040-392X See TERZO MONDO. 5264
0040-3946 See TEST BERLIN, WEST. ZEITSCHRIFT. 1300
0040-3989 See TESTIMONIANZE. 5003
0040-4020 See TETRAHEDRON. 1048
0040-4039 See TETRAHEDRON LETTERS. 1048
0040-4039 See TETRAHEDRON LETTERS. 1048
0040-4071 See TEVYNE. 2274
0040-411X See TEXANA. 2763
0040-4179 See TEXAS ARCHITECT. 310
0040-4187 See TEXAS BAR JOURNAL. 3063
0040-4209 See TEXAS BUSINESS REVIEW. 1586
0040-4233 See TEXAS CAVER, THE. 1411
0040-4241 See TEXAS COACH. 4926
0040-4284 See TEXAS DENTAL JOURNAL. 1336
0040-4322 See TEXAS FOOD MERCHANT. 2359
0040-4349 See TEXAS HIGHWAYS (AUSTIN, TEX.). 5492
0040-4365 See TEXAS INDUSTRIAL EXPANSION. 1629
0040-439X See TEXAS JEWISH POST, THE. 5755
0040-4403 See TEXAS JOURNAL OF SCIENCE, THE. 5165
0040-4411 See TEXAS LAW REVIEW. 3064
0040-442X See TEXAS LAWMAN, THE. 3178
0040-4446 See TEXAS LIBRARY JOURNAL. 3253
0040-4470 See TEXAS MEDICINE. 3645
0040-4543 See BULLETIN OF THE TEXAS ORNITHOLOGICAL SOCIETY. 5616
0040-4551 See TEXAS OUTLOOK, THE. 1787
0040-4586 See TEXAS PARKS & WILDLIFE. 4708
0040-4594 See TEXAS POLICE JOURNAL. 3178
0040-4640 See TEXAS PUBLIC EMPLOYEE. 1714
0040-4691 See TEXAS STUDIES IN LITERATURE AND LANGUAGE. 3445
0040-4705 See TEXAS STUDY OF SECONDARY EDUCATION RESEARCH JOURNAL. 1787
0040-4756 See TEXAS VETERINARY MEDICAL JOURNAL. 5522
0040-4829 See TEXTIL. 5357
0040-4853 See TEXTIL PRAXIS INTERNATIONAL. 5357
0040-487X See TEXTIL-WIRTSCHAFT (FRANKFURT). 5357
0040-490X See TEXTILE CHEMIST AND COLORIST. 5357
0040-4926 See TEXTILE DYER & PRINTER. 5357
0040-4969 See TEXTILE HISTORY. 5358
0040-4993 See TEXTILE INDUSTRY & TRADE JOURNAL. 5358

0040-5000 See JOURNAL OF THE TEXTILE INSTITUTE. 5353
0040-5043 See JOURNAL OF THE TEXTILE MACHINERY SOCIETY OF JAPAN. 5353
0040-5078 See TEXTILE MAGAZINE, THE. 5358
0040-5116 See TEXTILE MONTH. 5358
0040-5167 See TEXTILE PROGRESS. 5358
0040-5175 See TEXTILE RESEARCH JOURNAL. 5358
0040-5191 See TEXTILE TECHNOLOGY DIGEST. 5360
0040-5205 See TEXTILE TRENDS. 5358
0040-5213 See TEXTILE WORLD. 5358
0040-5248 See TEXTILES SUISSES. 5359
0040-5310 See TEXTILVEREDLUNG. 5359
0040-5329 See TEXT + KRITIK. 3445
0040-5418 See THEATER DER ZEIT. 5370
0040-5469 See THEATRE CRAFTS. 5370
0040-5493 See THEATRE EN POLOGNE, LE. 5370
0040-5507 See THEATER HEUTE. 5370
0040-5515 See THEATRE INFORMATION BULLETIN. 5370
0040-5523 See THEATRE NOTEBOOK. 5371
0040-5531 See THEATRE ORGAN (1970). 4156
0040-5574 See THEATRE SURVEY. 5371
0040-5612 See THEOLOGIA REFORMATA. 5003
0040-5620 See THEOLOGICAL EDUCATION. 5003
0040-5639 See THEOLOGICAL STUDIES (BALTIMORE). 5003
0040-5655 See THEOLOGIE UND PHILOSOPHIE. 5003
0040-5663 See THEOLOGISCH-PRAKTISCHE QUARTALSCHRIFT. 5037
0040-5671 See THEOLOGISCHE LITERATURZEITUNG. 5004
0040-568X See THEOLOGISCHE REVUE. 5004
0040-5698 See THEOLOGISCHE RUNDSCHAU. 5004
0040-5701 See THEOLOGISCHE ZEITSCHRIFT. 5004
0040-571X See THEOLOGY (LONDON). 5004
0040-5728 See THEOLOGY DIGEST. 5004
0040-5736 See THEOLOGY TODAY (EPHRATA, PA.). 5004
0040-5744 See THEORETICA CHIMICA ACTA. 1058
0040-5752 See THEORETICAL AND APPLIED GENETICS. 551
0040-5760 See THEORETICAL AND EXPERIMENTAL CHEMISTRY. 1058
0040-5779 See THEORETICAL AND MATHEMATICAL PHYSICS. 4423
0040-5787 See THEORETICAL CHEMICAL ENGINEERING. 2007
0040-5795 See THEORETICAL FOUNDATIONS OF CHEMICAL ENGINEERING. 2017
0040-5809 See THEORETICAL POPULATION BIOLOGY. 4560
0040-5817 See THEORIA (PIETERMARITZBURG). 2855
0040-5825 See THEORIA. 4363
0040-5833 See THEORY AND DECISION. 4363
0040-5841 See THEORY INTO PRACTICE. 1907
0040-585X See THEORY OF PROBABILITY AND ITS APPLICATIONS. 3538
0040-5884 See THEOSOPHICAL MOVEMENT, THE. 5045
0040-5892 See THEOSOPHIST, THE. 5004
0040-5906 See THEOSOPHY. 4363
0040-5914 See THERAPEUTIC RECREATION JOURNAL. 4394
0040-5922 See THERAPEUTIQUE. 3801
0040-5930 See THERAPEUTISCHE UMSCHAU. 3976
0040-5957 See THERAPIE. 4330

0040-5965 See THERAPIE DER GEGENWART. 3645
0040-5973 See THERAPIEWOCHE. 3645
0040-6015 See THERMAL ENGINEERING. 1998
0040-6031 See THERMOCHIMICA ACTA. 1058
0040-604X See THESAURUS - INSTITUTO CARO Y CUERVO. 3328
0040-6058 See THESE TIMES. 5004
0040-6066 See THETA (DURHAM). 4243
0040-6090 See THIN SOLID FILMS. 2084
0040-6120 See THIRD BRANCH, THE. 3143
0040-6171 See THIS ENGLAND. 2524
0040-6201 See THIS IS WEST TEXAS. 2547
0040-6325 See THOMIST, THE. 4363
0040-6376 See THORAX. 3952
0040-6406 See THOREAU SOCIETY BULLETIN, THE. 3446
0040-6457 See THOUGHT (NEW YORK). 5005
0040-6562 See THRESHOLD. 3446
0040-6708 See TIBETAN REVIEW. 2577
0040-6791 See TIDINGS (LOS ANGELES). 5037
0040-6872 See TIDSKRIFT FOR DOKUMENTATION. 3253
0040-6937 See TIDSKRIFT I FORTIFIKATION. 4059
0040-6953 See TIDSKRIFT (SUOMEN LAINOPILLINEN YHDISTYS). 3064
0040-702X See TIDSSKRIFT FOR DANSKE SYGEHUSE. 3793
0040-7038 See TIDSSKRIFT FOR DANSK FAAREAVL. 223
0040-7135 See TIDSSKRIFT FOR PLANTEAVL. 189
0040-7143 See TIDSSKRIFT FOR RETTSVIDENSKAP. 3064
0040-716X See TIDSSKRIFT FOR SAMFUNNSFORSKNING. 5224
0040-7186 See TIDSSKRIFT FOR SVSEN. 4184
0040-7194 See TIDSSKRIFT FOR TEOLOGI OG KIRKE. 5005
0040-7232 See TIE (LOUISVILLE), THE. 5005
0040-7356 See TIERS MONDE (PARIS). 1640
0040-7364 See TIERZUCHTER, DER. 223
0040-7380 See TIGER BEAT. 1070
0040-7437 See TIJDSCHRIFT VOOR BESTUURSWETENCHAPPEN EN PUBLEKRECHT. 3064
0040-7453 See TIJDSCHRIFT VOOR DIERGENEESKUNDE. 5523
0040-747X See TIJDSCHRIFT VOOR ECONOMISCHE EN SOCIALE GEOGRAFIE : TESG. 1524
0040-7496 See TIJDSCHRIFT VOOR ENTOMOLOGIE. 5614
0040-750X See TIJDSCHRIFT VOOR FILOSOFIE. 4364
0040-7518 See TIJDSCHRIFT VOOR GESCHIEDENIS (1920). 2631
0040-7550 See TIJDSCHRIFT VOOR NEDERLANDSE TAAL-EN LETTERKUNDE. 3328
0040-7585 See TIJDSCHRIFT VOOR RECHTSGESCHIEDENIS. 3064
0040-7615 See TIJDSCHRIFT VOOR SOCIALE WETENSCHAPPEN. 5224
0040-7623 See TIJDSCHRIFT VOOR VERVOERSWETENSCHAP. 5394
0040-7763 See TIMBER GROWER. 2396
0040-7798 See WOOD BASED PANELS INTERNATIONAL. 2406
0040-781X See TIME (CHICAGO, ILL.). 2493
0040-7836 See TIME & TIDE. 4078
0040-7887 See TIMES EDUCATIONAL SUPPLEMENT, THE. 1788
0040-7917 See TIMES OF THE AMERICAS, THE. 2552
0040-7941 See TIN AND ITS USES. 4022
0040-795X See TIN INTERNATIONAL. 2152
0040-7968 See TIN NEWS. 4022
0040-7984 See TINCTORIA. 5359
0040-8085 See TIRE REVIEW (1966). 5078

0040-8166 See TISSUE & CELL. 540
0040-8190 See TITLE NEWS. 2894
0040-8263 See TOASTMASTER, THE. 1123
0040-8271 See TOBACCO. 5373
0040-8298 See TOBACCO ABSTRACTS. 5373
0040-8328 See TOBACCO REPORTER. 5374
0040-8441 See TODAY'S CATHOLIC TEACHER. 1873
0040-8549 See TODAY'S PARISH. 5005
0040-859X See TODAY'S TRANSPORT INTERNATIONAL. 853
0040-8611 See TODO ES HISTORIA. 2763
0040-8670 See TOHO IGAKKAI ZASSHI. 3646
0040-8697 See HOKOKU (TOHOKU DAIGAKU. NOGAKU KENKYUJO). 92
0040-8719 See TOHOKU JOURNAL OF AGRICULTURAL RESEARCH. 141
0040-8727 See TOHOKU JOURNAL OF EXPERIMENTAL MEDICINE, THE. 3646
0040-8735 See TOHOKU MATHEMATICAL JOURNAL. 3538
0040-8743 See TOHOKU PSYCHOLOGICA FOLIA. 4620
0040-8808 See SCIENCE REPORTS OF THE RESEARCH INSTITUTES. SERIES A, PHYSICS, CHEMISTRY, AND METALLURGY. 5153
0040-8867 See TOKO-GINECOLOGIA PRACTICA. 3769
0040-8875 See TOKUSHIMA JOURNAL OF EXPERIMENTAL MEDICINE, THE. 3646
0040-8891 See BULLETIN OF TOKYO DENTAL COLLEGE, THE. 1318
0040-8905 See TOKYO IKA DAIGAKU ZASSHI. 3646
0040-8921 See BULLETIN OF TOKYO MEDICAL AND DENTAL UNIVERSITY, THE. 3561
0040-893X See TOKYO METROPOLITAN NEWS : A QUARTERLY JOURNAL OF THE TOKYO METROPOLITAN GOVERNMENT. 4691
0040-9006 See REPORT OF THE INSTITUTE OF INDUSTRIAL SCIENCE, UNIVERSITY OF TOKYO. 5146
0040-9014 See JOURNAL OF THE TOKYO UNIVERSITY OF FISHERIES. 2307
0040-9022 See TOKYO JOSHI IKA DAIGAKU ZASSHI. 3646
0040-9170 See TONEEL TEATRAAL. 389
0040-9243 See TOOLING & PRODUCTION. 2130
0040-9332 See TOPICAL TIME. 2788
0040-9340 See TOPICATOR. 1125
0040-9375 See TOPIQUE. 4620
0040-9383 See TOPOLOGY (OXFORD). 3539
0040-9588 See TORRE (RIO PIEDRAS (SAN JUAN), P.R.), LA. 3447
0040-9618 See BULLETIN OF THE TORREY BOTANICAL CLUB, THE. 505
0040-9634 See TOERTENELMI SZEMLE. 2631
0040-9669 See TOSHOKANKAI. 3253
0040-9723 See TOTEM (OLYMPIA). 2207
0040-9898 See TOWARD FREEDOM. 4536
0040-9952 See TOWN & COUNTRY (NEW YORK, N.Y.). 2548
0040-9960 See TOWN & COUNTRY PLANNING. 4691
0040-9979 See TOWN & VILLAGE. 5721
0040-9995 See TOWN-PLANNING AND LOCAL GOVERNMENT GUIDE, THE. 2837
0041-0020 See TOWN PLANNING REVIEW. 2837
0041-0063 See TOWSON STATE JOURNAL OF INTERNATIONAL AFFAIRS. 4536
0041-008X See TOXICOLOGY AND APPLIED PHARMACOLOGY. 3984
0041-0101 See TOXICON (OXFORD). 4331
0041-011X See TOY & HOBBY WORLD INTERNATIONAL. 2585
0041-0144 See TOYO SODA KENKYU HOKOKU. 3489
0041-0187 See TOYS AND PLAYTHINGS. 4867
0041-0284 See TRACK & FIELD NEWS. 4926
0041-0292 See TRACK & FIELD QUARTERLY REVIEW. 4926

0041-0306 See TRACK NEWSLETTER. 4927
0041-0330 See TRACKER, THE. 4157
0041-0438 See TRADE MARKS JOURNAL (OTTAWA). 1309
0041-0543 See TRADE WITH GREECE. 854
0041-056X See TRADE-MARK REPORTER, THE. 1308
0041-0608 See TRADITION (NEW YORK). 5053
0041-0683 See TRAFFIC ENGINEERING & CONTROL. 5394
0041-0691 See TRAFFIC MANAGEMENT. 5394
0041-0721 See TRAFFIC SAFETY (CHICAGO, ILL.). 5446
0041-073X See TRAFFIC WORLD, THE. 5394
0041-0748 See TRAIL & LANDSCAPE. 4173
0041-0756 See TRAIL AND TIMBERLINE. 4879
0041-0772 See TRAILER/BODY BUILD. 5394
0041-0780 See TRAILER LIFE. 4855
0041-0829 See TRAIN COLLECTORS QUARTERLY, THE. 2778
0041-0837 See TRAIN DISPATCHER (BERWYN), THE. 1715
0041-0861 See TRAINING & DEVELOPMENT (ALEXANDRIA, VA.). 947
0041-090X See TRAINING OFFICER, THE. 948
0041-0934 See TRAINS. 5437
0041-0950 See TRAITEMENT THERMIQUE. 4022
0041-1027 See TRANCIATURA STAMPAGGIO. 4022
0041-1108 See TRANSCULTURAL PSYCHIATRIC RESEARCH REVIEW. 3937
0041-1124 See TRANSFORMACION. 1630
0041-1132 See TRANSFUSION (PHILADELPHIA). 3774
0041-1175 See TRANSIT POSTMARK COLLECTOR. 1147
0041-1280 See TRANSMISSION & DISTRIBUTION. 2085
0041-1337 See TRANSPLANTATION. 3647
0041-1345 See TRANSPLANTATION PROCEEDINGS. 3977
0041-1434 See TRANSPORT ECONOMICS. 5395
0041-1442 See TRANSPORT ET TOURISME. 5494
0041-1450 See TRANSPORT THEORY AND STATISTICAL PHYSICS. 4430
0041-1469 See TRANSPORT HISTORY. 5395
0041-1515 See TRANSPORT MANAGEMENT; THE BRITISH JOURNAL OF TRADE AND TRANSPORT. 5395
0041-1558 See TRANSPORT TOPICS. 5396
0041-1612 See TRANSPORTATION JOURNAL. 5396
0041-1639 See TRANSLOG (WASHINGTON, D.C.). 4059
0041-1655 See TRANSPORTATION SCIENCE. 5397
0041-1698 See MOTRIX. 5421
0041-1752 See ANNALS OF THE TRANSVAAL MUSEUM. 4162
0041-1760 See TRAP & FIELD. 4927
0041-1787 See TRASFUSIONE DEL SANGUE. 3802
0041-1809 See TRASPORTI INDUSTRIALI. 5397
0041-1833 See TRATTAMENTI E FINITURA. 4022
0041-185X See TRAVAIL ET METHODES. 888
0041-1868 See TRAVAIL HUMAIN, LE. 4620
0041-1965 See TRAVAUX. 1999
0041-1973 See TRAVELAGE WEST. 5497
0041-1981 See TRAVEL AGENCY. 5494
0041-2007 See TRAVEL & LEISURE. 5495
0041-2066 See TRAVEL TRADE (NEW YORK, N.Y.). 5497
0041-2082 See TRAVEL WEEKLY. 5497
0041-2104 See TRAVELAGE EAST. 5497
0041-2155 See TREASURY BULLETIN. 814
0041-2171 See TREE. 3447
0041-2198 See TREE-RING BULLETIN. 2397
0041-2236 See TREES IN SOUTH AFRICA. 2397
0041-2279 See TREMPLIN AVERBODE. 1070

0041-2295 See TREND (POINTE-CLAIRE). **4239**
0041-2333 See TRENDLINE'S CURRENT MARKET PERSPECTIVES. **918**
0041-2449 See TRENTON. **855**
0041-2481 See TRI-OLOGY TECHNICAL REPORT. **142**
0041-249X See TRI-STATE FOOD NEWS. **2360**
0041-2511 See TRIAD (OHIO MUSIC EDUCATION ASSOCIATION). **4157**
0041-2538 See TRIAL. **3066**
0041-2546 See TRIAL LAWYER'S GUIDE, THE. **3066**
0041-2554 See TRIAL LAWYERS QUARTERLY. **3066**
0041-2597 See TRIANGLE (ENGLISH EDITION). **3647**
0041-2600 See TRIANGLE OF MU PHI EPSILON, THE. **4157**
0955-7040 See TRIBOLOGY AND CORROSION ABSTRACTS. **2017**
0041-2716 See TRIBUNE. **2632**
0041-2821 See TRIBUNE. **5813**
0041-283X See ENFANCE MAJUSCULE PARIS. **3164**
0041-2945 See TRIERER THEOLOGISCHE ZEITSCHRIFT. **5006**
0041-2953 See TRIERER ZEITSCHRIFT FUER GESCHICHTE UND KUNST DES TRIERER LANDES UND SEINER NACHBARGEBIETE. **2713**
0041-3011 See TRIMESTRE ECONOMICO, EL. **1640**
0041-3046 See QUARTERLY ECONOMIC REPORT. **1514**
0041-3054 See TRINITY COLLEGE RECORD. **1851**
0041-3097 See TRIQUARTERLY / NORTHWESTERN UNIVERSITY. **3447**
0041-3135 See TRIVENI (GUNTUR). **367**
0041-3151 See LA TROBE LIBRARY JOURNAL. **3222**
0041-3186 See TROPENLANDWIRT, DER. **142**
0041-3216 See TROPICAL AGRICULTURE. **142**
0041-3224 See TROPICAL AGRICULTURIST. **142**
0041-3232 See TROPICAL AND GEOGRAPHICAL MEDICINE. **3987**
0041-3240 See TROPICAL DISEASES BULLETIN. **3662**
0041-3259 See TROPICAL FISH HOBBYIST. **2315**
0041-3275 See TROPICAL MEDICINE AND HYGIENE NEWS. **3987**
0041-3291 See TROPICAL SCIENCE. **142**
0041-3372 See TROUT AND SALMON. **2315**
0041-3488 See TRUE CONFESSIONS (NEW YORK). **2494**
0041-350X See TRUE DETECTIVE. **5075**
0041-3615 See TRUE WEST. **2764**
0041-3674 See TRUSTEE. **3793**
0041-3682 See TRUSTS & ESTATES. **3119**
0041-3690 See TRUTH (PHILADELPHIA), THE. **2274**
0041-3712 See TRUTH SEEKER (SAN DIEGO, CALIF.), THE. **5006**
0041-3771 See TSITOLOGIIA. **540**
0041-3836 See TU CHE WEN CHAI. **2509**
0041-3860 See TUATARA. **475**
0041-3909 See TUBULAR STRUCTURES. **630**
0041-3917 See TUDOMANYOS ES MUSZAKI TAJEKOZTATAS. **3254**
0041-3984 See GROENTEN + FRUIT. VOLLEGRONDSGROENTEN. **2417**
0041-3984 See GROENTEN + FRUIT. FRUIT. **2417**
0041-3984 See GROENTEN + FRUIT. PADDESTOELEN. **2417**
0041-3984 See GROENTEN + FRUIT. ALGEMEEN. **2417**
0041-3984 See GROENTEN + FRUIT. GLASGROENTEN. **2417**
0041-3992 See TULANE LAW REVIEW. **3066**
0041-4018 See TULANE STUDIES IN GEOLOGY AND PALEONTOLOGY. **1400**

0041-4026 See TULANIAN, THE. **1095**
0041-4034 See TULIMULD. **3448**
0041-4050 See TULSA LAW JOURNAL. **3067**
0041-4093 See TUMOR RESEARCH. **3824**
0041-4131 See TUNISIE MEDICALE, LA. **3647**
0041-414X See TUNNELS & TUNNELLING. **2033**
0041-4158 See TURF AND SPORT DIGEST. **4927**
0041-4255 See BELLETEN. **2611**
0041-4271 See TURKEY WORLD (1968). **223**
0041-428X See TURKEYS. **223**
0041-4301 See TURKISH JOURNAL OF PEDIATRICS, THE. **3912**
0041-4360 See TURRIALBA : REVISTA INTERAMERICANO DE CIENCIAS AGRICOLAS. **143**
0041-4395 See TUTTI FOTOGRAFI. **4377**
0041-4530 See TV STAR PARADE. **1142**
0041-4565 See TVORCHESTVO. **332**
0041-462X See TWENTIETH CENTURY LITERATURE. **3355**
0041-4654 See CATHOLIC TWIN CIRCLE. **5026**
0041-4700 See TWO WHEELS. **4083**
0041-4727 See TWORCZOSC. **3448**
0041-4751 See TYDSKRIF VIR GEESTESWETENSKAPPE. **2856**
0041-476X See TYDSKRIF VIR LETTERKUNDE. **2315**
0041-4816 See TYO TERVEYS TURVALLISUUS. **2871**
0041-4859 See TYRES AND ACCESSORIES. **5078**
0041-4867 See TSEMENT. **630**
0041-4905 See CVETOVODSTVO. **2413**
0041-5065 See UE NEWS (U.S. EDITION). **1715**
0041-5146 See UITP BIBLIO-INDEX. TRANSPORT-VERKEHR. **5398**
0041-5278 See UNESCO COURIER, THE. **2856**
0041-5359 See UNISA ENGLISH STUDIES. **3449**
0041-543X See BULLETIN D'INFORMATION - URSI. **1128**
0041-5502 See USGA GREEN SECTION RECORD. **4928**
0041-5537 See U.S. NEWS & WORLD REPORT. **2494**
0041-5545 See USSR AND THIRD WORLD. **4537**
0041-5553 See COMPUTATIONAL MATHEMATICS AND MATHEMATICAL PHYSICS. **3501**
0041-560X See U-T LAWYER, THE. **3067**
0041-5650 See UCLA LAW REVIEW. **3067**
0041-5707 See UBERSEE RUNDSCHAU. **856**
0041-5715 See UFAHAMU. **2500**
0041-574X See UGANDA JOURNAL. **2644**
0041-5782 See UGESKRIFT FOR LAGER. **3648**
0041-5790 See UGOL. **2152**
0041-5812 See UHLI, RUDY. **2152**
0041-5995 See UKRAINIAN MATHEMATICAL JOURNAL. **3540**
0041-6002 See UKRAINSKI VISTI (EDMONTON). **5796**
0041-6010 See UKRAINIAN QUARTERLY, THE. **4498**
0041-6029 See UKRAINIAN REVIEW (LONDON, ENGLAND). **4499**
0041-6045 See UKRAINSKIJ HIMICESKIJ ZURNAL. **995**
0041-6061 See UKRAINSKYI ISTORYK. **2714**
0041-6118 See UKRAINSKYI BOTANICHNYI ZHURNAL. **529**
0041-6193 See ULSTER MEDICAL JOURNAL. **3648**
0041-624X See ULTRASONICS. **4424**
0041-6339 See UMPQUA TRAPPER, THE. **2764**
0041-6355 See UMWELT (DUSSELDORF). **2245**
0041-638X See ECONOMIC BULLETIN FOR EUROPE. **1634**
0041-6436 See UNASYLVA. **2397**
0041-6576 See UNDERSTANDING JAPAN. **2509**
0041-6592 See UNDERWATER LETTER, THE. **1458**
0041-6622 See UNDERWRITERS' REPORT. **2895**

0041-672X See UNIFORM COMMERCIAL CODE LAW JOURNAL. **3104**
0041-6762 See UNILIT (SECUNDERABAD). **3449**
0041-6924 See UNION LABOR NEWS (MADISON, WIS.). **1716**
0041-6932 See REVISTA DE LA UNION MATEMATICA ARGENTINA (1968). **3531**
0041-6940 See ARCHIVES. **3552**
0041-6959 See UNION MEDICALE DU CANADA. **3648**
0041-7017 See UNION RECORDER. **1096**
0041-7149 See UNITAS (MANILA). **1096**
0041-7173 See UNITED ASIA (BOMBAY). **2667**
0041-719X See BULLETIN - UNITED BIBLE SOCIETIES. **5015**
0041-7211 See JOURNAL OF CURRENT SOCIAL ISSUES. **4968**
0041-7238 See UNITED CHURCH OBSERVER, THE. **5006**
0041-7262 See UNITED EVANGELICAL. **5040**
0041-7270 See UNITED EVANGELICAL ACTION. **5006**
0041-7327 See UNITED MINE WORKERS JOURNAL. **1716**
0041-7343 See CURRENT BIBLIOGRAPHICAL INFORMATION / DAG HAMMARSKJOLD LIBRARY. **4502**
0041-7432 See MONTHLY BULLETIN OF STATISTICS - UNITED NATIONS. **5333**
0041-7475 See UNITED RUBBER WORKER: URW, THE. **5078**
0041-7548 See U.S. CATHOLIC. **5037**
0041-7637 See U.S. FARM NEWS. **143**
0041-7661 See U.S. GLASS, METAL & GLAZING. **2595**
0041-770X See JOURNAL OF THE UNITED SERVICE INSTITUTION OF INDIA, THE. **4048**
0041-7769 See ACCESSIONS LIST, MIDDLE EAST. **406**
0041-7904 See LIBRARY OF CONGRESS INFORMATION BULLETIN. **3226**
0041-7912 See L.C. CLASSIFICATION: ADDITIONS AND CHANGES. **3222**
0041-798X See PROCEEDINGS - UNITED STATES NAVAL INSTITUTE. **4182**
0041-8021 See OFFICIAL GAZETTE. **1306**
0041-803X See UNITED STATES PATENTS QUARTERLY, THE. **1309**
0041-8153 See UNITED SYNAGOGUE REVIEW. **5053**
0041-8226 See UNIVERSE MANCHESTER. **5813**
0041-8234 See UNIVERSIDAD (SANTA FE). **1851**
0041-8242 See UNIVERSIDAD (SAN SALVADOR, EL SALVADOR). **1851**
0041-8285 See REVISTA DE LA FACULTAD DE AGRONOMIA. **129**
0041-8307 See REVISTA DE LA FACULTAD DE FARMACIA. **4328**
0041-8420 See UNIVERSIDAD DE LA HABANA. **2553**
0041-851X See REVISTA JURIDICA DE LA UNIVERSIDAD INTERAMERICANA DE PUERTO RICO. **3042**
0041-8633 See BOLETIN MEXICANO DE DERECHO COMPARADO. **3124**
0041-8684 See PUBLICACIONES - INSTITUTO DE FISIOGRAFIA Y GEOLOGIA. **1392**
0041-8781 See REVISTA DO HOSPITAL DAS CLINICAS. **3635**
0041-8994 See RENDICONTI - SEMINARIO MATEMATICO DELLA UNIVERSITA DI PADOVA. **3531**
0041-9079 See UNIVERSITAS (STUTTGART). **2856**
0041-9109 See ANALELE STIINTIFICE ALE UNIVERSITATII "AL. I. CUZA" DIN IASI. SERIE NOUA. SECTIUNEA 1A, MATEMATICA. **3492**
0041-9133 See ANALELE STIINTIFICE ALE UNIVERSITATII "AL. I. CUZA" DIN IASI. SERIE NOUA. SECTIUNEA IIA, BIOLOGIE. **441**
0041-9257 See UNIVERSITY AFFAIRS / AFFAIRES UNIVERSITAIRES. **1852**
0041-9265 See UNIVERSITY BOOKMAN, THE. **1852**

0041-9354 See ANTHROPOLOGICAL PAPERS OF THE UNIVERSITY OF ALASKA. 229
0041-9419 See JOURNAL OF THE FACULTY OF MEDICINE, BAGHDAD. 3598
0041-9435 See BULLETIN OF THE SEISMOGRAPHIC STATIONS. 1403
0041-9494 See UNIVERSITY OF CHICAGO LAW REVIEW, THE. 3068
0041-9516 See UNIVERSITY OF COLORADO LAW REVIEW. 3068
0041-9524 See UNIVERSITY OF DAYTON REVIEW, THE. 3355
0041-9567 See UNIVERSITY OF EDINBURGH JOURNAL. 1852
0041-9605 See UNIVERSITY OF GHANA LAW JOURNAL. 3068
0041-9737 See UNIVERSITY OF LEEDS REVIEW, THE. 1096
0041-977X See BULLETIN OF THE SCHOOL OF ORIENTAL AND AFRICAN STUDIES. 3271
0041-9788 See LIBRARY REVIEW (LOUISVILLE, KY.). 3227
0041-9818 See UNIVERSITY OF MIAMI LAW REVIEW. 3069
0041-9907 See UNIVERSITY OF PENNSYLVANIA LAW REVIEW. 3069
0041-9915 See UNIVERSITY OF PITTSBURGH LAW REVIEW. 3069
0041-9923 See UNIVERSITY OF PORTLAND REVIEW. 2548
0041-994X See JOURNAL OF AGRICULTURE OF THE UNIVERSITY OF PUERTO RICO, THE. 99
0041-9966 See BULLETIN - QUEENSLAND. UNIVERSITY, BRISBANE. DEPT. OF CIVIL ENGINEERING. 2019
0042-0018 See UNIVERSITY OF SAN FRANCISCO LAW REVIEW. 3069
0042-0069 See UNIVERSITY OF SOUTH DAKOTA BULLETIN, THE. 1852
0042-0093 See OCCASIONAL PAPER - UNIVERSITY OF SYDNEY, AUSTRALIAN LANGUAGE RESEARCH CENTRE. 3307
0042-0123 See NAMAH-I DANISHKADAH-I DAMPIZISHKI. 5516
0042-0190 See UNIVERSITY OF TOLEDO LAW REVIEW, THE. 3069
0042-0204 See TECHNICAL REPORT (UNIVERSITY OF TORONTO. DEPT. OF COMPUTER SCIENCE). 1262
0042-0220 See UNIVERSITY OF TORONTO LAW JOURNAL, THE. 3069
0042-0247 See UNIVERSITY OF TORONTO QUARTERLY. 2856
0042-0271 See NEWS LETTER / THE UNIVERSITY OF VIRGINIA. 4669
0042-0328 See UNIVERSITY OF WESTERN AUSTRALIA LAW REVIEW. 3069
0042-0352 See UNIVERSITY OF WINDSOR REVIEW, THE. 3449
0042-0409 See UNIVERSO. 2578
0042-0409 See UNIVERSO [MICROFORM], L'. 2578
0042-0441 See UNLISTED DRUGS. 4331
0042-0468 See UNSCHEDULED EVENTS. 5264
0042-0476 See UNSEARCHABLE RICHES. 5020
0042-0506 See UNSER TSAYT. 2494
0042-059X See UNTERNEHMUNG. 889
0042-062X See UNTERRICHTSPRAXIS, DIE. 3331
0042-0735 See UPPER ROOM, THE. 5007
0042-0786 See URAL-ALTAISCHE JAHRBUCHER. 3331
0042-0786 See URAL-ALTAISCHE JAHRBUCHER (WIESBADEN, GERMANY : 1981). 3331
0042-0794 See URANIA. 401
0042-0816 See URBAN AFFAIRS QUARTERLY. 2837
0042-0859 See URBAN EDUCATION (BEVERLY HILLS, CALIF.). 1789
0042-0891 See URBAN LAND. 2838
0042-0905 See URBAN LAWYER, THE. 3070
0042-0972 See URBAN REVIEW, THE. 1789
0042-0999 See URBAN WEST. 2548
0042-1022 See URBANISTICA. 2838

0042-1065 See URDU NAMAH. 3449
0042-1084 See VFDB ZEITSCHRIFT. 2017
0042-1111 See UROLOGE. AUSGABE B. 3993
0042-1138 See UROLOGIA INTERNATIONALIS. 3993
0042-1154 See UROLOGIJA I NEFROLOGIJA. 3994
0042-1235 See US WURK. 3331
0042-1243 See USE OF ENGLISH, THE. 1789
0042-126X See USINE NOUVELLE. 1588
0042-1294 See USPEHI FIZICESKIH NAUK. 4424
0042-1308 See USPEKHI KHIMII. 995
0042-1316 See USPEHI MATEMATICESKIH NAUK. 3540
0042-1324 See USPEKHI SOVREMENNOI BIOLOGII. 475
0042-1359 See VESTNIK USTEDNIHO USTAVU GEOLOGICKEHO. 1401
0042-1405 See UTAH ECONOMIC AND BUSINESS REVIEW. 1525
0042-1413 See UEA ACTION. 1788
0042-143X See UTAH HISTORICAL QUARTERLY. 2764
0042-1448 See UTAH LAW REVIEW. 3070
0042-1502 See UTAH SCIENCE. 143
0042-1588 See UTILITY PURCHASING AND STORES. 952
0042-1685 See UZBEKSKII BIOLOGICHESKII ZHURNAL. 475
0042-1693 See UZBEKISTON GEOLOGIJA ZURNALI. 1400
0042-1707 See UZBEKSKII KHIMICHESKII ZHURNAL. 995
0042-1723 See VASLA. 3255
0042-174X See VDI-FORSHUNGSHEFT. 2000
0042-1758 See VDI NACHRICHTEN. 5168
0042-1766 See VDI-Z. 2131
0042-1790 See VEA NEWS. 1789
0042-1995 See VA-NYTT. 2183
0042-207X See VACUUM. 4430
0042-2096 See VADO E TORNO. 5399
0042-2169 See VAXTSKYDDSNOTISER. 4248
0042-2177 See VAG-OCH VATTEN BYGGAREN. 2033
0042-2363 See VALPARAISO UNIVERSITY LAW REVIEW. 3070
0042-238X See VALUATION (AMERICAN SOCIETY OF APPRAISERS). 815
0042-2401 See VALUE LINE INVESTMENT SURVEY (U.S. ED.), THE. 918
0042-2517 See VANDERBILT HUSTLER, THE. 1096
0042-2533 See VANDERBILT LAW REVIEW. 3070
0042-2568 See VANGUARD (VALPARAISO). 5007
0042-2592 See VANN. 2245
0042-2649 See VAR FAGELVARLD. 5620
0042-2657 See VAR FODA. 4199
0042-2703 See VARA PALSDJUR. 5523
0042-2738 See VARIETY. 4079
0042-2789 See VARSITY (TORONTO). 1096
0042-2800 See VART FORSVAR, TIDSKRIFT UTG. AF ALLMANNA FORSVARSFORENINGEN OCH FORENINGEN FOR NORRLANDS FASTA FORSVAR. 4060
0042-2835 See VASCULAR SURGERY. 3977
0042-2886 See VATTEN. 5541
0042-2932 See VE VENEZUELA. 5498
0042-2983 See VEDANTA KESARI, THE. 4364
0042-3106 See VEGETATIO. 529
0042-3114 See VEHICLE SYSTEM DYNAMICS. 2131
0042-3165 See VEJA. 2553
0042-3203 See VELD & FLORA. 530
0042-3211 See VELIGER, THE. 5599
0042-3254 See VELTRO, IL. 2524
0042-3327 See VENDING TIMES. 4214
0042-3378 See BOLETIN DEL ARCHIVO GENERAL DE LA NACION (CARACAS). 2480

0042-3386 See BOLETIN DEL ARCHIVO HISTORICO DE MIRAFLORES. 2480
0042-3491 See VENTURA COUNTY HISTORICAL SOCIETY QUARTERLY. 2476
0042-3580 See VENUS; JAPANESE JOURNAL OF MALACOLOGY. 5599
0042-3629 See MITTEILUNGSBLATT - VERBAND DER BIBLIOTHEKEN DES LANDES NORDRHEIN WESTFALEN. 3232
0042-370X See COMMUNION. 5028
0042-3718 See VERDAD Y VIDA. 5038
0042-3815 See MITTEILUNGEN DES VEREINIGUNG SCHWEIZERISCHER VERSICHERUNGSMATHEMATIKER. 2888
0042-384X See VEREINTE NATIONEN. 4537
0042-3874 See TIJDSCHRIFT VAN DE VERENIGING VOOR NEDERLANDSE MUZIEKGESCHIEDENIS. 4156
0042-3890 See VTB. VERFAHRENSTECHNISCHE BERICHTE. 2001
0042-3904 See VERFKRONIEK. 4570
0042-3920 See VERGLEICHENDE PAEDAGOGIK. 1789
0042-4021 See VERKEHRSMEDIZIN UND IHRE GRENZGEBIETE. 4806
0042-4056 See VERKSTADERNA. 2131
0042-4145 See VERMONT CATHOLIC TRIBUNE. 5038
0042-4161 See VERMONT HISTORY. 2764
0042-417X See VERMONT LIFE. 2549
0042-4188 See VERMONT MUSIC NEWS. 4158
0042-4234 See VERONA MISSIONS. 5007
0042-4269 See VERPACKUNG. 4222
0042-4358 See VERSICHERUNGSWIRTSCHAFT. 2895
0042-4439 See VERTICAL FILE INDEX. 427
0042-4447 See VERTICE (LISBOA). 3355
0042-4455 See VERTIFLITE. 39
0042-4498 See VERWALTUNG (BERLIN), DIE. 4693
0042-4501 See VERWALTUNGSARCHIV. 3071
0042-451X See VERWARMING EN VENTILATIE. 2608
0042-4609 See VESTNIK DERMATOLOGII I VENEROLOGII. 3723
0042-4625 See VESTNIK HIRURGII IM. I.I. GREKOVA. 3994
0042-4633 See VESTNIK MASINOSTROENIJA. 2152
0042-465X See VESTNIK OFTALMOLOGII. 3879
0042-4668 See VESTNIK OTORINOLARINGOLOGII. 3891
0042-4676 See VESTNIK RENTGENOLOGII I RADIOLOGII. 3947
0042-4684 See VESTNIK SELSKOHOZJAJSTVENNOJ NAUKI KAZAHSTANA. 144
0042-4692 See VESTNIK STATISTIKI. 5346
0042-4730 See VESTNIK USTREDNIHO USTAVU GEOLOGICKEHO. 1401
0042-4749 See VESTNIK VSESOJUZNOGO NAUCNO-ISSLEDOVATELSKOGO INSTITUTA ZELEZNODOROZNOGO TRANSPORTA. 5399
0042-4846 See VETERINARIJA (MOSKVA). 5524
0042-4854 See VETERINARY BULLETIN (LONDON). 5528
0042-4862 See VETERINARY ECONOMICS. 5525
0042-4870 See BULLETIN OF THE VETERINARY INSTITUTE IN PUAWY. 5506
0042-4897 See VETERINARY PRACTICE. 5526
0042-4900 See VETERINARY RECORD. 5526
0042-4935 See VETUS TESTAMENTUM. 5020
0042-5036 See VIATA MEDICALA. 3650
0042-5044 See VIATA ARMATEI : REVISTA ILUSTRATA DE LITERATURA SI ARTA EDITATA DE MINISTERUL APARARII NATIONALE. 4060
0042-5117 See LAW REVIEW (WELLINGTON). 2996
0042-5184 See VICTORIAN NATURALIST. 4173
0042-5192 See VICTORIAN NEWSLETTER, THE. 3355
0042-5206 See VICTORIAN POETRY. 3450

0042-5222 See VICTORIAN STUDIES. 3450

0042-5400 See VIE COMMUNALE ET DEPARTEMENTALE, LA. 4693

0042-5435 See VIE DES ARTS. 332

0042-546X See QUI TOURING. 5489

0042-5478 See VIE DU RAIL PARIS, LA. 5437

0042-5524 See VIE ET SANTE DAMMARIE-LES-LYS. 4806

0042-5583 See VIE MEDICALE, LA. 3650

0042-5605 See VIE SOCIALE. 5225

0042-5613 See VIE SPIRITUELLE, LA. 5007

0042-5648 See VIE WALLONNE. 2715

0042-5699 See VIERTELJAHRSCHRIFT FUER SOZIAL- UND WIRTSCHAFTSGESCHICHTE. 1588

0042-5702 See VIERTELJAHRSHEFTE FUER ZEITGESCHICHTE. 2632

0042-5710 See VIETNAM. 2667

0042-5818 See VIEWPOINTS (MONTREAL). 4499

0042-6024 See VIGILIA. 5038

0042-6032 See VIGILIAE CHRISTIANAE. 3451

0042-6083 See VIJESTI MUZEALACA I KONZERVATORA HRVATSKE. 4097

0042-6164 See VILLA DE MADRID : REVISTA DEL EXMO. AYUNTAMIENTO. 2715

0042-6180 See VILLAGE VOICE (NEW YORK), THE. 2549

0042-6199 See VILLAGER (BRONXVILLE, N.Y.), THE. 2549

0042-6210 See VILLAMOSSAG. 2085

0042-6229 See VILLANOVA LAW REVIEW. 3071

0042-6237 See VILLE GIARDINI. 2433

0042-6288 See VINDUET. 3451

0042-630X See VINI D'ITALIA. 2371

0042-6326 See VINOHRAD. 2372

0042-6350 See VINTAGE FORD, THE. 5427

0042-6369 See VINTAGE JAZZ MART. 4158

0042-6474 See VIRGINIA CAVALCADE. 2765

0042-6512 See VIRGINIA GEOGRAPHER, THE. 2579

0042-6571 See VIRGINIA JOURNAL OF INTERNATIONAL LAW. 3137

0042-658X See VIRGINIA JOURNAL OF SCIENCE. 5169

0042-6601 See VIRGINIA LAW REVIEW. 3071

0042-661X See VIRGINIA LAW WEEKLY. 3072

0042-6636 See VIRGINIA MAGAZINE OF HISTORY AND BIOGRAPHY, THE. 2765

0042-6652 See VIRGINIA MINERALS. 1445

0042-6709 See VIRGINIA PTA BULLETIN. 1874

0042-6717 See VIRGINIA PHARMACIST, THE. 4332

0042-6733 See VIRGINIA POULTRYMAN, THE. 223

0042-675X See VIRGINIA QUARTERLY REVIEW, THE. 3355

0042-6784 See VIRGINIA TOWN & CITY. 4693

0042-6792 See VIRGINIA WILDLIFE. 2208

0042-6806 See VIRITTAJA. 3332

0042-6822 See VIROLOGY (NEW YORK, N.Y.). 570

0042-6857 See UIRUSU. 3648

0042-6873 See VISAO. 2553

0042-6911 See VISION. 3355

0042-692X See VISION. 332

0042-6962 See VISION LETTER, THE. 4499

0042-6989 See VISION RESEARCH (OXFORD). 3879

0042-7004 See VISNYK. 4499

0042-7187 See VISVA-BHARATI JOURNAL OF PHILOSOPHY, THE. 4364

0042-7195 See VISVA-BHARATI QUARTERLY. 1309

0042-725X See VITA E PENSIERO. 4364

0042-7268 See VITA E SALUTE. 2495

0042-7306 See VITA LATINA. 3332

0042-7365 See VITA SOCIALE. 5038

0042-742X See VITAL SPEECHES OF THE DAY. 2495

0042-7470 See VITCHYZNA; LITERATURNO-KHUDOZHNII ZHURNAL. 3355

0042-7500 See VITIS. 475

0042-7519 See VITREOUS ENAMELLER. 2017

0042-7527 See VIVANT UNIVERS. 2579

0042-7543 See VIVARIUM. 4364

0042-7586 See RIVISTA DEL CLERO ITALIANO, LA. 4994

0042-7616 See VIZUGYI KOZLEMENYEK. 2096

0042-7683 See VLAANDEREN. 332

0042-773X See VNITRNI LEKARSTVI. 3802

0042-790X See VODOHOSPODARSKY CASOPIS. 1418

0042-7926 See VOEDING. 4200

0042-7934 See VOEDINGSMIDDELEN TECHNOLOGIE. 2361

0042-7993 See VOGELWELT, DIE. 5620

0042-8000 See VOGUE (NEW YORK). 5568

0042-8027 See VOGUE. 5568

0042-8108 See VOICE OF BUSINESS. 718

0042-8116 See VOICE OF FREEDOM (DALLAS, TEX.). 5008

0042-8132 See VOICE OF ISLAM, THE. 5045

0042-8175 See VOICE OF MISSIONS. 5069

0042-8191 See VOICE OF THE CEMENT, LIME, GYPSUM AND ALLIED WORKERS. 1717

0042-8256 See VOICE OF YOUTH (CHICAGO, ILL.), THE. 1921

0042-8264 See FULL GOSPEL BUSINESS MEN'S VOICE. 4960

0042-8272 See VOICES (AMERICAN ACADEMY OF PSYCHOTHERAPISTS). 3937

0042-8280 See VOICES INTERNATIONAL. 3473

0042-8442 See VOJNO-ISTORISKI GLASNIK. 4060

0042-8450 See VOJNOSANITETSKI PREGLED. 3650

0042-8639 See VOLTA REVIEW, THE. 4395

0042-8736 See VOPROSY EKONOMIKI. 718

0042-8744 See VOPROSY FILOSOFII. 4364

0042-8752 See VOPROSY IKHTIOLOGII. 2315

0042-8779 See VOPROSY ISTORII. 2633

0042-8787 See VOPROSY KURORTOLOGII, FIZIOTERAPII I LECEBNOJ FIZICESKOJ KULTURY. 3650

0042-8795 See VOPROSY LITERATURY. 3451

0042-8809 See VOPROSY MEDICINSKOJ HIMII. 494

0042-8817 See VOPROSY NEJROHIRURGII. 3977

0042-8825 See MATERINSTVO I DETSTVO / MINISTERSTVO ZDRAVOOKHRANENIIA ROSSIISKOI FEDERATSII. 3906

0042-8833 See VOPROSY PITANIIA. 4200

0042-8841 See VOPROSY PSIHOLOGII. 4621

0042-8957 See VOSPITANIE SHKOLNIKOV. 1790

0042-8965 See VOTRE BEAUTE, VOTRE SANTE. 406

0042-899X See VOX ROMANICA. 3332

0042-9007 See VOX SANGUINIS. 3774

0042-904X See VOYAGEUR. 2765

0042-9244 See DOKLADY VSESOUZNOJ ORDENA LENINA AKADEMII SELSKOHOZAJSTVENNYH NAUK IM. V.I. LENINA. 80

0042-9260 See ZAPISKI VSESOIUZNOGO MINERALOGICHESKOGO OBSHCHESTVA. 1445

0042-9368 See VYSOKOMOLEKULIARNYE SOEDINENIIA. SERIIA B. 995

0042-9384 See VYTIS. 5237

0042-9422 See VYZVOLNYI SHLIAKH. 3355

0042-9538 See WERBEN UND VERKAUFEN : W & V. 938

0042-9678 See WGO MONATSHEFTE FUER OSTEUROPAISCHES RECHT. 3075

0042-9686 See BULLETIN OF THE WORLD HEALTH ORGANIZATION. 3560

0042-9775 See WNYF. 2293

0042-9929 See WARME- UND STOFFUBERTRAGUNG. 2131

0042-9945 See WAFFEN- UND KOSTUMKUNDE. 252

0043-0013 See WAKAYAMA IGAKU. 3650

0043-003X See WAKE FOREST LAW REVIEW. 3072

0043-0048 See WALDARBEIT, DIE. 2398

0043-0099 See WALL STREET REPORTS. 919

0043-0102 See WALL STREET TRANSCRIPT, THE. 919

0043-0129 See WALLACES FARMER (1959). 145

0043-0161 See WALLS & CEILINGS. 631

0043-0218 See WAR CRY (OAKVILLE). 5008

0043-0234 See WAR CRY (NEW YORK, N.Y.), THE. 5314

0043-0315 See WARD'S AUTO WORLD. 5428

0043-0331 See WARENZEICHENBLATT. TEIL 1, (ANGEMELDETE ZEICHEN). AUSGABE A. 1929

0043-034X See WARENZEICHENBLATT. TEIL 2, (EINGETRAGENE ZEICHEN). AUSGABE A. 1930

0043-0374 See WARSHIP INTERNATIONAL. 4185

0043-0404 See WAS TUN. 4499

0043-0412 See WASCANA REVIEW. 3452

0043-0420 See WASHBURN LAW JOURNAL. 3072

0043-0439 See JOURNAL OF THE WASHINGTON ACADEMY OF SCIENCES. 5122

0043-0455 See WASHINGTON AND JEFFERSON LITERARY JOURNAL. 3452

0043-0463 See WASHINGTON AND LEE LAW REVIEW. 3072

0043-0501 See WASHINGTON COACH, THE. 4928

0043-0560 See WASHINGTON FOOD DEALER MAGAZINE, THE. 2361

0043-0587 See GRANGE NEWS, THE. 90

0043-0609 See WASHINGTON INTERNATIONAL ARTS LETTER. 2856

0043-0617 See WASHINGTON LAW REVIEW (1967). 3072

0043-0633 See WASHINGTON MONTHLY, THE. 4499

0043-0706 See WASHINGTON PURCHASER. 952

0043-0722 See WASHINGTON REPORT. 5314

0043-0749 See SCIENCE TRENDS. 5153

0043-0757 See WASHINGTON SOUNDS. 4395

0043-0773 See PROCEEDINGS OF THE WASHINGTON STATE ENTOMOLOGICAL SOCIETY. 5613

0043-0846 See WASHINGTON STATE VOTER. 4500

0043-0862 See WASHINGTON UNIVERSITY LAW QUARTERLY. 3073

0043-0897 See WASHINGTONIAN (WASHINGTON, D.C.), THE. 2549

0043-0900 See WASHINGTON'S HEALTH. 4807

0043-0927 See WASMANN JOURNAL OF BIOLOGY, THE. 476

0043-0951 See WASSER UND BODEN. 145

0043-0978 See WASSERWIRTSCHAFT. 5541

0043-0986 See WASSERWIRTSCHAFT-WASSERTECHNIK (BERLIN, DDR). 2096

0043-1001 See WASTE AGE. 2245

0043-1079 See WATCHMAKER, JEWELLER & SILVERSMITH (1941). 2915

0043-1087 See WATCHTOWER, THE. 5069

0043-1141 See WATER AND WASTES DIGEST. 5542

0043-1273 See WATER NEWSLETTER. 5543

0043-1346 See WATER QUALITY CONTROL DIGEST. 5543

0043-1354 See WATER RESEARCH (OXFORD). 5543

0043-1370 See WATER RESOURCES BULLETIN (URBANA). 5544

0043-1397 See WATER RESOURCES RESEARCH. 5547

0043-1443 See WATER WELL JOURNAL. 5548

0043-1486 See WATERSCHAPSBELANGEN. 5548

0043-1524 See WATERWAYS JOURNAL, THE. 5399

0043-1532 See WATSONIA. 530

0043-1575 See WAY, THE. 5008
0043-1621 See WAYNE LAW REVIEW. 3073
0043-1648 See WEAR. 2132
0043-1656 See WEATHER. 1436
0043-1664 See WEATHER VANE (CHARLESTON, W. VA.), THE. 3871
0043-1672 See WEATHERWISE. 1436
0043-1710 See WEE WISDOM; YOUNG FOLKS MAGAZINE DEVOTED TO PRACTICAL CHRISTIANITY. 1071
0043-1729 See WEED ABSTRACTS. 157
0043-1737 See WEED RESEARCH. 530
0043-1745 See WEED SCIENCE. 145
0043-1842 See WEEKLY LIVESTOCK REPORTER, THE. 223
0043-1850 See WEEKLY MARKET BULLETIN (CONCORD). 145
0043-1893 See WEEKLY PHARMACY REPORTS. 4332
0043-1923 See WEEKLY STATISTICAL SUGAR TRADE JOURNAL. 2362
0043-1974 See WEEKLY WEATHER AND CROP BULLETIN. 1437
0043-2040 See WEGE ZUM MENSCHEN. 5008
0043-2067 See WEGEN. 2033
0043-2156 See WEHRMEDIZINISCHE MONATSSCHRIFT. 3650
0043-2172 See WEHRTECHNIK. 4061
0043-2180 See WEIGHT WATCHERS. 2602
0043-2199 See WEIMARER BEITRAEGE. 3452
0043-2210 See WELCOME TO CZECHOSLOVAKIA. 5499
0043-2245 See WELDING AND METAL FABRICATION. 4028
0043-2245 See FAB GUIDE. 4027
0043-2253 See WELDING DESIGN & FABRICATION. 4028
0043-2288 See WELDING IN THE WORLD. 4028
0043-2296 See WELDING JOURNAL. 4028
0043-2318 See WELDING RESEARCH ABROAD. 4028
0043-2326 See BULLETIN - WELDING RESEARCH COUNCIL (U.S.). 4026
0043-2393 See WELL SERVICING. 4282
0043-2482 See WELT DER ARBEIT. 1717
0043-2520 See WELT DER SLAVEN. 3332
0043-2539 See WELT DES ISLAMS, DIE. 5045
0043-2547 See WELT DES ORIENTS, DIE. 3332
0043-2598 See WELTBUHNE, DIE. 2525
0043-261X See WELTKUNST, DIE. 368
0043-2636 See WELTWIRTSCHAFTLICHES ARCHIV. 5225
0043-2652 See WELTWIRTSCHAFT (TUBINGEN), DIE. 1588
0043-2695 See WENDING. 5009
0043-2792 See WERKSTATT UND BETRIEB. 2132
0043-2822 See WERKSTOFFE UND KORROSION. 4023
0043-289X See WESLEYAN ADVOCATE, THE. 5069
0043-2962 See WEST AFRICA (LONDON). 2500
0043-2989 See WEST AFRICAN JOURNAL OF BIOLOGICAL AND APPLIED CHEMISTRY. 995
0043-3047 See WEST & EAST. 2668
0043-308X See MONTHLY STATISTICAL DIGEST, WEST BENGAL. 1536
0043-3136 See WEST GEORGIA COLLEGE REVIEW. 1853
0043-3144 See WEST INDIAN MEDICAL JOURNAL, THE. 3650
0043-3225 See WEST VIRGINIA DENTAL JOURNAL. 1337
0043-325X See WEST VIRGINIA HISTORY. 2765
0043-3268 See WEST VIRGINIA LAW REVIEW. 3073
0043-3276 See WEST VIRGINIA LIBRARIES. 3256
0043-3284 See WEST VIRGINIA MEDICAL JOURNAL. 3650
0043-3292 See WEST VIRGINIA PHARMACIST, THE. 4332

0043-3373 See WESTCHESTER COUNTY PRESS, THE. 2550
0043-342X See WESTERLY. 3452
0043-3446 See PADAGOGIK (WEINHEIM AN DER BERGSTRASSE, GERMANY). 1771
0043-3462 See WESTERN AMERICAN LITERATURE. 3453
0043-3535 See WESTERN BUILDER. 631
0043-3624 See WCI : WESTERN CONSTRUCTION AND INDUSTRY MAGAZINE. 631
0043-3675 See EUROPEAN EDUCATION. 1745
0043-373X See WESTERN FOLKLORE. 2325
0043-3748 See WESTERN FRONT. 5763
0043-3799 See WESTERN GROWER & SHIPPER. 190
0043-3810 See WESTERN HISTORICAL QUARTERLY. 2636
0043-3837 See WESTERN HORSEMAN, THE. 2803
0043-3845 See WESTERN HUMANITIES REVIEW. 3453
0043-4000 See WESTERN OUTDOORS. 4880
0043-4019 See JOURNAL OF THE WESTERN PACIFIC ORTHOPAEDIC ASSOCIATION, THE. 3883
0043-4078 See WESTERN POLITICAL QUARTERLY, THE. 4500
0043-4094 See WESTERN PRODUCER. 146
0043-4132 See WESTERN RECORDER (MIDDLETOWN). 5009
0043-4191 See WESTERN SOCIALIST, THE. 4548
0043-4299 See WESTERN WORLD REVIEW. 3356
0043-4337 See WESTFALEN (MUNSTER). 2715
0043-4388 See WESTMINSTER THEOLOGICAL JOURNAL, THE. 5009
0043-4434 See WESTWAYS. 5428
0043-4442 See WETENSCHAP EN SAMENLEVING. 146
0043-4450 See WETTER UND LEBEN. 1437
0043-4558 See WHAT'S NEW IN ADVERTISING AND MARKETING. 767
0043-4590 See WHAT'S NEW IN HOME ECONOMICS. 2793
0043-4701 See WHEAT LIFE. 146
0043-4744 See WHEEL CLICKS. 5438
0043-4779 See WHEELS (AUSTRALIA). 5399
0043-4841 See WHICH? (LONDON). 1300
0043-4868 See WHITAKER'S BOOKS OF THE MONTH & BOOKS TO COME. 4833
0043-4876 See WHITE COLLAR. 1717
0043-4906 See WHITE COUNTY HERITAGE. 2766
0043-499X See WHITE TOPS, THE. 4867
0043-5007 See WHITE WING MESSENGER. 5009
0043-5082 See WIADOMOSCI ARCHEOLOGICZNE. 285
0043-5090 See WIADOMOSCI BOTANICZNE. 530
0043-5104 See WIADOMOSCI CHEMICZNE. 995
0043-5139 See WIADOMOSCI HUTNICZE. 4023
0043-5147 See WIADOMOSCI LEKARSKIE (1960). 3651
0043-5163 See WIADOMOSCI PARAZYTOLOGICZNE. 571
0043-5279 See WIEN AKTUELL. 2525
0043-5317 See WIENER GESCHICHTSBLATTER. 2716
0043-5325 See WIENER KLINISCHE WOCHENSCHRIFT. 3651
0043-5333 See WIENER LIBRARY BULLETIN, THE. 3256
0043-5341 See WIENER MEDIZINISCHE WOCHENSCHRIFT. 3651
0043-535X See WIENER TIERARZTLICHE MONATSSCHRIFT. 5527
0043-5457 See OUTDOOR EDGE. 4876
0043-5481 See WILDLIFE AUSTRALIA. 2209
0043-549X See WILDLIFE IN NORTH CAROLINA. 2209
0043-5511 See WILDLIFE REVIEW (FORT COLLINS). 2185
0043-5538 See ARIZONA WILDLIFE VIEWS. 2187

0043-5589 See WILLIAM AND MARY LAW REVIEW. 3075
0043-5597 See WILLIAM AND MARY QUARTERLY, THE. 2766
0043-5600 See WILLIAM AND MARY REVIEW, THE. 1854
0043-5627 See WILLIAMS' FAMILY BULLETIN, THE. 2477
0043-5643 See WILSON BULLETIN (WILSON ORNITHOLOGICAL SOCIETY), THE. 5621
0043-5651 See WILSON LIBRARY BULLETIN. 3256
0043-5716 See WINDLESS ORCHARD, THE. 3473
0043-5759 See HOUSE & GARDEN (BRITISH EDITION, 1948). 2901
0043-5775 See OFF LICENCE NEWS. 2370
0043-5791 See WINE. 2372
0043-583X See WINES & VINES. BUYER'S GUIDE ISSUE. 2373
0043-583X See WINES AND VINES. 2373
0043-5872 See WING FOOT CLAN, THE. 5078
0043-5937 See WINNER (WASHINGTON, D.C.), THE. 1350
0043-5953 See WINZER : FACHBLATT DES OSTERREICHISCHE WEINHAUS, DER. 2373
0043-5996 See WIRE. 4023
0043-6011 See WIRE INDUSTRY. 2086
0043-6046 See WIRE WORLD INTERNATIONAL. 2086
0043-6089 See WIRKENDES WORT (ZEITSCHRIFT). 3333
0043-6135 See WIRTSCHAFT UND RECHT. 1631
0043-6143 See WIRTSCHAFT UND STATISTIK. 5346
0043-6151 See WIRTSCHAFT UND WETTBEWERB. 857
0043-6275 See WIRTSCHAFTSDIENST (HAMBURG). 1526
0043-6291 See WIRTSCHAFTSPOLITISCHE BLAETTER. 1526
0043-6313 See WIRTSCHAFTSPRUFUNG, DIE. 753
0043-6356 See WISCONSIN AGRICULTURIST. 146
0043-6364 See WISCONSIN ARCHEOLOGIST, THE. 285
0043-6402 See WI CPA. 753
0043-6453 See WISCONSIN ENGINEER. 2001
0043-6488 See WISCONSIN JEWISH CHRONICLE, THE. 5053
0043-650X See WISCONSIN LAW REVIEW. 3075
0043-6534 See WISCONSIN MAGAZINE OF HISTORY. 2766
0043-6542 See WISCONSIN MEDICAL JOURNAL. 3651
0043-6585 See WISCONSIN PHARMACIST, THE. 4332
0043-6631 See WISCONSIN REVIEW (OSHKOSH). 3453
0043-6658 See WISCONSIN SCHOOL MUSICIAN, THE. 4159
0043-6666 See WISCONSIN SOCIOLOGIST, THE. 5265
0043-6720 See WISCONSIN TAXPAYER, THE. 4759
0043-678X See WISSENSCHAFT UND WEISHEIT. 5009
0043-6798 See WISSENSCHAFT UND WELTBILD; ZEITSCHRIFT FUER GRUNDFRAGEN DER FORSCHUNG UND WELTANSCHAUUNG. 4365
0043-6925 See WISSENSCHAFTLICHE ZEITSCHRIFT DER TECHNISCHEN UNIVERSITAT DRESDEN. 5170
0043-7085 See WITTERUNG IN UBERSEE, DIE. 1437
0043-7131 See WOCHENBLATT FUER PAPIERFABRIKATION. 4240
0043-7182 See WOJSKOWY PRZEGLAD HISTORYCZNY. 2716
0043-7255 See WOMAN BOWLER, THE. 4930
0043-728X See WOMAN CONSTITUTIONALIST. 5568
0043-7336 See WOMAN'S DAY. 5569

ISSN Index

0043-7344 *See* WOMAN'S JOURNAL. **5569**
0043-7379 *See* WOMAN'S PULPIT, THE. **5009**
0043-7417 *See* WOMAN'S WEEKLY LONDON. (1961). **5569**
0043-7441 *See* WOMEN IN BUSINESS (KANSAS CITY, MO.). **723**
0043-7468 *See* WOMEN LAWYERS' JOURNAL. **3076**
0043-7492 *See* WOMEN TO BY OF FOR AND ABOUT. **5570**
0043-7557 *See* WOMEN'S LEAGUE OUTLOOK. **5053**
0043-759X *See* WOMEN'S WORLD (WASHINGTON, D.C.). **5572**
0043-7662 *See* WOOD & WOOD PRODUCTS. **2406**
0043-7719 *See* WOOD SCIENCE AND TECHNOLOGY. **2406**
0043-7751 *See* WOODMEN OF THE WORLD MAGAZINE. **2896**
0043-776X *See* WOODWORKER (HEMEL HEMPSTEAD. (1910)). **635**
0043-7808 *See* WOOL & WOOLLENS OF INDIA. **5359**
0043-7840 *See* WOOL SACK, THE. **224**
0043-7859 *See* WOOL SCIENCE REVIEW. **5360**
0043-7875 *See* WOOL TECHNOLOGY AND SHEEP BREEDING. **224**
0043-7956 *See* WORD (WORCESTER). **3333**
0043-7964 *See* WORD (BROOKLYN), THE. **5009**
0043-7980 *See* WORD WAYS. **3333**
0043-8006 *See* WORDSWORTH CIRCLE. **3356**
0043-8014 *See* WORK BOAT, THE. **597**
0043-8022 *See* WORK STUDY. **889**
0043-8057 *See* WORKBENCH. **635**
0043-809X See WORKERS WORLD WW. **4500**
0043-8154 *See* WORLD (NEW YORK, N.Y. : 1967), THE. **3473**
0043-8170 *See* CANADA & THE WORLD. **5194**
0043-8200 *See* WORLD AFFAIRS (WASHINGTON). **4538**
0043-8219 *See* WORLD AGRICULTURAL ECONOMICS AND RURAL SOCIOLOGY ABSTRACTS. **157**
0043-8235 *See* WORLD AND THE SCHOOL, THE. **2633**
0043-8243 *See* WORLD ARCHAEOLOGY. **285**
0043-826X See WORLD AVIATION DIRECTORY. **40**
0043-8286 *See* WORLD BUDDHISM. **5022**
0043-8340 *See* WORLD COFFEE & TEA. **2373**
0043-8480 *See* WORLD FISHING. **2316**
0043-8502 *See* WORLD HEALTH. **4808**
0043-8529 *See* WORLD HIGHWAYS. **5446**
0043-8561 *See* WORLD INDUSTRIAL REPORTER. **4538**
0043-860X *See* WORLD JOURNAL OF PSYCHOSYNTHESIS. **3937**
0043-8618 *See* WORLD JURIST, THE. **4501**
0043-8677 *See* WORLD MEETINGS OUTSIDE UNITED STATES AND CANADA. **5170**
0043-8693 *See* WORLD MEETINGS: UNITED STATES AND CANADA. **5170**
0043-8758 *See* WORLD METAL STATISTICS. **4026**
0043-8774 *See* WORLD OF MUSIC (WILHELMSHAVEN). **4159**
0043-8790 *See* WORLD OIL (HOUSTON, TEX.). **4282**
0043-8804 *See* WORLD ORDER. **5010**
0043-8812 *See* NEW WORLD OUTLOOK. **5065**
0043-8839 *See* WORLD PARISH. **5010**
0043-8855 *See* INTERNATIONAL OIL NEWS. **4261**
0043-8871 *See* WORLD POLITICS. **4538**
0043-8901 *See* WORLD PROGRESS. **2550**
0043-8960 *See* WORLD REVIEW. **4501**
0043-8979 *See* WORLD REVIEW OF ANIMAL PRODUCTION. **147**
0043-8995 *See* WORLD SCOUTING. **5237**
0043-9045 See WORLD AVIATION DIRECTORY. **40**

0043-9088 *See* WORLD SURFACE COATINGS ABSTRACTS. **4226**
0043-9118 *See* WORLD TEXTILE ABSTRACTS. **5361**
0043-9126 *See* WORLD TOBACCO. **5374**
0043-9134 *See* WORLD TODAY, THE. **4539**
0043-9258 *See* WORLD WOOD. **2406**
0043-9339 *See* WORLD'S POULTRY SCIENCE JOURNAL. **224**
0043-9401 *See* WORMWOOD REVIEW, THE. **3454**
0043-941X *See* WORSHIP. **5010**
0043-9460 *See* WRECKING AND SALVAGE JOURNAL. **631**
0043-9517 *See* WRITER (BOSTON). **3454**
0043-9525 *See* WRITER'S DIGEST, THE. **3454**
0043-9533 *See* NEWSLETTER-WRITERS GUILD OF AMERICA, WEST. **3417**
0043-955X *See* WRITER'S NOTES & QUOTES. **3454**
0043-9630 *See* WYCHOWANIE FIZYCZNE I SPORT. **2602**
0043-9657 *See* WYNBOER. **2373**
0043-9665 *See* WYOMING ARCHAEOLOGIST, THE. **285**
0043-969X *See* WYOMING EDUCATOR, THE. **1792**
0043-9770 *See* WYOMING RURAL ELECTRIC NEWS. **2086**
0043-9800 *See* WYOMING STOCKMAN FARMER. **147**
0043-9819 *See* WYOMING WILDLIFE. **2210**
0043-9827 *See* WYOMING WOOL GROWER. **224**
0043-9932 *See* YACHT. **597**
0043-9940 *See* YACHTING (NEW YORK, N.Y.). **597**
0043-9983 *See* YACHTING MONTHLY, THE. **597**
0043-9991 *See* YACHTING WORLD. **597**
0044-0000 *See* YACHTS AND YACHTING. **597**
0044-0035 *See* YAKKYOKU. **4333**
0044-0078 *See* YALE FRENCH STUDIES. **2716**
0044-0086 *See* YALE JOURNAL OF BIOLOGY AND MEDICINE, THE. **3652**
0044-0094 *See* YALE LAW JOURNAL, THE. **3077**
0044-0124 *See* YALE REVIEW, THE. **5226**
0044-0175 *See* YALE UNIVERSITY LIBRARY GAZETTE, THE. **3256**
0044-0183 *See* YAMASHINA CHORUI KENKYUJO, KENKYU HOKOKU. **5621**
0044-0191 *See* YANKEE (DUBLIN, N.H.). **2550**
0044-0205 *See* YANKEE OILMAN. **4283**
0044-037X *See* YESTERYEARS. **2478**
0044-0426 *See* YIDDISHE KULTUR. **3456**
0044-0442 *See* YIDISHE SHPRAKH. **3334**
0044-0477 *See* YMER. **248**
0044-0507 *See* YOGA-MIMAMSA. **4186**
0044-0515 *See* YOJANA. **4695**
0044-0523 *See* YOKOHAMA MATHEMATICAL JOURNAL, THE. **3541**
0044-0531 *See* YOKOHAMA MEDICAL BULLETIN. **3652**
0044-0558 *See* YONAGO IGAKU ZASSHI. **3652**
0044-0604 *See* PROCEEDINGS OF THE YORKSHIRE GEOLOGICAL SOCIETY. **1391**
0044-0612 *See* YORKSHIRE JOURNAL. **5527**
0044-0728 *See* YOUNG CHILDREN. **1806**
0044-0809 See VIEWPOINT. **2896**
0044-0817 *See* YOUNG JUDAEAN. **5054**
0044-0841 *See* YOUNG MUSICIANS. **4159**
0044-1015 *See* YOUR EDMUNDITE MISSIONS NEWS LETTER. **5011**
0044-1031 *See* YOUR GARDEN CLAYTON. **2434**
0044-118X *See* YOUTH & SOCIETY. **5265**
0044-1341 *See* YUGOSLAV SURVEY. **2716**
0044-1368 *See* YUGOSLAVIA EXPORT. **858**
0044-1384 *See* UNAK (TORONTO). **1071**
0044-1449 *See* ZEITSCHRIFT FUER DIALEKTOLOGIE UND LINGUISTIK. **3335**
0044-1457 *See* INFORMATIONSDIENST BIBLIOTHEKSWESEN. **3217**
0044-1481 *See* Z OTCHANI WIEKOW. **285**

0044-149X *See* Z POLA WALKI. **4548**
0044-1570 *See* ZACCHIA. **3652**
0044-1597 *See* NONLINEAR VIBRATION PROBLEMS. **4413**
0044-1600 *See* ZAGADNIENIA EKONOMIKI ROLNEJ. **148**
0044-1619 *See* ZAGADNIENIA NAUKOZNAWSTWA. **5172**
0044-1643 *See* ZAHNAERZTLICHE MITTEILUNGEN. **1337**
0044-166X *See* ZWR. **1337**
0044-1740 *See* ZAMBIA NURSE (KITWE, ZAMBIA : 1978). **3871**
0044-1791 *See* ZAPISKI HISTORYCZNE. **2716**
0044-1805 See ZAPISKI VSEROSSIISKOGO MINERALOGICHESKOGO OBSHCHESTVA / ROSSIISKAIA AKADEMIIA NAUK. **1445**
0044-1856 *See* ZASCITA METALLOV. **4024**
0044-1864 *See* ZASHCHITA RASTENII. **530**
0044-1864 *See* ZASCITA RASTENIJ. **191**
0044-1899 *See* ZASTOSOWANIA MATEMATYKI. **3541**
0044-1945 *See* ZDOROVE. **3652**
0044-1961 *See* ZDRAVOOKHRANENIE BELORUSSII. **3652**
0044-197X *See* ZDRAVOOKHRANENIE ROSSIJSKOJ FEDERACII. **4809**
0044-2011 *See* ZDROWIE PUBLICZNE. **4809**
0044-2038 *See* ZEICHEN DER ZEIT (BERLIN, GERMANY). **5011**
0044-2054 See ZEISS INFORMATION WITH JENA REVIEW. **4442**
0044-2127 *See* ZEITSCHRIFT DES BERNISCHEN JURISTENVEREINS. **3077**
0044-2135 *See* ZEITSCHRIFT DES DEUTSCHER VEREINS FUER KUNSTWISSENSCHAFT (1963). **333**
0044-216X *See* ZEITSCHRIFT FUER AGYPTISCHE SPRACHE UND ALTERTUMSKUNDE. **286**
0044-2178 *See* ZEITSCHRIFT FUER ARZTLICHE FORTBILDUNG. **3739**
0044-2186 *See* ZEITSCHRIFT FUER ASTHETIK UND ALLGEMEINE KUNSTWISSENSCHAFT (BONN, GERMANY). **369**
0044-2194 *See* ZEITSCHRIFT FUER AGRARGESCHICHTE UND AGRARSOZIOLOGIE. **148**
0044-2240 *See* ZEITSCHRIFT FUER ANGEWANDTE ENTOMOLOGIE. **5614**
0044-2267 *See* ZEITSCHRIFT FUER ANGEWANDTE MATHEMATIK UND MECHANIK. **3541**
0044-2275 *See* ZEITSCHRIFT FUER ANGEWANDTE MATHEMATIK UND PHYSIK : ZAMP. **3541**
0044-2291 *See* ZEITSCHRIFT FUER ANGEWANDTE ZOOLOGIE. **5600**
0044-2305 *See* ZEITSCHRIFT FUER ANGLISTIK UND AMERIKANISTIK. **3456**
0044-2313 *See* ZEITSCHRIFT FUER ANORGANISCHE UND ALLGEMEINE CHEMIE. **1038**
0044-2321 *See* ZEITSCHRIFT FUER ARBEITSRECHT UND SOZIALRECHT. **3155**
0044-233X *See* ZEITSCHRIFT FUER ARCHAEOLOGIE. **286**
0044-2348 *See* ZEITSCHRIFT FUER AUSLAENDISCHES OEFFENTLICHES RECHT UND VOELKERRECHT. **3138**
0044-2356 *See* ZEITSCHRIFT FUER BALKANOLOGIE. **2717**
0044-2364 *See* ZEITSCHRIFT FUER BAYERISCHE LANDESGESCHICHTE. **2717**
0044-2372 *See* ZEITSCHRIFT FUER BETRIEBSWIRTSCHAFT. **1632**
0044-2380 *See* ZEITSCHRIFT FUER BIBLIOTHEKSWESEN UND BIBLIOGRAPHIE. **3257**
0044-2410 *See* ZEITSCHRIFT FUER DAS GESAMTE FAMILIENRECHT. **3122**
0044-2429 *See* ZEITSCHRIFT FUER DAS GESANTE GENOSSENSCHAFTSWESEN. **1544**

0044-2437 See ZEITSCHRIFT FUER DAS GESAMTE HANDELSRECHT UND WIRTSCHAFTSRECHT. 3078

0044-2445 See ZEITSCHRIFT FUER DAS GESAMTE KREDITWESEN. SCHRIFTENREIHE. 817

0044-2461 See ZEITSCHRIFT FUER DEN ERDKUNDEUNTERRICHT. 2579

0044-2496 See ZEITSCHRIFT FUER DEUTSCHE PHILOLOGIE. 3335

0044-2518 See ZEITSCHRIFT FUER DEUTSCHES ALTERTUM UND DEUTSCHE LITERATUR. 3335

0044-2526 See ZEITSCHRIFT FUER DIE ALTTESTAMENTLICHE WISSENSCHAFT. 5020

0044-2542 See ZEITSCHRIFT FUER DIE GESAMTE INNERE MEDIZIN UND IHRE GRENZGEBIETE. 3652

0044-2585 See ZEITSCHRIFT FUER DIE GESAMTE VERSICHERUNGS-WISSENSCHAFT. 2897

0044-2615 See ZEITSCHRIFT FUER DIE NEUTESTAMENTLICHE WISSENSCHAFT UND DIE KUNDE DER ALTEREN KIRCHE. 5011

0044-264X See ZEITSCHRIFT FUER ERNAHRUNGSWISSENSCHAFT. 4200

0044-2658 See ERZMETALL. 4001

0044-2666 See ZEITSCHRIFT FUER ETHNOLOGIE. 248

0044-2674 See ZEITSCHRIFT FUER EVANGELISCHE ETHIK. 5070

0044-2690 See ZEITSCHRIFT FUER EVANGELISCHES KIRCHENRECHT. 5070

0044-2712 See ZEITSCHRIFT FUER EXPERIMENTELLE UND ANGEWANDTE PSYCHOLOGIE. 4622

0044-2747 See ZEITSCHRIFT FUER FRANZOSISCHE SPRACHE UND LITERATUR. 3335

0044-2771 See ZEITSCHRIFT FUER GASTROENTEROLOGIE. 3748

0044-2798 See ZEITSCHRIFT FUER GEOMORPHOLOGIE. SUPPLEMENTBAND. 1401

0044-281X See ZEITSCHRIFT FUER GERONTOLOGIE. 3755

0044-2828 See ZEITSCHRIFT FUER GESCHICHTSWISSENSCHAFT. 2634

0044-2836 See ZEITSCHRIFT FUER GLETSCHERKUNDE UND GLAZIALGEOLOGIE. 1401

0044-2852 See ZEITSCHRIFT FUER HEERESKUNDE. 4061

0044-2887 See ZEITSCHRIFT FUER JAGDWISSENSCHAFT. 4931

0044-2895 See ZEITSCHRIFT FUER KATHOLISCHE THEOLOGIE. 5038

0044-2925 See ZEITSCHRIFT FUER KIRCHENGESCHICHTE. 5011

0044-2976 See ZEITSCHRIFT FUER KULTURAUSTAUSCH. 2717

0044-2992 See ZEITSCHRIFT FUER KUNSTGESCHICHTE. 369

0044-3026 See ZEITSCHRIFT FUER LEBENSMITTEL-UNTERSUCHUNG UND -FORSCHUNG. 2361

0044-3050 See ZEITSCHRIFT FUER MATHEMATISCHE LOGIK UND GRUNDLAGEN DER MATHEMATIK. 3541

0044-3093 See ZEITSCHRIFT FUER METALLKUNDE (STUTTGART, GERMANY). 4024

0044-3107 See ZEITSCHRIFT FUER MIKROSKOPISCH-ANATOMISCHE FORSCHUNG. 574

0044-3123 See ZEITSCHRIFT FUER MISSIONSWISSENSCHAFT UND RELIGIONSWISSENSCHAFT. 5011

0044-314X See ZEITSCHRIFT FUER MORPHOLOGIE UND ANTHROPOLOGIE. 248

0044-3220 See ZEITSCHRIFT FUER ORTHOPADIE UND IHRE GRENZGEBIETE. 3885

0044-3239 See ZEITSCHRIFT FUER OSTFORSCHUNG. 2717

0044-3247 See ZEITSCHRIFT FUER PAEDAGOGIK. 1792

0044-3263 See ZEITSCHRIFT FUER PFLANZENERHARUNG UND BODENKUNDE. 530

0044-3301 See ZEITSCHRIFT FUER PHILOSOPHISCHE FORSCHUNG. 4365

0044-331X See ZEITSCHRIFT FUER PHONETIK, SPRACHWISSENSCHAFT UND KOMMUNIKATIONSFORSCHUNG. 3335

0044-331x See SPRACHTYPOLOGIE UND UNIVERSALIENFORSCHUNG. 3323

0044-3336 See ZEITSCHRIFT FUER PHYSIKALISCHE CHEMIE (NEUE FOLGE). 1059

0044-3360 See ZEITSCHRIFT FUER POLITIK. 4501

0044-3409 See ZEITSCHRIFT FUER PSYCHOLOGIE MIT ZEITSCHRIFT FUER ANGEWANDTE PSYCHOLOGIE. 4622

0044-3441 See ZEITSCHRIFT FUER RELIGIONS- UND GEISTESGESCHICHTE. 5011

0044-3468 See ZEITSCHRIFT FUER SAUGETIERKUNDE. 476

0044-3476 See ZEITSCHRIFT FUER SCHWEIZERISCHE ARCHAEOLOGIE UND KUNSTGESCHICHTE. 286

0044-3484 See ZEITSCHRIFT FUR SCHWEIZERISCHE KIRCHENGESCHICHTE. REVUE D'HISTOIRE ECCLESIASTIQUE SUISSE. 5011

0044-3492 See ZEITSCHRIFT FUER SLAVISCHE PHILOLOGIE. 3335

0044-3506 See ZEITSCHRIFT FUER SLAWISTIK. 3335

0044-3514 See ZEITSCHRIFT FUER SOZIALPSYCHOLOGIE. 4622

0044-3549 See ZEITSCHRIFT FUER THEOLOGIE UND KIRCHE. 5011

0044-3565 See ZEITSCHRIFT FUER TIERPHYSIOLOGIE, TIERERNAHRUNG UND FUTTERMITTELKUNDE. 5600

0044-3581 See ZEITSCHRIFT FUR TIERZUCHTUNG UND ZUCHTUNGSBIOLOGIE (HAMBURG, GERMANY : 1939). 224

0044-3638 See ZEITSCHRIFT FUER VERGLEICHENDE RECHTSWISSENSCHAFT. 3138

0044-3654 See ZEITSCHRIFT FUR VERKEHRSSICHERHET. 5446

0044-3670 See ZEITSCHRIFT FUER VERKEHRSWISSENSCHAFT. 5400

0044-3697 See JOURNAL OF EXPERIMENTAL ANIMAL SCIENCE (1991). 5513

0044-3700 See ZEITSCHRIFT FUER VOLKSKUNDE. 2325

0044-3727 See ZEITSCHRIFT FUER WASSER- UND ABWASSER FORSCHUNG. 1419

0044-3751 See ZEITSCHRIFT FUER WIRTSCHAFTSGEOGRAPHIE. 2580

0044-3786 See ZEITSCHRIFT FUER WURTTEMBERGISCHE LANDESGESCHICHTE. 2717

0044-3808 See ZEITSCHRIFT FUER ZOOLOGISCHE SYSTEMATIK UND EVOLUTIONSFORSCHUNG. 5600

0044-3816 See ZEITSCHRIFT INTERNE REVISION. 725

0044-3867 See ZELLSTOFF UND PAPIER. 4240

0044-3883 See ZEMEDELSKA TECHNIKA. 161

0044-3913 See ZEMLEDELIE. 148

0044-3948 See ZEMLJA I VSELENNAJA. 401

0044-4018 See KENT RECUSANT HISTORY. 5031

0044-4030 See ZENTRALBLATT FUER PATHOLOGIE : GENERAL PATHOLOGY/PATHOLOGICAL ANATOMY. 3899

0044-409X See ZENTRALBLATT FUER CHIRURGIE. 3978

0044-409X See ZENTRALBLATT FUER CHIRURGIE. SONDERBAND. 3978

0044-4189 See ZENTRALBLATT FUER GEOLOGIE UND PALAONTOLOGIE. TEIL II: PALAONTOLOGIE. 4231

0044-4197 See ZENTRALBLATT FUER GYNAKOLOGIE. 3769

0044-4235 See ZENTRALBLATT FUER MATHEMATIK UND IHRE GRENZGEBIETE. 3543

0044-4251 See ZENTRALBLATT FUER NEUROCHIRURGIE. 3978

0044-4278 See ZENTRALBLATT FUER SOZIALVERSICHERUNG, SOZIALHILFE UND VERSORGUNG. 5315

0044-4391 See ZESZYTY HISTORYCZNE. 2717

0044-4405 See ZESZYTY NAUKOWE KATOLICKIEGO UNIWERSYTETU LUBELSKIEGO. 5172

0044-4413 See FASCICULI MATHEMATICI. 3505

0044-4448 See ZHELEZNODOROZHNYI TRANSPORT. 5438

0044-4456 See ZHENSHCHINY MIRA. 5572

0044-4464 See ZHILISHCHNOE I KOMMUNALNOE KHOZIAISTVO. 149

0044-4472 See ZHILISHCHNOE STROITELSTVO. 631

0044-4502 See ZURNAL ANALITICHESKOI HIMII. 1020

0044-4510 See ZURNAL EKSPERIMENTALNOJ I TEORETICESKOJ FIZIKI. 4426

0044-4529 See ZHURNAL EVOLIUTSIONNOI BIOKHIMII I FIZIOLOGII. 494

0044-4537 See ZHURNAL FIZICHESKOI KHIMII. 1059

0044-457X See ZHURNAL NEORGANICHESKOI KHIMII. 1038

0044-4588 See ZURNAL NEVROPATOLOGII I PSIHIATRII IM S.S. KORSAKOVA. 3847

0044-4596 See ZURNAL OBSCEJ BIOLOGI. 476

0044-460X See ZURNAL OBSEJ HIMII. 996

0044-4618 See ZURNAL PRIKLADNOI HIMII. 996

0044-4626 See PMTF. 4417

0044-4642 See ZURNAL TEHNICESKOJ FIZIKI. 4426

0044-4650 See ZURNAL USNYH, NOSOVYH I GORLOVYH BOLEZNEJ. 3891

0044-4669 See ZURNAL VYCISLITELNOJ MATEMATIKI I MATEMATICESKOJ FIZIKI. 4426

0044-4677 See ZHURNAL VYSSHEI NERVNOI DEIATELNOSTI IMENI I. P. PAVLOVA. 3847

0044-4715 See ZIEKENHUIS, HET. 3794

0044-4758 See SIYYON. 5052

0044-4812 See ZIVA. 4174

0044-4847 See ZIVOCISNA VYROBA. 224

0044-488X See ZNAK. 5011

0044-4901 See ZNAMJA ROSSII. 2717

0044-4952 See ZODIAQUE. 369

0044-4979 See ZONIERZ POLSKI. 4061

0044-4987 See ZONA FRANCA. 3456

0044-5029 See ZOO ANVERS. 5601

0044-5088 See ZOOLOGICA. 5601

0044-5096 See ZOOLOGICA AFRICANA. 5601

0044-510X See ZOOLOGICA POLONIAE; ARCHIVUM SOCIETATIS ZOOLOGORUM POLONIAE. 5601

0044-5134 See ZOOLOGICESKIJ ZURNAL. 5602

0044-5150 See ZOOLOGISCHE BEITRAEGE. 5602

0044-5169 See ZOOLOGISCHE GARTEN; ZEITSCHRIFT FUER DIE GESAMTE TIERGARTNEREI. 5603

0044-5177 See ZOOLOGISCHE JAHRBUCHER. ABTEILUNG FUER ANATOMIE UND ONTOGENIE DER TIERE. 5603

0044-5185 See ZOOLOGISCHE JAHRBUCHER. ABTEILUNG FUER ALLGEMEINE ZOOLOGIE UND PHYSIOLOGIE DER TIERE. 5603

0044-5193 See ZOOLOGISCHE JAHRBUCHER. ABTEILUNG FUER SYSTEMATIK, OKOLOGIE UND GEOGRAPHIE DER TIERE. 5603

0044-5223 See ENTOMOLOGISCHE MITTEILUNGEN AUS DEM ZOOLOGISCHEN MUSEUM HAMBURG. 5582

0044-5231 See ZOOLOGISCHER ANZEIGER. 5603

0044-5274 See ZOON. 5603

0044-5355 See ZPRAVODAJ VZLU. 5173

0044-5398 See ZUCKERRUEBE, DIE. 191

0044-5401 See ZUCHTUNGSKUNDE. 476

0044-555X See ZVUK (BEOGRAD). 4160

0044-5584 See ZYCIE I MYSL. 5011

0044-5622 See ABSEES. 2671
0044-5665 See AMERICAN FOREIGN LANGUAGE TEACHER. 3263
0044-5681 See AIM. AUTOMOTIVE INDUSTRY MATTERS. 5403
0044-5711 See ARIS. 337
0044-5851 See ACADIENSIS (FREDERICTON). 2717
0044-586X See ACAROLOGIA. 5573
0044-5878 See ACCIDENT PREVENTION. 2858
0044-5894 See ACCION EMPRESARIAL. 1460
0044-5959 See ACTA AGRONOMICA (PALMIRA). 43
0044-5967 See ACTA AMAZONICA. 439
0044-5975 See ACTA ANTIQUA ACADEMIAE SCIENTIARUM HUNGARICAE. 3261
0044-5983 See ACTA BOTANICA NEERLANDICA. 497
0044-5991 See ACTA HISTOCHEMICA ET CYTOCHEMICA. 531
0044-6009 See ACTA HOSPITALIA. 3775
0044-6025 See ACTA MEDICA IRANICA. 3544
0044-605X See ACTA VETERINARIA SCANDINAVICA. 5501
0044-6092 See ACTION ERA VEHICLE, THE. 5403
0044-6157 See ACTUALITE FIDUCIAIRE, L'. 2927
0044-6173 See AKTUELLE TRAUMATOLOGIE. 3547
0044-6203 See JOURNAL - ADDICTION RESEARCH FOUNDATION, THE. 4786
0044-6335 See ADOLESCENT MEDICINE (GLENVIEW). 3899
0044-636X See ADVANCED TECHNOLOGY LIBRARIES. 3187
0044-6378 See ADVANCES IN URETHANE SCIENCE AND TECHNOLOGY. 5081
0044-6394 See ADVERSE DRUG REACTION BULLETIN. 3978
0044-6416 See ADVOCATE (VANCOUVER). 2928
0044-6483 See AFRICA CONFIDENTIAL. 4514
0044-667X See AFRISCOPE. 2907
0044-6726 See AGORA MELBOURNE. 1887
0044-6793 See AGRICULTURA EM SAO PAULO. 48
0044-6807 See AGRICULTURAL ENGINEERING AUSTRALIA. 50
0044-6912 See AICHI-GAKUIN DAIGAKU SHIGAKKAI-SHI. 1315
0044-6947 See AIR (VANCOUVER). 3459
0044-6955 See AIR COMBAT. 7
0044-7005 See AIRFAIR. 5460
0044-7048 See AKRON BUSINESS AND ECONOMIC REVIEW. 637
0044-7064 See ALALUZ. 3359
0044-7072 See ALBANIA TODAY. 4462
0044-7250 See ALEXANDRIA JOURNAL OF AGRICULTURAL RESEARCH. 57
0044-7412 See AMANUENSIS. 3360
0044-7439 See AMBASSADOR, THE. 4515
0044-7447 See AMBIO. 2160
0044-7463 See AMENAGEMENT ET NATURE. 2186
0044-7471 See AMERASIA JOURNAL. 2254
0044-748X See LATINSKAIA AMERIKA. 2744
0044-751X See PROCEEDINGS OF THE AMERICAN ANTIQUARIAN SOCIETY. 2755
0044-7544 See AMERICAN BABY. 2276
0044-7560 See ALI-ABA CLE REVIEW. 1808
0044-7587 See ACS SINGLE ARTICLE ANNOUNCEMENT. 959
0044-7609 See ACA JOURNAL OF CHIROPRACTIC, THE. 3543
0044-7633 See AMERICAN CLASSICAL REVIEW. 1081
0044-7676 See AFTRA. 1148
0044-7749 See AMERICAN LABORATORY (FAIRFIELD). 960
0044-779X See DIRECTORY OF MEMBERS - AMERICAN PHILOLOGICAL ASSOCIATION. 3277

0044-7803 See AMERICAN POLITICS QUARTERLY. 4463
0044-7811 See AMERICAN POSTAL WORKER, THE. 1643
0044-7870 See PROCEEDINGS OF THE ASIS ANNUAL MEETING. 3242
0044-7889 See ASM NEWS (METALS PARK, OHIO). 3998
0044-7897 See ASM NEWS. 560
0044-7927 See ASTR, AMERICAN SOCIETY FOR THEATRE RESEARCH NEWSLETTER. 5361
0044-7943 See BULLETIN / AMERICAN SOCIETY OF CARTOGRAPHERS. 2580
0044-8060 See AMERICAN STUDIES IN SCANDINAVIA. 2719
0044-8095 See AMI DES JARDINS ET DE LA MAISON, L'. 2408
0044-8133 See BULLETIN DES AMIS D'ANDRE GIDE. 3369
0044-8222 See ANCESTOR. 2437
0044-8249 See ANGEWANDTE CHEMIE (WEINHEIM AN DER BERGSTRASSE, GERMANY). 961
0044-8265 See ANGLO-SOVIET JOURNAL, THE. 2673
0044-829X See NEWS BULLETIN - ANIMAL DEFENCE LEAGUE OF CANADA. 226
0044-8370 See JASO : JOURNAL OF THE ANTHROPOLOGICAL SOCIETY OF OXFORD. 238
0044-8435 See APIDOLOGIE. 5576
0044-8486 See AQUACULTURE. 2295
0044-8516 2316
0044-8591 See ARCHAEOLOGY IN MONTANA. 257
0044-8605 See ARCHEOLOGICKE ROZHLEDY. 259
0044-8613 See ARCHIPEL PARIS. 2501
0044-8621 See ARCHITECT. 288
0044-863X See ARCHITECTURA. 288
0044-8680 See ARCHITEKTURA A URBANIZMUS. 291
0044-8699 See ARCHIV ORIENTALNI. 3266
0044-8710 See ARCHIVES OF CHILD HEALTH. 3900
0044-8737 See ARCHIVIO STORICO SIRACUSANO. 2676
0044-8745 See ARCHIVIUM HIBERNICUM. 2480
0044-8753 See ARCHIVUM MATHEMATICUM. 3496
0044-8788 See AREAS OF CONCERN. 2187
0044-8885 See ARK RIVER REVIEW, THE. 3363
0044-8893 See ARKANSAS LP NEWS. 4251
0044-894X See ARMENIAN OBSERVER, THE. 5633
0044-9008 See ARS. 337
0044-9075 See ARTEFACT, THE. 260
0044-9202 See ASIAN MUSIC. 4101
0044-9237 See AJIA KENKYU (AJIA SEIKEI GAKKAI). 2645
0044-9288 See BOLETIN DE LA A.N.A.B.A. 3196
0044-9423 See ARCHIVES (QUEBEC). 2480
0044-961X See AGB REPORTS. 1807
0044-9652 See MINUTES OF THE MEETING - ASSOCIATION OF RESEARCH LIBRARIES. 3231
0044-9784 See ASTROLOGICAL REVIEW, THE. 390
0044-9873 See ATHLETIC ADMINISTRATION. 1855
0044-9881 See ATLANTIC CONTROL STATES BEVERAGE JOURNAL. 5070
0044-992X See ATLANTIC SALMON JOURNAL, THE. 2296
0044-9997 See AUDITOR, THE. 4937
0045-0049 See AUSBILDUNG UND BERATUNG IN LAND- UND HAUSWIRTSCHAFT / LAND- UND HAUSWIRTSCHAFTLICHER AUSWERTUNGS- UND INFORMATIONSDIENST. 2788
0045-0197 See AUSTRALIA NOW. 2668
0045-026X See AUSTRALIAN AUTHOR, THE. 3364
0045-0294 See AUSTRALIAN BEE JOURNAL. 63

0045-0308 See AUSTRALIAN BIBLICAL REVIEW. 5014
0045-0316 See AUSTRALIAN BIRD WATCHER. 5615
0045-0359 See CHIROPRACTIC JOURNAL OF AUSTRALIA. 4379
0045-0405 See AUSTRALIAN CURRENT LAW. LEGISLATION. 2938
0045-0405 See AUSTRALIAN CURRENT LAW. REPORTER. 2938
0045-0421 See AUSTRALIAN DENTAL JOURNAL. 1317
0045-0448 See AUSTRALIAN FILMS. 4064
0045-0618 See AUSTRALIAN JOURNAL OF FORENSIC SCIENCES, THE. 3740
0045-0685 See AUSTRALIAN MATHEMATICS TEACHER, THE. 3496
0045-0731 See A.N.C.O.L.D. BULLETIN. 1963
0045-0758 See AUSTRALIAN NURSES' JOURNAL. 3852
0045-0766 See AUSTRALIAN OCCUPATIONAL THERAPY JOURNAL. 1875
0045-0782 See AUSTRALIAN ORCHID REVIEW. 2409
0045-0855 See AUSTRALIAN SCIENCE TEACHERS' JOURNAL, THE. 5087
0045-0960 See AUSTRALIAN WELDING RESEARCH. 4026
0045-1150 See AVANT-SCENE DU CINEMA, L'. 4064
0045-1169 See AVANT-SCENE, THEATRE, L'. 5361
0045-1193 See INTERNATIONAL AVIATION MECHANICS JOURNAL. 24
0045-1304 See BADGER HERALD. 1089
0045-1312 See BADMINTON U S A. 4886
0045-1347 See BALLET-HOO. 1310
0045-1371 See BALTISTICA. 3268
0045-138X See BAMAH (JERUSALEM, ISRAEL). 5361
0045-1460 See BANK OF CANADA REVIEW. 775
0045-1487 See BANK TECHNOLOGY REPORT. 5087
0045-1568 See BAROMETER OF SMALL BUSINESS. 642
0045-1703 See BULLETIN DE STATISTIQUE - INSTITUT NATIONAL DE STATISTIQUE. 5324
0045-1932 See BIBLIOGRAPHY ON HIGH PRESSURE RESEARCH. 410
0045-1940 See BIBLIONEWS AND AUSTRALIAN NOTES AND QUERIES. 4824
0045-1983 See BIG BOOK OF METALWORKING MACHINERY. 3999
0045-1991 See BIG BYTE, THE. 1246
0045-2033 See SEIBUTSU KAGAKU / NIHON SEIBUTSU KAGAKUSHA KYOKAI HENSHU. 472
0045-205X See BIOLOGIE IN UNSERER ZEIT. 446
0045-2068 See BIOORGANIC CHEMISTRY. 1039
0045-2165 See BLACK GRAPHICS INTERNATIONAL. 316
0045-219X See BLACK LECHWE. 2188
0045-222X See BLACK MARIA. 3367
0045-2238 See BLACK NEWS DIGEST. 1655
0045-2300 See BOARDROOM REPORTS. 861
0045-2319 See BODYSHOP. 5408
0045-2351 See ROMANIAN NEWS AND WORLD REPORT. 2707
0045-2521 See BOOKPLATES IN THE NEWS. 2771
0045-2564 See BOOKS IN CANADA. 4825
0045-2572 See BOOKS IN ENGLISH. 411
0045-2629 See BOTANICA (NEW DELHI, INDIA). 503
0045-270X See BRASIL FLORESTAL. 2376
0045-2963 See B.C. HISTORICAL NEWS. 2722
0045-2998 See BC MOUNTAINEER, THE. 4869
0045-3005 See MUSEUM ROUND-UP. 4092
0045-3013 See BC OUTDOORS. 4869
0045-303X See SNOW SURVEY BULLETIN. 5539
0045-3102 See BRITISH JOURNAL OF SOCIAL WORK, THE. 5275

0045-3129 See B N A TOPICS. 2784
0045-3226 See BROKEN SPOKE, THE. 5408
0045-3285 See BUCKEYE REVIEW. 2257
0045-3307 See BUCKSKIN BULLETIN. 2724
0045-3501 See BULLETIN DE L'AFRIQUE NOIRE. 1466
0045-3536 See BULWARK, THE. 5057
0045-3544 See PUBLIC MANAGER (POTOMAC, MD.), THE. 4676
0045-3587 See BUSINESS & PROFESSIONAL WOMAN (OTTAWA). 5552
0045-3609 See BUSINESS AND SOCIETY REVIEW (1974). 645
0045-3846 See CALCUTTA REVIEW. 1090
0045-3900 See CALIFORNIA BUILDER & ENGINEER. 2020
0045-3978 See CALIFORNIA QUARTERLY. 3371
0045-4001 See CALIPER (TORONTO). 4385
0045-4109 See CAMPAIGNER (NEW YORK). 4540
0045-4168 See FORAGE NOTES. 88
0045-4192 See CANADA GAZETTE. PART 1. 2947
0045-4206 See CANADA GAZETTE. PART 2. 2947
0045-4214 See NEWSLETTER - CANADA JAPAN TRADE COUNCIL. 1638
0045-4222 See CANADA SKI. 4889
0045-4230 See CANADA SUPREME COURT REPORTS. 2947
0045-4257 See CANADA TODAY (WASHINGTON). 2529
0045-4303 See CANADA'S BUSINESS CLIMATE. 654
0045-432X See CANADIAN AGRICULTURAL ENGINEERING. 158
0045-4494 See CANADIAN BOATING. 592
0045-4575 See CANADIAN COIN BOX MAGAZINE. 655
0045-4648 See CANADIAN CURLING NEWS. 4889
0045-4737 See CANADIAN FAR EASTERN NEWSLETTER, THE. 4517
0045-477X See CANADIAN FICTION MAGAZINE. 3372
0045-4885 See CANADIAN FRUITGROWER. 2412
0045-4915 See CANADIAN HANDGUN. 2810
0045-4982 See DIALOGUE - CANADIAN INSTITUTE OF CHARTERED ACCOUNTANTS. 742
0045-5067 See CANADIAN JOURNAL OF FOREST RESEARCH. 2377
0045-5075 See CANADIAN JOURNAL OF OPTOMETRY. 4215
0045-5091 See CANADIAN JOURNAL OF PHILOSOPHY. 4343
0045-5156 See CANADIAN MANAGER. 863
0045-5164 See CMS NOTES. 3500
0045-5253 See CANADIAN PHILATELIST. 2784
0045-527X See CANADIAN RED BOOK. 5408
0045-544X See CANADIAN THEOSOPHIST, THE. 4942
0045-5466 See CANADIAN TRANSPORT. 5430
0045-5520 See CANADIAN VOCATIONAL JOURNAL. 1911
0045-5768 See CARE ON THE ROAD BIRMINGHAM. 5439
0045-5865 See CAROLINA TIPS. 5092
0045-5873 See CAROLINIAN (RALEIGH), THE. 5722
0045-6152 See CERAMURGIA. 2588
0045-625X See CHALLENGE IN EDUCATIONAL ADMINISTRATION. 1861
0045-639X See CHEMICAL INDUSTRY NOTES. 1011
0045-6403 See CHEMICAL INSIGHT. 1022
0045-6500 See CHEMICAL WEEKLY. 969
0045-6519 See CHEMISCHE TECHNIK. 2011
0045-6535 See CHEMOSPHERE (OXFORD). 2226
0045-656X See CHESAPEAKE BAY MAGAZINE. 593
0045-6608 See CHEVRE TOURS, LA. 209
0045-6705 See ORANA. 3239
0045-6713 See CHILDREN'S LITERATURE IN EDUCATION. 3374
0045-6764 See CHINA NOW. 2502
0045-6861 See CHURCH AND CLERGY FINANCE. 783
0045-6888 See CIENCIA AGRONOMICA. 74
0045-6896 See CIERVO, EL. 4948
0045-6926 See CINEMA. 4066
0045-6985 See CITY AND SUBURBAN TRAVEL. 5466
0045-7027 See CIVIC AFFAIRS (TORONTO). 4638
0045-7035 See CIVIL AFFAIRS JOURNAL AND NEWSLETTER. 4638
0045-7043 See CIVIL & MILITARY LAW JOURNAL. 3182
0045-7051 See CIVIL LIBERTIES. 5760
0045-7159 See CLIMBING (ASPEN, COLO.). 4871
0045-7167 See HORUMON TO RINSHO. 3731
0045-7205 See CLUB MANAGEMENT IN AUSTRALIA. 5230
0045-723X See COASTAL ZONE MANAGEMENT. 4253
0045-7256 See COCOA GROWERS' BULLETIN. 167
0045-737X See COLLEGE LAW DIGEST. 2952
0045-7590 See REPORT - COMMISSION ON ACCREDITATION OF REHABILITATION FACILITIES. 3792
0045-7663 See COMMUNICATION LONDON. 1967. 3923
0045-7736 See COMMUNITY EDUCATION JOURNAL. 1733
0045-7795 See COMPARATIVE LITERATURE IN CANADA. 3377
0045-7825 See COMPUTER METHODS IN APPLIED MECHANICS AND ENGINEERING. 1256
0045-7841 See COMPUTER PRICE GUIDE. 1244
0045-7906 See COMPUTERS & ELECTRICAL ENGINEERING. 1228
0045-7930 See COMPUTERS & FLUIDS. 2088
0045-7949 See COMPUTERS & STRUCTURES. 1228
0045-799X See CONCERNS (DON MILLS). 1342
0045-8007 See CONCRETE ABSTRACTS. 2003
0045-8120 See CONNECTICUT NUTMEGGER, THE. 2444
0045-8198 See CONSTRUCTION METALLIQUE. 4000
0045-8201 See CONSULTANTS NEWS. 659
0045-8325 See CONTACTS; REVUE FRANCAISE DE L'ORTHODOXIE. 4950
0045-8341 See CONTEMPORARY SURGERY. 3963
0045-835X See CONTENT FOR CANADIAN JOURNALISTS (1984). 2918
0045-8376 See CONTINENTAL FRANCHISE REVIEW. 660
0045-8422 See CONVENIENCE STORE NEWS. 660
0045-8511 See COPEIA. 5581
0045-8538 See CORE TEACHER. 1891
0045-8554 See CORMORANT NEWS BULLETIN, THE. 5412
0045-8597 See CORPORATION JOURNAL, THE. 3099
0045-8678 See CORROSION Y PROTECCION. 2012
0045-8732 See COSPAR INFORMATION BULLETIN. 17
0045-8856 See COUNTRY LIFE. 2514
0045-8872 See COURIER (CANADA. CANADIAN FORCES BASE (COLD LAKE, ALTA.)). 5782
0045-9038 See CRIMINAL JUSTICE NEWSLETTER (NEW YORK, N.Y.). 3105
0045-9070 See CRITICAL DIGEST. 5363
0045-9089 See CRITIQUE SOCIALISTE. 4470
0045-9127 See CROWN LONDON. 3275
0045-9186 See CUADERNOS DE HISTORIA EECONOMICA DE CATALUNA. 1554
0045-9208 See CUISINE COLLECTIVE. 2332
0045-9216 See CULTIVAR. 170
0045-9259 See CULTURED DAIRY PRODUCTS JOURNAL OF THE AMERICAN CULTURED DAIRY PRODUCTS INSTITUTE. 192
0045-9380 See CURRENT PROBLEMS IN PEDIATRICS (ENGLISH ED.). 3903
0045-9429 See CYPRUS TO-DAY. 2650
0045-9453 See CZASOPISMO GEOGRAFICZNE : KWARTALNIK ZRZESZENIA POL. NAUCZYCIELI GEOGRAFJI, TOWARZYSTWA GEOGRAFICZNEGO WE LWOWIE I TOWARZYSTWA GEOGRAFICZNEGO W POZNANIU. 2559
0045-9461 See CZECHOSLOVAK ECONOMIC DIGEST. 1479
0045-9518 See DAKOTA TERRITORY. 2444
0045-9550 See BULLETIN OF THE MEDICAL STAFF OF THE METHODIST HOSPITALS OF DALLAS. 3777
0045-9577 See DANCE/AMERICA. 1311
0045-9704 See DATAPRO 70. 1258
0045-9771 See DEACON. 5059
0045-978X See DEAF CATHOLIC, THE. 5028
0045-9852 See DELAWARE CONSERVATIONIST. 2191
0045-9917 See JOURNAL OF THE DENTAL ASSOCIATION OF THAILAND, THE. 1328
0045-9941 See DENTAL RADIOGRAPHY AND PHOTOGRAPHY. 1321
0046-001X See DESARROLLO ECONOMICO (BUENOS AIRES). 5198
0046-0036 See DESCENT WELLS. 1373
0046-0079 See DESPATCH. 4042
0046-0117 See DEUTSCHE BACKERZEITUNG. 2333
0046-0206 See DIALOGO SOCIAL. 2614
0046-029X See DINNY'S CALGARY DIGEST. 5581
0046-0400 See DIVIDEND. 667
0046-0419 See DIVIDEND RECORD. 4720
0046-0435 See DIXIE LOGGER AND LUMBERMAN MAGAZINE. 2400
0046-0451 See DOCTOR GUILDFORD. 3737
0046-0478 See DOCUMENTATION PAR L'IMAGE, LA. 5101
0046-0567 See DOMINION TAX CASES. 4721
0046-063X See DOSHISHA LITERATURE. 3382
0046-0702 See DRILLING CONTRACTOR. 4254
0046-0737 See DRUCKINDUSTRIE (ST. GALLEN). 4564
0046-0826 See DUODECIMAL BULLETIN, THE. 3504
0046-0885 See EXCERPTA INDONESICA. 5227
0046-0958 See EAST ANGLIAN BIBLIOGRAPHY / THE LIBRARY ASSOCIATION, EASTERN BRANCH, THE. 415
0046-0966 See EAST ST. LOUIS MONITOR. 5660
0046-0990 See EASYRIDERS. 4081
0046-1016 See EAU VIVE, L'. 5783
0046-1040 See ARTZAKANK. 2722
0046-1091 See ECHOES OF HISTORY. 2732
0046-1121 See ECOLOGY LAW QUARTERLY. 3110
0046-1202 See ECONOMIE DE L'ENERGIE. 1961
0046-1482 See EDUCATIONAL DIGEST (TORONTO). 1741
0046-1520 See EDUCATIONAL PSYCHOLOGIST. 4586
0046-1547 See ETS DEVELOPMENTS. 1745
0046-1628 See EIRENE; STUDIA GRAECA ET LATINA. 1076
0046-1709 See ELECTROMAGNETIC METROLOGY CURRENT AWARENESS SERVICE. 4443
0046-1733 See ELECTRONICS COMMUNICATOR. 2049
0046-1830 See ELLIPSE. 3384
0046-1946 See ENCHANTMENT. 2533
0046-1962 See ENFANCE ET LA MODE, L'. 1084
0046-1989 See ENGINEER (FORT BELVOIR), THE. 1972

0046-2012 See ENGINEERING DESIGN GRAPHICS JOURNAL. **1972**

0046-2098 See ENGLISH USAGE IN SOUTHERN AFRICA. **3279**

0046-2101 See ENSEIGNANTS (MONTREAL). **1744**

0046-225X See ENVIRONMENTAL ENTOMOLOGY. **5608**

0046-2276 See ENVIRONMENTAL LAW (PORTLAND, ORE.). **3111**

0046-2284 See ENVIRONMENTAL LAW REPORTER. **3111**

0046-2446 See ERGONOMICS ABSTRACTS. **1209**

0046-2497 See ESPACE GEOGRAPHIQUE. **2560**

0046-256X See EST-OVEST. **4473**

0046-2578 See ESTRATEGIA. **4043**

0046-2616 See ETHNOLOGIE FRANCAISE. **2261**

0046-2632 See ETNIA. **236**

0046-2772 See EUROPEAN JOURNAL OF SOCIAL PSYCHOLOGY. **5245**

0046-2802 See EUROPEAN STUDIES NEWSLETTER. **2687**

0046-3116 See FACTS AND REPORTS. **2639**

0046-3132 See FACTS FILE. **1561**

0046-3167 See FAG RAG. **2794**

0046-3213 See FAMILY PLANNING DIGEST. **588**

0046-3256 See FANFARES. **320**

0046-3272 See FAR EASTERN LAW REVIEW. **2968**

0046-3299 See FARM AND COUNTRY (TORONTO). **84**

0046-3337 See FARMER'S DIGEST. **85**

0046-3604 See FEED & FARM SUPPLY DEALER. **200**

0046-3663 See FEMINIST STUDIES. **5556**

0046-3728 See FIBRE MARKET NEWS. **5351**

0046-3736 See FICTION. **3387**

0046-3787 See FILM JOURNAL (HOLLINS), THE. **4070**

0046-3825 See FILMS A L'ECRAN. **4071**

0046-3841 See FILOLOGIA MODERNA. **3281**

0046-385X See FILOZOFIA (BRATISLAVA). **4347**

0046-3973 See BULLETIN - FISHERIES COUNCIL OF CANADA. **2297**

0046-4112 See FLORIDA CONTRACTOR. **2605**

0046-4171 See FLORIDA PSYCHOLOGIST, THE. **4587**

0046-418X See FLORIDA RESTAURATEUR & PURVEYOR NEWS. **5071**

0046-421X See FLOWER ARRANGER. **2435**

0046-4295 See FOCUS ON ASIAN STUDIES. **2651**

0046-4325 See FOCUS ON PAKISTAN. **5470**

0046-4333 See FOLIO : THE MAGAZINE FOR MAGAZINE MANAGEMENT. **4815**

0046-4384 See FOOD AND NUTRITION (WASHINGTON. 1971). **4191**

0046-4414 See FOOD INDUSTRY FUTURES. **2337**

0046-4481 See FORAGES. **2139**

0046-4546 See FOREIGN AGRICULTURAL TRADE OF THE UNITED STATES. **88**

0046-4589 See FOREST SCENE, THE. **2381**

0046-4651 See FRANKLIN COUNTY HISTORICAL REVIEW, THE. **2734**

0046-4686 See FORTHCOMING INTERNATIONAL SCIENTIFIC AND TECHNICAL CONFERENCES. **5106**

0046-4694 See FORTNIGHT (BELFAST). **3343**

0046-4708 See FORUM FOR PROMOTING 3-19 COMPREHENSIVE EDUCATION. **1747**

0046-4732 See FORUM LETTER. **5060**

0046-4767 See FOSTER PARENT. **2280**

0046-4910 See FRANCE FORUM. **2516**

0046-5038 See FREEDOM TO READ FOUNDATION NEWS. **3211**

0046-5070 See FRESHWATER BIOLOGY. **456**

0046-5259 See FULBRIGHT NEWSLETTER. **1747**

0046-5380 See GAMBIA WEEKLY, THE. **5801**

0046-5402 See GANITA. **3506**

0046-5437 See GARTNERYRKET. **89**

0046-5461 See GAS CHROMATOGRAPHY-MASS SPECTROMETRY ABSTRACTS. **1015**

0046-5577 See GEMEETEWERKEN. **2023**

0046-5607 See GENERAL PRACTITIONER. **3737**

0046-5755 See GEOMETRIAE DEDICATA. **3507**

0046-578X See GEORGIA JOURNAL OF INTERNATIONAL AND COMPARATIVE LAW, THE. **3128**

0046-5798 See GEORGIA MUSIC NEWS. **4119**

0046-581X See GEOSCOPE (OTTAWA). **2564**

0046-5828 See GEOTECHNICAL ENGINEERING. **2023**

0046-5917 See GHANA FARMER, THE. **90**

0046-5925 See GHANA SOCIAL SCIENCE JOURNAL. **5201**

0046-5933 See GIESSEREIFORSCHUNG. **4003**

0046-5968 See GIORNALE ITALIANO DI CARDIOLOGIA. **3705**

0046-6042 See GO (EDMONTON). **4850**

0046-6115 See GONZAGA LAW REVIEW. **2975**

0046-6158 See GOOD OLD DAYS. **3391**

0046-6174 See GOODFRUIT GROWER, THE. **2417**

0046-6220 See GOVERNMENT PURCHASING GUIDE (TORONTO). **950**

0046-631X See GRAPHOSCOPE, THE. **900**

0046-6387 See ELLENOKANADIKON VEMA. **5784**

0046-645X See GROUND WATER AGE. **5533**

0046-6468 See GROUP PROCESS. **4588**

0046-6506 See GROWING POINT. **1064**

0046-6514 See GRUPPENDYNAMIK. **4588**

0046-6654 See GUYANA JOURNAL. **4475**

0046-6700 See HABLEMOS DE CINE. **4071**

0046-6778 See HANDBALL (SKOKIE, ILL.). **4897**

0046-6832 See HAPPINESS HOLDING TANK. **3463**

0046-6891 See HARVARD DENTAL BULLETIN. **1324**

0046-6964 See HORTICULTURE DIGEST. **2419**

0046-7006 See HEALTH (CANBERRA). **4778**

0046-7022 See HEALTH DEVICES. **3581**

0046-7146 See HEAT PIPE TECHNOLOGY. **2605**

0046-7251 See HEMOPHILIA TODAY. **3705**

0046-7316 See HERON. **2024**

0046-7324 See HERZ-KREISLAUF. **3705**

0046-7413 See HIKOBIA / HIROSHIMA SHOKUBUTSUGAKU KENKYUKAI. **512**

0046-7472 See HIROSHIMA DAIGAKU SHIGAKU ZASSHI. **1324**

0046-757X See HISTORIENS ET GEOGRAPHES. **2618**

0046-7596 See HISTORISK TIDSKRIFT FOR FINLAND. **2691**

0046-760X See HISTORY OF EDUCATION (TAVISTOCK). **1750**

0046-7693 See HOCKEY DIGEST (EVANSTON, ILL.). **4899**

0046-7774 See HOME ECONOMICS RESEARCH JOURNAL. **2791**

0046-7847 See HONEYWELL COMPUTER JOURNAL, THE. **1259**

0046-7928 See HORN CALL, THE. **4121**

0046-7936 See HORSES (CARLSBAD, CALIF.). **2800**

0046-7979 See HOSPITAL FOOD SERVICE. **3784**

0046-8061 See GOTUJS' (TORONTO). **1064**

0046-8177 See HUMAN PATHOLOGY. **3895**

0046-8185 See HUMAN RIGHTS (CHICAGO, ILL.). **2979**

0046-8304 See HUNGARIAN LIBRARY AND INFORMATION SCIENCE ABSTRACTS. **3258**

0046-8339 See HUSDJUR : SVENSK HUSDJURSSKOTSEL, LADUGARDEN. **212**

0046-8371 See IEEE PUBLICATIONS BULLETIN. **2060**

0046-8428 See IWK INTERNATIONALE WISSENSCHAFTLICHE KORRESPONDENZ ZUR GESCHICHTE DER DEUTSCHEN ARBEITERBEWEGUNG. **1681**

0046-8444 See IBERO-AMERICANA. **5202**

0046-8452 See ICELANDIC CANADIAN. **2263**

0046-8541 See IDEALISTIC STUDIES. **4349**

0046-8622 See ILLINOIS STATE GENEALOGICAL SOCIETY QUARTERLY. **2454**

0046-8703 See IMPACT INTERNATIONAL. **4523**

0046-8746 See IMPRINT (SYRACUSE, N.Y.), THE. **3214**

0046-8843 See INDEPENDENT REPUBLIC QUARTERLY, THE. **2738**

0046-8908 See INDEX TO CURRENT URBAN DOCUMENTS. **4656**

0046-8932 See INDIA ABROAD. **2263**

0046-8967 See INDIAN AFFAIRS (NEW YORK). **2263**

0046-8983 See INDIAN GEOTECHNICAL JOURNAL. **2024**

0046-8991 See INDIAN JOURNAL OF MICROBIOLOGY. **563**

0046-9017 See INDIAN JOURNAL OF REGIONAL SCIENCE. **2825**

0046-9076 See INDIAN TRADER, THE. **2738**

0046-9092 See INDIAN WELDING JOURNAL. **4027**

0046-9157 See EXCEPTIONAL PARENT, THE. **2278**

0046-9181 See INDUSTRIA LECHERA : ORGANO DEL CENTRO NACIONAL DE LA INDUSTRIA LECHERA, LA. **195**

0046-9211 See INDUSTRIAL LAUNDERER. **5352**

0046-9262 See INDUSTRIAL WASTES. **2233**

0046-9351 See INFORMATION HISTORIQUE, L'. **2692**

0046-9459 See INFORMATIONS SOCIALES. **5247**

0046-9580 See INQUIRY (CHICAGO). **3587**

0046-9661 See INSITA. **353**

0046-970X See IPW BERICHTE. **1636**

0046-9750 See JOURNAL OF THE INSTITUTE OF BREWING. **2368**

0046-9777 See C.F.A. DIGEST, THE. **781**

0046-9920 See ICA INFORMA. **93**

0046-9939 See BOLETIM DO INSTITUTO DE PESCA. **2297**

0046-9963 See BOLETIM DO INSTITUTO ESTADUAL DE HEMATOLOGIA ARTHUR DE SEQUERIA CAVALCANTI. **3770**

0047-0376 See INSTRUMENTS INDIA. **3481**

0047-0414 See INTERCOM (DISTRICT OF COLUMBIA LIBRARY ASSOCIATION). **3217**

0047-0511 See INTERMOUNTAIN JEWISH NEWS. **5643**

0047-0554 See IACP LAW ENFORCEMENT LEGISLATION AND LITIGATION REPORT. **3107**

0047-0597 See INTERNATIONAL BARBED WIRE GAZETTE, THE. **159**

0047-0651 See ICMA NEWSLETTER. **4655**

0047-0724 See INTERNATIONAL JOURNAL OF GOVERNMENT AUDITING. **4732**

0047-0732 See INTERNATIONAL JOURNAL OF GROUP TENSIONS. **5248**

0047-0767 See INTERNATIONAL JOURNAL OF SPORT PSYCHOLOGY. **4900**

0047-0813 See INTERNATIONAL LAW NEWS, THE. **3130**

0047-083X See IMF SURVEY. **790**

0047-1119 See TEXTILES NEWS / INTERNATIONAL PRESS CUTTING SERVICE. **5359**

0047-116X See INTERNATIONAL PSYCHOLOGIST. **4591**

0047-1178 See INTERNATIONAL RELATIONS (LONDON). **4525**

0047-1259 See CHRONIQUE DE L'U.G.G.I. **1404**

0047-1291 See INTERPRETE, L'. **3288**

0047-1321 See INTERVENTION. **5290**

0047-1356 See INVESTOR'S DIGEST OF CANADA. **903**

0047-1437 See IRISH ANCESTOR, THE. **2454**

0047-1496 See IRON MAN. **2599**

0047-1518 See IRRIGATION JOURNAL. **159**

0047-1542 See ISLAS. **2321**

0047-1569 See HADASHOT ARKHEOLOGIYOT / AGAF HA-ATIKOT, MISRAD HA-HINUKH VEHA-TARBUT. **269**

0047-1607 See ISSUE (WALTHAM, MASS.). 2499
0047-1690 See JACK O'DWYER'S NEWSLETTER. 761
0047-1704 See JACKSON ADVOCATE. 5700
0047-1755 See JAPAN CHEMICAL WEEK. 1026
0047-1763 See NIPPON SHIKA ISHIKAI ZASSHI. 1331
0047-1801 See NIPPON DAICHO KOMONBYO GAKKAI ZASSHI. 3622
0047-181X See JAPANESE BUSINESS JOURNAL. 685
0047-1828 See JAPANESE CIRCULATION JOURNAL. 3706
0047-1852 See NIHON RINSHO. 3622
0047-1860 See RINSHO BYORI. 3897
0047-1879 See SANGYO IGAKU. 2870
0047-1887 See NIHON HOIGAKU ZASSHI. 3622
0047-1909 See JAPANESE JOURNAL OF SURGERY. 3966
0047-1917 See JAPANESE JOURNAL OF VETERINARY RESEARCH, THE. 5512
0047-2018 See JEWISH VETERAN, THE. 2265
0047-2085 See JORNAL BRASILEIRO DE PSIQUIATRIA. 3928
0047-2115 See JOURNAL CONSTRUCTO. 618
0047-2166 See JOURNAL DE PHARMACIE DE BELGIQUE. 4310
0047-2212 See JOURNAL FOR THE STUDY OF JUDAISM IN THE PERSIAN, HELLENISTIC AND ROMAN PERIOD. 5050
0047-2220 See JOURNAL OF APPLIED REHABILITATION COUNSELING. 1880
0047-2255 See JOURNAL OF CANADIAN FICTION. 3399
0047-2263 See JOURNAL OF CARIBBEAN HISTORY, THE. 2741
0047-228X See JOURNAL OF CLINICAL CHILD PSYCHOLOGY. 4594
0047-2301 See JOURNAL OF COLLECTIVE NEGOTIATIONS IN THE PUBLIC SECTOR. 1682
0047-231X See JOURNAL OF COLLEGE SCIENCE TEACHING. 5118
0047-2328 See JOURNAL OF COMPARATIVE FAMILY STUDIES. 2281
0047-2336 See JOURNAL OF CONTEMPORARY ASIA. 2655
0047-2352 See JOURNAL OF CRIMINAL JUSTICE. 3167
0047-2379 See JOURNAL OF DRUG EDUCATION. 1345
0047-2395 See JOURNAL OF EDUCATIONAL TECHNOLOGY SYSTEMS. 1224
0047-2425 See JOURNAL OF ENVIRONMENTAL QUALITY. 2217
0047-2433 See JOURNAL OF ENVIRONMENTAL SYSTEMS. 2176
0047-2441 See JOURNAL OF EUROPEAN STUDIES. 2694
0047-245X See JOURNAL OF FOOD DISTRIBUTION RESEARCH. 2346
0047-2468 See JOURNAL OF GEOMETRY. 3513
0047-2484 See JOURNAL OF HUMAN EVOLUTION. 239
0047-2492 See JOURNAL OF INTERGROUP RELATIONS. 5250
0047-2506 See JOURNAL OF INTERNATIONAL BUSINESS STUDIES. 687
0047-2514 See JOURNAL OF IRISH LITERATURE, THE. 3400
0047-2522 See JOURNAL OF KOREAN AFFAIRS. 2655
0047-2530 See JOURNAL OF LEGAL STUDIES, THE. 2988
0047-2557 See JOURNAL OF MATHEMATICAL AND PHYSICAL SCIENCES. 3513
0047-2565 See JOURNAL OF MEDICAL PRIMATOLOGY. 5513
0047-2573 See JOURNAL OF MEDIEVAL AND RENAISSANCE STUDIES, THE. 2695
0047-2581 See JOURNAL OF MEXICAN AMERICAN HISTORY, THE. 2741
0047-259X See JOURNAL OF MULTIVARIATE ANALYSIS. 3514

0047-262X See JOURNAL OF NURSING. 3859
0047-2638 See JOURNAL OF OPERATIONAL PSYCHIATRY. 3929
0047-2662 See JOURNAL OF PHENOMENOLOGICAL PSYCHOLOGY. 4599
0047-2689 See JOURNAL OF PHYSICAL AND CHEMICAL REFERENCE DATA. 4409
0047-2697 See JPMS; JOURNAL OF POLITICAL & MILITARY SOCIOLOGY. 5250
0047-2700 See JOURNAL OF POLITICAL STUDIES. 4479
0047-2727 See JOURNAL OF PUBLIC ECONOMICS. 4734
0047-2735 See JOURNAL OF RELIGIOUS STUDIES. 4970
0047-2751 See JOURNAL OF RURAL DEVELOPMENT AND ADMINISTRATION. 4659
0047-2778 See JOURNAL OF SMALL BUSINESS MANAGEMENT. 874
0047-2786 See JOURNAL OF SOCIAL PHILOSOPHY. 5206
0047-2794 See JOURNAL OF SOCIAL POLICY. 5293
0047-2816 See JOURNAL OF TECHNICAL WRITING AND COMMUNICATION. 1115
0047-2867 See JOURNAL OF THEOLOGY FOR SOUTHERN AFRICA. 4971
0047-2875 See JOURNAL OF TRAVEL RESEARCH. 5482
0047-2891 See JOURNAL OF YOUTH AND ADOLESCENCE. 5207
0047-2956 See J U C O REVIEW. 4901
0047-2972 See JUDGES' JOURNAL, THE. 3141
0047-3049 See KFZ I.E. KRAFTFAHRZEUG-BETRIEB UND AUTOMARKT. 5418
0047-312X See KALORI; JOURNAL OF THE MUSEUMS ASSOCIATION OF AUSTRALIA. 4090
0047-3251 See KARJATALOUS. 196
0047-3278 See KART OG PLAN. 2567
0047-3405 See KETTENWIRK-PRAXIS. 5353
0047-3766 See KUNSTSTOFF-JOURNAL. 4456
0047-3774 See L.A.S.I.E. 3222
0047-3839 See LABOR ARBITRATION IN GOVERNMENT. 3150
0047-3855 See LABORATORY PRODUCT NEWS. 5125
0047-3863 See LABORES DEL HOGAR. 4851
0047-3928 See LAMBDA ALPHA JOURNAL OF MAN. 240
0047-3936 See LAMP, THE. 3861
0047-4045 See LANGUAGE IN SOCIETY. 3295
0047-4053 See LANTERN'S CORE, THE. 3222
0047-4134 See LATIN AMERICAN LITERARY REVIEW. 3345
0047-4290 See LEBENSMITTELTECHNIK. 2348
0047-4509 See LIBERTARIAN ANALYSIS. 4480
0047-4606 See LIFE COMPANY TAX NEWSLETTER. 3003
0047-4630 See LIFELINER. 2458
0047-4800 See LITTERATURE (PARIS. 1971). 3408
0047-4851 See LIVING HISTORICAL FARMS BULLETIN. 2622
0047-486X See LIVING IN SOUTH CAROLINA. 1298
0047-4908 See LLOYD'S WEEKLY CASUALTY REPORTS. 4178
0047-4916 See GAI SABER (TOLOZA). 3389
0047-4959 See LOCUS (CAMBRIDGE, MASS.). 3408
0047-4991 See LOGISTICS AND TRANSPORTATION REVIEW, THE. 5386
0047-5149 See LOYALIST GAZETTE, THE. 2745
0047-5289 See MST ENGLISH QUARTERLY, THE. 3304
0047-536X See MACHINES PRODUCTION PARIS. 2121
0047-5378 See MACHINIST, THE. 1688
0047-5394 See MCKINSEY QUARTERLY, THE. 879

0047-5416 See REVUE DE GEOGRAPHIE. MADAGASCAR. 2575
0047-5432 See MADRONA. 3465
0047-5483 See MAGISTER (ST-NICOLAS). 1762
0047-5548 See MAINE TRAIL, THE. 5386
0047-5688 See MANAGEMENT EDUCATION AND DEVELOPMENT. 1617
0047-570X See MANAGEMENT IN GOVERNMENT. 4664
0047-5785 See VOCATIONAL TRAINING NEWS. 1917
0047-5793 See MANPOWER DOCUMENTATION. 1689
0047-5874 See MARATHON BALLINAMORE, CO. LEITRIM. 2538
0047-5912 See MARGA. 1573
0047-5955 See MER. MARINE ENGINEERS REVIEW. 1987
0047-6080 See MARYLAND NURSE, THE. 3861
0047-6099 See MARYLAND RESEARCHER, THE. 3007
0047-6161 See MASSACHUSETTS STUDIES IN ENGLISH. 3347
0047-6269 See MATHEMATICS EDUCATION, THE. 3520
0047-6374 See MECHANISMS OF AGEING AND DEVELOPMENT. 584
0047-6382 See MECHELECIV. 5127
0047-648X See MEDICAL DIMENSIONS. 3915
0047-651X See MEDICAL JOURNAL OF ZAMBIA. 3610
0047-6552 See MEDICAL PROGRESS THROUGH TECHNOLOGY. 3695
0047-6560 See NEWSLETTER - MEDICAL RESEARCH COUNCIL (OTTAWA). 3621
0047-6641 See MEETINGS ON ATOMIC ENERGY. 1950
0047-665X See MEIE ELU OUR LIFE. 5789
0047-6692 See MEMO: TO THE PRESIDENT. 1835
0047-6714 See MEMPHIS STATE UNIVERSITY LAW REVIEW. 3009
0047-6765 See MENTAL RETARDATION (WASHINGTON). 1882
0047-6773 See MERCURY (SAN FRANCISCO). 397
0047-6870 See METALETTER. 4009
0047-7125 See MICHIGAN READING JOURNAL, THE. 1900
0047-7222 See MIDDEN, THE. 274
0047-7230 See MEED. 1574
0047-7249 See MIDDLE EAST INTERNATIONAL. 4528
0047-729X See MIDLAND HISTORY. 2698
0047-732X See MIDWEST RACING NEWS. 4904
0047-7338 See MIGRANT ECHO. 2623
0047-7559 See MISSISSIPPI REVIEW. 3412
0047-7575 See UMKC LAW REVIEW. 3067
0047-7702 See BULLETIN OF THE MODERN GREEK STUDIES ASSOCIATION. 2681
0047-7729 See MODERN LANGUAGE STUDIES. 3303
0047-7796 See MK. MOBEL-KULTUR. 2906
0047-7923 See MONTAGNE ET ALPINISME, LA. 4875
0047-7931 See MONTANA FOOD DISTRIBUTOR. 2350
0047-794X See MONTANA OIL JOURNAL (1953). 4264
0047-8024 See MONTHLY BUSINESS ANALYSIS. 696
0047-8032 See MONTHLY SUMMARY OF STATISTICS, SOUTH AUSTRALIA. 4698
0047-8105 See MOREANA. 3413
0047-8121 See MORNING STAR PEOPLE, THE. 2268
0047-813X See MORTGAGE AND REAL ESTATE EXECUTIVES REPORT, THE. 4841
0047-8318 See MS. 5561

0047-8415 See MUSCULAR DEVELOPMENT. 2600
0047-8431 See MUSIC AND THE TEACHER. 4133
0047-8474 See MUSIKMARKT, DER. 4138
0047-8539 See MYSORE JOURNAL OF AGRICULTURAL SCIENCES. 110
0047-8717 See NARDA NEWS. 2812
0047-8733 See TUESDAY LETTER. 2207
0047-8997 See NOLPE NOTES. 3017
0047-9012 See NATIONAL PARKS JOURNAL. 2198
0047-9209 See NEBRASKA LAW REVIEW. 3014
0047-9403 See NEUE BERGBAUTECHNIK. 2147
0047-942X See NEUROELECTRIC NEWS. 584
0047-9454 See NEVADA ENGINEER, THE. 1988
0047-9462 See NEVADA HISTORICAL SOCIETY QUARTERLY (1961). 2748
0047-9500 See NEW AGE WEEKLY. 4483
0047-9551 See N. B. NATURALIST. 4168
0047-9586 See NEW COMMUNITY. 2269
0047-9624 See NEW ELECTRONICS. 2073
0047-9632 See NEW ENGINEER. 1988
0047-9705 See NEW FRONTIERS IN EDUCATION. 1837
0047-9772 See NEW JERSEY HISTORICAL COMMISSION NEWSLETTER. 2748
0047-9829 See NEW PATRIOT (CHICAGO, ILL. 1988). 3348
0048-0053 See NEW YORK STATE ENVIRONMENT. 2178
0048-0134 See NEW ZEALAND JOURNAL OF FORESTRY SCIENCE. 2389
0048-0169 See NEW ZEALAND VETERINARY JOURNAL. 5517
0048-0215 See NEWS & FARMER. 112
0048-0304 See NEWSPEACE. 4982
0048-0371 See NIGERIAN ACCOUNTANT, THE. 749
0048-038X See NIGERIAN BUSINESS DIGEST. 699
0048-0428 See NIHON IGAKU HOSHASEN GAKKAI ZASSHI. 3944
0048-0436 See NEC RESEARCH & DEVELOPMENT. 2073
0048-0444 See NIPPON IKA DAIGAKU ZASSHI. 3622
0048-0452 See NIPPON STEEL NEWS. 4013
0048-0495 See NORDISK JORDBRUGSFORSKNING. 114
0048-0509 See NORDISK TIDSSKRIFT FOR SPECIALPAEDAGOGIK. 1883
0048-0665 See NORTH CAROLINA RESEARCHER, THE. 3018
0048-0738 See NORTHEAST HISTORICAL ARCHAEOLOGY. 2751
0048-0967 See NOUVELLE ECOLE. 5253
0048-0975 See NOUVELLE REVUE INTERNATIONALE; PROBLEMES DE LA PAIX ET DU SOCIALISME, LA. 4544
0048-0983 See NOVA SCOTIA REPORTS (FREDERICTON). 3019
0048-1009 See NOVUM TESTAMENTUM. 5018
0048-1017 See NOVI DNI. 2270
0048-1033 See NUCLEAR MAGNETIC RESONANCE SPECTROMETRY ABSTRACTS. 4445
0048-105X See NUCLEONICS WEEK. 1952
0048-1084 See NUEVA NARRATIVA HISPANOAMERICANA. 3419
0048-1270 See OBERFLACHE - SURFACE. 4014
0048-1335 See OBSERVATIONS FROM THE TREADMILL. 4606
0048-1343 See OBZORJE PACIFIKA. 2751
0048-1440 See OESTERREICHISCHE MILITAERISCHE ZEITSCHRIFT. 4053
0048-153X See OHIO ARCHAEOLOGIST. 277
0048-1572 See OHIO STATE LAW JOURNAL. 3022
0048-1610 See OKLAHOMA RURAL NEWS. 117
0048-1637 See OLD CARS. 5422
0048-1742 See ARCH NOTES. 256

0048-1793 See MONOGRAPH / ONTARIO ASSOCIATION GEOGRAPHIC ENVIRONMENTAL EDUCATION, THE. 2569
0048-1815 See ONTARIO NUMISMATIST, THE. 2783
0048-1939 See OPEN LETTER (TORONTO). 3420
0048-1955 See OPHTHALMOLOGY DIGEST (1979). 3878
0048-2056 See OPUS INTERNATIONAL. 327
0048-2099 See ORBEN'S COMEDY FILLERS. 4864
0048-2129 See ORDO. 1511
0048-2161 See ORGANISTS' REVIEW. 4144
0048-2269 See ORTHODOX CHURCH, THE. 5039
0048-2285 See OSPEDALE PSICHIATRICO. 3932
0048-2331 See OTTAWA LAW REVIEW. 3024
0048-2366 See OUEST MEDICAL PARIS. 3625
0048-2420 See OUTDOOR GUIDE. 4876
0048-2609 See PR REPORTER (EXETER, N.H.). 764
0048-2641 See PACIFIC SUN. 5638
0048-265X See PACIFIST, THE. 4530
0048-2862 See PAPERPRINTPACK INDIA. 4236
0048-2870 See EAST ASIAN HISTORY. 2650
0048-2889 See PAPETIER (QUEBEC). 4236
0048-2897 See PAPIER UND KUNSTSTOFF VERARBEITER. 4237
0048-2935 See PARAGRAPHIC. 1883
0048-2951 See PARASSITOLOGIA. 468
0048-2994 See PARLIAMENTARY JOURNAL. 4486
0048-301X See PARNASSOS. 3310
0048-3028 See PARNASSUS : POETRY IN REVIEW. 3467
0048-3095 See PAZIFISCHE RUNDSCHAU. 5792
0048-3133 See PEDIATRIC CLINICS OF INDIA. 3908
0048-3214 See PENNSYLVANIA GEOLOGY. 1391
0048-3249 See PENNSYLVANIA RESEARCHER, THE. 3025
0048-3435 See PERSONAL INJURY RESEARCHER, THE. 3026
0048-3451 See PERSONNEL GUIDE TO CANADA'S TRAVEL INDUSTRY. 5488
0048-3486 See PERSONNEL REVIEW. 945
0048-3575 See PESTICIDE BIOCHEMISTRY AND PHYSIOLOGY. 4246
0048-3591 See PETROLEUM GAZETTE (MELBOURNE). 4272
0048-3664 See PHARMAZIE IN UNSERER ZEIT. 4324
0048-3672 See PHAROS. 5269
0048-3710 See PHILATELIC JOURNALIST, THE. 2786
0048-3761 See PHILIPPINE JOURNAL OF ANIMAL INDUSTRY, THE. 217
0048-377X See PHILIPPINE JOURNAL OF FISHERIES, THE. 2310
0048-3796 See PHILIPPINE JOURNAL OF LINGUISTICS. 3310
0048-3818 See PHILIPPINE JOURNAL OF NURSING, THE. 3867
0048-3842 See PHILIPPINE MINING & ENGINEERING JOURNAL. 1443
0048-3885 See LITTERARIA PRAGENSIA. 3408
0048-3893 See PHILOSOPHIA (RAMAT GAN). 4355
0048-3915 See PHILOSOPHY & PUBLIC AFFAIRS. 5212
0048-3931 See PHILOSOPHY OF THE SOCIAL SCIENCES. 5212
0048-4024 See PHYSICAL REVIEW ABSTRACTS. 4415
0048-4229 See PIROGUE (ISSY-LES-MOULINEAUX, FRANCE). 2521
0048-4245 See PITTURE E VERNICI. 3486
0048-4318 See PLANNING IN NORTHEASTERN ILLINOIS. 2831
0048-4326 See P I B C NEWS. 2830
0048-4334 See PLANT GENETIC RESOURCES NEWSLETTER. 120
0048-4350 See PLASTE UND KAUTSCHUK. 4457

0048-4415 See PLAYBOARD. 387
0048-4466 See PLERUS. 1512
0048-4474 See PLOUGHSHARES. 3424
0048-4482 See PLURAL SOCIETIES. 5213
0048-4520 See POEMES INEDITS. 3468
0048-4555 See POESIE; LA POESIE FRANCAISE DE BELGIQUE. 3468
0048-4563 See POESIE PRESENTE. 3468
0048-4717 See POLICLINICO, SEZIONE MEDICA. 3628
0048-4849 See POPULATION NEWSLETTER. 4557
0048-4903 See PORTUGALIAE PHYSICA. 4417
0048-4911 See POSITIF. 4076
0048-4954 See POTTERY IN AUSTRALIA. 2593
0048-5012 See PMI. POWDER METALLURGY INTERNATIONAL. 4015
0048-5020 See POWDER METALLURGY SCIENCE & TECHNOLOGY. 4015
0048-5055 See POWWOW TRAILS. 2754
0048-5144 See PRECISION SHOOTING. 4877
0048-5195 See PRESENCE FRANCOPHONE. 3425
0048-5284 See PRIMARY EDUCATION AUSTRALIA. 1805
0048-5314 See PRINT-EQUIP NEWS. 381
0048-5330 See PRINTER'S NEWS (WELLINGTON). 4568
0048-5535 See PROMETHEUS (WASHINGTON, D.C.). 1775
0048-5632 See PROUD. 3174
0048-5659 See PROUST RESEARCH ASSOCIATION NEWSLETTER. 3350
0048-5675 See PRZEGLAD PSYCHOLOGICZNY. 4609
0048-5713 See PSYCHIATRIC ANNALS. 3933
0048-573X See PSYCHIC OBSERVER. 4242
0048-5748 See PSYCHOLOGICAL ISSUES. 4611
0048-5756 See PSYCHOLOGIE MEDICALE. 4612
0048-5764 See PSYCHOPHARMACOLOGY BULLETIN. 4613
0048-5772 See PSYCHOPHYSIOLOGY. 586
0048-5829 See PUBLIC CHOICE. 1514
0048-5853 See PUBLIC FINANCE QUARTERLY. 4743
0048-5942 See PUBLISHERS' AUXILIARY. 4818
0048-5950 See PUBLIUS. 4492
0048-6000 See PULSE LONDON. 1959. 3631
0048-6019 See JOURNAL OF RESEARCH, PUNJAB AGRICULTURAL UNIVERSITY. 100
0048-6043 See PYRETHRUM POST. 470
0048-6078 See MUNICIPAL MANAGER, QUEENSLAND. 4667
0048-6086 See QUADERNI DI RADIOLOGIA. 3944
0048-6280 See QUEBEC PHARMACIE. 4327
0048-6302 See QUEENS BAR BULLETIN. 3033
0048-6361 See QUEENSLAND MASTER BUILDER. 625
0048-6418 See ADMINISTRATORS BULLETIN. 1859
0048-6493 See QUINZAINE LITTERAIRE, LA. 3427
0048-6604 See RADIO SCIENCE. 1409
0048-671X See RAMUS. 1079
0048-6868 See REAL ESTATE LAW JOURNAL. 3034
0048-6906 See REASON. 5214
0048-7066 See REEVES JOURNAL. 2608
0048-7104 See NURSING BC. 3863
0048-7120 See REHABILITACION (MADRID). 4382
0048-7139 See REHABILITATION DIGEST. 4393
0048-7155 See REIGN OF THE SACRED HEART. 5035
0048-7163 See TRAVAUX DE L'INSTITUT DE GEOGRAPHIE DE REIMS. 2577
0048-7171 See REINSURANCE. 2891
0048-721X See RELIGION (LONDON. 1971). 4991
0048-7317 See RESEARCH RECOMMENDATIONS. 707

0048-7325 See RESEARCH JOURNAL OF PHILOSOPHY & SOCIAL SCIENCES. 4358
0048-7333 See RESEARCH POLICY. 5147
0048-7376 See RESOURCES (WASHINGTON, D.C. 1959). 2204
0048-7384 See RESOURCES FOR AMERICAN LITERARY STUDY. 3351
0048-7449 See REUMATISMO. 3806
0048-7457 See REUSE/RECYCLE. 2242
0048-7481 See NEW YORK UNIVERSITY REVIEW OF LAW AND SOCIAL CHANGE. 3016
0048-749X See REVIEW OF REGIONAL STUDIES, THE. 2834
0048-7511 See REVIEWS IN AMERICAN HISTORY. 2757
0048-752X See REVIEWS IN ANALYTICAL CHEMISTRY. 1018
0048-7538 See CORROSION REVIEWS. 2011
0048-7554 See REVIEWS ON ENVIRONMENTAL HEALTH. 2181
0048-7651 See REVISTA CHILENA DE LITERATURA. 3430
0048-766X See REVISTA CHILENA DE OBSTETRICIA Y GINECOLOGIA. 3767
0048-7678 See REVISTA CUBANA DE CIENCIAS VETERINARIAS. 5520
0048-7694 See REVISTA DE ESTUDIOS POLITICOS. 4494
0048-7708 See REVISTA DE GEOGRAFIA. 2574
0048-7732 See REVISTA OBSTETRICIA Y GINECOLOGIA DE VENEZUELA. 3768
0048-7759 See REVISTA DE SOLDADURA. 4027
0048-7775 See REVISTA ECUATORIANA DE HIGIENE Y MEDICINA TROPICAL. 3986
0048-7791 See REVISTA ESPANOLA DE REUMATISMO Y ENFERMEDADES OSTEOARTICULARES. 3635
0048-7813 See REVISTA LTR. 3153
0048-7864 See REVISTA PAULISTA DE HOSPITAIS. 3636
0048-7937 See REVUE DE JURISPRUDENCE COMMERCIALE. 3043
0048-7953 See REVUE DE L'HABITAT FRANCAIS. 4846
0048-8003 See REVUE D'HISTOIRE MODERNE ET CONTEMPORAINE. 2628
0048-8062 See REVUE FRANCAISE D'ENDOCRINOLOGIE CLINIQUE, NUTRITION ET METABOLISME. 3733
0048-8143 See REVUE INTERNATIONALE DE PHILOSOPHIE. 4359
0048-8178 See REVUE ROUMAINE D'ETUDES INTERNATIONALES. 4534
0048-8267 See RICARDIAN. 5236
0048-8283 See RICERCA; MATEMATICHE PURE ED APPLICATE. 3532
0048-8305 See RIGHT ON (HOLLYWOOD, CALIF.). 1068
0048-8348 See RIVISTA DEL COLORE, VERNICIATURA INDUSTRIALE, LA. 4225
0048-8399 See RIVISTA DI IDROBIOLOGIA. 1417
0048-8402 See RIVISTA ITALIANA DI SCIENZA POLITICA. 4495
0048-8445 See ROCK & FOLK PARIS. 1966. 4150
0048-8453 See ROCK & GEM. 1444
0048-8534 See ROGUE DIGGER. 2470
0048-8550 See ROMANIA LITERARA. 3431
0048-8585 See ROMANIAN MEDICAL REVIEW. 3637
0048-8593 See ROMANTISME. 3432
0048-864X See ROUGHNECK, THE. 4277
0048-8658 See ROMANIA, DOCUMENTS, EVENTS / ROMANIAN NEWS AGENCY, AGERPRES. 2522
0048-8771 See RUNNING BOARD, THE. 5424
0048-878X See RURAL ARKANSAS. 2544
0048-8879 See RYDE RECORDER, THE. 2671
0048-9018 See SAISONS D'ALSACE STRASBOURG. 2522
0048-9107 See SANTE PUBLIQUE, LA. 4801
0048-9115 See SANTIAGO. 3433

0048-9182 See BULLETIN - SASKATCHEWAN GENEALOGICAL SOCIETY. 2441
0048-9190 See GUIDELINES (SASKATOON). 1749
0048-9239 See SATURDAY EVENING POST (1839), THE. 2492
0048-928X See SCANDINAVIAN CANADIAN BUSINESSMAN. 709
0048-9328 See SCHACH. 4866
0048-945X See JOURNAL OF SCHOOL NURSING, THE. 3860
0048-9492 See SCHUSS. 1904
0048-9522 See SCHWEIZER VOLKSKUNDE. 2324
0048-9581 See SCIENCE & GOVERNMENT REPORT. 5150
0048-9697 See SCIENCE OF THE TOTAL ENVIRONMENT, THE. 2181
0048-9778 See BULLETIN OF THE SCOTTISH INSTITUTE OF MISSIONARY STUDIES, THE. 4941
0048-9867 See SEA CLASSICS. 4183
0048-9913 See SEARCH (NASHVILLE). 5067
0049-0016 See SECURITY DISTRIBUTING & MARKETING. 5177
0049-0024 See SECURITY GAZETTE. 5177
0049-0164 See SEMINA. 4329
0049-0172 See SEMINARS IN ARTHRITIS AND RHEUMATISM. 3807
0049-0199 See SENIOR CITIZENS TODAY. 5181
0049-0202 See SENTINEL (TORONTO. 1957). 5067
0049-0210 See SRPSKI ARHIV ZA CELOKUPNO LEKARSTVO. / ARCHIVES SERBES DE MEDECINE GENERAL / SERBIAN ARCHIVES OF GENERAL MEDICINE. 3642
0049-0253 See SESAME STREET MAGAZINE. 1069
0049-0385 See SH'MA (PORT WASHINGTON, N.Y.). 4361
0049-0393 See SHOPPING CENTER WORLD. 4847
0049-0393= See SHOPPING CENTER WORLD PRODUCT AND SERVICE DIRECTORY. 957
0049-0415 See SHOTGUN NEWS. 4917
0049-0423 See SHUTTLE, SPINDLE & DYEPOT. 375
0049-0431 See SIC. 4496
0049-044X See NATIONAL NEWS REPORT. 2198
0049-0466 See SIGN WORLD. 766
0049-0490 See SILENT NEWS. 5721
0049-0512 See SIMMONS REVIEW, THE. 1095
0049-0520 See SIAJ - JOURNAL OF THE SINGAPORE INSTITUTE OF ARCHITECTS. 308
0049-0601 See SINTEZA. 364
0049-0628 See SIRJANA. 1584
0049-0849 See SOBRE LOS DERIVADOS DE LA CANA DE AZUCAR. 135
0049-0857 See SOCIAL CHANGE. 5308
0049-089X See SOCIAL SCIENCE RESEARCH. 5221
0049-0903 See ITEMS - SOCIAL SCIENCE RESEARCH COUNCIL (U.S.). 5205
0049-108X See BULLETIN - SOCIETE FRANCAISE DE PHOTOGRAMMETRIE ET DE TELEDETECTION. 4367
0049-1098 See CAHIERS--SOCIETE HISTORIQUE ACADIENNE, LES. 2725
0049-1101 See BULLETIN DE LA SOCIETE MEDICALE D'AFRIQUE NOIRE DE LANGUE FRANCAISE. 3559
0049-111X See ETUDES PREHISTORIQUES ORGNAC L'AVEN. 268
0049-1152 See SAN. 2783
0049-1160 See S.A.A.D. DIGEST. 1335
0049-1195 See NEWSLETTER - THE SOCIETY OF ARCHITECTURAL HISTORIANS. 304
0049-1225 See SOCIOLOGIA. 5260
0049-1241 See SOCIOLOGICAL METHODS & RESEARCH. 5261
0049-1446 See SOUTH AUSTRALIAN DAIRY FARMER'S JOURNAL, THE. 199
0049-1470 See SOUTH AUSTRALIAN STATE REPORTS, THE. 3056

0049-1527 See SOUTH EASTERN LATIN AMERICANIST. 2761
0049-1616 See SOUTHERN MOTORACING. 5425
0049-1624 See SOUTHERN PURCHASOR. 951
0049-1640 See SOUTHERN STARS. 400
0049-1659 See SOUTHERN UTAH NEWS. 5757
0049-1675 See SOUTHWESTERN AMERICAN LITERATURE. 3438
0049-1683 See SOUTHWESTERN JOURNAL OF SOCIAL EDUCATION. 5222
0049-1713 See SOVIET ANALYST. 4496
0049-173X See RUSSIAN JOURNAL OF DEVELOPMENTAL BIOLOGY. 472
0049-1748 See SOVIET JOURNAL OF QUANTUM ELECTRONICS. 2082
0049-1772 See SOWER, THE. 4999
0049-1802 See SPANISH TODAY. 3439
0049-1840 See DISABILITY NOW. 4387
0049-1845 See SPECIAL-INTEREST AUTOS. 5425
0049-1861 See ACADEMIE SPECTRUM. 5079
0049-206X See STANDARD-BEARER, THE. 4687
0049-2108 See CAMPUS REPORT (STANFORD). 1090
0049-2116 See STAR, THE. 4803
0049-2116 See STAR (CARVILLE), THE. 3716
0049-2205 See STEEL CONSTRUCTION : JOURNAL OF THE AUSTRALIAN INSTITUTE OF STEEL CONSTRUCTION. 628
0049-2353 See STROMATA. 4999
0049-2361 See STUDI E PROBLEMI DI CRITICA TESTUALE. 3324
0049-237X See STUDIES IN LOGIC AND THE FOUNDATIONS OF MATHEMATICS. 3537
0049-2388 See STUDIES IN THE LINGUISTIC SCIENCES. 3326
0049-2426 See SUB-STANCE. 3443
0049-2450 See SUD (MARSEILLE). 3443
0049-2477 See SUGAR NEWS. 188
0049-2507 See SUNDANCE. 2547
0049-2639 See SURFACE WAVE ABSTRACTS. 4453
0049-2647 See SURGELATION, LA. 1628
0049-2701 See SWEDISH JOURNAL OF AGRICULTURAL RESEARCH. 139
0049-2760 See SYNOPTIC. 1786
0049-2949 See TAMKANG REVIEW. 3354
See WORDS AND WINDMILLS. 1908
0049-3155 See TECHNICAL COMMUNICATION (WASHINGTON). 5162
0049-3449 See TEOLOGIA Y VIDA. 5002
0049-3481 See TETON. 4879
0049-3503 See TEXAS DENTAL ASSISTANTS ASSOCIATION BULLETIN. 1336
See SOUTHWEST STOCKMAN. 222
0049-3554 See TEXTILE ASIA. 5357
0049-3570 See TEXTILES PANAMERICANOS. 5359
0049-3589 See THAI JOURNAL OF AGRICULTURAL SCIENCE. 141
0049-366X See THEOLOGIE UND GLAUBE. 5003
0049-3740 See THIRD WORLD REPORTS. 4498
0049-3821 See THOROUGHBRED OF CALIFORNIA, THE. 2803
0049-3848 See THROMBOSIS RESEARCH. 3710
0049-3864 See TIERARZTLICHE UMSCHAU. 5523
0049-3910 See TIME OUT. 2524
0049-3945 See TOBACCO INTERNATIONAL. 5374
0049-397X See TOCHER; TALES, SONGS, TRADITION. 4156
0049-4127 See TOPIC (WASHINGTON). 2855
0049-4194 See TORONTO LIFE. 2548
0049-4208 See TORONTO MUSIC GUIDE. 4157
0049-4216 See TORONTO STOCK EXCHANGE REVIEW, THE. 917
0049-4321 See TRADE AND COMMERCE (WINNIPEG). 853
0049-4429 See TRANSITION (OTTAWA). 2286
0049-4437 See TRANSITION (WASHINGTON). 1524

0049-447X See TRANSPORT ROUTIER DU QUEBEC. 5396

0049-4488 See TRANSPORTATION (DORDRECHT). 5396

0049-450X See TRANSPORTATION LAW JOURNAL, THE. 3065

0049-4593 See TREASURE. 2779

0049-464X See TRIBUNA ITALIANA, LA. 2524

0049-4747 See TROPICAL ANIMAL HEALTH AND PRODUCTION. 5523

0049-4755 See TROPICAL DOCTOR. 3987

0049-4763 See TROPICAL GRASSLANDS. 189

0049-4801 See TUNDRA TIMES. 5629

0049-481X See TUNGSTEN NEWS. 4023

0049-4933 See TYDSKRIF VIR VOLKSKUNDE EN VOLKSTAAL. 2325

0049-5123 See UMENI. 367

0049-514X See UNABASHED LIBRARIAN, THE. 3254

0049-5387 See UNIDO NEWSLETTER. 1630

0049-5433 See JOURNAL - UNITED REFORMED CHURCH HISTORY SOCIETY. 5062

0049-5514 See SBORNIK VEDECKYCH PRACI LEKARSKE FAKULTY KARLOVY UNIVERSITY V HRADCI KRALOVE. 3638

0049-5522 See SUPPLEMENTUM SBORNIKU VEDECKYCH PRACI LEKARSKE FAKULTY UNIVERZITY KARLOVY V HRADCI KRALOVE. 3644

0049-5557 See UNMUZZLED OX. 3472

0049-5700 See URETHANE PLASTICS AND PRODUCTS. 5168

0049-5778 See VE6. 1142

0049-5832 See VANCOUVER STOCK EXCHANGE REVIEW. 919

0049-5891 See VASCULUM, THE. 4173

0049-612X See VICTORIA NATURALIST, THE. 4173

0049-6316 See VIEILLES MAISONS FRANCAISES PARIS. 310

0049-6456 See VINTAGE (NEW YORK, N.Y. 1971). 2360

0049-6472 See VIRGINIA DENTAL JOURNAL. 1337

0049-6480 See VIRGINIA GAZETTE (1930). 5760

0049-6499 See VIRGINIA RESEARCHER (CHARLOTTESVILLE VA). 3072

0049-6650 See VOGELWARTE, DIE. 5599

0049-6669 See VOICE (WESTCHESTER). 5008

0049-6723 See VOLKSWAGEN GREATS. 5427

0049-6804 See LIKARSKA SPRAVA. 3604

0049-691X See WASHINGTON INTERNATIONAL BUSINESS REPORT. 719

0049-6979 See WATER, AIR, AND SOIL POLLUTION. 2247

0049-7002 See WATER SKIER (WINTER HAVEN), THE. 4928

0049-7266 See WESTCHESTER HISTORIAN, THE. 2765

0049-7274 See WESTCHESTER LAW JOURNAL. 3073

0049-7282 See INFORMATION BULLETIN / WESTERN ASSOCIATION OF MAP LIBRARIES. 3215

0049-7347 See WESTERN AUSTRALIAN INSTITUTE OF TECHNOLOGY GAZETTE. 5169

0049-7371 See WESTERN CANADIAN LUMBER WORKER, THE. 2405

0049-7398 See WESTERN FLOORS. 2904

0049-741X See WESTERN CLEANER & LAUNDERER. 1031

0049-7479 See WESTERN OUTDOOR NEWS. 4880

0049-7487 See WESTERN OUTFITTER. 1088

0049-7525 See WESTERN WEEKLY REPORTS. 3074

0049-7541 See WHEEL, THE. 5022

0049-7592 See WHOOPER, THE. 2208

0049-7614 See WIDENING HORIZONS. 5568

0049-7649 See WILMINGTON JOURNAL (WILMINGTON, N.C.), THE. 5724

0049-7657 See WIND ROSE, THE. 4097

0049-7711 See WIRTSCHAFTSEIGENE FUTTER. 224

0049-7770 See WOMAN ACTIVIST, THE. 4500

0049-7835 See WOMEN STUDIES ABSTRACTS. 5572

0049-7878 See WOMEN'S STUDIES. 5571

0049-7959 See WORD AND WAY. 5009

0049-7991 See WORKING PAPERS IN CULTURAL STUDIES. 5265

0049-8025 See WORLD ANIMAL REVIEW / REVUE MONDIALE DE ZOOTECHNIE / REVISTA MUNDIAL DE ZOOTECNIA. 224

0049-8114 See WEEKLY EPIDEMIOLOGICAL RECORD. 3716

0049-8122 See WORLD MEDICAL JOURNAL. 3651

0049-8130 See WORLD PEACE NEWS. 4538

0049-8165 See WORLD TRIBUNE. 4378

0049-8246 See X-RAY SPECTROMETRY. 1020

0049-8254 See XENOBIOTICA. 3984

0049-836X See YOUNG ALLIANCE. 724

0049-8378 See YOUNG INDIAN. 2668

0049-8394 See YOUR CHURCH. 5010

0049-853X See JOURNAL - ZAMBIA LIBRARY ASSOCIATION. 3221

0049-8599 See ZEITSCHRIFT FUER AUSLANDISCHE LANDWIRTSCHAFT. 148

0049-8602 See ZEITSCHRIFT FUER BEWASSERUNGSWIRTSCHAFT. 148

0049-8610 See ZEITSCHRIFT FUER DIE GESAMTE HYGIENE UND IHRE GRENZGEBIETE. 4809

0049-8637 See ZEITSCHRIFT FUER ENTWICKLUNGSPSYCHOLOGIE UND PADAGOGISCHE PSYCHOLOGIE. 1792

0049-8653 See LILI, ZEITSCHRIFT FUER LITERATURWISSENSCHAFT UND LINGUISTIK. 3298

0049-8661 See ZEITSCHRIFT FUER ROMANISCHE PHILOLOGIE. 3335

0049-8696 See ZENTRALBLATT FUER PHARMAZIE, PHARMAKOTHERAPIE UND LABORATORIUMSDIAGNOSTIK. 4333

0049-8769 See JOURNAL OF THE ZOOLOGICAL SOCIETY OF INDIA. 5589

0065-0005 See AB BOOKMAN'S YEARBOOK. 4822

0065-003X See EUROP PRODUCTION. 833

0065-0129 See A.W. MELLON LECTURES IN THE FINE ARTS. 311

0065-0137 See ZEITSCHRIFT DES AACHENER GESCHICHTSVEREINS. 2716

0065-017X See LECTURE NOTES SERIES - AARHUS, DENMARK. UNIVERSITET. MATEMATISK INSTITUT. 3516

0065-0188 See VARIOUS PUBLICATIONS SERIES - AARHUS UNIVERSITET. MATEMATISK INSTITUT. 3540

0065-020X See ARSBOK FOR SVERIGES KOMMUNER. 4696

0065-0323 See ABHANDLUNGEN UND MATERIALIEN ZUR PUBLIZISTIK. 2609

0065-0382 See ABR-NAHRAIN. 5013

0065-0471 See BOLETIN DE LA ACADEMIE HONDURENA DE LA LENGUA. 3269

0065-0536 See COMPTES RENDUS DES SEANCES - ACADEMIE DES INSCRIPTIONS & BELLES-LETTRES. 2844

0065-0552 See ANNUAIRE - ACADEMIE DES SCIENCES. 5083

0065-0676 See ANPHI PAPERS, THE. 3851

0065-0684 See PROCEEDINGS OF THE ACADEMY OF POLITICAL SCIENCE. 4492

0065-0714 See QUADERNI DELL'ACCADEMIA CHIGIANA. 4148

0065-082X See ACCIDENTS IN NORTH AMERICAN MOUNTAINEERING. 4868

0065-0900 See ACTA AD ARCHAEOLOGIAM ET ARTIUM HISTORIAM PERTINENTIA. 335

0065-0919 See ACTA AGRARIA ET SILVESTRIA. SERIES AGRARIA. 43

0065-0927 See ACTA AGRARIA ET SILVESTRIA. SERIES SILVESTRIS. 2373

0065-0935 See ACTA AGRARIA ET SILVESTRIA. SERIES ZOOTECHNICA. 204

0065-0943 See ACTA AGRICULTURAE SCANDINAVICA. SUPPLEMENTUM. 43

0065-0951 See ACTA AGROBOTANICA. 496

0065-0986 See ACTA ARCHAEOLOGICA LODZIENSIA. 253

0065-101X See ACTA ARCHAEOLOGICA. 253

0065-1036 See ACTA ARITHMETICA. 3490

0065-1044 See ACTA BALTICO-SLAVICA. 2672

0065-1141 See ACTA CLASSICA. 1073

0065-1176 See ACTA DERMATOLOGICA. 3717

0065-1206 See ACTA FACULTATIS MEDICAE FLUMENENSIS. 3544

0065-1214 See GODISEN ZBORNIK NA MEDICINSKIOT FAKULTET VO SKOPJE. 3579

0065-1249 See ACTA GEOGRAPHICA LODZIENSIA. 2553

0065-1257 See ACTA GEOGRAPHICA LOVANIENSIA. 2553

0065-1265 See ACTA GEOLOGICA TAIWANICA. 1364

0065-1273 See ACTA GERMANICA. 3261

0065-1281 See ACTA HISTOCHEMICA. 531

0065-1311 See ACTA HISTORICA SCIENTIARUM NATURALIUM ET MEDICINALIUM. 5080

0065-132X See ACTA HYDROBIOLOGICA. 552

0065-1338 See ACTA HYDROPHYSICA (BERLIN). 1412

0065-1346 See ACTA JURIDICA (CAPE TOWN). 2927

0065-1354 See ACTA JUTLANDICA : AARSSKRIFT FOR UNIVERSITETSUNDERVISNINGEN I JYLLAND. 1807

0065-1389 See ACTA MEDICAE HISTORIAE PATAVINA. 3545

0065-1400 See ACTA NEUROBIOLOGIAE EXPERIMENTALIS. 3825

0065-1419 See ACTA NEUROCHIRURGICA : SUPPLEMENTUM. 3957

0065-1427 See ACTA NEUROLOGICA SCANDINAVICA. SUPPLEMENTUM. 3825

0065-1443 See ACTA NUNTIATURAE GALLICAE. 5022

0065-1524 See ACTA PHILOLOGICA. 3261

0065-1567 See ACTA PHYTOMEDICA. 497

0065-1583 See ACTA PROTOZOOLOGICA. 5573

0065-1591 See ACTA PSYCHIATRICA SCANDINAVICA. SUPPLEMENTUM. 3919

0065-1621 See ACTA RADIOBOTANICA ET GENETICA. BULLETIN OF THE INSTITUTE OF RADIATION BREEDING. 4432

0065-1672 See ACTA THEOLOGICA DANICA. 4931

0065-1699 See ACTA VETERINARIA SCANDINAVICA. SUPPLEMENTUM. 5501

0065-1710 See ACTA ZOOLOGICA CRACOVIENSIA. 5573

0065-1729 See ACTA ZOOLOGICA LILLOANA. 5573

0065-1737 See ACTA ZOOLOGICA MEXICANA. 5573

0065-1915 See ADELAIDE LAW REVIEW, THE. 2927

0065-2008 See ADOLESCENT PSYCHIATRY. 3899

0065-2032 See ADRESSBUCH DES DEUTSCHSPRACHIGEN BUCHHANDEL. 4823

0065-2113 See ADVANCES IN AGRONOMY. 44

0065-2156 See ADVANCES IN APPLIED MECHANICS. 2109

0065-2164 See ADVANCES IN APPLIED MICROBIOLOGY. 558

0065-2229 See ADVANCES IN BIOCHEMICAL PSYCHOPHARMACOLOGY. 3826

0065-227X See ADVANCES IN BIOPHYSICS. 494

0065-2296 See ADVANCES IN BOTANICAL RESEARCH. 497

0065-230X See ADVANCES IN CANCER RESEARCH. 3808

0065-2318 See ADVANCES IN CARBOHYDRATE CHEMISTRY AND BIOCHEMISTRY. 479

0065-2326 See ADVANCES IN CARDIOLOGY. 3697

0065-2377 See ADVANCES IN CHEMICAL ENGINEERING. 2007
0065-2385 See ADVANCES IN CHEMICAL PHYSICS. 1049
0065-2393 See ADVANCES IN CHEMISTRY SERIES. 959
0065-2407 See ADVANCES IN CHILD DEVELOPMENT AND BEHAVIOR. 4571
0065-2415 See ADVANCES IN CHROMATOGRAPHY (NEW YORK, N.Y.). 1038
0065-2423 See ADVANCES IN CLINICAL CHEMISTRY. 3892
0065-2458 See ADVANCES IN COMPUTERS. 1255
0065-2482 See ADVANCES IN CRYOGENIC ENGINEERING. 1963
0065-2490 See ADVANCES IN DRUG RESEARCH. 4289
0065-2504 See ADVANCES IN ECOLOGICAL RESEARCH. 2210
0065-2539 See ADVANCES IN ELECTRONICS AND ELECTRON PHYSICS. 2034
0065-2547 See ADVANCES IN ELECTRONICS AND ELECTRON PHYSICS. SUPPLEMENT. 2034
0065-2555 See ADVANCES IN ENGINEERING. 1964
0065-2563 See ADVANCES IN ENVIRONMENTAL SCIENCE AND TECHNOLOGY. 2223
0065-2571 See ADVANCES IN ENZYME REGULATION. 531
0065-258X See ADVANCES IN ENZYMOLOGY AND RELATED SUBJECTS. 479
0065-2598 See ADVANCES IN EXPERIMENTAL MEDICINE AND BIOLOGY. 3546
0065-2601 See ADVANCES IN EXPERIMENTAL SOCIAL PSYCHOLOGY. 4571
0065-2660 See ADVANCES IN GENETICS. 542
0065-2687 See ADVANCES IN GEOPHYSICS. 1402
0065-2695 See ADVANCES IN GEOPHYSICS. SUPPLEMENT. 1402
0065-2717 See ADVANCES IN HEAT TRANSFER. 4430
0065-2725 See ADVANCES IN HETEROCYCLIC CHEMISTRY. 1038
0065-275X See ADVANCES IN HUMAN GENETICS. 542
0065-2776 See ADVANCES IN IMMUNOLOGY. 3662
0065-2806 See ADVANCES IN INSECT PHYSIOLOGY. 5604
0065-2822 See ADVANCES IN INTERNAL MEDICINE. 3794
0065-2830 See ADVANCES IN LIBRARIANSHIP. 3187
0065-2849 See ADVANCES IN LIPID RESEARCH. 479
See ADVANCES IN MAGNETIC AND OPTICAL RESONANCE. 4443
0065-2881 See ADVANCES IN MARINE BIOLOGY. 552
0065-2911 See ADVANCES IN MICROBIAL PHYSIOLOGY. 558
0065-2938 See ADVANCES IN MICROCIRCULATION. 3698
0065-2954 See ADVANCES IN MOLTEN SALT CHEMISTRY. 1035
0065-2989 See ADVANCES IN NUCLEAR SCIENCE AND TECHNOLOGY. 2153
0065-3012 See ADVANCES IN OPTICAL AND ELECTRON MICROSCOPY. 572
0065-3055 See ADVANCES IN ORGANOMETALLIC CHEMISTRY. 1039
0065-3071 See ADVANCES IN OTO-RHINO-LARYNGOLOGY. 3885
0065-308X See ADVANCES IN PARASITOLOGY. 440
0065-3101 See ADVANCES IN PEDIATRICS. 3899
0065-3136 See ADVANCES IN PHARMACEUTICAL SCIENCES. 4289
See ADVANCES IN PHARMACOLOGY. 4289
0065-3152 See ADVANCES IN PHOTOCHEMISTRY. 1049

0065-3160 See ADVANCES IN PHYSICAL ORGANIC CHEMISTRY. 1049
0065-3179 See ADVANCES IN PLANNED PARENTHOOD. 587
0065-3195 See ADVANCES IN POLYMER SCIENCE. 1039
0065-3217 See ADVANCES IN PROBABILITY AND RELATED TOPICS. 3491
0065-3233 See ADVANCES IN PROTEIN CHEMISTRY. 1039
0065-325X See ADVANCES IN PSYCHOLOGICAL ASSESSMENT. 4572
0065-3268 See ADVANCES IN PSYCHOSOMATIC MEDICINE. 4572
0065-3276 See ADVANCES IN QUANTUM CHEMISTRY. 1049
0065-3292 See ADVANCES IN RADIATION BIOLOGY. 440
0065-3411 See ADVANCES IN SURGERY (CHICAGO). 3958
0065-3438 See ADVANCES IN THE ASTRONAUTICAL SCIENCES. 3
0065-3446 See ADVANCES IN THE BIOSCIENCES. 441
0065-3454 See ADVANCES IN THE STUDY OF BEHAVIOR. 4572
0065-3519 See ADVANCES IN VETERINARY SCIENCE AND COMPARATIVE MEDICINE. 5501
0065-3527 See ADVANCES IN VIRUS RESEARCH. 558
0065-3683 See AEROMEDICAL REVIEW. 4
0065-3802 See AFRICA. 2636
0065-3845 See AFRICA CONTEMPORARY RECORD. 2636
0065-387X See OCCASIONAL PAPERS. 2851
0065-3896 See AFRICA SOUTH OF THE SAHARA. 1923
0065-4000 See AFRICAN LITERATURE TODAY. 3358
0065-4019 See AFRICAN MUSIC. 4098
0065-406X See AFRICAN STUDIES SERIES. 2637
0065-4108 See AFRICAN WRITERS SERIES. 3358
0065-4299 See AGENTS AND ACTIONS. 4289
0065-4442 See AGRICULTURAL ECONOMICS REPORT (MICHIGAN STATE UNIVERSITY. DEPT. OF AGRICULTURAL ECONOMICS). 49
0065-4493 See AGRICULTURAL PROGRESS. 51
0065-4612 See AGRICULTURE HANDBOOK (UNITED STATES. DEPT. OF AGRICULTURE). 53
0065-4639 See AGRICULTURE INFORMATION BULLETIN. 54
0065-4663 See AGRONOMY. 56
0065-4868 See AIR TRAVEL BARGAINS / BY JIM WOODMAN. 8
0065-5287 See NACHRICHTEN DER AKADEMIE DER WISSENSCHAFTEN IN GOTTINGEN. PHILOLOGISCH-HISTORISCHE KLASSE. 3304
0065-5295 See NACHRICHTEN DER AKADEMIE DER WISSENSCHAFTEN IN GOTTINGEN. II, MATHEMATISCH-PHYSIKALISCHE KLASSE. 5130
0065-5309 See VEROFFENTLICHUNG. REIHE A, HOHERE GEODASIE / DEUTSCHE GEODATISCHE KOMMISSION BEI DER BAYERISCHEN AKADEMIE DER WISSENSCHAFTEN. 1412
0065-5759 See INFORMATION CIRCULAR - ALASKA. DIVISION OF GEOLOGICAL AND GEOPHYSICAL SURVEYS. 1356
0065-5813 See ALASKA PETROLEUM & INDUSTRIAL DIRECTORY. 4249
0065-616X See ALEXANDER LECTURES, THE. 3359
0065-6216 See REPORT - ALFRED P. SLOAN FOUNDATION. 1516
0065-6275 See ALISO. 498
0065-6364 See ALLAN HANCOCK MONOGRAPHS IN MARINE BIOLOGY. 552
0065-6429 See ALLIONIA. 498
0065-6445 See ALMA MATER. 1315
0065-650X See ALMANACH DU PEUPLE. 2527
0065-6569 See ALPINE JOURNAL, THE. 4868
0065-6585 See ALT-THURINGEN. 2673

0065-6631 See ALTENBURGER NATURWISSENSCHAFTLICHE FORSCHUNGEN. 4161
0065-6666 See ALUMINUM STATISTICAL REVIEW. 4025
0065-6755 See AMAZONIANA. 552
0065-678X See AMERICA VOTES. 4463
0065-6801 See MEMOIRS OF THE AMERICAN ACADEMY IN ROME. 1078
0065-681X See PAPERS AND MONOGRAPHS - AMERICAN ACADEMY IN ROME. 305
0065-6844 See RECORDS OF THE ACADEMY. 329
0065-6852 See MONOGRAPHS OF THE JOURNAL OF THE AMERICAN ACADEMY OF CHILD PSYCHIATRY. 3906
0065-6895 See INSTRUCTIONAL COURSE LECTURES. 3966
0065-6925 See AMERICAN ALPINE JOURNAL, THE. 4868
0065-6941 See SPECIAL PUBLICATION OF THE AMERICAN ANTHROPOLOGICAL ASSOCIATION, A. 245
0065-6968 See AMERICAN ART DIRECTORY. 335
0065-6968 See AMERICAN ART DIRECTORY. 333
0065-7069 See TECHNICAL REVIEW & REGISTER. 5356
0065-7107 See MONOGRAPH SERIES - AMERICAN ASSOCIATION OF CEREAL CHEMISTS. 2350
0065-7182 See PROCEEDINGS OF THE ANNUAL CONVENTION OF THE AMERICAN ASSOCIATION OF EQUINE PRACTITIONERS. 2801
0065-7352 See BUYER'S GUIDE - AMERICAN ASSOCIATION OF TEXTILE CHEMISTS AND COLORISTS. 5348
0065-7417 See AAS MICROFICHE SERIES. 3
0065-759X See AMERICAN BOOK TRADE DIRECTORY. 4821
0065-762X See AMERICAN CAMELLIA YEARBOOK, THE. 2408
0065-7638 See PROCEEDINGS OF THE AMERICAN CATHOLIC PHILOSOPHICAL ASSOCIATION. 4357
0065-7727 See ABSTRACTS OF PAPERS - AMERICAN CHEMICAL SOCIETY. 958
0065-7743 See ANNUAL REPORTS IN MEDICINAL CHEMISTRY. 4291
0065-7778 See TRANSACTIONS OF THE AMERICAN CLINICAL AND CLIMATOLOGICAL ASSOCIATION. 3647
0065-7859 See ACTIVITY. 1807
0065-7875 See ACI MANUAL OF CONCRETE PRACTICE. 598
0065-793X See AMERICAN COOPERATION. 1541
0065-8006 See TRANSACTIONS - AMERICAN CRYSTALLOGRAPHIC ASSOCIATION. 1033
0065-8006 See TRANSACTIONS OF THE AMERICAN CRYSTALLOGRAPHIC ASSOCIATION. 1033
0065-8073 See AMERICAN DENTAL DIRECTORY. 1315
0065-809X See AMERICAN DOCTORAL DISSERTATIONS. 1808
0065-8103 See AMERICAN DROP-SHIPPERS DIRECTORY. 822
0065-8111 See AMERICAN DRUG INDEX. 4290
0065-8162 See MEMOIRS OF THE AMERICAN ENTOMOLOGICAL INSTITUTE. 5611
0065-8170 See MEMOIRS OF THE AMERICAN ENTOMOLOGICAL SOCIETY. 5611
0065-8219 See AMERICAN EXPLORATION AND TRAVEL SERIES. 2718
0065-8278 See AMERICAN FARM & HOME ALMANAC, THE. 2527
0065-8375 See TRANSACTIONS OF THE AMERICAN FOUNDRYMEN'S SOCIETY (ANNUAL). 4022
0065-8448 See GEOPHYSICAL MONOGRAPH. 1406
0065-8456 See YEARBOOK / AMERICAN GOAT SOCIETY. 224
0065-8561 See ANNUAL REPORT OF THE AMERICAN HISTORICAL ASSOCIATION. 2610

0065-857X *See* AHA PAMPHLETS. 2717

0065-860X *See* AMERICAN IMAGO. 4572

0065-8693 *See* AIAA ROSTER. 6

0065-8766 *See* MANAGEMENT ADVISORY SERVICES: GUIDELINE SERIES. 876

0065-8804 *See* AICHE MONOGRAPH SERIES. 2007

0065-8812 *See* AICHE SYMPOSIUM SERIES. 2007

0065-8847 *See* BIBLIOGRAPHIC SERIES. 5012

0065-8987 *See* AMERICAN JEWISH YEAR BOOK. 5045

0065-8995 *See* AMERICAN JOURNAL OF JURISPRUDENCE (NOTRE DAME), THE. 2932

0065-9045 *See* PROCEEDINGS / AMERICAN LAW INSTITUTE. 3031

0065-910X *See* AMERICAN LIBRARY DIRECTORY. 3257

0065-9142 *See* AMERICAN LITERARY SCHOLARSHIP. 3360

0065-9207 *See* AMERICAN MARITIME LIBRARY, THE. 4174

0065-9258 *See* COLLOQUIUM PUBLICATIONS / AMERICAN MATHEMATICAL SOCIETY. 3500

0065-9266 *See* MEMOIRS OF THE AMERICAN MATHEMATICAL SOCIETY. 3522

0065-9274 *See* SELECTED TRANSLATIONS IN MATHEMATICAL STATISTICS AND PROBABILITY. 3533

0065-9282 *See* TRANSLATIONS OF MATHEMATICAL MONOGRAPHS. 3539

0065-9290 *See* TRANSLATIONS - AMERICAN MATHEMATICAL SOCIETY. 3539

0065-9401 *See* METEOROLOGICAL MONOGRAPHS (AMERICAN METEOROLOGICAL SOCIETY). 1431

0065-9452 *See* ANTHROPOLOGICAL PAPERS OF THE AMERICAN MUSEUM OF NATURAL HISTORY. 4162

0065-9495 *See* ANA CLINICAL SESSIONS. 3851

0065-9533 *See* TRANSACTIONS OF THE AMERICAN OPHTHALMOLOGICAL SOCIETY ANNUAL MEETING. 3879

0065-9541 *See* AMERICAN ORIENTAL SERIES, ESSAY. 2645

0065-955X *See* AMERICAN ORTHOPTIC JOURNAL. 3871

0065-9584 *See* BULLETIN OF THE AMERICAN PENSTEMON SOCIETY. 2411

0065-9703 *See* SPECIAL PUBLICATIONS / AMERICAN PHILOLOGICAL ASSOCIATION. 3323

0065-972X *See* PROCEEDINGS AND ADDRESSES OF THE AMERICAN PHILOSOPHICAL ASSOCIATION. 4357

0065-9738 *See* MEMOIRS OF THE AMERICAN PHILOSOPHICAL SOCIETY HELD AT PHILADELPHIA FOR PROMOTING USEFUL KNOWLEDGE. 4352

0065-9746 *See* TRANSACTIONS OF THE AMERICAN PHILOSOPHICAL SOCIETY. 4364

0065-9762 *See* YEAR BOOK - THE AMERICAN PHILOSOPHICAL SOCIETY. 4365

0065-9932 *See* SPECIAL REPORT - AMERICAN PUBLIC WORKS ASSOCIATION. 4686

0065-9940 *See* MANUAL OF THE AMERICAN RAILWAY ENGINEERING ASSOCIATION. 5432

0065-9959 *See* AMERICAN REFERENCE BOOKS ANNUAL. 1923

0065-9983 *See* REHABILITATION PUBLICATION. 4327

0065-9991 *See* JOURNAL OF THE AMERICAN RESEARCH CENTER IN EGYPT. 2641

0066-0000 *See* AMERICAN ROSE ANNUAL / AMERICAN ROSE SOCIETY, THE. 2408

0066-0035 *See* ANNUAL OF THE AMERICAN SCHOOLS OF ORIENTAL RESEARCH, THE. 255

0066-0132 *See* TRANSACTIONS OF THE AMERICAN SOCIETY FOR NEUROCHEMISTRY. 3847

0066-0558 *See* ASTM SPECIAL TECHNICAL PUBLICATION. 1966

0066-0558 *See* ASTM SPECIAL TECHNICAL PUBLICATION. 2100

0066-0566 *See* ASA SPECIAL PUBLICATION. 63

0066-0582 *See* PROCEEDINGS OF THE ... ANNUAL MEETING / AMERICAN SOCIETY OF BAKERY ENGINEERS. 2354

0066-0604 *See* TRANSACTIONS OF THE AMERICAN SOCIETY OF CIVIL ENGINEERS. 2007

0066-068X *See* YEARBOOK - AMERICAN SOCIETY OF SANITARY ENGINEERING. 2248

0066-0701 *See* PROCEEDINGS OF THE ANNUAL CONFERENCE - AMERICAN SOCIETY OF UNIVERSITY COMPOSERS. 4147

0066-071X *See* ASHA MONOGRAPHS. 4384

0066-0736 *See* PROCEEDINGS OF THE BUSINESS AND ECONOMIC STATISTICS SECTION. 1537

0066-0752 *See* PROCEEDINGS OF THE SOCIAL STATISTICS SECTION (WASHINGTON). 5336

0066-0833 *See* TRANSACTIONS OF THE MEETING OF THE AMERICAN SURGICAL ASSOCIATION. 3976

0066-0868 *See* SUMMARY OF PROCEEDINGS. ANNUAL CONFERENCE / AMERICAN THEOLOGICAL LIBRARY ASSOCIATION. 3251

0066-0884 *See* AMERICAN TRAIL SERIES. 2719

0066-0922 *See* AMERICAN UNIVERSITIES AND COLLEGES. 1808

0066-0957 *See* EAST ASIA SERIES. 2503

0066-0981 *See* NORTH AFRICA SERIES. 2642

0066-1058 *See* WEST AFRICA SERIES. 2644

0066-1090 *See* DEVELOPING WORLD : A UFS READINGS. 2908

0066-1198 *See* PROCEEDINGS, ... ANNUAL MEETING OF THE AMERICAN WOOD-PRESERVERS' ASSOCIATION. 2403

0066-1198 *See* PROCEEDINGS, ANNUAL MEETING OF THE AMERICAN WOOD-PRESERVERS' ASSOCIATION. 2403

0066-121X *See* AMERICANS BEFORE COLUMBUS. 2720

0066-1376 *See* ANALECTA GREGORIANA. 4934

0066-1392 *See* ANALECTA ROMANA INSTITUTI DANICI. 254

0066-1406 *See* ANALECTA ROMANA INSTITUTI DANICI. SUPPLEMENTUM. 254

0066-1465 *See* ANALES DE CIRUGIA. 3958

0066-1546 *See* ANATOLIAN STUDIES. 254

0066-1554 *See* ANATOLICA. 3264

0066-1562 *See* VERHANDLUNGEN DER ANATOMISCHEN GESELLSCHAFT. 3680

0066-1597 *See* ANCIENT CHRISTIAN WRITERS : THE WORKS OF THE FATHERS IN TRANSLATION. 4934

0066-1600 *See* ANCIENT PAKISTAN. 2645

0066-1619 *See* ANCIENT SOCIETY. 2610

0066-1759 *See* ANGEWANDTE BOTANIK. 499

0066-1805 *See* ANGLISTICA. 3264

0066-1813 *See* ANGLO AMERICAN TRADE DIRECTORY. 822

0066-183X *See* ANGLO-NORMAN TEXTS. 2673

0066-1945 *See* ROCZNIKI POMORSKIEJ AKADEMII MEDYCZNEJ IM. GEN. KAROLA SWIERCZEWSKIEGO W SZCZECINIE. 3987

0066-1953 *See* ANNALES ACADEMIAE SCIENTIARUM FENNICAE. SERIES A. I, MATHEMATICA (HELSINKI, FINLAND : 1975). 3493

0066-1961 *See* ANNALES ACADEMIAE SCIENTIARUM FENNICAE. SERIES A2: CHEMICA. 961

0066-197X *See* ANNALES ACADEMIAE SCIENTIARUM FENNICAE. SERIES A. III : GEOLOGICA-GEOGRAPHICA. 5083

0066-1988 *See* ANNALES ACADEMIAE SCIENTIARUM FENNICAE. SERIES A4: BIOLOGICA. 441

0066-1996 *See* ANNALES ACADEMIAE SCIENTIARUM FENNICAE. SER. A5: MEDICA. 3550

0066-2003 *See* ANNALES ACADEMIAE SCIENTIARUM FENNICAE. SERIES A. VI: PHYSICA. 4396

0066-2011 *See* ANNALES ACADEMIAE SCIENTIARUM FENNICAE. SERIES B. 254

0066-202X *See* ANNALES AFRICAINES. 2933

0066-2054 *See* ANNALES DE CHIRURGIE THORACIQUE ET CARDIOVASCULAIRE. 3959

0066-2062 *See* ANNALES DE DEMOGRAPHIE HISTORIQUE. 4549

0066-2070 *See* ANNALES DE GASTROENTEROLOGIE ET D'HEPATOLOGIE. 3743

0066-2097 *See* ANNALES DE PEDIATRIE (PARIS). 3900

0066-2216 *See* ANNALES POLONICI MATHEMATICI. 3493

0066-2224 *See* ANNALES SILESIAE. 2674

0066-2232 *See* ANNALES UNIVERSITATIS MARIAE CURIE-SKODOWSKA. SECTIO C. BIOLOGIA. 442

0066-2240 *See* ANNALES UNIVERSITATIS MARIAE CURIE-SKLODOWSKA. SECTION I: PHILOSOPHIA-SOCIOLOGIA. 4340

0066-2240 *See* ANNALES UNIVERSITATIS MARIAE CURIE-SKODOWSKA. SECTIO D, MEDICINA. 3550

0066-2275 *See* ANNALI DI SOCIOLOGIA. 5239

0066-2313 *See* ANNALS OF MATHEMATICS STUDIES. 3494

0066-2348 *See* ANNEE EPIGRAPHIQUE, L'. 1074

0066-2380 *See* ANNEE SOCIALE / INSTITUT DE SOCIOLOGIE, UNIVERSITE LIBRE DE BRUXELLES, L'. 5191

0066-2399 *See* ANNEE SOCIOLOGIQUE (1940/48). 5239

0066-2461 *See* ANNUAIRE ADMINISTRATIF ET JUDICIAIRE DE BELGIQUE. ADMINISTRATIEF EN GERECHTELIJK JAARBOEK VOOR BELGIE. 4626

0066-2488 *See* ANNUAIRE CATHOLIQUE DE FRANCE. 5023

0066-2607 *See* ANNUAIRE DE L'AFRIQUE DU NORD. 2498

0066-2623 *See* ANNUAIRE DE L'ARMEMENT A LA PECHE. 2294

0066-2658 *See* ANNUAIRE DE LEGISLATION FRANCAISE ET ETRANGERE / PUBLIE PAR LE CENTRE FRANCAIS DE DROIT COMPAREE. 3123

0066-3085 *See* ANNUAIRE FRANCAIS DE DROIT INTERNATIONAL. 3123

0066-3646 *See* ANNUAIRE STATISTIQUE DE LA BELGIQUE. 5321

0066-3654 *See* ANNUAIRE STATISTIQUE DE LA FRANCE. 1528

0066-3786 *See* ANNUAL BIBLIOGRAPHY OF ENGLISH LANGUAGE AND LITERATURE. 3457

0066-3808 *See* ANNUAL BULLETIN OF COAL STATISTICS FOR EUROPE. 1961

0066-3816 *See* ANNUAL BULLETIN OF ELECTRIC ENERGY STATISTICS FOR EUROPE. 2035

0066-3824 *See* ANNUAL BULLETIN OF GAS STATISTICS FOR EUROPE. 4283

0066-3832 *See* ANNUAL BULLETIN OF HISTORICAL LITERATURE. 2610

0066-3840 *See* ANNUAL BULLETIN OF HOUSING AND BUILDING STATISTICS FOR EUROPE. 2839

0066-3859 *See* ANNUAL BULLETIN OF TRANSPORT STATISTICS FOR EUROPE. BULLETIN ANNUEL DE STATISTIQUES DE TRANSPORTS POUR L'EUROPE. EZHEGODNYI BIULLETEN' EVROPEISKOI STATISTIKI TRANSPORTA. 5376

0066-4030 *See* ANNUAL PROGRESS IN CHILD PSYCHIATRY AND CHILD DEVELOPMENT. 3900

0066-4049 *See* ANNUAL REGISTER OF GRANT SUPPORT. 1809

0066-4057 *See* ANNUAL REGISTER (LONDON, ENGLAND : 1964). 2610

0066-409X *See* ANNUAL REPORTS IN ORGANIC SYNTHESIS. 1039

0066-4103 *See* ANNUAL REPORTS ON NMR SPECTROSCOPY. 4443

0066-4138 *See* ANNUAL REVIEW IN AUTOMATIC PROGRAMMING. 1278

0066-4146 See ANNUAL REVIEW OF ASTRONOMY AND ASTROPHYSICS. 391

0066-4154 See ANNUAL REVIEW OF BIOCHEMISTRY. 480

0066-4162 See ANNUAL REVIEW OF ECOLOGY AND SYSTEMATICS. 2211

0066-4170 See ANNUAL REVIEW OF ENTOMOLOGY. 5605

0066-4189 See ANNUAL REVIEW OF FLUID MECHANICS. 2087

0066-4197 See ANNUAL REVIEW OF GENETICS. 542

0066-4200 See ANNUAL REVIEW OF INFORMATION SCIENCE AND TECHNOLOGY. 3191

0066-4219 See ANNUAL REVIEW OF MEDICINE. 3551

0066-426X See ANNUAL REVIEW OF PHYSICAL CHEMISTRY. 1050

0066-4278 See ANNUAL REVIEW OF PHYSIOLOGY. 578

0066-4286 See ANNUAL REVIEW OF PHYTOPATHOLOGY. 500

0066-4308 See ANNUAL REVIEW OF PSYCHOLOGY. 4574

0066-4413 See ANNUAL SURVEY OF AMERICAN LAW. 2935

0066-4545 See ANNUARIO STATISTICO ITALIANO. 5322

0066-4596 See ANSCHRIFTEN DEUTSCHER VERLAGE, BUNDESREPUBLIK DEUTSCHLAND, DDR UND AUS DEM DEUTSCHSPRACHIGEN RAUM OSTERREICH, SCHWEIZ, SOWIE ANSCHRIFTEN WEITERER AUSLANDISCHER VERLAG MIT DEUTSCHEN AUSLIEFERUNGEN. 4812

0066-4626 See ANTARCTIC BIBLIOGRAPHY. 3457

0066-4634 See ANTARCTIC RESEARCH SERIES. 1402

0066-4677 See ANTHROPOLOGICAL FORUM. 229

0066-4693 See MITTEILUNGEN DER ANTHROPOLOGISCHEN GESELLSCHAFT IN WIEN. 241

0066-4715 See ANTHROPOLOGY OF THE NORTH. 230

0066-4758 See ANTIBIOTICS AND CHEMOTHERAPY. 4291

0066-4774 See ANTICHTHON. 1074

0066-4782 See ANTIKE KUNST. BEIHEFT. 337

0066-4804 See ANTIMICROBIAL AGENTS AND CHEMOTHERAPY. 559

0066-4812 See ANTIPODE. 2554

0066-4847 See ANTIQUITAS. REIHE 2. ABHANDLUNGEN AUS DEM GEBIETE DER VOR UND FRUHGESCHICHTE. 2610

0066-4863 See ANTIQUITAS. REIHE 4. BEITREAGE ZUR HISTORIA-AUGUSTA-FORSCHUNG. 2610

0066-4871 See ANTIQUITES AFRICAINES. 2637

0066-4987 See ANUAR DE LINGVISTICA SI ISTORIE LITERARA. 3265

0066-5045 See ANUARIO COLOMBIANO DE HISTORIA SOCIAL Y DE LA CULTURA. 5191

0066-5061 See ANUARIO DE ESTUDIOS MEDIEVALES. 2675

0066-507X See ANUARIO DE FILOLOGIA (CARACAS). 3266

0066-5088 See ANUARIO DE HISTORIA ECONOMICA Y SOCIAL / SEMINARIO DE HISTORIA SOCIAL Y ECONOMICA, FACULTAD DE FILOSOFIA Y LETRAS DE LA UNIVERSIDAD DE MADRID. 1546

0066-5096 See ANUARIO DE LA MINERIA DE CHILE / MINISTERIO DE ECONOMIA, SERVICO NACIONAL DE GEOLOGIA Y MINERIA. 2134

0066-510X See ANUARIO DE LA RELOJERIA Y ARTE EN METAL PARA ESPANA E HISPANOAMERICA. 3998

0066-5215 See ANUARIO FILOSOFICO. 4341

0066-5282 See ANZEIGER FUER SLAVISCHE PHILOLOGIE. 3266

0066-5347 See APOTHEKER-JAHRBUCH. 4292

0066-5355 See APPALACHIAN ADVANCE. 1726

0066-538X See PROCEEDINGS OF THE ... ANNUAL APPALACHIAN UNDERGROUND CORROSION SHORT COURSE. 2016

0066-5452 See APPLIED MATHEMATICAL SCIENCES. 3495

0066-5576 See APPROACHES TO SEMIOTICS. 3266

0066-5576 See APPROACHES TO SEMIOTICS. PAPERBACK SERIES. 3266

0066-5614 See AQUINAS LECTURE. 4341

0066-5657 See ARABIDOPSIS INFORMATION SERVICE. 500

0066-5673 See ARBEITEN ZUR ANGEWANDTEN STATISTIK. 3495

0066-5703 See ARBEITEN ZUR RECHTSVERGLEICHUNG. 1366

0066-5738 See ARBEITSBLATTER FUER RESTAURATOREN. 256

0066-5746 See ARD JAHRBUCH. 1149

0066-5754 See VORTRAGE - RHEINISCH-WESTFALISCHE AKADEMIE DER WISSENSCHAFTEN, N, NATUR-, INGENIEUR- UND WIRTSCHAFTSWISSENSCHAFTEN. 5169

0066-586X See ARBEITSRECHT DER GEGENWART, DAS. 3144

0066-5878 See ARBORETUM KORNICKIE. 500

0066-5894 See ARCHAEOLOGIA CANTIANA. 256

0066-5924 See ARCHAEOLOGIA POLONA / POLSKA AKADEMIA NAUK, INSTYTUT HISTORII KULTURY MATERIALNEJ. 256

0066-5983 See ARCHAEOLOGICAL JOURNAL, THE. 256

0066-6033 See ARCHAEOLOGISCHE MITTEILUNGEN AUS IRAN. 257

0066-605X See ARCHEOLOGIA (WARSAW. 1947). 258

0066-6157 See ARCHITECTS, CONTRACTORS, ENGINEERS GUIDE TO CONSTRUCTION COSTS. 599

0066-6203 See TRANSACTIONS OF THE ARCHITECTURAL AND ARCHAEOLOGICAL SOCIETY OF DURHAM AND NORTHUMBERLAND. 284

0066-622X See ARCHITECTURAL HISTORY. 289

0066-6262 See ARCHITEKTONIKA THEMATA. 290

0066-6270 See ARCHITEKTURA BUDAPEST. 1966. 291

0066-6297 See ARCHIV FUER DIPLOMATIK : SCHRIFTGESCHICHTE, SIEGEL, UND WAPPENKUNDE. 2675

0066-6327 See ARCHIV FUER GESCHICHTE DES BUCHWESENS. 4823

0066-6335 See ARCHIV FUER GESCHICHTE VON OBERFRANKEN. 2675

0066-6386 See ARCHIV FUER LITURGIEWISSENSCHAFT. 4935

0066-6432 See ARCHI FUER MITTELRHEINISCHE KIRCHENGESCHICHTE. 4935

0066-6440 See ARCHIV FUER ORIENTFORSCHUNG. 3266

0066-6459 See ARCHIV FUER PAPYRUSFORSCHUNG UND VERWANDTE GEBIETE. 3266

0066-6491 See ARCHIV FUER SCHLESISCHE KIRCHENGESCHICHTE. 5055

0066-6505 See ARCHIV FUER SOZIALGESCHICHTE. 2676

0066-6513 See ARCHIV FUER VOLKERKUNDE. 231

0066-6564 See ARCHIVES DE PHILOSOPHIE DU DROIT. 2936

0066-6637 See ARCHIVES OF ASIAN ART. 337

0066-670X See ARCHIVIO PUTTI DI CHIRURGIA DEGLI ORGANI DI MOVIMENTO. 3960

0066-6742 See ARCHIVO ESPANOL DE ARQUEOLOGIA. 259

0066-6750 See ARCHIVOS ARGENTINOS DE DERMATOLOGIA. 3718

0066-6769 See ARCHIVES OF MEDICAL RESEARCH. 3552

0066-6777 See ARCHIVOS DE OFTALMOLOGIA DE BUENOS AIRES. 3872

0066-6785 See ARCHIVUM HISTORIAE PONTIFICIAE. 4936

0066-6793 See ARCHIVUM (MUNCHEN). 2480

0066-684X See ARCHIWUM ENERGETYKI. 2036

0066-6882 See ARCHIWUM IURIDICUM CRACOVIENSE. 2936

0066-6912 See ARCHIWUM MINERALOGICZNE. 1438

0066-6939 See ARCTIC ANTHROPOLOGY. 231

0066-6998 See ARCTOS. 3266

0066-7358 See ARHEOLOGIA MOLDOVEI. 259

0066-7374 See PROCEEDINGS OF THE ARISTOTELIAN SOCIETY. 4358

0066-7412 See ARIZONA GEOLOGICAL SOCIETY DIGEST. 1366

0066-7501 See ANTHROPOLOGICAL PAPERS OF THE UNIVERSITY OF ARIZONA. 229

0066-7609 See OPTICAL SCIENCES CENTER NEWSLETTER. 4216

0066-7668 See ARKIV FOR NORDISK FILOLOGI. 3267

0066-7676 See ARKKITEHTUURIKILPAILUJA. 292

0066-7684 See ARLINGTON HISTORICAL MAGAZINE, THE. 2721

0066-782X See ARQUIVOS BRASILEIROS DE CARDIOLOGIA. 3699

0066-7870 See ARQUIVOS DE ZOOLOGIA. 5576

0066-7935 See ART BULLETIN OF VICTORIA. 338

0066-8036 See ARTHROPODS OF FLORIDA AND NEIGHBORING LAND AREAS. 5576

0066-8095 See ARTS / THE JOURNAL OF THE SYDNEY UNIVERSITY ARTS ASSOCIATION. 315

0066-8168 See ARTS PATRONAGE SERIES. 315

0066-8176 See ARV. 2318

0066-8192 See ARZNEI-TELEGRAMM : FAKTEN UND VERGLEICHE FUR DIE RATIONALE THERAPIE. 4292

0066-8281 See ASIAN AND AFRICAN STUDIES (JERUSALEM). 2638

0066-829X See ASIAN AND PACIFIC ARCHAEOLOGY SERIES. 260

0066-8370 See ANNUAL REPORT - ASIAN DEVELOPMENT BANK. 770

0066-8419 See ASIAN JOURNAL OF PHARMACY. 4293

0066-8435 See ASIAN PERSPECTIVES (HONOLULU). 260

0066-8443 See ASIAN PHILOSOPHICAL STUDIES. 4341

0066-8451 See ASIAN POPULATION STUDIES SERIES. 4549

0066-846X See ANNUAL REPORT - ASIAN PRODUCTIVITY ORGANIZATION. 1597

0066-8478 See ASIAN SOCIAL SCIENCE BIBLIOGRAPHY WITH ANNOTATIONS AND ABSTRACTS. 5226

0066-8486 See ASIAN STUDIES AT HAWAII. 2646

0066-8508 See ASIEN, AFRIKA, LATEINAMERIKA. 1547

0066-8672 See ASPECTS OF EDUCATION : JOURNAL OF THE INSTITUTE OF EDUCATION, THE UNIVERSITY OF HULL. 1726

0066-8702 See ASSEMBLY ENGINEERING MASTER CATALOG. 2110

0066-8710 See DIRECTORY / THE ASSOCIATED CHURCH PRESS. 4953

0066-8842 See ANNALES DE L'A C F A S. 5083

0066-8990 See ANNUAIRE - ASSOCIATION DES INSTITUTIONS D'ENSEIGNEMENT SECONDAIRE. 1724

0066-9458 See TRANSACTIONS OF THE ASSOCIATION OF AMERICAN PHYSICIANS. 3647

0066-9598 See TRANSACTIONS OF THE ASSOCIATION OF LIFE INSURANCE MEDICAL DIRECTORS OF AMERICA, ANNUAL MEETING. 2894

0066-961X See OFFICIAL METHODS OF ANALYSIS OF THE ASSOCIATION OF OFFICIAL ANALYTICAL CHEMISTS. 1018

0066-9628 See YEARBOOK - ASSOCIATION OF PACIFIC COAST GEOGRAPHERS. 2579

See ARL. 3191

0066-9814 See BULLETIN DE L'ASSOCIATION TECHNIQUE MARITIME ET AERONAUTIQUE. 4175

0066-9830 See ATTI A.G.I. 542

0066-9903 See ASSYRIOLOGICAL STUDIES. 3267

0066-992X See ASTICOU (HULL). 2722

0066-9997 See PROCEEDINGS - ASTRONOMICAL SOCIETY OF AUSTRALIA. 398

0067-0022 See ASTRONOMY AND ASTROPHYSICS ABSTRACTS. 402

0067-0049 See ASTROPHYSICAL JOURNAL. SUPPLEMENT SERIES, THE. 393

0067-0057 See ASTROPHYSICS AND SPACE SCIENCE LIBRARY. 393

0067-0081 See ANNUARIO DELLA SCUOLA ARCHEOLOGICA DI ATENE E DELLE MISSIONI ITALIANE IN ORIENTE. 255

0067-0286 See ATLAS DES STRUCTURES AGRAIRES AU SUD DU SAHARA. 63

0067-0340 See ATMOSPHERIC SCIENCE PAPER. 1420

0067-0464 See RECORDS OF THE AUCKLAND INSTITUTE AND MUSEUM. 5145

0067-0510 See AUCKLAND UNIVERSITY LAW REVIEW. 3089

0067-0561 See AUGUST VOLLMER CRIMINALISTIC SERIES. 3158

0067-0855 See NORTHERN TERRITORY IN FOCUS. 2670

See DEMOGRAPHY, SOUTH AUSTRALIA. 4561

See SUMMARY OF STATISTICS - AUSTRALIAN BUREAU OF STATISTICS. VICTORIAN OFFICE. 4701

0067-1223 See VICTORIAN YEAR-BOOK. 4701

0067-1525 See PROCEEDINGS OF THE ... AUSTRALIA-NEW ZEALAND CONFERENCE ON SOIL MECHANICS AND FOUNDATION ENGINEERING. 183

0067-1584 See YEAR BOOK / AUSTRALIAN ACADEMY OF SCIENCE. 5171

0067-1592 See PROCEEDINGS - THE AUSTRALIAN ACADEMY OF THE HUMANITIES. 2852

0067-1754 See AUSTRALIAN CAPITAL TERRITORY STATISTICAL SUMMARY. 5322

0067-1762 See ANNUAL REPORT / AUSTRALIAN COAL INDUSTRY RESEARCH LABORATORIES. 2133

0067-1827 See PROCEEDINGS OF THE AUSTRALIAN CONFERENCE ON ELECTROCHEMISTRY. 1035

0067-1843 See AUSTRALIAN DIGEST, THE. 2938

0067-1878 See AUSTRALIAN GOVERNMENT PUBLICATIONS. 4631

0067-1924 See AUSTRALIAN JOURNAL OF BOTANY. 501

0067-1940 See AUSTRALIAN JOURNAL OF MARINE AND FRESHWATER RESEARCH. 1446

0067-1975 See RECORDS OF THE AUSTRALIAN MUSEUM. 5596

0067-1983 See AUSTRALIAN NATIONAL ACCOUNTS : NATIONAL INCOME AND EXPENDITURE. 4696

0067-205X See FEDERAL LAW REVIEW. 2969

0067-2084 See PROCEEDINGS OF THE AUSTRALIAN PHYSIOLOGICAL AND PHARMACOLOGICAL SOCIETY. 585

0067-2149 See PROCEEDINGS OF THE AUSTRALIAN SOCIETY OF ANIMAL PRODUCTION. 219

0067-2173 See AUSTRALIAN SUGAR YEAR BOOK, THE. 2328

0067-2238 See AUSTRALIAN ZOOLOGIST, THE. 5577

0067-2343 See OSTERREICHISCHE HOCHSCHULSTATISTIK. 1839

0067-236X See OSTERREICHISCHE HISTORISCHE BIBLIOGRAPHIE. 2636

0067-2378 See AUSTRIAN HISTORY YEARBOOK. 2677

0067-2513 See AUTOMOBILE ALMANAC. 5405

0067-270X See AZANIA. 260

0067-2734 See BBA LIBRARY. BIOCHIMICA ET BIOPHYSICA ACTA LIBRARY. 3193

0067-284X See JAHRBUCH DER STAATLICHEN KUNSTSAMMLUNGEN IN BADEN-WURTTEMBERG. 354

0067-2904 See IRAQI JOURNAL OF SCIENCE. 5116

0067-2912 See BAHAMAS HANDBOOK AND BUSINESSMAN'S ANNUAL. 5462

0067-3080 See ANNUAL - BALTIMORE MUSEUM OF ART. 336

0067-3099 See BALTISCHE STUDIEN. 2677

0067-3129 See BAMPTON LECTURES IN AMERICA. 1811

0067-3226 See INFORME ANUAL / BANCO CENTRAL DE NICARAGUA. 791

0067-3234 See ANUARIO ESTADISTICO / JUNTA MONETARIA, SUPERINTENDENCIA DEL SISTEMA FINANCIERO, ASESORIA ACTUARIAL Y ESTADISTICA. 726

0067-3250 See INFORME ECONOMICO. 1495

0067-3277 See MEMORIA DEL GERENTE GENERAL DEL BANCO CENTRAL DEL ECUADOR. 798

0067-3315 See INFORME ANUAL - BANCO DE ESPANA. 1567

0067-3560 See ANNUAL REPORT - BANK FOR INTERNATIONAL SETTLEMENTS. 770

0067-3587 See BANK OF CANADA. ANNUAL REPORT OF THE GOVERNOR TO THE MINISTER OF FINANCE AND STATEMENT OF ACCOUNTS. 775

0067-3633 See ANNUAL ECONOMIC REVIEW (HONOLULU). 1545

0067-3692 See BANK OF JAPAN QUARTERLY BULLETIN. 775

0067-3811 See BANKING STATISTICS OF PAKISTAN. 726

0067-3951 See BANQUE DES MOTS (PARIS). 3268

0067-4087 See YEARBOOK - BAPTIST UNION OF WESTERN CANADA. 5069

0067-4222 See BAROQUE (MONTAUBAN). 3365

0067-4419 See BASIC FACTS ABOUT THE UNITED NATIONS. 3124

0067-4478 See BASLER BEITRAGE ZUR ETHNOLOGIE. 231

0067-4486 See BASLER BEITRAEGE ZUR GEOGRAPHIE. 2556

0067-4508 See BASLER STUDIEN ZUR DEUTSCHEN SPRACHE UND LITERATUR. 3268

0067-4524 See BASLER VEROFFENTLICHUNGEN ZUR GESCHICHTE DER MEDIZIN UND DER BIOLOGIE. 3555

0067-4540 See BASLER ZEITSCHRIFT FUER GESCHICHTE UND ALTERTUMSKUNDE. 2677

0067-4672 See BAYER SYMPOSIUM. 443

0067-4729 See BAYERISCHES JAHRBUCH FUER VOLKSKUNDE. 2843

0067-4737 See BEAU-COCOA. 3365

0067-4745 See BEAUFORTIA. 5577

0067-4826 See PUBLICATIONS OF THE BEDFORDSHIRE HISTORICAL RECORD SOCIETY. 2704

0067-5016 See BEITRAEGE ZUR GERICHTLICHEN MEDIZIN. 3740

0067-5024 See BEITRAGE ZUR GESCHICHTE DER PHILOSOPHIE UND THEOLOGIE DES MITTELALTERS. 3268

0067-5024 See BEITRAEGE ZUR GESCHICHTE DER PHILOSOPHIE UND THEOLOGIE DES MITTELALTERS. TEXTE UND UNTERSUCHUNGEN. 4342

0067-5083 See BEITRAEGE ZUR HYGIENE UND EPIDEMIOLOGIE. 3734

0067-5091 See BEITRAEGE ZUR INKUNABELKUNDE : IM AUFTRAGE DER DEUTSCHEN STAATSBIBLIOTHEK ZU BERLIN. 4564

0067-5121 See BEITRREAGE ZUR KUNST DES CHRISTLICHEN OSTENS. 343

0067-5148 See BEITRAEGE ZUR MEERESKUNDE. 1446

0067-5172 See BEITRAEGE ZUE OKUMENISCHEN THEOLOGIE. 4938

0067-5202 See BEITRAEGE ZUR ROMANISCHEN PHILOLOGIE DES MITTELALTERS. 3338

0067-5210 See BEITRAEGE ZUR SEXUALFORSCHUNG. 3921

0067-5245 See BEITRAEGE ZUR UR- UND FRUGESCHICHTLICHEN ARCHAOLOGIE DES MITTELMEER-KULTURRAUMES. 261

0067-5431 See ANNUAIRE STATISTIQUE DE POCHE - INSTITUT NATIONAL DE STATISTIQUE. 5321

0067-5490 See STATISTIQUES DEMOGRAPHIQUES. 4563

0067-5563 See STATISTIQUES SOCIALES. 1539

0067-5660 See VESNIK / VOJNI MUZEJ, BEOGRAD. 4060

0067-5768 See BERG- UND HUTTENMANNISCHE MONATSCHEFTE. SUPPLEMENTUM. 1438

0067-5830 See BERKELEY JOURNAL OF SOCIOLOGY. 5240

0067-5849 See MITTEILUNGEN AUS DER BIOLOGISCHEN BUNDESANSTALT FUER LAND- UND FORSTWIRTSCHAFT, BERLIN-DAHLEM. 2388

0067-5903 See FORSCHUNGEN ZUR OSTEUROPAISCHEN GESCHICHTE. 2688

0067-592X See VEROFFENTLICHUNGEN DER ABTEILUNG FUER SLAVISCHE SPRACHEN UND LITERATUREN DES OSTEUROPA-INSTITUTS (SLAVISCHES SEMINAR) AN DER FREIEN UNIVERSITAT BERLIN. 3450

0067-5938 See WIRTSCHAFTSWISSENSCHAFTLICHE VEROFFENTLICHUNGEN. 1526

0067-5954 See WISSENSCHAFTLICHE ZEITSCHRIFT DER HOCHSCHULE FUER OEKONOMIE. 1527

0067-5989 See VEROFFENTLICHUNGEN. ABTEILUNG SUDSEE. 2325

0067-6004 See FORSCHUNGEN UND BERICHTE - STAATLICHE MUSEEN BERLIN. 4088

0067-6055 See BERLINER BYZANTINISTISCHE ARBEITEN. 2678

0067-6179 See SPECIAL PUBLICATIONS. 4096

0067-6195 See BERYTUS; ARCHAEOLOGICAL STUDIES. 261

0067-6225 See BEST AMERICAN PLAYS. 5362

0067-6233 See BEST AMERICAN SHORT STORIES (BOSTON, MASS. : 1978). 3366

See BEST AMERICAN SHORT PLAYS, THE. 5362

0067-6322 See BEST'S SAFETY DIRECTORY. 2859

0067-6470 See PRACE BIAOSTOCKIEGO TOWARZYSTWA NAUKOWEGO. 1842

0067-6489 See ROCZNIKI AKADEMII MEDYCZNEJ W BIAYMSTOKU. 3637

0067-6535 See BIBLICAL RESEARCH. 5015

0067-6543 See BIBLIOGRAFI OVER DANMARKS OFFENTLIGE PUBLIKATIONER. 4696

0067-6586 See BIBLIOGRAFIA BRASILEIRA DE BOTANICA. 502

0067-6608 See BIBLIOGRAFIA BRASILEIRA DE CENCIAS SOCIAIS / INSTITUTO BRASILEIRO DE BIBLIOGRAFIA E DOCUMENTACAO. 408

0067-6640 See BIBLIOGRAFIA BRASILEIRA DE FISICA. 4398

0067-6691 See BIBLIOGRAFIA BRASILEIRA DE ZOOLOGIA. 5578

0067-6764 See BIBLIOGRAFIA SOBRE A ECONOMIA PORTUGUESA. 1530

0067-6829 See BIBLIOGRAPHIA SCIENTIAE NATURALIS HELVETICA. 5173

0067-6896 See PAPERS OF THE BIBLIOGRAPHICAL SOCIETY OF CANADA. 422

0067-6993 See FRANCIS BIBLIOGRAPHIE GEOGRAPHIQUE INTERNATIONALE. 531. 2561

0067-7000 See BIBLIOGRAPHIE INTERNATIONALE DE L'HUMANISME ET DE LA RENAISSANCE. 410

0067-706X See BIBLIOGRAPHIE ZUR SYMBOLIK, IKONOGRAPHIE UND MYTHOLOGIE. 4939

0067-7159 See BIBLIOGRAPHY OF ASIAN STUDIES. 2634

0067-7213 See BIBLIOGRAPHY OF OLD NORSE-ICELANDIC STUDIES. 3457

0067-7280 See BIBLIOGRAPHY OF THE HISTORY OF MEDICINE. 3655

0067-7329 See BIBLIOGRAPHY ON FOREIGN AND COMPARATIVE LAW, A. 3079

0067-7418 See BIBLIOTECA DI BIBLIOGRAFIA ITALIANA / DIRETTA DA CARLO FRATI. 410

0067-7477 See BIBLIOTHECA GERMANICA. 3269

0067-7833 See BIBLIOTHECA ANATOMICA. 3679

0067-7841 See BIBLIOTHECA ARNAMAGNANA. 3367

0067-7884 See BIBLIOTHECA BIBLIOGRAPHICA AURELIANA. 3457

0067-7892 See BIBLIOTHECA BOTANICA. 502

0067-7906 See BIBLIOTHECA CARDIOLOGICA. 3699

0067-7965 See BIBLIOTHECA HELVETICA ROMANA. 1074

0067-8023 See BIBLIOTHECA INDONESIA. 3195

0067-8031 See BIBLIOTHECA LATINA MEDII ET RECENTIORIS AEVI. 2678

0067-8112 See BIBLIOTHECA PHYCOLOGICA. 502

0067-8147 See BIBLIOTHECA PSYCHIATRICA. 3921

0067-8198 See BIBLIOTHECA NUTRITIO ET DIETA. 4188

0067-8244 See BIBLIOTH-EQUE ARCTIQUE ET ANTARCTIQUE. 2212

0067-8546 See BIJDRAGEN TOT DE DIERKUNDE. 5578

0067-8562 See BILATERAL STUDIES IN PRIVATE INTERNATIONAL LAW. 3124

0067-8643 See BINNENGEWASSER. 1352

0067-8694 See BIOCHEMICAL SOCIETY SYMPOSIA. 481

0067-8821 See BIOMATHEMATICS (BERLIN). 447

0067-8856 See BIOMEDICAL SCIENCES INSTRUMENTATION. 3687

0067-8864 See BIOMEMBRANES (NEW YORK, N.Y.). 532

0067-8899 See VERZEICHNIS LEIFERBARER BUCHER. EERGANZUNGSBAND. 4822

0067-8945 See PROCEEDINGS - BIRD CONTROL SEMINAR. 5619

0067-8961 See URBAN AND REGIONAL STUDIES. 2837

0067-902X See BIULETYN POLONISTYCZNY. 3367

0067-9038 See BIULETYN PERYGLACJALNY. 1367

0067-9100 See BLACK ORPHEUS. 3367

0067-9127 See BLAETTER FUER TECHNIKGESCHICHTE. 5089

0067-9208 See NAVORSINGE VAN DIE NASIONALE MUSEUM. 242

0067-9488 See BODLEIAN LIBRARY RECORD, THE. 3196

0067-9615 See BOLETIM DE INDUSTRIA ANIMAL. 207

0067-9666 See BOLETIN DE ESTUDIOS MEDICOS Y BIOLOGICOS. 449

0067-9674 See BOLETIN DE FILOLOGIA. 3269

0067-9720 See BOLETIN GENETICO. 543

0067-9879 See BOLLETTINO DELL'ATLANTE LINGUISTICO MEDITERRANEO. 3270

0067-9976 See BONNER JAHRBUCHER DES RHEINISCHEN LANDESMUSEUMS IN BONN (IM LANDSCHAFTSVERBAND RHEINLAND) UND DES VEREINS VON ALTERTUMSFREUNDEN IM RHEINLANDE. 262

0068-001X See BONNER ARBEITEN ZUR DEUTSCHEN LITERATUR. 3368

0068-0044 See BONNER BEITRAEGE ZUR SOZIOLOGIE / INSTITUT FUER SOZIOLOGIE DER UNIVERSITAT BONN. 5240

0068-0052 See BONNER GESCHICHTSBLATTER. 2679

0068-0095 See BOOK AUCTION RECORDS. 4824

0068-0125 See BOOK OF THE STATES, THE. 4634

0068-0141 See BOOKMAN'S PRICE INDEX. 253

0068-0192 See BOOKS FOR THE TEEN AGE. 1060

0068-0214 See BOOKS IN PRINT (NEW YORK). 411

0068-0303 See OCCASIONAL PUBLICATION - BOREAL INSTITUTE FOR NORTHERN STUDIES. 2751

0068-0346 See BOSTON STUDIES IN THE PHILOSOPHY OF SCIENCE. 5089

0068-0540 See BOWKER ANNUAL OF LIBRARY AND BOOK TRADE INFORMATION, THE. 3197

0068-063X See BRADFORD'S DIRECTORY OF MARKETING RESEARCH AGENCIES AND MANAGEMENT CONSULTANTS IN THE UNITED STATES AND THE WORLD. 921

0068-0737 See ABHANDLUNGEN DER BRAUNSCHWEIGISCHEN WISSENSCHAFTLICHEN GESELLSCHAFT. 5079

0068-0745 See BRAUNSCHWEIGISCHES JAHRBUCH. 2679

0068-1016 See GEOLOGY STUDIES. 1380

0068-1032 See TRANSACTIONS - BRISTOL AND GLOUCESTERSHIRE ARCHAEOLOGICAL SOCIETY. 284

0068-1075 See BRITAIN. 2514

0068-113X See BRITANNIA (SOCIETY FOR THE PROMOTION OF ROMAN STUDIES). 1075

0068-1156 See BRITANNICA BOOK OF THE YEAR. 1923

0068-1202 See PROCEEDINGS OF THE BRITISH ACADEMY. 1774

0068-1210 See BRITISH AID STATISTICS. 5323

0068-1288 See JOURNAL OF THE BRITISH ARCHAEOLOGICAL ASSOCIATION. 272

0068-130X See HANDBOOK OF THE BRITISH ASTRONOMICAL ASSOCIATION, THE. 395

0068-1407 See BRITISH CATALOGUE OF MUSIC, THE. 4105

0068-1571 See B.C. GEOGRAPHICAL SERIES. 2555

0068-161X See B. C. MUNICIPAL YEAR BOOK. 4712

0068-1628 See HANDBOOK - BRITISH COLUMBIA PROVINCIAL MUSEUM. 4088

0068-1636 See OCCASIONAL PAPERS OF THE BRITISH COLUMBIA PROVINCIAL MUSEUM. 4169

0068-1849 See UNIVERSITY OF BRITISH COLUMBIA LAW REVIEW. 3068

0068-2160 See COMPARATIVE LAW SERIES. 3126

0068-2276 See BRITISH MINIATURE ELECTRONIC COMPONENTS DATA ANNUAL. 2037

0068-2292 See BULLETIN OF THE BRITISH MUSEUM (NATURAL HISTORY) BOTANY. 505

0068-2306 See BULLETIN OF THE BRITISH MUSEUM (NATURAL HISTORY). HISTORICAL SERIES. 4164

0068-2314 See BRITISH ORTHOPTIC JOURNAL. 3873

0068-2454 See ANNUAL OF THE BRITISH SCHOOL AT ATHENS, THE. 2675

0068-2462 See PAPERS OF THE BRITISH SCHOOL AT ROME. 278

0068-2691 See BRITISH YEAR BOOK OF INTERNATIONAL LAW, THE. 3125

0068-2705 See SBORNIK PRACI FILOSOFICKE FACULTY BRNENSKE UNIVERSITY. 1904

0068-2748 See BROADSIDE (NEW YORK, N.Y. : 1940). 5362

0068-290X See BROWN'S NAUTICAL ALMANAC. 4175

0068-290X See BROWN'S NAUTICAL ALMANAC; DAILY TIDE TABLES. 4175

0068-3183 See ANALELE UNIVERSITATII BUCURESTI. GEOLOGIE. 1365

0068-3205 See ANALELE UNIVERSITATII BUCURESTI : ISTORIE. 2673

0068-3256 See ANALELE UNIVERSITATII BUCURESTI. LIMBA SI LITERATURA ROMANA. 3361

0068-3264 See ANALELE UNIVERSITATII BUCURESTI : LITERATURA UNIVERSALA SI COMPARATA. 3361

0068-3302 See ANALELE UNIVERSITATII BUCURESTI: SOCIOLOGIE. 5239

0068-3361 See BUCHEREI DES AUGENARZTES. 3873

0068-337X See BUCHEREI DES FRAUENARZTES. 3758

0068-3388 See BUCHEREI DES ORTHOPADEN. 3880

0068-3531 See MEANS BUILDING CONSTRUCTION COST DATA. 620

0068-371X See IZVESTIIA. 5117

0068-3787 See IZVESTIIA NA INSTITUTA ZA BULGARSKI EZIK. 3288

0068-3892 See IZVESTIJA NA INSTITUT PO TEHNICESKA MEHANIKA. 2117

0068-4015 See BULLETIN D'ARCHEOLOGIE MAROCAINE / ROYAUME DU MAROC, MINISTERE D'ETAT CHARGE DES AFFAIRES CULTURELLES, DIVISION DE L'ARCHEOLOGIE , DES MONUMENTS HISTORIQUES, DES SITES ET DES MUSEES, SERVICE DE L'ARCHEOLOGIE. 262

0068-4023 See BULLETIN DE PHILOSOPHIE MEDIEVALE. 4343

See BULLETIN D'HISTOIRE DE LA REVOLUTION FRANCAISE. 2681

0068-4236 See RAPPORT ANNUEL - BUREAU INTERNATIONAL DE L'HEURE. 399

0068-4341 See BURT FRANKLIN RESEARCH AND SOURCE WORKS SERIES. 2612

0068-4414 See BUSINESS EDUCATION INDEX. 727

0068-4503 See BUSINESS WHO'S WHO OF AUSTRALIA, THE. 727

0068-4945 See CAHIERS ARCHEOLOGIQUES. 265

0068-5011 See CAHIERS DE CIVILISATION MEDIEVALE. SUPPLEMENT. 2612

0068-5054 See CAHIERS DE MICROPALEONTOLOGIE. 4226

0068-5151 See CAHIERS DU TOURISME. SERIE A, LES. 5465

0068-516X See CAHIERS FERDINAND DE SAUSSURE. 3272

0068-5178 See CAHIERS JEAN-COCTEAU (PARIS). 3371

0068-5186 See CAHIERS MARCEL PROUST. 3371

0068-5372 See BULLETIN OF THE CALCUTTA SCHOOL OF TROPICAL MEDICINE. 3985

0068-5429 See CALEPINS DE BIBLIOGRAPHIE. 412

0068-5461 See OCCASIONAL PAPERS OF THE CALIFORNIA ACADEMY OF SCIENCES. 5136

0068-547X See PROCEEDINGS OF THE CALIFORNIA ACADEMY OF SCIENCES, 4TH SERIES. 5140

0068-5615 See CALIFORNIA HANDBOOK, THE. 2529

0068-5631 See BULLETIN OF THE CALIFORNIA INSECT SURVEY. 5606

0068-5720 See YEARBOOK - CALIFORNIA MACADAMIA SOCIETY. 2434

0068-5739 See CALIFORNIA MANUFACTURERS REGISTER. 3476

0068-5771 See CALIFORNIA PUBLIC SCHOOL DIRECTORY. 1923

0068-5798 See CALIFORNIA SLAVIC STUDIES. 2683

0068-5909 See CALIFORNIA STUDIES IN THE HISTORY OF ART. 346

0068-5933 See CONTRIBUTIONS OF THE UNIVERSITY OF CALIFORNIA ARCHAEOLOGICAL RESEARCH FACILITY. 266

0068-6093 See RESEARCH SERIES - UNIVERSITY OF CALIFORNIA, BERKELEY. INSTITUTE OF INTERNATIONAL STUDIES. 4534

0068-6190 See OCCASIONAL PAPER (UNIVERSITY OF CALIFORNIA, LOS ANGELES. AFRICAN STUDIES CENTER). 2642

0068-6344 See PUBLICATIONS: CLASSICAL STUDIES. 1079

0068-6379 See UNIVERSITY OF CALIFORNIA PUBLICATIONS IN ANTHROPOLOGY. 247

0068-6395 See UNIVERSITY OF CALIFORNIA PUBLICATIONS IN BOTANY. 529

0068-6417 See UNIVERSITY OF CALIFORNIA PUBLICATIONS IN ENTOMOLOGY. 5614

0068-6441 See UNIVERSITY OF CALIFORNIA PUBLICATIONS IN GEOGRAPHY. 2578

0068-645X See UNIVERSITY OF CALIFORNIA PUBLICATIONS IN GEOLOGICAL SCIENCES. 1400

0068-6484 See UNIVERSITY OF CALIFORNIA PUBLICATIONS IN LINGUISTICS. 3330

0068-6492 See UNIVERSITY OF CALIFORNIA PUBLICATIONS IN MODERN PHILOLOGY. 3331

0068-6506 See UNIVERSITY OF CALIFORNIA PUBLICATIONS IN ZOOLOGY. 5599

0068-6514 See UNIVERSITY OF CALIFORNIA PUBLICATIONS. NEAR EASTERN STUDIES. 2667

0068-6611 See TRANSACTIONS OF THE CAMBRIDGE BIBLIOGRAPHICAL SOCIETY. 426

0068-6638 See CAMBRIDGE CLASSICAL TEXTS AND COMMENTARIES. 1075

0068-6654 See CAMBRIDGE GEOGRAPHICAL STUDIES. 2558

0068-6689 See CAMBRIDGE LATIN AMERICAN STUDIES. 2726

0068-6719 See CAMBRIDGE PAPERS IN SOCIAL ANTHROPOLOGY. 233

0068-6735 See PROCEEDINGS OF THE CAMBRIDGE PHILOLOGICAL SOCIETY. 3312

0068-6743 See PROCEEDINGS OF THE CAMBRIDGE PHILOLOGICAL SOCIETY. SUPPLEMENT. 3312

0068-676X See CAMBRIDGE STUDIES IN LINGUISTICS. 3272

0068-6891 See ORIENTAL PUBLICATIONS. 2661

0068-7103 See CRUDE PETROLEUM AND NATURAL GAS INDUSTRY. 4254

0068-7189 See PRODUCTION OF POULTRY AND EGGS. 219

0068-7227 See SURVEY OF PRODUCTION. 1628

0068-7324 See LIVESTOCK MARKET REVIEW (ANNUAL ED.). 214

0068-7499 See ANNUAL REPORT - FISHERIES RESEARCH BOARD OF CANADA. 2294

0068-7626 See BULLETIN / GEOLOGICAL SURVEY OF CANADA. 1369

0068-7634 See MEMOIR - GEOLOGICAL SURVEY OF CANADA. 1387

0068-7642 See MISCELLANEOUS REPORT (GEOLOGICAL SURVEY OF CANADA). 1388

0068-7650 See PAPER - GEOLOGICAL SURVEY OF CANADA. 1390

0068-7715 See CLIMATOLOGICAL STUDIES (DOWNSVIEW). 1424

0068-7766 See ICE SUMMARY AND ANALYSIS: EASTERN CANADIAN SEABOARD. 1415

0068-7782 See METEOROLOGICAL TRANSLATIONS. 1431

0068-7863 See MINES BRANCH MONOGRAPH (OTTAWA). 2145

0068-8088 See REGISTER OF POST-GRADUATE DISSERTATIONS IN PROGRESS IN HISTORY AND RELATED SUBJECTS. 2627

0068-8134 See CANADA'S WHO'S WHO OF THE POULTRY INDUSTRY. 431

0068-8142 See CANADA YEARBOOK. 1923

0068-8185 See CANADIAN AGRICULTURAL INSECT PEST REVIEW, THE. 72

0068-8193 See CANADIAN ALMANAC & DIRECTORY. 1924

0068-8207 See CANADIAN ALPINE JOURNAL, THE. 4870

0068-8258 See C.A.R. SCOPE. 3561

0068-8347 See CANADIAN BANKRUPTCY REPORTS. 3086

0068-8398 See CANADIAN BOOKS IN PRINT. AUTHOR AND TITLE INDEX. 4827

0068-8401 See C B C ENGINEERING REVIEW. 1128

0068-8444 See JOURNAL OF THE CANADIAN CERAMIC SOCIETY. 2591

0068-8452 See LLOYD'S CANADIAN CHEMICAL, PHARMACEUTICAL, AND PRODUCT DIRECTORY. 4314

0068-8649 See CANADIAN DEPRECIATION GUIDE. 2948

0068-8657 See C E A HANDBOOK. 1861

0068-8665 See LLOYD'S CANADIAN ENGINEERING & INDUSTRIAL YEAR BOOK. 2099

0068-8762 See LLOYD'S CANADIAN FOOTWEAR AND LEATHER DIRECTORY. 3185

0068-8819 See CANADIAN GEOPHYSICAL BULLETIN. 1403

0068-8843 See CANADIAN GUNNER (SHILO. 1965). 4038

0068-886X See HISTORICAL BOOKLETS / THE CANADIAN HISTORICAL ASSOCIATION. 2737

See JOURNAL OF THE CANADIAN HISTORICAL ASSOCIATION. 2742

0068-8932 See CANADIAN HOSPITAL DIRECTORY. 3777

0068-8975 See YEARBOOK - CANADIAN INSTITUTE OF ACTUARIES. 2897

0068-9009 See CIM DIRECTORY. 2136

0068-9041 See LLOYD'S CANADIAN JEWELLERY AND GIFTWARE DIRECTORY. 2915

0068-9165 See CANADIAN LOCAL HISTORIES TO 1950: A BIBLIOGRAPHY. 2635

0068-9203 See CANADIAN MEDICAL DIRECTORY. 3913

0068-9238 See CANADIAN MERCHANDISE MART. 1082

0068-9270 See CANADIAN MINERALS YEARBOOK. 1438

0068-9289 See CANADIAN MINES HANDBOOK. 2136

0068-9394 See CANADIAN OIL REGISTER. 4253

0068-9459 See CANADIAN PLASTICS DIRECTORY & BUYER'S GUIDE. 4454

0068-9467 See CANADIAN PORTS AND SEAWAY DIRECTORY. 5448

0068-9475 See DIRECTORY OF THE CANADIAN PSYCHOLOGICAL ASSOCIATION. 4585

0068-9491 See CANADIAN PULP AND PAPER ASSOCIATION. NEWSPRINT DATA. 4233

0068-9521 See TECHNICAL SECTION PROCEEDINGS (MONTREAL). 4239

0068-970X See BULLETIN - CANADIAN SOCIETY OF BIBLICAL STUDIES. 5012

0068-9858 See LLOYD'S CANADIAN TEXTILE DIRECTORY. 5354

0068-9874 See CANADIAN THESES. 412

0068-9955 See LLOYD'S CANADIAN VARIETY MERCHANDISE DIRECTORY. 2584

0068-9963 See CANADIAN WHO'S WHO, THE. 431

0069-0023 See PROGRESS NOTES - CANADIAN WILDLIFE SERVICE. 470

0069-0058 See CANADIAN YEARBOOK OF INTERNATIONAL LAW. 3125

0069-0147 See CANCER FACTS AND FIGURES. 3811

0069-0171 See CANCER SEMINAR. 3812

0069-0384 See CARDIOVASCULAR CLINICS. 3701

0069-0481 See CARIBBEAN ECONOMIC ALMANAC. 1468

0069-0503 See ANNUAL REPORT. 5191

0069-0511 See CARIBBEAN MONOGRAPH SERIES. 2727

0069-0538 See CARIBBEAN SERIES. 2727

0069-0600 See CARLETON MATHEMATICAL SERIES. 3499

0069-0635 See ANNUAL REPORT - CARNEGIE CORPORATION OF NEW YORK. 4334

0069-066X See YEAR BOOK - CARNEGIE INSTITUTION OF WASHINGTON. 5171

0069-0740 See DIRECTORY AND REPORT / CARPET AND RUG INSTITUTE. 5350

0069-0767 See CARPET ANNUAL. 1601

0069-0805 See CARTOGRAPHY. 2581

0069-0813 See CARUS MATHEMATICAL MONOGRAPHS, THE. 3499

0069-0864 See JOURNAL OF SOCIOLOGY (CLEVELAND). 5250

0069-1003 See CAT FANCIERS' NEWS. 4286

0069-1011 See CATALOG FOR COLLEGE STORES, THE. 656

0069-116X See CATALOGUS MUSICUS. 4108

0069-1208 See CATHOLIC ALMANAC. 5025

0069-1267 See PROCEEDINGS OF THE ANNUAL CONVENTION. 4988

0069-1399 See CELTICA (DUBLIN). 3273

0069-1437 See CENSUS OF U.S. CIVIL AIRCRAFT. 16

0069-1461 See CENTERS OF CIVILIZATION SERIES. 2613

0069-1585 See ANNUAL REPORT / CENTRAL BANK OF THE PHILIPPINES. 771

0069-1593 See ANNUAL REPORT - CENTRAL BANK OF TRINIDAD AND TOBAGO. 1546

0069-1607 See CENTRAL CONFERENCE OF AMERICAN RABBIS ANNUAL CONVENTION. 5046

0069-178X See PUBLICATION - CENTRE DE RECHERCHES D'HISTOIRE ANCIENNE. 2626

0069-1968 See RAPPORT D'ACTIVITE - CENTRE NATIONAL DE DOCUMENTATION SCIENTIFIQUE ET TECHNIQUE. 5144

0069-2263 See CEREDIGION. 2683

0069-228X See ROZPRAVY. RADA MATEMATICKYCH A PRIRODNICH VED. 5149

0069-2298 See ROZPRAVY CESKOSLOVENSKE AKADEMIE VED. RADA SPOLECENSKYCH VED. 5217

0069-2328 See CESKOSLOVENSKA PEDIATRIE. 3901

0069-2336 See CESKOSLOVENSKA PSYCHIATRIE. 3923

0069-2344 See CESKOSLOVENSKA RADIOLOGIE. 3939

0069-2379 See CEYLON JOURNAL OF SCIENCE. BIOLOGICAL SCIENCES. 451

0069-2778 See CHART (CHICAGO. 1956). 3853

0069-2883 See CHEMICAL ANALYSIS. 1014

0069-3030 See ANNUAL REPORTS ON THE PROGRESS OF CHEMISTRY. SECTION B, ORGANIC CHEMISTRY. 1039

0069-3111 See CHEMISTRY AND BIOCHEMISTRY OF AMINO ACIDS, PEPTIDES, AND PROTEINS. 1040

0069-3138 See CHEMISTRY AND PHYSICS OF CARBON. 1035

0069-3154 See CHEMISTRY OF HETEROCYCLIC COMPOUNDS, THE. 971

0069-3227 See CHIBA DAIGAKU ENGEI GAKUBU GAKUJUTSU KOKOKU. 2412

0069-3235 See MUSEUM STUDIES (CHICAGO, ILL.). 359

0069-3286 See CHICAGO LECTURES IN MATHEMATICS. 3499

0069-3324 See PUBLICATIONS - UNIVERSITY OF CHICAGO. CENTER FOR MIDDLE EASTERN STUDIES. 2770

0069-3359 See SELECTED PAPERS. 710

0069-3367 See ORIENTAL INSTITUTE PUBLICATIONS. 277

0069-3391 See CHIGIANA. 4109

0069-343X See CHILDCRAFT ANNUAL. 1890

0069-3472 See CHILDREN'S BOOKS. AWARDS & PRIZES. 1061

0069-3480 See CHILDREN'S BOOKS IN PRINT (NEW YORK). 1072

0069-3561 See APARTADO. 1365

0069-3634 See CHILTON'S AUTO REPAIR MANUAL. 5410

0069-3693 See CHINA RESEARCH MONOGRAPHS / CENTER FOR CHINESE STUDIES, UNIVERSITY OF CALIFORNIA, BERKELEY. 2648

0069-3715 See CHIRON. 1075

0069-3758 See CHORD AND DISCORD. 4109

0069-3774 See RESEARCH PROJECT. 4615

0069-3871 See CHRISTIAN PERIODICAL INDEX. 5012

0069-3936 See CHROMATOGRAPHIC SCIENCE. 1014

0069-3987 See CHURCH OF ENGLAND YEAR BOOK, THE. 4947

0069-3995 See YEAR BOOK ... (... YEAR OF ISSUE) / THE CHURCH OF SCOTLAND. 5010

0069-4290 See CIVILISATIONS ET SOCIETES. 5268

0069-4355 See CIVILTA VENEZIANA. FONTI E TESTI. SER. 1 : FONTI E DOCUMENTI PER LA STORIA DELL'ARTE VENETA. 347

0069-4371 See CIVILTA VENEZIANA. SAGGI. 5268

0069-438X *See* CIVILTA VENEZIANA. STUDI. **2683**

0069-4428 *See* CLARK'S DIRECTORY OF SOUTHERN HOSPITALS. **3778**

0069-4495 *See* CLASSICS IN EDUCATION. **1732**

0069-4517 *See* CLASSIFIED BUSINESS DIRECTORY OF THE STATE OF CONNECTICUT. **657**

0069-4525 *See* CLASSIFIED DIRECTORY OF WISCONSIN MANUFACTURERS. **3476**

0069-4584 *See* CLAUSTHALER TEKTONISCHE HEFTE. **1353**

0069-4592 *See* CLAY RESOURCES BULLETIN. **2137**

0069-4657 *See* REPORT - WATER RESOURCES RESEARCH INSTITUTE, CLEMSON UNIVERSITY. **5538**

0069-4681 *See* ANNALES BIOLOGIE ANIMALE. **205**

0069-4770 *See* CLIN-ALERT. **3564**

0069-4797 *See* CLINICAL APPROACHES TO PROBLEMS OF CHILDHOOD. **3902**

0069-4827 *See* CLINICAL NEUROSURGERY. **3962**

0069-4835 *See* CLINICS IN DEVELOPMENTAL MEDICINE. **3830**

0069-5009 *See* ANNUAL REPORT - COLD SPRING HARBOR, NEW YORK. LABORATORY OF QUANTITATIVE BIOLOGY. **442**

0069-5211 *See* COLLANA DI STUDI PALESTRINIANI. **4110**

0069-5319 *See* COLLECTED WORKS ON CARDIO-PULMONARY DISEASES. **3703**

See JOURNAL OF COLLEGE AND ADULT READING AND LEARNING. **1832**

0069-5580 *See* ANNUAIRE DU COLLEGE DE FRANCE. **1809**

0069-5653 *See* COLLEGE HANDBOOK, THE. **1816**

0069-5688 *See* COLLEGE FACTS CHART. **1816**

0069-5696 *See* COLLEGE MUSIC SYMPOSIUM. **4110**

0069-5726 *See* MEDICAL DIRECTORY (VANCOUVER). **3915**

0069-5750 *See* PROCEEDINGS. **4988**

0069-5769 *See* PROCEEDINGS - INTERNATIONAL CONGRESS OF NEURO-PSYCHOPHARMACOLOGY. **3844**

0069-5807 *See* COLLOQUE DE METALLURGIE. **4000**

0069-5831 *See* PROCEEDINGS / COLLOQUIUM ON THE LAW OF OUTER SPACE. **3031**

0069-5971 *See* COLONIAL WILLIAMSBURG ARCHAEOLOGICAL SERIES. **266**

0069-598X *See* ANAIS - COLOQUIO DE ESTUDOS LUSO-BRASILEIROS. **2720**

0069-6099 *See* FLUID MECHANICS PAPERS. **2089**

0069-6102 *See* HYDRAULICS PAPERS. **2090**

0069-6129 *See* SANITARY ENGINEERING PAPERS. **2242**

0069-6145 *See* OCCASIONAL PAPER (UNIVERSITY OF COLORADO, BOULDER. INSTITUTE OF ARCTIC AND ALPINE RESEARCH). **5136**

0069-6218 *See* UNIVERSITY OF COLORADO STUDIES. SERIES IN EARTH SCIENCES. **1361**

0069-6277 *See* COLSTON PAPERS. **1817**

0069-6285 *See* COLUMBIA BIOLOGICAL SERIES. **452**

0069-6315 *See* COLUMBIA ESSAYS ON MODERN WRITERS. **3377**

0069-6331 *See* COLUMBIA STUDIES IN ECONOMICS. **1470**

0069-6358 *See* COLUMBIA UNIVERSITY STUDIES IN INTERNATIONAL ORGANIZATION. **1817**

0069-6366 *See* COLUMBIA UNIVERSITY STUDIES IN JEWISH HISTORY, CULTURE, AND INSTITUTIONS. **5047**

0069-6374 *See* COLUMBIA UNIVERSITY STUDIES IN LIBRARY SERVICE. **3203**

0069-6412 *See* COMITATUS. **3377**

0069-6552 *See* PETROLE. ELEMENTS STATISTIQUES (1968). **4271**

0069-6587 *See* COMMENTATIONES HUMANARUM LITTERARUM. **3274**

0069-6609 *See* COMMENTATIONES PHYSICO-MATHEMATICAE ET CHEMICO-MEDICAE. **4400**

0069-6749 *See* GENERAL REPORT ON THE ACTIVITIES OF THE COMMUNITIES. **1492**

See DIRECTORY OF RESEARCH WORKERS IN AGRICULTURE AND ALLIED SCIENCES. **153**

0069-7133 *See* COMMONWEALTH LAW REPORTS, THE. **2953**

0069-7141 *See* PHYTOPATHOLOGICAL PAPERS. **522**

0069-7362 *See* OCEANOGRAPHICAL STATION LIST. **1454**

0069-7435 *See* COMMONWEALTH SCIENTIFIC & INDUSTRIAL RESEARCH ORGANISATION. DIVISION OF HORTICULTURE. REPORT. **2412**

0069-7435 *See* REPORT / DIVISION OF HORTICULTURAL RESEARCH. **2430**

0069-7567 *See* DIVISION OF PLANT INDUSTRY TECHNICAL PAPER. **1413**

0069-7699 *See* DAIRY PRODUCE; A REVIEW OF PRODUCTION, TRADE, CONSUMPTION AND PRICES RELATING TO BUTTER, CHEESE, CONDENSED MILK, MILK POWDER, CASEIN, EGGS AND EGG PRODUCTS. **194**

0069-7745 *See* COMMONWEALTH UNIVERSITIES YEARBOOK. **1817**

0069-7818 *See* ANNUAL PRICE SURVEY: FAMILY BUDGET COSTS. **1462**

0069-7850 *See* COMMUNITY MENTAL HEALTH JOURNAL. MONOGRAPH SERIES. **4772**

0069-7893 *See* COMPARATIVE JURIDICAL REVIEW. **2954**

0069-8032 *See* COMPREHENSIVE BIOCHEMISTRY. **486**

0069-8040 *See* COMPREHENSIVE CHEMICAL KINETICS. **973**

0069-8148 *See* PROCEEDINGS OF THE ANNUAL COMPUTER PERSONNEL RESEARCH CONFERENCE. **1239**

0069-8288 *See* CONCRETE YEAR BOOK, THE. **608**

0069-8296 *See* CONDON LECTURES. **1818**

0069-8458 *See* STATISTICAL STANDARDS AND STUDIES. **2244**

0069-8644 *See* PROCEEDINGS OF THE CONFERENCE ON REMOTE SYSTEMS TECHNOLOGY. **5140**

0069-8652 *See* STUDIES IN INCOME AND WEALTH. **1523**

0069-8792 *See* CONFLICT STUDIES. **4518**

0069-8881 *See* CONGRES ARCHEOLOGIQUE DE FRANCE. **266**

0069-8938 *See* CONGRESSIONAL STAFF DIRECTORY. ADVANCE LOCATOR FOR CAPITOL HILL. **4640**

0069-8970 *See* MEMOIRS OF THE CONNECTICUT ACADEMY OF ARTS AND SCIENCES. **2850**

0069-9047 *See* GENERAL SERIES - CENTER FOR REAL ESTATE AND URBAN ECONOMIC STUDIES, SCHOOL OF BUSINESS ADMINISTRATION, UNIVERSITY OF CONNECTICUT. **4838**

0069-9063 *See* REPORT - UNIVERSITY OF CONNECTICUT. INSTITUTE OF WATER RESOURCES. **5538**

0069-911X *See* CONSERVATION DIRECTORY. **2190**

0069-9128 *See* CONSERVATION NOTE (WASHINGTON). **2190**

0069-9187 *See* CONSTRUCTION IN HAWAII. **609**

0069-9241 *See* CONSUMERS' RESEARCH MAGAZINE. HANDBOOK OF BUYING ISSUE. **1296**

0069-9365 *See* CONTEMPORARY AMERICAN PAINTING AND SCULPTURE. **348**

0069-9446 *See* CONTEMPORARY NEUROLOGY SERIES. **3830**

0069-9454 *See* CONTEMPORARY NEUROLOGY SYMPOSIA. **3830**

0069-9551 *See* CONTINUING ENGINEERING STUDIES SERIES. MONOGRAPHS. **1969**

0069-9616 *See* CONTRIBUTII BOTANICE. **507**

0069-9624 *See* CONTRIBUTIONS IN AFRO-AMERICAN AND AFRICAN STUDIES. **2638**

0069-9632 *See* SOUTHERN METHODIST UNIVERSITY CONTRIBUTIONS IN ANTHROPOLOGY. **245**

0069-9640 *See* CONTRIBUTIONS IN OCEANOGRAPHY. **1448**

0069-9667 *See* CONTRIBUTIONS TO INDIAN SOCIOLOGY. NEW SERIES. **5243**

0069-9780 *See* COOPER MONOGRAPHS ON ENGLISH AND AMERICAN LANGUAGE AND LITERATURE, THE. **3378**

0069-9896 *See* FUND OG FORSKNING I DET KONGELIGE BIBLIOTEKS SAMLINGER. **3211**

0069-9950 *See* COPYRIGHT LAW SYMPOSIUM. **1303**

0069-9969 *See* COPYRIGHT LAWS AND TREATIES OF THE WORLD. **1303**

0069-9977 *See* CORAL GABLES CONFERENCE ON FUNDAMENTAL INTERACTIONS AT HIGH ENERGY. PROCEEDINGS. **1936**

0070-0134 *See* BULLETIN (NEW YORK STATE SCHOOL OF INDUSTRIAL AND LABOR RELATIONS). **1657**

0070-0177 *See* ILR PAPERBACK. **1677**

0070-024X *See* CORNISH ARCHAEOLOGY. **266**

0070-0282 *See* CORPORATE MANAGEMENT TAX CONFERENCE. **4719**

0070-0320 *See* CORPUS CATHOLICORUM. **5028**

0070-0347 *See* CORPUS MEDICORUM GRAECORUM. **3569**

0070-0363 *See* CORPUS MENSURABILIS MUSICAE. **4112**

0070-0371 *See* CORPUS OF EARLY KEYBOARD MUSIC. **4112**

0070-0460 *See* CORPUS SCRIPTORUM DE MUSICA. **4112**

0070-0509 *See* CORRECTIONAL LITERATURE PUBLISHED IN CANADA. **3161**

0070-0673 *See* COTTON INTERNATIONAL. **5349**

0070-105X *See* EUROPEAN TREATY SERIES. **4473**

0070-1076 *See* PROCEEDINGS OF THE ANNUAL MEETING. **1842**

0070-1157 *See* SUGGESTED STATE LEGISLATION (1965). **3060**

0070-1262 *See* COUNTRY DANCE AND SONG. **1311**

0070-1327 *See* JOURNAL OF THE COUNTY LOUTH ARCHAEOLOGICAL AND HISTORICAL SOCIETY. **272**

0070-1416 *See* BULLETIN (CRANBROOK INSTITUTE OF SCIENCE). **5090**

0070-1459 *See* CREATIVE INTERFACE, THE. **4470**

0070-1467 *See* CREDIT MANUAL OF COMMERCIAL LAWS. **3099**

0070-1521 *See* CRIMINAL APPEAL REPORTS, THE. **3105**

0070-1548 *See* CRITICAL REVIEW (MELBOURNE), THE. **3340**

0070-1580 *See* CRONER'S REFERENCE BOOK FOR EMPLOYERS. **939**

0070-1599 *See* CRONER'S REFERENCE BOOK FOR EXPORTERS. **830**

0070-1602 *See* CRONER'S REFERENCE BOOK FOR IMPORTERS. **830**

0070-1610 *See* CRONER'S ROAD TRANSPORT OPERATION (OF GOODS VEHICLES IN THE UNITED KINGDOM AND ON THE CONTINENT OF EUROPE). **5380**

0070-1688 *See* CUADERNOS DE HISTORIA DEL ARTE. **348**

0070-1769 *See* CUADERNOS DEL SUR. **2730**

0070-1858 *See* CURRENT BRITISH DIRECTORIES. **663**

0070-1882 *See* CURRENT COINS OF THE WORLD. **2781**

0070-1998 *See* CURRENT LEGAL PROBLEMS. **2958**

0070-2021 *See* GELLIS & KAGAN'S CURRENT PEDIATRIC THERAPY. **3903**

0070-2064 *See* CURRENT PROBLEMS IN DERMATOLOGY. **3718**

0070-2129 See CURRENT TOPICS IN BIOENERGETICS. 453

0070-2137 See CURRENT TOPICS IN CELLULAR REGULATION. 535

0070-2153 See CURRENT TOPICS IN DEVELOPMENTAL BIOLOGY. 453

0070-2161 See CURRENT TOPICS IN MEMBRANES. 535

0070-217X See CURRENT TOPICS IN MICROBIOLOGY AND IMMUNOLOGY. 3669

0070-2188 See CURRENT TOPICS IN PATHOLOGY. 3894

0070-2218 See CURRENT VETERINARY THERAPY. 5508

0070-2234 See BUCHREIHE DER CUSANUS-GESELLSCHAFT. 5024

0070-2242 See SPECIAL PUBLICATION - CUSHMAN FOUNDATION FOR FORAMINIFERAL RESEARCH. 5597

0070-2307 See REVIEW FOR .../ AGRICULTURAL RESEARCH INSTITUTE. 128

0070-2315 See TECHNICAL BULLETIN - CYPRUS AGRICULTURAL RESEARCH INSTITUTE. 139

0070-2455 See CYSTIC FIBROSIS CLUB ABSTRACTS. 3570

0070-2471 See CZASOPISMO PRAWNO-HISTORYCZNE. 2958

0070-251X See DACIA. 266

0070-2536 See DAEDALUS LIBRARY, THE. 3205

0070-2625 See INITIATIONS ET ETUDES AFRICAINES. 2640

0070-2714 See DANIA POLYGLOTTA. 3458

0070-2749 See DANISH YEARBOOK OF PHILOSOPHY. 4344

0070-2781 See DANMARKS VAREINDFRSEL OG -UDFRSEL. 830

0070-2862 See DANTE STUDIES, WITH THE ANNUAL REPORT OF THE DANTE SOCIETY. 3380

0070-2951 See DAVISON'S TEXTILE "BLUE BOOK". 5350

0070-3060 See PROPRIETATIBUS LITTERARUM. SERIES MAIOR, DE. 3425

0070-3087 See PROPRIETATIBUS LITTERARUM. SERIES PRACTICA, DE. 3425

0070-3141 See DECEMBER. 3380

0070-315X See DECHEMA MONOGRAPHIEN. 974

0070-3176 See DECISIONS OF THE UNITED STATES COURTS INVOLVING COPYRIGHT. 1303

0070-3346 See DEMOCRAT (VANCOUVER). 4471

0070-3370 See DEMOGRAPHY. 4552

0070-3478 See BEFOLKNINGENS BEVGELSER. 5323

0070-3532 See INDUSTRISTATISTIK. 1534

0070-3656 See DENTAL GUIDE. 1320

0070-3664 See DENTAL IMAGES. 1321

0070-3710 See BULLETIN OF THE NINTH DISTRICT DENTAL SOCIETY. 1318

0070-3737 See DENTISTRY IN JAPAN. 1322

0070-3788 See DERBYSHIRE ARCHAEOLOGICAL JOURNAL, THE. 266

0070-3826 See DESCRIPTION AND ANALYSIS OF CONTEMPORARY STANDARD RUSSIAN. 3276

0070-3885 See DETROIT STUDIES IN MUSIC BIBLIOGRAPHY. 4160

0070-3893 See DEUTSCH-SLAWISCHE FORSCHUNGEN ZUR NAMENKUNDE UND SIEDLUNGSGESCHICHTE. 3276

0070-3923 See JAHRBUCH - DEUTSCHE AKADEMIE FUER SPRACHE UND DICHTUNG (DARMSTADT). 3398

0070-4067 See VERHANDLUNGEN DER DEUTSCHEN GESELLSCHAFT FUER INNERE MEDIZIN. 3802

0070-4113 See VERHANDLUNGEN DER DEUTSCHEN GESELLSCHAFT FUER PATHOLOGIE. 3898

0070-4121 See VERHANDLUNGEN DER DEUTSCHEN GESELLSCHAFT FUER RHEUMATOLOGIE. 3807

0070-413X See VERHANDLUNGSBERICHT DER DEUTSCHEN GESELLSCHAFT FUER UROLOGIE. 3994

0070-4296 See DPW. DEUTSCHE PAPIERWIRTSCHAFT. 4233

0070-4318 See JAHRBUCH DER DEUTSCHEN SCHILLERGESELLSCHAFT. 3398

0070-4326 See JAHRBUCH - DEUTSCHE SHAKESPEARE-GESELLSCHAFT WEST. 3398

0070-4334 See DEUTSCHE TEXTE DES MITTELALTERS. 3380

0070-4342 See VERHANGLUNGEN DER DEUTSCHEN ZOOLOGISCHEN GESELLSCHAFT. 5599

0070-4415 See JAHRBUCH DES DEUTSCHEN ARCHAOLOGISCHEN INSTITUTS. 270

0070-444X See DEUTSCHES DANTE - JAHRBUCH. 3380

0070-4563 See DEVELOPMENTS IN INDUSTRIAL MICROBIOLOGY. 562

0070-4571 See DEVELOPMENTS IN SEDIMENTOLOGY. 1373

0070-4717 See DICTIONARY OF CANADIAN BIOGRAPHY. 432

0070-4806 See DIDEROT STUDIES. 3381

0070-4903 See DINE ISRAEL. 3089

0070-4962 See DIPLOMAT'S ANNUAL, THE. 4472

0070-5012 See DIRECTORY FOR EXCEPTIONAL CHILDREN, THE. 1877

0070-5071 See DIRECTORY OF AMERICAN FIRMS OPERATING IN FOREIGN COUNTRIES. 666

0070-508X See DIRECTORY OF AMERICAN PHILOSOPHERS. 4345

0070-5209 See DIRECTORY OF CAMPUS MINISTRY. 4953

0070-5217 See DIRECTORY OF CANADIAN MAP COLLECTIONS. 2559

0070-5306 See DIRECTORY OF COMMUNITY SERVICES IN MARYLAND. 5282

0070-5330 See DIRECTORY OF COMPUTERIZED INFORMATION IN SCIENCE AND TECHNOLOGY. 5100

0070-5438 See DIRECTORY OF DIRECTORS, THE. 865

0070-5470 See INTERNATIONAL DIRECTORY OF ENGINEERING SOCIETIES AND RELATED ORGANIZATIONS. 1979

0070-5543 See DIRECTORY OF FOREIGN FIRMS OPERATING IN THE UNITED STATES. 666

0070-556X See DIRECTORY OF FRANCHISING ORGANIZATIONS. 954

0070-5586 See DIRECTORY OF GOVERNMENT AGENCIES SAFEGUARDING CONSUMER AND ENVIRONMENT. 4643

0070-5721 See DIRECTORY OF KANSAS MANUFACTURERS AND THEIR PRODUCTS. 3477

0070-5829 See DIRECTORY OF MEDICAL SPECIALISTS. 3913

0070-6000 See DIRECTORY OF ON-GOING RESEARCH IN SMOKING AND HEALTH. 4773

0070-6027 See DIRECTORY OF OREGON MANUFACTURERS. 3478

0070-6450 See DIRECTORY OF TENNESSEE MANUFACTURERS. 3478

0070-6477 See DIRECTORY OF THE FOREST PRODUCTS INDUSTRY. 2400

0070-6604 See DIRECTORY TO THE FURNISHING TRADE. 2905

0070-6728 See DISSERTATIONES BOTANICAE. 508

0070-6760 See DIX-HUITIEME SIECLE. 2615

0070-6906 See DOCUMENTI SULLE ARTI DEL LIBRO. 4828

0070-7007 See DOD'S PARLIAMENTARY COMPANION. 4645

0070-7031 See DOKUMENTE ZUR DEUTSCHLANDPOLITIK. 2685

0070-704X See DOLLARS & CENTS OF SHOPPING CENTERS, THE. 4837

0070-7112 See PROCEEDINGS - DORSET NATURAL HISTORY AND ARCHAEOLOGICAL SOCIETY. 4170

0070-7260 See MALAKOLOGISCHE ABHANDLUNGEN. 5590

0070-7279 See REICHENBACHIA / STAATLICHES MUSEUM FUER TIERKUNDE IN DRESDEN. 5613

0070-7295 See ABHANDLUNGEN UND BERICHTE DES STAATLICHEN MUSEUMS FUER VOLKERKUNDE, DRESDEN. 4083

0070-7325 See DROIT POLONAIS CONTEMPORAIN. 2964

0070-7333 See DROSOPHILA INFORMATION SERVICE. 454

0070-7414 See COMMUNICATIONS OF THE DUBLIN INSTITUTE FOR ADVANCED STUDIES. SERIES A. 3501

0070-7422 See COMMUNICATIONS OF THE DUBLIN INSTITUTE FOR ADVANCED STUDIES. SERIES D. GEOPHYSICAL BULLETIN. 1404

0070-7546 See DUMBARTON OAKS PAPERS. 2650

0070-7554 See DUMBARTON OAKS STUDIES. 2532

0070-7619 See MILLION DOLLAR DIRECTORY. 1505

0070-7694 See DUQUESNE STUDIES. PHILOLOGICAL SERIES. 3278

0070-7716 See DUQUESNE STUDIES. PSYCHOLOGICAL SERIES. 4585

0070-7872 See EARLY ENGLISH TEXT SOCIETY (PUBLICATION). 3383

0070-7961 See EAST AFRICAN GEOGRAPHICAL REVIEW, THE. 2560

0070-8089 See EAST CAROLINA UNIVERSITY PUBLICATIONS IN HISTORY. 2615

0070-8127 See EAST LAKES GEOGRAPHER, THE. 2560

0070-8232 See CONTRIBUTIONS IN ANTHROPOLOGY (PORTALES, N.M.). 234

0070-8356 See ECOLOGICAL STUDIES. 2214

0070-8488 See ANNUAL REVIEW - ECONOMIC COUNCIL OF CANADA. 1463

0070-8534 See ECONOMIC EDUCATION EXPERIENCES OF ENTERPRISING TEACHERS. 5199

0070-8550 See ECONOMIC HANDBOOK OF THE MACHINE TOOL INDUSTRY. 2113

0070-8682 See ECONOMIC SURVEY OF AFRICA. 1485

0070-8712 See ECONOMIC SURVEY OF EUROPE. 1485

0070-8798 See ECONOMIE ET FINANCES AGRICOLES. 81

0070-9131 See EDUCATION AUTHORITIES DIRECTORY AND ANNUAL, THE. 1862

0070-9263 See EDUCATIONAL AND PSYCHOLOGICAL INTERACTIONS. 1741

0070-9387 See EDUCATORS GRADE GUIDE TO FREE TEACHING AIDS. 1893

0070-9395 See EDUCATORS GUIDE TO FREE FILMS. 1893

0070-9417 See EDUCATORS GUIDE TO FREE GUIDANCE MATERIALS. 1913

0070-9425 See EDUCATORS GUIDE TO FREE SCIENCE MATERIALS / COMPILED AND EDITED BY MARY H. SATERSTROM. 1894

0070-9433 See EDUCATORS GUIDE TO FREE SOCIAL STUDIES MATERIALS / COMPILED AND EDITED BY PATRICIA H. SUTTLES AND STEVEN A. SUTTLES. 1894

0070-9662 See ELECTRICAL ENGINEERING RESEARCH ABSTRACTS. CANADIAN UNIVERSITIES. 2045

0070-9778 See ELECTROANALYTICAL CHEMISTRY. 1014

0070-9816 See ELECTRON TECHNOLOGY. 2046

0070-9972 See ELEMENTA AD FONTIUM EDITIONES. 2686

0070-9980 See ELEMENTARY TEACHERS' GUIDE TO FREE CURRICULUM MATERIALS. 1894

0071-0075 See EISENBAHN INGENIEUR KALENDER. 5431

0071-0164 See ENCORE. 5364

0071-0202 See ENCYCLOPEDIA OF ASSOCIATIONS. 1925

0071-0210 See ENCYCLOPEDIA OF BUSINESS INFORMATION SOURCES. 671

0071-0237 See ENCYCLOPEDIA OF SOCIAL WORK. 5284

0071-0288 See BUYERS GUIDE (ENGINEER (LONDON, ENGLAND)). 1967

0071-0393 See ENGINEERING AND TECHNOLOGY DEGREES. 1972

0071-0415 See ENGINEERS' SALARIES : SPECIAL INDUSTRY REPORT. 1974

0071-0601 See ENGLISH LANGUAGE AND ORIENTATION PROGRAMS IN THE UNITED STATES. 3279

0071-0636 See PUBLICATIONS - ENGLISH PLACE-NAME SOCIETY. 2574

0071-0709 See PROCEEDINGS OF THE ANNUAL MEETING OF THE ENTOMOLOGICAL SOCIETY OF ALBERTA. 5612

0071-0733 See JOURNAL OF THE ENTOMOLOGICAL SOCIETY OF BRITISH COLUMBIA. 5611

0071-0741 See BULLETIN - ENTOMOLOGICAL SOCIETY OF CANADA. 5579

0071-075X See MEMOIRS OF THE ENTOMOLOGICAL SOCIETY OF CANADA. 5591

0071-075X See MEMOIRS OF THE ENTOMOLOGICAL SOCIETY OF CANADA. 5612

0071-0768 See PROCEEDINGS OF THE ENTOMOLOGICAL SOCIETY OF ONTARIO. 5595

0071-0784 See MEMOIRES DE LA SOCIETE ENTOMOLOGIQUE DU QUEBEC. 5591

0071-0822 See ENTRETIENS SUR L'ANTIQUITE CLASSIQUE. 1076

0071-0857 See ENVIRONMENTAL GEOLOGY (MONTPELIER, VT.). 1375

0071-0954 See EPETERIS. 2650

0071-0989 See EPIGRAPHISCHE STUDIEN. 1076

0071-1012 See EPISCOPAL CHURCH ANNUAL, THE. 5059

0071-1039 See EQUAL OPPORTUNITY. 1822

0071-1063 See ERASMUS IN ENGLISH. 4346

0071-1071 See E.R.B.IVORE. 3383

0071-111X See ERGEBNISSE DER INNEREN MEDIZIN UND KINDERHEILKUNDE. 3796

0071-1128 See ERGEBNISSE DER LIMNOLOGIE. 1413

0071-1136 See ERGEBNISSE DER MATHEMATIK UND IHRER GRENZGEBIETE. 3505

0071-1152 See ERHVERVSHISTORISK AARBOG; MEDDELELSER FRA ERHVERVSARKIVET. 2686

0071-1160 See ERLANGER GEOLOGISCHE ABHANDLUNGEN. 1375

0071-1179 See ERNAHRUNGSFORSCHUNG. 4190

0071-1268 See ESAKIA. 5608

0071-1276 See ANAIS DA ESCOLA SUPERIOR DE AGRICULTURA LUIZ DE QUEIROZ. 4161

0071-1357 See ESSAYS AND STUDIES (LONDON, ENGLAND : 1950). 3385

0071-1365 See ESSAYS IN BIOCHEMISTRY. 487

0071-139X See ESSAYS IN FRENCH LITERATURE. 3385

0071-1411 See ESSAYS IN HISTORY. 2615

0071-1675 See ESTUDIOS DE CULTURA NAHUATL. 2732

0071-1713 See ESTUDIOS FILOLOGICOS. 3280

0071-1721 See ANEJOS DE ESTUDIOS FILOLOGICOS. 3264

0071-1772 See ETHIOPIAN PUBLICATIONS. 416

0071-1799 See ETHNIC TECHNOLOGY NOTES. 235

0071-1861 See ETNOGRAFIA POLSKA. 236

0071-190X See ETUDES DE LINGUISTIQUE APPLIQUEE. 3280

See ETUDES HISTORIQUES HONGROISES. 2687

0071-2124 See ETUDES LINGUISTIQUES (PARIS). 3280

0071-2248 See EUREKA : THE ARCHIMEDEANS' JOURNAL. 3505

0071-2396 See EPPO PUBLICATIONS. SERIES B. 509

0071-2477 See PUBLICATION / EUROPEAN ASSOCIATION FOR ANIMAL PRODUCTION. 219

0071-2507 See PROCEEDINGS OF THE TRIENNIAL CONFERENCE. 183

0071-2531 See PROCEEDINGS OF THE CONGRESS - EUROPEAN BREWERY CONVENTION. 2370

0071-2582 See EUROPEAN COMPANIES. 673

0071-2655 See EUROPEAN CONFERENCE ON MICROCIRCULATION. 3575

0071-2868 See ANNUAL REPORT - EUROPEAN INVESTMENT BANK. 891

0071-2930 See EUROPEAN MARKETING DATA AND STATISTICS. 728

0071-2973 See ANNUAL REPORT OF THE EUROPEAN ORGANIZATION FOR NUCLEAR RESEARCH. 4446

0071-3260 See EVOLUTIONARY BIOLOGY. 544

0071-3279 See EXCAVACIONES ARQUEOLOGICAS EN ESPANA. 268

0071-3309 See EXECUTIVE DIRECTORY OF THE U.S. PHARMACEUTICAL INDUSTRY. 4304

See ISSUES IN BIOMEDICINE. 459

0071-3473 See EXPLORATION GEOPHYSICS. 1405

0071-3597 See FACET BOOKS. BIBLICAL SERIES. 5016

0071-3619 See FACET BOOKS. SOCIAL ETHICS SERIES. 2250

0071-3651 See FACTS ABOUT NURSING. 3855

0071-3678 See FACTS AND FIGURES ON GOVERNMENT FINANCE. 4723

0071-3686 See TRANSACTIONS OF THE FACULTY OF ACTUARIES. 2894

0071-3783 See FAMOUS ARTISTS ANNUAL. 350

0071-3791 See FAR EAST AND AUSTRALASIA, THE. 1925

0071-4003 See FARM REAL ESTATE TAXES. 85

0071-4127 See FEDERAL EMPLOYEES ALMANAC. 4702

0071-450X See FEED ADDITIVE COMPENDIUM (1966). 86

0071-4607 See PROCEEDINGS OF THE ANNUAL MEETING - FERTILIZER INDUSTRY ROUND TABLE. 183

0071-4623 See FERTILIZER SCIENCE AND TECHNOLOGY SERIES. 87

0071-4682 See FIBER SCIENCE SERIES. 5105

0071-4739 See FIELDIANA. ANTHROPOLOGY. 236

0071-478X See FIELDING'S SELECTIVE SHOPPING GUIDE TO EUROPE. 954

0071-481X See FIGURA. 350

0071-4909 See FILM REFERENCE GUIDE FOR MEDICINE AND ALLIED SCIENCES. 3576

0071-495X See FILOLOGIA. 1076

0071-5042 See DIRECTORY OF DIRECTORS. [EXECUTIVES OF CANADA]. 728

0071-5042 See DIRECTORY OF DIRECTORS (TORONTO). 432

0071-5115 See FINANCIAL REPORTING IN CANADA. 744

0071-5220 See RADIOAKTIIVISUUSHAVAINTOJA. 1434

0071-5492 See FISH DISEASE LEAFLET. 2301

0071-5638 See FISKEN OG HAVET. 2303

0071-5697 See FIX YOUR VOLKSWAGEN. 5415

0071-576X See FLORA ET VEGETATIO MUNDI. 510

0071-5786 See FLORA MALESIANA. SERIES II, PTERIDOPHYTA. 510

0071-5794 See FLORA NEOTROPICA. 510

0071-5867 See FLORE DU CAMBODGE, DU LAOS ET DU VIETNAM. 511

0071-5875 See FLORE DU CAMEROUN. 511

0071-5972 See FLORIDA GOVERNMENT SERIES. 4649

0071-6022 See FLORIDA STATISTICAL ABSTRACT. 5327

0071-6146 See COOPERATIVE FOREST GENETICS RESEARCH PROGRAM. 2378

See BULLETIN OF THE FLORIDA MUSEUM OF NATURAL HISTORY. BIOLOGICAL SCIENCES. 4164

0071-6200 See PUBLICATION - FLORIDA WATER RESOURCES RESEARCH CENTER. 5538

0071-6340 See FODOR'S AUSTRIA. 5470

0071-6375 See FODOR'S EUROPE. 5471

0071-6405 See FODOR'S GREAT BRITAIN. 5471

0071-6413 See FODOR'S GREECE. 5471

0071-6421 See FODOR'S HAWAII. 5471

0071-643X See FODOR'S HOLLAND. 5471

0071-6464 See FODOR'S IRELAND. 5472

0071-6510 See FODOR'S PORTUGAL. 5473

0071-6529 See FODOR'S SCANDINAVIA. 5473

0071-6553 See FODOR'S SWITZERLAND. 5473

0071-657X See FODOR'S YUGOSLAVIA. 5474

0071-6588 See FODOR'S ISRAEL. 5472

0071-6618 See FODOR'S TURKEY. 5474

0071-6677 See FOLIA FORESTALIA POLONICA. SERIA A. LESNICTWO. 2379

0071-6693 See FOLIA GEOGRAPHICA DANICA. 2561

0071-6723 See FOLIA HISTORIAE ARTIUM. 350

0071-6774 See FOLKLORE AMERICANO. 2319

0071-6863 See FONTES ARCHAEOLOGICI POSNANIENSES. 268

0071-6871 See FONTES RERUM AUSTRIACARUM. OSTERREICHISCHE GESCHICHTS-QUELLEN. 1. ABTEILUNG. SCRIPTORES. 2688

0071-6952 See COMMODITY REFERENCE SERIES. 1602

0071-7002 See FAO COMMODITY REVIEW AND OUTLOOK. 83

0071-7029 See FAO FORESTRY DEVELOPMENT PAPER. 2379

0071-7037 See FAO FISHERIES STUDIES. 2300

0071-7045 See FAO LEGISLATIVE SERIES. 83

0071-707X See FAO NUTRITION MEETINGS REPORT SERIES. 4191

0071-7088 See FAO NUTRITIONAL STUDIES. 83

0071-710X See NATIONAL GRAIN POLICIES. 203

0071-7274 See FORD FOUNDATION ANNUAL REPORT. 4335

0071-7282 See FORECAST (LOS ANGELES). 1561

0071-7320 See FOREIGN CONSULAR OFFICES IN THE UNITED STATES. 4522

0071-7355 See FOREIGN RELATIONS OF THE UNITED STATES. 4522

0071-755X See FOREST RESOURCE REPORT - UNITED STATES. FOREST SERVICE. 2381

0071-7568 See FOREST SCIENCE. MONOGRAPH. 2381

0071-7665 See FORSCHUNGEN ZUE ANTIKEN SKLAVEREI. 4508

0071-7673 See FORSCHUNGEN ZUR MITTELALTERLICHEN GESCHICHTE. 2688

0071-7754 See PUBLICATION - FORT BURGWIN RESEARCH CENTER. 5143

0071-786X See PROGRESS IN DRUG RESEARCH. 4326

0071-7886 See FORTSCHRITTE DER CHEMIE ORGANISCHER NATURSTOFFE. 1041

0071-7916 See FORTSCHRITTE DER KIEFER- UND GESICHTS-CHIRURGIE. 1323

0071-7924 See FORTSCHRITTE DER PHYSIKALISCHEN CHEMIE. 1052

0071-7983 See FORTSCHRITTE DER WASSERCHEMIE UND IHRER GRENZGEBIETE. 5533

0071-7991 See FORTSCHRITTE DER ZOOLOGIE (STUTTGART). 5584

0071-8009 See FORTSCHRITTE IN DER GEOLOGIE VON RHEINLAND UND WESTFALEN. 1355

0071-8041 See SURGICAL FORUM. 3976

0071-8076 See FOTOINTERPRETACJA W GEOGRAFII. 2561

0071-8092 See FOUNDATION DIRECTORY, THE. 4336

0071-8394 See BULLETIN ARCHEOLOGIQUE DU COMITE DES TRAVAUX HISTORIQUES ET SCIENTIFIQUES. 262

0071-8823 See TRAVAUX ET DOCUMENTS / INSTITUT NATIONAL D'ETUDES DEMOGRAPHIQUES. 4560

0071-920X See NACHRICHTEN AUS DEM KARTEN- UND VERMESSUNGSWESEN. REIHE I. 2569

0071-9226 See FRANKFURTER BEITRAEGE ZUR GERMANISTIK. 3282

0071-9234 See FRANKFURTER GEOGRAPHISCHE HEFTE. 2561

0071-9277 See FRASER'S CANADIAN TRADE DIRECTORY. 729

0071-9382 See OCCASIONAL PAPERS - FREER GALLERY OF ART. 360

0071-9390 See FREIBERGER FORSCHUNGSHEFTE. REIHE A. 2139

0071-9404 See FREIBERGER FORSCHUNGSHEFTE. REIHE C. 1376

0071-9412 See FREIBERGER FORSCHUNGSHEFTE. REIHE D. 2139

0071-9420 See FREIBERGER FORSCHUNGSHEFTE. REIHE B. 4002

0071-9463 See JAHRBUCH DES FREIEN DEUTSCHEN HOCHSTIFTS. 3398

0071-9571 See NEW ZEALAND BUSINESS WHO'S WHO, THE. 699

0071-9587 See JOURNAL OF THE FRIENDS' HISTORICAL SOCIETY, THE. 5062

0071-9641 See FRONTIER MILITARY SERIES. 4044

0071-9676 See FRONTIERS OF RADIATION THERAPY AND ONCOLOGY. 3817

0071-9706 See FRUHMITTELALTERLICHE STUDIEN. 2689

0071-9889 See FUNDBERICHTE AUS HESSEN. 268

0071-9919 See FUNDHEFT FUR OFFENTLICHES RECHT. 2972

0071-9943 See FUNNYWORLD. 4861

0072-0038 See FYSIATRICKY A REUMATOLOGICKY VESTNIK. 3577

0072-0100 See GALLIA PREHISTOIRE. SUPPLEMENT. 269

0072-0119 See GALLIA, SUPPLEMENT. 2689

0072-0127 See JOURNAL - GALPIN SOCIETY. 4125

0072-0348 See GAZETTEER OF INDIA; INDIAN UNION, THE. 2504

0072-0534 See GEGENWARTSFRAGEN DER OST-WIRTSCHAFT. 1562

0072-0585 See GENAVA. 351

0072-0593 See GENEALOGICAL PERIODICAL ANNUAL INDEX. 2478

0072-0623 See BASIC INSTRUMENTS AND SELECTED DOCUMENTS. SUPPLEMENT / GENERAL AGREEMENTS ON TARIFFS AND TRADE. 1633

0072-0755 See REPORT OF THE ... SESSION / GENERAL FISHERIES COUNCIL FOR THE MEDITERRANEAN. 2311

0072-0771 See GENERAL SEMANTICS BULLETIN. 3283

0072-0798 See GENERAL SYSTEMS. 5200

0072-0879 See GENTES HERBARUM. 512

0072-0909 See GEOGRAPHER, THE. 2562

0072-0925 See GEOGRAPHICAL OBSERVER, THE. 2563

0072-0941 See MITTEILUNGEN DER GEOGRAPHISCHEN GESELLSCHAFT IN MUNCHEN. 2569

0072-0968 See GEOGRAPHISCHES TASCHENBUCH. 2564

0072-100X See GEOLOGIA SUDETICA. 1377

0072-1018 See GEOLOGICA ET PALAEONTOLOGICA. 1377

0072-1050 See GEOLOGICAL JOURNAL (CHICHESTER, ENGLAND). 1378

0072-1069 See MEMOIR / GEOLOGICAL SOCIETY OF AMERICA. 1387

0072-1077 See SPECIAL PAPER - GEOLOGICAL SOCIETY OF AMERICA. 1397

0072-1085 See SPECIAL PUBLICATION - GEOLOGICAL SOCIETY OF AUSTRALIA. 1397

0072-1115 See MITTEILUNGEN AUS DEM GEOLOGISCH-PALAEONTOLOGISCHEN INSTITUT DER UNIVERSITAET HAMBURG. 1388

0072-1298 See PUBLICATIONS - GEORGIA. UNIVERSITY. INSTITUTE OF COMMUNITY AND AREA DEVELOPMENT. 2832

0072-1328 See COLLECTED REPRINTS - UNIVERSITY OF GEORGIA MARINE INSTITUTE. 553

0072-1395 See GEOSCIENCE AND MAN. 2564

0072-1409 See PROCEEDINGS - GEOSCIENCE INFORMATION SOCIETY. 1359

0072-1468 See GERMAN OPINION ON PROBLEMS OF TODAY. 2517

0072-1484 See GERMANICA. 3391

0072-1492 See GERMANISTISCHE LINGUISTIK. 3284

0072-1670 See AUSSENHANDEL. REIHE 4: GENERALHANDEL. EIN- UND AUSFUHR VON MINERALOEL. 4251

0072-1883 See FINANZEN UND STEUEREN. REIHE 2 : STEUERHAUSHALT VON BUND, LANDERN UND GEMEINDEN. 4726

0072-2871 See LANDERKURZBERICHTE: KUBA. 5332

0072-3274 See LANDERKURZBERICHTE : PERU. 5332

0072-3665 See LAND- UND FORSTWIRTSCHAFT, FISCHEREI. REIHE 3 : VIEHWIRTSCHAFT. 2307

0072-369X See LANDERKURZBERICHTE : VENEZUELA. 5332

0072-3975 See UNTERNEHMEN UND ARBEITSSTATTEN. REIHE 1 : DIE KOSTENSTRUKTUR IN DER WIRTSCHAFT. V. GROSSHANDEL, HANDELVERTRETER UND HANDELSMAKLER, VERLAGSWESEN. 856

0072-4122 See ANNALEN DER METEOROLOGIE. 1419

0072-4130 See BERICHTE DES DEUTSCHEN WETTERDIENST. 1420

0072-4149 See BIBLIOGRAPHIEN DES DEUTSCHEN WETTERDIENSTES. 1421

0072-4203 See GESCHICHTLICHE LANDESKUNDE. 2689

0072-422X See JAHRBUCH / GESELLSCHAFT FUER DIE GESCHICHTE UND BIBLIOGRAPHIE DES BRAUWESENS E.V. 2368

0072-4238 See JAHRBUCH DER GESELLSCHAFT FUER NIEDERSACHSISCHE KIRCHENGESCHICHTE. 4967

0072-4378 See GHANA NATIONAL BIBLIOGRAPHY. 416

0072-4505 See GIFT AND DECORATIVE ACCESSORY BUYERS DIRECTORY, THE. 2584

0072-4513 See GIFU DAIGAKU NOGAKUBU KENKYU HOKOKU. 90

0072-4521 See GIFU DAIGAKU IGAKUBU KIYO. 3578

0072-4580 See GLADIOLUS ANNUAL : BEING THE YEARBOOK OF THE BRITISH GLADIOLUS SOCIETY, THE. 2417

0072-470X See ZESZYTY NAUKOWE - POLITECHNIKA SLASKA. MATEMATYKA. FIZYKA. 3542

0072-4750 See GLOSSARIA INTERPRETUM. 3284

0072-4769 See GLOTTODIDACTICA. 3284

0072-4793 See GOTEBORGER GERMANISTISCHE FORSCHUNGEN. 3284

0072-4874 See GOTTINGER ABHANDLUNGEN ZUR SOZIOLOGIE. 5246

0072-4947 See PROCEEDINGS. 4913

0072-5137 See GOVERNMENT CONTRACTS DIRECTORY. 1607

0072-5188 See GOVERNMENT REFERENCE BOOKS. 4652

0072-520X See DIRECTORY OF ORGANIZATIONS AND INDIVIDUALS PROFESSIONALLY ENGAGED IN GOVERNMENTAL RESEARCH AND RELATED ACTIVITIES. 4472

0072-5234 See GRADUATE ASSISTANTSHIP DIRECTORY IN THE COMPUTER SCIENCES. 1185

0072-5269 See GRADUATE STUDIES (LONDON, ENGLAND). 1826

0072-5285 See GRADUATE TEXTS IN MATHEMATICS. 3507

0072-5358 See GRAIN TRADE OF CANADA. 202

0072-5471 See GRANTS REGISTER, THE. 1826

0072-5498 See GRAPHIC ARTS TRADE DIRECTORY & REGISTER. 379

0072-5722 See CENTRAL OFFICE OF INFORMATION REFERENCE PAMPHLET. 4637

0072-5730 See ANNUAL ABSTRACT OF STATISTICS. 5321

See FAMILY SPENDING / CENTRAL STATISTICAL OFFICE. 1490

0072-6087 See ON THE STATE OF THE PUBLIC HEALTH (1963). 4795

0072-6109 See REPORT ON CONFIDENTIAL ENQUIRIES INTO MATERNAL DEATHS IN ENGLAND AND WALES. 3633

0072-6435 See HOME OFFICE RESEARCH STUDIES. 5479

0072-6729 See TECHNICAL BULLETIN - MINISTRY OF AGRICULTURE, FISHERIES AND FOOD. 139

0072-7008 See REPORT OF THE COUNCIL / NATURAL ENVIRONMENT RESEARCH COUNCIL. 2181

0072-7210 See TECHNICAL MONOGRAPH - GREAT BRITAIN. SOIL SURVEY. 189

0072-727X See GREAT DECISIONS. 4523

0072-7288 See GREAT IDEAS TODAY, THE. 1926

0072-7296 See ANNUAL REPORT - GREAT LAKES FISHERY COMMISSION. 2294

0072-7326 See GREAT LAKES RESEARCH CHECKLIST. 5549

0072-7342 See GREAT WEST AND INDIAN SERIES. 2735

0072-7431 See STATISTIKE EPETERIS TES HELLADOS. 5342

0072-7474 See GREEK, ROMAN AND BYZANTINE MONOGRAPHS. 1077

0072-7482 See GREEK, ROMAN AND BYZANTINE STUDIES. SCHOLARLY AIDS. 1077

0072-7490 See GREENWOOD'S GUIDE TO GREAT LAKES SHIPPING. 5449

0072-7741 See GROSSE NATURFORSCHER. 4166

0072-7865 See BUSINESS DIRECTORY (AGANA). 647

0072-8225 See GUIDE TO AMERICAN EDUCATIONAL DIRECTORIES. 1748

0072-8241 See GUIDE TO BIBLES IN PRINT. 5012

0072-8454 See GUIDE TO GOVERNMENT IN HAWAII. 4653

0072-8462 See GUIDE TO GOVERNMENT-LOAN FILMS. 4071

0072-8500 See GUIDE TO GRADUATE STUDY IN BOTANY FOR THE UNITED STATES AND CANADA. 512

0072-8535 See GUIDE TO INDUSTRIAL PARKS AND AREA DEVELOPMENT. 1565

0072-8551 See GUIDE TO JAPANESE TAXES. 4730

0072-8578 See GUIDE TO COLLECTIONS OF MANUSCRIPTS RELATING TO AUSTRALIA. 416

0072-8705 See GUIDE TO SUMMER CAMPS AND SUMMER SCHOOLS, THE. 4850

0072-8713 See GUIDE TO THE COALFIELDS. 2140

0072-8829 See GUIDE BOOK OF UNITED STATES COINS, A. 2781

0072-8853 See GUIDEBOOK TO LABOR RELATIONS. 3148

0072-8888 See GUIDEBOOK TO NEW JERSEY TAXES. 4730

0072-8896 See GUIDEBOOK TO NEW YORK TAXES. 4730

0072-890X See GUIDEBOOK TO PENNSYLVANIA TAXES. 4730

0072-8926 See GUIDES TO EUROPEAN TAXATION. 4730

0072-9000 See GUINNESS BOOK OF RECORDS (NEW YORK, N.Y.). 1926

0072-9027 See GULF RESEARCH REPORTS. 554

0072-9094 See GUTENBERG-JAHRBUCH. 4565

0072-9116 See BULLETIN - GEOLOGICAL SURVEY OF GUYANA. **1369**

0072-9280 See BERICHT / HAHN-MEITNER-INSTITUT BERLIN GMBH. **962**

0072-9469 See MITTEILUNGEN AUS DEM MUSEUM FUER VOLKERKUNDE HAMBURG. **241**

0072-9523 See HAMBURGER BEITRAEGE ZUR NUMISMATIK. **2781**

0072-9566 See HAMBURGER JAHRBUCH FUER WIRTSCHAFTS- UND GESELLSCHAFTSPOLITIK. **1493**

0072-9582 See HAMBURGER PHILOLOGISCHE STUDIEN. **3285**

0072-9612 See MITTEILUNGEN AUS DEM HAMBURGISCHEN ZOOLOGISCHEN MUSEUM UND INSTITUT. **5591**

0072-9833 See HANDBOOK OF LATIN AMERICAN STUDIES. **2735**

0072-9841 See HANDBOOK OF MEDICAL TREATMENT. **3580**

0072-9884 See HANDBOOK OF PRIVATE SCHOOLS, THE. **1749**

0073-0033 See HANDBUCH DER EXPERIMENTELLEN PHARMAKOLOGIE. **4306**

0073-0068 See HANDBUCH DER GROSSUNTERNEHMEN. **1493**

0073-0211 See HANDLOADER'S DIGEST. **3480**

0073-0327 See HANSISCHE GESCHICHTSBLATTER. **2690**

0073-0394 See HARMON MEMORIAL LECTURES IN MILITARY HISTORY, THE. **4045**

0073-0459 See HARVARD ARMENIAN TEXTS AND STUDIES. **2652**

0073-0467 See HARVARD BOOKS IN BIOLOGY. **456**

0073-0475 See HARVARD BOOKS IN BIOPHYSICS. **495**

0073-0483 See HARVARD EAST ASIAN MONOGRAPHS. **2652**

0073-0491 See HARVARD EAST ASIAN SERIES. **2652**

0073-0513 See HARVARD ENGLISH STUDIES. **3393**

0073-0521 See HARVARD HISTORICAL MONOGRAPHS. **2617**

0073-053X See HARVARD HISTORICAL STUDIES. **2617**

0073-0548 See HARVARD JOURNAL OF ASIATIC STUDIES. **2652**

0073-0564 See HARVARD LIBRARIAN, THE. **3213**

0073-0629 See HARVARD PUBLICATIONS IN MUSIC. **4120**

0073-0637 See HARVARD SEMITIC MONOGRAPHS. **5016**

0073-067X See HARVARD STUDIES IN BUSINESS HISTORY. **679**

0073-0688 See HARVARD STUDIES IN CLASSICAL PHILOLOGY. **1077**

0073-0696 See HARVARD STUDIES IN COMPARATIVE LITERATURE. **3393**

0073-0718 See HARVARD STUDIES IN ROMANCE LANGUAGES. **3393**

0073-0726 See HARVARD THEOLOGICAL STUDIES. **4962**

0073-0777 See PUBLICATION OF THE KRESS LIBRARY OF BUSINESS AND ECONOMICS. **705**

0073-0807 See OCCASIONAL PAPERS ON MOLLUSKS. **5593**

0073-0874 See HARVEY LECTURES, THE. **3580**

0073-0912 See HATTORI SHOKUBUTSU KENKYUJO HOKOKU. **512**

0073-0947 See HAUTES ETUDES ISLAMIQUES ET ORIENTALES D'HISTOIRE COMPAREE. **2652**

0073-0955 See HAUTES ETUDES MEDIEVALES ET MODERNES. **2690**

0073-0971 See HAUTES ETUDES ORIENTALES. **2652**

0073-1080 See STATE OF HAWAII DATA BOOK. **5339**

0073-1137 See REPORT OF THE OMBUDSMAN. **4681**

0073-1145 See HAWAII SERIES. **417**

0073-134X See PROCEEDINGS OF THE HAWAIIAN ENTOMOLOGICAL SOCIETY. **5613**

0073-1390 See HAYDN YEARBOOK, THE. **4121**

0073-148X See SOURCE BOOK OF HEALTH INSURANCE DATA. **2894**

0073-1560 See HEBBEL JAHRBUCH. **3393**

0073-1587 See HEGEL-STUDIEN. **4347**

0073-1595 See HEIDELBERG SCIENCE LIBRARY. **5109**

0073-1641 See HEIDELBERGER JAHRBUCHER. **5109**

0073-1684 See HEIDELBERGER TASCHENBUCHER. **4828**

0073-1692 See HEINE-JAHRBUCH. **3393**

0073-1706 See HELPING PERSON IN THE GROUP. **5287**

0073-1714 See HELPS FOR STUDENTS OF HISTORY. **2617**

0073-1811 See HELVETICA PAEDIATRICA ACTA. SUPPLEMENTUM. **3904**

0073-2001 See HESSISCHES JAHRBUCH FUER LANDESGESCHICHTE. **2690**

0073-201X See HEUTIGES DEUTSCH. REIHE 1: LINGUISTISCHE GRUNDLAGEN. **3285**

0073-2087 See HIDROBIOLOGIA. **554**

0073-2230 See HILGARDIA. **92**

0073-229X See HIROSAKI DAIGAKU NÂOGAKUBU GAKUJUTSU HOKOKU. **92**

0073-2311 See MEMOIRS OF THE FACULTY OF ENGINEERING, HIROSHIMA UNIVERSITY. **1987**

0073-2435 See HISTORIA (SANTIAGO). **2736**

0073-2486 See HISTORIA Y CULTURA (LIMA). **2617**

0073-2516 See BIBLIOTECA DEGLI "HISTORIAE MUSICAE CULTORES". **3194**

0073-2540 See HISTORIALLINEN ARKISTO. **2691**

0073-2567 See HISTORIC HOUSES, CASTLES, AND GARDENS IN GREAT BRITAIN AND IRELAND. **2691**

0073-2648 See TRANSACTIONS OF THE HISTORICAL SOCIETY OF GHANA. **2667**

0073-2680 See MITTEILUNGEN DES HISTORISCHEN VEREINS DER PFALZ. **2699**

0073-2702 See HISTORISKA OCH LITTERATURHISTORISKA STUDIER. **3394**

0073-2753 See HISTORY OF SCIENCE. **5110**

0073-277X See HISTORYKA. **2619**

0073-2788 See HITOTSUBASHI JOURNAL OF ARTS & SCIENCES. **321**

0073-2796 See HITOTSUBASHI JOURNAL OF LAW & POLITICS. **4476**

0073-280X See HITOTSUBASHI JOURNAL OF SOCIAL STUDIES. **5201**

0073-2842 See HOCHSCHULBUCHER FUER MATHEMATIK. **3507**

0073-2869 See HOCKEY STARS OF **4899**

0073-2885 See E.T.A. HOFFMANN-JAHRBUCH : MITTEILUNGEN DER E.T.A. HOFFMANN-GESELLSCHAFT. **3462**

0073-2907 See HOFSTRA UNIVERSITY YEARBOOK OF BUSINESS. **680**

0073-3059 See HOLLIS PRESS & PUBLIC RELATIONS ANNUAL. **760**

0073-3075 See HOME AND GARDEN BULLETIN. **2790**

0073-3253 See HSIANG-KANG FO CHIAO. **5021**

0073-3407 See HORNERO, EL. **5586**

0073-3776 See HUDSON INSTITUTE REPORT TO THE MEMBERS, THE. **5111**

0073-4071 See HUNTIA. **513**

0073-4209 See HYDROELECTRIC POWER RESOURCES OF THE UNITED STATES, DEVELOPED AND UNDEVELOPED. **2115**

0073-4225 See PROCEEDINGS OF HYDROLOGY SYMPOSIUM. **1417**

0073-4519 See BIENNIAL REPORT OF THE FISH AND GAME DEPARTMENT OF THE STATE OF IDAHO. **2297**

0073-4551 See OCCASIONAL PAPERS OF THE IDAHO MUSEUM OF NATURAL HISTORY. **4094**

0073-4586 See BULLETIN - FOREST, WILDLIFE AND RANGE EXPERIMENT STATION. **2189**

0073-4594 See STATION NOTE - UNIVERSITY OF IDAHO FOREST, WILDLIFE AND RANGE EXPERIMENT STATION. **2206**

0073-4667 See ETHNIES. **2261**

0073-4675 See IDESIA. **2195**

0073-4705 See IHERINGIA. SERIE BOTANICA. **513**

0073-4721 See IHERINGIA. SERIE ZOOLOGIA. **5586**

0073-4748 See ILLINOIS BIOLOGICAL MONOGRAPHS. **458**

0073-4918 See BULLETIN (ILLINOIS. NATURAL HISTORY SURVEY DIVISION). **4163**

0073-4926 See CIRCULAR - ILLINOIS NATURAL HISTORY SURVEY. **4164**

0073-4934 See SPECIAL REPORT (NORTHERN ILLINOIS UNIVERSITY. CENTER FOR SOUTHEAST ASIAN STUDIES). **2665**

0073-506X See CIRCULAR - ILLINOIS STATE GEOLOGICAL SURVEY. **2136**

0073-5086 See ENVIRONMENTAL GEOLOGY NOTES. **1375**

0073-5108 See ILLINOIS PETROLEUM. **4260**

0073-5167 See ILLINOIS STUDIES IN ANTHROPOLOGY. **238**

0073-5175 See ILLINOIS STUDIES IN LANGUAGE AND LITERATURE / UNIVERSITY OF ILLINOIS. **3286**

0073-5264 See T.& A.M. REPORT. **2130**

0073-5442 See WRC RESEARCH REPORT. **5549**

0073-5477 See ILLUSTRATORS. **373**

0073-5620 See IMPRIMATUR (MUNCHEN). **4829**

0073-5752 See INCUNABULA GRAECA. **1077**

0073-5817 See INDEX TO ARTICLES ON JEWISH STUDIES. **2263**

0073-5930 See INDEX TO HOW TO DO IT INFORMATION. **2779**

0073-599X See INDEX TO PHILIPPINE PERIODICALS. **2496**

0073-6066 See INDEX TO THESES WITH ABSTRACTS ACCEPTED FOR HIGHER DEGREES BY THE UNIVERSITIES OF GREAT BRITAIN AND IRELAND AND THE COUNCIL FOR NATIONAL ACADEMIC AWARDS. **1830**

0073-6074 See INDEX TRANSLATIONUM. **3286**

0073-6090 See INDIA, A REFERENCE ANNUAL. **2653**

0073-6244 See INDIA WHO'S WHO. **433**

0073-6279 See IASLIC SPECIAL PUBLICATION. **3214**

0073-6473 See ANNUAL REPORT - INDIAN INSTITUTE OF FOREIGN TRADE. **823**

0073-6600 See PROCEEDINGS OF THE INDIAN NATIONAL SCIENCE ACADEMY. PART B, BIOLOGICAL SCIENCES. **469**

0073-6619 See YEAR BOOK OF THE INDIAN NATIONAL SCIENCE ACADEMY, THE. **5171**

0073-6635 See INDIAN PHARMACEUTICAL GUIDE. **4307**

0073-6767 See PROCEEDINGS OF THE INDIANA ACADEMY OF SCIENCE. **5140**

0073-6902 See INDIANA HISTORICAL SOCIETY PUBLICATIONS. **2738**

0073-6953 See PUBLICATIONS. GEOGRAPHIC MONOGRAPH SERIES. **2574**

0073-7518 See MEDICAL SERIES, BULLETIN. **3611**

0073-7682 See PROCEEDINGS OF THE INDUSTRIAL WASTE CONFERENCE. **2239**

0073-7739 See INDUSTRIE ET ARTISANAT. **1611**

0073-7755 See INDUSTRIEABWASSER. **2233**

0073-7860 See INFORMATION PLEASE ALMANAC, ATLAS AND YEARBOOK. **1926**

0073-8212 See DOCUMENTS, ETUDES ET REPERTOIRES. **267**

0073-8301 See PUBLICATIONS MATHEMATIQUES. INSTITUT DES HAUTES ETUDES SCIENTIFIQUES. **3529**

0073-8360 See COLLECTION COLLOQUES ET SEMINAIRES. INSTITUT FRANCAIS DU PETROLE. **4253**

0073-8433 *See* PUBLIKATIONEN ZU WISSENSCHAFTLICHEN FILMEN, SEKTION TECHNISCHE WISSENSCHAFTEN, NATURWISSENSCHAFTEN. 5143

0073-8484 *See* MITTEILUNGEN DES INSTITUTS FUER OSTERREICHISCHE GESCHICHTSFORSCHUNG. 2699

0073-8530 *See* BULLETIN DE L'INSTITUT HISTORIQUE BELGE DE ROME. 2481

0073-8565 *See* ANNALES DE L'INSTITUT MICHEL PACHA. 552

0073-859X *See* ETUDES ET TRAVAUX. 1823

0073-8611 *See* INSTITUTA ET MONUMENTA. SERIE 2: INSTITUTA. 4122

0073-9006 *See* SPECIAL PUBLICATION--INSTITUTE OF BRITISH GEOGRAPHIES. 2576

0073-9146 *See* IEEE MEMBERSHIP DIRECTORY. 2060

0073-9294 *See* NYENGU BOGO - RIMMOG NYUGJON NYENGUSO. 2390

0073-9421 *See* POLICY PAPERS IN HUMAN RESOURCES AND INDUSTRIAL RELATIONS. 1702

0073-9464 *See* INSTITUTE OF METALS MONOGRAPH AND REPORT SERIES. 4004

0073-9677 *See* PROCEEDINGS - INSTITUTE OF REFRIGERATION. 2607

0073-9685 See FACTS (WASHINGTON). 4001

0073-9723 *See* LIBRARY BULLETIN (INSTITUTE OF SOUTHEAST ASIAN STUDIES). 3225

0073-9847 *See* SESSIONAL YEARBOOK ... AND DIRECTORY OF MEMBERS. 2030

0073-9855 *See* REVISTA DO INSTITUTO ADOLFO LUTZ. 4800

0073-9871 *See* SERIE CIENTIFICA. INSTITUTO ANTARTICO CHILENO. 1360

0073-9901 *See* MEMORIAS DO INSTITUTO BUTANTAN (SAO PAULO). 3674

0073-991X *See* PUBLICACIONES. SERIE BIBLIOGRAFICA. 423

0073-9928 *See* PUBLICACIONES. SERIES MINOR. 3312

0074-0195 *See* BOLETIN DEL INSTITUTO ESPANOL DE OCEANOGRAFIA (1983). 1447

0074-025X *See* MISCELANEA - FUNDACION MIGUEL LILLO. 4167

0074-0276 *See* MEMORIAS DO INSTITUTO OSWALDO CRUZ. 464

0074-039X *See* ANUARUL INSTITUTULUI DE ISTORIE SI ARHEOLOGIE A. D. XENOPOL. 256

0074-0411 *See* MEDEDELING - INSTITUUT VOOR CULTUURTECHNIEK EN WATERHUISHOUDING. 178

0074-042X *See* TECHNICAL BULLETIN - INSTITUTE FOR LAND AND WATER MANAGEMENT RESEARCH. 189

0074-0446 *See* JAARSVERSLAG - INSTITUUT VOOR PLANTENZEIKTENKUNDIG ONDERZOEK. 2421

0074-0551 *See* INSTRUMENTATION IN THE CHEMICAL AND PETROLEUM INDUSTRIES. 4260

0074-056X *See* INSTRUMENTATION IN THE POWER INDUSTRY. 2065

0074-0675 *See* INSURANCE ALMANAC (ENGLEWOOD. 1933), THE. 2882

0074-073X *See* INSURANCE PERIODICALS INDEX. 2897

0074-087X *See* ANNUAL REPORT / INTER-AMERICAN DEVELOPMENT BANK. 1462

0074-0993 *See* BULLETIN - INTER-AMERICAN TROPICAL TUNA COMMISSION. 449

0074-1000 *See* ANNUAL REPORT OF THE INTER-AMERICAN TROPICAL TUNA COMMISSION. 2295

0074-1035 *See* INTER-NORD. 2620

0074-1116 *See* INTERNATIONAL ABC AEROSPACE DIRECTORY. 24

0074-1132 *See* INTERDISCIPLINARY TOPICS IN GERONTOLOGY. 3752

0074-1175 *See* TECHNICAL SERIES / INTERGOVERNMENTAL OCEANOGRAPHIC COMMISSION. 1457

0074-1191 *See* THEMATA CHOROU + TECHNON. 310

0074-1388 *See* BULLETIN BIBLIOGRAPHIQUE DE LA SOCIETE INTERNATIONALE ARTHURIENNE. 3457

0074-1477 *See* PROCEEDINGS. 2094

0074-1612 *See* BULLETIN OF THE INTERNATIONAL ASSOCIATION OF ENGINEERING GEOLOGY. 2019

0074-1809 *See* SYMPOSIUM - INTERNATIONAL ASTRONOMICAL UNION. 401

0074-1868 *See* LEGAL SERIES. 1949

0074-1876 *See* PANEL PROCEEDINGS SERIES - INTERNATIONAL ATOMIC ENERGY AGENCY. 1952

0074-1892 *See* IAEA SAFETY SERIES. 4783

0074-1914 *See* TECHNICAL REPORTS SERIES / INTERNATIONAL ATOMIC ENERGY AGENCY. 1959

0074-1922 *See* INTERNATIONAL AUCTION RECORDS. 353

0074-2015 *See* INTERNATIONAL BIBLIOGRAPHY OF HISTORICAL SCIENCES. 2635

0074-2112 *See* PUBLICATIONS OF THE INTERNATIONAL BUREAU OF FISCAL DOCUMENTATION. 750

0074-2422 *See* DIGEST OF STATISTICS - INTERNATIONAL CIVIL AVIATION ORGANIZATION. SERIES AT, AIRPORT TRAFFIC. 17

0074-2449 *See* DIGEST OF STATISTICS - INTERNATIONAL CIVIL AVIATION ORGANIZATION. SERIES FP, FLEET-PERSONNEL. 17

0074-2457 *See* DIGEST OF STATISTICS - INTERNATIONAL CIVIL AVIATION ORGANIZATION. SERIES R, CIVIL AIRCRAFT ON REGISTER. 17

0074-249X *See* INDEX TO ICAO PUBLICATIONS. 23

0074-2740 *See* ICRP PUBLICATION. 3941

0074-2783 *See* BULLETIN D'INFORMATION - COMITE INTERNATIONAL DES SCIENCES HISTORIQUES. 5091

0074-3054 *See* TRANSACTIONS OF THE INTERNATIONAL CONFERENCE ON ENDODONTICS. 1337

0074-3992 *See* INTERNATIONAL JOURNAL OF UNIVERSITY ADULT EDUCATION. 1801

0074-4123 *See* PROCEEDINGS OF THE INTERNATIONAL CONGRESS ON METALLIC CORROSION. 2016

0074-4220 *See* INTERNATIONAL CONVOCATION ON IMMUNOLOGY. [PROCEEDINGS]. 3672

0074-4336 See ICES MARINE SCIENCE SYMPOSIA. 1449

0074-4417 *See* INTERNATIONAL CONGRESS OF THE INTERNATIONAL COUNCIL ON HEALTH, PHYSICAL EDUCATION, AND RECREATION. 1856

0074-445X *See* YEARBOOK / INTERNATIONAL COURT OF JUSTICE. 3138

0074-459X *See* INTERNATIONAL DIRECTORY OF MARKETING RESEARCH HOUSES AND SERVICE; GREEN BOOK. 926

0074-4603 *See* INTERNATIONAL DIRECTORY OF PHILOSOPHY AND PHILOSOPHERS. 4349

0074-5774 *See* INTERNATIONAL ENGINEERING DIRECTORY. 1979

0074-5804 *See* FID/CR REPORT. 3210

0074-5944 *See* BIBLIOGRAPHY : F I A F MEMBERS PUBLICATIONS. 4080

0074-6002 *See* IFLA DIRECTORY. 3214

0074-6142 *See* INTERNATIONAL GEOPHYSICS SERIES. 1407

0074-6215 See WORLD LIST OF UNIVERSITIES, OTHER INSTITUTIONS OF HIGHER EDUCATION AND UNIVERSITY ORGANISATIONS. LISTE MONDIALE DES UNIVERSITES, AUTRES ETABLISSEMENTS D'ENSEIGNEMENT SUPERIEUR ET ORGANISATIONS UNIVERSITAIRES. 1930

0074-6436 *See* BIBLIOGRAPHY - INTERNATIONAL INSTITUTE FOR LAND RECLAMATION AND IMPROVEMENT. 151

0074-6444 *See* BULLETIN - INTERNATIONAL INSTITUTE FOR LAND RECLAMATION AND IMPROVEMENT. 2189

0074-655X *See* BULLETIN OF THE INTERNATIONAL INSTITUTE OF SEISMOLOGY AND EARTHQUAKE ENGINEERING. 1403

0074-6681 *See* SPECIAL REPORT OF THE DIRECTOR-GENERAL ON THE APPLICATION OF THE DECLARATION CONCERNING ACTION AGAINST APARTHEID IN SOUTH AFRICA / INTERNATIONAL LABOUR OFFICE. 2643

0074-6681 *See* SUMMARY OF REPORTS (ARTICLES 19, 22 AND 35 OF THE CONSTITUTION). 1712

0074-6681 *See* REPORT / INTERNATIONAL LABOUR CONFERENCE. 1706

0074-6738 *See* REPORT OF THE ... CONFERENCE / THE INTERNATIONAL LAW ASSOCIATION. 3134

0074-6770 *See* INTERNATIONAL LESSON ANNUAL, THE. 4966

0074-6827 *See* INTERNATIONAL LITERARY MARKET PLACE. 4821

0074-7025 *See* SUMMARY PROCEEDINGS OF THE ANNUAL MEETING OF THE BOARD OF GOVERNORS. INTERNATIONAL MONETARY FUND. 1523

0074-7084 *See* INTERNATIONAL MOTION PICTURE ALMANAC (1956). 4073

0074-7157 *See* BULLETIN - INTERNATIONAL NORTH PACIFIC FISHERIES COMMISSION. 2298

0074-7203 *See* PROCEEDINGS OF THE ... CONFERENCE OF THE INTERNATIONAL ORGANIZATION OF CITRUS VIROLOGISTS. 183

0074-7211 *See* PROCEEDINGS OF THE INTERNATIONAL ORNITHOLOGICAL CONGRESS. 5595

0074-7238 *See* ANNUAL REPORT - INTERNATIONAL PACIFIC HALIBUT COMMISSION. 2294

0074-7289 *See* IPRA STUDIES IN PEACE RESEARCH. 4526

0074-7319 See INTERNATIONAL ENERGY ANNUAL. 1947

0074-7491 *See* COMPTE RENDU DU COLLOQUE DE L'INSTITUT INTERNATIONAL DE LA POTASSE. 1023

0074-7688 *See* INTERNATIONAL REVIEW OF CRIMINAL POLICY. 3166

0074-7696 *See* INTERNATIONAL REVIEW OF CYTOLOGY. 537

0074-7718 *See* INTERNATIONAL REVIEW OF EXPERIMENTAL PATHOLOGY. 3895

0074-7742 *See* INTERNATIONAL REVIEW OF NEUROBIOLOGY. 459

0074-7750 *See* INTERNATIONAL REVIEW OF RESEARCH IN MENTAL RETARDATION. 3927

0074-7769 *See* INTERNATIONAL REVIEW FOR THE SOCIOLOGY OF SPORT. 4901

0074-784X *See* PROCEEDINGS OF THE INTERNATIONAL SCHOOL OF PHYSICS "ENRICO FERMI". 4418

0074-7866 *See* INTERNATIONAL SCIENCE REVIEW SERIES. 5115

0074-7890 *See* INTERNATIONAL SECURITY DIRECTORY. 3166

0074-8218 *See* INTERNATIONAL SERIES OF MONOGRAPHS ON METAL PHYSICS AND PHYSICAL METALLURGY. 4004

0074-8609 *See* BULLETIN OF THE INTERNATIONAL STATISTICAL INSTITUTE. 5324

0074-8684 *See* INTERNATIONAL STUDIES IN SOCIOLOGY AND SOCIAL ANTHROPOLOGY. 5249

0074-8714 *See* ELECTRICAL RETAILING. 2045

0074-8919 *See* BABOON IN MEDICAL RESEARCH, THE. 3554

0074-896X *See* INTERNATIONAL TAX AGREEMENTS. 4732

0074-9125 *See* ANNUAL REPORT - INTERNATIONAL TIN COUNCIL. 3998

0074-9214 *See* UICC MONOGRAPH SERIES. 3825

0074-9273 *See* IUCN PUBLICATIONS NEW SERIES. 2196

0074-9508 *See* COMPTES RENDUS DE LA CONFERENCE - UNION INTERNATIONALE DE CHIMIE PURE ET APPLIQUE. 973

0074-9613 See INTERNATIONAL WHO'S WHO, THE. 433

0074-9621 See INTERNATIONAL YEAR BOOK AND STATESMEN'S WHO'S WHO, THE. 433

0074-9664 See INTERNATIONAL ZOO YEARBOOK. 5586

0074-9729 See VEROEFFENTLICHUNGEN DER INTERNATIONALEN GESELLSCHAFT FUER GESCHICHTE DER PHARMAZIE. NEUE FOLGE, DIE. 4332

0074-9745 See INTERNATIONALE ZEITSCHRIFTENSCHAU FUER BIBELWISSENSCHAFT UND GRENZGEBIETE. 5013

0074-9818 See INTERNATIONALES JAHRBUCH DER ERWACHSENENBILDUNG. 1801

0074-9834 See INTERNATIONALES JAHRBUCH FUER GESCHICHTS- UND GEOGRAPHIE-UNTERRICH. 2620

0074-9931 See INTERSCIENCE MONOGRAPHS AND TEXTS IN PHYSICS AND ASTRONOMY. 4406

0074-9958 See INTERSCIENCE TRACTS ON PHYSICS AND ASTRONOMY. 4406

0074-9982 See INTERSTATE PORT HANDBOOK. 5450

0074-9990 See INTRODUCTION TO SYSTEMATIC GEOMORPHOLOGY, AN. 1356

0075-0026 See INVENTARI DEI MANOSCRITTI DELLE BIBLIOTECHE D'ITALIA. 3218

0075-0050 See INVENTARIA ARCHAEOLOGICA. DENMARK. 270

0075-0115 See INVENTARIA ARCHAEOLOGICA. JUGOSLAVIJA. 270

0075-0271 See INVESTMENT COMPANIES (CDA/WIESENBERGER (FIRM)). 902

0075-0301 See POPULAR PHOTOGRAPHY'S INVITATION TO PHOTOGRAPHY. 4375

0075-0395 See IOWA PUBLICATIONS IN PHILOSOPHY. 4350

0075-0468 See IPEK. 270

0075-0700 See IRIS YEAR BOOK / BRITISH IRIS SOCIETY, THE. 2402

0075-0727 See IRISH BAPTIST HISTORICAL SOCIETY JOURNAL. 5061

0075-0735 See IRISH CATHOLIC DIRECTORY, THE. 5030

0075-0778 See IRISH GEOGRAPHY. 2566

0075-0867 See IRON AND STEEL INDUSTRY ANNUAL STATISTICS FOR THE UNITED KINGDOM. 4025

0075-0883 See IRON ORE (CLEVELAND, OHIO). 4005

0075-093X See ISLAMIC SURVEYS. 2768

0075-1243 See ISRAEL JOURNAL OF ENTOMOLOGY. 5610

0075-1391 See ISRAEL STUDIES IN CRIMINOLOGY. 3166

0075-1634 See ITALIAN STUDIES. 3397

0075-1782 See STATISTICHE DEL COMMERCIO INTERNO. 5500

0075-1820 See STATISTICHE DEI BILANCI DELLE AMMINISTRAZIONI REGIONALI, PROVINCIALI E COMUNALI. 4750

0075-1871 See STATISTICA ANNUALE DEL COMMERCIO CON L'ESTERO. 733

0075-188X See STATISTICA DEGLI INCIDENTI STRADALI. 5339

0075-1995 See RELAZIONE GENERALE SULLA SITUAZIONE ECONOMICA DEL PAESE. 1516

0075-2088 See SPECIAL PUBLICATION / J. L. B. SMITH INSTITUTE OF ICHTHYOLOGY. 5598

0075-2207 See JAHRBUCH DER BERLINER MUSEEN. 353

0075-2215 See JAHRBUCH DER BIBLIOTHEKEN, ARCHIVE UND INFORMATIONSSTELLEN DER DEUTSCHEN DEMOKRATISCHEN REPUBLIK. 3219

0075-2223 See JAHRBUCH DER DEUTSCHEN BIBLIOTHEKEN. 3219

0075-2266 See JAHRBUCH DER GRAPHISCHEN UNTERNEHMUNGEN OSTERREICHS. 4566

0075-2363 See JAHRBUCH DER PSYCHOANALYSE. 3927

0075-2371 See JAHRBUCH DER RAABE-GESELLSCHAFT. 3398

0075-2428 See JAHRBUCH DER WEHRTECHNIK. 4046

0075-2479 See JAHRBUCH DES EISENBAHNWESENS. 5432

0075-2517 See JAHRBUCH DES OFFENTLICHEN RECHTS DER GEGENWART. 4478

0075-2541 See JAHRBUCH FUER ANTIKE UND CHRISTENTUM. 4967

0075-2614 See JAHRBUCH FUER DIE GESCHICHTE MITTEL- UND OSTDEUTSCHLANDS. 2694

0075-2649 See JAHRBUCH FUER FREMDENVERKEHR. 5481

0075-2673 See JAHRBUCH FUER GESCHICHTE VON STAAT, WIRTSCHAFT UND GESELLSCHAFT LATEINAMERIKAS. 2740

0075-2681 See JAHRBUCH FUER LITURGIK UND HYMNOLOGIE. 4124

0075-2703 See JAHRBUCH FUER MUSIKALISCHE VOLKS- UND VOLKERKUNDE. 4124

0075-2711 See JAHRBUCH FUER NUMISMATIK UND GELDGESCHICHTE. 2781

0075-272X See JAHRBUCH FUER OPTIK UND FEINMECHANIK. 4435

0075-2738 See JAHRBUCH FUER OSTDEUTSCHE VOLKSKUNDE. 2321

0075-2746 See JAHRBUCH FUER OSTRECHT. 3131

0075-2770 See JAHRBUCH FUER SOZIALWISSENSCHAFT. 5205

0075-2789 See JAHRBUCH FUER VOLKSLIEDFORSCHUNG. 4124

0075-2800 See JAHRBUCH FUER WIRTSCHAFTSGESCHICHTE. 1568

0075-2819 See JAHRBUCH OBERFLACHENTECHNIK. 4005

0075-2851 See JAHRESBERICHT UBER DIE DEUTSCHE FISCHWIRTSCHAFT. 2306

0075-286X See JAHRESBERICHTE FUER DEUTSCHE GESCHICHTE. 418

0075-2878 See JAHRESBERICHTE UBER HOLZSCHUTA. 2402

0075-2886 See JAHRESFACHKATALOG: RECHT, WIRTSCHAFT, STEUERN. 2986

0075-2924 See JAHRESKATALOG PSYCHOLOGIE UND VERWANDTE WISSENSCHAFTEN. 4592

0075-2932 See JAHRESSCHRIFT FUER MITTELDEUTSCHE VORGESCHICHTE. 271

0075-3017 See JANE'S ALL THE WORLD'S AIRCRAFT (LONDON, ENGLAND). 4046

0075-3025 See JANE'S FIGHTING SHIPS. 4177

0075-3041 See JANE'S MAJOR COMPANIES OF EUROPE. 685

0075-3084 See JANE'S WORLD RAILWAYS. 5432

0075-3114 See JANUA LINGUARUM. SERIES MAIOR. 3289

0075-3203 See JAPAN CHEMICAL DIRECTORY. 1026

0075-3432 See JAPANESE JOURNAL OF MATHEMATICS. 3511

0075-3475 See JAPAN'S IRON & STEEL INDUSTRY. 1613

0075-3572 See JAZZFORSCHUNG (GRAZ). 4125

0075-3580 See JAHRBUCH DER JEAN-PAUL-GESELLSCHAFT. 3398

0075-3696 See JERUSALEM SYMPOSIA ON QUANTUM CHEMISTRY AND BIOCHEMISTRY, THE. 489

0075-3726 See JEWISH BOOK ANNUAL. 3399

0075-3750 See JEWISH TRAVEL GUIDE, THE. 5481

0075-3769 See JEWISH YEAR BOOK, THE. 5049

0075-3777 See JOBSON'S MINING YEAR BOOK. 2141

0075-3858 See JOHNS HOPKINS OCEANOGRAPHIC STUDIES, THE. 1450

0075-3874 See JOHNS HOPKINS SYMPOSIA IN COMPARATIVE HISTORY, THE. 2621

0075-3890 See JOHNS HOPKINS UNIVERSITY STUDIES IN GEOLOGY, THE. 1384

0075-3904 See JOHNS HOPKINS UNIVERSITY STUDIES IN HISTORICAL AND POLITICAL SCIENCE, THE. 5205

0075-3920 See JOHNSONIA. 5587

0075-4056 See JOUETS ET JEUX. 2584

0075-4102 See JOURNAL FUER DIE REINE UND ANGEWANDTE MATHEMATIK. 3511

0075-4161 See JOURNAL OF BYELORUSSIAN STUDIES. 3289

0075-417X See JOURNAL OF CHILD PSYCHOTHERAPY. 3928

0075-4218 See JOURNAL OF CROATIAN STUDIES. 3289

0075-4234 See JOURNAL OF EGYPTIAN ARCHAEOLOGY, THE. 271

0075-4242 See JOURNAL OF ENGLISH LINGUISTICS. 3290

0075-4250 See JOURNAL OF GLASS STUDIES. 2591

0075-4269 See JOURNAL OF HELLENIC STUDIES. 1078

0075-4277 See JOURNAL OF JURISTIC PAPYROLOGY, THE. 2988

0075-4285 See JOURNAL OF MALTESE STUDIES. 3400

0075-4293 See JOURNAL OF MATHEMATICS, TOKUSHIMA UNIVERSITY. 3514

0075-4315 See JOURNAL OF NUCLEAR MEDICINE. SUPPLEMENT. 3848

0075-4358 See JOURNAL OF ROMAN STUDIES, THE. 1078

0075-4366 See JOURNAL OF SCIENCE OF THE HIROSHIMA UNIVERSITY. SERIES B. DIVISION 2. BOTANY. 516

0075-4390 See JOURNAL OF THE WARBURG AND COURTAULD INSTITUTES. 2518

0075-4412 2921

0075-4439 See JOURNEES ANNUELLES DE DIABETOLOGIE DE L'HOTEL-DIEU. 3731

0075-4463 See ACQUISITIONS MEDICALES RECENTES. 3544

0075-4587 See JUST B'TWX US. 3221

0075-5001 See LIBRARY SERIES / UNIVERSITY OF KANSAS LIBRARIES. 3227

0075-5028 See MISCELLANEOUS PUBLICATION - UNIVERSITY OF KANSAS, MUSEUM OF NATURAL HISTORY. 4167

0075-5044 See UNIVERSITY OF KANSAS PALEONTOLOGICAL CONTRIBUTIONS. ARTICLE. 4231

0075-5052 See UNIVERSITY OF KANSAS PALEONTOLOGICAL CONTRIBUTIONS. PAPERS. 4231

0075-5168 See JOURNAL OF THE KARNATAK UNIVERSITY. SCIENCE. 5121

0075-5192 See WITTHAYASAN KASETSART. 146

0075-5222 See KASMERA. 3601

0075-5397 See KEMIA UJABB EREDMENYEI, A. 983

0075-5400 See KEMPE'S ENGINEERS YEAR-BOOK FOR 1984

0075-5400 See KEMPE'S ENGINEER'S YEAR-BOOK. 1984

0075-5494 See KENTUCKY DIRECTORY OF MANUFACTURERS. 3482

0075-5567 See COUNTY REPORT / KENTUCKY GEOLOGICAL SURVEY. 1372

0075-5591 See REPORT OF INVESTIGATIONS / KENTUCKY GEOLOGICAL SURVEY. 1394

0075-5605 See REPRINT / KENTUCKY GEOLOGICAL SURVEY. 1395

0075-5613 See SPECIAL PUBLICATION. KENTUCKY GEOLOGICAL SURVEY. 1398

0075-5621 See THESIS SERIES - KENTUCKY GEOLOGICAL SURVEY. 1399

0075-5893 See ANNUAL REPORT - KENYA. MINISTRY OF LABOUR. 1649

0075-5974 See KEW BULLETIN. 516

0075-6032 See KIERKEGAARDIANA. 4351

0075-6040 See KIME'S INTERNATIONAL LAW DIRECTORY. 3131

0075-6156 See REPRINT SERIES - INDUSTRIAL RELATIONS CENTRE. QUEEN'S UNIVERSITY. 1707

0075-6164 See RESEARCH SERIES - INDUSTRIAL RELATIONS CENTRE. QUEEN'S UNIVERSITY. 1708

0075-6199 See KIRCHENMUSIKALISCHES JAHRBUCH. 4128

0075-6210 See KIRCHLICHES JAHRBUCH FUER DIE EVANGELISCHE KIRCHE IN DEUTSCHLAND. 5062

0075-6245 See KIRTLANDIA. 4167

0075-6318 See KLEINE DEUTSCHE PROSADENKMALER DES MITTELALTERS. 3345

0075-6334 See KLIO (LEIPZIG, GERMANY : 1906). 2622

0075-6342 See KLUCZE DO OZNAZCZANIA KREGOWCOW POLSKI. 5589

0075-6407 See KOBE ECONOMIC & BUSINESS REVIEW. 1571

0075-6431 See KOBE DAIGAKU IGAKUBU KIYO. 3602

0075-6458 See KOEDOE. 5589

0075-6512 See KOLNER JAHRBUCH FUER VOR- UND FRUHGESCHICHTE. 2696

0075-6520 See KOLNER ROMANISTISCHE ARBEITEN. 3402

0075-6539 See KOLNER SCHRIFTEN ZUR POLITISCHEN WISSENSCHAFT. 4480

0075-6547 See KOLEOPTEROLOGISCHE RUNDSCHAU. 5589

0075-6636 See KOMPASS; MANUEL D'INFORMATIONS SUR L'ECONOMIE DE LA BELGIQUE ET DU GRAND-DUCHE DE LUXEMBOURG. 1502

0075-6687 See KOMPASS; REPERTORIO GENERALE DELL'ECONOMIA ITALIANA; REGISTER OF ITALIAN INDUSTRY AND COMMERCE. 843

0075-6709 See KOMPASS; INDEKS OVER NORGES INDUSTRI OG NRINGSLIV. 1571

0075-6733 See KOMPASS. 689

0075-6954 See KOSTEN EN FINANCIERING VAN DE GEZONDHEIDSZORG / CENTRAAL BUREAU VOOR DE STATISTIEK, HOOFDAFDELING GEZONDHEIDSSTATISTIEKEN. 4788

0075-7012 See AKADEMIA GORNICZP-HUTNICZA IM. STANISLAWA STASZICA. ZESZYTY NAUKOWE: CERAMIKA. 3997

0075-7055 See ZESZYTY NAUKOWE - POLITECHNIKA KRAKOWSKA. CHEMIA. 1020

0075-7063 See KRANKENHAUS (WIEN). 3787

0075-7209 See KULTURPFLANZE. 177

0075-725X See KUNST UND ALTERTUM AM RHEIN. 356

0075-7373 See KYOTO FURITSU DAIGAKU GAKUJUTSU HOKOKU, NOGAKU. 103

0075-7470 See LABOR RELATIONS AND PUBLIC POLICY SERIES. 1685

0075-7535 See LABORATORY TECHNIQUES IN BIOCHEMISTRY AND MOLECULAR BIOLOGY. 490

0075-7780 See LAMMERGEYER, THE. 4167

0075-7799 See JOURNAL OF THE LANCASHIRE DIALECT SOCIETY, THE. 3292

0075-787X See ZAHLENWERTE UND FUNKTIONEN AUS NATURWISSENSCHAFTEN UND TECHNIK GRUPPE 3. KRISTALL- UND FESTKORPERPHYSIK. 4425

0075-7896 See ZAHLENWERTE UND FUNKTIONEN AUS NATURWISSENSCHAFTEN UND TECHNIK GRUPPE 6. ASTRONOMIE, ASTROPHYSIK UND WELTRAUMFORSCHUNG. 401

0075-7918 See ZAHLENWERTE UND FUNKTIONEN AUS NATURWISSENSCHAFTEN UND TECHNIK GRUPPE 2. ATOM- UND MOLEKULARPHYSIK. 4425

0075-8159 See LATIN AMERICAN TRAVEL & PAN AMERICAN HIGHWAY GUIDE. 5482

0075-8167 See LATIN AMERICAN UURBAN RESEARCH. 2827

0075-823X See LAW IN EASTERN EUROPE. 2995

0075-8345 See LEATHER BUYERS GUIDE. 3185

0075-8396 See LEBARON RUSSELL BRIGGS PRIZE HONORS ESSAYS IN ENGLISH. 3404

0075-8442 See LECTURE NOTES IN ECONOMICS AND MATHEMATICAL SYSTEMS. 1503

0075-8450 See LECTURE NOTES IN PHYSICS. 4411

0075-8485 See LECTURES IN APPLIED MATHEMATICS. 3516

0075-8515 See LECTURES ON GAS CHROMATOGRAPHY. 984

0075-8523 See LECTURES ON MATHEMATICS IN THE LIFE SCIENCES. 3516

0075-8566 See LEEDS STUDIES IN ENGLISH. 3297

0075-8574 See LEEDS TEXTS AND MONOGRAPHS. 3297

0075-8647 See LEIDSE ROMANTISCHE REEKS. 3404

0075-8744 See YEAR BOOK (LEO BAECK INSTITUTE). 2275

0075-8787 See LEPIDOPTERA. 5590

0075-8833 See LESSING YEARBOOK. 3346

0075-8914 See LEVANT (LONDON). 273

0075-904X See LIBRARY ASSOCIATION OF ALBERTA OCCASIONAL PAPER, THE. 3224

0075-9139 See LIBRARY OF LIVING PHILOSOPHERS, THE. 4352

0075-918X See LIBROS EN VENTA EN HISPANOAMERICA Y ESPANA. 419

0075-9406 See LIFE INSURANCE FACT BOOK. 2886

0075-9414 See PROCEEDINGS OF THE ... ANNUAL MEETING OF THE LIFE INSURERS CONFERENCE. 2890

0075-9481 See LILLOA. 517

0075-949X See LILIES AND OTHER LILIACEAE. 2424

0075-9511 See LIMNOLOGICA. 463

0075-9546 See MITTEILUNGEN AUS DEM MAX-PLANCK-INSTITUT FUER AERONOMIE. 1431

0075-9597 See PROCEEDINGS OF THE LINGUISTIC CIRCLE OF MANITOBA AND NORTH DAKOTA. 3312

0075-966X See LINGUISTIQUE (PARIS. 1965), LA. 3299

0075-9708 See TRANSACTIONS OF THE LINNAEAN SOCIETY OF NEW YORK. 529

0075-9740 See LIONEL COHEN LECTURES. 1761

0075-9937 See LITERATUR UND WIRKLICHKEIT. 3406

0075-997X See LITERATURWISSENSCHAFTLICHES JAHRBUCH. 3407

0076-0048 See LITURGIEWISSENSCHAFTLICHE QUELLEN UND FORSCHUNGEN. 4974

0076-0072 See LIVING HISTORY OF THE WORLD; YEARBOOK. 2622

0076-0188 See LLEN CYMRU. 3346

0076-020X See LLOYD'S MARITIME ATLAS. 5451

0076-0234 See STATISTICAL TABLES. 5457

0076-0242 See LOCAL GOVERNMENT REPORTS OF AUSTRALIA, THE. 4663

0076-0390 See ROZPRAWY KOMISJI JEZYKOWEJ. ODZKIE TOWARZYSTWO NAUKOWE. 3318

0076-0501 See TRANSACTIONS OF THE LONDON & MIDDLESEX ARCHAEOLOGICAL SOCIETY. 284

0076-0552 See LONDON MATHEMATICAL SOCIETY LECTURE NOTE SERIES. 3517

0076-0579 See LONDON NATURALIST. 4167

0076-0625 See LONDON ORIENTAL SERIES. 2622

0076-0722 See BULLETIN OF THE INSTITUTE OF ARCHAEOLOGY / UNIVERSITY OF LONDON, INSTITUTE OF ARCHAEOLOGY. 264

0076-0730 See BULLETIN - INSTITUTE OF CLASSICAL STUDIES. 1075

0076-0765 See COMMONWEALTH PAPERS. 1090

0076-0773 See COLLECTED SEMINAR PAPERS / UNIVERSITY OF LONDON, INSTITUTE OF COMMONWEALTH STUDIES. 5195

0076-0943 See SCIENCE SERIES (LOS ANGELES). 4171

0076-0986 See PUBLICATIONS. 279

0076-0994 See SOUTHWEST MUSEUM PAPERS. 4096

0076-1109 See LSU WOOD UTILIZATION NOTES. 2387

0076-1184 See MEMORIAS DO INSTITUTO DE INVESTIGACAO CIENTIFICA DE MOCAMBIQUE. SERIES C, CIENCIAS HUMANAS. 5209

0076-132X See LOVEJOY'S COLLEGE GUIDE. 1834

0076-1435 See LUD. 2322

0076-1451 See LUND STUDIES IN ENGLISH. 3300

0076-146X See LUND STUDIES IN GEOGRAPHY. SERIES A. PHYSICAL GEOGRAPHY. 2568

0076-1478 See LUND STUDIES IN GEOGRAPHY. SERIES B. HUMAN GEOGRAPHY. 2568

0076-1508 See LUSITANIA SACRA. 2622

0076-1524 See JOURNAL OF THE LUTE SOCIETY OF AMERICA, INC. 4127

0076-1583 See BULLETIN DU STATEC / SERVICE CENTRAL DE LA STATISTIQUE ET DES ETUDES ECONOMIQUES. 1530

0076-1648 See LYCHNOS: LARDOMSHISTORISKA SAMFUNDETS ARSBOK. 5126

0076-1648 See LYCHNOS. 5126

0076-1656 See PUBLICATIONS DU DEPARTEMENT DE MATHEMATIQUES. 3529

0076-180X See SCIENTIFIC REPORT - MCGILL UNIVERSITY, STORMY WEATHER GROUP. 1434

0076-1982 See MCGILL SUB-ARCTIC RESEARCH PAPERS. 2568

0076-2016 See MCGRAW-HILL YEARBOOK OF SCIENCE AND TECHNOLOGY. 5127

0076-2091 See MACROMOLECULAR SYNTHESES. 985

0076-2148 See MADISON AVENUE HANDBOOK, THE. 762

0076-230X See MELANGES DE LA CASA DE VELAZQUEZ. 2698

0076-2342 See MAGAZINE OF ALBEMARLE COUNTY HISTORY, THE. 2745

0076-2725 See MAINFRANKISCHES JAHRBUCH FUER GESCHICHTE UND KUNST. 357

0076-2741 See JAHRBUCH DES ROEMISCH-GERMANISCHES ZENTRALMUSEUM MAINZ. 2620

0076-2776 See MAINZER PHILOSOPHISCHE FORSCHUNGEN. 4352

0076-2784 See MAINZER REIHE, DIE. 3465

0076-2792 See MAINZER ZEITSCHRIFT. 357

0076-2881 See MAJOR PROBLEMS IN PATHOLOGY. 3896

0076-289X See MAKEDONIKA (THESSALONIKA). 2850

0076-2997 See MALACOLOGIA. 5590

0076-3004 See MALACOLOGICAL REVIEW. 5590

0076-3136 See MEMOIR - MALAWI GEOLOGICAL SURVEY DEPARTMENT. 1387

0076-3373 See OFFICIAL YEAR BOOK - MALAYSIA. 2507

0076-3519 See MAMMALIAN SPECIES. 464

0076-3632 See MANAGEMENT INFORMATION GUIDE. 877

0076-3861 See MANITOBA LAW JOURNAL (1966). 3006

0076-390X See MANITOBA TRADE DIRECTORY. 845

0076-3934 See SERIES 2 : RESEARCH REPORTS - CENTER FOR SETTLEMENT STUDIES, UNIVERSITY OF MANITOBA. 5257

0076-4256 See MANUFACTURING MANAGEMENT SERIES. 879

0076-4418 See MARCONI'S INTERNATIONAL REGISTER. 1116

0076-4418 See MARCONI'S INTERNATIONAL REGISTER. 1159

0076-4795 See INFORMATION CIRCULAR (MARYLAND GEOLOGICAL SURVEY). 1382

0076-4809 See REPORT OF INVESTIGATIONS - MARYLAND GEOLOGICAL SURVEY. 1394

0076-4981 See PROCEEDINGS OF THE MASSACHUSETTS HISTORICAL SOCIETY. 2755

0076-5112 See MASTER'S THESES DIRECTORIES. EDUCATION. 1835

0076-5201 See MATERIALS SCIENCE RESEARCH. 5127

0076-521X See MATERIAY I PRACE ANTROPOLOGICZNE. 241

0076-5236 See MATERIAY ZACHODNIO POMORSKIE. 2697

0076-5252 See MATERIAUX POUR L'ETUDE DE L'EXTREME-ORIENT MODERNE ET CONTEMPORAIN. ETUDES LINGUISTIQUES. 3301

0076-5279 See MATERIAUX POUR L'ETUDE DE L'EXTREME-ORIENT MODERNE ET CONTEMPORAIN. TRAVAUX. 2658

0076-5325 See MATHEMATICAL ECONOMICS TEXTS. 1504

0076-5392 See MATHEMATICS IN SCIENCE AND ENGINEERING. 3521

0076-5430 See MATHEMATISCHE LEHRBUECHER UND MONOGRAPHIEN. ABTEILUNG 2. MATHEMATISCHE MONOGRAPHIEN. 3522

0076-5430 See MATHEMATISCHE LEHRBUECHER UND MONOGRAPHIEN. ABTEILUNG 1. MATHEMATISCHE LEHRBUECHER. 3522

0076-5449 See MATHEMATISCHE SCHULERBUCHEREI. 3522

0076-5465 See MAUDSLEY MONOGRAPHS. 3930

0076-5783 See MECHANICS (URBANA). 2122

0076-5821 See MEDIA SCANDINAVIA. 4816

0076-5864 See MEDIAEVAL SCANDINAVIA. 2697

0076-5872 See MEDIAEVAL STUDIES. 2697

0076-5880 See MEDIAEVALIA PHILOSOPHICA POLONORUM. 4352

0076-6011 See TRANSACTIONS OF THE MEDICAL SOCIETY. 3647

0076-6046 See MEDICINA RIBEIRAO PRETO. 3613

0076-6062 See MEDICINAL RESEARCH. 4315

0076-6097 See MEDIEVAL ARCHAEOLOGY. 274

0076-6100 See MEDIEVAL IBERIAN PENINSULA. TEXTS AND STUDIES. 2698

0076-6127 See MEDIEVALIA ET HUMANISTICA. 2698

0076-6151 See MEDIZINISCHE LANDERKUNDE. 3615

0076-6224 See MELANDERIA (PULLMAN, WASH.). 5611

0076-6232 See MELBOURNE HISTORICAL JOURNAL. 2670

0076-6321 See MELSHEIMER ENTOMOLOGICAL SERIES. 5591

0076-6372 See MEMORABILIA ZOOLOGICA. 5591

0076-6380 See REVISTA DE LA JUNTA DE ESTUDIOS HISTORICOS DE MENDOZA. 4171

0076-6461 See ... MENTAL MEASUREMENTS YEARBOOK, THE. 1763

0076-6518 See MERCK INDEX; AN ENCYCLOPEDIA OF CHEMICALS AND DRUGS, THE. 4315

0076-6526 See MERCK MANUAL OF DIAGNOSIS AND THERAPY, THE. 3616

0076-6542 See MERCK VETERINARY MANUAL, THE. 5516

0076-6658 See METAL STATISTICS (NEW YORK, N.Y.). 4026

0076-6682 See METALLSTATISTIK. 4010

0076-6828 See METHODS AND MODELS IN THE SOCIAL SCIENCES. 5209

0076-6879 See METHODS IN ENZYMOLOGY. 490

0076-6895 See METHODS IN GEOCHEMISTRY AND GEOPHYSICS. 1408

0076-6941 See METHODS OF BIOCHEMICAL ANALYSIS. 986

0076-695X See METHODS OF EXPERIMENTAL PHYSICS. 4412

0076-7115 See METROPOLITAN WASHINGTON REGIONAL DIRECTORY. 4665

0076-7131 See REVISTA DEL INSTITUTO NACIONAL DE CANCEROLOGIA. 3823

0076-7689 See MEYNIANA. 1388

0076-7948 See MICHIGAN GEOGRAPHICAL PUBLICATION. 2569

0076-8103 See MICHIGAN SLAVIC CONTRIBUTIONS. 3302

0076-812X See OCCASIONAL PAPERS. SOUTH ASIA SERIES. 2661

0076-8189 See LATIN AMERICAN STUDIES CENTER MONOGRAPH SERIES. 2744

0076-8367 See ANTHROPOLOGICAL PAPERS (UNIVERSITY OF MICHIGAN. MUSEUM OF ANTHROPOLOGY). 229

0076-8375 See MEMOIRS OF THE MUSEUM OF ANTHROPOLOGY, UNIVERSITY OF MICHIGAN. 241

0076-8391 See BULLETIN - UNIVERSITY OF MICHIGAN. MUSEUM OF ART. 4086

0076-8405 See MISCELLANEOUS PUBLICATIONS - MUSEUM OF ZOOLOGY, UNIVERSITY OF MICHIGAN. 5591

0076-8413 See OCCASIONAL PAPERS OF THE MUSEUM OF ZOOLOGY, UNIVERSITY OF MICHIGAN. 5593

0076-8502 See MIDDLE EAST AND NORTH AFRICA, THE. 1927

0076-8642 See MIKROCHIMICA ACTA. SUPPLEMENTUM (1966). 986

0076-8677 See PUBBLICAZIONI DELL'UNIVERSITA CATTOLICA DEL SACRO CUORE. CONTRIBUTI, SERIE III. SCIENZE FILOSOFICHE. 4358

0076-8782 See MILITARY YEAR-BOOK. 4051

0076-8820 See MILTON STUDIES. 3347

0076-8847 See MIMS DESK REFERENCE. 4316

0076-8936 See NEWSLETTER - MINERALOGICAL ASSOCIATION OF CANADA. 1443

0076-8952 See MINERALS YEARBOOK. 1442

0076-8995 See MINING ANNUAL REVIEW. 2145

0076-910X See MINNEAPOLIS INSTITUTE OF ARTS BULLETIN, THE. 325

0076-9142 See MINNESOTA DRAMA EDITIONS. 5366

0076-9169 See BULLETIN - MINNESOTA GEOLOGICAL SURVEY. 1370

0076-9177 See REPORT OF INVESTIGATIONS - MINNESOTA GEOLOGICAL SURVEY. 1394

0076-9193 See MINNESOTA HISTORICAL ARCHAEOLOGY SERIES. 2746

0076-9258 See MINNESOTA STUDIES IN THE PHILOSOPHY OF SCIENCE. 5129

0076-9266 See MINNESOTA SYMPOSIA ON CHILD PSYCHOLOGY. 4604

0076-9355 See MISCELLANEA MUSICOLOGICA (ADELAIDE). 4131

0076-9428 See MISSIONSWISSENSCHAFTLICHE FORSCHUNGEN. 4978

0076-9436 See JOURNAL OF THE MISSISSIPPI ACADEMY OF SCIENCES. 5121

0076-9576 See MISSOURI ARCHAEOLOGIST, THE. 275

0076-9614 See WATER RESOURCES REPORT (ROLLA). 5547

0076-9703 See UNIVERSITY OF MISSOURI STUDIES (1926). 1852

0076-9754 See MITTELLATEINISCHE STUDIEN UND TEXTE. 3412

0076-9762 See MITTELLATEINISCHES JAHRBUCH. 3302

0076-9789 See MOBIL TRAVEL GUIDE. GREAT LAKES AREA. 5485

0076-9797 See MOBIL TRAVEL GUIDE : MIDDLE ATLANTIC STATES. 5485

0076-9819 See MOBIL TRAVEL GUIDE. NORTHWEST AND GREAT PLAINS STATES. 5485

0076-9827 See MOBIL TRAVEL GUIDE : CALIFORNIA AND THE WEST. 5484

0076-9843 See MOBIL TRAVEL GUIDE. SOUTHWEST AND SOUTH CENTRAL AREA. 5485

0076-9894 See MODERN AMERICA. 2539

0076-9924 See MODERN ASPECTS OF ELECTROCHEMISTRY. 1034

0077-0027 See MODERN MIDDLE EAST SERIES (NEW YORK). 2770

0077-0094 See MODERN PROBLEMS OF PHARMACOPSYCHIATRY. 3931

0077-0159 See MODERN TRENDS IN ORTHOPAEDICS. 3883

0077-0221 See MOLECULAR BIOLOGY, BIOCHEMISTRY, AND BIOPHYSICS. 465

0077-0310 See MONDE D'OUTRE-MER, PASSE ET PRESENT. 2623

0077-0396 See MONGOLIA SOCIETY OCCASIONAL PAPERS, THE. 2659

0077-0507 See MONOGRAFIE MATEMATYCZNE. 3523

0077-0582 See MONOGRAPH SERIES IN WORLD AFFAIRS. 4529

0077-0590 See AERA MONOGRAPH SERIES ON CURRICULUM EVALUATION. 1887

0077-0639 See MONOGRAPHIAE BIOLOGICAE. 465

0077-0655 See MONOGRAPHIAE BOTANICAE. 518

0077-0671 See MONOGRAPHIEN AUS DEM GESAMTGEBIETE DER PSYCHIATRIE. 3838

0077-071X See MONOGRAPHIES FRANCAISES DE PSYCHOLOGIE. 4604

0077-0760 See MONOGRAPHS IN ALLERGY. 3675

0077-0809 See MONOGRAPHS IN CLINICAL CYTOLOGY. 539

0077-0825 See MONOGRAPHS IN DEVELOPMENTAL BIOLOGY. 466

0077-0876 See MONOGRAPHS IN HUMAN GENETICS. 549

0077-0892 See MONOGRAPHS IN ORAL SCIENCE. 1330

0077-0914 See PEDIATRIC AND ADOLESCENT MEDICINE. 3908

0077-0922 See MONOGRAPHS IN PATHOLOGY. 3896

0077-0930 See MONOGRAPHS IN POPULATION BIOLOGY. 466

0077-0965 See MONOGRAPHS IN VIROLOGY. 568

0077-0973 See MONOGRAPHS ON APPLIED OPTICS. 4438

0077-1015 See MONOGRAPHS ON ENDOCRINOLOGY. 3732

0077-104X See MONOGRAPHS ON OCEANOGRAPHIC METHODOLOGY. 1452

0077-1090 See BULLETIN / STATE OF MONTANA, BUREAU OF MINES AND GEOLOGY. 1370

0077-1120 See MEMOIR (MONTANA BUREAU OF MINES AND GEOLOGY). 2143

0077-1139 See SPECIAL PUBLICATION - STATE OF MONTANA, BUREAU OF MINES AND GEOLOGY. 1398

0077-118X See UNIVERSITY OF MONTANA CONTRIBUTIONS TO ANTHROPOLOGY. 247

0077-1198 See MONTANA VITAL STATISTICS. 4562

0077-1244 See COMUNICACIONES ANTROPOLOGICAS DEL MUSEO DE HISTORIA NATURAL DE MONTEVIDEO. 4087

0077-1384 See MONUMENTA AMERICANA. 275

0077-1473 See MONUMENTA MUSICAE SVECICAE / SVENSKA SAMFUNDET FOR MUSIKFORSKNING. 4132

0077-1503 See MONUMENTS OF RENAISSANCE MUSIC. 4132

0077-1554 See TRANSACTIONS OF THE MOSCOW MATHEMATICAL SOCIETY. 3539

0077-1805 See MOZART-JAHRBUCH. 4132

0077-1813 See MUELLERIA. 518

0077-1872 See MUNCHNER GERMANISTISCHE BEITRAEGE. 3348

0077-1899 See MUNCHNER JAHRBUCH DER BILDENDEN KUNST. 359

0077-1910 See MUNCHENER STUDIEN ZUR SPRACHWISSENSCHAFT. 3304

0077-1961 See SCHRIFTENREIHE DES MATHEMATISCHEN INSTITUTS DER UNIVERSITAT MUNSTER. 3533

0077-2070 See MITTEILUNGEN DER BAYERISCHE. 4228

0077-2186 See MUNICIPAL YEAR BOOK (WASHINGTON), THE. 4667

0077-2194 See MUSE (COLUMBIA). 4091

0077-2461 *See* MUSICA DISCIPLINA. **4135**

0077-247X *See* MUSICA MEDII AEVI. **4136**

0077-2496 *See* MUSICOLOGICAL STUDIES & DOCUMENTS. **4137**

0077-2526 *See* MUSIKALISCHE DENKMALER. **4138**

0077-2542 *See* MUSK-OX, THE. **2569**

0077-2550 *See* MUTUAL FUND FACT BOOK. **908**

0077-264X *See* PROCEEDINGS OF THE RESEARCH INSTITUTE OF ATMOSPHERICS, NAGOYA UNIVERSITY. **1433**

0077-2690 *See* NAMES IN SOUTH CAROLINA. **2570**

0077-2704 *See* NAMN OCH BYGD. **2570**

0077-2712 *See* MELANGES - CENTRE DE RECHERCHES ET D'APPLICATIONS PEDAGOGIQUES EN LANGUES. **3302**

0077-2879 *See* NASSAU REVIEW, THE. **2851**

0077-2887 *See* NASSAUISCHE ANNALEN. **2700**

0077-2933 *See* BIOGRAPHICAL MEMOIRS. **430**

0077-314X *See* NASA TECHNICAL REPORT. **29**

0077-3255 *See* PROCEEDINGS OF THE NATIONAL ASSOCIATION OF ANIMAL BREEDERS. **219**

0077-3662 *See* COLLECTED PAPERS FROM THE NATIONAL CANCER RESEARCH INSTITUTE. **3815**

0077-3794 *See* ANNUAL REPORTS OF THE NATIONAL COLLEGIATE ATHLETIC ASSOCIATION. **4883**

0077-3808 *See* PROCEEDINGS OF THE ANNUAL CONVENTION OF THE NATIONAL COLLEGIATE ATHLETIC ASSOCIATION (1967). **4913**

0077-4014 *See* SELECTED AND ANNOTATED BIBLIOGRAPHY OF REFERENCE MATERIAL IN CONSUMER FINANCE. **811**

0077-4049 *See* BULLETIN / NATIONAL COUNCIL FOR THE SOCIAL STUDIES. **5194**

0077-4093 *See* MONOGRAFIE DI ARCHEOLOGIA LIBICA. **275**

0077-4103 *See* YEARBOOK - NATIONAL COUNCIL OF TEACHERS OF MATHEMATICS. **3541**

0077-4278 *See* ESTIMATES OF SCHOOL STATISTICS. **1795**

0077-4332 *See* RANKINGS OF THE STATES. **1776**

0077-4472 *See* NATIONAL FACULTY DIRECTORY, THE. **1836**

0077-4529 *See* NATIONAL FINANCES, THE. **4738**

0077-4545 *See* NATIONAL FIRE CODES. **2292**

0077-4715 *See* EISEI SHIKENJO HOKOKU. **4774**

0077-4839 *See* NOGYO GIJUTSU KENKYUJO HOKOKU. RENZOKU B: DOJO HIRYO. **113**

0077-4847 *See* NOGYO GIJUTSU KENKYUJO HOKOKU. C : BYORI KONCHU. **2425**

0077-4863 *See* NOGYO GIJUTSU KENKYUJO HOKOKU. H : KEIEI TOCHI RIYO. **113**

0077-4928 *See* OCCASIONAL PAPERS / NATIONAL INSTITUTE OF ECONOMIC AND SOCIAL RESEARCH. **1509**

0077-4995 *See* REPORT OF THE NATIONAL INSTITUTE OF GENETICS. **551**

0077-5177 *See* NATIONAL LIST OF ADVERTISERS (TORONTO). **763**

0077-5266 *See* NEWSLETTER - NATIONAL OPINION RESEARCH CENTER. **5252**

0077-5339 *See* BULLETIN - NATIONAL PSYCHOLOGICAL ASSOCIATION FOR PSYCHOANALYSIS. **4579**

0077-5401 *See* PROCEEDINGS - NATIONAL RELAY CONFERENCE. **2076**

0077-5428 *See* TECHNICAL MEMORANDUM - ASSOCIATE COMMITTEE ON GEOTECHNICAL RESEARCH (OTTAWA). **2032**

0077-5541 *See* AERONAUTICAL REPORT LR. **4**

0077-5584 *See* PUBLICATIONS OF THE NATIONAL RESEARCH COUNCIL OF CANADA. **5143**

0077-5614 *See* NATIONAL COOPERATIVE HIGHWAY RESEARCH PROGRAM REPORT. **5442**

0077-5630 *See* ATOLL RESEARCH BULLETIN. **1366**

0077-5762 *See* ... YEARBOOK OF THE NATIONAL SOCIETY FOR THE STUDY OF EDUCATION, THE. **1792**

0077-5819 *See* YEN CHIU PAO KAO. **148**

0077-5835 *See* SHEHUI KEXUE LUNCONG. **5219**

0077-5843 *See* KAO KU JEN LEI HSUEH KAN / KUO LI TAIWAN TA HSUEH. **240**

0077-5851 *See* SHE HUI HSUEH KAN. **5258**

0077-586X *See* NATIONAL TANK TRUCK CARRIER DIRECTORY. **5388**

0077-5886 *See* NTDRA TIRE DEALERS SURVEY. **5076**

0077-5894 *See* NATIONAL TRADE-INDEX OF SOUTH AFRICA. **847**

0077-6033 *See* NATURA JUTLANDICA. **5592**

0077-6122 *See* VERHANDLUNGEN DER NATURFORSCHENDEN GESELLSCHAFT IN BASEL. **5168**

0077-6238 *See* NAVAL REVIEW (ANNAPOLIS). **4180**

0077-6262 *See* NAVIGATION. **4180**

0077-6270 *See* ANNUAIRE NAVIS. **5083**

0077-6297 *See* NAWPA PACHA. **275**

0077-6386 *See* UNIVERSITY OF NEBRASKA STUDIES. **2856**

0077-6599 *See* NEPRAJZI ERTESITO : NEPRAJZI MUZEUM EVKONYVE. **2269**

0077-6645 *See* JAARSTATISTIEK VAN DE IN-EN UITVOER PER LAND VAN DE NEDERLANDSE ANTILLEN. **842**

0077-670X *See* BELASTINGDRUK IN NEDERLAND. **4713**

0077-7579 *See* NETHERLANDS JOURNAL OF SEA RESEARCH. **556**

0077-7668 *See* NEUDRUCKE DEUTSCHER LITERATURWERKE. **3415**

0077-7749 *See* NEUES JAHRBUCH FUER GEOLOGIE UND PALAONTOLOGIE. ABHANDLUNGEN. **1389**

0077-7757 *See* NEUES JAHRBUCH FUER MINERALOGIE. ABHANDLUNGEN. **1443**

0077-7862 *See* NEUSSER JAHRBUCH. **326**

0077-7897 *See* ANTHROPOLOGICAL PAPERS (CARSON CITY). **229**

0077-7919 *See* OCCASIONAL PAPERS - NEVADA STATE MUSEUM. **4094**

0077-7927 *See* POPULAR SERIES (CARSON CITY, NEV.). **4095**

0077-796X *See* TECHNICAL REPORT SERIES P. PHYSICAL SCIENCES PUBLICATION. **5162**

0077-832X *See* RESEARCH REPORT / NEW HAMPSHIRE AGRICULTURAL EXPERIMENTAL STATION. **128**

0077-8338 *See* STATION BULLETIN - NEW HAMPSHIRE AGRICULTURAL EXPERIMENT STATION. **137**

0077-8346 *See* NEW HAMPSHIRE ARCHEOLOGIST, THE. **276**

0077-8389 *See* TECHNICAL CIRCULAR - NEW HAMPSHIRE FISH AND GAME DEPARTMENT. **4879**

0077-8435 *See* ANNUAL REPORT OF THE GEOLOGICAL SURVEY. NEW HEBRIDES CONDOMINIUM. **1365**

0077-8540 *See* NEW MEXICO AGRICULTURAL STATISTICS. **155**

0077-8567 *See* GUIDEBOOK - NEW MEXICO GEOLOGICAL SOCIETY. **1382**

0077-8575 *See* NEW MEXICO STATISTICAL ABSTRACT. **1536**

0077-8583 *See* BULLETIN - THE UNIVERSITY OF NEW MEXICO ART MUSEUM. **4086**

0077-8591 *See* NEW OFFICIAL GUIDE: JAPAN, THE. **2660**

0077-8605 *See* TRANSACTIONS OF THE NEW ORLEANS ACADEMY OF OPHTHALMOLOGY. **3879**

0077-8699 *See* MEMOIRS OF THE GEOLOGICAL SURVEY OF NEW SOUTH WALES. PALAEONTOLOGY. **4228**

0077-8737 *See* MINERAL RESOURCES. **2144**

0077-8842 *See* NEW TESTAMENT TOOLS AND STUDIES. **5018**

0077-8877 *See* NEW TRENDS IN BIOLOGY TEACHING. **467**

0077-8893 *See* NEW TRENDS IN MATHEMATICS TEACHING. **3524**

0077-8915 *See* PAPERS OF THE NEW WORLD ARCHAEOLOGICAL FOUNDATION. **278**

0077-8923 *See* ANNALS OF THE NEW YORK ACADEMY OF SCIENCES. **5083**

0077-8931 *See* MEMOIRS OF THE NEW YORK BOTANICAL GARDEN. **517**

0077-8958 *See* METROPOLITAN MUSEUM JOURNAL. **4091**

0077-9008 *See* MONOGRAPH - NEW YORK PSYCHOANALYTIC INSTITUTE. ERNST KRIS STUDY GROUP. **4604**

0077-9024 *See* NEW YORK PUBLICITY OUTLETS. **763**

0077-9156 *See* RESEARCH BULLETIN - NEW YORK (STATE). DEPT. OF COMMERCE. **850**

0077-9296 *See* CHECKLIST OF OFFICIAL PUBLICATIONS OF THE STATE OF NEW YORK, A. **413**

0077-9334 *See* NEW YORK STATE STATISTICAL YEARBOOK. **5334**

0077-9504 *See* STUDIES IN COMPARATIVE LITERATURE. **3441**

0077-961X *See* DSIR BULLETIN. **5102**

0077-9636 *See* DSIR INFORMATION SERIES. **5102**

0077-9644 *See* BULLETIN - NEW ZEALAND. SOIL BUREAU. **69**

0077-9954 *See* NEW ZEALAND ECONOMIC PAPERS. **1507**

0077-9962 *See* NEW ZEALAND ENTOMOLOGIST, THE. **5592**

0077-9970 *See* NEW ZEALAND FICTION. **3416**

0078-0022 *See* MISCELLANEOUS SERIES - NEW ZEALAND GEOGRAPHICAL SOCIETY. **2569**

0078-0251 *See* PROCEEDINGS OF THE UNIVERSITY OF NEWCASTLE-UPON-TYNE PHILOSOPHICAL SOCIETY. **4358**

0078-0316 *See* NEWFOUNDLAND MEDICAL DIRECTORY. **3916**

0078-0332 *See* NEWFOUNDLAND SOCIAL AND ECONOMIC PAPERS. **5211**

0078-0421 *See* NEWSLETTERS ON STRATIGRAPHY. **1389**

0078-0537 *See* NIEDERDEUTSCHE BEITRAEGE ZUR KUNSTGESCHICHTE. **360**

0078-0545 *See* NIEDERDEUTSCHES WORT. **3306**

0078-0561 *See* NIEDERSACHSISCHES JAHRBUCH FUER LANDESGESCHICHTE. **2624**

0078-0626 *See* ANNUAL ABSTRACT OF STATISTICS - NIGERIA. FEDERAL OFFICE OF STATISTICS. **5321**

0078-0685 *See* NIGERIA YEAR BOOK. **2500**

0078-0774 *See* NIGERIAN LAW JOURNAL, THE. **3017**

0078-0839 *See* NIHON DAIGAKU NOJUIGAKUBU GAKUJUTSU KENKYU HOKOKU. **113**

0078-0936 *See* NOCTES ROMANAE. **4353**

0078-0944 *See* REPORT OF THE NODA INSTITUTE FOR SCIENTIFIC RESEARCH. **493**

0078-0952 *See* NOMENCLATOR ZOOLOGICUS. **5593**

0078-0987 *See* NON-FERROUS METAL WORKS OF THE WORLD. **4013**

0078-1037 *See* NORDELBINGEN. **360**

0078-1045 *See* NORDFRIESISCHES JAHRBUCH. **2700**

0078-1053 *See* COLLECTION NORDICANA. **451**

0078-107X *See* NORDISK NUMISMATISK ARSSKRIFT. SCANDINAVIAN NUMISMATIC JOURNAL. **2782**

0078-1088 *See* YEARBOOK OF NORDIC STATISTICS. **5346**

0078-1193 *See* PUBLIKASJON - NORGES GEOTEKNISKE INSTITUTT. **1392**

0078-1266 *See* NORSK LITTERR ARBOK. **3418**

0078-1304 *See* NORTH AMERICAN FAUNA. **5593**

0078-1312 *See* NORTH AMERICAN FLORA. **520**

0078-1347 *See* NORTH AMERICAN RADIO-TV STATION GUIDE. **1135**

0078-1355 *See* TRANSACTIONS OF THE ... NORTH AMERICAN WILDLIFE AND NATURAL RESOURCES CONFERENCE. **2207**

0078-1444 See STUDENT PUBLICATION OF THE SCHOOL OF DESIGN. 309

0078-1525 See REPORT / WATER RESOURCES RESEARCH INSTITUTE OF THE UNIVERSITY OF NORTH CAROLINA. 5538

0078-1576 See MISCELLANEOUS SERIES (NORTH DAKOTA GEOLOGICAL SURVEY). 1388

0078-1630 See NORTH QUEENSLAND NATURALIST. 4169

0078-1681 See NORTHEAST FOLKLORE. 2323

0078-1703 See PROCEEDINGS OF THE ... ANNUAL MEETING OF THE NORTHEASTERN WEED SCIENCE SOCIETY. 2180

0078-172X See NORTHERN HISTORY. 2624

0078-1789 See NORTHWEST HISTORICAL SERIES. 2751

0078-1797 See PROCEEDINGS OF THE ANNUAL NORTHWEST WOOD PRODUCTS CLINIC. 2403

0078-1886 See INDUSTRISTATISTIKK. HEFTE 1, NRINGSTALL. 5328

0078-1924 See KONOMISK UTSYN. 1535

0078-1932 See STATISTISK ARBOK. 5343

0078-1983 See NORWEGIAN-AMERICAN STUDIES. 2751

0078-2009 See NOTAS DE ALGEBRA Y ANALISIS. 3524

0078-2092 See PROCEEDINGS OF THE EASTER SCHOOL IN AGRICULTURAL SCIENCE, UNIVERSITY OF NOTTINGHAM. 122

0078-2122 See NOTTINGHAM MEDIEVAL STUDIES. 2624

0078-2149 See RAPPORT SCIENTIFIQUE - INSTITUT FRANCAIS D'OCEANIE, SECTION OCEANOGRAPHIE. 1455

0078-2238 See BEIHEFTE ZUR NOVA HEDWIGIA. 501

0078-2505 See ANNUAL REPORT - TUBERCULOSIS CONTROL SERVICES, NOVA SCOTIA. 3948

0078-2521 See PROCEEDINGS OF THE NOVA SCOTIAN INSTITUTE OF SCIENCE. 5141

0078-2610 See BUYER'S GUIDE (HINSDALE, ILL.). 2154

0078-2653 See NURNBERGER FORSCHUNGEN. 2701

0078-2696 See NUMISMATIC CHRONICLE. 2782

0078-2718 See NUMISMATIC NOTES AND MONOGRAPHS (NEW YORK). 2782

0078-2904 See ANNUAL REPORT / OAK RIDGE ASSOCIATED UNIVERSITIES. 4446

0078-2947 See JAHRESBERICHTE UND MITTEILUNGEN DES OBERRHEINISCHEN GEOLOGISCHEN VEREINES. 1384

0078-298X See OBSTETRICS & GYNECOLOGY (NEW YORK. 1970). 3766

0078-3005 See OCCASIONAL PAPERS IN ANTHROPOLOGY. 242

0078-303X See OCCASIONAL PAPERS - DEPT. OF ENGLISH LOCAL HISTORY, LEICESTER UNIVERSITY. 2701

0078-3129 See OCCUPATIONAL SAFETY AND HEALTH SERIES. 2867

0078-3137 See OCEAN ENGINEERING INFORMATION SERIES. 2094

0078-317X See DOCKET SERIES. 2963

0078-3188 See OCEANIC LINGUISTICS. SPECIAL PUBLICATION. 3308

0078-320X See INVESTIGATIONAL REPORT - OCEANOGRAPHIC RESEARCH INSTITUTE (DURBAN). 555

0078-3218 See OCEANOGRAPHY AND MARINE BIOLOGY. 1454

0078-3234 See OCEANOLOGIA. 1454

0078-3250 See OCHRONA PRZYRODY. 4170

0078-3293 See ODENSE UNIVERSITY STUDIES IN ENGLISH. 3308

0078-3307 See STUDIES IN HISTORY AND SOCIAL SCIENCES. 2631

0078-3315 See STUDIES IN LINGUISTICS. 3326

0078-3323 See STUDIES IN LITERATURE (ODENSE). 3442

0078-3374 See O'DWYER'S DIRECTORY OF PUBLIC RELATIONS FIRMS. 763

0078-3579 See JAHRESHEFTE DES OSTERREICHISCHEN ARCHAOLOGISCHEN INSTITUTES IN WIEN. 271

0078-3633 See OSTERREICHISCHES JAHRBUCH FUER EXLIBRIS UND GEBRAUCHSGRAPHIK. 361

0078-3714 See OFFA. 2520

0078-3838 See OFFICIAL BASEBALL GUIDE. 4909

0078-3846 See OFFICIAL BASEBALL RULES. 4909

0078-3854 See OFFICIAL CATHOLIC DIRECTORY, THE. 5013

0078-3951 See RESEARCH BULLETIN / OHIO AGRICULTURAL RESEARCH AND DEVELOPMENT CENTER. 127

0078-3986 See BIOLOGICAL NOTES (COLUMBUS). 445

0078-3994 See BULLETIN OF THE OHIO BIOLOGICAL SURVEY. 450

0078-4052 See OHIO SPEECH JOURNAL, THE. 1119

0078-4303 See PROCEEDINGS OF THE OKLAHOMA ACADEMY OF SCIENCE. 5141

0078-432X See BULLETIN OF THE OKLAHOMA ANTHROPOLOGICAL SOCIETY. 233

0078-4389 See BULLETIN / OKLAHOMA GEOLOGICAL SURVEY. 1370

0078-4397 See CIRCULAR (OKLAHOMA GEOLOGICAL SURVEY). 1372

0078-4400 See GUIDE BOOK / OKLAHOMA GEOLOGICAL SURVEY. 1381

0078-4516 See OLD FARMER'S ALMANAC, THE. 1927

0078-463X See ONOMA. 3308

0078-4648 See ONOMASTICA (WROCAW). 2571

0078-4656 See ONOMASTICA CANADIANA. 3308

0078-4672 See ONTARIO ARCHAEOLOGY. 277

0078-4834 See ONTARIO FIELD BIOLOGIST, THE. 467

0078-4850 See ONTARIO GEOGRAPHY. 2571

0078-4923 See CURRICULUM SERIES. 1892

0078-5016 See MONOGRAPH SERIES - ONTARIO INSTITUTE FOR STUDIES IN EDUCATION. 1764

0078-5040 See ANNUAL CONFERENCE / THE ONTARIO PETROLEUM INSTITUTE. 4249

0078-5172 See OPEN DOORS (NEW YORK). 1796

0078-5237 See OPERA BOTANICA. 520

0078-5326 See OPHELIA. 556

0078-5342 See BULLETIN. 3873

0078-5458 See OPPORTUNITIES ABROAD FOR TEACHERS. 1902

0078-5466 See OPTICA APPLICATA. 4438

0078-5520 See OPUSCULA ATHENIENSIA. 1078

0078-5555 See ORBIS ANTIQUUS. 1078

0078-5679 See OREGON SCHOOL DIRECTORY. 1770

0078-5792 See OREGON STATE MONOGRAPHS. STUDIES IN EDUCATION AND GUIDANCE. 1770

0078-6071 See UNIVERSITY OF OREGON ANTHROPOLOGICAL PAPERS. 247

0078-6152 See ORGANIC PHOTOCHEMISTRY (NEW YORK). 1045

0078-6179 See ORGANIC REACTIONS. 1045

0078-6209 See ORGANIC SYNTHESES. 1045

0078-6217 See ORGANIC SYNTHESES. COLLECTIVE VOLUME. 1045

0078-6225 See ORGANISCHE CHEMIE IN EINZELDARSTELLUNGEN. 1045

0078-6241 See REVIEW OF FISHERIES IN OECD MEMBER COUNTRIES. 2311

0078-639x See REUNIONES BIBLIOTECOLOGICAS. 3246

0078-6403 See ANNUAL REPORT OF THE SECRETARY GENERAL TO THE GENERAL ASSEMBLY. 3123

0078-6500 See ORGANON. 5136

0078-6527 See ORIENS. 2661

0078-6578 See ORIENTALIA SUECANA. 2661

0078-6594 See ORNITHOLOGICAL MONOGRAPHS. 5619

0078-6608 See ORTHODONTIE FRANCAISE, L'. 1332

0078-6659 See MEMOIRS OF THE FACULTY OF ENGINEERING, OSAKA CITY UNIVERSITY. 1987

0078-6780 See REPORT - INSTITUTE OF THEORETICAL ASTROPHYSICS. 4419

0078-6845 See OSTBAIRISCHE GRENZMARKEN. 327

0078-6888 See OSTEUROPASTUDIEN DER HOCHSCHULEN DES LANDES HESSEN. REIHE I, GIESSENER ABHANDLUNGEN ZUR AGRAR- UND WIRTSCHAFTSFORSCHUNG DES EUROPAISCHEN OSTENS. 118

0078-6918 See OTAGO LAW REVIEW. 3024

0078-7191 See OXFORD GERMAN STUDIES. 3421

0078-7256 See OXFORD SLAVONIC PAPERS. 3336

0078-740X See PACIFIC ANTHROPOLOGICAL RECORDS. 243

0078-7442 See TRANSACTIONS OF THE PACIFIC COAST OBSTETRICAL AND GYNECOLOGICAL SOCIETY. 3769

0078-7469 See PACIFIC COAST PHILOLOGY. 3421

0078-754X See PACIFIC LINGUISTICS. SERIES B: MONOGRAPHS. 3309

0078-7558 See PACIFIC LINGUISTICS. SERIES C: BOOKS. 3309

0078-7566 See PACIFIC LINGUISTICS. SERIES D: SPECIAL PUBLICATIONS. 3309

0078-7582 See BULLETIN / PACIFIC MARINE FISHERIES COMMISSION. 2298

0078-7760 See QUADERNI PER LA STORIA DELL'UNIVERSITA DI PADOVA. 1843

0078-7795 See PAEDIATRISCHE FORTBILDUNGSKURSE FUER DIE PRAXIS. 3907

0078-7809 See PAIDEUMA (WIESBADEN). 243

0078-7817 See POLYMERS PAINT COLOUR YEAR BOOK. 4225

0078-7868 See PAKISTAN ARCHAEOLOGY. 277

0078-7892 See PAKISTAN -- BASIC FACTS. 4740

0078-8023 See PAKISTAN STATISTICAL YEARBOOK. 5335

0078-8163 See RECORDS OF THE GEOLOGICAL SURVEY OF PAKISTAN. 1393

0078-852X See PAKISTAN'S BALANCE OF PAYMENTS. 802

0078-8546 See PALAEONTOGRAPHICA AMERICANA. 4229

0078-8554 See PALAEONTOLOGIA AFRICANA. 4229

0078-8562 See PALAEONTOLOGIA POLONICA. 4229

0078-8597 See MEMOIR / THE PALEONTOLOGICAL SOCIETY. 4228

0078-866X See PAMIETNIK SOWIANSKI. 3309

0078-9062 See PAPERS IN AUSTRALIAN LINGUISTICS. 3309

0078-9127 See PAPERS IN LINGUISTICS OF MELANESIA. 3309

0078-9143 See PAPERS IN PHILIPPINE LINGUISTICS. 3309

0078-9178 See PAPERS IN SOUTH EAST ASIAN LINGUISTICS. 3309

0078-9402 See PAPYROLOGICA BRUXELLENSIA. 3422

0078-9410 See PAPYROLOGICA COLONIENSIA. 2702

0078-9410 See ABHANDLUNGEN DER RHEINISCH-WESTFAELISCHEN AKADEMIE DER WISSENSCHAFTEN. SONDERREIHE PAPYROLOGICA COLONIENSIA. 5079

0078-9437 See PARAPSYCHOLOGICAL MONOGRAPHS. 4242

0078-947X See STATISTIQUES DE TRAFIC : GRANDS AEROPORTS DE L'OUEST DE L'EUROPE. 42

0078-9585 See ETUDES ET MEMOIRES. 5469

0078-9747 See MEMOIRES DU MUSEUM NATIONAL D'HISTOIRE NATURELLE. SERIE A, ZOOLOGIE. 5591

ISSN Index

0078-9747 See MEMOIRES DU MUSEUM NATIONAL D'HISTOIRE NATURELLE. **4167**

0078-9755 See MEMOIRES DU MUSEUM NATIONAL D'HISTOIRE NATURELLE. **4167**

0078-9976 See BIBLIOTHEQUE RUSSE DE L'INSTITUT D'ETUDES SLAVES. **3367**

0079-001X See TEXTES PUBLIES PAR L'INSTITUT D'ETUDES SLAVES. **3328**

0079-0028 See TRAVAUX. **2713**

0079-0184 See PATHOLOGY ANNUAL. **3897**

0079-0230 See PATTERSON'S AMERICAN EDUCATION. **1772**

0079-0303 See PAPERS OF THE PEABODY MUSEUM OF ARCHAEOLOGY AND ETHNOLOGY, HARVARD UNIVERSITY. **278**

0079-032X See BULLETIN - PEABODY MUSEUM OF NATURAL HISTORY. **4164**

0079-0370 See PAEDAGOGICA BELGICA ACADEMICA. **1839**

0079-0400 See PEDIATRICS (NEW YORK, N.Y.). **3910**

0079-0419 See PEDOLOGIE. **181**

0079-0435 See MARINE RESEARCH IN INDONESIA. **556**

0079-063X See RESEARCH PUBLICATION. **2203**

0079-0737 See PEOPLES' APPALACHIA. **1578**

0079-0745 See PROCEEDINGS OF THE PEORIA ACADEMY OF SCIENCE. **4170**

0079-0893 See PERSICA. **2662**

0079-0958 See PERSPECTA. **305**

0079-1040 See PERSPECTIVES IN SOCIAL WORK. **5253**

0079-1091 See BOLETIN DE LA SOCIEDAD GEOLOGICA DEL PERU. **1367**

0079-1342 See PFLANZENSCHUTZ NACHRICHTEN. **181**

0079-1350 See PHAENOMENOLOGICA. **4355**

0079-1393 See PHARMACEUTICAL HISTORIAN. **4320**

0079-1466 See PHILIPPINE SCIENTIST, THE. **557**

0079-1628 See PHILOLOGICAL MONOGRAPHS. **3310**

0079-1636 See TRANSACTIONS OF THE PHILOLOGICAL SOCIETY. **3329**

0079-1679 See PHILOSOPHES MEDIEVAUX. **4355**

0079-1687 See PHILOSOPHIA ANTIQUA. **4355**

0079-1849 See PHOTOGRAPHY ANNUAL. **4374**

0079-192X See PHYSICIAN'S HANDBOOK. **3627**

0079-1938 See PHYSICS AND CHEMISTRY IN SPACE. **4415**

0079-1946 See PHYSICS AND CHEMISTRY OF THE EARTH. **1359**

0079-2020 See MONOGRAPHS OF THE PHYSIOLOGICAL SOCIETY. **584**

0079-2047 See PHYTON (HORN). **522**

0079-2071 See PILOT STUDIES APPROVED FOR STATE AID IN PUBLIC SCHOOL SYSTEMS IN VIRGINIA. **1902**

0079-2098 See PIONEER HERITAGE SERIES, THE. **2754**

0079-2357 See PLENUM PRESS HANDBOOKS OF HIGH-TEMPERATURE MATERIALS. **4015**

0079-2608 See MALY ROCZNIK STATYSTYCZNY. **5332**

0079-2640 See ROCZNIK STATYSTYCZNY FINANSOW. **4747**

0079-2667 See ROCZNIK STATYSTYCZNY GOSPODARKI MORSKIEJ. **4182**

0079-2985 See POLISH JOURNAL OF SOIL SCIENCE. **182**

0079-2993 See POLISH PSYCHOLOGICAL BULLETIN. **4608**

0079-3183 See SREDNIOWIECZE. **2710**

0079-3205 See PRACE INSTYTUTU MASZYN PRZEPYWOWYCH. **2125**

0079-323X See SCIENTIFIC ACTIVITIES OF THE POLISH ACADEMY OF SCIENCES, INSTITUTE OF FUNDAMENTAL TECHNOLOGICAL RESEARCH. **5155**

0079-3302 See POCZNIK KOMISJI HISTORYCZNOLITERACKIEJ. **3424**

0079-3310 See PRACE KOMISJI JEZYKOZNAWSTWA / POLSKA AKADEMIA NAUK--ODDZIA W KRAKOWIE. **3311**

0079-3450 See TEKA KOMISJI URBANISTYKI I ARCHITEKTURY. **309**

0079-3566 See ETUDES ET TRAVAUX - CENTRE D'ARCHEOLOGIE MEDITERRANEENNE DE L'ACADEMIE POLONAISE DES SCIENCES. **268**

0079-3620 See POLSKA 2000 / KOMITET BADAN I PROGNOZ "POLSKA 2000" POLSKIEJ AKADEMII NAUK. **2703**

0079-3663 See ROCZNIK POLSKIEGO TOWARZYSTWA GEOLOGICZNEGO. **1395**

0079-3701 See MECHANIKA TEORETYCZNA I STOSOWANA. **4429**

0079-4082 See REVISTA DO CENTRO DE ESTUDOS DEMOGRAFICOS. **4560**

0079-418X See ESTATISTICA INDUSTRIAL (LISBOA). **1532**

0079-421X See PORTUGIESISCHE FORSCHUNGEN DER GORRESGESELLSCHAFT. ERSTE REIHE, AUFSATZE. **2703**

0079-4236 See POST-MEDIEVAL ARCHAEOLOGY. **278**

0079-4252 See POSTEPY MIKROBIOLOGII. **568**

0079-4295 See POSTILLA. **4170**

0079-4376 See VEROFFENTLICHUNGEN DES MUSEUMS FUER UR- UND FRUHGESCHICHTE POTSDAM. **285**

0079-4570 See BULLETIN DE LA SOCIETE DES AMIS DES SCIENCES ET DES LETTRES DE POZNAN. SERIE D. SCIENCES BIOLOGIQUES. **449**

0079-466X See PRACE KOMISJI HISTORII SZTUKI. POZNANSKIE TOWARZYSTWO PRZYJACIO NAUK. **2626**

0079-4678 See PRACE KOMISJI JEZYKOZNAWCZEJ. **3311**

0079-4708 See PRACE KOMISJI NAUK ROLNICZYCH I KOMISJI NAUK LESNYCH. **121**

0079-4740 See LINGUA POSNANIENSIS. **3298**

0079-4791 See PRACE POLONISTYCZNE. **3424**

0079-4848 See PRAEHISTORISCHE ZEITSCHRIFT. **243**

0079-4856 See PRAGUE STUDIES IN MATHEMATICAL LINGUISTICS. **3527**

0079-4929 See PRAVNEHISTORICKE STUDIE. **2703**

0079-497X See PROCEEDINGS OF THE PREHISTORIC SOCIETY. **243**

0079-4988 See PREPARATIVE INORGANIC REACTIONS. **1037**

0079-4996 See ACTS AND PROCEEDINGS OF THE GENERAL ASSEMBLY OF THE PRESBYTERIAN CHURCH IN CANADA. **5054**

0079-5194 See PRINCETON MATHEMATICAL SERIES. **3527**

0079-5208 See PRINCETON MONOGRAPHS IN ART AND ARCHEOLOGY. **362**

0079-5240 See PRINCETON STUDIES IN MATHEMATICAL ECONOMICS. **1513**

0079-5259 See PRINCETON STUDIES IN MUSIC. **4147**

0079-5321 See JOURNAL OF THE PRINTING HISTORICAL SOCIETY. **3292**

0079-5399 See PRIVATE INDEPENDENT SCHOOLS. **1774**

0079-5445 See PRIZE COLLEGE STORIES. **3425**

0079-5453 See PRIZE STORIES. **3425**

0079-5607 See PROBABILITY AND MATHEMATICAL STATISTICS (NEW YORK, N.Y.). **3527**

0079-578X See PROBLEMY EKONOMICZNE. **1513**

0079-5836 See PRODEI. **3486**

0079-6050 See PROGRESS IN ASTRONAUTICS AND AERONAUTICS. **32**

0079-6085 See PROGRESS IN BIOCHEMICAL PHARMACOLOGY. **4326**

0079-6107 See PROGRESS IN BIOPHYSICS AND MOLECULAR BIOLOGY. **496**

0079-6123 See PROGRESS IN BRAIN RESEARCH. **3844**

0079-6255 See PROGRESS IN EXPERIMENTAL PERSONALITY AND PSYCHOPATHOLOGY RESEARCH. **3932**

0079-6263 See PROGRESS IN EXPERIMENTAL TUMOR RESEARCH. **3822**

0079-6271 See PROGRESS IN GASTROENTEROLOGY. **3747**

0079-6336 See PROGRESS IN HISTOCHEMISTRY AND CYTOCHEMISTRY. **540**

0079-6352 See PROGRESS IN INDUSTRIAL MICROBIOLOGY (AMSTERDAM, NETHERLANDS). **568**

0079-6379 See PROGRESS IN INORGANIC CHEMISTRY. **1037**

0079-6417 See PROGRESS IN LOW TEMPERATURE PHYSICS. **4418**

0079-6425 See PROGRESS IN MATERIALS SCIENCE. **2107**

0079-645X See PROGRESS IN MEDICAL VIROLOGY. **569**

0079-6468 See PROGRESS IN MEDICINAL CHEMISTRY. **990**

0079-6484 See PROGRESS IN MOLECULAR AND SUBCELLULAR BIOLOGY. **470**

0079-6565 See PROGRESS IN NUCLEAR MAGNETIC RESONANCE SPECTROSCOPY. **4450**

0079-6603 See PROGRESS IN NUCLEIC ACID RESEARCH AND MOLECULAR BIOLOGY. **470**

0079-6611 See PROGRESS IN OCEANOGRAPHY. **1455**

0079-6638 See PROGRESS IN OPTICS. **4440**

0079-6654 See PROGRESS IN PEDIATRIC SURGERY. **3911**

0079-6662 See PROGRESS IN PHYSICAL ORGANIC CHEMISTRY. **1046**

0079-6700 See PROGRESS IN POLYMER SCIENCE. **1047**

0079-6719 See ANNUAL POWDER METALLURGY CONFERENCE PROCEEDINGS. **3998**

0079-6727 See PROGRESS IN QUANTUM ELECTRONICS. **2077**

0079-6743 See PROGRESS IN REACTION KINETICS. **1057**

0079-6751 See PROGRESS IN RESPIRATION RESEARCH. **3951**

0079-6786 See PROGRESS IN SOLID STATE CHEMISTRY. **1057**

0079-6816 See PROGRESS IN SURFACE SCIENCE. **1057**

0079-6824 See PROGRESS IN SURGERY. **3972**

0079-6921 See PROGRESSIVE GROCER'S MARKETING GUIDEBOOK. **935**

0079-7030 See PROTECTIVE COATINGS ON METALS. **4017**

0079-7138 See PRZEGLAD ARCHEOLOGICZNY. **279**

0079-7189 See PRZESZOSC DEMOGRAFICZNA POLSKI. **2271**

0079-7227 See PSYCHIATRIA FENNICA. **3933**

0079-726X See PSYCHIATRIE DE L'ENFANT, LA. **3933**

0079-7294 See PSYCHOANALYTIC STUDY OF SOCIETY. **5214**

0079-7308 See PSYCHOANALYTIC STUDY OF THE CHILD, THE. **4610**

0079-7413 See PSYCHOLOGISCHE PRAXIS. **4612**

0079-7421 See PSYCHOLOGY OF LEARNING AND MOTIVATION, THE. **4613**

0079-7626 See PUBLIC PAPERS OF THE PRESIDENTS OF THE UNITED STATES. **4676**

0079-7758 See SAVANNA RESEARCH SERIES. **2575**

0079-7790 See PUBLICATIONS ON RUSSIA AND EASTERN EUROPE. **4492**

0079-7812 See PUBLICATIONS ROMANES ET FRANCAISES. **3426**

0079-7855 See PUBLISHERS' TRADE LIST ANNUAL, THE. **4822**

0079-7960 See ANNUAL REPORT - PULP AND PAPER RESEARCH INSTITUTE OF CANADA. **4232**

0079-8169 See PURE AND APPLIED MATHEMATICS (NEW YORK. 1949). **3529**

0079-8177 See PURE AND APPLIED MATHEMATICS. 3529

0079-8193 See PURE AND APPLIED PHYSICS. 4418

0079-8215 See PYRENAE. 279

0079-8258 See QUADERNI DI ARCHEOLOGIA DELLA LIBIA. 279

0079-8339 See TRAVAUX ET DOCUMENTS. 2763

0079-869X See REPERTOIRE DES MUNICIPALITES DU QUEBEC. 4679

0079-8797 See QUEEN'S PAPERS IN PURE AND APPLIED MATHEMATICS. 3530

0079-8835 See MEMOIRS OF THE QUEENSLAND MUSEUM. 4167

0079-8843 See QUEENSLAND NATURALIST. 4171

0079-8916 See PAPERS - QUEENSLAND. UNIVERSITY, BRISBANE. DEPT. OF ENTOMOLOGY. 5594

0079-8932 See PAPERS (UNIVERSITY OF QUEENSLAND. DEPT. OF GEOLOGY). 1390

0079-905X See QUELLENKATALOGE ZUR MUSIKGESCHICHTE. 4148

0079-9068 See QUELLEN UND FORSCHUNGEN AUS ITALIENISCHEN ARCHIVEN UND BIBLIOTHEKEN. 2627

0079-9114 See QUELLEN UND STUDIEN ZUR GESCHICHTE OSTEUROPAS. 2704

0079-9300 See OECUMENE : INTERNATIONAL BIBLIOGRAPHY 1975- INDEXED BY COMPUTER ; BIBLIOGRAPHIE INTERNATIONALE 1975- ETABLIE PAR ORDINATEUR. 421

0079-9335 See R L S, REGIONAL LANGUAGE STUDIES ... NEWFOUNDLAND. 3313

0079-9548 See RTR. RAILWAY TECHNICAL REVIEW. 5436

0079-9602 See RANCHI UNIVERSITY MATHEMATICAL JOURNAL. 3530

0079-9734 See RASSEGNA ITALIANA DI SOCIOLOGIA. 5255

0079-9890 See REAL ESTATE REPORT (STORR, CONN.). 4845

0079-9920 See RECENT ADVANCES IN PHYTOCHEMISTRY. 526

0079-9947 See RECENT DEVELOPMENTS IN THE CHEMISTRY OF NATURAL CARBON COMPOUNDS. 1047

0079-9955 See RECENT DEVELOPMENTS OF NEUROBIOLOGY IN HUNGARY. 3844

0079-9963 See RECENT PROGRESS IN HORMONE RESEARCH. 3733

0080-0015 See RECENT RESULTS IN CANCER RESEARCH. 3823

0080-0139 See VIE MUSICALE EN FRANCE SOUS LES ROIS BOURBONS. 2EME SERIE. RECHERCHES SUR LA MUSIQUE FRANCAISE CLASSIQUE, LA. 4158

0080-0163 See RECHTS- UND STAATSWISSENSCHAFTEN. 4493

0080-0260 See RECONSTRUCTION SURGERY AND TRAUMATOLOGY. 3973

0080-0287 See RECORDS OF CIVILIZATION, SOURCES AND STUDIES. 2627

0080-0325 See RECUEIL DES HISTORIENS DE LA FRANCE. OBITUAIRES. 434

0080-0473 See REFORMATIONSGESCHICHTLICHE STUDIEN UND TEXTE. 5035

0080-049X See REFRACTORY MATERIALS. 2149

0080-0619 See BIBLIOGRAPHY SERIES - REGIONAL SCIENCE RESEARCH INSTITUTE. 1530

0080-0627 See MONOGRAPH SERIES - REGIONAL SCIENCE RESEARCH INSTITUTE. 1506

0080-0694 See REGNUM VEGETABLE. 526

0080-0791 See REINE UND ANGEWANDTE METALLKUNDE IN EINZELDARSTELLUNGEN. 1993

0080-0821 See PROCEEDINGS - RELIABILITY PHYSICS SYMPOSIUM. 2077

0080-0848 See RELIGION AND REASON. 4990

0080-0953 See BIBLIOGRAPHY OF THE HISTORY OF ART : BHA. 334

0080-1348 See REPORTS AND PAPERS IN THE SOCIAL SCIENCES. 5215

0080-1356 See REPORTS AND PAPERS ON MASS COMMUNICATION. 1120

0080-1437 See REQUIREMENTS FOR TEACHING CERTIFICATES IN CANADA. 1778

0080-1461 See UNIQUE 3-IN-1 RESEARCH & DEVELOPMENT DIRECTORY. 5167

0080-1518 See RESEARCH CENTERS DIRECTORY. 3634

0080-178X See OCCASIONAL PAPER - RESERVE BANK OF AUSTRALIA. 732

0080-1844 See RESULTS AND PROBLEMS IN CELL DIFFERENTIATION. 540

0080-2050 See VOPROSY TEORII PLAZMY. 4424

0080-2085 See REVISTA CARTOGRAFICA. 2583

0080-2115 See REVISTA DE BIOLOGIA MARINA. 557

0080-2425 See REVISTA PERUANA DE ENTOMOLOGIA. 5613

0080-2484 See REVUE BIBLIOGRAPHIQUE DE SINOLOGIE. 2857

0080-2492 See REVUE CANADIENNE DE PSYCHO-EDUCATION. 1780

0080-2530 See REVUE DES ARCHEOLOGUES ET HISTORIENS D'ART DE LOUVAIN. 281

0080-2549 See REVUE DES ETUDES ARMENIENNES (PARIS). 2663

0080-2557 See REVUE DES ETUDES SLAVES. 2706

0080-259X See REVUE EGYPTIENNE DE DROIT INTERNATIONAL. 3135

0080-2603 See REVUE HITTITE ET ASIANIQUE. 2663

0080-262X See REVUE ROUMAINE D'HISTOIRE DE L'ART. SERIE BEAUX-ARTS. 330

0080-2654 See REVUE THEOLOGIQUE DE LOUVAIN. 4994

0080-2662 See RHEIN-MAINISCHE FORSCHUNGEN. 2575

0080-2670 See RHEINISCHE LEBENSBILDER. 2628

0080-2697 See RHEINISCHES JAHRBUCH FUER VOLKSKUNDE. 2324

0080-2727 See RHEUMATOLOGY. 3807

0080-2808 See LAW OF THE SEA INSTITUTE: OCCASIONAL PAPERS. 1451

0080-2964 See RICERCHE SULLE DIMORE RURALI IN ITALIA. 308

0080-3073 See RINASCIMENTO. 2853

0080-312X See BOLETIM DO MUSEU NACIONAL. NOVA SERIE, ZOOLOGIA. 5578

0080-3235 See RIVISTA ARCHEOLOGICA DELLA PROVINCIA E ANTICA DIOCESI DI COMO. 281

0080-3243 See RIVISTA DI CHIRURGIA DELLA MANO. 3974

0080-3278 See PROCEEDINGS - ROAD BUILDERS CLINIC. 1992

0080-3375 See ROCK MECHANICS. SUPPLEMENT. 1994

0080-3383 See PROCEEDINGS OF THE ROCKBRIDGE HISTORICAL SOCIETY. 2755

0080-3421 See ROCZNIK BIAOSTOCKI. 2707

0080-3456 See ROCZNIK GDANSKI. 2707

0080-3472 See ROCZNIK HISTORII SZTUKI. 363

0080-3499 See ROCZNIK KRAKOWSKI. 2707

0080-3545 See ROCZNIK ORIENTALISTYCZNY. 2663

0080-3588 See ROCZNIK SLAWISTYCZNY. 3317

0080-360X See ROCZNIK WARSZAWSKI. 2707

0080-3634 See ROCZNIKI DZIEJOW SPOECZNYCH I GOSPODARCZYCH. 1582

0080-3642 See ROCZNIKI GLEBOZNAWCZE. 185

0080-3650 See ROCZNIKI NAUK ROLNICZYCH. SERIA A, PRODUKCJA ROSLINNA / KOMITET UPRAWY I HODOWLI ROSLIN POLSKIEJ AKADEMII NAUK. 130

0080-3650 See ROCZNIKI NAUK ROLNICZYCH. SERIA A. PRODUKCJA ROSLINNA. 130

0080-3669 See ROCZNIKI NAUK ROLNICZYCH. SERIA B. ZOOTECHNICZNA. 130

0080-3677 See ROCZNIKI NAUK ROLNICZYCH. SERIA C. TECHNIKA ROLNICZA. 130

0080-3693 See ROCZNIKI NAUK ROLNICZYCH. SERIA E: OCHRONA ROSLIN. 527

0080-3723 See ROCZNIKI NAUK ROLNICZYCH. SERIA H. RYBACTWO. 2312

0080-3790 See ROMISCHE HISTORISCHE MITTEILUNGEN. 2707

0080-3855 See ROMANICA GANDENSIA. 3318

0080-3863 See ROMANICA GOTHOBURGENSIA. 3318

0080-3871 See ROMANICA HELVETICA. 3318

0080-3898 See ROMANISTISCHES JAHRBUCH. 3318

0080-391X See ANNUARIO - INSTITUTO GIAPPONESE DI CULTURA IN ROMA. 2645

0080-3987 See STUDIA MISSIONALIA. 5000

0080-4134 See JOURNAL OF THE ROYAL AGRICULTURAL SOCIETY OF ENGLAND. 101

0080-4193 See OBSERVER'S HANDBOOK, THE. 397

0080-4290 See CATALOGUE OF THE EXHIBITION - ROYAL CANADIAN ACADEMY OF ARTS. 347

0080-4363 See SYMPOSIA OF THE ROYAL ENTOMOLOGICAL SOCIETY OF LONDON. 5613

0080-4398 See GUIDES AND HANDBOOKS. 2617

0080-4401 See TRANSACTIONS OF THE ROYAL HISTORICAL SOCIETY. 2713

0080-4436 See ROYAL INSTITUTE OF PHILOSOPHY LECTURES. 4360

0080-4576 See YEAR BOOK OF THE ROYAL SOCIETY OF EDINBURGH. 5237

0080-4584 See ESSAYS BY DIVERS HANDS. 3385

0080-4606 See BIOGRAPHICAL MEMOIRS OF FELLOWS OF THE ROYAL SOCIETY. 430

0080-4622 See PHILOSOPHICAL TRANSACTIONS. BIOLOGICAL SCIENCES. 468

0080-4673 See YEAR-BOOK OF THE ROYAL SOCIETY OF LONDON. 5237

0080-469X See PROCEEDINGS OF THE ROYAL SOCIETY OF QUEENSLAND. 5141

0080-4703 See PAPERS AND PROCEEDINGS OF THE ROYAL SOCIETY OF TASMANIA. 5137

0080-4711 See YEAR BOOK - ROYAL SOCIETY OF TROPICAL MEDICINE AND HYGIENE. 3987

0080-4800 See RUSTUNGSBESCHRANKUNG UND SICHERHEIT. 4056

0080-4967 See ANNUAL RESEARCH CONFERENCES OF THE BUREAU OF BIOLOGICAL RESEARCH, THE. 442

0080-4983 See MONOGRAPHS OF THE RUTGERS CENTER OF ALCOHOL STUDIES. 1346

0080-5076 See SOUTH AFRICAN FISHING INDUSTRY HANDBOOK AND BUYER'S GUIDE, THE. 2313

0080-5084 See SIAM-AMS PROCEEDINGS. 3534

0080-5165 See ANNALES UNIVERSITATIS SARAVIENSIS. REIHE : MATHEMATISCH-NATURWISSENSCHAFTLICHE FAKULTAT. 4162

0080-5180 See SAARBRUCKER BEITRAEGE ZUR ALTERTUMSKUNDE. 245

0080-5262 See JAHRBUCH - SACHSISCHE AKADEMIE DER WISSENSCHAFTEN ZU LEIPZIG. 1831

0080-5297 See ABHANDLUNGEN DER SACHSISCHEN AKADEMIE DER WISSENSCHAFTEN ZU LEIPZIG, PHILOLOGISCH-HISTORISCHE KLASSE. 2671

0080-5300 See SITZUNGSBERICHTE DER SAECHSISCHE AKADEMIE DER WISSENSCHAFTEN, LEIPZIG, PHILOLOGISCH-HISTORISCHE KLASSE. 3321

0080-5319 See SAECULUM. 2628

0080-5459 See FRANCISCAN STUDIES. 5029

0080-5696 See SALZBURGER JAHRBUCH FUER PHILOSOPHIE. 4360

0080-5718 See SALZBURGER STUDIEN ZUR ANGLISTIK UND AMERIKANISTIK. 3319

0080-5823 See SAMMLUNG GELTENDER STAATSANGEHARIGKEITSGESETZE. 3045

0080-6064 See SANKYO KENKYUJO NENPO. 5149

0080-6331 See BOLETIM DO INSTITUTO OCEANOGRAFICO. 553

0080-6552 *See* SPECIAL PUBLICATION - SASKATCHEWAN NATURAL HISTORY SOCIETY. 4172

0080-6560 *See* SASKATCHEWAN POETRY BOOK. 3470

0080-6668 *See* UNIVERSITY LECTURES - UNIVERSITY OF SASKATCHEWAN. 1852

0080-6684 *See* SATHER CLASSICAL LECTURES. 1080

0080-6714 *See* RESEARCH REPORT. 5215

0080-6757 *See* SCANDINAVIAN POLITICAL STUDIES. 4495

0080-6765 *See* SCANDO-SLAVICA. 3319

0080-6951 *See* SCHRIFTEN DER MONUMENTA GERMANIAE HISTORICA (DEUTSCHES INSTITUT FUR ERFORSCHUNG DES MITTELALTERS). 2708

0080-696X *See* SCHRIFTEN UND QUELLEN DER ALTEN WELT. 1080

0080-715X *See* SCHRIFTENREIHE NEUROLOGIE. 3845

0080-7168 *See* SCHRIFTENREIHE ZUR GESCHICHTE UND POLITISCHEN BILDUNG. 4495

0080-7176 *See* SCHRIFTTUM ZUR DEUTSCHEN KUNST. 334

0080-7214 *See* SCHWEIZER ANGLISTISCHE ARBEITEN. 3434

0080-7273 *See* SCHWEIZERISCHE BEITRAGE ZUR ALTERTUMSWISSENSCHAFT. 2629

0080-732X *See* SCHRIFTEN DER SCHWEIZERISCHEN GESELLSCHAFT FUER VOLKSKUNDE. 2324

0080-7389 *See* SCHWEIZERISCHE PALAEONTOLOGISCHE ABHANDLUNGEN. 4230

0080-7478 *See* ANNUAL REPORT - SCIENCE COUNCIL OF CANADA. 5084

0080-7575 *See* SCIENCE OF CERAMICS. 2594

0080-7621 *See* SCIENCE YEAR. 5154

0080-7915 *See* ANNUAL REPORT / SCOTTISH LAW COMMISSION. 2935

0080-8024 *See* SCOTTISH GAELIC STUDIES. 3319

0080-8083 *See* SCOTTISH LAW DIRECTORY FOR ..., THE. 3047

0080-8202 *See* SCOTTISH SEA FISHERIES STATISTICAL TABLES. 2317

0080-8369 *See* SCRIPTA HIEROSOLYMITANA : PUBLICATIONS OF THE HEBREW UNIVERSITY, JERUSALEM. 1847

0080-8474 *See* SECURITIES LAW REVIEW. 3103

0080-8504 *See* SEED TRADE BUYERS' GUIDE. 186

0080-8539 *See* SEIKEN ZIHO. 473

0080-8784 *See* SEMICONDUCTORS AND SEMIMETALS. 2080

0080-8857 *See* MICROFILMING PROJECTS NEWSLETTER. 3231

0080-889X *See* SENCKENBERGIANA MARITIMA. 1456

0080-9004 *See* SERIES ON ROCK AND SOIL MECHANICS. 1397

0080-9012 *See* SERIES PAEDOPSYCHIATRICA. 3936

0080-9128 *See* SHAKESPEARE JAHRBUCH. 3435

0080-9152 *See* SHAKESPEARE SURVEY (CAMBRIDGE). 434

0080-9233 *See* SHEPARD'S ACTS AND CASES BY POPULAR NAMES, FEDERAL AND STATE. 3048

0080-9284 *See* SHIPPING MARKS ON TIMBER. 5456

0080-9292 *See* SHIPS AND AIRCRAFT OF THE UNITED STATES FLEET, THE. 4057

0080-9365 *See* SHOOTER'S BIBLE, THE. 4917

0080-9462 *See* NATURAL HISTORY BULLETIN (BANGKOK). 4168

0080-9462 *See* NATURAL HISTORY BULLETIN OF THE SIAM SOCIETY. 4168

0080-9594 *See* SILESIA ANTIQUA. 2709

0080-9624 *See* SIND UNIVERSITY RESEARCH JOURNAL. SCIENCE SERIES. 5158

0080-9640 *See* SINGAPORE ACCOUNTANT, THE. 751

0080-9659 *See* SINGAPORE BOOK WORLD. 4832

0080-9705 *See* SINGAPORE LAW REVIEW. 3055

0080-9713 *See* SINGAPORE NATIONAL BIBLIOGRAPHY. 424

0080-9993 *See* SLAVIA ANTIQUA. 282

0081-0002 *See* SLAVIA OCCIDENTALIS. 3321

0081-007X *See* SLOVANSKE HISTORICKE STUDIE. 2709

0081-0169 *See* SMALL MARKETERS AIDS. 936

0081-0177 *See* SMALL MARKETERS AIDS. 851

0081-0223 *See* SMITHSONIAN CONTRIBUTIONS TO ANTHROPOLOGY. 245

0081-024X *See* SMITHSONIAN CONTRIBUTIONS TO BOTANY. 528

0081-0258 *See* SMITHSONIAN STUDIES IN HISTORY AND TECHNOLOGY. 2629

0081-0266 *See* SMITHSONIAN CONTRIBUTIONS TO PALEOBIOLOGY. 4230

0081-0274 *See* SMITHSONIAN CONTRIBUTIONS TO THE EARTH SCIENCES. 1360

0081-0282 *See* SMITHSONIAN CONTRIBUTIONS TO ZOOLOGY. 5597

0081-0304 *See* CIRCULAR - CENTRAL BUREAU FOR ASTRONOMICAL TELEGRAMS, INTERNATIONAL ASTRONOMICAL UNION. 394

0081-0363 *See* SMOKING AND HEALTH BULLETIN. 4803

0081-0606 *See* SOCIALIST REGISTER. 4547

0081-0657 *See* BOLETIM DA SOCIEDADE BROTERIANA. 502

0081-0665 *See* MEMORIAS DA SOCIEDADE BROTERIANA. 518

0081-0746 *See* BULLETIN DE LA SOCIETE BELGE D'OPHTALMOLOGIE. 3873

0081-0754 *See* BULLETIN - SOCIETE CHATEAUBRIAND. 3370

0081-0932 *See* BULLETIN DE LA SOCIETE D'ETUDES POUR LA CONNAISSANCE D'EDOUARD MANET. 1729

0081-0991 *See* BULLETIN OF THE ENTOMOLOGICAL SOCIETY OF EGYPT. ECONOMIC SERIES. 5579

0081-1092 *See* BULLETINS ET MEMOIRES. 3873

0081-1130 *See* TEXTES - SOCIETE HISTORIQUE DE QUEBEC. 2763

0081-1270 *See* BULLETIN DES SOCIETES D'OPHTALMOLOGIE DE FRANCE. 3873

0081-1297 *See* BULLETIN OF THE SOCIETY FOR AFRICAN CHURCH HISTORY, THE. 4941

0081-136X *See* MEMOIRS OF THE SOCIETY FOR ENDOCRINOLOGY. 3731

0081-1386 *See* SYMPOSIA OF THE SOCIETY FOR EXPERIMENTAL BIOLOGY. 474

0081-1440 *See* BOOK LIST / SOCIETY FOR OLD TESTAMENT STUDY. 5012

0081-1475 *See* PROCEEDINGS OF THE SOCIETY FOR PSYCHICAL RESEARCH. 4609

0081-1483 *See* PROCEEDINGS OF THE CONFERENCE - SOCIETY FOR THE ADVANCEMENT OF FOOD SERVICE RESEARCH. 2354

0081-1548 *See* SYMPOSIA OF THE SOCIETY FOR THE STUDY OF INBORN ERRORS OF METABOLISM. 3644

0081-1564 *See* PROCEEDINGS OF THE SOCIETY OF ANTIQUARIES OF SCOTLAND. 279

0081-1580 *See* KUPRIAKAI SPOUDAI. 2696

0081-1610 *See* TRANSACTIONS OF SHASE JAPAN. 2608

0081-1661 *See* TRANSACTIONS - THE SOCIETY OF NAVAL ARCHITECTS AND MARINE ENGINEERS. 4184

0081-1718 *See* TRANSACTIONS OF THE SPWLA ANNUAL LOGGING SYMPOSIUM. 4280

0081-1750 *See* SOCIOLOGICAL METHODOLOGY. 5260

0081-1769 *See* SOCIOLOGICAL REVIEW MONOGRAPH, THE. 5261

0081-1947 *See* SOLID STATE PHYSICS (NEW YORK. 1955). 4421

0081-1955 *See* SOLID STATE PHYSICS : ADVANCES IN RESEARCH AND APPLICATIONS. SUPPLEMENT. 4421

0081-2056 *See* SOMERSET ARCHAEOLOGY AND NATURAL HISTORY. 282

0081-2455 *See* SOUTH AFRICAN JOURNAL OF ANTARCTIC RESEARCH. 2576

0081-2463 *See* SOUTH AFRICAN JOURNAL OF PSYCHOLOGY. 4619

0081-2528 *See* ANNUAL ECONOMIC REPORT / SOUTH AFRICAN RESERVE BANK. 770

0081-2692 *See* STATE PLAN FOR CONSTRUCTION AND MODERNIZATION OF HOSPITAL AND MEDICAL FACILITIES (COLUMBIA). 3792

0081-2838 *See* INFORMATION DOCUMENT (SOUTH PACIFIC COMMISSION). 2620

0081-2862 *See* TECHNICAL PAPER - SOUTH PACIFIC COMMISSION. 2671

0081-2951 *See* SECOLAS ANNALS. 2760

0081-2994 *See* SOUTHERN ANTHROPOLOGICAL SOCIETY PROCEEDINGS. 245

0081-3028 *See* SOUTHERN BAPTIST PERIODICAL INDEX. 5013

0081-3052 *See* SOUTHERN JOURNAL OF AGRICULTURAL ECONOMICS. 136

0081-315X *See* SOUTHWESTERN STUDIES. 2762

0081-3222 *See* STUDIEN ZUR MUSIKWISSENSCHAFT. 4155

0081-3559 *See* SPECIAL PAPERS IN INTERNATIONAL ECONOMICS. 1640

0081-3699 *See* SPEZIELLE PATHOLOGISCHE ANATOMIE. 3898

0081-3826 *See* SPRACHE UND DICHTUNG. 3439

0081-3834 *See* SPRAWOZDANIA ARCHEOLOGICZNE. 283

0081-3869 *See* SPRINGER TRACTS IN MODERN PHYSICS. 4422

0081-3877 *See* SPRINGER TRACTS IN NATURAL PHILOSOPHY. 4361

0081-3966 *See* GLAS. ODELJENJE MEDICINSKIH NAUKA. 3579

0081-3974 *See* GLAS - SRPSKA ADADEMIJA NAUKA I UMETNOSTI. ODELJENJE TEHNICKIH NAUKA. 5108

0081-4148 *See* STADLER GENETICS SYMPOSIA. 551

0081-4229 *See* STANDARD DIRECTORY OF ADVERTISERS (GEOGRAPHICAL ED.). 766

0081-4369 *See* JOURNAL - STANSTEAD COUNTY HISTORICAL SOCIETY. 2743

0081-4423 *See* STATE-APPROVED SCHOOLS OF NURSING, L.P.N./L.V.N. 3869

0081-4431 *See* STATE-APPROVED SCHOOLS OF NURSING-R.N. 3869

0081-4466 *See* INDEX NUMBERS OF STOCK EXCHANGE SECURITIES. 901

0081-4474 *See* STATE CONSTITUTIONAL CONVENTION STUDIES. 4687

0081-4539 *See* STATE OF FOOD AND AGRICULTURE, THE. 137

0081-4601 *See* STATESMAN'S YEAR-BOOK, THE. 4497

0081-4679 *See* STATISTICAL ABSTRACT OF ISRAEL. 5339

0081-4687 *See* STATISTICAL ABSTRACT OF LATIN AMERICA. 5339

0081-4695 *See* STATISTICAL ABSTRACT OF LOUISIANA / COMPILED UNDER THE DIRECTION OF JAMES R. BOBO. 5339

0081-4741 *See* STATISTICAL ABSTRACT OF THE UNITED STATES. 5339

0081-4776 *See* JOURNAL OF THE STATISTICAL AND SOCIAL INQUIRY SOCIETY OF IRELAND. 5330

0081-4873 *See* BASIC STATISTICS OF THE COMMUNITY. 5323

0081-5020 *See* STATISTICAL RESEARCH MONOGRAPHS. 5340

0081-5330 *See* STATISTISCHES JAHRBUCH DER SCHWEIZ. 5343

0081-5349 *See* STATISTISCHES JAHRBUCH DEUTSCHER GEMEINDEN. 5343

0081-5381 *See* STATISTISK ARSBOK FOER SVERIGE. 5343

0081-542X *See* STEAM PASSENGER SERVICE DIRECTORY. 5437

0081-5438 See TRUDY ORDENA LENINA MATEMATICHESKOGO INSTITUTA IMENI V. A. STEKLOVA. **3539**

0081-5462 See STEPPENWOLF. **3472**

0081-5624 See STOCK VALUES AND DIVIDENDS FOR TAX PURPOSES. **916**

0081-5691 See BULLETIN - MUSEUM OF FAR EASTERN ANTIQUITIES. **264**

0081-5888 See STRAHLENSCHUTZ IN FORSCHUNG UND PRAXIS. **3947**

0081-5896 See STRAHOVSKA KNIHOVNA. **3251**

0081-5993 See STRUCTURE AND BONDING (BERLIN). **1038**

0081-6027 See STRUCTURIST. **365**

0081-6051 See STUBS. **5369**

0081-6124 See STUDI CLASSICI E ORIENTALI. **1080**

0081-6140 See STUDI DI ARCHITETTURA ANTICA. **283**

0081-6205 See STUDI ROMAGNOLI. **2711**

0081-6248 See STUDI SECENTESCHI. **2711**

0081-6256 See STUDI TASSIANI. **3441**

0081-6272 See STUDIA ANGLICA POSNANIENSIA. **3324**

0081-6337 See STUDIA BIOPHYSICA. **496**

0081-6345 See STUDIA CAUCASICA. **2711**

0081-6353 See STUDIA CELTICA. **3324**

0081-637X See STUDIA ESTETYCZNE. **2855**

0081-6426 See STUDIA GEOLOGICA POLONICA. **1399**

0081-6434 See STUDIA GEOMORPHOLOGICA CARPATHO-BALCANICA. **2577**

0081-6442 See STUDIA GERMANICA GANDENSIA. **3441**

0081-6469 See STUDIA GRAMMATICA. **3324**

0081-6477 See STUDIA HIBERNICA. **3324**

0081-6485 See STUDIA HISTORIAE OECONOMICAE. **1585**

0081-6590 See STUDIA I MATERIAY Z DZIEJOW NAUKI POLSKIEJ. SERIA C : HISTORIA NAUK MATEMATYCZNYCH, FIZYKO-CHEMICZNYCH I GEOLOGICZNO-GEOGRAFICZNYCH. **5160**

0081-6736 See STUDIA MORALIA. **5000**

0081-6787 See STUDIA PALMYRENSKIE. ETUDES PALMYRENIENNES. **283**

0081-6809 See STUDIA PHILOLOGIAE SCANDINAVICAE UPSALIENSIA. **3325**

0081-685X See STUDIA PSYCHOLOGICZNE. **4619**

0081-6884 See STUDIA ROSSICA POSNANIENSIA. **3325**

0081-6906 See STUDIA SCIENTIARUM MATHEMATICARUM HUNGARICA. **3537**

0081-6949 See STUDIA STAROPOLSKIE. **3441**

0081-7104 See STUDIA Z HISTORII SZTUKI. **2631**

0081-7147 See STUDIA ZRODOZNAWCZE. COMMENTATIONES. **2631**

0081-7236 See STUDIEN ZUR DEUTSCHEN LITERATUR. **3441**

0081-7244 See STUDIEN ZUR ENGLISCHEN PHILOLOGIE. **3325**

0081-7295 See STUDIEN ZUR GESCHICHTE DER KATH. MORALTHEOLOGIE. **5000**

0081-7333 See STUDIEN ZUR MEDIZINGESCHICHTE DES NEUNZEHNTEN JAHRHUNDERTS. **3643**

0081-7341 See STUDIEN ZUR MUSIKGESCHICHTE DES 19. JAHRHUNDERTS. **4155**

0081-735X See STUDIEN ZUR PHILOSOPHIE UND LITERATUR DES NEUNZEHNTEN JAHRHUNDERTS. **4362**

0081-7449 See STUDIES AND REPORTS IN HYDROLOGY. **5540**

0081-7554 See STUDIES IN ANCIENT ORIENTAL CIVILIZATION. **283**

0081-7600 See STUDIES IN BIBLIOGRAPHY (CHARLOTTESVILLE, VA.). **425**

0081-7775 See UNIVERSITY OF NORTH CAROLINA. STUDIES IN COMPARATIVE LITERATURE. **3355**

0081-802X See STUDIES IN INTERNATIONAL AFFAIRS. **4536**

0081-8070 See PRINCETON STUDIES IN INTERNATIONAL FINANCE. **1639**

0081-8100 See STUDIES IN IRISH HISTORY. **2711**

0081-8194 See STUDIES IN MATHEMATICAL AND MANAGERIAL ECONOMICS. **1523**

0081-8224 See STUDIES IN MEDIEVAL AND RENAISSANCE HISTORY. **2711**

0081-8232 See STUDIES IN MEDITERRANEAN ARCHAEOLOGY. **283**

0081-8259 See STUDIES IN MUSEOLOGY. **4097**

0081-8267 See STUDIES IN MUSIC. **4155**

0081-8291 See STUDIES IN NEAR EASTERN CIVILIZATION. **2665**

0081-8321 See STUDIES IN ORIENTAL CULTURE. **2665**

0081-8399 See STUDIES IN PHILOSOPHY. **4362**

0081-8518 See STUDIES IN SOCIAL LIFE. **5223**

0081-8542 See STUDIES IN STATISTICAL MECHANICS. **4429**

0081-8593 See UNIVERSITY OF NORTH CAROLINA STUDIES IN GERMANIC LANGUAGES AND LITERATURES. STUDIES IN THE GERMANIC LANGUAGES AND LITERATURES (CHAPEL HILL, N.C.). **3331**

0081-8607 See STUDIES IN THE HISTORY OF CHRISTIAN THOUGHT. **5001**

0081-8682 See STUDIES IN THE SOCIAL SCIENCES (CARROLLTON, GA.). **5223**

0081-8720 See STUDIES IN TROPICAL OCEANOGRAPHY. **1457**

0081-8747 See STUDIES IN VERMONT GEOLOGY. **1399**

0081-895X See STUDY ABROAD. **1849**

0081-9077 See SUDOST-FORSCHUNGEN. **2712**

0081-9085 See SUDOSTDEUTSCHES ARCHIV. **2712**

0081-9131 See SUDOSTEUROPE-BIBLIOGRAPHIE. **425**

0081-9212 See SUGAR Y AZUCAR. YEARBOOK. **2359**

0081-9271 See SUMER (BAGHDAD). **283**

0081-928X See SUMITOMO SANGYO EISEI. **2870**

0081-931X See SUMMARY OF STATE LAWS AND REGULATIONS RELATING TO DISTILLED SPIRITS. **3061**

0081-9352 See SUMMER JOBS (PRINCETON, N.J.). **4209**

0081-9522 See FACTS ABOUT STORE DEVELOPMENT. **2334**

0081-9557 See SUPREME COURT REVIEW, THE. **3061**

0081-9573 See SURFACE AND COLLOID SCIENCE. **1058**

0081-9603 See SURFACTANT SCIENCE SERIES. **993**

0081-9638 See SURGERY ANNUAL. **3975**

0081-9808 See SVENSK GEOGRAFISK ARSBOK. **2577**

0081-9816 See SVENSK TIDSKRIFT FOR MUSIKFORSKNING. **4155**

0081-9980 See SWANSEA GEOGRAPHER. **2577**

0082-0008 See BULLETIN - SWAZILAND, GEOLOGICAL SURVEY AND MINES DEPARTMENT. **1370**

0082-0334 See STATISTISKA MEDDELANDEN. T. **5402**

0082-0415 See SYMPOSIA OF THE SWEDISH NUTRITION FOUNDATION. **4199**

0082-0431 See CANADIAN CONSTRUCTION CATALOGUE FILE. **606**

0082-0512 See SYDNEY LAW REVIEW, THE. **3062**

0082-0598 See SYDOWIA. **528**

0082-0644 See SYMBOLAE BOTANICAE UPSALIENSIS. **528**

0082-0660 See SYMBOLON. **5001**

0082-0695 See SYMPOSIA BIOLOGICA HUNGARICA. **474**

0082-0717 See PROCEEDINGS OF SYMPOSIA IN PURE MATHEMATICS. **3528**

0082-0725 See SYMPOSIA MATHEMATICA. **3537**

0082-0784 See SYMPOSIUM (INTERNATIONAL) ON COMBUSTION. PAPERS. **1997**

0082-0873 See SYMPOSIUM ON OCULAR THERAPY. **3879**

0082-0989 See PROCEEDINGS OF THE ... SYMPOSIUM ON THERMOPHYSICAL PROPERTIES. **1056**

0082-1101 See SYNOPSES OF THE BRITISH FAUNA. **5598**

0082-111X See SYNTHESE HISTORICAL LIBRARY. **3252**

0082-1144 See SYNTHETIC ORGANIC CHEMICALS. UNITED STATES PRODUCTION AND SALES. **1628**

0082-1470 See TAIWAN BUYERS' GUIDE. **3488**

0082-156X See TAMAGAWA DAIGAKU NOGAKUBU KENKYU HOKOKU. **139**

0082-2043 See GEOLOGICAL SURVEY BULLETIN (HOBART). **1378**

0082-2108 See UNIVERSITY OF TASMANIA LAW REVIEW. **3069**

0082-2116 See TASMANIAN YEAR BOOK. **2509**

0082-2183 See TAYLOR'S ENCYCLOPEDIA OF GOVERNMENT OFFICIALS, FEDERAL AND STATE. **4498**

0082-2213 See TEACHERS' ASSOCIATIONS. ASSOCIATIONS D'ENSEIGNANTS. ASOCIACIONES DE PERSONAL DOCENTE. **1906**

0082-2299 See PROCEEDINGS - TAGA. **381**

0082-2310 See TECHNICAL PAPERS IN HYDROLOGY. **1418**

0082-2523 See TECHNIQUES OF BIOCHEMICAL AND BIOPHYSICAL MORPHOLOGY. **474**

0082-2531 See TECHNIQUES OF CHEMISTRY. **994**

0082-2558 See TECHNIQUES OF METALS RESEARCH. **4021**

0082-2590 See TECHNISCHE PHYSIK IN EINZELDARSTELLUNGEN. **4423**

0082-2760 See TENNESSEE STATISTICAL ABSTRACT. **5345**

0082-2841 See TENNYSON RESEARCH BULLETIN. **1850**

0082-2884 See TERRAE INCOGNITAE. **2577**

0082-2930 See BULLETIN OF THE TEXAS ARCHEOLOGICAL SOCIETY. **264**

0082-2949 See TEXAS ARCHEOLOGY. **284**

0082-3023 See PUBLICATIONS OF THE TEXAS FOLK-LORE SOCIETY. **2324**

0082-3082 See MISCELLANEOUS PAPERS - TEXAS MEMORIAL MUSEUM. **4091**

0082-3120 See TEXAS PUBLIC LIBRARY STATISTICS. **3260**

0082-3198 See PHILOSOPHICAL INQUIRIES. **4355**

0082-3287 See ANNUAL REPORT - BUREAU OF ECONOMIC GEOLOGY, THE UNIVERSITY OF TEXAS AT AUSTIN. **1365**

0082-3309 See GEOLOGICAL CIRCULAR. **1377**

0082-3341 See PUBLICATIONS - UNIVERSITY OF TEXAS, BUREAU OF ECONOMIC GEOLOGY. **1392**

0082-3449 See CONTRIBUTIONS IN MARINE SCIENCE. **1448**

0082-3589 See TEXTE UND UNTERSUCHUNGEN ZUR GESCHICHTE DER ALTCHRISTLICHEN LITERATUR. **3445**

0082-3732 See TEXTS AND STUDIES IN THE HISTORY OF MEDIAEVAL EDUCATION. **1787**

0082-3759 See TEXTS FROM CUNEIFORM SOURCES. **2631**

0082-3767 See TEXTUS. **5020**

0082-3775 See TEXTUS PATRISTICI ET LITURGICI. **5003**

0082-3821 See THEATRE ANNUAL, THE. **5370**

0082-3880 See SCHRIFTEN DER THEODOR-STORM-GESELLSCHAFT. **3434**

0082-4151 See THOMAS FOOD INDUSTRY REGISTER. **2359**

0082-416X See THOMAS HARDY YEAR BOOK. **3446**

0082-4186 See BLATTER DER THOMAS MANN-GESELLSCHAFT. **3367**

0082-4232 See PUBLICATIONS OF THE THORESBY SOCIETY. **5235**

0082-4453 *See* ANALELE UNIVERSITATII DIN TIMISOARA. SERIA STINTE FIZICE-CHIMICE. 4396

0082-4526 *See* TITLES IN SERIES / A HANDBOOK FOR LIBRARIANS AND STUDENTS. 3253

0082-4658 *See* TOHOKU DAIGAKU RIGAKUBU CHISHITSUGAKU KOSEIBUTSUGAKU KYOSHITSU KENKYU HOBUN HOKOKU. 1399

0082-4720 *See* RINGYO SHIKENJO KENKYU HOKOKU. 2394

0082-4747 *See* MEMOIRS OF FACULTY OF TECHNOLOGY, TOKYO METROPOLITAN UNIVERSITY. 1987

0082-4763 *See* YUKIJIRUSHI NYUGYO KENKYUJO HOKOKU. 199

0082-4771 *See* TOKYO TORITSU EISEI KENKYUJO KENKYU NENPO. 4805

0082-478X *See* BULLETIN OF THE DEPARTMENT OF GEOGRAPHY, UNIVERSITY OF TOKYO. 2557

0082-4917 *See* AKTUELLE FRAGEN DER PSYCHIATRIE UND NEUROLOGIE. 3919

0082-495X *See* TOPICS IN INORGANIC AND GENERAL CHEMISTRY. 1038

0082-500X *See* TOPICS IN STEREOCHEMISTRY. 1058

0082-5042 *See* TORONTO MEDIEVAL BIBLIOGRAPHIES. 426

0082-5093 *See* LIFE SCIENCES MISCELLANEOUS PUBLICATION. 5590

0082-5107 *See* LIFE SCIENCES OCCASIONAL PAPERS. 5590

0082-5115 *See* ANNUAL REPORT - ROYAL ONTARIO MUSEUM. 4084

0082-5115 *See* ANNUAL REPORT / ROYAL ONTARIO MUSEUM. 4084

0082-514X *See* RESEARCH REPORT - DEPARTMENT OF ELECTRICAL ENGINEERING. UNIVERSITY OF TORONTO. 2079

0082-5182 *See* TECHNICAL PUBLICATION SERIES - DEPARTMENT OF MECHANICAL ENGINEERING, UNIVERSITY OF TORONTO. 2130

0082-5220 *See* REPORT - GREAT LAKES INSTITUTE, UNIVERSITY OF TORONTO. 1417

0082-5255 *See* UTIAS REPORT. 39

0082-5263 *See* UTIAS TECHNICAL NOTE. 39

0082-5328 *See* PONTIFICAL INSTITUTE OF MEDIAEVAL STUDIES. STUDIES AND TEXTS. 2703

0082-5336 *See* UNIVERSITY OF TORONTO ROMANCE SERIES. 3449

0082-5360 *See* JOURNAL OF THE FACULTY OF AGRICULTURE, TOTTORI UNIVERSITY. 101

0082-5433 *See* TOUNG PAO. 2666

0082-5514 *See* TEKA. 2631

0082-5549 *See* STUDIA SOCIETATIS SCIENTIARUM TORUNENSIS. SECTIO C. GEOGRAPHIA ET GEOLOGIA. 2577

0082-562X *See* MEMOIRS OF THE RESEARCH DEPARTMENT OF THE TOYO BUNKO (THE ORIENTAL LIBRARY). 1835

0082-5638 *See* TRABAJOS DE PREHISTORIA. 284

0082-5735 *See* DIPLOMATIC PRESS SUDAN TRADE DIRECTORY, THE. 831

0082-5786 *See* TRADEMARK REGISTER OF THE UNITED STATES, THE. 1309

0082-5891 *See* RAILWAY WORLD ANNUAL. 5436

0082-5921 *See* TRANSITION METAL CHEMISTRY. 1038

0082-6030 *See* TRAVAUX DE JURIDICTION INTERNATIONALE. 3137

0082-6073 *See* TRAVAUX D'HISTOIRE ETHICO-POLITIQUE. 2632

0082-6081 *See* TRAVAUX D'HUMANISME ET RENAISSANCE. 2713

0082-6146 *See* TRAVEL INDUSTRY PERSONNEL DIRECTORY. 5496

0082-6235 *See* TREATISE ON ADHESION AND ADHESIVES. 1058

0082-6340 *See* TREUBIA : RECUEIL DE TRAVAUX ZOOLOGIQUES, HYDROBIOLOGIQUES ET OCEANOGRAPHIQUES. 475

0082-6391 *See* TRIBOLIUM INFORMATION BULLETIN. 5604

0082-6413 *See* TRIBUS. 247

0082-660X *See* TRIVIUM (CARDIFF, WALES). 5225

0082-6731 *See* TUBINGER RECHTSWISSENSCHAFTLICHE ABHANDLUNGEN. 3066

0082-6744 *See* TULANE STUDIES IN POLITICAL SCIENCE. 4498

0082-6782 *See* TULANE STUDIES IN ZOOLOGY AND BOTANY. 5599

0082-6847 *See* TURCICA (PARIS). 3330

0082-6871 *See* ANNALI DELLA FACOLTA DI SCIENZE AGRARIE DELLA UNIVERSITA DEGLI STUDI DI TORINO. 59

0082-6979 *See* TURUN YLIOPISTON JULKAISUJA. SARJA A 2, BIOLOGICA. GEOGRAPHICA. GEOLOGICA. 475

0082-6987 *See* TURUN YLIOPISTON JULKAISUJA SARJA B: HUMANIORA. 2856

0082-710X *See* ANNUAL REPORT - METROPOLITAN TRANSIT COMMISSION. 5376

0082-7118 *See* TYNDALE BULLETIN (1966). 5006

0082-7347 *See* ULSTER FOLKLIFE. 2325

0082-7355 *See* ULSTER JOURNAL OF ARCHAEOLOGY. 285

0082-7541 *See* STATISTICAL YEARBOOK (UNESCO). 5341

0082-7592 *See* UNIFORM CRIME REPORTS FOR THE UNITED STATES. 3084

0082-7657 *See* UNION LIST OF SCIENTIFIC SERIALS IN CANADIAN LIBRARIES. 5176

0082-7800 *See* TRANSACTIONS OF THE UNITARIAN HISTORICAL SOCIETY. 5068

0082-7843 *See* YEAR BOOK OF THE UNITED BAPTIST CONVENTION OF THE ATLANTIC PROVINCES. 5069

0082-7878 *See* RECORD OF PROCEEDINGS - GENERAL COUNCIL. UNITED CHURCH OF CANADA. 5066

0082-7908 *See* HANDBOOK OF THE UNITED FREE CHURCH OF SCOTLAND, THE. 5061

0082-8041 *See* DEMOGRAPHIC YEARBOOK. 4561

0082-805X *See* POPULATION STUDIES - UNITED NATIONS. 4558

0082-8068 *See* REPORT ON THE WORLD SOCIAL SITUATION. 5255

0082-8084 *See* INDEX TO PROCEEDINGS OF THE ECONOMIC AND SOCIAL COUNCIL. 4523

0082-8092 *See* OFFICIAL RECORDS - ECONOMIC AND SOCIAL COUNCIL. 4530

0082-8114 *See* MINERAL RESOURCES DEVELOPMENT SERIES. 2144

0082-8122 *See* REGIONAL ECONOMIC CO-OPERATION SERIES. 1516

0082-8203 *See* REPORT OF THE ECONOMIC AND SOCIAL COUNCIL FOR THE YEAR ... UNITED NATIONS. 5215

0082-8262 *See* UNIDO MONOGRAPHS ON INDUSTRIAL DEVELOPMENT. 1641

0082-8289 *See* YEARBOOK OF THE INTERNATIONAL LAW COMMISSION. 3138

0082-8297 *See* UNITED NATIONS JURIDICAL YEARBOOK. 3137

0082-8300 *See* UNITED NATIONS LEGISLATIVE SERIES. 3137

0082-8408 *See* INDEX TO PROCEEDINGS OF THE SECURITY COUNCIL / DAG HAMMARSKJOLD LIBRARY. 4523

0082-8459 *See* STATISTICAL YEARBOOK / ANNUAIRE STATISTIQUE / DEPARTMENT OF ECONOMIC AND SOCIAL INFORMATION AND POLICY ANALYSIS, STATISTICAL DIVISION. 5341

0082-8521 *See* YEARBOOK OF THE UNITED NATIONS. 3138

0082-8548 *See* MINUTES - UNITED PRESBYTERIAN CHURCH IN THE U.S.A. 5064

0082-8599 *See* U.S.A. OIL INDUSTRY DIRECTORY. 4281

0082-8610 *See* ANNUAL REPORT - ADVISORY COMMISSION ON INTERGOVERNMENTAL RELATIONS. 4626

0082-8750 *See* PROCEEDINGS, ANNUAL MEETING OF THE UNITED STATES ANIMAL HEALTH ASSOCIATION. 5519

0082-8785 *See* DOCUMENTS ON DISARMAMENT. 4043

0082-9021 *See* BULLETIN - UNITED STATES. BUREAU OF LABOR STATISTICS. 1530

0082-9056 *See* HANDBOOK OF LABOR STATISTICS / U.S. DEPARTMENT OF LABOR, BUREAU OF LABOR STATISTICS. 1533

0082-9072 *See* OCCUPATIONAL OUTLOOK HANDBOOK. 4207

0082-9129 *See* BULLETIN / DEPARTMENT OF THE INTERIOR, BUREAU OF MINES. 2135

0082-9307 *See* ANNUAL SURVEY OF MANUFACTURES (WASHINGTON). 3475

0082-9382 *See* CENSUS OF MINERAL INDUSTRIES. 1438

0082-9439 *See* CITY GOVERNMENT FINANCES. 4717

0082-9455 *See* COUNTY AND CITY DATA BOOK. 2840

0082-9544 *See* TECHNICAL PAPER - U.S. DEPARTMENT OF COMMERCE, SOCIAL AND ECONOMICS STATISTICS ADMINISTRATION, BUREAU OF THE CENSUS. 5344

0082-9625 *See* OCEANOGRAPHIC REPORT (WASHINGTON). 1454

0082-9692 *See* CIRCULAR - COPYRIGHT OFFICE. 1303

0082-9714 *See* AGRICULTURAL STATISTICS (WASHINGTON, D.C.). 150

0082-9730 *See* ERS. 82

0082-9781 *See* MARKETING RESEARCH REPORT. 932

0082-979X *See* PRODUCTION RESEARCH REPORT - UNITED STATES DEPARTMENT OF AGRICULTURE. 122

0082-9803 *See* REPORT OF THE SECRETARY OF AGRICULTURE. 126

0082-9811 *See* TECHNICAL BULLETIN / UNITED STATES DEPARTMENT OF AGRICULTURE. 140

0082-9846 *See* OVERSEAS BUSINESS REPORTS. 848

0083-0062 *See* ECONOMIC COOPERATION SERIES. 1482

0083-0100 *See* GEOGRAPHIC BULLETIN. 2562

0083-016X *See* GEOGRAPHIC AND GLOBAL ISSUES QUARTERLY / UNITED STATES DEPARTMENT OF STATE, BUREAU OF INTELLIGENCE AND RESEARCH. 2562

0083-016X *See* GEOGRAPHIC NOTES / DEPARTMENT OF STATE, BUREAU OF INTELLIGENCE AND RESEARCH, THE GEOGRAPHER. 2562

0083-0186 *See* TREATIES AND OTHER INTERNATIONAL ACTS SERIES. 4537

0083-0208 *See* U.S. PARTICIPATION IN THE UN. 4537

0083-0445 *See* AGRICULTURAL ECONOMIC REPORT (WASHINGTON, D.C.). 49

0083-0534 *See* UNITED STATES EXCISE TAX GUIDE. 4757

0083-0585 *See* ANNUAL REPORT / FEDERAL COMMUNICATIONS COMMISSION. 1104

0083-0968 *See* U.S. FOAMED PLASTICS MARKETS & DIRECTORY. 4460

0083-1115 *See* GEOLOGICAL SURVEY RESEARCH. 1378

0083-1484 *See* TAX GUIDE FOR SMALL BUSINESS / DEPARTMENT OF THE TREASURY, INTERNAL REVENUE SERVICE. 4752

0083-1603 *See* LIBRARY OF CONGRESS PUBLICATIONS IN PRINT. 419

0083-1700 *See* US MASTER TAX GUIDE. 4757

0083-1816 *See* FEDERAL INFORMATION PROCESSING STANDARDS PUBLICATION. 4648

0083-1832 *See* NATIONAL BUREAU OF STANDARDS MONOGRAPH. 4413

0083-1840 *See* NATIONAL STANDARD REFERENCE DATA SERIES. 4031

0083-1972 *See* VITAL AND HEALTH STATISTICS. SERIES 10, DATA FROM THE NATIONAL HEALTH SURVEY. 4806

0083-1980 See VITAL AND HEALTH STATISTICS. SERIES 11, DATA FROM THE NATIONAL HEALTH SURVEY. 4806

0083-2014 See VITAL AND HEALTH STATISTICS. SERIES 1: PROGRAMS AND COLLECTION PROCEDURES. 4806

0083-2022 See VITAL AND HEALTH STATISTICS. SERIES 20, DATA FROM THE NATIONAL VITAL STATISTICS SYSTEM. 4806

0083-2057 See VITAL AND HEALTH STATISTICS. SERIES 2, DATA EVALUATION AND METHODS RESEARCH. 4806

0083-2073 See VITAL AND HEALTH STATISTICS. SERIES 4, DOCUMENTS AND COMMITTEE REPORTS. 5346

0083-209X See NCRP REPORT. 4793

0083-2103 See ANNUAL REPORT - NATIONAL ENDOWMENT FOR THE ARTS/NATIONAL COUNCIL ON THE ARTS. 313

0083-2154 See MENTAL HEALTH PROGRAM REPORTS. 4790

0083-2200 See ANNUAL REPORT OF THE NATIONAL LABOR RELATIONS BOARD. 1649

0083-2219 See COURT DECISIONS RELATING TO THE NATIONAL LABOR RELATIONS ACT. 3146

0083-2316 See NATIONAL PARK SERVICE SOURCE BOOK SERIES. 4852

0083-2332 See ANNUAL REPORT - NATIONAL SCIENCE FOUNDATION. 5084

0083-2448 See PUBLICATIONS OF THE UNITED STATES NAVAL OBSERVATORY. 1433

0083-2545 See BUSINESS STATISTICS (BIENNIAL). 727

0083-260X See RESEARCH AND DEVELOPMENT REPORT - OFFICE OF COAL RESEARCH, DEPARTMENT OF THE INTERIOR. 2150

0083-2898 See VOCATIONAL & TECHNICAL EDUCATION; ANNUAL REPORT. 1917

0083-2952 See GENERAL INFORMATION: THE VIRGIN ISLANDS OF THE UNITED STATES. 2533

0083-3274 See ANNUAL REPORT / SMALL BUSINESS ADMINISTRATION. 639

0083-3320 See SOIL SURVEY INVESTIGATIONS REPORT. 187

0083-3487 See UNITED STATES TREATIES AND OTHER INTERNATIONAL AGREEMENTS. 3137

0083-3495 See STANDARDBRED SIRES AND DAMS. 2802

0083-3517 See ANNUAL YEAR BOOK - UNITED STATES TROTTING ASSOCIATION, INC. 2797

0083-3541 See MEDICAL RESEARCH IN THE VETERANS' ADMINISTRATION. 3611

0083-3606 See BULLETIN - U.S. DEPT. OF LABOR, EMPLOYMENT STANDARDS ADMINISTRATION, WOMEN'S BUREAU. 1657

0083-4025 See UNIVERSITY OF KANSAS LAW REVIEW. 3068

0083-4041 See UNIVERSITY OF QUEENSLAND LAW JOURNAL, THE. 3069

0083-4106 See ZBORNIK FILOZOFICKEJ FAKULTY UNIVERZITY KOMENSKEHO. ETHNOLOGIA SLAVICA. 248

0083-419X See SBORNIK FILOZOFICKEJ FAKULTY UNIVERZITY KOMENSKEHO. PSYCHOLOGICA. 4617

0083-4300 See PRACE ARCHEOLOGICZNE. 278

0083-4343 See PRACE GEOGRAFICZNE. 2573

0083-4351 See STUDIA GALLO-POLONICA. 2711

0083-4424 See ZESZYTY NAUKOWE UNIWERSYTETU JAGIELLONSKIEGO. PRACE Z HISTORII SZTUKI. 2634

0083-4564 See UNTERSUCHUNGEN ZUR DEUTSCHEN LITERATURGESCHICHTE. 3449

0083-4580 See UNTERSUCHUNGEN ZUR SPRACH- UND LITERATURGESCHICHTE DER ROMANISCHEN VOLKER. 3449

0083-4661 See SKRIFTER UTGIVNA AV INSTITUTIONEN FOR NORDISKA SPRAK VID UPPSALA UNIVERSITET. 3321

0083-4688 See URBAN AFFAIRS ANNUAL REVIEWS. 5265

0083-4718 See TECHNICAL BULLETIN - URBAN LAND INSTITUTE. 2836

0083-4963 See UTRECHT MICROPALEONTOLOGICAL BULLETINS. 4231

0083-4998 See DISPUTATIONES RHENO-TRAJECTINAE. 3277

0083-5048 See VACATION STUDY ABROAD. 1789

0083-5161 See ANNUAL REPORT - VANCOUVER ART GALLERY. 336

0083-5234 See OCCASIONAL PAPER - GRADUATE CENTER FOR LATIN AMERICAN STUDIES (VANDERBILT UNIVERSITY). 2751

0083-5293 See VATICAN OBSERVATORY PUBLICATIONS. 401

0083-5390 See PETROLEO Y OTROS DATOS ESTADISTICOS. 4272

0083-5560 See VDI-BERICHTE. 2000

0083-5579 See MITTEILUNGEN DES VEREINS FUR GESCHICHTE DER STADT NURNBERG. 2623

0083-5587 See ZEITSCHRIFT DES VEREINS FUER HAMBURGISCHE GESCHICHTE. 2634

0083-5609 See ZEITSCHRIFT DES VEREINS FUER LUBECKISCHE GESCHICHTE UND ALTERTUMSKUNDE. 2717

0083-5617 See JAHRBUCH DES VEREINS FUER NIEDERDEUTSCHE SPRACHFORSCHUNG. 3288

0083-5684 See VERHANDLUNGEN DES DEUTSCHEN GEOGRAPHENTAGES. 2578

0083-5757 See BULLETIN / VERMONT GEOLOGICAL SURVEY. 1370

0083-5765 See SPECIAL PUBLICATION - VERMONT GEOLOGICAL SURVEY. 1398

0083-5781 See VERMONT YEAR BOOK. 718

0083-5846 See VERSTANDLICHE WISSENSCHAFT. 2632

0083-5870 See VETERINARY ANNUAL, THE. 5525

0083-5889 See SUPPLEMENTS TO VETUS TESTAMENTUM. 5001

0083-5897 See VIATOR (BERKELEY). 1080

0083-6109 See VIE MUSICALE EN FRANCE SOUS LES ROIS BOURBONS. ETUDES. 4158

0083-615X See MITTEILUNGEN DER OSTERREICHISCHEN GALERIE. 358

0083-6265 See VILAGTORTENET. 2632

0083-629X See PROCEEDINGS OF THE VIRGIL SOCIETY. 5235

0083-6311 See VIRGINIA BAPTIST REGISTER, THE. 5069

0083-6354 See VIRGINIA EDUCATIONAL DIRECTORY. 1790

0083-6389 See DOCUMENTS - VIRGINIA HISTORICAL SOCIETY. 2731

0083-6400 See CONTRIBUTION - VIRGINIA INSTITUTE OF MARINE SCIENCE. 554

0083-6524 See VIRGINIA STATE LIBRARY PUBLICATIONS. 2765

0083-6656 See VISTAS IN ASTRONOMY. 401

0083-6710 See VITAL STATISTICS OF THE UNITED STATES. 5346

0083-6729 See VITAMINS AND HORMONES; ADVANCES IN RESEARCH AND APPLICATIONS. 3733

0083-6745 See FILOLOGISKT ARKIV. 3281

0083-6796 See KUNGL. VITTERHETS-, HISTORIE- OCH ANTIKVITETSAKADEMIENS ARSBOK. 2849

0083-6915 See VOM WASSER. 5541

0083-6990 See MISCELLANEOUS PAPERS - LANDBOUWHOGESCHOOL WAGENINGEN. 109

0083-7105 See WALLRAF-RICHARTZ-JAHRBUCH. 368

0083-713X See WALTER PRESCOTT WEBB MEMORIAL LECTURES. 3452

0083-7156 See JOURNAL OF THE WALTERS ART GALLERY. 4090

0083-7199 See STUDIES OF THE WARBURG INSTITUTE. 2855

0083-7210 See WARD-PHILLIPS LECTURES IN ENGLISH LANGUAGE AND LITERATURE. 3332

0083-7229 See WARD'S AUTOMOTIVE YEARBOOK. 5428

0083-7393 See WASHINGTON. 4499

0083-7393 See WASHINGTON. 719

0083-7407 See TEXTILE MUSEUM JOURNAL. 4097

0083-7474 See TECHNICAL REPORT - WASHINGTON DEPARTMENT OF FISHERIES. 2314

0083-7547 See SPECIAL REPORT - UNIVERSITY OF WASHINGTON, DEPARTMENT OF OCEANOGRAPHY. 1457

0083-7555 See RESEARCH IN FISHERIES. 2311

0083-7571 See UNIVERSITY OF WASHINGTON PUBLICATIONS IN BIOLOGY. 475

0083-7709 See WATER RESOURCES SYMPOSIUM. 5547

0083-7792 See WEBBIA. 530

0083-7881 See WELLESLEY EDITION, THE. 4158

0083-7903 See NEW ZEALAND OCEANOGRAPHIC INSTITUTE MEMOIR. 1453

0083-7938 See REPORT - WELSH SOILS DISCUSSION GROUP. 184

0083-7989 See WENNER-GREN CENTER INTERNATIONAL SYMPOSIUM SERIES. 5169

0083-8004 See WENTWORTH BYGONES. 2765

0083-8039 See WERKE DER KUNST IN HEIDELBERG : EINE SCHRIFTENREIHE IM AUFTRAG DER JOSEPHINE UND EDVARD VON PORTHEIM-STIFTUNG FUR WISSENSCHAFT UND KUNST. 333

0083-8160 See WEST AFRICAN JOURNAL OF ARCHAEOLOGY. 285

0083-8500 See BULLETIN - WEST VIRGINIA GEOLOGICAL AND ECONOMIC SURVEY. 1371

0083-8543 See REPORT OF INVESTIGATIONS / STATE OF WEST VIRGINIA, GEOLOGICAL AND ECONOMIC SURVEY. 1395

0083-8675 See TECHNICAL BULLETIN / WESTERN AUSTRALIAN DEPARTMENT OF AGRICULTURE. 140

0083-8764 See WESTERN AUSTRALIAN REPORTS. 3073

0083-8772 See WESTERN AUSTRALIAN YEAR BOOK / COMMONWEALTH BUREAU OF CENSUS AND STATISTICS, WESTERN AUSTRALIAN OFFICE. 1930

0083-8799 See PAPERS PRESENTED AT THE ANNUAL CONVENTION. 2238

0083-8810 See REPORTS OF PROCEEDINGS OF ANNUAL MEETING - WESTERN CANADIAN SOCIETY FOR HORTICULTURE. 2430

0083-8837 See TECHNICAL PAPERS. 2083

0083-887X See WESTERN FRONTIER LIBRARY, THE. 2765

0083-8888 See WESTERN FRONTIERSMAN SERIES. 2765

0083-8934 See WESTERN LANDS AND WATER SERIES. 2766

0083-8969 See PROCEEDINGS OF THE WESTERN PHARMACOLOGY SOCIETY. 4326

0083-9027 See WESTFALISCHE FORSCHUNGEN. 2715

0083-9043 See WESTFAELISCHE ZEITSCHRIFT. 2715

0083-9108 See WHAT EVERY VETERAN SHOULD KNOW. 4061

0083-9167 See WHERE AMERICA'S LARGE FOUNDATIONS MAKE THEIR GRANTS. 2856

0083-9248 See WHIDDEN LECTURES. 2856

0083-9256 See ALMANACK FOR THE YEAR OF OUR LORD ... (LONDON, ENGLAND). 1923

0083-9345 See WHO WAS WHO. 435

0083-937X See WHO'S WHO (LONDON. 1849). 438

0083-9396 See WHO'S WHO IN AMERICA. 436

0083-9403 See "SHORT PLAY" SERIES, THE. 5368

0083-9523 See WHO'S WHO IN FINANCE AND INDUSTRY. 720

0083-9531 See WHO'S WHO IN FRANCE. 437

0083-9574 See WHO'S WHO IN INSURANCE. 437

0083-9612 See WHO'S WHO IN LEBANON. 437

0083-9671 See BARQUE'S PAKISTAN TRADE DIRECTORY AND WHO'S WHO. 824

0083-9736 See WHO'S WHO IN SWITZERLAND, INCLUDING THE PRINCIPALITY OF LIECHTENSTEIN. 438

0083-9752 See WHO'S WHO IN THE ARAB WORLD. 438

0083-9760 See WHO'S WHO IN THE EAST. 438

0083-9787 See WHO'S WHO IN THE MIDWEST. 438

0083-9809 See WHO'S WHO IN THE SOUTH AND SOUTHWEST. 438

0083-9825 See WHO'S WHO IN THE WORLD. 438

0083-9841 See WHO'S WHO OF AMERICAN WOMEN. 438

0083-9914 See WIENER BEITRAEGE ZUR ENGLISCHEN PHILOLOGIE. 3333

0083-9922 See WIENER BEITRAGE ZUR KULTURGESCHICHTE UND LINGUISTIK. 247

0083-9957 See WIENER GEOGRAPHISCHE SCHRIFTEN. 2579

0083-9965 See WIENER HUMANISTISCHE BLATTER. 1081

0083-999X See WIENER JAHRBUCH FUR PHILOSOPHIE. 4365

0084-0041 See WIENER SLAVISTISCHES JAHRBUCH. 3333

0084-005X See WIENER STUDIEN. 3333

0084-0068 See WIENER VOLKERKUNDLICHE MITTEILUNGEN. 247

0084-0076 See WIENER ZEITSCHRIFT FUER DIE KUNDE DES MORGENLANDES. 2633

0084-0084 See WIENER ZEITSCHRIFT FUR DIE KUNDE SUDASIENS UND ARCHIV FUR INDISCHE PHILOSOPHIE. 4365

0084-0122 See WILDLIFE BEHAVIOR AND ECOLOGY SERIES. 2222

0084-0173 See WILDLIFE MONOGRAPHS. 5600

0084-019X See WILEY SERIES ON SYSTEMS ENGINEERING AND ANALYSIS. 2001

0084-0254 See JOURNAL OF THE WILLIAM MORRIS SOCIETY, THE. 373

0084-0416 See WINTERTHUR PORTFOLIO. 368

0084-0424 See WIRE INDUSTRY YEARBOOK. 4023

0084-0467 See WIRKUNG DER LITERATUR. 3453

0084-0505 See TRANSACTIONS OF THE WISCONSIN ACADEMY OF SCIENCES, ARTS, AND LETTERS. 5167

0084-053X See WISCONSIN CHINA SERIES. 3453

0084-0556 See RESEARCH REPORT - WISCONSIN. DEPT. OF NATURAL RESOURCES. 2204

0084-0564 See TECHNICAL BULLETIN - WISCONSIN DEPARTMENT OF NATURAL RESOURCES. 2206

0084-0793 See LTC PAPER. 4663

0084-0823 See TRAINING & METHODS SERIES. 1524

0084-0998 See WISSENSCHAFTLICHE UND ANGEWANDTE PHOTAGRAPHIE, DIE. 4378

0084-1323 See WORKING PRESS OF THE NATION, THE. 2926

0084-1382 See WORLD ALMANAC AND BOOK OF FACTS, THE. 1930

0084-1439 See WORLD BOOK YEAR BOOK, THE. 1930

0084-1447 See WORLD BUDDHISM. 5022

0084-1471 See WORLD CARTOGRAPHY. 2583

0084-1498 See WORLD COLLECTORS ANNUARY. 369

0084-1641 See PROCEEDINGS OF THE WORLD CONGRESS. 3630

0084-1714 See WORLD ECONOMIC SURVEY (NEW YORK, N.Y.). 1641

0084-179X See WORLD FOOD PROBLEMS. 2361

0084-1889 See WORLD LIST OF UNIVERSITIES, OTHER INSTITUTIONS OF HIGHER EDUCATION AND UNIVERSITY ORGANISATIONS. LISTE MONDIALE DES UNIVERSITES, AUTRES ETABLISSEMENTS D'ENSEIGNEMENT SUPERIEUR ET ORGANISATIONS UNIVERSITAIRES. 1930

0084-1994 See REPORT - WORLD METEOROLOGICAL ORGANIZATION. 1434

0084-201X See TECHNICAL NOTE - WORLD METEOROLOGICAL ORGANIZATION. 1435

0084-2117 See WORLD OF LEARNING, THE. 1854

0084-2176 See PROCEEDINGS / WORLD PETROLEUM CONGRESS. 4275

0084-2230 See WORLD REVIEW OF NUTRITION AND DIETETICS. 4200

0084-2257 See WORLD STRENGTH OF THE COMMUNIST PARTY ORGANIZATIONS. 4548

0084-2273 See WORLD TOBACCO DIRECTORY. 5374

0084-2281 See AFRICA (WASHINGTON, D.C.). 2636

0084-2311 See MIDDLE EAST AND SOUTH ASIA, THE. 2769

0084-2338 See WESTERN EUROPE (WASHINGTON, D.C.: 1982). 2715

0084-2451 See WORLD WEATHER WATCH PLANNING REPORT. 1437

0084-2486 See WORLDWIDE REGISTER OF ADULT EDUCATION. 1802

0084-2508 See WORLD YEARBOOK OF EDUCATION. 1874

0084-2583 See WORLDWIDE PETROCHEMICAL DIRECTORY. 4282

0084-2699 See WRITERS DIRECTORY, THE. 2925

0084-2710 See WRITER'S HANDBOOK, THE. 2926

0084-2729 See WRITER'S MARKET, THE. 4820

0084-2737 See WRITER'S YEARBOOK. 3454

0084-2966 See ACTA UNIVERSITATIS WRATISLAVIENSIS. MATEMATYKA, FIZYKA, ASTRONOMIA. 3491

0084-2982 See ROZPRAWY KOMISJI HISTORII SZTUKI. 2707

0084-3156 See SCIENCE MONOGRAPH. 132

0084-3199 See UNIVERSITY OF WYOMING PUBLICATIONS (1935). 1853

0084-3210 See WATER RESOURCES SERIES (LARAMIE). 5547

0084-3296 See YAD VASHEM STUDIES. 2716

0084-330X See YALE CLASSICAL STUDIES. 1081

0084-3318 See YALE COLLEGE SERIES. 1096

0084-3334 See YALE GERMANIC STUDIES. 2716

0084-3342 See YALE HISTORICAL PUBLICATIONS. MANUSCRIPTS AND EDITED TEXTS. 2633

0084-3369 See YALE JUDAICA SERIES. 5054

0084-3415 See YALE PUBLICATIONS IN THE HISTORY OF ART. 369

0084-3458 See YALE SERIES OF YOUNGER POETS, THE. 3473

0084-3482 See YALE STUDIES IN ENGLISH. 3334

0084-3490 See YALE STUDIES IN POLITICAL SCIENCE. 4501

0084-3539 See BULLETIN - YALE UNIVERSITY ART GALLERY. 346

0084-3563 See YALE WESTERN AMERICANA SERIES. 2766

0084-358X See YEARBOOK AND DIRECTORY OF OSTEOPATHIC PHYSICIANS. 3652

0084-3601 See YEAR BOOK OF ADULT EDUCATION. 1802

0084-3652 See YEAR BOOK OF ANESTHESIA AND PAIN MANAGEMENT, THE. 3684

0084-3660 See YEARBOOK OF ASTRONOMY. 401

0084-3695 See YEARBOOK OF COMPARATIVE AND GENERAL LITERATURE. 3356

0084-3717 See YEAR BOOK OF DENTISTRY, THE. 1337

0084-3733 See YEAR BOOK OF DRUG THERAPY, THE. 4333

0084-3741 See YEAR BOOK OF ENDOCRINOLOGY, THE. 3733

0084-375X See YEARBOOK OF FISHERY STATISTICS. 2318

0084-3814 See YEARBOOK OF INTERNATIONAL ORGANIZATIONS. 1930

0084-3814 See YEARBOOK OF INTERNATIONAL ORGANIZATIONS. 4539

0084-3849 See YEARBOOK OF JEHOVAH'S WITNESSES. 5010

0084-3857 See YEAR-BOOK OF LABOUR STATISTICS / INTERNATIONAL LABOUR OFFICE. 1541

0084-3873 See YEAR BOOK OF MEDICINE, THE. 3652

0084-3903 See YEAR BOOK OF NUCLEAR MEDICINE, THE. 3849

0084-3911 See ... YEAR BOOK OF OBSTETRICS AND GYNECOLOGY, THE. 3769

0084-392X See YEAR BOOK OF OPHTHALMOLOGY, THE. 3880

0084-3946 See YEAR BOOK OF PATHOLOGY AND CLINICAL PATHOLOGY, THE. 3898

0084-3954 See YEAR BOOK OF PEDIATRICS, THE. 3912

0084-3970 See YEAR BOOK OF PSYCHIATRY AND APPLIED MENTAL HEALTH, THE. 3937

0084-4071 See YEAR BOOK OF UROLOGY, THE. 3994

0084-4144 See YEAR'S WORK IN ENGLISH STUDIES. 3455

0084-4152 See YEAR'S WORK IN MODERN LANGUAGE STUDIES. 3334

0084-4217 See YIVO BLETER. 3456

0084-4276 See YORKSHIRE ARCHAEOLOGICAL JOURNAL, THE. 285

0084-439X See YUBAL GOBES MEHQARIM SEL HA-MERKAZ LE-HEQER HA-MUSIQAH HA-YHUDIT. 4160

0084-4403 See Z BADAN KLASY ROBOTNICZEJ I INTELIGENCJI. 1720

0084-4411 See Z DZIEJOW FORM ARTYSTYCZNYCH W LITERATURZE POLSKIEJ. 3456

0084-4446 See ZAGADNIENIA RODZAJOW LITERACKICH. 3456

0084-473X See ANNUAL REPORT OF THE GEOLOGICAL SURVEY DEPARTMENT (LUSAKA). 1365

0084-5183 See ZBORNIK ISTORIJE KNJIZEVNOSTI. 3456

0084-5299 See ZEITSCHRIFT FUER ASSYRIOLOGIE UND VORDERASIATISCHE ARCHAOLOGIE. 286

0084-5302 See ZEITSCHRIFT FUER CELTISCHE PHILOLOGIE. 3335

0084-5310 See ZEITSCHRIFT FUER DIE GESAMTE STRAFRECHTSWISSENSCHAFT. 3109

0084-5337 See ZEITSCHRIFT FUER ERNAEHRUNGSWISSENSCHAFT. SUPPLEMENTUM. 4200

0084-5345 See ZEITSCHRIFT FUER KLINISCHE PSYCHOLOGIE. 4622

0084-5361 See METEOROLOGISCHE ZEITSCHRIFT / HERAUSGEGEBEN VON DER DEUTSCHEN METEOROLOGISCHEN GESELLSCHAFT, OSTERREICHISCHEN GESELLSCHAFT FEUR METEOROLOGIE, SCHWEIZERISCHEN GESELLSCHAFT FUER GEOPHYSIK. 1431

0084-537X See ZEITSCHRIFT FUER NATIONALOKONOMIE. SUPPLEMENTUM. 3542

0084-5388 See ZEITSCHRIFT FUER PAPYROLOGIE UND EPIGRAPHIK. 3456

0084-5396 See BEIHEFTE ZUR ZEITSCHRIFT FUER ROMANISCHE PHILOLOGIE. 3268

0084-540X See ZEITSCHRIFT FUER SCHWEIZERISCHES RECHT. 3078

0084-5442 See ZENITH. 5172

0084-5477 See ZESZYTY PROBLEMOWE POSTEPOW NAUK ROLNICZYCH. 149

0084-5507 See ZIEMIE ZACHODNIE. 2717

0084-5604 See VESTNIK ZOOLOGII. 5599

0084-5612 See SYMPOSIA OF THE ZOOLOGICAL SOCIETY OF LONDON. 5598

0084-5825 See ZWIERZETA LABORATORYJNE. 5604

0084-5841 See AMA. AGRICULTURAL MECHANIZATION IN ASIA, AFRICA AND LATIN AMERICA. 158

0084-5914 See ACTA PHYTOGEOGRAPHICA SUECICA. 497

0084-5957 See ADVANCES IN NEPHROLOGY FROM THE NECKER HOSPITAL. 3988

0084-6376 See PROFESSIONAL DIRECTORY / THE AMERICAN INSTITUTE OF CHEMISTS. 990

0084-6406 See ALA HANDBOOK OF ORGANIZATION. 3188

0084-6473 See ANNEE BALZACIENNE, L'. 3362

0084-6570 *See* ANNUAL REVIEW OF ANTHROPOLOGY. 228

0084-6597 *See* ANNUAL REVIEW OF EARTH AND PLANETARY SCIENCES. 1351

0084-6600 *See* ANNUAL REVIEW OF MATERIALS SCIENCE. 2100

0084-7089 *See* BULLETIN - AUSTRALIA, BUREAU OF MINERAL RESOURCES, GEOLOGY AND GEOPHYSICS. 1368

0084-7100 *See* REPORT / DEPARTMENT OF RESOURCES AND ENERGY, BUREAU OF MINERAL RESOURCES, GEOLOGY AND GEOPHYSICS. 1394

0084-7259 *See* JOURNAL OF THE AUSTRALIAN CATHOLIC HISTORICAL SOCIETY. 5031

0084-7348 *See* AUSTRALIAN ECONOMY: BUSINESS FORECASTS, THE. 1547

0084-7534 *See* APEA JOURNAL, THE. 4250

0084-7658 *See* AUSTRALIAN YEAR BOOK OF INTERNATIONAL LAW, THE. 3124

0084-7682 *See* BACH-JAHRBUCH. 4101

0084-7747 *See* ANNUAL REPORT OF THE BEAN IMPROVEMENT COOPERATIVE. 163

0084-7836 *See* BIBLIOGRAPHIA INTERNATIONALIS SPIRITUALITATIS / A PONTIFICIO INSTITUTO SPIRITUALITATIS O.C.D. EDITA. 4342

0084-7852 *See* BULLETIN / BIBLIOGRAPHICAL SOCIETY OF AUSTRALIA AND NEW ZEALAND. 3198

0084-800X *See* BRADEA. 504

0084-8018 *See* BBC MUSIC GUIDES. 4102

0084-8085 *See* CHECK LIST OF BRITISH OFFICIAL SERIAL PUBLICATIONS. 4468

0084-8174 *See* BULLETIN OF STATISTICS ON WORLD TRADE IN ENGINEERING PRODUCTS. 2002

0084-8212 *See* BY OG BYGD. 4086

0084-8239 *See* CAHIERS PAUL-LOUIS COURIER. 3371

0084-8263 *See* BULLETIN - CALIFORNIA. DEPT. OF WATER RESOURCES. 5531

0084-8271 *See* CALIFORNIA GOVERNMENT AND POLITICS ANNUAL. 4466

0084-8328 *See* CAMBRIAN LAW REVIEW, THE. 2947

0084-8425 *See* NATIONAL BULLETIN OF LITURGY. 4980

0084-8573 *See* CANADIAN LAW LIST (1951). 3139

0084-8808 *See* JAHRBUCH DER COBURGER LANDESSTIFTUNG. 2693

0084-8824 *See* ABSTRACTS OF PAPERS PRESENTED AT ... MEETINGS - LABORATORY OF QUANTITATIVE BIOLOGY. 439

0084-8875 *See* SPECIAL REPORT / COLORADO DIVISION OF WILDLIFE. 2205

0084-8921 *See* REPORT ON PUBLICATIONS OF THE SCHOOL OF INTERNATIONAL AFFAIRS AND THE REGIONAL INSTITUTES. 4533

0084-8956 *See* COMMENTARY (SINGAPORE). 2503

0084-9146 *See* PROCEEDINGS OF A CONFERENCE ON BANK STRUCTURE AND COMPETITION. 804

0084-9219 *See* CONTRIBUTIONS IN AMERICAN HISTORY. 2729

0084-9227 *See* CONTRIBUTIONS IN AMERICAN STUDIES. 2729

0084-9235 *See* CONTRIBUTIONS IN ECONOMICS AND ECONOMIC HISTORY. 1552

0084-9243 *See* CONTRIBUTIONS IN LIBRARIANSHIP AND INFORMATION SCIENCE. 3204

0084-9251 See CONTRIBUTIONS IN MILITARY STUDIES. 4040

0084-926X *See* CONTRIBUTIONS IN PHILOSOPHY. 4344

0084-9278 *See* CONTRIBUTIONS IN SOCIOLOGY. 5243

0084-9308 *See* NATIONALMUSEETS ARBEJDSMARK. 5234

0084-9499 *See* CURRENT BIOGRAPHY YEARBOOK. 432

0084-9529 *See* DACOTAH TERRITORY. 3462

0084-9537 *See* DADA SURREALISM. 318

0084-9596 *See* DANSK PERIODICAFORTEGNELSE. SUPPLEMENT. 414

0084-9650 *See* MONOGRAPH SERIES - DELAWARE MUSEUM OF NATURAL HISTORY. 4168

0084-9715 *See* ACCESSIONSKATALOG - DENMARK. RIGSBIBLIOTEKAREMBEDET. 3187

0084-9731 *See* DESCENT (SYDNEY). 2445

0084-9812 *See* DICKENS STUDIES ANNUAL. 3381

0084-9898 *See* DIRECTORY OF COLORADO MANUFACTURERS. 3477

0084-9944 *See* DIRECTORY OF GOVERNMENTS IN METROPOLITAN TORONTO. 4643

0084-9960 *See* DIRECTORY OF IRANIAN PERIODICALS. 415

0085-0039 *See* DIRECTORY OF THE PUBLIC AQUARIA OF THE WORLD. 5581

0085-0322 *See* ETUDES HAGUENOVIENNES. 2687

0085-0330 *See* EURAIL GUIDE. 5431

0085-0551 *See* DIRECTORY OF OBSOLETE SECURITIES. 896

0085-0624 *See* MAP SERIES (TALLAHASSEE, FLA.). 2582

0085-0640 *See* SPECIAL PUBLICATION - FLORIDA. BUREAU OF GEOLOGY. 1397

0085-0683 *See* MEMOIRS OF THE HOURGLASS CRUISES. 556

0085-0756 *See* FOLK (KBENHAVN). 236

0085-0888 *See* FRENCH XX BIBLIOGRAPHY. 3458

0085-0969 *See* GEOGRAPHICAL EDUCATION. 2563

0085-0985 *See* BULLETIN - GEOLOGICAL SURVEY OF IRELAND. 1369

0085-1043 *See* GEORGIA STATISTICAL ABSTRACT. 5328

0085-1280 *See* GROWTH (MELBOURNE, VIC.). 1564

0085-1302 *See* BEIHEFT ZUR ZEITSCHRIFT GRUPPENPSYCHOTHERAPIE UND GRUPPENDYNAMIK. 4577

0085-1353 *See* GUIDE TO BIOMEDICAL STANDARDS, THE. 3579

0085-1361 *See* HAFNIA. 351

0085-1418 *See* ARBOG - HANDELS- OG SFARTMUSEET PA KRONBORG. 823

0085-1442 *See* HARRIS SURVEY YEARBOOK OF PUBLIC OPINION, THE. 5246

0085-1469 *See* HEFTE FUR UNFALLHEILKUNDE. 2863

0085-1760 *See* INDEX OF ART IN THE PACIFIC NORTHWEST. 352

0085-1892 *See* BULLETIN (INSTITUT ROYAL DU PATRIMOINE ARTISTIQUE (BRUXELLES)). 345

0085-204X *See* INTERNATIONAL BIBLIOGRAPHY OF ECONOMICS. 1496

0085-2066 *See* INTERNATIONAL BIBLIOGRAPHY OF SOCIOLOGY. 5266

0085-2376 *See* JOURNAL OF ARABIC LITERATURE. 3399

0085-2392 *See* JOURNAL OF DEVELOPMENT PLANNING. 1637

0085-2414 *See* JOURNAL OF NORTHWEST SEMITIC LANGUAGES. 3291

0085-2473 *See* UNIVERSITY OF KANSAS PUBLICATIONS. HUMANISTIC STUDIES. 2856

0085-2538 *See* KIDNEY INTERNATIONAL. 3991

0085-2546 *See* KING'S GAZETTE. 3602

0085-2570 *See* ANNALS OF THE SCHOOL OF BUSINESS ADMINISTRATION, KOBE UNIVERSITY, THE. 638

0085-2619 *See* KYRKOHISTORISK AARSSKRIFT. 4972

0085-2635 *See* MEMOIRS OF THE FACULTY OF SCIENCE, KYUSHU UNIVERSITY. SERIES C. CHEMISTRY. 985

0085-2848 *See* PUBLICATIONS / LONDON RECORD SOCIETY. 2704

0085-2880 *See* LOUISIANA ANNUAL MILK MARKETING REPORT, THE. 929

0085-2899 *See* LOZANIA. 5590

0085-2953 *See* MAIL ORDER BUSINESS DIRECTORY : A COMPLETE GUIDE TO THE MAIL ORDER MARKET. 691

0085-297X *See* BIENNIAL REPORT - MAINE, SOIL AND WATER CONSERVATION COMMISSION. 2188

0085-2988 *See* JOURNAL OF THE MALACOLOGICAL SOCIETY OF AUSTRALIA. 5589

0085-3100 *See* MONOGRAPHS OF THE MARIO NEGRI INSTITUTE FOR PHARMACOLOGICAL RESEARCH. 4316

0085-3208 *See* MEDDELELSER FRA NY CARLSBERG GLYPTOTEK. 358

0085-3224 *See* MELBOURNE JOURNAL OF POLITICS. 4481

0085-3372 *See* ANNUAL DIRECTORY - DEPARTMENT OF NATURAL RESOURCES. GEOLOGICAL SURVEY DIVISION (LANSING). 1365

0085-3453 *See* MINE AND QUARRY MECHANISATION. 2144

0085-347X *See* MINNESOTA MEDICAL ASSISTANCE BIENNIAL REPORT DATA. 5296

0085-3488 *See* MINORITY STUDENT OPPORTUNITIES IN UNITED STATES MEDICAL SCHOOLS. 1836

0085-350X *See* MISSOURI JOURNAL OF RESEARCH IN MUSIC EDUCATION. 4131

0085-3518 *See* MODERN PLASTICS ENCYCLOPEDIA (1954). 4457

0085-3674 *See* NATALIA. 2642

0085-3739 *See* RESEARCH REPORT - NATIONAL COUNCIL OF TEACHERS OF ENGLISH. 3315

0085-378X *See* RESEARCH BULLETIN OF THE NATIONAL INSTITUTE FOR EDUCATIONAL RESEARCH. 1779

0085-3887 *See* NEMOURIA. 4169

0085-4077 *See* ANNUAL EDUCATIONAL SUMMARY NEW YORK STATE. 1724

0085-4166 *See* NEWS FROM THE RARE BOOK ROOM. 421

0085-4417 *See* NUYTSIA. 520

0085-4441 *See* NEW SOUTH WALES YEAR BOOK. 2510

0085-4468 *See* OHIO FISH AND WILDLIFE REPORT. 2201

0085-4522 *See* ORIENTALIA GOTHOBURGENSIA. 3308

0085-4522 *See* ORIENTALIA LOVANIENSIA PERIODICA. 3308

0085-4557 *See* OSLER LIBRARY NEWSLETTER. 3624

0085-4573 See CYPRIS. 4226

0085-4581 *See* PIE, PUBLICATIONS INDEXED FOR ENGINEERING. 1990

0085-459X *See* PACIFIC ISLANDS STUDIES AND NOTES. 2670

0085-462X *See* ANNUAL REPORT OF THE DIRECTOR - PAN AMERICAN SANITARY BUREAU. BUREAU. 3712

0085-4689 *See* PAPUA NEW GUINEA LAW REPORTS. 3024

0085-4786 *See* DOCUMENTS DE LINGUISTIQUE QUANTITATIVE. 3277

0085-4956 *See* TEKI HISTORYCZNE / POLSKIE TOWARZYSTWO HISTORYCZNE W WIELKIEJ BRYTANII. 2631

0085-5030 *See* PORT OF NEW ORLEANS ANNUAL DIRECTORY. 5454

0085-5227 *See* UNIVERSITY OF UTAH PUBLICATIONS IN THE AMERICAN WEST. 2764

0085-5243 *See* ARCHIVES DE FOLKLORE, LES. 2318

0085-5359 *See* QUEENSLAND YEAR BOOK. 1928

0085-5405 *See* REAL ESTATE TRENDS IN METROPOLITAN VANCOUVER. 4845

0085-543X *See* RECUEIL DES FILMS (MONTREAL). 4076

0085-5499 *See* REPERTOIRE BIBLIOGRAPHIQUE DES LIVRES IMPRIMES EN FRANCE AU SEIZIEME SIECLE. 423

0085-5553 *See* RESEARCH IN PHENOMENOLOGY. 4358

0085-5626 *See* REVISTA BRASILEIRA DE ENTOMOLOGIA. **5613**

0085-5642 *See* REVISTERO. INTERNATIONAL PERIODICALS DIRECTORY. **423**

0085-5693 *See* RAINFALL REPORT. **1434**

0085-5774 *See* JOURNAL OF THE HONG KONG BRANCH OF THE ROYAL ASIATIC SOCIETY. **5232**

0085-5839 *See* RURAL AFRICANA. **1582**

0085-5901 *See* REVISTA DO CENTRO DE CIENCIAS RURAIS. **129**

0085-5928 *See* SCANDINAVIAN JOURNAL OF GASTROENTEROLOGY. SUPPLEMENT. **3747**

0085-5944 *See* SCANDINAVIAN STUDIES IN LAW. **3135**

0085-6002 *See* SCOTTISH BUILDING AND CIVIL ENGINEERING YEAR BOOK. **627**

0085-6118 *See* SINGAPORE LIBRARIES. **3249**

0085-6304 *See* NEWSLETTER - SOCIETY FOR THE STUDY OF MIDWESTERN LITERATURE (U.S.). **3417**

0085-6320 *See* SOCIOLOSKI PREGLED. **5262**

0085-6398 *See* SOUTH AFRICAN JOURNAL OF PHOTOGRAMMETRY, THE. **2576**

0085-6401 *See* SOUTH ASIA. **2664**

0085-6428 *See* SOUTH AUSTRALIAN YEAR BOOK. **1929**

0085-6479 *See* BULLETIN / SOUTH DAKOTA GEOLOGICAL SURVEY. **1370**

0085-6487 *See* CIRCULAR / SOUTH DAKOTA GEOLOGICAL SURVEY. **1372**

0085-6509 *See* SOUTHEAST ASIAN ARCHIVES. **2484**

0085-6525 *See* SOUTHERN INDIAN STUDIES. **2761**

0085-6592 *See* SFI BULLETIN. **4917**

0085-6614 *See* STANDARD DIRECTORY OF ADVERTISING AGENCIES. **766**

0085-6630 *See* STANDARD PERIODICAL DIRECTORY, THE. **3251**

0085-6770 *See* STRAFFORD FESTIVAL. **388**

0085-6789 *See* STRATFORD FESTIVAL STORY, THE. **5369**

0085-6827 *See* STUDI E SAGGI LINGUISTICI. **3324**

0085-6835 See STUDIA FENNICA. FOLKLORISTICA. **2324**

0085-6878 *See* STUDIES IN MEDIEVAL CULTURE. **2711**

0085-6894 *See* STUDIES IN ROMANCE LANGUAGES (LEXINGTON, KY.). **3442**

0085-6940 *See* SUOMEN KALATALOUS. **2314**

0085-6991 *See* STATISTISKA MEDDELANDEN. SERIE BO. **628**

0085-7092 *See* TARLTON LAW LIBRARY LEGAL BIBLIOGRAPHY SERIES. **3083**

0085-7106 *See* TASMANIAN REPORTS, THE. **3062**

0085-7114 *See* TEACHERS OF HISTORY IN THE UNIVERSITIES AND POLYTECHNICS OF THE UNITED KINGDOM. **1849**

0085-7130 *See* TELEKTRONIKK. **2084**

0085-7157 *See* TELEVISION NEWS INDEX AND ABSTRACTS : ANNUAL INDEX. **1141**

0085-7157 *See* TELEVISION NEWS INDEX AND ABSTRACTS. **1167**

0085-7262 *See* MEDDELELSER FRA THORVALDSENS MUSEUM. **358**

0085-7289 *See* NANKYOKU SHIRYO. **2570**

0085-7351 *See* TRAVEL IDEAS. **5495**

0085-7440 *See* TURUN HISTORIALLINEN ARKISTO. **2713**

0085-7742 *See* BULLETIN - FORESTS COMMISSION, VICTORIA. **2376**

0085-7823 *See* VIETNAMESE STUDIES. HANOI, VIETNAM (1966). **2667**

0085-7947 *See* UNIVERSITY OF WASHINGTON PUBLICATIONS. LANGUAGE AND LITERATURE. **3331**

0085-8129 *See* BULLETIN - FORESTS DEPARTMENT. **2376**

0085-8137 *See* BULLETIN - GEOLOGICAL SURVEY OF WESTERN AUSTRALIA. **1369**

0085-8188 *See* WESTERN CANADIAN STEAM LOCOMOTIVE DIRECTORY. **5438**

0085-8269 *See* WOMEN'S RIGHTS LAW REPORTER. **3076**

0085-8293 *See* WORLD BANK ATLAS. **816**

0085-8307 *See* WORLD MOTOR VEHICLE DATA. **5428**

0085-8315 *See* WORLD POPULATION DATA SHEET OF THE POPULATION REFERENCE BUREAU, INC. **4561**

0090-0036 *See* AMERICAN JOURNAL OF PUBLIC HEALTH (1971). **4764**

0090-0044 *See* NATIONAL UNION CATALOG OF MANUSCRIPT COLLECTIONS. **3233**

0090-0141 *See* DIRECTORY OF DENTAL EDUCATORS. **1322**

0090-0222 *See* GREAT LAKES ENTOMOLOGIST, THE. **5609**

0090-0281 *See* RANCHER. SOUTHERN SAN JOAQUIN VALLEY EDITION. **124**

0090-0427 *See* ENVIRONMENTAL SCIENCE RESEARCH. **2170**

0090-0443 *See* CURRENT CONCEPTS IN NUTRITION. **4189**

0090-0486 *See* ENVIRONMENT FILM REVIEW. **2165**

0090-0508 *See* CURRENT CONTENTS. AGRICULTURE, BIOLOGY, & ENVIRONMENTAL SCIENCES. **152**

0090-0575 *See* INTERNATIONAL BIBLIOGRAPHY ON BURNS. **3660**

0090-0591 *See* CTFA COSMETIC JOURNAL. **403**

0090-0605 *See* NORTH AMERICAN LIBRARY EDUCATION DIRECTORY AND STATISTICS. **3259**

0090-0648 *See* FODOR'S IRELAND. **5472**

0090-0656 *See* FISHERY BULLETIN. **2303**

0090-0664 *See* TECHNICAL REPORT - SCHOOL OF FOREST RESOURCES. NORTH CAROLINA STATE UNIVERSITY. **2396**

0090-0702 *See* MATERNAL-CHILD NURSING JOURNAL. **3861**

0090-0729 *See* PROCEEDINGS / INSTITUTE OF ENVIRONMENTAL SCIENCES. **1991**

0090-0737 *See* PENNSYLVANIA ORCHARD AND VINEYARD SURVEY. **2427**

0090-0745 *See* PERSPECTIVES ON HUMAN EVOLUTION. **243**

0090-080X *See* WOMAN'S GUIDE TO WASHINGTON, D.C, A. **5499**

0090-0842 *See* CONSENSUS (BROOKLYN). **659**

0090-0893 *See* NFAIS NEWSLETTER. **3236**

0090-0907 *See* CHEMICAL MARKETING REPORTER. **968**

0090-1008 *See* AIR/GROUND SKY-WAVE PROPAGATION CHARTS FOR SELECTED WORLD WIDE STATIONS. **7**

0090-1016 *See* ANNUAL REPORT - ILLINOIS DEPARTMENT OF BUSINESS AND ECONOMIC DEVELOPMENT. **1546**

0090-1032 *See* HARVARD POLITICAL REVIEW. **4475**

0090-1059 *See* RACIAL AND ETHNIC SURVEY. **2271**

0090-1067 *See* STATE OF WISCONSIN STATE SUMMARY. TYPE AND AMOUNT OF AIDS PAID TO ALL GOVERNMENTAL UNITS AND COUNTIES. **5444**

0090-1075 *See* FACILITIES INVENTORY OF INSTITUTIONS OF HIGHER EDUCATION IN OREGON. **1823**

0090-1091 *See* JOURNAL OF CLINICAL COMPUTING. **3787**

0090-1156 *See* BRUCELLOSIS SURVEILLANCE (ANNUAL SUMMARY). **4769**

0090-1210 *See* STANDARDIZATION NEWS : SN. **4032**

0090-1229 *See* CLINICAL IMMUNOLOGY AND IMMUNOPATHOLOGY. **3668**

0090-1237 *See* CLAUDEL STUDIES. **3376**

0090-1326 *See* RECURRING BIBLIOGRAPHY OF HYPERTENSION. **3710**

0090-1334 *See* STAFF PAPER P. **137**

0090-1377 *See* CUMULATED ABRIDGED INDEX MEDICUS. **3656**

0090-1385 *See* ANESTHESIOLOGY BIBLIOGRAPHY. **3654**

0090-1393 *See* ANNUAL BIBLIOGRAPHY OF ORTHOPAEDIC SURGERY. **3880**

0090-1423 *See* CUMULATED INDEX MEDICUS. **3656**

0090-1474 *See* MEDICAL OPINION (NEW YORK, N.Y.). **3610**

0090-1482 *See* JOURNAL OF ALCOHOL AND DRUG EDUCATION. **1345**

0090-1520 *See* SUMMARY OF GENERAL LEGISLATION (TALLAHASSEE). **4689**

0090-1563 *See* MOTOR IMPORTED CAR REPAIR MANUAL. **5419**

0090-158X *See* US. **2548**

0090-1601 *See* FOUNDATION GRANTS INDEX, THE. **4336**

0090-1741 *See* NATIONAL ROSTER OF REALTORS. **4842**

0090-175X *See* DIGEST OF CITY LAWS (SEATTLE, WASH.). **2961**

0090-1830 *See* MARINE FISHERIES REVIEW. **2308**

0090-1911 *See* VIBRATIONAL SPECTRA AND STRUCTURE. **4442**

0090-1938 *See* JOURNAL OF ERIE STUDIES. **2741**

0090-1989 *See* DIRECTORY : NORTH DAKOTA CITY OFFICIALS. **4643**

0090-2020 *See* PENTHOUSE (NEW YORK). **3996**

0090-2039 *See* MOVIE X. **5188**

0090-2047 *See* OUI. **2491**

0090-2055 *See* BIBLIOGRAPHY OF WATER QUALITY RESEARCH REPORTS. **5531**

0090-2071 *See* PROTEUS (ALEXANDRIA, VA.). **328**

0090-2098 *See* METALLOGRAPHIC REVIEW, THE. **4009**

0090-2128 *See* MAINE CATALOG, THE. **2538**

0090-2144 *See* MOTOR RACING YEAR, THE. **4905**

0090-2152 *See* REPORT OF THE MICHIGAN EDUCATIONAL ASSESSMENT PROGRAM. **1870**

0090-2187 *See* GREAT LAKES WATER LEVELS. **1413**

0090-2233 *See* REPORT OF ACHIEVEMENTS OF PROGRAMS FOR THE AGING. **5305**

0090-2241 *See* TRAIL CAMPING. **4879**

0090-2276 *See* SMALL ARMS IN PROFILE (GARDEN CITY, N.Y.). **4057**

0090-2284 *See* ANALYTICAL MICROBIOLOGY. **558**

0090-2292 See COMPLETE HOCKEY BOOK. **4891**

0090-2349 *See* FODOR'S TUNISIA. **5474**

0090-2357 *See* REGISTER OF GRADUATES AND FORMER CADETS OF THE UNITED STATES MILITARY ACADEMY. **4055**

0090-2365 See DIRECTORY OF STUDENTS - HARVARD UNIVERSITY. **1821**

0090-239X *See* FOREST SERVICE RESEARCH ACCOMPLISHMENTS. **2381**

0090-2403 *See* REPORT OF THE CARCINOGENESIS PROGRAM. **3823**

0090-2411 *See* A.E. LEGAL NEWSLETTER. **286**

0090-242X *See* BUDGET - LOS ANGELES. **4714**

0090-2462 *See* COTTON DIGEST INTERNATIONAL, THE. **5349**

0090-256X *See* INFORMATION SHEET - MISSISSIPPI STATE UNIVERSITY. AGRICULTURAL AND FORESTRY EXPERIMENT STATION. **96**

0090-2594 *See* VANDERBILT JOURNAL OF TRANSNATIONAL LAW. **3137**

0090-2616 *See* ORGANIZATIONAL DYNAMICS. **881**

0090-2632 See POETS AND AUTHORS. **3424**

0090-2799 *See* ANNUAL REPORT FOR THE ADVISORY COUNCIL FOR TECHNICAL-VOCATIONAL EDUCATION IN TEXAS. **1910**

0090-2810 *See* WORLD CURRENCY CHARTS. **920**

0090-2829 *See* COUNTY OF ALLEGHENY BUDGET FOR OPERATING DEPARTMENTS, THE. 4719

0090-2845 *See* ANNUAL REPORT OF THE REGISTER OF COPYRIGHTS. 1301

0090-2896 *See* PHYSICAL CONDITION REPORT OF COMMERCIAL DRIVERS INVOLVED IN ACCIDENTS. 5389

0090-2934 *See* DIALYSIS & TRANSPLANTATION. 3571

0090-2977 *See* NEUROPHYSIOLOGY (NEW YORK). 3841

0090-2985 *See* CARNIVAL & CIRCUS BOOKING GUIDE. 4849

0090-3000 *See* CINEMAGIC (NEW YORK, N.Y.). 4067

0090-3019 *See* SURGICAL NEUROLOGY. 3976

0090-3051 *See* ANNUAL REPORT OF THE DIVISION OF SOCIAL SERVICES OF THE DEPARTMENT OF HEALTH AND SOCIAL SERVICES. 5272

0090-3078 *See* FVUS. 89

0090-3159 *See* CONTEMPORARY OB/GYN. 3759

0090-3167 *See* LEARNING (PALO ALTO, CALIF.). 1900

0090-3175 *See* CONFLUENCE (WASHINGTON). 1733

0090-3213 *See* PLANETARIAN, THE. 398

0090-323X *See* QUARTERLY - MIAMI MALACOLOGICAL SOCIETY. 5596

0090-3329 *See* ANNUAL REPORTS AND RESOLUTIONS - AMERICAN DENTAL ASSOCIATION. 1316

0090-3337 *See* BIOSCENE. (BIOSCENE / BIOSIS). 3196

0090-3353 *See* ROCK SCENE. 4151

0090-3361 *See* KEYBOARD ARTS. 4127

0090-3493 *See* CRITICAL CARE MEDICINE. 3723

0090-3507 *See* RECORD OF CONFERENCE PAPERS - PETROLEUM AND CHEMICAL INDUSTRY CONFERENCE. 2016

0090-3558 *See* JOURNAL OF WILDLIFE DISEASES. 5514

0090-3590 *See* AUERBACH DATA COMMUNICATIONS EQUIPMENT DIGEST. 2036

0090-3604 *See* JOURNAL OF THE AMERICAN ACADEMY OF PSYCHOANALYSIS, THE. 3930

0090-3612 *See* PUERTO RICO OFFICIAL INDUSTRIAL DIRECTORY. 3487

0090-3620 See CHICANO-LATINO LAW REVIEW. 2950

0090-3663 *See* MUSIC WORLD MAGAZINE (LOS ANGELES). 4135

0090-3671 *See* YEAR BOOK OF SURGERY, THE. 3977

0090-371X *See* ACCESSIONS LIST, EASTERN AFRICA. 406

0090-3752 *See* NUCLEAR DATA SHEETS (NEW YORK). 4448

0090-3779 *See* APPALACHIAN JOURNAL. 2721

0090-3787 *See* STATE OF ILLINOIS STATISTICAL REPORT. 5339

0090-3795 *See* ANNUAL REPORT - STATE OF NEBRASKA. DEPARTMENT OF HEALTH. 4767

0090-3809 *See* MONTANA STATE PLAN FOR ALCOHOL ABUSE AND ALCOHOLISM PREVENTION, TREATMENT, AND REHABILITATION, THE. 1347

0090-3817 *See* ESSAYS AND REPORTS - LUTHERAN HISTORICAL CONFERENCE. 5059

0090-3868 See RUSSIA, EURASIAN STATES, AND EASTERN EUROPE. 2508

0090-3884 *See* STEAM-ELECTRIC PLANT FACTORS. 1958

0090-3922 *See* VIDEOPLAYER. 5320

0090-3930 *See* IMPACT (PHILADELPHIA). 2263

0090-3965 *See* MEMBERSHIP DIRECTORY - NATIONAL ASSOCIATION OF COLLEGE ADMISSIONS COUNSELORS. 1835

0090-3973 *See* JOURNAL OF TESTING AND EVALUATION. 1983

0090-399X *See* REALTY BLUEBOOK. 4846

0090-4007 *See* COUNTRY MUSIC. 4112

0090-4015 *See* REPORT - N.H. STATE PLANNING PROJECT. 4854

0090-404X *See* SCULPTORS. 2783

0090-4066 *See* DIRECTORY OF CORPORATE URBAN AFFAIRS OFFICERS. 1604

0090-4082 *See* OUTSTANDING ELEMENTARY TEACHERS OF AMERICA. 1805

0090-4104 *See* JOURNAL OF SOVIET MATHEMATICS. 3514

0090-4171 *See* STATIONS. 3472

0090-418X *See* WHO'S WHO IN THE SECURITIES INDUSTRY. 438

0090-4198 *See* INDIANA LAW REVIEW. 2982

0090-4228 *See* TOUCHDOWN (PHOENIX, ARIZ.). 4926

0090-4236 See SOCIOLOGY (GUILFORD, CONN.). 5262

0090-4244 *See* JOURNAL OF ADULT EDUCATION. 1801

0090-4260 *See* LITERATURE FILM QUARTERLY. 4074

0090-4295 *See* UROLOGY (RIDGEWOOD, N.J.). 3994

0090-4309 *See* ANNUAL EDITIONS : READINGS IN BUSINESS. 639

0090-4317 *See* CURRENT EXPENSE DISBURSEMENTS BY SOURCE OF FUNDS. 1862

0090-4341 *See* ARCHIVES OF ENVIRONMENTAL CONTAMINATION AND TOXICOLOGY. 2161

0090-435X *See* QUARTER HORSE REFERENCE. 2802

0090-4368 *See* G.H.S. FOOT-NOTES. 2734

0090-4392 *See* JOURNAL OF COMMUNITY PSYCHOLOGY. 4595

0090-4414 *See* OFFICIAL A.A.U. BASKETBALL HANDBOOK. 4908

0090-4422 *See* ECONOMICS : ENCYCLOPEDIA. 1486

0090-4430 *See* ECONOMICS : TEXT. 1591

0090-4465 *See* VRA BULLETIN BOARD. 4694

0090-4473 *See* PROCEEDINGS; ANNUAL AAZPA CONFERENCE. 5595

0090-4481 *See* PEDIATRIC ANNALS. 3908

0090-449X *See* CLARK COUNTY HISTORY. 2728

0090-4503 *See* AERR. 44

0090-452X *See* CATSKILLS, THE. 2530

0090-4570 *See* RAG TIMES. 4148

0090-4600 *See* TAX MANAGEMENT INTERNATIONAL JOURNAL. 887

0090-4651 *See* OFFICIAL REPORT - ASSOCIATION OF CLASSROOM TEACHERS. 1868

0090-466X *See* JOURNAL OF PHARMACOKINETICS AND BIOPHARMACEUTICS. 4312

0090-4759 *See* SOVIET JOURNAL OF PARTICLES AND NUCLEI. 4451

0090-4775 *See* CYCLE GUIDE'S MOTORCYCLE ACCESSORIES GUIDE. 4081

0090-4805 *See* NATIONAL ASSOCIATION OF ELEMENTARY PRINCIPALS. 1867

0090-4813 *See* INTERNATIONAL ARMAMENTS MONTHLY. 4046

0090-483X *See* DUDLEY GENEALOGICAL REVIEW, THE. 2446

0090-4848 *See* HUMAN RESOURCE MANAGEMENT. 941

0090-4864 *See* NFEC DIRECTORY OF ENVIRONMENTAL INFORMATION SOURCES. 2219

0090-4937 *See* JR. AMERICAN MODELER. 27

0090-4945 *See* DIRECTORY OF CONSULTING SPECIALISTS. 865

0090-4953 *See* MULBERRY. 3466

0090-4996 *See* ANIMAL LEARNING & BEHAVIOR. 5575

0090-5003 *See* CHINA MEDICAL REPORTER. 3563

0090-502X *See* MEMORY & COGNITION. 4603

0090-5054 *See* BULLETIN OF THE PSYCHONOMIC SOCIETY. 4579

0090-5070 *See* GROUND WATER NEWSLETTER / WATER INFORMATION CENTER, WIC, THE. 5534

0090-5151 *See* WOODALL'S FLORIDA CAMPGROUND DIRECTORY. 4881

0090-516X *See* POLLUTION TECHNOLOGY REVIEW. 2239

0090-5186 *See* MADISON COUNTY GENEALOGIST, THE. 2459

0090-5224 *See* POE STUDIES. 434

0090-5232 *See* LC SCIENCE TRACER BULLET. 5175

0090-5267 *See* CONTROL AND DYNAMIC SYSTEMS. 1969

0090-5283 *See* VT RESEARCH SERIES. 1917

0090-5291 *See* ELECTRONICS BUYERS' GUIDE. 2049

0090-5321 *See* MISSISSIPPI COVERED EMPLOYMENT & WAGES. 1691

0090-5364 *See* ANNALS OF STATISTICS, THE. 5321

0090-5402 *See* PAINT RED BOOK. 4224

0090-5410 *See* HERPETON (GLENDORA, CALIF.). 5585

0090-5429 *See* ANNUAL REPORT - BUREAU OF POLLUTION CONTROL. STATE OF NEW JERSEY. DEPARTMENT OF ENVIRONMENTAL PROTECTION. 2224

0090-5453 *See* REPORT TO THE ADMINISTRATOR ON THE SKYLAB PROGRAM. 33

0090-547X *See* AMERICAN GOVERNMENT : TEXT. 4463

0090-5542 *See* BASIC LIFE SCIENCES. 443

0090-5550 *See* REHABILITATION PSYCHOLOGY. 4615

0090-5623 *See* OREGON SCHOOL COMMUNITY COLLEGE DIRECTORY. 1839

0090-5631 *See* PROCEEDINGS. ANNUAL MEAT SCIENCE INSTITUTE. 2353

0090-5658 *See* DIRECTORY OF PROGRAMS AND SERVICES FOR OLDER ADULTS : STATE OF OREGON BY COUNTIES. 5283

0090-5674 *See* PAIDEUMA (ORONO). 434

0090-5704 *See* NEWSLETTER OF THE LAMBERT-LAMBERTH ASSOCIATION. 2463

0090-5720 See JOURNAL OF SOCIO-ECONOMICS. 1570

0090-5747 *See* SAGE URBAN STUDIES ABSTRACTS. 2840

0090-5771 *See* CHRYSANTHEMUM. 2412

0090-5844 *See* NORTH CAROLINA FOLKLORE JOURNAL. 2323

0090-5860 *See* PROGRESS IN HAZARDOUS CHEMICALS HANDLING AND DISPOSAL. 2240

0090-5879 *See* TWENTY YEAR HIGHWAY NEEDS STUDY. 5446

0090-5895 *See* STATE GOVERNMENT FINANCES. 4749

0090-5917 *See* POLITICAL THEORY. 4490

0090-5992 *See* NATIONALITIES PAPERS. 2268

0090-600X *See* WHEELER'S TRAILER RESORT AND CAMPGROUND GUIDE. SUN BELT EDITION. 4880

0090-6034 *See* CRICKET (LA SALLE). 1062

0090-6093 *See* NEWSLETTER - COWAN CLAN UNITED. 2463

0090-6107 *See* PROGRESS REPORT - MAINE LAW ENFORCEMENT PLANNING AND ASSISTANCE AGENCY. 3173

0090-6182 *See* ANNUAL REPORT - ARIZONA STATE ECONOMIC OPPORTUNITY OFFICE. 1546

0090-6239 *See* ANNUAL REPORT - NATIONAL ASSOCIATION OF INDEPENDENT SCHOOLS. 1725

0090-6247 *See* ANNUAL REPORT - OFFICE OF DIRECTOR. OREGON DEPARTMENT OF TRANSPORTATION. 5376

0090-6352 *See* ASSESSMENT AND VALUATION LEGAL REPORTER. 4711

0090-6379 *See* BLI BULLETIN. 1655

0090-6468 *See* BETTER WAYS TO DO IT. 370

ISSN Index

0090-6484 See DIRECTORY OF EXECUTIVE RECRUITERS. 939

0090-6484 See DIRECTORY OF EXECUTIVE RECRUITERS (STANDARD ED.). 940

0090-6492 See GRANT AWARDS - U.S. DEPARTMENT OF TRANSPORTATION. 5383

0090-6506 See MAJOR MEDICAL PLANS : SELECTED COLLECTIVE BARGAINING AGREEMENTS, CALIFORNIA. 2887

0090-6514 See TELOS (ST. LOUIS). 5224

0090-6565 See STATISTICAL REPORT - CITY OF LOS ANGELES. SOCIAL SERVICE DEPARTMENT. 5267

0090-6654 See EVALUATIONS OF DRUG INTERACTIONS. 4303

0090-6700 See OFFICIAL MUSEUM DIRECTORY, THE. 4094

0090-6743 See DESCRIPTIVE REPORT OF PROGRAM ACTIVITIES FOR VOCATIONAL EDUCATION. 1912

0090-6778 See IEEE TRANSACTIONS ON COMMUNICATIONS. 1157

0090-6786 See STEREO DIRECTORY & BUYING GUIDE. 5319

0090-6808 See SELECTED IRRIGATION RETURN FLOW QUALITY ABSTRACTS. 2095

0090-6816 See U.S.A.N. AND THE U.S.P. DICTIONARY OF DRUG NAMES. 4331

0090-6875 See MUNICIPAL POLICY STATEMENT - LEAGUE OF ARIZONA CITIES & TOWNS. 4667

0090-6905 See JOURNAL OF PSYCHOLINGUISTIC RESEARCH. 3291

0090-6964 See ANNALS OF BIOMEDICAL ENGINEERING. 3685

0090-6980 See PROSTAGLANDINS. 585

0090-7030 See MEDICAL EXAMINATION REVIEW BOOK. VOLUME 11. PEDIATRICS. 3906

0090-7065 See MEDICAL EXAMINATION REVIEW BOOK. PATHOLOGY SPECIALTY BOARD REVIEW. 3896

0090-7073 See MEDICAL EXAMINATION REVIEW BOOK. NEUROLOGY SPECIALTY BOARD REVIEW. 3837

0090-7081 See FISH DIRECTORY. 5285

0090-709X See HYDROLOGIC REPORT (NEW MEXICO. BUREAU OF MINES AND MINERAL RESOURCES). 1414

0090-7111 See CENSUS OF MAINE MANUFACTURES. 1601

0090-712X See WATERWAY GUIDE. NORTHERN EDITION. 597

0090-7138 See PUBLIC ASSISTANCE FOR MINNESOTA INDIANS. 2271

0090-7154 See STATISTICS OF MISSOURI NONPUBLIC ELEMENTARY AND SECONDARY SCHOOLS. 1798

0090-7162 See UTAH STATE PLAN FOR THE ADMINISTRATION OF VOCATIONAL EDUCATION. 1917

0090-7170 See RESEARCH PAPER (UNIVERSITY OF WISCONSIN--MADISON. TENURE CENTER). 1517

0090-7197 See BLACK PHOTOGRAPHERS ANNUAL, THE. 4367

0090-7219 See COMPLETE INCOME TAX GUIDE, THE. 4718

0090-7286 See TOPICAL NEW ISSUES. 2788

0090-7308 See FLAG. 4117

0090-7324 See REFERENCE SERVICES REVIEW. 1928

0090-7359 See DIRECTOR'S REPORT - PAPANICOLAOU CANCER RESEARCH INSTITUTE AT MIAMI FLORIDA. 3816

0090-7375 See FINANCIAL REPORT OF THE GENERAL SUPERINTENDENT - BOARD OF SCHOOL COMMISSIONERS OF THE CITY OF INDIANAPOLIS. 1864

0090-7391 See DEPARTMENT OF AGRICULTURAL EDUCATION REPORT. 78

0090-7421 See JOURNAL OF ALLIED HEALTH. 3593

0090-7456 See MONTHLY STATISTICAL SUMMARY REPORT - STATE OF OHIO, DEPARTMENT OF MENTAL HEALTH AND MENTAL RETARDATION, DIVISION OF BUSINESS ADMINISTRATION, BUREAU OF STATISTICS. 4810

0090-7480 See BEST'S SAFETY DIRECTORY. 2859

0090-7812 See DIRECTORY OF MISSOURI'S REGIONAL PLANNING SYSTEM, A. 2821

0090-7847 See RAILROAD HISTORY. 5435

0090-7855 See PAABS REVISTA. 491

0090-7871 See EQUILIBRIUM (WASHINGTON, D.C.). 4552

0090-788X See LET'S GO : THE STUDENT GUIDE TO THE UNITED STATES AND CANADA. 5483

0090-7944 See COLUMBIA HUMAN RIGHTS LAW REVIEW. 4506

0090-7987 See CHILDREN'S BOOK REVIEW SERVICE. 3339

0090-8010 See REPORTS OF OFFICERS AND PROCEEDINGS OF THE SUPREME LODGE OF THE ANCIENT ORDER OF UNITED WORKMEN. 5236

0090-8029 See AUTO RACING DIGEST. 4885

0090-8037 See OKLAHOMA RURAL MANPOWER REPORT. 1700

0090-8045 See ASTM YEAR BOOK. 2101

0090-8053 See COMPARATIVE GUIDE TO AMERICAN COLLEGES : FOR STUDENTS, PARENTS, AND COUNSELORS. 1818

0090-8061 See CONGRESSIONAL DISTRICT ATLAS. 2559

0090-8088 See GREEN AMERICA. 2384

0090-8134 See RESEARCH DIVISION BULLETIN (VIRGINIA POLYTECHNIC INSTITUTE AND STATE UNIVERSITY. RESEARCH DIVISION). 1845

0090-8142 See RESEARCH PROGRESS REPORT - WESTERN SOCIETY OF WEED SCIENCE. 185

0090-8177 See BIENNIAL REPORT - MINNESOTA DEPARTMENT OF NATURAL RESOURCES. 2188

0090-8207 See GRAPHIC ARTS BULLETIN OF THE INSTITUTE OF PAPER SCIENCE AND TECHNOLOGY. 334

0090-8215 See KNITTER'S JOURNAL. 5184

0090-824X See CURRENT OPINION. 5244

0090-8258 See GYNECOLOGIC ONCOLOGY. 3817

0090-8290 See CANADIAN-AMERICAN SLAVIC STUDIES. 2683

0090-8312 See ENERGY SOURCES. 1942

0090-8320 See OCEAN DEVELOPMENT AND INTERNATIONAL LAW. 3182

0090-8363 See CHEMICAL ABSTRACTS. APPLIED CHEMISTRY AND CHEMICAL ENGINEERING SECTIONS. 1021

0090-838X See ALCOHOL HEALTH AND RESEARCH WORLD. 1339

0090-841X See EXECUTIVE CAPITAL CONSTRUCTION BUDGET. 4723

0090-8428 See MAJOR GOALS OF VOCATIONAL EDUCATION IN MAINE. 1914

0090-8460 See CONNECTICUT MASTER TRANSPORTATION PLAN. 5380

0090-8517 See BULLETIN - CONNECTICUT RIVER VALLEY COVERED BRIDGE SOCIETY. 2019

0090-8533 See INCENTIVE TRAVEL AND BUSINESS MEETINGS. 1677

0090-855X See MINORITY BUILDER. 621

0090-8614 See ALA SIGHTS TO SEE BOOK. 5403

0090-8657 See TIRE SCIENCE & TECHNOLOGY. 5426

0090-8681 See BOECKH BUILDING COST INDEX NUMBERS. 601

0090-8711 See CUTTING HORSE. 2798

0090-8738 See JOURNAL OF THE BROMELIAD SOCIETY. 516

0090-8762 See PRACTICAL HORSEMAN. 2801

0090-8770 See AIRLINERS INTERNATIONAL. 10

0090-8789 See CARBON COUNTY LAW JOURNAL, THE. 2948

0090-8800 See CONTEMPORARY TOPICS IN MOLECULAR IMMUNOLOGY. 3668

0090-8878 See HOUSEHOLD & PERSONAL PRODUCTS INDUSTRY : HAPPI. 977

0090-8932 See RENDER. 2355

0090-8967 See ANNUAL REPORT - ILLINOIS INSTITUTE FOR ENVIRONMENTAL QUALITY. 2160

0090-8991 See STATISTICAL YEARBOOK - NEW YORK MERCANTILE EXCHANGE. 733

0090-9009 See SWIZZLE STICK. 852

0090-9033 See BUYER'S GUIDE TO THE WORLD OF TAPE. 5316

0090-905X See IOWA GENEALOGICAL SOCIETY SURNAME INDEX. 2454

0090-9114 See AMERICANA. 2527

0090-9122 See FISCAL YEAR REPORT - STATE OF MONTANA. BOARD OF INVESTMENTS. 899

0090-9130 See INDEX OF AMERICAN PERIODICAL VERSE. 3458

0090-9157 See RADIO CONTROL PRODUCTS DIRECTORY. 375

0090-9211 See ART INVESTMENT REPORT, THE. 891

0090-9238 See ON SITE (WASHINGTON, D.C.). 623

0090-9262 See REGIONAL ECONOMIC PROJECTIONS SERIES. 1516

0090-9300 See MARYLAND GEOGRAPHER, THE. 2568

0090-9327 See PENNY STOCK HANDBOOK. 910

0090-9335 See WALL ST. U.S.A. 919

0090-9351 See TUBERCULOSIS PROGRAMS. 3952

0090-9378 See SCIENCE QUEST. 5153

0090-9408 See MEH LADY. 1835

0090-9416 See LATIN AMERICAN INDEX. 4480

0090-9459 See SUPPLEMENTARY DIRECTORY OF THE AMERICAN BAPTIST CHURCHES IN THE U.S.A. 5068

0090-9467 See FOREIGN ECONOMIC TRENDS AND THEIR IMPLICATIONS FOR THE UNITED STATES. 1561

0090-9483 See NATURAL RESOURCES, SCIENCE AND TECHNOLOGY NEWSLETTER. 2199

0090-9513 See FOCUS : BLACK AMERICAN BIBLIOGRAPHY SERIES. SUPPLEMENT. 2276

0090-9521 See ARCHITECTURE PLUS. 290

0090-9556 See DRUG METABOLISM AND DISPOSITION. 4300

0090-967X See FLORIDA HORSE, THE. 2799

0090-9688 See FOOD AND HOME NOTES. 88

0090-9769 See LOUISIANA FOLKLORE MISCELLANY. 2322

0090-9793 See COSMIC SOFTWARE CATALOG. 1228

0090-9831 See CRITIC (NEW YORK). 4067

0090-9874 See ANNUAL REPORT TO THE GOVERNOR AND MEMBERS OF THE GENERAL ASSEMBLY - MISSOURI COMMISSION ON HIGHER EDUCATION. 1809

0090-9882 See JOURNAL OF APPLIED COMMUNICATION RESEARCH : JACR. 1114

0090-9890 See MUSEUM PROGRAM GUIDELINES. 4092

0091-0082 See MOLECULAR COMPLEXES. 1056

0091-0090 See OFFICIAL CANDIDATES PAMPHLET. 4485

0091-018X See FOOD MANAGEMENT. 2338

0091-0260 See PUBLIC PERSONNEL MANAGEMENT. 946

0091-0287 See YALE SCIENTIFIC. 5171

0091-0368 See ANNUAL REPORT OF THE DEPARTMENT OF MILITARY AFFAIRS TO THE GOVERNOR OF MONTANA. 4035

0091-0376 See PRAIRIE NATURALIST, THE. 4170

0091-0392 See BANK PROTECTION BULLETIN. 775

0091-0406 See NEBRASKA STATE PUBLICATIONS CHECKLIST. 420

0091-0422 See PSYCHIATRIC OUTPATIENT PROGRAM. 3933

0091-0430 See LAWYER-TO-LAWYER CONSULTATION PANEL. 2997

0091-0457 See ANNUAL REPORT - ENVIRONMENTAL QUALITY COUNCIL. 2160

0091-0473 See COLLECTABLE OLD ADVERTISING. 757

0091-049X See DYNAMIC ASPECTS OF HOST-PARASITE RELATIONSHIPS. 454

0091-0511 See PROGRAM INFORMATION SERIES REPORT. 5302

0091-052X See MISSOURI MINERAL NEWS. 1442

0091-0554 See SPACE AGE NEWS. 35

0091-0562 See AMERICAN JOURNAL OF COMMUNITY PSYCHOLOGY. 4573

0091-0619 See ION EXCHANGE AND MEMBRANES. 1053

0091-0627 See JOURNAL OF ABNORMAL CHILD PSYCHOLOGY. 4593

0091-0651 See FIELD & STREAM SPORTSMAN. 4872

0091-066X See COMPREHENSIVE MANPOWER PLAN. 1660

0091-0678 See ANNUAL REPORT - STATE PLANNING OFFICE. EXECUTIVE DEPARTMENT. STATE OF MAINE. 2815

0091-0686 See ANNUAL REPORT - STATE INVESTMENT COUNCIL. STATE OF NEBRASKA. 4710

0091-0694 See CATALOGUE OF STATE PROGRAMS (CARSON CITY). 1551

0091-0716 See GUIDE TO NEBRASKA STATE AGENCIES. 4653

0091-0724 See ANNUAL CAUSES & CONDITIONS OF POVERTY IN SOUTH DAKOTA. 5272

0091-0775 See KENTUCKY SCHOOL DIRECTORY, THE. 1760

0091-0783 See NTA-TIA BOOKSHELF. 4739

0091-0821 See OFFICIAL NATIONAL FOOTBALL LEAGUE GUIDE. 4909

0091-0996 See ANNUAL REPORT OF THE DEPARTMENT OF SOCIAL AND REHABILITATION SERVICES TO THE GOVERNOR OF MONTANA. 5272

0091-1003 See DIRECTORY : DIOCESAN AGENCIES OF CATHOLIC CHARITIES, UNITED STATES, PUERTO RICO, AND CANADA. 5282

0091-1011 See FOR THE DEFENSE (AUSTIN). 3107

0091-102X See INDIAN VOICE (SANTA CLARA). 2738

0091-1038 See MODEL CITIES BULLETIN. 1764

0091-1046 See MODERN ASTRONOMY (BUFFALO). 397

0091-1062 See SAMPE JOURNAL. 1995

0091-1070 See NORTH DAKOTA STATE PLAN FOR DEVELOPMENTAL DISABILITIES SERVICES AND FACILITIES CONSTRUCTION. 5299

0091-1178 See TAX PRACTICE AND PROCEDURE. 4754

0091-1267 See COLD STORAGE. 167

0091-1305 See FARMFUTURES. 86

0091-1313 See FORESTRY RESEARCH REPORT. 2382

0091-1348 See NEWS OF THE LEPIDOPTERISTS' SOCIETY. 5592

0091-1372 See SOAP, COSMETICS, CHEMICAL SPECIALTIES. 1030

0091-1399 See BRIEFS OF AIRCRAFT ACCIDENTS INVOLVING TURBINE POWERED AIRCRAFT, U.S. GENERAL AVIATION. 15

0091-1402 See STATEHOUSE OBSERVER, THE. 4688

0091-1410 See TRANSPORTATION; CURRENT LITERATURE. 5396

0091-1429 See UNITED STATES EARTHQUAKES. 1400

0091-1461 See SKI RACING REDBOOK. 4918

0091-1488 See BACHY. 316

0091-150X See PHARMACEUTICAL CHEMISTRY JOURNAL. 4320

0091-1542 See NEW AND EXPANDED INDUSTRIES ANNOUNCED IN ALABAMA. 1619

0091-1550 See TEXAS LIVESTOCK STATISTICS. 157

0091-1577 See ANNUAL REPORT - CINCINNATI CITY PLANNING COMMISSION. 2814

0091-1585 See STATE PLAN FOR HOSPITAL AND MEDICAL FACILITIES CONSTRUCTION. 3792

0091-1593 See TRIENNIAL REPORT ON WATER RESOURCES DEVELOPMENT. 5541

0091-1607 See AKIKI, THE. 2436

0091-164X See NORTH CAROLINA DENTAL GAZETTE. 1331

0091-1658 See AMERICAN STATISTICS INDEX. 4696

0091-1666 See CDS REVIEW. 1318

0091-1674 See CLINICAL SOCIAL WORK JOURNAL. 5279

0091-1682 See CLINICAL TRENDS IN UROLOGY. 3989

0091-1720 See PUBLIC SCIENCE NEWSLETTER. 5143

0091-1798 See ANNALS OF PROBABILITY, THE. 3494

0091-181X See MARINE BEHAVIOUR AND PHYSIOLOGY. 583

0091-1852 See WORLD PROGRESS YEARBOOK. 2633

0091-1860 See CONTRIBUTIONS FROM THE UNIVERSITY OF MICHIGAN HERBARIUM. 507

0091-1879 See SIMPLICITY FASHIONS. 5186

0091-1933 See MICHIGAN MANUAL. 4665

0091-1984 See CATV SYSTEMS DIRECTORY, MAP SERVICE & HANDBOOK. 1130

0091-200X See PHYSICIAN'S WORLD. 3916

0091-2018 See WOODALL'S BETTER CAMPING. 4881

0091-2034 See LAWRENCE. ALUMNI EDITION. 1092

0091-2131 See ETHOS. 4586

0091-2174 See INTERNATIONAL JOURNAL OF PSYCHIATRY IN MEDICINE, THE. 3927

0091-2182 See JOURNAL OF NURSE-MIDWIFERY. 3859

0091-2204 See COPPER STUDIES. 4000

0091-2212 See C.U.S.I.P. DIRECTORY. 893

0091-2271 See HISTORY; ANNUAL SUPPLEMENT. 4045

0091-2328 See INVESTMENT ADVISER DIRECTORY. 902

0091-2336 See HEMATOLOGY CASE STUDIES. 3772

0091-2344 See ALL LOW-RENT PUBLIC HOUSING PROGRAMS, REGION 10: SEATTLE. 2813

0091-2352 See ALL LOW-RENT PUBLIC HOUSING PROGRAMS, REGION 1: BOSTON. 2813

0091-2360 See TODAY'S CHIROPRACTIC. 3646

0091-2387 See NATIONAL SPOKESMAN. 3839

0091-2433 See ALL LOW-RENT PUBLIC HOUSING PROGRAMS, REGION 2: NEW YORK. 2813

0091-2441 See ALL LOW-RENT PUBLIC HOUSING PROGRAMS, REGION 9: SAN FRANCISCO. 2813

0091-245X See ALL LOW-RENT PUBLIC HOUSING PROGRAMS, REGION 6: FORT WORTH. 2813

0091-2492 See INTERNATIONAL ECONOMIC REPORT OF THE PRESIDENT. 1636

0091-2514 See ALL LOW-RENT PUBLIC HOUSING PROGRAMS, REGION 3: PHILADELPHIA. 2813

0091-2522 See ALL LOW-RENT PUBLIC HOUSING PROGRAMS, REGION 4: ATLANTA. 2813

0091-2530 See ALL LOW-RENT PUBLIC HOUSING PROGRAMS, REGION 7: KANSAS CITY. 2813

0091-2549 See MEMBER BANK CONDITION, TENTH FEDERAL RESERVE DISTRICT. 797

0091-2565 See OPERATING RATIOS OF SECOND DISTRICT MEMBER BANKS. 802

0091-2581 See BUSINESS FIRMS DIRECTORY OF THE DELAWARE VALLEY. 648

0091-259X See ANNUAL REPORT - TENNESSEE ARTS COMMISSION. 313

0091-2700 See JOURNAL OF CLINICAL PHARMACOLOGY, THE. 4310

0091-2719 See TRANSPLANTATION TODAY. 3977

0091-2751 See JCU : JOURNAL OF CLINICAL ULTRASOUND. 3591

0091-2786 See RESEARCH AND DEVELOPMENT - AMERICAN GAS ASSOCIATION. 4276

0091-2816 See INCOME TAX PROCEDURE. 4731

0091-2840 See A. I. D. MEMORY DOCUMENTS. 1528

0091-2867 See CHRISTIAN EDUCATOR. 4944

0091-2875 See PERSPECTIVE (TRENTON). 1773

0091-2883 See PROGRESS REPORT - MICHIGAN DEPARTMENT OF SOCIAL SERVICES. OFFICE OF YOUTH SERVICES. 5302

0091-2921 See PERSPECTIVES IN PEDIATRIC PATHOLOGY. 3910

0091-2948 See LOST GENERATION JOURNAL. 3408

0091-2980 See INTRODUCING SYRACUSE TO YOU. 2535

0091-3030 See METHODS IN PHARMACOLOGY. 4315

0091-3057 See PHARMACOLOGY, BIOCHEMISTRY AND BEHAVIOR. 4322

0091-3154 See WHO'S WHO IN ECOLOGY. 436

0091-3162 See WIRE JOURNAL DIRECTORY/CATALOG. 4023

0091-3170 See TELEX DIRECTORY. 1168

0091-3189 See MISSISSINEWA GENEALOGICAL QUARTERLY. 2460

0091-3197 See INTRODUCING COLUMBUS TO YOU. 2535

0091-3200 See INTRODUCING BUFFALO TO YOU. 2535

0091-3219 See JOURNAL OF ETHNIC STUDIES, THE. 2266

0091-3235 See DIRECTORY OF LATIN AMERICANISTS. 2512

0091-3251 See INDEX TO THE PUBLIC SCHOOLS (ALBANY). 1752

0091-3278 See JUVENILE COURT STATISTICS (WASHINGTON). 3081

0091-3286 See OPTICAL ENGINEERING. 4439

0091-3367 See JOURNAL OF ADVERTISING. 761

0091-3383 See AMERICAN SQUARE DANCE. 1310

0091-3405 See OFFICIAL HANDBOOK OF THE AAU CODE. 4909

0091-3413 See OFFICIAL RULES FOR COMPETITIVE SWIMMING. 4910

0091-3421 See C.L.C. CONTEMPORARY LITERARY CRITICISM. 3339

0091-3456 See VIGNETTES. 1096

0091-3480 See AIDJEX BULLETIN. 1412

0091-3502 See AGRICULTURAL FINANCE STATISTICS. 726

0091-3510 See ANNUAL REPORT - CAPITAL AREA PLANNING COUNCIL. 2814

0091-3529 See ANNUAL BENZENE & DERIVATIVES. 4249

0091-3537 See BUSINESS JOURNAL (WICHITA). 650

0091-3545 See CALIFORNIA EMPLOYER CONTRIBUTIONS TO THE UNEMPLOYMENT FUND. 1658

0091-357X See REGISTER OF RETIREMENT BENEFIT PLANS REPORTED UNDER THE WELFARE AND PENSION PLANS DISCLOSURE ACT. 1705

0091-3588 See STATE OF IOWA SCHOLARSHIPS, TUITION GRANTS, MEDICAL TUITION LOANS : BIENNIUM REPORT. 1785

0091-360X See A.V. GUIDE. 1887

0091-3642 See FRUIT VARIETIES JOURNAL. 2415

0091-3669 See MOSQUITO SYSTEMATICS. 2177

0091-3693 See NORTH CAROLINA AGRICULTURAL STATISTICS. 115

0091-3707 See SOCIAL SCIENCES CITATION INDEX (PRINT ED.). 5228

0091-3715 See POLITICAL SCIENCE REVIEWER, THE. 4490

0091-3723 See JOURNAL OF CHINESE LINGUISTICS. 3289

0091-3758 See RESOURCE-DATA BOOK. 5337

0091-3774 See MOTORCYCLE BLUE BOOK. 4082

0091-3804 See C.U.S.I.P. DIRECTORY. CORPORATE DIRECTORY. 893

0091-3812 See AGENCY ACCOUNTABILITY SURVEY. 1642

0091-3820 See AUDIT OF THE RURAL TELEPHONE BANK, DEPARTMENT OF AGRICULTURE (WASHINGTON). 1150

0091-3847 See PHYSICIAN AND SPORTSMEDICINE, THE. 3955

0091-3863 See UTAH ANNUAL EVALUATION REPORT; TITLE I ESEA. 1873

0091-3901 See ILLUSTRATED DIGEST OF BASEBALL. 4899

0091-391X See SEMICONDUCTOR SILICON. 2080

0091-3952 See ADVANCES IN NEUROLOGY. 3826

0091-3960 See AMERICAN JOURNAL OF ACUPUNCTURE. 3548

0091-3995 See SIECUS REPORT. 5188

0091-4002 See BIRK'S. 2942

0091-4010 See GUIDEBOOK TO OHIO TAXES. 4730

0091-4029 See HOFSTRA LAW REVIEW. 2978

0091-4037 See INTERNATIONAL JOURNAL OF POLYMERIC MATERIALS. 978

0091-4053 See PLANNING LEGISLATION IN NEW YORK STATE. 3029

0091-4061 See SEC DOCKET. 913

0091-407X See U.S./JAPAN OUTLOOK. 855

0091-4118 See REPORT - PENNSYLVANIA CRIME COMMISSION. 3174

0091-4150 See INTERNATIONAL JOURNAL OF AGING & HUMAN DEVELOPMENT, THE. 5247

0091-4169 See JOURNAL OF CRIMINAL LAW & CRIMINOLOGY. 3107

0091-4169 See JOURNAL OF CRIMINAL LAW & CRIMINOLOGY. [MICROFILM], THE. 3107

0091-4223 See MEDICAL EXAMINATION REVIEW BOOK. OBSTETRICS AND GYNECOLOGY SPECIALTY BOARD REVIEW. 3765

0091-424X See DACAS : DRUG ABUSE CURRENT AWARENESS SYSTEM. 1342

0091-4258 See DIRECTORY OF THE AMERICAN OPTOMETRIC ASSOCIATION. 4215

0091-4347 See LIETUVIU TAUTOS PRAEITIS. 2696

0091-4355 See ESTIMATES OF EMPLOYMENT, HOURS, AND EARNINGS IN NONAGRICULTURAL ESTABLISHMENTS. SPRINGFIELD STANDARD METROPOLITAN STATISTICAL AREA. 1668

0091-438X See ANNUAL GRAZING STATISTICAL REPORT. 2398

0091-4401 See ARIZONA THOROUGHBRED, THE. 2797

0091-441X See CALIFORNIA HORSE REVIEW. 2797

0091-4460 See MAFES RESEARCH HIGHLIGHTS. 106

0091-4487 See PROCEEDINGS OF THE WESTERN SOCIETY OF WEED SCIENCE. 183

0091-4509 See CONTEMPORARY DRUG PROBLEMS. 1342

0091-4517 See ESTIMATES OF EMPLOYMENT, HOURS, AND EARNINGS IN NONAGRICULTURAL ESTABLISHMENTS: DECATUR STANDARD METROPOLITAN STATISTICAL AREA. 1668

0091-4533 See INVESTMENT COMPANIES INTERNATIONAL YEARBOOK. 902

0091-4541 See WATER POLLUTION CONTROL PLAN (SPRINGFIELD). 5543

0091-4576 See CONSUMER GUIDE PHOTOGRAPHIC EQUIPMENT TEST REPORTS. 4368

0091-4584 See HOW FEDERAL AGENCIES HAVE SERVED THE HANDICAPPED. 4388

0091-4622 See U. S. BLACK BUSINESS. 716

0091-4630 See PROGRESS REPORT. THE MINORITY BUSINESS ENTERPRISE PROGRAM. 705

0091-469X See RECORD - I.E.E.E. SYMPOSIUM ON COMPUTER SOFTWARE RELIABILITY. 1281

0091-4711 See LOUISIANA LABOR MARKET. 1688

0091-4770 See ALL LOW-RENT PUBLIC HOUSING PROGRAMS, REGION 5: CHICAGO. 2813

0091-4789 See COLORADO CITY RETAIL SALES BY STANDARD INDUSTRIAL CLASSIFICATION. 952

0091-4789 See COLORADO STATE AND COUNTY RETAIL SALES BY STANDARD INDUSTRIAL CLASSIFICATION (ANNUAL). 953

0091-4843 See MILLING AND BAKING NEWS. 202

0091-4908 See ANNUAL MANPOWER PLANNING REPORT. CHICAGO STANDARD METROPOLITAN STATISTICAL AREA. 1645

0091-4916 See JOURNAL OF NUCLEAR MEDICINE TECHNOLOGY. 3848

0091-4924 See FLANNERY O'CONNOR BULLETIN. 432

0091-4932 See F.H.A. HOMES. 2822

0091-4959 See NEW BOOKS QUARTERLY CHECKLIST SERIES : AFRO-AMERICAN HISTORY AND CULTURE. 2748

0091-4975 See CORPORATE REPORTS ON FILE. 895

0091-4991 See DIRECTORY OF MEMBERS / SOCIETY OF AMERICAN TRAVEL WRITERS. 5468

0091-5009 See AREA WAGE SURVEY : AUSTIN, TEXAS, METROPOLITAN AREA. 1652

0091-5025 See DRUG ABUSE PREVENTION REPORT. 1343

0091-5033 See ECONOMIC CONDITIONS IN NEW HAMPSHIRE LOCAL OFFICE AREAS. 1664

0091-5041 See MEMORIALS - GEOLOGICAL SOCIETY OF AMERICA. 1387

0091-5106 See NEVADA STATE PLAN FOR CAREER EDUCATION. 1914

0091-5114 See PENNSYLVANIA STATE PLAN FOR THE ADMINISTRATION OF VOCATIONAL-TECHNICAL EDUCATION PROGRAMS, A. 1915

0091-5122 See PROCEEDINGS - COMMITTEE ON COMPUTER TECHNOLOGY. 5442

0091-5149 See VIRGINIA HIGH SCHOOL DROPOUTS. 1798

0091-5157 See POPULAR PSYCHOLOGY (SHERMAN OAKS). 4608

0091-522X See ENVIOS. 3384

0091-5386 See EXTERNAL TRADE STATISTICS (SAN JUAN). 728

0091-5440 See UNIVERSITY OF BALTIMORE LAW REVIEW. 3068

0091-5459 See UNION LABOR REPORT. 3155

0091-5467 See ANNUAL REPORT / NATIONAL TRUST FOR HISTORIC PRESERVATION. 2720

0091-5475 See REPORT - CINCINNATI BAR ASSOCIATION. 3037

0091-5483 See AUDIT OF THE UNITED STATES CAPITOL HISTORICAL SOCIETY FOR THE YEAR ENDED 2722

0091-5491 See AMERICAN MARINE REGISTER. 5447

0091-5505 See WOODALL'S MOBILE HOME LIFESTYLE. 2839

0091-5513 See WEST VIRGINIA COAL FACTS. 2153

0091-5521 See COMMUNITY COLLEGE REVIEW. 1817

0091-5572 See RAILROAD CAR JOURNAL. 5435

0091-5599 See SALARY SURVEY OF STATE GOVERNMENT EMPLOYERS (PHOENIX). 1709

0091-5610 See POPULATION : PERSPECTIVE. 4557

0091-5637 See JOURNAL OF SOUTH ASIAN LITERATURE. 3400

0091-5661 See PERSONAL INCOME TAX IN OREGON, THE. 4740

0091-567X See SEASON SUMMARY - OREGON BARTLETT PEAR COMMISSION. 2431

0091-5734 See WASHINGTON TRANSPORTATION NEWSLETTER. 5399

0091-5823 See RESEARCH REPORT AFDC. 5306

0091-5882 See ANNUAL DESCRIPTIVE REPORT OF PROGRAM ACTIVITIES FOR VOCATIONAL EDUCATION. 1910

0091-5939 See HOUSING & DEVELOPMENT REPORTER. 2824

0091-5971 See SAA NEWSLETTER. 2483

0091-6064 See STATE AID TO MUNICIPALITIES FOR HIGHWAYS AND STREETS (BOSTON). 5444

0091-6110 See FINANCIAL REPORT - UNIVERSITY OF VIRGINIA. 1824

0091-6145 See PROGRESS IN EXTRACTIVE METALLURGY. 4016

0091-6196 See WEST VIRGINIA'S STATE SYSTEM OF HIGHER EDUCATION. 1853

0091-6226 See SELF-PUBLISHING WRITER, THE. 4819

0091-6234 See SOCIAL DEVELOPMENT ACTIVITIES IN LATIN AMERICA PROMOTED BY THE INTER-AMERICAN FOUNDATION. 1584

0091-6242 See MANAGEMENT REPORT - GENERAL SERVICES ADMINISTRATION. 4664

0091-6323 See SOUL JOURNEY. 5491

0091-6331 See EXERCISE AND SPORT SCIENCES REVIEWS. 3954

0091-634X See BULLETIN OF THE AMERICAN ACADEMY OF PSYCHIATRY AND THE LAW. 3922

0091-6358 See ASTRONOMY (MILWAUKEE). 393

0091-6439 See SURNAME INDEX (WICHITA). 2474

0091-6447 See OUR FAMILY HERITAGE. 2466

0091-6455 See TRAILS AND TALES. 2475

0091-6471 See JOURNAL OF PSYCHOLOGY AND THEOLOGY. 4600

0091-648X See INDEX OF EMPLOYMENT OPPORTUNITIES. PROFESSIONAL CAREERS EDITION. 4205

0091-6544 See FAMILY THERAPY. 3925

0091-6552 See JOURNAL OF MECHANOCHEMISTRY & CELL MOTILITY. 538

0091-6625 See GLASS (PRINCETON). 2590

0091-6641 See STUDIO POTTER. 2594

0091-6692 See PEST CONTROL TECHNOLOGY. 4246

0091-6706 See WOOD-WOODS FAMILY MAGAZINE, THE. 2477

0091-6730 See NEBRASKA MEDICAL JOURNAL, THE. 3619

0091-6749 See JOURNAL OF ALLERGY AND CLINICAL IMMUNOLOGY. 3673

0091-6765 See ENVIRONMENTAL HEALTH PERSPECTIVES. 4774

0091-679X See METHODS IN CELL BIOLOGY. 538

0091-6803 See PHYSICIANS' DESK REFERENCE FOR OPHTHALMOLOGY. 3878

0091-6846 See STRATEGIC REVIEW. 4058

0091-6854 See SPECTRUM 1: STOCK HOLDINGS SURVEY. 914

0091-6862 See SPECTRUM 2: INVESTMENT COMPANY PORTFOLIOS. 914

0091-6897 See PASTFINDER (SAINT JOSEPH, MICH.). 2466

0091-6943 See VINTAGE AIRPLANE, THE. 39

0091-6951 See RESIDENT AND OFF-CAMPUS ENROLLMENT, VIRGINIA STATE-CONTROLLED INSTITUTIONS OF HIGHER EDUCATION. 1845

0091-6986 See INTERNATIONAL DIVER INDEX. WORLD INDIVEX EDITION. 4900

0091-6994 See IN (IOWA CITY). 322

0091-701X See CONSORTIUM DIRECTORY. 1818

0091-7052 See GUIDE TO GRADUATE DEPARTMENTS OF SOCIOLOGY. 5246

0091-7079 See HAROLD L. LYON ARBORETUM LECTURE. 456

0091-7168 See DIRECTORY FOR THE EASTERN ASSOCIATION OF STUDENT FINANCIAL AID ADMINISTRATORS. 1820

0091-7176 See ANCIENT TIMES. 4100

0091-7214 See MATHEMATICS INTERNATIONAL. 3521

0091-7222 See ANNUAL REPORT - NATIONAL GALLERY OF ART (U.S.). 336

0091-7230 See POT-HOOKS & HANGERS. 3470

0091-7257 See VERTEX (LOS ANGELES). 3450

0091-729X See ADMISSION REQUIREMENTS OF U.S. AND CANADIAN DENTAL SCHOOLS. 1315

0091-7311 See WASHINGTON REPORT ON LONG TERM CARE. 3793

0091-732X See REVIEW OF RESEARCH IN EDUCATION. 1904

0091-7338 See STUDIES IN THE HISTORY OF ART. 366

0091-7370 See ANNALS OF CLINICAL AND LABORATORY SCIENCE. 3893

0091-7397 See CURRENT TOPICS IN EXPERIMENTAL ENDOCRINOLOGY. 3727

0091-7435 See PREVENTIVE MEDICINE (1972). 3629

0091-7443 See RESEARCH PUBLICATIONS - ASSOCIATION FOR RESEARCH IN NERVOUS AND MENTAL DISEASE. 3845

0091-7451 See COLD SPRING HARBOR SYMPOSIA ON QUANTITATIVE BIOLOGY. 451

0091-7508 See NORTH CAROLINA AGRICULTURAL CHEMICALS MANUAL. 115

0091-7516 See QUARTER RACING RECORD, THE. 2802

0091-7583 See DIRECTORY OF WOMEN IN THE MATHEMATICAL SCIENCES. 3503

0091-7591 See FIND CATALOG. 4117

0091-7605 See FOOD PURITY PERSPECTIVES. 2339

0091-7613 See GEOLOGY (BOULDER). 1380

0091-7648 See WILDLIFE SOCIETY BULLETIN. 2209

0091-7664 See WHISKEY, WOMEN, AND 4159

0091-7672 See DIRECTORY OF STATE - USDA RURAL DEVELOPMENT COMMITTEES. 5198

0091-7680 See GIFFORD PINCHOT NATIONAL FOREST. 2383

0091-7699 See FINAL CONTROL ELEMENTS; PROCEEDINGS. 2114

0091-7702 See PROCEEDINGS OF INTERNATIONAL WIRE AND CABLE SYMPOSIUM. 2076

0091-7710 See JOURNAL OF ANTHROPOLOGICAL RESEARCH. 238

0091-7729 See SCIENCE-FICTION STUDIES. 3434

0091-7877 See MEDICAL BOOK GUIDE. 3608

0091-7885 See TECHNOLOGY BOOK GUIDE. 5163

0091-7915 See GOVERNMENT PUBLICATIONS GUIDE. 416

0091-7958 See OCCASIONAL PAPERS OF THE MUSEUM OF NATURAL HISTORY (LAWRENCE). 4169

0091-8059 See HEADLIGHTS (NEW YORK). 5431

0091-8083 See STUDIES IN AMERICAN FICTION. 3354

0091-8156 See INDUSTRY WAGE SURVEY. INDUSTRIAL CHEMICALS. 1679

0091-8199 See FOREIGN ANIMAL DISEASE REPORT. 5510

0091-8229 See REPORT OF THE COMMISSION ON TAXATION AND PRODUCTION OF IRON ORE AND OTHER MINERALS. 4745

0091-8261 See EMPLOYEE COMPENSATION IN THE PRIVATE NONFARM ECONOMY. 1665

0091-8296 See MISSIOLOGY. 4977

0091-8342 See ECONOMIC STABILIZATION PROGRAM. 1485

0091-8369 See JOURNAL OF HOMOSEXUALITY. 2795

0091-8377 See MACHINERY & EQUIPMENT PRICING GUIDE. 2120

0091-8393 See U.S. MEDICAL DIRECTORY. 3793

0091-8407 See WORLD MANUFACTURING. 4024

0091-8458 See DIRECTORY : FLORIDA PORTS AND WATERWAYS. 5448

0091-8482 See REPORT - WORKSHOP FOR CHILD CARE STAFF OF FLORIDA'S CHILD CARING FACILITIES. 5305

0091-8601 See INDUSTRIAL EDUCATION. 1913

0091-861X See COOKING FOR PROFIT. 2332

0091-8644 See TECHNICAL ABSTRACT REPORT - DEPT. OF TRANSPORTATION. CLIMATIC IMPACT ASSESSMENT PROGRAM. 1435

0091-8652 See SINGLE. 5258

0091-8660 See EBONY JR. 1063

0091-8687 See AUTOHARP. 4101

0091-8695 See REPORT ON FEDERAL FUNDS RECEIVED IN IOWA. 4746

0091-875X See ANNUAL SUMMARY REPORT. PROGRESS AND PLANS - AMES LABORATORY, U.S.A.E.C. 2154

0091-8784 See BIENNIAL REPORT - OREGON BOARD OF EDUCATION. 1727

0091-8822 See MOTOR SPORT YEARBOOK. 4905

0091-8857 See BULLETIN OF THE WATAUGA ASSOCIATION OF GENEALOGISTS. 2440

0091-8903 See RHODE ISLAND DENTAL JOURNAL, THE. 1335

0091-8954 See PRODUCT SAFETY UP TO DATE. 4796

0091-9004 See EDUCATIONAL SERIES - NORTH DAKOTA GEOLOGICAL SURVEY. 1374

0091-9012 See INFORMATION PAMPHLET - SOUTH DAKOTA GEOLOGICAL SURVEY. 1383

0091-9055 See LICENSED ATTORNEYS OF NORTH DAKOTA. 3003

0091-9128 See CRIMINAL JUSTICE COMPREHENSIVE PLAN. 3162

0091-9160 See DATAMEX. WESTERN HEMISPHERE. 5468

0091-9209 See CITY EMPLOYMENT. 4638

0091-9217 See BEST SCIENCE FICTION. 3366

0091-9233 See EMPLEO, HORAS Y SALARIOS EN LOS ESTABLECIMIENTOS MANUFACTUREROS PROMOVIDOD POR LA ADMINISTRACION DE FOMENTO ECONOMICO O LA COMPANIA DE FOMENTO INDUSTRIAL DE PUERTO RICO. 1664

0091-925X See POPULATION REPORTS. SERIES J, FAMILY PLANNING PROGRAMS (ENGLISH ED.) 4558

0091-9357 See AMERICAN BOOK PRICES CURRENT. 4823

0091-9381 See DIRECTORY OF THE AMERICAN BAPTIST CHURCHES IN THE U.S.A. 5059

0091-942X See REPORT - OFFICE OF ATHLETIC COMMISSIONER (LINCOLN). 4915

0091-9462 See INTERNATIONAL DIRECTORY OF NURSES WITH DOCTORAL DEGREES. 3857

0091-9497 See DIRECTORY OF THE LABOR RESEARCH ADVISORY COUNCIL TO THE BUREAU OF LABOR STATISTICS. 1663

0091-9519 See TRADE DIRECTORY, MEMBERSHIP LIST - ELECTRONIC INDUSTRIES ASSOCIATION. 2084

0091-9527 See NCEA-GANLEY'S CATHOLIC SCHOOLS IN AMERICA. 5033

0091-9535 See GOVERNOR'S MANPOWER PLAN (JUNEAU). 1676

0091-9578 See PLASTICS ENGINEERING. 4458

0091-9632 See GRADUATE FACULTY AND PROGRAMS IN POLITICAL SCIENCE. 4475

0091-9640 See JOURNAL OF CURRITUCK COUNTY HISTORICAL SOCIETY, THE. 2741

0091-9667 See RAIL PASSENGER STATISTICS IN THE NORTHEAST CORRIDOR. 5435

0091-9691 See UTAH BAR JOURNAL. 3070

0091-9705 See WENCO INTERNATIONAL TRADE DIRECTORY, THE. 857

0091-9721 See CONTRACEPTIVE TECHNOLOGY. 588

0091-9748 See REPORT - ADVISORY COUNCIL ON HISTORIC PRESERVATION. 2757

0091-9756 See METROPOLITAN ATLANTA BUSINESS DIRECTORY. 693

0091-9764 See NEWSLETTER - HUNTSVILLE ASSOCIATION OF FOLK MUSICIANS. 4141

0091-9837 See ANNUAL REPORT - ENVIRONMENTAL DEFENSE FUND. 2160

0091-9845 See HAWAII OBSERVER. 2534

0091-9993 See NO-TILL FARMER. 179

0092-0002 See INTERNATIONAL DECADE OF OCEAN EXPLORATION. 1450

0092-0053 See FARM CHEMICALS (1973). 84

0092-007X See FLORIDA SUMMARY OF ACCIDENT DATA. 5440

0092-0126 See FEDERAL FINANCIAL MANAGEMENT DIRECTORY. 4723

0092-0142 See CLASSIFICATION AND PAY PLAN - (TALLAHASSEE) DIVISION OF PERSONNEL. 4638

0092-0169 See INCIDENTS OF SUSPECTED CHILD ABUSE IN MARYLAND. 5289

0092-0193 See ION EXCHANGE AND SOLVENT EXTRACTION. 1053

0092-0215 See ARKANSAS SOCIAL SERVICES ANNUAL REPORT. 5273

0092-0258 See STANFORD REVIEW. 1848

0092-0304 See WISCONSIN DAIRY FACTS. 199

0092-0320 See POLLUTING INCIDENTS IN AND AROUND U.S. WATERS. 2238

0092-0355 See BASIN BIBLIOGRAPHY (OLYMPIA). 5549

0092-0371 See AAMC CURRICULUM DIRECTORY. 1806

0092-0398 See STANYAN NEWS. 4154

0092-0401 See ROCK (NEW YORK). 4150

0092-0436 See DISC AND THAT. 4115

0092-0479 See POWDER COATING CONFERENCE. 4015

0092-0517 See JOURNAL OF COUNTRY MUSIC, THE. 4126

0092-0525 See JAZZ DIGEST. 4124

0092-055X See TEACHING SOCIOLOGY. 5264

0092-0576 See POWDER DIFFRACTION FILE SEARCH MANUAL : ORGANIC. 1046

0092-0592 See GRAPEVINE (SARATOGA). 4119

0092-0606 See JOURNAL OF BIOLOGICAL PHYSICS. 495

0092-0614 See LOUISIANA DIRECTORY OF CITIES, TOWNS, AND VILLAGES. 2745

0092-0622 See AQUEDUCT (LOS ANGELES). 5530

0092-069X See GAMBLERS WORLD. 4861

0092-0703 See JOURNAL OF THE ACADEMY OF MARKETING SCIENCE. 929

0092-072X See PROCEEDINGS OF THE ANNUAL CONVENTION - CHRISTIAN ASSOCIATION FOR PSYCHOLOGICAL STUDIES. 4988

0092-0770 See REPORT OF PROGRESS BY THE ILLINOIS ENVIRONMENTAL PROTECTION AGENCY. 2181

0092-0789 See DEVIL'S BOX. 4114

0092-0819 See BANDMASTERS REPORT. 4102

0092-0843 See DIGEST OF OFFICIAL OPINIONS - ATTORNEY GENERAL (TALLAHASSEE). 3140

0092-0851 See PUBLICATION - HISTORICAL SOCIETY OF WASHINGTON COUNTY, VIRGINIA. 2755

0092-0908 See WORLD DIRECTORY OF ENVIRONMENTAL ORGANIZATIONS. 2210

0092-0959 See BALDWIN'S OHIO LEGISLATIVE SERVICE. 2939

0092-0991 See COUNTRY SQUIRE. 4112

0092-1041 See MUSIC CAPITOL NEWS. COUNTRYWIDE. 4133

0092-1068 See AMERICAN HUNTER, THE. 4868

0092-119X See AMERICAN JOURNAL (NEW YORK). 2527

0092-1254 See MASTER PLAN FOR TRANSPORTATION (TRENTON). 5386

0092-1262 See NOTICE TO MARINERS. 4181

0092-1289 See CAMP FIRE LEADERSHIP. 5229

0092-1300 See POWDER DIFFRACTION FILE SEARCH MANUAL (FINK METHOD) : INORGANIC. 1018

0092-1319 See POWDER DIFFRACTION FILE SEARCH MANUAL, HANAWALT METHOD: INORGANIC. 1037

0092-1327 See AMERICAN ART REVIEW. 336

0092-1491 See NATIONAL DEFENSE (WASHINGTON). 4052

0092-1505 See LEGISLATIVE REPORTER (LINCOLN). 3108

0092-1548 See BROOKHAVEN HIGHLIGHTS. 4446

0092-1661 See PROCEEDINGS. ANNUAL SYMPOSIUM. INCREMENTAL MOTION CONTROL SYSTEMS AND DEVICES. 2076

0092-170X See JEALOUS MISTRESS, THE. 2986

0092-1734 See NEW FISHING (NEW YORK). 2309

ISSN Index

0092-1769 See INTERNATIONAL SKI TRAILS. 4901

0092-1777 See EDUCATIONAL DIRECTORY. STATE & DISTRICT OFFICES (HONOLULU). 1741

0092-1793 See FREMONTIA (SACRAMENTO, CALIF.). 511

0092-1815 See INTERNATIONAL JOURNAL OF INSTRUCTIONAL MEDIA. 1897

0092-1882 See LOS ANGELES COUNTY ALMANAC. 4663

0092-1904 See UNITED STATES GOVERNMENT MANUAL (1974). 4692

0092-1912 See FICTION INTERNATIONAL. 3387

0092-1939 See A.R.S. S. AGRICULTURAL RESEARCH SERVICE. SOUTHERN REGION. 42

0092-2005 See TEXAS FRUIT AND PECAN STATISTICS. 2362

0092-2021 See NORTH STAR. 4142

0092-2056 See NATIONAL HURRICANE OPERATIONS PLAN. 1432

0092-2102 See INTERFACES (PROVIDENCE). 871

0092-2145 See CALIFORNIA AND WESTERN STATES GRAPE GROWER. 166

0092-2234 See TECHNOLOGY ASSESSMENT (NEW YORK, N.Y.). 5163

0092-2250 See MICHIGAN CENTENNIAL FARMS DIRECTORY. 108

0092-2315 See AMERICAN JOURNAL OF CRIMINAL LAW. 3105

0092-2323 See JOURNAL OF INDO-EUROPEAN STUDIES, THE. 3290

0092-2366 See INDIANA WATERSHED PROGRESS. 2091

0092-2404 See DIRECTORY OF PRIVATE ELEMENTARY SCHOOLS AND HIGH SCHOOLS IN CALIFORNIA THAT HAVE COMPLIED WITH EDUCATION CODE SECTION 29009.5. 1736

0092-2447 See JOURNAL OF APPLIED MEASUREMENTS. 5118

0092-2455 See DIRECTORY OF SPECIFIC LEARNING DISABILITY SERVICES. 1878

0092-248X See PRACTICAL LAWYER'S LAW OFFICE MANAGEMENT MANUAL, THE. 3030

0092-2501 See ELECTRICAL WORLD DIRECTORY OF ELECTRIC UTILITIES IN LATIN AMERICA, BERMUDA AND THE CARIBBEAN ISLANDS. 4761

0092-2560 See WEEKLY CALIFORNIA CITATOR. 3073

0092-2633 See PROCEEDINGS - NATIONAL PEACH COUNCIL. 2353

0092-2676 See YEAR REPORT - TEMPORARY STATE COMMISSION ON THE WATER SUPPLY NEEDS OF SOUTHEASTERN NEW YORK. 5549

0092-2684 See COLORADO WATER RESOURCES CIRCULAR. 5532

0092-2781 See SUMMARY OF ACCIDENTS INVESTIGATED BY THE FEDERAL RAILROAD ADMINISTRATION. 5437

0092-2803 See RAND PAPER SERIES. 5144

0092-2811 See AMERICAN COIN-OP. 5347

0092-2862 See AVIATION DAILY'S AIRLINE STATISTICAL ANNUAL. 41

0092-2870 See AIR FREIGHT DIRECTORY. 5375

0092-2986 See JOURNAL OF THE MIDWEST HISTORY OF EDUCATION SOCIETY. 1759

0092-2994 See ENGINEERING AND TECHNOLOGY GRADUATES. 5103

0092-3036 See PROCEEDINGS - NATIONAL PEACH COUNCIL. 2353

0092-3079 See ANNUAL REPORT OF THE VIOLENT CRIMES COMPENSATION BOARD (NEWARK). 3157

0092-3095 See MOTORCYCLE RIDER'S GUIDE. 4082

0092-3222 See INDIANA RURAL MANPOWER REPORT. 1678

0092-3389 See HIGHWAY TRANSPORTATION RESEARCH AND DEVELOPMENT STUDIES. 5441

0092-3419 See CATALOGUE - NATIONAL INDIAN LAW LIBRARY. 3079

0092-3478 See YEARBOOK OF THE AMERICAN BAPTIST CHURCHES IN THE U.S.A. 5069

0092-3524 See IUSTITIA (BLOOMINGTON). 2985

0092-3532 See FEDERAL AVIATION REGULATIONS & AIRMAN'S INFORMATION MANUAL : BASIC REFERENCE BOOK. 19

0092-3567 See IFR AIRCRAFT HANDLED. 23

0092-3583 See RESEARCH REPORT - DEPARTMENT OF MOTOR VEHICLES. RESEARCH AND TECHNOLOGY DIVISION (OLYMPIA). 5424

0092-3605 See PENNSYLVANIA JUVENILE COURT DISPOSITIONS. 3082

0092-3656 See FLORIDA AGRICULTURAL STATISTICS. COMMERCIAL CITRUS INVENTORY. 87

0092-3672 See REAL ESTATE VENTURE ANALYSIS. 4845

0092-3680 See TECHNICAL DIGEST - I.E.E.E. VEHICULAR TECHNOLOGY ANNUAL CONFERENCE. 5426

0092-3699 See WATER RESOURCES RESEARCH SERIES (NASHVILLE). 5547

0092-3745 See ANNUAL ROSTER - TEXAS STATE BOARD OF LANDSCAPE ARCHITECTS. 2409

0092-3761 See DATA ON IOWA'S AREA SCHOOLS AND PUBLIC JUNIOR COLLEGE. 1819

0092-380X See WASHINGTON STATE. 4694

0092-3818 See ILLINOIS SERVICES DIRECTORY. 1609

0092-3850 See GIFTS YOU CAN MAKE FOR CHRISTMAS. 2584

0092-3877 See BAR (AUSTIN). 2939

0092-3893 See COUPLES (NEW YORK). 2278

0092-3907 See CRIMINAL JUSTICE QUARTERLY, THE. 3105

0092-3931 See JOURNAL OF RESEARCH AND TRAINING, THE. 3929

0092-3974 See INTERNATIONAL DIRECTORY OF LITTLE MAGAZINES & SMALL PRESSES. 1926

0092-4016 See CONTRIBUTIONS TO PRIMATOLOGY. 5581

0092-4059 See COUNTRY RECORDING VOICE. 4112

0092-4067 See DIRECTORY OF MISSOURI LIBRARIES. 3207

0092-4113 See MUSELETTER (WASHINGTON, D.C.). 4132

0092-413X See ANNUAL REPORT - NEW MEXICO. REAL ESTATE COMMISSION. 4834

0092-4148 See LATIN AMERICA (WASHINGTON). 2743

0092-4164 See WHERE THE TRAILS CROSS. 2477

0092-4180 See CRAFTS & SEWING. 371

0092-4199 See DAY CARE AND EARLY EDUCATION. 1803

0092-4199 See DAY CARE AND EARLY EDUCATION. [MICROFILM]. 1803

0092-4202 See DIRECTORY OF PRIVATE TRADE, TECHNICAL, AND ART SCHOOLS (TRENTON). 1912

0092-4229 See SPEED (BELOIT). 1349

0092-4245 See WESLEYAN THEOLOGICAL JOURNAL. 5009

0092-4253 See ANNUAL REPORT - CALIFORNIA JOB DEVELOPMENT CORPORATION LAW EXECUTIVE BOARD. 639

0092-430X See PEPPERDINE LAW REVIEW. 3026

0092-4318 See PLATTE VALLEY REVIEW. 2543

0092-4407 See MANAGERS (NEW YORK). 906

0092-4415 See PRIMITIVE BAPTIST YEARBOOK. 5066

0092-4423 See RESOURCE GUIDE TO READING & LANGUAGE ARTS PROGRAMS & MATERIALS. 3336

0092-4458 See LDA JOURNAL. 1329

0092-4466 See HEARING INSTRUMENTS. 3888

0092-4512 See PETERSEN'S COMPLETE BOOK OF PLYMOUTH, DODGE, CHRYSLER. 5423

0092-4520 See EQUITY NEWS. 385

0092-4563 See SYNTAX AND SEMANTICS. 3327

0092-458X See RESEARCH BULLETIN - OHIO EDUCATION ASSOCIATION. 1779

0092-4598 See WHO'S WHO IN TRAINING AND DEVELOPMENT. 438

0092-4601 See N.A.D.A. RECREATION VEHICLE APPRAISAL GUIDE. 5388

0092-4644 See PUPIL TRANSPORTATION STATISTICS, ILLINOIS PUBLIC SCHOOLS. 1796

0092-4660 See YEARBOOK AND MINUTES OF THE ANNUAL CONFERENCE - EVANGELICAL FREE CHURCH OF AMERICA. 5069

0092-4687 See STATUTORY SALARIES, MISSOURI STATE OFFICIALS. 4689

0092-4709 See PHOTOGRAPHIC TECHNOLOGY USSR. 4374

0092-4717 See DIRECTORY OF BANKING INSTRUCTORS. 788

0092-4725 See VICTORIAN LITERATURE & CULTURE. 3450

0092-4741 See POPULAR MUSIC NEWS. 4147

0092-4857 See MEI MARKETING ECONOMICS GUIDE. 933

0092-4873 See REPORTER - AMERICAN PUBLIC WORKS ASSOCIATION. 4682

0092-4938 See BIENNIAL REPORT, OREGON'S SUBMERGED AND SUBMERSIBLE LANDS. 4632

0092-4954 See CREDIT UNION DIRECTORY AND BUYERS' GUIDE. 786

0092-4962 See CLASSIFIED INDEX OF NATIONAL LABOR RELATIONS BOARD DECISIONS AND RELATED COURT DECISIONS. 3145

0092-4970 See ELECTRIC GENERATING AND DISTRIBUTING COMPANIES. 2043

0092-5047 See ACUPUNCTURE (LOS ANGELES). 3546

0092-5055 See ANNUAL OF PSYCHOANALYSIS, THE. 3920

0092-5063 See C.B.M.S. NEWSLETTER. 4106

0092-5128 See SOCIAL AND REHABILITATIVE SERVICES (CRANSTON). 5308

0092-5136 See SEARCH AND RESCUE MAGAZINE. 4802

0092-5144 See VERMONT FACTS AND FIGURES. 5345

0092-5209 See IOWA FARM OUTLOOK. 97

0092-5268 See GRANTS AND AWARDS AVAILABLE TO AMERICAN WRITERS. 3392

0092-5306 See BEST OF NATIONAL LAMPOON, THE. 2528

0092-5322 See FUSILIER (LA PUENTE). 4044

0092-5357 See SALARIES OF CERTIFICATED EMPLOYEES IN CALIFORNIA PUBLIC SCHOOLS. 1709

0092-5365 See HERE'S HOW (NEW YORK). 4370

0092-5454 See COUNTRYWIDE ANNUAL YEARBOOK. 4113

0092-5470 See DEVELOPMENTS IN HUMAN SERVICES. 5282

0092-5497 See PAPER CONSERVATION NEWS. 3240

0092-5500 See RESEARCH MEMORANDUM - MUNICIPAL RESEARCH AND SERVICES CENTER OF WASHINGTON (SEATTLE). 4683

0092-5519 See AMERICAN FOLKLIFE. 2318

0092-5543 See STATE FACILITIES PLAN (OLYMPIA). 5311

0092-556X See VENTURES IN RESEARCH. 5168

0092-5594 See CONGENITAL MALFORMATIONS SURVEILLANCE. 3759

0092-5616 See BENCHMARK PAPERS IN BIOLOGICAL CONCEPTS. 443

0092-5659 See BULLETIN - AMERICAN LUNG ASSOCIATION. 3948

0092-5756 See BIBLIOGRAPHY OF NOISE, A. 2161

0092-5764 See CONNECTICUT WALK BOOK. 4871

0092-5802 See SUPERVISORY AND MIDDLE MANAGEMENT SALARY SURVEY (LOS ANGELES). 1713

0092-5810 See VERMONT'S FISHERIES ANNUAL. 2315

0092-5853 See AMERICAN JOURNAL OF POLITICAL SCIENCE. 4463

0092-5969 See POPULAR SPORTS FACE-OFF. 4912

0092-5977 See PROGRAM MATERIALS FOR SEMINAR FOR GEORGIA DISTRICT ATTORNEYS. 3108

0092-6000 See CURRENT LITERATURE IN FAMILY PLANNING. 2287

0092-6019 See IMMUNOLOGY SERIES. 3671

0092-6027 See MICROBIOLOGY SERIES. 567

0092-6051 See ANNUAL REPORT - STATE OF MARYLAND. CRIMINAL INJURIES COMPENSATION BOARD. 3157

0092-6078 See DIRECTORY OF FULL YEAR HEAD START PROGRAMS. 1736

0092-6086 See INTER ALIA (RENO). 2983

0092-6094 See ORGANIC COMPOUNDS : REACTIONS AND METHODS. 1045

0092-6108 See TITLE VARIES. 3253

0092-6140 See IMPROVEMENT IDEAS. 300

0092-6159 See PROGRESS REPORT ON TRIP ENDS GENERATION RESEARCH COUNTS (SAN FRANCISCO). 5390

0092-6213 See CIRCULATORY SHOCK. 3702

0092-623X See JOURNAL OF SEX & MARITAL THERAPY. 5187

0092-6264 See BOOKSTORE JOURNAL REVIEWS. 4826

0092-6272 See ENDURO (COMPTON). 4081

0092-6280 See HANDBOOK AND DIRECTORY - ASSOCIATION FOR EDUCATIONAL DATA SYSTEMS. 1749

0092-6302 See SEMICONDUCTOR HEAT SINK, SOCKET & ASSOCIATED HARDWARE D.A.T.A. BOOK. 2080

0092-6353 See HORSE PLAY. 2799

0092-6361 See CURRENT CONTENTS. SOCIAL & BEHAVIORAL SCIENCES. 5227

0092-640X See ATOMIC DATA AND NUCLEAR DATA TABLES. 4446

0092-6418 See DIRECTORY OF THE LEADING FIRMS IN THE JOB PLATING AND ENAMELING INDUSTRY. 4001

0092-6426 See LIMITS IN THE SEAS. 3181

0092-6442 See STATE WATER PLAN PUBLICATION (LINCOLN). 5539

0092-6515 See AUTO-TRAIN MAGAZINE. 5429

0092-6558 See JOURNAL OF THE INTERDENOMINATIONAL THEOLOGICAL CENTER, THE. 4971

0092-6566 See JOURNAL OF RESEARCH IN PERSONALITY. 4601

0092-6620 See PROJECTS, PRODUCTS, AND SERVICES OF THE NATIONAL CENTER FOR EDUCATIONAL STATISTICS. 1796

0092-6639 See WOMEN'S ORGANIZATIONS & LEADERS DIRECTORY. 5571

0092-668X See NATIONAL DIRECTORY OF MODULAR BUILDING MANUFACTURERS. 622

0092-6698 See NEW WRITERS (NEW YORK). 3416

0092-671X See RES PUBLICA (CLAREMONT). 4683

0092-6752 See PESTICIDES (SACRAMENTO). 4247

0092-6825 See LIST OF INTERCEPTED PLANT PESTS. 2424

0092-6876 See AUTOMATIC TAXFINDER AND TAX PREPARER'S HANDBOOK. 4712

0092-6884 See DAILY TAX REPORT (WASHINGTON). 2958

0092-6914 See GOLF & CLUB YEARBOOK. 4896

0092-6930 See PROCEEDINGS OF THE CAJAL CLUB. 3680

0092-7031 See STATE PLAN FOR VOCATIONAL EDUCATION IN NORTH DAKOTA / STATE BOARD FOR VOCATIONAL EDUCATION. 1916

0092-7082 See SPORTS AFIELD OUTDOOR ALMANAC, THE. 4879

0092-7147 See DAILY BREAD. 4952

0092-718X See LETTERS & PAPERS ON THE SOCIAL SCIENCES. 5208

0092-7201 See LINEAR INTEGRATED CIRCUITS AND MOS DEVICES. 2071

0092-7228 See THYRISTORS, RECTIFIERS, AND DIACS. 2084

0092-7422 See ANNUAL DIRECTORY AND REPORT - AMERICAN DEFENSE PREPAREDNESS ASSOCIATION. 4034

0092-7449 See DIRECTION. 5381

0092-7481 See ANNUAL REPORT / THE URBAN INSTITUTE. 5191

0092-7627 See ASIA-PACIFIC REGIONAL COMPENSATION SURVEY. AUSTRALIA. 1654

0092-7643 See ANNUAL REPORT - OVERSEAS DEVELOPMENT COUNCIL. 1598

0092-7651 See ARCHIVES OF PODIATRIC MEDICINE AND FOOT SURGERY. 3917

0092-7678 See ASIAN AFFAIRS (NEW YORK). 4516

0092-7686 See BOOKLEGGER MAGAZINE. 3196

0092-7694 See CASON QUARTERLY, THE. 2442

0092-7708 See CONCH REVIEW OF BOOKS, THE. 3340

0092-7732 See PRODUCT SAFETY & LIABILITY REPORTER. 4796

0092-7740 See SECURITY REGISTER. 5307

0092-7767 See SOURCE DIRECTORY OF PREDICASTS, INC, THE. 425

0092-7791 See AUDIT OF THE FINANCIAL STATEMENTS OF FEDERAL CROP INSURANCE CORPORATION. 2874

0092-7856 See ARCHITECTURAL SCHOOLS IN NORTH AMERICA. 289

0092-7872 See COMMUNICATIONS IN ALGEBRA. 3500

0092-7880 See DEPARTMENT OF THE ARMY HISTORICAL SUMMARY (WASHINGTON). 4042

0092-7899 See EDUCATIONAL DIRECTORY OF MISSISSIPPI SCHOOLS. 1741

0092-7910 See REPORT OF EVALUATION OF STUDENT FINANCIAL AID (HELENA). 1844

0092-7929 See ANNUAL OF NEW ART AND ARTISTS, AN. 336

0092-7937 See ANNUAL REPORT - CITIZENS ADVISORY COUNCIL (HARRISBURG). 2160

0092-7953 See BULLETIN - GENEALOGICAL SOCIETY OF OLD TYRON COUNTY. 2440

0092-8089 See ADSORPTION AND ADSORBENTS. 1049

0092-8208 See CHILDREN'S LITERATURE (STORRS). 1061

0092-8216 See CORD SPORTSFACTS HUNTING. 4871

0092-8240 See BULLETIN OF MATHEMATICAL BIOLOGY. 450

0092-8348 See ACTIVITY REPORT OF THE VIRGINIA STATE APPLE COMMISSION. 2407

0092-8372 See DISCIPLE (ST. LOUIS, MO.). 5059

0092-8380 See ENCYCLOPEDIA OF GOVERNMENTAL ADVISORY ORGANIZATIONS. 4646

0092-8445 See PROCEEDINGS OF THE ANNUAL GOVERNOR'S WORKSHOP ON INTERGOVERNMENTAL RELATIONS AND REGIONAL PLANNING (SAN ANTONIO). 2832

0092-847X See RESEARCH REPORT - INSTITUTE FOR RESEARCH ON POVERTY (MADISON). 5215

0092-8526 See DIRECTORY LISTING CURRICULUMS OFFERED IN THE COMMUNITY COLLEGES OF PENNSYLVANIA. 1820

0092-8607 See BIOMEDICAL COMMUNICATIONS. 1105

0092-8615 See DRUG INFORMATION JOURNAL. 4300

0092-8623 See JOURNAL OF MENTAL HEALTH ADMINISTRATION. 5292

0092-8658 See APSA DIRECTORY OF DEPARTMENT CHAIRPERSONS. 4464

0092-8666 See BELL TOWER, THE. 4102

0092-8674 See CELL (CAMBRIDGE). 533

0092-8682 See CURRENT MEDICAL DIAGNOSIS & TREATMENT. 3570

0092-8720 See PAMPHLET - DEPARTMENT OF EMPLOYMENT AND SOCIAL SERVICES (BALTIMORE). 5300

0092-8763 See SWEET'S PLANT ENGINEERING EXTENSION INDUSTRIAL CONSTRUCTION AND RENOVATION FILE. 2099

0092-881X See COLLEGE FOOTBALL MODERN RECORD BOOK. 4890

0092-8828 See P.B.X. SYSTEMS GUIDE. 2074

0092-8887 See CREATIVE GUITAR INTERNATIONAL. 4113

0092-8909 See LADY GOLFER (SCOTTSDALE). 4903

0092-8933 See POLICE AND LAW ENFORCEMENT. 3171

0092-9077 See BULLETIN - COOPERATIVE EXTENSION SERVICE (ATHENS). 1541

0092-9158 See INVENTORY OF WASTE WATER PRODUCTION AND WASTE WATER RECLAMATION PRACTICES IN CALIFORNIA. 2233

0092-9166 See CREATION RESEARCH QUARTERLY. 5097

0092-9174 See DIRECTORY OF SAN FRANCISCO ATTORNEYS. 2962

0092-9212 See MICHIGAN STATE EMPLOYEES' RETIREMENT SYSTEM. 4698

0092-9239 See AUDIT REPORT - STATE OF NEVADA. PUBLIC SERVICE COMMISSION. 4631

0092-9263 See TLF QUARTERLY. 4079

0092-9336 See OSTEOPATHIC ANNALS. 3624

0092-9344 See POPULATION REPORTS. SERIES B, INTRAUTERINE DEVICES (ENGLISH ED.). 4557

0092-9425 See SCHIST (WILLIMANTIC). 3470

0092-9433 See CLEAN WATER (WASHINGTON). 5532

0092-9476 See INFORMATION PAMPHLET - DEPARTMENT OF EMPLOYMENT AND SOCIAL SERVICES (BALTIMORE). 5290

0092-9530 See COST OF STORING AND HANDLING COTTON AT PUBLIC STORAGE FACILITIES. 77

0092-9549 See JOURNAL - OSWEGO COUNTY HISTORICAL SOCIETY. 2743

0092-9565 See CURRENT GEOLOGICAL AND GEOPHYSICAL STUDIES IN MONTANA / STATE OF MONTANA, BUREAU OF MINES AND GEOLOGY. 1354

0092-959X See TUBERCULOSIS IN INDIANA. 3952

0092-9638 See RC AND D RELEASE. 2392

0092-9719 See SANGO (BRONX). 2759

0092-9727 See POPULAR PERIODICAL INDEX. 422

0092-9735 See POLITICAL INQUIRY. 4489

0092-9786 See ANNUAL REPORT OF THE DEPARTMENT OF AGRICULTURE (MONTANA). 61

0092-9794 See MASSACHUSETTS AGRICULTURAL STATISTICS. 155

0092-9824 See F.A.S. PUBLIC INTEREST REPORT. 5104

0092-9883 See C.S.S. NEED ANALYSIS. 1813

0092-9891 See ACTIVE RESEARCH TASKS REPORT (CINCINNATI). 2159

0092-9956 See OFFENDERS RELEASED FROM ADULT CORRECTIONAL INSTITUTIONS (MADISON). 3171

0092-9980 See ANNUAL REPORT / OKLAHOMA. AERONAUTICS COMMISSION. 11

0093-0008 See EDUCATIONAL PERSONNEL IN DELAWARE PUBLIC SCHOOLS. 1863

0093-0083 See FORESTRY BULLETIN (CLEMSON, S.C.). 2381

0093-013X See EGGS, CHICKENS AND TURKEYS. 210

0093-0164 See LYONS TEACHER-NEWS. 4129

0093-0180 See FEDERAL MOTOR VEHICLE FLEET REPORT FOR THE FISCAL YEAR ENDING 5382

0093-0202 See AUDIT REPORT - STATE OF NEVADA. DEPARTMENT OF ADMINISTRATION. PERSONNEL DIVISION. 4631

0093-0229 See OFFICIAL BRAND LAWS (LINCOLN). 3021

0093-0237 See NEWSLETTER OF THE A.A.P.S.C. 3907

0093-0253 See COMPUTATIONAL MUSICOLOGY NEWSLETTER. 4111

0093-0288 See 1810 OVERTURE. 4098

0093-0296 See POWER TRANSISTORS AND POWER HYBRID CIRCUITS. 2075

0093-0334 See HASTINGS CENTER REPORT, THE. 3580

0093-0407 See SLEEP RESEARCH. 4618

0093-0415 See WESTERN JOURNAL OF MEDICINE, THE. 3650

0093-0431 See CHILDREN'S LITERARY ALMANAC. 3374

0093-044X See CRIME PREVENTION REVIEW. 3162

0093-0466 See AUTOMOBILE INSURANCE LOSSES COLLISION COVERAGES VARIATIONS BY MAKE AND SERIES. 2875

0093-0482 See M.E. MEETINGS & EXPOSITIONS. 691

0093-0520 See SYNOPSIS OF LAWS ENACTED BY THE STATE OF MARYLAND. 3062

0093-0539 See SUMMARY OF GROUND WATER DATA FOR TENNESSEE. 5540

0093-0679 See LANDSLIDE (EUREKA). 1386

0093-0709 See SYRACUSE JOURNAL OF INTERNATIONAL LAW AND COMMERCE. 3136

0093-0717 See ARIZONA BUSINESS. 1463

0093-0741 See REGULATED ELECTRIC STUDY (JEFFERSON CITY). 4679

0093-075X See AUDIT REPORT - STATE OF NEVADA. NEVADA STATE COUNCIL ON THE ARTS. 315

0093-0768 See COUNTY ASSESSMENT STATUS REPORT (SALEM). 4719

0093-0776 See SOMETHING ELSE YEARBOOK. 331

0093-0784 See UNION WAGES AND HOURS : GROCERY STORES. 1716

0093-0881 See FREE LOAN FILMS. 4071

0093-089X See AMERICAN DOWSER. 4240

0093-0938 See BUILDING IDEAS (DES MOINES). 294

0093-0997 See MERIDIAN (LOS ANGELES). 3616

0093-1047 See COLLECTORS' AUCTION (BALTIMORE). 4087

0093-1071 See REPORT OF THE STATE BOARD OF INDEPENDENT COLLEGES AND UNIVERSITIES (TALLAHASSEE). 1915

0093-1179 See ATLANTA CONSTITUTION : A GEORGIA INDEX, THE. 408

0093-1217 See REPORT OF THE LEGISLATIVE INTERIM COMMITTEE ON EDUCATION (SALEM). 1778

0093-1225 See INVENTORY OF NONPURCHASED FOREIGN CURRENCIES. 792

0093-1233 See WHO'S WHO IN GEORGIA. 437

0093-1314 See MEDICAL MEETINGS. 3610

0093-1365 See PHOTO INFORMATION ALMANAC. 4373

0093-1381 See FINAL REPORT - TEXAS LEGISLATIVE SERVICE. 2970

0093-142X See ARKANSAS ANIMAL MORBIDITY REPORT. 5504

0093-1446 See DAIRY PRODUCTS (WASHINGTON, D.C.). 194

0093-1489 See NEBRASKA TRACTOR TEST. 160

0093-1551 See CORRECTIVE AND SOCIAL PSYCHIATRY AND JOURNAL OF BEHAVIOR TECHNOLOGY METHODS AND THERAPY. 3924

0093-1586 See AUDIT REPORT - STATE OF NEVADA. NEVADA STATE MUSEUM. 4084

0093-1616 See ABATEMENT AND POLLUTION CONTROL TRAINING AND EDUCATIONAL PROGRAMS PRESENTED BY THE UNITED STATES ENVIRONMENTAL PROTECTION AGENCY. 2222

0093-1683 See RESEARCH NOTE FPL. 2392

0093-1691 See WASHINGTON STATE PROGRAM FOR MIGRANT CHILDREN'S EDUCATION. 1790

0093-1705 See WORLD LITERATURE WRITTEN IN ENGLISH. 3356

0093-1780 See DIRECTORY - FEDERAL COMMUNICATIONS BAR ASSOCIATION. 2961

0093-1829 See DEVELOPMENTS IN CORPORATE, BANKING, AND SECURITIES LAW. 3099

0093-1845 See GAVEL (BISMARCK). 2973

0093-1853 See JOURNAL OF PSYCHIATRY & LAW, THE. 2989

0093-1888 See LIBRARIANS' HANDBOOK (BIRMINGHAM). 3223

0093-1896 See CRITICAL INQUIRY. 318

0093-190X See BABSON'S INVESTMENT DIGEST. 891

0093-1918 See CLASSIC COLLECTOR, THE. 347

0093-1926 See I.R.C.A. FOREIGN LOG. 1133

0093-1950 See SHINDIG IN THE BARN. 4153

0093-1977 See SOUTHWESTERN CAMPING & TRAILERING. 4878

0093-1985 See ADVERTISING LAW ANTHOLOGY. 2928

0093-2108 See FEDERAL CARRIERS CASES (CHICAGO). 2969

0093-2124 See ON SCENE. 4181

0093-2140 See RAILROAD ACCIDENTS IN OREGON. 5401

0093-2159 See REPORT OF THE OFFICE OF THE PUBLIC DEFENDER FOR THE STATE OF MARYLAND. 3108

0093-2175 See CHILD PERSONALITY AND PSYCHOPATHOLOGY. 3901

0093-2213 See INTEGRATIVE PHYSIOLOGICAL AND BEHAVIORAL SCIENCE. 4590

0093-2221 See TOPICS IN CARBON-13 NMR SPECTROSCOPY. 1019

0093-2248 See PMBR, PHYSICIANS'S MEDICAL BOOK REFERENCE. 3628

0093-2256 See PROTECT (GREAT BARRINGTON). 625

0093-2280 See LEGISLATION AFFECTING SOUTH DAKOTA MUNICIPALITIES. 4661

0093-2396 See ANNUAL REPORT - INTERIM COMPLIANCE PANEL (WASHINGTON). 2934

0093-240X See CURRENT GEOLOGICAL RESEARCH IN WEST VIRGINIA. 1372

0093-2418 See STATISTICAL REPORT OF ACCIDENTS (CHARLESTON). 5402

0093-2477 See WORLD-WIDE GOLF DIRECTORY. 4930

0093-2485 See ECONOMIC BOOKS : CURRENT SELECTIONS. 1482

0093-2558 See MINNESOTA ALCOHOL PROGRAMS FOR HIGHWAY SAFETY. 4791

0093-2574 See PROCEEDINGS - CONSORTIUM ON REVOLUTIONARY EUROPE. 2703

0093-2582 See ST. CROIX REVIEW, THE. 5223

0093-2736 See MARKETING BULLETIN (SYRACUSE). 930

0093-2825 See FOR YOUNGER READERS. 4388

0093-3023 See COURT DECISIONS AND LEGAL OPINIONS (SEATTLE). 2957

0093-3058 See DUQUESNE LAW REVIEW. 2964

0093-3074 See PUBLIC USE OF THE NATIONAL PARKS SYSTEMS (WASHINGTON). 2202

0093-3090 See SOUTHERN CALIFORNIA BUSINESS DIRECTORY AND BUYERS GUIDE. 712

0093-3104 See THEORY AND RESEARCH IN SOCIAL EDUCATION. 5224

0093-3139 See COLLEGE LITERATURE. 3376

0093-3155 See FOREST H. BELT'S YEARBOOK OF CONSUMER ELECTRONICS. 2055

0093-3163 See GRANTS AND AWARDS AVAILABLE TO FOREIGN WRITERS. 3392

0093-321X See OFFENDERS ADMITTED TO ADULT CORRECTIONAL INSTITUTIONS (MADISON). 3171

0093-3236 See ELECTRICAL PRODUCTS YEARBOOK. 2045

0093-3279 See ALCOHOLISM DIGEST ANNUAL, THE. 1340

0093-3287 See ENVIRONMENT ABSTRACTS. 2184

0093-3341 See NETWORK (TEMPE). 3233

0093-3368 See TEXAS INSURANCE FACT BOOK. 2894

0093-3465 See OPPORTUNITIES IN IOWA'S AREA SCHOOLS. 1839

0093-3481 See R & S REPORT (HONOLULU). 5337

0093-352X See FAMILY PLANNING RESEARCH AND EVALUATION MANUAL. 588

0093-3597 See JOURNAL OF BIO-FEEDBACK, THE. 4594

0093-3619 See YEAR BOOK OF DERMATOLOGY, THE. 3723

0093-3651 See SEA TECHNOLOGY. 1456

0093-3708 See METRIC NEWS. 4031

0093-3813 See IEEE TRANSACTIONS ON PLASMA SCIENCE. 3693

0093-3821 See LIST OF JOURNALS INDEXED IN INDEX MEDICUS. 3660

0093-383X See REFERENCE TABLES. DRUG ARRESTS AND DISPOSITIONS (SACRAMENTO). 3174

0093-3864 See LAND USE LAW REPORT. 2993

0093-3929 See SOUTHERN HORSEMAN. 2802

0093-3961 See JOURNAL OF FINANCIAL EDUCATION. 794

0093-397X See LEGAL NOTES FOR EDUCATION. 3000

0093-3988 See BIENNIAL REPORT - NORTH CAROLINA. STATE DEPARTMENT OF SOCIAL SERVICES OF THE DEPARTMENT OF HUMAN RESOURCES. 5274

0093-4046 See APPLICATION AND ENROLLMENT PATTERNS OF TRANSFER STUDENTS (ALBANY). 1810

0093-4054 See CONTEMPORARY TOPICS IN IMMUNOBIOLOGY. 3668

0093-4062 See DIGEST OF MOTOR LAWS. 2961

0093-4070 See FINANCIAL DAILY CARD SERVICE, CUMULATIVE. 898

0093-4089 See FLORIDA SENATE, THE. 4649

0093-4135 See ANNUAL REPORT ON THE QUALITY OF THE AIR IN WASHINGTON, D.C. 2224

0093-416X See COMPUTER REVIEW. 1264

0093-4178 See WHO'S WHO IN NORTH CAROLINA. 437

0093-4186 See STATISTICAL COMPILATION - ADMINISTRATIVE OFFICE OF THE COURTS (ANNAPOLIS). 3083

0093-4208 See OPERATING FINANCIAL DATA FOR ILLINOIS PUBLIC JUNIOR COLLEGES. 1839

0093-4240 See GRADUATE FACULTY PHILOSOPHY JOURNAL. 4347

0093-4259 See OUTSTANDING EDUCATORS IN AMERICA. 1771

0093-4313 See COTTON GINNINGS. A10. 168

0093-4321 See COTTON GINNINGS. A10. 168

0093-433X See COTTON GINNINGS IN THE UNITED STATES. 168

0093-4364 See MEAT AND POULTRY INSPECTION. 215

0093-4429 See UNITED STATES COTTON QUALITY REPORT FOR GINNINGS. 190

0093-4437 See ANESTHESIOLOGY REVIEW. 3681

0093-4445 See JOURNAL OF LONG TERM CARE ADMINISTRATION, THE. 3787

0093-4461 See PHYSICIANS' DESK REFERENCE (PRINT ED.). 4325

0093-4496 See POPULATION REPORTS. SERIES H, BARRIER METHODS (ENGLISH ED.). 4558

0093-450X See PROCEEDINGS - PHILIP MORRIS SCIENCE SYMPOSIUM. 5142

0093-4518 See JOURNAL OF THE AMERICAN SOCIETY FOR PREVENTIVE DENTISTRY. 1328

0093-4631 See SELECTED LIST OF FEDERAL LAWS AND TREATIES RELATING TO SPORT FISH AND WILDLIFE. 3116

0093-4658 See JOURNAL OF COATED FABRICS. 5353

0093-4666 See MYCOTAXON. 518

0093-4674 See CRIMINAL LAW COMMENTATOR (NEW YORK). 3106

0093-4690 ISSN Index

0093-4690 *See* JOURNAL OF FIELD ARCHAEOLOGY. 271

0093-4747 *See* CURRENT TOPICS IN NEUROBIOLOGY. 3831

0093-4798 *See* RESEARCH IN PARAPSYCHOLOGY. 4243

0093-500X *See* ENERGY TODAY. 1942

0093-5018 *See* EUROPE : BASIC OIL LAWS AND CONCESSION CONTRACTS. ORIGINAL TEXTS. SUPPLELMENT. 2967

0093-5026 *See* GOOD NEWS OF TOMORROW'S WORLD. 4961

0093-5034 *See* LABOR RESEARCH REPORT (ALBANY). 1685

0093-5085 *See* ANNUAL REPORT - NORTH CAROLINA HUMAN RELATIONS COMMISSION. 5191

0093-5093 *See* COURSE ANNOUNCEMENT - DIVISION OF TRAINING. NATIONAL INSTITUTE FOR OCCUPATIONAL SAFETY AND HEALTH. 2861

0093-5107 *See* JOURNAL OF REAL ESTATE TAXATION. 4734

0093-5166 *See* CONTEMPORARY PROBLEMS IN CARDIOLOGY. 3703

0093-5220 *See* INSIDERS' GUIDE TO THE COLLEGES, THE. 1830

0093-5247 *See* STATE BUDGET - OFFICE OF FISCAL ANALYSIS (HARTFORD). 4749

0093-5263 *See* CREATIVITY IN ACTION. 4583

0093-528X *See* HCL CATALOGING BULLETIN. 3213

0093-5301 *See* JOURNAL OF CONSUMER RESEARCH, THE. 927

0093-531X *See* PERSPECTIVES IN RELIGIOUS STUDIES. 4986

0093-5328 *See* PHI KAPPA PHI NEWSLETTER. 5235

0093-5352 *See* RETIREMENT LETTER. 5181

0093-5379 *See* T.E.L. THE ELECTRIC LETTER. 2083

0093-5387 *See* UNDERSEA BIOMEDICAL RESEARCH. 3697

0093-5476 *See* DIRECTORY OF AIR QUALITY MONITORING SITES. 2227

0093-5557 *See* BENCHMARK PAPERS IN HUMAN PHYSIOLOGY. 578

0093-5603 *See* POPULATION ANALYSIS OF THE ILLINOIS ADULT PRISON SYSTEM. 3172

0093-5611 *See* MINIMUM WAGE AND MAXIMUM HOURS STANDARDS UNDER THE FAIR LABOR STANDARDS ACT. 1690

0093-5697 *See* BLACK PRESS PERIODICAL DIRECTORY, THE. 2917

0093-5719 *See* CHEMICAL ABSTRACTS. INDEX GUIDE. 967

0093-5735 *See* ENGINEERING, SCIENTIFIC AND TECHNICAL SALARY SURVEY. 1974

0093-5778 *See* MONTCLAIR JOURNAL OF SOCIAL SCIENCES AND HUMANITIES, THE. 5209

0093-5816 *See* DIRECTORY OF PUBLISHED PROCEEDINGS. SERIES PCE : POLLUTION CONTROL/ECOLOGY. 2227

0093-5832 *See* FARMLAND NEWS. 86

0093-5859 *See* HYDROMETEOROLOGICAL REPORT (WASHINGTON). 1426

0093-5867 *See* MARYLAND AGRI-ECONOMICS. 107

0093-5891 *See* TOXIC MATERIALS NEWS. 2245

0093-6014 *See* ARMS AND ARMOR ANNUAL. 4036

0093-6057 *See* HOWARD UNIVERSITY REVIEWS OF SCIENCE, THE. 5110

0093-609X *See* ORIGINS (WASHINGTON). 5033

0093-6146 *See* MARRIAGE & DIVORCE. 2283

0093-6170 *See* WEB (WALTHAM). 4158

0093-6200 *See* BIENNIAL REPORT - ARKANSAS WATERWAYS COMMISSION. 5447

0093-6219 *See* SPRING TESTING PROGRAM IN INDEPENDENT SCHOOLS AND SUPPLEMENTARY STUDIES. 1784

0093-6243 *See* ANNUAL REPORT OF THE OKLAHOMA ALCOHOLIC BEVERAGE CONTROL BOARD. 1341

0093-6251 *See* DIRECTORY OF CROSS-CULTURAL RESEARCH AND RESEARCHERS. 5198

0093-6367 *See* ANNUAL REPORT - DEPARTMENT OF COMMISSIONERS OF THE LAND OFFICE (OKLAHOMA CITY). 4627

0093-6413 *See* MECHANICS RESEARCH COMMUNICATIONS. 4429

0093-6421 *See* MICHIGAN LICENSED OCCUPATIONS. 4206

0093-6456 *See* TRANSACTIONS OF THE DELAWARE ACADEMY OF SCIENCE. 5166

0093-6464 *See* NEWSPAPERS RECEIVED CURRENTLY IN THE LIBRARY OF CONGRESS. 5647

0093-6502 *See* COMMUNICATION RESEARCH. 1107

0093-6596 *See* AUDIT REPORT - STATE OF NEVADA. DEPARTMENT OF CONSERVATION AND NATIONAL RESOURCES. DIVISION OF STATE PARKS. 2187

0093-660X *See* ANNUAL REPORT OF THE OFFICE OF REVENUE SHARING (WASHINGTON). 4710

0093-6634 *See* FAIT-FEIGHT-FATE. 2446

0093-6642 *See* MONOGRAPHS ON MUSIC IN HIGHER EDUCATION. 4132

0093-6685 *See* UNITED STATES TRADE ASSOCIATIONS. 1630

0093-6693 *See* CHARITABLE TRUST DIRECTORY, OFFICE OF ATTORNEY GENERAL. 3140

0093-6715 *See* ANNUAL STATISTICAL REPORT - DIVISION OF FAMILY SERVICES. 5266

0093-6758 *See* FILM LITERATURE INDEX. 4080

0093-6812 *See* BULLETIN OF THE UNIVERSITY OF NEBRASKA STATE MUSEUM. 4164

0093-6855 *See* CHEMICAL MUTAGENS. 543

0093-691X *See* THERIOGENOLOGY. 5522

0093-6928 *See* WALKING HORSE REPORT. 2803

0093-6960 *See* KINESIOLOGY (WASHINGTON). 583

0093-6987 *See* RIDGE RUNNERS, THE. 2470

0093-707X *See* PERSIMMON HILL. 2754

0093-7118 *See* ANNUAL REPORT. THE STATUS OF WOMEN IN FLORIDA. 5551

0093-7126 *See* FLORIDA STATE MANPOWER PLAN. 1675

0093-7150 *See* SURVEY OF INCOME OF CIVIL SERVICE ANNUITANTS (WASHINGTON). 4689

0093-7177 *See* RIVER FORECASTS PROVIDED BY THE NATIONAL WEATHER SERVICE. 1417

0093-7207 *See* ANNUAL REPORT - DEPARTMENT OF REVENUE AND TAXATION. AD VALOREM TAX DIVISION (CHEYENNE). 4710

0093-7274 *See* WOODALL'S MOBILE/MODULAR LIVING. 2839

0093-7290 *See* DATA CHANNELS. 1257

0093-7320 *See* JOURNAL FOR GERIATRIC CARE STAFF MEMBER. 3752

0093-7339 *See* JOURNAL OF PODIATRIC MEDICAL EDUCATION. 3918

0093-7347 *See* JOURNAL OF THE NEW JERSEY DENTAL ASSOCIATION. 1328

0093-7355 *See* LAB ANIMAL. 5515

0093-741X *See* REPORT ON VISUAL IMPAIRMENT SERVICES TEAMS. 4393

0093-7487 *See* MULTINATIONAL EXECUTIVE TRAVEL COMPANION. 5485

0093-7495 *See* ORIGINS (LOMA LINDA). 5136

0093-7517 *See* USC/FAR CONSOLIDATED PLAN FOR FOREIGN AFFAIRS RESEARCH. 4537

0093-7630 *See* FEP GUIDELINES. 3148

0093-7665 *See* ANNUAL REPORT - WAYNE COUNTY DEPARTMENT OF SOCIAL SERVICES. 5273

0093-7673 *See* PEOPLE (CHICAGO. 1974). 2543

0093-7711 *See* IMMUNOGENETICS (NEW YORK). 3670

0093-7754 *See* SEMINARS IN ONCOLOGY. 3824

0093-7835 *See* PROGRAM STATISTICS - MICHIGAN DEPARTMENT OF SOCIAL SERVICES. 5266

0093-7851 *See* PETROLEO INTERNACIONAL. 4272

0093-786X *See* DESERET NEWS CHURCH ALMANAC. 5059

0093-7878 *See* PROCEEDINGS OF THE NATIONAL CONFERENCE ON PUBLIC GAMING. 3173

0093-7932 *See* UTAH PROSECUTOR, THE. 3109

0093-7991 *See* RESEARCH NEWS - DIVISION OF RESEARCH DEVELOPMENT AND ADMINISTRATION. 5147

0093-8009 *See* CHILD DEVELOPMENT STATE PLAN (PENNSYLVANIA). 5278

0093-8017 *See* ANNUAL EVALUATION OF THE NEW YORK STATE UNEMPLOYMENT INSURANCE FUND. 1645

0093-8076 *See* CLINICAL LABORATORY REFERENCE. 3566

0093-8106 *See* PROGRAM AND PROJECT ACCOMPLISHMENTS (NEW ORLEANS). 2239

0093-8157 *See* REVIEWS IN ANTHROPOLOGY. 244

0093-8165 *See* AIR QUALITY DATA. 2223

0093-8238 *See* QUARTER HORSE OF THE PACIFIC COAST, THE. 2801

0093-8246 *See* ANNUAL REPORT OF THE DEPARTMENT OF BUSINESS REGULATION (HELENA). 823

0093-8254 *See* AWARD WINNING ARCHITECTURE/USA. 293

0093-8270 *See* C.O.S.-M.O.S. DIGITAL INTEGRATED CIRCUITS. 2037

0093-8297 *See* ESQ. 3385

0093-8300 *See* FEDERAL GRANT-IN-AID PROGRAMS (PHOENIX). 4723

0093-8335 *See* SMITHSONIAN OPPORTUNITIES FOR RESEARCH AND STUDY IN HISTORY, ART, SCIENCE. 2854

0093-8408 *See* ENGINEERING INDEX ENERGY ABSTRACTS. 2004

0093-8440 *See* SOLDIERS (WASHINGTON). 4057

0093-8483 *See* JOURNAL OF CAMEROON AFFAIRS. 2640

0093-8505 *See* RAILWAY HISTORY MONOGRAPH, THE. 5436

0093-8548 *See* CRIMINAL JUSTICE AND BEHAVIOR. 4583

0093-8556 *See* CURRENT PEDIATRIC DIAGNOSIS & TREATMENT. 3903

0093-8580 *See* PROFESSIONAL SELF-EVALUATION AND CONTINUING EDUCATION PROGRAM. 3944

0093-8637 *See* GUIDEBOOK TO FLORIDA TAXES. 4730

0093-8645 *See* GUIDEBOOK TO WISCONSIN TAXES. 4730

0093-8653 *See* ANNUAL PUBLIC DEFENDERS' WORKSHOP. 3105

0093-867X *See* AREA WAGE SURVEY : FORT LAUDERDALE-HOLLYWOOD AND WEST PALM BEACH, FLORIDA, METROPOLITAN AREAS. 1652

0093-8688 *See* JOURNAL OF COLLEGE AND UNIVERSITY LAW, THE. 2987

0093-8718 *See* DIRECTORY OF HOME CENTERS. 2811

0148-5318 *See* PROCESSED FISHERY PRODUCTS, ANNUAL SUMMARY. 2311

0093-8742 *See* SALARIES SCHEDULED FOR ADMINISTRATIVE AND SUPERVISORY PERSONNEL IN PUBLIC SCHOOLS. 1870

0093-8769 *See* CLINICAL DENTISTRY. 1319

0093-8815 *See* APPLICATIONS OF CRYOGENIC TECHNOLOGY. 5085

0093-8823 *See* DIRECT LEVIES ON GAMING IN NEVADA. 4720

0093-8831 *See* FACT BOOK AND REPORT OF THE WEST VIRGINIA STATE SYSTEM OF HIGHER EDUCATION. 1823

0093-884X *See* PHYSICAL FACILITIES AT INSTITUTIONS OF HIGHER EDUCATION IN WEST VIRGINIA. 1841

0093-8858 *See* PRO SE. 3031

0093-8912 *See* COMPREHENSIVE PLAN FOR CRIMINAL JUSTICE. 3160

0093-8947 *See* REPORT NO. TES. **2241**

0093-9056 *See* ARCHIVES INFORMATION CIRCULAR. **2479**

0093-9064 *See* CHANGES MAGAZINE (BISBEE). **3374**

0093-917X *See* TEEN-AGE DRIVERS (OLYMPIA). **5445**

0093-9196 *See* BIBLIOGRAPHY ON ATOMIC TRANSITION PROBABILITIES. **4033**

0093-9226 *See* SUMMARY OF PUBLIC ACTS (HARTFORD). **3061**

0093-9307 *See* TRANSLATION (NEW YORK). **3447**

0093-934X *See* BRAIN AND LANGUAGE. **3828**

0093-9374 *See* LEICA MANUAL. **4371**

0093-9404 *See* OVERVIEW OF BLOOD. **3773**

0093-9412 *See* REPORT OF THE NATIONAL MARINE FISHERIES SERVICE. **2311**

0093-9501 *See* DIRECTORY OF SPECIAL PROGRAMS FOR MINORITY GROUP MEMBERS; CAREER INFORMATION SERVICES, EMPLOYMENT SKILLS BANKS, FINANCIAL AID. **5283**

0093-951X *See* DIRECTORY OF TRUST INSTITUTIONS. **788**

0093-9528 *See* DUN & BRADSTREET REFERENCE BOOK OF TRANSPORTATION. **5381**

0093-9560 *See* MHS REVIEW. **5591**

0093-9579 *See* SEMIOTEXTE (NEW YORK). **5257**

0093-9625 *See* HAWAII REVIEW. **3393**

0093-9668 *See* MINNESOTA STATISTICAL ABSTRACT. **5333**

0093-9676 *See* NATIONAL UNION CATALOG. MOTION PICTURES AND FILMSTRIPS. **3259**

0093-9714 *See* RESEARCH ADVANCES IN ALCOHOL AND DRUG PROBLEMS. **1348**

0093-9722 *See* UROLOGY TIMES. **3994**

0093-9781 *See* AVERAGE RETAIL PRICES OF SELECTED COMMODITIES AND SERVICES. **1590**

0093-979X *See* ANALYSIS OF ANNUAL REPORTS OF LICENSEES. **770**

0093-9811 *See* PARROTT TALK. **2466**

0093-9854 *See* HEART OF TEXAS RECORDS. **2452**

0093-9889 *See* INFORMATION SERIES - TENNESSEE STATE BOARD OF VOCATIONAL EDUCATION. **1913**

0093-9900 *See* MODERN NURSING HOME DIRECTORY OF NURSING HOMES IN THE UNITED STATES, U.S. POSSESSIONS AND CANADA. **3789**

0093-9951 *See* ROSTER OF BLACK ELECTED OFFICIALS IN THE SOUTH. **4684**

0093-996X *See* TAPE RECORDING & BUYING GUIDE. **5319**

0093-9994 *See* IEEE TRANSACTIONS ON INDUSTRY APPLICATIONS. **2062**

0094-0003 *See* PHYSICAL REVIEW AND PHYSICAL REVIEW LETTERS INDEX. **4415**

0094-002X *See* AMERICAN INDIAN LAW REVIEW. **2932**

0094-0054 *See* CAMPER'S GUIDE TO AREA CAMPGROUNDS. **4870**

0094-0097 *See* YEH TSAO. **2510**

0094-0143 *See* UROLOGIC CLINICS OF NORTH AMERICA, THE. **3993**

0094-0178 *See* OLD-HOUSE JOURNAL, THE. **623**

0094-0186 #y 0094-0816 *See* OFF-LEAD. **4287**

0094-0291 *See* HIKING (HIGHLAND PARK). **4873**

0094-0321 *See* MECCA (NEW ORLEANS). **4130**

0094-033X *See* NEW GERMAN CRITIQUE. **3415**

0094-0348 *See* POPULATION MOBILITY IN HAWAII. **4557**

0094-0372 *See* COCKSHAW'S CONSTRUCTION LABOR NEWS & OPINION. **607**

0094-0399 *See* YOUR SCHOOL & THE LAW. **3077**

0094-0429 *See* MISSOURI C.H.P. IN RETROSPECT. **4791**

0094-0445 *See* ROGUES 'N RASCALS. **1846**

0094-0453 *See* SHELDON'S RETAIL DIRECTORY OF THE UNITED STATES AND CANADA AND PHELON'S RESIDENT BUYERS AND MERCHANDISE BROKERS. **957**

0094-047X *See* AIRMAN'S INFORMATION MANUAL (FALLBROOK, CALIF.). **10**

0094-0496 *See* AMERICAN ETHNOLOGIST. **228**

0094-0518 *See* BEAUTY (NEW YORK). **402**

0094-0534 *See* CONSUMERS INDEX TO PRODUCT EVALUATIONS AND INFORMATION SOURCES. **1300**

0094-0569 *See* INVENTORY OF INTERSTATE CARRIER WATER SUPPLY SYSTEMS BY STATES AND ENVIRONMENTAL PROTECTION AGENCY REGIONS. **5535**

0094-0593 *See* JOURNAL OF CORPORATE TAXATION, THE. **4734**

0094-0623 *See* LEGAL NOTES FOR INSURANCE. **3000**

0094-064X *See* PLANNING REVIEW. **882**

0094-0771 *See* MIDDLE SCHOOL JOURNAL. **1764**

0094-078X *See* NORTHWESTERN TOUR BOOK. **5486**

0094-0798 *See* ORAL HISTORY REVIEW, THE. **2625**

0094-0844 *See* THORNY TRAIL, THE. **2475**

0094-0860 *See* DROPOUT REPORT : DELAWARE PUBLIC SCHOOLS. **1737**

0094-0887 *See* FAR-WESTERN FORUM. **3387**

0094-0933 *See* ABORTION SURVEILLANCE. **587**

0094-095X *See* DIRECTORY OF CONTINUING EDUCATION OPPORTUNITIES IN NEW YORK CITY. **1800**

0094-1123 *See* NEVADA STATE PLAN FOR VOCATIONAL EDUCATION. **1914**

0094-1131 See TRUCK CAMPER TRADE-IN GUIDE. **5398**

0094-114X *See* MECHANISM AND MACHINE THEORY. **2122**

0094-1166 *See* ARKANSAS COMPREHENSIVE MANPOWER PLAN. **1654**

0094-1182 *See* CIVIL WAR COLLECTORS' DEALER DIRECTORY, THE. **250**

0094-1190 *See* JOURNAL OF URBAN ECONOMICS. **1501**

0094-1255 *See* BOOK OF NAMES, THE. **756**

0094-1263 *See* FESTIVAL USA. **2733**

0094-1271 *See* IDAHO AGRICULTURAL STATISTICS. **154**

0094-1298 *See* CLINICS IN PLASTIC SURGERY. **3962**

0094-1344 *See* COUNTRY MUSIC WORLD. **4112**

0094-1352 *See* INDUSTRISCOPE (RICHMOND). **901**

0094-1360 *See* JEFFERSONIAN REVIEW, THE. **3399**

0094-1387 *See* GRANTS - U.S. DEPARTMENT OF HEALTH, EDUCATION, AND WELFARE. OFFICE OF HUMAN DEVELOPMENT. OFFICE OF YOUTH DEVELOPMENT. **5286**

0094-1417 *See* ASTROGRAPH (ARLINGTON), THE. **391**

0094-1433 *See* DIRECTORY OF ECONOMIC RESEARCH IN MISSISSIPPI. **1479**

0094-1441 *See* DIRECTORY OF RESOURCES FOR OLDER PEOPLE IN NEW HAMPSHIRE. **5283**

0094-1476 *See* JOURNAL OF THE PHILADELPHIA ASSOCIATION FOR PSYCHOANALYSIS. **3930**

0094-1484 *See* MAGYAR NAPTAR (NEW YORK). **2489**

0094-1492 *See* MATERIALS PERFORMANCE. **2105**

0094-1514 *See* MOTOR HANDBOOK. **5419**

0094-1611 *See* WORLD GUIDE TO TRADE ASSOCIATIONS. **858**

0094-162X *See* TENTH MUSE, THE. **3472**

0094-1646 *See* INDUSTRIAL ENERGY. **4260**

0094-1662 See STATISTICAL REPORT ON MERGERS AND ACQUISITIONS. **1539**

0094-1670 *See* CONSERVATION IN KANSAS. **2190**

0094-1697 *See* ANNUAL REPORT ON THE QUALITY OF THE ENVIRONMENT (ST. PAUL). **2161**

0094-1700 *See* JOURNAL OF SPORT HISTORY. **4902**

0094-1735 *See* SELECTED DECISIONS OF THE INTERNATIONAL MONETARY FUND AND SELECTED DOCUMENTS. **811**

0094-1794 *See* ESTATE PLANNING (TAMPA). **3118**

0094-1832 *See* HYDRAULIC RESEARCH IN THE UNITED STATES AND CANADA. **2090**

0094-1891 *See* WOODALL'S DIRECTORY OF MOBILE HOME COMMUNITIES. **2839**

0094-1905 *See* REGISTER PLANNED EMERGENCY PRODUCERS. **4055**

0094-1921 *See* CAMPAIGN LAW REPORTER. **4467**

0094-1956 *See* JOURNAL OF INSTRUCTIONAL PSYCHOLOGY. **4597**

0094-1964 *See* PAINTBRUSH (LARAMIE). **3467**

0094-2057 *See* CALIFORNIA SCHOOL LAW DIGEST. **2946**

0094-2065 *See* COMMUNIO (SPOKANE, WASH.). **4949**

0094-209X *See* DIRECTORIES OF HAWAII. **2559**

0094-2227 *See* HANDBOOK FOR FINANCIAL AID ADMINISTRATORS. **1827**

0094-2251 *See* NEWSLETTER - VIRGINIA STATE BAR. YOUNGER MEMBERS CONFERENCE. **3017**

0094-226X *See* NEWSLETTER & DIGEST OF SELECTED OPINIONS OF STATE ATTORNEYS GENERAL. **3142**

0094-2278 *See* RAILWAY PASSENGER CAR ANNUAL. **5436**

0094-2316 *See* WORLD OF POLITICS. **4501**

0094-2324 *See* COMMUNITY DEVELOPMENT DIGEST (WASHINGTON). **2818**

0094-2375 *See* FANTASIAE. **5074**

0094-2383 See JOURNAL OF ABSTRACTS (AND ARTICLES) IN INTERNATIONAL EDUCATION. **1795**

0094-2391 See JOURNAL OF NATURAL RESOURCES AND LIFE SCIENCES EDUCATION. **100**

0094-2405 *See* MEDICAL PHYSICS (LANCASTER). **4412**

0094-2413 *See* JUVENILE JUSTICE DIGEST. **3168**

0094-2421 *See* CELEBRATION (KANSAS CITY, MO.). **5027**

0094-243X *See* AIP CONFERENCE PROCEEDINGS. **4396**

0094-2464 *See* SMALL BUSINESSMAN'S CLINIC. **711**

0094-2499 *See* JOURNAL OF BIOCOMMUNICATION, THE. **3593**

0094-2502 *See* BUSINESS REGULATION LAW REPORT: WAGE AND PRICE CONTROL. **3097**

0094-2510 *See* MARKETING CALIFORNIA DRIED FRUITS. **2349**

0094-2553 *See* UNITED STATES JUDICIAL REPORTER. **3068**

0094-2561 *See* DISCLOSURE RECORD. **788**

0094-260X *See* AABC NEWSLETTER. **1806**

0094-2626 *See* LIBRARY STATISTICS OF ILLINOIS COLLEGES AND UNIVERSITIES. **3259**

0094-2707 *See* IRT DIGEST. **5384**

0094-2715 *See* INSCAPE (PASADENA). **3396**

0094-2782 *See* NEW MEXICO FOREST PRODUCTS DIRECTORY. **2389**

0094-2790 *See* MOVEMENT OF CALIFORNIA FRUITS AND VEGETABLES BY RAIL, TRUCK, AND AIR. **846**

0094-2863 See SOVIET AND POST-SOVIET REVIEW, THE. **4496**

0094-2871 *See* STATE AIR POLLUTION IMPLEMENTATION PLAN PROGRESS REPORT. **2182**

0094-288X *See* RUSSIAN HISTORY (PITTSBURGH). **2707**

0094-2898 *See* PROCEEDINGS OF THE ANNUAL SOUTHEASTERN SYMPOSIUM ON SYSTEM THEORY. **1200**

0094-291X See MENTAL HEALTH, RETARDATION AND HOSPITALS (CRANSTON). **3789**

0094-2987 See PUBLICATIONS RESOURCE MANUAL (SPRINGFIELD). **3243**

0094-3029 See FINANCIAL REPORT - CARNEGIE ENDOWMENT FOR INTERNATIONAL PEACE. **4521**

0094-3037 See EAST CENTRAL EUROPE. **2846**

0094-3061 See CONTEMPORARY SOCIOLOGY (WASHINGTON). **5243**

0094-3096 See AMERICAN METRIC JOURNAL. **4029**

0094-3118 See DOGSOLDIER (SPOKANE). **3382**

0094-3134 See PROBE DIRECTORY OF FOREIGN DIRECT INVESTMENT IN THE UNITED STATES. **912**

0094-3142 See SUMMARIES OF FOREIGN GOVERNMENT ENVIRONMENTAL REPORTS. **2182**

0094-3150 See BEST'S EXECUTIVE DATA SERVICE. REPORT A6- COMPARATIVE EXPERIENCE BY STATE (STATE LEADERS). **2875**

0094-3258 See BULLETIN - KODALY MUSICAL TRAINING INSTITUTE INC. **4106**

0094-3282 See EMPRESS CHINCHILLA BREEDER (1974). **3183**

0094-3320 See 13TH MOON. **3357**

0094-3355 See HORSE AND HORSEMAN. **2799**

0094-3452 See PLACE (INDIANA). **5489**

0094-3509 See JOURNAL OF FAMILY PRACTICE, THE. **3738**

0094-3517 See ICTA ROSTER. **5480**

0094-3525 See COMPREHENSIVE FACILITIES INVENTORY REPORT (HARTFORD). **1818**

0094-3584 See AMERICAN BAR REFERENCE HANDBOOK, THE. **2932**

0094-3606 See EDUCATION IN WASHINGTON. **1739**

0094-3630 See ABSTRACTS OF FISHERY RESEARCH REPORTS. **2293**

0094-3649 See DRUM CORPS REVIEW. **4115**

0094-3673 See BEHAVIOR SCIENCE RESEARCH. **5192**

0094-372X See SOUTH DAKOTA INDIAN RECIPIENTS OF SOCIAL WELFARE. **5310**

0094-3770 See AMERICAN BIBLIOGRAPHY OF SLAVIC AND EAST EUROPEAN STUDIES. **2634**

0094-3789 See APHIS 81. **2409**

0094-3797 See APHIS 91. **62**

0094-3800 See CALIFORNIA PLANT PATHOLOGY. **505**

0094-3819 See CATTLE (WASHINGTON). **209**

0094-3851 See SHEEP AND GOATS. **221**

0094-3878 See RESEARCH REPORT - AGRICULTURAL EXPERIMENT STATION, UTAH STATE UNIVERSITY. **127**

0094-3932 See ADVANCES IN FIRE RETARDANTS. **2287**

0094-3967 See FAIRFAX COUNTY GOVERNMENT ORGANIZATION MANUAL. **4647**

0094-3975 See FUNDAMENTALS OF AEROSPACE INSTRUMENTATION. **22**

0094-3991 See NARCOTICS AND DRUG ABUSE. **1347**

0094-4033 See UNION CATALOG OF MAPS (BERKELEY). **2578**

0094-4076 See EMORY LAW JOURNAL. **2966**

0094-4084 See INTERNATIONAL DIRECTORY OF BEHAVIOR AND DESIGN RESEARCH. **5204**

0094-4092 See LIST OF LOCAL BOARDS OF THE SELECTIVE SERVICE SYSTEM. **4049**

0094-4106 See MANPOWER PLANNING DATA (WASHINGTON). **944**

0094-4181 See FORESTRY RESEARCH NOTE (CAMAS). **2382**

0094-4211 See GAIU HANDBOOK OF WAGES, HOURS, AND FRINGE BENEFITS. **1675**

0094-422X See TRANSCRIBINGS, ANNUAL CONFERENCE - AMERICAN SOCIETY OF PENSION ACTUARIES. **1715**

0094-4238 See ANNUAL REPORT - GOVERNOR'S COMMITTEE ON CRIME, DELINQUENCY AND CORRECTIONS (CHARLESTON). **3157**

0094-4246 See ARIZONA LEGISLATIVE SERVICE. **2937**

0094-4289 See JOURNAL OF ENGINEERING MATERIALS AND TECHNOLOGY. **2118**

0094-4319 See RULES AND PROCEDURES FOR OPERATION OF TEACHERS' RETIREMENT SYSTEM OF OKLAHOMA. **1709**

0094-4424 See FAMILY PLANNING SERVICES. ANNUAL SUMMARY. **589**

0094-4459 See PROCEEDINGS OF THE SPECIAL CONVENTION OF THE NATIONAL COLLEGIATE ATHLETIC ASSOCIATION. **4913**

0094-4467 See SOUTHEASTERN EUROPE (PITTSBURGH). **2523**

0094-4483 See PERSPECTIVES - CENTER FOR HEALTH ADMINISTRATION STUDIES, UNIVERSITY OF CHICAGO. **4795**

0094-4491 See MARYLAND MANUAL. **4664**

0094-4645 See NEW VOICES (NEW PALTZ). **3416**

0094-470X See EXAMINATION OF FINANCIAL STATEMENTS OF OVERSEAS PRIVATE INVESTMENT CORPORATION. **897**

0094-4726 See REPORT OF THE GOVERNOR'S YOUTH COUNCIL (RICHMOND). **1068**

0094-4742 See WORLD ENVIRONMENTAL DIRECTORY. **2183**

0094-4920 See SOCIAL SCIENCES INDEX. **5228**

0094-4955 See BLUE BOOK OFFICIAL LAWN EQUIPMENT TRADE-IN GUIDE. **2810**

0094-498X See LAISVE, I. **2696**

0094-4998 See POINT OF REFERENCE. **2625**

0094-5021 See ANNUAL REPORT - DIVISION OF FORESTRY, FISHERIES, AND WILDLIFE DEVELOPMENT, TENNESSEE VALLEY AUTHORITY. **2374**

0094-503X See YOUTH CONSERVATION CORPS PROGRAM. **2210**

0094-5056 See EASTERN ECONOMIC JOURNAL. **1480**

0094-5072 See INTER DEPENDENT, THE. **4524**

0094-5145 See JOURNAL OF COMMUNITY HEALTH. **4786**

0094-5153 See WINE NOW. **2372**

0094-517X See STATE OF NEVADA REVENUE SHARING TRUST FUND AUDIT REPORT. **4749**

0094-5218 See OFFICIAL RAILWAY GUIDE. NORTH AMERICAN TRAVEL EDITION. UNITED STATES, CANADA AND MEXICO, THE. **5433**

0094-5242 See OFFICIAL MEETING FACILITIES GUIDE. **2808**

0094-5277 See BARRISTER (CHICAGO). **2940**

0094-5293 See AIR QUALITY ABSTRACTS. **2223**

0094-5315 See AMERICAN MEN AND WOMEN OF SCIENCE: ECONOMICS. **5173**

0094-5323 See AUGUSTINIAN STUDIES. **5024**

0094-534X See OHIO NORTHERN UNIVERSITY LAW REVIEW. **3021**

0094-5366 See BILINGUAL REVIEW. **3269**

0094-5374 See CAREER DEVELOPMENT, DROPOUT PREVENTION PROGRAM, EXPERIMENTAL PROGRAMS, TEACHER LEADERSHIP PROGRAM, REGIONAL SERVICE UNITS. **1911**

0094-5390 See DIRECTORY OF OKLAHOMA AIRPORTS. **18**

0094-5404 See ESSAYS IN LITERATURE. **3342**

0094-5439 See MAINE PROSECUTOR BULLETIN, THE. **3108**

0094-5447 See METALLURGY/MATERIALS EDUCATION YEARBOOK. **4011**

0094-5455 See NORTH DAKOTA ACADEMIC LIBRARY STATISTICS. **3259**

0094-5463 See PRODUCT SAFETY & THE LAW. **3032**

0094-5595 See DIRECTORIO INDUSTRIAL U.S.A. **1604**

0094-5609 See EXAMINATION OF FINANCIAL STATEMENTS, INTER-AMERICAN FOUNDATION. **4722**

0094-5617 See HASTINGS CONSTITUTIONAL LAW QUARTERLY. **3093**

0094-5625 See LE-TORAH VE-HORA AH. **5050**

0094-5633 See MEASURING MORMONISM. **4976**

0094-5641 See MINNESOTA HEALTH STATISTICS. **4791**

0094-5706 See STATE OF IDAHO ANNUAL WORK PROGRAM. **5444**

0094-5714 See SYNTHESIS AND REACTIVITY IN INORGANIC AND METAL-ORGANIC CHEMISTRY. **994**

0094-5765 See ACTA ASTRONAUTICA. **3**

0094-5781 See TEXTILE CLEANING TECHNOLOGY. **5357**

0094-579X See STONE SOUP (SANTA CRUZ, CALIF.). **1069**

0094-5803 See RESEARCH IN THE SCHOOL OF BUSINESS (MADISON). **1517**

0094-5811 See MEDICAL WORLD NEWS REVIEW. **3612**

0094-582X See LATIN AMERICAN PERSPECTIVES. **4542**

0094-5838 See INTERFACE (ATLANTA). **5232**

0094-5846 See FUNDAMENTALS OF COSMIC PHYSICS. **395**

0094-5862 See FAMILY ALBUM, THE. **3387**

0094-5889 See CAPTAIN'S MATE. **4889**

0094-5927 See ACCIDENTAL POISONING IN WISCONSIN. **4763**

0094-5943 See READER'S ADVISER, THE. **3459**

0094-596X See ANNUAL REPORT AND PROCEEDINGS OF THE ANNUAL ENCAMPMENT (LANSING). **4034**

0094-5994 See DIRECTORY: SUB-STATE PLANNING DISTRICTS IN OKLAHOMA. **2821**

0094-6044 See PROCEEDINGS OF THE CLINICAL DIALYSIS AND TRANSPLANT FORUM. **3992**

0094-6087 See CAREERS (PORTLAND). **1912**

0094-6133 See MALPRACTICE DIGEST. **3005**

0094-6176 See SEMINARS IN THROMBOSIS AND HEMOSTASIS. **3774**

0094-6206 See ORIGINS OF BEHAVIOR, THE. **4606**

0094-6249 See CHEMICAL REFERENCE MANUAL. **1014**

0094-629X See CATALOG OF NATIONAL ARCHIVES MICROFILM PUBLICATIONS. **2481**

0094-6303 See GLOBAL DIRECTORY OF GAS COMPANIES. **4259**

0094-6338 See SOUTH CAROLINA VITAL AND MORBIDITY STATISTICS. **5338**

0094-6354 See AANA JOURNAL. **3849**

0094-6362 See ALGAE ABSTRACTS. **5529**

0094-6478 See MLA INDEX AND BIBLIOGRAPHY SERIES. **4131**

0094-6559 See ASIA & AUSTRALASIA. BASIC OIL LAWS AND CONCESSION CONTRACTS, ORIGINAL TEXTS. SUPPLEMENT (PHOTOCOPY). **4251**

0094-6567 See CHEM SOURCES U.S.A. **967**

0094-6591 See ORTHOPAEDIC REVIEW. **3883**

0094-6613 See COLLEGE MONTHLY. **1816**

0094-6680 See WHO'S WHO IN TEXAS. **438**

0094-6710 See WESTERN LIVESTOCK JOURNAL. CENTRAL EDITION. **223**

0094-6893 See ECONOMIC REVIEW (RICHMOND, VA.). **1485**

0094-6907 See CANTWELL TAPESTRY, A. **2441**

0094-6915 See BACKTRACKER, THE. **2438**

0094-6923 See INTERNATIONAL TELEX BOOK. AMERICAS EDITION. **1158**

0094-6958 See SAGE PUBLIC ADMINISTRATION ABSTRACTS. **4699**

0094-7083 See EARLY AMERICAN LIFE. YEARBOOK. **2731**

0094-7113 See OREGON WILDLIFE. **2201**

0094-7148 See REPORT OF CASES DETERMINED IN THE SUPREME COURT AND COURT OF APPEALS OF THE STATE OF NEW MEXICO. **3038**

0094-7156 See REPORT OF THE FEDERAL HOME LOAN MORTGAGE CORPORATION. **808**

0094-7180 See SPECIAL MANAGEMENT BULLETIN. **812**

0094-7237 See ENVIRONMENTAL BIOLOGY. **454**

0094-730X See JOURNAL OF FLUENCY DISORDERS. **3595**

0094-7326 See REPORT OF THE NEW MEXICO VETERANS' SERVICE COMMISSION. 4681

0094-7342 See JOURNAL OF MORMON HISTORY. 4969

0094-7415 See AVERAGE DAILY TRAFFIC VOLUMES ON INTERSTATE, ARTERIAL AND PRIMARY ROUTES. 5439

0094-744X See BULLETIN - U.S. COAST GUARD ACADEMY ALUMNI ASSOCIATION. 1101

0094-7466 See MINERALS TRANSPORTATION. 1442

0094-7474 See PROCEEDINGS OF THE SUMMER COMPUTER SIMULATION CONFERENCE. 1283

0094-7490 See AMERICAN PRINTMAKERS. 4563

0094-7512 See DIRECTORY OF COUNSELING SERVICES. 1912

0094-7555 See BANKING LEGISLATION IN THE CONGRESS. 3085

0094-7598 See LAND USE LAW & ZONING DIGEST. 2993

0094-761X See NATIONAL TRANSPORTATION SAFETY BOARD DECISIONS. 5388

0094-7628 See NEW HAMPSHIRE COMPREHENSIVE LAW ENFORCEMENT PLAN. 3170

0094-7636 See WATER-RESOURCES BULLETIN (SALT LAKE CITY). 5544

0094-7660 See ILLINOIS INSURANCE. 2882

0094-7679 See JOURNALISM HISTORY. 2921

0094-7709 See RAS NEWSLETTER. 423

0094-7741 See SUMMARY OF GRANTS AND CONTRACTS ACTIVE ON 4804

0094-7768 See INTERNATIONAL STUDIES NOTES. 4525

0094-7776 See OSAHRC REPORTS. 3023

0094-7784 See WHO'S WHO IN FLORIDA. 437

0094-7814 See INVENTORY OF MARRIAGE AND FAMILY LITERATURE. 2281

0094-7849 See TORT LAW LETTER, THE. 3065

0094-7881 See GRADUATE SCIENCE EDUCATION STUDENT SUPPORT AND POSTDOCTORALS. 5108

0094-7903 See DEMOCRATIC FOCUS, THE. 4471

0094-792X See CPA LETTER, THE. 742

0094-7954 See APSA DEPARTMENTAL SERVICES PROGRAM, SURVEY OF DEPARTMENTS. 4464

0094-7970 See AAP-AUPS UNIVERSITY PRESS STATISTICS. 5320

0094-8004 See DIRECTORY OF MINORITY OWNED BUSINESSES IN TEXAS. 667

0094-8020 See ICP SOFTWARE GUIDE : BANKING. 790

0094-8039 See JOURNAL OF MUSCLE SHOALS HISTORY, THE. 2741

0094-8047 See MINNESOTA STUDIES IN VOCATIONAL REHABILITATION. 1690

0094-8063 See ENERGY REVIEW (SANTA BARBARA). 1942

0094-8071 See NEWS BULLETIN (DETROIT). 2292

0094-8098 See READERS ADVISORY SERVICE : SELECTED TOPICAL BOOKLISTS. 423

0094-8136 See YACHTING YEAR BOOK OF NORTHERN CALIFORNIA. 597

0094-8160 See AIR RESEARCH SUMMARY. 2223

0094-8233 See ALLOYS INDEX. 3997

0094-8241 See VIRGINIA'S APPROPRIATIONS FOR HIGHER EDUCATION. 1853

0094-825X See SWEET'S INDUSTRIAL CONSTRUCTION & RENOVATION FILE WITH PLANT ENGINEERING EXTENSION MARKET LIST. 630

0094-8276 See GEOPHYSICAL RESEARCH LETTERS. 1406

0094-8292 See UNCLASSIFIED ACCESSION LIST. 426

0094-8322 See DIRECTORY OF HIGHER EDUCATION. 1821

0094-8373 See PALEOBIOLOGY. 4229

0094-8381 See AIR FORCE LAW REVIEW, THE. 3182

0094-839X See COME FLY WITH US. 16

0094-8438 See LAW ENFORCEMENT REPORT. 3169

0094-8454 See OFFICIAL SOUTHERN CALIFORNIA PORTS MARITIME DIRECTORY AND GUIDE. 5453

0094-8462 See PEOPLE (ST. PAUL). 5301

0094-8500 See ENZYME ENGINEERING. 3692

0094-8519 See ABSTRACTS OF THE ... GENERAL MEETING OF THE AMERICAN SOCIETY FOR MICROBIOLOGY. 476

0094-8594 See INTERNATIONAL JOURNAL OF PURCHASING AND MATERIALS MANAGEMENT. 950

0094-8667 See DIRECTORY OF HOME CENTER OPERATORS & HARDWARE CHAINS. 2811

0094-8683 See INVESTMENT REVIEW. 903

0094-8705 See JOURNAL OF THE PHILOSOPHY OF SPORT. 4902

0094-8713 See LUSK'S PRINCE WILLIAM COUNTY REAL ESTATE DIRECTORY SERVICE. 4840

0094-873X See MONTANA LIBRARY DIRECTORY, WITH STATISTICS OF MONTANA PUBLIC LIBRARIES. 3259

0094-8748 See NATIONAL EMISSIONS REPORT. 2237

0094-8764 See OFFICIAL PUBLICATION - ASSOCIATION OF AMERICAN PLANT FOOD CONTROL OFFICIALS. 116

0094-8837 See SELECTED TABLES IN MATHEMATICAL STATISTICS. 3542

0094-8853 See ANNUAL REPORT - COUNCIL OF BETTER BUSINESS BUREAUS. 1293

0094-8918 See NEW PRODUCT DIRECTORY OF NEW YORK STOCK EXCHANGE LISTED COMPANIES, THE. 1619

0094-8934 See FOLK HARP JOURNAL. 4118

0094-8942 See ANNUAL HEALTH MANPOWER CONFERENCE. 3913

0094-8969 See AMERICAN HOSPITAL ASSOCIATION GUIDE TO THE HEALTH CARE FIELD. 3548

0094-8985 See JOURNAL - THE LOS ANGELES INSTITUTE OF CONTEMPORARY ART. 354

0094-9000 See THEORY OF PROBABILITY AND MATHEMATICAL STATISTICS. 3538

0094-9086 See HOPKINS QUARTERLY. 3344

0094-9094 See CHIEF EXECUTIVES AND MEMBERS OF GOVERNING BOARDS OF ALABAMA INSTITUTIONS OF HIGHER EDUCATION. 1815

0094-9124 See OFFSHORE TECHNOLOGY YEARBOOK. 4268

0094-9140 See INVESTIGATION OF FLOODS IN HAWAII. 1415

0094-9167 See CAPE ISLAND SOUND. 3461

0094-9175 See BASKETBALL BULLETIN, THE. 4886

0094-9183 See SOCIAL PROBLEMS (GUILFORD). 5259

0094-9191 See APCA DIRECTORY AND RESOURCE BOOK. 2224

0094-9264 See PRINCIPLES AND TECHNIQUES OF HUMAN RESEARCH AND THERAPEUTICS. 4325

0094-9361 See EUROHEALTH HANDBOOK. 3780

0094-9426 See BOOK FORUM. 3338

0094-9434 See ELECTRICAL PRACTICE. 2045

0094-9450 See NASSAU COUNTY HISTORICAL SOCIETY JOURNAL, THE. 2747

0094-9477 See PREVIEWS OF HEAT AND MASS TRANSFER. 4432

0094-9515 See ANNUAL REPORT - JOINT FEDERAL-STATE LAND USE PLANNING COMMISSION FOR ALASKA. 4627

0094-9531 See SHEPARD'S FEDERAL LAW CITATIONS IN SELECTED LAW REVIEWS. 3050

0094-954X See WHO'S WHO IN NATIONAL ATHLETICS HIGH SCHOOL FOOTBALL. 437

0094-9620 See AMERICAN OPTOMETRIC ASSOCIATION NEWS. 4215

0094-9655 See JOURNAL OF STATISTICAL COMPUTATION AND SIMULATION. 1282

0094-9701 See METIVTA, HA-. 5051

0094-9736 See ARMY RECREATION AND TRAVEL GUIDE. 4036

0094-9744 See BASENJI, THE. 4285

0094-9787 See OLYMPIAN (NEW YORK, N.Y.), THE. 4910

0094-9833 See HOSPITALS, NURSING HOMES AND RELATED HEALTH FACILITIES. 3786

0094-9892 See SOVIET SHIPBUILDING. 4183

0094-9914 See YOUR HIGHWAY DEPARTMENT, ARKANSAS. 5446

0094-9930 See JOURNAL OF PRESSURE VESSEL TECHNOLOGY. 2118

0094-9973 See BEST'S AGENTS GUIDE. LIFE-HEALTH. 2875

0094-9981 See SOURCES (ALBUQUERQUE). 3250

0094-999X See PROBATE LAWYER, THE. 3031

0095-0033 See DATA BASE. 1257

0095-005X See ARIZONA EDUCATIONAL DIRECTORY. 1726

0095-0130 See COMPUTERIZED SERIALS SYSTEMS SERIES. 3203

0095-0157 See FLORIDA MARINE RESEARCH PUBLICATIONS. 455

0095-019X See OSIRIS (SCHENECTADY, N.Y.). 3467

0095-036X See TEXAS NURSING. 3870

0095-0378 See INTERNATIONAL ASTROLOGICAL REGISTER. 390

0095-0394 See PERSONNEL REPORT. 945

0095-0416 See SUPPLEMENTAL YEAR BOOK - STATE BOARD OF PROFESSIONAL ENGINEERS AND LAND SURVEYORS. 1997

0095-0432 See INJURY EXPERIENCE IN COAL MINING. 2863

0095-0459 See SPIT IN THE OCEAN. 3439

0095-0483 See INFORME ANUAL - ESTADO LIBRE ASOCIADO DE PUERTO RICO, POLICIA DE PUERTO RICO. 3166

0095-053X See NLR: NATIONAL LIBRARY REPORTER. 3237

0095-0548 See ETHNIC MINORITY AFFAIRS DIRECTORY. 2260

0095-0572 See SPECIAL BIBLIOGRAPHIES (ROCKVILLE). 1350

0095-0637 See FACT BOOK : ALABAMA INSTITUTIONS OF HIGHER EDUCATION, UNIVERSITIES AND COLLEGES. 1823

0095-0645 See BIENNIAL REPORT - STATE OF MINNESOTA, DEPARTMENT OF REVENUE. 4713

0095-067X See WOODENBOAT, THE. 597

0095-0696 See JOURNAL OF ENVIRONMENTAL ECONOMICS AND MANAGEMENT. 1499

0095-0742 See DMAAC TECHNICAL TRANSLATIONS LIST. 4043

0095-0777 See INSTRUMENTATION IN THE FOOD AND BEVERAGE INDUSTRY. 2345

0095-0815 See RELAY MINIATURE AND SUBMINIATURE D.A.T.A. BOOK. 2079

0095-0831 See REPORT TO THE CONGRESS - LISTER HILL NATIONAL CENTER FOR BIOMEDICAL COMMUNICATIONS. 3633

0095-0866 See WESTERN PENNSYLVANIA GENEALOGICAL SOCIETY QUARTERLY. 2477

0095-0874 See SYMBOLS OF AMERICAN LIBRARIES. 3252

0095-0920 See DIRECTORY OF OKLAHOMA. 4644

0095-0963 See AUTOMEDICA (NEW YORK). 3686

0095-0971 See BIO-MEDICAL SCOREBOARD. 3556

0095-1005 See SEARCH AND SEIZURE LAW REPORT. 3047

0095-1013 See LIFESTYLE. 2537

0095-1048 See FOOTWEAR MANUAL. 1084

0095-1056 See SALES RATIO STUDY; RESIDENTIAL AND COMMERCIAL PROPERTIES. 4747

0095-1129 See TUBERCULOSIS BEDS IN HOSPITALS. 3952

0095-1137 See JOURNAL OF CLINICAL MICROBIOLOGY. 565

0095-1145 See PSYCHOLOGY (MENTOR). 4613

0095-1161 See DIGEST OF OREGON LAWS. 2961
0095-1188 See WOMEN LAW REPORTER. 3076
0095-1234 See NEWSLETTER - FRIENDS OF MICRONESIA. 2670
0095-1315 See GREAT PLAINS-ROCKY MOUNTAIN GEOGRAPHICAL JOURNAL. 2565
0095-1358 See FODOR'S ... RUSSIA, THE REPUBLICS AND THE BALTICS. 5473
0095-1366 See NEWSLETTER - CASSETTE INFORMATION SERVICES. 1901
0095-1382 See STATISTICAL TABLES - DEPARTMENT OF EMPLOYMENT SECURITY. 2898
0095-1390 See ALBION (BOONE). 2672
0095-1439 See CENTRAL KENTUCKY RESEARCHER. 2442
0095-1447 See CINEFAN. 4066
0095-1471 See INTERNATIONAL YEARBOOK OF FOREIGN POLICY ANALYSIS, THE. 4526
0095-1498 See KENTUCKY LOCAL DEBT REPORT. 4735
0095-151X See PROFILE (LOS ANGELES, CALIF. 1974). 4913
0095-1528 See URBAN PLANNING QUARTERLY. 2838
0095-1536 See WOMEN (WASHINGTON). 5570
0095-1579 See BRITISH ISLES AND IRELAND TRAVEL GUIDE. 5465
0095-1587 See FOSTER NATURAL GAS REPORT FROM WASHINGTON. 4256
0095-1625 See RIDER. 4082
0095-165X See EL DORADO. 235
0095-1676 See MANAGEMENT SERIES (INDIANAPOLIS). 2198
0095-1692 See CIVIL ENGINEERING REPORT SERIES. 2021
0095-1730 See SEEMS. 3470
0095-179X See ANNUAL REPORT - CRIMINAL JUSTICE TRAINING AND STANDARDS COUNCIL. 3157
0095-1811 See AMERICAN CLEAN CAR. 638
0095-182X See AMERICAN INDIAN QUARTERLY. 2255
0095-1854 See BRAKES. 4769
0095-1862 See DIRECTORY OF UNITED STATES CEMETERIES. 2407
0095-1897 See MONTHLY ENERGY REVIEW. 1950
0095-1927 See TEXAS CERTIFIED SEED DIRECTORY. 2432
0095-196X See G.C.B. BULLETIN. 3165
0095-1994 See ANNUAL REPORT - DEPARTMENT OF SAFETY. 5438
0095-2001 See TIRES. 4805
0095-2028 See NATIONAL COLLEGE OF THE STATE JUDICIARY. 3013
0095-2036 See MISSION HAND BOOK. 4978
0095-2044 See ENVIRONMENTAL QUALITY (WASHINGTON). 2169
0095-2095 See PROCEEDINGS OF THE DIGITAL EQUIPMENT COMPUTER USERS SOCIETY. 1200
0095-2109 See ANNUAL REPORT TO THE CONGRESS BY THE OFFICE OF TECHNOLOGY ASSESSMENT. 5084
0095-2117 See COMPTROLLER GENERAL'S PROCUREMENT DECISIONS. 949
0095-2184 See INTEGRITY FORUM. 5204
0095-2206 See ANNUAL REPORT - ARKANSAS ENVIRONMENTAL PRESERVATION COMMISSION. 2186
0095-2222 See CONSUMERS' RESEARCH MAGAZINE. 1296
0095-2230 See REPORT OF ACTIVITIES FOR THE STATE DEPARTMENT OF ART, HISTORICAL AND CULTURAL PRESERVATION. 2853
0095-2338 See JOURNAL OF CHEMICAL INFORMATION AND COMPUTER SCIENCES. 980
0095-2427 See HARVARD MAGAZINE. 1092
0095-2443 See JOURNAL OF ELASTOMERS AND PLASTICS, THE. 4456

0095-2451 See PROCEEDINGS OF THE NATIONAL SEMINAR ON YEAR-ROUND EDUCATION. 1869
0095-2486 See A.G.R. 42
0095-2583 See ECONOMIC INQUIRY. 1483
0095-2591 See JOURNAL - THE INTERNATIONAL NETSUKE COLLECTORS SOCIETY. 373
0095-2613 See ORFF ECHO, THE. 4144
0095-263X See RARE COIN REVIEW. 2783
0095-2664 See TUNNELING TECHNOLOGY NEWSLETTER. 2033
0095-2680 See NEWS PREVIEWS. 4817
0095-2699 See AGRICULTURAL LIBRARIES INFORMATION NOTES. 3188
0095-2737 See COMPUTERS & SOCIETY. 1179
0095-2753 See TAXABLE SALES IN CALIFORNIA. SALES AND USE TAX (ANNUAL). 4754
0095-2788 See VOGUE PATTERNS. 5186
0095-2796 See SUMMARY OF ELECTION LAWS ENACTED BY THE LEGISLATIVE ASSEMBLY - OREGON. 3061
0095-280X See STUDIES IN AMERICAN HUMOR. 3441
0095-2842 See HANDBOOK OF ILLINOIS GOVERNMENT. 4475
0095-2850 See ECONOMIC AND SOCIAL PROGRESS IN LATIN AMERICA. 1556
0095-2893 See INVENTORY OF THE COLLECTIONS. 4089
0095-2907 See DICKSON MOUNDS MUSEUM ANTHROPOLOGICAL STUDIES. 235
0095-2923 See INSURANCE FORUM, THE. 2883
0095-294X See FORECASTER. 1491
0095-2958 See BIOLOGY DIGEST. 477
0095-2990 See AMERICAN JOURNAL OF DRUG AND ALCOHOL ABUSE, THE. 1340
0095-3016 See ANNUAL ECONOMIC REPORT - WISCONSIN DEPARTMENT OF REVENUE. 4709
0095-3032 See REAL ESTATE ASSESSMENT/SALES RATIO STUDY. 4843
0095-3083 See BUYERS GUIDE TO INDIAN ART. 346
0095-3105 See NEBRASKA STATISTICAL REPORT OF ABORTIONS. 591
0095-3164 See REPORT OF THE SOUTH DAKOTA STATE PHARMACEUTICAL ASSOCIATION AND THE SOUTH DAKOTA BOARD OF PHARMACY. 4327
0095-3180 See RESOLUTION OF CORRECTIONAL PROBLEMS AND ISSUES. 3175
0095-3199 See REPORT OF THE STATE AUDITOR OF MINNESOTA ON THE REVENUES, EXPENDITURES, AND DEBT OF THE CITIES AND VILLAGES IN MINNESOTA. 4746
0095-3237 See OCCUPATIONAL SAFETY & HEALTH REPORTER. 2867
0095-327X See ARMED FORCES AND SOCIETY. 4035
0095-3318 See REPORT - OFFICE OF ALCOHOLISM, DEPARTMENT OF HEALTH AND SOCIAL SERVICES, STATE OF ALASKA. 1348
0095-3334 See MASSACHUSETTS LANDINGS, ANNUAL SUMMARY. 2308
0095-3350 See SUMMARY OF ACCIDENTS INVOLVING THE DRINKING DRIVER. 5445
0095-3369 See DIGEST OF UNITED STATES PRACTICE IN INTERNATIONAL LAW. 3127
0095-3385 See ANNUAL WORK PROGRAM - WASHINGTON TRAFFIC SAFETY COMMISSION. 4767
0095-3423 See COMMERCE BUSINESS DAILY. 949
0095-3431 See ALABAMA'S VITAL EVENTS. 5320
0095-344X See HIGHWAY STATISTICS. 5441
0095-3474 See A.C.A. INDUSTRY GUIDE TO HEARING AIDS. INTERNATIONAL EDITION. 4382
0095-3482 See SUMMARY AND ANALYSIS OF INTERNATIONAL TRAVEL TO THE U.S. 5491

0095-3520 See AMORTIZATION, INSURANCE PREMIUM AND OUTSTANDING PRINCIPAL BALANCE TABLES FOR HOME MORTGAGES AND LOANS INSURED UNDER THE NATIONAL HOUSING ACT. 769
0095-3539 See HEALTH INFORMATION FOR INTERNATIONAL TRAVEL. 3713
0095-3555 See RAPPORT (LOS ANGELES, CALIF.). 388
0095-3563 See VINIFERA WINE GROWERS JOURNAL, THE. 190
0095-361X See BASIC STATE PLAN AND ANNUAL PROGRAM. 3193
0095-3628 See MICROBIAL ECOLOGY. 2218
0095-3644 See WISCONSIN LABOR FORCE. 1718
0095-3660 See STATE AND REGIONAL DATA, FEDERALLY FUNDED COMMUNITY MENTAL HEALTH CENTERS. 5311
0095-3679 See PEANUT SCIENCE. 180
0095-3709 See FEDERAL AID PAID TO NEW YORK STATE SCHOOL DISTRICTS. 1864
0095-3717 See DRIVING WHEEL. 4115
0095-3725 See DIRECTORY OF CLINICAL LABORATORIES, CLINICAL LABORATORY PERSONNEL. 3894
0095-3776 See REPORT - TEXAS MAPPING ADVISORY COMMITTEE. 2583
0095-3792 See HEALTH CARE LABOR MANUAL. 1676
0095-3814 See TOPICS IN HEALTH CARE FINANCING. 814
0095-3865 See ANNUAL REPORT - STATE OF ALASKA, LEGISLATIVE BUDGET AND AUDIT COMMITTEE. 4710
0095-389X See FARM LABOR REPORT (CASPER). 1669
0095-3903 See FOREIGN TRADE ANNUAL REPORT; VIRGINIA PORTS. 836
0095-3911 See JOURNAL OF THE ST. CLAIR COUNTY HISTORICAL SOCIETY. 2742
0095-3946 See PROLOG (LOS ANGELES). 4913
0095-3962 See SALES TRAINING & DEVELOPMENT. 936
0095-3997 See ADMINISTRATION & SOCIETY. 4624
0095-4004 See ADULT PROBATION ADMISSIONS. 3156
0095-4063 See COMMUNICATIONS WORLD. 1130
0095-4128 See PROPYLENE ANNUAL. 1047
0095-4144 See REPORTS ON INTERNATIONAL COMPENSATION : ARGENTINA. 1707
0095-4179 See TRW SOFTWARE SERIES : INDEX TO PUBLICATIONS IN PRINT. 1210
0095-4195 See ACTA BOTANICA SINICA. 497
0095-4284 See NORTH CAROLINA DATA FILE. 1576
0095-4314 See WISCONSIN TRAILS. 2550
0095-4330 See WASHINGTON AGRICULTURAL STATISTICS. 157
0095-4349 See DOD DIRECTORY OF CONTRACT ADMINISTRATION SERVICES COMPONENTS. 4043
0095-4373 See CLIMATOLOGICAL DATA. HAWAII AND PACIFIC. 1422
0095-439X See PHOTOGRAPHY MARKET PLACE. 4374
0095-4403 See BULLETIN OF THE AMERICAN SOCIETY FOR INFORMATION SCIENCE. 3198
0095-4411 See CAMPBOOK. NORTHWESTERN. 4870
0095-4438 See COLUMBAN MISSION. 4948
0095-4446 See DIRECTORY OF IOWA MANUFACTURERS. 3477
0095-4470 See JOURNAL OF PHONETICS. 3291
0095-4489 See STUDIES IN BROWNING AND HIS CIRCLE. 435
0095-4497 See COMPOSITE MATERIALS. 973
0095-4519 See INNOVATIONS (PALO ALTO). 5290
0095-4527 See CYTOLOGY AND GENETICS. 535
0095-4543 See PRIMARY CARE. 3738
0095-4608 See BYZANTINE STUDIES. 2682
0095-4616 See APPLIED MATHEMATICS AND OPTIMIZATION. 3495

0095-4640 *See* BENCHMARK PAPERS IN ECOLOGY. 2212

0095-4659 *See* ANNUAL REPORT ON THE COMPREHENSIVE WATER RESOURCES PLAN. 5529

0095-4683 *See* AIRLINE HANDBOOK. 5460

0095-4705 *See* HOW TO (INDIANAPOLIS). 616

0095-4810 *See* ANNUAL WORK PROGRAM - SOUTHWEST NEW MEXICO COUNCIL OF GOVERNMENTS. 2815

0095-4829 *See* ADVANCES AND TECHNICAL STANDARDS IN NEUROSURGERY. 3957

0095-4837 *See* CHARTBOOK ON PRICES, WAGES, AND PRODUCTIVITY. 1590

0095-4861 *See* CLINICAL AND BIOCHEMICAL ANALYSIS. 485

0095-487X *See* CONDOMINIUM WORLD. 2819

0095-4888 *See* DIRECTORY OF MINNESOTA'S AREA MENTAL HEALTH, MENTAL RETARDATION, INEBRIETY PROGRAMS. 4773

0095-4918 *See* JOURNAL OF PORTFOLIO MANAGEMENT. 904

0095-4926 *See* SOUTHERN CREATIVITY ANNUAL. 766

0095-506X *See* INTERNATIONAL FOUNDATIONS OF EDUCATION QUARTERLY, THE. 1753

0095-5086 *See* PUBLIC UTILITIES LAW ANTHOLOGY. 3033

0095-5108 *See* CLINICS IN PERINATOLOGY. 3759

0095-5124 *See* PETERSEN'S HUNTING ANNUAL. 4877

0095-5159 *See* RESTAURANT EXECUTIVE. 5072

0095-5205 *See* DIRECTORY : NEW JERSEY AGRICULTURAL ORGANIZATIONS. 79

0095-5213 *See* KALEIDOSCOPE (BOSTON). 1759

0095-5248 *See* NEW FRONTIERS (SEATTLE). 5252

0095-5264 *See* REPORT / NEVADA BUREAU OF MINES AND GEOLOGY. 1394

0095-5272 *See* INSTITUTIONAL CHARACTERISTICS OF COLLEGES AND UNIVERSITIES. 1830

0095-5337 *See* ILLINOIS HANDCRAFTS DIRECTORY. 373

0095-537X *See* WEIGHING & MEASUREMENT. 4033

0095-5388 *See* VOYAGES TO THE INLAND SEA. 3473

0095-5396 *See* NATIONAL OPERATIONS AND AUTOMATION CONFERENCE PROCEEDINGS, THE. 801

0095-5418 *See* STRICTLY U.S. 2787

0095-5485 *See* U.S. IMPORTS. CONSUMPTION AND GENERAL SIC-BASED PRODUCTS BY WORLD AREAS. 855

0095-5531 *See* BUYERS GUIDE TO OUTDOOR ADVERTISING, THE. 756

0095-5558 *See* COUNTRY PLACE. 77

0095-5574 *See* ANNUAL REPORT - KENTUCKY MANPOWER DEVELOPMENT, INC. 3913

0095-5663 *See* NEW YORK TIMES SCHOOL MICROFILM COLLECTION INDEX BY REELS, THE. 5711

0095-5698 *See* ACCESS (SYRACUSE). 2496

0095-571X *See* SEMEIA. 5019

0095-5752 *See* UNIFORM CRIME REPORTS, COMMONWEALTH OF PENNSYLVANIA. 3084

0095-5760 *See* ALASKA HUNTING GUIDE. 4868

0095-5817 *See* AUDIT OF NEW YORK STATE AGENCIES. 739

0095-5868 *See* OPT, THE MAGAZINE ON PEOPLE AND THINGS. 5211

0095-5876 *See* PROCEEDINGS OF THE SAN DIEGO BIOMEDICAL SYMPOSIUM. 3696

0095-5892 *See* TRAINING (MINNEAPOLIS). 948

0095-5949 *See* LOUISIANA HISTORICAL QUARTERLY. 2745

0095-5981 *See* HUMANITIES INDEX. 2857

0095-5981 *See* HUMANITIES INDEX. CD-ROM. 2847

0095-6007 *See* CONGRESSIONAL QUARTERLY ALMANAC. 4640

0095-6074 *See* POLLUTION CONTROL JOURNAL. 2238

0095-6112 *See* WEST VIRGINIA WORK FORCE ANNUAL AVERAGES. 1717

0095-6147 *See* CALIFORNIA ACCOUNTANCY ACT WITH RULES AND REGULATIONS. 740

0095-6171 *See* GRANT AWARDS - UNITED STATES CIVIL SERVICE COMMISSION, BUREAU OF INTERGOVERNMENTAL PERSONNEL PROGRAMS. 4704

0095-6430 *See* STATE OF FLORIDA COMPREHENSIVE MANPOWER PLAN. 1712

0095-6457 *See* CARPET SPECIFIER'S HANDBOOK, THE. 5348

0095-6562 *See* AVIATION SPACE AND ENVIRONMENTAL MEDICINE. 3554

0095-6643 *See* ANNUAL AUDIT - ARIZONA STATE PARKS BOARD. 738

0095-666X *See* TECHNICAL BULLETIN - IFI RESEARCH CENTER. 5356

0095-6686 *See* PHYSICAL RESEARCH REPORT. 2028

0095-6694 *See* OSSC BULLETIN. 1771

0095-6783 *See* ANNUAL REPORT - MISSISSIPPI MARINE RESOURCES COUNCIL. 1446

0095-6813 *See* EXPENDITURES FOR STAFF DEVELOPMENT AND TRAINING ACTIVITIES. 5285

0095-6848 *See* JOURNAL OF JAPANESE STUDIES, THE. 2655

0095-6856 *See* KENTUCKY PRIMARY AND GENERAL ELECTION. 4480

0095-6910 *See* HOMEGROWN (ROHNERT PARK). 2321

0095-6945 *See* INTERSECTIONS. 5249

0095-6953 *See* N. A. D. A. MOTORCYCLE & MOPED APPRAISAL GUIDE. 4082

0095-697X *See* JUVENILE LAW NEWSLETTER. 3121

0095-702X *See* RENDEZVOUS OF WESTERN ART. 363

0095-7046 *See* U.S. INDUSTRIAL DIRECTORY. 1630

0095-7100 *See* BNA PENSION REPORTER. 1656

0095-7119 *See* BEST SCIENCE FICTION OF THE YEAR, THE. 3366

0095-7178 *See* DISNEY NEWS. 4850

0095-7240 *See* WORLD ALMANAC GUIDE TO PRO HOCKEY, THE. 4930

0095-7291 *See* FOREIGN TAX LAW BI-WEEKLY BULLETIN. 3128

0095-7321 *See* FISCAL YEAR HIGHER EDUCATION BUDGET RECOMMENDATIONS : CAPITAL IMPROVEMENTS. 1824

0095-7348 *See* MINNESOTA AND ENVIRONS WEATHER ALMANAC. 1431

0095-7356 *See* MONTHLY ENERGY REVIEW. 1950

0095-7380 *See* THEORY OF STOCHASTIC PROCESSES. 3538

0095-7461 *See* SPOTS. 388

0095-7496 *See* CRIMINAL JUSTICE NEWSLETTER (BLOOMINGTON). 3162

0095-7577 *See* JOURNAL OF SPACE LAW. 2989

0095-7607 *See* EUROPEAN PARLIAMENT DIGEST. 4647

0095-7615 *See* HORIZONS. 23

0095-7682 *See* FISHERY STATISTICS OF THE UNITED STATES. 2317

0095-7712 *See* NORTH DAKOTA ACCIDENT FACTS. 5442

0095-7763 *See* UA JOURNAL. 1715

0095-7798 *See* TAXABLE SALES IN VIRGINIA COUNTIES & CITIES BASED ON RETAIL SALES TAX REVENUES. 4754

0095-7917 *See* CURRENT CONTENTS. ENGINEERING, TECHNOLOGY & APPLIED SCIENCES. 2003

0095-7925 *See* DIRECTORY OF HEALTH SCIENCES LIBRARIES IN THE UNITED STATES. 3207

0095-7968 *See* REPORT ON SALARIES, FRINGE BENEFITS, AND RELATED PRACTICES AFFECTING CLASSIFIED SERVICE EMPLOYEES OF NEW YORK STATE. 1707

0095-7984 *See* JOURNAL OF BLACK PSYCHOLOGY, THE. 4594

0095-7992 *See* IDAHO STATE TESTING PROGRAM : TABLES OF STANDARD SCORES WITH CORRESPONDING PERCENTILE NORMS FOR THE IOWA TESTS OF EDUCATIONAL DEVELOPMENT. 1751

0095-8034 *See* CALIFORNIA UNION LIST OF PERIODICALS. 412

0095-8050 *See* EXPENDITURES REPORT OF THE MASSACHUSETTS REHABILITATION COMMISSION. 1668

0095-8069 *See* U.S. BUDGET RECOMMENDATIONS. 4757

0095-8190 *See* ANNUAL REPORT TO CONGRESS / UNITED STATES CONSUMER PRODUCT SAFETY COMMISSION. 1293

0095-8204 *See* STATE DATA PROFILES, CALENDAR YEAR. 137

0095-8220 *See* LEGISLATION CHECK LIST. 3001

0095-8263 *See* STATUS REPORT : CAPITAL IMPROVEMENTS PROGRAM, CONSTRUCTION SUMMARY. 1627

0095-828X *See* DIRECTORY OF PRIVATE SCHOOLS IN NEW YORK STATE. 1736

0095-8301 *See* DIABETES FORECAST. 3727

0095-8387 *See* DEL-CHEM BULLETIN, THE. 974

0095-8484 *See* CHEMIST-ANALYST. 1014

0095-8638 *See* BULLETIN - STATE GEOLOGICAL AND NATURAL HISTORY SURVEY OF CONNECTICUT. 4164

0095-8808 *See* DU PONT MAGAZINE. 1024

0095-8948 *See* ENGINEERING AND MINING JOURNAL (1926). 2138

0095-8956 *See* JOURNAL OF COMBINATORIAL THEORY. SERIES B. 3512

0095-8964 *See* JOURNAL OF ENVIRONMENTAL EDUCATION, THE. 2175

0095-8972 *See* JOURNAL OF COORDINATION CHEMISTRY. 981

0095-9243 *See* WOODALL'S TRAILERING PARKS & CAMPGROUNDS. WESTERN EDITION. 4881

0095-926X *See* CPI DETAILED REPORT. 1590

0095-9669 *See* COMSAT TECHNICAL REVIEW. 1152

0095-9782 *See* JOURNAL OF SOLUTION CHEMISTRY. 1055

0095-9960 *See* CERAMIC ABSTRACTS. 2595

0096-0128 *See* PROCEEDINGS / ELECTRIC FURNACE CONFERENCE. 4016

0096-0268 *See* PROCEEDINGS OF THE ANNUAL CONVENTION - AMERICAN RAILWAY ENGINEERING ASSOCIATION. 5434

0096-0411 *See* CONTRIBUTIONS FROM THE LABORATORY OF VERTEBRATE BIOLOGY. 452

0096-0551 *See* COMPUTER LANGUAGES. 1278

0096-0764 *See* FLUID MECHANICS : SOVIET RESEARCH. 2089

0096-0802 *See* HEAT TRANSFER. JAPANESE RESEARCH. 4431

0096-1078 *See* STATION BULLETIN - OREGON STATE UNIVERSITY, AGRICULTURAL EXPERIMENT STATION. 137

0096-1191 *See* JOURNAL OF FORAMINIFERAL RESEARCH. 5588

0096-1264 *See* STATISTICAL SUMMARY OF THE OFFICE OF REGISTRATION AND RECORDS. 1798

0096-1280 *See* LIST OF LIGHTS AND FOG SIGNALS. 4178

0096-1329 *See* LENGTH OF STAY IN PAS HOSPITALS, UNITED STATES, EASTERN REGION. 3788

0096-1337 *See* JOURNAL OF UNDERGRADUATE PSYCHOLOGICAL RESEARCH. 4602

0096-1345 *See* INDEX AND CUMULATIVE LIST OF PAPERS ON RADIATION CHEMISTRY. 978

0096-1353 *See* FORD'S DECK PLAN GUIDE. 5474

0096-140X *See* AGGRESSIVE BEHAVIOR. 4572

0096-1426 *See* VOCATIONAL REHABILITATION INDEX. 5313

0096-1442 *See* JOURNAL OF URBAN HISTORY. 2621

0096-1469 *See* ASHLEYS OF AMERICA QUARTERLY. 2438

0096-1485 See ALCOHOL, DRUG ABUSE, MENTAL HEALTH, RESEARCH GRANT AWARDS. 1339

0096-1493 See ADMINISTRATIVE REGISTER OF KENTUCKY. 2928

0096-1507 See A.I.D. RESEARCH AND DEVELOPMENT ABSTRACTS. 2913

0096-1523 See JOURNAL OF EXPERIMENTAL PSYCHOLOGY : HUMAN PERCEPTION AND PERFORMANCE. 4597

0096-1531 See RESEARCH DIRECTORY OF THE REHABILITATION RESEARCH AND TRAINING CENTERS. 4382

0096-1728 See PUBLICATION - CALIFORNIA STATE WATER RESOURCES CONTROL BOARD. 5537

0096-1736 See JOURNAL OF OCCUPATIONAL MEDICINE. 2864

0096-221X See EASTMAN ORGANIC CHEMICAL BULLETIN. 1041

0096-2341 See ACCESSIONS LIST, SOUTHEAST ASIA. 406

0096-2651 See FIELDIANA : GEOLOGY. 1375

0096-2708 See HORIZONS IN BIOCHEMISTRY AND BIOPHYSICS. 457

0096-2716 See CONTACT LENS JOURNAL. 3873

0096-2740 See PERSPECTIVE ON AGING. 3754

0096-2902 See RESEARCH METHODS IN NEUROCHEMISTRY. 3844

0096-3003 See APPLIED MATHEMATICS AND COMPUTATION. 3495

0096-3054 See DIRECTORY OF COMMUNITY-BASED MENTAL RETARDATION SERVICES. 5282

0096-3070 See FLORIDA STATE UNIVERSITY LAW REVIEW. 2971

0096-3089 See GEOCHIMICA. 1376

0096-3151 See MONTANA HUMAN SERVICES DIRECTORY. 5297

0096-3208 See STATE OF NORTH CAROLINA UNIFORM CRIME REPORT. 3083

0096-3216 See KARTER NEWS. 4903

0096-3224 See FINANCES OF EMPLOYEE-RETIREMENT SYSTEMS OF STATE AND LOCAL GOVERNMENTS. 1669

0096-3291 See YEARBOOK OF SCIENCE AND THE FUTURE. 5171

0096-3313 See SPORTS CARS IN REVIEW. 5425

0096-333X See MISSISSIPPI FINANCIAL STATISTICS FOR HIGHWAY PLANNING ON STATE HIGHWAYS COUNTY ROADS CITY STREETS. 5401

0096-3399 See ARIZONA ASSOCIATION OF COUNTIES SALARY AND BENEFIT SURVEY. 1653

0096-3402 See BULLETIN OF THE ATOMIC SCIENTISTS. 5091

0096-3445 See JOURNAL OF EXPERIMENTAL PSYCHOLOGY : GENERAL. 4596

0096-3488 See BANK MIDYEAR REVIEW. TEXAS. 775

0096-3496 See QUARTERLY - INTERNATIONAL PLASTIC MODELERS' SOCIETY. UNITED STATES BRANCH. 4460

0096-3518 See IEEE TRANSACTIONS ON SIGNAL PROCESSING. 2064

0096-378X See PROCEEDINGS OF THE SOUTH DAKOTA ACADEMY OF SCIENCE. 5142

0096-3895 See TURTOX NEWS. 475

0096-3917 See CANCER LETTER, THE. 3811

0096-3925 See MOSCOW UNIVERSITY BIOLOGICAL SCIENCES BULLETIN. 466

0096-3941 See EOS (WASHINGTON, D.C.). 1404

0096-4131 See BULLETIN OF THE BUFFALO SOCIETY OF NATURAL SCIENCES. 4164

0096-4158 See MARYLAND NATURALIST, THE. 4167

0096-4166 See PROCEEDINGS OF THE ROCHESTER ACADEMY OF SCIENCE. 5141

0096-4255 See JOURNAL OF THE MISSOURI WATER AND SEWERAGE CONFERENCE. 2234

0096-4263 See PROCEEDINGS OF THE WEST VIRGINIA ACADEMY OF SCIENCE. 5142

0096-4417 See AMERICAN HORTICULTURIST (ALEXANDRIA). 2408

0096-4522 See PROCEEDINGS / THE SOIL AND CROP SCIENCE SOCIETY OF FLORIDA. 183

0096-4581 See BULLETIN - NEW MEXICO BUREAU OF MINES & MINERAL RESOURCES. 2135

0096-4859 See MINES MAGAZINE. 1442

0096-5197 See TECHNICAL PUBLICATION (UTAH. DEPT. OF NATURAL RESOURCES). 2206

0096-5502 See HOSPITAL & COMMUNITY PSYCHIATRY. MICROFILM. 3926

0096-5960 See YEARBOOK OF THE CALIFORNIA AVOCADO SOCIETY. 2434

0096-6053 See BULLETIN (GEOLOGICAL SURVEY OF WYOMING). 1369

0096-6061 See BULLETIN - TEXAS AGRICULTURAL EXPERIMENT STATION. 70

0096-607X See BULLETIN - UNIVERSITY OF FLORIDA, AGRICULTURAL EXPERIMENT STATIONS. 70

0096-6088 See BULLETIN / VIRGINIA AGRICULTURAL EXPERIMENT STATION. 70

0096-6304 See WATER QUALITY INSTRUMENTATION. 5543

0096-6398 See BULLETIN - NEW JERSEY AGRICULTURAL EXPERIMENT STATION, RUTGERS UNIVERSITY. 69

0096-6851 See TRANSACTIONS OF THE AMERICAN OTOLOGICAL SOCIETY. 3891

0096-7238 See INSTRUMENTATION IN THE AEROSPACE INDUSTRY. 24

0096-736X See SAE TRANSACTIONS. 5425

0096-7580 See PROCEEDINGS OF THE INTERNATIONAL SOCIETY OF SUGARCANE TECHNOLOGISTS. 183

0096-7629 See WELDING RESEARCH (MIAMI). 4028

0096-7688 See ANNUAL REPORT OF THE SECRETARY OF THE STATE HORTICULTURAL SOCIETY OF MICHIGAN. 2409

0096-7750 See MONOGRAPHS - ACADEMY OF NATURAL SCIENCES OF PHILADELPHIA. 4168

0096-7769 See NORTHWEST GEOLOGY. 1390

0096-7807 See SOVIET JOURNAL OF ECOLOGY, THE. 2221

0096-7866 See BULLETIN - DIVISION OF GEOLOGY. 1369

0096-7874 See BULLETIN OF THE AGRICULTURAL EXPERIMENT STATION OF THE LOUISIANA STATE UNIVERSITY AND A & M COLLEGE. 69

0096-7963 See PROCEEDINGS - ANNUAL SYMPOSIUM ON INSTRUMENTATION FOR THE PROCESS INDUSTRIES. 3486

0096-8056 See ANNALS OF OTOLOGY, RHINOLOGY & LARYNGOLOGY. SUPPLEMENT, THE. 3886

0096-848X See YEARBOOK OF PHYSICAL ANTHROPOLOGY (WASHINGTON). 248

0096-8498 See SOUTHERN COOPERATIVE SERIES BULLETIN. 136

0096-8676 See ANNUAL REPORT - MARYLAND AGRICULTURAL EXPERIMENT STATION. 61

0096-8684 See BEGONIAN, THE. 2410

0096-8714 See TREE PLANTERS' NOTES. 2397

0096-879X See CURRENT ANTARCTIC LITERATURE. 2559

0096-882X See JOURNAL OF STUDIES ON ALCOHOL. 1346

0096-8846 See ITALIAN AMERICANA. 2264

0096-8854 See ANNUAL REPORT / FEDERAL JUDICIAL CENTER. 2934

0096-8870 See PROCEEDINGS, ANNUAL CONVENTION - GAS PROCESSORS ASSOCIATION. 4275

0096-9117 See NEWS BULLETIN (AUSTIN, TEX.). 4228

0096-9192 See PROCEEDINGS OF THE LOUISIANA ACADEMY OF SCIENCES, THE. 5141

0096-9206 See PROCEEDINGS OF THE MONTANA ACADEMY OF SCIENCES. 5141

0096-9214 See PROCEEDINGS OF THE NORTH DAKOTA ACADEMY OF SCIENCE. 5141

0096-9419 See NAVY CIVIL ENGINEER. 2027

0096-9796 See ARIZONA TRAFFIC ACCIDENT SUMMARY. 5439

0096-980X See CALIFORNIA MANPOWER. 1658

0096-9893 See EXAMINATION OF THE RURAL TELEPHONE BANK'S FINANCIAL STATEMENTS. 743

0096-9990 See DIRECTORY OF U.S.S.R. MINISTRY OF DEFENSE AND ARMED FORCES OFFICIALS. 4042

0097-000X See STATE OF COLORADO ANNUAL HIGHWAY SAFETY WORK PROGRAM. 5444

0097-0050 See JOURNAL OF HEALTH EDUCATION. ASSOCIATION FOR THE ADVANCEMENT OF HEALTH EDUCATION. 4786

0097-0166 See NUTRITION RESEARCH. 4196

0097-0212 See MISCELLANEOUS PUBLICATION - UNITED STATES DEPARTMENT OF AGRICULTURE. 109

0097-0263 See HIAS BULLETIN. 1919

0097-0298 See BULLETIN OF THE BIOLOGICAL SOCIETY OF WASHINGTON. 4164

0097-031X See CETOLOGY. 5580

0097-0336 See UNITED STATES NAVAL OBSERVATORY CIRCULAR. 401

0097-0387 See MONOGRAPHS OF THE WESTERN FOUNDATION OF VERTEBRATE ZOOLOGY. 5592

0097-0484 See BULLETIN - KANSAS AGRICULTURAL EXPERIMENT STATION. 69

0097-0549 See NEUROSCIENCE AND BEHAVIORAL PHYSIOLOGY. 584

0097-059X See PROCEEDINGS OF THE HEAT TRANSFER AND FLUID MECHANICS INSTITUTE. 2125

0097-062X See SPECIAL CIRCULAR - OHIO AGRICULTURAL RESEARCH AND DEVELOPMENT CENTER. 136

0097-0638 See SPECIAL PUBLICATION - AMERICAN FISHERIES SOCIETY. 2313

0097-0832 See CONTRIBUTION - UNIVERSITY OF MARYLAND, NATURAL RESOURCES INSTITUTE. 2191

0097-0883 See BULLETIN - MOUNT DESERT ISLAND BIOLOGICAL LABORATORY (1934). 450

0097-0905 See BULLETIN / CONNECTICUT AGRICULTURE EXPERIMENT STATION. 68

0097-1065 See METHODS IN SUBNUCLEAR PHYSICS. 4448

0097-1138 See ABSOLUTE SOUND, THE. 5315

0097-1146 See ANIMA (CHAMBERSBURG). 4185

0097-1154 See INDIAN LAW REPORTER. 2981

0097-1197 See REGIONAL SCIENCE PERSPECTIVES. 1516

0097-1367 See BULLETIN - UNIVERSITY OF DELAWARE, AGRICULTURAL EXPERIMENT STATION. 70

0097-1731 See PROCEEDINGS - CALIFORNIA WEED CONFERENCE. 2428

0097-1782 See VIRGINIA FRUIT. 2433

0097-191X See BULLETIN - NEVADA BUREAU OF MINES AND GEOLOGY. 1370

0097-2126 See PROCEEDINGS OF THE AMERICAN POWER CONFERENCE. 2125

0097-2169 See TAPPI MONOGRAPH SERIES. 4239

0097-2290 See ECONOMIC PAPER (RALEIGH). 1483

0097-2312 See LOSS PREVENTION. 2014

0097-2495 See FABRICS-FASHIONS. 5350

0097-2509 See INTERNATIONAL PULP & PAPER DIRECTORY. 4234

0097-2525 See INTERNATIONAL TELEX BOOK. EUROPEAN EDITION. 1158

0097-2533 See MODERN HI-FI AND MUSIC. 5317

0097-255X See PEOPLE'S YELLOW PAGES OF AMERICA. 5301

0097-2576 See BULLETIN (OHIO. DIVISION OF WATER). 5531

0097-2622 See MEMOIRS OF THE SOUTHERN CALIFORNIA ACADEMY OF SCIENCES. 5128

0097-2924 See CIRCULAR / UTAH GEOLOGICAL AND MINERAL SURVEY. 1372

0097-305X See COUNTRY PROFILES. 4551

0097-3149 See CIRCULAR / GEOLOGICAL SURVEY OF ALABAMA. 1372

0097-3157 See PROCEEDINGS OF THE ACADEMY OF NATURAL SCIENCES OF PHILADELPHIA. 4170

0097-3165 See JOURNAL OF COMBINATORIAL THEORY. SERIES A. 3512

0097-3211 See BULLETIN OF THE ALLYN MUSEUM. 4086

0097-3254 See SPECIAL PUBLICATION - ACADEMY OF NATURAL SCIENCES OF PHILADELPHIA. 1360

0097-3262 See BULLETIN - GEOLOGICAL SURVEY OF ALABAMA. 1369

0097-3270 See SPECIAL PUBLICATION / SOCIETY FOR SEDIMENTARY GEOLOGY. 4231

0097-3491 See BULLETIN - UNIVERSITY OF ARKANSAS, FAYETTEVILLE. AGRICULTURAL EXPERIMENT STATION. 70

0097-3556 See CONTRIBUTIONS FROM THE MUSEUM OF PALEONTOLOGY. 4226

0097-3564 See D.A.T.A.'S MICROWAVE TUBE. 2040

0097-3793 See MAP AND CHART SERIES. 1357

0097-3807 See MEMOIRS OF THE TORREY BOTANICAL CLUB. 518

0097-3866 See SPECIAL PUBLICATION - U.N.M. INSTITUTE OF METEORITICS. 1434

0097-4218 See MID-WEST CONTRACTOR. 621

0097-4374 See PROCEEDINGS OF THE ARKANSAS ACADEMY OF SCIENCE. 5140

0097-4412 See STUDIES IN NATURAL SCIENCES. 4172

0097-4463 See ANNALS OF THE CARNEGIE MUSEUM. 4162

0097-4471 See BULLETIN (KANSAS GEOLOGICAL SURVEY). 1369

0097-4536 See CROSSTIES. 2378

0097-4560 See INFORMATION SERIES - ASPHALT INSTITUTE. 2024

0097-4668 See ANTIBIOTICS (NEW YORK. 1967). 4291

0097-4749 See AMERICAN PAINT & COATINGS JOURNAL. CONVENTION DAILY. 4222

0097-479X See NATIONAL DIRECTORY OF CHILD ABUSE SERVICES AND INFORMATION. 5297

0097-4803 See R.U.S.I. AND BRASSEY'S DEFENCE YEARBOOK. 4054

0097-4951 See ANGLICAN THEOLOGICAL REVIEW. SUPPLEMENTARY SERIES. 4934

0097-496X See PEMBROKE MAGAZINE, THE. 3423

0097-5176 See MAGIC MAGAZINE (NEW YORK). 4863

0097-5184 See NINETEENTH CENTURY. 360

0097-5214 See READING AND LITERATURE : GENERAL INFORMATION YEARBOOK. 1903

0097-5249 See MYCOPLASMATALES. 568

0097-5257 See PEDIATRIC NEPHROLOGY. 3909

0097-5273 See BULLETIN - UNIVERSITY OF ARKANSAS (FAYETTEVILLE CAMPUS). ENGINEERING EXPERIMENT STATION. 1967

0097-5281 See BULLETIN - NEVADA BUREAU OF MINES AND GEOLOGY. 1370

0097-5338 See NORTH DAKOTA FARM RESEARCH. 115

0097-5370 See REPORT SERIES - AGRICULTURAL EXPERIMENT STATION, DIVISION OF AGRICULTURE, UNIVERSITY OF ARKANSAS. 126

0097-5397 See SIAM JOURNAL ON COMPUTING. 1262

0097-5419 See SOUTHERN MEDICINE. 3642

0097-5478 See BULLETIN - OHIO. DIVISION OF GEOLOGICAL SURVEY. 1370

0097-5486 See BULLETIN - AGRICULTURAL EXPERIMENT STATION, RIO PIEDRAS. 68

0097-5605 See INFORMATION CIRCULAR - STATE OF OHIO, DEPARTMENT OF NATURAL RESOURCES, DIVISION OF GEOLOGICAL SURVEY. 1383

0097-5672 See REPORT OF INVESTIGATION (ILLINOIS STATE WATER SURVEY). 5538

0097-5680 See REPORT OF INVESTIGATIONS - STATE OF OHIO, DEPARTMENT OF NATURAL RESOURCES, DIVISION OF GEOLOGICAL SURVEY. 1394

0097-5729 See WRRI BULLETIN. 5549

0097-5982 See PEDIATRIC CONFERENCES FROM THE CHILDREN'S HOSPITAL OF NEWARK. 3908

0097-5990 See QRB. QUALITY REVIEW BULLETIN. 3791

0097-6008 See SONIX. 3801

0097-6032 See ANNUAL REPORT - EAST-WEST POPULATION INSTITUTE. 4549

0097-6075 See CREATIVITY. 758

0097-6083 See DIRECTORY OF LAW ENFORCEMENT AND CRIMINAL JUSTICE EDUCATION. 3163

0097-6091 See HISTORY OF PSYCHOLOGY IN AUTOBIOGRAPHY. 4588

0097-6105 See MESA REPORT. 1452

0097-6156 See ACS SYMPOSIUM SERIES. 959

0097-6202 See NATIONAL REVIEW OF CORPORATE ACQUISITIONS, THE. 697

0097-6245 See INSURANCE MAGAZINE'S GOLD BOOK OF INSURANCE MARKETING. 2883

0097-6253 See JOURNAL OF THE NORTH AMERICAN FALCONERS' ASSOCIATION, THE. 4874

0097-627X See MONOGRAPH - AMERICAN DANCE THERAPY ASSOCIATION. 1882

0097-6288 See PRINCIPAL INTERNATIONAL BUSINESSES. 704

0097-6326 See FEDERAL REGISTER. 2969

0097-6326 See FEDERAL REGISTER [MICROFORM]. 2970

0097-6334 See MISCELLANEOUS PUBLICATION - TEXAS AGRICULTURAL EXPERIMENT STATION. 109

0097-6474 See CHEMICAL ABSTRACTS. COLLECTIVE INDEX. 1011

0097-6482 See ANALOG SOUNDS. 4100

0097-6539 See HYPE. 4122

0097-6547 See DIRECTORY OF MEMBERS - INSTITUTE OF MANAGEMENT CONSULTANTS. 865

0097-6555 See ISSUES IN EGO PSYCHOLOGY. 4592

0097-6563 See SIGMA PHI EPSILON JOURNAL. 1872

0097-6571 See YOUR COLLEGE-BOUND STUDENTS. 1854

0097-6784 See UNDERGROUND EVANGELISM MAGAZINE. 5006

0097-6822 See TRANSACTIONS OF THE AMERICAN SOCIETY OF MECHANICAL ENGINEERS. 2130

0097-6997 See MOODY'S STOCK SURVEY. 908

0097-7004 See MODERN CHINA. 2659

0097-7012 See GUIDE TO THE CRAFT WORLD. 373

0097-7020 See BIBLIOGRAPHIE COURANTE D'ARTICLES DE PERIODIQUES POSTERIEURS A 1944 SUR LES PROBLEMES POLITIQUES, ECONOMIQUES, ET SOCIAUX. SUPPLEMENT. 5192

0097-7055 See ASTRONOMICAL PAPERS. 392

0097-7136 See AUDUBON. 2187

0097-7195 See CITYSCAPE. 2728

0097-7209 See CRYSTAL MIRROR. 5021

0097-7241 See P/M LITERATURE REFERENCE GUIDE. 4014

0097-725X See STANDARD MAGAZINE. 2547

0097-7276 See ASSOCIATION OF COLLEGE, UNIVERSITY AND COMMUNITY ARTS ADMINISTRATORS, INC. 315

0097-7330 See MAGNETIC RESONANCE REVIEW. 4444

0097-7349 See NEBRASKA STATE PLAN FOR THE ADMINISTRATION OF VOCATIONAL EDUCATION. 1914

0097-7403 See JOURNAL OF EXPERIMENTAL PSYCHOLOGY : ANIMAL BEHAVIOR PROCESSES. 4596

0097-7411 See KEXUE TONGBAO (SCIENTIA). 5123

0097-7438 See COMMUNITY EDUCATION. 1891

0097-7497 See TITLE III ESEA MINI-GRANT PROJECT ABSTRACTS. 1788

0097-7519 See WATER QUALITY MONITORING DATA FOR GEORGIA STREAMS. 5543

0097-7543 See BIENNIAL REPORT OF THE MASSACHUSETTS CIVIL DEFENSE AGENCY AND OFFICE OF EMERGENCY PREPAREDNESS TO THE GOVERNOR AND GENERAL COURT. 1072

0097-7551 See MONTANA AGING SERVICES PROGRAM BOOK. 5296

0097-7594 See ANNUAL REPORT - OFFICE OF BOATING WATER SAFETY (WASHINGTON (STATE)). 591

0097-7667 See STATISTICAL DATA ON PERSONS RELEASED FROM PAROLE BY DISCHARGE AND VIOLATION. 3083

0097-7683 See FISCAL YEAR HIGHER EDUCATION BUDGET RECOMMENDATIONS : OPERATIONS AND GRANTS. 1824

0097-7721 See GTE JOURNAL OF RESEARCH AND DEVELOPMENT. 2056

0097-7780 See INTERGOVERNMENTAL AFFAIRS FELLOWSHIP PROGRAM. 4657

0097-7799 See CATALOG OF FEDERAL DOMESTIC ASSISTANCE. 1468

0097-7810 See COMPENDIUM OF RESEARCH CONTRACTS AND REPORTS - (DEPT. OF HOUSING AND URBAN DEVELOPMENT). 2819

0097-7837 See WEST VIRGINIA LABOR FORCE ANNUAL AVERAGES HOURS & EARNINGS : WEST VIRGINIA STANDARD METROPOLITAN STATISTICAL AREAS. 1540

0097-7853 See NORTH DAKOTA VOCATIONAL AGRICULTURE FARM BUSINESS MANAGEMENT EDUCATION. 115

0097-7861 See NUMBER OF ADMINISTRATORS AND SUPERVISORS, CLASSROOM TEACHERS, AND SPECIAL SERVICES PERSONNEL EMPLOYED IN EACH NEW JERSEY PUBLIC SCHOOL DISTRICT BY COUNTY. 1867

0097-7950 See POVERTY IN TEXAS. 5254

0097-8035 See PAID MY DUES. 4145

0097-8043 See RESTAURANT BUSINESS. 5072

0097-8051 See SAN JOSE STUDIES. 2854

0097-806X See EXPLORATION (NORMAL, ILL.). 3387

0097-8078 See WATER RESOURCES. 1419

0097-8116 See ASTERISK. 4101

0097-8175 See GEBBIE PRESS ALL-IN-ONE DIRECTORY. 1111

0097-8213 See NEW SETTLER'S GUIDE FOR WASHINGTON, D.C. AND COMMUNITIES IN NEARBY MARYLAND AND VIRGINIA, THE. 2829

0097-8221 See OCCASIONAL REVIEW, THE. 2541

0097-823X See OPERATING PLAN - STATE LIBRARY OF OHIO. 3239

0097-8280 See REPORT TO THE GOVERNOR OF IDAHO AND THE LEGISLATURE FROM THE IDAHO POTATO COMMISSION. 184

0097-8329 See CONSUMER ELECTRONICS PRODUCT NEWS. 2039

0097-8337 See CONSUMER GUIDE : AUTO. 5412

0097-8345 See CREDIT (WASHINGTON). 786

0097-8418 See SIGCSE BULLETIN. 1262

0097-8442 See ANCIENT INTERFACE, THE. 591

0097-8477 See U. S. COAL PRODUCTION BY COMPANY : BITUMINOUS, ANTHRACITE, LIGNITE. 1630

0097-8485 See COMPUTERS & CHEMISTRY. 973

0097-8493 See COMPUTERS & GRAPHICS. 1232

0097-8507 See LANGUAGE (BALTIMORE). 3295

0097-8582 See BIENNIAL REPORT OF THE COMMISSIONER OF FINANCIAL INSTITUTIONS AND SUPERVISOR OF HOMESTEAD AND BUILDING AND LOAN ASSOCIATIONS. 778

0097-8620 See CURRENT PRESCRIBING. 4298

0097-8639 See DIRECTORY OF NATIONAL AND INTERNATIONAL UNIONS AND ASSOCIATIONS WITH EXCLUSIVE RECOGNITION IN THE FEDERAL SERVICE. 1663

0097-8655 See DRIVERS LICENSES. 5381

ISSN Index

0097-8663 *See* ESTRENO. 5364

0097-868X *See* GOVERNMENTAL FINANCES AND EMPLOYMENT AT A GLANCE. 4728

0097-8698 *See* GROSS NATIONAL PRODUCT GROWTH RATES AND TREND DATA BY REGION AND COUNTRY. 1564

0097-871X *See* INTERSCHOLASTIC ATHLETIC ADMINISTRATION. 4901

0097-8744 *See* MICHIGAN SCHOOL BUS ACCIDENTS. 5386

0097-8779 *See* OAG WORLDWIDE CRUISE & SHIPLINE GUIDE. 5487

0097-8787 *See* PLANT PROTECTION AND QUARANTINE PROGRAMS. 2427

0097-8817 *See* REPORT AND ROSTER : REGISTERED LAND SURVEYORS. 2030

0097-8825 *See* STATE OF NEVADA BOND TRUST FUND AUDITOR REPORT. 2894

0097-8833 *See* TIMES MAGAZINE (WASHINGTON), THE. 2547

0097-8892 *See* JOURNAL OF DEVELOPMENTAL DISABILITIES, THE. 4389

0097-8906 *See* OSAWATOMIE. 4544

0097-8930 *See* COMPUTER GRAPHICS. 1232

0097-8965 *See* INTERNATIONAL STUDIES NEWSLETTER. 4525

0097-8973 *See* ACTIVITY SUMMARY DRUG AND NARCOTIC CASES. 1338

0097-9007 *See* GOVERNMENT REPORTS ANNOUNCEMENTS & INDEX. 5175

0097-9074 *See* POPULATION REPORTS. SERIES A, ORAL CONTRACEPTIVES (ENGLISH ED.). 4557

0097-9082 *See* POPULATION REPORTS. SERIES E, LAW AND POLICY (ENGLISH ED.). 4558

0097-9090 *See* POPULATION REPORT. SERIES I, PERIODIC ABSTINENCE (ENGLISH ED.). 4557

0097-9104 *See* POPULATION REPORTS. SERIES K, INJECTABLES AND IMPLANTS (ENGLISH ED.). 4558

0097-9147 *See* ROSTER OF REGISTERED PRACTITIONERS OF THE HEALING ARTS LICENSED AND REGISTERED IN THE STATE OF VIRGINIA. 3917

0097-9163 *See* WORKMEN'S COMPENSATION DATA. 1719

0097-918X *See* STUDENT FINANCIAL AID ACTIVITY REPORT. 1848

0097-9198 *See* TELEPHONE STATISTICS : SELECTED FINANCIAL DATA FOR WISCONSIN TELEPHONE COMPANIES. 1125

0097-9236 *See* ANNUAL REPORT - CALIFORNIA. COMMISSION FOR ECONOMIC DEVELOPMENT. 1462

0097-9244 *See* SESQUIANNUAL REPORT - FLORIDA COMMISSION ON HUMAN RELATIONS. 4513

0097-9309 *See* CATALOG OF STATE ASSISTANCE PROGRAMS. 4637

0097-9341 *See* INVENTORY OF AMERICAN INTERMODAL EQUIPMENT. 5450

0097-9368 *See* MESA SAFETY REVIEWS. 2865

0097-9449 *See* VITAL STATISTICS OF NEW YORK STATE. 5346

0097-9457 *See* FATAL MOTOR VEHICLE ACCIDENT COMPARATIVE DATA REPORT. 5440

0097-9473 *See* GUIDEBOOK - STATE OF OHIO, DEPARTMENT OF NATURAL RESOURCES, DIVISION OF GEOLOGICAL SURVEY. 1382

0097-9503 *See* ARABIAN HORSE JOURNAL, THE. 2797

0097-952X *See* CULTURAL INFORMATION SERVICE. 4952

0097-9546 *See* ORCHID ADVOCATE, THE. 2426

0097-9554 *See* SECURITIES REGULATION LAW JOURNAL. 3047

0097-9562 *See* SOROPTIMIST OF THE AMERICAS, THE. 5566

0097-966X *See* DIGEST OF TECHNICAL PAPERS. 2041

0097-9708 *See* TENNESSEE VALLEY HISTORICAL REVIEW. 2762

0097-9732 *See* MEDOC. 3660

0097-9740 *See* SIGNS (CHICAGO, ILL.). 5566

0097-9767 *See* BEST OF GOAL, THE. 4887

0097-9783 *See* HUMAN LIFE REVIEW, THE. 589

0097-9805 *See* PEDIATRIC NURSING. 3866

0097-9805 *See* PEDIATRIC NURSING [MICROFORM]. 3866

0097-9813 *See* LITIGATION. 3003

0097-9902 *See* CALIFORNIA LIBRARY LAWS. 2946

0097-9910 *See* COMMISSARYMAN 1 & C. 4175

0097-9937 *See* JOURNAL OF CONTEMPORARY LAW. 2987

0098-0005 *See* LIST OF LEGAL INVESTMENTS FOR SAVINGS BANKS IN CONNECTICUT. 905

0098-0021 *See* NEW SKILLS FOR PROGRESS : MDTA. 1694

0098-003X *See* KANSAS STATE PLAN FOR COMPREHENSIVE ALCOHOL ABUSE AND ALCOHOLISM PREVENTION, TREATMENT AND REHABILITATION. 1346

0098-0056 *See* STATISTICAL REPORT OF PROPERTY ASSESSMENT AND TAXATION. 4848

0098-0099 *See* ANNUAL REPORT OF THE MARYLAND BOARD OF PHARMACY. 4291

0098-0129 *See* TRANSPORTATION FOCUS. 5396

0098-0153 *See* CARLE SELECTED PAPERS. 3562

0098-0196 *See* ANNUAL CONFERENCE REPORT ON COTTON INSECT RESEARCH AND CONTROL. 4244

0098-020X *See* AREA WAGE SURVEY. DAYTONA BEACH, FLORIDA, METROPOLITAN AREA. 1652

0098-0307 *See* MICHIGAN LABOR MARKET REVIEW. 1690

0098-0315 *See* ROSTER OF LICENSED REAL ESTATE BROKERS AND SALESMEN BY COMPANY. 4847

0098-0331 *See* JOURNAL OF CHEMICAL ECOLOGY. 2217

0098-0358 *See* NURSING RESEARCH (BOSTON). 3865

0098-0382 *See* ULTRASOUND IN MEDICINE. 3648

0098-0463 *See* PROGRESS IN AIR POLLUTION CONTROL. 2240

0098-0471 *See* FILM REVIEW DIGEST (MILLWOOD). 4070

0098-0498 *See* NORTH DAKOTA COMPREHENSIVE CRIMINAL JUSTICE PLAN. 3170

0098-0579 *See* HUMAN RIGHTS ORGANIZATIONS & PERIODICALS DIRECTORY. 4509

0098-0617 *See* REPORT TO THE CONGRESS OF THE UNITED STATES ON URBAN TRANSPORTATION POLICIES & ACTIVITIES. 5391

0098-0668 *See* KEEPING UP WITH KODALY CONCEPTS IN MUSIC EDUCATION. 4127

0098-0706 *See* PROFESSIONAL KARATE. 4913

0098-0722 *See* REMOTE COMPUTING DIRECTORY. 1239

0098-0730 *See* SOUL IN REVIEW. 4153

0098-0765 *See* DATA REPORT - U.S. DEPARTMENT OF COMMERCE, NATIONAL OCEANIC AND ATMOSPHERIC ADMINISTRATION NATIONAL MARINE FISHERIES SERVICE. 2300

0098-079X *See* MAINE PROSECUTOR, CRIMINAL LEGISLATION MANUAL, THE. 3169

0098-0803 *See* MISSISSIPPI LANDINGS, ANNUAL SUMMARY. 2308

0098-0846 *See* WYOMING STATE PLAN. 5549

0098-0897 *See* RESOURCES IN EDUCATION. 1779

0098-0900 *See* PROTOCOL OF THE COLLOQUY OF THE CENTER FOR HERMENEUTICAL STUDIES IN HELLENISTIC AND MODERN CULTURE. 1079

0098-0986 *See* EUROPEAN REGISTER OF RESEARCH ON VISUAL IMPAIRMENT. 4388

0098-1052 *See* TEXAS FAMILY PHYSICIAN. 3739

0098-1095 *See* DIRECTORY OF LOCAL HOUSING AUTHORITIES. 2821

0098-1109 *See* DIRECTORY OF U.S. GOVERNMENT AUDIOVISUAL PERSONNEL. 4644

0098-1125 *See* NOTABLE READING PROJECTS. 1901

0098-1133 *See* OFFICIAL GAZETTE OF THE UNITED STATES PATENT AND TRADEMARK OFFICE. PATENTS. 1306

0098-115X *See* SPECIAL STUDIES - UTAH GEOLOGICAL AND MINERAL SURVEY. 1398

0098-1222 *See* INSECTS OF VIRGINIA, THE. 5610

0098-1257 *See* ERS RESEARCH MEMO. 1745

0098-1338 *See* REPORT OF THE PLANNING DIVISION, STATE DEPARTMENT OF FINANCE. 4681

0098-1354 *See* COMPUTERS & CHEMICAL ENGINEERING. 2011

0098-1389 *See* SOCIAL WORK IN HEALTH CARE. 5309

0098-1435 *See* CALIFORNIA EMPLOYER. 1658

0098-1443 *See* REPORT TO THE NATION ON THE MANAGEMENT OF METRIC IMPLEMENTATION, A. 4032

0098-1486 *See* AMERICAN NURSE, THE. 3850

0098-1516 *See* ENLB, EMERGENCY NURSE LEGAL BULLETIN. 3855

0098-1524 *See* EPLB. EMERGENCY PHYSICIAN LEGAL BULLETIN. 3724

0098-1532 *See* MEDICAL AND PEDIATRIC ONCOLOGY. 3906

0098-1559 *See* PROGRAM NOTES - ASSOCIATION OF UNIVERSITY PROGRAMS IN HEALTH ADMINISTRATION. 3791

0098-1605 *See* ANTHROPOLOGY NEWSLETTER. 230

0098-163X *See* HISTORY IN NEWSPAPER FRONT PAGES, A. 2619

0098-1656 *See* MOTOR PARTS AND TIME GUIDE. 5420

0098-1672 *See* YEAR BOOK OF DIAGNOSTIC RADIOLOGY, THE. 3947

0098-1710 *See* ELEMENTS (MIDLAND). 1605

0098-1729 *See* INCOME TAX GUIDE FOR MILITARY PERSONNEL. 745

0098-1745 *See* MOTOR AUTO REPAIR MANUAL. 5419

0098-1753 *See* PENSION WORLD. 1701

0098-177X *See* POLICE CALL, FIRE EMERGENCY RADIO DIRECTORY. 1136

0098-1788 *See* RING (WASHINGTON), THE. 4150

0098-1796 *See* YESTERDAY'S MEMORIES. 4159

0098-180X *See* HOSPITAL INFECTION CONTROL. 3584

0098-1818 *See* MONTHLY LABOR REVIEW. 1691

0098-1834 *See* ANNUAL REPORT - CRIMINAL COURT OF THE CITY OF NEW YORK. 3078

0098-1974 *See* MISSOURI VITAL STATISTICS. 5333

0098-2016 *See* STATISTICAL REPORT - STATE OF NEW YORK OFFICE OF COURT ADMINISTRATION. 3083

0098-2040 *See* ANNUAL REPORT - INDIANA ARTS COMMISSION. 312

0098-2113 *See* CURRENTS IN THEOLOGY AND MISSION. 4952

0098-2164 *See* BIOLOGY BULLETIN OF THE RUSSIAN ACADEMY OF SCIENCES. 446

0098-2172 *See* DIESEL FUEL DIRECTORY. 5413

0098-2199 *See* JOHN BERRYMAN STUDIES. 3464

0098-2202 *See* JOURNAL OF FLUIDS ENGINEERING. 2092

0098-2210 *See* METAL DISTRIBUTION. 4009

0098-2245 *See* EXECUTIVE AND OWNERSHIP REPORT. CLASS I & II MOTOR CARRIERS OF PROPERTY. 673

0098-2296 *See* ANNUAL REPORT OF FEDERAL PREVAILING RATE ADVISORY COMMITTEE. 4628

0098-2318 *See* BEVERAGE WORLD. 2364

0098-2326 *See* HEBERT'S CATALOGUE OF USED PLATE NUMBER SINGLES. 2785

0098-2377 *See* DIRECTORY - AMERICAN GROUP PRACTICE ASSOCIATION. 3779

0098-2393 See INTERNATIONAL BIBLIOGRAPHY OF THE FORENSIC SCIENCES, THE. 3660

0098-2431 See ANNUAL REPORT - THE INSTITUTE FOR CERTIFICATION OF COMPUTER PROFESSIONALS. 1255

0098-2466 See DUN & BRADSTREET'S GUIDE TO YOUR INVESTMENTS. 897

0098-2474 See EXPLORATIONS IN RENAISSANCE CULTURE. 2846

0098-2547 See FODOR'S BERMUDA. 5471

0098-2571 See AUTOMOTIVE ENGINEERING. 2110

0098-2598 See CARDINAL YEARBOOK, THE. 1814

0098-2601 See EIGHTEENTH-CENTURY LIFE. 5268

0098-261X See JUSTICE SYSTEM JOURNAL, THE. 3141

0098-2644 See YEARBOOK OF HERPETOLOGY. 5600

0098-2679 See ANNUAL REPORT - WYOMING STATE BOARD OF NURSING. 3851

0098-2709 See DIRECTORY OF SENIOR CENTERS AND CLUBS. 5179

0098-2717 See REPORT OF THE GOVERNOR'S EARTHQUAKE COUNCIL. 5305

0098-2725 See SUMMARY OF GENERAL STATISTICS. 4811

0098-2741 See CLASSIC MG YEARBOOK, THE. 5411

0098-275X See STUDIES IN MODERN EUROPEAN HISTORY AND CULTURE. 2711

0098-2784 See BIBLIOGRAPHY AND INDEX OF GEOLOGY. 1361

0098-2822 See ART AND ARCHITECTURE BOOK GUIDE. 338

0098-2873 See ESTATE PLANNING REVIEW. 3118

0098-2946 See ARS-H. 63

0098-2997 See MOLECULAR ASPECTS OF MEDICINE. 3618

0098-3004 See COMPUTERS & GEOSCIENCES. 1178

0098-3063 See IEEE TRANSACTIONS ON CONSUMER ELECTRONICS. 2061

0098-3071 See GEORGIA STATE UNIVERSITY FACT BOOK. 1825

0098-308X See NCPC QUARTERLY. 2829

0098-311X See HEALTH CONSEQUENCES OF SMOKING, THE. 4779

0098-3128 See FINANCIAL CONDITION OF PENN CENTRAL TRANSPORTATION COMPANY, THE. 5431

0098-3225 See OPERATING REVENUE AND EXPENSE STATISTICS CLASS A AND B PRIVATE GAS UTILITIES IN WISCONSIN. 4699

0098-3276 See FIRE INDEPENDENT, THE. 2289

0098-3284 See GRADUATE, THE. 1091

0098-3314 See NEW PATRIOT, THE. 4052

0098-3330 See XENHARMONIKON. 4159

0098-3381 See NEW ENGLAND MUSICIAN'S GUIDE, THE. 4140

0098-3403 See ANNUAL REPORT - MARYLAND HISTORICAL TRUST. 2720

0098-342X See SCIENCE BOOKS & FILMS. 5151

0098-3500 See ACM TRANSACTIONS ON MATHEMATICAL SOFTWARE. 1283

0098-3519 See CRUISING WORLD. 593

0098-3527 See DULCIMER PLAYER NEWS, THE. 4115

0098-3535 See ILLINOIS MUSIC COUNTRY MAGAZINE. 4122

0098-3543 See PROCEEDINGS OF ... ANNUAL MEETING - AMERICAN ASSOCIATION OF VETERINARY LABORATORY DIAGNOSTICIANS. 5519

0098-3578 See ADMINISTRATIVE AND TECHNICAL SALARY SURVEY. 1642

0098-3624 See MOTOR TRUCK REPAIR MANUAL. 5420

0098-3632 See NEWSLETTER - BLUEGRASS CLUB OF NEW YORK. 4140

0098-3640 See YUGNTRUF. 3456

0098-3691 See GROUND-WATER DATA FOR MICHIGAN. 5533

0098-3845 See SPECIAL REPORT - DIVISION OF CORRECTION, A. 3177

0098-3896 See REPORT ON FOREIGN CURRENCIES HELD BY THE U.S. GOVERNMENT. 808

0098-390X See ANNUAL STATISTICAL SUMMARY OF THE STATE OF MARYLAND FAMILY PLANNING PROGRAM. 2287

0098-3993 See ANNUAL BOOKLET - MINNESOTA, DIVISION OF VOCATIONAL REHABILITATION, DEPARTMENT OF EDUCATION. 1644

0098-4035 See REPORT - ADVISORY COUNCIL ON HISTORIC PRESERVATION. 2757

0098-4043 See ANNUAL PRODUCTION BY ACTIVE FIELDS, OIL AND GAS DIVISION. 4250

0098-4094 See IEEE TRANSACTIONS ON CIRCUITS & SYSTEMS. PART 1, FUNDAMENTAL THEORY AND APPLICATIONS. 2061

0098-4094 See IEEE TRANSACTIONS ON CIRCUITS AND SYSTEMS. PART 2, ANALOG AND DIGITAL SIGNAL PROCESSING. 2061

0098-4108 See JOURNAL OF TOXICOLOGY AND ENVIRONMENTAL HEALTH. 3982

0098-4132 See STATE DIRECTORY OF HIGHER EDUCATION INSTITUTIONS AND AGENCIES IN MARYLAND. 1848

0098-4167 See ANNUAL REPORT - STATE OF CONNECTICUT HEALTH & EDUCATIONAL FACILITIES AUTHORITY. 3776

0098-4205 See ANNUAL REPORT OF THE INDIANA DEPARTMENT OF MENTAL HEALTH, THE. 4766

0098-423X See DISTRIBUTION OF HIGH SCHOOL GRADUATES. 1736

0098-4256 See SELECTED EDUCATIONAL OPPORTUNITIES. 1915

0098-4329 See MISSISSIPPI DENTAL ASSOCIATION JOURNAL. 1330

0098-4345 See POINT OF VIEW (SOMERVILLE). 3867

0098-4469 See DIRECTORY OF AQUARIUM SPECIALISTS. 2300

0098-4477 See DIRECTORY OF ARTS ORGANIZATIONS IN MISSISSIPPI. 319

0098-4485 See DOCTORAL DISSERTATIONS ON ASIA. 2650

0098-4515 See SACRAMENTO MEDICINE. 3638

0098-4566 See COUNTRYSIDE (BLAINE). 4112

0098-4582 See COLUMBIA JOURNAL OF ENVIRONMENTAL LAW. 3110

0098-4590 See FLORIDA SCIENTIST. 5105

0098-4612 See JOURNAL OF POLITICAL SCIENCE (CLEMSON). 4479

0098-4671 See MULTISTATE BAR REVIEW MANUAL. 3012

0098-471X See DETROIT MEDICAL NEWS. 3571

0098-4752 See CONDITION OF EDUCATION, THE. 1733

0098-4817 See ANNUAL EXHIBITION - NATIONAL SCULPTURE SOCIETY. 336

0098-4825 See BULLETIN - UTAH GEOLOGICAL AND MINERAL SURVEY. 1370

0098-4833 See MEDICAL LAW LETTER FOR PHYSICIANS, SURGEONS & HEALTH PROFESSIONALS, THE. 3008

0098-4841 See COPPER STATE BULLETIN. 2444

0098-485X See RARE AMERICANA. 423

0098-4949 See METHODOLOGY REPORTS. 4810

0098-4957 See COMMERCIAL BAR, THE. 2953

0098-4981 See JOURNAL OF THE AMERICAN PORTUGUESE SOCIETY, THE. 2695

0098-5147 See CALIFORNIA PRIVATE SCHOOL DIRECTORY. 1730

0098-5163 See GEORGIA STATE UNIVERSITY'S APPROACH TO AFFIRMATIVE ACTION. 1825

0098-518X See ENERGY RESEARCH PROGRAM OF THE U.S. DEPARTMENT OF THE INTERIOR. 1941

0098-5228 See AAN ANNUAL CONVENTION REPORT. 2416

0098-5236 See ANDERSON'S CAMPGROUND DIRECTORY. 4869

0098-5279 See DATA BOOK ON ILLINOIS HIGHER EDUCATION. 1819

0098-5287 See INVENTORY OF DEGREE PROGRAMS IN CONNECTICUT'S COLLEGES AND UNIVERSITIES, AN. 1831

0098-5325 See U.S. EXPORTS. DOMESTIC MERCHANDISE, SIC-BASED PRODUCTS BY WORLD AREA. 855

0098-5368 See DIRECTORY OF STATE, REGIONAL AND COMMERCIAL ORGANIZATIONS. 831

0098-5376 See EQUIPMENT & TECHNOLOGY INTERNATIONAL. 5103

0098-5384 See FLOW, ITS MEASUREMENT AND CONTROL IN SCIENCE AND INDUSTRY. 2089

0098-5406 See PET AGE. 4287

0098-5422 See SPUR (DELAPLANE). 2802

0098-5430 See AMERICAN PAINT & COATINGS JOURNAL. 4222

0098-5449 See FAITH & REASON. 4958

0098-5570 See NSA MAGAZINE. 1838

0098-5589 See IEEE TRANSACTIONS ON SOFTWARE ENGINEERING. 1286

0098-5589 See IEEE TRANSACTIONS ON SOFTWARE ENGINEERING. 1286

0098-5597 See REVIEW OF EDUCATION, THE. 1779

0098-5600 See SCIENCE OF BIOLOGY JOURNAL. 472

0098-5635 See DIRECTORY OF WASHINGTON BUSINESS ASSOCIATIONS. 667

0098-5643 See INTERNATIONAL RESEARCH DOCUMENT. 5329

0098-5651 See OKLAHOMA HEALTH STATISTICS. 4810

0098-566X See PUBLICATIONS AND PATENTS OF THE EASTERN UTILIZATION RESEARCH AND DEVELOPMENT DIVISION. 123

0098-5740 See COMPREHENSIVE CRIMINAL JUSTICE PLAN, CRIMINAL JUSTICE PROGRAMS. 3160

0098-5783 See NORTH CAROLINA LOCAL HEALTH DEPARTMENTS : BUDGETARY, ECONOMIC, AND OTHER PERTINENT DATA. 4794

0098-5872 See BULLETIN - MARION COUNTY MEDICAL SOCIETY. 3560

0098-5880 See BULLETIN - LUZERNE COUNTY MEDICAL SOCIETY, THE. 3560

0098-5910 See YEARBOOK - SOCIETY OF WIRELESS PIONEERS. 2087

0098-5937 See UTU NEWS. 1716

0098-5961 See LAW & PSYCHOLOGY REVIEW. 2994

0098-597X See JOURNAL OF COMPUTER-BASED INSTRUCTION. 1223

0098-5988 See BASKETBALL DIGEST. 4886

0098-6054 See ROMANIAN SOURCES. 2707

0098-6062 See INDEX TO ST. LOUIS NEWSPAPERS. 5703

0098-6070 See ACR BULLETIN. 3938

0098-6089 See ADVANCES IN NEUROCHEMISTRY. 3826

0098-6119 See ANNUAL MEETING - AMERICAN INSTITUTE OF ORAL BIOLOGY. 1316

0098-6127 See ARTERY. 3795

0098-6135 See DIRECTORY OF HEALTH CARE FACILITIES. 3779

0098-6151 See JOURNAL OF THE AMERICAN OSTEOPATHIC ASSOCIATION, THE. 3598

0098-6275 See SALALM NEWSLETTER. 3247

0098-6283 See TEACHING OF PSYCHOLOGY. 4620

0098-6291 See TEACHING ENGLISH IN THE TWO-YEAR COLLEGE. 1850

0098-6305 See ENR DIRECTORY OF DESIGN FIRMS. 1975

0098-6356 See ACADEMIC YEAR ABROAD IN EUROPE-AFRICA-AUSTRALIA. 1721

0098-6364 See ANNUAL REPORT OF THE BOARD OF EXAMINERS FOR COUNTY HIGHWAY AND CITY STREET SUPERINTENDENTS. 5438

0098-6402 See EXPERIENCE OF FEDERAL AGENCIES UNDER THE PROGRAM OF SELF-INSURING FIDELITY LOSSES PURSUANT TO PUBLIC LAW 92-310. **2879**

0098-6437 See ABSTRACTS. SYMPOSIA PAPERS PRESENTED BEFORE THE APHA ACADEMY OF PHARMACEUTICAL SCIENCES AT THE ANNUAL MEETING OF THE AMERICAN PHARMACEUTICAL ASSOCIATION. **4288**

0098-6445 See CHEMICAL ENGINEERING COMMUNICATIONS. **2009**

0098-6453 See ENR DIRECTORY OF CONTRACTORS. WEST REGION. **614**

0098-6453 See ENR DIRECTORY OF CONTRACTORS. MIDWEST REGION. **614**

0098-6453 See ENR DIRECTORY OF CONTRACTORS. SOUTH REGION. **614**

0098-6461 See MIDEAST MARKETS. **846**

0098-647X See RESEARCH OPPORTUNITIES IN RENAISSANCE DRAMA. **3429**

0098-6488 See TIDE TABLES, HIGH AND LOW WATER PREDICTIONS, EAST COAST OF NORTH AND SOUTH AMERICA, INCLUDING GREENLAND. **1457**

0098-6526 See CALIFORNIA SCHOOL DISTRICT FINANCIAL ANALYSES. **1730**

0098-6534 See GENERAL ASSEMBLY OF GEORGIA, THE. **4650**

0098-6569 See CATHETERIZATION AND CARDIOVASCULAR DIAGNOSIS. **3702**

0098-6577 See KIDNEY INTERNATIONAL. SUPPLEMENT. **3991**

0098-6615 See ECOLOGY USA (HOUSTON). **2214**

0098-664X See DIRECTORY OF MUSIC FACULTIES IN COLLEGES AND UNIVERSITIES, U.S. AND CANADA. **4114**

0098-6658 See SOVIET MICROELECTRONICS. **2082**

0098-6690 See DAIRY MARKET STATISTICS, ANNUAL SUMMARY. **152**

0098-678X See COUNTY GOVERNMENT FINANCES. **4719**

0098-6798 See EXAMINATION OF FINANCIAL STATEMENTS OF THE PENNSYLVANIA AVENUE DEVELOPMENT CORPORATION. **4647**

0098-681X See QUARTERLY FINANCIAL REPORT FOR MANUFACTURING, MINING AND TRADE CORPORATIONS. **1623**

0098-6836 See REPORT OF RANDOM SAMPLE EGG PRODUCTION TESTS, UNITED STATES AND CANADA. **126**

0098-6860 See TECHNICAL NOTE (UNITED STATES. BUREAU OF LAND MANAGEMENT). **5598**

0098-6909 See HOSPITAL FORMULARY. **4306**

0098-6917 See OPTOMETRIC EDUCATION. **4216**

0098-6917 See JOURNAL OF OPTOMETRIC EDUCATION. **4216**

0098-6925 See MODERN PHARMACOLOGY-TOXICOLOGY. **4316**

0098-6933 See INCORPORATED MUNICIPALITIES, MUNICIPAL OFFICIALS AND STATE STREET AID ALLOCATIONS. **4655**

0098-6976 See WISCONSIN JOURNAL OF PUBLIC INSTRUCTION. **1791**

0098-7026 See COTTON QUALITY CROP. **5350**

0098-7069 See PROGRESS IN THE IMPLEMENTATION OF MOTOR VEHICLE EMISSION STANDARDS. **2240**

0098-714X See SURVEY OF PHARMACY LAW. **3061**

0098-7174 See PENNSYLVANIA POLICE CRIMINAL LAW BULLETIN, THE. **3171**

0098-7328 See AMERICAN FRANCHISE & BUSINESS OPPORTUNITY DIRECTORY. **638**

0098-7336 See BANKRUPTCY COURT DECISIONS. **3085**

0098-7344 See CONSUMER'S REGISTER OF AMERICAN BUSINESS, THE. **659**

0098-7360 See MARKETING CALIFORNIA ARTICHOKES. **2348**

0098-7379 See ANNUAL REVIEW OF ENGLISH BOOKS ON ASIA. **4823**

0098-7395 See DICTIONARY CATALOG OF THE COLUMBIA UNIVERSITY LAW LIBRARY. SUPPLEMENT. **3206**

0098-745X See ANNUAL REPORT TO THE SECRETARY, DEPARTMENT OF THE INTERIOR. **1446**

0098-7468 See STATE OF ILLINOIS REPORT ON TITLE I, PUBLIC LAW 89-313. **1885**

0098-7484 See JAMA : THE JOURNAL OF THE AMERICAN MEDICAL ASSOCIATION. **3591**

0098-7530 See PRODUCT SAFETY LETTER. **1299**

0098-7573 See DEVICES & DIAGNOSTICS LETTER. **3571**

0098-759X See SUMMARY OF ENACTMENTS. **3061**

0098-7611 See TORTS. **3065**

0098-762X See CONTRACTS. **2956**

0098-7638 See CONSTITUTIONAL LAW. **3092**

0098-7646 See EXAMINATION OF FINANCIAL STATEMENTS OF STUDENT LOAN INSURANCE FUND. **1823**

0098-7670 See CRIMINAL JUSTICE NEWSLETTER (SPRINGFIELD). **3162**

0098-7727 See ON SITE (WASHINGTON, D.C.). **623**

0098-7743 See PETROLEUM/ENERGY BUSINESS NEWS INDEX. **4272**

0098-7751 See U.S. EXPORTS AND IMPORTS OF GOLD. **855**

0098-776X See PENSEE (PORTLAND). **5137**

0098-7786 See MODERN PAINT AND COATINGS. **4224**

0098-7816 See UNIVERSITY AND COLLEGE LIBRARIES. **3260**

0098-7913 See SERIALS REVIEW. **3249**

0098-7921 See POPULATION AND DEVELOPMENT REVIEW. **4556**

0098-793X See ALLIED LANDSCAPE INDUSTRY MEMBER DIRECTORY. **2408**

0098-7956 See COMBAT DATA SUBSCRIPTION SERVICE. **4039**

0098-7964 See FACT SHEET BOOKLET. **5285**

0098-7999 See REMEDIES. **3037**

0098-8030 See MICHIGAN GERMANIC STUDIES. **3302**

0098-8049 See CRIMINAL LAW (LOS ANGELES, CALIF.). **3106**

0098-8057 See STATISTICAL REPORT - LOUISIANA, HEALTH AND SOCIAL AND REHABILITATION SERVICES ADMINISTRATION (ANNUAL). **3661**

0098-8103 See MANUAL OF THE GENERAL ASSEMBLY OF THE STATE OF GEORGIA. **4664**

0098-8111 See MENTAL RETARDATION AND THE LAW. **3009**

0098-812X See PUBLICATIONS REPORT - NATIONAL CENTER FOR HEALTH SERVICES RESEARCH AND DEVELOPMENT. **4811**

0098-8154 See POTOMAC APPALACHIAN (MAY 1972). **4877**

0098-8235 See WORLD ENVIRONMENT REPORT. **2248**

0098-8243 See COMPREHENSIVE THERAPY. **3567**

0098-8251 See FOCUS : BIOLOGY. **455**

0098-8278 See IASSW DIRECTORY. **5289**

0098-8294 See COSTS OF FOODS PURCHASED BY USDA AND LOCAL SCHOOL SYSTEMS. **1862**

0098-8324 See ANNUAL ADAPSO INDUSTRY REPORT. **1235**

0098-8359 See CUMULATIVE RECORDS - EXPORT-IMPORT BANK OF THE UNITED STATES. **786**

0098-8413 See U.S. ALPHABETICAL PHYSICIAN REFERENCE LISTING. **3917**

0098-8421 See JOURNAL OF THE AMERICAN MEDICAL WOMEN'S ASSOCIATION (1972). **3597**

0098-8472 See ENVIRONMENTAL AND EXPERIMENTAL BOTANY. **509**

0098-8545 See LOUISIANA REGISTER. **3004**

0098-8553 See MULTIDISCIPLINARY RESEARCH. **4605**

0098-857X See SCANDINAVIAN REVIEW. **2272**

0098-8588 See AMERICAN JOURNAL OF LAW & MEDICINE. **2932**

0098-8634 See SYNTHESIS (REDWOOD CITY). **4619**

0098-8707 See SOCCER WORLD. **4919**

0098-874X See FLORIDA ADMINISTRATIVE WEEKLY. **2970**

0098-8774 See PROSECUTORS' BULLETIN, THE. **3108**

0098-8847 See EARTHQUAKE ENGINEERING & STRUCTURAL DYNAMICS. **2022**

0098-8863 See EXPOSURE (NEW YORK, N.Y.). **4369**

0098-8898 See EMPLOYEE RELATIONS LAW JOURNAL. **3146**

0098-891X See LENDING LAW FORUM, THE. **3087**

0098-8928 See MARKETING CALIFORNIA PEARS. **2349**

0098-8936 See REAL ESTATE DIRECTORY OF MANHATTAN. **4844**

0098-8960 See UPSHAW FAMILY JOURNAL, THE. **2476**

0098-8995 See TRENDS IN LEGAL SERVICES. **3066**

0098-9029 See SELECTED SCHOOL CHARACTERISTICS. REPORT ON THE CITY-WIDE TESTING PROGRAM. REPORT ON PER PUPIL STAFFING COSTS : ELEMENTARY SCHOOLS. **1783**

0098-9037 See COUNTRY MUSIC NEWS (TURBOTVILLE, PA.). **4112**

0098-9053 See LINGUISTIC ANALYSIS. **3298**

0098-9134 See JOURNAL OF GERONTOLOGICAL NURSING. **3858**

0098-9134 See JOURNAL OF GERONTOLOGICAL NURSING. **3858**

0098-9150 See ACTA MICROBIOLOGICA SINICA. **558**

0098-9177 See LOTTERY WORLD. **4736**

0098-9207 See QUALIFIED REMODELER. **625**

0098-9215 See RADIO CONTROL BUYERS GUIDE. **2777**

0098-9223 See REFLECTIONS (OKLAHOMA CITY). **3801**

0098-924X See CENTERPOINT. **5195**

0098-9258 See ADVANCES IN CONSUMER RESEARCH. **1293**

0098-9266 See JOURNAL OF EARLY SOUTHERN DECORATIVE ARTS. **373**

0098-9282 See ZION'S HERALD (1975). **5070**

0098-9355 See FRENCH FORUM. **3343**

0098-9363 See ASCENT (URBANA, ILL.). **3364**

0098-9371 See CHILDREN'S BOOK SHOWCASE, THE. **1061**

0098-941X See ANNUAL REPORT - SOUTH DAKOTA HOUSING DEVELOPMENT AUTHORITY. **2815**

0098-9436 See COLUMBIA STUDIES IN PHILOSOPHY. **4344**

0098-9444 See BIBLICAL ARCHAEOLOGY REVIEW, THE. **261**

0098-9452 See CHARITON REVIEW, THE. **3374**

0098-9479 See EARTHBOND. **2965**

0098-9487 See IAJRC JOURNAL. **4122**

0098-9495 See JOURNAL OF EDUCATION FINANCE. **1865**

0098-9509 See MARXISM AND THE MASS MEDIA. **4502**

0098-9517 See SABBATH WATCHMAN, THE. **5067**

0098-9525 See UNION (CRANFORD). **2548**

0098-9584 See JOURNAL OF SCHOOL SOCIAL WORK, THE. **1865**

0098-9657 See LIST OF COMPANIES REGISTERED UNDER THE INVESTMENT COMPANY ACT OF 1940. **905**

0098-9738 See 'AHA' ILONO. **3138**

0098-9746 See ARIZONA DIRECTORY OF STATE REGULATORY AGENCIES FOR BUSINESSES AND OCCUPATIONS. **4630**

0098-9819 See CURRENT PHYSICS INDEX. **4426**

0098-9827 *See* EDUCATIONAL OPPORTUNITY PROGRAM NOTES. **1878**

0098-9843 *See* NEWSLETTER - COURT PRACTICE INSTITUTE. **3142**

0098-986X *See* U.S. PHYSICIAN REFERENCE LISTING. **3917**

0098-9886 *See* INTERNATIONAL JOURNAL OF CIRCUIT THEORY AND APPLICATIONS. **2066**

0099-0027 *See* PROFESSIONAL SAFETY. **2868**

0099-0043 *See* ENGRAVERS JOURNAL, THE. **4564**

0099-0124 *See* CONNECTICUT MANUFACTURING DIRECTORY. **3477**

0099-0159 *See* GOLDENSEAL. **2320**

0099-0175 *See* STATE DIRECTORY OF PUBLIC OFFICIALS IN GEORGIA, THE. **4687**

0099-0191 *See* TRAILER LIFE'S RV CAMPGROUND & SERVICES DIRECTORY. **4879**

0099-0221 CALLIGRAFREE SCRIBE. **377**

0099-0256 *See* ACCREDITATION. **1807**

0099-0264 *See* MOONS AND LION TAILES. **3466**

0099-0280 *See* MOMENT (NEW YORK). **5051**

0099-0302 *See* SPECIAL EDUCATION PROGRAMS/SERVICES. **1885**

0099-0329 *See* PROCEEDINGS OF THE ANNUAL MEETING OF THE WESTERN SOCIETY FOR FRENCH HISTORY. **2703**

0099-037X *See* PROGRESS IN BEHAVIOR MODIFICATION. **4609**

0099-0388 *See* SPORTSWOMAN, THE. **4923**

0099-0396 *See* TIME BARRIER EXPRESS. **4156**

0099-0418 *See* CONFLICTS OF LAW. **2955**

0099-0426 *See* HOUSTON'S PUBLIC COMPANIES. **790**

0099-0450 *See* PLASTICS MANUFACTURING CAPABILITIES IN MISSISSIPPI. **4458**

0099-0477 *See* SALARY PLAN, STATE OF NORTH CAROLINA. **4684**

0099-0485 *See* SELECTED STATISTICS ON STUDENTS AND STAFF IN NEW YORK CITY SCHOOL DISTRICTS. **1797**

0099-054X *See* ISSUE PAPER - OFFICE OF STATE PLANNING. **1568**

0099-0655 *See* STATISTICS OF SOUTH DAKOTA PUBLIC LIBRARIES. **3260**

0099-0728 *See* KANSAS EDUCATIONAL DIRECTORY. **1759**

0099-0744 *See* READING ACHIEVEMENT TEST REPORT. **1903**

0099-0779 *See* ALPHABETICAL CATALOG OF THE BOOKS AND PAMPHLETS OF THE INTERNATIONAL INSTITUTE OF SOCIAL HISTORY, AMSTERDAM. SUPPLEMENT. **407**

0099-0809 *See* INDEX OF TRADEMARKS ISSUED FROM THE UNITED STATES PATENT AND TRADEMARK OFFICE. **1304**

0099-0817 *See* RECORD COLLECTORS JOURNAL, THE. **5318**

0099-085X *See* ANNUAL REPORT - SOUTHEASTERN LIBRARY NETWORK. **3191**

0099-0876 *See* INDEX TO PRAVDA. **2920**

0099-0892 *See* NEVADA HISTORICAL REVIEW. **2748**

0099-0906 *See* NEW DIMENSIONS SCIENCE FICTION. **3415**

0099-0914 MONTHLY ENERGY REVIEW. **1950**

0099-0922 *See* SUBJECT CATALOG OF THE LIBRARY. SUPPLEMENT. **3251**

0099-0965 *See* INDEX TO ART PERIODICALS. SUPPLEMENT. **352**

0099-0973 *See* SURVEY OF BUSINESS. **1586**

0099-1023 *See* INDIANA PUBLIC MANAGEMENT. **4656**

0099-1031 *See* BAR LEADER. **2940**

0099-104X *See* LUSK'S BALTIMORE COUNTY REAL ESTATE DIRECTORY, PROPERTY TRANSFERS. **4840**

0099-1066 *See* AGRICULTURAL OUTLOOK (WASHINGTON, D.C. : 1975). **51**

0099-1090 *See* IFPA COMMUNICATOR. **4072**

0099-1104 *See* MANPOWER INFORMATION FOR AFFIRMATIVE ACTION PROGRAMS. **1689**

0099-1112 *See* PHOTOGRAMMETRIC ENGINEERING AND REMOTE SENSING. **1990**

0099-1147 *See* ADVANCES IN PATHOBIOLOGY. **440**

0099-118X OKLAHOMA HEALTH STATISTICS. **4810**

0099-1198 *See* ANNUAL REPORT - BUCKNELL UNIVERSITY. **1809**

0099-1228 *See* CRIMINAL PROCEDURE. **3106**

0099-1236 *See* CORPORATIONS. **3099**

0099-1244 *See* CIVIL PROCEDURE. **3089**

0099-1260 *See* ANNUAL REPORT - EMPLOYMENT DIVISION. **1649**

0099-1287 *See* ANNUAL REPORT OF THE MARYLAND BICENTENNIAL COMMISSION TO THE GOVERNOR, THE GENERAL ASSEMBLY, AND THE SECRETARY, DEPARTMENT OF ECONOMIC AND COMMUNITY DEVELOPMENT. **2720**

0099-1333 *See* JOURNAL OF ACADEMIC LIBRARIANSHIP. **3219**

0099-1341 *See* RESEARCH REPORT - ILLINOIS COMMUNITY COLLEGE BOARD. **1845**

0099-135X *See* DETROIT COLLEGE OF LAW REVIEW. **2960**

0099-1368 *See* INDEX TO IEEE PUBLICATIONS. **2004**

0099-1384 *See* VIDEOSOCIOLOGY. **5265**

0099-1414 *See* SAGE ANNUAL REVIEWS OF COMMUNICATIONS RESEARCH. **1121**

0099-1457 *See* LOUISIANA TECH UNIVERSITY FACULTY PUBLICATIONS. ANNUAL SUPPLEMENT. **419**

0099-1465 *See* SOUTHERN UNIVERSITY LAW REVIEW. **3057**

0099-1473 *See* UNDERWOOD ANNALS. **2476**

0099-1546 *See* PROGRESS IN ANESTHESIOLOGY. **3684**

0099-1589 *See* DIRECTORY OF NURSERYMEN AND OTHERS LICENSED TO SELL NURSERY STOCK IN CALIFORNIA, AND SUMMARY OF LAWS AND REGULATIONS. **2413**

0099-1600 *See* BIENNIAL REPORT - STATE OF FLORIDA DEPARTMENT OF STATE. **4632**

0099-1627 *See* ANNUAL REPORT - STATE OF OHIO, LEGISLATIVE BUDGET OFFICE OF THE LEGISLATIVE SERVICE COMMISSION, LEGISLATIVE BUDGET COMMITTEE. **4710**

0099-1635 *See* ANNUAL REPORT - OKLAHOMA WATER RESOURCES BOARD. **5529**

0099-1643 *See* DIRECTORY OF MEMBERS - STATE BAR OF ARIZONA. **2962**

0099-166X *See* DEFENSE SURVEY & DIRECTORY. **4042**

0099-1686 *See* LUSK'S ANNE ARUNDEL COUNTY REAL ESTATE DIRECTORY, PROPERTY TRANSFERS. **4840**

0099-1694 DESARROLLO NACIONAL. **5099**

0099-1767 *See* JOURNAL OF EMERGENCY NURSING. **3858**

0099-1783 *See* GOLF GUIDE (SANTA MONICA). **4896**

0099-1791 *See* LUPTONIAN, THE. **2458**

0099-183X *See* SOCIAL THOUGHT (WASHINGTON, D.C.). **4997**

0099-1848 *See* COLLIER BANKRUPTCY CASES. **3086**

0099-1856 *See* ACTIVE NAMES OF BUREAU PROJECTS AND MAJOR STRUCTURES. **2087**

0099-1864 *See* MARTIN FAMILY QUARTERLY. **2459**

0099-1899 *See* AREA WAGE SURVEY. SACRAMENTO, CALIFORNIA, METROPOLITAN AREA. **1653**

0099-1910 *See* AFFIRMATIVE ACTION INFORMATION. **1642**

0099-1929 *See* ANALYSIS OF OFFICIAL PESTICIDE SAMPLES. **4243**

0099-1961 *See* DCAS MANUFACTURING COST CONTROL DIGEST. **3477**

0099-197X *See* DIRECTORY OF OKLAHOMA'S CITY AND TOWN OFFICIALS. **4644**

0099-1988 *See* FAMILY LAW. BENDER PAMPHLET EDITION. **3120**

0099-2046 *See* WASHINGTON REGION. **4560**

0099-2054 *See* WAGE & FRINGE BENEFITS FOR SELECTED OCCUPATIONS PAID BY VIRGINIA MANUFACTURERS. **1717**

0099-2070 *See* SOCIAL SERVICES PERSONNEL IN NORTH CAROLINA COUNTIES. **5309**

0099-2089 *See* SELECTED STATISTICAL DATA - MARYLAND STATE BOARD FOR COMMUNITY COLLEGES. **1797**

0099-2135 *See* FLORIDA STATE PLAN FOR THE EDUCATION OF EXCEPTIONAL STUDENTS. **1879**

0099-2151 *See* NATIONAL REGISTER OF HEALTH SERVICE PROVIDERS IN PSYCHOLOGY. **4605**

0099-2178 *See* ENROLLMENT REPORT OF APPRENTICES IN CALIFORNIA PUBLIC SECONDARY AND ADULT SCHOOLS AND COMMUNITY COLLEGES. **1913**

0099-2186 *See* VIRGINIA ASSESSMENT/SALES RATIO STUDY. **4758**

0099-2240 *See* APPLIED AND ENVIRONMENTAL MICROBIOLOGY. **559**

0099-2275 *See* ENVIRONMENTAL PROGRAM ADMINISTRATORS. **2169**

0099-2399 *See* JOURNAL OF ENDODONTICS. **1327**

0099-2410 *See* PUBLIC DOCUMENTS (BATON ROUGE, LA.). **4699**

0099-2445 *See* FINANCIAL ANALYSIS OF THE MOTOR CARRIER INDUSTRY. **5382**

0099-2453 *See* HUMAN RESOURCES ABSTRACTS. **1533**

0099-2461 *See* INTERNATIONAL TELEX BOOK. AFRICAN-ASIAN-AUSTRALASIAN EDITION, THE. **1158**

0099-2496 *See* VIRGINIA TIDEWATER GENEALOGY. **2476**

0099-250X *See* ABSTRACTS, ANNUAL MEETING - AMERICAN SOCIETY FOR ARTIFICIAL INTERNAL ORGANS. **3957**

0099-2615 *See* AUTOMOBILE INTERNATIONAL. **5405**

0099-3468 *See* RESEARCH NOTE INT. **2392**

0099-3492 *See* TECHNICAL PAPERS, REGIONAL TECHNICAL CONFERENCE. **4460**

0099-409X *See* PROCEEDINGS, INTERNATIONAL WATER CONFERENCE, ENGINEERS SOCIETY OF WESTERN PENNSYLVANIA. **2094**

0099-4227 *See* REPORT OF INVESTIGATION - NORTH DAKOTA GEOLOGICAL SURVEY. **1394**

0099-426X *See* NEW ENGLAND FRUIT MEETINGS. **111**

0099-4480 *See* JOURNAL OF THE ILLUMINATING ENGINEERING SOCIETY. **2069**

0099-5223 *See* NEW YORK'S FOOD AND LIFE SCIENCES BULLETIN. **112**

0099-5355 *See* LANCET (NORTH AMERICAN EDITION), THE. **3603**

0099-5428 *See* ANALYTICAL PROFILES OF DRUG SUBSTANCES. **1050**

0099-5444 *See* NEMATROPICA. **5592**

0099-5541 *See* SPECIAL REPORT - MONTANA FISH AND GAME DEPARTMENT. **2313**

0099-5851 *See* IOWA STATE UNIVERSITY VETERINARIAN. **5512**

0099-5908 *See* SOCIETY OF AUTOMOTIVE ENGINEERS. **1996**

0099-6246 *See* ADVANCES IN BEHAVIORAL BIOLOGY. **440**

0099-6459 *See* SPECIAL PUBLICATION - COLORADO GEOLOGICAL SURVEY. **1397**

0099-6874 *See* PROCEEDINGS - IRONMAKING CONFERENCE. **4016**

0099-6882 *See* ISOCHRON/WEST. **1383**

0099-7676 *See* CIRCULAR (FLORIDA COOPERATIVE EXTENSION SERVICE). **1541**

0099-7730 *See* TEXAS AGRICULTURAL EXPERIMENT STATION LEAFLET. **141**

0099-7749 *See* MINERAL RESOURCE CIRCULAR. **1441**

0099-7838 *See* ANNUAL REPORT OF THE NORTHERN NUT GROWERS ASSOCIATION. **61**

0099-8508 *See* TECHNICAL REPORT AFML-TR. **4058**

0099-8745 *See* OKIKA O HAWAII, NA. **2426**

0099-9016 See PROGRESS IN NEUROPATHOLOGY. 3844
0099-9032 See PUBLICATION OF TECHNICAL PAPERS AND PROCEEDINGS OF THE ANNUAL MEETING OF SUGAR INDUSTRY TECHNOLOGISTS, INC. 2354
0099-9512 See ANNUAL PROCEEDINGS, RELIABILITY PHYSICS SYMPOSIUM. 4397
0099-9598 See ALKALOIDS. CHEMISTRY AND PHARMACOLOGY, THE. 1039
0099-9660 See WALL STREET JOURNAL. EASTERN EDITION, THE. 5690
0018-0599 See HERBA POLONICA. 512
0100-0039 See CIENTIFICA (JABOTICABAL). 5507
0100-0195 See REVISTA MEDICA DO ESTADO DO RIO DE JANEIRO. 3636
0100-0365 See INFORME CIENCIA E ARTE : BOLETIM. 2848
0100-0462 See CADERNOS DE CIRURGIA (SAO BERNARDO DO CAMPO). 3961
0100-0519 See JORNAL BRASILEIRO DE UROLOGIA. 3990
0100-0551 See PESQUISA E PLANEJAMENTO ECONOMICO (RIO DE JANEIRO). 1512
0100-0608 See ENGENHARIA NA INDUSTRIA (SAO PAULO). 5103
0100-0683 See REVISTA BRASILEIRA DE CIENCIA DO SOLO. 185
0100-0705 See BIBLIOGRAFIA BRASILEIRA DE ENGENHARIA. 1966
0100-0756 See BIBLIOGRAFIA BRASILEIRA DE QUIMICA (RIO DE JANEIRO, BRAZIL : 1984). 962
0100-0829 See REVISTA DA ESCOLA DE BIBLIOTECONOMIA DA UFMG. 3246
0100-0888 See REVISTA LETRAS (CURITIBA). 3316
0100-0934 See MONOGRAFIAS DE MATEMATICA. 3523
0100-0993 See ALIMENTACAO (SAO PAULO). 2326
0100-1213 See ARQUIVOS DO MINISTERIO DA JUSTICA. 2937
0100-1299 See ANUARIO ESTATISTICO DO BRASIL / MINISTERIO DA AGRICULTURA, INDUSTRIA E COMMERCIO, DIRECTORIA GERAL DE ESTATISTICA. 5322
0100-1752 See REVISTA DO INSTITUTO DOS ADVOGADOS BRASILEIROS. 3042
0100-185X See MULTIDISCIPLINAR. REVISTA DO ICNPF. 1765
0100-1949 See BOLETIM TECNICO CEPED. 5089
0100-1965 See CIENCIA DA INFORMACAO. 3202
0100-2007 See MEMORIAS DO INSTITUTO DE BIOCIENCIAS (RECIFE). 464
0100-204X See PESQUISA AGROPECUARIA BRASILEIRA. 119
0100-2104 See ELETRICIDADE MODERNA (SAO PAULO). 2052
0100-2481 See ARQUIVOS DA UNIVERSIDADE FEDERAL RURAL DO RIO DE JANEIRO. 63
0100-2570 See MERCADO COMUM BRASILEIRO : SAO PAULO. 846
0100-2597 See ARQUIVOS DA ESCOLA DE MEDICINA VETERINARIA DA UNIVERSIDADE FEDERAL DA BAHIA. 5504
0100-2910 See BRAZILIAN ECONOMIC STUDIES. 1465
0100-3003 See CIRCULAR TECNICA / EMPRESA GOIANA DE PESQUISA AGROPECUARIA. 74
0100-3054 See BOLETIN TECNICO - IAPAR. 68
0100-3127 See ACTA ONCOLOGICA BRASILEIRA. 3808
0100-3232 See REVISTA BRASILEIRA DE CLINICA E TERAPEUTICA. 3634
0100-3267 See CIENCIA E PRATICA. 74
0100-3283 See HANSENOLOGIA INTERNATIONALIS. 3580
0100-3313 See COMUNICACOES CIENTIFICAS DA FACULDADE DE MEDICINA VETERINARIA E ZOOTECNIA DA UNIVERSIDADE DE SAO PAULO. 5508
0100-3356 See CIRCULAR - FUNDACAO INSTITUTO AGRONOMICO DO PARANA. 74
0100-3364 See INFORME AGROPECUARIO. 96

0100-3364 See INFORME AGROPECUARIO (BELO HORIZONTE). 96
0100-350X See COLETANEA DO INSTITUTO DE TECNOLOGIA DE ALIMENTOS. 2331
0100-3526 See BIOGEOGRAFIA. 2556
0100-3569 See BOLETIM DA SOCIEDADE BRASILEIRA DE MATEMATICA. 3497
0100-3593 See ENERGIA NUCLEAR E AGRICULTURA. 2154
0100-3674 See REVISTA DO INSTITUTO DE LATICINIOS CANDIDO TOSTES. 2356
0100-378X See LEGISLACAO DO ESTADO DO RIO DE JANEIRO / SECRETARIA DE ESTADO DE JUSTICA, DIVISAO DE DIVULGACAO. 3001
0100-4042 See QUIMICA NOVA. 990
0100-4107 See ECOSSISTEMA / FACULDADE DE AGRONOMIA E ZOOTECNIA "MANOEL CARLOS GONCALVES.". 81
0100-4158 See FITOPATOLOGIA BRASILEIRA. 172
0100-4298 See AGROANALYSIS. 55
0100-4409 See INFORMACOES ECONOMICAS - INSTITUTO DE ECONOMIA AGRICOLA. 1495
0100-4417 See BOLETIM TECNICO - COORDENDORIA DE ASSISTENCIA TECNICA INTEGRAL. 67
0100-4557 See IPEF, INSTITUTO DE PESQUISAS E ESTUDOS FLORESTAIS. 2385
0100-4670 See ECLETICA QUIMICA. 974
0100-4743 See INDEX MEDICUS LATINO-AMERICANO. 3586
0100-4859 See REVISTA DA SOCIEDADE BRASILEIRA DE ZOOTECNIA. 5596
0100-4921 See GEOLOGIA E METALURGIA. 4002
0100-4956 See REVISTA ECONOMICA DO NORDESTE. 1582
0100-512X See KRITERION. 4351
0100-5375 See PESQUISAS - INSTITUTO DE GEOCIENCIAS. UNIVERSIDADE FEDERAL DO RIO GRANDE DU SUL. 1391
0100-5405 See SUMMA PHYTOPATHOLOGICA. 2432
0100-5472 See PALEOCLIMAS. 4229
0100-6045 See MANUSCRITO. 4352
0100-6061 See COMUNICADO TECNICO (CENTRO DE PESQUISA AGROPECUARIA DO TROPICO SEMI-ARIDO). 76
0100-607X See REVISTA DO SECTOR DE CIENCIAS AGRARIAS. 129
0100-6223 See SACCHARUM STAB. 992
0100-6711 See REVISTA BRASILEIRA DE TECNOLOGIA. 5147
0100-6762 See REVISTA ARVORE. 2394
0100-6886 See CIRCULAR TECNICA - UNIDADE DE EXECUCAO DE PESQUISA DE AMBITO ESTADUAL DE DOURADOS. 167
0100-6908 See MINERACAO METALURGIA (1968). 4012
0100-6916 See ENGENHARIA AGRICOLA. 82
0100-6932 See HISTORIA, QUESTOES & DEBATES. 2736
0100-6991 See REVISTA DO COLEGIO BRASILEIRO DE CIRURGIOES. 3973
0100-7092 See PUBLICACAO ACIESP. 5143
0100-7157 See REVISTA DE BIBLIOTECONOMIA DE BRASILIA. 3246
0100-7319 See JORNAL SUL-AMERICANO DE BIOCIENCIAS. 5118
0100-7343 See REVISTA BRASILEIRA DE MEDICINA. PSIQUIATRIA. 3935
0100-736X See PESQUISA VETERINARIA BRASILEIRA. 5518
0100-7416 See BOLETIM TECNICO - EMPASC. 67
0100-7947 See ENGARRAFADOR MODERNO. 2334
0100-8102 See BOLETIM DE PESQUISA. 67
0100-8307 See CIENCIA E NATURA. 5094
0100-8404 See REVISTA BRASILEIRA DE BOTANICA. 526
0100-8455 See REVISTA BRASILEIRA DE GENETICA. 551
0100-8587 See RELIGIAO E SOCIEDADE. 4990

0100-8617 See COMUNICADO TECNICO - UEPAE DE DOURADOS. 168
0100-8625 See CIRCULAR TECNICA - CENTRO NACIONAL DE PESQUISA DE TRIGO. 200
0100-8730 See ANUARIO ESTATISTICO DO ESTADO DE SAO PAULO. 5322
0100-8765 See COMUNICADO TECNICO - UNIDADE DE EXECUCAO DE PESQUISA DE AMBITO TERRITORIAL DE PORTO VELLIO. 168
0100-879X See BRAZILIAN JOURNAL OF MEDICAL AND BIOLOGICAL RESEARCH. 3558
0100-8854 See COMUNICADO TECNICO (CENTRO NACIONAL DE PESQUISA DE MANDIOCA E FRUTICULTURA (BRAZIL)). 2412
0100-896X See COMUNICADO TECNICO - EMPRESA DE PESQUISA AGROPECUARIA DO ESTADO DO RIO DE JANEIRO. 76
0100-8986 See DOCUMENTOS - EMPRESA CATARINENSE DE PESQUISA AGROPECUARIA 1978-. 80
0100-9303 See ANUARIO MINERAL BRASILEIRO. 1361
0100-9397 See ALIMENTACAO (SAO PAULO). 2326
0100-9443 See DOCUMENTOS (CENTRO NACIONAL DE PESQUISA DE GADO DE CORTE (BRAZIL)). 210
0100-9508 See INFORME DA PESQUISA - INSTITUTO AGRONOMICO DO PARANA. 96
0100-9508 See INFORME DA PESQUISA. 2385
0100-9729 See DOCUMENTOS (CENTRO DE PESQUISA AGROPECUARIA DO TROPICO SEMI-ARIDO). 79
0101-0697 See BANCO DE BIBLIOGRAFIAS / EMBRAPA, EMPRESA BRASILEIRA DE PESQUISA AGROPECUARIA, DEPARTAMENTO DE INFORMACAO E DOCUMENTACAO. 64
0101-1057 See BOLETIM DE PESQUISA FLORESTAL. 2376
0101-1723 See ENSAIOS FEE. 1488
0101-1766 See PROJETO. 306
0101-1774 See REVISTA DE ODONTOLOGIA DA UNESP. 1334
0101-1782 See CEARA MEDICO. 3562
0101-1847 See CIRCULAR TECNICA. 2377
0101-1944 See NATURALIA (SAO JOSE DO RIO PRETO). 4168
0101-2061 See CIENCIA E TECNOLOGIA DE ALIMENTOS. 4188
0101-2177 See NORDESTE, CONJUNTURA INDUSTRIAL. 1620
0101-2991 See CADERNOS DE TECNOLOGIA E CIENCIA. 5092
0101-3033 See ESTATISTICAS DA SAUDE. ASSISTENCIA MEDICO-SANITARIA. 3780
0101-3084 See PUBLICACAO IPEN. 4418
0101-3130 See ESTUDOS TEOLOGICOS. 4956
0101-3157 See REVISTA DE ECONOMIA POLITICA (CENTRO DE ECONOMIA POLITICA (SAO PAULO, BRAZIL). 1518
0101-3173 See TRANSFORMACAO. 4364
0101-3211 See CADERNOS FUNDAP. 4466
0101-3289 See REVISTA BRASILEIRA DE CIENCIAS DO ESPORTE. 4915
0101-3300 See NOVOS ESTUDOS CEBRAP. 4485
0101-3335 See LETRAS DE HOJE. 3297
0101-3351 See SONDAGEM CONJUNTURAL, INDUSTRIA DE TRANSFORMACAO / FUNDACAO INSTITUTO TECNICO DE ECONOMIA E PLANEJAMENTO. 1627
0101-3394 See REVISTA LATINOAMERICANA DE DOCUMENTACION. 3246
0101-3459 See PERSPECTIVAS / UNIVERSIDADE ESTADUAL PAULISTA. 5212
0101-3505 See REVISTA DE LETRAS (MARILIA). 3316
0101-3548 See CADERNOS DE LINGUISTICA E TEORIA DA LITERATURA. 3271
0101-3580 See BOLETIM DE ZOOLOGIA. 5578
0101-3742 See SEMINA (LONDRINA). 133
0101-3793 See REVISTA DE CIENCIAS FARMACEUTICAS. 4328
0101-3858 See PEDIATRIA (SAO PAULO). 3907

0101-4064 *See* ESTUDOS IBERO-AMERICANOS. 2687

0101-4161 *See* ESTUDOS ECONOMICOS - INSTITUTO DE PESQUISAS ECONOMICAS. 1592

0101-4242 *See* BOLETIM DE FISIOLOGIA ANIMAL. 578

0101-4366 *See* REVISTA DO INSTITUTO HISTORICO E GEOGRAFICO BRASILEIRO. 2552

0101-4501 *See* CIENCIAS MEDICAS (NITEROI). 3564

0101-451X *See* ANAIS DO MUSEU DE ANTROPOLOGIA. 228

0101-4684 *See* GUIA BRASILEIRO DE INSTITUCOES DE PESQUISA EM AGRICULTURA / MINISTERIO DA AGRICULTURA, BINAGRI. 91

0101-4862 *See* LINGUA E LITERATURA. 3298

0101-5354 *See* ACTA BIOLOGICA LEOPOLDENSIA. 531

0101-5494 *See* DOCUMENTOS / EMPRESA BRASILEIRA DE PESQUISA AGROPECUARIA, VINCULADA AO MINISTERIO DA AGRICULTURA, CENTRO NACIONAL DE PESQUISA DE SOJA. 170

0101-5508 *See* COMUNICADO TECNICO - CENTRO DE TECNOLOGIA AGRICOLA E ALIMENTAR. 76

0101-5575 *See* REVISTA DO HCPA & FACULDADE DE MEDICINA DA UNIVERSIDADE FEDERAL DO RIO GRANDE DO SUL. 3635

0101-563X *See* RBM, REVISTA BRASILEIRA DE MANDIOCA. 125

0101-5664 *See* PORTOS E NAVIOS. 4181

0101-5907 *See* REVISTA PARAENSE DE MEDICINA. 3636

0101-6016 *See* PSICOLOGIA. 4609

0101-6431 *See* BOLETIM DE PESQUISA - UNIDADE DE EXECUCAO DE PESQUISA DE AMBITO ESTADUAL DE PORTO VELHO. 67

0101-6628 *See* SERVICO SOCIAL E SOCIEDADE. 5307

0101-6644 *See* DOCUMENTOS - CENTRO NACIONAL DE PESQUISA DE TRIGO. 200

0101-7217 *See* REVISTA DOCPOP. 4560

0101-7268 *See* BOLETIM ABDF. 3196

0101-7438 *See* PESQUISA OPERACIONAL. 5138

0101-7616 *See* ROESSLERIA. 2204

0101-7683 *See* COMUNICADO TECNICO - EMCAPA. 76

0101-8051 *See* REVISTA DE LETRAS (FORTALEZA). 3351

0101-8175 *See* REVISTA BRASILEIRA DE ZOOLOGIA. 5596

0101-8205 *See* MATEMATICA APLICADA E COMPUTACIONAL. 3517

0101-8248 *See* REVISTA BRASILEIRA DE LINGUA E LITERATURA. 3315

0101-8434 *See* REB. REVISTA ECLESIASTICA BRASILEIRA. 5035

0101-8469 *See* REVISTA BRASILEIRA DE NEUROLOGIA : ORGAO OFICIAL DO INSTITUTO DE NEUROLOGIA DEOLINDO COUTO, UNIVERSIDADE FEDERAL DO RIO DE JANEIRO. 3845

0101-8477 *See* ANUARIO DE INFORMATICA CWB. 1170

0101-8515 *See* CIENCIA HOJE : REVISAT DE DIVULGACAO CIENTIFICA DA SOCIEDADE BRASILEIRA PARA O PROGRESSO DA CIENCIA. 5094

0101-8612 *See* PESQUISA MUNICIPAL / FUNDACAO SISTEMA ESTADUAL DE ANALISE DE DADOS, SEADE. 2830

0101-8698 *See* UNILETRAS. 3449

0101-8868 *See* REVISTA DE DOUTRINA E JURISPRUDENCIA / TRIBUNAL DE JUSTICA DO DISTRITO FEDERAL E DOS TERRITORIOS. 3041

0101-8949 *See* DOCUMENTOS - EMCAPA. 80

0101-9570 *See* TRAVESSIA. 3447

0101-9597 *See* HILEIA MEDICA. 3583

0101-9600 *See* HILEIA MEDICA. SUPLEMENTO. 3583

0101-9619 *See* PESQUISAS. HISTORIA. 2625

0101-9635 *See* LEOPOLDIANUM. 1834

0101-9651 *See* PESQUISA EM ANDAMENTO - EMPAER. 119

0101-966X *See* BOLETIM DE PESQUISA - EMPAER. 67

0101-9678 *See* CIRCULAR TECNICA - EMPAER. 74

0101-9872 *See* REVIEW OF IBERIAN LATIN AMERICAN DERMATOLOGY. 3722

0102-0048 *See* BOLETIM DE PESQUISA - UEPAE DOURADOS. 200

0102-0226 *See* RESENHA ESTATISTICA DO RIO GRANDE DO SUL / SECRETARIA DE COORDENACAO E PLANEJAMENTO, FUNDACAO DE ECONOMIA E ESTATISTICA. 1538

0102-0617 *See* ENSAYOS ECIEL. 1488

0102-0803 *See* REVISTA BRASILEIRA DE REPRODUCAO ANIMAL. 5520

0102-0811 *See* REVISTA DE MATEMATICA E ESTATISTICA / UNIVERSIDADE ESTADUAL PAULISTA. 3531

0102-0897 *See* REVISTA COMUNICACOES E ARTES. 1121

0102-0935 *See* ARQUIVO BRASILEIRO DE MEDICINA VETERINARIA E ZOOTECNIA. 5504

0102-1184 *See* REFORMA AGRARIA. 125

0102-1249 *See* ACTA GEOLOGICA LEOPOLDENSIA. 1364

0102-1656 *See* ATLANTICA. 553

0102-1931 *See* PLASTICO MODERNO. 4457

0102-1958 *See* MONOGRAFIAS (INSTITUTO DE PESQUISAS TECNOLOGICAS). 5129

0102-2105 *See* REVISTA AMRIGS. 3634

0102-2334 *See* ANAIS DO CBEN. 3851

0102-2423 *See* DOCUMENTOS / EMPA-MT. 80

0102-2504 *See* RELATORIO ANUAL / MINISTERIO DA INDUSTRIA E DO COMERCIO, CONSELHO DE DESENVOLVIMENTO INDUSTRIAL, SECRETARIA EXECUTIVA. 4679

0102-2571 *See* REVISTA DO PATRIMONIO HISTORICO E ARTISTICO NACIONAL. 308

0102-2636 *See* POLITICA E ESTRATEGIA. 4532

0102-2687 *See* REVISTA BRASILEIRA DE ENGENHARIA. CADERNO DE ENGENHARIA QUIMICA / ASSOCIACAO BRASILEIRA DE ENGENHARIA QUIMICA. 2017

0102-292X *See* BOLETIM DE PESQUISA. 165

0102-2997 *See* NEMATOLOGIA BRASILEIRA. 5592

0102-3098 *See* REVISTA BRASILEIRA DE ESTUDOS DE POPULACAO. 4560

0102-311X *See* CADERNOS DE SAUDE PUBLICA / MINISTERIO DA SAUDE, FUNDACAO OSWALDO CRUZ, ESCOLA NACIONAL DE SAUDE PUBLICA. 4770

0102-3411 See JOURNAL OF APPLIED NON-CLASSICAL LOGICS. 3511

0102-3586 *See* JORNAL DE PNEUMOLOGIA : PUBLICACAO OFICIAL DA SOCIEDADE BRASILEIRA DE PNEUMOLOGIA E TISIOLOGIA. 3949

0102-3691 *See* CIRCULAR TECNICA - EMPA-MT. 74

0102-3772 *See* PSICOLOGIA. TEORIA E PESQUISA. 4609

0102-4264 *See* ACTA SEMIOTICA ET LINGUISTICA. 3261

0102-4272 *See* ARQUIVOS DO MUSEU DE HISTORIA NATURAL. 4162

0102-4418 *See* ARTICULACAO PESQUISA-EXTENSAO / EMPRESA CAPIXABA DE PESQUISA AGROPECUARIA, EMPRESA DE ASSISTENCIA TECNICA E EXTENSAO RURAL DE ESTADO DE ESPIRITO SANTO. 63

0102-4450 *See* REVISTA DE DOCUMENTACAO DE ESTUDOS EM LINGUISTICA TEORICA E APLICADA. 3315

0102-4469 *See* PERSPECTIVA TEOLOGICA. 4986

0102-4876 *See* AVIACAO EM REVISTA. 12

0102-4906 *See* ESTUDOS ANGLO-AMERICANOS. 3280

0102-4914 *See* MATHEMATICAL AND DYNAMICAL ASTRONOMY SERIES. 397

0102-5171 *See* BOLETIM MENSAL / BANCO CENTRAL DO BRASIL. 779

0102-5511 *See* BOLETIM TECNICO - COMISSAO EXECUTIVA DO PLANO DA LAVOURA CACAUEIRA, DEPARTAMENTO ESPECIAL DA AMAZONIA. 67

0102-5651 *See* DOCUMENTOS / UEPAE DOURADOS. 80

0102-5716 *See* VETERINARIA E ZOOTECNIA. 5523

0102-5767 *See* CADERNOS DE ESTUDOS LINGUISTICOS / UNIVERSIDADE ESTADUAL DE CAMPINAS, INSTITUTO DE ESTUDOS DA LINGUAGEM, DEPARTAMENTO DE LINGUISTICA. 3271

0102-6380 *See* ARS VETERINARIA. 5504

0102-6526 *See* SERIE LINGUISTICA. 3320

0102-6615 *See* ESCRITA. 3385

0102-6720 *See* ARQUIVOS BRASILEIROS DE CIRURGIA DIGESTIVA ABCD: BRAZILIAN ARCHIVES OF DIGESTIVE SURGERY. 3960

0102-695X *See* REVISTA BRASILEIRA DE FARMACOGNOSIA. 4328

0102-6968 *See* BOLETIM - CENTRO DE LETRAS E CIENCIAS HUMANAS. 2843

0102-6992 *See* SOCIEDADE E ESTADO : REVISTA SEMESTRAL DO DEPARTAMENTO DE SOCIOLOGIA DA UNB. 5259

0102-7344 *See* CABRA & BODES. 165

0102-7646 *See* REVISTA ABP-APAL. 3935

0102-7794 *See* ARQUIVOS FLUMINENSES DE MEDICINA VETERINARIA. 5504

0102-8774 *See* REVISTA DE DIREITO DO TRABALHO (SAO PAULO). 3153

0102-8979 *See* AU. ARQUITETURA E URBANISMO. 293

0102-9185 *See* DOCUMENTOS - CENTRO NACIONAL DE PESQUISA DE COCO. 80

0102-9290 *See* BOLETIM BIBLIOGRAFICO. 2840

0102-9304 *See* BOLETIM DE GEOCIENCIAS DA PETROBRAS. 1367

0102-9479 *See* HUMANIDADES (BRASILIA, BRAZIL). 5231

0102-9541 *See* CVRD REVISTA. 1970

0102-9711 *See* CADERNOS DO CEAS. 5241

0102-9738 *See* PESQUISA EM ANDAMENTO - CENTRO NACIONAL DE PESQUISA DE UVA E VINHO. 2370

0102-9797 *See* REVISTA BRASILEIRA DE MERCADO DE CAPITAIS. 913

0102-9800 *See* GEOCHIMICA BRASILIENSIS. 1376

0102-9843 *See* REVISTA BRASILEIRA DE ENGENHARIA QUIMICA. 2017

0103-006X *See* CIENCIA VETERINARIA JABOTICABAL. 5507

0103-0078 *See* CIS DOCUMENTACAO / CENTRO DE INFORMACOES SIDERURGICAS. 4000

0103-054X *See* JORNAL SUL-TROPICAL DE MEDICINA / SOUTH TROPICAL JOURNAL OF MEDICINE. 3986

0103-0663 *See* REVISTA DE ODONTOLOGIA DA UNIVERSIDADE DE SAO PAULO. 1334

0103-0779 *See* AGROPECUARIA CATARINENSE. 56

0103-1562 *See* FACE (SAO PAULO, BRAZIL). 3281

0103-1767 *See* BOLETIM TECNICO - INSTITUTO DE PESCA. 2297

0103-1813 *See* TRABALHOS EM LINGUISTICA APLICADA. 3329

0103-1821 *See* ESTUDOS PORTUGUESES E AFRICANOS : EPA. 3385

0103-2070 *See* TEMPO SOCIAL : REVISTA DE SOCIOLOGIA DA USP / UNIVERSIDADE DE SAO PAULO, FACULDADE DE FILOSOFIA, LETRAS E CIENCIAS HUMANAS, DEPARTAMENTO DE SOCIOLOGIA. 5264

0103-2402 *See* REVISTA BRASILEIRA DE SOCIOLOGIA. 5256

0103-2674 *See* REVISTA DO INSTITUTO FLORESTAL. 2394

0103-3131 *See* REVISTA BRASILEIRA DE FISIOLOGIA VEGETAL. 526

0103-3247 *See* COLECAO CLE. 5095

0103-3700 *See* HORTI SUL. 2418

0103-3816 See AGROTROPICA. 57
0103-4014 See ESTUDOS AVANCADOS. 2732
0103-4138 See PLANEJAMENTO E POLITICAS PUBLICAS. 4673
0103-4235 See ALIMENTOS E NUTRICAO / UNIVERSIDADE ESTADUAL PAULISTA. 4187
0103-4332 See SINTESE. 5219
0103-491X See TEXTOS DE METODOS MATEMATICOS. 3538
0103-5053 See JOURNAL OF THE BRAZILIAN CHEMICAL SOCIETY. 982
0103-5266 See PETROBRAS NEWS. 4271
0103-5673 See CADERNOS DO CEDI. 5241
0103-626X See HERITAGE NEWS (CANBERRA, A.C.T.). 2510
0103-6440 See RHEOLOGY GERMANY. 1335
0103-6963 See REVISTA BRASILEIRA DE LITERATURA COMPARADA. 3429
0103-751X See BRASIL PORTO ALEGRE. 3369
0103-7641 See PERFIL DO ESTADO DA BAHIA : ESTATISTICAS SELECIONADAS / GOVERNO DO ESTADO DA BAHIA, SECRETARIA DO PLANEJAMENTO, CIENCIA E TECNOLOGIA, CENTRO DE ESTATISTICA E INFORMACOES, CEI. 2202
0103-8478 See CIENCIA RURAL : REVISTA CIENTIFICA DO CENTRO DE CIENCIAS RURAIS DA UNIVERSIDADE FEDERAL DE SANTA MARIA. 74
0103-8915 See MARGEM. 5208
0103-9016 See SCIENTIA AGRICOLA. 4171
0103-9318 See BRAZILIAN COMMUNICATION RESEARCH YEARBOOK. 1105
0103-9733 See BRAZILIAN JOURNAL OF PHYSICS. 4398
0104-0030 See ECORIO. 2164
0104-0111 See REVISTA DE CIENCIAS HUMANAS : REVISTA DA UFPR. 2853
0104-026X See ESTUDOS FEMINISTAS. 5555
0104-1290 See SAUDE E SOCIEDADE. 4801
0105-0257 See KOPENHAGENER BEITRAEGE ZUR GERMANISTISCHEN LINGUISTIK. 3293
0105-032X See LO-BLADET. 1688
0105-0397 See SCANDINAVIAN AUDIOLOGY. 3891
0105-0583 See CRAS. 348
0105-0621 See ODENSE UNIVERSITY STUDIES IN PSYCHIATRY AND MEDICAL PSYCHOLOGY. 3932
0105-0648 See DANSKE FYSIOTERAPEUTER. 4380
0105-0710 See POLITICA. 4488
0105-0761 See LINDBERGIA. 517
0105-1024 See FOLK OG KULTUR. 2319
0105-1121 See RETFRD ARHUS. 3039
0105-1164 See SKATTER OG AFGIFTER. 4748
0105-1423 See HISTORIA MEDICINAE VETERINARIAE. 5511
0105-1512 See NORTH. 360
0105-1539 See NORDISK TIDSSKRIFT FOR LOGOPEDI OG FONIATRI. SCANDINAVIAN JOURNAL OF LOGOPEDICS AND PHONIATRICS. 3889
0105-175X See INTER-NOISE. 2174
0105-1873 See CONTACT DERMATITIS. 3718
0105-2403 See SCIENTIFUR. 3186
0105-2624 See NORTH-INFORMATION. 360
0105-2896 See IMMUNOLOGICAL REVIEWS. 3671
0105-3191 See DANSK TEOLOGISK TIDSSKRIFT. 4952
0105-3205 See INGENIREN (KBENHAVN. 1975). 1978
0105-3213 See COOPERATIVE RESEARCH REPORT - INTERNATIONAL COUNCIL FOR THE EXPLORATION OF THE SEA (1972). 1448
0105-3639 See ALFRED BENZON SYMPOSIUM. 3547
0105-4139 See PUBLIKATION - INSTITUT FOR SOCIAL MEDICIN, KBENHAVNS UNIVERSITET. 3631
0105-4503 See IWGIA DOCUMENTS. 238

0105-4570 See LANDINSPEKTREN; TIDSSKRIFT FOR OPMALINGSOG MATRIKELVAESEN. 2027
0105-6255 See ACTA CAMPANOLOGICA. 3544
0105-6263 See INTERNATIONAL JOURNAL OF ANDROLOGY. 3588
0105-6387 See IWGIA NEWSLETTER. 5205
0105-6883 See BERETNING FRA STATENS HUSDYRBRUGSFORSG. 65
0105-6972 See MM. 4131
0105-7014 See TEXT & KONTEXT. 3328
0105-712X See FOLK OG FORSKNING / UDG. AF UNIVERSTETSFORENINGEN FOR DET SYDLIGE OG VESTLIGE JYLLAND. 2846
0105-7200 See DANSK AUDIOLOGOPDI. 3887
0105-7510 See ORBIS LITTERARUM. 3420
0105-7618 See SFINX. 2629
0105-791X See NYT FRA MILJSTYRELSENS REFERENCELABORAFORIUM. 1018
0105-8258 See GEOKOMPENDIER. 2564
0105-9238 See MODSPIL. 4131
0105-9254 See AARBOG / KOEBSTADMUSEET "DEN GAMLE BY". 2671
0105-9327 See ECOGRAPHY. 2213
0105-984X See NORTH-DEBAT. 360
0105-9858 See ARSSKRIFT - CARLSBERGFONDET, FREDERIKSBORGMUSEET, NY CARLSBERGFONDET. 1074
0105-9912 See DATA (KBENHAVN. 1971). 1257
0105-9963 See ANGLICA ET AMERICANA. 3264
0106-004X See FRUGTAVLEREN. 2342
0106-0244 See ENERGIOVERSIGT. 1938
0106-035X See NOVELLEREGISTER. 3459
0106-0392 See HANDBOG I DANSK POLITIK. 1565
0106-0481 See HISTORISK-FILOSOFISKE MEDDELELSER. 2619
0106-0767 See DANSK KONOMISK BIBLIOGRAFI. 1479
0106-0805 See CDR PROJECT PAPERS. 2908
0106-0821 See ROLIG-PAPIR. 3317
0106-0880 See ARCHAEOLOGY OF SVENDBORG, DENMARK, THE. 257
0106-102X See MEDIAEVAL SCANDINAVIA SUPPLEMENTS. 2697
0106-1046 See MEDDELELSER OM GRNLAND. GEOSCIENCE. 1358
0106-1054 See MEDDELELSER OM GRNLAND. BIOSCIENCE. 464
0106-1062 See MEDDELELSER OM GRNLAND. MAN & SOCIETY. 2519
0106-1313 See SLAVICA OTHINIENSIA. 3321
0106-1348 See ICO. 352
0106-1372 See NEWSLETTER FROM THE COMMISSION FOR SCIENTIFIC RESEARCH IN GREENLAND. 5133
0106-147X See DANSK ARTIKELINDEKS. 414
0106-1542 See BERETNING - FAELLESUDVALGET FOR STATENS MEJERI- OG HUSDYRBRUGSFORSG. 207
0106-1607 See INTERNATIONAL JOURNAL OF ANDROLOGY. SUPPLEMENT. 3588
0106-2301 See SCANDINAVIAN PSYCHOANALYTIC REVIEW, THE. 4617
0106-2581 See STATENS PLANTEAVLSUDVALG BERETNING / UDARBEJDET AF INFORMATIONSTJENESTEN. 188
0106-2778 See ARSBERETNING / ROSKILDE UNIVERSITETSCENTER, INSTITUT FOR GEOGRAFI, SAMFUNDSANALYSE OG DATALOGI. 5191
0106-2840 See RIS-R. 1956
0106-3030 See ARCHITECTURA. 288
0106-3308 See BRNEKLINIKENS VEJLEDNINGER. 4385
0106-3324 See FABRIK OG BOLIG. 2688
0106-3715 See BYGNINGSSTATISKE MEDDELELSER. 2020
0106-4487 See DOLPHIN (ARRHUS, DENMARK). 3382
0106-4525 See DANSKE STUDIER. 3341
0106-4622 See DANSK UDSYN. 2685

0106-469X See MEDDELELSER OM KONSERVERING. 358
0106-4797 See FORTID OG NUTID. 2616
0106-4940 See HYMNOLOGISKE MEDDELELSER. 4121
0106-5173 See MARXISTISK ANTROPOLOGI. 241
0106-519X See LANDBRUGETS PRISFORHOLD. 104
0106-5378 See SVANTEVIT. 3327
0106-5408 See LIGNINGSVEJLEDNINGEN. SELSKABER / STATSSKATTEDIREKTORATET, LIGNINGSAFDELINGEN, SELSKABSSKATTEKONTORET. 4736
0106-553X See DANA (DANMARKS FISKERI- OG HAVUNDERSGELSER). 554
0106-5629 See DMT. DANSK MUSIK TIDSSKRIFT. 4115
0106-5734 See KUNAPIPI. 3403
0106-6072 See BRANDVAERN. 2288
0106-620X See LITTERATUR & SAMFUND. 3408
0106-6854 See DANSK VETERINAERTIDSSKRIFT. 5508
0106-7303 See CENTRING SLAGELSE. 4849
0106-7559 See FARG OCH LACK SCANDINAVIA. 4223
0106-7818 See MARITIM KONTAKT. 4179
0106-8040 See NYS. NYDANSKE STUDIER & ALMEN KOMMUNIKATIONSTEORI. 3307
0106-8202 See ARSBERETNING - AARHUS UNIVERSITET. GEOLOGISK INSTITUT. 1366
0106-8350 See SYGEPLEJERSKEN. 3870
0106-8377 See FAUNA ENTOMOLOGICA SCANDINAVICA. 5608
0106-8393 See GARTNER-TIDENDE : ORGAN FOR ALMINDELIG DANSK GARTNERFORENING. 2416
0106-9543 See LIVER (COPENHAGEN). 3799
0106-9896 See ARBEJDSMARKEDSUDDANNELSERNE STATISTIK. TABELMATERIALE VEDRRENDE OMSKOLING OG ERHVERVSINTRODUKTION. 1651
0107-055X See NORDIC JOURNAL OF BOTANY. 520
0107-0851 See STATISTIKKEN. ARBEJDERLN. 5343
0107-0967 See VARESTATISTIK FOR INDUSTRI. SERIE A, ANIMALSKE OG VEGETABILSKE PRODUKTER, SAMT ANDRE NRINGS OG NYDELSESMIDLER. 2360
0107-0975 See VARESTATISTIK FOR INDUSTRI. SERIE B, MINERALSKE OG KEMISKE PRODUKTER, TROG PAPIR SAMT VARER DERAF. 2360
0107-0983 See VARESTATISTIK FOR INDUSTRI. SERIE C, TEKSTILVARER, FODTJ, SPORTSARTIKLER M.V. 2360
0107-0991 See VARESTATISTIK FOR INDUSTRI. SERIE D, METALLER, METALVARER, MASKINER, APPARATER OG INSTRUMENTER, SAMT TRANSPORTMIDLER. 2360
0107-1009 See VEJVISER I STATISTIKKEN. 5345
0107-1033 See FILMSSONEN, DANSK FILMFORTEGNELSE / UDGIVIT AF BIBLIOTEKSCENTRALEN OG DET DANSKE FILMMUSEUM. 4071
0107-1211 See PSYKE & LOGOS. 4614
0107-2919 See OPUS (COPENHAGEN, DENMARK). 4144
0107-3117 See BERETNING FOR PERIODEN ... / FRA FLLESRADET VEDRRENDE MINERALSKE RASTOFFER I GRNLAND. 2135
0107-4083 See VARD I NORDEN. 3870
0107-4164 See GRUNDTVIG STUDIER. 4961
0107-4849 See FRA BORNHOLMS MUSEUM. 4088
0107-4857 See DANSK ORGELAARBOG. 4113
0107-4997 See OVERSIGT OVER RAPPORTER M.M. VEDRRENDE VANDKRAFTUNDERSGELSEL I GRNLAND PR. 30 JUNI. 1417
0107-5675 See LANDBRUGSREGNSKABSSTATISTIK. 104
0107-6329 See OBJEKTIV HELLERUP. 4372
0107-6442 See PIST PROTTA. 3468

0107-699X See JURISTEN / DANMARKS JURIST- OG KONOMFORBUND. 2991

0107-7031 See VARESTATISTIK FOR INDUSTRI (ANNUAL). 1630

0107-7139 See DANMARK I TAL. 5326

0107-7430 See REPORT OF THE MARINE POLLUTION LABORATORY. 2220

0107-7481 See DISPLAY. 1241

0107-833X See SCANDINAVIAN JOURNAL OF PRIMARY HEALTH CARE. 3739

0107-8461 See ARBEJDERHISTORIE. 1651

0107-8593 See SCANDINAVIAN AUDIOLOGY. SUPPLEMENTUM. 3891

0107-8666 See RAPPORT OM KONTROLLEN MED KONSUMMLKPRODUKTER FOR ARET. 198

0107-8909 See BOLIGTLLINGEN. 4550

0107-9212 See STUDIER FRA SPROG- OG OLDTIDSFORSKNING. 3325

0107-9328 See MIV: MUSEERNE I VIBORG AMT. 2699

0107-9700 See BERETNING FOR UNDERVISNINGSARET ... / DANMARKS BIBLIOTEKSSKOLE. 3194

0107-9786 See BERETNING FOR ... / DEN CENTRALE VIDENSKABSETISKE KOMITE. 3555

0108-0288 See BULLETIN OF THE EUROPEAN ASSOCIATION OF FISH PATHOLOGISTS. 2298

0108-0695 See DESIGN FROM SCANDINAVIA. 372

0108-0954 See GAMMA (KBENHAVN). 4434

0108-1284 See TIDSSKRIFT FOR TANDLGER (COPENHAGEN, DENMARK : 1981). 1336

0108-1675 See ALLERGY SUPPLEMENTUM. 3666

0108-1993 See RELIGIONSVIDENSKABELIGT TIDSSKRIFT. 4991

0108-2086 See PESTICIDRESTER I DANSKE LEVNEDSMIDLER. 4247

0108-2701 See ACTA CRYSTALLOGRAPHICA. SECTION C, CRYSTAL STRUCTURE COMMUNICATIONS. 1031

0108-271X See NORDISK SEXOLOGI. 4606

0108-2914 See NORDIC SOUNDS. 5318

0108-3627 See DJF HANDBOGEN. 3146

0108-4135 See LIVING ARCHITECTURE. 302

0108-464X See JOURNAL OF DANISH ARCHAEOLOGY. 271

0108-5344 See OFTALMOLOG. 3624

0108-545X See STATISTISKE EFTERRETNINGER. NATIONALREGNSKAB, OFFENTLIGE FINANSER, BETALINGSBALANCE. 4700

0108-5468 See STATISTISKE EFTERRETNINGER. INDUSTRI OG ENERGI / DANMARKS STATISTIK. 1540

0108-5476 See STATISTISKE EFTERRETNINGER. PENGE- OG KAPITALMARKED. 734

0108-5484 See STATISTISKE EFTERRETNINGER. SAMFRDSEL OG TURISME. 5393

0108-5492 See STATISTISKE EFTERRETNINGER. UDDANNELSE OF KULTUR. 1798

0108-5506 See STATISTISKE EFTERRETNINGER. UDENRIGSHANDEL / DANMARKS STATISTIK. 5344

0108-5514 See STATISTISKE EFTERRETNINGER. ARBEJDSMARKED. 1540

0108-5522 See STATISTISKE EFTERRETNINGER. LANDBRUG. 157

0108-5530 See STATISTISKE EFTERRETNINGER. BEFOLKNING OG VALG. 5344

0108-5549 See STATISTISKE EFTERRETNINGER. BYGGE- OG ANLGSVIRKSOMHED. 5344

0108-5557 See STATISTISKE EFTERRETNINGER. FRERNE OG GRNLAND. 5344

0108-5565 See STATISTISKE EFTERRETNINGER. INDKOMST, FORBRUG OG PRISER. 1540

0108-5573 See STATISTISKE EFTERRETNINGER. GENEREL ERHVERVSSTATISTIK OG HANDEL. 5344

0108-5603 See STATISTISK MANEDSOVERSIGT. 1539

0108-5697 See LEVENDE BILLEDER. 4073

0108-6561 See HELTIDSLANDBRUGETS KONOMI / JORDBRUGSKONOMISK INSTITUT. 92

0108-6596 See CDR RESEARCH REPORT. 5195

0108-6898 See INUIT. 2739

0108-7398 See RAPPORT - STATENS JORDBRUGS KONOMISKE INSTITUT. 124

0108-7401 See RAPPORT / STATENS JORDBRUGSKONOMISK INSTITUT. 124

0108-7681 See ACTA CRYSTALLOGRAPHICA. SECTION B, STRUCTURAL SCIENCE. 1031

0108-7827 See SCANDINAVIAN ATLAS OF HISTORIC TOWNS. 2708

0108-8076 See BEFOLKNINGEN I KOMMUNERNE. 4550

0108-8408 See VIKING COLLECTION, THE. 2715

0108-8416 See NORTH-WESTERN EUROPEAN LANGUAGE EVOLUTION. 3306

0108-8777 See FREDERIKSBERG GENNEM TIDERNE. 2688

0109-1182 See JYLLANDS-POSTEN. 5799

0109-2502 See ENDODONTICS & DENTAL TRAUMATOLOGY. 1323

0109-2529 See FICHES D'IDENTIFICATION DU PLANCTON. 5583

0109-2537 See COPENHAGEN WORKING PAPERS IN LINGUISTICS. 3275

0109-2731 See ARSSKRIFT - LOLLAND-FALSTERS STIFTSMUSEUM 1983. 4084

0109-3967 See NORDICA. 3418

0109-5110 See DANISH HYDRAULICS. 2088

0109-5641 See DENTAL MATERIALS. 1321

0109-6249 See BYGNINGSARKOLOGISKE STUDIER. 294

0109-7318 See WINDPOWER MONTHLY. 1960

0109-8314 See VEJVISER I STATISTIKKEN. 5345

0109-9485 See OM GYMNASIET STUDENTERKURSUS OG HF. 1770

0110-0068 See MIORITA. 2699

0110-022X See NEW ZEALAND FAMILY PHYSICIAN, THE. 3738

0110-0246 See TAX REPORTS, NEW ZEALAND. 3062

0110-0262 See NEW ZEALAND INTERNATIONAL REVIEW. 4530

0110-0343 See N.Z.A.S.I.A.N. 2659

0110-0416 See YEAR BOOK AND PROCEEDINGS OF THE GENERAL ASSEMBLY - PRESBYTERIAN CHURCH OF NEW ZEALAND. 5069

0110-0424 See FLOW OF RESOURCES FROM NEW ZEALAND TO DEVELOPING COUNTRIES, THE. 2909

0110-0610 See TECHNICAL REPORT / PLANT PHYSIOLOGY DIVISION. 529

0110-0637 See NEW ZEALAND JOURNAL OF INDUSTRIAL RELATIONS. 1694

0110-070X See BUTTERWORTHS CURRENT LAW. 3125

0110-0718 See BULLETIN OF THE NEW ZEALAND NATIONAL SOCIETY FOR EARTHQUAKE ENGINEERING. 2019

0110-0815 See WISPAS. 5549

0110-0831 See NEW ZEALAND ANNUAL. 2510

0110-0858 See ISLANDS. 3397

0110-098X See NEW ZEALAND HOME AND BUILDING. 2902

0110-1048 See WHAT'S NEW IN FOREST RESEARCH. 2398

0110-1072 See OFFICE EQUIPMENT NEWS. 3485

0110-1102 See ART NEW ZEALAND. 339

0110-1242 See STATISTICAL HANDBOOK / NEW ZEALAND WOOD BOARD. 5360

0110-1277 See NEW ZEALAND ADMINISTRATIVE REPORTS : NZAR. 3016

0110-1439 See LANDSCAPE, THE. 2422

0110-1447 See NATIONAL MUSEUM OF NEW ZEALAND MISCELLANEOUS SERIES. 4093

0110-1471 See NEW ZEALAND WINGS. 30

0110-148x See NEW ZEALAND LAW REPORTS, THE. 3133

0110-1625 See TURNBULL LIBRARY RECORD, THE. 3254

0110-165X See NEW ZEALAND SOIL BUREAU BIBLIOGRAPHIC REPORT. 155

0110-1668 See NEW ZEALAND ENERGY JOURNAL. 1951

0110-1730 See COMMERCIAL FISHING. 2299

0110-1943 See REDUNDANCY IN NEW ZEALAND. 1705

0110-1951 See UNITED NATIONS HANDBOOK. 4537

0110-1978 See CROP RESEARCH NEWS. 169

0110-201X See NEW ZEALAND REPRESENTATIVES OVERSEAS. 4530

0110-2044 See DISCUSSION PAPER IN NATURAL RESOURCE ECONOMICS / DEPARTMENT OF AGRICULTURAL ECONOMICS AND FARM MANAGEMENT, MASSEY UNIVERSITY. 79

0110-2079 See N.Z. SOIL SURVEY REPORT. 179

0110-4187 See PROCEEDINGS OF THE NUTRITION SOCIETY OF NEW ZEALAND. 4198

0110-4373 See LIBRARY LIFE : NEW ZEALAND LIBRARY ASSOCIATION NEWSLETTER. 3226

0110-4381 See BUILD (WELLINGTON). 602

0110-4403 See TECHNICAL PAPER P - BUILDING RESEARCH ASSOCIATION OF NEW ZEALAND. 630

0110-4454 See OUT AUCKLAND. 2795

0110-4527 See BULLETIN - ENTOMOLOGICAL SOCIETY OF NEW ZEALAND. 5579

0110-4578 See PATIENT MANAGEMENT. 3626

0110-4691 See WATER AND SOIL MANAGEMENT PUBLICATION. 190

0110-4705 See WATER & SOIL MISCELLANEOUS PUBLICATION. 190

0110-4888 See BULLETIN OF NEW ZEALAND ART HISTORY. 345

0110-5124 See NEW ZEALAND ANTARCTIC RECORD. 2570

0110-5159 See ACCOUNTING AND FINANCE. 736

0110-5191 See PUBLIC SECTOR (WELLINGTON). 4677

0110-5205 See NZOI OCEANOGRAPHIC FIELD REPORT. 1453

0110-5221 See D. S. I. R. DISCUSSION PAPER. 5098

0110-540x See NEW ZEALAND JOURNAL OF ARCHAEOLOGY. 276

0110-5493 See JOURNAL - AVIATION HISTORICAL SOCIETY OF NEW ZEALAND. 25

0110-5566 See CHEMISTRY IN NEW ZEALAND. 971

0110-5647 See HISTORICAL JOURNAL / OTAKI HISTORICAL SOCIETY. 2669

0110-5698 See SHIPPING AND CARGO MOVEMENTS. 5456

0110-571X See NEW ZEALAND SPEECH-LANGUAGE THERAPISTS' JOURNAL, THE. 3889

0110-5787 See LISTENER WELLINGTON. 1134

0110-6007 See NEW ZEALAND CARTOGRAPHY AND GEOGRAPHIC INFORMATION SYSTEMS : THE JOURNAL OF THE NEW ZEALAND CARTOGRAPHIC SOCIETY. 2582

0110-6015 See WOOL (PALMERSTON NORTH). 5360

0110-6155 See RAILS (WELLINGTON). 5435

0110-6260 See ORCHARDIST OF NEW ZEALAND, THE. 180

0110-6295 See AUTOMATION AND CONTROL. 1217

0110-635X See JOURNAL - NEW ZEALAND DIETETIC ASSOCIATION. 4192

0110-6384 See NEW ZEALAND JOURNAL OF SPORTS MEDICINE, THE. 3955

0110-6465 See NEW ZEALAND JOURNAL OF ECOLOGY. 2219

0110-6589 See PROCEEDINGS ... ANNUAL CONFERENCE / AGRONOMY SOCIETY OF NEW ZEALAND. 121

0110-6813 See NATIONAL BUSINESS REVIEW. 697

0110-6929 See REPORT - HOSPITAL DESIGN AND EVALUATION UNIT, DEPARTMENT OF HEALTH. 3792

0110-7089 See TECHNICAL NOTE - GEOPHYSICS DIVISION. 1411
0110-7321 See INTER-INDUSTRY STUDY OF THE NEW ZEALAND ECONOMY. 1534
0110-7380 See NEW ZEALAND JOURNAL OF FRENCH STUDIES. 3416
0110-7747 See COMMUNITY MOVES. 4385
0110-7968 See NEW ZEALAND NURSING FORUM. 3862
0110-7992 See DEER FARMER, THE. 210
0110-8719 See URBAN SERIES MAP. 1400
0110-943X See RECORDS - NATIONAL MUSEUM OF NEW ZEALAND. 4095
0110-9510 See NEW ETHICALS CATALOGUE. 4334
0110-9561 See REPORT IPD.TS - INDUSTRIAL PROCESSING DIVISION, DEPARTMENT OF SCIENTIFIC AND INDUSTRIAL RESEARCH. 5145
0110-9596 See NEW ZEALAND JOURNAL OF BUSINESS. 699
0110-9618 See REPORT OF THE NEW ZEALAND FISHING INDUSTRY BOARD. 2311
0110-9901 See ANNUAL REPORT - NATIONAL HYDATIDS COUNCIL. 5503
0110-9944 See ENVIRONMENTAL RADIOACTIVITY ANNUAL REPORT. 2229
0111-0020 See NEW ETHICALS (AUCKLAND. 1976). 4317
0111-0608 See NEWZINDEX. 732
0111-1485 See JOURNAL OF THE NEW ZEALAND SOCIETY OF PERIODONTOLOGY. 1328
0111-1582 See NEW ZEALAND EDUCATION GAZETTE (WELLINGTON, N.Z. : 1980). 1768
0111-1957 See ALPHA (WELLINGTON, N.Z.). 5082
0111-199X See NEW ZEALAND POPULATION REVIEW. 4555
0111-2694 See NEW ZEALAND TREE GROWER. 2389
0111-3232 See FRESHWATER CATCH. 2304
0111-4239 See DISTRICT COURT REPORTS. 2963
0111-431X See NEW ZEALAND PHARMACY. 4318
0111-4506 See GREENPEACE NEWS. 2216
0111-5383 See FAUNA OF NEW ZEALAND. 5608
0111-5871 See TU TANGATA. 2671
0111-6304 See NEW ZEALAND HEALTH REVIEW. 4793
0111-6339 See AGRICULTURAL POLICY PROCEEDINGS. 51
0111-686X See NEWSLETTER - NEW ZEALAND NATURE CONSERVATION COUNCIL. 2200
0111-7351 See SOCIAL WORK REVIEW (NEWTON, AUCKLAND, N.Z.). 5310
0111-7653 See AUCKLAND-WAIKATO HISTORICAL JOURNAL. 2611
0111-8129 See FRI BULLETIN / FOREST RESEARCH INSTITUTE, NEW ZEALAND FOREST SERVICE. 2383
0111-8234 See CURRENT PUBLICATIONS / NEW ZEALAND AGRICULTURAL ENGINEERING INSTITUTE. 158
0111-8854 See MENTALITIES. 4604
0111-915X See DAIRY EXPORTER. 193
0111-9176 See NEW ZEALAND STATISTICIAN, THE. 5334
0111-9184 See SPECIAL PUBLICATION / AGRONOMY SOCIETY OF NEW ZEALAND. 137
0111-932X See TECHNICAL REPORT SOUTHERN SOUTH ISLAND REGION, AGRICULTURAL RESEARCH DIVISION, MINISTRY OF AGRICULTURE & FISHERIES. 140
0111-946X See TRANSACTIONS OF THE INSTITUTION OF PROFESSIONAL ENGINEERS NEW ZEALAND, ELECTRICAL/MECHANICAL/CHEMICAL ENGINEERING SECTION. 1999
0111-9508 See TRANSACTIONS OF THE INSTITUTION OF PROFESSIONAL ENGINEERS NEW ZEALAND, CIVIL ENGINEERING SECTION. 2033
0111-977X See STREAMLAND. 188
0112-0212 See NEW ZEALAND JOURNAL OF ENVIRONMENTAL HEALTH. 4793

0112-0581 See CANTERBURY LAW REVIEW, THE. 2948
0112-0603 See AGRICULTURAL POLICY DISCUSSION PAPER. 51
0112-109X See NEW ZEALAND JOURNAL OF PSYCHOLOGY (CHRISTCHURCH. 1983). 4605
0112-1227 See JOURNAL OF NEW ZEALAND LITERATURE : JNZL. 3400
0112-1642 See SPORTS MEDICINE (AUCKLAND). 3956
0112-224X See NEW ZEALAND JOURNAL OF ADULT LEARNING. 1801
0112-2789 See ON FILM. 4075
0112-3599 See COMMUNITY MENTAL HEALTH IN NEW ZEALAND. 5280
0112-398X See WASTELINES. 2183
0112-465X See RECORD / NEW ZEALAND GEOLOGICAL SURVEY. 1393
0112-4927 See SURVEILLANCE (WELLINGTON). 5522
0112-4951 See DANCE NEWS WELLINGTON. 1312
0112-6059 See WOOL REPORT NEW ZEALAND. 5360
0112-6210 See NEW ZEALAND MUSEUMS JOURNAL. 359
0112-739X See ANNUAL REVIEW OF THE NEW ZEALAND SHEEP AND BEEF INDUSTRY. 206
0112-7438 See NURSING PRAXIS IN NEW ZEALAND INC. 3865
0112-8191 See WORKING PAPERS IN ECONOMICS HAMILTON. 1527
0112-8787 See NEW ZEALAND HERALD, THE. 5807
0112-8868 See NEW ZEALAND MEDICAL WORKFORCE STATISTICS 3661
0112-8949 See NEW ZEALAND FLIGHT SAFETY. 30
0112-9120 See NEW ZEALAND MONTHLY REVIEW 1986. 2510
0112-921X See NEW ZEALAND SOCIOLOGY. 5252
0112-9341 See ILLUSIONS. 4072
0112-9376 See ARTS ADVOCATE WELLINGTON. 342
0112-9392 See GOODS AND SERVICES TAX LEGISLATION. 4727
0112-949X See SUPERMARKETING AUCKLAND. 2359
0112-9597 See NEW ZEALAND FORESTRY. 2389
0112-9643 See PUBLICATION - VETERINARY CONTINUING EDUCATION, MASSEY UNIVERSITY. 5519
0112-9724 See NZTP OVERSEAS MARKET RESEARCH SERIES. 5486
0112-9767 See NZTD DOMESTIC RESEARCH SERIES. 5486
0112-9783 See NZTD REGIONAL RESEARCH SERIES. 5486
0112-9910 See SOUTHLAND TIMES. 5807
0113-0501 See PETROLEUM EXPLORATION IN NEW ZEALAND NEWS. 4272
0113-051X See INVERMAY TECHNICAL REPORT. 5116
0113-0846 See PACIFIC WORLD. 2201
0113-0994 See STUDIES IN RESOURCE MANAGEMENT. 2206
0113-1044 See OCCASIONAL PAPER / NEW ZEALAND INSTITUTE OF INTERNATIONAL AFFAIRS. 4485
0113-1060 See BIO-INPHARMA. 3686
0113-1133 See STATISTICS PUBLICATIONS CATALOGUE. 5342
0113-1206 See CUISINE AUCKLAND. 2789
0113-1850 See GROCERS' REVIEW. 2342
0113-1982 See NEW ZEALAND OUTLOOK. 2510
0113-1990 See FRONTLINE DUNEDIN. 3724
0113-2180 See NEW ZEALAND FISHERIES TECHNICAL REPORT. 2309
0113-2261 See NEW ZEALAND FISHERIES RESEARCH BULLETIN. 2309
0113-227X See NEW ZEALAND FISHERIES OCCASIONAL PUBLICATION. 2309

0113-2288 See NEW ZEALAND FISHERIES DATA REPORT. 2309
0113-2326 See CATERING MANAGEMENT (AUCKLAND, N.Z.). 2330
0113-2415 See ANTIPODAS : JOURNAL OF HISPANIC STUDIES OF THE UNIVERSITY OF AUCKLAND. 3362
0113-2431 See GRINZ YEARBOOK. 2452
0113-2792 See NEW ZEALAND WOOL MARKET REVIEW. 5354
0113-3128 See NEW ZEALAND FOREST INDUSTRIES. 2403
0113-3667 See DEMOGRAPHIC TRENDS. 4552
0113-4485 See RESEARCH REPORT. 127
0113-4507 See DISCUSSION PAPER - AGRIBUSINESS & ECONOMICS RESEARCH UNIT, LINCOLN COLLEGE. 79
0113-4566 See ARCHITECTURE NEW ZEALAND. 290
0113-4957 See NZ BUSINESS. 700
0113-5201 See LMS ALERT. NEUROPSYCHOTHERAPEUTICS. 4314
0113-5376 See ORAL HISTORY IN NEW ZEALAND. 2670
0113-583X See POTTER. 2593
0113-6526 See INDEX NEW ZEALAND [MICROFORM] : INNZ. 417
0113-6895 See MARKETING BULLETIN - DEPARTMENT OF MARKETING, MASSEY UNIVERSITY. 930
0113-7441 See MUSIC IN NEW ZEALAND. 4133
0113-7492 See NEW ZEALAND NATURAL SCIENCES. 1358
0113-7832 See ARCHAEOLOGY IN NEW ZEALAND. 257
0113-7867 See ENGLISH IN AOTEAROA. 1894
0113-8138 See NEW ZEALAND INTERNATIONAL BUSINESS. 699
0113-8286 See ASMAL NEW ZEALAND TRAVEL. 5462
0113-8901 See FOOD INDUSTRY NEWS AUCKLAND. 2337
0113-9320 See NEW ZEALAND MANUFACTURER 1992. 3485
0113-9606 See NEW ZEALAND FISHERMAN. 4908
0114-0655 See NEW ZEALAND RECENT LAW REVIEW. 3016
0114-0671 See NEW ZEALAND JOURNAL OF CROP AND HORTICULTURAL SCIENCE. 2425
0114-0892 See CLINICAL PHARMACOKINETICS. DRUG DATA HANDBOOK. 4296
0114-1090 See TE PUNA MATAURANGA: THE NATIONAL LIBRARY OF NEW ZEALAND NEWSLETTER. 3252
0114-1562 See TRANSACTIONS OF THE INSTITUTION OF PROFESSIONAL ENGINEERS NEW ZEALAND. GENERAL SECTION. 2182
0114-2119 See KEY STATISTICS / DEPARTMENT OF STATISTICS, NEW ZEALAND. 5330
0114-2402 See DRUG INVESTIGATION. 4300
0114-2550 See GP WEEKLY. 3738
0114-3670 See ASMAL AUSTRALIA TRAVEL. 5462
0114-3727 See NEW ZEALAND HEALTH & HOSPITAL. 3789
0114-4022 See NEW ZEALAND AGRICHEMICAL AND PLANT PROTECTION MANUAL. 112
0114-412X See SENTINEL WELLINGTON. 1989. 133
0114-4138 See TAKAHE CHRISTCHURCH. 3444
0114-4189 See NEW ZEALAND LEGACY : JOURNAL OF THE NEW ZEALAND FEDERATION OF HISTORICAL SOCIETIES. 2670
0114-4553 See PROCEEDINGS OF THIS SOCIETY'S SEMINAR - SHEEP & BEEF CATTLE SOCIETY OF THE NEW ZEALAND VETERINARY ASSOCIATION. 219
0114-4596 See NEW ZEALAND JOURNAL OF COMPUTING. 1197
0114-5916 See DRUG SAFETY. 4301
0114-6106 See AUSTRALASIAN INDUSTRY REPORTER. 1598
0114-6912 See ECONOMY WIDE CENSUS. 613
0114-6971 See OVERSEAS POSTS. 4672

0114-7366 *See* REVIEW (NEW ZEALAND MOUNTAIN LANDS INSTITUTE). 2204
0114-7579 *See* LANDLINE WELLINGTON. 1386
0114-8087 *See* PARKS & RECREATION AUCKLAND. 4707
0114-8257 *See* IRHACE JOURNAL. 2606
0114-9954 *See* REACTIONS WEEKLY. 4327
0115-0022 *See* SYLVATROP. 2396
0115-0073 *See* PHILIPPINE DEVELOPMENT. 1578
0115-0235 *See* BUSINESS OUTLOOK IN THE PHILIPPINES AND ASIA. 651
0115-0243 *See* PHILIPPINE QUARTERLY OF CULTURE AND SOCIETY. 5253
0115-0324 *See* PHILIPPINE JOURNAL OF MICROBIOLOGY AND INFECTIOUS DISEASES, THE. 568
0115-0405 *See* CLSU SCIENTIFIC JOURNAL. 75
0115-0456 *See* FPRDI JOURNAL : A PUBLICATION OF THE FOREST PRODUCTS RESEARCH AND DEVELOPMENT INSTITUT, NATIONAL SCIENCE AND TECHNOLOGY AUTHORITY. 2400
0115-0553 *See* KALIKASAN, THE PHILIPPINE JOURNAL OF BIOLOGY. 462
0115-074X *See* ADB QUARTERLY REVIEW. 768
0115-0804 *See* PHILIPPINE PHYTOPATHOLOGY. 521
0115-0928 *See* PHILIPPINE FARMERS' JOURNAL. 120
0115-0944 *See* INTERNATIONAL RICE RESEARCH NEWSLETTER. 174
0115-0960 *See* CANOPY INTERNATIONAL. 2377
0115-1029 *See* PHILIPPINE JOURNAL OF CARDIOLOGY. 3709
0115-138X *See* JOURNAL - INTEGRATED BAR OF THE PHILIPPINES. 2986
0115-1401 *See* C. B. REVIEW. 1467
0115-1541 *See* COCONUT FARMERS BULLETIN, THE. 167
0115-1657 *See* MONTHLY BUSINESS & TAX BULLETIN. 3102
0115-1746 *See* PHILIPPINE BUSINESS REVIEW. 703
0115-1746 *See* POLICY ANALYSIS. 703
0115-1851 *See* YEARBOOK OF LABOR STATISTICS (MANILA). 1541
0115-2009 *See* NORTHWESTERN MINDANAO RESEARCH JOURNAL. 2660
0115-2025 *See* PHILIPPINE JOURNAL OF CROP SCIENCE, THE. 181
0115-2181 *See* INITIATIVES IN POPULATION. 4553
0115-2203 *See* COMPILATION OF PRESIDENTIAL DECREES - (PHILIPPINES). 2954
0115-222X *See* GRAINS JOURNAL. 202
0115-2254 *See* ASIAN PRESS AND MEDIA DIRECTORY, THE. 756
0115-2408 *See* JOURNAL OF NORTHERN LUZON. 1758
0115-2440 *See* AGRIASIA / PRODUCED BY AGRICULTURAL INFORMATION BANK FOR ASIA. 48
0115-2467 *See* IRRI REPORTER, THE. 97
0115-2483 *See* PHILIPPINE LAW GAZETTE. 3142
0115-2629 *See* PHILIPPINE LABOR REVIEW. 1701
0115-2742 *See* MINDANAO JOURNAL. 2658
0115-2807 *See* CENTRAL BANK CIRCULARS AND MEMORANDA. 782
0115-3153 *See* PHILIPPINE JOURNAL OF PSYCHOLOGY. 4608
0115-3226 *See* BULLETIN OF THE AMERICAN HISTORICAL COLLECTION. 2647
0115-3757 *See* ATOMEDIA, PHILIPPINES. 2154
0115-3862 *See* IRRI RESEARCH PAPER SERIES. 97
0115-3870 *See* REVIEW, THE. 2508
0115-4389 *See* ICLARM STUDIES AND REVIEWS. 2305
0115-4419 *See* INDUSTRY DIGEST. 1612
0115-4435 *See* ICLARM CONFERENCE PROCEEDINGS. 2305
0115-4443 *See* FISHERIES TODAY. 2302

0115-4494 *See* ICLARM REPORT. 2305
0115-4516 *See* NUTRISYON. 4195
0115-4974 *See* ASIAN AQUACULTURE. 2296
0115-5547 *See* ICLARM TECHNICAL REPORTS. 2305
0115-5679 *See* AGHAM. 5081
0115-5784 *See* ANIMAL FEED SERVICE BULLETIN. 200
0115-5997 *See* ICLARM BIBLIOGRAPHIES. 2317
0115-6500 *See* PHILIPPINE JOURNAL OF COCONUT STUDIES, THE. 181
0115-690X *See* JOURNAL OF FISHERIES & AQUACULTURE. 2306
0115-7809 *See* SCIENCE DILIMAN. 5151
0115-8007 *See* IBON FACTS AND FIGURES. 1494
0115-8724 *See* PHILIPPINE SCIENCE & TECHNOLOGY ABSTRACTS. 5175
0115-8805 *See* PHILIPPINE YEARBOOK OF INTERNATIONAL LAW, THE. 3133
0115-8848 *See* TRANSACTIONS OF THE NATIONAL ACADEMY OF SCIENCE AND TECHNOLOGY. 5166
0115-8864 *See* SINAG-AGHAM. 5157
0115-9003 *See* PHILIPPINE SEAS. 3182
0115-9011 *See* PHILIPPINE REVIEW OF ECONOMICS & BUSINESS, THE. 1512
0115-9143 *See* JOURNAL OF PHILIPPINE DEVELOPMENT. 1614
0115-9321 *See* BAGONG PAMANA. 3365
0116-0257 *See* EAST ASIAN PASTORAL REVIEW. 4954
0116-0443 *See* PHILIPPINE INQUIRER. 5807
0116-0516 *See* STUDIES IN PHILIPPINE LINGUISTICS. 3326
0116-0710 *See* ANNALS OF TROPICAL RESEARCH. 5083
0116-0923 *See* KASARINLAN. 2656
0116-1105 *See* ASIAN DEVELOPMENT REVIEW. 1547
0116-1377 *See* BRACKISHWATER AQUACULTURE ABSTRACTS. 2297
0116-2470 *See* NATIONAL MIDWEEK. 2659
0116-2675 *See* VITAL STATISTICS REPORT. 5346
0116-290X *See* NAGA, THE ICLARM QUARTERLY. 2308
0116-2993 *See* ASIAN ENVIRONMENT. 2161
0116-3000 *See* KEY INDICATORS OF DEVELOPING ASIAN AND PACIFIC COUNTRIES. 1571
0116-3140 *See* PCARRD MONITOR, THE. 119
0116-3655 *See* HISTORICAL BULLETIN / PHILIPPINE HISTORICAL ASSOCIATION. 2652
0116-4252 *See* NCCP NEWSLETTER. 4483
0116-4260 *See* TUGON. 5006
0116-4325 *See* ROOT CROPS DIGEST. 130
0116-5038 *See* PHILIPPINE NEWS & FEATURES. 2662
0116-5461 *See* WCCI FORUM. 1908
0116-5747 *See* PEACEMAKER. 2270
0116-6107 *See* NRCP DIRECTORY. 5135
0116-6360 *See* JUSTICE & PEACE REVIEW. 4510
0116-6514 *See* ASIAN FISHERIES SCIENCE. 2296
0116-709X *See* PRAXIS: JOURNAL OF POLITICAL SCIENCE. 4492
0116-7294 *See* PHILIPPINE TECHNOLOGY JOURNAL. 5138
0116-7847 *See* CMU JOURNAL OF SCIENCE. 5095
0116-7960 *See* PHILIPPINE POPULATION JOURNAL. 590
0116-8657 *See* BARRISTERS BULLETIN. 2940
0117-0171 *See* CONSUMERS' FORUM. 1296
0117-0481 *See* ASIAN DEVELOPMENT OUTLOOK : ADO. 1547
0117-0503 *See* PHILIPPINE JOURNAL OF BIOTECHNOLOGY. 3695
0117-0686 *See* NATIONAL MUSEUM PAPERS. 4168
0117-0880 *See* PROGRAM REPORT - INTERNATIONAL RICE RESEARCH INSTITUTE. 183

0117-1577 *See* ALTERNATIVE LAW FORUM. 2932
0117-3138 *See* SOLIDARIDAD SAN JUAN, METRO MANILA. 4496
0120-0097 *See* REVISTA DEL INSTITUTO NACIONAL DE MEDICINA LEGAL DE COLOMBIA. 3742
0120-0143 *See* FITOPATOLOGIA COLOMBIANA. 510
0120-0216 *See* ALEPH (MANIZALES, COLOMBIA). 3359
0120-033X *See* REVISTA UNIVERSIDAD EAFIT. 4683
0120-0534 *See* REVISTA LATINOAMERICANA DE PSICOLOGIA. 4616
0120-0542 *See* BOLETIN CIENTIFICO - CENTRO DE INVESTIGACIONES OCEANOGRAFICAS E HIDROGRAFICAS. 1447
0120-0550 *See* IMPUESTO A LA RENTA; REGIMEN LEGAL TRIBUTARIO. 4731
0120-0747 *See* ESTUDIOS RURALES LATINOAMERICANOS. 82
0120-0755 *See* DIRECTORIO FINANCIERO NACIONAL. 787
0120-0976 *See* REVISTA INTERAMERICANA DE BIBLIOTECOLOGIA / UNIVERSIDAD DE ANTIOQUIA, ESCUELA INTERAMERICANA DE BIBLIOTECOLOGIA. 3246
0120-0992 *See* CUADERNOS DE FILOSOFIA Y LETRAS. 4344
0120-1034 *See* NEUROLOGIA EN COLOMBIA. 3840
0120-1115 *See* REVISTA UNIVERSIDAD PONTIFICIA BOLIVARIANA. 2492
0120-1182 *See* REVISTA DE LA SOCIEDAD COLOMBIANA DE ENDOCRINOLOGIA. 3733
0120-1204 *See* BOLETIN BIBLIOGRAFICO (REGIONAL CENTER FOR BOOK PROMOTION IN LATIN AMERICA AND THE CARIBBEAN). 4824
0120-1395 *See* CORREO DE LOS ANDES. 1818
0120-1433 *See* ORQUIDEOLOGIA. 2427
0120-1468 *See* FRANCISCANUM. 4347
0120-159X *See* REVISTA COLOMBIANA DE SOCIOLOGIA / DEPARTAMENTO DE SOCIOLOGIA, UNIVERSIDAD NACIONAL. 5256
0120-1743 *See* CIRCULAR (INGEOMINAS). 1372
0120-1751 *See* REVISTA COLOMBIANA DE ESTADISTICA. 5337
0120-1824 *See* CASSAVA NEWSLETTER. 166
0120-193X *See* CARTA ADMINISTRATIVA. 4702
0120-1980 *See* LECTURAS MATEMATICAS. 3516
0120-2367 *See* REVISTA UNIVERSIDAD DE ANTIOQUIA. 1094
0120-2448 *See* AMC. ACTA MEDICA COLOMBIANA. 3794
0120-2510 *See* BOLETIN DE ANTROPOLOGIA. 232
0120-2537 *See* HUELLAS : REVISTA DE LA UNIVERSIDAD DEL NORTE. 1092
0120-2596 *See* LECTURAS DE ECONOMIA. 1572
0120-2634 *See* ARROZ EN LAS AMERICAS. 63
0120-2804 *See* REVISTA COLOMBIANA DE QUIMICA. 991
0120-2812 *See* ACTA AGRONOMICA (UNIVERSIDAD NACIONAL DE COLOMBIA. FACULTAD DE CIENCIAS AGROPECUARIAS). 43
0120-288X *See* ABSTRACTS ON CASSAVA (MANIHOT ESCULENTA CRANTZ). 161
0120-2944 *See* RESUMENES ANALITICOS SOBRE PASTOS TROPICALES. 128
0120-3045 *See* MAGUARE : REVISTA DEL DEPARTAMENTO DE ANTROPOLOGIA DE LA UNIVERSIDAD NACIONAL DE COLOMBIA. 240
0120-3088 *See* REVISTA JAVERIANA (BOGOTA). 2552
0120-338X *See* FORMA Y FUNCION. 3282
0120-3479 *See* LENGUAJE CALI. 3297
0120-3495 *See* ANUARIO ESTADISTICO DE ANTIOQUIA. 5322
0120-3576 *See* COYUNTURA ECONOMICA. 1554
0120-3584 *See* DESARROLLO Y SOCIEDAD. 1555
0120-3797 *See* AVANCES EN PSICOLOGIA CLINICA LATINOAMERICANA. 4575

0120-386X See REVISTA DE LA FACULTAD NACIONAL DE SALUD PUBLICA. 4799

0120-3878 See PERSPECTIVAS EN PSICOLOGIA. 4607

0120-3959 See ANALES DEL INSTITUTO DE INVESTIGACIONES MARINAS DE PUNTA DE BETIN. 552

0120-4157 See BIOMEDICA. 3556

0120-4203 See CONTADURIA UNIVERSIDAD DE ANTIOQUIA. 741

0120-4289 See REVISTA / CAMARA DE COMERCIO DE BOGOTA. 4683

0120-4335 See COLOMBIA, CIENCIA Y TECNOLOGIA. 5095

0120-4807 See UNIVERSITAS HUMANISTICA. 1851

0120-5099 See SERIE MEMORIAS DE EVENTOS CIENTIFICOS COLOMBIANOS. 527

0120-5307 See INVESTIGACION Y EDUCACION EN ENFERMERIA : REVISTA DE LA FACULTAD DE ENFERMERIA, UNIVERSIDAD DE ANTIOQUIA. 3857

0120-5323 See UNIVERSITAS PHILOSOPHICA. 4364

0120-5331 See CIFRAS. 5799

0120-5587 See LINGUISTICA Y LITERATURA : REVISTA DEL DEPARTAMENTO DE ESPANOL. 3299

0120-5722 See NOTICIERO TECNICO SOBRE INCENDIOS. 2292

0120-6281 See BOLETIN DE ESTADISTICA (BOGOTA, COLOMBIA). 5323

0120-6478 See INDICE HISPANOAMERICANO DE CIENCIAS SOCIALES. 5203

0120-6516 See GLOTTA. 3284

0120-7040 See BANCA Y FINANZAS. 773

0120-7067 See NUCLEARES (BOGOTA). 1952

0120-7458 See REVISTA LATINOAMERICANA DE SEXOLOGIA. 4616

0120-7504 See UNIMETRO : ORGANO DE INFORMACION E INVESTIGACION. 3648

0120-8098 See TRIMESTRE GEOGRAFICO. 2578

0120-8195 See NUEVA REVISTA COLOMBIANA DE FOLCLOR. 2323

0120-8268 See REVISTA DE LA ACADEMIA COLOMBIANA DE HISTORIA ECLESIASTICA. 2758

0120-8322 See COLOMBIA MEDICA : CM. 3567

0120-8446 See EDUCACION HOY. 1737

0120-8462 See CUADERNOS DE FILOSOFIA LATINOAMERICANA / ORGANO DE DIVULGACION DE LA FACULTAD DE FILOSOFIA Y EL CENTRO DE ENSENANZA DESESCOLARIZADA DE LA UNIVERSIDAD SANTO TOMAS. 4344

0120-9299 See INDICADORES DE COYUNTURA. 1566

0120-9493 See BOLETIN DE LA ACADEMIA DE HISTORIA DEL VALLE DEL CAUCA. 2723

0120-9523 See BOLETIN DE MINAS Y ENERGIA. 2135

0120-9906 See ACTA CLINICA ODONTOLOGICA. 1315

0120-9965 See AGRONOMIA COLOMBIANA. 56

0121-0017 See REVISTA ANTIOGUENA DE ECONOMIA Y DESARROLLO. 1518

0121-0203 See REVISTA DE ASCOLBI / ASOCIATION COLOMBIANA DE BIBLIOTECOLOGOS Y DOCUMENTALISTAS, ASCOLBI. 3246

0121-0254 See SERIE DE DOCUMENTACION / CORPORACION NACIONAL DE INVESTIGACION Y FOMENTO FORESTAL. 2395

0121-0335 See FORO DEL JURISTA. 2972

0121-0793 See IATREIA MEDELLIN. 3585

0121-1242 See LIBRO EN AMERICA LATINA Y EL CARIBE, EL. 4830

0121-2079 See INFORMES ANTROPOLOGICOS / INSTITUTO COLOMBIANO DE ANTROPOLOGIA. 238

0121-2354 See UNIDAD INDIGENA. 247

0121-2613 See INDICE COLOMBIANO DE ECONOMIA Y NEGOCIOS. 682

0121-3776 See KINETOSCOPIO, EL. 4073

0121-4802 See ESTRATEGIA ECONOMICA Y FINANCIERA. 1489

0121-5183 See BEYOND LAW / MAS ALLA DEL DERECHO. 2941

0121-6279 See EXTERNADISTA : REVISTA DE LA UNIVERSIDAD EXTERNADO DE COLOMBIA. 2968

0125-0140 See BUSINESS IN THAILAND. 649

0125-0477 See BUSINESS REVIEW. 652

0125-0485 See KAEN KASET. 101

0125-0492 See STUDIA ISLAMIKA. 5045

0125-1570 See WARASAN PHESATCHESAT MAHA WITTHAYALAI MAHIDON. 4332

0125-1643 See WARASAN KROMKANPAET LAE ANAMAI. 3650

0125-1759 See JOURNAL OF FERROCEMENT. 632

0125-1783 See ENFO. 2165

0125-2488 See PASAA. 3310

0125-4111 See ISDS-SEA BULLETIN. 4815

0125-5088 See ENVIRONMENTAL SANITATION REVIEWS. 5533

0125-605X See QUARTERLY BULLETIN - BANK OF THAILAND. 805

0125-6068 See THAI JOURNAL OF SURGERY. 3976

0125-6459 See THAILAND FOREIGN AFFAIRS NEWSLETTER / INFORMATION DEPARTMENT, MINISTRY OF FOREIGN AFFAIRS. 4498

0125-6491 See WETCHASAN SATTAWAPHAET. 5527

0125-6637 See THAI LIFE. 2770

0125-6718 See ASIAN-PACIFIC POPULATION PROGRAMME NEWS. 4549

0125-6726 See BUFFALO BULLETIN. 5579

0125-7382 See ASEAN INVESTOR. 891

0125-8370 See WITTHAYASAN KASETSAT. SAKHA SANGKHOMMASAT. 5226

0125-877X See ASIAN PACIFIC JOURNAL OF ALLERGY AND IMMUNOLOGY. 3666

0125-9008 See BACA. 3193

0125-9156 See BERITA IPTEK. 5088

0125-9318 See MENARA PERKEBUNAN. 108

0125-9407 See ACTA PHARMACEUTICA. 4288

0125-9644 See LEMBARAN PUBLIKASI PUSAT PENGEMBANGAN TEKNOLOGI MINYAK DAN GAS BUMI LEMIGAS. 4263

0125-9660 See BULLETIN (LEMBAGA PENELITIAN PETERNAKAN (INDONESIA)). 208

0125-975X See BIOTROP SPECIAL PUBLICATION. 448

0125-992X See JURNAL KEPENDIDIKAN. 1899

0126-0057 See TRUBUS. 142

0126-0251 See MAJALAH DEMOGRAFI INDONESIA. 4554

0126-0537 See AGRIVITA. 55

0126-0901 See MEDIKA. 4315

0126-0979 See KESEHATAN MASYARAKAT. 4788

0126-0979 See MAJALAH KESEHATAN MASYARAKAT. 4789

0126-1010 See BERITA INDUSTRI. 1548

0126-1061 See GEOLOGI INDONESIA. 1377

0126-1118 See DUTA RIMBA / PERUM PERHUTANI. 2378

0126-1126 See PROCEEDINGS OF THE ANNUAL CONVENTION - INDONESIAN PETROLEUM ASSOCIATION. 4275

0126-1436 See BULLETIN PENELITIAN HORTIKULTURA. 2411

0126-155X See EKONOMI DAN KEUANGAN INDONESIA. 1488

0126-1568 See ATOM INDONESIA. 4446

0126-1924 See BULLETIN OF THE BRACKISHWATER AQUACULTURE DEVELOPMENT CENTRE. 2298

0126-222X See ANALISIS CSIS. 4515

0126-2491 See KOMUNIKA. 3293

0126-2696 See ENERGI INDONESIA. 1938

0126-2912 See STATISTIK INDONESIA. STATISTICAL YEARBOOK OF INDONESIA. 5342

0126-3692 See PELITA BPKS. 5300

0126-3919 See KEADAAN ANGKATAN KERJA DI INDONESIA. 1682

0126-4397 See STATISTIK KEUANGAN DESA JAWA DAN MADURA. 4700

0126-4613 See DIRECTORY PERUSAHAAN BIS (ANTAR PROPINSI). 5381

0126-4737 See MAJALAH PEMBINAAN BAHASA INDONESIA. 3300

0126-494X See STRUKTUR BIAYA BUS DAN TRUK UMUM. 5426

0126-5016 See JURNAL ANTROPOLOGI DAN SOSIOLOGI. 239

0126-5059 See DEWAN SASTERA. 3381

0126-513X See JURNAL INSTITUSI JURUTERA MALAYSIA. 1984

0126-5164 See JERNAL BAHAGIAN PERANCANG DAN PENYELIDIKAN PELAJARAN. 1755

0126-5172 See JERNAL SEJARAH. 2654

0126-5180 See DISKUSI. 2503

0126-5245 See ASEAN REVIEW. 2645

0126-5318 See NATURE MALAYSIANA. 4169

0126-5539 See WARTA GEOLOGI. 1401

0126-561X See FEDERATION MUSEUMS JOURNAL. 4087

0126-5644 See JEBAT. 2654

0126-5652 See MALAYSIAN VETERINARY JOURNAL, THE. 5516

0126-575X See PLANTER, THE. 120

0126-5865 See MONTHLY BULLETIN. 5076

0126-5885 See MONTHLY STATISTICAL BULLETIN / MAJLIS PENGELUAR-PENGELUAR GETAH MALAYSIA. 5078

0126-5903 See WARTA PASARAN LADA / PEPPER MARKET BULLETIN. 2361

0126-5938 See DAKWAH. 5042

0126-6039 See SAINS MALAYSIANA. 5149

0126-6101 See GEOGRAPHICA (KUALA LUMPUR). 2562

0126-6128 See PERTANIKA. 119

0126-6160 See LAND DEVELOPMENT DIGEST. 4840

0126-6187 See BULETIN PERSATUAN GEOLOGI MALAYSIA. 1368

0126-6209 See ABU TECHNICAL REVIEW. 1125

0126-625X See ACCOUNTING JOURNAL, THE. 737

0126-6322 See JERNAL UNDANG-UNDANG. 3131

0126-6373 See TENGGARA. 3444

0126-6403 See ASIAN DEFENCE JOURNAL. 4037

0126-642X See MALAYSIAN GEOGRAPHERS. 2568

0126-6705 See BULLETIN OF THE MALAYSIAN MATHEMATICAL SOCIETY. 3498

0126-7000 See ILMU ALAM. 2653

0126-7280 See ALAM SEKITAR. 2223

0126-7353 See JOURNAL OF THE MALAYSIAN BRANCH OF THE ROYAL ASIATIC SOCIETY. 2656

0126-7663 See JOURNAL OF SCIENCE AND MATHEMATICS EDUCATION IN SOUTHEAST ASIA. 1758

0126-7752 See JOURNAL OF MEDICAL AND HEALTH LABORATORY TECHNOLOGY, MALAYSIA. 3596

0126-7809 See MAJALAH PERPUSTAKAAN MALAYSIA. 3229

0126-7906 See MALAYSIAN JOURNAL OF SCIENCE. 5127

0126-7930 See BUSINESSCOPE. 654

0126-7957 See JOURNAL - KEMENTERIAN PELAJARAN MALAYSIA. 1756

0126-8023 See DENTAL JOURNAL OF MALAYSIA. 1321

0126-8252 See LAPORAN TAHUNAN ... KETUA PENGARAH INSURANS. 2886

0126-8309 See LAPURAN TAHUNAN - MAJLIS PENGELUAR-PENGELUAR GETAH MALAYSIA. 5076

0126-852X See ISLAMIC HERALD. 5043

0126-8635 See MALAYSIAN JOURNAL OF PATHOLOGY, THE. 3896

0126-8643 See MALAYSIAN APPLIED BIOLOGY. 463

0126-8856 See PERANGKAAN TAHUNAN PERIKANAN. 2317

0126-8988 See JURNAL SEJARAH MELAKA. 2656

0126-9070 See KIMIA. 983

0126-9089 See ULASAN GETAH MALAYSIA. 5078

0126-9208 See PROCEEDINGS OF THE MALAYSIAN BIOCHEMICAL SOCIETY CONFERENCE. 492

0126-9223 See KUKILA. 5618

0126-950X See UTUSAN KONSUMER. 1300

0126-9569 See JURNAL SAINS - INSTITUT PENYELIDIKAN GETAH MALAYSIA. 5122

0126-9682 See STANDARD CATALOGUE OF MALAYSIA-SINGAPORE-BRUNEI COINS AND PAPER MONEY. 2783

0126-9801 See DIRECTORY - PERSEKUTUAN PEKILANG-PEKILANG MALAYSIA. 3478

0126-9860 See SEATRAD BULLETIN. 2150

0127-0095 See NEGARA. 5210

0127-0192 See MAPPS NEWSLETTER. 517

0127-0206 See MALAYAN NATURALIST. 4167

0127-0249 See PORIM BULLETIN. 2353

0127-0257 See PORIM TECHNOLOGY. 120

0127-0362 See LABOUR AND MANPOWER REPORT / MINISTRY OF LABOUR AND MANPOWER. 1685

0127-046X See SOUTHEAST ASIAN REVIEW OF ENGLISH. 3322

0127-0605 See PALMOIL UPDATE. 1621

0127-1164 See BIBLIOGRAFI BUKU-BUKU DALAM BAHASA MALAYSIA. 408

0127-1253 See PETUNJUK-PETUNJUK BURUH. 1701

0127-1474 See MALAYSIAN JOURNAL OF TROPICAL GEOGRAPHY. 2568

0127-1563 See SINGAPORE STAMP CATALOGUE IN FULL COLOUR. 2787

0127-1857 See PURBA. 2662

0127-2012 See INFOFISH INTERNATIONAL. 2305

0127-2179 See DIRECTORY OF AMERICAN BUSINESS IN MALAYSIA. 666

0127-2209 See OCCASIONAL PAPER - PORIM. 1027

0127-2284 See AL-NAHDAH. 5041

0127-2462 See ANNUAL COMPANIES HANDBOOK / THE KUALA LUMPUR STOCK EXCHANGE. 890

0127-2969 See MALAYSIAN RUBBER REVIEW. 5076

0127-3051 See INDUSTRIAL LAW REPORTS (KUALA LUMPUR, MALAYSIA). 3149

0127-306X See PLANTI NEWS. 2428

0127-3957 See JURNAL BAHASA MODEN : JURNAL PUSAT BAHASA, UNIVERSITI MALAYA. 3293

0127-4082 See KAJIAN MALAYSIA : JOURNAL OF MALAYSIAN STUDIES. 2656

0127-5127 See ALIRAN MONTHLY. 5190

0127-5720 See TROPICAL BIOMEDICINE. 3987

0127-6581 See BERITA ISOPB. 2410

0127-6883 See JOURNAL OF PLANT PROTECTION IN THE TROPICS. 100

0127-7065 See JOURNAL OF NATURAL RUBBER RESEARCH. 5076

0127-7170 See ASIAN-PACIFIC ENVIRONMENT. 2161

0127-7324 See ASEAN FOOD JOURNAL. 2327

0127-7979 See TEKNOLOGI KOKO-KELAPA. 140

0127-8428 See BULETIN SUKU TAHUNAN. 1549

0127-8436 See OPTIONS SERDANG. 117

0127-9793 See FRIM TECHNICAL INFORMATION. 2383

0128-0538 See ASIAN WETLAND NEWS. 2187

0128-0686 See JURNAL PENYELIDIKAN MARDI. 101

0128-1143 See CONSUMER CURRENTS. 1294

0128-1283 See JOURNAL OF TROPICAL FOREST SCIENCE. 2386

0128-1828 See ELAEIS. 5102

0128-357X See THIRD WORLD RESURGENCE. 2855

0128-3715 See PERIODICA ISLAMICA : AN INTERNATIONAL CONTENTS JOURNAL. 5044

0128-3863 See JOURNAL OF DEVELOPMENT COMMUNICATION, THE. 1114

0128-4134 See THIRD WORLD ECONOMICS. 1524

0129-0169 See BEFORE I GET OLD. 4102

0129-0533 See INTERNATIONAL JOURNAL OF HIGH SPEED COMPUTING. 1260

0129-0541 See INTERNATIONAL JOURNAL OF FOUNDATIONS OF COMPUTER SCIENCE. 1190

0129-055X See REVIEWS IN MATHEMATICAL PHYSICS. 4419

0129-0568 See CONCEPTS IN NEUROSCIENCE. 3830

0129-0657 See INTERNATIONAL JOURNAL OF NEURAL SYSTEMS. 1190

0129-0835 See INTERNATIONAL JOURNAL OF PIXE. 3942

0129-1122 See PETROMIN (SINGAPORE). 4274

0129-1262 See SOUTH EAST ASIAN PRINTER MAGAZINE. 4569

0129-1564 See INTERNATIONAL JOURNAL OF HIGH SPEED ELECTRONICS. 2066

0129-167X See INTERNATIONAL JOURNAL OF MATHEMATICS. 3509

0129-1815 See AEROSPACE SINGAPORE. 5

0129-1831 See INTERNATIONAL JOURNAL OF MODERN PHYSICS. C. 4406

0129-2021 See SOUTHEAST ASIAN BULLETIN OF MATHEMATICS. 3536

0129-2838 See PLANEWS. 2830

0129-2862 See IMPACT SINGAPORE. 4964

0129-2900 See ASEAN BUSINESS QUARTERLY. 639

0129-2951 See SINGAPORE BUSINESS. 851

0129-3273 See SINGAPORE JOURNAL OF OBSTETRICS & GYNAECOLOGY. 3768

0129-3281 See JOURNAL OF NUMERICAL LINEAR ALGEBRA WITH APPLICATIONS. 3514

0129-3729 See JOURNAL OF THE SINGAPORE NATIONAL ACADEMY OF SCIENCE. 5121

0129-3826 See SINGAPORE VETERINARY JOURNAL. 5522

0129-4172 See ASIAN JOURNAL OF PHARMACEUTICAL SCIENCES. 4293

0129-4431 See SINGAPORE BOOKS IN PRINT. 4832

0129-4679 See BUDGET FOR THE FINANCIAL YEAR / REPUBLIC OF SINGAPORE, THE. 780

0129-4776 See SINGAPORE JOURNAL OF EDUCATION. 1784

0129-4881 See ASEAN JOURNAL OF CLINICAL SCIENCES. 3553

0129-5276 See INVESTOR'S GUIDE (SINGAPORE). 903

0129-5411 See ASIA-PACIFIC ENGINEERING JOURNAL. PART A, ELECTRICAL ENGINEERING. 2036

0129-5721 See SEAISI QUARTERLY. 4019

0129-5829 See ARCHITECTURE JOURNAL / SCHOOL OF ARCHITECTURE, NATIONAL UNIVERSITY OF SINGAPORE. 290

0129-5896 See ASIA COMPUTER WEEKLY. 1235

0129-6078 See INSIGHT (SINGAPORE). 4784

0129-6175 See SOUTHEAST ASIA BUILDING. 627

0129-6256 See SINGAPORE STANDARDS YEARBOOK. 4032

0129-6264 See PARALLEL PROCESSING LETTERS. 1280

0129-6485 See SINGAPORE JOURNAL OF PRIMARY INDUSTRIES. 134

0129-6612 See MEDIA ASIA. 1116

0129-6965 See REPORT ON THE LABOUR FORCE SURVEY OF SINGAPORE. 1707

0129-7023 See BULLETIN - REGIONAL INSTITUTE OF HIGHER EDUCATION AND DEVELOPMENT. 1813

0129-704X See IMAGE. 4964

0129-7457 See SINGAPORE COMMUNITY HEALTH BULLETIN, THE. 4803

0129-7619 See SINGAPORE JOURNAL OF TROPICAL GEOGRAPHY. 2576

0129-7767 See GUIDELINES. 3284

0129-797X See CONTEMPORARY SOUTHEAST ASIA. 2649

0129-8372 See MIMAR (SINGAPORE). 303

0129-8534 See PAPINEAU'S GUIDE TO THAILAND. 5488

0129-8682 See PAPINEAU'S GUIDE TO SINGAPORE. 5488

0129-9387 See SINGA. 5258

0129-9743 See PAPINEAU'S GUIDE TO SRI LANKA. 5488

0129-9891 See CCA NEWS / CHRISTIAN CONFERENCE OF ASIA. 4943

0130-0059 See LATVIESU VALODAS KULTURAS JAUTAJUMI. 3296

0130-0075 See VESTNIK MOSKOVSKOGO UNIVERSITETA. SERIA IX : FILOLOGIIA. 3331

0130-0091 See VESTNIK MOSKOVSKOGO UNIVERSITETA. SERIIA VII : FILOSOFIIA. 4364

0130-0105 See VESTNIK MOSKOVSKOGO UNIVERSITETA. SERIIA VI, EKONOMIKA. 1525

0130-0172 See LIETUVIU KALBOTYROS KLAUSIMAI. 3297

0130-0415 See VOPROSY TEORII SISTEM AVTOMATICESKOGO UPRAVLENIJA. 2131

0130-0911 See VDNKH SSSR. 144

0130-0997 See GELIOTEHNIKA (TASKENT). 1945

0130-1098 See GEOLOGIJA SIBIRI I DALNEGO VOSTOKA. 1379

0130-1128 See GEOHIMIA I RUDOOBRAZOVANIE. 1355

0130-1616 See ZNAMJA (MOSKVA). 3356

0130-1640 See ZNANIE--SILA. 5173

0130-2019 See IMMUNOLOGIJA I ALLERGIJA. 3671

0130-2051 See KALENDAR ZNAMENATELNYKH I PAMIATNYKH DAT. 2621

0130-2272 See KLIMAT I GIDROLOGIIA SIBIRI I DALNEGO VOSTOKA. 1416

0130-2329 See KNIZHNAIA LETOPIS. DOPOLNITELNYI VYPUSK. KNIGI I BROSHIURY / GOSUDARSTVENNYI KOMITET SSSR PO DELAM IZDATELSTV, POLIGRAFII I KNIZHNOI TORGOVLI, VSESOIUZNAIA ORDENA "ZNAK POCHETA" KNIZHNAIA PALATA. 418

0130-2337 See KODRY. 3402

0130-2426 See NAROD I DEMOKRATIIA. 4482

0130-2434 See KOMUNIST UKRAINY. 4542

0130-2507 See POTREBITELSKAIA KOOPERATSIIA KAZAKHSTANA. 1543

0130-2515 See KORMA. 103

0130-2620 See KRATKIE SOOBSENIA - INSTITUT ARHEOLOGII. 272

0130-2671 See KROKODIL. 3345

0130-2701 See KRYLIA RODINY. 27

0130-2884 See METALLURGICESKAJA TEPLOTEHNIKA. 4010

0130-2906 See METEOROLOGIIA I GIDROLOGIIA; NAUCHNO-TEKHNICHESKII ZHURNAL. 1431

0130-3031 See DEKORATIVNOE ISKUSSTVO / UCHREDITELI SKH SSSR. 372

0130-3066 See DETALI MASIN (KIEV). 2112

0130-3074 See DEFEKTOLOGIJA. 1877

0130-3082 See DEFEKTOSKOPIIA. 1970

0130-3090 See DENGI I KREDIT. 787

0130-318X See DINAMIKA SISTEM. 3503

0130-3198 See DIFFERENCIALNAJA GEOMETRIJA. 3503

0130-321X See DNIPRO. 3382

0130-3562 See DON. 3382

0130-3589 See ZHURNALIST. 2926

0130-3597 See LITERATURNAJA ARMENIJA. 3346

0130-3740 See MATERIALY PO ARHEOLOGII EVROPEJSKOGO SEVERO-VOSTOKA. 274

0130-3864 See NOVAJA I NOVEJSAKA ISTORIJA (MOSKVA). 2624

0130-5247 *See* UKRAINSKIJ ISTORICNIJ ZURNAL. **2632**

0130-5263 *See* UKRAINSKA MOVA I LITERATURA V SHKOLI. **3449**

0130-5395 *See* UPRAVLJAJUSCIE SISTEMY I MASINY (KIEV, 1972). **1262**

0130-5522 *See* FIZIKA V SHKOLE : NAUCHNO-METODICHESKII ZHURNAL MINISTERSTVO PROSVESHCHENIIA SSSR. **4403**

0130-5824 *See* FORMIROVANIE I KONTROL KACESTVA POVERHNOSTNYH VOD. **455**

0130-5972 *See* HIMIJA I ZIZN. **488**

0130-6073 *See* INOSTRANNYE JAZYKI V SKOLE. **3287**

0130-6359 *See* IONNYE RASPLAVY. **1036**

0130-6405 *See* ISKUSSTVO KINO. **4073**

0130-6634 *See* ISKATEL. **3397**

0130-6685 *See* ISTORICESKIE ZAPISKI. **2620**

0130-6758 *See* ITOGI NAUKI I TEKHNIKI : SERIIA MIKROBIOLOGIIA. **564**

0130-6774 *See* ITOGI NAUKI I TEKHNIKI. SERIIA TEKHNICHESKAIA KIBERNETIKA. **1251**

0130-6812 *See* PATMA-BANASIRAKAN HANDES. **3310**

0130-6863 *See* NABLIUDENIIA ISKUSSTVENNYKH NEBESNYKH TEL. **29**

0130-6898 *See* NADEZHNOST I KONTROL KACHESTVA. **4220**

0130-6936 *See* NARODNA TVORCHIST TA ETNOGRAFIIA. **374**

0130-7045 *See* NAUKA I RELIGIJA. **4980**

0130-7371 *See* USPEHI BIOLOGICESKOJ HIMII. **494**

0130-7673 *See* NOVYJ MIR. **3349**

0130-7754 *See* NUMIZMATIKA I EPIGRAFIKA / AKADEMIIA NAUK SSSR, INSTITUT ARKHEOLOGII. **2782**

0130-8246 *See* POLIMERY V MELIORACII I VODNOM HOZJAJSTVE. **2094**

0130-8483 *See* POEZIJA (KIIV). **3470**

0130-8734 *See* SBORNIK NAUCHNYKH (VETERINARNAIA AKADEMIIA). **5521**

0130-884X *See* ZIBRANNIA POSTANOV URIADU UKRAINY. **3078**

0130-9099 *See* LESOVODSTVO, LESNYE KULTURY I POCHVOVEDENIE. **2387**

0130-9277 *See* LINGVISTICHESKIE PROBLEMY FUNKTSIONALNOGO MODELIROVANIIA RECHEVOI DEIATELNOSTI. **3300**

0130-9412 *See* ANALIZ NA PROBLEMNYKH SETIAKH / AKADEMIIA NAUK SSSR, INSTITUT MIROVOI EKONOMIKI I MEZHDUNARODNYKH OTNOSHENII. **3493**

0130-9641 *See* INTERNATIONAL AFFAIRS (MOSCOW). **4524**

0130-9803 *See* NAUCNYE OSNOVY RAZVITIA ZIVOTNOVODSTVA V BELORUSSII. **216**

0131-0062 *See* OVOCHIVNYTSTVO I BASHTANNYTSTVO. **180**

0131-0097 *See* OGONEK. **2520**

0131-1301 *See* REFERATIVNYI ZHURNAL : OBSHCHIE VOPROSY PATOLOGII. **3897**

0131-1328 *See* ENERGETICHESKOE STROITELSTVO ZA RUBEZHOM : ORGAN MINISTERSTVA ENERGETIKI I ELEKTROTEKHNICHESKOI PROMYSHLNNOSTI. **1937**

0131-1344 *See* EPIGRAFIKA VOSTAKA. **267**

0131-1611 *See* PROBLEMY SPECIALNOJ ELEKTROMETALLURGII. **4016**

0131-1638 *See* SBORNIK ANNOTACIJ NAUCNO-ISSLEDOVATELSKIH RABOT - TOMSKIJ POLITEHNICESKIJ INSTITUT IM. S.M. KIROVA. **5149**

0131-1646 *See* FIZIOLOGIJA CELOVEKA. **580**

0131-1670 *See* NEFTEPERERABOTKA, NEFTEHIMIJA I SLANCEPERERABOTKA. **4266**

0131-1689 *See* TRUDY - GOSUDARSTVENNYJ NAUCNO-ISSLEDOVATELSKIJ I PROEKTNYJ INSTITUT NEFTJANOJ PROMYSLENNOSTI. **4280**

0131-1697 *See* GIGIENICESKIE ASPEKTY OHRANY OKRUZAJUSCEJ SREDY. **2172**

0131-1719 *See* LITOLOGIJA I PALEOGEOGRAFIJA. **1459**

0131-1751 *See* ITOGI NAUKI I TEHNIKI - VSESOUZNYJ INSTITUT NAUCNOJ I TEHNICESKOJ INFORMACII. SERIJA CITOLOGIJA. **537**

0131-176X *See* FIZIKA MOLEKUL (KIEV). **1052**

0131-2278 *See* PERSPEKTIVY. **4545**

0131-2332 *See* MOSKVA. **3413**

0131-2367 *See* MUZYKA (KIEV, UKRAINE). **4139**

0131-2383 *See* MUZYKALNAIA ZHIZN. **4139**

0131-2561 *See* VITCYZNA (KIIV). **3451**

0131-2618 *See* OKHRANA TRUDA I SOTSIALNOE STRAKHOVANIE. **2867**

0131-2642 *See* PALESTINSKII SBORNIK. **2770**

0131-2677 *See* PAMIATNIKI TURKMENISTANA. **2702**

0131-2928 *See* PROBLEMY MASINOSTROENIJA. **2125**

0131-3142 *See* PROBLEMY JADERNOJ FIZIKI I KOSMICESKIH LUCHEJ. **4450**

0131-3150 *See* ISTORIJA SSSR. **2693**

0131-3266 *See* ZDES I TEPER. **3456**

0131-3533 *See* REFERATIVNYJ ZURNAL - VSESOJUZNYJ INSTITUT NAUCNOJ I TEHNICESKOJ INFORMACII. 66, KORROZIJA I ZASCITA OT KORROZII. **4017**

0131-355X *See* REFERATIVNYJ ZURNAL - VSESOJUZNYJ INSTITUT NAUCNOJ I TEHNICESKOJ INFORMACII. 70. RADIACIONNAJA BIOLOGIJA. **471**

0131-3568 *See* SADOVODSTVO. **2430**

0131-3940 *See* TRUDY ASTROFIZICESKOGO INSTITUTA. **38**

0131-4122 *See* KNIZHNAIA TORGOVLIA. REFERATIVNAIA INFORMATSIIA. **4829**

0131-5145 *See* NAUCHNYE TRUDY (MOSKOVSKII INSTITUT STALI I SPLAVOV). **4013**

0131-5560 *See* PROMYSHLENNYI TRANSPORT. **3487**

0131-6044 *See* ROMAN-GAZETA. **3352**

0131-6095 *See* RUSSKAJA LITERATURA (LENINGRAD. 1958). **3432**

0131-6273 *See* SELSKIE ZORI. **133**

0131-6311 *See* KHOZIAIN. **102**

0131-6370 *See* SELSKOE KHOZIAISTVO UZBEKISTANA. **133**

0131-6397 *See* SELSKOHOZJAJSTVENNAJA BIOLOGIJA. **473**

0131-6761 *See* SOVETSKAJA JUSTICIJA. **3057**

0131-677X *See* SOVETSKAA TURKOLOGIJA. **3322**

0131-6842 *See* NEJROHIRURGIJA. **3970**

0131-694X *See* TELEVIDENIE, RADIOVESHCHANIE. **1123**

0131-694X *See* EFIR. **1131**

0131-7377 *See* SEMJA I SKOLA. **1783**

0131-7482 *See* KHLIBOROB UKRAINY. (KHLEBOROB UKRAINY). **177**

0131-7555 *See* HUDOZNIK. **322**

0131-8012 *See* IZVESTIIA AKADEMII NAUK UZSSR. SERIIA FIZIKO-MATEMATICHESKIKH NAUK. **4407**

0131-8039 *See* IZVESTIIA VYSSHIKH UCHEBNYKH ZAVEDENII. PRAVOVEDENIE. **2985**

0131-8098 *See* RADIOSPEKTROSKOPIIA. **4441**

0131-8314 *See* ORGANIC REACTIVITY. **1045**

0131-8721 *See* SPUTNIK (ANGL. JAZ.). **2523**

0131-8780 *See* SREDNIE VEKA. **2710**

0131-9140 *See* STEPNYE PROSTORY. **138**

0131-9582 *See* STEKLO I KERAMIKA. **2594**

0132-0114 *See* TRUDY FIZICHESKOGO INSTITUTA / AKADEMIIA NAUK SSSR, FIZICHESKII INSTITUT IM. P.N. LEBEDEVA. **4424**

0132-0696 *See* PREPODAVANIE ISTORII V SHKOLE. **2626**

0132-0742 *See* EKRAN. **4068**

0132-0777 *See* LINGUISTICA URALICA. **3299**

0132-0947 *See* SHAKHMATY V SSSR. **4866**

0132-1196 *See* PROFSOIUZY. **1704**

0132-1366 *See* SOVETSKOE SLAVIANOVEDENIE. **2710**

0132-1544 *See* UKRAINSKA KULTURA. **2524**

0132-1625 *See* SOTSIOLOGICHESKIE ISSLEDOVANIIA. **5263**

0132-2095 *See* BIBLIOTEKA "OGONEK.". **3367**

0132-2133 *See* BIBLIOTEKA "KOMSOMOLSKOI PRAVDY". **3194**

0132-2354 *See* EKSTRAKTSIIA, IONNYI OBMEN. **1052**

0132-2818 *See* LITOVSKIJ MATEMATICESKIJ SBORNIK. **3517**

0132-3423 *See* BIOORGANICHESKAIA KHIMIIA. **1039**

0132-344X *See* KOORDINACIONNAJA HIMIJA. **1055**

0132-3458 *See* OBSHCHESTVENNYE NAUKI I SOVREMENNOST : ONS. **5211**

0132-3474 *See* PROGRAMMIROVANIE. **1281**

0132-358X *See* REFERATIVNYI ZHURNAL: PCHELOVODSTVO, SHELKOVODSTVO. **125**

0132-4160 *See* AVTOMATIKA I VYCISLITEL'NAYA TEHNIKA (RIGA). **1218**

0132-4713 *See* METROLOGIIA / GOSUDARSTVENNYI KOMITET SSSR PO STANDARTAM. **4031**

0132-5183 *See* PROIZVODSTVO OGNEUPOROV. **4017**

0132-5949 *See* POLITYKA I CHAS : ZHURNAL T SK KOMPARTII UKRAINY. **4545**

0132-6074 *See* IZVESTIIA AKADEMII NAUK GRUZINSKOI SSR : SERIIA KHIMICHESKAIA. **979**

0132-6112 *See* IZVESTIIA AKADEMIIA NAUK AZERBAIDZHANSKOI SSR. SERIIA BIOLOGICHESKIKH NAUK. **459**

0132-6244 *See* HIMIJA GETEROCIKLICESKIH SOEDINENIJ. **977**

0132-6295 *See* KAROGS (RIGA). **2518**

0132-6414 *See* FIZIKA NIZKIH TEMPERATUR (KIEV). **4430**

0132-6627 *See* MOLDOVA SI LUMEA. **4543**

0132-6651 *See* FIZIKA I HIMIJA STEKLA. **2589**

0132-7003 *See* GEOLOGICESKOE STROENIE I POLEZNYE ISKOPAEMYE NIZNEGO POVOLZJA. **1379**

0132-7046 *See* HIMIJA I TEHNOLOGIJA CELLJULOZY. **1025**

0132-7070 *See* ISSLEDOVANIJA V OBLASTI HIMII I TEHNOLOGII PRODUKTOV PERERABOTKI GORJUCIH ISKOPAEMYH. **978**

0132-7267 *See* NEORGANICHESKIE STEKLA, POKRYTIIA I MATERIALY. **2592**

0132-8425 *See* ZHURNALIST UKRAINY. **2926**

0132-862X *See* ZURNAL MOSKOVSKOJ PATRIARHII. **5040**

0132-8743 *See* LESOVEDEIE I LESNOE KHOZIAISTVO. **5126**

0133-011X *See* BAROMFITENYESZTES ES FELDOLGOZAS. **207**

0133-0276 *See* HUNGARIAN JOURNAL OF INDUSTRIAL CHEMISTRY. **977**

0133-0306 *See* DAILY NEWS BUDAPEST. **5802**

0133-0314 *See* VAROSI KOZLEKEDES. **5399**

0133-0365 *See* HUNGARIAN ECONOMY (BUDAPEST. 1972), THE. **1566**

0133-0748 *See* SOPRONI SZEMLE. **2630**

0133-0829 *See* NOVENYVEDELEM. **520**

0133-090X *See* UJ MAGYAR HIREK. **2524**

0133-0918 *See* GABONAIPAR. **201**

0133-1027 *See* SCIENCAJ KOMUNIKAJOJ - BUDAPESTA TERITORIA KOMITATO DE HUNGARA ESPERANTO-ASOCIO. **5150**

0133-1531 *See* ARS HUNGARICA. **337**

0133-1620 *See* AUTOMATIZALAS. **1218**

0133-1752 *See* NEPSZABADSAG. **5802**

0133-185X *See* MAGYAR NEMZET. **5802**

0133-1892 *See* BUDAPEST REGISEGEI. **2680**

0133-1906 *See* MAGYAR HIRLAP. **5802**

0133-2023 *See* FOLIA ARCHAEOLOGICA BUDAPEST. **268**

0133-2082 *See* TEXTILIPARI KUTATO INTEZET KOZLEMENYEI. **5359**

0133-2368 See LITERATURA (BUDAPEST). 3406

0133-2392 See MUZSAK. 4093

0133-2430 See GALAKTIKA. 5107

0133-2546 See KORROZIOS FIGYELO. 4007

0133-2767 See PARLANDO. 4145

0133-3046 See STUDIA COMITATENSIA BUDAPEST. 4096

0133-333X See KULFOLDI MAGYAR NYELVU KIADVANYOK. 418

0133-3399 See ALKALMAZOTT MATEMATIKAI LAPEK. 3492

0133-3461 See SZOCIOLOGIA (BUDAPEST. 1972). 5264

0133-3682 See ZOLDSEGTERMESZTESI KUTATO INTEZET BULLETINJE. 2434

0133-3720 See CEREAL RESEARCH COMMUNICATIONS. 200

0133-3844 See BIOLOGIA (BUDAPEST). 444

0133-3852 See ANALYSIS MATHEMATICA (BUDAPEST). 3493

0133-3909 See THERAPIA HUNGARICA (ENGLISH EDITION). 3645

0133-4565 See KISTENYESZTOK LAPJA. 5589

0133-4875 See MEZOGAZDASAGI ES ELELMISZERIPARI KONYVTAROSOK TAJEKOZTATOJA. 3231

0133-4883 See HAEMATOLOGIA (BUDAPEST. 1976. SOROZAT). 3772

0133-4921 See MUZEUMI KOZLEMENYEK - MUVELODESI MINISZTERIUM MUZEUMI OSZTALY. 4093

0133-5332 See UJ FORRAS. 3449

0133-5405 See ANAESTHESIOLOGIA ES INTENSIV THERAPIA. 3680

0133-5839 See KULFOLDI TARSADALOMTUDOMANYI KEZIKONYVEK. 5227

0133-6088 See CUMANIA. 2684

0133-6215 See ABSTRACTA BOTANICA. 496

0133-6622 See FOLIA HISTORICA. 2688

0133-6894 See MAGYAR NEMZETI BIBLIOGRAFIA. IDOSZAKI KIADVANYOK REPERTORIUMA. 419

0133-705X See CSONGRAD MEGYEI KONYVTAROS. 3205

0133-7351 See VAS MEGYEI KONYVTARAK ERTESITOJE, A. 3255

0133-736X See MAGYAR KONYVTARI SZAKIRODALOM BIBLIOGRAFIAJA, A. 3259

0133-7599 See THEOLOGIAI SZEMLE. 5003

0133-8358 See TOLNA MEGYEI KONYVTAROS. 3253

0133-9095 See MIKOLOGIAI KOZLEMENYEK. 575

0133-9214 See LUDAS EVKONYV. 2519

0134-0352 See MIKROFILMEK CIMJEGYZEKE. MODERN NYOMTATVANYOK / ORSZAGOS SZECHENYI KONYVTAR. 3231

0134-126X See PROCEEDINGS OF THE ... TIHANY SYMPOSIUM ON RADIATION CHEMISTRY. 989

0134-1790 See STUDIES IN ENGLISH AND AMERICAN. 3325

0134-2258 See UZBEK TILI VA ADABIETI / UZBEKISTON SSR FANLAR AKADEMIIASI, A.S. PUSHKIN NOMIDAGI TIL VA ADABIET INSTITUTI. 3450

0134-2673 See ITOGI NAUKI I TEHNIKI - VSESOJUZNYI INSTITUT NAUCNOJ I TEHNICESKOJINFORMACI SERIJA FIZIOLOGIJA CELOVEKA I ZIVOTNYH. 581

0134-2681 See ITOGI NAUKI I TEHNIKI - VSESOUZNYJ INSTITUT NAUCNOJ I TEHNICESKOJ INFORMACII. SERIA ZIVOTNOVODSTVO I VETERINARIJA. 5512

0134-2754 See NOVAIA OTECHESTVENNAIA LITERATURA PO OBSHCHESTVENNYM NAUKAM. NAUKOVEDENIE / ROSSIISKAIA AKADEMIIA NAUK, INSTITUT NAUCHNOI INFORMATSII PO OBSHCHESTVENNYM NAUKAM. 5135

0134-2835 See NOVAIA INOSTRANNAIA LITERATURA PO OBSHCHESTVENNYM NAUKAM: EKONOMIKA. 1593

0134-2878 See REFERATIVNYI ZHURNAL. SERIIA 2, ZEMLEDELIE.--. 125

0134-2924 See NOVAIA SOVETSKAIA I INOSTRANNAIA LITERATURA PO OBSHCHESTVENNYM NAUKAM. POLSKAIA NARODNAIA RESPUBLIKA. 2701

0134-2932 See NOVAIA OTECHESTVENNAIA I INOSTRANNAIA LITERATURA PO OBSHCHESTVENNYM NAUKAM. RELIGIOVEDENIE / ROSSIISKAIA AKADEMIIA NAUK, INSTITUT NAUCHNOI INFORMATSII PO OBSHCHESTVENNYM NAUKAM. 4982

0134-3106 See KULTUROS BARAI. 2518

0134-3211 See METAI : LIETUVOS RASYTOJU SAJUNGOS MENRASTIS. 3411

0134-3475 See BIOLOGIA MORA (VLADIVOSTOK). 553

0134-3580 See ZHULDYZ. 3456

0134-3963 See PROBLEMY SEVERA / AKADEMIIA NAUK SSSR, SIBIRSKOE OTDELENIE, GOSUDARSTVENNAIA PUBLICHNAIA NAUCHNO-TEKHNICHESKAIA BIBLIOTEKA. 422

0134-3998 See OPTIMIZACIJA. 3526

0134-4307 See UZBEKISTON RESPUBLIKASI FANLAR AKADEMIIASINING MABRUZALARI. 5168

0134-4315 See SOVETIS HEYMLAND. 3438

0134-4536 See LOOMING. 3408

0134-4978 See EKOLOGIIA I ZASHCHITA LESA : MEZHVUZOVSKII SBORNIK NAUCHNYKH TRUDOV / LENINGRADSKAIA LESOTEKHNICHESKAIA AKADEMIIA IMENI S.M. KIROVA. 2215

0134-5052 See FIZIKA PLAZMY (MOSKVA. 1975). 4403

0134-5400 See VOPROSY ATOMNOJ NAUKI I TEHNIKI. FIZIKA RADIACIONNYH POVREZDENIJ I RADIACIONNOE MATERIALOVEDENIE. 4442

0134-5486 See SOCIAL SCIENCES. 5221

0134-5710 See LESOSECHNYE, LESOSKLADSKIE RABOTY I SUKHOPUTNYI TRANSPORT LESA : MEZHVUZOVSKII SBORNIK NAUCHNYKH TRUDOV / LENINGRADSKAIA LESOTEKHNICHESKAIA AKADEMIIA IMENI S.M. KIROVA. 2387

0134-580X See REFERATIVNYI ZHURNAL FARMAKOLOGIIA OBSHCHAYA FARMAKOLOGIYA NERVNOI SISTEMY. 471

0134-6350 See PRIKLADNAA MATEMATIKA. 3527

0134-6695 See SOVETSKOE BIBLIOTEKOVEDENIE. 3250

0134-7071 See FIZIKA I KHIMIIA STEKLOOBRAZUIUSHCHIKH SISTEM. 1015

0134-7780 See ITOGI NAUKI I TEKHNIKI. SERIIA ZASHCHITA RASTENII / VSESOIUZNYI INSTITUT NAUCHNOI I TEKHNICHESKOI INFORMATSII. 4245

0134-7799 See ITOGI NAUKI I TEKHNIKI. SERIIA ORGANIZATSIIA UPRAVLENIIA TRANSPORTOM. 5384

0134-8140 See SOVETSKII VOIN. 4057

0134-837X See KNIGA. ISSLEDOVANIIA I MATERIALY. 2622

0134-8442 See ZHURNALIST, PRESSA, AUDITORIIA / LENINGRADSKII GOSUDARSTVENNYI UNIVERSITET IM. A.A. ZHDANOVA. 2926

0134-8469 See VNESHNIAIA TORGOVLIA. 857

0134-8752 See GOSUDARSTVENNYE STANDARTY SSSR : UKAZATEL / GOSUDARSTVENNYI KOMITET STANDARTOV SOVETA MINISTROV SSSR. 4030

0134-8817 See GEOMETRICHESKII SBORNIK. 3507

0134-8876 See PROBLEMY METODA I ZHANRA. 3425

0134-9007 See SPEKTROSKOPIJA GAZORAZRJADNOJ PLAZMY. 4445

0134-9147 See POLIGRAFICESKAJA PROMYSLENNOST. OBZORNAJA INFORMACIJA. 4567

0134-9236 See MORSKOI SBORNIK. 4179

0134-9392 See KONSTRUKCIONNYE MATERIALY NA OSNOVE UGLERODA. 619

0134-9570 See MASINY I TEHNOLOGIJA TORFJANOGO PROIZVODSTVA. 2143

0134-9619 See ROMANSKOE I GERMANSKOE IAZYKOZNANIE. 3318

0135-0420 See TSIRKULIAR-ASTROFIZICHESKAIA OBSERVATORIIA, SHEMAKHA, RUSSIA. 401

0135-0617 See DEPONIROVANNYE RUKOPISI / GOSUDARSTVENNYI KOMITET SSSR PO NAUKE I TEKHNIKE, AKADEMIIA NAUK SSSR, VSESOIUZNYI INSTITUT NAUCHNOI I TEKHNICHESKOI INFORMATSII, SEKTOR TEORII I METODIKI DEPONIROVANIIA NAUCHNYKH RABOT. 5099

0135-1117 See VESTNIK KIEVSKOGO UNIVERSITETA. ROMANO-GERMANSKAIA FILOLOGIIA. 3331

0135-129X See ZVAIGZNOTA DEBESS. 401

0135-1419 See FIZIKA ATMOSFERY. 1425

0135-1605 See GEOLOGIJA I NEFTEGAZONOSNOST TURKMENISTANA. 4259

0135-2164 See GEOLOGIIA I GEOKHIMIIA GORIUCHIKH ISKOPAEMYKH (KIEV, UKRAINE : 1974). 2139

0135-2202 See ISTORYCHNI DOSLIDZHENNIA. ISTORIIA ZARUBIZHNYKH KRAIN / AKADEMIIA NAUK UKRAINSKOI RSR, INSTYTUT ISTORII. 2620

0135-2210 See ISTORYCHNI DOSLIDZHENNIA : VITCHYZNIANA ISTORIIA. 2693

0135-2466 See METSANDUSLIKUD UURIMUSED. 2388

0135-3861 See ACTA ORNITHOLOGICA LITUANICA / AKADEMIIA NAUK LITOVSKOI SSR, INSTITUT ZOOLOGII I PARAZITOLOGII [AND] LITOVSKOE ORNITOLOGICHESKOE OBSHCHESTVO--OTDELENIE VSESOIUZNOGO ORNITOLOGICHESKOGO OBSHCHESTVA. 5614

0135-5813 See TRUDY KOMI NAUCHNOGO TSENTRA URO AN SSSR / AKADEMIIA NAUK SSSR, URALSKOE OTDELENIE, KOMI NAUCHNYI TSENTR. 5599

0135-6569 See FINNO-UGRISTIKA / MINISTERSTVO VYSSHEGO I SREDNEGO SPETSIALNOGO OBRAZOVANIIA RSFSR, MORDOVSKII GOSUDARSTVENNYI UNIVERSITET IMENI N.P. OGAREVA. 3281

0135-7832 See DRUZHBA (IOSHKAR-OLA, R.S.F.S.R.). 3382

0136-1228 See METODY DISKRETNOGO ANALIZA V ...; SBORNIK TRUDOV. 3523

0136-1732 See ADGEZIA RASPLAVOV I PAJHA MATERIALOV. 4026

0136-1813 See VOPROSY GEOKHIMII I TIPOMORFIZM MINERALOV. 1401

0136-3360 See IZVESTIIA VYSSHIKH UCHEBNYKH ZAVEDENII. ELEKTROMEKHANIKA. 2067

0136-3638 See FIZICESKIE SVOJSTVA METALLOV I SPLAVOV. 4002

0136-3751 See SBORNIK NAUCHNYKH TRUDOV (VSESOIUZNYI NAUCHNO-ISSLEDOVATELSKII INSTITUT FIZIOLOGII, BIOKHIMII I PITANIIA). 221

0136-491X See MOLEKULJARNAJA GENETIKA I BIOFIZIKA. 549

0136-7439 See PROTOZOOLOGIJA. 569

0136-7447 See RUSSKIJ FOLKLOR. 2324

0136-7455 See USPEKHI SREDNEAZIATSKOI ARKHEOLOGII. 2714

0136-7463 See ZHURNAL STRUKTURNOJ HIMII. 1059

0136-7595 See ZAPOVEDNIKI BELORUSSII / GOSUDARSTVENNOE ZAPOVEDNO-OKHOTNICHE KHOZIAISTVO BELOVEZHSKAIA PUSHCHA. 4174

0136-7773 See STROITELNYE MATERIALY I KONSTRUKTSII. 629

0136-8079 See PROBLEMY SOVREMENNOJ ANALITICESKOJ KHIMII. 1018

0136-8109 See UCHENYE ZAPISKI LENINGRADSKOGO ORDENA LENINA GOSUDARSTVENNOGO UNIVERSITETA IMENI A.A. ZHDANOVA. SERIIA MATEMATICHESKIKH NAUK. 5167

0136-9121 See EKOLOGICHESKAIA I EKSPERIMENTALNAIA PARAZITOLOGIIA. 5582

0136-9172 See PISCEVAJA PROMYSLENNOST (KIEV. 1977). 2353

0136-9377 See BIOKHIMIHA ZHIVOTNYKH I CHELOVEKA. 578

0137-0057 See RADIATSIONNAIA BEZOPASNOST I ZASHCHITA AES. 2158

0137-0162 See VOPROSY AKUSHERSTVA I PEDIATRII. 3912

0137-0235 See TEORETICESKAJA I PRIKLADNAJA MEHANIKA (MINSK). 2130

0137-0243 See ITOGI NAUKI I TEKHNIKI. SERIIA POZHARNAIA OKHRANA / GOSUDARSTVENNYI KOMITET SSSR PO NAUKE I TEKHNIKE, AKADEMIIA NAUK SSSR, VSESOIUZNYI INSTITUT NAUCHNOI I TEKHNICHESKOI INFORMATSII. 2291

0137-0251 See ITOGI NAUKI I TEKHNIKI. SERIIA ORGANICHESKAIA KHIMIIA. 1042

0137-0340 See HIMIJA TVERDOGO TELA. 977

0137-0618 See VOPROSY KLINICESKOJ MEDICINY (DUSANBE). 3650

0137-0723 See NOVOE VREMIA. 4530

0137-0723 See NOVOE VIEMIA (MOSCOW, R.S.F.S.R.). 4530

0137-0782 See VESTNIK MOSKOVSKOGO UNIVERSITETA. SERIIA XV: VYCHISLITELNAIA MATEMATIKA I KIBERNETIKA. 1262

0137-0936 See VESTNIK MOSKOVSKOGO UNIVERSITETA. SERIIA XIV : PSIKHOLOGIIA. 4621

0137-0936 See VESTNIK MOSKOVSKOGO UNIVERSITETA SERIA 14 PSIHOLOGIA. 4621

0137-0952 See VESTNIK MOSKOVSKOGO UNIVERSITETA. SERIA 16. BIOLOGIA. 475

0137-1053 See DIELEKTRYCZNE I OPTYCZNE ASPEKTY ODDZIAYWAN MIEDZYCZASTECZKOWYCH. 1051

0137-1169 See ACTA UNIVERSITATIS WRATISLAVIENSIS. STUDIA LINGUISTICA. 3261

0137-1223 See SYSTEMS SCIENCE. 1249

0137-1266 See LOWIEC POLSKI. 4874

0137-1282 See FIZYKOCHEMICZNE PROBLEMY MINERALURGII. 1439

0137-1347 See PRACE INSTYTUTU METEOROLOGII I GOSPODARKI WODNEJ. 1433

0137-1479 See FRUIT SCIENCE REPORTS. 172

0137-155X See BIULETYN OCENY ODMIAN - CENTRALNY OSRODEK BADANIA ODMIAN ROSLIN UPRAWNYCH W SUPI WIELKIEJ POW. SRODA WLKP. 66

0137-1576 See BIULETYN INSTYTUTU ZIEMNIAKA. 2329

0137-1592 See ACTA ICHTHYOLOGICA ET PISCATORIA. 2293

0137-1649 See PRACE I MATERIAY ZOOTECHNICZNE / INSTYTUT GENETYKE I HODOWLI ZWIERZAT POLSKIEJ AKADEMII NAUK. 5594

0137-1657 See ROCZNIKI NAUKOWE ZOOTECHNIKI. 5521

0137-1665 See ROCZNIKI NAUKOWE ZOOTECHNIKI. MONOGRAFIE I ROZPRAWY. 5521

0137-1738 See ROCZNIKI AKADEMII ROLNICZEJ W POZNANIU. OGRODNICTWO. 130

0137-1886 See ZESZYTY NAUKOWE AKADEMII ROLNICZEJ W KRAKOWIE. ROLNICTWO. 149

0137-1916 See ZESZYTY NAUKOWE. AKADEMIA ROLNICZA W KRAKOWIE, ZOOTECHNIKA. 224

0137-1940 See ZOOTECHNIKA / AKADEMIA ROLNICZA W SZCZECINIE. 224

0137-1959 See ZESZYTY NAUKOWE AKADEMII ROLNICZEJ WE WROCAWAIU. ROLNICTWO. 149

0137-1975 See ZESZYTY NAUKOWE. WETERYNARIA. 5528

0137-2017 See ZESZYTY NAUKOWE AKADEMII ROLNICZEJ WE WROCAWIU. ZOOTECHNIKA. 149

0137-222X See SPOTKANIA Z ZABYTKAMI. 283

0137-2335 See PRACE NAUKOWE - POLITECHNIKA WARSZAWSKA. MECHANIKA. 2125

0137-2351 See ZESZYTY NAUKOWE UNIWERSYTETU JAGIELLONSKIEGO. PRACE Z BIOLOGII MOLEKULARNEJ. 476

0137-2378 See ZESZYTY NAUKOWE UNIWERSYTETU JAGIELLONSKIEGO. PRACE Z NAUK POLITYCZNYCH. 4501

0137-2386 See ZESZYTY NAUKOWE UNIWERSYTETU JAGIELLONSKIEGO. ACTA COSMOLOGICA. 401

0137-2459 See PAPERS AND STUDIES IN CONTRASTIVE LINGUISTICS. 3309

0137-2467 See STUDIA GERMANICA POSNANIENSIA. 3324

0137-2475 See STUDIA ROMANICA POSNANIENSIA. 5075

0137-2548 See LITERATURA. 3406

0137-2645 See PRZEMYS FERMENTACYJNY I OWOCOWO-WARZYWNY. 1028

0137-2866 See ROCZNIK MUZEUM NARODOWEGO W KIELCACH. 4096

0137-2890 See ROCZNIKI POLSKIEGO TOWARZYSTWA MATEMATYCZNEGO, SERIA 3: MATEMATYKA STOSOWANA. 3532

0137-2904 See REPORTS ON MATHEMATICAL LOGIC. 3531

0137-2998 See KWARTALNIK HISTORII PRASY POLSKIEJ. 4816

0137-3013 See HUMANIZACJA PRACY. 1608

0137-3080 See ESTUDIOS LATINOAMERICANOS / POLSKA AKADEMIA NAUK, INSTYTUT HISTORII. 2551

0137-320X See MATERIAY MUZEUM BUDOWNICTWA LUDOWEGO W SANOKU. 4091

0137-3234 See PAMIETNIKARSTWO POLSKIE. 434

0137-3595 See POSTEPY CYBERNETYKI. 1221

0137-3668 See AURA. 2211

0137-3714 See OCHRONA POWIETRZA. 5136

0137-3722 See USPEKHI MEKHANIKI. 4430

0137-3838 See WIADOMOSCI ZIELARSKIE. 146

0137-3846 See POWOKI OCHRONNE. 1991

0137-4214 See PRZEGLAD HODOWLANY. 219

0137-4249 See GOSPODYNI WARSZAWA. 5558

0137-4680 See KONKRETY. 2518

0137-4710 See PIKA NOZNA. 4912

0137-4788 See SAD NOWOCZESNY. 185

0137-4796 See SLUZBA ROLNA. 135

0137-480X See W DRODZE. 5008

0137-4877 See FILM NA SWIECIE 1974. 4070

0137-4982 See PROBLEMY SZKOLNICTWA I NAUK MEDYCZNYCH. 3629

0137-4990 See ERGONOMIA WROCAW. 2114

0137-5067 See MECHANIKA I KOMPUTER / POLSKA AKADEMIA NAUK, INSTYTUT PODSTAWOWYCH PROBLEMOW TECHNIKI. 2107

0137-5075 See ARCHIVES OF ACOUSTICS. 4452

0137-5083 See POLISH JOURNAL OF CHEMISTRY. 988

0137-5261 See KOSZALINSKIE ZESZYTY MUZEALNE. 4090

0137-5318 See STUDIA MUZEALNE. 4097

0137-5474 See ZAGADNIENIA EKSPLOATACJI MASZYN. 2132

0137-5482 See KRAS I SPELEOLOGIA. 1385

0137-5490 See PRZEGLAD USTAWODAWSTWA GOSPODARCZEGO. 3102

0137-5849 See DZIENNIK URZEDOWY CEN. 1591

0137-5857 See SPRAWOZDANIA - POZNANSKIE TOWARZYSTWO PRZYJACIO NAUK. WYDZIA HISTORII I NAUK SPOECZNYCH. 2630

0137-5881 See ACTA PHYSIOLOGIAE PLANTARUM. 497

0137-6187 See DZIENNIK URZEDOWY GOWNEGO KOMITETU KULTURY FIZYCZNEJ I SPORTU. 2596

0137-6365 See STUDIA GEOTECHNICA ET MECHANICA. 1997

0137-6616 See ACTA UNIVERSITATIS NICOLAI COPERNICI. NAUKI HUMANISTYCZNO-SPOECZNE. ARCHEOLOGIA. 253

0137-6810 See ZYCIE WETERYNARYJNE. 5528

0137-6853 See ANNALES UNIVERSITATIS MARIAE CURIE-SKODOWSKA. SECTIO AA, CHEMIA. 961

0137-6861 See ANNALES UNIVERSITATIS MARIAE CURIE-SKODOWSKA. SECTIO AAA: PHYSICA. 4397

0137-6934 See BANACH CENTER PUBLICATIONS. 3496

0137-6985 See COLLECTANEA THEOLOGICA. 5028

0137-7566 See GEOGRAFIA W SZKOLE. 2562

0137-7604 See GOSC NIEDZIELNY. 4961

0137-7663 See KRZYZOWKA. 4862

0137-7698 See MIS. 1066

0137-7930 See DZIALKOWIEC. 2413

0137-8112 See WIADOMOSCI SPORTOWE. 4929

0137-8171 See SZKOLA ZAWODOWA. 4209

0137-8252 See ROZRYWKA. 4865

0137-8287 See RODZINA. 2285

0137-8295 See REWIA ROZRYWKI. 4865

0137-8511 See POMYCZEK. 1068

0137-8546 See OPOLE OPOLE. 2520

0137-8570 See AUSRA. 2256

0137-8686 See SUZBA ZDROWIA. 4804

0137-8694 See SEZAM. 5566

0137-8783 See PRZEGLAD (NACZELA ORGANIZACJA TECHNICZNA (POLAND)). 1704

0137-883X See MAY MODELARZ. 2774

0137-8996 See FIZYKA DIELEKTRYKOW I RADIOSPEKTROSKOPIA. 4443

0137-9011 See ECHO KRAKOWA. 5807

0137-902X See ECHO DNIA. 5807

0137-9038 See DZIENNIK ZACHODNI. 5807

0137-9046 See DZIENNIK WIECZORNY. 5807

0137-9062 See DZIENNIK BALTYCKI. 5807

0137-9070 See CHOPSKA DROGA. 73

0137-9089 See DZIENNIK POLSKI. 5807

0137-9097 See EXPRESS ILUSTROWANY. 5808

0137-9100 See EP. EXPRESS POZNANSKI. 5808

0137-9127 See GAZETA OLSZTYNSKA. 5808

0137-9143 See GAZETA ROBOTNICZA. 5808

0137-9178 See GOS SZCZECINSKI. 5808

0137-9186 See GOS WIELKOPOLSKI. 5808

0137-9194 See GOS WYBRZEZA. 5808

0137-9208 See GROMADA ROLNIK POLSKI. 91

0137-9224 See KURIER LUBELSKI. 5808

0137-9240 See KURIER SZCZECINSKI. 5808

0137-9259 See NOWOSCI TORUN. 5808

0137-9267 See PRZEGLAD SPORTOWY. 4913

0137-9275 See SOWO LUDU. 5808

0137-9291 See SOWO POLSKIE. 5808

0137-9305 See SPORT KATOWICE. 4920

0137-9321 See SWIAT MODYCH WARSZAWA. 1949. 1070

0137-933X See TEMPO KRAKOW. 4925

0137-9364 See WIECZOR KATOWICE. 5808

0137-9372 See WIECZOR WROCAWIA. 5808

0137-9380 See WIECZOR WYBRZEZA. 5808

0137-9399 See ZIELONY SZTANDAR. 2525

0137-9410 See ZYCIE CZESTOCHOWY. 5808

0137-9488 See GAZETA WSPOCZESNA. 5808

0137-9518 See GAZETA LUBUSKA 1975. 5808

0137-9526 See GOS POMORZA. 5808

0137-9534 See NOWINY. 5808

0137-9674 See FIRMA. 1607

0137-9690 See ZAGADNIENIA BIOFIZYKI WSPOCZESNEJ. 496

0137-9798 See QUATERNARY STUDIES IN POLAND / POLISH ACADEMY OF SCIENCES, BRANCH OFFICE IN POZNAN, COMMITTEE OF QUATERNARY RESEARCH. 1393

0137-9860 See STUDIES ON THE DEVELOPING COUNTRIES. 1628

0137-9941 See PRACE INSTYTUTU METALURGII ZELAZA IM, ST. STASZICA. 4015

0138-0125 See PUBLICATIONS OF THE INSTITUTE OF GEOPHYSICS. D. 1409

0138-0184 *See* ATMOSPHERIC OZONE ... SOLAR RADIATION. 4433

0138-0311 *See* PRAXIOLOGY. 5254

0138-032X *See* ARCHIWUM NAUKI O MATERIAACH. 2100

0138-0338 *See* POLISH POLAR RESEARCH. 5138

0138-0478 *See* PROBLEMY TURYSTYKI. 5489

0138-0540 *See* INZYNIERIA MORSKA. 1981

0138-0702 *See* BIBLIOGRAFIA POMORZA ZACHODNIEGO. PISMIENNICTWO ZAGRANICZNE. 409

0138-0710 *See* TYGODNIK PILSKI. 2524

0138-0729 *See* TZ. TYGODNIK ZAMOJSKI. 2524

0138-0745 *See* ZBLIZENIA KOSZALIN. 2525

0138-0796 *See* PRACE INSTYTUTU TECHNIKI BUDOWLANEJ. 2028

0138-0893 *See* PRZEGLAD KONINSKI. 2521

0138-0907 *See* PANORAMA LESZCZYNSKA. 2521

0138-0915 *See* PRACE INSTYTUTU TECHNOLOGII ELEKTRONOWEJ CEMI. 2075

0138-0974 *See* GEOLOGIA. 1377

0138-0990 *See* GORNICTWO. 2140

0138-1067 *See* WISSENSCHAFTLICHE ZEITSCHRIFT - ERNST-MORITZ-ARNDT-UNIVERSITAT GRIEFSWALD. MEDIZINISCHE REIHE. 3651

0138-1091 *See* HALLESCHE STUDIEN ZUR GESCHICHTE DER SOZIALDEMOKRATIE. 4542

0138-1504 *See* WISSENSCHAFTLICHE ZEITSCHRIFT - MARTIN-LUTHER-UNIV. HALLE-WITTENBERG. MATHEMATISCH-NATURWISSENSCHAFTLICHE REIHE. 5170

0138-1547 *See* TISCHTENNIS. 4926

0138-1555 *See* ARBEITSSCHUTZ, ARBEITSHYGIENE. 2859

0138-1679 *See* STAHLBERATUNG. 4020

0138-1725 *See* SCHRIFTENREIHE BEITRAGE ZUM SONDERSCHULWESEN UND ZUR REHABILITATIONSPADAGOGIK. 1885

0138-2179 *See* WISSENSCHAFTLICHE BERICHTE - ZENTRALINSTITUT FUER FESTKORPERPHYSIK UND WERKSTOFFORSCHUNG. 4425

0138-2357 *See* GEOPHYSIK UND GEOLOGIE (BERLIN, DDR). 1406

0138-290X *See* WISSENSCHAFTLICHE ZEITSCHRIFT DER PADAGOGISCHEN HOCHSCHULE "KARL LIEBKNECHT" POTSDAM. 5170

0138-2934 *See* MODERNE RONTGENFOTOGRAPHIE / ORWO. 3944

0138-3019 *See* MATHEMATICAL RESEARCH. 3520

0138-3140 *See* ROSTOCKER PHYSIKALISCHE MANUSKRIPTE. 4420

0138-3299 *See* ROSTOCKER AGRARWISSENSCHAFTLICHE BEITRAEGE. 131

0138-3957 *See* SITZUNGSBERICHTE DER SACHSISCHEN AKADEMIE DER WISSENSCHAFTEN ZU LEIPZIG, PHILOLOGISCH-HISTORISCHE KLASSE. 4361

0138-4104 *See* BEITRAEGE ZUR GESCHICHTE DER HUMBOLDT-UNIVERSITAT ZU BERLIN. 1811

0138-4198 *See* POTSDAMER FORSCHUNGEN. REIHE A. 1774

0138-4309 *See* TIERERNAHRUNG UND FUTTERUNG. 204

0138-4694 *See* SUDASIATISCHE SPRACHWISSENSCHAFTLICHE STUDIEN / AKADEMIE DER WISSENSCHAFTEN DER DDR, ZENTRALINSTITUT FUR SPRACHWISSENSCHAFT. 3326

0138-4988 *See* ACTA BIOTECHNOLOGICA. 3685

0138-5097 *See* BEITRAEGE ZUR KLINISCHEN NEUROLOGIE UND PSYCHIATRIE. 3828

0138-5658 *See* ABHANDLUNGEN DES METEOROLOGISCHEN DIENSTES DER DEUTSCHEN DEMOKRATISCHEN REPUBLIK. 1419

0138-5798 *See* KOMMENTARE ZUM ARZNEIBUCH DER DEUTSCHEN DEMOKRATISCHEN REPUBLIK. 4313

0138-6247 *See* ACPA. 204

0138-6425 *See* REVISTA CUBANA DE CIENCIAS SOCIALES. 4546

0138-6441 *See* REVISTA FORESTAL BARACOA. 2394

0138-7154 *See* CIENCIAS BIOLOGICAS. 451

0138-7324 *See* ACTUALIDADES DE LA INFORMACION CIENTIFICA Y TECNICA. 3187

0138-7669 *See* LEGALIDAD SOCIALISTA : BOLETIN DE INFORMACION JURIDICA EDITADO POR LA FISCALIA GENERAL DE LA REPUBLICA. 3001

0138-7766 *See* CUBA, HALF-YEARLY ECONOMIC REPORT. 1478

0138-7871 *See* REFERATIVA DE EDUCACION : RE. 1777

0138-8452 *See* REVISTA CUBANA DE INVESTIGACIONES PESQUERAS / CENTRO DE INVESTIGACIONES PESQUERAS, MIRAMAR, LA HABANA, CUBA. 2312

0138-8770 *See* GACETA DE CUBA. 320

0138-8800 *See* TECNICA POPULAR. 5165

0138-9092 *See* AQUACULTURA HUNGARICA. 2295

0138-9130 *See* SCIENTOMETRICS. 5156

0138-9491 *See* ANNALES UNIVERSITATIS SCIENTIARUM BUDAPESTINENSIS DE ROLANDO EOTVOS NOMINATAE. SECTIO COMPUTATORICA. 3493

0138-9947 *See* SZOLNOK MEGYEI MUZEUMI EVKONYV. 4097

0139-0090 *See* BEKES MEGYEI MUZEUMOK KOZLEMENYEI. 2678

0139-0252 *See* DUNAKANYAR. 4850

0139-1054 *See* ANYAGGAZDALKODAS ES RAKTARGAZDALKODAS. 1598

0139-1682 *See* HETI VILAGGAZDASAG : HVG. 1635

0139-2115 *See* FEJER MEGYEI KONYVTAROS. 3210

0139-3006 *See* ACTA ALIMENTARIA (BUDAPEST). 2325

0139-3499 *See* SZABOLCS-SZATMAR MEGYEI KONYVTARI HIRADO. 3252

0139-3510 *See* BERUHAZASI, EPITOIPARI, LAKASEPITESI ZSEBKONYV. 600

0139-4215 *See* PEST MEGYEI ORVOS-GYOGYSZERESZ NAPOK TUDOMANYOS KOZLEMENYEI. 3627

0139-4509 *See* KORHAZ- ES ORVOSTECHNIKA. 3602

0139-4932 *See* INTERNATIONAL BASKETBALL. 4900

0139-4983 *See* SOMOGYI MUZEUMOK KOZLEMENYEI. 2710

0139-5033 *See* VYSKUMNE PRACE Z ODBORU PAPIERA A CELULOZY. 4239

0139-5297 *See* SBORNIK VEDECKYCH PRACI USTREDNIHO STATNIHO VETERINARNIHO USTAVU. 5521

0139-5378 *See* ZBORNIK SLOVENSKEHO NARODNEHO MUZEA. HISTORIA. ANNALES MUSEI NATIONALIS SLOVACI. 2716

0139-570X *See* VEDECKY CASOPIS ZEMEDELSKA EKONOMIKA. 144

0139-5807 *See* PRACE VYZKUMNEHO USTAVU LESNIHO HOSPODARSTVI A MYSLIVOSTI. 2390

0139-5815 *See* UMENI A REMESLA. 376

0139-598X *See* CZECHOSLOVAK BIBLIOGRAPHY ON EPIDEMIOLOGY AND MICROBIOLOGY. 3734

0139-6005 *See* SPRAVNI PRAVO. 3094

0139-6013 *See* URODA. 190

0139-6501 *See* STOP (BRATISLAVA). 5426

0139-6544 *See* PRIRODNI VEDY. 5139

0139-682X *See* SBORNIK VYSOKE SKOLY CHEMICKO-TECHNOLOGICKE V PRAZE. FIZIKALNI CHEMIE. SBORNIK PRAZHSKOGO KHIMIKO- TECHNOLOGICHESKOGO INSTITUTA. FIZICHESKAIA KHIMIIA. SCIENTIFIC PAPERS OF THE PRAGUE INSTITUTE OF CHEMICAL TECHNOLOGY. PHYSICAL CHEMISTRY. 1057

0139-701X See PRUMYSLOVE VLASTNICTVI / VYDAVA FEDERALNI URAD PRO VYNALEZY. 1308

0139-7036 *See* REVUE OBHCODU, PRUMYSLU, HOSPODARSTVI. 1582

0139-7214 *See* VYTVARNY ZIVOT. 368

0139-7265 *See* VYZKUM V CHOVU SKOTU. 145

0139-7575 *See* SBORNIK VYSOKE SKOLY CHEMICKO-TECHNOLOGICKE V PRAZE. FIZIKA MATERIALU A MERICI TECHNIKA. SBORNIK PRAZHSKOGO KHIMIKO-TECHNOLOGICHESKOGO INSTITUTA. FIZIKA MATERIALOV I IZMERITELNAIA TEKHNIKA. SCIENTIFIC PAPERS OF THE PRAGUE INSTITUTE OF CHEMICAL TECHNOLOGY. MATERIAL SCIENCE AND MEASUREMENT TECHNIQUE. 2108

0139-7583 *See* ZAPADNE KARPATY. SERIA HYDROGEOLOGIA A INZINIERSKA GEOLOGIA. 1419

0139-763X *See* PRACE VYZKUMNEHO USTAVU GEOLOGICKEHO INZENYRSTVI. 4275

0139-7834 *See* SBORNIK GPO. 1396

0139-7893 *See* FOLIA ZOOLOGICA (BRNO). 5584

0139-8288 *See* ZAPADNE KARPATY. SERIA GEOLOGIA. 1401

0139-8717 *See* EVA BRATISLAVA. 1084

0139-8822 *See* HYDINARSTVO. 212

0139-8946 *See* ZAPADNE KARPATY. MINERALOGIA, PETROGRAFIA, GEOCHEMIA, METALOGENEZA. 1401

0139-908X *See* SBORNIK VYSOKE SKOLY CHEMICKO-TECHNOLOGICKE V PRAZE. POLYMERY-CHEMIE, VLASTNOSTI A ZPRACOVANI. 1047

0139-9365 *See* VYTVARNA KULTURA. 368

0139-939X *See* FOLIA PHARMACEUTICA (PRAHA). 4305

0139-9683 *See* SBORNIK VYSOKE SKOLY CHEMICKO-TECHNOLOGICKE V PRAZE. A. 992

0139-973X *See* SBORNIK VYSOKE SKOLY CHEMICKO-TECHNOLOGICKE V PRAZE. AUTOMATIZOVANE SYSTEMY RIZENI A VYPOCETNI METODY. SBORNIK PRAZHSKOGO KHIMIKO-TEKHNOLOGICHESKOGO INSTITUTA. AVTOMATIZIROVANNYE SISTEMY UPRAVLENIIA I VYCHISLITELNYE METODY. SCIENTIFIC PAPERS OF THE PRAGUE INSTITUTE OF CHEMICAL TECHNOLOGY. AUTOMATIC CONTROL SYSTEMS AND COMPUTING METHODS. 2017

0139-9853 *See* PAMATKY A PRIRODA. 2702

0139-9918 *See* MATHEMATICA SLOVACA. 3518

0140-0096 *See* CONSERVATOR (LONDON). 348

0140-0118 *See* MEDICAL & BIOLOGICAL ENGINEERING & COMPUTING. 3695

0140-041X *See* RAPRA NEWS. 5077

0140-0428 *See* EDUCATIONAL ADMINISTRATION AND HISTORY. MONOGRAPH. 1863

0140-0460 *See* TIMES (LONDON, ENGLAND: 1788). 5813

0140-0568 *See* CATALYSIS. 1050

0140-0835 *See* TOPICS IN ENZYME AND FERMENTATION BIOTECHNOLOGY. 3696

0140-0843 *See* TOPICS IN ANTIBIOTIC CHEMISTRY. 4331

0140-1033 *See* PAPER CONSERVATION NEWS (LONDON). 4235

0140-1084 *See* COMMUNITY NEWS - WELSH OFFICE OF THE EUROPEAN COMMUNITIES. 4639

0140-1211 *See* MEDIEVAL SERMON STUDIES NEWSLETTER. 4976

0140-1599 *See* ACOUSTICS LETTERS. 4452

0140-1610 *See* EUROPEAN JOURNAL OF RHEUMATOLOGY AND INFLAMMATION (ENGLISH EDITION). 3804

0140-1750 See JOURNAL OF SOCIAL AND EVOLUTIONARY SYSTEMS. 5250

0140-1890 *See* ANTENNA. 5576

0140-1912 *See* NEWS LETTER - CUMBRIA FAMILY HISTORY SOCIETY. 2462

0140-1963 *See* JOURNAL OF ARID ENVIRONMENTS. 1357

0140-1971 *See* JOURNAL OF ADOLESCENCE (LONDON, ENGLAND). 3904

ISSN Index

0140-2196 See SAGE ANNUAL REVIEW OF SOCIAL AND EDUCATIONAL CHANGE. 1781

0140-2285 See JAZZ JOURNAL INTERNATIONAL. 4125

0140-2315 See SCOTTISH JOURNAL OF PHYSICAL EDUCATION. 1858

0140-2382 See WEST EUROPEAN POLITICS. 4500

0140-2390 See JOURNAL OF STRATEGIC STUDIES, THE. 4048

0140-2447 See NEW LITERATURE ON OLD AGE. 5180

0140-2722 See BRITISH MEDICINE (LONDON : 1972). 3559

0140-2935 See ENVOY INTERNATIONAL (ASHFORD, KENT : 1981). 4520

0140-2986 See HEALTH AND HYGIENE (LONDON). 4777

0140-3028 See MEDICAL LABORATORY WORLD. 3610

0140-3222 See NATURAL GAS FOR INDUSTRY AND COMMERCE. 4265

0140-3249 See COMPUTERS AND LAW. 1178

0140-332X See TRANSACTIONS OF THE HISTORIC SOCIETY OF LANCASHIRE AND CHESHIRE FOR THE YEAR. 2713

0140-3397 See QUINQUEREME. 3313

0140-3435 See WHICH COMPUTER?. 1207

0140-346X See WORDS WORTH. 1908

0140-3664 See COMPUTER COMMUNICATIONS. 1240

0140-3990 See TRANSACTIONS - LEICESTERSHIRE ARCHAEOLOGICAL AND HISTORICAL SOCIETY. 284

0140-4040 See WHO OWNS WHOM: UNITED KINGDOM AND REPUBLIC OF IRELAND. 720

0140-4067 See NUCLEAR ENERGY (1978). 1951

0140-4237 See INTERNATIONAL BUILDING SERVICES ABSTRACTS. 617

0140-4253 3216

0140-427X See MAP COLLECTOR, THE. 2582

0140-4415 See MIMS AFRICA. 4315

0140-4539 See TREASURE HUNTING. 2779

0140-4571 See VOLE. 310

0140-458X See CLIMATE MONITOR. 1422

0140-4768 See RURAL DEVELOPMENT ABSTRACTS / [PREPARED BY THE COMMONWEALTH BUREAU OF AGRICULTURAL ECONOMICS]. 2840

0140-4784 See FOREST PRODUCTS ABSTRACTS. 2399

0140-4822 See AGRICULTURAL SUPPLY INDUSTRY. 158

0140-489X See ECONOMIC OUTLOOK (LONDON. 1977). 1483

0140-492X See EUROPEAN BIBLIOGRAPHY OF SOVIET, EAST EUROPEAN AND SLAVONIC STUDIES. 2635

0140-5039 See EAR. EDINBURGH ARCHITECTURAL RESEARCH. 298

0140-5047 See FAIRPLAY WORLD SHIPPING DIRECTORY. 5449

0140-5098 See MIDDLE EAST WATER & SEWAGE. 5536

0140-511X See JOURNAL OF AUDIOVISUAL MEDIA IN MEDICINE, THE. 3593

0140-525X See BEHAVIORAL AND BRAIN SCIENCES, THE. 4576

0140-5314 See ABORTION STATISTICS. ENGLAND & WALES. 591

0140-5365 See TOXICOLOGY ABSTRACTS. 3662

0140-5373 See AQUATIC SCIENCES AND FISHERIES ABSTRACTS. PART 1 : BIOLOGICAL SCIENCES AND LIVING RESOURCES. 2316

0140-5381 See AQUATIC SCIENCES AND FISHERIES ABSTRACTS. PART 2 : OCEAN TECHNOLOGY, POLICY AND NON-LIVING RESOURCES. 2316

0140-5403 See NORFOLK ANCESTOR : JOURNAL OF THE NORFOLK & NORWICH GENEALOGICAL SOCIETY, THE. 2464

0140-5721 See COUNTRY MUSIC ROUND UP. 4112

0140-5748 See HEALTH CARE BUYERS GUIDE. 950

0140-5772 See SELL'S BRITISH EXPORTERS (1980). 851

0140-5799 See AMERICAN BUSINESS IN BRITAIN. 638

0140-5977 See MODEL BOATS. 594

0140-6000 See DARTS WORLD. 4892

0140-6078 See MUSICA ASIATICA. 4135

0140-6388 See MLC ECONOMIC INFORMATION SERVICE. MEAT DEMAND TRENDS. 216

0140-654X See STONEHENGE VIEWPOINT. 283

0140-6582 See WHO OWNS WHOM: CONTINENTAL EUROPE. 720

0140-6647 See PENSION FUNDS AND THEIR ADVISERS. 911

0140-668X See INTERNATIONAL MONOGRAPH SERIES ON EARLY CHILD CARE. 2281

0140-6701 See FUEL AND ENERGY ABSTRACTS. 1944

0140-671X See JOURNAL OF SOURCES IN EDUCATIONAL HISTORY. 1758

0140-6728 See WESTMINSTER STUDIES IN EDUCATION. 1791

0140-6736 See LANCET (BRITISH EDITION). 3603

0140-6787 See NSCA MEMBERS' HANDBOOK. 2179

0140-7007 See INTERNATIONAL JOURNAL OF REFRIGERATION. 2606

0140-7082 See EDINBURGH BIBLIOGRAPHICAL SOCIETY TRANSACTIONS. 415

0140-7430 See NATIONAL GALLERY TECHNICAL BULLETIN. 359

0140-7503 See ESSEX FAMILY HISTORIAN, THE. 2446

0140-7570 See GREAT OUTDOORS. 4873

0140-7686 See BRITISH JOURNAL OF OBSTETRICS AND GYNAECOLOGY. SUPPLEMENT. 3758

0140-7708 See PHYSICAL EDUCATION REVIEW. 1857

0140-7724 See POSTGRADUATE DOCTOR. MIDDLE EAST EDITION. 3628

0140-7740 See ANIMATIONS. 5361

0140-7775 See JOURNAL OF FISH DISEASES. 2306

0140-7783 See JOURNAL OF VETERINARY PHARMACOLOGY AND THERAPEUTICS. 5514

0140-7791 See PLANT, CELL AND ENVIRONMENT. 523

0140-7805 See BOOKS IN THE EARTH SCIENCES AND RELATED TOPICS. 1352

0140-7813 See BRITISH GEOLOGICAL LITERATURE. 1368

0140-8321 See MIDDLE EAST TRAVEL. 5484

0140-8445 See POWDER COATINGS BULLETIN. 4225

0140-8488 See BUILDING WITH STEEL (LONDON. 1969). 605

0140-8534 See HEALTH & SAFETY MONITOR. 2862

0140-8798 See WATERBORNE & HIGH SOLIDS COATINGS BULLETIN. 4225

0140-895X See IRISH LITERARY STUDIES. 3397

0140-9018 See WELSH SOCIAL TRENDS / WELSH OFFICE / TUEDDIADAU CYMDEITHASOL / Y SWYDDFA GYMREIG. 1526

0140-9123 See RECENT ADVANCES IN ENDOCRINOLOGY AND METABOLISM. 3733

0140-9174 See MANAGEMENT RESEARCH NEWS : MRN. 878

0140-9220 See AERIAL ARCHAEOLOGY. 253

0140-9883 See ENERGY ECONOMICS. 1940

0141-0016 See ... VOLUME OF THE WALPOLE SOCIETY, THE. 368

0141-0156 See COLLECTED PAPERS ON SOUTH ASIA. 2649

0141-0164 See RICE ABSTRACTS. 1012

0141-0172 See SOYABEAN ABSTRACTS. 156

0141-0180 See SEED ABSTRACTS. 156

0141-0229 See ENZYME AND MICROBIAL TECHNOLOGY. 3692

0141-0296 See ENGINEERING STRUCTURES. 2023

0141-0326 See HANDBOOK OF ASTRONOMY, ASTROPHYSICS, AND GEOPHYSICS. 395

0141-0415 See IN TRUST. 301

0141-0423 See JOURNAL OF RESEARCH IN READING. 1898

0141-061X See ELECTRONIC TECHNOLOGY (LONDON). 2048

0141-0687 See CARGO HANDLING ABSTRACTS / INTERNATIONAL CARGO HANDLING CO-ORDINATION ASSOCIATION. 5400

0141-075X See METHODS FOR THE EXAMINATION OF WATERS AND ASSOCIATED MATERIALS. 2236

0141-0768 See JOURNAL OF THE ROYAL SOCIETY OF MEDICINE. 3599

0141-0814 See JOURNAL OF THE SOCIETY FOR UNDERWATER TECHNOLOGY. 1450

0141-1004 See STUDIES IN OPERATIONS RESEARCH. 1204

0141-1012 See LIBRARY OF ANTHROPOLOGY. 240

0141-1047 See CURRENCY CONFIDENTIAL. 786

0141-1047 See EUROPEAN & MIDDLE EAST TAX REPORT, THE. 4722

0141-1128 See MONOGRAPHS ON ASTRONOMICAL SUBJECTS. 397

0141-1136 See MARINE ENVIRONMENTAL RESEARCH. 2177

0141-1144 See COMPANY. 5553

0141-1187 See APPLIED OCEAN RESEARCH. 1446

0141-1403 See HEALTH EQUIPMENT NOTE. 3581

0141-1594 See PHASE TRANSITIONS. 4414

0141-1675 See ANNUAL REPORT - SOIL SURVEY. ENGLAND AND WALES. 163

0141-1748 See INTERNATIONAL BROADCASTING. 1133

0141-1896 See JOURNAL OF MUSICOLOGICAL RESEARCH, THE. 4126

0141-1918 See INTERNATIONAL POWER GENERATION. 2067

0141-1926 See BRITISH EDUCATIONAL RESEARCH JOURNAL. 1728

0141-1942 See ANNUAL BULLETIN - SOCIETE JERSIAISE. 2675

0141-1969 See BRITISH SUGAR NEWS. 165

0141-2140 See GENERAL AND SYNTHETIC METHODS. 1041

0141-2175 See PLANNED INNOVATION. 882

0141-2191 See ARCHITECTURAL MONOGRAPHS. 289

0141-2205 See APEX (KIDDERMINSTER). 5273

0141-2221 See AGRA EUROPE. POTATO MARKETS. 46

0141-223X See AGRA EUROPE. PRESERVED MILK. 191

0141-2256 See MEDICAL RESEARCH COUNCIL ANNUAL REPORT. 3611

0141-2302 See CANAL & RIVERBOAT. 4870

0141-237X See DOUBLE TRESSURE : JOURNAL OF THE HERALDRY SOCIETY OF SCOTLAND, THE. 2445

0141-2604 See ANNUAL LIST OF PUBLICATIONS - DEPARTMENT OF THE ENVIRONMENT. DEPARTMENT OF TRANSPORT. LIBRARY SERVICES. 2160

0141-2647 See WORKING PAPER SERIES - HEALTH SERVICES MANAGEMENT UNIT. DEPARTMENT OF SOCIAL ADMINISTRATION. UNIVERSITY OF MANCHESTER. 4808

0141-2760 See JOURNAL OF CLINICAL & LABORATORY IMMUNOLOGY. 3673

0141-2841 See PHYSIOLOGY AND PATHOPHYSIOLOGY OF THE SKIN, THE. 585

0141-2876 See BRITISH TAX REPORT. 4714

0141-2949 See POLICE STUDIES. 3172

0141-299X See CELL NUCLEUS. 534

0141-3228 See FINANCIAL TIMES OIL AND GAS INTERNATIONAL YEAR BOOK. 4256

0141-3236 See FINANCIAL TIMES WHO'S WHO IN WORLD OIL AND GAS. 1607

0141-3244 *See* FINANCIAL TIMES MINING INTERNATIONAL YEAR BOOK. 2139

0141-3317 *See* JOURNAL OF CHRONIC DISEASES AND THERAPEUTICS RESEARCH. 3594

0141-335X *See* LITERATURE OF ART, THE. 3407

0141-3368 *See* CURRENT SURGICAL PRACTICE. 3963

0141-3376 *See* PROSPECTING IN AREAS OF GLACIATED TERRAIN. 2148

0141-3473 *See* BEHAVIOURAL PSYCHOTHERAPY. 4577

0141-3600 *See* SPECIAL PUBLICATION ... OF THE INTERNATIONAL ASSOCIATION OF SEDIMENTOLOGISTS. 1398

0141-3619 *See* OPEN EARTH. 1359

0141-3635 *See* FACTOTUM (LONDON, ENGLAND). 3210

0141-3805 *See* BIRMINGHAM SLAVONIC MONOGRAPHS. 3269

0141-3821 *See* NOTTINGHAMSHIRE FAMILY HISTORY SOCIETY : JOURNAL. 2465

0141-3899 *See* NURSING RESEARCH ABSTRACTS. 3865

0141-3910 *See* POLYMER DEGRADATION AND STABILITY. 988

0141-3929 *See* AFRICAN BUSINESS. 637

0141-4151 *See* ARAB SHIPPING. 5447

0141-4259 *See* DEER. 226

0141-4305 *See* U.K. PETROLEUM INDUSTRY STATISTICS. CONSUMPTION AND REFINERY PRODUCTION. 4285

0141-4577 *See* WORCESTERSHIRE HISTORICAL SOCIETY (PUBLICATIONS). 5237

0141-4585 *See* EEC SHIPPING. 5449

0141-4615 *See* RAIL ENGINEERING INTERNATIONAL (1981). 5434

0141-4739 *See* BRITISH REVIEW OF ECONOMIC ISSUES. 1465

0141-4836 *See* INTERNATIONAL ENVIRONMENT & SAFETY. 2174

0141-4909 *See* REGISTER OF SHIPS (LLOYD'S REGISTER OF SHIPPING). 5455

0141-5085 *See* GRAINGER SOCIETY JOURNAL, THE. 4119

0141-5387 *See* EUROPEAN JOURNAL OF ORTHODONTICS. 1323

0141-5425 *See* JOURNAL OF BIOMEDICAL ENGINEERING. 3694

0141-5492 *See* BIOTECHNOLOGY LETTERS. 3689

0141-5530 *See* INTERNATIONAL JOURNAL OF MATERIALS IN ENGINEERING APPLICATIONS. 2103

0141-5573 *See* ENGINEERING DESIGN GUIDES. 1972

0141-5581 *See* RECENT ADVANCES IN GASTROENTEROLOGY. 3747

0141-559X *See* NEWSLETTER - CHARLES RENNIE MACKINTOSH SOCIETY. 304

0141-5735 *See* TTJ TELEPHONE ADDRESS BOOK. 2405

0141-5859 *See* JUSTICE OF THE PEACE (CHICHESTER). 2991

0141-5972 *See* BRITISH QUALIFICATIONS. 4210

0141-6200 *See* BRITISH JOURNAL OF RELIGIOUS EDUCATION. 4940

0141-6219 *See* ELECTRONIC COMPONENTS & APPLICATIONS. 2047

0141-6278 *See* ABC GUIDE TO INTERNATIONAL TRAVEL. 5459

0141-6286 *See* EAST LONDON RECORD. 2686

0141-6340 *See* NOMINA. 3306

0141-6359 *See* PRECISION ENGINEERING. 2125

0141-6421 *See* JOURNAL OF PETROLEUM GEOLOGY. 4262

0141-6561 *See* LIBRARY AND INFORMATION RESEARCH NEWS. 3224

0141-6707 *See* AFRICAN JOURNAL OF ECOLOGY. 2211

0141-6723 *See* MUSEUMS AND ART GALLERIES IN GREAT BRITAIN AND IRELAND. 4093

0141-6790 *See* ART HISTORY. 339

0141-6979 *See* URBAN DESIGN FORUM. 2837

0141-7037 *See* JOURNAL OF THE BRITISH CONTACT LENS ASSOCIATION. 3876

0141-7134 *See* TRAINING DIGEST. 947

0141-7258 *See* COMMERCIAL LAWS OF EUROPE. 3098

0141-7266 *See* EUROPEAN COMMERCIAL CASES. 3100

0141-7282 *See* EDUCARE LONDON. 1878

0141-7592 *See* DIRECTORY / ENGINEERING EMPLOYERS' FEDERATION. 1970

0141-7614 *See* JOURNAL / CORNWALL FAMILY HISTORY SOCIETY. 2455

0141-7711 *See* CSA NEUROSCIENCES ABSTRACTS. 3656

0141-7789 *See* FEMINIST REVIEW. 5556

0141-8009 *See* NEWSLETTER - GLASGOW & WEST OF SCOTLAND FAMILY HISTORY SOCIETY. 2463

0141-8017 *See* INTERNATIONAL SECURITY REVIEW. 872

0141-8033 *See* JOURNAL OF SOCIAL WELFARE & FAMILY LAW. 3121

0141-8130 *See* INTERNATIONAL JOURNAL OF BIOLOGICAL MACROMOLECULES. 581

0141-8149 *See* OXFORD GERMAN STUDIES : BOOK SUPPLEMENT. 2702

0141-8211 *See* EUROPEAN JOURNAL OF EDUCATION. 1745

0141-8246 *See* HEALTH & SAFETY AT WORK (CROYDON). 2862

0141-8459 *See* EDUCA. 1912

0141-8513 *See* COMMONWEALTH CURRENTS. 2908

0141-8521 *See* FOOD SURVEILLANCE PAPER. 2340

0141-8602 *See* METALLURGIA (1978). 4010

0141-8610 *See* PHILOSOPHICAL MAGAZINE. A, PHYSICS OF CONDENSED MATTER, DEFECTS AND MECHANICAL PROPERTIES. 4414

0141-867X *See* BRITISH JOURNAL FOR EIGHTEENTH-CENTURY STUDIES, THE. 3369

0141-8955 *See* JOURNAL OF INHERITED METABOLIC DISEASE. 3798

0141-8963 *See* LABORATORY EQUIPMENT DIRECTORY. 5125

0141-9064 *See* MOSSBAUER SPECTROSCOPY ABSTRACTS. 4438

0141-9072 *See* SCOTTISH EDUCATIONAL REVIEW. 1783

0141-9285 *See* MARKETING WEEK. 932

0141-9331 *See* MICROPROCESSORS AND MICROSYSTEMS. 1230

0141-9382 *See* DISPLAYS. 1228

0141-9455 *See* FLEET STREET REPORTS. 1304

0141-9536 *See* AFRICA HEALTH. 3547

0141-9544 *See* JOURNAL OF THE NORTH MIDDLESEX FAMILY HISTORY SOCIETY. 2456

0141-965X *See* EPILEPSY. 3832

0141-9668 *See* TROPICAL FORESTRY PAPERS. 2397

0141-9676 *See* REPORT - WATT COMMITTEE ON ENERGY. 1955

0141-9684 *See* BNF NUTRITION BULLETIN. 4188

0141-9811 *See* ELECTRIC VEHICLE DEVELOPMENTS. 5381

0141-982X *See* TEACHING STATISTICS. 1798

0141-9838 *See* PARASITE IMMUNOLOGY. 3675

0141-9846 *See* JOURNAL OF DEVELOPMENTAL PHYSIOLOGY. 3763

0141-9854 *See* CLINICAL AND LABORATORY HAEMATOLOGY. 3771

0141-9870 *See* ETHNIC AND RACIAL STUDIES. 2260

0141-9889 *See* SOCIOLOGY OF HEALTH & ILLNESS. 5262

0141-9951 *See* CURRENT MEDICAL RESEARCH AND OPINION SUPPLEMENT. 3570

0142-0143 *See* IFCC NEWS. 977

0142-0232 *See* PERSONAL COMPUTER WORLD. 1272

0142-0305 *See* MIDDLE EAST ARCHITECTURAL DESIGN. 303

0142-0372 *See* NURSING (OXFORD). 3865

0142-0410 *See* CONSTRUCTION (LONDON, 1977). 609

0142-0453 *See* JOURNAL OF AUTOMATIC CHEMISTRY, THE. 1016

0142-0461 *See* EUROPEAN INTELLECTUAL PROPERTY REVIEW. 1304

0142-0496 *See* COMPUTER FRAUD & SECURITY BULLETIN. 1225

0142-0550 *See* CONSTRUCTION PLANT & EQUIPMENT INTERNATIONAL ANNUAL. 610

0142-0615 *See* INTERNATIONAL JOURNAL OF ELECTRICAL POWER & ENERGY SYSTEMS. 2066

0142-064X *See* JOURNAL FOR THE STUDY OF THE NEW TESTAMENT. 5017

0142-0674 *See* BIOENGINEERING CURRENT AWARENESS NOTIFICATION : BECAN. 3686

0142-0704 *See* HOME IMPROVEMENTS JOURNAL. 616

0142-0763 *See* COMECON REPORTS. 1470

0142-0771 y 0307-0379 *See* INTERNATIONAL ECONOMIC DATA SERVICE. 1636

0142-0798 *See* HALI. 5351

0142-1042 *See* CLICK LONDON. 1973. 3273

0142-1050 *See* CURRENT (LONDON, ENGLAND). 2514

0142-1123 *See* INTERNATIONAL JOURNAL OF FATIGUE. 2102

0142-1557 *See* ICL TECHNICAL JOURNAL. 1187

0142-159X *See* MEDICAL TEACHER. 3611

0142-1832 *See* CAVES & CAVING. 1371

0142-1867 *See* CARMARTHENSHIRE ANTIQUARY, THE. 2683

0142-1883 *See* FRUIT AND TROPICAL PRODUCTS. 172

0142-1913 *See* TOBACCO QUARTERLY. 5374

0142-1921 *See* WOOL QUARTERLY. 5361

0142-193X *See* TSETSE AND TRYPANOSOMIASIS INFORMATION QUARTERLY. 5599

0142-2278 *See* NEWS LETTER OF THE SOCIETY OF ARCHIVISTS. 2482

0142-2324 *See* EARTH SCIENCE CONSERVATION. 2192

0142-2367 *See* INTERNATIONAL CONGRESS AND SYMPOSIUM SERIES / ROYAL SOCIETY OF MEDICINE. 3588

0142-2391 *See* RESOURCE MANAGEMENT AND OPTIMIZATION. 2204

0142-2413 *See* SURVEYS IN HIGH ENERGY PHYSICS. 4451

0142-2421 *See* SURFACE AND INTERFACE ANALYSIS : SIA. 1019

0142-2510 *See* FIRE (TUNBRIDGE WELLS). 2290

0142-2782 *See* BIOPHARMACEUTICS & DRUG DISPOSITION. 4293

0142-288X *See* UNITED KINGDOM ATOMIC ENERGY AUTHORITY NORTHERN DIVISION REPORT. 1959

0142-2952 *See* ENCYCLOPEDIA OF HIGHWAY LAW AND PRACTICE. 2966

0142-2987 *See* ENCYCLOPEDIA OF U.K. AND EUROPEAN PATENT LAW. 2966

0142-310X *See* BUILDING SERVICES & ENVIRONMENTAL ENGINEER. 2019

0142-3134 *See* REPORT ASSISTANT MASTERS AND MISTRESSES ASSOCIATION. 1778

0142-3304 *See* HISTORICAL METALLURGY. 4003

0142-3312 *See* TRANSACTIONS OF THE INSTITUTE OF MEASUREMENT AND CONTROL. 2131

0142-3363 *See* BWLETIN Y BWRDD GWYBODAU CELTAIDD. 3271

0142-338X *See* VOGUE PATTERNS (BRITISH EDITION). 5186

0142-3401 *See* CHEMICAL PHYSICS OF SOLIDS AND THEIR SURFACES. 4399

0142-3487 *See* NATIONAL TRUST STUDIES. 325

0142-422X *See* AGRA EUROPE SPECIAL REPORT. 46

0142-4319 *See* JOURNAL OF MUSCLE RESEARCH AND CELL MOTILITY. 538

0142-4688 See SOUTHERN HISTORY. 2710
0142-4742 See CARIBBEAN INSIGHT. 2726
0142-4793 See OFFSHORE ENGINEERING INFORMATION BULLETIN. 3238
0142-4823 See CURRENCY FORECASTING SERVICE. 895
0142-4857 See PETITS PROPOS CULINAIRES. 4197
0142-5048 See KEY BRITISH ENTERPRISES : KBE / COMPILED AND PUBLISHED BY PUBLICATIONS DIVISION, DUN & BRADSTREET LIMITED. 688
0142-5137 See RATE SUPPORT GRANT STATISTICS / SOCIETY OF COUNTY TREASURERS. 4699
0142-517X See WEST MIDDLESEX FAMILY HISTORY SOCIETY JOURNAL. 2477
0142-5196 See CHARTERED QUANTITY SURVEYOR. 2020
0142-5218 See BRITISH ALTERNATIVE THEATRE DIRECTORY. 5362
0142-5242 See GRASS AND FORAGE SCIENCE. 90
0142-5447 See MEMBERSHIP LIST - ROYAL COLLEGE OF PSYCHIATRISTS. 3930
0142-5455 See EMPLOYEE RELATIONS. 940
0142-5463 See INTERNATIONAL JOURNAL OF COSMETIC SCIENCE. 404
0142-5471 See INFORMATION DESIGN JOURNAL. 3215
0142-5625 See CHANNEL ISLANDS SPECIALISED CATALOGUE OF STAMPS AND POSTAL HISTORY. 2784
0142-5633 See CAP MONITOR. 72
0142-5692 See BRITISH JOURNAL OF SOCIOLOGY OF EDUCATION. 5241
0142-5803 See TRANSACTIONS - ASSOCIATION FOR STUDIES IN THE CONSERVATION OF HISTORIC BUILDINGS. 310
0142-5811 See SYMPOSIUM PAPERS / INSTITUTION OF CHEMICAL ENGINEERS, NORTH WESTERN BRANCH. 2017
0142-5854 See COMMUNICATION TECHNOLOGY IMPACT. 1152
0142-5889 See ADVANCES IN DESERT AND ARID LAND TECHNOLOGY AND DEVELOPMENT. 5081
0142-5900 See ECONOMIC PERSPECTIVES (CHUR). 1484
0142-5919 See INTERNATIONAL JOURNAL OF SOLAR ENERGY. 1948
0142-5927 See PRACTICAL APPROACH TO PATENTS, TRADEMARKS AND COPYRIGHTS, A. 1308
0142-5951 See JOURNAL CONTENTS IN QUANTITATIVE METHODS. 3511
0142-6001 See APPLIED LINGUISTICS. 3266
0142-6028 See STUDIES ON ASIAN TOPICS. 2508
0142-615X See STONEHAM CATALOGUE OF BRITISH STAMPS, THE. 2787
0142-6184 See DEFENCE (ETON). 4040
0142-6192 See HOBBY ELECTRONICS. 2056
0142-6230 See HI-FI NEWS & RECORD REVIEW. 5317
0142-6265 See INSURANCE AGE. 2882
0142-632X See PCR / PRODUCTION AND CASTING REPORT. 1621
0142-6338 See JOURNAL OF TROPICAL PEDIATRICS (1980). 3905
0142-6397 See LANDSCAPE RESEARCH. 2423
0142-6516 See GEOSYSTEMS NEWS. 1380
0142-6540 See OXFORD ART JOURNAL. 361
0142-6567 See NEWS FROM XINHUA NEWS AGENCY, CHINA. WEEKLY ISSUE. 2507
0142-6591 See ANNUAL REPORT OF THE ANIMAL HEALTH TRUST. 5503
0142-6680 See SHIPBROKER, THE. 5456
0142-6702 See ART MONTHLY. 339
0142-694X See DESIGN STUDIES. 2097
0142-7164 See APPLIED PSYCHOLINGUISTICS. 3266
0142-7210 See COMPUTING TODAY (LONDON). 1266

0142-7237 See FIRST LANGUAGE. 3281
0142-7253 See ARCHAEOASTRONOMY. 256
0142-727X See INTERNATIONAL JOURNAL OF HEAT AND FLUID FLOW, THE. 2116
0142-7466 See TV WORLD. 1142
0142-7490 See LAWYER'S REMEMBRANCER. 2998
0142-7547 See SOCIETY FOR GENERAL MICROBIOLOGY QUARTERLY, THE. 570
0142-7571 See MASTER BAKERS' HANDBOOK AND BUYERS GUIDE. 2349
0142-7695 See TECHNICAL NOTE - SCOTTISH AGRICULTURAL COLLEGES. 140
0142-7849 See THIRD WORLD PLANNING REVIEW. 2836
0142-7873 See JOURNAL OF PLANKTON RESEARCH. 5588
0142-7938 See DELICHON URBICA. 2445
0142-7946 See POSTGRADUATE DOCTOR. AFRICA. 3628
0142-7962 See NORFOLK ARCHAEOLOGY. 276
0142-8004 See BIOLOGICAL RHYTHMS. 578
0142-8012 See CARDIOVASCULAR PHYSIOLOGY. 579
0142-8020 See CELL CALCIUM. 3562
0142-8039 See CELL CONTACT PHENOMENA. 533
0142-8047 See CELL MEMBRANES. 533
0142-8055 See CYCLIC AMP (SHEFFIELD, ENGLAND). 486
0142-8063 See CELL TRANSFORMATION. 534
0142-8071 See ENZYME REGULATION. 487
0142-8098 See GASTRIC SECRETION. 3744
0142-8101 See GASTROINTESTINAL HORMONES. 3746
0142-811X See HUMAN SEXUALITY. 3585
0142-8136 See IMMUNOHISTOCHEMISTRY. 537
0142-8144 See INSULIN AND GLUCAGON. 3731
0142-8152 See IRON METABOLISM. 3590
0142-8160 See LEUCOCYTES. 3674
0142-8179 See LYMPHOCYTES SHEFFIELD. 490
0142-8195 See MACROPHAGES SHEFFIELD. 3605
0142-8217 See MITOCHONDRIA / ISSUED MONTHLY BY UNIVERSITY OF SHEFFIELD BIOMEDICAL INFORMATION SERVICE. 3617
0142-8225 See NERVE CELL BIOLOGY / UNIVERSITY OF SHEFFIELD BIOMEDICAL INFORMATION SERVICE. 466
0142-8233 See NEUROPEPTIDES (SHEFFIELD). 3841
0142-8241 See NEUROPHYSIOLOGY SHEFFIELD. 584
0142-825X See PANCREATIC AND SALIVARY SECRETION. 3732
0142-8268 See PLATELETS SHEFFIELD. 3773
0142-8276 See PROLACTIN SHEFFIELD. 3732
0142-8284 See PROSTAGLANDINS-BIOLOGY. 3732
0142-8314 See RELEASING HORMONES. 3733
0142-8330 See STEROID RECEPTORS. 540
0142-8349 See THYROID HORMONES. 3645
0142-8357 See RENAL TRANSPLANTATION AND DIALYSIS. 3633
0142-8365 See AUTOIMMUNE DISEASES. 3667
0142-8403 See NEUROCHEMISTRY SHEFFIELD. 491
0142-8543 See VISION. 1143
0142-8640 See DNA SHEFFIELD. 3573
0142-8780 See RESPIRATORY SYSTEM. 3951
0142-8810 See TISSUE CULTURE SHEFFIELD. 540
0142-8853 See GRAPHICS WORLD. 379
0142-887X See AIM. 4083
0142-890X See CLASSIC BIKE. 1294
0142-8950 See PROCEEDINGS OF THE HAMPSHIRE FIELD CLUB AND ARCHAEOLOGICAL SOCIETY. 279
0142-9310 See EGYPT NEWSLETTER. 4520

0142-9345 See NEW AFRICAN (LONDON. 1978). 2499
0142-9361 See SIMULATION/GAMES FOR LEARNING. 1905
0142-937X See EUROPEAN SUPPLIES BULLETIN / FISHERY ECONOMICS RESEARCH UNIT, WHITE FISH AUTHORITY. 2300
0142-9418 See POLYMER TESTING. 4459
0142-9434 See ROYAL SHAKESPEARE COMPANY; A COMPLETE RECORD OF THE YEAR'S WORK. 5368
0142-9612 See BIOMATERIALS. 3556
0142-9663 See TEN.8. 4377
0142-9698 See INORGANIC BIOCHEMISTRY. 488
0142-9752 See STANLEY GIBBONS STAMP CATALOGUE. PART 1: BRITISH COMMONWEALTH. 2787
0143-005X See JOURNAL OF EPIDEMIOLOGY AND COMMUNITY HEALTH (1979). 3735
0143-0106 See PLANTSMAN, THE. 2428
0143-0114 See LONDON OIL REPORTS. 4263
0143-0130 See MRC NEWS. 3618
0143-0203 See MEDICAL PHYSICS HANDBOOKS. 4412
0143-0238 See CYCLING WORLD. 4892
0143-0289 See CAS. CURRENT AWARENESS SERVICE - BRITISH INSTITUTE OF MENTAL HANDICAP. 1793
0143-0343 See SCHOOL PSYCHOLOGY INTERNATIONAL. 4618
0143-0386 See RESEARCH REPORTS DIGEST / NATURE CONSERVANCY COUNCIL. 2204
0143-0394 See SOVIET SCIENTIFIC REVIEWS. SECTION A, PHYSICS REVIEWS. 4422
0143-0408 See CHEMISTRY REVIEWS. 971
0143-0416 See SOVIET SCIENTIFIC REVIEWS. SECTION C, MATHEMATICAL PHYSICS REVIEWS. 4422
0143-0432 See SOVIET SCIENTIFIC REVIEWS. SECTION E, ASTROPHYSICS AND SPACE PHYSICS REVIEWS. 400
0143-0513 See GLOUCESTERSHIRE FAMILY HISTORY SOCIETY JOURNAL. 2451
0143-0556 See REVIEW OF SECURITY AND THE STATE. 4683
0143-0610 See PROCEEDINGS OF THE ... CONVENTION. 3425
0143-0637 See METALS ANALYSIS AND OUTLOOK. 4011
0143-0750 See INTERNATIONAL JOURNAL OF AMBIENT ENERGY. 1947
0143-0769 See CURRENCY PROFILES. 786
0143-0807 See EUROPEAN JOURNAL OF PHYSICS. 4402
0143-0815 See CLINICAL PHYSICS AND PHYSIOLOGICAL MEASUREMENT. 4400
0143-084X See JOURNAL OF INDUSTRIAL AFFAIRS. 687
0143-0955 See ORAL HISTORY (COLCHESTER). 2625
0143-0963 See CLEANING MAINTENANCE AND BIG BUILDING MANAGEMENT. 607
0143-1005 See HELICOPTER. 22
0143-1145 See AEROSPACE EUROPE. 5
0143-1161 See INTERNATIONAL JOURNAL OF REMOTE SENSING. 1980
0143-117X See HYPERTENSION SHEFFIELD. 3585
0143-1250 See TRANSACTIONS OF THE MONUMENTAL BRASS SOCIETY. 284
0143-1285 See BOOKS IN SCOTLAND. 4826
0143-1315 See AVON CONSERVATION NEWS. 2677
0143-1374 See MIND YOUR OWN BUSINESS. 695
0143-1404 See BIOCONTROL NEWS AND INFORMATION. 151
0143-1412 See SLOW DANCER. 3471
0143-1463 See STATISTICS OF THE MISUSE OF DRUGS UNITED KINGDOM, SUPPLEMENTARY TABLES / HOME OFFICE. 1350
0143-1536 See NPL NEWS. 4413
0143-2044 See CRYO LETTERS. 452

0143-2087 See OPTIMAL CONTROL APPLICATIONS & METHODS. 1220

0143-2095 See STRATEGIC MANAGEMENT JOURNAL. 887

0143-2192 See LABELS & LABELLING INTERNATIONAL. 4219

0143-2214 See WHERE TO LEARN ENGLISH IN GREAT BRITAIN. 3333

0143-2249 See BUILDING CONSERVATION. 603

0143-2257 See AIRFINANCE JOURNAL. 9

0143-2389 See TRANSACTIONS OF THE WORCESTERSHIRE ARCHAEOLOGICAL SOCIETY. 284

0143-2826 See QUATERNARY NEWSLETTER. 1393

0143-2885 See INTERNATIONAL ENDODONTIC JOURNAL. 1325

0143-2974 See LOCAL POPULATION STUDIES. 4554

0143-3032 See BAR BRITISH SERIES. 261

0143-3067 See BAR INTERNATIONAL SERIES. 261

0143-3083 See RESEARCH AND CLINICAL FORUMS. 3634

0143-3245 See BLOCK (EAST BARNET, HERTFORDSHIRE). 2513

0143-3296 See ECOLOGY ABSTRACTS. 2184

0143-3334 See CARCINOGENESIS (NEW YORK). 3814

0143-3369 See INTERNATIONAL JOURNAL OF VEHICLE DESIGN. 5417

0143-3377 See ROSPA BULLETIN. 4800

0143-3474 See INTERNATIONAL DIRECTORY OF VOLUNTARY WORK. 4338

0143-3482 See DIRECTORY OF JOBS & CAREERS ABROAD. 4203

0143-3490 See SUMMER JOBS, BRITAIN. 4209

0143-3563 See NOVA HRVATSKA. 2660

0143-3598 See FOULING PREVENTION RESEARCH DIGEST. 1976

0143-361X See AMSSEE NEWS. 4083

0143-3636 See NUCLEAR MEDICINE COMMUNICATIONS. 3848

0143-3709 See MARINE PROPULSION INTERNATIONAL. 5452

0143-3717 See ASHLAR. 292

0143-3768 See LANDSCAPE HISTORY. 2423

0143-3784 See MEDIEVAL ENGLISH THEATRE. 5366

0143-3857 See ERGODIC THEORY AND DYNAMICAL SYSTEMS. 3505

0143-389X See ADVENTURE HOLIDAYS. 5460

0143-3911 See TUNNELLING. 2152

0143-4004 See PLACENTA (EASTBOURNE). 539

0143-4136 See NATE NEWS HUDDERSFIELD. 3305

0143-4160 See CELL CALCIUM (EDINBURGH). 533

0143-4179 See NEUROPEPTIDES (EDINBURGH). 3841

0143-4187 See MUNICIPAL JOURNAL (LONDON. 1970). 4667

0143-4217 See LECTINS SHEFFIELD. 490

0143-4225 See POLYPEPTIDES SHEFFIELD. 3628

0143-4233 See MEMBRANE PROTEINS. 490

0143-4241 See TRANSMITTERS RECEPTORS & SYNAPSES. 4331

0143-4276 See NEUROHYPOPHYSIAL HORMONES. 3732

0143-4284 See RENIN, ANGIOTENSIN & KININS. 471

0143-4632 See JOURNAL OF MULTILINGUAL AND MULTICULTURAL DEVELOPMENT. 3291

0143-4853 See INTERNATIONAL MEDICINE (LONDON). 3589

0143-4853 See INTERNATIONAL MEDICINE. SUPPLEMENT. 3589

0143-4861 See RLJ. ROSKILL'S LETTER FROM JAPAN. 4018

0143-4977 See BRITISH JOURNAL OF ACUPUNCTURE. 3558

0143-5000 See DRYDOCK. 5449

0143-5043 See BRADFORD STUDIES ON YUGOSLAVIA. 2679

0143-5051 See SOCIAL BIOLOGY AND HUMAN AFFAIRS. 5258

0143-5108 See JOURNAL FOR THE STUDY OF THE NEW TESTAMENT. SUPPLEMENT SERIES. 5017

0143-5124 See LIBRARY MANAGEMENT (MCB PUBLICATIONS (FIRM)). 3226

0143-5140 See INTERNATIONAL LABMATE. 1015

0143-5175 See TRANSACTIONS OF THE SHROPSHIRE ARCHAEOLOGICAL AND HISTORICAL SOCIETY. 284

0143-5221 See CLINICAL SCIENCE (1979). 485

0143-523X See LATIN AMERICA REGIONAL REPORTS. CARIBBEAN. 1572

0143-5248 See LATIN AMERICA REGIONAL REPORTS. ANDEAN GROUP. 1572

0143-5256 See LATIN AMERICA REGIONAL REPORTS. SOUTHERN CONE. 1572

0143-5264 See LATIN AMERICA REGIONAL REPORTS. MEXICO & CENTRAL AMERICA. 1572

0143-5272 See LATIN AMERICA REGIONAL REPORTS. BRAZIL. 1572

0143-5272 See BRAZIL REPORT. 1549

0143-5280 See LATIN AMERICAN WEEKLY REPORT. 2489

0143-5329 See CREDIT CONTROL. 785

0143-5337 See FIRE ENGINEERS JOURNAL. 2289

0143-5353 See OCCUPATIONAL SAFETY & HEALTH (BIRMINGHAM). 2867

0143-5426 See FIGHT RACISM, FIGHT IMPERIALISM! : ANTI-IMPERIALIST BULLETIN OF THE REVOLUTIONARY COMMUNIST GROUP. 4474

0143-5450 See AIR ENTHUSIAST. 7

0143-5469 See EDUCATION YEAR BOOK. 1741

0143-5531 See PULS (LONDON, ENGLAND). 3426

0143-5663 See INTERNATIONAL INDEX TO TELEVISION PERIODICALS. 1133

0143-5671 See FISCAL STUDIES. 4726

0143-5698 See INTERNATIONAL TREE CROPS JOURNAL, THE. 2385

0143-5795 See CHATHAM HOUSE PAPERS. 4517

0143-5906 See HEREFORD'S NORTH AMERICA. 23

0143-5922 See KING'S THEOLOGICAL REVIEW. 4972

0143-5949 See STREET MACHINE (LONDON, ENGLAND). 5426

0143-6147 See TROPICAL PEST MANAGEMENT. 4248

0143-6228 See APPLIED GEOGRAPHY (SEVENOAKS). 2554

0143-6244 See BUILDING SERVICES ENGINEERING RESEARCH & TECHNOLOGY. 604

0143-6287 See COAL CALENDAR. 1935

0143-6295 See BUSINESS LAW REVIEW LONDON. 3096

0143-6333 See JAMES JOYCE BROADSHEET. 3398

0143-6503 See OXFORD JOURNAL OF LEGAL STUDIES. 3024

0143-652X See COMMERCIAL FISHING. 2299

0143-6570 See MDE. MANAGERIAL AND DECISION ECONOMICS. 1504

0143-6597 See THIRD WORLD QUARTERLY. 1587

0143-6619 See WESTINDIAN DIGEST. 2525

0143-6767 See RECENT ADVANCES IN CLINICAL BIOCHEMISTRY. 493

0143-6775 See RECENT ADVANCES IN CLINICAL VIROLOGY. 3632

0143-6791 See RECENT ADVANCES IN MEDICINE (EDINBURGH). 3633

0143-6813 See RECENT ADVANCES IN OTOLARYNGOLOGY. 3891

0143-6848 See RECENT ADVANCES IN OBSTETRICS AND GYNAECOLOGY. 3767

0143-6864 See HAZARDOUS CARGO BULLETIN. 5450

0143-6910 See HAIRDRESSERS JOURNAL INTERNATIONAL. 404

0143-6953 See RECENT ADVANCES IN HISTOPATHOLOGY. 540

0143-6961 See RECENT ADVANCES IN RADIOLOGY AND MEDICAL IMAGING. 3946

0143-697X See RECENT ADVANCES IN HAEMATOLOGY. 3773

0143-702X See IEE PROCEEDINGS. A, SCIENCE, MEASUREMENT AND TECHNOLOGY. 2057

0143-7038 See IEE PROCEEDINGS. PART B. ELECTRIC POWER APPLICATIONS. 2058

0143-7046 See IEE PROCEEDINGS. C, GENERATION, TRANSMISSION, AND DISTRIBUTION. 2057

0143-7054 See IEE PROCEEDINGS. D, CONTROL THEORY AND APPLICATIONS. 2057

0143-7062 See IEE PROCEEDINGS. PART E. COMPUTERS AND DIGITAL TECHNIQUES. 1229

0143-7100 See IEE PROCEEDINGS. PART I. SOLID-STATE AND ELECTRON DEVICES. 2058

0143-7151 See EMULSION POLYMERISATION. 975

0143-716X 4223

0143-7178 See ADVANCES IN NUCLEAR QUADRUPOLE RESONANCE. 4445

0143-7208 See DYES AND PIGMENTS. 4223

0143-7240 See AEROPLANT MONTHLY. 5

0143-7275 See TRANSDUCER TECHNOLOGY. 5167

0143-7453 See INTERNATIONAL BAR NEWS (LONDON, ENGLAND). 3129

0143-7496 See INTERNATIONAL JOURNAL OF ADHESION AND ADHESIVES. 1053

0143-750X See TEMPERATURE CONTROLLED STORAGE AND DISTRIBUTION. 2359

0143-750X See TEMPERATURE CONTROLLED STORAGE AND DISTRIBUTION. 1629

0143-7526 See SENSORY PERCEPTION AND INFORMATION PROCESSING. 4618

0143-7534 See LEARNING AND MEMORY / ISSUED BY UNIVERSITY OF SHEFFIELD BIOMEDICAL INFORMATION SERVICE. 3930

0143-7623 See TYPOGRAPHIC SOCIETY OF TYPOGRAPHIC DESIGNERS. 4570

0143-7690 See SCRIP (RICHMOND). 4329

0143-7720 See INTERNATIONAL JOURNAL OF MANPOWER. 1680

0143-7739 See LEADERSHIP & ORGANIZATION DEVELOPMENT JOURNAL. 875

0143-7755 See TABLEWARE INTERNATIONAL. 2594

0143-7798 See STEEL TIMES INTERNATIONAL. 4021

0143-781X See HISTORY OF POLITICAL THOUGHT. 4476

0143-7836 See GLASS INTERNATIONAL. 2590

0143-7941 See TAX MANAGEMENT INTERNATIONAL FORUM, THE. 4753

0143-7968 See HAIR (LONDON). 404

0143-7984 See RESEARCH PUBLICATIONS OF THE WELLCOME UNIT FOR THE HISTORY OF MEDICINE. 3634

0143-8042 See JOURNAL OF CHINESE MEDICINE, THE. 3594

0143-8050 See ANGEL EXHAUST. 3460

0143-8123 See COMMENTS ON MOLECULAR AND CELLULAR BIOPHYSICS. 535

0143-814X See JOURNAL OF PUBLIC POLICY. 4479

0143-8166 See OPTICS AND LASERS IN ENGINEERING. 4439

0143-8204 See SUSSEX ARCHAEOLOGICAL COLLECTIONS. 284

0143-8263 See INTERNATIONAL AUTHORS AND WRITERS WHO'S WHO, THE. 433

0143-8301 See SCOTTISH JOURNAL OF RELIGIOUS STUDIES, THE. 4995

0143-831X See ECONOMIC AND INDUSTRIAL DEMOCRACY. 1664

0143-8328 See PAY & BENEFITS BULLETIN. 944

0143-8395 See RECENT ADVANCES IN SURGERY. 3973

0143-8484 See PLUNKETT DEVELOPMENT SERIES. 1543
0143-8689 See CURRICULUM (DRIFFIELD). 1892
0143-8700 See REPORT OF THE INTERNATIONAL WHALING COMMISSION. 5596
0143-8751 See TARGET GUN. 4925
0143-8883 See PROSPECT EDINBURGH. 1978. 306
0143-8956 See BRITISH NUMISMATIC JOURNAL. 2780
0143-8980 See ENTERTAINMENT & ARTS MANAGEMENT. 5364
0143-9014 See PIG NEWS AND INFORMATION. 155
0143-9073 See ECOS BRITISH ASSOCIATION OF NATURE CONSERVATIONISTS. 2192
0143-9073 See ECOS. 2192
0143-926X See COSMATOM. 4401
0143-9294 See CLINICAL AND EXPERIMENTAL PHARMACOLOGY & PHYSIOLOGY. SUPPLEMENT. 4296
0143-9405 See CHINA BUSINESS REPORT. 656
0143-9553 See KEYWORD INDEX TO SERIAL TITLES. 2489
0143-9669 See REREPORT, THE. 2892
0143-9677 See TAX HAVEN & SHELTER REPORT. NORTH AMERICAN EDITION. 4752
0143-9685 See HISTORICAL JOURNAL OF FILM, RADIO, AND TELEVISION. 4071
0143-974X See JOURNAL OF CONSTRUCTIONAL STEEL RESEARCH. 618
0143-9774 See NEWS OF MUSLIMS IN EUROPE. 5044
0143-9782 See JOURNAL OF TIME SERIES ANALYSIS. 3516
0143-991X See INDUSTRIAL ROBOT, THE. 1219
0143-9952 See JANE'S ARMOUR AND ARTILLERY. 4046
0144-0004 See JANE'S MILITARY COMMUNICATIONS. 4047
0144-0071 See MONTGOMERYSHIRE COLLECTIONS. 2699
0144-008X See JOURNAL OF THE EIGHTEEN NINETIES SOCIETY. 3400
0144-0098 See TRANSACTIONS - CAERNARVONSHIRE HISTORICAL SOCIETY. 2713
0144-0179 See CONFERENCE TRANSACTIONS - BRITISH ARCHAEOLOGICAL ASSOCIATION. 266
0144-0209 See IDS FOCUS. 1609
0144-0241 See HENRY BRADSHAW SOCIETY (SERIES). 4962
0144-025X See ONLINE & CD NOTES. 3239
0144-0314 See LAC MANUAL SERIES. 5515
0144-0322 See JOURNAL OF THE SOCIETY OF LEATHER TECHNOLOGISTS AND CHEMISTS. 3184
0144-0330 See JOURNAL OF CLINICAL PATHOLOGY. SUPPLEMENT. ROYAL COLLEGE OF PATHOLOGISTS SYMPOSIA. 3895
0144-0357 See PROSE STUDIES. 3425
0144-0365 See JOURNAL OF LEGAL HISTORY, THE. 2988
0144-0381 See ARMS CONTROL (LONDON, ENGLAND). 4036
0144-039X See SLAVERY & ABOLITION. 4513
0144-0403 See MEDICINE INTERNATIONAL. THE MONTHLY ADD-ON JOURNAL. UK EDITION. 3613
0144-0411 See MEDICINE INTERNATIONAL. THE QUARTERLY ADD-ON JOURNAL. 3613
0144-0519 See RECENT ADVANCES IN GERIATRIC MEDICINE. 3754
0144-0535 See RECENT ADVANCES IN NEUROPATHOLOGY. 3844
0144-0551 See MUSHROOM JOURNAL. 2424
0144-0594 See MAJOR COMPANIES OF THE ARAB WORLD. 691
0144-0713 See RADIO MODELLER. 2777
0144-0969 See SOCIAL WORK INFORMATION BULLETIN. 5309

0144-1019 See SEAWAYS (1980). 4183
0144-1027 See COMPANY LAWYER, THE. 3098
0144-1078 See RECENT ADVANCES IN INFECTION. 3715
0144-1205 See YEARBOOK (ROYAL BALLET). 1314
0144-1256 See RECENT ADVANCES IN COMMUNITY MEDICINE. 4798
0144-1329 See BRITISH PUBLIC OPINION. 5241
0144-1485 See MONOGRAPH - MINERALOGICAL SOCIETY. 1442
0144-1493 See PROCEEDINGS - INSTITUTE OF FOOD SCIENCE AND TECHNOLOGY (U.K.). 2353
0144-1647 See TRANSPORT REVIEWS. 5396
0144-1795 See JOURNAL OF AUTONOMIC PHARMACOLOGY. 4310
0144-1825 See CERAMIC REVIEW. 2587
0144-2015 See HAMBRO COMPANY GUIDE, THE. 678
0144-2074 See SCIENTIFIC AND TECHNICAL SURVEYS - BRITISH FOOD MANUFACTURING INDUSTRIES RESEARCH ASSOCIATION. 2357
0144-2147 See SPECIAL PUBLICATION - BRITISH CERAMIC RESEARCH ASSOCIATION. 2594
0144-221X See TRANSACTIONS OF THE NATURAL HISTORY SOCIETY OF NORTHUMBRIA. 4173
0144-235X See INTERNATIONAL REVIEWS IN PHYSICAL CHEMISTRY. 1053
0144-2384 See REFER. 3244
0144-2449 See ZEOLITES. 1038
0144-249X See STANLEY GIBBONS POSTCARD CATALOGUE. 2778
0144-2600 See JOURNAL OF THE INSTITUTE OF ENERGY. 1949
0144-2813 See BUSINESS EDUCATION. 647
0144-2872 See POLICY STUDIES. 4488
0144-2910 See MODEL BOATS. 594
0144-2937 See POPULAR CRAFTS. 374
0144-2945 See JOURNAL OF LARYNGOLOGY AND OTOLOGY. SUPPLEMENT, THE. 3889
0144-2988 See MACROMOLECULAR CHEMISTRY (ROYAL SOCIETY OF CHEMISTRY (GREAT BRITAIN)). 1044
0144-3054 See EUROPEAN COMPETITION LAW REVIEW : ECLR. 3100
0144-3097 See COMPUTING (LONDON. 1980). 1237
0144-3143 See ITRI PUBLICATION. 4005
0144-3194 See NAVY INTERNATIONAL. 4180
0144-3321 See CRIMINAL APPEAL REPORTS (SENTENCING), THE. 3105
0144-333X See INTERNATIONAL JOURNAL OF SOCIOLOGY & SOCIAL POLICY, THE. 5248
0144-3410 See EDUCATIONAL PSYCHOLOGY (DORCHESTER-ON-THAMES). 4586
0144-3453 See TRANSPORT (LONDON. 1980). 5395
0144-3569 See BRITISH JOURNAL OF PHYSICAL EDUCATION. 1855
0144-3577 See INTERNATIONAL JOURNAL OF OPERATIONS & PRODUCTION MANAGEMENT. 871
0144-3585 See JOURNAL OF ECONOMIC STUDIES (BRADFORD). 1499
0144-3593 See STATUTE LAW REVIEW. 3059
0144-3607 See ZOOLOGICAL RECORD (LONDON). 5604
0144-3615 See JOURNAL OF OBSTETRICS AND GYNAECOLOGY. 3763
0144-3631 See TECHNICAL NOTE BRITISH CERAMIC RESEARCH ASSOCIATION. 2594
0144-3690 See AUCTION PRICES OF AMERICAN ARTISTS. 343
0144-3909 See HUMAN LYMPHOCYTE DIFFERENTIATION. 537
0144-4034 See BOAT TECHNOLOGY INTERNATIONAL. 592
0144-4212 See PSLG. PUBLIC SERVICE & LOCAL GOVERNMENT. 4675
0144-4271 See MEDECONOMICS. 3607

0144-4360 See LITERARY REVIEW (EDINBURGH). 3346
0144-4425 See PAINT TITLES. 4226
0144-4549 See LLOYD'S SHIPPING INDEX. 5452
0144-4557 See LLOYD'S VOYAGE RECORD. 5452
0144-4565 See BIORESOURCE TECHOLOGY. 2225
0144-4646 See COMMUNICATION RESEARCH TRENDS. 1107
0144-5081 See STAFF OF SCOTTISH SOCIAL WORK DEPARTMENTS. 5311
0144-5138 See HISTORY OF UNIVERSITIES. 1829
0144-5154 See ASSEMBLY AUTOMATION. 1217
0144-5170 See JOURNAL OF GARDEN HISTORY. 2421
0144-5243 See MILTRONICS. 4051
0144-5294 See GEOLOGICAL CURATOR / GCG, THE. 4088
0144-5537 See OPCS MONITOR. CENSUS MONITORS. 4555
0144-557X See ANALYTICAL PROCEEDINGS. 1013
0144-5596 See SOCIAL POLICY & ADMINISTRATION. 4686
0144-5774 See SOUNDS. 4154
0144-5871 See HIGH PERFORMANCE TEXTILES. 5351
0144-588X See BCG NEWSLETTER BOLTON. 4084
0144-5979 See CLINICAL PHYSIOLOGY (OXFORD). 579
0144-5987 See ENERGY EXPLORATION & EXPLOITATION. 1940
0144-6037 See SOUND INTERNATIONAL. 5319
0144-6045 See PLASTICS, RUBBER AND COMPOSITES PROCESSING AND APPLICATIONS. 4458
0144-6096 See BUSINESS SCOTLAND. 652
0144-6126 See BRAD ADVERTISER & AGENCY LIST. 756
0144-6193 See CONSTRUCTION MANAGEMENT AND ECONOMICS. 610
0144-6266 See RECENT ADVANCES IN CROSSLINKING & CURING. 4225
0144-6347 See BSHS NEWSLETTER. 5090
0144-6592 See RECENT ADVANCES IN NURSING. 3868
0144-6622 See RUSSIAN ENGINEERING RESEARCH. 2128
0144-6657 See BRITISH JOURNAL OF CLINICAL PSYCHOLOGY, THE. 4578
0144-6665 See BRITISH JOURNAL OF SOCIAL PSYCHOLOGY, THE. 4578
0144-6673 See LLOYD'S SHIPPING ECONOMIST. 5452
0144-6789 See INTERNATIONAL X-RAY EMISSION SPECTROMETRY. 1016
0144-686X See AGEING AND SOCIETY. 3748
0144-7076 See PN REVIEW (MANCHESTER, GREATER MANCHESTER : 1979). 3350
0144-7084 See ANNUAL REPORT / EASTERN HEALTH AND SOCIAL SERVICES BOARD, NORTHERN IRELAND. 4765
0144-7394 See TEACHING PUBLIC ADMINISTRATION : TPA. 4690
0144-7475 See THOMAS COOK OVERSEAS TIMETABLE. 5492
0144-7505 See BULLETIN / PRINTING HISTORICAL SOCIETY. 4564
0144-7521 See AFRICAN TEXTILES. 5347
0144-7556 See INDEX OF CONFERENCE PROCEEDINGS / THE BRITISH LIBRARY, DOCUMENT SUPPLY CENTRE. 3214
0144-7564 See COMPARATIVE CRITICISM. 3340
0144-7599 See NEWSLETTER MARC. USERS GROUP. 3235
0144-7726 See 9H. 286
0144-7750 See WORLD RADIO TV HANDBOOK. 1143
0144-7777 See CLINICA. 3564
0144-7785 See NVB. NOISE & VIBRATION BULLETIN. 2179
0144-7815 See IAHS-AISH PUBLICATION. 1415

0144-8153 See EVANGELICAL REVIEW OF THEOLOGY. 4957

0144-8188 See INTERNATIONAL REVIEW OF LAW AND ECONOMICS. 1636

0144-8196 See SCOTTISH PLANNING & ENVIRONMENTAL LAW. 2835

0144-8196 See SCOTTISH PLANNING LAW & PRACTICE. 3047

0144-8218 See FAR EASTERN TECHNICAL REVIEW. 835

0144-8234 See AED (LONDON, ENGLAND). 1544

0144-8420 See RADIATION PROTECTION DOSIMETRY. 4440

0144-8447 See SCIENCE FOR PEOPLE (LONDON). 5151

0144-8463 See BIOSCIENCE REPORTS. 532

0144-8587 See CONSTRUCTION PAPERS. 610

0144-8609 See AQUACULTURAL ENGINEERING. 2295

0144-8617 See CARBOHYDRATE POLYMERS. 1040

0144-8625 See BRITISH JOURNAL OF FAMILY PLANNING, THE. 588

0144-865X See PROGRESS IN STROKE RESEARCH. 3709

0144-8684 See CURRENT TOPICS IN ANAESTHESIA. 3682

0144-8722 See SOBORNOST. 5040

0144-8765 See BIOLOGICAL AGRICULTURE & HORTICULTURE. 66

0144-8811 See DEVELOPMENTS IN MEAT SCIENCE. 2333

0144-8846 See PROCEEDINGS OF THE ... EUROPEAN CONFERENCE ON MIXING. 2016

0144-9281 See ENVIRONMENTAL EDUCATION AND INFORMATION. 2167

0144-929X See BEHAVIOUR & INFORMATION TECHNOLOGY. 5087

0144-932X See LIVERPOOL LAW REVIEW, THE. 3003

0144-9370 See ANNUAL REPORT AND ACCOUNTS - WATER RESEARCH CENTRE. 2224

0144-946X See PURVADESH. 2662

0144-9613 See ASSOCIATION MANAGEMENT WATFORD. 860

0144-963X See PHYSICAL CHEMISTRY OF FAST REACTIONS. 1056

0144-9753 See ASIAN DIGEST. 2501

0144-9958 See BRITISH LIBRARY REFERENCE DIVISION NEWSPAPER LIBRARY NEWSLETTER. 3197

0145-0034 See BEHAVIOR & SOCIETY. 5240

0145-0042 See MOUTH OF THE DRAGON. 3466

0145-0050 See CLIMATOLOGICAL DATA. ALABAMA. 1422

0145-0069 See CLIMATOLOGICAL DATA. CALIFORNIA. 1422

0145-0093 See REPORT - CENTER FOR ENERGY STUDIES, KANSAS STATE UNIVERSITY. 1994

0145-0123 See TJS SPEC. PUBL. 5166

0145-0220 See ASIAN LAW FORUM. 2937

0145-0239 See DAILY TREASURY STATEMENT. 787

0145-0263 See TECHNICAL NOTES - OCCUPATIONAL SAFETY AND HEALTH ADMINISTRATION. 2871

0145-0301 See RESEARCH LIBRARY, RECENT ACQUISITIONS. 3245

0145-0352 See U.S. EXPORT SALES. 855

0145-0360 See WEEKLY COTTON MARKET REVIEW. 190

0145-0379 See BERKELEY PAPERS IN HISTORY OF SCIENCE. 5088

0145-0387 See CLIMATOLOGICAL DATA. ARIZONA. 1422

0145-0395 See CLIMATOLOGICAL DATA. MONTANA. 1423

0145-0409 See CLIMATOLOGICAL DATA. LOUISIANA. 1423

0145-0417 See CLIMATOLOGICAL DATA. KANSAS. 1423

0145-0425 See CLIMATOLOGICAL DATA. MISSISSIPPI. 1423

0145-0433 See CLIMATOLOGICAL DATA. KENTUCKY. 1423

0145-0441 See CLIMATOLOGICAL DATA. NEBRASKA. 1423

0145-045X See CLIMATOLOGICAL DATA. MICHIGAN. 1423

0145-0468 See CLIMATOLOGICAL DATA. IOWA. 1423

0145-0476 See CLIMATOLOGICAL DATA. MINNESOTA. 1423

0145-0484 See CLIMATOLOGICAL DATA. FLORIDA. 1422

0145-0492 See CLIMATOLOGICAL DATA. GEORGIA. 1422

0145-0506 See CLIMATOLOGICAL DATA. COLORADO. 1422

0145-0514 See CLIMATOLOGICAL DATA. IDAHO. 1422

0145-0522 See CLIMATOLOGICAL DATA. ILLINOIS. 1423

0145-0530 See CLIMATOLOGICAL DATA. INDIANA. 1423

0145-0549 See CLIMATOLOGICAL DATA. MARYLAND AND DELAWARE. 1423

0145-0646 See DAILY DEPOSITORY SHIPPING LIST. 5448

0145-0662 See MOLASSES MARKET NEWS. 109

0145-0670 See BULLETIN (NATIONAL SCIENCE FOUNDATION (U.S.)). 5091

0145-0689 See RIVER CURRENTS (ST. LOUIS, MO. : 1981). 4182

0145-0700 See APPEARANCES OF SOVIET LEADERS. 4630

0145-0735 See CALIFORNIA INDIAN EDUCATION CENTERS. 1730

0145-0786 See INTERNATIONAL POETRY REVIEW (GREENSBORO). 3344

0145-0794 See CLIMATOLOGICAL DATA. NORTH CAROLINA. 1423

0145-0824 See ANNUAL REPORT - UNITED CHURCH BOARD FOR WORLD MINISTRIES. 4935

0145-1014 See AVIATION MONTHLY. 13

0145-1049 See INTERAGENCY TRAINING CALENDAR OF COURSES. 943

0145-1073 See SURFACE WARFARE. 4183

0145-1081 See FINANCIAL STATEMENTS - DEPARTMENT OF HOUSING AND URBAN DEVELOPMENT, OFFICE OF FINANCE AND ACCOUNTING. 2822

0145-112X See PROFILE (NORFOLK, VA.). 4054

0145-1189 See EPA JOURNAL. 2171

0145-126X See FDA QUARTERLY ACTIVITIES REPORT. 4647

0145-1294 See CUMULATED ANNOTATIONS / CLEARINGHOUSE ON HEALTH INDEXES. 4809

0145-1308 See U.S. GREAT LAKES PORTS. 5398

0145-1340 See MIGRANT HEALTH PROJECTS. 4791

0145-1359 See HOUSING PERFORMANCE INDICATORS. 2825

0145-1391 See EPOCH (ITHACA). 3384

0145-1421 See EAST/WEST TECHNOLOGY DIGEST. 5102

0145-1456 See SOVIET JOURNAL OF MARINE BIOLOGY, THE. 557

0145-1472 See COLLEGE STUDENT AND THE COURTS, THE. 2952

0145-1545 See CLEVELAND-MARSHALL LAW NOTES. 2951

0145-1561 See IAIABC JOURNAL. 2863

0145-1715 See DOWNTOWN PLANNING & DEVELOPMENT ANNUAL. 2821

0145-1731 See CALLIGRAFREE SCRIBE. 377

0145-1782 See DISTRIBUTION OF MOTOR VEHICLE REGISTRATION FEES AND FUEL TAXES TO OHIO CITIES. 5413

0145-1790 See ILLUSTRATED ENCYCLOPAEDIA YEARBOOK, THE. 1926

0145-1855 See COMMUNITY DESIGN CENTERS : PROFILE. 295

0145-188X See INDUSTRIAL RELATIONS LAW JOURNAL. 3149

0145-1928 See REPORT OF THE SECRETARY OF THE COMMONWEALTH TO THE GOVERNOR AND GENERAL ASSEMBLY OF VIRGINIA. 4681

0145-2037 See ANNUAL REPORT - EDUCATIONAL COMMISSION FOR FOREIGN MEDICAL GRADUATES. 3550

0145-2096 See DIPLOMATIC HISTORY. 2731

0145-2126 See LEUKEMIA RESEARCH. 3820

0145-2134 See CHILD ABUSE & NEGLECT. 5277

0145-2134 See CHILD ABUSE & NEGLECT [MICROFORM]. 5277

0145-2150 See SCHOOL ACHIEVEMENT IN EARLY CHILDHOOD EDUCATION. 1805

0145-2169 See RESEARCH, PROGRAM DEVELOPMENT, AND EVALUATION IN CALIFORNIA SPECIAL EDUCATION. 1884

0145-2193 See ENROLLMENT OF CHILDREN IN EDUCATIONALLY HANDICAPPED PROGRAMS IN EXCESS OF LEGAL LIMITATION. 1878

0145-2207 See HIGHER EDUCATION IN MONTANA DIRECTORY. 1828

0145-2215 See REPORT - SPECIAL STUDIES SECTION, FIELD OPERATIONS DIVISION, TEXAS WATER QUALITY BOARD. 4762

0145-2223 See MEMBERSHIP DIRECTORY - AMERICAN SOCIETY FOR PUBLIC ADMINISTRATION, NATIONAL CAPITAL AREA CHAPTER. 4664

0145-2258 See AFRICAN ECONOMIC HISTORY. 1544

0145-2282 See FEDERAL SCIENTIFIC AND TECHNICAL COMMUNICATION ACTIVITIES : PROGRESS REPORT. 5105

0145-2290 See NEWS DIGEST - INTERNATIONAL INSTITUTE OF MUNICIPAL CLERKS. 4669

0145-2320 See RS-SERIES. 1709

0145-238X See IASSIST QUARTERLY. 3258

0145-2398 See KALOS. 2795

0145-2401 See DIRECTORY - ASSOCIATION OF HALFWAY HOUSE ALCOHOLISM PROGRAMS OF NORTH AMERICA. 1342

0145-2436 See SELECTED STATISTICS ON THE OFFICE OF ATTORNEY GENERAL. 3083

0145-2517 See INSTRUCTIONAL DISC RECORDINGS CATALOG. 4122

0145-2525 See INSTRUCTIONAL CASSETTE RECORDINGS CATALOG. 4122

0145-2584 See INTERNATIONAL COUNTERMEASURES HANDBOOK, THE. 4046

0145-2665 See NEW MEXICO DIGEST (CLOVIS), THE. 1575

0145-269X See SOCIETY OF BIBLICAL LITERATURE MONOGRAPH SERIES. 5019

0145-2711 See SOCIETY OF BIBLICAL LITERATURE SEMINAR PAPERS. 5019

0145-2770 See SOCIETY OF BIBLICAL LITERATURE DISSERTATION SERIES. 5019

0145-2789 See AAR STUDIES IN RELIGION. 4931

0145-2797 See JRE STUDIES IN RELIGIOUS ETHICS. 2252

0145-2800 See WATER OPERATION AND MAINTENANCE BULLETIN. 5543

0145-2851 See LEGAL CIRCLE, THE. 2999

0145-2886 See WIRE TECHNOLOGY BUYER'S GUIDE. 4023

0145-2908 See VERMONT LAW REVIEW. 3071

0145-2924 See FINANCIAL STATEMENT AFTER ALLOCATION. 5382

0145-2932 See PEOPLE (RALEIGH). 5301

0145-2991 See GEORGIA LEGAL DIRECTORY, THE. 3141

0145-3009 See FORGET ME NOT (ANCHORAGE). 2320

0145-3017 See CORPORATE BUYERS OF DESIGN SERVICES USA. 296

0145-3025 See CHILD ABUSE AND NEGLECT RESEARCH. 5277

0145-305X See DEVELOPMENTAL AND COMPARATIVE IMMUNOLOGY. 3669

0145-3076 See STATE COURT JOURNAL. 3058

0145-3084 See BIN. BIBLIOGRAPHY NEWSLETTER. 410

0145-3149 See BRAILLE SCORES CATALOG. ORGAN. 4104

0145-3165 See BRAILLE SCORES CATALOG. INSTRUMENTAL. 4104

0145-319X See NASA TECH BRIEFS (WASHINGTON, D.C. 1976). 5130

0145-3203 See TEXTS AND TRANSLATIONS. 1080

0145-3297 See CHRISTIAN COMMUNITY (COLUMBUS), THE. 4944

0145-336X See HEALTH ISSUES ON CAPITOL HILL. 4780

0145-3378 See JOURNAL OF PSYCHOHISTORY, THE. 4599

0145-3416 See IMMIGRATION NEWSLETTER. 1919

0145-3432 See SOUTHERN ILLINOIS UNIVERSITY LAW JOURNAL. 3057

0145-3483 See CINEGRAM. 4066

0145-3491 See PHILADELPHIA BAR REPORTER. 3029

0145-3491 See RETAINER, THE. 3039

0145-3505 See PROFESSIONAL LIABILITY REPORTER. 3032

0145-3513 See ITA JOURNAL. 4124

0145-3521 See DIRECTORY OF REGULATED LOAN COMPANIES, PAWNBROKERS, INSURANCE PREMIUM FINANCE COMPANIES. 788

0145-353X See COMMUNITY ACTIVITIES (SALEM). 4039

0145-3556 See FOREMOST FILM OF 4071

0145-3599 See CHARTBOOK ON OCCUPATIONAL INJURIES AND ILLNESSES. 2860

0145-3610 See FOOD INDUSTRY DIRECTORY, THE. 2337

0145-3637 See ECONOMIC REPORT, THE STATE OF SOUTH CAROLINA. 1558

0145-370X See INTERNATIONAL OPHTHALMOLOGICAL REPORTER. 3875

0145-3726 See PROGRESS IN CANCER RESEARCH AND THERAPY. 3822

0145-3734 See FOLK LETTER, THE. 4118

0145-3750 See GUTHRIE NEW THEATER. 5364

0145-3785 See TRAVEL TRAILERS, 5TH WHEEL TRAILERS, CAMPING TRAILERS RV GUIDE, NEW & USED VALUES. 5397

0145-3815 See ENVIRONMENTAL PERIODICALS BIBLIOGRAPHY. 2184

0145-3866 See DIRECTORY - NATIONAL FLUID POWER ASSOCIATION. 2113

0145-3890 See BULLETIN OF THE INTERNATIONAL ORGANIZATION FOR SEPTUAGINT AND COGNITE STUDIES. 5046

0145-3904 See EGG PRODUCTS. 210

0145-3920 See AMERICAN POSTCARD JOURNAL. 1144

0145-3947 See SALARY SURVEY (NEW YORK). 1709

0145-4064 See FIREHOUSE. 2290

0145-4072 See EXCHANGE (COLUMBIA). 385

0145-4110 See THUNDERBIRD ILLUSTRATED. 5426

0145-4129 See HEALTH LAWYERS NEWS REPORT. 2978

0145-4137 See CIVILIAN LABOR FORCE, EMPLOYMENT, UNEMPLOYMENT AND UNEMPLOYMENT RATE. 1659

0145-4145 See YEAR BOOK OF CARDIOLOGY, THE. 3711

0145-417X See COAL DATA. 1935

0145-4218 See NAWGA DIRECTORY OF MEMBERS. 2351

0145-4226 See CRIMINAL JUSTICE JOURNAL (SAN DIEGO, CALIF.). 3162

0145-4242 See TEXAS COLLEGIATE EDUCATION DIRECTORY. 1850

0145-4250 See AMERICAN HANDGUNNER, THE. 4882

0145-4269 See OREGON PROPERTY TAX STATISTICS. 4699

0145-4331 See FOUNDATIONAL STUDIES. 1747

0145-434X See PAL, PACKAGING AND LABELING. FEDERAL LEGISLATIVE AND REGULATORY SUPPLEMENT. 4221

0145-4366 See PROCEEDINGS OF THE ANNUAL CONVENTION OF THE NATIONAL ASSOCIATION OF SYNAGOGUE ADMINISTRATORS. 5052

0145-4374 See DIRECTORY OF FEDERAL PROGRAMS ADMINISTERED BY THE NEW JERSEY DEPARTMENT OF EDUCATION, A. 1862

0145-4390 See ALABAMA LEGAL DIRECTORY, THE. 2929

0145-4420 See BEST'S EXECUTIVE DATA SERVICE: LIFE-HEALTH INDUSTRY MARKETING RESULTS. 2875

0145-4455 See BEHAVIOR MODIFICATION. 4576

0145-4463 See CALIFORNIA MASTER PLAN FOR SPECIAL EDUCATION, ANNUAL EVALUATION REPORT. 1876

0145-4471 See POWDER. 4913

0145-448X See NEW YORK LAW SCHOOL LAW REVIEW. 3016

0145-4595 See SUMMARY REPORT ON REAL PROPERTY OWNED BY THE UNITED STATES THROUGHOUT THE WORLD AS OF 4847

0145-4609 See PROPRIETARY SCHOOL DIRECTORY. 1775

0145-4633 See AIRPORT DIRECTORY OF THE STATE OF COLORADO. 10

0145-4668 See FLORIDA ESTIMATES OF POPULATION / PREPARED BY THE POPULATION PROGRAM, BUREAU OF ECONOMIC AND BUSINESS RESEARCH, COLLEGE OF BUSINESS ADMINISTRATION, UNIVERSITY OF FLORIDA. 4553

0145-4684 See STEP UP YOUR AWARENESS. 3251

0145-4714 See CHICAGO METRO BOOK, THE. 757

0145-4781 See PROCEEDINGS OF NATIONAL WASTE PROCESSING CONFERENCE (1976). 2239

0145-479X See JOURNAL OF BIOENERGETICS AND BIOMEMBRANES. 565

0145-4811 See ADVANCES IN MASS SPECTROMETRY IN BIOCHEMISTRY AND MEDICINE. 960

0145-482X See JOURNAL OF VISUAL IMPAIRMENT & BLINDNESS. 4390

0145-4870 See SWEET'S CATALOG FILE : PRODUCTS FOR INDUSTRIAL CONSTRUCTION AND RENOVATION. 629

0145-4889 See SWEET'S CATALOG FILE : PRODUCTS FOR INDUSTRIAL CONSTRUCTION AND RENOVATION, RENOVATION EXTENSION. 629

0145-4900 See KNIT FABRIC PRODUCTION. 5353

0145-4951 See PLUMBING FIXTURES. 2607

0145-496X See SHEETS, PILLOWCASES, AND TOWELS. 5355

0145-5001 See TRUCK TRAILERS. 3489

0145-5044 See N.J. STATE BAR ASSOCIATION. 3012

0145-5060 See BOONE SCOUT OF THE BOONE FAMILY ASSOCIATION OF WASHINGTON, THE. 2439

0145-5079 See REPORT OF ANNUAL SEMINAR ON ESTATE PLANNING. 3119

0145-5184 See FLUORESCENT LAMP BALLASTS. 2055

0145-5249 See TRACTORS, EXCEPT GARDEN TRACTORS. 1629

0145-532X See GOVERNMENT REPORTS ANNUAL INDEX. 5108

0145-5338 See BENCHMARK PAPERS IN ANALYTICAL CHEMISTRY. 1013

0145-5397 See LIBRARY DEVELOPMENTS (AUSTIN, TEX.). 3225

0145-5400 See GPU NEWS. 2794

0145-5435 See SYNAPSE (SAN FERNANDO). 4156

0145-5443 See TOLEDO AREA ABORIGINAL RESEARCH BULLETIN. 2763

0145-5451 See NATIONAL PRESCRIPTION AUDIT: THERAPEUTIC CATEGORY REPORT. 4317

0145-5494 See ENDANGERED FAECES. 3384

0145-5516 See JOURNAL OF THE ILLINOIS SPEECH & THEATRE ASSOCIATION. 5365

0145-5532 See SOCIAL SCIENCE HISTORY. 5220

0145-5559 See TRADESHOW (LOS ANGELES, CALIF.). 767

0145-5575 See THORNDYKE FILE, THE. 3446

0145-5583 See MEDICAL DIRECTORY (WATERVILLE). 3915

0145-5613 See EAR, NOSE & THROAT JOURNAL. 3887

0145-5648 See FHA MONTHLY REPORT OF OPERATIONS. HOME MORTGAGE PROGRAMS. 2822

0145-5656 See FHA MONTHLY REPORT OF OPERATIONS. PROJECT MORTGAGE INSURANCE PROGRAMS. 2822

0145-5680 See CELLULAR AND MOLECULAR BIOLOGY. 534

0145-5710 See MAZINGIRA (EDITION FRANCAISE). 2177

0145-5729 See MAZINGIRA (EDICION EN ESPANOL). 2177

0145-5753 See ROHMER REVIEW, THE. 3431

0145-5761 See WORKING WOMAN. 5572

0145-577X See WOODALL'S RETIREMENT AND RESORT COMMUNITIES. EASTERN EDITION. 4855

0145-5788 See TEACHING PHILOSOPHY. 4363

0145-5796 See SOUTH CAROLINA FOOD AND AGRICULTURAL PRODUCTS : EXPORT DIRECTORY. 2358

0145-5818 See CRIMINAL JUSTICE PERIODICAL INDEX. 3080

0145-5850 See BANKERS SCHOOLS DIRECTORY. 776

0145-5907 See CONNIE DATA SUMMARIES. 2226

0145-5915 See BUYERS' GUIDE & DEALER DIRECTORY: NORTHEASTERN AREA. 826

0145-5982 See BIBLIOGRAPHY OF THE HISTORY OF ART : BHA. 334

0145-6008 See ALCOHOLISM : CLINICAL AND EXPERIMENTAL RESEARCH. 1340

0145-6016 See HOBBY ARTIST NEWS. 2774

0145-6032 See CINEFANTASTIQUE. 4066

0145-6067 See FOUNDATION 500. 5286

0145-6083 See HUGHES ESTATE, SUMMARY OF PROBATE PROCEEDINGS. 2979

0145-613X See DAIWA FISHING ANNUAL. 2299

0145-6180 See MPLA NEWSLETTER (1975). 3232

0145-6202 See FEDERAL YELLOW BOOK. 1926

0145-6237 See SOUNDBOARD. 4154

0145-627X See BOOK TALK (ALBUQUERQUE). 4825

0145-6288 See INFOLETTER - INTERNATIONAL PLANT PROTECTION CENTER. 174

0145-6296 See VETERINARY AND HUMAN TOXICOLOGY. 5524

0145-630X See MEETING NEWS. 692

0145-6334 See ASSUR. 2646

0145-6342 See ALI-ABA COURSE MATERIALS JOURNAL. 2930

0145-6393 See AREA MANPOWER REVIEW : SACRAMENTO-YOLO PLANNING AREA. 1652

0145-6396 See MARKETING LETTUCE FROM SALINAS-WATSONVILLE, OTHER CENTRAL CALIFORNIA DISTRICTS AND COLORADO. 2349

0145-6407 See AREA MANPOWER REVIEW : SOLANO COUNTY. 1652

0145-6415 See AREA MANPOWER REVIEW : CITY OF RICHMOND. 1652

0145-6490 See MEMBERSHIP DIRECTORY - SOCIETY OF AMERICAN ARCHIVISTS. 2482

0145-6520 See BOARD OF TAX APPEALS DECISIONS. 4713

0145-6539 See DIRECTORY OF STUDENTS - HARVARD UNIVERSITY. 1821

0145-6571 See LAW OFFICER'S BULLETIN, THE. 3107

0145-658X See KENTUCKY LEGAL DIRECTORY, THE. 2992

0145-6598 See GOVERNMENT CONTRACTS SERVICE. 2975
0145-661X See DIRECTORY - MASSACHUSETTS DEPARTMENT OF FOOD AND AGRICULTURE. 79
0145-6636 See PASTORAL MUSIC NOTEBOOK. 4145
0145-6776 See AUTO INDEX, THE. 5404
0145-6784 See SOLDIER OF FORTUNE. 4057
0145-6792 See GLASSWORKS. 3463
0145-6806 See CB VOICE. 1151
0145-6814 See CURRENT AWARENESS PROFILE ON QUANTUM CHEMISTRY. 974
0145-6857 See ALABAMA'S HEALTH. 4764
0145-689X See NATIONAL DISEASE AND THERAPEUTIC INDEX. 3619
0145-6911 See MCCUTCHEON'S DETERGENTS & EMULSIFIERS : FUNCTIONAL MATERIALS. 985
0145-6970 See INTERNATIONAL PENTECOSTAL HOLINESS ADVOCATE, THE. 5061
0145-7012 See CREPE COOKBOOK FOR DINNERS & DESSERTS. 2789
0145-7055 See MCCUTCHEON'S DETERGENTS & EMULSIFIERS. NORTH AMERICAN EDITION. 1044
0145-708X See AREA MANPOWER REVIEW : VALLEJO-FAIRFIELD-NAPA SMSA. NAPA COUNTY SUPPLEMENT. 1529
0145-7101 See AREA MANPOWER REVIEW : SAN MATEO COUNTY. 1652
0145-7128 See AREA MANPOWER REVIEW : SAN FRANCISCO CITY AND COUNTY. 1652
0145-7144 See AREA MANPOWER REVIEW : SACRAMENTO STANDARD METROPOLITAN STATISTICAL AREA. PLACER COUNTY SUPPLEMENT. 1652
0145-7160 See AREA MANPOWER REVIEW : MARIN COUNTY. 1652
0145-7179 See AREA MANPOWER REVIEW: CITY OF OAKLAND. 1652
0145-7187 See ANNUAL PLANNING REPORT : SEATTLE-EVERETT, WASHINGTON AREA. 1648
0145-7217 See DIABETES EDUCATOR, THE. 3727
0145-7233 See CONCORDIA JOURNAL. 4949
0145-7241 See ARTNEWSLETTER, THE. 342
0145-7306 See REPORT TO THE GOVERNOR - NEW YORK STATE FACILITIES DEVELOPMENT CORPORATION. 4799
0145-7314 See SUMMARY INFORMATION ON MASTER OF SOCIAL WORK PROGRAMS. 5312
0145-7322 See CRIMINAL LAW OUTLINE. 3106
0145-7330 See GEOGRAPHIC PROFILE OF EMPLOYMENT AND UNEMPLOYMENT. 1675
0145-7381 See KRISTEN VITENSKAPS KVARTALSHEFTE. BIBELSTUDIER. 5017
0145-739X See KRISTEN VIDENSKABS KVARTALSHEFTE. BIBELSTUDIER. 5017
0145-7411 See VIERTELJAHRSHEFT DER CHRISTLICHEN WISSENSCHAFT. BIBELLEKTIONEN. 5020
0145-7454 See LIVRETE TRIMESTRAL DA CIENCIA CRISTA. LICOES BIBLICAS. 5018
0145-7470 See HERAUT DE LA SCIENCE CHRETIENNE, LE. 4962
0145-7489 See ARAUTO DA CIECIA CRISTA, O. 4935
0145-7519 See ARALDO DELLA SCIENZA CRISTIANA, L'. 4935
0145-7527 See KIRISUTOKYO KAGAKU KOTARI. SEISHO KYOKA. 5062
0145-7551 See KRISTEN VIDENSKABS HEROLD. 4972
0145-756X See HERAUT VAN DE CHRISTELIJKE WETENSCHAP, DE. 4962
0145-7578 See HEROLD DER CHRISTLICHEN WISSENSCHAFT, DER. 4962
0145-7586 See PEOPLE'S REPUBLIC OF CHINA BIOGRAPHICAL APPEARANCES. 4673
0145-7594 See PROCEEDINGS OF THE INTERNATIONAL SCHOOL OF HYDROCARBON MEASUREMENT. 989
0145-7632 See HEAT TRANSFER ENGINEERING. 2012

0145-7659 See PRIVACY JOURNAL. 1227
0145-7667 See LIBERTY BELL (REEDY, W. VA.). 4481
0145-7675 See OTHER SIDE (SAVANNAH), THE. 4984
0145-7705 See LIST OF INSPECTED TANK BARGES & TANKSHIPS. 5451
0145-7721 See INSTITUTIONS OF HIGHER EDUCATION INDEX, BY STATE AND CONGRESSIONAL DISTRICT. 1830
0145-773X See ANNUAL REPORT - NEW CASTLE STATE HOSPITAL. 3776
0145-7780 See GRAHAM HOUSE REVIEW. 3463
0145-7802 See WOMEN IN THE WORKING WORLD. 5570
0145-7810 See TRAVEL MASTER. 2809
0145-7829 See FLORIDA LEGAL DIRECTORY, THE. 2971
0145-7837 See BUDGET AS ADOPTED BY THE BOARD OF COMMISSIONERS. 4634
0145-7861 See NEWSLETTER OF THE SSIS. 2660
0145-787X See MIME JOURNAL. 5366
0145-7888 See STUDIES IN 20TH CENTURY LITERATURE. 3354
0145-7934 See B.T.I. NEWSLETTER. 4937
0145-7950 See YEARBOOK AND CHURCH DIRECTORY OF THE ORTHODOX CHURCH IN AMERICA. 5040
0145-7977 See OFFICIAL UNITED STATES TENNIS TOURNAMENT DIRECTORY. 4910
0145-7985 See WIN NEWS. 5568
0145-7993 See AMERICAN INDIAN JOURNAL. 2932
0145-8000 See BIZARRE CLASSIX. 4367
0145-8019 See KIRISUTOKYO KAGAKU SAKIGAKE. 4972
0145-8124 See ELECTION ADMINISTRATION REPORTS. 4472
0145-8132 See DATA REPORT ON PROGRAMS FOR THE HANDICAPPED. 1877
0145-8159 See GUIDE TO AMUSEMENT RIDES. 4862
0145-8167 See CB RADIO JOURNAL. 1105
0145-8183 See OHIO INSTRUCTIONAL GRANTS ANNUAL REPORT. 1838
0145-8191 See REPORT OF THE VIRGINIA ATHLETIC COMMISSION TO THE GOVERNOR OF VIRGINIA. 4915
0145-8213 See SCALE CABINETMAKER, THE. 2777
0145-8264 See JOURNAL OF THE MILKING SHORTHORN AND ILLAWARRA BREEDS. 213
0145-8345 See BARRY BERNDES' ANNUAL EDITION OF SAN DIEGO GUIDE. 5462
0145-8353 See SCHOOL RACIAL-ETHNIC CENSUS. 1782
0145-8388 See NEW LAUREL REVIEW. 3415
0145-8396 See NEWSLETTER - INSTITUTE FOR STUDIES IN AMERICAN MUSIC. 4141
0145-840X See KOREAN STUDIES. 2657
0145-8426 See SOUTHERN ELECTRICAL BUYERS' GUIDE. 2082
0145-8442 See CUSTOMER SERVICE NEWSLETTER. 865
0145-8450 See CUSTOMER COMMUNICATOR, THE. 663
0145-8477 See BATTELLE TODAY. 5087
0145-8485 See CONTRIBUTIONS TO LIBRARIANSHIP. 3204
0145-8493 See PROCEEDINGS OF THE AMERICAN ACADEMY AND INSTITUTE OF ARTS AND LETTERS. 328
0145-8515 See RANCH MAGAZINE, THE. 220
0145-8531 See STATISTICAL DATA. 1350
0145-8558 See UTAH BAR LETTER. ANNUAL ROSTER OF ACTIVE RESIDENT UTAH ATTORNEYS. 3070
0145-8566 See RECORD (WASHINGTON, D.C. : 1975). 3036
0145-8574 See AMICUS CURIARUM. 3138
0145-8604 See LEGISLATIVE REVIEW. 3002
0145-8620 See LAND USE PLANNING IN NEBRASKA. 4840

0145-8647 See BIENNIAL REPORT - STATE OF WISCONSIN, DEPARTMENT OF REGULATION AND LICENSING. 4632
0145-8655 See WISCONSIN PUBLIC EMPLOYMENT DECISIONS DIGEST. 1718
0145-8744 See SEC SPEAKS IN ..., THE. 3047
0145-8752 See MOSCOW UNIVERSITY GEOLOGY BULLETIN. 1388
0145-8760 See LARGE EMPLOYERS IN MASSACHUSETTS, THE. 1687
0145-8825 See GREATER LLANO ESTACADO SOUTHEAST HERITAGE, THE. 2735
0145-885X See GNOSTICA. 4241
0145-8876 See JOURNAL OF FOOD PROCESS ENGINEERING. 2346
0145-8884 See JOURNAL OF FOOD BIOCHEMISTRY. 2346
0145-8892 See JOURNAL OF FOOD PROCESSING AND PRESERVATION. 2346
0145-8973 See CHASQUI (WILLIAMSBURG, VA.). 3374
0145-8981 See PN. PRACTICAL NURSING CAREER. 3867
0145-899X See COMBINATIONS. 4368
0145-9031 See SPECIAL PUBLICATION - CARNEGIE MUSEUM OF NATURAL HISTORY. 4172
0145-9058 See BULLETIN OF CARNEGIE MUSEUM OF NATURAL HISTORY. 4164
0145-9090 See WORLD COIN NEWS. 2783
0145-9112 See NORTHEAST IMPROVER, THE. 197
0145-9120 See KENTUCKY COLLEGES AND UNIVERSITIES : DEGREES CONFERRED. 1833
0145-9155 See PIMA COUNTY EMPLOYER WAGE SURVEY. 1702
0145-9171 See ANNUAL REPORT TO THE GOVERNOR AND LEGISLATURE ON PREPAID HEALTH PLANS, PHPS. 2874
0145-9198 See AMERICAN OIL & GAS REPORTER, THE. 4249
0145-9236 See ENDANGERED SPECIES TECHNICAL BULLETIN. 2165
0145-9309 See SELECTED LIBRARY ACQUISITIONS. 3248
0145-935X See CHILD & YOUTH SERVICES. 5278
0145-9376 See FLORIDA VOCATIONAL JOURNAL. 1913
0145-9392 See OKLAHOMA FARMER-STOCKMAN, THE. 117
0145-9406 See SECURITY MANAGEMENT (ARLINGTON, VA.). 885
0145-9457 See BP REPORT ON THE BUSINESS OF BOOK PUBLISHING. 4827
0145-9503 See TRIMENIAIO PERIODIKO TES CHRISTIANIKES EPISTEMES. BIBLIKA MATHEMATA. 5006
0145-9546 See HOROLOGICAL TIMES. 2916
0145-9589 See PROCEEDINGS OF THE ANNUAL ASSEMBLY MEETING. 32
0145-9597 See MAINE REGISTER, STATE YEAR-BOOK AND LEGISLATIVE MANUAL. 4663
0145-9627 See LIBRARY NETWORKS. 3226
0145-9635 See INDEPENDENT SCHOOL (BOSTON, MASS.). 1751
0145-9651 See MEDIA REPORT TO WOMEN. 1117
0145-9686 See CLEMENTS' ENCYCLOPEDIA OF WORLD GOVERNMENTS. 4468
0145-9694 See BACCALAUREATE EDUCATION IN NURSING. KEY TO A PROFESSIONAL CAREER IN NURSING. 3852
0145-9724 See TRAINEES AND FELLOWS SUPPORTED BY THE NATIONAL INSTITUTE OF DENTAL RESEARCH AND TRAINED DURING FISCAL YEAR 1336
0145-9740 See MEDICAL ANTHROPOLOGY. 241
0145-9783 See MAN AND MEDICINE. 2252
0145-9791 See HORSE ILLUSTRATED. 2799
0145-9813 See TRAFFIC VOLUMES ON THE CALIFORNIA STATE HIGHWAY SYSTEM. 5446
0145-9848 See WORLD WINE ALMANAC & WINE ATLAS. 2373
0145-9880 See APPLICATIONS PROGRAMS. 1278

0145-9899 See PROGRAM BUDGET REQUEST - EDUCATIONAL COMMUNICATIONS BOARD. 1842

0145-9902 See BUDGET REQUEST - STATE DEPARTMENT OF PUBLIC INSTRUCTION. 1812

0145-9910 See AMERICAN INDIAN EARLY CHILDHOOD EDUCATION. 1802

0145-9929 See DOCTORAL DISSERTATIONS IN HISTORY. 2615

0145-9937 See ENDOMETRIUM. 3760

0145-9996 See AMERICAN MEN AND WOMEN OF SCIENCE: MEDICAL AND HEALTH SCIENCES. 5173

0146-0005 See SEMINARS IN PERINATOLOGY. 3768

0146-003X See AMERICAN MEN AND WOMEN OF SCIENCE: PHYSICS, ASTRONOMY, MATHEMATICS, STATISTICS, AND COMPUTER SCIENCE. 5173

0146-0048 See AMERICAN MEN AND WOMEN OF SCIENCE: BIOLOGY. 5173

0146-0056 See AMERICAN MEN AND WOMEN OF SCIENCE: CHEMISTRY. 5173

0146-0064 See AMERICAN MEN AND WOMEN OF SCIENCE: CONSULTANTS. 5173

0146-0072 See PAY TV NEWSLETTER, THE. 1136

0146-0110 See BROADCAST INVESTOR. 1127

0146-0137 See TECHNICAL EDUCATION NEWS. 1916

0146-0153 See PHOTO ELECTRONIC IMAGING. 4373

0146-0161 See IMP, INDUSTRIAL MODELS & PATTERNS. 3481

0146-017X See STATE LEGISLATION ON SMOKING AND HEALTH. 4804

0146-0196 See JOURNAL OF THE SOUTH CAROLINA BAPTIST HISTORICAL SOCIETY. 5062

0146-0269 See GRAVES FAMILY NEWSLETTER, THE. 2452

0146-0315 See SANTA CLARA LAW REVIEW. 3046

0146-0331 See HISTORY OF PSYCHOLOGY SERIES. 4588

0146-034X See INTERAMERICAN PSYCHOLOGIST. 4590

0146-0366 See JOURNAL OF CHRISTIAN COUNSELING. 4968

0146-0382 See LEGAL RESEARCH JOURNAL. 3000

0146-0404 See INVESTIGATIVE OPHTHALMOLOGY & VISUAL SCIENCE. 3875

0146-0447 See MONOGRAPH SERIES OF THE EUROPEAN ORGANIZATION FOR RESEARCH ON TREATMENT OF CANCER. 3821

0146-0463 See XANADU (WANTAGH). 3473

0146-0501 See PESTICIDE & TOXIC CHEMICAL NEWS. 4246

0146-0544 See URBAN AMERICA. 2837

0146-0579 See AOR REPORTER. 4630

0146-0587 See BUSINESS TAX INTERPRETATIONS. 4715

0146-0595 See REAL ESTATE ISSUES. 4844

0146-0617 See DEVELOPMENT ASSISTANCE PROGRAMS OF U. S. NON-PROFIT ORGANIZATIONS IN EL SALVADOR. 2908

0146-0625 See BMWE JOURNAL. 1655

0146-0633 See STATE HIGHWAY IMPROVEMENT PROGRAM: PRIMARY SYSTEM. 2031

0146-065X See STATE OF IOWA CLASSIFIED SERVICE PAY PLAN. 1712

0146-0668 See ILLINOIS TEACHER SALARY SCHEDULE AND POLICY STUDY. 1864

0146-0676 See MARKETING CALIFORNIA CARROTS. 2349

0146-0706 See ELASTOMERICS. 5075

0146-0714 See ELASTOMERICS NEWS-LOG. 5075

0146-0722 See ADVANCES IN PAIN RESEARCH AND THERAPY. 3826

0146-0749 See MICROBIOLOGICAL REVIEWS. 567

0146-0811 See AMERICAN MCD. NEW ENGLAND EDITION. 5375

0146-082X See AMERICAN MCD. PACIFIC STATES EDITION. 5375

0146-0838 See CHECKLIST OF OFFICIAL NEW JERSEY PUBLICATIONS. 413

0146-0846 See SERIES IN CLINICAL AND COMMUNITY PSYCHOLOGY, THE. 4618

0146-0862 See ISSUES IN COMPREHENSIVE PEDIATRIC NURSING. 3857

0146-0889 See SPORTING GOODS BUSINESS. 713

0146-0919 See MULTI-HOUSING NEWS. 2828

0146-096X See MUSIC AT YALE. 4133

0146-0994 See JAPANESE PHILATELY. 2785

0146-1028 See ALASKA LIBRARY DIRECTORY. 3189

0146-1044 See SEXUALITY AND DISABILITY. 4393

0146-1079 See BIBLICAL THEOLOGY BULLETIN. 5015

0146-1109 See MIDCONTINENTAL JOURNAL OF ARCHAEOLOGY, MCJA. 274

0146-1117 See COUNCIL NOTES - INDIANA FAMILY HEALTH COUNCIL, INC. 3569

0146-1133 See WOMEN'S COACHING CLINIC. 4930

0146-1176 See READING CLINIC, THE. 1777

0146-1192 See SUMMARY OF ACCIDENTS INVOLVING THE DRINKING DRIVER. 5445

0146-1214 See TECHNOLOGY & CONSERVATION. 366

0146-1222 See R. I. BULLETIN. 2923

0146-1265 See COACHING : MEN'S ATHLETICS. 4890

0146-1273 See PROCEEDINGS OF SUMMER INSTITUTE ON PARTICLE PHYSICS. 4418

0146-1362 See WOODALL'S CAMPGROUND DIRECTORY. NORTH AMERICAN EDITION. 4881

0146-1397 See STONE COUNTRY. 3472

0146-1419 See ROCKBOTTOM. 3431

0146-1451 See NEW DIMENSIONS IN MENTAL HEALTH. 4793

0146-146X See PROCEEDINGS OF THE ANNUAL AAMI/FDA CONFERENCE ON MEDICAL DEVICE REGULATION. 3696

0146-1516 See LOCAL HEALTH DEPARTMENTS IN OREGON. 4789

0146-1524 See ANNUAL REPORT - NATIONAL BOARD OF MEDICAL EXAMINERS. 3913

0146-1540 See PROGRESS IN PEDIATRIC HEMATOLOGY/ONCOLOGY. 3773

0146-1621 See DIRECTORY OF ANIMAL DISEASE DIAGNOSTIC LABORATORIES. 5509

0146-163X See SECOND CIRCUIT REDBOOK. 3143

0146-1664 See JOURNAL OF UNDERGRADUATE ECONOMICS, THE. 1501

0146-1672 See PERSONALITY & SOCIAL PSYCHOLOGY BULLETIN. 4607

0146-1753 See BIENNIAL ROSTER OF REGISTERED PROFESSIONAL ENGINEERS AND LAND SURVEYORS AND ALABAMA LAW REGULATING PRACTICE OF ENGINEERING AND LAND SURVEYING. 1966

0146-1796 See TOUR BOOK, THE. 4926

0146-1826 See CALIFORNIA PROPERTY TAX CONFERENCE. 4716

0146-1842 See NEWS FOR SOUTH CAROLINA LIBRARIES. 3234

0146-1850 See FERTILIZER SUMMARY DATA. 87

0146-1869 See RIO GRANDE HISTORY. 2759

0146-1877 See NORTHWEST INDIAN NEWS. 2270

0146-1885 See ROCKINGCHAIR. 4151

0146-1893 See PIT & QUARRY HANDBOOK AND BUYERS GUIDE FOR THE NONMETALLIC MINERALS INDUSTRIES. 2148

0146-1907 See SUMMARY OF RATE SCHEDULES OF NATURAL GAS PIPELINE COMPANIES AS FILED WITH THE FEDERAL ENERGY REGULATORY COMMISSION AND THE NATIONAL ENERGY BOARD OF CANADA. 4284

0146-1931 See FOSSIL ENERGY PROGRAM REPORT. 1944

0146-1958 See JOURNAL OF THE FLAGSTAFF INSTITUTE. 1637

0146-1966 See WWIM. WHO'S WHERE IN MUSIC. 4159

0146-1990 See BRYANT BACKTRAILS. 2440

0146-2008 See REPLICA (MIAMI, FLA. 1970). 2492

0146-2067 See STONY HILLS. 3354

0146-2075 See PIMIENTA. 3996

0146-2083 See TUUMBA. 3448

0146-2091 See MEDIA DIGEST (FINKSBURG). 1763

0146-2105 See STAR-WEB PAPER. 3439

0146-2113 See AFFIRMATIVE ACTION REGISTER. 938

0146-2148 See ANNUAL STATISTICAL REPORT. MENTAL HEALTH SERVICES. MENTAL RETARDATION SERVICES. VETERANS' HOMES SERVICE (NEBRASKA). 5266

0146-2172 See REFERENCE DATA REPORT. 5145

0146-2199 See CAPE ROCK, THE. 3461

0146-2210 See RETAIL BAKING TODAY. 2356

0146-2229 See GENEALOGICAL JOURNAL (SALT LAKE CITY, UTAH). 2450

0146-2296 See FACULTY CHARACTERISTICS, PUBLIC COLLEGES AND UNIVERSITIES IN WEST VIRGINIA. 1823

0146-230X See MARYLAND BANK MONITOR. 797

0146-2318 See YOU (NEW YORK. 1976). 4622

0146-2334 See LILITH (NEW YORK). 5050

0146-2342 See ARTVIEW. 342

0146-2415 See AREA MANPOWER REVIEW : CITY OF BERKELEY. 1652

0146-2423 See BIENNIAL REPORT - GOVERNOR'S ADVOCACY COMMITTEE FOR CHILDREN AND YOUTH. 5274

0146-2431 See DIRECTORY OF SCHOOLS AND ESTABLISHMENTS APPROVED FOR VETERANS TRAINING. 1736

0146-244X See NATIONAL SECURITY AFFAIRS FORUM, THE. 4052

0146-2458 See YEARBOOK - ENSIGN CLASS ASSOCIATION. 4931

0146-2520 See IN SITU. 1440

0146-2539 See SENIOR WORLD. 5182

0146-258X See DISCUSSION PAPER - CENTER FOR LATIN AMERICA IN THE UNIVERSITY OF WISCONSIN, MILWAUKEE. 1821

0146-2628 See SUPER CHEVY. 5426

0146-2652 See POPULAR CYCLING. 429

0146-2679 See COLLECTION MANAGEMENT. 3202

0146-2709 See JURIS QUAESITOR. 2990

0146-275X See LONG-TERM CARE ADMINISTRATOR. 3788

0146-2768 See HEALTH IN WISCONSIN. 4780

0146-2806 See CURRENT PROBLEMS IN CARDIOLOGY. 3704

0146-2814 See COTH REPORT. 3778

0146-2857 See FACTORY OUTLET NEWSLETTER, THE. 1296

0146-2873 See FACTORY OUTLET SHOPPING GUIDE. WASHINGTON, D.C., MARYLAND, VIRGINIA, DELAWARE. 1296

0146-292X See S.S. HUEBNER FOUNDATION MONOGRAPH SERIES. 2893

0146-2938 See EQUAL OPPORTUNITY REPORT USDA PROGRAMS. 1667

0146-2954 See PARA-LEGAL UPDATE. 3025

0146-2962 See JOURNAL OF CHEROKEE STUDIES. 2266

0146-2970 See COMMENTS ON ASTROPHYSICS. 394

0146-2989 See BULLETIN OF MEDIEVAL CANON LAW. 2944

0146-3055 See NLM TECHNICAL BULLETIN, THE. 3237

0146-3071 See JOURNAL OF SEED TECHNOLOGY. 176

0146-3128 See PHARMCHEM NEWSLETTER, THE. 4324

ISSN Index

0146-3136 See POETS ON. 3470

0146-3160 See MYSTERY FANCIER, THE. 3414

0146-3217 See KANSAS WRITER'S MARKET. 3401

0146-3233 See AREA WAGE SURVEY : STAMFORD, CONNECTICUT, METROPOLITAN AREA. 1653

0146-3241 See SOUTH DAKOTA UNIFIED COURTS. 3143

0146-3292 See MOTOCROSS ACTION MAGAZINE. 4082

0146-3314 See FACTORY MANAGEMENT (NEW YORK). 868

0146-3365 See CAO TIMES. 390

0146-3373 See COMMUNICATION QUARTERLY. 1107

0146-3411 See HERESIES. 5558

0146-342X See EXPERIMENTAL EDUCATION PROGRAMS IN SPECIAL EDUCATION. 1879

0146-3438 See LOWER BUCKS COUNTY REAL ESTATE DIRECTORY. 4840

0146-3489 See RELIX. 4149

0146-3543 See FOREIGN SERVICE JOURNAL. 4522

0146-3586 See STUDIES IN HUMAN RIGHTS. 4513

0146-3632 See OCCUPATIONAL SAFETY AND HEALTH (NEW YORK). 2867

0146-3659 See PLANTS ALIVE. 2428

0146-3683 See COAL DEMONSTRATION PLANTS. TECHNICAL REPORT. 972

0146-3691 See COAL CONVERSION AND UTILIZATION. TECHNICAL REPORT. 972

0146-3705 See AIAA PAPER. 6

0146-3721 See AMERICAN JOURNAL OF DANCE THERAPY. 4573

0146-3845 See INTERNATIONAL COAL. 1636

0146-3934 See COLLEGE STUDENT JOURNAL. 1817

0146-3942 See BULLETIN - INSTITUTE OF MATHEMATICAL STATISTICS. 5324

0146-3950 See NATIONAL DIRECTORY OF BUDGET MOTELS. 2808

0146-3969 See BATTERIES (NEW YORK). 4398

0146-3977 See ANNUAL MEETING PROCEEDINGS - INTERNATIONAL INSTITUTE OF SYNTHETIC RUBBER PRODUCERS, INC. 5075

0146-3985 See SHELL (WABAN). 3471

0146-4000 See EXCHANGE (PROVO). 1091

0146-4043 See ALBRIGHT JOURNAL, THE. 391

0146-406X See BARRON'S REGENTS EXAMS AND ANSWERS: 11TH YEAR MATHEMATICS. 3497

0146-4094 See HEBREW STUDIES. 5048

0146-4108 See SOVIET METEOROLOGY AND HYDROLOGY. 1434

0146-4116 See AUTOMATIC CONTROL AND COMPUTER SCIENCES. 1217

0146-4124 See TOPOLOGY PROCEEDINGS. 3539

0146-4140 See JOURNAL OF BALLISTICS. 2014

0146-4159 See FOREST STATISTICS FOR IOWA. 2399

0146-4183 See OUI ALBUM. 4372

0146-4213 See MARITAL STATUS AND LIVING ARRANGEMENTS. 2283

0146-4248 See WORLD BOOK & TRAVEL REPORT. 5499

0146-4264 See SEMI DIRECTORY. 2080

0146-4302 See MONTANA ECONOMIC INDICATORS. 1574

0146-4310 See JOURNAL OF APPLIED SOCIAL SCIENCES, THE. 5291

0146-437X See NEW YORK HISTORY. 2748

0146-4396 See CA SELECTS: CATALYSIS (ORGANIC REACTIONS). 999

0146-440X See CA SELECTS: CATALYSIS (APPLIED AND PHYSICAL ASPECTS). 999

0146-4426 See CA SELECTS: COAL SCIENCE & PROCESS CHEMISTRY. 999

0146-4434 See CA SELECTS: CORROSION. 1000

0146-4442 See CA SELECTS: ELECTROCHEMICAL REACTIONS. 1001

0146-4450 See CA SELECTS: ELECTRON & AUGER SPECTROSCOPY. 1001

0146-4469 See CA SELECTS: ELECTRON SPIN RESONANCE (CHEMICAL ASPECTS). 1001

0146-4477 See CA SELECTS: GAS CHROMATOGRAPHY. 1003

0146-4485 See CA SELECTS: GEL PERMEATION CHROMATOGRAPHY. 1003

0146-4493 See CA SELECTS: ION EXCHANGE. 1004

0146-4515 See CA SELECTS: PAPER & THIN-LAYER CHROMATOGRAPHY. 1007

0146-4523 See CA SELECTS: RADIATION CHEMISTRY. 1009

0146-4531 See CA SELECTS: SOLVENT EXTRACTION. 1009

0146-454X See CA SELECTS: SURFACE CHEMISTRY (PHYSICOCHEMICAL ASPECTS). 1010

0146-4574 See POLO (GAITHERSBURG, MD.). 4912

0146-4582 See RED BOOK OF OPHTHALMOLOGY, THE. 3878

0146-4639 See REGULATORY WATCHDOG SERVICE. ALERT BULLETIN. 4679

0146-4647 See NEWS DIGEST - ITA. 5133

0146-4671 See PETERSEN'S HUNTING. 4912

0146-4698 See SURVEY OF TRAVEL IN KENTUCKY. 5492

0146-4701 See AUDIO CRITIC, THE. 5315

0146-4728 See DATZ PHILATELIC INDEX OF UNITED STATES POSTAGE STAMPS. 2785

0146-4744 See BUSINESS ASSISTANCE MONOGRAPH SERIES, THE. 646

0146-4752 See HIGH SOLIDS COATINGS. 977

0146-4760 See JOURNAL OF ANALYTICAL TOXICOLOGY. 3981

0146-4809 See NOISE NEWS. 2179

0146-4833 See COMPUTER COMMUNICATION REVIEW. 1240

0146-485X See SEC ACCOUNTING REPORT. 751

0146-4892 See WOODALL'S RETIREMENT AND RESORT COMMUNITIES. NATIONAL EDITION. 4855

0146-4914 See STATE OF MONTANA OFFICE OF THE SUPERINTENDENT OF PUBLIC INSTRUCTION AND BOARD OF PUBLIC EDUCATION : REPORT ON AUDIT. 4688

0146-4930 See NEW LETTERS. 3416

0146-4957 See JOHN PETER ZENGER AWARD FOR FREEDOM OF THE PRESS AND THE PEOPLE'S RIGHT TO KNOW, THE. 2921

0146-4965 See ALA BULLETIN : A PUBLICATION OF THE AFRICAN LITERATURE ASSOCIATION. 3359

0146-4981 See INTERNATIONAL JOURNAL OF FUSION ENERGY. 495

0146-499X See POTATO GROWER OF IDAHO. 182

0146-5015 See SALARIES OF SCIENTISTS, ENGINEERS AND TECHNICIANS. 1709

0146-5066 See 5-YEAR CUMULATED BIBLIOGRAPHY OF ORTHOPAEDIC SURGERY. 3654

0146-5171 See EUROPEAN ACCOMMODATIONS DIRECTORY. 2805

0146-521X See REGIONAL ANESTHESIA. 3684

0146-5236 See AUTOMOTIVE FUEL ECONOMY PROGRAM. ANNUAL REPORT TO THE CONGRESS. 4251

0146-5244 See STUDIES IN ART HISTORY PRESENTED AT THE MIDDLE ATLANTIC SYMPOSIUM IN THE HISTORY OF ART. 366

0146-5295 See GEORGIA MUNICIPAL YEARBOOK, THE. 2823

0146-5325 See TENNESSEE INDUSTRIES GUIDE, THE. 1629

0146-5341 See DIRECTORY OF TRADE AND INDUSTRIAL EDUCATION : SOUTH CAROLINA. 1912

0146-5368 See MONTANA POSTAL CACHE. 1145

0146-5414 See HARVEST QUARTERLY. 5246

0146-5422 See ONLINE (WESTON, CONN.). 1275

0146-5457 See CONSCIOUSNESS AND SELF-REGULATION. 4582

0146-5473 See PUBLIC WORKS NEWS. 4677

0146-5481 See NAIC MALPRACTICE CLAIMS. 2888

0146-5503 See AUDIT REPORT, DEPARTMENT OF PARKS AND TOURISM, MONUMENTS AND HISTORICAL SITES DIVISION, ARKANSAS TERRITORIAL CAPITOL RESTORATION. 4712

0146-5546 See JUMP CUT. 1115

0146-5554 See CUMULATIVE INDEX TO NURSING & ALLIED HEALTH LITERATURE. 3656

0146-5562 See INTERRACIAL BOOKS FOR CHILDREN BULLETIN. 1065

0146-5589 See INTERNATIONAL SERIES IN THE SCIENCE OF THE SOLID STATE. 5115

0146-5597 See LIQUID CRYSTALS AND ORDERED FLUIDS. 1032

0146-5600 See BIOCHEMISTRY OF DISEASE, THE. 482

0146-5635 See BIENNIAL REPORT OF THE TEXAS LIBRARY AND HISTORICAL COMMISSION. 3195

0146-5651 See MONOGRAPH SERIES - UNITED STATES HISTORICAL SOCIETY. 2747

0146-566X See FLAT GLASS. 2589

0146-5740 See STATE PLAN FOR CHILD WELFARE SERVICES. 5311

0146-5791 See STAFF NOTES. 4154

0146-5848 See FAULT, THE. 350

0146-5856 See JOURNAL OF THE ARNOLD SCHOENBERG INSTITUTE. 4126

0146-5902 See HIGHER EDUCATION DATA BOOK. 1828

0146-5945 See POLICY REVIEW (WASHINGTON). 5213

0146-597X See PERSONNEL FORUM. 945

0146-5988 See TRAVELER'S TOLL-FREE TELEPHONE DIRECTORY. 5497

0146-6046 See ANNUAL REPORT OF THE NATIONAL CREDIT UNION ADMINISTRATION. 771

0146-6062 See OPERA REVIEW. 4144

0146-6119 See EMSA BULLETIN. 572

0146-6143 See MUZZLELOADERS' ANNUAL. 3485

0146-616X See GENEALOGICAL & LOCAL HISTORY BOOKS IN PRINT. 4828

0146-6216 See APPLIED PSYCHOLOGICAL MEASUREMENT. 4574

0146-6232 See FOREFRONT (BERKELEY). 1975

0146-6267 See PROCEEDINGS OF ... SYNTHETIC PIPELINE GAS SYMPOSIUM. 4275

0146-6283 See CEREAL FOODS WORLD. 2331

0146-6348 See NEWSLETTER - WAYNE STATE UNIVERSITY LIBRARIES. 3236

0146-6380 See ORGANIC GEOCHEMISTRY. 1390

0146-6402 See ADVANCES IN BEHAVIOUR RESEARCH AND THERAPY. 4571

0146-6410 See PROGRESS IN PARTICLE AND NUCLEAR PHYSICS. 4450

0146-6429 See BULLETIN OF THE SOCIETY OF VECTOR ECOLOGISTS. 2212

0146-6437 See AMERICAN SHOEMAKING DIRECTORY OF SHOE MANUFACTURERS. 1081

0146-6453 See ANNALS OF THE ICRP. 3938

0146-6518 See INTERNATIONAL JOURNAL FOR HOUSING SCIENCE AND ITS APPLICATIONS. 2825

0146-6585 See WESTERN CANADA : ALASKA CAMPING. 4880

0146-6593 See PEOPLE (RENO). 4795

0146-6607 See CRAFTS 'N THINGS. 371

0146-6615 See JOURNAL OF MEDICAL VIROLOGY. 565

0146-6623 See JOURNAL OF AQUATIC PLANT MANAGEMENT. 515

0146-6690 See NATIONAL INSTITUTES OF HEALTH ANNUAL REPORT OF INTERNATIONAL ACTIVITIES. 3619

0146-678X See ORIENTAL INSTITUTE COMMUNICATIONS. 3308

0146-6801 *See* TOLL FREE BUSINESS. **1168**

0146-681X *See* CHEMICAL PROCESSING AND ENGINEERING (NEW YORK). **2010**

0146-6836 See DIRECTORY OF INDUSTRIAL HEAT PROCESSING AND COMBUSTION EQUIPMENT. UNITED STATES MANUFACTURERS, THE. **613**

0146-6852 *See* RADIO CONTACTS. **1137**

0146-6887 *See* LINN'S WORLD STAMP ALMANAC. **2785**

0146-6895 *See* BARRON'S REGENTS EXAMS AND ANSWERS : FRENCH LEVEL 3, COMPREHENSIVE FRENCH. **3268**

0146-6909 *See* SOLAR THERMAL ENERGY UTILIZATION. CUMULATIVE VOLUME. **1957**

0146-6941 *See* NORTHWEST CHESS. **4864**

0146-695X *See* SEVEN STARS. **3471**

0146-6968 *See* LISTING OF PEER REVIEWERS USED BY NSF DIVISIONS. **5126**

0146-6984 *See* TITLE I IN ACTION. **1788**

0146-700X *See* WYOMING OFFICIAL DIRECTORY. **4695**

0146-7026 *See* SAFETY RELATED RECALL CAMPAIGNS FOR MTOR VEHICLES AND MOTOR VEHICLE EQUIPMENT, INCLUDING TIRES: DETAILED REPORTS. **5425**

0146-7034 *See* FLORIDA AD VALOREM VALUATIONS AND TAX DATA. **4727**

0146-7042 *See* BIG DEAL. **3367**

0146-7077 *See* ANNUAL REPORT TO THE GOVERNOR AND GENERAL ASSEMBLY - STATE OF CONNECTICUT, COMMISSION ON HOSPITALS & HEALTH CARE. **3776**

0146-7115 *See* COMPUTERS IN CHEMISTRY AND INSTRUMENTATION. **1023**

0146-7174 *See* HERALD OF CHRISTIAN SCIENCE, THE. **4962**

0146-7182 *See* BUTT. **4827**

0146-7190 *See* POWELL MONETARY ANALYST, THE. **1513**

0146-7204 *See* POWELL GOLD INDUSTRY GUIDE AND INTERNATIONAL MINING ANALYST, THE. **2148**

0146-7220 *See* EUDORA WELTY NEWSLETTER. **3386**

0146-7239 *See* MOTIVATION AND EMOTION. **4604**

0146-731X *See* MARKET STATISTICS. **906**

0146-7328 *See* FINANCIAL PLANNING GUIDE FOR MILITARY PERSONNEL. **4044**

0146-7336 *See* DIRECTORY OF RESEARCH GRANTS. **1821**

0146-7360 *See* HOSPITAL AND HEALTH CARE REPORT. **3783**

0146-7387 *See* REPORT OF THE COMPTROLLER TO THE GOVERNOR OF VIRGINIA. **4745**

0146-7409 *See* STATE OF FLORIDA: LOCAL GOVERNMENT FINANCIAL REPORT. **4749**

0146-7425 *See* BUSINESS CONDITIONS (NEW YORK). **646**

0146-7433 *See* ALUMNI DIRECTORY - UNIVERSITY OF NORTH CAROLINA AT CHAPEL HILL. **1100**

0146-7468 *See* SUMMARY OF ACCIDENT DATA (RICHMOND). **5445**

0146-7506 *See* EXPENDITURE REPORT - STATE OF COLORADO, DEPARTMENT OF HIGHWAYS. **5440**

0146-7549 *See* LOCAL SERVICE CARRIERS PASSENGER ENPLANEMENTS. **27**

0146-7557 *See* AMERICAN PROFESSIONAL CONSTRUCTOR, THE. **2018**

0146-7603 *See* NEW JERSEY SCHOOL LAW DECISIONS (INDEX). **3015**

0146-7646 *See* PRB REPORT. **4559**

0146-7662 *See* EYEPIECE. **395**

0146-7808 *See* HYPOTHETICAL ADVISORY OPINIONS. **2251**

0146-7816 *See* INSTITUTE OF JUDICIAL ADMINISTRATION REPORT. **2983**

0146-7824 See VEGETARIAN TIMES. **4200**

0146-7832 *See* NEW THOUGHT (SCOTTSDALE, ARIZ.). **4981**

0146-7875 *See* NEBRASKA SYMPOSIUM ON MOTIVATION. **4605**

0146-7883 *See* MUSIC-IN-PRINT SERIES. **4133**

0146-7891 *See* NINETEENTH-CENTURY FRENCH STUDIES. **3349**

0146-7905 *See* MENTAL HEALTH STATE PLAN. **5296**

0146-7921 *See* CHRISTOPHER STREET. **2793**

0146-7956 *See* SCIENTIFIC AND TECHNICAL PUBLICATIONS OF THE ENVIRONMENTAL RESEARCH LABORATORIES. **2181**

0146-8014 *See* WORLDWIDE GUIDE TO MEDICAL ELECTRONICS MARKETING REPRESENTATION, THE. **3256**

0146-8030 *See* FIBER AND INTEGRATED OPTICS. **4434**

0146-8049 *See* ENZYMOLOGY. **487**

0146-8081 *See* WHO WAS WHO IN AMERICA. **435**

0146-809X *See* SOUTHERN EXPOSURE (DURHAM, N.C.). **2761**

0146-8235 *See* TAX GUIDE FOR ENGINEERS. **4752**

0146-8243 *See* SWEET'S INTERIORS MARKET. **2903**

0146-8251 *See* SOUTHERN GOLF. **4919**

0146-8308 *See* SWEET'S LIGHT RESIDENTIAL CONSTRUCTION MARKET. **630**

0146-8316 *See* SWEET'S ENGINEERING MARKET. **2032**

0146-8324 *See* SWEET'S INDUSTRIAL CONSTRUCTION AND RENOVATION MARKET/RENOVATION EXTENSION. **630**

0146-8332 *See* ALCOHOL TECHNICAL REPORTS. **1339**

0146-8340 *See* GLAD DIRECTORY OF RESOURCES AVAILABLE TO DEAF & HARD-OF-HEARING PERSONS IN THE SOUTHERN CALIFORNIA AREA. **5286**

0146-8359 *See* STATE ROAD ANNUAL REPORT. **5444**

0146-8383 *See* RACING PIGEON BULLETIN. **4914**

0146-8405 *See* GOVERNMENT AFFAIRS REPORT. **4651**

0146-8456 *See* SWEET'S GENERAL BUILDING MARKET. **630**

0146-8480 See SOUTH CAROLINA ANNUAL STATE PLAN FOR VOCATIONAL-TECHNICAL EDUCATION. **1915**

0146-8510 *See* UROBOROS. **3472**

0146-8553 *See* MAKTABA AFRIKANA SERIES. **2641**

0146-857X *See* DATABOOK - U.S. DEPT. OF HEALTH, EDUCATION, AND WELFARE, NATIONAL INSTITUTE OF EDUCATION, DISSEMINATION AND RESOURCES GROUP, R & D SYSTEM SUPPORT DIVISION. **1892**

0146-8618 *See* ANNUAL DESCRIPTIVE REPORT: VOCATIONAL TECHNICAL EDUCATION IN PENNSYLVANIA. **1910**

0146-8626 See NATIONAL FEDERATION HANDBOOK. **4906**

0146-8677 *See* QUEENS COLLEGE STUDIES IN LIBRARIANSHIP. **3243**

0146-8685 *See* RILA BULLETIN. **3247**

0146-8693 *See* JOURNAL OF PEDIATRIC PSYCHOLOGY. **4599**

0146-8707 *See* BAXTER'S EURAILPASS TRAVEL GUIDE. **5429**

0146-874X *See* CURRENTS (PHILADELPHIA). **5281**

0146-8758 *See* MUNICIPAL PROGRESS. **4667**

0146-8766 *See* SCHOOL DISTRICTS THAT WERE GRANTED WAIVERS OF ADMINISTRATOR-TEACHER RATIO LIMITS. **1871**

0146-8782 *See* U.S. FATS AND OILS STATISTICS. **157**

0146-8790 *See* ADVANCES IN THE MANAGEMENT OF CLINICAL HEART DISEASE. **3698**

0146-8812 *See* FIGHTING WOMAN NEWS. **2597**

0146-8855 *See* MOUNTAIN DIGGINGS. **2747**

0146-8863 *See* CHARACTERISTICS OF REGISTERED APPRENTICES IN CALIFORNIA. **1659**

0146-8871 *See* ANNUAL REPORT OF THE OFFICE OF COMMISSIONER OF BANKING. **772**

0146-888X *See* POLYDOXY. **5052**

0146-891X *See* ANNUAL SUMMARY OF ACTIVITIES - ARIZONA DEPARTMENT OF ECONOMIC SECURITY. **1650**

0146-8928 *See* ISSUES - EXECUTIVE OFFICE OF THE PRESIDENT, OFFICE OF MANAGEMENT AND BUDGET. **4734**

0146-8952 *See* CAPITAL PROJECTS. **4716**

0146-8979 *See* PROJECT SKYWATER; BIENNIAL REPORT. **1433**

0146-9002 *See* SIGNIFICANT FEATURES OF FISCAL FEDERALISM. **4748**

0146-9029 *See* CRIME IN HAWAII. **3080**

0146-9037 *See* BID OPENING REPORT. **5439**

0146-9053 *See* ANNUAL UPDATE TO THE ALASKA STATE PLAN FOR THE REDUCTION OF ALCOHOLISM AND ALCOHOL ABUSE. **1341**

0146-907X *See* BUDGET REVISIONS - EXECUTIVE OFFICE OF THE PRESIDENT, OFFICE OF MANAGEMENT AND BUDGET. **4715**

0146-9088 *See* DIGEST OF SELECTED REPORTS - UNITED WAY OF AMERICA. **5282**

0146-910X *See* LAIFS. **2422**

0146-9118 *See* OCCURRENCE. **3467**

0146-9126 *See* OCEAN RESOURCES ENGINEERING. **2094**

0146-9134 See POWER TRANSMISSION DESIGN ... GUIDE TO PT PRODUCTS. **2124**

0146-9150 *See* BIENNIAL REPORT - NORTH CAROLINA MANPOWER COUNCIL. **1655**

0146-9169 *See* FOLKNIK, THE. **4118**

0146-9177 *See* CRIMINAL JUSTICE ABSTRACTS. **3080**

0146-924X See VESTNIK ST. PETERSBURG UNIVERSITY: MATHEMATICS. **3540**

0146-9266 *See* SMOKESHOP. **712**

0146-9274 *See* IAM (NEW YORK). **2738**

0146-9282 *See* EDUCATIONAL CONSIDERATIONS. **1913**

0146-9304 *See* FOODS ADLIBRA (1975). **2362**

0146-9312 *See* SEA HISTORY. **4183**

0146-9339 *See* MYTHLORE. **3414**

0146-9347 *See* MYTHPRINT. **3414**

0146-9398 *See* ALA-ARTS. **312**

0146-9428 *See* JOURNAL OF FOOD QUALITY. **2346**

0146-9479 *See* CONSTRUCTION CONTRACTOR, THE. **609**

0146-9487 *See* HOMEMAKER OF THE NATIONAL EXTENSION HOMEMAKERS COUNCIL, THE. **2791**

0146-9517 *See* NSS BULLETIN, THE. **1359**

0146-955X *See* PROCEEDINGS OF THE ... INTERSOCIETY ENERGY CONVERSION ENGINEERING CONFERENCE. **1953**

0146-9568 *See* TOLEDOT. **2475**

0146-9576 *See* SAN FRANCISCO THEATRE. **5368**

0146-9584 *See* JOURNAL OF LEGISLATION. **2989**

0146-9592 *See* OPTICS LETTERS. **4439**

0146-9606 *See* AMERICAN ARTIST DIRECTORY OF ART SCHOOLS AND WORKSHOPS. **312**

0146-9622 *See* TRUCKS 26,000 PLUS. **5398**

0146-9649 *See* SIMMONS KINFOLK. **2472**

0146-9657 *See* KOREA NEWSREVIEW. **2506**

0146-9665 *See* CHILD ABUSE AND NEGLECT PROGRAMS. **5277**

0146-9673 *See* EMPLOYMENT AND TRAINING REPORTER. **4204**

0146-9681 *See* BEST HOME PLANS. **293**

0146-9703 *See* FLORIDA EXPORT GUIDE. **836**

0146-9738 *See* DENTAL LAB PRODUCTS. **1321**

0146-9797 *See* STATEMENT OF TAX POLICY. **4750**

0146-9800 *See* ACCOUNTING RESEARCH MONOGRAPH. **737**

0146-9819 *See* AUDITING RESEARCH MONOGRAPH. **739**

0146-9916 See RECOMMENDED SALARIES AND BENEFITS FOR CAREER SERVICE EMPLOYEES. 4678

0146-9924 See CIRCUIT RIDER (NASHVILLE), THE. 5058

0146-9959 See METEOR NEWS. 397

0146-9975 See NSOA BULLETIN. 4142

0147-0000 See STATE PLAN FOR THE ADMINISTRATION OF VOCATIONAL EDUCATION UNDER THE VOCATIONAL EDUCATION AMENDMENTS OF 1968, AND PART F OF THE HIGHER EDUCATION ACT OF 1965 (SALEM). 1916

0147-0019 See BROWN FAMILY NEWS AND GENEALOGICAL SOCIETY, THE. 2440

0147-0027 See BULLETIN - RAILROAD STATION HISTORICAL SOCIETY, THE. 5430

0147-0043 See ASPEN VACATION GUIDE. 5462

0147-0051 See FIRE & MOVEMENT. 4861

0147-006X See ANNUAL REVIEW OF NEUROSCIENCE. 3827

0147-0078 See RECENT RESEARCHES IN AMERICAN MUSIC. 4148

0147-0086 See RECENT RESEARCHES IN THE MUSIC OF THE CLASSICAL ERA. 4148

0147-0191 See ILLINOIS CONFERENCE ON MEDICAL INFORMATION SYSTEMS. 3585

0147-0205 See ESSAYS IN NEUROCHEMISTRY AND NEUROPHARMACOLOGY. 3832

0147-0221 See INFORME ANUAL; SERVICIOS ODONTOLOGICOS. 1325

0147-0256 See ANNUAL REPORT; DENTAL EDUCATION. 1316

0147-0272 See CURRENT PROBLEMS IN CANCER. 3815

0147-0310 See EXHIBITS DIRECTORY - ASSOCIATION OF AMERICAN PUBLISHERS. 4815

0147-0353 See HEALTH VALUES. 4782

0147-037X See MING STUDIES. 2658

0147-0388 See LISTENERS' GUIDE - WGMS. 4129

0147-0396 See REBIS CHAPBOOK SERIES, THE. 3470

0147-0418 See JOURNAL OF INTERIOR DESIGN EDUCATION AND RESEARCH. 2901

0147-0434 See STATE OF THE STATES ON CRIME AND JUSTICE. 3177

0147-0477 See STATUS (WASHINGTON). 1540

0147-0507 See ANNUAL REPORT OF THE LEGISLATIVE BUDGET AND FINANCE COMMITTEE FOR THE REGULAR SESSION OF THE GENERAL ASSEMBLY OF THE COMMONWEALTH OF PENNSYLVANIA. 4710

0147-0515 See NIAAA-RUCAS ALCOHOLISM TREATMENT SERIES. 1347

0147-0531 See NORTH CAROLINA LABOR FORCE ESTIMATES BY COUNTY, DEFINED MULTI-COUNTY LABOR AREAS, STATE MULTI-COUNTY PLANNING REGIONS. 1695

0147-0566 See STATE COASTAL ZONE MANAGEMENT ACTIVITIES. 4687

0147-0639 See MAINE ANTIQUE DIGEST. 251

0147-0663 See BLUE BOOK ILLUSTRATED PRICE GUIDE TO COLLECTABLE CAMERAS. 4367

0147-0698 See THRUPUT. 814

0147-071X See ADVANCES IN BEHAVIORAL PHARMACOLOGY. 4571

0147-0728 See GAY COMMUNITY NEWS (BOSTON, MASS.). 2794

0147-0779 See MODERN GREEK SOCIETY. 5209

0147-0787 See BOOKS AT BROWN. 4821

0147-0809 See LIGHT METALS (NEW YORK). 4007

0147-0817 See REFERENCE INFORMATION PAPER. 2483

0147-0833 See JOURNAL OF EQUINE MEDICINE AND SURGERY, THE. 2800

0147-0868 See WITTENBERG REVIEW OF LITERATURE & ART. 3356

0147-0876 See ANNUAL REPORTS OF PROGRESS - REHABILITATION ENGINEERING CENTER AT RANCHO LOS AMIGOS HOSPITAL. 3685

0147-0914 See STATE VOCATIONAL REHABILITATION AGENCY PROGRAM DATA. 5311

0147-0922 See RESEARCH PROGRAMS - NATIONAL ENDOWMENT FOR THE HUMANITIES. 2853

0147-0949 See HEALTH STATISTICS PLAN. 4810

0147-0957 See PATIENT ORIGIN DATA FOR NORTH DAKOTA HOSPITALS AND NURSING HOMES. 3790

0147-099X See MEDICAL SUBJECT HEADINGS. TREE STRUCTURES. 3230

0147-1015 See UKRAINIAN ORTHODOX WORD. 5040

0147-1023 See CONTRIBUTIONS IN FAMILY STUDIES. 2278

0147-1031 See CONTRIBUTIONS IN INTERCULTURAL AND COMPARATIVE STUDIES. 2845

0147-104X See CONTRIBUTIONS IN WOMEN'S STUDIES. 5553

0147-1066 See CONTRIBUTIONS IN POLITICAL SCIENCE. 4470

0147-1082 See CONTEMPORARY PROBLEMS OF CHILDHOOD. 4582

0147-1112 See DAX MONEY-MAKER. 664

0147-1120 See PROCEEDINGS OF THE ANNUAL CONFERENCE OF THE ASSOCIATION OF COLLEGE UNIONS - INTERNATIONAL. 1842

0147-1139 See DIGNITY. 5187

0147-1147 See DESIGN METHODS. 297

0147-1163 See RUFUS, THE. 3470

0147-1201 See MAIN. 4186

0147-121X See LIGHT (NEW YORK. 1973). 3465

0147-1228 See HOOSIER JOURNAL OF ANCESTRY, THE. 2454

0147-1236 See ACTFL FOREIGN LANGUAGE EDUCATION SERIES, THE. 3261

0147-1244 See AIRCRAFT INDEX MAGAZINE. 9

0147-1260 See CHILD PROTECTION REPORT. 4771

0147-1287 See DAVE CAMPBELL'S TEXAS FOOTBALL. 4892

0147-1295 See DAVE CAMPBELL'S ARKANSAS FOOTBALL. 4892

0147-1309 See ANNUAL IMMIGRATION AND NATURALIZATION INSTITUTE. 2934

0147-1325 See DIRECTORY OF OFFICERS, COUNCIL, AND COMMITTEES. 2962

0147-1333 See OCCUPATIONAL PROFILES OF OREGON'S MANUFACTURING INDUSTRIES. 1699

0147-135X See REAL PROPERTY LAW SECTION NEWSLETTER. 4845

0147-1376 See LAW LIBRARY NEWSLETTER. 3222

0147-1384 See KING'S LETTER, THE. 4128

0147-1392 See HAWAII LEGAL REPORTER. 2977

0147-1406 See CALIFORNIA TEACHERS SALARIES AND SALARY SCHEDULES. 1861

0147-1422 See TRAVEL NORTH AMERICA. 5496

0147-1449 See ORAL AND MAXILLOFACIAL SURGERY DIRECTORY OF THE WORLD. 3971

0147-1473 See SOCIAL DEVELOPMENT ISSUES. 5308

0147-1481 See OFFSHORE RIG NEWSLETTER, THE. 4267

0147-149X See COTTONWOOD (LAWRENCE, KAN.). 3378

0147-1503 See SELECTED DATA ON MIXTURES. SER. A. THERMODYNAMIC PROPERTIES OF NON-REACTING BINARY SYSTEMS OF ORGANIC SUBSTANCES. 1057

0147-152X See OFFSHORE INTERNATIONAL NEWSLETTER, THE. 4267

0147-1538 See BRANCH DIRECTORY AND SUMMARY OF DEPOSITS FOR THE STATES OF INDIANA, MICHIGAN. 780

0147-1546 See BRANCH DIRECTORY AND SUMMARY OF DEPOSITS FOR THE STATE OF OHIO. 780

0147-1554 See ACROSS THE BOARD. 636

0147-1570 See COMPFLASH. 1660

0147-1619 See CORPORATION LAW AND TAX REPORT (1975). 3099

0147-1627 See CALYX (CORVALLIS). 3371

0147-1635 See JOURNAL OF BASIC WRITING. 3289

0147-1686 See FLOATING ISLAND. 3463

0147-1694 See CONTEMPORARY JEWRY. 2259

0147-1708 See COAL PROCESSING TECHNOLOGY. 2137

0147-1724 See SOUTHWESTERN ENTOMOLOGIST, THE. 5613

0147-1740 See URBAN LEAGUE REVIEW, THE. 2274

0147-1759 See WOMEN & LITERATURE. 3454

0147-1767 See INTERNATIONAL JOURNAL OF INTERCULTURAL RELATIONS. 5248

0147-1783 See INFORMATION CIRCULAR - STATE OF WASHINGTON, DEPARTMENT OF NATURAL RESOURCES, DIVISION OF GEOLOGY AND EARTH RESOURCES. 1383

0147-1821 See GRADUATE PROGRAMS IN PHYSICS, ASTRONOMY AND RELATED FIELDS. 4404

0147-1902 See BULLETIN - GEORGIA MUSEUM OF ART, THE UNIVERSITY OF GEORGIA. 4085

0147-1929 See OPERATIONS MANUAL OF THE NATIONAL ASSOCIATION OF REALTORS. 4842

0147-1937 See REAL ANALYSIS EXCHANGE. 3530

0147-1945 See ADVANCE BUDGETING. A REPORT TO THE CONGRESS. 4624

0147-1953 See MEMBERSHIP DIRECTORY CLASSIFIED BY SPECIALTY. 906

0147-197X See CURRENT PROBLEMS IN ANESTHESIA AND CRITICAL CARE MEDICINE. 3963

0147-1996 See YEAR BOOK OF FAMILY PRACTICE, THE. 3739

0147-2011 See SOCIETY (NEW BRUNSWICK). 5222

0147-2046 See JAMES MADISON JOURNAL, THE. 745

0147-2089 See OLD TIMER. 2752

0147-2097 See BIRMINGHAM AREA INDUSTRIAL DIRECTORY. 1599

0147-2119 See WHO'S WHO IN THE PICTURE FRAMING INDUSTRY. 438

0147-2127 See CAS FORUM. 1814

0147-2135 See ARL STATISTICS. 3257

0147-2151 See OUTSTANDING LEADERS IN ELEMENTARY AND SECONDARY EDUCATION. 1771

0147-2178 See INTERSTATE COMMERCE COMMISSION'S REPORT TO THE PRESIDENT AND THE CONGRESS. EFFECTIVENESS OF THE ACT. AMTRAK. 5432

0147-2186 See RESEARCH REPORT - MISSISSIPPI AGRICULTURAL & FORESTRY EXPERIMENT STATION. 128

0147-2208 See LAVENTHOL & HORWATH PERSPECTIVE. 747

0147-2305 See SALARIES & BENEFITS IN BOAT MANUFACTURING. 1709

0147-2356 See GEORGE D. HALL'S THE NEW ENGLAND INDUSTRIAL SERVICE DIRECTORY. 1607

0147-2364 See HUNGATE. 2454

0147-2380 See UTAH BLACK BEAR HARVEST. 2208

0147-2429 See PLASTICS IN BUILDING CONSTRUCTION. 624

0147-2453 See CURRICULUM REVIEW. 1892

0147-247X See PHOTOGRAPHER'S MARKET. 4374

0147-2488 See RICHARDSON FAMILY RESEARCHER AND HISTORICAL NEWS. 2470

0147-250X See BIBLIOGRAPHY. BOOKS FOR CHILDREN. 1072

0147-2542 See OHIO DOCUMENTS. 4671

0147-2550 See MASSACHUSETTS MUSIC NEWS. 4130

0147-2569 See CHESS HORIZONS. 4858

0147-2585 See MAINE MENTAL HEALTH PLAN. 4789

0147-2593 See LION AND THE UNICORN (BROOKLYN), THE. 3346
0147-2607 See REPORT OF THE MISSISSIPPI STATE HOSPITAL COMMISSION. 3792
0147-264X See DENTAL RESEARCH IN THE UNITED STATES AND OTHER COUNTRIES. 1321
0147-2682 See BIOMEDICAL TECHNOLOGY INFORMATION SERVICE. 3687
0147-2720 See NEW QUARTERLY (NEW YORK), THE. 2490
0147-2771 See NATIONAL HEALTH DIRECTORY. 4792
0147-2828 See BLACK PRESS INFORMATION HANDBOOK. 5647
0147-2836 See BRANCH DIRECTORY AND SUMMARY OF DEPOSITS FOR THE STATES OF SOUTH CAROLINA, NORTH CAROLINA. 780
0147-2844 See NEW JERSEY TAX HANDBOOK. 4738
0147-2887 See REPORT ON ENVIRONMENTAL RADIATION SURVEILLANCE IN NORTH CAROLINA. 2242
0147-2909 See NUCLEAR REGULATORY COMMISSION ISSUANCES. 1952
0147-2968 See RUNNING TIMES. 4916
0147-2976 See CATALOG OF MEMBERSHIP PROGRAMS AND SERVICES. 818
0147-2984 See BUDGET - STATE OF NORTH CAROLINA, THE. 4715
0147-300X See INTERNATIONAL GLASS/METAL CATALOG. 2591
0147-3026 See INTERNATIONAL OTORHINOLARYNGOLOGICAL REPORTER. 3888
0147-3042 See INTERNATIONAL CARDIOLOGICAL REPORTER. 3706
0147-3077 See PERIODICAL GUIDE FOR COMPUTERISTS. 1261
0147-3085 See CELESTINESCA. 3373
0147-3093 See MOODY'S COMPLETE CORPORATE INDEX. 696
0147-3115 See BRANCH DIRECTORY AND SUMMARY OF DEPOSITS FOR THE STATES OF CALIFORNIA, NEW MEXICO, ARIZONA. 780
0147-3123 See BRANCH DIRECTORY AND SUMMARY OF DEPOSITS FOR THE STATES OF MARYLAND, DISTRICT OF COLUMBIA, VIRGINIA. 780
0147-3131 See BRANCH DIRECTORY AND SUMMARY OF DEPOSITS FOR THE STATE OF NEW YORK. 780
0147-314X See BRANCH DIRECTORY AND SUMMARY OF DEPOSITS FOR THE STATES OF IDAHO, NEVADA, WASHINGTON, OREGON, UTAH. 780
0147-3166 See WINESBURG EAGLE, THE. 439
0147-3174 See REPORT OF THE PRESIDENT - UNIVERSITY OF MARYLAND. 1844
0147-3190 See LECOURT. 2999
0147-3247 See NUESTRO. 2270
0147-3263 See REPORT OF ACCOMPLISHMENTS, RHODE ISLAND. 126
0147-328X See LIQUID CHROMATOGRAPHY LITERATURE, ABSTRACTS AND INDEX. 1017
0147-3336 See PROGRAM-CURRICULUM PLANS. 5066
0147-3344 See REVENUE NEWS. 4747
0147-3352 See TELEVISION CONTACTS. 1140
0147-3360 See CONSUMER PRODUCT HAZARD INDEX. 4772
0147-3387 See ABSTRACTS OF PAPERS - BYZANTINE STUDIES CONFERENCE. 2671
0147-3395 See NEW ENGLAND JOURNAL OF PARAPSYCHOLOGY. 4242
0147-3417 See NEWSLETTER - SEARL NATIONAL SPACE RESEARCH CONSORTIUM, UNITED KINGDOM DIVISION. 30
0147-3433 See MANAGEMENT OF HOUSING. 2827
0147-3441 See SPARTAN, THE. 4866
0147-345X See EASTMAN NOTES. 4116
0147-3476 See NATIONAL DIRECTORY OF MEDICARE HOME HEALTH AGENCIES. 2889

0147-3492 See BIENNIAL BUDGET REQUEST - WISCONSIN DEPARTMENT OF HEALTH AND SOCIAL SERVICES. 5274
0147-3506 See SCOUT FOUR WHEEL DRIVE ANNUAL. 5425
0147-3522 See OCEAN RESOURCES ENGINEERING. 2094
0147-3557 See CONNECTICUT AIR QUALITY SUMMARY. 2226
0147-3565 See PORSCHE PANORAMA. 5423
0147-3573 See NUDIS VERBIS. 3142
0147-3581 See UTAH JUDICIAL BRIEFS. 3070
0147-359X See PUBLIC UTILITIES AND TRANSPORTATION NEWSLETTER. 4677
0147-3603 See ADMINISTRATION OF JUSTICE MEMORANDA. 2927
0147-3611 See REPORT OF CASE DECISIONS. 3153
0147-3638 See LEGISLATIVE CALENDAR / UNITED STATES HOUSE OF REPRESENTATIVES, COMMITTEE ON THE BUDGET. 4736
0147-3654 See SCIENCELAND. 5154
0147-3689 See JOHN MARSHALL LAW JOURNAL. 2986
0147-3697 See HYDROLOGIC REPORT (LOS ANGELES). 5534
0147-3719 See DEBTOR & CREDITOR. BENDER PAMPHLET EDITION. 2959
0147-3743 See SAFETY SADISTICS. 4801
0147-3778 See BRANCH DIRECTORY AND SUMMARY OF DEPOSITS FOR THE STATES OF NEW JERSEY, DELAWARE. 780
0147-3808 See COMMUNITY COLLEGE FINANCES. 1817
0147-3824 See VA EDUCATION LOAN DEFAULTS : ANNUAL REPORT. 1853
0147-3891 See GREEN BOOK BUYERS' GUIDE FOR GARDEN MERCHANDISE. 2417
0147-3905 See CHRONICLE GRADUATE & PROFESSIONAL MAJORS : FINANCING GRADUATE STUDY. 1815
0147-3913 See PATIENT CARE REVIEW. 3790
0147-3921 See DIRECTORY OF INPATIENT FACILITIES FOR THE MENTALLY RETARDED. 3779
0147-3948 See ABSTRACTS - INTERNATIONAL FERTILITY RESEARCH PROGRAM. 587
0147-3956 See ADVANCE DATA FROM VITAL AND HEALTH STATISTICS OF THE NATIONAL CENTER FOR HEALTH STATISTICS. 4809
0147-3964 See MULTIVARIATE EXPERIMENTAL CLINICAL RESEARCH. 4605
0147-4006 See CARCINOGENESIS. A COMPREHENSIVE SURVEY. 3814
0147-409X See EXPORT GRAFICS USA. 834
0147-4103 See LEGISLATIVE CALENDAR - UNITED STATES SENATE. COMMITTEE ON AGRICULTURE, NUTRITION, AND FORESTRY. 4661
0147-4154 See SURGICAL FORUM (BIRMINGHAM). 3976
0147-4197 See WYOMING WATER POLLUTION CONTROL PROGRAM PLAN. 5549
0147-4243 See ECONOMIC ANALYSIS OF UNITED STATES SKI AREAS. 4893
0147-4251 See PUBLIC ADVISORY COMMITTEES, AUTHORITY, STRUCTURE, FUNCTIONS, MEMBERS. 4797
0147-4294 See END OF YEAR REPORT - NORTHWEST FEDERAL REGIONAL COUNCIL. 4646
0147-4316 See ISRAEL SECURITIES REVIEW (1975). 904
0147-4359 See ENERGY CONSERVATION ANNUAL REPORT. 1939
0147-4367 See VOICE OF WASHINGTON MUSIC EDUCATORS. 4158
0147-4383 See AGENCY DIRECTORY - AMERICAN HUMANE. 5270
0147-4405 See DIRECTORY OF CHILD CARE CENTERS. 5282
0147-4413 See JOURNAL OF THE AMERICAN LISZT SOCIETY. 4126

0147-4464 See LOUISIANA INTERNATIONAL TRADE DIRECTORY. 844
0147-4553 See DIRECTORY OF WOMEN-OWNED BUSINESSES. WASHINGTON-BALTIMORE METROPOLITAN AREA. 688
0147-457X See FIELD CROPS PRODUCTION, DISPOSITION, VALUE. 171
0147-4596 See MAINE WATER QUALITY STATUS. 5536
0147-4618 See NAAM. 4139
0147-4626 See STATISTICS FOR MUNICIPAL AUTHORITIES IN PENNSYLVANIA. 4700
0147-4642 See COMMUNICATION YEARBOOK. 1107
0147-4669 See ASTRONOMY AND ASTROPHYSICS MONTHLY INDEX. 392
0147-4693 See ON THE LINE MAGAZINE. 4485
0147-4723 See POPULAR GARDENING INDOORS. 2428
0147-474X See SOUTH DAKOTA GOVERNOR'S ADVISORY COMMITTEE ON EMPLOYMENT OF THE HANDICAPPED. 4394
0147-4758 See LABOR FORCE STATISTICS (HONOLULU). 1535
0147-4766 See MANPOWER PLANNING AND UTILIZATION. 1689
0147-4774 See UNDERSTANDING FINANCIAL STATEMENTS. 752
0147-4782 See TODAY'S CLINICIAN. 3646
0147-4804 See WORLD-WIDE PRINTER. 4570
0147-4839 See ANNALS OF THE NYINGMA LINEAGE IN AMERICA. 5020
0147-4847 See AASHTO QUARTERLY. 5375
0147-4855 See AURA (BUFFALO). 4367
0147-4863 See ADVANCES IN MICROBIAL ECOLOGY. 2211
0147-4871 See FEEDBACK (WASHINGTON). 1132
0147-4898 See ALUMNI DIRECTORY - TEXAS CHRISTIAN UNIVERSITY, THE. 1099
0147-4901 See ANNUAL PLANNING REPORT - STATE OF FLORIDA, DEPARTMENT OF COMMERCE, DIVISION OF EMPLOYMENT SECURITY. 1648
0147-4936 See INVISIBLE CITY. 3464
0147-4995 See QUALITY AND RELIABILITY ASSURANCE. 883
0147-5002 See BRANCH DIRECTORY AND SUMMARY OF DEPOSITS FOR THE STATES OF CONNECTICUT, MAINE, MASSACHUSETTS, NEW HAMPSHIRE, RHODE ISLAND, VERMONT. 780
0147-510X See US (NEW YORK, N.Y. 1985). 2548
0147-5169 See AMERICAN HOME'S BEST PROJECTS. 369
0147-5185 See AMERICAN JOURNAL OF SURGICAL PATHOLOGY, THE. 3892
0147-5207 See MON-KHMER STUDIES. 3303
0147-5223 See MONOGRAPH - SIGMA THETA TAU. 3862
0147-5231 See SOMATICS. 4361
0147-524X See ADMINISTRATIVE BRIEFS. 3775
0147-5258 See PROCEEDINGS - ANNUAL CONTRACTOR'S CONFERENCE OF THE ARTIFICIAL KIDNEY PROGRAM OF THE NATIONAL INSTITUTE OF ARTHRITIS, METABOLISM, AND DIGESTIVE DISEASES. 3800
0147-5274 See PROSIT. 375
0147-5282 See SWEET POTATO. 4155
0147-5304 See PROFITABLE CRAFT MERCHANDISING. 375
0147-5339 See EEO YEARBOOK. 4043
0147-5355 See REPORT ON FRINGE BENEFITS AND RELATED PRACTICES AFFECTING POLICEMEN. 3174
0147-538X See NEW YORK TIMES INDEX, THE. 5814
0147-5401 See INDUSTRIAL HYGIENE NEWS (PITTSBURGH). 2863
0147-5436 See ALOHA (HONOLULU). 5460
0147-5460 See JOURNAL OF HISPANIC PHILOLOGY. 3290
0147-5479 See INTERNATIONAL LABOR AND WORKING CLASS HISTORY. 1680

0147-5525 See STATISTICAL SOURCE DIRECTORY FOR NEW JERSEY STATE GOVERNMENT. 5340

0147-555X See ROSTER OF WOMEN AND MINORITY ENGINEERING AND TECHNOLOGY STUDENTS. 1995

0147-5568 See ANNUAL REPORT / UNITED STATES INTERNATIONAL TRADE COMMISSION. 823

0147-5606 See FUNPARKS DIRECTORY. 4861

0147-5614 See REPORT OF VITAL STATISTICS FOR OHIO. 4811

0147-5622 See PSYCHOSOCIAL REHABILITATION JOURNAL. 3934

0147-5630 See INDEX TO FREE PERIODICALS. 2496

0147-5649 See DOW JONES STOCK OPTIONS HANDBOOK, THE. 897

0147-5657 See DIRECTORIO PROFESIONAL HISPANO. 1663

0147-5665 See DRI ENERGY BULLETIN. 1936

0147-5673 See COMMITTEE HANDBOOK - AICPA. 741

0147-5681 See CHILDREN'S BOOK REVIEW INDEX. 3339

0147-569X See REPORT FROM ASPEN INSTITUTE BERLIN. 2853

0147-5711 See MEDICAL SUBJECT HEADINGS. ANNOTATED ALPHABETIC LIST. 3230

0147-572X See MRIS ABSTRACTS. 4179

0147-5738 See COUNTRY SOUNDS OF THE SOUTHWEST. 4112

0147-5754 See INTERMEDIA (LOS ANGELES). 322

0147-5886 See PENJERDEL LOCATION & MARKET GUIDE OF THE DELAWARE VALLEY, THE. 1578

0147-5894 See COLLEGE AND UNIVERSITY ADMISSIONS AND ENROLLMENT, NEW YORK STATE. 1816

0147-5908 See PUERTO RICO (WASHINGTON. 1976). 1579

0147-5916 See COGNITIVE THERAPY AND RESEARCH. 4581

0147-5924 See INFO FRANCHISE NEWSLETTER, THE. 840

0147-5959 See CATHOLIC TELEPHONE GUIDE. 5026

0147-5967 See JOURNAL OF COMPARATIVE ECONOMICS. 1592

0147-5975 See EXPERIMENTAL MYCOLOGY. 574

0147-5991 See OFFICIAL SOUVENIR PROGRAM OF SPOLETO FESTIVAL U.S.A, THE. 386

0147-6009 See PSYCHOEDUCATIONAL JOURNAL FOR THE TREATMENT OF CHILDREN. 1884

0147-6041 See STATE LEGISLATURES. 4688

0147-605X See PUBLICATION INDEX - COLLEGE OF ARTS & SCIENCES, UNIVERSITY OF FLORIDA. 1843

0147-6068 See SYSTEMS ENGINEERING FOR POWER. 2083

0147-6122 See SILVER VAIN. 3437

0147-6149 See UNIVERSITY JOURNAL, THE. 1096

0147-6157 See PROPOSED COMPREHENSIVE ANNUAL SERVICES PLAN (INDIANAPOLIS). 5302

0147-6173 See PATENT OFFICE EXAMINATION REVIEW COURSE. 3025

0147-619X See PLASMID. 550

0147-6211 See SPECIAL PUBLICATION - CALIFORNIA DIVISION OF MINES AND GEOLOGY. 1397

0147-6262 See CRC HANDBOOK OF CHEMISTRY AND PHYSICS. 973

0147-6270 See CITY AND COUNTRY AMERICAN ELSEWHEN ALMANAC, THE. 2530

0147-636X See STANDARD & POOR'S STATISTICAL SERVICE CURRENT STATISTICS. 733

0147-6378 See PACKER'S PRODUCE AVAILABILITY AND MERCHANDISING GUIDE, THE. 118

0147-6432 See TAP ROOTS (SHREVEPORT). 2474

0147-6467 See ANNUAL STATISTICAL REPORT - SOUTH DAKOTA DEPARTMENT OF SOCIAL SERVICES. 5266

0147-6475 See ANNUAL REPORT - MASSACHUSETTS LABOR RELATIONS COMMISSION. 3144

0147-6491 See BIBLIOGRAPHIC GUIDE TO NORTH AMERICAN HISTORY. 2634

0147-6505 See BIBLIOGRAPHIC GUIDE TO EDUCATION. 1793

0147-6513 See ECOTOXICOLOGY AND ENVIRONMENTAL SAFETY. 2214

0147-6521 See ENERGY INFORMATION ABSTRACTS. 1962

0147-6572 See LEGISLATIVE CALENDAR - UNITED STATES SENATE. COMMITTEE ON GOVERNMENTAL AFFAIRS. 4661

0147-6580 See QUARTERLY REVIEW - FEDERAL RESERVE BANK OF NEW YORK. 805

0147-6629 See SEATTLE REVIEW, THE. 3435

0147-6637 See ANALYSIS - TEXAS. COMPTROLLER'S OFFICE. 4709

0147-6645 See BIG APPLE JAZZ. 4103

0147-6653 See MONOLITH. 4132

0147-6696 See COMMENTARIES. 2953

0147-6734 See STATE & AREA FORECASTING SERVICE. 1522

0147-6769 See DEMOCRATIC PARTY. YEAR BOOK. 4471

0147-6777 See YOUNG LAWYERS NEWSLETTER. 3077

0147-6807 See STATISTICAL AND ACCOUNTING REPORT. 4811

0147-6823 See RESEARCH NOTE - BUREAU OF ECONOMIC GEOLOGY, UNIVERSITY OF TEXAS AT AUSTIN. 1395

0147-6874 See MOSCOW UNIVERSITY SOIL SCIENCE BULLETIN. 179

0147-6882 See SCIENTIFIC AND TECHNICAL INFORMATION PROCESSING. 3248

0147-6912 See DHEW OBLIGATIONS TO INSTITUTIONS OF HIGHER EDUCATION AND OTHER NONPROFIT ORGANIZATIONS. 1820

0147-6971 See VALUE OF PUBLIC UTILITY REAL AND PERSONAL PROPERTY BY COUNTY. 4693

0147-698X See JOURNAL OF POWDER & BULK SOLIDS TECHNOLOGY. 2014

0147-6998 See PLUMBING, HEATING, PIPING. 2607

0147-7048 See THEY MULTIPLIED. 2475

0147-7064 See DATA USER EDUCATION & TRAINING ACTIVITIES. 5326

0147-7080 See SALARIES, WAGES AND FRINGE BENEFITS OF OKLAHOMA CITIES AND TOWNS. 1538

0147-7110 See MICHIGAN FREE PRESS. 5693

0147-7161 See GEORGIA COURTS JOURNAL. 3141

0147-7196 See (LAGUNA), A. 3403

0147-7250 See CLASSIFIED INDEX OF DISPOSITIONS OF ULP CHARGES BY THE GENERAL COUNSEL OF THE NATIONAL LABOR RELATIONS BOARD. 1659

0147-7277 See NIAID MANUAL OF TISSUE TYPING TECHNIQUES. 3675

0147-7293 See INTERNATIONAL BUSINESSMAN'S GUIDE TO OFFICIAL WASHINGTON, THE. 683

0147-7307 See LAW AND HUMAN BEHAVIOR. 2994

0147-7315 See WEST'S MILITARY JUSTICE REPORTER. 3183

0147-7374 See BARRON'S REGENTS EXAMS AND ANSWERS : CHEMISTRY. 962

0147-7382 See BUDGET - NATIONAL TRANSPORTATION SAFETY BOARD. 5378

0147-7439 See SATELLITE COMMUNICATIONS. 1163

0147-7447 See ORTHOPEDICS (THOROFARE). 3884

0147-7528 See NATIONAL NEWSPAPER ASSOCIATION DIRECTORY. 4817

0147-7536 See MUSICA JUDAICA. 4136

0147-7544 See DIALOGUE IN INSTRUMENTAL MUSIC EDUCATION. 4114

0147-7587 See END OF YEAR REPORT. REGIONAL PROGRAM PLANS ASSESSMENT. 4646

0147-7617 See STATE OF MONTANA DEPARTMENT OF NATURAL RESOURCES AND CONSERVATION : REPORT ON EXAMINATION OF FINANCIAL STATEMENT. 2206

0147-7633 See CHILTON'S REVIEW OF OPTOMETRY. 4215

0147-7641 See PUBLICATIONS OF THE INSTITUTE OF GOVERNMENT. CUMULATIVE SUPPLEMENT. 4699

0147-7668 See AEROPHILE (SAN ANTONIO). 5

0147-7676 See SPEAKERS. 5319

0147-7706 See SSI, SHORT STORY INTERNATIONAL. 3439

0147-7714 See ENVIRONMENTAL LAW HANDBOOK. 3111

0147-7730 See OPERATIONS REPORT - STATE CORPORATION COMMISSION, DIVISION OF AERONAUTICS. 31

0147-7749 See CAPITAL IMPROVEMENT PROGRAM (FAIRFAX). 4636

0147-7781 See MECHANICAL WORKING & STEEL PROCESSING. 4008

0147-7803 See YEARBOOK - WORLD COUNCIL OF CREDIT UNIONS. 1544

0147-7811 See GOAL ATTAINMENT REVIEW. 4777

0147-7889 See NEWSLETTER - ASSOCIATION OF SYSTEMATICS COLLECTIONS. 4094

0147-7919 See FODOR'S IRAN. 5472

0147-7935 See MICROSTATE STUDIES. 4482

0147-7951 See DRESSAGE & CT. 2798

0147-796X See DRESSAGE & CT. 2798

0147-7986 See FLORIDA OUTLOOK, THE. 1533

0147-8044 See NCEA-GANLEY'S CATHOLIC SCHOOLS IN AMERICA. 5033

0147-8052 See OKLAHOMA OCCUPATIONAL EMPLOYMENT STATISTICS. 1537

0147-8060 See POST ALLOCATION OF FUNDS AND TRAINING ACTIVITY SUMMARY. 3173

0147-8087 See PHARMACEUTICAL TECHNOLOGY. 4321

0147-8117 See AUDIT REPORT, COMMISSION ON AGING. 5178

0147-8125 See AUDIT REPORT, DEPARTMENT OF EDUCATION, TENNESSEE SCHOOL FOR THE BLIND. 1726

0147-8133 See AUDIT REPORT, DEPARTMENT OF EDUCATION, TENNESSEE SCHOOL FOR THE DEAF. 1726

0147-8176 See FODOR'S EGYPT. 5471

0147-8184 See VIA (BERKELEY). 3450

0147-8257 See HELR. THE HARVARD ENVIRONMENTAL LAW REVIEW. 3113

0147-8265 See WHO'S WHO IN CHIROPRACTIC, INTERNATIONAL. 436

0147-8281 See MANPOWER TRAINING NEEDS, PUERTO RICO. 1689

0147-8354 See ADULT BASIC EDUCATION (ATHENS, GA.). 1799

0147-8362 See BIENNIAL REPORT - STATE DEPARTMENT OF HIGHWAYS AND PUBLIC TRANSPORTATION. 5377

0147-8389 See PACING AND CLINICAL ELECTROPHYSIOLOGY. 3708

0147-8397 See EASTWEST MARKETS. 832

0147-8419 See ALABAMA PLANNING RESOURCE CHECKLIST : COUNTY/REGIONAL SERIES. 2813

0147-8427 See GLASS (PORTLAND, OR.). 2590

0147-8486 See STANDARD COMMERCIAL DIRECTORY. 851

0147-8494 See GRAMOPHONE NEWS, THE. 5317

0147-8508 See FINANCIAL REPORT ON REGISTERED CHARITABLE ORGANIZATIONS. 5285

0147-8559 See SOUTH ATLANTIC URBAN STUDIES. 2836

0147-8613 See CAMPBOOK. NORTH CENTRAL. 4870

0147-8648 See UPDATE ON LAW-RELATED EDUCATION. 3070

0147-8680 See FODOR'S SOUTH. 5473

0147-8702 See COLLECTED REPRINTS - WEATHER MODIFICATION PROGRAM OFFICE. 1424

0147-8729 See LIAS NEWSLETTER. 3003

0147-877X See NACUBO BUSINESS OFFICER. 696

0147-8796 See FOUNDRY OPERATIONS PLANBOOK. 4002

0147-8826 See COLLEGE PLANNING/SEARCH BOOK. 1817

0147-8834 See FLYFISHER, THE. 2304

0147-8850 See ENERGY AND ENVIRONMENT ANNUAL REPORT. 1939

0147-8877 See POLICE BADGE, THE. 3171

0147-8885 See JOURNAL OF HISTOTECHNOLOGY. 538

0147-8974 See LOCAL AUTHORITIES PARTICIPATING IN LOW-RENT HOUSING PROGRAMS. 2827

0147-8982 See REGISTER OF RESERVE OFFICERS. 4182

0147-9016 See ANNUAL REPORT - PARKLAWN COMPUTER CENTER. 4766

0147-9032 See REVIEW - FERNAND BRAUDEL CENTER FOR THE STUDY OF ECONOMIES, HISTORICAL SYSTEMS, AND CIVILIZATIONS. 1517

0147-9059 See RAM DIGEST, THE. 2832

0147-9091 See REGULATORY ALERT. 3037

0147-9113 See DIRECTORY OF POSTSECONDARY EDUCATIONAL INSTITUTIONS IN ALASKA. 1821

0147-9121 See RESEARCH IN LABOR ECONOMICS. 1707

0147-9156 See CONTEMPORARY FRENCH CIVILIZATION. 2684

0147-9164 See CALIFORNIA WATER PLAN OUTLOOK, THE. 5531

0147-9229 See REVIEW OF TAXATION OF INDIVIDUALS, THE. 3119

0147-927X See BROWN JUDAIC STUDIES. 5046

0147-9334 See NEWSLETTER - MARYLAND DEPARTMENT OF STATE PLANNING. 2829

0147-9342 See HARVARD SEMITIC STUDIES. 5048

0147-9369 See GEORGIA JOURNAL OF SCIENCE. 5107

0147-9385 See NATIONAL SURVEY OF SALARIES AND WAGES IN PUBLIC SCHOOLS. 1693

0147-9415 See COMPUTER TERMINALS REVIEW. 1264

0147-9458 See LEGAL AID NEWS (NEW YORK), THE. 3180

0147-9490 See LEGAL NOTES (WASHINGTON). 3087

0147-9504 See INDEX OF ACTIVE REGISTERED INVESTMENT COMPANIES UNDER THE INVESTMENT COMPANY ACT OF 1940 AND RELATED INVESTMENT ADVISERS, PRINCIPAL UNDERWRITERS, SPONSORS (I.E. DEPOSITORS) AND UNDERLYING COMPANIES. 901

0147-9539 See HIGHWAY SUFFICIENCY REPORT. 5441

0147-9547 See WORK STOPPAGES IN GOVERNMENT. 1718

0147-9555 See PHILIPPINE TIMES, THE. 2662

0147-9563 See HEART & LUNG. 3856

0147-9571 See COMPARATIVE IMMUNOLOGY, MICROBIOLOGY AND INFECTIOUS DISEASES. 561

0147-958X See CLINICAL AND INVESTIGATIVE MEDICINE. 3565

0147-9640 See LEGISLATIVE SUMMARY - DEPARTMENT OF COMMUNITY AND REGIONAL AFFAIRS, DIVISION OF COMMUNITY AND RURAL DEVELOPMENT. 3002

0147-9652 See JAMMER'S HANDBOOK. 4081

0147-9660 See ENERGY REVIEW (LEXINGTON). 1942

0147-9695 See VINTAGE TRIUMPH, THE. 5427

0147-9725 See MARYLAND BIRDLIFE. 5618

0147-9733 See COLORADO LIBRARIES. 3203

0147-975X See REPORT OF OUTSTANDING INDEBTEDNESS OF COUNTIES, CITIES, VILLAGES, TOWNSHIPS, SCHOOLS, SPECIAL DISTRICTS, AUTHORITIES, STATE BONDS. 4745

0147-9784 See YEAR BOOK COLOR ATLAS SERIES. 2583

0147-9806 See CALIFORNIA WATER PLAN OUTLOOK, SUMMARY REPORT, THE. 5531

0147-9822 See WARD'S WHO'S WHO AMONG U.S. MOTOR VEHICLE MANUFACTURERS. 435

0147-9857 See LOYOLA OF LOS ANGELES LAW REVIEW. 3004

0147-9865 See GEORGIA LABOR MARKET TRENDS. 1675

0147-9873 See WITTENBERG HISTORY JOURNAL, THE. 2633

0147-9881 See CHILDREN IN CUSTODY. 3160

0147-9903 See API INDEXES : INDEX TERM USE STATISTICS. 4250

0147-9911 See AVIATION CONSUMER, THE. 13

0147-992X See MCELROY FAMILY NEWSLETTER, THE. 2459

0147-9938 See NATIONAL BLUEGRASS MUSIC NEWS, THE. 4139

0147-9946 See REAL ESTATE AND CONSTRUCTION REPORT. 4843

0147-9962 See ORAL ENGLISH. 3308

0147-9970 See LITIGATION NEWS. 3003

0147-9989 See RESTAURANT HOSPITALITY. 5072

0148-0014 See RED BOOK CONSTRUCTION REGISTER. 625

0148-0030 See PEOPLE POWER. 1298

0148-0057 See MEASUREMENTS & CONTROL. 5127

0148-009X See CONSOLIDATED TAX RETURNS. 4718

0148-0162 See RACCOON. 3470

0148-0189 See LEN BUCKWALTER'S NORTH AMERICAN CB CHANNEL DIRECTORY. 1159

0148-0200 See RAILROAD ACCIDENT REPORT. BRIEF FORMAT. 5435

0148-0227 See JOURNAL OF GEOPHYSICAL RESEARCH. 1407

0148-0243 See AMERICAN GO JOURNAL, THE. 4856

0148-026X See FOCUS (CHICAGO. 1977). 2971

0148-0324 See CALIFORNIA ENVIRONMENTAL DIRECTORY. 2162

0148-0340 See BROWARD LEGACY. 2724

0148-0359 See MAINE DIRECTORY OF NATURAL RESOURCE ORGANIZATIONS. 2197

0148-0375 See INTERNATIONAL PETROLEUM ENCYCLOPEDIA. 4261

0148-0413 See PLANNING GUIDE ESEA IV, PART B: LIBRARIES AND LEARNING RESOURCES. 1868

0148-0421 See AUDIT REPORT, DEPARTMENT OF EDUCATION CENTRAL OFFICE. 1726

0148-043X See AUDIT REPORT, DEPARTMENT OF EDUCATION, TENNESSEE ASSOCIATION OF THE FUTURE FARMERS OF AMERICA. 63

0148-0448 See AUDIT REPORT, DEPARTMENT OF INSURANCE, STATE BOARD OF ACCOUNTANCY. 739

0148-0456 See AUDIT REPORT, DEPARTMENT OF EDUCATION, DIVISION OF VOCATIONAL TECHNICAL EDUCATION. 1910

0148-0464 See AUDIT REPORT, DEPARTMENT OF INSURANCE, TENNESSEE BOARD OF BARBER EXAMINERS. 4712

0148-0480 See AUDIT REPORT, CLEVELAND STATE COMMUNITY COLLEGE (TENNESSEE). 1810

0148-0529 See MATERIALS PERFORMANCE : CORROSION ENGINEERING BUYER'S GUIDE. 2015

0148-0545 See DRUG AND CHEMICAL TOXICOLOGY (NEW YORK, N.Y. 1978). 3980

0148-0553 See LAW LINES. 3222

0148-0588 See GUILD NOTES. 4508

0148-0596 See REPORT TO THE PRESIDENT AND TO THE COUNCIL ON ENVIRONMENTAL QUALITY. 2181

0148-0693 See SUMMARY OF ACTIVITIES - COMMITTEE ON ARMED SERVICES, UNITED STATES SENATE. 3183

0148-0715 See RADIO FREQUENCY PLAN. 1137

0148-0731 See JOURNAL OF BIOMECHANICAL ENGINEERING. 3694

0148-0766 See LODGING HOSPITALITY. 2807

0148-0782 See DIRECTORY OF VIRGINIA'S POSTSECONDARY EDUCATION AND TRAINING OPPORTUNITIES. 1821

0148-0812 See JOURNAL OF DERMATOLOGIC SURGERY AND ONCOLOGY, THE. 3967

0148-0820 See NEW YORK ANNUAL PROGRAM SUMMARY. 112

0148-0839 See NORTH CAROLINA MINORITY BUSINESS DIRECTORY. 699

0148-0847 See SOCIAL WORK RESEARCH & ABSTRACTS. 5267

0148-0863 See PUBLIC REVENUES FROM ALCOHOL BEVERAGES. 2370

0148-0871 See SOLAR ENERGY & RESEARCH DIRECTORY. 1957

0148-0901 See SPERRY LAWYER, THE. 3103

0148-0928 See SOVIET ARMED FORCES REVIEW ANNUAL. 4057

0148-0944 See OCCASIONAL PAPER - MISSOURI ACADEMY OF SCIENCE. 5135

0148-0960 See OCCASIONAL PAPERS - UNIVERSITY OF ARKANSAS MUSEUM. 4094

0148-0987 See LASER INTERACTION AND RELATED PLASMA PHENOMENA. 4411

0148-0995 See MUSLIM SCIENTIST. 5210

0148-1002 See PROCEEDINGS OF THE ANNUAL ROCKY MOUNTAIN BIOENGINEERING SYMPOSIUM. 469

0148-1010 See CONTINUING EDUCATION LECTURES. 3568

0148-1029 See STUDIES IN ICONOGRAPHY. 5000

0148-1037 See MINORITY VOICES. 358

0148-1045 See MEDIA LAW REPORTER. 3008

0148-1061 See EDUCATION LIBRARIES. 3209

0148-107X See EMPLOYMENT DISCRIMINATION DIGEST. 3147

0148-1169 See INTERNATIONAL JOURNAL OF HUMAN RELATIONS, THE. 5248

0148-1185 See FINANCIAL DIRECTORY OF PENSION FUNDS. MICHIGAN, SOUTHERN, EXCLUDING DETROIT & SUBURBS (FLINT, GRAND RAPIDS, KALAMAZOO & OTHERS). 1671

0148-1223 See FINANCIAL DIRECTORY OF PENSION FUNDS. MINNESOTA (EXCLUDING MINNEAPOLIS-ST. PAUL AREA). 1671

0148-1371 See FINANCIAL DIRECTORY OF PENSION FUNDS. OHIO, NORTHERN, CLEVELAND AREA. 1673

0148-1401 See FINANCIAL DIRECTORY OF PENSION FUNDS. KENTUCKY. 1671

0148-1479 See FINANCIAL DIRECTORY OF PENSION FUNDS. MICHIGAN, DETROIT CITY PROPER. 1671

0148-1614 See FINANCIAL DIRECTORY OF PENSION FUNDS. GEORGIA, EXCLUDING ATLANTA AREA. 1670

0148-1665 See FINANCIAL DIRECTORY OF PENSION FUNDS. OHIO, SOUTHERN, EXCLUDING CINCINNATI AREA (COLUMBUS, DAYTON, ATHENS & OTHERS). 1673

0148-1665 See FINANCIAL DIRECTORY OF PENSION FUNDS. OHIO, SOUTHERN, CINCINNATI AREA. 1673

0148-1762 See DIRECTORY OF MEMBERS - MUNICIPAL FINANCE OFFICERS ASSOCIATION. 4720

0148-1797 See WATER QUALITY MANAGEMENT DIRECTORY. 5543

0148-1819 See DIRECTORY OF CONTRACT SERVICE FIRMS. 1970

0148-1843 *See* MISSISSIPPI STATE GOVERNMENT PUBLICATIONS. **420**

0148-1851 *See* MISSOURI OCCUPATIONAL STAFFING PATTERNS OF SELECTED NON-MANUFACTURING INDUSTRIES SURVEYED. **4206**

0148-1878 *See* MOODY'S BOND RECORD. **907**

0148-1886 *See* BULLETIN OF THE MASSACHUSETTS ARCHAEOLOGICAL SOCIETY. **264**

0148-1940 *See* IRS LETTER RULINGS. **4734**

0148-1967 *See* SOCIAL SECURITY MANUAL. **5308**

0148-1983 *See* TEXAS HERITAGE (FORT WORTH). **2475**

0148-1991 *See* WEST'S LOUISIANA SESSION LAW SERVICE. **3074**

0148-2009 *See* LONERGAN WORKSHOP. **4974**

0148-2068 *See* OCCASIONAL RESEARCH PAPER (BRIGHAM YOUNG UNIVERSITY. SCHOOL OF LIBRARY AND INFORMATION SCIENCES). **3238**

0148-2076 *See* 19TH CENTURY MUSIC. **4098**

0148-2092 *See* FREEBIES (SANTA MONICA). **1297**

0148-2122 *See* NARROW GAUGE AND SHORT LINE GAZETTE. **5433**

0148-2157 *See* UPPER TEXAS COAST REPORT. **4281**

0148-2181 *See* JOURNAL OF PENSION PLANNING AND COMPLIANCE. **904**

0148-2203 *See* SPINOFF. **5159**

0148-222X *See* NATIONAL TRUCK CHARACTERISTIC REPORT. **5388**

0148-2289 *See* A-95 CLEARINGHOUSE REPORT. **2812**

0148-2300 *See* INTERNATIONAL ADVENTURE TRAVELGUIDE. **5480**

0148-2319 *See* RECENT ADVANCES IN ULTRASOUND IN BIOMEDICINE. **3633**

0148-2327 *See* CA SELECTS: FLAVORS & FRAGRANCES. **1002**

0148-2335 *See* CA SELECTS: PHOTOBIOCHEMISTRY. **1007**

0148-2343 *See* CA SELECTS: PROSTAGLANDINS. **1008**

0148-2351 *See* CA SELECTS: LIQUID CRYSTALS. **1004**

0148-236X *See* CA SELECTS: SOLAR ENERGY. **1009**

0148-2378 *See* CA SELECTS: ATHEROSCLEROSIS & HEART DISEASE. **998**

0148-2386 *See* CA SELECTS: ANTITUMOR AGENTS. **997**

0148-2394 *See* CA SELECTS: ANTI-INFLAMMATORY AGENTS & ARTHRITIS. **997**

0148-2408 *See* CA SELECTS: CARCINOGENS, MUTAGENS & TERATOGENS. **998**

0148-2416 *See* CA SELECTS: NEW BOOKS IN CHEMISTRY. **1005**

0148-2432 *See* CA SELECTS: RAMAN SPECTROSCOPY. **1009**

0148-2440 *See* CA SELECTS: SILVER CHEMISTRY. **1009**

0148-2459 *See* CA SELECTS: B-LACTAM ANTIBIOTICS. **998**

0148-2521 *See* ANNUAL PRESERVATION PROGRAM, THE. **2186**

0148-2564 *See* MINUTES OF THE TRUSTEES OF THE COLLEGE, ACADEMY AND CHARITABLE SCHOOLS, UNIVERSITY OF PENNSYLVANIA. **1866**

0148-2572 *See* PROCEEDINGS AND MINUTES, ANNUAL MEETING OF THE AGRICULTURAL RESEARCH INSTITUTE. **121**

0148-2580 *See* FURMAN UNIVERSITY ALUMNI DIRECTORY. **1102**

0148-2599 *See* SUMMARY OF OPEN GAO RECOMMENDATIONS FOR LEGISLATIVE ACTION. **752**

0148-2602 *See* MARYLAND POLICE AND CORRECTIONAL TRAINING COMMISSIONS REPORT TO THE GOVERNOR, THE SECRETARY OF PUBLIC SAFETY AND CORRECTIONAL SERVICES, AND MEMBERS OF THE GENERAL ASSEMBLY. **3169**

0148-2653 *See* SELF DETERMINATION QUARTERLY JOURNAL, THE. **4685**

0148-267X *See* MOBILITY OF UNDERGRADUATE COLLEGE STUDENTS BETWEEN WASHINGTON COLLEGES AND UNIVERSITIES. **1836**

0148-2688 *See* INSURANCE LAW. **2983**

0148-2696 *See* USSR : HARD CURRENCY TRADE AND PAYMENTS. **856**

0148-270X *See* TEXAS FIDDLER, THE. **4156**

0148-2718 *See* REAL ESTATE CLOSINGS. **4844**

0148-2726 See DAIRY (SAINT PAUL, MINN.). **194**

0148-2742 *See* STATISTICAL PROFILE, NORTH CAROLINA PUBLIC SCHOOLS. **1797**

0148-2750 *See* LEGAL MALPRACTICE REVIEW. **3000**

0148-2769 *See* TSA LA GI. **1851**

0148-2777 *See* AUDIT REPORT, DEPARTMENT OF EDUCATION, ALVIN C. YORK AGRICULTURAL INSTITUTE. **63**

0148-2785 *See* WATER AND SEWER PROGRAMS FOR OHIO. **5542**

0148-2807 *See* STEEL MILL PRODUCTS (LEXINGTON). **1628**

0148-2823 *See* WINDY CITY SPELEONEWS, THE. **1412**

0148-284X *See* M-G FINANCIAL WEEKLY. INDUSTRISCOPE EDITION, THE. **905**

0148-2882 *See* RECREATION AND PARK EDUCATION CURRICULUM CATALOG. **4708**

0148-2890 *See* OCCUPATIONAL PROFILES OF SELECTED NON-MANUFACTURING INDUSTRIES IN OREGON. **4207**

0148-2920 *See* AGRICULTURAL ECONOMICS STATISTICAL SERIES. **150**

0148-2947 *See* HIGH INCOME TAX RETURNS. **4731**

0148-2963 *See* JOURNAL OF BUSINESS RESEARCH. **686**

0148-298X *See* DEPARTMENT OF TRANSPORTATION, STATE OF RHODE ISLAND. **5381**

0148-2998 *See* COMMUNIST STATES AND DEVELOPING COUNTRIES, AID AND TRADE. **4541**

0148-3005 *See* HOUSE BILL SUMMARIES. **4654**

0148-3013 *See* YEARBOOK - NEW YORK YEARLY MEETING, RELIGIOUS SOCIETY OF FRIENDS. **5069**

0148-3021 *See* BRANCH DIRECTORY AND SUMMARY OF DEPOSITS FOR THE STATE OF PENNSYLVANIA. **780**

0148-3064 *See* BEST'S KEY RATING GUIDE : PROPERTY-CASUALTY. **2876**

0148-3072 *See* CONSUMER BUSINESS REVIEW. **1552**

0148-3102 *See* CHEVRON WORLD. **4253**

0148-3129 *See* GRANTS FOR RESEARCH ON EDUCATION AND WORK. **1913**

0148-3145 *See* ACTUARIAL TABLES EFFECTIVE FOR TERMINATIONS. **2872**

0148-3153 *See* PETERSEN'S PRO BASEBALL. **4912**

0148-317X *See* PROPOSED COMPREHENSIVE ANNUAL SERVICE PROGRAM PLAN FOR THE STATE OF HAWAII. **5302**

0148-3188 *See* CHARITABLE TRUST DIRECTORY, OFFICE OF ATTORNEY GENERAL. **3140**

0148-3218 *See* BEST'S INSURANCE REPORTS, PROPERTY-CASUALTY. **2876**

0148-3234 *See* SUPPLEMENTAL SALARY STUDY, SELECTED SCHOOL, DISTRICT, AND COUNTY PERSONNEL. **1873**

0148-3242 *See* MILWAUKEE LAWYER, THE. **3010**

0148-3250 *See* LOUISVILLE REVIEW, THE. **3408**

0148-3285 *See* SECONDARY RECOVERY REPORT. **2150**

0148-3293 *See* DCAS MANAGEMENT SYNOPSIS EXECUTIVE SUMMARY. **4040**

0148-3331 *See* CHRISTIANITY & LITERATURE. **3375**

0148-3358 *See* HONOLULU WHOLESALE PRICES EGGS, POULTRY, PORK, BEEF AND RICE. **93**

0148-3412 See UFO REPORT (BROOKLYN). **38**

0148-3420 *See* AUDIT REPORT. BOARD OF PSYCHOLOGY. **4575**

0148-3439 *See* AUDIT REPORT. BOARD OF MEDICAL EXAMINERS. **3554**

0148-3447 *See* AUDIT REPORT, DEPARTMENT OF MILITARY - TENNESSEE DIVISION OF STATE AUDIT. **4037**

0148-3498 *See* TM, TRADEMARK DIRECTORY. **1308**

0148-3501 *See* RUSHLIGHT (VERNON), THE. **2080**

0148-3544 *See* LISTENING POST (CITY OF INDUSTRY). **4129**

0148-3560 *See* OFFICIAL AAU PHYSIQUE HANDBOOK : OFFICIAL RULES. **2600**

0148-3579 *See* OFFICIAL DIRECTORY OF REGISTERED DOCTORS OF MEDICINE, MEDICAL CORPORATIONS AND DOCTORS OF CHIROPODY-PODIATRY. **3916**

0148-3595 *See* TECHNOLOGY TODAY. **1916**

0148-3609 *See* WHOLE WORLD OIL DIRECTORY, THE. **4282**

0148-3633 *See* REPORT AND RECOMMENDATIONS TO THE GOVERNOR AND THE GENERAL ASSEMBLY. **3153**

0148-3668 *See* AMERICAN PRESERVATION. **2719**

0148-3706 *See* GOLF BUSINESS (1976). **4896**

0148-3714 *See* INSIDE OUT (NEW YORK). **3166**

0148-3730 *See* ROAD/HOUSE. **3470**

0148-3765 *See* PRICE TRENDS. **2593**

0148-3773 *See* WHO'S WHO (CHICAGO). **436**

0148-3781 *See* BEHAVIORAL PRIMATOLOGY. **5577**

0148-379X *See* OREGON LEGISLATION. **3023**

0148-3811 *See* MID-PACIFIC REGION REPORT. **2093**

0148-3838 *See* PAPERS ON PALEONTOLOGY. **4230**

0148-3846 *See* JOURNAL OF REHABILITATION ADMINISTRATION. **4390**

0148-3854 *See* AUDIT REPORT, DEPARTMENT OF JUDICIAL, STATE PROSECUTIONS. **3158**

0148-3862 *See* AUDIT REPORT, DIVISION OF PRINTING. **4631**

0148-3870 *See* AUDIT REPORT, COMMISSION TO CONTROL THE SUPREME COURT BUILDING AT NASHVILLE. **4631**

0148-3897 *See* ORNAMENT (LOS ANGELES, CALIF.). **2915**

0148-3919 *See* JOURNAL OF LIQUID CHROMATOGRAPHY. **1017**

0148-3951 *See* PACKAGED FLUID MILK SALES IN FEDERAL MILK ORDER MARKETS. **197**

0148-396X *See* NEUROSURGERY. **3970**

0148-3994 *See* NEWS LETTER OF THE PARKE SOCIETY. **2462**

0148-4001 *See* MODERN SALON. **404**

0148-401X *See* OUTDOOR RECREATION IN GEORGIA. **4877**

0148-4036 *See* PENNSYLVANIA MENNONITE HERITAGE. **2467**

0148-4052 *See* SUCCESSFUL MEETINGS : SM. **714**

0148-4079 *See* JOB SAFETY & HEALTH REPORT. **2864**

0148-4087 *See* PUBLIC TRANSIT REPORT. **5390**

0148-4109 *See* FEDERAL RESEARCH REPORT. **4724**

0148-4125 *See* SLUDGE. **2243**

0148-4133 *See* MENUS OF THE VALLEY'S FINEST RESTAURANTS. **5071**

0148-4141 *See* PLAIN TALK. **3241**

0148-4168 *See* PUBLIC ADMINISTRATION UPDATE. **4676**

0148-4176 *See* PROCEEDINGS OF THE ANNUAL MEETING - NATIONAL ACADEMY OF ARBITRATORS. MEETING. **2868**

0148-4184 *See* ACCOUNTING HISTORIANS JOURNAL, THE. **737**

0148-4192 *See* NBS. REACTOR. SUMMARY OF ACTIVITIES. **4448**

0148-4214 *See* MISSOURI AREA LABOR TRENDS. **1691**

0148-4230 See VOCAL MAJORITY, THE. 5568
0148-4249 See WESLEYAN (MIDDLETOWN). 1103
0148-4265 See CURRENT NEPHROLOGY. 3989
0148-4273 See SUMMARY OF THE SOUTH DAKOTA CRIMINAL JUSTICE PLAN FOR ACTION, A. 3177
0148-4303 See EQUAL OPPORTUNITY ASSESSMENT AND AFFIRMATIVE ACTION PLAN. 1323
0148-432X See AMERICAN EDUCATOR. 1723
0148-4338 See ANNUAL STATISTICAL DIGEST - BOARD OF GOVERNORS OF THE FEDERAL RESERVE SYSTEM. 772
0148-4346 See CLE BULLETIN. 2951
0148-4354 See LOBBYING IN THE FLORIDA HOUSE OF REPRESENTATIVES. 4662
0148-4419 See SOUTHERN JOURNAL OF APPLIED FORESTRY. 2395
0148-4427 See MONOGRAPHS OF THE PHYSIOLOGICAL SOCIETY OF PHILADELPHIA. 584
0148-4435 See POLLUTION ENGINEERING AND TECHNOLOGY. 2238
0148-4478 See CHILTON'S FOOD ENGINEERING INTERNATIONAL. 2331
0148-4494 See LAWS RELATED TO THE DEPARTMENT OF SOCIAL SERVICES, PASSED DURING THE LEGISLATIVE SESSION. 2997
0148-4508 See NATIONAL DIRECTORY OF EDUCATIONAL PROGRAMS IN GERONTOLOGY AND GERIATRICS. 3754
0148-4516 See CAPITAL FEASTS. 5070
0148-4567 See STATE MANPOWER REVIEW. 1712
0148-4591 See INDICATORS OF EDUCATIONAL QUALITY, SUMMARY. 1752
0148-4648 See INTERNATIONAL DRUG REPORT. 3166
0148-4664 See GOVERNMENTAL SERVICES NEWSLETTER (ASHLAND, MO.). 4652
0148-4710 See FORUM ON INFECTION. 3577
0148-4737 See PALEOPATHOLOGY NEWSLETTER. 278
0148-4761 See HEALTH LABOR RELATION REPORTS. 1677
0148-480X See RECOMBINANT DNA RESEARCH. 551
0148-4818 See U.S. PHARMACIST. 4331
0148-4834 See JOURNAL OF NURSING EDUCATION, THE. 3859
0148-4869 See JOURNAL - ASSOCIATION FOR HOSPITAL MEDICAL EDUCATION. 3592
0148-4885 See AFFIRMATIVE ACTION PLAN FOR EQUAL EMPLOYMENT OPPORTUNITY. 1807
0148-4893 See JOURNAL OF THE WESTERN SOCIETY OF PERIODONTOLOGY / PERIODONTAL ABSTRACTS, THE. 1329
0148-494X See MONTHLY ENERGY REVIEW. 1950
0148-4966 See MARKETING CALIFORNIA BROCCOLI. 2349
0148-4974 See MARKETING CALIFORNIA CELERY. 2349
0148-4982 See JUDICIAL FUNCTION OUTLINE. 2990
0148-4990 See MICHIGAN SCHOOL BOND LOAN PROGRAM : ANNUAL BULLETIN. 1836
0148-5016 See ARCHIVES OF ANDROLOGY. 3678
0148-5032 See MAYFLOWER QUARTERLY, THE. 2745
0148-5067 See ALLIED HEALTH EDUCATION PROGRAMS IN JUNIOR AND SENIOR COLLEGES. HEALTH PLANNERS EDITION. 4764
0148-5075 See ANNUAL PLANNING REPORT : FALL RIVER, MASSACHUSETTS-RHODE ISLAND LABOR MARKET AREA. 1648
0148-5091 See DIRECTORY OF FEDERAL DROUGHT ASSISTANCE. 79
0148-5121 See INTERNATIONAL FILE OF MICROGRAPHICS EQUIPMENT & ACCESSORIES. 4370
0148-513X See SCHOOL AND DISTRICT REPORTS. EXPLANATORY MATERIALS. 1870

0148-5202 See AUDIT REPORT, DEPARTMENT OF GENERAL SERVICES, MOTOR VEHICLE MANAGEMENT DIVISION. 4631
0148-5229 See ANNUAL REPORT OF THE ATTORNEY GENERAL OF THE UNITED STATES. 3139
0148-5245 See GEORGIA LANDINGS, ANNUAL SUMMARY. 2304
0148-5296 See PROCESSED FISHERY PRODUCTS, ANNUAL SUMMARY. 2311
0148-5318 See U.S. PRODUCTION OF FISH FILLETS AND STEAKS, ANNUAL SUMMARY. 2315
0148-5326 See SOUTH CAROLINA LANDINGS, ANNUAL SUMMARY. 1457
0148-5342 See PROGRESS IN COMMUNICATION. 4392
0148-5350 See ADCA, AMERICAN DIRECTORY OF COLLECTION AGENCIES AND ATTORNEYS. 768
0148-5369 See DAILY PLANET ALMANAC, THE. 390
0148-5385 See HEALTH FACILITIES COURT DIGEST, THE. 2977
0148-5393 See AZACA. 2771
0148-5415 See COMMISSIONER'S REPORT ON THE EDUCATION PROFESSIONS. 1891
0148-5423 See CASH DISPENSERS AND AUTOMATED TELLERS. 727
0148-5458 See STUDIES IN EDUCATION (WICHITA). 1786
0148-5490 See PHYSICIAN MANPOWER IN OREGON DATA BOOK. 3916
0148-5520 See REQUESTS FOR INTERPRETATIONS AND POLICY STATEMENTS. 4705
0148-5539 See MOSSTYPER, THE. 4566
0148-5547 See RESEARCH PROGRAMS / NATIONAL INSTITUTE OF ENVIRONMENTAL HEALTH SCIENCES. 2242
0148-5555 See PUBLIC HEALTH STATISTICS (NEW ORLEANS). 4811
0148-558X See JOURNAL OF ACCOUNTING AUDITING & FINANCE. 746
0148-5598 See JOURNAL OF MEDICAL SYSTEMS. 3787
0148-5601 See CHILD ABUSE REPORT (HARRISBURG, PA.). 5277
0148-561X See DEGRE SECOND. 3341
0148-5628 See CLIMATOLOGICAL DATA FOR AMUNDSEN-SCOTT, ANTARCTICA. 1422
0148-5687 See WASHINGTON MANUFACTURERS REGISTER. 3489
0148-5717 See SEXUALLY TRANSMITTED DISEASES. 4802
0148-5733 See PACIFIC INFORMATION SERVICE ON STREET-DRUGS. 4319
0148-5741 See YALE FOREST SCHOOL NEWS. 2398
0148-575X See OLD TRAILS. 2752
0148-5768 See ARIZONA'S FIVE-YEAR TRANSPORTATION CONSTRUCTION PROGRAM. 2018
0148-5784 See NABTE REVIEW. 696
0148-5792 See JOBBER RETAILER. 5417
0148-5814 See PUBLIC WORKS PROGRESS. 4677
0148-5822 See EGO (SAN FRANCISCO). 2532
0148-5865 See ARABESQUE (NEW YORK, N.Y.). 4100
0148-5881 See NEVADA REVIEW OF BUSINESS & ECONOMICS. 698
0148-5903 See AMERICAN BOOKSELLER (NEW YORK. 1977). 4823
0148-5911 See TUROV ON OPTIONS AND HEDGING. 918
0148-5938 See JAPANESE REVIEW. 1498
0148-5997 See DOCKET REPORT - CENTER FOR CONSTITUTIONAL RIGHTS. 3092
0148-6004 See ENVIRONMENTAL MONITORING AT MAJOR U.S. ENERGY RESEARCH & DEVELOPMENT ADMINISTRATION CONTRACTOR SITES. 2168
0148-6012 See MARYLAND ARCHEOLOGY. 273

0148-6039 See ACCIDENT FACTS (CHICAGO). 4763
0148-6055 See JOURNAL OF RHEOLOGY (NEW YORK, N.Y.). 4428
0148-6063 See UNITED STATES POLITICAL SCIENCE DOCUMENTS. 4503
0148-6071 See JPEN, JOURNAL OF PARENTERAL AND ENTERAL NUTRITION. 4194
0148-608X See EXXON EDUCATION FOUNDATION REPORT. 1746
0148-6128 See WPI JOURNAL. 5171
0148-6136 See LAW AND POPULATION PROGRAMME NEWSLETTER. 2994
0148-6160 See LOUISIANA PLANNING DIRECTORY. 2827
0148-6179 See AFRICAN AMERICAN REVIEW. 3358
0148-6187 See BEVERAGE INDUSTRY. 2364
0148-6195 See JOURNAL OF ECONOMICS AND BUSINESS. 1499
0148-6225 See COMMITTEE ON EAST ASIAN LIBRARIES BULLETIN. 3203
0148-6233 See MINNESOTA NEW AND EXPANDING INDUSTRY. 1618
0148-625X See SUMMARY OF SELECTED LEGISLATION RELATED TO THE HANDICAPPED, A. 3061
0148-6276 See ANNUAL NATIONAL VEHICLE POPULATION PROFILE : LIGHT TRUCKS. 5403
0148-6284 See DEMOGRAPHIC REPORT, HEW. 4552
0148-6292 See CRIME IN MAINE (ANNUAL). 3080
0148-6306 See STATE OF MONTANA, BOARD OF EXAMINERS, REPORT ON EXAMINATION OF FINANCIAL STATEMENTS. 4749
0148-6322 See DIRECTORY OF PROVIDERS OF FAMILY PLANNING AND ABORTION SERVICES. 588
0148-639X See MUSCLE & NERVE. 3838
0148-6411 See IEEE TRANSACTIONS ON COMPONENTS, HYBRIDS AND MANUFACTURING TECHNOLOGY. 2061
0148-6438 See UFO REPORT (BROOKLYN). 38
0148-6470 See COMBINE FACTS. 158
0148-6489 See PUBLIC LAND AND RESOURCES LAW DIGEST, THE. 3115
0148-6519 See ANNUAL REPORT OF THE TREASURER (STATE OF NEW HAMPSHIRE). 4710
0148-6535 See STUDIES IN ECONOMICS (MENLO PARK). 1523
0148-6594 See COMPANIES HOLDING BOILER AND PRESSURE VESSEL CERTIFICATES OF AUTHORIZATION FOR USE OF CODE SYMBOL STAMPS. 2112
0148-6632 See PROFESSIONAL DESIGN SUPPLEMENT. 624
0148-6659 See ROOTS (ST. PAUL, MINN.). 2759
0148-6675 See FIRE TECHNOLOGY ABSTRACTS. 2290
0148-6683 See MULKEY JOURNAL. 2461
0148-6691 See AEROPHILE EXTRA. 5
0148-673X See TRUMPETER (LONDON). 2788
0148-6799 See ARMY OFFICER'S GUIDE, THE. 4036
0148-6802 See INVEST YOURSELF. 5290
0148-6845 See JOURNAL OF THE VIOLIN SOCIETY OF AMERICA. 4127
0148-6861 See ANNUAL NATIONAL VEHICLE POPULATION PROFILE : IMPORT CARS. 5403
0148-6934 See EEO REVIEW, THE. 1664
0148-6977 See PERSONNEL RESEARCH AND DEVELOPMENT CENTER OF THE U. S. CIVIL SERVICE COMMISSION, THE. 4704
0148-6985 See STATE OF BLACK AMERICA, THE. 2273
0148-7000 See GEOGRAPHICAL LOCATION CODES (WASHINGTON. 1976). 2563
0148-7043 See ANNALS OF PLASTIC SURGERY. 3959
0148-7132 See WALLACE STEVENS JOURNAL, THE. 3473

0148-7140 See COMPREHENSIVE MANPOWER PLAN AND GRANT APPLICATION. **1660**

0148-7191 See SAE TECHNICAL PAPER SERIES. **2128**

0148-7213 See OFFICE OF RESEARCH PROGRAMS LIST OF SELECTED PUBLICATIONS & RESEARCH PROJECTS IN PROGRESS. **3171**

0148-723X See CIRCULAR - ASSOCIATION OF AMERICAN RAILROADS, MECHANICAL DIVISION. **5430**

0148-7264 See NEW YORK AFRICAN STUDIES ASSOCIATION NEWSLETTER. **2642**

0148-7299 See AMERICAN JOURNAL OF MEDICAL GENETICS. **542**

0148-7345 See DIRECTORY OF OPPORTUNITIES IN INTERNATIONAL LAW. **3127**

0148-7353 See EXECUTIVE COMPENSATION ANALYSIS OF PROFESSIONAL SERVICES' FIRMS. **1668**

0148-7361 See NEW DIMENSIONS IN PSYCHIATRY. **3931**

0148-7388 See TURNABOUT. **5188**

0148-7396 See BLUEGRASS DIRECTORY, THE. **4104**

0148-7442 See DIRECTORY OF MICHIGAN MUNICIPAL OFFICIALS. **4643**

0148-7450 See HEALTH IN THE UNITED STATES. **4780**

0148-7485 See NORTH DAKOTA EDUCATIONAL FACTS. **1769**

0148-7493 See ROCKY MOUNTAIN MUSICAL EXPRESS. **4151**

0148-7566 See GET READY SHEET, THE. **3212**

0148-7590 See REPORT OF ... COMMISSIONER OF AGRICULTURE, FOOD AND RURAL RESOURCES TO THE ... REGULAR SESSION OF THE ... MAINE STATE LEGISLATURE. **126**

0148-7639 See ADFL BULLETIN. **3261**

0148-7655 See LOUISIANA GENEALOGICAL REGISTER, THE. **2458**

0148-771X See GRASS ROOTS PERSPECTIVES ON AMERICAN HISTORY. **2735**

0148-7728 See WISCONSIN ANNUAL HIGHWAY SAFETY WORK PROGRAM. **5446**

0148-7736 See TEXAS MONTHLY (AUSTIN). **2547**

0148-7752 See MISSOURI STATE PLAN FOR THE IMPLEMENTATION OF THE COMPREHENSIVE ALCOHOL ABUSE AND ALCOHOLISM PREVENTION, TREATMENT AND REHABILITATION ACT OF 1970. **1346**

0148-7760 See USSR FACTS & FIGURES ANNUAL. **5345**

0148-7795 See PANHANDLE-PLAINS HISTORICAL REVIEW. **2753**

0148-7841 See GUIDE TO SERVICES. **4653**

0148-7868 See AFRICANA LIBRARIES NEWSLETTER (URBANA, ILL.). **3188**

0148-7876 See LIBRARY BULLETIN - TEXAS DEPARTMENT OF WATER RESOURCES. **5536**

0148-7884 See DISCOVER RENO/TAHOE. **2532**

0148-7906 See LAWN, GARDEN AND HOME SHOWTIME. **2423**

0148-7914 See SEXUAL HEALTH AND RELATIONSHIPS. **5188**

0148-7922 See FAMILY LAW REPORTER, THE. **3120**

0148-7949 See GOVERNMENT MANAGER, THE. **4704**

0148-7965 See BNA'S PATENT, TRADEMARK & COPYRIGHT JOURNAL. **1301**

0148-7973 See CHEMICAL REGULATION REPORTER. **2949**

0148-7981 See LABOR RELATIONS REPORTER. **3151**

0148-8007 See POCKET BOOK OF PRO FOOTBALL, THE. **4912**

0148-8015 See VILLAGE LAW. **3071**

0148-8023 See R & D MONOGRAPH. **1705**

0148-8082 See IOWA ELDERLY AND DISABLED PROPERTY TAX RELIEF REPORT. **4733**

0148-8090 See NORTH CAROLINA BOATING ACCIDENT STATISTICS. **597**

0148-8139 See UNITED STATES LAW WEEK, THE. **3068**

0148-8147 See AFFIRMATIVE ACTION COMPLIANCE MANUAL FOR FEDERAL CONTRACTORS. **1642**

0148-8155 See DAILY REPORT FOR EXECUTIVES. **664**

0148-8171 See NEW HAMPSHIRE STATE PLAN, THE ADMINISTRATION OF VOCATIONAL TECHNICAL EDUCATION. **1914**

0148-818X See AUTOMATIC MUSICAL INSTRUMENTS PRICING GUIDE. **4101**

0148-8198 See BIENNIAL REPORT - NEVADA INDIAN COMMISSION. **2256**

0148-821X See PENNSYLVANIA WORK INJURIES. **2868**

0148-8287 See JOURNAL OF THERMAL INSULATION. **2606**

0148-8295 See TAX MANAGEMENT MEMORANDUM. **4753**

0148-8317 See ENVIRONMENTAL IMPACT NEWS. **2168**

0148-8333 See ANNUAL REPORT - NATIONAL CANCER INSTITUTE, DIVISION OF CANCER BIOLOGY AND DIAGNOSIS. **3808**

0148-8341 See NASA TECHNICAL PAPER. **29**

0148-8368 See FACILITIES INVENTORY & UTILIZATION STUDY. **1746**

0148-8376 See JOURNAL OF SOCIAL SERVICE RESEARCH. **5293**

0148-8406 See TROLLEY TALK. **5437**

0148-8414 See AMERICAN SPECTATOR (ARLINGTON, VA.), THE. **3337**

0148-8449 See NATIONAL OPINION POLL. **5252**

0148-8457 See NEW CONCEPTS IN URBAN TRANSPORTATION. **5388**

0148-8473 See INFORMATION SERIES. GROUP 2: DESIGN AND CONSTRUCTION OF TRANSPORTATION FACILITIES. **5384**

0148-849X See BIBLIOGRAPHY (NATIONAL RESEARCH COUNCIL (U.S.) TRANSPORTATION RESEARCH BOARD). **5400**

0148-8511 See NEWSLINE (WASHINGTON). **5388**

0148-8538 See GUIDE TO LOCATION INFORMATION. **4071**

0148-8546 See MINNESOTA CITIES. **4665**

0148-8554 See NATIONAL GENEALOGICAL INQUIRER. **2462**

0148-8562 See NIAID CATALOG OF TISSUE TYPING ANTISERA. **568**

0148-8570 See YEAR OF ACHIEVEMENT. **5314**

0148-8589 See NASA REFERENCE PUBLICATION. **29**

0148-8619 See U.S. JOURNAL OF DRUG AND ALCOHOL DEPENDENCE, THE. **1350**

0148-8686 See HUMAN BEHAVIOR AND ENVIRONMENT. **5247**

0148-8732 See SAILBOAT & EQUIPMENT DIRECTORY. **596**

0148-8740 See MOTORBOAT & EQUIPMENT DIRECTORY. **594**

0148-8813 See STUDENT HANDBOOK - PRINCE GEORGE'S COMMUNITY COLLEGE. **1849**

0148-8848 See UNITED STATES BANKER (COS COB). **815**

0148-8856 See ACE INTERNATIONAL. ENGLISH EDITION. **5315**

0148-8872 See SNACK FOOD BLUE BOOK. **2358**

0148-8899 See PROFESSIONAL AGENT, THE. **2890**

0148-8902 See ZEROWORK. **1720**

0148-8996 See BIBLIOSCAN Q-Z. **410**

0148-902X See PLAINSWOMAN. **5564**

0148-9038 See FUNGICIDE AND NEMATICIDE TESTS. **172**

0148-9046 See ELECTRO-OPTICS SERIES. **1972**

0148-9054 See PRACTICAL SPECTROSCOPY. **1018**

0148-9062 See INTERNATIONAL JOURNAL OF ROCK MECHANICS AND MINING SCIENCES & GEOMECHANICS ABSTRACTS. **2141**

0148-9089 See WORLD OF HOUSE PLANTS, THE. **2434**

0148-9097 See ADMISSIONS DECISIONS STUDY - FLORIDA. UNIVERSITY, GAINESVILLE. GRADUATE SCHOOL. **1792**

0148-9119 See PLASTICS COMPOUNDING. **4458**

0148-9127 See CRAFTS (PEORIA, ILL.). **371**

0148-9135 See AMBIANCE. **1081**

0148-9143 See FLORIDA MONTHLY. **2533**

0148-916X See INTERNATIONAL JOURNAL OF LEPROSY AND OTHER MYCOBACTERIAL DISEASES. **4785**

0148-9194 See INDUSTRY WAGE SURVEY : NONFERROUS FOUNDRIES. **1679**

0148-9208 See INDUSTRY WAGE SURVEY. CORRUGATED AND SOLID FIBER BOXES. **1679**

0148-9240 See STATE PLAN FOR PROGRAMS ON AGING UNDER TITLE III AND TITLE VII OF THE OLDER AMERICANS ACT OF 1965 AS AMENDED FOR THE STATE OF NEW HAMPSHIRE. **5311**

0148-9267 See COMPUTER MUSIC JOURNAL. **1240**

0148-9275 See BIENNIAL REPORT TO LEGISLATURE - BUREAU OF PUBLIC LANDS. **4632**

0148-9283 See ANNUAL REPORT / COMMODITY FUTURES TRADING COMMISSION. **891**

0148-9291 See FUNDING REPORT - CONNECTICUT JUSTICE COMMISSION. **3165**

0148-9321 See NEBRASKA HEALTH MANPOWER REPORTS: NURSING HOME ADMINISTRATORS. **3789**

0148-933X See CONSTRUCTION & SURETY LAW DIVISION NEWSLETTER. **2956**

0148-9348 See MEMBERSHIP DIRECTORY - APPRAISERS ASSOCIATION OF AMERICA, INC. **4840**

0148-9356 See TRUNKLINE CARRIER DOMESTIC PASSENGER ENPLANEMENTS. **38**

0148-9364 See FANFARE (TENAFLY, N.J.). **4117**

0148-9380 See APPROVED WELDING ELECTRODE WIRE-FLUX AND WIRE-GAS COMBINATIONS. **4026**

0148-9399 See SUMMARY REPORT OF CAMPAIGN CONTRIBUTIONS AND EXPENDITURES, PRIMARY ELECTION. **4497**

0148-9445 See NORTH DAKOTA JUDICIAL MASTER PROGRAM, THE. **3142**

0148-9461 See WILDLIFE MANAGEMENT LEAFLET. **2209**

0148-9542 See JAX FAX TRAVEL MARKETING MAGAZINE. **5481**

0148-9607 See TECH, THE. **5690**

0148-9623 See GARGOYLE (MADISON), THE. **2973**

0148-9704 See OREGON TRANSPORTATION COMMISSION POLICIES. **5389**

0148-9720 See SMALL PRESS RECORD OF BOOKS IN PRINT. **4832**

0148-9739 See CAROLINA BIOLOGY READERS. **450**

0148-9747 See INDUSTRY WAGE SURVEY. SHIPBUILDING AND REPAIRING. **1679**

0148-9763 See PRACTICING FAMILY LAWYER, THE. 3122
0148-9771 See DIRECTORY OF ALCOHOLISM COUNCILS IN AMERICA. 1343
0148-981X See OHIO FARMER COUNTY LINE RURAL DIRECTORY : HURON COUNTY, THE. 2752
0148-9828 See EGG MARKETING GUIDE. 2334
0148-9836 See NORTHEAST GULF SCIENCE. 1453
0148-9844 See QUEST WHO'S WHO. 434
0148-9887 See EDUCATION DIRECTORY. STATE EDUCATION AGENCY OFFICIALS. 1863
0148-9917 See JOURNAL OF AMBULATORY CARE MANAGEMENT, THE. 3786
0148-9925 See REPORT - ADMINISTRATIVE OFFICE OF PENNSYLVANIA COURTS. 3142
0148-9968 See CARIBE. 3373
0148-9976 See ALL STATES TAX HANDBOOK. 4709
0148-9992 See NEWS LETTER OF THE ASTRONOMICAL SOCIETY OF NEW YORK. 397
0149-0109 See FINANCING THE OREGON UNEMPLOYMENT INSURANCE PROGRAM. 1532
0149-0125 See ATHELINGS. 2528
0149-015X See STUDIES IN THE AMERICAN RENAISSANCE. 3354
0149-0168 See COMPLETE HANDBOOK OF COLLEGE FOOTBALL, THE. 4891
0149-0184 See ANNUAL REPORT ON THE GEOTHERMAL RESOURCES ACT OF 1975 (TEXAS). 2554
0149-0192 See ANTIQUE SHOP GUIDE. 249
0149-0230 See UNPUBLISHED WRITINGS ON WORLD RELIGIONS. 5007
0149-0257 See HOMES INTERNATIONAL. 2824
0149-0281 See WHO AUDITS AMERICA. 753
0149-029X See WATER INDUSTRY STATISTICAL PROFILE, A. 5549
0149-0303 See VEHICLE REGISTRATION AND MOTOR FUEL TAXES, AMOUNTS DISTRIBUTED TO LOCAL GOVERNMENTS, BY COUNTY. 4693
0149-032X See NARROW FABRICS. 3485
0149-0338 See BUYER'S GUIDE REPORTS : SHOPPER'S GUIDE. 1294
0149-0354 See BARATARIA. 3338
0149-0370 See EVALUATION ENGINEERING. 2054
0149-0389 See STUDIES IN CONFLICT AND TERRORISM. 5263
0149-0397 See MARINE GEORESOURCES & GEOTECHNOLOGY. 1986
0149-0400 See LEISURE SCIENCES. 5208
0149-0419 See MARINE GEODESY. 1358
0149-0451 See GEOMICROBIOLOGY JOURNAL. 563
0149-046X See MEMBRANE BIOCHEMISTRY. 490
0149-0486 See ROSTER OF REGISTERED ARCHITECTS (AUSTIN). 308
0149-0508 See PEACE AND CHANGE. 4531
0149-0516 See PEQUOD. 3423
0149-0540 See PLANNING REPORT - MINNESOTA HIGHER EDUCATION COORDINATING BOARD. 1841
0149-0567 See WVLC NEWSLETTER. 3256
0149-0583 See STOCKS OF WOOL AND RELATED FIBERS. 5356
0149-0605 See ENGINEERING RESEARCH HIGHLIGHTS. 1974
0149-0613 See COSTS AND RETURNS FROM VEGETABLE CROPS IN FLORIDA, WITH COMPARISONS. 168
0149-0656 See TRANSIT LAW REVIEW. 5395
0149-0672 See EQUUS. 2799
0149-0699 See SELF (NEW YORK). 5566
0149-0737 See NEWS MEDIA & THE LAW, THE. 3017
0149-0788 See DIRECTORY OF HALFWAY HOUSES AND GROUP HOMES FOR TROUBLED CHILDREN. 5283

0149-080X See MANPOWER AND HUMAN RESOURCES STUDIES. 1689
0149-0818 See MULTINATIONAL INDUSTRIAL RELATIONS SERIES. 1692
0149-0826 See BUSINESS REVIEW AND ECONOMIC NEWS FROM ISRAEL. 1467
0149-0842 See HANDBOOK - ALABAMA LAW INSTITUTE. 2976
0149-0885 See PMD, PHARMACEUTICAL MARKETERS DIRECTORY. 4325
0149-0893 See POTOMAC (CHICAGO). 4545
0149-0907 See BIORESEARCH TODAY. PESTICIDES. 4244
0149-0915 See BIORESEARCH TODAY. POPULATION, FERTILITY & BIRTH CONTROL. 4550
0149-0923 See BIORESEARCH TODAY. INDUSTRIAL HEALTH & TOXICOLOGY. 2859
0149-094X See BIORESEARCH TODAY. HUMAN & ANIMAL PARASITOLOGY. 447
0149-0958 See BIORESEARCH TODAY. FOOD ADDITIVES & RESIDUES. 2329
0149-0966 See BIORESEARCH TODAY. HUMAN & ANIMAL AGING. 3750
0149-0974 See BIORESEARCH TODAY. FOOD MICROBIOLOGY. 560
0149-0982 See BIORESEARCH TODAY. BIRTH DEFECTS. 3557
0149-0990 See BIORESEARCH TODAY. BIO-ENGINEERING & INSTRUMENTATION. 447
0149-1008 See BIORESEARCH TODAY. ADDICTION. 3557
0149-1016 See BIORESEARCH TODAY. CANCER A. CARCINOGENESIS. 3809
0149-1024 See BIORESEARCH TODAY. CANCER B. ANTICANCER AGENTS. 3809
0149-1032 See BIORESEARCH TODAY. CANCER C. IMMUNOLOGY. 3809
0149-1040 See NEW YORK LITERARY FORUM. 3416
0149-1059 See CAPITAL IMPROVEMENTS PROGRAM FOR CHICAGO. 4716
0149-1067 See INTERNATIONAL SECURITIES REGULATION. 902
0149-1091 See O'DWYER'S DIRECTORY OF CORPORATE COMMUNICATIONS. 763
0149-1113 See PHARMACY SCHOOL ADMISSION REQUIREMENTS. 4323
0149-1148 See COMPREHENSIVE IMMUNOLOGY. 3668
0149-1199 See ACM GUIDE TO COMPUTING LITERATURE. 1208
0149-1210 See 33 METAL PRODUCING. 3996
0149-1245 See STRUCTURES AND ENVIRONMENT HANDBOOK. 629
0149-1253 See HOOSIER FAMILY ARCHIVES. 2454
0149-1288 See FODOR'S PARIS. 5472
0149-1296 See SEED ANALYSIS REPORT. 2431
0149-1342 See URETHANE ABSTRACTS. 4460
0149-1423 See AAPG BULLETIN. 4248
0149-1431 See FAMILY LAW REVIEW. 3120
0149-144X See PROCEEDINGS : ANNUAL RELIABILITY AND MAINTAINABILITY SYMPOSIUM. 4221
0149-1458 See SRA "OUTFIT" NEWSLETTER. 36
0149-1474 See BIENNIAL REPORT - MINNESOTA BOARD OF DENTISTRY. 1317
0149-1520 See OHIO POPULATION ESTIMATES. 4555
0149-1539 See ANNUAL REPORT - DIVISION OF LONG-TERM CARE. 5272
0149-1547 See PEASANT STUDIES. 5212
0149-1598 See REPORT ON THE AMERICAS. 2757
0149-1601 See INDEX TO BILLS INTRODUCED IN UTAH LEGISLATIVE SESSION. 2981
0149-161X See SENIOR TEXANS EMPLOYMENT PROGRAM ANNUAL REPORT TO GOVERNOR'S COMMITTEE ON AGING. 1710
0149-1679 See BUILDING TECHNOLOGY PROJECT SUMMARIES. 605
0149-1695 See LEGAL BRIEFS FOR EDITORS, PUBLISHERS, AND WRITERS. 2999

0149-1717 See PHARMACY LAW DIGEST. 3029
0149-1725 See CLUES (LINCOLN). 2728
0149-175X See OCCASIONAL PAPERS - THE MUSEUM, TEXAS TECH UNIVERSITY. 4094
0149-1768 See SPECIAL PUBLICATIONS - THE MUSEUM, TEXAS TECH UNIVERSITY. 4096
0149-1776 See GLACIOLOGICAL DATA. 1413
0149-1784 See JOURNAL OF SOUTH ASIAN AND MIDDLE EASTERN STUDIES. 2769
0149-1792 See CHARACTERISTICS OF STATE PLANS FOR AID TO FAMILIES WITH DEPENDENT CHILDREN UNDER THE SOCIAL SECURITY ACT, TITLE IV-A, AND FOR GUAM, PUERTO RICO, & VIRGIN ISLANDS. 5277
0149-1830 See VELVET LIGHT TRAP, THE. 4079
0149-1865 See SOUTH CAROLINA STATEWIDE TESTING PROGRAM, SUMMARY REPORT. 1872
0149-189X See KAWEAH RIVER FLOWS, DIVERSIONS AND STORAGE. 1416
0149-1903 See AUDIT REPORT, BOARD OF PODIATRY. 3554
0149-192X See QUANTITATIVE APPLICATIONS IN THE SOCIAL SCIENCES. 5214
0149-1938 See SUNWORLD. 1958
0149-1954 See NEW MEXICO PROFESSIONAL ENGINEER (1977). 1988
0149-1962 See ANNUAL STATISTICAL REPORT OF EXPENDITURES MADE IN CONNECTION WITH ELECTIONS, THE. 4501
0149-1970 See PROGRESS IN NUCLEAR ENERGY (NEW SERIES). 2158
0149-1989 See COLLECTED ALGORITHMS FROM ACM. SUPPLEMENT. 1175
0149-1997 See ALLEGHENY LUDLUM HORIZONS. 3997
0149-2012 See STATE OF NEVADA, DEPARTMENT OF PAROLE AND PROBATION, AUDIT REPORT. 3177
0149-2020 See BRIEF OUTLINE OF THE OKLAHOMA REVENUE SYSTEM, A. 4713
0149-2039 See INTERNATIONAL DIRECTORY OF MEMBERS. 4839
0149-2055 See SUPERINTENDENT'S NEWSLETTER. 1873
0149-2063 See JOURNAL OF MANAGEMENT. 873
0149-208X See PORT OF BOSTON HANDBOOK. 5454
0149-2101 See NEBRASKA STATE PLAN FOR ALCOHOLISM, THE. 1347
0149-2136 See JOURNAL OF PETROLEUM TECHNOLOGY. 4262
0149-2144 See STATE OF NEVADA, DEPARTMENT OF PAROLE AND PROBATION, RESTITUTION TRUST FUND, AUDIT REPORT. 3177
0149-2160 See STATE OF NEVADA, CONSOLIDATED BOND AND INTEREST REDEMPTION FUND, AUDIT REPORT. 4749
0149-2179 See STATE OF NEVADA, COMPUTER ACQUISITION SINKING FUND, AUDIT REPORT. 4749
0149-2195 See MORBIDITY AND MORTALITY WEEKLY REPORT. 4792
0149-225X See AUDIT REPORT, STATE OF NEVADA DEPARTMENT OF PAROLE AND PROBATION, PAROLEE'S REVOLVING LOAN FUND; PRISONER'S WORK RELEASE REVOLVING LOAN FUND. 3158
0149-2322 See SUPERINTENDENT'S NEWSLETTER. 1873
0149-2365 See SOCCER DIGEST (EVANSTON). 4919
0149-2381 See CHEMICAL TIMES & TRENDS. 969
0149-239X See EXPERIMENTAL YACHT SOCIETY JOURNAL. 4176
0149-2403 See ANNUAL REPORT - MISSOURI ELECTIONS COMMISSION. 4628
0149-242X See MONOGRAPHS OF THE HIGH/SCOPE EDUCATIONAL RESEARCH FOUNDATION. 1765
0149-2438 See TUFTS KINSMEN. 2476
0149-2446 See NEWS - ASSOCIATION OF COLLEGIATE SCHOOLS OF ARCHITECTURE. 304

0149-2454 See CURRENT CONCEPTS IN RADIOLOGY. 3940

0149-2470 See GEOLOGICAL SURVEY OCCASIONAL PAPER. 1378

0149-2500 See SBIC DIGEST. 913

0149-2551 See NEARA JOURNAL. 2748

0149-2578 See WASHINGTON SOCIAL LEGISLATION BULLETIN. 4694

0149-2586 See STUDIES IN WELFARE POLICY. 5312

0149-2608 See ALUMNI MAGAZINE - ALUMNI ASSOCIATION OF THE JOHNS HOPKINS HOSPITAL SCHOOL OF NURSING, THE. 1100

0149-2632 See HOSPITAL PEER REVIEW. 3785

0149-2667 See NUTRITION AND THE BRAIN. 4196

0149-2675 See PERSONNEL MANAGEMENT. 945

0149-2691 See WAGES AND HOURS. 1717

0149-2829 See ACTIVITIES OF THE FEDERAL COUNCIL FOR SCIENCE AND TECHNOLOGY AND THE FEDERAL COORDINATING COUNCIL FOR SCIENCE, ENGINEERING AND TECHNOLOGY. 5080

0149-2837 See WHITE HOUSE FELLOWSHIPS, THE. 4705

0149-2853 See DENTAL REFLECTIONS. 1321

0149-2918 See CLINICAL THERAPEUTICS. 4297

0149-2934 See OHIO FARMER COUNTY LINE RURAL DIRECTORY : CRAWFORD COUNTY, THE. 2752

0149-2942 See MISSOURI REGISTER. 3011

0149-2950 See RESPIRATORY PHYSIOLOGY. 3951

0149-3019 See PROCEEDINGS OF THE TECHNICAL PROGRAM - NATIONAL NOISE AND VIBRATION CONTROL CONFERENCE. 2239

0149-3027 See MOTORCYCLE STATISTICAL ANNUAL. 4083

0149-3035 See ROSTER OF LICENSED PROFESSIONAL ENGINEERS. 1994

0149-3043 See EPOCHE (LOS ANGELES). 4956

0149-3078 See TECHNICAL REPORT - COLLEGE OF MARINE STUDIES, UNIVERSITY OF DELAWARE. 1457

0149-3094 See EQL REPORT. 2230

0149-3108 See JOURNAL OF THE ADHESIVE AND SEALANT COUNCIL, THE. 1026

0149-3132 See TRANSIT FACT BOOK (WASHINGTON, D.C.). 5395

0149-3175 See WNY MOTORIST. 5428

0149-3205 See BOARDS AND COMMISSIONS, STATE OF ALASKA. 4633

0149-323X See NATIONAL TAX TRAINING PROGRAM : TAX PRACTICE FUNDAMENTALS FOR NONTAX PROFESSIONALS. 3102

0149-3272 See ADMINISTRATIVE LAW (GARDENA). 3091

0149-3299 See SCHOLAR AND EDUCATOR. 1781

0149-3302 See YEAR-ROUND EDUCATION ACTIVITIES IN THE UNITED STATES. 1792

0149-3329 See WORK IN FLORIDA. 1718

0149-337X See DIRECTORY OF ADMINISTRATIVE SERVICES. 4643

0149-337X See AMERICAN CITY & COUNTY, THE. 5238

0149-340X See BIENNIAL REPORT - KANSAS ADULT AUTHORITY. 3158

0149-3434 See IFDC REPORT. 94

0149-3442 See TACK 'N TOGS MERCHANDISING. 2802

0149-354X See ANNUAL MEETING, TECHNICAL COMMITTEE REPORTS. 2288

0149-3574 See NUCLEARFUEL. 2157

0149-3582 See SECURITIES WEEK. 913

0149-3620 See SLO PITCH. 4919

0149-3639 See HOTEL & RESORT INDUSTRY. 2806

0149-3698 See APPROVAL OF AWARDS FOR INSTITUTIONS PARTICIPATING IN THE COLLEGE WORK-STUDY PROGRAM. 1651

0149-371X See WORKERS COVERED BY KENTUCKY UNEMPLOYMENT INSURANCE LAW BY COUNTY. 2896

0149-3744 See POST ROCK. 4795

0149-3760 See DIRECTORY OF DOCTORS OF OSTEOPATHY LICENSED AND REGISTERED IN TENNESSEE. 3572

0149-3779 See ANNUAL AREA LABOR REVIEW. 1644

0149-3825 See BIBLIOGRAPHY ON COLD REGIONS SCIENCE AND TECHNOLOGY. 5088

0149-3965 See ANNUAL REPORT - UNITED TECHNOLOGIES. 2096

0149-4023 See IFYGL BULLETIN. 839

0149-4082 See ADDVANTAGE. 4881

0149-4120 See AVERAGE MONTHLY WORKERS COVERED BY KENTUCKY UNEMPLOYMENT INSURANCE LAW BY INDUSTRIAL DIVISION AND COUNTY. 2875

0149-4147 See TURBOMACHINERY INTERNATIONAL. 2131

0149-4228 See GRUB STREET. 3392

0149-4244 See NEW OXFORD REVIEW. 4981

0149-4279 See MODERN GOLD COINAGE. 2781

0149-4309 See SALARY SURVEY (LOS GATOS). 1709

0149-4368 See DIRECTORIO DE MIEMBROS - SOCIEDAD INTERAMERICANA DE PSICOLOGIA. 4585

0149-4376 See PHILOSOPHY OF RELIGION AND THEOLOGY : PROCEEDINGS. 4986

0149-4392 See ANNUAL REPORT OF THE INHALATION TOXICOLOGY RESEARCH INSTITUTE. 3979

0149-4465 See DIESEL & GAS TURBINE WORLDWIDE. 2112

0149-4473 See VIVA (NEW YORK). 2549

0149-4481 See PUBLICATIONS OF THE FOOD AND RESOURCE ECONOMICS DEPARTMENT, UNIVERSITY OF FLORIDA. 123

0149-4503 See CHICOREL INDEX TO SHORT STORIES IN ANTHOLOGIES AND COLLECTIONS. 3374

0149-4538 See SECONDARY SCHOOLS FOR INTERNATIONAL STUDENTS, U.S.A. 1847

0149-4635 See HUSTLER (COLUMBUS). 3995

0149-466X See PLAYERS. 3996

0149-4694 See REGISTER OF INDEXERS. 3244

0149-4724 See AFRICAN DIRECTIONS. 2636

0149-4732 See ADVANCES IN CLINICAL CHILD PSYCHOLOGY. 4571

0149-4740 See NATIONAL NOW TIMES. 5562

0149-4864 See ANNUAL REPORT - DEPARTMENT OF COMMERCE AND ECONOMIC DEVELOPMENT. 822

0149-4872 See SOCIOLOGICAL OBSERVATIONS. 5261

0149-4880 See PAPERS IN INTERNATIONAL STUDIES : LATIN AMERICAN SERIES. 2753

0149-4899 See PLASTICS MACHINERY & EQUIPMENT. 4458

0149-4902 See MOTA. 4091

0149-4910 See NACTA JOURNAL. 110

0149-4929 See MARRIAGE & FAMILY REVIEW. 2283

0149-4953 See MONEY (CHICAGO, ILL.). 906

0149-4961 See DIRECTORY OF LABOR MARKET INFORMATION REPORTS AND PUBLICATIONS. 1663

0149-4988 See ANNUAL FINANCIAL ANALYSIS FOR PENNSYLVANIA SCHOOLS. 1860

0149-4996 See WESTERN RAILROADER AND WESTERN RAILFAN. 5438

0149-502X See EXECUTIVE PERSONNEL IN THE FEDERAL SERVICE. 4647

0149-5046 See HEARD HERITAGE. 2736

0149-5054 See COMPUTER PERIPHERALS REVIEW. 1264

0149-5070 See WESTERN NEW YORK. 719

0149-5097 See PROPOSED, STATE OF CALIFORNIA, ANNUAL STATEWIDE SOCIAL SERVICES PLAN. 5302

0149-516X See SOUTHERN ACCENTS. 2903

0149-5186 See ALPHABETIZED DIRECTORY OF AMERICAN JOURNALISTS. 2917

0149-5208 See COUNTYWIDE ANNUAL PLAN REVIEW / FAIRFAX COUNTY, VA. OFFICE OF COMPREHENSIVE PLANNING. 2819

0149-5216 See DIRECTORY - AMERICAN RECOVERY ASSOCIATION, INC. 666

0149-5267 See NATIONAL PETROLEUM NEWS. 4265

0149-5275 See E/MJ INTERNATIONAL DIRECTORY MINING ACTIVITY DIGEST. 2138

0149-5372 See CHECKLIST OF HUMAN RIGHTS DOCUMENTS. 4505

0149-5380 See WWD. 1088

0149-5402 See ANNUAL REPORT TO THE GOVERNOR AND THE GENERAL ASSEMBLY OF MARYLAND. 1809

0149-547X See LIBRARIES FOR COLLEGE STUDENTS WITH HANDICAPS. 3223

0149-5496 See CHICOREL INDEX TO READING AND LEARNING DISABILITIES. 1877

0149-5542 See ELECTRONICS INTERNATIONAL. 2049

0149-5550 See ENERGY LEGISLATIVE SERVICE. 2966

0149-5569 See GREEN MARKETS. 90

0149-5585 See INTERNATIONAL CONSTRUCTION WEEK. 618

0149-5712 See MAARAV. 3300

0149-5739 See JOURNAL OF THERMAL STRESSES. 2119

0149-5747 See ADVANCED LIGHTER THAN AIR REVIEW. 1103

0149-5771 See ELECTRICAL MARKETING. 2045

0149-578X See COAL WEEK. 2137

0149-5801 See KEYSTONE NEWS BULLETIN. 2142

0149-581X See PLATT'S OILGRAM PRICE REPORT. 4275

0149-5852 See IFCD REPORT (SPANISH EDITION). 93

0149-5860 See CHICOREL INDEX TO VIDEO TAPES AND CASSETTES. 5316

0149-5879 See SEWAGE TREATMENT CONSTRUCTION GRANTS MANUAL. 2243

0149-5933 See COMPARATIVE STRATEGY. 4518

0149-5941 See STUDIES IN CONFLICT AND TERRORISM. 5263

0149-5992 See DIABETES CARE. 3727

0149-600X See AREA WAGE SURVEY. NORFOLK-VIRGINIA BEACH-PORTSMOUTH AND NEWPORT NEWS-HAMPTON, VIRGINIA-NORTH CAROLINA METROPOLITAN AREA. 1653

0149-6034 See PROGRAMS AND PLANS / ENVIRONMENTAL RESEARCH LABORATORIES. 5142

0149-6077 See WASHOUT REVIEW. 3356

0149-6085 See JOURNAL OF FOOD SAFETY. 2346

0149-6115 See ASTM GEOTECHNICAL TESTING JOURNAL. 1965

0149-6123 See CEMENT, CONCRETE AND AGGREGATES. 606

0149-6131 See PERSONAL LIABILITY DIGEST. 3028

0149-6166 See INDEX TO FEDERAL TAX ARTICLES. SUPPLEMENT. 4731

0149-6174 See ELECTRICAL BLUE BOOK, THE. 2044

0149-6190 See EXTRA PAY FOR EXTRA SERVICES IN NEW JERSEY SCHOOL DISTRICTS. 1863

0149-6255 See EMPLOYMENT PRACTICES DECISIONS. 3147

0149-6263 See ENERGY RESOURCES (DENVER). 1941

0149-6301 See NOMAD NEWS. 5421

0149-631X See FODOR'S LONDON. 5472

0149-6328 See PROGRESS REPORT TO THE GOVERNOR'S HIGHWAY SAFETY OFFICE. 5390

0149-6387 See TRADEMARK RULES OF PRACTICE OF THE PATENT AND TRADEMARK OFFICE WITH FORMS AND STATUTES. 1309

0149-6395 See SEPARATION SCIENCE AND TECHNOLOGY. 1029

0149-6409 See HENRY L. DOHERTY SERIES. 4259

0149-6417 See PLAFSEP. PROCESSING (LIBRARIES)--ANECDOTES, FACETIAE, SATIRE, ETC.--PERIODICALS. 3241

0149-6425 See RODEO NEWS. 4915

0149-6433 See TRANSACTIONS OF THE ANNUAL MEETING OF THE ORTHOPAEDIC RESEARCH SOCIETY. 3885

0149-6441 See WEST BRANCH. 3452

0149-645X See IEEE MTT-S INTERNATIONAL MICROWAVE SYMPOSIUM DIGEST. 2060

0149-6468 See TRUST FUNDS. 5068

0149-6492 See VOLUNTARY ACTION LEADERSHIP. 5313

0149-6557 See ON WATCH (WASHINGTON). 3183

0149-662X See IDAHO STATE PARKS AND RECREATION. 4706

0149-6662 See FINANCIAL REPORT - STATE OF NEVADA, DIVISION OF COLORADO RIVER RESOURCES. 2089

0149-6670 See QUEST (REDONDO BEACH). 5144

0149-6697 See DIRECTORY OF POSTSECONDARY OCCUPATIONAL EDUCATION OPPORTUNITIES IN LOUISIANA. 1912

0149-6727 See MEDICAL IMAGING. 3943

0149-6735 See MONTEFIORE MEDICINE. 3618

0149-676X See AMERICAN WINE SOCIETY MANUAL, THE. 2363

0149-6786 See SERVICES HANDBOOK - ARIZONA DEPARTMENT OF EDUCATION. 1783

0149-6808 See SCHOOL FOODSERVICE RESEARCH REVIEW. 2356

0149-6824 See SOUTH SHORE. 331

0149-6840 See FOLKLIFE CENTER NEWS. 2319

0149-6905 See PROCEEDINGS, ANNUAL MEETING - WASHINGTON STATE HORTICULTURAL ASSOCIATION. 2428

0149-6913 See GEORGE D. HALL'S DIRECTORY OF MASSACHUSETTS MANUFACTURERS. 3479

0149-6948 See CASE ANALYSIS IN SOCIAL SCIENCE IN SOCIAL THERAPY. 5241

0149-6956 See CRAIN'S CHICAGO BUSINESS. 662

0149-6980 See MEDIA & VALUES. 1116

0149-7006 See CHICOREL INDEX TO ABSTRACTING AND INDEXING SERVICES : PERIODICALS IN HUMANITIES AND THE SOCIAL SCIENCES. 2844

0149-7014 See ON LOCATION. 4075

0149-7081 See WOMEN ARTISTS NEWS. 333

0149-709X See RFD (WOLF CREEK). 2796

0149-7162 See DOWN'S SYNDROME. 544

0149-7189 See EVALUATION AND PROGRAM PLANNING. 5285

0149-7197 See RETIRED MILITARY ALMANAC. 4055

0149-7219 See YEARBOOK OF ROMANIAN STUDIES. 2716

0149-7308 See NEWSLETTER - AMERICAN SOCIETY OF BREWING CHEMISTS. 987

0149-7359 See TELEVISION NETWORK MOVIES. 4078

0149-7375 See TELEVISION INDEX: NETWORK FUTURES, PROGRAM DEBUTS, RETURNS, SPECIALS AND CHANGES. 1141

0149-7413 See SENIOR TRIBUNE, THE. 5182

0149-7421 See DEVELOPMENTS IN MARKETING SCIENCE. 923

0149-7464 See BILINGUAL TEACHER CORPS PROGRAM, THE. 1876

0149-7510 See JOB SAFETY & HEALTH (WASHINGTON. 1977). 2864

0149-7510 See JOB SAFETY & HEALTH; AN ADVISORY BULLETIN ON GOVERNMENT AND INDUSTRY SAFETY POLICIES, PROCEDURES AND PRACTICES. 2864

0149-7537 See WHO'S WHO IN ENGINEERING (NEW YORK. 1977). 436

0149-7553 See DIRECTORY OF U.S. FIRMS AND ORGANIZATIONS IN INDONESIA. 1605

0149-7596 See ANNUAL REPORT - GOVERNOR'S COUNCIL ON DRUG AND ALCOHOL ABUSE. 1341

0149-7626 See MEDIA MARKET GUIDE. TOP 100 MARKETING AREAS. 762

0149-7634 See NEUROSCIENCE AND BIOBEHAVIORAL REVIEWS. 3842

0149-7642 See RED BOOK OF HOUSING MANUFACTURERS, THE. 625

0149-7677 See DANCE RESEARCH JOURNAL. 1312

0149-7685 See PROCEEDINGS OF THE PLANT GROWTH REGULATOR WORKING GROUP. 2429

0149-7707 See MODERN SILVER COINAGE. 2782

0149-7723 See MIDDLE ELEMENTARY CLASS PACKET, THE. 1764

0149-7863 See PUSHCART PRIZE, THE. 3426

0149-7901 See JOURNAL OF APPLIED MANAGEMENT. 873

0149-7944 See CURRENT SURGERY. 3963

0149-7952 See GERMAN STUDIES REVIEW. 2689

0149-7987 See ARIZONA BICENTENNIAL REVIEW. 1653

0149-8029 See OPFLOW. 5537

0149-8045 See QUILT WORLD. 5185

0149-807X See DATA REPORT, HIGH ALTITUDE METEOROLOGICAL DATA. INTERNATIONAL DELAYED DATA ISSUE. 1425

0149-8088 See INDEX TO SCIENTIFIC & TECHNICAL PROCEEDINGS. 5112

0149-8096 See MOUNTAIN MUSIC AND WHERE TO FIND IT. 4132

0149-8126 See DUN & BRADSTREET EXPORT DOCUMENTATION DIGEST. 832

0149-8258 See MANUAL OF MANAGEMENT ASSUMPTIONS FOR PLANNING BUSINESS STRATEGIES. 879

0149-8282 See SUMMARY OF ACCOUNTS AND DEPOSITS IN ALL MUTUAL SAVINGS BANKS. 813

0149-8304 See DIRECTORY OF-- PERSONNEL RESPONSIBLE FOR RADIOLOGICAL HEALTH PROGRAMS. 4773

0149-8320 See EQUAL EMPLOYMENT OPPORTUNITY COMMISSION AFFIRMATIVE ACTION PLAN. 1667

0149-8347 See ADULT BIBLE STUDIES. 5014

0149-8363 See LECCIONES CRISTIANAS. 4973

0149-8428 See RELIGION INDEX ONE. PERIODICALS. 5013

0149-8436 See RELIGION INDEX TWO : MULTI-AUTHOR WORKS. 4991

0149-8444 See KEYSTONE FOLKLORE. 2321

0149-8452 See STATUS REPORT - FINANCIAL ACCOUNTING STANDARDS BOARD. 751

0149-8495 See LABOREGISTER, THE. 1685

0149-8509 See MONTANA WATER POLLUTION CONTROL PROGRAM PLAN. 5536

0149-8517 See MUGWUMPS. 4132

0149-8584 See EXPLORING THE BIBLE. AGES 8-12. PACKET. 5016

0149-869X See WORK IN AMERICA INSTITUTE STUDIES IN PRODUCTIVITY. 1631

0149-8711 See OMNI (NEW YORK, N.Y.). 2542

0149-8738 See INTERNATIONAL ENVIRONMENT REPORTER. CURRENT REPORT. 3113

0149-8754 See REPORTER (GRANADA HILLS), THE. 5236

0149-8770 See ANNUAL REPORT - OKLAHOMA TOURISM AND RECREATION DEPARTMENT. 5500

0149-8797 See PUBLIC ADMINISTRATION TIMES. 4676

0149-8851 See RIVER STYX. 3431

0149-886X See JOURNAL OF OPTOMETRIC VISION DEVELOPMENT (1976). 4216

0149-8886 See JOURNAL OF THE ACADEMY OF REHABILITATIVE AUDIOLOGY. 3889

0149-8894 See SUPERMARKET MANAGEMENT. 887

0149-8932 See INTERVIEW (NEW YORK, N.Y. 1977). 2535

0149-8959 See WOMEN AND MINORITY MANPOWER STATISTICS. 1540

0149-8975 See MICROGRAPHICS INDEX, THE. 4371

0149-9009 See CONTEMPORARY DIAGNOSTIC RADIOLOGY. 3940

0149-9106 See ARCHITECTURE MINNESOTA. 290

0149-9114 See KANSAS HISTORY. 2743

0149-9149 See COLONY VISITOR. 2729

0149-9165 See NEBRASKA VISITOR SURVEY. 1507

0149-9203 See ELECTRONICS RETAILING. 954

0149-9211 See NEW HAMPSHIRE AFFIRMATIVE ACTION DATA. 1536

0149-9238 See SOLAR ENERGY HANDBOOK. 1957

0149-9246 See HASTINGS INTERNATIONAL AND COMPARATIVE LAW REVIEW. 3129

0149-9254 See LABOR MARKET INFORMATION DIRECTORY FOR VIRGINIA EMPLOYMENT COMMISSION. 1683

0149-9270 See PRINCETON ALUMNI WEEKLY. 1102

0149-9300 See MICROGRAPHICS TODAY. 4371

0149-9319 See SHORTHORN COUNTRY. 221

0149-9327 See NOSTALGIA ILLUSTRATED. 2541

0149-9351 See NATO CONFERENCE SERIES : III, HUMAN FACTORS. 584

0149-9378 See COMPENDIUM OF ORGANIC SYNTHETIC METHODS. 1041

0149-9386 See ENERGY (STAMFORD, CONN. 1975). 1942

0149-9394 See NEWS RELEASE FROM THE CHESS PRESS SYNDICATE. 4864

0149-9408 See AMERICAN BOOK REVIEW, THE. 3337

0149-9483 See ADVANCES IN NUTRITIONAL RESEARCH. 4186

0149-9505 See STATE OF OREGON COMPREHENSIVE DEVELOPMENTAL DISABILITIES PLAN. 4394

0149-9521 See MANUFACTURING IN MINNESOTA. 3483

0149-9556 See DATA/COMM INDUSTRY REPORT. 1257

0149-9564 See LAKE POWELL FISHERIES INVESTIGATIONS. 2307

0149-9599 See NEBRASKA HEALTH MANPOWER REPORTS : OPTOMETRISTS. 4216

0149-9602 See HEALTH FOODS BUSINESS. 2343

0149-9610 See MISSOURI OVERALL PROGRAM DESIGN AND ANNUAL WORK PROGRAM. 2828

0149-9637 See PONTIAC; CHASSIS SHOP MANUAL. 5423

0149-9653 See POLISH MUSEUM OF AMERICA QUARTERLY, THE. 4095

0149-967X See FORUM (DEVON). 1747

0149-9688 See MULTIVARIATE EXPERIMENTAL CLINICAL RESEARCH. 4605

0149-9718 See TAR, TENNESSEE ADMINISTRATIVE REGISTER. NOTICE SECTION. 3062

0149-9734 See MEDICAL ELECTRONICS (PITTSBURGH, PA.). 3609

0149-9742 See EXTRAMURAL RESEARCH PROGRAMS SUPPORTED BY THE FOOD AND DRUG ADMINISTRATION. 3576

0149-9831 See POETS AND AUTHORS. 3424

0149-9866 See BULLETIN / NEW MEXICO STATE UNIVERSITY, AGRICULTURAL EXPERIMENT STATION. 69

0149-9882 See MICROGRAPHICS INDEX. SUPPLEMENT, THE. 4371

0149-9890 See PAPER - AMERICAN SOCIETY OF AGRICULTURAL ENGINEERS. 1990

0149-9920 See TEXAS HORSE-TRADER, THE. 2802

0149-9939 See NATIONAL LIBRARY OF MEDICINE AUDIOVISUALS CATALOG. 3233

0149-9963 See PROCEEDINGS OF THE STATISTICAL COMPUTING SECTION. 3528

0149-9971 *See* REVIEW OF INTERNATIONAL BROADCASTING. 1138

0150-0104 *See* DOSSIERS ARCHEOLOGIQUES, HISTORIQUES ET CULTURELS DU NORD ET DU PAS-DE-CALAIS. 2685

0150-0112 *See* DOSSIERS DE L'ELEVAGE, LES. 5509

0150-1313 *See* RAIL SYNDICALISTE, LE. 5435

0150-1844 *See* POINTS DE VENTE PARIS. 934

0150-262X *See* SAHARA INFO. 4495

0150-3146 *See* ECHO DE L'AFRIQUE, L'. 4472

0150-536X *See* JOURNAL OF OPTICS. 4436

0150-5505 *See* GEOSTANDARDS NEWSLETTER. 1380

0150-5726 *See* ACTIVITES (CHAMBRE DE COMMERCE ET D'INDUSTRIE DE NICE ET DES ALPES-MARITIMES). 4623

0150-5998 *See* BIBLIOGRAPHIE DE LA FRANCE. SUPPLEMENT 4. ATLAS, CARTES ET PLANS. 2580

0150-6021 *See* BULLETIN - ASSOCIATION FRANCIASE DES PONTS ET CHARPENTES. 605

0150-6439 *See* MAISON INDIVIDUELLE, LA. 4206

0150-6463 *See* PETROLE ET LE GAZ ARABES. 4272

0150-6617 *See* INDUSTRIES ET TECHNIQUES. 1611

0150-6854 *See* ARGUS ET LA SEMAINE, L'. 2874

0150-6943 *See* CAHIERS JEAN GIRAUDOUX. 3371

0150-7206 *See* REVUE TECHNIQUE CARROSSERIE. 5424

0150-7214 *See* REVUE MOTO TECHNIQUE BOULOGNE-SUR-SEINE. 1625

0150-7230 *See* AUTO EXPERTISE. 5404

0150-7540 *See* TOUTES LES NOUVELLES DE L'HOTELLERIE ET DU TOURISME. 2809

0150-7583 *See* BULLETIN TRIMESTRIEL DE LA BANQUE DE FRANCE. 781

0150-939X *See* AVICULTEUR, L'. 5577

0150-9535 *See* CAHIERS DE LA RECHERCHE ARCHITECTURALE, LES. 294

0150-9861 *See* JOURNAL OF NEURORADIOLOGY. 3942

0151-0193 *See* GERONTOLOGIE ET SOCIETE (PARIS). 3751

0151-0282 *See* SCIENCE ET VIE. NUMERO HORS SERIE. 5151

0151-0770 *See* BULLETIN MENSUEL DE STATISTIQUE IINDUSTRIELLE. 1530

0151-0827 *See* DOCUMENTS STRASBOURG. 2615

0151-1637 *See* SCIENCE ET TECHNIQUE DU FROID / REFRIGERATION SCIENCE AND TECHNOLOGY. 2608

0151-1904 *See* VERS L'EDUCATION NOUVELLE. 1789

0151-2323 *See* VIE PARIS. 1976, LA. 5038

0151-4040 *See* CHAUSSER 1968. 1082

0151-4105 *See* REVUE D'HISTOIRE DES SCIENCES. 5148

0151-4989 *See* CANAL PARIS. 317

0151-5055 *See* ECONOMIA. 1556

0151-5845 *See* PSYCHOMOTRICITE, LA. 4613

0151-6086 *See* PICTON, LE. 2702

0151-6353 *See* SPORT AUTO, VIRAGE AUTO, CHAMPION. 5425

0151-6981 *See* AQUARAMA. 4285

0151-6981 *See* AQUARAMA. 2771

0151-7848 *See* PHOT ARGUS EDITION GENERALE. 4372

0151-8801 *See* LETTRE DE MICHEL DEBRE, LA. 3405

0151-9093 *See* ACTUALITE CHIMIQUE, L'. 959

0151-9107 *See* ANNALES DE CHIMIE (PARIS. 1914). 961

0151-9638 *See* ANNALES DE DERMATOLOGIE ET DE VENEREOLOGIE. 3717

0151-979X *See* SHOW MAGAZINE. 5368

0152-0032 *See* POSIE I.E. POESIE. 3470

0152-0741 *See* PAGES DE L'EVENEMENT, LES. 2491

0152-0768 *See* POUVOIRS. 4532

0152-139X *See* FOI AUJOURD HUI. 5029

0152-1977 *See* ACTION FAMILIALE ET SCOLAIRE. 1722

0152-2108 *See* PROSPECTIVE ET SANTE. 3543

0152-2981 *See* DEMAIN L'AFRIQUE. 2639

0152-3058 *See* CUNICULTURE (PARIS). 210

0152-5425 *See* PETROLE ET TECHNIQUES. 4272

0152-593X *See* CAHIERS SPINOZA. 4343

0152-6189 *See* TOTAL INFORMATION. 4280

0152-6790 *See* FRANCE FRUITS ET LEGUMES. 172

0152-7401 *See* REVUE FRANCAISE D'ADMINISTRATION PUBLIQUE. 4684

0152-8505 *See* LECTURE JEUNESSE. 1066

0152-9668 *See* ANNALES DES PONTS ET CHAUSSEES. 2018

0153-0216 *See* FORET PRIVEE (1977), LA. 2382

0153-0313 *See* LENGAS. 3297

0153-0747 *See* TELE 7 JOURS. 1164

0153-1069 *See* EQUIPE. PARIS, L'. 4894

0153-114X *See* MAGHREB-DEVELOPPEMENT. 1638

0153-1700 *See* ETUDES CANADIENNES. 2732

0153-2448 *See* ACTUALITE DE LA FORMATION PERMANENTE. REPERTOIRE D'ADRESSES UTILES. 1807

0153-288X *See* BULLETIN INTERNATIONAL D'INFORMATIONS. 4295

0153-3320 *See* CAHIERS DE LINGUISTIQUE. ASIE ORIENTALE. 3271

0153-3401 *See* AL-MUSTAQBAL. 2525

0153-3762 *See* NHAN BAN. 5801

0153-3851 *See* BULLETIN DE LA CATHEDRALE DE STRASBOURG. 294

0153-4092 *See* POUR LA SCIENCE. 5139

0153-419X *See* MONDE. DOSSIERS ET DOCUMENTS, LE. 2519

0153-4459 *See* ECONOMIE DU CENTRE-EST, L'. 1558

0153-4661 *See* ESCRIME. 4894

0153-4742 *See* LETTRE MEDICALE, LA. 3604

0153-4831 *See* ECHOS PARIS. 1928, LES. 1737

0153-5471 *See* ACIER POUR CONSTRUIRE, L'. 598

0153-5552 *See* CAHIERS - S.E.M.A. 2860

0153-6184 *See* CAHIERS DE L'INSTITUT D'AMENAGEMENT ET D'URBANISME DE LA REGION D'ILE-DE-FRANCE. 2816

0153-6281 *See* BULLETIN TECHNIQUE DE L INSEMINATION ARTIFICIELLE. 5506

0153-7121 *See* ANNALES DES PAYS NIVERNAIS. 2674

0153-789X *See* MONDE. REIMPRESSION EN MINIFORMAT, LE. 5800

0153-8756 *See* ECOLOGIA MEDITERRANEA. 2213

0153-9027 *See* NOUS VOULONS LIRE PESSAC. 3349

0153-9167 *See* MONDE ET LES MINERAUX, LE. 1442

0153-9175 *See* BULLETIN DE LA SOCIETE D'ETUDES SCIENTIFIQUES DE L'AUDE. 5090

0153-9221 *See* ETUDES VAUCLUSIENNES. 2846

0153-9329 *See* CONFRONTATIONS PSYCHIATRIQUES PARIS. 3923

0153-9337 *See* ARCHEOLOGIE MEDIEVALE. 259

0153-9345 *See* PALEORIENT. 2770

0153-9353 *See* SOCIETE DES AMIS DES ARTS ET SCIENCES DE TOURNUS. 2854

0153-937X *See* BULLETIN DE LA SOCIETE D'ETUDES SCIENTIFIQUES ET ARCHEOLOGIQUES DE DRAGUIGNAN ET DU VAR. 263

0153-9442 *See* ENERPRESSE. 1943

0153-9620 *See* VAGABONDAGES. 3472

0153-9841 *See* ANALYSE FINANCIERE. 770

0153-985X *See* COURRIER DU CNRS, LE. 5097

0154-0262 *See* BIOLOGIE VEGETALE, SCIENCES AGRICOLES. LEXIQUE. 66

0154-0300 *See* PHYSIQUE, CHIMIE. LEXIQUE. 3241

0154-0319 *See* SCIENCES DE LA VIE. LEXIQUE. 5154

0154-0327 *See* CHIMIE PURE ET CHIMIE APPLIQUEE. LEXIQUE. 3201

0154-0335 *See* ENERGIE. LEXIQUE. 3209

0154-0351 *See* SCIENCES DE L'INGENIEUR. LEXIQUE. 5154

0154-036X *See* METALLURGIE. LEXIQUE. 4010

0154-0505 *See* SOCIETE HISTORIQUE ET ARCHEOLOGIQUE DE L'ORNE. 2710

0154-2656 *See* ARCHEOLOGIA CORSA. 258

0154-3229 *See* REVUE D'ECONOMIE INDUSTRIELLE. 1582

0154-473X *See* THERAPIE ET REEDUCATION PSYCHOMOTRICE. 3846

0154-5280 *See* ECHOS DU CENTRE INTERNATIONAL D'ETUDES PEDAGOGIQUES DE SEVRES. 2686

0154-5639 *See* CONFLUENTS. 2614

0154-5752 *See* BAROMETRE PORC. 207

0154-5868 *See* ALMA. 3263

0154-6902 *See* SEMIOTIQUE ET BIBLE. 4996

0154-9049 *See* MONDE DE LA BIBLE, LE. 5018

0155-025X *See* ANNUAL REPORT / ADMINISTRATIVE REVIEW COUNCIL. 2934

0155-0306 *See* SOCIAL ALTERNATIVES. 5258

0155-0438 *See* CORELLA. 5617

0155-0535 *See* BUSHDRIVER. 5408

0155-0543 *See* NEWSLETTER / MUSICOLOGICAL SOCIETY OF AUSTRALIA. 4141

0155-0640 *See* AUSTRALIAN REVIEW OF APPLIED LINGUISTICS. 3267

0155-0802 *See* REPORT / FOREIGN INVESTMENT REVIEW BOARD. 912

0155-1019 *See* GETTING TOGETHER. 1063

0155-1078 *See* RESCENT. 1845

0155-1507 *See* REPORT / CSIRO, DIVISION OF HUMAN NUTRITION. 4198

0155-1531 *See* REPORT - DIRECTOR OF MINES (HOBART). 2149

0155-2112 *See* ANNUAL REPORT / AUSTRALIAN NATIONAL UNIVERSITY RESEARCH SCHOOL OF EARTH SCIENCES. 1351

0155-2147 *See* ENGLISH IN AUSTRALIA. 3279

0155-2171 *See* CONTEMPORARY ISSUES. 1733

0155-218X *See* READING TIME. 3428

0155-2341 *See* EDUCATIONAL ENQUIRY. 1741

0155-2589 *See* INDUSTRIAL ARBITRATION REPORTS, NEW SOUTH WALES, THE. 3149

0155-2643 *See* AUSTRALIAN WATER RESOURCES COUNCIL - TECHNICAL PAPER. 5530

0155-2821 *See* PERSPECTIVES SYDNEY. 1773

0155-2864 *See* AUSTRALIAN BOOK REVIEW. 3337

0155-2996 *See* GRANTEE REPORTS - FULBRIGHT EDUCATIONAL DEVELOPMENT PROGRAM. 1748

0155-3259 *See* SAJER. 1781

0155-3410 *See* QUARTERLY NOTES / GEOLOGICAL SURVEY OF NEW SOUTH WALES. 1392

0155-3437 *See* ANNUAL REPORT - AMDEL. 3998

0155-3453 *See* RESEARCH REPORT - AUSTRALIAN ARMY PSYCHOLOGICAL RESEARCH UNIT. 4615

0155-3720 *See* BROADCAST ENGINEERING NEWS. 1127

0155-400X *See* QUEENSLAND GEOGRAPHICAL JOURNAL. NEW SERIES. 2574

0155-4131 *See* AUSTROBAILEYA. 501

0155-4204 *See* ANNUAL REPORT / LIBRARY COUNCIL OF NEW SOUTH WALES. 3190

0155-4255 *See* NOTES AND MISCELLANY SYDNEY. 1769

0155-4395 *See* PRIMARY SCIENCE BULLETIN CANBERRA. 1902

0155-4611 *See* MODE AUSTRALIA. 1086

ISSN Index

0155-5367 *See* QUARTERLY MAGAZINE / MUSIC TEACHERS' ASSOCIATION OF NEW SOUTH WALES. **4148**

0155-5561 *See* BULLETIN - GEOLOGICAL SURVEY OF NEW SOUTH WALES. **1369**

0155-588X *See* SECONDARY TEACHER. **1905**

0155-6002 *See* CORROSION AUSTRALASIA. **2011**

0155-6290 *See* PARLIAMENTARY DEBATES SYDNEY. **4672**

0155-641X *See* REPORT OF THE NEW SOUTH WALES STATE FISHERIES FOR THE YEAR ENDED **2311**

0155-7084 *See* ANNUAL REPORT / COMMISSIONER FOR MAIN ROADS. **5438**

0155-7742 *See* RESEARCH REPORT - CSIRO DIVISION OF ANIMAL PRODUCTION. **220**

0155-7785 *See* SPECULATIONS IN SCIENCE AND TECHNOLOGY. **5159**

0155-8072 *See* ANNUAL REPORT / THE GREAT BARRIER REEF MARINE PARK AUTHORITY. **2187**

0155-8471 *See* LIBRARY NEWS - LA TRABE UNIVERSITY LIBRARY. **3226**

0155-8722 *See* RECORDER. **1705**

0155-8986 *See* GRANTEE REPORTS - FULBRIGHT UNIVERSITY ADMINISTRATOR PROGRAM. **1748**

0155-9060 *See* PACIFIC RESEARCH MONOGRAPH. **2670**

0155-9362 *See* QUEENSLAND GOVERNMENT INDUSTRIAL GAZETTE, THE. **3153**

0155-9567 *See* NATIONAL DIRECTORY OF INTERNSHIPS, RESIDENCIES & REGISTRARSHIPS, AUSTRALIA. **3619**

0155-9648 *See* TRUCKIN' LIFE. **5398**

0155-9672 *See* RESEARCH PAPER. **2393**

0155-977X *See* SOCIAL ANALYSIS (ADELAIDE, S. AUST.). **5219**

0155-9796 *See* PROCEEDINGS OF THE AUSTRALIAN CERAMIC CONFERENCE. **2593**

0155-9982 *See* ACCOUNTING FORUM (ADELAIDE, S. AUST.). **737**

0156-0069 *See* INNOVATION IN AUSTRALIAN TECHNOLOGY / AUSTRALIAN ACADEMY OF TECHNOLOGICAL SCIENCES. **5114**

0156-0204 *See* ANNUAL REPORT - EARTH RESOURCES FOUNDATION. UNIVERSITY OF SYDNEY. **2186**

0156-0301 *See* AUSTRALIAN JOURNAL OF LANGUAGE AND LITERACY / ARA, THE. **3267**

0156-0417 *See* AUSTRALIAN JOURNAL OF CLINICAL AND EXPERIMENTAL HYPNOSIS. **2857**

0156-0832 *See* OVERLANDER. **4853**

0156-1103 *See* LINKS BRISBANE. **1804**

0156-1316 *See* INDO-PACIFIC PREHISTORIC ASSOCIATION BULLETIN. **270**

0156-1383 *See* BIRD BEHAVIOUR. **5615**

0156-1650 *See* RELIGIOUS TRADITIONS. **4992**

0156-224X *See* CHURCH HERITAGE. **4947**

0156-2452 *See* BULK WHEAT. **68**

0156-2681 *See* AUSTRALIAN MEAT INDUSTRY BULLETIN, THE. **206**

0156-2703 *See* INPHARMA WEEKLY. **4308**

0156-2878 *See* COMMUNITY EDUCATION NEWSLETTER. **1733**

0156-3491 *See* ACORN JOURNAL : OFFICIAL JOURNAL OF THE AUSTRALIAN CONFEDERATION OF OPERATING ROOM NURSES. **3850**

0156-4706 *See* VAT. VICTORIAN ASSOCIATION OF TEACHERS. **1908**

0156-4722 *See* PUBLICATIONS ADVICE. **423**

0156-5044 *See* PARENT. **1771**

0156-5087 *See* BIBLIOGRAPHY - BUREAU OF MINERAL RESOURCES, GEOLOGY AND GEOPHYSICS. **1352**

0156-5184 *See* BULLETIN / AUSTRALIAN MUSIC THERAPY ASSOCIATION. **4105**

0156-5281 *See* SLACAD NEWSLETTER. **3250**

0156-5419 *See* SYDNEY STUDIES IN ENGLISH. **3443**

0156-5788 *See* AUSTRALIAN HEALTH REVIEW. **3777**

0156-5826 *See* JOURNAL OF AUSTRALIAN POLITICAL ECONOMY, THE. **1498**

0156-6245 *See* ENVIRONMENTAL RESEARCH BULLETIN. **2169**

0156-6490 *See* WINESTATE. **2373**

0156-6717 *See* GUIDELINES. **3258**

0156-708X *See* OCCASIONAL PAPER - DEPARTMENT OF EDUCATION, UNIVERSITY OF SYDNEY. **1769**

0156-7268 *See* ENVIRONMENTAL RESEARCH NOTE. **2169**

0156-7365 *See* AUSTRALIAN JOURNAL OF CHINESE AFFAIRS, THE. **2501**

0156-7799 *See* REFLECTIONS. **3530**

0156-8698 *See* GREAT CIRCLE. **4176**

0156-9287 *See* PUBLICATION (UNIVERSITY OF WESTERN AUSTRALIA. DEPT. OF GEOLOGY). **1392**

0156-949X *See* PACE. PROCESS AND CHEMICAL ENGINEERING. **1027**

0156-9600 *See* OPENING. **1770**

0156-9821 *See* AUSTRALIAN BEAUTY THERAPIST. **402**

0157-0641 *See* PRINCIPAL AGRICULTURAL COMMODITIES, TASMANIA / AUSTRALIAN BUREAU OF STATISTICS. **121**

0157-065X *See* NUMBER OF RURAL ESTABLISHMENTS, IRRIGATION AND FERTILISER USAGE, TASMANIA / AUSTRALIAN BUREAU OF STATISTICS. **116**

0157-1338 *See* GEO (DEE WHY WEST, A.C.T.). **2561**

0157-1532 *See* AUSTRALIAN JOURNAL OF AUDIOLOGY, THE. **3886**

0157-1672 *See* SURVEYING AUSTRALIA. **2032**

0157-1729 *See* GUNS AUSTRALIA. **4897**

0157-1826 *See* HERDSA NEWS. **1828**

0157-2067 *See* COMPENDIUM OF LOCAL GOVERNMENT AREA STATISTICS / AUSTRALIAN BUREAU OF STATISTICS, TASMANIAN OFFICE. **4697**

0157-2156 *See* CENSUS OF MANUFACTURING ESTABLISHMENTS. DETAILS OF OPERATIONS AND SMALL AREA STATISTICS, TASMANIA / [AUSTRALIAN BUREAU OF STATISTICS, TASMANIA]. **3489**

0157-2229 *See* NEWSLETTER - LIBRARY ASSOCIATION OF AUSTRALIA. NORTHERN TERRITORY BRANCH. **3235**

0157-244X *See* RESEARCH IN SCIENCE EDUCATION. **1779**

0157-2547 *See* CANCER IN NEW SOUTH WALES : INCIDENCE AND MORTALITY. **3811**

0157-3039 *See* AUSTRALIAN CANEGROWER. **63**

0157-308X *See* BULLETIN OF THE AUSTRALIAN LITTORAL SOCIETY. **2189**

0157-3314 *See* UNIVERSITY OF ADELAIDE LIBRARY NEWS. **3254**

0157-3357 *See* PRACTISING ADMINISTRATOR, THE. **1868**

0157-3470 *See* RELEASE. **3174**

0157-3705 *See* REVIEWS JOURNAL. **3351**

0157-3950 *See* GOING DOWN SWINGING. **3391**

0157-4043 *See* ARLIS/ANZ NEWS. **408**

0157-4094 *See* FACTS AND FIGURES. AUSTRALIAN DENTISTRY. **1323**

0157-4388 *See* TAFE VIEW. **1786**

0157-4566 *See* AUSTRALIAN COAL REPORT. **1933**

0157-4701 *See* WORKING PAPERS - CENTRE FOR APPLIED ECONOMIC RESEARCH. UNIVERSITY OF NEW SOUTH WALES. **1527**

0157-471X *See* MONASH NINETEENTH-CENTURY DRAMA SERIES. **5366**

0157-5295 *See* FUN RUNNER. **4895**

0157-5317 *See* JUSTINIAN. **2992**

0157-5503 *See* MONOGRAPH SERIES (AUSTRALIA. DEPT. OF HEALTH. POLICY AND PLANNING DIVISION). **4791**

0157-5856 *See* REPORT FOR YEAR ENDED 30TH JUNE ... / VICTORIAN DAIRY INDUSTRY AUTHORITY. **198**

0157-6011 *See* JUSTICE TRENDS. **4510**

0157-6038 *See* JOURNAL OF TERTIARY EDUCATIONAL ADMINISTRATION. **1758**

0157-6283 *See* ACLALS BULLETIN. **3357**

0157-6321 *See* AUSTRALIAN JOURNAL OF SOCIAL ISSUES, THE. **5274**

0157-6429 *See* AUSTRALIAN MARINE SCIENCE BULLETIN. **553**

0157-6461 *See* NON-DESTRUCTIVE TESTING - AUSTRALIA. **1989**

0157-6488 *See* SCIOS. **5156**

0157-6542 *See* AUSTRALIAN SPORTS DIRECTORY. **4885**

0157-6895 *See* ARCHIVES AND MANUSCRIPTS. **2479**

0157-7271 *See* REACTIONS. **3632**

0157-728X *See* AUSTRALIAN OIL & GAS DIRECTORY. **4251**

0157-7344 *See* TRANSITION. **310**

0157-745X *See* RESEARCH AND DEVELOPMENT MONOGRAPH - UNIVERSITY OF NEW SOUTH WALES, CENTRE FOR MEDICAL EDUCATION, RESEARCH AND DEVELOPMENT. **3634**

0157-759X *See* VINCULUM. **3540**

0157-7662 *See* NEW ZEALAND BOOKS IN PRINT / NEW ZEALAND BOOK PUBLISHERS ASSOCIATION. **4822**

0157-7832 *See* STRINGYBARK & GREENHIDE. **4155**

0157-8243 *See* AGNOTE. **2293**

0157-8944 *See* GOULCAE JOURNAL OF EDUCATION. **1748**

0157-8952 *See* LAW SOCIETY BULLETIN. **2997**

0157-9347 *See* REVIEW PAPER - UNIVERSITY OF NEW SOUTH WALES, CENTRE FOR MEDICAL EDUCATION RESEARCH AND DEVELOPMENT. **3634**

0157-9509 *See* ETHICAL TABLET & CAPSULE HANDBOOK. **4303**

0157-9711 *See* TM. TROPICAL AGRONOMY TECHNICAL MEMORANDUM. **529**

0157-9762 *See* CHEMICAL ENGINEERING IN AUSTRALIA : CEA. **2010**

0158-037X *See* STUDIES IN CONTINUING EDUCATION. **1802**

0158-040X *See* ANNUAL REPORT - DEPARTMENT OF TRADE & RESOURCES. **822**

0158-071X *See* ARRB RESEARCH REPORT ARR. **5377**

0158-0760 *See* GENERAL AND APPLIED ENTOMOLOGY. **5609**

0158-0876 *See* INCITE (SYDNEY). **3214**

0158-099X *See* LOWDOWN 1982. **386**

0158-149X *See* AUSTRALIAN HISTORICAL GEOGRAPHY : A BULLETIN OF THE REFERENCE SECTION OF AUSTRALIA 1788-1988 : A BICENTENNIAL HISTORY. **2555**

0158-1570 *See* ANNALS OF THE ROYAL AUSTRALASIAN COLLEGE OF DENTAL SURGEONS. **1316**

0158-1589 *See* VICTORIAN GOVERNMENT DIRECTORY. **4693**

0158-1953 *See* SEARMG NEWSLETTER. **2854**

0158-1996 *See* STATE REPORTS, WESTERN AUSTRALIA. **4688**

0158-2631 *See* BULLETIN - STUDENT COUNSELLING AND RESEARCH UNIT, UNIVERSITY OF NEW SOUTH WALES. **4201**

0158-2658 *See* AUSTRALIAN CAMERA CRAFT MAGAZINE. **4367**

0158-2755 *See* TECHNOTE DARWIN. **5164**

0158-2763 *See* TECHNICAL BULLETIN / NORTHERN TERRITORY, DEPARTMENT OF PRIMARY PRODUCTION. **140**

0158-2836 *See* YOUR MONEY WEEKLY. **817**

0158-3026 *See* LITERACY LINK. **1881**

0158-3921 *See* VICTORIAN FICTION RESEARCH GUIDES. **3450**

0158-3999 *See* AUSTRALIAN STANDARD. **64**

0158-4030 *See* ANNUAL REPORT - SUPERVISING SCIENTIST FOR THE ALLIGATOR RIVERS REGION. **5084**

0158-4154 *See* CANTRILL'S FILMNOTES. **4065**

0158-4197 *See* EMU. **5617**

0158-4960 See AUSTRALIAN JOURNAL OF MEDICAL SCIENCE. 3554
0158-4995 See CONNECT. BRUNSWICK. 1733
0158-5088 See REPORT - URANIUM ADVISORY COUNCIL. 4017
0158-5231 See BIOCHEMISTRY INTERNATIONAL. 482
0158-5312 See NEWSLETTER OF THE AUSTRALIAN ASSOCIATION FOR MARITIME HISTORY. 4181
0158-5428 See TECHNICAL EDUCATION, VICTORIA. 1916
0158-5460 See LINK-UP. 3228
0158-572X See FISHING WORLD SYDNEY. 4872
0158-6270 See NATIONAL OUTLOOK SYDNEY. 5252
0158-6335 See MAJOR MANUFACTURING AND MINING INVESTMENT PROJECTS. 3483
0158-6912 See JOURNAL OF THE HOME ECONOMICS ASSOCIATION OF AUSTRALIA. 2791
0158-7048 See CRAFT VICTORIA. 371
0158-7102 See REGIONAL JOURNAL OF SOCIAL ISSUES. 5255
0158-720X See GEOLOGICAL EXCURSION HANDBOOK. 1377
0158-7366 See ORAL HISTORY ASSOCIATION OF AUSTRALIA JOURNAL. 2670
0158-7404 See ANNUAL REPORT / INSTITUTE OF BIOLOGICAL RESOURCES. 2186
0158-7439 See ANNUAL REPORT (INSTITUTE OF PHYSICAL SCIENCES (COMMONWEALTH SCIENTIFIC AND INDUSTRIAL RESEARCH ORGANIZATION)). 4397
0158-7447 See AUSTRALIAN ADMINISTRATOR. 1860
0158-7765 See ZINC TODAY. 2153
0158-7919 See DISTANCE EDUCATION. 1736
0158-8273 See MONOGRAPH SERIES (JAMES COOK UNIVERSITY OF NORTH QUEENSLAND. DEPARTMENT OF GEOGRAPHY). 2569
0158-9431 See MULTICULTURAL LIBRARIES NEWSLETTER. 3232
0158-9571 See MUSE. ARTS AND ENTERTAINMENT IN CANBERRA. 359
0158-9938 See AUSTRALASIAN PHYSICAL & ENGINEERING SCIENCES IN MEDICINE. 3685
0159-0030 See AUSTRALIAN HI-FI. 4367
0159-0340 See GUIDING IN AUSTRALIA. 1064
0159-0677 See TASMANIAN ANCESTRY. 2474
0159-1193 See PRACTISING MANAGER. 882
0159-1290 See AUSTRALIAN COTTON GROWER. 164
0159-1878 See WHO'S DRILLING. 4282
0159-2033 See LAB TALK. 5125
0159-2068 See TRANSACTIONS OF THE INSTITUTION OF ENGINEERS, AUSTRALIA. CIVIL ENGINEERING. 2033
0159-2483 See LEGAL REPORTER, THE. 3000
0159-3285 See VICTORIAN BAR NEWS. 3071
0159-3935 See PROCESS ENGINEERING. 1992
0159-6071 See GENETIC RESOURCES COMMUNICATION. 173
0159-625X See INTERVIEW. 1754
0159-6306 See DISCOURSE. 1736
0159-6322 See AUSTRALIAN GEM & TREASURE HUNTER. 4869
0159-6365 See AUSTRALIAN AQUACULTURE. 2297
0159-656X See INTERNATIONAL CAMELLIA JOURNAL. 2420
0159-6586 See BOGONG. 2188
0159-7191 See MOROCCO BOUND. 4830
0159-7302 See NETWORK (MELBOURNE (VIC.). 5433
0159-7868 See CURRICULUM PERSPECTIVES. 1892
0159-8090 See CLINICAL BIOCHEMIST REVIEWS. 485
0159-818X See NOMEN NUDUM. 1390
0159-8376 See NEWSLETTER - AUSTRALIAN AND NEW ZEALAND SOCIETY OF NUCLEAR MEDICINE. 3848

0159-8430 See PUBLICATION - ENVIRONMENT PROTECTION AUTHORITY OF VICTORIA. 2180
0159-8910 See AUSTRALIAN JOURNAL OF GEODESY, PHOTOGRAMMETRY, AND SURVEYING. 2018
0159-9100 See MIMS HOSPITAL EQUIPMENT AND SUPPLIES. 3789
0159-9135 See INTERACTA. 1896
0159-9321 See POCKET YEAR BOOK OF NEW SOUTH WALES, AUSTRALIA, THE. 1928
0160-0028 See DRUG ABUSE & ALCOHOLISM NEWSLETTER. 1343
0160-0087 See EXPANSION ARTS. 320
0160-0095 See NORTH DAKOTA STATE PLAN FOR LIBRARY DEVELOPMENT. 3237
0160-0109 See CAPITAL IMPROVEMENTS PROGRAM STATUS REPORT, FINANCIAL SUMMARY. 894
0160-0141 See IEEE POWER ENGINEERING SOCIETY DISCUSSIONS AND CLOSURES OF ABSTRACTED PAPERS FROM THE SUMMER MEETING. 2060
0160-0168 See BIBLION (NEW YORK, N.Y.). 2843
0160-0176 See INTERNATIONAL REGIONAL SCIENCE REVIEW. 1497
0160-0184 See PEDIATRIC ALERT. 3908
0160-0192 See TOLUENE XYLENES ANNUAL. 1030
0160-0206 See PROCEEDINGS OF THE MINERAL WASTE UTILIZATION SYMPOSIUM. 1444
0160-0273 See DIRECTORY OF TENNESSEE COUNTY OFFICIALS. 4644
0160-0281 See AMERICAN JOURNAL OF TRIAL ADVOCACY, THE. 2932
0160-0362 See PROFESSIONAL MARKETING REPORT. 935
0160-0370 See MARKETING FLORIDA AVOCADOS, LIMES, MANGOS. 2349
0160-0400 See SSI. 1272
0160-0451 See ANNUAL PLANNING REPORT : SAN FRANCISCO-OAKLAND STANDARD METROPOLITAN STATISTICAL AREA, BALANCE OF ALAMEDA COUNTY, ALAMEDA COUNTY EXCEPT CITIES OF OAKLAND AND BERKELEY. 1648
0160-0494 See ANNUAL PLANNING REPORT : VALLEJO-FAIRFIELD-NAPA STANDARD METROPOLITAN STATISTICAL AREA, NAPA COUNTY. 1648
0160-0559 See INTERNATIONAL SERIES ON SPORT SCIENCES. 3954
0160-0583 See NEW YORK TIMES THEATER REVIEWS, THE. 5366
0160-0656 See INDEX OF LEGISLATION. 2981
0160-0664 See COLLECTIONS (BUFFALO). 4165
0160-0680 See SULPHUR IN AGRICULTURE. 188
0160-0699 See UMBRELLA (GLENDALE). 367
0160-0745 See ANNUAL PLANNING INFORMATION: SAN FRANCISCO-OAKLAND STANDARD METROPOLITAN STATISTICAL AREA, CITY OF BERKELEY. 1647
0160-0761 See ANNUAL PLANNING INFORMATION : SAN FRANCISCO-OAKLAND STANDARD METROPOLITAN STATISTICAL AREA, CITY OF RICHMOND. 1647
0160-0818 See REVENEWS. 4746
0160-0826 See GEOLOGICAL SURVEY GUIDEBOOK. 1378
0160-0842 See DISTRIBUTORS OF ELECTRONIC PARTS. 2042
0160-0850 See FIDDLE & A BOW. 4117
0160-0869 See YEAR END REPORT - KANSAS ECONOMIC OPPORTUNITY OFFICE. 1528
0160-0885 See CURRICULUM PLANS. 5059
0160-0907 See FRENCH SETTLEMENT HISTORICAL REGISTER, THE. 2734
0160-0915 See DIGEST OF ENACTMENTS, GENERAL ASSEMBLY. 2961
0160-0923 See HELIOS (LUBBOCK). 1077
0160-0958 See JOURNAL OF THE FLUORESCENT MINERAL SOCIETY. 1440
0160-0966 See SEPM SHORT COURSE NOTES. 4230

0160-1032 See REPORT / CENTER FOR SOCIAL ORGANIZATION OF SCHOOLS, THE JOHNS HOPKINS UNIVERSITY. 1778
0160-1040 See IA, THE JOURNAL OF THE SOCIETY FOR INDUSTRIAL ARCHEOLOGY. 269
0160-1067 See SOCIETY FOR INDUSTRIAL ARCHEOLOGY NEWSLETTER. 282
0160-1075 See NEW DIRECTIONS FOR WOMEN. 5562
0160-1091 See REVIEW OF CURRENT RESEARCH. 3175
0160-1121 See WESTERN BIRDS. 5620
0160-1148 See ELECTRONOTES. 4116
0160-1156 See PROCEEDINGS OF THE ANNUAL MEETING, WESTERN WASHINGTON HORTICULTURAL ASSOCIATION. 2429
0160-1199 See ILLINOIS REPORTS. 2980
0160-1245 See LEGISLATIVE APPROPRIATIONS REPORT. 3001
0160-1253 See SCHIESSPORTSCHULE DIALOGUES. 4916
0160-1261 See RAILROAD ACCIDENT INVESTIGATION REPORTS. 5435
0160-1296 See EDUCATORS GUIDE TO FREE VIDEOTAPES. 1743
0160-130X See BANK EXPANSION QUARTERLY. 774
0160-1318 See GUIDE MOTOR CLUB'S ANNUAL EMERGENCY ROAD SERVICE GUIDE. 5415
0160-1326 See LAWS RELATING TO THE PRACTICE OF OPTOMETRY, WITH RULES AND REGULATIONS. 2997
0160-1334 See MULTISTATE BAR REVIEW SERIES. 3012
0160-1377 See DIGEST OF BILLS ENACTED BY THE GENERAL ASSEMBLY. 2961
0160-1415 See ANNUAL REPORT OF THE MISSISSIPPI DEPARTMENT OF ARCHIVES AND HISTORY. 2479
0160-1520 See ANNUAL REPORT - OFFICE OF THE SECRETARY OF STATE. 4629
0160-1555 See ANNUAL SECURITIES SEMINAR COURSE HANDBOOK. 2935
0160-1598 See CLEVELAND BAR JOURNAL (1968). 2951
0160-161X See ANNUAL REPORT, STATE OF ILLINOIS ALCOHOLISM PLANS AND PROGRAMS. 1341
0160-1636 See ADVANCED EXERCISES IN DIAGNOSTIC RADIOLOGY. 3938
0160-1644 See MOTOR EARLY MODEL CRASH ESTIMATING GUIDE. 5419
0160-1652 See COMMUNICATING NURSING RESEARCH. 3854
0160-1660 See CUMITECH. 561
0160-1792 See ARISE. 1875
0160-1806 See MOPED BIKING. 4081
0160-1830 See SPORTS AFIELD DEER. 4879
0160-1857 See LEFT CURVE. 4480
0160-1873 See ABSTRACTS OF THE ANNUAL MEETING - AMERICAN ANTHROPOLOGICAL ASSOCIATION. 227
0160-189X See TEACHER EDUCATION CENTERS IN WEST VIRGINIA. 1906
0160-1970 See STATISTICAL PROFILE - IOWA DEPARTMENT OF TRANSPORTATION. 5402
0160-2047 See LOG (BROOKLYN). 1688
0160-2063 See NEW INDUSTRIES AND PLANT EXPANSIONS REPORTED IN WISCONSIN. 1619
0160-2071 See MICROPALEONTOLOGY SPECIAL PUBLICATION. 4228
0160-2098 See JOURNAL OF JUVENILE LAW. 3121
0160-2101 See PROPOSED CONNECTICUT STATE PLAN ON AGING. 5302
0160-211X See NEBRASKA ANNUAL HOUSING REPORT. 2829
0160-2136 See NATIONAL CONFERENCE ON RADIATION CONTROL. 4438
0160-2144 See GREAT RIVER REVIEW. 3392
0160-2225 See CONSUMER COMPLAINT GUIDE. 1294

0160-2284 See PRIMARY FOREST INDUSTRY OF WEST VIRGINIA, THE. 2391
0160-2330 See NEW MEXICO FOLKLORE RECORD, THE. 2323
0160-2365 See NEWSLETTER - AMERICAN MUSICAL INSTRUMENT SOCIETY. 4140
0160-2373 See GLEANINGS (CAMBRIDGE). 4960
0160-239X See GREAT BASIN NATURALIST MEMOIRS. 4166
0160-242X See COMPREHENSIVE ENDOCRINOLOGY. 3727
0160-2446 See JOURNAL OF CARDIOVASCULAR PHARMACOLOGY. 4310
0160-2489 See SEMINARS IN NEUROLOGICAL SURGERY. 3974
0160-2497 See COMPUTER PERSONNEL. 1279
0160-2519 See PUBLICATIONS OF THE LEANDER MCCORMICK OBSERVATORY OF THE UNIVERSITY OF VIRGINIA. 399
0160-2527 See INTERNATIONAL JOURNAL OF LAW AND PSYCHIATRY. 2984
0160-2543 See CYNEGETICUS. 4892
0160-256X See AWIS MAGAZINE. 5087
0160-2578 See AMERICAN BENCH, THE. 3138
0160-2586 See NATIONAL DIRECTORY OF PROGRESSIVE AND RANK & FILE LABOR LAWYERS. 3152
0160-2594 See OFFICERS OF PENNSYLVANIA AGRICULTURAL ORGANIZATIONS. 116
0160-2667 See VERDI NEWSLETTER. 4158
0160-2721 See AGING (NEW YORK, N.Y.). 3749
0160-273X See MARINE SCIENCE (PLENUM). 1452
0160-2764 See MESTER (LOS ANGELES). 3411
0160-2829 See GUIDEBOOK - WYOMING GEOLOGICAL ASSOCIATION. 1382
0160-2896 See INTELLIGENCE (NORWOOD). 4590
0160-290X See CHILD ADVOCACY PROGRAMS. 3901
0160-2934 See CHARACTERISTICS OF MAJOR COLLECTIVE BARGAINING AGREEMENTS. 1659
0160-2950 See PROCEEDINGS OF THE ANNUAL NORTHEASTERN FOREST INSECT WORK CONFERENCE. 2239
0160-2985 See MAJOR PROGRAMS, BUREAU OF LABOR STATISTICS. 1536
0160-3019 See AIRSTREAM SERVICE MANUAL. 5403
0160-3051 See GEOLOGICAL SURVEY BULLETIN (BLOOMINGTON, IND.). 1378
0160-306X See SCIENCE SCOPE (WASHINGTON, D.C.). 5153
0160-3086 See RESEARCH SERIES (UNIVERSITY OF OKLAHOMA. ARCHAEOLOGICAL RESEARCH AND MANAGEMENT CENTER). 280
0160-3094 See RESOURCE ATLAS - UNIVERSITY OF NEBRASKA, CONSERVATION AND SURVEY DIVISION. 2574
0160-3124 See PUBLICATIONS OF THE ARKANSAS PHILOLOGICAL ASSOCIATION. 3312
0160-3159 See PROCEEDINGS - NEW ENGLAND-ST. LAWRENCE VALLEY GEOGRAPHICAL SOCIETY. 2573
0160-3167 See ECONOMIC DEVELOPMENT PROJECTS IN THE ARAB WORLD AND IRAN. 1557
0160-3183 See TOPICS IN BIOELECTROCHEMISTRY AND BIOENERGETICS. 493
0160-323X See STATE & LOCAL GOVERNMENT REVIEW. 4687
0160-3299 See WOODSTOVE FIREPLACE AND EQUIPMENT DIRECTORY. 2812
0160-3302 See ILLINOIS MANUFACTURERS DIRECTORY. 3480
0160-3337 See ANNUAL REPORT - STATE COMPENSATION FUND (ARIZONA). 1650
0160-3345 See ALASKA ECONOMIC TRENDS. 1461
0160-337X See ENHANCED OIL-RECOVERY FIELD REPORTS. 4255
0160-3450 See AMERICAN PHARMACY. 4290

0160-3477 See JOURNAL OF POST KEYNESIAN ECONOMICS. 1593
0160-354X See MICHIGAN PAPERS ON SOUTH AND SOUTHEAST ASIA. 2658
0160-3582 See KIT - ASSOCIATION OF RESEARCH LIBRARIES. SYSTEMS AND PROCEDURES EXCHANGE CENTER. 3221
0160-3604 See ENERGY RESEARCH ABSTRACTS. 1962
0160-3612 See BELTSVILLE SYMPOSIA IN AGRICULTURAL RESEARCH. 65
0160-3647 See CIRCULAR - ENGINEERING EXPERIMENT STATION, OREGON STATE UNIVERSITY. 1968
0160-3655 See PUBLIC INFORMATION CIRCULAR - GEOLOGICAL SURVEY OF WYOMING. 1392
0160-3663 See PROCEEDINGS - OFFSHORE TECHNOLOGY CONFERENCE. 2095
0160-3701 See PERINATAL CARE. 3766
0160-3728 See WHO'S WHO IN RELIGION. 5009
0160-3736 See NEWORLD. 326
0160-3779 See MINERAL ECONOMICS ABSTRACTS. 2144
0160-3787 See ISOZYMES. 488
0160-3825 See STUDENT PRESS LAW CENTER REPORT. 3060
0160-3906 See FODOR'S CANADA. 5471
0160-3914 See FODOR'S CRUISES AND PORTS OF CALL. 5471
0160-3922 See NUTRITIONAL PERSPECTIVES. 4197
0160-3949 See DELTA PI EPSILON RAPID READER. 1735
0160-3957 See DELTA PI EPSILON SERVICE BULLETIN. 1735
0160-3965 See GREEN THUMB (OAKLAND). 2417
0160-404X See DIRECTORY OF SECURITY ANALYST SOCIETIES, ANALYST SPLINTER GROUPS, STOCKBROKER CLUBS. 896
0160-4120 See ENVIRONMENT INTERNATIONAL. 2165
0160-4163 See PROCEEDINGS OF THE SEMINAR OF THE CONFERENCE OF INSURANCE LEGISLATORS. 2890
0160-418X See THOROUGHBREDS. 2803
0160-4198 See JOURNAL OF HEALTH AND HUMAN RESOURCES ADMINISTRATION. 5292
0160-4201 See VOICE OF YOUTH ADVOCATES. 3451
0160-4228 See NEWSLETTER - PENNSYLVANIA ACADEMY OF SCIENCE. 5133
0160-4236 See ATLAS SERIES - GEOLOGICAL SURVEY OF ALABAMA. 1366
0160-4279 See KINDERGARTEN CLASS PACKET, THE. 1760
0160-4287 See YOUNGER ELEMENTARY CLASS PACKET, THE. 1792
0160-4309 See EXCEPTIONAL CHILD EDUCATION RESOURCES. 1795
0160-4317 See FRESHWATER AND MARINE AQUARIUM. 2304
0160-4333 See PRAEGER SPECIAL STUDIES IN INTERNATIONAL BUSINESS, FINANCE, AND TRADE. 704
0160-4341 See HUMBOLDT JOURNAL OF SOCIAL RELATIONS. 5202
0160-435X See EQUAL EMPLOYMENT COMPLIANCE UPDATE. 3147
0160-4422 See PERSPECTIVES IN LAW & PSYCHOLOGY. 3029
0160-4430 See SELF-IN-PROCESS SERIES. 4618
0160-4457 See PLATT'S OIL PRICE HANDBOOK AND OILMANAC. 4274
0160-449X See LABOR STUDIES JOURNAL. 1685
0160-4562 See MISSOURI AIRPORT DIRECTORY. 28
0160-4570 See MOTOR CARRIER ANNUAL REPORTS. 5387
0160-4589 See OUTER-ISLAND PRICES OF WHOLESALE FRESH FRUITS AND VEGETABLES. 180
0160-4619 See EXTENDED ABSTRACTS - ELECTROCHEMICAL SOCIETY. 1034

0160-4643 See VIRGINIA DIVISION OF MINERAL RESOURCES PUBLICATION. 1445
0160-4694 See BOMBAY GIN. 3368
0160-4708 See CANADIAN TAX AND TRADE BRIEFS. 4716
0160-4716 See CHATTANOOGA AND TRI-STATE AREA DIRECTORY OF MANUFACTURERS. 3476
0160-4724 See CHIEF EXECUTIVE (NEW YORK, N.Y. 1977). 863
0160-4732 See CORPORATE AND PERSONAL TAXATION IN THE ARAB WORLD. 3098
0160-4740 See FISH AND WILDLIFE REFERENCE SERVICE NEWSLETTER. 4872
0160-4783 See SENIOR LIFE. 5181
0160-4856 See DIRECTORY OF PUBLIC HOUSING AGENCIES. 2821
0160-4872 See WEEKLY INSIDERS POULTRY REPORT. 157
0160-4880 See FICTION CATALOG. 416
0160-4899 See STANDARD & POOR'S STOCK REPORTS: NEW YORK STOCK EXCHANGE. 915
0160-4910 See WEEKLY INSIDERS TURKEY LETTER. 157
0160-4929 See POLITICS TODAY (SANTA BARBARA). 4491
0160-4937 See BULLETIN OF THE SOUTHERN CALIFORNIA PALEONTOLOGICAL SOCIETY. 4226
0160-4953 See COLLECTION BUILDING. 3202
0160-4961 See HEALTH SERVICES ADMINISTRATION EDUCATION. 4781
0160-502X See CALTECH. 5092
0160-5070 See KENTUCKY WARBLER, THE. 5618
0160-5119 See NEWSLETTER - FLORIDA FRIENDS OF BLUEGRASS SOCIETY. 4141
0160-5143 See FOREST INSECT AND DISEASE CONDITIONS IN THE UNITED STATES. 2380
0160-5151 See MINERAL COMMODITY SUMMARIES. 2006
0160-516X See SALARIES AND RELATED MATTERS IN THE SERVICE DEPARTMENT. 1709
0160-5216 See POWER ENGINEERING (NEW YORK). 2124
0160-5232 See WILLIAM AND MARY BUSINESS REVIEW. 723
0160-5240 See WORK RELEASE FOR MISDEMEANANTS IN MINNESOTA. 3179
0160-5267 See OFFICIAL DIRECTORY - VIRGINIA BANKERS ASSOCIATION. 802
0160-5283 See AUDIT REPORT, STATE OF NEVADA DEPARTMENT OF COMMERCE, BANKING AND SAVINGS AND LOAN DIVISIONS. 773
0160-5291 See AUDIT REPORT, STATE OF NEVADA DEPARTMENT OF COMMERCE, STATE FIRE MARSHAL DIVISION. 2288
0160-5313 See CONTRIBUTIONS IN BIOLOGY AND GEOLOGY. 452
0160-5321 See AUDIT REPORT, STATE OF NEVADA DEPARTMENT OF COMMERCE, DIRECTOR'S OFFICE. 823
0160-533X See AUDIT REPORT, STATE OF NEVADA, DEPARTMENT OF COMMERCE, REAL ESTATE EDUCATION RESEARCH AND RECOVERY FUND. 4631
0160-5348 See AUDIT REPORT, STATE OF NEVADA, DEPARTMENT OF COMMERCE, REAL ESTATE DIVISION. 4631
0160-5356 See AUDIT REPORT, STATE OF NEVADA, CLARK COUNTY TAXICAB AUTHORITY. 4631
0160-5380 See AUDIT REPORT, STATE OF NEVADA, DEPARTMENT OF COMMERCE, HOUSING DIVISION. 4631
0160-5402 See JOURNAL OF PHARMACOLOGICAL AND TOXICOLOGICAL METHODS. 4312
0160-5429 See INTERNATIONAL EDUCATION. 1753
0160-5518 See PROCEEDINGS OF THE ANNUAL MISSOURI RIVER BASIN GOVERNORS' CONFERENCE. 5537

ISSN Index

0160-5526 *See* PORT OF DETROIT WORLD HANDBOOK. 5454

0160-5550 *See* PEOPLE'S FOLK DANCE DIRECTORY. 1314

0160-5585 *See* SCHOOL PSYCHOLOGIST, THE. 4618

0160-5607 *See* CONSTRUCTION NEWS (LITTLE ROCK). 610

0160-5623 *See* OUTLINE OF PTO PATENT INTERFERENCE PRACTICE. 1307

0160-564X *See* ARTIFICIAL ORGANS. 3960

0160-5658 *See* ANNUAL SURVEY OF COLORADO LAW. 2935

0160-5674 *See* ATALA. 5605

0160-5682 *See* JOURNAL OF THE OPERATIONAL RESEARCH SOCIETY, THE. 3515

0160-5720 *See* MLA NEWSLETTER (NEW YORK). 3303

0160-5739 *See* FLORIDA RETIREMENT LIVING. 5179

0160-5747 *See* BASKETBALL FORECAST. 4887

0160-5755 *See* AUDIT REPORT, STATE OF NEVADA DEPARTMENT OF GENERAL SERVICES, PURCHASING DIVISION, DONATED COMMODITIES REVOLVING FUND. 4712

0160-5771 *See* YOUNG WRESTLER, THE. 4931

0160-581X *See* SCIENTIFIC PUBLICATIONS AND PRESENTATIONS RELATING TO PLANETARY QUARANTINE. 41

0160-5836 *See* DEFENSE & FOREIGN AFFAIRS HANDBOOK. 4041

0160-5860 *See* LOAN GROWTH CREDIT RISK REVIEW. 796

0160-5941 *See* COAL (DENVER). 2137

0160-595X *See* MONTANA HUMAN SERVICES DIRECTORY. 5297

0160-5968 *See* SELECTED TRADE AND ECONOMIC DATA OF THE CENTRALLY PLANNED ECONOMIES. 851

0160-5976 *See* HUMANITY & SOCIETY. 5247

0160-5992 *See* IN THESE TIMES. 5203

0160-6034 *See* ARTIFACTS (DAYTON). 2721

0160-6077 *See* DIRECTORY OF LIBRARY REPROGRAPHIC SERVICES. 3207

0160-614X *See* MADE IN USA. 844

0160-6166 *See* CLUB LIVING. 4890

0160-6271 *See* SCHOOL FOOD SERVICE JOURNAL. 2356

0160-628X *See* BLAKE. 316

0160-6298 *See* GORDON'S PRINT PRICE ANNUAL. 378

0160-6336 *See* KNITOVATIONS. 5353

0160-6344 *See* ATLAS OF TUMOR PATHOLOGY. 3809

0160-6352 *See* PASSENGER TRAIN JOURNAL. 5433

0160-6360 *See* CHEMICAL NEW PRODUCT DIRECTORY, THE. 1022

0160-6379 *See* FAMILY & COMMUNITY HEALTH. 4775

0160-6395 *See* NAEA NEWS. 359

0160-6409 *See* SYSTEMS, MAN, AND CYBERNETICS REVIEW. 1252

0160-6425 *See* DIMENSIONS (LITTLE ROCK, ARK. 1973). 1892

0160-6425 *See* DIMENSIONS OF EARLY CHILDHOOD. 1803

0160-6433 *See* TIMBER HARVESTING. 2405

0160-6441 *See* AUTOMATION SURVEY. 773

0160-6468 *See* DIRECTORY OF MEDICAL SCHOOLS WORLDWIDE. 1821

0160-6492 *See* FOREST PEST CONDITIONS IN THE NORTHEAST. 2380

0160-6565 *See* GUEST AUTHOR. 3392

0160-659X *See* COMMON LAW LAWYER, THE. 2953

0160-6654 *See* DEVOTIONAL SPEECHES OF THE YEAR. 5059

0160-6662 *See* INDIVIDUAL ONSITE WASTEWATER SYSTEMS. 2232

0160-6689 *See* JOURNAL OF CLINICAL PSYCHIATRY, THE. 3928

0160-6697 *See* DRUG FATE AND METABOLISM. 4300

0160-6727 *See* CONTEMPORARY TOPICS IN POLYMER SCIENCE. 1041

0160-6751 *See* PROCEEDINGS AND PAPERS OF THE ANNUAL CONFERENCE OF THE CALIFORNIA MOSQUITO AND VECTOR CONTROL ASSOCIATION. 2239

0160-676X *See* U.S. FACILITIES AND PROGRAMS FOR CHILDREN WITH SEVERE MENTAL ILLNESSES : DIRECTORY. 3912

0160-6778 *See* SECONDARY EDUCATION TODAY. 1783

0160-6786 *See* AMC. AMERICAN MARITIME CASES. 3180

0160-6794 *See* COUNSELING INTERVIEWER, THE. 4583

0160-6808 *See* GOLF ILLUSTRATED (COVINA, CALIF.). 4896

0160-6816 *See* W.W. 1 AERO. 39

0160-6824 *See* GOLF INDUSTRY. 4896

0160-6840 *See* WIDE ANGLE. 4080

0160-6875 *See* STANDARD TRANSPORTATION COMMODITY CODE. 5437

0160-6891 *See* RESEARCH IN NURSING & HEALTH. 3868

0160-6905 *See* STATE OF TEXAS WATER QUALITY MANAGEMENT PROGRAM. 5539

0160-6913 *See* PASSENGER TRAIN JOURNAL. 5433

0160-6921 *See* TOUR BOOK : HAWAII. 5492

0160-6948 *See* NUTRIENT REQUIREMENTS OF DOMESTIC ANIMALS. 5517

0160-6972 *See* JOURNAL OF ORAL IMPLANTOLOGY, THE. 1327

0160-6980 *See* CONTINUING EDUCATION FOR HEALTH CARE PROVIDERS. 1800

0160-6999 *See* AADE EDITORS' JOURNAL. 4811

0160-7006 *See* HEALTH CARE EDUCATION. 4778

0160-7057 *See* REPORT - CONFERENCE OF PRESIDENTS OF MAJOR AMERICAN JEWISH ORGANIZATIONS. 5236

0160-7065 *See* DIESEL CAR DIGEST. 5413

0160-7081 *See* ARCHIVES OF THE FOUNDATION OF THANATOLOGY (1976). 4341

0160-7103 *See* CRIME IN MONTANA. 3080

0160-7162 *See* NEW VISTAS IN COUNSELING SERIES. 3620

0160-7200 *See* ANNUAL REPORT - WILLIAM T. GRANT FOUNDATION. 5273

0160-7219 *See* PERINATAL PRESS. 3766

0160-7243 *See* STONE IN AMERICA. 365

0160-726X *See* MOUNTAIN GAZETTE. 4905

0160-7278 *See* ARMY/NAVY STORE & OUTDOOR MERCHANDISER. 1081

0160-7308 *See* TRIAL DIPLOMACY JOURNAL. 3066

0160-7340 *See* GUIDE TO MANUFACTURED HOMES. 615

0160-7367 *See* SPIRIT (WASHINGTON). 4999

0160-7383 *See* ANNALS OF TOURISM RESEARCH. 5191

0160-7456 *See* POLICY POSITIONS. 4674

0160-7456 *See* POLICY POSITIONS. WINTER MEETING SUPPLEMENT. 4674

0160-7464 *See* EXTENDED ABSTRACTS AND PROGRAM - BIENNIAL CONFERENCE ON CARBON. 1975

0160-7472 *See* INTERNATIONAL TELEPHONE DIRECTORY OF THE DEAF. 1158

0160-7480 *See* MODERN HEALTHCARE (1977). 3789

0160-7499 *See* TECHNICAL CONFERENCE PROCEEDINGS / IRRIGATION ASSOCIATION. 2095

0160-7510 *See* GOOD OLD DAYS. SPECIAL ISSUES. 2735

0160-7537 *See* SALT (KENNEBUNK). 1094

0160-7545 *See* ELLEN GLASGOW NEWSLETTER, THE. 3384

0160-7561 *See* PHILOSOPHICAL STUDIES IN EDUCATION. 4356

0160-757X *See* INFUSION (ANDOVER). 3587

0160-7626 *See* INFERTILITY. 3762

0160-7642 *See* REGIONAL CONFERENCE SERIES IN MATHEMATICS. 3530

0160-7650 *See* CRAFTS REPORT, THE. 372

0160-7677 *See* SLACKWATER REVIEW, THE. 3437

0160-7715 *See* JOURNAL OF BEHAVIORAL MEDICINE. 4594

0160-7731 *See* BILL OF RIGHTS IN ACTION. 4504

0160-7774 *See* JOURNAL OF SUPERVISION AND TRAINING IN MINISTRY. 4970

0160-7782 *See* BULLETIN / GEOTHERMAL RESOURCES COUNCIL. 1934

0160-7804 *See* JOURNAL FOR GROWTH IN MARRIAGE, THE. 2281

0160-788X *See* RECLAMATION REVIEW. 125

0160-791X *See* TECHNOLOGY IN SOCIETY. 5164

0160-7960 *See* COUNSELING AND VALUES. 4583

0160-8029 *See* CATALOGING SERVICE BULLETIN. 3200

0160-8037 *See* DEVELOPING COUNTRY COURIER, THE. 4471

0160-8053 *See* FNP NEWSLETTER : FOOD, NUTRITION AND HEALTH. 4191

0160-8061 *See* JOURNAL OF ORGANIZATIONAL BEHAVIOR MANAGEMENT. 4599

0160-807X *See* REPORTER - NATIONAL CENTER FOR RESEARCH RESOURCES (U.S.). 3634

0160-8126 *See* PUBLIC EDUCATION DIRECTORY. 1775

0160-8150 *See* AM-FM RADIO GUIDE NEW YORK. 1126

0160-8185 *See* POOR JOE'S OHIO STATE ALMANACK. 2543

0160-8193 *See* POOR JOE'S INDIANA ALMANACK. 2543

0160-8207 *See* POOR JOE'S WASHINGTON ALMANACK. 2543

0160-8231 *See* ADOLESCENT MEDICINE (NEW YORK). 3899

0160-824X *See* MINERAL RESOURCE REPORT (HARRISBURG). 1388

0160-8266 *See* REPORT - PLANNING ADVISORY SERVICE. 2833

0160-8290 *See* SAFETY AND ENVIRONMENTAL PROTECTION DIVISION PROGRESS REPORT. 2181

0160-8312 *See* VOCATIONAL EVALUATION AND WORK ADJUSTMENT BULLETIN. 4395

0160-8320 *See* JOURNAL OF ATHLETIC TRAINING. 1856

0160-8347 *See* ESTUARIES. 554

0160-8371 *See* CONFERENCE RECORD OF THE ... IEEE PHOTOVOLTAIC SPECIALISTS CONFERENCE. 2039

0160-838X *See* PULPIT DIGEST (1978). 4988

0160-8428 *See* PROCEEDINGS OF THE NATIONAL CONFERENCE ON FLUID POWER. 2095

0160-8460 *See* ANNOTATION. 2720

0160-8495 *See* PENNSYLVANIA LAW JOURNAL-REPORTER. 3025

0160-8533 *See* CLEVELAND MAGAZINE. 2486

0160-8584 *See* LABORATORY AND RESEARCH METHODS IN BIOLOGY AND MEDICINE. 463

0160-8614 *See* STREM CHEMIKER, THE. 993

0160-8657 *See* MANAGEMENT COMPENSATION, RAILROADS. 5432

0160-8681 *See* THANATOS. 4363

0160-8703 *See* LITERARY ONOMASTICS STUDIES. 3406

0160-8711 *See* CCIS NEWSLETTER. 1173

0160-872X *See* WAFL BOOK, THE. 4079

0160-8797 *See* MASTER'S THESES DIRECTORIES. THE ARTS AND SOCIAL SCIENCES. 324

0160-8819 *See* BIBLIOGRAPHY OF CORPORATE SOCIAL RESPONSIBILITY. 1599

0160-8835 *See* AMD (NEW YORK, N.Y.). 2109

0160-8843 *See* CONTRIBUTIONS SERIES - AMERICAN ASSOCIATION OF STRATIGRAPHIC PALYNOLOGISTS. 1372

0160-8851 See REPORT - STATE ENGINEER'S OFFICE, WYOMING WATER PLANNING PROGRAM. 5538

0160-8886 See MOTOR TREND NEW CAR BUYER'S GUIDE. 5420

0160-8894 See GR. GROCERS REPORT. 2342

0160-8932 See KEY (GOREVILLE). 929

0160-8959 See CA SELECTS: ANALYTICAL ELECTROCHEMISTRY. 997

0160-8967 See CA SELECTS: COLLOIDS (APPLIED ASPECTS). 1000

0160-8975 See CA SELECTS: COLLOIDS (PHYSICOCHEMICAL ASPECTS). 1000

0160-8991 See FODOR'S SOUTH-EAST ASIA. 5473

0160-9009 See FRONTIERS (BOULDER). 5557

0160-9025 See CA SELECTS: COMPUTERS IN CHEMISTRY. 1000

0160-9041 See CA SELECTS: ENVIRONMENTAL POLLUTION. 1002

0160-905X See CA SELECTS: ORGANOFLUORINE CHEMISTRY. 1006

0160-9068 See CA SELECTS: FUNGICIDES. 1003

0160-9076 See CA SELECTS: GASEOUS WASTE TREATMENT. 1003

0160-9084 See CA SELECTS: HERBICIDES. 1003

0160-9092 See CA SELECTS: INSECTICIDES. 1004

0160-9106 See CA SELECTS: LIQUID WASTE TREATMENT. 1004

0160-9114 See CA SELECTS: METALLO ENZYMES & METALLO COENZYMES. 1005

0160-9130 See CA SELECTS: ORGANO-TRANSITION METAL COMPLEXES. 1006

0160-9149 See CA SELECTS: POLLUTION MONITORING. 1008

0160-9157 See CA SELECTS: RECOVERY & RECYCLING OF WASTES. 1009

0160-9165 See CA SELECTS: SOLID & RADIOACTIVE WASTE TREATMENT. 1009

0160-9173 See CA SELECTS: STEROIDS (BIOCHEMICAL ASPECTS). 1009

0160-9181 See CA SELECTS: STEROIDS (CHEMICAL ASPECTS). 1009

0160-919X See CA SELECTS: TRACE ELEMENT ANALYSIS. 1010

0160-9203 See UPDATE (LIBRARY OF CONGRESS. NATIONAL LIBRARY SERVICE FOR THE BLIND AND PHYSICALLY HANDICAPPED). 3255

0160-9238 See IFC GENERAL POLICIES. 790

0160-9270 See JOURNAL - WISCONSIN STATE READING ASSOCIATION. 1899

0160-9289 See CLINICAL CARDIOLOGY (MAHWAH, N.J.). 3703

0160-9327 See ENDEAVOUR (NEW SERIES). 5103

0160-9440 See ROSTER OF MEMBERS - ASSOCIATION FOR HOSPITAL MEDICAL EDUCATION. 3637

0160-9475 See SPINA BIFIDA THERAPY. 3807

0160-9483 See MICHIGAN MUSIC. 4131

0160-9491 See GENERAL INFORMATION CONCERNING PATENTS. 1304

0160-9513 See SOCIAL WORK WITH GROUPS (NEW YORK. 1978). 5310

0160-9548 See BASIC DATA SERIES. GROUND-WATER RELEASE. 5531

0160-9599 See PUBLICATIONS IN CLIMATOLOGY. 1433

0160-9602 See QUARTERLY - NORTHEASTERN NEVADA HISTORICAL SOCIETY. 2756

0160-9645 See ANCIENT WORLD, THE. 254

0160-9688 See CRIMINAL JUSTICE AND THE PUBLIC. 3162

0160-970X See BOOK INDUSTRY TRENDS. 4824

0160-9742 See NETWORK PLANNING PAPER. 3233

0160-9769 See HIGH PERFORMANCE (LOS ANGELES). 385

0160-9823 See THUNDERBIRD INTERNATIONAL, THE. 888

0160-9831 See FOLKLORE WOMEN'S COMMUNICATION. 2320

0160-984X See PALESTINE-ISRAEL BULLETIN. 4511

0160-9882 See RETAIL PRICES AND INDEXES OF FUELS AND UTILITIES. 4683

0160-9890 See OFFICIAL CONGRESSIONAL DIRECTORY. 4670

0160-9904 See FOREST SERVICE ORGANIZATIONAL DIRECTORY. 2381

0160-9912 See PACKAGE X. 4740

0160-9920 See STATISTICS OF INCOME. CORPORATION INCOME TAX RETURNS. 4700

0160-9963 See APPLIED RADIOLOGY (1976). 3939

0161-0023 See ASSOCIATIONS OF DELAWARE VALLEY. 5228

0161-004X See SPOTLIGHT (NEW YORK). 2762

0161-0090 See PRIESTHOOD AND BROTHERHOOD. 4987

0161-0112 See BREAST CANCER. 3809

0161-0120 See INTERFACE (SOCIETY FOR ENVIRONMENTAL GEOCHEMISTRY AND HEALTH). 2233

0161-0139 See PSYCHOPHARMACOLOGY (NEW YORK). 4326

0161-0260 See WASHINGTON CALENDAR MAGAZINE. 5499

0161-0295 See TIMS/ORSA BULLETIN. 1629

0161-0325 See HIGHWAY & VEHICLE SAFETY REPORT. 5440

0161-0376 See AEB, ANALYTICAL & ENUMERATIVE BIBLIOGRAPHY. 3457

0161-0384 See BUSINESS INTERNATIONAL MONEY REPORT. 781

0161-0392 See BULLETIN - WEST VIRGINIA SPELEOLOGICAL SURVEY. 1403

0161-0406 See REFRACTORIES (BUREAU OF THE CENSUS). 4441

0161-0414 See PRAXIS (ITHACA). 3350

0161-0457 See SCANNING. 574

0161-0511 See SAR MAGAZINE, THE. 5236

0161-0546 See ARTIST'S MARKET (1979). 376

0161-0562 See CURRENT CAREER AND OCCUPATIONAL LITERATURE. 4203

0161-0589 See PROCEEDINGS OF THE WESTERN SNOW CONFERENCE. 1359

0161-0627 See IRAN ECONOMIC NEWS. 1497

0161-0708 See UNIVERSITY OF PUGET SOUND LAW REVIEW. 3069

0161-0716 See DOWN SYNDROME NEWS / THE NEWSLETTER OF THE NATIONAL DOWN SYNDROME CONGRESS. 544

0161-0716 See DOWN'S SYNDROME NEWS. 544

0161-0740 See NEW PRODUCT, NEW BUSINESS DIGEST. 699

0161-0759 See ANNUAL REPORT TO CONGRESS ON THE IMPLEMENTATION OF PUBLIC LAW 94-413, THE ELECTRIC & HYBRID VEHICLE RESEARCH, DEVELOPMENT & DEMONSTRATION ACT OF 1976. 5377

0161-0775 See THEATER (NEW HAVEN, CONN.). 5370

0161-0783 See AMICUS JURIS. 2933

0161-0805 See INTERNATIONAL DEFENSE BUSINESS : REPORT. 4046

0161-0813 See INTERNATIONAL DEFENSE BUSINESS: DEFENSE SURVEY. 4046

0161-0961 See OIL AND GAS FIELD STUDIES. 4268

0161-0988 See AAUP BOOK SHOW CATALOGUE. 4563

0161-0996 See EIGHTEENTH CENTURY, THE. 2635

0161-1003 See INDIANA UNIVERSITY ART MUSEUM BULLETIN. 4089

0161-1038 See IEEE INSTRUMENTATION AND MEASUREMENT SOCIETY NEWSLETTER. 2059

0161-1054 See SKI X-C. 4918

0161-1097 See NAIS MEMBER SCHOOL TUITION FEES, FACULTY SALARIES, AND ADMINISTRATIVE SALARIES. 1866

0161-1100 See JOURNAL OF APPLIED MANAGEMENT. 873

0161-1119 See ADVENTIST REVIEW (WEEKLY). 5054

0161-1127 See GOVERNMENT R & D REPORT. 5108

0161-1151 See AGED CARE & SERVICES REVIEW. 5270

0161-1178 See AMERICAN FAMILY (WASHINGTON), THE. 2276

0161-1194 See CRYPTOLOGIA. 1226

0161-1232 See ART-ANTIQUES INVESTMENT REPORT, THE. 891

0161-1372 See SURGICAL ROUNDS. 3976

0161-1380 See INTEGRAL YOGA. 4965

0161-1461 See LANGUAGE, SPEECH & HEARING SERVICES IN SCHOOLS. 1881

0161-147X See HERPETOLOGICAL CIRCULAR. 5585

0161-1542 See MONOGRAPHS IN SYSTEMATIC BOTANY FROM THE MISSOURI BOTANICAL GARDEN. 518

0161-1550 See GEODEX SYSTEM/S. 3212

0161-1569 See GEODEX SYSTEM-A. 299

0161-1577 See BRILLIANT CORNERS. 316

0161-1585 See ON FILM (SANTA BARBARA). 4075

0161-1607 See NHRC REPORT. 3621

0161-1666 See MONTANA AIR QUALITY DATA AND INFORMATION SUMMARY FOR 2236

0161-1674 See ANNUAL REPORT TO THE PRESIDENT AND THE CONGRESS ON THE STATE ENERGY CONSERVATION PROGRAM. 1932

0161-1704 See NEWSLETTER - MUSIC OCLC USERS GROUP. 4141

0161-1712 See INTERNATIONAL JOURNAL OF MATHEMATICS AND MATHEMATICAL SCIENCES. 3509

0161-178X See TAXATION FOR LAWYERS. 3062

0161-1798 See VELO-NEWS. 429

0161-1801 See SOCIALIST REVIEW (SAN FRANCISCO). 4547

0161-1828 See OVERSEAS OUTLOOK. 4392

0161-1836 See BIRDING. 5578

0161-1852 See TECHNICAL PAPER - SOCIETY OF MANUFACTURING ENGINEERS. EM. 1998

0161-1887 See TECHNICAL PAPER - SOCIETY OF MANUFACTURING ENGINEERS. TE. 1998

0161-1895 See I.D.E.A.S. INTERIORS, DESIGN, ENVIRONMENT, ARTS, STRUCTURES. 2901

0161-1909 See WEST VIRGINIA STATE BAR CONTINUING LEGAL EDUCATION BULLETIN. 3073

0161-1917 See REPORT OF THE NATIONAL HEART, LUNG, AND BLOOD ADVISORY COUNCIL. 3710

0161-1925 See MOTEL ECONOMY GUIDE : FLORIDA & I-95. 2808

0161-1992 See BRIDE'S & YOUR NEW HOME. 2277

0161-2042 See SUCCESSFUL BUSINESS. 714

0161-2077 See GRADUATE COMMUNICATION STUDIES. 1112

0161-2115 See NCJW JOURNAL. 2268

0161-2123 See SIMMENTAL SHIELD. 221

0161-2174 See MAP, MONITORING ATTITUDES OF THE PUBLIC. 2887

0161-2212 See BALANCED PERSPECTIVE ON : THE HEALTH OF KANSANS. 4768

0161-2220 See FINNIGAN SPECTRA. 4434

0161-2298 See DIRECTORY OF CONSTITUENT ORGANIZATIONS. 2259

0161-2328 See ANALOG SCIENCE FICTION & FACT. 3361

0161-2344 See WOMAN'S DAY VEGETABLE GARDENING, CANNING & FREEZING. 2433

0161-2352 See WORLD GOODWILL NEWSLETTER. 2913

0161-2387 See ECONOMIC REVIEW (KANSAS CITY). 1485

0161-2417 See HEARINGS IN PUBLIC ASSISTANCE. 5287

0161-2425 See PERSONNEL CONSULTANT. 945

0161-2433 See NEW YORK TIMES BIOGRAPHICAL SERVICE, THE. **434**
0161-2492 See CALLALOO. **3371**
0161-2506 See BLOODROOT. **3367**
0161-2522 See INTERNATIONAL MEALS ON WHEELS DIRECTORY. **5290**
0161-2549 See GALLIMAUFRY. **3389**
0161-2557 See UNITED STATES UNDERWATER FATALITY STATISTICS. **4811**
0161-2573 See TESTS IN MICROFICHE : ANNOTATED INDEX. **1873**
0161-2581 See EXPANSION SURVEY, RETAIL TRADE INDUSTRY. **954**
0161-2654 See MUSIC CLUBS MAGAZINE (1963). **4133**
0161-2670 See CIRCULAR. **1372**
0161-2697 See PHILLIPS SHIELD. **4274**
0161-2719 See TULL TRACING. **2476**
0161-2727 See NEW DRIVER (HIGHLAND PARK, ILL.). **5421**
0161-2735 See KISS. **5074**
0161-2786 See EARNSHAW'S INFANTS-GIRLS-BOYS WEAR REVIEW. **1083**
0161-2794 See BRADFORD BOOK OF COLLECTOR'S PLATES, THE. **2586**
0161-2824 See GOLDEN'S DIAGNOSTIC RADIOLOGY. **3941**
0161-2840 See ISSUES IN MENTAL HEALTH NURSING. **3858**
0161-2867 See WATER RESOURCES SPECIAL REPORT. **5547**
0161-2875 See WORLD MEETINGS. MEDICINE. **3651**
0161-2883 See MEMBRANE PROTEINS (NEW YORK, N.Y.). **464**
0161-2921 See INFORMATION BULLETIN OF THE CENTRAL BUREAU FOR SATELLITE GEODESY. **1407**
0161-2964 See PAY STRUCTURE OF THE FEDERAL CIVIL SERVICE. **1701**
0161-2972 See WEEKLY REGULATORY MONITOR, THE. **3073**
0161-3081 See TUNE UP. **4157**
0161-309X See PUBLIC ACCOUNTING REPORT. **750**
0161-3103 See NATIONAL AIRPORT SYSTEM PLAN. **30**
0161-3138 See EVIDENTIA. **3148**
0161-3146 See GEOGRAPHIC SALARY DIFFERENTIALS. **1675**
0161-3154 See DIRECTORY, PROFESSIONAL REAL ESTATE MANAGEMENT WHO'S WHO. **4837**
0161-3189 See MISSISSIPPI PHARMACIST. **4316**
0161-3219 See PROCEEDINGS - BIENNIAL CORNELL ELECTRICAL ENGINEERING CONFERENCE. **2076**
0161-3251 See MEDICAL TRIAL TECHNIQUE QUARTERLY ANNUAL. **3009**
0161-3278 See MEDICAL SUBJECT HEADINGS. TREE ANNOTATIONS. **3611**
0161-3324 See GRAPH THEORY NEWSLETTER. **3507**
0161-3332 See PROCEEDINGS OF THE CONVENTION - INTERNATIONAL ASSOCIATION OF FISH AND WILDLIFE AGENCIES. **2202**
0161-3367 See ICE, INSIDE CODE ENFORCEMENT. **2979**
0161-3405 See CONSTRUCTION EMPLOYMENT GUIDE IN THE NATIONAL AND INTERNATIONAL FIELD. **609**
0161-3448 See SATELLITE NEWS. **1163**
0161-3499 See VETERINARY SURGERY. **5527**
0161-3618 See REPORT FROM THE DIRECTOR, NATIONAL INSTITUTE OF ALLERGY AND INFECTIOUS DISEASES. **3715**
0161-3642 See INTERNATIONAL JOURNAL OF QUANTUM CHEMISTRY. QUANTUM CHEMISTRY SYMPOSIUM. **1053**
0161-3669 See WHO'S WHO IN DISPLAY HOLOGRAPHY. **436**
0161-3715 See RADIONAVIGATION JOURNAL. **4182**

0161-3863 See ASRT SCANNER. **3939**
0161-3871 See TENNESSEE SPORTSMAN. **4879**
0161-3901 See AIR POLLUTION CONTROL. **2223**
0161-3979 See MAINE'S STATE PLAN ON DEVELOPMENTAL DISABILITIES. **5295**
0161-4002 See PROCEEDINGS OF THE ANNUAL INSTITUTE ON SECURITIES LAWS AND REGULATIONS. **3031**
0161-4118 See MISSOURI RIVER BASIN, STATE AND FEDERAL WATER AND RELATED LAND RESOURCE PROGRAMS. **2093**
0161-4126 See COMMUNICATION OUTLOOK. **1107**
0161-4169 See SUMMARIES OF PROJECTS COMPLETED. **5160**
0161-4177 See INDIVIDUAL AND THE FUTURE OF ORGANIZATIONS, THE. **5203**
0161-4223 See LIGHTWORKS. **357**
0161-424X See CHRONICLE GUIDE TO EXTERNAL & CONTINUING EDUCATION. **1800**
0161-4290 See NASBA DIGEST OF STATE ACCOUNTANCY LAWS AND STATE BOARD REGULATIONS. **3013**
0161-4320 See MOPED DEALER. **4081**
0161-4347 See FARM INDUSTRY NEWS SUNBELT. **84**
0161-4363 See BACON'S INTERNATIONAL PUBLICITY CHECKER. **756**
0161-4371 See HIGH FIDELITY'S BUYING GUIDE TO TAPE SYSTEMS. **5317**
0161-4401 See AAMA PERSONNEL POLICIES AND BENEFITS SURVEY. **938**
0161-4444 See UNITED STATES COAST PILOT. 6, GREAT LAKES, LAKES ONTARIO, ERIE, HURON, MICHIGAN, AND SUPERIOR AND ST. LAWRENCE RIVER. **4184**
0161-4452 See SCIENTIFIC PUBLICATIONS OF THE SCIENCE MUSEUM OF MINNESOTA. **5155**
0161-4533 See NEIGHBORHOOD HEALTH CENTERS : SUMMARY OF PROJECT DATA. REPORT. **4793**
0161-4541 See EQUAL EMPLOYMENT OPPORTUNITY COMPLIANCE. **3147**
0161-4568 See WEEKLY PSYCHIATRY UPDATE SERIES. **3937**
0161-4576 See JOURNAL OF SEX EDUCATION AND THERAPY. **5187**
0161-4681 See TEACHERS COLLEGE RECORD (1970). **1849**
0161-4703 See HORN OF AFRICA. **2640**
0161-4754 See JOURNAL OF MANIPULATIVE AND PHYSIOLOGICAL THERAPEUTICS. **4380**
0161-4762 See BEST OF PHOTOJOURNALISM, THE. **4367**
0161-4770 See BUDGET PROPOSED FOR THE DEPARTMENT OF LABOR AND RELATED AGENCIES, THE. **1656**
0161-4851 See GAS DIGEST. **4257**
0161-486X See COLUMBIA, A MAGAZINE OF POETRY AND PROSE. **3377**
0161-4886 See DENVER MAGAZINE, THE. **2532**
0161-4894 See ANNUAL SURVEY - NATIONAL CONFERENCE OF CATHOLIC CHARITIES. **5023**
0161-4924 See PROCEEDINGS OF THE ANNUAL NEW MEXICO WATER CONFERENCE. **5537**
0161-4932 See FLORIDA GENEALOGIST, THE. **2448**
0161-4940 See CATALYSIS REVIEWS : SCIENCE AND ENGINEERING. **2009**
0161-4967 See DATA FROM THE CLIENT ORIENTED DATA ACQUISITION PROCESS. STATE OFFICIALS. **1350**
0161-5009 See PUBL HERPETOL. **5595**
0161-5033 See DATA FROM THE CLIENT ORIENTED DATA ACQUISITION PROCESS. SMSA STATISTICS. **1350**
0161-5041 See SUMMARY REPORT, DATA FORM THE NATIONAL DRUG ABUSE TREATMENT UTILIZATION SURVEY (NDATUS). **1349**
0161-5068 See EXECUTIVE REPORT, DATA FROM THE NATIONAL DRUG ABUSE TREATMENT UTILIZATION SURVEY (NDATUS). **1344**

0161-5084 See SCOTT STANDARD POSTAGE STAMP CATALOGUE. **2787**
0161-5114 See RE-VIEW (NEW YORK). **363**
0161-5122 See CURRENT MUNICIPAL PROBLEMS (CUMULATION). **4641**
0161-5149 See METAL IONS IN BIOLOGICAL SYSTEMS. **490**
0161-5173 See STATISTICS OF COMMUNICATIONS COMMON CARRIERS. **1164**
0161-5181 See GOVERNMENT PRINTING & BINDING REGULATIONS. **4565**
0161-5203 See AMERICAN HOME'S TREASURY OF AMERICANA. **248**
0161-522X See MARINE RECREATIONAL FISHERIES. **2308**
0161-5238 See BRETHREN MISSIONARY HERALD. **4940**
0161-5270 See SMALL FARM, THE. **3471**
0161-5289 See PSYCHOANALYSIS AND CONTEMPORARY THOUGHT. **4610**
0161-5351 See SPORT AEROBATICS. **4920**
0161-5378 See HIGHLANDER (BARRINGTON), THE. **2262**
0161-5408 See AG ALERT. **45**
0161-5440 See HISTORICAL METHODS. **5201**
0161-5459 See THERMOTROL TECHNICIAN, THE. **1336**
0161-5483 See ICUIS BIBLIOGRAPHY SERIES. **5012**
0161-5505 See JOURNAL OF NUCLEAR MEDICINE (1978), THE. **3848**
0161-5513 See NJPC BULLETIN. **3862**
0161-5556 See BOOK-MART (DECATUR), THE. **4825**
0161-5580 See FALK SYMPOSIUM. **3576**
0161-5645 See U.S. ENVIRONMENTAL PROTECTION AGENCY LIBRARY SYSTEM BOOK CATALOG. **3214**
0161-5653 See SCHOOL SOCIAL WORK JOURNAL. **1871**
0161-5688 See RETAILER (RALEIGH), THE. **957**
0161-5718 See NEWSLETTER / IEEE PROFESSIONAL COMMUNICATION SOCIETY. **2073**
0161-5734 See CARDIOVASCULAR DRUGS. **3701**
0161-5769 See PROCEEDINGS - WORLD MAGNESIUM CONFERENCE. **4016**
0161-5793 See DIRECTORY OF CLINICAL FELLOWSHIPS IN MEDICINE : UNITED STATES AND CANADA. **3572**
0161-5815 See PRORODEO SPORTS NEWS. **4913**
0161-5823 See BROADCASTING AND THE LAW. **2943**
0161-584X See MAINE LEGIONNAIRE, THE. **5233**
0161-5858 See CONNECTICUT MARKET BULLETIN. **76**
0161-5882 See EXISTING HOME SALES. **4837**
0161-5890 See MOLECULAR IMMUNOLOGY. **3675**
0161-5912 See WASHINGTON STATE'S WATER. **5541**
0161-5920 See SURVEY OF SECONDARY AND ENHANCED RECOVERY OPERATIONS IN TEXAS, A. **4280**
0161-5971 See SONGWRITER'S MARKET. **4153**
0161-6080 See SUCCESSFUL DEALER, THE. **5393**
0161-6102 See BUSINESS TIMES (EAST HARTFORD, CONN.), THE. **653**
0161-6110 See EASTERN FINANCIAL TIMES. **788**
0161-6196 See BOARD OF DIRECTORS ANNUAL STUDY. **861**
0161-6218 See LIST OF ART NEEDLEWORK, YARN KNITTING STORES. **5184**
0161-6234 See LINN'S STAMP NEWS. **2785**
0161-6293 See BPC, BUILDING PRODUCTS CATALOG. **602**
0161-6307 See ATTORNEY GENERAL'S REPORT ON FEDERAL LAW ENFORCEMENT AND CRIMINAL JUSTICE ASSISTANCE ACTIVITIES. **3158**
0161-6331 See WINGS (NEVADA CITY). **39**

0161-6366 See LINNEAN SOCIETY SYMPOSIUM SERIES. 5233

0161-6374 See PROCEEDINGS - ELECTROCHEMICAL SOCIETY. 1034

0161-6404 See PROCEEDINGS OF THE ... IEEE FREQUENCY CONTROL SYMPOSIUM. 4418

0161-6412 See NEUROLOGICAL RESEARCH (NEW YORK). 3840

0161-6420 See OPHTHALMOLOGY (ROCHESTER, MINN.). 3878

0161-6463 See AMERICAN INDIAN CULTURE AND RESEARCH JOURNAL. 2254

0161-6471 See PROMOTING COMMUNITY HEALTH. 3630

0161-6536 See ENCORE AMERICAN & WORLDWIDE NEWS. 2260

0161-6587 See BOSTON COLLEGE LAW REVIEW. 2943

0161-6595 See ENERGY CONSERVATION NEWS. 1939

0161-6625 See INFORMATION BULLETIN - NATIONAL CENTER FOR ATMOSPHERIC RESEARCH. 1426

0161-6641 See CURRENT ISSUES (WASHINGTON). 4470

0161-6668 See CONNOISSEURS' GUIDE TO CALIFORNIA WINE. 2366

0161-6692 See ARTISTS EQUITY NEWS. 341

0161-6706 See SPORTS 'N SPOKES. 4923

0161-6749 See INTERACTION (WASHINGTON. 1977). 3926

0161-6765 See HEALTH, SAFETY & EDUCATION. 4781

0161-6811 See CABLE TELEVISION LAW : MUNICIPAL LAW OFFICERS EDITION. 2945

0161-682X See ROMANTIST, THE. 3432

0161-6846 See PUBLIC LIBRARY QUARTERLY (NEW YORK, N.Y.). 3243

0161-6862 See COMPUTER PRODUCTS. 1244

0161-6889 See ADVERTISING DIGEST. CLASSIFIED EDITION. 754

0161-6900 See CALVIN SYNOD HERALD. 5727

0161-6935 See COMPARATIVE PATHOBIOLOGY. 3894

0161-6951 See ICP INFORMATION NEWSLETTER. 1015

0161-7028 See INDEX OF FDA REGULATORY LETTERS. 4656

0161-7036 See FTC FREEDOM OF INFORMATION LOG. 837

0161-7044 See FDA FREEDOM OF INFORMATION LOG. 4647

0161-7079 See PULP & PAPER REVIEW. 4238

0161-7109 See JUVENILE & FAMILY COURT JOURNAL. 3121

0161-7125 See ROUND THE TABLE. 2893

0161-7133 See MISSIONARY MONTHLY. 4978

0161-7141 See YEAR IN PICTURES, THE. 2633

0161-715X See SIBYL-CHILD. 330

0161-7176 See WASHINGTON PHYSICIANS DIRECTORY, THE. 3917

0161-7214 See PROFESSIONAL'S TIRE HANDBOOK, THE. 5423

0161-7222 See STUDIA MYSTICA. 3441

0161-7230 See RESEARCH IN POLITICAL ECONOMY. 1581

0161-7249 See RESEARCH IN PHILOSOPHY & TECHNOLOGY. 5147

0161-7257 See CURRENT CONSTRUCTION COSTS. 612

0161-7273 See RURAL DEVELOPMENT PROGRESS. 5256

0161-7338 See NEW YORK RUNNING NEWS. 4907

0161-7346 See ULTRASONIC IMAGING. 3802

0161-7362 See SIERRA. 2205

0161-7370 See POPULAR SCIENCE (NEW YORK, N.Y.). 5139

0161-7389 See USA TODAY (NEW YORK, N.Y.). 2548

0161-7397 See BULLETIN - INTERNATIONAL ASSOCIATION OF ORIENTALIST LIBRARIANS. 3198

0161-7419 See FAIRFIELD COUNTY EXECUTIVE. 674

0161-7427 See MICROELECTRONICS MANUFACTURING TECHNOLOGY. 2072

0161-7435 See GEORGE HERBERT JOURNAL. 3390

0161-7494 See PUBLIC EMPLOYEE MAGAZINE, THE. 4705

0161-7508 See DISTRIBUTED PROCESSING PRODUCT REPORTS. 1183

0161-7524 See INTERNATIONAL WORKSHOP ON DIABETES AND CAMPING. 3731

0161-7540 See DENTAL ADMISSION TESTING PROGRAM REPORT. 1320

0161-7648 See TOWSON STATE UNIVERSITY JOURNAL OF PSYCHOLOGY. 4620

0161-7656 See BENCHMARK PAPERS IN GENETICS. 543

0161-7672 See WORLD SMOKING & HEALTH. 5374

0161-7680 See RYAN ADVISORY FOR HEALTH SERVICES GOVERNING BOARDS, THE. 4800

0161-7699 See ANNUAL REPORT / NATIONAL EYE INSTITUTE. 3872

0161-7702 See JOURNAL OF INTERNATIONAL PHYSICIANS. 3595

0161-7710 See BFLO. 4887

0161-7729 See SCHOLARS' FACSIMILES AND REPRINTS (SERIES). 3319

0161-7745 See BEST'S REVIEW (PROPERTY/CASUALTY INSURANCE ED.). 2876

0161-7753 See ARKANSAS EDUCATOR. 1888

0161-7761 See ANTHROPOLOGY & EDUCATION QUARTERLY. 230

0161-7796 See RADIATION PROTECTION ACTIVITIES. 2240

0161-780X See CURRENT NEUROLOGY. 3831

0161-7818 See CURRENT RADIOLOGY. 3940

0161-7834 See GATER RACING PHOTO NEWS. 4896

0161-7842 See SADDLE HORSE REPORT. 2802

0161-7893 See WOODBOOK, THE. 2406

0161-7931 See DELAP'S F & SF REVIEW. 3380

0161-7982 See NYEA ADVOCATE. 1769

0161-7990 See NAEB BULLETIN. 950

0161-8016 See NATIONAL REPORTER (BIXBY). 5732

0161-8032 See PROMT / PREDICASTS OVERVIEW OF MARKETS AND TECHNOLOGY. 1537

0161-8059 See PRACTICAL SAILOR, THE. 595

0161-8075 See TRAVELER'S ALMANAC. 5497

0161-8105 See SLEEP (NEW YORK, N.Y.). 3641

0161-8113 See ZONING AND PLANNING LAW REPORT. 3078

0161-813X See NEUROTOXICOLOGY (PARK FOREST SOUTH). 3843

0161-8164 See PARENTS' CHOICE. 2284

0161-8199 See GEOGRAPHIC DISTRIBUTION OF FEDERAL FUNDS IN IOWA. 1562

0161-8202 See JOURNAL OF ARACHNOLOGY, THE. 5587

0161-8237 See AMERICAN AGRICULTURIST (1976). 58

0161-827X See JOURNAL OF COLLEGE AND UNIVERSITY STUDENT HOUSING, THE. 1832

0161-8288 See TRAINING AND MANPOWER DEVELOPMENT ACTIVITIES. 5312

0161-8318 See ASSEMBLING. 343

0161-8342 See ANTIQUE TRADER WEEKLY, THE. 249

0161-8350 See FLETCHER. 1102

0161-8415 See PR. PHARMACEUTICAL REPRESENTATIVE. 4325

0161-8423 See THEODORE ROOSEVELT ASSOCIATION JOURNAL. 435

0161-8490 See EPA ACTIVITIES UNDER THE RESOURCE CONSERVATION AND RECOVERY ACT OF 1976. 2193

0161-8504 See CURRENTS IN ALCOHOLISM. 1342

0161-8512 See GEOGRAPHIC DISTRIBUTION OF FEDERAL FUNDS IN OREGON. 1563

0161-8520 See GEOGRAPHIC DISTRIBUTION OF FEDERAL FUNDS IN WASHINGTON. 1564

0161-8539 See GEOGRAPHIC DISTRIBUTION OF FEDERAL FUNDS IN MINNESOTA. 1563

0161-8547 See GEOGRAPHIC DISTRIBUTION OF FEDERAL FUNDS IN LOUISIANA. 1563

0161-8598 See VFW, VETERANS OF FOREIGN WARS MAGAZINE. 4060

0161-8628 See NATIONAL TRANSPORTATION STATISTICS. 5401

0161-8636 See GEOGRAPHIC DISTRIBUTION OF FEDERAL FUNDS IN WEST VIRGINIA. 1564

0161-8741 See DALLAS-FORT WORTH HOME GARDEN. 2789

0161-8776 See PRIMARY PREVENTION OF PSYCHOPATHOLOGY. 3932

0161-8822 See PAPERS IN SLAVIC PHILOLOGY. 3309

0161-8830 See UNITED STATES OCEANBORNE FOREIGN TRADE ROUTES. 5458

0161-8849 See GEOGRAPHIC DISTRIBUTION OF FEDERAL FUNDS IN RHODE ISLAND. 1563

0161-8873 See GEOGRAPHIC DISTRIBUTION OF FEDERAL FUNDS IN PENNSYLVANIA. 1563

0161-8881 See GEOGRAPHIC DISTRIBUTION OF FEDERAL FUNDS IN TEXAS. 1564

0161-889X See GEOGRAPHIC DISTRIBUTION OF FEDERAL FUNDS IN WYOMING. 1564

0161-8903 See TURKEY YEAR BOOK. 2713

0161-8911 See GEOGRAPHIC DISTRIBUTION OF FEDERAL FUNDS IN NEW HAMPSHIRE. 1563

0161-892X See GEOGRAPHIC DISTRIBUTION OF FEDERAL FUNDS IN VIRGINIA. 1564

0161-8938 See JOURNAL OF POLICY MODELING. 5206

0161-8962 See GEOGRAPHIC DISTRIBUTION OF FEDERAL FUNDS IN OHIO. 1563

0161-8970 See GEOGRAPHIC DISTRIBUTION OF FEDERAL FUNDS IN SOUTH CAROLINA. 1563

0161-8989 See GEOGRAPHIC DISTRIBUTION OF FEDERAL FUNDS IN INDIANA. 1562

0161-8997 See GEOGRAPHIC DISTRIBUTION OF FEDERAL FUNDS IN COLORADO. 1562

0161-9012 See GEOGRAPHIC DISTRIBUTION OF FEDERAL FUNDS IN HAWAII. 1562

0161-9020 See FOOTBALL NEWS (DETROIT). 4895

0161-9039 See CAMPAIGNER SPECIAL REPORT, THE. 4636

0161-9055 See HOME VIDEO REPORT, THE. 4370

0161-9063 See BROADCAST FINANCIAL JOURNAL. 1127

0161-9101 See GEOGRAPHIC DISTRIBUTION OF FEDERAL FUNDS IN SOUTH DAKOTA. 1563

0161-9128 See GEOGRAPHIC DISTRIBUTION OF FEDERAL FUNDS IN NEBRASKA. 1563

0161-9136 See PENNSYLVANIA LAW ENFORCEMENT JOURNAL. 3171

0161-9152 See AGE (OMAHA). 3748

0161-9187 See GEOGRAPHIC DISTRIBUTION OF FEDERAL FUNDS IN WISCONSIN. 1564

0161-9195 See GEOGRAPHIC DISTRIBUTION OF FEDERAL FUNDS IN UTAH. 1564

0161-9233 See STATE OF CIVIL RIGHTS, THE. 4513

0161-9268 See ADVANCES IN NURSING SCIENCE. 3850

0161-9284 See MAGAZINE ANTIQUES (1971), THE. 251

0161-9292 See UNION LEADER. 2548

0161-9373 See MARITIME NEWSLETTER. 1690

0161-9411 See NAVSEA JOURNAL. 4180

0161-9446 See OCCUPATIONAL SAFETY AND HEALTH TRAINING GRANTS. 2867

0161-9470 See INDEX TO THE U.S. PATENT CLASSIFICATION. 1304

0161-9500 See EXECUTIVE EDUCATOR, THE. 1863

0161-9535 See EVALUATION OF THE URBAN HOMESTEADING DEMONSTRATION PROGRAM, ANNUAL REPORT. 2822

0161-9551 See MTM, MOTORCOACH TOUR MART. 5485

0161-956X See PEABODY JOURNAL OF EDUCATION. 1772

0161-9632 See PRISON LAW MONITOR. 3173

0161-9640 See CLINICAL CHEMISTRY NEWS. 972

0161-9705 See CHINESE LITERATURE (MADISON). 3375

0161-9713 See TEXTILE WEEK. 5358

0161-9772 See COMMERCIAL NEWS USA. 829

0161-9799 See GEOGRAPHIC DISTRIBUTION OF FEDERAL FUNDS IN ARIZONA. 1562

0161-9802 See GEOGRAPHIC DISTRIBUTION OF FEDERAL FUNDS IN NORTH CAROLINA. 1563

0161-9810 See AMMO. 1643

0161-9845 See PROGRAM GUIDE - SOUTH DAKOTA PUBLIC TELEVISION. 1136

0161-9861 See UNITED FLY TYERS' ROUNDTABLE. 2315

0161-987X See NOTRE DAME MAGAZINE. 1838

0161-990X See CONSTRUCTION LABOR NEWS. 1661

0161-9926 See ALCOHOLISM AND DRUG ABUSE FACILITIES IN THE STATE OF SOUTH DAKOTA. 1339

0161-9934 See CONTEMPORARY ISSUES IN NEPHROLOGY. 3989

0161-9969 See GEOGRAPHIC DISTRIBUTION OF FEDERAL FUNDS IN ILLINOIS. 1562

0161-9985 See GEOGRAPHIC DISTRIBUTION OF FEDERAL FUNDS IN MISSOURI. 1563

01612573 See TESTS IN MICROFICHE. 1886

0162-0002 See TEACHER WRITER. 2924

0162-0010 See COLORADO EDITOR. 2918

0162-0037 See DIRECTORY - AMERICAN ACADEMY OF DERMATOLOGY. 3720

0162-0053 See PROCEEDINGS OF THE ANNUAL CONVENTION OF THE DAUGHTERS OF THE REPUBLIC OF TEXAS. 2755

0162-0061 See PAWN REVIEW, THE. 3422

0162-0088 See WWS, WORLD WIDE SHIPPING GUIDE. 5458

0162-010X See OCCUPATIONAL INJURIES AND ILLNESSES IN THE UNITED STATES BY INDUSTRY. 2867

0162-0126 See CINEMONKEY. 4067

0162-0134 See JOURNAL OF INORGANIC BIOCHEMISTRY. 489

0162-0150 See BUREAU MEMORANDUM. 4385

0162-0177 See CENTENNIAL REVIEW, THE. 2844

0162-0266 See HIT PARADER. 2534

0162-0282 See SHORELINER. 5436

0162-0290 See DIRECTORY AND STATISTICS OF OREGON LIBRARIES. 3206

0162-0304 See GREENHOUSE REVIEW. 3343

0162-0312 See AMERICAN PHONOGRAPH JOURNAL. 5315

0162-0320 See ANNUAL REPORT - LOWER COLORADO RIVER AUTHORITY. 2087

0162-0339 See MEMBERSHIP DIRECTORY - NATIONAL COUNCIL FOR RESOURCE DEVELOPMENT. 1763

0162-0347 See GEOGRAPHIC DISTRIBUTION OF FEDERAL FUNDS IN MICHIGAN. 1563

0162-0355 See GEOGRAPHIC DISTRIBUTION OF FEDERAL FUNDS IN MAINE. 1563

0162-0363 See CATHOLIC SENTINEL - CATHOLIC CHURCH. DIOCESE OF BAKER (OR.). 5026

0162-0371 See ALUMNI DIRECTORY - THE UNIVERSITY OF CHICAGO LAW SCHOOL. 1099

0162-0398 See GEOGRAPHIC DISTRIBUTION OF FEDERAL FUNDS IN ARKANSAS. 1562

0162-0436 See QUALITATIVE SOCIOLOGY. 5254

0162-0452 See GEOGRAPHIC DISTRIBUTION OF FEDERAL FUNDS IN NORTH DAKOTA. 1563

0162-0460 See GEOGRAPHIC DISTRIBUTION OF FEDERAL FUNDS IN MONTANA. 1563

0162-0479 See GEOGRAPHIC DISTRIBUTION OF FEDERAL FUNDS IN CALIFORNIA. 1562

0162-0487 See GEOGRAPHIC DISTRIBUTION OF FEDERAL FUNDS IN KANSAS. 1562

0162-0495 See GEOGRAPHIC DISTRIBUTION OF FEDERAL FUNDS IN FLORIDA. 1562

0162-0509 See GEOGRAPHIC DISTRIBUTION OF FEDERAL FUNDS IN NEW MEXICO. 1563

0162-0568 See AMERICAN STEEPLECHASING. 2796

0162-0576 See GEOGRAPHIC DISTRIBUTION OF FEDERAL FUNDS IN ALASKA. 1563

0162-0584 See RELATIVE VALUE ANALYSIS. 912

0162-0592 See WORK EXPERIENCE OF THE POPULATION. 1718

0162-0622 See GEOGRAPHIC DISTRIBUTION OF FEDERAL FUNDS IN MASSACHUSETTS. 1563

0162-0657 See PROCEEDINGS OF THE ANNUAL SEMINAR OF THE CALIFORNIA COMMUNITY HEALTH INSTITUTE. 4796

0162-0703 See REPORT FROM HEADQUARTERS. 1706

0162-0711 See GEOGRAPHIC DISTRIBUTION OF FEDERAL FUNDS IN DELAWARE. 1562

0162-0738 See BIRDING NEWS SURVEY. 5578

0162-0746 See SHORELINER SUPPLEMENT. 5436

0162-0754 See GEOGRAPHIC DISTRIBUTION OF FEDERAL FUNDS IN GEORGIA. 1562

0162-0800 See OLMSTE(A)D'S GENEALOGY RECORDED. 2465

0162-0827 See CATALOGUE OF ACCESSIONED PUBLICATIONS. SUPPLEMENT. 1447

0162-0843 See HEALTH SCIENCES SERIALS. 3213

0162-0851 See L'HERITAGE (CHALMETTE). 2458

0162-0886 See CLINICAL INFECTIOUS DISEASES. 3712

0162-0908 See YEAR BOOK OF SPORTS MEDICINE, THE. 3957

0162-0932 See VERBATIM. 3331

0162-0975 See UPDATE : CARDIOLOGY. 3711

0162-0991 See GEOGRAPHIC DISTRIBUTION OF FEDERAL FUNDS IN NEVADA. 1563

0162-1033 See COLLECTORS NEWS & THE ANTIQUE REPORTER. 250

0162-1068 See SPOTLIGHT ON CAREER PLANNING, PLACEMENT AND RECRUITMENT. 4209

0162-1076 See GOVERNMENT CONTRACTS REPORTS. 4651

0162-1122 See FOOD DRUG COSMETIC LAW REPORTS (RX EDITION). 3100

0162-122X See PRODUCTS LIABILITY REPORTS. 3032

0162-1270 See SA. 2512

0162-1297 See RUGBY (NEW YORK). 4915

0162-1300 See IMPACT JOURNAL. 4655

0162-1319 See ROBERT FINIGAN'S PRIVATE GUIDE TO RESTAURANTS. 5073

0162-1327 See PENINSULA MAGAZINE. 2543

0162-1343 See PLAY METER MAGAZINE. 4864

0162-1378 See MODE INTERNATIONAL. 1086

0162-1424 See HOME HEALTH CARE SERVICES QUARTERLY. 5288

0162-1440 See TREE TRACERS, THE. 2475

0162-1459 See JOURNAL OF THE AMERICAN STATISTICAL ASSOCIATION. 5329

0162-1467 See NCAA DIRECTORY. 4906

0162-1475 See ENERGY CONSERVATION UPDATE. 1939

0162-153X See AMERICAN SHOTGUNNER, THE. 4883

0162-1548 See GEOGRAPHIC DISTRIBUTION OF FEDERAL FUNDS IN TENNESSEE. 1564

0162-1564 See TENNESSEE LIBRARIAN. 3252

0162-1599 See NEW ENGLAND STATES LIMITED, THE. 5433

0162-1602 See N.A.R.D. JOURNAL. 4316

0162-1688 See GEOGRAPHIC DISTRIBUTION OF FEDERAL FUNDS IN MARYLAND. 1563

0162-1726 See BOYCOTT LAW BULLETIN. 2943

0162-1769 See GEOGRAPHIC DISTRIBUTION OF FEDERAL FUNDS IN NEW JERSEY. 1563

0162-1831 See NATIONAL FORUM (ANN ARBOR). 1836

0162-1874 See GEOGRAPHIC DISTRIBUTION OF FEDERAL FUNDS IN MISSISSIPPI. 1563

0162-1882 See GEOGRAPHIC DISTRIBUTION OF FEDERAL FUNDS IN OKLAHOMA. 1563

0162-1890 See EVANGEL (WINONA LAKE). 4957

0162-1904 See ZONE (BROOKLYN). 3456

0162-1912 See JOURNAL OF AGRICULTURAL AND RESOURCE ECONOMICS. 99

0162-1955 See ACCENT. 4931

0162-1963 See GENERAL SCIENCE INDEX. CD-ROM. 5107

0162-1963 See GENERAL SCIENCE INDEX. 5175

0162-1971 See CONTEMPO (BIRMINGHAM, ALA.). 4950

0162-198X See DISCOVERY (BIRMINGHAM, ALA.). 5059

0162-2005 See WEST'S FEDERAL CASE NEWS. 3074

0162-2013 See AMERICAN KENNEL CLUB STUD BOOK REGISTER. 4285

0162-2080 See MONTGOMERY JOURNAL, THE. 5759

0162-2099 See PRINCE GEORGE'S JOURNAL, THE. 5759

0162-2129 See NRA. NAVAL RESERVE ASSOCIATION NEWS. 4181

0162-2137 See PENNSYLVANIA BULLETIN (HARRISBURG). 3025

0162-220X See CANCER NURSING. 3853

0162-2234 See ASSEMBLIES OF GOD HOME MISSIONS. 4936

0162-2242 See SPORT STYLE. 1087

0162-2315 See DOWNSTATE SERIES OF RESEARCH IN PSYCHIATRY AND PSYCHOLOGY, THE. 3924

0162-2374 See STATE MENTAL HOSPITALS. 3792

0162-2382 See MEDICAL COMPUTING SERIES. 3608

0162-2439 See SCIENCE, TECHNOLOGY & HUMAN VALUES. 5153

0162-2447 See SAMS TAPE RECORDER SERVICE DATA. 5318

0162-2528 See PHYSICAL TECHNIQUES IN MEDICINE. 3695

0162-2692 See YOUNG SPARTACUS. 1071

0162-2706 See CPCU JOURNAL. 2878

0162-2714 See COAL OUTLOOK. 1935

0162-2722 See CHARLESTON MAGAZINE. 2486

0162-2765 See GOODFELLOW REVIEW OF CRAFTS, THE. 373

0162-2781 See MILK MARKETER. 197

0162-279X See PROCEEDINGS PLP. PRODUCT LIABILITY PREVENTION SEMINAR. 4221

0162-2811 See COMMUNICATION ABSTRACTS. 1124

0162-282X See MEMPHIS. 2538

0162-2838 See SEC NO-ACTION LETTERS INDEX AND SUMMARIES. 4685

0162-2870 See OCTOBER (CAMBRIDGE, MASS.). 327

0162-2889 See INTERNATIONAL SECURITY. 4525

0162-2897 See CALIFORNIA HISTORY (SAN FRANCISCO). 2726

0162-2900 See LOS ANGELES LAWYER. 3004

0162-2919 See PROCEEDINGS PLP. PRODUCT LIABILITY PREVENTION CONVENTION. 4221

0162-2927 See STATUS OF ELECTRIC POWER IN THE MISSOURI RIVER BASIN. 2082

0162-2951 See CHIEFS OF STATE AND CABINET MEMBERS OF FOREIGN GOVERNMENTS. 4637

0162-2986 See ALA BRIEF. 2929

0162-3052 See LAE NEWS. 1760

0162-3060 See POST SCRIPTS (INDIANAPOLIS). 4865

0162-3079 See JURISDOCS. 2990

0162-3095 See ETHOLOGY AND SOCIOBIOLOGY. 4586

0162-3109 See IMMUNOPHARMACOLOGY. 3672

0162-3117 See THOROUGHBRED RECORD (1967). 2803

0162-3125 See BACON'S PUBLICITY CHECKER. 756

0162-3176 See CONSTRUCTION BRIEFINGS. 608

0162-3184 See EXTRAORDINARY CONTRACTUAL RELIEF REPORTER. 674
0162-3214 See PETERSEN'S 4 WHEEL & OFF-ROAD. 4912
0162-3257 See JOURNAL OF AUTISM AND DEVELOPMENTAL DISORDERS. 3928
0162-3346 See MANAGING (PITTSBURGH). 878
0162-3370 See BETTER LIVING MAGAZINE (SUNNYVALE). 2485
0162-3397 See AMERICAN LAWYER (NEW YORK. 1979), THE. 2933
0162-3419 See GEOGRAPHIC DISTRIBUTION OF FEDERAL FUNDS IN TERRITORIES & OTHER AREAS ADMINISTERED BY THE U.S. 1564
0162-3427 See TRACTOR AND FARM IMPLEMENT LUBRICATION GUIDE. 161
0162-3435 See TRUCK LUBRICATION GUIDE. 5398
0162-3443 See CAR CARE GUIDE. 5409
0162-3508 See STRUCTURES COST MANUAL; SQUARE FOOT COSTS FOR RESIDENTIAL, COMMERCIAL, INDUSTRIAL, AGRICULTURAL AND MILITARY BUILDINGS. 629
0162-3532 See JOURNAL FOR THE EDUCATION OF THE GIFTED. 1880
0162-3540 See OFFICIAL MUSIC & RECORD DIRECTORY. 4143
0162-3559 See PSBA BULLETIN. 1869
0162-3567 See UNITY (UNITY VILLAGE). 5006
0162-3583 See RIFLE. 4915
0162-3605 See BLUE SHEET, THE. 4294
0162-363X See COMMUNITY AND THE BANK. 783
0162-3702 See KELLNER'S MONEYGRAM. 4371
0162-3796 See WOODALL'S CAMPGROUND MANAGEMENT. 889
0162-3842 See IEEE BULLETIN. 2059
0162-3869 See UNITED RUBBER WORKER: URW, THE. 5078
0162-3885 See BUSINESS COMMUNICATIONS REVIEW. 646
0162-3893 See COLUMBIA (NEW YORK, N.Y. 1978). 1090
0162-3907 See PROGRESS REPORT - AMERICAN PHYSICAL THERAPY ASSOCIATION. 4382
0162-3923 See SUPERCYCLE (HUNTINGTON BEACH). 4083
0162-3974 See NEIGHBORS. 2889
0162-3982 See PREACHER'S MAGAZINE, THE. 4987
0162-4075 See CONCRETE INTERNATIONAL. 608
0162-4105 See DATABASE (WESTON). 1253
0162-413X See JOSEPH CONRAD TODAY. 433
0162-4237 See CEMETERY BUSINESS & LEGAL GUIDE. 2407
0162-4261 See LIVING WITH TEENAGERS. 2283
0162-427X See MATURE LIVING (NASHVILLE). 5180
0162-4296 See OPEN WINDOWS. 4983
0162-4326 See PROCLAIM (NASHVILLE). 4988
0162-4334 See SOUTHERN BAPTIST HANDBOOK (1991). 4998
0162-4350 See LIVING WITH PRESCHOOLERS. 2282
0162-4377 See MUSIC MAKERS (NASHVILLE). 4134
0162-4423 See EXPLORING 1 FOR LEADERS. 5060
0162-4431 See EXPLORING B. 5060
0162-461X See CHILDREN'S LEADERSHIP. 1061
0162-4652 See CHURCH RECREATION MAGAZINE. 4849
0162-4687 See BIBLE DISCOVERERS TEACHER. 5014
0162-4695 See BIBLE DISCOVERERS. 5014
0162-4830 See BIBLE BOOK STUDY FOR YOUTH TEACHERS. 5014
0162-4962 See BIOGRAPHY (HONOLULU). 430
0162-4989 See IMPACT (WASHINGTON). 2980
0162-5047 See LIVESTOCK WEEKLY (SAN ANGELO). 215

0162-5063 See BANKING INDUSTRY CONFERENCE. 777
0162-5136 See CANDY WHOLESALER. 2330
0162-5144 See EAGLE (UNITED STATES FIELD HOCKEY ASSOCIATION, INC.), THE. 4893
0162-5152 See INSIDERS' CHRONICLE, THE. 791
0162-5160 See PA. TOWNSHIP NEWS. 4672
0162-5179 See OREGON FARM BUREAU NEWS. 117
0162-5225 See ST. JOSEPH JOURNAL OF LIVESTOCK AND AGRICULTURE. 222
0162-5233 See FOOD INSTITUTE REPORT, THE. 2337
0162-5241 See PROFILE (OMAHA). 705
0162-5276 See KIWANIS. 5232
0162-5314 See BIBLIOGRAPHIC GUIDE TO LATIN AMERICAN STUDIES. 2634
0162-5322 See BIBLIOGRAPHIC GUIDE TO SOVIET AND EAST EUROPEAN STUDIES. 2634
0162-5349 See EMORY ALUMNUS, THE. 1102
0162-5403 See ALASKA REVIEW OF SOCIAL AND ECONOMIC CONDITIONS. 1545
0162-542X See OFFICIAL BASEBALL REGISTER. 4856
0162-5462 See FINNISH AMERICANA. 2733
0162-5519 See HADRONIC JOURNAL. 4447
0162-5543 See DIRECTORY OF PHYSICAL THERAPISTS AND PHYSICAL THERAPISTS ASSISTANTS LICENSED AND REGISTERED IN TENNESSEE. 4380
0162-5551 See SHORT NOTES ON ALASKAN GEOLOGY. 1397
0162-5616 See FLORIDA FOLK ARTS DIRECTORY. 320
0162-5667 See HEARING & SPEECH ACTION. 4388
0162-5675 See OIL, GAS, MARINE DIRECTORY OF THE GULF SOUTH/ATLANTIC COAST. 4269
0162-5691 See CORPORATE PRACTICE SERIES. 3099
0162-5748 See REVIEW OF HIGHER EDUCATION. 1845
0162-5764 See LICENSING LAW AND BUSINESS REPORT. 3101
0162-5780 See CURRENT INTERESTS OF THE FORD FOUNDATION. 5281
0162-5888 See JOINT ECONOMIC REPORT, THE. 1498
0162-5918 See ALPHA (MEMPHIS). 1808
0162-5934 See ASWLC. 1126
0162-5942 See EMERGENCY. 4774
0162-5950 See ON-YOUR-OWN GUIDE TO ASIA, THE. 5487
0162-5977 See CSP DIRECTORY OF SUPPLIERS OF EDUCATIONAL FOREIGN LANGUAGE MATERIALS. 1892
0162-5993 See DISCUS NEWS LETTER. 2366
0162-6140 See PROCESSED FISHERY PRODUCTS, ANNUAL SUMMARY. 2311
0162-6191 See CONSTRUCTOR (WASHINGTON). 611
0162-6280 See FOLKLORE AND MYTHOLOGY STUDIES (LOS ANGELES, CALIF. : 1977). 2320
0162-6337 See DEFENDERS. 2191
0162-6353 See CAROLINAS COMPANIES. 655
0162-6361 See SOCIAL SECURITY EXPLAINED. 5308
0162-637X See CHEMICAL WORKER, THE. 1659
0162-640X See MALMGREN'S WORLD TRADE OUTLOOK. 845
0162-6434 See JOURNAL OF SPECIAL EDUCATION TECHNOLOGY. 1881
0162-6442 See CUSTOMS BULLETIN AND DECISIONS. 2958
0162-6450 See IMAGINE (WATERBURY, CONN.). 4122
0162-6477 See COLLECTED LETTERS / CORRESPONDENCE SOCIETY OF SURGEONS. 3962
0162-6493 See INFECTIOUS DISEASE PRACTICE. 3587
0162-6507 See MONEY MANAGEMENT FOR PHYSICIANS. 799

0162-6523 See MOUNTAIN VACATION & TRAVEL GUIDE COVERING WESTERN NORTH CAROLINA. 5485
0162-6531 See STANDARD AND POOR'S REGISTERED BOND INTEREST RECORD. 915
0162-6604 See AFTERMARKET EXECUTIVE. 5403
0162-6612 See ALSC NEWSLETTER. 3189
0162-6620 See ACTION IN TEACHER EDUCATION. 1887
0162-6647 See FOUR CORNERS ADVISOR, THE. 1491
0162-6655 See MPLS. ST. PAUL. 2747
0162-6671 See PRIMROSES. 2428
0162-6701 See BOWLING GREEN TIMES, THE. 5702
0162-6728 See AMERICAN FISHERIES DIRECTORY & REFERENCE BOOK, THE. 2294
0162-6744 See COLORADO CONSTRUCTION INDUSTRY REFERENCE BOOK. 608
0162-6760 See SPIRITUALITY TODAY. 5036
0162-6779 See CONTINGENT FOREIGN LIABILITIES OF THE UNITED STATES GOVERNMENT. 4719
0162-6795 See JOURNAL OF ASIAN CULTURE. 2505
0162-6809 See OFFICIAL GUIDE, TRACTORS AND FARM EQUIPMENT. 160
0162-6817 See MARKET LOGIC FROM THE INSTITUTE FOR ECONOMETRIC RESEARCH. 906
0162-6825 See DIMENSION. 4953
0162-6833 See AWARE. 4937
0162-6841 See START (BIRMINGHAM, ALA.). 4999
0162-6892 See WOMEN IN MEDICAL ACADEMIA. 3651
0162-6906 See MONOGRAPHS IN DEVELOPMENTAL PEDIATRICS. 3906
0162-6922 See ARIZONA COMPREHENSIVE BEHAVIORAL HEALTH PLAN. 4767
0162-6973 See CADENCE. 4106
0162-699X See TRANSPORTATION MONITORING REPORT. 5396
0162-7015 See WOODALL'S RV BUYER'S CATALOG. 5400
0162-7023 See CATHOLIC UNIVERSE-BULLETIN, THE. 5027
0162-7031 See CATHOLIC EXPONENT, THE. 5025
0162-704X See CONFERENCE PAPERS INDEX. 5096
0162-7104 See INDIANA PRAIRIE FARMER. 95
0162-7112 See CAS REPORT (COLUMBUS). 966
0162-7139 See DECADE. 318
0162-7163 See LACMA PHYSICIAN. 3914
0162-7171 See SYNOPSIS OF FAMILY THERAPY PRACTICE. 3937
0162-7201 See CQ, CONTEMPORARY QUARTERLY. 3462
0162-721X See FOLLIES. 3343
0162-7260 See FOREFRONT (NEW YORK). 3817
0162-7279 See CRANIOFACIAL GROWTH SERIES. 3569
0162-7325 See NATIONAL LAW JOURNAL, THE. 3013
0162-7341 See JOURNAL OF SPORT BEHAVIOR. 4902
0162-7368 See WOODALL'S RV BUYER'S GUIDE. 5400
0162-7406 See WOODALL'S CAMPGROUND DIRECTORY. EASTERN EDITION. 4881
0162-7414 See WOODALL'S CAMPGROUND DIRECTORY. WESTERN EDITION. 4881
0162-7457 See BANK SECURITY REPORT. 776
0162-7465 See BANK TAX REPORT, THE. 776
0162-7473 See BANK TELLER'S REPORT. 776
0162-7481 See BRANCH BANKER'S REPORT. 780
0162-7511 See KESS TAX PRACTICE REPORT. 4735
0162-752X See REAL ESTATE LAW REPORT. 3035
0162-7538 See REAL ESTATE TAX IDEAS. 4845
0162-7635 See YACHTSMAN'S GUIDE TO THE GREATER ANTILLES. 5500

0162-7643 See OPTICAL INFORMATION PROCESSING. 4439

0162-7651 See ANNOTATED DIRECTORY OF SELF-PUBLISHED TEXTILE BOOKS. 5347

0162-766X See MIDDLE EAST, ABSTRACTS AND INDEX. 2635

0162-7686 See CA SELECTS: ADHESIVES. 997

0162-7694 See CA SELECTS: ANIMAL LONGEVITY & AGING. 997

0162-7708 See CA SELECTS: BATTERIES & FUEL CELLS. 998

0162-7716 See CA SELECTS: BIOGENIC AMINES & THE NERVOUS SYSTEM. 998

0162-7724 See CA SELECTS: BIOLOGICAL INFORMATION TRANSFER. 998

0162-7732 See CA SELECTS: BLOOD COAGULATION. 998

0162-7740 See CA SELECTS: CRYSTAL GROWTH. 1000

0162-7767 See CA SELECTS: DETERGENTS, SOAPS, & SURFACTANTS. 1001

0162-7775 See CA SELECTS: DRUG & COSMETIC TOXICITY. 1001

0162-7783 See CA SELECTS: ELECTRODEPOSITION. 1001

0162-7791 See CA SELECTS: ENERGY REVIEWS & BOOKS. 1002

0162-7805 See CA SELECTS: FLAMMABILITY. 1002

0162-7813 See CA SELECTS: FOOD TOXICITY. 1003

0162-7821 See CA SELECTS: HEAT-RESISTANT & ABLATIVE POLYMERS. 1003

0162-783X See CA SELECTS: ORGANOPHOSPHORUS CHEMISTRY. 1006

0162-7848 See CA SELECTS: ORGANIC REACTION MECHANISMS. 1006

0162-7864 See CA SELECTS: THERMOCHEMISTRY. 1010

0162-7872 See CA SELECTS: X-RAY ANALYSIS & SPECTROSCOPY. 1010

0162-7880 See WHO'S WHO IN AMERICAN LAW. 3075

0162-7899 See GROUNDSWELL. 2155

0162-7910 See AAHE BULLETIN. 1806

0162-7929 See CONCORDIA COMMENTATOR. 4828

0162-7953 See POLLED HEREFORD WORLD (1965). 217

0162-7996 See ANTITRUST (CHICAGO, ILL.). 3095

0162-8038 See AFFIRMATIONS. 4932

0162-8046 See UFO ANNUAL (BROOKLYN). 38

0162-8089 See ANNUAL REPORT / DEPARTMENT OF AGRICULTURE. 60

0162-8097 See STATISTICAL REVIEW (NEW YORK). 4222

0162-8127 See HORSECARE. 2800

0162-8151 See MCGRAW-HILL HOMEBOOK, THE. 2902

0162-816X See MEDICAL EQUIPMENT CLASSIFIED, THE. 3609

0162-8178 See ITE JOURNAL. 5384

0162-8208 See ALTADENA REVIEW, THE. 3337

0162-8216 See COMMUNICATION THEORY IN THE CAUSE OF MAN. 234

0162-8267 See HERITAGE REVIEW. 2690

0162-8275 See CDE STOCK OWNERSHIP DIRECTORY: TRANSPORTATION INDUSTRY. 5379

0162-8283 See JOURNAL OF THE AMERICAN HISTORICAL SOCIETY OF GERMANS FROM RUSSIA. 2695

0162-8291 See SEA WORLD. 557

0162-8321 See MONOGRAPHS OF MARINE MOLLUSCA. 5591

0162-8372 See UNIVERSITY OF ARKANSAS AT LITTLE ROCK LAW JOURNAL. 3068

0162-8380 See JEEPERS KREEPERS REFUND PEEPERS. 2791

0162-8402 See HYDROGEN PROGRESS. 2090

0162-8445 See ARTS & HUMANITIES CITATION INDEX. PERMUTERM SUBJECT INDEX. 2842

0162-8445 See ARTS & HUMANITIES CITATION INDEX (PRINT ED.). 2857

0162-8461 See LOUISIANA STATE PLAN FOR COMPREHENSIVE MENTAL HEALTH SERVICES. 4789

0162-8615 See LINCOLN LORE. 2744

0162-8623 See WIND ENERGY REPORT. 1960

0162-8674 See UNITED STATES COURT DIRECTORY (UNITED STATES. ADMINISTRATIVE OFFICE OF THE UNITED STATES COURTS). 3143

0162-8712 See CALIFORNIA SOCIOLOGIST. 5241

0162-8739 See DIFFERENT DRUMMER (TOMS RIVER, N.J.), A. 3381

0162-8771 See NEW ENGLAND PRINTER & PUBLISHER. 4567

0162-881X See FLOORING (NEW YORK, N.Y.). 615

0162-8828 See IEEE TRANSACTIONS ON PATTERN ANALYSIS AND MACHINE INTELLIGENCE. 1229

0162-8879 See MALLET, THE. 634

0162-8887 See COMMUNITY PUBLICATION RATES AND DATA. 757

0162-8941 See EQUINE PRACTICE. 2798

0162-895X See POLITICAL PSYCHOLOGY. 4608

0162-8968 See INC. (BOSTON, MASS.). 681

0162-8976 See PRAIRIE SUN. 5661

0162-9026 See WESTERN MINING DIRECTORY. 2153

0162-9034 See MINORITY ORGANIZATIONS: A NATIONAL DIRECTORY. 2267

0162-9050 See NEW ISSUES (FORT LAUDERDALE, FLA.). 909

0162-9077 See HOME LIGHTING & ACCESSORIES. 2906

0162-9085 See NAHUATZEN, EL. 3466

0162-9093 See COMMUNICATIONS AND THE LAW. 2954

0162-9115 See W. 1088

0162-9123 See WORKBASKET AND HOME ARTS MAGAZINE, THE. 376

0162-9131 See ENERGY USER NEWS. 1942

0162-914X See FOOTWEAR NEWS. 1084

0162-9158 See HFD. 2906

0162-9174 See UNIVERSITY OF DAYTON LAW REVIEW. 3068

0162-9212 See ADULT TEACHER'S GUIDE. 1887

0162-9220 See BIBLE ADVENTURES (ELGIN, ILL.). 5014

0162-9255 See CHRISTIAN LIVING (ELGIN). 4945

0162-9298 See SENIOR HIGH TEACHER'S GUIDE. 1905

0162-9328 See RIGHT WOMAN, THE. 5565

0162-9352 See PROSTAGLANDINS & THERAPEUTICS. 3631

0162-9360 See JOURNAL OF CLINICAL HEMATOLOGY AND ONCOLOGY. 3772

0162-9379 See ORTHOPAEDIC TRANSACTIONS. 3884

0162-9387 See DIRECTORY OF PRECEPTORSHIP PROGRAMS IN THE HEALTH PROFESSIONS, A. 4773

0162-9417 See ANNUAL REPORT - CENTER FOR LAW AND HEALTH SCIENCES. 3739

0162-945X See UPDATE (ARLINGTON). 1917

0162-9492 See GEOGRAPHIC DISTRIBUTION OF FEDERAL FUNDS IN NEW YORK. 1563

0162-9573 See BIBLE-IN-LIFE STORIES. 5014

0162-962X See COMPREHENSIVE BIBLE STUDY. 5016

0162-9662 See JOURNAL OF PRE-COLLEGE PHILOSOPHY, THE. 4351

0162-9689 See BUS WORLD. 5378

0162-9697 See SELECTED PAPERS IN SCHOOL FINANCE. 1783

0162-976X See NEWSLETTER - ASSOCIATION FOR THE ADVANCEMENT OF BALTIC STUDIES, INC. 5211

0162-9778 See JOURNAL OF BALTIC STUDIES. 2694

0162-9816 See TRAVLTIPS. 5497

0162-9840 See KEITHWOOD DIRECTORY OF HOSPITAL & SURGICAL SUPPLY DEALERS. 3602

0162-9859 See JUVENILE AND FAMILY COURT NEWSLETTER. 3121

0162-9905 See RESTORATION (KNOXVILLE). 3429

0162-9913 See PRIVATE PSYCHIATRIC HOSPITALS. 3791

0162-9972 See HOTEL & TRAVEL INDEX. 2806

0163-0008 See OHIO MONTHLY RECORD. 3021

0163-0059 See TULIP TIDINGS. 2433

0163-0075 See CINCINNATI MEDICINE. 3564

0163-0202 See RESEARCH AND DEVELOPMENT PROGRAMS GUIDE. 4055

0163-0210 See DOING BUSINESS ABROAD. JOYNER'S GUIDE TO OFFICIAL WASHINGTON. 667

0163-0229 See KOREAN REVIEW, THE. 2657

0163-027X See AVON PARK SUN. 5649

0163-0288 See LEDGER (LAKELAND), THE. 5650

0163-0334 See DIET & EXERCISE. 2596

0163-0350 See REVISTA DE MUSICA LATINOAMERICANA. 4149

0163-0369 See NEW FARM, THE. 111

0163-0415 See DIECIOCHO. 3381

0163-0423 See ITALIAN-AMERICAN IDENTITY. 2739

0163-0458 See HEALTH DEVICES ALERTS. 3659

0163-0466 See INDEX TO NEW ENGLAND PERIODICALS. 417

0163-0512 See FACETS (CHICAGO, ILL.). 3737

0163-0547 See COMPUTERS & MEDICINE. 1179

0163-0563 See NUMERICAL FUNCTIONAL ANALYSIS AND OPTIMIZATION. 3525

0163-0601 See JOURNAL OF ANTHROPOLOGY (DEKALB), THE. 238

0163-0628 See FODOR'S BRAZIL. 5471

0163-0652 See LIMITED PARTNERS LETTER. 3003

0163-0679 See CEM, CHILTON'S CONTROL EQUIPMENT MASTER. 2111

0163-0687 See ROOF. 3470

0163-0695 See TIERRA (SOUTHERN TEXAS ARCHAEOLOGICAL ASSOCIATION), LA. 284

0163-075X See KENYON REVIEW, THE. 3345

0163-0768 See FORUM LINGUISTICUM. 3282

0163-0784 See MASSACHUSETTS NURSE, THE. 3861

0163-0873 See BIBLIOGRAPHIES AND LITERATURE OF AGRICULTURE. 151

0163-0881 See PHILOSOPHY OF SCIENCE ASSOCIATION NEWSLETTER. 5138

0163-092X See PORTFOLIO (NEW YORK. 1979). 362

0163-0946 See ODYSSEY (PETERBOROUGH, N.H.). 398

0163-0954 See ICARUS. 3464

0163-0970 See REFERENCES TO CONTEMPORARY PAPERS ON ACOUSTICS. 4453

0163-0989 See EARTH'S DAUGHTERS. 3383

0163-0997 See INTERSEARCH. 4478

0163-1047 See BEHAVIORAL AND NEURAL BIOLOGY. 5577

0163-1055 See HANDBOOK AND DIRECTORY - CLASSIC CAR CLUB OF AMERICA. 5416

0163-1101 See SHEPARD'S MILITARY JUSTICE CITATIONS. 3183

0163-111X See AUTOMATIC DATA PROCESSING ACTIVITIES SUMMARY IN THE UNITED STATES GOVERNMENT. 4631

0163-1128 See BOOKWOMAN, THE. 4827

0163-1136 See CONNECTICUT MAGAZINE (FAIRFIELD, CONN.). 2531

0163-1152 See MAINE HISTORICAL SOCIETY QUARTERLY. 2745

0163-1160 See REPORT - TEXAS TECH UNIVERSITY, WATER RESOURCES CENTER. 5538

0163-1209 See CUMBERLANDS (PIKEVILLE. 1977). 3379

0163-1241 See ABINGDON CLERGY INCOME TAX GUIDE. 4708
0163-1284 See PLATT'S OILGRAM NEWS. 4274
0163-1292 See PLATT'S OILGRAM PRICE REPORT. 4275
0163-1314 See ACUPUNCTURE LETTER, THE. 3546
0163-139X See SUMMARY OF PUBLIC SECTOR LABOR RELATIONS POLICIES. 3154
0163-1403 See STATISTICS ON SOCIAL WORK EDUCATION IN THE UNITED STATES. 5267
0163-1411 See MASSACHUSETTS LAW REVIEW. 3007
0163-1438 See NATURAL RESOURCES & EARTH SCIENCES. 2199
0163-1462 See ELECTROTECHNOLOGY (SPRINGFIELD, VA.). 2050
0163-1500 See NTIS ALERT. BUILDING INDUSTRY TECHNOLOGY. 623
0163-1519 See CHEMISTRY (SPRINGFIELD). 971
0163-1543 See PSYCHOTHERAPY FINANCES. 4614
0163-156X See CURRENT HEALTH 2. 4772
0163-1578 See ADVANCES IN ASTHMA & ALLERGY. 3948
0163-1608 See AMERICAN REVENUER, THE. 2784
0163-1632 See NOTES ON VIRGINIA. 305
0163-1640 See 18 ALMANAC. 1088
0163-1675 See CARDIOLOGY UPDATE. 3701
0163-1691 See DERMATOLOGY UPDATE. 3719
0163-1705 See DRUG THERAPEUTICS. 4301
0163-1721 See PSYCHIATRIC MEDICINE UPDATE. 3933
0163-1780 See WORLD TRAVELING. 5500
0163-1799 See TODAY'S CHRISTIAN WOMAN. 5005
0163-1802 See MEDICAL PHYSICS MONOGRAPH. 4412
0163-1829 See PHYSICAL REVIEW B : CONDENSED MATTER. 4415
0163-1861 See KENT COLLECTOR, THE. 355
0163-1888 See MOLYBDENUM MOSAIC. 4013
0163-1918 See TECHNICAL DIGEST / INTERNATIONAL ELECTRON DEVICES MEETING. 2083
0163-1926 See CAT WORLD. 4286
0163-1942 See AMERICAN JOURNAL OF FORENSIC PSYCHIATRY, THE. 3919
0163-1969 See SPEARS REPORT, DRILLING. 4279
0163-1993 See STANDARD & POOR'S STOCK REPORTS: OVER THE COUNTER. 915
0163-2000 See BUDGET OF THE UNITED STATES GOVERNMENT. 4714
0163-2035 See COGNITIVE THEORY. 4581
0163-206X See STEEL INDUSTRY REVIEW. 1628
0163-2108 See CONTEMPORARY NEUROSURGERY. 3963
0163-2116 See DIGESTIVE DISEASES AND SCIENCES. 3744
0163-2132 See ON STAGE (WASHINGTON). 386
0163-2183 See SYNERJY. 1959
0163-2191 See NATIONAL MANUFACTURERS REGISTER. 3485
0163-2205 See LINKS (SACRAMENTO). 5295
0163-2213 See CARCH NEWS. 3778
0163-223X See NURSINGWORLD JOURNAL. 3866
0163-2248 See NEW ENGLAND SENIOR CITIZEN. 5180
0163-2299 See NEW VIRGINIA REVIEW. 3348
0163-2302 See U.S. SCIENTISTS AND ENGINEERS. 5167
0163-2345 See PROCEEDINGS OF THE INDUSTRIAL WASTE, ADVANCED WATER AND SOLID WASTE CONFERENCE. 2239
0163-2361 See WORLD POPULATION ESTIMATES. 4561
0163-2396 See STUDIES IN SYMBOLIC INTERACTION. 5263
0163-2418 See QUALITY CONTROL REPORTS. 3487

0163-2426 See MEDICAL DEVICES, DIAGNOSTICS & INSTRUMENTATION REPORTS. 3608
0163-2469 See MILFORD SERIES, POPULAR WRITERS OF TODAY, THE. 3411
0163-2566 See EDF LETTER. 2192
0163-2574 See CURRENT CONTENTS. PHYSICAL, CHEMICAL & EARTH SCIENCES. 1362
0163-2582 See PHYSICAL FITNESS/SPORTS MEDICINE. 2600
0163-2604 See TENNESSEE RESEARCHER (CHARLOTTESVILLE), THE. 3063
0163-268X See ANDERSON'S CAMPGROUND DIRECTORY. 4869
0163-2698 See TECHNOLOGY EXCHANGE BULLETIN. 5163
0163-2787 See EVALUATION & THE HEALTH PROFESSIONS. 3576
0163-2809 See CHILDREN'S LANGUAGE. 3273
0163-2817 See OFFICIAL NATIONAL COLLEGIATE ATHLETIC ASSOCIATION BASKETBALL RULES & INTERPRETATIONS, THE. 4909
0163-2825 See MOUNTAIN STATE GEOLOGY. 1388
0163-2833 See SAR STATISTICS. 5402
0163-2841 See MODERN PSYCHOTHERAPY. 4604
0163-2876 See COMMERCIAL AND FINANCIAL CHRONICLE (1978), THE. 895
0163-2884 See SWIMMING AND DIVING RULES. 4925
0163-2930 See FIRA NAFM. 2905
0163-2965 See STUDIA AFRICANA. 2643
0163-299X See TODAY'S PROFESSIONALS. 4209
0163-3015 See BOSTON PHOENIX, THE. 5688
0163-3031 See CORPORATE FINANCE SOURCEBOOK, THE. 785
0163-304X See HEALTH FOODS RETAILING MERCHANDISING HANDBOOK. 2343
0163-3058 See MAGILL'S LITERARY ANNUAL. 4821
0163-3082 See DAILY LOCAL NEWS (WEST CHESTER). 5735
0163-3090 See DISPATCH (LEXINGTON), THE. 5723
0163-3147 See LAWYER'S REGISTER INTERNATIONAL BY SPECIALTIES AND FIELDS OF LAW INCLUDING A DIRECTORY OF CORPORATE COUNSEL. 3101
0163-3155 See CURRENT CONTENTS. ARTS & HUMANITIES. 334
0163-3171 See GLOBAL TECTONICS AND METALLOGENY. 1356
0163-3201 See OCALA STAR-BANNER. 5650
0163-321X See R.F. DESIGN. 1993
0163-3228 See DIAGNOSIS (ORADELL, N.J.). 3571
0163-3244 See WOMAN LOCALLY. 5569
0163-3252 See JOURNAL OF STUDIES IN TECHNICAL CAREERS. 1914
0163-3287 See EMPLOYMENT INFORMATION IN THE MATHEMATICAL SCIENCES. 1666
0163-3333 See POCKET DIRECTORY OF THE CALIFORNIA LEGISLATURE. 4673
0163-3341 See ENTREPRENEUR (SANTA MONICA, CALIF.). 672
0163-335X See GEOGRAPHIC DISTRIBUTION OF FEDERAL FUNDS IN VERMONT. 1564
0163-3376 See RESEARCH PAPER FPL. 2393
0163-3392 See JOURNAL OF CURRENT ISSUES AND RESEARCH IN ADVERTISING. 761
0163-3422 See TEAM TORIZONS. 5002
0163-3430 See WHITE HOUSE NEWS PHOTOGRAPHERS ANNUAL AWARDS. 4378
0163-3465 See HOSPITAL ENGINEERING (CHICAGO). 1977
0163-3473 See OPERATIVE DENTISTRY. SUPPLEMENT. 1332
0163-352X See KEEPING POSTED. TEACHER'S/LEADER'S EDITION (NEW YORK). 1759
0163-3562 See DYNAMITE (NEW YORK). 1063

0163-3570 See SCHOLASTIC ACTION. 1904
0163-3627 See SAMS AUTO RADIO SERVICE DATA. 2080
0163-3635 See LEADERS. 1572
0163-3643 See RESEARCH NOTE FPL. 2392
0163-3716 See PALESTINE PERSPECTIVES. 4531
0163-3724 See INTERNATIONAL ENERGY STATISTICAL REVIEW. 1963
0163-3732 See CHRONOLOG (PALO ALTO, CALIF.). 3202
0163-3759 See JOURNAL OF POSTGRADUATE PHARMACY. COMMUNITY EDITION, THE. 4313
0163-3767 See SEMICONDUCTOR INTERNATIONAL. 2080
0163-3805 See ADDRESS LIST, REGIONAL AND SUBREGIONAL LIBRARIES FOR THE BLIND AND PHYSICALLY HANDICAPPED. 3187
0163-3813 See CONTRIBUTIONS IN COMPARATIVE COLONIAL STUDIES. 2729
0163-3821 See CONTRIBUTIONS IN DRAMA AND THEATRE STUDIES. 5363
0163-383X See GUIDE TO GIFTS AND BEQUESTS, CALIFORNIA, THE. 4338
0163-3848 See EDWARD SAPIR MONOGRAPH SERIES IN LANGUAGE, CULTURE, AND COGNITION. 3278
0163-3856 See FUSION ENERGY UPDATE. 2155
0163-3864 See JOURNAL OF NATURAL PRODUCTS. 1043
0163-3872 See PORCH. 3470
0163-3899 See FACTS (WASHINGTON). 4001
0163-3910 See JOURNAL OF POSTGRADUATE PHARMACY. HOSPITAL EDITION, THE. 4313
0163-3945 See NATIONAL GUARD (WASHINGTON. 1978). 4052
0163-3988 See NEWS-SUN (SEBRING, FLA.), THE. 5650
0163-3996 See HEALTH LAW PROJECT LIBRARY BULLETIN. 2978
0163-4003 See COMPUTER YEARBOOK (DETROIT). 1257
0163-4011 See NEWS-LEADER. 5650
0163-4038 See SUNDAY STAR-NEWS, THE. 5724
0163-4046 See ACCESSIONS LIST, SOUTHEAST ASIA. CUMULATIVE LIST OF MALAYSIA, SINGAPORE AND BRUNEI SERIALS. 406
0163-4054 See ACCESSIONS LIST, SOUTHEAST ASIA. CUMULATIVE LIST OF INDONESIAN SERIALS. 406
0163-4070 See SOCCER AMERICA. 4919
0163-4089 See AMERICAN DEMOGRAPHICS. 4549
0163-4097 See U.S. GEOLOGICAL SURVEY IN ALASKA ..., PROGRAMS, THE. 1400
0163-4119 See FEED & GRAIN TIMES. 200
0163-4143 See STUDIES IN CONTEMPORARY SATIRE. 3441
0163-416X See ZOO GOER, THE. 5601
0163-4275 See ENVIRONMENTAL ETHICS. 2167
0163-4313 See WOODALL'S FLORIDA & SOUTHERN STATES RETIREMENT AND RESORT COMMUNITIES. 4855
0163-4356 See THERAPEUTIC DRUG MONITORING. 4330
0163-4364 See MANUFACTURING CONFECTIONER, THE. 3483
0163-4372 See JOURNAL OF GERONTOLOGICAL SOCIAL WORK. 5292
0163-4402 See GEOMAGNETIC DATA. 4443
0163-4429 See NONWOVENS INDUSTRY. 1620
0163-4437 See MEDIA, CULTURE & SOCIETY. 5251
0163-4445 See JOURNAL OF FAMILY THERAPY. 3928
0163-4453 See JOURNAL OF INFECTION, THE. 3714
0163-447X See B C & T NEWS. 1654
0163-4496 See ALMANACK - INSTITUTE OF ELECTRICAL AND ELECTRONICS ENGINEERS, INC. PHILADELPHIA SECTION. 2034
0163-4518 See FARM SHOW. 159

0163-4526 See JOURNAL OF WATER BORNE COATINGS. 4224
0163-4542 See POWDER COATINGS. 4225
0163-4569 See NATIONAL LIBRARY OF MEDICINE PROGRAMS AND SERVICES. 3233
0163-4577 See SAGA NATIONAL PRINT EXHIBITION. 382
0163-4585 See LET'S GO: THE BUDGET GUIDE TO EUROPE. 5482
0163-4607 See SOUND TRAX. 4154
0163-4615 See HANDBOOK OF BUSINESS FINANCE AND CAPITAL SOURCES. 790
0163-4623 See GUIDE TO CALIFORNIA FOUNDATIONS. 5287
0163-4631 See PRECISELY. 3425
0163-4666 See TEXAS FACT BOOK. 1586
0163-4674 See ACCIDENT/INCIDENT BULLETIN. 4763
0163-4682 See ECONOMIC WORLD DIRECTORY OF JAPANESE COMPANIES IN USA. 832
0163-4720 See SCIENCE UPDATE. 5154
0163-4755 See REPORT TO CONGRESS ON ADMINISTRATION OF OCEAN DUMPING ACTIVITIES. PUBLIC LAW 92-532, MARINE PROTECTION, RESEARCH, AND SANCTUARIES ACT OF 1972. 2242
0163-4771 See TEXAS RIVERS AND RAPIDS. 4879
0163-4798 See SCHOLASTIC SEARCH. 1781
0163-4801 See RESOURCE PUBLICATION - U.S. FISH AND WILDLIFE SERVICE. 2204
0163-481X See JOURNAL OF CONTINUING EDUCATION IN HOSPITAL & CLINICAL PHARMACY, THE. 4311
0163-4844 See KNOW YOUR WORLD EXTRA. 1899
0163-4925 See GAINESVILLE SUN. 5649
0163-4941 See AERONAUTICAL ENGINEERING (WASHINGTON, DC.). 4
0163-4976 See PLANTING TO HARVEST; ANNUAL CROP WEATHER SUMMARY. 182
0163-4984 See BIOLOGICAL TRACE ELEMENT RESEARCH. 483
0163-4992 See CELL BIOPHYSICS. 495
0163-5042 See FIELD & STREAM DEER HUNTING ANNUAL. 4871
0163-5050 See PALATKA DAILY NEWS. 5650
0163-5069 See FILM CRITICISM. 4069
0163-5085 See WORLD DEVELOPMENT REPORT. 1589
0163-5123 See ANNUAL INDEX TO MOTION PICTURE CREDITS. 4063
0163-5158 See AGEING INTERNATIONAL. 5270
0163-5182 See PROCEEDINGS OF THE HUMAN FACTORS SOCIETY ANNUAL MEETING. 2125
0163-528X See FOLK DANCE DIRECTORY. 1313
0163-5328 See WOODALL'S MISSOURI/ARKANSAS CAMPGROUND DIRECTORY. 4881
0163-5360 See T.U.B.A. MEMBERSHIP ROSTER. 4156
0163-5379 See ADVANCES IN INSTRUCTIONAL PSYCHOLOGY. 4572
0163-5425 See FOCUS: TEACHING ENGLISH LANGUAGE ARTS. 3281
0163-5433 See WYOMING ISSUES. 1589
0163-545X See ENVIRONMENTAL LAW NEWSLETTER. 3111
0163-5468 See FIELD & STREAM BASS FISHING ANNUAL. 2301
0163-5476 See MIDDLE EAST CONTEMPORARY SURVEY. 2769
0163-5506 See PUBLIC LIBRARIES. 3243
0163-5557 See ANNUAL REPORT / THE JAPAN-UNITED STATES FRIENDSHIP COMMISSION. 5239
0163-5581 See NUTRITION AND CANCER. 4195
0163-559X See BULLETIN OF MAGNETIC RESONANCE. 4443
0163-5603 See CHICOREL INDEX TO POETRY IN ANTHOLOGIES AND COLLECTIONS IN PRINT. 3461

0163-5611 See RECRUITING TRENDS (EAST LANSING). 1705
0163-562X See PAW PRINTS. 1067
0163-5689 See PROGRESS IN COMMUNICATION SCIENCES. 1120
0163-5697 See SIGBIO NEWSLETTER. 1203
0163-5700 See SIGACT NEWS. 1202
0163-5727 See SIGCAPH NEWSLETTER. 1225
0163-5743 See SIGDA NEWSLETTER. 1221
0163-5778 See SIGNUM NEWSLETTER. 1203
0163-5808 See SIGMOD RECORD. 1255
0163-5824 See SIGSAM BULLETIN. 1203
0163-5840 See SIGIR FORUM. 1276
0163-5883 See WATER FOR WESTERN ENERGY DEVELOPMENT UPDATE. 1960
0163-5891 See STONE AGE. 713
0163-5905 See NORDIC. 4908
0163-5921 See DEVELOPMENTS IN IMMUNOLOGY. 3669
0163-5948 See SOFTWARE ENGINEERING NOTES. 1230
0163-5964 See COMPUTER ARCHITECTURE NEWS. 1232
0163-5980 See OPERATING SYSTEMS REVIEW. 1248
0163-5999 See PERFORMANCE EVALUATION REVIEW. 1289
0163-6006 See APL QUOTE QUAD. 1278
0163-6065 See DIRECTORY OF BLOOD ESTABLISHMENTS REGISTERED UNDER SECTION 510 OF THE FOOD, DRUG, AND COSMETIC ACT. 5282
0163-6111 See PETERSON'S ANNUAL GUIDES/GRADUATE STUDY. 1840
0163-612X See NAMIT JOURNAL. 4139
0163-6146 See DEVELOPMENTS IN CANCER RESEARCH. 3816
0163-6154 See VOLGA TRIBUNE, THE. 5744
0163-6189 See MACROMOLECULAR SYNTHESES. COLLECTIVE VOLUME. 1044
0163-6197 See ELECTRONIC BUSINESS. 2046
0163-6200 See FOOTBALL CASE BOOK. 4895
0163-6219 See FOOTBALL OFFICIALS MANUAL. 4895
0163-6227 See GOMER'S BUDGET TRAVEL DIRECTORY. 5478
0163-6235 See STOCKS IN THE STANDARD & POOR'S 500. 916
0163-6251 See NEWCASTLE FORGOTTEN FANTASY LIBRARY, THE. 3416
0163-6278 See CURRENT CHEMICAL REACTIONS. 1011
0163-6383 See INFANT BEHAVIOR & DEVELOPMENT. 4590
0163-6391 See CANADA-UNITED STATES LAW JOURNAL. 3125
0163-6405 See READER'S DIGEST. LARGE-TYPE EDITION. 2491
0163-643X See REMOTELY PILOTED MAGAZINE. 33
0163-6448 See AUTOMOTIVE WHOLESALING : FINANCIAL OPERATION AND PERFORMANCE ANALYSIS. 1599
0163-6480 See MORAL EDUCATION FORUM. 1765
0163-6510 See URBAN EDGE (ENGLISH ED.), THE. 2837
0163-6537 See DIRECTORY OF PERSONAL IMAGE CONSULTANTS. 758
0163-6545 See RADICAL HISTORY REVIEW. 4545
0163-6553 See B.C.S. BUSINESS CHANGE SERVICE : PENNSYLVANIA. 641
0163-6561 See BULLETIN - CENTER FOR THE STUDY OF WORLD RELIGIONS, HARVARD UNIVERSITY. 4940
0163-657X See STANFORD FRENCH REVIEW. 3353
0163-660X See WASHINGTON QUARTERLY, THE. 4538
0163-6626 See INTERFACE. 1223
0163-6642 See FAMILY PRACTICE RECERTIFICATION. 3737

0163-6669 See DESIGNFAX. 2097
0163-6707 See SAVE PROCEEDINGS. 1626
0163-6723 See WORLDCASTS. PRODUCT. 1632
0163-6731 See WORLDCASTS. REGIONAL. 1632
0163-6774 See ACRONYMS. 1170
0163-6782 See SAVINGS AND LOAN MARKET STUDY. 810
0163-6804 See IEEE COMMUNICATIONS MAGAZINE. 1157
0163-6820 See RECORD - GARLAND COUNTY HISTORICAL SOCIETY, THE. 2756
0163-6847 See PROCEEDINGS - WESTERN HEMISPHERE NUTRITION CONGRESS. 4198
0163-6898 See STATISTICAL REPORT - SOUTH CAROLINA DEPARTMENT OF SOCIAL SERVICES. 5267
0163-6952 See PEOPLE & ENERGY. 1952
0163-6995 See DEVELOPMENTS IN MARINE BIOLOGY. 453
0163-7010 See OXBRIDGE DIRECTORY OF NEWSLETTERS. 2923
0163-7029 See CARDIAC/THORACIC SURGERY. 3961
0163-7053 See NEWSWEEK (INTERNATIONAL, ATLANTIC EDITION). 2490
0163-7061 See NEWSWEEK (INTERNATIONAL, PACIFIC EDITION). 2490
0163-7088 See NOTES ON TEACHING ENGLISH. 3307
0163-710X See FAMILY ADVOCATE. 3120
0163-7150 See INDEX TO ACCOUNTING AND AUDITING TECHNICAL PRONOUNCEMENTS. 745
0163-7169 See CHINA BUSINESS REVIEW, THE. 657
0163-7177 See INTERNAL REVENUE CODE. 4732
0163-7207 See BOATING REGISTRATION STATISTICS. 597
0163-7223 See INTERCOM (WASHINGTON. EDICION ESPANOL). 4554
0163-7258 See PHARMACOLOGY & THERAPEUTICS (OXFORD). 4322
0163-7266 See RAILFAN & RAILROAD. 5435
0163-7282 See EXETASIS. 3386
0163-7290 See CATALOG OF COPYRIGHT EENTRIES, FOURTH SERIES. PART 1, NONDRAMATIC LITERARY WORKS [MICROFORM]. 1302
0163-7304 See CATALOG OF COPYRIGHT ENTRIES. FOURTH SERIES. PART 2. SERIALS & PERIODICALS. 1302
0163-7312 See CATALOG OF COPYRIGHT ENTRIES. FOURTH SERIES. PART 3. PERFORMING ARTS. 1302
0163-7320 See CATALOG OF COPYRIGHT ENTRIES, FOURTH SERIES. PART 4, MOTION PICTURES & FILMSTRIPS MICROFORM. 4065
0163-7339 See CATALOG OF COPYRIGHT ENTRIES. FOURTH SERIES. PART 5. VISUAL ARTS. 1302
0163-7347 See CATALOG OF COPYRIGHT ENTRIES. FOURTH SERIES. PART 6. MAPS. 1302
0163-7355 See CATALOG OF COPYRIGHT ENTRIES. FOURTH SERIES. PART 7. SOUND RECORDINGS. 1302
0163-7363 See CATALOG OF COPYRIGHT ENTRIES. FOURTH SERIES. PART 8. RENEWALS. 1302
0163-7460 See ART & DESIGN NEWS. 376
0163-7479 See TEXAS INTERNATIONAL LAW JOURNAL. 3136
0163-7517 See SALES & MARKETING MANAGEMENT. 936
0163-7525 See ANNUAL REVIEW OF PUBLIC HEALTH. 4767
0163-755X See MELUS. 3410
0163-7592 See HYDROLOGIC DATA REDUCTION AND ANALYSIS SERIES. 1414
0163-7606 See FEDERAL COMMUNICATIONS LAW JOURNAL. 2969
0163-7622 See MILWAUKEE HISTORY. 2746
0163-7649 See STABLE & KENNEL NEWS OF THE SOUTH. 2802

0163-7665 *See* FEDERAL PERSONNEL GUIDE. 4702

0163-7673 *See* REVIEWS IN BIOCHEMICAL TOXICOLOGY. 3983

0163-769X *See* ENDOCRINE REVIEWS. 3729

0163-772X *See* TCA REPORT. 570

0163-772X *See* NCA/TCS NEWSLETTER. 539

0163-7800 *See* CURRENT PULMONOLOGY. 3704

0163-7819 *See* OHIONETWORK. 2541

0163-7827 *See* PROGRESS IN LIPID RESEARCH. 1046

0163-7843 *See* PACIFIC HORTICULTURE. 2427

0163-7851 *See* HORTICULTURAL REVIEWS. 2419

0163-786X *See* RESEARCH IN SOCIAL MOVEMENTS, CONFLICTS AND CHANGE. 5255

0163-7878 *See* RESEARCH IN POPULATION ECONOMICS. 4559

0163-7916 *See* UNTITLED (CARMEL). 4377

0163-8084 *See* MILL'S PHARMACY STATE BOARD REVIEW. 4315

0163-8211 *See* AMERICAN RAG, THE. 3360

0163-822X *See* ILLINOIS SCHOOL RESEARCH AND DEVELOPMENT. 1751

0163-8262 *See* IMPACT (SYRACUSE). 5187

0163-8270 *See* FEDERAL CIVILIAN WORK FORCE STATISTICS. 1532

0163-8297 *See* PUBLIC WELFARE DIRECTORY, THE. 5303

0163-8300 *See* W-MEMO. 4694

0163-8343 *See* GENERAL HOSPITAL PSYCHIATRY. 3925

0163-8378 *See* CELEBRITY. 2530

0163-8386 *See* GUIDE TO MICROFORMS IN PRINT. SUBJECT. 3212

0163-8475 *See* COMMUNITY REVIEW (NEW BRUNSWICK). 1818

0163-8505 *See* SOCIOLOGICAL PRACTICE. 5261

0163-853X *See* DISCOURSE PROCESSES. 3277

0163-8548 *See* HUMAN STUDIES. 4348

0163-8602 *See* PRESIDENT'S NATIONAL URBAN POLICY REPORT, THE. 2831

0163-8610 *See* CONSER. 3204

0163-8688 *See* CRADLE ROLL PROGRAM HELPS. 5058

0163-8718 *See* KINDERGARTEN PROGRAM HELPS. 5062

0163-8769 *See* EARLITEEN-JUNIOR PROGRAM HELPS. 5059

0163-8831 *See* REVIEW OF LEGAL EDUCATION IN THE UNITED STATES, A. 3040

0163-8866 *See* ADVENTIST REVIEW (MONTHLY, INTER-AMERICAN EDITION). 5054

0163-8874 *See* FIRE CASUALTY & SURETY BULLETINS 325. COMPLETE SERVICE. 2881

0163-8882 *See* FIRE CASUALTY & SURETY BULLETINS 301. STANDARD LINES SET. 2880

0163-8920 *See* POLICY STATISTICS SERVICE. 2897

0163-8939 *See* ADVANCED SALES REFERENCE SERVICE. 2872

0163-8971 *See* GROUP (LOVELAND, COLO.). 1064

0163-898X *See* OCLC NEWSLETTER. 3238

0163-8998 *See* ANNUAL REVIEW OF NUCLEAR AND PARTICLE SCIENCE. 4446

0163-9005 *See* THERMAL CONDUCTIVITY (1975). 4432

0163-9013 *See* TRANSACTIONS OF THE NEBRASKA ACADEMY OF SCIENCES AND AFFILIATED SOCIETIES. 5167

0163-9021 *See* LIVER, NORMAL FUNCTION AND DISEASE. 3799

0163-903X *See* WASHINGTON REVIEW. 333

0163-9072 *See* WRITERS FORUM (COLORADO SPRINGS). 3454

0163-9099 *See* HAZARDOUS AND TOXIC SUBSTANCES. 2231

0163-9102 *See* HANDBOOK OF LIPID RESEARCH. 1041

0163-9110 *See* MOTOR IMPORTED CAR REPAIR MANUAL. PROFESSIONAL SERVICE TRADE EDITION. 5419

0163-9153 *See* COLORADO SCHOOL OF MINES QUARTERLY. 2137

0163-917X *See* PROCEEDINGS OF THE TECHNICAL PROGRAM - INTERNATIONAL MICROELECTRONICS CONFERENCE. 2077

0163-9188 *See* FEMS SYMPOSIUM. 563

0163-9218 *See* RLE PROGRESS REPORT. 2079

0163-9269 *See* BEHAVIORAL & SOCIAL SCIENCES LIBRARIAN. 3193

0163-9366 *See* JOURNAL OF NUTRITION FOR THE ELDERLY. 4193

0163-9374 *See* CATALOGING & CLASSIFICATION QUARTERLY. 3200

0163-9382 *See* FOREIGN TRADE : THE PORT OF NEW YORK AND NEW JERSEY. 836

0163-9439 *See* CBMS-NSF REGIONAL CONFERENCE SERIES IN APPLIED MATHEMATICS. 3499

0163-9447 *See* WATER RESOURCES DATA. TENNESSEE. 5545

0163-9471 *See* UNITED STATES COAST PILOT. 8, PACIFIC COAST. ALASKA, DIXON ENTRANCE TO CAPE SPENCER. 4184

0163-948X *See* INSIDE F.E.R.C. 1947

0163-9501 *See* CURRENT CARDIOLOGY. 3704

0163-9528 *See* SUPERMARKET SHOPPER. 2359

0163-9544 *See* U.S. WINE MARKET. 2371

0163-9587 *See* MOSSBAUER EFFECT REFERENCE AND DATA JOURNAL. 4426

0163-9595 *See* THERMAL ANALYSIS APPLICATION STUDY. 1019

0163-9617 *See* AMSTAT NEWS. 5320

0163-9625 *See* DEVIANT BEHAVIOR. 4584

0163-9633 *See* CLINICAL PREVENTIVE DENTISTRY. 1319

0163-9641 *See* INFANT MENTAL HEALTH JOURNAL. 4590

0163-9684 *See* WHITE BOOK OF SKI AREAS. U.S. AND CANADA, THE. 4929

0163-9706 *See* VIEW (OAKLAND). 367

0163-9757 *See* GEOLOGICAL NOTE (COLUMBUS, OHIO). 1378

0163-9765 *See* WRRI. 5549

0163-9811 See ELECTRONIC MAIL & MICRO SYSTEMS. 1154

0163-982X *See* GTE LENKURT DEMODULATOR. 2056

0163-9838 *See* RAC NEWSLETTER. 2006

0163-9854 *See* TELECOMMUNICATIONS REPORTS. 1166

0163-9900 *See* HERB QUARTERLY, THE. 2418

0163-9935 *See* OFFICE PRODUCTS, MASTER CATALOG & BUYING GUIDE. 4213

0163-9943 *See* CLAYMORE (CONVENT STATION), THE. 2728

0163-996X *See* FEDERAL TAX COORDINATOR 2D. WEEKLY ALERT. 4724

0163-9978 *See* TAX YEAR IN REVIEW, THE. 752

0163-9994 *See* RESEARCH INSTITUTE LAWYERS TAX ALERT, THE. 3039

0164-0011 *See* LIGHTNING FLASH (PITTSFIELD, MASS.), THE. 1427

0164-0070 *See* CAROLINA PLANNING. 2817

0164-0151 *See* VITAL STATISTICS (EUGENE). 5346

0164-0178 *See* AMERICAN JEWISH HISTORY. 2255

0164-0208 *See* CARMICHAEL'S ANNUAL FRANCHISE DIRECTORY. 655

0164-0240 *See* CRIMINOLOGIST (COLUMBUS), THE. 3163

0164-0259 *See* KNOWLEDGE (BEVERLY HILLS, CALIF.). 5207

0164-0275 *See* RESEARCH ON AGING. 3754

0164-0283 *See* SAGE FAMILY STUDIES ABSTRACTS. 2287

0164-0291 *See* INTERNATIONAL JOURNAL OF PRIMATOLOGY. 5586

0164-0313 *See* JOURNAL OF FUSION ENERGY. 1949

0164-0364 *See* AMERICAN CRIMINAL LAW REVIEW, THE. 3105

0164-0372 *See* PROBATE AND PROPERTY (CHICAGO, ILL. : 1987). 3118

0164-0402 *See* PROCEEDINGS OF THE WATER-BORNE AND HIGHER-SOLIDS COATINGS SYMPOSIUM. 4459

0164-0429 *See* AAAS SELECTED SYMPOSIA SERIES. 5079

0164-0453 *See* ANALYSIS OF DRUGS AND METABOLITES BY GAS CHROMATOGRAPHY-MASS SPECTROMETRY. 1012

0164-0496 *See* MISSOURI UNION LIST OF SERIAL PUBLICATIONS. 3231

0164-0526 *See* REGISTRY OF THE AMERICAN BOARD FOR CERTIFICATION IN ORTHOTICS AND PROSTHETICS, INC. 3884

0164-0550 *See* DIRECTORY OF SERVICES - TEXAS DEPARTMENT OF MENTAL HEALTH AND MENTAL RETARDATION. 5283

0164-0577 *See* MULTIPLE RISK FACTOR INTERVENTION TRIAL. PUBLIC ANNUAL REPORT. 3708

0164-0585 *See* MONOGRAPHS OF THE AMERICAN COLLEGE OF NUTRITION. 4194

0164-0593 *See* RENTAL RATES COMPILATION. 626

0164-0666 *See* BULLETIN OF THE SOUTHERN ASSOCIATION OF AFRICANISTS, THE. 2638

0164-0674 *See* CATHOLIC NEAR EAST MAGAZINE. 5026

0164-0704 *See* JOURNAL OF MACROECONOMICS. 1500

0164-0712 *See* NATIONAL WETLANDS NEWSLETTER. 3114

0164-0739 *See* GUIDE TO MICROFORMS IN PRINT. SUPPLEMENT. 416

0164-0747 *See* GUIDE TO MICROFORMS IN PRINT. AUTHOR, TITLE. 416

0164-0755 *See* PROCEEDINGS - AWWA WATER QUALITY TECHNOLOGY CONFERENCE. 5537

0164-081X *See* GLYCOCONJUGATES, THE. 487

0164-0828 *See* BANK NOTE REPORTER. 2780

0164-0852 *See* CLINICAL EXERCISES IN INTERNAL MEDICINE. 3796

0164-0917 *See* AEE DIRECTORY OF ENERGY PROFESSIONALS, THE. 2109

0164-0925 *See* ACM TRANSACTIONS ON PROGRAMMING LANGUAGES AND SYSTEMS. 1278

0164-0933 *See* FIFTEENTH CENTURY STUDIES. 2616

0164-0941 *See* FISHING IN MARYLAND. 2303

0164-1085 *See* SILVERFISH REVIEW. 3437

0164-1212 *See* JOURNAL OF SYSTEMS AND SOFTWARE, THE. 1280

0164-1220 *See* FUTURICS. 5107

0164-1239 See IEEE ANNALS OF THE HISTORY OF COMPUTING. 1187

0164-1255 *See* FUNDAMENTAL CONCEPTS OF ESTATE ADMINISTRATION. 3118

0164-1263 *See* PEDIATRIC DENTISTRY. 1332

0164-1298 *See* ARTPARK. 342

0164-1344 *See* JOURNAL OF TRAFFIC SAFETY EDUCATION. 5441

0164-145X *See* HIGGINSON JOURNAL. 3464

0164-1492 *See* DICKINSON STUDIES. 3462

0164-1514 *See* WASHINGTON HEALTH RECORD. 4807

0164-1522 *See* COLLABORATION (HIGH FALLS). 4344

0164-1662 *See* FLORIDA JOURNAL OF ANTHROPOLOGY, THE. 236

0164-1700 *See* PROCEEDINGS - AMERICAN SOCIETY FOR THE ADVANCEMENT ANESTHESIA IN DENTISTRY. 3684

0164-1743 *See* MEDIA GUIDE INTERNATIONAL. EDITION : BUSINESS/PROFESSIONAL PUBLICATIONS. 762

0164-176X *See* P.I.P.E.R., PENSIONS & INVESTMENT'S PERFORMANCE EVALUATION REPORT. 910

0164-1816 *See* ABSTRACTS / AMERICAN ACADEMY OF RELIGION. 4931

0164-1824 *See* FOREIGN MEAT INSPECTION. 211
0164-1999 *See* SCIENTIFIC PRESENTATIONS OF THE ANNUAL MEETING - AMERICAN ANIMAL HOSPITAL ASSOCIATION. 5521
0164-2006 *See* CONFERENCE RECORD OF IEEE INTERNATIONAL SYMPOSIUM ON ELECTRICAL INSULATION. 2039
0164-2030 *See* CLEARWATERS. 5532
0164-2049 *See* GEOSCIENCE WISCONSIN. 1380
0164-2057 *See* NATO CONFERENCE SERIES. IV. MARINE SCIENCES. 556
0164-2111 *See* FANGORIA. 4068
0164-212X *See* OCCUPATIONAL THERAPY IN MENTAL HEALTH. 2867
0164-2340 *See* TOPICS IN EMERGENCY MEDICINE. 3725
0164-2472 *See* SOCIAL TEXT. 5259
0164-2510 *See* SUPPLEMENT TO THE DIRECTORY OF THE AMERICAN RIGHT. 4497
0164-2529 *See* ... SURVEY OF BUYING POWER FORECASTING SERVICE, THE. 1523
0164-2537 *See* KARIKAZO. 2321
0164-2553 *See* ARCHIVES OF PODIATRIC MEDICINE AND FOOT SURGERY. SUPPLEMENT. 3917
0164-2650 *See* MENTAL HYGIENE LAW (NEW YORK). 3009
0164-2804 *See* ELECTRICIAN'S GUIDE. 2045
0164-2812 *See* EXECUTIVE COMPENSATION IN THE HIGH-TECHNOLOGY INDUSTRIES. 1668
0164-2820 *See* FRANKLIN COUNTY LEGAL JOURNAL. 2972
0164-2847 *See* HANDBOOK - NATIONAL ASSOCIATION OF SCHOOLS OF MUSIC. 4120
0164-2863 *See* AIR GUN. 4882
0164-3037 *See* BIRD WATCHER'S DIGEST. 5615
0164-3096 *See* BASKETBALL TIMES. 4887
0164-310X *See* CURRENT REVIEWS FOR NURSE ANESTHETISTS. 3855
0164-3134 *See* NORTHWESTERN SPORTSMAN. 4908
0164-3150 *See* AMERICAN ORGANIST (1979), THE. 4099
0164-3169 *See* PERSPECTIVA MUNDIAL. 1701
0164-3207 *See* DEMOCRATIC LEFT. 4471
0164-3215 *See* SHOWCASE U.S.A. 851
0164-3223 *See* DRUM CORPS WORLD (MADISON). 4115
0164-324X *See* FIBERARTS. 5184
0164-3290 *See* NUTSHELL NEWS. 374
0164-3304 *See* OREGON GEOLOGY. 1390
0164-3320 *See* SECURITY DEALER. 5177
0164-3339 *See* CALIFORNIA SUPREME COURT SERVICE. 3139
0164-3355 *See* TEXAS PUBLIC UTILITY NEWS. 4762
0164-338X *See* NATURAL FOODS MERCHANDISER. 2351
0164-341X *See* REVIEWERS' CONSENSUS. 3351
0164-3428 *See* FOODREVIEW (WASHINGTON, D.C.). 2341
0164-3460 *See* COUNTED THREAD. 5183
0164-3495 *See* EMMY. 1131
0164-3509 *See* SKINNED KNUCKLES. 5425
0164-3525 *See* ECONOMIC WORLD (LOS ANGELES). 1486
0164-3533 *See* NEW ENGLAND BUSINESS. 698
0164-3568 *See* MY FRIEND. 1066
0164-3576 *See* MICHIGAN BAR JOURNAL, THE. 3009
0164-3584 *See* SOAP OPERA DIGEST. 2546
0164-3592 *See* NADA NEWSLETTER. 5421
0164-3606 *See* VOICE OF EVANGELICAL METHODISM, THE. 5069
0164-3622 *See* LOUISIANA MUNICIPAL REVIEW. 4663
0164-3649 *See* WISCONSERVATION. 2210
0164-3665 *See* NORTH COUNTY LIVING. 2541
0164-3681 *See* GRAIN & FEED JOURNALS (1978). 201

0164-369X *See* AUTO RACING USA (FRANKLIN LAKES, N.J.). 4885
0164-3703 *See* HARNESS HORSEMEN INTERNATIONAL. 2799
0164-3711 *See* GAME BIRD BREEDERS, AVICULTURISTS, ZOOLOGISTS AND CONSERVATIONISTS GAZETTE. 211
0164-372X *See* SETTER MAGAZINE, THE. 4288
0164-3762 *See* ELECTRONIC FIELD ENGINEER, THE. 2047
0164-3851 *See* SCHOOLS AND THE COURTS, THE. 1872
0164-3886 *See* US-CHINA REVIEW. 4537
0164-3916 *See* AMERICAN RABBI (CANOGA PARK, LOS ANGELES, CALIF.), THE. 5045
0164-3932 *See* COUNTY AGENT, THE. 77
0164-3940 *See* BULLETIN DE LA SOCIETE DES SCIENCES HISTORIQUES ET NATURELLES DE L'YONNE. 2680
0164-3959 *See* KEA NEWS. 1759
0164-3975 *See* STREET MACHINE (CANOGA PARK, LOS ANGELES, CALIF.). 4866
0164-3991 *See* VIRGINIA EXTENSION. 1543
0164-4033 *See* GOOD TIMES. 2534
0164-4114 *See* WOODSMITH. 635
0164-4130 *See* TENNESSEE LEGISLATIVE RESEARCHER. 3063
0164-4211 *See* VERONA MISSIONS. 5007
0164-4238 *See* SURGICAL TECHNOLOGIST, THE. 3644
0164-4254 *See* NORTH CAROLINA RECREATIONAL AND PARK REVIEW. 4853
0164-4289 *See* KENNEL REVIEW. 4287
0164-4297 *See* ARIZONA STATE LAW JOURNAL. 2937
0164-4343 *See* POTENTIALS IN MARKETING. 935
0164-4351 591
0164-453X *See* CLEVELAND BUSINESS REVIEW. 657
0164-4564 *See* FEDERAL RULES SERVICE. 3140
0164-4580 *See* NAVAL STORES REVIEW (1979). 2403
0164-4602 *See* TAPE DECK. 5319
0164-4610 *See* WASHINGTON SERVICE BUREAU SUPREME COURT BRIEF SERVICE. ANTITRUST AND SECURITIES. 3104
0164-4645 *See* GLAUCOMA (MIAMI). 3875
0164-4661 *See* FORESTRY NEWSLETTER (AVONDALE ESTATES). 2382
0164-4696 *See* MISSION-FOCUS. 5064
0164-470X *See* NASA NADA. 5665
0164-4742 *See* WORDS (WILLOW GROVE). 4214
0164-4769 *See* PHOTO LAB MANAGEMENT. 4373
0164-4815 *See* CLO NEWS. 3160
0164-4831 *See* BEER STATISTICS NEWS. 2362
0164-4912 *See* GU, THE JOURNAL OF GENITOURINARY MEDICINE. 3990
0164-4939 *See* MARKING INDUSTRY MAGAZINE. 933
0164-498X *See* TODAY IN HEALTH PLANNING. 4805
0164-5056 *See* PRIMAL INSTITUTE NEWSLETTER, THE. 4608
0164-5102 *See* MERCHANT (HARRISBURG), THE. 5737
0164-5145 *See* WHITE TRIANGLE NEWS. 5237
0164-5188 *See* FLORIDA FISHING NEWS. 2304
0164-5218 *See* BLACK ODYSSEY. 5465
0164-5234 *See* 20 DE MAYO. 5631
0164-5285 *See* NEW ERA (SALT LAKE CITY), THE. 4981
0164-5293 *See* HISTORIC ILLINOIS. 2737
0164-5315 *See* BIWEEKLY LIST OF PAPERS ON RADIATION CHEMISTRY AND PHOTOCHEMISTRY. 962
0164-5331 *See* CALIFORNIA-ARIZONA FARM PRESS. 71
0164-534X *See* CAUSE/EFFECT. 1814
0164-5366 *See* NORTH SHORE. 2541
0164-5382 *See* SMALL BUSINESS REPORT (MONTEREY, CALIF.). 711

0164-5390 *See* LAW OFFICE INFORMATION SERVICE. 3081
0164-5447 *See* CIRCUIT NEWS (JERICHO). 2038
0164-5536 *See* OREGON CONIFER. 2390
0164-5552 *See* CAR COLLECTOR & CAR CLASSICS MAGAZINE. 5409
0164-5560 *See* CLASSIC IMAGES. 4067
0164-5587 *See* BIBLE-SCIENCE NEWSLETTER. 5014
0164-5609 *See* CBE VIEWS. 451
0164-5625 *See* CHURCH EDUCATOR. 4947
0164-5668 *See* COLLEGE AND JUNIOR TENNIS. 4890
0164-5706 *See* PAINT HORSE JOURNAL (1979). 2801
0164-5749 *See* FLOTATION SLEEP INDUSTRY. 2905
0164-5757 *See* ALI REPORTER, THE. 2931
0164-5765 *See* LAUNDRY NEWS. 5354
0164-5773 *See* PALMETTO BANKER. 802
0164-5803 *See* WESTERN ROOFING INSULATION AND SIDING. 631
0164-5811 *See* PERSONNEL ADVISORY BULLETIN. 945
0164-5862 *See* VIDEOPHILE, THE. 1143
0164-5927 *See* COUNTY LIFE (READING). 2531
0164-5935 *See* NATION'S CITIES WEEKLY. 4668
0164-5951 *See* OFFICE WORLD NEWS. 4213
0164-5994 *See* STAR & SKY. 37
0164-6001 *See* WESTERN FRUIT GROWER. 146
0164-6052 *See* CAMBRIDGE REPORT ON CORPORATE MERGERS AND CORPORATE POLICY, THE. 782
0164-6168 *See* TEXAS THOROUGHBRED (WICHITA FALLS, KAN.). 2802
0164-6206 *See* INTERCOM. 1113
0164-6214 *See* COLONIAL HOMES. 295
0164-6222 *See* PENNSYLVANIA GOLDEN GUERNSEY NEWS. 197
0164-6257 *See* FEDERAL VETERINARIAN, THE. 5510
0164-6273 *See* ARKANSAS TIMES. 3363
0164-6281 *See* ARIZONA BEVERAGE ANALYST. 2363
0164-629X *See* WHEELER'S DESERT LETTER. 719
0164-6303 *See* WORSHIP TIMES. 5010
0164-632X *See* OCEAN WORLD. 1454
0164-6338 *See* PRO SOUND NEWS (INTERNATIONAL ED.). 5318
0164-6338 *See* PRO SOUND NEWS (U.S. ED.). 5318
0164-6346 *See* MOTOR IMPORTED CAR CRASH ESTIMATING GUIDE. 5419
0164-6362 *See* ELECTRONIC BUYERS' NEWS. 2046
0164-6389 *See* WASHINGTON STATE REGISTER. 4694
0164-6397 *See* FIRE AND POLICE PERSONNEL REPORTER. 4775
0164-6427 *See* FLORIDA BAR CASE SUMMARY SERVICE, THE. 2970
0164-6451 *See* CHURCH TEACHERS. 4948
0164-6478 *See* WHIPPET, THE. 4288
0164-6508 *See* AFTERNOON TV. 1125
0164-6524 *See* OHIO REPUBLICAN NEWS. 4485
0164-6559 *See* SHELTER (GERMANTOWN). 627
0164-6656 *See* QUARTER HORSE JOURNAL (1953), THE. 2801
0164-6710 *See* NORTHERN VIRGINIAN. 2541
0164-6745 *See* SPRINGFIELD MAGAZINE. 2546
0164-6796 *See* NEW MEXICO BUSINESS JOURNAL. 698
0164-680X *See* AMERISKA DOMOVINA. 5726
0164-6826 *See* PHARMACEUTICAL TECHNOLOGY INTERNATIONAL. 4321
0164-6850 *See* NORTH CAROLINA STATE BAR QUARTERLY. 3018
0164-6915 *See* COLLECTORS JOURNAL (VINTON). 5669

ISSN Index

0164-6931 See FORUM (NORTH HOLLYWOOD). 3107

0164-6966 See NINGAS. 2270

0164-7008 See AMERICAN COLLECTOR'S JOURNAL, THE. 248

0164-7016 See IRE JOURNAL, THE. 2921

0164-7024 See CANYON ECHO. 2530

0164-7032 See CNSW NEWSLETTER. 3989

0164-7040 See CALIFORNIA FAMILY LAW REPORT. 3119

0164-7075 See ADVANCES IN ASTHMA ALLERGY & PULMONARY DISEASES. 3947

0164-7148 See SQUASH NEWS (HOPE VALLEY, R.I.). 4924

0164-7202 See NUTRITION HEALTH REVIEW. 4196

0164-7237 See ANTIQUE CAR TIMES. 248

0164-7253 See MOUNTAIN MOVERS. 4979

0164-7288 See VIRTUE. 5007

0164-7296 See MUNICIPAL MANAGEMENT. 4667

0164-7318 See DEER AND DEER HUNTING. 4871

0164-7369 See WASHINGTON SCIENCE TEACHERS' JOURNAL. 5169

0164-7407 See MONEY FINDER. 799

0164-7415 See NATIONAL RIGHT TO LIFE NEWS. 589

0164-7423 See BAPTIST PROGRESS (BROOKLYN). 5056

0164-7482 See GARDENING NEWSLETTER. 2416

0164-7539 See IZARD COUNTY HISTORIAN, THE. 2739

0164-758X See HIGH BLOOD PRESSURE HIGHLIGHTS. 3705

0164-7598 See HEALTH PATHWAYS. 4780

0164-761X See BILLIARDS DIGEST. 4857

0164-7660 See INDIANA MEDIA JOURNAL. 3215

0164-7709 See INSIGHTS (SPRINGFIELD, OHIO). 4965

0164-775X See COMMUNIQUE (KENT). 4582

0164-7768 See PERSONAL FINANCE (ARLINGTON, VA.). 803

0164-7822 See PENNSYLVANIA NATURALIST, THE. 4170

0164-789X #y 0164-789 See BRIEF TIMES REPORTER, THE. 2943

0164-7911 See WOMEN'S AD REVIEW. 5570

0164-7954 See INTERNATIONAL JOURNAL OF ACAROLOGY. 5586

0164-7962 See CROCHET WORLD. 5183

0164-7970 See NEW DIRECTIONS FOR STUDENT SERVICES. 1767

0164-7989 See NEW DIRECTIONS FOR PROGRAM EVALUATION. 5298

0164-8071 See ATLANTA BUSINESS CHRONICLE. 640

0164-808X See CHESAPEAKE BOATMAN, THE. 593

0164-8152 See NEW HAMPSHIRE BUSINESS REVIEW. 698

0164-8292 See D (DALLAS. 1978). 2532

0164-8306 See DAYTIME SERIAL NEWSLETTER. 1131

0164-8322 See PETROLEUM ENGINEER INTERNATIONAL. 4272

0164-8330 See ALASKA FISHERMAN'S JOURNAL. 2293

0164-8349 See MOTORCYCLE PRODUCT NEWS. 4082

0164-8357 See OHIO POLICE CHIEF, THE. 3171

0164-8365 See POLICE MARKSMAN, THE. 3172

0164-8381 See NEW DAWN (NEW YORK). 2795

0164-8470 #y 0148-012x See INTERIORS (NEW YORK, N.Y. : 1978). 2901

0164-8497 See VEGETARIAN TIMES. 4200

0164-8527 See CHILD CARE INFORMATION EXCHANGE. 5278

0164-8535 See TALK (NEW YORK). 5264

0164-856X See SOLIDARITY (DETROIT, MICH.). 1711

0164-8578 See RURAL MISSOURI. 2544

0164-8594 See CAMEL'S CALF, THE. 4185

0164-8608 See GEORGIA WILDLIFE. 2194

0164-8632 See KANSAS BUSINESS REVIEW (LAWRENCE. 1977). 688

0164-8640 See FARMWEEK (EASTERN ED.). 86

0164-8683 See MISSISSIPPI EDUCATOR, THE. 1764

0164-8691 See FLIGHTLOG. 1674

0164-8748 See CALIFORNIA EXPLORER. 5465

0164-8756 See COMPUTER/LAW JOURNAL. 2954

0164-8780 See RANCH & COAST. 5489

0164-8985 See AUDIO & ELECTRONICS DIGEST. 5315

0164-8993 See SYNERGY (DALLAS). 3252

0164-9027 See DENHAM SPRINGS AND LIVINGSTON PARISH NEWS. 5683

0164-9078 See MOHAVE VALLEY NEWS. 5630

0164-9086 See NEWS MESSENGER, THE. 5759

0164-9108 See NORTH JACKSON PROGRESS. 5627

0164-9124 See ROUND ROCK LEADER. 5754

0164-9183 See BOWLERS JOURNAL. 4888

0164-9221 See TEXAS GOVERNMENT NEWSLETTER. 4498

0164-923X See UNITED STATES SPECIALIST, THE. 1147

0164-9256 See MOTORCYCLIST'S POST, THE. 5387

0164-9345 See KENTUCKY BENCH & BAR. 2992

0164-9353 See UNITED CAPRINE NEWS. 223

0164-9418 See CATHOLIC LIGHT, THE. 5735

0164-9442 See OKLAHOMA DENTAL ASSOCIATION JOURNAL. 1331

0164-9450 See MINNESOTA (ST. PAUL. 1978). 1102

0164-9477 See JONQUIL. 5232

0164-9507 See DIALOGUES IN PEDIATRIC UROLOGY. 3903

0164-9515 See WOMAN'S EXECUTIVE BULLETIN. 723

0164-9531 See ANIMAL KEEPERS' FORUM. 5575

0164-9558 See ALASKA'S RESOURCES. 2186

0164-9566 See LIBRARY PR NEWS. 3226

0164-9574 See PRODUCT LIABILITY TRENDS. 3032

0164-9655 See MILLIMETER. 4074

0164-968X See MANUFACTURING TODAY. 3484

0164-9833 See DYNAMIC BUSINESS : A PUBLICATION OF THE SMALLER MANUFACTURER'S COUNCIL. 670

0164-985X See CLINICAL CANCER LETTER, THE. 3815

0164-9906 See AVIATION INTERNATIONAL NEWS. 13

0164-9914 See CHAIN DRUG REVIEW. 656

0164-9957 See MIX (BERKELEY, CALIF.), THE. 5317

0165-0009 See CLIMATIC CHANGE. 1422

0165-0041 See INFORMATIE VOOR DE BUITENDIENST. 942

0165-005X See CULTURE, MEDICINE AND PSYCHIATRY. 3924

0165-0076 See PROCES ARNHEM. 3173

0165-0106 See ERKENNTNIS. 4346

0165-0114 See FUZZY SETS AND SYSTEMS. 3506

0165-0157 See LINGUISTICS AND PHILOSOPHY. 3299

0165-0203 See NATURAL RESOURCES FORUM. 2199

0165-022X See JOURNAL OF BIOCHEMICAL AND BIOPHYSICAL METHODS. 489

0165-0254 See INTERNATIONAL JOURNAL OF BEHAVIORAL DEVELOPMENT. 4591

0165-0262 See OUTLOOK ON SCIENCE POLICY. 5137

0165-0270 See JOURNAL OF NEUROSCIENCE METHODS. 3837

0165-0289 See GIDS VOOR PERSONEELSMANAGEMENT. 941

0165-0300 See REVIEW OF CENTRAL AND EAST EUROPEAN LAW. 3135

0165-0327 See JOURNAL OF AFFECTIVE DISORDERS. 3593

0165-0378 See JOURNAL OF REPRODUCTIVE IMMUNOLOGY. 3674

0165-0394 See EUCLIDES (GRONINGEN, NETHERLANDS). 3505

0165-0424 See AQUATIC INSECTS. 5605

0165-0505 See BIJDRAGEN EN MEDEDELINGEN BETREFFENDE DE GESCHIEDENIS DER NEDERLANDEN. 2678

0165-0513 See RECUEIL DES TRAVAUX CHIMIQUES DES PAYS-BAS (1920). 991

0165-0521 See STUDIES ON NEOTROPICAL FAUNA AND ENVIRONMENT. 5598

0165-0572 See RESOURCES AND ENERGY. 1517

0165-0645 See PAEDAGOGISCHE STUDIEN. 1771

0165-0653 See INTERNATIONAL JOURNAL FOR THE ADVANCEMENT OF COUNSELLING. 4591

0165-070X See NETHERLANDS INTERNATIONAL LAW REVIEW. 3133

0165-0734 See PS. PERIODIEK VOOR SOCIALE VERZEKERNIG, SOCIALE VOORZIENINGEN EN ARBEIDSRECHT. 2891

0165-0750 See COMMON MARKET LAW REVIEW. 2953

0165-084X See SPEKTATOR. 3439

0165-0858 See BZZLLETIN. 3461

0165-0890 See TIKKER. 3446

0165-1005 See CORE JOURNALS IN OPHTHALMOLOGY. 3873

0165-1048 See BIBLIOTHEEK EN SAMENLEVING. 3195

0165-1056 See CORE JOURNALS IN CLINICAL NEUROLOGY. 3830

0165-1064 See TECHNIQUES IN THE LIFE SCIENCES. CELL BIOLOGY. 540

0165-1064 See TECHNIQUES IN THE LIFE SCIENCES. PHYSIOLOGY. 587

0165-1064 See TECHNIQUES IN THE LIFE SCIENCES. BIOCHEMISTRY. 493

0165-1110 See MUTATION RESEARCH. REVIEWS IN GENETIC TOXICOLOGY. 3982

0165-1137 See TIJDSCHRIFT VOOR MILIEU EN RECHT. 3116

0165-1153 See ITINERARIO. 2693

0165-1188 See TIJDSCHRIFT VOOR PSYCHOTHERAPIE. 4620

0165-1196 See BOBO. 1060

0165-1250 See DEVELOPMENTS IN GEOTECHNICAL ENGINEERING. 1970

0165-1307 See GEOPHYSICS AND ASTROPHYSICS MONOGRAPHS. 1406

0165-1358 See GUA PAPERS OF GEOLOGY. SERIES 1. 1381

0165-1404 See HYDROBIOLOGICAL BULLETIN. 457

0165-1528 See BOUWRECHT. 2943

0165-1587 See EUROPEAN REVIEW OF AGRICULTURAL ECONOMICS. 82

0165-1633 See SOLAR ENERGY MATERIALS AND SOLAR CELLS : AN INTERNATIONAL JOURNAL DEVOTED TO PHOTOVOLTAIC, PHOTOTHERMAL, AND PHOTOCHEMICAL SOLAR ENERGY CONVERSION. 1957

0165-1684 See SIGNAL PROCESSING. 2081

0165-1714 See DEVELOPMENTS IN BIOCHEMISTRY. 486

0165-1722 See M&O. 1617

0165-1765 See ECONOMICS LETTERS. 1486

0165-1773 See KENNIS EN METHODE. 4351

0165-1781 See PSYCHIATRY RESEARCH. 3934

0165-1803 See ANNUAL REPORT - INTERNATIONAL INSTITUTE FOR LAND RECLAMATION AND IMPROVEMENT. 4627

0165-182X See TIJDSCHRIFT VOOR CRIMINOLOGIE. 3178

0165-1838 See JOURNAL OF THE AUTONOMIC NERVOUS SYSTEM. 3837

0165-1854 See CURRENT TOPICS IN MATERIALS SCIENCE. 2022

0165-1889 See JOURNAL OF ECONOMIC DYNAMICS & CONTROL. 1499

0165-196X See MONOGRAPHS IN FETAL PHYSIOLOGY. 584

0165-2087 See RSG. RICHTING SPORT-GERICHT. 1904

0165-2117 See ENERGIESPECTRUM. 2113

0165-2125 See WAVE MOTION. 3541

0165-2176 See VETERINARY QUARTERLY, THE. 5526

0165-2192 See KOSMETIEK. 404

0165-2214 See DEVELOPMENTS IN TOXICOLOGY AND ENVIRONMENTAL SCIENCE. 3980

0165-2230 See TRANSAKTIE : PUBLIKATIE VAN HET POLEMOLOGISCH INSTITUUT VAN DE RIJKSUNIVERSITEIT GRONINGEN. 4536

0165-2265 See DEVELOPMENTS IN CELL BIOLOGY. 536

0165-232X See COLD REGIONS SCIENCE AND TECHNOLOGY. 1968

0165-2362 See PROGRESS IN THEORETICAL ORGANIC CHEMISTRY. 1057

0165-2370 See JOURNAL OF ANALYTICAL AND APPLIED PYROLYSIS. 1016

0165-2419 See MATHEMATICAL PHYSICS AND APPLIED MATHEMATICS. 3519

0165-2427 See VETERINARY IMMUNOLOGY AND IMMUNOPATHOLOGY. 5525

0165-2478 See IMMUNOLOGY LETTERS. 3671

0165-2516 See INTERNATIONAL JOURNAL OF THE SOCIOLOGY OF LANGUAGE. 3287

0165-2524 See ESPERANTO - DOKUMENTOJ. 3279

0165-2540 See BEHEER EN ONDERHOUD. 600

0165-2575 See ESPERANTO DOCUMENTS. 3279

0165-2621 See DOCUMENTS SUR L'ESPERANTO. 3277

0165-2753 See UTRECHT MICROPALEONTOLOGICAL BULLETINS. SPECIAL PUBLICATION. 4231

0165-280X See MEDEDELINGEN VAN DE WERKGROEP VOOR TERTIAIRE EN KWARTAIRE GEOLOGIE. 1387

0165-2826 See INTERTAX. 4733

0165-2958 See BIBLIOGRAFIE VAN IN NEDERLAND VERSCHENEN OFFICIELE UITGAVEN BIJ RIJKSOVERHEID EN PROVINCIALE BESTUREN. 409

0165-2982 See GELUID ALPHEN AAN DEN RIJN. 5316

0165-313X See FRIESLAND POST. 4850

0165-3253 See STUDIES IN ORGANIC CHEMISTRY (AMSTERDAM). 1047

0165-3806 See DEVELOPMENTAL BRAIN RESEARCH. 3831

0165-4004 See FOLIA LINGUISTICA. 3282

0165-4055 See INTERNATIONAL JOURNAL OF PSYCHOLINGUISTICS. 3287

0165-4101 See JOURNAL OF ACCOUNTING & ECONOMICS. 746

0165-4179 See RECREATIE EN TOERISME. 5490

0165-4373 See PRANA. 2852

0165-4608 See CANCER GENETICS AND CYTOGENETICS. 3811

0165-4675 See BRAND & BRANDWEER. 756

0165-4888 See TEXT (THE HAGUE). 3328

0165-4896 See MATHEMATICAL SOCIAL SCIENCES. 5208

0165-5094 See TIRADE. 5237

0165-5108 See AANDRIJFTECHNIEK. 2108

0165-5299 See ARTS & WERELD. 3553

0165-5302 See MOBILIA (AMSTERDAM). 2906

0165-5515 See JOURNAL OF INFORMATION SCIENCE. 3220

0165-5531 See FOTO & DOKA. 4369

0165-5655 See FEM. FINANCIEEL-ECONOMISCH MAGAZINE. 1490

0165-5701 See INTERNATIONAL OPHTHALMOLOGY. 3875

0165-5728 See JOURNAL OF NEUROIMMUNOLOGY. 3836

0165-5752 See SYSTEMATIC PARASITOLOGY. 5598

0165-5817 See PHILIPS JOURNAL OF RESEARCH. 2075

0165-5876 See INTERNATIONAL JOURNAL OF PEDIATRIC OTORHINOLARYNGOLOGY. 3904

0165-6031 See AARDAPPELWERELD. 161

0165-6074 See MICROPROCESSING AND MICROPROGRAMMING. 1269

0165-6090 See THYMUS. 3677

0165-6147 See TRENDS IN PHARMACOLOGICAL SCIENCES (REGULAR ED.). 4331

0165-6457 See BOUWTIPS. ED. GRON, FRIESLAND, DRENTHE. 601

0165-6465 See OVERIJSSELSE HISTORISCHE BIJDRAGEN : VERSLAGEN EN MEDEDELINGEN VAN DE VEREENIGING TOT BEOEFENING VAN OVERIJSSELSCH REGT EN GESCHIEDENIS. 2702

0165-6554 See BOUWTIPS. ED. NOORD-HOLLAND EN ZUID-HOLLAND. 602

0165-6775 See CONSUMENTENGIDS. 1294

0165-7003 See DEVELOPMENTS IN NEUROSCIENCE. 3831

0165-7054 See HUISARTS & PRAKTIJK. 3738

0165-7062 See ELEKTRONICA + I.E. EN ELEKTROTECHNIEK. 2051

0165-7100 See HUMAN REPRODUCTIVE MEDICINE. 3762

0165-716X See AMSTERDAM STUDIES IN THE THEORY AND HISTORY OF LINGUISTIC SCIENCE. SERIES 2. CLASSICS IN PSYCHOLINGUISTICS. 3263

0165-7208 See PHARMACOCHEMISTRY LIBRARY. 4321

0165-7259 See PUBLIKATIES VAN DE GEZONDHEIDSORGANISATIE T. N. O. SERIE A : ALGEMENE ONDERWERPEN. 3631

0165-7267 See AMSTERDAM STUDIES IN THE THEORY AND HISTORY OF LINGUISTIC SCIENCE. SERIES V, LIBRARY AND INFORMATION SOURCES IN LINGUISTICS. 3264

0165-7380 See VETERINARY RESEARCH COMMUNICATIONS. 5527

0165-7569 See LINGVISTICAE INVESTIGATIONES. SUPPLEMENTA. 3300

0165-7712 See LINGUISTIC & LITERARY STUDIES IN EASTERN EUROPE. 3298

0165-7763 See STUDIES IN LANGUAGE COMPANION SERIES : SLCS. 3326

0165-7836 See FISHERIES RESEARCH. 2302

0165-7992 See MUTATION RESEARCH. MUTATION RESEARCH LETTERS. 550

0165-8107 See NEURO-OPHTHALMOLOGY (AMSTERDAM : AEOLUS PRESS. 1980). 3876

0165-8204 See LAMPAS. 3294

0165-8352 See JANSSEN RESEARCH FOUNDATION SERIES. 4309

0165-8573 See ZUIVELZICHT. 199

0165-8719 See CORE JOURNALS IN GASTROENTEROLOGY. 3743

0165-8743 See PURDUE UNIVERSITY MONOGRAPHS IN ROMANCE LANGUAGES. 3313

0165-9227 See GRAZER PHILOSOPHISCHE STUDIEN. 4347

0165-9367 See BULLETIN ANTIEKE BESCHAVING : BABESCH. 2612

0165-9405 See CORE JOURNALS IN CARDIOLOGY. 3703

0165-9464 See BULLETIN ZOOLOGISCH MUSEUM, UNIVERSITEIT VAN AMSTERDAM. 5580

0165-9510 See BULLETIN VAN HET RYKSMUSEUM. 4086

0165-9618 See COSTERUS. 3275

0165-988X See WERELD EN ZENDING. 5009

0165-9936 See TRAC, TRENDS IN ANALYTICAL CHEMISTRY (PERSONAL EDITION). 1019

0166-008X See EHBO VOORPOST VAN DE DOKTER. 3574

0166-0314 See MAASGOUW, DE. 2697

0166-0381 See KRONIEK VAN HET REMBRANDTHUIS, DE. 355

0166-0462 See REGIONAL SCIENCE AND URBAN ECONOMICS. 2833

0166-0462 See REGIONAL SCIENCE AND URBAN ECONOMICS [MICROFORM]. 2833

0166-0470 See BULLETIN - KNOB. 5806

0166-0535 See MUZIEK & DANS. 4139

0166-056X See SELECTED PAPERS. 3952

0166-0586 See NEDERLANDSE BOEK. 3348

0166-0616 See STUDIES IN MYCOLOGY. 576

0166-0829 See LINGUISTIK AKTUELL. 3299

0166-0861 See DEVELOPMENTS IN BIOENERGETICS AND BIOMEMBRANES. 453

0166-0918 See DEVELOPMENTS IN SOIL SCIENCE. 170

0166-0934 See JOURNAL OF VIROLOGICAL METHODS. 566

0166-106X See PUBLICATION SERIES / NETHERLANDS INSTITUTE FOR SEA RESEARCH. 557

0166-1116 See STUDIES IN ENVIRONMENTAL SCIENCE (AMSTERDAM). 2221

0166-1167 See SYMPOSIA OF THE GIOVANNI LORENZINI FOUNDATION. 3644

0166-1280 See JOURNAL OF MOLECULAR STRUCTURE. THEOCHEM. 1054

0166-1809 See ONS AMSTERDAM. 2701

0166-1957 See TRANSPORT POLICY AND DECISION MAKING. 5395

0166-2074 See MUSEUMVISIE. 4093

0166-2082 See TOPICS IN ENVIRONMENTAL HEALTH. 4805

0166-2236 See TRENDS IN NEUROSCIENCES (REGULAR ED.). 3847

0166-2287 See DEVELOPMENTS IN AGRICULTURAL AND MANAGED FOREST ECOLOGY. 2213

0166-2430 See JONXIS LECTURES, THE. 3592

0166-2481 See DEVELOPMENTS IN PSYCHIATRY. 3924

0166-252X See LOGOPEDIE EN FONIATRIE. 4391

0166-2635 See DEVELOPMENTS IN PRECAMBRIAN GEOLOGY. 1373

0166-2651 See REKREAKSIE. 4854

0166-2694 See AFRICAN STUDIES ABSTRACTS : THE ABSTRACTS JOURNAL OF THE AFRICAN STUDIES CENTRE, LEIDEN. 5226

0166-2740 See EXCHANGE. 4958

0166-3518 See NEUROONCOLOGY. 3841

0166-3534 See GROEN. 2417

0166-3542 See ANTIVIRAL RESEARCH. 3551

0166-3615 See COMPUTERS IN INDUSTRY. 1228

0166-3658 See INZET. 2885

0166-3755 See MOER. 1764

0166-3925 See TIJDSCHRIFT KANKER. 3824

0166-4115 See ADVANCES IN PSYCHOLOGY. 4572

0166-4298 See RAAKPUNT (MAARSSEN). 2285

0166-4301 See WESTERHEEM. 285

0166-4328 See BEHAVIOURAL BRAIN RESEARCH. 3828

0166-445X See AQUATIC TOXICOLOGY (AMSTERDAM, NETHERLANDS). 3979

0166-4492 See TABLEAU (UTRECHT). 366

0166-4751 See NEDERLANDS TIJDSCHRIFT VOOR ERGOTHERAPIE. 5297

0166-4786 See AARDE & I.E. EN KOSMOS. 5079

0166-4972 See TECHNOVATION. 1629

0166-5162 See INTERNATIONAL JOURNAL OF COAL GEOLOGY. 1383

0166-5189 See STUDIES ON THE FAUNA OF CURACAO AND OTHER ISLANDS. 5598

0166-5316 See PERFORMANCE EVALUATION. 1261

0166-5766 See PORTS AND DREDGING. 5454

0166-5790 See GLOT. 3284

0166-5839 See LANDEIGENAAR. 4840

0166-591X See TIJDSCHRIFT VOOR ONDERWIJSRESEARCH. 5165

0166-5987 See NEDERLANDS TIJDSCHRIFT VOOR NATUURKUNDE (AMSTERDAM. 1991). 5132

0166-6010 See MATERIALS SCIENCE MONOGRAPHS. 1986

0166-6061 See STUDIES IN MODERN THERMODYNAMICS. 1058
0166-6231 See CRIMINOLOGY, PENOLOGY AND POLICE SCIENCE ABSTRACTS. 3080
0166-6282 See CRIMINOLOGY, PENOLOGY AND POLICE SCIENCE ABSTRACTS. 3080
0166-6304 See DOCUMENTATIEBLAD WERKGROEP ACHTTIENDE EEUW. 319
0166-6363 See BOUWEN MET STAAL. 5089
0166-641X See BOUWMARKT ROTTERDAM. 1599
0166-6495 See GEWASBESCHERMING. 512
0166-6584 See NOTULAE ODONATOLOGICAE. 467
0166-6622 See COLLOIDS AND SURFACES. 1051
0166-6851 See MOLECULAR AND BIOCHEMICAL PARASITOLOGY. 465
0166-6991 See SYNTHESE LIBRARY. 4363
0166-7602 See AZANIA VRIJ. 4465
0166-7688 See ANALYSE. 3549
0166-8129 See MEDELINGEN - LANDBOUW-ECONOMISCH INSTITUUT. 107
0166-8439 See H2O. 5534
0166-8544 See REVIEWS IN CANCER EPIDEMIOLOGY. 3823
0166-8595 See PHOTOSYNTHESIS RESEARCH. 521
0166-8641 See TOPOLOGY AND ITS APPLICATIONS. 3539
0166-9087 See CONJUNCTUURTEST. 1552
0166-9338 See MAANDSTATISTIEK BOUWNIJVERHEID. 633
0166-9370 See BOS, BERICHTEN OVER STADSVERNIEUWING. 2816
0166-946X See BUITENLANDSE PROJECTEN / EXPORTBEVORDERINGS- EN VOORLICHTINGSDIENST, EVD. 1549
0166-9834 See APPLIED CATALYSIS A : GENERAL. 2008
0166-9834 See APPLIED CATALYSIS. B : ENVIRONMENTAL. 2161
0166-9842 See DEVELOPMENTS IN CARDIOVASCULAR MEDICINE. 3704
0166-9966 See BIBLIOGRAFIE VAN NEDERLANDSE PROEFSCHRIFTEN / DUTCH THESES. 409
0167-0026 See PROFIEL VAN BEROEPSONDERWIJS EN VOLWASSENENEDUCATIE. 1775
0167-0115 See REGULATORY PEPTIDES. 1047
0167-0581 See TIJDSCHRIFT FINANCIEEL MANAGEMENT. 814
0167-0913 See RAADSADVIEZEN / RAAD VOOR DE KUNST. 328
0167-1146 See BINNENLANDS BESTUUR. 861
0167-1359 See TIJDSCHRIFT VOOR ARBITRAGE. 3064
0167-1731 See FERTILIZER RESEARCH. 171
0167-174X See IFOR REPORT. 4509
0167-1782 See WORLD CROPS : PRODUCTION, UTILIZATION, AND DESCRIPTION. 530
0167-188X See INTERNATIONAL JOURNAL OF PRODUCTION ECONOMICS. 1612
0167-1987 See SOIL & TILLAGE RESEARCH. 186
0167-2231 See CARNEGIE-ROCHESTER CONFERENCE SERIES ON PUBLIC POLICY. 1468
0167-2320 See SOCIOLOGY OF THE SCIENCES. 5158
0167-2487 See EUROPEAN JOURNAL OF SURGERY, THE. 3964
0167-2533 See HUMAN SYSTEMS MANAGEMENT. 5111
0167-2584 See SURFACE SCIENCE LETTERS. 5161
0167-2681 See JOURNAL OF ECONOMIC BEHAVIOR & ORGANIZATION. 1498
0167-2738 See SOLID STATE IONICS. 4421
0167-2746 See CHEMISCH MAGAZINE. 970
0167-2789 See PHYSICA. D. 4414
0167-2878 See DUTCH BIRDING. 5582
0167-2894 See DEVELOPMENTS IN PETROLOGY. 1458

0167-2932 See GRASDUINEN. 512
0167-2940 See TRAC, TRENDS IN ANALYTICAL CHEMISTRY. 1019
0167-2991 See STUDIES IN SURFACE SCIENCE AND CATALYSIS. 1058
0167-3696 See INS AND OUTS. 3396
0167-3785 See HANDBOOK OF POWDER TECHNOLOGY. 5109
0167-3890 See DURABILITY OF BUILDING MATERIALS. 613
0167-3939 See ELAN (DEVENTER, NETHERLANDS). 866
0167-398X See INFORMATIE VOOR DE VERKOOPBINNENDIENST. 682
0167-3998 See QUARTERLY BULLETIN / DE NEDERLANDSCHE BANK N.V. 805
0167-4048 See COMPUTERS & SECURITY. 1226
0167-4110 See NATURAL RESOURCES FORUM LIBRARY. 2199
0167-4137 See DEVELOPMENTS IN AGRICULTURAL ENGINEERING. 79
0167-4188 See CHEMICAL ENGINEERING MONOGRAPHS. 2010
0167-4242 See AGRARISCH RECHT. 2928
0167-4366 See AGROFORESTRY SYSTEMS. 2211
0167-4412 See PLANT MOLECULAR BIOLOGY. 550
0167-4439 See ORTHOVISIES. 1883
0167-4501 See DEVELOPMENTS IN FOOD SCIENCE. 2333
0167-4528 See DEVELOPMENTS IN MINERAL PROCESSING. 1439
0167-4544 See JOURNAL OF BUSINESS ETHICS. 2251
0167-4587 See NUTRICIA SYMPOSIUM. 467
0167-465X See SERIES IN RADIOLOGY. 3947
0167-4706 See VERPLEEGKUNDIGE STUDIES. 3870
0167-4730 See STRUCTURAL SAFETY. 629
0167-4757 See SELECTED ANNOTATED BIBLIOGRAPHY OF POPULATION STUDIES IN THE NETHERLANDS. 4562
0167-4765 See BOEKBLAD. 4812
0167-4773 See TTT, INTERDISCIPLINAIR TIJDSCHRIFT VOOR TAAL- & TEKSTWETENSCHAP. 3330
0167-4781 See BIOCHIMICA ET BIOPHYSICA ACTA. GENE STRUCTURE AND EXPRESSION. 543
0167-482X See JOURNAL OF PSYCHOSOMATIC OBSTETRICS AND GYNAECOLOGY. 3764
0167-4838 See BIOCHIMICA ET BIOPHYSICA ACTA. PROTEIN STRUCTURE AND MOLECULAR ENZYMOLOGY. 482
0167-4870 See JOURNAL OF ECONOMIC PSYCHOLOGY. 1593
0167-4889 See BIOCHIMICA ET BIOPHYSICA ACTA. MOLECULAR CELL RESEARCH. 532
0167-4927 See DEVELOPMENTS IN ONCOLOGY. 3816
0167-4943 See ARCHIVES OF GERONTOLOGY AND GERIATRICS. 3749
0167-4978 See DEVELOPMENTS IN CLINICAL BIOCHEMISTRY. 486
0167-5001 See KLEI, GLAS, KERAMIEK. 2592
0167-5028 See PROGRESS IN CLINICAL PHARMACY. 4326
0167-5060 See ANNALS OF DISCRETE MATHEMATICS. 4326
0167-5117 See DEVELOPMENTS IN ATMOSPHERIC SCIENCE. 1425
0167-5133 See JOURNAL OF SEMANTICS (NIJMEGEN). 3291
0167-5168 See DEVELOPMENTS IN ANIMAL AND VETERINARY SCIENCES. 5509
0167-5249 See LAW AND PHILOSOPHY. 2994
0167-5257 See NAAMKUNDE. 3304
0167-5265 See INFORMATION SERVICES & USE. 3216
0167-5273 See INTERNATIONAL JOURNAL OF CARDIOLOGY. 3706

0167-5311 See SPANISH-LANGUAGE PSYCHOLOGY. 4619
0167-5389 See MAINTENANCE MANAGEMENT INTERNATIONAL. 876
0167-5427 See AQUATIC MAMMALS. 5576
0167-5567 See HANDBOOK OF INFLAMMATION. 3580
0167-5648 See DEVELOPMENTS IN WATER SCIENCE. 1413
0167-5699 See IMMUNOLOGY TODAY (AMSTERDAM. REGULAR ED.). 3671
0167-5710 See INFORMATION TECHNOLOGY & PEOPLE (WEST LINN, OR.). 870
0167-5729 See SURFACE SCIENCE REPORTS. 2083
0167-577X See MATERIALS LETTERS. 2105
0167-5796 See CORE JOURNALS IN DERMATOLOGY. 3718
0167-5834 See DEVELOPMENTS IN SOLAR SYSTEM AND SPACE SCIENCE. 395
0167-5877 See PREVENTIVE VETERINARY MEDICINE. 5518
0167-5885 See MEYLER AND PECK'S DRUG-INDUCED DISEASES. 3616
0167-5907 See PAIDIKA. 2796
0167-5915 See TIJDSCHRIFT VOOR SEKSUOLOGIE. 5188
0167-5923 See POPULATION RESEARCH AND POLICY REVIEW. 4558
0167-5931 See NORTH-HOLLAND SERIES IN APPLIED MATHEMATICS AND MECHANICS. 2123
0167-594X See JOURNAL OF NEURO-ONCOLOGY. 3819
0167-6091 See RESEARCH MONOGRAPHS IN IMMUNOLOGY. 3676
0167-6105 See JOURNAL OF WIND ENGINEERING AND INDUSTRIAL AERODYNAMICS. 1983
0167-6164 See JOURNAL OF AFRICAN LANGUAGES AND LINGUISTICS. 3289
0167-6245 See INFORMATION ECONOMICS AND POLICY. 1157
0167-6253 See NEUROSCIENCE LETTERS. SUPPLEMENT. 3842
0167-6296 See JOURNAL OF HEALTH ECONOMICS. 1499
0167-6318 See LINGUISTIC REVIEW, THE. 3298
0167-6334 See DEVELOPMENTS IN ENDOCRINOLOGY (THE HAGUE). 3727
0167-6350 See ANALYTICAL CHEMISTRY SYMPOSIA SERIES. 1013
0167-6369 See ENVIRONMENTAL MONITORING AND ASSESSMENT. 2168
0167-6377 See OPERATIONS RESEARCH LETTERS. 5136
0167-6385 See DEVELOPMENTS IN PERINATAL MEDICINE. 3760
0167-6393 See SPEECH COMMUNICATION. 1122
0167-6423 See SCIENCE OF COMPUTER PROGRAMMING. 1281
0167-6458 See DEVELOPMENTS IN GENETICS. 544
0167-6482 See PAIN. SUPPLEMENT (AMSTERDAM). 3625
0167-6504 See DEVELOPMENTS IN NUTRITION AND METABOLISM. 4189
0167-6520 See BUMPER. 3370
0167-6555 See PHARMACEUTISCH WEEKBLAD. SCIENTIFIC EDITION. 4321
0167-6563 See CRUSTACEANA. SUPPLEMENT. 5581
0167-6598 See PSYCHOLOGIE LISSE. 4612
0167-6601 See MEDISCH JAAR, HET. 3614
0167-6636 See MECHANICS OF MATERIALS. 2106
0167-6644 See ONDERWIJSLITERATUUR. 1796
0167-6652 See PUBLICATIONS DE LA SOCIETE HISTORIQUE ET ARCHEOLOGIQUE DANS LE LIMBOURG. 306
0167-6687 See INSURANCE MATHEMATICS & ECONOMICS. 2884
0167-6695 See ISOTOPE GEOSCIENCE. 1383

0167-6695 See ISOTOPE GEOSCIENCE. 1042

0167-6768 See NETHERLANDS YEARBOOK OF INTERNATIONAL LAW. 3133

0167-6784 See OPHTHALMIC PAEDIATRICS AND GENETICS. 550

0167-6806 See BREAST CANCER RESEARCH AND TREATMENT. 3809

0167-6830 See ORBIT (AMSTERDAM). 3878

0167-6857 See PLANT CELL, TISSUE AND ORGAN CULTURE. 523

0167-6865 See INTERNATIONAL JOURNAL OF MICROCIRCULATION: CLINICAL AND EXPERIMENTAL. 3798

0167-6881 See STUDIES IN PHYSICAL AND THEORETICAL CHEMISTRY. 1058

0167-6903 See PLANT GROWTH REGULATION. 523

0167-6911 See SYSTEMS & CONTROL LETTERS. 1998

0167-692X See ENERGY RESEARCH. 1941

0167-6938 See PROGRESS IN FILTRATION AND SEPARATION. 1028

0167-6970 See MOLECULAR ASPECTS OF CELLULAR REGULATION. 539

0167-6997 See INVESTIGATIONAL NEW DRUGS. 3818

0167-7004 See FERNSTROM FOUNDATION SERIES. 3576

0167-7012 See JOURNAL OF MICROBIOLOGICAL METHODS. 566

0167-7055 See COMPUTER GRAPHICS FORUM : A JOURNAL OF THE EUROPEAN ASSOCIATION FOR COMPUTER GRAPHICS. 1232

0167-7063 See JOURNAL OF NEUROGENETICS. 549

0167-7101 See TOPICS IN MOLECULAR PHARMACOLOGY. 4331

0167-7152 See STATISTICS & PROBABILITY LETTERS. 3536

0167-7187 See INTERNATIONAL JOURNAL OF INDUSTRIAL ORGANIZATION. 871

0167-7209 See CURRENT REVIEWS IN BIOMEDICINE. 3570

0167-725X See METABOLIC ASPECTS OF CARDIOVASCULAR DISEASE. 3708

0167-7306 See NEW COMPREHENSIVE BIOCHEMISTRY. 987

0167-7314 See INTERNATIONAL JOURNAL OF PHARMACOGNOSY. 4308

0167-7322 See JOURNAL OF MOLECULAR LIQUIDS. 982

0167-7373 See TYPOLOGICAL STUDIES IN LANGUAGE. 3330

0167-739X See FUTURE GENERATIONS COMPUTER SYSTEMS : FGCS. 1247

0167-7411 See TOPOI. 4364

0167-7594 See NEDERLANDS INTERNATIONAAL PRIVATRECHT : REPERTORIUM OP VERDRAGENRECHT, WETGEVING, RECHTSPRAAK EN LITERATUUR. 3014

0167-7640 See TRENDS IN BIOCHEMICAL SCIENCES (AMSTERDAM. REGULAR ED.). 493

0167-7659 See CANCER AND METASTASIS REVIEWS. 3810

0167-7691 See TRENDS IN PHARMACOLOGICAL SCIENCES (REFERENCE ED.). 4331

0167-7764 See JOURNAL OF ATMOSPHERIC CHEMISTRY. 1426

0167-7799 See TRENDS IN BIOTECHNOLOGY (PERSONAL EDITION). 3697

0167-790X See MATERIALS PROCESSING, THEORY AND PRACTICES. 2105

0167-7926 See PRZEWALSKI HORSE. 2801

0167-7942 See ECONOMISCH- EN SOCIAAL-HISTORISCH JAARBOEK. 1559

0167-8000 See STATISTICAL JOURNAL OF THE UNITED NATIONS ECONOMIC COMMISSION FOR EUROPE. 5340

0167-8019 See ACTA APPLICANDAE MATHEMATICAE. 3490

0167-806X See NATURAL LANGUAGE AND LINGUISTIC THEORY. 3305

0167-8094 See ORDER (DORDRECHT). 3526

0167-8116 See INTERNATIONAL JOURNAL OF RESEARCH IN MARKETING. 926

0167-8140 See RADIOTHERAPY AND ONCOLOGY. 3823

0167-8191 See PARALLEL COMPUTING. 1248

0167-8205 See DEVELOPMENTS IN NEPHROLOGY. 3989

0167-8256 See DEVELOPMENTS IN MOLECULAR VIROLOGY. 562

0167-8272 See BIBLIOGRAFIE NEDERLANDSE SOCIOLOGIE. 5240

0167-8302 See DEVELOPMENTS IN OBSTETRICS AND GYNECOLOGY. 3760

0167-8310 See THEORETISCHE GESCHIEDENIS. 2631

0167-8329 See EDUCATION FOR INFORMATION. 1739

0167-8353 See EXCERPTA MEDICA. SECTION 52. TOXICOLOGY. 3659

0167-8396 See COMPUTER AIDED GEOMETRIC DESIGN. 1232

0167-8418 See DEVELOPMENTS IN HEMATOLOGY AND IMMUNOLOGY. 3771

0167-8442 See THEORETICAL AND APPLIED FRACTURE MECHANICS. 4430

0167-8477 See JURIDISCHE BIBLIOTHECARIS, DE. 3221

0167-8477 See SOCIAL RESEARCH METHODOLOGY ABSTRACTS. 5227

0167-8507 See MULTILINGUA. 3304

0167-8523 See SECRETORY PROCESS, THE. 3640

0167-8574 See PROGRESS IN PHYCOLOGICAL RESEARCH. 525

0167-8655 See PATTERN RECOGNITION LETTERS. 1234

0167-8744 See DIALOGOS HISPANICOS DE AMSTERDAM. 3277

0167-8760 See INTERNATIONAL JOURNAL OF PSYCHOPHYSIOLOGY. 581

0167-8809 See AGRICULTURE, ECOSYSTEMS & ENVIRONMENT. 53

0167-8892 See DEVELOPMENTS IN ENVIRONMENTAL MODELLING. 2163

0167-8965 See CORE JOURNALS IN CLINICAL PHARMACOLOGY. 3569

0167-9023 See DEVELOPMENTS IN MOLECULAR AND CELLULAR BIOCHEMISTRY. 486

0167-9074 See DEVELOPMENTS IN NUCLEAR MEDICINE. 3848

0167-9082 See ITEMS. 301

0167-9090 See EXCERPTA MEDICA. SECTION 38. ADVERSE REACTIONS TITLES. 3659

0167-9104 See PERSPEKTIEF. 4372

0167-9171 See EXCERPTA MEDICA. SECTION 37. DRUG LITERATURE INDEX. 3659

0167-9198 See PSYCHOPHARMACOLOGY (AMSTERDAM). 4326

0167-9228 See TIJDSCHRIFT VOOR GERONTOLOGIE EN GERIATRIE. 3755

0167-9236 See DECISION SUPPORT SYSTEMS. 865

0167-9244 See TECHNIQUES AND INSTRUMENTATION IN ANALYTICAL CHEMISTRY. 1019

0167-9260 See INTEGRATION (AMSTERDAM). 2066

0167-9287 See EDUCATION & COMPUTING. 1223

0167-9295 See EARTH, MOON, AND PLANETS. 395

0167-9309 See DEVELOPMENTS IN AQUACULTURE AND FISHERIES SCIENCE. 2300

0167-9317 See MICROELECTRONIC ENGINEERING. 2072

0167-9392 See FAUX TITRE: ETUDES DE LANGUE ET LITTERATURE FRANCAISES PUBLIEES. 3281

0167-9406 See TASKS FOR VEGETATION SCIENCE. 5161

0167-9430 See TRENDS IN BIOTECHNOLOGY (REFERENCE ED.). 3697

0167-9449 See COAL SCIENCE AND TECHNOLOGY. 2137

0167-9457 See HUMAN MOVEMENT SCIENCE. 5202

0167-9473 See COMPUTATIONAL STATISTICS & DATA ANALYSIS. 3502

0167-9597 See KUNSTSTOF EN RUBBER. 5076

0167-9619 See ERFGOED VAN INDUSTRIE EN TECHNIEK. 2686

0167-966X See VRIJETIJD EN SAMENLEVING. 4855

0167-9732 See SUPPLEMENTS TO NOVUM TESTAMENTUM. 5001

0167-9767 See ZUIDAFRIKAANSE KOERIER. 4501

0167-9775 See HISTORISCH GEOGRAFISCH TIJDSCHRIFT. 2565

0167-9848 See HUSSERL STUDIES. 4348

0167-9899 See INTERNATIONAL JOURNAL OF CARDIAC IMAGING. 3706

0167-9902 See THEORETICAL MEDICINE. 3645

0167-9945 See INTERNATIONAL JOURNAL OF CLINICAL MONITORING AND COMPUTING. 1190

0168-0021 See DETAILHANDEL MAGAZINE. 831

0168-0072 See ANNALS OF PURE AND APPLIED LOGIC. 3494

0168-0102 See NEUROSCIENCE RESEARCH. 3842

0168-051X See BONE AND MINERAL RESEARCH. 3803

0168-0617 See NEUROENDOCRINE PERSPECTIVES. 3732

0168-1176 See INTERNATIONAL JOURNAL OF MASS SPECTROMETRY AND ION PROCESSES. 4405

0168-1222 See FUNDAMENTAL THEORIES OF PHYSICS. 4403

0168-132X See NATO ASI SERIES. SERIES E, APPLIED SCIENCE. 5130

0168-1591 See APPLIED ANIMAL BEHAVIOUR SCIENCE. 5504

0168-1605 See INTERNATIONAL JOURNAL OF FOOD MICROBIOLOGY. 2345

0168-1699 See COMPUTERS AND ELECTRONICS IN AGRICULTURE. 76

0168-1702 See VIRUS RESEARCH. 571

0168-1753 See NORTH SEA MONITOR. 5453

0168-1796 See PRIORITY ISSUES IN MENTAL HEALTH : A BOOK SERIES PUBLISHED UNDER THE AUSPICES OF THE WORLD FEDERATION FOR MENTAL HEALTH. 4796

0168-1923 See AGRICULTURAL AND FOREST METEOROLOGY. 1419

0168-1974 See NORTH-HOLLAND SERIES IN STATISTICS AND PROBABILITY. 3524

0168-2121 See VERSUS. 4079

0168-2148 See TIJDSCHRIFT VOOR SKANDINAVISTIEK. 3328

0168-2555 See FOUNDATIONS OF SEMIOTICS. 3282

0168-2563 See BIOGEOCHEMISTRY. 2188

0168-2601 See OPEN HOUSE INTERNATIONAL. 305

0168-2857 See AS. MAANDBLAD AKTIVITEITENSEKTOR. 5274

0168-3020 See BASIS-METAALINDUSTRIE / CENTRAAL BUREAU VOOR DE STATISTIEK, HOOFDAFDELING STATISTIEKEN VAN INDUSTRIE EN BOUWNIJVERHEID. 3998

0168-3128 See GROFSMEDERIJEN, STAMP- EN PERSBEDRIJVEN / CENTRAAL BUREAU VOOR DE STATISTIEK, HOOFDAFDELING STATISTIEKEN VAN INDUSTRIE EN BOUWNIJVERHEID. 1608

0168-3179 See TANK-, RESERVOIR- EN PIJPLEIDINGBOUW / CENTRAAL BUREAU VOOR DE STATISTIEK, HOOFDAFDELING STATISTIEKEN VAN INDUSTRIE EN BOUWNIJVERHEID. 1628

0168-3187 See ZEEVAARTVERWANTE BEDRIJVEN / CENTRAAL BUREAU VOOR DE STATISTIEK, HOOFDAFDELING STATISTIEKEN VAN VERKEER EN VERVOER. 5458

0168-3225 See CONSTRUCTIEWERKPLAATSEN, EXCL. TANK-, RESERVOIR- EN PIJPLEIDINGBOUW / CENTRAAL BUREAU VOOR DE STATISTIEK, HOOFDAFDELING STATISTIEK VAN INDUSTRIE EN BOUWNIJVERHEID. 1552

0168-325X See FOOD MANAGEMENT AMERSFOORT. 2338

0168-342X See METTALBEWERKINGSMACHINE - INDUSTRIE EN MACHINEGEREEDSCHAPPENFABRIEKEN / CENTRAAL BUREAU VOOR DE STATISTIED, HOOFDAFDELING STATISTIEKEN VAN INDUSTRIE EN BOUWNIFVERHEID. 2122

0168-3462 See STATISTIEK VAN DE OPENBARE BIBLIOTHEKEN / CENTRAAL BUREAU VOOR DE STATISTIEK, HOOFDAFDELING SOCIAAL-CULTURELE STATISTIEKEN. 3260

0168-3489 See NATIONALE REKENINGEN / CENTRAAL BUREAU VOOR DE STATISTIEK. 4668

0168-3527 See FABRIEKEN VAN MACHINES EN APPARATEN VOOR HOUT- EN MEUBELINDUSTRIE, TEXTIEL- EN KLEDINGINDUSTRIE, WASSERIJEN EN CHEMISCHE REINIGING, LEDER- EN LEDERVERWERKENDE INDUSTRIE, PAPIER- EN GRAFISCHE INDUSTRIE / CENTRAAL BUREAU VOOR DE STATISTIEK, HOOFDAFDELING STATISTIEKEN VAN INDUSTRIE EN BOUWNIJVERHEID. 2114

0168-3578 See STOOMKETEK- EN KRACHTWERKTUIGENINDUSTRIE / CENTRAAL BUREAU VOOR DE STATISTITEK, HOOFDAFDELING STATISTIEKEN VAN INDUSTRIE EN BOUWNIFVERHEID. 2129

0168-3659 See JOURNAL OF CONTROLLED RELEASE. 981

0168-3837 See STATISTIEK DER PROVINCIALE FINANCIEN / CENTRAAL BUREAU VOOR DE STATISTIEK. 4700

0168-3845 See OP PAD (DEN HAAG). 5487

0168-4094 See NAAMLIJSTEN VOOR DE STATISTIEK VAN DE BUITENLANDSE HANDEL. 696

0168-437X See GENEES- EN VERBANDMIDDELENINDUSTRIE / CENTRAAL BUREAU VOOR DE STATISTIEK, HOOFDAFDELING STATISTIEKEN VAN INDUSTRIE EN BOUWNIJVERHEID. 3578

0168-4418 See KUNSTSTOFVERWERKENDE INDUSTRIE / CENTRAAL BUREAU VOOR DE STATISTIEK, HOOFDKAFDELING STATISTIEKEN VAN INDUSTRIE EN BOUWNIJVERHEID. 1615

0168-4469 See TRICOT- EN KOUSENINDUSTRIE / CENTRAAL BUREAU VOOR DE STATISTIEK, HOOFDAFDELING STATISTIEDEN VAN INDUSTRIE EN BOUWNIJVERHEID. 1088

0168-454X See ONDERZOEK HUISHOUDENS MET EENMALIGE UITKERING / CENTRAAL BUREAU VOOR DE STATISTIEK, HOOFDAFDELING STATISTIEKEN VAN INKOMEN EN CONSUMPTIE. 5335

0168-4604 See INTRAMURALE GEZONDHEIDSZORG / CENTRAAL BUREAU VOOR DE STATISTIK, HOOFDAFDELING GEZINDHEIDSSTATISTIEKEN. 4785

0168-4639 See STATISTIEK DER BRANDEN / CENTRAAL BUREAU VOOR DE STATISTIEK, HOOFDAFDELING STATISTIEKEN VAN RECHTSBESCHERMING EN VEILIGHEID. 2293

0168-4647 See GROOTHANDEL IN VOEDINGS- EN GENOTMIDDELEN / CENTRAAL BUREAU VOOR DE STATISTIEK, HOOFDAFDELING STATISTIEKEN VAN BINNENLANDSE HANDEL EN DIENSTVERLENING. 838

0168-4663 See HOUT- EN MEUBELINDUSTRIE, EXCL. METALEN MEUBELEN / CENTRAAL BUREAU VOOR DE STATISTIEK, HOOFDAFDELING STATOSTOELM VAN INDUSTRIE EN BOUWNIJVERHEID. 2906

0168-468X See SPEUR- EN ONTWIKKELINGSWERK IN NEDERLAND / CENTRAAL BUREAU VOOR DE STATISTIEK, HOOFDAFDELING STATISTIEKEN VAN ONDERWIJS EN WETENSCHAPPEN. 5159

0168-471X See LEDERINDUSTRIE / CENTRAAL BUREAU VOOR DE STATISTIEK, HOOFDAFDELING STATISTIEKEN VAN INDUSTRIE EN BOUWNIJVERHEID. 3185

0168-4809 See NEDERLANDSE JEUGD EN HAAR ONDERWIJS / CENTRAAL BUREAU VOOR DE STATISTIEK, HOOFDAFDELING STATISTIEKEN VAN ONDERWIJS EN WETENSCHAPPEN, DE. 1767

0168-4841 See CEMENT-, KALK- EN OVERIGE MINERALE PRODUKTENINDUSTRIE, GLASINDUSTRIE EN -BEWERKINGSINRICHTINGEN / CENTRAAL BUREAU VOOR DE STATISTIEK, HOOFDAFDELING STATISTIEKEN VAN INDUSTRIE EN BOUWNIJVERHEID. 2587

0168-4914 See BANDINDUSTRIE EN OVERIGE TEXTIELINDUSTRIE / CENTRAAL BUREAU VOOR DE STATISTIEK, HOOFDAFDELING STATISTIEKEN VAN INDUSTRIE EN BOUWNIJVERHEID. 5348

0168-4949 See FABRIEKEN VAN TANDWIELEN, LAGERS EN ANDERE DRIJFWERKELEMENTEN / CENTRAAL BUREAU VOOR DE STATISTIEK, HOOFDAFDELING STATISTIEK I.E. STATISTIEKEN VAN INDUSTRIE EN BOUWNIJVERHEID. 1606

0168-4965 See RUBBERVERWERKENDE INDUSTRIE / CENTRAAL BUREAU VOOR DE STATISTIEK, HOOFDAFDELING STATISTIEKEN VAN INDUSTRIE EN BOUWNIJVERHEID. 3487

0168-5058 See STATISTIEK VAN HET WETENSCHAPPELIJK ONDERWIJS / CENTRAAL BUREAU VOOR DE STATISTIEK, HOOFDAFDELING STATISTIEKEN VAN ONDERWIJS EN WETENSCHAPPEN. 1798

0168-5066 See MEELFABRIEKEN, GORT- EN RIJSTPELLERIJEN E.D. / CENTRAAL BUREAU VOOR DE STATISTIEK, HOOFDAFDELING STATISTEIKEN VAN INDUSTRIE EN BOUWNIJVERHEID. 202

0168-5139 See LEDERWARENINDUSTRIE, EXCL. KLEDING / CENTRAAL BUREAU VOOR DE STATISTIEK, HOOFDAFDELING STATISTIEKEN VAN INDUSTRIE EN BOUWNIJVERHEID. 3185

0168-5163 See STATISTIEK VAN DE ELEKTRICITEITS--VOORZIENING IN NEDERLAND / CENTRAAL BUREAU VOOR DE STATISTIEK, HOOFDAFDELING STATISTIEKEN VAN INDUSTRIE EN BOUWNIJVERHEID. 4700

0168-518X See ZUIVELINDUSTRIE. 199

0168-5295 See ONDERHOUD WATERGANGEN / CENTRAAL BUREAU VOOR DE STATISTIEK, AFDELING NATUURLIJK MILIEU. 2094

0168-5481 See FINANCIELE GEGEVENS KERKGENOOTSCHAPPEN / CENTRAAL BUREAU VOOR DE STATISTIEK, HOOFDAFDELING FINANCIELE STATISTIEKEN. 4959

0168-5538 See STATISTIEK VREEMDELINGENVERKEER / CENTRAAL BUREAU VOOR DE STATISTIEK, HOOFDAFDELING SOCIAAL-CULTURELE STATISTIEKEN. 5500

0168-5597 See ELECTROENCEPHALOGRAPHY AND CLINICAL NEUROPHYSIOLOGY EVOKED POTENTIALS. 580

0168-5716 See MARGARINE- EN OILEFABRIEKEN / CENTRAAL BUREAU VOOR DE STATISTIEK, HOOFDAFDELING STATISTIEKEN VAN INDUSTRIE EN BOUWNIJVERHEID. 1617

0168-5775 See TRAM- EN AUTOBUSBEDRIJVEN / CENTRAAL BUREAU VOOR DE STATISTIEK, HOOFDAFDELING STATISTIEKEN VAN VERKEER EN VERVOER. 5394

0168-5783 See JUSTICIELE KINDERBESCHERMING. 3081

0168-5813 See PRODUKTIESTATISTIEKEN : BROOD-, BESCHUIT-, BANKET-, KOEKEN BISCUITFABRIEKEN (W.O. BROOD- EN BANKETBAKKERIJEN). 2354

0168-583X See NUCLEAR INSTRUMENTS & METHODS IN PHYSICS RESEARCH. SECTION B, BEAM INTERACTIONS WITH MATERIALS AND ATOMS. 4449

0168-5961 See GIETERIJEN / CENTRAAL BUREAU VOOR DE STATISTIEK, HOOFDAFDELING STATISTIEKEN VAN INDUSTRIE EN BOUWNIJVERHEID. 1607

0168-6151 See MODERN QUATERNARY RESEARCH IN SOUTHEAST ASIA. 4228

0168-6178 See DEVELOPMENTS IN ECONOMIC GEOLOGY. 1373

0168-6208 See PALAEOECOLOGY OF AFRICA AND THE SURROUNDING ISLANDS. 4228

0168-6291 See IRRIGATION AND DRAINAGE SYSTEMS. 2091

0168-6429 See METAALPRODUKTENINDUSTRIE, EXCL. MACHINES EN TRANSPORTMIDDELEN / CENTRAAL BUREAU VOOR DE STATISTIEK, HOOFDAFDELING STATISTIEKEN VAN INDUSTRIE EN BOUWNIJVERHEID. 4008

0168-647X See FOLIA LINGUISTICA HISTORICA. 3282

0168-6496 See FEMS MICROBIOLOGY, ECOLOGY. 562

0168-6577 See EUROPEAN JOURNAL OF POPULATION. 4553

0168-6917 See CURRENT CLINICAL PRACTICE SERIES. 3570

0168-6976 See ZIEKENHUISHYGIENE EN INFEKTIEPREVENTIE. 3794

0168-7034 See JOURNAL OF CONSUMER POLICY. 1297

0168-7212 See BATAVIA ACADEMICA : BULLETIN VAN DE NEDERLANDSE WERKGROEP UNIVERSITEITSGESCHIEDENIS. 1811

0168-7298 See BOLLETTINO DI ITALIANISTICA. 2513

0168-7433 See JOURNAL OF AUTOMATED REASONING. 1220

0168-7565 See VEETEELT. 223

0168-7670 See MEDISCH-FARMACEUTISCHE MEDEDELINGEN. 4315

0168-7697 See NEW IN CHESS YEARBOOK. 4864

0168-7778 See JOURNAL OF MANAGEMENT CONSULTING (AMSTERDAM). 873

0168-7840 See ELEKTRONICA. 2051

0168-7875 See SUPERCOMPUTER. 1204

0168-7913 See NEWSLETTER - DEPARTMENT OF POTTERY TECHNOLOGY, UNIVERSITY OF LEIDEN. 276

0168-7972 See DEVELOPMENTS IN PLANT GENETICS AND BREEDING. 508

0168-8022 See ADVANCES IN VEGETATION SCIENCE. 498

0168-8162 See EXPERIMENTAL & APPLIED ACAROLOGY. 5583

0168-8227 See DIABETES RESEARCH AND CLINICAL PRACTICE. 3728

0168-8227 See DIABETES RESEARCH AND CLINICAL PRACTICE. 3728

0168-8235 See MEDIAMARKT. 933

0168-8278 See JOURNAL OF HEPATOLOGY. 3798

0168-8332 See MONTHLY BULLETIN NORTH SEA. 1358

0168-8375 See REVIEWS OF OCULOMOTOR RESEARCH. 3879

0168-8405 See STATISTIEK FINANCIEN VAN ONDERNEMINGEN, HANDEL / CENTRAAL BUREAU VOOR DE STATISTIEK, HOOFDAFDELING STATISTIEKEN VAN KAPITAALGOEDERENVOORRAAD EN BALANSEN. 733

0168-8421 See INZET AMSTERDAM. 2910

0168-8448 See ALTERNATIVE MEDICINE. 3548

0168-8456 See SUPPLEMENT BIJ DE SOCIAAL-ECONOMISCHE MAANDSTATISTIEK / CENTRAL BUREAU VOOR DE STATISTIEK. 5228

0168-8472 See TIJDSCHRIFT VAN DE NEDERLANDSE VERENIGING VOOR KLINISCHE CHEMIE. 994

0168-8510 See HEALTH POLICY (AMSTERDAM). 3582

0168-8529 See BUITENSCHOOLS MONDELING ONDERWIJS / CENTRAAL BUREAU VOOR DE STATISTIEK, HOOFDAFDELING STATISTIEKEN VAN ONDERWIJS EN WETENSCHAPPEN. 1729

0168-8561 See BIOGENIC AMINES. 483

0168-8626 See TIJDSCHRIFT VOOR AGOLOGIE. 5224

0168-8634 See JOURNAL OF CLINICAL AND EXPERIMENTAL NEUROPSYCHOLOGY. 3834

0168-8693 See HN MAGAZINE. 4963

0168-874X See FINITE ELEMENTS IN ANALYSIS AND DESIGN. 1233

0168-9002 See NUCLEAR INSTRUMENTS & METHODS IN PHYSICS RESEARCH. SECTION A, ACCELERATORS, SPECTROMETERS, DETECTORS AND ASSOCIATED EQUIPMENT. 4449

0168-9029 See CRIMINALITEIT EN STRAFRECHTSPELEGING. 3080

0168-9045 See KORT BESTEK. 4660

0168-9193 See JONG HOLLAND. 354

0168-9274 See APPLIED NUMERICAL MATHEMATICS : TRANSACTIONS OF IMACS. 3495

0168-9428 See BIJBLIJVEN. 3556

0168-9444 See HARVARD BUSINESS REVIEW. 1565

0168-9452 See PLANT SCIENCE (LIMERICK). 524

0168-9479 See TRENDS IN GENETICS (LIBRARY ED.). 552

0168-9533 See PIGS. 217

0168-9614 See PROGRESS IN PROTEIN-LIPID INTERACTIONS. 990

0168-9673 See ACTA MATHEMATICAE APPLICATAE SINICA. 3490

0168-9711 See BEWEGEN & HULPVERLENING. 4379

0168-9789 See MISSION STUDIES. 4978

0168-9878 See CHLOE AMSTERDAM. 3375

0168-9908 See BETER. 4768

0168-9959 See TIJDSCHRIFT VOOR THEOLOGIE. 5005

0169-0078 See COLLECTION MONOGRAPHIQUE RODOPI EN LITTERATURE FRANCAISE CONTEMPORAINE. 3376

0169-0124 See STUDIES IN SLAVIC AND GENERAL LINGUISTICS. 3326

0169-0175 See STUDIES IN SLAVIC LITERATURE AND POETICS. 3442

0169-0221 See AMSTERDAMER PUBLIKATIONEN ZUR SPRACHE UND LITERATUR. 3361

0169-023X See DATA & KNOWLEDGE ENGINEERING. 1253

0169-0566 See ADVANCES IN AGRICULTURAL BIOTECHNOLOGY. 44

0169-0639 See WELZYNSWEEKBLAD 1981. 5314

0169-0833 See RESTORATIVE NEUROLOGY. 3845

0169-0965 See LANGUAGE AND COGNITIVE PROCESSES. 3294

0169-1015 See SPATIAL VISION. 3536

0169-1066 See JAPANESE ANAESTHESIA JOURNALS' REVIEW. 3683

0169-1074 See INTELLECTUELE EIGENDOM & RECLAMERECHT. 1305

0169-1112 See PAIN CLINIC, THE. 3625

0169-1163 See JAPANESE JOURNAL OF RHEUMATOLOGY. 3805

0169-121X See MATHEMATICAL ENGINEERING IN INDUSTRY. 3518

0169-1317 See APPLIED CLAY SCIENCE. 5085

0169-1341 See SHARE INTERNATIONAL. 4186

0169-1368 See ORE GEOLOGY REVIEWS. 1390

0169-1570 See TIJDSCHRIFT VOOR CONSUMENTENRECHT. 1300

0169-1767 See ECONOMIC FORECASTS. 1557

0169-1821 See NATO'S SIXTEEN NATIONS. 4052

0169-1864 See ADVANCED ROBOTICS. 1210

0169-1872 See NEDERLANDS TIJDSCHRIFT VOOR OPVOEDING, VORMING EN ONDERWIJS. 1767

0169-1910 See PRAKTIJKMANAGEMENT. 4325

0169-2046 See LANDSCAPE AND URBAN PLANNING. 2827

0169-2070 See INTERNATIONAL JOURNAL OF FORECASTING. 684

0169-2143 See PUBLIKATIE - INSTITUUT VOOR MECHANISATIE, ARBEID EN GEBOUWEN. 123

0169-2216 See TIJDSCHRIFT VOOR ARBEIDSVRAAGSTUKKEN. 947

0169-2267 See MESTSTOFFEN. 2424

0169-2607 See COMPUTER METHODS AND PROGRAMS IN BIOMEDICINE. 3691

0169-2720 See ZIEKENHUISFARMACIE. 4334

0169-2763 See INFOMEDIARY. 3215

0169-2895 See RUSSIAN JOURNAL OF NUMERICAL ANALYSIS AND MATHEMATICAL ANALYSIS. 3532

0169-2968 See FUNDAMENTA INFORMATICAE. 1185

0169-3158 See STUDIES IN INORGANIC CHEMISTRY. 1038

0169-328X See MOLECULAR BRAIN RESEARCH. 3838

0169-3298 See SURVEYS IN GEOPHYSICS. 1411

0169-3395 See ZEITSCHRIFT FUR PSYCHOANALYTISCHE THEORIE UND PRAXIS. 4622

0169-3662 See STYGOLOGIA. 1418

0169-3816 See JOURNAL OF CROSS-CULTURAL GERONTOLOGY. 3753

0169-3867 See BIOLOGY & PHILOSOPHY. 446

0169-3913 See TRANSPORT IN POROUS MEDIA. 994

0169-3956 See NEWSLETTER ON THE OIL EMBARGO AGAINST SOUTH AFRICA. 4266

0169-409X See ADVANCED DRUG DELIVERY REVIEWS. 4289

0169-4146 See JOURNAL OF INDUSTRIAL MICROBIOLOGY. 565

0169-4197 See INTERNATIONAL JOURNAL OF PANCREATOLOGY. 3798

0169-4200 See I2-PROCESTECHNOLOGIE. 1977

0169-4243 See JOURNAL OF ADHESION SCIENCE AND TECHNOLOGY. 1053

0169-4286 See NEW FORESTS. 2389

0169-4332 See APPLIED SURFACE SCIENCE. 4397

0169-4375 See BELMONTIA. 501

0169-4421 See ARCHITECTUUR, BONWEN. 290

0169-4669 See CWI MONOGRAPHS. 3502

0169-4707 See PARASITOLOGY TODAY (REFERENCE ED.). 468

0169-4839 See NEDERLANDSE GEOGRAFISCHE STUDIES. 2570

0169-4855 See LEIDS KUNSTHISTORISCH JAARBOEK. 357

0169-5002 See LUNG CANCER (AMSTERDAM, NETHERLANDS). 3820

0169-5037 See STAATSCOURANT. 4687

0169-5150 See AGRICULTURAL ECONOMICS. 49

0169-5347 See TRENDS IN ECOLOGY & EVOLUTION (AMSTERDAM). 2221

0169-5363 See ABN ECONOMIC REVIEW. 768

0169-5436 See RECUEIL DES COURS - ACADEMIE DE DROIT INTERNATIONAL. 3134

0169-5509 See EXCERPTA INFORMATICA. 1219

0169-5533 See STUDIES IN THE HISTORY OF MODERN SCIENCE. 5160

0169-555X See GEOMORPHOLOGY. 1380

0169-5568 See ADVANCED TEXTBOOKS IN ECONOMICS. 1460

0169-5606 See VISIBLE RELIGION / INSTITUTE OF RELIGIOUS INCONOGRAPHY, STATE UNIVERSITY GRONINGEN. 5008

0169-5983 See FLUID DYNAMICS RESEARCH. 5105

0169-6009 See BONE AND MINERAL. 3726

0169-605X See ABSTRACTS ON RURAL DEVELOPMENT IN THE TROPICS. 5189

0169-6149 See ORIGINS OF LIFE AND EVOLUTION OF THE BIOSPHERE. 467

0169-6165 See BOCHUMER ANGLISTISCHE STUDIEN. 3269

0169-622X See TECHNIEK IN DE GGEZONDHEIDSZORG : BEHEER EN TOEPASSING. 5162

0169-6548 See COMMUNICATIONS ON HYDRAULIC AND GEOTECHNICAL ENGINEERING. 2088

0169-6572 See MEDEDELINGEN VAN HET NEDERLANDS INSTITUUT TE ROME. 358

0169-6726 See NEDERLANDS KUNSTHISTORISCH JAARBOEK. 359

0169-6777 See NIEUWE STEM. 2520

0169-6882 See PHARMA SELECTA. 4319

0169-7161 See HANDBOOK OF STATISTICS. 5328

0169-7226 See OUDTESTAMENTISCHE STUDIEN. 5018

0169-7285 See KBM. KANTOORMARKT. 4212

0169-7439 See CHEMOMETRICS AND INTELLIGENT LABORATORY SYSTEMS. 971

0169-7447 See ANALECTA PRAEHISTORICA LEIDENSIA. 2610

0169-7528 See CORRUPTION AND REFORM. 4470

0169-7552 See COMPUTER NETWORKS AND ISDN SYSTEMS. 1240

0169-7722 See JOURNAL OF CONTAMINANT HYDROLOGY. 1415

0169-796X See JOURNAL OF DEVELOPING SOCIETIES. 2621

0169-8095 See ATMOSPHERIC RESEARCH. 1420

0169-8141 See INTERNATIONAL JOURNAL OF INDUSTRIAL ERGONOMICS. 2099

0169-8346 See VERSLAGEN EN MEDEDEELINGEN VAN DE PLANTENZIEKTENKUNDIGE DIENST, WAGENINGEN. 530

0169-8354 See JEWISH LAW ANNUAL, THE. 2986

0169-8451 See KERKHISTORISCHE BIJDRAGEN. 4972

0169-8834 See STUDIES IN THE HISTORY OF RELIGIONS. 5001

0169-8958 See MNEMOSYNE. SUPPLEMENTUM. 1078

0169-9261 See KWALITEIT IN BEDRIJF. 689

0169-9385 See MAANDSTATISTIEK RECHTSBESCHERMING EN VEILIGHEID. 3082

0169-9423 See HANDBUCH DER ORIENTALISTIK, 1. ABT. DER NAHE UND DER MITTLERE OSTEN. 2768

0169-9563 See SINICA LEIDENSIA. 2664

0169-9729 See OLS NEWS : THE INDEPENDENT VOICE OF OPEN LEARNING. 1770

0169-9865 See STUDIES IN SOUTH ASIAN CULTURE. 2665

0170-0243 See EAST-WEST EUROPEAN ECONOMIC INTERACTION. 1480

0170-026X See ZEITSCHRIFT FUER ARABISCHE LINGUISTIK. 3335

0170-0391 See KHIPU. 323

0170-0405 See PFLANZENSCHUTZ-NACHRICHTEN BAYER (ENGLISH ED.). 2427

0170-057X See GESTALT THEORY. 4588

0170-0596 See SCHMERZSTUDIEN. 3639

0170-060X See PRAXIS DER PSYCHOMOTORIK. 1884

0170-0693 See KUNSTHARZ NACHRICHTEN. 4456

0170-0839 See POLYMER BULLETIN (BERLIN, WEST). 1056

0170-0944 See SACHUNTERRICHT UND MATHEMATIK IN DER PRIMARSTUFE. 3532

0170-1002 See DEUTSCHE BIBLIOGRAPHIE. ZEITSCHRIFTEN-VERZEICHNIS. 414

0170-1037 See DEUTSCHE NATIONALBIBLIOGRAPHIE UND BIBLIOGRAPHIE DES IM AUSLAND ERSCHIENENEN DEUTSCHSPRACHIGEN VEROFFENTLICHUNGEN. REIGE A. ESCHIENENE. 414

0170-1053 See DEUTSCHE NATIONALBIBLIOGRAPHIE UND BIBLIOGRAPHIE DER IM AUSLAND ERSCHIENENEN DEUTSCHSPRACHIGEN VEROFFENTLICHUNGEN. REIHE B, MONOGRAPHIEN UND PERIODIKA AUSSERHALB DES VERLAGSBUCHHANDELS. WOCHENTLICHES VERZEICHNIS / BEARBEITER UND HERAUSGEBER, DIE DEUTSCHE BIBLIOTHEK. 414

0170-107X See DEUTSCHE NATIONALBIBLIOGRAPHIE UND BIBLIOGRAPHIE DER IM AUSLAND ERSCHIENENEN DEUTSCHSPRACHIGEN VEROFFENTLICHUNGEN. REIHE C, KARTEN, VIERTELJAHRLICHES VERZEICHNIS / BEARBEITER UND HERAUSGEBER, DIE DEUTSCHE BIBLIOTHEK. 4813

0170-110X See ZEITSCHRIFT FUER MYKOLOGIE. 576

0170-1452 See JURA : JURISTISCHE AUSBILDUNG. 2990
0170-1703 See EUROPEAN TRANSACTIONS ON ELECTRICAL POWER ENGINEERING. 2054
0170-1711 See ETZ. ELEKROTECHNISCHE ZEITSCHRIFT (BERLIN, WEST). 2054
0170-1738 See BERLINER SIGELVERZEICHNIS / BERLINER GESAMTKATALOG ; DEUTSCHE STAATSBIBLIOTHEK, INSTITUT FUER LEIHVERKEHR UND ZENTRALKATALOGE ; DEUTSCHES BIBLIOTHEKSINSTITUT. 3194
0170-1754 See MEDIA PERSPEKTIVEN. 1117
0170-1789 See ZEITSCHRIFT FUER DIFFERENTIELLE UND DIAGNOSTISCHE PSYCHOLOGIE. 4622
0170-1827 See ELRAD. 2053
0170-2033 See ELEKTRISCHE ENERGIE-TECHNIK. 1937
0170-2041 See LIEBIGS ANNALEN DER CHEMIE. 984
0170-205X See LABOR-MEDIZIN (GIT-VERLAG GIEBELER). 3603
0170-219X See SEMIOSIS. 3320
0170-2327 See ERGO-MED. 3575
0170-2513 See MAGAZIN FUER AMERIKANISTIK. 2745
0170-2602 See PRAVENTION. 4795
0170-2696 See AMTLICHE NACHRICHTEN DER BUNDESANSTALT FUER ARBEIT. ARBEITSSTATISTIK ... JAHRESZAHLEN. 5320
0170-2890 See SPORTDOKUMENTATION : LITERATUR DER SPORTWISSENSCHAFT. 4921
0170-2955 See AUSSENDANDEL. REIHE 2, AUSSENHANDEL NACH WAREN UND LANDERN (SPEZIALHANDEL). 824
0170-2971 See SPEKTRUM DER WISSENSCHAFT. 5159
0170-3064 See HAMBURGER KREBSDOKUMENTATION. 3817
0170-3153 See DEUTSCHE SPRACHE IN EUROPA UND UBERSEE. 3276
0170-3188 See ERDWISSENSCHAFTLICHE FORSCHUNG. 2560
0170-3250 See GEOECOLOGICAL RESEARCH. 2216
0170-3331 See FORTSCHRITT UND FORTBILDUNG IN DER MEDIZIN. 3577
0170-3609 See SCHRIFTEN DER MAINZER PHILOSOPHISCHEN FAKULTATSGESELLSCHAFT E. V. 4360
0170-3617 See IFO SPIEGEL DER WIRTSCHAFT. 1533
0170-3668 See MUNCHENER OSTASIATISCHE STUDIEN. 3413
0170-3722 See PRAXIS GRUNDSCHULE. 1094
0170-4060 See AVR. ALLGEMEINER VLIESSTOFF-REPORT. 4232
0170-4176 See MEDIA DATEN, ZEITSCHRIFTEN MIT AUSLANDSTEIL. 1116
0170-4184 See MEDIA DATEN ZEITUNGEN, ANZEIGENBLATTER. 4816
0170-4192 See MEDIA DATEN, FACHZEITSCHRIFTEN. 1116
0170-4214 See MATHEMATICAL METHODS IN THE APPLIED SCIENCES. 3519
0170-4613 See SPW. 4547
0170-4664 See INFOBRIEF RESEARCH AND TECHNOLOGY. 5113
0170-4818 See ENGLERA. 509
0170-5121 See COMPUTERWOCHE. 1179
0170-5148 See CHRIST IN DER GEGENWART. 4943
0170-5156 See JAHRESBERICHT DER BUNDESANSTALT FUR GEWASSERKUNDE / BFG. 1415
0170-5334 See ANAESTHESIOLOGIE UND INTENSIVMEDIZIN (ERLANGEN). 3680
0170-5431 See FORSCHUNGSPROGRAMM - BUNDESANSTALT FUR STRASSENWESEN, BEREICH UNFALLFORSCHUNG. 5440
0170-5792 See MOTORIK. 4792
0170-5814 See ARCHAOLOGISCHE MITTEILUNGEN AUS IRAN. ERGANZUNGSBAND. 258

0170-589X See MATERIALKUNDLICH-TECHNISCHE REIHE. 5127
0170-5903 See HORMONE AND METABOLIC RESEARCH. SUPPLEMENT SERIES. 3730
0170-5911 See BASF-STUDIE. 2859
0170-5946 See SUGIA, SPRACHE UND GESCHICHTE IN AFRIKA. 3326
0170-6012 See INFORMATIK-SPEKTRUM. 1259
0170-608X See DATEN UND DOKUMENTE ZUM UMWELTSCHUTZ. 2191
0170-6233 See BERICHTE ZUR WISSENSCHAFTSGESCHICHTE. 5088
0170-6241 See ZEITSCHRIFT FUER SEMIOTIK. 5172
0170-6322 See SCHRIFTENREIHE DES DEUTSCHEN WOLLFORSCHUNGS INSTITUTES AN DER TECHNISCHEN HOCHSCHULE AACHEN. 5150
0170-6632 See CHIP. 1266
0170-6659 See BANKFACHKLASSE, DIE. 776
0170-7256 See DATENSCHUTZ-BERATER. 1226
0170-7434 See PHYSICS BRIEFS. 4427
0170-7809 See ZMP BILANZ. GETREIDE-FUTTERMITTEL. 204
0170-7825 See AUSSENHANDEL. REIHE 3: AUSSENHANDEL NACH LAENDERN UND WARENGRUPPEN, SPEZIALHANDEL. 824
0170-8007 See BALKAN-ARCHIV. 3267
0170-8147 See SCHRIFTENREIHE DES DEUTSCHEN VERBANDES FUER WASSERWIRTSCHAFT UND KULTURBAU. 5539
0170-8287 See EEG-LABOR, DAS. 3831
0170-8406 See ORGANIZATION STUDIES. 5211
0170-8414 See IMMERGRUNE BLATTER. 2420
0170-8570 See HISPANISTISCHE STUDIEN. 3394
0170-8643 See LECTURE NOTES IN CONTROL AND INFORMATION SCIENCES. 3223
0170-8694 See SIFKU-INFORMATIONEN. 5307
0170-8791 See NZ. NEUE ZEITSCHRIFT FUER MUSIK (1979). 4142
0170-8805 See KASSELER ARBEITEN ZUR SPRACHE UND LITERATUR. 3293
0170-8821 See HEIDELBERGER BEITRAEGE ZUR ROMANISTIK. 3285
0170-8872 See REGENSBURGER BEITRAEGE ZUR DEUTSCHEN SPRACH- UND LITERATURWISSENSCHAFT: REIHE B, UNTERSUCHUNGEN. 3428
0170-8929 See MUNCHNER ZEITSCHRIFT FUER BALKANKUNDE. 2699
0170-9135 See MAINZER STUDIEN ZUR AMERIKANISTIK. 3409
0170-9267 See BAUTENSCHUTZ + BAUSANIERUNG. 600
0170-9291 See AMTSBLATT DES EUROPAISCHEN PATENTAMTS. 1301
0170-9305 See EUROPAISCHES PATENTBLATT. 1304
0170-9321 See METHODEN UND VERFAHREN DER MATHEMATISCHEN PHYSIK. 3523
0170-9348 See INTERNATIONAL BOOKS IN PRINT. 4821
0170-9364 See ALTE STADT, DIE. 2673
0170-9518 See BEITRAEGE ZUR ALLGEMEINEN UND VERGLEICHENDEN ARCHAEOLOGIE. 261
0170-9526 See INFORMATIONSDIENST - VEREIN DEUTSCHER INGENIEURE. BLECHBEARBEITUNG. 4004
0170-9550 See INFORMATIONSDIENST - VEREIN DEUTSCHER INGENIEURE. KALTMASSIVUMFORMUNG. 1978
0170-9569 See INFORMATIONSDIENST - VEREIN DEUTSCHER INGENIEURE. ELEKTRISCH ABTRAGENDE FERTIGUNGSVERFAHREN. 2064
0170-9577 See TZ FUER METALLBEARBEITUNG. 4023
0170-9739 See ZEITSCHRIFT FUER PHYSIK. C, PARTICLES AND FIELDS. 4425
0170-9933 See ME I AL STATISTICS (FRANKFURT). 4026

0170-9976 See DEUTSCHES GEWASSERKUNDLICHES JAHRBUCH. RHEINGEBIET. TEIL III, MITTEL- UND NIEDERRHEIN MIT IJSSELGEBIET. 5532
0171-0079 See ATALANTA (MUNCHEN). 5605
0171-0184 See BEITRAGE ZUR DERMATOLOGIE. 3718
0171-0834 See KODIKAS. 3293
0171-1091 See UROLOGIC RADIOLOGY. 3994
0171-1113 See VERHANDLUNGEN / GESELLSCHAFT FUER OKOLOGIE. 2222
0171-1288 See PERSPEKTIVEN DER PHILOSOPHIE. 4355
0171-1458 See PAPIER- UND ZELLSTOFF-DIENST. 4237
0171-1814 See ANASTHESIOLOGIE UND INTENSIVMEDIZIN (BERLIN, WEST). 3681
0171-1873 See SPRINGER SERIES IN SOLID-STATE SCIENCES. 993
0171-2004 See HANDBOOK OF EXPERIMENTAL PHARMACOLOGY. 4306
0171-2144 See BERICHT UBER DAS ... INTERNATIONALE KOLLOQUIUM UBER DIE VERHUTUNG VON ARBEITSUNFALLEN UND BERUFSKRANKHEITEN IN DER CHEMISCHEN INDUSTRIE. 2859
0171-2268 See UNI HANNOVER. 1851
0171-2446 See MITTEILUNGEN DER VERSUCHSANSTALT FUER PILZANBAU DER LANDWIRTSCHAFTSKAMMER RHEINLAND, KREFELD-GROSSHUTTENHOF. 2388
0171-2985 See IMMUNOBIOLOGY (1979). 3670
0171-3434 See PSYCHOSOZIAL. 4613
0171-3647 See INFORMATIONSDIENST - VEREIN DEUTSCHER INGENIEURE. SCHMIEDEN UND PRESSEN. 1978
0171-4155 See BEITRAEGE ZUR FREMDSPRACHENVERMITTLUNG AUS DEM KONSTANZER SLI. 3268
0171-4198 See ELEKTRONIK HEUTE. 2051
0171-4279 See LABORPRAXIS IN DER MEDIZIN. 3603
0171-4511 See METALLURGICAL PLANT AND TECHNOLOGY : MPT. 4010
0171-4546 See GSI-REPORT. 976
0171-4694 See JAHRBUCH DES VEREINS ZUM SCHUTZ DER BERGWELT. 2196
0171-4937 See SEKRETARIAT. 710
0171-4996 See ITALIENISCH. 3288
0171-5216 See JOURNAL OF CANCER RESEARCH AND CLINICAL ONCOLOGY. 3819
0171-5410 See AAA, ARBEITEN AUS ANGLISTIK UND AMERIKANISTIK. 3260
0171-5445 See BAUPHYSIK. 2019
0171-5496 See LICHT (MUNCHEN). 2070
0171-5860 See ANALYSE & KRITIK. 5190
0171-6123 See HEPATOLOGY. 3797
0171-6425 See THORACIC AND CARDIOVASCULAR SURGEON, THE. 3976
0171-645X See BEITRAEGE ZUR HOCHSCHULFORSCHUNG. 1811
0171-6468 See OR-SPEKTRUM. 5136
0171-6530 See AURORA-BUCHREIHE. 430
0171-6662 See BRITISH AND IRISH STUDIES IN GERMAN LANGUAGE AND LITERATURE. 3270
0171-6859 See CANADIAN STUDIES IN GERMAN LANGUAGE AND LITERATURE. 3372
0171-6867 See AUSTRALIAN AND NEW ZEALAND STUDIES IN GERMAN LANGUAGE AND LITERATURE. 3364
0171-7111 See HAEMATOLOGY AND BLOOD TRANSFUSION. 3772
0171-712X See RECHT DER ELEKTRIZITATSWIRTSCHAFT. 1954
0171-7219 See STANFORD GERMAN STUDIES. 3323
0171-7235 See TUBINGER STUDIEN ZUR DEUTSCHEN LITERATUR. 3448
0171-7243 See AMUSEMENT-INDUSTRIE. 4848
0171-726X See UTAH STUDIES IN LITERATURE AND LINGUISTICS. 3450
0171-791X See PRAXIS DER PSYCHOTHERAPIE UND PSYCHOSOMATIK. 4608

0171-7928 See ARCHITEKTUR & WOHNEN. 291

0171-7952 See BAUEN FUER DIE LANDWIRTSCHAFT (ZEITSCHRIFT). 600

0171-8045 See DIABETOLOGIE-INFORMATIONEN. 3728

0171-8096 See TECHNISCHES MESSE : TM. 4033

0171-8177 See ENTOMOLOGIA GENERALIS. 5607

0171-8630 See MARINE ECOLOGY. PROGRESS SERIES (HALSTENBEK). 2218

0171-8649 See GEOGRAPHIE UND SCHULE. 2564

0171-8932 See ZEITSCHRIFTEN-DATENBANK : ZDB. 427

0171-9033 See MILITARPOLITIK. 4050

0171-9289 See FREIBEUTER. 2517

0171-9327 See SOZIALPAEDIATRIE IN PRAXIS UND KLINIK. 3911

0171-9335 See EUROPEAN JOURNAL OF CELL BIOLOGY. 536

0171-9599 See CONTACTOLOGIA. DEUTSCHE AUSGABE. 4215

0171-9602 See CONTACTOLOGIA ED. FRANCAISE. 3873

0171-967X See CALCIFIED TISSUE INTERNATIONAL. 578

0171-9734 See HANDCHIRURGISCHE TASCHENBUCHER. 3965

0171-9750 See ARCHIVES OF TOXICOLOGY. SUPPLEMENT. 3979

0171-9904 See JAHRBUCH FUER VOLKSKUNDE. 2321

0172-0104 See PHARMA DIALOG. 4319

0172-018X See BLATTER FUER VORGESETZTE. 1599

0172-049X See WETTBEWERB IN RECHT UND PRAXIS : WRP. 3104

0172-0589 See BRAUEREI-JOURNAL. 2365

0172-0597 See INTERNATIONAL SOCIETY FOR MUSIC EDUCATION YEARBOOK. 4123

0172-0643 See PEDIATRIC CARDIOLOGY. 3908

0172-0910 See BEIHEFT ZUM BULLETIN JUGEND + LITERATUR. 3365

0172-1003 See DDH. DAS DACHDECKER-HANDWERK. 612

0172-1062 See BAYREUTHER MATHEMATISCHE SCHRIFTEN. 3497

0172-116X See RECHT UND MEDIZIN. 3742

0172-1232 See CURRENT DIAGNOSTIC PEDIATRICS. 3902

0172-1364 See SCRIPTUM GERIATRICUM. 3755

0172-1518 See FORSCHUNG (BOPPARD). 5105

0172-1526 See GERMAN RESEARCH : REPORTS OF THE DFG. 5107

0172-1984 See KLIMA, KALTE, HEIZUNG. 2606

0172-1992 See ENGLISCH AMERIKANISCHE STUDIEN. 3384

0172-2131 See SCHRIFTENREIHE DER AKADEMIE FUR OEFFENTLICHES GESUNDHEITSWESEN IN DUSSELDORF. 4801

0172-2190 See WORLD PATENT INFORMATION. 1309

0172-2409 See HAUSTEX. 5351

0172-2727 See JAHRBUCH FUER HAUSFORSCHUNG. 301

0172-2778 See FUNKSCHAU. SONDERHEFT. 2055

0172-2867 See DLW-NACHRICHTEN. 613

0172-2875 See ZEITSCHRIFT FUER BERUFS- UND WIRTSCHAFTSPADAGOGIK 1980. 1918

0172-3006 See MITTEILUNGEN - INSTITUT FUER BAUTECHNIK. 621

0172-3235 See STEREO. 5319

0172-3286 See LICHT-FORSCHUNG. 4438

0172-3723 See DATEN DES GESUNDHEITSWESENS. 4809

0172-3790 See HYGIENE + MEDIZIN. 3585

0172-4029 See STADION (COLOGNE, GERMANY). 4924

0172-4185 See OFF ROAD MUNCHEN. 5388

0172-4207 See ADVANCED SERIES IN AGRICULTURAL SCIENCES. 44

0172-4568 See APPLICATIONS OF MATHEMATICS. 3494

0172-4576 See ARBEITS- UND SOZIALRECHTLICHE SCHRIFTENREIHE. 3144

0172-4606 See AKTUELLE ENDOKRINOLOGIE UND STOFFWECHSEL. 3726

0172-4614 See ULTRASCHALL IN DER MEDIZIN. 3648

0172-4622 See INTERNATIONAL JOURNAL OF SPORTS MEDICINE. 3954

0172-4770 See BEITRAEGE ZUM AUSLAENDISCHEN OEFFENTLICHEN RECHT UND VOELKERRECHT. 2941

0172-4797 See SOZIOLOGENKORRESPONDENZ. 5263

0172-4843 See COMPREHENSIVE MANUALS IN RADIOLOGY. 3940

0172-5076 See CRYSTALS. 1032

0172-5300 See VOX LATINA. 3332

0172-5505 See MUSIKTHERAPEUTISCHE UMSCHAU. 4138

0172-570X See STUDIES IN THE HISTORY OF MATHEMATICS AND PHYSICAL SCIENCES. 3537

0172-5726 See SPRINGER SERIES IN COMPUTATIONAL PHYSICS. 4422

0172-5742 See STUDIES OF BRAIN FUNCTION. 3846

0172-5912 See SONNENENERGIE & WARMEPUMPE. 1957

0172-5998 See TEXTS AND MONOGRAPHS IN PHYSICS. 4423

0172-603X See TEXTS AND MONOGRAPHS IN COMPUTER SCIENCE. 1205

0172-6048 See TOPICS IN ENVIRONMENTAL PHYSIOLOGY AND MEDICINE. 2182

0172-6056 See UNDERGRADUATE TEXTS IN MATHEMATICS. 3540

0172-6099 See ACTA MEDICOTECHNICA (1979). 3545

0172-6145 See GEOTECHNIK. 2023

0172-6153 See ELEKTRONIK ENTWICKLUNG. 2051

0172-6161 See SPRINGER SERIES ON ENVIRONMENTAL MANAGEMENT. 2206

0172-6188 See SPRINGER SERIES IN EXPERIMENTAL ENTOMOLOGY. 5613

0172-6196 See BETRIEBSWIRT GERNSBACH, DER. 642

0172-620X See SPRINGER SERIES IN LANGUAGE AND COMMUNICATION. 3323

0172-6218 See SPRINGER SERIES IN CHEMICAL PHYSICS. 4442

0172-6250 See ELEKTRONIK-PRODUKTION & PRUFTECHNIK. 2051

0172-6315 See SOURCES IN THE HISTORY OF MATHEMATICS AND PHYSICAL SCIENCES. 3536

0172-6331 See SPRINGER SERIES IN MICROBIOLOGY. 570

0172-6374 See KUNSTSTOFFBERATER (1979). 4456

0172-6390 See HEPATO-GASTROENTEROLOGY. 3746

0172-6404 See HISTORICAL SOCIAL RESEARCH (QUANTUM (ASSOCIATION) : 1979). 5201

0172-6404 See HISTORICAL SOCIAL RESEARCH (KOLN). 5246

0172-665X See SCHRIFTENREIHE DES BAYERISCHEN LANDESAMTES FUER WASSERWIRTSCHAFT. 1417

0172-6897 See BERLINER SEMINAR. 4293

0172-7028 See EUROPEAN PHOTOGRAPHY (GOTTINGEN, GERMANY). 4369

0172-7265 See KUNSTREPORT. 356

0172-7362 See VARIETIES OF ENGLISH AROUND THE WORLD : GENERAL SERIES. 3331

0172-7389 See SPRINGER SERIES IN SYNERGETICS. 5159

0172-7400 See KREDITPRAXIS 1979. 796

0172-7419 See ANLAGEPRAXIS. 770

0172-7788 See LECTURE NOTES IN MEDICAL INFORMATICS. 3604

0172-780X See NEURO ENDOCRINOLOGY LETTERS. 3732

0172-7893 See KIELER MEERESFORSCHUNGEN. SONDERHEFT. 555

0172-7966 See INORGANIC CHEMISTRY CONCEPTS. 1036

0172-8083 See CURRENT GENETICS. 544

0172-8113 See PATHOLOGE, DER. 3896

0172-8172 See RHEUMATOLOGY INTERNATIONAL. 3807

0172-8180 See BROT & BACKWAREN. 2329

0172-8237 See INTERNATIONALE SCHULBUCHFORSCHUNG. 1754

0172-8261 See AUDIOLOGISCHE AKUSTIK. AUDIOLOGICAL ACOUSTICS. 4384

0172-8288 See TEXTEN + SCHREIBEN. 1205

0172-8350 See KUNSTSPIEGEL. 324

0172-8490 See BERLINER ARZTEBLATT. 3555

0172-8512 See JAHRBUCH UBERBLICKE MATHEMATIK. 3511

0172-8717 See KONTAKTE. 2070

0172-8741 See UNIVERSITAT BONN, PHYSIKALISCHES INSTITUT. IR. 4424

0172-8784 See BERLINER GEOWISSENSCHAFTLICHE ABHANDLUNGEN. REIHE A. GEOLOGIE UND PALAONTOLOGIE. 1367

0172-8865 See ENGLISH WORLD-WIDE. 3279

0172-9047 See LOHN + GEHALT. 690

0172-908X See MAGNESIUM-BULLETIN. 4007

0172-9098 See VIOLA : JAHRBUCH DER INTERNATIONALEN VIOLA-FORSCHUNGSGESELLSCHAFT, DIE. 4158

0172-9160 See MEDICA (STUTTGART). 3607

0172-9179 See FACIES. 4227

0172-9187 See MORPHOLOGIA MEDICA. 3679

0172-9225 See NEURALTHERAPIE NACH HUNEKE. 3620

0172-9314 See CARGOWORLD. 5448

0172-9322 See AKUPUNKTURARZT, AURIKULOTHERAPEUT, DER. 3547

0172-9446 See GSF-BERICHT. P. 2517

0172-9578 See HANDBUCH DER GEFAHRLICHEN GUTER. 2230

0172-9683 See GITARRE + LAUTE. 4119

0172-9721 See ANIMATION HANNOVER. 2596

0173-0274 See INGENIEURWISSENSCHAFTLICHE BIBLIOTHEK. 1978

0173-0452 See MVP-BERICHTE. 4792

0173-0487 See BIA REPORT. 2859

0173-0568 See ZEITSCHRIFT FUER SCHADENSRECHT : ZFS / HERAUSGEGEBEN VON DEN RECHTSANWAELTEN ALFRED FLEISCHMANN, HANAU ... [ET AL.]. 3078

0173-0711 See OKOLOGIE DER VOGEL. 5593

0173-0835 See ELECTROPHORESIS. 1015

0173-0886 See HAMMABURG : VOR- U. FRUHGESCHICHTLICHE FORSCHUNGEN AUS DEM NIEDERELBISCHEN RAUM. 2690

0173-170X See DISORDERS OF HUMAN COMMUNICATION. 3887

0173-1726 See SIEMENS COMPONENTS. DEUTSCHE AUSGABE. 2081

0173-1734 See SIEMENS COMPONENTS. ENGLISH AUSGABE. 2081

0173-1831 See BIBLIOGRAPHIEN ZUR PHILOSOPHIE. 4342

0173-1882 See APOTHEKE HEUTE. 921

0173-1890 See PHARMAZEUTISCHE VERFAHRENSTECHNIK HEUTE. 4324

0173-2145 See HISTORISCHE SOZIALFORSCHUNG. 5201

0173-2315 See INTENSIVMEDIZINISCHE PRAXIS. 3683

0173-2501 See STRASSENVERKEHRSZAHLUNGEN. 5426

0173-2595 See ZPA. ZEITSCHRIFT FUER PRAKTISCHE AUGENHEILKUNDE. 3880

0173-2781 See ART (HAMBURG). 339

0173-2803 See MAKROMOLEKULARE CHEMIE. RAPID COMMUNICATIONS, DIE. **1044**
0173-2986 See ABSTRACTS IN GERMANY ANTHROPOLOGY. **227**
0173-301X See PATHOLINGUISTICA. **3891**
0173-3028 See CHRIST UND WELT / RHEINISCHER MERKUR. **5027**
0173-3303 See WIRTSCHAFTSSCHUTZ + SICHERHEITSTECHNIK. **3179**
0173-3338 See ZENTRALBLATT FUER ARBEITSMEDIZIN, ARBEITSSCHUTZ, PROPHYLAXE UND ERGONOMIE. **3653**
0173-3532 See MOTIVATIONSFORSCHUNG. **4604**
0173-363X See UMWELTMAGAZIN WURZBURG. **2182**
0173-3869 See GESUNDHEITSWESEN. REIHE 2.3, SONSTIGE MELDEPFLICHTIGE KRANKHEITEN (STUTTGART. KOHLHAMMER. 1977). **3713**
0173-394X See SOZIALLEISTUNGEN. REIHE 1: VERSICHERTE IN DER KRANKEN- UND RENTENVERSICHERUNG. **5310**
0173-4865 See TEXTE DER HETHITER. **1080**
0173-4911 See JOURNAL OF OPTICAL COMMUNICATIONS. **4436**
0173-5187 See FORUM MUSIKBIBLIOTHEK. **3211**
0173-5373 See AMPHIBIA-REPTILIA. **5575**
0173-539X See G. GESCHICHTE MIT PFIFF. **2616**
0173-5764 See ARZT UND PATIENT (BADEN-BADEN). **3553**
0173-5896 See STATISTICAL SOFTWARE NEWSLETTER. **3536**
0173-6213 See LOGISTIK HEUTE. **5386**
0173-6264 See LUFT- UND RAUMFAHRT. **28**
0173-6280 See DVW HESSEN MITTEILUNGEN. **2022**
0173-6396 See WERKZEUG MACHINEN FUER DIE METALLBEARBEITUNG, HANDBUCH. **4023**
0173-6574 See KURZBERICHTE / INSTITUT FUER ARBEITSMARKT- UND BERUFSFORSCHUNG. **1683**
0173-6760 See KERAMIK AUGSBURG. **2592**
0173-6868 See NIEDERSACHSISCHES ZAHNARZTEBLATT. **1331**
0173-7082 See CURRENT RESEARCH IN OPHTHALMIC ELECTRON MICROSCOPY. **3874**
0173-749X See VERHANDLUNGEN DES NATURWISSENSCHAFTLICHEN VEREINS IN HAMBURG (1979). **4173**
0173-752X See METHODS OF OPERATIONS RESEARCH (1980). **1987**
0173-7597 See KRANKENHAUSPHARMAZIE. **4313**
0173-7600 See JAHRBUCH FUER REGIONALWISSENSCHAFT / HERAUSGEGEBEN VOM VORSTAND DER GESELLSCHAFT FUER REGIONALFORSCHUNG E. V. (DEUTSCHSPRACHIGE GRUPPE DER REGIONAL SCIENCE ASSOCIATION). **2694**
0173-7619 See APPLIED GEOGRAPHY AND DEVELOPMENT. **2554**
0173-7767 See DATENSCHUTZ-NACHRICHTEN. **4507**
0173-783X See BEITRAEGE ZUR TABAKFORSCHUNG INTERNATIONAL. **5372**
0173-7937 See PSYCHOTHERAPIE, PSYCHOSOMATIK, MEDIZINISCHE PSYCHOLOGIE. **4614**
0173-8046 See AIT. ARCHITEKTUR, INNENARCHITEKTUR, TECHNISCHER AUSBAU. **287**
0173-8062 See ZEITSCHRIFT FUER LOGISTIK. **890**
0173-8607 See PIANO-JAHRBUCH. **4146**
0173-8712 See VDLUFA-SCHRIFTENREIHE. **144**
0173-8720 See UMWELT UND ENERGIE. **1959**
0173-9220 See RATIONELL REINIGEN. **625**
0173-9522 See ZIELSPRACHE RUSSISCH. **3336**
0173-9565 See MARINE ECOLOGY (BERLIN, WEST). **2218**
0173-9859 See HNO PRAXIS HEUTE. **3888**
0173-9913 See CFI, CERAMIC FORUM INTERNATIONAL. **2588**

0173-9980 See BULK SOLIDS HANDLING. **1967**
0174-0008 See ERNAHRUNGS-UMSCHAU 1977. **2334**
0174-0202 See ZEITSCHRIFT FUER RECHTSSOZIOLOGIE. **5265**
0174-0474 See TEXTE ZUR FORSCHUNG. **3445**
0174-0652 See URAL-ALTAISCHE JAHRBUCHER NEUE FOLGE. **3331**
0174-108X See KRANKENPFLEGE JOURNAL. **3861**
0174-1098 See ZEITSCHRIFT FUER LARMBEKAMPFUNG. **2248**
0174-1357 See MARKSCHEIDEWESEN, DAS. **2143**
0174-1446 See RECYCLING. **2180**
0174-1551 See CARDIOVASCULAR AND INTERVENTIONAL RADIOLOGY. **3939**
0174-1578 See JOURNAL OF COMPARATIVE PHYSIOLOGY. B, BIOCHEMICAL, SYSTEMIC, AND ENVIRONMENTAL PHYSIOLOGY. **582**
0174-1616 See ERGEBNISSE DER GASTROENTEROLOGIE. **3744**
0174-1756 See LWF DOCUMENTATION. **4975**
0174-1799 See GLUCKAUF. WITH ENGLISH TRANSLATION (ESSEN). **2140**
0174-1810 See FORSTLICHE FORSCHUNGSBERICHTE MUNCHEN. **2383**
0174-1837 See ANASTHESIOLOGIE, INTENSIVMEDIZIN, NOTFALLMEDIZIN, SCHMERZTHERAPIE : AINS. **3681**
0174-1993 See VERZEICHNIS DER WISSENSCHAFTLICHEN FILME. TEILVERZEICHNIS B. **144**
0174-2086 See HEPHAISTOS (BAD BRAMSTEDT). **269**
0174-2108 See INFORMATIONSBRIEF AUSLANDERRECHT. **2982**
0174-2450 See COLO-PROCTOLOGY, INTERNATIONAL EDITION. **3962**
0174-254X See APPARENT PLACES OF FUNDAMENTAL STARS. **391**
0174-2752 See KLINISCHE UND EXPERIMENTELLE UROLOGIE. **3991**
0174-2817 See VERHANDLUNGEN DER DEUTSCHEN GESELLSCHAFT FUER HERZ- UND KREISLAUFFORSCHUNG. **3711**
0174-304X See NEUROPEDIATRICS. **3841**
0174-3082 See EUROPEAN JOURNAL OF PEDIATRIC SURGERY : OFFICIAL JOURNAL OF AUSTRIAN ASSOCIATION OF PEDIATRIC SURGERY ... ZEITSCHRIFT FUER KINDERCHIRURGIE. **3964**
0174-3244 See UMWELTHYGIENE (ESSEN). **2245**
0174-3279 See MOMBERGER AIRPORT INFORMATION. **29**
0174-3287 See JAHRESBERICHT / GESELLSCHAFT FUR INFORMATION UND DOKUMENTATION. **3219**
0174-3384 See BRAUNSCHWEIGER NATURKUNDLICHE SCHRIFTEN. **4163**
0174-3511 See KUNSTPREISJAHRBUCH. **356**
0174-3597 See HELGOLAENDER MEERESUNTERSUCHUNGEN. **554**
0174-4003 See SCHRIFTENREIHE KUNSTOFF -FORSCHUNG. **4460**
0174-4224 See EARLY MAN NEWS. **4227**
0174-4410 See STUDIEN UND TEXTE ZUR SOZIALGESCHICHTE DER LITERATUR. **3441**
0174-4704 See HUMAN RIGHTS LAW JOURNAL : HRLJ. **3129**
0174-4720 See JAHRBUCH ZUR LITERATUR IN DER DDR / HERAUSGEGEBEN IM AUFTRAG DES ARBEITSKREISES LITERATUR UND GERMANISTIK IN DER DDR VON PAUL GERHARD KLUSSMANN UND HEINRICH MOHR. **3398**
0174-4771 See SCHRIFTENREIHE DER DEUTSCHEN GESELLSCHAFT FUER MEDIZINISCHE DOKUMENTATION, INFORMATIK UND STATISTIK E. V. **3639**
0174-481X See GIESSENER STUDIENREIHE HEIL - UND SONDERPADAGOGIK. **1879**
0174-4879 See INTERNATIONAL JOURNAL OF CLINICAL PHARMACOLOGY, THERAPY AND TOXICOLOGY (1980). **4308**

0174-4909 See FRANKFURTER ALLGEMEINE. **5801**
0174-4917 See SUEDDEUTSCHE ZEITUNG. **5802**
0174-4933 See GKSS JAHRESBERICHT. **4176**
0174-5026 See HANDBUCH DER GROSSFORSCHUNG / ARBEITSGEMEINSCHAFT DER GROSSFORSCHUNGSEINRICHTUNGEN (AGR). **5109**
0174-5506 See DIAKRISIS. **4953**
0174-559X See TRANSPORTRECHT. **3066**
0174-6162 See VERWALTUNGSWIRT, DER. **3071**
0174-6170 See WIRTSCHAFT UND ERZIEHUNG. **1791**
0174-6189 See ELEKTROWARME INTERNATIONAL. EDITION A : ELEKTOWARME IM TECHNISCHEN AUSBAU. **2604**
0174-7363 See FINANCIAL TIMES (FRANKFURT ED.). **675**
0174-7371 See TRACE ELEMENTS IN MEDICINE. **3647**
0174-738X See VERDAUUNGSKRANKHEITEN. **3748**
0174-7398 See VIRCHOWS ARCHIV. A, PATHOLOGICAL ANATOMY AND HISTOPATHOLOGY. **3898**
0175-0496 See PC-WELT. **1199**
0175-274X See S + F. **4534**
0175-3851 See INTENSIVMEDIZIN + NOTFALLMEDIZIN. **3588**
0175-4211 See WABOLU-HEFTE. **2183**
0175-4467 See STREIT. **3060**
0175-4548 See F & W, FUHREN UND WIRTSCHAFTEN IM KRANKENHAUS. **3780**
0175-5676 See BEITRAEGE ZUR OKONOMISCHEN FORSCHUNG. **1464**
0175-5811 See ARZTE-ZEITUNG. **3553**
0175-6133 See AUSGRABUNGEN UND FUNDE IN WESTFALEN-LIPPE / IM AUFTRAG DES LANDSCHAFTSVERBANDES WESTFALEN-LIPPE HERAUSGEGEBEN VON WESTFALISCHES MUSEUM FUER ARCHAOLOGIE, AMT FUER BODENDENKMALPFLEGE. **2677**
0175-6346 See KANADIER. **5801**
0175-6508 See PHILOSOPHISCHE ABHANDLUNGEN. **4356**
0175-6524 See BIBLIOTHEKSRECHTLICHE VORSCHRIFTEN. **3195**
0175-6869 See MITTEILUNGEN - DEUTSCHE FORSCHUNGSGESELLSCHAFT FUER DRUCK- UND REPRODUKTIONSTECHNIK E.V. **4566**
0175-713X See BERUGSBILDUNG, WIETERBILDUNG, BILDUNGSPOLITIK. **1727**
0175-7326 See MATERIALIEN DES FORSCHUNGSINSTITUTS FUR DIE ZAHNARZTLICHE VERSORGUNG. **1329**
0175-7350 See STATISTISCHE MITTEILUNGEN. **5343**
0175-7571 See EUROPEAN BIOPHYSICS JOURNAL. **495**
0175-7598 See APPLIED MICROBIOLOGY AND BIOTECHNOLOGY. **559**
0175-7601 See LOGBUCH, DAS. **2774**
0175-7652 See BEITRAEGE AUS DER EV. MILITARSEELSORGE. **4938**
0175-7784 See ZEITSCHRIFT FUER STOMATOLOGIE. **3716**
0175-7814 See ARZT IM KRANKENHAUS UND IM GESUNDHEITSWESEN (1981), DER. **3553**
0175-8292 See VITIS, VITICULTURE AND ENOLOGY ABSTRACTS. **2362**
0175-8314 See ALLES UBER WEIN. **2363**
0175-8330 See EUROPEAN ECONOMIES IN GRAPHS AND FIGURES / IFO, THE. **1489**
0175-8438 See PROGRAMM-BUDGET. **4742**
0175-8446 See BERLIN IN GESCHICHTE UND GEGENWART. **2678**
0175-8659 See JOURNAL OF APPLIED ICHTHYOLOGY. **2306**
0175-9264 See LEXICOGRAPHICA. SERIES MAIOR. **3297**
0175-9299 See PERSONALRAT, DER. **4704**

0175-9388 See GERMANISTISCHE TEXTE UND STUDIEN. 3284

0176-0769 See GEOBOTANISCHE KOLLOQUIEN. 2216

0176-0920 See EX MAGAZINE. 2054

0176-0971 See ZUPFMUSIK MAGAZIN. 4160

0176-1226 See MANA, MANNHEIMER ANALYTIKA. 324

0176-1439 See THEOLOGY IN CONTEXT. 5004

0176-1617 See JOURNAL OF PLANT PHYSIOLOGY. 516

0176-1625 See GUMMI, FASERN, KUNSTSTOFFE. 5076

0176-1714 See SOCIAL CHOICE AND WELFARE. 5308

0176-1749 See LUNG & RESPIRATION. 3950

0176-2354 See DAMASZENER MITTEILUNGEN. 266

0176-2389 See LAND AGRARWIRTSCHAFT UND GESELLSCHAFT. 103

0176-2540 See ABHANDLUNGEN ZUR KARST- UND HOHLENKUNDE. REIHE F : GESCHICHTE DER SPELAOLOGIE, BIOGRAPHIEN, VOLKSKUNDE. 1402

0176-2575 See BIBLIOGRAPHIE PADAGOGIK. REIHE B, BUCHER. 4809

0176-2621 See HELDIA. 5585

0176-2753 See FUNDEVOGEL. 3389

0176-2818 See LATEINAMERIKA. 2743

0176-3261 See PKV PUBLIK. 2890

0176-3288 See DATACOM. 1296

0176-3296 See MICROFAUNA MARINA. 465

0176-3474 See HIGH TECH DEUTSCHE AUSG. 5109

0176-3679 See PHARMACOPSYCHIATRY. 4323

0176-3695 See DEUTSCHES ARZTEBLATT AUSG. C. 3571

0176-3733 See INKLINGS. 3396

0176-3857 3576

0176-3997 See CAROLINEA. 4164

0176-4152 See P. M. PETER MOOSLEITNERS INTERESSANTES MAGAZIN. 2491

0176-4179 See KONTINENT (BERLIN, GERMANY). 4480

0176-4225 See DIACHRONICA. 3277

0176-4241 See MEDIENWISSENSCHAFT, REZENSIONEN. 1117

0176-4268 See JOURNAL OF CLASSIFICATION. 3512

0176-4276 See CONSTRUCTIVE APPROXIMATION. 3502

0176-4284 See MEDIZIN IN RECHT UND ETHIK. 3742

0176-4616 See PRAXIS KURIER, KONGRESS-SYNOPSE AKTUELL : PK. 3629

0176-473X See KEHRWIEDER. 5451

0176-4829 See KLINISCHE CHEMIE IN EINZELDARSTELLUNGEN. 984

0176-5035 See LECTURE NOTES IN ENGINEERING. 1985

0176-6104 See VOGUE MUNCHEN. 5568

0176-6112 See FASHION GUIDE DUSSELDORF. 1084

0176-6449 See ZENTRALBLATT FUER JUGENDRECHT. 3122

0176-7062 See NEUE KUNST IN MUNCHEN. 359

0176-7151 See MEDICOLEGAL LIBRARY. 3742

0176-7593 See LIBRARIES, INFORMATION CENTERS AND DATABASES IN SCIENCE AND TECHNOLOGY : A WORLD GUIDE. 3258

0176-7615 See MODERN SYNTHETIC METHODS. 1027

0176-7771 See FINANZ-RUNDSCHAU FUER EINKOMMENSTEUER UND KORPERSCHAFTSTEUER : FR. 3128

0176-7984 See FORTSCHRITTE IN DER ATOMSPEKTROMETRISCHEN SPURENANALYTIK. 4434

0176-8654 See UNIX/MAIL. 1206

0176-8824 See 64'ER. 1169

0176-8905 See KLEINE SCHRIFTEN DER GESELLSCHAFT FUER THEATERGESCHICHTE. 5365

0176-9030 See JAHRESBERICHT / VON DER HEYDT-MUSEUM KUNST- UND MUSEUMSVEREIN. 354

0176-912X QUINOLONES BULLETIN : REPORTS ON GYRASE INHIBITORS. 3632

0176-9340 See ADVANCES IN SOIL SCIENCE (NEW YORK). 161

0176-9472 See SCHRIFTEN DES ARBEITSKREISES SELBSTANDIGER KULTUR-INSTITUTE. 2492

0177-0608 See K-PLASTIC- & KAUTSCHUK-ZEITUNG EXPORT ISSUE. 5076

0177-0667 See ENGINEERING WITH COMPUTERS. 1974

0177-0950 See MUNCHNER GEOWISSENSCHAFTLICHE ABHANDLUNGEN. REIHE A, GEOLOGIE UND PALAONTOLOGIE. 1389

0177-0977 See PC-MAGAZIN. 1199

0177-1205 See LEITERPLATTEN. 1193

0177-1469 See CP + T INTERNATIONAL CASTING PLANT AND TECHNOLOGY. 4000

0177-1477 See STUCK, PUTZ, TROCKENBAU. 3488

0177-2082 See GEMEINDEWACHSTUM. 4553

0177-2309 See NOTARZT, DER. 3725

0177-2392 See TROPICAL MEDICINE AND PARASITOLOGY. 3987

0177-2503 See STUDIEN ZUR INTEGRIERTEN LANDLICHEN ENTWICKLUNG. 138

0177-2570 See VINUM. 2372

0177-3062 See AMTLICHE MITTEILUNGEN DER BUNDESANSTALT FUER ARBEITSSCHUTZ. 2858

0177-3348 See ZEITSCHRIFT FUER ZAHNARZTLICHE IMPLANTOLOGIE. 1337

0177-350X See MUSIK PSYCHOLOGIE : JAHRBUCH DER DEUTSCHEN GESELLSCHAFT FUER MUSIKPSYCHOLOGIE. 4137

0177-3593 See BIOLOGICAL CHEMISTRY HOPPE-SEYLER. 483

0177-3674 See KUNSTFORUM INTERNATIONAL. 356

0177-4182 See MUSIKTHEORIE. 4138

0177-4204 See CURRENT TOPICS IN MEDICAL MYCOLOGY. 574

0177-4212 See BILDUNG UND WISSENSCHAFT. 5088

0177-4247 See JUGENDBUCHMAGAZIN. 3400

0177-4565 See KES : ZEITSCHRIFT FUER KOMMUNIKATIONS UND EDV SICHERHEIT. 1115

0177-4832 See STEEL RESEARCH. 4020

0177-5014 See TASPO MAGAZIN. 2432

0177-5103 See DISEASES OF AQUATIC ORGANISMS. 554

0177-5146 See ENVIRONMENTAL GEOLOGY AND WATER SCIENCES. 1375

0177-5235 See MICRO COMPUTER COLLEG. 1195

0177-5499 See NET. NACHRICHTEN ELEKTRONIK + TELEMATIK (1984). 1160

0177-5537 See UNFALLCHIRURG, DER. 3725

0177-6363 See STATISTISCHE RUNDSCHAU NORDRHEIN-WESTFALEN. 1522

0177-6495 See SPRINGER SERIES ON ATOMS + PLASMAS. 4422

0177-6673 See SCHRIFTENREIHE DES FACHBEREICHS INTERNATIONALE AGRARENTWICKLUNG. 132

0177-6738 See NEUE GESELLSCHAFT, FRANKFURTER HEFTE, DIE. 5210

0177-6754 See NATURHEILPRAXIS MIT NATURMEDIZIN. 3619

0177-6762 See ZUM : ZEITSCHRIFT FUER URHEBER- UND MEDIENRECHT/FILM UND RECHT. 4080

0177-7114 See WOODWORKING INTERNATIONAL NURNBERG. 635

0177-7246 See MAENNER-VOGUE. 3995

0177-7424 See SPIXIANA. SUPPLEMENT. 5598

0177-7440 See CONFRUCTA. 2366

0177-7505 See VHF COMMUNICATIONS. 1123

0177-7513 See UKW-BERICHTE. 4442

0177-7726 See PFERDEHEILKUNDE. 5518

0177-7955 See NEURO-ORTHOPEDICS. 3839

0177-7963 See FEW-BODY SYSTEMS. 4447

0177-7971 See METEOROLOGY AND ATMOSPHERIC PHYSICS. 1431

0177-798X See THEORETICAL AND APPLIED CLIMATOLOGY. 1436

0177-8161 See PATIENTORIENTIERTE ALLGEMEINMEDIZIN. 3626

0177-8293 See DMSG AKTIV. 4387

0177-8358 See MITTEILUNGSBLATT DER ARBEITSGEMEINSCHAFT KATHOLISCH-THEOLOGISCHER BIBLIOTHEKEN, AKTHB. 3231

0177-8374 See PRAXIS DER NATURWISSENSCHAFTEN PHYSIK. 4417

0177-8382 See PRAXIS DER NATURWISSENSCHAFTEN BIOLOGIE. 469

0177-8706 See EVANGELIKALE MISSIOLOGIE. 4957

0177-8757 See PROGRESS IN CLINICAL BIOCHEMISTRY AND MEDICINE. 492

0177-8811 See FEW-BODY SYSTEMS. SUPPLEMENTUM. 4447

0177-8978 See JAHRBUCH DES ZENTRALINSTITUTS FUER KUNSTGESCHICHTE. 354

0177-9095 See GIATROSPAEDIATRIE. 3903

0177-9109 See GIATROSGYNAKOLOGIE. 3761

0177-9214 See ACTA BIOLOGICA BENRODIS. 4161

0177-9370 See FORSCHUNGEN ZUR GESCHICHTE DER ALTEREN DEUTSCHEN LITERATUR. 3388

0177-9516 See PRAXIS DER NATURWISSENSCHAFTEN CHEMIE. 989

0177-9591 See APOTHEKE UND KRANKENHAUS : ZEITSCHRIFT DES VERBANDES DER KRANKENHAUSVERSORGENDEN OFFIZIN-APOTHEKER E.V. 4292

0177-9990 See CHIRURGISCHE GASTROENTEROLOGIE MIT INTERDISZIPLINAREN GESPRACHEN. 3743

0178-0026 See ROBOTERSYSTEME. 1216

0178-045X See ARCHAOLOGISCHE NACHRICHTEN AUS BADEN. 258

0178-0999 See A + S AKTUELL. 4763

0178-1197 See OFFSET-TECHNIK. 4567

0178-126X See STUDIEN ZUR THEORETISCHEN LINGUISTIK. 3325

0178-1715 See OP-JOURNAL. 3624

0178-1987 See AMERICAN STUDIES (MUNICH, GERMANY). 5190

0178-2010 See RFL. RUNDSCHAU FUER FLEISCHUNTERSUCHUNG UND LEBENSMITTELUBERWACHUNG. 5521

0178-2029 See BIOENGINEERING (GRAFELFING, GERMANY). 3686

0178-2134 See ADVANCES IN IMMUNITY AND CANCER THERAPY. 3662

0178-2320 See AUTOMATISIERUNGSTECHNISCHE PRAXIS : ATP. 2110

0178-2525 See RETTUNGSDIENST. 3634

0178-2762 See BIOLOGY AND FERTILITY OF SOILS. 164

0178-2770 See DISTRIBUTED COMPUTING. 1258

0178-2789 See VISUAL COMPUTER, THE. 1235

0178-2835 See SIEBDRUCK, DER. 4569

0178-2916 See MITTEILUNGEN DES OBSTBAUVERSUCHSRINGES DES ALTEN LANDES. 2424

0178-2967 See BIBLISCHE NOTIZEN. 5015

0178-2983 See HANDBALL-MAGAZIN. 4897

0178-3084 See WEHRAUSBILDUNG. 4061

0178-3165 See MITTEILUNGEN DER FORSTLICHEN VERSUCHS- UND FORSCHUNGSANSTALT BADEN-WRTTEMBERG. 2388

0178-3335 See DISKUSSIONSBEITRAGE - UNIVERSITAT KIEL, INSTITUT FUER AGRARPOLITIK UND MARKTLEHRE. 79
0178-3351 See DEUTSCHE MEDIZIN. 3571
0178-3556 See MANIPULATOR, THE. 5801
0178-3564 See INFORMATIK - FORSCHUNG UND ENTWICKLUNG. 1188
0178-4609 See FORTSCHRITTE AUF DEM GEBIETE DER RONTGENSTRAHLEN UND DER NUKLEARMEDIZIN. ERGANZUNGSBAND. 3941
0178-4617 See ALGORITHMICA. 1170
0178-4641 See KEYBOARDS. 4128
0178-4862 See APOTHEKER-ZEITUNG STUTTGART. 4292
0178-4927 See MITTEILUNGSBLATT / GESELLSCHAFT DEUTSCHER CHEMIKER, FACHGRUPPE CHEMIE-INFORMATION. 986
0178-515X See BIOPROCESS ENGINEERING (BERLIN, WEST). 2008
0178-5893 See VERKAUFSLEITER-SERVICE. 718
0178-594X See KMI. BUEROWIRTSCHAFT, LEHRE UND PRAXIS. 1899
0178-692X See SCHMERZDIAGNOSTIK UND THERAPIE. 3639
0178-7128 See AUFKLARUNG. 2677
0178-725X See AFRIKANISTISCHE ARBEITSPAPIERE. 3262
0178-7284 See JOURNAL FUER DIE FRAU. 5559
0178-7527 See GIATROSUROLOGIE. 3990
0178-7586 See HARD AND SOFT. 1186
0178-7667 See FORUM DER PSYCHOANALYSE. 4587
0178-7675 See COMPUTATIONAL MECHANICS. 2112
0178-7683 See ZEITSCHRIFT FUER PHYSIK. D, ATOMS, MOLECULES AND CLUSTERS. 4425
0178-7764 See INTERNATIONALES SAUNA-ARCHIV. 2599
0178-7810 See GEOGRAPHIE AKTUELL. 2563
0178-7888 See MYCOTOXIN RESEARCH. 519
0178-7896 See MITTEILUNGEN DER BERLINER GESELLSCHAFT FUER ANTHROPOLOGIE, ETHNOLOGIE UND URGESCHICHTE. 241
0178-7969 See SALIX. 3638
0178-8051 See PROBABILITY THEORY AND RELATED FIELDS. 3527
0178-8116 See SCHRIFTENREIHE ANGEWANDTE VERSICHERUNGSMATHEMATIK. 3533
0178-8345 See DIAGNOSE & LABOR. 3571
0178-8515 See ABHANDLUNGEN ZUR SPRACHE UND LITERATUR. 3357
0178-8728 See COGITO DARMSTADT. 1175
0178-8930 See RECHT DER DATENVERARBEITUNG : RDV. 1227
0178-8957 See BLICKPUNKT SCHMERZ. 3557
0178-9090 See INFEKTIONEN UND KLINIKHYGIENE. 3587
0178-9600 See FORTSCHRITT-BERICHTE VDI. REIHE 17, BIOTECHNIK. 456
0178-9775 See GESAMTKATALOG DER DUSSELDORFER KULTURINSTITUTE (GDK) [MICROFORM] / BIBLIOTHEKSSTELLE DER DUSSELDORFER KULTURINSTITUTE. 351
0178-9805 See TOP HAIR. 405
0178-9902 See SPECULUM ORBIS. 2583
0179-0080 See WISSENSCHAFTLICHER BUCH BESPRECHUNGSDIENST : WIBB. 5009
0179-0358 See PEDIATRIC SURGERY INTERNATIONAL. 3909
0179-051X See DYSPHAGIA. 3887
0179-1389 See ANGLISTISCHE FORSCHUNGEN. 3264
0179-1613 See ETHOLOGY. 5583
0179-1796 See FERTILITAT. 3760
0179-1826 See MEDICAL CORPS INTERNATIONAL. 3608
0179-1834 See GOPPINGER ARBEITEN ZUR GERMANISTIK. 3284
0179-1958 See INTERNATIONAL JOURNAL OF COLORECTAL DISEASE. 3589
0179-1990 See COMPUTER UND RECHT (KOLN). 2955

0179-2148 See ASPECTS OF MATHEMATICS. D. 3496
0179-2156 See ASPECTS OF MATHEMATICS. E. 3496
0179-2180 See LINGUISTISCHE ARBEITEN UND BERICHTE. 3299
0179-2466 See BRAUEREI FORUM. 2365
0179-2482 See STUTTGARTER ARBEITEN ZUR GERMANISTIK. 3443
0179-2679 See CIM-MANAGEMENT. 1174
0179-2784 See HANNOVERSCHE STUDIEN UBER DEN MITTLEREN OSTEN. 2504
0179-2830 See KRITISCHE VIERTELJAHRESSCHRIFT FUER GESETZGEBUNG UND RECHTSWISSENSCHAFT. 2993
0179-2938 See RECHTSRHEINISCHES KOLN. 2704
0179-2997 See DEUTSCHE NATIONALBIBLIOGRAPHIE UND BIBLIOGRAPHIE DER IM AUSLAND ERSCHIENENEN DEUTSCHSPRACHIGEN VEROFFENTLICHUNGEN. MONOGRAPHIEN UND PERIODIKA DES VERLAGSBUCHHANDELS UND AUSSERHALB DES VERLAGSBUCHHANDELS. WOCHENTLICHES VERZEICHNIS. WOCHENREGISTER ZU REIHE A UND REIHE B / BEARBEITER UND HERAUSGEBER, DIE DEUTSCHE BIBLIOTHEK. 414
0179-3063 See THAT'S YUGOSLAVIA. 2524
0179-3098 See AIDS-FORSCHUNG. 3663
0179-3187 See ERDOL, ERDGAS, KOHLE. 4255
0179-3462 See IWL UMWELTBRIEF. 2196
0179-3551 See GLAUBE UND LERNEN. 4960
0179-3616 See QUANTITATIVE LINGUISTICS. 3313
0179-3632 See SPRINGER SERIES IN COMPUTATIONAL MATHEMATICS. 1262
0179-3780 See COLLOQUIUM HELVETICUM. 3376
0179-4027 See BEITRAEGE ZUR NEUEREN LITERATURGESCHICHTE. 3366
0179-4043 See NJW-RECHTSPRECHUNGS-REPORT, ZIVILRECHT. 3090
0179-4051 See ZEITSCHRIFT FUER GESETZGEBUNG : ZG. 3078
0179-4167 See RESEARCH IN TEXT THEORY. 3315
0179-4485 See SCHRIFTENREIHE DER FORSCHUNGSGESELLSCHAFT FUER AGRARPOLITIK UND AGRARSOZIOLOGIE E.V. BONN. 5257
0179-4515 See LIBERIA-FORUM. 2641
0179-4639 See ZEITSCHRIFT FUER GESCHICHTE DER ARABISCH-ISLAMISCHEN WISSENSCHAFTEN. 1792
0179-5066 See BETRIEBSWIRTSCHAFTLICHE NACHRICHTEN FUER DIE LANDWIRTSCHAFT. 66
0179-5376 See DISCRETE & COMPUTATIONAL GEOMETRY. 3503
0179-5724 See MEDIENSPIEGEL. 2490
0179-5775 See IPN-BLATTER. 1755
0179-5953 See REVIEWS OF ENVIRONMENTAL CONTAMINATION AND TOXICOLOGY. 2242
0179-6844 See TEXTCONTEXT. 3328
0179-714X See DEUTSCHE ZEITSCHRIFT FUER BIOLOGISCHE VETERINAR-MEDIZIN. 5508
0179-7158 See STRAHLENTHERAPIE UND ONKOLOGIE. 3824
0179-7166 See CARDIOLOGISCH-ANGIOLOGISCHES BULLETIN. 3700
0179-7239 See KIRCHE UND ISRAEL. 5050
0179-7247 See ANALYSES OF HAZARDOUS SUBSTANCES IN BIOLOGICAL MATERIALS. 2224
0179-7417 See LISTEN (FRANKFURT AM MAIN, GERMANY). 3346
0179-7549 See LANDERBERICHT. BRASILIEN / STATISTISCHES BUNDESAMT. 5331
0179-8367 See FEMINIST, DER. 5556
0179-8669 See THEORETICAL SURGERY. 3976

0179-8812 See EW. ERNAHRUNGSWIRTSCHAFT. 2334
0179-9541 See PLANT BREEDING. 523
0179-9738 See INFORMATIONSTECHNIK. 1188
0179-9746 See REGENSBURGER MATHEMATISCHE SCHRIFTEN. 3530
0179-9932 See ENERGIE SPEKTRUM. 1938
0180-0078 See VERRE ACTUALITES. 2595
0180-0612 See SAGES FEMMES. 3768
0180-3468 See AILLEURS PARIS. 3358
0180-3840 See SUIVRE, A. 3354
0180-4103 See NOTES BIBLIOGRAPHIQUES CARAIBES. 421
0180-4200 See ANNALES DE L'INSTITUT D'ETUDES OCCITANES. 3264
0180-4278 See NOTE D'INFORMATION / ASSOCIATION DES BIBLIOTHECAIRES FRANCAIS. 3237
0180-4979 See B.A.T. BON A TIRER. 4563
0180-5738 See EUROPEAN JOURNAL OF PEDIATRIC SURGERY : OFFICIAL JOURNAL OF AUSTRIAN ASSOCIATION OF PEDIATRIC SURGERY ... ZEITSCHRIFT FUER KINDERCHIRURGIE. 3964
0180-6424 See STRATEGIES PARIS. 767
0180-8214 See COMMENTAIRE (JULLIARD). 3377
0180-8524 See HOMMES ET LIBERTES. 4508
0180-8567 See BULLETIN D'INFORMATIONS ET DE RECHERCHES. 3369
0180-9040 See HANDICAPS ET INADAPTATIONS PARIS. 4388
0180-9288 See DIEU EST AMOUR SAINT-CENERE. 5028
0180-9296 See FRANCIS BULLETIN SIGNALETIQUE. 527, HISTOIRE ET SCIENCES DES RELIGIONS. 4959
0180-930X See ANNALES DE LA RECHERCHE URBAINE, LES. 5239
0180-9423 See REVUE DES LETTRES MODERNES. JEAN GIONO, LA. 3430
0180-961X See TRAUVUX SCIENTIFIQUES DU PARC NATIONAL DE LA VANOISE. 4173
0180-9857 See GROUPE FAMILIAL, LE. 2280
0180-9869 See REVUE DE DROIT IMMOBILIER. 3042
0180-9938 See AVIS AUX NAVIGATEURS. 4175
0181-0006 See BULLETIN SIGNALETIQUE. 364, PROTOZOAIRES ET INVERTEBRES, ZOOLOGIE GENERALE ET APPLIQUEE. 5580
0181-009X See ARES (LYON, FRANCE). 3124
0181-0162 See ILE-DE-FRANCE, NOTE DE CONJONCTURE REGIONALE. 1566
0181-0448 See REVUE D'ALSACE. 2706
0181-0529 See REVUE FRANCAISE DE GEOTECHNIQUE. 3264
0181-057X See MASSES OUVRIERES. 1690
0181-0626 See BULLETIN DU MUSEUM NATIONAL D'HISTOIRE NATURELLE. SECTION A : ZOOLOGIE, BIOLOGIE ET ECOLOGIE ANIMALES. 5579
0181-0642 See BULLETIN DU MUSEUM NATIONAL D'HISTOIRE NATURELLE. SECTION C : SCIENCES DE LA TERRE : PALEONTOLOGIE, GEOLOGIE, MINERALOGIE. 4163
0181-0790 See CAHIERS LEON TROTSKY. 4540
0181-0839 See CAHIERS GEOGRAPHIQUES DE ROUEN. 2557
0181-0855 See REVUE DU SCOM. 4683
0181-0979 See ACTUALITES SCIENTIFIQUES ET AGRONOMIQUES DE L'I.N.R.A. 44
0181-1010 See NOTE FINANCIERE ANNUELLE. ILE-DE-FRANCE. 801
0181-1126 See CAHIERS SIMONE WEIL. 4343
0181-1223 See LETTRE D'INFORMATION METAUX DE LA REVUE LA RECUPERATION. 4007
0181-1517 See BULLETIN STATISTIQUE DE LA DGAC / MINISTERE DES TRANSPORTS, AVIATION CIVILE. 41
0181-1525 See CAHIERS DU MUSEE NATIONAL D'ART MODERNE. 346
0181-1568 See CRYPTOGAMIE. ALGOLOGIE. 452

0181-1576 See CRYPTOGAMIE. BRYOLOGIE, LICHENOLOGIE. 507

0181-1584 See CRYPTOGAMIE. MYCOLOGIE (1979). 507

0181-1789 See BULLETIN DE LA SOCIETE BOTANIQUE DE FRANCE. ACTUALITES BOTANIQUES. 504

0181-1797 See LETTRES BOTANIQUES (PARIS). 517

0181-3048 See CONNAISSANCE DES TEMPS. 4175

0181-3684 See NOUVEAU BIOLOGISTE, LE. 467

0181-4095 See LANGAGE ET SOCIETE. 3294

0181-4141 See FILM ECHANGE. 4069

0181-4400 See TRAVAUX DE L'INSTITUT D'HISTOIRE DE L'ART DE LYON. 367

0181-4788 See CIMADE INFORMATION. 4468

0181-5512 See JOURNAL FRANCAIS D'OPHTALMOLOGIE. 3875

0181-6764 See TECHNI-PORC. 222

0181-7205 See ANALYSES, THEORIE. 3264

0181-7582 See REVUE DE CYTOLOGIE ET DE BIOLOGIE VEGETALES - LE BOTANISTE. 526

0181-7671 See LIBRESENS PARIS. 5062

0181-7779 See CAHIERS SAINT-JOHN PERSE. 3371

0181-7949 See MONDE DE LA MUSIQUE, LE. 4132

0181-7981 See DEPECHE DU MIDI TOULOUSE, LA. 5800

0181-9739 See HISTOIRE DES ACCIDENTS DU TRAVAIL. 2863

0181-9801 See FEUILLETS DE RADIOLOGIE. 3941

0182-0745 See OCEANIS : SERIE DE DOCUMENTS OCEANOGRAPHIQUES. 1454

0182-1377 See PRACTICIENS ET 3 EME AGE. 3629

0182-2373 See CAHIERS OBSIDIANE, LES. 2514

0182-2411 See HISTOIRE, L'. 2617

0182-3280 See INDICATEUR OFFICIEL VILLE A VILLE. 2982

0182-3329 See BUILDING RESEARCH AND INFORMATION : THE INTERNATIONAL JOURNAL OF RESEARCH, DEVELOPMENT AND DEMONSTRATION. 604

0182-3876 See BULLETIN DE LA SOCIETE ARCHEOLOGIQUE ET HISTORIQUE DES HAUTS CANTONS DE L'HERAULT. 263

0182-4295 See ANNALES DE LA FONDATION LOUIS DE BROGLIE. 4396

0182-4708 See SAVOIR MARIN, LE. 4854

0182-564X See CHRONIQUE DE LA RECHERCHE MINIERE. 1371

0182-6220 See POMME D'API. 2852

0182-628X See MEMOIRES - ACADEMIE DES SCIENCES, BELLES LETTRES ET ARTS D'ANGERS. 2850

0182-6557 See ANNUAIRE - LES AMIS DE LA BIBLIOTHEQUE HUMANISTE DE SELESTAT. 3190

0182-7146 See NATURE ET PROGRES PARIS. 111

0182-7634 See PELERIN D'ARES, LE. 3310

0182-855X See ANNALES PUBLIEES PAR L'UNIVERSITE DE TOULOUSE - LE MIRAIL. 1808

0183-3014 See IL, L'. 352

0183-3189 See POUR LA DANSE, CHAUSSONS ET PETITS RATS. 387

0183-3235 See BULLETIN D'INFORMATION - M.I.D.I.S.T. 5091

0183-4568 See GENERALISTE PARIS, LE. 3578

0183-5009 See BFCE MULTIDEVISES. 1464

0183-5017 See ACTUALITES (PARIS). 821

0183-5084 See MICRO SYSTEMES PARIS. 1978. 1269

0183-5173 See JOURNAL D'AGRICULTURE TRADITIONNELLE ET DE BOTANIQUE APPLIQUEE. 98

0183-536X See CAHIERS DE LA ROTONDE. 1075

0183-6552 See LETTRE DE L'EQUIPEMENT ELECTRIQUE ET ELECTRONIQUE L. 3 E, LA. 2070

0183-7656 See A.G.R.A. FRANCE. 42

0183-9187 See FUNDAMENTAL AND APPLIED NEMATOLOGY. 456

0183-973X See ETUDES IRLANDAISES. 2687

0183-9950 See ANNEE ... DE LA SCIENCE-FICTION ET DU FANTASTIQUE, L'. 3362

0184-0266 See MEMOIRES DE BIOSPEOLOGIE. 464

0184-1068 See DOCUMENTS D'ARCHEOLOGIE MERIDIONALE. 266

0184-2595 See MONTAGNES MAGAZINE GRENOBLE. 4875

0184-5926 See DROIT ET AFFAIRES INTERNATIONAL. 2964

0184-6345 See ACTION MISSIONNAIRE PARIS. 4932

0184-6531 See ANNEES. DOCUMENTS CLEIRPPA. 3749

0184-6906 See ENSEIGNEMENT TECHNIQUE PARIS. 1938, L'. 1894

0184-6949 See ANNEE PHILOLOGIQUE (PARIS), L'. 1081

0184-6957 See BULLETIN DE L'ASSOCIATION GUILLAUME BUDE. 3270

0184-7015 See REVUE DES ETUDES MAISTRIENNES. 3430

0184-7155 See COLLECTION DES UNIVERSITES DE FRANCE. 1815

0184-7473 See COMBAT NATURE PERIGUEUX. 2163

0184-7570 See LANGUES NEO-LATINES, LES. 3296

0184-7651 See BULLETIN DE LA SOCIETE ARCHEOLOGIQUE ET HISTORIQUE DU LIMOUSIN. 263

0184-7678 See CAHIERS ELISABETHAINES. 3339

0184-7732 See FRANCAIS AUJOURD'HUI: REVUE DE L'ASSOCIATION FRANCAISE DES ENSEIGNANTS DE FRANCAIS, LE. 3282

0184-7783 See POPULATION ET SOCIETES. 4557

0184-9697 See EQUIP-AFRIQUE. 1975

0184-9719 See BANQUE AFRIQUE PARIS. 778

0185-0008 See CIENCIA Y DESARROLLO. 5094

0185-0059 See BOLETIN DEL INSTITUTO DE INVESTIGACIONES ELECTRICAS. 2037

0185-0121 See NUEVA REVISTA DE FILOLOGIA HISPANICA. 3307

0185-013X See FORO INTERNACIONAL. 4474

0185-0164 See ESTUDIOS DE ASIA & AFRICA. 2503

0185-0172 See HISTORIA MEXICANA. 2736

0185-0261 See INFORMACION CIENTIFICA Y TECNOLOGICA. 5113

0185-0326 See BIOTICA. 448

0185-0334 See CIENCIA PESQUERA / DIRECCION GENERAL DEL INSTITUTO NACIONAL DE LA PESCA. 2299

0185-0539 See MEMORIA DE EL COLEGIO NACIONAL. 1835

0185-0601 See COMERCIO EXTERIOR. 828

0185-0628 See INFECTOLOGIA. 3714

0185-0644 See ANALES DEL INSTITUTO DE MATEMATICAS. 3492

0185-075X See CIENCIA (MEXICO CITY, MEXICO). 5094

0185-0814 See RELACIONES INTERNACIONALES. 4533

0185-0830 See TEXTO CRITICO / CENTRO DE INVESTIGACIONES LINGUISTICO-LITERARIAS. 3445

0185-0849 See ECONOMIA INFORMA. 1481

0185-0873 See BOLETIN DEL DEPARTAMENTO DE GEOLOGIA, UNI-SON. 1367

0185-0903 See CITAS LATINOAMERICANAS EN CIENCIAS SOCIALES Y HUMANIDADES : CLASE. 5195

0185-0962 See INSTITUTO DE GEOLOGIA REVISTA. 1383

0185-0970 See ENFERMERA AL DIA. 3855

0185-0989 See TLALOCAN. 246

0185-0997 See BOLETIN BIBLIOGRAFICO DE LA ESCUELA NACIONAL DE CIENCIAS BIOLOGICOS. 449

0185-1004 See PERIODICA. 5175

0185-1012 See REVISTA MEXICANA DE ANESTESIOLOGIA Y REANIMACION. 3684

0185-1039 See TRIMESTRE POLITICO. 4498

0185-1101 See REVISTA MEXICANA DE ASTRONOMIA Y ASTROFISICA. 399

0185-1136 See MONETARIA. 799

0185-1179 See AMERICA INDIGENA. 227

0185-1225 See ANALES DE ANTROPOLOGIA / INSTITUTO DE INVESTIGACIONES ANTROPOLOGICAS. 228

0185-1276 See ANALES DEL INSTITUTO DE INVESTIGACIONES ESTETICAS. 336

0185-1284 See REVISTA LATINOAMERICANA DE ESTUDIOS EDUCATIVOS. 1780

0185-1314 See GEOMIMET. 2139

0185-1330 See UNIVERSIDAD DE MEXICO : REVISTA DE LA UNIVERSIDAD NACIONAL AUTONOMA DE MEXICO. 1851

0185-1373 See ANUARIO DE LETRAS (MEXICO). 3362

0185-1586 See VUELTA. 2512

0185-1594 See ENSENANZA E INVESTIGACION EN PSICOLOGIA. 4586

0185-1616 See ESTUDIOS POLITICOS (MEXICO CITY, MEXICO). 4473

0185-1659 See CUICUILCO. 234

0185-1810 See REVISTA DE LA FACULTAD DE DERECHO DE MEXICO. 3041

0185-1861 See REVISTA INTERAMERICANA DE PLANIFICACION. 2834

0185-1918 See REVISTA MEXICANA DE CIENCIAS POLITICAS Y SOCIALES. 5216

0185-1934 See COMPENDIUM DE INVESTIGACIONES CLINICAS LATINOAMERICANAS. 3567

0185-2027 See BOLETIN BIBLIOGRAFICO MEXICANO. 3457

0185-2167 See ACTAS DE LA FACULTAD DE MEDICINA, UNIVERSIDAD AUTONOMA DE GUADALAJARA. 3545

0185-2264 See SPM. SALUD PUBLICA DE MEXICO. 4803

0185-2310 See BOLETIN TECNICO. 2376

0185-237X See DUALISMO. 1591

0185-240X See BIBLIOGRAFIA FILOSOFICA MEXICANA. 4365

0185-2418 See CIENCIA FORESTAL. 2377

0185-2426 See CARIBE CONTEMPORANEO, EL. 1550

0185-2523 See ESTUDIOS DE HISTORIA NOVOHISPANA. 2732

0185-254X See ANALES DEL INSTITUTO DE BIOLOGIA. SERIE BOTANICA. 498

0185-2590 See ANALES DEL INSTITUTO DE BIOLOGIA. SERIE ZOOLOGIA. 5502

0185-2620 See ESTUDIOS DE HISTORIA MODERNA Y CONTEMPORANEA DE MEXICO. 2615

0185-2647 See ESTUDIOS DE LINGUISTICA APLICADA. 3280

0185-2973 See INFORMACION SISTEMATICA. 5806

0185-3287 See ANALES DEL INSTITUTO DE CIENCIAS DEL MAR Y LIMNOLOGIA, UNIVERSIDAD NACIONAL AUTONOMA DE MEXICO. 552

0185-3295 See ANUARIO JURIDICO. 2935

0185-3309 See REVISTA MEXICANA DE FITOPATOLOGIA. 526

0185-3325 See SALUD MENTAL (MEXICO). 3936

0185-3481 See REVISTA DE FILOSOFIA. 4359

0185-3570 See REVISTA DE BELLAS ARTES (MEXICO, D.F.). 363

0185-3716 See GACETA (MEXICO CITY, MEXICO : 1954). 5231

0185-3880 See CIENCIAS MARINAS. 553

0185-3899 See INGENIERIA PETROLERA. 2013

0185-3929 *See* RELACIONES / COLEGIO DE MICHOACAN. **2756**

0185-4038 *See* DERMATOLOGIA. **3719**

0185-4178 *See* MEXICO FINANCIAL MONTHLY REPORT. **798**

0185-4186 *See* ESTUDIOS SOCIOLOGICOS. **5245**

0185-4275 *See* CASA DEL TIEMPO. **2511**

0185-4356 *See* GACETA INFORMATIVA DE LEGISLACION NACIONAL. **2973**

0185-4569 *See* MEXICO EN EL ARTE (MEXICO CITY, MEXICO). **358**

0185-4666 *See* FEM. **5555**

0185-4925 *See* PLURAL. **328**

0185-5093 *See* QUIPU. **5144**

0185-5131 *See* CUADERNOS DE ARQUITECTURA MESOAMERICANA. **296**

0185-5271 *See* ESTUDIOS DE CULTURA MAYA. **2732**

0185-5727 *See* PALABRA Y EL HOMBRE, LA. **2851**

0185-5905 *See* PRACTICA ODONTOLOGICA. **1333**

0185-6022 *See* REVISTA MEXICANA DE POLITICA EXTERIOR. **2758**

0185-6235 *See* ATENCION MEDICA. **3553**

0185-6278 *See* INDIAN NEWS OF THE AMERICAS / INTER-AMERICAN INDIAN INSTITUTE. **2264**

0185-6286 *See* TRACE (MEXICO CITY, MEXICO). **5224**

0185-6375 *See* LOGOS (MEXICO). **4352**

0185-6456 *See* BOLETIN ESTADISTICO DE BANCA MULTIPLE. **779**

0185-8572 *See* CUADERNOS DE ARQUITECTURA VIRREINAL. **296**

0185-9811 *See* ARMAS Y LETRAS - UNIVERSIDAD DE NUEVO LEON. **1089**

0186-1840 *See* COTIDIANO, EL. **1661**

0186-1891 *See* GEOS - UNION GEOFISICA MEXICANA. **1406**

0186-3231 *See* REVISTA CHAPINGO. **128**

0186-3738 *See* LIBRO Y EL PUEBLO, EL. **3259**

0186-5102 *See* INVESTIGACIONES MARINAS CICIMAR. **555**

0186-5617 *See* CUESTION SOCIAL (MEXICO CITY, MEXICO : 1985). **5281**

0186-7210 *See* ESTUDIOS DEMOGRAFICOS Y URBANOS. **4553**

0186-9418 *See* VOICES OF MEXICO. **2512**

0186-9787 *See* ANTROPOLOGIA Y TECNICA. **231**

0187-0173 *See* SOCIOLOGICA. **5260**

0187-1455 *See* BUSINESS MEXICO. **650**

0187-3180 *See* REVISTA MEXICANA DE MICOLOGIA. **576**

0187-358X *See* INVESTIGACION BIBLIOTECOLOGICA. **3218**

0187-4640 *See* REVISTA LATINOAMERICANA DE MICROBIOLOGIA (1970). **569**

0187-4780 *See* MONOGRAFIAS DEL INSTITUTO DE MATEMATICAS. UNIVERSIDAD NACIONAL AUTONOMA DE MEXICO. **3523**

0187-6074 *See* ARQUEOLOGIA. **260**

0187-6112 *See* 'AMATL. **1089**

0187-6236 *See* ATMOSFERA. **1420**

0187-7151 *See* ACTA BOTANICA MEXICANA. **497**

0187-7372 *See* FRONTERA NORTE. **5200**

0187-7674 *See* CARTA ECONOMICA REGIONAL : CER. **1468**

0187-7690 *See* REVISTA INTERCONTINENTAL DE PSICOLOGIA Y EDUCACION. **4616**

0187-7895 *See* CONSTRUCCION Y TECNOLOGIA. **608**

0187-8190 *See* REVISTA MEXICANA DE COMUNICACION. **1121**

0187-8468 *See* REVISTA INTERAMERICANA DE SOCIOLOGIA. **5256**

0187-8565 *See* CRM, BOLETIN DE INFORMACION : ORGANO DE COMUNICACION INTERNO. **2138**

0188-0128 *See* ARCHIVES OF MEDICAL RESEARCH. **3552**

0188-0683 *See* TV Y NOVELAS. **2494**

0188-1477 *See* REVISTA GENERAL DE MARINA. **4182**

0188-1744 *See* MEMORIA. **358**

0188-1833 *See* LLOYD'S MEXICAN ECONOMIC REPORT. **905**

0188-2546 *See* LITERATURA MEXICANA. **3406**

0188-2724 *See* MARIE CLAIRE EN ESPANOL. **1085**

0188-2848 *See* NORTE (MEXICO, D.F.). **3467**

0188-302X *See* AGROCIENCIA. SERIE FITOCIENCIA. **55**

0188-3038 *See* AGROCIENCIA. SERIE CIENCIA ANIMAL. **55**

0188-3046 *See* AGROCIENCIA. SERIE PROTECCION VEGETAL. **55**

0188-3054 *See* AGROCIENCIA. SERIE MATEMATICAS APLICADAS, ESTADISTICA Y COMPUTACION. **3491**

0188-3062 *See* AGROCIENCIA. SERIE RECURSOS NATURALES RENOVABLES. **55**

0188-3070 *See* AGROCIENCIA. SERIE SOCIOECONOMIA. **1461**

0188-3089 *See* AGROCIENCIA. SERIE SUELO, AGUA Y CLIMA. **55**

0188-3631 *See* REVISTA DE ARQUEOLOGIA AMERICANA / INSTITUTO PANAMERICANO DE GEOGRAFIA E HISTORIA. **280**

0188-4360 *See* BOLETIN MENSUAL DE INFORMACION BASICA DEL SECTOR AGROPECUARIO Y FORESTAL / SECRETARIA DE AGRICULTURA Y RECURSOS HIDRAULICOS, SUBSECRETARIA DE PLANEACION, DIRECCION GENERAL DE ESTADISTICA. **67**

0188-4492 *See* BOLETIN DEL SISTEMA ESTATAL DE DOCUMENTACION DEL ESTADO DE MEXICO. **4633**

0188-4611 *See* INVESTIGACIONES GEOGRAFICAS : BOLETIN DEL INSTITUTO DE GEOGRAFIA. **2566**

0188-476X *See* BIBLIOTECA DE MEXICO. **3366**

0188-4824 *See* MEMORIA DE PAPEL. **325**

0188-4999 *See* REVISTA INTERNACIONAL DE CONTAMINACION AMBIENTAL. **2242**

0188-5022 *See* MEDICINA Y ETICA. **2252**

0188-5340 *See* INSEH INFORMA. **5247**

0188-7890 *See* AVANCES EN INVESTIGACION AGROPECUARIA. **64**

0189-0085 *See* RESEARCH FOR DEVELOPMENT : THE JOURNAL OF THE NIGERIAN INSTITUTE OF SOCIAL & ECONOMIC RESEARCH. **1517**

0189-0514 *See* JOURNAL OF ANIMAL PRODUCTION RESEARCH. **213**

0189-0913 *See* NIGERIAN JOURNAL OF NUTRITIONAL SCIENCES. **4195**

0189-0964 *See* NIGERIAN MEDICAL PRACTITIONER, THE. **3986**

0189-1162 *See* NIA JOURNAL. **305**

0189-160X *See* WEST AFRICAN JOURNAL OF MEDICINE. **3650**

0189-2029 *See* BI-LINGUAL MAGAZINE. **5447**

0189-207X *See* NIGERIAN CURRENT LAW REVIEW : THE JOURNAL OF THE NIGERIAN INSTITUTE OF ADVANCED LEGAL STUDIES. **3017**

0189-2320 *See* UWA NDI IGBO. **3450**

0189-322X *See* NIGERIAN JOURNAL OF PHARMACEUTICAL SCIENCES. **4318**

0189-4412 *See* NIGERIAN LIBRARY AND INFORMATION SCIENCE REVIEW. **3236**

0189-5222 *See* JOURNAL OF LEATHER RESEARCH. **3184**

0189-5680 *See* JOURNAL OF THE LINGUISTIC ASSOCIATION OF NIGERIA : JOLAN. **3292**

0189-5923 *See* NIGERIAN JOURNAL OF POLICY AND STRATEGY. **4484**

0189-6709 *See* AFRICAN JOURNAL OF ACADEMIC LIBRARIANSHIP. **3188**

0189-7233 *See* NIGERIAN PETROLEUM NEWS. **4266**

0189-7705 *See* PHARMACY WORLD. **4323**

0189-8892 *See* NEWSWATCH (LAGOS). **2499**

0189-8965 *See* JOURNAL OF THE NIGERIAN MATHEMATICAL SOCIETY. **3515**

0189-9023 *See* APPROVED REVENUE, RECURRENT AND CAPITAL ESTIMATES (NIGERIA). **4711**

0189-9392 *See* BULLETIN AFRICAIN DE GEOSCIENCE. **1352**

0190-0005 *See* CITY HALL DIGEST. **4638**

0190-0013 *See* PHILOSOPHY AND LITERATURE. **4356**

0190-0218 *See* ADVANCES IN INORGANIC BIOCHEMISTRY. **479**

0190-0226 *See* BOARDING KENNEL PROPRIETOR. **4286**

0190-0234 *See* INKLINGS. **3396**

0190-0250 *See* EIS CUMULATIVE. **2164**

0190-0277 *See* BULLETIN OF THE 8TH DISTRICT DENTAL SOCIETY. **1318**

0190-0382 *See* LANGUAGE INTERVENTION SERIES. **3295**

0190-0412 *See* GESTALT JOURNAL, THE. **4588**

0190-048X *See* PUBLISHING EDUCATION NEWSLETTER. **4819**

0190-0498 See CAMPAIGN FINANCE LAW. **2947**

0190-0536 *See* PHILOSOPHICAL INVESTIGATIONS. **4355**

0190-0579 *See* ANALYSIS OF PROVISIONS IN SELECTED ARTICLES OF AGREEMENTS. **1860**

0190-0617 *See* WORLDWIDE BIOMEDICAL MEETINGS, CONFERENCES, AND EXHIBITIONS. **3651**

0190-0625 *See* THYROID TODAY. **3733**

0190-0692 *See* INTERNATIONAL JOURNAL OF PUBLIC ADMINISTRATION. **4657**

0190-0749 *See* MEAD JOHNSON SYMPOSIUM ON PERINATAL AND DEVELOPMENTAL MEDICINE. **3606**

0190-0757 *See* MATERNAL/NEWBORN ADVOCATE. **3764**

0190-0935 *See* QUILTING AND RELATED NEEDLEWORK. **5185**

0190-0943 *See* INTERFERENCE TECHNOLOGY ENGINEER'S MASTER. **2066**

0190-0951 *See* BIOMEDICAL ENGINEERING AND HEALTH SYSTEMS. **3686**

0190-096X *See* CHEMISTRY OF ORGANOMETALLIC COMPOUNDS, THE. **1040**

0190-0986 *See* CONTEMPORARY RELIGIOUS MOVEMENTS. **4950**

0190-1079 *See* COMPARATIVE STUDIES IN BEHAVIORAL SCIENCE. **4582**

0190-1109 *See* WILEY SERIES IN URBAN RESEARCH, THE. **2839**

0190-1141 *See* FOSSIL ENERGY RESEARCH AND DEVELOPMENT PROGRAM OF THE U.S. DEPARTMENT OF ENERGY. **1944**

0190-1168 *See* NEW SPIRIT. **5298**

0190-1176 *See* PAIDEIA (BUFFALO). **4354**

0190-1192 *See* COMMUNITY ASSOCIATION LAW REPORTER. **2954**

0190-1230 *See* GEOGRAPHIC DISTRIBUTION OF FEDERAL FUNDS IN CONNECTICUT. **1562**

0190-1249 *See* SPORTS AFIELD OUTDOOR ALMANAC, THE. **4879**

0190-1257 *See* FORSIM REVIEW. **2400**

0190-1281 *See* RESEARCH IN ECONOMIC ANTHROPOLOGY. **244**

0190-1370 *See* ELECTRICAL APPARATUS. **2044**

0190-1389 *See* SPORT AMERICANA BASEBALL CARD PRICE GUIDE, THE. **2778**

0190-1400 *See* PHOTOLETTER, THE. **4375**

0190-1419 *See* EMPLOYMENT AND UNEMPLOYMENT TRENDS. **1666**

0190-146X *See* CELLULAR SENESCENCE AND SOMATIC CELL GENETICS. **534**

0190-1486 *See* CURRENT TOPICS IN HEMATOLOGY. **3771**

0190-1559 *See* BANJO NEWSLETTER. **4102**

0190-1567 *See* FREE STOCK PHOTOGRAPHY DIRECTORY, THE. **4369**

0190-1591 *See* CALIFORNIA CRIPPLED CHILDREN SERVICES STATISTICAL REPORT. **5266**

0190-1656 *See* KURZWEIL REPORT, THE. **4390**

0190-1672 See MENTAL HEALTH AUDIT CRITERIA SERIES. 4790
0190-1729 See ELECTRIC UTILITY STATISTICAL REFERENCE. 2003
0190-1737 See STREET MAGAZINE. 2547
0190-1796 See PROFESSIONAL WOMEN AND MINORITIES. 5564
0190-1818 See JHP, JOURNAL OF HOMEOPATHIC PRACTICE. 3591
0190-1990 See NEW YORK TIMES CURRENT EVENTS EDITION, THE. 2540
0190-2008 See JOURNAL OF CARIBBEAN STUDIES. 2741
0190-2075 See SPEECH COMMUNICATION DIRECTORY. 1122
0190-2083 See WORLD FINANCIAL MARKETS. 816
0190-2148 See EXPERIMENTAL LUNG RESEARCH. 3949
0190-2199 See COUNSELOR PREPARATION. 1877
0190-2210 See STATE CONSUMER ACTION. 1300
0190-2245 See REPORT OF THE MIGRATORY BIRD CONSERVATION COMMISSION. 5620
0190-2253 See GUSTO (BRONX). 3463
0190-227X See REPORTS OF THE PRESIDENT AND THE TREASURER - JOHN SIMON GUGGENHEIM MEMORIAL FOUNDATION. 5236
0190-2350 See LEGAL ASPECTS OF MEDICAL PRACTICE. 2999
0190-2377 See TENNESSEE OUT OF DOORS. 2207
0190-2407 See STUDIES IN THE AGE OF CHAUCER. 435
0190-2458 See IN BUSINESS. 2232
0190-2474 See LABCHOWS DIGEST. 5515
0190-2504 See CONGENITAL MALFORMATIONS SURVEILLANCE. 3759
0190-2555 See DIRECTORY, JUVENILE & ADULT CORRECTIONAL DEPARTMENTS, INSTITUTIONS, AGENCIES & PAROLING AUTHORITIES / AMERICAN CORRECTIONAL ASSOCIATION. 3163
0190-2563 See CORRECTIONS TODAY. 3161
0190-2571 See ON THE LINE (COLLEGE, PARK MD.). 3171
0190-261X See KINDERGARTEN CREATIVE TEACHING AIDS. 1899
0190-2644 See JUNIOR HIGH CREATIVE TEACHING AIDS. 1899
0190-2679 See READ 'N DO STORIES. 1777
0190-2709 See ASTROFIZICHESKIE ISSLEDOVANIIA. 391
0190-2717 See IZVESTIIA ORDENA TRUDOVOGO ASTROFIZICH ESKOI OBSERVATORII. 396
0190-2725 See SOCIAL PSYCHOLOGY QUARTERLY. 5259
0190-2792 See TECHNICAL ASSISTANCE BULLETIN (ANN ARBOR). 4879
0190-2911 See MIDAMERICA (EAST LANSING). 3411
0190-292X See POLICY STUDIES JOURNAL. 4488
0190-2938 See CONSUMER INFORMATION SERIES (WASHINGTON. 1971). 1295
0190-2946 See ACADEME (WASHINGTON. 1979). 1806
0190-2997 See SUMMARY OF RATE SCHEDULES OF NATURAL GAS PIPELINE COMPANIES AS FILED WITH THE FEDERAL ENERGY REGULATORY COMMISSION AND THE NATIONAL ENERGY BOARD OF CANADA. 4284
0190-3012 See NORTHERN NEW ENGLAND REVIEW. 3418
0190-3047 See DIRECTORY OF MANUFACTURERS, STATE OF HAWAII. 3477
0190-3055 See RHODE ISLAND GENEALOGICAL REGISTER. 2470
0190-3063 See CONTRACT MANAGEMENT. 2956
0190-3144 See MEMO (CINCINNATI). 1690
0190-3187 See INTERNATIONAL FAMILY PLANNING PERSPECTIVES. 2281
0190-3195 See PERSPECTIVAS INTERNACIONALES EN PLANIFICACION FAMILIAR. 2285

0190-3217 See DIRECTORY OF LABOR MARKET INFORMATION. 1663
0190-3233 See REVIEW (CHARLOTTESVILLE). 3351
0190-3241 See FUTURE SURVEY. 1533
0190-3322 See APPALACHIAN VOICE, THE. 2187
0190-3330 See THINKING. 1907
0190-3349 See FOOD MARKETING INDUSTRY SPEAKS, THE. 2338
0190-3373 See ANTHROPOLOGICAL LITERATURE. 248
0190-3381 See THRUST. 1714
0190-339X See CHRONICLE FINANCIAL AID GUIDE. 1815
0190-3454 See HANDBOOK OF ANTIMICROBIAL THERAPY. 4306
0190-3500 See INVENTORY OF HEALTH CARE FACILITY SURVEYORS, UNITED STATES. 3590
0190-3527 See RESOURCE DIRECTORY, HEALTH INFORMATION SHARING PROJECT. 4799
0190-3535 See VIEWPOINT (NEW YORK. 1968). 2896
0190-3608 See CONSER TABLES. 3204
0190-3632 See ARRL REPEATER DIRECTORY. 1126
0190-3640 See SEZ. 3435
0190-3659 See BOUNDARY 2. 3368
0190-3667 See MONGOLIAN STUDIES. 2659
0190-3802 See HIGH ADVENTURE. 1064
0190-3810 See HI-TEEN STUDENT GUIDE. 4962
0190-3829 See HI-TEEN TEACHER GUIDE. 4962
0190-387X See ALI-ABA COURSE OF STUDY MATERIALS. CONSTRUCTION CONTRACTING IN THE MIDDLE EAST: PROBLEMS AND SOLUTIONS. 2931
0190-3888 See ALI-ABA COURSE OF STUDY MATERIALS. PRACTICE AND PROCEDURE IN FEDERAL TAX CONTROVERSIES: TAX COURT AND ELSEWHERE. 2931
0190-3896 See ELDERLY POPULATION: ESTIMATES BY COUNTY, THE. 4552
0190-3918 See PROCEEDINGS OF THE INTERNATIONAL CONFERENCE ON PARALLEL PROCESSING. 1261
0190-3926 See ANNUAL REVIEW FOR THE YEAR RELATING TO OIL AND GAS. 4250
0190-3934 See ANNUAL REPORT - STATE ENVIRONMENTAL IMPROVEMENT AUTHORITY. 2224
0190-3950 See BEGINNER TEACHER. 4938
0190-4000 See ADULT STUDENT GUIDE. 4932
0190-4132 See PROCEEDINGS OF THE INTERNATIONAL CONFERENCE ON LASERS. 5140
0190-4167 See JOURNAL OF PLANT NUTRITION. 515
0190-4175 See ELECTRIC VEHICLE PROGRESS. 2044
0190-4205 See ST. LOUIS HOME/GARDEN. 2903
0190-4280 See AT EASE. 4936
0190-4310 See CLASSIFIED INDEX OF DECISIONS OF THE REGIONAL DIRECTORS OF THE NATIONAL LABOR RELATIONS BOARD IN REPRESENTATION PROCEEDINGS. 3145
0190-4329 See NATIONAL COLLEGIATE CHAMPIONSHIPS (1978). 4906
0190-440X See GROUP PRACTICE (NEWSLETTER). 3780
0190-4507 See BOATING PRODUCT NEWS. 592
0190-4531 See PROCEEDINGS OF THE TECHNICAL CONFERENCE ON ARTIFICIAL INSEMINATION AND REPRODUCTION. 219
0190-4566 See YOUTH LEADER (SPRINGFIELD, MO.), THE. 5011
0190-4574 See TEEN TEACHER GUIDE (SPRINGFIELD, MO.). 5002
0190-4590 See TEEN STUDENT GUIDE (SPRINGFIELD, MO.). 1070
0190-4620 See WOMAN'S TOUCH. 5569
0190-4639 See PARACLETE (SPRINGFIELD, MO.). 5065

0190-4655 See COOPERATIVE EDUCATION QUARTERLY. 1733
0190-4671 See GEOLINGUISTICS. 3283
0190-4701 See FURMAN STUDIES. 2846
0190-4760 See CEC CENSUS OF BUYERS IN THE CHEMICAL PROCESS INDUSTRIES. 1601
0190-4787 See DIRECTORY AND GUIDE - BUILDING CONSTRUCTION EMPLOYERS' ASSOCIATION OF CHICAGO, INC. 2961
0190-4795 See BUC USED BOAT PRICE GUIDE. 592
0190-4817 See ADVANCES IN CANCER CHEMOTHERAPY. 3808
0190-4906 See BLACK REVIEW, THE. 3367
0190-4914 See BUSINESS OWNER (HICKSVILLE, N.Y.), THE. 651
0190-4922 See CONTRIBUTIONS TO MUSIC EDUCATION. 4112
0190-4949 See CA SELECTS: ZEOLITES. 1011
0190-4981 See COMBINED CUMULATIVE INDEX TO PEDIATRICS. 3655
0190-5031 See ANNUAL REPORTS ON THE EXCHANGE OF MEDICAL INFORMATION AND SHARING MEDICAL RESOURCES. 3551
0190-504X See FOOD MARKETING INDUSTRY SPEAKS : DETAILED TABULATIONS, THE. 2338
0190-5066 See SAME-DAY SURGERY. 3974
0190-5112 See CANCER REPORT (NEW YORK). 3812
0190-5139 See RATE REVIEW TOPICS. 3632
0190-5163 See SURVEY OF GRANT-MAKING FOUNDATIONS WITH ASSETS OF OVER $1,000,000 OR GRANTS OF OVER $200,000. 4689
0190-5171 See KANSAS DIRECTORY. 4659
0190-5244 See WHAT'S NEW IN COLLECTIVE BARGAINING NEGOTIATIONS & CONTRACTS. 3155
0190-5252 See LAW WEEK'S SUMMARY & ANALYSIS OF CURRENT LAW. 2997
0190-5260 See UNION LABOR REPORT WEEKLY NEWSLETTER. 3155
0190-5279 See AMERICAN DRUGGIST (1974). 4290
0190-5295 See ABSTRACTS - SOCIETY FOR NEUROSCIENCE. 3825
0190-535X See ONCOLOGY NURSING FORUM. 3866
0190-5368 See TOXICON. SUPPLEMENT (OXFORD). 4331
0190-5384 See UNITED STATES PHARMACOPEIA. NATIONAL FORMULARY. SUPPLEMENT, THE. 4331
0190-5406 See FAMILY PHARMACY NEWSLETTER, THE. 4304
0190-5449 See PHOTO ROSTER. 4842
0190-5457 See DAILY GUIDEPOSTS. 4952
0190-5473 See LEGISLATIVE CALENDAR / UNITED STATES HOUSE OF REPRESENTATIVES, COMMITTEE ON BANKING, FINANCE, AND URBAN AFFAIRS. 4661
0190-5481 See BOATING SAFETY TRAINING MANUAL. 4768
0190-5511 See RANGE SCIENCE SERIES (DENVER). 5144
0190-552X See AIR TRANSPORT (WASHINGTON). 8
0190-5597 See POST-SUMMER ELECTRIC POWER SURVEY. 1953
0190-5627 See MONOGRAPHS OF THE HEBREW UNION COLLEGE. 5051
0190-5678 See LIVESTOCK AND MEAT STATISTICS. SUPPLEMENT. 154
0190-5732 See SALARY SURVEY OF SUPERVISORY AND NON-SUPERVISORY PROFESSIONAL ENGINEERS. 1709
0190-5805 See LEGISLATIVE CALENDAR / UNITED STATES HOUSE OF REPRESENTATIVES, COMMITTEE ON RULES. 4661
0190-5848 See PROCEEDINGS - FRONTIERS IN EDUCATION CONFERENCE. 1991
0190-5880 3101

0190-5988 See CURRENT BUSINESS REPORTS. ADVANCE MONTHLY RETAIL SALES. 953
0190-5996 See BUILDERS (WASHINGTON, D.C. 1979), THE. 602
0190-6011 See JOURNAL OF ORTHOPAEDIC AND SPORTS PHYSICAL THERAPY, THE. 3882
0190-602X See CHINA FACTS & FIGURES ANNUAL. 2502
0190-6038 See FINANCIAL DIRECTORY OF PENSION FUNDS. ALASKA. 1669
0190-6070 See RED BOOK (CHICAGO), THE. 849
0190-6097 See WESLEYAN CHRISTIAN ADVOCATE. 5069
0190-6135 See HAMPDEN-SYDNEY POETRY REVIEW, THE. 3463
0190-6208 See BUSINESS LEADS AND SALES TARGETS. 650
0190-6240 See FINANCIAL DIRECTORY OF PENSION FUNDS. NEW JERSEY, SOUTHERN. TRENTON, CAMDEN, ATLANTIC CITY & OTHERS. 1672
0190-6259 See FINANCIAL DIRECTORY OF PENSION FUNDS. ALABAMA. 1669
0190-6267 See FINANCIAL DIRECTORY OF PENSION FUNDS. FLORIDA, SOUTHERN. WEST PALM BEACH, MIAMI, FT. MYER & OTHERS. 1670
0190-6275 See BUSINESS AMERICA. 825
0190-6283 See DIRECTORY OF SOUTH CAROLINA SCHOOLS. 1736
0190-6291 See FINANCIAL DIRECTORY OF PENSION FUNDS. DISTRICT OF COLUMBIA. 1670
0190-6305 See FINANCIAL DIRECTORY OF PENSION FUNDS. FLORIDA, NORTHERN. JACKSONVILLE, TALLAHASSEE, GAINESVILLE & OTHERS. 1670
0190-6534 See FINANCIAL DIRECTORY OF PENSION FUNDS. ARKANSAS. 1669
0190-6542 See FINANCIAL DIRECTORY OF PENSION FUNDS. COLORADO. 1670
0190-6550 See FINANCIAL DIRECTORY OF PENSION FUNDS. ARIZONA. 1669
0190-6569 See LIGHT 'N' HEAVY. 4973
0190-6577 See FOLK MUSIC MAGAZINE. 4118
0190-6585 See AUERBACH DATA WORLD. 1256
0190-6593 See WESTERN NEW ENGLAND LAW REVIEW. 3073
0190-6615 See PROCEEDINGS OF THE ANNUAL MEETING - NATIONAL ASSOCIATION OF SCHOOLS OF MUSIC. 4147
0190-6682 See POET PEU A PEU, THE. 3468
0190-6690 See OFFICIAL INTERMODAL EQUIPMENT REGISTER, THE. 5388
0190-6704 See OFFICIAL RAILWAY GUIDE (NORTH AMERICAN FREIGHT SERVICE EDITION). 5433
0190-6755 See DESIGN AND CONTROL OF CONCRETE MIXTURES. 612
0190-6763 See RAILWAY LINE CLEARANCES. 5436
0190-6771 See CURRENT PRACTICE IN NURSING CARE OF THE ADULT. 3855
0190-678X See FORMAT (ST. CHARLES). 350
0190-6798 See SPEEDY BEE. 5598
0190-6887 See ILLINOIS DOCUMENTS LIST. 417
0190-7034 See BOSTON COLLEGE ENVIRONMENTAL AFFAIRS LAW REVIEW. 3110
0190-7085 See INTERNATIONAL ECONOMIC CONDITIONS. 1496
0190-7093 See DRAGONFLIES. 4585
0190-7115 See UKRAINSKA KNYHA. 426
0190-7123 See FINANCIAL DIRECTORY OF PENSION FUNDS. IOWA. 1671
0190-7131 See FINANCIAL DIRECTORY OF PENSION FUNDS. IDAHO. 1670
0190-7166 See AD $ SUMMARY. 753
0190-7174 See BACKGROUND PAPER - CONGRESS OF THE UNITED STATES, CONGRESSIONAL BUDGET OFFICE. 4712
0190-7190 See CPR POPULATION RESEARCH. 4551

0190-7220 See DANCE (NEW YORK, N.Y. 1980). 1312
0190-7239 See FINANCIAL DIRECTORY OF PENSION FUNDS. MAINE. 1671
0190-7247 See FINANCIAL DIRECTORY OF PENSION FUNDS. NEVADA. 1672
0190-7263 See FINANCIAL DIRECTORY OF PENSION FUNDS. MONTANA. 1672
0190-7271 See FINANCIAL DIRECTORY OF PENSION FUNDS. NEBRASKA. 1672
0190-731X See SCRIBLERIAN AND THE KIT-CATS, THE. 2854
0190-7360 See BASIC EDUCATIONAL OPPORTUNITY GRANT PROGRAM HANDBOOK. 1727
0190-7379 See SAWMILL TECHNIQUES FOR SOUTHEAST ASIA. 2404
0190-7395 See ANNUAL ADVANCED FAMILY LAW COURSE. 3119
0190-7409 See CHILDREN AND YOUTH SERVICES REVIEW. 5278
0190-7433 See FLEETWOOD'S STANDARD FIRST DAY COVER CATALOG. 2785
0190-745X See BULLETIN OF BIBLIOGRAPHY (1979). 412
0190-7468 See JOURNAL INDEX TO THE ALBUQUERQUE JOURNAL. 5712
0190-7476 See NATIONAL DIRECTORY OF CHILDREN, YOUTH & FAMILIES SERVICES. 5297
0190-7522 See TAX GUIDE FOR COLLEGE TEACHERS AND OTHER COLLEGE PERSONNEL. 4752
0190-7565 See TALON ANNUAL REPORT. SOUTH CENTRAL REGIONAL MEDICAL LIBRARY PROGRAM. 3252
0190-7670 See SANITARY LANDFILLS. 2185
0190-7700 See FINANCIAL DIRECTORY OF PENSION FUNDS. LOUISIANA. 1671
0190-7794 See CIA PUBLICATIONS RELEASED TO THE PUBLIC THROUGH LIBRARY OF CONGRESS DOCEX. 4638
0190-7816 See FINANCIAL DIRECTORY OF PENSION FUNDS. OREGON. 1673
0190-7867 See COAL MINING AND QUARRYING. 2137
0190-7948 See SEED CROPS. VEGETABLE SEED REPORT. 186
0190-7972 See FINANCIAL DIRECTORY OF PENSION FUNDS. VERMONT. 1674
0190-7980 See FINANCIAL DIRECTORY OF PENSION FUNDS. TENNESSEE. 1673
0190-7999 See FINANCIAL DIRECTORY OF PENSION FUNDS. UTAH. 1674
0190-8006 See FINANCIAL DIRECTORY OF PENSION FUNDS. RHODE ISLAND. 1673
0190-8014 See FINANCIAL DIRECTORY OF PENSION FUNDS. NEW HAMPSHIRE. 1672
0190-8022 See FINANCIAL DIRECTORY OF PENSION FUNDS. NORTH DAKOTA. 1673
0190-8146 See PRIVACY ACT ISSUANCES ... COMPILATION. 3031
0190-8189 See FOLK AND KINFOLK OF HARRIS COUNTY. 2448
0190-8200 See SOURCES OF SUPPLY : BUYERS GUIDE. 4239
0190-8219 See FINANCIAL DIRECTORY OF PENSION FUNDS. SOUTH DAKOTA. 1673
0190-8235 See COLORADO LABOR ADVOCATE. 5642
0190-8251 See FINANCIAL DIRECTORY OF PENSION FUNDS. INDIANA, NORTHERN. SOUTH BEND, FT. WAYNE, MUNCIE & OTHERS. 1671
0190-826X See SOUTH CAROLINA MAGAZINE OF ANCESTRAL RESEARCH, THE. 2473
0190-8278 See FINANCIAL DIRECTORY OF PENSION FUNDS. PENNSYLVANIA, EASTERN. PHILADELPHIA CITY PROPER. 1673
0190-8286 See WASHINGTON POST (WASHINGTON, D.C. : 1974). 5648
0190-8308 See FINANCIAL DIRECTORY OF PENSION FUNDS. MISSISSIPPI. 1672

0190-8324 See FINANCIAL DIRECTORY OF PENSION FUNDS. NORTH CAROLINA, EASTERN. RALEIGH, FAYETTEVILLE, WILMINGTON & OTHERS. 1673
0190-8367 See YOUTH CONSERVATION CORPS PROGRAM. 2210
0190-8480 See INTERNATIONAL NUTRITION POLICY SERIES. 4192
0190-8669 See FINANCIAL DIRECTORY OF PENSION FUNDS. CALIFORNIA, SOUTHERN. LOS ANGELES CITY PROPER. 1670
0190-8677 See FINANCIAL DIRECTORY OF PENSION FUNDS. CALIFORNIA, NORTHERN, EXCLUDING SAN FRANCISCO. OAKLAND, SAN JOSE, FRESNO & OTHERS. 1670
0190-8685 See YEAR BOOK - CINCINNATI SYMPHONY ORCHESTRA. 4159
0190-8715 See REPORTS ON RESEARCH ASSISTED BY THE PETROLEUM RESEARCH FUND. 1029
0190-8723 See SPECIAL PUBLICATION - CALIFORNIA NATIVE PLANT SOCIETY. 2431
0190-874X See MINERALS IN THE ECONOMY OF FLORIDA. 1442
0190-8758 See MINERALS IN THE ECONOMY OF NEW MEXICO. 1442
0190-8766 See PRO FILE: THE OFFICIAL DIRECTORY OF THE AMERICAN INSTITUTE OF ARCHITECTS. 306
0190-9061 See MINERALS IN THE ECONOMY OF MAINE. 1618
0190-9177 See JOURNAL OF HEAT TREATING. 4006
0190-9185 See MONITORING THE FUTURE. 5209
0190-9193 See PREPRINTS / CONFERENCE ON SEVERE LOCAL STORMS. 1433
0190-9215 See CARNIVOROUS PLANT NEWSLETTER. 506
0190-9290 See FINANCIAL DIRECTORY OF PENSION FUNDS. NEW YORK, EASTERN UPSTATE. POUGHKEEPSIE, ALBANY, GLENS FALLS & OTHERS. 1672
0190-9304 See FINANCIAL DIRECTORY OF PENSION FUNDS. CONNECTICUT, SOUTHERN. STAMFORD, NEW HAVEN, NEW LONDON & OTHERS. 1670
0190-9312 See FINANCIAL DIRECTORY OF PENSION FUNDS. CONNECTICUT, NORTHERN. HARTFORD, WILLIMANTIC, WATERBURY & OTHERS. 1670
0190-9320 See POLITICAL BEHAVIOR. 4488
0190-9339 See ALI-ABA COURSE OF STUDY. EMINENT DOMAIN : MATERIALS. 2930
0190-9347 See ALI-ABA COURSE OF STUDY. REAL ESTATE CONDOMINIUMS AND PUDS : MATERIALS. 2931
0190-9355 See ALI-ABA COURSE OF STUDY. TAX AND BUSINESS PLANNING FOR THE SMALL BUT GROWING BUSINESS : MATERIALS. 3095
0190-938X See AVIATION NEWS (RENO). 13
0190-9398 See CA SELECTS: CHEMICAL HAZARDS, HEALTH, & SAFETY. 999
0190-9401 See CA SELECTS: CARBON & HETEROATOM NMR. 998
0190-941X See CA SELECTS: PROTON MAGNETIC RESONANCE. 1008
0190-9428 See CA SELECTS: INFRARED SPECTROSCOPY (ORGANIC ASPECTS). 1004
0190-9436 See CA SELECTS: INFRARED SPECTROSCOPY (PHYSICOCHEMICAL ASPECTS). 1004
0190-9444 See CA SELECTS: COLLOIDS (MACROMOLECULAR ASPECTS). 1000
0190-9541 See INTERNATIONAL SPORT SCIENCES. 3954
0190-955X See FINANCIAL DIRECTORY OF PENSION FUNDS. PENNSYLVANIA, EASTERN, EXCLUDING PHILADELPHIA AREA. HARRISBURG, WILKESBARRE & OTHERS. 1673
0190-9584 See ALI-ABA COURSE OF STUDY : ESTATE PLANNING UNDER THE NEW ESTATE AND GIFT TAX LAW : MATERIALS. 3117
0190-9592 See ALI-ABA COURSE OF STUDY. LAND USE LITIGATION, CRITICAL ISSUES FOR ATTORNEYS, DEVELOPERS, AND PUBLIC OFFICIALS : MATERIALS. 2930

0190-9622 *See* JOURNAL OF THE AMERICAN ACADEMY OF DERMATOLOGY. **3721**

0190-9657 *See* ALI-ABA COURSE OF STUDY. SELECTED PROBLEMS IN TAX PLANNING FOR AGRICULTURE : MATERIALS. **2931**

0190-9665 *See* ALI-ABA COURSE OF STUDY. BUSINESS WORKOUTS: MATERIALS. **3094**

0190-9673 *See* ALI-ABA COURSE OF STUDY. ATOMIC ENERGY LICENSING AND REGULATION : MATERIALS. **2153**

0190-969X *See* CALIFORNIA JOURNAL ALMANAC OF STATE GOVERNMENT AND POLITICS. **4636**

0190-9703 *See* ADVANCES IN THE STUDY OF COMMUNICATION AND AFFECT. **4572**

0190-9789 *See* GREEN SCENE, THE. **2417**

0190-9835 *See* WHITEWALLS (CHICAGO, ILL.). **368**

0190-9851 *See* PRIVATE LABEL (GENERAL ED.). **882**

0190-9886 See FINANCIAL DIRECTORY OF PENSION FUNDS. NORTH CAROLINA, WESTERN. WINSTON-SALEM, LEXINGTON, GREENSBORO, CHARLOTTE & OTHERS. **1673**

0190-9894 See FINANCIAL DIRECTORY OF PENSION FUNDS. INDIANA, SOUTHERN (INDIANAPOLIS, TERRE HAUTE, EVANSVILLE & OTHERS). **1671**

0190-9908 See FINANCIAL DIRECTORY OF PENSION FUNDS. NEW YORK, WESTERN UPSTATE. ROCHESTER, BUFFALO, ELMIRA & OTHERS. **1672**

0190-9916 See FINANCIAL DIRECTORY OF PENSION FUNDS. PENNSYLVANIA, WESTERN, EXCLUDING PITTSBURGH AREA. ERIE, NEW CASTLE, GREENSBURG & OTHERS. **1673**

0190-9924 See FINANCIAL DIRECTORY OF PENSION FUNDS. PENNSYLVANIA, WESTERN (PITTSBURGH AREA). **1673**

0190-9932 See FINANCIAL DIRECTORY OF PENSION FUNDS. NEW YORK, MANHATTAN-MIDTOWN, 41 ST. TO 50 ST. **1672**

0190-9940 See ARCHAEOASTRONOMY (COLLEGE PARK). **256**

0190-9975 *See* ALI-ABA COURSE OF STUDY. THE SUPREME COURT AND THE FEDERAL SECURITIES LAWS, IMPLICATIONS FOR LIABILITIES : MATERIALS. **2931**

0190-9983 *See* MARYLAND PUBLIC & PRIVATE POST SECONDARY EDUCATION INSTITUTIONS, AGENCIES, AND BOARDS. DIRECTORY. **1835**

0191-0000 See FINANCIAL DIRECTORY OF PENSION FUNDS. WISCONSIN, SOUTHERN, EXCLUDING MILWAUKEE AREA. MADISON, LACROSSE, OSHKOSH & OTHERS. **1674**

0191-0051 *See* O'DWYER'S DIRECTORY OF PUBLIC RELATIONS EXECUTIVES. **763**

0191-0132 *See* ASIAN WALL STREET JOURNAL. WEEKLY, THE. **1547**

0191-0167 *See* RESTORATION WITNESS. **4993**

0191-0183 *See* AMERICAN BAPTIST WOMAN, THE. **5055**

0191-0221 *See* MARTINDALE-HUBBELL LAW DIRECTORY (PRINT). **3006**

0191-0256 *See* TAM TAY. **2509**

0191-0272 *See* ALI-ABA COURSE OF STUDY. BASIC LAW OF PENSIONS AND DEFERRED COMPENSATION: MATERIALS. **2930**

0191-0280 *See* ALI-ABA COURSE OF STUDY : BANK DEFENSE OF NEGOTIABLE INSTRUMENT CASES : MATERIALS. **3084**

0191-0302 *See* PERISCOPE (OXFORD). **3153**

0191-0310 *See* STATISTICAL ABSTRACT OF OKLAHOMA (1972). **5339**

0191-0345 See FINANCIAL DIRECTORY OF PENSION FUNDS. NEW YORK, MANHATTAN-DOWNTOWN. WALL ST. TO 40 ST. **1672**

0191-037X *See* PUBLICATIONS OF THE NEBRASKA STATE HISTORICAL SOCIETY. **2755**

0191-0396 *See* OIL PRODUCING INDUSTRY IN YOUR STATE, THE. **4270**

0191-0434 *See* FOREIGN COMMERCE STATISTICAL REPORT : PORT OF BALTIMORE AND OTHER MARYLAND PORTS. **729**

0191-0442 See FINANCIAL DIRECTORY OF PENSION FUNDS. NEW YORK. BROOKLYN, S.I., BRONX, QUEENS. **1672**

0191-0493 See FINANCIAL DIRECTORY OF PENSION FUNDS. NEW YORK, MANHATTAN-UPTOWN. 51 ST. TO HARLEM RIVER. **1672**

0191-0531 *See* FARM PRODUCTION EXPENDITURES / UNITED STATES DEPARTMENT OF AGRICULTURE, STATISTICAL REPORTING SERVICE, CROP REPORTING BOARD. **85**

0191-0574 *See* INDEX TO SOCIAL SCIENCES & HUMANITIES PROCEEDINGS. **5203**

0191-0639 *See* OPTICAL INDUSTRY & SYSTEMS ENCYCLOPEDIA & DICTIONARY, THE. **4439**

0191-0841 *See* TECHNICAL PAPER - SOCIETY OF MANUFACTURING ENGINEERS. EE. **2130**

0191-085X *See* TECHNICAL PAPER - SOCIETY OF MANUFACTURING ENGINEERS (MF). **3488**

0191-0930 *See* TEXAS JOURNAL OF POLITICAL STUDIES. **4498**

0191-0965 *See* YOGA JOURNAL. **2602**

0191-1031 *See* KENTUCKY REVIEW (LEXINGTON. 1979), THE. **2849**

0191-1090 *See* WINTER WHEAT AND RYE SEEDINGS. **191**

0191-1104 *See* SOUTH DAKOTA REGISTER. **3057**

0191-1112 *See* STANDARD & POOR'S STOCK REPORTS. AMERICAN STOCK EXCHANGE. **915**

0191-118X *See* ANALYSIS OF WORKMEN'S COMPENSATION LAWS. **3144**

0191-1368 *See* CRC HANDBOOK SERIES IN NUTRITION AND FOOD. SECTION G : DIETS, CULTURE MEDIA, FOOD SUPPLEMENTS. **4189**

0191-1392 *See* APPAREL OUTLOOK. **1081**

0191-1422 *See* CONGRESSIONAL YELLOW BOOK (QUARTERLY ED.). **1924**

0191-1457 *See* ANNUAL REPORT - STATE OF ARKANSAS, PUBLIC SERVICE COMMISSION. **4759**

0191-152X *See* OAG AIR CARGO GUIDE. **5388**

0191-1538 See OAG POCKET FLIGHT GUIDE (NORTH AMERICAN EDITION). **5486**

0191-1546 See OAG POCKET FLIGHT GUIDE (EUROPE & MIDDLE EAST ED.). **5486**

0191-1554 *See* PERFORMING WOMAN, THE. **4145**

0191-1570 *See* ALI-ABA COURSE OF STUDY. POSTGRADUATE COURSE IN FEDERAL SECURITIES LAW: MATERIALS. **3084**

0191-1589 *See* ALI-ABA COURSE OF STUDY. LEGAL ISSUES IN THE COAL INDUSTRY : MATERIALS. **2931**

0191-1619 See OAG DESKTOP FLIGHT GUIDE (NORTH AMERICAN ED.). **5486**

0191-1635 *See* UTAH SYMPHONY. **4157**

0191-1651 *See* ALI-ABA COURSE OF STUDY. ADVANCED BUSINESS TAX PLANNING : MATERIALS. **3094**

0191-166X *See* ALI-ABA COURSE OF STUDY. ENVIRONMENTAL LITIGATION : MATERIALS. **3109**

0191-1686 *See* NUCLEAR SCIENCE APPLICATIONS. **4449**

0191-1686 *See* NUCLEAR SCIENCE APPLICATIONS. **4449**

0191-1708 *See* FUNDAMENTALS OF PURE AND APPLIED ECONOMICS. **1592**

0191-1716 *See* TB (SOUTH DAKOTA AGRICULTURAL EXPERIMENT STATION). **139**

0191-1724 *See* POLLUTION ABSTRACTS. ANNUAL INDEX. **2185**

0191-1775 *See* HERCULES MIXER, THE. **679**

0191-1791 *See* NEWSLETTER - SALT CITY SONG MINERS TRADITIONAL FOLK MUSIC CLUB OF CENTRAL NEW YORK. **4141**

0191-1813 *See* JOURNAL OF AMERICAN CULTURE. **2740**

0191-183X *See* FLORIDA BUSINESS PUBLICATIONS INDEX. **676**

0191-1856 *See* PROCEEDINGS OF THE ANNUAL COCCIDIOIDOMYCOSIS STUDY GROUP MEETING. **3630**

0191-1864 *See* LONG LIFE MAGAZINE. **3754**

0191-1880 *See* VERMONT REGISTERED NURSE. **3870**

0191-1902 *See* BYLAWS, RULES, AND SPECIFICATIONS - WOMEN'S INTERNATIONAL BOWLING CONGRESS. **4888**

0191-1929 See JEDNOTA ANNUAL FURDEK. **2740**

0191-1937 *See* RESEARCH IN CORPORATE SOCIAL PERFORMANCE AND POLICY. **5255**

0191-1945 *See* ALI-ABA COURSE OF STUDY : LEGAL ASPECTS OF MUSEUM OPERATIONS : MATERIALS. **2930**

0191-1953 *See* FULL BLAST. **4119**

0191-1961 *See* MISSOURI REVIEW, THE. **3412**

0191-2003 *See* ALI-ABA COURSE OF STUDY : MODERN REAL ESTATE TRANSACTIONS : MATERIALS. **2931**

0191-2011 *See* ALI-ABA COURSE OF STUDY. CLASS AND DERIVATIVE ACTIONS AND OTHER MULTIPARTY COMPLEX LITIGATION : MATERIALS. **3088**

0191-202X *See* ALI-ABA COURSE OF STUDY. CONDOMINIUM CONVERSIONS: MATERIALS. **2930**

0191-2038 *See* ALI-ABA COURSE OF STUDY : OIL SPILLS AND THE LAW : MATERIALS. **3109**

0191-2046 *See* ALI-ABA COURSE OF STUDY. LITIGATION UNDER THE FEDERAL SECURITIES LAWS : MATERIALS. **2931**

0191-2054 *See* SHELLFISH MARKET REVIEW. **2313**

0191-2097 *See* TIEN PHONG. **2509**

0191-2135 *See* EXECUTIVE PERSPECTIVE. **1237**

0191-2178 *See* ALI-ABA COURSE OF STUDY. FRAUD, INSIDE INFORMATION, AND FIDUCIARY DUTY UNDER RULE 10B-5 : MATERIALS. **3094**

0191-2194 *See* MARYLAND STATE YEARLY AIR QUALITY DATA REPORT. **28**

0191-2208 *See* EXPENSE ANALYSIS, CONDOMINIUMS, COOPERATIVES, & PLANNED UNIT DEVELOPMENTS. **4837**

0191-2224 *See* ALI-ABA COURSE OF STUDY. ERISA AND THE FEDERAL SECURITIES LAWS : MATERIALS. **2930**

0191-2232 *See* POLYNUCLEAR AROMATIC HYDROCARBONS. **3822**

0191-2240 *See* ALI-ABA COURSE OF STUDY : SECTION 8 HUD-SUBSIDIZED HOUSING, NEW TAX-EXEMPT FINANCING TECHNIQUES : MATERIALS. **2931**

0191-2291 *See* NURSES' DRUG ALERT. **3863**

0191-2305 *See* COMPUTER AIDED DESIGN OF DIGITAL SYSTEMS. **1232**

0191-2321 *See* FODOR'S AUSTRALIA, NEW ZEALAND AND THE SOUTH PACIFIC. **5470**

0191-233X *See* PRENTICE-HALL 1040 HANDBOOK. **4741**

0191-2364 *See* FEDERAL INCOME TAX (RESTON, VA.). **4724**

0191-2372 *See* ALI-ABA COURSE OF STUDY. FEDERAL ELECTION LAW: MATERIALS. **2930**

0191-2380 *See* ALI-ABA COURSE OF STUDY : STATE AND LOCAL TAXATION AND FINANCE : MATERIALS. **2931**

0191-2399 *See* ALI-ABA COURSE OF STUDY. THE ECONOMICS OF ANTITRUST : MATERIALS. **3095**

0191-2453 *See* CURRENT TOPICS IN NUTRITION AND DISEASE. **4189**

0191-2461 *See* FAMILY PRACTICE JOURNAL. **3737**

0191-2488 *See* CONTRIBUTIONS TO MEDICAL PSYCHOLOGY. **4583**

0191-2534 *See* UNDERWATER MEDICINE AND RELATED SCIENCES. **3648**

0191-2542 *See* DENTAL DIMENSIONS. **1320**

0191-2550 *See* DIRECTORY - AMERICAN SOCIETY FOR CLINICAL PHARMACOLOGY AND THERAPEUTICS. **4299**

0191-2577 *See* ARABIAN HORSE JOURNAL, THE. **2797**

0191-2585 *See* ALI-ABA COURSE OF STUDY : ENERGY AND THE LAW, PROBLEMS AND CHALLENGES OF THE LATE 70'S : MATERIALS. **2930**

0191-2607 See TRANSPORTATION RESEARCH. PART A, POLICY AND PRACTICE. 5397

0191-2615 See TRANSPORTATION RESEARCH. PART B : METHODOLOGICAL. 5397

0191-2623 See ALI-ABA COURSE OF STUDY. DOMESTIC TAXATION OF HARD MINERALS : MATERIALS. 2930

0191-2631 See WASHINGTON PUBLIC POWER SUPPLY SYSTEM ANNUAL REPORT. 1960

0191-264X See WHO'S WHO IN MUSIC (TUSCALOOSA). 437

0191-281X See SUNDAY REPUBLICAN (SPRINGFIELD, MASS.). 5690

0191-2836 See ARTHRITIS FOUNDATION ANNUAL REPORT. 3803

0191-2879 See DIRECTORY OF NURSING HOME ADMINISTRATORS LICENSED AND REGISTERED IN TENNESSEE. 3779

0191-2917 See PLANT DISEASE. 181

0191-2933 See PLANTS, SITES & PARKS. 703

0191-2941 See NATURE AND SYSTEM. 4168

0191-2984 See WEYERHAEUSER SCIENCE SYMPOSIUM. 2398

0191-3026 See RESEARCH IN MARKETING. 935

0191-3042 See INDEPENDENT STUDY. 1752

0191-3069 See ALI-ABA COURSE OF STUDY : LEGAL PROBLEMS OF MUSEUM ADMINISTRATION : MATERIALS. 2931

0191-3077 See ALI-ABA COURSE OF STUDY. THE COPYRIGHT ACT OF 1976 : MATERIALS. 1301

0191-3085 See RESEARCH IN ORGANIZATIONAL BEHAVIOR. 5255

0191-3123 See ULTRASTRUCTURAL PATHOLOGY. 3898

0191-3166 See CHINA AND US. 5195

0191-3247 See WORLD FREE FLIGHT REVIEW. 40

0191-328X See ALASKA TODAY. 2917

0191-3298 See YOGA RESEARCH. 4186

0191-3379 See INTERNATIONAL FORUM FOR LOGOTHERAPY, THE. 4349

0191-3387 See PACIFIC BASIN QUARTERLY. 1577

0191-3409 See BARRON'S REGENTS EXAMS AND ANSWERS : SPANISH LEVEL 3, COMPREHENSIVE SPANISH. 3268

0191-3425 See BARRON'S REGENTS EXAMS AND ANSWERS: 10TH YEAR MATHEMATICS. 3496

0191-3433 See WAGE & SALARY HANDBOOK. 1717

0191-3484 See BARRON'S QUESTIONS AND ANSWERS. COMPREHENSIVE ENGLISH, 3 AND 4. 3268

0191-3522 See MAN AT ARMS. 4049

0191-3549 See UNDERGROUND SHOPPER. NEW YORK CITY, THE. 2793

0191-3557 See JOURNAL OF CALIFORNIA AND GREAT BASIN ANTHROPOLOGY. 238

0191-359X See NATIONAL LIBRARIAN : THE NLA NEWSLETTER. 3233

0191-3638 See MSTA HANDBOOK. 1900

0191-3646 See DEWEY DECIMAL CLASSIFICATION ADDITIONS, NOTES, AND DECISIONS. 3206

0191-3654 See TURTLE MAGAZINE FOR PRESCHOOL KIDS. 1071

0191-3662 See CHRONICLE TWO-YEAR COLLEGE DATABOOK. 1815

0191-3670 See CHRONICLE FOUR-YEAR COLLEGE DATABOOK. 1815

0191-3689 See ALI-ABA CONFERENCE. CONFERENCE ON FEDERAL INCOME TAX SIMPLIFICATION: PAPERS. 2930

0191-3697 See ALI-ABA SYMPOSIUM. REGIONAL SYMPOSIUM ON THE STRUCTURE AND GOVERNANCE OF CORPORATIONS : MATERIALS. 3095

0191-3719 See DIRECTORY OF WASHINGTON CREATIVE SERVICES. 319

0191-3743 See PENSION, PROFIT-SHARING, WELFARE, AND OTHER COMPENSATION PLANS. 3153

0191-3794 See CANCER CONTROL JOURNAL. 3811

0191-3859 See ALI-ABA COURSE OF STUDY. FEDERAL RULES OF EVIDENCE : MATERIALS. 2930

0191-3875 See PROCEEDINGS OF SYMPOSIUM - DESERT TORTOISE COUNCIL. 5595

0191-3913 See JOURNAL OF PEDIATRIC OPHTHALMOLOGY AND STRABISMUS. 3905

0191-3972 See COMMUNITY HEALTH INSTITUTE CLEARINGHOUSE NEWS, THE. 4772

0191-4006 See BUSINESS LIBRARY NEWSLETTER. 3199

0191-4022 See MODULUS. 303

0191-4030 See STEREO WORLD. 4377

0191-4049 See ANNUAL REPORT - VIRGINIA ENVIRONMENTAL ENDOWMENT. 2161

0191-4057 See SCHEDULE C-I, CLASSIFICATION OF COUNTRY AND TERRITORY DESIGNATIONS FOR U.S. IMPORT STATISTICS. 733

0191-4073 See ALI-ABA COURSE OF STUDY. WATER AND AIR POLLUTION: MATERIALS. 3109

0191-4103 See COAL REVIEW (LEXINGTON). 2137

0191-412X See ALI-ABA COURSE OF STUDY : ABA SECTION OF TAXATION, ADVANCED STUDY SESSIONS, ADVANCED ESTATE PLANNING TECHNIQUES : MATERIALS. 3117

0191-4138 See MAN IN THE NORTHEAST. 240

0191-4146 See UNIVERSITY PUBLISHING. 4833

0191-4162 See PCA MESSENGER, THE. 4986

0191-4170 See CHEMICAL REVIEW. 1022

0191-4219 See STUDYING ADULT LIFE AND WORK LESSONS. 2286

0191-4278 See ADIX. 1103

0191-4294 See CHRISTIAN SINGLE. 4946

0191-4308 See ALI-ABA COURSE OF STUDY. ERISA-PHASE II : MATERIALS. 2930

0191-4316 See ANNUAL REPORT - BIBLIOGRAPHICAL CENTER FOR RESEARCH. 3190

0191-4367 See WEEKLY COAL PRODUCTION. 2153

0191-4383 See SULFUR (UNITED STATES. BUREAU OF MINES). 1445

0191-4510 See BEST'S UNDERWRITING GUIDE FOR COMMERCIAL LINES. 2876

0191-4537 See PHILOSOPHY & SOCIAL CRITICISM. 4357

0191-4545 See EUROPE (WASHINGTON, D.C.). 833

0191-4561 See CLEARINGHOUSE ADELL'S CATALOG OF ADULT EDUCATION PROJECTS. 1800

0191-4588 See QUICK PRINTING. 4569

0191-460X See DOLL NEWS. 2773

0191-4618 See FLORIDA FORUM. 615

0191-4642 See BUSINESS AND COMMERCIAL AVIATION. 15

0191-4677 See MIRROR NEWS. 3484

0191-4723 See NEVADA BEVERAGE INDEX. 2369

0191-4731 See BAY & DELTA YACHTSMAN. 591

0191-4766 See PET BUSINESS. 4287

0191-4839 See CODIFICATION OF PRESIDENTIAL PROCLAMATIONS AND EXECUTIVE ORDERS. 2952

0191-4847 See RADICAL TEACHER (CAMBRIDGE). 1776

0191-4871 See CABLE GUIDE. 1129

0191-4936 See NORTH JERSEY SUBURBANITE, THE. 5711

0191-4960 See WORCESTER MAGAZINE (WORCESTER). 4855

0191-4979 See NEW YORK AUTO REPAIR NEWS. 5421

0191-4995 See GOOD TIMES (GREENVILLE, NY.). 2534

0191-5029 See EAST COBB NEIGHBOR, THE. 5653

0191-5037 See DOVER POST. 5647

0191-5096 See JOURNAL OF SOCIOLOGY AND SOCIAL WELFARE. 5293

0191-5134 See CITIZEN NEWS. 5645

0191-5169 See PENNYSAVER SHOPPING GUIDE. 1298

0191-5223 See NATIONAL BUSINESS ASSOCIATION. 697

0191-5290 See IDAHO BEVERAGE ANALYST. 2367

0191-5304 See BEVERAGE ANALYST. MONTANA. 2364

0191-5312 See BEVARAGE ANALYST. OREGON. 2364

0191-5347 See BEVARAGE ANALYST. WASHINGTON. 2364

0191-5398 See ENVIRONMENTAL PROFESSIONAL, THE. 2169

0191-5401 See BEHAVIORAL ASSESSMENT. 4576

0191-541X See LIGHTING DIMENSIONS. 4074

0191-5436 See TWO-WAY RADIO DEALER. 1142

0191-5444 See CHAROLAIS JOURNAL. 209

0191-5460 See HIGHLAND PARK LIFE. 5660

0191-5479 See BONITA BANNER. 5649

0191-5487 See SMYRNA NEIGHBOR, THE. 5655

0191-5525 See POWDER SPRINGS NEIGHBOR. 5654

0191-5622 See SOLUBILITY DATA SERIES. 992

0191-5657 See HIGH COUNTRY NEWS. 2195

0191-5665 See MECHANICS OF COMPOSITE MATERIALS. 2106

0191-5789 See SALUBRITAS (ENGLISH EDITION). 4801

0191-5851 See TENNIS INDUSTRY. 4925

0191-586X See FLORIDA GROCER. 2335

0191-5886 See JOURNAL OF NONVERBAL BEHAVIOR. 4598

0191-5908 See NEWS TRANSCRIPT. 5711

0191-5940 See ORNAMENTAL/MISCELLANEOUS METAL FABRICATOR. 4014

0191-5959 See GRAIN & FEED REVIEW (DES MOINES, IOWA). 201

0191-6106 See TRY US. 2274

0191-6114 See BAKER'S DIGEST. 2328

0191-6122 See PALYNOLOGY. 1390

0191-6181 See FOOD PRODUCTION MANAGEMENT. 2339

0191-619X See FOOD WORLD (COLUMBIA). 2340

0191-6238 See PROFESSIONAL PILOT. 32

0191-6246 See U.S. MEDICINE. 3917

0191-6270 See SPOTLIGHT (WASHINGTON), THE. 5648

0191-6297 See HISPANIC NOTABLES IN THE UNITED STATES OF NORTH AMERICA. 2262

0191-6300 See NORTHBROOK LIFE. 5661

0191-6319 See SAFE JOURNAL. 34

0191-6327 See SONOMA BUSINESS. 712

0191-6335 See OFFICIAL CALIFORNIA APARTMENT JOURNAL. 2829

0191-6394 See PHARMACY WEST. 4323

0191-6408 See ROTOR & WING INTERNATIONAL. 34

0191-6459 See AUTOMOTIVE BOOSTER OF CALIFORNIA, THE. 5406

0191-6521 See AFRICA NEWS (DURHAM). 4514

0191-6599 See HISTORY OF EUROPEAN IDEAS. 2691

0191-6629 See NEW YORK PUBLIC LIBRARY DIRECTORY OF COMMUNITY SERVICES, THE. 5298

0191-6637 See CARROLL COUNTY HISTORICAL SOCIETY QUARTERLY, THE. 2727

0191-6653 See HOSE & NOZZLE (SHREVEPORT). 4260

0191-6688 See ACCESS REPORTS, PRIVACY. 2926

0191-6696 See ACCESS REPORTS REFERENCE FILE. 2926

0191-6750 See MENTAL HEALTH REPORTS. 4790

0191-6785 See HURDY GURDY. 4121

0191-6823 See PROFESSIONAL CARWASHING. 935

0191-6904 See MODEL RETAILER (CLIFTON, VA.). 2775

ISSN Index

0191-6920 *See* FOWLERVILLE REVIEW, THE. 5692

0191-6939 *See* GENERATIONS (BALTIMORE). 5047

0191-6955 *See* ENCEPHALITIS SURVEILLANCE. 3832

0191-6963 *See* DRAWING (NEW YORK, N.Y. 1979). 349

0191-703X *See* RANDOLPH REPORTER, THE. 5711

0191-7056 *See* TOWN TOPICS (PRINCETON, N.J.). 5711

0191-7064 *See* ADVISOR NEWSPAPER. UTICA-SHELBY EDITION, THE. 5685

0191-7072 *See* KENNESAW NEIGHBOR, THE. 5654

0191-7080 *See* BERKELEY MONTHLY, THE. 3338

0191-7145 *See* TEMPLE CITY TIMES. 5640

0191-717X *See* GOLF TRAVELER, THE. 4897

0191-7269 *See* ACWORTH NEIGHBOR, THE. 5651

0191-7307 *See* MALIBU SURFSIDE NEWS, THE. 5636

0191-7323 *See* COLLIER COUNTY STAR NEWS, THE. 5649

0191-7366 *See* PLEASURE BOATING. 595

0191-7382 *See* AUSTELL NEIGHBOR, THE. 5652

0191-7439 *See* COMMAND POST. 5659

0191-7463 *See* FOOTHILLS TRADER. 5645

0191-7587 *See* DRUG STORE NEWS. 4301

0191-7617 *See* ROLLER SKATING BUSINESS. 4854

0191-7633 *See* GREYHOUND BREEDER'S JOURNAL. 4286

0191-7684 *See* TRAWICK'S FLORIDA PRACTICE AND PROCEDURE. 3066

0191-7714 *See* EASTERN/WESTERN QUARTER HORSE JOURNAL. 2798

0191-7722 *See* DALMO'MA. 3462

0191-7757 *See* HARVARD MEDICAL ALUMNI BULLETIN. 1102

0191-7811 *See* NASA CONFERENCE PUBLICATION. 29

0191-782X *See* ELECTROCHEMICAL INDUSTRIES AND TECHNOLOGY. 1024

0191-7838 *See* GUIDE TO VINTAGE WINE PRICES. 2367

0191-7854 *See* AOA OCCASIONAL PAPERS IN GERONTOLOGY. 3749

0191-7870 *See* CLINICAL BIOMECHANICS. 3917

0191-7900 *See* PALESTINE (NEW YORK. 1976). 4531

0191-7927 *See* DUBLIN VILLAGER. 5728

0191-7935 *See* PHOTO STAR. 5730

0191-7951 *See* PCSO BULLETIN. 1332

0191-8079 *See* CLARION (NEW YORK. 1972). 1815

0191-8095 *See* SNOW GOER. 4919

0191-8117 *See* MASTERS (AUGUSTA). 4904

0191-8125 *See* ALI-ABA COURSE OF STUDY. LAND PLANNING AND REGULATION OF DEVELOPMENT : MATERIALS. 2930

0191-8133 *See* NATIONAL DEAN'S LIST, THE. 1836

0191-8141 *See* JOURNAL OF STRUCTURAL GEOLOGY. 1385

0191-8184 *See* WHO'S WHO AT THE ABA. 436

0191-8192 *See* SAN FRANCISCO PROGRESS, THE. 5639

0191-8249 *See* ALI-ABA COURSE OF STUDY. ABA SECTION OF TAXATION, ADVANCED STUDY SESSIONS, ESTATE AND INCOME TAX PLANNING FOR EXECUTIVES AND SMALL BUSINESS OWNERS : MATERIALS. 3117

0191-8273 *See* PRINTING JOURNAL. 4568

0191-8311 *See* HAWAII ARCHITECT. 299

0191-8494 *See* ALPHARETTA NEIGHBOR, THE. 5652

0191-8516 *See* LEGAL ASPECTS OF PHARMACY PRACTICE. 2999

0191-8524 *See* APPELLATE COURT ADMINISTRATION REVIEW. 3139

0191-8540 *See* PROGRESS OF EDUCATION IN THE UNITED STATES OF AMERICA. 1775

0191-8567 *See* CONSUMER PROTECTION NEWSLETTER. 2956

0191-8575 *See* OCEAN YEARBOOK. 1454

0191-8621 *See* DIRECTORY OF USSR MINISTRY OF FOREIGN AFFAIRS OFFICIALS. 3127

0191-863X *See* ALTMAN WEIL PENSA REPORT TO LEGAL MANAGEMENT, THE. 2932

0191-8656 *See* ALI-ABA COURSE OF STUDY. ESTATE PLANNING IN DEPTH : MATERIALS. 3117

0191-8664 *See* ADENA. 2717

0191-8699 *See* SOJOURNER (CAMBRIDGE). 5566

0191-8761 *See* INTERNATIONAL TRAVEL NEWS (SACRAMENTO, CALIF.). 5481

0191-877X *See* DEFENSE MANUAL. 3089

0191-8818 *See* CONNECTICUT BEVERAGE JOURNAL. 2366

0191-8834 *See* PIG INTERNATIONAL (EUROPE, ASIA, AFRICA, LATIN AMERICA AND OCEANIA EDITION. 217

0191-8869 *See* PERSONALITY AND INDIVIDUAL DIFFERENCES. 4607

0191-8982 *See* WISCONSIN ESCAPE. 5499

0191-9016 *See* REVIEW OF AGRICULTURAL ECONOMICS. 128

0191-9032 *See* ARAB MARKETS. 823

0191-9040 *See* INSECT SCIENCE AND ITS APPLICATION. 5609

0191-9059 *See* PCH. PHYSICOCHEMICAL HYDRODYNAMICS. 1056

0191-9091 *See* NORWALK WEEKLY TRADER. 2541

0191-9148 *See* INSTRUCTIONAL MATERIALS ADOPTION DATA FILE. 1896

0191-9199 *See* FRENCH 17. 3458

0191-9202 *See* PHYSICAL EDUCATION INDEX (CAPE GIRARDEAU). 1796

0191-9210 *See* COFFEE BREAK. 2531

0191-9237 *See* PURCHASOR, NEW YORK STATE. 951

0191-927X *See* GENERAL AVIATION NEWS. 22

0191-9288 *See* HUDSON VALLEY. 2535

0191-9407 *See* PROGRAM MANAGER. 883

0191-9423 *See* STATE ADMINISTRATIVE OFFICIALS CLASSIFIED BY FUNCTIONS. 4687

0191-9466 *See* STATE ELECTIVE OFFICIALS AND THE LEGISLATURES (1977). 4687

0191-9482 *See* MOUNTAINWEST MAGAZINE. 2539

0191-9512 *See* OZONE : SCIENCE & ENGINEERING. 1037

0191-9539 *See* JOURNAL OF ENGINEERING AND APPLIED SCIENCES. 1982

0191-9601 *See* PEDIATRICS IN REVIEW. 3910

0191-9636 *See* INTERNATIONAL DIRECTORY OF CONSULTING ENVIRONMENTAL AND CIVIL ENGINEERS. 2025

0191-9660 *See* PAY LESS TAX LEGALLY. 4740

0191-9776 *See* COMPUTER AND INFORMATION SYSTEMS ABSTRACTS JOURNAL. 1208

0191-9806 *See* CALIFORNIA STATE PLAN FOR COMMUNITY MENTAL HEALTH CENTERS. 4770

0191-9814 *See* BULLETIN - U.S. COAST GUARD ACADEMY ALUMNI ASSOCIATION. 1101

0191-9822 *See* WILLAMETTE LAW REVIEW. 3075

0191-9849 *See* GULF STATES OIL AND GAS DIRECTORY. 4259

0191-9857 *See* FLORIDA FOOD DEALER. 2335

0192-0014 *See* COMTEC CABLE TELEVISION VIEWERS GUIDE. 1130

0192-0030 *See* APARTMENT AGE. 2815

0192-0073 *See* DEERFIELD LIFE. 5659

0192-009X *See* O & A MARKETING NEWS. 5421

0192-0111 *See* COUNTRY ALMANAC, THE. 5634

0192-0197 *See* CANYON COURIER WEEKENDER, THE. 5642

0192-0219 *See* MOTORCYCLE DEALERNEWS MERCHANDISER. 4082

0192-0235 *See* CONTRA COSTA TIMES. 5634

0192-0278 *See* SUNNYVALE VALLEY JOURNAL. 5640

0192-0286 *See* WHEELING LIFE. 5662

0192-0316 *See* AUTOMOTIVE RECYCLING. 5407

0192-0324 *See* LA MIRADA LAMPLIGHTER. 5636

0192-0359 *See* NATIONAL UTILITY CONTRACTOR, THE. 622

0192-0367 *See* FROZEN FOOD REPORT. 2342

0192-0375 *See* UNICORN TIMES. 2548

0192-0421 *See* ORANGE COUNTY NEWS. 5638

0192-0561 *See* INTERNATIONAL JOURNAL OF IMMUNOPHARMACOLOGY. 4308

0192-0596 *See* TRAINING AND DEVELOPMENT ALERT. 947

0192-060X *See* WASHINGTON REPRESENTATIVES. 4499

0192-0618 *See* C/O : JOURNAL OF ALTERNATIVE HUMAN SERVICES. 5276

0192-0642 *See* TIMBER/WEST. 2405

0192-0669 *See* FAYETTE NEIGHBOR, THE. 5653

0192-0677 *See* HENRY NEIGHBOR, THE. 5653

0192-0685 *See* PAULDING NEIGHBOR, THE. 5654

0192-0693 *See* SOUTH FULTON NEIGHBOR, THE. 5655

0192-0707 *See* DORAVILLE DEKALB NEIGHBOR, THE. 5653

0192-0715 *See* SANDY SPRINGS NEIGHBOR, THE. 5655

0192-0731 *See* NORTHSIDE NEIGHBOR, THE. 5654

0192-074X *See* CLAYTON NEIGHBOR, THE. 5652

0192-0758 *See* DOUGLAS NEIGHBOR, THE. 5653

0192-0774 *See* SOUTHSIDE AND FAYETTE SUN. 5655

0192-0782 *See* CLAYTON SUN. 5652

0192-0790 *See* JOURNAL OF CLINICAL GASTROENTEROLOGY. 3746

0192-0812 *See* RESEARCH IN COMMUNITY AND MENTAL HEALTH. 4615

0192-0820 *See* ALI-ABA COURSE OF STUDY. ENVIRONMENTAL LAW: MATERIALS. 3109

0192-0847 *See* FRUIT SOUTH. 172

0192-0855 *See* BUSINESS ATLANTA. 646

0192-0871 *See* UNDERCURRENT (NEW YORK). 4927

0192-0995 *See* AUTOMOTIVE BODY REPAIR NEWS. 5406

0192-1002 *See* LIFE SAFETY CODE HANDBOOK. 2291

0192-1088 *See* ACADEMY FORUM (NEW YORK), THE. 3918

0192-1126 *See* COUNTRY SHOPPER, THE. 5715

0192-1134 *See* KARTING DIGEST. 5418

0192-1142 *See* NEWMONTH. 4484

0192-1150 *See* DOMESTIC BASE FACTORS REPORT. 4043

0192-1169 *See* NORTHWEST BOAT TRAVEL. 594

0192-1193 *See* JOURNAL OF CLINICAL AND EXPERIMENTAL GERONTOLOGY. 3753

0192-1207 *See* KELTICA. 2696

0192-1215 *See* IRISH ECHO. 2264

0192-1223 *See* NAPSAC NEWS. 589

0192-1231 *See* NEWSPAPERS IN MICROFORM: FOREIGN COUNTRIES. 5647

0192-1266 *See* BIOMEDICAL PRODUCTS. 3687

0192-1282 *See* CLINICAL LAB PRODUCTS. 3565

0192-1290 *See* ENGINEER'S DIGEST (WILLOW GROVE). 1974

0192-1304 *See* 20/20. 4214

0192-1312 *See* DEVELOPMENT COMMUNICATION REPORT. 1110

0192-1347 *See* FASTFACTS EUROPEAN HOTEL LOCATOR. 2805

0192-1355 *See* WESTERN ILLINOIS REGIONAL STUDIES. 2766

0192-1371 *See* COLLEGE ADMINISTRATOR AND THE COURTS, THE. 2952

0192-1401 *See* PIERCE COUNTY HERALD (PUYALLUP, WASH.). 5761

0192-1460 *See* MACNEIL/LEHRER REPORT. BROADCAST REVIEW AND INDEX, THE. 4528

0192-1487 See DESIGNERS WEST. 2900

0192-1541 See ELECTRONIC ENGINEERING TIMES. 2047

0192-155X See TRAVEL 800. 5494

0192-1576 See WESTERN LOS ANGELES COUNTY APARTMENT OWNER/BUILDER. 2839

0192-1630 See SOUTHEAST REAL ESTATE NEWS. 4847

0192-1649 See YACHTING NEWS. 597

0192-1657 See INSTALLATION & CLEANING SPECIALIST. 2901

0192-1711 See PLUMBING ENGINEER. 2607

0192-1738 See SAN FERNANDO VALLEY APARTMENT OWNER BUILDER. 2835

0192-1835 See SOUTHERN CALIFORNIA BEVERAGE BULLETIN. 2371

0192-186X See AUTO MERCHANDISING NEWS. 641

0192-1878 See APPAREL INDUSTRY MAGAZINE. 1081

0192-1932 See WILSHIRE CENTER'S LARCHMONT CHRONICLE. 5641

0192-1940 See L.A. WEEKLY. 5636

0192-1967 See STREET MACHINES & BRACKET RACING. 5426

0192-2009 See DALLAS COUNTY BUSINESS GUIDE, THE. 664

0192-2017 See PERSPECTIVES ON WRITING AND SPEECH : RESEARCH, INSTRUCTION, AND CURRICULUM DEVELOPMENT. 3310

0192-2211 See FEDERAL MEDICAL CENTERS, HOSPITALS, AND MEDICAL CLINICS WITH REPORTED MORBIDITY DATA. 3780

0192-2262 See HOSPITAL MATERIEL MANAGEMENT QUARTERLY. 3784

0192-2289 See FIRSTCLASS (IRVING, TEX.). 5470

0192-2300 See INFORMATIONAL BULLETIN - MARINE BIOLOGICAL LABORATORY. 554

0192-2351 See KOVELS' COMPLETE ANTIQUES PRICE LIST, THE. 251

0192-236X See ANNUAL REPORT - COUNCIL ON FOREIGN RELATIONS, INC. 4515

0192-2378 See FODOR'S CHINA. 5471

0192-2394 See NURSING CAREER DIRECTORY. 3863

0192-2424 See BULLETIN OF THE SCIENCE FICTION WRITERS OF AMERICA. 3370

0192-2440 See FINANCIAL DIRECTORY OF PENSION FUNDS. VIRGINIA, NORTHERN. (ARLINGTON, WINCHESTER, HARRISONBURG & OTHERS). 1674

0192-2467 See OHIO VALLEY RETAILER. 934

0192-2483 See MABLETON NEIGHBOR, THE. 5654

0192-2491 See M B NEWS. 357

0192-2505 See PARK & GROUNDS MANAGEMENT. 4707

0192-253X See DEVELOPMENTAL GENETICS. 544

0192-2556 See FINANCIAL DIRECTORY OF PENSION FUNDS. MINNESOTA, MINNEAPOLIS-ST. PAUL AREA. 1672

0192-2564 See GUIDE TO MIDDLE STATES SCHOOLS IN NEW YORK. 1749

0192-2572 See GUIDE TO MIDDLE STATES SCHOOLS IN DELAWARE, DISTRICT OF COLUMBIA, MARYLAND, PUERTO RICO, CANAL ZONE, VIRGIN ISLANDS, OVERSEAS. 1749

0192-2580 See GUIDE TO MIDDLE STATES SCHOOLS IN NEW JERSEY. 1749

0192-2599 See GUIDE TO MIDDLE STATES SCHOOLS IN PENNSYLVANIA. 1749

0192-2602 See INDEX-DIGEST - UNITED STATES DEPARTMENT OF THE INTERIOR, OFFICE OF HEARINGS AND APPEALS. 3081

0192-2629 See OFFICIAL DIRECTORY OF INDUSTRIAL AND COMMERCIAL TRAFFIC EXECUTIVES, THE. 5388

0192-2637 See ROSWELL NEIGHBOR, THE. 5655

0192-270X See COMPREHENSIVE ENVIRONMENT, HEALTH, AND SAFETY PROGRAM REPORT. 4772

0192-2718 See MILITARY CLUBS & RECREATION. 4050

0192-2734 See ADVANCES IN THERMAL ENGINEERING. 1964

0192-2742 See SMOKIE REVIEW. 5662

0192-2858 See ANNALS OF SCHOLARSHIP. 2842

0192-2882 See THEATRE JOURNAL (WASHINGTON, D.C.). 5371

0192-2912 See CONSERVATION ADMINISTRATION NEWS. 3204

0192-2947 See FINANCIAL DIRECTORY OF PENSION FUNDS. GEORGIA, ATLANTA AREA. 1670

0192-2963 See PHYSICIAN EAST. 3627

0192-298X See RN IDAHO. 3868

0192-2998 See ANNUAL BOOK OF ASTM STANDARDS. 2100

0192-303X See INTECH. 2065

0192-3048 See GOLF COURSE MANAGEMENT. 4896

0192-3056 See MISSOURI BEEF CATTLEMAN. 216

0192-3072 See SIMMENTAL SHIELD. 221

0192-3080 See TOPEKA MAGAZINE. 2548

0192-3110 See FAIRPRESS. 5645

0192-3129 See NORTH LAKE TAHOE BONANZA. 5708

0192-3137 See DIRECT MARKETING MARKET PLACE, THE. 728

0192-3145 See FORENSIC SERVICES DIRECTORY. 2972

0192-3218 See GEOGRAPHIC DISTRIBUTION OF FEDERAL FUNDS IN ALABAMA. 1562

0192-3226 See FINANCIAL DIRECTORY OF PENSION FUNDS. MASSACHUSETTS, EXCLUDING BOSTON & SUBURBS. WORCESTER, SPRINGFIELD, PITTSFIELD & OTHERS. 1671

0192-3234 See CRIME AND JUSTICE (CHICAGO, ILL.). 3161

0192-3242 See INDEX OF MAJORS AND GRADUATE DEGREES. 1830

0192-3315 See AAII JOURNAL, THE. 890

0192-3323 See CRIMINAL LAW REVIEW (NEW YORK, N.Y. : 1979). 3106

0192-334X See DISCOGRAPHIES (WESTPORT). 4115

0192-3374 See WATER, WASTEWATER-CHEMICAL AND RADIOLOGICAL ANALYSES : TABULATION. 5548

0192-3412 See FODOR'S NEW ENGLAND. 5472

0192-3439 See KITELINES. 4851

0192-3455 See ALPHABETIC LIST OF LENDERS. 1723

0192-3463 See FINANCIAL DIRECTORY OF PENSION FUNDS. ILLINOIS, CHICAGO CITY PROPER. 1670

0192-348X See FLORIDA RESTAURATEUR. 5071

0192-3536 See KEY. THIS WEEK IN MIAMI BEACH. 5482

0192-3579 See SOUTHERN BOATING. 596

0192-3633 See WATER TECHNOLOGY. 5548

0192-3641 See BULLETIN OF THE HUNT INSTITUTE FOR BOTANICAL DOCUMENTATION. 505

0192-3692 See R - RAND CORPORATION. 5144

0192-3722 See GEOGRAPHIC DISTRIBUTION OF FEDERAL FUNDS IN DISTRICT OF COLUMBIA. 1562

0192-3730 See FODOR'S FAR WEST. 5471

0192-3749 See CHINESE MUSIC. 4109

0192-3757 See BLACK COLLEGIAN (NEW ORLEANS), THE. 1811

0192-3765 See FODOR'S BERMUDA. 5471

0192-3773 See INDEX TO TITLE 40 OF THE CODE OF FEDERAL REGULATIONS : PROTECTION OF ENVIRONMENT. 3113

0192-379X See ANNUAL FINANCIAL REVIEW - FOOD MARKETING INSTITUTE. 2327

0192-3803 See GEOGRAPHIC DISTRIBUTION OF FEDERAL FUNDS IN IDAHO. 1562

0192-382X See WEEKLY BULLETIN. PORT OF NEW ORLEANS. 5458

0192-3838 See LOUISIANA PHARMACIST, THE. 4314

0192-3854 See CONDENSED CPA TAX REVIEW. 2955

0192-3862 See FEDERAL COAL MANAGEMENT REPORT. 2139

0192-3889 See PRACTICAL WILL DRAFTING. 3118

0192-3897 See COMMERCIAL REAL ESTATE LEASES. 4835

0192-3900 See MONTAGUE'S MODERN BOTTLE IDENTIFICATION AND PRICE GUIDE. 2592

0192-3919 See FODOR'S MID-ATLANTIC. 5472

0192-3978 See CONSTRUCTION EQUIPMENT (1970). 609

0192-3986 See DATA PROCESSING IN ALASKA. 1257

0192-401X See ORTESOL JOURNAL, THE. 3308

0192-4036 See INTERNATIONAL JOURNAL OF COMPARATIVE AND APPLIED CRIMINAL JUSTICE. 3166

0192-415X See AMERICAN JOURNAL OF CHINESE MEDICINE, THE. 3548

0192-4184 See SEVEN COUNTY FARM AND HOME NEWS. 134

0192-4192 See PERFORMING ARTS (HOUSTON). 387

0192-4214 See SOUTHWEST ART. 365

0192-4273 See NATIONAL DIRECTORY OF STATE & LOCAL GOVERNMENT TRAINERS. 4668

0192-4281 See BULLETIN OF THE ASSOCIATION OF NORTH DAKOTA GEOGRAPHERS. 2557

0192-429X See JOURNAL OF ELECTRONIC DEFENSE. 4048

0192-4338 See HIGHER EDUCATION DESKBOOK, THE. 1828

0192-4346 See ADVANCES IN EXPERIENTIAL SOCIAL PROCESSES. 5189

0192-4400 See GRIFFIN REPORT OF FOOD MARKETING, THE. 2342

0192-4486 See CARPET & RUG INDUSTRY. 2899

0192-4516 See DAVISON INDEX, THE. 5691

0192-4524 See COASTAL JOURNAL. 5685

0192-4532 See WOODALL'S RV OWNER'S HANDBOOK. 5400

0192-4540 See FODOR'S MID-ATLANTIC. 5472

0192-4559 See ANNUAL REVIEW / CHIEF, NATIONAL GUARD BUREAU. 4035

0192-4591 See UNITED STATES ZIP CODE MARKETING BUSINESS MAP ATLAS. NATIONAL EDITION. 1147

0192-4613 See FINANCIAL ASSISTANCE BY GEOGRAPHIC AREA. REGION II, NEW YORK, N.Y. 4725

0192-4621 See YEAR-END REPORT - HERITAGE CONSERVATION AND RECREATION SERVICE. 2210

0192-4680 See IMMR (INSTITUTE FOR MINING AND MINERALS RESEARCH, UNIVERSITY OF KENTUCKY). 2140

0192-477X See TRANSATLANTIC PERSPECTIVES. 4339

0192-4788 See ACTIVITIES, ADAPTATION & AGING. 3748

0192-4842 See COOPERATION (JEFFERSON CITY). 3569

0192-4869 See SOUTH SHORE NEWS (WEST HANOVER, MASS.). 5690

0192-4885 See OFFSHORE (WEST NEWTON). 594

0192-4893 See NEW HOMES MAGAZINE. 4842

0192-494X See PROCEEDINGS OF POWERCON. 2076

0192-4966 See FINANCIAL ASSISTANCE BY GEOGRAPHIC AREA. REGION V, CHICAGO, ILLINOIS. 4725

0192-4982 See FINANCIAL ASSISTANCE BY GEOGRAPHIC AREA. REGION III, PHILADELPHIA, PENNA. 4725

0192-4990 See WEAR OF MATERIALS. 2132

0192-5008 See EPA PUBLICATIONS. 2229

0192-5016 See VOLUNTARY INDUSTRIAL ENERGY CONSERVATION. 1960

ISSN Index

0192-5024 *See* GEOGRAPHIC DISTRIBUTION OF FEDERAL FUNDS IN KENTUCKY. **1563**

0192-5032 *See* MINING PERSONNEL PRACTICES SURVEY. **1690**

0192-5040 *See* CITY AND REGIONAL MAGAZINE DIRECTORY. **2918**

0192-5067 *See* ASLA MEMBERS' HANDBOOK. **2409**

0192-5075 *See* PRODUCT LIABILITY UPDATE. **3032**

0192-5083 *See* LINCOLN REVIEW. **2744**

0192-5121 *See* INTERNATIONAL POLITICAL SCIENCE REVIEW. **4477**

0192-513X *See* JOURNAL OF FAMILY ISSUES. **2282**

0192-5180 *See* SOUND OF VIENNA, THE. **2546**

0192-5210 *See* YANKEE HORSETRADER. **2803**

0192-5253 *See* COMMERCIAL NEWS. **5715**

0192-5261 *See* VERMONT NEWS GUIDE. **5758**

0192-5326 *See* FIELDING'S EUROPE. **5470**

0192-5334 *See* KIPS BOOK, THE. **1274**

0192-5342 *See* WASHINGTON D. C. METROPOLITAN AREA FOUNDATION DIRECTORY, THE. **4694**

0192-5385 *See* INDEX OF FEDERALLY SUPPORTED PROGRAMS IN HEART, BLOOD VESSEL, LUNG, AND BLOOD DISORDERS. **3706**

0192-5458 *See* KRUSE REPORT. **5418**

0192-5504 *See* MINNESOTA BUSINESS JOURNAL. **695**

0192-5512 *See* WORLDWIDE PROJECTS. **2001**

0192-5539 *See* FRIENDSCRIPT. **3211**

0192-5547 *See* PROTECTING THE CORPORATE OFFICER AND DIRECTOR FROM LIABILITY. **3102**

0192-5563 *See* SPECIAL PUBLICATION SERIES - PYMATUNING LABORATORY OF ECOLOGY, UNIVERSITY OF PITTSBURGH. **2221**

0192-558X *See* ADVANCES IN THE ECONOMICS OF ENERGY AND RESOURCES. **1931**

0192-5598 *See* FINANCIAL ASSISTANCE BY GEOGRAPHIC AREA. REGION VI, DALLAS, TEXAS. **4725**

0192-5652 *See* ABSTRACTS - SYMPOSIUM ON MOLECULAR SPECTROSCOPY. **4432**

0192-5660 *See* INSTITUTIONAL INVESTOR (INTERNATIONAL ED.). **901**

0192-5709 *See* AMERICAN TOOL, DIE & STAMPING NEWS. **3475**

0192-5717 *See* ANN ARBOR OBSERVER. **2484**

0192-5741 *See* ATOM TABLOID. MIDDLESEX COUNTY EDITION, THE. **5709**

0192-5768 *See* LINCOLN PARKER, THE. **5692**

0192-5784 *See* OFFICIAL (LOS ANGELES). **2607**

0192-5792 *See* SOUTHERN PHARMACY JOURNAL. **4329**

0192-5857 *See* ABSTRACTS OF PAPERS PRESENTED TO THE AMERICAN MATHEMATICAL SOCIETY. **3490**

0192-5865 *See* WHEELWRIGHTINGS. **3453**

0192-5881 *See* COMIC ART STUDIES. **377**

0192-5903 *See* AMERICAN COMMUNITIES TOMORROW. **5190**

0192-592X *See* THE JOURNAL. **1225**

0192-5938 *See* BIG BEAUTIFUL WOMAN. **1082**

0192-5946 *See* OAKLAND. **2541**

0192-5997 *See* CLASSIFICATION, ASSETS AND LOCATION OF REGISTERED INVESTMENT COMPANIES UNDER THE INVESTMENT COMPANY ACT OF 1940. **894**

0192-6020 *See* BIOLOGICAL MAGNETIC RESONANCE. **4443**

0192-6055 *See* NEWSLETTER - AMBULANCE & MEDICAL SERVICES ASSOCIATION OF AMERICA. **3725**

0192-608X *See* REPORT OF THE NATIONAL MEETING OF THE CENTURY III LEADERS, THE. **1870**

0192-6098 *See* CHILTON'S FOOD ENGINEERING MASTER. **2331**

0192-6101 *See* HEALTH MANPOWER PILOT PROJECTS PROGRAM. ANNUAL REPORT TO THE LEGISLATURE AND THE HEALING ARTS LICENSING BOARDS. **3914**

0192-611X *See* ANNUAL MANAGEMENT COMPENSATION STUDY. **1645**

0192-6128 *See* DIVISIONS. **4115**

0192-6152 *See* LEGAL MEMORANDUM (RESTON), A. **3000**

0192-6160 *See* PRACTITIONER (RESTON), THE. **1868**

0192-6187 *See* AMERICAN JOURNAL OF FAMILY THERAPY, THE. **4573**

0192-6209 *See* TELECOMMUNICATIONS (EURO-GLOBAL ED.). **1165**

0192-6217 *See* MICROWAVE JOURNAL (EURO-GLOBAL ED.). **2072**

0192-6225 *See* MICROWAVE JOURNAL (INTERNATIONAL ED.). **4412**

0192-6233 *See* TOXICOLOGIC PATHOLOGY. **3898**

0192-625X *See* FEDERAL JUDICIAL WORKLOAD STATISTICS. **3080**

0192-6268 *See* GUIDEBOOK SERIES-MINNESOTA GEOLOGICAL SURVEY. **1382**

0192-6314 *See* PRINTERS HOT LINE. **4568**

0192-6322 *See* FARMERS HOT LINE. **86**

0192-6349 *See* COMPUTER HOT LINE. **1176**

0192-6365 *See* NASSP BULLETIN. **1866**

0192-6446 *See* CANTON EAGLE, THE. **5691**

0192-6462 *See* NEW HAMPSHIRE BEVERAGE JOURNAL. **2369**

0192-6497 *See* WESTLAND EAGLE, THE. **5694**

0192-6519 *See* PRESS ADVERTISER (PONTIAC), THE. **5693**

0192-6535 *See* ROCHESTER TIMES, THE. **5720**

0192-6543 *See* MISSOURI HOSPITAL PROFILES. **3789**

0192-6578 *See* FINANCIAL ASSISTANCE BY GEOGRAPHIC AREA. REGION VIII, DENVER, COLORADO. **4725**

0192-6586 *See* FINANCIAL ASSISTANCE BY GEOGRAPHIC AREA. REGION IX, SAN FRANCISCO, CALIFORNIA. **4725**

0192-6608 *See* FINANCIAL ASSISTANCE BY GEOGRAPHIC AREA. REGION X, SEATTLE, WASHINGTON. **4725**

0192-6640 *See* QUARTERLY BIBLIOGRAPHY OF MAJOR TROPICAL DISEASES. **3986**

0192-673X *See* SUBCONTRACTING. **3060**

0192-6764 *See* BRAHMAN JOURNAL, THE. **207**

0192-6772 *See* NATIONAL HOME CENTER NEWS. **2792**

0192-6802 *See* CURRENT WORLD LEADERS. **4519**

0192-6837 *See* NATIONAL OBSERVER BOOK OF CROSSWORDS, THE. **4863**

0192-687X *See* SHINING MOUNTAIN SENTINEL. **2545**

0192-6942 *See* OHIO MEDIA SPECTRUM. **3239**

0192-6969 *See* INDEX TO AMERICAN REFERENCE BOOKS ANNUAL. **1926**

0192-6985 *See* BIOLOGICAL ABSTRACTS / RRM. **477**

0192-6993 *See* BULLETIN - EARLY SITES RESEARCH SOCIETY. **5229**

0192-7019 *See* MOODY'S DIVIDEND RECORD. **907**

0192-7027 *See* MY LITTLE SALESMAN TRUCK CATALOG. **5421**

0192-706X *See* CRIMES AGAINST BUSINESS. **3162**

0192-7124 *See* LOGGER AND LUMBERMAN MAGAZINE, THE. **2402**

0192-7159 *See* PACIFIC COAST NURSERYMAN & GARDEN SUPPLY DEALER. **2427**

0192-7167 *See* MOODY'S OTC INDUSTRIAL MANUAL. **907**

0192-7302 *See* ORION MARKETING TRADE-IN GUIDE. **934**

0192-7361 *See* SKYDIVING. **4918**

0192-7388 *See* ACCESSIONS LIST, EASTERN AFRICA. ANNUAL SERIAL SUPPLEMENT. **406**

0192-7442 *See* MADISON MAGAZINE. **2537**

0192-7450 *See* BUSINESS (MADISON). **650**

0192-7469 *See* EXHAUST NEWS. **5104**

0192-7507 *See* ACCENT. **2913**

0192-7582 *See* FINANCIAL DIRECTORY OF PENSION FUNDS. MISSOURI, EASTERN. ST. LOUIS, JEFFERSON CITY & OTHERS. **1672**

0192-7590 *See* BUILDING CONSTRUCTION NEWS. **603**

0192-7639 *See* DOMESTIC AND INTERNATIONAL COMMERCIAL LOAN CHARGE-OFFS. **788**

0192-7663 *See* PUBLISHING TRENDS & TRENDSETTERS. **4819**

0192-7671 *See* WELDING DISTRIBUTOR (1966). **938**

0192-7698 *See* LAB (RIDGEWOOD). **3603**

0192-7701 *See* LONG TERM CARE. **3788**

0192-771X *See* MINUTES OF MEETING / NATIONAL ADVISORY EYE COUNCIL. **3876**

0192-7736 *See* CURRENT STATUS OF MODERN THERAPY. **4298**

0192-7841 *See* COLUMBIA FLIER. **5686**

0192-7906 *See* PINCKNEY POST AND WHITMORE LAKER, THE. **5693**

0192-7973 *See* METROPOLITAN PURCHASOR. **950**

0192-8007 *See* AXIS (WASHINGTON). **3193**

0192-8023 *See* CHILTON'S GOING PLACES. **5466**

0192-8031 *See* YELLOWSTONE GRIZZLY BEAR INVESTIGATIONS. **5600**

0192-8058 *See* FDM, FURNITURE DESIGN & MANUFACTURING. **634**

0192-8074 *See* FINANCIAL ASSISTANCE BY GEOGRAPHIC AREA. REGION VII, KANSAS CITY, MISSOURI. **4725**

0192-8082 *See* ROMEO-WASHINGTON ADVISOR NEWSPAPER, THE. **5693**

0192-8090 *See* FOOM. **3388**

0192-8104 *See* DIRECTORY OF SUBSPECIALTY FELLOWSHIP TRAINING PROGRAMS. **3572**

0192-8163 *See* COMPENSATION AND WORKING CONDITIONS. **1660**

0192-8171 *See* RANGER, THE. **5762**

0192-8198 *See* PATENT LAW HANDBOOK. **1307**

0192-821X *See* ALI-ABA COURSE OF STUDY. ALI-ABA CONFERENCE ON ERISA : MATERIALS. **2930**

0192-8228 *See* NATIONAL JAIL AND ADULT DETENTION DIRECTORY. **3170**

0192-8295 *See* LABOR MARKET REVIEW : SAN FRANCISCO-OAKLAND STANDARD METROPOLITAN STATISTICAL AREA. **1684**

0192-8309 *See* LAND USE & ENVIRONMENT LAW REVIEW. **3114**

0192-8317 *See* FARM MACHINERY & TRACTOR FACTS. **159**

0192-8376 *See* RESEARCH OUTLOOK / UNITED STATES ENVIRONMENTAL PROTECTION AGENCY, RESEARCH AND DEVELOPMENT. **2203**

0192-8406 *See* PENNY SAVER (LANCASTER), THE. **5738**

0192-8457 *See* CONTRACTORS GUIDE (LOMBARD, ILL.). **611**

0192-8465 *See* CAPE COD NEWS (SANDWICH, MASS.). **5688**

0192-8503 *See* HARTFORD ADVOCATE. **5645**

0192-8511 *See* NEW HAVEN ADVOCATE. **5646**

0192-8562 *See* AMERICAN JOURNAL OF PEDIATRIC HEMATOLOGY/ONCOLOGY, THE. **3900**

0192-8589 *See* VALLEY SUN (WASILLA), THE. **5629**

0192-8597 *See* 1590 BROADCASTER. **5707**

0192-8600 *See* TRI-COUNTY FREE-PRESS, THE. **2494**

0192-8627 *See* MUSICAL HERITAGE REVIEW. **4136**

0192-8643 *See* ANNUAL CONFERENCE OF STATE MEDICAID DIRECTORS. CONFERENCE REPORT. **2873**

0192-8651 *See* JOURNAL OF COMPUTATIONAL CHEMISTRY. **981**

0192-8686 See SOCIAL PRACTICE. 5220
0192-8716 See PIKESTAFF FORUM, THE. 2543
0192-8732 See STORES OF THE YEAR. 2903
0192-8740 See PROCEEDINGS OF THE ANNUAL AIR TRAFFIC CONTROL ASSOCIATION FALL CONFERENCE. 32
0192-8821 See Y-NOT ANTIQUE & FLEA MARKET DIRECTORY, THE. 252
0192-8856 See ENVIRONMENTAL CONTROL TECHNOLOGY ACTIVITIES OF THE DEPARTMENT OF ENERGY. 2167
0192-8902 See BUS RIDE. 5378
0192-8910 See AMESBURY NEWS. 5684
0192-8988 See SUNFLOWER (FARGO), THE. 188
0192-9046 See INTERFACE. INSURANCE INDUSTRY. 2884
0192-9097 See BUDDY (DALLAS, TEX.). 4105
0192-9151 See RETAILER AND MARKETING NEWS. 936
0192-916X See SHELBY REPORT OF THE SOUTHWEST. 2357
0192-9194 See SOUTHWEST REAL ESTATE NEWS. 4847
0192-9216 See TEXAS CONTRACTOR. 630
0192-9267 See FISHING IN NEW YORK. 2303
0192-9275 See PRINTING HISTORY. 4568
0192-9305 See PROGRAM REPORT / NATIONAL HEART, LUNG, AND BLOOD INSTITUTE, DIVISION OF LUNG DISEASES. 3951
0192-9356 See WESTOSHA REPORT. 5772
0192-9399 See MONEY MAKING OPPORTUNITIES. 696
0192-9410 See STOW SENTRY. 5730
0192-9437 See FARM, RANCH & SUBURBAN ACREAGE. 85
0192-9453 See LAND AND WATER (FORT DODGE). 2197
0192-9461 See BUSINESS NEWS (MACOMB). 651
0192-9550 See TILE & DECORATIVE SURFACES. 2907
0192-9593 See OKLAHOMA BUSINESS. 701
0192-9631 See SOUTHERN DUTCHESS NEWS. 5721
0192-9658 See COUNTRY TODAY, THE. 5766
0192-9666 See WORTHWHILE PRICE GUIDE, THE. 4833
0192-9674 See AUTOWEEK. 5407
0192-9690 See SURVEY OF THE MINI/MICROCOMPUTER MARKET. 1274
0192-9720 See LOYOLA LAW REVIEW. 3004
0192-9739 See LABOR MARKET REVIEW : SAN JOSE STANDARD METROPOLITAN STATISTICAL AREA. 1684
0192-9747 See PROGRAM BUDGET STATEMENT. 4796
0192-9755 See SEMINARS IN RESPIRATORY MEDICINE. 3952
0192-9763 See AMERICAN JOURNAL OF OTOLOGY (NEW YORK, N.Y.), THE. 3886
0192-9771 See RURAL-URBAN RECORD. 5730
0192-978X See NATIONAL HIGH SCHOOL SPORTS RECORD BOOK. 4906
0192-9801 See POTOMAC LAW REVIEW. 3030
0192-9844 See LABOR MARKET REVIEW: SALINAS-SEASIDE-MONTEREY STANDARD METROPOLITAN STATISTICAL AREA. 1684
0192-9879 See RACIAL, ETHNIC, AND SEX ENROLLMENT DATA FROM INSTITUTIONS OF HIGHER EDUCATION. 1843
0192-9887 See CCLM NEWSLETTER. 3373
0192-9909 See MEMBERSHIP/COMMITTEE DIRECTORY - BUILDING OWNERS AND MANAGERS ASSOCIATION INTERNATIONAL. 4840
0192-9917 See JOURNAL OF MAGIC HISTORY, THE. 4862
0192-9925 See FODOR'S CALIFORNIA. 5471
0192-9968 See AMERICAN INDIAN ART MAGAZINE. 336
0193-0192 See SEC CORPORATION INDEX. 913
0193-0230 See DEARBORN TIMES-HERALD. 5691

0193-0249 See VASSAR PIONEER TIMES, THE. 5694
0193-0311 See SALMON RIVER NEWS. 5720
0193-032X See OPHTHALMOLOGY TIMES. 3878
0193-0362 See BUDGET REQUEST - U.S. CONSUMER PRODUCT SAFETY COMMISSION. 4634
0193-0389 See BELLEVUE LEADER. 5706
0193-0443 See FRIENDLY FAIRWAYS OF MICHIGAN. 4895
0193-0486 See PROCEEDINGS OF THE ... ANNUAL CONFERENCE OF THE HOSPITAL MANAGEMENT SYSTEMS SOCIETY. 3791
0193-0494 See REPORT OF THE ADMINISTRATOR / ALCOHOL, DRUG ABUSE, AND MENTAL HEALTH ADMINISTRATION. 1348
0193-0516 See INSURANCE CONFERENCE PLANNER. 2883
0193-0613 See SOUTHERN BEVERAGE JOURNAL. 2371
0193-063X See AGE DISCRIMINATION IN EMPLOYMENT ACT OF 1967. 1642
0193-0761 See GROUND-WATER SERIES (LAWRENCE, KAN.). 1414
0193-077X See COMMUNITY CRIER, THE. 5691
0193-0818 See RESEARCH COMMUNICATIONS IN SUBSTANCES OF ABUSE. 1348
0193-0826 See JOURNAL OF LIBRARY ADMINISTRATION. 3220
0193-0850 See AWC NEWS/FORUM. 4160
0193-0885 See MUMPS COMPUTING. 1196
0193-0907 See AUTO & TRUCK INTERNATIONAL EN ESPANOL. 5404
0193-0923 See NEW ENGLAND FARMER (ST. JOHNSBURY). 111
0193-0931 See AMERICAN JEWELRY MANUFACTURER. 2913
0193-1008 See RESERVE FORCES MANPOWER CHARTS. 4055
0193-1016 See BRANSON TRI-LAKES DAILY NEWS. 5702
0193-1032 See RICE CROP QUALITY. 185
0193-1040 See U.S. DEPARTMENT OF ENERGY BUDGET TO CONGRESS : BUDGET HIGHLIGHTS. 4692
0193-1075 See SLOVENE STUDIES. 2710
0193-1091 See AMERICAN JOURNAL OF DERMATOPATHOLOGY, THE. 3717
0193-113X See VOLUNTEERS WHO PRODUCE BOOKS. 4395
0193-1180 See ECONOMIC REPORT OF THE PRESIDENT TRANSMITTED TO THE CONGRESS. 1484
0193-1202 See DANCEMAGAZINE COLLEGE GUIDE. 1312
0193-1245 See SPECIAL PUBLICATION - DIVISION OF FISH AND WILDLIFE, SECTION OF FISHERIES. 2313
0193-1385 See TOWARD INTERAGENCY COORDINATION: FEDERAL RESEARCH AND DEVELOPMENT ON ADOLESCENCE. 2286
0193-1415 See CANCER MANAGEMENT. 3812
0193-1423 See STATE PLAN FOR DEVELOPMENTAL DISABILITIES (HARRISBURG, PA.). 4688
0193-1458 See TELOCATOR. 1168
0193-1474 See VOICES (SOUTHBURY). 5646
0193-1490 See INLAND EMPIRE MAGAZINE. 682
0193-1504 See WHOLE FOODS. 2361
0193-1520 See INDIANA REGISTER. 2982
0193-158X See ANNUAL REPORT - MISSISSIPPI AIR AND WATER POLLUTION CONTROL COMMISSION. 2224
0193-1598 See MEMBERSHIP DIRECTORY - GYPSY LORE SOCIETY, NORTH AMERICAN CHAPTER. 2322
0193-1601 See CHRONICLE SUMMARY REPORT. 1815
0193-1628 See LABOR LAW REPORT. 3150
0193-1644 See SEA REPORTER. 1872
0193-1652 See PROFILE OF ENVIRONMENTAL QUALITY. REGION 8: COLORADO, MONTANA, NORTH DAKOTA, SOUTH DAKOTA, UTAH, WYOMING. 2239

0193-1660 See CHARACTERISTICS OF FHA SINGLE-FAMILY MORTGAGES, SELECTED SECTIONS OF NATIONAL HOUSING ACT. 4717
0193-1687 See U.S. FOREIGN TRADE: CONCORDANCE OF STATISTICAL CLASSIFICATIONS OF DOMESTIC AND FOREIGN COMMODITIES EXPORTED FROM THE UNITED STATES. 734
0193-175X See POLITICAL HANDBOOK OF THE WORLD (1975). 4489
0193-1784 See ACRL PUBLICATIONS IN LIBRARIANSHIP. 3187
0193-1814 See NEWS CIRCLE, THE. 2269
0193-1849 See AMERICAN JOURNAL OF PHYSIOLOGY : ENDOCRINOLOGY AND METABOLISM. 577
0193-1857 See AMERICAN JOURNAL OF PHYSIOLOGY : GASTROINTESTINAL AND LIVER PHYSIOLOGY. 578
0193-1865 See REGISTERED REPRESENTATIVE, THE. 912
0193-1873 See CAREERS (SARATOGA). 4203
0193-1903 See COMPENDIUM ON CONTINUING EDUCATION FOR THE PRACTICING VETERINARIAN, THE. 5508
0193-1911 See KINESIS REPORT, THE. 4602
0193-1970 See REVIEW AND EVALUATION OF THE NUCLEAR REGULATORY COMMISSION SAFETY RESEARCH PROGRAM. 2158
0193-2004 See HAP. HEART OF AMERICA PURCHASER. 950
0193-2047 See MID-AMERICA COMMERCE & INDUSTRY. 950
0193-211X See PILOT NEWS. 31
0193-2128 See SERVICE REPORTER. 2608
0193-2136 See TRAINING WORLD. 1123
0193-2179 See VOLUNTARY EFFORT QUARTERLY. 3650
0193-2209 See RESEARCH REPORT - OKLAHOMA MEDICAL RESEARCH FOUNDATION. 3634
0193-2241 See WALL STREET JOURNAL. WESTERN EDITION, THE. 5690
0193-225X See WALL STREET JOURNAL. SOUTHWEST EDITION, THE. 816
0193-2276 See GRADUATING ENGINEER. 1976
0193-2306 See RESEARCH IN EXPERIMENTAL ECONOMICS. 1517
0193-2314 See BROOKS' STANDARD RATE BOOK, THE. 1656
0193-2322 See TEXAS LEGISLATIVE HANDBOOK. 4498
0193-2349 See CONTINUING EDUCATION IN ORTHOPAEDIC SURGERY. SOUND RECORDING. 3568
0193-242X See MARKETING FLORIDA VEGETABLES : SUMMARY. 2349
0193-2438 See SPEARS REPORT, PRODUCTION. 4279
0193-2446 See SOUTHERN CHANGES. 4513
0193-2527 See PUBLICATION SP. 625
0193-2551 See GIFTWARE NEWS. 2584
0193-2586 See INTERIOR CONSTRUCTION. 617
0193-2691 See JOURNAL OF DISPERSION SCIENCE AND TECHNOLOGY. 4428
0193-2721 See FINANCIAL STATUS OF MAJOR FEDERAL ACQUISITIONS. 4649
0193-273X See SOLINEWS. 3250
0193-2748 See STUDIES IN FORMATIVE SPIRITUALITY. 5037
0193-2802 See TWIN CITIES READER. 2548
0193-2810 See PHOTOGRAPHY INDEX. 4374
0193-2853 See AGRICULTURAL RESEARCH RESULTS. (SOUTHERN SERIES). 51
0193-2861 See SATELLITE WEEK. 1163
0193-2918 See AUDIT OF THE FINANCIAL STATEMENTS OF FEDERAL CROP INSURANCE CORPORATION. 2874
0193-2926 See SUMMARIES OF CONCLUSIONS AND RECOMMENDATIONS ON THE OPERATIONS OF CIVIL DEPARTMENTS AND AGENCIES. 4689
0193-2950 See HORSE & RIDER ALL-WESTERN YEARBOOK. 2799

0193-3000 See BURNSVILLE CURRENT, THE. 5694

0193-306X See PROCEEDINGS OF THE INTERNATIONAL CONFERENCE ON FIRE SAFETY. 2292

0193-3086 See ODL SOURCE. 3238

0193-3108 See NEW FLORIDA. 2748

0193-3183 See SAN DIEGO LOG. 2544

0193-3221 See BUSINESS OPPORTUNITIES JOURNAL. 893

0193-323X See CHILTON'S FOOD ENGINEERING. 2331

0193-3264 See CHILTON'S AUTOMOTIVE MARKETING. 5410

0193-3302 See SOCIO-ECONOMIC FACTBOOK FOR SURGERY. 3975

0193-3310 See REPORT OF PROGRESS - MERL. 2241

0193-3329 See WORLD OPINION UPDATE. 4538

0193-3337 See REPORT ON SURVEY OF U.S. SHIPBUILDING AND REPAIR FACILITIES. 4182

0193-3388 See LIABILITY LEDGER. 3002

0193-3418 See PROCEEDINGS OF NEW YORK UNIVERSITY ANNUAL NATIONAL CONFERENCE ON LABOR. 3153

0193-3477 See CLEAR TRACK. 5430

0193-3485 See REVOLUTIONARY WORKER. 5661

0193-3507 See PACIFIC BOATING ALMANAC. SOUTHERN CALIFORNIA, ARIZONA & BAJA. 595

0193-3515 See PACIFIC BOATING ALMANAC. NORTHERN CALIFORNIA & NEVADA. 595

0193-3558 See FISH KILLS CAUSED BY POLLUTION IN ... (1975). 2301

0193-3604 See JOURNAL OF RELIGIOUS STUDIES (CLEVELAND, OHIO). 4970

0193-3612 See REVOLUTION (CHICAGO). 4494

0193-3655 See EARLY WARNING REPORT. 670

0193-3663 See PUBLIC BROADCASTING REPORT, THE. 1136

0193-3671 See AM-FM FACILITIES CHANGES ADDENDA. 1148

0193-3701 See ADVANCES IN AGRICULTURAL TECHNOLOGY (NORTH CENTRAL SERIES). 44

0193-3728 See ADVANCES IN AGRICULTURAL TECHNOLOGY (SOUTHERN SERIES). 44

0193-3736 See ADVANCES IN AGRICULTURAL TECHNOLOGY (WESTERN SERIES). 44

0193-3752 See AGRICULTURAL REVIEWS AND MANUALS (NORTHEASTERN SERIES). 52

0193-3760 See AGRICULTURAL REVIEWS AND MANUALS. WESTERN SERIES. 52

0193-385X See DIRECTORY OF UNIONS AND ASSOCIATIONS WITH EXCLUSIVE RECOGNITION IN THE FEDERAL SERVICE. 1663

0193-3884 See WHOLE CLASSROOM, THE. 1791

0193-3892 See CORONICA, LA. 3275

0193-3906 See MILITARY LAW REPORTER. 3183

0193-3922 See JOURNAL FOR SPECIALISTS IN GROUP WORK, THE. 4592

0193-3973 See JOURNAL OF APPLIED DEVELOPMENTAL PSYCHOLOGY. 4593

0193-3981 See ALCOHOL AND DRUG ABUSE YEARBOOK/DIRECTORY, THE. 1339

0193-4007 See DELAWARE LAW MONTHLY, THE. 2959

0193-4015 See PRETRIAL REPORTER, THE. 3173

0193-4120 See TEST (OAKHURST, N.J.). 2130

0193-4139 See ASEE PRISM. 1965

0193-4171 See OIL PRICE DATABOOK. 4270

0193-4198 See WATER FLYING ANNUAL. 39

0193-4201 See SIGNIFICANT ISSUES FACING DIRECTORS. 886

0193-4244 See CICERONE (MIAMI). 5466

0193-4252 See UTAH REPORT OF MEDICAID STATISTICS. 5267

0193-4260 See STATE PLAN FOR COMPREHENSIVE MENTAL HEALTH SERVICES : ANNUAL REVIEW AND PROGRESS REPORTS FOR THE STATE OF OKLAHOMA. 4804

0193-4279 See DIRECTORSHIP (WESTPORT). 865

0193-4325 See EXAMINATION OF FINANCIAL STATEMENTS OF THE PENSION BENEFIT GUARANTY CORPORATION. 1668

0193-4384 See SEARS. 1299

0193-4392 See FARMERS' BULLETIN. 85

0193-4406 See BRIMLEYANA. 5578

0193-4414 See BUSINESS ADVOCATE, THE. 3096

0193-4457 See ACT. ADVERTISING/COMMUNICATIONS TIMES. 753

0193-4538 See AIRTRAN NEWS. 11

0193-4546 See AEROSPACE DAILY. 5

0193-4562 See APF REPORTER. 2917

0193-4570 See NEWS - AMERICAN IMMIGRATION AND CITIZENSHIP CONFERENCE. 1920

0193-4597 See AVIATION DAILY. 13

0193-4600 See BLUE CHIP ECONOMIC INDICATORS. 1548

0193-4627 See CONGRESS IN PRINT. 4640

0193-4635 See NEWS - CONSUMER FEDERATION OF AMERICA. 1298

0193-4651 See ELEMENTS (WASHINGTON), THE. 2192

0193-466X See HIRSCH REPORT, THE. 1186

0193-4686 See REGULATORY EYE. 4679

0193-4716 See WAYS & MEANS (WASHINGTON, D.C.). 4694

0193-4724 See WEEKLY BPN PROPANE NEWSLETTER. 4281

0193-4775 See GOVERNMENTAL FLEET MANAGEMENT. 4652

0193-4783 See UNITED KINGDOM, THE COMMONWEALTH OF NATIONS, A DIRECTORY OF GOVERNMENTS, THE. 4499

0193-4821 See PENNSYLVANIA LAWYER, THE. 3025

0193-4856 See IOWA GEOLOGY. 1383

0193-4864 See INTELLECTUAL PROPERTY LAW REVIEW. 1305

0193-4872 See HARVARD JOURNAL OF LAW & PUBLIC POLICY. 2976

0193-4880 See CORPORATE COUNSEL, THE. 3098

0193-4902 See PS, POSTSECONDARY EDUCATION IN NEW YORK STATE. 1775

0193-4929 See REVIEWS IN INORGANIC CHEMISTRY (LONDON, ENGLAND). 1037

0193-4953 See TOWERS CLUB USA NEWSLETTER. 2925

0193-497X See WINE SPECTATOR, THE. 2372

0193-5011 See DIRECTORY OF GRADUATE RESEARCH. 974

0193-5046 See PHILOSOPHIC EXCHANGE. 4355

0193-5070 See DECISIONS OF THE UNITED STATES DEPARTMENT OF THE INTERIOR. 4642

0193-5097 See LILLY DIGEST. 4314

0193-5127 See MUSIC WORKS (SAN FRANCISCO, CALIF.). 4135

0193-5143 See HENDERSONVILLE STAR NEWS. 5745

0193-5151 See THESAURUS - AMERICAN PETROLEUM INSTITUTE. 3253

0193-5178 See BULLSEYE (NORTH LAS VEGAS). 2529

0193-5216 See HILLSIDE JOURNAL OF CLINICAL PSYCHIATRY, THE. 3926

0193-5224 See ANNUAL PROGRESS REPORT - UNIVERSITY OF CALIFORNIA, LABORATORY OF NUCLEAR MEDICINE AND RADIATION BIOLOGY. 3847

0193-5232 See HEALTH EDUCATION REPORTS. 4779

0193-533X See GAZETTE (NEW YORK. 1979), THE. 3390

0193-5356 See NEW MEXICO INDEPENDENT, THE. 5712

0193-5364 See RECENT RESEARCHES IN THE MUSIC OF THE NINETEENTH AND EARLY TWENTIETH CENTURIES. 4149

0193-5372 See AMERICAN SUZUKI JOURNAL. 4100

0193-5380 See EIGHTEENTH CENTURY (LUBBOCK), THE. 2686

0193-5437 See COMMUNICATOR (NORTHWEST COMMUNICATION ASSOCIATION), THE. 1108

0193-547X See NORTH CAROLINA INFORMATION AND FACT BOOK, THE. 2750

0193-5518 See FLUID POWER INDUSTRY OUTLOOK SURVEY. 3479

0193-5526 See SWANN GALLERIES, INC. 4832

0193-5585 See GRAIN STOCKS. 201

0193-5593 See COUNTY GOVERNMENT EMPLOYMENT. 1661

0193-5615 See ANTHROPOLOGY AND HUMANISM QUARTERLY. 230

0193-5658 See UNDERGROUND STORAGE OF NATURAL GAS BY INTERSTATE PIPELINE COMPANIES. 4281

0193-5720 See BIBLIOGRAPHY OF AMERICAN PALEOBOTANY. 502

0193-5739 See LABOR & EMPLOYMENT LAW. 3150

0193-5771 See TAX ANGLES. 4752

0193-5798 See ENCLITIC. 3342

0193-5801 See CATALOG OF TELEVISION AND AUDIOVISUAL MATERIALS. 1130

0193-581X See ALMANAC (MCMURRAY), THE. 5734

0193-5895 See RESEARCH IN LAW AND ECONOMICS. 3039

0193-5909 See CONNECTICUT, RHODE ISLAND DIRECTORY OF MANUFACTURERS. 3477

0193-5933 See TRANSACTIONS - GEOTHERMAL RESOURCES COUNCIL. 1959

0193-5968 See LIVING CITY (NEW YORK). 4974

0193-5992 See MISCELLANEOUS REPORT - U.S. ARMY, CORPS OF ENGINEERS, COASTAL ENGINEERING RESEARCH CENTER. 2093

0193-600X See JOURNAL OF THE INTERNATIONAL ASSOCIATION OF BUDDHIST STUDIES, THE. 5021

0193-6085 See TODAY'S FILM MAKER. 4079

0193-614X See CHILTON'S ELECTRONIC COMPONENT NEWS. 2038

0193-6166 See MALPRACTICE PREVENTION FOR HOSPITALS. 3005

0193-6174 See CHILTON'S IAN (1977). 1968

0193-6182 See CHILTON'S PD&D. 1601

0193-6212 See PRESBYTERION. 5066

0193-6271 See BEHAVIOR IMPROVEMENT NEWS. 4576

0193-6301 See BLACK WARRIOR REVIEW, THE. 3338

0193-6387 See ENVIRONS (DAVIS). 3112

0193-6425 See PROCEEDINGS OF THE SOUTHERN PASTURE AND FORAGE CROP IMPROVEMENT CONFERENCE. 183

0193-6468 See ECONOSCOPE VIEW, THE. 1559

0193-6484 See CHEMISTRY INTERNATIONAL. 971

0193-6492 See SUBURBAN NEWS. 5711

0193-6514 See TOBACCO MARKET REVIEW. FLUE-CURED. 5374

0193-6530 See DIGEST OF TECHNICAL PAPERS / IEEE INTERNATIONAL SOLID-STATE CIRCUITS CONFERENCE. 2041

0193-6557 See OFFICIAL ARMY NATIONAL GUARD REGISTER. 4053

0193-6603 See VEGETABLES (WASHINGTON). 190

0193-6654 See VIRGINIA CONTINUING LEGAL EDUCATION BULLETIN. 3071

0193-6700 See WESTERN JOURNAL OF COMMUNICATION. 1124

0193-6808 See MANAGING HOUSING LETTER. 2827

0193-6816 See HOSPICE LETTER. 3783

0193-6824 See INTERCOLLEGIATE PRESS BULLETINS. 1831

0193-6832 See BUSS. 1265

0193-6840 See DIRECTORY OF ONLINE DATABASES. 3207

0193-6859 See AMERICAN POPULAR CULTURE. 5268

0193-6867 See ART REFERENCE COLLECTION. 334

0193-6875 See CONTRIBUTIONS TO THE STUDY OF SCIENCE FICTION AND FANTASY. 3378

0193-6905 See ALI-ABA COURSE OF STUDY. BUSINESS TAX PLANNING : MATERIALS. 3094

0193-6956 See ARTSPACE. 342

0193-6999 See CONVENTION ON INTERNATIONAL TRADE IN ENDANGERED SPECIES OF WILD FAUNA AND FLORA. 2191

0193-7014 See S9 HOBBY RADIO. 1138

0193-7022 See CHILTON'S MOTOR/AGE (1970). 5411

0193-7081 See STATE OF THE COLORADO JUDICIARY, THE. 3143

0193-7138 See HEALTH EDUCATION REPORT (OJAI). 4779

0193-7162 See HEBREW ANNUAL REVIEW. 5017

0193-7197 See JOURNAL OF VINYL TECHNOLOGY. 4456

0193-7200 See GILBERT LAW SUMMARIES. CRIMINAL LAW. 3107

0193-7235 See JOURNAL OF SPORT AND SOCIAL ISSUES. 5250

0193-7251 See MORTON GROVE CHAMPION. 5661

0193-726X See BRAKE & FRONT END. 5408

0193-7278 See SPECIALTY & CUSTOM DEALER. 5425

0193-7324 See NATIONAL ELECTRICAL CODE HANDBOOK (1978), THE. 2292

0193-7332 See SAN DIEGO SPORTS DIGEST. 4916

0193-7340 See REPORT OF THE DIRECTOR, NATIONAL HEART, LUNG, AND BLOOD INSTITUTE. 4798

0193-7359 See REKINDLE. 2292

0193-7367 See JUDICIAL CONDUCT REPORTER. 3141

0193-7375 See COUNSELING AND HUMAN DEVELOPMENT. 5281

0193-7383 See EDITORIAL EYE, THE. 4814

0193-7391 See OUTPUT MODE. 4818

0193-743X See CLINICS IN DIAGNOSTIC ULTRASOUND. 3566

0193-7448 See EMERGENCY MEDICAL SERVICES RESEARCH METHODOLOGY WORKSHOP. 3724

0193-7480 See ARIZONA BUSINESS/INDUSTRY. 639

0193-7510 See THIS WEEK IN THE VALLEY OF THE SUN. KEY. 2547

0193-7545 See CIRCULATORY SHOCK. SUPPLEMENT. 3702

0193-7561 See DIRECTORY, HANDBOOK - CALIFORNIA STATE PSYCHOLOGICAL ASSOCIATION. 4585

0193-7588 See LAGNIAPPE. 3403

0193-7596 See CHICAGO CREATIVE DIRECTORY, THE. 1130

0193-7642 See NATIONAL FARM TRACTOR AND IMPLEMENT BLUE BOOK. 160

0193-7693 See NEW YORK NO-FAULT ARBITRATION REPORTS. 3016

0193-7707 See MASS COMM REVIEW. 1116

0193-7758 See IRB. 2251

0193-7774 See CHINOPERL PAPERS. 3375

0193-7782 See BILL-DALE MARCINKO'S AFTA. 3338

0193-7804 See MICHIGAN DISCUSSIONS IN ANTHROPOLOGY. 241

0193-7820 See LA-BAS. 3465

0193-7855 See FASB INTERPRETATION. 744

0193-7871 See WORLD EAGLE. 5228

0193-791X See NEIGHBORHOOD WORKS, THE. 2829

0193-7928 See HEALTH FUNDS DEVELOPMENT LETTER. 3581

0193-7960 See ACC BASKETBALL. 4881

0193-7979 See ELECTRONIC DATA PROCESSING SALARY SURVEY. 1664

0193-7987 See DECISIONS - FEDERAL MINE SAFETY AND HEALTH REVIEW COMMISSION. 2861

0193-8010 See GILBERT LAW SUMMARIES: CRIMINAL PROCEDURE. 3107

0193-8061 See PHOEBUS. 362

0193-8096 See GLOBAL AGENDA, A. 4522

0193-8126 See MONTANA ENVIRONMENTAL SCIENCES. 2236

0193-8134 See REPORTER (WASHINGTON. 1977), THE. 3183

0193-8150 See EXECUTIVE LETTER (DALLAS). 867

0193-8177 See BICYCLE FORUM. 428

0193-8207 See AMERICAN INDIAN LIBRARIES NEWSLETTER. 3189

0193-8223 See DEPARTMENT OF FORESTRY TECHNICAL PAPER. 2378

0193-8274 See SHARING THE PRACTICE. 4997

0193-8290 See LAW & HOUSING JOURNAL. 2994

0193-8355 See NATURAL HAZARDS OBSERVER. 1358

0193-8371 See CITY & TOWN (NORTH LITTLE ROCK, ARK.). 4638

0193-8401 See SPORTING GOODS MARKET IN ..., THE. 4879

0193-841X See EVALUATION REVIEW. 5245

0193-8495 See PROCEEDINGS - HARDWOOD SYMPOSIUM OF THE HARDWOOD RESEARCH COUNCIL. 2403

0193-8509 See JOURNAL OF THE ARIZONA-NEVADA ACADEMY OF SCIENCE. 1357

0193-8568 See UROLOGIC SURGERY (MT. KISCO). 3977

0193-8592 See SUMMARY INSPECTION REPORT OF OFFICIAL SAMPLES ON SEED, FEED, FERTILIZER & AG-LIME. 203

0193-8614 See HILLS AND HARBORS. 2534

0193-8649 See NEWSLETTER - BULGARIAN STUDIES ASSOCIATION. 2624

0193-8657 See U.S. CENTRAL STATION NUCLEAR ELECTRIC GENERATING UNITS, SIGNIFICANT MILESTONES. 2159

0193-8673 See STATE/CITY LIST OF LENDERS. 1848

0193-8738 See LATIN AMERICA PETROLEUM DIRECTORY. 4263

0193-8762 See FACTFINDER FOR THE NATION. 4553

0193-8770 See NEWSLETTER OF THE CHICAGO GENEALOGICAL SOCIETY. 2463

0193-8835 See CHERRIES (ALBANY, N.Y.). 166

0193-886X See KNIGHT LETTER (CHARLOTTESVILLE). 2457

0193-8991 See MELVILLE SOCIETY EXTRACTS. 3411

0193-9009 See HUMAN SERVICES IN THE RURAL ENVIRONMENT. 5288

0193-9017 See FRANCHISING IN THE ECONOMY. 954

0193-9025 See FOOD RESEARCH INSTITUTE STUDIES (1975). 88

0193-9041 See CONTRIBUTIONS TO THE STUDY OF MUSIC AND DANCE. 4112

0193-905X See INDEX TO INTERNATIONAL PUBLIC OPINION. 5247

0193-9084 See DIRECTORY OF FUNDED PROJECTS. 1821

0193-9106 See GREEN MARKETS FERTILIZER PRICE HANDBOOK. 1607

0193-9114 See FODOR'S JORDAN AND THE HOLY LAND. 5472

0193-9130 See GUIDE TO TRAVEL AND RESIDENCE EXPENSES FOR THE MULTINATIONAL EXECUTIVE. 5479

0193-9181 See DEFENSE & FOREIGN AFFAIRS' WEEKLY REPORT ON STRATEGIC AFRICAN AFFAIRS. 4519

0193-9211 See WORD AND SPIRIT. 5038

0193-9254 See NEWSLETTER - IAMSLIC. 1453

0193-9262 See LOWE INVESTMENT & FINANCIAL LETTER. 905

0193-9270 See INTERNATIONAL PETROLEUM FINANCE. 4261

0193-9300 See ATTORNEYS' DIRECTORY OF SAN DIEGO COUNTY. 3078

0193-9327 See SURVEY OF CONTRACTING STATISTICS. 4062

0193-936X See EPIDEMIOLOGIC REVIEWS. 3734

0193-9394 See CASE STUDIES IN HEALTH ADMINISTRATION. 3778

0193-9416 See NEW DIRECTIONS FOR MENTAL HEALTH SERVICES. 5298

0193-9424 See NORTH CAROLINA STATE PLAN FOR ALCOHOL AND DRUG ABUSE. 1347

0193-9432 See CHECKLIST OF OFFICIAL NORTH CAROLINA STATE PUBLICATIONS. 413

0193-9459 See WESTERN JOURNAL OF NURSING RESEARCH. 3871

0193-9467 See TULSALETTER (1976). 4281

0193-9483 See MEDICAL ASSISTANCE, MEDICAID (LANSING). 5295

0193-9513 See REGIONAL COTTON VARIETY TESTS. 184

0193-953X See PSYCHIATRIC CLINICS OF NORTH AMERICA, THE. 3933

0193-9548 See FIELD OF VISION (PITTSBURGH). 320

0193-9556 See FODOR'S FLORIDA. 5471

0193-9602 See VIDEOLOG : PROGRAMS FOR GENERAL INTEREST AND ENTERTAINMENT, THE. 1143

0193-9610 See OFFICIAL BLACKBOOK PRICE GUIDE OF UNITED STATES COINS, THE. 2782

0193-9653 See OFFICIAL PGA TOUR BOOK. 4910

0193-9661 See INTERNATIONAL MARKETING REPORT. 926

0193-967X See RULES GOVERNING THE COURTS OF THE STATE OF NEW JERSEY, 1969 REVISION, AS AMENDED. 3143

0193-9688 See PROCEEDINGS, A&WMA ANNUAL MEETING. 2239

0193-9718 See WHAT IT COSTS. 2896

0193-9734 See BUSINESS DATA PROCESSING: A WILEY SERIES. 646

0193-9742 See CLINICAL PEDIATRICS, MATERNAL AND CHILD HEALTH. 3902

0193-9815 See RENAISSANCE AND RENASCENCES IN WESTERN LITERATURE. 3428

0193-9831 See VACATION & TRAVEL GUIDE. 5498

0193-984X See FEED GRAIN, WHEAT, UPLAND COTTON AND RICE PROGRAMS, DISASTER AND DEFICIENCY PROVISIONS. 200

0193-9866 See MILITARY IMAGES. 4050

0193-9874 See NORTH AMERICAN DIRECTORY OF MONTESSORI SCHOOLS. 1901

0193-9904 See LAS VIRGENES ENTERPRISE. 5636

0193-9939 See HEALTHCARE FUNDRAISING NEWSLETTER. 3782

0193-9939 See HOSPITAL FUND RAISING NEWSLETTER. 3784

0193-9947 See BALKAN INVESTMENT REPORT. 892

0193-998X See HERITAGE TALES. 2736

0193-9998 See REPORT TO THE SECRETARY, DEPARTMENT OF HEALTH, EDUCATION, AND WELFARE (U.S. INTERAGENCY COORDINATING COMMITTEE). 3806

0194-0015 See NORTHERN NEW ENGLAND LEGAL DIRECTORY, MAINE, NEW HAMPSHIRE, AND VERMONT, THE. 3019

0194-0023 See AUTOMOTIVE AIR CONDITIONING AND HEATING SERVICE MANUAL : BOOK SUPPLEMENT. 5406

0194-004X See AMWA FREELANCE DIRECTORY, THE. 2917

0194-0074 See NOR KIANK. 5637

0194-0104 See NOLOAD FUND X. 910

0194-0112 See LIBRARIANS' NEWSLETTER. 3223

0194-0139 See REFUNDLE BUNDLE. 1299

0194-0163 See BASIC MICROBIOLOGY. 560

0194-018X See SOURCE BOOK OF MINICOMPUTERS. 1274

0194-0252 See INSIDE N.R.C. **1947**
0194-0287 See ENVIRONMENTAL SCIENCE AND TECHNOLOGY (NEW YORK). **2170**
0194-0295 See BUILDING COST FILE. WESTERN EDITION. **603**
0194-035X See PUBLICATIONS OF THE MISSOURI PHILOLOGICAL ASSOCIATION. **3313**
0194-0376 See REGULATORY REPORTER. **3116**
0194-0384 See WHEELERS RV RESORT & CAMPGROUND GUIDE. **4880**
0194-0406 See CALIFORNIA GOLD BOOK. **2365**
0194-0422 See IMPACT (CLAREMONT). **4964**
0194-049X See RUTGERS ART REVIEW, THE. **363**
0194-0511 See COUNTY VETERAN POPULATION. **4034**
0194-0538 See BIOCHEMISTRY (NEW YORK, N.Y. 1980). **482**
0194-0546 See CONFERENCE PAPERS ANNUAL INDEX. **5096**
0194-0554 See DIRECTORY - STATE BOARD OF MEDICAL EXAMINERS OF SOUTH CAROLINA. **3914**
0194-0562 See FREIGHT COMMODITY STATISTICS. MOTOR CARRIERS OF PROPERTY. **5401**
0194-0589 See COLORADO-NORTH REVIEW. **3377**
0194-0600 See PRINCIPLES AND PRESENTATION : SAVINGS AND LOAN. **750**
0194-0627 See HOME PLAN IDEAS. **616**
0194-0686 See NATIONAL INDUSTRIAL COUNCIL DIRECTORY. **1619**
0194-0694 See INFORMATION INTELLIGENCE ONLINE NEWSLETTER. **1274**
0194-0724 See SAN FRANCISCO REVIEW OF BOOKS. **330**
0194-0740 See CONFERENCE PAPERS QUARTERLY INDEX. **414**
0194-0767 See BULLETIN, NATIONAL EMPLOYMENT LISTING SERVICE FOR THE CRIMINAL JUSTICE SYSTEM. **4201**
0194-0775 See NATIONAL EMPLOYMENT LISTING SERVICE FOR HUMAN SERVICES. **1692**
0194-0805 See NATIONAL EMPLOYMENT LISTING SERVICE FOR THE CRIMINAL JUSTICE SYSTEM. SPECIAL EDITION: EDUCATIONAL OPPORTUNITIES. **4206**
0194-0880 See HANDBOOK OF BEHAVIORAL NEUROBIOLOGY. **3833**
0194-0910 See NATIONAL HARDWOOD MAGAZINE. **634**
0194-0929 See RICE FARMING AND RICE INDUSTRY NEWS. **185**
0194-0937 See SOUTHEAST FARM PRESS. **136**
0194-0945 See SOUTHWEST FARM PRESS. **136**
0194-0953 See CRIMINAL JUSTICE HISTORY. **3162**
0194-0961 See AIRLINE INDUSTRY DIRECTORY. **10**
0194-1046 See SOLAR, GEOTHERMAL, ELECTRIC AND STORAGE SYSTEMS PROGRAM, SUMMARY DOCUMENT. **1957**
0194-1070 See ART/WORLD (NEW YORK. 1976). **340**
0194-1100 See HENRY E. SIGERIST SUPPLEMENTS TO THE BULLETIN OF THE HISTORY OF MEDICINE, THE. **3583**
0194-1127 See ANNUAL ADVANCED ANTITRUST WORKSHOP. **3095**
0194-116X See ANNUAL REPORT OF THE MALDEN PUBLIC LIBRARY. **3191**
0194-1186 See IMPORT/EXPORT WOOD PURCHASING NEWS. **2401**
0194-1194 See WATER EQUIPMENT NEWS. **5542**
0194-1240 See TENNESSEE JOURNAL, THE. **4498**
0194-1259 See TENNESSEE ATTORNEYS MEMO. **3063**
0194-1291 See WASHINGTON DRUG LETTER (WASHINGTON. 1979). **4332**
0194-1313 See MICKLE STREET REVIEW, THE. **3411**

0194-1348 See PHOTO CRAFT NEWS. **4373**
0194-1356 See ARCHITECTURE SERIES--BIBLIOGRAPHY. **311**
0194-1356 See INDEX TO ARCHITECTURE SERIES--BIBLIOGRAPHY. **301**
0194-1399 See BUREAU OF RADIOLOGICAL HEALTH PUBLICATIONS SUBJECT INDEX. **3939**
0194-1410 See CHILTON'S TRUCK & OFF-HIGHWAY INDUSTRIES. **5379**
0194-1429 See SPECIALTY FOOD MERCHANDISING. **2358**
0194-1453 See NORTHEASTERN GEOLOGY. **1390**
0194-1461 See MEASUREMENT & CONTROL NEWS. **4031**
0194-147X See MEDICAL ELECTRONIC PRODUCTS. **3609**
0194-1488 See ADMINISTRATION OF THE MARINE MAMMAL PROTECTION ACT OF 1972. (UNITED STATES. FISH AND WILDLIFE SERVICE.) **2185**
0194-1534 See AMERICAN SHOWMAN, THE. **860**
0194-1542 See BARRY COUNTY ADVERTISER. **5702**
0194-1569 See BUILDING AND REMODELING. **603**
0194-1593 See OBRERO REBELDE, EL. **1696**
0194-1607 See MEDIA SCIENCE NEWSLETTER. **1117**
0194-1623 See PUBLIC TECHNOLOGY. **5143**
0194-164X See HUNGARIAN STUDIES NEWSLETTER. **2692**
0194-1658 See JOURNAL OF INTRAVENOUS THERAPY (LOS ANGELES). **3595**
0194-1682 See CALIFORNIA CORRECTIONAL NEWS. **3159**
0194-1712 See OUR TOWN. **5769**
0194-1771 See TALENT & BOOKING'S DISCO. **4156**
0194-178X See DIRECTORY OF NIGHTCLUBS, HOTELS, THEATRES, LOUNGES & DISCOTHEQUES. **5363**
0194-1798 See FEDERAL TAX VALUATION DIGEST. **4724**
0194-1844 See STEREO TEST REPORTS. **5319**
0194-1879 See HOUSTON JOURNAL OF INTERNATIONAL LAW. **3129**
0194-1887 See DMA AERONAUTICAL CHART MONTHLY BULLETIN. **18**
0194-1917 See ROCHESTER ECCENTRIC. **5693**
0194-1968 See SHELBY REPORT OF THE SOUTHEAST, THE. **2357**
0194-2050 See MULTI-COUNTY STAR. **5654**
0194-2069 See AIM FOR RACIAL HARMONY & PEACE. **5238**
0194-2131 See UPPER ARLINGTON NEWS, THE. **5731**
0194-214X See FIRE MANAGEMENT NOTES. **2289**
0194-2158 See JOURNAL OF COMMUNITY COMMUNICATION, THE. **1114**
0194-2182 See POTOMAC ALMANAC. **5687**
0194-2212 See STUDENT AID NEWS. **1785**
0194-2239 See EDUCATION DAILY. **1739**
0194-2247 See FEDERAL GRANTS & CONTRACTS WEEKLY. **1746**
0194-2255 See EDUCATION OF THE HANDICAPPED. **1878**
0194-2271 See SCHOOL LAW NEWS. **1871**
0194-228X See TAX EXEMPT NEWS. **4752**
0194-2352 See HEALTH GRANTS & CONTRACTS WEEKLY. **4780**
0194-2425 See METRO NEWARK. **820**
0194-245X See REMINDER. ZONE ONE. BRANDON, GROVELAND, ATLAS AND HADLEY TOWNSHIPS, THE. **5693**
0194-2468 See GAS INDUSTRIES (1978). **4257**
0194-2476 See CONSTRUCTION DIGEST. **609**
0194-2514 See DIAGNOSTIC IMAGING (SAN FRANCISCO, CALIF.). **3940**
0194-2522 See HOLLY HOBBIE'S HOME TIMES. **2790**

0194-2530 See PDQ. **4567**
0194-2557 See CARDIAC ALERT. **3700**
0194-259X See JOURNAL OF RESPIRATORY DISEASES, THE. **3950**
0194-2603 See LOS ANGELES BUSINESS JOURNAL. **690**
0194-2611 See PRIME TIME (NEW YORK). **5181**
0194-262X See SCIENCE & TECHNOLOGY LIBRARIES (NEW YORK, N.Y.). **3248**
0194-2638 See PHYSICAL & OCCUPATIONAL THERAPY IN PEDIATRICS. **4381**
0194-2735 See SMALL CITY AND REGIONAL COMMUNITY, THE. **2835**
0194-2751 See SUBURBAN NEWS (FLINT), THE. **5694**
0194-276X See SUBURBAN NEWS (READING), THE. **5690**
0194-2778 See BIOMEDICAL ENGINEERING AND COMPUTATION SERIES. **3686**
0194-2794 See T-SHIRT TIMES, THE. **1087**
0194-2824 See PROGRESS IN IMPROVING PROGRAM AND BUDGET INFORMATION FOR CONGRESSIONAL USE. **4742**
0194-2832 See ARGENTINA OUTREACH. **4504**
0194-2859 See TEACHER UPDATE. **1786**
0194-2913 See CALIFORNIA COMMUNITIES. **2816**
0194-2964 See DELMARVA FARMER, THE. **78**
0194-2972 See FNP NEWSLETTER : PRICE TRENDS OF FOOD INGREDIENTS. **2335**
0194-2980 See FNP NEWSLETTER, FOOD PACKAGING AND LABELING. **4219**
0194-3014 See NORTHERN MICHIGAN NEWS. **5693**
0194-3030 See WILDERNESS RECORD. **2209**
0194-3049 See HEALTH SYSTEMS REPORT ALMANAC ON FEDERAL HEALTH ISSUES, PROPOSALS, ADMINISTRATIVE ACTIONS, LEGISLATION, PUBLIC LAWS. **2978**
0194-3057 See RESEARCH IN LABOR ECONOMICS. SUPPLEMENT. **1707**
0194-3073 See CALIFORNIA PUBLIC EMPLOYEE RELATIONS : CPER SERIES. **1658**
0194-3081 See NEW DIRECTIONS FOR COMMUNITY COLLEGES. **1837**
0194-3111 See BLUE RIBBON FILL-IT-INS. **4858**
0194-312X See BLUE RIBBON WORD-FINDS. **4858**
0194-3146 See CIRCLE-A-WORD PUZZLES. **4859**
0194-3154 See CROSSWORD TREAT. **4859**
0194-3162 See CROSSWORD VARIETIES. **4859**
0194-3170 See FEATURED FILL-IT-INS. **4861**
0194-3189 See RING-A-WORD PUZZLES. **4865**
0194-3197 See SOAP OPERA WORD-FIND HIDDEN WORD PUZZLES. **4866**
0194-3227 See SUPERB FILL-IT-INS. **4866**
0194-3235 See SUPERB WORD-FIND PUZZLES. **4866**
0194-3243 See PRESSTIME. **4818**
0194-3278 See VARIETY CROSSPATCHES. **4867**
0194-3286 See VARIETY WORD-FIND PUZZLES. **4867**
0194-3294 See VETTE'N USA. **5427**
0194-3324 See CUSTOM HOMES. **612**
0194-3340 See WORLD RECORD GAME FISHES. **2316**
0194-3391 See INDIAN REVIEW (CHICAGO), THE. **2653**
0194-3413 See ARCHAEOLOGICAL NEWS. **257**
0194-3448 See AMERICAN JOURNAL OF THEOLOGY & PHILOSOPHY. **4340**
0194-3456 See AMERICAN FUCHSIA SOCIETY BULLETIN. **2408**
0194-3464 See NUGGETS (YREKA). **2323**
0194-3499 See EMPLOYEE BENEFITS. **1665**
0194-3537 See SENTINEL (EAST BRUNSWICK, N.J. : 1973). **5711**
0194-3545 See BANNER-GAZETTE, THE. **5662**
0194-357X See COMPUTE (GREENSBORO). **1266**
0194-3588 See DM NEWS. **923**
0194-360X See FURNITURE/TODAY. **2905**

0194-3642 See EMPLOYMENT BULLETIN (AMERICAN SOCIOLOGICAL ASSOCIATION : 1976). 4204

0194-3650 See HARVARD ARCHITECTURE REVIEW, THE. 299

0194-3669 See POLITICS (BATON ROUGE). 4491

0194-3677 See SOLON TIMES, THE. 5730

0194-3707 See BULLETIN FROM WISCONSIN LIVE STOCK BREEDERS' ASSOCIATION, THE. 208

0194-3723 See RON JANOFF'S GUIDE TO COMMERCIAL REAL ESTATE. 4847

0194-3766 See ALLIED HEALTH EDUCATION DIRECTORY. 1923

0194-3790 See HANDBOOK OF THE NATIONS. 4475

0194-3820 See LOGOS JOURNAL. 4974

0194-3839 See EQUIPMENT LEASING. 2967

0194-3847 See PREVIEW (WASHINGTON). 4076

0194-3871 See PROGRAM ADMINISTRATION REVIEW OF THE SOCIAL SECURITY DISABILITY INSURANCE AND THE SUPPLEMENTAL SECURITY INCOME VOCATIONAL REHABILITATION PROGRAMS. 1704

0194-388X See MISSISSIPPI LIBRARIES. 3231

0194-3898 See POSTGRADUATE OBSTETRICS & GYNECOLOGY. 3767

0194-3960 See RESEARCH IN HUMAN CAPITAL AND DEVELOPMENT. 1517

0194-3979 See YEARBOOK - AMERICAN SOCIETY OF PENSION ACTUARIES. 1720

0194-4010 See LANDMARK BRIEFS AND ARGUMENTS OF THE SUPREME COURT OF THE UNITED STATES : CONSTITUTIONAL LAW. 3093

0194-4029 See GRAMERCY REVIEW, THE. 3391

0194-4045 See CHRONICLE GUIDE TO GRADUATE & PROFESSIONAL STUDY. 1815

0194-407X See SPECIAL PUBLICATION - COUNCIL FOR AGRICULTURAL SCIENCE AND TECHNOLOGY. 137

0194-4142 See FACTBOOK - BUREAU OF HIGHER AND CONTINUING EDUCATION. 1823

0194-4177 See RAND MCNALLY CAMPGROUND & TRAILER PARK GUIDE, EASTERN. 4708

0194-4231 See QUARTERLY WEST. 3427

0194-424X See KUDZU (CAYCE). 3465

0194-4282 See BEEFMASTER COWMAN, THE. 207

0194-4290 See GEORGIA PHARMACEUTICAL JOURNAL. 4306

0194-4320 See NORTH AMERICAN HUNTER. 4876

0194-4347 See DENTALPRACTICE. 1322

0194-4363 See JOURNAL OF THE AMERICAN PLANNING ASSOCIATION. 2826

0194-4398 See WESTERN BACKCOUNTRY MAGAZINE. 4880

0194-4401 See WISCONSIN HOLSTEIN NEWS. 199

0194-4452 See AGRICULTURE ACROSS MICHIGAN. 53

0194-4495 See SEEDS (DECATUR, GA.). 2912

0194-4525 See MIDLANDS BUSINESS JOURNAL. 694

0194-4533 See MODERN DRUMMER. 4131

0194-455X See AGING & LEISURE LIVING. 3749

0194-4622 See GREAT LAKES SAILING SCANNER. 593

0194-4681 See WORLD PORTS (1978). 5458

0194-469X See AIRCRAFT FORECAST. 9

0194-472X See JOURNAL OF MARITAL AND FAMILY THERAPY. 2282

0194-4754 See NATIONAL HOOKUP. 4391

0194-4800 See FLORIDA ADMINISTRATIVE LAW REPORTS. 3093

0194-4835 See PREMIER HOG PRODUCER. 219

0194-4851 See TYPE WORLD. 4570

0194-4894 See TOURIST ATTRACTIONS & PARKS. 4855

0194-4959 See ERISA UPDATE, THE. 1667

0194-5025 See 68 MICRO JOURNAL. 1265

0194-5084 See PACIFIC NEWS SERVICE. 2491

0194-5106 See JOURNAL OF KANSAS PHARMACY, THE. 4311

0194-5149 See NCSL NEWSLETTER. 4031

0194-5165 See CALIFORNIA COUNTRY. 2529

0194-5173 See AMERICAN CHOW CHOW INC, THE. 4285

0194-5181 See TODAY'S OR NURSE. 3870

0194-519X See PROFESSIONALS. 3725

0194-5289 See VIEWPOINT (MARLOW HEIGHTS). 5568

0194-5319 See HOOSIER BUSINESS WOMAN, THE. 5558

0194-5327 See DAILY RECORD (NEW ORLEANS), THE. 5683

0194-5343 See HEALTH FOODS COMMUNICATOR, THE. 2343

0194-5351 See POOL & SPA NEWS. 703

0194-536X See MOUNTAINEER POSTMASTER. 2539

0194-5386 See EARTHTONE. 80

0194-5394 See TRAILS-A-WAY. OHIO EDITION. 4879

0194-5467 See PHOTOGRAPHER'S FORUM. 4374

0194-5564 See GREAT LAKES FISHERMAN (COLUMBUS, OHIO). 2304

0194-567X See KENTUCKY PHARMACIST, THE. 4313

0194-5742 See COAST WATCH. 1448

0194-5769 See DAKOTA COUNTRY. 4871

0194-5785 See CIVITAN MAGAZINE, THE. 5230

0194-5793 See BAM. 4102

0194-5912 See MAINTENANCE SUPERVISOR'S BULLETIN. 876

0194-5947 See ABA BANKING JOURNAL. 768

0194-5955 See TIMBER MART-SOUTH. 2405

0194-5998 See OTOLARYNGOLOGY AND HEAD AND NECK SURGERY. 3971

0194-6021 See HUNTINGTON BEACH INDEPENDENT. 5635

0194-6137 See CHRISTIAN LIFE COMMUNITIES HARVEST. 4945

0194-6161 See WORLD MEETINGS. SOCIAL & BEHAVIORAL SCIENCES, HUMAN SERVICES & MANAGEMENT. 5226

0194-6196 See PAYROLL EXCHANGE. 1701

0194-620X See TRAVEL AGENT INTERNACIONAL, EL. 5495

0194-6218 See PROPELLER (EAST DETROIT). 4913

0194-6307 See BEACHCOMBER, THE. 5709

0194-6366 See GERONTOLOGY SPECIAL INTEREST SECTION NEWSLETTER. 3752

0194-6382 See MENTAL HEALTH SPECIAL INTEREST SECTION NEWSLETTER. 4790

0194-6390 See DEVELOPMENTAL DISABILITIES SPECIAL INTEREST SECTION NEWSLETTER. 1877

0194-6404 See OLD CARS PRICE GUIDE. 5422

0194-6412 See EASY READER. 5634

0194-6439 See ROTARY ROCKET. 5424

0194-6498 See AWP NEWSLETTER (NORFOLK). 3365

0194-651X See HAWAII FISHING NEWS. 2305

0194-6536 See AMERICAN CHIROPRACTOR, THE. 4379

0194-6595 See INTERNATIONAL JOURNAL OF THE SOCIOLOGY OF LAW. 2984

0194-6625 See AG. REVIEW (PUTNAM, CONN.). 45

0194-6684 See WORD OF LIFE LIFE LINES. 5009

0194-6706 See DOG SPORTS. 4286

0194-6730 See SKEPTICAL INQUIRER, THE. 4243

0194-6749 See POPULAR CROSSWORDS (NEW YORK, N.Y.). 4865

0194-6803 See ARABIAN HORSE EXPRESS. 2797

0194-6854 See BALLOONING. 14

0194-6927 See VOICE OF THE TRAPPER. 4880

0194-7176 See AMERICAN HOME ECONOMICS ASSOCIATION ACTION. 2788

0194-7176 See A.H.E.A. ACTION. 2788

0194-7222 See CREATIVE REAL ESTATE MAGAZINE. 4836

0194-7230 See SUFFOLK BANNER, THE. 222

0194-7249 See BOBINA, LA. 1082

0194-7257 See LANDSCAPE CONTRACTOR, THE. 2423

0194-7303 See DOWNRIVER NEWS-HERALD, THE. 5691

0194-732X See BOSTON MONTHLY, THE. 2529

0194-7354 See NEW YORK WORKER'S COMPENSATION COMMENTS. 3152

0194-7397 See MICROWAVES PRODUCT DATA DIRECTORY. 2072

0194-7443 See ILLINOIS AGRI-NEWS. 94

0194-7508 See IMMUNOLOGY & ALLERGY PRACTICE. 3671

0194-7575 See METRO BUSINESS. 693

0194-7648 See JOURNAL OF LEGAL MEDICINE (CHICAGO. 1979), THE. 3741

0194-7710 See WESTWORD. 5644

0194-7729 See FISHING HOLES. 4872

0194-780X See SCALE SHIP MODELER. 4183

0194-7818 See HANDICAPPED REQUIREMENTS HANDBOOK. SUPPLEMENT. 4388

0194-7826 See MEGIDDO MESSAGE. 5018

0194-7834 See ALASKA BAPTIST MESSENGER. 5054

0194-7869 See COMICS JOURNAL, THE. 377

0194-7893 See LACROSSE (BALTIMORE, MD.). 4903

0194-7990 See AMERIKAI MAGYAR SZO. 5713

0194-8008 See AMERICAN CRAFT. 369

0194-8032 See HEARTBEAT (LOS ANGELES). 589

0194-8083 See KNITTING WORLD (SEABROOK, N.H.) 5184

0194-8121 See FORUM (AL-ANON), THE. 1344

0194-813X See NEW MEXICO BEVERAGE ANALYST. 2370

0194-8148 See BLACK HILLS NATIONAL FOREST PRODUCTS NEWS. 2376

0194-8172 See ARGUS (SAN FRANCISCO). 3872

0194-8210 See IRS PRACTICE AND PROCEDURES. 4734

0194-8237 See SPIDELL'S CALIFORNIA TAXLETTER. 3058

0194-8253 See WOODS 'N' WATER. 4881

0194-8261 See CAHPERD JOURNAL TIMES. 4770

0194-8326 See CARIBBEAN BUSINESS. 655

0194-8369 See SOUNDINGS. TRADE ONLY. 596

0194-844X See MEDICAL DEVICE & DIAGNOSTIC INDUSTRY. 3608

0194-8458 See CONTEMPORARY ORTHOPAEDICS. 3881

0194-8490 See DOLLAR$ENSE (LOS ANGELES). 1296

0194-8504 See CALIFORNIA STRAWBERRY REPORT. 2330

0194-8520 See MOTOR NEWS (CHICAGO). 4082

0194-8628 See NILES LIFE, THE. 5661

0194-8652 See A/C FLYER, THE. 3

0194-8679 See AUTOSOUND & COMMUNICATIONS. 5315

0194-8717 See SUPERVISOR'S SAFETY CLINIC. 4804

0194-8733 See CONVENIENCE STORE NEWS. 660

0194-8784 See NLRB ADVICE MEMORANDUM REPORTER. 3152

0194-8822 See TAX, FINANCIAL AND ESTATE PLANNING FOR THE OWNER OF A CLOSELY-HELD CORPORATION. 3119

0194-8849 See AEA ADVOCATE. 1860

0194-889X See NATIONAL PUBLIC EMPLOYMENT REPORTER. 3152

0194-8903 See CONSTRUCTION DIMENSIONS. 609

0194-8911 See SOUTH FLORIDA SPORTSCENE MAGAZINE. 4919

0194-892X See TRI-COUNTY NEWS (FENTON). 5694

0194-8954 See CASCADES EAST. 4870

ISSN Index

0194-9039 See FLIGHT REPORTS. 21
0194-9055 See QUICK FOOT. 4376
0194-9063 See SCIENTIFIC AMERICAN MEDICINE. 3639
0194-9071 See ART INSIGHT. 339
0194-908X See LAKE UNION HERALD. 5062
0194-9098 See TENNIS WEEK. 4926
0194-9101 See MERCER BUSINESS : A PUBLICATION OF MERCER COUNTY CHAMBER. 693
0194-911X See HYPERTENSION (DALLAS, TEX. 1979). 3705
0194-9160 See VISITANTE DOMINICAL, EL. 5038
0194-9179 See SONFLOWERS DISCIPLESHIP JOURNAL. 4998
0194-9225 See BUSINESS TRENDS (PETALUMA, CALIF.). 653
0194-9276 See OHIO ENGINEER, THE. 1989
0194-9314 See SURFING (SAN CLEMENTE, CALIF.). 4924
0194-9349 See YESTERYEAR (PRINCETON). 252
0194-9381 See MORTON GROVE LIFE. 5661
0194-939X See NATIONAL BUS TRADER. 5388
0194-9411 See MOTOR CRASH ESTIMATING GUIDE. 5419
0194-9535 See ESQUIRE (1979). 2533
0194-9543 See ANGUS JOURNAL. 205
0194-9640 See TIDINGS, WEST LINN. 5734
0194-9683 See PRINTED CIRCUIT FABRICATION. 2075
0194-9748 See PRESCOTT'S WEEKLY. 5630
0194-9772 See COTTON GROWER. 168
0194-9799 See LEAVEN (KANSAS CITY), THE. 5677
0194-9802 See TPA MESSENGER. 4820
0194-9993 See ATLANTIC CITY MAGAZINE. 2485
0195-0002 See MISSISSIPPI BUSINESS JOURNAL, THE. 695
0195-0037 See POOP SHEET, THE. 4912
0195-0045 See COLORADO GREEN. 2412
0195-007X See MARYLAND ANGLER, THE. 2308
0195-0088 See CONSTRUCTION PROJECT NEWS. GREATER DETROIT EDITION. 610
0195-0126 See COSTA MESA NEWS. 5634
0195-0134 See PASO ROBLES COUNTRY NEWS, THE. 5638
0195-0142 See FAVORITE CROSSWORD PUZZLES. 4861
0195-0207 See EXETER. 1091
0195-0223 See EASTERN BASKETBALL. 4893
0195-0290 See LAW ENFORCEMENT LEGAL REPORTER INCORPORATED, THE. 3168
0195-0304 See IFOAM BULLETIN. 94
0195-0320 See BMX PLUS. 428
0195-0347 See AVIATORS HOT LINE. 14
0195-0363 See UFCW ACTION. 1715
0195-0398 See GOLD BUG, THE. 789
0195-0444 See BEEF DIGEST. 207
0195-0495 See SPECIALTY ADVERTISING BUSINESS. 766
0195-0533 See REDWOOD CITY ALMANAC. 5639
0195-0576 See OIL EXPRESS. 4269
0195-0622 See LEADER (RESEARCH TRIANGLE PARK, N.C.), THE. 5723
0195-0673 See WASHINGTON AGRICULTURAL RECORD, THE. 145
0195-0681 See EPISCOPAL NEWS, THE. 4956
0195-072X See GALLERY (NEW YORK, N.Y.). 3995
0195-0746 See EXECUTIVE WEALTH ADVISORY. 674
0195-0770 See PUBLIC EMPLOYMENT PERSPECTIVE. PENNSYLVANIA. 1704
0195-0819 See CHICAGO APPAREL NEWS. 1082
0195-0843 See CITY PAPER. 5686
0195-0851 See ASTROLOGY (NEW YORK). 390
0195-0894 See SPRINGFIELD MAGAZINE (SPRINGFIELD, MO.). 2546
0195-0908 See B.A.S. SPEAKER, THE. 5316

0195-0932 See ABRASIVE ENGINEERING SOCIETY MAGAZINE. 2109
0195-0975 See 'BAMA. 4886
0195-0983 See NEW JERSEY LAWYER (MAGAZINE). 3015
0195-105X See MEMBERS CALENDAR - MUSEUM OF MODERN ART. 4091
0195-1076 See FINISHING INTERNATIONAL. 1975
0195-1157 See COMMUNITY JOBS. 1660
0195-1238 See ESTATE PLANNING & TAXATION COORDINATOR. 3118
0195-1297 See GOSPEL ADVOCATE (NASHVILLE). 4961
0195-1300 See SKIERS ADVOCATE. 4918
0195-1351 See BIBLICAL ILLUSTRATOR. 4938
0195-1416 See COLONIAL HOMES. 295
0195-1459 See SUBCONTRACTOR, THE. 629
0195-1467 See MILITARY MODELER. 4051
0195-1548 See PULPIT RESOURCE. 4988
0195-1556 See AMERICAN ISSUE (DES MOINES), THE. 1340
0195-1564 See AUTOMOTIVE EXECUTIVE (1979). 5406
0195-1580 See BUILDING BLOCKS. 3369
0195-1599 See NEW GUN WEEK, THE. 4907
0195-1661 See CORVETTE FEVER MAGAZINE. 5412
0195-1688 See WOMEN'S POLITICAL TIMES. 4500
0195-1696 See OBSCENITY LAW BULLETIN. 3020
0195-1750 See VIDEO STORE. 1142
0195-1815 See PENN JERSEY BAPTIST. 5065
0195-1874 See HOME ENERGY DIGEST, WOOD BURNING QUARTERLY. 1946
0195-1904 See PRODUCTION NEWS. 1622
0195-1920 See PHALANX (ALEXANDRIA). 2107
0195-1947 See HOG DIGEST. 212
0195-1955 See LONE STAR SIERRAN. 2177
0195-1963 See MINNESOTA REALTOR. 4841
0195-1971 See PENNSYLVANIA DAIRY FARMSHINE. 197
0195-2021 See DAILY GRAPHS. STOCK OPTION GUIDE. 896
0195-2056 See ASIANWEEK. 5633
0195-2064 See JOURNAL OF RETAIL BANKING. 795
0195-2080 See HAPPY WANDERER, THE. 5479
0195-2099 See ILLINOIS PHARMACIST (1979). 4307
0195-220X See AG. MARKET CHARTS. 45
0195-2250 See GLOBAL COMMUNICATIONS. 1112
0195-2269 See NEW DIRECTIONS FOR CHILD DEVELOPMENT. 4605
0195-2285 See MS QUARTERLY REPORT. 3838
0195-2307 See JOURNAL OF THE AMERICAN PARAPLEGIA SOCIETY. 3598
0195-2366 See MATERIAL HANDLING PRODUCT NEWS. 2104
0195-2439 See HOME COOKING. 2790
0195-2447 See GAITHERSBURG GAZETTE, THE. 5686
0195-2463 See SHOW STEER, THE. 221
0195-2498 See MT. OLIVE CHRONICLE. 5710
0195-251X See PROVISO STAR-SENTINEL. 5661
0195-2528 See LEYDEN STAR-SENTINEL. 5661
0195-2552 See YANKEE FOOD SERVICE. 2361
0195-2617 See FEDERAL GRANTS MANAGEMENT HANDBOOK. 4723
0195-2633 See BRITISH HERITAGE. 2485
0195-2641 See NEW YORK HERALD TIMES CROSSWORD PUZZLES ONLY. 4864
0195-265X See CHRISTIAN CRUSADE. 4944
0195-2692 See LOST TREASURE. 5074
0195-2714 See CULTURE & HISTORY. 2730
0195-2781 See PTA TODAY. 1775
0195-2854 See PRAIRIE STATER. 2543
0195-2870 See MAINE SNOWMOBILER. 4904

0195-2889 See JOURNAL FRANCAIS D'AMERIQUE. 5636
0195-2927 See ARIZONA STATESMAN OUTLOOK. 1101
0195-2986 See AAPG EXPLORER. 1364
0195-3117 See TRUE STORY (NEW YORK). 5075
0195-3125 See PETROLEUM/C-STORE PRODUCTS. 4272
0195-315X See INTERNAL MEDICINE ALERT. 3797
0195-3184 See HOME TEXTILES TODAY. 5351
0195-3192 See NEW JERSEY REPORTER. 4669
0195-3311 See INSIDER'S BANKING & CREDIT ALMANAC, THE. 791
0195-3346 See FCX CAROLINA COOPERATOR. 86
0195-3354 See NURSING ABSTRACTS. 3661
0195-3400 See ANISHINAABE GIIGIDOWIN. 3264
0195-3443 See MARYLAND DOCUMENTS. 419
0195-346X See BUC ... NEW BOAT PRICE GUIDE. 592
0195-3478 See INSIDE SPORTS. 4900
0195-3516 See EXIT (GLENMONT). 3386
0195-3524 See OIL SPILL INTELLIGENCE REPORT. 4270
0195-3540 See OFFICIAL BLACKBOOK PRICE GUIDE OF UNITED STATES PAPER MONEY, THE. 2782
0195-3559 See OFFICIAL BLACKBOOK PRICE GUIDE OF UNITED STATES POSTAGE STAMPS, THE. 2786
0195-3591 See CFTC DATABOOK. 894
0195-3605 See NEW ORLEANS MARDI GRAS GUIDE. 5485
0195-3613 See JOURNAL OF LABOR RESEARCH. 1682
0195-3656 See PRACTICAL LABOR LAW: COURSE MANUAL. 3153
0195-3664 See CIVIL ENGINEERING (NEW YORK, N.Y. 1979). 2021
0195-3672 See COAL SERVICE REFERENCE MANUAL. 1602
0195-3680 See ANNUAL INSTITUTE FOR CORPORATE COUNSEL. 3095
0195-3702 See DMA AERONAUTICAL CHART UPDATING MANUAL, CHUM. 18
0195-3737 See JUSTICIA (NEW YORK). 1682
0195-377X See LACUS FORUM. 3294
0195-3869 See HRAF NEWSLETTER. 5202
0195-3958 See COLEMAN GUIDE TO CAMPING & THE GREAT OUTDOORS. 4871
0195-3966 See MMI PRESS SYMPOSIUM SERIES. 986
0195-3982 See GRIFFITH OBSERVER. 395
0195-4008 See WILEY SERIES ON PERSONALITY PROCESSES. 4621
0195-4016 See NEWSLETTER - FINGER LAKES LIBRARY SYSTEM. 3235
0195-4040 See JOEL WHITBURN'S TOP POP SINGLES. 4160
0195-4105 See 3-2-1 CONTACT. 1059
0195-413X See COAL CONVERSION. 1023
0195-4148 See ART CRITICISM. 338
0195-4180 See AMCA NEWSLETTER. 2160
0195-4237 See PROGRESS IN MACROCYCLIC CHEMISTRY. 1046
0195-4253 See SPACE SCIENCE TEXT SERIES. 400
0195-4261 See BASIC AND CLINICAL IMMUNOLOGY (NEW YORK). 3667
0195-4296 See MEDIAWEEK (NEW YORK, N.Y.). 933
0195-430X See STUDIES IN THE HISTORY OF AMERICAN EDUCATION. 1786
0195-4318 See INFORMER (RALEIGH), THE. 3217
0195-4482 See DISABILITY NEWSLETTER. 2879
0195-4520 See CALIFORNIA POLL, THE. 4561
0195-4520 See FIELD POLL, THE. 5245
0195-4555 See MARINE FISH MANAGEMENT. 2308
0195-4563 See LUNDBERG LETTER. 4263

0195-4636 See WORKBOOK, THE. 1300
0195-4644 See WEST VIRGINIA BUSINESS INDEX. 719
0195-4695 See URBAN TRANSPORT NEWS. 5399
0195-4709 See QUARTERLY REPORT - STATE GAMING CONTROL BOARD. 4677
0195-475X See JOURNAL OF MAYAN LINGUISTICS. 3291
0195-4768 See FEDERAL INCOME TAX (ENGLEWOOD CLIFFS), THE. 4723
0195-4776 See LIST OF PLANTS OPERATING UNDER USDA POULTRY AND EGG GRADING AND EGG PRODUCTS INSPECTION PROGRAMS. 214
0195-4784 See READINGS IN MANAGEMENT : ANNUAL EDITIONS. 884
0195-4806 See ANNUAL REPORT TO THE PRESIDENT AND THE CONGRESS ON THE WEATHERIZATION ASSISTANCE PROGRAM. 1932
0195-4822 See IRVINE WORLD NEWS, THE. 5636
0195-4857 See TECHNICAL SERVICES LAW LIBRARIAN. 3252
0195-489X See LANDSCAPE SYSTEMS. 2423
0195-4911 See CA SELECTS: ATOMIC SPECTROSCOPY. 998
0195-4938 See CA SELECTS: CHEMICAL INSTRUMENTATION. 999
0195-4946 See CA SELECTS: CHEMICAL PROCESSING APPARATUS. 999
0195-4962 See CA SELECTS: ELECTROPHORESIS. 1001
0195-4970 See CA SELECTS: EMULSION POLYMERIZATION. 1001
0195-4989 See CA SELECTS: FLUIDIZED SOLIDS TECHNOLOGY. 1002
0195-4997 See CA SELECTS: FUEL & LUBRICANT ADDITIVES. 1003
0195-5012 See CA SELECTS: INORGANIC & ORGANOMETALLIC REACTION MECHANISMS. 1004
0195-5020 See CA SELECTS: ION-CONTAINING POLYMERS. 1004
0195-5039 See CA SELECTS: LASER APPLICATIONS. 1004
0195-5063 See CA SELECTS: OPTICAL & PHOTOSENSITIVE MATERIALS. 1006
0195-5071 See CA SELECTS: OPTIMIZATION OF ORGANIC REACTIONS. 1006
0195-508X See CA SELECTS: ORGANIC STEREOCHEMISTRY. 1006
0195-5101 See CA SELECTS: ORGANOTIN CHEMISTRY. 1006
0195-511X See CA SELECTS: PLASTIC FILMS. 1007
0195-5128 See CA SELECTS: POLYMER MORPHOLOGY. 1008
0195-5136 See CA SELECTS: PORPHYRINS. 1008
0195-5152 See CA SELECTS: SURFACE ANALYSIS. 1010
0195-5160 See CA SELECTS: SYNFUELS. 1010
0195-5179 See CA SELECTS: SYNTHETIC MACROCYCLIC COMPOUNDS. 1010
0195-5187 See CA SELECTS: THERMAL ANALYSIS. 1010
0195-5195 See CA SELECTS: ULTRAFILTRATION. 1010
0195-5209 See CA SELECTS: ULTRAVIOLET & VISIBLE SPECTROSCOPY. 1010
0195-5217 See CA SELECTS: HIGH PERFORMANCE LIQUID CHROMATOGRAPHY. 1003
0195-5225 See SUREPAY UPDATE. 813
0195-5233 See WASHINGTON ACTION REPORTER. 4694
0195-5241 See REPORT - NATIONAL CENTER FOR STATE COURTS. 3142
0195-5276 See REFUGEES & HUMAN RIGHTS NEWSLETTER. 1921
0195-5292 See CAPITAL ENERGY LETTER. 1935
0195-5322 See WASHINGTON REPORT (AMERICAN ADVERTISING FEDERATION). 767
0195-5365 See SCIENCE FICTION CHRONICLE. 3434

0195-5373 See ATOMIC SPECTROSCOPY. 1013
0195-539X See WHO'S WHO IN CALIFORNIA BUSINESS AND FINANCE. 436
0195-5411 See FIRMS IN THE 8(A) BUSINESS DEVELOPMENT PROGRAM. 2261
0195-542X See PHARMACY & THERAPEUTICS FORUM. 4323
0195-5551 See ISSUE PAPER / UNIVERSITY OF PENNSYLVANIA, NATIONAL HEALTH CARE MANAGEMENT CENTER. 4785
0195-5594 See GENESIS OF BEHAVIOR. 4587
0195-5616 See VETERINARY CLINICS OF NORTH AMERICA. SMALL ANIMAL PRACTICE, THE. 5525
0195-5632 See ARMY MOTORS. 4036
0195-5640 See SKI RUN. 4918
0195-5705 See FOCUS (MADISON). 1491
0195-5713 See HOUSE OF DELEGATES REPORTS (1966). 3856
0195-573X See PSITTACOSIS SURVEILLANCE. 4797
0195-5756 See ANNUAL INSTITUTE ON SECURITIES REGULATION. 890
0195-5780 See PLATE WORLD. 2593
0195-5799 See PIEGAN STORYTELLER, THE. 2754
0195-5810 See MASSACHUSETTS DIRECTORY OF MANUFACTURERS. 3484
0195-5845 See MASSACHUSETTS LEGAL DIRECTORY, WITH RHODE ISLAND SECTION. 3007
0195-5861 See FORESTRY RESEARCH WEST. 2382
0195-5888 See CONSTITUTION, JEFFERSON'S MANUAL, AND RULES OF THE HOUSE OF REPRESENTATIVES OF THE UNITED STATES. 4640
0195-5896 See EDUCATIONAL MARKETER YELLOW PAGES. 4564
0195-5926 See PEDIATRIC SOCIAL WORK. 5300
0195-5934 See PRIME TIMES (MADISON). 5181
0195-5942 See CONFERENCE NOTES - AMERICAN INDUSTRIAL DEVELOPMENT COUNCIL, INC. 1602
0195-5969 See STEPFAMILIES. 2286
0195-5985 See MEMBER ROSTER - ROBERT MORRIS ASSOCIATES. 797
0195-6000 See JOURNAL OF PUBLIC AND INTERNATIONAL AFFAIRS. 5206
0195-6043 See CONTINUUM (L. D. PANKEY INSTITUTE). 1319
0195-6051 See JOURNAL OF POPULAR FILM AND TELEVISION, THE. 4073
0195-6086 See SYMBOLIC INTERACTION. 5264
0195-6108 See AMERICAN JOURNAL OF NEURORADIOLOGY. 3827
0195-6124 See DIRECTORY - OUTDOOR WRITERS ASSOCIATION OF AMERICA. 2919
0195-6132 See PROGRAM REPORT (NATIONAL SCIENCE FOUNDATION (US)). 5142
0195-6159 See MISSOURI ECONOMIC INDICATORS. 1574
0195-6167 See MUSIC THEORY SPECTRUM. 4135
0195-6175 See CALIFORNIA POLITICAL WEEK. 4636
0195-6183 See WOMAN POET. 3473
0195-6191 See MEAN MOUNTAIN MUSIC. 4130
0195-6221 See WHO'S WHO IN THE DENTAL LABORATORY INDUSTRY. 1337
0195-623X See PROCEEDINGS - INTERNATIONAL SYMPOSIUM ON MULTIPLE-VALUED LOGIC. 1230
0195-6264 See PRINCIPLES AND PRESENTATION : BANKING. 803
0195-6272 See PREAKNESS, THE. 2801
0195-6299 See WOMAN'S DAY GREAT HOLIDAY BAKING IDEAS. 2793
0195-6310 See COMPARATIVE SOCIAL RESEARCH. 5242
0195-6329 See OCCASIONAL PAPERS - VIRGINIA LIBRARY ASSOCIATION. 3238
0195-6418 See BELL & HOWELL'S NEWSPAPER INDEX TO THE LOS ANGELES TIMES. 5691

0195-6450 See DEFENSE MONITOR, THE. 4041
0195-6515 See PACIFIC FISHING. 2310
0195-6531 See TAX GUIDE. WEEKLY ALERT. 4752
0195-6574 See ENERGY JOURNAL (CAMBRIDGE, MASS.). 1940
0195-6620 See STANGER REPORT, THE. 916
0195-6639 See STATE LEGISLATIVE LEADERSHIP, COMMITTEES, AND STAFF. 4688
0195-6655 See INTER-AMERICAN MUSIC REVIEW. 4123
0195-6663 See APPETITE. 4187
0195-6671 See CRETACEOUS RESEARCH. 4226
0195-668X See EUROPEAN HEART JOURNAL. 3704
0195-6698 See EUROPEAN JOURNAL OF COMBINATORICS. 3505
0195-6701 See JOURNAL OF HOSPITAL INFECTION, THE. 3714
0195-671X See WORKERS' COMPENSATION MANUAL FOR UNION REPRESENTATIVES. 3155
0195-6728 See DISCOTHEQUE MAGAZINE. 1313
0195-6744 See AMERICAN JOURNAL OF EDUCATION (CHICAGO). 1724
0195-6752 See JOURNAL OF HISTORICAL REVIEW, THE. 2621
0195-6779 See MEDIA HISTORY DIGEST. 2922
0195-6795 See MEMBERSHIP DIRECTORY - NATIONAL SOCIETY OF FUND RAISING EXECUTIVES. 798
0195-6809 See CONNECTICUT LEGAL DIRECTORY, THE. 2955
0195-6825 See TEXT OF "A" PAPERS FROM THE WINTER MEETING - IEEE POWER ENGINEERING SOCIETY. 2084
0195-6876 See ENGINEERING TIMES (WASHINGTON, D.C.). 1974
0195-6922 See PUBLIC LIBRARY PROGRAM GUIDELINES. 3243
0195-6965 See WORLD NATURAL GAS. 4282
0195-699X See ENERGY RESEARCH PROGRAMS. 1941
0195-7015 See CLINICAL APHASIOLOGY. 3830
0195-7023 See WHEELMEN, THE. 429
0195-7074 See LOUISIANA CONTRACTOR. 619
0195-7163 See ARCADIA BIBLIOGRAPHICA VIRORUM ERUDITORUM. 407
0195-7171 See MULTIPLE LINEAR REGRESSION VIEWPOINTS. 3523
0195-7228 See SELECTED INDUSTRIAL AIR POLLUTION CONTROL EQUIPMENT. 2243
0195-7236 See ANL-HEP-CP (ARGONNE NATIONAL LABORATORY, HIGH ENERGY PHYSICS DIVISION). 4396
0195-7252 See NEWSLETTER - INTERNATIONAL PRISONERS AID ASSOCIATION. 3170
0195-7260 See PAPERS IN ROMANCE. 3309
0195-7295 See VIDEOLOG : PROGRAMS FOR THE HEALTH SCIENCES, THE. 4806
0195-7317 See FODOR'S CIVIL WAR SITES. 5471
0195-7333 See LEFT REVIEW (KENT). 4543
0195-7341 See SUMMARIES OF FY ... RESEARCH IN THE CHEMICAL SCIENCES. 993
0195-735X See GERMAN AND CENTRAL EUROPEAN EMIGRATION. 1918
0195-7384 See JE ME SOUVIENS. 2455
0195-7392 See STATE AND LOCAL GRANT AWARDS. 4749
0195-7414 See RETAIL CREDIT SURVEY FOR SEVENTH FEDERAL RESERVE DISTRICT. 809
0195-7449 See RESEARCH IN RACE AND ETHNIC RELATIONS. 2272
0195-7473 See POLITICAL COMMUNICATION. 4489
0195-7481 See HOLLYWOOD REPORTER TV SPECIAL, THE. 4072
0195-749X See FEDERAL REGULATORY DIRECTORY. 4648
0195-7503 See EAST-WEST TRADE, WORLD MARKETS. 832
0195-7511 See MOVING FORCE. 3012

0195-752X *See* MISSOURI WATER QUALITY REPORT. 1416

0195-7538 *See* SCI RECORD BOOK OF TROPHY ANIMALS, THE. 4878

0195-7546 *See* FILMROW. 4071

0195-7597 *See* JOURNAL FOR VOCATIONAL SPECIAL NEEDS EDUCATION, THE. 1880

0195-7627 *See* NEW JERSEY BELL JOURNAL. 1160

0195-7643 *See* WHITTIER LAW REVIEW. 3075

0195-766X *See* MENTAL HEALTH YEARBOOK/DIRECTORY, THE. 4791

0195-7678 *See* COMPARATIST, THE. 3377

0195-7686 *See* URBAN, STATE AND LOCAL LAW NEWSLETTER. 3070

0195-7732 *See* WOMEN & POLITICS. 4500

0195-7740 *See* PROCEEDINGS OF THE ... ANNUAL MEETING OF THE NATIONAL COUNCIL ON RADIATION PROTECTION AND MEASUREMENTS. 3944

0195-7759 *See* MYRA WALDO'S TRAVEL GUIDE TO THE ORIENT AND ASIA. 5485

0195-7767 *See* MYRA WALDO'S TRAVEL GUIDE TO THE SOUTH PACIFIC. 5485

0195-7775 *See* PATIENT ACCOUNTS. 3790

0195-7791 *See* SOCIAL SCIENCE MONITOR. 5220

0195-7805 *See* INDIANA UNDERWRITER, THE. 2882

0195-7813 *See* MANUSCRIPT SOCIETY NEWS, THE. 2774

0195-7848 *See* CUMBERLAND JOURNAL. 318

0195-7910 *See* AMERICAN JOURNAL OF FORENSIC MEDICINE AND PATHOLOGY, THE. 3739

0195-7953 *See* COSMOPOLITAN LIVING. 2789

0195-7996 *See* UNITED STATES PHARMACOPEIA, THE. 4331

0195-8011 *See* AMS STUDIES IN THE RENAISSANCE. 2673

0195-802X *See* HOFSTRA UNIVERSITY CULTURAL & INTERCULTURAL STUDIES. 3394

0195-8054 *See* SILVER & GOLD REPORT. 914

0195-8097 *See* ASIAN VOICE. 2722

0195-8100 *See* SPORTS LITERATURE INDEX. 4923

0195-8135 *See* CUBAN CHRONOLOGY. 4519

0195-8194 *See* MOBILITY (WASHINGTON). 695

0195-8208 *See* ART & ANTIQUES. 337

0195-8224 *See* RESEARCH REVIEW - LITTLE BIG HORN ASSOCIATES. 2757

0195-8232 *See* ARMAMENT & DEFENSE SURVEY. 4035

0195-8259 *See* COMPARATIVE CLIMATIC DATA FOR THE UNITED STATES. 1424

0195-833X *See* INSIDE SEMC. 4089

0195-8402 *See* HEALTH EDUCATION QUARTERLY. 4779

0195-8410 *See* FOREST INSECT AND DISEASE CONDITIONS IN THE NORTHERN REGION. 2380

0195-8437 *See* FARM, RANCH & COUNTRY VACATIONS. 5469

0195-8453 *See* JOURNAL OF THE ROCKY MOUNTAIN MEDIEVAL AND RENAISSANCE ASSOCIATION. 2621

0195-8461 *See* BLUE BOOK OF MAJOR HOMEBUILDERS, THE. 601

0195-8526 *See* COMPU-FAX. 1175

0195-8593 *See* PHOENIX (STANFORD, CALIF.). 243

0195-8623 *See* SPORTS LAW REPORTER. 3058

0195-8631 *See* HEALTH CARE FINANCING REVIEW. 2897

0195-864X *See* QUARTERLY / SAN BERNARDINO COUNTY MUSEUM ASSOCIATION. 4095

0195-8658 *See* CALIFORNIA WATER. 5531

0195-8674 *See* CUNA NATIONAL MEMBER SURVEY. 786

0195-8747 *See* STAINLESS STEEL AND ALLOY TOOL STEEL: U.S. IMPORTERS' PRICES, UNSHIPPED ORDERS, AND INVENTORIES, ANNUAL SURVEY. 4020

0195-8836 *See* CHILD ABUSE AND NEGLECT GRANTS PROGRAM. 5277

0195-8895 *See* WORLD PRESS REVIEW. 4539

0195-8917 *See* PROCEEDINGS OF THE CONGRESS OF THE INTERNATIONAL INSTITUTE OF PUBLIC FINANCE. 4742

0195-895X *See* BEST NEWSPAPER WRITING. 2917

0195-8984 *See* ELECTRONIC NEW PRODUCT DIRECTORY, THE. 2047

0195-9018 *See* HANDBOOK OF ECONOMIC STATISTICS (WASHINGTON). 1533

0195-9034 *See* YEARBOOK OF AMERICAN AND CANADIAN CHURCHES. 5010

0195-9050 *See* CSA JOURNAL, THE. 5230

0195-9077 *See* BULLETIN - SPECIAL LIBRARIES ASSOCIATION, NORTH CAROLINA CHAPTER. 3198

0195-9085 *See* HORIZONS IN BIBLICAL THEOLOGY. 5017

0195-9093 *See* NAME AUTHORITIES. CUMULATIVE MICROFORM EDITION. 3232

0195-9131 *See* MEDICINE AND SCIENCE IN SPORTS AND EXERCISE. 3955

0195-9174 *See* PROBE TELECOMMUNICATIONS JOURNAL. 1162

0195-9182 *See* REPORT ON EXECUTIVE PREREQUISITES. 1707

0195-9190 *See* STATUS (SCOTTSDALE). 2082

0195-9204 *See* LEADERSHIP (WASHINGTON). 875

0195-9212 *See* BAHAI NEWS (WILMETTE). 5042

0195-9247 *See* CONTRACTING FOR SERVICES; COURSE MANUAL. 3146

0195-9255 *See* ENVIRONMENTAL IMPACT ASSESSMENT REVIEW. 2167

0195-9271 *See* INTERNATIONAL JOURNAL OF INFRARED AND MILLIMETER WAVES. 4435

0195-928X *See* INTERNATIONAL JOURNAL OF THERMOPHYSICS. 4406

0195-9298 *See* JOURNAL OF NONDESTRUCTIVE EVALUATION. 2104

0195-931X *See* STATISTICAL YEARBOOK OF THE WESTERN LUMBER INDUSTRY. 2399

0195-9328 *See* ANALISIS LATINOAMERICANO. 4515

0195-9344 *See* QUARTERLY INJURY & ILLNESS INCIDENCE REPORT. 2868

0195-9352 *See* NEW JERSEY DIRECTORY OF MANUFACTURERS. 3485

0195-9387 *See* CHRISTIAN ANTI-COMMUNISM CRUSADE. 4540

0195-9409 *See* MONTHLY F.O.B. PRICE SUMMARY PAST SALES. INLAND MILLS. 2403

0195-9425 *See* JOURNAL OF SECURITY ADMINISTRATION. 3168

0195-9468 *See* SPENSER STUDIES. 3471

0195-9476 *See* POPULAR SPORTS. SOCCER ILLUSTRATED. 4912

0195-9484 *See* AMERICAN CONSTRUCTION INDUSTRY DIRECTORY. 598

0195-9492 *See* INDEX TO GOVERNMENT REGULATION. 2981

0195-9549 *See* INTERCHANGE (PHILADELPHIA). 4784

0195-9557 *See* MULTIPLE IMAGING PROCEDURES. 3944

0195-9565 *See* SAUNDERS MONOGRAPHS IN CLINICAL ORTHOPAEDICS. 3884

0195-9581 *See* WASHINGTON CREDIT LETTER PRIVACY REPORT. 3072

0195-959X *See* WASHINGTON CREDIT LETTER DIGEST. 3072

0195-962X *See* GALLUP POLL, THE. 5246

0195-9638 *See* CHICAGO FACES. 2727

0195-9700 *See* EDUCATION'S FEDERAL FUNDING ALERT. 1743

0195-9727 *See* BAGNALL'S VPO INDUSTRY NEWS. 5377

0195-9735 *See* CONTEST HOTLINE. 4859

0195-9743 *See* WOMAN IN HISTORY. 5569

0195-976X *See* PROCEEDINGS OF THE HEALTH POLICY FORUM. 4796

0195-9794 *See* NATIONAL ENVIRONMENTAL IMPACT PROJECTION. 2237

0195-9824 *See* HOSPITAL PUBLIC RELATIONS. 760

0195-9840 *See* CONGRESS AND HEALTH. 4772

0195-9859 *See* DIRECTORY OF ADULT DAY CARE CENTERS. 5282

0196-0008 *See* AVERY INDEX TO ARCHITECTURAL PERIODICALS. SUPPLEMENT [MICROFORM] / COLUMBIA UNIVERSITY. 293

0196-0008 *See* AVERY INDEX TO ARCHITECTURAL PERIODICALS. SECOND EDITION. REVISED AND ENLARGED. SUPPLEMENT. 311

0196-0016 *See* FTC : WATCH. 2972

0196-0024 *See* MYRA WALDO'S TRAVEL GUIDE TO SOUTH AMERICA. 5485

0196-0032 *See* MYRA WALDO'S RESTAURANT GUIDE TO NEW YORK CITY AND VICINITY. 5072

0196-0040 *See* NATIONAL SQUARE DANCE DIRECTORY. 1314

0196-0075 *See* LIBRARY & ARCHIVAL SECURITY. 3224

0196-0091 *See* EPA PUBLICATIONS BIBLIOGRAPHY. 2184

0196-0121 *See* THANATOLOGY ABSTRACTS. 4620

0196-0156 *See* AUTOMOTIVE Q & A. 5407

0196-0164 *See* REPORTING ON READING. 1778

0196-0180 *See* AMERICANA ANNUAL, THE. 1923

0196-0202 *See* EAR AND HEARING. 3887

0196-0229 *See* RECOMBINANT DNA TECHNICAL BULLETIN. 3696

0196-0237 *See* MUSEOLOGY / TEXAS TECH UNIVERSITY. 4092

0196-0369 *See* POLICY RESEARCH PROJECT REPORT. 4674

0196-0377 *See* NEWSLETTER - TENNESSEE ANTHROPOLOGICAL ASSOCIATION. 242

0196-0407 *See* PROFESSIONAL STANDARDS REVIEW ORGANIZATIONS. 4796

0196-0555 *See* DIRECTORY OF WORLD CHEMICAL PRODUCERS. 1024

0196-058X *See* OCCUPATIONAL HEALTH AND SAFETY LETTER. 2866

0196-0598 *See* ENVIRONMENTAL HEALTH LETTER. 2228

0196-0636 *See* NEVADA AGRICULTURAL STATISTICS. 155

0196-0644 *See* ANNALS OF EMERGENCY MEDICINE. 3723

0196-0652 *See* ABIRA DIGEST. 429

0196-0709 *See* AMERICAN JOURNAL OF OTOLARYNGOLOGY. 3885

0196-0717 *See* SOUTHWEST & TEXAS WATER WORKS JOURNAL. 5539

0196-0725 *See* SISKIYOU PIONEER IN FOLKLORE, FACT AND FICTION, THE. 2324

0196-075X *See* WATER LINE NEWSLETTER. 5543

0196-0768 *See* SMITHSONIAN CONTRIBUTIONS TO THE MARINE SCIENCES. 1457

0196-0776 *See* ALASKA OPEN-FILE REPORT. 1365

0196-0784 *See* CONGRESSIONAL INSIGHT. 4469

0196-0792 *See* TECHNOLOGY NEWS - UNITED STATES. BUREAU OF MINES. 2152

0196-0830 *See* CUBA UPDATE. 4541

0196-0857 *See* AG IMPACT. 45

0196-0881 *See* MAPLINE. 2582

0196-0911 *See* EQUIPPING YOUTH. 1063

0196-092X *See* YOUNG SUPERSTARS. 1072

0196-1004 *See* CPC SALARY SURVEY. 4203

0196-1039 *See* BULLETIN (ALABAMA MUSEUM OF NATURAL HISTORY). 4163

0196-1055 *See* FODOR'S SUNBELT LEISURE GUIDE. 5473

0196-1063 *See* NORTHERN SOCIAL SCIENCE REVIEW. 5211

0196-1098 *See* STATE INVESTMENT PLAN. 2836

0196-1136 *See* PRINCETON RECOLLECTOR. 2755

0196-1152 See RESEARCH IN SOCIAL PROBLEMS AND PUBLIC POLICY. 5255

0196-1179 See POLYGRAPH LAW REPORTER. 3029

0196-125X See ARMS CONTROL TODAY. 3124

0196-1292 See CONSULTANTS AND CONSULTING ORGANIZATIONS DIRECTORY. 659

0196-1306 See COLUMNS (MADISON). 2729

0196-1349 See FEDERAL INCOME TAX GUIDE. 4723

0196-1357 See WATER-RESOURCES INVESTIGATIONS OF THE U.S. GEOLOGICAL SURVEY NEW MEXICO DISTRICT. 5547

0196-1365 See INTERNATIONAL JOURNAL OF THERAPEUTIC COMMUNITIES. 3589

0196-1381 See WINE TRADE (SAN FRANCISCO), THE. 2373

0196-1497 See OPEN FILE REPORT MICROFORM / U.S. GEOLOGICAL SURVEY. 1390

0196-1500 See WYOMING CONTRIBUTIONS TO ANTHROPOLOGY. 247

0196-1527 See MODERN AVIATION LIBRARY. 29

0196-1551 See JOB OPENINGS FOR ECONOMISTS. 4205

0196-1586 See SHOWCASE (MINNEAPOLIS). 4153

0196-1594 See BLACK BAG (WASHINGTON), THE. 3557

0196-1608 See CHECKLIST OF OFFICIAL PENNSYLVANIA PUBLICATIONS. 413

0196-1683 See SMALL TOWN. 2835

0196-1705 See STOCK PICTURE, THE. 916

0196-173X See RESEARCH LIBRARIES GROUP NEWS, THE. 3245

0196-1772 See SULFUR REPORTS. 1038

0196-1780 See CURRENT LAW INDEX. 3080

0196-1799 See LITA NEWSLETTER. 3228

0196-1845 See DIRECTORY OF SUPERMARKET, GROCERY, AND CONVENIENCE STORE CHAINS. 2333

0196-1853 See SINISTER WISDOM. 2796

0196-187X See FIGA. 4117

0196-1934 See ADVANCES IN THANATOLOGY. 4572

0196-1942 See ASSOCIATION TRENDS. 640

0196-1950 See TAX MONTHLY FOR ASSOCIATIONS. 4753

0196-1977 See LIPP. LIBRARY INSIGHTS, PROMOTION & PROGRAMS. 3228

0196-1993 See RESEARCH PAPER PSW. 2393

0196-2000 See JOURNAL OF SOCIAL RECONSTRUCTION. 5207

0196-2019 See JOURNAL OF THE MODOC COUNTY HISTORICAL SOCIETY. 2742

0196-2035 See DENVER JOURNAL OF INTERNATIONAL LAW AND POLICY. 3126

0196-2043 See OREGON LAW REVIEW. 3023

0196-2051 See PENNSYLVANIA BAR ASSOCIATION QUARTERLY. 3025

0196-206X See JOURNAL OF DEVELOPMENTAL AND BEHAVIORAL PEDIATRICS. 3904

0196-2078 See MCCONNAUGHEY BULLETIN (MCCONNAUGHEY AND VARIANTS) OF THE MCCONNAUGHEY SOCIETY OF AMERICA, INC, THE. 5233

0196-2086 See AMERICAN CLASSICAL LEAGUE NEWSLETTER. 2527

0196-2094 See GENERAL TECHNICAL REPORT PSW. 2383

0196-2140 See FERNALD CLUB YEARBOOK. 5583

0196-2175 See WEST VIRGINIA FOLKLORE JOURNAL. 2325

0196-2221 See ANTHOLOGY OF MAGAZINE VERSE AND YEARBOOK OF AMERICAN POETRY (1980). 3460

0196-2272 See WARMAN'S ANTIQUES AND THEIR PRICES. 252

0196-2353 See CORRECTIONAL SERVICES NEWS. 3161

0196-2361 See SPECIAL REPORT (STATE UNIVERSITY OF NEW YORK AT STONY BROOK. MARINE SCIENCES RESEARCH CENTER). 473

0196-2485 See PACIFIC DAILY NEWS. 5802

0196-2493 See NRDC WORLD ENVIRONMENT ALERT. 2201

0196-2515 See MARINE RESOURCE BULLETIN. 1452

0196-2523 See HIGHLIGHTS (SAIPAN). 4654

0196-254X See TIE REPORT. 1714

0196-2558 See PUBLIC GAMING NEWSLETTER. 4865

0196-2604 See MOODY STREET IRREGULARS. 3413

0196-2655 See VETERANS BENEFITS UNDER CURRENT EDUCATIONAL PROGRAMS. INFORMATION BULLETIN. 1789

0196-2671 See HEART OF TEXAS RECORDS. 2452

0196-2728 See CHAIRMAN'S REPORT - NATIONAL ARTHRITIS ADVISORY BOARD. 3804

0196-2752 See CANA, INC. 3852

0196-2809 See COUNTRIES OF THE WORLD AND THEIR LEADERS YEARBOOK. 2559

0196-2884 See SAN FERNANDO POETRY JOURNAL. 3470

0196-2892 See IEEE TRANSACTIONS ON GEOSCIENCE AND REMOTE SENSING. 1406

0196-2981 See FACTS ON FILE YEARBOOK. 2616

0196-3007 See PERSPECTIVES ON FILM. 4076

0196-3023 See LLA BULLETIN. 3228

0196-304X See FORENSIC QUARTERLY, THE. 1111

0196-3090 See GEOLOGICAL MILESTONES. 1378

0196-3120 See HORIZONS. 23

0196-3163 See MEMBERSHIP DIRECTORY - NATIONAL ABORTION FEDERATION. 3765

0196-318X See SUFFOLK UNIVERSITY LAW SCHOOL ALUMNI DIRECTORY. 1103

0196-3198 See TEXAS BUSINESS EDUCATION ASSOCIATION YEARBOOK. 715

0196-321X See GENERAL TECHNICAL REPORT FPL. 2401

0196-3228 See NORTHWESTERN JOURNAL OF INTERNATIONAL LAW & BUSINESS. 3102

0196-3236 See WASHINGTON OPERA MAGAZINE, THE. 4158

0196-3295 See NSFRE JOURNAL. 5299

0196-3309 See CMLEA JOURNAL. 3202

0196-3317 See LITIGATING AN ANTITRUST CASE. 3101

0196-3376 See RESEARCH NOTE PSW. 2393

0196-3457 See INTER-CITY WAGE & SALARY DIFFERENTIALS. 1680

0196-3465 See AMERICA'S OUTSTANDING NAMES AND FACES. 429

0196-3481 See PRAIRIE STATE PATRIOT. 2755

0196-3511 See DIRECTORY OF THE AGRICULTURAL RESEARCH SERVICE. 79

0196-3538 See ARAB-ASIAN AFFAIRS. 4464

0196-3546 See GOLD & SILVER SURVEY. 4003

0196-3554 See CHINA ECONOMIC REPORT. 1469

0196-3562 See NEAR EAST SERIES. 2659

0196-3570 See WORLD LITERATURE TODAY. 3454

0196-3589 See ROPER REPORTS. 5256

0196-3597 See ARMED FORCES JOURNAL INTERNATIONAL. 4035

0196-3619 See TECHNICAL MONOGRAPH - PARENTERAL DRUG ASSOCIATION, INC. 4330

0196-3627 See VETERINARY RADIOLOGY & ULTRASOUND. 5526

0196-3635 See JOURNAL OF ANDROLOGY. 581

0196-3643 See INFORMATION CHICAGO. 2535

0196-3651 See MYRA WALDO'S TRAVEL GUIDE TO SOUTHERN EUROPE. 5485

0196-3678 See CREDIT UNION DIRECTORY. 786

0196-3716 See GENETIC ENGINEERING. 545

0196-3767 See ENVIRONMENTAL REGULATORY ADVISOR. 3112

0196-3813 See CHAN. CONSUMER HEALTH ACTION NETWORK. 1294

0196-3821 See RESEARCH IN FINANCE. 808

0196-383X See ROADRUNNER REFUNDER. 1299

0196-3856 See NEWS FROM ABMAC. 3621

0196-3880 See PROCEEDINGS OF THE TOPOLOGY CONFERENCE, THE. 3528

0196-3953 See U.S. TRADE WITH THE COMMUNIST COUNTRIES BY SEVEN DIGIT COMMODITY CODE FOR 856

0196-402X See RECORD (NORWOOD). 1993

0196-4119 See LUSK'S DISTRICT OF COLUMBIA REAL ESTATE DIRECTORY SERVICE. 4840

0196-4143 See D-LIST. 4298

0196-416X See NORTH CENTRAL NEW MEXICO SALARY SURVEY. 1695

0196-4194 See FAYETTE LEGAL JOURNAL. 2968

0196-4224 See PRIVATE ACTS OF THE STATE OF TENNESSEE PASSED BY THE GENERAL ASSEMBLY. 4674

0196-4259 See GENEALOGIST (MANCHESTER, N.H.), THE. 2450

0196-4283 See JOURNAL OF FOODSERVICE SYSTEMS. 2347

0196-4399 See CLINICAL MICROBIOLOGY NEWSLETTER. 561

0196-4410 See ITS ANNUAL TECHNICAL PROGRESS REPORT. 1158

1067-3849 See PHILLIPS BUSINESS INFORMATION'S INTERACTIVE VIDEO NEWS. 4372

0196-4437 See PUBLIC EMPLOYMENT (1965). 4676

0196-4577 See OREGON BLUE BOOK. 4671

0196-4585 See MANUAL FOR THE GENERAL COURT. 4664

0196-4593 See GRANTS FOR RESEARCH ON LAW AND GOVERNMENT IN EDUCATION. 1748

0196-4607 See SINO-US TRADE STATISTICS. 733

0196-4623 See NEW YORK RED BOOK, THE. 4484

0196-4658 See STANDARD & POOR'S DIVIDEND RECORD. 915

0196-4666 See STANDARD & POOR'S INDUSTRY SURVEYS. 1522

0196-4674 See STANDARD & POOR'S CORPORATION RECORDS. CURRENT NEWS EDITION. 915

0196-4682 See WPA, WRITING PROGRAM ADMINISTRATION. 3454

0196-4704 See DIRECTORY OF COLLEGES OFFERING COURSES AND DEGREES BY MAIL. 1820

0196-4712 See NONRUBBER FOOTWEAR: ANNUAL SURVEY OF PRODUCERS AND IMPORTERS. 847

0196-4720 See HISTORICAL REPORT OF THE SECRETARY OF STATE, ARKANSAS. 4476

0196-4739 See OFF. MAN., STATE MO. 4670

0196-4755 See MISSISSIPPI OFFICIAL AND STATISTICAL REGISTER. 4698

0196-4763 See CYTOMETRY (NEW YORK, N.Y.). 535

0196-4801 See SOCIAL ANARCHISM. 4546

0196-4852 See NEW MEXICO STATE MEDICAL FACILITIES PLAN. 3620

0196-4879 See DATA FROM THE CLIENT ORIENTED DATA ACQUISITION PROCESS. ANNUAL DATA. 1342

0196-4895 See NEW JERSEY NURSE (1978). 3862

0196-4909 See FORWARD PLAN FOR THE HEALTH SERVICES ADMINISTRATION. 4776

0196-4925 See ICPM. SERIES 1. 3918

0196-4933 See JOURNAL - ASSOCIATION FOR HEALTHCARE PHILANTHROPY (U.S.). 3786

0196-4976 See MEMBERSHIP LIST - VIRGINIA GENEALOGICAL SOCIETY. 2460

0196-4984 See BASIC EDUCATION (WASHINGTON, D.C.). 1727

0196-5034 See FOUNDATION BULLETIN (NEW YORK). 2785

0196-5042 See EDUCATIONAL RESEARCH QUARTERLY. 1742

0196-5050 See SIGNAGE QUARTERLY. 766

0196-5069 See U.S. PUBLICITY DIRECTORY. RADIO & TV. 1142

0196-5077 See U.S. PUBLICITY DIRECTORY. NEWSPAPERS. 2925

0196-5085 See U.S. PUBLICITY DIRECTORY. MAGAZINES. 2925

0196-5093 See U.S. PUBLICITY DIRECTORY. BUSINESS & FINANCE. 2925

0196-5107 See U.S. PUBLICITY DIRECTORY. COMMUNICATION SERVICES. 2925

0196-514X See FINANCIAL FREEDOM REPORT. 898

0196-5174 See VIRGINIA CONTINUING LEGAL EDUCATION BULLETIN. 3071

0196-5204 See SIAM JOURNAL ON SCIENTIFIC AND STATISTICAL COMPUTING. 3535

0196-5220 See SEYMOUR BRITCHKY'S RESTAURANT LETTER. 5073

0196-5239 See MISSOURI GEOCODE LIST. 2569

0196-5247 See MISSOURI HEALTH MANPOWER. 3915

0196-5255 See APSA DIRECTORY OF DEPARTMENT CHAIRPERSONS. 4464

0196-5263 See GUIDE TO THE USE OF THE GRADUATE RECORD EXAMINATIONS. 1827

0196-5352 See MOTOR CARRIER STATISTICAL SUMMARY. 5401

0196-5395 See GUIDES TO FOREST AND CONSERVATION HISTORY OF NORTH AMERICA. 2194

0196-5409 See ARCHAEOLOGICAL SERIES (TUCSON). 257

0196-5425 See OFFICIAL UNITED STATES TENNIS ASSOCIATION YEARBOOK AND TENNIS GUIDE WITH THE OFFICIAL RULES, THE. 4910

0196-5433 See ANNUAL REPORT - NATIONAL CENTER FOR STATE COURTS. 3139

0196-5530 See QUARTERLY INDEX TO CURRENT CONTENTS. LIFE SCIENCES. 3632

0196-5603 See INSTITUTE SCHOLAR. 4349

0196-5611 See WRITERS GUILD DIRECTORY. 2925

0196-562X See MENTAL HEALTH STATISTICS (JEFFERSON CITY). 4810

0196-5654 See AMERICAN BOOK COLLECTOR (1980). 2770

0196-5662 See JOURNAL - TEXAS SOCIETY FOR ELECTRON MICROSCOPY. 572

0196-5700 See SUPERMARKET BUSINESS. 2359

0196-5743 See INTERCHANGE (SACRAMENTO). 4389

0196-5778 See MUNICIPAL LAW SECTION NEWSLETTER. 3012

0196-5786 See PAPERWORK AND RED TAPE. 4672

0196-5905 See VIDEO WEEK. 1142

0196-5913 See PUDDING MAGAZINE. 3470

0196-5921 See ZYMURGY. 2373

0196-593X See MINNESOTA VOLUNTEER, THE. 2198

0196-5980 See ECONOMIC REPORT OF THE GOVERNOR (LANSING). 1484

0196-5999 See FODOR'S MEXICO. 5472

0196-6006 See SCITECH BOOK NEWS. 5156

0196-6103 See ANNUAL REPORT OF THE OHIO DEPARTMENT OF TAXATION. 4710

0196-612X See ... CQ GUIDE TO CURRENT AMERICAN GOVERNMENT, THE. 4641

0196-6138 See PARKER DIRECTORY OF CALIFORNIA ATTORNEYS. 3025

0196-6170 See BULLETIN (MICHIGAN HISTORICAL COLLECTIONS). 2724

0196-6197 See DERMATOLOGY TIMES. 3719

0196-6200 See CONTEMPORARY MUSIC ALMANAC. 4111

0196-6219 See CERAMIC ENGINEERING AND SCIENCE PROCEEDINGS. 2587

0196-626X See GMP LETTER, THE. 3479

0196-6286 See WILLIAM CARLOS WILLIAMS REVIEW. 3356

0196-6294 See FACTS AT YOUR FINGERTIPS. 4775

0196-6316 See AWARDS, HONORS, AND PRIZES. 5229

0196-6324 See AMERICAN JOURNAL OF MATHEMATICAL AND MANAGEMENT SCIENCES. 3492

0196-6340 See DIRECTORY - TEXAS OSTEOPATHIC MEDICAL ASSOCIATION. 3572

0196-6375 See FINITE ELEMENTS IN FLUIDS. 2089

0196-6383 See CLINICAL AND EXPERIMENTAL NEUROLOGY. 3830

0196-6405 See SERVICE AND METHODS DEMONSTRATION PROGRAM ANNUAL REPORT. EXECUTIVE SUMMARY. 5392

0196-6421 See DIRECTORY OF CERTIFIED PSYCHIATRISTS AND NEUROLOGISTS. 3924

0196-6448 See ANNUAL STATISTICS OF MEDICAL SCHOOL LIBRARIES IN THE UNITED STATES AND CANADA. 3257

0196-6456 See CAMPBOOK. NORTHEASTERN. 4870

0196-6537 See WASHINGTON PSYCHIATRIC SOCIETY DIRECTORY, THE. 3937

0196-6545 See DIRECTORY OF THE AMERICAN PSYCHOLOGICAL ASSOCIATION (1978). 1925

0196-6553 See AMERICAN JOURNAL OF INFECTION CONTROL. 3734

0196-6561 See AMS STUDIES IN THE EIGHTEENTH CENTURY. 3361

0196-657X See AMS STUDIES IN THE NINETEENTH CENTURY. 3361

0196-6685 See ANNUAL REPORT - PUBLIC EMPLOYEES' RETIREMENT ASSOCIATION OF NEW MEXICO. 1649

0196-6707 See NEWSLETTER - PITTSBURGH REGIONAL LIBRARY CENTER, INC. 3236

0196-6715 See EDUCATION LAW AND THE PUBLIC SCHOOLS. BULLETIN AND UPDATE SUBSCRIPTION SERVICE. 1863

0196-6723 See ANNUAL REPORT - STATE OF NEW YORK, DEPARTMENT OF MOTOR VEHICLES. 5403

0196-6774 See JOURNAL OF ALGORITHMS. 3511

0196-6782 See PLEADER, THE. 3029

0196-6790 See NURSE, THE PATIENT & THE LAW, THE. 3020

0196-6847 See CAMINOS (SAN BERNARDINO). 2529

0196-6871 See NEW YORK MEDICAL QUARTERLY, THE. 3620

0196-6901 See R.H.M. SURVEY OF WARRANTS, OPTIONS & LOW-PRICE STOCKS, THE. 912

0196-691X See ARTFUL DODGE. 3363

0196-7010 See HOT ROD PERFORMANCE AND CUSTOM DIRECTORY. 5416

0196-7045 See OLD FORT NEWS. 2752

0196-7053 See CONTRIBUTIONS TO THE STUDY OF RELIGION. 4950

0196-7061 See NEWSLETTER - PHARMACEUTICAL MANUFACTURERS ASSOCIATION. 4318

0196-707X See CONTRIBUTIONS TO THE STUDY OF EDUCATION. 1733

0196-7088 See CONTRIBUTIONS IN ETHNIC STUDIES. 2259

0196-7134 See DOCUMENTARY EDITING. 2919

0196-7185 See GEORGE D. HALL'S MASSACHUSETTS SERVICE DIRECTORY. 1607

0196-7207 See GEORGETOWN UNIVERSITY ROUND TABLE ON LANGUAGES AND LINGUISTICS. 3283

0196-7215 See FIBRE BOX HANDBOOK. 4219

0196-7223 See BRS BULLETIN. 1172

0196-7231 See SIMON AND SCHUSTER CROSSWORD PUZZLE BOOK. 4866

0196-7258 See LISTENING (WASHINGTON). 4390

0196-7282 See ANNUAL MEETING - AMERICAN INSTITUTE OF CHEMICAL ENGINEERS. 2007

0196-7355 See NEVADA PUBLIC AFFAIRS REVIEW. 4668

0196-7487 See JOURNAL OF THE LEGAL PROFESSION, THE. 2989

0196-7509 See MASSACHUSETTS LAWYERS WEEKLY. 3007

0196-7517 See BRITISH DIGEST ILLUSTRATED. 2514

0196-7533 See ROSTER OF REGISTERED FORESTERS OF MISSISSIPPI. 2394

0196-7576 See GUIDE TO THE ADMISSIONS TESTING PROGRAM. 1827

0196-7614 See U.S. CONGRESS HANDBOOK, THE. 4691

0196-7622 See DIRECTORY - BELGIAN AMERICAN CHAMBER OF COMMERCE IN THE UNITED STATES, INC, THE. 819

0196-7630 See GENERAL COMPETITION RULES (DENVER). 5415

0196-7649 See MICHIGAN APPELLATE DIGEST. 3009

0196-7681 See DIRECTORY OF KANSAS PUBLIC OFFICIALS. 4643

0196-7703 See OCCASIONAL PAPERS OF THE IDAHO MUSEUM OF NATURAL HISTORY. 4094

0196-772X See NUCLEAR WASTE MANAGEMENT PROGRAM SUMMARY DOCUMENT. 2237

0196-7746 See ANNUAL RESEARCH REVIEW - CALIFORNIA DEPARTMENT OF CORRECTIONS. 3158

0196-7754 See ENERGY REPORT - TEXAS. COMPTROLLER'S OFFICE. 1941

0196-7762 See THORNDIKE ENCYCLOPEDIA OF BANKING AND FINANCIAL TABLES. YEARBOOK. 814

0196-7827 See OFFICIAL RULES FOR PROFESSIONAL FOOTBALL. 4910

0196-7843 See PUBLIC UTILITIES REPORTS. 4762

0196-786X See PROFESSIONAL EDUCATOR, THE. 1903

0196-7878 See LAND AREAS OF THE NATIONAL FOREST SYSTEM. 2386

0196-7886 See CANADIAN STRATEGIC REPORT. 4039

0196-7975 See GUIDEBOOK TO FAIR EMPLOYMENT PRACTICES. 3148

0196-8092 See LASERS IN SURGERY AND MEDICINE. 3969

0196-8114 See WORD PROCESSING (FRANKLIN LAKES). 1292

0196-8122 See ARKANSAS SOCIAL STUDIES TEACHER, THE. 5191

0196-8203 See DISCLOSURE (CHICAGO). 1296

0196-8211 See MATERIALS MANAGEMENT & PHYSICAL DISTRIBUTION ABSTRACTS. 879

0196-8254 See DIRECTORY OF MEMBERS - AMERICAN SOCIETY FOR MICROBIOLOGY. 562

0196-8270 See GEORGE D. HALL'S DIRECTORY OF CONNECTICUT MANUFACTURERS. 3479

0196-8297 See TECHNICAL REPORTS (UNIVERSITY OF MICHIGAN. MUSEUM OF ANTHROPOLOGY). 4097

0196-8319 See BULLETIN OF THE ARCHAEOLOGICAL SOCIETY OF NEW JERSEY. 264

0196-8327 See CITY RECORD (CLEVELAND), THE. 4638

0196-8386 See TRANSLATIONS ON NORTH KOREA. 2667

0196-8394 See WOMEN & WORK. 1718

0196-8440 See SCIENTIFIC HONEYWELLER. 5155

0196-8459 See PRATT INSTITUTE CREATIVE ARTS THERAPY REVIEW. 3932

0196-8475 See DIRECTORY OF HISTORIANS OF LATIN AMERICAN ART. 349

0196-8491 See DENVER METROPOLITAN MEDIA DIRECTORY. 1110

0196-8505 See MILWAUKEE AREA MEDIA DIRECTORY. 1117

0196-8513 See FINDER BINDER. WILLAMETTE VALLEY'S UPDATED MEDIA DIRECTORY. 759

0196-853X See FINDERBINDER. 759

0196-8548 See FINDER BINDER. ARIZONA'S UPDATED MEDIA DIRECTORY. 2919

0196-8564 See SAN DIEGO SOURCE BOOK. 5236

0196-8572 See WASHINGTON STATE MEDIA DIRECTORY. 1124

0196-8599 See JOURNAL OF COMMUNICATION INQUIRY, THE. 1114

0196-8610 See DUN'S CENSUS OF AMERICAN BUSINESS. 728

0196-8653 See CONTEMPORARY ENDOCRINOLOGY. 3727

0196-867X See SALARY & BENEFITS SURVEY. 1709

0196-8696 See ADVANCES IN DATA PROCESSING MANAGEMENT. 1255

0196-8718 See ADVANCES IN DATA BASE MANAGEMENT. 1252

0196-8726 See FINDER BINDER. NORTHEAST OHIO/GREATER CLEVELAND. 759

0196-8734 See FINDER BINDER. OKLAHOMA CITY METROPOLITAN UPDATED MEDIA DIRECTORY. 759

0196-8793 See VIDEO REVIEW (NEW YORK, N.Y.). 4377

0196-884X See CRANBERRIES (WASHINGTON). 168

0196-8858 See ADVANCES IN APPLIED MATHEMATICS. 3491

0196-8866 See YEAR BOOK - PERQUIMANS COUNTY HISTORICAL SOCIETY. 2766

0196-8882 See TAX ALERT FOR MANAGEMENT. 4751

0196-8904 See ENERGY CONVERSION AND MANAGEMENT. 1939

0196-8947 See CHRISTIAN CROSE FAMILY NEWSLETTER. 2443

0196-8998 See NEWSLETTER - BYRON SOCIETY. 5234

0196-9021 See CEP REPORT. 1469

0196-9064 See MIDWEST REGIONAL SOLAR ENERGY PLANNING VENTURE. 1950

0196-9072 See JOURNAL OF PASTORAL PRACTICE, THE. 5017

0196-9099 See CONTRIBUTIONS IN BLACK STUDIES. 2845

0196-9110 See ENCYCLIA. 5102

0196-9137 See BUFFALO (CUSTER). 208

0196-9161 See SPECIAL BULLETIN - MUNICIPAL FINANCE OFFICERS ASSOCIATION OF THE UNITED STATES AND CANADA. 4748

0196-9226 See FINANCIAL ASSISTANCE BY GEOGRAPHIC AREA. REGION I, BOSTON, MASS. 4725

0196-9307 See DIRECTORY OF HIGHER EDUCATION INSTITUTIONS IN MISSOURI. 1821

0196-9323 See PETER DAG INVESTMENT LETTER, THE. 911

0196-9366 See HANDBOOK OF CYCLICAL INDICATORS. 4404

0196-9382 See REPORT ON REPORTS. 935

0196-9420 See NEWSLETTER - NATIONAL COUNCIL FOR INTERNATIONAL VISITORS. 2911

0196-948X See NEW MEXICO GEOLOGY. 1389

0196-9560 See ASSEMBLIES OF GOD EDUCATOR. 1726

0196-9641 See THRESHOLDS IN EDUCATION. 1787

0196-9668 See YOUTH-SERVING ORGANIZATIONS DIRECTORY. 5314

0196-9684 See DISTINGUISHED LECTURERS SERIES. 3382

0196-9722 See CYBERNETICS AND SYSTEMS. 1250

0196-9730 See PROCEEDINGS AND REPORTS - FLORIDA STATE UNIVERSITY, CENTER FOR YUGOSLAV-AMERICAN STUDIES, RESEARCH AND EXCHANGES. 2703

0196-9757 See DIRECTORY - NATIONAL BAND ASSOCIATION. 4114

0196-9773 See STUDENT GUIDE TO: GRADUATE LAW STUDY PROGRAMS. 3060

0196-9781 See PEPTIDES (NEW YORK, N.Y, : 1980). 492

0196-9870 See GREEN PAGES REHAB SOURCEBOOK, THE. 5286

0196-9897 See NORTH DAKOTA FARM REPORTER. 115

0196-9986 See MUNICIPAL MARYLAND. 4667

0197-0070 See JOURNAL OF ADOLESCENT HEALTH. 3593

0197-0100 See JOURNAL OF JEWISH MUSIC AND LITURGY. 4126

0197-016X See ANNUAL MEETING OF THE AMERICAN ASSOCIATION FOR CANCER RESEARCH PROCEEDINGS. 3808

0197-0178 See IDP REPORT. 1254

0197-0186 See NEUROCHEMISTRY INTERNATIONAL. 3839

0197-0216 See JOURNAL OF PHASE EQUILIBRIA. 4006

0197-0232 See PUBLIC EMPLOYEE RELATIONS COUNSELLOR. 3153

0197-0259 See DATA FROM THE CLIENT ORIENTED DATA ACQUISITION PROCESS. TREND REPORT. 1342

0197-0291 See YEAR BOOK - HISTORICAL SOCIETY OF HOPKINS COUNTY. 2766

0197-0305 See LUSK'S FAIRFAX COUNTY, VIRGINIA REAL ESTATE DIRECTORY SERVICE. 4840

0197-0313 See CDE STOCK OWNERSHIP DIRECTORY : BANKING & FINANCE. 782

0197-0321 See CDE STOCK OWNERSHIP DIRECTORY : ENERGY. 782

0197-0364 See ANTIQUARIAN TRADE LIST ANNUAL. 4823

0197-0380 See MLA DIRECTORY OF PERIODICALS. 3259

0197-0429 See CHARTBOOK OF FEDERAL PROGRAMS IN AGING. 5277

0197-0437 See BOOK MARKS. 3196

0197-0496 See ANNUAL REPORT - WYOMING ENERGY CONSERVATION OFFICE. 1932

0197-0526 See TECHNICAL REPORT - CORNELL UNIVERSITY WATER RESOURCES AND MARINE SCIENCES CENTER. 5540

0197-0666 See JOURNAL OF THE NUTRITIONAL ACADEMY. 4194

0197-0674 See OTO REVIEW. 3890

0197-0704 See DIRECTORY OF FULL-TIME COUNTY AND URBAN HEALTH DEPARTMENTS, A. 4773

0197-0755 See WATER RESOURCES DATA FOR PENNSYLVANIA. 5544

0197-0909 See ANNUAL REPORT - AMERICAN BUREAU FOR MEDICAL ADVANCEMENT IN CHINA, INC. 3550

0197-0968 See NASSAU COUNTY BAR ASSOCIATION ANNUAL DIRECTORY. 3013

0197-0976 See FIELD TRIP GUIDEBOOK (COLUMBIA). 1375

0197-1050 See NORTH CAROLINA STATE PLAN FOR DRUG ABUSE PREVENTION FUNCTIONS, THE. 1347

0197-1069 See PULP & PAPER BULLETIN. 4237

0197-1093 See ART & AUCTION (NEW YORK, N.Y.). 250

0197-1174 See WINGS (MANLIUS). 1886

0197-1212 See UNIVERSITAS (ALBANY). 2548

0197-1220 See MAINE, VERMONT, NEW HAMPSHIRE DIRECTORY OF MANUFACTURERS. 3483

0197-1239 See ANNUAL REPORT - AMERICAN CIVIL LIBERTIES UNION. 4504

0197-1360 See JOURNAL OF THE AMERICAN INSTITUTE FOR CONSERVATION. 323

0197-1387 See WEST VIRGINIA FORESTRY NOTES. 2398

0197-1433 See ADVANCES IN DISTRIBUTED PROCESSING MANAGEMENT. 1255

0197-1441 See COMUNIUNEA ROMANEASCA. 3377

0197-1468 See GENEALOGIST (NEW YORK), THE. 2450

0197-1476 See ADVANCES IN DATA COMMUNICATIONS MANAGEMENT. 1255

0197-1484 See PSYCSCAN. CLINICAL PSYCHOLOGY. 4623

0197-1492 See PSYCSCAN. DEVELOPMENTAL PSYCHOLOGY. 4623

0197-1506 See PIPELINE DIGEST. 4274

0197-1514 See ADVANCES IN COMPUTER SECURITY MANAGEMENT. 1225

0197-1522 See JOURNAL OF IMMUNOASSAY. 3673

0197-1565 See ROSTER/INDUSTRY DIRECTORY. 2370

0197-1581 See ANALYSIS OF SINGLE EMPLOYER DEFINED BENEFIT PLAN TERMINATIONS. 1643

0197-162X See GIRLS GYMNASTICS JUDGING MANUAL. NATIONAL FEDERATION EDITION. 4896

0197-1654 See DRI INDUSTRY FINANCIAL SERVICE. 788

0197-1662 See ASAE PUBLICATION. 1965

0197-1689 See TMS PAPER SELECTION. 4022

0197-1700 See ABSTRACTS, ANNUAL MEETING - ASSOCIATION OF AMERICAN GEOGRAPHERS. 2553

0197-1751 See SPECIAL PUBLICATIONS OF THE SOCIETY FOR GENERAL MICROBIOLOGY. 570

0197-1778 See ENVIRONMENTAL GEOLOGY SERIES (LAWRENCE). 1375

0197-1816 See MANUFACTURED HOUSING NEWSLETTER. 2828

0197-1859 See CLINICAL IMMUNOLOGY NEWSLETTER. 3668

0197-1875 See DIRECT MARKETING NEWS DIGEST. 923

0197-1883 See ROYAL RED BALL OUTDOOR SPORTSMAN. 4878

0197-193X See CAVEAT VENDOR. 2949

0197-1948 See INTERNATIONAL ACTIVITIES. 1979

0197-1956 See ENVIRONMENTAL ASSESSMENT. ELECTRIC HYBRID VEHICLE RESEARCH, DEVELOPMENT AND DEMONSTRATION PROGRAM. 2228

0197-1980 See N. A. D. A. MOTORCYCLE & MOPED APPRAISAL GUIDE. 4082

0197-2022 See SOLAR COLLECTOR MANUFACTURING ACTIVITY. 1963

0197-2103 See CONNECTICUT ANCESTRY. 2444

0197-2138 See PSI-M. 4242

0197-2197 See PENINSULA (SAN MATEO), LA. 2754

0197-2219 See RUBBER & PLASTICS NEWS II. 5077

0197-2227 See CLASSICAL AND MODERN LITERATURE. 1075

0197-2243 See INFORMATION SOCIETY, THE. 3216

0197-2316 See NEWS - ADMINISTRATIVE CONFERENCE OF THE UNITED STATES. 4669

0197-2340 See TEXAS NATURAL RESOURCES REPORTER. 4280

0197-2375 See CRAIN'S CLEVELAND BUSINESS. 663

0197-2405 See BEST'S RETIREMENT INCOME GUIDE. 2876

0197-2456 See CONTROLLED CLINICAL TRIALS. 3568

0197-2472 See NEW YORK STATE REGISTER, THE. 4669

0197-2510 See JEMS. 3724

0197-2529 See EXPENDITURES OF GENERAL REVENUE SHARING AND ANTIRECESSION FISCAL ASSISTANCE FUNDS. 4723

0197-2545 See PERSPECTIVE (LUBBOCK). 2830

0197-2596 See POLICY AND PROCEDURES HANDBOOK. 3029

0197-260X See CHESS LIFE (1980). 4858

0197-2626 See DON CLEARY'S RECORD COLLECTORS DIRECTORY. 5316

0197-2685 See ELECTRONIC NEW PRODUCT DIRECTORY, THE. 2047

0197-2707 See NEWSLETTER-STATE, COURT, AND COUNTY LAW LIBRARIES SECTION. 3236

0197-2723 See MANUFACTURERS GUIDE : OHIO. 3483

0197-2731 See DIVISION OF ENVIRONMENTAL CONTROL TECHNOLOGY PROGRAM. 2227

0197-2766 See FRACTURE MECHANICS OF CERAMICS. 2589

0197-2790 See SAGAMORE ARMY MATERIALS RESEARCH CONFERENCE PROCEEDINGS. 4056

0197-2804 See PROGRAMS AND SCHOOLS. 1915

0197-2847 See INFORMATION INTERCHANGE (ATLANTA, GA.). 3216

0197-2863 See ARMS GAZETTE. 4036

0197-288X See FISCAL LETTER, THE. 4726

0197-2901 See PUBLIC SCHOOL ENROLLMENT AND STAFF, NEW YORK STATE. 1776

0197-2936 See ASRC REPORT. 1420

0197-2944 See ASRC REPORT. 1420

0197-2979 See AAVSO CIRCULAR. 391

0197-2987 See CASH MANAGEMENT FORUM. 782

0197-3002 See CONNECTICUT MANUFACTURING DIRECTORY. 3477

0197-3029 See SIBBALD GUIDE, THE. 811

0197-3037 See PRAIRIE ROOTS. 2468

0197-3045 See BRIDE OF CHRIST, THE. 5057

0197-3096 See HUMAN DEVELOPMENT (NEW YORK). 4589

0197-3118 See CARDIOVASCULAR REVIEWS & REPORTS. 3702

0197-3169 See RECORDS OF VERMONT BIRDS. 5620

0197-3177 See HAZARDOUS MATERIALS TRANSPORTATION (BOSTON). 2231

0197-3320 See TRANSPORTATION AND TRAVEL : OFFICIAL TABLE OF DISTANCES, FOREIGN TRAVEL. 5494

0197-3363 See CAMEO (NEW YORK). 5074

0197-3479 See SKI INDUSTRY LETTER, THE. 4918

0197-3525 See SHEET MUSIC MAGAZINE. STANDARD PIANO/GUITAR. 4153

0197-3541 See SCHOOL LAWYER, THE. 1871

0197-355X See LOOK HERE. 1834

0197-3614 See FINANCIAL DIRECTORY OF PENSION FUNDS. MISSOURI, WESTERN. KANSAS CITY, ST. JOSEPH, SPRINGFIELD & OTHERS. 1672

0197-3622 See UMAP JOURNAL, THE. 3540

0197-3630 See HOUSTON INTERNATIONAL BUSINESS DIRECTORY. 680

0197-3649 See CONTEMPORARY HEMATOLOGY/ONCOLOGY. 3771

0197-3657 See PROGRESS REPORT - EAR RESEARCH INSTITUTE. 3891

0197-3665 See NORTHWEST EXPERIENCE, THE. 1576

0197-3703 See ASPHALT SALES. 599

0197-372X See MICROWAVE TIMES, THE. 2792

0197-3762 See VISUAL RESOURCES. 368

0197-3851 See PRENATAL DIAGNOSIS. 3767

0197-3886 See LAW IN AMERICAN SOCIETY. 2995

0197-3967 See MANAGING CORROSION WITH PLASTICS. 2014

0197-3975 See HABITAT INTERNATIONAL. 2823

0197-3983 See NEW YORK STATE LEGISLATIVE ANNUAL. 4669

0197-4009 See POETRY EAST. 3469

0197-4033 See AROIDEANA. 2409

0197-4041 See LIGAND REVIEW, THE. 3674

0197-4076 See ASCE NEWS. 2018

0197-4114 See TEXAS CRUISING GUIDE. 4184

0197-4149 See WOODWORKER (NEW YORK, N.Y. 1980). 635

0197-4173 See MUSIC USA. 4135

0197-4181 See LARGE CORPORATE BANKING. 796

0197-419X See TRANSPORTATION REVIEW. 5397

0197-4238 See MANUAL - THE STATE OF RHODE ISLAND AND PROVIDENCE PLANTATIONS. 4664

0197-4246 See HEALTH CARE FINANCING ADMINISTRATION RULINGS ON MEDICARE, MEDICAID, PROFESSIONAL STANDARDS REVIEW, AND RELATED MATTERS. 2882

0197-4254 See ATLANTIC ECONOMIC JOURNAL. 1464

0197-4327 See WESTERN JOURNAL OF BLACK STUDIES, THE. 2275

0197-4335 See AREA WAGE SURVEY. PROVIDENCE-WARWICK-PAWTUCKET, RHODE ISLAND-MASSACHUSETTS, METROPOLITAN AREA. 1653

0197-4424 See AREA WAGE SURVEY : BIRMINGHAM, ALABAMA, METROPOLITAN AREA. 1652

0197-4475 See NATO CONFERENCE SERIES. I. ECOLOGY. 2219

0197-4483 See SURFACE DESIGN JOURNAL. 5356

0197-453X See PROCEEDINGS OF THE INTERNATIONAL CONFERENCE ON FLUIDIZED BED COMBUSTION. 4418

0197-4556 See ARTS IN PSYCHOTHERAPY, THE. 3921

0197-4564 See U.C. DAVIS LAW REVIEW. 3067

0197-4572 See GERIATRIC NURSING (NEW YORK). 3856

0197-4580 See NEUROBIOLOGY OF AGING. 3839

0197-4602 See OFFICE PRODUCTS ANALYST, THE. 4213

0197-4610 See JERSEY WOMAN. 5559

0197-4637 See MULTINATIONAL MONITOR. 846

0197-470X See DURBIN DATA SHEETS. 378

0197-4742 See RESOURCES IN LIBRARY AND INFORMATION SCIENCE. 3246

0197-4777 See WATERWAYS (NEW YORK, N.Y.). 3473

0197-4815 See NEWSLETTER - ASSOCIATION OF LAW LIBRARIES OF UPSTATE NEW YORK. 3235

0197-4874 See NEW WILDERNESS LETTER. 4875

0197-4904 See RURAL DEVELOPMENT COUNCIL PUBLICATION (FAIRBANKS). 2834

0197-4947 See DISCOVERY (AUSTIN). 2532

0197-4955 See BUFFALO LAW JOURNAL. 2944

0197-498X See MADISON COUNTY HERITAGE. 2745

0197-4998 See FODOR'S BUDGET EUROPE. 5471

0197-5013 See PROCEEDINGS OF GOLD AND MONEY SESSION AND GOLD TECHNICAL SESSION. 2783

0197-5021 See LOS ANGELES COUNTY MUSEUM OF ART REPORT. 4090

0197-5056 See HORIZONS (CHICAGO. 1980). 1324

0197-5080 See RESEARCH IN SOCIOLOGY OF EDUCATION AND SOCIALIZATION. 5255

0197-5099 See MANHATTAN MENUS. 5071

0197-5110 See JOURNAL OF RECEPTOR RESEARCH. 538

0197-5129 See SUMMARY OF INVESTIGATIONS RELATING TO READING. 3327

0197-5137 See FEASTS & SEASONS. 3387

0197-5145 See NATO CONFERENCE SERIES : VI, MATERIALS SCIENCE. 5130

0197-5242 See SEATTLE ART MUSEUM NEWSLETTER. 4096

0197-5307 See SOUTHERN A.R.C. 2761

0197-534X See CATALYSIS IN ORGANIC SYNTHESES. 1040

0197-5366 See SOUTH ASIA LIBRARY NOTES & QUERIES. 3250

0197-5382 See FUTURES INDUSTRY'S MANAGED ACCOUNT REPORTS. 899

0197-5412 See ARIZONA PROGRESS. 1546

0197-5439 See WORLD REFUGEE SURVEY. 1921

0197-5455 See MEMBERSHIP DIRECTORY / AMERICAN COLLEGE OF PHYSICIANS. 1927

0197-5587 See LIBRARY IMAGINATION PAPER, THE. 3225

0197-5617 See FARM BUREAU NEWS (WASHINGTON). 84

0197-5633 See NEW GARDENS NEWSLETTER. 2425

0197-5641 See ANNUAL REVIEW OF CALIFORNIA OIL AND GAS PRODUCTION. 4250

0197-5668 See STATE PUBLICATIONS INDEX. 4497

0197-582X See CURRENT OBSTETRIC & GYNECOLOGIC DIAGNOSIS & TREATMENT. 3759

0197-5838 See POPULATION REPORTS. SERIES L, ISSUES IN WORLD HEALTH (ENGLISH ED.). 4558

0197-5889 See BIBLIOGRAPHIC GUIDE TO MAPS AND ATLASES. 2580

0197-5897 See JOURNAL OF PUBLIC HEALTH POLICY. 4787

0197-5978 See NEGOTIATIONS. 3152

0197-5986 See MODERN PHOTOGRAPHY'S GUIDE TO THE WORLD'S BEST CAMERAS. 4371

0197-5994 See NEW MUSIC NEWS. 4140

0197-6044 See HIGH ROLLER. 3213

0197-6060 See RAGAN REPORT, THE. 706

0197-6109 See GENERAL TECHNICAL REPORT WO. 2383

0197-6176 See ABSTRACTS ON MANAGEMENT & ADMINISTRATION OF PHARMACY. 4288

0197-6214 See GUIDE TO QUALITY CONSTRUCTION PRODUCTS. 616

0197-6265 See BULLETIN - THE MARIE SELBY BOTANICAL GARDENS. 505

0197-6281 See MUSHROOMS. 179

0197-6346 See MAURICE EWING SERIES. 1358

0197-6354 See COAL AGE LIBRARY OF OPERATING HANDBOOKS. 2137

0197-6559 See HANDS ON! (DAYTON, OHIO). 634

0197-663X See WILLA CATHER PIONEER MEMORIAL NEWSLETTER. 3453

0197-6656 See STUDENT GUIDE TO: SUMMER LAW STUDY PROGRAMS. 3060

0197-6664 See FAMILY RELATIONS. 2279

0197-6680 See FARMWEEK (BLOOMINGTON). 86

0197-6699 See PIACT PAPERS. 590

0197-6729 See JOURNAL OF ADVANCED TRANSPORTATION. 5385

0197-6737 See BILINGUAL RESOURCES. 1876

0197-6745 See DICTIONARIES. 3277

0197-6753 See TMR, TRAVEL MARKETING REPORT. 1999

0197-6761 See SPS CHAPTER LIST. 4422

0197-6788 See SOVIET MATHEMATICS - DOKLADY. 3536

0197-6796 See CONTACT II. 3461

0197-680X See PHANTASMAGORIA (UNIVERSITY HEIGHTS). 2491

0197-6818 See SNIPPETS. 936

0197-6850 See CLARION (NEW YORK, 1971), THE. 347

0197-6869 See AMERICAN DANCE DIRECTORY. 1310

0197-6877 See SURVEY OF GENERATION AND TRANSMISSION COOPERATIVES. 1543

0197-6885 See PAMPHLET - OFFICE OF PERSONNEL MANAGEMENT. 4704

0197-6893 See C-L/CLL. COUNSELING-LEARNING COMMUNITY LANGUAGE LEARNING NEWSLETTER. 3271

0197-6923 See REPRESENTATIVE AMERICAN SPEECHES. 3429

0197-6958 See CLINICAL AND SCIENTIFIC SESSIONS. 3853

0197-6966 See REVIEW OF THE U.S. ECONOMY. 1518

0197-6974 See FAMILY MEDICINE REVIEW, THE. 3737

0197-7016 See BLUE UNICORN. 3460

0197-7024 See POLYGRAPH (LINTHICUM HEIGHTS). 3172

0197-7032 See NATIONAL RIGHT TO WORK NEWSLETTER. 1692

0197-7040 See ANDERSON REPORT, THE. 1231

0197-7083 See DONOGHUE'S MONEYLETTER. 897

0197-7105 See CORD SPORTFACTS PRO FOOTBALL GUIDE. 4891

0197-7156 See RUSSIAN MATHEMATICS. 3532

0197-7172 See CONTROL OF BANKING. 3086
0197-7202 See FRANCE ... SPECIALIZED CATALOGUE OF ARTIST PROOFS, DE LUXE SHEETS, IMPERFORATES, COLOR ESSAYS, FIRST DAY COVERS, COLLECTIVE PROOFS, PRINTERS INSPECTION PROOFS, ILLUSTRATIONS. 2785
0197-7210 See SCHISTO UPDATE. 3661
0197-7229 See MCGREGOR FUND REPORT. 797
0197-7253 See INDUSTRY AND DEVELOPMENT (NEW YORK. ENGLISH EDITION). 1611
0197-7261 See LITHIC TECHNOLOGY. 273
0197-727X See PROCEEDINGS - PACIFIC CHEMICAL ENGINEERING CONGRESS. 2016
0197-7342 See KEYWORDS. 1288
0197-7377 See COMMON SENSE (PORTSMOUTH). 4469
0197-7423 See REPORT OF THE PATIENT REGISTRY. 3801
0197-7458 See METADATA'S LEGALGRAM FOR THE COMMUNICATIONS INDUSTRY. 3009
0197-7466 See WORLD ECONOMIC REVIEW (PHILADELPHIA, PA.). 1527
0197-7474 See WPIX EDITORIALS. 1143
0197-7482 See GEOREF (CD-ROM). 1363
0197-7490 See RESOURCE SERIES - COLORADO GEOLOGICAL SURVEY, DEPARTMENT OF NATURAL RESOURCES, STATE OF COLORADO. 1395
0197-7539 See RISK REPORT, THE. 2892
0197-7571 See BIOSOURCES DIGEST. 448
0197-7636 See HARVARD COLLEGE ECONOMIST. 1493
0197-7679 See CARNIVOROUS PLANTS DIGEST. 2412
0197-7717 See BEHAVIORAL MEDICINE ABSTRACTS. 3654
0197-7768 See BITS. 3460
0197-7776 See KOREAN CHURCH DIRECTORY OVERSEAS. 4972
0197-7784 See DEVOTEE. 4114
0197-7806 See ILLUSTRATED HOUSE PLANS. 300
0197-7849 See ASCAP IN ACTION. 4101
0197-789X See WORLD ENERGY OUTLOOK. 1961
0197-7903 See ART HAZARDS NEWS. 383
0197-7938 See NATIONAL DELINQUENCY SURVEY. 800
0197-7954 See SHO-BAN NEWS, THE. 5657
0197-7962 See CUE (HOLLAND PATENT), THE. 5363
0197-7997 See SWIMMING POOL WEEKLY AND SWIMMING POOL AGE REPLACEMENT PARTS GUIDE. 630
0197-8004 See NEW YORK TIMES ANNUAL REVIEW, THE. 2624
0197-8012 See AFRICA BUSINESS & ECONOMIC REVIEW. 1632
0197-8039 See RADIATION CURING BUYER'S GUIDE. 3944
0197-8055 See DAILY RECORDER, THE. 2958
0197-8071 See NEWS-LETTER OF THE SOCIETY FOR THE STUDY OF SOUTHERN LITERATURE, THE. 3416
0197-8098 See BROWN'S DIRECTORY OF NORTH AMERICAN AND INTERNATIONAL GAS COMPANIES. 4252
0197-811X See WORLD ECONOMIC BULLETIN. 1589
0197-8128 See BIG TEN FOOTBALL ALMANAC. 4887
0197-8160 See HUMAN GENETICS. SUPPLEMENT (ROCKVILLE). 547
0197-8187 See PROGRAM AND RESOURCE DIGEST, THE. 4675
0197-8195 See AMERICAN CIVIL LIBERTIES UNION RECORDS AND PUBLICATIONS UPDATE, THE. 2932
0197-8209 See HANDBOOK OF CONTRACT FLOOR COVERING. 616
0197-8322 See ADVANCES IN INFLAMMATION RESEARCH. 3546

0197-8349 See NORM EVANS' SEAHAWK REPORT. 4908
0197-8357 See JOURNAL OF INTERFERON RESEARCH. 565
0197-8373 See RESEARCH NOTE SO. 2393
0197-8403 See WEEKLY CONGRESSIONAL MONITOR, THE. 4694
0197-8454 See CLINICAL LAB LETTER. 3893
0197-8462 See BIOELECTROMAGNETICS. 3556
0197-8519 See NEXUS (WILMINGTON). 3170
0197-8535 See APPLIED OPTICS AND OPTICAL ENGINEERING. 4433
0197-8543 See ESL-TR (UNITED STATES. AIR FORCE. AIR FORCE ENGINEERING AND SERVICES CENTER. ENGINEERING AND SERVICES LABORATORY). 5103
0197-873X See ANNUAL VOLUME OF PEDIATRICS CLUB BY CONTRIBUTING MEMBERS. 3900
0197-8748 See PROCEEDINGS OF AMERICAN PEANUT RESEARCH AND EDUCATION SOCIETY, INC. 183
0197-8829 See LITERATURE (WASHINGTON). 3407
0197-887X See ISOZYME BULLETIN, THE. 548
0197-8896 See WITNESS (AMBLER), THE. 5069
0197-890X See TENDRIL. 3444
0197-8969 See ANNUAL PROCEEDINGS OF THE PHYTOCHEMICAL SOCIETY OF EUROPE. 480
0197-9027 See NEWSLETTER - CUBA HISTORICAL SOCIETY, THE. 2749
0197-906X See MINING RESEARCH REVIEW. 2146
0197-9140 See WATER POLLUTION RESEARCH JOURNAL OF CANADA. 2247
0197-9159 See DUMBARTON OAKS. 2685
0197-9183 See INTERNATIONAL MIGRATION REVIEW : IMR. 1919
0197-9299 See PLA BULLETIN. 3241
0197-9337 See EARTH SURFACE PROCESSES AND LANDFORMS. 1374
0197-9361 See OLSEN'S AGRIBUSINESS REPORT. 117
0197-937X See CORPORATE 500. THE DIRECTORY OF CORPORATE PHILANTHROPY. 4335
0197-9450 See LOCAL CLIMATOLOGICAL DATA. BIRMINGHAM, ALABAMA. NAT. WEATHER SERVICE FCST. OFC. MONTHLY SUMMARY. 1428
0197-9477 See FASTFACTS HOTEL MOTEL LOCATOR, UNITED STATES & CANADA. 2805
0197-9523 See LOCAL CLIMATOLOGICAL DATA. MONTGOMERY, ALABAMA, ANNUAL SUMMARY WITH COMPARATIVE DATA. 1429
0197-9531 See LOCAL CLIMATOLOGICAL DATA. MONTGOMERY, ALABAMA, MONTHLY SUMMARY. 1429
0197-954X See LOCAL CLIMATOLOGICAL DATA. ANCHORAGE, ALASKA. ANNUAL SUMMARY WITH COMPARATIVE DATA. 1427
0197-9620 See LOCAL CLIMATOLOGICAL DATA. BETHEL, ALASKA, ANNUAL SUMMARY WITH COMPARATIVE DATA. 1427
0197-971X See LOCAL CLIMATOLOGICAL DATA. GULKANA, ALASKA, MONTHLY SUMMARY. 1428
0197-9728 See LOCAL CLIMATOLOGICAL DATA. FAIRBANKS, ALASKA. ANNUAL SUMMARY WITH COMPARATIVE DATA. 1428
0197-9841 See LOCAL CLIMATOLOGICAL DATA. MCGRATH, ALASKA, ANNUAL SUMMARY WITH COMPARATIVE DATA. 1429
0197-9884 See PROGRAM OF THE ANNUAL MEETING - ORGANIZATION OF AMERICAN HISTORIANS. 2755
0197-9892 See SUBSCRIBER AND PRIMARY AUDIENCE STUDY DIGEST, THE. 2924
0197-9922 See STUDIES IN AVIAN BIOLOGY. 474
0197-9930 See EARLY MAN. 267
0197-9949 See DIRECTORY OF MEMBERS & MUSEUMS. 4114
0197-9965 See MINES DIRECTORY. 2145
0197-9973 See RESOURCES IN EDUCATION. ANNUAL CUMULATION. 1797

0198-0009 See CONTEMPORARY NUTRITION. 4189
0198-0068 See BANBURY REPORT. 443
0198-0092 See MODELING AND SIMULATION. 1282
0198-0130 See PROCEEDINGS - LIGHTWOOD RESEARCH CONFERENCE. 2403
0198-0149 See DEEP-SEA RESEARCH. PART A. OCEANOGRAPHIC RESEARCH PAPERS. 1362
0198-0181 See ACTIVITIES REPORT OF THE R & D ASSOCIATES. 2326
0198-0211 See FOOT & ANKLE. 3881
0198-0254 See DEEP-SEA RESEARCH. PART B. OCEANOGRAPHIC LITERATURE REVIEW. 1362
0198-0270 See ANNUAL CONFERENCE ON CATV RELIABILITY. 1126
0198-0289 See CONNECTICUT LAW TRIBUNE, THE. 2955
0198-0297 See WOMAN'S DAY COOKING FOR TWO. 2793
0198-0300 See WORLD POLITICS (GUILFORD). 4501
0198-0319 See ALABAMA RULES OF COURTS. 3138
0198-0351 See CONGRESSIONAL BUDGET REQUEST. 1936
0198-0386 See ROAD & TRACK ROAD ATLAS & TRAVEL GUIDE. 5490
0198-0475 See LOCAL CLIMATOLOGICAL DATA. PHOENIX, ARIZONA, MONTHLY SUMMARY. 1429
0198-0483 See LOCAL CLIMATOLOGICAL DATA. TUCSON, ARIZONA, MONTHLY SUMMARY. 1430
0198-0521 See LOCAL CLIMATOLOGICAL DATA. TALKEETNA, ALASKA, ANNUAL SUMMARY WITH COMPARATIVE DATA. 1430
0198-0602 See LOCAL CLIMATOLOGICAL DATA. YUMA, ARIZONA. MONTHLY SUMMARY. 1430
0198-0610 See LOCAL CLIMATOLOGICAL DATA. FORT SMITH, ARKANSAS. MONTHLY SUMMARY. 1428
0198-0629 See LOCAL CLIMATOLOGICAL DATA. LITTLE ROCK, ARKANSAS, MONTHLY SUMMARY. 1429
0198-0653 See LOCAL CLIMATOLOGICAL DATA. YUMA, ARIZONA, ANNUAL SUMMARY WITH COMPARATIVE DATA. 1430
0198-0874 See LOCAL CLIMATOLOGICAL DATA. BLUE CANYON, CALIFORNIA, ANNUAL SUMMARY WITH COMPARATIVE DATA. 1428
0198-0939 See LOCAL CLIMATOLOGICAL DATA. MOUNT SHASTA, CALIFORNIA, ANNUAL SUMMARY WITH COMPARATIVE DATA. 1429
0198-1056 See CINEFEX. 4066
0198-1064 See CINEMACABRE. 4066
0198-1099 See HARD CRABS. 3343
0198-1110 See WOODALL'S FLORIDA (GERMAN ED.). 5499
0198-1161 See LOCAL CLIMATOLOGICAL DATA. HARTFORD, CONNECTICUT, MONTHLY SUMMARY. 1428
0198-1188 See LOCAL CLIMATOLOGICAL DATA. WASHINGTON, D.C., WASHINGTON NATIONAL AIRPORT, MONTHLY SUMMARY. 1430
0198-1269 See LOCAL CLIMATOLOGICAL DATA. MIAMI, FLORIDA. ANNUAL SUMMARY WITH COMPARATIVE DATA. 1429
0198-1374 See LOCAL CLIMATOLOGICAL DATA. KEY WEST, FLORIDA, MONTHLY SUMMARY. 1429
0198-1390 See LOCAL CLIMATOLOGICAL DATA. ORLANDO, FLORIDA, MONTHLY SUMMARY. 1429
0198-1447 See INSTREAM FLOW INFORMATION PAPER. 1415
0198-151X See LITERARY MARKET REVIEW. 3406
0198-1587 See LOCAL CLIMATOLOGICAL DATA. AUGUSTA, GEORGIA. ANNUAL SUMMARY WITH COMPARATIVE DATA. 1427
0198-1781 See LOCAL CLIMATOLOGICAL DATA. LEWISTON, IDAHO, ANNUAL SUMMARY WITH COMPARATIVE DATA. 1429

0198-1838 See LOCAL CLIMATOLOGICAL DATA. CAIRO, ILLINOIS, MONTHLY SUMMARY. 1428

0198-1870 See LOCAL CLIMATOLOGICAL DATA. MOLINE, ILLINOIS, MONTHLY SUMMARY. 1429

0198-1919 See LOCAL CLIMATOLOGICAL DATA. ROCKFORD, ILLINOIS, MONTHLY SUMMARY. 1430

0198-1978 See LOCAL CLIMATOLOGICAL DATA. FORT WAYNE, INDIANA, MONTHLY SUMMARY. 1428

0198-1994 See ANNUAL PROGRESS REPORT - WATER MANAGEMENT RESEARCH PROJECT. 5529

0198-2060 See LOCAL CLIMATOLOGICAL DATA. DES MOINES, IOWA, MONTHLY SUMMARY. 1428

0198-215X See LOCAL CLIMATOLOGICAL DATA. DODGE CITY, KANSAS, ANNUAL SUMMARY WITH COMPARATIVE DATA. 1428

0198-2419 See LOCAL CLIMATOLOGICAL DATA. BOSTON, MASSACHUSSETS, ANNUAL SUMMARY WITH COMPARATIVE DATA. 1428

0198-2478 See MCCALL'S (PATTERN BOOK). 5185

0198-2532 See LOCAL CLIMATOLOGICAL DATA. DETROIT, MICHIGAN, METROPOLITAN AIRPORT, ANNUAL SUMMARY WITH COMPARATIVE DATA. 1428

0198-2575 See LOCAL CLIMATOLOGICAL DATA. GRAND RAPIDS, MICHIGAN, ANNUAL SUMMARY WITH COMPARATIVE DATA. 1428

0198-2613 See LOCAL CLIMATOLOGICAL DATA. LANSING, MICHIGAN, ANNUAL SUMMARY WITH COMPARATIVE DATA. 1429

0198-280X See LOCAL CLIMATOLOGICAL DATA. JACKSON, MISSISSIPPI, MONTHLY SUMMARY. 1429

0198-3156 See LOCAL CLIMATOLOGICAL DATA. NORTH PLATTE, NEBRASKA. ANNUAL SUMMARY WITH COMPARATIVE DATA. 1429

0198-3202 See LOCAL CLIMATOLOGICAL DATA. OMAHA, NEBRASKA (NORTH). MONTHLY SUMMARY. 1429

0198-327X See LOCAL CLIMATOLOGICAL DATA. ELKO, NEVADA, MONTHLY SUMMARY. 1428

0198-3318 See LOCAL CLIMATOLOGICAL DATA. LAS VEGAS, NEVADA, MONTHLY SUMMARY. 1429

0198-3350 See LOCAL CLIMATOLOGICAL DATA. WINNEMUCCA, NEVADA, MONTHLY SUMMARY. 1430

0198-3377 See LOCAL CLIMATOLOGICAL DATA. CONCORD, NEW HAMPSHIRE, MONTHLY SUMMARY. 1428

0198-3393 See LOCAL CLIMATOLOGICAL DATA. MOUNT WASHINGTON OBSERVATORY, GORHAM, NEW HAMPSHIRE. MONTHLY SUMMARY. 1429

0198-3474 See LOCAL CLIMATOLOGICAL DATA. ALBUQUERQUE, NEW MEXICO, ANNUAL SUMMARY WITH COMPARATIVE DATA. 1427

0198-3660 See LOCAL CLIMATOLOGICAL DATA. ROCHESTER, NEW YORK, MONTHLY SUMMARY. 1430

0198-3709 See LOCAL CLIMATOLOGICAL DATA. ASHEVILLE, NORTH CAROLINA. MONTHLY SUMMARY. 1427

0198-3768 See LOCAL CLIMATOLOGICAL DATA. GREENSBORO, HIGH POINT, WINSTON-SALEM AP, N.C, MONTHLY SUMMARY. 1428

0198-3849 See LOCAL CLIMATOLOGICAL DATA. FARGO, NORTH DAKOTA, MONTHLY SUMMARY. 1428

0198-3938 See LOCAL CLIMATOLOGICAL DATA. CLEVELAND, OHIO, ANNUAL SUMMARY WITH COMPARATIVE DATA. 1428

0198-4128 See LOCAL CLIMATOLOGICAL DATA. BURNS, OREGON, MONTHLY SUMMARY. 1428

0198-4179 See LOCAL CLIMATOLOGICAL DATA. PENDLETON, OREGON, ANNUAL SUMMARY WITH COMPARATIVE DATA. 1429

0198-4373 See LOCAL CLIMATOLOGICAL DATA. PONAPE ISLAND, PACIFIC, ANNUAL SUMMARY WITH COMPARATIVE DATA. 1429

0198-442X See LOCAL CLIMATOLOGICAL DATA. WAKE ISLAND, PACIFIC, MONTHLY SUMMARY. 1430

0198-4470 See LOCAL CLIMATOLOGICAL DATA. AVOCA, PENNSYLVANIA. ANNUAL SUMMARY WITH COMPARATIVE DATA. 1427

0198-4527 See LOCAL CLIMATOLOGICAL DATA. MIDDLETOWN/HARRISBURG INTL. APT. MONTHLY SUMMARY. 1429

0198-4543 See LOCAL CLIMATOLOGICAL DATA. PHILADELPHIA, PENNSYLVANIA, MONTHLY SUMMARY. 1429

0198-4586 See LOCAL CLIMATOLOGICAL DATA. BLOCK ISLAND, RHODE ISLAND, MONTHLY SUMMARY. 1428

0198-4659 See LOCAL CLIMATOLOGICAL DATA. COLUMBIA, SOUTH CAROLINA, MONTHLY SUMMARY. 1428

0198-4675 See LOCAL CLIMATOLOGICAL DATA. GREENVILLE-SPARTANBURG AP. GREER, S.C., MONTHLY SUMMARY. 1428

0198-4721 See LOCAL CLIMATOLOGICAL DATA. RAPID CITY, SOUTH DAKOTA, ANNUAL SUMMARY WITH COMPARATIVE DATA. 1430

0198-4802 See LOCAL CLIMATOLOGICAL DATA. KNOXVILLE, TENNESSEE, ANNUAL SUMMARY WITH COMPARATIVE DATA. 1429

0198-487X See LOCAL CLIMATOLOGICAL DATA. OAK RIDGE, TENNESSEE. MONTHLY SUMMARY. 1429

0198-4888 See LOCAL CLIMATOLOGICAL DATA. ABILENE, TEXAS, ANNUAL SUMMARY WITH COMPARATIVE DATA. 1427

0198-4896 See LOCAL CLIMATOLOGICAL DATA. ABILENE, TEXAS, MONTHLY SUMMARY. 1427

0198-5000 See PELVIC SURGEON, THE. 3971

0198-5140 See LOCAL CLIMATOLOGICAL DATA. PORT ARTHUR, TEXAS, ANNUAL SUMMARY WITH COMPARATIVE DATA. 1429

0198-5256 See LOCAL CLIMATOLOGICAL DATA. WICHITA FALLS, TEXAS. MONTHLY SUMMARY. 1430

0198-5302 See LOCAL CLIMATOLOGICAL DATA. BURLINGTON, VERMONT, ANNUAL SUMMARY WITH COMPARATIVE DATA. 1428

0198-5310 See LOCAL CLIMATOLOGICAL DATA. BURLINGTON, VERMONT, MONTHLY SUMMARY. 1428

0198-5337 See LOCAL CLIMATOLOGICAL DATA. LYNCHBURG, VIRGINIA. MONTHLY SUMMARY. 1429

0198-5396 See LOCAL CLIMATOLOGICAL DATA. ROANOKE, VIRGINIA. MONTHLY SUMMARY. 1430

0198-5418 See LOCAL CLIMATOLOGICAL DATA. OLYMPIA, WASHINGTON. MONTHLY SUMMARY. 1429

0198-5493 See LOCAL CLIMATOLOGICAL DATA. SPOKANE, WASHINGTON. MONTHLY SUMMARY. 1430

0198-5639 See LOCAL CLIMATOLOGICAL DATA. ELKINS, WEST VIRGINIA. MONTHLY SUMMARY. 1429

0198-5655 See LOCAL CLIMATOLOGICAL DATA. HUNTINGTON, WEST VIRGINIA. MONTHLY SUMMARY. 1428

0198-5744 See LOCAL CLIMATOLOGICAL DATA. MILWAUKEE, WISCONSIN. ANNUAL SUMMARY WITH COMPARATIVE DATA. 1429

0198-5795 See LOCAL CLIMATOLOGICAL DATA. CHEYENNE, WYOMING. MONTHLY SUMMARY. 1428

0198-5833 See LOCAL CLIMATOLOGICAL DATA. SHERIDAN, WYOMING. MONTHLY SUMMARY. 1430

0198-585X See LATENT IMAGE. 302

0198-6120 See NATIONAL DEFENSE EXECUTIVE RESERVE ANNUAL REPORT TO THE PRESIDENT, THE. 4052

0198-6155 See JOURNAL OF OPHTHALMIC PHOTOGRAPHY, THE. 3876

0198-6171 See DAKOTA FARMER, THE. 78

0198-6252 See UKRAINSKYI FILATELIST / SOIUZ UKRAINSKYKH FILATELISTIV I NUMIZMATYKIV. 2788

0198-6325 See MEDICINAL RESEARCH REVIEWS. 4315

0198-6341 See PEDIATRICS DIGEST (1979). 3910

0198-6384 See HOSPITAL WAGE, SALARY, AND BENEFITS SURVEY. 3785

0198-6414 See PAPERBOUND BOOKS FOR YOUNG PEOPLE. 1072

0198-6422 See DIRECTORY OF FIELD CONTACTS FOR THE COORDINATION OF THE USE OF RADIO FREQUENCIES. 1153

0198-6449 See HALCYON (RENO). 2847

0198-6457 See MCCALL'S PATTERNS. 5185

0198-6465 See NUCLEAR POWER PLANT OPERATING EXPERIENCE ... ANNUAL REPORT. 2157

0198-6546 See NATIONAL CRIMINAL JUSTICE THESAURUS. 3170

0198-6554 See C:JET. 2918

0198-6562 See FISCAL SURVEY OF THE STATES. 4726

0198-6600 See PROCEEDINGS OF THE WESTERN ASSOCIATION OF FISH AND WILDLIFE AGENCIES AND THE WESTERN DIVISION AMERICAN FISHERIES ASSOCIATION. 2202

0198-6627 See DIAGNOSTIC DIALOG. 974

0198-6635 See FEEDBACK (MILLBRAE). 1894

0198-6643 See DERMATOLOGY DIGEST (1979). 3719

0198-666X See GRACE THEOLOGICAL JOURNAL. 4961

0198-6716 See STATUS OF ACTIVE FOREIGN CREDITS OF THE U.S. GOVT.: FOREIGN CREDITS BY U.S. GOVT. AGENCIES. 4750

0198-6805 See JAZZOLOGIST, THE. 4125

0198-6848 See ICPSR BULLETIN. 5202

0198-6856 See THEOLOGICAL EDUCATOR, THE. 5003

0198-6899 See MEASLES SURVEILLANCE REPORT. 4790

0198-6953 See WHO'S WHO IN RICHMOND BUSINESS. 437

0198-6996 See ANNOTATED BIBLIOGRAPHY OF BIBLIOGRAPHIES ON SELECTED GOVERNMENT PUBLICATIONS AND SUPPLEMENTARY GUIDES TO THE SUPERINTENDENT OF DOCUMENTS CLASSIFICATION SYSTEM. SUPPLEMENT. 407

0198-702X See NEWS BULLETIN - ARKANSAS BAR ASSOCIATION. 3017

0198-7070 See CUMULATED INDEX TO THE U.S. DEPARTMENT OF STATE PAPERS RELATING TO THE FOREIGN RELATIONS OF THE UNITED STATES, THE. 4641

0198-7097 See RADIOLOGY MANAGEMENT. 3946

0198-7143 See FOLIO. PUBLIC RELATIONS, THE. 2971

0198-7194 See PROCEEDINGS OF THE NORTH AMERICAN SOCIETY FOR OCEANIC HISTORY. 4182

0198-7216 See ARTHRITIS INTERAGENCY COORDINATING COMMITTEE ANNUAL REPORT TO THE SECRETARY, U.S. DEPARTMENT OF HEALTH, EDUCATION, AND WELFARE. 3803

0198-7224 See HIGH FIDELITY'S BUYING GUIDE TO STEREO COMPONENTS. 5317

0198-7232 See IT'S YOUR BUSINESS (ROCKVILLE CENTER). 2985

0198-7259 See PROGRESS IN BATTERIES & SOLAR CELLS. 2077

0198-7267 See PROCEEDINGS, ANNUAL MEETING - NEW JERSEY MOSQUITO CONTROL ASSOCIATION, INC. 2239

0198-7283 See ACCOUNTING JOURNAL (NEW YORK), THE. 737

0198-7356 See BARTONIA. 501

0198-7364 See HAMLINE LAW REVIEW. 2976

0198-7399 See SOCIOECONOMIC ISSUES OF HEALTH. 4803

0198-7429 See BEHAVIORAL DISORDERS. 1875

0198-7445 See PIACT PRODUCT NEWS. 590

0198-7496 See WAGNER LATIN AMERICAN NEWSLETTER, THE. 2765

0198-7518 See EDUCATING EXCEPTIONAL CHILDREN. 1878

0198-7569 See INTERNATIONAL JOURNAL OF PERIODONTICS & RESTORATIVE DENTISTRY, THE. 1325

0198-7577 See MONOGRAPHS IN UROLOGY. 3991

0198-7666 See LOCAL CLIMATOLOGICAL DATA. GRAND JUNCTION, COLORADO, ANNUAL SUMMARY WITH COMPARATIVE DATA. 1428
0198-7739 See LOCAL CLIMATOLOGICAL DATA. ALAMOSA, COLORADO, MONTHLY SUMMARY. 1427
0198-7763 See MUSEUM OF THE GREAT PLAINS NEWSLETTER. 4092
0198-7771 See OCCUPATIONAL INJURIES AND ILLNESSES IN MAINE. 2866
0198-7798 See MATERIALS SCIENCES PROGRAMS. 2106
0198-781X See AUTOMOBILE INDUSTRY TRENDS. 5405
0198-7895 See TWIN CITIES EPICURE. 2548
0198-7941 See OFFICIAL AAU TAE KWON DO RULES. 2600
0198-7992 See THAI PHILATELY. 2787
0198-800X See THIRD EYE. 3472
0198-8018 See FOREST INSECT AND DISEASE CONDITIONS IN THE PACIFIC NORTHWEST. 2380
0198-8026 See INTERNATIONAL CORPORATE BANKING REPORT TO PARTICIPANTS. 792
0198-8034 See ANNUAL REPORT OF THE BOARD OF VISITORS OF THE BUFFALO PSYCHIATRIC CENTER TO THE DEPARTMENT OF MENTAL HYGIENE. 3920
0198-8042 See IMPAC REPORTS. 870
0198-8085 See CURRENT GASTROENTEROLOGY. 3743
0198-8093 See CURRENT HEPATOLOGY. 3796
0198-8107 See WRIT (WASHINGTON), THE. 3076
0198-8158 See POPULAR MUSIC MAGAZINE. 4147
0198-8174 See CAMPBELL LAW REVIEW. 2947
0198-8212 See HANDWOVEN. 5351
0198-8220 See HANDWOVEN. 5351
0198-8239 See SPIN-OFF (LOVELAND, COLO.). 5356
0198-8263 See STUDIES IN ECONOMIC ANALYSIS. 1595
0198-8344 See RASD UPDATE. 3244
0198-8379 See SCHOLASTIC MATH MAGAZINE. 3532
0198-8387 See FIBERSCOPE. 5351
0198-8417 See NONRUBBER FOOTWEAR : U.S. PRODUCTION, IMPORTS FOR CONSUMPTION, APPAREL U.S. CONSUMPTION, EMPLOYMENT, WHOLESALE PRICE INDEX, AND CONSUMER PRICE INDEX. 1086
0198-8433 See CALIFORNIA ACADEMIC LIBRARIES LIST OF SERIALS MICROFORM. 3199
0198-8468 See CITIZEN PARTICIPATION (MEDFORD). 4468
0198-8476 See NEW ENGLAND ENVIRONMENTAL NETWORK NEWS. 2178
0198-8549 See NORTHERN KENTUCKY LAW REVIEW. 3018
0198-859X See INLAND RIVER GUIDE. 5450
0198-8654 See DOUBLE PLATINUM CIRCUS. 4115
0198-8662 See ANNUAL PLANNING INFORMATION : SAN FRANCISCO-OAKLAND STANDARD METROPOLITAN STATISTICAL AREA, CONTRA COSTA COUNTY, EXCLUDING THE CITY OF RICHMOND. 1647
0198-8670 See BITS AND PIECES (DENVER). 2723
0198-8700 See FEDERAL FUNDS FOR RESEARCH AND DEVELOPMENT. 5104
0198-8719 See POLITICAL POWER AND SOCIAL THEORY. 4489
0198-8735 See INFORMATION SERIES - COLORADO WATER RESOURCES RESEARCH INSTITUTE. 2195
0198-8794 See ANNUAL REVIEW OF GERONTOLOGY & GERIATRICS. 3749
0198-8816 See AMERICAN CHIANINA JOURNAL. 205
0198-8859 See HUMAN IMMUNOLOGY. 3670
0198-8867 See PAPERBOARD PACKAGING'S OFFICIAL CONTAINER DIRECTORY. 4221

0198-8875 See IREX OCCASIONAL PAPERS. 5204
0198-8891 See TRIBAL AND BUREAU LAW ENFORCEMENT SERVICES AUTOMATED DATA REPORT: NAVAJO AREA. 3178
0198-8905 See TRIBAL AND BUREAU LAW ENFORCEMENT SERVICES AUTOMATED DATA REPORT: TOTAL ALL AREAS. 3178
0198-8921 See NEWSLETTER OF THE MUSIC CRITICS ASSOCIATION, INC. 4141
0198-893X See REAL PROPERTY (GARDENA). 3035
0198-8999 See PROCEEDINGS OF THE ANNUAL RECIPROCAL MEAT CONFERENCE OF THE AMERICAN MEAT SCIENCE ASSOCIATION. 219
0198-9014 See INDEX TO THE CODE OF FEDERAL REGULATIONS. 2981
0198-9049 See EDUCATIONAL PROGRAMS THAT WORK (SAN FRANCISCO, CALIF.). 1742
0198-9073 See JOURNAL OF THE AMERICAN TAXATION ASSOCIATION, THE. 4735
0198-9103 See COMPENDIUM NEWSLETTER, THE. 2190
0198-912X See READINGS IN PERSONAL GROWTH AND ADJUSTMENT. 4615
0198-9138 See INDEX OF FEDERAL SPECIFICATIONS, STANDARDS AND COMMERCIAL ITEM DESCRIPTIONS. 4656
0198-9154 See PSE OUTDOOR ADVENTURES BOWHUNTING ANNUAL. 4878
0198-9162 See RED BOOK (WORTHINGTON). 2407
0198-9251 See BANKING LAW: NEW YORK BANKING LAW. 3085
0198-9278 See AFRICAN AND AFRO-AMERICAN STUDIES AND RESEARCH CENTER REPRINTS. 2636
0198-9308 See D PROJECT. 2532
0198-9340 See MW NEWSLETTER, THE. 2461
0198-9359 See MIDWEST ANCESTREE QUARTERLY, THE. 2460
0198-9375 See GATEWAY HERITAGE. 2734
0198-9383 See JOURNAL FOR CONSTRUCTIVE CHANGE. 873
0198-9391 See AMIE. 2484
0198-9405 See MEDIEVAL PROSOPOGRAPHY. 2698
0198-9448 See ADVANCED REAL ESTATE LAW COURSE. 2928
0198-9510 See CORNELL INTERNATIONAL NUTRITION MONOGRAPH SERIES. 4189
0198-9553 See BEST'S EXECUTIVE DATA SERVICE. REPORT A7-, FIVE YEAR EXPERIENCE BY STATE. 2875
0198-9561 See INTERNATIONAL BONSAI. 2420
0198-9618 See MARINER'S CATALOG, THE. 4179
0198-9626 See VICTORIAN TRAVELER'S COMPANION. 5498
0198-9634 See CONTACT QUARTERLY. 1311
0198-9650 See COMMERCIAL BUYERS GUIDE : PUERTO RICO, VIRGIN ISLANDS, THE. 949
0198-9669 See COUNTRY REPORTS ON HUMAN RIGHTS PRACTICES. 4506
0198-9677 See ANNUAL REPORT / POLYMER SCIENCE AND STANDARDS DIVISION. 2100
0198-9693 See CAPITAL UNIVERSITY LAW REVIEW. 3160
0198-9715 See COMPUTERS, ENVIRONMENT AND URBAN SYSTEMS. 2819
0198-9731 See ANNUAL REVIEW OF FAMILY THERAPY. 3921
0198-9774 See RESOURCES IN HUMAN NURTURING MONOGRAPH. 3767
0198-9839 See JOURNAL OF INFORMATION MANAGEMENT. 2885
0198-9855 See SING HEAVENLY MUSE!. 3437
0198-9863 See ABSTRACTS - AMERICAN SOCIETY OF ANIMAL SCIENCE. 5501
0198-9871 See CONTRIBUTIONS TO THE STUDY OF POPULAR CULTURE. 5243
0198-988X See ANNUAL REPORT - OKLAHOMA EDUCATIONAL TELEVISION AUTHORITY. 1888

0198-9898 See MINNESOTA WOMAN'S YEARBOOK. 5296
0198-9901 See BLUELINE (POTSDAM, N.Y.). 3367
0198-9928 See FOUR ZOAS JOURNAL. 3388
0198-9936 See POWELL ALERT, THE. 1299
0198-9960 See MANHATTAN BOOK HOUND. 4830
0199-0004 See TRUE LOVE (NEW YORK). 5075
0199-0012 See TRUE EXPERIENCE (NEW YORK). 2494
0199-0020 See TRUE ROMANCE (NEW YORK). 5075
0199-0039 See POPULATION AND ENVIRONMENT. 4556
0199-0071 See ZPG REPORTER. 2287
0199-0101 See ENGINEER'S DIGEST (WILLOW GROVE). 1974
0199-0128 See BASEBALL BULLETIN. 4886
0199-0144 See PYTHIAN INTERNATIONAL. 5235
0199-0217 See CHRISTMAS TREES. 2377
0199-025X See TRAVEL HOLIDAY. 5495
0199-0284 See NATIONAL JESUIT NEWS. 4980
0199-0292 See WORLDWIDE MISSIONS. 5010
0199-0306 See NEW HAMPSHIRE MAGAZINE (DURHAM). 1093
0199-0330 See CITY LIMITS. 2818
0199-0349 See HISPANIC BUSINESS. 679
0199-0357 See GOURMET RETAILER, THE. 2342
0199-0365 See MAINE SPORTSMAN, THE. 4904
0199-042X See SCREW WEST. 2492
0199-0438 See RECORD ADVERTISER. 5739
0199-0586 See ALASKA FEST. 5460
0199-0705 See PREDICAMENT, THE. 4913
0199-0802 See CIVIL LITIGATION REPORTER. 3089
0199-0853 See INTERNATIONAL TENNIS WEEKLY. 4901
0199-0861 See PALMETTO STAR NEWS. 5235
0199-087X See SEA CLASSICS. 4183
0199-0918 See OHIO PARENTS AND TEACHERS ASSOCIATION NEWS. 1770
0199-0926 See MARYLAND ADVANCE REPORTS. 3006
0199-0950 See AUCTION EXCHANGE, THE. 5691
0199-0969 See PALM BEACH REVIEW. 3024
0199-106X See INNOVATION ABSTRACTS. 1896
0199-1159 See PALO ALTO WEEKLY. 5638
0199-1248 See NEVADA (CARSON CITY, NEV.). 2540
0199-1256 See BULLETIN - UNIVERSITY OF KANSAS MEDICAL CENTER, THE. 3777
0199-1299 See CALIFORNIA LIBRARIES. 3199
0199-1329 See OFFICE PRODUCTS DEALER (WHEATON). 4213
0199-1337 See SEA POWER (1971). 4183
0199-1388 See AQUACULTURE MAGAZINE. 2295
0199-1507 See WASHINGTON SERVICE BUREAU SUPREME COURT BRIEF SERVICE. SECURITIES. 3072
0199-1531 See AUSTIN HOMES & GARDENS. 2898
0199-1639 See WISCONSIN MASTER PLUMBER. 2609
0199-1671 See AGRIBUSINESS WORLDWIDE. 48
0199-1744 See GOVERNMENT FINANCIAL MANAGEMENT TOPICS. 4728
0199-1795 See DANCE TEACHER NOW. 1312
0199-1833 See MEDICAL LIABILITY REPORTER. 3008
0199-1876 See ADVOCATE (LOS ANGELES TRIAL LAWYERS ASSOCIATION). 2928
0199-1892 See WOODWORKER'S JOURNAL (NEW MILFORD), THE. 635
0199-1914 See MODEL RAILROADING. 2775
0199-2074 See INDUSTRIAL PRODUCT BULLETIN. 3481
0199-218X See SUPERB WORD-TWISTS. 4866
0199-221X See WAS, WESTERN APICULTURAL SOCIETY JOURNAL. 5600
0199-2287 See GRAIN & FEED MERCHANT, THE. 201

0199-2317 See MILK AND LIQUID FOOD TRANSPORTER. 5387

0199-2376 See KLIATT (WELLESLEY, MASS.). 3221

0199-2406 See BALLS AND STRIKES. 4886

0199-2414 See CALUNDERWRITER. 2877

0199-2422 See NEWS PHOTOGRAPHER. 4372

0199-2465 See MID AMERICAN AUTO RACING NEWS. 4904

0199-2481 See ACPM NEWS. 3544

0199-2546 See COUNTY COMMISSIONER (MONTGOMERY), THE. 4641

0199-2554 See AANA NEWSBULLETIN. 3849

0199-2708 See HUMMER, THE. 4851

0199-2805 See SOUTHEAST FOOD SERVICE NEWS. 2358

0199-2864 See ADWEEK (EASTERN ED.). 755

0199-2880 See EXECUTIVE FEMALE, THE. 867

0199-2899 See LONG ISLAND JEWISH WORLD. 2267

0199-2910 See INTERMOUNTAIN CATHOLIC. 4965

0199-2929 See JEWISH LIVING. 2265

0199-2945 See FORT MYERS BEACH OBSERVER. 5649

0199-2953 See GOSPEL MISSION OF SOUTH AMERICA. 4961

0199-2988 See TAXIDERMY REVIEW. 2778

0199-3003 See SOAP OPERA STARS. 1139

0199-3038 See NAE WASHINGTON INSIGHT (NEWSLETTER ED.). 4979

0199-3062 See TEXAS GOLF. 4926

0199-3100 See BENEFITS NEWS ANALYSIS. 642

0199-3178 See TOXIC SUBSTANCES JOURNAL. 2871

0199-3186 See DIRECTOR (MADISON, WIS.), THE. 2407

0199-3267 See ABILENE REPORTER-NEWS. 5746

0199-3291 See BASS MASTER MAGAZINE. 2297

0199-3313 See KEYBOARD WORLD. 4128

0199-3356 See WEST COAST PEDDLAR. 2550

0199-3372 See SOUTHERN OUTDOORS (MONTGOMERY). 4878

0199-3429 See GOD'S WORD TODAY. 5016

0199-3445 See RAILROADIANA EXPRESS, THE. 2777

0199-347X See LA VERNE MAGAZINE. 2536

0199-350X See PEOPLE (PALO ALTO. 1979), THE. 4544

0199-3534 See RESSI REVIEW. 4846

0199-3607 See KANSAS BUSINESS NEWS. 688

0199-3666 See OUTDOORS TODAY. 4877

0199-3844 See BAKER STREET MISCELLANEA. 1923

0199-3887 See MASTER SALESMANSHIP. 933

0199-4018 See WEAR. 857

0199-4050 See SHORT LINE, THE. 5436

0199-4212 See IOWA VOTER. 4478

0199-4220 See AMERICAN COWBOY. 4882

0199-4239 See HOLSTEIN WORLD. 195

0199-4336 See GRAIN STORAGE & HANDLING. 202

0199-4395 See WEEKLY NEWS (MIAMI, FLA.), THE. 2796

0199-4441 See JEWISH WORLD (ALBANY), THE. 2265

0199-4468 See IMPORT AUTOMOTIVE PARTS & ACCESSORIES. 5416

0199-4484 See TV WORLD. 1142

0199-4514 See TOLE WORLD. 332

0199-4565 See FLORIDA REAL ESTATE COMMISSION NEWS & REPORTS. 4838

0199-462X See SAN FRANCISCO JOURNAL. CHINESE EDITION, THE. 5639

0199-4646 See FORDHAM URBAN LAW JOURNAL, THE. 2971

0199-4654 See SENSIBLE SOUND, THE. 5318

0199-4697 See CURRENT CONCEPTS IN ONCOLOGY. 3815

0199-4743 See ADWEEK. WESTERN ADVERTISING NEWS. 755

0199-4751 See FLOWERS&. 2435

0199-4786 See OCCUPATIONAL OUTLOOK QUARTERLY. 1699

0199-4883 See FEDERAL LABOR RELATIONS REPORTER. 1669

0199-4905 See MEDICAL SCIENCES BULLETIN. 4315

0199-4913 See PETERSEN'S PHOTOGRAPHIC. 4372

0199-4972 See ACTION SPORTS (SOUTH LAGUNA, CALIF.). 4881

0199-5030 See SUPREME COURT BULLETIN (MANCHESTER, N.H.). 3061

0199-5049 See SHARE THE WORD. 5019

0199-5073 See INLAND EMPIRE MAGAZINE. 682

0199-5103 See GROUP PRACTICE JOURNAL. 3780

0199-5111 See CRUISE TRAVEL MAGAZINE. 5467

0199-5197 See COBBLESTONE. 1062

0199-5200 See CRAFT RANGE. 371

0199-5235 See MASSACHUSETTS DISCRIMINATION LAW REPORTER. 3007

0199-526X See RHODE ISLAND MAGAZINE. 2544

0199-5286 See FOOD FREEZING AND PROCESSING EQUIPMENT. 2337

0199-5316 See SAFARI (TUCSON, ARIZ.). 4916

0199-5405 See HUSTLER HUMOR. 3995

0199-5421 See MAINLINE MODELER. 5432

0199-543X See AFA WATCHBIRD, THE. 4285

0199-5464 See GNSI NEWSLETTER. 5108

0199-5537 See PONY JOURNAL, THE. 2801

0199-5588 See CLASSIC CROSSWORD PUZZLES. 4859

0199-5596 See APPROVED CROSSWORD PUZZLES. 4857

0199-5626 See INDEX TO RECENT NEW HAMPSHIRE CASES. 2981

0199-5634 See STRIPER. 2314

0199-5669 See FIA WEEKLY BULLETINS. 1606

0199-5677 See MISSISSIPPI MAGAZINE (JACKSON). 2539

0199-5731 See PROSPECTUS. 4217

0199-574X See WEEKLY WORLD NEWS. 5651

0199-5782 See WEST'S BANKRUPTCY REPORTER. 3088

0199-5804 See EJAG NEWS MAGAZINE, THE. 5414

0199-5839 See FLORIDA REALTOR. 4838

0199-5928 See DERBY (NORMAN, OKLA.). 2798

0199-5979 See BIRD WORLD (NORTH HOLLYWOOD). 5615

0199-6010 See DECATUR DEKALB NEIGHBOR, THE. 5653

0199-6029 See SOUTH DEKALB NEIGHBOR, THE. 5655

0199-6037 See ACADEMY REPORTER (WASHINGTON). 4288

0199-6045 See MAILBOX (GREENSBORO), THE. 1900

0199-6096 See BUS TOURS MAGAZINE. 5465

0199-6134 See MUNICIPAL FINANCE JOURNAL. 4738

0199-6177 See SIGNIFICANT SEC FILINGS REPORTER. 3055

0199-6193 See SISA NEWS. 2493

0199-6231 See JOURNAL OF SOLAR ENERGY ENGINEERING. 1949

0199-6258 See WRESTLING USA (LAHABRA). 4931

0199-6266 See HOOSIER EQUESTRIAN. 2799

0199-6282 See ROCKDALE NEIGHBOR, THE. 5654

0199-6290 See BACK HOME IN KENTUCKY. 2722

0199-6304 See EMPLOYEE HEALTH & FITNESS. 1665

0199-6312 See HOSPITAL RISK MANAGEMENT. 869

0199-6363 See PACIFIC NORTHWEST. 2542

0199-6371 See PRINCIPAL (EAST LANSING). 1805

0199-6401 See RURAL MONTANA. 131

0199-6436 See HORSEMEN'S YANKEE PEDLAR. 2800

0199-6517 See GEORGIA SPORTSMAN. 4872

0199-6533 See MANDOLIN WORLD NEWS. 4129

0199-6606 See RADIO GUIDE (MADISON). 1137

0199-6649 See INFOWORLD. 1268

0199-669X See CALIFORNIA BUSINESS LAW REPORTER. 3097

0199-669X See FORO ARCHIVISTICO : REVISTA TECNICA DEL SISTEMA NACIONAL DE ARCHIVOS. 2481

0199-672X See NEBRASKA FERTILIZER & AG-CHEMICAL DIGEST. 111

0199-6770 See AMERICAN MARKSMAN, THE. 4883

0199-6819 See SLOVAK V AMERIKE. 5739

0199-6827 See RISK MANAGEMENT REPORTS. 2892

0199-686X See CBIA NEWS. 656

0199-6886 See USA POLONIA. 5722

0199-6894 See HOOSIER CONSERVATION. 2216

0199-6983 See RUNNER'S GAZETTE. 4916

0199-7009 See HOME & AWAY (OMAHA, NEB.). 5479

0199-7025 See CALIFORNIA PEACE OFFICER, THE. 3159

0199-7041 See TEXAS LIVESTOCK MARKET NEWS. 222

0199-7068 See MODEL SHIP BUILDER. 4179

0199-7106 See ANNIE'S QUICK & EASY PATTERN CLUB. 5347

0199-7114 See PROGRAM MANAGER. 883

0199-7122 See DAKOTA FAMILY. 78

0199-7130 See MARKETPLACE (SCOTTDALE), THE. 1504

0199-7165 See MIDNIGHT HOROSCOPE. 390

0199-7238 See CAPE COD LIFE. 2530

0199-7254 See LAS VEGAN. 2537

0199-7270 See CLAYTON SUN. 5652

0199-7289 See DORAVILLE DEKALB NEIGHBOR, THE. 5653

0199-7300 See FILM JOURNAL (NEW YORK), THE. 4070

0199-7327 See SCALE R/C MODELER. 2778

0199-7343 See COLORADO MEDICINE (1980). 3567

0199-736X See DENTALPRACTICE. 1322

0199-7378 See BULLETIN OF THE OCMA, THE. 3560

0199-7394 See GOVERNMENT BUYER. 950

0199-7408 See DUNWOODY DEKALB NEIGHBOR, THE. 5653

0199-7416 See CHAMBLEE DEKALB NEIGHBOR, THE. 5652

0199-7424 See ISRAEL SCENE (AMERICAN EDITION). 5048

0199-7459 See COMICS FEATURE. 4859

0199-7483 See WINE WORLD. 2373

0199-7521 See HOME & AWAY (CHICAGO, ILL.). 4081

0199-7564 See CORNELL COOPERATIVE EXTENSION AGRICULTURAL NEWS. 76

0199-7580 See OHIO HOLSTEIN NEWS. 197

0199-7602 See INSIDE (PHILADELPHIA, PA.). 2264

0199-7661 See LEADERSHIP (CAROL STREAM). 4973

0199-7696 See FOODSERVICE PRODUCT NEWS. 2341

0199-770X See HISPANIC TIMES MAGAZINE. 4204

0199-7734 See OHIO TEAMSTER, THE. 1700

0199-7823 See ILLINOIS TIMES. 5660

0199-7858 See BAY STATE BUSINESS WORLD. 642

0199-7890 See VETTE. 5427

0199-7912 See DRUG METABOLISM NEWSLETTER. 4301

0199-7920 *See* SPEAKER BUILDER. **5319**

0199-8013 *See* PLANT SERVICES. **2124**

0199-8072 *See* AMERICAN WAR MOTHER, THE. **2720**

0199-8137 *See* MCDOWELL EXPRESS, THE. **5723**

0199-8153 *See* SEQUOIA (SAN FRANCISCO). **4996**

0199-817X *See* NEMATOLOGY NEWSLETTER. **5592**

0199-820X *See* CURRENT HEALTH 1. **4772**

0199-8269 *See* SOUTHERN BAPTIST JOURNAL. **5067**

0199-8293 *See* WORLD AROUND YOU, THE. **4395**

0199-8315 *See* BICHON FRISE REPORTER, THE. **4285**

0199-8366 *See* GROOM & BOARD. **4286**

0199-8374 *See* CHICAGO LAWYER. **2950**

0199-8404 *See* BARTENDER. **2364**

0199-8463 *See* NORTH EAST OUT DOORS. **4876**

0199-8498 *See* SUGAR PRODUCER, THE. **2359**

0199-8501 *See* INSIDE KUNG-FU. **2598**

0199-8536 *See* POWERLIFTING USA. **4913**

0199-8595 *See* ENERGY ENGINEERING : JOURNAL OF THE ASSOCIATION OF ENERGY ENGINEERS. **1940**

0199-8668 *See* SOUTHERN STRUGGLE. **5263**

0199-8730 *See* BIZ. **4201**

0199-8757 *See* CURRENT CONCEPTS IN SKIN DISORDERS. **3718**

0199-8803 *See* TODAY'S MISSAL. **5037**

0199-8919 *See* CLUW NEWS. **1659**

0199-8951 *See* SYSTEMS USER. **1262**

0199-896X *See* SOUTHERN CALIFORNIA HOME & GARDEN. **309**

0199-8986 *See* HUMAN RESOURCE PLANNING. **942**

0199-8994 *See* NCEE REGISTRATION BULLETIN. **1988**

0199-901X *See* NEWS INDIA (NEW YORK). **2269**

0199-9044 *See* SNEA IMPACT. **1784**

0199-9060 *See* SOIL & WATER CONSERVATION NEWS. **186**

0199-9117 *See* GUITAR & LUTE. **4120**

0199-9184 *See* MINIATURE COLLECTOR. **2774**

0199-9206 *See* ARIZONA REALTOR DIGEST. **4834**

0199-9214 *See* DAYTON. **2730**

0199-9311 *See* CREDIT UNION NEWS. **1542**

0199-932X *See* ALLIANCE UPDATE. **1854**

0199-9346 *See* COMMUNITIES (LOUISA). **2818**

0199-9362 *See* LOW RIDER. **5418**

0199-9370 *See* SUNSHINE ARTISTS, U.S.A. **375**

0199-9400 *See* FOODSERVICE DISTRIBUTION NEWS. **2341**

0199-946X *See* BASEBALL HOBBY NEWS. **2771**

0199-9559 *See* ORCHID DIGEST, THE. **2426**

0199-9583 *See* HUGUENOT HISTORIAN, THE. **2738**

0199-9591 *See* ACADIAN GENEALOGY EXCHANGE. **2436**

0199-963X *See* BASE REPORT: BUDGETING, ACCOUNTABILITY, AND STAFFING EVALUATION, PERSONNEL. **938**

0199-9664 *See* HISTORICAL NEWS LETTER. **2737**

0199-9753 *See* DIAMOND REGISTRY BULLETIN, THE. **2914**

0199-977X *See* COAL PRODUCTION & TRANSPORTATION : ANNUAL CONFERENCE. **1602**

0199-9788 *See* GAMES (BASIC ED.). **4861**

0199-9826 *See* ALBANY STATE COLLEGE JOURNAL OF ARTS AND SCIENCES. **1808**

0199-9850 *See* MUNICIPAL WAGE AND SALARY SURVEY. **1692**

0199-9869 *See* SOLUTIONS (1980). **136**

0199-9885 *See* ANNUAL REVIEW OF NUTRITION. **4187**

0199-9931 *See* DARTMOUTH, THE. **1091**

0199-994X *See* GEOGRAPHICAL PERSPECTIVES. **2563**

0199-9990 *See* GOVERNMENT RELATIONS STATUS REPORT. **3087**

0201-4211 *See* SELSKOE STROITELSTVO. **627**

0201-4564 *See* ELEKTRICHESKIE STANTSII. **2051**

0201-6354 *See* EZHEGODNIK KNIGI SSSR. **3387**

0201-6745 *See* TRUDY ASTRONOMICHESKOI OBSERVATORII (LENINGRAD, R.S.F.S.R.). **401**

0201-6982 *See* SOVETSKAIA ZHENSHCHINA. **5566**

0201-7296 *See* KUZNECNO-STAMPOVOCNOE PROIZVODSTVO (1959). **4007**

0201-7318 *See* JOURNAL OF THE MOSCOW PATRIARCHATE, THE. **5039**

0201-7369 *See* BIULLETEN VSESOIUZNOGO KARDIOLOGICHESKOGO NAUCHNOGO TSENTRA AMN SSSR. **3699**

0201-7474 *See* HIMIJA DREVESINY. **2401**

0201-7490 *See* TEKHNIKA I VOORUZHENIE : ORGAN NACHALNIKA VOORUZHENII RKKA. **4059**

0201-7563 *See* ANESTEZIOLOGIJA I REANIMATOLOGIJA. **3681**

0201-7997 *See* SBORNIK NAUCHNYKH TRUDOV / VSESOIUZNAIA ORDENA LENINA I ORDENA TRUDOVOGO KRASNOGO ZNAMENI AKADEMIIA SELSKOKHOZIAISTVENNYKH NAUK IMENI V.I. LENINA, GOUDARSTVENNYI ORDENA TRUDOVOGO KRASNOGO ZNAMENI NIKITSKII BOTANICHESKII SAD. **527**

0201-8136 *See* EESTI TEADUSTE AKADEEMIA TOIMETISED. GEOLOOGIA. **1374**

0201-8268 *See* MODELIROVANIE V MEKHANIKE / AKADEMIIA NAUK SSSR, SIBIRSKOE OTDELENIE, VYCHISLITELNYI TSENTR [I] INSTITUT TEORETICHESKOI I PRIKLADNOI MEKHANIKI. **4429**

0201-8373 *See* SOVIET FILM. **4078**

0201-8454 *See* DOKLADY AKADEMII NAUK UKRAINSKOI SSR. SERIIA B, GEOLOGICHESKIE, KHIMICHESKIE I BIOLOGICHESKIE NAUKI. **5101**

0201-8462 *See* MIKROBIOLOGICHESKII ZHURNAL. **567**

0201-8470 *See* UKRAINSKII BIOKHIMICHESKII ZHURNAL. **494**

0201-8489 *See* FIZIOLOGICESKIJ ZURNAL. **580**

0201-8500 *See* BOOKS AND ART IN THE USSR. **4825**

0201-8691 See ETYKA, ESTETYKA I TEORIIA KULTURY / MINISTERSTVO VYSHCHOI I SEREDNOI SPETSIALNOI OSVITY URSR, KYIVSKYI ORDENA LENINA I ORDENA ZHOVTNEVOI REVOLIUTSII DERZHAVNYI UNIVERSYTET IM. T.H. SHEVCHENKA. **2250**

0201-873X *See* PROIZVODSTVO STALI V KISLORODNO-KONVERTORNYH I MARTENOVSKIH CEHAH. **4017**

0201-9280 *See* EZHEGODNIK. **4227**

0201-9957 *See* TRUDY VSESOJUZNOGO NAUCNO-ISSLEDOVATELSKOGO INSTITUTA GIDROMETEOROLOGICESKOJ INFORMACII-MIROVOGO CENTRA DANNYH. **1436**

0202-0726 *See* ITOGI NAUKI I TEKHNIKI : SERIIA GEODEZIIA I AEROSEMKA. **396**

0202-1447 *See* TRUDY INSTITUTA IMENI PASTERA. **3736**

0202-1927 *See* MEKHANIZATSIIA I ELEKTRIFIKASIIA SEL'SKOGO KHOZIAISTVA. **1987**

0202-2036 *See* OBSHCHESTVENNYE NAUKI V SSSR. SERIIA 1 : PROBLEMY NAUCHNOGO KOMMUNIZMA. **5211**

0202-2117 *See* OBSHCHESTVENNYE NAUKI ZA RUBEZHOM. SERIIA 7: LITERATUROVEDENIE. **3419**

0202-2141 *See* SOTSIALNYE I GUMANITARNYE NAUKI. SERIIA 8, NAUKOVEDENIE : OTECHESTVENNAIA I ZARUBEZHNAIA LITERATURA / ROSSIISKAIA AKADEMIIA NAUK, INSTITUT NAUCHNOI INFORMATSII PO OBSHCHESTVENNYM NAUKAM. **5158**

0202-2273 *See* POLITICHESKAIA ORGANIZATSIIA OBSHCHESTVA I UPRAVLENIE PRI SOTSIALIZME. **4490**

0202-2435 *See* ANALIZ STILEI ZARUBEZHNOI KHUDOZHESTVENNOI LITERATURY. **3264**

0202-2478 *See* VOPROSY REGIONALNOJ GEOLOGII. **1401**

0202-2540 *See* NOVAIA SOVETSKAIA I INOSTRANNAIA LITERATURA PO OBSHCHESTVENNYM NAUKAM. RUMYNIIA. **421**

0202-2915 *See* FIZIKA TVERDOGO TELA (DONETSKII GOSUDARSTRENNYI UNIVERSITET). **4427**

0202-3288 *See* LIETUVOS TSR AUKSTUJU MOKYKLU MOKSLO DARBAI: GEOGRAFIJA. **2568**

0202-3296 *See* KALBOTYRA / VILNIUSSKII UNIVERSITET. **3293**

0202-3318 *See* LIETUVOS TSR AUKSTUJU MOKYKLU MOKSLO DARBAI: PSICHOLOGIJA. **4602**

0202-3326 *See* LIETUVOS TSR AUKSTUJU MOKYKLU MOKSLO DARBAI: PEDAGOGIKA. **1761**

0202-3334 *See* LIETUVOS VETERINARIJOS AKADEMIJOS MOKSLO DARBAI. **5515**

0202-3342 *See* LIETUVOS ISTORIJOS METRASTIS. **2697**

0202-5132 *See* REFERATIVNYJ ZURNAL - VSESOUZNYJ INSTITUT NAUCNOJ I TEHNICESKOJ INFORMACII. 77, FARMAKOLOGIA EFFEKTORNYH SISTEM, HIMIOTERAPEVTICESKIE SREDSTVA. **471**

0202-5361 *See* NAUCHNO-TEKHNICHESKII BIULLETEN VSESOIUZNOGO ORDENA LENINA I ORDENA DRUZHBY NARODOV NAUCHNO-ISSELDOVATELSKOGO INSTITUTA RASTENIEVODSTVA IMENI N.I. VAVILOVA / VSESOIUZNAIA ORDENA LENTINA I ORDENA TRUDOGO KRASNOGO ZNAMENI AKADEMIIA SELSKOKHOZIAISTVENNYKH NAUK IMENI V.I. LENINA. **2425**

0202-5418 *See* RUSSKII IAZYK V MOLDAVSKOI SHKOLE : [UCHEBNO-METODICHESKII ZHURNAL MINISTERSTVA PROSVESHCHENIIA MOLDAVSKOI SSR]. **3319**

0202-5442 *See* BIULLETEN MEZHDUNARODNYKH NAUCHNYKH SEZDOV, KONFERENTSII, KONGRESSOV, VYSTAVOK / VSESOIUZNYI INSTITUT NAUCHNOI I TEKHNICHESKOI INFORMATSII, MEZHDUNARODNYI TSENTR NAUCHNOI I TEKHNICHESKOI INFORMATSII. **5088**

0202-5531 *See* BIULLETEN NAUCNO-TEHNICESKOJ INFORMACII VSESOUZNOGO NAUCNO-ISSLEDOVATELSKOGO INSTITUTA RISA. **164**

0202-6538 *See* MATERIALY I ISSLEDOVANIA - GOSUDARSTVENNYE MUZEI MOSKOVSKOGO KREMLA. **4091**

0202-702X *See* ITOGI NAUKI I TEKHNIKI. SERIIA ZOOLOGIIA POZVONOCHNYH. **5587**

0202-7135 *See* ITOGI NAUKI I TEKHNIKI. SERIIA PATOLOGICHESKAIA ANATOMIIA. **3895**

0202-7143 *See* ITOGI NAUKI I TEKHNIKI. POCHVOVEDENIE I AGROKHIMIIA. **98**

0202-716X *See* ITOGI NAUKI I TEKHNIKI. SERIIA RASTENIEVODSTVO. **514**

0202-7186 *See* ITOGI NAUKI I TEKHNIKI. SERIIA FIZIOLOGIIA RASTENII. **514**

0202-7275 *See* ITOGI NAUKI I TECHNIKI. SERIIA GEOMAGNETIZM I VYSOKIE SLOI ATMOSFERY. **390**

0202-7305 *See* ITOGI NAUKI I TEKHNIKI. OKEANOLOGIIA. **1450**

0202-7321 *See* ITOGI NAUKI I TEHNIKI - VSESOUZNYJ INSTITUT NAUCNOJ I TEHNICESKOJ INFORMACII. SERIA OHRANA PRIRODY I VOSPROIZVODSTVO PRIRODNYH RESURSOV. **2196**

0202-7364 *See* ITOGI NAUKI I TEKHNIKI. SERIIA NEMETALLICHESKIE POLEZNYE ISKOPAEMYE. **1440**

0202-7445 *See* ITOGI NAUKI I TEHNIKI - VSESOJUZNYJ INSTITUT NAUCHOJ I TEHNICESKO J INFORMACII. SERIJA ALGEBRA, TOPOLOGIJA, GEOMETRIJA. **3510**

0202-7453 *See* ITOGI NAUKI I TEKHNIKI. SERIIA MATEMATICHESKII ANALIZ / GOSUDARSTVENNYI KOMITET SSSR PO NAUKE I TEKHNIKE, AKADEMIIA NAUK SSSR, VSESOIUZNYI INSTITUT NAUCHNOI I TEKHNICHESKOI INFORMATSII. **3510**

ISSN Index

0202-7461 *See* ITOGI NAUKI I TEHNIKI - VSESOJUZNYJ INSTITUT NAUCNOJ I TEHNICESKOJ INFORMACII. SERIJA PROBLEMY GEOMETRII. 3510

0202-7488 *See* ITOGI NAUKI I TEHNIKI - VSESOJUZNYJ INSTITUT NAUCNOJ I TEHNICESKOJ INFORMACII. SERIJA TEORIJA VEROJATNOSTEJ, MATEMATICESKAJA STATISTIKA, TEORETICESKAJA KIBERNETIKA. 3510

0202-7623 *See* ITOGI NAUKI I TEKHNIKI. REZANIE METALLOV, STANKI I INSTRUMENTY. 2117

0202-7690 *See* ITOGI NAUKI I TEKHNIKI: TEKHNOLOGIIA I OBORUDOVANIE KUZNECHNO-SHTAMPOVOCHNOGO PROIZVODSTVA. 4005

0202-781X *See* ITOGI NAUKII TEKHNIKI SERIIA MEKHANIKA ZHIDKOSTEI I GAZA. 2117

0202-7933 *See* ITOGI NAUKI I TEHNIKI - VSESOJUZNYJ INSTITUT NA UCNOJ I TEHNICESKOJ INFORMACII, SERIJA FIZIKA PLAZMY. 4406

0202-795X *See* ITOGI NAUKI I TEKHNIKI. SERIIA BIOLOGICHESKAIA KHIMIIA. 489

0202-7968 *See* ITOGI NAUKI I TEKHNIKI. SERIIA KINETIKA I KATALIZ / GOSUDARSTVENNYI KOMITET SSSR PO NAUKE I TEKHNIKE, AKADEMIIA NAUK SSSR, VSESOIUZNYI INSTITUT NAUCHNOI I TEKHNICHESKOI INFORMATSII. 978

0202-7984 *See* IGOTI NAUKI I TEKHNIKI. SERIIA KRISTALLOKHIMIIA. 1032

0202-8042 *See* ITOGI NAUKI I TEKHNIKI. SERIIA TEKHNOLOGIIA ORGANICHESKIKH VESHCHESTV / GOSUDARSTVENNYI KOMITET SSSR PO NAUKE I TEKHNIKE, AKADEMIIA NAUK SSSR, VSESOIUZNYI INSTITUT NAUCHNOI I TEKHNICHESKOI INFORMATSII. 1042

0202-8093 *See* ITOGI NAUKI I TEKHNIKI. SERIIA ELEKTROKHIMIIA / GOSUDARSTVENNYI KOMITET SSSR PO NAUKE I TEKHNIKE, AKADEMIIA NAUK SSSR, VSESOIUZNYI INSTITUT NAUCHNOI I TEKHNICHESKOI INFORMATSII. 1034

0202-8158 *See* ITOGI NAUKI I TEKHNIKI. SERIIA EKONOMIKA, ORGANIZATSIIA, TEKHNOLOGIIA I OBORUDOVANIE POLIGRAFICHESKOGO PROIZVODSTVA / VSESOIUZNYI INSTITUT NAUCHNOI I TEKHNICHESKOI INFORMATSII. 5117

0202-9030 *See* REFERATIVNYJ ZURNAL - VSESOJUZNYJ INSTITUT NAUCNOJ I TEHNICESKOJ INFORMACII. 53. IMMUNOLOGIJA. ALLERGOLOGIJA. 3676

0203-0292 *See* INZHENERNAIA GEOLOGIIA / AKADEMIIA NAUK SSSR. 1383

0203-1272 *See* MEHANIKA KOMPOZITNYH MATERIALOV. 2107

0203-2198 *See* CHELOVEK I STIKHIIA. 2212

0203-2805 *See* PRIBOROSTROENIE (MINSK). 3486

0203-3054 *See* INFORMATICS ABSTRACTS. 3215

0203-3100 *See* GEOFIZICHESKII ZHURNAL. 1405

0203-3119 *See* SVERH-TVERDYE MATERIALY. 1997

0203-3275 *See* KOMPOZITSIONNYE POLIMERNYE MATERIALY / AKADEMIIA NAUK UKRAINSKOI SSR, INSTITUT KHIMII VYSOKOMOLEKULIARNYKH SOEDINENII. 1044

0203-4638 *See* SCIENCE IN USSR. 5152

0203-4654 *See* FIZIKA I TEHNIKA VYSOKIH DAVLENIJ. 4403

0203-4883 *See* KAVKAZ I VIZANTIIA. 2696

0203-493X *See* NEIROKHIMIIA. 987

0203-4972 *See* AKTUALNYE VOPROSY BIBLIOTECHNOI RABOTY / GOSUDARSTVENNAIA BIBLIOTEKA SSSR IMENI V.I. LENINA. 3188

0203-5189 *See* REFERATIVNYI ZHURNAL. ELEKTROTEKHNIKA / GOSUDARSTVENNYI KOMITET SSSR PO NAUKE I TEKHNIKE, AKADEMIIA NAUK SSSR, VSESOIUZNYI INSTITUT NAUCHNOI I TEKHNICHESKOI INFORMATSII. 2079

0203-5308 *See* REFERATIVNYI ZHURNAL. ENERGETIKA / GOSUDARSTVENNYI KOMITET SSSR PO NAUKE I TEKHNIKE, AKADEMIIA NAUK SSSR, VSESOIUZNYI INSTITUT NAUCHNOI I TEKHNICHESKOI INFORMATSII. 2079

0203-5626 *See* NOVYE DANNYE O MINERALAKH / AKADEMIIA NAUK SSSR, MINERALOGICHESKIĔI MUZEI IM. A.E. FERSMANA. 1443

0203-5650 *See* MODELI I SISTEMY OBRABOTKI INFORMATSII. 3232

0203-5839 *See* BRATSKII VESTNIK. 5057

0203-5936 *See* MUSLIMS OF THE SOVIET EAST. 4979

0203-6703 *See* TRUDY VIEV. 5523

0203-6827 *See* NAUCNYE TRUDY - VSESOJUZNYJ NAUCNO-ISSLEDOVATELSKIJ INSTITUT FIZIOLOGII BIOHIMII I PITANIJA SELSKO-HOZJAJSTEVENNYH ZIVOTNYH. 5516

0203-8722 *See* KOMPLEKSNYE METALLOORGANICESKIE KATALIZATORY POLIMERIZACII OLEFINOV. 4007

0204-0476 *See* ARGUMENTY I FAKTY : BIULLETEN ORDENA LENINA VSESOIUZNOGO OBSHCHESTVA "ZNANIE," LEKTORAM, PROPAGANDISTAM, POLITINFORMATORAM, AGITATORAM. 2676

0204-0670 *See* KIRGIZIIA V PECHATI SSSR I ZARUBEZHNYKH SOTSIALISTICHESKIKH STRAN. 418

0204-2061 *See* KNYGOTYRA. 3221

0204-3548 *See* MINERALOGICESKIJ ZURNAL. 1442

0204-3556 *See* HIMIJA I TEHNOLOGIJA VODY. 5534

0204-3564 *See* EKSPERIMENTALNAJA ONKOLOGIJA. 3816

0204-3572 *See* ELEKTRONNOE MODELIROVANIE. 1259

0204-3580 *See* METALLOFIZIKA (KIEV). 4009

0204-3599 *See* TEHNICESKAJA ELEKTRODINAMIKA. 2084

0204-3602 *See* PROMYSLENNAJA TEPLOTEHNIKA. 2127

0204-3998 *See* HIMICESKAJA PROMYSLENNOST. SERIJA, FOSFORNAJA PROMYSLENNOST. 1025

0204-4080 *See* VOENNO-ISTORICHESKI SBORNIK. 4060

0204-4110 *See* SERDIKA. 3533

0204-4560 *See* STROEZ I FUNKCII NA MOZKA. 3846

0204-5060 *See* NASH DOM : [IZDANIE NA KOMITETA ZA KULTURA]. 2902

0204-5311 *See* RUDOOBRAZOVATELNI PROCESI I MINERALNI NAHODISCA. 1444

0204-577X *See* ABSTRACTS OF BULGARIAN SCIENTIFIC LITERATURE. INDUSTRY, BUILDING AND TRANSPORT. STATE COMMITTEE FOR SCIENCE AND TECHNICAL PROGRESS, CENTRAL INSTITUTE FOR SCIENTIFIC AND TECHNICAL INFORMATION. 1963

0204-5958 *See* FIZIKO-HIMICESKA MEHANIKA. 1052

0204-6091 *See* IZVESTIA NA NARODNATA BIBLIOTEKA KIRIL I METODIJ. 3219

0204-6377 *See* CELULOZA I KHARTIYA. 4233

0204-6385 *See* NAUCHNI TRUDOVE - VISSH SELSKOSTOPANSKI INSTITUT "VASIL KOLAROV" PLOVDIV. 111

0204-6725 *See* MEDIKO-BIOLOGICESKAJA INFORMACIJA. 3614

0204-6946 *See* FIZIKA (SOFIA). 4403

0204-7209 *See* PROBLEMI NA GEOGRAFIIATA. 2573

0204-7535 *See* MATERIALOZNANIE I TEKNOLOGIYA. 4008

0204-7675 *See* EKOLOGIA (SOFIA). 2215

0204-823X *See* BULGARSKO MUZIKOZNANIE (SOFIA, BULGARIA : 1979). 4105

0204-8523 *See* OBSHTESTVO I PRAVO. 3020

0204-8531 *See* ALO, 160. 2287

0204-8620 *See* PROBLEMS OF CULTURE / COMMITTEE FOR CULTURE, RESEARCH INSTITUTE FOR CULTURE AT THE COMMITTEE FOR CULTURE, AND THE BULGARIAN ACADEMY OF SCIENCES. 5254

0204-8701 *See* SUPOSTAVITELNO EZIKOZNANIE. 3327

0204-8809 *See* ACTA MICROBIOLOGICA BULGARICA. 558

0204-8817 *See* BIOLOGIA ET IMMUNOLOGIA REPRODUCTIONIS. 3556

0204-8884 *See* BULGARIAN FILMS. 4064

0204-9104 *See* SPACE RESEARCH IN BULGARIA. 400

0204-9155 *See* PROBLEMS OF INFECTIOUS AND PARASITIC DISEASES. 3715

0204-9562 *See* NOVOSTI V TSELULOZNO-KHARTIENATA PROMISHLENOST / MINISTERSTVO NA GORITE I GORSKATA PROMISHLENOST, DSO, "TSELULOZA I KHARTIIA"-NIITSKH. 4235

0204-9848 *See* PROBLEMI NA TEKHNICHESKATA KIBERNETIKA I ROBOTIKATA. 1252

0204-9864 *See* BYZANTINO BULGARICA. 2682

0205-003X *See* PROBLEMI NA HRANENETO. 4197

0205-0390 *See* SRAVNITELNO LITERATUROZNANIE / [BULGARSKA AKADEMIIA NA NAUKITE, INSTITUT ZA LITERATURA]. 3439

0205-0439 *See* GODISNIK NA VISSIJA INSTITUT PO ARHITEKTURA I STROITELSTVO. SVITK II HISROTEHNIKA. 1976

0205-0617 *See* NASELENIE. 4555

0205-0625 *See* USPEHI NA MOLEKULARNATA BIOLOGIA. 475

0205-0838 *See* ABV. 4822

0205-1400 *See* ECONOMIC NEWS OF BULGARIA. 1483

0205-1656 *See* SUVREMENNA ZHURNALISTIKA / [SBZH, NAUCHNO-INFORMATSIONEN TSENTUR]. 2924

0205-1710 *See* OVOSHTARSTVO, GRADINARSTVO I KONSERVNA PROMISHLENOST. 180

0205-177X *See* HRANITELNOPROMISHLENA NAUKA. 2343

0205-2512 *See* BALKANISTIKA / BULGARSKA AKADEMIIA NA NAUKITE, INSTITUT PO BALKANISTIKA. 2677

0205-2679 *See* SBORNIK ZA NARODNI UMOTVORENIJA I NARODOPIS. 3319

0205-2741 *See* PROBLEMI NA METEOROLOGIATA I HIDROLOGIATA. 1417

0205-3209 *See* BULGARISTIKA. 2680

0205-3799 *See* ABSTRACTS OF BULGARIAN SCIENTIFIC LITERATURE. CULTURE / BULGARIAN ACADEMY OF SCIENCES, SCIENTIFIC INFORMATION CENTRE. 335

0205-3829 *See* VETERINARNA SBIRKA. 5524

0205-3845 *See* IKONOMIKA I UPRAVLENIE NA SELSKOTO STOPANSTVO. 94

0205-5295 *See* HUDOZESTVENNOE NASLEDIE. 322

0205-9592 *See* PSIHOLOGICESKIJ ZURNAL. 4609

0205-9614 *See* ISSLEDOVANIE ZEMLI IZ KOSMOSA. 2566

0206-0477 *See* TRUDY ZOOLOGICHESKOGO INSTITUTA. 5599

0206-1074 *See* TRUDY INSTITUTA - NAUCNO-ISSLEDOVATELSKIJ INSTITUT PROMYSLENNOGO STROITELSTVA. 630

0206-1473 *See* NEW TIMES. 4529

0206-314X *See* KPSS XXVI SEZDI QARORLARINI HAETGA TATBIQ ETISHDA UZBEKISTON MATBUOTI. 5251

0206-4251 *See* TAVAN ATAL. 3444

0206-4715 *See* VOPROSY SISTEMOTEKHNIKI. 1255

0206-4731 *See* VOPROSY EKOLOGII I OKHRANY PRIRODY. 2208

0206-4952 *See* IMMUNOLOGIJA (MOSKVA). 3671

0206-572X *See* ME, MEHANIZACIA I ELEKTRIFIKACIA SELSKOGO HOZAISTVA (MOSKVA). 107

0206-6335 *See* VESTNIK SELSKOHOZAJSTVENNOJ NAUKI. 144

0206-6548 *See* KONSTRUKTIVNAIA TEROIIA FUNKTSII I FUNKTSIONALNYI ANALIZ. 3516

0207-0111 *See* GIBRIDNYE VYCHISLITELNYE MASHINY I KOMPLEKSY. 1251

0207-0472 *See* VOPROSY ATOMNOI NAUKI I TEKHNIKI. SERIIA OBSHCHAIA I IADERNAIA FIZIKA. 4451

0207-0480 *See* VOPROSY ATOMNOI NAUKI I TEKHNIKI. SERIIA TEKHNIKA FIZICHESKOGO EKSPERIMENTA. 4451

0207-1258 *See* LITUANISTIKA V SSSR: ISKUSSTVOVEDENIE. 324

0207-3676 *See* OBSHCHESTVO I EKONOMIKA. 1576

0207-4001 *See* DAUGAVA. 3380

0207-401X *See* HIMICESKAJA FIZIKA. 1052

0207-4028 *See* TIKHOOKEANSKAIA GEOLOGIA. 1399

0207-6756 *See* UPRAVLENIE I NAUCHNO-TEKHNICHESKII PROGRESS. 5168

0207-6861 *See* INFORMATSIONNYE MATERIALY / AKADEMIIA NAUK SSSR, FILOSOFSKOE OBSHCHESTVO SSSR. 4349

0207-6918 *See* KANTOVSKII SBORNIK / MINISTERSTVO VYSSHEGO I SREDNEGO SPETSIALNOGO OBRAZOVANIIA RSFSR, KALININGRADSKII GOSUDARSTVENNYI UNIVERSITET. 4351

0207-7280 *See* SSSR KHALQ DEPUTATLARI SEZDI VA SSSR OLII SOVETINING AKHBOROTNOMASI. 4497

0207-9224 *See* SUBTROPICHESKIE KULTURY. 188

0207-9739 *See* ZRELISHCHNYE ISKUSSTVA. 389

0207-9941 *See* TEORIIA OPERATOROV I TEORIIA FUNKTSII. 3538

0208-0087 *See* BIBLIOGRAFICHESKAIA INFORMATSIIA. SREDSTVA OBUCHENIIA V VYSSHEI I SREDNEI SPETSIALNOI SHKOLE / MINISTERSTVO VYSSHEGO I SREDNEGO SPETSIALNOGO OBRAZOVANIIA SSSR, NAUCHNO-ISSLEDOVATELSKII INSTITUT PROBLEM VYSSHEI SHKOLY. 1793

0208-0613 *See* MOLEKULIARNAIA GENETIKA, MIKROBIOLOGIIA I VIRUSOLOGIIA. 568

0208-1245 *See* ITOGI NAUKI I TEKHNIKI. SERIIA ATMOSFERA, OKEAN, KOSMOS PROGRAMMA RAZREZY. 1450

0208-189X *See* GORIUCHIE SLANTSY. 1381

0208-2330 *See* ITOGI NAUKI I TEHNIKI - VSESOUZNYJ INSTITUT NAUCNOJ I TEHNICESKOJ INFORMACII. SERIA BIOTEHNOLOGIA. 3693

0208-2403 *See* SOVETSKII MUZEI (1984). 4096

0208-287X *See* IZOBRETENIIA : OFITSIALNYI PATENTNYI BIULLETEN. 1305

0208-2888 *See* PROMYSHLENNYE OBRAZTSY, TOVARNYE ZNAKI : OFITSIALNYI BIULLETEN GOSUDARSTVENNOGO KOMITETA SSSR PO DELAM IZOBRETENII I OTKRYTII. 1308

0208-4074 *See* STUDIA GRAMATYCZNE / POLSKA AKADEMIA NAUK, INSTYTUT JEZYKA POLSKIEGO. 3324

0208-4147 *See* PROBABILITY AND MATHEMATICAL STATISTICS. 3542

0208-4163 *See* SOWO PODLASIA. 2523

0208-418X *See* ARCHIWUM TERMODYNAMIKI. 4430

0208-4198 *See* ARCHIVUM COMBUSTIONIS. 4430

0208-421X *See* STUDIA I MATERIAY OCEANOLOGICZNE. 5160

0208-4228 *See* LINGUISTICA SILESIANA. 3299

0208-4333 *See* BIBLIOTEKARZ. 3194

0208-4449 *See* BIOLOGIA (POZNAN, POLAND). 444

0208-4902 *See* ZESZYTY NAUKOWE. SERIA I. 1528

0208-4961 See ZESZYTY NAUKOWE. BIOLOGIA / UNIWERSYTET GDANSKI. 476

0208-5216 *See* BIOCYBERNETICS AND BIOMEDICAL ENGINEERING / POLISH ACADEMY OF SCIENCES, INSTITUTE OF BIOCYBERNETICS AND BIOMEDICAL ENGINEERING. 3686

0208-5437 *See* PRACE Z NAUK SPOECZNYCH. 5213

0208-5607 *See* ANNALES ACADEMIAE MEDICAE SILESIENSIS. 3550

0208-5704 *See* ANNALS OF WARSAW AGRICULTURAL UNIVERSITY - SGGW-AR. FORESTRY AND WOOD TECHNOLOGY. 2374

0208-5712 *See* ANNALS OF WARSAW AGRICULTURAL UNIVERSITY, SGGW--AR. AGRICULTURE. 59

0208-5739 *See* ANNALS OF WARSAW AGRICULTURAL UNIVERSITY, SGGW-AR. ANIMAL SCIENCE. 205

0208-5747 *See* ANNALS OF WARSAW AGRICULTURAL UNIVERSITY, SGGW-AR. HORTICULTURE. 2409

0208-5763 *See* ANNALS OF WARSAW AGRICULTURAL UNIVERSITY, SGGW-AR. VETERINARY MEDICINE. 5503

0208-5771 *See* ANNALS OF WARSAW AGRICULTURAL UNIVERSITY SGGW-AR. LAND RECLAMATION. 59

0208-595X *See* ANNUAL REPORT - NATIONAL INSTITUTE OF HYGIENE. 4766

0208-600X *See* ACTA UNIVERSITATIS LODZIENSIS. FOLIA SOCIOLOGICA. 5238

0208-6034 *See* ACTA UNIVERSITATIS LODZIENSIS. FOLIA ARCHAEOLOGICA. 253

0208-6069 *See* ACTA UNIVERSITATIS LODZIENSIS. FOLIA IURIDICA. 2927

0208-6220 *See* AKCENT : A. 312

0208-6247 *See* IM. INZYNIERIA MATERIALOVA. 1977

0208-6263 *See* WIADOMOSCI INSTYTUTU METEOROLOGII I GOSPODARKI WODNEJ. 1437

0208-6360 *See* ZESZYTY NAUKOWE - AKADEMIA TECHNICZNO-ROLNICZA IM. JANA I JEDRZEJA SNIADECKICH W BYDGOSZCZY. CHEMIA I TECHNOLOGIA CHEMICZNA. 996

0208-6425 *See* INZYNIERIA CHEMICZNA I PROCESOWA. 2013

0208-645X *See* PRACE INSTYTUTU GEOLOGICZNEGO. 1391

0208-6573 *See* FUNCTIONES ET APPROXIMATIO COMMENTARII MATHEMATICI. 3506

0208-6603 *See* BIULETYN (INSTYTUT GEOLOGICZNY (POLAND)). 1367

0208-6786 *See* NAD WARTA BODZ. 2519

0208-6883 *See* NOWINY JELENIOGORSKIE. 2520

0208-6956 *See* TRYBUNA WABRZYSKA. 2524

0208-6964 *See* ZYCIE PRZEMYSKIE. 2525

0208-6972 *See* TYGODNIK POCKI. 2524

0208-6980 *See* TYGODNIK PIOTRKOWSKI. 2524

0208-6999 *See* ZIEMIA GORZOWSKA. 2525

0208-7006 *See* TEMI. TARNOWSKI MAGAZYN INFORMACYJNY. 2523

0208-7243 *See* POLISH ART STUDIES. 328

0208-7286 *See* INFORMATYKA / POLITECHNIKA SLASKA. 3217

0208-7375 *See* POLISH POLITICAL SCIENCE / POLISH ASSOCIATION OF POLITICAL SCIENCE. 4488

0208-7421 *See* ZIEMIA KALISKA. 5808

0208-7448 *See* MECHANIZACJA I AUTOMATYZACJA GORNICTWA. 2143

0208-7499 *See* WOKNA CHEMICZNE. 995

0208-7669 *See* ZESZYTY NAUKOWE NAUK SPOECZNYCH I EKONOMICZNYCH. 5226

0208-7693 *See* GAZETA KRAKOWSKA 1980. 5808

0208-7707 *See* DZIENNIK LODZKI 1980. 5807

0208-7723 *See* LAD WARSZAWA. 4972

0208-7782 *See* ANTENA. 1126

0208-7944 *See* ZESZYTY NAUKOWE (AKADEMIA EKONOMICZNA W KRAKOWIE). 5808

0208-8045 *See* TYGODNIK SOLIDARNOSC. 5808

0208-8061 *See* PUBLICATIONS OF THE INSTITUTE OF GEOPHYSICS. G. 1409

0208-8274 *See* PODSTAWY GOSPODARKI W SRODOWISKU MORSKIM / POLSKA AKADEMIIA NAUK, KOMITET BADAN MORZA. 1455

0208-838X *See* ROCZNIK STATYSTYCZNY MIAST / GOWNY URZAD STATYSTYCZNY. 5337

0208-841X *See* ARTIFICIAL SATELLITES. PLANETARY GEODESY / POLISH ACADEMY OF SCIENCES, SPACE RESEARCH CENTRE. 1402

0208-8525 *See* PUBLICATIONS OF THE INSTITUTE OF GEOPHYSICS. 1409

0208-8584 *See* CONFERENCE ON APPLIED CRYSTALLOGRAPHY. PROCEEDINGS. 1031

0208-8622 *See* TYGODNIK NADWISLANSKI. 2524

0208-8746 *See* GAZETA POZNANSKA 1981. 5808

0208-9068 *See* ANNALES SOCIETATIS GEOLOGORUM POLONIAE. 1365

0208-9092 *See* PRACE OSRODKA BADAWCZO-ROZWOJOWEGO PRZETWORNIKOW OBRAZU. 5139

0208-9130 *See* RZECZPOSPOLITA WARSZAWA. 5808

0208-9300 *See* ROCZNIK STATYSTYCZNY WOJEWODZTW. 5337

0208-9386 *See* KRZEPNIECIE METALI I STOPOW. 4007

0209-0023 *See* PRZEGLAD TYGODNIOWY. 2521

0209-0031 *See* WIEDZA OBRONNA : DWUMIESIECZNIK TOWARZYSTWA WIEDZY OBRONNEJ. 4061

0209-0058 *See* MATERIAY ELEKTRONICZNE. 2071

0209-0333 *See* TRANSPORT MIEJSKI. 5395

0209-0554 *See* VETO WARSZAWA. 718

0209-0600 *See* ZESZYTY NAUKOWE - POLITECHNIKA IODZKA. TECHNOLOGIA I CHEMIA SPOZYWCZA. 1031

0209-0708 *See* BIULETYN MORSKIEGO INSTYTUTU RYBACKIEGO. 2297

0209-1291 *See* KATECHETA. 4971

0209-147X *See* DOM. 319

0209-164X *See* ZYWIENIE CZOWIEKA I METABOLIZM. 4200

0209-2166 *See* TYGODNIK LUDOWY. 2524

0209-2182 *See* ORZECZNICTWO SADU NAJWYZSZEGO. IZBA CYWILNA I ADMINISTRACYJNA ORAZ IZBA PRACY I UBEZPIECZEN SPOECZNYCH. 5300

0209-2492 *See* BIULETYN INFORMACYJNY - INSTYTUT ZOOTECHNIKI. 207

0209-3537 *See* ILUZJON WARSZAWA. 4072

0209-3871 *See* RAPORT O STANIE, ZAGROZENIU I OCHRONIE SRODOWISKA 2180

0209-4541 *See* OXIDATION COMMUNICATIONS. 1045

0209-4835 *See* STUDIA GEOGRAPHICA DEBRECEN. 2577

0209-4894 *See* KONYVTARI JEGYZESEK. 3222

0209-6137 *See* MATHEMATICAL METHODS OF OPERATIONS RESEARCH. 3519

0209-6145 *See* PEST MEGYEI KONYVTAROS. 3241

0209-682X *See* SPORTORVOSI SZEMLE. 3956

0209-732X *See* MEDICOR NEWS. 3944

0209-7788 *See* KISALFOLDI KONYVTAROS. 3221

0209-9004 *See* ACTA GEOGRAPHICA AC GEOLOGICA ET METEOROLOGICA DEBRECINA. 1351

0209-9306 *See* ERDESZETI ES FAIPARI TUDOMANYOS KOZLEMENYEK. 2379

0209-9578 *See* TEXTIL- ES TEXTILRUHAZATI IPARI SZAKIRODALMI TAJEKOZTATO. 5357

0209-9683 *See* COMBINATORICA (BUDAPEST. 1981). 3500

0210-0010 *See* REVISTA DE NEUROLOGIA. 3845

0210-0061 *See* CUADERNOS PARA INVESTIGACION DE LA LITERATURA HISPANICA. 3379

0210-0088 *See* BASILISCO (OVIEDO, SPAIN). 4342

0210-010X *See* CERAMICA MADRID. 2587

0210-0118 *See* NOVAMAQUINA 2000. 2123

0210-0150 *See* AVENC, L'. 2677

0210-0223 *See* SISTEMA (MADRID). 5219

0210-0266 *See* CUADERNOS DE ECONOMIA. 1554

0210-0363 *See* ESTUDIOS TRINITARIOS. 4956

ISSN Index

0210-038X See REVISTA DE ESTUDIOS HISTORICOS DE LA GUARDIA CIVIL. **2627**

0210-0398 See CIENCIA TOMISTA. **5027**

0210-0460 See ANALES VALENTINOS. **4934**

0210-0479 See CIMBRA. **295**

0210-0525 See ESTUDIOS MADRID. **3385**

0210-0581 See MORALIA. **5209**

0210-0614 See REVISTA ESPANOLA DE DOCUMENTACION CIENTIFICA. **3246**

0210-0630 See CUADERNOS DE PEDAGOGIA. **1734**

0210-0657 See CLINICA Y ANALISIS GRUPAL. **4581**

0210-0665 See FRIO, CALOR, AIRE ACONDICIONADO. **2605**

0210-0681 See ANALES DE LA SOCIEDAD ERGOFTALMOLOGICA ESPANOLA. **3872**

0210-0819 See CIENCIA & INDUSTRIA FARMACEUTICA. **4296**

0210-0908 See DIRECCION Y PROGRESO. **665**

0210-0924 See REVISTA DE INSTITUCIONES EUROPEAS. **1582**

0210-0940 See BOLETIN DE LA ASOCIACION ESPANOLA DE COLO-PROTOLOGIA. **3558**

0210-1041 See CONCILIUM (MADRID). **4949**

0210-1130 See CITOLOGIA : REVISTA OFICIAL DE LE SOCIEDAD ESPANOLA DE CITOLOGIA, EN COLABORACION CON LAS SOCIEDADES LATINOAMERICANAS DE CITOLOGIA. **535**

0210-119X See CIMAL. **317**

0210-122X See PROCESO DE DATOS. **1261**

0210-1262 See BOLETIN DE LA ASOCIACION ESPANOLA DE ENDOSCOPIA DIGESTIVA. **3795**

0210-1270 See PASTOS. **118**

0210-1300 See ANTOLOGIA DERMATOLOGICA. **3717**

0210-136X See INVESTIGACION Y CIENCIA. **5116**

0210-1424 See COMUNICACION PSIQUIATRICA. **3923**

0210-1475 See BOLETIN DE LA SOCIEDAD CASTELLONENSE DE CULTURA. **2843**

0210-1521 See INVESTIGACIONES ECONOMICAS. **1568**

0210-1602 See TEOREMA. **4363**

0210-1610 See ESTUDIOS ECLESIASTICOS. **5029**

0210-1629 See ARCHIVO TEOLOGICO GRANADINO. **5023**

0210-1653 See BOLETIN EPIDEMIOLOGICO SEMANAL - MINISTERIO DE SANIDAD Y CONSUMO. PUBLICACIONES. DOCUMENTACION Y BIBLIOTECA. **3558**

0210-1688 See BANCA ESPANOLA. **773**

0210-1718 See LABOREO. **1685**

0210-1742 See REVISTA DE EXTENSION AGRARIA. **129**

0210-1777 See IMHE. INFORMACION DE MAQUINAS-HERRAMIENTA, EQUIPOS Y ACCESORIOS. **2115**

0210-1793 See REVISTA DE PSIQUIATRIA DE LA FACULTAD DE MEDICINA DE BARCELONA. **3936**

0210-184X See M.I. MONTAJES E INSTALACIONES. **2606**

0210-1874 See REVISTA ESPANOLA DE LINGUISTICA. **3316**

0210-1912 See CUNICULTURAL. **210**

0210-1947 See BOLETIN ECONOMICO DE LA CONSTRUCCION 1956. **601**

0210-1963 See ARBOR. **5085**

0210-2056 See ENERGIA MADRID. **1938**

0210-2064 See INGENIERIA QUIMICA (MADRID). **2013**

0210-2137 See GACETA NUMISMATICA. **2781**

0210-2145 See EME DOS. **614**

0210-220X See JANO. MEDICINA Y HUMANIDADES. **3591**

0210-2307 See INDUSTRIA MINERA. **2140**

0210-2323 See REVISTA ESPANOLA DE CIRUGIA DE LA MANO. **3973**

0210-2366 See FONAMENTS. **2688**

0210-2439 See BOLETIN BIBLIOGRAFICO DE LA PREVENCION. **1656**

0210-2560 See COMUNICACIONES I.N.I.A. SERIE TECNOLOGIA AGRARIA. **76**

0210-2692 See ZONA ABIERTA. **5226**

0210-279X See ACTUALIDAD DERMATOLOGICA. **3717**

0210-2854 See REVISTA DE ESTUDIOS EXTREMENOS. **2705**

0210-2870 See DIALOGO ECUMENICO. **4953**

0210-3133 See ESCRITOS DEL VEDAT. **4956**

0210-3230 See ARCHIVO DE PREHISTORIA LEVANTINA. **2611**

0210-3311 See COMUNICACIONES I.N.I.A. SERIE GENERAL. **76**

0210-3338 See COMUNICACIONES I.N.I.A. SERIE RECURSOS NATURALES. **76**

0210-3397 See AVANCES EN TERAPEUTICA. **4293**

0210-3451 See REVISTA DE LA SOCIEDAD ESPANOLA DE DIALISIS Y TRANSPLANTE. **3635**

0210-3516 See LETRAS DE DEUSTO. **2849**

0210-3524 See TERUEL. **2712**

0210-3702 See INFANCIA Y APRENDIZAJE. **4590**

0210-3761 See TG. TAPICERIAS GANCEDO. **376**

0210-380X See RECERQUES. **1580**

0210-4067 See ARCHIVO HISPALENSE. **2676**

0210-4083 See MONSALVAT. **4132**

0210-4164 See BOLETIN DE LA ANABAD. **2480**

0210-4199 See BIOMETRICA. **3893**

0210-4466 See ASCLEPIO : ARCHIVO IBEROAMERICANO DE HISTORIA DE LA MEDICINA Y ANTROPOLOGIA MEDICA. **3553**

0210-4598 See ESTADISTICA DE ESTABLECIMIENTOS SANITARIOS CON REGIMEN DE INTERNADO. **3780**

0210-4660 See CLINICA ANESTESIOLOGICA. **3565**

0210-4695 See ACTA ESTRABOLOGICA. **3871**

0210-4806 See ACTAS UROLOGICAS ESPANOLAS. **3988**

0210-4814 See PUBLICATIONES DEL DEPARTAMENTO DE ZOOLOGIA / UNIVERSIDAD DE BARCELONA, FACULTAD DE BIOLOGIA. **5595**

0210-4822 See BOLETIN DE LA REAL ACADEMIA ESPANOLA. **3269**

0210-4830 See ESTUDIS D'HISTORIA AGRARIA. **82**

0210-4903 See MISCELANEA MEDIEVAL MURCIANA. **2699**

0210-4946 See BOLLETIN DE ARCHIVOS. **2480**

0210-5020 See REVISTA ROL DE ENFERMERIA. **3868**

0210-5187 See MEDICINA CUTANEA IBERO-LATINO-AMERICANA. **3721**

0210-5209 See BIBLIA Y FE. **5015**

0210-5233 See REVISTA ESPANOLA DE INVESTIGACIONES SOCIOLOGICAS. **5256**

0210-5268 See MONOGRAFIA DEL COLEGIO IBERO-LATINO-AMERICANO DE DERMATOLOGIA. **3722**

0210-5403 See ANALES - INSTITUTO MEDICO BENEFICENCIA. **3549**

0210-5527 See ARCHIVOS DE LA FACULTAD DE MEDICINA DE OVIEDO. **3552**

0210-5543 See CARNICA 2000. **2366**

0210-5551 See REVISTA CATALANA DE TEOLOGIA. **4993**

0210-5659 See NUESTRA CABANA. **217**

0210-5691 See MEDICINA INTENSIVA / SOCIEDAD ESPANOLA DE MEDICINA INTENSIVA Y UNIDADES CORONARIAS. **3613**

0210-5705 See GASTROENTEROLOGIA Y HEPATOLOGIA. **3745**

0210-5713 See AMERICAN JOURNAL OF MEDICINE. EDICION ESPANOLA. **3548**

0210-5721 See PEDIATRICS. EDICION ESPANOLA. **3910**

0210-573X See CLINICA E INVESTIGACION EN GINECOLOGIA Y OBSTETRICIA. **3758**

0210-5810 See ANUARIO DE ESTUDIOS AMERICANOS. **2721**

0210-5969 See MOTOR MUNDIAL. **5420**

0210-5977 See PRESUPUESTO Y GASTO PUBLICO. **4741**

0210-6035 See REVISTA DE ESTUDIOS PENITENCIARIOS (1961). **3175**

0210-6086 See ESTUDIOS FILOSOFICOS (VALLADOLID). **4346**

0210-6272 See CUADERNOS DE INVESTIGACION HISTORICA. **2684**

0210-6302 See ACTUALIDAD ELECTRONICA. **2034**

0210-6310 See TOLETUM. **2855**

0210-6329 See REVISTA DE LA ASOCIACION ESPANOLA DE FARMACEUTICOS DE HOSPITALES. **4328**

0210-6337 See LEVIATAN (MADRID, SPAIN). **4528**

0210-6353 See HISTORIA 16. **2691**

0210-6361 See CENTRO MEDICO. **3562**

0210-6523 See ANALES DE LA REAL ACADEMIA DE MEDICINA Y CIRUGIA DE VALLADOLID. **3958**

0210-6531 See BOLETIN DE BELLAS ARTES. **344**

0210-6604 See REVISTA IBEROAMERICANA DE CORROSION Y PROTECCION. **2017**

0210-6612 See SALUD Y TRABAJO (MADRID). **2870**

0210-685X See DEFORMACION METALICA. **4000**

0210-6868 See PISCINAS. **623**

0210-7058 See ANALES DE LA REAL ACADEMIA DE MEDICINA Y CIRUGIA DE CADIZ. **3958**

0210-7112 See REVISTA ESPANOLA DE TEOLOGIA. **4993**

0210-7171 See AVANCES EN OBSTETRICIA Y GINECOLOGIA. **3757**

0210-721X See BUTLLETI DE LA SOCIETAT CATALANA DE PEDIATRIA. **3901**

0210-7228 See BOLETIN DEL INSTITUTO GEMOLOGICO ESPANOL. **2913**

0210-7260 See ESTUDIOS SEGOVIANOS. **2687**

0210-7279 See INFORMACIONES PSIQUIATRICAS. **3926**

0210-7309 See O.R.L.-DIPS. **3890**

0210-7481 See BOLETIN DE LA REAL ACADEMIA DE BUENAS LETRAS DE BARCELONA. **2843**

0210-7554 See QUADERNS D'ALLIBERAMENT. **4493**

0210-7562 See REVISTA DE DERECHO POLITICO. **3094**

0210-7708 See LAGASCALIA. **517**

0210-7716 See HISTORIA, INSTITUCIONES, DOCUMENTOS. **2691**

0210-7821 See STOCHASTICA. **3536**

0210-7872 See POLITICA Y SOCIEDAD (MADRID, SPAIN). **5213**

0210-7945 See CLINICA RURAL. **3565**

0210-8054 See QUESTIIO. **1993**

0210-8135 See MTA. PEDIATRIA. **3906**

0210-8143 See BOLETIN DEL MUSEO DEL PRADO. **4085**

0210-8240 See JORNADAS DE TRABAJO SOBRE SUSTITUCIONES ARTICULARES. **3805**

0210-8275 See NUEVA ENFERMERIA. **3862**

0210-8348 See PSIQUIS. **3933**

0210-8372 See BIBLIOGRAFIA ESPANOLA. SUPLEMENTO DE PUBLICACIONES PERIODICAS. **408**

0210-8445 See BOLETIN AURIENSE. **262**

0210-8461 See CIVITAS. REVISTA ESPANOLA DE DERECHO ADMINISTRATIVO. **3092**

0210-847X See CUADERNOS DE ESTUDIOS GALLEGOS. **2684**

0210-8496 See JABEGA : REVISTA DE LA DIPUTACION PROVINCIAL DE MALAGA. **2693**

0210-8518 See REVISTA GENERAL DE LEGISLACION Y JURISPRUDENCIA. **3042**

0210-8550 See BERCEO. **2678**

0210-8615 See LLULL: BOLETIN DE LA SOCIEDAD ESPANOLA DE HISTORIA DE LAS CIENCIAS. **5126**

ISSN Index

0210-8704 *See* ESTUDIS D'HISTORIA CONTEMPORANIA DEL PAIS VALENCIA. **2687**

0210-8755 *See* REVISTA LATINA DE CARDIOLOGIA EUROAMERICANA. **3710**

0210-895X *See* BIOLOGIA & CLINICA HEMATOLOGICA. **3770**

0210-8984 *See* BOLETIN DE LA ASOCIACION ESPANOLA DE ENTOMOLOGIA. **5606**

0210-900X *See* HARVARD - DEUSTO BUSINESS REVIEW. **679**

0210-9085 *See* BOLETIN DE INFORMACION DEL LABORATORIO DE CARRETERAS Y GEOTECNIA. **5439**

0210-9107 *See* PAPELES DE ECONOMIA ESPANOLA. **1577**

0210-9174 *See* REVISTA DE FILOLOGIA ESPANOLA. **3316**

0210-9344 *See* MERCADO (MADRID, SPAIN). **798**

0210-9352 *See* OECOLOGIA AQUATICA. **2219**

0210-9395 *See* ESTUDIOS DE PSICOLOGIA. **4586**

0210-9409 *See* INDICE ESPANOL DE CIENCIA Y TECNOLOGIA. **5112**

0210-945X *See* VIERAEA. **4173**

0210-9506 *See* ACTA BOTANICA MALACITANA. **497**

0210-9522 *See* MISCELANEA COMILLAS. **4977**

0210-9603 *See* ANUARIO DE HISTORIA CONTEMPORANEA. **2675**

0210-962X *See* CUADERNOS DE ARTE DE LA UNIVERSIDAD DE GRANADA. **318**

0210-9697 *See* ESTIMULACION CARDIACA. **3704**

0210-9743 *See* BOLETIN DEL CENTRO DE CALCULO DE LA UNIVERSIDAD COMPLUTENSE. **1172**

0210-9778 *See* LAZAROA. **517**

0210-9832 *See* ACTA OBSTETRICA Y GINECOLOGICA HISPANO-LUSITANA. **3756**

0210-9980 *See* SAITABI. **2708**

0210-9999 *See* TIEMPOS MEDICOS DE ESPANA. **1788**

0211-0040 *See* REVISTA DE HISTORIA DE LA PSICOLOGIA. **4616**

0211-0547 *See* CUADERNOS DE INVESTIGACION FILOLOGICA. **3276**

0211-058X *See* GASTRUM. **3746**

0211-0768 *See* D'ART. **349**

0211-0776 *See* IBERICA. ACTUALIDAD CIENTIFICA. **5111**

0211-0873 *See* SANT PAU. **3638**

0211-089X *See* REVISTA ESPANOLA DE CIRUGIA CARDIACA, TORACICA Y VASCULAR. **3973**

0211-108X *See* BOLETIN DE SISMOS PROXIMOS. **1402**

0211-1128 *See* BOLETIN DEL CENTRO NACIONAL DE ALIMENTACION Y NUTRICION. **4188**

0211-1136 *See* FLUIDOS. **2090**

0211-125X *See* ANUARIO ESPANOL DE SEGUROS. **891**

0211-1322 *See* ANALES DEL JARDIN BOTANICO DE MADRID (1979). **499**

0211-1381 *See* CUENTA Y RAZON. **2514**

0211-139X *See* REVISTA ESPANOLA DE GERIATRIA Y GERONTOLOGIA. **3755**

0211-1535 *See* BOLETIN / CIRCULO DE EMPRESARIOS. **861**

0211-2051 *See* BOLETIN DE LA SOCIEDAD ARAGONESA DE PEDIATRIA. **3901**

0211-2078 *See* CORDUBA / MUSEO ARQUEOLOGICO PROVINCIAL. **2684**

0211-2159 *See* PSICOLOGICA. **4609**

0211-2213 *See* COYUNTURA ENERGETICA. **1936**

0211-2299 *See* ENDOCRINOLOGIA (BARCELONA). **2**

0211-2310 *See* ALMENARA (MADRID). **2645**

0211-2329 *See* ANALES DEL INSTITUTO DE ESTUDIOS GERUNDENSES. **2673**

0211-2558 *See* FOLIA NEUROPSIQUIATRICA GRANADA. **3833**

0211-2663 *See* REVISTA DE GIRONA. **2705**

0211-2698 *See* ARCHIVOS DE LA SOCIEDAD CANARIA DE OFTALMOLOGIA. **3872**

0211-2744 *See* REVISTA JURIDICA ESPANOLA LA LEY. **5810**

0211-2841 *See* CHIP MADRID. **1174**

0211-2892 *See* ROTACION. **5455**

0211-2973 *See* EUROFACH ELECTRONICA. **2054**

0211-3058 *See* MUNDO CIENTIFICO. **5130**

0211-3171 *See* BOLETIN DEL MUSEO E INSTITUTO CAMON AZNAR. **344**

0211-3325 *See* QUIMERA (BARCELONA, SPAIN). **3351**

0211-3333 *See* R.P. INTERNACIONAL DE RELACIONES PUBLICAS. **765**

0211-3473 *See* MEDIEVALIA / INSTITUTO UNIVERSITARIO DE ESTUDIOS MEDIEVALES. **2698**

0211-3481 *See* CUADERNOS DE PSICOLOGIA (BARCELONA, SPAIN). **4583**

0211-3538 *See* ANUARIO MUSICAL. **4100**

0211-3589 *See* AL-QANTARA (MADRID). **2672**

0211-3732 *See* DEFENSA MADRID. **17**

0211-3759 *See* ESTUDIOS - DEPARTAMENTO DE HISTORIA MODERNA, UNIVERSIDAD DE ZARAGOZA. **2615**

0211-4003 *See* ALTAMIRA. **2673**

0211-402X *See* ENRAHONAR. **4345**

0211-4143 *See* ACTUALIDAD BIBLIOGRAFICA DE FILOSOFIA Y TEOLOGIA. **4339**

0211-4364 *See* REVISTA DE ESTUDIOS DE JUVENTUD. **1068**

0211-4437 *See* HOSPITAL COMARCAL. **3584**

0211-4445 *See* JAMA EN ESPANOL. **3591**

0211-450X *See* MUSEO CANARIO, EL. **4091**

0211-4526 *See* PERSONA Y DERECHO. **3090**

0211-4623 *See* STUDIA OECOLOGICA. **2221**

0211-464X *See* SENARA. **3320**

0211-478X *See* QUADERNS D'ARQUEOLOGIA I HISTORIA DE LA CIUTAT / AJUNTAMENT DE BARCELONA, MUSEU D'HISTORIA DE LA CIUTAT, SEMINARI D'INVESTIGACIO "A. DURAN I SANPERE.". **279**

0211-5239 *See* ALXEBRA. **3492**

0211-5271 *See* ARTEGUIA. **341**

0211-528X *See* COMUNICACIONES UROLOGICAS. **3796**

0211-5441 *See* IMAGENES DE LA FE. **5030**

0211-5492 *See* MISSIONALIA HISPANICA. **5032**

0211-5549 *See* PSICOPATOLOGIA. **3932**

0211-5557 *See* QUADERNS DE L'INSTITUT CATALA D'ANTROPOLOGIA. **243**

0211-5581 *See* REVISTA DE POLITICA COMPARADA. **4494**

0211-5611 *See* ANTHROPOS (BARCELONA, SPAIN). **2842**

0211-5638 *See* FISIOTERAPIA. **4380**

0211-5735 *See* REVISTA DE LA ASOCIACION ESPANOLA DE NEUROPSIQUIATRIA. **3935**

0211-5743 *See* REVISTA ESPANOLA DE DERECHO CONSTITUCIONAL. **3094**

0211-5808 *See* ARCHIVO DE ARTE VALENCIANO; PUBLICACION DE LA REAL ACADEMIA DE BELLAS ARTES DE SAN CARLOS. **337**

0211-5905 *See* OHITURA. **242**

0211-5913 *See* REVISTA CANARIA DE ESTUDIOS INGLESES. **3315**

0211-6057 *See* NUTRICION CLINICA DIETETICA HOSPITALARIA. **4195**

0211-6111 *See* REVISTA COMPLUTENSE DE HISTORIA DE AMERICA / DEPARTAMENTO DE HISTORIA DE AMERICA I. **2757**

0211-6243 *See* ANALES DE FISICA. SERIE A, FENOMENOS E INTERACCIONES. **4396**

0211-6243 *See* ANALES DE FISICA. **4396**

0211-6340 *See* BUTLLETI EPIDEMIOLOGIC DE CATALUNYA. **3561**

0211-6529 *See* MISCELLANIA ZOOLOGICA. **5591**

0211-6553 *See* CARDIOVASCULAR REVIEWS & REPORTS EDICION ESPANOL. **3702**

0211-660X *See* ACTA CHIRURGICA CATALONIAE. **3957**

0211-6871 *See* ESTUDIOS TERRITORIALES. **2822**

0211-6901 *See* GINE-DIPS. **3761**

0211-6995 *See* NEFROLOGIA. **3991**

0211-7029 *See* PHOTOVISION. **4375**

0211-7045 *See* STEREOFONIA. **5319**

0211-7215 *See* ANGLO AMERICAN STUDIES. **2610**

0211-7274 *See* RHEUMA (MADRID). **3637**

0211-7339 *See* ANALISIS Y MODIFICACION DE CONDUCTA. **4573**

0211-7649 *See* CUADERNOS DE ESTUDIOS CASPOLINOS / GRUPO CULTURAL CASPOLINO, INSTITUCION FERNANDO EL CATOLICO. **2684**

0211-772X *See* ETNOGRAFIA ESPANOLA. **236**

0211-8173 *See* TECNOLOGIA DEL AGUA. **5541**

0211-8238 *See* BIBLIOMATICA. **3194**

0211-8262 *See* LABOR HOSPITALARIA. **3787**

0211-8319 *See* ATEMCOP. **599**

0211-8335 *See* INTERNATIONAL BULLETIN OF BIBLIOGRAPHY ON EDUCATION (QUARTERLY). **1795**

0211-8343 *See* TRABAJOS DEL INSTITUTO CAJAL. **540**

0211-8351 *See* PROGRESOS EN PSICOARMACOLOGIA. **4326**

0211-8483 *See* BOLETIN DE ARTE MALAGA. **344**

0211-8688 *See* GUIA CHIP. **678**

0211-9005 *See* ENFERMERIA CIENTIFICA. **3855**

0211-9099 *See* ULTRASONIDOS. **2000**

0211-9358 *See* ANALECTA MALACITANA. **3264**

0211-9536 *See* DYNAMIS (GRANADA). **3573**

0211-9552 *See* FOTO PROFESIONAL. **4369**

0211-9560 *See* HERRI-ARDURALARITZAKO EUSKAL ALDIZKARIA. **3093**

0211-9595 *See* QUADERNS D'ARQUITECTURA I URBANISME. **307**

0211-9714 *See* STUDIA BOTANICA. **528**

0211-9803 *See* ANALES DE GEOGRAFIA DE LA UNIVERSIDAD COMPLUTENSE / SECCION DE GEOGRAFIA. **2553**

0211-9811 *See* ARXIU DE TEXTOS CATALANS ANTICS. **408**

0211-9919 *See* CIC INFORMA. **607**

0212-0054 *See* QUERCUS. **2180**

0212-0062 *See* REVISTA DE ARQUEOLOGIA (MADRID, SPAIN). **280**

0212-0208 *See* PENSAMIENTO IBEROAMERICANO. **1512**

0212-0267 *See* HISTORIA DE LA EDUCACION. **1750**

0212-0283 *See* ESCUELA MEDICA. **4775**

0212-0348 *See* ECYM. ENDOCRINOLOGIA CLINICA Y METABOLISMO. **3729**

0212-047X *See* OFFARM. **4318**

0212-0550 *See* CUADERNOS DE TRADUCCION E INTERPRETACION. **3276**

0212-0569 *See* QUIMICA ANALITICA SALAMANCA. **1018**

0212-0607 *See* HORIZONTE EMPRESARIAL. **1566**

0212-0747 *See* ANUARIO DE DERECHO INTERNACIONAL. **3124**

0212-0771 *See* REVISTA DE LA SOCIEDAD ANDALUZA DE TRAUMATOLOGIA Y ORTOPEDIA. **3635**

0212-078X *See* MAINAKE. **273**

0212-100X *See* FORTSCHRITTE DER NEUROLOGIE - PSYCHIATRIE EDICION ESPANOLA. **3925**

0212-1514 *See* MTA. MEDICINA INTERNA. **3799**

0212-1565 *See* INFORMES TECNICOS / INSTITUTO ESPANOL DE OCEANOGRAFIA. **1450**

0212-1573 *See* DOCUMENTS D'ANALISI GEOGRAFICA / [PUBLICACIONS DEL DEPARTAMENT DE GEOGRAFIA, UNIVERSITAT AUTONOMA DE BARCELONA]. **2560**

0212-1611 *See* NUTRICION HOSPITALARIA. **4195**

0212-1689 *See* ALIMENTACION, EQUIPOS Y TECNOLOGIA. **4187**

0212-1700 *See* LAPIZ : REVISTA MENSUAL DE ARTE. **356**

0212-1786 *See* AFERS INTERNACIONALS. **4461**

0212-1808 See CLINICA CARDIOVASCULAR. 3703
0212-1824 See CUADERNOS DE PREHISTORIA Y ARQUEOLOGIA CASTELLONENSES. 266
0212-1867 See ESIC MARKET. 1489
0212-1891 See NUCLEAR ESPANA. 5253
0212-193X See REVISTA IBERO-AMERICANA DE ORTODONICA. 1334
0212-2146 See CAMPO, EL. 72
0212-2618 See CANCER TOPICS. VERSION ESPANOLA. 3812
0212-2820 See MUSEOS. 4092
0212-3673 See REVISTA GALLEGA DE PATOLOGIA DIGESTIVA. 3897
0212-3754 See REVISTA DE ROBOTICA. 2128
0212-3800 See INFECTOLOGIKA. 3672
0212-3819 See ESTUDIS ESCENICS. 5364
0212-3940 See CHIBRET INTERNATIONAL JOURNAL OF OPHTHALMOLOGY EDICION ESPANOLA. 3873
0212-4157 See ERA SOLAR. 1943
0212-4386 See ECONOMISTAS (MADRID, SPAIN). 1487
0212-4521 See ENSENANZA DE LAS CIENCIAS. 5103
0212-4572 See ANALISIS CLINICOS. 3549
0212-4637 See SENPE. REVISTA DE LA SOCIEDAD ESPANOLA DE NUTRICION PARENTERAL Y ENTERAL. 4199
0212-4750 See BOLETIN DE LEGISLACION DE LAS COMUNIDADES AUTONOMAS : BCA. 4633
0212-5056 See REVISTA DE LLENGUA I DRET. 1079
0212-5382 See NURSING. EDICION ESPANOLA. 3864
0212-548X See BOLETIN / MUSEO DE ZARAGOZA. 4085
0212-5544 See BOLETIN DEL MUSEO ARQUEOLOGICO NACIONAL. 262
0212-5617 See BLE. BOLETIN DE LEGISLACION EXTRANJERA. 3124
0212-5633 See CROQUIS. 296
0212-5730 See AULA ORIENTALIS. 2646
0212-5994 See SUPLEMENTOS SOBRE EL SISTEMA FINANCIERO. 1586
0212-6052 See CIENCIA MEDICA. 3564
0212-6095 See CIVITAS. REVISTA ESPANOLA DE DERECHO DEL TRABAJO. 2951
0212-6109 See REVISTA DE HISTORIA ECONOMICA. 1582
0212-6117 See ABRENTE. 311
0212-6176 See BUTLLETI EPIDEMIEOLOGIC GENERALITAT VALENCIANA. 3561
0212-632X See BITACORA. 591
0212-6524 See PANORAMA PANADERO. 2352
0212-6567 See ATENCION PRIMARIA. 3736
0212-6583 See FARMACIA CLINICA. 4304
0212-6591 See GACETA FISCAL : REVISTA MENSUAL DE ORIENTACION JURIDICO-TRIBUTARIA. 4727
0212-6605 See INVESTIGACION Y CLINICA LASER : ORGANO DEL GRUPO DE EXPERIMENTACION E INVESTIGACION CLINICA LASER (GRUPO LASER-ESPANA). 3590
0212-6753 See RAICES (MADRID, SPAIN). 2271
0212-7113 See REVISTA DE TOXICOLOGIA. 3983
0212-7180 See BOLETIN DE ESTADISTICAS LABORALES. 1656
0212-7199 See ANALES DE MEDICINA INTERNA : ORGANO OFICIAL DE LA SOCIEDAD ESPANOLA DE MEDICINA INTERNA. 3794
0212-7210 See R T S. REVISTA DE TREBALL SOCIAL. 5254
0212-7350 See EXPANSION COMERCIAL. 833
0212-7458 See BOLLETI DE LA SOCIETAT ARQUEOLOGICA LULIANA 1978. 262
0212-7466 See COMUNICACIONES PRESENTADAS A LAS ... JORNADAS DEL COMITE ESPANOL DE LA DETERGENCIA. 1023
0212-7601 See ATENCION MEDICA MADRID. 3553
0212-7636 See ESTUDIOS DE LINGUISTICA. 3280

0212-8241 See HIPERTENSION. 3705
0212-8292 See MEDICINA VETERINARIA (BARCELONA, SPAIN). 5516
0212-8322 See ANALES DE PEDAGOGIA. 1724
0212-8519 See INSTALACIONES DEPORTIVAS XXI. 617
0212-8578 See ARTE Y CEMENTO. 599
0212-8608 See ACTAS CLINICAS DELFOS. 3545
0212-8799 See ARCHIVOS DE MEDICINA DEL DEPORTE : PUBLICACION DE LA FEDERACION ESPANOLA DE MEDICINA DEL DEPORTE / FEMEDE. 3953
0212-8985 See LAIETANIA. 273
0212-9000 See MOTOR 16. 5419
0212-9051 See BOLETIN DE LA ACADEMIA GALEGA DE CIENCIAS. 5089
0212-9108 See RUIZIA. 527
0212-9183 See BOLETIN OFICIAL DEL MINISTERIO DE SANIDAD Y CONSUMO. 1293
0212-9205 See REVISTA CATALANA DE PSICOANALISI. 4616
0212-923X See GARCILLA. 4165
0212-9442 See HORA DE POESIA. 3464
0212-9515 See ESTUDIOS DE HISTORIA Y DE ARQUEOLOGIA MEDIEVALES. 2687
0212-9744 See GERIATRIKA. 3751
0212-9787 See NEOPLASIA. 3821
0212-9965 See FORUM BARCELONA. 3577
0213-005X See ENFERMEDADES INFECCIOSAS Y MICROBIOLOGIA CLINICA. 3713
0213-019X See INDICE ESPANOL DE CIENCIAS SOCIALES. SERIE A, PSICOLOGIA Y CIENCIAS DE LA EDUCACION. 5203
0213-0246 See ESTUDIOS DE PREHISTORIA Y ARQUEOLOGIA MADRILENAS. 267
0213-0400 See ELECTRONICA HOY. 2048
0213-053X See ANUARIO DE LINGUISTICA HISPANICA. 3266
0213-0556 See RELACIONES LABORALES. 1706
0213-0580 See ACTA PAEDIATRICA SCANDINAVICA ED. ESPANOLA. 3899
0213-0599 See ANALES DE PSIQUIATRIA. 3920
0213-0645 See APARATO LOCOMOTOR. 3880
0213-0815 See CUADERNOS DE SECCION. MUSICA / EUSKO-IKASKUNTZA, SOCIEDAD DE ESTUDIOS VASCOS. 4113
0213-1110 See URBANISMO REVISTA. 2838
0213-1137 See REVISATA DE DERECHO PROCESAL. 3040
0213-1145 See BOLETIN DE LA ASOCIACION DE DEMOGRAFIA HISTORICA. 4550
0213-1196 See DIALOGO FILOSOFICO. 4345
0213-120X See JOYAS & JOYEROS. 2915
0213-1307 See PC WORLD MADRID. 1271
0213-1315 See REVISTA INTERNACIONAL DE METODOS NUMERICOS PARA CALCULO Y DISEƒNO EN INGENIERIA. 1994
0213-1315 See REVISTA INTERNACIONAL DE METODOS NUMERICOS PARA CALCULO Y DISENO EN INGENIERIA. 2099
0213-1382 See ESTUDIOS HUMANISTICOS. FILOLOGIA. 3280
0213-1463 See REVISTA DE LA ASOCIACION CASTELLANA DE APARATO DIGESTIVO. 3801
0213-1811 See ANALES DE LA ASOCIACION DE PALINOLOGOS DE LENGUA ESPAƒNOLA. 3264
0213-201X See EPOS / UNIVERSIDAD NACIONAL DE EDUCACION A DISTANCIA, FACULTAD DE FILOLOGIA. 3279
0213-2052 See STUDIA HISTORICA. HA. ANTIQUA. 2630
0213-2087 See STUDIA HISTORICA. HA. CONTEMPORANEA. 2631
0213-2214 See NORBA-ARTE. 360
0213-2230 See REVISTA MATEMATICA IBEROAMERICANA. 3531
0213-2338 See LUCENTUM. 273
0213-2397 See MANUSCRITS. 2697
0213-246X See EUTOPIAS. 3281
0213-2613 See HOJAS DIVULGADORAS - MINISTERIO DE AGRICULTURA, PESCA Y ALIMENTACION. 92

0213-2672 See AUTOMATIZACION DE LA PRODUCCION. 1599
0213-2885 See ACTAS DE LA FUNDACION PUIGVERT : UROLOGIA, NEFROLOGIA, ANDROLOGIA / INSTITUTO DE UROLOGIA, NEFROLOGIA, ANDROLOGIA, HOSPITAL DE LA SANTA CRUZ Y SAN PABLO. 3987
0213-2966 See AL-GEZIRA. 2609
0213-2990 See HISTOLOGIA MEDICA. 537
0213-3105 See NOSA TERRA, A. 5269
0213-3113 See AUTOMATICA E INSTRUMENTACION. 1217
0213-3156 See COLLECCION LEGISLATIVA DEL MINISTERIO DE DEFENSA. ANO 1988. 4039
0213-3407 See BOLETIN DE PRECIOS AGRARIOS ED. SEMANAL. 67
0213-3660 See REIGOS Y DRENAJES XXI. 2095
0213-3709 See NORBA. REVISTA DE GEOGRAFIA. 2570
0213-3717 See APUNTS. MEDICINA DE L'ESPORT. 3953
0213-375X See NORBA. REVISTA DE HISTORIA. 2624
0213-3865 See EKONOMIAZ. 1559
0213-3911 See HISTOLOGY AND HISTOPATHOLOGY. 537
0213-3954 See BRITISH MEDICAL JOURNAL ED. ESPANOLA. 3795
0213-4004 See ANALES DE BIOLOGIA. SECCION BIOLOGIA AMBIENTAL. 2211
0213-4101 See MICROBIOLOGIA (MADRID). 567
0213-411X See NEW METHODS IN DRUG RESEARCH. 4317
0213-4144 See ARCHIVOS DE ODONTOESTOMATOLOGIA. 1316
0213-4152 See QUIMICA 2000. 990
0213-4233 See REVISTA ESPANOLA DE NEUROLOGIA. 3845
0213-4241 See REVISTA ESPANOLA DE EPILEPSIA. 3845
0213-4365 See ANALES DE FILOLOGIA HISPANICA / UNIVERSIDAD DE MURCIA. 3264
0213-4373 See TURIA. 3448
0213-4462 See QUADERN CAPS. 3632
0213-4489 See PARQUES Y JARDINES. 4707
0213-4497 See CUADERNOS DO LABORATORIO XEOLOXICO DE LAXE. 2559
0213-4748 See REVISTA DE PSICOLOGIA SOCIAL. 4616
0213-4829 See REVISTA ESPANOLA DE MICROBIOLOGIA CLINICA. 569
0213-4845 See HOSPITAL PRACTICE (ED. EN ESPANOL). 3584
0213-4853 See NEUROLOGIA (BARCELONA, SPAIN). 3840
0213-487X See A & V, MONOGRAFIAS DE ARQUITECTURA Y VIVIENDA. 286
0213-5000 See INVESTIGACION AGRARIA. PRODUCCION Y PROTECCION VEGETALES. 175
0213-5035 See INVESTIGACION AGRARIA. PRODUCCION Y SANIDAD ANIMALES. 213
0213-5302 See FONTILLES. 3720
0213-5353 See CIRUGIA DE URGENCIA. 3723
0213-5434 See ANALES DE VETERINARIA DE MURCIA. 5502
0213-5469 See ANALES DE CIENCIAS - UNIVERSIDAD DE MURCIA. 960
0213-5574 See INDUSTRIA FARMACEUTICA. 4307
0213-5612 See CUADERNOS DE ACCION SOCIAL. 5197
0213-5663 See ANALES DE PREHISTORIA Y ARQUEOLOGIA. 254
0213-5760 See PUBLICACIONES OFICIALES. 4677
0213-5787 See DIABETES NEWS ED. ESPANOLA. 3728
0213-5884 See COMUNIDAD Y DROGAS. 3568
0213-5949 See CATALAN REVIEW. 2258
0213-6163 See EUROPEAN JOURNAL OF PSYCHIATRY, THE. 3925
0213-6171 See PROYECTO 2000. 2127

0213-6228 See ANNLAS DE L'INSTITUT D'ESTUDIS GIRONINS. 2674

0213-6252 See ABACO. 5189

0213-635X See INVESTIGACION AGRARIA. ECONOMIA. 97

0213-6449 See SABER LEER. 3352

0213-6465 See CUADERNOS DE LA BIBLIOTECA ISLAMICA "FELIX MARIA PAREJA". 414

0213-6562 See ACTUALIDAD PENAL. 2927

0213-6635 See AWRAQ : ESTUDIOS SOBRE EL MUNDO ARABE E ISLAMICO CONTEMPORANEO. 2677

0213-6716 See CUADERNOS DE ARTE COLONIAL. 348

0213-6856 See POLITICA EXTERIOR. 4532

0213-6910 See BOLETIN DE SANIDAD VEGETAL. PLAGAS. 4244

0213-6929 See ACTUALIDAD FINANCIERA. 2927

0213-6945 See BCE. BOLETIN DE DERECHO DE LAS COMUNIDADES EUROPEAS. 4516

0213-7097 See ACTUALIDAD LABORAL. 2927

0213-7100 See ACTUALIDAD CIVIL. 3088

0213-7119 See RBC. REVISIONES SOBRE BIOLOGIA CELULAR. 540

0213-7275 See LAB 2000. 5125

0213-7585 See REVISTA DE ESTUDIOS REGIONALES. 5216

0213-7615 See REVISTA ESPANOLA DE DROGODEPENCENCIAS. 1348

0213-7828 See QUIMICA HOY. 990

0213-7895 See CANENTE. 3372

0213-8093 See C.I.R.I.E.C. ESPANA. 1467

0213-8115 See CARDIOLOGIA ... BARCELONA. 3700

0213-814X See REVISTA ESPANOLA DE MEDICINA NUCLEAR. SUPLEMENTO. 3849

0213-8190 5345

0213-8204 See TRABAJOS DE INVESTIGACION OPERATIVA. 3539

0213-831X See SOPRODEN. 1335

0213-8328 See CONTROL DE CALIDAD ASISTENCIAL. 3568

0213-8468 See INGENIERIA CIVIL MADRID. 2024

0213-8514 See REVISTA DE LA SOCIEDAD ESPANOLA DE QUIMICA CLINICA. 1018

0213-8530 See ITINERA GEOBOTANICA. 514

0213-8948 See RE. REVISTA DE EDIFICACION. 307

0213-9111 See GACETA SANITARIA. 4776

0213-9146 See ANALES ESPANOLES DE PEDIATRIA. SUPLEMENTO. 3900

0213-9391 See URBANISMO / COAM. 2838

0213-9510 See MADRID, UNE. 3605

0213-9626 See INMUNOLOGIA (1987). 3672

0213-9634 See MINERVA : REVISTA DE FILOLOGIA CLASICA. 1078

0213-9693 See ACTUALIDAD... EN EL LABORATORICO CLINICO F. SUNER CASADEVALL, LA. 5080

0213-9715 See CARABELA. 3272

0214-0039 See COMUNICACION Y SOCIEDAD. 1109

0214-0055 See ARDI. 2676

0214-0322 See COMUNICACIONES I.N.I.A. SERIE ECONOMIA. 76

0214-0349 See ITEM. 3219

0214-0381 See ALGO 2000. 2513

0214-0578 See FRUT. 172

0214-0659 See DOLOR. 3573

0214-0896 See ECOLOGIA (MADRID). 2213

0214-0934 See DRUG NEWS & PERSPECTIVES. 4301

0214-1256 See ARQUITECTURA VIVA. 292

0214-1353 See ELYTRON. 5582

0214-1388 See CUADERNOS DE TEATRO CLASICO. 5363

0214-1396 See ESPANA CONTEMPORANEA : EC. 3385

0214-140X See BOLETIN DE LA SOCIEDAD MICOLOGICA DE MADRID. 574

0214-1477 See REVISTA ESPANOLA DE ALERGOLOGIA E INMUNOLOGIA CLINICA : ORGANO OFICIAL DE LA SOCIEDAD ESPANOLA DE ALERGOLOGIA E INMUNOLOGIA CLINICA. 3676

0214-1485 See DOLOR & INFLAMACION : FARMACOTERAPIA, INVESTIGACION Y CLINICA MEDICA / PATROCINADA POR LIGA REUMATOLOGICA ESPANOLA (LIRE). 3804

0214-1493 See PUBLICACIONS MATEMATIQUES / DEPARTAMENT DE MATEMATIQUES, UNIVERSITAT AUTONOMA DE BARCELONA. 3529

0214-1868 See CABLE MADRID. 1129

0214-2244 See FV. FOTO-VIDEO ACTUALIDAD. 4369

0214-2406 See BOLETIN DEL MINISTERIO DE TRABAJO Y SEGURIDAD SOCIAL. 3144

0214-2422 See HOSPITAL 2000. 300

0214-2570 See HISTORIA SOCIAL (VALENCIA, SPAIN). 5201

0214-2813 See BOLETIN DE LA SOCIEDAD ESPANOLA DE HIDROLOGIA MEDICA. 3558

0214-2880 See JOURNAL OF CLINICAL NUTRITION & GASTROENTEROLOGY, THE. 3746

0214-297X See BOOGIE MADRID. 4104

0214-3038 See LA ESPANA MEDIEVAL, EN. 2696

0214-3089 See CATALAN WRITING. 3373

0214-3127 See RENOVATEC BARCELONA. 626

0214-3135 See PROMECANICA BARCELONA. 2127

0214-3151 See ANIMALIA (BARCELONA). 4285

0214-3240 See ESTADISTICO DE ENCUESTAS. 5327

0214-3429 See REVISTA ESPANOLA DE QUIMIOTERAPIA : PUBLICACION OFICIAL DE LA SOCIEDAD ESPANOLA DE QUIMIOTERAPIA. 3823

0214-3550 See COGNITIVA MADRID. 4581

0214-3577 See REVISTA MATEMATICA DE LA UNIVERSIDAD COMPLUTENSE DE MADRID / FACULTAD DE CIENCIAS MATEMATICAS, UNIVERSIDAD COMPLUTENSE DE MADRID. 3531

0214-3755 See CORE JOURNALS EN ALERGIA E INMUNOLOGIA. 3668

0214-3771 See FGL : BOLETIN DE LA FUNDACION FEDERICO GARCIA LORCA. 3387

0214-3852 See BOLETIN EPIDEMIOLOGICO DE CASTILLA Y LEON. 4769

0214-3917 See APUNTES DE CARDIOLOGIA. 3699

0214-3925 See ACTEME. ACTUALIZACION DE TEMAS MEDICOS. 3545

0214-400X See CUADERNOS DE HISTORIA CONTEMPORANEA. 2614

0214-4018 See CUADERNOS DE HISTORIA MODERNA. 2614

0214-4034 See INSTALACIONES Y TECNICAS DEL CONFORT. 2606

0214-4042 See REVISTA DE DERECHO AMBIENTAL. 3040

0214-4077 See AVANCES EN TRAUMATOLOGIA, CIRUGIA, REHABILITACION, MEDICINA PREVENTIVA Y DEL DEPORTE. 3554

0214-4123 See CLIJ. 3376

0214-4220 See MONOGRAFIAS DE DERMATOLOGIA : M.D.D. 3722

0214-4344 See MANTENIMIENTO BARCELONA. 4008

0214-4441 See BIBLIOGRAFIA ESPANOLA. SUPLEMENTO DE CARTOGRAFIA. 2556

0214-4514 See FAIG ARTS. 320

0214-4662 See TECNOLOGIA Y ARQUITECTURA. 5165

0214-4670 See CUADERNOS DE INVESTIGACION HISTORICA BROCAR. 2614

0214-4697 See FARMACEUTICO HOSPITALES, EL. 4304

0214-4727 See ANALES DE ARQUITECTURA : REVISTA DEL DEPARTAMENTO DE TEORIA DE LA ARQUITECTURA Y PROYECTOS ARQUITECTONICOS, ESCUELA TECNICA SUPERIOR DE ARQUITECTURA DE VALLADOLID. 287

0214-4808 See REVISTA ALICANTINA DE ESTUDIOS INGLESES. 3315

0214-4832 See COMPOSICION ARQUITECTONICA / FUNDACION FAUSTINO ORBEGOZO EIZAGUIRRE, INSTITUTO DE ARTE Y HUMANIDADES. 295

0214-4840 See ADICCIONES PALMA DE MALLORCA. 1338

0214-4905 See ANUNCIOS MADRID. 921

0214-5987 See RESEARCH IN SURGERY. 3973

0214-5995 See RESEARCH IN SURGERY. SUPLEMENTO. 3973

0214-6185 See REVISTA DEL CENTRO DE ESTUDIOS CONSTITUCIONALES. 3094

0214-6282 See INTERNATIONAL JOURNAL OF DEVELOPMENTAL BIOLOGY, THE. 541

0214-6363 See MEDICO MADRID, EL. 3614

0214-6436 See HIPERTENSION Y ARTERIOESCLEROSIS. 3705

0214-6568 See ACTA ESTOMATOLOGICA VALENCIANA. 3544

0214-6738 See CUADERNOS DE FILOLOGIA. III, LITERATURAS, ANALISIS. 3379

0214-6746 See CUADERNOS DE FILOLOGIA. II, STUDIA LINGUISTICA HISPANICA. 3276

0214-6908 See DELINCUENCIA VALENCIA. 5244

0214-736X See STUDIA ZAMORENSIA. 3325

0214-7378 See PUBLICACIONES ESPECIALES - INSTITUTO ESPANOL DE OCEANOGRAFIA. 1455

0214-7602 See ALAZET : REVISTA DE FILOLOGIA. 3262

0214-7955 See KOBIE. BELLAS ARTES / DIPUTACION FORAL DE BIZKAIA. 355

0214-8021 See PAPERS DE TURISME. 5488

0214-803X See ALIMENTALEX (MADRID). 2326

0214-820X See TRASPLANTE OF ORGANS AND TISSUES. 3977

0214-8307 See BOLETIN ICE ECONOMICO. 1966

0214-8358 See SCIENTIA MARINA. 557

0214-8714 See MEDICINA DE REHABILITACION. 4381

0214-8919 See GESTION HOSPITALARIA. 3856

0214-8935 See FARMACOTERAPIA MADRID. 4305

0214-9206 See MT. MAQUINAS Y TRACTORES AGRICOLAS. 160

0214-9249 See DOCUMENTOS DE ARQUITECTURA ALMERIA. 298

0214-9370 See CORE JOURNALS EN ANESTESIOLOGIA. 3682

0214-9915 See PSICOTHEMA OVIEDO. 4609

0214-9923 See ANDALUCIA COOPERATIVA. 1541

0214-9931 See PC ACTUAL. 1198

0215-0190 See BULETIN PENELITIAN KEHUTANAN. 2376

0215-028X See BULETIN PENELITIAN HUTAN. 2376

0215-1162 See CORD. COCONUT RESEARCH & DEVELOPMENT. 168

0215-1367 See WEEDWATCHER. 2433

0215-1502 See COCOMUNITY NEWSLETTER. 75

0215-1561 See INDONESIAN ECONOMY, THE. 1495

0215-1618 See ASEAN NEWSLETTER / ASSOCIATION OF SOUTHEAST ASIAN NATIONS. 2645

0215-255X See AMANAH (JAKARTA, INDONESIA). 4933

0215-2711 See PALAWIJI NEWS. 118

0215-2770 See JAKARTA JAKARTA. 2510

0215-8981 See INDUSTRIAL CROPS RESEARCH JOURNAL. 95

0216-1273 See BERITA BIBLIOGRAFI (JAKARTA, INDONESIA : 1984). 408

0216-2563 See BHAYANGKARA. 3158

0216-3411 See BULLETIN KFT : MEDIA KARYAWAN FILM DAN TELEVISI INDONESIA. 1128

0216-3500 See BULETIN PENELITIAN INSTITUT PERTANIAN BOGOR. 68

0216-4051 See MAJALAH BULANAN KORPRI. 1689

0216-4167 *See* SARI KARANGAN INDONESIA. 5149

0216-5023 *See* BIOTROPIA. 2376

0216-616X *See* ACTA PHARMACEUTICA INDONESIA. 4289

0216-6216 *See* INDEKS MAJALAH ILMIAH INDONESIA / INDEX OF INDONESIAN LEARNED PERIODICALS. 417

0216-6909 *See* STATISTIK PERHUBUNGAN - BIRO PUSAT STATISTIK (LALU LINTAS ANGKUTAN BARANG ANTAR PULAU MENURUT JENIS PELAYARAN). 5457

0216-700X *See* DIREKTORI PERUSAHAAN TRUK (ANTAR PROPINSI) DI JAWA. 5381

0216-7050 *See* TINJAUAN EKONOMI. 814

0216-7107 *See* ECONOMIC REVIEW (JAKARTA, INDONESIA). 1558

0216-7204 *See* BERKALA BIOANTHROPOLOGI INDONESIA. 232

0216-7727 *See* JURNAL PENELITIAN PERIKANAN LAUT. 2307

0216-7867 *See* BULLETIN PERKARETAN. 70

0216-8170 *See* INDONESIAN JOURNAL OF CROP SCIENCE. 174

0216-8219 *See* AKADEMIKA (SALA, INDONESIA). 1544

0216-8316 *See* JURNAL PENELITIAN PASCA PANEN PERIKANAN. 2307

0216-9053 *See* HASIL-HASIL RAPAT KERDJA KESEHATAN NASIONAL. 4777

0216-9525 *See* JURNAL PENELITIAN DAN PENGEMBANGAN KEHUTANAN. 2386

0216-9657 *See* PEMBERITAAN PENELITIAN TANAMAN INDUSTRI. 119

0217-1120 *See* LLOYD'S MARITIME ASIA. 5451

0217-1139 *See* SHIPPERS' TIMES. 5456

0217-1260 *See* WHAT'S NEW IN BUILDING SINGAPORE. 631

0217-1287 *See* MASS COM PERIODICAL LITERATURE INDEX. 1116

0217-1880 *See* SINGAPORE SCIENTIST. 5158

0217-1910 *See* WHO'S WHO IN MALAYSIA & SINGAPORE (PETALING JAYA, SELANGOR). 437

0217-2070 *See* CHECKLIST OF CURRENT PERIODICALS / NATIONAL UNIVERSITY OF SINGAPORE LIBRARY. 413

0217-2976 *See* MATHEMATICAL MEDLEY. 3519

0217-2992 *See* CONTRIBUTIONS TO SOUTHEAST ASIAN ETHNOGRAPHY. 234

0217-3239 *See* SURVEY OF MALAYSIAN LAW. 3061

0217-4251 *See* SINGAPORE JOURNAL OF PHYSICS. 4421

0217-4316 *See* SINGAPORE STATISTICAL NEWS : SSN. 5338

0217-4421 *See* ASIAN TIMBER (SINGAPORE). 2375

0217-4472 *See* ASEAN ECONOMIC BULLETIN. 1463

0217-4561 *See* ASIA PACIFIC JOURNAL OF MANAGEMENT. 860

0217-4715 *See* PSA NEWS. 849

0217-4820 *See* PERFORMING ARTS (SINGAPORE). 387

0217-5460 *See* ASEAN JOURNAL ON SCIENCE & TECHNOLOGY FOR DEVELOPMENT. 5086

0217-5541 *See* BUILDING & CONSTRUCTION NEWS. 602

0217-5908 *See* SINGAPORE ECONOMIC REVIEW. 1584

0217-5959 *See* ASIA-PACIFIC JOURNAL OF OPERATIONAL RESEARCH. 1598

0217-6181 *See* SINGAPORE INPUT-OUTPUT TABLES. 1584

0217-6602 *See* OIL & GAS NEWS YEARBOOK. 4268

0217-6661 *See* APTIRC BULLETIN. 4711

0217-7323 *See* MODERN PHYSICS LETTERS A. 4448

0217-751X *See* INTERNATIONAL JOURNAL OF MODERN PHYSICS A. 4405

0217-8281 *See* SERIES IN MODERN APPLIED MATHEMATICS. 3534

0217-8362 *See* COMPUTERWORLD SINGAPORE. 1180

0217-8451 *See* INDOCHINA REPORT. 4524

0217-913X *See* JOURNAL OF THE HISTORY SOCIETY (1979). 2621

0217-9520 *See* SOJOURN (SINGAPORE, SINGAPORE). 5222

0217-9687 *See* ASIA PACIFIC JOURNAL OF PHARMACOLOGY. 4293

0217-9695 *See* HOTELIER SINGAPORE. 2806

0217-9792 *See* INTERNATIONAL JOURNAL OF MODERN PHYSICS B. 4406

0217-9822 *See* JOURNAL OF ELECTRONICS (CHINA). 2069

0217-9849 *See* MODERN PHYSICS LETTERS. B, CONDENSED MATTER PHYSICS, STATISTICAL PHYSICS, APPLIED PHYSICS. 4412

0218-0014 *See* INTERNATIONAL JOURNAL OF PATTERN RECOGNITION AND ARTIFICIAL INTELLIGENCE. 1213

0218-0812 *See* ASIA JOURNAL OF THEOLOGY. 4936

0218-1029 *See* REVIEWS OF THE SOLID STATE SCIENCE. 4419

0218-1169 *See* VIETNAM COMMENTARY / INFORMATION & RESOURCE CENTER. 2667

0218-1266 *See* JOURNAL OF CIRCUITS, SYSTEMS, AND COMPUTERS. 2068

0218-1274 *See* INTERNATIONAL JOURNAL OF BIFURCATION AND CHAOS IN APPLIED SCIENCES AND ENGINEERING. 1979

0218-1444 *See* JOURNAL OF CHINESE GEOGRAPHY, THE. 2567

0218-1932 *See* INTERNATIONAL JOURNAL OF GENOME RESEARCH. 548

0218-1940 *See* INTERNATIONAL JOURNAL OF SOFTWARE ENGINEERING AND KNOWLEDGE ENGINEERING. 1229

0218-1959 *See* INTERNATIONAL JOURNAL OF COMPUTATIONAL GEOMETRY & APPLICATIONS. 3509

0218-1967 *See* INTERNATIONAL JOURNAL OF ALGEBRA AND COMPUTATION. 3509

0218-1991 *See* INTERNATIONAL JOURNAL OF NONLINEAR OPTICAL PHYSICS. 4435

0218-2025 *See* MATHEMATICAL MODELS & METHODS IN APPLIED SCIENCES : MP3SAS. 3519

0218-2130 *See* INTERNATIONAL JOURNAL ON ARTIFICIAL INTELLIGENCE TOOLS. 1213

0218-2157 *See* INTERNATIONAL JOURNAL OF INTELLIGENT & COOPERATIVE INFORMATION SYSTEMS : IJICIS. 1213

0218-2165 *See* JOURNAL OF KNOT THEORY AND ITS RAMIFICATIONS. 3513

0218-2173 *See* SINGAPORE JOURNAL OF LEGAL STUDIES. 3055

0218-2696 *See* ASIA INSURANCE REVIEW. 2874

0218-2718 *See* INTERNATIONAL JOURNAL OF MODERN PHYSICS. D, GRAVITATION, ASTROPHYSICS, COSMOLOGY. 4406

0218-3013 *See* INTERNATIONAL JOURNAL OF MODERN PHYSICS. E, NUCLEAR PHYSICS. 4447

0218-3056 *See* REGIONAL OUTLOOK, SOUTHEAST ASIA. 2663

0218-3161 *See* SINGAPORE LAW REPORTS, THE. 3055

0218-3382 *See* INTERNATIONAL JOURNAL OF MANUFACTURING SYSTEMS AND DESIGN. 3481

0218-3390 *See* JOURNAL OF BIOLOGICAL SYSTEMS. 460

0218-348X *See* FRACTALS. 3506

0218-396X *See* JOURNAL OF COMPUTATIONAL ACOUSTICS. 4452

0218-4885 *See* INTERNATIONAL JOURNAL OF UNCERTAINTY, FUZZINESS AND KNOWLEDGE BASED SYSTEMS. 1190

0218-4958 *See* JOURNAL OF ENTERPRISING CULTURE. 687

0218-5393 *See* INTERNATIONAL JOURNAL OF RELIABILITY, QUALITY & SAFETY ENGINEERING. 1980

0218-5563 *See* ACCOUNTING AND BUSINESS REVIEW. 736

0220-1186 *See* ASTRAPI PARIS. 1978. 5192

0220-2018 *See* BULLETIN DU CENTRE DE RECHERCHES D'HISTOIRE DES MOUVEMENTS SOCIAUX ET DU SYNDICALISME. 5194

0220-2220 *See* ARTS DE L'OUEST. 342

0220-2352 *See* BULLETIN COMPTABLE & FINANCIER. 740

0220-2476 *See* INFORMATION CARDIOLOGIQUE, L'. 3706

0220-3332 *See* ARGUS DES METAUX PARIS. 3998

0220-4592 *See* AMITIES ACADIENNES. 2255

0220-5858 *See* VIE FRANCAISE (PARIS, FRANCE: 1978). 1588

0220-6358 *See* COTE OFFICIELLE. 895

0220-6617 *See* REVUE ARCHEOLOGIQUE DU CENTRE DE LA FRANCE. 281

0220-6765 *See* MOI AUVERGNE, A. 2461

0220-7346 *See* CANCEROLOGIE. 3814

0220-7591 *See* ARCHITECTURE (PARIS 1979). 290

0220-7796 *See* REVUE ARCHEOLOGIQUE DE 'EST ET DU CENTRE EST SUPPLEMENT. 281

0220-813X See R.I.A. (PARIS, 1977). 2355

0220-8245 *See* GEO ED. FRANCAISE. 2517

0220-8245 *See* GEO (ED. FRANCAISE). 2488

0220-9896 *See* REVUE DE LA CONCURRENCE ET DE LA CONSOMMATION. 3103

0221-0363 *See* JOURNAL DE RADIOLOGIE. 3942

0221-0436 *See* MONDES ET CULTURES : COMPTES RENDUS TRIMESTRIELS DES SEANCES DE L'ACADEMIE DES SCIENCES D'OUTRE-MER. 5129

0221-0703 *See* OBJECTIF EUROPE STRASBOURG. 2520

0221-2536 *See* DOCUMENTS - B.R.G.M. 1439

0221-2781 *See* POLITIQUE INTERNATIONALE. 4532

0221-3664 *See* CAHIERS D'HISTOIRE ET DE PHILOSOPHIE DES SCIENCES. 5092

0221-3796 *See* ANNALES MEDICALES DE NANCY ET DE L'EST. 3550

0221-4792 *See* ARCHEOLOGIE EN LANGUEDOC. 259

0221-5004 *See* STUDIA IRANICA. 2665

0221-5047 *See* CAHIERS D'HISTOIRE DE L'INSTITUT DE RECHERCHES MARXISTES. 2682

0221-5772 *See* AFRIQUE ENTREPRISE. 1544

0221-5896 *See* KTEMA. 1078

0221-6280 *See* HISTOIRE DE L'EDUCATION. 1750

0221-7678 *See* JAMA JOURNAL OF THE AMERICAN MEDICAL ASSOCIATION. EDITION FRANCAISE. 3591

0221-7945 *See* BULLETIN DE LA SOCIETE THEOPHILE GAUTIER. 3369

0221-7996 *See* BIBA. 1082

0221-8321 *See* BULLETIN ARCHEOLOGIQUE DE PROVENCE. 262

0221-833X *See* SPEAKEASY. 3353

0221-8852 *See* AMERINDIA. 3263

0222-0334 *See* FRANCE LATINE, LA. 3282

0222-0377 *See* CHARCUTERIE ET GASTRONOMIE PARIS. 2331

0222-0776 *See* RBM. REVUE EUROPEENNE DE BIOTECHNOLOGIE MEDICALE. 5145

0222-1543 *See* RUSSKOE VOZROZHDENIE. 5040

0222-1578 *See* CAHIERS GERARD DE NERVAL. 3371

0222-2027 *See* ARCHIVERT. 291

0222-3856 *See* AUDITION & PAROLE. 4384

0222-3996 *See* AUTO VERTE PARIS. 1979. 5405

0222-4194 *See* DROIT OUVRIER, LE. 3146

0222-5123 *See* MET-MAR. 1430

0222-559X *See* SECURITE CIVILE ET INDUSTRIELLE. 1073

0222-6588 See FLASH INFORMATIONS - CHAMBRE DE COMMERCE FRANCO-SOVIETIQUE. 819

0222-6618 See COMMERCE ET COOPERATION PARIS. 828

0222-8394 See RAPPORT DE RECHERCHE LPC. 2030

0222-8599 See MANUEL PRATIQUE DES DOUANES C.F.T.C. 1920

0222-9617 See NEUROPSYCHIATRIE DE L'ENFANCE ET DE L'ADOLESCENCE. 3841

0222-9714 See CAHIERS EVANGILE. 4942

0222-9838 See INFORMATION GRAMMATICALE (PARIS), L'. 3287

0223-0038 See AIR FAN. 4033

0223-0135 See REVUE TECHNIQUE MACHINISME AGRICOLE. 5424

0223-2928 See ACTUALITES EN MEDECINE DU SPORT. 3953

0223-3053 See COMMUNAUTE EUROPEENNE INFORMATIONS. 1470

0223-3711 See REVUE DES LANGUES ROMANES. 3316

0223-4246 See BULLETIN SIGNALETIQUE. 891: INDUSTRIES MECANIQUES. 2111

0223-4289 See LIVRES JEUNES AUJOURD'HUI. 3408

0223-4300 See TRESORS MONETAIRES. 2783

0223-4335 See VIDE, LES COUCHES MINCES, LE. 4424

0223-4386 See CULTURE TECHNIQUE. 5098

0223-4661 See ACTUALITES GYNECOLOGIQUES (PARIS. 1971). 3756

0223-4726 See LEGI SOCIAL. 3151

0223-4734 See CROIRE AUJOURD'HUI. 5028

0223-4866 See ENJEUX. 4030

0223-5102 See MELANGES DE L'ECOLE FRANCAISE DE ROME. ANTIQUITE. 2698

0223-5234 See EUROPEAN JOURNAL OF MEDICINAL CHEMISTRY. 3575

0223-5242 See DOSSIER DU CENTRE NATIONAL D'INFORMATION SUR LE MEDICAMENT HOSPITALIER. 4299

0223-5331 See BULLETIN D'INFORMATIONS ARCHITECTURALES. 294

0223-5404 See REVUE INTERNATIONALE DE DROIT PENAL / DIRIGEE PAR J.A. ROUX, L. HUGUENEY, H. DONNEDIEU DE VABRES. 3109

0223-5439 See ADMINISTRATION PARIS. 1962. 4461

0223-5587 See TECHNIQUES TRESOR. 887

0223-5625 See DOCUMENTS D'INFORMATION ET DE GESTION. 866

0223-5633 See METROPOLIS (PARIS). 2828

0223-565X See NOUVELLE REVUE DE PSYCHANALYSE. 4606

0223-5978 See ECONOMISTE DU TIERS MONDE, L'. 1559

0223-6335 See COMPTES RENDUS DES TRAVAUX DES COLLOQUES. 4400

0223-7164 See SOMMAIRES DE DROIT DU TRAVAIL. 3154

0223-7237 See GENEALOGIES BOURBONNAISES ET DU CENTRE / CERCLE GENEALOGIQUE ET HERALDIQUE DU BOURBONNAIS. 2450

0223-9434 See LETTRE DU PSYCHIATRE PARIS, LA. 3930

0224-0254 See COMMUNION ET DIACONIE WATTRELOS. 4949

0224-0424 See STRATEGIQUE. 4058

0224-0475 See GROUPE D'ETUDE DES MONUMENTS ET OEUVRES D'ART DU BEAUVAISIS. 351

0224-0718 See ASSOCIATION LEONARD-DE-VINCI. 343

0224-3016 See NOREX INFORMATION PARIS-LA DEFENSE. 1197

0224-3911 See DIAGRAMMES. 3503

0224-4365 See TRAVAIL ET EMPLOI. 3154

0224-5027 See BOULANGER PATISSIER 1979, LE. 2329

0224-5264 See ANNALES SCIENTIFIQUES DE L'UNIVERSITE DE FRANCHE-COMTE-BESANCON. MEDECINE ET PHARMACIE. 4291

0224-7518 See CATALOGUE DE LA PRODUCTION CINEMATOGRAPHIQUE FRANCAISE. 4065

0224-9928 See J MAGAZINE. 1755

0225-0292 See PRAVOSLAVNOE OBOZRENIE. 5040

0225-0306 See HANDBOOK AND DIRECTORY - CANADIAN WOMEN'S FIELD HOCKEY ASSOCIATION. 4898

0225-0314 See HANDBOOK AND DIRECTORY - CANADIAN FIELD HOCKEY ASSOCIATION. 4898

0225-0403 See PROCEEDINGS - CANADIAN LABOUR CONGRESS, CONSTITUTIONAL CONVENTION. 1703

0225-0411 See PROCES-VERBAL - CONGRES DU TRAVAIL DU CANADA, ASSEMBLEE STATUTAIRE. 1703

0225-0446 See NEWS FROM THE CENTRE - INSTITUTE FOR NONPROFIT ORGANIZATIONS. 5298

0225-0454 See QUEBEC VOYAGES. 5489

0225-0500 See CANADIAN JOURNAL OF NETHERLANDIC STUDIES. 2683

0225-0519 See ALBERTA REPORT. 2527

0225-0535 See COLLINS BAY CON. T. A. C. T. 3160

0225-0594 See NEA PATRIDA. 5790

0225-0608 See CANADIAN TAXPAYER. 4716

0225-0632 See REPERTOIRE VIDEO FEMMES. 423

0225-0721 See MAGAZINE - CANADIAN ORNAMENTAL PHEASANT AND GAME BIRD ASSOCIATION. 2774

0225-0888 See FOOT NOTES - BEEF AND SHEEP BRANCH (EDMONTON). 836

0225-0969 See MON JOURNAL LAURIER DES LAURENTIDES. 5790

0225-0977 See RECUEIL DES MEMBRES - LA FEDERATION DE L'AGRICULTURE DE L'ONTARIO. 125

0225-0985 See MEMBERS' DIGEST - ONTARIO FEDERATION OF AGRICULTURE. 107

0225-0993 See PRATIQUE PRIVEE, LA. 306

0225-1078 See NOUS LES ENSEIGNANTS DE L'ONTARIO. 1867

0225-1094 See ICE THICKNESS DATA FOR CANADIAN SELECTED STATIONS. FREEZE-UP, BREAK-UP. 1415

0225-1140 See ITAL COMMERCE. 842

0225-1205 See MINCHUNG SINMUN. 5789

0225-1248 See NEWSCALL NEWSLETTER, THE. 2749

0225-1272 See NUTRIPLAN. 2792

0225-1574 See CANADIANA AUTHORITIES. 3200

0225-1582 See MOEBIUS. 3412

0225-1604 See INNISFIL SCOPE, THE. 5786

0225-1760 See UTLAS NEWSLETTER (1979). 3255

0225-1795 See ONTARIO CORPORATION AND INCOME TAX LEGISLATION INCLUDING MINING TAXES AND SMALL BUSINESS DEVELOPMENT CORPORATIONS. 701

0225-1876 See SPORTS CLUB MAGAZINE. 4922

0225-1965 See AU FIL DES EVENEMENTS. 1726

0225-1981 See TERMINOLOGIE. 3328

0225-199X See TECHNIQUES DE PECHE. 2314

0225-2066 See PETIT PROMENEUR, LE. 5792

0225-2074 See SCARBORO CONSUMER. 5794

0225-2082 See NORTH YORK CONSUMER, THE. 5791

0225-2104 See REENBOU. 3470

0225-2112 See FEUILLET BIBLIQUE, LE. 5016

0225-2260 See ONTARIO GRADUATE SCHOLARSHIP PROGRAM. 1839

0225-2279 See CANADIAN NATIVE LAW REPORTER. 2948

0225-2287 See LEGAL INFORMATION SERVICE - NATIVE LAW CENTRE. 2999

0225-2333 See ALUMNI DIRECTORY - UNIVERSITY OF TORONTO. 1100

0225-2376 See REPORT OF THE PRESIDENT / NATURAL SCIENCES AND ENGINEERING RESEARCH COUNCIL CANADA. 4681

0225-2392 See CANADIAN BOOKSELLER (TORONTO). 4827

0225-2449 See FELLOWSHIP PROGRAM - INSURANCE INSTITUTE OF CANADA. 2880

0225-2600 See GUIDE DE LA ROUTE, PROVINCES DE L'ATLANTIQUE ET DU QUEBEC. 5478

0225-2627 See TRAIT D'UNION (OTTAWA). 4691

0225-2643 See NEW USES FOR SULPHUR TECHNOLOGY SERIES. 1027

0225-2651 See RESUMES DES DECISIONS RECENTES RENDUES PAR LA COMMISSION D'APPEL DE L'IMMIGRATION. 1921

0225-2686 See DIRECTORY & CONSUMER GUIDE - BETTER BUSINESS BUREAU GREATER TORONTO. 1296

0225-2708 See CRADLE CLUB MAGAZINE. 2278

0225-2716 See ANNUAIRE ET RAPPORT D'ACTIVITES - DEPARTEMENT DE DEMOGRAPHIE, UNIVERSITE DE MONTREAL. 4549

0225-2724 See PAPERS ON PLANNING AND DESIGN. 2830

0225-2732 See CENTRE FOR EAST ASIAN STUDIES OCCASIONAL PAPERS. 2648

0225-2783 See REAL ESTATE NEWS (TORONTO). 4844

0225-2899 See CANADIAN FOLKLORE (FOLKLORE STUDIES ASSOCIATION OF CANADA). 2318

0225-3089 See JOURNAL DE L'ASSOCIATION OUVRIERE CANADIENNE. 1681

0225-3100 See NEWSPAPER OF THE CANADIAN WORKERS' ASSOCIATION. 1695

0225-3151 See CINEMA AU QUEBEC, REPERTOIRE, LE. 4066

0225-316X See QUEBEC FILM INDUSTRY HANDBOOK. 4076

0225-3194 See TERMINOGRAMME. 3328

0225-3208 See RAPPORT ANNUEL DU SURINTENDANT DES ASSURANCES (QUEBEC. 1977). 2891

0225-3291 See ANNUAL REPORT / WORKERS' COMPENSATION BOARD, NEWFOUNDLAND AND LABRADOR. 1650

0225-3488 See WESTERN HOG JOURNAL. 223

0225-3550 See S P E A Q JOURNAL. 3319

0225-3569 See ENTREMETTEUR. 5784

0225-3577 See UP FRONT. 3472

0225-3593 See PORTE-VOIX, LE. 5301

0225-3704 See SALARIES AND SALARY SCALES OF FULL-TIME TEACHING STAFF AT CANADIAN UNIVERSITIES (SUPPLEMENT TO PRELIMINARY ED.). 1846

0225-3739 See MONTHLY RECORD. METEOROLOGICAL OBSERVATIONS IN CANADA. SUPPLEMENT. 1431

0225-3798 See RESEARCHER (SUDBURY). 5019

0225-3801 See MISSIONNAIRES CATHOLIQUES CANADIENS, STATISTIQUES. 5013

0225-381X See GRATIS (SCARBOROUGH, ONT.). 4862

0225-3828 See WORKING PAPER - CANADIAN ENERGY RESEARCH INSTITUTE. 1960

0225-3860 See CAHIER DE RECHERCHE - FACULTE DES SCIENCES SOCIALES. DEPARTMENT DE SCIENCE ECONOMIQUE. UNIVERSITE D'OTTAWA. 1467

0225-3895 See MEDICINE NORTH AMERICA. 3614

0225-395X See FUTURE HEALTH. 3577

0225-3992 See CROSSWORLD (LONDON, ONT.). 2908

0225-4034 See DCS NEWSLETTER. 2040

0225-4042 See S. O. N. G. SHEET. 1709

0225-4115 See JUSTICE. 3168

0225-414X See NOTICE TO IMPORTERS. 848

0225-4190 See HANDBOOK OF CANADIAN CONSUMER MARKETS. 1297

0225-4255 See WEST COAST LIFELINER. 4807

0225-4271 See GERONTOPHILE (SAINTE-FOY). 5179
0225-4484 See LIBRARY BULLETIN - BOREAL INSTITUTE FOR NORTHERN STUDIES. 3224
0225-4530 See PENSION PLANS IN QUEBEC. 1701
0225-4786 See DONNA (DOWNSVIEW). 5554
0225-4913 See HORSES ALL. 2800
0225-5014 See QUORUM (OTTAWA). 2544
0225-5081 See Y U L SERIALS LIST. 3256
0225-512X See SENTINEL (RIDGEWAY). 4996
0225-5162 See AECQ STRATEGY. 598
0225-5189 See REVUE CANADIENNE D'ETUDES DU DEVELOPPEMENT. 1639
0225-5235 See MUSEUMS IN NOVA SCOTIA. 4093
0225-5316 See GEOSCIENCE RESEARCH GRANT PROGRAM, SUMMARY OF RESEARCH. 1380
0225-5359 See CAHIERS D'HISTOIRE DE LA SOCIETE D'HISTOIRE DE BELOEIL-MONT-SAINT-HILAIRE, LES. 2612
0225-5367 See CHRISTIANS, JEWS TODAY. 4946
0225-5375 See CHRISTIANS, JEWS TODAY (FRENCH EDITION). 5047
0225-5391 See LEGAL SHOCK. 3000
0225-543X See ERE ATLANTEENNE. 4241
0225-5456 See PORTS ANNUAL. CANADIAN PORTS EDITION. 5454
0225-5472 See DIRECTORY OF INDUSTRIAL RELATIONS LIBRARIES IN CANADA. 3207
0225-5480 See VEHICLE (QUEBEC). 3255
0225-5510 See INFORMAG. 2535
0225-5529 See MINI JOURNAL, LE. 1804
0225-5545 See ENTRELLES, L'. 5555
0225-5677 See HEARTLAND OF SOUTHERN ONTARIO DIRECTORY. 839
0225-5693 See B. C. COUNSELLOR, THE. 1875
0225-5707 See CLIMATIC PERSPECTIVES. 1422
0225-5723 See TALKING BOOKS. 4832
0225-5758 See NEWSLETTER - PRAIRIE RELIGIOUS LIBRARY ASSOCIATION. 4982
0225-5774 See CROP PROTECTION NEWSLETTER. 169
0225-5782 See ONTARIO SPORTSCENE. 4911
0225-5790 See WORLD PRESS DIGEST. 2925
0225-5804 See RESILOG. 5306
0225-5871 See HOME OWNERS'. 2791
0225-5898 See NORTHWEST TERRITORIES GAZETTE. PART 1. 4670
0225-5952 See ECONOMIC AND FINANCIAL OUTLOOK. 1556
0225-6096 See FORUM (ONTARIO CONFEDERATION OF UNIVERSITY FACULTY ASSOCIATIONS). 1825
0225-610X See WRITER'S LIFELINE. 2926
0225-6193 See BANAR. 2528
0225-6207 See TRAVELWEEK BULLETIN. 5497
0225-6339 See SEASONS NORTH. 2760
0225-6355 See OPUS (ST. JOHN'S). 4144
0225-6363 See COATINGS. 4223
0225-638X See TORONTO THEATRE REVIEW. 5372
0225-6398 See LANDSCAPE TRADES. 2423
0225-6452 See FUR CHIC. 3184
0225-6533 See ADVENTURING IN CONSERVATION. 2185
0225-655X See PROCES-VERBAL DU CONGRES DE LA CSN (1978). 1703
0225-6592 See PANORAMA - NORANDA (ENGLISH ED.). 2147
0225-686X See MUSICWORKS. 4137
0225-6959 See RAPPORT ET TRAVAUX - GROUPE DE RECHERCHE SUR LA SOCIETE MONTREALAISE AU 19E SIECLE. 2756
0225-6975 See LIFELINES (SHERWOOD PARK. 1979). 589
0225-6991 See ADTALK. 754
0225-7009 See HAPPENINGS IN KAMLOOPS. 4851
0225-7017 See CHELSEY OVERVIEW. 5781

0225-7025 See DALMENY REVIEW. 5783
0225-7033 See CORD (HAMILTON). 5280
0225-7068 See MANDATE (TORONTO. 1979). 4975
0225-7114 See PICA. 4170
0225-7203 See LIVRE OFFICIEL DES RECORDS - LIGUE CANADIENNE DE FOOTBALL. 4903
0225-7211 See SIMMENTAL COUNTRY. 221
0225-7238 See IMPLANTATION D'UNE ENTREPRISE AU CANADA, L'. 1609
0225-7335 See NEWSLETTER - BLUE MOUNTAINS BRUCE TRAIL CLUB. 4875
0225-7416 See TRAIT D'UNION JEUNESSE, LE. 5005
0225-7459 See CANADIAN NEWS INDEX TORONTO. 5781
0225-7459 See CANADIAN NEWS INDEX (TORONTO). 5781
0225-7629 See ATLANTIC LIFE BUSINESS. 641
0225-7645 See ONTARIO TEACHERS' FEDERATION SUBMISSION TO THE CABINET, THE. 1770
0225-7874 See DEVIL'S ARTISAN, THE. 4564
0225-8013 See DISCUSSION PAPER - ECONOMIC COUNCIL OF CANADA. 1480
0225-8285 See MEETINGS & INCENTIVE TRAVEL. 5484
0225-8307 See LIBRARY OWNER'S MANUAL (1980). 3226
0225-8536 See NEW HORIZONS (TORONTO. 1972). 4242
0225-8579 See ANNUAL REPORT OF THE SUPERINTENDENT OF INSURANCE (QUEBEC. 1977). 2873
0225-901X See REPORT - DIVISION OF HEALTH SERVICES RESEARCH AND DEVELOPMENT, UNIVERSITY OF BRITISH COLUMBIA. 3917
0225-9044 See SPIRALE (MONTREAL). 365
0225-9044 See SPIRALE (MONTREAL). 331
0225-9060 See PROCEEDINGS, ANNUAL CONVENTION - NEW BRUNSWICK FEDERATION OF LABOUR. 1702
0225-9168 See INDUSTRIAL CORPORATIONS, FINANCIAL STATISTICS, PRELIMINARY DATA. 1610
0225-9206 See BATH & KITCHEN MARKETER. 2898
0225-9214 See FUEL CONSUMPTION GUIDE. 5415
0225-9222 See ENONCES DE PRINCIPE - ASSOCIATION CANADIENNE DES AUTOMOBILISTES. 5414
0225-9273 See MANITOBA HIGH SCHOOLS ATHLETIC DIRECTORY. 4904
0225-9303 See CAHIERS GEN-HISTO. 2441
0225-9346 See FARM MACHINERY CUSTOM AND RENTAL RATES, DETAILED SUPPLEMENT. 159
0225-9354 See NEWS - INTERMEDIATE TEACHERS ASSOCIATION. 1867
0225-9370 See CRESCENDO (CHARLOTTETOWN). 4113
0225-9389 See BOECKH BUILDING COST GUIDE. COMMERCIAL. 601
0225-9397 See BOECKH BUILDING COST GUIDE. INSTITUTIONAL. 601
0225-9400 See BOECKH BUILDING COST GUIDE. LIGHT INDUSTRIAL. 601
0225-9419 See BOECKH BUILDING COST GUIDE. RESIDENTIAL. 601
0225-9443 See DIRECTORY OF RETAIL CHAINS IN CANADA. 954
0225-9451 See CANADIAN MEDICAL EDUCATION STATISTICS. 3655
0225-9532 See APARTMENT WORLD IN WINNIPEG. 2815
0225-9583 See DIRECTORY - INDEPENDENT CANADIAN BUSINESSMEN ASSOCIATION OF BRITISH COLUMBIA. 5516
0225-9591 See MEDECIN VETERINAIRE DU QUEBEC, LE. 5516
0225-9648 See STATISTIQUES DE L'INSCRIPTION - UNIVERSITE DE MONTREAL, BUREAU DU REGISTRAIRE. 1848
0225-9745 See QUEBEC INTER. 4533

0225-9753 See PECU REVIEW, THE. 1512
0225-9761 See AT HOME IN CANADA'S CAPITAL. 4834
0225-9796 See DESTINY. 4953
0225-9818 See FISHERIES DATA REPORT. 2302
0225-9842 See GO SYSTEM TIMETABLE. 5383
0225-9850 See SUBMISSION TO THE ONTARIO COUNCIL ON UNIVERSITY AFFAIRS (CARLETON UNIVERSITY). 1849
0225-9877 See JOURNAL OF THE CANADIAN ATHLETIC THERAPISTS ASSOCIATION, THE. 3954
0225-9885 See REVUE QUEBECOISE DE PSYCHOLOGIE. 4617
0225-9907 See STATISTICS QUARTERLY - BUREAU OF STATISTICS (YELLOWKNIFE). 5342
0225-9923 See ANNUAL REVIEW - LABOUR CANADA. 1650
0225-9990 See DANGEROUS AND/OR UNUSUAL OCCURRENCES. 2861
0226-000X See CALGARY, ALBERTA, CITY DIRECTORY. 2557
0226-0115 See LUSOLT TALK. 3229
0226-0174 See MOYEN FRANCAIS. 3413
0226-0263 See CANADIAN EXPORTER (SCARBORO). 826
0226-0344 See COTTAGER MAGAZINE, THE. 2819
0226-0409 See CANADIAN BOOK OF CHARITIES. 5276
0226-0425 See PROVINCE OF NOVA SCOTIA, CANADA, THE. 1513
0226-0441 See GAY CHRISTIAN WITNESS. 2794
0226-0484 See FATAL ACCIDENT SUMMARY (VICTORIA). 2862
0226-0492 See REPERTOIRE DES CENTRES RESIDENTIELS COMMUNAUTAIRES AU CANADA. 5304
0226-0522 See CANADIAN COMMUNITY COLLEGE PROGRAMMES (NATIONAL EDITION). 1814
0226-0530 See CANADIAN COMMUNITY COLLEGE PROGRAMMES. INTERNATIONAL EDITION. 1814
0226-0565 See LISTE DES PERIODIQUES REGULIEREMENT RECUS - UNIVERSITE DE MONTREAL. BIBLIOTHEQUE DES SCIENCES HUMAINES ET SOCIAL. 419
0226-0816 See ANNUAL REPORT - THE ALBERTA FOUNDATION FOR THE PERFORMING ARTS. 383
0226-0840 See POTTERSFIELD PORTFOLIO, THE. 3424
0226-0891 See MONDE NOUVEAU (THURSO). 2283
0226-0905 See DIRECTORY OF SOCIAL SERVICE ADMINISTRATORS OF LOCAL MUNICIPALITIES. 5283
0226-1014 See BULLETIN ROUTIER; QUEBEC. 4635
0226-1081 See OTTAWA JOURNAL (INDEX). 2542
0226-112X See OCTOBER (MONTREAL). 4544
0226-1138 See OCTOBRE (MONTREAL). 4544
0226-1219 See STATUTES OF NEW BRUNSWICK. 3059
0226-1278 See NOUVELLES / CONSEIL DES MONUMENTS ET SITES DU QUEBEC. 2751
0226-1383 See COIFFURE DU CANADA. 403
0226-1391 See REPORT - VISUAL ARTS (EDMONTON). 363
0226-1456 See CONTACT (BRITISH COLUMBIA HOSPITAL/HOMEBOUND TEACHERS' ASSOCIATION). 1877
0226-1472 See INTERNATIONAL JOURNAL OF ENERGY SYSTEMS. 1947
0226-1499 See HARVEST (EDMONTON). 3165
0226-1510 See HEALTHSHARING. 4782
0226-1561 See ONTARIO WRESTLER. 4911
0226-157X See CANADIAN RAILWAY CLUB NEWS. 5430
0226-1685 See ASTIS BIBLIOGRAPHY. 5173
0226-1758 See TODAY'S BRIDE (DON MILLS). 2286

0226-1766 See CONNECTIONS (TORONTO). 5242

0226-1774 See WORKING PAPER SERIES (UNIVERSITY OF TORONTO. STRUCTURAL ANALYSIS PROGRAMME). 5265

0226-1944 See NEWS - FEMINIST PARTY OF CANADA. 5562

0226-1979 See CANADIAN PODIUM, THE. 1550

0226-1995 See MARCHE INTERNATIONAL (PIERREFONDS). 2911

0226-2002 See NIKKA TAIMUSU. 5790

0226-2053 See PROCEEDINGS - CANADIAN SOCIETY FOR CIVIL ENGINEERING. 2029

0226-2061 See INSTANTANES MATHEMATIQUES. 3509

0226-210X See QUEBECENSIA. 2756

0226-2169 See SAGAMIEN. 2575

0226-2177 See CANADIAN HUMAN RIGHT REPORTER. 4505

0226-224X See AU COURANT (OTTAWA. ENGLISH EDITION). 1547

0226-2258 See AU COURANT (OTTAWA. EDITION FRANCAIS). 1464

0226-2290 See LABOUR COMMENTARY. 1685

0226-2304 See INPUT-OUTPUT STRUCTURE OF THE CANADIAN ECONOMY. 1612

0226-2320 See RESTAURANT, CATERER AND TAVERN STATISTICS. 5073

0226-2347 See CANDID FACTS. 3795

0226-2428 See MAIEUTICS. 5208

0226-2436 See CLANDIGGER (EDMONTON). 2443

0226-2452 See INSPECTEUR DE GTA (1975). 2233

0226-2460 See IAO INSPECTOR. 2232

0226-2509 See ACQUISITIONS / METROPOLITAN TORONTO LIBRARY, GENERAL REFERENCE DEPARTMENT. 3187

0226-2533 See MUNICIPAL REFERENCE LIBRARY ACQUISITIONS. 3232

0226-2541 See ACQUISITIONS - METROPOLITAN TORONTO LIBRARY, MUSIC DEPARTMENT. 4098

0226-255X See METROPOLITAN TORONTO LIBRARY. SCIENCE & TECHNOLOGY DEPT. ACQUISITIONS. 3231

0226-2568 See ACQUISITIONS / METROPOLITAN TORONTO LIBRARY, SOCIAL SCIENCES DEPARTMENT. 5189

0226-2576 See MARCHE DU TRAVAIL (QUEBEC). 1690

0226-2649 See REPERTOIRE DES MEMBRES - CORPORATION PROFESSIONNELLE DES DIETETISTES DU QUEBEC. 4198

0226-272X See HIGHLIGHTS (MISSISSAUGA). 385

0226-2770 See NEWSLETTER - HUMAN RIGHTS COMMISSION OF BRITISH COLUMBIA. 4511

0226-2789 See NEWSLETTER - MINISTRY OF HEALTH (VICTORIA). 4793

0226-286X See ORGANIZATION OF THE GOVERNMENT OF ALBERTA. 4671

0226-2878 See INTERACTION (INTERGOVERNMENTAL COMMITTEE ON URBAN AND REGIONAL RESEARCH). 4657

0226-2894 See MONITEUR DES AFFAIRES ET DE LA FINANCE, LE. 907

0226-3033 See BULLETIN D'INFORMATION. RETAIL SALES TAX ACT. LOI SUR LA TAXE DE VENTE AU DETAIL. 2944

0226-3068 See ZAPAD. 2275

0226-3084 See RAPPORT D'ACTIVITES - OFFICE DE LA CONSTRUCTION DU QUEBEC. 4678

0226-3165 See INFORMATION CIRCULAR - EXPORT DEVELOPMENT CORPORATION. 840

0226-3300 See COLLECTION UPDATE. 3203

0226-3351 See INTERIM REPORT - B. C. HYDRO. 4657

0226-3424 See SIMCOE REVIEW. 3352

0226-3432 See QUALITE (DOLLARD-DES-ORMEAUX). 883

0226-3440 See U. C. REVIEW. 3449

0226-3467 See CADUCEE, LE. 862

0226-3513 See TOUR BRITISH COLUMBIA. 5493

0226-3556 See COMMUNICATIONS - AMNISTIE INTERNATIONALE, SECTION CANADIENNE. 3126

0226-3564 See PAPERS OF THE CANADIAN SOCIETY OF CHURCH HISTORY. 4985

0226-3572 See PIERRES VIVANTES. 5034

0226-3580 See JOURNAL LA REPUBLIQUE. 5787

0226-367X See PRETEXTE (MONTREAL). 3425

0226-3688 See ATULU, L'. 3192

0226-3726 See FEDERAL SCIENCE EXPENDITURES AND PERSONNEL. 4648

0226-3742 See FOREST INSECT AND DISEASE CONDITIONS: VANCOUVER FOREST REGION. 2380

0226-3750 See FOREST INSECT AND DISEASE CONDITIONS: PRINCE RUPERT FOREST REGION. 2380

0226-3769 See FOREST INSECT AND DISEASE CONDITIONS : PRINCE GEORGE FOREST REGION. 2380

0226-3777 See FOREST INSECT AND DISEASE CONDITIONS : KAMLOOPS FOREST REGION. 2380

0226-3785 See FOREST INSECT AND DISEASE CONDITIONS: NELSON FOREST REGION. 2380

0226-3793 See FOREST INSECT AND DISEASE CONDITIONS : CARIBOO FOREST REGION. 2380

0226-3947 See ECONOMICS OF MILK PRODUCTION IN ALBERTA. 194

0226-4188 See FOREST INSECT AND DISEASE CONDITIONS : YUKON TERRITORY. 2380

0226-4196 See ALBERTA COURT CALENDAR. 3138

0226-4390 See BUDGET. COMMUNIQUES (QUEBEC). 4634

0226-4552 See WATER WELL RECORDS FOR ONTARIO. 5548

0226-4560 See HOUSEHOLD FACILITIES BY INCOME AND OTHER CHARACTERISTICS. 1493

0226-4609 See NON-METAL MINES. 1363

0226-4617 See QUARRIES AND SAND PITS. 1363

0226-482X See SUMMARY OF THE HUNTING REGULATIONS (TORONTO). 4879

0226-5001 See PASTOR'S BULLETIN. 4985

0226-5036 See MANITOBA HISTORICAL SOCIETY NEWSLETTER. 2745

0226-5044 See MANITOBA HISTORY. 2745

0226-5109 See CHIA HUA CH'IAO PAO. 2727

0226-5117 See EASTERN NEWS (MISSISSAUGA). 5783

0226-5389 See ALUMNINEWS - CARLETON UNIVERSITY. 1101

0226-5400 See FRANCISATION EN MARCHE. 4650

0226-5419 See DIRECTORY OF LONG TERM CARE CENTRES IN CANADA. 3779

0226-5443 See POLOISTE, LE. 4912

0226-5540 See BULLETIN D'INFORMATION - CONSEIL REGIONAL DE DEVELOPPEMENT DE L'OUTAOUAIS (07). 1466

0226-5575 See ADC DU CREDIT. 768

0226-5648 See CANADIAN GENERAL AVIATION NEWS. 16

0226-5702 See ONTARIO WATER SKIER, THE. 4911

0226-5729 See CONCERTACTION. 5280

0226-5737 See MARIGOLD REPORT. 3230

0226-5761 See THEATRE HISTORY IN CANADA. 5370

0226-5877 See ANNUAIRE - ASSOCIATION DES CAMPS DU QUEBEC. 4869

0226-5893 See POLICY OPTIONS. 4488

0226-5907 See VILLAGER (MISSISSAUGA). 5797

0226-5923 See C. H. A. C. REVIEW. 3777

0226-5931 See REVUE A. C. C. S. 3792

0226-5958 See NOUVELLES DES SWINGERS. 5188

0226-5982 See JAPAN REPORT (CANADIAN EDITION). 842

0226-6040 See APT. REVIEW. EGLINTON EDITION. 383

0226-6075 See ALBERTA CATTLEMAN, THE. 205

0226-6083 See CROC. 3379

0226-6091 See DATA PRODUCT NEWS (TORONTO). 1245

0226-6105 See GENERATIONS (WINNIPEG). 2451

0226-6210 See CHANTIER. 607

0226-6245 See ENTRAIDE GENEALOGIQUE. 2446

0226-6253 See ECRITIQUE. 3462

0226-627X See ATLANTIC POST CALLS. 2797

0226-6296 See ATLIN NUGGET, THE. 5780

0226-6318 See HAWKESBURY EXPRESS. 5786

0226-6326 See GUELPH THIS WEEK. 5785

0226-6350 See ELK POINT REFLECTIONS. 5784

0226-6369 See ELK POINT SENTINEL. 5784

0226-6377 See BATTLEFORD TELEGRAPH. 5780

0226-6385 See CONTINUUM (MONTREAL). 5782

0226-6407 See HAVRE (CHANDLER). 5786

0226-6415 See GRAND TRUNK POPLAR PRESS, THE. 5785

0226-6458 See FINANCIAL SUMMARY AND BUDGETARY REVIEW. 4726

0226-6520 See PEEL FARM NEWS. 119

0226-658X See RURAL UTILITIES NEWSLETTER. 4684

0226-6598 See INFO-QUEBEC. 1259

0226-661X See ALERTA (TORONTO). 4503

0226-6644 See HEMOPHILIE DE NOS JOURS, L'. 3583

0226-6857 See MAISONS D'ICI. 2827

0226-6873 See EGALITE (MONCTON). 4472

0226-6881 See DIALOGUES ET CULTURES. 3277

0226-7063 See CAHIERS D'HISTOIRE DE DEUX-MONTAGNES. 2725

0226-7071 See CANADIAN JOURNAL OF EARLY CHILDHOOD EDUCATION. 1803

0226-7144 See LANGUES ET LINGUISTIQUE. 3296

0226-7152 See BONJOUR (TROIS-RIVIERES-OUEST). 5024

0226-7160 See ALMAGESTE. 391

0226-7187 See QUEBEC ROCK. 4148

0226-7195 See A. C. C. L. UNION LIST OF SERIALS. 3186

0226-7233 See ILE LETTREE, L'. 5786

0226-7284 See REVUE AUTOCHTONE. 3042

0226-7292 See PASSEPORT GASTRONOMIQUE. MONTREAL ET ALENTOURS. 5072

0226-7403 See PERMIS ACCORDES AUX COMPAGNIES ETRANGERES. 4740

0226-7411 See PHOTOMAG (VILLE LEMOYNE). 4375

0226-7446 See CANADIAN GEMMOLOGIST. 2913

0226-7454 See UNIVERSITES (MONTREAL). 1852

0226-7454 See UNIVERSITES (MONTREAL). 1852

0226-7500 See MEETINGS CANADA. 5233

0226-7535 See MINCE ET SVELTE. 4194

0226-7551 See SHOPPING CENTRE CANADA. 958

0226-7586 See REGISTER (MONTREAL, 1980). 2627

0226-7616 See WORKING PAPER (QUEEN'S UNIVERSITY (KINGSTON, ONT.). CENTRE FOR RESOURCE STUDIES). 2153

0226-7667 See JOINTURE. 1832

0226-7683 See OEIC INFORMATION BULLETIN. 1454

0226-7691 See B. C. ARCHER, THE. 4885

0226-773X See RULES BOOK OF THE FEDERATION OF CANADIAN ARCHERS. 4916

0226-7748 See E I C, ELECTRONIQUE, INDUSTRIELLE & COMMERCIALE. 2056

0226-7764 See LEGENDE. 1761

0226-7772 See VIVRE (GRANBY). 5008

0226-7810 See ACTIVE LIVING (TORONTO). 2595

0226-7837 See MOVING TO OTTAWA/HULL (1978). 4841

0226-7845 See ACCORD (CALGARY). 2254

0226-7861 See VIATEURS EN MISSION. 5007

0226-7934 See GAZETTE - LAURENTIAN UNIVERSITY. 1825

0226-7950 See POINT D'INTERROGATION (MONTREAL). 1702

0226-8019 See RAPPORT ANNUEL - CORPORATION DES BIBLIOTHECAIRES PROFESSIONNELS DU QUEBEC. 3243

0226-8043 See QUADERNI D'ITALIANISTICA. 3426

0226-8124 See NOYAU, LE. 115

0226-8205 See GLOBAL OUTLOOK. 4475

0226-823X See APPARENT PER CAPITA FOOD CONSUMPTION IN CANADA. PART 1. 2327

0226-8248 See APPARENT PER CAPITA FOOD CONSUMPTION IN CANADA. PART 2. 2327

0226-8361 See MARINE AFFAIRS BIBLIOGRAPHY. 3181

0226-840X See SAMISDAT. 3352

0226-8418 See SCRIPTA MEDITERRANEA. 2854

0226-8434 See BULLETIN - ASSOCIATION DES CONSEILLERS EN ORGANISATION ET METHODES DE QUEBEC, LE. 862

0226-8442 See C. W. E. A. NEWS. 4399

0226-8531 See CO-OPSERVATIONS. 1541

0226-8558 See DIRECTORY OF HOUSING CO-OPERATIVES. 1542

0226-8566 See KRAGOZORI. 2696

0226-8620 See MUSICK. 4137

0226-8655 See CAISSE-EXPRESS. 1541

0226-8663 See BOUEILLE, LA. 5781

0226-868X See LUTRIN. 4129

0226-8701 See COMMUNIQUE - SYNCHRO SWIM CANADA. 4891

0226-8728 See SELECTION DE PRESSE / CLUB MULTI-SPORTS INTERNATIONAL DE MONTREAL. 4917

0226-8760 See CANADIAN NETWORK PAPERS. 3200

0226-8841 See HEALTH LAW IN CANADA. 2977

0226-8868 See DIRECTORY OF MEMBERS OF THE ASSOCIATION OF TRANSLATORS AND INTERPRETERS OF ONTARIO. 3277

0226-8868 See DIRECTORY OF MEMBERS OF THE ASSOCIATION OF TRANSLATORS AND INTERPRETERS OF ONTARIO. 3277

0226-8922 See CONVENTIONS & MEETINGS CANADA (1981). 2804

0226-8949 See CONTINENTAL REFLECTIONS. 4950

0226-9023 See EFFECTIFS HUMAINS - COMMISSION SCOLAIRE L'ISLET-SUD. 1743

0226-9031 See DIRECTORY OF MEMBERS - FREELANCE EDITORS' ASSOCIATION OF CANADA. 4814

0226-9074 See CONTACT WEST ISLAND. 5782

0226-9120 See SPEC (NEW CARLISLE). 5795

0226-9139 See COURRIER DE LOTBINIERE, LE. 5782

0226-9171 See TOPOLOGIE STRUCTURALE STRUCTURAL TOPOLOGY. 3539

0226-9201 See COMPUTING NEWS / YORK UNIVERSITY. 1180

0226-9228 See SPECTRUM (TORONTO. 1981). 5311

0226-9317 See INDIAN LIFE MAGAZINE. 2264

0226-9325 See OSC BULLETIN. 910

0226-9368 See RESEARCH NOTE - PROVINCE OF BRITISH COLUMBIA, MINISTRY OF FORESTS. 2393

0226-9376 See MATERIEL DIDACTIQUE AGREE PAR LE MINISTERE DE L'EDUCATION POUR LES ECOLES PRIMAIRES ET SECONDAIRES DE LANGUE FRANCAISE. SUPPLEMENT. 1866

0226-9392 See ONTARIO ENERGY REVIEW. 1952

0226-9422 See AT THE CENTRE (HAMILTON). 2859

0226-9449 See PURE BEAUTE, LA. 2544

0226-9465 See GLOBAL FUTURES DIGEST. 1592

0226-952X See COOPERATIVE ENERGY. 1936

0226-9554 See TANGENCE. 3444

0226-9635 See ETUDES SUR LE FUTURISME ET LES AVANT-GARDES. 3386

0226-9686 See SUBURBAN (COTE-SAINT-LUC ED.). 5795

0226-9783 See ETINCELLE (LAVAL). 5285

0226-9791 See EX LIBRIS (OTTAWA). 3210

0226-9848 See LOOK INSIDE. 5065

0226-9864 See CANADIAN RETAILER. 952

0226-9880 See BULLETIN DE L'AQDR, LE. 5275

0226-9902 See FEMMES D'ACTION. 5556

0226-9945 See REVUE DE PAPINEAU, LA. 5794

0226-9961 See INFORMATEUR (LONGUEUIL). 682

0226-9988 See NOTES DE RECHERCHE (UNIVERSITE DE MONTREAL. FACULTE DE L'AMENAGEMENT). 2829

0226-9996 See ORDRE HOSPITALIER. 4984

0227-0021 See NOEUD. 5033

0227-0072 See UNIVERSITY OF MANITOBA ANTHROPOLOGY PAPERS. 247

0227-0129 See ANNUAL CONFERENCE. CONFERENCE SUMMARIES - CANADIAN NUCLEAR SOCIETY. 2153

0227-017X See RETAIL CHAIN AND DEPARTMENT STORES. 956

0227-0242 See LEB. 1834

0227-0250 See BOEUF DE L'EST. 207

0227-0315 See FILLES D'AUJOURD'HUI. 1063

0227-0331 See BUSINESSBEAT. 654

0227-034X See SERVICE (TORONTO). 5307

0227-0390 See FEDERAL COURT OF APPEAL DECISIONS. 2969

0227-0404 See NOS SOURCES. 2464

0227-0455 See NEW QUARTERLY. 3416

0227-0579 See ALBERTA WILD ROSE QUARTER HORSE JOURNAL. 2796

0227-0595 See BUILDCORE INDEX. 602

0227-0609 See MCINTOSH GALLERY. 358

0227-0668 See STATISTIQUE - BUREAU DE LA STATISTIQUE DU QUEBEC (1981). 5343

0227-0722 See VEUX-TU-SAVOIR. 1873

0227-0730 See OPTO PRESSE. 4216

0227-0773 See ISLAND (LANTZVILLE). 3464

0227-0781 See COGNITION (SCARBOROUGH). 167

0227-079X See COMMERCE MONCTON (1981). 828

0227-0803 See CRIEE. 2532

0227-0862 See WHISTLE (VANCOUVER). 4929

0227-0897 See ALPHA ACTION REPORTER. 4383

0227-0900 See CHASE ALMANAC. CANADIAN EDITION. 2530

0227-0927 See PROPOS PEDAGOGIQUES. 1775

0227-096X See DAILY PRAYER REMINDER. 4952

0227-0978 See MICHAEL FIGHTING. 4977

0227-1001 See WOOD TECHNOLOGY NOTES. 2406

0227-1044 See BULLETIN TRIMESTRIEL ECONOMIQUE (MONTREAL). 606

0227-1095 See PASTORALE SCOLAIRE (QUEBEC). 4985

0227-1109 See DIRECTORY OF NATIVE COMMUNITIES AND ORGANIZATIONS IN ONTARIO. 2259

0227-1141 See ECHO DE LA COUR. 2965

0227-115X See PLEIN CADRE. 4375

0227-1176 See INTERNATIONAL TELEX. 1158

0227-1184 See RIPOSTE (1980). 1299

0227-1192 See CARDSTON CHRONICLE, THE. 5781

0227-1206 See GAZETTE DU C. L. S. C, LA. 5785

0227-1222 See JOURNAL LE ST-FRANCOIS. 5787

0227-1249 See JOURNAL (LACHUTE). 5787

0227-1265 See TAX PRINCIPLES TO REMEMBER. 4754

0227-1311 See CONFLICT QUARTERLY. 4518

0227-1338 See IASC BULLETIN. 3214

0227-1346 See MAGOOK (EDITION FRANCAISE). 1066

0227-1370 See GASPESIE (GASPE. 1979). 2734

0227-1397 See ONTARIO BUSINESS. 701

0227-1400 See ANNUAL BIBLIOGRAPHY OF VICTORIAN STUDIES. 3356

0227-1435 See ACCESS (HALIFAX). 4383

0227-1532 See NEWFOUNDLAND TV TOPICS. 1160

0227-1540 See OBLIGATION, L'. 2751

0227-1559 See U F O UPDATE. 38

0227-1567 See BENEVOLE, LE. 1341

0227-1575 See BULLETIN GEOLOGIQUE (SAINTE-FOY). 1369

0227-1761 See PRODUCTION OF SELECTED BISCUITS. 2354

0227-1834 See SOCCER CANADA. 4919

0227-1842 See INFORM - A P I Q, L'. 3914

0227-1850 See AUTOMATIC MERCHANDISING IN CANADA. 1599

0227-1907 See ANNUAL CONFERENCE. PROCEEDINGS - CANADIAN NUCLEAR SOCIETY. 2154

0227-2040 See ACTION (LIMOILOU). 4932

0227-2059 See GUIDE TO CANADIAN MANUFACTURERS. 3480

0227-2067 See VOIX MULTICULTURELLE, LA. 2765

0227-2121 See NUNS' ISLAND JOURNAL. 5791

0227-2180 See REVUE CANADIENNE DU DROIT D'AUTEUR. 1308

0227-2202 See NEWSTODAY. 1867

0227-2261 See SABINE/MAGAZINE. 3247

0227-227X See LIAISON (THEATRE-ACTION). 5365

0227-2288 See POINT (BATHURST). 5793

0227-2296 See PONT, LE. 5793

0227-2377 See LINNEEN, LE. 4167

0227-2423 See ZINOTAJS. 2717

0227-244X See TURNOUT, THE. 5437

0227-2458 See MILEPOST (WINNIPEG). 5432

0227-2512 See NORTHERN TIMES (WHITEHORSE). 5791

0227-2547 See INDIRECTIONS. 3287

0227-2598 See NEWS (MAPLE RIDGE). 5790

0227-261X See 2000, AN. 4856

0227-2628 See ONTARIO GOVERNMENT PUBLICATIONS ANNUAL CATALOGUE 421

0227-2644 See IMPACT 80. 1609

0227-2687 See LIBERATION (MILTON). 4973

0227-2741 See BOOKS IN PERSIAN (1980). 4826

0227-2776 See BOOKS IN VIETNAMESE (1980). 4826

0227-2806 See GRAPHIC MONTHLY, THE. 4565

0227-2822 See CAHIERS DE CAP-ROUGE. 1090

0227-2881 See PATHFINDER (CALGARY). 4877

0227-2911 See JOURNAL DE LA COTE. 5787

0227-2938 See CONTACT (ASSOCIATION OF TEACHERS OF ENGLISH AS A SECOND LANGUAGE OF ONTARIO). 3274

0227-2962 See B. C. AREA ANNUAL DOCKET. 5055

0227-3020 See TRANSPORT-ACTION. 5395

0227-3160 See HELICOPTERS. 23

0227-3187 See UNION LIST OF SERIALS IN THE SOCIAL SCIENCES AND HUMANITIES HELD BY CANADIAN LIBRARIES. 5228

0227-3233 See CENTREGRAMME. 4108

0227-3268 See ORDERS IN COUNCIL (OTTAWA). 3023

0227-3357 See ALBERTA DRILLING PROGRESS AND PIPELINE RECEIPTS WEEKLY REPORT. 4249

0227-3411 See WHO'S WHO IN CANADIAN BUSINESS. 436

0227-3438 See QUEBEC SPECTRUM. 1843

0227-3462 See BULLETIN - ENVIRONMENT COUNCIL OF ALBERTA. 2162

0227-3470 See GRAND BEND SUN. 5785

0227-3489 See KELOWNA TODAY. 5788

0227-3535 See CASE HISTORY - MINERAL EXPLORATION RESEARCH INSTITUTE. 1438

0227-3543 See NOTE DE RECHERCHE - INSTITUT DE RECHERCHE EN EXPLORATION MINERALE. 1443
0227-3713 See GEOLOG (GEOLOGICAL ASSOCIATION OF CANADA). 1377
0227-3748 See C H R A RECORDER. 4770
0227-3772 See VANCOUVER EXPRESS. 5797
0227-3780 See SCHOOL LIBRARIES IN CANADA. 3248
0227-3837 See WINE & DINE. 2361
0227-3853 See MID-NORTH MONITOR, THE. 5789
0227-4175 See ONTARIO SPECTRUM. 1839
0227-4302 See DIRECTORY OF RESTAURANT AND FAST FOOD CHAINS IN CANADA. 5070
0227-4310 See AMATEUR MUSICIEN (1980). 4099
0227-4310 See AMATEUR MUSICIEN (1980). 4099
0227-4337 See PROCEEDINGS OF THE ... TRIENNIAL ASSEMBLY (... MEETING) OF THE CANADIAN COUNCIL OF CHURCHES, THE. 4988
0227-437X See "BROWN CHART" FOR ALL LINES OF GENERAL INSURANCE, PROVINCIAL RESULTS : ... REPORT, THE. 2876
0227-4442 See REPERTOIRE DES RESSOURCES FRANCO-ONTARIENNES. 2757
0227-4450 See JACQUES. 4862
0227-4523 See PROFANE. 243
0227-4558 See REFLET. 5391
0227-4604 See FLASH 10. 1864
0227-4752 See NOVA SCOTIA HISTORICAL REVIEW. 2751
0227-4760 See STRATEGY (LIBRARIES & LEARNING, INC.). 3251
0227-4787 See CANADA WATER ACT : ANNUAL REPORT, THE. 5531
0227-4906 See NOS LUTTES EXPRESS. 1695
0227-499X See AS THE SPIRIT MOVES. 4936
0227-5015 See NEWSLETTER - FILM STUDIES ASSOCIATION OF CANADA. 4075
0227-5023 See CHANSONS D'AUJOURD'HUI. 4108
0227-5090 See SCRIVENER. 3435
0227-5341 See MONTMORENCY. 1836
0227-535X See COOPERATIVEMENT VOTRE. 1541
0227-5368 See GUIDE (HAWKESBURY). 5785
0227-5406 See INFORMER (CALGARY). 4965
0227-5414 See INTERNATIONAL HOPKINS ASSOCIATION NEWSLETTER, THE. 3464
0227-5422 See NEW WYCLIF SOCIETY NEWSLETTER, THE. 4981
0227-5430 See IMAGE DE LA RIVE SUD, L'. 5786
0227-5449 See LOVE MAKES THE WORLD GO AWRY. 3409
0227-5457 See ECHO NOTRE-DAME. 2732
0227-5503 See MCMASTER SYMPOSIUM ON IRON AND STEELMAKING. 4008
0227-552X See CIRCULAIRE AUX PRETRES ET AUTRES AGENTS DE PASTORALE. 5027
0227-5538 See DENT POUR DENT. 1320
0227-5554 See BEREAN AMBASSADOR, THE. 5056
0227-5562 See TRAIT D'UNION (MASCOUCHE). 5796
0227-5708 See CITT NEWS. 5379
0227-5864 See ANNUAL REPORT / ONTARIO SHARE AND DEPOSIT INSURANCE CORPORATION. 2873
0227-5872 See SASKATCHEWAN ARCHAEOLOGY. 282
0227-5880 See CANPARA (1976). 4889
0227-5899 See INFORMATION - FEDERATION QUEBECOISE DES DIRECTEURS D'ECOLE. 1864
0227-5910 See CRISIS (TORONTO). 4583
0227-5953 See ROBERT CAMPBELL'S SOUP TO NUTS. 4865
0227-5961 See BULLETIN DE LA BANQUE ROYALE. 780
0227-5996 See MANUEL - ASSOCIATION CANADIENNE DE BADMINTON. 4904
0227-6046 See COL BLANC. 1659

0227-6062 See MARKET (TORONTO). 2121
0227-6089 See ROAD OF THE PARTY. 4546
0227-6119 See PARAPSYCHOLOGY (OTTAWA). 4242
0227-6127 See CASSIOPEIA (BRAMPTON). 3373
0227-6143 See SERIALS LIST MICROFORM / UNIVERSITY OF SASKATCHEWAN LIBRARY. 424
0227-6267 See HAMILTON GUIDEBOOK. 5479
0227-6291 See NEWSLETTER / FEDERATION OF CATHOLIC PARENT-TEACHER ASSOCIATIONS OF ONTARIO. 1768
0227-6313 See RESSOURCES (TORONTO). 1625
0227-633X See INTERNATIONAL FORUM (EN LUTTE (ORGANISATION)). 4542
0227-6364 See EGLISE DE TROIS--RIVIERES. 5029
0227-6372 See EGLISE DE TROIS-RIVIERES. DOCUMENT. 5029
0227-6402 See EDITION SPECIALE - CHASSE-GALERIE. 319
0227-6526 See TORONTO ARGONAUTS FACT BOOK. 4926
0227-6550 See SKYLINE (HAMILTON). 2760
0227-6569 See NEWSLINE - MANITOBA LIBRARY ASSOCIATION. 3236
0227-6593 See CHAMBER (WINNIPEG, MAN.). 819
0227-6631 See BUILDING OPERATING MANAGER. 603
0227-6658 See ORIENTEERING CANADA. 4911
0227-6747 See REPORT ON COUNCIL ACTIVITY - CANADIAN ADVERTISING ADVISORY BOARD. ADVERTISING STANDARDS COUNCIL. 765
0227-6755 See VIBRATIONS (TORONTO). 4394
0227-681X See REVIEW / BURLINGTON CHAMBER OF COMMERCE. 850
0227-6836 See SWINGTIME NEWS. 5188
0227-6879 See NEWSLETTER / ONTARIO COMMITTEE ON THE STATUS OF WOMEN. 5562
0227-6909 See COUP D'OEIL SUR L'HALTEROPHILIE. 4891
0227-7409 See NEWSPAPER (TORONTO). 5790
0227-7417 See SPORT PRESTIGE. 4921
0227-7514 See NEWSLETTER - SASKATCHEWAN ARCHAEOLOGICAL SOCIETY. 276
0227-7611 See RAPPORT ANNUEL / LA CORPORATION PROFESSIONNELLE DES PHYSIOTHERAPEUTES DU QUEBEC. 4382
0227-7751 See FITNESS AND LIFESTYLE RESEARCH REVIEWS. 2597
0227-793X See SEASONS. 4171
0227-7964 See LAVALIN (ENGLISH EDITION). 1985
0227-7980 See PROCEEDINGS OF THE ANNUAL MEETING - CANADIAN PEST MANAGEMENT SOCIETY. 4247
0227-7999 See INFORMER, THE. 5786
0227-8030 See NEW ERA (LANARK). 5790
0227-8073 See ANNUAL REPORT OF THE CHIEF ELECTORAL OFFICER ADMINISTERING THE ELECTION FINANCES AND CONTRIBUTIONS DISCLOSURE ACT. 4628
0227-8138 See MARCHE BYWARD. 5483
0227-8375 See CANADIAN TAX PLANNER'S NEWSLETTER. 740
0227-8464 See TRURO AND DISTRICT, NOVA SCOTIA, CITY DIRECTORY. 2578
0227-8472 See NOUVELLES D'OUTREMENT. 5791
0227-8480 See VOICE OF THE ELGIN FARMER. 145
0227-8499 See LOOK AT LONDON. 5483
0227-8529 See DENTAL SPECTRUM (OTTAWA). 1321
0227-8561 See MONOGRAPH - CHILDREN'S PSYCHIATRIC RESEARCH INSTITUTE. 3931
0227-8626 See VILLE DE HAMPSTEAD REPERTOIRE. 2579
0227-8669 See CANADIAN BUSINESS INDEX. 727
0227-8715 See MOT A MOT (QUEBEC). 4529

0227-874X See CHINESE-CANADIAN BULLETIN (1980). 2727
0227-8782 See CANADIAN ECUMENICAL NEWS. 4942
0227-8804 See CANADIAN INFORMATION INDUSTRY ASSOCIATION. 3199
0227-8863 See SMALL FRUIT INFORMATION LETTER. 135
0227-9142 See BUDGET / VILLE DE MONTREAL. 4715
0227-9304 See SMOKY RIVER NEWS, THE. 5794
0228-0043 See IMPORT EXPORT BULLETIN. 839
0228-0108 See SUPREME COURT LAW REVIEW, THE. 3061
0228-0124 See ELOIZES. 3384
0228-0205 See ROMANCE. 5074
0228-0213 See OFFICIEL DE LA PUBLICITE AU QUEBEC, L'. 763
0228-0221 See KANATA SOSIG. 5788
0228-0337 See COLLECTION ENCRE. 3376
0228-037X See MILE ZERO NEWS. 5789
0228-0469 See O R G A NEWSLINE. 5422
0228-0515 See CONFLUENCE (FORT SIMPSON). 5782
0228-0523 See PIONEER (CHETWYND). 5793
0228-0531 See NORTHUMBERLAND NEWS. 5791
0228-054X See MANNVILLE REFLECTIONS. 5789
0228-0558 See MACKENZIE DRIFT. 5789
0228-0566 See LINDSAY THIS WEEK. 5788
0228-0604 See OUTDOOR ATLANTIC. 4876
0228-0612 See QUARTER CIRCLE. 2801
0228-0655 See RECENT AND RECOMMENDED MEDICAL BOOKS. 3633
0228-0663 See MON MEILLEUR. 2801
0228-0671 See FOR THE LEARNING OF MATHEMATICS : AN INTERNATIONAL JOURNAL OF MATHEMATICS EDUCATION. 3505
0228-0698 See BADMINTONIEN. 4886
0228-071X See ENTREFILET. 4894
0228-0744 See BULLETIN / SOCIETY FOR THE STUDY OF ARCHITECTURE IN CANADA. 294
0228-0787 See ONTARIO NEST RECORDS SCHEME. 5593
0228-0825 See MINUTES OF PROCEEDINGS AND EVIDENCE OF THE STANDING COMMITTEE ON MANAGEMENT AND MEMBERS' SERVICES. 3010
0228-0868 See PRENONS NOTRE MUSIQUE EN MAIN!. 4147
0228-0914 See CANADIAN SCHOOL EXECUTIVE (1982). 1861
0228-0922 See CONDITIONS DE TRAVAIL CONTENUES DANS LES CONVENTIONS COLLECTIVES AU QUEBEC. 1661
0228-0930 See CAHIERS DE LA SEIGNEURIE DE CHAMBLY. 2725
0228-1074 See INTERCOM (ONTARIO UNIVERSITY REGISTRARS' ASSOCIATION). 1831
0228-1090 See AGRICULTURAL SOCIETIES NEWSLETTER. 52
0228-1139 See AU COURANT (PUBLIC SERVICE COMMISSION. NATIONAL CAPITAL REGIONAL OFFICE). 4631
0228-1171 See MILITANT CHRETIEN INTERNATIONAL, LE. 5032
0228-1244 See ENNUI. 319
0228-1252 See BULLETIN DE NOUVELLES - PRESSE ETUDIANTE DU QUEBEC. 1089
0228-1325 See SOCIAL RESOURCES INVENTORY. NORTHEASTERN REGION. 5308
0228-1333 See SOCIAL RESOURCES INVENTORY. EDMONTON REGION. 5308
0228-1422 See ALMANACH DU BAS-DU-FLEUVE. 2527
0228-1457 See ORIENTATION-NOUVELLES. 1770
0228-1503 See BULLETIN DE L'ANIMATEUR, LE. 5229
0228-1511 See CONSEIL DU PATRONAT DU QUEBEC. 1661
0228-152X See CHARLTON CANADIAN TRADE DOLLAR GUIDE, THE. 2780

0228-1538 See DIRECTORY & SERVICES GUIDE - CANADIAN ASSOCIATION OF WAREHOUSING AND DISTRIBUTION SERVICES. 1604

0228-1538 See DIRECTORY & SERVICES GUIDE - CANADIAN ASSOCIATION OF WAREHOUSING AND DISTRIBUTION SERVICES. 1604

0228-1554 See MEDIA WEST. 5251

0228-1619 See DIRECTORY - CANADIAN ROOFING CONTRACTORS' ASSOCIATION. 613

0228-1635 See JOURNAL OF UKRAINIAN STUDIES. 2849

0228-1686 See PRODUCTEUR DE LAIT QUEBECOIS, LE. 198

0228-1759 See CONTACT (KEMPTVILLE COLLEGE OF AGRICULTURAL TECHNOLOGY). 76

0228-1767 See CANADIAN DANCE NEWS. 1311

0228-1821 See C R S PERSPECTIVES. 2136

0228-1937 See WASTELANDS. 3452

0228-1953 See SASKATCHEWAN BUSINESS BULLETIN. 709

0228-1961 See CANADIAN COMPETITION POLICY RECORD. 1600

0228-2011 See WORKING PAPER - ROLE OF THE AUTOMOBILE STUDY, TRANSPORT CANADA. 5428

0228-202X See NEWSLETTER - ONTARIO MINISTRY OF AGRICULTURE AND FOOD. 112

0228-2038 See AGRICULTURAL NEWSLETTER (SUDBURY). 50

0228-2046 See BOREAL INSTITUTE VERTICAL FILES ON NORTHERN AFFAIRS, KWIC INDEX TO CLIPPING SERVICE ON MICROFICHE. 2724

0228-2119 See OSEILLEUR, L'. 2752

0228-2151 See LISTE DES MEMBRES DU CLUB DES ORNITHOLOGUES DE SIC QUEBEC. 5618

0228-2232 See COMPETITIONS, SUMMARIES, PROJECTS, TRIALS. 75

0228-2283 See JEWISH STAR (CALGARY). 5787

0228-2305 See SURVEY OF AGRICULTURAL LOST TIME INJURIES. 138

0228-2313 See INSTRUCTIONAL DEVELOPMENT AT WATERLOO. 1896

0228-2321 See BOOMERANG, THE. 3158

0228-2348 See EASTERN ZONE NEWSLETTER - ONTARIO ASSOCIATION OF ARCHERS. 4893

0228-2364 See MUSEUM NOTES (VANCOUVER). 4092

0228-2380 See LOUSAVORITCH. 2745

0228-2399 See HONES MUTUAL MONTHLY. 2534

0228-2410 See PLANNING GUIDELINE SERIES. 2831

0228-2429 See FORESIGHT (SACKVILLE). 1824

0228-2453 See INFO 9. 5289

0228-2488 See PRESENTATION TO THE PREMIER AND PROVINCIAL CABINET. 1579

0228-250X See TRICOLORUL. 2713

0228-2518 See IN SUMMARY. 5203

0228-2542 See BOURSE D'EMPLOIS EN REVUE, LA. 1656

0228-2550 See ARGILE BLEUE, L'. 1860

0228-2569 See JOURNAL LA MITIS. 5787

0228-2577 See KOL YAAKOV. 5050

0228-2585 See NEUVE EGLISE. 5234

0228-2593 See NEGOCIATIONS 79. 1693

0228-2607 See NEGOTIATIONS 79. 1693

0228-2623 See VIEIL ART, LE. 5182

0228-2631 See PASSEPORT. 5488

0228-2690 See BULLETIN, CONVERSION AU SYSTEME METRIQUE. 4029

0228-2747 See AVEC LE CHRIST ET LE SAINT-PERE. 5024

0228-2763 See MAQUIGNON DE LEVRARD. 2538

0228-278X See JOURNAL LE NORD. 5787

0228-2828 See MESSENGER (SCARBOROUGH). 5789

0228-2933 See SHEEP FOCUS "N" FACTS. 221

0228-3115 See SHADES. 4152

0228-3123 See INFORMATION FOR SENIORS. 5290

0228-314X See REPORT OF THE AUDITOR GENERAL (EDMONTON). 4745

0228-3212 See PERFORMANCE COMPARISON, CANADIAN POOLED PENSION FUNDS. 1701

0228-3263 See BRITISH COLUMBIA SPORTS HALL OF FAME AND MUSEUM. 4888

0228-3344 See POTBOILER (RICHMOND). 3424

0228-3409 See CANADIAN CUSTOMS AND EXCISE REPORTS. 2948

0228-3425 See JOURNAL - CONSEIL REGIONAL DE LA SANTE ET DES SERVICES SOCIAUX, REGION 01. 5291

0228-3441 See DIRECTORY - NORTHWESTERN ONTARIO REGION, MINISTRY OF EDUCATION. 1735

0228-3484 See NEWSLETTER - THE INNUIT GALLERY OF ESKIMO ART. 360

0228-3492 See P.S. POST-SCRIPTUM. 2542

0228-3530 See PLONGEE. 4912

0228-3573 See TRAVAUX DE RECHERCHE - BANQUE DU CANADA. 814

0228-3689 See JARNIGOINE. 2321

0228-3778 See GALERIE JOLLIET. 350

0228-3808 See REFERENCE SERIES - EXTERNAL AFFAIRS CANADA. 4679

0228-3824 See SIGNAL (WINNIPEG). 5393

0228-3867 See ACQUISITIONS LIST / MANITOBA, DEPT. OF EDUCATION, LIBRARY. 1792

0228-3875 See REPORT TO MEMBERS - MANITOBA TEACHERS' RETIREMENT ALLOWANCES FUND. 1870

0228-3891 See FUND RAISING EVENT REPORT. 5286

0228-409X See MEDECINE TRADITIONNELLE CHINOISE ET ACUPUNCTURE. 3607

0228-4111 See KEWA. 272

0228-4138 See ASIATHEQUE. 2646

0228-4146 See AUTRE PAROLE, L'. 4937

0228-4189 See TIME MANAGEMENT REPORT. 888

0228-4235 See WORKING PAPER (UNIVERSITY OF WESTERN ONTARIO.) CENTRE FOR THE STUDY OF INTERNATIONAL ECONOMIC RELATIONS). 1641

0228-4278 See LAND ASSESSMENT/SALES RATIO STUDY AND EQUALIZED ASSESSMENTS. 4660

0228-4413 See BETOIRE, LA. 1402

0228-4448 See BIVOUAC. 5229

0228-4723 See ANNUAL REPORT / CAPE BRETON DEVELOPMENT CORPORATION. 4627

0228-4839 See CLUB DES AMIS DE GILLES VILLENEUVE INC. 4890

0228-488X See DEMOCRATE (PARTI NOUVEAU DEMOCRATIQUE DU QUEBEC). 4471

0228-491X See CANADIAN PHILOSOPHICAL REVIEWS. 4343

0228-5037 See CHENE. 4637

0228-5045 See CHAPEAU. 1541

0228-5134 See LISTING OF SUPPLEMENTARY DOCUMENTS / STATISTICS CANADA, LIBRARY. 3259

0228-5266 See EMPLOYMENT LAW REPORT, THE. 3147

0228-5347 See AU LENDEMAIN DE L'ECOLE SECONDAIRE. 1910

0228-5401 See COMMUNICATION - CANADIAN CO-ORDINATING COUNCIL ON DEAFNESS. 4385

0228-541X See LIBRARY BINDINGS (WEYBURN). 3224

0228-5479 See VIE EN ROSE, LA. 5567

0228-5517 See VIVRE +. 5182

0228-5584 See AGRIWEEK. 199

0228-5622 See MONTHLY OIL AND GAS PRODUCTION REPORT. 4264

0228-5630 See DRILLING ACTIVITY REPORT. 4254

0228-5657 See SUMMARY OF INVESTIGATIONS BY THE SASKATCHEWAN GEOLOGICAL SURVEY. 1399

0228-5681 See MOT MYSTERE. 4863

0228-569X See MOT A TROUVER MYSTERIEUX. 4863

0228-5703 See PEUPLE (ST-AGAPIT). 5792

0228-572X See EARTH & TIDE. 2731

0228-5819 See CURRENT ECONOMIC ANALYSIS (OTTAWA). 1478

0228-586X See ALIVE (VANCOUVER). 4187

0228-5908 See ECHO DES BASQUES. 2446

0228-5916 See TRAVELIFE. 5497

0228-6017 See JEWISH STAR (EDMONTON EDITION). 5787

0228-6114 See ANNUAL REPORT - SASKATCHEWAN HOG MARKETING COMMISSION. 206

0228-6157 See WINE TIDINGS. 2372

0228-6203 See INTERNATIONAL JOURNAL OF MODELLING & SIMULATION. 1282

0228-6238 See QUOI DE 9. 5303

0228-6246 See ANNUAL REVIEW - SCIENCE COUNCIL OF CANADA. 5084

0228-6262 See PORTAGE (RIVIERE-DU-LOUP). 5793

0228-6289 See JOURNAL ACTON REGIONAL. 5787

0228-6297 See COURRIER DE PORTNEUF, LE. 5782

0228-6351 See QUEBEC SOCCER. 4914

0228-636X See REVEIL A JONQUIERE, LE. 5794

0228-6475 See MOTS A TROUVER POPULAIRES. 4863

0228-6483 See MOTS ENTRE-CROISES POPULAIRES. 4863

0228-653X See CORPUS CHEMICAL REPORT. 1023

0228-6556 See CAHIERS DE BIBLIOLOGIE. 4827

0228-6599 See PERIODIQUES - BIBLIOTHEQUE. CEGEP DE MAISONNEUVE. 422

0228-6610 See ANALYSE DE LA CAMPAGNE / CENTRAIDE CANADA. 5271

0228-6629 See TEMPS LIBRE (LAUZON). 4925

0228-6637 See ARPENTEURS & GEOMETRES. 2555

0228-6645 See COURRIER DE GRAND'MERE, LE. 5782

0228-6653 See REVEIL A CHICOUTIMI, LE. 5794

0228-6661 See REVEIL A LA BAIE, LE. 5794

0228-667X See ECHO DES VOYAGES, L'. 5469

0228-670X See SEMENCE, LA. 5019

0228-6726 See VIDEO GUIDE (VANCOUVER). 1142

0228-6831 See FREEWHEELIN'. 4081

0228-684X See LUTTES URBAINES. 2827

0228-6858 See TOWNSHIPS CROSSROADS. 5224

0228-6939 See JOURNAL OF HISTORY AND POLITICS. 2621

0228-6947 See CHARLTON STANDARD CATALOGUE OF ROYAL DOULTON FIGURINES, THE. 2772

0228-6963 See LANDSCAPE ARCHITECTURAL REVIEW. 2422

0228-698X See VOILA QUEBEC. 5499

0228-7005 See ANNUAIRE DU SPORT UNIVERSITAIRE QUEBECOIS ET CALENDRIERS DES ACTIVITES. 4883

0228-7021 See COIFFBEC. 402

0228-703X See PEUPLE DE LA CHAUDIERE. 5792

0228-7099 See POLYSCOPE (SAINT-LEONARD D'ASTON, QUEBEC). 1774

0228-7137 See FLAG : THE FOOTHILLS LIBRARY ASSOCIATION GAZETTE, THE. 3211

0228-7161 See B.C. DEAF ADVOCATE, THE. 4384

0228-717X See NOVA SCOTIA WORKER, THE. 1695

0228-7226 See PLAYBOY COLLECTORS GUIDE & PRICE LIST, THE. 3996

0228-7293 See BREAKTHROUGH FOR WOMEN. 5552

0228-7498 See CRAFT FACTOR. 371

0228-7633 See STATEMENT OF FINANCIAL OPERATIONS. 812

0228-7684 See COMMISSAIRE D'ECOLES. 1861

0228-7730 See ANNUAIRE - ASSOCIATION DES COLLEGES DU QUEBEC (1979). 1808
0228-7749 See MADE IN CANADA. ARTISTS IN BOOKS. 357
0228-7781 See SOUND HERITAGE SERIES. 1997
0228-782X See VANCOUVER POETRY CENTRE NEWSLETTER. 3472
0228-7838 See MAL DE BLOCS. 3005
0228-7846 See ST-LAURENT. 375
0228-7897 See KENNEBECASIS VALLEY POST. 5788
0228-7927 See MANITOBA INSECT CONTROL GUIDE. 107
0228-7935 See OFFENSIVES COMMUNAUTAIRES ET CULTURELLES. 1699
0228-7951 See ECRITURE FRANCAISE DANS LE MONDE. 3383
0228-8044 See REPORT TO THE PEOPLE / YOUTH FOR CHRIST/VANCOUVER. 4992
0228-8079 See BULLETIN PROVINCIAL (CANADIAN CHILD AND YOUTH DRAMA ASSOCIATION. NEW BRUNSWICK). 5362
0228-8095 See RUPERT'S LAND NEWS. 4994
0228-8168 See WESTCOAST MUSIC. 4158
0228-8206 See CHANNEL (ST. CATHARINES). 2530
0228-8222 See MANUEL DE PRATIQUE DE L'ARCHITECTURE. 303
0228-8230 See PANJAB AFFAIRS. 2662
0228-829X See FASHION IMAGES. 1084
0228-8435 See RAPPORT ANNUEL - COMMISSION QUEBECOISE DES LIBERATIONS CONDITIONNELLES. 5303
0228-8494 See OMH. OFFICES MUNICIPAUX D'HABITATION. 2830
0228-8656 See OTTAWA CO-OPERATIVE DIRECTORY. 1543
0228-8699 See CHRONIC DISEASES IN CANADA. 3563
0228-8702 See MALADIES CHRONIQUES AU CANADA. 3606
0228-8710 See BREF (ASSOCIATION DES TISSERANDS D'ICI), EN. 5348
0228-8753 See CANADIAN ISBN PUBLISHER'S DIRECTORY. 4827
0228-877X See ONTARIO MEDICAL TECHNOLOGIST / ONTARIO SOCIETY OF MEDICAL TECHNOLOGISTS. 3624
0228-8788 See CONSTRUCTION CANADA. 609
0228-8826 See TRUSTEE NEWS / SASKATCHEWAN SCHOOL TRUSTEES ASSOCIATION. 1873
0228-8842 See B.C. NATURALIST. 2187
0228-8907 See CANADIAN HOSPITAL ASSOCIATION COMMITTEE RESEARCH REPORT. 3777
0228-8923 See MARINE AND INSURANCE NEWS. 2887
0228-894X See NATIONAL LOSS PREVENTION. 880
0228-8958 See CANADIAN LOSS PREVENTION. 863
0228-8966 See MANITOBA FOOD PRODUCTS DIRECTORY. 2348
0228-8982 See SPECTRUM (MONTREAL. 1981). 5223
0228-9016 See SUR L'EMPREMIER. 2762
0228-9024 See U OF T WOMAN'S NEWSMAGAZINE. 5567
0228-9059 See JOURNAL ETUDIANT - COLLEGE DE JONQUIERE. 1092
0228-9067 See COCKTAIL MOLOTOV, LE. 1090
0228-9075 See ONTARIO FENCER. 4911
0228-9083 See CONDUCTEUR AVERTI. 5412
0228-9113 See RAPPORT ANNUEL - MINISTERE DE L'ENERGIE ET DES RESSOURCES (QUEBEC). 2203
0228-913X See NEOLOGY / EDMONTON SCIENCE FICTION AND COMIC ARTS SOCIETY. 3415
0228-9148 See AURORE. TRAITE, L'. 4937
0228-9156 See SERIALS RECORD FILE / UNIVERSITY OF LETHBRIDGE LIBRARY. 424

0228-9164 See GAZETTE (GRAND FALLS). 5785
0228-9199 See POINT (ALEXANDRIA). 5793
0228-9229 See CALGARY EVANGELICAL DIRECTORY. 4942
0228-9288 See ALBERTA FAMILY HISTORIES SOCIETY QUARTERLY. 2436
0228-9296 See HML NEWS. 457
0228-9326 See STARDOCK (OTTAWA). 3439
0228-9474 See OFFICERS / ALBERTA SOCIETY OF ARTISTS. 361
0228-9504 See CANADIAN CRICKETER, THE. 4889
0228-9512 See DATA SCOPE (OAKVILLE). 1603
0228-9539 See YEARBOOK - ROYAL CANADIAN COLLEGE OF ORGANISTS (1978). 4159
0228-9547 See FAITS ET CHIFFRES, LES MINES AU CANADA. 1606
0228-9555 See CRANE LIBRARY W.I.P. 3204
0228-9571 See CRANE LIBRARY UPDATE. 3204
0228-9636 See DIPLOMES - UNIVERSITE DE MONTREAL. 1820
0228-9652 See READING MANITOBA. 1903
0228-9695 See SASKATOON, SASKATCHEWAN, CITY DIRECTORY. 2575
0228-975X See BULLETIN - SOCIETE BOTANIQUE DU QUEBEC. 505
0228-9776 See GUIDE DE L'AUTOMOBILE AMERICAINE, LE. 5415
0228-9830 See IMPRESSION (VALLEYFIELD). 5786
0228-9873 See BARATAINKNAK A MAGYAR JEZSUITAK. 4938
0228-9938 See PARAVOICE. 4911
0228-9954 See PETITE NATION, LA. 5792
0228-9962 See INTERNATIONAL CORRESPONDANCE (MONTREAL). 4542
0229-0065 See THIS BUSINESS OF TRUCKING. 5394
0229-0081 See DIRECTORY OF PROGRAMS IN STATISTICS AND RELATED AREAS IN CANADIAN UNIVERSITIES / STATISTICAL SOCIETY OF CANADA. 3503
0229-009X See CULTURE (QUEBEC. 1981). 234
0229-012X See MAL-I-MIC (1979). 2745
0229-0154 See CULTURAL GUIDE (OTTAWA). 318
0229-0219 See CHRISTIAN INFO COMMUNIGRAM. 4945
0229-0235 See BCATML NEWSLETTER, THE. 3268
0229-0243 See ROYAL BANK LETTER, THE. 1582
0229-0324 See REVIEW OF PROFESSIONAL MANPOWER. 1708
0229-0383 See YUKON KOMIX. 4868
0229-0391 See NORTHERN PEN. 5791
0229-0413 See PLASTICS BUSINESS. 4457
0229-0510 See STRATEGY (TORONTO). 916
0229-0553 See BRMNA JOURNAL. 5430
0229-0618 See ANNUAL - KAJAKS TRACK AND FIELD CLUB. 4883
0229-0685 See PROLETARIAN REVOLUTION (MONTREAL). 4545
0229-0693 See REVOLUTION PROLETARIENNE (MONTREAL). 4546
0229-0715 See THIRD EYE (TORONTO). 4394
0229-0723 See GOLD POST. 4838
0229-074X See SEIGNEURIE DE LAUZON. 2760
0229-0766 See BULLETIN STATISTIQUE - DIRECTION GENERALE DE L'ENSEIGNEMENT COLLEGIAL. 1793
0229-0804 See WHIZ FUNNIES. 3453
0229-0812 See DIGEST ON GAY RIGHTS. 4507
0229-0871 See UQACTUALITE. 1853
0229-088X See ON THE RUN. 4911
0229-0898 See BONJOUR QUEBEC. 5465
0229-091X See GOOD NEWS FROM NARAMATA CENTRE. 4961
0229-0928 See MISSIONS DES ILES. 4978
0229-0936 See REVEIL DU PONTIAC, LE. 5794
0229-0995 See PROCEEDINGS / CANADIAN INSTITUTE OF ACTUARIES. 2890

0229-1096 See OUR SCHOOLS (OTTAWA). 5033
0229-110X See NOS ECOLES (OTTAWA). 5033
0229-1142 See DIRECTORY / CANADIAN GAS ASSOCIATION. 4760
0229-1185 See CORRESPONDANCE INTERNATIONALE (MONTREAL). 4541
0229-1215 See HORIZONS SF. 3394
0229-1223 See RESEARCH ANIMALS IN CANADA. 226
0229-1231 See SCRIPT USER'S GUIDE. 1281
0229-124X See VM/370 CMS EXEC USER'S GUIDE. 1281
0229-1320 See ONTARIO CRAFT. 374
0229-1347 See A.N.CH.A. AGENCIA NOTICIOSA CHILENA ANTIFASCISTA (EDICION INGLESA). 4539
0229-1398 See HOUSE OF COMMONS DEBATES (OTTAWA. RETROSPECTIVE COMPILATION). 4654
0229-1428 See O.N.E. NEWSLETTER. 4197
0229-1495 See ICHOR. 3395
0229-1509 See CHEER. 4109
0229-1533 See CUE TRACK. 4113
0229-1541 See SPORT MEDICINE DIRECTORY. 3956
0229-155X See LIST OF MEMBERS / AUCTIONEERS' ASSOCIATION OF ALBERTA. 929
0229-1622 See LAND MANAGEMENT HANDBOOKS / PROVINCE OF BRITISH COLUMBIA, MINISTRY OF FORESTS. 2386
0229-1630 See COMMUNITY MARKETS CANADA : THE COMPREHENSIVE GUIDE TO THE LATEST COMMUNITY NEWSPAPER MARKET DATA. 757
0229-1681 See SERIALS LIST / ERINDALE COLLEGE LIBRARY. 424
0229-1711 See B.C. ADMINISTRATOR. 1860
0229-172X See FORO INTERNACIONAL (IN STRUGGLE (ORGANIZATION)). 4542
0229-1738 See WHO IS DOING WHAT IN HISTORIC PRESERVATION. 310
0229-1770 See FOCUS ON FOOD SERVICE. 2335
0229-1886 See FIVE YEAR FOREST AND RANGE RESOURCE PROGRAM. 2379
0229-1908 See MINERAL INDUSTRY QUARTERLY REPORT. 1441
0229-1916 See QUAKER CONCERN. 5066
0229-1924 See FISH SUPPLIES INTERNATIONAL : PROCESSING & MARKETING NEWS. 2301
0229-1940 See SKI INDUSTRY BULLETIN. 4918
0229-1959 See SOLWEST. 1957
0229-1967 See WAGES FOR HOUSEWORK : CAMPAIGN BULLETIN, THE. 1717
0229-1975 See SURVIVE (VANCOUVER, B.C.). 5001
0229-1983 See NORTHERN ONTARIO CONSTRUCTION & RESOURCE INDUSTRIES DIRECTORY, PURCHASING GUIDE. 622
0229-1991 See CORNWALL, ONTARIO CITY DIRECTORY. 2559
0229-2068 See INFOMANE. 5786
0229-2092 See FARM LIGHT & POWER (MANITOBA EDITION). 85
0229-2106 See FARM LIGHT & POWER (ALBERTA EDITION). 85
0229-2130 See DESTINATION (TORONTO, ONT.). 5468
0229-2181 See NEWSLETTER (INTERNATIONAL OMBUDSMAN INSTITUTE). 3017
0229-2203 See JAMBOREE COUNTRY MUSIC MAGAZINE. 4124
0229-2297 See REVUE LITTERAIRE DU C.E.G.E.P. DE GRANBY. 3351
0229-2319 See FRIDAY (TORONTO). 4850
0229-2351 See SQUASH REVIEW. 4924
0229-253X See CREATION SCIENCE DIALOGUE. 5097
0229-2548 See CANADIAN PARLIAMENTARY REVIEW. 4636
0229-2556 See REVUE PARLEMENTAIRE CANADIENNE. 4684

ISSN Index

0229-2572 *See* PROGRAMME SOUVENIR. FESTIVAL DU VOYAGEUR, ST. BONIFACE, MANITOBA. **4853**

0229-2599 *See* RESEARCH INVENTORY / MEMORIAL UNIVERSITY OF NEWFOUNDLAND, OFFICE OF RESEARCH. **1845**

0229-2602 *See* TOP GENERATION NEWSLETTER. **5182**

0229-2637 *See* SEARCHLIGHT (BLOOMFIELD, ONT.). **2472**

0229-2645 *See* NEWSLETTER / ONTARIO ASSOCIATION OF LIBRARY TECHNICIANS. **3236**

0229-2653 *See* ACTION FOR CANADA'S CHILDREN. **1059**

0229-2661 *See* CONCERN (NEW WESTMINSTER). **4772**

0229-2718 *See* NOTES DU CENTRE D'ETUDES DU TOURISME, LES. **5486**

0229-2726 *See* LABOUR REVIEW / ST. CATHARINES AND DISTRICT LABOUR COUNCIL. **1686**

0229-2742 *See* NEWSLETTER / NIAGARA CHILDREN'S SERVICES COMMITTEE. **5299**

0229-2750 *See* NOTES FROM NIAGARA. **2465**

0229-2807 *See* ARC (MONTREAL). **5055**

0229-2858 *See* RAPPORT ANNUEL DES ACTIVITES (ASSOCIATION TOURISTIQUE REGIONALE RICHELIEU RIVE-SUD). **1623**

0229-2866 *See* NATIONAL NEWSLETTER - CANSPA. **622**

0229-2971 *See* SUBURBAN. NOTRE DAME DE GRACE EDITION. **5795**

0229-298X *See* SUBURBAN. DOLLARD DES ORMEAUX EDITION. **5795**

0229-2998 *See* SUBURBAN. COTE DES NEIGES EDITION. **5795**

0229-3005 *See* SUBURBAN (WESTMOUNT EDITION). **5795**

0229-3013 *See* SUBURBAN. NEW BORDEAUX, CARTIERVILLE EDITION. **5795**

0229-3021 *See* SUBURBAN. TOWN OF MOUNT ROYAL EDITION. **5795**

0229-303X *See* SUBURBAN. ST. LAURENT EDITION. **5795**

0229-3048 *See* SUBURBAN (LAVAL EDITION). **2547**

0229-3099 *See* ALBERTA SCIENCE TEACHER, THE. **5082**

0229-3110 *See* FEEDBACK (CALGARY). **2822**

0229-3129 *See* CANADIAN INDEPENDENT SCHOOL JOURNAL. **1730**

0229-3153 *See* ANNUAL CBAC SURVEY OF PERFORMING ARTS ORGANIZATIONS. **383**

0229-3161 *See* DIRECTORY - SPORTS FEDERATION OF CANADA. **4893**

0229-3196 *See* TORONTO CLARION. **5796**

0229-320X *See* POSTILLON DE CHAMPLAIN. **5793**

0229-3234 *See* INFLATION IN CANADA. **791**

0229-3277 *See* POINT DE VUE (SENNETERRE). **5793**

0229-3285 *See* MIRABEL-- A VOL D'OISEAU. **4666**

0229-3390 *See* CEGEP-INTER. **1814**

0229-3404 *See* AFFAIRES (MONTREAL. 1981). **636**

0229-3463 *See* PACER (WINNIPEG, MAN.). **4911**

0229-3471 *See* BASELINE, THE. **4886**

0229-348X *See* PROFILS D'ENTREPRISES QUEBECOISES. **705**

0229-3560 *See* REFLET DE MON MILIEU. **5793**

0229-3587 *See* AUBE. **3827**

0229-365X *See* SUMMARY OF PROCEEDINGS. ANNUAL CONVENTION - B.C. FEDERATION OF LABOUR (CLC). **1712**

0229-3684 *See* 4 FOR 20. **4881**

0229-379X *See* CAREERS (EDMONTON). **4202**

0229-3803 *See* VIE OUVRIERE (MONTREAL, QUEBEC). **1716**

0229-3862 *See* BADMINTON NEW-NOUVEAU BRUNSWICK : NEWSLETTER. **4886**

0229-3870 *See* CPRS CROSS-REFERENCE LIST. **758**

0229-3889 *See* SOLEIL DE TRIEST. **5310**

0229-3943 *See* CITOYEN (NORMETAL). **5782**

0229-4001 *See* BULLETIN (MONTREAL CITIZENSHIP COUNCIL). **5194**

0229-4028 *See* TALKING BOOKS CATALOGUE SUPPLEMENT. **4832**

0229-4044 *See* WORLD MARKET PERSPECTIVE. **817**

0229-4052 *See* TEMPS FORT. **4855**

0229-4141 *See* TRUSTEE (EDMONTON, ALTA.). **1873**

0229-415X *See* HOMES FOR THE AGED. **3783**

0229-4273 *See* CANADIAN TEACHERS' FEDERATION, ITS OBJECTIVES, ITS POLICY. **1890**

0229-4338 *See* INFORMACCUEIL, L'. **5289**

0229-4362 *See* TRANSPORTEUR, LE. **5005**

0229-4370 *See* LARGE PRINT BOOKS / GEORGIAN BAY REGIONAL LIBRARY SYSTEM. **4829**

0229-4397 *See* UNISSON. **1873**

0229-4442 *See* CANADIAN HOSPITALITY. **2804**

0229-4540 *See* ONTARIO NEWS BULLETIN / WCTU. **4983**

0229-4567 *See* LABOUR SURVEY (SOCIETY OF THE PLASTICS INDUSTRY OF CANADA). **1687**

0229-4575 *See* SALARY SURVEY (SOCIETY OF THE PLASTICS INDUSTRY OF CANADA). **1709**

0229-4605 *See* SOURCES & RESOURCES (BRITISH COLUMBIA SCHOOL LIBRARIANS' ASSOCIATION). **3250**

0229-463X *See* AJAR. **3358**

0229-4680 *See* UNB PERSPECTIVES. **1851**

0229-4699 *See* HUMANITIES ASSOCIATION OF CANADA NEWSLETTER. **2847**

0229-4702 *See* PAS GRAPHIC, THE. **5792**

0229-480X *See* WOMEN AND ENVIRONMENTS. **5569**

0229-4834 *See* VOICE OF THE YOUTH. **4548**

0229-4842 *See* VOIX DES JEUNES (TORONTO. 1979). **4548**

0229-4915 *See* TALKING BOOKS CATALOGUE / LAKE ONTARIO REGIONAL LIBRARY SYSTEM. **426**

0229-4966 *See* ATHLETICS (TORONTO. 1981). **4884**

0229-5059 *See* PRAIRIE WOMAN. **5564**

0229-5113 *See* REFUGE (TORONTO. ENGLISH EDITION). **5304**

0229-5156 *See* CONGRESS ... PROCEEDINGS - FEDERATION DES SPORTS DU CANADA. **4891**

0229-5229 *See* COUNTRY VACATIONS IN ALBERTA. **4849**

0229-5253 *See* PROVINCE OF BRITISH COLUMBIA BUDGET. **4742**

0229-5261 *See* LIVING WORD (SWAN RIVER). **5018**

0229-527X *See* NEWSLETTER / BRITISH COLUMBIA GENEALOGICAL SOCIETY. **2463**

0229-5296 *See* NOW (RIVERVIEW). **386**

0229-5334 *See* U.S.G. NEWSLETTER. **2578**

0229-5385 *See* HYSTERIA (KITCHENER). **5558**

0229-5393 *See* LEGAL SUPPORT STAFF NEWSLETTER. **3001**

0229-5407 *See* ADVOCATE (TORONTO. 1976). **4383**

0229-5415 *See* SPARTACIST CANADA. **4547**

0229-5520 *See* EYE OPENER (YORKTON). **5784**

0229-5628 *See* C-CORE PUBLICATION. **1967**

0229-5636 *See* LIGHT (TORONTO. 1978). **5043**

0229-5644 *See* AHMADIYYA GAZETTE. **5041**

0229-5776 *See* SI QUE. **3436**

0229-5806 *See* HANDBOOK - CANADIAN BADMINTON ASSOCIATION. **4898**

0229-5814 *See* BULLETIN MATCH. **5552**

0229-5903 *See* GOOD HEALTH (DON MILLS). **1297**

0229-5954 *See* UBC LIBRARY BULLETIN. **3254**

0229-6012 *See* WEST ENDER. **5797**

0229-6047 *See* OOMPHALOSKEPSIS. **2542**

0229-6071 *See* SCHOMBERG-NOBLETON NEWS. **5794**

0229-6098 *See* MINERAL WOOL INCLUDING FIBROUS GLASS INSULATION. **621**

0229-611X *See* WHO'S WHO DIRECTORY OF SPORTS, RECREATION AND PHYSICAL EDUCATION. **4929**

0229-6128 *See* MOTOR MINIATURES. **5420**

0229-6152 *See* KALENDAR KSL (1980). **2695**

0229-6268 *See* WESTERN TRUCK NEWS. **5399**

0229-6330 *See* STUDIA BIBLIOLOGICA. **425**

0229-6470 *See* HEBDO POLICE. **3165**

0229-6497 *See* TRAFIC ROUTIER (MONTREAL. 1981). **5394**

0229-6519 *See* STRATHCLAIR & DISTRICT REVIEW. **5795**

0229-6535 *See* SPEAQ-OUT. **3323**

0229-6543 *See* GLOBAL REPORT (VANCOUVER). **869**

0229-6551 *See* CANADIAN ENTREPRENEUR MAGAZINE. **826**

0229-6594 *See* THAMES VALLEY TIMES. **5796**

0229-6616 *See* ANNUAIRE DES LOISIRS SCIENTIFIQUES. **5083**

0229-6632 *See* PRAIRIE WEED. **525**

0229-6640 *See* SORT IT OUT. **4153**

0229-6659 *See* HUGH LE CAINE PROJECT NEWSLETTER, THE. **4121**

0229-6667 *See* HEADLAMP (ARMDALE). **5416**

0229-6705 *See* GLENGARRY HISTORICAL SOCIETY. **2734**

0229-6713 *See* WEST CARLETON BANNER. **5797**

0229-673X *See* DAN-QUYEN. **2650**

0229-6756 *See* UB NEWS. **223**

0229-6799 *See* GUELPH EXAMINER, THE. **5785**

0229-6802 *See* BEACON (PARRY SOUND). **5780**

0229-6829 *See* QUESTIONS DE CULTURE. **5214**

0229-6861 *See* SURREY TIMES. **5795**

0229-690X *See* NOW AND THEN (DOWNSVIEW). **3020**

0229-6942 *See* WORLD POLICY. **4538**

0229-6993 *See* PASTIMES (ARMDALE). **252**

0229-7000 *See* OCCASIONAL PAPERS - DEPARTMENT OF POLITICAL SCIENCE. CARLETON UNIVERSITY. **4485**

0229-7043 *See* ECRITOIRE (MONTREAL). **3383**

0229-7094 *See* FIFTH COLUMN. **298**

0229-7108 *See* ANNUAL REPORT / SUPERINTENDENT OF INSURANCE. **2873**

0229-7175 *See* HIS DOMINION (REGINA). **4963**

0229-7183 *See* WORKING FOR WILDLIFE. **2210**

0229-7191 *See* OFA FOOD BASKET. **180**

0229-7205 *See* SAAMIS SEEKER. **2471**

0229-7221 *See* LIBRAIRIE ILLUSTREE, LA. **324**

0229-7248 *See* THORNHILL MONTH. **2547**

0229-7256 *See* NEWSLETTER - CANADIAN RESEARCH INSTITUTE FOR THE ADVANCEMENT OF WOMEN. **5562**

0229-7302 *See* MONCTON CITY DIRECTORY (1992). **2569**

0229-7337 *See* VERNON'S CITY OF KITCHENER-WATERLOO (ONTARIO) DIRECTORY. **2578**

0229-7345 *See* NURSING PROGRAMS AND ENTRANCE REQUIREMENTS AT CANADIAN UNIVERSITIES. **3865**

0229-737X *See* SUGAR WORLD. **2359**

0229-7396 *See* RACQUETBALL CANADA (1981). **4914**

0229-740X *See* RAPPORT (TORONTO. 1981). **1515**

0229-7450 *See* ELITE SPORTIVE QUEBECOISE, L'. **4894**

0229-7477 *See* M.A.A.E. JOURNAL. **357**

0229-7493 *See* IOTA (LASALLE). **1831**

0229-7507 *See* MIM (SAINT-AUGUSTIN-DE-DESMAURES, QUEBEC). **4665**

0229-7655 *See* SPHQ NOUVELLES. **2762**

0229-768X *See* HOODOOS HIGHLANDER, THE. **5786**

0229-7698 See SAGAMIE. 4854
0229-7701 See PETROLIA-ENNISKILLEN GAZETTE, THE. 5792
0229-7728 See NEWS SPREADER, THE. 112
0229-7744 See OSHAWA THIS WEEKEND. 5792
0229-7752 See NEWS (ROBLIN). 5790
0229-7779 See CCMS BUSINESS PAGES. 863
0229-7795 See TINIG. 2509
0229-7817 See JOURNAL WEST (DUNDAS). 5787
0229-7833 See MESSENGER (WASAGA BEACH). 4481
0229-7876 See PRODUCTEUR DE PORC QUEBECOIS. 219
0229-7892 See O ELLEN AGGELIAPHOROS. 5791
0229-7906 See DESPORTO (TORONTO, ONT.). 4892
0229-7930 See SPIRIT CANADA. 4154
0229-7949 See SMOKY LAKE SIGNAL. 5794
0229-7957 See TWO MOUNTAINS JOURNAL. 5796
0229-7965 See PERFORMANCE (TORONTO). 387
0229-799X See ANTIGONISH SPECTATOR, THE. 5780
0229-8023 See ODYSSEE (MONTREAL). 5300
0229-8031 See CANADIAN TAX DIGEST (ANNUAL EDITION). 4716
0229-8066 See MASTER TAPE LIST OF EDUCATIONAL TEXTS FOR THE VISUALLY AND PHYSICALLY HANDICAPPED 1882
0229-8090 See GRAINEWS. 173
0229-8104 See OPSEU NEWS. 1700
0229-8139 See RAPPORT ANNUEL / COMMISSION MUNICIPALE DU QUEBEC. 4678
0229-821X See CANADIAN TRAVEL SURVEY. DOMESTIC TRAVEL. 5466
0229-8244 See NOUVELLES DE LA DDIPE, LES. 1901
0229-8422 See TOY REPORT. 2585
0229-8538 See RAPPORT ANNUEL / INSTITUT NATIONAL DE PRODUCTIVITE. 4678
0229-8546 See ALBERTA'S RESERVES OF GAS. 4249
0229-8627 See SELECTED PAPERS FROM THE TRANSPORTATION SEMINAR SERIES. 5392
0229-8643 See RAPPORT ANNUEL ... / REGIE DES ENTREPRISES DE CONSTRUCTION DU QUEBEC. 625
0229-8651 See RSSI. RECHERCHES SEMIOTIQUES. SEMIOTIC INQUIRY. 3318
0229-866X See BULLETIN DE L'AGE D'OR, LE. 5178
0229-8694 See CP RAIL SYSTEM NEWS. 5430
0229-8759 See NEWSLETTER - MONTREAL JOINT HOSPITAL INSTITUTE. 5298
0229-8937 See AU-COURANT (HYDRO-QUEBEC. BIBLIOTHEQUE). 408
0229-8961 See CANADIAN ART SALES INDEX ..., THE. 346
0229-9062 See LISTE ANNOTEE D'ARBITRES DE GRIEFS. 1688
0229-9089 See KEY PERSONNEL DIRECTORY (LAW SOCIETY OF ALBERTA). 2992
0229-9259 See RAPPORT ANNUEL - CONSEIL DE LA LANGUE FRANCAISE. 3314
0229-9283 See PERMIS ACCORDES AUX COMPAGNIES ETRANGERES. 4740
0229-9429 See ACTUALITE MEDICALE, L'. 3912
0229-9437 See RELEASE (CALGARY). 329
0229-9461 See BULLETIN DES C.G.A. 740
0229-9534 See REPERTOIRE DES LABORATOIRES D'ESSAIS ET D'ANALYSES DU QUEBEC 1993
0229-9631 See TFP NEWSLETTER. 5003
0229-964X See TFP INFORME. 5003
0229-9704 See OCCASIONAL STUDENT PAPER (UNIVERSITY OF BRITISH COLUMBIA. CENTRE FOR TRANSPORTATION STUDIES). 5388
0229-9712 See POSITIVE (LONDON, ONT.). 3241
0229-9720 See PUBLICITAIRE (MONTREAL). 765
0229-978X See "QUOTE UNQUOTE". 1094

0229-9798 See UW NOTES. 1853
0229-981X See JOURNAL DU SAMEDI, LE. 5787
0229-9844 See RACKETT. 4148
0229-9852 See COOPERATIVE GAMES NEWSLETTER. 4859
0229-9887 See HEBDO JOURNAL. 5786
0229-9909 See BOITE A OUTILS. 1800
0230-0508 See PSZICHOLOGIA: AZ MTA PSZICHOLOGIAI INTEZETENEK FOLYOIRATA. 4614
0230-0648 See MALAKOLOGIAI TAJEKOZTATO. 5590
0230-1814 See ALLATTENYESZTES ES TARKARMANYOZAS. 205
0230-1954 See SAVARIA. 2708
0230-2241 See SZOLOTERMEZTESES BORASZAT. 2371
0230-2810 See MEZOGAZDASAGI GEPUZEMELTETES. 108
0230-2896 See MUSZAKI INFORMACIO. KORSZERU MUNKAFELTETELEK, MUNKAVEDELEM. 2865
0230-3035 See WORLD WEIGHTLIFTING. 2602
0230-418X See YEARBOOK OF INVESTMENT STATISTICS. 735
0230-4414 See IDEGENFORGALMI EVKONYV / OSSZEALLITOTTA A KSH KERESKEDELMI ES KOZLEKEDESI STATISZTIKAI FOOSZTALY, IDEGENFORGALMI OSZTALY. 5480
0230-4805 See TELEPULESFEJLESZTES. 2836
0230-5348 See ANYAGMOZGATASI ES CSOMAGOLASI SZAKIRODALMI TAJEKOZTATO. 4217
0230-5755 See HUNGARY, STATISTICAL DATA / CENTRAL STATISTICAL OFFICE OF HUNGARY. 5328
0230-6514 See OMIKK HIRADO. 3239
0230-7065 See GEOLOGIAI ES GEOFIZIKAI SZAKIROLDALMI TAJEKOZTATO. 1377
0230-788X See MAGYAR EREMGYUJTOK EGYESULETE CSONGRAD MEGYEI SZERVEZETENEK KIADVANYAI, A. 2781
0230-9017 See MISCELLANEA ZOOLOGICA HUNGARICA. 5591
0231-035X See FOLIA MUSEI HISTORICO-NATURALIS BAKONYIENSIS. 4165
0231-0643 See AUTOMATIZALASI, SZAMTASTECHNIKAI ES MERESTECHNIKAI SZAKIRODALMI TAJEKOZTATO. 1218
0231-0651 See BANYASZATI SZAKIRODALMI TAJEKOZTATO. 2135
0231-066X See ELEKTRONIKAI ES HRADASTECHNIKAI SZAKIRODALMI TAJEKOZTATO. 2052
0231-0678 See ENERGIAIPARI ES ENERGIAGAZDALKODASI SZAKIRODALMI TAJEKOZTATO. 1938
0231-0686 See GEPESZETI SZAKIRODALMI TAJEKOZTATO. 2115
0231-0694 See GEPGYARTASTECHNOLOGIAI ES SZERSZAMGEPIPARI SZAKIRODALMI TAJEKOZTATO. 2115
0231-0708 See KOHASZATI ES ONTESZETI SZAKIRODALMI TAJEKOZTATO. 4007
0231-0716 See KORNYEZETVEDELMI SZAKIRODALMI TAJEKOZTATO. 2218
0231-0724 See KOZUTI KOZLEKEDESI SZAKIRODALMI TAJEKOZTATO. 5441
0231-0732 See MELYEPITESI ES VIZEPITESI SZAKIRODALMI TAJEKOZTATO. 2027
0231-0740 See PAPRIPARI ES NYOMDAIPARI SZAKIRODALMI TAJEKOZTATO. 4237
0231-0759 See VALLALATSZERVEZESI ES IPARGAZDASAGI SZAKIRODALMI TAJEKOZTATO. 889
0231-0767 See VASUTI KOZLEKEDESI SZAKIRODALMI TAJEKOZTATO. 5437
0231-0775 See VEGYIPARI SZAKIRODALMI TAJEKOZTATO MUANYAG- ES GUMIIPARI KULONLENYOMATA. 995
0231-0783 See ELEKTROTECHNIKAI SZAKIRODALMI TAJEKOZTATO. 2052
0231-1941 See HAJOZASI SZAKIRODALMI TAJEKOZTATO. 5450

0231-195X See IPARI FORMATERVEZESI SZAKIRODALMI TAJEKOZTATO. 2901
0231-2522 See TARSADALOMKUTATAS. 5224
0231-2662 See FINOMMECHANIKA-MIKROTECHNIKA. 3479
0231-3146 See ACTA CHIMICA HUNGARICA. 959
0231-3928 See REPULESI SZAKIRODALMI TAJEKOZTATO. 33
0231-424X See ACTA PHYSIOLOGICA HUNGARICA. 577
0231-441X See ACTA PAEDIATRICA HUNGARICA. 3899
0231-4428 See ACTA PHYSICA HUNGARICA. 4395
0231-4592 See MAGYAR NEMZETI BIBLIOGRAFIA: IDOSZAKI KIADVANYOK BIBLIOGRAFIAJA. 419
0231-4614 See ACTA CHIRURGICA HUNGARICA. 3957
0231-4622 See ACTA MICROBIOLOGICA HUNGARICA. 558
0231-5025 See SBORNIK PRACI FILOZOFICKE FAKULTY BRNENSKE UNIVERZITY. RADA UMENOVEDNA. 364
0231-5297 See TECHNICKE PRIUCKY (STATNI VYZKUMNY USTAV PRO STAVBU STROJU). 2130
0231-5300 See SBORNIK CESKE GEOGRAFICKE SPOLECNOSTI. 2576
0231-5335 See ACTA DENDROBIOLOGICA. 497
0231-5386 See INFORMACNI PRIRUCKA / CESKOSLOVENSKA AKADEMIE VED. 5232
0231-5394 See KNIZNICE ODBORNYCH A VEDECKYCH SPISU VYSOKEHO UCENI TECHNICKEHO V BRNE. SVAZEK A. 5123
0231-5513 See POPULACNI ZPRAVY. 4556
0231-567X See SBORNIK UVTI. ZAHRADNICTVI. 2431
0231-5777 See SCRIPTA FACULTATIS SCIENTIARUM NATURALIUM UNIVERSITATIS PURKYNIANAE BRUNENSIS. BIOLOGIA. 472
0231-5785 See ACTA FACULTATIS FORESTALIS, ZVOLEN. 2373
0231-5823 See ARCHEOLOGIA HISTORICA. 258
0231-5882 See GENERAL PHYSIOLOGY AND BIOPHYSICS. 580
0231-5890 See ARS VITRARIA. 2586
0231-5904 See LITERARNI ARCHIV. 3406
0231-6005 See ACTA HISTORIAE RERUM NATURALIUM NECNON TECHNICARUM. SPECIAL ISSUE. 5080
0231-6056 See STALETA PRAHA. 309
0231-6900 See VEDECKE PRACE OVOCNARSKE. 5168
0231-715X See ACTA FACULTATIS RERUM NATURALIUM UNIVERSITATIS COMENIANAE. 2553
0231-7362 See OPUS MUSICUM. 4144
0231-7567 See SBORNIK PRACI FILOSOFICKE FAKULTY BRNENSKE UNIVERSITY. A, RADY JAZYKOVEDNE. 3319
0231-7710 See SBORNIK PRACI FILOSOFICKE FAKULTY BRNENSKE UNIVERSITY. C, RADY HISTORICKA. 2629
0231-7753 See SBORNIK PEDAGOGICKE FAKULTY UNIVERZITY KARLOVY. BIOLOGIE. 472
0231-7834 See ZBORNIK PRAC USTAVU EXPERIMENTALNEJ FARMAKOLOGIE SAV. 4333
0231-7915 See SBORNIK PRACI FILOZOFICKE FAKULTY BRNENSKE UNIVERZITY. RADA ARCHEOLOGICKO-KLASICKA. 282
0231-889X See ACTA PHYSICA UNIVERSITATIS COMENIANAE. 4395
0231-9004 See CONTRIBUTIONS OF THE GEOPHYSICAL INSTITUTE OF THE SLOVAK AKADEMY OF SCIENCES. SERIES OF METEOROLOGY. 1424
0231-908X See ARS POPULI. 337
0231-9470 See METODIKY PRO ZAVADENI VYSLEDKU VYZKUMU DO ZEMEDELSKE PRAXE. 108
0231-956X See VYZKUMY V CECHACH. SUPPLEMENTUM. 2715

0231-973X See SLOVENSKA NARODNA BIBLIOGRAFIA. SERIA B-J, PERIODIKA, MAPY, DIZERTACNE PRACE, SPECIALNE TLACE, FIREMNA LITERATURA. GRAFIKA, HUDOBNINY, OFICIALNE DOKUMENTY, AUDIOVIZUALNE DOKUMENTY. 424

0231-9942 See VESTNIK FEDERALNIHO URADU PRO VYNALEZY. CAST A, VYNALEZY. 1309

0231-9969 See TRANSACTIONS OF THE ... PRAGUE CONFERENCE ON INFORMATION THEORY, STATISTICAL DECISION FUNCTIONS, RANDOM PROCESSES. 3539

0231-9985 See VESTNIK FEDERALNIHO URADU PRO VYNALEZY. CAST B, OCHRANNE ZNAMKY, PRUMYSLOVE UZORY. 1309

0232-0487 See ACTA MUSEI REGINAEHRADECENSIS. SERIE B, SCIENTIAE SOCIALES. 5189

0232-0878 See ACTA COMENIANA. 1722

0232-1300 See CRYSTAL RESEARCH AND TECHNOLOGY (1979). 1031

0232-1513 See EXPERIMENTAL PATHOLOGY (1981). 3894

0232-2064 See ZEITSCHRIFT FUER ANALYSIS UND IHRE ANWENDUNGEN. 3541

0232-3915 See METROLOGISCHE ABHANDLUNGEN. 4031

0232-4393 See ZENTRALBLATT FUER MIKROBIOLOGIE. 571

0232-4814 See DEUTSCHES SPORTECHO AUSGABE B. 4892

0232-4849 See GESETZBLATT DER DEUTSCHEN DEMOKRATISCHEN REPUBLIC. SONDERDRUCK. 2974

0232-4865 See BIBLIOGRAPHIE ZUR ARCHAO-ZOOLOGIE UND GESCHICHTE DER HAUSTIERE. 286

0232-5535 See ENTOMOLOGISCHE NACHRICHTEN UND BERICHTE. 5582

0232-5683 See TAGUNGSBAND - KAMMER DER TECHNIK SUHL. 5161

0232-704X See ANNALS OF GLOBAL ANALYSIS AND GEOMETRY. 3494

0232-7090 See CHARITE-ANNALEN. 3563

0232-7384 See EXPERIMENTAL AND CLINICAL ENDOCRINOLOGY. 3730

0232-766X See BIOMEDICA BIOCHIMICA ACTA. 447

0232-9298 See SYSTEMS ANALYSIS, MODELLING, SIMULATION. 3537

0232-9387 See ZEITGENOSSISCHES MUSIKSCHAFFEN IN DER DEUTSCHEN DEMOKRATISCHEN REPUBLIK. 4160

0233-0202 See PSYCHOLOGIE FUER DIE PRAXIS : ORGAN DER GESELLSCHAFT FUER PSYCHOLOGIE DER DEUTSCHEN DEMOKRATISCHEN REPUBLIK. 4612

0233-0652 See ARBEITEN ZUR MECHANISIERUNG DER PFLANZEN- UND TIERPRODUKTION. 2327

0233-111X See JOURNAL OF BASIC MICROBIOLOGY. 564

0233-1594 See DDR-LITERATUR ... IM GESPRACH. 3380

0233-1608 See ZEITSCRHIFT FUR KLINISCHE MEDIZIN (BERLIN, DDR). 3653

0233-1888 See STATISTICS (BERLIN, DDR). 3543

0233-2337 See KULTURBAUTEN. 302

0233-237X See PHARMACOKINETICS. 4321

0233-2655 See AGROSELEKT. REIHE 1, LANDTECHNIK. 56

0233-2736 See START BERLIN, DDR. 1986. 4924

0233-2752 See AGROSELEKT. REIHE 3, TIERPRODUKTION. 204

0233-2809 See AGROSELEKT. REIHE 4, VETERINARMEDIZIN. 5502

0233-2957 See UNTERSUCHUNGEN ZUR LOGIK UND ZUR METHODOLOGIE : BEITRAEGE DES KOOPERATIONSRATES LOGIK AN DER KARL-MARX-UNIVERSITAT / HERAUSGEGEBEN IM AUFTRAG DES REKTORS DER KARL-MARX-UNIVERSITAT LEIPZIG VOM KOOPERATIONSRAT LOGIK AN DER KARL-MARX-UNIVERSITAT LEIPZIG. 4364

0233-4755 See BIOLOGICHESKIE MEMBRANY. 446

0233-528X See AVIAKOSMICHESKAIA I EKOLOGICHESKAIA MEDITSINA. 3554

0233-6723 See ITOGI NAUKI I TEKHNIKI. SERIIA SOVREMENNYE PROBLEMY MATEMATIKI FUNDAMENTALNYE NAPRAVLENIIA. 3510

0233-6944 See SBORNIK TRUDOV (VSESOIUZNYI NAUCHNO-ISSLEDOVATELSKII INSTITUT PRIKLADNYKH AVTOMATIZIROVANNYKH SISTEM (SOVIET UNION). 1221

0233-7568 See MATEMATICHESKAIA FIZIKA I NELINEINAIA MEKHANIKA. 4412

0233-7584 See MORSKOI GIDROFIZICHESKII ZHURNAL. 1452

0233-7657 See BIOPOLIMERY I KLETKA. 447

0233-7665 See KINEMATIKA I FIZIKA NEBESNYH TEL. 4411

0233-7754 See RYBOLOV. 2312

0233-7770 See KUKURUZA I SORGO. 177

0234-0577 See MOSKOVSKII ZHURNAL. 304

0234-0852 See ALGEBRA I ANALIZ. 3491

0234-0860 See DISKRETNAIA MATEMATIKA. 1183

0234-0879 See MATEMATICHESKOE MODELIROVANIE. 3517

0234-1360 See BELARUSKAIA MOVA I LITERATURA U SHKOLE. 3268

0234-1670 See EKHO PLANETY. 4520

0234-1727 See ROSSIIA MOLODAIA. 130

0234-2758 See BIOTEHNOLOGIA (MOSKVA). 3690

0234-4483 See IONNYE RASPLAVY I TVERDYE ELEKTROLITY. 4406

0234-4823 See VOPROSY ALGEBRY / GOMELSKIFI GOSUDARSTVENNYI UNIVERSITET. 3541

0234-6540 See OBZORNAIA INFORMATSIIA. RESTAVRATSIIA PAMIATNIKOV ISTORII I KULTURY / MINISTERSTVO KULTURY SSSR, GOSUDARSTVENNAIA ORDENA LENINA BIBLIOTEKA SSSR IMENI V.I. LENINA. 327

0234-7059 See ENVIRONMENTAL MANAGEMENT ABSTRACTS. 2193

0234-8004 See SPORT ZA RUBEZHOM. 4921

0234-8098 See POTREBITELSKAIA KOOPERATSIIA : PK. 1298

0234-8179 See RADUGA. 2521

0234-9140 See MONITORING FONOVOGO ZAGRIAZNENIIA PRIRODNYKH SRED / GOSUDARSTVENNYI KOMITET SSSR PO GIDROMETEOROLOGII I KONTROLIU PRIRODNOI SREDY, AKADEMIIA NAUK SSSR, LABORATORIIA MONITORINGA PRIRODNOI SREDY I KLIMATA. 1431

0234-968X See SIGNALNAYA INFORMATSIYA KHIMIYA VYSOKIKH ENERGII. 992

0234-9698 See SIGNALNAYA INFORMATSIYA SORBENTY POVERKHNOSTNO-AKTIVNYE VESHCHESTVA. 992

0234-9701 See SIGNALNAYA INFORMATSIYA OCHISTKA I UTILIZATSIYA OTKHODOV KHIMICHESKIK PROIZVODSTV. 992

0234-971X See SIGNALNAYA INFORMATSIYA NAPOLNENNYE I ARMIROVANNYE PLASTIKI. 992

0234-9736 See SIGNALNAYA INFORMATSIYA KATALIZ I KATALIZATORY. 1058

0234-9752 See SIGNALNAYA INFORMATSIYA NEIROPEPTIDY. 587

0235-0041 See AKHBOROTI AKADEMIIAI FANHOI RSS TOJIKISTON. SERIIAI SHARQSHINOSI TARIKH FILOLOGIIA. 3262

0235-0114 See METALLOORGANICHESKAIA KHIMIIA / AKADEMIIA NAUK SSSR. 1044

0235-0122 See VYSOKOCHISTYE VESHCHESTVA / AKADEMIIA NAUK SSSR. 995

0235-1188 See FILOSOFSKIE NAUKI. 4347

0235-2265 See ITOGI NAUKI I TEKHNIKI. SERIIA SVIAZ / GOSUDARSTVENNYI KOMITET SSSR PO NAUKE I TEKHNIKE, AKADEMIIA NAUK SSSR, VSESOIUZNYI INSTITUT NAUCHNOI I TEKHNICHESKOI INFORMATSII, 10 SVIAZ. 1158

0235-2273 See ITOGI NAUKI I TEKHNIKI. SERIIA TEKHNOLOGIIA SILIKATNYKH I TUGOPLAVKIKH NEMETALLICHESKIKH MATERIALOV. 1440

0235-229X See ITOGI NAUKI I TEKHNIKI. SERIIA FIZICHESKIE OSNOVY LAZERNOI I PUCHKOVOI TEKHNOLOGII. 2067

0235-2443 See APK-EKONOMIKA, UPRAVLENIE / GOSUDARSTVENNYI AGROPROMYSHLENNYI KOMITET SSSR. 62

0235-2478 See ZOOTEKHNIIA. 225

0235-2486 See PISHCHEVAIA PROMYSHLENNOST. 2353

0235-2494 See EKONOMIKA SELSKOKHOZIAISTVENNYKH I PERERABATYVAIUSHCHIKH PREOPRIIATII. 81

0235-2508 See KHLEBOPRODUKTY : EZHEMESIACHNYI TEORETICHESKII I NAUCHNO-PRAKTICHESKII ZHURNAL MINISTERSTVA KHLEBOPRODUKTOV SSSR I GOSUDARSTVENNOGO AGROPROMYSHLENNOGO KOMITETA SSSR. 2347

0235-2516 See HIMIZACI A SELSKOGO HOZAJSTVA. 92

0235-2524 See MELIORATSIIA I VODNOE KHOZIAISTVO (MOSCOW, R.S.F.S.R.). 2093

0235-2532 See ZERNOVYE KULTURY. 149

0235-2540 See KORMOVYE KULTURY. 202

0235-2559 See TEKHNICHESKIE KULTURY. 189

0235-2567 See KHLOPOK. 177

0235-2583 See SAKHARNAIA SVEKLA--PROIZVODSTVO I PERERABOTKA. 2356

0235-2591 See SADOVODSTVO I VINOGRADARSTVO. 2430

0235-2605 See KOMBIKORMOVAIA PROMYSHLENNOST. 202

0235-2958 See AGROPROMYSHLENNYI KOMPLEKS KAZAKHSTANA. 2326

0235-2990 See ANTIBIOTIKI I HIMIOTERAPIA. 4291

0235-3490 See ARKHEOLOHIIA. 260

0235-4233 See PROBLEMY METALLURGICESKOGO PROIZVODSTVA. 4016

0235-4276 See SLOVO. 3437

0235-5043 See KLUB (MOSCOW, R.S.F.S.R. : 1989). 5207

0235-6007 See ITOGI NAUKI I TEKHNIKI. SERIIA NARKOLOGIIA. 1345

0235-6740 See ORIENTAL STUDIES IN THE USSR. 2661

0235-6813 See FAR EAST, STUDIES BY SOVIET SCHOLARS SERIES, THE. 2503

0235-7089 See RODINA. 3352

0235-7097 See IZVESTIIA TSK TPSS. 4658

0235-7119 See PROBLEMY MASHINOSTROENIIA I NADEZHNOSTI MASHIN / AKADEMIIA NAUK SSSR. 2125

0235-716X See LITUANISTICA / LIETUVOS MOKSLU AKADEMIJA. 2697

0235-7186 See FILOSOFIJA, SOCIOLOGIJA / LIETUVOS MOKSLU AKADEMIJA. 4346

0235-7208 See ENERGETIKA. 2053

0235-7216 See CHEMIJA / LIETUVOS MOKSLU SKADEMIJA. 5093

0235-7224 See EKOLOGIJA / LIETUVOS MOKSLU AKADEMIJA / EKOLOGIIA / LITOVSKAIA AKADEMIIA NAUK / ECOLOGY / THE LITHUANIAN ACADEMY OF SCIENCES. 2215

0235-7232 See LIETUVOS MOKSLU AKADEMIJA. EKSPERIMENTINE BIOLOGIJA. 463

0235-7259 See ARKHITEKTURA I STROITELSTVO ROSSII : AS. 291

0235-764X See BUSINESS CONTACT. 826

0235-8573 See TRAKTORY I SELSKOKHOZIAISTVENNYE MASHINY. 161

0235-8964 See SUPERCONDUCTIVITY: PHYSICS, CHEMISTRY, TECHNIQUE. 4423

0236-0268 See PUL'S. 1068

0236-0918 See NARODNYI DEPUTAT. 4668

0236-0942 See DIALOG (MOSCOW, R.S.F.S.R.). 4541

0236-1485 See KOLUMNA. 3402

0236-2767 See NAUKA I MY. 5131

ISSN Index

0236-2791 See GRUDNAIA I SERDECHNO-SOSUDISTAIA KHIRURGIIA. 3705

0236-5278 See ACTA GEOLOGICA HUNGARICA. 1364

0236-5286 See ACTA MEDICA HUNGARICA. 3544

0236-5294 See ACTA MATHEMATICA HUNGARICA. 3490

0236-5383 See ACTA BIOLOGICA HUNGARICA. 439

0236-5391 See ACTA MORPHOLOGICA HUNGARICA. 3545

0236-5731 See JOURNAL OF RADIOANALYTICAL AND NUCLEAR CHEMISTRY. 1017

0236-5731 See JOURNAL OF RADIOANALYTICAL AND NUCLEAR CHEMISTRY. 1017

0236-5731 See JOURNAL OF RADIOANALYTICAL AND NUCLEAR CHEMISTRY. LETTERS. 1017

0236-5758 See ACTA GEODAETICA, GEOPHYSICA ET MONTANISTICA HUNGARICA. 1402

0236-6290 See ACTA VETERINARIA HUNGARICA (BUDAPEST. 1983). 5501

0236-6495 See ACTA BOTANICA HUNGARICA. 496

0236-6568 See HUNGARIAN STUDIES : HS. 2692

0236-7130 See ACTA ZOOLOGICA HUNGARICA. 5573

0236-929X See HISTORIA INFANTIAE. 1804

0237-0301 See ETUDES HISTORIQUES HONGROISES. 2687

0237-0743 See FOLIA BIOTECHNOLOGICA. 3692

0237-1545 See UNGARISCHE WIRTSCHAFTSHEFTE. 937

0237-1995 See MARKETING BUDAPEST. 930

0237-2169 See SZILIKATIPARI ES SZILIKATTUDOMANYI KONFERENCIA. 2594

0237-2525 See SAKKELET. 4865

0237-2576 See KOZUTI KOZLEKEDESI SZAKIRODALMI TAJEKOZTATO. UTUGYI SZAKKIADAS. 5441

0237-3831 See BUSINESS PARTNER HUNGARY. 826

0237-4323 See FALU, A. 2822

0237-5265 See SZABVANY ES VILAG. 4032

0237-5478 See GESCHAEFTSPARTNER UNGARN. 838

0237-6261 See ACTA BIOCHIMICA ET BIOPHYSICA HUNGARICA. 479

0237-8930 See BULLETIN OF THE UNIVERSITY OF AGRICULTURAL SCIENCES, GODOLLO. 70

0237-9740 See AV KOMMUNIKACIO. 1104

0238-0161 See ACTA AGRONOMICA HUNGARICA. 43

0238-0412 See MAGYAR OLIMPIAI AKADEMIA EVKONYVE, A. 4904

0238-1249 See ACTA PHYTOPATHOLOGICA ET ENTOMOLOGICA HUNGARICA. 497

0238-1486 See EUROPEAN REVIEW OF NATIVE AMERICAN STUDIES. 2261

0238-180X See BUSINESS GUIDE HUNGARY. 648

0238-2512 See HAJDU-BIHAR MEGYEI KONYVTARI TEKA. 3213

0238-602X See HUNGARIAN ECONOMIC REVIEW : HER. 839

0238-6178 See ABSTRACT REVIEW IN SCIENCE EXTENSION. 5079

0238-6852 See KERTESZETI ES ELELMISZERIPARI EGYETEM KOEZLEMENYEI / PUBLICATIONES UNIVERSITATIS HORTICULTURAE INDUSTRIAEQUE ALIMENTARIAE, A. 2422

0238-7891 See MEZOGAZDASAGI ELELMISZERIPARI STATISZTIKAI ZSEBKONYU / LOZPONTI STATISZTIKAI HIVATAL. 5333

0238-888X See KAPU. 2695

0238-9401 See HUNGARIAN MUSIC QUARTERLY. 4121

0238-9746 See SWIAT CISZY. 4394

0238-9932 See HUNGARIAN OBSERVER, THE. 2488

0239-0639 See MAI NAP. 5802

0239-1260 See GEORGICON FOR AGRICULTURE. 90

0239-1929 See INVEST IN HUNGARY. 902

0239-202X See ARTIUM QUAESTIONES / UNIWERSYTET IM. ADAMA MICKIEWICZA W POZNANIU. 342

0239-2089 See PROBLEMY PROJEKTOWE. 4016

0239-3611 See MAGAZYN HUTNICZY. 4007

0239-4243 See ANNALES UNIVERSITATIS MARIAE CURIE-SKODOWSKA. SECTIO EE, ZOOTECHNICA. 5575

0239-4405 See SPORT WYCZYNOWY. 4921

0239-4421 See BIBLIOGRAFIA WYDAWNICTW CIAGYCH / BIBLIOGRAPHY OF POLISH SERIALS / BIBLIOTEKA NARODOWA, INSTYTUT BIBLIOGRAFICZNY. 409

0239-5061 See ZESZYTY NAUKOWE WYZSZEJ SZKOY PEDAGOGICZNEJ W BYDGOSZCZY. STUDIA TECHNICZNE. 476

0239-5096 See STAN HODOWLI I WYNIKI OCENY SWIN W ROKU. 5522

0239-5320 See ZESZYTY NAUKOWE AKADEMII GORNICZO-HUTNICZEJ IM. STANISAWA STASZICA. MECHANIKA. 4024

0239-622X See BIBLIOGRAFIA GOSPODARKI I INZYNIERII WODNEJ. 5531

0239-6246 See BIBLIOGRAFIA HYDROLOGII I OCEANOLOGII. 1412

0239-6270 See BIBLIOGRAFIA METEOROLOGII: POLSKA. 1421

0239-6297 See MATERIALY BADAWCZE - INSTYTUT METEOROLOGII I GOSPODARKI WODNEJ. SERIA, HYDROLOGIA I OCEANOLOGIA. 1416

0239-6629 See KWARTA. 3403

0239-6653 See SZKIEKO I OKO. 1070

0239-6661 See ACTA UNIVERSITATIS WRATISLAVIENSIS. 2841

0239-6807 See TYGODNIK CIECHANOWSKI. 2524

0239-684X See TYGODNIK SIEDLECKI. 2524

0239-6874 See OKOLICE. 3420

0239-7048 See BIBLIOGRAFIA PEDAGOGIKI SZKOY WYZSZEJ ZA ROK 1811

0239-7269 See BULLETIN OF THE POLISH ACADEMY OF SCIENCES. MATHEMATICS. 3499

0239-7277 See BULLETIN OF THE POLISH ACADEMY OF SCIENCES. EARTH SCIENCES. 1352

0239-7285 See BULLETIN OF THE POLISH ACADEMY OF SCIENCES. CHEMISTRY. 963

0239-7471 See PRZEGLAD KATOLICKI. 5034

0239-751X See BULLETIN OF THE POLISH ACADEMY OF SCIENCES. BIOLOGY. 450

0239-7528 See BULLETIN OF THE POLISH ACADEMY OF SCIENCES. TECHNICAL SCIENCES. 5091

0239-7978 See PRACE MATEMATYCZNE. 3527

0239-8028 See NEOTERM : JOURNAL OF THE INTERNATIONAL ORGANIZATION FOR UNIFICATION OF TERMINOLOGICAL NEOLOGISMS, AND WORLD BANK OF INTERNATIONAL TERMS. 3305

0239-832X See STUDIA DO DZIEJOW DAWNEGO UZBROJENIA I UNIFORMU WOJSKOWEGO. 2630

0239-8435 See SAT AUDIO VIDEO. 5318

0239-8508 See FOLIA HISTOCHEMICA ET CYTOBIOLOGICA. 536

0239-8796 See REBUS. 4865

0239-8818 See HEMISPHERES / [POLISH ACADEMY OF SCIENCES, INSTITUTE OF HISTORY, CENTER FOR STUDIES ON NON-EUROPEAN COUNTRIES]. 2617

0239-930X See ZESZYTY NAUKOWE AKADEMII ROLNICZEJ IM. H. KOATAJA W KRAKOWIE LESNICTWO. 149

0239-9326 See OGRODNICTWO. 2426

0239-9342 See SESJA NAUKOWA. 134

0239-958X See BIBLIOGRAFIA AGROMETEOROLOGII. 1420

0239-9989 See OPUSCULA MUSEALIA. 4095

0240-2963 See ANNALES DE LA FACULTE DES SCIENCES DE TOULOUSE. 3493

0240-396X See ECHANGE TRAVAIL PARIS. 1664

0240-3994 See ETUDES DROMOISES. 350

0240-4656 See CELEBRER PARIS. 2844

0240-4672 See ANNALES DE HAUTE-PROVENCE. 2674

0240-4729 See REPERTOIRE MENSUEL DU MINISTERE DE L'INTERIEUR. 4680

0240-5555 See UNIVERS DU FRANCAIS SEVRES, L'. 1788

0240-6411 See AVENIR & SANTE. 3852

0240-7914 See JOURNAL FRANCAIS D'ORTHOPTIQUE. 3875

0240-8260 See MEMOIRES DE LA SOCIETE ARCHEOLOGIQUE ET HISTORIQUE DE NANTES ET DE LOIRE-ATLANTIQUE. 274

0240-8392 See DOUBLE PAGE. 4369

0240-8465 See BULLETIN SIGNALETIQUE. 171, CHIMIE GENERALE ET CHIMIE PHYSIQUE / CENTRE NATIONAL DE LA RECHERCHE SCIENTIFIQUE. 1050

0240-8473 See BULLETIN SIGNALETIQUE. 172, CHIMIE ANALYTIQUE / CENTRE NATIONAL DE LA RECHERCHE SCIENTIFIQUE. 1014

0240-849X See BULLETIN SIGNALETIQUE. 120, GEOPHYSIQUE EXTERNE, ASTRONOMIE ET ASTROPHYSIQUE / CENTRE NATIONAL DE LA RECHERCHE SCIENTIFIQUE. 402

0240-866X See NOUVEUX OUVRAGES DE REFERENCE, LISTE ANNUELLE / BIBLIOTHEQUE NATIONALE, DEPARTMENT DES LIVRES IMPRIMES, SALLE DES CATALOGUES ET DES BIBLIOGRAPHIES. 421

0240-8678 See CAHIERS DE CIVILISATION MEDIEVALE. BIBLIOGRAPHIE. 2635

0240-8759 See VIE ET MILIEU (1980). 2222

0240-8783 See REVUE D'HYDROBIOLOGIE TROPICALE. 471

0240-8805 See BULLETIN DES ANGLICISTES MEDIEVISTES. 3270

0240-8813 See SCIENCES DES ALIMENTS. 2356

0240-883X See ALLER SIMPLE. 312

0240-8864 See C.A.R.A. CENTRE AIXOIS DE RECHERCHES ANGLAISES. 3271

0240-8910 See ABSTRACTA IRANICA. 406

0240-8937 See BULLETIN DU MUSEUM NATIONAL D'HISTOIRE NATURELLE. SECTION B : ADANSONIA, BOTANIQUE, PHYTOCHIMIE. 504

0240-9925 See INTER REGIONS. 2825

0241-0109 See JOURNAL INTERNATIONAL DE MEDECINE, LE. 3592

0241-0257 See CAMEROUN SELECTION. 826

0241-0362 See INF TELECOM ET TELEMATIQUE PARIS. 1157

0241-0389 See VIANDES ET PRODUITS CARNES AUBIERE. 2360

0241-2284 See BULLETIN D'INFORMATION SUR L'ALCOOLISME. 1342

0241-2640 See INFOTECTURE. 1275

0241-2799 See CAHIERS PHILOSOPHIQUES. 4343

0241-2977 See BULLETIN DE L'OEUVE DE LA CATHEDRALE DE METZ. 294

0241-5089 See A.H. AUMONERIES DES HOPITAUX. 3543

0241-6646 See VOIE D'AVALLON, LA. 5008

0241-6794 See CAHIERS TECHNIQUES DU BATIMENT. 606

0241-6972 See SOINS. PSYCHIATRIE. 3937

0241-7413 See REVUE DE PAU ET DU BEARN. 363

0242-0627 See CAHIERS JURIDIQUES ET FISCAUX DE L'EXPORTATION. 826

0242-1283 See COMMUTATION & TRANSMISSION. 1152

0242-1623 See REVUE INTERNATIONALE DE LA PROPRIETE INDUSTRIELLE ET ARTISTIQUE : RIPIA. 1308

0242-1968 See BULLETIN SIGNALETIQUE UCD DE JOUY-EN-JOSAS. 5580

0242-2085 See GRAPH-AGRI : ANNUAIRE DE GRAPHIQUES AGRICOLES. 90

0242-2565 See MACHINISME AGRICOLE TROPICAL. 159

0242-2921 *See* BASE DE DONNEES ECONOMIQUES, FINANCIERES ET SOCIALES RESEDA. **65**

0242-2999 *See* INTER CDI ETAMPES. **683**

0242-3960 *See* INTER BLOC. **3966**

0242-4959 *See* QUATRE SAISONS DU JARDINAGE, LES. **2429**

0242-5149 *See* IMPREVUE (MONTPELLIER). **3395**

0242-5629 *See* REVUE DES LOYERS ET DES FERMAGES, DE LA PROPRIETE COMMERCIALE, DES FONDS DE COMMERCE, DE LA CONSTRUCTION ET DE LA COPROPRIETE IMMOBILIERES. **4846**

0242-5769 *See* MONDE INFORMATIQUE, LE. **1195**

0242-5912 *See* BULLETIN FISCAL FRANCIS LEFEBVRE. **4715**

0242-6110 *See* ANNALES DES FALSIFICATIONS, DE L'EXPERTISE CHIMIQUE ET TOXICOLOGIQUE. **3978**

0242-6277 *See* R.G.S. REVUE GENERALE DE SECURITE. **2868**

0242-648X *See* JOURNAL DE READAPTATION MEDICALE. **3882**

0242-6498 *See* ANNALES DE PATHOLOGIE. **3893**

0242-6536 *See* BULLETIN D'INFORMATION DU CENTRE DE DONNEES STELLAIRES. **394**

0242-6595 *See* REVUE DE L'ALIMENTATION ANIMALE. **220**

0242-6757 *See* JOURNAL OFFICIEL DE LA REPUBLIQUE FRANCAISE. DEBATS PARLEMENTAIRES, ASSEMBLEE NATIONALE. QUESTIONS ECRITES ET REPONSES DES MINISTRES. **4659**

0242-6765 *See* JOURNAL OFFICIEL DE LA REPUBLIQUE FRANCAISE. DEBATS PARLIAMENTAIRES, ASSEMBLEE NATIONALE. COMPTE RENDU INTEGRAL. **4659**

0242-6870 *See* HUMANITE PARIS, L'. **2847**

0242-6986 *See* PLANCHE MAGAZINE. **4912**

0242-7818 *See* ECONOMIE PROSPECTIVE INTERNATIONALE. **1634**

0242-830X *See* MONUMENTS HISTORIQUES (1980). **304**

0242-8466 *See* BULLETIN DE LIAISON - GROUPE POLYPHENOLS. **963**

0242-8903 *See* REVUE DE L'AMEUBLEMENT, LA. **2907**

0242-8962 *See* DIALOGUE PARIS. 196?. **5244**

0242-9225 *See* JOURNAL DE MICKEY 1952, LE. **1065**

0242-9454 *See* REVUE D'EDUCATION MEDICALE. **3636**

0242-9616 *See* PSYCHANALYSTES. **3933**

0242-9780 *See* REVUE FRANCAISE DE GESTION INDUSTRIELLE. **885**

0243-0088 *See* JOURNEES DE LA RECHERCHE OVINE ET CAPRINE. **213**

0243-1203 *See* JOURNAL EUROPEEN DE RADIOTHERAPIE. **3942**

0243-1327 *See* CASSUS BELLI. **4889**

0243-1335 *See* CA M'INTERESSE. **2514**

0243-1947 *See* LETTRE DU C.E.P.I.I. / CENTRE D'ETUDES PROSPECTIVES ET D'INFORMATIONS INTERNATIONALES, LA. **1637**

0243-2226 *See* CAHIERS DE L'IMAGINAIRE, LES. **3371**

0243-3664 *See* BULLETIN D'INFORMATION - M.I.D.I.S.T. **5091**

0243-4504 *See* CINEMACTION. **4066**

0243-4695 *See* INFORMATIQUE U.S. EN DIRECT, L'. **5113**

0243-4938 *See* SONO PARIS. **4453**

0243-5314 *See* BULLETIN ANALYTIQUE - CIE. **2329**

0243-6299 *See* CAHIERS - SYSTEMA. **5092**

0243-6450 *See* MOTS. **4482**

0243-6507 *See* ANNUAIRE DE STATISTIQUE AGRICOLE (FRANCE. SERVICE REGIONAL DE STATISTIQUE AGRICOLE, POITOU-CHARENTES). **151**

0243-6566 *See* ACTIVITE DES ABATTOIRS EN ... / REPUBLIQUE FRANCAISE, MINISTERE DE L'AGRICULTURE, DIRECTION GENERALE DE L'ADMINISTRATION ET DU FINANCEMENT, SERVICE DES ENQUETES ET ETUDES STATISTIQUES. **204**

0243-6795 *See* ROUTIERS, LES. **5444**

0243-6884 *See* CHAMPAGNE-ARDENNE, STATISTIQUE AGRICOLE. **73**

0243-7155 *See* STATISTIQUE AGRICOLE. PRINCIPAUX RENSEIGNEMENTS, REGIONS NORD-PAS DE CALAIS ET PICARDIE / MINISTERE DE L'AGRICULTURE, SERVICE REGIONAL DE STATISTIQUE AGRICOLE. **156**

0243-7228 *See* INNOVATION ET TECHNOLOGIE EN BIOLOGIE ET MEDECINE. **3693**

0243-7686 *See* BULLETIN DE LA SOCIETE D'ETUDES DES HAUTES-ALPES. **2680**

0243-7694 *See* SCIENCE ET RECHERCHE. **5151**

0243-7880 *See* BULLETIN D'INFORMATION DES LABORATOIRES DES SERVICES VETERINAIRES. **5506**

0243-8283 See AGRESTE. SERIES, COMMERCE EXTERIEUR BOIS ET DERIVES. **2399**

0243-8410 *See* REVUE DE L'ACADEMIE DU CENTRE. **2706**

0243-8941 *See* RESEAU D'INFORMATION COMPTABLE AGRICOLE. REGION CENTRE. **128**

0244-4623 *See* NORD SUD EXPORT. **847**

0244-6014 *See* BULLETIN - SOCIETE FRANCAISE DE PHOTOGRAMMETRIE ET DE TELEDETECTION. **4367**

0244-6103 *See* CAHIERS D'ETUDES ROMANES : C.E.R. **1075**

0244-710X *See* FRANCEXPORT. **837**

0244-7118 *See* IMPLANTATION ETRANGERE DANS L'INDUSTRIE AU 1ER JANVIER, L'. **901**

0244-7118 *See* ENQUETE ANNUELLE DE BRANCHE. INGENIERIE, ETUDES ET CONSEILS / MINISTERE DE L'INDUSTRIE ET DE LA RECHERCHE, SERVICE D'ETUDE DES STRATEGIES ET DES STATISTIQUES INDUSTRIELLES. **2004**

0244-7827 *See* POLITIQUE AFRICAINE (PARIS, FRANCE : 1981). **4491**

0244-8327 *See* ABBAY. **2636**

0244-9056 *See* RECHERCHE AEROSPATIALE (TECHNICAL TRANSLATION). **33**

0244-9358 *See* REVUE TRIMESTRIELLE DE DROIT COMMERCIAL ET DE DROIT ECONOMIQUE. **3103**

0244-9676 *See* AFGHANISTAN EN LUTTE. **2644**

0244-9811 *See* PERLIN 1980. **1067**

0245-0283 *See* CATALOGUE DE L'INGENIERIE. **1967**

0245-1875 *See* EDITEURS ET DIFFUSEURS DE LANGUE FRANCAISE, LES. **4814**

0245-3827 *See* RAPPORT D'ACTIVITE / MINISTERE DE LA SANTE, MINISTERE DU TRAVAIL, INSERM, SERVICE CENTRAL DE PROTECTION CONTRE LES RAYONNEMENTS IONISANTS. **4441**

0245-4505 *See* INDUSTRIES DES CEREALES. **202**

0245-4548 *See* AUTO STEREO PARIS. **5405**

0245-484X *See* FORET MEDITERRANEENNE. **2382**

0245-5196 *See* CAESARODUNUM : BULLETIN DE L'INSTITUT D'ETUDES LATINES DE LA FACULTE DES LETTRES ET SCIENCES HUMAINES D'ORLEANS-TOURS. **1075**

0245-5552 *See* JOURNAL D'ECHOGRAPHIE ET DE MEDECINE ULTRASONORE : JEMU. **3592**

0245-5676 *See* ART PRESS (PARIS, FRANCE : 1981). **313**

0245-5781 *See* CONFECTION 2000 NOUVELLES TECHNIQUES DE L'HABILLEMENT. **1083**

0245-5811 *See* JOURNAL DE TRAUMATOLOGIE. **3592**

0245-5919 *See* MOTRICITE CEREBRALE, READAPTATION, NEUROLOGIE DU DEVELOPPEMENT. **3838**

0245-6001 *See* MESSAGES DES PTT. **1145**

0245-7458 *See* SE COMPRENDRE PARIS. **4996**

0245-7466 *See* BULLETIN EPIDEMIOLOGIQUE HEBDOMADAIRE : BEH / REPUBLIQUE FRANCAISE, MINISTERE DE LA SOLIDARITE, DE LA SANTE ET DE LA PROTECTION SOCIALE, DIRECTION GENERALE DE LA SANTE. **3734**

0245-8160 *See* AFRIQUE LITTERAIRE, L'. **3358**

0245-8292 *See* MEMOIRES ET ETUDES SCIENTIFIQUES DE LA REVUE DE METALLURGIE. **4008**

0245-8411 *See* PAYS D'ALSACE. **2702**

0245-8438 *See* EURO P.V. **833**

0245-8608 *See* ICHTYOPHYSIOLOGICA ACTA. **457**

0245-8969 *See* EPS. EDUCATION PHYSIQUE ET SPORT. **4894**

0245-8977 *See* E.P.S. 1. **2596**

0245-9132 *See* ECONOMIE ET HUMANISME. **1634**

0245-9337 *See* BULLETIN OF THE INTERNATIONAL PEDIATRIC ASSOCIATION. **3901**

0245-940X *See* CHIMIE MAGAZINE. **972**

0245-9442 *See* POUR. **5254**

0245-9469 *See* REVUE DE DROIT SANITAIRE ET SOCIAL. **4800**

0245-9507 *See* PEUPLE BRETON, LE. **2271**

0245-9523 *See* PREHISTOIRE ARIEGEOISE : BULLETIN DE LA SOCIETE PREHISTORIQUE DE L'ARIEGE. **1409**

0245-9574 *See* TECHNIQUES DE L'INGENIEUR. PLASTIQUES. **4460**

0245-985X *See* INDUSTRIES AGRO-ALIMENTAIRES. **2344**

0245-9930 *See* ANNUAIRE CNRS SCIENCES DE L'HOMME ET DE LA SOCIETE. **5239**

0246-0122 *See* NOUVELLE REVUE DE MEDECINE DE TOULOUSE. **3623**

0246-0149 *See* PROGRES EN HEMATOLOGIE. **3773**

0246-0203 *See* ANNALES DE L'I.H.P. PROBABILITES ET STATISTIQUES. **3493**

0246-0211 *See* ANNALES DE L'I.H.P. PHYSIQUE THEORIQUE. **4396**

0246-0831 *See* REVUE INTERNATIONALE DU TRACHOME ET DE PATHOLOGIE OCULAIRE TROPICALE ET SUBTROPICALE ET DE SANTE PUBLIQUE. **3879**

0246-0874 *See* GEOLOGIE DE LA FRANCE. **1379**

0246-0882 *See* VERITE STENOGRAPHIQUE, LA. **718**

0246-0971 *See* ECOMINE. **1355**

0246-1226 *See* NOUVELLES DE L'ACADEMIE / ACADEMIE DES SCIENCES, LES. **5135**

0246-1234 *See* REANIMATION ET MEDECINE D'URGENCE. **3725**

0246-1315 See VERITE STENOGRAPHIQUE, LA. **718**

0246-1331 *See* CHRONIQUES D'ART SACRE. **347**

0246-1528 *See* HYDROLOGIE CONTINENTALE. **1415**

0246-1641 *See* HYDROGEOLOGIE (ORLEANS). **1414**

0246-1900 *See* SOUDER. **4027**

0246-1919 *See* SOUVENIR NAPOLEONIEN, LE. **2630**

0246-2346 *See* DEBAT, LE. **2845**

0246-2591 *See* 30 MILLIONS D'AMIS, LA VIE DES BETES. **1059**

0246-2648 *See* CAHIERS ROGER NIMIER. **3371**

0246-2826 *See* ANALYTICA. **4573**

0246-4438 *See* EDUCATION PAR LE JEU ET L'ENVIRONNEMENT, L'. **1740**

0246-5582 *See* CAHIERS DU QUATERNAIRE. **1371**

0246-5825 *See* BULLETIN DE LA COMMISSION DEPARTEMENTALE DES ANTIQUITES DE LA SEINE-MARITIME. **2680**

0246-5957 *See* MAGIC CROCHET. **5184**

0246-6341 *See* LINGUISTIQUE ET SEMIOLOGIE. **3299**

0246-8298 *See* J.D.I. **1755**

0246-9367 See RECHERCHES EN DIDACTIQUE DES MATHEMATIQUES REVUE. 3530
0246-9561 See RECUEIL D'EVALUATIONS DES OUVRAGES COURANTS DU BATIMENT. 625
0247-0101 See BULLETIN DE L'INSTITUT D'HISTOIRE DU TEMPS PRESENT (PARIS, FRANCE : 1981). 2612
0247-0357 See PAROLES ET MUSIQUE MENSUEL. 4145
0247-039X See CARACTERE 1980. 4564
0247-1906 See NEIGE, LA. 4907
0247-2406 See PREVENIR MARSEILLE. 5489
0247-3372 See ECONOMIE PAPETIERE. 1487
0247-3739 See ALTERNATIVES ECONOMIQUES DIJON. 1589
0247-400X See ANNUAIRE DES PAYS DE L'OCEAN INDIEN. 2637
0247-4069 See NOTE FINANCIERE ANNUELLE. MIDI-PYRENEES. 801
0247-4352 See VIDEOTEX PARIS. 1235
0247-4808 See OPTO ELECTRONIQUE. 2074
0247-6800 See PREVENTION SANTE. 4796
0247-6886 See 4X4 MAGAZINE. 4848
0247-7114 See PTT INFO. 1120
0247-7750 See REVUE PRESCRIRE, LA. 3637
0247-7769 See HIFI VIDEO MAGAZINE. 4071
0247-8277 See ECO 3. 2227
0247-8315 See GABON SELECTION PARIS. 837
0247-9095 See DIFFERENCES PARIS. 1980. 4471
0247-915X See CONTRASTES (PARIS). 3275
0247-9788 See DROIT ET CULTURES : CAHIERS DU CENTRE DE RECHERCHE DE L'U.E.R. DE SCIENCES JURIDIQUES. 3127
0248-0018 See JOURNAL D'UROLOGIE. 3990
0248-0573 See ANNUAIRE DES COLLECTIVITES LOCALES / C.N.R.S., G.R.A.L. 4626
0248-1855 See CREEZ!. 663
0248-2339 See TOBOGGAN TOULOUSE. 4926
0248-3351 See ETUDES DE LA REVUE DU LOUVRE ET DES MUSEES DE FRANCE. 4087
0248-3521 See LITTERATURE, MEDECINE, SOCIETE. 3605
0248-3912 See ARCHIVES ET DOCUMENTS, MICRO-EDITION. SCIENCES HUMAINES. 2857
0248-4579 See TEXTES ET LANGAGES. 3445
0248-4900 See BIOLOGY OF THE CELL. 532
0248-4951 See NOUVELLES QUESTIONS FEMINISTES. 5563
0248-496X See TRACES. 3447
0248-6016 See TECHNIQUES & CULTURE. 5162
0248-6644 See MEMOIRES / SOCIETE D'HISTOIRE ET D'ARCHEOLOGIE DE BEAUNE (COTE-D'OR). 274
0248-742X See COLLECTION DE MONOGRAPHIES DE MEDECINE DU TRAVAIL. 2860
0248-7845 See AVANT-SCENE. BALLET/DANSE, L'. 1310
0248-8515 See SEKSA KHMER. 2664
0248-8663 See REVUE DE MEDECINE INTERNE, LA. 3801
0248-8868 See CAMERA STYLO. 4065
0248-9635 See N.P.N. MEDECINE. 3618
0248-9643 See EST MEDECINE. 3575
0249-0420 See SUPPLEMENT AU BULLETIN ANALYTIQUE PETROLIER. 4280
0249-2571 See COMMUNICATIONS & STRATEGIES MONTPELLIER. 1175
0249-3047 See PENINSULE. 2662
0249-3136 See FONDERIE, FONDEUR D'AUJOURD'HUI. 4002
0249-3381 See INFORMATIQUE DOCUMENTAIRE PARIS, L'. 1189
0249-3756 See PROBLEMES AUDIOVISUELS. 1136
0249-4418 See BULLETIN BIBLIOGRAPHIQUE FONDERIE. 4025
0249-4744 See ECONOMIE & PREVISION. 1487

0249-4779 See BULLETIN D'INFORMATION (CENTRE NATIONAL DU MACHINISME AGRICOLE, DU GENIE RURAL, DES EAUX ET DES FORETS (FRANCE). 158
0249-4914 See VOIES FERREES. 857
0249-5627 See AGRONOMIE. 56
0249-5635 See CAHIERS ETHNOLOGIQUES. 233
0249-5643 See TRANSPORT PUBLIC. 5395
0249-5708 See BIC-CODE. 4218
0249-5902 See BULLETIN / CENTRE PIERRE LEON D'HISTOIRE ECONOMIQUE ET SOCIALE. 1549
0249-6046 See BULLETIN OFFICIEL DES SERVICES DU PREMIER MINISTRE. 4702
0249-6208 See JOURNAL DE MEDECINE LEGALE, DROIT MEDICAL. 3741
0249-6267 See MODELES LINGUISTIQUES. 3303
0249-6275 See NOTA BENE (PARIS, FRANCE). 3418
0249-633X See MEMOIRE DE LA SOCIETE MATHEMATIQUE DE FRANCE. 3522
0249-6356 See ETUDES SOCIOCRITIQUES. CO-TEXTES. 5245
0249-6402 See TOXICOLOGICAL EUROPEAN RESEARCH. 3984
0249-6410 See MEMOIRE HORS-SERIE ... DE LA SOCIETE GEOLOGIQUE DE FRANCE. 1387
0249-6429 See SONS, CHIRURGIE (PARIS, FRANCE : 1982). 3975
0249-6526 See PROMOCLIM A. 2607
0249-6550 See JOURNAL D'ERGOTHERAPIE PARIS. 4380
0249-664X See MEMOIRES DE LA SOCIETE DES SCIENCES NATURELLES ET ARCHEOLOGIQUES DE LA CREUSE. 274
0249-6704 See FILS, TUBES, BANDES, PROFILES. 2114
0249-6739 See ORIENTATION SCOLAIRE ET PROFESSIONNELLE. 1839
0249-6747 See MEMOIRES DE LA COMMISSION DES ANTIQUITES DU DEPARTEMENT DE LA COTE-D'OR. 2850
0249-6763 See BULLETIN DE LA SOCIETE ARCHEOLOGIQUE DU FINISTERE. 263
0249-6879 See GRAND MAGHREB : REVUE MENSUELLE DU CENTRE D'INFORMATION SUR LE GRAND MAGHREB (CIGMA). 2499
0249-728X See BULLETIN DES ETUDES AFRICAINES. 2498
0249-7344 See REVUE DE LA BIBLIOTHEQUE NATIONALE. 3246
0249-7395 See REVUE D'ECOLOGIE. 2220
0249-7557 See REUNION DES SCIENCES DE LA TERRE. 1360
0249-7581 See RHUMATOLOGIE (AIX-LES-BAINS). 3807
0249-762X See BIBLIOGRAPHIE PALYNOLOGIE. 5088
0249-7921 See ETUDES DE PHILOSOPHIE MEDIEVALE. 4346
0249-8138 See PHOSPHORE PARIS. 1068
0249-8316 See DOCUMENTS D'ARCHEOLOGIE MERIDIONALE. NUMERO SPECIAL, SERIE METHODES ET TECHNIQUES. 266
0249-9185 See CAHIERS DE PSYCHOLOGIE COGNITIVE. 4579
0249-9320 See BULLETIN DE LA REVUE DE LA SOCIETE D'ARCHEOLOGIE ET D'HISTOIRE DU PAYS DE LORIENT. 263
0249-9975 See COURRIER - O.C.C, LE. 5467
0250-0035 See CRUX (PRETORIA). 3275
0250-0280 See DIENSPLIG. 4042
0250-0329 See REBUS, DE. 3035
0250-0418 See ANNUAL CONFERENCE, PROCEEDINGS - ELECTRON MICROSCOPY SOCIETY OF SOUTHERN AFRICA. 572
0250-054X See ARCHITECTURE SA. 290
0250-0787 See TERRESTRIAL ECOSYSTEMS NEWSLETTERS. 474
0250-0817 See AFRICAN BUSINESS & CHAMBER OF COMMERCE REVIEW. 817
0250-0868 See INTERNATIONAL JOURNAL OF TISSUE REACTIONS. 537
0250-152X See EDUCAMUS. 1738

0250-1554 See ERNAHRUNG (VIENNA, AUSTRIA). 4190
0250-1619 See CAHIERS DU CEDAF, LES. 5194
0250-1651 See KEXUE FAZHAN. 5123
0250-2135 See REVISTA LATINOAMERICANA DE ACUICULTURA. 2312
0250-2348 See ANNUAL REPORT / NATIONAL INSTITUTE FOR COAL RESEARCH. 2133
0250-2933 See ANUARUL INSTITUTULUI DE GEOLOGIE SI GEOFIZICA. 1365
0250-2992 See COOKEIA : SERIES OF MISCELLANEOUS PUBLICATIONS IN THE HUMAN SCIENCES BY THE NATIONAL MUSEUMS AND MONUMENTS OF ZIMBABWE. 2639
0250-3018 See ZIMBABWEA. 2644
0250-3190 See REVISTA AIBDA. 3246
0250-3212 See BEITRAEGE ZUR UROLOGIE. 3988
0250-3220 See BEITRAEGE ZUR ONKOLOGIE. 3809
0250-3255 See SOOCHOW JOURNAL OF MATHEMATICS. 3536
0250-3263 See DONGWUXUE ZAZHI. 5582
0250-3298 See THALASSOGRAFIKA. 2314
0250-3301 See HUANJING KEXUE. 2173
0250-3336 See SENUR DAIHAGGYO NYAGHAG KOMMUNJIB. 4329
0250-3395 See NYENGU BOGO - NYENNAM DAIHAGGYO GONNEB GISUR NYENGUSO. 5135
0250-362X See KUWAIT BULLETIN OF MARINE SCIENCE. 1451
0250-3670 See REVISTA UNIVERSITARIA. 1846
0250-3751 See DEVELOPMENTS IN OPHTHALMOLOGY. 3874
0250-3794 See WORLD HEALTH STATISTICS ANNUAL. 4811
0250-3891 See EIB-INFORMATION / EUROPEAN INVESTMENT BANK. 897
0250-4057 See SOCIAL SECURITY DOCUMENTATION. ASIAN SERIES. 2893
0250-4219 See RISCPT BULLETIN. 2181
0250-4227 See IRPTC BULLETIN. 2233
0250-4278 See INDICATORS OF INDUSTRIAL ACTIVITY. 1609
0250-4294 See NEWSLETTER - IFLA. SECTION OF BIOLOGICAL AND MEDICAL SCIENCES LIBRARIES. 3235
0250-4340 See PAKISTAN BUSINESS & SHOPPING GUIDE. 702
0250-4359 See PAKISTAN HOTEL & RESTAURANT GUIDE. 2808
0250-4367 See MEDICINAL & AROMATIC PLANTS ABSTRACTS. 517
0250-4375 See NUCLEAR SCIENCE RESEARCH CONFERENCE SERIES. 4449
0250-4413 See ENTOMOFAUNA. 5582
0250-4421 See BLUES LIFE JOURNAL. 4104
0250-4421 See BLUES LIFE. 4104
0250-4499 See CONNECT: UNESCO-UNEP ENVIRONMENTAL EDUCATION NEWSLETTER. 2163
0250-4650 See AFER. 4932
0250-4677 See ATHEROGENESE (WIEN). 3699
0250-4685 See BIYOKIMYA DERGISI. 484
0250-4693 See BULLETIN DU GROUPEMENT INTERNATIONAL POUR LA RECHERCHE SCIENTIFIQUE EN STOMATOLOGIE & ODONTOLOGIE. 1318
0250-4707 See BULLETIN OF MATERIALS SCIENCE. 5091
0250-474X See INDIAN JOURNAL OF PHARMACEUTICAL SCIENCES. 4307
0250-4758 See INDIAN JOURNAL OF VETERINARY PATHOLOGY. 5512
0250-488X See REVUE BELGE D'ACUPUNCTURE. 3636
0250-4936 See WIENER ZEITSCHRIFT FUER SUCHTFORSCHUNG. 1350
0250-4952 See THERAPIE FAMILIALE. 4620
0250-4960 See NEPHROLOGIE. 3991

ISSN Index

0250-5002 See AMPI MEDICAL PHYSICS BULLETIN. 4396

0250-5010 See ANNALEN VAN DE BELGISCHE VERENIGING VOOR STRALINGSBESCHERMING. 4433

0250-5037 See ARCHIVOS DE BIOLOGIA ANDINA. 442

0250-5045 See AVIATION MEDICINE (BANGALORE). 3554

0250-507X See BIOVIGYANAM. 448

0250-5118 See BULLETIN (INTERNATIONAL DAIRY FEDERATION). 192

0250-5193 See GUJARAT AGRICULTURAL UNIVERSITY RESEARCH JOURNAL. 91

0250-524X See INDIAN JOURNAL OF FORESTRY. 2384

0250-5266 See INDIAN VETERINARY MEDICAL JOURNAL. 5512

0250-5304 See IRMA JOURNAL. 2591

0250-5339 See JOURNAL OF SCIENCE AND TECHNOLOGY. 5119

0250-5347 See JOURNAL OF SHIVAJI UNIVERSITY. SCIENCE. 5120

0250-5363 See KARACHI UNIVERSITY JOURNAL OF SCIENCE. 5122

0250-5371 See LEGUME RESEARCH. 105

0250-538X See MAADINI. 2143

0250-541X See NATIONAL ACADEMY SCIENCE LETTERS. 5130

0250-5460 See REVISTA BOLIVIANA DE QUIMICA. 991

0250-5479 See REVISTA LATINOAMERICANA DE CIENCIAS AGRICOLAS. 129

0250-5517 See REVUE ROUMAINE DE BIOLOGIE. SERIE DE BIOLOGIE VEGETALE. 526

0250-5525 See SCHWEIZERISCHE MEDIZINISCHE WOCHENSCHRIFT. SUPPLEMENTUM. 3639

0250-5584 See UNDOC: CURRENT INDEX. UNITED NATIONS DOCUMENTS INDEX. 4503

0250-5649 See CIENCIAS VETERINARIAS (HEREDIA). 5507

0250-5754 See EP NEWS. 4646

0250-5762 See EUROPA FORUM LUXEMBOURG. 4521

0250-5886 See GREEN EUROPE (BRUSSELS, BELGIUM). 90

0250-5991 See JOURNAL OF BIOSCIENCES. 461

0250-605X See REVISTA INTERNACIONAL DE SEGURIDAD SOCIAL. 1708

0250-6092 See BOLETIN ESTADISTICO DE LA OEA. 1548

0250-6114 See CHIEFS OF STATE AND CABINET MINISTERS OF THE AMERICAN REPUBLICS. 4637

0250-6157 See FINANCIAMIENTO DEL DESARROLLO. 4726

0250-6203 See OAS CECON TRADE NEWS. 848

0250-6211 See DIRECTORY / ORGANIZATION OF AMERICAN STATES. 4644

0250-6319 See SUMMARY OF THE DECISIONS TAKEN AT THE MEETINGS AND TEXTS OF THE RESOLUTIONS APPROVED. 3136

0250-6335 See JOURNAL OF ASTROPHYSICS AND ASTRONOMY. 396

0250-6343 See HUWA WA-HIYA. 1064

0250-636X See TROPICAL GASTROENTEROLOGY. 3987

0250-6394 See STATISTICAL BULLETIN / NORTHWEST ATLANTIC FISHERIES ORGANIZATION. 2317

0250-6408 See JOURNAL OF NORTHWEST ATLANTIC FISHERY SCIENCE. 2307

0250-6416 See SCIENTIFIC COUNCIL REPORTS. 2312

0250-6432 See SCIENTIFIC COUNCIL STUDIES. 2312

0250-6459 See ZEITSCHRIFT FUER NEUERE RECHTSGESCHICHTE. 3078

0250-6505 See REGIONAL DEVELOPMENT DIALOGUE. 2833

0250-6602 See OCCUPATIONAL HEALTH FOUNDATION, INSTITUTE OF OCCUPATIONAL HEALTH. 2866

0250-6807 See ANNALS OF NUTRITION & METABOLISM. 4187

0250-6831 See BELIZEAN STUDIES. 2723

0250-6882 See EMIRATES MEDICAL JOURNAL. 3574

0250-6912 See DRUGS AND PHARMACEUTICALS, CURRENT HIGHLIGHTS (R & D). 4302

0250-6920 See DRUGS AND PHARMACEUTICALS. INDUSTRY HIGHLIGHTS. 4302

0250-6971 See CAHIERS DE LA REVUE DE THEOLOGIE ET DE PHILOSOPHIE. 4941

0250-7005 See ANTICANCER RESEARCH. 3809

0250-7072 See NATUROPA (ENGLISH EDITION). 2200

0250-7161 See EURE. 2822

0250-7196 See HAMDARD ISLAMICUS. 5042

0250-7277 See GEOTHERMAL REPORT. MINERAL RESOURCES DIVISION, FIJI. 1945

0250-7307 See BY-LAWS, RULES AND REGULATIONS. INTERNATIONAL MONETARY FUND. 4635

0250-7315 See REGLEMENTATION GENERALE, REGLES ET REGLEMENTS / FONDS MONETAIRE INTERNATIONAL. 1516

0250-7323 See ESTATUTOS Y REGLAMENTO / FONDO MONETARIO INTERNACIONAL. 1489

0250-7366 See ANNUAL REPORT ON EXCHANGE ARRANGEMENTS AND EXCHANGE RESTRICTIONS - INTERNATIONAL MONETARY FUND. 823

0250-7374 See GOVERNMENT FINANCE STATISTICS YEARBOOK. 4698

0250-7412 See BULLETIN DU FMI. 780

0250-7420 See BOLETIN DEL FMI. 779

0250-7455 See AL-TAMWIL WA-AL-TANMIYAH. 4708

0250-7463 See INTERNATIONAL FINANCIAL STATISTICS YEARBOOK - INTERNATIONAL MONETARY FUND. 730

0250-7471 See INTERNATIONAL FINANCIAL STATISTICS ANUARIO. 730

0250-7498 See ANNUAL REPORT OF THE EXECUTIVE BOARD - INTERNATIONAL MONETARY FUND. 1632

0250-7501 See RAPPORT ANNUEL DU CONSEIL D'ADMINISTRATION - FONDS MONETAIRE INTERNATIONAL. 1515

0250-751X See INFORME ANUAL DEL DIRECTORIO EJECUTIVO - FONDO MONETARIO INTERNACIONAL. 1495

0250-7528 See JAHRESBERICHT DER EXECUTIVDIREKTOREN - INTERNATIONALER WAHRUNGSFONDS. 1497

0250-765X See MEMBERS - INTERNATIONAL FOLK MUSIC COUNCIL. 4130

0250-7668 See ANNALES DE GEOGRAPHIE (BEIRUT, LEBANON). 2553

0250-7692 See CLEO-SCHRIFTEN. 75

0250-7730 See BULLETIN DES DESSINS ET MODELES INTERNATIONAUX : PUBLICATION MENSUELLE DU BUREAU INTERNATIONAL DE L'ORGANISATION MONDIALE DE LA PROPRIETE INTELLECTUELLE. 3476

0250-7803 See AARDKUNDIGE MEDEDELINGEN. 1364

0250-7811 See LIST OF FISHING VESSELS - NORTHWEST ATLANTIC FISHERIES ORGANIZATION. 2307

0250-7838 See NUMISMATISCHE ZEITSCHRIFT. 2782

0250-8036 See ANNALES DE PHILOSOPHIE. 4340

0250-8044 See FUROR. 2517

0250-8052 See BULLETIN OEPP. 165

0250-8060 See WATER INTERNATIONAL. 5542

0250-8095 See AMERICAN JOURNAL OF NEPHROLOGY. 3988

0250-8257 See KENYA JOURNAL OF SCIENCES. SERIES B, BIOLOGICAL SCIENCES. 462

0250-829X See INDIAN JOURNAL OF BOTANY. 513

0250-8303 See INGENIERIA Y CIENCIA QUIMICA. 2013

0250-832X See DENTO MAXILLO FACIAL RADIOLOGY. 1322

0250-8338 See I P H INFORMATION. 4234

0250-8621 See AFRO TECHNICAL PAPERS. 4764

0250-863X See ENVIRONMENTAL HEALTH CRITERIA. 4774

0250-8869 See HSIN SHIH / LIEN-HO-KUO CHIAO KO WEN TSU CHIH. 4655

0250-9083 See HANGUG NUIHAG DOSEGWAN. 3580

0250-9326 See SANTE DU MONDE. 4801

0250-9377 See UNDRO NEWS. 2912

0250-944X See INTERNATIONAL FRUIT WORLD. 2345

0250-9628 See JOURNAL OF COMBINATORICS, INFORMATION & SYSTEM SCIENCES. 3512

0250-9660 See ICSSR JOURNAL OF ABSTRACTS AND REVIEWS : POLITICAL SCIENCE. 4476

0250-9768 See JOURNAL OF ECONOMIC AND TAXONOMIC BOTANY. 515

0250-9954 See TECHNIKA CHRONIKA EPISTEMONIKE EKDOSE. T.E.E. EPISTEMONIKE PERIOCHE A. 2032

0250-9970 See HAWLIYAT FAR AL-ADAB AL-ARABIYAH. 3285

0250-9989 See ECOFORUM ENGLISH EDITION. 2164

0251-012X See JOURNAL OF THE INDIAN MUSICOLOGICAL SOCIETY. 4127

0251-0251 See WORKING PAPER - WORLD EMPLOYMENT PROGRAMME RESEARCH. 1719

0251-0316 See TECHNIKA CHRONIKA EPISTEMONIKE EKDOSE T.E.E. EPISTEMONIKE PERIOCHE B. 2130

0251-0324 See TECHNIKA CHRONIKA EPISTEMONIKE EKODSE T.E.E. EPISTEMONIKE PERIOCHE C. 2017

0251-0391 See TRANSAFRICAN JOURNAL OF HISTORY. 2644

0251-0405 See JOURNAL OF EASTERN AFRICAN RESEARCH & DEVELOPMENT. 2640

0251-0421 See JOURNAL OF THE LANGUAGE ASSOCIATION OF EASTERN AFRICA. 3292

0251-0464 See IGU NEWSLETTER. 2565

0251-0480 See PAKISTAN JOURNAL OF AGRICULTURAL RESEARCH. 118

0251-0758 See REVUE MAROCAINE DE MEDECINE ET SANTE. 3636

0251-0790 See GAODENG XUEXIAO HUAXUE XUEBAO. 976

0251-0804 See FANGZHI KEXUE. 5350

0251-0952 See SEED SCIENCE AND TECHNOLOGY. 186

0251-0960 See SCHWEIZER INGENIEUR UND ARCHITEKT. 1995

0251-0960 See SCHWEIZER INGENIEUR UND ARCHITEKT. 2030

0251-1029 See VASA. SUPPLEMENTUM. 3802

0251-1045 See ZIMBABWE JOURNAL OF AGRICULTURAL RESEARCH, THE. 149

0251-107X See TRANSACTIONS OF THE INTERNATIONAL ASTRONOMICAL UNION. 401

0251-1088 See ENVIRONMENTALIST, THE. 2193

0251-1096 See JOURNAL OF THE INSTITUTION OF ENGINEERS (INDIA). ELECTRONICS & TELECOMMUNICATION ENGINEERING DIVISION. 2070

0251-110X See JOURNAL OF THE INSTITUTION OF ENGINEERS (INDIA). PART EN CALCUTTA, ENVIRONMENTAL ENGINEERING DIVISION, THE. 2176

0251-1126 See CHEMIE, KUNSTSTOFFE AKTUELL. 1022

0251-1193 See GERFAUT, LE. 5617

0251-1207 See FACHSPRACHE. 3281

0251-1223 See GEOBIOS (JODHPUR). 456

0251-1258 See ICHTHYOLOGICAL BULLETIN OF THE J.L.B. SMITH INSTITUTE OF ICHTHYOLOGY. 5586

0251-1266 See INTERNATIONAL JOURNAL ON POLICY AND INFORMATION. 5204

0251-1460 See SITUATION MONDIALE DE L'ALIMENTATION ET DE L'AGRICULTURE, LA. 135

0251-1495 See TRAINING FOR AGRICULTURE AND RURAL DEVELOPMENT. 142

0251-1649 See INTERNATIONAL JOURNAL OF CLINICAL PHARMACOLOGY RESEARCH. 4308

0251-1657 See SWISS DENT. 1336

0251-1665 See SWISS MED. 3644

0251-1673 See SWISS PHARMA. 4330

0251-1681 See SWISS FOOD. 2359

0251-169X See SWISS PLASTICS. 2108

0251-1703 See SWISS CHEM. 993

0251-1711 See REVISTA DA BIBLIOTECA NACIONAL (LISBOA). 3260

0251-172X See ODONTO-STOMATOLOGIE TROPICALE. 1331

0251-1789 See INVASION & METASTASIS. 537

0251-1894 See LAND REFORM, LAND SETTLEMENT AND COOPERATIVES. 1542

0251-2068 See CONCEPTS IN PEDIATRIC NEUROSURGERY. 3902

0251-2432 See WORLD HEALTH FORUM. 4808

0251-2483 See ESTUDIOS PARAGUAYOS. 2732

0251-2491 See ANDEAN REPORT, THE. 1545

0251-2521 See ASEAN BRIEFING. 2501

0251-2912 See BENELUX. 1548

0251-2920 See CEPAL REVIEW. 1551

0251-2955 See TURKISH PUBLIC ADMINISTRATION ANNUAL. 4691

0251-298X See ZAIRE-AFRIQUE. 2644

0251-303X See INDIAN JOURNAL OF POLITICAL STUDIES, THE. 4476

0251-3048 See INDIA QUARTERLY. 4523

0251-3072 See KOREA & WORLD AFFAIRS. 4528

0251-3102 See REVUE DE TOURISME. 5490

0251-3110 See ASIAN & PACIFIC QUARTERLY OF CULTURAL AND SOCIAL AFFAIRS. 2842

0251-3137 See BEIJING INFORMATION. 4465

0251-3498 See REVUE OLYMPIQUE. 4915

0251-3552 See NUEVA SOCIEDAD. 2751

0251-3722 See REVUE DE L'OTAN. 4494

0251-3986 See ANNUAL ECE/FAO PRICE REVIEW. 2327

0251-401X See COMMODITY TRADE AND PRICE TRENDS. 829

0251-4079 See MINES, GEOLOGIE ET ENERGIE. 1358

0251-4133 See MITTEILUNGEN DER EIDGENOSSISCHEN FORSCHUNGSANSTALT FUER WALD, SCHNEE UND LANDSCHAFT. 2388

0251-4184 See ACTA MATHEMATICA VIETNAMICA. 3490

0251-4230 See ESTUDOS MATEMATICA E INFORMATICA, INSTITUTO GULBENKIAN DE CIENCIA. 1259

0251-4265 See YEARBOOK / UNITED NATIONS COMMISSION ON INTERNATIONAL TRADE LAW. 3138

0251-4451 See BULLETIN INTERNATIONAL DES SCIENCES DE LA MER. 1447

0251-4478 See REVISTA TECNICA INTEVEP. 4277

0251-4494 See DISASTER PREPAREDNESS IN THE AMERICAS. AMERICAN SANITARY BUREAU. 4773

0251-4710 See EPI NEWSLETTER. 3713

0251-4729 See PAI BOLETIN INFORMATIVO. 4795

0251-4761 See REVUE JURIDIQUE, POLITIQUE, ET ECONOMIQUE DU MAROC. 3043

0251-4788 See TAIWAN SHENXUE LUNKAN. 5002

0251-4877 See WORLD LIST OF SOCIAL SCIENCE PERIODICALS. 5226

0251-5253 See TERMNET NEWS : JOURNAL OF THE INTERNATIONAL NETWORK FOR TERMINOLOGY (TERMNET). 3328

0251-5342 See FRONTIERS IN DIABETES. 3730

0251-5350 See NEUROEPIDEMIOLOGY. 3840

0251-5547 See CHILD REFERENCE BULLETIN. 5278

0251-5601 See PROGRES EN NEONATOLOGIE / JOURNEES NATIONALES DE NEONATOLOGIE. 3911

0251-575X See STUDIES AND DOCUMENTS ON CULTURAL POLICIES. 1885

0251-6365 See OCCASIONAL PAPER / INTERNATIONAL MONETARY FUND. 801

0251-6438 See MONTHLY COMMODITY PRICE BULLETIN. 110

0251-6497 See UNHCR INFORMATION. 1921

0251-6500 See REFUGEE UPDATE ENGLISH ED. 4512

0251-6519 See YEARBOOK ON HUMAN RIGHTS FOR 4514

0251-6616 See MONTHLY BIBLIOGRAPHY. PT 1 : BOOKS, OFFICIAL DOCUMENTS, SERIALS. 420

0251-6624 See MONTHLY BIBLIOGRAPHY. PART II, SELECTED ARTICLES / UNITED NATIONS, LIBRARY. 4529

0251-6632 See DEVELOPMENT FORUM - UNITED NATIONS. 1479

0251-6861 See POPULI (ENGLISH ED.). 4559

0251-690X See EVERYONE'S UNITED NATIONS. 3128

0251-7205 See HABITAT NEWS. 2823

0251-723X See NATURAL RESOURCES & ENERGY. 2199

0251-7329 See UN CHRONICLE. 4537

0251-737X See PSYCHOTHERAPIES (GENEVA, SWITZERLAND). 3935

0251-7388 See LECTURES LIEGE. 3346

0251-7604 See POPULATION BULLETIN OF THE UNITED NATIONS. 4556

0251-7787 See NOTES AND DOCUMENTS - UNITED NATIONS, CENTRE AGAINST APARTHEID. 4511

0251-7833 See REPORTS OF INTERNATIONAL ARBITRAL AWARDS - UNITED NATIONS. 3134

0251-8716 See FORUM MONDIAL DE LA SANTE. 4776

0251-8996 See POPULATION - UNITED NATIONS FUND FOR POPULATION ACTIVITIES. 4559

0251-9518 See DISARMAMENT - UNITED NATIONS. 4520

0251-9569 See WORKSHOP REPORT - UNESCO. INTERGOVERNMENTAL OCEANOGRAPHIC COMMISSION. 1458

0251-981X See MAB TECHNICAL NOTES. 463

0252-0176 See WORLD ANIMAL REVIEW / REVUE MONDIALE DE ZOOTECHNIE / REVISTA MUNDIAL DE ZOOTECNIA. 224

0252-0184 See WORLD ANIMAL REVIEW / REVUE MONDIALE DE ZOOTECHNIE / REVISTA MUNDIAL DE ZOOTECNIA. 224

0252-029X See STATISTIQUES FINANCIERES INTERNATIONALES ANNUAIRE - FONDS MONETAIRE INTERNATIONAL. 812

0252-0524 See PUBLICATIONS / COUNCIL OF EUROPE. 4532

0252-0540 See OFFICIAL REPORT OF DEBATES / COUNCIL OF EUROPE, STANDING CONFERENCE OF LOCAL AND REGIONAL AUTHORITIES OF EUROPE. 4671

0252-0613 See STOCK-TAKING ON THE EUROPEAN CONVENTION ON HUMAN RIGHTS. 4513

0252-063X See INTERNATIONAL EXCHANGE OF INFORMATION ON CURRENT CRIMINOLOGICAL RESEARCH PROJECTS IN MEMBER STATES OF THE COUNCIL OF EUROPE / DIRECTORATE OF LEGAL AFFAIRS, COUNCIL OF EUROPE, DIVISION OF CRIME PROBLEMS, COUNCIL OF EUROPE. 3166

0252-0656 See DOCUMENTS, WORKING PAPERS - COUNCIL OF EUROPE, PARLIAMENTARY ASSEMBLY. 3127

0252-0664 See OFFICIAL REPORT OF DEBATES - COUNCIL OF EUROPE, PARLIAMENTARY ASSEMBLY. 4671

0252-0842 See FUTURE FOR OUR PAST / COUNCIL OF EUROPE, A. 299

0252-0877 See INFORMATION BULLETIN ON LEGAL ACTIVITIES WITHIN THE COUNCIL OF EUROPE AND IN MEMBER STATES. 3129

0252-0958 See FORUM - COUNCIL OF EUROPE. 2516

0252-1032 See ACTA DE ODONTOLOGIA PEDIATRICA. 1315

0252-1091 See REVUE ZAIROISE DES SCIENCES NUCLEAIRES. 4451

0252-1792 See NOMENCLATURE DES VOIES DE TELECOMMUNICATION UTILISEES POUR LA TRANSMISSION DES TELEGRAMMES. LIST OF TELECOMMUNICATION CHANNELS USED FOR THE TRANSMISSION OF TELEGRAMS. NOMENCLATOR DE LA VIAS DE TELECOMUNICACION EMPLEADAS PARA LA TRANSMISION DEL TELEGRAMAS. 1161

0252-1865 See APUNTES. 5191

0252-1873 See FUTURE (NEW DELHI, INDIA). 2280

0252-1881 See JAHRBUCH DER SCHWEIZERISCHEN GESELLSCHAFT FUER UR- UND FRUHGESCHICHTE. 270

0252-1962 See REVISTA DE INVESTIGACIONES MARINAS. 557

0252-2047 See ANNUAL REPORT - UNITED NATIONS, ECONOMIC COMMISSION FOR AFRICA. 1462

0252-2217 See ESTUDIO ECONOMICO DE AMERICA LATINA Y EL CARIBE / COMISION ECONOMICA PARA AMERICA LATINA Y EL CARIBE. 1489

0252-239X See EUROPA TRANSPORT. KONJUNKTURERHEBUNG. 5382

0252-2659 See WEEKLY ANALYSIS OF ECUADOREAN ISSUES. 1526

0252-2667 See JOURNAL OF INFORMATION & OPTIMIZATION SCIENCES. 3513

0252-2942 See ANNUAL REPORT - WORLD BANK. 2907

0252-2977 See STATISTIQUES FINANCIERES INTERNATIONALES / FONDS MONETAIRE INTERNATIONAL. 734

0252-2993 See SERIE DE FOLLETOS - FONDO MONETARIO INTERNACIONAL. 1520

0252-3019 See DIRECTION OF TRADE STATISTICS. YEARBOOK - INTERNATIONAL MONETARY FUND. 728

0252-3035 See BALANCE OF PAYMENTS STATISTICS. YEARBOOK / INTERNATIONAL MONETARY FUND. 726

0252-306X See DIRECTION OF TRADE STATISTICS - INTERNATIONAL MONETARY FUND (MONTHLY EDITION). 728

0252-3078 See ESTADISTICAS FINANCIERAS INTERNACIONALES / FONDO MONETARIO INTERNACIONAL. 728

0252-3116 See LIBRARY AND INFORMATION SERVICE. 3224

0252-3353 See DATE PALM JOURNAL, THE. 170

0252-337X See ANALES DE LA ACADEMIA DE GEOGRAFIA E HISTORIA DE GUATEMALA. 228

0252-3426 See SMALL INDUSTRY BULLETIN FOR ASIA AND THE PACIFIC. 711

0252-354X See ESCAP AGRICULTURE DIVISION, ARSAP/FADINAP, REGIONAL INFORMATION SUPPORT SERVICE (RISS). 153

0252-3582 See RNAM NEWSLETTER. 161

0252-5097 See REPORT - WORLD BANK. 808

0252-5119 See IDEAS FORUM. 5811

0252-5356 See BIHADASHT-I JAHAN. 2596

0252-5380 See GENERAL INFORMATION PROGRAMME, UNISIST NEWSLETTER. SUPPLEMENT ON BIBLIOGRAPHICAL SERVICES THROUGHOUT THE WORLD IN 416

0252-7014 See RESOLUTIONS AND DECISIONS ADOPTED BY THE GENERAL ASSEMBLY DURING ITS ... SESSION - UNITED NATIONS. 3134

0252-791X See REFUGEES - UNITED NATIONS HIGH COMMISSIONER FOR REFUGEES. 1921

0252-7987 See REPINDEX : INDICE COMPUTARIZADO DE LA RED PANAMERICANA DE INFORMACION Y DOCUMENTACION EN INGENIERIA SANITARIA Y CIENCIAS DEL AMBIENTE (REPIDISCA). 2181

0252-8150 See ZYGOS (ATHENS, GREECE : 1982). 369

0252-8169 See JOURNAL OF COMPARATIVE LITERATURE & AESTHETICS. 354

ISSN Index

0252-8231 See INTERNATIONAL ARCHIVES OF PHOTOGRAMMETRY AND REMOTE SENSING. 1979

0252-8266 See EUROSTATISTIK, DATEN ZUR KONJUNKTURANALYSE / STATISTISCHES AMT DER EUROPAISCHEN GEMEINSCHAFTEN. 1532

0252-8290 See REVUE D'ETUDES PALESTINIENNES. 4534

0252-8347 See PAPUA NEW GUINEA NATIONAL BIBLIOGRAPHY. 422

0252-841X See BOLETIN DE ANTROPOLOGIA AMERICANA. 232

0252-8754 See INFORPRESS CENTROAMERICANA (SERIES). 1567

0252-8762 See REVISTA DE LA INTEGRACION Y EL DESARROLLO DE CENTROAMERICA. 1518

0252-8835 See ALLPANCHIS. 5022

0252-8843 See REVISTA DE CRITICA LITERARIA LATINOAMERICANA. 3351

0252-886X See AMAZONIA PERUANA. 2718

0252-8894 See HISTORICA (LIMA). 2737

0252-8908 See HOMINES. 5201

0252-8983 See REVISTA HISTORICA. 2758

0252-8983 See REVISTA HISTORICA (MONTEVIDEO). 2758

0252-8991 See BOLETIN MENSUAL - BANCO CENTRAL DE VENEZUELA. 779

0252-9041 See GRUPO ANDINO. 2735

0252-905X See ACTUALIDADES - CENTRO DE ESTUDIOS LATINOAMERICANOS ROMULO GALLEGOS. 3358

0252-9076 See MONTALBAN. 2699

0252-9203 See SOCIAL SCIENCES IN CHINA. 5221

0252-9254 See INDIAN JOURNAL OF PHYSICS B AND PROCEEDINGS OF THE INDIAN ASSOCIATION FOR THE CULTIVATION OF SCIENCE B. 4405

0252-9262 See INDIAN JOURNAL OF PHYSICS A AND PROCEEDINGS OF THE INDIAN ASSOCIATION FOR THE CULTIVATION OF SCIENCE A. 4405

0252-9289 See ARCHIVES DES SCIENCES ET COMPTE RENDU DES SEANCES DE LA SOCIETE. 4162

0252-9386 See CAHIERS IVOIRIENS DE RECHERCHE LINGUISTIQUE / INSTITUT DE LINGUISTIQUE APPLIQUU.N.A.C.I-ABIDJAN. 3272

0252-9416 See MAUSAM. 1430

0252-9424 See VERMESSUNG, PHOTOGRAMMETRIE, KULTURTECHNIK. 2000

0252-9459 See EVENTS (BEIRUT). 2651

0252-9556 See BIBLIOGRAPHIE ZUR SCHWEIZER KUNST, BIBLIOGRAPHIE ZUR DENKMALPFLEGE / BIBLIOGRAPHIE DE L'ART SUISSE, BIBLIOGRAPHIE DE LA CONSERVATION DES BIENS CULTURELS / ETH, EIDGENOESSISCHE TECHNISCHE HOCHSCHULE ZUERICH, INSTITUT FUER DENKMALPFLEGE. 344

0252-9599 See CHINESE ANNALS OF MATHEMATICS. SER. B. 3500

0252-9602 See SHUXUE WULI XUEBAO. 3534

0252-9610 See CARGONEWS ASIA. 5379

0252-9629 See TRAVELNEWS ASIA. 5497

0252-9742 See BULLETIN OF THE EUROPEAN ASSOCIATION FOR THEORETICAL COMPUTER SCIENCE. 1172

0252-9769 See REVISTA GEOFISICA. 1410

0252-9777 See HANGUK JAKMUL HAKHOE CHI. 173

0252-9785 See BULLETIN - INTERNATIONAL COUNCIL ON ARCHIVES. 2481

0252-9793 See ARMADA INTERNATIONAL. 4035

0252-9939 See CARIBBEAN GEOGRAPHY. 2558

0252-9955 See BILDUNGSFORSCHUNG UND BILDUNGSPRAXIS. 1728

0252-9963 See MESOAMERICA (ANTIGUA, GUATEMALA). 2746

0253-0015 See BOLETIN DE LIMA. 5193

0253-0031 See TA-LIEN KUNG HSUEH YUAN HSUEH PAO. 5111

0253-004X See PHONOGRAPHIC BULLETIN. 5318

0253-0201 See MATERIALE DE CONSTRUCTII. 620

0253-0279 See FOREIGN SCOUTING SERVICE. LATIN AMERICA. 4256

0253-0333 See EULAR BULLETIN. MONOGRAPH SERIES. 3804

0253-0341 See ARZTE. 3553

0253-0406 See BIENNIAL REPORT - LEAGUE OF RED CROSS SOCIETIES. 5274

0253-0457 See NESTLE FOUNDATION PUBLICATION SERIES. 4195

0253-0465 See KRANKENPFLEGE. 3861

0253-052X See AFRICAN JOURNAL OF CLINICAL AND EXPERIMENTAL IMMUNOLOGY. 3985

0253-0538 See CLEC. CARIB-LATIN ENERGY CONSULTANT. 1935

0253-0562 See ACTA MEDICA PORTUGUESA. 3545

0253-0597 See GARCIA DE ORTA : SERIE DE ZOOLOGIA. 5584

0253-0600 See STATISTIQUES DE LA JUSTICE : CONTINENT ET ILES ADJACENTES. 3083

0253-0643 See EXPERIENTIA OPHTHALMOLOGICA. 3874

0253-066X See CARIBBEAN JOURNAL OF RELIGIOUS STUDIES. 4942

0253-0678 See INGENIERIA HIDRAULICA (LA HABANA). 2091

0253-0716 See IRANIAN JOURNAL OF MEDICAL SCIENCES. 3590

0253-0759 See MEDICAL JOURNAL OF BASRAH UNIVERSITY, THE. 3610

0253-0775 See PETROLEUM NEWS. 4273

0253-0783 See ENERGY ASIA. 1939

0253-0899 See INNSBRUCKER HISTORISCHE STUDIEN. 2620

0253-0961 See MEDICOM. 3614

0253-097X See ARCHIV FUER LAGERSTATTENFORSCHUNG DER GEOLOGISCHEN BUNDESANSTALT. 1366

0253-1097 See MAJALLAT AL-ULUM AL-IJTIMAIYAH. 5208

0253-1151 See REVISTA CUBANA DE HIGIENE Y EPIDEMIOLOGIA. 3736

0253-1208 See JOURNAL DE LA SOCIETE CHIMIQUE DE TUNISIE. 979

0253-1232 See ANALELE INSTITUTULUI DE GEODEZIE, FOTOGRAMMETRIE, CARTOGRAFIE SI ORGANIZAREA TERITORIULUI. 1351

0253-1445 See REFUGEE ABSTRACTS : A PUBLICATION OF THE INTERNATIONAL REFUGEE INTEGRATION RESOURCE CENTRE. 1921

0253-1453 See BOTANICA HELVETICA. 503

0253-1496 See AGRICULTURAL REVIEWS. 51

0253-150X See AGRICULTURAL SCIENCE DIGEST (AGRICULTURAL RESEARCH COMMUNICATION CENTER.). 161

0253-1550 See ANUARUL INSTITUTULUI DE ISTORIE SI ARHEOLOGIE CLUJ-NAPOCA. 2675

0253-1593 See ANALECTA CARTUSIANA. 4934

0253-1607 See MONUMENTET. 303

0253-1623 See BULLETIN D'ETUDES ORIENTALES. 2647

0253-164X See MELANGES DE L'UNIVERSITE SAINT-JOSEPH. 1078

0253-1658 See REVISTA PORTUGUESA DE HISTORIA. 2706

0253-1666 See BELAS-ARTES. 343

0253-1674 See DIDASKALIA (LISBOA). 4953

0253-1682 See ANALELE INSTITUTULUI DE CERCETARI PENTRU CEREALE SI PLANTE TEHNICE, FUNDULEA. 58

0253-1798 See DARI DE SEAMA ALE SEDINTELOR - INSTITUTUL DE GEOLOGIE SI GEOFIZICA. 5. TECTONICA SI GEOLOGIE REGIONALA. 1373

0253-1860 See ANALELE UNIVERSITATII DIN CRAIOVA. MATHEMATICA, FIZICA-CHIMIE. 3492

0253-1879 See OCROTIREA NATURII SI A MEDIULUI INCONJURATOR. 4170

0253-1933 See REVUE - OFFICE INTERNATIONAL DES EPIZOOTIES. 5521

0253-200X See THEILHEIMER'S SYNTHETIC METHODS OF ORGANIC CHEMISTRY. 1048

0253-2042 See WOMEN, WORK AND DEVELOPMENT. 5570

0253-2050 See FAO SOILS BULLETIN. 171

0253-2069 See BIOLOGY INTERNATIONAL. 447

0253-2131 See WORLD BANK REPRINT SERIES. 816

0253-2239 See GUANGXUE XUEBAO. 4434

0253-2263 See CHENGDU KEJI DAXUE XUEBAO. 5093

0253-228X See DONGBEI NONGXUEYUAN XUEBAO. 80

0253-2298 See FEIJINSHUKUANG. 1439

0253-2301 See FU-CHIEN NUNG YEH KO CHI. 89

0253-2301 See FUJIAN NONGYE KEJI. 89

0253-231X See GONGCHENG REWULI XUEBAO. 4430

0253-2336 See MEITAN KEXUE JISHU. 2143

0253-2352 See ZHONGHUA GUKE ZAZHI. 3885

0253-2379 See TIANTI WULI XUEBAO. 4423

0253-2387 See TAIYUAN GONGYE DAXUE XUEBAO. 5161

0253-2395 See SHANXI DAXUE XUEBAO. ZIRAN KEXUE BAN. 5157

0253-2409 See RANLIAO HUAXUE XUEBAO. 990

0253-2417 See LINCHAN HUAXUE YU GONGYE. 2387

0253-245X See HAIYANG WENJI. 1449

0253-2468 See HUANJING KEXUE XUEBAO. 1977

0253-2484 See ENTOMOLOGICA BASILIENSIA. 5607

0253-2581 See VIZANTIJSKIJ VREMENNIK. 2633

0253-259X See TRUDY OTDELA DREVNERUSSKOJ LITERATURY. AKADEMIJA NAUK SSSR; INSTITUT RUSSKOJ LITERATURY. PUSKINSKIJ DOM. 3448

0253-2654 See WEISHENGWUXUE TONGBAO. 571

0253-2662 See ZHONGHUA MINGUO WEI SHENGWU JI MIANYIXUE ZAZHI. 572

0253-2670 See ZHONGCAOYAO. 4333

0253-2697 See SHIYOU XUEBAO. 4278

0253-2700 See YUNNAN ZHIWU YANJIU. 530

0253-2719 See JILINYIKE DAXUE XUEBAO. 3592

0253-2727 See ZHONGHUA XUEYEXUE ZAZHI. 3774

0253-276X See TAI-WAN NUNG YEH (NAN-TOU HSIEN, TAIWAN : 1979). 139

0253-2778 See ZHONGGUO KEXUE JISHU DAXUE XUEBAO. 5172

0253-2786 See YOUJI HUAXUE. 1049

0253-2859 See WORLD DEBT TABLES. 1540

0253-2883 See PAKISTAN AGRICULTURE. 118

0253-2913 See POINT SERIES. 4987

0253-2921 See CATALYST (GOROKA, PAPUA NEW GUINEA). 2669

0253-2948 See REVISTA COSTARRICENSE DE CIENCIAS MEDICAS. 3635

0253-2964 See BULLETIN OF THE KOREAN CHEMICAL SOCIETY. 963

0253-2980 See HANGUG RAGNON HAGHOI JI. 195

0253-3065 See CEN MUN HAGHOI JI. 394

0253-3073 See SAINNYAG HAGHOI JI (SENUR). 4329

0253-3081 See GUMSOG PYOMYEN CERI. 4003

0253-3103 See TAINYAN NEINJI. 1959

0253-3111 See SUNCEN HYAN DAIHAG NONMUNJIB. 1095

0253-312X See HANGUG BUSIG HAGHOI JI. 1976

0253-3138 See GOMU HAGHOI JI. 5075

0253-3146 See HAN'GUK NONGGONG HAKHOE CHI. 91

0253-3154 See HANGUG NYENNYAN SIGRYAN HAGHOI JI. 4191

0253-3162 See DAIHAN MISAINMUR HAGHOI JI. 561

0253-3197 See GUOLI ZHONGGUO YIYAO YANJIUSUO YANJIU BAOGAO. 3579

0253-3200 See PARPU, JONNI GISUR. 4237

0253-3219 See HEJISHU. 2155
0253-3219 See JISHU, HE. 1981
0253-3243 See BULLETIN DE L'INSTITUT SCIENTIFIQUE (RABAT). 5090
0253-3251 See NOTES DU LABORATOIRE DE PALEONTOLOGIE DE L'UNIVERSITE DE GENEVA. 4228
0253-3324 See URBAN DEVELOPMENT DEPARTMENT TECHNICAL PAPER. 2837
0253-3405 See CARIBBEAN JOURNAL OF MATHEMATICAL AND COMPUTING SCIENCES. 3499
0253-3537 See STAFF COMMODITY WORKING PAPER - WORLD BANK. 812
0253-357X See SHENGZHI YU BIYUN. 591
0253-3588 See SHANDONG HAIYANGXUE YUAN XUEBAO. 1457
0253-3596 See YUANZINENG NONGYE YINGYONG. 1961
0253-360X See HANJIE XUEBAO. 4027
0253-3618 See HANGZHOU DAXUE XUEBAO. ZIRAN KEXUE BAN. 5109
0253-3626 See CHONGQING DAXUE XUEBAO. 5229
0253-3642 See PIGE KEJI. 3185
0253-3669 See SENGONG KEJI TONGXUN. 2395
0253-3677 See FENZI KEXUE YUEBAO. 1052
0253-3685 See JIANGSU YIYAO. 3591
0253-3707 See BAIQUIEN YIKE DAXUE XUEBAO. 3555
0253-3758 See CHUNG-HUA HSIN HSUEH KUAN PING TSA CHIH. 3702
0253-3766 See ZHONGHUA ZHONGLIU ZAZHI. 3825
0253-3774 See ZHONGGUO YIXUE KEXUEYUAN XUEBAO. 3653
0253-3782 See DIZHEN XUEBAO. 1404
0253-3790 See YUANZIHE WULI. 4451
0253-3804 See TU MU SHUI LI. 2033
0253-3812 See THEOLOGY & LIFE (HONG KONG). 5004
0253-3820 See FENXI HUAXUE. 1015
0253-3839 See CHUNG-KUO KUNG CH'ENG HSUEH KAN. 1968
0253-3847 See DAIHAN GUMSOG HAGHOI JI. 4000
0253-3863 See JOSA NYENGU BOGO - JANWEN GAIBAR NYENGUSO. 2141
0253-3901 See O.C.C.G.E. INFORMATIONS / OCCGE, SECRETARIAT GENERAL. 3736
0253-391X See EPETERIS ETAIREIAS BUZANTINON SPOUDON. 2686
0253-3952 See SOCIAL DYNAMICS. 5258
0253-3987 See VIE ECONOMIQUE (BERNE), LA. 1526
0253-3995 See JOURNAL FUER SOZIALFORSCHUNG. 5249
0253-4010 See IUSSP PAPERS. 4554
0253-410X See PROCEEDINGS OF THE INDIAN ACADEMY OF SCIENCES. PLANT SCIENCES. 525
0253-4118 See PROCEEDINGS OF THE INDIAN ACADEMY OF SCIENCES. ANIMAL SCIENCES. 5595
0253-4126 See PROCEEDINGS OF THE INDIAN ACADEMY OF SCIENCE. EARTH AND PLANETARY SCIENCES. 1359
0253-4134 See PROCEEDINGS OF THE INDIAN ACADEMY OF SCIENCES. CHEMICAL SCIENCES. 989
0253-4142 See PROCEEDINGS OF THE INDIAN ACADEMY OF SCIENCES. MATHEMATICAL SCIENCES. 3528
0253-4177 See BANDAOTI XUEBAO. 2036
0253-4193 See HAIYANG XUEBAO (ZHONGGUOHUA). 1449
0253-4258 See DONGBEI GONGXUEYUAN XUEBAO. 5101
0253-4312 See TULIAO GONGYE. 4225
0253-4320 See XIANDAI HUAGONG. 1031
0253-4339 See ZHILENG XUEBAO. 2609
0253-4347 See ZHONGNAN KUANGYE XUEYUAN XUEBAO. 2153

0253-4355 See INDIAN JOURNAL OF PLANT PROTECTION. 513
0253-4436 See INDIAN REVIEW OF LIFE SCIENCES. 458
0253-4525 See APPROPRIATE TECHNOLOGY FOR WATER SUPPLY AND SANITATION. 2224
0253-4533 See SPRACHE & KOGNITION. 3323
0253-4606 See IRCWD NEWS. 2233
0253-4649 See NYMPHAEA. 1359
0253-4754 See INTERNATIONAL JOURNAL OF STRUCTURES. 2099
0253-4827 See APPLIED MATHEMATICS AND MECHANICS. 3495
0253-4851 See TROPICAL VETERINARIAN. 3987
0253-486X See CHINESE JOURNAL OF GEOCHEMISTRY. 1050
0253-4878 See SCHWEIZER WAFFEN-MAGAZIN. 4056
0253-4886 See DIGESTIVE SURGERY. 3963
0253-4924 See FOOD TECHNOLOGY ABSTRACTS. 2362
0253-4932 See JOURNAL OF NANJING UNIVERSITY. 1833
0253-4959 See DICENGXUE ZAZHI. 1373
0253-4967 See DIZHEN DIZHI. 1404
0253-4975 See GUOJI DIZHEN DONGTAI. 1406
0253-5025 See INDIAN FOOD INDUSTRY. 2344
0253-505X See HAIYANG XUEBAO (ENGLISH ED.). 1449
0253-5068 See BLOOD PURIFICATION. 3770
0253-5106 See JOURNAL OF THE CHEMICAL SOCIETY OF PAKISTAN. 982
0253-5122 See CURRENT PRACTICES IN GEOTECHNICAL ENGINEERING. 2022
0253-5238 See OAZ, OSTERREICHISCHE APOTHEKER-ZEITUNG. 4318
0253-5254 See PERSONATION AND PSYCHOTHERAPY. 3932
0253-5262 See SCHWEISSTECHNIK (VIENNA). 1995
0253-5297 See AKTUELLE PROBLEME DER NEUROPATHOLOGIE. 3892
0253-5327 See OESTERREICHISCHES PATENBLATT. 1306
0253-5386 See ANNUAL REPORT - INTERNATIONAL CENTRE FOR DIARRHOEAL DISEASE RESEARCH. 3743
0253-5408 See BANGLADESH JOURNAL OF AGRICULTURE. 64
0253-5416 See BANGLADESH JOURNAL OF BOTANY. 501
0253-5424 See BANGLADESH JOURNAL OF JUTE & FIBRE RESEARCH. 5348
0253-5440 See BANGLADESH JOURNAL OF SOIL SCIENCE. 164
0253-5459 See CHITTAGONG UNIVERSITY STUDIES. PART II, SCIENCE. 5094
0253-5475 See FRP REPORT. 3761
0253-5513 See ACTA GASTROENTEROLOGICA BOLIVIANA. 3743
0253-5521 See INDICE BOLIVIANO DE CIENCIAS DE LA SALUD. 4784
0253-5580 See CARDIOLOGIE TROPICALE. 3985
0253-5637 See CIENCIAS DE LA TIERRA Y DEL ESPACIO. 1353
0253-5645 See INGENIERIA ENERGETICA. 1947
0253-5653 See MINERIA EN CUBA, LA. 2145
0253-5688 See REVISTA CENIC. 471
0253-5696 See REVISTA DEL JARDIN BOTANICO NACIONAL. 526
0253-570X See REVISTA DE SALUD ANIMAL. 4799
0253-5718 See SERIE DE GEOFISICA. 1411
0253-5742 See BOLETIN DE PSICOLOGIA. 4577
0253-5750 See CIENCIA Y TECNICA EN LA AGRICULTURA. VETERINARIA. 5507
0253-5777 See CENTRO AZUCAR. 2331
0253-5785 See CENTRO AGRICOLA. 73
0253-5815 See CUBAN JOURNAL OF AGRICULTURAL SCIENCE. 77
0253-5890 See JOURNAL OF THE EGYPTIAN SOCIETY OF PARASITOLOGY. 462

0253-5955 See AFRICAN JOURNAL OF AGRICULTURAL SCIENCES. 45
0253-5963 See POST, KENYA. 5139
0253-5971 See MAKTABA. 3229
0253-6005 See BOLETIN TECNICO - ARPEL. 4252
0253-6072 See CHANG-CHUN TI CHIH HSUEH YUAN HSUEH PAO. 1371
0253-6080 See TIAOWEI FUSHIPIN KEJI. 4199
0253-6099 See KUANGYE GONGCHENG. 2143
0253-6102 See COMMUNICATIONS IN THEORETICAL PHYSICS. 4400
0253-620X See INDIAN THEOLOGICAL STUDIES. 4964
0253-6226 See ADVANCES IN BRYOLOGY. 498
0253-6250 See JUNNAN NUIDAIJI. 3601
0253-6269 See ARCHIVES OF PHARMACAL RESEARCH. 4292
0253-6277 See JANYEN GWAHAG DAIHAG NONMUNJIB. 5117
0253-6315 See RONMUNJIB - CUNNAM DAIHAGGYO GONNEB GYONYUG NYENGUSO. 5148
0253-634X See GARYOUNIS SCIENTIFIC BULLETIN. 5107
0253-6390 See ANNALES DE L'UNIVERSITE DE MADAGASCAR. BIOLOGIE, CLINIQUE, SANTE PUBLIQUE. 441
0253-6420 See HANGUG SEMNYU GONHAGHOIJI. 5351
0253-6498 See HANGUK WONYE HAKHOE CHI. 2418
0253-6501 See HANGUG SAINHWAR GWAHAG NYENGUNWEN RONCON. 456
0253-651X See HANGUG GYNNHAGHOI JI. 575
0253-6595 See ASIAN JOURNAL OF DAIRY RESEARCH. 192
0253-6625 See JOURNAL OF MEDITERRANEAN ANTHROPOLOGY & ARCHAEOLOGY. 239
0253-6684 See SCIENCE REVIEW (CALCUTTA). 5153
0253-6749 See MISCELLANEOUS REPORTS - MINISTRY OF AGRICULTURE AND NATURAL RESOURCES. AGRICULTURAL RESEARCH INSTITUTE. 109
0253-679X See GEOVIEWS (SECUNDERABAD). 1356
0253-6803 See HEALTH AND POPULATION. PERSPECTIVES AND ISSUES. 4777
0253-682X See AROGYA. 3552
0253-6838 See INDIAN CHEMICAL ABSTRACTS. 978
0253-6897 See BULLETIN OF RADIATION PROTECTION. 4399
0253-7125 See CURRENT RESEARCH ON MEDICINAL & AROMATIC PLANTS. 2413
0253-7133 See CURRENT RESEARCH - UNIVERSITY OF AGRICULTURAL SCIENCES. 78
0253-7141 See INDIAN JOURNAL OF ENVIRONMENTAL PROTECTION. 2174
0253-7168 See INDIAN JOURNAL OF PARASITOLOGY. 563
0253-7176 See INDIAN JOURNAL OF PSYCHOLOGICAL MEDICINE. 3926
0253-7184 See INDIAN JOURNAL OF SEXUALLY TRANSMITTED DISEASES. 4784
0253-7206 See INTERNATIONAL BIOSCIENCE MONOGRAPH. 458
0253-7214 See JOURNAL OF ADVANCED ZOOLOGY. 5587
0253-7222 See JOURNAL OF DHARMA. 4968
0253-7230 See JOURNAL OF SCIENTIFIC RESEARCH (BHOPAL). 5120
0253-7257 See JOURNAL OF THE ACOUSTICAL SOCIETY OF INDIA. 4410
0253-7265 See JOURNAL OF THERMAL ENGINEERING, THE. 2119
0253-732X See ACTA CIENCIA INDICA. PHYSICS. 4395
0253-7338 See ACTA CIENCIA INDICA. CHEMISTRY. 959
0253-7370 See WEST INDIAN LAW JOURNAL. 3073

0253-7389 See WORLD BANK CATALOG OF PUBLICATIONS, THE. **1540**

0253-7400 See ARCHIV DER GESCHICHTE DER NATURWISSENSCHAFTEN. **5085**

0253-7419 See MEDEQUIP. **3607**

0253-7494 See WORLD BANK TECHNICAL PAPER. **5170**

0253-7567 See PROCEEDINGS OF THE NUTRITION SOCIETY OF INDIA. **4198**

0253-7605 See JOURNAL OF CYTOLOGY AND GENETICS, THE. **537**

0253-7613 See INDIAN JOURNAL OF PHARMACOLOGY. **4307**

0253-7621 See HANDBOOK OF MEDICAL EDUCATION. **3580**

0253-7656 See DIRECTORY OF PARA-MEDICAL INSTITUTIONS OF INDIA. **3572**

0253-8040 See INDIAN JOURNAL OF WEED SCIENCE. **95**

0253-8229 See SRI LANKA JATIKA GRANTHA NAMAVALIYA. **425**

0253-8288 See JOURNAL OF PHARMACY. **4312**

0253-8296 See BULLETIN BIBLIOGRAPHIQUE SPELEOLOGIQUE. **5173**

0253-830X See NATURAL SCIENCES. **5131**

0253-8318 See PAKISTAN VETERINARY JOURNAL. **5518**

0253-8326 See INFORME ANUAL DE ACTIVIDADES - SERVICIO ESPECIAL DE SALUD PUBLICA. **4784**

0253-8482 See JOURNAL OF THE SIERRA LEONE MEDICAL & DENTAL ASSOCIATION. **1329**

0253-8512 See MEDICAL LETTER ON DRUGS AND THERAPEUTICS EDITION FRANCAISE, THE. **4314**

0253-858X See IMPORTS AND EXPORTS STATISTICS. **5328**

0253-9071 See LANGUAGE FORUM. **3295**

0253-9128 See HUIBAO - TAIWAN UMU SHOUYI XUEHUI. **5511**

0253-9179 See ZHONGHUA MINGUO SHOUYI XUEHUI ZAZHI. **5528**

0253-9268 See REVISTA CUBANA DE FISICA. **4420**

0253-9306 See RESEARCH JOURNAL. SCIENCE / UNIVERSITY OF INDORE. **5147**

0253-9314 See MATSYA. **2308**

0253-9322 See AFRICA THEOLOGICAL JOURNAL. **4933**

0253-9349 See BULLETIN / CROIX-ROUGE LIBANAISE. **4769**

0253-9365 See BANGALORE THEOLOGICAL FORUM. **4937**

0253-939X See SOUTH AFRICAN JOURNAL FOR ENOLOGY AND VITICULTURE. **2371**

0253-9446 See NEUROLOGIA ET PSYCHIATRIA. **3840**

0253-9543 See CHINA DAILY (INTERNATIONAL EDITION). **5798**

0253-9608 See ZIRAN ZAZHI. **5172**

0253-9616 See FFTC BOOK SERIES. **2414**

0253-9624 See ZHONGHUA YUFANG-YIXUE ZAZHI. **3654**

0253-9659 See AL-SULB AL-ARABI. **1596**

0253-9675 See SWISS BIOTECH. **3696**

0253-9683 See HUADONG HUAGONG XUEYUAN XUEBAO. **1025**

0253-9691 See AL HAKEEM. **3547**

0253-9705 See HUANJING BAOHU (BEIJING). **2232**

0253-9713 See BEIJING YIXUE. **3555**

0253-9721 See FANGZHI XUEBAO. **5350**

0253-973X See ZHONGHUA YIXUE JIANYAN ZAZHI. **5172**

0253-9748 See ZHENKONG KEXUE YU JISHU. **5172**

0253-9756 See ZHONGGUO YAOLI XUEBAO. **4333**

0253-9772 See YICHUAN. **552**

0253-9780 See ZHONGHUA HEYIXUE ZAZHI. **3849**

0253-9799 See JIANGSU ZHONGYI ZAZHI. **3592**

0253-9829 See TU JANG. **190**

0253-9837 See CHIHUA XUEBAO. **1050**

0253-9853 See SHANXI XIN YIYAO. **3641**

0253-987X See HSI-AN CHIAO TUNG TA HSUEH. **1977**

0253-9888 See WUHAN DAXUE XUEBAO. ZIRAN. KEXUE. **5171**

0253-9896 See TIANJIN YIYAO. **3645**

0253-990X See SHIPIN YU FAXIAO GONGYE. **2357**

0253-9918 See SHENGWU HUAXUE YU SHENGWU WULI JINZHAN. **473**

0253-9934 See SHANGHAI YIXUE. **3640**

0253-9942 See SHANGHAI JIAOTONG DAXUE XUEBAO. **5157**

0253-9950 See HE HUAXUE YU FANGSHE HUAXUE. **976**

0253-9969 See BULLETIN DE THEOLOGIE AFRICAINE. **4941**

0253-9977 See XIBAO SHENGWUXUE ZAZHI. **541**

0253-9985 See SHIYOU YU TIANRANQI DIZHI. **4278**

0254-0002 See DAQI KEXUE. **1424**

0254-0037 See BEIJING GONGYE DAXUE XUEBAO. **5087**

0254-0061 See KOUQIANG YIXUE. **1329**

0254-0088 See SILI ZHONGGUO YIYAO XUEYUAN YANJIU NIANBAO. **3641**

0254-0096 See TAIYANG NENG XUEBAO. **1959**

0254-0126 See INTERNATIONAL JOURNAL OF TROPICAL PLANT DISEASES. **514**

0254-0142 See SHOU I KO CHI TSA CHIH. **3641**

0254-0150 See RUNHUA YU MIFENG. **1995**

0254-0223 See CIENCIA E TECNICA VITIVINICOLA. **5094**

0254-0282 See RELATORIO - DIRECCAO PROVINCIAL DOS SERVICOS DE SAUDE E ASSISTENCIA. **4798**

0254-0304 See MINING AND ENGINEERING. **2145**

0254-0436 See SPECIAL PUBLICATION SERIES / GEOLOGICAL SURVEY OF INDIA. **1398**

0254-0509 See LUCRARI STIINTIFICE - INSTITUTUL AGRONOMIC "NICOLAE BALCESCU," BUCURESTI, SERIA C, MEDICINA VETERINARA. **5515**

0254-0517 See AFRO-ASIAN JOURNAL OF OPHTHALMOLOGY. **3871**

0254-0533 See TEXTILE INDUSTRIES DYEGEST OF SOUTHERN AFRICA. **5358**

0254-0568 See SCIENTIFIC REVIEWS ON ARID ZONE RESEARCH. **2220**

0254-0584 See MATERIALS CHEMISTRY AND PHYSICS. **1055**

0254-0657 See MELANESIAN LAW JOURNAL. **3009**

0254-0665 See RESEARCH IN MELANESIA. **244**

0254-072X See ACTAS PROCESALES DEL DERECHO VIVO. **2927**

0254-0770 See REVISTA TECNICA DE LA FACULTAD DE INGENIERIA, UNIVERSIDAD DEL ZULIA. **1994**

0254-0789 See SUDAN JOURNAL OF FOOD SCIENCE AND TECHNOLOGY. **2358**

0254-0819 See ACUTE CARE. **3850**

0254-0924 See REPORT OF THE REGISTRAR-GENERAL OF CEYLON ON VITAL STATISTICS FOR **5337**

0254-105X See PROGRESS IN REPRODUCTIVE BIOLOGY AND MEDICINE. **470**

0254-1092 See CURRENT AGRICULTURE. **78**

0254-1114 See ASIAN SOURCES ELECTRONICS. **2036**

0254-1173 See ASIAN SOURCES TIMEPIECES. **2916**

0254-1246 See MAGGLINGEN. **4903**

0254-1319 See MAZUIXEE ZAZHII. **3606**

0254-1408 See ZHONGHUA LILIAO ZAZHI. **4382**

0254-1416 See ZHONGHUA MAZUIXUE ZAZHI. **3684**

0254-1424 See ZHONGHUA WULIYIXUE ZAZHI. **3654**

0254-1432 See ZHONGHUA XIAOHUA ZAZHI. **3748**

0254-1440 See ZHONG SHAN YIXUEYUAN XUEBAO. **3653**

0254-1475 See DOCUMENTS - COMMISSION OF THE EUROPEAN COMMUNITIES. **4645**

0254-1572 See ARTESANIA Y FOLKLORE DE VENEZUELA. **341**

0254-1769 See ZHONGHUA HULI ZAZHI. **3871**

0254-1785 See CHUNG-HUA CH'I KUAN I CHIH TSA CHIH. **3564**

0254-1793 See YAOWU FENXI ZAZHI. **4333**

0254-1807 See SCRIPTURA. **5019**

0254-1815 See REPORT (COUNCIL FOR MINERAL TECHNOLOGY (SOUTH AFRICA)). **1444**

0254-1858 See SOUTH AFRICAN JOURNAL OF ZOOLOGY. **5597**

0254-1912 See JAARLIKSE SEMINAAR OOR TEORETIESE FISIKA. **4428**

0254-1971 See COURSES AND LECTURES / INTERNATIONAL CENTRE FOR MECHANICAL SCIENCES. **2112**

0254-2005 See PROCES-VERBAUX - INTERNATIONAL ASSOCIATION FOR THE PHYSICAL SCIENCES OF THE OCEAN. **1455**

0254-2021 See SHUPIHUI. **2273**

0254-217X See ASIAN COMPUTER MONTHLY. **1235**

0254-2188 See COMPUTER WEEK. **1178**

0254-2218 See RAILWAYS. **5436**

0254-2242 See ELECTROTECHNICA, ELECTRONICA, AUTOMATICA. AUTOMATICA SI ELECTRONICA. **2050**

0254-2293 See PROBLEME DE PROTECTIA PLANTELOR. **4247**

0254-2307 See ROMANIAN JOURNAL OF GERONTOLOGY AND GERIATRICS. **3755**

0254-2420 See BOLETIN CINTERFOR, OIT. **1911**

0254-2471 See CENTRAL AMERICA REPORT (GUATEMALA CITY). **1551**

0254-2552 See STATISTICAL BULLETIN - CIPEC DOCUMENTATION CENTRE. **1627**

0254-2595 See HELLIS NEWSLETTER. **3213**

0254-2609 See GRADUATE MEDICAL EDUCATION IN THE EUROPEAN REGION. SUPPLEMENTARY REPORT. **3579**

0254-2765 See TRANSACTIONS OF THE ZIMBABWE SCIENTIFIC ASSOCIATION. **5167**

0254-2870 See SEAMIC INFORMATION RETRIEVAL ON CURRENT LITERATURE. SERIES F: HEALTH STATUS INDICATORS. **4802**

0254-2897 See PUBLICATION - INTERNATIONAL UNION OF GEOLOGICAL SCIENCES. **1392**

0254-2900 See BIOLOGICAL BULLETIN OF INDIA. **444**

0254-2935 See CELL AND CHROMOSOME RESEARCH. **533**

0254-301X See REALITES DE LA FOI. DIGEST. **4989**

0254-3052 See GAONENG WULI YU HE WULI. **4447**

0254-3087 See YIQI YIBIAO XUEBAO. **5171**

0254-3133 See ACCIS NEWSLETTER. **1170**

0254-3176 See ZHONGGUO DIZHI KEXUEYUAN YUANBAO. **1402**

0254-3214 See NEWSLETTER (CYPRUS POPULAR BANK). **801**

0254-3214 See ECONOMIC REVIEW (CYPRUS POPULAR BANK). **1484**

0254-3419 See PAHODOC. **4795**

0254-3427 See CSNI REPORT. **2154**

0254-3435 See REVISTA DE LA SANIDAD DE LAS FUERZAS POLICIALES. **3635**

0254-3478 See JOURNAL OF RESEARCH IN AYURVEDA & SIDDHA. **4185**

0254-3486 See SUID-AFRIKAANSE TYDSKRIF VIR NATUURWETENSKAP EN TEGNOLOGIE. **5160**

0254-3494 See PAPER. SOUTHERN AFRICA. **4236**

0254-3567 See FUEL SCIENCE AND TECHNOLOGY. **4257**

0254-3591 See PLANT PHYSIOLOGY BIOCHEMISTRY. **524**

0254-3729 See ASIAN BUSINESS. **640**

0254-3893 See WWF NEWS. 2210
0254-3915 See IAWA BULLETIN. 2401
0254-3923 See ANIMALS INTERNATIONAL. 5503
0254-3931 See STUDIES AND RESEARCH - INTERNATIONAL SOCIAL SECURITY ASSOCIATION. 1712
0254-4059 See CHINESE JOURNAL OF OCEANOLOGY AND LIMNOLOGY. 1447
0254-4091 See INDIAN BOTANICAL REPORTER. 513
0254-4105 See INDIAN JOURNAL OF VETERINARY SURGERY. 5512
0254-4113 See CERRAHPASA MEDICAL REVIEW. 3562
0254-4121 See BULLETIN OF THE TECHNICAL UNIVERSITY OF ISTANBUL. 5091
0254-413X See KING ABDULAZIZ MEDICAL JOURNAL. 3602
0254-4156 See TZU TUNG HUA HSUEH PAO. 1221
0254-4164 See JISUANJI XUEBAO. 1191
0254-4172 See JENGI HAGHOI RONMUN JI. 2068
0254-4210 See REVISTA CENTROAMERICANA DE ECONOMIA. 1581
0254-4296 See ANNALES AEQUATORIA. 228
0254-4318 See ES. ELEKTRONIKSCHAU. 1132
0254-4385 See BULETINUL UNIVERSITATII DIN GALATI. FASCICULA II, MATEMATICA, FIZICA, MECANICA TEORETICA. 3497
0254-4407 See ZWINGLIANA. 5011
0254-4415 See ECONOMIA (LIMA). 1556
0254-4466 See HAN HSUEH YEN CHIU. 2652
0254-4474 See LANGUAGE RESEARCH. 3296
0254-4539 See BANO BIGGYAN PATRIKA. 2375
0254-4547 See MAJALLAH-I DANISHKADAH-I DARUSAZI. 4314
0254-4571 See MAJALLAH-I NIZAM-I PIZISHKI-I IRAN. 3606
0254-4636 See CERAMICS TODAY. 2588
0254-4679 See PROCEEDINGS / EUROPEAN CONFERENCE ON SOIL MECHANICS AND FOUNDATION ENGINEERING. 2125
0254-4725 See FAO FOOD AND NUTRITION PAPER. 4190
0254-4903 See CHINESE SCIENCE ABSTRACTS. PART B. 5093
0254-4946 See GETEROGENNYJ KATALIZ. 1015
0254-4962 See PSYCHOPATHOLOGY. 3934
0254-5020 See MEDICINE AND SPORT SCIENCE. 3955
0254-5063 See ZHONGGUO DIZHI KEXUEYUAN, YICHANG DIZHI KUANGCHAN YANJIUSUO SUOKAN. 1402
0254-5071 See ZHONGGUO NIANGZAO. 2373
0254-508X See ZHONGGUO ZAOZHI. 4240
0254-5098 See ZHONGHUA FANGSHE YIXUE YU FANGHU ZAZHI. 3947
0254-5101 See ZHONGHUA WEISHENGWUXUE HE MIANYIXUE ZAZHI. 3677
0254-5128 See COMPTES-RENDUS DE L'ASSEMBLEE GENERALE DE LA COMMISSION INTERNATIONALE TECHNIQUE DE SUCRERIE. 5096
0254-5179 See CHINESE SCIENCE ABSTRACTS. PART A. 5093
0254-5225 See PENOLOGICAL INFORMATION BULLETIN / COUNCIL OF EUROPE. 3171
0254-5233 See PENOLOGICAL INFORMATION BULLETIN / COUNCIL OF EUROPE. 3171
0254-5268 See BUSINESS INDIA. 649
0254-5276 See BULETINI I SHKENCAVE GJEOLOGJIKE. 1368
0254-5284 See FAO IRRIGATION AND DRAINAGE PAPER. 2089
0254-5330 See ANNALS OF OPERATIONS RESEARCH. 5083
0254-5357 See YANKUANG CESHI. 1445
0254-5381 See ENTOMOLOGIA HELLENICA. 5582
0254-5446 See TURKISH JOURNAL OF NUCLEAR SCIENCES. 4451
0254-5454 See TURKIYE BITKI KORUMA DERGISI. 143

0254-5462 See DIS HEKIMLIGI YUKSEK OKULU BULTENI. 1322
0254-5527 See EGE UNIVERSITESI FEN FAKULTESI DERGISI. SERI A. 5102
0254-5543 See BULETINUL UNIVERSITATII DIN GALATI. FASCICULA V, TEHNOLOGII IN CONSTRUCTII SIC DE MASINI, METALURGIE. 3999
0254-5586 See ASIAN SOURCES COMPUTER PRODUCTS. 1235
0254-5616 See SOIL RESEARCH REPORT. 187
0254-5799 See PAPERS PRESENTED AT THE ... TECHNICAL CONFERENCE ON OCEANOGRAPHIC CARTOGRAPHY. 1455
0254-5837 See NEWSLETTER - INTERNATIONAL ASSOCIATION FOR CEREAL CHEMISTRY. 2351
0254-5853 See DONGWUXUE YANJIU. 5582
0254-5861 See JIEGOU HUAXUE. 979
0254-587X See JINSHU RECHULI XUEBAO. 4005
0254-5888 See JISHU YU XUNLIAN. 4006
0254-5896 See ZHONGGUO KEXUE. A, SHUXUE, WULIXUE, TIANWENXUE, JISHUKEXUE. 5172
0254-590X See ZHONGGUO KEXUE. B, HUAXUE, SHENGWUXUE, NONGXUE, YIXUE, DIXUE. 5172
0254-5934 See HANGUG NYUJEN HAGHOI JI. 547
0254-5942 See HANNYAN NUI-DAI HAGSUR JI. 3580
0254-5985 See NYEIBAN NUIHAG HOI JI. 3623
0254-6019 See FAO ANIMAL PRODUCTION AND HEALTH PAPER. 226
0254-6051 See JINSHU RECHULI. 4005
0254-6086 See HE JUBIAN YU DENGLIZITI WULI. 4447
0254-6094 See HUAGONG JIXIE. 2013
0254-6108 See HUANJING HUAXUE. 2173
0254-6116 See KANG SHENG SU. 4313
0254-6124 See KONGJIAN KEXUE XUEBAO. 27
0254-6132 See KUANGCHUANG DIZHI KEXUEYUAN, KUANGCHUANG DIZHI YANJIUSUO SUOKAN. 1386
0254-6140 See MO FENLI KEXUE YU JISHU. 5129
0254-6167 See XIBEI SHIFAN XUEYUAN XUEBAO. ZIRAN KEXUE BAN. 5171
0254-6221 See DASEINSANALYSE (BASEL). 3924
0254-6272 See JOURNAL OF TRADITIONAL CHINESE MEDICINE. 3600
0254-6280 See LAND AND WATER ROME. 5536
0254-6299 See SOUTH AFRICAN JOURNAL OF BOTANY. 528
0254-6337 See SWISS VET. 5522
0254-6361 See SURGERY (SOUTHERN AFRICAN ED.). 3975
0254-6396 See EPITHEORESE KYPRIAKOU DIKAIOU. 2967
0254-6426 See EVERGREEN (PEECHI, INDIA). 2379
0254-6442 See MOSCOSOA : CONTRIBUCIONES CIENTIFICAS DEL JARDIN BOTANICO NACIONAL "DR. RAFAEL M. MOSCOSO". 518
0254-6450 See ZHONGHUA LIUXINGBING ZAZHI. 3717
0254-6469 See FANGZHI GONGCHENG XUEKAN. 5350
0254-7279 See PROBLEM DE AGROFITOTEHNIE TEORETICA SI APLICATA. 121
0254-7287 See ROMANIAN JOURNAL OF MINERAL DEPOSITS. 1396
0254-7295 See ROMANIAN JOURNAL OF PALEONTOLOGY. 4230
0254-7309 See DARI DE SEAMA ALE SEDINTELOR - INSTITUTUL DE GEOLOGIE SI GEOFIZICA. 4, STRATIGRAFIE. 1373
0254-7325 See BOLETIN DE LA ACADEMIA NACIONAL DE LA HISTORIA (CARACAS). 2723
0254-7449 See BOLETIN DE LA SOCIEDAD GEOGRAFICA Y DE HISTORIA "SUCRE". 2556
0254-7600 See NATURAL IMMUNITY. 3675
0254-7678 See MISCELANEA ANTROPOLOGICA ECUATORIANA. 241
0254-7813 See COMPUTER SCIENCE AND INFORMATICS. 1177

0254-7821 See MEHRAN UNIVERSITY RESEARCH JOURNAL OF ENGINEERING AND TECHNOLOGY. 1987
0254-7988 See REGIONAL STUDIES (INSTITUTE OF REGIONAL STUDIES (ISLAMABAD, PAKISTAN)). 2833
0254-8038 See CARIBBEAN QUARTERLY. 2486
0254-8240 See GACETA ARQUEOLOGICA ANDINA. 268
0254-8275 See BEITRAEGE ZUR INTENSIV- UND NOTFALLMEDIZIN. 3555
0254-833X See ARAB NEWS. 5809
0254-8356 See NEOTESTAMENTICA. 4980
0254-8364 See LEUCAENA RESEARCH REPORTS. 105
0254-8372 See JOURNAL OF ECONOMIC DEVELOPMENT. 1498
0254-8399 See INDIA TODAY. 2653
0254-8607 See MEMORIILE SECTIILOR STIINTIFICE / ACADEMIA REPUBLICII SOCIALISTE ROMANIA. 5128
0254-8623 See SRI LANKAN FAMILY PHYSICIAN. 3739
0254-8704 See JOURNAL OF ENVIRONMENTAL BIOLOGY. 2233
0254-8720 See SEAMIC INFORMATION RETRIEVAL ON CURRENT LITERATURE. SERIES L. VENEREAL DISEASE, GONORRHEA. 4802
0254-8747 See ADVANCES IN AUDIOLOGY. 4383
0254-8755 See INTERNATIONAL JOURNAL OF TROPICAL AGRICULTURE. 97
0254-8801 See AGRINDEX. 150
0254-8844 See NEWSLETTER - INTERNATIONAL ORGANIZATION OF PLANT BIOSYSTEMATISTS. 519
0254-8852 See DISCUSSIONS IN NEUROSCIENCES. 3831
0254-8860 See INDIAN JOURNAL OF GASTROENTEROLOGY. 3746
0254-8895 See ANALELE UNIVERSITATII BUCURESTI. FIZICA (1977). 4396
0254-8992 See STEUERENTSCHEID : STE / HERAUSGEBER, PRAXIS IN DER WISSENSCHAFT, DER. 1522
0254-9026 See ZHONGHUA LAONIAN YIXUE ZAZHI. 3755
0254-9042 See ZHONGGUO YIXUE WENZHAI. ZHONGYI. 3653
0254-9182 See BULLETIN OF THE CHRISTIAN INSTITUTE OF SIKH STUDIES. 4941
0254-9204 See PAKISTAN JOURNAL OF APPLIED ECONOMICS. 1511
0254-9212 See ANTHROPOLOGICA DEL DEPARTAMENTO DE CIENCIAS SOCIALES. 228
0254-9239 See LEXIS. 3297
0254-9263 See HEALTH FOR ALL SERIES. 5287
0254-9298 See LEBENSMITTEL- UND BIOTECHNOLOGIE. 2348
0254-9379 See PROCHE-ORIENT, ETUDES ECONOMIQUES. 1513
0254-9395 See INDIAN JOURNAL OF LEPROSY. 4784
0254-9409 See JOURNAL OF COMPUTATIONAL MATHEMATICS. 3512
0254-9433 See VEROFFENTLICHUNGEN DES GEOBOTANISCHEN INSTITUTS DER ETH, STIFTUNG RUBEL, ZURICH. 530
0254-959X See WORKING PAPER (INTERNATIONAL CENTRE FOR DIARRHOEAL DISEASE RESEARCH, BANGLADESH). 4808
0254-9670 See EXPERIMENTAL AND CLINICAL IMMUNOGENETICS. 3669
0254-9719 See IARC INTERNAL TECHNICAL REPORT. 3818
0254-9808 See TIBETAN BULLETIN. 5005
0254-9824 See UIS BULLETIN. 1400
0254-9948 See MONUMENTA SERICA. 2623
0255-0008 See ILCA BULLETIN. 212
0255-0105 See ANNALEN DES NATURHISTORISCHEN MUSEUMS IN WIEN. SERIE B, FUER BOTANIK UND ZOOLOGIE. 499
0255-013X See INA NEWSLETTER. 4227

0255-0148 See JOURNAL OF WATER RESOURCES. 5535
0255-030X See HANDI-COMMUNICATIONS. 1186
0255-0334 See INTERAMERICA (ED. ESPANOLA). 1830
0255-0342 See INTERAMERICA (ENGLISH ED.). 1831
0255-0350 See INTERAMERICA (ED. FRANCAISE). 1830
0255-0369 See INTERAMERICAN (ED. PORTUGUESA). 1831
0255-0393 See ETUDES LINGUISTIQUES. 3280
0255-058X See SOUTH AFRICAN TUNNELLING. 2031
0255-0776 See SOCIAL EUROPE. 1711
0255-0806 See INNOVATION AND TECHNOLOGY TRANSFER/ DG XIII. 5114
0255-0822 See OECD ECONOMIC STUDIES. 1576
0255-0830 See REVUE ECONOMIQUE DE L'OCDE (PARIS). 1956
0255-0849 See BIBLIOGRAPHIE INTERNATIONALE DE LA DEMOGRAPHIE HISTORIQUE. 4561
0255-0857 See INDIAN JOURNAL OF MEDICAL MICROBIOLOGY. 563
0255-2701 See CHEMICAL ENGINEERING AND PROCESSING. 2009
0255-2779 See LITERARY ENDEAVOUR, THE. 3406
0255-2795 See BIBLIOTERM. 3269
0255-2876 See TAP CHI KHOA HOC KY THUAT. 5161
0255-2930 See ZHONGGUO ZHENJIU. 3653
0255-3074 See MITTEILUNGEN DER GEODATISCHEN INSTITUTE DER TECHNISCHEN UNIVERSITAT GRAZ. 1388
0255-3104 See BAUEN IN STAHL. 293
0255-3147 See COMITE CONSULTATIF POUR LES ETALONS DE MESURE DES RAYONNEMENTS IONISANTS : RAPPORT. 4030
0255-3449 See BAOGAO - GUOJI LAOGONG JU. GUOJI LAOGONG DAHUI. 1654
0255-349X See REPORT - INTERNATIONAL LABOUR ORGANISATION, AFRICAN REGIONAL CONFERENCE. 1706
0255-3627 See QUARTERLY LABOUR FORCE STATISTICS. 1537
0255-3643 See JOURNAL OF PURE AND APPLIED SCIENCES BAHAWALPUR. 5119
0255-3813 See NATO REVIEW. 4529
0255-3910 See PAIN AND HEADACHE. 3844
0255-3953 See EUROSTAT, GENERAL GOVERNMENT ACCOUNTS AND STATISTICS. 4697
0255-4070 See AHFAD JOURNAL, THE. 5550
0255-4100 See COCOS : JOURNAL OF THE COCONUT RESEARCH INSTITUTE OF SRI LANKA. 167
0255-4119 See COCONUT BULLETIN (LUNUWILA, SRI LANKA). 167
0255-4216 See TRANSNATIONAL CORPORATIONS. 716
0255-4356 See TIMBER BULLETIN. 2405
0255-4429 See WORLD BADMINTON. 4930
0255-4585 See ILRAD REPORTS. 5511
0255-5476 See MATERIALS SCIENCE FORUM. 2106
0255-5506 See TRAVAIL DANS LE MONDE, LE. 5494
0255-5514 See WORLD LABOUR REPORT. 1720
0255-5905 See YEN CHIU HUI PAO. 148
0255-6014 See QUARTERLY JOURNAL OF THE EXPERIMENTAL FOREST OF NATIONAL TAIWAN UNIVERSITY. 2391
0255-6103 See TAIWAN NONGYE. 139
0255-6448 See FABIS. 171
0255-6472 See LESOTHO LAW JOURNAL. 3002
0255-6588 See PROCEEDINGS OF THE NATIONAL SCIENCE COUNCIL, REPUBLIC OF CHINA. PART A, PHYSICAL SCIENCE AND ENGINEERING. 5141
0255-6596 See PROCEEDINGS OF THE NATIONAL SCIENCE COUNCIL, REPUBLIC OF CHINA. PART B, LIFE SCIENCES. 3630
0255-660X See PHOTONIRVACHAK (DEHRA DUN). 1391
0255-6677 See QATAR UNIVERSITY SCIENCE BULLETIN. 5143
0255-688X See SCHWEIZER BAUMARKT. 308
0255-6928 See DENTAL-REVUE. 1321
0255-6979 See OECD FINANCIAL STATISTICS. PART 2, FINANCIAL ACCOUNTS OF OECD COUNTRIES. ITALY. 802
0255-7045 See MONOGRAPH / EUROPEAN BREWERY CONVENTION. 2369
0255-7053 See ZHONGHUA YISHI ZAZHI. 3654
0255-7118 See CARIBBEAN JOURNAL OF LEGAL INFORMATION : BULLETIN OF THE CARIBBEAN ASSOCIATION OF LAW LIBRARIANS, THE. 2948
0255-7126 See SPECIAL PUBLICATION / INTERNATIONAL CENTRE FOR DIARRHOEAL DISEASE RESEARCH, BANGLADESH. 3801
0255-7150 See INDIAN JOURNAL OF COMPARATIVE ANIMAL PHYSIOLOGY. 5586
0255-7177 See PAFAI JOURNAL. 1027
0255-7193 See CLAY RESEARCH. 1353
0255-7207 See BULLETIN / RAJENDRA MEMORIAL RESEARCH INSTITUTE OF MEDICAL SCIENCES. 3561
0255-7290 See FASHION ACCESSORIES. 1084
0255-7312 See BUSINESS TRAVELLER ASIA-PACIFIC ED. 5465
0255-7568 See RIAZI. 3532
0255-7673 See VERKAUF UND MARKETING. 937
0255-7789 See MATHEMATICAL RESEARCH REPORT. 3520
0255-7800 See TA TZU JAN. 4172
0255-7924 See BOLETIN DE BIOTECNOLOGIA : ORGANO DE DIFUSION DEL COMITE PERMANENTE DE BIOTECNOLOGIA DE LA ASOCIACION INTERCIENCIA. 3690
0255-7940 See ZIZANIOLOGIA. 531
0255-7975 See PEDIATRIC NEUROSURGERY. 3909
0255-7983 See CONCEPTS IN IMMUNOPATHOLOGY. 3668
0255-8106 See JOURNAL OF INTERNATIONAL ARBITRATION. 3131
0255-8114 See MEMBERSHIP DIRECTORY / INTERNATIONAL ASSOCIATION OF MARINE SCIENCE LIBRARIES AND INFORMATION CENTERS. 3230
0255-8173 See AGROFORESTRY TODAY. 55
0255-8270 See CHANGGENG YIXUE. 3562
0255-8297 See YINGYONG KEXUE XUEBAO. 5171
0255-8319 See CAGRINDEX / CAGRIS, CARIBBEAN INFORMATION SYSTEM FOR THE AGRICULTURAL SCIENCES. 71
0255-8327 See REVISTA DE PSICOTERAPIA PSICOANALITICA. 4616
0255-8386 See LABOUR STATISTICS. 1686
0255-8726 See ANNUAL REPORT / CENTRAL COUNCIL FOR RESEARCH IN UNANI MEDICINE. 3550
0255-8777 See MINISTERIAL FORMATION. 4977
0255-884X See WORLD HANDBALL MAGAZINE. 4930
0255-9072 See SCHWEIZERISCHE ZEITSCHRIFT FUER SOZIALVERSICHERUNG UND BERUFLICHE VORSORGE. 2893
0255-9293 See ANNUAL REVIEW OF ENGINEERING INDUSTRIES AND AUTOMATION 1965
0255-9587 See BULLETIN OF THE ZOOLOGICAL SURVEY OF INDIA. 5580
0255-9609 See TECHNICAL REVIEW - IETE. 2083
0255-9625 See INTERNATIONAL JOURNAL OF IMMUNOTHERAPY. 3672
0255-9641 See TRAVAIL SOCIAL 1981. 5313
0255-9773 See SOFTART PRESS. 364
0255-982X See ARAB JOURNAL OF PLANT PROTECTION. 2409
0255-9994 See OLIVAE (MADRID, SPAIN : ENGLISH EDITION). 2352
0256-0011 See JOURNAL OF CURRENT BIOSCIENCES. 489
0256-0038 See CHROMIUM REVIEW. 4000
0256-0046 See CRITICAL ARTS. 1109
0256-0054 See ECQUID NOVI. 2919
0256-0100 See SOUTH AFRICAN JOURNAL OF EDUCATION. 1784
0256-0119 See GATT FOCUS (ENGLISH ED.). 837
0256-0151 See REVISTA URUGUAYA DE DERECHO CONSTITUCIONAL Y POLITICO. 3094
0256-0844 See CERCETARI NUMISMATICE. 2780
0256-0909 See VIKALPA. 889
0256-0917 See PARKETT. 361
0256-0933 See CROP IMPROVEMENT. 169
0256-1115 See KOREAN JOURNAL OF CHEMICAL ENGINEERING, THE. 2014
0256-1425 See FIZIOLOGIJA I BIOHIMIJA KULTURNYH RASTENIJ. 510
0256-1492 See HAIYANG DIZHI YU DISIJI DIZHI. 1382
0256-1514 See ENDOCYTOBIOSIS AND CELL RESEARCH. 536
0256-1530 See ADVANCES IN ATMOSPHERIC SCIENCES / EDITED BY CHINESE COMMITTEE OF METEOROLOGY AND ATMOSPHERIC PHYSICS AND INSTITUTE OF ATMOSPHERIC PHYSICS, ACADEMIA SINICA. 1419
0256-1565 See CAHIERS DU DEPARTEMENT DES LANGUES ET DES SCIENCES DU LANGAGE. 3272
0256-1654 See BULLETIN OF ELECTROCHEMISTRY. 1034
0256-1670 See PALYNOS. 521
0256-1840 See INTERNATIONAL ARCHIVES OF PHOTOGRAMMETRY AND REMOTE SENSING. 1979
0256-1859 See EPIDEMIOLOGICAL BULLETIN - PAN AMERICAN HEALTH ORGANIZATION. 3734
0256-1883 See ZHENJUN XUEBAO. 576
0256-2235 See INDUSTRY AND FINANCE SERIES. 791
0256-2308 See YEAR IN IMMUNOLOGY, THE. 3677
0256-2316 See PULA. 4533
0256-2324 See MONTHLY BULLETIN OF STATISTICS, THE REPUBLIC OF CHINA. 5333
0256-2332 See ENERGY PRICES AND TAXES. 1941
0256-2480 See HAMLET STUDIES. 3392
0256-2499 See SADHANA (BANGALORE). 1995
0256-2529 See BAU, UM. 293
0256-257X See JOURNAL OF TAIWAN MUSEUM. 4166
0256-2596 See SOVETSKOE DEKORATIVNOE ISKUSSTVO. 365
0256-260X See SOVETSKAA GRAFIKA. 365
0256-2804 See AFRICA INSIGHT. 5189
0256-2863 See TEMAS DE TRABAJO SOCIAL. 5312
0256-2928 See EUROPEAN JOURNAL OF PSYCHOLOGY OF EDUCATION. 1878
0256-307X See CHINESE PHYSICS LETTERS. 4400
0256-310X See MYCOLOGIA HELVETICA. 575
0256-3118 See SHP NEWS. 2095
0256-3193 See AIRPORT HANDLING MANUAL. 10
0256-3223 See DANGEROUS GOODS REGULATIONS. 4773
0256-3231 See REGLEMENTATION POUR LE TRANSPORT DES MARCHANDISES DANGEREUSES. 2180
0256-3282 See PASSENGER SERVICES CONFERENCE RESOLUTIONS MANUAL / IATA. 31
0256-341X See TRUDY GEOMETRICHESKOGO SEMINARA. 3539
0256-3517 See IAB. 352
0256-3525 See ECONOMIC AND FINANCIAL PROSPECTS. 788

0256-3592 See DELTION STATISTIKE DEMASION OIKONOMIKON. 4697

0256-419X See TRAVEL BUSINESS ANALYST EUROPE ED. 5495

0256-422X See JOURNAL OF STATISTICAL RESEARCH - UNIVERSITY OF DACCA. INSTITUTE OF STATISTICAL RESEARCH AND TRAINING. 5329

0256-4246 See DISSERTATIONEN DER UNIVERSITAT FUER BODENKULTUR IN WIEN. 79

0256-4270 See BERATER-INFORMATION - LBL. 65

0256-4319 See PROTECTOR. 3174

0256-4327 See SPORT SCIENCE REVIEW (CHAMPAIGN, ILL.). 4921

0256-436X See JOURNAL OF PLANT ANATOMY AND MORPHOLOGY. 515

0256-4378 See SUBSTANCES ET SPECIALITES PHARMACEUTIQUES CLASSEES COMME STUPEFIANTS EN VENTE DANS 16 PAYS EUROPEENS. 4330

0256-4459 See TICKETING HANDBOOK. 37

0256-4467 See ELLIS (ENGLISH EDITION). 2965

0256-4718 See JOURNAL OF LITERARY STUDIES (PRETORIA, SOUTH AFRICA). 3345

0256-4742 See LIVE ANIMALS REGULATIONS / IATA. 5386

0256-4947 See ANNALS OF SAUDI MEDICINE. 3550

0256-5145 See IUFRO NEWS. 2402

0256-520X See PEDAGOGIEKJOERNAAL. 1772

0256-5250 See ZEITGESCHICHTE. 2634

0256-5293 See MEMORIILE SECTIEI DE STIINTE ISTORICE. 2698

0256-5471 See RESOURCE MATERIAL SERIES. 3175

0256-5528 See REVMATOLOGIJA. 3636

0256-5552 See ETUDES ET DOCUMENTS - INSTITUT DE RELATIONS INTERNATIONALES. 4521

0256-5846 See BULLETIN / ECONOMIC AND SOCIAL COMMITTEE OF THE EUROPEAN COMMUNITIES. 1549

0256-596X See EARTH OBSERVATION QUARTERLY. 1354

0256-5985 See DIABETES RESEARCH (EDINBURGH, LOTHIAN). 3728

0256-6028 See PULSE (KLOOF). 2078

0256-6095 See TOKTOKKIE AFRIKAANSE ED. 2207

0256-6141 See ENERGY IN EUROPE. 1940

0256-6303 See AGRARWIRTSCHAFTLICHE STUDIEN. 1460

0256-663X See COGNITIVE SYSTEMS. 4581

0256-6672 See INTERNATIONAL QUARTERLY OF ENTOMOLOGY. 5610

0256-6702 See JOURNAL OF THE GRASSLAND SOCIETY OF SOUTHERN AFRICA, THE. 101

0256-6869 See THERAPIEWOCHE SCHWEIZ. 3645

0256-6877 See WORLD ECONOMIC OUTLOOK (WASHINGTON). 1641

0256-6885 See CURRENT RESEARCH REPORTER. 78

0256-7008 See VECTOR KLOOF. 2796

0256-7040 See CHILD'S NERVOUS SYSTEM. 3902

0256-7245 See SYNTHESIS (BUCURESTI). 3444

0256-7253 See GEOMUNDO. 2564

0256-7679 See CHINESE JOURNAL OF POLYMER SCIENCE. 972

0256-7822 See INTERNATIONAL DEFENSE DIRECTORY. 4046

0256-7865 See COMMUNICATIONS: SERIES C BIOLOGY AND GEOLOGICAL ENGINEERING. 452

0256-7873 See TERMINOLOGIE ET TRADUCTION / COMMISSION DES COMMUNAUTES EUROPEENES, DIRECTION TRADUCTION, SERVICE TERMINOLOGIE ET APPLICATIONS INFORMATIQUES. 3328

0256-7911 See JOURNAL OF SOLAR ENERGY RESEARCH / SOLAR ENERGY RESEARCH CENTER, SCIENTIFIC RESEARCH COUNCIL, BAGHDAD. 1949

0256-8047 See ANNUAL ABSTRACTS OF STATISTICS - CENTRAL OFFICE OF STATISTICS (VALLETTA). 5321

0256-808X See SRI LANKA YEAR BOOK. 2526

0256-8462 See ARBOK HINS ISLENZKA FORNLEIFAFELAGS. 256

0256-8535 See ANNUAL REPORT OF THE DEPARTMENT OF POSTAL SERVICES (CYPRUS). 1144

0256-8543 See JOURNAL OF RESEARCH IN CHILDHOOD EDUCATION. 1758

0256-8551 See JOURNAL OF MICROBIAL BIOTECHNOLOGY. 3694

0256-8632 See CIP CIRCULAR (ENGLISH ED.). 167

0256-8829 See EDUCARE (PRETORIA). 1738

0256-8861 See SOUTH AFRICAN JOURNAL OF LIBRARY AND INFORMATION SCIENCE. 3250

0256-8888 See REGISTRE DE L'ISDS ED. SUR BANDE MAGNETIQUE. 3244

0256-9043 See GUANGHUA (ZHONG-YINGWEN BAN). 2262

0256-9175 See BONTEBOK. 2188

0256-9361 See BIBLE DISTRIBUTOR. ENGLISH. 5014

0256-9507 See MISSIONALIA. 5013

0256-9574 See SAMJ. SOUTH AFRICAN MEDICAL JOURNAL. 3638

0256-9647 See CARIBBEAN FINANCE AND MANAGEMENT. 863

0256-9701 See SOILLESS CULTURE. 187

0256-9957 See ASIA PACIFIC TECH MONITOR. 5086

0257-0009 See NEWS FROM ISDS. 3234

0257-0130 See QUEUEING SYSTEMS. 1993

0257-019X See DILI ZHISHI. 2559

0257-1404 See CONTRIBUTIONS TO SOUTH ASIAN STUDIES. 2650

0257-1412 See JOURNAL OF ASSOCIATION OF EXPLORATION GEOPHYSICISTS. 1407

0257-1676 See DROITS ET LIBERTES EN SYRIE. 4507

0257-1862 See SOUTH AFRICA JOURNAL OF PLANT AND SOIL. 187

0257-201X See S.A.P.A. POULTRY BULLETIN, THE. 220

0257-2028 See PHARMACEUTICAL & COSMETIC REVIEW. 4320

0257-2095 See CITRUS AND SUB-TROPICAL FRUIT JOURNAL, THE. 167

0257-2168 See NOTAS SOBRE LA ECONOMIA Y EL DESARROLLO / CEPAL, COMISION ECONOMICA PARA AMERICA LATINA Y EL CARIBE. 1508

0257-2184 See ECONOMIC SURVEY OF LATIN AMERICA AND THE CARIBBEAN / ECONOMIC COMMISSION FOR LATIN AMERICA AND THE CARIBBEAN. 1485

0257-2222 See REGISTRE DE L'ISDS (ED. SUR MICROFICHE). 4819

0257-2389 See SANNEB MISAINMURHAG HOIJI. 3638

0257-2605 See ETHIOPIAN JOURNAL OF AGRICULTURAL SCIENCES. 82

0257-2753 See DIGESTIVE DISEASES (BASEL). 3744

0257-277X See IMMUNOLOGIC RESEARCH. 3670

0257-3032 See WORLD BANK RESEARCH OBSERVER, THE. 1631

0257-3148 See STUDY PAPER - CGIAR. 138

0257-3245 See RESEARCH AND DEVELOPMENT REPORTER. 5146

0257-3385 See REVUE SCIENCE ET TECHNIQUE. SERIE SCIENCES AGRONOMIQUES ET ZOOTECHNIQUES. 185

0257-3415 See EMPLOYMENT, ADJUSTMENT, AND INDUSTRIALISATION. 1666

0257-3423 See JOURNAL OF THE INSTITUTION ENGINEERS (INDIA). AEROSPACE ENGINEERING DIVISION. 26

0257-3431 See JOURNAL OF THE INSTITUTION OF ENGINEERS (INDIA). AGRICULTURAL ENGINEERING DIVISION. 101

0257-3490 See BANGLADESH JOURNAL OF CHILD HEALTH. 3900

0257-3512 See CONDITIONS OF WORK DIGEST. 1661

0257-3636 See HONG KONG COUNTDOWN. 680

0257-4063 See TEXTES LITTERAIRES FRANCAIS. 3445

0257-4217 See MITTEILUNGEN DER ABTEILUNG FUER MINERALOGIE AM LANDESMUSEUM JOANNEUM. 1442

0257-4314 See REVISTA CUBANA DE EDUCACION SUPERIOR : RCES. 1846

0257-4322 See REVISTA CUBANA DE PSICOLOGIA / UNIVERSIDAD DE LA HABANA. 4616

0257-442X See JOURNAL OF THE INSTITUTION OF ENGINEERS (INDIA). MINING ENGINEERING. 2142

0257-4799 See CANYE KEXUE. 5606

0257-4829 See CHIH WU SHENG LI HSUEH PAO. 579

0257-4985 See PAKISTAN JOURNAL OF OTOLARYNGOLOGY. 3890

0257-4993 See JOURNAL OF POTASSIUM RESEARCH. 176

0257-5264 See EUROSTAT. REGNSKABER. LANDBRUG, SKOVBRUG, ENHEDSVRDIER. 82

0257-5426 See WIEL. 5428

0257-5574 See XUMU SHOUYI XUEBAO. 5527

0257-5639 See SHANG-HAI I SHU CHIA. 364

0257-5655 See KAO-HSIUNG I HSUEH KO HSUEH TSA CHIH. 3601

0257-6074 See CULTURE POPULAIRE ALBANAISE. 5268

0257-6333 See IRC NEWSLETTER. 4785

0257-6376 See NUCLEAR DATA NEWSLETTER. 1951

0257-6384 See ESCAP REMOTE SENSING NEWSLETTER. 1355

0257-6430 See STUDIES IN HISTORY NEW DELHI. 2665

0257-6449 See WINAK. 1791

0257-6457 See CUADERNOS DE POETICA. 3379

0257-6554 See NEWSLETTER - IATEFL. 3306

0257-7135 See SOCIOLINGUISTICS. 3322

0257-7151 See CLAT REPORT. 1659

0257-716X See JOURNAL OF TONGJI MEDICAL UNIVERSITY. 3600

0257-7305 See MANUSHI. 5560

0257-7348 See SOUTH ASIAN ANTHROPOLOGIST. 245

0257-7526 See CAHIERS ROUMAINS D'ETUDES LITTERAIRES. 3339

0257-7550 See LEAST DEVELOPED COUNTRIES ... REPORT / PREPARED BY THE UNCTAD SECRETARIAT, THE. 1572

0257-7712 See HUA-HSI I KO TA HSUEH HSUEH PAO. 3585

0257-7755 See CAHIERS BEI / BANQUE EUROPEENNE D'INVESTISSEMENT. 893

0257-7801 See QUARTERLY NATIONAL ACCOUNTS (PARIS, FRANCE : 1983). 1514

0257-7828 See INTERNATIONAL JOURNAL OF SCIENCE & ENGINEERING. 1980

0257-7941 See ANCIENT SCIENCE OF LIFE. 499

0257-7968 See JOURNAL OF THE INDIAN GEOPHYSICAL UNION. 1408

0257-7992 See ARDC NEWS. 62

0257-8018 See EXPORT TIMES (NEW DELHI), THE. 834

0257-8050 See POLLUTION RESEARCH. 2239

0257-8069 See ASCI JOURNAL OF MANAGEMENT. 860

0257-8131 See SHANGHAI YIKE DAXUE XUEBAO. 3640

0257-8166 See TAIWAN ELECTRONICS INDUSTRY. 2083

0257-8301 See KENYA PAST AND PRESENT. 2641

0257-8328 See BUREAUX ET SYSTEMES. 862

0257-8441 *See* RESEARCH BULLETIN - INTERNATIONAL CROPS RESEARCH INSTITUTE FOR THE SEMI-ARID TROPICS. **184**

0257-8700 *See* WATER SEWAGE & EFFLUENT. **5548**

0257-8727 *See* PACT : REVUE DU GROUPE EUROPEEN D'ETUDES POUR LES TECHNIQUES PHYSIQUES, CHIMIQUES ET MATHEMATIQUES APPLIQUEES A L'ARCHEOLOGIE. **277**

0257-8867 *See* FOOD REVIEW. **2339**

0257-8891 *See* SKRIF EN KERK. **4997**

0257-8921 *See* WOORD EN DAAD WORD AND ACTION. **5009**

0257-893X *See* ASIAN ADVERTISING & MARKETING. **756**

0257-8972 *See* SURFACE & COATINGS TECHNOLOGY. **2108**

0257-9162 *See* REVISTA AVICULTURA. **220**

0257-9421 *See* CRYPTOGAMICA HELVETICA. **507**

0257-9472 *See* DACHAUER HEFTE. **2685**

0257-960X *See* ANNALES MONEGASQUES. **2674**

0257-9731 *See* ZHONGGUO JIXIE GONGCHENG XUEKAN. **2132**

0257-9774 *See* ANTHROPOS FRIBOURG. **230**

0257-9928 *See* PROBLEMY TEORII I PRAKTIKI UPRAVLENIIA. **882**

0258-0136 *See* SOUTH AFRICAN JOURNAL OF PHILOSOPHY. **4361**

0258-0144 *See* SUID-AFRIKAANSE TYDSKRIF VIR SOSIOLOGIE, DIE. **5263**

0258-0314 *See* BULLETIN OF THE INSTITUTE OF EARTH SCIENCES, ACADEMIA SINICA. **1352**

0258-0322 *See* MAKROMOLEKULARE CHEMIE. MACROMOLECULAR SYMPOSIA, DIE. **1044**

0258-0330 *See* CURRENT STUDIES IN HEMATOLOGY AND BLOOD TRANSFUSION. **3771**

0258-0357 *See* ACTA ANTHROPOGENETICA. **227**

0258-0365 *See* ALIGARH JOURNAL OF ENGLISH STUDIES, THE. **3359**

0258-0373 *See* ANDHRA PRADESH JOURNAL OF ARCHAEOLOGY, THE. **254**

0258-0381 *See* NEW QUEST. **5252**

0258-042X *See* MANAGEMENT AND LABOUR STUDIES. **943**

0258-0438 *See* MAN & DEVELOPMENT. **1617**

0258-0446 *See* MAN & ENVIRONMENT. **1386**

0258-0543 *See* STRATEGIC DIRECTION. **713**

0258-0551 *See* TECHNOLOGY STRATEGIES. **5164**

0258-0659 *See* JOURNAL OF XIAN MEDICAL UNIVERSITY. **3600**

0258-0748 *See* QUARTERLY NEWSLETTER - INTERNATIONAL COMMISSION ON OCCUPATIONAL HEALTH. **2868**

0258-0764 *See* BULLETIN ARBIDO. **3198**

0258-0772 *See* REVUE ARBIDO. **3246**

0258-0780 *See* NARODNOE HOZAJSTVO UKRAINSKOJ SSR. STATISTICESKIJ EZEGODNIK. **5334**

0258-0853 *See* NYADARSA PAMJIKARANA BULETINA. **5335**

0258-0926 *See* HEDONGLI GONGCHENG. **2155**

0258-0934 *See* DIANZIXUE YU TANCE JISHU, HE. **2041**

0258-1213 *See* NATO ASI SERIES. SERIES A, LIFE SCIENCES. **466**

0258-1248 *See* NATO ASI SERIES. SERIES F, COMPUTER AND SYSTEM SCIENCES. **1196**

0258-1256 *See* NATO ASI SERIES. SERIES G, ECOLOGICAL SCIENCES. **2219**

0258-1302 *See* BULLETIN DE L'ALCAM. **3270**

0258-1442 *See* MAGALLAT MAGMA AL-LUGAT AL-ARABIYYAT BI-DIMASQ. **1834**

0258-1647 *See* NURSING RSA. **3865**

0258-1698 *See* STUDIES IN HISTORY (SAHIBABAD). **2665**

0258-1701 *See* REVIEW JOURNAL OF PHILOSOPHY & SOCIAL SCIENCE. **4359**

0258-1728 *See* JOURNAL OF RESEARCH / ASSAM AGRICULTURAL UNIVERSITY. **100**

0258-1736 *See* ISI LECTURE NOTES. **5329**

0258-1744 *See* CHRISTIAN ORIENT. **5039**

0258-1825 *See* KUNG CHI TUNG LI HSUEH HSUEH PAO. **4411**

0258-1922 *See* INDUSTRIEKONJUNKTUR / INDUSTRIAL TRENDS / [EUROSTAT]. **1611**

0258-1965 *See* EF NEWS / EUROPEAN FOUNDATION FOR THE IMPROVEMENT OF LIVING AND WORKING CONDITIONS. **1664**

0258-1965 *See* NEWS FROM THE FOUNDATION / FOUNDATION FOR THE IMPROVEMENT OF LIVING AND WORKING CONDITIONS. **1694**

0258-2015 *See* FUNKTIONSKRANKHEITEN DES BEWEGUNGSAPPARATES. **3804**

0258-2023 *See* NATO ASI SERIES. SERIES C, MATHEMATICAL AND PHYSICAL SCIENCES. **3524**

0258-2066 *See* QUARTERLY NATIONAL ACCOUNTS--ESA / COMPTES NATIONAUX TRIMESTRIELS--SEC / EUROSTAT. **1580**

0258-2236 *See* PERSPECTIVES IN EDUCATION (JOHANNESBURG, SOUTH AFRICA). **1773**

0258-2244 *See* SA WATER BULLETIN. **5539**

0258-2279 *See* LITERATOR. **3406**

0258-235X *See* HINWEISE UND STUDIEN ZUM LEBENSWERK VON ALBERT STEFFEN. **3393**

0258-2368 *See* KOREAN JOURNAL OF TOXICOLOGY, THE. **3982**

0258-2384 *See* JOURNAL FUER ENTWICKLUNGSPOLITIK : JEP. **1569**

0258-2457 *See* PARKS AND. GROUNDS. **4707**

0258-252X *See* TYDSKRIF VIR REGSWETENSKAP. **3067**

0258-2678 *See* ACCION CRITICA. **5269**

0258-2708 *See* TAIWAN-SHENG TAIZHONG-QU NONGYE GAILIANG CHANG TEKAN ... HAO. **139**

0258-2708 *See* SPECIAL REPORT. **137**

0258-3062 *See* CHINA COAL INDUSTRY YEARBOOK. **2136**

0258-3089 *See* PROGRESS REPORT / ASIAN VEGETABLE RESEARCH AND DEVELOPMENT CENTER. **123**

0258-3097 *See* SOYBEAN RUST NEWSLETTER. **528**

0258-3097 *See* PROGRESS REPORT SUMMARIES - ASIAN VEGETABLE RESEARCH AND DEVELOPMENT CENTER. **183**

0258-3143 *See* WORLD BANK RESEARCH PROGRAM (1986), THE. **1631**

0258-3178 *See* HEALTH MANPOWER DIRECTORY. **3914**

0258-3186 *See* ASIAN JOURNAL OF SURGERY. **3960**

0258-3275 *See* ASSIUT JOURNAL OF AGRICULTURAL SCIENCES. **63**

0258-3283 *See* HUAXUE SHIJI. **5365**

0258-3291 *See* DANGDAI YIXUE. **3570**

0258-3313 *See* CONSERVA. **2163**

0258-3321 *See* SOUTH AFRICAN JOURNAL OF DAIRY SCIENCE. **198**

0258-3348 *See* BRYOPHYTORUM BIBLIOTHECA. **504**

0258-3577 *See* CA QUARTERLY. **1467**

0258-3690 *See* ICSID REVIEW. **3129**

0258-3828 *See* STUDIA ISLANDICA. **3441**

0258-414X *See* JOURNAL OF FORENSIC ODONTO-STOMATOLOGY, THE. **1327**

0258-4190 *See* PROCEEDINGS / INDO-PACIFIC FISHERY COMMISSION. **2310**

0258-4425 *See* AMERICAN JOURNAL OF NONINVASIVE CARDIOLOGY. **3698**

0258-4476 *See* ANNUAL REPORT FOR THE YEAR ... / TEA RESEARCH FOUNDATION OF KENYA. **163**

0258-4565 *See* SAWTRI SPECIAL PUBLICATION. **5355**

0258-462X *See* ZHONGHVA KUNCHONG. **5600**

0258-4638 *See* MAGALLAT TIBB AL-ASNAN AL-URDUNNIYYAT. **1329**

0258-4646 *See* ZHONGGUO YIKE DAXUE XUEBAO. **3653**

0258-4697 *See* LIN CHUANG I HSUEH. **3605**

0258-4751 *See* PARLEMENTS ET FRANCOPHONIE. **4486**

0258-4913 *See* AFRICA MEDIA REVIEW. **1103**

0258-509X *See* SOUTH AFRICAN JOURNAL OF MUSICOLOGY. **4154**

0258-5200 *See* INDUSTRIAL PSYCHOLOGY. **4590**

0258-526X *See* TAIWAN HSU MU SHOU I HSUEH HUI HUI PAO. **5522**

0258-5308 *See* CIVILTA CIBERNETICA. **5095**

0258-5316 *See* MIMARLIK FAKULTESI DERGISI. **303**

0258-5936 *See* CULTIVOS TROPICALES. **77**

0258-5987 *See* PASTOS Y FORRAJES. **118**

0258-5995 *See* REVISTA CUBANA DE QUIMICA. **991**

0258-610X *See* ONE IN TEN. **1067**

0258-6150 *See* FAO FORESTRY PAPER. **2379**

0258-6169 *See* WOMEN OF EUROPE. **5570**

0258-6185 *See* PROCEEDINGS OF THE EUROPEAN PROSTHODONTIC ASSOCIATION, THE. **3630**

0258-624X *See* SRI LANKA FORESTER, THE. **2396**

0258-6428 *See* CHINESE JOURNAL OF PHYSIOLOGICAL SCIENCES. **579**

0258-6495 *See* REVISTA CUBANA DE REPRODUCCION ANIMAL. **220**

0258-6568 *See* SA PUBLIEKREG. **3045**

0258-6754 *See* GUIDE TO THE ECONOMY / NEDBANK GROUP. **1493**

0258-6770 *See* WORLD BANK ECONOMIC REVIEW, THE. **1631**

0258-6819 *See* WIENER SLAWISTISCHER ALMANACH. **3333**

0258-6959 *See* ANALELE INSTITUTULUI DE CERCETARI PEDOLOGIE SI AGROCHIMIE. **162**

0258-7025 *See* ZHONGGUO JIGUANG. **4442**

0258-7033 *See* ZHONGGUO XUMU ZAZHI. **5528**

0258-7041 *See* SHANGHAI KEJI DAXUE XUEBAO. **5157**

0258-7076 *See* XIYOU JINSHU. **4024**

0258-7106 *See* KUANGCHUANG DIZHI. **1441**

0258-7122 *See* BANGLADESH JOURNAL OF AGRICULTURAL RESEARCH. **64**

0258-7203 *See* SOUTH AFRICAN JOURNAL ON HUMAN RIGHTS. **4513**

0258-7254 *See* ACCOUNTANCY SA. **735**

0258-7270 *See* INTERNATIONAL AFFAIRS BULLETIN. **4524**

0258-7327 *See* BIULETENI - ABASTUMNIS ASTROPIZIKURI OBSERVATORIA. MTA QANOBILI. **393**

0258-7440 *See* WORLD ECONOMIC AND FINANCIAL SURVEYS. **1527**

0258-7602 *See* PESTICIDES-CIPAC METHODS AND PROCEEDINGS SERIES : COLLABORATIVE INTERNATIONAL PESTICIDES ANALYTICAL COUNCIL PUBLICATIONS. **4247**

0258-7831 *See* EDUCATION. WHITES / REPUBLIC OF SOUTH AFRICA, DEPARTMENT OF STATISTICS. **1741**

0258-7947 *See* AL-MILAFF. **4515**

0258-8013 *See* ZHONGGUO DIANJI GONGCHENG XUEBAO. **2087**

0258-8021 *See* CHUNG-KUO SHENG WU I HSUEH KUNG CHENG HSUEH PAO. **3564**

0258-8064 *See* MUZEJ. **4093**

0258-837X *See* STANDARDTERM. **3323**

0258-8382 *See* NEUES AUS ALT-VILLACH. **4094**

0258-8412 *See* SI YU YAN. **2854**

0258-848X *See* THERAPIEWOCHE OSTERREICH. **3645**

0258-8501 *See* JOURNAL OF WEST INDIAN LITERATURE. **3400**

0258-851X *See* IN VIVO (ATHENS). **458**

0258-8536 *See* BOLETIN DEL INSTITUTO DE ESTUDIOS AYMARAS. **2724**

0258-8730 *See* STUDIA UNIVERSITATIS BABES-BOLYAI. PHYSICA. **4423**

0258-8757 *See* CHINESE MEDICAL SCIENCES JOURNAL. **3563**

0258-8803 *See* TRADITIONAL CHINESE MEDICINE DIGEST. **3647**

0258-8811 *See* BEIJING ZHONGYI XUEYUAN XUEBAO. 3555
0258-8900 *See* BULLETIN OF VOLCANOLOGY. 1403
0258-8927 *See* CHILD CARE WORKER, THE. 5242
0258-9001 *See* JOURNAL OF CONTEMPORARY AFRICAN STUDIES : JCAS. 2848
0258-9168 *See* SOUTHERN AFRICAN UPDATE. 2500
0258-929X *See* UPDATE CAPE TOWN. 3649
0258-9346 *See* POLITIKON. 4491
0258-9494 *See* INFORMATIONS MONDIALES - UNDA. 1133
0258-9524 *See* JAHRBUCH / SCHWEIZERISCHES INSTITUT FUER KUNSTWISSENSCHAFT. 354
0258-9672 *See* EMP NEWSLETTER. 1110
0258-9680 *See* JOURNAL OF EUROPEAN STUDIES (KARACHI). 2694
0258-9710 *See* SRI LANKA JOURNAL OF SOCIAL SCIENCES. 5223
0259-000X *See* LISTE D'ABREVIATIONS DE MOTS DES TITRES DE PUBLICATIONS EN SERIE. 3228
0259-0018 *See* LISTE D'ABREVIATIONS DE MOTS DES TITRES DE PUBLICATIONS EN SERIE. SUPPLEMENT. 3228
0259-0123 *See* JOURNAL OF NATAL AND ZULU HISTORY. 2640
0259-0190 *See* KRONOS. 2641
0259-0247 *See* FRENCH STUDIES IN SOUTHERN AFRICA. 3389
0259-0336 *See* GLEANER INDEX / NATIONAL LIBRARY OF JAMAICA, THE. 5805
0259-0492 *See* RETRIBUCIONES, INDUSTRIA Y SERVICIOS VERDIENSTE, PRODUZIERENDES GEWERBE UND DIENSTLEISTUNGEN EARNINGS, INDUSTRY AND SERVICES / [EUROSTAT]. 1708
0259-0786 *See* QUELLEN ZUR THEATERGESCHICHTE. 5367
0259-0816 *See* LAW & ANTHROPOLOGY. 2993
0259-0859 *See* BHUTAN JOURNAL OF ANIMAL HUSBANDRY. 5505
0259-1081 *See* THRACO-DACIA. 2712
0259-1278 *See* BRAIN DYSFUNCTION. 3828
0259-1340 *See* MODELS IN DERMATOLOGY. 3722
0259-191X *See* ORION JOHANNESBURG. 1989
0259-2010 *See* NAMIBIANA. 2642
0259-210X *See* WORLD BANK DISCUSSION PAPERS. 1527
0259-2282 *See* HACETTEPE MEDICAL JOURNAL. 3580
0259-2371 *See* REVISTA DEL ARCHIVO GENERAL DE LA NACION (LIMA). 2483
0259-238X *See* ASIA-PACIFIC POPULATION JOURNAL. 4549
0259-2517 *See* FAO PLANT PRODUCTION AND PROTECTION PAPER. 509
0259-2525 *See* FAO PLANT PRODUCTION AND PROTECTION SERIES. 171
0259-272X *See* ETLIK VETERINER MIKROBIYOLOJI ENSITITUSU DERGISI. 5510
0259-2843 *See* BULETINI I SHKENCAVE ZOOTEKNIKE E VETERINARE. 5579
0259-2878 *See* PAPER (INTERNATIONAL ORGANIZATION FOR THE ELIMINATION OF ALL FORMS OF RACIAL DISCRIMINATION). 4511
0259-2894 *See* FOREST GENETIC RESOURCES INFORMATION. 2380
0259-2924 *See* CIENCIA Y TECNICA EN LA AGRICULTURA. PASTOS Y FORRAJES. 74
0259-2932 *See* CIENCIA Y TECNICA EN LA AGRICULTURA. GANADO PORCINO. 5094
0259-2940 *See* EVALUATION REPORT : REPORT OF THE EXECUTIVE DIRECTOR. 2193
0259-322X *See* EAAP PUBLICATION. 210
0259-3548 *See* MESOLITHIC MISCELLANY. 274
0259-3599 *See* SCHAFFHAUSER BEITRAGE ZUR GESCHICHTE. 2708
0259-3629 *See* DISARMAMENT TIMES. 4043
0259-3637 *See* TSUNAMI NEWSLETTER. 1412

0259-3696 *See* INTERNATIONAL CHILDREN'S RIGHTS MONITOR. 4477
0259-3785 *See* TUNG WU SHE HUI HSUEH PAO. 5264
0259-4064 *See* FOOD AID IN FIGURES. 2909
0259-4137 *See* MITTEILUNGEN DES OBEROSTERREICHISCHEN LANDESARCHIVS. 2699
0259-4374 *See* ENVIO. 2732
0259-4412 *See* KONTEKST. 3402
0259-4897 *See* PUBLICATIONS DU CENTRE DE RECHERCHES EN MATHEMATIQUES PURES. SERIE I. 3529
0259-5133 *See* MOSKVA V CIFRAH. 5333
0259-5559 *See* ENTREPRENEUR POTCHEFSTROOM. 672
0259-5591 *See* UNIE GOODWOOD, DIE. 1908
0259-5605 *See* APPLIED PLANT SCIENCE. 163
0259-563X *See* DENTEKSA. 1322
0259-6199 *See* CAHIERS DE LINGUISTIQUE FRANCAISE. 3271
0259-6334 *See* NUFUSBILIM DERGISI. THE TURKISH JOURNAL OF POPULATION STUDIES. 4555
0259-6415 *See* SIMPLICIANA. 3437
0259-6563 *See* ANNALES DE LA SOCIETE JEAN-JACQUES ROUSSEAU. 3361
0259-6776 *See* BALANCE OF PAYMENTS OF JAMAICA. 773
0259-7268 *See* HEALTH AND SAFETY GUIDE. 2232
0259-7284 *See* WORKSHOP CONFERENCES HOECHST. 3651
0259-7357 *See* INDEX OF PUBLICATIONS - WORLD BANK. 1533
0259-7365 *See* DACCA UNIVERSITY STUDIES. PART B, THE. 5098
0259-7373 *See* BULLETIN CRITIQUE DES ANNALES ISLAMOLOGIQUES. 5042
0259-8213 *See* WORLD MARKET FOR DAIRY PRODUCTS, THE. 199
0259-8264 *See* WORLD TRANSLATIONS INDEX : A JOINT PUBLICATION OF INTERNATIONAL TRANSLATIONS CENTRE [AND] CENTRE NATIONAL DE LA RECHERCHE SCIENTIFIQUE IN CO-OPERATION WITH THE NATIONAL TRANSLATIONS CENTER AT THE JOHN CRERAR LIBRARY OF THE UNIVERSITY OF CHICAGO. 5171
0259-8434 *See* BULLETIN - INTERNATIONAL DAIRY FEDERATION. 192
0259-8582 *See* REVUE INTERNATIONALE DES SERVICES DE SANTE DES FORCES ARMEES : ORGANE DU COMITE INTERNATIONAL DE MEDECINE ETUDE PHARMACIE MILITAIRES. 3636
0259-9082 *See* MAJALLAH-I ZABANSHINASI. 3301
0259-9090 *See* NASHR-I DANISH. 5044
0259-9147 See DISABILITY AND REHABILITATION. 4387
0259-9651 *See* AFRICANA RESEARCH BULLETIN. 5189
0259-9775 *See* ECONOMIC REVIEW (COLOMBO). 1484
0259-9791 *See* JOURNAL OF MATHEMATICAL CHEMISTRY. 981
0259-9880 *See* TRADE WINDS MONTHLY. 854
0260-0005 *See* SERIALS IN THE BRITISH LIBRARY. 424
0260-0064 *See* BUTTERWORTHS INTERNATIONAL MEDICAL REVIEWS. CARDIOLOGY. 3700
0260-0099 *See* BUTTERWORTHS INTERNATIONAL MEDICAL REVIEWS. CLINICAL PHARMACOLOGY AND THERAPEUTICS. 4295
0260-0196 *See* BUTTERWORTHS INTERNATIONAL MEDICAL REVIEWS. UROLOGY. 3988
0260-0226 *See* MULTIRACIAL EDUCATION. 1765
0260-0226 *See* MULTIRACIAL SCHOOL. 1765
0260-0315 *See* BOOKMARK (EDINBURGH, LOTHIAN). 4825
0260-0358 *See* JAMAHIRIYA REVIEW. 2640

0260-0420 *See* ENGLISH HERITAGE MONITOR. 2515
0260-0668 *See* TIMES INDEX, THE. 5813
0260-0749 *See* FINANCIAL AID FOR FIRST DEGREE STUDY AT COMMONWEALTH UNIVERSITIES. 1824
0260-0854 *See* OXFORD REVIEWS OF REPRODUCTIVE BIOLOGY. 584
0260-0862 *See* DEVELOPMENTS IN ENVIRONMENTAL CONTROL AND PUBLIC HEALTH. 4773
0260-0935 *See* BIBLE TRANSLATOR, THE. 5015
0260-1060 *See* NUTRITION AND HEALTH (BERKHAMSTED). 4195
0260-1079 *See* JOURNAL OF INTERDISCIPLINARY ECONOMICS. 1499
0260-1087 *See* INTERNATIONAL BULK JOURNAL : IBJ. 5384
0260-1222 *See* BIMH MENTAL HANDICAP BULLETIN. 3921
0260-1230 *See* JOURNAL OF MOLLUSCAN STUDIES. 5588
0260-1265 *See* YEARBOOK AND PHILATELIC SOCIETIES' DIRECTORY. 2788
0260-1362 *See* SCHOOL ORGANISATION. 1871
0260-1370 *See* INTERNATIONAL JOURNAL OF LIFELONG EDUCATION. 1801
0260-1508 *See* EXHIBITOR'S HANDBOOK, THE. 759
0260-1656 *See* ELECTRICAL PRODUCTS TUNBRIDGE WELLS, KENT. 2045
0260-1702 *See* YEAR BOOK & REGISTER OF MEMBERS / CLARINET AND SAXOPHONE SOCIETY. 4159
0260-1753 *See* HEL ACHAU. MICROFORM. : JOURNAL OF THE CLWYD FAMILY HISTORY SOCIETY. 2453
0260-1818 *See* ANNUAL REPORTS ON THE PROGRESS OF CHEMISTRY. SECTION A, INORGANIC CHEMISTRY. 1035
0260-1826 *See* ANNUAL REPORTS ON THE PROGRESS OF CHEMISTRY. SECTION C, PHYSICAL CHEMISTRY. 1050
0260-1974 *See* FOOD WORLD NEWS. 2340
0260-2067 *See* IRISH SLAVONIC STUDIES. 2692
0260-2105 *See* REVIEW OF INTERNATIONAL STUDIES. 4534
0260-2288 *See* SENSOR REVIEW. 5157
0260-2342 *See* MEDICINE IN PRACTICE. 3738
0260-2385 *See* INSURANCE BROKERS' MONTHLY AND INSURANCE ADVISER. 2883
0260-2431 *See* CONFERENCE BLUE BOOK. 5467
0260-2873 *See* HANDBOOK OF BRITISH ANAESTHESIA. 3683
0260-2938 *See* ASSESSMENT AND EVALUATION IN HIGHER EDUCATION. 1810
0260-3004 *See* SMASH HITS. 1300
0260-3055 *See* ANNALS OF GLACIOLOGY. 1412
0260-3063 *See* MUSLIM WORLD BOOK REVIEW, THE. 5044
0260-3233 *See* VEGETARIAN (ALTRINCHAM, CHESHIRE : 1980). 4200
0260-3322 *See* RUTLAND RECORD. 2708
0260-3438 *See* INTERNATIONAL DIRECTORY OF SOFTWARE. 1287
0260-3594 *See* COMMENTS ON MODERN CHEMISTRY. PART A, COMMENTS ON INORGANIC CHEMISTRY. 1036
0260-373X *See* YEARBOOK / INSTITUTE OF MANAGEMENT CONSULTANTS. 889
0260-3748 *See* INNOVATION AND MANAGEMENT. 870
0260-3772 *See* RESEARCH PAPERS (CENTRE FOR THE STUDY OF ISLAM AND CHRISTIAN-MUSLIM RELATIONS (BIRMINGHAM, WEST MIDLANDS, ENGLAND)). 5044
0260-3780 *See* NEWSLETTER - BEATRIX POTTER SOCIETY. 3416
0260-4027 *See* WORLD FUTURES. 4365
0260-408X *See* DEFENCE INDUSTRY DIGEST. 4040
0260-4116 *See* TRADITIONAL KENT BUILDINGS. 310

0260-4248 *See* DEVELOPMENTS IN PETROLEUM GEOLOGY. **4254**

0260-4280 *See* PERSPECTIVE OF PHYSICS. **4413**

0260-4299 *See* INTERNATIONAL COAL REPORT. **1947**

0260-4310 *See* DEVELOPMENTS IN POLYMER DEGRADATION. **1041**

0260-4337 *See* DEVELOPMENTS IN POLYMERISATION. **974**

0260-4353 *See* FLUID MECHANICS OF ASTROPHYSICS AND GEOPHYSICS, THE. **1405**

0260-437X *See* JOURNAL OF APPLIED TOXICOLOGY. **3981**

0260-4450 *See* ADHESION (LONDON). **1049**

0260-4736 *See* SANDGROUSE. **5620**

0260-4752 *See* PRACTICAL ENGLISH TEACHING. **1902**

0260-485X *See* CROP PROTECTION IN NORTHERN BRITAIN. **169**

0260-4868 *See* EUROPEAN HUMAN RIGHTS REPORTS. **4508**

0260-5473 *See* CHILDREN IN CARE OR UNDER SUPERVISION, SCOTLAND. **5278**

0260-5503 *See* MANCHESTER GEOGRAPHER : JOURNAL OF THE MANCHESTER GEOGRAPHICAL SOCIETY, THE. **2568**

0260-5511 *See* ABSTRACTS ON HYGIENE AND COMMUNICABLE DISEASES. **4809**

0260-5600 *See* CAMBRIDGE MEDIEVAL CELTIC STUDIES. **3272**

0260-5619 *See* CATALOGUE OF BRITISH OFFICIAL PUBLICATIONS NOT PUBLISHED BY HMSO. **412**

0260-5872 *See* CLINICAL CYTOGENETICS. **535**

0260-5902 *See* PLANT BIOTECHNOLOGY. **523**

0260-597X *See* TURNER STUDIES. **367**

0260-6267 *See* INTERNATIONAL JOURNAL OF PHARMACEUTICAL TECHNOLOGY & PRODUCT MANUFACTURE. **4308**

0260-6275 *See* JOURNAL OF SEPARATION PROCESS TECHNOLOGY. **982**

0260-6291 *See* SPECIAL PUBLICATION / ROYAL SOCIETY OF CHEMISTRY. **993**

0260-6313 *See* CROSS CURRENT. **1734**

0260-647X See ADVERSE DRUG REACTIONS AND TOXICOLOGICAL REVIEWS. **3978**

0260-6518 See TEXTILE HORIZONS INTERNATIONAL. **5358**

0260-6593 *See* CURRENT TECHNOLOGY INDEX : CTI. **5174**

0260-6666 *See* MONITOR ABINGDON. **1275**

0260-6739 *See* BASES (SAO PAULO, BRAZIL). **2551**

0260-6739 *See* PHILATELIST AND PJGB, THE. **2786**

0260-6755 *See* PARLIAMENTS, ESTATES & REPRESENTATION. **4487**

0260-6763 *See* TRENDS AND PERSPECTIVES IN PARASITOLOGY. **475**

0260-6879 *See* INFORMATION AND LIBRARY MANAGER. **3215**

0260-6917 *See* NURSE EDUCATION TODAY. **3862**

0260-7239 *See* INSTITUTE OF HOUSING YEAR BOOK, THE. **2825**

0260-7247 *See* INFOMATICS. **1259**

0260-7352 *See* CANADEAN WORLD NEW PRODUCTS. **2330**

0260-7409 *See* INTERNATIONAL PACKAGING ABSTRACTS. **4222**

0260-7417 *See* JOURNAL OF EDUCATIONAL TELEVISION. **1757**

0260-7425 *See* TONIC (ROBERT SIMPSON SOCIETY). **4156**

0260-7468 *See* EUROPEAN RACEHORSE, THE. **2799**

0260-7476 *See* JET. JOURNAL OF EDUCATION FOR TEACHING. **1897**

0260-7514 *See* PARENTS (LONDON). **2284**

0260-7530 *See* WHAT VIDEO? LONDON. 1980. **4079**

0260-759X *See* LIVERPOOL FAMILY HISTORIAN. **2458**

0260-7840 *See* MODERN POWER SYSTEMS. **1950**

0260-8170 *See* RECENT ADVANCES IN CLINICAL NUTRITION. **4198**

0260-8316 *See* CONFERENCES & EXHIBITIONS INTERNATIONAL. **5096**

0260-8464 *See* LENTIL ABSTRACTS. **105**

0260-8642 *See* PLANNING AND DEVELOPMENT STATISTICS ... ACTUALS / CIPFA, STATISTICAL INFORMATION SERVICE. **4699**

0260-8693 *See* HANDGUNNER. **4898**

0260-8774 *See* JOURNAL OF FOOD ENGINEERING. **2346**

0260-8790 *See* CORRELATION. **390**

0260-8820 *See* DIRECTORY OF INDEPENDENT HOSPITALS AND HEALTH SERVICES, THE. **3779**

0260-8847 *See* JOURNAL OF SYNTHETIC METHODS. **1043**

0260-9169 *See* BARBOUR COMPENDIUM. BUILDING PRODUCTS. **599**

0260-9185 *See* DEVELOPMENTS IN REINFORCED PLASTICS. **4454**

0260-924X *See* IRELAND, PORTS & SHIPPING HANDBOOK. **5450**

0260-9541 *See* ARCHIVES OF NATURAL HISTORY. **4162**

0260-9568 *See* JOURNAL OF THE DECORATIVE ARTS SOCIETY 1890-1940. **373**

0260-9576 *See* LOSS PREVENTION BULLETIN. **2865**

0260-9592 *See* LONDON REVIEW OF BOOKS, THE. **3346**

0260-9606 *See* ANTIQUES ACROSS THE WORLD. **249**

0260-9770 *See* MULTICULTURAL EDUCATION ABSTRACTS. **1795**

0260-9827 See POLITICAL GEOGRAPHY. **2572**

0260-9894 *See* HIGHWAYS AND TRANSPORTATION STATISTICS ... ESTIMATES. **5401**

0260-9967 *See* UNITED KINGDOM AIRPORTS - ACCOUNTS AND STATISTICS. **42**

0260-9991 *See* JOURNAL OF ART & DESIGN EDUCATION. **354**

0261-0116 *See* LANGUAGES OF ASIA AND AFRICA. **3296**

0261-0140 *See* PROGRESS IN OBSTETRICS AND GYNAECOLOGY. **3767**

0261-0159 *See* EQUAL OPPORTUNITIES INTERNATIONAL. **1667**

0261-0175 *See* LLOYD'S BANK ECONOMIC BULLETIN. **796**

0261-0183 *See* CSP. CRITICAL SOCIAL POLICY. **4541**

0261-0272 *See* REVIEWING SOCIOLOGY : A REVIEW JOURNAL FROM THE SCHOOL OF SOCIOLOGICAL STUDIES. **5256**

0261-0280 *See* HOUSING (LONDON. 1978). **2824**

0261-0329 *See* GLAZED EXPRESSIONS. **299**

0261-0345 *See* TRANSACTIONS OF DIESEL ENGINEERS & USERS ASSOCIATION. **2100**

0261-0361 *See* CB. CITIZENS BAND. **1151**

0261-0590 *See* INFORMATION BULLETIN - ASH. **4784**

0261-0736 *See* HEALTH EQUIPMENT INFORMATION. **3781**

0261-0876 *See* MAJALLA (LONDON), AL. **2489**

0261-118X *See* PULVERTAFT PAPERS. **2468**

0261-1279 *See* EARLY MUSIC HISTORY. **4116**

0261-135X *See* SHROPSHIRE FAMILY HISTORY JOURNAL. **2472**

0261-1376 *See* EXPLORATIONS IN KNOWLEDGE. **4346**

0261-1392 *See* LEISURE, RECREATION, AND TOURISM ABSTRACTS. **4856**

0261-1430 *See* POPULAR MUSIC (CAMBRIDGE UNIVERSITY PRESS). **4147**

0261-1449 *See* RECENT ADVANCES IN OCCUPATIONAL HEALTH. **3633**

0261-1473 *See* MIDDLE EAST INDUSTRY & TRANSPORT. **5387**

0261-1538 *See* LIVERPOOL MONOGRAPHS IN HISPANIC STUDIES. **3408**

0261-1562 *See* AFRICA TODAY (LONDON, ENGLAND). **2497**

0261-1570 *See* AFRICA WHO'S WHO. **429**

0261-1589 *See* FIRE RESEARCH NEWS. **2289**

0261-1651 *See* DRAMA BROADSHEET. **5363**

0261-1732 *See* INFORMATION TECHNOLOGY AND PEOPLE. **3217**

0261-1740 *See* RETAIL BANKER INTERNATIONAL (LONDON EDITION). **809**

0261-1910 *See* PROFESSIONAL VIDEO INTERNATIONAL YEARBOOK. **1136**

0261-1929 *See* ATLA : ALTERNATIVES TO LABORATORY ANIMALS. **3979**

0261-1988 *See* HERITAGE OUTLOOK. **300**

0261-2097 *See* EUREKA (BECKENHAM). **2098**

0261-2151 *See* LLOYD'S REGISTER OF SHIPPING. **5451**

0261-2194 *See* CROP PROTECTION (GUILDFORD, SURREY). **169**

0261-2267 *See* INTERNATIONAL AUTOMOTIVE REVIEW. **5417**

0261-233X *See* DEFENSE LATIN AMERICA. **4041**

0261-2356 *See* FAIRPLAY WORLD PORTS DIRECTORY. **5449**

0261-2399 *See* WORLD AIRNEWS. **40**

0261-2429 *See* CANCER SURVEYS. **3812**

0261-2747 *See* EUROPEAN INFORMATION SERVICE. **2516**

0261-2755 *See* SCHOOL ORGANISATION & MANAGEMENT ABSTRACTS. **1797**

0261-2763 *See* ADVANCED GERIATRIC MEDICINE. **3748**

0261-2917 *See* LABORATORY HAZARDS BULLETIN. **2872**

0261-2925 *See* ARAB BANKER. **772**

0261-2933 *See* BMCIS BUILDING MAINTENANCE PRICE BOOK. **601**

0261-3050 *See* BULLETIN OF LATIN AMERICAN RESEARCH. **2725**

0261-3077 *See* GUARDIAN (LONDON). **5812**

0261-3093 *See* MATRIX : A REVIEW FOR PRINTERS AND BIBLIOPHILES. **334**

0261-3131 *See* ECOLOGIST (1979). **2214**

0261-3166 *See* NUCLEIC ACIDS SYMPOSIUM SERIES. **491**

0261-3204 *See* PERIOD HOME. **305**

0261-3344 *See* RISK MEASUREMENT SERVICE. **1519**

0261-3360 *See* CURRENT MEDICAL LITERATURE. RHEUMATOLOGY. **3804**

0261-3409 *See* ARCHAEOLOGIA, OR MISCELLANEOUS TRACTS RELATING TO ANTIQUITY. **256**

0261-3417 *See* ARCHAEOLOGIA AELIANA. **256**

0261-3468 *See* WAGNER NEWS (LONDON, ENGLAND). **389**

0261-3565 *See* LINCOLNSHIRE FAMILY HISTORIAN. **2458**

0261-3646 *See* MEDICAL FORUM (OXFORD, OXFORDSHIRE). **3609**

0261-3697 *See* COMPUTER & VIDEO GAMES. **1230**

0261-3794 *See* ELECTORAL STUDIES. **4645**

0261-3875 *See* LEGAL STUDIES (LONDON. 1981). **3000**

0261-4103 *See* INFORMATION AGE. **1226**

0261-4154 *See* ISSUES IN SOCIAL WORK EDUCATION / ASSOCIATION OF TEACHERS IN SOCIAL WORK EDUCATION. **5291**

0261-4189 *See* EMBO JOURNAL. **454**

0261-4286 *See* JOURNAL OF WORLD FOREST RESOURCE MANAGEMENT. **2386**

0261-4294 *See* GIFTED EDUCATION INTERNATIONAL. **1879**

0261-4316 *See* CATHOLIC ARCHIVES : THE JOURNAL OF THE CATHOLIC ARCHIVES SOCIETY. **5025**

0261-4332 *See* ARCHAEOLOGICAL REVIEW FROM CAMBRIDGE. **257**

0261-4340 *See* ITALIANIST. **3397**

0261-4367 *See* LEISURE STUDIES. **4852**

ISSN Index

0261-4413 See INTERNATIONAL AGRICULTURAL DEVELOPMENT (CROWBOROUGH, EAST SUSSEX). 96

0261-4448 See LANGUAGE TEACHING. 3336

0261-4472 See AFTERIMAGE (LONDON, ENGLAND). 4062

0261-4553 See ATPASES. 3553

0261-4596 See BLOOD TRANSFUSION. 3795

0261-4707 See HIGH PERFORMANCE LIQUID CHROMATOGRAPHY SHEFFIELD. 1011

0261-4928 See SMOOTH MUSCLE. 3807

0261-4952 See INVERTEBRATE NEUROBIOLOGY. 3590

0261-4960 See MONOCLONAL ANTIBODIES. 3675

0261-4979 See RECOMBINANT DNA. 551

0261-4995 See INTESTINAL FUNCTION. 3746

0261-507X See OMNIBUS (LONDON). 1770

0261-510X See BRITISH JOURNAL OF DEVELOPMENTAL PSYCHOLOGY, THE. 4578

0261-5142 See MICRO DECISION. 1269

0261-5169 See PIMS MEDIA DIRECTORY. 763

0261-5177 See TOURISM MANAGEMENT (1982). 888

0261-5282 See THEATRE RECORD. 5371

0261-5363 See NEW BOOKBINDER, THE. 4830

0261-5479 See SOCIAL WORK EDUCATION. 5309

0261-5487 See IRPI. INTERNATIONAL REINFORCED PLASTICS INDUSTRY. 4455

0261-5568 See RESEARCH HIGHLIGHTS IN SOCIAL WORK. 5255

0261-5606 See JOURNAL OF INTERNATIONAL MONEY AND FINANCE. 795

0261-5614 See CLINICAL NUTRITION. 4188

0261-5681 See WEST SURREY FAMILY HISTORY SOCIETY RECORD SERIES. 2633

0261-572X See GRAMPIAN DIRECTORY. 1926

0261-5746 See PAINT & RESIN. 4224

0261-586X See FORT. 4044

0261-6661 See CBI NEWS. 5093

0261-6777 See OCEAN VOICE. 4181

0261-6823 See AA FILES. 287

0261-6904 See BIOTECHNOLOGY BULLETIN. 3688

0261-6939 See 2 D DRAMA, DANCE. 383

0261-7005 See REPORT OF THE COUNCIL FOR THE YEAR ... / SCIENCE AND ENGINEERING RESEARCH COUNCIL. 5145

0261-7021 See PAEDIATRIC CARDIOLOGY. 3907

0261-7080 See BULLETIN OF THE FRIENDS OF JADE, THE. 370

0261-7374 See EUROPEAN ENERGY PROFILE. 1635

0261-8028 See JOURNAL OF MATERIALS SCIENCE LETTERS. 2103

0261-8214 See EUROPEAN POWER NEWS. 1944

0261-8412 See NEUROMUSCULAR DISEASES. 3841

0261-8788 See RECENT ADVANCES IN UROLOGY/ANDROLOGY. 3992

0261-9180 See MATERIALS AT HIGH TEMPERATURES. 2105

0261-9261 See CIVIL JUSTICE QUARTERLY. 3089

0261-927X See JOURNAL OF LANGUAGE AND SOCIAL PSYCHOLOGY. 3290

0261-9288 See IMMIGRANTS & MINORITIES. 1919

0261-9768 See EUROPEAN JOURNAL OF TEACHER EDUCATION. 1894

0261-989X See LIFE SUPPORT SYSTEMS. 3604

0261-9997 See MENTAL HANDICAP : JOURNAL OF THE BRITISH INSTITUTE OF MENTAL HANDICAP. 5296

0262-0200 See MATERNAL & CHILD HEALTH (RICHMOND, SURREY). 3738

0262-0421 See HM CUSTOM AND EXCISE TARIFF AMENDMENT. 4731

0262-0448 See HELICOPTER WORLD (LONDON, 1982). 23

0262-0456 See EAST EUROPEAN MARKETS. 897

0262-0634 See MONTHLY BULLETIN OF INDICES PRICE ADJUSTMENT FORMULAE FOR CONSTRUCTION CONTRACTS. 633

0262-0642 See MONTHLY BULLETIN OF INDICES PRICE ADJUSTMENT FORMULAE FOR CONSTRUCTION CONTRACTS. 633

0262-0669 See TURF MANAGEMENT. 2433

0262-0820 See FISH FARMING INTERNATIONAL. 2301

0262-0855 See INTERNATIONAL DEVELOPMENT ABSTRACTS. 2913

0262-0898 See CLINICAL & EXPERIMENTAL METASTASIS. 3815

0262-1037 See CREATIVE REVIEW LONDON. 1980. 922

0262-1495 See LAW SOCIETY'S GAZETTE. 2997

0262-155X See DEVELOPMENTS IN POLYMER STABILISATION. 4454

0262-1576 See DEVELOPMENTS IN ADHESIVES. 2012

0262-1592 See DEVELOPMENTS IN RUBBER AND RUBBER COMPOSITES. 5075

0262-1606 See DEVELOPMENTS IN FOOD COLOURS... . 2333

0262-1630 See PORTS / ASSOCIATED BRITISH PORTS. 5454

0262-1711 See JOURNAL OF MANAGEMENT DEVELOPMENT, THE. 943

0262-1762 See WORLD PUMPS. 2132

0262-1797 See IEE CONTROL ENGINEERING SERIES. 2057

0262-219X See ARCHITECTURAL PRESERVATION AND NEW DESIGN IN CONSERVATION. 289

0262-2238 See ANIMAL PHARM. 5502

0262-2262 See SPECIALTY CHEMICALS (REDHILL). 993

0262-2580 See SNACK FOOD INTERNATIONAL. 936

0262-2734 See WHAT'S NEW IN COMPUTING. 1207

0262-2750 See FRENCH STUDIES BULLETIN. 3389

0262-2955 See LABORATORY MICROCOMPUTER. 1268

0262-3145 See HOSPITAL DOCTOR. 3584

0262-317X See INTERNATIONAL AUTO INDUSTRY NEWSLETTER. 5417

0262-3226 See INDUSTRIAL SAFETY DATA FILE. 2863

0262-3234 See ANTHONY & BERRYMAN'S MAGISTRATES' COURT GUIDE. 2935

0262-3269 See HOUSEHOLD FISH CONSUMPTION IN GREAT BRITAIN. 2305

0262-3617 See EVERYDAY ELECTRONICS. 2054

0262-3781 See BRIEFING PAPER ON SOUTHERN AFRICA / INTERNATIONAL DEFENCE & AID FUND. 4038

0262-401X See BRITISH TELECOMMUNICATIONS ENGINEERING. 1150

0262-4079 See NEW SCIENTIST (1971). 5132

0262-4087 See EDUCATION SECTION REVIEW - BRITISH PSYCHOLOGICAL SOCIETY. 4585

0262-4125 See TRUE STORY LONDON. 2494

0262-415X See TRUE ROMANCES. 5075

0262-4168 See LIQUID CHROMATOGRAPHY MASS SPECTROMETRY ABSTRACTS. 984

0262-4230 See MANUFACTURING CHEMIST (LONDON: 1981). 985

0262-4273 See MODERN MEDICINE (BECKENHAM). 3617

0262-4389 See SCOTTISH ARCHAEOLOGICAL REVIEW : SAR. 282

0262-4397 See TTG. TRAVEL TRADE GAZETTE. U.K. AND IRELAND. 5498

0262-4524 See TEMENOS. 332

0262-4591 See SEARCHLIGHT (LONDON). 5257

0262-480X See SMALL SHIPS. 5457

0262-4842 See JOURNAL OF ONE-NAME STUDIES, THE. 2455

0262-4893 See CELLULAR POLYMERS. 4454

0262-4966 See CHURCHSCAPE. 295

0262-5067 See ECONOMIC PROGRESS REPORT. 1557

0262-5091 See NUCLEAR ENGINEER, THE. 2156

0262-5253 See OXFORD JOURNAL OF ARCHAEOLOGY. 277

0262-5318 See DERWENT BIOTECHNOLOGY ABSTRACTS. 3691

0262-5334 See COMMERCIAL AND INDUSTRIAL FLOORSPACE STATISTICS, WALES. 5325

0262-5377 See PSYCHIATRY IN PRACTICE. 3934

0262-5504 See DERMATOLOGY IN PRACTICE (LONDON). 3719

0262-5547 See CARDIOLOGY IN PRACTICE. 3701

0262-5601 See MATCH WEEKLY. 1298

0262-5628 See DIRT BIKE RIDER. 4081

0262-5644 See STUDIES ON WOMEN ABSTRACTS. 5572

0262-5709 See TTG. TRAVEL TRADE GAZETTE. EUROPA. 5497

0262-5814 See HORSE & PONY. 2799

0262-5849 See PPM. PET PRODUCT MARKETING. 4287

0262-5865 See CHIEF EXECUTIVE. 863

0262-5881 See CHEMIST & DRUGGIST DIRECTORY. 4296

0262-5938 See COFFEE & COCOA INTERNATIONAL. 2366

0262-6004 See PROCEEDINGS OF THE SUFFOLK INSTITUTE OF ARCHAEOLOGY AND HISTORY. 279

0262-6330 See PROGRESS IN MIGRAINE RESEARCH. 3844

0262-642X See WELDING REVIEW INTERNATIONAL. 4029

0262-6438 See PROCESS AND CHEMICAL ENGINEERING. 2006

0262-6608 See WILTSHIRE ARCHAEOLOGICAL AND NATURAL HISTORY MAGAZINE (1982). 285

0262-6624 See KERRANG!. 1298

0262-6632 See TECHNICAL INFORMATION SERVICE - CHARTERED INSTITUTE BUILDING. 630

0262-6667 See HYDROLOGICAL SCIENCES JOURNAL. 1415

0262-6950 See FLYPAST. 21

0262-6969 See INTERNATIONAL FINANCIAL LAW REVIEW. 3100

0262-7027 See SPECIAL PUBLICATION ... OF THE BRITISH ECOLOGICAL SOCIETY,. 2221

0262-7043 See RESPIRATORY DISEASE IN PRACTICE. 3951

0262-7108 See ENERGY ECONOMIST. 1940

0262-7183 See BIOMASS BULLETIN. 1933

0262-7280 See SOUTH ASIA RESEARCH. 2854

0262-7299 See ABORTION REVIEW. 3755

0262-7612 See ENLIGHTENMENT AND DISSENT. 4473

0262-7701 See CAPTIVE INSURANCE COMPANY REVIEW. 2877

0262-7841 See LIBRARY TECHNOLOGY NEWS LTN. 3227

0262-7922 See END PAPERS. 4473

0262-7965 See MINING DIRECTORY, THE. 2145

0262-7981 See FIRE SURVEYOR. 2290

0262-8015 See DITCHLEY NEWSLETTER, THE. 5198

0262-8104 See WATERLINES. 5548

0262-821X See JOURNAL OF MICROPALEONTOLOGY. 4227

0262-8260 See MUSIC & AUTOMATA. 4132

0262-8279 See ELECTRIC LIVING JOURNAL : ELECTRICAL ASSOCIATION FOR WOMEN. 2811

0262-8325 See WELSH AGRICULTURAL STATISTICS / WELSH OFFICE / YSTADEGAU AMAETHYDDOL CYMRU / Y SWYDDFA GYMREIG. 145

0262-8333 See WELSH HOUSING STATISTICS / WELSH OFFICE / YSTADEGAU TAI CYMRU / Y SWYDDFA GYMREIG. 2839

0262-8732 See BRISTOL ADVANCES IN THERAPEUTICS. 3558

0262-8740 See IMMUNOASSAY. SUPPLEMENT. 3670

0262-8759 See COMMUNITY OUTLOOK. 3854

0262-8767 See BRITISH JOURNAL OF CLINICAL PRACTICE. SYMPOSIUM SUPPLEMENT. 3559

0262-8783 See PRACTICAL METHODS IN CLINICAL IMMUNOLOGY SERIES. 3675

0262-8805 See RAILPOWER. 5435

0262-8856 See IMAGE AND VISION COMPUTING. 1233

0262-9224 See TENNIS LONDON. 1981. 4925

0262-9240 See TRADING LAW. 3136

0262-9291 See DISCUSSION PAPERS IN GEOLINGUISTICS. 2559

0262-9534 See PUBLIC RELATIONS YEAR BOOK. 765

0262-9615 See FISH FARMER INTERNATIONAL FILE. 2301

0262-9798 See YOUTH AND POLICY. 1072

0262-9836 See SELECTED ABSTRACTS ON OCCUPATIONAL DISEASES. 2872

0262-9909 See WATERBULLETIN. 5548

0262-995X See CANTERBURY AND YORK SOCIETY (SERIES). 5229

0263-0257 See CIVIL ENGINEERING SYSTEMS. 2021

0263-0281 See ANNUAL REPORT / HORTICULTURE RESEARCH INTERNATIONAL. 2409

0263-0338 See AFRICAN ARCHAEOLOGICAL REVIEW, THE. 253

0263-0346 See LASER AND PARTICLE BEAMS. 4437

0263-0850 See CLASSIC MOTOR CYCLE, THE. 5379

0263-0869 See MULTICULTURAL TEACHING TO COMBAT RACISM IN SCHOOL AND COMMUNITY. 1901

0263-0885 See YOUR COMPUTER. 1273

0263-0915 See WIND ENGINEERING ABSTRACTS. 2001

0263-0923 See JOURNAL OF LOW FREQUENCY NOISE AND VIBRATION. 2234

0263-1008 See APPAREL INTERNATIONAL. 1081

0263-1016 See MIDDLE EAST HEALTH (1981). 3616

0263-1024 See OILMAN. NEWSLETTER. 4270

0263-1180 See WOOD & EQUIPMENT NEWS + WOODWORKING MATERIALS. 2405

0263-1210 See FACE (LONDON, ENGLAND). 4117

0263-1377 See RETAIL AUTOMATION. 707

0263-1474 See ELECTRONIC PRODUCT DESIGN. 2048

0263-1512 See ANAESTHESIA (EDINBURGH). 3680

0263-1776 See WELLSIAN (EDWALTON, NOTTINGHAMSHIRE : 1976). 3452

0263-1784 See WINDOW INDUSTRIES. 2595

0263-2098 See WELFARE RIGHTS BULLETIN. 5314

0263-211X See EDUCATIONAL MANAGEMENT & ADMINISTRATION : JOURNAL OF THE BRITISH EDUCATIONAL MANAGEMENT AND ADMINISTRATION SOCIETY. 1863

0263-2136 See FAMILY PRACTICE. 3737

0263-2160 See LITIGATION (CHICHESTER, ENGLAND). 3003

0263-2217 See INTERNATIONAL MEAT MARKET REVIEW. 213

0263-2241 See MEASUREMENT : JOURNAL OF THE INTERNATIONAL MEASUREMENT CONFEDERATION. 4031

0263-2306 See NEWS OF HYMNODY. 4981

0263-2373 See EUROPEAN MANAGEMENT JOURNAL. 867

0263-2535 See ANNUAL REPORT OF THE OXFORD ORTHOPAEDIC ENGINEERING CENTRE. 3685

0263-2543 See BLITZ LONDON. 316

0263-2659 See CURRENT MEDICAL LITERATURE. GASTROENTEROLOGY / THE ROYAL SOCIETY OF MEDICINE. 3743

0263-2667 See CHILDREN LOOKED AFTER BY LOCAL AUTHORITIES IN WALES / WELSH OFFICE / PLANT Y GOFELIR AM DANYNT GAN AWDURDODAU LLEOL CYMRU / Y SWYDDFA GYMREIG. 5278

0263-2764 See THEORY, CULTURE & SOCIETY. 5224

0263-2772 See FACILITIES (BRADFORD, WEST YORKSHIRE, ENGLAND). 3478

0263-2985 See CAPITAL EXPENDITURE AND DEBT FINANCING STATISTICS / CIPFA, STATISTICAL INFORMATION SERVICE. 4697

0263-3167 See BOILING POINT. 5089

0263-323X See JOURNAL OF LAW AND SOCIETY. 2988

0263-3248 See COMPUTERS IN GENEALOGY. 1266

0263-3507 See ST. THOMAS'S HOSPITAL GAZETTE (1981). 3792

0263-3523 See BRITISH ECONOMY SURVEY. 1465

0263-3639 See HOUSE PRICES. 4838

0263-3728 See DEVELOPMENTS IN FOOD PRESERVATIVES. 2333

0263-3736 See DEVELOPMENTS IN WATER TREATMENT. 5532

0263-3752 See DEVELOPMENTS IN FOOD PACKAGING. 4218

0263-3957 See POLITICS (MANCHESTER (GREATER MANCHESTER)). 4491

0263-4236 See CARPET & FLOORCOVERINGS REVIEW. 5348

0263-4368 See INTERNATIONAL JOURNAL OF REFRACTORY METALS & HARD MATERIALS. 4004

0263-4376 See DEVELOPMENTS IN FOOD PRESERVATION. 2333

0263-4422 See CLINICAL SURGERY INTERNATIONAL. 3962

0263-4503 See MARKETING INTELLIGENCE & PLANNING. 931

0263-4678 See MANAGEMENT IN GOVERNMENT (LONDON, ENGLAND). 4704

0263-4708 See DEVELOPMENTS IN FOOD PROTEINS. 2333

0263-4759 See ENGINEERING COMPUTERS. 1184

0263-4848 See CLINICAL ALLERGY. SUPPLEMENT. 3667

0263-4929 See JOURNAL OF METAMORPHIC GEOLOGY. 1458

0263-4937 See CENTRAL ASIAN SURVEY. 2648

0263-497X See INK & PRINT INTERNATIONAL. 4566

0263-497X See INK & PRINT. 4566

0263-5046 See FIRST BREAK. 1405

0263-5054 See ABERDEEN PETROLEUM REPORT. 4249

0263-5062 See DEFENCE HELICOPTER WORLD. 17

0263-5070 See OIL & GAS (OXFORD, OXFORDSHIRE). 3022

0263-5143 See RESEARCH IN SCIENCE & TECHNOLOGICAL EDUCATION. 5147

0263-5178 See TECHNICAL BULLETIN (EGGS AUTHORITY). 5162

0263-5232 See BULLETIN OF THE HEGEL SOCIETY OF GREAT BRITAIN, THE. 4343

0263-5372 See INFORME LATNOAMERICANO. 2489

0263-5429 See NEW GENERATION. 4555

0263-5488 See INTERNATIONAL TAX-FREE TRADER. BUYERS GUIDE & DIRECTORY. 4733

0263-550X See BBC ENGLISH. 3268

0263-5534 See AQUALINE ABSTRACTS. 2002

0263-5577 See INDUSTRIAL MANAGEMENT & DATA SYSTEMS. 1259

0263-5712 See 1851 CENSUS INDEX SERIES. 2436

0263-5720 See PC USER (LONDON, ENGLAND). 1271

0263-5747 See ROBOTICA. 1216

0263-5852 See IFF TELECOMMUNICATIONS SERIES. 1156

0263-5879 See INTERNATIONAL TEXTILE CALENDAR / TEXTILE INSTITUTE. 5352

0263-5909 See JOURNAL OF COMMUNITY EDUCATION. 1756

0263-5917 See CRITICAL REPORTS ON APPLIED CHEMISTRY. 973

0263-5933 See TRANSACTIONS OF THE ROYAL SOCIETY OF EDINBURGH. EARTH SCIENCES. 1361

0263-6050 See WORLD CEMENT. 631

0263-6115 See JOURNAL OF THE AUSTRALIAN MATHEMATICAL SOCIETY. SERIES A : PURE MATHEMATICS AND STATISTICS. 3515

0263-6131 See WOOL RECORD (BRADFORD, WEST YORKSHIRE : 1982). 5360

0263-6174 See ADSORPTION SCIENCE & TECHNOLOGY. 2007

0263-6190 See CAD/CAM DIGEST. 1231

0263-6204 See DEVELOPMENTS IN CRYSTALLINE POLYMERS. 1032

0263-6263 See TRUCK & BUS BUILDER. 3489

0263-6271 See SCIENCE IN PARLIAMENT. 5152

0263-6344 See THEATRE IRELAND. 5370

0263-6352 See JOURNAL OF HYPERTENSION. 3707

0263-6484 See CELL BIOCHEMISTRY AND FUNCTION. 484

0263-6522 See INTEGRATED CIRCUITS INTERNATIONAL. 2065

0263-6530 See DEC USER. 1182

0263-662X See ECUM BULLETIN. 4955

0263-6697 See COMPASS SPORT/THE ORIENTEER. 4891

0263-6751 See ANGLO-SAXON ENGLAND. 2673

0263-676X See THEMES IN DRAMA. 389

0263-6778 See ABSTRACTS IN BIOCOMMERCE. 3654

0263-6786 See VOX EVANGELICA. 5008

0263-6794 See TUBE INTERNATIONAL. 4023

0263-6824 See ACOLAM NEWSLETTER / STANDING CONFERENCE OF NATIONAL AND UNIVERSITY LIBRARIES, ADVISORY COMMITTEE ON LATIN AMERICAN MATERIALS. 3187

0263-7065 See ECONOMIC INDICATORS, FORECASTS FOR COMPANY PLANNING. 1483

0263-7103 See BRITISH JOURNAL OF RHEUMATOLOGY. 3803

0263-7197 See HMSO MONTHLY CATALOGUE. 4654

0263-7200 See ANNUAL REPORT / SCOTTISH CROP RESEARCH INSTITUTE. 163

0263-7243 See CARDIOVASCULAR PHARMACOLOGY. 3701

0263-7251 See CELL CYCLE. 533

0263-726X See CELL DIFFERENTIATION SHEFFIELD. 533

0263-7294 See DIABETES MELLITUS. 3571

0263-7383 See ANNALES BENJAMIN CONSTANT. 3361

0263-743X See DAILY LIST / HMSO BOOKS. 4697

0263-7472 See PROPERTY MANAGEMENT. (LONDON). 4843

0263-7499 See RENT REVIEW & LEASE RENEWAL. 4846

0263-7553 See PICTURE HOUSE. 4076

0263-7561 See BEEBUG. 1171

0263-760X See CAVE SCIENCE (1982). 1404

0263-7618 See INTERNATIONAL MARINE SAFETY DIRECTORY. 4177

0263-7677 See SPINK NUMISMATIC CIRCULAR. 2783

0263-7707 See MEDAL LONDON. 2781

0263-774X See ENVIRONMENT AND PLANNING. C, GOVERNMENT & POLICY. 4646

0263-7758 See ENVIRONMENT AND PLANNING. D, SOCIETY & SPACE. 5199

0263-7855 See JOURNAL OF MOLECULAR GRAPHICS. 1234

0263-7863 See INTERNATIONAL JOURNAL OF PROJECT MANAGEMENT. 1980

0263-788x See PROCEEDINGS OF THE INSTITUTION OF CIVIL ENGINEERS, TRANSPORT. **2029**

0263-788x See PROCEEDINGS OF THE INSTITUTION OF CIVIL ENGINEERS. STRUCTURES AND BUILDINGS. **2029**

0263-7944 See SHIPCARE & MARITIME MANAGEMENT. **5456**

0263-7960 See BUILT ENVIRONMENT (LONDON, 1978). **2816**

0263-7995 See GILBERT & SULLIVAN NEWS. **385**

0263-8118 See ADVERTISING FORECAST, THE. **754**

0263-8223 See COMPOSITE STRUCTURES. **2101**

0263-8231 See THIN-WALLED STRUCTURES. **2032**

0263-8355 See RUTHERFORD APPLETON LABORATORY. **5149**

0263-8371 See CHANGES : AN INTERNATIONAL JOURNAL OF PSYCHOLOGY AND PSYCHOTHERAPY. **4580**

0263-841X See IN PRACTICE (LONDON 1979). **5511**

0263-8568 See MEDICAL LABORATORY SCIENTIFIC OFFICERS REGISTER, THE. **3610**

0263-8614 See ITE SYMPOSIUM. **2217**

0263-8630 See STUDIES IN LAW AND PRACTICE FOR HEALTH SERVICE MANAGEMENT. **3060**

0263-8762 See CHEMICAL ENGINEERING RESEARCH & DESIGN. **2010**

0263-8878 See MAIL ON SUNDAY. **5812**

0263-9106 See WHICH CAMERA?. **4378**

0263-9114 See EUROPEAN JOURNAL OF CHIROPRACTIC. **3575**

0263-9149 See PORT STATISTICS. **5401**

0263-9254 See CURRENT RESEARCH IN LIBRARY & INFORMATION SCIENCE. **3205**

0263-9319 See SURGERY (OXFORD). **3975**

0263-9335 See PROCEEDINGS OF THE NORTH OF ENGLAND SOILS DISCUSSION GROUP. **183**

0263-9424 See CAMBRIDGE STUDIES IN MATHEMATICAL BIOLOGY. **450**

0263-9459 See CRUCIFERAE NEWSLETTER. **77**

0263-9467 See BIRA JOURNAL. **4633**

0263-9475 See CIRCA (BELFAST, NORTHERN IRELAND). **347**

0263-9513 See MINERALOGICAL SOCIETY BULLETIN. **1441**

0263-9653 See ROAD ACCIDENTS, WALES. **5443**

0263-967X See BSAP OCCASIONAL PUBLICATION. **5506**

0263-9815 See BP STATISTICAL REVIEW OF WORLD ENERGY. **1961**

0263-9904 See ROMANCE STUDIES : A JOURNAL OF THE UNIVERSITY OF WALES. **1846**

0263-9947 See VAT INTELLIGENCE. **717**

0264-0198 See SCOTTISH LANGUAGE. **3319**

0264-0236 See CONCRETE PLANT AND PRODUCTION. **608**

0264-0325 See JOURNAL OF THE ROYAL SOCIETY OF HEALTH. **4787**

0264-0414 See JOURNAL OF SPORTS SCIENCES. **4902**

0264-0473 See ELECTRONIC LIBRARY. **3209**

0264-049X See CHARTERED SURVEYOR WEEKLY. **4835**

0264-0732 See WORLD LEASING YEARBOOK. **1631**

0264-0767 See ENDOCRINOLOGY AND METABOLISM SERIES. **3729**

0264-0775 See FLUID ABSTRACTS. CIVIL ENGINEERING. **2004**

0264-0821 See JOURNAL OF PROPERTY RESEARCH. **4839**

0264-083X See WORLD OF INTERIORS, THE. **2904**

0264-0872 See WORLD VIEW (NEW YORK, N.Y.). **2633**

0264-0937 See TREASURER. **1524**

0264-1097 See LAW REPORTS. CHANCERY DIVISION (1972). **2996**

0264-1119 See LAW REPORTS. FAMILY DIVISION. **3121**

0264-1135 See LAW REPORTS. HOUSE OF LORDS. **2996**

0264-1275 See MATERIALS & DESIGN. **2104**

0264-1410 See MEAD JOHNSON ADVANCES IN THERAPEUTICS. **3606**

0264-1615 See INTERLENDING & DOCUMENT SUPPLY. **3217**

0264-1801 See PSYCHOLOGICAL MEDICINE. MONOGRAPH SUPPLEMENT. **4611**

0264-2050 See LOCAL GOVERNMENT POLICY MAKING. **4663**

0264-2069 See SERVICE INDUSTRIES JOURNAL, THE. **1626**

0264-2190 See BULLETIN OF THE SOCIETY FOR ITALIAN STUDIES. **3271**

0264-2247 See INTERNATIONAL PHARMACEUTICAL TECHNOLOGY & PRODUCT MANUFACTURE ABSTRACTS. **4309**

0264-2417 See RECENT ADVANCES IN PERINATAL MEDICINE. **3767**

0264-2425 See READING IN A FOREIGN LANGUAGE. **3314**

0264-2506 See FINISHING. **4224**

0264-2522 See SCOTT NEWSLETTER, THE. **3434**

0264-2557 See AMATEUR RADIO (BICESTER). **1126**

0264-259X See AQUANAUT. **1351**

0264-2603 See NEW SERVICE STATION AND PARTS BUYER. **699**

0264-2670 See DEVELOPMENTS IN FOOD MICROBIOLOGY. **562**

0264-2689 See BRITISH ASSOCIATION FOR PSYCHOPHARMACOLOGY MONOGRAPH. **3922**

0264-2697 See MARICHEM. **5386**

0264-2751 See CITIES (LONDON, ENGLAND). **2817**

0264-2778 See PERMANENT REVOLUTION (LONDON, ENGLAND : 1983). **1701**

0264-2786 See MEDIEVAL ENGLISH THEATRE MODERN SPELLING TEXTS. **3301**

0264-2824 See PARLIAMENTARY HISTORY : A YEARBOOK. **4672**

0264-2867 See LATIN AMERICAN SPECIAL REPORTS. **2512**

0264-2867 See LATIN AMERICAN SPECIAL REPORTS. **2552**

0264-2875 See DANCE RESEARCH. **1312**

0264-3014 See TOPICAL REVIEWS IN VASCULAR SURGERY. **3976**

0264-3022 See DEVELOPMENTS IN ORIENTED POLYMERS. **1041**

0264-3081 See RECENT ADVANCES IN RENAL MEDICINE. **3992**

0264-3138 See CASTME JOURNAL. **1890**

0264-3294 See COGNITIVE NEUROPSYCHOLOGY. **4581**

0264-3340 See ASIAN ELECTRICITY. **2036**

0264-3375 See JOURNAL OF SEMI-CUSTOM ICS. **2069**

0264-3391 See CURRENT BIOTECHNOLOGY. **3656**

0264-3405 See BRITISH CACTUS & SUCCULENT JOURNAL. **504**

0264-3499 See OCCASIONAL PAPERS SERIES - DEPARTMENT OF GEOGRAPHY, UNIVERSITY OF GLASGOW. **2571**

0264-3596 See INTERZONE. **3397**

0264-3693 See BOOKPLATE JOURNAL, THE. **4825**

0264-3707 See JOURNAL OF GEODYNAMICS. **1384**

0264-3723 See J.P. WEEKLY LAW DIGEST, THE. **2986**

0264-3731 See JUSTICE OF THE PEACE REPORTS (CHICHESTER, WEST SUSSEX). **2991**

0264-3758 See JOURNAL OF APPLIED PHILOSOPHY. **4350**

0264-3812 See JAPANSCAN. FOOD SCIENCE AND THE FOOD INDUSTRY. **2345**

0264-3847 See MICRO-SCOPE AYLESBURY. **1195**

0264-3944 See PASTORAL CARE IN EDUCATION. **1772**

0264-410X See VACCINE. **3649**

0264-4185 See BRITISH ASTRONOMICAL ASSOCIATION CIRCULAR. **393**

0264-4193 See COMPUTER SYSTEMS. **1246**

0264-441X See WHAT MICRO?. **1273**

0264-4509 See COMMUNICATE (HIGH WYCOMBE). **1151**

0264-4517 See CURRENT ISSUES IN EUROPEAN SOCIAL PSYCHOLOGY. **4584**

0264-4568 See TELECOMMUNICATIONS NEWS. **1165**

0264-4584 See ARCHIMEDES WORLD. **1171**

0264-4703 See PRECISION TOOLMAKER. **2125**

0264-4754 See ANIMAL TECHNOLOGY. **5503**

0264-4770 See TEXAS PERSONAL INJURY LAW REPORTER. **3064**

0264-4827 See FIRE DIRECTORY, THE. **2289**

0264-4835 See DREDGING + PORT CONSTRUCTION. SERIES II. **613**

0264-4924 See ARCHIVES OF EMERGENCY MEDICINE. **3723**

0264-5041 See EUROPEAN TABLEWARE BUYERS GUIDE. **2589**

0264-5130 See FISHERIES RESEARCH DATA REPORT. **2302**

0264-5157 See JOURNAL OF THE TILES & ARCHITECTURAL CERAMICS SOCIETY. **302**

0264-519X See RESEARCH, POLICY AND PLANNING : THE JOURNAL OF THE SOCIAL SERVICES RESEARCH GROUP. **5215**

0264-5254 See ANGLO-SAXON STUDIES IN ARCHAEOLOGY AND HISTORY. **254**

0264-5319 See FOUNDRY YEAR BOOK. **4002**

0264-5424 See PRINT BUYER (1982). **4568**

0264-5475 See DISABILITY NEWS. **4387**

0264-5491 See OXFORD AGRARIAN STUDIES. **118**

0264-5564 See VINAVER STUDIES IN FRENCH. **3451**

0264-5769 See FRENCH RAILWAY REVIEW. **5431**

0264-5807 See NEWSLETTER OF THE SOCIETY FOR ENVIRONMENTAL THERAPY. **2178**

0264-5904 See LONDON ENVIRONMENTAL BULLETIN. **2177**

0264-5947 See MEMBERS DIRECTORY / THE INSTITUTION OF ENVIRONMENTAL HEALTH OFFICERS. **4790**

0264-598X See CHRISTIAN ARENA. **4944**

0264-6021 See BIOCHEMICAL JOURNAL (LONDON. 1984). **481**

0264-6196 See BRITISH JOURNAL OF VISUAL IMPAIRMENT, THE. **4385**

0264-6307 See TEXAS INSURANCE LAW REPORTER. **3064**

0264-6315 See GREATER LONDON INTELLIGENCE JOURNAL. **2823**

0264-6404 See CLINICIAN (MACCLESFIELD, ENGLAND). **4297**

0264-6412 See RAD HARLOW. **3944**

0264-6420 See MARITIME GUIDE / LLOYD'S REGISTER OF SHIPPING. **5452**

0264-6501 See UNCENSORED POLAND NEWS BULLETIN / INFORMATION CENTRE FOR POLISH AFFAIRS (U.K.), STUDIUM SPRAW POLSKICH (WLK. BRYTANIA). **2714**

0264-6544 See PROBATION SERVICE STATISTICS ... ESTIMATES. **3082**

0264-6552 See ADMINISTRATION OF JUSTICE STATISTICS ... ESTIMATES. **3078**

0264-6811 See JOURNAL OF ENERGY & NATURAL RESOURCES LAW. **2987**

0264-6838 See JOURNAL OF REPRODUCTIVE AND INFANT PSYCHOLOGY. **3764**

0264-6854 See CONSTRUCTION COMPUTING. **1180**

0264-6900 See CIRCULATION ET METABOLISME DU CERVEAU. **3564**

0264-7052 See EMPLOYMENT GAZETTE. **1666**

0264-7060 See FAN. FEMINIST ARTS NEWS. **320**

ISSN Index

0264-7133 *See* TABLE (LONDON. 1953). **4689**
0264-7141 *See* INSCAPE LONDON. **353**
0264-715X *See* CONVERTING TODAY. **2039**
0264-7176 *See* PROCESS ENGINEERING INDEX. **2016**
0264-729X *See* FIZIKA I KHIMIIA OBRABOTKI MATERIALOV. **4403**
0264-7303 *See* METALLIC MATERIALS. **4009**
0264-732X *See* LITHOWEEK. **4566**
0264-7362 *See* EUROPEAN ACCESS. **4473**
0264-7397 *See* RECENT ADVANCES IN DIABETES. **3733**
0264-7400 *See* RECENT ADVANCES IN EPILEPSY. **3844**
0264-7478 *See* GASTROENTEROLOGY IN PRACTICE. **3745**
0264-7532 *See* RECENT ADVANCES IN HEPATOLOGY. **3801**
0264-763X *See* TROPICAL DEVELOPMENT AND RESEARCH INSTITUTE (SERIES G). **142**
0264-7753 *See* HIGH PERFORMANCE PLASTICS. **4455**
0264-7834 See CAPITAL TAXES NEWS AND REPORTS. **4717**
0264-7982 *See* DEVELOPMENTS IN IONIC POLYMERS. **1041**
0264-8067 *See* MODERN AFRICA. **696**
0264-8121 *See* NEW LAW FOR SURVEYORS. **4842**
0264-8148 *See* DESIGNERS' JOURNAL. **297**
0264-8164 *See* ASIAN BUILDING & CONSTRUCTION. **292**
0264-8172 *See* MARINE AND PETROLEUM GEOLOGY. **1386**
0264-8334 *See* PARAGRAPH (MODERN CRITICAL THEORY GROUP). **3309**
0264-8377 *See* LAND USE POLICY. **1502**
0264-8393 *See* DEVELOPMENTS IN BLOCK COPOLYMERS. **1041**
0264-8407 *See* DEVELOPMENTS IN DAIRY CHEMISTRY. **194**
0264-8423 *See* ADVANCES IN LASER SPECTROSCOPY (LONDON, ENG.). **4432**
0264-8431 *See* REVIEWS IN CHEMICAL ENGINEERING. **2017**
0264-844X *See* DEVELOPMENTS IN GEOPHYSICAL EXPLORATION METHODS. **1404**
0264-8490 *See* ASIAN TIMES. **2485**
0264-8563 *See* HOUSEWARES TONBRIDGE. **2812**
0264-861X *See* OXFORD SURVEYS OF PLANT MOLECULAR AND CELL BIOLOGY. **584**
0264-8709 *See* REPORT / INSTITUTE OF HYDROLOGY. **1417**
0264-8717 *See* SCOLAG : SCOTTISH LEGAL ACTION GROUP BULLETIN. **3046**
0264-8725 *See* BIOTECHNOLOGY & GENETIC ENGINEERING REVIEWS. **3688**
0264-8733 *See* PORT CONSTRUCTION AND OCEAN TECHNOLOGY. **624**
0264-8822 *See* COUNTRYSIDE COMMISSION NEWS. **4641**
0264-9047 *See* EUROPEAN ADHESIVES AND SEALANTS. **4223**
0264-9136 *See* BOAT INTERNATIONAL. **592**
0264-9144 *See* HERITAGE SCOTLAND : THE MAGAZINE OF THE NATIONAL TRUST FOR SCOTLAND. **2690**
0264-9160 *See* DANCE THEATRE JOURNAL. **1312**
0264-9187 *See* GEC JOURNAL OF RESEARCH. **1976**
0264-9217 *See* NORTH IRISH ROOTS. **2464**
0264-9241 *See* TECHNICAL GUIDE (QUATERNARY RESEARCH ASSOCIATION (GREAT BRITAIN)). **1399**
0264-9381 *See* CLASSICAL AND QUANTUM GRAVITY. **4400**
0264-9454 *See* THOMAS HARDY ANNUAL (LONDON, ENGLAND). **3446**
0264-9462 *See* FOOD PROCESSING (BROMLEY, LONDON, ENGLAND). **2339**
0264-9624 *See* PHOSPHOLIPIDS. **492**
0264-9640 *See* CHLOROPLASTS. **3563**

0264-9659 *See* LIPOSOMES. **490**
0264-9683 *See* MODUS. **2792**
0264-9691 *See* DOCKLANDS NEWS. **667**
0264-9799 *See* COAL INTERNATIONAL (REDHILL, SURREY, ENGLAND). **1438**
0264-9861 *See* INNOVATION ST. ANDREWS. **1979**
0264-9977 *See* COUNSELLING. **4583**
0264-9993 *See* ECONOMIC MODELLING. **1591**
0265-0002 *See* OILSEEDS. **116**
0265-0029 *See* QUARTERLY DRY BULK MARKET REPORT. **849**
0265-0088 *See* GREEN BOOK BATH. **321**
0265-0215 *See* EUROPEAN JOURNAL OF ANAESTHESIOLOGY. **3682**
0265-0223 *See* INTERNATIONAL ACCOUNTING BULLETIN. **745**
0265-0290 *See* ECONOMIC REVIEW (DEDDINGTON). **1485**
0265-041X *See* LIBRARY CONSERVATION NEWS. **3225**
0265-0460 *See* NATIONAL PARKS TODAY. **4707**
0265-0487 *See* INTERNATIONAL JOURNAL OF ADVERTISING. **760**
0265-0517 *See* BRITISH JOURNAL OF MUSIC EDUCATION : BJME. **4105**
0265-0525 *See* SOCIAL PHILOSOPHY & POLICY. **5219**
0265-0533 *See* JOURNAL OF SOCIAL WORK PRACTICE. **5293**
0265-0568 *See* NATURAL PRODUCT REPORTS. **491**
0265-0584 *See* INDUSTRIAL CORROSION. **2102**
0265-0665 *See* ECONOMIC AFFAIRS (LONDON, ENGLAND). **1482**
0265-0673 *See* PHARMACEUTICAL MEDICINE (BASINGSTOKE). **4320**
0265-072X *See* OXFORD SURVEYS IN EVOLUTIONARY BIOLOGY. **468**
0265-0746 *See* IMA JOURNAL OF MATHEMATICS APPLIED IN MEDICINE AND BIOLOGY. **3508**
0265-0754 *See* IMA JOURNAL OF MATHEMATICAL CONTROL AND INFORMATION. **3508**
0265-086X *See* BRADLEYA. **504**
0265-0886 *See* LATIN AMERICAN TIMES (BOGOTA). **2744**
0265-0916 *See* INTERNATIONAL JOURNAL OF RAPID SOLIDIFICATION. **4004**
0265-1033 See CONTEMPORARY HYPNOSIS : THE JOURNAL OF THE BRITISH SOCIETY OF EXPERIMENTAL AND CLINICAL HYPNOSIS. **2857**
0265-1068 *See* SEVENTEENTH-CENTURY FRENCH STUDIES. **3435**
0265-1211 *See* LAW REPORTS. CHANCERY DIVISION, FAMILY DIVISION. **3121**
0265-1238 *See* LAW REPORTS. INDEX, THE. **2996**
0265-1335 *See* INTERNATIONAL MARKETING REVIEW. **926**
0265-1416 *See* INTERNATIONAL CONSTRUCTION LAW REVIEW, THE. **3129**
0265-1459 *See* CHILDRIGHT. **1062**
0265-1491 *See* ASPECTS OF APPLIED BIOLOGY. **443**
0265-1548 *See* MUSIC WEEK (1983). **4135**
0265-1564 *See* BUSINESS COMPUTING & COMMUNICATIONS. **1172**
0265-1602 *See* EDUCATION AND HEALTH : JOURNAL OF THE HEA SCHOOLS HEALTH EDUCATION UNIT, UNIVERSITY OF EXETER. **1855**
0265-1645 *See* FARMING NEWS LONDON. 1982. **86**
0265-1661 *See* FINANCIAL TECHNOLOGY INTERNATIONAL BULLETIN. **5105**
0265-1866 *See* CLAIMANTS UNDER THREAT. **1225**
0265-203X *See* FOOD ADDITIVES AND CONTAMINANTS. **2335**
0265-2048 *See* JOURNAL OF MICROENCAPSULATION. **4311**
0265-2099 *See* CREDIT MANAGEMENT. **785**

0265-2323 *See* INTERNATIONAL JOURNAL OF BANK MARKETING. **792**
0265-2455 *See* LLOYD'S SHIP MANAGER : LSM. **5452**
0265-2587 *See* ASSIGNATION. **5192**
0265-2609 *See* THEATREPHILE. **5371**
0265-2625 *See* JOURNAL (THIRTIES SOCIETY (LONDON, ENGLAND)). **302**
0265-2730 *See* GUIDE TO POSTGRADUATE DEGREES, DIPLOMAS AND COURSES IN MEDICINE. **3579**
0265-296X *See* WHAT TO BUY FOR BUSINESS. **4214**
0265-2986 *See* IEE TOPICS IN CONTROL SERIES. **2058**
0265-2994 *See* MONOGRAPHS ON CRYOGENICS. **4431**
0265-301X *See* ELECTRONICS MANUFACTURE & TEST. **2049**
0265-3028 *See* HYBRID CIRCUITS : JOURNAL OF THE INTERNATIONAL SOCIETY FOR HYBRID MICROELECTRONICS-UK / INTERNATIONAL SOCIETY FOR HYBRID ELECTRONICS, UNITED KINGDOM. **2056**
0265-3036 See INTERNATIONAL BIODETERIORATION & BIODEGRADATION. **1356**
0265-3214 *See* INDUSTRIAL RESEARCH IN THE UNITED KINGDOM. **5113**
0265-3273 *See* SCOTTISH SLAVONIC REVIEW. **3319**
0265-3389 *See* AMERICAN STUDIES LIBRARY NEWSLETTER. **3189**
0265-3400 *See* PHLS MICROBIOLOGY DIGEST. **568**
0265-3435 *See* ANALYTICAL INSTRUMENT INDUSTRY REPORT. **1597**
0265-3443 *See* NEW MATERIALS/JAPAN. **2107**
0265-3656 *See* BBC WILDLIFE. **2188**
0265-3664 *See* HERITAGE INTERPRETATION. **2690**
0265-3788 *See* TRANSFORMATION (EXETER). **5005**
0265-3818 *See* JANE'S DEFENCE WEEKLY. **4047**
0265-3842 *See* KEW MAGAZINE, THE. **516**
0265-3923 *See* MINERALS HANDBOOK (LONDON, ENGLAND). **2145**
0265-3990 *See* PIPELINES ABSTRACTS : BHRA ABSTRACTS JOURNAL. **2124**
0265-4075 *See* JOURNAL OF SOCIAL AND PERSONAL RELATIONSHIPS. **4601**
0265-4199 *See* LANDSCAPE INSTITUTE YEARBOOK AND DIRECTORY. **302**
0265-4210 *See* LAND AND MINERALS SURVEYING. **2027**
0265-4245 *See* METHODS IN ORGANIC SYNTHESIS. **1012**
0265-427X *See* CARGO CLAIMS ANALYSIS. **3180**
0265-430X *See* URANIUM AND NUCLEAR ENERGY. **1960**
0265-4377 *See* TOPICS IN MOLECULAR AND STRUCTURAL BIOLOGY. **475**
0265-4385 *See* UNIVERSITY COMPUTING : THE BULLETIN OF THE IUCC. **1852**
0265-444X *See* MAURITIAN INTERNATIONAL. **2642**
0265-4458 *See* CONFERENCE & COMMON ROOM. **1733**
0265-4490 *See* DATABASE AND NETWORK JOURNAL. **1253**
0265-4504 *See* COMMUTER WORLD. **16**
0265-4539 *See* SCOTTISH BULLETIN OF EVANGELICAL THEOLOGY, THE. **4995**
0265-4547 *See* EVANGEL : QUARTERLY REVIEW OF BIBLICAL, PRACTICAL AND CONTEMPORARY THEOLOGY. **4957**
0265-4644 *See* PROJECTS REVIEW (LONDON, ENGLAND). **306**
0265-4881 *See* SALISBURY REVIEW, THE. **3352**
0265-5063 *See* MUSICAL TRADITIONS. **4137**
0265-511X *See* OPENMIND (LONDON. 1983). **4795**
0265-5209 *See* CHARITY LONDON. 1983. **4335**

0265-5217 See BRITISH JOURNAL OF HEALTHCARE COMPUTING, THE. 1172
0265-5241 See INTENSIVE & CRITICAL CARE DIGEST. 3588
0265-5322 See LANGUAGE TESTING. 3296
0265-5373 See FARM BUILDINGS AND ENGINEERING : JOURNAL OF THE FARM BUILDINGS INFORMATION CENTRE AND THE FARM BUILDINGS ASSOCIATION. 614
0265-539X See COMMUNITY DENTAL HEALTH. 1319
0265-5527 See HOWARD JOURNAL OF CRIMINAL JUSTICE, THE. 3165
0265-5551 See IT'S NEWS LONDON. 1983. 1191
0265-5640 See DODO (TRINITY). 5581
0265-5721 See CHEMICAL HAZARDS IN INDUSTRY. 2872
0265-573X See PROBATION STATISTICS, ENGLAND AND WALES / HOME OFFICE. 3082
0265-5772 See AS-SARQ AL-AWSAT. 5811
0265-5780 See SAYYIDATI. 2601
0265-5799 See INTERNATIONAL SAUDI-REPORT. 2505
0265-5934 See HULL CLAIMS ANALYSIS. 2882
0265-5942 See JOURNAL OF NEWSPAPER AND PERIODICAL HISTORY. 2921
0265-6019 See IDS PAY DIRECTORY. 1677
0265-6183 See PERFORMANCE CAR. 5423
0265-6191 See SPEECH, HEARING AND LANGUAGE. 3323
0265-637X See URETHANES TECHNOLOGY. 4460
0265-6469 See MIDDLE EAST FOOD TRADE & CATERING EQUIPMENT. 2350
0265-6485 See FROZEN & CHILLED FOODS. 2341
0265-6493 See BUILDING CONTROL. 603
0265-6590 See CHILD LANGUAGE TEACHING AND THERAPY. 1877
0265-6647 See HEALTH LIBRARIES REVIEW. 3213
0265-6701 See CONTEMPORARY ISSUES IN CLINICAL BIOCHEMISTRY. 486
0265-671X See INTERNATIONAL JOURNAL OF QUALITY & RELIABILITY MANAGEMENT, THE. 871
0265-6736 See INTERNATIONAL JOURNAL OF HYPERTHERMIA. 3589
0265-6833 See BULLETIN / YORKSHIRE NATURALISTS' UNION. 4164
0265-6868 See HIGHWAYS AND TRANSPORTATION. 5441
0265-6914 See EUROPEAN HISTORY QUARTERLY. 2687
0265-6957 See SOCIAL SERVICES RESEARCH JOURNAL. 5309
0265-7007 See COMMUNITY PSYCHIATRIC NURSING JOURNAL. 3854
0265-718X See STATE OF THE WORLD'S CHILDREN (OXFORD). 5311
0265-7295 See NORTH WIND. 3418
0265-7406 See SUGAR CANE (1983). 188
0265-7511 See GALLERIES. 4088
0265-7651 See OXFORD STUDIES IN ANCIENT PHILOSOPHY. 4354
0265-7775 See WHITAKER'S ISBN LISTING. 4833
0265-7880 See WHEAT, BARLEY AND TRITICALE ABSTRACTS. 157
0265-7937 See ROAD TRAFFIC LAW BULLETIN. 5443
0265-797X See CURRENT MEDICAL LITERATURE. DIABETES. 3727
0265-7988 See BANKING & FINANCIAL TRAINING. 777
0265-7996 See BULLETIN (CENTRE FOR ECONOMIC POLICY RESEARCH (GREAT BRITAIN)). 1466
0265-8003 See DISCUSSION PAPER SERIES / CENTRE FOR ECONOMIC POLICY RESEARCH. 1480
0265-8038 See DURHAM ARCHAEOLOGICAL JOURNAL. 267
0265-8119 See SWEDISH BOOK REVIEW. SUPPLEMENT. 4832

0265-8119 See SWEDISH BOOK REVIEW. 3354
0265-8135 See ENVIRONMENT AND PLANNING. B, PLANNING & DESIGN. 2821
0265-8143 See GLAD RAG : JOURNAL OF THE TRANSVESTITE/TRANSSEXUAL SOCIAL GROUP (UK), THE. 5187
0265-8240 See LAW & POLICY. 2994
0265-8305 See PRINT QUARTERLY. 4568
0265-8321 See METALS INDUSTRY NEWS. 4011
0265-8356 See LONDON MARKET NEWSLETTER. 2887
0265-8364 See UK VENTURE CAPITAL JOURNAL. 815
0265-8410 See MARINE & AVIATION INSURANCE REPORT. 2887
0265-847X See ENGLISH LANGUAGE RESEARCH JOURNAL. 3279
0265-8712 See WHITE DWARF. 2779
0265-8887 See BL/BSD NAME AUTHORITY LIST. 410
0265-9220 See CONTENTS PAGES IN EDUCATION. 1794
0265-9247 See BIOESSAYS. 532
0265-9301 See TRANSPORT RESEARCH & CONSULTANCY BRIEFING. 5396
0265-931X See JOURNAL OF ENVIRONMENTAL RADIOACTIVITY. 2233
0265-9387 See REVIEW OF THE ECONOMY AND EMPLOYMENT. 1708
0265-9441 See TCS&D BUYERS' GUIDE. 2359
0265-9484 See WORLD BANKING ABSTRACTS. 816
0265-9581 See RESEARCH PAPER (GREAT BRITAIN. HEALTH AND SAFETY EXECUTIVE). 2869
0265-9611 See BRE NEWS OF CONSTRUCTION RESEARCH. 602
0265-962X See BRE NEWS OF FIRE RESEARCH. 2288
0265-9646 See SPACE POLICY. 36
0265-9697 See PROGRESS IN MEDICAL AND ENVIRONMENTAL PHYSICS. 4418
0265-9735 See TOPICAL LAW. 3065
0265-9743 See PEM NEWS. 4319
0265-9808 See SIGHTLINE : JOURNAL OF THE ASSOCIATION OF BRITISH THEATRE TECHNICIANS. 388
0265-9883 See BRITISH JOURNAL OF PSYCHOTHERAPY. 3922
0265-9921 See FIELD ARCHAEOLOGIST, THE. 268
0265-9999 See SENIOR NURSE. 3869
0266-0032 See SOIL USE AND MANAGEMENT. 187
0266-0245 See M & M, D & D. 4314
0266-0288 See PRESTEL DIRECTORY, THE. 1162
0266-030X See WHAT KEYBOARD?. 4159
0266-0342 See SOUTHAMPTON MEDICAL JOURNAL. 3642
0266-0512 See INTERNATIONAL MONOGRAPHS ON RISK. 3981
0266-0539 See HARDWARE & GARDEN REVIEW. 2418
0266-0628 See BUILDING LAW MONTHLY. 2944
0266-0776 See WELSH HOSPITAL WAITING LIST BULLETIN / WELSH OFFICE / BWLETIN RHESTR AROS YSBYTAI CYMRU / Y SWYDDFA GYMREIG. 3793
0266-0784 See ENGLISH TODAY. 3279
0266-0806 See TEXAS HEALTH LAW REPORTER. 3063
0266-0814 See TEXAS EVIDENCE REPORTER. 3063
0266-0830 See STUDIES IN THE EDUCATION OF ADULTS. 1802
0266-0865 See BANKING TECHNOLOGY. 777
0266-0946 See NEWS - MUSEUM PROFESSIONALS GROUP. 4094
0266-0954 See LANDSCAPE SCOTLAND QUARTERLY. 2423
0266-0970 See CARE OF THE CRITICALLY ILL. 3562

0266-1144 See GEOTEXTILES AND GEOMEMBRANES. 495
0266-1217 See CHRISTIE'S INTERNATIONAL MAGAZINE. 347
0266-139X See CIVIL ENGINEERING SURVEYOR. 2021
0266-1500 See LINEN HALL REVIEW. 3405
0266-156X See DEVELOPMENTS IN PRESSURE VESSEL TECHNOLOGY. 3477
0266-1640 See PTERIDOLOGIST. 525
0266-1721 See IEE HISTORY OF TECHNOLOGY SERIES. 2057
0266-1756 See TOOLS & TRADES. 635
0266-206X See OCCASIONAL PAPERS / SCANDINAVIAN INSTITUTE OF ASIAN STUDIES. 2661
0266-2078 See MEDICAL TEXTILES. 3612
0266-2124 See BIOLOGICAL PSYCHIATRY (LONDON, ENGLAND). 3922
0266-2132 See AIRFINANCE ANNUAL. 9
0266-2159 See RESEARCH SUPPORTED BY THE ECONOMIC AND SOCIAL RESEARCH COUNCIL. 5215
0266-2183 See JOURNAL OF THE MUHYIDDIN IBN ARABI SOCIETY. 5043
0266-2205 See SUBSEA ENGINEERING NEWS. 2095
0266-2329 See BRITISH MUSIC EDUCATION YEARBOOK. 4105
0266-2426 See INTERNATIONAL SMALL BUSINESS JOURNAL. 684
0266-2442 See BULLETIN OF THE ANGLO-ISRAEL ARCHAEOLOGICAL SOCIETY. 264
0266-2493 See CONTROL SYSTEMS TONBRIDGE. 1180
0266-2558 See BRITISH JEWELLER 1983. 2913
0266-2671 See ECONOMICS AND PHILOSOPHY. 1486
0266-268X See COMPUTING DECISIONS / NATIONAL COMPUTING CENTRE. 1180
0266-2698 See LOCAL HISTORY. 2697
0266-2914 See INFORME ESPECIAL - LATIN AMERICAN NEWSLETTERS. 1495
0266-304X See BINARY COMPUTING IN MICROBIOLOGY. 560
0266-304X See BINARY. 560
0266-3104 See QUALITY TECHNOLOGY HANDBOOK. 5143
0266-3198 See FERRO-ALLOY DIRECTORY. 4001
0266-3198 See FERRO-ALLOY DIRECTORY & DATABOOK. 4002
0266-3368 See EDUCATIONAL TECHNOLOGY ABSTRACTS. 1794
0266-352X See COMPUTERS AND GEOTECHNICS. 1372
0266-3538 See COMPOSITES SCIENCE AND TECHNOLOGY. 2101
0266-3554 See GERMAN HISTORY : THE JOURNAL OF THE GERMAN HISTORY SOCIETY. 2689
0266-3570 See AGRA-BRIEFING. 46
0266-3597 See HAZELL'S GUIDE AND THE BAR LIST. 2977
0266-3597 See HAZELL'S GUIDE TO THE JUDICIARY AND THE COURTS. 3141
0266-3775 See RECENT ADVANCES IN TROPICAL MEDICINE. 3986
0266-3791 See KELLY'S POST OFFICE LONDON BUSINESS DIRECTORY. 688
0266-3821 See BUSINESS INFORMATION REVIEW. 3199
0266-3953 See LEGAL ACTION. 2999
0266-3996 See REFERENCE BOOK & BUYERS GUIDE / ICHCA, INTERNATIONAL CARGO HANDLING CO-ORDINATION ASSOCIATION. 849
0266-4062 See JOURNAL OF THE BRITISH ASSOCIATION OF TEACHERS OF THE DEAF, THE. 1881
0266-4151 See EUROPEAN RUBBER JOURNAL (LONDON, ENGLAND : 1982). 5075
0266-4283 See COMPUTING EQUIPMENT. 1180

ISSN Index

0266-4348 *See* GENITOURINARY MEDICINE. 4776

0266-4356 *See* BRITISH JOURNAL OF ORAL & MAXILLOFACIAL SURGERY, THE. 3961

0266-4380 *See* API. ARCHITECTURAL PERIODICALS INDEX. 311

0266-447X *See* PRACTICAL DIABETES. 3732

0266-4488 *See* TAMIL TIMES. 2666

0266-4615 *See* WATER SCIENCE REVIEWS. 1038

0266-4623 *See* INTERNATIONAL JOURNAL OF TECHNOLOGY ASSESSMENT IN HEALTH CARE. 3589

0266-464X *See* NEW THEATRE QUARTERLY : NTQ. 5366

0266-4658 *See* ECONOMIC POLICY. 1484

0266-4666 *See* ECONOMETRIC THEORY. 1591

0266-4674 *See* JOURNAL OF TROPICAL ECOLOGY. 2218

0266-4720 *See* EXPERT SYSTEMS. 1212

0266-4763 *See* JOURNAL OF APPLIED STATISTICS. 5329

0266-4801 *See* TOLLEY'S COMPUTER LAW AND PRACTICE. 1227

0266-481X *See* FOOTBALL MONTHLY (1980). 4895

0266-4909 *See* JOURNAL OF COMPUTER ASSISTED LEARNING. 1223

0266-4992 *See* STAFFORDSHIRE ARCHAEOLOGICAL STUDIES. 283

0266-5182 *See* FAST LANE. 2487

0266-5247 *See* RESEARCH REPORT - TRANSPORT AND ROAD RESEARCH LABORATORY. 5391

0266-5433 *See* PLANNING PERSPECTIVES : PP. 2831

0266-545X *See* ATARI USER. 1264

0266-5611 *See* INVERSE PROBLEMS. 3510

0266-5794 *See* BEACHWEAR FORECAST INTERNATIONAL. 1081

0266-6030 *See* SOUTH ASIAN STUDIES (SOCIETY FOR SOUTH ASIAN STUDIES). 2665

0266-6057 *See* AND. JOURNAL OF ART AND ART EDUCATION. 336

0266-6073 *See* DENTAL ANNUAL (BRISTOL, ENGLAND). 1320

0266-612X See INTENSIVE & CRITICAL CARE NURSING : THE OFFICIAL JOURNAL OF THE BRITISH ASSOCIATION OF CRITICAL CARE NURSES. 3857

0266-6138 *See* MIDWIFERY. 3765

0266-6189 *See* LLOYD'S MONTHLY LIST OF LAID UP VESSELS. 5451

0266-6286 *See* WORD & IMAGE (LONDON. 1985). 1124

0266-6294 *See* BLOOD COAGULATION FACTORS. 449

0266-6308 *See* DNA PROBES. 453

0266-6499 *See* REPRODUCTIVE PHYSIOLOGY. 586

0266-6669 *See* INFORMATION DEVELOPMENT. 3215

0266-6731 *See* AFRICA BIBLIOGRAPHY. 407

0266-6863 *See* ISSUES IN CRIMINOLOGICAL AND LEGAL PSYCHOLOGY. 4592

0266-6871 *See* AIR CONDITIONING & REFRIGERATION NEWS. 2602

0266-688X *See* ETHICS & MEDICINE : A CHRISTIAN PERSPECTIVE ON ISSUES IN BIOETHICS. 3575

0266-6952 *See* JOURNAL / INSTITUTE OF MUSLIM MINORITY AFFAIRS. 2265

0266-6979 *See* GEOLOGY TODAY. 1380

0266-7037 *See* INTENSIVE CARE WORLD (BALDOCK). 3588

0266-7045 *See* CONTRACTOR REPORT - TRANSPORT AND ROAD RESEARCH LABORATORY. 611

0266-7053 *See* UPDATE (LONDON. 1984). 753

0266-7061 *See* COMPUTER APPLICATIONS IN THE BIOSCIENCES. 1176

0266-7169 *See* LABORATORY NEWS. 463

0266-7177 *See* MODERN THEOLOGY. 4978

0266-7185 *See* METALS AND MATERIALS (BURY ST. EDMONDS). 4011

0266-7193 *See* TURKISH SHIPPING. 5458

0266-7215 *See* EUROPEAN SOCIOLOGICAL REVIEW. 5245

0266-7320 *See* PROGRESS IN RUBBER AND PLASTICS TECHNOLOGY. 5077

0266-7347 *See* WORLD WROUGHT COPPER STATISTICS. 4024

0266-7355 *See* WORLD METAL STATISTICS YEARBOOK. 4024

0266-7363 *See* EDUCATIONAL PSYCHOLOGY IN PRACTICE. 4586

0266-7398 *See* CRICKETER INTERNATIONAL. 4891

0266-7401 *See* CRICKETER QUARTERLY FACTS AND FIGURES. 4891

0266-7428 *See* SCOTTISH INDUSTRIAL HISTORY. 1626

0266-7606 *See* BRITISH CERAMIC TRANSACTIONS AND JOURNAL. 2586

0266-7681 *See* JOURNAL OF HAND SURGERY, BRITISH VOLUME. 3967

0266-7797 *See* FINTECH. 2, ELECTRONIC OFFICE. 2055

0266-7800 *See* EUROPEAN PAINT AND RESIN NEWS. 4223

0266-7991 *See* PROMOTIONS & INCENTIVES. 883

0266-8025 *See* FAR EASTERN AGRICULTURE. 84

0266-8033 *See* MEMORY LANE (LEIGH-ON-SEA, ESSEX). 4130

0266-8068 *See* NATIONAL TRUST. 304

0266-8130 *See* PROFESSIONAL NURSE (LONDON, ENGLAND). 3867

0266-8254 *See* LETTERS IN APPLIED MICROBIOLOGY. 566

0266-836X *See* BULLETIN OF THE AMATEUR ENTOMOLOGISTS' SOCIETY, THE. 5606

0266-8394 *See* KNITTING INTERNATIONAL. 5353

0266-8483 *See* PC BUSINESS WORLD. 1245

0266-8505 *See* MACHINE KNITTING NEWS. 5354

0266-8513 *See* INFORMATION TECHNOLOGY & PUBLIC POLICY. 1188

0266-8599 *See* SHADOW : THE NEWSLETTER OF THE TRADITIONAL COSMOLOGICAL SOCIETY. 399

0266-8653 *See* REINSURANCE MARKET REPORT. 2891

0266-8688 *See* MEDIA INTERNATIONAL. 762

0266-8734 *See* PSYCHOANALYTIC PSYCHOTHERAPY. 3934

0266-8769 *See* LAMPADA. 3861

0266-8874 *See* MIDDLE EAST DENTISTRY & ORAL HEALTH. 1330

0266-8920 *See* PROBABILISTIC ENGINEERING MECHANICS. 2125

0266-8971 *See* 100 A1. 5447

0266-903X *See* OXFORD REVIEW OF ECONOMIC POLICY. 1511

0266-9056 *See* THS HEALTH SUMMARY. 4805

0266-9080 *See* IRISH PHILOSOPHICAL JOURNAL. 4350

0266-9102 *See* LEISURE MANAGEMENT. 4852

0266-9366 *See* FOOD & DRUGS INDUSTRY BULLETIN. 2336

0266-9536 *See* ANTI-CANCER DRUG DESIGN. 3809

0266-9838 *See* ENVIRONMENTAL SOFTWARE. 2170

0266-996X *See* AQUACULTURE AND FISHERIES MANAGEMENT. 2295

0267-0003 *See* LECTURES IN ANAESTHESIOLOGY. 3683

0267-0194 *See* AL-MUSAFIR AL-ARABI. 5460

0267-0216 *See* ARAB WORLD AGRIBUSINESS. 62

0267-0267 *See* ATHLETICS COACH. 4884

0267-0275 *See* POSTGRADUATE DOCTOR. CARIBBEAN. 3628

0267-0348 *See* SELECTED BIBLIOGRAPHIES ON AGEING. 3661

0267-0429 *See* MACHINE INTELLIGENCE NEWS. 1215

0267-0445 *See* CURRENT MEDICAL LITERATURE. NEUROLOGY. 3830

0267-0631 *See* BRITISH MEDICAL JOURNAL (PRACTICE OBSERVED ED.). 3559

0267-0712 *See* SOCIAL STUDIES REVIEW. 5259

0267-0739 *See* POLICING. 3172

0267-0763 *See* ADVERTISING LAW & PRACTICE. 2928

0267-0771 *See* INSOLVENCY LAW & PRACTICE. 3087

0267-078X *See* PROFESSIONAL NEGLIGENCE. 3032

0267-0836 *See* MATERIALS SCIENCE AND TECHNOLOGY. 2105

0267-0844 *See* SURFACE ENGINEERING. 1997

0267-0887 *See* FREE ASSOCIATIONS. 3925

0267-1085 *See* INTERNATIONAL UNDERWATER SYSTEMS DESIGN. 2091

0267-1131 *See* FAMILY TREE MAGAZINE. 2447

0267-1255 *See* MOBILE TELECOMMUNICATIONS NEWS. 1160

0267-1336 *See* PROSTAGLANDIN PERSPECTIVES. 3631

0267-1379 *See* CURRENT OPINION IN GASTROENTEROLOGY. 3744

0267-1409 *See* MINERAL PLANNING. 1441

0267-1459 See CRITICAL REVIEWS IN MULTIPHASE SCIENCE AND TECHNOLOGY. 5097

0267-1484 *See* FIN TECH. 1, TELECOM MARKETS. 1155

0267-1506 *See* FOOD MANUFACTURE INTERNATIONAL. 2338

0267-1522 *See* RESEARCH PAPERS IN EDUCATION. 1779

0267-1611 *See* EDUCATIONAL AND CHILD PSYCHOLOGY. 4585

0267-1816 *See* WHICH VAN?. 5428

0267-1905 *See* ANNUAL REVIEW OF APPLIED LINGUISTICS. 3265

0267-1948 *See* CURRENT RESEARCH IN BRITAIN. PHYSICAL SCIENCES. 414

0267-1956 *See* CURRENT RESEARCH IN BRITAIN. BIOLOGICAL SCIENCES. 453

0267-1964 *See* CURRENT RESEARCH IN BRITAIN. SOCIAL SCIENCES. 5197

0267-1972 *See* CURRENT RESEARCH IN BRITAIN. THE HUMANITIES. 2845

0267-2073 See INTERNATIONAL JOURNAL OF PAEDIATRIC DENTISTRY / THE BRITISH PAEDONDONTIC SOCIETY [AND] THE INTERNATIONAL ASSOCIATION OF DENTISTRY FOR CHILDREN. 1325

0267-2146 *See* COMMITTEE REPORTS PUBLISHED BY HMSO INDEXED BY CHAIRMAN. 4639

0267-2170 *See* HEALTH & LIBERATION : ANTI-APARTHEID MOVEMENT HEALTH COMMITTEE NEWSLETTER. 3581

0267-2359 *See* CONSTRUCTION LAW JOURNAL. 609

0267-2375 *See* RESEARCH INFORMATION NOTE - FORESTRY COMMISSION RESEARCH & DEVELOPMENT DIVISION. 2392

0267-2561 *See* BUILDING MARKET REPORT. 603

0267-257X *See* JOURNAL OF MARKETING MANAGEMENT. 928

0267-2618 *See* NEMS NEWS. 4093

0267-2634 *See* PUBLICATIONS OF THE LINCOLN RECORD SOCIETY, THE. 2704

0267-2715 *See* MODEL AUTO REVIEW. 2775

0267-2928 *See* IMLS GAZETTE. 3586

0267-2987 *See* MAIZE ABSTRACTS. 154

0267-3037 *See* HOUSING STUDIES. 2825

0267-3061 *See* BULLETIN OF THE ANNA FREUD CENTRE. 3922

0267-3088 *See* VERNACULAR BUILDING. 310

0267-310X *See* ENVIRONMENTAL DIGEST FOR WALES / WELSH OFFICE / CRYNHOAD O YSTADEGAU'R AMGYLCHEDD / Y SWYDDFA GYMREIG. 2167

0267-3142 *See* WINNICOTT STUDIES. 4621

0267-3223 *See* HEALTH CARE UK. 3581

0267-3231 See EUROPEAN JOURNAL OF COMMUNICATION (LONDON). 1111
0267-3290 See MUSIC WEEK DIRECTORY. 4135
0267-3320 See COMMUNICATIONS IN LABORATORY MEDICINE. 3567
0267-3347 See SERIAL PUBLICATIONS IN THE BRITISH MUSEUM, NATURAL HISTORY LIBRARY ON MICROFICHE. 4172
0267-3606 See TRAVEL MEDICINE INTERNATIONAL. 3647
0267-3754 See LEISURE MANAGER : THE JOURNAL OF THE INSTITUTE OF LEISURE & AMENITY MANAGEMENT, THE. 4852
0267-3770 See INVESTMENT MANAGEMENT. 903
0267-3789 See SPECTRUM : THE QUARTERLY MAGAZINE OF THE INDEPENDENT TELEVISION COMMISSION. 1139
0267-3843 See INTERNATIONAL JOURNAL OF ADOLESCENCE AND YOUTH. 2281
0267-3851 See CATERING & HEALTH. 2330
0267-3932 See IEE PROCEEDINGS. PART J, OPTOELECTRONICS. 2058
0267-3991 See ART & DESIGN / ARCHITECTURAL DESIGN PUBLICATIONS. 338
0267-4009 See ADVANCES IN SPECIAL ELECTROMETALLURGY. 3997
0267-4130 See CENTRAL AMERICA REPORT. 4505
0267-4297 See TRAFFIC BULLETIN - WILDLIFE TRADE MONITORING UNIT. 2207
0267-4386 See INTERNATIONAL JOURNAL OF INNOVATIVE HIGHER EDUCATION : THE OFFICIAL JOURNAL OF THE UNIVERSITY WITHOUT WALLS INTERNATIONAL COUNCIL. 1831
0267-4424 See FINANCIAL ACCOUNTABILITY & MANAGEMENT IN GOVERNMENTS, PUBLIC SERVICES, AND CHARITIES. 4649
0267-4645 See DISABILITY, HANDICAP & SOCIETY. 5284
0267-4653 See SEXUAL AND MARITAL THERAPY. 2286
0267-4718 See CONTEMPORARY ERGONOMICS : PROCEEDINGS OF THE ERGONOMICS SOCIETY'S ANNUAL CONFERENCE. 1969
0267-4823 See PORT DEVELOPMENT INTERNATIONAL. 5454
0267-484X See ATLAS (LONDON, ENGLAND : 1985). 343
0267-4874 See ADVANCES IN CONTRACEPTION. 587
0267-5099 See LATIN AMERICAN MINING LETTER. 2143
0267-5307 See TECHNICAL REVIEW MIDDLE EAST. 5162
0267-5315 See PORTUGUESE STUDIES. 2625
0267-534X See MANX LAW REPORTS. 3006
0267-5374 See EMPLOYMENT AFFAIRS REPORT. 1666
0267-5382 See MEDIA BULLETIN / EUROPEAN INSTITUTE FOR THE MEDIA. 1116
0267-5447 See DATA STORAGE REPORT. 1257
0267-5471 See DIVISIONAL NOTE - NATIONAL INSTITUTE OF AGRICULTURAL ENGINEERING. 79
0267-5498 See LINGUISTICS ABSTRACTS. 3299
0267-5501 See MICROMATH : A JOURNAL OF THE ASSOCIATION OF TEACHERS OF MATHEMATICS. 3523
0267-565X See BROADCAST SYSTEMS ENGINEERING. 1128
0267-5730 See INTERNATIONAL JOURNAL OF TECHNOLOGY MANAGEMENT. 5115
0267-5889 See CHEMICAL BUSINESS BULLETIN. SPECIALITY CHEMICALS. 968
0267-5900 See ADVANCED MATERIALS FOR OPTICS AND ELECTRONICS. 5080
0267-5943 See RAILWATCH. 5435
0267-5994 See EPC PUBLICATION. 4775
0267-6044 See NORTHERN IRELAND ANNUAL ABSTRACT OF STATISTICS. 5335
0267-6087 See PR WEEK. 764
0267-6117 See PACKAGING WEEK. 4221

0267-6141 See ANARCHIST ENCYCLOPAEDIA. 4539
0267-615X See MUSLIM EDUCATION QUARTERLY. 1765
0267-6192 See COMPUTER SYSTEMS SCIENCE AND ENGINEERING. 1228
0267-6303 See WORLD COMMODITY FORECASTS / THE ECONOMIST INTELLIGENCE UNIT. 1527
0267-6338 See BRITISH FARMER 1985. 68
0267-6362 See AFRICA EVENTS. 2497
0267-6389 See SATELLITE TECHNOLOGY. 34
0267-6583 See SECOND LANGUAGE RESEARCH. 3320
0267-6591 See PERFUSION. 3709
0267-6605 See CLINICAL MATERIALS. 3566
0267-6621 See APPLIED COMPUTER AND COMMUNICATIONS LAW. 2936
0267-6648 See UNIVERSALIST - QUAKER UNIVERSALIST GROUP. 5068
0267-6672 See EDINBURGH REVIEW (EDINBURGH : 1985). 3383
0267-680X See ADVANCES IN ULTRAHARD MATERIALS APPLICATION TECHNOLOGY. 5081
0267-6834 See REVIEW OF SCOTTISH CULTURE. 2705
0267-7253 See PIANO JOURNAL / EUROPEAN PIANO TEACHERS ASSOCIATION. 4146
0267-7261 See SOIL DYNAMICS AND EARTHQUAKE ENGINEERING (1984). 1996
0267-7296 See HAZARDS. 2862
0267-7334 See PHARMACY UPDATE. 4323
0267-7563 See GEOFILE. 2517
0267-7768 See CONSTRUCTION HISTORY : JOURNAL OF THE CONSTRUCTION HISTORY GROUP. 609
0267-808X See EAST EUROPEAN REPORTER. 2686
0267-8160 See WELSH TRANSPORT STATISTICS / YSTADEGAU TRAFNIDIAETH CYMRU. 5399
0267-8179 See JQS. JOURNAL OF QUATERNARY SCIENCE. 1385
0267-8225 See INTERNATIONAL MOTOR BUSINESS. 5417
0267-8233 See EUROPEAN MOTOR BUSINESS. 5414
0267-8292 See LIQUID CRYSTALS. 1032
0267-8306 See TEXAS LAWYER, THE. 3064
0267-8314 See EMPLOYMENT BULLETIN AND IR DIGEST. 1666
0267-8349 See BULLETIN - JOINT ASSOCIATION OF CLASSICAL TEACHERS. 1729
0267-8357 See MUTAGENESIS. 549
0267-8373 See WORK AND STRESS. 4621
0267-842X See AFKAR INQUIRY. 4932
0267-8446 See FINTECH. 3, PERSONAL COMPUTER MARKETS. 1267
0267-8489 See AFRC NEWS. 45
0267-8519 See COMPANY CAR. 5412
0267-8519 See COMPANY CAR. 5380
0267-8594 See MUSEUM ABSTRACTS. 4098
0267-8691 See UNITED KINGDOM NATIONAL ACCOUNTS. 1525
0267-8852 See OILS & FATS INTERNATIONAL. 1620
0267-8853 See OILS & FATS INTERNATIONAL. 1620
0267-8896 See TEXAS REAL ESTATE LAW REPORTER. 3064
0267-8950 See TRANSITION (LONDON, ENGLAND). 1917
0267-9078 See FINTECH. 5, SOFTWARE MARKETS. 1286
0267-9337 See GEC REVIEW. 2055
0267-937X See JOURNAL OF INTERNATIONAL BANKING LAW. 3087
0267-9477 See JOURNAL OF ANALYTICAL ATOMIC SPECTROMETRY. 1016
0267-9515 See ONLINE BUSINESS INFORMATION. 701
0267-954X See SPACE (BEACONSFIELD). 35

0267-9612 See FINNEGANS WAKE CIRCULAR, A. 3388
0267-9655 See INTERNATIONAL JOURNAL OF MORAL AND SOCIAL STUDIES. 2251
0267-9671 See LASER DISC REVIEW. 5125
0267-9949 See ARGENTINA (LONDON, ENGLAND). 639
0267-9957 See VENEZUELA (LONDON. 1985). 2494
0267-9965 See BRAZIL (LONDON, ENGLAND). 2485
0267-9973 See MEXICO (LONDON, ENGLAND). 2490
0267-999X See ANNUAL REGISTER OF MERCHANTS' PREMISES. 60
0268-0033 See CLINICAL BIOMECHANICS (BRISTOL). 3565
0268-005X See FOOD HYDROCOLLOIDS. 1041
0268-0106 See INTERNATIONAL JOURNAL OF ESTUARINE AND COASTAL LAW. 3181
0268-0130 See HERPETOLOGICAL JOURNAL, THE. 5585
0268-0165 See GEODRILLING. 1405
0268-0181 See JACT REVIEW. 1077
0268-0408 See FOOD MARKET ABSTRACTS. 2338
0268-0459 See HEALTH SERVICE ABSTRACTS. 3659
0268-0513 See OPEN LEARNING. 1801
0268-0556 See ARAB LAW QUARTERLY. 2936
0268-0653 See LITIGATION LETTER. 3003
0268-0661 See SOUTH AMERICA, CENTRAL AMERICA, AND THE CARIBBEAN. 2761
0268-0696 See LLOYD'S MARITIME LAW NEWSLETTER. 3181
0268-0750 See VIDEO MAKER. 4079
0268-0815 See CASUALTY RETURN / LLOYD'S REGISTER OF SHIPPING. 2877
0268-0882 See JOURNAL OF INTERVENTIONAL RADIOLOGY. 3942
0268-0890 See CURRENT ORTHOPAEDICS. 3881
0268-0920 See PACKAGING TODAY LONDON. 4221
0268-0939 See JOURNAL OF EDUCATION POLICY. 1756
0268-1056 See POLIN. 5052
0268-1064 See MIND & LANGUAGE. 3302
0268-1072 See NEW TECHNOLOGY, WORK, AND EMPLOYMENT. 1694
0268-1080 See HEALTH POLICY AND PLANNING. 4780
0268-109X See ECLAT. 3278
0268-1110 See DYNAMICS AND STABILITY OF SYSTEMS. 1246
0268-1137 See OXFORD MAGAZINE. 1102
0268-1145 See LITERARY AND LINGUISTIC COMPUTING. 1193
0268-1153 See HEALTH EDUCATION RESEARCH. 4779
0268-1161 See HUMAN REPRODUCTION (OXFORD). 541
0268-117X See SEVENTEENTH CENTURY, THE. 2709
0268-1218 See JOURNAL OF MEDICAL AND VETERINARY MYCOLOGY. 575
0268-1242 See SEMICONDUCTOR SCIENCE AND TECHNOLOGY. 4420
0268-1293 See SEAFOOD INTERNATIONAL. 2313
0268-1315 See INTERNATIONAL CLINICAL PSYCHOPHARMACOLOGY. 4308
0268-1323 See BUILDERS MERCHANTS JOURNAL (TONBRIDGE AND MALLING, KENT : 1985). 602
0268-1374 See FLUID ABSTRACTS. CIVIL ENGINEERING. 2004
0268-1544 See AGING. 3749
0268-1552 See PEPTIDE HORMONE RECEPTORS. 492
0268-1595 581
0268-1617 See EXTRACELLULAR MATRIX. 536
0268-1625 See CYTOSKELETON SHEFFIELD. 3570

0268-1641 See ATRIAL NATRIURETIC FACTORS. 3699

0268-1781 See BUTCHER & PROCESSOR. 2329

0268-1900 See INTERNATIONAL JOURNAL OF MATERIALS & PRODUCT TECHNOLOGY. 1980

0268-1927 See MARINE INSURANCE INTERNATIONAL. 2887

0268-1935 See INSURANCE SYSTEMS BULLETIN. 2884

0268-201X See GERIATRIC MEDICINE (HORTON KIRBY. 1985). 3751

0268-2028 See PLAYS INTERNATIONAL. 5367

0268-2087 See JEWELLERY STUDIES. 2914

0268-2125 See LEARNING RESOURCES JOURNAL. 1834

0268-2141 See SUPPORT FOR LEARNING. 1786

0268-215X See CABLE & SATELLITE EXPRESS. 1128

0268-2176 See PRIMARY TEACHING STUDIES. 1902

0268-2222 See BIBRA BULLETIN. 3979

0268-232X See MAJOR FINANCIAL INSTITUTIONS OF EUROPE. 797

0268-2400 See BRITISH BULLETIN OF PUBLICATIONS ON LATIN AMERICA, THE CARIBBEAN, PORTUGAL AND SPAIN / CANNING HOUSE, HISPANIC AAN LUSO-BRAZILIAN COUNCIL. 4827

0268-2575 See JOURNAL OF CHEMICAL TECHNOLOGY AND BIOTECHNOLOGY (1986). 1026

0268-2605 See APPLIED ORGANOMETALLIC CHEMISTRY. 961

0268-2613 See PROGRESS IN TRANSFUSION MEDICINE. 3773

0268-2621 See BEREAVEMENT CARE. 5274

0268-2966 See ICB. INTERNATIONAL CARPET BULLETIN. 5351

0268-3091 See ROUND TABLE SERIES / ROYAL SOCIETY OF MEDICINE SERVICES. 3637

0268-3105 See KELLY'S U.K. EXPORTS. 843

0268-313X See AGROW. 57

0268-327X See LLOYD'S MARITIME DIRECTORY. 5451

0268-3369 See BONE MARROW TRANSPLANTATION (BASINGSTOKE). 3558

0268-3393 See BCIRA ABSTRACTS OF INTERNATIONAL LITERATURE ON METAL CASTINGS PRODUCTION. 3998

0268-3555 See PHLEBOLOGY / VENOUS FORUM OF THE ROYAL SOCIETY OF MEDICINE. 3800

0268-3644 See PLANNING APPEAL DECISIONS (ANDOVER, ENGLAND). 2831

0268-3679 See TEACHING MATHEMATICS AND ITS APPLICATIONS. 3538

0268-3709 See INTERIGHTS BULLETIN. 4509

0268-375X See DIRECTORY OF MANAGEMENT CONSULTANTS IN THE UK. 865

0268-3768 See INTERNATIONAL JOURNAL, ADVANCED MANUFACTURING TECHNOLOGY, THE. 3481

0268-3784 See COUNSEL : THE JOURNAL OF THE BAR OF ENGLAND & WALES. 2957

0268-3830 See VERSE (OXFORD, OXFORDSHIRE). 3473

0268-3938 See INTERNATIONAL JOURNAL OF CONSTRUCTION MANAGEMENT & TECHNOLOGY. 618

0268-3946 See JOURNAL OF MANAGERIAL PSYCHOLOGY. 4598

0268-3962 See JOURNAL OF INFORMATION TECHNOLOGY : JIT. 1192

0268-4012 See INTERNATIONAL JOURNAL OF INFORMATION MANAGEMENT. 3218

0268-4055 See COMPLEMENTARY MEDICAL RESEARCH. 5096

0268-4160 See CONTINUITY AND CHANGE. 5243

0268-4179 See AISB QUARTERLY. 1211

0268-4225 See H & V ENGINEER. 2605

0268-425X See CIRCAEA : BULLETIN OF THE ASSOCIATION FOR ENVIRONMENTAL ARCHAEOLOGY. 266

0268-4268 See HENSTON VETERINARY VADE MECUM. SMALL ANIMALS, THE. 5511

0268-4276 See HENSTON VETERINARY VADE MECUM. LARGE ANIMALS, THE. 5511

0268-4306 See FRAME NEWS. 226

0268-4373 See BRITISH CERAMIC PROCEEDINGS. 2586

0268-4519 See ELEKTOR ELECTRONICS. 2051

0268-4527 See INTELLIGENCE AND NATIONAL SECURITY. 4524

0268-4535 See JOURNAL OF COMMUNIST STUDIES, THE. 4542

0268-4705 See CURRENT OPINION IN CARDIOLOGY. 3704

0268-4764 See TEXTILE OUTLOOK INTERNATIONAL. 5358

0268-490X See SCIENCE AND PUBLIC AFFAIRS (LONDON, ENGLAND). 5218

0268-4926 See BLUEPRINT (LONDON. 1983). 293

0268-4942 See PERFORMANCE BIKES. 5389

0268-4969 See LOOKS LONDON. 2489

0268-4977 See TODAY'S RUNNER. 4926

0268-523X See WHAT'S NEW IN PROCESSING. 1263

0268-5248 See RADIO CONTROL BOAT MODELLER. 2777

0268-5256 See DIRECTORY OF INTERNATIONAL FILM AND VIDEO FESTIVALS. 4068

0268-5280 See ALUMINIUM INDUSTRY. 3997

0268-537X See JOURNAL OF IRISH ARCHAEOLOGY, THE. 271

0268-540X See ANTHROPOLOGY TODAY. 230

0268-5418 See THOMAS HARDY JOURNAL, THE. 3446

0268-5485 See OPTOMETRY TODAY (LONDON). 4217

0268-5507 See CONSTRUCTION TODAY. 2021

0268-5558 See CARAVAN BUSINESS. 5466

0268-5639 See ERGONOMIST. 2114

0268-5809 See INTERNATIONAL SOCIOLOGY. 5248

0268-5965 See LINGUIST (LONDON, ENGLAND : 1986). 3298

0268-5981 See RIALTO, THE. 3470

0268-6112 See IRISH BIBLICAL STUDIES. 5017

0268-6171 See IEE MANAGEMENT OF TECHNOLOGY SERIES. 5111

0268-6252 See CURRENT PROBLEMS IN NEUROLOGY. 3831

0268-6287 See CHROMATOGRAPHY ABSTRACTS. 1014

0268-6325 See WHERE TO BUY CONSTRUCTION & MAINTENANCE SERVICES FOR BUILDINGS. 631

0268-652X See ADA USER. 1278

0268-6538 See BOOKS AT BOSTON SPA. MICROFORM. 4825

0268-6554 See OLD WEST RIDING. 2625

0268-6708 See SOFTWARE USER'S YEAR BOOK, THE. 1203

0268-6716 See HISTORICAL RESEARCH FOR HIGHER DEGREES IN THE UNITED KINGDOM. PART I, THESES COMPLETED. 1829

0268-6724 See HISTORICAL RESEARCH FOR HIGHER DEGREES IN THE UNITED KINGDOM. PART II, THESES IN PROGRESS. 2618

0268-6821 See COMPUTER USERS' YEAR BOOK. 1245

0268-6872 See EXE. 1184

0268-6902 See MANAGERIAL AUDITING JOURNAL. 748

0268-6961 See SOFTWARE ENGINEERING JOURNAL. 1996

0268-7038 See APHASIOLOGY. 3551

0268-7151 See MOTORCYCLE INTERNATIONAL. 4082

0268-716X See COMPUTERGRAM INTERNATIONAL. 1178

0268-7364 See PROGRESS IN THE PSYCHOLOGY OF LANGUAGE. 3312

0268-7372 See CURRENT RESEARCH FOR THE INFORMATION PROFESSION. 3205

0268-7402 See BULLETIN - UK CENTRE FOR ECONOMIC AND ENVIRONMENTAL DEVELOPMENT. 1466

0268-7429 See LIGHTING + SOUND INTERNATIONAL. 5126

0268-747X See RHEUMATOLOGY FORUM. 3807

0268-7518 See CHURCH MONUMENTS. 4947

0268-7615 See AIRLINE BUSINESS. 9

0268-764X See BENEFITS & COMPENSATION INTERNATIONAL. 2875

0268-7658 See CHURCH GROWTH DIGEST. 4947

0268-7844 See WEEKLY PETROLEUM ARGUS. 4282

0268-8050 See CONDITION MONITOR. 2112

0268-808X See ERYTHROCYTES. 536

0268-8212 See IMPACT INTERNATIONAL (NEW YORK, N.Y.). 2367

0268-8247 See PLASTICS INDUSTRY EUROPE. 4458

0268-8328 See MILITARY ILLUSTRATED : PAST & PRESENT. 4050

0268-8336 See LAW LIBRARY INFORMATION REPORTS. 3222

0268-8360 See AIDS NEWSLETTER (LONDON, ENGLAND). 3664

0268-8395 See FRANCHISE MAGAZINE. 677

0268-8425 See SATELLITE TV EUROPE. 1121

0268-8433 See FINANCIAL TIMES LAW REPORTS. 2970

0268-8670 See WORLD AEROSPACE PROFILE : THE INTERNATIONAL REVIEW OF AEROSPACE DESIGN AND DEVELOPMENT. 40

0268-8697 See BRITISH JOURNAL OF NEUROSURGERY. 3829

0268-8867 See PROJECT APPRAISAL. 912

0268-8921 See LASERS IN MEDICAL SCIENCE. 3604

0268-893X See PUBLIC LIBRARY JOURNAL. 3243

0268-9111 See CONSORT (DOLMETSCH FOUNDATION), THE. 4111

0268-9146 See ANIMAL GENETICS. 542

0268-9189 See VETERINARY PRACTICE MANAGEMENT (EPSOM AND EWELL, SURREY). 5526

0268-9219 See LIQUIDS HANDLING. 4263

0268-9235 See JOURNAL OF MANAGEMENT IN MEDICINE. 3596

0268-9499 See FIBRINOLYSIS. 455

0268-960X See BLOOD REVIEWS. 3770

0268-9650 See BMT ABSTRACTS : BRITISH MARITIME TECHNOLOGY ABSTRACTS. 4185

0268-9669 See LLOYD'S PROFESSIONAL LIABILITY TODAY. 3004

0268-9707 See BRITISH LIBRARY BIBLIOGRAPHIC SERVICES NEWSLETTER. 411

0268-9766 See SURFACE COATING & RAW MATERIAL DIRECTORY. 4225

0268-9812 See POLYMERS & RUBBER ASIA. 4459

0268-9847 See ADVANCED CERAMICS REPORT. 2585

0268-9855 See MUSEUM DESIGN. 4092

0268-9936 See ANNUAL BIBLIOGRAPHY OF THE HISTORY OF NATURAL HISTORY. 4174

0268-9960 See ITI. INTERNATIONAL TELECOMMUNICATIONS INTELLIGENCE. 1158

0268-9987 See JOURNAL OF EDUCATIONAL GERONTOLOGY. 3753

0269-0039 See CONSTRUCTION INDUSTRY LAW LETTER. 2956

0269-0055 See WASAFIRI. 3452

0269-0071 See ADVANCES IN PINEAL RESEARCH. 440

0269-0136 See INTERNATIONAL JOURNAL OF MINING AND GEOLOGICAL ENGINEERING. 2141

0269-0225 See DIAGNOSTIC ENGINEERING : NEWSLETTER OF THE INSTITUTION OF DIAGNOSTIC ENGINEERS. 1970

0269-0357 See INTERNATIONAL PUBLIC RELATIONS REVIEW. 761

0269-0365 See MOD CONTRACTS BULLETIN. 695

0269-0403 See JOURNAL OF THE ROYAL MUSICAL ASSOCIATION. 4127

0269-0497 See BRITISH JOURNAL OF ACADEMIC LIBRARIANSHIP. 3197

0269-0500 See INTERNATIONAL REVIEW OF CHILDREN'S LITERATURE AND LIBRARIANSHIP. 3218
0269-0535 See BRITISH COMPANY CASES. 3096
0269-0543 See AGRICULTURAL ZOOLOGY REVIEWS. 53
0269-0616 See WOMAN ALIVE. 5009
0269-0802 See EUROPEAN PATENT OFFICE REPORTS. 1304
0269-0942 See LOCAL ECONOMY. 1573
0269-1159 See SUN AT WORK IN EUROPE. 1958
0269-1183 See QUARTERLY JOURNAL OF TECHNICAL PAPERS. 4276
0269-1191 See FRENCH HISTORY. 2689
0269-1205 See LITERATURE & THEOLOGY. 3407
0269-1213 See RENAISSANCE STUDIES. 2705
0269-1302 See ATHLETICS TODAY. 4884
0269-1396 See PRATIQUE LONDON. 3715
0269-1418 See LEATHER IN ASIA. 3185
0269-1450 See ICB CARPET DIRECTORY. 5351
0269-1469 See SHEPPARD'S BOOK DEALERS IN NORTH AMERICA. 4832
0269-1728 See SOCIAL EPISTEMOLOGY. 4361
0269-1787 See SCOTTISH PHOTOGRAPHY BULLETIN. 4376
0269-185X See CURRENT MEDICAL LITERATURE. GROWTH AND GROWTH FACTORS. 3570
0269-1922 See DENNING LAW JOURNAL, THE. 2959
0269-2058 See WHAT'S NEW IN MARKETING. 938
0269-2104 See HEALTH CARE MANAGEMENT. 3781
0269-2139 See PROTEIN ENGINEERING. 492
0269-2155 See CLINICAL REHABILITATION. 4380
0269-2163 See PALLIATIVE MEDICINE. 3625
0269-2171 See INTERNATIONAL REVIEW OF APPLIED ECONOMICS. 1497
0269-2244 See ROYAL HISTORICAL SOCIETY STUDIES IN HISTORY. 2707
0269-2309 See ELECTRONICS SHOWCASE. 2050
0269-2325 See ARAB JOURNAL OF THE SOCIAL SCIENCES, THE. 5191
0269-2333 See POST-MARKETING SURVEILLANCE. 935
0269-2414 See NEW BEACON REVIEW. 3415
0269-2430 See OFFICE TRADE NEWS. 700
0269-2457 See AGRICULTURE INTERNATIONAL. 54
0269-2465 See PRIMARY SCIENCE REVIEW. 5139
0269-249X See DIATOM RESEARCH. 508
0269-2511 See CONSTITUTIONAL REFORM : THE QUARTERLY REVIEW. 3092
0269-2562 See JOURNAL OF ACCESS STUDIES / FORUM FOR ACCESS STUDIES. 1801
0269-2694 See BUTTERWORTHS JOURNAL OF INTERNATIONAL BANKING AND FINANCIAL LAW. 3086
0269-2716 See IPSWICH & SUFFOLK DIRECTORY OF INDUSTRY & COMMERCE, THE. 684
0269-2813 See ALIMENTARY PHARMACOLOGY & THERAPEUTICS. 4290
0269-2821 See ARTIFICIAL INTELLIGENCE REVIEW, THE. 1211
0269-283X See MEDICAL AND VETERINARY ENTOMOLOGY. 5611
0269-2848 See SURFACING JOURNAL INTERNATIONAL. 993
0269-297X See QUALITY ASSURANCE ABSTRACTS. 5303
0269-3003 See PUBLISHER (HODDESDON, ENGLAND). 4818
0269-3011 See PC WEEK (UK ED.). 1271
0269-3046 See OFFICE MAGAZINE WILMINGTON, KENT. 4213
0269-3089 See NETWORK (LONDON. 1985). 1196
0269-3216 See ELECTRONIC PRODUCT REVIEW. 2048
0269-3275 See MACUSER LONDON. 1268

0269-3518 See JOURNAL OF CELL SCIENCE. SUPPLEMENT. 537
0269-3615 See INTERSPACE FLEET. 1114
0269-3666 See PITMAN MONOGRAPHS AND SURVEYS IN PURE AND APPLIED MATHEMATICS. 3526
0269-3674 See PITMAN RESEARCH NOTES IN MATHEMATICS SERIES. 3526
0269-3712 See INTERNATIONAL YEARBOOK OF LAW, COMPUTERS, AND TECHNOLOGY. 2984
0269-3720 See TAX PRACTITIONER'S DIARY. 4754
0269-3747 See INTERNATIONAL TOURISM REPORTS. 5481
0269-3755 See TRAVEL & TOURISM ANALYST. 5495
0269-378X See INTERNATIONAL MINING. 2141
0269-3798 See INTERNATIONAL JOURNAL OF GEOGRAPHICAL INFORMATION SYSTEMS. 2566
0269-381X See COALTRANS WORCESTER PARK. 1935
0269-3852 See EUROPE REVIEW. 4473
0269-3879 See BMC. BIOMEDICAL CHROMATOGRAPHY. 449
0269-3933 See RESEARCH PAPERS IN BANKING AND FINANCE. 808
0269-4042 See ENVIRONMENTAL GEOCHEMISTRY AND HEALTH. 2167
0269-4123 See NEWSLETTER - GARDEN HISTORY SOCIETY (1981). 2425
0269-4158 See COUNTRY REPORT. BELGIUM, LUXEMBOURG. 1472
0269-4166 See COUNTRY REPORT. CANADA. 1472
0269-4174 See COUNTRY REPORT. SRI LANKA. 1476
0269-4204 See COUNTRY REPORT. NIGERIA. 1475
0269-4212 See COUNTRY REPORT. ARGENTINA. 1472
0269-4239 See COUNTRY REPORT. KENYA. 1475
0269-4263 See COUNTRY REPORT. SPAIN. 1476
0269-428X See COUNTRY REPORT. PHILIPPINES. 1476
0269-4301 See COUNTRY REPORT. HUNGARY. 1474
0269-431X See COUNTRY REPORT. BANGLADESH. 1472
0269-4336 See COUNTRY REPORT. CAMEROON, CAR, CHAD. 1472
0269-4417 See COUNTRY PROFILE. THE GAMBIA, MAURITANIA / EIU, THE ECONOMIST INTELLIGENCE UNIT. 1554
0269-4565 See EPITHELIA. 5583
0269-4662 See JEWISH BOOK NEWS & REVIEWS. 5048
0269-4697 See ARTIST'S AND ILLUSTRATOR'S MAGAZINE. 341
0269-4727 See JOURNAL OF CLINICAL PHARMACY AND THERAPEUTICS. 4310
0269-4735 See PRO SOUND NEWS (EUROPEAN ED.). 5318
0269-4859 See YOUTH LIBRARY REVIEW. 3257
0269-4905 See CRIME PREVENTION TECHNOLOGY. 3162
0269-493X See BROADCAST HARDWARE INTERNATIONAL. 1127
0269-5022 See PAEDIATRIC AND PERINATAL EPIDEMIOLOGY. 3736
0269-5030 See SCOTTISH ECONOMIC & SOCIAL HISTORY. 5218
0269-5073 See COUNTRY PROFILE. SRI LANKA. 1553
0269-5138 See COUNTRY PROFILE. DENMARK, ICELAND. 1553
0269-5154 See COUNTRY REPORT. MADAGASCAR, MAURITIUS, SEYCHELLES, COMOROS. 1475
0269-5162 See COUNTRY REPORT. UNITED ARAB EMIRATES. 1477
0269-5170 See COUNTRY REPORT. AUSTRIA. 1472
0269-5197 See COUNTRY REPORT. CHILE. 1473

0269-5251 See COUNTRY REPORT. CUBA, DOMINICAN REPUBLIC, HAITI, PUERTO RICO. 1473
0269-526X See COUNTRY REPORT. EGYPT. 1473
0269-5278 See COUNTRY REPORT. IRELAND. 1474
0269-5286 See COUNTRY REPORT. FRANCE. 1473
0269-5294 See COUNTRY REPORT. INDIA, NEPAL. 1474
0269-5413 See COUNTRY REPORT. INDONESIA. 1474
0269-5421 See COUNTRY REPORT. ITALY. 1474
0269-543X See COUNTRY REPORT. PERU, BOLIVIA. 1476
0269-5448 See COUNTRY REPORT. IRAN. 1474
0269-5456 See COUNTRY REPORT. PORTUGAL. 1476
0269-5464 See COUNTRY REPORT. TURKEY. 1477
0269-5472 See COUNTRY REPORT. UNITED KINGDOM. 1477
0269-5502 See COUNTRY REPORT. IRAQ. 1474
0269-5588 See COUNTRY PROFILE. MALAYSIA, BRUNEI. 1553
0269-5642 See RECENT ADVANCES IN ANIMAL NUTRITION. 5520
0269-5669 See COUNTRY REPORT. ROMANIA, BULGARIA, ALBANIA. 1476
0269-5677 See COUNTRY REPORT. INDOCHINA: VIETNAM, LAOS, CAMBODIA. 1474
0269-5693 See COUNTRY REPORT. LEBANON, CYPRUS. 1554
0269-5715 See COUNTRY REPORT. KUWAIT. 1475
0269-5731 See COUNTRY REPORT. BRAZIL. 1472
0269-574X See COUNTRY REPORT. DENMARK, ICELAND. 1473
0269-5774 See TOLLEY'S IMMIGRATION AND NATIONALITY LAW AND PRACTICE. 1921
0269-5782 See TRUST LAW INTERNATIONAL : PENSION FUNDS, COMMERCIAL TRUSTS, AND CHARITIES. 918
0269-5790 See O.F.I. OCCASIONAL PAPERS. 2390
0269-5839 See INTERNATIONAL REVIEWS OF ERGONOMICS. 2117
0269-591X See COUNTRY REPORT. GREECE. 1474
0269-5936 See COUNTRY REPORT. MEXICO. 1475
0269-5960 See COUNTRY PROFILE. IRAN. 1553
0269-6037 See COUNTRY PROFILE. THE GAMBIA, GUINEA-BISSAU, CAPE VERDE. 1554
0269-6126 See COUNTRY REPORT. MOROCCO. 1475
0269-6134 See COUNTRY REPORT. NETHERLANDS. 1475
0269-6142 See COUNTRY REPORT. SWEDEN. 1477
0269-6150 See COUNTRY REPORT. SUDAN. 1477
0269-6169 See COUNTRY REPORT. SWITZERLAND. 1477
0269-6177 See COUNTRY REPORT. URUGUAY, PARAGUAY. 1478
0269-6185 See COUNTRY REPORT. USA. 1554
0269-6193 See COUNTRY REPORT. POLAND. 1476
0269-6215 See COUNTRY REPORT. SAUDI ARABIA. 1476
0269-6231 See COUNTRY REPORT. CHINA, NORTH KOREA. 1473
0269-6355 See COUNTRY PROFILE. SAUDI ARABIA. 1553
0269-6363 See COUNTRY PROFILE. CONGO, SAO TOME AND PRINCIPE, GUINEA-BISSAU, CAPE VERDE / THE ECONOMIST INTELLIGENCE UNIT. 1552
0269-6533 See JET CUTTING TECHNOLOGY. 2068
0269-6606 See COUNTRY PROFILE. UNITED ARAB EMIRATES. 1554
0269-6630 See COUNTRY PROFILE. TANZANIA. 1553

0269-6630 See COUNTRY REPORT. TANZANIA, MOZAMBIQUE. 1477

0269-6681 See COUNTRY REPORT. JAPAN. 1474

0269-669X See COUNTRY REPORT. SOUTH KOREA. 1476

0269-6703 See COUNTRY REPORT. MALAYSIA, BRUNEI. 1475

0269-6711 See COUNTRY REPORT. SINGAPORE. 1476

0269-672X See COUNTRY REPORT. TAIWAN. 1477

0269-6738 See COUNTRY REPORT. SOUTH AFRICA. 1476

0269-6746 See COUNTRY REPORT. NAMIBIA, BOTSWANA, LESOTHO, SWAZILAND. 1475

0269-6762 See COUNTRY REPORT. HONG KONG, MACAU. 1474

0269-6797 See ARABLE FARMING. 62

0269-6959 See CURRENT MEDICAL LITERATURE. ANAESTHESIOLOGY / THE ROYAL SOCIETY OF MEDICINE. 3682

0269-7017 See COUNTRY PROFILE. MOZAMBIQUE. 1553

0269-7041 See COUNTRY PROFILE. SINGAPORE. 1553

0269-7092 See COUNTRY PROFILE. CONGO, SAO TOME AND PRINCIPE, GUINEA-BISSAU, CAPE VERDE / THE ECONOMIST INTELLIGENCE UNIT. 1552

0269-7114 See COUNTRY REPORT. NEW ZEALAND. 1475

0269-7122 See COUNTRY REPORT. PACIFIC ISLANDS: PAPUA NEW GUINEA, FIJI, SOLOMON ISLANDS, WESTERN SAMOA, VANUATU, TONGA. 1476

0269-7149 See COUNTRY REPORT. TRINIDAD, TOBAGO, GUYANA, BARBADOS, WINDWARD & LEEWARD ISLANDS. 1477

0269-7157 See COUNTRY REPORT. COLOMBIA. 1473

0269-7165 See COUNTRY REPORT. ECUADOR. 1473

0269-7173 See COUNTRY REPORT. PAKISTAN, AFGHANISTAN. 1476

0269-7211 See COUNTRY REPORT. SYRIA. 1477

0269-722X See COUNTRY REPORT. JORDAN. 1475

0269-7262 See COUNTRY REPORT. TOGO, NIGER, BENIN, BURKINA. 1477

0269-7270 See PROCEEDINGS OF THE ROYAL SOCIETY OF EDINBURGH. SECTION B, BIOLOGICAL SCIENCES. 470

0269-7351 See COUNTRY PROFILE. LEBANON, CYPRUS / EIU, THE ECONOMIST INTELLIGENCE UNIT. 1553

0269-736X See COUNTRY PROFILE. MADAGASCAR, COMOROS. 1553

0269-7378 See COUNTRY PROFILE. MAURITIUS, SEYCHELLES. 1553

0269-7459 See PLANNING PRACTICE + RESEARCH. 2831

0269-7483 See BIORESOURCE TECHOLOGY. 2225

0269-7491 See ENVIRONMENTAL POLLUTION (1987). 2229

0269-7572 See BIORECOVERY (BERKHAMSTED). 3687

0269-7580 See INTERNATIONAL REVIEW OF VICTIMOLOGY. 3166

0269-7653 See EVOLUTIONARY ECOLOGY. 2216

0269-7696 See CATERING UPDATE. 2331

0269-7726 See CONTAINER MANAGEMENT. 5448

0269-7777 See EXPORT GUIDE TO EUROPE, THE. 834

0269-7858 See ART AND DESIGN NEWSLETTER. 338

0269-8005 See COUNTRY PROFILE. USA. 1554

0269-8161 See LIBRARY AND INFORMATION NEWS. 3224

0269-817X See LAW & JUSTICE. 2994

0269-8188 See HEALTH & SAFETY AT WORK. 2862

0269-8196 See DIGEST OF REPORT - TRANSPORT AND ROAD RESEARCH LABORATORY. 5440

0269-8269 See HAM RADIO TODAY. 1156

0269-8307 See RADIO CONTROL MODELS & ELECTRONICS : RCM AND E. 2777

0269-834X See SCALE MODELS INTERNATIONAL. 2778

0269-8390 See SOUTH WESTERN CATHOLIC HISTORY. 5036

0269-8404 See EASTERN ART REPORT : FORTNIGHTLY SURVEY OF THE ARTS OF THE MIDDLE EAST, SOUTH ASIA, CHINA & JAPAN. 349

0269-8463 See FUNCTIONAL ECOLOGY. 2216

0269-8498 See HERPETOFAUNA NEWS. 5585

0269-8595 See INTERNATIONAL STUDIES IN THE PHILOSOPHY OF SCIENCE : I.S.P.S. 5116

0269-8773 See COSMOS. 2319

0269-879X See WELFARE MANCHESTER. 5314

0269-8803 See JOURNAL OF PSYCHOPHYSIOLOGY. 4600

0269-8811 See JOURNAL OF PSYCHOPHARMACOLOGY (OXFORD, ENGLAND). 4313

0269-8854 See BULLETIN - RAPAL. 1800

0269-8862 See ABSTRACTS IN ARTIFICIAL INTELLIGENCE / THE TURING INSTITUTE. 1210

0269-8889 See KNOWLEDGE ENGINEERING REVIEW, THE. 1214

0269-8897 See SCIENCE IN CONTEXT. 5152

0269-8951 See MEDICAL SCIENCE RESEARCH. 3611

0269-8986 See IOP SHORT MEETINGS SERIES. 4406

0269-9052 See BRAIN INJURY. 3828

0269-915X See MYCOLOGIST, THE. 576

0269-9206 See CLINICAL LINGUISTICS & PHONETICS. 3274

0269-9222 See BRITISH JOURNAL OF CANADIAN STUDIES. 2724

0269-9265 See KELLY'S BUSINESS DIRECTORY. 843

0269-9370 See AIDS (LONDON). 3664

0269-946X See AUTOSPORT (TEDDINGTON). 5407

0269-9478 See HORTICULTURE WEEK. 2419

0269-9567 See MIDDLE EAST COMMUNICATIONS. 1160

0269-963X See LIBRARY EQUIPMENT REPORT. 3225

0269-9648 See PROBABILITY IN THE ENGINEERING AND INFORMATIONAL SCIENCES. 1991

0269-9656 See REMNANTS. 2705

0269-9702 See BIOETHICS. 3556

0269-9761 See MACHINE KNITTING MONTHLY. 5184

0269-977X See CAYMAN ISLANDS LAW REPORTS, THE. 2949

0269-980X See TROPICAL TIMBERS. 2399

0269-9834 See PACKAGING INDUSTRY DIRECTORY. 4220

0269-9931 See COGNITION & EMOTION. 4581

0269-994X See APPLIED PSYCHOLOGY. 4574

0270-000X See GUIDE TO PRACTICE AND PROCEDURE, U.S. DEPARTMENT OF ENERGY, BOARD OF CONTRACT APPEALS, CONTRACT ADJUSTMENT BOARD, FINANCIAL ASSISTANCE APPEALS BOARD, INVENTION LICENSING APPEALS BOARD. 1945

0270-0034 See WATER RESOURCES COORDINATION DIRECTORY. 5544

0270-0042 See INJURY EXPERIENCE IN METALLIC MINERAL MINING. 2864

0270-0050 See MCCALL'S BOOK FOR BRIDES. 2283

0270-0077 See TAX COMPANION, THE. 4752

0270-0085 See GAYOSO STREET REVIEW, THE. 3390

0270-0093 See ELECTRONIC MARKET DATA BOOK. 2047

0270-0107 See ANNUAL REPORT OF OHIONET. 3190

0270-0115 See ENERGY RESOURCE NOTES. 1941

0270-0123 See TMO UPDATE. 4033

0270-0131 See MONOGRAPHS IN PSYCHOBIOLOGY AND DISEASE. 466

0270-0344 See BALTIMORE COUNTY HERITAGE PUBLICATION, A. 2722

0270-0352 See CUMULATIVE INDEX - FOOD MARKETING INSTITUTE, INFORMATION SERVICE. 2332

0270-0409 See SMALL GRAINS. 186

0270-0417 See WORKING. 1719

0270-0425 See ARIZONA SENIOR WORLD, THE. 5629

0270-045X See INTERNATIONAL ECONOMIC SCOREBOARD. 1636

0270-045X See INTERNATIONAL ECONOMIC SCOREBOARD. 1636

0270-0484 See JOURNAL OF THE AMERICAN REAL ESTATE AND URBAN ECONOMICS ASSOCIATION. 4839

0270-0492 See CGCR. COMPRESSED GASES AND CRYOGENICS REPORT. 4399

0270-0506 See D.C. CIRCUIT HANDBOOK. 2958

0270-0514 See LOCAL CLIMATOLOGICAL DATA. PITTSBURGH, PENNSYLVANIA, GREATER PITTSBURGH AIRPORT. ANNUAL SUMMARY WITH COMPARATIVE DATA. 1429

0270-0522 See LOCAL CLIMATOLOGICAL DATA. PITTSBURGH, PENNSYLVANIA. WEA. SVS. CONTRACT MET. OBSY. GREATER PITTSBURGH INTL. AP. MONTHLY SUMMARY. 1429

0270-0573 See REVIEW OF CURRENT DHHS, DOE, AND EPA RESEARCH RELATED TO TOXICOLOGY. 3983

0270-059X See LIBRARY LECTURES (KNOXVILLE). 3226

0270-0603 See HEALTH EDUCATION BULLETIN. 4779

0270-0611 See PUBLICATION - AMERICAN INSTITUTE OF THE HISTORY OF PHARMACY. 4327

0270-062X See KIDNEY DISEASE. 3991

0270-0646 See GUIDELINES IN MEDICINE. 3579

0270-0654 See JUDICIAL FELLOWS PROGRAM, THE. 3141

0270-0662 See NEWS FROM THE HILL (WASHINGTON). 3102

0270-0697 See ANALYTICAL STUDIES FOR THE U.S. ENVIRONMENTAL PROTECTION AGENCY. 2160

0270-0743 See ELECTRIC UTILITY GENERATION PLANBOOK, THE. 2044

0270-0751 See ENVIROLINE USER'S MANUAL. 2228

0270-0786 See TEXTILE CHALLENGER. 1714

0270-0808 See STATE GOVERNMENT TAX COLLECTIONS IN 4749

0270-0816 See NATIONAL GARDENING SURVEY. 2425

0270-0824 See JOURNAL - NEW MEXICO HIGHLANDS UNIVERSITY. 1832

0270-0832 See HARMONICA HAPPENINGS. 4120

0270-0999 See CONSUMER AFFAIRS LETTER, THE. 1294

0270-1022 See IGT GASCOPE. 4260

0270-1111 See DIRECTORY OF ENVIRONMENTAL ORGANIZATIONS (LOS ANGELES). 2213

0270-1138 See INTERNATIONAL PETROCHEMICAL DEVELOPMENT. 4261

0270-1146 See METALSMITH. 374

0270-1154 See STATUS OF THE FAMILY FARM, ANNUAL REPORT TO THE CONGRESS. 138

0270-1170 See JOURNAL OF ET NURSING. 3858

0270-1197 See BUILDING STANDARDS. 604

0270-126X See PUERTO RICO BUSINESS REVIEW. 705

0270-1294 See ENERGY RESOURCES SERIES. 1942

0270-1367 See RESEARCH QUARTERLY FOR EXERCISE AND SPORT. 1858

0270-1448 See READINGS ON EQUAL EDUCATION. 1884
0270-1456 See HARVARD WOMEN'S LAW JOURNAL. 2977
0270-1464 See ANNUAL SURVEY OF BANKRUPTCY LAW. 3084
0270-1480 See PROCEEDINGS OF THE ANNUAL STUDENT SYMPOSIUM ON MARINE AFFAIRS. 557
0270-1510 See RULES OF CONDUCT. BYLAWS AND IMPLEMENTING RESOLUTIONS OF COUNCIL. 751
0270-1537 See BASEBALL RULE BOOK. NATIONAL FEDERATION EDITION. 4886
0270-1553 See PATIENT CARE FLOW CHART MANUAL. 3738
0270-1561 See EXECUTIVE COMPENSATION REPORT FOR SMALL TO MEDIUM SIZED COMPANIES. 674
0270-1596 See BIENNIAL REPORT PREPARED IN ACCORDANCE WITH THE OZONE PROTECTION PROVISION, SECTION 153 (G), OF THE CLEAN AIR ACT AMENDMENTS OF 1977. 2225
0270-160X See WHO'S WHO IN THE FISH INDUSTRY. 2316
0270-1618 See KOREAN CULTURE (LOS ANGELES). 2657
0270-1626 See ENGELSMAN'S GENERAL CONSTRUCTION COST GUIDE. 614
0270-1707 See PHILATELIC LITERATURE REVIEW. 2786
0270-1715 See ACCREDITED INSTITUTIONS OF POSTSECONDARY EDUCATION, PROGRAMS, CANDIDATES. 1807
0270-174X See NOUVELLES, LES. 1306
0270-1766 See SPECIAL SERIES / SOCIETY FOR ETHNOMUSICOLOGY. 4154
0270-1812 See SPORT SCENE. 4921
0270-1847 See COLD SPRING HARBOR MONOGRAPH SERIES. 451
0270-188X See ETTORE MAJORANA INTERNATIONAL SCIENCE SERIES : PHYSICAL SCIENCE. 5103
0270-1898 See PROCEEDINGS OF THE INTERNATIONAL PYROTECHNICS SEMINAR. 989
0270-1960 See GERONTOLOGY & GERIATRICS EDUCATION. 3752
0270-1987 See REVIEW OF PERSONALITY AND SOCIAL PSYCHOLOGY. 4615
0270-1995 See WORLD HERITAGE WORLD. 2478
0270-2002 See LIBRO VERDE, EL. 1616
0270-2010 See JOURNAL OF SOVIET LASER RESEARCH. 4437
0270-2053 See INJURY EXPERIENCE IN SAND AND GRAVEL MINING. 2864
0270-2061 See INCL JOURNAL. 2980
0270-207X See OUTREACH (CHICAGO). 3725
0270-210X See BULLETIN OF THE EGYPTOLOGICAL SEMINAR. 264
0270-2118 See ROLE OF VIRUSES IN HUMAN CANCER, THE. 3823
0270-2223 See NEWSPAPER GUILD, AFL-CIO, CLC CONSTITUTION, THE. 1695
0270-2266 See BUSINESS INSIGHTS : SCHOOL OF BUSINESS ADMINISTRATION QUARTERLY MAGAZINE, CALIFORNIA STATE UNIVERSITY, LONG BEACH. 649
0270-2282 See NORTH AMERICAN HUMAN RIGHTS DIRECTORY. 4511
0270-2304 See FAMILY PRACTICE RESEARCH JOURNAL, THE. 3737
0270-2398 See TRAVELORE REPORT, THE. 5497
0270-2401 See NEWSLETTER FOR INVENTORS, A. 5133
0270-241X See ANDREW SEYBOLD'S REPORT ON MOBILE EMERGENCY COMMUNICATIONS. 1104
0270-2436 See ALABAMA AGRICULTURAL STATISTICS. 151
0270-2479 See EMPLOYMENT LAW UPDATE. 3147
0270-2487 See GOVERNMENT UNION REVIEW. 3148

0270-2495 See JOURNAL OF AFRICAN CIVILIZATIONS. 2640
0270-2541 See NEW DESIGNS FOR YOUTH DEVELOPMENT. 1067
0270-255X See NMM WEEKLY. 4842
0270-2584 See INTERNATIONAL CONFERENCE ON ENVIRONMENTAL PROBLEMS OF THE EXTRACTIVE INDUSTRIES. 2174
0270-2592 See JOURNAL OF FINANCIAL RESEARCH, THE. 794
0270-2614 See SKENECTADA. 4172
0270-2630 See SURF REPORT, THE. 4924
0270-2673 See NEWSLETTER - AMERICAN ASSOCIATION OF TISSUE BANKS. 3621
0270-2681 See APPAREL SALES/MARKETING COMPENSATION SURVEY. 921
0270-2703 See PRISON DECISIONS. 3173
0270-2711 See READING PSYCHOLOGY. 4615
0270-272X See WILLIAM MITCHELL LAW REVIEW. 3075
0270-2746 See CYCLE WORLD TEST ANNUAL & BUYER'S GUIDE. 4081
0270-2762 See RETAIL BANKING REPORT. 809
0270-2770 See NASADAD ALCOHOL AND DRUG ABUSE REPORT. MONTHLY REPORT. 1347
0270-2789 See NASADAD ALCOHOL AND DRUG ABUSE REPORT. SPECIAL REPORT. 1347
0270-2797 See AGENCY LIST, GEOGRAPHIC. 5460
0270-2835 See NATIONAL ASSOCIATION OF CONSUMER AGENCY ADMINISTRATORS NEWS. 1298
0270-2894 See CONTINENTAL BIRDLIFE. 5617
0270-2908 See GILBERT LAW SUMMARIES. CONFLICT OF LAWS. 2974
0270-2924 See ALTERNATIVES (NEW MARKET). 2527
0270-2932 See ASPHALT PAVING TECHNOLOGY. 2018
0270-2959 See FLYING NEEDLE, THE. 5184
0270-2983 See AMS STUDIES IN MODERN LITERATURE. 3361
0270-2991 See AMS STUDIES IN CRIMINAL JUSTICE. 3156
0270-3009 See NATIONAL MEETING - AMERICAN CHEMICAL SOCIETY, DIVISION OF ENVIRONMENTAL CHEMISTRY. 987
0270-3017 See NEW MEXICO JOURNAL OF SCIENCE. 5132
0270-3068 See FIBER OPTICS DIRECTORY UPDATE SERVICE. 1155
0270-3076 See FIBER OPTICS CROSS-REFERENCE PATENT ABSTRACTS SERVICE. 1304
0270-3084 See FIBER OPTICS PATENT ABSTRACTS SERVICE. 1304
0270-3106 See JOURNAL OF ADDICTIVE DISEASES. 1345
0270-3114 See PREVENTION IN HUMAN SERVICES. 4810
0270-3149 See WOMEN & THERAPY. 5569
0270-3157 See PRIMARY SOURCES AND ORIGINAL WORKS. 3241
0270-3181 See PHYSICAL & OCCUPATIONAL THERAPY IN GERIATRICS. 4381
0270-319X See LEGAL REFERENCE SERVICES QUARTERLY. 3000
0270-3203 See MUSIC INDUSTRY BULLETIN. 4134
0270-3211 See TERATOGENESIS, CARCINOGENESIS, AND MUTAGENESIS. 3824
0270-3246 See CURRENT ISSUES IN THE AMERICAN ECONOMY. 1478
0270-3289 See FILM AND VIDEO MAKERS DIRECTORY, THE. 4069
0270-3300 See ANNUAL REPORT - MENTAL HYGIENE ADMINISTRATION. 4766
0270-3343 See HEALTH LAW VIGIL. 2978
0270-3386 See FORECAST (SILVER SPRING). 1425
0270-3424 See LEGAL CONNECTION; CORPORATIONS & LAW FIRMS, THE. 3101
0270-3432 See DEFENDER (COLUMBUS), THE. 3106

0270-3467 See PRESIDENTS REPORT - COLONIAL WILLIAMSBURG FOUNDATION, THE. 5235
0270-3521 See MVR. 3414
0270-353X See POLITICAL FINANCE LOBBY REPORTER. 4489
0270-3572 See BUSINESS AND THE MEDIA. 1105
0270-3599 See SEVENTH-DAY ADVENTIST PERIODICAL INDEX. 5013
0270-3629 See MICHIGAN ROMANCE STUDIES. 3302
0270-3637 See NETWORK (RESEARCH TRIANGLE PARK). 589
0270-3653 See BORGO REFERENCE LIBRARY, THE. 3197
0270-3750 See DICTIONARY ENCYCLOPEDIA HANDBOOK REVIEW. 1925
0270-3777 See DANGEROUS PROPERTIES OF INDUSTRIAL MATERIALS REPORT. 2861
0270-3807 See DISCUSSIONS AND CLOSURES OF ABSTRACTED PAPERS FROM THE WINTER MEETING. 2042
0270-3815 See DIRECTORY OF NEW ENGLAND SKI TOURING CENTERS, A. 4892
0270-3823 See MONTANA AGING SERVICES PROGRAM BOOK. 5296
0270-3831 See ENTERTAINMENT LAW REPORTER. 2966
0270-384X See CALIFORNIA FRESH FRUIT AND VEGETABLE SHIPMENTS BY RAIL, TRUCK, AND AIR. 2330
0270-3920 See ADVANCES IN SCHOOL PSYCHOLOGY. 4572
0270-3955 See VERMONT ECONOMIC ALMANAC, THE. 1525
0270-4005 See MONETARY POLICY REPORT FROM THE COMMITTEE ON BANKING, HOUSING, AND URBAN AFFAIRS, UNITED STATES SENATE. 799
0270-4013 See ADVANCES IN SPECIAL EDUCATION. 1874
0270-4021 See ADVANCES IN EARLY EDUCATION AND DAY CARE. 1802
0270-403X See AIR FORCE JOURNAL OF LOGISTICS. 4033
0270-4048 See JAZZ RAG. 4125
0270-4064 See JOURNAL OF THE KANAWHA VALLEY GENEALOGICAL SOCIETY, THE. 2455
0270-4072 See FOODBORNE DISEASE SURVEILLANCE. ANNUAL SUMMARY. 4776
0270-4080 See REPORT OF ACTIVITIES - NEW MEXICO FORESTRY DIVISION. 2392
0270-4137 See PROSTATE, THE. 3800
0270-4145 See JOURNAL OF CRANIOFACIAL GENETICS AND DEVELOPMENTAL BIOLOGY. 3805
0270-4153 See WEEKLY INSIDERS DAIRY & EGG LETTER. 199
0270-4161 See RESTAURANT BUYERS GUIDE. 951
0270-417X See SEAFOOD PRICE - CURRENT. 2357
0270-4188 See ANNUAL PRICE REVIEW. 60
0270-4196 See DETERMINATIONS OF THE NATIONAL MEDIATION BOARD. 3146
0270-4218 See BASEBALL CASE BOOK. 4886
0270-4226 See BASKETBALL OFFICIALS MANUAL. 4887
0270-4234 See REPORT - NATIONAL SOCIETY TO PREVENT BLINDNESS. 3878
0270-4242 See INDEX TO DECISIONS OF THE OCCUPATIONAL SAFETY AND HEALTH REVIEW COMMISSION. 2863
0270-4250 See NEED ANALYSIS REQUIREMENTS, PLUS THE COMPLETE CSS CODE LIST. 1837
0270-4269 See TELEPHONE ANGLES. 1167
0270-4331 See REPORT ON KANSAS LEGISLATIVE INTERIM STUDIES TO THE LEGISLATURE. 3038
0270-4358 See GREECE AND YUGOSLAVIA ON $15 & $20 A DAY. 5478
0270-4366 See ANNUAL BLACK CONSUMER BUYING SURVEY, FOOD SALES. 1462

0270-4404 See ACRONYMS, INITIALISMS & ABBREVIATIONS DICTIONARY. 3261

0270-4412 See NEBRASKA REVIEW (FAIRBURY, NEB.). 1093

0270-4447 See SAFETY NEWS (DENVER). 2869

0270-4463 See NEBRASKA ANCESTREE. 2462

0270-448X See COMMUTER AIR CARRIER TRAFFIC STATISTICS. 41

0270-4528 See PREDICASTS F & S INDEX INTERNATIONAL. 732

0270-4536 See PREDICASTS F & S INDEX EUROPE. 704

0270-4544 See PREDICASTS F & S INDEX UNITED STATES. 704

0270-4552 See DIRECT INVESTMENT LAW REPORT. 3127

0270-4579 See MICHIGAN CRITICAL MATERIALS REGISTER. 2236

0270-4595 See MEMBERSHIP DIRECTORY - FLORIDA LIBRARY ASSOCIATION. 3230

0270-4609 See COME FOR TO SING. 4111

0270-4625 See COINAGE MAGAZINE'S GOLD & SILVER. 2780

0270-4633 See BOSTON MYCOLOGICAL CLUB BULLETIN. 574

0270-4641 See MEMBERSHIP DIRECTORY - SUBURBAN NEWSPAPERS OF AMERICA. 5661

0270-465X See UPCHURCH BULLETIN. 2476

0270-4668 See HOME WINE AND BEER MAKERS INFORMATION. 2367

0270-4676 See BULLETIN OF SCIENCE, TECHNOLOGY & SOCIETY. 5091

0270-4730 See STUDIES IN HIGH ENERGY PHYSICS. 4423

0270-4757 See SIGNCRAFT. 382

0270-4765 See JOURNAL OF THE WEST VIRGINIA HISTORICAL ASSOCIATION, THE. 2743

0270-4803 See CARIBBEAN BARGAIN BOOK, THE. 5466

0270-4838 See U.S. METRIC BOARD ANNUAL REPORT. 4033

0270-4846 See COMPUTER LITERATURE INDEX. 1208

0270-4862 See CALIFORNIA INTERNATIONAL TRADE REGISTER. 1467

0270-4900 See NET RESULTS. 4980

0270-4919 See HISTORICAL INTELLIGENCER. 5061

0270-4935 See ELECTROMAGNETIC NEWS REPORT. 2046

0270-496X See SOURCEWORLD. 1276

0270-4978 See BASIC AND CLINICAL NUTRITION. 4187

0270-4986 See KODAK LABORATORY CHEMICALS BULLETIN. 984

0270-5001 See BULLETIN - NORTH CAROLINA, DEPARTMENT OF NATURAL RESOURCES AND COMMUNITY DEVELOPMENT, DIVISION OF LAND RESOURCES, GEOLOGICAL SURVEY SECTION. 1370

0270-5060 See JOURNAL OF FRESHWATER ECOLOGY. 2218

0270-5079 See AIR TAXI CHARTER & RENTAL DIRECTORY OF NORTH AMERICA. 8

0270-5095 See DOCUMENTS TO THE PEOPLE. 3208

0270-5117 See ACOUSTICAL IMAGING. 4451

0270-5176 See INTERNATIONAL AIR SAFETY SEMINAR PROCEEDINGS. 24

0270-5184 See EXPORT-IMPORT MARKETS. 834

0270-5192 See CARDOZO LAW REVIEW. 2948

0270-5206 See BENDER'S DICTIONARY OF 1040 DEDUCTIONS. 2941

0270-5214 See JOHNS HOPKINS APL TECHNICAL DIGEST. 1981

0270-5230 See TOPICS IN HEALTH INFORMATION MANAGEMENT. 3793

0270-5249 See COMMERCIAL AIRCRAFT FLEETS. 16

0270-5257 See PROCEEDINGS - INTERNATIONAL CONFERENCE ON SOFTWARE ENGINEERING. 1289

0270-5265 See WEST'S FEDERAL TAXATION. CORPORATIONS, PARTNERSHIPS, ESTATES AND TRUSTS. 4758

0270-5273 See STATE DATA ON OCCUPATIONAL INJURIES AND ILLNESSES. 2870

0270-5281 See CEMETERY MANAGEMENT. 2407

0270-529X See TEXAS BRIEFCASE SHEPARD'S. 3063

0270-5303 See ANNUAL REPORTS OF THE NORTH CAROLINIANA SOCIETY, INC. AND THE NORTH CAROLINA COLLECTION. 2721

0270-5311 See DIRECTORY AND YEARBOOK - HUMAN FACTORS SOCIETY. 1970

0270-5338 See STOKVIS STUDIES IN HISTORICAL CHRONOLOGY & THOUGHT. 2630

0270-5346 See CAMERA OBSCURA (BERKELEY). 4065

0270-5400 See OIL AND GAS PRODUCTION REPORT. NORTHERN ROCKIES. 4268

0270-5419 See OIL AND GAS PRODUCTION REPORT. SOUTHERN ROCKIES. 4268

0270-5427 See PROCEEDINGS OF THE INTERNATIONAL CONFERENCE ON BASEMENT TECTONICS. 1391

0270-5443 See INFORMATIVE CIRCULAR - OHIO BIOLOGICAL SURVEY. 458

0270-5451 See GEOLOGICAL NEWSLETTER (PORTLAND). 1378

0270-5486 See RESEARCH PAPER - NEVADA ARCHEOLOGICAL SURVEY. 280

0270-5494 See TAX NOTES (ARLINGTON). 4753

0270-5508 See SZIVARVANY. 3444

0270-5516 See PETTIT REPORT ON THE POLITICS OF SAN FRANCISCO, THE. 4487

0270-5524 See SEA HERITAGE NEWS. 2545

0270-5575 See ANNUAL REPORT - GRADUATE DEPT. OF LIBRARY AND INFORMATION SCIENCE, THE CATHOLIC UNIVERSITY OF AMERICA. 3190

0270-5583 See BITS OF BARK FROM THE FAMILY TREE. 2439

0270-5605 See FINANCIAL FACTS ON WYOMING TAXING UNITS. 4725

0270-5621 See PURCHASING MANAGERS REPORT ON BUSINESS. 1623

0270-563X See FEDERAL EXECUTIVE DIRECTORY. 4648

0270-5656 See FINANCIAL REVIEW OF ALIEN INSURERS. 2880

0270-5664 See INTERNATIONAL STUDIES IN PHILOSOPHY. 4349

0270-5672 See FARMLINE. 86

0270-5680 See LAKE LOG CHIPS. 844

0270-5702 See CQ. CONNECTICUT QUARTERLY. 3378

0270-5877 See ASA NEWSLETTER (PARK RIDGE). 3682

0270-5923 See AREA WAGE SURVEY. YORK, PENNSYLVANIA, METROPOLITAN AREA. 1653

0270-5974 See BEST'S AGGREGATES & AVERAGES. PROPERTY-CASUALTY. 2875

0270-5982 See VERMONT NATURAL HISTORY. 4173

0270-6075 See INTERNATIONAL AND INTERCULTURAL COMMUNICATION ANNUAL. 1113

0270-6210 See SAN FRANCISCO JUNG INSTITUTE LIBRARY JOURNAL, THE. 4617

0270-6245 See REGISTER AND MANUAL - STAGE OF CONNECTICUT. 4679

0270-6253 See AMS STUDIES IN SOCIAL HISTORY. 2610

0270-6261 See AMS STUDIES IN THE MIDDLE AGES. 2673

0270-627X See COMPLETE BUYER'S GUIDE TO STEREO/HI-FI EQUIPMENT, THE. 5316

0270-6288 See PRIMARY-JUNIOR KID-CRAFTS. 1068

0270-6318 See PRIMARY KID-CRAFTS. 1068

0270-6326 See ANNUAL REPORT AND FINANCIAL STATEMENTS - ALASKA MUNICIPAL BOND BANK. 891

0270-6350 See VIBES (NEW YORK). 4158

0270-6377 See GENETIC ENGINEERING NEWS. 545

0270-6474 See JOURNAL OF NEUROSCIENCE, THE. 3836

0270-6504 See UKY BU (UNIVERSITY OF KENTUCKY). 2000

0270-6512 See DOE/ER (UNITED STATES. DEPT. OF ENERGY. OFFICE OF ENERGY RESEARCH). 1936

0270-6571 See MICHIGAN MIDDLE SCHOOL JOURNAL. 1764

0270-658X See NUTRITION AND HEALTH (NEW YORK). 4195

0270-661X See JOURNAL OF TRADITIONAL ACUPUNCTURE, THE. 3600

0270-6644 See CLINICAL PSYCHIATRY NEWS. 3923

0270-6660 See CURRENT POPULATION REPORTS. SERIES P-28, SPECIAL CENSUSES. 4551

0270-6679 See FEMINIST ISSUES. 5556

0270-6687 See CORONA (BOZEMAN). 3378

0270-6717 See INTERFACE (CHICAGO). 3217

0270-6768 See NATIONAL INTELLIGENCE REPORT. CLINICAL LABS/BLOOD BANKS. 3619

0270-6792 See LIBRARY INSTRUCTION ROUND TABLE NEWS. 3225

0270-6814 See ECONOMIC TRENDS IN COLOR (1978). 1485

0270-6822 See MUFON UFO JOURNAL, THE. 29

0270-6865 See FROM THE HORSE'S MOUTH (PITTSBURGH). 1675

0270-6881 See NAEN BULLETIN. 1766

0270-7098 See IOWA JOURNAL OF RESEARCH IN MUSIC EDUCATION. 4124

0270-7101 See GEMSHORN. 4119

0270-7179 See ANTARCTIC METEORITE NEWSLETTER. 1420

0270-7195 See ADVISORY REPORT - UNIVERSITY OF WISCONSIN SEA GRANT COLLEGE PROGRAM. 1807

0270-7284 See SNA PERSPECTIVE. 1249

0270-7306 See MOLECULAR AND CELLULAR BIOLOGY. 568

0270-7314 See JOURNAL OF FUTURES MARKETS, THE. 904

0270-739X See PITTMAN-ROBERTSON GAME MANAGEMENT TECHNICAL SERIES. 2202

0270-7462 See CRITICAL CARE. 3569

0270-7497 See GREAT ISSUES OF THE DAY. 2488

0270-7500 See PENNSYLVANIA HERITAGE (1974). 2754

0270-7527 See RESUME (DENVER). 4277

0270-7543 See DIRECTORS ENCYCLOPEDIA OF NEWSPAPERS, THE. 1925

0270-7578 See ACHIEVEMENTS (WASHINGTON). 4701

0270-7586 See ANNUAL COLLECTION AND STORAGE OF SOLAR ENERGY FOR THE HEATING OF BUILDINGS. 1931

0270-7594 See ALI-ABA COURSE OF STUDY. ESTATE PLANNING FOR RETIRING OR DYING CLIENTS : MATERIALS. 3117

0270-7683 See REAL ESTATE & THE LAW. 4843

0270-7691 See STATISTICAL SUMMARY - FLORIDA CITRUS PROCESSORS ASSOCIATION. 2358

0270-7705 See CAREER EDUCATION (WASHINGTON). 1911

0270-7713 See DUN & BRADSTREET'S KEY BUSINESS RATIOS. 669

0270-7721 See REALTY. RELOCATION. REVIEW. 4846

0270-773X See ADVANCES IN CHROMATOGRAPHY (HOUSTON). 1020

0270-7748 See NEW IMAGE OF MAN IN MEDICINE, A. 3620

0270-7772 See RESEARCH MONOGRAPH - NATIONAL INSTITUTE ON ALCOHOL ABUSE AND ALCOHOLISM. 1348

0270-7780 See VIRGINIA NURSE. 3870

0270-7799 See BAYLOR NURSING EDUCATOR. 3852

0270-7837 See ANNUAL MEETING OF THE MINNESOTA SECTION, AIME AND ANNUAL MINING SYMPOSIUM. 2133

0270-7918 See ULTRANUTRITION DIGEST. 4199

0270-7926 See CHRYSLER MUSEUM, THE. 4086

0270-7950 See NCI FACT BOOK. 3821

0270-7969 See BUSINESS TRAVELER'S REPORT. 5465

0270-7985 See FOREIGN TOURIST ARRIVALS BY SELECTED STATES- AND PORTS-OF-ENTRY. 5474

0270-7993 See WOMAN'S ART JOURNAL. 368

0270-8019 See WORLDWATCH PAPER. 2210

0270-8035 See CHAPTERS (CAMBRIDGE). 2530

0270-8043 See AAPG CONTINUING EDUCATION COURSE NOTE SERIES. 4248

0270-8094 See PUBLIC LANDS NEWS. 2202

0270-8183 See FODOR'S CENTRAL AMERICA. 5471

0270-8205 See SHORT-TERM ENERGY OUTLOOK. VOLUME II, METHODOLOGY. 1956

0270-823X See ECD. ENERGY CONSERVATION DIGEST. 1937

0270-8272 See DESCRIPTOR FREQUENCY LIST. 3205

0270-8280 See OFFICIAL NATIONAL FEDERATION BASKETBALL RULE BOOK. 4909

0270-8299 See CITIZENS LAW ADVISOR. 2950

0270-8329 See BULLETIN ... OF SEISMICITY OF THE SOUTHEASTERN UNITED STATES. 1403

0270-8337 See NEWSLETTER - EARTHQUAKE ENGINEERING RESEARCH INSTITUTE. 1409

0270-8345 See MAINE GEOLOGIST, THE. 1386

0270-837X See VIRGINIA JOURNAL OF EDUCATION (1980). 1908

0270-8388 See ART OF NEGOTIATING NEWSLETTER, THE. 1654

0270-840X See IRANIAN STUDIES SEMINAR, ANNUAL PROCEEDINGS. 2768

0270-8434 See EXXON TRAVEL CLUB MEXICO VACATION TRAVEL GUIDE. 2805

0270-8469 See DISTRIBUTION OF OCCUPATIONAL EMPLOYMENT IN STATES AND AREAS BY RACE AND SEX. 1663

0270-8493 See COLLEGE COST BOOK, THE. 1816

0270-8507 See VLSI UPDATE. 1239

0270-854X See JOHN MARSHALL LAW REVIEW, THE. 2986

0270-8558 See HISPANIC AMERICAN PERIODICALS INDEX (LOS ANGELES, CALIF.). 2496

0270-8647 See PSA (EAST LANSING, MICH.). 5143

0270-8655 See U.S. DEPARTMENT OF THE INTERIOR NATIONAL PARK SERVICE TRANSACTIONS AND PROCEEDINGS SERIES. 2207

0270-8698 See HERB IRELAND'S SALES PROSPECTOR. NEW ENGLAND. 925

0270-8701 See HERB IRELAND'S SALES PROSPECTOR. NEW YORK, NEW JERSEY AND SOUTHERN CONNECTICUT. 925

0270-871X See HERB IRELAND'S SALES PROSPECTOR. PENNSYLVANIA, DELAWARE AND SOUTHERN NEW JERSEY. 925

0270-8728 See HERB IRELAND'S SALES PROSPECTOR. OHIO AND MICHIGAN. 925

0270-8736 See HERB IRELAND'S SALES PROSPECTOR. ILLINOIS AND INDIANA. 925

0270-8744 See HERB IRELAND'S SALES PROSPECTOR. OHIO RIVER VALLEY. 925

0270-8752 See HERB IRELAND'S SALES PROSPECTOR. GEORGIA, FLORIDA, ALABAMA AND NORTH AND SOUTH CAROLINA. 925

0270-8760 See HERB IRELAND'S SALES PROSPECTOR. MARYLAND, VIRGINIA, WEST VIRGINIA, NORTH AND SOUTH CAROLINA, AND DISTRICT OF COLUMBIA. 925

0270-8779 See HERB IRELAND'S SALES PROSPECTOR. LOUISIANA, MISSISSIPPI, ARKANSAS, OKLAHOMA, KENTUCKY AND TENNESSEE. 925

0270-8787 See HERB IRELAND'S SALES PROSPECTOR. TEXAS, OKLAHOMA AND NEW MEXICO. 925

0270-8795 See HERB IRELAND'S SALES PROSPECTOR. MISSOURI, KANSAS, IOWA AND NEBRASKA. 925

0270-8809 See HERB IRELAND'S SALES PROSPECTOR. WISCONSIN, MINNESOTA, IOWA, NORTH AND SOUTH DAKOTA. 925

0270-8817 See HERB IRELAND'S SALES PROSPECTOR. CANADA. 616

0270-8825 See HERB IRELAND'S SALES PROSPECTOR. COLORADO, IDAHO, MONTANA, OREGON, UTAH, WASHINGTON, WYOMING AND ALASKA. 925

0270-8833 See HERB IRELAND'S SALES PROSPECTOR. CALIFORNIA, ARIZONA, NEVADA AND HAWAII. 925

0270-885X See CABLE TV ADVERTISING. 756

0270-8876 See SUPPLEMENTAL TIDAL PREDICTIONS, ANCHORAGE, NIKISHKA, SELDOVIA, AND VALDEZ, ALASKA. 4183

0270-8884 See NOLSLETTER. 3180

0270-8892 See ANNUAL REPORT ON MARKETING, IRRIGATION, PRODUCTION. 163

0270-8906 See INSCOM JOURNAL. 4046

0270-8930 See BIENNIAL REPORT - CALIFORNIA ENERGY COMMISSION. 1933

0270-8949 See EDMUND'S UNITED STATES COIN PRICES. 2781

0270-8965 See INSIDE E.P.A. WEEKLY REPORT. 2174

0270-8973 See PUBLIC SECTOR HEALTH CARE RISK MANAGEMENT. 3791

0270-899X See 16 MAGAZINE. 1059

0270-9074 See ARCHIVES OF FAMILY PRACTICE. 3736

0270-9104 See RIVER CITY LIBRARY TIMES. 3247

0270-9139 See HEPATOLOGY (BALTIMORE, MD.). 3797

0270-9163 See ENERGY LAW JOURNAL. 2966

0270-9228 See ADVANCES IN FAMILY INTERVENTION, ASSESSMENT AND THEORY. 3919

0270-9287 See QUARTERLY REVIEW - UNITED METHODIST BOARD OF HIGHER EDUCATION AND MINISTRY (U.S.). 5066

0270-9295 See SEMINARS IN NEPHROLOGY. 3993

0270-9317 See BUILDING-PERMIT ACTIVITY IN FLORIDA (ANNUAL). 603

0270-9325 See GUITAR & MANDOLIN. 4120

0270-9341 See PHOENIX HOME/GARDEN. 2902

0270-9368 See SHAKER MESSENGER, THE. 2760

0270-9376 See REPORT OF THE PROCEEDINGS - NATIONAL CENTER FOR A BARRIER FREE ENVIRONMENT, A. 2181

0270-9406 See MODERN JEWISH STUDIES ANNUAL. 3412

0270-9422 See SAS COMMUNICATIONS. 1121

0270-9473 See MINERAL PERSPECTIVES. 1441

0270-9481 See WATER RESOURCES PLANNING SERIES. 5547

0270-9503 See WATER QUALITY SERIES (LOGAN). 5543

0270-9538 See SCS-TP (UNITED STATES. SOIL CONSERVATION SERVICE). 185

0270-9554 See TAILING DISPOSAL TODAY. 4021

0270-9600 See WATER RESOURCES MONOGRAPH. 5547

0270-9678 See ALLIANCE WORLD (CAMP HILL, PA.), THE. 4933

0270-9686 See ALI-ABA COURSE OF STUDY. INVESTMENT ADVISER REGULATION : MATERIALS. 2930

0270-9694 See ALI-ABA COURSE OF STUDY. ESTATE PLANNING : MATERIALS. 3117

0270-9708 See ALI-ABA COURSE OF STUDY. FOREIGN INVESTMENT IN U.S. REAL ESTATE : MATERIALS. 4833

0270-9732 See N.L.R.B ELECTION REPORT. CASES CLOSED. 1692

0270-9783 See NEWSWIRE. 2923

0270-9805 See JOURNAL / SUPREME COURT OF THE UNITED STATES. 3141

0270-9848 See ARMY CLUB SYSTEM ANNUAL REPORT, FISCAL YEAR 4036

0270-9856 See SURNAME AND PUBLICATION INDEX. 2474

0270-9864 See MEMORANDUM - AMERICAN NEWSPAPER PUBLISHERS ASSOCIATION. 4816

0270-9872 See DATAGUIDE. 1237

0270-9910 See WALL STREET FINAL, THE. 718

0270-9953 See DIRECTORY OF RURAL HEALTH CARE PROGRAMS. 4773

0271-0137 See JOURNAL OF MIND AND BEHAVIOR, THE. 4598

0271-0145 See LAS VEGAS INSIDER, THE. 2537

0271-0188 See ROSTER - AMERICAN INSTITUTE OF CERTIFIED PLANNERS. 1582

0271-0196 See DIRECTORY - FORUM COMMITTEE ON HEALTH LAW, AMERICAN BAR ASSOCIATION. 2961

0271-020X See ACADEMY NEWSLETTER, THE. 5079

0271-0218 See TOMLINSON'S LONE STAR BOOK OF TEXAS RECORDS. 2763

0271-0226 See FOREIGN AFFAIRS RESEARCH SPECIAL PAPERS AVAILABLE, UNION OF SOVIET SOCIALIST REPUBLICS. 416

0271-0277 See DIRECTORY OF JEWISH FAMILY & CHILDREN'S AGENCIES. 5283

0271-0285 See INFORMATION SERIES / COLORADO GEOLOGICAL SURVEY. 1383

0271-0315 See OIL SHALE SYMPOSIUM PROCEEDINGS. 4270

0271-0323 See REPORT - EARTHQUAKE ENGINEERING RESEARCH CENTER, COLLEGE OF ENGINEERING, UNIVERSITY OF CALIFORNIA, BERKELEY, CALIFORNIA. 2030

0271-0331 See AQUATIC SERIES. 2187

0271-0358 See TECHNICAL REPORT - LAMAR-MERIFIELD. 1399

0271-0366 See OCCASIONAL PUBLICATIONS OF THE DEPARTMENT OF GEOGRAPHY (URBANA). 2571

0271-0420 See COMPUTERS & GEOLOGY. 1372

0271-0447 See MINERAL RESOURCES SERIES (LAWRENCE). 1441

0271-0498 See MIDDLE EAST EXECUTIVE REPORTS. 3132

0271-0528 See OCCASIONAL PAPER - COUNCIL ON ECONOMIC PRIORITIES. 1509

0271-0560 See NEW DIRECTIONS FOR HIGHER EDUCATION. 1837

0271-0579 See NEW DIRECTIONS FOR INSTITUTIONAL RESEARCH. 1767

0271-0633 See NEW DIRECTIONS FOR TEACHING AND LEARNING. 1901

0271-0641 See ANTHROPOLOGICAL RESEARCH PAPER. 229

0271-0692 See NATIONAL WATER LINE. 5536

0271-0706 See NUCLEAR INDEX, THE. 4449

0271-0730 See ARBA SICULA. 3363

0271-0749 See JOURNAL OF CLINICAL PSYCHOPHARMACOLOGY. 4310

0271-0781 See ERN. EXECUTIVE RECRUITER NEWS. 940

0271-082X See GASAVERS NEWS. 4258

0271-0838 See PHOTOGRAPH COLLECTOR, THE. 4374

0271-0846 See LUZ (NEW YORK). 5188

0271-0897 See PRIVATE REAL ESTATE LIMITED PARTNERSHIPS. 4843

0271-0919 See HOT ROD MAGAZINE CHEVROLET. 5416

0271-0927 See BEST'S DIRECTORY OF RECOMMENDED INSURANCE ADJUSTERS. 2875

0271-0986 See HISPANIC JOURNAL. 3394

0271-1044 See NEWSLETTER / NATIONAL WEATHER ASSOCIATION. 1432

0271-1052 See NATIONAL WEATHER DIGEST. 1432

0271-1079 See NC SHOPOWNER. 2123

0271-1095 *See* CALIFORNIA OPINION INDEX. 5241

0271-1133 *See* NATIONAL DIRECTORY OF SHORTHAND REPORTERS. 3013

0271-1141 *See* INTELLIGENCE REPORTS IN CARDIOVASCULAR DISEASE. 3706

0271-1192 *See* SPRINGER SERIES ON DEATH AND SUICIDE, THE. 4361

0271-1206 *See* TOPICS IN HOSPITAL PHARMACY MANAGEMENT. 4331

0271-1214 *See* TOPICS IN EARLY CHILDHOOD SPECIAL EDUCATION. 1886

0271-1265 *See* ANESTHESIOLOGY (GLENDALE, CALIF.). 3681

0271-1281 *See* OPHTHALMOLOGY (GLENDALE, CALIF.). 3878

0271-1303 *See* INTERNAL MEDICINE (GLENDALE, CALIF.). 3797

0271-1311 *See* PSYCHIATRY (GLENDALE, CALIF.). 3934

0271-132X *See* ORTHOPAEDICS (GLENDALE, CALIF.). 3884

0271-1338 *See* UROLOGY (GLENDALE, CALIF.). 3994

0271-1346 *See* PEDIATRICS (GLENDALE, CALIF.). 3910

0271-1362 *See* FAMILY PRACTICE (GLENDALE, CALIF.). 3737

0271-1370 *See* ALI-ABA COURSE OF STUDY. QUALIFIED PLANS, INSURANCE, AND PROFESSIONAL CORPORATIONS : MATERIALS. 3094

0271-1478 *See* CHEMICAL SUBSTANCES CONTROL. 969

0271-1486 *See* SPECIAL REPORT - UNITED STATES DEPARTMENT OF STATE, BUREAU OF PUBLIC AFFAIRS. 4535

0271-1508 See SPECIAL REPORT - UNITED STATES DEPARTMENT OF STATE, BUREAU OF PUBLIC AFFAIRS. 4535

0271-1532 *See* ACCOMPLISHMENTS OF FISCAL YEAR - NORTHEASTERN AREA, STATE AND PRIVATE FORESTRY. 2373

0271-1567 *See* EMPLOYEE RETIREMENT INCOME SECURITY ACT : REPORT TO CONGRESS. 3147

0271-1591 *See* VEGETARIAN VOICE. 4806

0271-1621 *See* ANNUAL REPORT - MASSACHUSETTS HOME MORTGAGE FINANCE AGENCY. 771

0271-1699 *See* NEWSLETTER, GRAVURE ENVIRONMENTAL. 4567

0271-1710 *See* RAPPORT SUR LE DEVELOPPEMENT DANS LE MONDE. 806

0271-1737 *See* INFORME SOBRE EL DESARROLLO MUNDIAL. 791

0271-1753 *See* DEPARTMENT OF HOUSING AND URBAN DEVELOPMENT ANNUAL REPORT TO CONGRESS ON INDIAN AND ALASKA NATIVE HOUSING AND COMMUNITY DEVELOPMENT PROGRAMS. 2820

0271-1834 *See* TAQRIR AN AL-TANMIYAH FI AL-ALAM. 1586

0271-1842 *See* FUNDAMENTAL RESEARCH IN HOMOGENEOUS CATALYSIS. 1052

0271-1869 *See* EXPERIMENTAL MAGNETISM. 4443

0271-1877 *See* ELECTRON MICROSCOPY IN HUMAN MEDICINE. 3574

0271-1893 *See* MINNESOTA NUTRITION CONFERENCE. 5516

0271-1923 *See* TEXAS ANTITRUST BULLETIN. 3104

0271-1931 *See* DRI-FACS, FINANCIAL AND CREDIT STATISTICS INFORMATION SERVICE : APPLIED REPORTS AND GRAPHICS LIBRARY. 728

0271-1966 *See* CLASSICAL CALLIOPE. 1062

0271-1982 *See* MATHEMATICS OF FINITE ELEMENTS AND APPLICATIONS, THE. 3521

0271-1990 *See* KOBRIN LETTER, THE. 3345

0271-2024 *See* BAR REPORT. 2940

0271-2032 *See* LAW OF THE LAND. 3179

0271-2040 *See* JOHNSON OUTBOARDS BOATING. 593

0271-2075 *See* PUBLIC ADMINISTRATION AND DEVELOPMENT. 4675

0271-2091 *See* INTERNATIONAL JOURNAL FOR NUMERICAL METHODS IN FLUIDS. 2091

0271-2172 *See* RURAL DEVELOPMENT PERSPECTIVES. 131

0271-2202 *See* TILR. TRANSNATIONAL IMMIGRATION LAW REPORTER. 1921

0271-2210 *See* MECHANICS & HOME REPAIR. 621

0271-2229 *See* AAAS PUBLICATION. 5079

0271-2334 *See* ADVANCES IN TRANSPORT PROCESSES. 4430

0271-2342 *See* SARCOPHAGUS. 3470

0271-2350 *See* PROGRESS IN SURGICAL PATHOLOGY. 3972

0271-2385 *See* COUNSELING CLIENTS IN THE ENTERTAINMENT INDUSTRY. 2957

0271-2393 *See* RATIOS OF CALIFORNIA PUBLIC SCHOOL NONTEACHING EMPLOYEES TO CLASSROOM TEACHERS. 1869

0271-2504 *See* ALI-ABA COURSE OF STUDY. TRIAL EVIDENCE IN FEDERAL AND STATE COURTS, A CLINICAL STUDY OF RECENT DEVELOPMENTS: MATERIALS. 2931

0271-2571 *See* HANDBOOK - OKLAHOMA BAR ASSOCIATION. 2976

0271-2598 *See* SPEEDNEWS. 36

0271-2628 *See* INSURANCE SERVICE: REGIONAL REVIEW. 2884

0271-2644 *See* POLISH FAMILY TREE SURNAMES. 2468

0271-2652 *See* POWER DIRECTORY. 2075

0271-2660 *See* TOLUENE XYLENES ANNUAL. 1030

0271-2741 *See* CALIFORNIA GOVERNMENT CONTRACTS. 2946

0271-2776 *See* FODOR'S ALASKA. 5470

0271-2784 *See* RESEARCH AND DEVELOPMENT PROJECTS IN AGING. 5305

0271-2792 *See* SURVEY OF LAW. 3061

0271-2830 *See* TITUS TRAIL, THE. 2475

0271-2857 *See* SPORTS MEDICINE (MOUNT KISCO). 3956

0271-2873 *See* CITATOR OF THE DECISIONS OF THE OCCUPATIONAL SAFETY AND HEALTH REVIEW COMMISSION. 2860

0271-2881 *See* HOUSE & GARDEN PLANS GUIDE (1979). 2420

0271-2911 *See* METAL IONS IN BIOLOGY. 490

0271-3098 *See* FOLK ART SAMPLER. 373

0271-3128 *See* BERGER BUILDING COST FILE, UNIT PRICES. WESTERN EDITION. 600

0271-3144 *See* ROLE OF BEHAVIORAL SCIENCE IN PHYSICAL SECURITY, THE. 3175

0271-3152 *See* FOCUS ON HEALTH (NEW YORK, N.Y.). 4776

0271-3160 *See* MIDDLE EAST (NEW YORK, N.Y.), THE. 2658

0271-325X *See* TECHNICAL METHODS BULLETIN - PARENTERAL DRUG ASSOCIATION. 4330

0271-3276 *See* ALASKA JOURNAL OF COMMERCE & PACIFIC RIM REPORTER. 822

0271-3284 *See* IMMUNOLOGY TRIBUNE. 3672

0271-3373 *See* GUIDE TO SPECIFICATIONS FOR INTERIOR LANDSCAPING, A. 2418

0271-3381 *See* GEOGRAPHIC COST OF LIVING DIFFERENTIALS : LARGE CITIES. 1492

0271-339X *See* ANNUAL REPORT - CITY OF CHICAGO/HSA. 4765

0271-3438 *See* COTA NEWSLETTER. 1130

0271-3462 *See* DISCIPLINE AND GRIEVANCES. WHITE COLLAR EDITION. 940

0271-3470 *See* DRI-FACS : REFERENCE GUIDE TO U.S. WEEKLY BANKING STATISTICS. 728

0271-3489 *See* ANNUAL LICENSING LAW AND BUSINESS INSTITUTE. 3095

0271-3497 *See* GOVERNING NORTH DAKOTA. 4651

0271-3519 *See* ARAB STUDIES QUARTERLY. 2645

0271-3527 *See* PETERSEN'S HOW TO TUNE YOUR CAR. 5423

0271-3535 *See* ALI-ABA COURSE OF STUDY. BROKER-DEALER REGULATION: MATERIALS. 2930

0271-3543 *See* ALI-ABA COURSE OF STUDY. ESTATE PLANNING FOR THE CLOSELY HELD BUSINESS : MATERIALS. 3117

0271-3551 *See* ALI-ABA COURSE OF STUDY. BASIC ESTATE AND GIFT TAXATION: MATERIALS. 3117

0271-356X *See* ALI-ABA COURSE OF STUDY. BANKING AND COMMERCIAL LENDING LAW : MATERIALS. 3084

0271-3578 *See* ALI-ABA COURSE OF STUDY : ABA SECTION OF TAXATION, ANNUAL ADVANCED STUDY SESSIONS, BUSINESS AND ESTATE PLANNING WITH LIFE AND DISABILITY INSURANCE : MATERIALS. 3117

0271-3586 *See* AMERICAN JOURNAL OF INDUSTRIAL MEDICINE. 3548

0271-3659 *See* EXECUTIVE SPEAKER, THE. 867

0271-3667 *See* SCHOOL LIBRARIAN'S WORKSHOP, THE. 3247

0271-3683 *See* CURRENT EYE RESEARCH. 3874

0271-3705 *See* SAXOPHONE SYMPOSIUM, THE. 4152

0271-3888 *See* BULLETIN / HOLMES SAFETY ASSOCIATION. 2860

0271-3942 *See* CRITTENDEN MORTGAGE DIRECTORY. 786

0271-3969 *See* U.S. COINS OF VALUE. 2783

0271-3993 *See* SYLLOGE NUMMORUM GRAECORUM (NEW YORK). 2783

0271-406X *See* HOSPITAL FINANCIAL MANAGEMENT ASSOCIATION ANNUAL REPORT. 3784

0271-4086 *See* SOCIAL SERVICE DELIVERY SYSTEMS. 5221

0271-4094 *See* CODE OF FEDERAL REGULATIONS. 40, PROTECTION OF ENVIRONMENT. 2163

0271-4132 *See* CONTEMPORARY MATHEMATICS (AMERICAN MATHEMATICAL SOCIETY). 3502

0271-4159 *See* COMPUTER GRAPHICS WORLD. 1232

0271-4280 *See* SENATE ISSUES YEARBOOK. 4685

0271-4477 *See* COMPUTER-READABLE DATA BASES. 1236

0271-4558 *See* PROCEEDINGS OF THE CONFERENCE OF THE AMERICAN COUNTRY LIFE ASSOCIATION, INC. 5254

0271-4698 *See* PROJECT OUTCOMES REPORTING. 1775

0271-4779 *See* CARDIOVASCULAR REVIEW (BALTIMORE). 3702

0271-4795 *See* CRI COMMUNICATIONS UPDATE SERVICE. 1109

0271-4809 *See* TELEVISION/RADIO AGE COMMUNICATIONS COURSEBOOK. 1141

0271-4817 *See* JOURNAL OF CLINICAL CHIROPRACTIC. 4380

0271-4868 *See* DRI INDUSTRY FINANCIAL SERVICES: ANNUAL LONG-TERM REVIEW. 788

0271-4965 *See* REPORT SE (WORLD DATA CENTER A FOR SOLID EARTH GEOPHYSICS). 1410

0271-4973 *See* ANNUAL FALL FIELD CONFERENCE - BIG RIVERS AREA GEOLOGICAL SOCIETY. 1365

0271-4981 *See* TECHNICAL REPORT - COASTAL ENGINEERING RESEARCH CENTER (U.S.). 1998

0271-499X *See* TECHNICAL PAPER - U.S. ARMY, CORPS OF ENGINEERS, COASTAL ENGINEERING RESEARCH CENTER. 1998

0271-5015 *See* DEPARTMENT AND SPECIALTY STORE MERCHANDISING AND OPERATING RESULTS. 953

0271-5023 *See* EN PASSANT, POETRY. 3468

0271-5031 *See* SCOTTISH-AMERICAN GENEALOGIST. 2471

0271-5058 *See* RESEARCHER (JACKSON, MISS.). 1845

0271-5082 *See* MEMBERSHIP DIRECTORY AND CERTIFICATION REGISTRY. 2198

0271-5104 *See* SCIENTIFIC ANGLERS FLY FISHING HANDBOOK. 2312

0271-5139 *See* JOURNAL OF AMERICAN ROMANIAN CHRISTIAN LITERARY STUDIES. 2740

0271-5147 *See* NORTHERN OHIO LIVE. 2541

0271-5163 *See* MUSIC RESEARCHER'S EXCHANGE, THE. 4134

0271-5198 *See* CLINICAL HEMORHEOLOGY. 3771

0271-5228 *See* LANDLORD TENANT LAW BULLETIN. 2993

0271-5287 *See* QUARTERLY REVIEW - FEDERAL RESERVE BANK OF MINNEAPOLIS. 805

0271-5309 *See* LANGUAGE & COMMUNICATION. 3294

0271-5317 *See* NUTRITION RESEARCH (NEW YORK, N.Y.). 4196

0271-5333 *See* RADIOGRAPHICS. 3945

0271-5341 *See* ANNUAL REPORT TO CONGRESS ON THE USE OF ALCOHOL IN MOTOR FUELS. 1020

0271-535X *See* INSIDER'S GUIDE TO PREP SCHOOLS, THE. 1753

0271-5368 *See* COUNSELOR PREPARATION. 1877

0271-5376 *See* COASTAL RESEARCH. 1353

0271-5414 *See* LANDMARK (EL MONTE), THE. 2743

0271-5422 *See* AWWA SEMINAR PROCEEDINGS. 4760

0271-5430 *See* TELEPHONE NEWS. 1167

0271-5481 *See* LIABILITY REPORTER. 3169

0271-5511 *See* CONTRACTOR BUSINESS REPORT. 660

0271-5589 *See* OCCUPATIONAL DEVELOPMENTS MAGAZINE. 4207

0271-5732 *See* MESSAGE (CHERRY HILL), THE. 4976

0271-5864 *See* BADGER COMMON TATER, THE. 164

0271-5937 *See* VENDING MACHINES, COIN OPERATED. 1631

0271-5953 *See* VIDEO PRODUCT NEWS. 4079

0271-6011 *See* WILEY SERIES OF PRACTICAL CONSTRUCTION GUIDES. 631

0271-602X *See* WILEY SERIES IN PLASMA PHYSICS. 4425

0271-6046 *See* WILEY SERIES IN MANAGEMENT. 889

0271-6062 *See* PRINCIPAL (ARLINGTON, VA.). 1868

0271-6100 *See* FLORIDA KEYS MAGAZINE. 2733

0271-6119 *See* WELCOME TO THE TAX REVOLT. 4758

0271-6127 *See* FINAL GRAPE CRUSH REPORT. 87

0271-6135 *See* ELLIS HORWOOD SERIES IN COMPUTERS AND THEIR APPLICATIONS, THE. 1184

0271-6151 *See* ELLIS HORWOOD SERIES IN MATHEMATICS & ITS APPLICATIONS. 3504

0271-616X *See* FIESER AND FIESER'S REAGENTS FOR ORGANIC SYNTHESIS. 1041

0271-6208 *See* TRANSPORT IN THE LIFE SCIENCES. 540

0271-6283 *See* NEW YORK STATE CRIMINAL LAW REVIEW. 3108

0271-633X *See* CULTURAL RESOURCES SERIES (DENVER). 2191

0271-6348 *See* STUDIES ON THE MORPHOLOGY AND SYSTEMATICS OF SCALE INSECTS. 5613

0271-6437 *See* BROOKLYN ENGINEER, THE. 1966

0271-6445 *See* ACCESSIONS LIST. SOUTH ASIA. 406

0271-6453 *See* ST. LOUIS BUSINESS JOURNAL. 713

0271-6461 *See* GUIDE TO RECORD RETENTION REQUIREMENTS. 2976

0271-6577 *See* CARIBBEAN STUDIES NEWSLETTER. 2727

0271-6607 *See* FRENCH LITERATURE SERIES. 3343

0271-6615 *See* CALIFORNIA SERVICES REGISTER. 654

0271-6690 *See* COASTAL ENGINEERING TECHNICAL AID. 1448

0271-678X *See* JOURNAL OF CEREBRAL BLOOD FLOW AND METABOLISM. 582

0271-6909 *See* BANKING LAW JOURNAL DIGEST. 3085

0271-6925 *See* RIPLEY P. BULLEN MONOGRAPHS IN ANTHROPOLOGY AND HISTORY. 245

0271-6941 *See* OKLAHOMA SERIES, THE. 2752

0271-7069 *See* SEA GRANT REPORT (COLLEGE). 2313

0271-7085 *See* ENHANCED ENERGY RECOVERY NEWS. 1943

0271-7107 *See* APPLIED GENETICS NEWS. 542

0271-7166 *See* PLS LISTING. POWER FACILITIES OPERATED BY THE BUREAU OF RECLAMATION. 2075

0271-7212 *See* RESEARCH BULLETIN / MASSACHUSETTS AGRICULTURAL EXPERIMENT STATION. 127

0271-7220 *See* OLD-HOUSE JOURNAL CATALOG, THE. 623

0271-7263 *See* AMERICAN BROADCASTING COMPANIES ANNUAL REPORT. 1126

0271-731X *See* GTE SYLVANIA NEWS. 2056

0271-7328 *See* GF NEWS. 2342

0271-7379 *See* INTERNATIONAL SERIES ON APPLIED SYSTEMS ANALYSIS. 1190

0271-7395 *See* PROGRESS IN RESOURCE MANAGEMENT AND ENVIRONMENTAL PLANNING. 2240

0271-7417 *See* TMSA AEROSPACE MARKET OUTLOOK. 37

0271-7506 *See* PSYCSCAN. APPLIED PSYCHOLOGY. 4623

0271-7522 *See* NEWS-LETTER - NATIONAL SOCIETY OF UNITED STATES DAUGHTERS OF 1812. 5234

0271-7603 *See* SAMP CATALOG : SUPPLEMENT. 3247

0271-7638 *See* FLAGS, DIAMONDS, AND STATUES. 5431

0271-7654 *See* OVERVIEW - FARMERS HOME ADMINISTRATION. 118

0271-7662 *See* DIRECTORY OF FOOD SERVICE DISTRIBUTORS (BUSINESS GUIDES, INC.). 2333

0271-7735 *See* LITTLE BALKANS REVIEW, THE. 357

0271-7751 *See* MONEY MARKET FUND SURVEY'S COMPLETE DIRECTORY OF MONEY MARKET FUNDS. 907

0271-776X *See* JOURNAL OF THE NATIONAL TECHNICAL ASSOCIATION. 5121

0271-7808 *See* FANTASY VOICES. 3387

0271-793X *See* NATIONAL POULTRY IMPROVEMENT PLAN. DIRECTORY OF PARTICIPANTS HANDLING EGG-TYPE AND MEAT-TYPE CHICKENS AND TURKEYS. 216

0271-7948 *See* NATIONAL POULTRY IMPROVEMENT PLAN. DIRECTORY OF PARTICIPANTS HANDLING WATERFOWL, EXHIBITION POULTRY, AND GAME BIRDS. 216

0271-7956 *See* YEAR BOOK OF CLINICAL PHARMACY, THE. 4333

0271-7964 *See* YEAR BOOK OF EMERGENCY MEDICINE, THE. 3726

0271-7999 *See* AMUSEMENT PARK JOURNAL. 4857

0271-8014 *See* ENTERTAINMENT INDUSTRY DIRECTORY, THE. 384

0271-8022 *See* INDIANA THEORY REVIEW. 4122

0271-8049 *See* WATER AND LAND RESOURCE ACCOMPLISHMENTS. FEDERAL RECLAMATION PROJECTS, SUMMARY REPORT. 2208

0271-8057 *See* JOURNAL OF TISSUE CULTURE METHODS. 538

0271-8197 *See* NEW PAGES. 4817

0271-8200 *See* JOURNAL OF PRECISION TEACHING. 1898

0271-8227 *See* IOWA WOMAN. 5559

0271-8235 *See* SEMINARS IN NEUROLOGY. 3846

0271-8286 *See* ANODIC BEHAVIOR OF METALS AND SEMICONDUCTOR SERIES, THE. 3998

0271-8294 *See* TOPICS IN LANGUAGE DISORDERS. 3329

0271-8308 *See* IEEE IECI PROCEEDINGS. 2059

0271-8448 *See* NEW JERSEY LEGISLATIVE INDEX. 3015

0271-8472 *See* NT. NEWS ON TESTS. 1769

0271-8480 *See* SOLAR BULLETIN (RAMSEY). 400

0271-8510 *See* AAPG STUDIES IN GEOLOGY. 4248

0271-8529 *See* AAPG MEMOIR. 1364

0271-8537 *See* BULLETIN - MISSISSIPPI DEPARTMENT OF ENVIRONMENTAL QUALITY, BUREAU OF GEOLOGY. 1370

0271-8545 *See* BULLETIN - WASHINGTON DEPARTMENT OF NATURAL RESOURCES, DIVISION OF GEOLOGY AND EARTH RESOURCES. 1371

0271-8561 *See* DATA ON EARNED DEGREES CONFERRED BY INSTITUTIONS OF HIGHER EDUCATION BY RACE, ETHNICITY AND SEX. 1819

0271-8588 *See* LOCAL AREA PERSONAL INCOME. 1503

0271-8669 *See* GETTING AHEAD IN DP. 1259

0271-8685 *See* MIDWEST HISTORICAL AND GENEALOGICAL REGISTER. 2460

0271-8707 *See* DRUG INTERACTIONS NEWSLETTER. 4300

0271-888X *See* COLORADO GEOLOGICAL SURVEY OPEN-FILE REPORT. 1372

0271-8987 *See* ALASKA SHIPPERS GUIDE. 5447

0271-9053 *See* JOURNAL OF THE AMERICAN ASSOCIATION OF VARIABLE STAR OBSERVERS, THE. 396

0271-9096 *See* CALENDAR OF FESTIVALS. 5268

0271-9126 *See* LANDSCAPING, LAWNS AND GARDENS. 2423

0271-9134 *See* DICKINSON MAGAZINE. 1091

0271-9142 *See* JOURNAL OF CLINICAL IMMUNOLOGY. 3673

0271-9150 *See* NATIONAL CONSULTOR. 748

0271-9177 *See* CROSS-CULTURAL RESEARCH AND METHODOLOGY SERIES. 5197

0271-9193 *See* COMPLEX HUMAN BEHAVIOR. 4582

0271-9223 *See* CENTURY PSYCHOLOGY SERIES. 4580

0271-9231 *See* ASPECTS OF MODERN LAND SURVEYING. 2018

0271-9266 *See* ADVANCES IN MENTAL HANDICAP RESEARCH. 3919

0271-9274 *See* STUDIES IN AMERICAN JEWISH LITERATURE (ALBANY, N.Y.). 3441

0271-9282 *See* TOPICS IN HORMONE CHEMISTRY. 587

0271-9312 *See* PROCEEDINGS OF THE CALIFORNIA CONFERENCE ON RUBBER-TOUGHENED PLASTICS. 4459

0271-9347 *See* WISTAR SYMPOSIUM SERIES. 587

0271-9355 *See* BIOLOGICAL REGULATION AND DEVELOPMENT. 445

0271-9371 *See* TOXIC AND HAZARDOUS WASTE DISPOSAL. 2245

0271-9460 *See* JOURNAL OF APPLIED POLYMER SCIENCE. APPLIED POLYMER SYMPOSIUM. 1042

0271-9509 *See* GREENWOOD ENCYCLOPEDIA OF AMERICAN INSTITUTIONS, THE. 1926

0271-9517 *See* NACADA JOURNAL / NATIONAL ACADEMIC ADVISING ASSOCIATION. 1836

0271-9517 *See* NACADA JOURNAL. 762

0271-955X *See* FRONTIERS IN AGING SERIES. 3751

0271-9649 *See* EVENT (NEW YORK), THE. 2616

0271-969X *See* TECHNICAL HIGHLIGHTS - NATIONAL MEASUREMENT LABORATORY. 4032

0271-9703 *See* NTIA REPORT. 1161

0271-972X *See* SCOPE (CHICHESTER). 2221

0271-9738 See ADVANCES IN ANALYSIS OF BEHAVIOUR. 4571
0271-9746 See ACCT TRUSTEE QUARTERLY. 1807
0271-9754 See ANNUAL STATUS REPORT ON THE INACTIVE URANIUM MILL TAILINGS SITES REMEDIAL ACTION PROGRAM. 2224
0271-9789 See DIRECTORY OF THE AMERICAN SOCIETY OF PLANT PHYSIOLOGISTS. 508
0271-9800 See ANNUAL OF ARMENIAN LINGUISTICS. 3265
0271-9819 See EIDOS (CAZENOVIA). 2732
0271-9827 See ARTHUR FROMMER'S DOLLARWISE GUIDE TO NEW ENGLAND. 5461
0271-9835 See UNIVERSITY OF HAWAII LAW REVIEW. 3068
0271-9851 See DIRECTORY OF KOREAN PHYSICIANS: DISTRICT OF COLUMBIA, MARYLAND, AND VIRGINIA. 3913
0271-9894 See BEVERAGE INDUSTRY NEWS MERCHANDISER. 2364
0271-9908 See INFORMATION TEXT SERIES / HAWAII INSTITUTE OF TROPICAL AGRICULTURE AND HUMAN RESOURCES. 96
0271-9916 See RESEARCH EXTENSION SERIES / HAWAII INSTITUTE OF TROPICAL AGRICULTURE AND HUMAN RESOURCES. 127
0271-9940 See DANCE BOOK FORUM. 1311
0271-9959 See ENGINEERING CONFERENCE. 4233
0271-9967 See ANNUAL MEETING - NATIONAL MASTITIS COUNCIL, INC. 191
0272-0000 See RETAIL BANK CREDIT REFERRAL DIRECTORY. 809
0272-006X See CIVIL SERVICE COURT DIGEST, THE. 4702
0272-0086 See CHINA EXCHANGE NEWS. 5195
0272-0108 See NUCLEAR MEDICINE ANNUAL. 3848
0272-0116 See CONSTRUCTION LAWYER, THE. 2956
0272-0167 See DIRECTORY OF HOME CENTER OPERATORS & HARDWARE CHAINS. 2811
0272-0175 See CLARK'S GUIDE TO AMERICA'S ANTIQUE SHOPS. 250
0272-0205 See COAL WEEK INTERNATIONAL. 1439
0272-0264 See GREENWOOD ENCYCLOPEDIA OF BLACK MUSIC, THE. 4119
0272-0280 See NIEPODLEGOSC. 2700
0272-0299 See CORPORATE EFT REPORT. 784
0272-0310 See INTERNATIONAL IMAGING SOURCE BOOK. 1190
0272-0329 See WEST'S FEDERAL TAXATION. INDIVIDUAL INCOME TAXES. 4758
0272-0337 See ESSAYS IN HISTORY (ARLINGTON). 2615
0272-0345 See UPDATE (SMITHSONIAN INSTITUTION. TRAVELING EXHIBITION SERVICE). 4097
0272-0353 See RUNNER YEARBOOK, THE. 4916
0272-0361 See HIGH ROADS FOLIO. 2534
0272-037X See DLA BULLETIN (OAKLAND, CALIF.). 3208
0272-0396 See ENTREPRENEURIAL MANAGER'S NEWSLETTER. 672
0272-0418 See RSCJ: A JOURNAL OF REFLECTION. 5035
0272-0426 See ANCESTORING. 2437
0272-0434 See ADVANCES IN THE MECHANICS AND PHYSICS OF SURFACES. 2100
0272-0469 See WASHINGTON CONSUMER'S CHECKBOOK. 1300
0272-0515 See ROUNDTABLE REPORT. 4800
0272-0523 See PRODUCTIVITY REPORT FOR ALL PRODUCERS BY STATE, COUNTY, & TYPE MINING. 2148
0272-054X See BIOLOGICAL SCIENCE TEXTS. 5088
0272-0566 See ASA STUDIES. 231
0272-0574 See PRIMER OF LABOR RELATIONS. 1702
0272-0590 See FUNDAMENTAL AND APPLIED TOXICOLOGY. 3980

0272-0620 See SEASONS IN ART. 364
0272-0671 See POLICY PUBLISHERS AND ASSOCIATIONS DIRECTORY. 5213
0272-068X See ADVANCES IN HUMAN PSYCHOPHARMACOLOGY. 4289
0272-0701 See FREE INQUIRY (BUFFALO). 4347
0272-0736 See ANNUAL GAMING CONFERENCE. 3156
0272-0787 See ADVANCES IN NEUROGERONTOLOGY. 3826
0272-0825 See BARNES ASSOCIATES NATIONAL FUND RAISER. 4334
0272-0868 See MARK SKOUSEN'S FORECASTS & STRATEGIES ON INFLATION, TAXES AND GOVERNMENT CONTROLS. 4736
0272-0884 See TECHNICALITIES. 3252
0272-0892 See DIRECTORY, LICENSED HOSPITALS AND AMBULATORY SURGICAL TREATMENT CENTERS IN TENNESSEE. 3779
0272-0914 See STANDARD & POOR'S STATISTICAL SERVICE: SECURITY PRICE INDEX RECORD. 915
0272-0922 See JD (WASHINGTON). 2986
0272-0930 See COMMUNICATION GRAPHICS. 377
0272-0957 See OCCUPATIONAL INJURIES AND ILLNESSES. SUMMARY (WASHINGTON). 2867
0272-0965 See PNEUMA (SPRINGFIELD). 5066
0272-1007 See REPORT OF THE FOREST SERVICE (WASHINGTON). 2392
0272-1058 See SOUTH CAROLINA ANNUAL STATE PLAN FOR VOCATIONAL-TECHNICAL EDUCATION. 1915
0272-1066 See GUIDE TO JEWISH CHICAGO, AND YEARBOOK. 2262
0272-1074 See GEORGE D. HALL'S NEW YORK MANUFACTURERS DIRECTORY. 3479
0272-1082 See CENTURY (ALBUQUERQUE). 3339
0272-1120 See ENVIROSOUTH. 2171
0272-1163 See AMERICAN EXPORT REGISTER. 822
0272-1198 See DIRECTORY - FORUM COMMITTEE ON FRANCHISING. 3099
0272-1201 See WBA NEWSLETTER (BOSTON, MASS.). 3073
0272-1236 See VIDEO PROGRAMS INDEX, THE. 4377
0272-1252 See FOTO FINDER. 4369
0272-1279 See ST. LOUIS. 2546
0272-1309 See DIRECTORY OF CERTIFIED PETROLEUM GEOLOGISTS. 1373
0272-1368 See REFLECTIONS (LOS ANGELES). 3725
0272-1384 See LANDMARKS OBSERVER. 2743
0272-1406 See TAMPA BAY HISTORY. 2762
0272-1511 See AAPG REPRINT SERIES. 1364
0272-1562 See MCCALL'S DECORATING BOOK. 2906
0272-1570 See NORTHWEST DISCOVERY. 4169
0272-1589 See EAST ASIAN EXECUTIVE REPORTS. 3099
0272-1635 See ANALES DE LA LITERATURA ESPANOLA CONTEMPORANEA. 3361
0272-166X See COMPARATIVE POLITICAL ECONOMY AND PUBLIC POLICY SERIES. 1470
0272-1686 See ARTIFICIAL INTELLIGENCE SERIES, THE. 1212
0272-1694 See BIPAC ACTION REPORT. 4465
0272-1716 See IEEE COMPUTER GRAPHICS AND APPLICATIONS. 1233
0272-1724 See IEEE POWER ENGINEERING REVIEW. 2060
0272-1732 See IEEE MICRO. 1267
0272-1740 See ADVANCES IN SUBSTANCE ABUSE, BEHAVIORAL AND BIOLOGICAL RESEARCH. 1339
0272-1767 See PRODUCTS LIABILITY AND TRANSPORTATION LEGAL DIRECTORY. 3032
0272-1775 See INTERNATIONAL GOLF DIRECTORY, THE. 4900
0272-1856 See OFFICE OF THE STATE ARCHEOLOGIST REPORTS. 277

0272-1864 See DIRECTORY OF ORGANIZATIONS WORKING FOR WOMEN'S EDUCATIONAL EQUITY. 1736
0272-1910 See SHARDS NEWSLETTER, THE. 2594
0272-1937 See JOURNAL OF THE AFRO-AMERICAN HISTORICAL AND GENEALOGICAL SOCIETY. 2455
0272-1961 See LEGAL ASSISTANTS: UPDATE. 2999
0272-1988 See REFERENCE BOOK REVIEW, THE. 1928
0272-1996 See WLW JOURNAL. 3256
0272-2003 See SOUTHERN LIVING ... ANNUAL RECIPES. 2792
0272-2011 See AMERICAN REVIEW OF CANADIAN STUDIES, THE. 2719
0272-202X See SPRINGER SERIES, FOCUS ON WOMEN. 5566
0272-2038 See STANDARDS FOR BLOOD BANKS AND TRANSFUSION SERVICES. 3774
0272-2089 See FAMILY JOURNAL (PUTNEY, VT.). 2279
0272-2097 See ART VOICES (WEST PALM BEACH, FLA.). 340
0272-2119 See CASE REGISTER. 949
0272-2186 See CPC SALARY SURVEY FOR REGION MAPA. 1819
0272-2216 See CPC SALARY SURVEY FOR REGION MCPA. 4203
0272-2291 See BUYING GUIDE TO CAR STEREO SYSTEMS. 5316
0272-2305 See WEST AFRICA SERIES. 2644
0272-2410 See PACE LAW REVIEW. 3024
0272-2429 See CENTER FOR STRATEGIC AND INTERNATIONAL STUDIES, GEORGETOWN UNIVERSITY, THE. 4517
0272-2445 See BLUE BOOK OF PENSION FUNDS, THE. 1655
0272-2488 See CONTEMPORARY CONCEPTS IN PHYSICS. 4401
0272-2623 See TRIENNIAL ASSESSMENT OF THE TENNESSEE VALLEY AUTHORITY. 4691
0272-2631 See STUDIES IN SECOND LANGUAGE ACQUISITION. 3326
0272-264X See RESOURCE MATERIALS : ESTATE PLANNING IN DEPTH. 3119
0272-2658 See PUBLIC EDUCATION SERIES. 5595
0272-2666 See PERFUMER & FLAVORIST. 1028
0272-2674 See DIRECTORY OF MEMBERS, LOT EXCHANGE, MAUSOLEUM CRYPT EXCHANGE, DOLLAR CREDIT PLANS. 2407
0272-2690 See LANGUAGE PROBLEMS & LANGUAGE PLANNING. 3295
0272-2712 See CLINICS IN LABORATORY MEDICINE. 3566
0272-2720 See DRAMA-LOGUE. 5364
0272-2739 See WRITE-OFF. 4759
0272-2747 See RAM'S HORN (HANOVER, N.H.), THE. 3314
0272-2755 See MOSSBAUER HANDBOOK. 1012
0272-2771 See TOBACCO MARKET REVIEW. FIRE-CURED AND DARK AIR-CURED. 5374
0272-2836 See ANNUAL REPORT ON CARCINOGENS. 3808
0272-2917 See SYRACUSE NEWS. 2083
0272-3212 See GE NEWS. 2055
0272-3271 See BANK PERSONNEL NEWS. 775
0272-3298 See STUDIES IN CULTURAL RESOURCE MANAGEMENT. 2396
0272-3344 See VIETNAM DIGEST (BERKELEY). 2667
0272-3387 See DIRECTORY OF PROFESSIONAL GENEALOGISTS AND RELATED SERVICES. 2445
0272-3395 See MVMA MOTOR VEHICLE FACTS & FIGURES. 5421
0272-3433 See PUBLIC HISTORIAN, THE. 2626
0272-3441 See PROCEEDINGS OF THE ANNUAL PACIFIC ISLANDS STUDIES CONFERENCE, UNIVERSITY OF HAWAII, THE. 2670
0272-3468 See RULES FOR INBOARD, INBOARD ENDURANCE, UNLIMITED RACING. 595

0272-3476 See RULES FOR STOCK OUTBOARD, PRO OUTBOARD, MODIFIED OUTBOARD. 595

0272-3484 See SERVICE CORPORATION DIRECTORY. 811

0272-3506 See RECOMMENDED RULES FOR CARE OF POWER BOILERS. 2127

0272-3514 See RULES FOR OUTBOARD PERFORMANCE, CRAFT AND DRAG RACING. 595

0272-3522 See AUDIT OF SAINT LAWRENCE SEAWAY DEVELOPMENT CORPORATION FINANCIAL STATEMENTS. 739

0272-3530 See DRUG-NUTRIENT INTERACTIONS. 4301

0272-3581 See TODAY'S EDUCATION. SOCIAL STUDIES EDITION. 1907

0272-3603 See BIOGRAPHICAL DIRECTORY OF THE AMERICAN PODIATRY ASSOCIATION. 3655

0272-3611 See DIESEL FUEL DIRECTORY. 5413

0272-3638 See URBAN GEOGRAPHY. 2578

0272-3646 See PHYSICAL GEOGRAPHY. 2572

0272-3654 See PERIODICALS AND SOURCES. 422

0272-3689 See LABOR-MANAGEMENT RELATIONS IN STATE AND LOCAL GOVERNMENTS. 1683

0272-3700 See IFPRI REPORT. 94

0272-3743 See INVENTORY OF POWER PLANTS IN THE UNITED STATES. 2005

0272-3778 See LABORATORY REGULATION MANUAL. 2993

0272-3786 See STALLION DIRECTORY. 2802

0272-3794 See PSYCHOLOGY (GUILFORD). 4612

0272-3808 See AGING (GUILFORD, CONN.). 3749

0272-3816 See CRIMINAL JUSTICE (GUILFORD, CONN.). 3162

0272-3840 See ADVANCES IN BIOMATERIALS. 3546

0272-3948 See REPORT ON SHAREHOLDER PROPOSALS. 1624

0272-3980 See SERIES IN GEOTECHNICAL ENGINEERING. 1996

0272-4014 See THEORIES IN MARKETING SERIES. 937

0272-4022 See WILEY SERIES ON STUDIES IN ENVIRONMENTAL MANAGEMENT AND RESOURCE DEVELOPMENT. 948

0272-4030 See HOUSTON REVIEW, THE. 2738

0272-4057 See CHEMICAL ENGINEERING EQUIPMENT BUYERS' GUIDE. 2009

0272-4065 See LAW & BUSINESS DIRECTORY OF CORPORATE COUNSEL. 3101

0272-4170 See MATERIALS TECHNOLOGY (COLUMBUS). 2106

0272-4219 See WHO'S WHO IN PROFESSIONAL PEST CONTROL. 437

0272-4294 See SEAFOOD AMERICA. 2357

0272-4308 See INTERNATIONAL JOURNAL OF PARTIAL HOSPITALIZATION. 3786

0272-4316 See JOURNAL OF EARLY ADOLESCENCE, THE. 4596

0272-4324 See PLASMA CHEMISTRY AND PLASMA PROCESSING. 2015

0272-4332 See RISK ANALYSIS. 4800

0272-4340 See CELLULAR AND MOLECULAR NEUROBIOLOGY. 534

0272-4359 See ANOTHER CHICAGO MAGAZINE. 3362

0272-4367 See FREEDOM SOCIALIST, THE. 4542

0272-4391 See DRUG DEVELOPMENT RESEARCH. 4300

0272-4405 See EAST TEXAS FAMILY RECORDS. 2446

0272-4448 See PROGRAMS PROVIDING SERVICES TO BATTERED WOMEN. 5302

0272-4456 See EARLY CHILDHOOD EDUCATION (GUILFORD). 1803

0272-4464 See SOCIAL PROBLEMS (GUILFORD). 5259

0272-4472 See BOUNDARY AND ANNEXATION SURVEY. 4634

0272-4480 See AMERICAN MILITARY INSTITUTE DIRECTORY OF MEMBERS. 4034

0272-4499 See MCCALL'S COUNTRY DECORATING. 374

0272-4502 See GENERAL AVIATION ACTIVITY AND AVIONICS SURVEY. 22

0272-4510 See SCIENCE & LIVING TOMORROW. 5150

0272-4529 See ANNUAL REPORT, PUBLIC WATER SUPPLIES FOR THE STATE OF OKLAHOMA, NORTHWEST DISTRICT. 2224

0272-4537 See FAXON ... LIBRARIANS' GUIDE TO CONTINUATIONS. 3210

0272-4553 See COMPUTER AND COMMUNICATIONS BUYER. 1244

0272-4561 See CONSTRUCTION CLAIMS MONTHLY. 609

0272-457X See HYBRIDOMA. 3670

0272-4596 See MUNICIPAL DIRECTORY (AUGUSTA). 4667

0272-4626 See EUROPEAN APPLIED RESEARCH REPORTS. ENVIRONMENT AND NATURAL RESOURCES SECTION. 2171

0272-4634 See JOURNAL OF VERTEBRATE PALEONTOLOGY. 4227

0272-4650 See ORGANO OFICIAL DE LA JUNTA CIVICO-MILITAR CUBANA. 2752

0272-4669 See VETERINARY PHARMACEUTICALS & BIOLOGICALS. 5526

0272-4677 See PROCEEDINGS, REGION 6 CONFERENCE. 2077

0272-4685 See IEEE CONFERENCE RECORD OF ... ANNUAL CONFERENCE OF ELECTRICAL ENGINEERING PROBLEMS IN THE RUBBER AND PLASTICS INDUSTRIES. 2059

0272-4693 See ANTENNAS AND PROPAGATION. 2035

0272-4723 See PAPER SUMMARIES - AMERICAN SOCIETY FOR NONDESTRUCTIVE TESTING. 1990

0272-4774 See REPORT ORO. 1955

0272-4782 See BRITISH DEFENCE DIRECTORY. 4038

0272-4790 See ADVANCES IN DRYING. 2096

0272-4855 See OFFICE AUTOMATION CONFERENCE DIGEST. 4213

0272-4863 See NATURAL GAS FROM CALIFORNIA FIELDS. 4265

0272-4936 See ANNALS OF TROPICAL PAEDIATRICS. 3985

0272-4944 See JOURNAL OF ENVIRONMENTAL PSYCHOLOGY. 4596

0272-4960 See IMA JOURNAL OF APPLIED MATHEMATICS. 3508

0272-4979 See IMA JOURNAL OF NUMERICAL ANALYSIS. 3508

0272-4987 See QUARTERLY JOURNAL OF EXPERIMENTAL PSYCHOLOGY. A, HUMAN EXPERIMENTAL PSYCHOLOGY, THE. 4614

0272-4995 See QUARTERLY JOURNAL OF EXPERIMENTAL PSYCHOLOGY. B, COMPARATIVE AND PHYSIOLOGICAL PSYCHOLOGY, THE. 4614

0272-5010 See EDUCATION (GUILFORD). 1893

0272-5037 See PROCEEDINGS OF THE ANNUAL MEETING - AMERICAN SOCIETY OF INTERNATIONAL LAW. 3134

0272-507X See REVIEWS OF HEMATOLOGY. 3773

0272-5088 See ACCELERATORS AND STORAGE RINGS. 5403

0272-5231 See CLINICS IN CHEST MEDICINE. 3566

0272-5290 See FORD FERGIE FARMER. 88

0272-5339 See YEARBOOK - NATIONAL ASSOCIATION OF CONGREGATIONAL CHRISTIAN CHURCHES, THE. 5010

0272-5363 See POSTAGE STAMP PRICES OF THE UNITED STATES, UNITED NATIONS, AND CANADA AND PROVINCES. 2786

0272-5371 See WESTERN BANK DIRECTORY. 816

0272-538X See ADMINISTRATION OF PUBLIC LAWS 81-874 & 81-815. 1859

0272-5398 See TENSION CONTROL. 4620

0272-5401 See BERGER BUILDING COST FILE, UNIT PRICES. CENTRAL EDITION, THE. 600

0272-5452 See CALIFORNIA ANTHROPOLOGIST. 233

0272-5460 See INTERNSHIPS. 4205

0272-5509 See FINISHED FABRICS. PRODUCTION, INVENTORIES, AND UNFILLED ORDERS. 3479

0272-5525 See AUGUSTAN SOCIETY OMNIBUS, THE. 2438

0272-5541 See MASSON TODAY. 4816

0272-555X See STAT (SANTA MONICA). 3725

0272-5622 See FOUNDATION ONE. 4776

0272-569X See TRAVEL EXPENSE MANAGEMENT. 5495

0272-5711 See FOLKLORE AND FOLKLIFE IN VIRGINIA. 2320

0272-572X See JAZZ TIMES (WASHINGTON). 4125

0272-5800 See COMPENDIUM OF RESEARCH REPORTS. 2819

0272-5827 See SEARCH (MIAMI), THE. 2664

0272-5835 See SPRINGER SERIES ON ADULTHOOD AND AGING. 3755

0272-586X See ARKANSAS HEALTH MANPOWER STATISTICS : LICENSED PRACTICAL NURSES. 3654

0272-5878 See ARKANSAS HEALTH MANPOWER STATISTICS : REGISTERED NURSES. 3654

0272-5916 See IDAHO DEPARTMENT OF HEALTH & WELFARE ANNUAL REPORT. 4783

0272-5940 See DIRECTORY - COUNCIL OF SPECIALISTS IN PSYCHIATRIC AND MENTAL HEALTH NURSING. 3855

0272-5959 See LIBERTARIAN DIGEST, THE. 4480

0272-6017 See CHANGING PUBLIC ATTITUDES ON GOVERNMENTS AND TAXES. 4717

0272-6025 See NATIONAL ASSOCIATION FOR LAW PLACEMENT MEMBERSHIP DIRECTORY. 3013

0272-6068 See LAND AND WATER REPORT. 2197

0272-6084 See SEDIMENTA. 557

0272-6106 See HYDROLOGY AND WATER RESOURCES IN ARIZONA AND THE SOUTHWEST. 1415

0272-6122 See INTERNATIONAL BULLETIN OF MISSIONARY RESEARCH. 4965

0272-619X See SPYGLASS. 596

0272-6246 See BUYERS BOOK OF AMERICAN CRAFTS, THE. 370

0272-6289 See INTERNATIONAL ESSAYS FOR BUSINESS DECISION MAKERS, THE. 683

0272-6327 See PERSPECTIVES IN BIOMECHANICS. 3626

0272-6335 See POLYMERS IN BIOLOGY AND MEDICINE. 469

0272-6343 See ELECTROMAGNETICS. 2046

0272-6351 See PARTICULATE SCIENCE AND TECHNOLOGY. 2015

0272-6378 See MARK TWAIN SOCIETY BULLETIN. 3410

0272-6386 See AMERICAN JOURNAL OF KIDNEY DISEASES. 3988

0272-6394 See NEW WORLD JOURNAL. 2748

0272-6408 See EXPERIMENTAL AND CLINICAL PSYCHIATRY. 3925

0272-6459 See SO & SO. 3471

0272-6467 See ELLIS HORWOOD SERIES IN ANALYTICAL CHEMISTRY. 1015

0272-6513 See CONNECTIONS (NEW YORK, N.Y.). 1062

0272-6521 See PYROTECHNICA. 1028

0272-6548 See STRIKES, STOPPAGES, AND BOYCOTTS. 3154

0272-6602 See HOUSTON MONTHLY. 5071

0272-6637 See JOURNAL OF THE MIDWEST FINANCE ASSOCIATION. 905

0272-6696 See ANNUAL MCGRAW-HILL SURVEY : BUSINESS' SPENDING PLANS FOR PLANTS AND EQUIPMENT. 1546

0272-6777 See COMPANIES HOLDING NUCLEAR CERTIFICATES OF AUTHORIZATION. 2154

0272-6793 See FLORICULTURE CROPS. 2414

0272-6815 See ANNUAL PLANNING INFORMATION: SAN FRANCISCO-OAKLAND STANDARD METROPOLITAN STATISTICAL AREA, CITY OF BERKELEY. 1647

0272-684X See INTERNATIONAL QUARTERLY OF COMMUNITY HEALTH EDUCATION. 4785

0272-6890 See MEXICAN REVOLUTION REPORTER, THE. 2746

0272-6904 See COLORADO HOMES & LIFESTYLES. 2904

0272-6912 See MOTHERS AND CHILDREN (WASHINGTON). 2283

0272-6963 See JOURNAL OF OPERATIONS MANAGEMENT. 1614

0272-7013 See EXAMINATION OF FISCAL ... PRESIDENTIAL AND VICE PRESIDENTIAL CERTIFIED EXPENDITURES. 4647

0272-7021 See EXAMINATION OF UNITED STATES RAILWAY ASSOCIATION'S FINANCIAL STATEMENTS. 5431

0272-703X See ANNUAL PLANNING INFORMATION : SAN FRANCISCO-OAKLAND STANDARD METROPOLITAN STATISTICAL AREA, CITY OF RICHMOND. 1647

0272-7064 See OSTEOPATHIC PHYSICIAN'S COMPENDIUM OF DRUG THERAPY, THE. 4318

0272-7129 See LEGAL OPINIONS OF THE OFFICE OF GENERAL COUNSEL - UNITED STATES. DEPT. OF HOUSING AND URBAN DEVELOPMENT. 3000

0272-7145 See CHILDREN'S DIGEST (INDIANAPOLIS. : 1981). 1061

0272-7161 See LAWYERS TITLE NEWS. 2998

0272-717X See MID-HUDSON LANGUAGE STUDIES. 3302

0272-7250 See ALBANIAN CATHOLIC BULLETIN. 5022

0272-7358 See CLINICAL PSYCHOLOGY REVIEW. 4581

0272-7374 See JOURNAL OF HOUSING (1979). 2826

0272-7404 See COMEDY. 3377

0272-7439 See TEXTURED YARN PRODUCTION. 3488

0272-7552 See HANDBOOK / NATIONAL ASSOCIATION OF SCHOOLS OF ART AND DESIGN. 351

0272-7560 See SOUTHEASTERN LAW LIBRARIAN. 3250

0272-7579 See SPORTSCAPE. 4923

0272-765X See SOCIAL ACTION & THE LAW. 3056

0272-7692 See DIALOGUE (WASHINGTON, D.C. : ENGLISH ED.). 1110

0272-7714 See ESTUARINE, COASTAL AND SHELF SCIENCE. 1449

0272-7730 See STARMONT READER'S GUIDES. 3353

0272-7757 See ECONOMICS OF EDUCATION REVIEW. 1737

0272-779X See INDEX TO THE GRAND FORKS HERALD. 2535

0272-7838 See U.S. WOMAN ENGINEER. 2000

0272-7854 See NAVY ARMS MUZZLELOADERS' JOURNAL. 2812

0272-7862 See STATE BUDGET TRENDS. 4749

0272-7889 See COUNTRY SAMPLER : NORTH AMERICAN FOLK ART. 371

0272-7897 See MARRIAGE & FAMILY. 2283

0272-7919 See INTERNATIONAL JOURNAL OF TURKISH STUDIES. 2692

0272-7943 See CAR STEREO (NEW YORK). 2038

0272-796X See GREAT RECIPES OF THE WORLD. 2342

0272-7978 See ABSTRACTS. STATE APPALACHIAN DEVELOPMENT PLANS AND INVESTMENT PROGRAMS. 2813

0272-7994 See NEWSLETTER / INTERNATIONAL CONGRESS ON HIGH SPEED PHOTOGRAPHY AND PHOTONICS. 4372

0272-8060 See HOUSTON MONTHLY. 2535

0272-8079 See S/N. SPEECHWRITER'S NEWSLETTER. 1121

0272-8087 See SEMINARS IN LIVER DISEASE. 3801

0272-8095 See NCAA SWIMMING; ANNUAL GUIDE. 4907

0272-8109 See WAGE DIFFERENCES AMONG METROPOLITAN AREAS : SUMMARY. 1717

0272-8117 See DELAWARE DIRECTORY OF COMMERCE AND INDUSTRY. 1603

0272-8125 See DOMESTIC AND IMPORTED VEHICLES TOWING MANUAL. 5413

0272-8133 See ALI-ABA COURSE OF STUDY. TAX PLANNING FOR AGRICULTURE : MATERIALS. 2931

0272-8141 See ISA DIRECTORY OF INSTRUMENTATION (TRADE EDITION). 3481

0272-8214 See MEMPHIS MUSIC DIRECTORY, THE. 4130

0272-8230 See FIRST TUESDAY. 4837

0272-8249 See SOMBRAS DEL PASADO. 2761

0272-832X See DIGEST OF COUNCIL BILLS - WISCONSIN. LEGISLATIVE COUNCIL. 2961

0272-8362 See SETTING MUNICIPAL PRIORITIES. 4747

0272-8370 See LANDMEN'S DIRECTORY. 4263

0272-8389 See MACHINE MANUAL OF INSTRUCTIONS FOR JUDGES OF ELECTION. PRIMARY ELECTION. 4663

0272-8397 See POLYMER COMPOSITES. 4459

0272-8400 See TEXAS FAMILY LAND HERITAGE REGISTRY. 141

0272-8427 See U.S. GOVERNMENT AGENCY SECURITY MARKET REPORT : FORECASTS AND ANALYSES, THE. 815

0272-8435 See BUDGET IN BRIEF / U.S. DEPARTMENT OF ENERGY. 4714

0272-8443 See HEALTH FACILITIES ENERGY REPORT. 1946

0272-846X See JOURNAL OF CLINICAL NEURO-OPHTHALMOLOGY. 3875

0272-8478 See CONSTRUCTION LABOR RATE TRENDS AND OUTLOOK. 1661

0272-8486 See BULLETIN ON TRAINING. 939

0272-8494 See FOLKLORE BIBLIOGRAPHY. 2325

0272-8516 See BICYCLE BLUE BOOK. BICYCLE SPECIFICATION GUIDE. 428

0272-8524 See BICYCLE BLUE BOOK. UNITED STATES BICYCLE TRADE INDEX. 428

0272-8532 See BASE LINE (GOLDEN, COLO.). 2580

0272-8540 See CHICAGO HISTORY. 2727

0272-8591 See HEAVY TRUCK COLLISION ESTIMATING GUIDE: CHEVROLET, DIAMOND REO, DODGE, FORD, FREIGHTLINER, GMC, INTERNATIONAL, KENWORTH, MACK, PETERBILT, WHITE. 5383

0272-8621 See PATENT ANTITRUST. 1307

0272-8656 See TRIENNIAL REPORT : A SURVEY OF PUBLIC EDUCATION IN THE NATION'S URBAN SCHOOL DISTRICTS, THE. 1788

0272-8699 See NATIONAL DIRECTORY AND ATLAS OF BUDGET MOTELS. 2808

0272-8710 See PROCEEDINGS OF THE PMR CONFERENCE. 1079

0272-8729 See TECHNICAL REPORT - WATER RESOURCES RESEARCH CENTER, UNIVERSITY OF HAWAII. 5540

0272-8737 See FOREST INSECT AND DISEASE CONDITIONS. INTERMOUNTAIN REGION. 2380

0272-880X See PROCEEDINGS OF THE INTERNATIONAL CENTRE FOR HEAT AND MASS TRANSFER. 4418

0272-8842 See CERAMICS INTERNATIONAL. 2588

0272-8850 See PERIODICALS DIGEST, DENTISTRY. 1333

0272-8869 See BIBLIOGRAPHY OF FOSSIL VERTEBRATES. 4231

0272-8885 See MATH NOTEBOOK. 1882

0272-8893 See FOCUS ON LEARNING PROBLEMS IN MATHEMATICS. 1879

0272-8915 See TEXAS OIL REGISTER. 4280

0272-8923 See CYCLE STREET AND TOURING GUIDE. 4081

0272-8966 See SANCTUARY (LINCOLN, MASS.). 4171

0272-8974 See ANNUAL REPORT TO CONGRESS - URBAN INITIATIVES ANTI-CRIME PROGRAM. 3157

0272-8982 See ALI-ABA COURSE OF STUDY. PRODUCTS LIABILITY : PREVENTION, LITIGATION, AND LAW REFORM : MATERIALS. 2931

0272-8990 See ALI-ABA COURSE OF STUDY. ENERGY LAW : MATERIALS. 2930

0272-9008 See ENVIRONMENT (GUILFORD). 2165

0272-9016 See SOCIAL WORK PAPERS OF THE SCHOOL OF SOCIAL WORK, UNIVERSITY OF SOUTHERN CALIFORNIA. 5309

0272-9024 See WAGE CHRONOLOGY : BERKSHIRE HATHAWAY AND THE CLOTHING AND TEXTILE WORKERS. 1717

0272-9032 See GENETIC TECHNOLOGY NEWS. 5107

0272-9059 See BULLETIN OF THE OCMA, THE. 3560

0272-9067 See ARTICULATOR (COLUMBUS), THE. 1317

0272-9172 See MATERIALS RESEARCH SOCIETY SYMPOSIA PROCEEDINGS. 2071

0272-9199 See PEDALPOINT. 4145

0272-9210 See WATER CHLORINATION. 5542

0272-9237 See ADVANCES IN CLINICAL CARDIOLOGY. 3698

0272-9296 See LEGAL RESOURCE INDEX. 3082

0272-930X See MERRILL-PALMER QUARTERLY (1960). 4604

0272-9318 See SUMMARY OF TAXES IN ARKANSAS, A. 4751

0272-9334 See WEST'S MILITARY JUSTICE DIGEST. 3183

0272-9342 See OUTDOOR SPORTSMAN (POINT PLEASANT). 4877

0272-9377 See COLORADO HERITAGE. 2729

0272-9385 See ANNUAL REPORT - GRADUATE DEPT. OF LIBRARY AND INFORMATION SCIENCE, THE CATHOLIC UNIVERSITY OF AMERICA. 3190

0272-9393 See ALI-ABA COURSE OF STUDY. LABOR RELATIONS AND EMPLOYMENT LAW FOR THE CORPORATE COUNSEL AND THE GENERAL PRACTITIONER: MATERIALS. 3143

0272-9407 See FINANCIAL REPORT AND PROGRESS REPORT ON SPRUCE BUDWORM PROGRAMS. 2379

0272-9490 See AMERICAN JOURNAL OF OCCUPATIONAL THERAPY, THE. 1874

0272-9512 See NURSING MATTERS. 3864

0272-9520 See TARAKAN MUSIC LETTER, THE. 4156

0272-9555 See TECHNICAL REPORT - WATER AND ENERGY RESEARCH INSTITUTE, UNIVERSITY OF GUAM. 5540

0272-958X See GLOVES AND MITTENS. 3479

0272-9598 See RIVERSEDGE. 3431

0272-9601 See PROOFTEXTS. 3425

0272-961X See WOMAN'S WORLD (ENGLEWOOD, N.J.). 5569

0272-9628 See HAZARDOUS MATERIALS INTELLIGENCE REPORT. 2231

0272-9644 See RIO GRANDE CHAPTER BULLETIN. 3247

0272-9695 See NCI GRANTS AWARDED. 3821

0272-9768 See PRODUCTION CREDIT ASSOCIATIONS, OPERATING STATISTICS. 732

0272-9776 See SOLAR CENSUS. 1957

0272-9873 See SOUTH CAROLINA GEOLOGY. 1397

0272-9881 See CLINICAL BIOCHEMISTRY REVIEWS (ELMSFORD, N.Y.). 485

0272-989X See MEDICAL DECISION MAKING. 1215

0272-9903 See SELECTA MATHEMATICA SOVIETICA. 3533

0272-9911 See NEWSLETTER - AUGUST DERLETH SOCIETY. 3416

0272-992X See FAMILY (BOCA RATON). 2279

0272-9962 See MENTAL HEALTH (BOCA RATON). 4790

0272-9970 See MONEY (BOCA RATON). 1574
0273-0014 See WOMEN (BOCA RATON). 5570
0273-0022 See WORK (BOCA RATON). 1718
0273-0049 See WASHINGTON INTERNATIONAL ORGANIZATIONAL GUIDE. 857
0273-0057 See MULTINATIONAL CORPORATION REGULATORY GUIDEBOOK, THE. 3012
0273-009X See FOCUS ON RENEWABLE NATURAL RESOURCES. 2194
0273-0111 See WIDE WORLD OF CANOEING. 597
0273-012X See JDR 3RD FUND REPORT, THE. 323
0273-0138 See FUTURE SURVEY ANNUAL. 5107
0273-0162 See BLUE BOOK (TULSA), THE. 1341
0273-0197 See BULLETIN OF THE NEEDLE AND BOBBIN CLUB, THE. 5183
0273-0227 See LINDA HALL LIBRARY MISCELLANY. 3228
0273-026X See EXAMINATION OF THE FINANCIAL STATEMENTS OF FHA INSURANCE OPERATIONS. 2879
0273-0278 See POSTGRADUATE RADIOLOGY. 3944
0273-0332 See MANAGEMENT COMPENSATION, RAILROADS. 5432
0273-0340 See HENRY JAMES REVIEW, THE. 3344
0273-0359 See NEU-BRAUNFELSER JAHRBUCH. 2748
0273-0367 See ASSOCIATION EXECUTIVE COMPENSATION STUDY. 640
0273-0383 See HOT ROD MAGAZINE CORVETTE. 5416
0273-0391 See KITH AND KIN OF BOONE COUNTY, WEST VIRGINIA. 2457
0273-0499 See NONALIGNED THIRD WORLD ANNUAL. 1576
0273-0553 See DIRECTORY OF ACTIVE MINES IN ARIZONA. 2138
0273-0561 See MEDICAL DIRECTORY OF NEW YORK STATE. 3608
0273-0618 See HOTTEST NEW BUSINESS IDEAS, THE. 680
0273-0642 See CASE DIGEST (LANSING). 4505
0273-0685 See SECURITIES AND FEDERAL CORPORATE LAW REPORT. 3103
0273-0693 See SCOTIA. 2709
0273-0782 See CONAN THE BARBARIAN. 4859
0273-0820 See SAFE, EFFECTIVE AND THERAPEUTICALLY EQUIVALENT PRESCRIPTION DRUGS. 4329
0273-0898 See ICI TRENDS IN MUTUAL FUND ACTIVITY. 900
0273-0936 See SCHOOL TRANSPORTATION. 5392
0273-0960 See OCCASIONAL PAPERS - UNITED METHODIST BOARD OF HIGHER EDUCATION AND MINISTRY. 1838
0273-0979 See BULLETIN (NEW SERIES) OF THE AMERICAN MATHEMATICAL SOCIETY. 3498
0273-0995 See BRIEF (CHICAGO. 1980), THE. 2943
0273-1029 See MOTOR VACUUM & WIRING DIAGRAM DIAGNOSTIC MANUAL. PROFESSIONAL SERVICE TRADE EDITION. 5420
0273-1169 See BUDGET GUIDELINES : CONDOMINIUMS, PLANNED DEVELOPMENTS, STOCK COOPERATIVES, COMMUNITY ASSOCIATIONS. 2816
0273-1177 See ADVANCES IN SPACE RESEARCH. 3
0273-1223 See WATER SCIENCE AND TECHNOLOGY. 5548
0273-124X See CONTRIBUTIONS TO THE STUDY OF CHILDHOOD AND YOUTH. 4583
0273-1274 See DISNEY'S YEAR BOOK. 1063
0273-1355 See QUARTERLY REPORT - MIT SEA GRANT PROGRAM. 5143
0273-1371 See GEOPOLITICS OF ENERGY. 1945
0273-1398 See FINE HOMEBUILDING. 615
0273-1525 See DIRECTORY OF SOLAR ENERGY RESEARCH ACTIVITIES IN THE UNITED STATES. 1936

0273-1622 See NEWS FROM DUN & BRADSTREET, INC. BUSINESS ECONOMICS DIVISION. WEEKLY FAILURES. 1508
0273-1657 See DRINKERS, DRINKING AND ALCOHOL-RELATED MORTALITY AND HOSPITALIZATIONS. 1343
0273-1762 See WESTERN PETROLEUM REGISTER. 4282
0273-1843 See SOHIO NEWS. 4278
0273-1916 See STATISTICAL REPORT - STATE OF ALASKA, ALASKA OIL AND GAS CONSERVATION COMMISSION. 2206
0273-1991 See WESTERN ROUNDUP COUNTRY MUSIC TRADE DIRECTORY & NEWS REPORT. 4158
0273-2017 See SURVIVAL TOMORROW. 5264
0273-2033 See ONE SHOW - ONE CLUB FOR ART & COPY (NEW YORK, N.Y.), THE. 763
0273-205X See MISSOURI STATE PLAN ON ALCOHOL AND DRUG ABUSE PREVENTION AND TREATMENT. 1346
0273-2114 See MOTIF (SPRINGFIELD). 4132
0273-2173 See SOCIOLOGICAL SPECTRUM. 5261
0273-2181 See COMMUNIQUE (OVERSEAS DEVELOPMENT COUNCIL). 2908
0273-2203 See ANNUAL IMPLEMENTATION PLAN (WATERBURY). 4765
0273-2211 See RCUH ANNUAL REPORT. 5145
0273-2238 See WATER ENGINEERING & MANAGEMENT. 2096
0273-2254 See DERMATOLOGY & ALLERGY. 3719
0273-2289 See MOLECULAR BIOTECHNOLOGY. 3695
0273-2297 See DEVELOPMENTAL REVIEW. 4584
0273-2300 See REGULATORY TOXICOLOGY AND PHARMACOLOGY. 4327
0273-2343 See SHARE (BERKELEY, CALIF.). 3249
0273-236X See EMPLOYEE BENEFITS CASES. 3146
0273-2424 See FACULTY PAPERS OF MIDWESTERN STATE UNIVERSITY. 1864
0273-2459 See JOURNAL OF THE SOCIETY FOR ACCELERATIVE LEARNING AND TEACHING, THE. 1881
0273-2467 See AGING (BOCA RATON). 5178
0273-2475 See CONSUMERISM (BOCA RATON). 1296
0273-2483 See DEATH & DYING (BOCA RATON, FLA.). 4344
0273-2491 See DEFENSE (BOCA RATON). 4041
0273-2505 See DRUGS (BOCA RATON). 1344
0273-2513 See ETHICS (BOCA RATON). 2250
0273-2521 See HUMAN RIGHTS. 4508
0273-253X See POLLUTION (BOCA RATON). 2238
0273-2548 See POPULATION (BOCA RATON). 4556
0273-2556 See RELIGION (BOCA RATON). 4991
0273-2564 See SEXUALITY (BOCA RATON). 5188
0273-2572 See SPORTS (BOCA RATON). 4922
0273-2580 See TECHNOLOGY (BOCA RATON). 5163
0273-2599 See THIRD WORLD (BOCA RATON). 2912
0273-2602 See TRANSPORTATION (BOCA RATON). 5396
0273-2610 See YOUTH (BOCA RATON). 1072
0273-270X See NEW JERSEY MONTHLY. 2540
0273-2858 See METROPOLITAN HOME. 2902
0273-2874 See BARRY FAIN'S PRIVATE BLUE BOOK OF GUN VALUES. 4037
0273-2912 See PROCEEDINGS OF THE LEHIGH COUNTY HISTORICAL SOCIETY. 2755
0273-2939 See MONOGRAPHS IN TOXICOLOGY : ENVIRONMENTAL AND SAFETY ASPECTS. 3982
0273-2955 See WILEY SERIES IN MARKETING. 938
0273-2963 See WILEY SERVICE MANAGEMENT SERIES. 889
0273-2971 See SYNTHETIC FUELS UPDATE. 4280

0273-298X See CURRENT ENERGY PATENTS. 1936
0273-303X See HOME PLANET NEWS. 3394
0273-3048 See ASBESTOS LITIGATION REPORTER. 2937
0273-3072 See CATO JOURNAL, THE. 5195
0273-3080 See SCAN NEWSLETTER. 1221
0273-3102 See ENERGY CLEARINGHOUSE. 1939
0273-3137 See DEVICE TECHNIQUES. 3571
0273-3188 See DEFENSE WEEK. 4042
0273-320X See NURSING ... DRUG HANDBOOK. 3864
0273-3218 See AWWA MAINSTREAM. 5531
0273-3226 See BIOTECHNOLOGY NEWS. 3689
0273-3234 See WORK RELATED ABSTRACTS. 1540
0273-3269 See COPTIC CHURCH REVIEW. 5039
0273-3315 See CCLM NEWSLETTER. 3373
0273-3323 See CENTRAL PARK. 2844
0273-334X See PROCEEDINGS, ANNUAL CONVENTION - OHIO COUNCIL ON FAMILY RELATIONS. 2285
0273-3366 See FANON CENTER JOURNAL. 5285
0273-3374 See HOROLOGICAL DIALOGUES. 2916
0273-3412 See PENNSYLVANIA HISTORICAL BIBLIOGRAPHY. 422
0273-3420 See POINT SPREAD PLAYBOOK. 4912
0273-3439 See PUBLIC EMPLOYEES CONFERENCE PROCEEDINGS. 1704
0273-3447 See SAN DIEGO COUNTY DIRECTORY OF MANUFACTURERS AND INDUSTRIAL DISTRIBUTORS. 1625
0273-3498 See MENTAL HEALTH SERVICE SYSTEM REPORTS. SERIES GN, METHODOLOGY / U.S. DEPARTMENT OF HEALTH AND HUMAN SERVICES, PUBLIC HEALTH SERVICE, ALCOHOL, DRUG ABUSE, AND MENTAL HEALTH ADMINISTRATION, NATIONAL INSTITUTE OF MENTAL HEALTH. 3930
0273-3536 See STUDIES IN MICROBIOLOGY (BERKELEY, CALIF.). 570
0273-3544 See FAMILY-CENTERED COMMUNITY NURSING. 3856
0273-3560 See FAIRSHARE. 3120
0273-3617 See RISK MANAGEMENT REPORT, MEDICAL RECORDS, THE. 3637
0273-3633 See DONNELLEY SEC HANDBOOK. 3099
0273-3641 See FEDERAL LAW JOURNAL (OVIEDO). 2969
0273-3676 See NATIONAL NEWSPAPER INDEX. 5814
0273-3684 See BUSINESS INDEX. 727
0273-3692 See SUBJECT INDEX TO THE ILLINOIS REGISTER, WITH TABLES. 3083
0273-3714 See SOURCE BOOK OF PROJECTS, SCIENCE EDUCATION DEVELOPMENT AND RESEARCH. 1872
0273-3730 See NAPSAC DIRECTORY OF ALTERNATIVE BIRTH SERVICES AND CONSUMER GUIDE. 3765
0273-3749 See INTERNATIONAL DIRECTORY OF ASTROLOGERS & PSYCHICS, THE. 390
0273-3757 See PUBLIC RELATIONS ALMANAC FOR EDUCATORS, THE. 764
0273-3765 See WAY MARKINGS. 1148
0273-3803 See MEANS COLORADO DIRECTORY, THE. 4074
0273-3811 See OIL AND GAS PRODUCTION IN KANSAS. 4268
0273-382X See OCCUPATIONAL PROJECTIONS AND TRAINING DATA. 4207
0273-3838 See ANNUAL TRADITIONAL CRAFT DAYS. 370
0273-396X See TEXAS ENERGY ISSUES. 1959
0273-4001 See ARKANSAS GAZETTE INDEX. 2528
0273-4117 See NEVADA RNFORMATION. 3862
0273-4125 See FINDEX. 924
0273-4168 See SEAWORLD (MYSTIC). 1456

ISSN Index

0273-4230 *See* CORRECTIONS YEARBOOK, THE. **3161**

0273-429X *See* CHINESE PHYSICS. **4399**

0273-4303 *See* SOUTHERN EXPORTER, THE. **851**

0273-432X *See* LOCKHEED AIRCRAFT CORPORATION. **1536**

0273-4362 *See* NASA SPACE SYSTEMS TECHNOLOGY MODEL. **29**

0273-4370 *See* AIR FORCE REPORT. **4034**

0273-4397 *See* FATS AND OILS. PRODUCTION, CONSUMPTION, AND FACTORY AND WAREHOUSE STOCKS (ANNUAL). **1606**

0273-4400 *See* ELECTRIC LAMPS (ANNUAL). **2043**

0273-4419 *See* WHALEWATCHER. **5600**

0273-4435 *See* GUIDE TO FEDERAL FUNDING FOR GOVERNMENTS AND NONPROFITS. **4653**

0273-4443 *See* EDUCATION FUNDING NEWS. **1739**

0273-446X *See* RURAL EDUCATOR (FORT COLLINS), THE. **1781**

0273-4532 *See* SPRING-AUTUMN PAPERS. **2665**

0273-4540 *See* TOILETRY AND BEAUTY AIDS MARKET. **405**

0273-4605 *See* ALA HANDBOOK OF ORGANIZATION AND MEMBERSHIP DIRECTORY. **3188**

0273-4613 *See* CONSULTING OPPORTUNITIES JOURNAL. **659**

0273-4672 *See* WORKER FOR THE NORTHWEST, THE. **1718**

0273-4680 *See* WORKER FOR THE MARYLAND-D.C.-VIRGINIA AREA, THE. **1718**

0273-4737 *See* ASSE SOCIETY UPDATE. **1965**

0273-4753 *See* JOURNAL OF MARKETING EDUCATION. **928**

0273-480X *See* WORLD'S FAIR (CORTE MADERA, CALIF.). **5226**

0273-4923 *See* PEANUT MARKETING SUMMARY CROP. **180**

0273-4931 *See* ARMSTRONG OIL DIRECTORIES, LOUISIANA, TEXAS GULF COAST, EAST TEXAS, ARK. AND MISS. **4251**

0273-494X *See* DIRECTORY OF BAR ACTIVITIES. **2961**

0273-4966 *See* JOURNAL OF EVERETT & SNOHOMISH COUNTY HISTORY. **2741**

0273-4974 *See* NATIONAL REPORT COMPUTERS AND HEALTH. **1196**

0273-4982 *See* SMITHSONIAN YEAR (1980). **5158**

0273-4990 *See* HOT TOPICS. **2535**

0273-5016 *See* URNER BARRY'S PRICE-CURRENT. WEST COAST EDITION. **143**

0273-5024 *See* JOURNAL OF TEACHING IN PHYSICAL EDUCATION. **1856**

0273-5040 *See* BABY & TODDLER TEACHER GUIDE. **4937**

0273-5059 *See* CHURCH PROGRAMS FOR MIDDLERS & JUNIORS. **4947**

0273-5113 *See* CHURCH PROGRAMS FOR PRIMARIES. **4947**

0273-5148 *See* PRIMARY ONE. **5019**

0273-5164 *See* PRIMARY TWO STUDENT GUIDE. **5066**

0273-5172 *See* DIRECTORY - FORUM COMMITTEE ON THE ENTERTAINMENT AND SPORTS INDUSTRIES. **2961**

0273-5180 *See* DIRECTORY - FORUM COMMITTEE ON THE CONSTRUCTION INDUSTRY, AMERICAN BAR ASSOCIATION. **2961**

0273-5202 *See* REPORTED MORBIDITY AND MORTALITY IN TEXAS, ANNUAL SUMMARY. **4799**

0273-5229 *See* ARMSTRONG OIL DIRECTORIES, ROCKY MOUNTAIN AND CENTRAL UNITED STATES. **4251**

0273-5237 *See* SMALL FARM PROGRAMS AND ACTIVITIES, STATE REPORTS. **135**

0273-5253 *See* ANNUAL INSTITUTE ON MINERAL LAW. **2934**

0273-5261 *See* DEUTSCHAMERIKANER (CHICAGO), DER. **2532**

0273-530X *See* IMPACTO. **2551**

0273-5415 *See* PRECANCEL FORUM. **1147**

0273-5423 *See* EXECUTIVE JEWELER. **2914**

0273-5504 *See* GUARDIAN OF TRUTH. **4961**

0273-5520 *See* RESTAURANTS & INSTITUTIONS (CHICAGO, ILL.). **5073**

0273-5598 *See* PHILATELIC OBSERVER. **2786**

0273-5601 *See* GOAL (NEW YORK, N.Y.). **4896**

0273-5644 *See* SEE THE TREASURE COAST. **5490**

0273-5652 *See* ART BUSINESS NEWS. **338**

0273-5687 *See* WESTERN HVACR NEWS. **2608**

0273-5695 *See* HEARTH AND HOME (GILFORD, N.H. : 1989). **1946**

0273-5695 *See* WOOD 'N ENERGY (CONCORD, N.H. : 1980). **1960**

0273-5709 *See* NATURESCAPE. **466**

0273-5717 *See* ENCOUNTERS (ST. PAUL, MINN.). **5102**

0273-5768 *See* BREWING INDUSTRY NEWS, THE. **2365**

0273-5776 *See* STOCK SHOW, THE. **222**

0273-5822 *See* MINI STORAGE MESSENGER, THE. **695**

0273-5857 *See* SANTA ROSA FREE PRESS. **5651**

0273-5865 *See* DISCIPLESHIP JOURNAL. **4954**

0273-5946 *See* HOTLINE (SPRINGFIELD, ILL.). **5288**

0273-5954 *See* CONTRACTORS GUIDE (LOMBARD, ILL.). **611**

0273-6004 *See* SAN FRANCISCO WHOLESALE ORNAMENTAL CROPS REPORT. **2430**

0273-608X *See* 99 NEWS, THE. **3**

0273-6136 *See* CATHOLIC TWIN CIRCLE. **5026**

0273-6160 *See* BETTER LIVING (NEW YORK. 1981). **2528**

0273-6187 *See* INTERMOUNTAIN CATHOLIC. **4965**

0273-6225 *See* BUILDER DEVELOPER WEST. **602**

0273-6284 *See* ATPCO PASSENGER TARIFF SET. **12**

0273-6314 *See* EXECUTIVE INTELLIGENCE REVIEW. **1490**

0273-6357 *See* CAMBRIDGE REPORT ON CORPORATE MERGERS AND CORPORATE POLICY, THE. **782**

0273-6381 *See* ARLINGTON JOURNAL (ALEXANDRIA. 1980), THE. **5758**

0273-639X *See* ALEXANDRIA JOURNAL (ALEXANDRIA. 1980), THE. **5758**

0273-6403 *See* FAIRFAX JOURNAL (SPRINGFIELD. 1980), THE. **5758**

0273-6438 *See* NEW YORK ENVIRONMENTAL NEWS : NYEN. **2178**

0273-6454 *See* POLKA NEWS, THE. **1314**

0273-6462 *See* SHEET MUSIC MAGAZINE. STANDARD PIANO/GUITAR. **4153**

0273-6527 *See* THIS PEOPLE. **5004**

0273-6551 *See* BROKER WORLD. **2876**

0273-656X *See* CHILTON'S AUTOMOTIVE INDUSTRIES (1976). **5410**

0273-6586 *See* LEISURE TIME ELECTRONICS. **2070**

0273-6608 *See* INTERNAL MEDICINE (PLAINSBORO, N.J.). **3797**

0273-6667 *See* REAL ESTATE NEWS (BALTIMORE). **4844**

0273-6683 *See* MIAA NEWSLETTER, THE. **4904**

0273-6691 *See* GRAY'S SPORTING JOURNAL. **4873**

0273-6705 *See* QUOTE (ATLANTA, GA.). **3427**

0273-6713 *See* COMMERCIAL FISHERIES NEWS. **2299**

0273-6748 *See* EUROPEAN CAR. **5414**

0273-6780 *See* MISSIONARY EVANGEL. **4978**

0273-6837 *See* WALL PAPER (NEW YORK, N.Y.), THE. **2903**

0273-6861 *See* VIRGINIA CONTRACTOR. **2033**

0273-6896 *See* CAHPERD JOURNAL TIMES. **4770**

0273-6950 *See* ARIZONA BUSINESS GAZETTE. **639**

0273-6993 *See* WINFIELD PRESS, THE. **5662**

0273-7000 *See* ANNUAL ENERGY LITIGATION INSTITUTE : EFFECTIVE STRATEGIES & TECHNIQUES. **2934**

0273-7027 *See* ESTATE PLANNING & CALIFORNIA PROBATE REPORTER. **3118**

0273-7078 *See* STAMP AUCTION NEWS. **2787**

0273-7116 *See* LOS ALAMOS SCIENCE. **5126**

0273-7167 *See* GOSPEL HERALD (JELLICO), THE. **4961**

0273-7175 *See* BRANDEIS QUARTERLY, THE. **1812**

0273-7191 *See* AVIATION TRAVEL AND TIMES. **14**

0273-7280 *See* FILIPINO CATHOLIC. **5029**

0273-7310 *See* AVIATION LAW REPORTS. **2939**

0273-7353 *See* ESA NEWSLETTER - ENTOMOLOGICAL SOCIETY OF AMERICA. **5608**

0273-7434 *See* BOWHUNTER (FORT WAYNE). **4869**

0273-7477 *See* AUTOMOTIVE SERVICE REPORTS. **5407**

0273-7485 *See* IS. INTER SERVICE. **955**

0273-7515 *See* MIDWEST FLYER MAGAZINE. **28**

0273-7590 *See* HUMPTY DUMPTY'S MAGAZINE. **1064**

0273-7612 *See* EXECUTIVE COMPENSATION & TAXATION COORDINATOR. **2968**

0273-7639 *See* AVIONICS (POTOMAC, MD.). **14**

0273-7671 *See* SUNFLOWER WORLD. **2432**

0273-768X *See* EMPLOYEE BENEFITS COMPLIANCE COORDINATOR. **940**

0273-7736 *See* CITY ON A HILL. **1090**

0273-7752 *See* LOW PRICED STOCK SURVEY, THE. **905**

0273-7841 *See* ALBEMARLE MAGAZINE, THE. **2527**

0273-7906 *See* SCEA EMPHASIS. **1870**

0273-7930 *See* INDIANA BUSINESS MAGAZINE. **682**

0273-7965 *See* BUILDER & CONTRACTOR. **602**

0273-8015 *See* MONEY FINDER. **799**

0273-8023 *See* ALLIANCE UPDATE. **1854**

0273-8031 *See* HAN'GUK ILBO NEW YORK PAN. **5717**

0273-804X *See* CALIFORNIA OPTOMETRY. **4215**

0273-8120 *See* SEW NEWS. **5186**

0273-8139 *See* PHARMACEUTICAL ENGINEERING. **4320**

0273-8163 *See* ALTERNATIVE ENERGY RETAILER. **1931**

0273-8201 *See* PRINTOUT (SAINT CLOUD, MINN.). **1239**

0273-8287 *See* CALIFORNIA HORSEMAN'S NEWS. **2797**

0273-8295 *See* WAY OF ST. FRANCIS (1980). **5008**

0273-8309 *See* VIRGINIA LIFELINE. **3650**

0273-835X *See* OUTLOOK (PALO ALTO). **749**

0273-8457 *See* POLAR GEOGRAPHY AND GEOLOGY. **1391**

0273-8481 *See* JOURNAL OF BURN CARE & REHABILITATION, THE. **3594**

0273-8511 *See* MODERN RECORDING & MUSIC. **5317**

0273-8546 *See* NEW SENSE BULLETIN. **4605**

0273-8570 *See* JOURNAL OF FIELD ORNITHOLOGY. **5618**

0273-8589 *See* DIVER (PORTLAND CONN.), THE. **4893**

0273-8619 *See* DALLAS ORNAMENTAL CROPS MARKET NEWS. **170**

0273-8635 *See* ILLINOIS WEATHER & CROPS. **174**

0273-883X *See* LOUISIANA FARM REPORTER. **105**

0273-8848 *See* LOUISIANA CROP-WEATHER SUMMARY. **178**

0273-8910 *See* EAP DIGEST. **1344**

0273-8929 *See* MASSACHUSETTS MEDICAL NEWS. **3606**

0273-8961 *See* CALIFORNIA GRAPEVINE. **2365**

0273-9054 *See* FAMILY LIFE TODAY. **2279**
0273-9100 *See* JUNIOR BOWLER. **4902**
0273-9135 *See* CROSSFACE, THE. **4892**
0273-9186 *See* DOWN HOME (BIRMINGHAM). **5468**
0273-9240 *See* CREATIVE PRODUCTS NEWS. **1603**
0273-9259 *See* SAN MARCOS COURIER. **5640**
0273-9267 *See* CREDIT UNION MANAGEMENT. **786**
0273-9348 *See* UKRAINIAN WEEKLY, THE. **2274**
0273-9372 *See* MIAMI MENSUAL. **2538**
0273-9399 *See* SPECIALIST (NEW YORK, N.Y.). **3251**
0273-9402 *See* TRUCK BLUE BOOK. **5426**
0273-9518 *See* IAR HOTLINE. **5317**
0273-9550 *See* PRINT & GRAPHICS. **4568**
0273-9593 *See* ALABAMA MESSENGER, THE. **5625**
0273-9615 *See* CHILDREN'S HEALTH CARE. **3901**
0273-964X *See* OFFICE GUIDE. **700**
0273-9658 *See* OFFICIAL RAILWAY GUIDE. NORTH AMERICAN TRAVEL EDITION. UNITED STATES, CANADA AND MEXICO, THE. **5433**
0273-9747 *See* FLORIDA FUNERAL DIRECTOR, THE. **2407**
0273-9755 *See* WISCONSIN ESCAPE. **5499**
0273-9895 *See* KANSAS CITY AVIATION. **27**
0273-9917 *See* JOURNAL FOR EDUCATION IN PHOTOJOURNALISM, THE. **4371**
0273-9933 *See* INDIANA MUSICATOR. **4122**
0273-9941 *See* WINONA DAILY NEWS. **5699**
0273-9976 See JOURNAL OF AHIMA. **3786**
0273-9992 *See* URNER BARRY'S PRICE-CURRENT. **223**
0274-0001 *See* FLICKERTALES (ERIE, N.D.). **5725**
0274-4783 *See* MICHIGAN FISHERMAN, THE. **2308**
0274-4805 *See* BOTTOM LINE, PERSONAL. **644**
0274-4813 *See* CYCLING U.S.A. **428**
0274-483X See SAN DIEGO HOME/GARDEN LIFESTYLES. **2792**
0274-4856 *See* FOLIO (NORTH HOLLYWOOD). **1132**
0274-4872 *See* KEEPER'S VOICE. **3168**
0274-4929 *See* INDIANAPOLIS BUSINESS JOURNAL. **682**
0274-497X *See* JOURNAL OF BIOLOGICAL PHOTOGRAPHY. **460**
0274-5003 *See* V-8 TIMES. **5427**
0274-502X *See* REPORT - AUDUBON SOCIETY OF RHODE ISLAND. **2203**
0274-5054 *See* BEAN COMMISSION JOURNAL, THE. **164**
0274-5097 *See* PRINTS (ALTON). **4569**
0274-5100 *See* FASHION GALLERIA, THE. **1084**
0274-5143 *See* PENTHOUSE VARIATIONS. **3996**
0274-5151 *See* TC. TWIN CITIES. **2547**
0274-5186 *See* FOUNDATION DRILLING. **615**
0274-5232 *See* AMAZING SPIDER-MAN, THE. **4856**
0274-5240 *See* AVENGERS, THE. **4857**
0274-5267 *See* CAPTAIN AMERICA. **1061**
0274-5275 *See* INCREDIBLE HULK, THE. **4862**
0274-5291 *See* FANTASTIC FOUR. **4861**
0274-533X *See* MIGHTY THOR, THE. **4863**
0274-5372 *See* THE UNCANNY X-MEN. **4867**
0274-5410 *See* SURVEY ANNOUNCEMENT - KENTUCKY CROP & LIVESTOCK REPORTING SERVICE. **222**
0274-547X *See* INDIANA BEVERAGE JOURNAL. **2367**
0274-5496 *See* GREATER WASHINGTON BOARD OF TRADE NEWS, THE. **1564**
0274-5526 *See* PLEXUS (OAKLAND, CALIF.). **5564**
0274-5542 *See* INTERNAL MEDICINE NEWS & CARDIOLOGY NEWS. **3746**
0274-5569 *See* INCREASE. **4964**
0274-5577 *See* DEPRESSION GLASS NATIONAL MARKET APPRAISAL REPORT, THE. **2588**

0274-5615 *See* OHIO CIVIL LIBERTIES. **4511**
0274-564X *See* ORNITHOLOGICAL NEWSLETTER. **5619**
0274-5704 *See* ARC (ARLINGTON, TEX. : MAY 20, 1980). **4884**
0274-5720 *See* MUZZLELOADER, THE. **4905**
0274-5771 *See* FEED INTERNATIONAL. **201**
0274-5798 *See* FLYING REVIEW. **21**
0274-5801 *See* HANGUK ILBO (CHICAGO, ILL.). **5660**
0274-5852 *See* WILLIAM WINTER COMMENTS (1976). **4538**
0274-5917 *See* SONGWRITER (HOLLYWOOD). **4153**
0274-5933 *See* SAN FRANCISCO FOCUS. **2545**
0274-595X *See* JOINT PERSPECTIVES. **4047**
0274-5976 *See* GRAPHIC ARTS PRODUCT NEWS (CHICAGO). **379**
0274-600X *See* PRAYERS FOR WORSHIP. **4987**
0274-6018 *See* STUDENT DOCTOR. **3643**
0274-6050 *See* BIG FARMER ENTREPRENEUR. **66**
0274-6085 *See* ANTIQUES & COLLECTIBLES (GREENVALE, N.Y.). **249**
0274-6093 *See* CALIFORNIA INNTOUCH. **2804**
0274-6115 *See* MARBLEHEAD MAGAZINE. **2538**
0274-614X *See* MEDICAL HOTLINE. **3609**
0274-6220 *See* DELL PENCIL PUZZLES & WORD GAMES. **4860**
0274-6239 *See* DELL OFFICIAL CROSSWORD PUZZLES. **4860**
0274-6271 See FIBER OPTICS AND COMMUNICATIONS. **1155**
0274-6301 *See* DELL CROSSWORD PUZZLES. **4859**
0274-631X *See* COMPUTERS IN HOSPITALS. **1179**
0274-6336 *See* PENNSYLVANIA SPORTSMAN, THE. **4877**
0274-6425 *See* DELL POCKET CROSSWORD PUZZLES. **4860**
0274-6441 *See* SECOND BOAT, THE. **2472**
0274-645X *See* SUPERVISORY SENSE. **947**
0274-6484 *See* NEW ENGLAND ENGINEERING JOURNAL. **1988**
0274-6522 *See* FLASHLIGHT (PASADENA, CALIF.). **4959**
0274-6530 *See* COMMUNICATION QUARTERLY (EAST LANSING). **1891**
0274-6549 *See* OREGON OPTOMETRY. **4217**
0274-6565 *See* AMERICAN FARRIERS' JOURNAL. **2796**
0274-6581 *See* VISION. **5008**
0274-6662 *See* VOLLEYBALL MAGAZINE. **4928**
0274-6697 *See* TENNES-SIERRAN, THE. **5237**
0274-6743 *See* TOTAL HEALTH. **4805**
0274-6824 *See* USAF FIGHTER WEAPONS REVIEW. **4060**
0274-6859 *See* TIJUANA MAGAZINE. **2547**
0274-6956 *See* OLD DOMINION GARDENER. **2426**
0274-6964 *See* SVOBODA (JERSEY CITY). **5711**
0274-6980 *See* MISSISSIPPI OIL & GAS PRODUCTION REPORT. **4264**
0274-7014 *See* ARIZONA FARM BUREAU NEWS. **62**
0274-7073 *See* ART NEW ENGLAND. **339**
0274-7111 *See* BANK ADVERTISING NEWS. **774**
0274-712X *See* QUILTER'S NEWSLETTER MAGAZINE. **5185**
0274-7138 *See* GRAIN JOURNAL (DECATUR, ILL.). **201**
0274-7219 *See* WESTERN BOWHUNTER. **4880**
0274-726X *See* CONTRACEPTIVE TECHNOLOGY UPDATE. **588**
0274-7286 *See* SIBERIAN QUARTERLY, THE. **4288**
0274-7294 *See* OHIO DISTRICT COURT REVIEW. **3021**
0274-7308 *See* FENCE POST, THE. **5642**
0274-7383 *See* SOAP OPERA MAGAZINE. **2546**

0274-7405 *See* WINGS OF GOLD (PENSACOLA, FLA.). **39**
0274-7448 *See* ALABAMA POLICE JOURNAL. **3156**
0274-7464 *See* INTER-CITY EXPRESS (OAKLAND, CALIF.). **5636**
0274-7472 *See* WISCONSIN RESTAURATEUR, THE. **5073**
0274-7502 *See* CYCLE NEWS EAST. **428**
0274-7529 *See* DISCOVER (CHICAGO, ILL.). **5101**
0274-7707 *See* YOUTH'S LIVING IDEALS. **1072**
0274-7723 *See* CAROLINA BLUE. **2486**
0274-774X *See* SOUTHERN GRAPHICS. **382**
0274-7774 *See* AV MAGAZINE, THE. **226**
0274-7960 *See* ROB TUCKER'S MEMORY LANE. **4077**
0274-7979 *See* BOXING TODAY. **4888**
0274-8010 *See* VELVET TALKS. **3996**
0274-8037 *See* EUROPE REPORT, THE. **2516**
0274-8096 *See* PRINTED CIRCUIT FABRICATION. **2075**
0274-8207 *See* IEEE IMPACT. **2059**
0274-8215 *See* AMERICAN TOWMAN, THE. **5403**
0274-8231 See EXTENSION NEWS & ADVISOR. **83**
0274-8274 *See* TRAIL BLAZER (PASO ROBLES). **2803**
0274-8282 See NEW ALASKA OUTDOORS, THE. **4875**
0274-8304 *See* COMPLIANCE GUIDE FOR PLAN ADMINISTRATORS. **1660**
0274-8363 *See* SNOWMOBILE (MILWAUKEE). **4919**
0274-8401 *See* STUDENT PRESS BULLETIN, THE. **1095**
0274-8460 *See* MUSTANG MONTHLY MAGAZINE. **5421**
0274-8533 *See* FLORIDA LAW WEEKLY, THE. **2971**
0274-8541 *See* RADIO WORLD (FALLS CHURCH, VA.). **1138**
0274-8584 *See* JUNIOR LEAGUE REVIEW. **5559**
0274-8622 *See* MINNESOTA SPORTSMAN. **4874**
0274-8657 *See* RED THE NET, LA. **1777**
0274-8762 *See* ACORN (PLATTEVILLE), THE. **1887**
0274-8770 *See* MONTEREY LIFE. **2539**
0274-8797 *See* FLORIDA FIREMAN. **2290**
0274-8800 *See* SOUTHWEST PURCHASING. **951**
0274-8851 *See* CUTTER, THE. **663**
0274-886X *See* IT'S SPORTS. **4901**
0274-8894 *See* TURNING POINTS (CHESHIRE). **716**
0274-9009 *See* PAN Z WAMI. **4985**
0274-9017 *See* MINNEAPOLIS LABOR REVIEW, THE. **1690**
0274-9181 *See* SUNBURST (ROSEVILLE). **5224**
0274-9262 *See* DAKOTA STUDENT, THE. **1819**
0274-9319 *See* LPBA JOURNAL. **3005**
0274-9394 *See* OFFSHORE (WEST NEWTON). **594**
0274-9408 *See* SHAWNEE-CRIDERSVILLE PRESS. **5730**
0274-9459 *See* OMS OUTREACH. **4983**
0274-9556 *See* PRESSURE. **2094**
0274-9696 *See* COST ENGINEERING (MORGANTOWN. 1980). **1969**
0274-970X *See* UNION REGISTER, THE. **2405**
0274-9734 *See* ROANOKER, THE. **2544**
0274-9742 *See* LANSING STATE JOURNAL. **5692**
0274-9777 *See* SPS NEWSREPORT. **2924**
0274-9955 *See* MONTANA MAGAZINE. **2539**
0274-9998 *See* I/O NEWS. **1267**
0275-0031 *See* WISE GIVING GUIDE. **4339**
0275-004X *See* RETINA (PHILADELPHIA, PA.). **3878**
0275-0066 *See* CARDIOLOGY (NEW YORK, N.Y.). **3701**
0275-0074 *See* PLAINSONG (BOWLING GREEN, KY.). **3468**

ISSN Index

0275-0120 See TOPICS IN GEOBIOLOGY. **475**

0275-0147 See RADIX (BERKELEY, CALIF.). **4989**

0275-021X See INSIDE/OUT (NEW YORK, N.Y. : 1980). **3396**

0275-0236 See INFECTION CONTROL DIGEST. **3587**

0275-0244 See HAZARDOUS WASTE LITIGATION REPORTER. **3112**

0275-0252 See NATIONAL BANKRUPTCY REPORTER. **3087**

0275-0279 See REVIEWS IN MINERALOGY. **1444**

0275-0287 See BRITISH MYCOLOGICAL SOCIETY SYMPOSIUM SERIES. **574**

0275-0317 See BUSINESS INSURANCE. EDITORIAL INDEX. **2877**

0275-0333 See PENSIONS & INVESTMENT AGE. EDITORIAL INDEX. **911**

0275-0384 See COST OF CLEAN AIR AND CLEAN WATER, THE. **2227**

0275-0392 See HUMAN RIGHTS QUARTERLY. **4509**

0275-0457 See FIBER OPTICS AND COMMUNICATIONS. **1155**

0275-0473 See INTELEC. **1157**

0275-049X See HUMAN RIGHTS INTERNET REPORTER. **4502**

0275-0503 See PROFESSIONAL LIABILITY. **3032**

0275-0589 See GAMUT (CLEVELAND, OHIO), THE. **2533**

0275-0597 See WASHINGTON FACT BOOK. **2549**

0275-0600 See CIRCULAR - NEW JERSEY DEPARTMENT OF AGRICULTURE. **74**

0275-0716 See EMS COMMUNICATOR. **3724**

0275-0732 See SPORTING NEWS ... BASEBALL YEARBOOK, THE. **4921**

0275-0740 See AMERICAN REVIEW OF PUBLIC ADMINISTRATION. **4625**

0275-0791 See MONROE LEGAL REPORTER. **3011**

0275-0805 See NEW CHURCH LIFE. **5065**

0275-0813 See DATAPRO REPORTS ON MINICOMPUTERS. **1274**

0275-0872 See ANNUAL REPORT / LOS ANGELES POLICE DEPARTMENT. **3157**

0275-0902 See REGULATORY WATCHDOG SERVICE. ALERT BULLETIN. **4679**

0275-0910 See IUPAC CHEMICAL DATA SERIES. **979**

0275-0929 See SPECIAL PUBLICATION / OKLAHOMA GEOLOGICAL SURVEY. **1398**

0275-1062 See CHINESE ASTRONOMY AND ASTROPHYSICS. **394**

0275-1070 See NURSING HOME SALARY & BENEFITS REPORT. **3790**

0275-1100 See PUBLIC BUDGETING & FINANCE. **4743**

0275-1119 See UPDATES AND SUPPLEMENTS TO ACCOMPANY WEST'S FEDERAL TAXATION. **4757**

0275-1127 See REAL ESTATE SECURITIES LETTER. **4845**

0275-1178 See MENNONITE YEARBOOK & DIRECTORY. **5064**

0275-1216 See WASHINGTON WATCH (FOREST HILLS, NEW YORK, N.Y.). **4500**

0275-1267 See FHA HOMES. DATA FOR STATES AND SELECTED AREAS ON CHARACTERISTICS OF FHA OPERATIONS UNDER SECTION 245, GRADUATED PAYMENT MORTGAGE PROGRAM. **2822**

0275-1275 See JOURNAL OF THE EARLY REPUBLIC. **2742**

0275-133X See TOWARD INTERAGENCY COORDINATION: FEDERAL RESEARCH AND DEVELOPMENT ON EARLY CHILDHOOD. **1788**

0275-1356 See PROCEEDINGS ... ANNUAL CONFERENCE OF THE AMERICAN COUNCIL ON CONSUMER INTERESTS. **1299**

0275-1402 See JOURNAL OF RELIGION AND THE APPLIED BEHAVIORAL SCIENCES. **4970**

0275-1410 See THREEPENNY REVIEW, THE. **3446**

0275-1453 See TEXAS DO. **3645**

0275-1461 See MEDICAL INDUSTRY ANALYSIS SERVICE. **3609**

0275-1488 See SITE REPORT, THE. **3488**

0275-1569 See YEAR BOOK (AMERICAN SOCIETY OF BOOKPLATE COLLECTORS AND DESIGNERS). **2779**

0275-1607 See RARITAN. **3351**

0275-1690 See BUSINESSMAN'S GUIDE TO THE ARAB WORLD. **654**

0275-1712 See BIOGRAPHICAL DIRECTORY OF THE AMERICAN ACADEMY OF PEDIATRICS. **3655**

0275-1720 See BENSON MAGAZINE OF RESEARCH. **2439**

0275-1739 See POETRY/LA. **3469**

0275-1755 See ... U.S. INVESTMENT TAX CREDIT INDEX, THE. **918**

0275-178X See LOCAL CLIMATOLOGICAL DATA. BIRMINGHAM, ALABAMA, MUNICIPAL AIRPORT, ANNUAL SUMMARY WITH COMPARATIVE DATA. **1428**

0275-1798 See LOCAL CLIMATOLOGICAL DATA. BIRMINGHAM, ALABAMA, CITY OFFICE, ANNUAL SUMMARY WITH COMPARATIVE DATA. **1428**

0275-1879 See SPECIAL CARE IN DENTISTRY. **1335**

0275-1887 See OHIO STATE MANUFACTURERS GUIDE, THE. **3485**

0275-1895 See ALASKA DIRECTORY OF ATTORNEYS. **2929**

0275-1917 See ANNUAL REPORT / MASSACHUSETTS TECHNOLOGY DEVELOPMENT CORPORATION. **5084**

0275-1968 See HISTORICAL BULLETIN (MADISON, WIS.). **2618**

0275-1992 See MASTER SHOE REBUILDER, THE. **1086**

0275-200X See ANNUAL REPORT OF THE FEDERAL LABOR RELATIONS AUTHORITY AND THE FEDERAL SERVICE IMPASSES PANEL FOR THE FISCAL PERIOD **1649**

0275-2050 See REPORT ON FAMILY PLANNING SERVICES AND POPULATION RESEARCH, A. **590**

0275-2077 See AIRPORTS OF MEXICO AND CENTRAL AMERICA. **11**

0275-2158 See OCCASIONAL PUBLICATIONS IN CLASSICAL STUDIES. **1078**

0275-2166 See WINDOW (BETHESDA, MD.). **3453**

0275-2174 See YOUR NEW ECONOMY HOME PLANS. **311**

0275-2182 See GREAT CONTEMPORARY ISSUES. GROUP 1, UPDATE, THE. **2617**

0275-2204 See ELECTRON MICROSCOPY AND X-RAY APPLICATIONS TO ENVIRONMENTAL AND OCCUPATIONAL HEALTH ANALYSIS. **3941**

0275-2239 See STEEL PRODUCTS MANUAL. **4020**

0275-2298 See END-STAGE RENAL DISEASE ANNUAL REPORT TO CONGRESS. **3989**

0275-2514 See GEOGRAPHIES FOR ADVANCED STUDIES. **2564**

0275-2565 See AMERICAN JOURNAL OF PRIMATOLOGY. **5574**

0275-259X See INTRODUCTORY MATHEMATICS FOR SCIENTISTS AND ENGINEERS. **3510**

0275-2689 See WATER RESOURCES DATA FOR FLORIDA. **5544**

0275-2735 See MEDICAL 911. **3725**

0275-2743 See CORNERSTONE (CHICAGO, ILL.). **4950**

0275-2751 See CENTED MONOGRAPH SERIES. **2226**

0275-2778 See GENE AMPLIFICATION AND ANALYSIS. **545**

0275-2840 See MICHIGAN ANNUAL AIR QUALITY REPORT. **2236**

0275-2875 See AFRICAN/AMERICAN DIRECTORY. **637**

0275-2883 See CARIBBEAN/AMERICAN DIRECTORY. **655**

0275-2913 See SPECIAL COURT NEWS. **3143**

0275-2956 See INTERNATIONAL DEFENSE INTELLIGENCE. **4046**

0275-3014 See DEPARTMENT OF ENERGY RED BOOK. **1936**

0275-3030 See VOLUNTEERING. **5313**

0275-3049 See ADVANCES IN DEVELOPMENTAL PSYCHOLOGY. **4571**

0275-309X See COVERTACTION INFORMATION BULLETIN. **4519**

0275-312X See ANTARA KITA. **5191**

0275-3162 See ANNUAL REPORT - NYS PROJECT FINANCE AGENCY. **4628**

0275-3170 See POLICY GUIDE OF THE AMERICAN CIVIL LIBERTIES UNION. **4511**

0275-3243 See SHELL NEWS. **4278**

0275-3286 See NATIONAL HIGHWAY AND AIRWAY CARRIERS AND ROUTES. **5401**

0275-3340 See NTDPMA BUYERS GUIDE, THE. **951**

0275-3529 See RELIGIOUS FREEDOM REPORTER. **3093**

0275-3545 See TRAVEL MARKETING AND AGENCY MANAGEMENT GUIDELINES. **5496**

0275-3553 See ARIZONA ANTHROPOLOGIST. **231**

0275-357X See PIEDMONT LITERARY REVIEW. **3423**

0275-3588 See JOURNAL OF ARAB AFFAIRS. **4527**

0275-3596 See PACIFIC STUDIES. **2670**

0275-360X See MODERN AGING RESEARCH. **3754**

0275-3626 See BEHIND THE WHISTLE. **4887**

0275-3677 See PR CASEBOOK. **763**

0275-3707 See RADIOACTIVE WASTE MANAGEMENT (OAK RIDGE, TENN.). **2240**

0275-374X See HAZARDOUS WASTE NEWS. **2231**

0275-3758 See U.S. RAIL NEWS. **5437**

0275-3766 See TOXIC MATERIALS TRANSPORT. **5394**

0275-3782 See EMERGENCY PREPAREDNESS NEWS. **1073**

0275-3863 See PROCEEDINGS AND PAPERS OF THE GEORGIA ASSOCIATION OF HISTORIANS, THE. **2626**

0275-3871 See EUROPEAN PETROLEUM DIRECTORY. **4256**

0275-3898 See NORTH AMERICAN ENERGY REVIEW, THE. **1951**

0275-3901 See UV/EB NEWS. **4442**

0275-391X See CAR CARE. **5409**

0275-3960 See GEOLOGY OF PETROLEUM (NEW YORK, N.Y.). **4259**

0275-3987 See PSYCHOMUSICOLOGY. **4147**

0275-3995 See AAG NEWSLETTER. **2553**

0275-4088 See LEGAL LOOSELEAFS IN PRINT. **3082**

0275-4096 See ILLINOIS INSIGHTS. **5289**

0275-410X See LAMAR JOURNAL OF THE HUMANITIES. **2849**

0275-4118 See JOURNAL OF SUNG-YUAN STUDIES. **2505**

0275-4207 See BIOENGINEERING NEWS. **444**

0275-4282 See SEDIMENTOLOGY RESEARCH LABORATORY CONTRIBUTION. **1396**

0275-4304 See RES PUBLICA LITTERARUM. **1079**

0275-4371 See VALUE ENGINEERING & MANAGEMENT DIGEST. **2000**

0275-441X See READING INSTRUCTION JOURNAL, THE. **1843**

0275-4428 See SOUTH JERSEY MAGAZINE. **2761**

0275-4436 See FRENCH-ENGLISH TRANSLATORS EXCHANGE. **3282**

0275-4444 See TEXAS SCHOOL LAW NEWS (AUSTIN, TEX. : 1980). **3064**

0275-4452 See LABOR NOTES (DETROIT, MICH.). **1684**

0275-4487 See SPORTING NEWS SUPER BOWL BOOK, THE. **4922**

0275-4509 See SOYA BLUEBOOK. **188**

0275-4525 See SPUR AND PHOENIX, THE. **2473**

0275-4533 See SHIPMENTS TO FEDERAL GOVERNMENT AGENCIES. **3488**

0275-4541 *See* CLINICAL ULTRASOUND REVIEW. 3796

0275-455X *See* BEST OF PERSONAL COMPUTING, THE. 1273

0275-4681 *See* COSMETIC INSIDER'S REPORT. 403

0275-469X *See* NEW GLASS REVIEW. 2592

0275-4703 *See* FLYING DISC MAGAZINE. 21

0275-4924 *See* FOCUS ON THE CENTER FOR RESEARCH LIBRARIES. 3211

0275-4932 *See* SWITCHGEAR, SWITCHBOARD APPARATUS, RELAYS, AND INDUSTRIAL CONTROLS. 2083

0275-4940 *See* MEDICAL PRODUCTS MARKETERS DIRECTORY. 3695

0275-4959 *See* RESEARCH IN THE SOCIOLOGY OF HEALTH CARE. 5255

0275-4967 *See* GERSHON'S ... SPECIALIZED CATALOGUE OF ISRAEL AND THE HOLY LAND. 2785

0275-4975 *See* BEST'S EXECUTIVE DATA SERVICE. REPORT A2, EXPERIENCE OF PUERTO RICO. PROPERTY AND CASUALTY INSURANCE. 2875

0275-4983 *See* AIRCRAFT PROPELLERS. 9

0275-4991 *See* MEMBERSHIP DIRECTORY / AMERICAN INSTITUTE OF PROFESSIONAL GEOLOGISTS. 1387

0275-505X *See* PUBLICATION - AMERICAN ACADEMY AND INSTITUTE OF ARTS AND LETTERS. 328

0275-5076 *See* SEMIANNUAL REPORT - UNITED STATES. DEPT. OF LABOR. OFFICE OF THE INSPECTOR GENERAL. 1710

0275-5114 *See* NYAC NEWS. 4670

0275-5157 *See* SOURCES OF COMPILED LEGISLATIVE HISTORIES. 3083

0275-5181 *See* U.S. PHARMACEUTICAL MARKET. DRUG STORES. 4331

0275-519X *See* PANDORA (DENVER, COLO.). 3422

0275-5203 *See* SONORA REVIEW. 3353

0275-522X *See* INFORM REPORTS. 2195

0275-5262 *See* ELECTRON MICROSCOPY IN BIOLOGY. 572

0275-5270 *See* WORD & WORLD. 5009

0275-5297 *See* SAGE YEARBOOKS IN POLITICS AND PUBLIC POLICY. 4495

0275-5300 *See* SAGE YEARBOOKS IN WOMEN'S POLICY STUDIES. 5565

0275-5319 *See* RESEARCH IN INTERNATIONAL BUSINESS AND FINANCE. 1639

0275-5327 *See* JOURNAL OF SOUTHERN AFRICAN AFFAIRS. 4479

0275-5351 *See* TRIALOGUE. 1640

0275-5394 *See* FIELD HOCKEY RULES. NATIONAL FEDERATION ED. 4894

0275-5408 *See* OPHTHALMIC & PHYSIOLOGICAL OPTICS. 4216

0275-5483 *See* TECHNICAL REPORT - TEXAS WATER RESOURCES INSTITUTE. 5540

0275-5505 See PROCEEDINGS OF THE INTERNATIONAL SYMPOSIUM ON REMOTE SENSING AND GLOBAL ENVIRONMENTAL CHANGE. 1409

0275-5513 *See* UNIVERSITY OF LOUISVILLE STUDIES IN PALEONTOLOGY AND STRATIGRAPHY. 4231

0275-5564 *See* AMOCO TRAVELER. 5461

0275-5599 *See* WASHINGTON REPORT ON THE HEMISPHERE. 2912

0275-5610 *See* ASSETS. 640

0275-5629 *See* MAENAD. 5560

0275-5734 *See* GOLF DIRECTORY. 4896

0275-5742 *See* ADVANCES IN MEDICAL SOCIAL SCIENCE. 5238

0275-5777 *See* POLYMER MONOGRAPHS (NEW YORK, N.Y. : 1981). 1046

0275-5793 *See* CARIBBEAN STUDIES (NEW YORK N.Y.). 2727

0275-5807 *See* STUDIES IN CYBERNETICS. 1252

0275-5823 *See* MILITARY OPERATIONS RESEARCH. 4051

0275-584X See TOPICS ON THE CULTURE OF THE AMERICAN SOUTH. 2548

0275-5866 *See* MUSICOLOGY. 4137

0275-5947 *See* NORTH AMERICAN JOURNAL OF FISHERIES MANAGEMENT. 2309

0275-598X See FITNESS AND SPORTS REVIEW INTERNATIONAL. 1855

0275-6013 *See* MID-AMERICA FOLKLORE. 2322

0275-6048 *See* TURKISH STUDIES ASSOCIATION BULLETIN. 3355

0275-6056 3355

0275-6072 *See* JOURNAL OF LAW & EDUCATION. 1865

0275-6129 *See* PCH. PETROLEUM CONCESSION HANDBOOK. 4271

0275-6137 *See* SUMMARY OF WEATHER MODIFICATION ACTIVITIES REPORTED IN 1435

0275-6145 *See* MINUTES OF THE ANNUAL MEETING OF THE FIRST CATHOLIC SLOVAK UNION OF THE UNITED STATES OF AMERICA AND CANADA. 2747

0275-6161 *See* LAND RESOURCES LABORATORY SERIES. 2197

0275-617X See PROCEEDINGS OF THE JOHNS HOPKINS WORKSHOP ON CURRENT PROBLEMS IN PARTICLE THEORY. 4418

0275-6196 *See* WASTE MANAGEMENT. 2246

0275-6226 *See* MAZAMA. 5233

0275-6250 *See* MINUTES OF THE SEMI-ANNUAL MEETING OF THE BOARD OF DIRECTORS OF THE FIRST CATHOLIC SLOVAK UNION OF THE UNITED STATES AND CANADA. 5032

0275-6323 *See* ANNUAL MEETING PAPERS - AMERICAN PETROLEUM INSTITUTE. PRODUCTION DEPT. 4249

0275-634X See IN DEFENSE OF THE ALIEN. 1919

0275-6382 *See* VETERINARY CLINICAL PATHOLOGY. 5525

0275-6404 *See* FEDERAL CAPITAL IMPROVEMENTS PROGRAM FOR THE NATIONAL CAPITAL REGION. 898

0275-6501 *See* SOUL SEARCHER. 4243

0275-6528 *See* WELLWOMAN. 5069

0275-6587 *See* BEAR & COMPANY. 4938

0275-6595 *See* MICRO WAVE NEWS. 2350

0275-6617 *See* SYSTEM DEVELOPMENT. 1262

0275-6625 *See* ALABAMA FORESTS. 2374

0275-665X See OBSTETRIC ANESTHESIA DIGEST. 3683

0275-6668 *See* JOURNAL OF BUSINESS STRATEGY, THE. 686

0275-6692 *See* AID BULLETIN (KENT, OHIO). 5238

0275-6714 *See* INSIDE CONGRESS. 617

0275-6773 *See* WOOD IBIS. 3473

0275-6811 *See* SOURCEBOOK OF LIBRARY TECHNOLOGY, THE. 3250

0275-6862 *See* STEEL MILL PRODUCTS (WASHINGTON, D.C.). 4020

0275-6870 *See* TYPOGRAPHY (NEW YORK, N.Y.). 4570

0275-6889 *See* MANHATTAN REVIEW (NEW YORK, N.Y. : 1980), THE. 3465

0275-6900 *See* PERSONAL COMPUTING INDUSTRY REPORT. 1272

0275-6919 *See* SAGUAROLAND BULLETIN. 527

0275-6935 *See* REVISION (CAMBRIDGE, MASS.). 3429

0275-6943 *See* METALWORKING SALES LEADS. 4012

0275-701X See CA SELECTS: AMINO ACIDS, PEPTIDES & PROTEINS. 997

0275-7028 *See* CA SELECTS: ANTIOXIDANTS. 997

0275-7036 *See* CA SELECTS: COATINGS, INKS, & RELATED PRODUCTS. 999

0275-7044 *See* CA SELECTS: COSMETIC CHEMICALS. 1000

0275-7052 *See* CA SELECTS: DISTILLATION TECHNOLOGY. 1001

0275-7060 *See* CA SELECTS: EPOXY RESINS. 1002

0275-7079 *See* CA SELECTS: FATS & OILS. 1002

0275-7087 *See* CA SELECTS: INORGANIC ANALYTICAL CHEMISTRY. 1004

0275-7095 *See* CA SELECTS: INORGANIC CHEMICALS & REACTIONS. 1004

0275-7109 *See* CA SELECTS: NOVEL SULFUR HETEROCYCLES. 1005

0275-7117 *See* CA SELECTS: ORGANIC ANALYTICAL CHEMISTRY. 1006

0275-7125 *See* CA SELECTS: PLASTICS FABRICATION & USES. 1007

0275-7133 *See* CA SELECTS: PLASTICS MANUFACTURING & PROCESSING. 1008

0275-7168 *See* CA SELECTS: SYNTHETIC HIGH POLYMERS. 1010

0275-7176 *See* CONTEMPORARY AUTHORS. NEW REVISION SERIES. 414

0275-7184 *See* COMMERCIAL FOOD PATENTS, U.S. 2332

0275-7206 *See* HISTORY AND ANTHROPOLOGY. 237

0275-7214 *See* MATHEMATICAL REPORTS (CHUR, SWITZERLAND). 3520

0275-7222 *See* COMPREHENSIVE PSYCHOTHERAPY. 3923

0275-7230 *See* ELECTROCOMPONENT SCIENCE MONOGRAPHS. 2046

0275-7249 *See* WATER-RELATED DISEASE OUTBREAKS SURVEILLANCE. ANNUAL SUMMARY. 2248

0275-7257 *See* REMOTE SENSING REVIEWS. 1993

0275-7265 *See* MMI PRESS POLYMER MONOGRAPH SERIES. 986

0275-7273 *See* RADIOACTIVE WASTE MANAGEMENT (CHUR, SWITZERLAND : 1981). 2240

0275-7281 *See* SOVIET SCIENTIFIC REVIEWS SUPPLEMENT SERIES. ASTROPHYSICS AND SPACE PHYSICS REVIEWS. 35

0275-7303 See ENGINEERING AND TECHNOLOGY DEGREES. 1972

0275-7346 *See* NEW YORK LAWYER'S LETTER. 3016

0275-7389 *See* SCOPE MISCELLANEOUS PUBLICATION. 2181

0275-746X See CONGRESSIONAL DISTRICT BUSINESS PATTERNS. 1470

0275-7486 *See* COMPANY RECOGNITION STUDY. RETAILER EDITION. 1969

0275-7494 *See* REPORT OF HEALTH, PHYSICAL EDUCATION, AND RECREATION RESEARCH PROJECTS COMPLETED OR IN PROGRESS IN THE STATE OF INDIANA, A. 1857

0275-7516 *See* COUNTERPROOF. 377

0275-7540 *See* CHEMISTRY IN ECOLOGY. 2212

0275-7559 *See* BIOTECHNOLOGY (NEW YORK, N.Y. : 1983). 3689

0275-7567 *See* C1 MOLECULE CHEMISTRY. 1035

0275-7583 *See* MLC UPDATE. 3232

0275-7613 *See* RELOCATION REPORT, THE. 4846

0275-7656 *See* TANNER LECTURES ON HUMAN VALUES, THE. 2253

0275-7664 *See* GREAT PLAINS QUARTERLY. 2735

0275-7672 *See* VANDERBILT STREET REVIEW. 3450

0275-7699 *See* ALLIED HEALTH TRENDS. 4764

0275-777X See INDIANA LIBRARIES. 3215

0275-7893 *See* SOVIET TECHNOLOGY REVIEWS. SECTION A, ENERGY REVIEWS. 1957

0275-794X See DISARMAMENT NEWS & INTERNATIONAL VIEWS. 4520

0275-7982 *See* STUDIES IN COMMUNICATIONS. 1122

0275-8008 *See* ANNUAL REPORT OF THE NEBRASKA STATE BOARD OF EXAMINERS FOR PROFESSIONAL ENGINEERS AND ARCHITECTS. 1965

0275-8024 *See* DESTINATIONS (KNOXVILLE, TENN.). 5468

0275-8040 *See* PRODUCTIVITY (STAMFORD, CONN.). 883

0275-8059 *See* FMI ISSUES BULLETIN. 924

ISSN Index

0275-8075 *See* SCIENCE, TECHNOLOGY & SOCIETY. **5153**

0275-8083 *See* MAPS ON FILE. **2582**

0275-8091 *See* COLLECTIONS (PHILADELPHIA, PA.). **3567**

0275-8113 *See* MILKWEED CHRONICLE. **325**

0275-8180 *See* MICHIGAN NATURAL RESOURCES MAGAZINE, THE. **2198**

0275-827X *See* CENTRAL NEW YORK ENVIRONMENT. **2162**

0275-8326 *See* NATIONAL MONTHLY STOCK SUMMARY, THE. **909**

0275-8369 *See* GREATER BOSTON MEDIA DIRECTORY. **1112**

0275-8385 *See* HISTORICALLY SPEAKING. **2737**

0275-8393 *See* GUIDE TO FEDERAL FUNDING FOR EDUCATION. **1748**

0275-8407 *See* AMS STUDIES IN MODERN SOCIETY. **5190**

0275-8423 *See* CLASSIC IMAGES. **4067**

0275-8555 *See* MISSISSIPPI GEOLOGY. **1388**

0275-8652 *See* MARYLAND ENTOMOLOGIST. **5591**

0275-8660 *See* VICTORIAN STUDIES BULLETIN. **3450**

0275-8679 *See* MBL LECTURES IN BIOLOGY. **464**

0275-8687 *See* IRON & STEELMAKER. **4005**

0275-8768 *See* PROGRESS IN CONTEMPORARY CARTOGRAPHY. **2583**

0275-8873 *See* APPAREL PLANT WAGES SURVEY. **1650**

0275-8954 *See* IN POLITICS. **4476**

0275-9098 *See* CURRENT TOPICS OF CONTEMPORARY THOUGHT. **5098**

0275-9101 *See* BODY BULLETIN. **2596**

0275-911X *See* ISSLEDOVANIE ZEMLI IZ KOSMOSA. **1981**

0275-9128 *See* GEOPHYSICAL JOURNAL. **1405**

0275-9136 *See* ELECTRONIC MODELING. **2047**

0275-9144 *See* PHYSICS OF METALS. **4014**

0275-9152 *See* DATABASES ONLINE. **1253**

0275-9179 *See* WYTHE COUNTY HISTORICAL REVIEW. **2766**

0275-9195 *See* A PROPOS - AMERICAN CENTER OF UNIMA. **388**

0275-9233 *See* NATIONAL LEGAL CENTER NEWS. **3013**

0275-9306 *See* PESC RECORD. **2075**

0275-9314 *See* SWEDISH AMERICAN GENEALOGIST. **2474**

0275-9357 *See* DIRECTORY OF EDUCATIONAL PROGRAMS. **1735**

0275-9373 *See* STATEMENT OF FOREIGN CURRENCIES PURCHASED WITH DOLLARS. **4750**

0275-939X *See* APPLIED RESEARCH SUMMARY OF AWARDS. **5085**

0275-942X *See* COLORADO WEST SALARY SURVEY. **1660**

0275-9438 *See* MOUNTAIN STATES MINING SURVEY. **1442**

0275-9527 *See* SOUTH ASIAN REVIEW - SOUTH ASIAN LITERARY ASSOCIATION. **3353**

0275-9543 *See* TUITION AND REQUIRED FEES AND ROOM AND BOARD CHARGES AT INSTITUTIONS OF HIGHER EDUCATION IN PENNSYLVANIA. **1851**

0275-9578 *See* NEW PATTERNS OF LEARNING. **4605**

0275-9594 *See* DEMOGRAPHIC MONOGRAPHS. **4552**

0275-9608 *See* FERROELECTRICS AND RELATED PHENOMENA. **1032**

0275-9616 *See* LIBRARY OF CONGRESS ACQUISITIONS. MANUSCRIPT DIVISION. **3226**

0275-9640 *See* HANDMADE (ASHEVILLE, N.C.). **5184**

0275-9675 *See* ARTICULATION. **1810**

0275-9691 *See* SURVEY OF ARCHITECTURAL DRAFTING & DESIGNERS' SALARIES. **309**

0275-9713 *See* OZARK PERIODICAL INDEX. **2636**

0275-9748 *See* WDS FORUM. **3452**

0275-9829 *See* AMTRAK'S INVENTORY AND PROPERTY CONTROLS NEED STRENGTHENING. **5429**

0275-9837 *See* LET'S GO. THE BUDGET GUIDE TO THE USA. **5483**

0275-9985 *See* MINERAL INDUSTRY, EXPLORATION, PRODUCTION AND PROCESSING SURVEY. **1441**

0275-9993 *See* HEBREW UNION COLLEGE ANNUAL. SUPPLEMENTS. **5048**

0276-0029 *See* JAMAICAN VIEW. **2536**

0276-0045 *See* REVIEW OF CONTEMPORARY FICTION. **3351**

0276-0061 *See* IPI DATA SERVICE. EXPLORATION, PRODUCTION, TRANSPORTATION, REFINING & MARKETING (NORTH AMERICA). **4261**

0276-0096 *See* IPI DATA SERVICE. EXPLORATION, PRODUCTION, TRANSPORTATION, REFINING & MARKETING (WORLD). **4261**

0276-0150 *See* DIGEST OF RICO INVESTIGATIONS. **2961**

0276-0177 *See* ANNUAL REPORT - CENTER FOR RESEARCH IN WATER RESOURCES, THE UNIVERSITY OF TEXAS AT AUSTIN. **5529**

0276-0231 *See* DIVISION REPORT / COLORADO DIVISION OF WILDLIFE. **2191**

0276-0320 *See* FOOD STAMP PROGRAM : STATISTICAL SUMMARY OF OPERATIONS. **5266**

0276-0355 *See* CHRONICLE CAREER INDEX. **4203**

0276-0371 *See* CHRONICLE VOCATIONAL SCHOOL MANUAL. **1912**

0276-0398 *See* UNDERLINE. **310**

0276-0401 *See* RESEARCH AND INVENTION. **5146**

0276-0460 *See* GEO-MARINE LETTERS. **554**

0276-0495 *See* MALPRACTICE PREVENTION FOR PHYSICIANS. **3005**

0276-0509 *See* RESEARCH DIGEST - LATINO INSTITUTE (RESTON, VA.). **2757**

0276-0525 *See* CHALLENGE TO CHANGE : LIBRARY APPLICATIONS OF CONCEPTS. **3201**

0276-055X *See* RECENT ETHICS OPINIONS. **2253**

0276-0746 *See* WORKERS VANGUARD (NEW YORK, N.Y.). **1719**

0276-0800 *See* SANTA BARBARA SENIOR WORLD, THE. **5181**

0276-0819 *See* EXTRUSION DIGEST. **4455**

0276-0835 *See* VIDEO (SAN FRANCISCO, CALIF.). **4079**

0276-0851 *See* PAWLEYS ISLAND PERSPECTIVE, THE. **3350**

0276-0878 *See* JOURNAL OF CONTINUING SOCIAL WORK EDUCATION. **1756**

0276-0886 *See* PHILOSOPHICAL SPECULATIONS IN SCIENCE FICTION & FANTASY. **3423**

0276-0908 *See* COMMUNITY BANK PRESIDENT, THE. **783**

0276-1017 *See* NCAA BASKETBALL. **4906**

0276-1025 *See* ALASKA BAR RAG, THE. **2929**

0276-1092 *See* YEAR BOOK OF ORTHOPEDICS, THE. **3885**

0276-1114 *See* MODERN JUDAISM. **5051**

0276-119X *See* NBER REPORTER. **1507**

0276-1270 *See* CONSUMER FEDERATION OF AMERICA. **1295**

0276-1319 *See* WATER RESOURCES DATA. VIRGINIA. **5546**

0276-1386 *See* COMMUNIQUE - SOCIETY FOR INTERCULTURAL EDUCATION, TRAINING AND RESEARCH. **1733**

0276-1432 *See* JEWISH JURISPRUDENCE. **2986**

0276-1459 *See* MULTIPHASE SCIENCE AND TECHNOLOGY. **5130**

0276-1467 *See* JOURNAL OF MACROMARKETING. **928**

0276-1483 *See* PROCEEDINGS OF THE ... ANNUAL MEETING OF THE SOCIETY OF PROSPECTIVE MEDICINE. **3630**

0276-1505 *See* BENCH AND BAR OF MINNESOTA, THE. **2941**

0276-1521 *See* SCHNAUZER SHORTS. **4288**

0276-153X *See* SCREEN (CHICAGO, ILL.). **4077**

0276-1564 *See* BLOOMSBURY REVIEW, THE. **3338**

0276-1599 *See* OCCUPATIONAL THERAPY JOURNAL OF RESEARCH. **1883**

0276-1629 *See* SADEX. **1583**

0276-1645 *See* MANUFACTURED HOMES APPRAISAL GUIDE, OFFICIAL VALUATION GUIDE. **2827**

0276-1653 *See* RESEARCH IN DOMESTIC AND INTERNATIONAL AGRIBUSINESS MANAGEMENT. **707**

0276-170X *See* FARM & RANCH LIVING. **84**

0276-1726 *See* ST. LOUIS METRO MEDIA GUIDE. **1122**

0276-1769 *See* OCCASIONAL PAPERS - UNIVERSITY OF ILLINOIS (URBANA-CHAMPAIGN CAMPUS). GRADUATE SCHOOL OF LIBRARY AND INFORMATION SCIENCE. **3238**

0276-1785 *See* FEDERAL AVIATION REGULATIONS. N.PART 39, P. AIRWORTHINESS DIRECTIVES. **19**

0276-1858 *See* ENERGY NEWSLETTER INDEX. **1941**

0276-1882 *See* GENETIC ENGINEERING LETTER. **545**

0276-1890 *See* COAL STATISTICS INTERNATIONAL. **1438**

0276-1904 *See* AM-POL EAGLE. **5713**

0276-1920 *See* CORNELL DESKBOOK. **1818**

0276-1971 *See* PALETTE TALK. **361**

0276-203X *See* NEWSNOTES - CENTER FOR LAW AND EDUCATION (U.S.). **3017**

0276-2048 *See* RURAL LIBRARIES. **3247**

0276-2056 *See* ISTF NEWS. **2385**

0276-2072 *See* FAT TUESDAY. **5268**

0276-2080 *See* PHILOSOPHICAL TOPICS. **4356**

0276-2110 *See* NEW HAMPSHIRE MARKETING DIRECTORY. **934**

0276-2129 *See* PETERSEN'S ... COLLEGE FOOTBALL. **4912**

0276-2137 *See* SHELL MANAGEMENT ANNUAL REPORT. **2313**

0276-2153 *See* FINDER BINDER. DALLAS/FORT WORTH METROPLEX AREA NEWS MEDIA. **759**

0276-2196 *See* FINDER BINDER. DETROIT AREA UPDATED MEDIA DIRECTORY. **759**

0276-220X *See* CURRENT CONTENTS. COMPUMATH. **3502**

0276-2234 *See* ONCOLOGY TIMES. **3822**

0276-2242 *See* TOXIC CONTROL. **3983**

0276-2250 *See* LIST OF REGISTERED DOCTORS OF MEDICINE AND SURGERY, DOCTORS OF OSTEOPATHY LICENSED TO PRACTICE MEDICINE AND SURGERY, DOCTORS OF OSTEOPATHY LICENSED TO PRACTICE OSTEOPATHY, DOCTORS OF CHIROPRACTIC, DOCTORS OF PODIATRY. **3914**

0276-2277 *See* WORLD PHARMACEUTICALS DIRECTORY. **4333**

0276-2285 *See* JOURNAL OF RURAL COMMUNITY PSYCHOLOGY. **4601**

0276-2293 *See* JOURNAL OF THE NATIONAL REYE'S SYNDROME FOUNDATION. **3599**

0276-2307 *See* SPORTING NEWS ... PRO FOOTBALL YEARBOOK, THE. **4922**

0276-2315 *See* INTERNATIONAL PERSPECTIVES IN UROLOGY. **3990**

0276-2323 *See* HOSPITAL SAFETY INFORMATION SERVICE. **3785**

0276-2358 *See* ACCENT ON WORSHIP. **4931**

0276-2366 *See* IMAGINATION, COGNITION AND PERSONALITY. **4589**

0276-2374 *See* EMPIRICAL STUDIES OF THE ARTS. **319**

0276-2382 *See* MITCHELL TECHNICAL SERVICE BULLETIN, COLLISION. **5419**

0276-2412 *See* ADVANCES IN HYDROGEN ENERGY. **1931**

0276-2463 *See* SURVEY OF JUDICIAL SALARIES. **3143**

0276-2471 *See* NEWSLETTER - NATIONAL TECHNICAL ASSOCIATION. **5133**

ISSN Index

0276-2544 See PUMPS AND COMPRESSORS. 2127

0276-2560 See FODOR'S ROME. 5473

0276-2676 See JOHN M. ECHOLS COLLECTION ON SOUTHEAST ASIA ACCESSIONS LIST, THE. 2496

0276-2714 See KAHANE. 2266

0276-2730 See PRINCETON HISTORY. 2755

0276-2749 See SECURITIES INDUSTRY TRENDS. 913

0276-2803 See DEALER'S AND TRAPPER'S LISTING BOOK. 3183

0276-2811 See COMPUTER GRAPHICS NEWS (WASHINGTON, D.C.). 1232

0276-2854 See ERASMUS OF ROTTERDAM SOCIETY YEARBOOK. 1076

0276-2897 See NUCLEAR WASTE NEWS (SILVER SPRING, MD.). 2237

0276-2900 See AMERICAN MARKETPLACE. 1293

0276-2919 See FUSION POWER REPORT. 1945

0276-3052 See INTERVAL (SAN DIEGO, CALIF.). 4123

0276-3060 See OLD FARMER'S ALMANAC. SPECIAL CANADIAN EDITION, THE. 1927

0276-3079 See SPECIALTY LAW DIGEST. HEALTH CARE (ANNUAL). 3742

0276-329X See ZOOSOUNDS. 5603

0276-3303 See ZOO VIEW. 5601

0276-3338 See OLD MILL NEWS. 305

0276-3362 See HEMINGWAY REVIEW, THE. 3344

0276-3389 See FINISHED BROADWOVEN FABRIC PRODUCTION. 3479

0276-3397 See TAMARIND PAPERS, THE. 382

0276-3478 See INTERNATIONAL JOURNAL OF EATING DISORDERS, THE. 3798

0276-3486 See JOURNAL OF SOLAR SCIENCES. 1949

0276-3508 See ADVANCES IN OPHTHALMIC PLASTIC AND RECONSTRUCTIVE SURGERY. 3958

0276-3516 See MOODY'S HANDBOOK OF NASDAQ STOCKS. 907

0276-3567 See DIGEST OF SIGNIFICANT CLASSIFICATION DECISIONS AND OPINIONS. 939

0276-3583 See BOSTON COLLEGE THIRD WORLD LAW JOURNAL. 3125

0276-3605 See BLACK MUSIC RESEARCH JOURNAL. 4103

0276-3613 See ALCOHOLISM REPORT, THE. 1340

0276-363X See WORKER'S ADVOCATE, THE. 4548

0276-3656 See INSECTICIDE & ACARICIDE TESTS. 4245

0276-3672 See SANDIA SCIENCE NEWS. 5149

0276-3680 See OFFSHORE FIELD DEVELOPMENT INTERNATIONAL. 1620

0276-3729 See HOSANNA (PHOENIX, ARIZ.). 4963

0276-3737 See POE MESSENGER, THE. 3424

0276-3788 See MONTANA LAWYER, THE. 3012

0276-3834 See WEST VIRGINIA WILDLIFE RESEARCH. 2208

0276-3850 See JOURNAL OF SOCIAL WORK & HUMAN SEXUALITY. 5293

0276-3869 See MEDICAL REFERENCE SERVICES QUARTERLY. 3230

0276-3877 See REFERENCE LIBRARIAN, THE. 3244

0276-3893 See JOURNAL OF HOUSING FOR THE ELDERLY. 2826

0276-3915 See COMMUNITY & JUNIOR COLLEGE LIBRARIES. 3203

0276-3923 See BUSINESS/MANAGEMENT (GUILFORD, CONN.). 862

0276-3974 See CANCER NEWSLINE. 3812

0276-4008 See ANALYSIS OF MARYLAND SALES AND USE TAX ... REVENUES COLLECTED IN MONTGOMERY COUNTY / MONTGOMERY COUNTY GOVERNMENT, DEPARTMENT OF FINANCE. 4709

0276-4040 See INTERNATIONAL GAS TECHNOLOGY HIGHLIGHTS. 4261

0276-4091 See GW WASHINGTON STUDIES. 1827

0276-4105 See LOCAL HISTORY STUDIES. 2744

0276-4164 See PALMETTO (ORLANDO, FLA.), THE. 2427

0276-4237 See MEYER MIRROR, THE. 2460

0276-4296 See CARDIOLOGIST'S COMPENDIUM OF DRUG THERAPY, THE. 3700

0276-430X See DERMATOLOGIST'S COMPENDIUM OF DRUG THERAPY, THE. 3719

0276-4350 See ORTHOPEDIC SURGEON'S COMPENDIUM OF DRUG THERAPY, THE. 3884

0276-4393 See PSYCHIATRIST'S COMPENDIUM OF DRUG THERAPY, THE. 3934

0276-444X See ADDRESS DIRECTORY / SOCIETY OF VERTEBRATE PALEONTOLOGY. 4226

0276-4458 See ANNUAL DIRECTORY / TEXAS RETAIL GROCERS ASSOCIATION. 2327

0276-4482 See SCHOOLS IN THE MIDDLE. 1872

0276-4520 See NATIONAL RADIO PUBLICITY DIRECTORY. 1135

0276-4539 See ANNUAL REPORT, PUBLIC WATER SUPPLIES FOR THE STATE OF OKLAHOMA, SOUTH CENTRAL DISTRICT. 5529

0276-4547 See AMERICAN MINING CONGRESS LEGISLATIVE BULLETIN. 2133

0276-4563 See DIALOGUE ON LIBERTY. 4471

0276-4601 See SAN DIEGO CONSUMER'S VOICE. 1299

0276-4644 See COSTA RICA REPORT. 2512

0276-4652 See DISCHARGE PLANNING UPDATE. 3780

0276-4687 See VINEYARD ALMANAC & WINE GAZETTEER, THE. 2371

0276-4709 See UNITED STATES VIEWS ON MEXICO. 2764

0276-4741 See MOUNTAIN RESEARCH AND DEVELOPMENT. 241

0276-475X See LORE (MILWAUKEE, WIS.). 4090

0276-4768 See SAXOPHONE JOURNAL. 4152

0276-4784 See DATA (CHICAGO, ILL.). 1734

0276-4792 See REAL ESTATE BOARD REPORT, THE. 4843

0276-4822 See SALARY SURVEY OF MIDDLE MANAGEMENT AND SUPERVISORY PERSONNEL. SOUTHERN CALIFORNIA. 1709

0276-4830 See PRO REGE. 1842

0276-4849 See PROCEEDINGS OF THE NATIONAL OCEAN SURVEY HYDROGRAPHIC SURVEY CONFERENCE, ... ANNUAL MEETING. 4182

0276-4857 See KNOX COUNTY, KENTUCKY KINFOLK. 2457

0276-4865 See WORLDWIDE HUNTING ANNUAL. 4881

0276-4881 See ... FIREHOUSE MAGAZINE. BUYER'S GUIDE, THE. 2290

0276-5047 See ARTERIOSCLEROSIS AND THROMBOSIS. 3699

0276-5055 See BIOCYCLE. 2225

0276-5063 See ADVANCES IN MODERN ENVIRONMENTAL TOXICOLOGY. 2858

0276-5098 See MICROCOMPUTER SYSTEMS. 1269

0276-5241 See NEWPORT REVIEW, THE. 2541

0276-5284 See NURSING & HEALTH CARE. 3863

0276-5306 See WORLD DIRECTORY OF NEUROLOGICAL SURGEONS. PART 1, UNITED STATES OF AMERICA AND CANADA. 3977

0276-5322 See SMALL BUSINESS TAX REVIEW, THE. 4748

0276-5330 See CRITICAL PERSPECTIVES ON CONTEMPORARY PSYCHOLOGY. 4583

0276-5349 See ANNUAL REPORT / ASSOCIATION OF AMERICAN PUBLISHERS. 4812

0276-5357 See TRENDS IN THE HOTEL INDUSTRY. USA EDITION. 2809

0276-5365 See ... DIRECTORY OF LEGAL AID AND DEFENDER OFFICES IN THE UNITED STATES, THE. 3179

0276-539X See OPD CHEMICAL BUYERS DIRECTORY. 1027

0276-5519 See AMERICAN REGISTER OF PRINTING AND GRAPHIC ARTS SERVICES, THE. 4563

0276-5535 See SELECTED ELECTRONIC AND ASSOCIATED PRODUCTS, INCLUDING TELEPHONE AND TELEGRAPH APPARATUS. 2080

0276-5543 See SOUTH DAKOTA ARCHAEOLOGY. 282

0276-5551 See LUMBER PRODUCTION AND MILL STOCKS. 2402

0276-5616 See SUMMARY OF PROCEEDINGS. MANAGEMENT INSTITUTE. 3143

0276-5624 See RESEARCH IN SOCIAL STRATIFICATION AND MOBILITY. 5255

0276-5632 See MIDDLE EAST POLICY SURVEY. 4482

0276-5659 See ART SCAPE. 340

0276-5667 See LOGOS (SANTA CLARA, CALIF.). 4352

0276-5675 See DES LITIGATION REPORTER. 2960

0276-5683 See THOMAS WOLFE REVIEW, THE. 3446

0276-5691 See AMERICAN ARTISTS OF RENOWN. 336

0276-5713 See CABLE TV TECHNOLOGY. 1129

0276-5756 See COMPUTING RESOURCES FOR THE PROFESSIONAL. 659

0276-5837 See BAKERSFIELD CALIFORNIAN, THE. 5633

0276-5845 See CREATIVE SECRETARY. 663

0276-5853 See EEO REPORT, THE. 940

0276-590X See OPINION (LOS ANGELES, CALIF.), LA. 5638

0276-5918 See LNG DIGEST. 4263

0276-5926 See DAILY REPORT (BAKERSFIELD, CALIF.), THE. 2958

0276-5934 See DAILY MUNGER OILOGRAM. 4254

0276-5977 See OIL/ENERGY STATISTICS BULLETIN AND CANADIAN OIL REPORTS. 1963

0276-5985 See OIL IN THE ROCKIES. 4269

0276-6043 See RESPONSE (WASHINGTON, D.C.). 4277

0276-606X See HEALTH OF KANSANS CHART BOOK, THE. 4780

0276-6078 See RECORDING INDUSTRY INDEX. 5318

0276-6094 See PREPARATION OF ANNUAL DISCLOSURE DOCUMENTS. 3030

0276-6108 See LAWYER DIRECTORY (ROCKVILLE, MD.). 2997

0276-6272 See GUARDIANSHIP NEWS. 3121

0276-6280 See INSURANCE THEFT LOSSES. VANS, PICKUPS AND UTILITY VEHICLES, ... MODELS. 2884

0276-6310 See JEWISH EDUCATION DIRECTORY. 5049

0276-6361 See INSURANCE SERVICE QUARTERLY REVIEW. 2884

0276-637X See OFFICIAL MUSEUM PRODUCTS AND SERVICES DIRECTORY, THE. 4094

0276-640X See ILLINOIS AVIATION (SPRINGFIELD, ILL. : 1979). 23

0276-6418 See MATTRESSES AND FOUNDATIONS. 3484

0276-6434 See OFFICIAL DIRECTORY OF DATA PROCESSING, COMPUTER USERS SOUTHERN USA. 1261

0276-6442 See OFFICIAL DIRECTORY OF DATA PROCESSING, COMPUTER USERS EASTERN USA. 1261

0276-6450 See OFFICIAL DIRECTORY OF DATA PROCESSING, EDP SYSTEM USERS MIDWESTERN USA. 1261

0276-6469 See CONGRESSIONAL PRESENTATION, FISCAL YEAR. 4518

0276-6515 See RICHMOND QUARTERLY, THE. 3431

0276-6531 See CDF REPORTS. 5276

0276-6566 See STATE AND METROPOLITAN AREA DATA BOOK. 5339

0276-6574 See COMPUTERS IN CARDIOLOGY. 3703

0276-6582 See SURFBOARD. 4924

0276-6590 See DIRECTORY - ASSOCIATION OF ACADEMIC HEALTH CENTERS (U.S.). 3779

0276-6604 See TWENTIETH CENTURY WATCH. 5068

0276-6612 See ADWEEK (MIDWEST ED.). 755

0276-6639 See REPRESENTING PUBLICLY TRADED CORPORATIONS. 3102

0276-6655 See FOLK MUSIC MINISTRY. 4118

0276-6671 See MCCALL'S CHRISTMAS KNIT & CROCHET. 5185

0276-668X See AMERICAN INSTITUTE OF ARCHITECTS MEMBERSHIP DIRECTORY. 287

0276-6701 See SAVE ON SHOPPING DIRECTORY. 957

0276-6736 See LOCOMOTIVE QUARTERLY. 5432

0276-6744 See YEARBOOK OF PODIATRIC MEDICINE AND SURGERY. 3918

0276-6760 See AERO ARMOR-SERIES. 4033

0276-6787 See STANDARDS FOR OBSTETRIC, GYNECOLOGIC, AND NEONATAL NURSING. 3768

0276-6795 See EX TEMPORE. 4117

0276-6884 See MENTAL HEALTH SERVICE SYSTEM REPORTS. SERIES AN, EPIDEMIOLOGY. 3736

0276-6906 See CODE OF FEDERAL REGULATIONS. CFR INDEX AND FINDING AIDS. 2952

0276-6922 See ANNUAL PLAN ... OF THE ILLINOIS DEPARTMENT OF MENTAL HEALTH AND DEVELOPMENTAL DISABILITIES. 4765

0276-6965 See PROBATION AND PAROLE LAW REPORTS. 3173

0276-6973 See CALIFORNIA STATE LIBRARY NEWSLETTER. 3199

0276-699X See PROCEEDINGS OF THE MUMPS USERS' GROUP MEETING. 1200

0276-7015 See UPDATE TO THE OKLAHOMA DEVELOPMENT PLAN FOR THE OZARKS REGIONAL COMMISSION. 1630

0276-7023 See UPDATE TO THE OKLAHOMA DEVELOPMENT PLAN FOR THE OZARKS REGIONAL COMMISSION. 1630

0276-7031 See NEW ON THE CHARTS. 4140

0276-704X See MONOGRAPHS ON FRAGRANCE RAW MATERIALS. 404

0276-7090 See TOURNAMENT CHESS. 4867

0276-7120 See QC (FOREST HILLS, N.Y.). 2544

0276-7155 See SOUTHWESTERN REVIEW (LAFAYETTE, LA.), THE. 3353

0276-7163 See STATE EXECUTIVE DIRECTORY. 4687

0276-718X See EDUCATION LAW BULLETIN. 1863

0276-7201 See AMICUS JOURNAL, THE. 2186

0276-7228 See MEMBERS IN GOOD STANDING AS OF ... / SOCIETY FOR ITALIAN HISTORICAL STUDIES. 2698

0276-7244 See UNITED STATES POSTAL CARD CATALOG. 1147

0276-7317 See INDUSTRY INTERNATIONAL. 682

0276-7325 See YEAR'S WORK - INSURANCE INSTITUTE FOR HIGHWAY SAFETY, THE. 5446

0276-7333 See ORGANOMETALLICS. 1045

0276-7414 See INVESTIGATE NEWSLETTER. 902

0276-7430 See EUROPEAN REVIEW (LEXINGTON, MASS.). 1560

0276-7449 See JOURNAL OF THE ALLEGHENIES. 2742

0276-7457 See UNITED STATES GOVERNMENT ... TELEPHONE DIRECTORY. REGION 1. 4692

0276-7481 See WATER UTILITY OPERATING DATA. 5548

0276-749X See COMPUTER AIDED DESIGN REPORT. 1232

0276-752X See CLIENT COUNSELING UPDATE : CCU. 2951

0276-7546 See NATIONAL LAW REVIEW REPORTER. 3013

0276-7570 See UCMP QUARTERLY. 3254

0276-7597 See AIRBRUSH DIGEST. 376

0276-7627 See REPRESENTING PROFESSIONAL ATHLETES AND TEAMS. 3039

0276-7643 See SACRED HEART UNIVERSITY REVIEW. 1094

0276-7651 See STATE LAWS AND PUBLISHED ORDINANCES, FIREARMS. 3058

0276-7724 See PROCEEDINGS OF THE ANNUAL MEETING AND REGIONAL MEETING - AMERICAN ASSOCIATION OF RAILROAD SUPERINTENDENTS. 5434

0276-7740 See STOCKS & BONDS ON THE NEW YORK STOCK EXCHANGE. 916

0276-7775 See CDE STOCK OWNERSHIP DIRECTORY : FORTUNE 500. 782

0276-7783 See MANAGEMENT INFORMATION SYSTEMS QUARTERLY. 1194

0276-7805 See DIRECTORY OF FACULTY CONTRACTS AND BARGAINING AGENTS IN INSTITUTIONS OF HIGHER EDUCATION. 1663

0276-7813 See WHOLESALER PRODUCTS CATALOG. 631

0276-7872 See BURRELLE'S ... PENNSYLVANIA MEDIA DIRECTORY. 1105

0276-7899 See SECOND CENTURY (ABILENE, TEX.), THE. 4996

0276-7902 See BARRIO (WASHINGTON, D.C.), EL. 2256

0276-7910 See GAVEA-BROWN. 3390

0276-7929 See PROCEEDINGS OF THE ... ANNUAL CONFERENCE SOUTHEASTERN ASSOCIATION OF FISH AND WILDLIFE AGENCIES. 4913

0276-7961 See MICROWAVE WORLD. 2072

0276-8038 See PT (ALEXANDRIA, VA.). 4382

0276-8127 See NEW MEXICO CIVIL TRIAL REPORTER. 3090

0276-8151 See ANNUAL JOURNAL / PETER W. RODINO INSTITUTE OF CRIMINAL JUSTICE. 3156

0276-816X See SOMETHING ABOUT THE AUTHOR. 435

0276-8178 See TWENTIETH-CENTURY LITERARY CRITICISM. 3355

0276-8186 See NATIONAL PARKS (WASHINGTON, D.C.). 4707

0276-8232 See DRIP/TRICKLE IRRIGATION. 170

0276-8267 See STATE OF THE ART REPORT. 5160

0276-8275 See WASHINGTON TARIFF AND TRADE LETTER. 857

0276-8283 See PHYSICIANS' CURRENT PROCEDURAL TERMINOLOGY. 1928

0276-8291 See ABBEY NEWSLETTER, THE. 2478

0276-8313 See HISTORICAL JOURNAL OF MASSACHUSETTS. 2737

0276-8321 See REPORT OF THE ADMINISTRATOR - UNITED STATES. HEALTH SERVICES ADMINISTRATION. 4798

0276-8429 See CHEMICAL ENGINEERING CATALOG. 2009

0276-8445 See CODE OF FEDERAL REGULATIONS. 30, MINERAL RESOURCES. 2952

0276-8453 See SUMMARY OF OIL FIELDS WELL CHANGES. 4280

0276-8488 See WEEKLY BULLETIN - NEW YORK (STATE). BANKING DEPT. 816

0276-8593 See MULTICHANNEL NEWS. 1135

0276-8607 See OCCASIONAL PUBLICATIONS IN NORTHEASTERN ANTHROPOLOGY. 242

0276-864X See UCLA HISTORICAL JOURNAL. 2632

0276-8739 See JOURNAL OF POLICY ANALYSIS AND MANAGEMENT. 4479

0276-8887 See MILIEU THERAPY. 4604

0276-8895 See HUNTING (NEW YORK, N.Y.). 4899

0276-8909 See UPDATE (WASHINGTON, D.C. 1976). 4692

0276-8917 See YACHTSMAN'S POCKET ALMANAC, THE. 597

0276-8968 See ANNUAL CONFERENCE / TRAVEL AND TOURISM RESEARCH ASSOCIATION. 5461

0276-8976 See APPLICATIONS OF MANAGEMENT SCIENCE. 860

0276-8992 See COLORADO WILDLIFE RESEARCH REVIEW. 4871

0276-9018 See FODOR'S COLORADO. 5471

0276-9034 See FROMMER'S HOW TO LIVE IN FLORIDA ON $10,000 A YEAR. 1492

0276-9042 See KNIFE WORLD. 2774

0276-9069 See 1001 CRAFT IDEAS. 369

0276-9077 See ATLANTIC (BOSTON, MASS. : 1981), THE. 2528

0276-9085 See ENDLESS VACATION - RESORT CONDOMINIUMS INTERNATIONAL, THE. 5469

0276-9123 See NHEA/NEA EDUCATOR. 1768

0276-9212 See FAA AVIATION FORECASTS. 19

0276-9220 See BORDERLANDS JOURNAL, THE. 1812

0276-9239 See MODERN RECORDING & MUSIC'S BUYER'S GUIDE. 5317

0276-9247 See WORK FORCE PROFILE AS OF SEPTEMBER 30 1718

0276-9271 See YOUTH CONSERVATION CORPS. 2210

0276-928X See JOURNAL OF STAFF DEVELOPMENT, THE. 1801

0276-9298 See URBAN ACADEMIC LIBRARIAN. 3255

0276-9433 See GROWER TALKS. 2418

0276-9468 See ANNUAL REPORT - ILLINOIS. GENERAL ASSEMBLY. LEGISLATIVE INVESTIGATING COMMITTEE. 4627

0276-9565 See NEWSLETTER - CAMPUS MINISTRY WOMEN (ORGANIZATION). 5562

0276-9581 See REPORTS OF CASES DECIDED IN THE APPELLATE DIVISION OF THE SUPREME COURT, STATE OF NEW YORK. 3039

0276-9603 See JUVENILE LAW REPORTS. 3121

0276-9654 See SOCIAL POLICY RESEARCH MONOGRAPHS SERIES. 5219

0276-9662 See SERIES IN THERMAL AND TRANSPORT SCIENCES. 5157

0276-9670 See SCRIPTA SERIES IN MATHEMATICS. 3533

0276-9700 See ELLIS HORWOOD SERIES IN CHEMICAL SCIENCE. 975

0276-9719 See JOHANNESBURG QUARTERLY GOLD STOCK REPORT. 2141

0276-9743 See BRIEFING BOOK ON MAJOR POLICY ISSUES. 1656

0276-9778 See NEW HAMPSHIRE POLITICAL ALMANAC, THE. 4484

0276-9786 See MINING MACHINERY AND MINERAL PROCESSING EQUIPMENT. 2146

0276-9891 See GUIDE TO FEDERAL PROCUREMENT. 4653

0276-9905 See IN-FISHERMAN, THE. 2305

0276-9913 See ADVANCES IN DESCRIPTIVE PSYCHOLOGY. 4571

0276-9948 See UNIVERSITY OF ILLINOIS LAW REVIEW. 3068

0276-9956 See ENFO. 2165

0276-9964 See FLORIDA SOLAR COALITION NEWSLETTER. 1944

0276-9972 See COMPUTER PUBLICITY NEWS. 758

0276-9980 See ALMANAC OF VIRGINIA POLITICS, THE. 4462

0277-0008 See PHARMACOTHERAPY. 4323

0277-0032 See BENCHMARK PAPERS IN BEHAVIOR. 4577

0277-0059 See MICRO MOONLIGHTER. 1245

0277-0121 See RESEARCH IN URBAN ECONOMICS. 1517

0277-0148 See SUMMARY REPORT FOR THE PROFESSIONAL DEVELOPMENT AND PROGRAM IMPROVEMENT CENTERS PROGRAM. 1873

0277-0164 See DIRECTORY OF ILLINOIS VISUAL ARTISTS. 349

0277-0180 See OPEC REVIEW. 4270

0277-0245 See NRBA SALES AND PROMOTION NEWS. 1135

0277-027X See PVP - AMERICAN SOCIETY OF MECHANICAL ENGINEERS. PRESSURE VESSELS AND PIPING DIVISION. **2127**

0277-0288 See LIBRARY SYSTEMS. **3227**

0277-030X See TEXAS MATHEMATICS TEACHER. **3538**

0277-0326 See SEMINARS IN ANESTHESIA. **3684**

0277-0334 See HOW TO DOUBLE YOUR INCOME. **404**

0277-0393 See CLINICAL ENGINEERING INFORMATION SERVICE. **3691**

0277-0407 See CCAN. **606**

0277-0415 See PLATT'S OIL MARKETING BULLETIN. **934**

0277-0423 See EUROPA (NEW YORK, N.Y.). **2687**

0277-0431 See WAY MAGAZINE, THE. **5020**

0277-0458 See ST. CLAIR SERIES IN MANAGEMENT AND ORGANIZATIONAL BEHAVIOR, THE. **886**

0277-0474 See BIBLICAL SCHOLARSHIP IN NORTH AMERICA. **5015**

0277-0482 See MORE MINNESOTA GUIDE MAGAZINE. **2539**

0277-0504 See ANNUAL STATUS REPORT ON THE URANIUM MILL TAILINGS REMEDIAL ACTION PROGRAM. **2224**

0277-0512 See NEW YORK LAW FINDER. **3082**

0277-0520 See ANNUAL DIRECTORY / HAWAII STATE BAR ASSOCIATION. **2934**

0277-0539 See SOCIAL SECURITY EXPLAINED. **5308**

0277-0555 See EXPERT WITNESS JOURNAL. **2968**

0277-0563 See ANNUAL REPORT / TEXAS COASTAL AND MARINE COUNCIL. **2815**

0277-0571 See ANNUAL REPORT / TEXAS BOARD OF LICENSURE FOR NURSING HOME ADMINISTRATORS. **3776**

0277-0598 See SELECTA (CORVALLIS, OR.). **3320**

0277-0628 See UNCOVERINGS. **5186**

0277-0660 See BIENNIAL REPORT - WISCONSIN. DEPT. OF AGRICULTURE, TRADE AND CONSUMER PROTECTION. **66**

0277-0679 See COMMUNICATIONS DAILY. **1152**

0277-0687 See ADVANCES IN DISEASE PREVENTION. **3546**

0277-0695 See NASW REGISTER OF CLINICAL SOCIAL WORKERS. **5297**

0277-0717 See FANTASY BOOK. **3387**

0277-0725 See KNIVES. **4007**

0277-0733 See SPUN YARN PRODUCTION. **3488**

0277-0776 See LIST OF PUBLICATIONS - UNITED STATES. CONGRESSIONAL BUDGET OFFICE. **4736**

0277-0792 See KEYNOTES (DALLAS, TEX.). **2812**

0277-0806 See MICHIGAN SOCIAL STUDIES TEXTBOOK STUDY. **1764**

0277-0865 See COMPUTER SECURITY JOURNAL. **1226**

0277-0873 See DIRECTORY OF EVALUATION TRAINING. **5283**

0277-089X See EXPLORATION (SANTA FE, N.M.) **236**

0277-0903 See JOURNAL OF ASTHMA, THE. **3950**

0277-0911 See MSRB REPORTS. **3012**

0277-092X See INTERNATIONAL YOGA GUIDE. **2598**

0277-0938 See PEDIATRIC PATHOLOGY. **3897**

0277-0946 See MEXICO REPORT (EL PASO, TEX.). **1574**

0277-0962 See WORLDWIDE REFINING AND GAS PROCESSING DIRECTORY (1978). **4283**

0277-0989 See NEW YORK TIMES CURRENT EVENTS INDEX, THE. **2490**

0277-0997 See NORTHERN RAVEN, THE. **4169**

0277-1004 See AAA WORLD (TEXAS, NEW MEXICO, OKLAHOMA ED.). **5459**

0277-1012 See AAA WORLD. NEW HAMPSHIRE. **5459**

0277-1020 See AAA WORLD (TEXAS, NEW MEXICO, OKLAHOMA ED.). **5459**

0277-1039 See AAA WORLD. MASSACHUSETTS. **5459**

0277-1055 See AAA WORLD (TEXAS, NEW MEXICO, OKLAHOMA ED.). **5459**

0277-1071 See AMERICAN ACADEMY OF RELIGION ACADEMY SERIES. **4933**

0277-108X See GROUP HQ DIRECTORY. **5231**

0277-1098 See PLAY THE RED. **3468**

0277-1128 See CHEMICAL AND PHYSICAL PROCESSES IN COMBUSTION. **968**

0277-1136 See DELAWARE VALLEY GUIDE TO TRANSPORTATION. **5381**

0277-1152 See MISSISSIPPI COLLEGE LAW REVIEW. **3010**

0277-1160 See DECORATOR (GLENS FALLS, N.Y.), THE. **372**

0277-1187 See ITHACA TIMES. **5717**

0277-1233 See ENGINEER OF CALIFORNIA. **1972**

0277-1268 See CSM'S ... EQUIPMENT BUYERS' GUIDE FOR THE FOOD INDUSTRY. **2332**

0277-1276 See EMPLOYEE BENEFITS AND PERSONNEL PRACTICES SURVEY. SAN FRANCISCO BAY AREA, NORTHWEST, COLORADO, ARIZONA, AND TEXAS. **940**

0277-1314 See MASSACHUSETTS POLITICAL ALMANAC, THE. **4664**

0277-1322 See RES (CAMBRIDGE, MASS.). **244**

0277-1330 See ICBP TECHNICAL PUBLICATION. **2195**

0277-1349 See HINDU TEXT INFORMATION. **417**

0277-1357 See HIGH PERFORMANCE REVIEW. **5317**

0277-1365 See NEWS BULLETIN / NATIONAL COUNCIL OF TEACHERS OF MATHEMATICS. **3524**

0277-1373 See AFRICANA DIRECTIONS. **1923**

0277-139X See LIGHT ON THE WORD. TEACHER. **1900**

0277-1411 See AAA WORLD. WISCONSIN. **5459**

0277-1446 See CONTINUITY. **2614**

0277-1454 See CORRESPONDENT BANKING. **785**

0277-1462 See CABLE TV MAGAZINE. **1129**

0277-1489 See MARKETING CALIFORNIA PEARS. **2349**

0277-1500 See DIRECTORY OF BLACK FILM/TV TECHNICIANS & ARTISTS, WEST COAST. **4067**

0277-1519 See DIRECTORY OF SMALL PRESS & MAGAZINE EDITORS & PUBLISHERS, THE. **4814**

0277-1527 See WORLD FACTBOOK (WASHINGTON, D.C.). **2579**

0277-1535 See PALABRA, LA. **3421**

0277-1551 See BEST'S DIRECTORY OF RECOMMENDED INSURANCE ATTORNEYS. **2941**

0277-1616 See ELECTRIC OUTPUT. **2043**

0277-1659 See A-E-C AUTOMATION NEWSLETTER. **286**

0277-1691 See INTERNATIONAL JOURNAL OF GYNECOLOGICAL PATHOLOGY. **3895**

0277-1713 See BUSINESS LAW REPORTER. **3096**

0277-173X See IDSA PAPERS. **2098**

0277-1764 See AVIATION SAFETY (RIVERSIDE, CONN.). **14**

0277-1845 See ACTIVITIES AND SUMMARY REPORT OF THE COMMITTEE ON THE DISTRICT OF COLUMBIA, HOUSE OF REPRESENTATIVES. **4623**

0277-1853 See BUTYLENES ANNUAL. **1600**

0277-1918 See JOURNAL OF THE ALASKA GEOLOGICAL SOCIETY. **1385**

0277-1926 See GROUND WATER MONITORING REVIEW. **1413**

0277-1969 See DIRECTORY OF RETAILER OWNED COOPERATIVES, WHOLESALER SPONSORED VOLUNTARIES, WHOLESALE GROCERS, SERVICES MERCHANDISERS. **1604**

0277-2000 See RENTAL RATE BLUE BOOK FOR OLDER EQUIPMENT. **626**

0277-2027 See BUSINESS & PROFESSIONAL ETHICS JOURNAL. **645**

0277-2086 See CHAMPAIGN COUNTY GENEALOGICAL SOCIETY QUARTERLY. **2442**

0277-2116 See JOURNAL OF PEDIATRIC GASTROENTEROLOGY AND NUTRITION. **3905**

0277-2124 See BULLETIN - SPECIAL LIBRARIES ASSOCIATION. SAN FRANCISCO BAY REGION CHAPTER. **3199**

0277-2140 See WIND ENERGY ABSTRACTS. **1960**

0277-2191 See SUMMARY PROGRESS REPORT / U.S. GRAIN MARKETING RESEARCH LABORATORY. **188**

0277-2213 See EMPLOYEE BENEFITS AND PERSONNEL PRACTICES SURVEY. SOUTHERN CALIFORNIA. **1665**

0277-2248 See TOXICOLOGICAL AND ENVIRONMENTAL CHEMISTRY. **3984**

0277-2256 See EMPLOYEE BENEFITS AND PERSONNEL PRACTICES SURVEY. MINNESOTA, NEW ENGLAND, NEW YORK, AND UNASSIGNED. **1665**

0277-2280 See ARMSTRONG OIL DIRECTORIES, TEXAS AND SOUTHEASTERN NEW MEXICO. **4251**

0277-2302 See INSTAURATION. **4477**

0277-2310 See HIGHWAY SAFETY STEWARDSHIP REPORT, THE. **5441**

0277-2353 See HOSPITAL SALARY SURVEY REPORT. **3785**

0277-2361 See SECTION OF TAXATION NEWSLETTER / ABA. **3047**

0277-237X See NEXUS (NEWARK, N.J.). **763**

0277-2388 See GEOGRAPHICAL RESEARCH STUDIES SERIES. **2563**

0277-2418 See ALTERNATE SOURCE, THE. **1264**

0277-2426 See LANDSCAPE JOURNAL. **2423**

0277-2434 See PHILOSOPHY IN SCIENCE. **5138**

0277-2442 See INTERNATIONAL LIVING (WASHINGTON, D.C.). **5481**

0277-2469 See PSYCHOLOGY & SOCIAL THEORY. **4612**

0277-2477 See WILEY MONOGRAPHS IN CHEMICAL PHYSICS. **4425**

0277-2493 See WILEY SERIES IN PURE AND APPLIED OPTICS. **4442**

0277-2507 See WILEY MONOGRAPHS IN CRYSTALLOGRAPHY. **1033**

0277-2566 See WILEY SERIES IN DIAGNOSTIC AND THERAPEUTIC RADIOLOGY. **3947**

0277-2639 See TUTORIAL ESSAYS IN PSYCHOLOGY. **4621**

0277-2647 See WILEY SERIES IN COMPUTING. **1207**

0277-268X See WILEY WORD PROCESSING SERIES. **1292**

0277-2736 See DISCUSSIONS ON TEACHING. **2615**

0277-2752 See NEW POETS SERIES, THE. **3467**

0277-2825 See WIRELESS REGISTER. WORLD WIDE EDITION, THE. **1143**

0277-2833 See RESEARCH IN THE SOCIOLOGY OF WORK. **5255**

0277-2868 See REPORT TO THE CONGRESS ON OCEAN POLLUTION AND OFFSHORE DEVELOPMENT. **1456**

0277-2914 See ADULT CINEMA REVIEW. **4062**

0277-2922 See IRANIAN ASSETS LITIGATION REPORTER. **3131**

0277-2930 See COMMODITIES LAW LETTER. **2953**

0277-2949 See CAI NEWS / WASHINGTON METROPOLITAN CHAPTER. **654**

0277-3007 See MUSCULOSKELETAL UPDATE. **3806**

0277-3015 See NEW METHODS (SAN FRANCISCO, CALIF.). **5517**

0277-3066 See BLACK BELT (BURBANK, CALIF.). **4887**

0277-3074 See DOE NEW TECHNOLOGY. **1936**

0277-3082 See NEW ERA (BARRYTOWN, N.Y.). **4981**

0277-3090 See RESEARCH GRANTS, TRAINING AWARDS, SUMMARY TABLES. **3844**

0277-3139 See WORLD AGRICULTURAL SUPPLY AND DEMAND ESTIMATES. **147**

0277-318X See RUTGERS LAW JOURNAL. **3045**

ISSN Index

0277-3252 See ALI-ABA COURSE OF STUDY. ABA SECTION OF TAXATION, ANNUAL OF TAXATION, ANNUAL ADVANCED STUDY SESSIONS, ADVANCED TAX PLANNING FOR REAL ESTATE TRANSACTIONS: MATERIALS. 2930

0277-3325 See WORK YEARS AND PERSONNEL COSTS, EXECUTIVE BRANCH, UNITED STATES GOVERNMENT. 1718

0277-335X See SOUTH ATLANTIC REVIEW. 3322

0277-3406 See TECHNICAL REPORT - PARENTERAL DRUG ASSOCIATION. 4330

0277-3414 See DIRECTORY OF MEMBERS / AMERICAN ASSOCIATION FOR CANCER RESEARCH. 3816

0277-3481 See VIDEO X. 1142

0277-349X See QUALITY CRAFTS MARKET, THE. 375

0277-3511 See WHO'S WHO IN AMERICAN LAW ENFORCEMENT. 436

0277-352X See WALL STREET JOURNAL MAGAZINE, THE. 2549

0277-3538 See DESIGN SOLUTIONS. 297

0277-3554 See COUNTRY SONG ROUNDUP. SPECIAL. 4112

0277-3570 See FINANCIAL ASSISTANCE BY GEOGRAPHIC AREA (UNITED STATES. DEPT. OF EDUCATION. OFFICE OF FINANCIAL MANAGEMENT). 1824

0277-3597 See BIBLIOTHECA PRESS UPDATE. 3195

0277-3619 See ASDA HANDBOOK. 1317

0277-3627 See ASDA NEWS (1981). 1317

0277-3635 See DENTISTRY (CHICAGO, ILL.). 1322

0277-3643 See COMMERCIAL LAW. GOLD BOOK. BENDER PAMPHLET EDITION. NEW YORK UNIFORM COMMERCIAL CODE, GENERAL OBLIGATIONS LAW. 3097

0277-366X See SURNAME RESEARCH DIRECTORY. 2474

0277-3694 See DIRECTORY OF COMPUTER DEALERS. INTERNATIONAL EDITION. 1237

0277-3708 See COLORADO LEGISLATIVE ALMANAC. 4468

0277-3716 See DRUG STORE MARKET GUIDE. 4301

0277-3724 See STATISTICAL SUMMARY, FEDERAL MEAT AND POULTRY INSPECTION FOR FISCAL YEAR. 2362

0277-3732 See AMERICAN JOURNAL OF CLINICAL ONCOLOGY. 3808

0277-3740 See CORNEA. 3873

0277-3791 See QUATERNARY SCIENCE REVIEWS. 1393

0277-3813 See JOURNAL OF WOOD CHEMISTRY AND TECHNOLOGY. 1055

0277-3899 See STAMP COLLECTOR. 2787

0277-3945 See RHETORIC SOCIETY QUARTERLY. 3317

0277-3988 See BOND GUIDE. 892

0277-402X See U.S. TAX CASES. 4757

0277-4038 See CHEMICAL ENGINEERING ASPECTS OF BIOMEDICINE RESEARCH STUDIES SERIES. 3690

0277-4054 See MEMBERSHIP DIRECTORY / CHAMBER MUSIC AMERICA. 4130

0277-4070 See WILDLIFE RESEARCH REPORT (DENVER, COLO.). 2209

0277-4097 See TRAVEL GUIDE FLORIDA. 5495

0277-4100 See TEXAS FAMILY JOURNAL. 2286

0277-4119 See PRODUCTION EMPLOYEES COST SURVEY. 1703

0277-4135 See WORLD-WIDE OFFICIAL ORGAN BLUE BOOK. 4159

0277-4194 See PRIMARY CARE MEDICINE DRUG ALERTS. 4325

0277-4208 See PRACTICAL GASTROENTEROLOGY. 3747

0277-4216 See PERIODONTAL CLINICAL INVESTIGATIONS : OFFICIAL PUBLICATION OF THE NORTHEASTERN SOCIETY OF PERIODONTISTS. 1333

0277-4232 See EDUCATION WEEK 1741

0277-4240 See RUTGERS PROFESSIONAL PSYCHOLOGY REVIEW. 4617

0277-4267 See SYMPOSIUM ON SALT. 1399

0277-4275 See WIRE JOURNAL INTERNATIONAL. 4023

0277-4305 See SPECIAL PUBLICATION IFDC. 188

0277-4356 See LETRAS FEMENINAS. 3404

0277-4445 See MASSON MONOGRAPHS IN DENTISTRY. 1329

0277-4461 See DAWN (HONESDALE, PA.). 4185

0277-4518 See FAMILY MINISTRIES. 4958

0277-4569 See VICTORIA, CROSSROADS OF SOUTH TEXAS. 2476

0277-464X See COMMUNITY UPO. 2818

0277-4690 See NEW ENGLAND CONSERVATIONIST, THE. 2200

0277-4720 See ST. JOHNS REVIEW (1981), THE. 1847

0277-4747 See BENCHMARK PAPERS IN PHYSICAL CHEMISTRY AND CHEMICAL PHYSICS. 1050

0277-4771 See DRAG RULES. 4893

0277-478X See ANNUAL PROGRAM INFORMATION NOTICE. 1932

0277-4844 See VIEW FROM SPRINGFIELD. 4693

0277-4860 See RADIO & RECORDS. 1137

0277-4887 See SONORENSIS. 4096

0277-4909 See JOTS FROM THE POINT. 2455

0277-4917 See DAILY LEGISLATIVE REPORT. 4641

0277-4933 See DEFENSE & FOREIGN AFFAIRS. 4041

0277-495X See LEGAL INTELLIGENCER, THE. 2999

0277-4968 See TRENDLINE DAILY ACTION STOCK CHARTS. 917

0277-4976 See HOUSTON BUSINESS JOURNAL. 680

0277-4984 See DATAPRO REPORTS ON OFFICE SYSTEMS. 4211

0277-4992 See WALL STREET LETTER. 919

0277-500X See STANDARD CORPORATION DESCRIPTIONS. 916

0277-514X See NEW PERFORMANCE. 1314

0277-5158 See WEST'S FEDERAL TAX SYSTEM. 3074

0277-5166 See NEGATIVE CAPABILITY. 3414

0277-5204 See VISIONS IN LEISURE AND BUSINESS. 4855

0277-5212 See WETLANDS (WILMINGTON, N.C.). 2208

0277-5220 See EXPOSURE (WASHINGTON, D.C.). 455

0277-5247 See BRAILLE BOOKS. 4827

0277-5263 See NEWS MONITORING SERVICE. 2749

0277-5301 See DIRECTORY OF MEMBERS / SOCIETY OF AMERICAN TRAVEL WRITERS. 5468

0277-5336 See WHO'S WHO IN BLACK CORPORATE AMERICA. 436

0277-5344 See SOUTH BUSINESS. 712

0277-5360 See QUEST STAR. 3427

0277-5387 See POLYHEDRON. 1037

0277-5395 See WOMEN'S STUDIES INTERNATIONAL FORUM. 5571

0277-5417 See LOYOLA OF LOS ANGELES INTERNATIONAL AND COMPARATIVE LAW JOURNAL. 3132

0277-545X See LIFE STYLES HEALTH SERIES. 4789

0277-5506 See TECHNICAL BULLETIN - MISSISSIPPI AGRICULTURAL AND FORESTRY EXPERIMENT STATION. 139

0277-5565 See LOTTERY PLAYER'S MAGAZINE. 4863

0277-5581 See SEA GRANT BIENNIAL REPORT / U.S. DEPARTMENT OF COMMERCE, NATIONAL OCEANIC AND ATMOSPHERIC ADMINISTRATION, NATIONAL SEA GRANT COLLEGE PROGRAM. 1456

0277-5646 See CDE STOCK OWNERSHIP DIRECTORY : AGRIBUSINESS. 656

0277-5700 See CONNECTICUT DIGEST OF ADMINISTRATIVE REPORTS TO THE GOVERNOR. 4469

0277-5727 See SEARCH (NILES, ILL.). 2472

0277-5735 See STREET RODDER. 4924

0277-5743 See TRUCKIN. 5398

0277-5778 See BOSTON COLLEGE INTERNATIONAL AND COMPARATIVE LAW REVIEW. 3125

0277-5786 See GENERAL TECHNICAL REPORT RM. 2383

0277-5794 See RESEARCH NOTE RM. 2393

0277-5816 See MEMBERSHIP DIRECTORY / GEOLOGICAL SOCIETY OF AMERICA. 1387

0277-5840 See PAYROLL ACCOUNTING. 749

0277-5859 See SUMMARY OF UMTA'S TRANSIT ASSISTANCE PROGRAM. 5393

0277-5883 See TOPICS IN CHEMICAL ENGINEERING. 2017

0277-5913 See GENEALOGICAL COMPUTING. 2450

0277-5921 See CONTRIBUTIONS TO POLITICAL ECONOMY. 1590

0277-5948 See RECOMMENDED REFERENCE BOOKS FOR SMALL AND MEDIUM-SIZED LIBRARIES AND MEDIA CENTERS. 1928

0277-5956 See CONNECTICUT NEWS HANDBOOK. 2918

0277-609X See NATURALISTS' DIRECTORY AND ALMANAC, INTERNATIONAL, THE. 5131

0277-6103 See ENERGY COST CUTTER, THE. 1939

0277-612X See FOR PARENTS. 2280

0277-6138 See NEW ARTS REVIEW. 326

0277-6162 See WRITER'S & PHOTOGRAPHER'S GUIDE TO NEWSPAPER MARKETS. 4378

0277-6189 See COMMUNITY SERVICE NEWSLETTER. 2818

0277-6197 See OCEANOGRAPHIC MONTHLY SUMMARY. 1454

0277-6219 See RECORD INTERIORS. 2903

0277-6286 See CAUSEWAYS & THEATRE PROJECTS; ANNUAL REPORT. 5439

0277-6294 See MUNICIPAL ATTORNEYS' OPINIONS. 3012

0277-6308 See ARKANSAS ARCHEOLOGICAL SURVEY RESEARCH REPORT. 259

0277-6332 See PROCEEDINGS, ANNUAL CONFERENCE OF GUIDANCE PERSONNEL IN OCCUPATIONAL EDUCATION. 1915

0277-643X See ATSIS JOURNAL. 2874

0277-6464 See FAMILY THERAPY NEWS. 4587

0277-6499 See AERONAUTICS AND SPACE REPORT OF THE PRESIDENT. ACTIVITIES. 4

0277-6537 See REPORTER (UTICA, N.Y.). 3245

0277-6553 See TECHNICAL PUBLICATIONS OF THE STATE BIOLOGICAL SURVEY OF KANSAS. 474

0277-660X See REPORT TO COUNCIL ON AGING. 5305

0277-6618 See PRENTICE-HALL ACCOUNTING FACULTY DIRECTORY. 750

0277-6650 See PETROLEUM EXPLORATION MAP. 4272

0277-6669 See GEODYNAMICS SERIES. 1376

0277-6693 See JOURNAL OF FORECASTING. 5249

0277-6715 See STATISTICS IN MEDICINE. 3661

0277-6758 See MCGRAW-HILL'S NATIONAL ELECTRICAL CODE HANDBOOK. 2071

0277-6766 See LYMPHOKINE AND CYTOKINE RESEARCH. 538

0277-6774 See COMMUNITY/JUNIOR COLLEGE. 1817

0277-6790 See YEARBOOK OF THE INTERNATIONAL ASSOCIATION FOR CHILD AND ADOLESCENT PSYCHIATRY AND ALLIED PROFESSIONS. 3937

0277-6863 See CRIT. 296

0277-6936 See FAMILY FOOTPRINTS. 2447

0277-6987 See DON'T MISS OUT. 1822

0277-6995 See CERVANTES (GAINESVILLE, FLA.). 431

0277-7010 See INDIVIDUAL PSYCHOLOGY. 4590

0277-7037 See MASS SPECTROMETRY REVIEWS. 1017

0277-7061 See IMPRINT (NEW YORK, N.Y. : 1976). 380

0277-7096 See SAVE THE SCHOOLS. 1781

0277-710X See KAIROS (OAKLAND, CALIF.). 3345

0277-7126 See AMERICAN JOURNAL OF SEMIOTICS. 3263

0277-7215 See CANCER IN ILLINOIS. 3811

0277-7223 See CHIRICU (BLOOMINGTON, IND. : 1981). 2613

0277-7266 See MEDICAL MALPRACTICE LITIGATION. 3008

0277-7282 See RELEASES FROM JUVENILE INSTITUTIONS (1979). 3174

0277-7290 See RESEARCH AND TECHNOLOGY ANNUAL REPORT. 5146

0277-7312 See BRICKER'S INTERNATIONAL DIRECTORY. VOL. 1, LONG-TERM UNIVERSITY-BASED EXECUTIVE PROGRAMS. 862

0277-7347 See PROCEEDINGS OF THE ANNUAL MEETING - INDUSTRIAL RELATIONS RESEARCH ASSOCIATION (1978). 1703

0277-7355 See SCIENTIFIC, ENGINEERING, AND MEDICAL SOCIETIES PUBLICATIONS IN PRINT. 5155

0277-7398 See MANAGING THE HUMAN CLIMATE. 762

0277-7401 See HOME CARE SERVICES IN NEW YORK STATE. 4783

0277-7452 See NORDIC SKIING COMPETITION GUIDE. 4908

0277-7460 See NSCLC WASHINGTON WEEKLY. 3020

0277-7533 See BIG MAMA RAG. 5551

0277-7541 See BROWN COMPANY ANNUAL REPORT. 644

0277-7576 See PROCEEDINGS OF THE INTERNATIONAL INSTRUMENTATION SYMPOSIUM. 32

0277-7746 See COMPLICATIONS IN SURGERY. 3963

0277-7770 See CONNECTICUT POETRY REVIEW, THE. 3461

0277-7789 See WRITING INSTRUCTOR, THE. 3334

0277-7800 See THRESHOLD OF FANTASY. 3446

0277-7819 See RESOURCE REVIEW. 5762

0277-7827 See FROMMER'S SOUTH AMERICA ON $ ... A DAY. 5478

0277-7851 See ENERGY FROM BIOMASS AND WASTES. 4255

0277-786X See PROCEEDINGS OF SPIE--THE INTERNATIONAL SOCIETY FOR OPTICAL ENGINEERING. 1991

0277-7886 See BASIC AND CLINICAL ENDOCRINOLOGY. 3726

0277-7924 See MANUFACTURED HOUSING DEALER. ANNUAL DIRECTORY & BUYER'S GUIDE. 2827

0277-8017 See INTERMUSE. 322

0277-8025 See ACS SERVICE REPORT. 1541

0277-8033 See JOURNAL OF PROTEIN CHEMISTRY. 490

0277-8041 See CONTEMPORARY PSYCHIATRY (NEW YORK, N.Y.). 3923

0277-8068 See JOURNAL OF CRYSTALLOGRAPHIC AND SPECTROSCOPIC RESEARCH. 1032

0277-8076 See NORTHLIGHT (TEMPE, ARIZ.). 4372

0277-8130 See JIVE. 2536

0277-8165 See CATHOLIC YOUTH MINISTRY. 5027

0277-8173 See AMERICAN JOURNAL OF SOCIAL PSYCHIATRY, THE. 3920

0277-8203 See DNA - UNITED STATES. DEFENSE NUCLEAR AGENCY. 4446

0277-8211 See PROCEEDINGS / INTERNATIONAL CEMENT SEMINAR. 5140

0277-8246 See TECHNICAL DOCUMENT - UNITED STATES. NAVAL OCEAN SYSTEMS CENTER. 1457

0277-8270 See INTERNATIONAL JOURNAL OF MICROCIRCUITS AND ELECTRONIC PACKAGING, THE. 4219

0277-8289 See ANNUAL REPORT - OKLAHOMA. DEPT. OF HUMAN SERVICES. 5272

0277-8300 See TRANSMISSION DIGEST. 5426

0277-836X See BETTER HOMES AND GARDENS DECORATING IDEAS. WINDOW & WALL IDEAS. 2899

0277-8378 See BOATING INDUSTRY STATISTICAL YEARBOOK. 597

0277-8394 See EDITIONS CATALOG. 319

0277-8416 See ... DISCOVERAMERICARD DIRECTORY OF CITIES & HOTELS, THE. 2805

0277-8424 See INDEX TO AUDIO EQUIPMENT REVIEWS. 5317

0277-8432 See IMPRIMIS. 1494

0277-8459 See LAW, MEDICINE & HEALTH CARE. 2995

0277-8467 See CLEAN WATER ACTION NEWS. 5532

0277-8475 See WG & L REAL ESTATE OUTLOOK. 4848

0277-8491 See HOUSING LAW BULLETIN. 2979

0277-8521 See HEALTH HAZARD EVALUATION SUMMARIES. 2863

0277-853X See SAUNDERS MONOGRAPHS IN CLINICAL RADIOLOGY. 3946

0277-8556 See NATIONAL PRODUCTIVITY REVIEW. 880

0277-8599 See METHODS IN HEMATOLOGY. 3773

0277-8610 See MEANS HISTORICAL COST INDEXES. 620

0277-8637 See MIT PRESS SERIES IN HEALTH AND PUBLIC POLICY. 5296

0277-867X See BACKPACKER. 4869

0277-870X See INTERNATIONAL SOLID FUEL BUYER'S GUIDE DIRECTORY. 2606

0277-8718 See MARIN KIN TRACER, THE. 2459

0277-8726 See MARKERS. 357

0277-8815 See BULLETIN - COASTAL SOCIETY. 1352

0277-8955 See COMMUNICATOR (CHICAGO, ILL. : 1981), THE. 3203

0277-898X See EUPHONY. 2054

0277-9102 See ACCENT/REVIEWS. 4931

0277-9145 See MIDDLER STUDENT GUIDE. 4977

0277-9153 See MIDDLER TEACHER. 1900

0277-9161 See JUNIOR TEACHER (SPRINGFIELD, MO.). 1899

0277-917X See JUNIOR STUDENT. 4971

0277-9188 See PRIMARY TEACHER. 1902

0277-9196 See LAURISTON S. TAYLOR LECTURES IN RADIATION PROTECTION AND MEASUREMENTS. 4788

0277-920X See SIG SECURITY, AUDIT & CONTROL REVIEW. 1262

0277-9218 See NEW JERSEY MUNICIPAL DATA BOOK, THE. 2829

0277-9269 See JOURNAL OF MUSICOLOGY (ST. JOSEPH, MICH.), THE. 4126

0277-9277 See MARKET WATCH (NEW YORK, N.Y.). 2369

0277-9285 See CANADIAN VIEWPOINT (WILLOW GROVE, PA.). 3200

0277-9293 See WATER-RESOURCES INVESTIGATIONS IN NEVADA. 5546

0277-9307 See STATE DATA PROFILES, CALENDAR YEAR. 137

0277-9315 See SOCIOLOGY (GUILFORD, CONN.). 5262

0277-9358 See AMERICAN MOTORCYCLIST. 4080

0277-9390 See GOVERNMENT PUBLICATIONS REVIEW (1982). 3212

0277-9404 See RANGE SCIENCE SERIES (FORT COLLINS, COLO.). 124

0277-9455 See ARID LANDS NEWSLETTER. 2187

0277-948X See OPEN-FILE REPORT (ATLANTA, GA.). 1390

0277-9536 See SOCIAL SCIENCE & MEDICINE (1982). 5220

0277-9544 See LAWYER'S ALMANAC, THE. 2998

0277-9552 See CATALOG (ARTHRITIS INFORMATION CLEARINGHOUSE (U.S.). 3804

0277-9560 See CONCERT MAGAZINE (WALPOLE, MASS.). 4111

0277-9579 See ANNUAL HOSPITAL REPORT. 3776

0277-9595 See COLORADO INSURANCE INDUSTRY STATISTICAL REPORT. 2897

0277-9617 See DIRECTORY OF WOMEN'S & CHILDREN'S WEAR SPECIALTY STORES. 1083

0277-9625 See DIRECTORY OF MEN'S & BOYS' WEAR SPECIALTY STORES. 1083

0277-9633 See RELIABILITY REVIEW (MILWAUKEE, WIS.). 1993

0277-9668 See YELLOWJACKET (QUINCY, ILL.). 2478

0277-9676 See PREDICASTS F&S INDEX. UNITED STATES ANNUAL EDITION. 422

0277-9684 See PREDICASTS F & S INDEX EUROPE ANNUAL. 1579

0277-9692 See PREDICASTS F&S INDEX. INTERNATIONAL ANNUAL. 1621

0277-9714 See DRUG FACTS AND COMPARISONS. 4300

0277-9773 See BIOTECHNOLOGY INVESTMENT OPPORTUNITIES. 3689

0277-979X See FINESCALE MODELER. 2773

0277-9811 See ZURNALS (LITTLETON, MASS.). 2276

0277-982X See FORENSIC BULLETIN. 3164

0277-9870 See INTERNATIONAL GUIDE TO PSI PERIODICALS AND ORGANIZATIONS. 4243

0277-9889 See PROCEEDINGS OF THE ANNUAL CONVENTION - CANON LAW SOCIETY OF AMERICA. 5034

0277-9897 See POST SCRIPT (JACKSONVILLE, FLA.). 4076

0277-9943 See ADVERTISING COMPLIANCE SERVICE. 754

0277-9951 See MODERN APPLICATIONS NEWS. 4012

0277-996X See NEW ENGLAND JOURNAL OF HUMAN SERVICES. 5298

0278-0038 See GOING PUBLIC, THE IPO REPORTER. 789

0278-0046 See IEEE TRANSACTIONS ON INDUSTRIAL ELECTRONICS (1982). 2062

0278-0062 See IEEE TRANSACTIONS ON MEDICAL IMAGING. 3941

0278-0070 See IEEE TRANSACTIONS ON COMPUTER-AIDED DESIGN OF INTEGRATED CIRCUITS AND SYSTEMS. 2061

0278-0089 See UNITED STATES COAST PILOT. 9, PACIFIC AND ARCTIC COASTS. ALASKA, CAPE SPENCER TO BEAUFORT SEA. 4184

0278-0097 See IEEE TECHNOLOGY & SOCIETY MAGAZINE. 5111

0278-0119 See DIRECTORY OF INDUSTRY DATA SOURCES. THE UNITED STATES OF AMERICA AND CANADA. 1531

0278-0135 See PREDICASTS FORECASTS. 1537

0278-0143 See PUBLICATION CATALOG OF THE U.S. DEPARTMENT OF HEALTH AND HUMAN SERVICES. 5303

0278-016X See SOCIAL COGNITION. 5258

0278-0178 See JLAG REVIEW. 323

0278-0194 See ROCKY MOUNTAIN MAGAZINE ... WINTER GUIDE, THE. 4878

0278-0208 See GOLDFINCH, THE. 1063

0278-0224 See PARITY. 1701

0278-0232 See HEMATOLOGICAL ONCOLOGY. 3772

0278-0240 See DISEASE MARKERS. 3713

0278-0275 See FINANCIAL DIRECTORY OF PENSION FUNDS. OHIO, NORTHWESTERN (TOLEDO, MANSFIELD, LIMA & OTHERS). 1673

0278-0283 See FINANCIAL DIRECTORY OF PENSION FUNDS. MARYLAND, EASTERN (BALTIMORE, ANNAPOLIS, EASTERN SHORE & OTHERS). **1671**

0278-0291 See FINANCIAL DIRECTORY OF PENSION FUNDS. NEW YORK, WEST CENTRAL UPSTATE (UTICA, SYRACUSE, BINGHAMTON & OTHERS). **1672**

0278-0305 See FINANCIAL DIRECTORY OF PENSION FUNDS. NEW YORK (NASSAU & SUFFOLK COUNTIES ONLY). **1672**

0278-0313 See FINANCIAL DIRECTORY OF PENSION FUNDS. WASHINGTON, EASTERN (SPOKANE, YAKIMA, PASCO & OTHERS). **1674**

0278-0321 See FINANCIAL DIRECTORY OF PENSION FUNDS. OHIO, MIDEASTERN (AKRON, YOUNGSTOWN, ZANESVILLE, CANTON & OTHERS). **1673**

0278-033X See FINANCIAL DIRECTORY OF PENSION FUNDS. WISCONSIN, NORTHERN (GREENBAY, WAUSAU, EAU CLAIRE & OTHERS). **1674**

0278-0348 See FINANCIAL DIRECTORY OF PENSION FUNDS. FLORIDA, CENTRAL (TAMPA, LAKELAND, ORLANDO & OTHERS). **1670**

0278-0356 See FINANCIAL DIRECTORY OF PENSION FUNDS. NEW YORK, WESTCHESTER COUNTY AREA (YONKERS, WHITE PLAINS, MIDDLETOWN & OTHERS). **1672**

0278-0364 See FINANCIAL DIRECTORY OF PENSION FUNDS. PENNSYLVANIA, EASTERN, SUBURBAN PHILADELPHIA (UPPER DARBY, WEST CHESTER, KING OF PRUSSIA & OTHERS). **1673**

0278-0372 See JOURNAL OF CRUSTACEAN BIOLOGY. **555**

0278-0380 See AUDITING. **739**

0278-0488 See FEDERAL PRODUCTIVITY MEASUREMENT. **4648**

0278-050X See DIRECTORY OF MEMBERS - NATIONAL SOFT DRINK ASSOCIATION. **2366**

0278-0518 See SELECTED FEDERAL AND STATE BOOK PROGRAM INFORMATION. **3248**

0278-0526 See ANNUAL REPORT OF THE JUSTICE SYSTEM IMPROVEMENT ACT AGENCIES / BUREAU OF JUSTICE STATISTICS, LAW ENFORCEMENT ASSISTANCE ADMINISTRATION, NATIONAL INSTITUTE OF JUSTICE, OFFICE OF JUSTICE ASSISTANCE, RESEARCH, AND STATISTICS. **3157**

0278-0569 See NASSP NEWSLEADER. **1866**

0278-0577 See ANNUAL REPORT / NATIONAL HEART, LUNG, AND BLOOD INSTITUTE. **3699**

0278-0585 See AMERICAN SENTINEL (WASHINGTON, D.C.), THE. **4463**

0278-0593 See CHARITABLE GIVING AND SOLICITATION. **4335**

0278-0739 See PRINCIPLES AND PRESENTATION. MINING. **2148**

0278-0747 See U.S. GEOLOGICAL SURVEY IN ALASKA ..., PROGRAMS, THE. **1400**

0278-0763 See MORAVIAN MUSIC JOURNAL. **4132**

0278-0771 See JOURNAL OF ETHNOBIOLOGY. **238**

0278-0801 See CARGO FACTS. **5379**

0278-081X See CIRCUITS, SYSTEMS, AND SIGNAL PROCESSING. **2039**

0278-0828 See PASSAGES NORTH. **3422**

0278-0844 See 1001 HOME IDEAS. **2898**

0278-0909 See DUPAGE CONSERVATIONIST, THE. **2191**

0278-0933 See LIPS (MONTCLAIR, N.J.). **3465**

0278-0941 See FEDERAL TRAVEL DIRECTORY (WASHINGTON, D.C. : 1981). **5469**

0278-095X See JOURNAL OF PRIMARY PREVENTION, THE. **4787**

0278-0976 See NEW PARENT ADVISER. **2284**

0278-0984 See ADVANCES IN APPLIED MICROECONOMICS. **1460**

0278-1018 See SOVIET CHRISTIAN PRISONER LIST. **4999**

0278-1026 See WOMAN'S DAY DESSERT LOVER'S COOKBOOK. **2793**

0278-1034 See CAREER SCHOOL DIRECTORY. **4202**

0278-1042 See JOURNAL OF PROBATION AND PAROLE : THE JOURNAL OF THE NEW YORK STATE PROBATION OFFICERS ASSOCIATION. **3167**

0278-1050 See ANNUAL CONFERENCE ON FIRE RESEARCH. **2287**

0278-1069 See FROMMER'S SCANDINAVIA ON $ ... A DAY. **5477**

0278-1077 See COMPLEX VARIABLES THEORY AND APPLICATION. **3501**

0278-1174 See CATHOLIC NEW YORK. **5026**

0278-1182 See DIRECTORY OF COLLEGE SEMINARS AND SHORT COURSES IN ENGINEERING AND MANAGEMENT. **1820**

0278-1204 See CURRENT PERSPECTIVES IN SOCIAL THEORY. **5244**

0278-1247 See HMO EXECUTIVE SALARY SURVEY. **1677**

0278-1263 See PAN AM CLIPPER. **31**

0278-1301 See MUNICIPAL LITIGATION REPORTER. **3012**

0278-1328 See NATIONAL PARK STATISTICAL ABSTRACT. **2185**

0278-1352 See LEGISLATOR'S HANDBOOK (DETROIT, MICH.), THE. **4736**

0278-1360 See DAILY REPORT: LATIN AMERICA, INDEX. **1131**

0278-1379 See AMATEUR CALL BOOK, THE. **1148**

0278-1387 See SPEAKERS. **5319**

0278-1425 See PROFESSIONAL SURVEYOR. **2029**

0278-1433 See OUTSIDE (1980). **4877**

0278-1441 See ART PAPERS. **340**

0278-145X See SEMINARS IN DERMATOLOGY. **3722**

0278-1468 See OCCASIONAL PAPERS (GROUP OF THIRTY). **1638**

0278-1484 See ANNUAL REPORT - ARKANSAS-WHITE-RED BASINS INTER-AGENCY COMMITTEE. **2087**

0278-1514 See SHAREOWNERSHIP. **913**

0278-1522 See DESIGN ARTS (NEW YORK, N.Y.). **318**

0278-1557 See KNOWLEDGE AND SOCIETY, STUDIES IN THE SOCIOLOGY OF CULTURE PAST AND PRESENT. **5251**

0278-1573 See ANNUAL OBITUARY, THE. **429**

0278-1603 See WILDROWS. **2766**

0278-1611 See GRANTS FOR RESEARCH ON DESEGREGATION. **1748**

0278-1646 See EXPORT TRADE REPORTER. **834**

0278-1670 See NUREG/CR (UNITED STATES. NUCLEAR REGULATORY COMMISSION). **2158**

0278-1700 See CONTEMPORARY NEPHROLOGY. **3989**

0278-1719 See PSYCHOBIOLOGY AND PSYCHOPATHOLOGY. **4610**

0278-1727 See MICROBEAM ANALYSIS. **1012**

0278-1743 See RESEARCH SERVICES DIRECTORY. **5147**

0278-1824 See CHEMICAL SCREENING, INITIAL EVALUATIONS OF SUBSTANTIAL RISK NOTICES, SECTION 8(E). **4244**

0278-1832 See CHEMICAL ABSTRACTS. PHYSICAL, INORGANIC, AND ANALYTICAL CHEMISTRY SECTIONS. **968**

0278-1859 See STATE (WASHINGTON, D.C.). **4688**

0278-1867 See NATIONAL BASEBALL HALL OF FAME AND MUSEUM YEARBOOK. **4906**

0278-1875 See FEDERAL INCOME TAX PROCEDURES. **4724**

0278-1891 See PYNCHON NOTES. **3426**

0278-193X See WORKING MOTHER (NEW YORK, N.Y. 1981). **2287**

0278-1956 See DMA AERONAUTICAL CHART MONTHLY BULLETIN. **18**

0278-2065 See BERGER BUILDING & DESIGN COST FILE. UNIT PRICES. WESTERN EDITION, THE. **600**

0278-2073 See FINANCIAL DIRECTORY OF PENSION FUNDS. WASHINGTON, WESTERN, EXCLUDING SEATTLE AREA (TACOMA, OLYMPIA & OTHERS). **1674**

0278-2081 See FINANCIAL DIRECTORY OF PENSION FUNDS. MASSACHUSETTS, BOSTON CITY PROPER. **1671**

0278-209X See FINANCIAL DIRECTORY OF PENSION FUNDS. MASSACHUSETTS, SUBURBAN BOSTON (LYNN, FRAMINGHAM & OTHERS). **1671**

0278-2103 See FINANCIAL DIRECTORY OF PENSION FUNDS. TEXAS, NORTHWESTERN (FORT WORTH, AMARILLO, LUBBOCK, MIDLAND, EL PASO). **1674**

0278-2111 See FINANCIAL DIRECTORY OF PENSION FUNDS. WASHINGTON, WESTERN (SEATTLE AREA ONLY). **1674**

0278-212X See FINANCIAL DIRECTORY OF PENSION FUNDS. VIRGINIA, SOUTHERN (RICHMOND, NORFOLK, ROANOKE & OTHERS). **1674**

0278-2146 See BERGER BUILDING & DESIGN COST FILE. UNIT PRICES. CENTRAL EDITION, THE. **600**

0278-2154 See FINANCIAL DIRECTORY OF PENSION FUNDS. WISCONSIN, MILWAUKEE (SHEBOYGAN, WAUWATOSA, RACINE & OTHERS). **1674**

0278-2162 See FINANCIAL DIRECTORY OF PENSION FUNDS. MARYLAND, WESTERN (FREDERICK, ROCKVILLE, WALDORF & OTHERS). **1671**

0278-2170 See FINANCIAL DIRECTORY OF PENSION FUNDS. MICHIGAN, SUBURBAN DETROIT (PONTIAC, ANN ARBOR, MONROE & OTHERS). **1671**

0278-2189 See FINANCIAL DIRECTORY OF PENSION FUNDS. TEXAS, NORTH CENTRAL & EASTERN (WACO, BRYAN, CONROE, LUFKIN, TYLER, LONGVIEW, TEXARKANA). **1673**

0278-2219 See ASA NEWS (LOS ANGELES, CALIF.). **2498**

0278-2286 See MOTIF (COLUMBUS, OHIO). **2322**

0278-2308 See INTERNATIONAL SOCIAL SCIENCE REVIEW. **5204**

0278-2316 See INFECTIOUS DISEASES NEWSLETTER (NEW YORK, N.Y.). **3714**

0278-2324 See CONJUNCTIONS (NEW YORK, N.Y.). **3340**

0278-2359 See ADVANCES IN THE PSYCHOLOGY OF HUMAN INTELLIGENCE. **4572**

0278-2367 See ADVANCES IN PERSONALITY ASSESSMENT. **4572**

0278-2375 See PROCEEDINGS OF THE ... ANNUAL CONFERENCE OF THE ASSOCIATION FOR BUSINESS SIMULATION AND EXPERIENTIAL LEARNING. **704**

0278-2383 See INFORMATION AND REFERRAL. **5289**

0278-2391 See JOURNAL OF ORAL AND MAXILLOFACIAL SURGERY. **3968**

0278-2405 See FINANCIAL DIRECTORY OF PENSION FUNDS. CALIFORNIA, UPPER NORTHERN (STOCKTON, SACRAMENTO & OTHERS). **1670**

0278-2480 See MEDIGUIDE TO ONCOLOGY. **3821**

0278-2502 See FACT BOOK / NATIONAL INSTITUTE OF NEUROLOGICAL AND COMMUNICATIVE DISORDERS AND STROKE. **3833**

0278-2529 See SUBJECT INDEX OF EXTRAMURAL RESEARCH ADMINISTERED BY THE NATIONAL CANCER INSTITUTE. **3824**

0278-2618 See WASHINGTON LETTER ON LATIN AMERICA. **1526**

0278-2626 See BRAIN AND COGNITION. **4577**

0278-2650 See ECONOMY HOME PLANS FOR TODAY!. **298**

0278-2677 See CLINICAL PHARMACY. **4297**

0278-2693 See SPORTS COLLECTORS DIGEST. **4922**

0278-2715 See HEALTH AFFAIRS (MILLWOOD, VA.). **4777**

0278-2731 See INTERNATIONAL RESEARCH CENTERS DIRECTORY. **5115**

0278-2766 See RECRUIT & RETAIN. **3868**

0278-2774 See COMPUTER GRAPHICS MARKETPLACE. 1232
0278-2782 See MESSIANIC OUTREACH, THE. 5051
0278-2804 See TRANSITIONS (CINCINNATI, OHIO). 5395
0278-2839 See HOME (ORADELL, N.J.). 2900
0278-2847 See JOURNAL OF CHINESE STUDIES. 2655
0278-2863 See COMMUNITY ANIMAL CONTROL. 226
0278-2871 See NEWSLETTER OF THE AMERICAN COMMITTEE TO ADVANCE THE STUDY OF PETROGLYPHS AND PICTOGRAPHS. 242
0278-291X See PROCEEDINGS - ROCKY MOUNTAIN SYMPOSIUM ON MICROCOMPUTERS: SYSTEMS, SOFTWARE, ARCHITECTURE. 1272
0278-2960 See ALPINE SKIING COMPETITION GUIDE. ROCKY MOUNTAIN EDITION. 4882
0278-2987 See FISCAL YEAR BUDGET ESTIMATES - DEPT. OF TRANSPORTATION, OFFICE OF THE SECRETARY. 5382
0278-2995 See CONTROL OF WASTE AND WATER POLLUTION FROM POWER PLANT FLUE GAS CLEANING SYSTEMS. 2227
0278-3029 See MILITARY ASSISTANCE PROGRAM ADDRESS DIRECTORY. 4050
0278-3037 See TYPE CERTIFICATE DATA SHEETS AND SPECIFICATIONS. VOLUME VI, AIRCRAFT LISTING & AIRCRAFT ENGINE & PROPELLER LISTING. 38
0278-310X See UNIVERSITY OF MISSISSIPPI STUDIES IN ENGLISH, THE. 3449
0278-3126 See SCHOOL AGE NOTES. 1782
0278-3134 See SMITH PAPERS. 2472
0278-3193 See ROEPER REVIEW. 1885
0278-3223 See NASHVILLE AREA CHAMBER OF COMMERCE BUSINESS DIRECTORY. 696
0278-324X See CORAL REEF NEWSLETTER. 1448
0278-3258 See ELECTRONIC LEARNING. 1223
0278-3266 See SIBBALD GUIDE TO THE TEXAS TOP TWO-FIFTY, THE. 710
0278-3274 See NOVITATES ARTHROPODAE. 5593
0278-3304 See RETIREMENT PROCEEDINGS. 5181
0278-3355 See BULLETIN - NEW YORK STATE MUSEUM (1976). 4086
0278-3436 See GOSPEL WORLD. 4119
0278-3452 See HEALTH DEVICES SOURCEBOOK. 3581
0278-3479 See DEFENSE ELECTRONICS. 2040
0278-3487 See LICENSED OPERATING REACTORS, STATUS SUMMARY REPORT. 2156
0278-3509 See MOODY'S INTERNATIONAL MANUAL. 907
0278-3517 See MOODY'S INTERNATIONAL NEWS REPORTS. 907
0278-3576 See GUIDE TO U.S. TAXES FOR CITIZENS ABROAD. 4730
0278-3584 See ACADEMIC YEAR & SUMMER PROGRAMS ABROAD. 1721
0278-3649 See INTERNATIONAL JOURNAL OF ROBOTICS RESEARCH, THE. 1220
0278-3711 See PROCEEDINGS - JOINT SPE/DOE SYMPOSIUM ON ENHANCED OIL RECOVERY. 4275
0278-372X See HOW TO FIND INFORMATION ABOUT COMPANIES. 680
0278-3738 See NEUROSCIENCE NEWSLETTER. 4605
0278-3746 See CHILDREN'S BIBLE STUDIES. ELEMENTARY B. STUDENT BOOK. 5016
0278-3789 See NRCSA PROGRAM DIRECTORY. EUROPE. 1769
0278-3827 See ARTEXTREME. 341
0278-3835 See OCCASIONAL PAPER / WESTERN ASSOCIATION OF MAP LIBRARIES. 2582
0278-386X See ALASKA MINES & GEOLOGY. 1365
0278-3916 See LAW/TECHNOLOGY. 5125

0278-3924 See YESTERDAYS. 2478
0278-3932 See YOUNG WOMAN. 5572
0278-3940 See AUSTRALIAN-AMERICAN BUSINESS REVIEW, THE. 641
0278-3983 See TRENDS IN THE HOTEL INDUSTRY. INTERNATIONAL EDITION. 2809
0278-4009 See ESTATE PLANNING (LOS ANGELES, CALIF.). 3118
0278-4017 See SCIENCE AND TECHNOLOGY SERIES. 34
0278-4084 See DIRECTORY OF INTERCULTURAL EDUCATION NEWSLETTERS. 1736
0278-4092 See CONNECTICUT NURSING NEWS (1980). 3854
0278-4114 See LOOSE CHANGE. 2774
0278-4122 See COMPARABLE WORTH PROJECT NEWSLETTER. 658
0278-4157 See CARDIOLOGY TIMES. 3701
0278-4165 See JOURNAL OF ANTHROPOLOGICAL ARCHAEOLOGY. 271
0278-4203 See FAMOUS MONSTERS. 4068
0278-422X See SURVEY AND ANALYSIS OF BUSINESS CAR POLICIES & COSTS. 714
0278-4238 See TRANSLATIONS INDEX (AMERICAN SOCIETY FOR METALS). 4022
0278-4254 See JOURNAL OF ACCOUNTING AND PUBLIC POLICY. 746
0278-4297 See JOURNAL OF ULTRASOUND IN MEDICINE. 3943
0278-4319 See INTERNATIONAL JOURNAL OF HOSPITALITY MANAGEMENT. 2807
0278-4327 See PROGRESS IN RETINAL RESEARCH. 585
0278-4343 See CONTINENTAL SHELF RESEARCH. 1354
0278-4351 See QUARTERLY NEWSLETTER OF THE LABORATORY OF COMPARATIVE HUMAN COGNITION, THE. 4615
0278-436X See JAPOS BULLETIN. 2785
0278-4386 See SOURCE II, THE. 5491
0278-4394 See MOUNTAIN MESSENGER, THE. 5637
0278-4416 See POLICY STUDIES REVIEW. 4488
0278-4432 See MENDY AND THE GOLEM. 5018
0278-4467 See A.I.R. DIRECTORY OF RADIO PROGRAMMING. 1125
0278-4491 See ENVIRONMENTAL PROGRESS. 2229
0278-4513 See PLANT/OPERATIONS PROGRESS. 2015
0278-4580 See FEDERAL FAST FINDER. 4648
0278-4602 See PSYCHIATRY DIGEST (1979). 3934
0278-4653 See HEALTH (GUILFORD, CONN.). 4780
0278-4661 See HUMAN DEVELOPMENT (GUILFORD, CT.). 4589
0278-467X See TOURS AND VISITS DIRECTORY. 5494
0278-4726 See AUTOMOTIVE LITIGATION REPORTER. 2939
0278-4734 See LOUISIANA LEGAL DIRECTORY, THE. 3004
0278-4750 See PROBLEMY OSVOENIIA PUSTYN. 2202
0278-4807 See REHABILITATION NURSING. 3868
0278-4815 See SUMMARY OF PROCEEDINGS : ANNUAL MEETING OF THE SOUTHERN GOVERNORS' ASSOCIATION. 4689
0278-4823 See SCHOOL LIBRARY MEDIA QUARTERLY. 3248
0278-4831 See TELECOMMUNICATIONS (NORTH AMERICAN EDITION). 1166
0278-484X See TELECOMMUNICATIONS (GLOBAL ED.). 1165
0278-4912 See CATALOG OF PUBLICATIONS OF THE NATIONAL CENTER FOR HEALTH STATISTICS. 4809
0278-4939 See VIEWS AND ESTIMATES OF THE COMMITTEE ON FOREIGN AFFAIRS ON THE BUDGET. 3137
0278-4955 See COMPLETE HOCKEY BOOK. 4891

0278-4963 See HOUSTON CORPORATE DIRECTORY. 680
0278-4971 See NORTH CAROLINA EDUCATION DIRECTORY. 1769
0278-4998 See PEDIATRIC MENTAL HEALTH. 3909
0278-5013 See VIDEO AGE INTERNATIONAL. 1142
0278-5021 See CONSTELLATION / MIDDLE ATLANTIC PLANETARIUM SOCIETY. 394
0278-503X See CABLE TV PROGRAMMING. 1129
0278-5048 See SALES REP'S ADVISOR, THE. 885
0278-5064 See GUIDE TO FEDERAL ASSISTANCE. NEWSLETTER, THE. 4730
0278-5129 See ALCOHOL, DRUGS, AND AGING. USAGE AND PROBLEMS. 1339
0278-5137 See ANNUAL REPORT / HOWARD UNIVERSITY COLLEGE OF MEDICINE. 1809
0278-5145 See FLOW SYSTEMS NEWSLETTERS. 536
0278-5153 See HOSPITAL PHONE BOOK, THE. 3785
0278-517X See REPORT FROM THE WHITE HOUSE CONFERENCE ON AGING. 3754
0278-520X See IEEE TECHNICAL ACTIVITIES GUIDE. 2061
0278-5226 See JOURNAL OF ARBORICULTURE. 2421
0278-5234 See VITAL AND HEALTH STATISTICS. SERIES 23. DATA FROM THE NATIONAL SURVEY OF FAMILY GROWTH. 4560
0278-5277 See CRIMINAL JUSTICE CAREER DIGEST. 4203
0278-5307 See LIBERTAS MATHEMATICA. 3517
0278-5323 See HEALTH GROUPS IN WASHINGTON : A DIRECTORY. 4780
0278-5374 See PROGRAM HIGHLIGHTS. 3630
0278-5382 See PROGRESS REPORT / THE UNITED STATES-JAPAN COOPERATIVE CANCER RESEARCH PROGRAM. 3822
0278-5404 See FREIGHT SERVICE DIRECTORY. CHICAGO EDITION. 5383
0278-5420 See JOURNAL OF AGENT AND MANAGEMENT SELECTION AND DEVELOPMENT, THE. 2885
0278-5439 See INTERNATIONAL BUSINESS REPORT (NEW YORK, N.Y.). 841
0278-5447 See WATER RESOURCES DEVELOPMENT IN MINNESOTA. 5546
0278-5455 See VINYL EDITION, THE. 4158
0278-5501 See MAVERICK GUIDE TO NEW ZEALAND, THE. 5484
0278-551X See AXIOS (LOS ANGELES, CALIF.). 3338
0278-5587 See NEWSDAY. NASSAU EDITION. 5719
0278-565X See POCKETS. 1068
0278-5684 See DIRECTORY OF LIBRARIES AND INFORMATION SOURCES IN THE PHILADELPHIA AREA. 3207
0278-5706 See JOB CATALOG, THE. 4205
0278-5722 See PLUMBING-HEATING-COOLING CATALOG : PHC. 2607
0278-5730 See ANNUAL REPORT / U.S. DEPARTMENT OF EDUCATION. 1725
0278-5749 See TRAINING AND DEVELOPMENT ORGANIZATIONS DIRECTORY. 888
0278-5757 See WHO'S WHO IN THE INTERNATIONAL PERSONNEL MANAGEMENT ASSOCIATION. 948
0278-5781 See WATER RESOURCES DEVELOPMENT IN MICHIGAN (1981). 5546
0278-579X See FINANCIAL DIRECTORY OF PENSION FUNDS. NEW JERSEY, NORTHERN, NEWARK AND ENVIRONS (NEWARK, PASSAIC, JERSEY CITY & OTHERS). 1672
0278-5803 See VETERANS READJUSTMENT APPOINTMENTS IN THE FEDERAL GOVERNMENT. 4705
0278-5811 See OUT HEALTH. 4795
0278-5846 See PROGRESS IN NEURO-PSYCHOPHARMACOLOGY & BIOLOGICAL PSYCHIATRY. 4326

0278-5889 See OFFICIAL DIRECTORY OF DATA PROCESSING, COMPUTER USERS WESTERN USA. 1261

0278-5900 See INDEX (TULSA, OKLA.), THE. 4900

0278-5919 See CLINICS IN SPORTS MEDICINE. 3953

0278-5927 See JOURNAL OF AMERICAN ETHNIC HISTORY. 2265

0278-5943 See AMERICAN CLASSICAL STUDIES. 1073

0278-5951 See ANNUAL ENERGY BALANCE (U.S.). 1931

0278-596X See RIDERANNUAL. 4082

0278-5986 See PROCEEDINGS - NORTH AMERICAN MOTOR VEHICLE EMISSIONS CONTROL CONFERENCE. 2239

0278-5994 See DIESEL & GAS TURBINE WORLDWIDE. 2112

0278-6001 See FINANCIAL DIRECTORY OF PENSION FUNDS. NEW JERSEY, NORTHERN, EXCLUDING NEWARK AND ENVIRONS (HACKENSACK, PATTERSON, SUMMIT & OTHERS). 1672

0278-601X See SERI JOURNAL. 1956

0278-6036 See NASHVILLE CITY GUIDE. 2747

0278-6087 See JOURNAL OF BUSINESS FORECASTING METHODS & SYSTEMS, THE. 1592

0278-6117 See SULFUR LETTERS. 1038

0278-6125 See JOURNAL OF MANUFACTURING SYSTEMS. 3482

0278-6133 See HEALTH PSYCHOLOGY. 4588

0278-615X See RULE BOOK - MIDWEST 4 WHEEL DRIVE ASSOCIATION. 4915

0278-6168 See REPORT / NATIONAL COUNCIL ON FAMILY RELATIONS. 2285

0278-6192 See MARKET GUIDE, LATIN AMERICA. 1574

0278-6206 See TECHNICAL PROCEEDINGS / ANNUAL CONFERENCE AND INTERNATIONAL TRADE FAIR OF THE NATIONAL WATER SUPPLY IMPROVEMENT ASSOCIATION. 5540

0278-6273 See LASER CHEMISTRY. 984

0278-6281 See LIFE CHEMISTRY REPORTS. 490

0278-6303 See WLN PARTICIPANT. 3256

0278-632X See KIDSTUFF. 1065

0278-6346 See TRENDS--CONSUMER ATTITUDES AND THE SUPERMARKET ... UPDATE. 2360

0278-6354 See REPORT / NATIONAL COUNCIL ON HEALTH CARE TECHNOLOGY. 3633

0278-6389 See OFFICIAL EXPORT GUIDE. 848

0278-6397 See RERUNS. 1138

0278-6400 See TEXTBOOK SERIES / AMERICAN PHILOLOGICAL ASSOCIATION. 3328

0278-6419 See VESTNIK MOSKOVSKOGO UNIVERSITETA. SERIIA XV, VYCHISLITELNAIA MATEMATIKA I KIBERNETIKA. ENGLISH. 1252

0278-6435 See UNDERSTANDING HEALTH. 4805

0278-6443 See TRADE SHOW & CONVENTION GUIDE. 767

0278-6478 See WHO'S WHO AMONG AMERICAN LAW STUDENTS. 3075

0278-6486 See PRINCIPLES AND PRESENTATION. RETAILING. 956

0278-6516 See WHO'S WHO IN THE MOTION PICTURE INDUSTRY. 438

0278-6524 See MARKET GUIDE (NEW YORK, N.Y.). 797

0278-6559 See OFFICIAL DIRECTORY / U.S. ARMY CORPS OF ENGINEERS. 4053

0278-6575 See EDUCATION AT ISSUE. 1862

0278-6605 See AFRICAN NEWSPAPER INDEX, THE. 5685

0278-6613 See MAVERICK GUIDE TO HAWAII, THE. 5484

0278-663X See TERRORISM (MINNEAPOLIS, MINN.). 3177

0278-6648 See IEEE POTENTIALS. 2060

0278-6656 See CLASSICAL ANTIQUITY. 1075

0278-6680 See INTERNATIONAL COUNTRY RISK GUIDE. 901

0278-6729 See SPRINGER SERIES ON BEHAVIOR THERAPY AND BEHAVIORAL MEDICINE. 4619

0278-6826 See AEROSOL SCIENCE AND TECHNOLOGY. 1020

0278-6834 See NATIONAL INSTITUTES OF HEALTH RESEARCH PLAN. 4792

0278-6850 See PHARMALERT (BALTIMORE, MD.). 4324

0278-6877 See MENTAL HEALTH SERVICE SYSTEM REPORTS. SERIES CN, MENTAL HEALTH NATIONAL STATISTICS. 4810

0278-6915 See FOOD AND CHEMICAL TOXICOLOGY. 3980

0278-6923 See NETWORK NEWS (STANFORD, CALIF.). 1118

0278-694X See STATISTICAL REFERENCE INDEX ... ANNUAL. 5340

0278-6990 See AMERICAN FRESHMAN: NATIONAL NORMS, THE. 1808

0278-7016 See RAISE THE STAKES. 2491

0278-7040 See AMERICAN POWER BOAT ASSOCIATION ROSTER. 591

0278-7059 See NURSING HOMES IN WASHINGTON STATE. 3790

0278-7067 See WELDING & FABRICATING DATA BOOK. 4028

0278-7091 See GEOSCIENCE TEXTS. 1356

0278-7156 See VETERANOTES. 4060

0278-7202 See INDIAN TIMES. 5643

0278-7210 See CHILDREN'S LEGAL RIGHTS JOURNAL. 3120

0278-7245 See BAKING IDEAS. 2788

0278-7253 See URBAN TRANSPORTATION OFFICIALS. 5399

0278-7261 See CRITICA HISPANICA. 3275

0278-7318 See HEALTH SCIENCES AUDIOVISUALS. 4781

0278-7350 See SAMUEL BUTLER NEWSLETTER, THE. 3433

0278-7393 See JOURNAL OF EXPERIMENTAL PSYCHOLOGY. LEARNING, MEMORY, AND COGNITION [MICROFORM]. 4597

0278-7393 See JOURNAL OF EXPERIMENTAL PSYCHOLOGY. LEARNING, MEMORY, AND COGNITION. 4597

0278-7407 See TECTONICS (WASHINGTON, D.C.). 1411

0278-7415 See BETTER HOMES AND GARDENS CREATIVE IDEAS. 370

0278-7431 See WESTERN PENNSYLVANIA GENEALOGICAL SOCIETY QUARTERLY. 2477

0278-744X See YOUR FAMILY PET. 4288

0278-7466 See SWEATERS AND AFGHANS. 5186

0278-7474 See DO-IT-YOURSELF PROJECTS. 372

0278-7490 See HOLIDAY CRAFTS. 373

0278-7504 See 100'S OF NEEDLEWORK & CRAFT IDEAS. 5182

0278-7571 See REPORT OF THE COMMISSIONER OF BANKS OF DEBT PRORATE COMPANIES LICENSED UNDER MINNESOTA STATUTES, CHAPTER 332. 807

0278-761X See MINNESOTA FAMILY LAW JOURNAL. 3122

0278-7628 See MINNESOTA REAL ESTATE LAW JOURNAL. 3010

0278-7636 See NEBRASKA WORKMEN'S COMPENSATION REHEARING DECISIONS. 3152

0278-7644 See BANK INSURANCE SURVEY. 2875

0278-7652 See WASHBURN UNIVERSITY SCHOOL OF LAW ALUMNI DIRECTORY. 1103

0278-7660 See VISTAS (MERION, PA.). 367

0278-7679 See RIDNA SHKOLA (NEW YORK, N.Y.). 1781

0278-7687 See YEATS ANNUAL (LONDON, ENGLAND). 3455

0278-7695 See DECISIONS OF THE FEDERAL LABOR RELATIONS AUTHORITY. 3146

0278-7784 See RELIGIOUS SOCIALISM. 4992

0278-7806 See NEWSLETTER OF THE HAWK MIGRATION ASSOCIATION OF NORTH AMERICA, THE. 5592

0278-7970 See DENVER WESTERNERS ROUNDUP, THE. 2730

0278-7989 See LATIN MUSIC YEARBOOK, THE. 4128

0278-8039 See EMPLOYEE EMPLOYER FEDERAL EMPLOYMENT TAX GUIDE. 3146

0278-8047 See WORLD TECHNOLOGY PATENT LICENSING GAZETTE. 1310

0278-8071 See BLUE GRASS ROOTS. 2439

0278-808X See MEDICAL DEVISE REGISTER. 3788

0278-8101 See KOSMOS (TORRANCE, CALIF.). 390

0278-8128 See AMERICAN ILLUSTRATION SHOWCASE. 376

0278-8187 See CHRISTIANITY & CIVILIZATION. 4946

0278-8209 See PATIENT EDUCATION NEWSLETTER. 4795

0278-8225 See MAINSTREAM (SAN DIEGO, CALIF.). 4391

0278-8314 See AMERICAN PHOTOGRAPHY SHOWCASE. 4366

0278-8330 See 100S OF IDEAS. 369

0278-8365 See CHRONOLOGIES OF MAJOR DEVELOPMENTS IN SELECTED AREAS OF FOREIGN AFFAIRS (CUMULATIVE EDITION). 4518

0278-8373 See LANDSCAPE ARCHITECTURE. HOME LANDSCAPE. 2423

0278-8381 See ECONOMIC INDICATORS (CHARLESTON, W. VA.). 1557

0278-8403 See BEHAVIOR THERAPIST, THE. 4576

0278-842X See WHO'S WHO IN SPECIAL LIBRARIES. 437

0278-8683 See AMERICAN SHOWCASE OF ILLUSTRATION AND PHOTOGRAPHY. 4366

0278-8748 See OCEANOGRAPHIC DATA EXCHANGE. 1454

0278-8772 See SAUDI REPORT. 2663

0278-8780 See EASTERN KENTUCKY UNIVERSITY ALUMNI DIRECTORY. 1102

0278-8799 See DUN'S INDUSTRIAL GUIDE, THE METALWORKING DIRECTORY. 4001

0278-8802 See PROCEEDINGS OF THE ... ANNUAL DREDGING SEMINAR. 2094

0278-8810 See BEAUTIFUL HOME PLANS. 293

0278-8829 See DIRECTORY / AMERICAN SOCIETY OF JOURNALISTS AND AUTHORS. 2919

0278-8845 See ALUMNI DIRECTORY - WEST GEORGIA COLLEGE. 1100

0278-8861 See FRIENDS OF FINANCIAL HISTORY. 899

0278-887X See ALUMNI DIRECTORY (AMHERST, MASS.). 1097

0278-8896 See BONDWEEK. 892

0278-8926 See HOW, WHEN, & WHERE IN TENNESSEE. 2535

0278-8942 See FLASHMAPS INSTANT GUIDE TO DALLAS, FORT WORTH. 2560

0278-8950 See LIGHT PLANE MAINTENANCE. 27

0278-8969 See AFRO-HISPANIC REVIEW. 3262

0278-8985 See ENGINEERING AND TECHNOLOGY ENROLLMENTS. 1972

0278-9000 See DIRECTORY - AMERICAN ACADEMY OF DERMATOLOGY. 3720

0278-9035 See FARM MACHINERY AND LAWN AND GARDEN EQUIPMENT. 159

0278-9051 See MUSIC CIRCULAR. 4133

0278-9078 See ETHNIC FORUM. 2260

0278-9108 See PPG INDUSTRIES FOUNDATION : REPORT. 5301

0278-9124 See GEORGE D. HALL'S NEW JERSEY MANUFACTURERS DIRECTORY. 3479

0278-9132 See GLOBAL ATMOSPHERIC BACKGROUND MONITORING FOR SELECTED ENVIRONMENTAL PARAMETERS BAPMON DATA FOR 2172

0278-9140 See LOCAL CLIMATOLOGICAL DATA. JACKSON, KENTUCKY, ANNUAL SUMMARY WITH COMPARATIVE DATA. 1428

0278-9175 See COMPUTING TEACHER, THE. 1222

0278-9213 See CROSS COUNTRY SKIER. 4892

0278-9221 See ANNOTATED BIBLIOGRAPHY OF STATISTICAL METHODOLOGY. 5321

0278-9299 See ROCKY MOUNTAIN PETROLEUM DIRECTORY. 4277

0278-9302 See INTERNAL COMBUSTION ENGINES. 2116

0278-9329 See NEW MEXICO LIBRARY STATISTICS. 3259

0278-9337 See INSULATED WIRE AND CABLE. 1612

0278-9345 See USDC APPROVED LIST OF FISH ESTABLISHMENTS AND PRODUCTS. 2315

0278-937X See WASHINGTON PAPERS, THE. 919

0278-9396 See PROCEEDINGS OF THE ... ANNUAL MEETING / INTERNATIONAL OMEGA ASSOCIATION. 4181

0278-940X See CRITICAL REVIEWS IN BIOMEDICAL ENGINEERING. 3691

0278-9418 See MOTOR AGE MECHANICS NEWSLETTER. 5419

0278-9426 See JOURNAL / GLASS ART SOCIETY. 2591

0278-9434 See TRANSPORTATION QUARTERLY. 5397

0278-9450 See MAINLINES (INDIANAPOLIS, IND.). 3861

0278-9469 See PALINET NEWS. 3240

0278-9507 See AMERICAN CERAMICS. 2586

0278-9566 See BI-ANNUAL REVIEW OF ALLERGY. 3667

0278-9612 See WRESTLING'S MAIN EVENT. 4931

0278-9620 See SCIENCE AND ENGINEERING PERSONNEL. 5150

0278-9639 See AIRWAVES. 1125

0278-9647 See COMPUTER TECHNOLOGY REVIEW. 1246

0278-9655 See MAPS AND PUBLICATIONS ... PRICE LIST. 2582

0278-9663 See DIRECTORY OF WORD PROCESSING MANAGEMENT. 1292

0278-9671 See LITERATURE AND MEDICINE. 3605

0278-9744 See UNIVERSITY OF KANSAS PALEONTOLOGICAL CONTRIBUTIONS. MONOGRAPHS. 4231

0278-9752 See BORGO POLITICAL SCENARIOS. 4465

0278-9779 See MEDICO INTERAMERICANO. 3614

0278-9795 See RUG NEWS. 5355

0278-9809 See IT'S GOD'S WORLD. 4966

0278-9817 See LAWYER'S ALERT. 2998

0278-9884 See OFFICIAL PENCIL PUZZLES & WORD GAMES. 4864

0278-9922 See ELECTRONIC SERVICING & TECHNOLOGY. 2048

0278-9930 See TEXAS FIREMEN. 2293

0278-9957 See RAH-I ZINDAGI. 2508

0278-9973 See BROWNS NEWS/ILLUSTRATED. 4888

0279-0025 See OSU QUEST. 1839

0279-0033 See PENNSYLVANIA JOURNAL OF HEALTH, PHYSICAL EDUCATION, RECREATION, DANCE. 1902

0279-0041 See AMERICAN PREMIERE. 4063

0279-0106 See ARBOR AGE. 2375

0279-0165 See BULLETIN - WORKERS LEAGUE (U.S.). CENTRAL COMMITTEE. 4540

0279-0238 See GIANTS NEWSWEEKLY, THE. 4896

0279-0246 See CALIFORNIA EYE, THE. 4466

0279-0254 See OPEN WHEEL. 4911

0279-0270 See AAA WORLD. POTOMAC. 5459

0279-0297 See FLORIDA PLANNING (TALLAHASSEE, FLA. : 1981). 2823

0279-0300 See RENEWAL (WINCHESTER, VA.). 4493

0279-0394 See MONTANA CROP & LIVESTOCK REPORTER. 178

0279-0408 See IMPRINT (HILLSDALE, N.J.). 4589

0279-0459 See RELIGIOUS LIFE (CHICAGO, ILL.). 4992

0279-0467 See LABOR & INVESTMENTS. 1683

0279-0483 See ORANGE COAST. 2542

0279-0491 See ILLINOIS VOCATIONAL EDUCATION JOURNAL. 1913

0279-053X See TABLOID (FAIRFAX, VA.), THE. 4569

0279-0548 See SERVICES (VIENNA, VA.). 4214

0279-0580 See WEST VIRGINIA HILLS & STREAMS. 2208

0279-0602 See WESTERN PLANNER, THE. 4695

0279-0610 See STRIPED BASS MAGAZINE. 2314

0279-0645 See CATHOLIC VOICE (OAKLAND, CALIF.), THE. 5027

0279-067X See ESSEX GENEALOGIST, THE. 2446

0279-070X See COMPUTERS AND PROGRAMMING. 1279

0279-0718 See BLACK FAMILY. 2256

0279-0750 See PACIFIC PHILOSOPHICAL QUARTERLY. 4354

0279-0858 See CLAVIER'S PIANO EXPLORER. 4110

0279-0874 See OREGON AGRI-FACTS. 117

0279-0882 See RHODE ISLAND LAWYERS WEEKLY. 3044

0279-0939 See COMMODEX. 829

0279-0971 See MOVING HOUSE AND HOME (NEW YORK, N.Y.). 5387

0279-1005 See OFFICIAL DECISIONS, OPINIONS AND RELATED MATTERS OF THE PUBLIC EMPLOYMENT RELATIONS BOARD OF THE STATE OF NEW YORK. 3021

0279-1021 See CPA MARKETING REPORT. 922

0279-103X See OBJECTOR (SAN FRANCISCO, CALIF.). 3183

0279-1072 See JOURNAL OF PSYCHOACTIVE DRUGS. 1346

0279-1102 See CONSTRUCTION LITIGATION REPORTER. 2956

0279-1110 See FDC REPORTS. TOILETRIES, FRAGRANCES AND SKIN CARE. 404

0279-1137 See NEWSLETTER (SPINAL CORD SOCIETY (U.S.)). 3843

0279-1153 See COLLEGE AND JUNIOR TENNIS. 4890

0279-1161 See CALIFORNIA ENGLISH. 3371

0279-1196 See COMMUNICARE. 4949

0279-1226 See AVENUE (NEW YORK, N.Y.). 2528

0279-1234 See GREEK ACCENT. 2689

0279-1277 See MEDIA GENERAL MARKET DATAGRAPHICS. 906

0279-1293 See SRPSKA BORBA. 2273

0279-1323 See ORLANDO MAGAZINE. 2542

0279-1382 See EXECUTIVE REPORT (PITTSBURGH, PA.). 674

0279-1412 See AGRICULTURE IN IDAHO. 54

0279-1447 See ROBB REPORT, THE. 2492

0279-1498 See FROZEN FOOD EXECUTIVE, THE. 2341

0279-1579 See UNISPHERE. 1249

0279-1633 See LAND (MANKATO, MINN.), THE. 103

0279-165X See TEXAS FARMER STOCKMAN. 141

0279-1749 See SPORTSMAN PILOT (HALES CORNERS, WIS.). 36

0279-1773 See MICHIGAN RUNNER, THE. 4904

0279-182X See YISRAEL SELLANU. 2770

0279-1862 See COASTLINES (SANTA BARBARA, CALIF.). 1101

0279-1889 See BOTTOM LINE (CHARLESTON, S.C.), THE. 739

0279-1943 See ROUSTABOUT, THE. 1956

0279-1978 See WOMENS CIRCLE CROCHET. 5186

0279-2028 See SKILL (DETROIT, MICH.). 1710

0279-2109 See TAX IDEAS. 4753

0279-2133 See STATEWAYS. 852

0279-2184 See SUPER FORD MAGAZINE. 5426

0279-2249 See SOUTH COAST SPORTFISHING. 4854

0279-2257 See JUVENILE AND FAMILY LAW DIGEST. 3121

0279-2273 See INSIDE THE AUBURN TIGERS (AUBURN, ALA.). 4900

0279-2311 See WESTERN RETAILER NEWS. 958

0279-2338 See SAVING ENERGY. 1956

0279-2370 See METRO TIMES (DETROIT, MICH.), THE. 5692

0279-2435 See GW TIMES. 1827

0279-2443 See TEXAS WOMAN (FORT WORTH, TEX.). 5567

0279-2451 See SOONER JAYCEE. 5236

0279-246X See EPIC ILLUSTRATED. 4860

0279-2486 See SOUTH TEXAS AGRINEWS. 136

0279-2540 See VANDERBILT TODAY. 1096

0279-2583 See WISCONSIN REALTOR, THE. 4848

0279-2613 See CALIFORNIA VEGETABLE REVIEW. 71

0279-2621 See CALIFORNIA LIVESTOCK REVIEW. 208

0279-263X See CALIFORNIA FRUIT & NUT REVIEW. 71

0279-2648 See CALIFORNIA FIELD CROP REVIEW. 166

0279-2664 See INTERACT (LOS ALTOS, CALIF.). 1260

0279-2737 See ON TRACK (SANTA ANA, CALIF.). 4911

0279-2869 See ETHICS IN GOVERNMENT REPORTER. 2250

0279-2893 See NSM REPORT. 934

0279-2958 See DESARROLLO NACIONAL. 5099

0279-3083 See NATIONAL MOTORIST. 5485

0279-3105 See FOOD MERCHANDISING FOR NON-FOOD RETAILERS. 2338

0279-313X See CLARIDAD (SANTURCE, P.R.). 3376

0279-3148 See STAPLREVIEW. 188

0279-3172 See IN OTHER WORDS. 5017

0279-3229 See ZONTIAN. 5572

0279-3261 See MISSOURI ENTERPRISE. 2539

0279-3326 See JOURNAL / COLORADO EDUCATION ASSOCIATION. 1755

0279-3415 See B'NAI B'RITH INTERNATIONAL JEWISH MONTHLY, THE. 5046

0279-3490 See MARYLAND CLUB WOMAN, THE. 5561

0279-3504 See OHIO. 2541

0279-3547 See HEALTH (SAN FRANCISCO, CALIF.). 4781

0279-3555 See AMERICAN CITIZEN, THE. 2527

0279-3628 See WESTERNER, THE. 1096

0279-3652 See COMBONI MISSIONS. 4949

0279-3695 See JOURNAL OF PSYCHOSOCIAL NURSING AND MENTAL HEALTH SERVICES. 3860

0279-3741 See MILWAUKEE LABOR PRESS. 1690

0279-3857 See GEORGIA BUSINESS AND ECONOMIC CONDITIONS. 677

0279-389X See COLORADO POTATO GROWER. 167

0279-3911 See MESSENGER, THE. 2538

0279-3962 See NEW TIMES (PHOENIX, ARIZ.). 5630

0279-3997 See HOUSTON BAR BULLETIN. 2979

0279-4039 See DYNAMIC BUSINESS : A PUBLICATION OF THE SMALLER MANUFACTURER'S COUNCIL. 670

0279-4063 See CALIFORNIA LAWYER. 2946

0279-4071 See CONTRACTING BUSINESS. 2604

0279-408X See DIRECTIONS AT RIDER COLLEGE. 1101

0279-4098 See DEVELOPMENTAL DISABILITIES SPECIAL INTEREST SECTION NEWSLETTER. 1877

0279-4101 See GERONTOLOGY SPECIAL INTEREST SECTION NEWSLETTER. 3752

0279-411X See PHYSICAL DISABILITIES SPECIAL INTEREST SECTION NEWSLETTER. 1883

0279-4128 See SENSORY INTEGRATION SPECIAL INTEREST SECTION NEWSLETTER. 1885
0279-4136 See MENTAL HEALTH SPECIAL INTEREST SECTION NEWSLETTER. 4790
0279-4144 See DOG SPORTS. 4286
0279-4152 See LO-POWER COMMUNITY TV. 1134
0279-4160 See ACQUISITION/DIVESTITURE WEEKLY REPORT. 636
0279-4195 See DAILY COMMERCE. 830
0279-4209 See PENNYSAVER SHOPPING GUIDE. 1298
0279-4217 See CORN GROWER. 168
0279-425X See USED CAR DEALER, THE. 5427
0279-4276 See BUSINESS, NORTH CAROLINA. 651
0279-4322 See ULTRA (HOUSTON, TEX.). 2548
0279-4357 See NATIONAL ENERGY JOURNAL, THE. 1950
0279-4438 See FACILITIES DESIGN & MANAGEMENT. 2900
0279-4446 See TAX HOTLINE. 4753
0279-4462 See LUTHERAN PERSPECTIVE. 5063
0279-4489 See COURIER (LEXINGTON, KY.). 5467
0279-4519 See REVISTA AEREA. 33
0279-4527 See NEW ORLEANS CITIBUSINESS. 698
0279-4535 See NEVADA BAPTIST, THE. 4980
0279-4543 See MARKET NEWS. LIVESTOCK, MEAT, GRAIN AND SEED DIVISION. 107
0279-4551 See CALIFORNIA HONEY REPORT. 71
0279-456X See EXPORTADOR, EL. 835
0279-4616 See ROOFER MAGAZINE, THE. 3487
0279-4659 See WINDRIDER. 4929
0279-4691 See FEDERAL BAR NEWS & JOURNAL. 2969
0279-473X See DECA DIMENSIONS. 1912
0279-4799 See HOSPITAL PURCHASING NEWS. 3785
0279-4802 See MEDICAL PRODUCTS SALES. 3611
0279-4829 See SURGICAL PRODUCT NEWS. 3684
0279-4853 See ENDLESS VACATION - RESORT CONDOMINIUMS INTERNATIONAL, THE. 5469
0279-4888 See DALLAS APPAREL NEWS. 1083
0279-490X See AMERICAN BABY'S CHILDBIRTH EDUCATOR. 3756
0279-4918 See DRAPERIES & WINDOW COVERINGS. 2905
0279-4969 See COLTSFOOT. 507
0279-4977 See METROPOLIS (NEW YORK, N.Y.). 358
0279-4985 See MINIATURE HORSE JOURNAL, THE. 2801
0279-5078 See KANSAS ENVIRONMENT. 2235
0279-5086 See GUN DOG. 4873
0279-5124 See IRONTON TRIBUNE, THE. 5728
0279-5167 See ADVOCATE (STAMFORD, CONN.), THE. 5644
0279-5175 See ALABAMA PEACE OFFICERS' JOURNAL. 3156
0279-5183 See ARIZONA STATESMAN OUTLOOK. 1101
0279-5272 See PHARMACY STUDENT, THE. 4323
0279-5299 See CORPORATE REPORT MINNESOTA. 662
0279-5310 See CHRISTIAN FAMILY (BLOWNTVILLE, TEX.). 4945
0279-5337 See WESTERN CITY (SACRAMENTO, CALIF. : 1976). 4694
0279-5345 See MISSIONS USA. 5064
0279-5388 See KENTUCKY JOURNAL OF COMMERCE AND INDUSTRY, THE. 843
0279-5442 See CRITICAL CARE NURSE. 3854
0279-5507 See NRA NEWSLETTER (ALEXANDRIA, VA.). 4381
0279-5566 See CONTRACTORS HOT LINE EQUIPMENT ESTIMATOR. 611
0279-5604 See WHOLE LIFE TIMES. 4200
0279-5639 See HEALTH FACT NEWS. 2598
0279-5647 See ORTHOPEDICS TODAY. 3884
0279-568X See DIALOGUE (MUNROE FALLS, OHIO). 319
0279-5701 See SYNC. 1272
0279-571X See VIDEO BUSINESS. 4377
0279-5779 See AAA TRAVELER. MUSKINGUM AAA EDITION, THE. 5403
0279-5957 See RURAL SOCIOLOGIST, THE. 5257
0279-5965 See REGARDIE'S. 4846
0279-6015 See SCHOOL PSYCHOLOGY REVIEW. 4618
0279-6023 See VIRGINIA LIFELINE. 3650
0279-6058 See FORMAT (MINNETONKA, MINN.). 759
0279-6090 See ROD SERLING'S THE TWILIGHT ZONE MAGAZINE. 3431
0279-6198 See WATCH & CLOCK REVIEW. 2916
0279-6201 See AMERICA UKRAINIAN CATHOLIC DAILY. 2254
0279-621X See ENERGY UNLIMITED. 1942
0279-6244 See UNDER WESTERN SKIES. 4079
0279-6309 See REALTOR NEWS. 4846
0279-6325 See OIL IN CALIFORNIA. 4269
0279-6376 See ARIZONA LIVING. 2528
0279-6384 See NEW DRIVER (HIGHLAND PARK, ILL.). 5421
0279-6422 See JOURNAL OF THE ILLINOIS OPTOMETRIC ASSOCIATION. 4216
0279-6449 See CALIFORNIA CAL-LIOPE. 1658
0279-6511 See IT'S ME. 1085
0279-6562 See PHONOLOG REPORTS. 4146
0279-6570 See PHARMACEUTICAL EXECUTIVE. 4320
0279-6589 See GAMBIT (NEW ORLEANS, LA.). 5684
0279-6651 See YOUTH (PASADENA, CALIF.). 1072
0279-666X See AGSCENE. 57
0279-6783 See ALABAMA GAME & FISH. 4868
0279-6848 See DRAGON (LAKE GENEVA, WIS.). 4860
0279-6856 See FRIENDLY EXCHANGE. 5474
0279-6929 See AJL NEWSLINE. 5271
0279-6945 See CAA MAGAZINE. 4889
0279-7011 See SCOTTISH RITE JOURNAL. 5236
0279-7038 See PENTECOSTAL MINISTER, THE. 4986
0279-7046 See TAX PREPARERS LIABILITY SERVICE. 3062
0279-7070 See BEVERAGE MARKET, THE. 2364
0279-7097 See ADVOCATE (MUNCIE, IND.), THE. 5228
0279-7119 See AERO INDEX. 4
0279-7208 See WRITING (HIGHLAND PARK, ILL.). 1792
0279-7216 See ANCLA (EL PASO, TEX.). 4934
0279-7712 See OKLAHOMA FARM STATISTICS. 155
0279-7720 See RDH. 1334
0279-7739 See NATIONAL DRILLERS BUYERS GUIDE. 5536
0279-7771 See INDUSTRIA PORCINA. 213
0279-7801 See OIL PRICE INFORMATION SERVICE. 4270
0279-7828 See PARISH COMMUNICATION. 4985
0279-7844 See NEW YORK APPAREL NEWS. 1086
0279-7895 See MARYLAND FARMER (BALTIMORE, MD. : 1979). 107
0279-7933 See BANTHA TRACKS. 5229
0279-795X See WASHINGTON COUNTY NEWS (CHIPLEY, FLA.). 5651
0279-7968 See AMERICAN AERONAUT. 1643
0279-7976 See JOURNAL OF PARENTERAL SCIENCE AND TECHNOLOGY. 4311
0279-7984 See JAX FAX TRAVEL MARKETING MAGAZINE. 5481
0279-800X See BULLETIN - NORTH DAKOTA LEAGUE OF CITIES. 4634
0279-8042 See RESTORER (ROWLETT, TEX.), THE. 4993
0279-8069 See BIBLE NEWSLETTER, THE. 5014
0279-8077 See DX BULLETIN, THE. 1154
0279-8107 See OUTDOOR RETAILER. 956
0279-8158 See BULLETIN / AMERICAN SUNBATHING ASSOCIATION, THE. 4849
0279-8166 See PENNSYLVANIA LAW JOURNAL-REPORTER. 3025
0279-8182 See BIBLICAL RECORDER. 5057
0279-8190 See OREGON BUSINESS. 701
0279-8204 See COW COUNTRY. 209
0279-8247 See GOURMET'S NOTEBOOK, A. 2342
0279-8271 See DAREDEVIL. 4859
0279-8360 See CFA CALIFORNIA PROFESSOR. 1890
0279-8425 See ARABIAN HORSE TIMES, THE. 2797
0279-8433 See LIVING ORTHODOXY. 5039
0279-8468 See DESTINATIONS. 5381
0279-8476 See VETTE VUES MAGAZINE. 5427
0279-8549 See SEAFOOD LEADER. 2313
0279-8557 See NEW JERSEY EDUCATION LAW REPORT, THE. 3015
0279-8611 See NEW YORK HOLSTEIN NEWS. 216
0279-8689 See ACTION NOW (SAN JUAN CAPISTRANO, CALIF.). 4848
0279-8700 See OUTDOOR HIGHLIGHTS. 4876
0279-8778 See NEW YORK STATE JOURNAL OF PHARMACY, THE. 4318
0279-8816 See KART-TECH. 4903
0279-8840 See FOCAL POINT (ENGLEWOOD, COLO.). 5060
0279-8867 See COUNTY VIEWPOINT. 4641
0279-8875 See TEXAS SPORTSMAN. 4879
0279-8913 See NATIONAL CHRISTIAN REPORTER, THE. 4980
0279-8964 See IDAHO MOUNTAIN EXPRESS. 5656
0279-8999 See MEN'S AD REVIEW. 762
0279-9006 See AUSTIN INSURANCE REPORT. ADMINISTRATIVE EDITION. 2874
0279-9014 See AG UPDATE /. 191
0279-9065 See OUTDOOR NEWS (OKLAHOMA CITY, OKLA.). 2201
0279-9111 See BOND (MINNEAPOLIS, MINN.). 5057
0279-9200 See SHEEP MAGAZINE. 221
0279-9278 See PLACE IN THE COUNTRY, A. 2830
0279-9308 See FLYING SAFETY (1981). 21
0279-9316 See ASME NEWS (1981). 2110
0279-9324 See YOUR HEALTH & FITNESS. 4808
0279-9340 See MEDICAL TRIBUNE. MICROFORM. 3612
0279-9340 See MEDICAL TRIBUNE (1980). 3612
0279-9405 See CROPS (TOPEKA, KAN.). 169
0279-9413 See REPORTS OF MASSACHUSETTS APPELLATE DIVISION (MONTHLY). 3039
0279-9472 See AMERICAN HIKER. 4868
0279-9529 See OBSERVER (PHILADELPHIA, PA.). 3623
0279-9553 See AMERICAN SAILOR. 591
0279-960X See MARPLE'S BUSINESS NEWSLETTER. 692
0279-9618 See ILLINOIS FOODSERVICE NEWS. 5071
0279-9626 See COUNTY BAR UPDATE. 2957
0279-9634 See OHIO RUNNER, THE. 4910
0279-9642 See ATPCO CARGO TARIFF SET. 12
0279-9707 See WHAT'S BREWING?. 4929
0279-9731 See TAXIDERMY TODAY. 2778
0279-9758 See CHUGAN KWANGGO. 5634
0279-9766 See STATEN ISLAND MAGAZINE. 2547
0279-9804 See APUNTES (DALLAS, TEX.). 4935
0279-9812 See NATIONAL WOODLANDS. 2388
0279-9839 See FOOD PEOPLE AND THEIR COMPANIES. 2338
0279-9847 See CREATIVE COOK'S DIGEST, THE. 2789

0279-9863 See INFOAAU. 2598
0279-9871 See POULTRY AND EGG MARKET NEWS REVIEW. 218
0279-9960 See KANSAS REALTOR. 4840
0279-9979 See TENNIS LIFE. 4925
0280-1418 See VALFARDS BULLETINEN / SCB. 5313
0280-1892 See RESULTS (FORSKNINGSSTIFTELSEN SKOGSARBETEN). 2394
0280-2414 See ABRAKADABRA. 3357
0280-2686 See ARSBOK / ARKITEKTURMUSEET. 292
0280-2791 See SCANDINAVIAN JOURNAL OF DEVELOPMENT ALTERNATIVES. 4535
0280-4026 See PUBLIKATION / CHALMERS TEKNISKA HOGSKOLA, GOTEBORG, INSTITUTIONEN FOR VATTENFORSORJNINGS- OCH AVLOPPSTEKNIK. 2240
0280-4123 See OMVARDAREN. 3866
0280-4158 See ARBETSRAPPORT / SVERIGES LANTBRUKSUNIVERSITET, INSTITUTIONEN FOR SKOGSEKONOMI. 2375
0280-4344 See SWEDISH EXPORT DIRECTORY. 852
0280-4549 See STAD OCH LAND. 2432
0280-4638 See HJARTA, KARL, LUNGOR. 3949
0280-526X See WORKING PAPERS - LUND UNIVERSITY, DEPARTMENT OF LINGUISTICS, GENERAL LINGUISTICS, PHONETICS. 3333
0280-6487 See GARDAR. 3389
0280-6495 See TELLUS. SERIES A, DYNAMIC METEOROLOGY AND OCEANOGRAPHY. 1436
0280-6509 See TELLUS. SERIES B, CHEMICAL AND PHYSICAL METEOROLOGY. 1436
0280-719X See RAPPORT (SVENSKA BIBLIOTEKARIESAMFUNDET). 3244
0280-7270 See INTERNATIONAL JOURNAL OF MASS EMERGENCIES AND DISASTERS. 1073
0280-7645 See ALCOHOL, DRUGS, AND TRAFFIC SAFETY : CURRENT RESEARCH LITERATURE. 1339
0280-7750 See SCANDINAVIAN WORKING PAPERS ON BILINGUALISM. 3319
0280-7823 See LEDARSKAP, EKONOMEN. 1503
0280-8331 See SYSTEMA ASCOMYCETUM. 528
0280-8633 See STUDIA ANTHROPONYMICA SCANDINAVICA. 2474
0280-9982 See COMPUTER SWEDEN. 1178
0281-0018 See SEMINAR PROCEEDINGS FROM THE SCANDINAVIAN INSTITUTE OF AFRICAN STUDIES. 2500
0281-0662 See JOURNAL OF SOCIAL AND ADMINISTRATIVE PHARMACY : JSAP. 4313
0281-0999 See BULLETIN FROM SADRAC. 4295
0281-286X See KYRKOMUSIKERNAS TIDNING. 4128
0281-3432 See SCANDINAVIAN JOURNAL OF PRIMARY HEALTH CARE. SUPPLEMENT. 3739
0281-3505 See ADVOKATEN (STOCKHOLM). 2928
0281-5087 See ACID NEWS STOCKHOLM. 2223
0281-5087 See ACID RAIN. 2185
0281-5478 See STOCKHOLM STUDIES IN BALTIC LANGUAGES. 3324
0281-5737 See SCANDINAVIAN HOUSING AND PLANNING RESEARCH. 2835
0281-5877 See ARCHAEOLOGY AND ENVIRONMENT. 257
0281-658X See BYGG & TEKNIK. 606
0281-6733 See NORDISK CELLULOSA. 4235
0281-6814 See WORKING PAPERS IN AFRICAN STUDIES. 2644
0281-7446 See ARBETARHISTORIA : MEDDELANDE FRAN ARBETARRORELSENS ARKIV OCH BIBLIOTEK. 1651
0281-7985 See CAMEL FORUM. 5507
0281-8353 See NORDIC JOURNAL OF SOVIET AND EAST EUROPEAN STUDIES. 2700
0281-9015 See SVENSKA PC-WORLD. 1204
0282-0080 See GLYCOCONJUGATE JOURNAL. 1025
0282-0196 See ACID MAGAZINE. 2222

0282-423X See JOURNAL OF OFFICIAL STATISTICS. 5329
0282-4485 See LANDSTINGSVARLDEN. 4661
0282-5449 See HASSELBLAD FORUM. 4370
0282-5902 See KULTURENS VARLD. 2696
0282-6011 See SIDA RAPPORT. 2912
0282-633X See LAEKARMATRIKELN. 3914
0282-6364 See AUDIO VIDEO. 5315
0282-6674 See TEKNIK FOR LANTBRUKET. 140
0282-7476 See ACTA UNIVERSITATIS UPSALIENSIS. COMPREHENSIVE SUMMARIES OF UPPSALA DISSERTATIONS FROM THE FACULTY OF MEDICINE. 3545
0282-7581 See SCANDINAVIAN JOURNAL OF FOREST RESEARCH. 2394
0282-762X See MEDDELANDEN FRAN SVENSKA RIKSARKIVET. 2482
0282-7913 See TIDSKRIFT FOR LITTERATURVETENSKAP. 3446
0282-8006 See STRINDBERGIANA. 3440
0282-8677 See STUDIES IN PLANT ECOLOGY. 528
0282-941X See SIP NEWSLETTER FROM SWEDEN (ENGLISH EDITION). 2522
0283-0280 See SCPF INFORMATION. 4239
0283-0698 See RAPPORT (SVERIGES LANTBRUKSUNIVERSITET. INSTITUTIONEN FOR HUSDJURSHYGIEN). 5519
0283-1007 See SMALL SCALE FORESTRY. 2395
0283-1899 See KULTURRADET : STATENS KULTURRAD INFORMERAR. 2696
0283-1929 See SOCIONOMEN 1987. 5310
0283-2380 See ACTA PHILOSOPHICA GOTHOBURGENSIA. 4339
0283-2631 See NORDIC PULP & PAPER RESEARCH JOURNAL. 4235
0283-4529 See BORSMEDDELANDEN. 4634
0283-653X See OPSIS KALOPSIS. 3420
0283-748X See HOTELL & PENSIONAT. 2806
0283-7536 See BULLETIN FOR COLLEGES OF TEACHER EDUCATION IN COOPERATION, THE. 1813
0283-7560 See FRIA TIDER. 4850
0283-7692 See STUDIES OF HIGHER EDUCATION AND RESEARCH. 1849
0283-8060 See SWEDISH DEFENCE MATERIEL ADMINISTRATION QUALIFIED PRODUCT LIST OF ELECTRONIC COMPONENTS : SE-MIL-QPL. 2083
0283-8117 See DRUG ABUSE / THE SWEDISH COUNCIL FOR INFORMATION ON ALCOHOL AND OTHER DRUGS (CAN) ; NATIONAL DIRECTORATE FOR THE PREVENTION OF ALCOHOL AND DRUG PROBLEMS. 1343
0283-8486 See JOURNAL OF PREHISTORIC RELIGION. 4969
0283-8494 See STUDIES IN MEDITERRANEAN ARCHAEOLOGY AND LITERATURE. POCKET-BOOK. 283
0283-8708 See VETSKAP. 1096
0283-8974 See IUI YEARBOOK / INDUSTRIAL INSTITUTE FOR ECONOMIC AND SOCIAL RESEARCH. 1497
0283-9318 See SCANDINAVIAN JOURNAL OF CARING SCIENCES. 3869
0284-0200 See LIFE & PEACE REVIEW. 4973
0284-0448 See BERGSMANNEN. 2135
0284-1754 See ALLT I HEMMET 1987. 1293
0284-1851 See ACTA RADIOLOGICA (STOCKHOLM, SWEDEN : 1987). 3938
0284-186X See ACTA ONCOLOGICA (STOCKHOLM, SWEDEN). 3808
0284-2998 See NORDISK ARKITEKTURFORSKNING. 305
0284-3153 See RAPPORT (SVERIGES LANTBRUKSUNIVERSITET. INSTITUTIONEN FOR EKONOMI). 124
0284-351X See FORSKNINGSRAPPORT (STOCKHOLMS UNIVERSITET. SOCIOLOGISKA INSTITUTIONEN). 5245
0284-3757 See SKB TECHNICAL REPORT. 5158
0284-4311 See SCANDINAVIAN JOURNAL OF PLASTIC AND RECONSTRUCTIVE SURGERY AND HAND SURGERY. 3974

0284-5717 See SCANDINAVIAN JOURNAL OF BEHAVIOUR THERAPY. 4617
0284-6454 See SCANDINAVIAN PULP & PAPER MAGAZINE. 4239
0284-6578 See GOTEBORG STUDIES IN CONSERVATION. 2194
0284-8015 See GLOBAL CHANGE / IGBP. 1356
0284-8422 See COMPOSITAE NEWSLETTER. 4165
0284-9224 See WORKING PAPER - DEVELOPMENT STUDY UNIT, DEPARTMENT OF SOCIAL ANTHROPOLOGY, UNIVERSITY OF STOCKHOLM. 247
0284-9232 See REPORT - DEVELOPMENT STUDY UNIT, DEPARTMENT OF SOCIAL ANTHROPOLOGY, UNIVERSITY OF STOCKHOLM. 244
0285-0028 See TAIKABUTSU OVERSEAS. 5161
0285-0125 See KOKURITSU KYOIKU KENKYUJO KENKYU SHUROKU. 1760
0285-0192 See NIHON OYO JIKI GAKKAISHI. 4444
0285-0206 See GAIKO TO BUNKA. 2651
0285-0362 See SHARP GIHO. 5157
0285-0427 See SHIZUOKA DAIGAKU KYOYOBU KENKYU HOKOKU. JINBUN SHAKAI KAGAKU HEN. 2854
0285-0567 See KIITO KENSA KENKYU HOKOKU. 5353
0285-1601 See AFRICAN STUDY MONOGRAPHS. 2498
0285-1903 See DENSHI TOKYO. 2041
0285-192X See PURE CHEMICALS DAIICHI. 990
0285-2543 See NOGYO KIKAI GAKKAISHI. 160
0285-2853 See UCHU KAGAKU KENKYUJO HOKOKU. TOKUSHU. 401
0285-3175 See ANNUAL REPORT OF THE INSTITUTE OF GEOSCIENCE, THE UNIVERSITY OF TSUKUBA. 1351
0285-3191 See HACHU RYOSEIRUIGAKU ZASSHI. 5585
0285-3299 See SEIRIGAKU GIJUTSU KENKYUKAI HOKOKU. 5156
0285-3507 See NIHON SAKUMOTSU GAKKAI KYUSHU SHIBUKAIHO. 179
0285-3582 See LATIN AMERICAN STUDIES (SAKURA-MURA, IBARAKI-KEN, JAPAN). 2744
0285-3604 See HOSHASEN. 4434
0285-3663 See NIIGATA YAKKA DAIGAKU KENKYU HOKOKU. 4318
0285-3817 See TOHOKU KOGYO DAIGAKU KIYO. SERIES 1. RIKOGAKUEN. 2033
0285-3833 See NIHON DENSHI ZAIRYO GIJUTSU KYOKAI KAIHO. 2074
0285-4015 See SHAKAIGAKU KENKYUJO KIYO. 5218
0285-4031 See SEKIYU TO SHOHI DOTAI TOKEI GEPPO. SHO-KO-KOGYO / [HENSHU] TSUSHO SANGYO DAIJIN KANBO CHOSA TOKEIBU. 710
0285-4139 See NEC GIHO. 5132
0285-4406 See RAFIDAN. 2770
0285-4619 See NIKKEI KONPYUTA. 1238
0285-4821 See HISTORIA SCIENTIARUM. 5110
0285-4937 See PHARMA JAPAN. 4319
0285-5275 See NISSEKI REBYU. 5134
0285-5283 See KITAKYUSHU KOGYO KOTO SENMON GAKKO KENKYU HOKOKU. 5123
0285-5313 See YAKUBUTSU, SEISHIN, KODO. 4622
0285-5364 See KENKYU KIYO - AKITA KOGYO KOTO SENMON GAKKO. 5123
0285-5380 See SANGYO TO KANKYO. 2242
0285-5437 See ENERUGI (TOKYO. 1968). 1943
0285-5801 See OSAKA SHIRITSU KANKYO KAGAKY KENKYUJO HOKOKU. CHOSA KENKYU NENPO. 4795
0285-5895 See KANKYO KAGAKU SOGO KENKYUJO NENPO. 2176
0285-6107 See EHIME DAIGAKU KOGAKUBU KIYO. 2022
0285-6174 See NIHON DAIGAKU KOGAKUBU KIYO. BUNRUI A. 1989

0285-6182 See NIHON DAIGAKU KOGAKUBU KIYO. BUNRUI B, IPPAN KYOIKU HEN. **1989**

0285-6220 See GEKKAN HAIKIBUTSU. **2230**

0285-6506 See INTERNATIONAL JOURNAL OF AESTHETIC SURGERY / INTERNATIONAL SOCIETY OF AESTHETIC SURGERY. **3966**

0285-6689 See KINKI ARUMINIUMU HYOMEN SHORI KENKYUKAI KAISHI. **4006**

0285-6808 See REPORT - INSTITUTE OF SPACE AND ASTRONAUTICAL SCIENCE, TOKYO. **33**

0285-6905 See KISO, KANKYO KAGAKU KENKYU. **1357**

0285-6921 See KYUSHU DAIGAKU NOGAKUBU FUZOKU SUISAN JIKKENJO HOKOKU. **2307**

0285-7006 See BIFIDUS, FLORES ET FRUCTUS. **477**

0285-7049 See MOKUZAI KENKYU SHIRYO. **634**

0285-726X See JAPAN PULP AND PAPER. **4234**

0285-7685 See OKAYAMA RIKA DAIGAKU KIYO. A, SHIZEN KAGAKU. **5136**

0285-8096 See NIHON SANKA FUJINKA GAKKAI KANTO RENGO CHIHO BUKAI KAIHO. **3765**

0285-8177 See SUMITOMO BYOIN IGAKU ZASSHI. **3643**

0285-8282 See CHUGOKU MONDAI. **1551**

0285-8452 See KINZOKU HAKUBUTSUKAN KIYO. **4006**

0285-8576 See MIYAZAKI DAIGAKU KYOIKUGAKUBU KIYO : SHIZEN KAGAKU. **1866**

0285-8592 See MIYAZAKI DAIGAKU KYOIKU GAKUBU KIYO. GEIJUTSU, HOKEN TAIIKU, KASEI, GIJUTSU. **1764**

0285-869X See ISHIKAWA-KEN KOGYO SHIKENJO SHIKENJO HOKOKU. **5353**

0285-8800 See SHIBAKUSA KENKYU. **134**

0285-9211 See WASEDA BULLETIN OF COMPARATIVE LAW. **3137**

0285-922X See SHOWA SHIGAKKAI ZASSHI. **1335**

0285-9394 See DETA TSUSHIN. **1258**

0285-9521 See FIRE SCIENCE AND TECHNOLOGY. **2290**

0285-9556 See JOURNAL OF JAPANESE TRADE & INDUSTRY. **687**

0285-9610 See TOYAMA DAIGAKU KYOIKU GAKUBU KIYO. B, RIKAKEI. **5166**

0285-9815 See SANKEN GIHO. **5149**

0286-0406 See SCIENCE & TECHNOLOGY IN JAPAN (TOKYO. 1982). **5150**

0286-0511 See JOSHI EIYO DAIGAKU KIYO. **4192**

0286-0635 See JAPAN AVIATION DIRECTORY. **25**

0286-0902 See KENKYU HOKOKU / NAGASAKI DAIGAKU KOGAKUBU. **1984**

0286-0945 See KOKKAIDO KOGAI BOSHI KENKYUJO HO. **2235**

0286-102X See NAGANO-KEN SHOKUHIN KOGYO SHIKENJO KENKYU HOKOKU. **2350**

0286-1127 See RATEN AMERIKA KENKYU NENPO. **2756**

0286-1275 See WASEDA JINBUN SHIZEN KAGAKU KENKYU. **5169**

0286-1283 See WASEDA SHAKAI KAGAKU KENKYU. **5225**

0286-1291 See DOSHISHA DAIGAKU EIGO EIBUNGAKU KENKYU. **3277**

0286-1933 See KANZEI CHUO BUNSEKISHOHO. **5122**

0286-2018 See KYUSHU KOGYO GIJUTSU SHIKENJO HOKOKU. TOKUSHUGO. **5125**

0286-2093 See GENGO BUNKA KENKYU (MATSUYAMA-SHI, JAPAN). **3283**

0286-2190 See BYOTAI SEIRI (OSAKA. 1982). **4343**

0286-2212 See SHOHIN KENKYU. **851**

0286-262X See AICHI-KEN KOGYO GIJUTSU SENTA HOKOKU. **5081**

0286-2743 See NIIHAMA KOGYO KOTO SENMON GAKKO KIYO. RIKOGAKU HEN. **5134**

0286-2794 See NUMAZU KOGYO KOTO SENMON GAKKO KENKYU HOKOKU. **5135**

0286-2999 See PROGRESS IN POLYMER SCIENCE, JAPAN. **1047**

0286-3383 See SHIZUOKA DAIGAKU DENSHI KOGAKU KENKYUJO KENKYU HOKOKU. **2081**

0286-3553 See LIBERAL STAR. **2658**

0286-3707 See MIYAGI KOGYO KOTO SENMON GAKKO KENKYU KIYO. **5129**

0286-3855 See GENGO BUNKABU KIYO. **3283**

0286-4002 See KYUSHU TOKAI DAIGAKU KIYO. KOGAKUBU. **1985**

0286-4185 See SHITENNOJI KOKUSAI BUKKYO DAIGAKU BUNGAKUBU KIYO. **5022**

0286-4215 See KEIO SCIENCE AND TECHNOLOGY REPORTS. **1984**

0286-438X See NINGEN TO KANKYO. **2178**

0286-4835 See KINO ZAIRYO. **1984**

0286-522X See BULLETIN OF INFORMATICS AND CYBERNETICS. **1250**

0286-5408 See ENVIRONMENTAL RESEARCH CENTER PAPERS. **1404**

0286-5858 See SHIKA ZAIRYO, KIKAI. **1335**

0286-5890 See HIROSAKI DAIGAKU HOKEN KANRI GAIYO. **2882**

0286-5971 See JAMA FORUM, THE. **5417**

0286-6188 See RESEARCH LETTERS ON ATMOSPHERIC ELECTRICITY. **1434**

0286-6250 See SAGAMI JOSHI DAIGAKU KIYO. **1094**

0286-6366 See SEITOKU EIYO TANKI DAIGAKU KIYO. **4199**

0286-6501 See NENSHO KENKYU. **1951**

0286-6536 See SUISAN FUKAJO KENKYU HOKOKU. **2314**

0286-6943 See KOGYO TOSO. **984**

0286-6951 See TAIIKU KENKYUJO KIYO. **1858**

0286-7052 See NIHON RINSHO SEIRI GAKKAI ZASSHI. **584**

0286-7117 See TACHIKAWA TANDAI KIYO. **5161**

0286-7370 See NIHON DAIGAKU RIKO GAKUBU IPPAN KYOIKU KYOSHITSU IHO. **1838**

0286-7400 See KOKURITSU REKISHI MINZOKU HAKUBUTSUKAN KENKYU HOKOKU. **4090**

0286-7826 See KYUSHU SANGYO DAIGAKU KOGAKUBU KENKYU HOKOKU. **1985**

0286-8237 See KINJO GAKUIN DAIGAKU RONSHU, KASEIGAKU HEN. **2791**

0286-8539 See ROJIN MONDAI KENKYU. **5181**

0286-8733 See UTSUNOMIYA DAIGAKU NOGAKUBU ENSHURIN HOKOKU. **2397**

0286-9306 See BIFIDOBACTERIA AND MICROFLORA. **560**

0286-9314 See KOKYU. **3950**

0286-9322 See JAPANESE JOURNAL OF SPORTS SCIENCES. **4901**

0286-9640 See RYUKYU DAIGAKU RIGAKUBU KIYO. **1456**

0286-9659 See OPUTORONIKUSU. **4440**

0286-9667 See AFRICAN STUDY MONOGRAPHS. SUPPLEMENTARY ISSUE. **2498**

0286-9675 See TSUKUBA CHUGOKU BUNKA RONSO / TSUKUBA DAIGAKU CHUGOKU BUNKA KENKYU PUROJEKUTO. **3448**

0286-9713 See SOSHIKI KAGAKU / ORGANIZATION SCIENCE / HENSHU, SOSHIKI GAKKAI. **5158**

0286-987X See SENI KAGAKU. **5355**

0287-0010 See TOSHOKAN JOHO DAIGAKU KENKYU HOKOKU. **3253**

0287-0029 See NOGYO DOBOKU SHIKENJO GIHO. HE, SUIKO. **113**

0287-0029 See NOGYO DOBOKU SHIKENJO GIHO. LI, NOCHI SEIBI. **113**

0287-0029 See NOGYO DOBOKU SHIKENJO GIHO. WM, SUIRI. **113**

0287-0150 See MACHI & SUMAI. **2827**

0287-0223 See DOBUTSU BUNRUI GAKKAI SHI. **5581**

0287-041X See TRANSACTIONS OF THE JAPAN FOUNDRYMEN'S SOCIETY. **4022**

0287-0517 See ENVIRONMENTAL MEDICINE : ANNUAL REPORT OF THE RESEARCH INSTITUTE OF ENVIRONMENTAL MEDICINE, NAGOYA UNIVERSITY. **3574**

0287-069X See SHOKEN IHO. **3055**

0287-0894 See IYAKUHIN KENKYU. **3591**

0287-1408 See TOYAMA DAIGAKU TORICHIUMU KAGAKU SENTA KENKYU HOKOKO. **1038**

0287-1645 See BESSATSU SEIKEI GEKA. **3960**

0287-1734 See SHOKU NO KAGAKU. **2357**

0287-1793 See ANNUAL REPORT / KAWASAKI HEAVY INDUSTRIES, LTD. **1597**

0287-2145 See ECHOES OF PEACE. **2249**

0287-2218 See BIJUTSU TECHO. **344**

0287-2226 See BESSATSU BIJUTSU TECHO. **344**

0287-2323 See WASEDA FORAMU. **1853**

0287-2404 See LTCB RESEARCH. **797**

0287-2641 See SEIMEI HOKEN KEIEI. **2893**

0287-2951 See KAIJO HOAN DAIGAKKO KENKYU HOKOKU. RIKOGAKU-KEI. **5122**

0287-3516 See NIHON EIYO SHOKURYO GAKKAI SHI. **4195**

0287-3796 See SAIBO KOGAKU. **472**

0287-4547 See DENTAL MATERIALS JOURNAL. **1321**

0287-5071 See KENKYU HOKOKU / KANKYO KAGAKU KENKYUJO. **2235**

0287-5136 See RINBOKU IKUSHUJO KENKYU HOKOKU. **2394**

0287-5357 See SOPHIA LINGUISTICA. **3322**

0287-6485 See KUSIRI NO CHISHIKI. **4313**

0287-7406 See SUMITOMO BANK ECONOMIC SURVEY. **1586**

0287-7414 See PURETINGU TO KOTINGU. **1028**

0287-7651 See KISO SHINRIGAKU KENKYU. **4602**

0287-7805 See TSUDA-JUKU DAIGAKU KIYO. **2855**

0287-8429 See ANNALS OF PHYSIOLOGICAL ANTHROPOLOGY, THE. **228**

0287-8461 See JIDOKA GIJUTSU. **1220**

0287-8607 See JOURNAL OF IRRIGATION ENGINEERING AND RURAL PLANNING. **176**

0287-8712 See TOKISHIKOROJI FORAMU. **3983**

0287-9131 See HOBUNSHU / KYOTO DAIGAKU GENSHIRO JIKKENJO GAKUJUTSU KOENKAI. **1053**

0287-9530 See JAPAN DIRECTORY OF PROFESSIONAL ASSOCIATIONS. **685**

0287-9840 See KOZAN. **2143**

0287-9980 See MATHEMATICAL REPORTS OF COLLEGE OF GENERAL EDUCATION, KYUSHU UNIVERSITY. **3520**

0288-0032 See HYPERTENSION RESEARCH, CLINICAL AND EXPERIMENTAL. **3706**

0288-0490 See NETSU SHORI. **4013**

0288-1012 See SHIKA YAKUBUTSU RYOHO. **4329**

0288-2043 See RADIATION MEDICINE. **3944**

0288-2493 See DAIGAKU NYUSHI FORAMU. **1819**

0288-2876 See EIGO EIBUNGAKU KENKYU HIROSHIMA. 1954. **3278**

0288-3031 See NIHON JOSHI DAIGAKU KIYO. BUNGAKUBU. **2507**

0288-3503 See ACTA SLAVICA IAPONICA. **2672**

0288-3619 See EIJINGU. **5179**

0288-3635 See NEW GENERATION COMPUTING. **1270**

0288-3708 See KAIGI DAIGAKKO KENKYU HOKOKU. **1833**

0288-3864 See PACKAGING JAPAN. **4220**

0288-3953 See FUKUOKA JOSHI DAIGAKU KASEI GAKUBU KIYO. **456**

0288-4623 See NIHON NO TEIRYU. **2660**

0288-4771 See YOSETSU GAKKAI RONBUNSHU. **4029**

0288-5417 See ENERUGI HENKAN GIJUTSU. **1943**

0288-5867 See KINOSHI KENKYUKAI SHI / ANNALS OF THE HIGH PERFORMANCE PAPER SOCIETY, JAPAN. **4235**

0288-6065 See OBERON. **3419**

0288-6103 See DEMPA DIGEST. **2040**

0288-6154 See SHOIN LITERARY REVIEW. **3352**

0288-6502 See TOCHI ZOSEI KOGAKU KENKYU SHISETSU HOKOKU. **1999**

0288-6510 See KANTO RINBOKU IKUSHUJO NENPO. **2386**

0288-691X See FOTON FAKUTORI NYUSU. **1944**

0288-738X See KINKI DAIGAKU KYUSHU KOGAKUBU KENKYU HOKOKU. RIKAGAKU-HEN. 1984

0288-7622 See LOCAL GOVERNMENT REVIEW IN JAPAN. 4663

0288-7878 See NIHON RINSHO KAGAKKAI NENKAI KIROKU. 987

0288-8262 See NIHON KAIMEN IGAKKAI ZASSHI. 467

0288-8432 See BANK OF JAPAN MONETARY AND ECONOMIC STUDIES. 775

0289-0003 See ZOOLOGICAL SCIENCE. 5602

0289-0011 See BIOTRONICS. 2410

0289-0143 See PHOTO INTERNATIONAL TOKYO. 1969. 4373

0289-0569 See AICHI KYOIKU DAIGAKU KENKYU HOKOKU. SOSAKU HEN. 312

0289-0615 See KANAZAWA DAIGAKU KEIZAI RONSHU. 1501

0289-0739 See SAITAMA MATHEMATICAL JOURNAL. 3532

0289-0747 See KENKYU NENPO (TAKUSHOKU DAIGAKU. KENKYUJO). 5207

0289-0771 See JOURNAL OF ETHOLOGY. 239

0289-0917 See RYUKOKU KIYO. 2853

0289-1239 See CROSS CURRENTS. 3275

0289-1522 See FINANCIAL STATISTICS OF JAPAN. 4697

0289-1530 See RYUKYU DAIGAKU IGAKKAI ZASSHI. 3638

0289-1956 See JAPAN TIMES (TOKYO. 1956), THE. 5805

0289-2111 See BAMBOO JOURNAL. 164

0289-2405 See SEIRI SHINRIGAKU TO SEISHIN SEIRIGAKU. 4618

0289-3207 See NOGYO KENKYU SENTA KENKYU HOKOKU. 113

0289-3371 See MEN'EKI YAKURI SHINPOJUMU. 4315

0289-3568 See TSUKUBA JIKKEN SHOKUBUTSUEN KENKYU HOKOKU. 2432

0289-3827 See KYOTO JOSHI DAIGAKU SHOKUMOTSU GAKKAI SHI. 2348

0289-4424 See MIYAGI KYOIKU DAIGAKU KIYO. DAI 2-BUNSATSU, SHIZEN KAGAKU, KYOIKU KAGAKU. 1358

0289-4610 See GUNMA NOGYO KENKYU. A, SOGO. 91

0289-5102 See SUNAGAWA SHIRITSU BYOIN IGAKU ZASSHI. 3643

0289-5420 See RAIBURARIANZU FORAMU. 3243

0289-5447 See TUMOUR BIOLOGY. 475

0289-6001 See GEOGRAPHICAL REVIEW OF JAPAN. SERIES B. 2563

0289-6079 See NAVI. 4180

0289-6508 See NIKKEI BAITO. 1197

0289-6508 See NIKKEI BAITO: NIKKEI BYTE. 1270

0289-6672 See NSG TECHNICAL REPORT. 2592

0289-7024 See SHINKEI GANKA. 3879

0289-730X See WAKAN IYAKU GAKKAISHI. 3650

0289-7512 See KAGOSHIMA-KEN EISEI KENKYUJOHO (1983). 4788

0289-7520 See SCIENTIFIC PAPERS OF THE COLLEGE OF ARTS AND SCIENCES, THE UNIVERSITY OF TOKYO. 5155

0289-7938 See LANGUAGE TEACHER / JAPAN ASSOCIATION OF LANGUAGE TEACHERS, THE. 3296

0289-8020 See SERAPYUTIKKU RISACHI. 3640

0289-8055 See IRYO JOHOGAKU. 3590

0289-8063 See STRUCTURAL ENGINEERING/EARTHQUAKE ENGINEERING. 2031

0289-9051 See KOBE JOURNAL OF MATHEMATICS. 3516

0289-9582 See IWATE SHIGAKU KENKYU. 2620

0290-0106 See ALARMES, PROTECTION, SECURITE. 2858

0290-0378 See FAITS & CHIFFRES. 1532

0290-0556 See BULLETIN MENSUEL D'INFORMATION (FRANCE. SERVICE DE CONSERVATION DES GISEMENTS). 4252

0290-1188 See DECOUVERTES ARCHEOLOGIQUES EN TOURNUGEOIS. 266

0290-4500 See PUBLICATIONS DE LA SORBONNE. HISTOIRE ANCIENNE ET MEDIEVALE. 2626

0290-5736 See COURRIER DE LA SCLEROSE EN PLAQUES, LE. 3569

0290-9693 See R.C.M. RADIO COMMANDE MAGAZINE. 1120

0291-0764 See BOUTIQUES DE FRANCE. 952

0291-1191 See DEMEURES & CHATEAUX. 296

0291-1655 See SYNTHESE (EDITIONS RECHERCHE SUR LES CIVILISATIONS). 2712

0291-1795 See VIVRE ENSEMBLE LILLE. 5008

0291-1981 See JOURNAL DE PHARMACIE CLINIQUE. 4310

0291-2066 See IRIS (MONTPELLIER). 3397

0291-2120 See CAHIERS COLETTE. 3371

0291-2430 See BIO / LA LETTRE DES BIOTECHNOLOGIES. 444

0291-2708 See AFGHAN REALITIES. 4503

0291-3798 See 17 - 18. 3357

0291-5871 See BULLETIN OFFICIEL DU MINISTERE DE L'EDUCATION NATIONALE (PARIS, FRANCE : 1981). 1729

0291-6207 See BULLETIN OFFICIEL DU MINISTERE DE L'EDUCATION NATIONALE. NO SPECIAL : BO. 1729

0291-8374 See BULLETIN DE LA SOCIETE DE PHARMACIE DE L'OUEST. 4294

0291-851X See STATISTIQUE MEDICALE DANS LES ARMEES. 4062

0291-8897 See NOTES VERTES ECONOMIQUE. SERIE INFORMATIONS RAPIDES. 1508

0291-8900 See NOTES VERTES ECONOMIQUES. SERIE CONJONCTURE. 1508

0292-1731 See ENERGIE PLUS. 1938

0292-1782 See ECODOC : REVUE BIBLIOGRAPHIQUE BIMESTRIELLE PUBLIEE PAR LE RESEAU D'INFORMATION EN ECONOMIE GENERALE. 1531

0292-1979 See CAHIER - CENTRE DE RECHERCHES SUR L'ANTIQUITE TARDIVE ET LE HAUT MOYEN-AGE. 2682

0292-2215 See PRATIQUES DE FORMATION SAINT-DENIS. 1802

0292-2290 See NOTE FINANCIERE ANNUELLE / BANQUE DE FRANCE, SECRETARIAT REGIONAL, REGION ALSACE. 801

0292-4625 See ART ET ARTISTES. 338

0292-4943 See CAHIERS DU C.E.R.M.T.R.I, LES. 412

0292-5354 See DOSSIERS DU CANARD, LES. 4472

0292-5370 See ACTION GUNS. 4881

0292-5451 See QUAND DIEU PARLE AUX HOMMES. 4989

0292-8418 See BIO-SCIENCES. 3686

0292-8477 See GEOCHRONIQUE. 1376

0292-8515 See BULLETIN BIBLIOGRAPHIQUE AMERIQUE LATINE / RESEAU DOCUMENTAIRE AMERIQUE LATINE, GRECO 26, CNRS. 411

0292-9651 See PRATIQUES CORPORELLES. 3844

0293-0196 See CREATIONS CANNES LA BOCCA. 5097

0293-0277 See GENRE HUMAIN, LE. 237

0293-082X See ESF COMMUNICATIONS. 2171

0293-1915 See COLLOQUES DE L'INRA, LES. 75

0293-2148 See MELANGES DE LA BIBLIOTHEQUE DE LA SORBONNE. 419

0293-2547 See TE AVEIA. 1586

0293-3055 See COURRIER DE LA PLANETE PARIS. 5097

0293-373X See LOU TERRAIRE. 2697

0293-4906 See ART ET THERAPIE. 1875

0293-5090 See ARTERES ET VEINES. 3699

0293-5945 See SANTE 2000 MEDECINE. 3638

0293-6186 See NOUVELLES D'ORLEANS, LES. 2520

0293-6852 See LIEN HORTICOLE. 2424

0293-7166 See BRISES. BULLETIN DE RECHERCHES SUR L'INFORMATION EN SCIENCES ECONOMIQUES HUMAINES ET SOCIALES. 2485

0293-843X See GEOBIOS (LYON, FRANCE). 4227

0293-9134 See ARCHEOLOGIE EN BRETAGNE. SUPPLEMENT. 259

0293-9495 See NOUVELLE GAZETTE DE LA TRANSFUSION : BULLETIN D'INFORMATION DE L'ADTS, LA. 3623

0293-9789 See ACTUALITE DES ARTS PLASTIQUES. 335

0293-9908 See COMPTES RENDUS DE THERAPEUTIQUE ET DE PHARMACOLOGIE CLINIQUE. 4297

0294-0000 See LIVRES HEBDO. 419

0294-0027 See LIVRES DU MOIS, LES. 4816

0294-0035 See TROIS MOIS DE NOUVEAUTES. 4833

0294-0078 See C.F. RAMUZ. 3370

0294-0086 See PIERRE JEAN JOUVE. 3423

0294-0264 See SCIENCES ET TECHNIQUES EN PERSPECTIVE. 5154

0294-0337 See SCIENCES SOCIALES ET SANTE. 4801

0294-0442 See CAHIERS DE LA NOUVELLE, LES. 3371

0294-0531 See PARTIE PRENANTE. 1772

0294-0620 See INDUSTRIES PARIS. 1611

0294-0671 See MISES AU POINT DE BIOCHIMIE PHARMACOLOGIQUE. 4316

0294-0701 See GUIDE EUROPEEN DES PROGICIELS. EDITION COMPLEMENTAIRE / CXP. 1286

0294-0736 See JOURNAL D'ECONOMIE MEDICALE. 3592

0294-0787 See OFFICE DES PRIX DU BATIMENT. TOUS CORPS D'ETAT. 1511

0294-0817 See MEDECINE AERONAUTIQUE ET SPATIALE. 3607

0294-0833 See REVUE FRANCAISE DE FINANCES PUBLIQUES. 4747

0294-0868 See EDUCATION ET FORMATIONS / REALISTE PAR LA SOUS-DIRECTION DES ENQUETES STATISTIQUES ET DES ETUDES DU SERVICE DE L'INFORMATIQUE DE GESTION ET DES STATISTIQUES (S.I.G.E.S.) DU MINISTERE DE L'EDUCATION NATIONALE. 1739

0294-0922 See REEDUCATION POSTURALE GLOBALE. 3806

0294-0965 See REVUE D'ARCHEOLOGIE MODERNE ET D'ARCHEOLOGIE GENERALE : RAMAGE. 281

0294-1007 See MEDSUBHYP. 3615

0294-1090 See UN AN DE NOUVEAUTES. 4833

0294-1155 See AGE D'OR, L'. 4933

0294-1228 See ANNALES FRANCAISES DES MICROTECHNIQUES ET DE CHRONOMETRIE. 4397

0294-1341 See ISRAEL & PALESTINE POLITICAL REPORT : I & P. 4526

0294-135X See ARTRACES. BULLETIN. 334

0294-1414 See NOUVELLE REVUE DU XVIE SIECLE. 3418

0294-1449 See ANNALES DE L'INSTITUT HENRI POINCARE. ANALYSE NON LINEAIRE. 3493

0294-1759 See VINGTIEME SIECLE (PARIS, FRANCE : 1984). 2632

0294-1805 See PHILOSOPHIE (PARIS, FRANCE : 1984). 4356

0294-1813 See REVUE FRANCAISE D'ENDODONTIE. 1334

0294-1910 See SATMER ED. FRANCAISE. 1434

0294-202X See REVUE DE LA CERAMIQUE ET DU VERRE, LA. 2593

0294-2925 See INTERNATIONAL VIEWPOINT. 4477

0294-3484 See BULLETIN DE LA SOCIETE D'ETUDES ET DE RECHERCHES HISTORIQUES DU PAYS DE RETZ. 2680

0294-3506 See BIOFUTUR. 3686

0294-4030 See NOUVELLE TOUR DE FEU, LA. 3467

0294-4049 See CAHIERS DE LA MUTUALITE DANS L'ENTREPRISE, LES. **1467**

0294-474X See REVUE INTERNATIONALE DE RHUMATOLOGIE. **3807**

0294-4782 See AME ET LA CORDE, L'. **4099**

0294-6475 See INDIAN OCEAN NEWSLETTER / LA LETTRE DE L'OCEAN INDIEN, THE. **1494**

0294-6939 See CAHIERS DE LA GUITARE, LES. **4106**

0294-7080 See SYSTEMES DE PENSEE EN AFRIQUE NOIRE. **5002**

0294-7390 See CIRCULAIRES DE LA FEDERATION NATIONALE DES PROMOTEURS-CONSTRUCTEURS. **4296**

0294-7544 See INFOTECTURE (EUROPEAN ED.). **1275**

0294-8052 See INTERNATIONAL HERALD TRIBUNE. **5800**

0294-8168 See LIAISONS SOCIALES. BREF SOCIAL. **5208**

0294-8176 See LIAISONS SOCIALES. LEGISLATION SOCIALE. **3003**

0294-8567 See ARCHITECTURE INTERIEURE-C.R.E.E. **290**

0295-0448 See AQUA REVUE. **2295**

0295-1630 See PLEINE MARGE. **362**

0295-1967 See SPECTRA BIOLOGIE. **3696**

0295-2319 See POLITIX. **4491**

0295-2556 See ABSTRACT RHUMATO PARIS. **3802**

0295-317X See PISCICULTURE FRANCAISE D'EAU VIVE ET D'ETANG SAUMATRE ET MARINE, LA. **469**

0295-3722 See ANALYSE MUSICALE. **4100**

0295-3943 See MIDI MEDIA. **1117**

0295-4303 See RIA, LE TECHNICIEN DU LAIT. **198**

0295-4591 See CAHIERS HOSPITALIERS: PERSONNEL AND FORMATION. **3777**

0295-5024 See ROMAN 20-50. **3431**

0295-5075 See EUROPHYSICS LETTERS. **4402**

0295-5385 See LUTTE DE CLASSE 1986. **4543**

0295-5717 See REVUE DOCUMENTAIRE - CENTRE TECHNIQUE DU BOIS ET DE L'AMEUBLEMENT. **5337**

0295-5725 See PISCINES, SPAS MAGAZINE. **306**

0295-5830 See REVUE DE DROIT DES AFFAIRES INTERNATIONALES. **3102**

0295-5849 See REVUE DES INDUSTRIES D'ART. **363**

0295-5873 See SYSTEMES SOLAIRES. **1959**

0295-608X See BULLETIN DES AUTOROUTES FRANCAISES. **5439**

0296-1350 See CONTACT & URGENCES 92. **3723**

0296-1598 See AUTOMATIQUE-PRODUCTIQUE INFORMATIQUE INDUSTRIELLE. **2110**

0296-3140 See BULLETIN D'INFORMATION SUR LES ETOILES BE. **1729**

0296-3698 See BUSEFAL. BULLETIN POUR LES SOUS ENSEMBLES FLOUS ET LEURS APPLICATIONS. **1089**

0296-3981 See NEURO-PSY. **3839**

0296-4074 See LETTRE D'INFORMATION DU COMITE CONSULTATIF NATIONAL D'ETHIQUE POUR LES SCIENCES DE LA VIE ET DE LA SANTE. **2252**

0296-5321 See REVUE DES LABORATOIRES D'ESSAIS, LA. **5148**

0296-807X See HAITI INFORMATION LIBRE. **4475**

0296-8517 See BUREAU D'ETUDES AUTOMATISMES. **1218**

0296-8576 See WINNIE. **1071**

0296-8630 See ARTS ET LIVRES. **342**

0296-8754 See LOGICIELS ET SERVICES. **1193**

0296-9009 See LETTRE DE L'INFECTIOLOGUE, LA. **3604**

0296-9386 See PNEUMATIQUE PARIS, LE. **5077**

0296-9947 See ABSTRACT GYNECO PARIS. **3755**

0296-9955 See ABSTRACT NEURO ET PSY PARIS. **3825**

0297-2557 See ART DU THEATRE (PARIS, FRANCE : 1985). **5361**

0297-2638 See QUI-VIVE INTERNATIONAL. **3313**

0297-2964 See RECHERCHE EN SOINS INFIRMIERS. **3868**

0297-4444 See ETUDES ET SYNTHESES DE L'I.E.M.V.T. **5510**

0297-4592 See REVUE FRANCAISE DE LOGISTIQUE. **5148**

0297-4932 See OSTREICULTEUR FRANCAIS, L'. **2310**

0297-5785 See L'OISEAU MAGAZINE : REVUE DE LA LIGUE FRANCAISE POUR LA PROTECTION DES OISEAUX. **5618**

0297-6005 See KINESITHERAPEUTE PRATICIEN. **3806**

0297-7486 See NOUVEAUX CAHIERS MARIALS. **4982**

0297-8148 See MARINE MICROBIAL FOOD WEBS. **566**

0297-8156 See ABSTRACT PEDIATRIE PARIS. **3899**

0298-0924 See REVUE INTERNATIONALE DE C.F.A.O. ET D'INFOGRAPHIE. **1121**

0298-119X See ROUSSILLON AGRICOLE. **131**

0298-2285 See 01 INFORMATIQUE (HEBDOMADAIRE). **1246**

0298-3850 See REVUE DE MEDECINE PSYCHOSOMATIQUE (1985). **4616**

0298-3958 See LETTRE D'EUROPE AVENIR, LA. **4480**

0298-6027 See PETROSTRATEGIES ENGLISH ED. **1953**

0298-6248 See CLEFS C.E.A. **4446**

0298-6957 See RECUEIL DES ACTES ADMINISTRATIFS - ARDENNES, PREFECTURE. **4678**

0298-6965 See RECUEIL DES ACTES ADMINISTRATIFS DU DEPARTEMENT DES ARDENNES. **4678**

0298-7902 See NOTEBOOKS FOR STUDY AND RESEARCH - INTERNATIONAL INSTITUTE FOR RESEARCH AND EDUCATION. **4484**

0298-7929 See ANNALES D'HISTOIRE DES ENSEIGNEMENTS AGRICOLES. **59**

0298-8879 See TRAVAUX ET DOCUMENTS. **4536**

0298-895X See ANNUAIRE EUROPEEN DE DEFENSE. **4034**

0298-9018 See PERISCOPE. SPHERES. **5137**

0298-9507 See PETROSTRATEGIES (FRENCH EDITION). **4274**

0299-2213 See ANNALES DE CHIRURGIE VASCULAIRE. **3959**

0299-2507 See ALZHEIMER ACTUALITES. **3826**

0299-3147 See POPI. **1068**

0299-3600 See ARCHOZOOLOGIA. **259**

0299-4690 See PANORAMA (LEVALLOIS). **956**

0299-5948 See 01 INFORMATIQUE. ANNUAIRE. **1169**

0299-6898 See PANORAMA PARIS. 1986. **5034**

0299-7258 See TECHNIQUES, SCIENCES, METHODES : TSM. **2244**

0299-7827 See GRIFFON. **1748**

0299-8556 See SOCIETE D'HISTOIRE DU VAL DE LIEPVRE. **2710**

0299-9781 See PAPERCAST. **4236**

030-794X See NEWSBEAT. **5298**

0300-0087 See ANNALI DI OSTETRICIA, GINECOLOGIA, MEDICINA PERINATALE. **3757**

0300-0168 See SBORNIK NAUCNYH TRUDOV - KLINIKA NERVNYH BOLEZNEJ IRKUTSKOGO MEDICINSKOGO INSTITUTA. **3638**

0300-0508 See PHYSIOTHERAPY CANADA. **3627**

0300-0559 See REVUE DE MEDECINE DU TRAVAIL. **3636**

0300-0605 See JOURNAL OF INTERNATIONAL MEDICAL RESEARCH, THE. **3595**

0300-0664 See CLINICAL ENDOCRINOLOGY (OXFORD). **3727**

0300-0702 See MISES A JOUR CARDIOLOGIQUES. **3708**

0300-0729 See RHINOLOGY. **3891**

0300-0753 See DAIRY REVIEW, THE. **152**

0300-0818 See JINKO ZOKI. **3592**

0300-0923 See WHO FOOD ADDITIVES SERIES. **2361**

0300-0974 See CHEST DISEASES. **3563**

0300-1059 See HANDWERK IM LANDE NORDRHEIN-WESTFALEN, DAS. **679**

0300-1067 See STUDIA PHONOLOGICA. **3325**

0300-1237 See EUROPEAN JOURNAL OF FOREST PATHOLOGY. **2379**

0300-1245 See PEDIATRICIAN. **3910**

0300-1261 See CHEMORECEPTION ABSTRACTS. **477**

0300-1296 See REVUE DE PODOLOGIE. **3918**

0300-1598 See BIBLIOGRAPHY OF FAMILY PLANNING & POPULATION. **591**

0300-1628 See INTERNATIONAL TAX REPORT, THE. **902**

0300-1644 See BERLIN MAGAZIN. **2513**

0300-1652 See NIGERIAN MEDICAL JOURNAL. **3622**

0300-1695 See PILOT (CLAYGATE). **31**

0300-1717 See JOURNAL OF AGRICULTURAL ECONOMICS AND DEVELOPMENT. **99**

0300-1725 See CURRENT PROBLEMS IN CLINICAL BIOCHEMISTRY. **486**

0300-1741 See ECONOMIC SURVEY - UNITED REPUBLIC OF TANZANIA. **1558**

0300-1792 See PUBBLICAZIONI DELL'UNIVERSITA CATTOLICA DEL SACRO CUORE. **422**

0300-1989 See JAHRBUCH DER KARL-MAY-GESELLSCHAFT. **3398**

0300-2012 See WOLFENBUTTELER BEITRAEGE. **3256**

0300-2039 See BRUCKE-ARCHIV. **345**

0300-2055 See FORTECKNING OVER ADVOKATER OCH ADVOKATBYRAER AR JAMIE STADGAR FOR SVERIGES ADVOKATSAMFUND. **2972**

0300-2098 See ANNUAL STATISTICAL BULLETIN - SWAZILAND. CENTRAL STATISTICAL OFFICE. **5321**

0300-211X See RADICAL PHILOSOPHY. **4358**

0300-2144 See MANAGEMENT JOURNAL. **877**

0300-2217 See NEW ZEALAND REGISTER OF SPECIALISTS. **3916**

0300-2314 See FIKIR VE SAN'ATTA HAREKET. **2503**

0300-2330 See NEMZETKOZI VASUTI OESSEZEKOETTETESEK KIVONATOS MENETRENDJE. **5433**

0300-2438 See BIULETYN PRZEMYSKOWEGO INSTYTUTE AUTOMATYKI I POMIAROW. **2111**

0300-2462 See UNUTRASNJA TRGOVINA. **734**

0300-2535 See LICNI DOHOCI. **1535**

0300-2543 See ANKETA O PORODICNIM BUDZETIMA RADNICKIH DOMACINSTAVA. **5321**

0300-2608 See ENSEIGNEMENT DU RUSSE, L'. **3279**

0300-2659 See PREVENT. **3629**

0300-2667 See MANAGEMENT INFORMATION SERVICE. **877**

0300-2810 See I.C.I.D. BULLETIN. **2090**

0300-2896 See ARCHIVOS DE BRONCONEUMOLOGIA. **3948**

0300-2977 See NETHERLANDS JOURNAL OF MEDICINE. **3800**

0300-3124 See TEOLLISUUSSANOMAT. **3488**

0300-3140 See ANNUAL REPORT - ROYAL BOTANICAL GARDENS. **499**

0300-3159 See TEKAWENNAKE. **2547**

0300-3167 See UMFORMTECHNIK. **2131**

0300-3256 See ZOOLOGICA SCRIPTA. **5601**

0300-3264 See YOUNG SOLDIER. **1071**

0300-3310 See SKIP. **5457**

0300-3329 See SICHERHEITSINGENIEUR. **2870**

0300-3337 See SICHERHEITSBEAUFTRAGTER. **3176**

0300-337X See SCOTTISH GENEALOGIST, THE. **2472**

0300-340X See RIVISTA STORICA DELL'ANTICHITA. **2628**

0300-3418 See REVISTA DE QUIMICA TEXTIL. **5355**

0300-3434 See RENAL PHYSIOLOGY. 3993

0300-3450 See RECHENTECHNIK DATENVERARBEITUNG. 1262

0300-3485 See RASSEGNA DI DIRITTO LEGISLAZIONE E MEDICINA LEGALE VETERINARIA. 5519

0300-3515 See RALLY (MELBOURNE). 5303

0300-3523 See PROTEE. 3312

0300-3558 See PRISON SERVICE JOURNAL. 3173

0300-3574 See POLLUSTOP. 2238

0300-3604 See PHOTOSYNTHETICA. 492

0300-3620 See CIVIL SERVICE REPORTER (QUEZON CITY). 4702

0300-3639 See PHENIX. 4864

0300-3655 See PERSONALHISTORISK TIDSSKRIFT. 2467

0300-3698 See PROCEEDINGS OF THE CONFERENCE ON PUBLIC RELATIONS IN PUBLIC UNDERTAKINGS. 764

0300-3701 See ORQUIDEA (MEXICO. 1971). 520

0300-371X See NOTES ON THE SCIENCE OF BUILDING. 623

0300-3760 See KUANG YE JI SHU. 2143

0300-3787 See MUNDO ELECTRONICO. EDICION INTERNACIONAL. 2073

0300-3833 See MEDICINA DE POSTGRADO. 3613

0300-3884 See MUNDO FINANCIERO. 1506

0300-3922 See MULTINATIONAL BUSINESS. 1638

0300-3930 See LOCAL GOVERNMENT STUDIES. 876

0300-3981 See INFORMATIONEN ZUR ORTS-, REGIONAL- UND LANDESPLANUNG. 96

0300-4015 See DAI HAN SENG RI HAK HUI JI. 580

0300-4090 See H.K.I.M.S. HONG KONG INDEX OF MEDICAL SPECIALTIES. 3579

0300-4112 See FORSTARCHIV. 2383

0300-4147 See IIMS, INDONESIA INDEX OF MEDICAL SPECIALITIES. 4307

0300-4155 See IMPACT (MANILA). 5203

0300-418X See HONG KONG MONTHLY DIGEST OF STATISTICS. 4698

0300-4228 See FLEET STREET LETTER. 899

0300-4236 See EVANGELISCHE KOMMENTARE. 4957

0300-4279 See EDUCATION 3-13. 1804

0300-4287 See ECONOMICS (LONDON). 1486

0300-4341 See JAPAN 21ST. 685

0300-435X See CANADIAN GUIDER. 1730

0300-4376 See CURRENT TITLES IN ELECTROCHEMISTRY. 1011

0300-4406 See CMN. COMMON MARKET NEWS. 1470

0300-4414 See DEJINY VED A TECHNIKY. 5099

0300-4422 See BOLLETTINO DELLA DEPUTAZIONE DI STORIA PATRIA PER L'UMBRIA. 4633

0300-4430 See EARLY CHILD DEVELOPMENT AND CARE. 2278

0300-4481 See CERVEZA Y MALTA. 2366

0300-4511 See CANADA RIDES. 2529

0300-4554 See BIP. BULLETIN DE L'INDUSTRIE PETROLIERE. 4252

0300-4627 See BLATT FUER SORTENWESEN. 2780

0300-4651 See AFRICAN, THE. 2497

0300-466X See ARTBIBLIOGRAPHIES MODERN. 334

0300-4678 See BROTHERHOOD ACTION. 5229

0300-483X See TOXICOLOGY (AMSTERDAM). 3984

0300-4864 See JOURNAL OF NEUROCYTOLOGY. 538

0300-4937 See MEDECINE ET ARMEES. 4049

0300-4953 See ARTES DE MEXICO. 314

0300-5062 See ACTAS LUSO-ESPANOLAS DE NEUROLOGIA, PSIQUIATRIA Y CIENCIAS AFINES. 3826

0300-5127 See BIOCHEMICAL SOCIETY TRANSACTIONS. 481

0300-5143 See CLEAN AIR. 2226

0300-5178 See WIENER KLINISCHE WOCHENSCHRIFT. SUPPLEMENTUM. 3651

0300-5186 See MONOGRAPHS IN NEURAL SCIENCES. 3838

0300-5194 See EXCERPTA MEDICA. SECTION 46. ENVIRONMENTAL HEALTH AND POLLUTION CONTROL. 3659

0300-5208 See CIBA FOUNDATION SYMPOSIUM. 485

0300-5224 See NIEREN- UND HOCKDRUCKKRANKHEITEN. 3622

0300-5267 See SHILAP. SOCIEDAD HISPANO-LUSO-AMERICANA DE LEPIDOPTEROLOGIA. 5613

0300-5275 See ONTARIO DENTIST. 1332

0300-5283 See MEDICAL JOURNAL OF MALAYSIA. 3610

0300-5305 See ARCHITEKTURA CSR. 291

0300-5356 See ARHITECTURA. 291

0300-5364 See BRITISH JOURNAL OF AUDIOLOGY. 3887

0300-5372 See EXCERPTA MEDICA. SECTION 29. CLINICAL BIOCHEMISTRY. 478

0300-5402 See ACTA UNIVERSITATIS CAROLINAE. GEOGRAPHICA. 2553

0300-5453 See AL-HUDA AL-JADIDAH. 5713

0300-5526 See INTERVIROLOGY. 564

0300-5550 See REVISTA ESPANOLA DE LECHERIA. 198

0300-5577 See JOURNAL OF PERINATAL MEDICINE. 3764

0300-5623 See UROLOGICAL RESEARCH. 3994

0300-5666 See MONOGRAPH SERIES (GREAT BRITAIN. PUBLIC HEALTH LABORATORY SERVICE). 4791

0300-5712 See JOURNAL OF DENTISTRY. 1326

0300-5720 See HOSPITAL DEVELOPMENT. 3784

0300-5755 See ALIMENTARIA. 4764

0300-5771 See INTERNATIONAL JOURNAL OF EPIDEMIOLOGY. 3735

0300-581X See ARBEITSMEDIZIN, SOZIALMEDIZIN, PRAVENTIVMEDIZIN. 2859

0300-5844 See PUBLICATION - CANADIAN FORESTRY SERVICE. 2391

0300-5860 See ZEITSCHRIFT FUER KARDIOLOGIE. 3711

0300-5909 See CARE IN THE HOME. 4771

0300-5968 See HOSPITALS & HEALTH SERVICES YEAR BOOK AND DIRECTORY OF HOSPITAL SUPPLIERS, THE. 3785

0300-6026 See TRENDS IN HOUSING. 2837

0300-6034 See CONSUMER CREDIT AND TRUTH-IN-LENDING COMPLIANCE REPORT. 2956

0300-6069 See NEW JERSEY REGISTER. 4669

0300-6093 See ROYALTON REVIEW. 1846

0300-6123 See RUBBER & PLASTICS NEWS. 5077

0300-6182 See SOUTH DAKOTA MUNICIPALITIES. 4686

0300-6239 See SOUTHERN TOBACCO JOURNAL. 5373

0300-6247 See TALKING LEAF (LOS ANGELES, CALIF. : 1972). 2274

0300-6271 See PIB'S BUSINESS & INCENTIVES. 703

0300-6301 See MOTOR NORTH. 5420

0300-631X See BIBLIOGRAPHY OF PAPER AND THIN-LAYER CHROMATOGRAPHY, AND SURVEY OF APPLICATIONS. 996

0300-6344 See RED CLOUD COUNTRY. 2271

0300-6379 See VESELKA. 1071

0300-6387 See SPORTS CAR. 5425

0300-6425 See RECOVERING LITERATURE. 3351

0300-6433 See TEPSA JOURNAL. 1873

0300-645X See VIRGINIA GENEALOGIST, THE. 2476

0300-6557 See TRAILER BOATS. 596

0300-6565 See WHISPERING WIND. 2275

0300-662X See WESTERN MINING NEWS. 919

0300-6638 See VOLUNTARY ACTION LEADERSHIP. 5313

0300-6646 See NATIONAL ON-CAMPUS REPORT. 1836

0300-676X See OSHKOSH ADVANCE-TITAN. 5769

0300-6794 See NOSTALGIA NEWSLETTER. 2541

0300-6808 See UTE BULLETIN, THE. 2274

0300-6816 See P.A.A. AFFAIRS. 4555

0300-6859 See URBAN AFFAIRS ABSTRACTS. 4701

0300-6875 See AAHS NEWSLETTER. 3

0300-6921 See CHICAGO REPORTER, THE. 4505

0300-693X See DAPHNIS. 3380

0300-7006 See WORLD EDUCATION REPORTS. 1792

0300-7022 See ADRIS NEWSLETTER. 4932

0300-7073 See FAMILY PRACTICE NEWS. 3737

0300-7081 See RECENT ADDITIONS / MUNICIPAL REFERENCE LIBRARY, CITY OF CHICAGO. 3244

0300-7111 See FASHION NEWSLETTER. 1084

0300-7138 See DU PONT CONTEXT. 1605

0300-7162 See DIACRITICS. 3341

0300-7227 See BIBLIOGRAPHY AND INDEX OF MICROPALEONTOLOGY. 4231

0300-7324 See DOW THEORY FORECASTS. 897

0300-7405 See INTERMOUNTAIN LOGGING NEWS. 2401

0300-743X See CORE. 4506

0300-7448 See AMERICAN DANCE GUILD NEWSLETTER. 1310

0300-7464 See NEWS BULLETIN - BRAZILIAN-AMERICAN CHAMBER OF COMMERCE. 1638

0300-7472 See AFTERIMAGE. 4366

0300-7480 See BEER MARKETER'S INSIGHTS. 2364

0300-7499 See BUFFALO SPREE. 2529

0300-7502 See MARYLAND TRAVEL SCENE. 5484

0300-7561 See CRAB, THE. 3204

0300-757X See INSIDE R & D : THE WEEKLY REPORT ON TECHNICAL INNOVATION. 1025

0300-7588 See NEWSLETTER - INTER-SOCIETY COLOR COUNCIL. 5133

0300-7626 See AMERICAN WHITEWATER. 4883

0300-774X See POPULAR ARCHAEOLOGY. 278

0300-7766 See POPULAR MUSIC AND SOCIETY. 4147

0300-788X See SUN TRACKS. 3443

0300-7928 See RIPON COLLEGE MAGAZINE. 1094

0300-7936 See ROBINSON JEFFERS NEWSLETTER. 434

0300-7944 See SURVIVAL (NORTH AMERICAN EDITION). 4497

0300-7995 See CURRENT MEDICAL RESEARCH AND OPINION. 3570

0300-8010 See ACTES DU ... CONGRES NATIONAL DES SOCIETES SAVANTES. SECTION DES SCIENCES. 5080

0300-8037 See SCANDINAVIAN JOURNAL OF SOCIAL MEDICINE. 3639

0300-8045 See REPORTS ON HEALTH AND SOCIAL SUBJECTS. 4799

0300-807X See GEOGRAPHIA MEDICA (BUDAPEST). 3735

0300-8126 See INFECTION. 3714

0300-8134 See JOURNAL OF HUMAN ERGOLOGY. 583

0300-8142 See LIBRI ONCOLOGICI. 3820

0300-8169 See MEDICINA & HISTORIA. 3612

0300-8177 See MOLECULAR AND CELLULAR BIOCHEMISTRY. 491

0300-8185 See PAKISTAN JOURNAL OF BIOCHEMISTRY. 491

0300-8207 See CONNECTIVE TISSUE RESEARCH. 580

0300-8223 See M.I.M.S. IRELAND. 3605

0300-824X See ENVIRONMENTAL QUALITY AND SAFETY. 2169

0300-8258 See CONNECTICUT FIRESIDE. 2531

0300-8274 See ACTUALITES PSYCHIATRIQUES. 3919

0300-8371 See NEUE MUNCHNER BEITRAGE ZUR GESCHICHTE DER MEDIZIN UND NATURWISSENSCHAFTEN. MEDIZINHISTORISCHE REIHE. 3620

0300-838X See MICROBIOLOGY ABSTRACTS. SECTION A : INDUSTRIAL & APPLIED MICROBIOLOGY. 478

0300-8398 See MICROBIOLOGY ABSTRACTS. SECTION B, BACTERIOLOGY. 478

0300-8428 See BASIC RESEARCH IN CARDIOLOGY. 3699

0300-8452 See FORECAST (SILVER SPRING). 1425

0300-8495 See AUSTRALIAN FAMILY PHYSICIAN. 3737

0300-8509 See FORE (NORTH HOLLYWOOD, CALIF.). 4895

0300-8533 See OYO YAKURI. 4319

0300-8584 See MEDICAL MICROBIOLOGY AND IMMUNOLOGY. 566

0300-8592 See AKTUELLE RADIOLOGIE. 3938

0300-8622 See LEBER, MAGEN, DARM. 3747

0300-8630 See KLINISCHE PADIATRIE. 3906

0300-8665 See SCHRIFTENREIHE DES VEREINS FUER WASSER-, BODEN- UND LUFTHYGIENE. 1360

0300-8738 See REVISTA MEDICO-CHIRURGICALA A SOCIETATII DE MEDICI SI NATURALISTI DIN IASI. 3973

0300-8800 See HOLLAND REPORTER, THE. 5635

0300-8827 See ACTA ORTHOPAEDICA SCANDINAVICA. SUPPLEMENTUM. 3880

0300-8835 See ACTA OBSTETRICIA ET GYNECOLOGICA SCANDINAVICA. SUPPLEMENTUM. 3756

0300-8843 See ACTA PAEDIATRICA SCANDINAVICA. SUPPLEMENT. 3899

0300-8851 See HEROLD DER WAHRHEIT. 4962

0300-8878 See SCANDINAVIAN JOURNAL OF INFECTIOUS DISEASES. SUPPLEMENTUM. 3716

0300-8886 See SCANDINAVIAN JOURNAL OF UROLOGY AND NEPHROLOGY. SUPPLEMENT. 3993

0300-8916 See TUMORI. 3824

0300-8932 See REVISTA ESPANOLA DE CARDIOLOGIA. 3710

0300-8959 See NEW ALASKAN. 2540

0300-8967 See ACTA PSYCHIATRICA BELGICA. 3919

0300-9009 See ACTA NEUROLOGICA BELGICA. 3825

0300-9033 See ACTA GASTROENTEROLOGICA LATINOAMERICANA. 3794

0300-9041 See GINECOLOGIA Y OBSTETRICIA DE MEXICO. 3761

0300-9068 See REVISTA LATINOAMERICANA DE PATOLOGIA. 3897

0300-9084 See BIOCHIMIE. 483

0300-9130 See RESEARCH IN EXPERIMENTAL MEDICINE. 3634

0300-9149 See KOKUBYO GAKKAI ZASSHI. 3602

0300-9157 See RYUMACHI. 3807

0300-9165 See NIPPON SANKA FUJINKA GAKKAI ZASSHI. 3766

0300-9173 See NIHON RONEN IGAKKAI ZASSHI. 3754

0300-922X See PERKIN TRANSACTIONS 1. 1046

0300-9246 See DALTON TRANSACTIONS. 1036

0300-9254 See JOURNAL OF THE NATIONAL SCIENCE COUNCIL OF SRI LANKA. 5121

0300-9440 See PROGRESS IN ORGANIC COATINGS. 4225

0300-9475 See SCANDINAVIAN JOURNAL OF IMMUNOLOGY. 3676

0300-9483 See BOREAS. 1368

0300-9491 See FOSSILS AND STRATA. 1376

0300-9513 See REVUE FRANCAISE D'HISTOIRE D'OUTRE-MER. 2706

0300-953X See JOURNAL DE LA SOCIETE DES OCEANISTES. 238

0300-953X See JOURNAL DE LA SOCIETE DES OCEANISTES MICROFILM. 271

0300-9556 See PADIATRIE UND PADOLOGIE. SUPPLEMENTUM. 3907

0300-9564 See JOURNAL OF NEURAL TRANSMISSION. GENERAL SECTION : JNT. 3835

0300-9572 See RESUSCITATION. 3951

0300-9580 See PERKIN TRANSACTIONS. 2. 1046

0300-9629 See COMPARATIVE BIOCHEMISTRY AND PHYSIOLOGY. A, COMPARATIVE PHYSIOLOGY. 579

0300-9645 See JOURNAL OF BIOSOCIAL SCIENCE. SUPPLEMENT. 5205

0300-967X See ZEITSCHRIFT FUER GEBURTSHILFE UND PERINATOLOGIE. 3769

0300-9726 See UPSALA JOURNAL OF MEDICAL SCIENCES. SUPPLEMENT. 3649

0300-9734 See UPSALA JOURNAL OF MEDICAL SCIENCES. 3649

0300-9742 See SCANDINAVIAN JOURNAL OF RHEUMATOLOGY. 3807

0300-9750 See ACTA ENDOCRINOLOGICA. SUPPLEMENTUM. 3726

0300-9815 See REVUE D'ODONTO-STOMATOLOGIE. 1334

0300-9823 See BULLETIN - OFFICE INTERNATIONAL DES EPIZOOTIES (PARIS). 5506

0300-9831 See INTERNATIONAL JOURNAL FOR VITAMIN AND NUTRITION RESEARCH (SUPPLEMENT). 4192

0300-9831 See INTERNATIONAL JOURNAL FOR VITAMIN AND NUTRITION RESEARCH. 4192

0300-9858 See VETERINARY PATHOLOGY. 5526

0300-9947 See NURSING BIBLIOGRAPHY. 421

0300-9963 See SELECTED ANNUAL REVIEWS OF THE ANALYTICAL SCIENCES. 1019

0301-0023 See OCCUPATIONAL MEDICINE. 3623

0301-0066 See PERCEPTION (LONDON). 4607

0301-0074 See ORGANOMETALLIC CHEMISTRY (LONDON. 1972). 1045

0301-0082 See PROGRESS IN NEUROBIOLOGY. 3844

0301-0104 See CHEMICAL PHYSICS. 1050

0301-0139 See PIGMENT CELL. 539

0301-0147 See HAEMOSTASIS. 3580

0301-0163 See HORMONE RESEARCH. 3730

0301-0171 See CYTOGENETICS AND CELL GENETICS. 544

0301-0244 See POLISH JOURNAL OF PHARMACOLOGY AND PHARMACY. 4325

0301-0252 See SOVETSKAIA BIBLIOGRAFIA (MOSKVA, R.S.F.S.R. : 1946). 425

0301-035X See BANGLADESH MEDICAL JOURNAL. 3555

0301-0368 See ASIAN ARCHIVES OF ANAESTHESIOLOGY & RESUSCITATION. 3960

0301-0384 See HEALTH OF THE PEOPLE, THE. 4780

0301-0406 See REVISTA DE PATOLOGIA TROPICAL. 3986

0301-0422 See PUBLIC HEALTH REVIEWS. 4797

0301-0430 See CLINICAL NEPHROLOGY. 3989

0301-0449 See PEDIATRIC RADIOLOGY. 3944

0301-0457 See BEHRING INSTITUTE MITTEILUNGEN. 3667

0301-0481 See H + G ZEITSCHRIFT FUER HAUTKRANKHEITEN. 3720

0301-0511 See BIOLOGICAL PSYCHOLOGY. 4577

0301-0546 See ALLERGOLOGIA ET IMMUNOPATHOLOGIA. 3665

0301-0597 See CESKOSLOVENSKA NEUROLOGIE A NEUROCHIRURGIE. 3829

0301-0643 See EPOCH (CROYDON). 5244

0301-0724 See FOLIA VETERINARIA LATINA. 5510

0301-0732 See JOURNAL OF THE SOUTH AFRICAN VETERINARY ASSOCIATION. 5513

0301-083X See MEDICINSKA ISTRAZIVANJA. SUPPLEMENTUM. 3614

0301-0899 See NIPPON SHIKA MASUI GAKKAI ZASSHI. 1331

0301-0902 See AICHI IKA DAIGAKU IGAKKAI ZASSHI. 3547

0301-102X See BULLETIN OF THE JOHN RYLANDS UNIVERSITY LIBRARY OF MANCHESTER. 2843

0301-1143 See BOLETIN DE LA SOCIEDAD VALENCIANA DE PATOLOGIA DIGESTIVA. 3558

0301-1208 See INDIAN JOURNAL OF BIOCHEMISTRY & BIOPHYSICS. 488

0301-1216 See INDIAN JOURNAL OF PREVENTIVE AND SOCIAL MEDICINE. 3586

0301-1348 See PHARMA INTERNATIONAL (TRI-LINGUAL EDITION). 4319

0301-150X See ELECTROMYOGRAPHY AND CLINICAL NEUROPHYSIOLOGY. 3796

0301-1526 See VASA. 3802

0301-1542 See NIHON KYOBU SHIKKAN GAKKAI ZASSHI. 3800

0301-1569 See ORL; JOURNAL FOR OTO-RHINO-LARYNGOLOGY AND ITS BORDERLANDS. 3890

0301-1623 See INTERNATIONAL UROLOGY AND NEPHROLOGY. 3990

0301-1798 See USPEHI FIZIOLOGICESKIH NAUK. 587

0301-1909 See SBORNIK NAUCHNYKH TRUDOV MONIIAG. 5149

0301-1933 See MATERIALY NAUCNOJ STUDENCESKOJ KONFERENCII. 5127

0301-2123 See ACTA BIOLOGICA PARANAENSE. 439

0301-2131 See SOUTH AFRICAN ARCHIVES OF OPHTHALMOLOGY. 3879

0301-2204 See GYNECOLOGIE. 3761

0301-2212 See SOCIAL BEHAVIOR AND PERSONALITY. 5258

0301-228X See BRITISH JOURNAL OF ORTHODONTICS. 1317

0301-2298 See ACTA FACULTATIS PHARMACEUTICAE UNIVERSITATIS COMENIANAE. 4288

0301-2328 See MICROBIOLOGY ABSTRACTS. SECTION C, ALGOLOGY, MYCOLOGY & PROTOZOOLOGY. 478

0301-2468 See GIGIENA NASELENIH MISC. 4777

0301-2514 See ACTA UNIVERSITATIS PALACKIANAE OLOMUCENSIS FACULTATIS MEDICAE. 3545

0301-2522 See ACTA UNIVERSITATIS PALACKIANAE OLOMUCENSIS FACULTATIS MEDICAE SUPPLEMENTUM. 3545

0301-2549 See POLYTHEMATICAL COLLECTED REPORTS OF THE MEDICAL FACULTY OF THE PALACKY UNIVERSITY. 3628

0301-2581 See NISSEI BYOIN IGAKU ZASSHI. 3622

0301-2603 See NO SHINKEI GEKA. 3843

0301-2611 See KENSA TO GIJUTSU. 3602

0301-2689 See BERICHTE UBER LANDWIRTSCHAFT. SONDERHEFT. 65

0301-2727 See FORTSCHRITTE DER PFLANZENZUCHTUNG. 172

0301-2735 See FORTSCHRITTE IM ACKER- UND PFLANZENBAU. 88

0301-2778 See MAMMALIA DEPICTA. 5590

0301-2794 See FORTSCHRITTE DER VETERINARMEDIZIN. 5510

0301-2867 See TAEHAN PANGSASON HAKHOE CHI. 3947

0301-3006 See ANALYTISCHE PSYCHOLOGIE. 4573

0301-3073 See FRONTIERS OF HORMONE RESEARCH. 487

0301-3081 See CONTRIBUTIONS TO MICROBIOLOGY AND IMMUNOLOGY. 3668

0301-3294 See ZGL. ZEITSCHRIFT FUER GERMANISTISCHE LINGUISTIK. 3335

0301-3308 See BULLETIN SIGNALETIQUE. [SECTION] 140. ELECTROTECHNIQUE. 2037

0301-3499 See BULLETIN SIGNALETIQUE. 885: NUISANCES. 2225

0301-3626 See SANT PAU. 3638

0301-3642 See PROSPETTIVE IN PEDIATRIA. 3911

0301-374X See NEW TECHNIQUES IN BIOPHYSICS AND CELL BIOLOGY. 495

0301-3847 See SCANDINAVIAN JOURNAL OF RHEUMATOLOGY. SUPPLEMENT. 3807

0301-3952 See JOURNAL DE BIOLOGIE BUCCALE. 1326

0301-4126 See BULLETIN DE LA SOCIETE DE L'HISTOIRE DE L'ART FRANCAIS. 345

0301-4184 See DIGITAL PROCESSES. 2042

0301-4193 See CONTRIBUTIONS TO HUMAN DEVELOPMENT. 4583

0301-4207 See RESOURCES POLICY. 2204

0301-4215 See ENERGY POLICY. 1941

0301-4223 See NEW ZEALAND JOURNAL OF ZOOLOGY. 5592

0301-4282 See ENCYCLOPEDIE ENTOMOLOGIQUE PARIS. 5582

0301-441X See EXCELSA. 509

0301-4428 See THEORETICAL LINGUISTICS. 3328

0301-4460 See ANNALS OF HUMAN BIOLOGY. 442

0301-4487 See ANAIS DA ACADEMIA MINEIRA DE MEDICINA. 3549

0301-4606 See BANGLADESH PHARMACEUTICAL JOURNAL. 4293

0301-4622 See BIOPHYSICAL CHEMISTRY. 483

0301-4681 See DIFFERENTIATION (LONDON). 536

0301-472X See EXPERIMENTAL HEMATOLOGY. 3771

0301-4738 See INDIAN JOURNAL OF OPHTHALMOLOGY. 3875

0301-4746 See INDUSTRIAL SAFETY CHRONICLE. 2863

0301-4762 See JOURNAL DE PHARMACOLOGIE CLINIQUE. 4310

0301-4770 See JOURNAL OF CHROMATOGRAPHY LIBRARY. 981

0301-4797 See JOURNAL OF ENVIRONMENTAL MANAGEMENT. 2175

0301-4800 See JOURNAL OF NUTRITIONAL SCIENCE AND VITAMINOLOGY. 4193

0301-4835 See KRANKENVERSICHERUNG (BERLIN), DIE. 2886

0301-4851 See MOLECULAR BIOLOGY REPORTS. 465

0301-486X See MYCOPATHOLOGIA (1975). 576

0301-4894 See NIHON GEKA GAKKAI ZASSHI. 3970

0301-4924 See REPORT BY THE SUB-COMMITTEE ON NUTRITIONAL SURVEILLANCE (LONDON). 4198

0301-5041 See TOKYO-TO SHINKEI KAGAKU SOGO KENKYUJO NEMPO. 3846

0301-5068 See EGYPTIAN JOURNAL OF PHARMACEUTICAL SCIENCES. 4302

0301-5092 See VETERINARIA (MEXICO). 5523

0301-5149 See DEVELOPMENTS IN BIOLOGICAL STANDARDIZATION. 453

0301-536X See FRONTIERS OF ORAL PHYSIOLOGY. 1323

0301-5386 See NEKOTORYE FILOSOFSKIE VOPROSY SOVREMENNOGO ESTESTVOZNANIJA. 4353

0301-5394 See FARMACIJA (KIEV). 4304

0301-5548 See EUROPEAN JOURNAL OF APPLIED PHYSIOLOGY AND OCCUPATIONAL PHYSIOLOGY. 580

0301-5556 See ADVANCES IN ANATOMY, EMBRYOLOGY AND CELL BIOLOGY. 3678

0301-5564 See HISTOCHEMISTRY (BERLIN). 536

0301-5572 See BRITISH JOURNAL OF SEXUAL MEDICINE. 3559

0301-5602 See MAJOR PROBLEMS IN NEUROLOGY. 3837

0301-5629 See ULTRASOUND IN MEDICINE & BIOLOGY. 3648

0301-5645 See PEOPLE (ENGLISH ED.). 590

0301-5661 See COMMUNITY DENTISTRY AND ORAL EPIDEMIOLOGY. 1319

0301-567X See BEITRAEGE ZUR TROPISCHEN LANDWIRTSCHAFT UND VETERINARMEDIZIN. 3985

0301-5718 See UPDATE. 3739

0301-5742 See JOURNAL OF INDIAN ORTHODONTIC SOCIETY, THE. 1327

0301-5750 See BULLETIN OF THE PAN AMERICAN HEALTH ORGANIZATION. 4769

0301-5785 See AUSTRALIAN OUTLOOK. LONDON. 2510

0301-603X See SUID.-AFRIKAANSE TYDSKRIF VIR LANDBOUVOORLIGTING. 138

0301-620X See JOURNAL OF BONE AND JOINT SURGERY. BRITISH VOLUME. 3966

0301-6226 See LIVESTOCK PRODUCTION SCIENCE. 214

0301-6269 See PRISMA (JAKARTA, INDONESIA). 2662

0301-6307 See QUADERNI STORICI. 2704

0301-6315 See REPORT / HANNAH RESEARCH INSTITUTE. 198

0301-6323 See SCANDINAVIAN JOURNAL OF IMMUNOLOGY. SUPPLEMENT. 3676

0301-6331 See PROCEEDINGS OF THE UNIVERSITY OF OTAGO MEDICAL SCHOOL. 3630

0301-634X See RADIATION AND ENVIRONMENTAL BIOPHYSICS. 496

0301-6404 See NORTH EASTERN AFFAIRS. 2660

0301-6412 See NEUROLINGUISTICS (AMSTERDAM). 3305

0301-6455 See STUDI E DOCUMENTI DI ARCHITETTURA. 309

0301-6463 See MUSEOLOGIA (AMSTERDAM). 4168

0301-6552 See ESTATISTICA DA ACTIVIDADE MINEIRA NO ESTADO DE ANGOLA. 2004

0301-6579 See COMENTARIOS BIBLIOGRAFICOS AMERICANOS. 3340

0301-6587 See ANTHROPOLOGICA (BARCELONA). 228

0301-6668 See FISKE (STOCKHOLM). 2303

0301-6692 See MICHEL EUROPA-KATALOG. 2786

0301-679X See TRIBOLOGY INTERNATIONAL. 2108

0301-6811 See ZEITSCHRIFT FUER KINDER- UND JUGENDPSYCHIATRIE. 3937

0301-6943 See VETERINARY HISTORY. 5525

0301-7001 See STUDIA BOTANICA HUNGARICA. 528

0301-7028 See WATER SERVICES. 2248

0301-7036 See PROBLEMAS DEL DESARROLLO. 1639

0301-7052 See REVISTA DE FARMACIA E BIOQUIMICA BELO HORIZONTE. 4328

0301-7117 See ASIAN MANUFACTURING. 3475

0301-7176 See PROGRESS REPORT - INSTITUTE OF HYDRODYNAMICS AND HYDRAULIC ENGINEERING (LYNGBY). 2095

0301-7257 See BYRON JOURNAL. 3339

0301-7311 See SCANDINAVIAN JOURNAL OF SOCIAL MEDICINE. SUPPLEMENTUM. 3639

0301-732X See ARCHIVOS DE MEDICINA VETERINARIA. 5504

0301-7362 See ISTANBUL TP FAKULTESI MECMUASI. 3590

0301-7516 See INTERNATIONAL JOURNAL OF MINERAL PROCESSING. 2140

0301-7567 See GUIA DE REUNIONES CIENTIFICAS Y TECNICAS EN ARGENTINA. 5108

0301-7575 See ELECTRON SPIN RESONANCE SPECTROSCOPY ABSTRACTS. 4443

0301-7605 See CRITIQUE (GLASGOW). 4470

0301-7737 See ANNALES UNIVERSITATIS MARIAE CURIE-SKODOWSKA. SECTIO DD, MEDICINA VETERINARIA. 5503

0301-7842 See MAJOR PROBLEMS IN DERMATOLOGY. 3721

0301-8059 See ANAIS DA SOCIEDADE ENTOMOLOGICA DO BRASIL. 5605

0301-8121 See JOURNAL OF CHINESE PHILOSOPHY. 4350

0301-8164 See EGYPTIAN JOURNAL OF HORTICULTURE. 2413

0301-8172 See EGYPTIAN JOURNAL OF MICROBIOLOGY. 562

0301-8180 See EGYPTIAN JOURNAL OF PHYTOPATHOLOGY. 509

0301-8199 See EGYPTIAN JOURNAL OF VETERINARY SCIENCE. 5509

0301-8202 See HART BULLETIN. 3705

0301-8288 See MONTHLY REPORT - MINISTRY OF LABOUR & MANPOWER (KUALA LUMPUR). 1691

0301-8296 See MAYURQA. 2697

0301-8539 See GUIDE DU TRAVAIL DES METAUX. 4003

0301-8571 See EGYPTIAN JOURNAL OF FOOD SCIENCE. 2334

0301-8628 See COMPENDIO STATISTICO ITALIANO. 5325

0301-8679 See CARBOHYDRATE CHEMISTRY & METABOLISM ABSTRACTS. 966

0301-8695 See ANIMAL BEHAVIOR ABSTRACTS. 5604

0301-8849 See EGYPTIAN JOURNAL OF BILHARZIASIS. 3796

0301-8857 See MICHEL EUROPA-KATALOG. 2786

0301-8881 See LET'S SQUARE DANCE. 1313

0301-9020 See BOTSWANA. 644

0301-9047 See DEMOCRATIC WORLD. 1591

0301-908X See FINNISH FISHERIES RESEARCH. 2301

0301-9101 See IDEAS (HYDERABAD). 2738

0301-9187 See TRAVAUX DE L'INSTITUT DE SPEOLOGIE EMILE RACOVITZA. 4173

0301-9195 See BRITISH PTERIDOLOGICAL SOCIETY BULLETIN. 504

0301-9225 See HANDBUCH DER OFFENTLICHEN BIBLIOTHEKEN. 3213

0301-9233 See IRONMAKING & STEELMAKING. 4005

0301-9268 See PRECAMBRIAN RESEARCH. 1391

0301-9314 See METAL STOCKHOLDING SERVICES & EQUIPMENT. 1505

0301-9322 See INTERNATIONAL JOURNAL OF MULTIPHASE FLOW. 2067

0301-9330 See BULLETIN OF QUANTITATIVE AND COMPUTER METHODS IN SOUTH ASIAN STUDIES. 2647

0301-9489 See DOUSOU SHUANGYUEKAN. 2503

0301-9837 See HATTEN TOJO KOKU NO TOKEI SHIRYO MOKUROKU. 416

0301-9845 See DENSHI GIJUTSU SOGO KENKYUJO YORAN. 2041

0301-9934 See KANCHI KENCHIKU. 618

0302-0029 See HANZAIGAKU ZASSHI. 3740

0302-0665 See FRONTIERS OF GASTROINTESTINAL RESEARCH. 3744

0302-0681 See SOUTH AFRICA. 2643

0302-0738 See JOURNAL DE PHYSIQUE. II (LES ULIS). 4408

0302-0738 See JOURNAL DE PHYSIQUE. I (LES ULIS). 4408

0302-0738 See JOURNAL DE PHYSIQUE. III (LES ULIS). 4408

0302-0762 See HOT BUTTERED SOUL. 4121

0302-0770 See BORSE (WIEN). 892

0302-0797 See CHEMICAL ENGINEER (LONDON). 2009

0302-0800 See MEDECINE, BIOLOGIE, ENVIRONNEMENT. 464

0302-0924 See ANNALES DE L'UNIVERSITE D'ABIDJAN. SERIE G : GEOGRAPHIE. 2554

0302-0940 See BOLETIM ESTATISTICO - BANCO REGIONAL DE DESENVOLVIMENTO DO EXTREMO SUL. 779

0302-0959 See REVISTA DA FACULDADE SALESIANA. 2552

0302-0983 See MARINA YEARBOOK. 594

0302-1033 See ANNALES MUSEI GOULANDRIS. 4161

0302-1041 See EUTHYNE. 2516

0302-1122 See ANTHROPINES SHESEIS. 5191

0302-1319 See JOURNAL OF INDIAN WRITING IN ENGLISH, THE. 3400

0302-1343 See BULLETIN DE LA CHAMBRE DE COMMERCE D'INDUSTRIE ET AGRICULTURE DE MAURITANIE. 818

0302-136X See HRONIKO (ATHENAI). 322

0302-1475 See SIGN LANGUAGE STUDIES. 3321

0302-1610 See INDIAN JOURNAL OF PSYCHIATRIC SOCIAL WORK. 5289

0302-1653 See BLOOD PLATELETS. 410

0302-167X See PTA HEUTE. 4326

0302-2013 See DATA KREDIT PERBANKAN. 787

0302-2196 See INTERNATIONALES VERZEICHNIS DER WIRTSCHAFTSVERBANDE. 842

0302-2277 See BOLETIN - OBSERVATORIO ASTRONOMICO MUNICIPAL DE ROSARIO. 393

0302-2366 See ADVANCES IN NEUROSURGERY. 3957

0302-2404 See BULLETIN OF POSTGRADUATE INSTITUTE OF MEDICAL EDUCATION AND RESEARCH, CHANDIGARH. 3560

0302-2498 See CHRONICLE OF PARLIAMENTARY ELECTIONS. 4637

0302-251X See SIEMENS ZEITSCHRIFT. 2081

0302-2528 See SIEMENS REVIEW. 2081

0302-2560 See ELIN-ZEITSCHRIFT. 1972

0302-2609 See INDUSTRIES ELECTRIQUES ET ELECTRONIQUES (PARIS, 1973). 2064

0302-2676 See BULLETIN SCIENTIFIQUE DE L'ASSOCIATION DES INGENIEURS ELECTRICIENS SORTIS DE L'INSTITUT ELECTROTECHNIQUE MONTEFIORE. 2037

0302-2684 See SCIENCES GEOLOGIQUES. 1396

0302-2692 See SCIENCES GEOLOGIQUES. BULLETIN. 1396

0302-2749 See BULLETIN OF THE GEOLOGICAL INSTITUTIONS OF THE UNIVERSITY OF UPPSALA. 1370

0302-282X See NEUROPSYCHOBIOLOGY. 3842

0302-2838 See EUROPEAN UROLOGY. 3989

0302-2870 See PUMPS AND OTHER FLUIDS MACHINERY ABSTRACTS. 2127

0302-2935 See MALAYSIAN FORESTER, THE. 2387

0302-2994 See ACTA PHYSIOLOGICA SCANDINAVICA. SUPPLEMENTUM. 577

0302-3052 See MONDES EN DEVELOPPEMENT. 1505

0302-3087 See CUADERNOS COLOMBIANOS. 2551

0302-3141 See HANDBOOK OF VEGETATION SCIENCE. 512

0302-3184 See BAPTIST UNION DIRECTORY, THE. 5056

0302-3303 See DIRECTORY OF ALTERNATIVE PERIODICALS (BRIGHTON). 415

0302-3427 See SCIENCE & PUBLIC POLICY. 4685

0302-3451 See AUDIOVISUAL LIBRARIAN, THE. 3192

0302-4091 See WHO OWNS WHOM: AUSTRALASIA AND FAR EAST. 720

0302-4148 See MERSEYSIDE CHAMBER OF COMMERCE AND INDUSTRY DIRECTORY. 820

0302-4172 See MIMS MIDDLE EAST. 3617

0302-4210 See PHOTOGRAPHIC TECHNIQUES IN SCIENTIFIC RESEARCH. 4374

0302-4288 See CZECHOSLOVAK BIBLIOGRAPHY ON INDUSTRIAL HYGIENE AND OCCUPATIONAL DISEASES. 2872

0302-4296 See CATALOGO DE ESPECIALIDADES FORMACEUTICOS. 4295

0302-4342 See ANALES ESPANOLES DE PEDIATRIA. 3900

0302-4350 See AKTUELLE NEUROLOGIE. 3826

0302-4423 See INDICATEURS DE L'ECONOMIE TOGOLAISE. 1567

0302-4520 See EGYPTIAN JOURNAL OF ANIMAL PRODUCTION. 210

0302-4563 See PORK INDUSTRY GAZETTE. 218

0302-4598 See BIOELECTROCHEMISTRY AND BIOENERGETICS. 2036

0302-4660 See NIGERIAN JOURNAL OF PAEDIATRICS. 3907

0302-4717 See RIVISTA DI PATOLOGIA E CLINICA DELLA TUBERCOLOSI E DI PNEUMOLOGIA. 3952

0302-4784 See ANNUAL REPORT - TRADE DEVELOPMENT AUTHORITY (NEW DELHI). 823

0302-4830 See INFORMATIVO - SNI. 5113

0302-4873 See ANNUAL REPORT - WESTERN STATE LIBRARY. 3191

0302-5020 See AGARD HIGHLIGHTS. 6

0302-5144 See CONTRIBUTIONS TO NEPHROLOGY. 3989

0302-5160 See HISTORIOGRAPHIA LINGUISTICA. 3285

0302-5268 See INVESTIGACION E INFORMACION TEXTIL Y DE TENSIOACTIVOS. 5353

0302-5276 See JAARVERSLAG / RIJKSINSTITUUT VOOR NATUURBEHEER. 4166

0302-5349 See HANDBOG - DANSK MASKINHANDLERFORENING. 159

0302-5470 See FIZIKA ZHIDKOGO SOSTOIANIIA. 4403

0302-5640 See CULTURES AU ZAIRE ET EN AFRIQUE. 234

0302-5691 See ANTARTIDA (BUENOS AIRES). 2554

0302-6086 See CISLENNYE METODY V DINAMIKE RAZREZENNYH GAZOV. 4427

0302-6221 See BAZAK GUIDE TO SPAIN. 5462

0302-6248 See QRQ. 4843

0302-6256 See VEDERE INTERNATIONAL. 4217

0302-6353 See BERICHT DES KULTUSMINISTERIUMS BADEN-WURTTEMBERG ZUR BERATUNG DES HAUSHALTSPLANES. 1860

0302-6469 See VERHANDELINGEN - KONINKLIJKE ACADEMIE VOOR GENEESKUNDE VAN BELGIE. 3649

0302-6477 See GALVANO-ORGANO. 4002

0302-6566 See KARKA (TEL AVIV). 2197

0302-6701 See EGYPTIAN JOURNAL OF SOIL SCIENCE. 170

0302-6795 See ANNUAL REPORT - BANK EKSPOR IMPOR INDONESIA. 770

0302-6868 See ANNUAIRE - ACADEMIE D'ATHENES. 1808

0302-6930 See PROBLEMY STOMATOLOGII (TASKENT). 1333

0302-6973 See NATIONAL DEBATE, THE. 4483

0302-7074 See DECIDUOUS FRUIT GROWER, THE. 2413

0302-7260 See HOKKEJ (MOSKVA). 4899

0302-7465 See DEVELOPMENTS IN THE EUROPEAN COMMUNITIES (DUBLIN). 1555

0302-752X See FOLCLORICA (GOIANIA). 2319

0302-7538 See GUIDELINES FOR INDUSTRIES (NEW DELHI). 1608

0302-7554 See INDIAN BIOLOGIST. 458

0302-7562 See INDIAN JOURNAL OF ZOOLOGY. 5586

0302-766X See CELL AND TISSUE RESEARCH. 533

0302-7716 See ZIEMNIAK. 191

0302-7724 See RS. CUADERNOS DE REALIDADES SOCIALES. 5256

0302-7767 See COOPERATIVE PERSPECTIVE. 1541

0302-7775 See INGEGNERIA AMBIENTALE INQUINAMENTO E DEPURAZIONE. 4784

0302-7813 See RONTGEN-BERICHTE. 3946

0302-8054 See ABHANDLUNGEN DER AKADEMIE DER WISSENSCHAFTEN DER DDR. 5079

0302-8070 See BALNEOLOGIA BOHEMICA. 4379

0302-8089 See GATEWAYS OF EASTERN AFRICA. 5449

0302-8119 See OFEQ (TEL-AVIV). 1577

0302-8127 See IMANUEL. 5048

0302-8178 See BAY ZIK. 3365

0302-8186 See FOLQ UN MEDINAH. 2651

0302-8194 See BI-YEAF. 14

0302-8348 See ARSSKRIFT - SYDSVENSKA ORTNAMNSSALLSKAPETS. 3267

0302-8402 See TRUDY INSTITUTA - NAUCNO-ISSLEDOVATELSKIJ INSTITUT KLINICESKOJ I EKSPERIMENTALNOJ HIRURGII M.Z. S.S.S.R. 3977

0302-8445 See KNIZHKA PARTIINOGO AKTIVISTA. 4660

0302-8453 See RASCETY ATOMNYH I JADERNYH KONSTANT. 4450

0302-8542 See NUCLEON. 2157

0302-8577 See EKSPONEN. 2503

0302-8585 See ZESZYTY KAUKOWE UNIWERYSTETU JAGIELLONSKIEGO. PRACE BOTANICZNE. 531

0302-8607 See BULLETIN STATISTIQUE DU SECRETARIAT GENERAL A L'AVIATION CIVILE. 41

0302-8623 See ILLUSTRATED WEEKLY OF INDIA ANNUAL, THE. 2504

0302-8720 See K.G.M.T.I. KOZLEMENYEI. 1984

0302-8801 See KENKYU NENKAN. 3293

0302-8852 See REVISOR (AMSTERDAM). 3429

0302-8879 See SERI PMST. 4685

0302-8887 See DIAN (KOTA BHARU). 2503

0302-8933 See ARCHIVES OF MICROBIOLOGY. 559

0302-9034 See RAPORT - INSTYTUT FIZYKI I TECHNIKI JADROWEJ AGH. 4450

0302-9069 See LITEINCE PROIZVODSTVO, METALLOVEDENIE I OBRABOTKA METALLOV DAVLENIEM. 4007

0302-9107 See MATERIALY PO ISTORII KIRGIZOV I KIRGIZII. 2697

0302-9247 See HAMBURG HANDBUCH. 4475

0302-9255 See GASTROENTEROLOGISCHE FORTBILDUNGSKURSE FUER DIE PRAXIS. 3745

0302-9263 See MEDITERRANEE MEDICALE. 3614

0302-9271 See SEMAINE DES HOPITAUX. THERAPEUTIQUE. 3792

0302-9328 See SPECIAL ENVIRONMENTAL REPORT - WORLD METEOROLOGICAL ORGANIZATION. 1434

0302-9409 See MOVIMIENTO DE PRODUCTOS AGRICOLAS ALIMENTICIOS INGRESADOS A LIMA METROPOLITANA. 110

0302-9468 See BGS, ZEITSCHRIFT DES BUNDESGRENZSCHUTZES. 2513

0302-9646 See MAWAS DIRI. 2506

0302-9654 See BERICHT AUS DEM HAUS DER NATUR IN SALZBURG. 4162

0302-9743 See LECTURE NOTES IN COMPUTER SCIENCE. 1214

0302-9751 See HIMICESKAJA TERMODINAMIKA I RAVNOVESIJA. 1052

0302-9778 See UGYVITEL ES INFORMACIO AZ ALLAMIGAZGATASBAN. 4692

0302-9794 See NOVUM GEBRAUCHSGRAPHIK. 381

0302-9808 See JOURNAL OF THE FOOD MARKETING CENTRE. 2347

0302-9859 See MANAGEMENT DAN USAHAWAN INDONESIA. 876

0303-013X See KISHO KENKYUJO KENKYU GYOSEKI GAIYO SHU. 1427

0303-0245 See NIIGATA-KEN SUISAN SHIKENJO NEMPO. 2309

0303-0350 See KANAGAWA-KEN EISEI KENKYUJO KENKYU HKOKU. 4788

0303-0377 See HATTATSU SHOGAI KENKYUJO NEMPO. 547

0303-0512 See DAIYAMONDO GENDAI EIGO NO KISO CHISHIKI. 3276

0303-0857 See CHIEN WEI. 2502

0303-0881 See XING GUANG. 2510

0303-089X See XIN GINGNIAN KEXUE. 5171

0303-0954 See DAOYU JIKAN. 3380

0303-1136 See PROCEEDINGS OF THE FULL BOARD MEETING - ISCU AB. 5140

0303-1152 See MANO EN EL CAJON, LA. 3465

0303-1179 See ASTERISQUE. 3496

0303-125X See ONE WORLD (GENEVA). 4983

0303-1276 See BULLETIN DE LIAISON DE LA RECHERCHE EN INFORMATIQUE ET AUTOMATIQUE. 1218

0303-1381 See YEDION LE-TEKNOLOGYAH SEL MEDA U-MAHSEVIM. 1263

0303-139X See QIYYUM. 2180

0303-1497 See EMEQ, HA-. 5047
0303-1500 See ALON HA-ONATI - NEOT QEDUMIM, HA-. 5014
0303-1519 See HITHADSHUT. 2652
0303-1527 See HINUK MERUGARIM BE-YISRAEL. 1800
0303-1594 See DIRECTORY OF THE UNITED NATIONS ORGANIZATION AND SPECIALIZED AGENCIES IN IRAQ. 3127
0303-1675 See BOLETIM TRIMESTRAL DE ESTATISTICA - INSTITUTO NACIONAL DE ESTATISTICA. DELEGACAO SE S. TOME E PRINCIPE. 5323
0303-1705 See BOLETIM TRIMESTRAL DE ESTATISTICA (FUNCHAL). 5323
0303-1721 See BULLETIN TECHNIQUE D'INFORMATION (FRANCE. MINISTERE DE L'AGRICULTURE ET DU DEVELOPPEMENT RURAL). 70
0303-1799 See PRIX INFORMATION (ALGER). 1594
0303-1829 See NOTAS DE POBLACION. 4555
0303-1853 See AGREKON. 46
0303-2000 See ANYAMOZGATAS GEPESITESE A GEPIRPARBAN, AZ. 1598
0303-2264 See PROBLEMY MEDYCYNY WIEKU ROZWOJOWEGO. 3629
0303-2272 See POLSKA BIBLIOGRAFIA NAUK KOSCIELNYCH. 4987
0303-2310 See ARSBERETNING - GEOLOGISK CENTRALINSTITUT (KBENHAVN). 1366
0303-240X See REVUE DE L'ENERGIE. 1956
0303-2418 See NORMALE UND PATHOLOGISCHE ANATOMIE. 3679
0303-2434 See ITC JOURNAL, THE. 1356
0303-2442 See TERVEYDENHUOLTO. 4804
0303-2485 See KUUKAUSIKATSAUS SUOMEN ILMASTOON. 1427
0303-2493 See INFORMATIONEN ZUR RAUMENTWICKLUNG. 2825
0303-2507 See DRAHTHERSTELLUNG UND BEARBEITUNG, DRAHTERZEUGNISSE. 3478
0303-2515 See ANNALS OF THE SOUTH AFRICAN MUSEUM. 4083
0303-2582 See INDIAN JOURNAL OF CLINICAL PSYCHOLOGY. 4589
0303-2647 See BIO SYSTEMS. 444
0303-2930 See CITRANA. 2503
0303-3007 See INTERNATIONAL JOURNAL OF KOREAN STUDIES. 2654
0303-3066 See MAYA MARATHI. 3410
0303-3171 See MANUSIA DAN MASYARAKAT. 240
0303-3236 See BULLETIN PENELITIAN KESEHATAN. 4769
0303-3309 See ISO CATALOGUE. 4030
0303-3821 See BHARTIYA KRISHI ANUSANDHAN PATRIKA. 66
0303-3848 See BRASS BULLETIN. 4105
0303-3899 See BULLETIN DU BUREAU INTERNATIONAL D'EDUCATION. 1729
0303-3902 See INTERFACE (AMSTERDAM). 4123
0303-3910 See IRISH JOURNAL OF PSYCHOLOGY, THE. 4592
0303-3937 See ORBIS MUSICAE. 4144
0303-4011 See PLASTICOS UNIVERSALES. 4457
0303-402X See COLLOID AND POLYMER SCIENCE. 1050
0303-4097 See INDIAN JOURNAL OF MYCOLOGY AND PLANT PATHOLOGY. 575
0303-4119 See BIOLOGICESKIE NAUKI. 4163
0303-4135 See ANNALES ACADEMIAE MEDICAE GEDANENSIS. 3549
0303-4178 See POETICA (MUNCHEN). 3424
0303-4186 See CONTRIBUTIONS TO ATMOSPHERIC PHYSICS. 1424
0303-4216 See TOPICS IN APPLIED PHYSICS. 4423
0303-4232 See SCALA. 2522
0303-4240 See REVIEWS OF PHYSIOLOGY, BIOCHEMISTRY AND PHARMACOLOGY. 586
0303-4259 See PSYCHIATRISCHE PRAXIS. 3934

0303-4283 See LEBEN UND UMWELT. 463
0303-4305 See INNERE MEDIZIN. 3797
0303-4380 See BASLER ZAHLENSPIEGEL. 1548
0303-4410 See ESTIMATED INTERNAL MIGRATION BULLETIN (PORT OF SPAIN). 4552
0303-4445 See MARINERS' (SINGAPORE). 4179
0303-4534 See ZEITSCHRIFT FUER GEOLOGISCHE WISSENSCHAFTEN. 1401
0303-4569 See ANDROLOGIA (BERLIN, WEST). 3549
0303-4615 See STUDI NOVECENTESCHI. 5223
0303-4690 See ANALES DE LA FUNDACION PUIGVERT. 3988
0303-4763 See ANUARIO ESTADISTICO DE SEGUROS. 2897
0303-4909 See FAUNA POLSKI. 5583
0303-4933 See ITALIA NELLA POLITICA INTERNAZIONALE, L'. 4526
0303-4992 See KETAHANAN NASIONAL. 4048
0303-5042 See MAGYAR PEDIATER. 3906
0303-5093 See METEOROS (BOGOTA). 1431
0303-5190 See PURNAWIRAWAN (JAKARTA). 2662
0303-5220 See REPRODUCCION (MADRID). 3767
0303-5239 See REVISTA CUBANA DE CIENCIA AVICOLA. 220
0303-5247 See RIVISTA INTERNAZIONALE DI ECONOMIA DEI TRASPORTI. 1519
0303-5476 See CHIBA IGAKU ZASSHI. 3563
0303-5514 See DNIAS ANNUAL REPORT + 1. 5101
0303-5689 See MUZYKA I ZIZN. 4139
0303-5840 See SBORNIK RABOT TOLJATTINSKOJ GIDROMETEOROLOGICESKOJ OBSERVATORII. 1417
0303-5859 See SEIKABUTSU SEISAN SHUKKA TOKEI. 1520
0303-5964 See ABHA. ANNUAL BIBLIOGRAPHY OF THE HISTORY OF THE PRINTED BOOK AND LIBRARIES. 3257
0303-5980 See STUDIA LEIBNITIANA. SUPPLEMENTA. 4362
0303-5999 See BIBLIOGRAPHIE DER DEUTSCHSPRACHIGEN PSYCHOLOGISCHEN LITERATUR. 4622
0303-6065 See NIHON HYOJUN SANGYO BUNRUI; GOJUON SAKUIN HYO. 5334
0303-6227 See CHIRURGISCHES FORUM FUER EXPERIMENTELLE UND KLINISCHE FORSCHUNG. 3962
0303-6286 See TIERAERZTLICHE PRAXIS. 5523
0303-6405 See DOCUMENTA OPHTHALMOLOGICA. PROCEEDINGS SERIES. 3874
0303-6448 See STATISTICAL YEARBOOK OF THE NETHERLANDS. 5341
0303-6456 See TVZ : VAKBLAD VOOR DE VERPLEGKUNDIGEN. 3870
0303-6464 See DEUTSCHE ZAHN-, MUND-, UND KIEFERHEILKUNDE MIT ZENTRALBLATT. 1322
0303-6480 See NORDISK MEDICINHISTORISK AARSBOK. 3623
0303-657X See ZEITSCHRIFT FUER ERKRANKUNGEN DER ATMUNGSORGANE. 3952
0303-6758 See JOURNAL OF THE ROYAL SOCIETY OF NEW ZEALAND. 5121
0303-6812 See JOURNAL OF MATHEMATICAL BIOLOGY. 461
0303-6847 See JOURNAL OF VASCULAR RESEARCH. 3707
0303-688X See PARASITOLOGIA HUNGARICA. 468
0303-6898 See SCANDINAVIAN JOURNAL OF STATISTICS. 5338
0303-691X See WEST AFRICAN JOURNAL OF PHARMACOLOGY AND DRUG RESEARCH. 4332
0303-6960 See INDIAN JOURNAL OF NEMATOLOGY : OFFICIAL PUBLICATION OF THE NEMATOLOGICAL SOCIETY OF INDIA. 5586

0303-6979 See JOURNAL OF CLINICAL PERIODONTOLOGY. 1326
0303-6987 See JOURNAL OF CUTANEOUS PATHOLOGY. 3721
0303-6995 See JOURNAL OF NEURAL TRANSMISSION. SUPPLEMENTUM. 3835
0303-7193 See NEW ZEALAND JOURNAL OF PHYSIOTHERAPY. 4381
0303-7207 See MOLECULAR AND CELLULAR ENDOCRINOLOGY. 3732
0303-7215 See MAN-MADE FIBERS OF JAPAN. 5354
0303-7339 See TIJDSCHRIFT VOOR PSYCHIATRIE. 3937
0303-7460 See BULLETIN MENSUEL - CHAMBRE DE COMMERCE, D'AGRICULTURE ET D'INDUSTRIE DE LA REPUBLIQUE TOGOLAISE. 1549
0303-7495 See BULLETIN DE L'INSTITUT FRANCAIS D'ETUDES ANDINES. 2724
0303-7525 See BRAZILIAN JOURNAL OF VETERINARY RESEARCH AND ANIMAL SCIENCE : REVISTA DA FACULDADE DE MEDICINA VETERINARIA E ZOOTECNIA DA UNIVERSIDADE DE SAO PAULO. 5506
0303-7584 See BOLETIN DEL INSTITUTO DE TONANTZINTLA. 393
0303-7622 See AUDIOVISIONE (ROMA). 5315
0303-7657 See REVISTA BRASILEIRA DE SAUDE OCUPACIONAL. 2869
0303-7762 See ANAIS DO INSTITUTO DE HIGIENE E MEDICINA TROPICAL. 3549
0303-7800 See PERIODICA POLYTECHNICA : TRANSPORTATION ENGINEERING. TRANSPORT. 5389
0303-7819 See ENCYCLOPAEDIA JUDAICA YEAR BOOK. 5047
0303-7908 See SOCIJALNA PSIHIJATRIJA. 3937
0303-7940 See ARCHIFACTS. 2479
0303-805X See ISO BULLETIN. 4030
0303-8122 See JOURNAL OF THE SCIENCE SOCIETY OF THAILAND. 5121
0303-8130 See SUHDANNE. 1586
0303-8157 See POZNAN STUDIES IN THE PHILOSOPHY OF THE SCIENCES AND THE HUMANITIES. 4357
0303-8173 See ACTA MEDICA AUSTRIACA. 3794
0303-8181 See ACTA MEDICA AUSTRIACA. SUPPLEMENT. 3794
0303-8300 See SOCIAL INDICATORS RESEARCH. 5219
0303-8351 See OUTPUT. 1261
0303-8408 See SOZIAL- UND PRAEVENTIVMEDIZIN. 4803
0303-8432 See GIORNALE ITALIANO DI ALLERGOLOGIA E IMMUNOLOGIA CLINICA. 3670
0303-8440 See REVISTA DE IGIENA, BACTERIOLOGIE, VIRUSOLOGIE, PARAZITOLOGIE, EPIDEMIOLOGIE, PNEUMOFTIZIOLOGIE. SERIA : IGIENA. 4799
0303-8459 See EXCERPTA MEDICA. SECTION 50. EPILEPSY ABSTRACTS. 3659
0303-8467 See CLINICAL NEUROLOGY AND NEUROSURGERY. 3830
0303-8505 See NAGALAND BUDGET. SOME FACTS AND CHARTS. 4699
0303-853X See ECONOMIC SURVEY OF LIBERIA. 1558
0303-8556 See C. E. G. BULLETIN. 2136
0303-8564 See ARCHIPELAGO. 2768
0303-8629 See DETAILED DEMAND FOR GRANTS OF INDUSTRIES & COMMERCE DEPARTMENT. GOVERNMENT OF JAMMU AND KASHMIR. 831
0303-8637 See DETAILED DEMAND FOR GRANTS OF LADAKH AFFAIR DEPARTMENT. GOVERNMENT OF JAMMU AND KASHMIR. 1479
0303-8645 See DETAILED DEMAND FOR GRANTS OF FOOD SUPPLIES AND TRANSPORT DEPARTMENT. GOVERNMENT OF JAMMU AND KASHMIR. 4642

0303-8653 See DETAILED DEMAND FOR GRANTS OF EDUCATION DEPARTMENT. GOVERNMENT OF JAMMU AND KASHMIR. 1735

0303-8696 See COUNCIL FOR MUTUAL ECONOMIC ASSISTANCE. 1472

0303-884X See PEDIATRIC AND ADOLESCENT MEDICINE. 3908

0303-8866 See TERAPEVTICHESKAIA STOMATOLOGIIA. 1336

0303-8874 See ANALES OTORRINOLARINGOLOGICOS IBERO-AMERICANOS. 3886

0303-8890 See DERMOFARMACIA. 3720

0303-9021 See VLAAMS DIERGENEESKUNDIG TIJDSCHRIFT. 5527

0303-9056 See MEDEDELINGEN VAN HET RIJKSSTATION VOOR LANDBOUWTECHNICK. 107

0303-9099 See ANNALES DE GEMBLOUX. 59

0303-9110 See BULLETIN - INSTITUT ROYAL DES SCIENCES NATURELLES DE BELGIQUE. SCIENCES DE LA TERRE. 1352

0303-9129 See BULLETIN - INSTITUT ROYAL DES SCIENCES NATURELLES DE BELGIQUE. ENTOMOLOGIE. 5579

0303-9137 See BULLETIN - INSTITUT ROYAL DES SCIENCES NATURELLES DE BELGIQUE. BIOLOGIE. 449

0303-9153 See BULLETIN DU JARDIN BOTANIQUE NATIONAL DE BELGIQUE. 504

0303-9226 See CENSUS OF BOARDS OF EXECUTORS AND TRUST COMPANIES. 782

0303-9293 See JOURNAL OF COMMERCE, INDUSTRY & TRANSPORTATION. 842

0303-9463 See WORLD BANK CATALOG. ACCESSION LIST. 816

0303-948X See DETAILED DEMAND FOR GRANTS OF WORKS DEPARTMENT. GOVERNMENT OF JAMMU AND KASHMIR. 4720

0303-9609 See SOCIETE ROYALE D'ECONOMIE POLITIQUE DE BELGIQUE (SERIES). 1521

0303-9617 See REVUE DES PAYS DE L'EST. 4534

0303-9625 See RECHERCHES SOCIOLOGIQUES. 5215

0303-9676 See ESTUDIOS SOCIALES CENTROAMERICANOS. 5245

0303-9692 See SCHWEIZERISCHE ZEITSCHRIFT FUER VOLKSWIRTSCHAFT UND STATISTIK. 1538

0303-9722 See AMMINISTRAZIONE ITALIANA. 4625

0303-9862 See REVISTA DE CIENCIAS SOCIAIS. 5216

0303-9889 See REVISTA DE ESTUDIOS SOCIALES (MADRID, SPAIN). 5256

0303-9935 See TIJDSCHRIFT VOOR SOCIALE GESCHIEDENIS. 4548

0303-9951 See INDIAN JOURNAL OF POLITICS. 4476

0304-0003 See LIAS. 2518

0304-0089 See ENCYCLOPEDIA OF WORLD PROBLEMS AND HUMAN POTENTIAL / EDITED BY UNION OF INTERNATIONAL ASSOCIATIONS. 1925

0304-016X See SCIENTIFIC REPORT / INTERNATIONAL PACIFIC HALIBUT COMMISSION. 2312

0304-0208 See NORTH-HOLLAND MATHEMATICS STUDIES. 3524

0304-0224 See EUROPEAN RESEARCH LIBRARIES COOPERATION : THE LIBER QUARTERLY. 3209

0304-0313 See PATOLOGIA E CLINICA OSTETRICA E GINECOLOGICA. 3766

0304-033X See DESIGN (BERGAMO). 372

0304-0364 See ANNUARIO DEL COMMERCIO ESTERO. 823

0304-0534 See ANNALI DELL' ISTITUTO SPERIMENTALE PER L'OLIVICOLTURA. 59

0304-0550 See ANNALI DELL'ISTITUTO SPERIMENTALE PER LA FLORICOLTURA. 2408

0304-0569 See ANNALI DELL'ISTITUTO SPERIMENTALE PER LA FRUTTICOLTURA. 2326

0304-0577 See ANNALI DELL'ISTITUTO SPERIMENTALE PER LA VALLORIZZAZIONE TECNOLOGICA DEI PRODOTTI AGRICOLI. 2326

0304-0585 See ANNALI DELL'ISTITUTO SPERIMENTALE PER LA PATOLOGIA VEGETALE. 2408

0304-0593 See RIVISTA DI INGEGNERIA AGRARIA. 34

0304-0607 See RIVISTA DI ZOOTECNIA E VETERINARIA. 5521

0304-0615 See ANNALI DELL'ISTITUTO SPERIMENTALE AGRONOMICO. 59

0304-064X See GIORNALE DI AGRICOLTURA. 90

0304-0666 See ANNUARIO DELL'AGRICOLTURA ITALIANA. 62

0304-0712 See AMSTERDAM STUDIES IN THE THEORY AND HISTORY OF LINGUISTIC SCIENCE. SERIES 1, AMSTERDAM CLASSICS IN LINGUISTICS, 1800-1925. 3264

0304-0720 See AMSTERDAM STUDIES IN THE THEORY AND HISTORY OF LINGUISTIC SCIENCE. SERIES III, STUDIES IN THE HISTORY OF THE LANGUAGE SCIENCES. 3263

0304-0763 See AMSTERDAM STUDIES IN THE THEORY AND HISTORY OF LINGUISTIC SCIENCE. SERIES IV, CURRENT ISSUES IN LINGUISTIC THEORY. 3264

0304-0798 See ANNALS OF THE NATAL MUSEUM, PIETERMARITZBURG. 4162

0304-0925 See HYDROLOGICAL ANNUAL. 1414

0304-0933 See EXPLANATORY MEMORANDUM ON THE BUDGET (ISLAMABAD). 4723

0304-0941 See DECISION (CALCUTTA). 865

0304-095X See BANGLADESH DEVELOPMENT STUDIES, THE. 1547

0304-100X See SERVICES LAW CASES. 4705

0304-1042 See JAPANESE JOURNAL OF RELIGIOUS STUDIES. 4967

0304-1123 See LITERARY REVIEW (LUCKNOW). 3346

0304-1166 See CHEMICAL INDIA ANNUAL. 2010

0304-1174 See CHEMICAL INDUSTRY BUYER'S GUIDE FOR SOUTHERN AFRICA. 1601

0304-1204 See FREE CHINA TODAY. 2503

0304-1220 See HAITI-CULTURE. 2534

0304-1239 See IMPULSE (WIEN). 3395

0304-1247 See MANJARI. 3409

0304-1298 See BULLETIN SIGNALETIQUE. 161, STRUCTURE DE L'ETAT CONDENSE, CRISTALLOGRAPHIE / CENTRE NATIONAL DE LA RECHERCHE SCIENTIFIQUE. 1031

0304-1417 See BUFANDA DEL SOL, LA. 3369

0304-1484 See DIRECTORY HOTEL PARIWISATA & TRAVEL BUREAU. 2805

0304-1603 See HANDBOOK, ANNUAL CONFERENCE - ASSOCIATED CHURCHES OF CHRIST IN NEW ZEALAND. 4962

0304-162X See INDEX TO THE TIMES OF INDIA. 5803

0304-1654 See JAPANESE AEROSPACE DIRECTORY. 25

0304-1727 See MODERN RATIONALIST, THE. 4978

0304-1735 See NEW ZEALAND SOIL BUREAU SCIENTIFIC REPORT. 179

0304-1964 See TAXES AND PLANNING. 4755

0304-2065 See ENERGIE (PFAFFHAUSEN). 1938

0304-2138 See REVISTA DA FUNDACAO SESP. 4799

0304-2146 See NIPPON NETTAI IGAKKAI ZASSHI. 3986

0304-2154 See JAHRBUCH DER AKADEMIE DER WISSENSCHAFTEN DER DDR. 5232

0304-2162 See MOIS, LE. 799

0304-2189 See IRIAN. 238

0304-2227 See JOURNAL OF THE BURMA RESEARCH SOCIETY. 2656

0304-2243 See JOURNAL OF ETHIOPIAN STUDIES. 2640

0304-2294 See LINGUISTICA ANTVERPIENSIA. 3299

0304-2367 See REVISTA DEL MUSEO NACIONAL (LIMA). 244

0304-2421 See THEORY AND SOCIETY. 5264

0304-2529 See ACTIVIDADES EN TURRIALBA / CATIE. 44

0304-2596 See ANUARIO INDIGENISTA. 231

0304-260X See ASIAN ECONOMIES. 1547

0304-2707 See CAHIERS ZAIROIS D'ETUDES POLITIQUES ET SOCIALES. 1550

0304-274X See ECONOMIC BULLETIN - NATIONAL BANK OF EGYPT. 789

0304-2782 See EUROPAEISCHE RUNDSCHAU. 4521

0304-2790 See HACETTEPE SOSYAL VE BESERI BILIMLER DERGISI. 1749

0304-2820 See DERECHO Y REFORMA AGRARIA; REVISTA. 2960

0304-2847 See REVISTA FACULTAD NACIONAL DE AGRONOMIA, MEDELLIN. 129

0304-2855 See MAGALLA AL-AKADIMIYYA AL-ARABIYYA LI-N-NAQL AL-BAHRI. 4178

0304-288X See CERN COURIER. 4446

0304-2928 See BULLETIN DU DROIT D'AUTEUR. 1302

0304-2944 See IMPACT, SCIENCE ET SOCIETE. 5112

0304-2995 See NATURE ET RESSOURCES. 2200

0304-3002 See MUSEUM ED. FRANCAISE. 4092

0304-3037 See REVUE INTERNATIONALE DES SCIENCES SOCIALES. 5217

0304-3045 See PERSPECTIVES - UNESCO. 1773

0304-3053 See PERSPECTIVAS : REVISTA TRIMESTRAL DE EDUCACION. 1773

0304-310X See CORREO, EL. 2845

0304-3118 See COURRIER DE L'UNESCO, LE. 2908

0304-3134 See CORRIERE UNESCO. 234

0304-3169 See UNESCO KOERIER. 332

0304-324X See GERONTOLOGY (BASEL). 3752

0304-3320 See RECHERCHE EN MATIERE D'ECONOMIE DES TRANSPORTS. 1515

0304-3371 See OECD FINANCIAL STATISTICS. METHODOLOGICAL SUPPLEMENT / STATISTIQUES FINANCIERES DE L'OCDE. SUPPLEMENT METHODOLOGIQUE. 1510

0304-3371 See OECD FINANCIAL STATISTICS. PART 2, FINANCIAL ACCOUNTS OF OECD COUNTRIES. ITALY. 802

0304-3398 See OBSERVATEUR DE L'OCDE, L'. 1509

0304-341X See NUCLEAR LAW BULLETIN. 3020

0304-3428 See NUCLEAR LAW BULLETIN. 3020

0304-3479 See RUSSIAN LITERATURE. 3432

0304-3487 See RUSSIAN LINGUISTICS. 3318

0304-3606 See IRRINEWS. 175

0304-3622 See BULLETIN OF THE INTERNATIONAL ASSOCIATION FOR SHELL AND SPATIAL STRUCTURES. 605

0304-3703 See VINCULOS. 247

0304-3711 See BRENESIA. 4163

0304-3754 See ALTERNATIVES (AMSTERDAM). 1545

0304-3770 See AQUATIC BOTANY. 500

0304-3789 See EXCERPTA MEDICA. SECTION 65. CANCER IMMUNOLOGY. LITERATURE INDEX. 3659

0304-3797 See EUROPEAN JOURNAL OF ENGINEERING EDUCATION. 1975

0304-3800 See ECOLOGICAL MODELLING. 2214

0304-3835 See CANCER LETTERS. 3811

0304-3843 See HYPERFINE INTERACTIONS. 4443

0304-386X See HYDROMETALLURGY. 4003

0304-3878 See JOURNAL OF DEVELOPMENT ECONOMICS. 1569

0304-3886 See JOURNAL OF ELECTROSTATICS. 2069

0304-3894 See JOURNAL OF HAZARDOUS MATERIALS. 2234

0304-3932 See JOURNAL OF MONETARY ECONOMICS. 1500

0304-3940 See NEUROSCIENCE LETTERS. 3842

0304-3959 See PAIN (AMSTERDAM). 3896
0304-3975 See THEORETICAL COMPUTER SCIENCE. 1205
0304-3991 See ULTRAMICROSCOPY. 574
0304-4017 See VETERINARY PARASITOLOGY. 5526
0304-4033 See REVISTA CENTROAMERICANA DE NUTRICION Y CIENCIAS DE ALIMENTOS. 4198
0304-4041 See EXCERPTA MEDICA. SECTION 40. DRUG DEPENDENCE, ALCOHOL ABUSE, AND ALCOHOLISM. 3659
0304-405X See JOURNAL OF FINANCIAL ECONOMICS. 794
0304-4068 See JOURNAL OF MATHEMATICAL ECONOMICS. 1500
0304-4076 See JOURNAL OF ECONOMETRICS. 1592
0304-4092 See DIALECTICAL ANTHROPOLOGY. 235
0304-4122 See REACTION KINETICS AND CATALYSIS LETTERS. 1057
0304-4130 See EUROPEAN JOURNAL OF POLITICAL RESEARCH. 4473
0304-4149 See STOCHASTIC PROCESSES AND THEIR APPLICATIONS. 3536
0304-4157 See BIOCHIMICA ET BIOPHYSICA ACTA (MR). REVIEWS ON BIOMEMBRANES. 962
0304-4165 See BIOCHIMICA ET BIOPHYSICA ACTA (G). 482
0304-4173 See BIOCHIMICA ET BIOPHYSICA ACTA (BR) - REVIEWS ON BIOENERGETICS. 444
0304-4181 See JOURNAL OF MEDIEVAL HISTORY. 2695
0304-4181 See JOURNAL OF MEDIEVAL HISTORY MICROFORM. 2695
0304-419X See REVIEWS ON CANCER. 3823
0304-4203 See MARINE CHEMISTRY. 1451
0304-422X See POETICS (AMSTERDAM). 3468
0304-4238 See SCIENTIA HORTICULTURAE. 2431
0304-4246 See CONTRIBUTIONS TO GYNECOLOGY AND OBSTETRICS. 3759
0304-4254 See PEDIATRIC AND ADOLESCENT ENDOCRINOLOGY. 3908
0304-4289 See PRAMANA. 4417
0304-4300 See ANALECTA SACRA TARRACONENSIA. 4934
0304-4319 See ANUARIO DE HISTORIA DEL DERECHO ESPANOL. 2935
0304-4343 See REVISTA / UNIVERSIDAD DE LA REPUBLICA, ESCUELA UNIVERSITARIA DE BIBLIOTECOLOGIA Y CIENCIAS AFINES "ING. FEDERICO E. CAPURRO," BIBLIOTECA. 3246
0304-4432 See SCHWEIZER SPITAL. 3792
0304-4475 See BARCELONA QUIRURGICA. 3960
0304-4513 See JOURNAL OF THE DIABETIC ASSOCIATION OF INDIA. 3731
0304-4556 See IRANIAN JOURNAL OF PUBLIC HEALTH. 4785
0304-4602 See ANNALS OF THE ACADEMY OF MEDICINE, SINGAPORE. 3550
0304-4629 See GENEESMIDDELENBULLETIN. 4305
0304-4815 See REVISTA ESPANOLA DE REUMATOLOGIA : ORGANO OFICIAL DE LA SOCIEDAD ESPANOLA DE REUMATOLOGIA. 3806
0304-4823 See MEDIKON. 3614
0304-484X See GAZETTE OF THE EGYPTIAN PAEDIATRIC ASSOCIATION. 3903
0304-4858 See GACETA MEDICA DE BILBAO. 3578
0304-4866 See GALICIA CLINICA. 3578
0304-4920 See CHINESE JOURNAL OF PHYSIOLOGY, THE. 579
0304-4939 See AEGEAN MEDICAL JOURNAL. 3546
0304-5013 See PROGRESOS DE OBSTETRICIA Y GINECOLOGIA. 3767
0304-5102 See JOURNAL OF MOLECULAR CATALYSIS. 1054
0304-5110 See SAMIKSA. 4617

0304-5196 See BOLETIM - INSTITUTO DO AZEITE E PRODUTOS OLEAGINOSOS. 5089
0304-5242 See JOURNAL OF PLANTATION CROPS. 176
0304-5250 See INDIAN JOURNAL OF ECOLOGY. 2217
0304-5277 See HWAHAK KYOYUK. CHEMICAL EDUCATION. 977
0304-5293 See ANNUAL REPORT OF THE INSTITUTE OF PHYSICS, ACADEMIA SINICA. 4397
0304-5439 See CIMMYT REPORT ON WHEAT IMPROVEMENT. 200
0304-5463 See CIMMYT REVIEW. 167
0304-548X See CIMMYT REPORT ON MAIZE IMPROVEMENT. 74
0304-5552 See BOLETIN TECNICO - UNIVERSIDAD DE CHILE, FACULTAD DE AGRONOMIA. 68
0304-5560 See BOLETIN TECNICO / UNIVERSIDAD DE CHILE, FACULTAD DE CIENCIAS AGRARIAS, VETERINARIAS Y FORESTALES, ESCUELA DE CIENCIAS FORESTALES. 2376
0304-5609 See CIENCIA E INVESTIGACION AGRARIA. 74
0304-5692 See ANNUAIRE DES STATISTIQUES DU COMMERCE EXTERIEUR (KINSHASA). 5321
0304-5714 See MEMOIRES DE L'INSTITUT OCEANOGRAPHIQUE. 1452
0304-5722 See BULLETIN DE L'INSTITUT OCEANOGRAPHIQUE (MONACO). 1447
0304-5757 See CONJONCTION. 2729
0304-5773 See BULLETIN PERPUSTAKAAN DAN DOKUMENTASI. 3198
0304-5854 See BULLETIN DE LIAISON - ASEQUA. 1369
0304-5919 See ABRIDGED TRADE STATISTICS FOR TANZANIA, UGANDA, AND KENYA. 725
0304-5951 See ABSTRACTS ON TROPICAL AGRICULTURE. 149
0304-6028 See ADMINISTRATION FOR DEVELOPMENT. 4624
0304-6257 See AMSTERDAMER BEITRAEGE ZUR NEUEREN GERMANISTIK. 3361
0304-6486 See ANNUAL REPORT AND ACCOUNTS - INDUSTRIAL DEVELOPMENT BANK LIMITED. 770
0304-6516 See ANNUAL FINANCIAL STATEMENT AND EXPLANATORY MEMORANDUM ON THE BUDGET OF THE PUNJAB GOVERNMENT. 4709
0304-6710 See ANNUAL REPORT AND ACCOUNTS - KARNATAKA STATE FINANCIAL CORPORATION. 770
0304-6796 See ANNUAL REPORT - CENTRAL BANK OF BARBADOS. 1546
0304-694X See ANNUAL REPORT - DEPARTMENT OF THE INTERIOR. 4627
0304-6966 See ANNUAL REPORT: DIRECTORS' REPORT, BALANCE SHEET AND ACCOUNTS. 2873
0304-7091 See ANNUAL REPORT - INTERNATIONAL CENTRE FOR THEORETICAL PHYSICS. 4397
0304-7652 See AIR NAVIGATION PLAN, EUROPEAN REGION. 7
0304-8101 See ANNUAL REPORT - PUNJAB NATIONAL BANK. 772
0304-8292 See ANNUAL REPORT - TECHNISCH-PHYSISCHE DIENST TNO-TH. 4397
0304-8349 See ANNUAL REPORT - UNITED PLANTING ASSOCIATION OF MALAYSIA. 61
0304-8489 See ANNUAL SUPPLEMENT TO HONG KONG TRADE STATISTICS, COUNTRY BY COMMODITY IMPORTS. 726
0304-8497 See ANUARIO CONSULTIVO DE TRABAJO. 3144
0304-8551 See ARAB OIL & GAS DIRECTORY. 4250
0304-8594 See ARCHITECTS TRADE JOURNAL. 288
0304-8608 See ARCHIVES OF VIROLOGY. 560

0304-8616 See ARCHIVOS DE FARMACOLOGIA Y TOXICOLOGIA. 4292
0304-8624 See ARMENIAN STUDIES. 2645
0304-8640 See ARTIST (CALCUTTA). 314
0304-8659 See ARUNA. 2501
0304-8667 See ASIAN PRESS, THE. 2917
0304-8675 See ASIAN PROFILE. 5192
0304-8683 See ASIRYADA. 2501
0304-8705 See ASTRONAUTICAL RESEARCH. 12
0304-8713 See AUSTRIA TODAY. 2513
0304-8721 See AUTOMOBIL (JOHANNESBURG). 5405
0304-8799 See BOSQUE. 2376
0304-8802 See AGRO SUR. 55
0304-8853 See JOURNAL OF MAGNETISM AND MAGNETIC MATERIALS. 4444
0304-8888 See BEVOLKINGSSTATISTIEKEN - NATIONAAL INSTITUUT VOOR DE STATISTIEK. 4561
0304-8918 See ALINORM. 2326
0304-8977 See BALANCE OF PAYMENTS. 773
0304-8993 See BALANCE PREVENTIVO - SOCIEDAD PRIVADA MUNICIPAL TRANSPORTES DE BARCELONA. 5377
0304-9027 See BANGLADESH JOURNAL OF ZOOLOGY. 5577
0304-9116 See BHARATA VARSHA. 5240
0304-9272 See BRAHMANA-GAURAVA. 5040
0304-9345 See BULLETIN - BANGLADESH BANK. 780
0304-9426 See BULLETIN DE STATISTIQUE - DIRECTION DE LA STATISTIQUE ET DE LA DOCUMENTATION (RWANDA). 5324
0304-9450 See BULLETIN DU MINISTERE DE LA SANTE PUBLIQUE ET DE LA FAMILLE. 4769
0304-9485 See BULLETIN MENSUEL DE STATISTIQUE - DIRECTION DE LA STATISTIQUE ET DES ETUDES ECONOMIQUES (GABON). 1530
0304-9515 See BULLETIN OF HAFFKINE INSTITUTE. 3712
0304-9523 See BULLETIN OF THE ASTRONOMICAL SOCIETY OF INDIA. 394
0304-9558 See BULLETIN OF THE INDIAN INSTITUTE OF HISTORY OF MEDICINE. 3560
0304-9590 See BULLETIN OF THE UNESCO REGIONAL OFFICE OF SCIENCE AND TECHNOLOGY FOR AFRICA. 5091
0304-9612 See BULLETIN P 3 - INSTITUT KEGURUAN DAN ILMU PENDIDIKAN, YOGYAKARTA, INDONESIA. PUSAT PENELITIAN PENDIDIKAN. 1729
0304-9647 See BUSINESS AND DEVELOPMENT NEWS. 1600
0304-9701 See INTERNATIONAL FORUM ON INFORMATION AND DOCUMENTATION. 3218
0304-971X See REVISTA DE BIOLOGIA DEL URUGUAY. 471
0304-9809 See BANGLADESH JOURNAL OF SCIENTIFIC AND INDUSTRIAL RESEARCH. 5087
0304-9825 See BULLETIN OF THE INSTITUTE OF MATHEMATICS, ACADEMIA SINICA. 3498
0304-9841 See CSIO COMMUNICATIONS. 5097
0304-985X See DELFT PROGRESS REPORT. 2022
0304-9876 See ELECTRONICS INFORMATION & PLANNING. 2049
0304-9914 See JOURNAL OF THE KOREAN MATHEMATICAL SOCIETY. 3515
0305-0009 See JOURNAL OF CHILD LANGUAGE. 3289
0305-0033 See ASLIB INFORMATION (LONDON, ENGLAND : 1973). 3192
0305-0041 See MATHEMATICAL PROCEEDINGS OF THE CAMBRIDGE PHILOSOPHICAL SOCIETY. 3519
0305-0068 See COMPARATIVE EDUCATION. 1733
0305-0173 See NORTHERN ARCHITECT. 305
0305-0270 See JOURNAL OF BIOGEOGRAPHY. 2567
0305-0319 See COSMETIC WORLD NEWS. 403

ISSN Index

0305-0378 *See* DISTRIBUTION DEVELOPMENTS. 2042

0305-0483 *See* OMEGA (OXFORD). 880

0305-0491 *See* COMPARATIVE BIOCHEMISTRY AND PHYSIOLOGY. B, COMPARATIVE BIOCHEMISTRY. 486

0309-4944 See INTERNATIONAL PETROLEUM ABSTRACTS INCORPORATING OFFSHORE ABSTRACTS. 4261

0305-0548 *See* COMPUTERS & OPERATIONS RESEARCH. 1179

0305-0629 *See* INTERNATIONAL INTERACTIONS. 4524

0305-0661 *See* ANBAR MARKETING & DISTRIBUTION ABSTRACTS. 726

0305-067X *See* PERSONNEL + TRAINING ABSTRACTS. 732

0305-0718 *See* COMMONWEALTH LAW BULLETIN. 2953

0305-0734 *See* MIDDLE EAST (LONDON, ENGLAND : 1985). 1505

0305-0785 *See* SCOTTISH LITERARY JOURNAL. 3434

0305-0831 *See* AEROSPACE (LONDON, 1974). 5

0305-0920 *See* APPROPRIATE TECHNOLOGY. 5085

0305-0998 *See* YEAR BOOK. 821

0305-103X *See* URBAN ABSTRACTS. 2837

0305-1048 *See* NUCLEIC ACIDS RESEARCH. 491

0305-1218 *See* RATEL. 5596

0305-1498 *See* OXFORD LITERARY REVIEW, THE. 3349

0305-1641 *See* ASIDES. ABERDEEN STUDIES IN DEFENCE ECONOMICS. 1464

0305-1706 *See* FILM DOPE. 4069

0305-1765 *See* LOUGHTON REVIEW. 5812

0305-179X *See* TANKER REGISTER. 5457

0305-1803 *See* LIQUID GAS CARRIER REGISTER. 4263

0305-1811 See EUROPEAN JOURNAL OF IMMUNOGENETICS : OFFICIAL JOURNAL OF THE BRITISH SOCIETY FOR HISTOCOMPATABILITY AND IMMUNOGENETICS. 3669

0305-182X *See* JOURNAL OF ORAL REHABILITATION. 1327

0305-1838 *See* MAMMAL REVIEW. 5590

0305-1846 *See* NEUROPATHOLOGY AND APPLIED NEUROBIOLOGY. 3896

0305-1862 *See* CHILD CARE, HEALTH AND DEVELOPMENT. 3901

0305-1870 *See* CLINICAL AND EXPERIMENTAL PHARMACOLOGY & PHYSIOLOGY. 4296

0305-196X *See* ECOLOGICAL ABSTRACTS. 2184

0305-1978 *See* BIOCHEMICAL SYSTEMATICS AND ECOLOGY. 481

0305-2109 *See* COMMUNICATIONS INTERNATIONAL. 1152

0305-2133 *See* JOURNAL OF THE PLAYING-CARD SOCIETY. 4862

0305-215X *See* ENGINEERING OPTIMIZATION. 1973

0305-2206 *See* RESEARCH BULLETIN - INSTITUTE FOR THE STUDY OF WORSHIP AND RELIGIOUS ARCHITECTURE. 307

0305-2249 *See* AUDIO VISUAL. 1104

0305-2370 *See* ANNUAL BULLETIN OF STATISTICS. 2362

0305-2443 *See* ANNOTATED BIBLIOGRAPHY (WEED RESEARCH ORGANIZATION). 2409

0305-3245 *See* MEMBERSHIP DIRECTORY - PHILATELIC TRADERS' SOCIETY. 2785

0305-3342 *See* MEDICAL DIRECTORY. 3915

0305-4055 *See* REPORT - CIRIA UNDERWATER ENGINEERING GROUP. 1994

0305-4136 *See* HOSPITAL UPDATE. 3585

0305-4179 *See* BURNS : JOURNAL OF THE INTERNATIONAL SOCIETY FOR BURN INJURIES. 3561

0305-4233 *See* COMMUNICATION. 1106

0305-4349 *See* DRUGLINK INFORMATION LETTER. 1343

0305-439X *See* PROCESSING. 2016

0305-4403 *See* JOURNAL OF ARCHAEOLOGICAL SCIENCE. 271

0305-4438 *See* MUSIC AND LITURGY. 4133

0305-4470 *See* JOURNAL OF PHYSICS. A : MATHEMATICAL AND GENERAL. 4409

0305-4756 *See* CAMDEN HISTORY REVIEW. 2683

0305-4829 *See* HEAT TREATMENT OF METALS. 4003

0305-4934 *See* ORNAMENTAL HORTICULTURE. 2434

0305-4985 *See* OXFORD REVIEW OF EDUCATION. 1771

0305-5000 *See* DENTAL UPDATE. 1321

0305-5167 *See* BRITISH LIBRARY JOURNAL, THE. 3197

0305-5477 *See* VERNACULAR ARCHITECTURE. 310

0305-5698 *See* EDUCATIONAL STUDIES. 1743

0305-5701 *See* NATIONAL PORTS COUNCIL BULLETIN. 5453

0305-5728 *See* VINE. VERY INFORMAL NEWSLETTER ON LIBRARY AUTOMATION. 3255

0305-5736 *See* POLICY AND POLITICS. 4487

0305-5795 *See* PROCEEDINGS - DEVON ARCHAEOLOGICAL SOCIETY. 279

0305-5906 *See* MUNICIPAL YEAR BOOK AND PUBLIC SERVICES DIRECTORY, THE. 4667

0305-5914 *See* GEOGRAPHICAL PAPERS. DEPARTMENT OF GEOGRAPHY, UNIVERSITY OF READING. 2563

0305-6031 *See* OHE BRIEFING. 4794

0305-6120 *See* CIRCUIT WORLD. 2038

0305-6244 *See* REVIEW OF AFRICAN POLITICAL ECONOMY. 1581

0305-6252 *See* REPORTS / MINORITY RIGHTS GROUP. 4512

0305-635X *See* OFFICE EQUIPMENT INDEX. 4213

0305-6376 *See* HANDBOOK OF POLYTECHNIC COURSES. 1913

0305-6562 *See* SCOTLANDS REGIONS. 4685

0305-6643 *See* REGISTERS AND DIRECTORY - ROYAL COLLEGE OF VETERINARY SURGEONS. 5520

0305-7070 *See* JOURNAL OF SOUTHERN AFRICAN STUDIES. 2641

0305-7194 *See* CEGB RESEARCH. 2038

0305-7232 *See* CANCER BIOCHEMISTRY BIOPHYSICS. 3810

0305-7240 *See* JOURNAL OF MORAL EDUCATION. 1758

0305-7259 *See* MATHEMATICS IN SCHOOL. 3520

0305-7267 *See* STUDIES IN SCIENCE EDUCATION. 5160

0305-733X *See* BLINDS AND SHUTTERS. 2904

0305-7356 *See* PSYCHOLOGY OF MUSIC. 4147

0305-7364 *See* ANNALS OF BOTANY. 499

0305-7372 *See* CANCER TREATMENT REVIEWS. 3812

0305-7380 *See* DIRECTORY / ART LIBRARIES SOCIETY. 349

0305-7410 *See* CHINA QUARTERLY (LONDON). 2648

0305-7445 See INTERNATIONAL JOURNAL OF NAUTICAL ARCHAEOLOGY, THE. 270

0305-7453 *See* JOURNAL OF ANTIMICROBIAL CHEMOTHERAPY, THE. 564

0305-7488 *See* JOURNAL OF HISTORICAL GEOGRAPHY. 2567

0305-750X *See* WORLD DEVELOPMENT. 1641

0305-7518 *See* LEPROSY REVIEW. 3604

0305-7615 *See* APPLIED HEALTH PHYSICS ABSTRACTS AND NOTES. 4433

0305-764X *See* CAMBRIDGE JOURNAL OF EDUCATION. 1890

0305-7712 *See* ENVIRONMENTAL CHEMISTRY. 975

0305-7798 *See* SHEET METAL INDUSTRIES YEARBOOK. 4019

0305-781X *See* BULLETIN OF THE ASSOCIATION OF BRITISH THEOLOGICAL AND PHILOSOPHICAL LIBRARIES. 3198

0305-7879 *See* VOCATIONAL ASPECT OF EDUCATION, THE. 1917

0305-7887 *See* ANNUAL REPORT - BRITISH LIBRARY. 3190

0305-7925 *See* COMPARE. 1891

0305-8034 *See* LONDON JOURNAL, THE. 2697

0305-8107 See JOURNAL OF OCCUPATIONAL AND ORGANIZATIONAL PSYCHOLOGY. 4598

0305-8182 *See* JABBERWOCKY. 3398

0305-8298 *See* MILLENNIUM. 4529

0305-8417 *See* PRIMATE EYE. 5594

0305-8441 *See* COOMBE LODGE REPORT. 1818

0305-8468 *See* FOCUS ON INTERNATIONAL & COMPARATIVE LIBRARIANSHIP. 3211

0305-8476 See EUROPEAN CURRENT LAW : MONTHLY DIGEST. 2967

0305-8549 *See* DEVON HISTORIAN, THE. 2614

0305-862X *See* AFRICAN RESEARCH & DOCUMENTATION. 3188

0305-8719 *See* GEOLOGICAL SOCIETY SPECIAL PUBLICATION. 1378

0305-8727 *See* PUBLICATIONS 5235

0305-8751 See HOME COOKING. 2790

0305-876X *See* OFFSHORE ENGINEER. 2094

0305-893X *See* TOLLEY'S INCOME TAX. 4756

0305-9006 *See* PROGRESS IN PLANNING. 2832

0305-9014 *See* PUBLIC FINANCE AND ACCOUNTANCY. 4743

0305-9049 *See* OXFORD BULLETIN OF ECONOMICS AND STATISTICS. 1577

0305-9154 *See* PLANT GROWTH REGULATOR ABSTRACTS. 155

0305-9189 *See* STATE LIBRARIAN. 3251

0305-9219 *See* SAGA-BOOK. 3432

0305-9235 See FLUID ABSTRACTS. PROCESS ENGINEERING. 2004

0305-926X *See* HOUSMAN SOCIETY JOURNAL. 3394

0305-9286 *See* ACT DIGEST. 4931

0305-9332 *See* INDUSTRIAL LAW JOURNAL (LONDON). 3149

0305-9359 *See* KENT FAMILY HISTORY SOCIETY JOURNAL. 2456

0305-9456 See FLUID ABSTRACTS. CIVIL ENGINEERING. 2004

0305-9529 *See* NEW INTERNATIONALIST. 4529

0305-960X *See* RELIGIOUS BOOKS IN PRINT. 4991

0305-9669 *See* FAMILY PRACTITIONER SERVICES, THE. 3737

0305-9758 *See* ELECTRON SPIN RESONANCE. 1015

0305-9766 *See* ELECTRONIC STRUCTURE AND MAGNETISM OF INORGANIC COMPOUNDS. 1036

0305-9804 *See* NUCLEAR MAGNETIC RESONANCE. 4444

0305-9871 *See* RESEARCH BULLETIN (GREAT BRITAIN. HOME OFFICE. RESEARCH AND PLANNING UNIT). 3175

0305-9987 *See* MASS SPECTROMETRY. 1017

0306-0012 *See* CHEMICAL SOCIETY REVIEWS. 969

0306-0020 *See* MANTATOPHOROS. 3301

0306-0128 *See* DANCE GAZETTE. 1312

0306-0152 *See* CONSTRUCTION REFERENCES. 632

0306-0209 *See* NAVAL ARCHITECT, THE. 5453

0306-0209 *See* SMALL CRAFT. 596

0306-0225 *See* SUB-CELLULAR BIOCHEMISTRY. 540

0306-0322 *See* AFRICAN BOOK PUBLISHING RECORD, THE. 4811

0306-0349 *See* AIRTRADE. 821

0306-0373 *See* DELIUS SOCIETY JOURNAL, THE. 4113

0306-0381 *See* OEM DESIGN. 3485

0306-0403 *See* SWIMMING TEACHER. 4925

0306-0519 *See* FURNITURE MANUFACTURER. 3479

0306-0632 See PROGRESS IN FOOD & NUTRITION SCIENCE. 4198
0306-0713 See ORGANOPHOSPHORUS CHEMISTRY. 1045
0306-0748 See TEXTILES. 5359
0306-0837 See LLAFUR. 1688
0306-0845 See URBAN HISTORY. 2838
0306-0926 See TRANSACTIONS OF THE ORIENTAL CERAMIC SOCIETY. 2595
0306-0985 See CARGO SYSTEMS INTERNATIONAL. 5379
0306-1078 See EARLY MUSIC. 4116
0306-1426 See WOMEN'S REPORT. 5571
0306-1582 See POULTRY ABSTRACTS. 156
0306-1612 See BULLETIN OF MONUMENTAL BRASS SOCIETY. 264
0306-168X See FOLDING CARTON INDUSTRY. 4219
0306-1817 See SHIPPING STATISTICS AND ECONOMICS. 5402
0306-1922 See PROCUREMENT WEEKLY. 704
0306-1973 See LITERATURE & HISTORY. 3407
0306-2015 See CHILDREN'S LITERATURE ABSTRACTS. 3458
0306-204X See BUYERS' GUIDE. 2587
0306-2074 See SPORE RESEARCH. 570
0306-2104 See LIQUID CHROMATOGRAPHY ABSTRACTS. 1017
0306-2163 See INDUSTRIAL CASES REPORTS. 3149
0306-2406 See CERTIFIED ACCOUNTANT. 740
0306-2473 See YEARBOOK OF ENGLISH STUDIES, THE. 3334
0306-2619 See APPLIED ENERGY. 1932
0306-2643 See INTERNATIONAL REVIEW OF PSYCHO-ANALYSIS, THE. 4592
0306-2775 See WATER SPACE. 5548
0306-2848 See INDONESIA CIRCLE : [JOURNAL]. 2505
0306-2880 See REPROGRAPHICS QUARTERLY. 4569
0306-2910 See IBCAM. 5416
0306-2945 See LLOYD'S MARITIME AND COMMERCIAL LAW QUARTERLY. 3181
0306-2988 See STAINLESS STEEL INDUSTRY. 1627
0306-3070 See JOURNAL OF GENERAL MANAGEMENT. 873
0306-3127 See SOCIAL STUDIES OF SCIENCE. 5221
0306-3178 See CHARTERED SURVEYOR : URBAN QUARTERLY. 2817
0306-3224 See CONTENTS PAGES IN MANAGEMENT. 728
0306-3232 See CONSTRUCTION NEWS MAGAZINE. 610
0306-3240 See DISTRICT COUNCILS REVIEW. 4645
0306-3380 See TECHNICAL BULLETIN - BRITISH GEOMORPHOLOGICAL RESEARCH GROUP. 1361
0306-3461 See MERIDIAN POETRY MAGAZINE. 3466
0306-3488 See INTERNATIONAL WHO'S WHO IN COMMUNITY SERVICE. 433
0306-3534 See EUROPEAN PLASTICS NEWS. 4455
0306-3615 See MARKETING AND ADVERTISING NEWS. 930
0306-3623 See GENERAL PHARMACOLOGY. 4306
0306-3631 See JOURNAL OF COMMONWEALTH & COMPARATIVE POLITICS, THE. 4478
0306-364X See RENEWABLE ENERGY BULLETIN. 1954
0306-3666 See MEN OF ACHIEVEMENT. 433
0306-3674 See BRITISH JOURNAL OF SPORTS MEDICINE. 3953
0306-3747 See ADDITIVES FOR POLYMERS. 1038
0306-395X See PETROLEUM ECONOMIST (ENGLISH EDITION). 4272

0306-3968 See RACE & CLASS. 2271
0306-400X See INTERNATIONAL WATER POWER & DAM CONSTRUCTION. 2091
0306-4026 See PSI NEWS & VIEWS. 1704
0306-4123 See BOARD MANUFACTURE AND PROCESSING. 2399
0306-414X See EUROPEAN RUBBER DIRECTORY. 5075
0306-4190 See INTERNATIONAL JOURNAL OF MECHANICAL ENGINEERING EDUCATION, THE. 2116
0306-4220 See INDEX ON CENSORSHIP. 3344
0306-4352 See SPECIAL PUBLICATION - BRITISH CARBONIZATION RESEARCH ASSOCIATION. 992
0306-4379 See INFORMATION SYSTEMS (OXFORD). 1254
0306-4409 See RECORDER MAGAZINE, THE. 4149
0306-4484 See CURRENT ADVANCES IN PLANT SCIENCE. 507
0306-4522 See NEUROSCIENCE. 3842
0306-4530 See PSYCHONEUROENDOCRINOLOGY. 3732
0306-4549 See ANNALS OF NUCLEAR ENERGY. 2153
0306-4565 See JOURNAL OF THERMAL BIOLOGY. 462
0306-4573 See INFORMATION PROCESSING & MANAGEMENT. 3216
0306-4603 See ADDICTIVE BEHAVIORS. 1338
0306-4875 See ANNUAL REPORT OF COUNCIL AND ACCOUNTS - CHEMICAL SOCIETY. 961
0306-4964 See FOUNDATION (DAGENHAM). 3388
0306-4964 See FOUNDATION. 3388
0306-4980 See IDF BULLETIN. 3731
0306-5049 See BUSINESS ECONOMIST. 647
0306-512x See NEW HUMANIST (LONDON, ENGLAND). 4353
0306-5251 See BRITISH JOURNAL OF CLINICAL PHARMACOLOGY. 4294
0306-5278 See NORTHERN SCOTLAND. 2700
0306-5286 See ROAD TRAFFIC REPORTS. 5444
0306-5456 See BRITISH JOURNAL OF OBSTETRICS AND GYNAECOLOGY. 3758
0306-5464 See NDC PAPER. 3619
0306-5472 See BMA NEWS REVIEW. 3557
0306-5480 See H. G. WELLS NEWSLETTER, THE. 3392
0306-557X See KEY ABSTRACTS. ELECTRONIC CIRCUITS. 2005
0306-5634 See AIR INTERNATIONAL. 7
0306-5677 See CATHOLIC DIRECTORY FOR SCOTLAND, THE. 5025
0306-5758 See MANCHESTER CHAMBER OF COMMERCE AND INDUSTRY YEARBOOK. 820
0306-5774 See YEARBOOK OF WORLD ELECTRONICS DATA ... VOL. 1, WEST EUROPE. 2086
0306-5782 See FREEZE. 2341
0306-5790 See TRANSACTIONS - ANGLESEY ANTIQUARIAN SOCIETY AND FIELD CLUB. 2713
0306-5812 See DEGREE COURSE OFFERS. 1819
0306-5898 See INTERNATIONAL MOTOR-CYCLE RACING BOOK. 4081
0306-5928 See BRITISH MUSIC YEARBOOK. 4105
0306-6045 See INTERNATIONAL TAX-FREE TRADER & DUTY-FREE WORLD. 4733
0306-610X See CRAFTS (CRAFTS ADVISORY COMMITTEE). 371
0306-6142 See CONCEPTS AND TECHNIQUES IN MODERN GEOGRAPHY. 2559
0306-6150 See JOURNAL OF PEASANT STUDIES, THE. 5250
0306-624X See INTERNATIONAL JOURNAL OF OFFENDER THERAPY AND COMPARATIVE CRIMINOLOGY. 3166
0306-6274 See MOTOR REPORT INTERNATIONAL. 5420
0306-6444 See GAS ENGINEERING AND MANAGEMENT. 4257
0306-6479 See NEW LAW JOURNAL, THE. 3015

0306-6657 See MODERN MEDICINE OF IRELAND. 3618
0306-6800 See JOURNAL OF MEDICAL ETHICS. 3596
0306-686X See JOURNAL OF BUSINESS FINANCE & ACCOUNTING. 746
0306-6924 See ARCHAEOLOGIA CAMBRENSIS. 256
0306-7076 See BRITISH CERAMIC REVIEW. 2586
0306-7262 See REFORM. 5067
0306-7297 See JOURNAL OF HUMAN MOVEMENT STUDIES. 583
0306-7319 See INTERNATIONAL JOURNAL OF ENVIRONMENTAL ANALYTICAL CHEMISTRY. 1015
0306-7327 See IRRIGATION AND DRAINAGE ABSTRACTS / COMMONWEALTH AGRICULTURAL BUREAUX. 2005
0306-7343 See OCCASIONAL PAPERS ON TECHNOLOGY. 4094
0306-7440 See TRADITIONAL MUSIC. 4157
0306-7467 See CHRISTIAN BRETHREN REVIEW : THE JOURNAL OF THE CHRISTIAN BRETHREN RESEARCH FELLOWSHIP. 4944
0306-7475 See ANTIQUARIAN BOOK MONTHLY REVIEW. 4823
0306-7556 See CROP PHYSIOLOGY ABSTRACTS. 152
0306-7610 See POULTRY SCIENCE SYMPOSIUM. 218
0306-7661 See FRAMEWORK. 4071
0306-770X See OIL WORLD STATISTICS. 4284
0306-7718 See COMMERCIAL TELEVISION AND RADIO YEAR BOOK. 1130
0306-7734 See INTERNATIONAL STATISTICAL REVIEW. 5329
0306-7742 See SOCIAL TRENDS. 5267
0306-7866 See QUARTERLY ECONOMIC COMMENTARY (GLASGOW). 1579
0306-7874 See CONFERENCE - INTERNATIONAL SOLAR ENERGY SOCIETY UK SECTION. 1936
0306-7971 See SPARE RIB. 5566
0306-8145 See CANADA TODAY (LONDON). 2529
0306-8218 See HANDBOOK - RUGBY FOOTBALL UNION. 4898
0306-8234 See PAPER (LONDON). 4236
0306-8293 See INTERNATIONAL JOURNAL OF SOCIAL ECONOMICS. 1496
0306-8307 See BULLETIN / BRITISH ECOLOGICAL SOCIETY. 2162
0306-8331 See PEUPLES. 590
0306-8358 See IRISH GENEALOGIST. 2454
0306-8374 See ASIAN AFFAIRS (LONDON). 2646
0306-8390 See LIST OF MEMBERS - INTERNATIONAL INSTITUTE FOR STRATEGIC STUDIES. 4049
0306-8455 See NEWSLETTER - STUDY GROUP ON EIGHTEENTH-CENTURY RUSSIA. 2700
0306-848X See TRANSACTIONS OF THE RADNORSHIRE SOCIETY, THE. 2713
0306-8501 See ANNUAL REVIEW - THE JUNIOR CHAMBER OF COMMERCE FOR LONDON. 818
0306-8544 See COAL AND ENERGY QUARTERLY. 1935
0306-8552 See ELECTROTECHNOLOGY (LONDON). 2050
0306-882X See FLORA (LONDON). 2435
0306-8919 See OPTICAL AND QUANTUM ELECTRONICS. 4439
0306-9192 See FOOD POLICY. 2339
0306-9206 See NORTH CHESHIRE FAMILY HISTORIAN 1975. 2464
0306-9222 See OXYRHYNCHUS PAPYRI, THE. 3421
0306-9397 See CONFERENCES & EXHIBITIONS INTERNATIONAL. 5096
0306-9400 See LAW TEACHER, THE. 2997
0306-9419 See INTERNATIONAL JOURNAL OF FORENSIC DENTISTRY. 1325
0306-9443 See BRITISH JOURNAL OF CANCER. SUPPLEMENT, THE. 3809
0306-9516 See AFRICAN BOOKS IN PRINT. 407

0306-9575 See CONTACT LENS JOURNAL (THORNTON HEATH, SURREY), THE. 4215

0306-9699 See PROFESSIONAL CARE OF MOTHER AND CHILD. 3767

0306-9788 See CITY OF LONDON LAW REVIEW. 2950

0306-9796 See CAMBRIA. 2557

0306-9869 See ELECTRON MICROSCOPY ABSTRACTS. 454

0306-9877 See MEDICAL HYPOTHESES. 3609

0306-9885 See BRITISH JOURNAL OF GUIDANCE & COUNSELLING. 1911

0306-9907 See ACCOUNTS OF THE NORTHERN IRELAND HOUSING EXECUTIVE. 2813

0306-9958 See ROOT AND BRANCH. 2470

0307-0018 See CRANES TODAY. 2112

0307-0131 See BYZANTINE AND MODERN GREEK STUDIES. 2682

0307-028X See WALCOT FAMILY BULLETIN. 2477

0307-0336 See ACCOUNTANTS DIGEST (LONDON, ENGLAND). 735

0307-0360 See LONDON CURRENCY REPORT. 797

0307-0387 See MIDDLE EAST CURRENCY REPORTS. 1638

0307-0409 See ANBAR YEARBOOK. 638

0307-0492 See INSTITUTION OF CHEMICAL ENGINEERS SYMPOSIUM SERIES, THE. 2013

0307-0514 See EDUCATION STATISTICS ... ESTIMATES / CIPFA, STATISTICAL INFORMATION SERVICE. 1794

0307-0522 See PUBLIC LIBRARY STATISTICS ... ESTIMATES. 3259

0307-0603 See DIGEST OF UNITED KINGDOM ENERGY STATISTICS. 1961

0307-0697 See POWER & WORKS ENGINEERING (1974). 1991

0307-0778 See PAPER & BOARD ABSTRACTS. 4240

0307-0824 See HEALTH AND PERSONAL SOCIAL SERVICES STATISTICS FOR ENGLAND WITH SUMMARY TABLES FOR GREAT BRITAIN. 5266

0307-0840 See HEALTH AND PERSONAL SOCIAL SERVICES STATISTICS FOR WALES. 5266

0307-0956 See EASTERN DAILY PRESS. 5812

0307-1022 See SOCIAL HISTORY (LONDON). 2630

0307-112X See IMMUNOLOGY ABSTRACTS. 3660

0307-1146 See ANNUAL REPORT / THE ELECTRICITY COUNCIL. 4696

0307-1219 See BRITISH COMBUSTION. 2111

0307-1243 See GARDEN HISTORY. 2415

0307-1375 See ARBORICULTURAL JOURNAL, THE. 2375

0307-1391 See DATA ARCHIVE BULLETIN / SSRC. 2481

0307-1448 See DONIZETTI SOCIETY JOURNAL. 4115

0307-1456 See SALG NEWSLETTER. 3247

0307-157X See ENDOCRINOLOGY. 3729

0307-160X See BRAZILIAN GAZETTE, THE. 2485

0307-1723 See JOURNAL OF THE SOMERSET INDUSTRIAL ARCHAEOLOGICAL SOCIETY. 272

0307-174X See INTERNATIONAL POLYMER SCIENCE AND TECHNOLOGY. 1011

0307-1766 See FINANCIAL TIMES (LONDON ED.). 5812

0307-1782 See WATER SERVICES YEARBOOK. 5548

0307-1790 See YOUTH IN SOCIETY. 5314

0307-191X See PENSIONS WORLD. 2889

0307-2118 See FITECH. 2290

0307-238X See REVIEWS OF RESEARCH AND PRACTICE OF THE INSTITUTE FOR RESEARCH INTO MENTAL AND MULTIPLE HANDICAP. 3935

0307-2606 See LOCKE NEWSLETTER, THE. 4352

0307-2657 See BSBI ABSTRACTS. 449

0307-2770 See NEW GERMAN STUDIES. 3305

0307-2851 See MIDLAND ANCESTOR : JOURNAL OF THE BIRMINGHAM AND MIDLAND SOCIETY FOR GENEALOGY AND HERALDRY, THE. 2460

0307-2894 See INTERNATIONAL WHO'S WHO IN MUSIC AND MUSICIANS' DIRECTORY. 433

0307-3017 See DINGHY SAILING. 593

0307-3084 See GAS DIRECTORY AND WHO'S WHO. 4257

0307-3165 See RADIO AND TELEVISION SERVICING. 2078

0307-322X See INTERNATIONAL DENDROLOGY SOCIETY YEARBOOK. 514

0307-3238 See YORK PAPERS IN LINGUISTICS. 3334

0307-3246 See SEMINAR PAPERS - DEPARTMENT OF GEOGRAPHY. UNIVERSITY OF NEWCASTLE UPON TYNE. 2576

0307-3262 See IBERIAN STUDIES. 2517

0307-3289 See JOURNAL OF THE INSTITUTE OF HEALTH EDUCATION. 4787

0307-3335 See NEWSLETTER - BRITISH SCIENCE FICTION ASSOCIATION. 3417

0307-3343 See SHAW'S DIRECTORY OF COURTS IN ENGLAND AND WALES. 3048

0307-3378 See BULLETIN OF ECONOMIC RESEARCH. 1590

0307-4358 See MANAGERIAL FINANCE. 797

0307-4412 See BIOCHEMICAL EDUCATION. 481

0307-4420 See STRATEGY & DEFENCE. 4058

0307-4455 See NORTHERN CATHOLIC HISTORY. 5033

0307-4463 See POPULATION TRENDS. 4562

0307-4617 See SCREEN INTERNATIONAL. 4077

0307-4722 See ART LIBRARIES JOURNAL. 3192

0307-4765 See JOURNAL OF THE BALINT SOCIETY. 3930

0307-4803 See NEW LIBRARY WORLD. 3234

0307-4870 See JOURNAL OF PLANNING AND ENVIRONMENT LAW. 3113

0307-4927 See REPORT OF THE HOUGHTON POULTRY RESEARCH STATION. 220

0307-5095 See JOURNAL OF ELECTROPHYSIOLOGICAL TECHNOLOGY. 3595

0307-5117 See ARCHAEOLOGICAL SURVEY OF EGYPT. MEMOIR. 257

0307-5125 See TEXTS FROM EXCAVATIONS. 284

0307-5400 See EUROPEAN LAW REVIEW. 2967

0307-5451 See HISTORY OF TECHNOLOGY. 5110

0307-5494 See BIOMEDICAL LETTERS. 3556

0307-5508 See COMMUNITY CARE. 5279

0307-5664 See BELFAST TELEGRAPH [MICROFORM]. 5811

0307-5664 See BELFAST TELEGRAPH. 5811

0307-5966 See JOURNAL OF METEOROLOGY. 1426

0307-5974 See RELIGION, STATE & SOCIETY : THE KESTON JOURNAL. 4991

0307-6067 See COMMUNITY WORK. 5280

0307-6164 See BP&R BRITISH PLASTICS AND RUBBER. 4454

0307-6334 See CHURCH MUSIC QUARTERLY. 4109

0307-6490 See AUTOMOTIVE ENGINEER. 5406

0307-6571 See COIN YEARBOOK. 2780

0307-6598 See TOPICS IN GASTROENTEROLOGY. 3748

0307-661X See TLS. TIMES LITERARY SUPPLEMENT. 4820

0307-6628 See CHESHIRE ARCHAEOLOGICAL BULLETIN. 265

0307-6679 See STAMP MAGAZINE. 2787

0307-6768 See MANAGEMENT SERVICES (ENFIELD). 878

0307-6857 See ANNUAL REPORT - INTERNATIONAL PLANNED PARENTHOOD FEDERATION. 2276

0307-692X See AUSTRALIAN JOURNAL OF ECOLOGY. 2211

0307-6938 See CLINICAL AND EXPERIMENTAL DERMATOLOGY. 3718

0307-6946 See ECOLOGICAL ENTOMOLOGY. 5607

0307-6962 See PHYSIOLOGICAL ENTOMOLOGY. 5612

0307-6970 See SYSTEMATIC ENTOMOLOGY. 5613

0307-7144 See LORE AND LANGUAGE. 2322

0307-7195 See PRINTING INDUSTRIES. 4568

0307-7241 See BLUES-LINK. 4104

0307-7403 See RECENT ADVANCES IN CLINICAL NEUROLOGY. 3844

0307-7411 See AIR EXTRA. 7

0307-7462 See LIST OF THE MEMBERS OF THE ROYAL COLLEGES OF PHYSICIANS OF THE UNITED KINGDOM. 3915

0307-7523 See FABIAN PAMPHLET / FABIAN SOCIETY. 1490

0307-7535 See FABIAN TRACT. 4474

0307-7608 See INTERNATIONAL STEEL STATISTICS, UNITED KINGDOM. 4025

0307-7640 See MEDICAL INFORMATICS. 1261

0307-7675 See MUSEUMS YEARBOOK. 4093

0307-7772 See CLINICAL OTOLARYNGOLOGY AND ALLIED SCIENCES. 3887

0307-7780 See SECURITECH. 2080

0307-7863 See NEW CIVIL ENGINEER. 2027

0307-7942 See ENERGY WORLD. 1943

0307-7950 See HAC. THE HEATING AND AIR CONDITIONING JOURNAL. 2605

0307-8035 See ANNUAL REPORT OF STUDIES IN ANIMAL NUTRITION AND ALLIED SCIENCES. 206

0307-8086 See COURTAULD INSTITUTE ILLUSTRATION ARCHIVES. ARCHIVE 4, LATE 18TH & 19TH CENTURY SCULPTURE IN THE BRITISH ISLES. 2481

0307-8337 See ENGLISH LANGUAGE TEACHING JOURNAL. 3279

0307-8353 See PROCEEDINGS OF THE INSTITUTION OF CIVIL ENGINEERS, TRANSPORT. 2029

0307-8353 See PROCEEDINGS OF THE INSTITUTION OF CIVIL ENGINEERS. CIVIL ENGINEERING. 2029

0307-8353 See PROCEEDINGS OF THE INSTITUTION OF CIVIL ENGINEERS. MUNICIPAL ENGINEER. 2029

0307-8353 See PROCEEDINGS OF THE INSTITUTION OF CIVIL ENGINEERS. STRUCTURES AND BUILDINGS. 2029

0307-8353 See PROCEEDINGS OF THE INSTITUTION OF CIVIL ENGINEERS. WATER, MARITIME AND ENERGY. 2094

0307-8361 See PROCEEDINGS OF THE INSTITUTION OF CIVIL ENGINEERS, TRANSPORT. 2029

0307-8361 See PROCEEDINGS OF THE INSTITUTION OF CIVIL ENGINEERS. CIVIL ENGINEERING. 2029

0307-8361 See PROCEEDINGS OF THE INSTITUTION OF CIVIL ENGINEERS. MUNICIPAL ENGINEER. 2029

0307-8361 See PROCEEDINGS OF THE INSTITUTION OF CIVIL ENGINEERS. STRUCTURES AND BUILDINGS. 2029

0307-8361 See PROCEEDINGS OF THE INSTITUTION OF CIVIL ENGINEERS. WATER, MARITIME AND ENERGY. 2094

0307-8388 See THEMELIOS. 5003

0307-8515 See CLOTHING INSTITUTE YEAR BOOK & MEMBERSHIP REGISTER, THE. 1083

0307-8523 See MUSIC TRADES INTERNATIONAL DIRECTORY. 4135

0307-8531 See RARE EARTH BULLETIN. 5145

0307-854X See BOOKTALK. 4826

0307-8647 See BAR QUARTERLY. 4824

0307-868X See YEAR BOOK - ROYAL YACHTING ASSOCIATION. 597

0307-8698 See RINGING & MIGRATION. 5620

0307-8833 See THEATRE RESEARCH INTERNATIONAL. 5371

0307-904X See APPLIED MATHEMATICAL MODELLING. 3495

0307-9058 See MISCELLANEOUS REPORT - CENTRE FOR OVERSEAS PEST RESEARCH. 109

0307-9066 See MINING DEPARTMENT MAGAZINE. 2145

0307-9082 See REPORT - CENTRE FOR OVERSEAS PEST RESEARCH. 4247
0307-9201 See SAGE RACE RELATIONS ABSTRACTS. 5266
0307-9325 See BRICK BULLETIN. 602
0307-9414 See PLASTICS AND RUBBER: MATERIALS AND APPLICATIONS. 5077
0307-9457 See AVIAN PATHOLOGY. 5505
0307-9481 See BRITISH LIBRARY NEWS. 3197
0307-9562 See THAMES POETRY. 3472
0307-9945 See ACTIVATION ANALYSIS ABSTRACTS. 1012
0307-9961 See ARTBIBLIOGRAPHIES. CURRENT TITLES. 334
0308-0021 See WHERE TO BUY CHEMICALS AND CHEMICAL PLANT. 995
0308-0110 See MEDICAL EDUCATION. 3609
0308-0161 See INTERNATIONAL JOURNAL OF PRESSURE VESSELS AND PIPING, THE. 2116
0308-0188 See INTERDISCIPLINARY SCIENCE REVIEWS : ISR. 5114
0308-0226 See BRITISH JOURNAL OF OCCUPATIONAL THERAPY, THE. 1876
0308-0234 See HOSPITAL AND HEALTH SERVICES REVIEW, THE. 3783
0308-0242 See POLICE SURGEON, THE. 3742
0308-0382 See EPWORTH REVIEW. 5059
0308-0390 See BUSINESS WHO'S WHO, THE. 431
0308-0501 See FIRE AND MATERIALS. 615
0308-051X See PHARMATHERAPEUTICA. 4324
0308-0587 See MODERN ENGLISH TEACHER. 1900
0308-0684 See IEE NEWS. 2057
0308-0803 See PUBLISHED BY CSD. 4705
0308-082X See ANNUAL REPORT - TOWN AND COUNTRY PLANNING ASSOCIATION. 2815
0308-0838 See FERN GAZETTE, THE. 510
0308-0951 See CHARLES LAMB BULLETIN, THE. 3339
0308-1060 See TRANSPORTATION PLANNING AND TECHNOLOGY. 5396
0308-1079 See INTERNATIONAL JOURNAL OF GENERAL SYSTEMS. 1247
0308-1087 See LINEAR AND MULTILINEAR ALGEBRA. 3517
0308-1176 See SCOTS MERCANTILE LAW STATUTES. 3103
0308-1192 See UNITED KINGDOM ANTARCTIC RESEARCH REPORT. 1361
0308-1222 See ENERGY TRENDS. 1942
0308-1265 See BREWING & DISTILLING INTERNATIONAL. 2365
0308-1451 See YEAR BOOK - THE ROYAL INSTITUTION OF CHARTERED SURVEYORS. 2579
0308-1664 See BALL BEARING JOURNAL (LUTON). 2111
0308-1907 See NATFHE JOURNAL. 1836
0308-1958 See IMPACT OF TAX CHANGES ON INCOME DISTRIBUTION, THE. 4731
0308-1990 See NEW ORLEANS MUSIC. 4140
0308-2105 See PROCEEDINGS OF THE ROYAL SOCIETY OF EDINBURGH. SECTION A. MATHEMATICA. 3528
0308-2172 See MANAGEMENT AND MARKETING ABSTRACTS. 731
0308-2237 See CV NEWS LETTER. 1479
0308-2342 See JOURNAL OF CHEMICAL RESEARCH. SYNOPSES. 980
0308-2350 See JOURNAL OF CHEMICAL RESEARCH. MINIPRINT. 980
0308-2458 See RECENT ADVANCES IN CLINICAL NUCLEAR MEDICINE. 3849
0308-2482 See NEWSLETTER - BRITISH INSTITUTE OF INTERNATIONAL AND COMPARATIVE LAW. 3133
0308-2555 See BROADSHEET - ASSOCIATION OF CLINICAL PATHOLOGISTS. 3893
0308-275X See CRITIQUE OF ANTHROPOLOGY. 234
0308-2776 See PROSPICE. 3426
0308-2938 See INTERNATIONAL MARKETING DATA AND STATISTICS. 730
0308-2938 See INTERNATIONAL MARKETING DATA AND STATISTICS. 926
0308-3233 See ISSUES IN RACE AND EDUCATION. 1755
0308-3322 See REPORT - ROYAL GREENWICH OBSERVATORY. 399
0308-3446 See MARKET RESEARCH EUROPE. 731
0308-3462 See ESSEX ARCHAEOLOGY AND HISTORY : THE TRANSACTIONS OF THE ESSEX ARCHAEOLOGICAL SOCIETY. 2686
0308-3594 See LOCAL COUNCIL REVIEW. 4662
0308-3616 See MEDICAL LABORATORY SCIENCES. 3610
0308-3845 See JOURNAL - CAMBORNE SCHOOL OF MINES. 2141
0308-4035 See NEWSLETTER - SOUTH-EAST ASIA LIBRARY GROUP. 3236
0308-406X See SCOTTISH TEACHERS' SALARIES MEMORANDUM. 1710
0308-4167 See PROCEEDINGS OF SYMPOSIUM ... OF THE ASSOCIATION OF BRITISH WILD ANIMAL KEEPERS. 2202
0308-4183 See JOURNAL OF THE BRISTOL AND AVON FAMILY HISTORY SOCIETY. 2455
0308-4205 See PROFESSIONAL PRINTER. 4569
0308-4221 See COMPUTER APPLICATIONS. 5096
0308-4272 See RADIOLOGICAL PROTECTION BULLETIN. 4419
0308-4353 See CONSUMER EUROPE. 922
0308-437X See ACOUSTICS BULLETIN. 4452
0308-4388 See HALSBURY'S LAWS OF ENGLAND ANNUAL ABRIDGEMENT. 2976
0308-4450 See WEST AFRICAN JOURNAL OF SOCIOLOGY AND POLITICAL SCIENCE, THE. 5265
0308-4469 See QUARTERLY BULLETIN OF COCOA STATISTICS / BULLETIN TRIMESTRIEL DE STATISTIQUES DU CACAO. 2362
0308-454X See TELEVISION (LONDON). 1141
0308-4558 See ANNUAL BIBLIOGRAPHY OF BRITISH AND IRISH HISTORY. PUBLICATIONS OF ... / ROYAL HISTORICAL SOCIETY. 2634
0308-4574 See BRACTON LAW JOURNAL, THE. 2943
0308-4698 See BRITISH COUNTRY MUSIC ASSOCIATION YEARBOOK. 4105
0308-4884 See COMMONWEALTH IN WORLD TRADE, THE. 829
0308-4906 See RECENT ADVANCES IN PAEDIATRIC SURGERY. 3911
0308-4914 See RECENT ADVANCES IN ORTHOPAEDICS. 3884
0308-4930 See ARCHITECT & SURVEYOR. 288
0308-4949 See JOURNAL - ROYAL BRITISH LEGION. 5232
0308-4957 See VIDA HISPANICA (1972). 3332
0308-5147 See ECONOMY AND SOCIETY. 5199
0308-518X See ENVIRONMENT & PLANNING A. 2821
0308-521X See AGRICULTURAL SYSTEMS. 52
0308-5279 See REPORT AND ACCOUNTS - BANK OF ENGLAND. 807
0308-5392 See TECHNIQUES OF PHYSICS. 4423
0308-5406 See ANCIENT MYSTERIES. 4240
0308-5422 See PROCEEDINGS OF THE ... INTERNATIONAL CRYOGENIC ENGINEERING CONFERENCE. 1992
0308-5457 See GARDEN (LONDON 1975). 2415
0308-549X See DAVID FIELD ALL-WORLD MINIATURE SHEET CATALOGUE. 2785
0308-5589 See TECHNICAL REPORT SERIES - FISHERIES LABORATORY. 2314
0308-5694 See IMAGO MUNDI (LYMPNE). 2582
0308-5708 See PUBLICATION - THE SCOTTISH AGRICULTURAL COLLEGES. 123
0308-5732 See AGRICULTURAL ENGINEER, THE. 50
0308-5759 See ADOPTION & FOSTERING. 5270
0308-5961 See TELECOMMUNICATIONS POLICY. 1166
0308-597X See MARINE POLICY. 1452
0308-6194 See CHRISTIAN PARAPSYCHOLOGIST, THE. 4241
0308-6275 See DYSLEXIA REVIEW. 3573
0308-6321 See WINCHESTER CATHEDRAL RECORD. 2716
0308-6437 See GEARTEST. 4176
0308-6534 See JOURNAL OF IMPERIAL AND COMMONWEALTH HISTORY, THE. 2695
0308-6569 See ANGLO-AMERICAN LAW REVIEW, THE. 2933
0308-6593 See JOURNAL OF CLINICAL PHARMACY. 4310
0308-6623 See RECENT ADVANCES IN RESPIRATORY MEDICINE. 3951
0308-6631 See MINING MAGAZINE (LONDON). 2146
0308-6674 See MALLORN. 3409
0308-6712 See BRITISH TOYS & HOBBIES. 2772
0308-6739 See LIST OF MEMBERS / FRESHWATER BIOLOGICAL ASSOCIATION. 463
0308-6747 See ARCHITECTURE WEST MIDLANDS. 290
0308-6801 See JOURNAL OF CENTRE FOR ADVANCED TV STUDIES : JCATS. 1134
0308-6860 See ETHNIC GROUPS. 2260
0308-6887 See AMNESTY INTERNATIONAL NEWSLETTER. 4503
0308-6909 See CORE. COLLECTED ORIGINAL RESOURCES IN EDUCATION. 1734
0308-7050 See MEAT HYGIENIST, THE. 2349
0308-7093 See COMMENT LONDON. 1971. 4518
0308-7174 See ELECTRICAL CONTRACTOR. 2044
0308-7298 See HISTORY OF PHOTOGRAPHY. 4370
0308-7344 See POTATO ABSTRACTS. 156
0308-7395 See QUARTERLY INDEX ISLAMICUS. 5013
0308-7476 See AUTOTRADE. 5407
0308-7506 See TERTIARY RESEARCH SPECIAL PAPER. 1399
0308-762X See INTERNATIONAL NEWSLETTER. 2692
0308-7654 See GAS WORLD (LONDON, ENGLAND : 1974). 4258
0308-8073 See ESTIMATING INFORMATION SERVICE. 614
0308-8146 See FOOD CHEMISTRY. 1024
0308-8154 See IN-HOUSE. 300
0308-8197 See DAIRY INDUSTRIES INTERNATIONAL. 193
0308-8448 See DESIGN ENGINEERING (LONDON, ENGLAND). 1970
0308-8464 See FINANCIAL TIMES WORLD HOTEL DIRECTORY, THE. 2805
0308-8480 See CAB INTERNATIONAL NEWS. 71
0308-8502 See WHO OWNS WHOM. NORTH AMERICA. 720
0308-8596 See ARCHITECT & SURVEYOR. 288
0308-8839 See MARITIME POLICY AND MANAGEMENT. 5452
0308-8863 See AGRICULTURAL ENGINEERING ABSTRACTS. 150
0308-888X See ESSAYS IN POETICS. 3385
0308-9002 See INTEREST RATE SERVICE. 791
0308-9126 See NDT & E INTERNATIONAL : INDEPENDENT NONDESTRUCTIVE TESTING AND EVALUATION. 1988
0308-9290 See RESEARCH FIELDS IN PHYSICS AT UNITED KINGDOM UNIVERSITIES AND POLYTECHNICS. 4419
0308-9312 See IDS BRIEF. 1677
0308-9339 See IDS STUDY. 1677
0308-9541 See EUROPEAN JOURNAL OF INFORMATION SYSTEMS. 1184
0308-9568 See LAC NEWS. 5515
0308-9649 See TERTIARY RESEARCH. 1399
0308-9819 See HOUSING AND CONSTRUCTION STATISTICS (ANNUAL). 632
0308-9827 See SPOTLIGHT. ACTRESSES. 388

03082970 See SORGHUM AND MILLETS ABSTRACTS. 156
0309-0019 See PRS NEWS. 5235
0309-0051 See AIA BULLETIN. 253
0309-0132 See MEDICAL RESEARCH COUNCIL HANDBOOK. 3611
0309-0140 See RECENT ADVANCES IN PAEDIATRICS. 3911
0309-0167 See HISTOPATHOLOGY. 3894
0309-0183 See SPOTLIGHT. ACTORS. 388
0309-040X See OFFSHORE SERVICE VESSEL REGISTER / COMPILED AND PUBLISHED BY H. CLARKSON & COMPANY LIMITED, THE. 5453
0309-0426 See HOUSE MAGAZINE. 4476
0309-0477 See INTERNATIONAL TEA COMMITTEE MONTHLY STATISTICAL SUMMARY. 2362
0309-0558 See MANAGERIAL LAW. 3151
0309-0566 See EUROPEAN JOURNAL OF MARKETING. 924
0309-0582 See MANAGEMENT BIBLIOGRAPHIES & REVIEWS. 731
0309-0590 See JOURNAL OF EUROPEAN INDUSTRIAL TRAINING. 873
0309-0671 See INTERNATIONAL LAW REPORTS. 3130
0309-0728 See INDUSTRIAL ARCHAEOLOGY REVIEW. 270
0309-0787 See JOURNAL FOR THE STUDY OF THE OLD TESTAMENT. SUPPLEMENT SERIES. 5017
0309-0817 See AUTOMOBILE ABSTRACTS (NUNEATON. 1975). 5405
0309-0884 See PRS YEARBOOK. 4147
0309-0892 See JOURNAL FOR THE STUDY OF THE OLD TESTAMENT. 5017
0309-1112 See FAMILY PLANNING TODAY. 589
0309-1120 See ASHINGTONIA. 500
0309-1139 See CADMIUM ABSTRACTS. 3999
0309-118X See INTERMEDIA (LONDON). 1157
0309-1287 See PROTOZOOLOGICAL ABSTRACTS. 5604
0309-1295 See NUTRITION ABSTRACTS AND REVIEWS. SERIES A: HUMAN & EXPERIMENTAL. 4201
0309-1309 See MERVYN PEAKE REVIEW, THE. 3411
0309-1317 See INTERNATIONAL JOURNAL OF URBAN AND REGIONAL RESEARCH. 2825
0309-1325 See PROGRESS IN HUMAN GEOGRAPHY. 2573
0309-1333 See PROGRESS IN PHYSICAL GEOGRAPHY. 2573
0309-135X See NUTRITION ABSTRACTS AND REVIEWS. SERIES B. LIVESTOCK FEEDS AND FEEDING. 155
0309-1384 See PLANNER (LONDON). 2830
0309-1414 See POLICE REVIEW (LONDON). 3172
0309-152X See IRCS MEDICAL SCIENCE. PSYCHOLOGY AND PSYCHIATRY. 3927
0309-1619 See POWYS REVIEW, THE. 3350
0309-1651 See CELL BIOLOGY INTERNATIONAL REPORTS. 533
0309-166X See CAMBRIDGE JOURNAL OF ECONOMICS. 1467
0309-1708 See ADVANCES IN WATER RESOURCES. 5528
0309-1740 See MEAT SCIENCE. 215
0309-1791 See APPLIED BOTANY. 500
0309-1805 See BRITISH SOCIETY FOR CELL BIOLOGY SYMPOSIUM. 449
0309-1813 See ATOMIC ABSORPTION AND EMISSION SPECTROMETRY ABSTRACTS. 1013
0309-1848 See RAT NEWS LETTER. 5519
0309-1902 See JOURNAL OF MEDICAL ENGINEERING & TECHNOLOGY. 3694
0309-1929 See GEOPHYSICAL AND ASTROPHYSICAL FLUID DYNAMICS. 1405
0309-2097 See OE REPORT. 5354
0309-2135 See PENTAGRAM PAPERS. 305
0309-2216 See INTERNATIONAL COPPER INFORMATION BULLETIN. 4025

0309-2224 See CONSERVATION NEWS (LONDON). 4087
0309-2240 See REPORT / POTATO MARKETING BOARD. 184
0309-2283 See RECENT ADVANCES IN RHEUMATOLOGY. 3806
0309-2305 See RECENT ADVANCES IN ANAESTHESIA AND ANALGESIA. 3684
0309-2399 See CAREERS IN NURSING AND OTHER HEALTH SERVICE PROFESSIONS. 3853
0309-2402 See JOURNAL OF ADVANCED NURSING. 3858
0309-2410 See MAJOR PROBLEMS IN OPHTHALMOLOGY. 3876
0309-2437 See RECENT ADVANCES IN OPHTHALMOLOGY. 3878
0309-2445 See PUBLISHING HISTORY. 4819
0309-2534 See ADVANCES IN RAMAN SPECTROSCOPY. 4396
0309-2666 See MEDICAL TECHNOLOGIST AND SCIENTIST, THE. 3612
0309-2674 See RECENT ADVANCES IN PLASTIC SURGERY. 3973
0309-2690 See PERKIN-ELMER ANALYTICAL NEWS. 5137
0309-2747 See RECENT ADVANCES IN DERMATOLOGY. 3722
0309-2984 See HISTORY WORKSHOP. 2619
0309-3093 See BERKSHIRE ARCHAEOLOGICAL JOURNAL, THE. 261
0309-314X See ON-LINE REVIEW. 1275
0309-3247 See JOURNAL OF STRAIN ANALYSIS FOR ENGINEERING DESIGN, THE. 2118
0309-331X See COFFEE INTERNATIONAL. 2366
0309-3492 See THIRD WAY. 5004
0309-3603 See PROCEEDINGS OF THE CAMBRIDGE ANTIQUARIAN SOCIETY. 2626
0309-3646 See PROSTHETICS AND ORTHOTICS INTERNATIONAL. 4392
0309-3700 See LIVERPOOL CLASSICAL MONTHLY : LCM. 251
0309-3743 See YORK HISTORIAN. 311
0309-3891 See JOURNAL OF CONSUMER STUDIES AND HOME ECONOMICS. 1298
0309-3964 See ESTUARIES AND COASTAL WATERS OF THE BRITISH ISLES : A BIBLIOGRAPHY OF RECENT SCIENTIFIC PAPERS. 554
0309-4111 See FARM BUILDING PROGRESS. 158
0309-4170 See CHRISTIAN LIBRARIAN. 3202
0309-4189 See OFFSHORE RESEARCH FOCUS. 4267
0309-4227 See PAPER CONSERVATOR. 4235
0309-427X See ANNALES DE KINESITHERAPIE. 4379
0309-4294 See FISHERIES ECONOMICS NEWSLETTER. 2317
0309-4308 See NATIONAL REVIEW FOR LITURGY. 4980
0309-4375 See EXETER LINGUISTIC STUDIES. 3281
0309-4529 See SOUTH AMERICAN HANDBOOK. 5491
0309-4561 See PLASTICS AND RUBBER INTERNATIONAL. 4457
0309-457X See MAGHREB REVIEW, THE. 2641
0309-4693 See SOCIAL SERVICE ABSTRACTS (LONDON). 5267
0309-4707 See MIDDLE EAST ELECTRICITY. 2072
0309-4715 See EUROPEAN SCIENCE EDITING : BULLETIN OF THE EUROPEAN ASSOCIATION OF SCIENCE EDITORS. 4815
0309-4944 See INTERNATIONAL PETROLEUM ABSTRACTS. 4283
0309-4979 See COAL ABSTRACTS. 1961
0309-5118 See HATCHER REVIEW, THE. 2690
0309-524X See WIND ENGINEERING. 1437
0309-5347 See CIIG REVIEW. 607
0309-5428 See LONDON PASSENGER TRANSPORT. 5432

0309-5487 See DIRECTORY OF BRITISH ASSOCIATIONS & ASSOCIATIONS IN IRELAND. 5230
0309-5770 See CATALYSTS IN CHEMISTRY. 967
0309-5800 See JOURNAL OF THE CAMBRIDGESHIRE FAMILY HISTORY SOCIETY. 2455
0309-5991 See SEMICONDUCTORS AND INSULATORS. 4421
0309-622X See FIRE SERVICE STATISTICS ... ACTUALS. 2290
0309-6270 See LOGOPHILE. 3300
0309-6505 See UNIVERSITY OF CAMBRIDGE. DEPARTMENT OF ENGINEERING. CUED/C-MAT. 2000
0309-6521 See UNIVERSITY OF CAMBRIDGE. DEPARTMENT OF ENGINEERING. CUED/A-TURBO. 2000
0309-6564 See DUTCH CROSSING. 3382
0309-6653 See M D A INFORMATION. 4091
0309-6688 See FEN. FINITE ELEMENT NEWS. 5105
0309-6831 See SEMINAR SERIES (SOCIETY FOR EXPERIMENTAL BIOLOGY (GREAT BRITAIN)). 473
0309-6858 See INTERNATIONAL JOURNAL OF PAEDIATRIC DENTISTRY / THE BRITISH PAEDONDONTIC SOCIETY [AND] THE INTERNATIONAL ASSOCIATION OF DENTISTRY FOR CHILDREN. 1325
0309-6866 See FIRE PREVENTION (LONDON, 1971). 2289
0309-6904 See IPPF CO-OPERATIVE INFORMATION SERVICE. 589
0309-698X See ACADEMIC AND CLINICAL REPORTS - INSTITUTE OF LARYNGOLOGY AND OTOLOGY ASSOCIATED WITH THE ROYAL NATIONAL THROAT, NOSE AND EAR HOSPITAL. 3885
0309-7013 See SUPPLEMENTARY VOLUME - ARISTOTELIAN SOCIETY. 4363
0309-703X See COMPANY SECRETARY'S REVIEW. 3098
0309-7234 See EUROPEAN INDUSTRIAL RELATIONS REVIEW. 1668
0309-7242 See PURCHASING & SUPPLY MANAGEMENT / INSTITUTE OF PURCHASING AND SUPPLY. 951
0309-7269 See INDUSTRIAL RELATIONS REVIEW AND REPORT. 1678
0309-7471 See MATERIAL MATTERS. 1066
0309-7544 See SOCIAL SCIENCE TEACHER. 1905
0309-7676 See INTERNATIONAL BUSINESS LAWYER. 3129
0309-7684 See INTERNATIONAL LEGAL PRACTITIONER. 3130
0309-7765 See BRONTE SOCIETY PUBLICATIONS. TRANSACTIONS. 3369
0309-7846 See HYDROGRAPHIC JOURNAL. 1414
0309-7900 See TAX PLANNING INTERNATIONAL REVIEW. 4754
0309-7986 See TRANSACTIONS OF THE CUMBERLAND & WESTMORLAND ANTIQUARIAN & ARCHAEOLOGICAL SOCIETY. 2713
0309-7994 See REPORT AND TRANSACTIONS - THE DEVONSHIRE ASSOCIATION FOR THE ADVANCEMENT OF SCIENCE, LITERATURE AND ART. 329
0309-8001 See TRENDS IN INTERNATIONAL BANKING AND CAPITAL MARKETS. 814
0309-8044 See YEAR BOOK - BRITISH FEDERATION OF MUSIC FESTIVALS. 389
0309-8117 See PROCEEDINGS OF THE INSTITUTE OF ACOUSTICS. 4453
0309-8133 See SYNTHETIC CRYSTALS NEWSLETTER. 1033
0309-8141 See PRAGMATICS. MICROFICHE. 3311
0309-8168 See CAPITAL & CLASS. 1590
0309-8249 See JOURNAL OF PHILOSOPHY OF EDUCATION. 1898
0309-8265 See JOURNAL OF GEOGRAPHY IN HIGHER EDUCATION. 2567
0309-8559 See FAMILY HISTORY NEWS AND DIGEST. 2447

0309-8710 See ANNALS OF THE ISRAEL PHYSICAL SOCIETY. 5228
0309-877X See JOURNAL OF FURTHER AND HIGHER EDUCATION. 1832
0309-8826 See PARLIAMENTARY DEBATES (HANSARD). HOUSE OF COMMONS OFFICIAL REPORT. 4672
0309-8834 See PARLIAMENTARY DEBATES (HANSARD). HOUSE OF LORDS OFFICIAL REPORT, THE. 4672
0309-8885 See COMPUTING JOURNAL ABSTRACTS. 1208
0309-8958 See TOURISM INTELLIGENCE QUARTERLY. 5493
0309-9105 See SCOTTISH FISHERIES INFORMATION PAMPHLET. 2312
0309-913X See HERTFORDSHIRE PEOPLE. 2453
0309-9210 See TRANSACTIONS OF THE THOROTON SOCIETY OF NOTTINGHAMSHIRE. 2713
0309-930X See B.S.B.I. NEWS. 501
0310-0014 See AUSTRALIAN LAW REPORTS. 2939
0310-0049 See AUSTRALIAN MAMMALOGY. 5577
0310-0367 See WATER (MELBOURNE). 2247
0310-057X See ANAESTHESIA AND INTENSIVE CARE. 3680
0310-1053 See AUSTRALIAN BUSINESS LAW REVIEW. 3096
0310-1258 See AUSTRALIAN PIPELINER. 4251
0310-1304 See AUSTRALIAN SHELL NEWS. 5577
0310-138X See AUSTRALIAN VETERINARY PRACTITIONER. 5505
0310-1452 See BELLE (SYDNEY, N.S.W.). 293
0310-1584 See CABBAGES AND KINGS. 2669
0310-1797 See CLEO. 5553
0310-1878 See CCEA NEWSLETTER. 1861
0310-2076 See COSMOPOLITAN AUSTRALIAN EDITION. 5554
0310-222x See EARTH GARDEN. 5244
0310-2556 See ORAL HISTORY (PORT MORESBY, PAPUA NEW GUINEA). 2625
0310-2890 See GRASS ROOTS SHEPPARTON. 90
0310-2939 See HABITAT (MELBOURNE). 2194
0310-3242 See LEARNING EXCHANGE. 1761
0310-365X See NEW JOURNALIST. 2922
0310-3773 See NIUGINI CAVER. 1409
0310-4044 See PROBE (MELBOURNE). 1774
0310-4168 See REFRACTORY GIRL. 5565
0310-4184 See PEX. 4274
0310-4303 See SCIENCE IN NEW GUINEA. 5152
0310-4559 See ANNUAL REPORT AND STATEMENT OF ACCOUNTS - RURAL RECONSTRUCTION BOARD (HOBART). 2814
0310-4664 See TRAINING AND DEVELOPMENT IN AUSTRALIA. 716
0310-4729 See RECORD SYDNEY. 2483
0310-4796 See ANNUAL REPORT - ENVIRONMENT PROTECTION AUTHORITY MELBOURNE. 2160
0310-4834 See VICTORIAN ORGAN JOURNAL. 4158
0310-4869 See WELFARE IN AUSTRALIA. 5314
0310-5148 See ANNUAL REPORT - AUSTRALIAN ARBITRATION INSPECTORATE. 1648
0310-5369 See WESTERN TEACHER. 1908
0310-5660 See INSIDE RETAILING. 955
0310-5695 See NOTES ON HIGHER EDUCATION. 1838
0310-5709 See DEVELOPING EDUCATION. 1735
0310-5776 See MENTAL HEALTH IN AUSTRALIA (1973). 4790
0310-5814 See ANCIENT HISTORY: RESOURCES FOR TEACHERS. 2610
0310-6020 See FILTER PERTH. 1895
0310-6659 See INDONESIAN ACQUISITIONS LIST. 3215
0310-6802 See CONTINUO (BRISBANE, QLD.). 4112
0310-6810 See AUSTRALIAN JOURNAL OF HOSPITAL PHARMACY. 4293

0310-6853 See AUSTRALIAN JOURNAL OF HUMAN COMMUNICATION DISORDERS. 4384
0310-7175 See INDEPENDENT EDUCATION. 1751
0310-7205 See RHOMBUS. 3532
0310-723X See ABORIGINAL NEWS (CANBERRA). 2253
0310-7477 See NEWSRAIL. 5433
0310-7817 See AUSTRALIAN FEDERAL TAX REPORTER. 4712
0310-7833 See WILDLIFE RESEARCH. 5600
0310-7841 See AUSTRALIAN JOURNAL OF PLANT PHYSIOLOGY. 501
0310-7949 See INTERACTION MELBOURNE. 1897
0310-8260 See KEY VIVE. 4127
0310-8279 See CATTLE. 208
0310-8767 See EDUCATIONAL ADMINISTRATOR MELBOURNE. 1863
0310-9011 See LANDSCAPE AUSTRALIA. 2423
0310-9186 See IRIS AND RES NOVISSIMAE. 1077
0311-0192 See INSURANCE & BANKING RECORD, THE. 791
0311-0370 See AGRIBUSINESS DECISION. 48
0311-0435 See DAVID LORD'S WORLD OF CRICKET. 4859
0311-0699 See DENTAL ANAESTHESIA AND SEDATION. 1320
0311-0729 See GAZETTE - AUSTRALIAN MATHEMATICAL SOCIETY. 3506
0311-0877 See ANNUAL REPORT - IONOSPHERE PREDICTION SERVICE (CANBERRA). 1420
0311-0893 See REPORT OF RESEARCH ACTIVITIES - DIVISION OF TECHNICAL SERVICES, QUEENSLAND DEPARTMENT OF FORESTRY. 2392
0311-0893 See RESEARCH REPORT / DIVISION OF TECHNICAL SERVICES (RESEARCH AND UTILIZATION), QUEENSLAND DEPARTMENT OF FORESTRY. 2393
0311-094X See AUSTRALIAN TAX REVIEW. 2939
0311-1784 See WORDS AND WINDMILLS. 1908
0311-1881 See AUSTRALIAN ENTOMOLOGICAL MAGAZINE. 5605
0311-1903 See CHARTERED BUILDER. 607
0311-1911 See POWER FARMING MAGAZINE. 160
0311-2101 See ANNUAL REPORT - THE WATER QUALITY COUNCIL OF QUEENSLAND. 5530
0311-2136 See SOUTH PACIFIC JOURNAL OF TEACHER EDUCATION. 1847
0311-2225 See ADBRIEF. 754
0311-2543 See EDUCATION, RESEARCH AND PERSPECTIVES. 1822
0311-2756 See SOUTH AUSTRALIAN GENEALOGIST. 2473
0311-2772 See TEACHER FEEDBACK. 1906
0311-2799 See ASIA TEACHERS' BULLETIN. 1726
0311-2934 See BULLETIN. 1302
0311-306X See CANCER FORUM. 3811
0311-3140 See MONASH UNIVERSITY LAW REVIEW. 3011
0311-3531 See EARTH SCIENCE AND RELATED INFORMATION. 1354
0311-3558 See WASTE DISPOSAL AND WATER MANAGEMENT IN AUSTRALIA. 2246
0311-3612 See AUSTRALIAN PODIATRIST. 3917
0311-3639 See CINEMA PAPERS. 4066
0311-3760 See MIGRATION ACTION. 1920
0311-3930 See GLOBE (MELBOURNE). 2565
0311-4198 See HECATE. 5558
0311-4546 See ECOS. 2227
0311-4627 See CANBERRA LINGUIST. 3272
0311-4775 See UNICORN (CARLTON, TAS.). 1788
0311-4805 See COASTLINE. 1353
0311-5518 See ALCHERINGA (SYDNEY). 4226
0311-5836 See CSIRO INDEX. 5097
0311-5984 See NEWSLETTER / AUSTRALIAN LAW LIBRARIANS' GROUP. 3235
0311-6166 See NUOVO PAESE. 2701
0311-6336 See AUSTRALIAN BULLETIN OF LABOUR. 1654

0311-662X See NATA NEWS SYDNEY. 2123
0311-6999 See AUSTRALIAN EDUCATIONAL RESEARCHER. 1810
0311-7197 See ANNUAL REPORT - PIPELINE AUTHORITY. 4250
0311-8002 See AUSTRALIAN JOURNAL OF PHARMACY. 4293
0311-8150 See AUSTRALIAN BIRDS : JOURNAL OF THE N. S. W. FIELD ORNITHOLOGISTS CLUB. 5615
0311-8185 See NATA DIRECTORY SYDNEY. 2123
0311-8223 See AUSTRALIAN PARKS AND RECREATION. 4706
0311-8479 See WOMANSPEAK. 5569
0311-8576 See TECHNICAL BULLETIN (NEW SOUTH WALES. DEPT. OF AGRICULTURE). 139
0311-8959 See ANNUAL REPORT - FISHING INDUSTRY RESEARCH COMMITTEE. 2294
0311-905X See CURRENT THERAPEUTICS. 4298
0311-9254 See HEALTH BULLETIN (MELBOURNE). 4778
0311-9297 See PROCEEDINGS OF THE AUSTRALIAN ASSOCIATION OF GERONTOLOGY. 3754
0311-9513 See CONFERENCE OF PRESIDING OFFICERS AND CLERKS OF THE PARLIAMENTS OF AUSTRALIA, FIJI, NAURU, PAPUA NEW GUINEA AND WESTERN SAMOA. 4640
0311-953X See ANNUAL REPORT - EXPORT PAYMENTS INSURANCE CORPORATION. 2873
0311-9882 See AUSTRALIAN WOOL SALE STATISTICS; STATISTICAL ANALYSIS. 5360
0312-0317 See BALTIC NEWS. 4504
0312-1267 See VOLUME OF PAPERS - ANNUAL CONFERENCE AUSTRALIAN INSTITUTE OF HEALTH SURVEYORS SOUTH AUSTRALIAN DIVISION. 4807
0312-1372 See CHAIN-REACTION (CARLTON, VIC.). 2189
0312-1658 See QUEENSLAND LAWYER, THE. 3034
0312-1674 See NEW SOUTH WALES LAW REPORTS. 3016
0312-1844 See SOCIAL SCIENCE TEACHER SYDNEY. 5221
0312-1933 See PROCEEDINGS - NATIONAL CONFERENCE OF THE AUSTRALIAN SOCIETY FOR OPERATIONS RESEARCH. 1991
0312-2417 See AUSTRALIAN ARCHAEOLOGY. 260
0312-2530 See AUSTRALIAN HISTORY TEACHER. 1888
0312-2654 See METRO (MELBOURNE). 4074
0312-3162 See RECORDS OF THE WESTERN AUSTRALIAN MUSEUM. 4171
0312-3278 See ALPHABETICAL INDEX OF CONSTITUENT PARTICULARS OF TRADE MARKS. 1301
0312-3685 See MATHEMATICAL SCIENTIST. 3520
0312-3766 See MINERAL RESOURCES REPORT CANBERRA. 1358
0312-3774 See EXPORT HANDBOOK SYDNEY. 674
0312-407X See AUSTRALIAN SOCIAL WORK. 5274
0312-4371 See CATALOGUING AUSTRALIA. 3200
0312-455X See WORK AND PEOPLE. 948
0312-4592 See AGIS : ATTORNEY-GENERAL'S INFORMATION SERVICE. 2928
0312-4681 See FLEETLINE. 5382
0312-4711 See AUSTRALIAN GEOLOGIST, THE. 1366
0312-4738 See PROCEEDINGS - ENDOCRINE SOCIETY OF AUSTRALIA. 3732
0312-4819 See PUBLICATIONS OF THE AUSTRALIAN BUREAU OF STATISTICS. 5336
0312-4886 See TEACHER EDUCATION. 1905
0312-5033 See AUSTRALIAN JOURNAL OF EARLY CHILDHOOD. 1802
0312-5211 See CSIRO TEXTILE NEWS. 5350
0312-5270 See NEWSLIB BRISBANE. 3236
0312-5327 See AUSTRALIAN GIFTGUIDE. 2583

0312-567X *See* REPORT - DIVISION OF ENVIRONMENTAL MECHANICS. CSIRO (CANBERRA). 2181

0312-5688 *See* ANNUAL REPORT - PUBLIC SERVICE BOARD (PERTH). 4701

0312-5807 *See* JOURNAL OF THE AUSTRALIAN NAVAL INSTITUTE. 4178

0312-5963 *See* CLINICAL PHARMACOKINETICS. 4296

0312-6056 *See* ANNUAL SUMMARY OF AUSTRALIAN NOTICES TO MARINERS. 4174

0312-6137 *See* HANDBOOK - FACULTY OF MEDICINE, UNIVERSITY OF NEW SOUTH WALES. 3580

0312-6145 *See* EARLY DAYS. 2669

0312-617X *See* BUILDING RESEARCH. 604

0312-6358 *See* REPORT - JOINT COAL BOARD. 2149

0312-6579 *See* COMMUNITY HEALTH BULLETIN. 4772

0312-6757 *See* COVER NOTE SYDNEY. 2878

0312-6765 *See* ARTFORCE. 341

0312-6862 *See* PARLIAMENT OF WESTERN AUSTRALIA DIGEST, THE. 3025

0312-8008 *See* AUSTRALIAN PRESCRIBER. 3554

0312-8393 *See* ELECTRICITY SUPPLY INDUSTRY IN AUSTRALIA. 2046

0312-8466 *See* RESEARCH REPORT - DIVISION OF APPLIED ORGANIC CHEMISTRY. 1047

0312-8857 *See* AUSTRALIAN AUTISM REVIEW. 4575

0312-8962 *See* AUSTRALIAN JOURNAL OF MANAGEMENT. 860

0312-8970 *See* AUSTRALIAN CHILD AND FAMILY WELFARE. 5274

0312-9519 *See* CHRISTIAN BROTHERS STUDIES. 1732

0312-9543 *See* READING EDUCATION. 1777

0312-9608 *See* BMR JOURNAL OF AUSTRALIAN GEOLOGY AND GEOPHYSICS. 1367

0312-9616 *See* MEDIA INFORMATION AUSTRALIA. 1116

0312-9640 *See* JOURNAL OF THE HISTORICAL SOCIETY OF SOUTH AUSTRALIA. 2669

0312-9764 *See* TELOPEA. 2432

0312-9837 *See* PETROLEUM NEWSLETTER, THE. 4273

0312-9950 *See* AUSTRALIAN STRING TEACHER. 4101

0313-0096 *See* UNIVERSITY OF NEW SOUTH WALES LAW JOURNAL, THE. 3069

0313-0568 *See* THOMSON'S LIQUOR GUIDE. 2371

0313-0797 *See* STEREO FM RADIO. 1139

0313-1459 *See* SPAN. 3439

0313-1688 *See* GEOLOGICAL SURVEY PAPER. 1378

0313-1696 *See* AGIA NEWSLETTER. 1351

0313-2153 *See* NEW DOCTOR. 3916

0313-2382 *See* ADVERTISING EXPENDITURE IN MAIN MEDIA. 1103

0313-363X *See* SKYSAILOR. 4919

0313-3656 *See* QUEENSLAND GOVERNMENT DIRECTORY. 4677

0313-377X *See* AGRICULTURAL ECONOMICS BULLETIN (ARMIDALE, N.S.W.). 49

0313-3796 *See* PLANNING NEWS SOUTH MELBOURNE. 2831

0313-380X *See* A.P.C. REVIEW. 1720

0313-4083 *See* JOURNAL OF THE ADELAIDE BOTANIC GARDENS. 516

0313-4133 *See* NCOSS NEWS. 5297

0313-4202 *See* YEARBOOK - AUSTRALIAN SOCIETY OF EDUCATIONAL TECHNOLOGY. 1792

0313-4253 *See* QUEENSLAND LAW SOCIETY JOURNAL, THE. 3034

0313-4393 See COMMERCIAL PHOTOGRAPHY IN AUSTRALIA. 4368

0313-4423 *See* SCARLET WOMAN. 5566

0313-4555 See RANGELAND JOURNAL, THE. 2391

0313-5373 *See* AUSTRALIAN JOURNAL OF TEACHER EDUCATION, THE. 1888

0313-5527 *See* CHEMICAL ENGINEERING IN AUSTRALIA / THE INSTITUTION OF ENGINEERS, AUSTRALIA. 2010

0313-5543 *See* RESEARCH AND DEVELOPMENT PAPER - TERTIARY EDUCATION RESEARCH CENTRE. UNIVERSITY OF NEW SOUTH WALES. 1845

0313-5861 *See* SOUTHERN CROSS SYDNEY. 1961. 4998

0313-5926 *See* ECONOMIC ANALYSIS AND POLICY. 1591

0313-5934 *See* JASSA. 793

0313-5942 *See* BHP JOURNAL. 3999

0313-5977 *See* CANBERRA HISTORICAL JOURNAL. 2669

0313-6086 *See* MINERAL INDUSTRY QUARTERLY. 2144

0313-6124 *See* CONTEMPORARY SOCIAL WORK EDUCATION. 5280

0313-6221 *See* PARERGON. 1079

0313-623X *See* AUSTRALIAN TRADE PRACTICES REPORTER 1975. 824

0313-6353 *See* LAND RIGHTS NEWS. 4840

0313-6485 *See* WOMAN WRITER. 3454

0313-6647 *See* AUSTRALIAN JOURNAL OF PUBLIC ADMINISTRATION. 4631

0313-6728 *See* SPECIAL EDUCATION BULLETIN BRISBANE. 1885

0313-6736 *See* ANNUAL REPORT - AUSTRALIAN ACADEMY OF TECHNOLOGICAL SCIENCES. 5083

0313-6825 *See* FUNCTION. 3506

0313-6833 *See* ANNUAL REPORT - AUSTRALIAN ROAD RESEARCH BOARD. 5376

0313-685x *See* SCOPP : SATURDAY CENTRE OF PROSE & POETRY. 3470

0313-6922 *See* NATIONAL CONFERENCE PUBLICATION - INSTITUTION OF ENGINEERS, AUSTRALIA. 1988

0313-704x *See* AESIS QUARTERLY. 1361

0313-766X *See* AUSTRALIAN POWERBOAT. 591

0313-7732 *See* CONSUMER SURVEYS. INTERIM REPORT. 1296

0313-7767 *See* TEACHING MATHEMATICS. 3538

0313-7791 *See* WORKING PAPERS / SHLRC. 3333

0313-7872 *See* BEACH CONSERVATION. 2188

0313-8445 *See* AUSTRALIAN COMPANY LAW REPORTS. 3096

0313-8496 *See* INSIDE WELFARE BULLETIN. 1496

0313-8860 *See* WESTERN GEOGRAPHER. 2579

0313-895X *See* TECHNICAL MANUAL ATM. 5445

0313-9093 *See* BIENNIAL REPORT / CSIRO DIVISION OF FOREST RESEARCH. 2376

0314-0520 *See* ANNUAL REPORT / TRADE PRACTICES COMMISSION. 3095

0314-0679 *See* GRADUATE OUTLOOK. 1826

0314-1004 *See* PROCEEDINGS OF THE NUTRITION SOCIETY OF AUSTRALIA. 4198

0314-1039 *See* AUSTRALIAN DEFENCE FORCE JOURNAL : JOURNAL OF THE AUSTRALIAN PROFESSION OF ARMS. 4037

0314-1160 *See* CRIMINAL LAW JOURNAL. 3106

0314-1543 *See* SCHOOL AND COMMUNITY NEWS CANBERRA. 1782

0314-2094 *See* MONTHLY SUMMARY OF STATISTICS, TASMANIA / AUSTRALIAN BUREAU OF STATISTICS. 5333

0314-2523 *See* AUSTRALIAN REPRESENTATIVE BASINS PROGRAM REPORT SERIES. 5530

0314-2531 *See* PANORAMA. 1771

0314-254X *See* BIENNIAL REPORT / DIVISION OF PROTEIN CHEMISTRY, INSTITUTE OF INDUSTRIAL TECHNOLOGY. 962

0314-2779 *See* LABOUR STATISTICS ... AUSTRALIA. 1535

0314-2825 *See* EAST TIMOR NEWS : BULLETIN OF THE EAST TIMOR NEWS AGENCY. 4507

0314-3155 *See* SIMPLY LIVING. 2182

0314-3171 *See* ANNUAL REPORT AND STATEMENTS OF ACCOUNT. AUSTRALIAN INSTITUTE OF PETROLEUM. 4250

0314-3767 *See* AUSTRALIAN SOCIETY OF INDEXERS NEWSLETTER. 3193

0314-3902 *See* EDUCATION CAPITAL. 1738

0314-3937 *See* OCCASIONAL PAPERS - APPLIED LINGUISTICS ASSOCIATION OF AUSTRALIA. 3307

0314-4240 *See* CHEMISTRY IN AUSTRALIA. 970

0314-4275 *See* AUSTRALIAN SECRETARY. 641

0314-4607 *See* MINING REVIEW CANBERRA 1977. 2146

0314-4984 *See* SCIENCE AND TECHNOLOGY INFORMATION BULLETIN. B10. FISH DISEASES. 2312

0314-528X *See* PROCEEDINGS OF THE ... NATIONAL CONFERENCE OF THE AUSTRALIAN MUSIC THERAPY ASSOCIATION HELD IN ..., THE. 4147

0314-5956 *See* SHEET - CSIRO, DIVISION OF BUILDING RESEARCH. 627

0314-6464 *See* AUSTRALIAN JOURNAL OF ART. 343

0314-657X *See* THEMATIC MAPPING BULLETIN. 2583

0314-660X *See* PATIENT MANAGEMENT (SEAFORTH). 3626

0314-6677 *See* SCIENCE FICTION. 3434

0314-6685 *See* GRAPHIX PRAHRAN. 379

0314-6820 *See* NEWSLETTER - STATISTICAL SOCIETY OF AUSTRALIA. 5334

0314-6855 *See* POETRY MONASH. 3469

0314-7320 *See* CURRENCY. 5281

0314-7495 *See* NEW LITERATURE REVIEW. 3348

0314-7606 *See* SIGMA. 3535

0314-769X *See* JOURNAL OF AUSTRALIAN STUDIES. 2669

0314-7797 *See* DJAWAL IDI. 1803

0314-8211 *See* CANBERRA BIRD NOTES. 5616

0314-8580 *See* A.I.I. JOURNAL. 2872

0314-8769 *See* ABORIGINAL HISTORY. 227

0314-9021 See AUSTRALIAN JOURNAL OF PUBLIC HEALTH. 4768

0314-9099 *See* CANBERRA ANTHROPOLOGY. 233

0314-9307 *See* DIRECTORY OF STATE AND PUBLIC LIBRARY SERVICES IN QUEENSLAND. 3208

0314-9781 *See* ENVIRONMENTAL REPORT CLAYTON. 2169

0314-989X *See* NORTHERN PERSPECTIVE. 3418

0314-9919 *See* ANNUAL REPORT / AUSTRALIAN NATIONAL GALLERY. 4083

0314-9935 *See* PRESIDENTIAL ADDRESS OF THE AUSTRALIAN ACADEMY OF TECHNOLOGICAL SCIENCES. 5139

0315-0151 *See* GO INFO. 5231

0315-0151 *See* GO INFO. 2794

0315-0208 *See* SPEAR (TORONTO). 2273

0315-0380 *See* ECO/LOG WEEK. 2227

0315-047X *See* DECORMAG. 2899

0315-0542 *See* OUTDOOR CANADA. 4876

0315-0631 *See* DIRECTORY OF COMMUNITY SERVICES IN METROPOLITAN TORONTO. 5282

0315-0801 *See* DINOSAURIAN WHO'S-WHO. 432

0315-0836 *See* CANADIAN THEATRE REVIEW. 5362

0315-0860 *See* HISTORIA MATHEMATICA. 3507

0315-0879 *See* CANADIAN KEY BUSINESS DIRECTORY. 655

0315-0941 *See* GEOSCIENCE CANADA. 1380

0315-1042 *See* O C P, ON CONTINUING PRACTICE. 4318

0315-1131 *See* MS CANADA. 3838

0315-1204 *See* CO-OPERATEUR AGRICOLE, LE. 75

0315-1301 *See* COSMETICS (DON MILLS). 403

0315-1409 *See* CANADIAN AND INTERNATIONAL EDUCATION. 1730

0315-1417 *See* C O R S BULLETIN. 1236

0315-1433 See CANADIAN ANNUAL REVIEW OF POLITICS AND PUBLIC AFFAIRS. 4467

0315-1468 See CANADIAN JOURNAL OF CIVIL ENGINEERING. 2020

0315-1557 See PREVENIR (MONTREAL). 2521

0315-162X See JOURNAL OF RHEUMATOLOGY, THE. 3805

0315-1654 See ENERGY ANALECTS. 1938

0315-1697 See ACFO INFO. 2526

0315-1700 See WORLD DIRECTORY OF HISTORIANS OF MATHEMATICS. 3541

0315-1808 See T A S A, TEACHING ATYPICAL STUDENTS IN ALBERTA. 1886

0315-1867 See CONSOMMATEUR CANADIEN, LE. 1294

0315-1948 See NOS JEUNES (ENGLISH EDITION). 1769

0315-1999 See CANADIAN BOOKS IN PRINT. SUBJECT INDEX. 4821

0315-2022 See WESTERN GEOGRAPHICAL SERIES. 2579

0315-212X See REGINA. 2544

0315-2146 See PROCEEDINGS OF THE ENTOMOLOGICAL SOCIETY OF MANITOBA. 5613

0315-2286 See NATIONAL (OTTAWA). 3013

0315-2340 See DOCUMENTATION ET BIBLIOTHEQUES. 3208

0315-2383 See UNITT'S CANADIAN PRICE GUIDE TO ANTIQUES & COLLECTABLES. 252

0315-2561 See INFORMATION NORTH. 2535

0315-2669 See DENTAL EDUCATION REGISTER. 1320

0315-2685 See JEWISH DIALOGUE. 3399

0315-2715 See CANADIAN FILM-MAKERS DISTRIBUTION CENTRE CATALOGUE. 4065

0315-2774 See DIRECTORY - LAKE ONTARIO REGIONAL LIBRARY SYSTEM. 3206

0315-2782 See HIGH AND LOW. 900

0315-2804 See RAINCOAST CHRONICLES. 2756

0315-2871 See WARPATH (OTTAWA). 333

0315-2898 See ALMANACH MODERNE. 2484

0315-2944 See UP TO THE NECK. 5313

0315-2979 See BULLETIN - CORPORATION PROFESSIONNELLE DES MEDECINS DU QUEBEC. 3559

0315-2979 See BULLETIN - PROFESSIONAL CORPORATION OF PHYSICIANS OF QUEBEC. 3561

0315-2995 See NEWSLETTER - GUIDANCE AND COUNSELLING ASSOCIATION. 1882

0315-3088 See WHERE TO EAT IN CANADA. 5073

0315-3150 See INFORMATION - CANADIAN ASSOCIATION OF SOCIAL WORKERS. 5289

0315-3495 See CANADIAN DEFENCE QUARTERLY (TORONTO). 4038

0315-3509 See NEWSLETTER - SPECIAL EDUCATION COUNCIL OF THE ALBERTA TEACHERS' ASSOCIATION. 1882

0315-3525 See EMPLOYMENT BULLETIN (TORONTO. 1971). 1666

0315-3649 See M5V MAGAZINE. 324

0315-3681 See UTILITAS MATHEMATICA. 3540

0315-369X See REPORTING CLASSROOM RESEARCH. 1778

0315-3754 See CAPILANO REVIEW, THE. 3372

0315-3770 See EVENT (NEW WESTMINSTER). 3386

0315-3835 See BRITISH COLUMBIA GENEALOGIST, THE. 2440

0315-3916 See CARNET MUSICAL. 4108

0315-3967 See CAHIERS LINGUISTIQUES D'OTTAWA. 3272

0315-3975 See VIDEO-PRESSE. 1071

0315-4130 See LIBRE COURS. 1834

0315-4149 See INTERNATIONAL FICTION REVIEW. 3396

0315-4165 See EXIL (TROIS- RIVIERES). 5364

0315-4297 See JOURNAL OF CANADIAN ART HISTORY. 323

0315-4920 See C P A C REVIEW. 2816

0315-5021 See WATERLOO HISTORICAL SOCIETY. 2765

0315-5226 See VANGUARD (VANCOUVER). 367

0315-5412 See JOURNAL OF AUTOMATIC WRITING, THE. 4241

0315-5420 See MANAGEMENT COMPENSATION IN CANADA. 943

0315-5463 See FOOD RESEARCH INTERNATIONAL. 2339

0315-5501 See TRUCK CANADA. 5398

0315-5900 See COMMUNIQUE - INTERMET. 5242

0315-5943 See REPERTOIRE DE L'EDITION AU QUEBEC. 423

0315-5986 See INFOR. INFORMATION SYSTEMS AND OPERATIONAL RESEARCH. 1259

0315-6036 See ACTION (TORONTO. 1970). 4932

0315-6168 See CANADIAN PARLIAMENTARY GUIDE. 4636

0315-6311 See REPORT ON THE CANADIAN DRUG STORE MARKET, A. 4327

0315-6451 See ROYAL CANADIAN MILITARY INSTITUTE YEARBOOK. 4056

0315-6532 See CHRISTIAN INQUIRER (NATIONAL EDITION). 4945

0315-6559 See CHRISTIAN INQUIRER (TORONTO EDITION). 4945

0315-6575 See VOTRE REGIME DER RENTES DU QUEBEC (1973). 718

0315-6850 See PRAIRIE GARDEN. 2428

0315-6877 See PROCEEDINGS OF THE CANADIAN SOCIETY FOR HORTICULTURAL SCIENCE. 2429

0315-7253 See MINUTES OF PROCEEDINGS OF THE ANNUAL CONFERENCE - ASSOCIATION OF SUPERINTENDENTS OF INSURANCE OF THE PROVINCES OF CANADA. 3010

0315-7288 See GUIDE TO PERIODICALS AND NEWSPAPERS (TORONTO). 416

0315-7326 See 16MM FILMS AVAILABLE FROM THE PUBLIC LIBRARIES OF METROPOLITAN TORONTO. 4062

0315-7423 See GRAIN. 3391

0315-7946 See HORIZON SEPHARDI. 2619

0315-7997 See HISTORICAL REFLECTIONS. 2618

0315-8098 See CANADIAN INSURANCE. 2877

0315-811X See DIGEST BUSINESS & LAW JOURNAL. 3099

0315-8179 See ASCENT (KOOTENAY BAY). 4936

0315-8322 See CANADA LEGAL DIRECTORY. 3139

0315-8357 See REPERTOIRE DES SERVICES COMMUNAUTAIRES DE GRANBY ET DES ENVIRONS. 5304

0315-8535 See ONTARIO SCHOOL COUNSELLORS' ASSOCIATION REVIEW. 1770

0315-8624 See UP TO THE NECK, ACTION. 5313

0315-8705 See BULLETIN - CANADIAN ETHNIC STUDIES ASSOCIATION. 2257

0315-8764 See ANNUAIRE - ASSOCIATION DES INSTITUTIONS DE NIVEAUX PRESCOLAIRE ET ELEMENTAIRE DU QUEBEC. 1724

0315-8888 See EMERGENCY LIBRARIAN. 3209

0315-8977 See TRANSACTIONS OF THE CANADIAN SOCIETY FOR MECHANICAL ENGINEERING. 2130

0315-8985 See TELENATION. 1140

0315-906X See CLASSMATE. 1732

0315-9116 See MANITOBA MUSIC EDUCATOR. 4130

0315-9124 See M.S.L.A.V.A. JOURNAL. 3229

0315-9159 See MANITOBA SCIENCE TEACHER. 5127

0315-9167 See MATH JOURNAL, THE. 3518

0315-9205 See GUIDE DE L' AUTO (MONTREAL). 5415

0315-9329 See M.H.E.T.A. JOURNAL. 2791

0315-9388 See EDUCATIONAL PLANNING. 1742

0315-940X See JOURNAL - UNIVERSITIES ART ASSOCIATION OF CANADA. 355

0315-954X See FAMILLE AVERTIE. 4775

0315-9655 See M I C MISSION NEWS. 4975

0315-9701 See ROLL OF THE ORDER - THE PRIORY OF CANADA. 3175

0315-9779 See REPORT ON ADVERTISING REVENUES IN CANADA, A. 765

0315-9892 See INTERCOM (SASKATOON). 1753

0315-9906 See RACAR. 362

0315-9914 See DA VINCI. 3462

0315-9930 See ARGUS (MONTREAL). 3191

0315-9930 See ARGUS (MONTREAL). 726

0315-9981 See I D R C REPORTS. 2910

0315-999X See B. C. SPORTS ANNUAL. 4886

0316-0041 See CRIMINOLOGIE (MONTREAL). 3162

0316-0041 See CRIMINOLOGIE (MONTREAL). 3163

0316-0068 See RESEARCH PAPER - CENTRE FOR URBAN AND COMMUNITY STUDIES. UNIVERSITY OF TORONTO. 2833

0316-0076 See ENCYCLOPEDIE ARTISTIQUE. 1131

0316-0106 See LOTUS NEWSLETTER. 105

0316-019X See NOVA (MIDDLETON). 5791

0316-0203 See NORTH DELTA SENTINEL. 5790

0316-0211 See CLARION (CAPREOL). 5782

0316-022X See TOWNSHIPS SUN, THE. 5796

0316-0238 See NEWS ADVERTISER (KITIMAT). 5790

0316-0254 See MOUNT BRYDGES BULLETIN, THE. 5790

0316-0262 See COURIER (ORLEANS). 5782

0316-0270 See BENITO STANDARD. 5780

0316-0300 See ESSAYS ON CANADIAN WRITING. 3385

0316-0343 See CANADIAN PLAINS BULLETIN. 2726

0316-0386 See NOTES ON UNIONS. 1695

0316-0432 See NOUVELLES DE LA BIBLIOTHEQUE CENTRALE DE PRET. REGION DU SAGUENAY-LAC-SAINT-JEAN. 3237

0316-0513 See ANCETRE (QUEBEC). 2437

0316-0556 See POLK'S SAGUENAY DIRECTORY. 2572

0316-0645 See STORY SO FAR, THE. 3440

0316-070X See RESEARCH REPORT - YORK UNIVERSITY. SOCIAL PSYCHOLOGY RESEARCH PROGRAMME. INSTITUTE FOR BEHAVIOURAL RESEARCH. 5256

0316-0734 See DIRECTORY OF ASSOCIATIONS IN CANADA. 5230

0316-0785 See MON FRERE ET MOI. 4978

0316-0823 See BRITISH COLUMBIA GOVERNMENT PUBLICATIONS MONTHLY CHECKLIST. 411

0316-0963 See NOUVELLES - ASTED. 3237

0316-1064 See CONSTRUCTION MATERIALS SPECIFIER, THE. 610

0316-1099 See DIRECTORY OF COMMUNITY (HAMILTON). 5282

0316-1137 See CANADIAN CERAMICS. 2587

0316-1218 See CANADIAN JOURNAL OF HIGHER EDUCATION (1975). 1814

0316-1226 See DIRECTORY OF ACCREDITED CAMPS. 4871

0316-1234 See COURS DE PERFECTIONNEMENT DU NOTARIAT. 3089

0316-1269 See HISTORY, TECHNOLOGY, AND ART MONOGRAPH. 5110

0316-1285 See ARCHAEOLOGY MONOGRAPH. 257

0316-1331 See CANADIAN MASTER TAX GUIDE. 4716

0316-1447 See MEDIA FREE TIMES. 2538

0316-151X See OFFICIAL PLAYING RULES FOR THE CANADIAN FOOTBALL LEAGUE, THE. 4910

0316-1536 See REGLEMENT OFFICIEL DE JEU POUR LA LIGUE CANADIENNE DE FOOTBALL. 4914

0316-1552 See ALBERTA HISTORY. 2718

0316-1560 See CATALOGUE DE L'EDITEUR OFFICIEL DU QUEBEC. 4813

0316-1609 See ROOM OF ONE'S OWN. 3432

0316-1617 See ONTARIO GOVERNMENT PUBLICATIONS MONTHLY CHECKLIST. 4671

0316-1633 See MARINE SCIENCES RESEARCH LABORATORY TECHNICAL REPORT. 556

0316-1641 See LIST OF MEMBERS OF THE HOUSE OF COMMONS OF CANADA. 4662

0316-1765 See VERNON'S CITY OF HAMILTON (ONTARIO) DIRECTORY. 2578

0316-1986 See LONDON BROADSIDE. 2744

0316-2001 See ONTARIO LAND SURVEYOR, THE. 2028

0316-2052 See QUEBEC FRANCAIS. 3427

0316-2079 See NEWSLETTER - EARLY CHILDHOOD EDUCATION COUNCIL. 1768

0316-2141 See HEALTH CARE DIGEST. 3581

0316-2281 See FACTS AND FIGURES : MINING IN CANADA. 2139

0316-2532 See BOWLINE. 592

0316-2559 See YEAR BOOK - CANADIAN RACING PIGEON UNION. 4931

0316-2702 See GRAND MANAN HISTORIAN, THE. 2735

0316-2753 See BLACK I. 3367

0316-280X See CANADIAN CAMPER, THE. 4870

0316-2907 See CANADIAN GIDEON. 4942

0316-2923 See PHILOSOPHIQUES. 4356

0316-3040 See COME AND SEE. 5016

0316-3083 See CANADIAN COMMUNICATIONS REPORTS. 1129

0316-330X See CHRONICLE - CANADIAN FEDERATION OF UNIVERSITY WOMEN. 5553

0316-3334 See PERSPECTIVES (SASKATOON). 5212

0316-3350 See WILDLAND NEWS. 2209

0316-3369 See NEWSLETTER - NATIONAL FARMERS UNION. 112

0316-3393 See L. A. W. G. LETTER. 4480

0316-3504 See FACTS AND FIGURES OF THE AUTOMOTIVE INDUSTRY (ANNUAL EDITION). 5401

0316-3547 See CANADIAN GAS FACTS. 4760

0316-3571 See REPORT OF PROCEEDINGS OF THE TAX CONFERENCE CONVENED BY THE CANADIAN TAX FOUNDATION. 4745

0316-361X See SIGNAL (QUEBEC). 4997

0316-3733 See AUBELLE, L'. 2375

0316-3768 See WRIT (TORONTO). 3454

0316-3849 See PHILANTHROPIST, THE. 4338

0316-4055 See ONTARIO REVIEW (WINDSOR, ONT.). 3420

0316-4128 See ANNUAL REPORT - SASKATCHEWAN WHEAT POOL. 163

0316-4209 See SCARLET & GOLD. 3176

0316-4241 See ANNUAL NEWSPRINT SUPPLEMENT - CANADIAN PULP AND PAPER ASSOCIATION. 4232

0316-4357 See BULLETIN - GENETICS SOCIETY OF CANADA. 543

0316-4454 See BULLETIN DE L'INSTITUT DE READAPTATION DE MONTREAL, LE. 5275

0316-4691 See BIBLIOGRAPHIC SERIES - CENTRE FOR URBAN AND COMMUNITY STUDIES. UNIVERSITY OF TORONTO. 2840

0316-473X See ALBERTA CATHOLIC DIRECTORY. 5022

0316-4764 See FOR YOUR CAREER INFORMATION. 1824

0316-4837 See ACCESSION LIST - NATIONAL INDIAN BROTHERHOOD, LIBRARY. 2254

0316-4888 See Q.A.S.A. BULLETIN. 1869

0316-490X See DIRECTORY OF THE ASSOCIATION OF PROFESSIONAL ENGINEERS AND GEOSCIENTISTS OF THE PROVINCE OF BRITISH COLUMBIA. 1971

0316-4934 See NEWSLETTER - CANADIAN SOCIETY OF MICROBIOLOGISTS / BULLETIN DE NOUVELLES - SOCIETET CANADIENNE DES MICROBIOLOGISTES. 568

0316-4942 See PATRICIAN, THE. 4053

0316-4969 See CANADIAN SOCIAL STUDIES : THE HISTORY AND SOCIAL SCIENCE TEACHER. 1890

0316-4985 See PRO MOTION NEWSLETTER. 1857

0316-5043 See UNION LIST OF SERIALS IN MONTREAL HOSPITAL LIBRARIES. 426

0316-5051 See 1+1. 2784

0316-5078 See DISCUSSION PAPER - INSTITUTE FOR ECONOMIC RESEARCH. QUEEN'S UNIVERSITY. KINGSTON, ONTARIO. 1480

0316-5094 See NEWSMAGAZINE - CENTRE FOR WOMEN. HUMBER COLLEGE OF APPLIED ARTS AND TECHNOLOGY. CENTRE FOR CONTINUOUS LEARNING. 1838

0316-5140 See BULLETIN D'INFORMATION - UNION DES MUNICIPALITES DE LA PROVINCE DE QUEBEC. 4634

0316-5159 See FAPUQ NOUVELLES BREVES. 1823

0316-5167 See SAND PATTERNS. 3433

0316-5175 See CDS. CONSEIL DE DEVELOPPEMENT SOCIAL DU MONTREAL METROPOLITAIN. 5242

0316-5183 See KINGSTON RELATIONS. 2457

0316-5256 See AL MITZPE HAHINUCH. 5045

0316-5310 See SPECIAL LECTURES OF THE LAW SOCIETY OF UPPER CANADA. 3058

0316-5345 See SCIENCE ET ESPRIT. 4360

0316-5388 See PERSPECTIVE (EDMONTON). 4673

0316-5418 See PATRICIA NEWS BULLETIN. 4053

0316-5434 See WESTON TIMES REVIEW. 2550

0316-5442 See REXDALE TIMES REVIEW. 5794

0316-5620 See SITREP. 4057

0316-5639 See FALCON FLYER. 5784

0316-5795 See NEW BRUNSWICK FEDERATION OF LABOUR. ANNUAL SUBMISSION TO THE PREMIER AND MEMBERS OF THE CABINET OF THE GOVERNMENT OF NEW BRUNSWICK. 1693

0316-5892 See MEMORANDUM TO THE GOVERNMENT OF CANADA BY THE CANADIAN LABOUR CONGRESS. 1690

0316-5906 See MEMOIRE PRESENTE AU GOUVERNEMENT DU CANADA PAR LE CONGRES DU TRAVAIL DU CANADA. 1618

0316-5922 See PUBLICATION SERIES - TRANSPORT GROUP. DEPARTMENT OF CIVIL ENGINEERING. UNIVERSITY OF WATERLOO. 5793

0316-5949 See UNIVERSITY OF WATERLOO LIBRARY SERIALS LIST. 3255

0316-5965 See GLITTER. 2534

0316-5981 See ATLANTIC PROVINCES BOOK REVIEW, THE. 3337

0316-599X See NEWSLETTER - ALBERTA TEACHERS' ASSOCIATION. 1867

0316-6015 See CANADIAN ARTISTS IN EXHIBITION. 346

0316-6031 See ONTARIO SECURITIES LEGISLATION. 701

0316-6120 See ANNUAIRE TELEPHONIQUE JUDICIAIRE DU QUEBEC. 2934

0316-618X See GNOSIS (MONTREAL). 4347

0316-6198 See MOTOR VEHICLE DATA BOOK. 5420

0316-6317 See AMATEUR ENOLOGIST, THE. 2363

0316-6325 See NOVA SCOTIA LAW NEWS. 3019

0316-6368 See REVUE DE L'UNIVERSITE DE MONCTON (1976). 1846

0316-6384 See OLYMPRESS 1976. 4910

0316-6414 See MADISON'S CANADIAN LUMBER DIRECTORY. 2402

0316-6473 See MANITOBA SOCIAL SCIENCE TEACHER, THE. 5208

0316-6481 See ONTARIO BUSINESS CORPORATIONS ACT WITH REGULATIONS (CCH CANADIAN). 3102

0316-6546 See MONTHLY STATEMENT - INSTITUTE OF CHARTERED ACCOUNTANTS OF ALBERTA, A. 748

0316-6635 See GOULBOURN MIRROR. 5785

0316-6724 See CHARLOTTES, THE. 2727

0316-6759 See JABBERWOCKY (TORONTO). 1065

0316-6791 See CUSSNEWS. 5244

0316-683X See DIDSBURY BOOSTER AND MOUNTAIN VIEW COUNTY NEWS. 5783

0316-6864 See DIAKONIA TES BASILEIAS. 4953

0316-6872 See TIMMINS PORCUPINE NEWS. 5796

0316-6902 See LITTLE BEND. 5788

0316-6953 See NORTH WIND (VANCOUVER). 5299

0316-697X See BOW VALLEY VIEWS. 5781

0316-7046 See CHANGES (TORONTO). 2530

0316-7232 See PONTE (WILLOWDALE). 5254

0316-7283 See ACCIDENT FATALITIES, CANADA. 4763

0316-7372 See CRANE LIBRARY NEWS. 3204

0316-7429 See LANGUAGES OF SOUTH INDIA. 3296

0316-7526 See PHARMACOLOGIE PRATIQUE. 4322

0316-7534 See HIGH PRAIRIE REPORTER. 5786

0316-7542 See FORT MCMURRAY TODAY. 5784

0316-7569 See DIRECTORY - ONTARIO PSYCHOLOGICAL ASSOCIATION. 4585

0316-7739 See GRAND NEWS. 2785

0316-778X See QUEEN'S LAW JOURNAL. 3033

0316-7798 See NEWFOUNDLAND AND LABRADOR BUSINESS DIRECTORY AND BUYERS GUIDE. 699

0316-7852 See POINT (MONTREAL). 849

0316-7909 See FELLOWSHIP OF BELIEVERS BULLETIN. 4958

0316-7933 See ANNUAL MEETING. PROCEEDINGS. CANADIAN URBAN TRANSIT ASSOCIATION. 5376

0316-7968 See PUBLICATION (UNIVERSITY OF TORONTO. DEPT. OF CIVIL ENGINEERING). 2029

0316-7984 See RESEARCH REPORT - UNIVERSITY OF MANITOBA, CENTRE FOR TRANSPORTATION STUDIES. 5391

0316-7992 See ANNUAIRE POLK DE HULL. 2554

0316-800X See DIRECTORY: LUTHERAN CHURCHES IN CANADA. 5059

0316-8077 See OFFICIAL ARROW STREET GUIDE OF OTTAWA AND DISTRICT. 5487

0316-8123 See DIRECTORY OF FIRMS AND CORPORATIONS AUTHORIZED TO PRACTISE PROFESSIONAL ENGINEERING IN THE PROVINCE OF ONTARIO. 1971

0316-8131 See CANADIAN AND PROVINCIAL GOLF RECORDS. 4889

0316-8158 See POLICY, ORGANIZATION AND RULES - GIRL GUIDES OF CANADA. 5235

0316-8166 See LAKEHEAD UNIVERSITY SUMMER SESSION. 1834

0316-8182 See MEMBERS' GUIDE TO THE BCTF. 1900

0316-8271 See ANNUAIRE POLK DE BAIE-COMEAU. 2554

0316-8298 See WRIGLEY'S HOTEL DIRECTORY. 2810

0316-8336 See MCGILL UNIVERSITY. FACULTY OF DENTISTRY. 1329

0316-8379 See SERIAL TITLES IN THE HUMANITIES AND SOCIAL SCIENCES (WINDSOR). 2854

0316-8395 See SERIAL TITLES IN THE PURE AND APPLIED SCIENCES (WINDSOR). 5157

0316-8409 See NEWSLETTER - ASSOCIATION FOR NATIVE DEVELOPMENT IN THE PERFORMING AND VISUAL ARTS. 326

0316-8417 See JUBILEE (GORRIE). 3400

0316-8530 See MONTREAL CE MOIS-CI. 4852

0316-8549 See DIRECTORY OF EDUCATION (TORONTO). 1735

0316-8573 See SCHOOL OF COMPUTER SCIENCE. UNIVERSITY OF WINDSOR. 1202

0316-8581 See MAINELINE. 215

0316-8603 See GERMAN-CANADIAN YEARBOOK. 2734

0316-8638 See CALENDAR - BRANDON UNIVERSITY. 1813

0316-8654 ISSN Index

0316-8654 *See* WESTERN NEWS (LONDON). 1853

0316-8743 *See* BULLETIN - CANADIAN RELIGIOUS CONFERENCE. 4940

0316-8751 *See* BULLETIN - CONFERENCE RELIGIEUSE CANADIENNE. 4940

0316-8786 *See* RESEARCH SERVICE - RESEARCH DEPARTMENT. BOARD OF EDUCATION FOR THE CITY OF TORONTO. 1779

0316-8808 *See* EXTENSION BULLETIN - DEPARTMENT OF AGRICULTURAL ECONOMICS AND FARM MANAGEMENT FACULTY OF AGRICULTURE. UNIVERSITY OF MANITOBA. 83

0316-8816 *See* RESEARCH BULLETIN - DEPARTMENT OF AGRICULTURAL ECONOMICS AND FARM MANAGEMENT. FACULTY OF AGRICULTURE. UNIVERSITY OF MANITOBA. 127

0316-8832 *See* BULLETIN AMQ. 3497

0316-8891 *See* INDEX TO CANADIAN LEGAL PERIODICAL LITERATURE. 3081

0316-8913 *See* MY BROTHER AND I. 4979

0316-893X *See* CONTEMPORARY SHOWCASE. SYLLABUS. 4111

0316-8964 *See* EMPLOYMENT OPPORTUNITIES HANDBOOK CANADA. WESTERN EDITION. 4204

0316-9030 *See* BASILIAN ANNALS, THE. 5024

0316-9057 *See* ANTICON. 1860

0316-9103 *See* MIRABEL, LE. 5789

0316-9138 *See* INSTANT (TORONTO). 2781

0316-9332 *See* ASSOCIATION FOR RETARDED CHILDREN OF BRITISH COLUMBIA. ANNUAL CONFERENCE (MINUTES). 5274

0316-9448 *See* COUTTS LIBRARY SERVICES. CURRENT CANADIAN BOOKS. 414

0316-9537 *See* BLUE BOOK OF FOOD STORE OPERATORS AND WHOLESALERS. 2329

0316-9707 *See* ARCTIC GAS. BIOLOGICAL REPORT SERIES. 443

0316-9782 *See* NEDERLANDSE COURANT (WILLOWDALE). 2268

0316-9839 *See* DIRECTORY OF DESIGNATED MEMBERS - APPRAISAL INSTITUTE OF CANADA. 4836

0316-9871 *See* COSMETICS HANDBOOK. 403

0316-9898 *See* GUIDE DES COSMETIQUES. 404

0316-991X *See* VACATION (TORONTO). 5498

0317-0039 *See* SPLIT LEVEL. 3439

0317-0055 *See* CANADIAN COMMUNICATIONS LAW REVIEW. 2947

0317-0144 *See* DISCUSSION PAPER (UNIVERSITY OF BRITISH COLUMBIA. DEPT. OF ECONOMICS). 1480

0317-0179 *See* PRESENTATION - SOCIETE ROYALE DU CANADA. 5235

0317-0187 *See* BROKEN CUE NEWS, THE. 4858

0317-0292 *See* CANADIAN ELECTRONICS ENGINEERING ANNUAL BUYERS' GUIDE AND CATALOG DIRECTORY. 2037

0317-0306 *See* MANITOBA AND SASKATCHEWAN SUCCESSION DUTY AND GIFT TAX LEGISLATION. 4736

0317-0322 *See* SERTEK. 3249

0317-039X *See* ACCESS (VANCOUVER). 3186

0317-0489 *See* JMC BULLETIN. 4125

0317-0500 *See* CHESTERTON REVIEW, THE. 3374

0317-0527 *See* NEWSLETTER - ORGANIC GROWERS CO-OPERATIVE. 112

0317-0535 *See* CANADIAN LABOUR RELATIONS BOARDS REPORTS. 3145

0317-056X *See* FROM THE GROUND UP. 22

0317-0659 *See* THIRD WORLD FORUM. 4498

0317-0683 *See* PLEIN-JOUR SUR CHARLEVOIX. 5793

0317-073X *See* CARLETON UNIVERSITY STUDENT JOURNAL OF PHILOSOPHY, THE. 4343

0317-0772 *See* CHRISTIANS AGAINST TERRORISM. 4946

0317-0780 *See* CPAC BOOKSHOPPE. 2819

0317-0861 *See* CANADIAN PUBLIC POLICY. 1468

0317-087X *See* MUSCLE MAG INTERNATIONAL. 2600

0317-0926 *See* CIM BULLETIN. 2136

0317-0934 *See* REFERENCE TABLES - CANADIAN PULP AND PAPER ASSOCIATION. 4238

0317-0977 *See* NOUVELLES. RELATIONS OUVRIERES. ASSOCIATION DE LA CONSTRUCTION DE MONTREAL ET DU QUEBEC. 1695

0317-0993 *See* NEWSLETTER. LABOUR RELATIONS. CONSTRUCTION ASSOCIATION OF MONTREAL AND THE PROVINCE OF QUEBEC. 1695

0317-1078 *See* GREAT LAKER, THE. 4233

0317-1264 *See* CANADIAN UNDERWRITER. ANNUAL STATISTICAL REVIEW. 2897

0317-1272 *See* INSURANCE MARKETER, THE. 2884

0317-1388 *See* PEOPLE'S FOREST, THE. 2390

0317-1442 *See* NOUVEAU DIALOGUE. 4354

0317-1493 *See* CONSENSUS (WINNIPEG). 4950

0317-1507 *See* AFANAF. 1807

0317-1515 *See* ANNUAIRE POLK DE GRANBY QUEBEC. 2554

0317-1604 *See* REPORT / ALBERTA LAW REFORM INSTITUTE. 3037

0317-1663 *See* DALHOUSIE LAW JOURNAL. 2959

0317-1671 *See* CANADIAN JOURNAL OF NEUROLOGICAL SCIENCES. 3829

0317-1965 *See* CYNOMAG. 4286

0317-1981 *See* LISTE DES ACQUISITIONS - INFORMATHEQUE DE LINGUISTIQUE. UNIVERSITE D'OTTAWA. 3300

0317-2058 *See* CONSUMER FOOD BULLETIN. 2332

0317-2074 *See* CANADIAN RATIOS FOR PROFIT PLANNING. 1600

0317-2090 See CANADIAN INDIA STAR, THE. 2648

0317-2104 *See* NEBULA (NORTH BAY). 3414

0317-2139 *See* QUARTERLY OF CANADIAN STUDIES FOR THE SECONDARY SCHOOL, THE. 1776

0317-2155 *See* DIRECTORY OF THE CANADIAN ASSOCIATION OF UNIVERSITY SCHOOLS OF MUSIC. 4115

0317-2163 *See* FOOTBALL JOURNAL. 4895

0317-2198 *See* DIMANCHE ET FETE. 4953

0317-221X *See* DECISIONS DU CONGRES DE LA C. E. Q. 1662

0317-2279 *See* UNION DES PRODUCTEURS AGRICOLES. 1716

0317-2309 *See* NEWFOUNDLAND SIGNAL, THE. 5790

0317-2341 *See* PRISM (OTTAWA). 5301

0317-2406 *See* BOOKS IN MARATHI. 4826

0317-2465 *See* DIRECTORY OF LIBRARIES IN NEWFOUNDLAND AND LABRADOR. 3207

0317-2481 *See* FLYPAPER (CALGARY). 4895

0317-2546 *See* RESEARCH AND CURRENT ISSUES SERIES - INDUSTRIAL RELATIONS CENTRE. QUEEN'S UNIVERSITY. 1707

0317-2627 *See* DRUG INDEX (TORONTO). 4300

0317-2635 *See* CHATELAINE (EDITION FRANCAISE). 5553

0317-266X *See* FELLOWSHIP YEARBOOK. 5060

0317-2740 *See* EDUCATION MARKET IN CANADA, THE. 1740

0317-2821 *See* CANADA. TAX APPEAL BOARD CASES. INDEX. SUPPLEMENT. 2947

0317-2899 *See* VERNON'S CITY OF CAMBRIDGE (ONTARIO) DIRECTORY. 2578

0317-2910 *See* LEMKIVSKYJ KALENDAR. 2744

0317-2996 *See* B C T F INFORMATIONAL REPORT. 1727

0317-3011 *See* ETHNIC SCENE. 2260

0317-3100 *See* POPULATION REPRINTS. 4558

0317-3143 *See* VITAL STATISTICS. PRELIMINARY ANNUAL REPORT (OTTAWA). 4563

0317-3178 *See* DAILY COMMERCIAL NEWS AND CONSTRUCTION RECORD. 612

0317-3186 See PRINCE GEORGE CITY DIRECTORY (BUSINESS ED.). 2573

0317-3240 *See* ATLANTIC SPECTRUM. 1810

0317-333X *See* WESTERN SPECTRUM. 1853

0317-3348 *See* UNIVERSITY OF WATERLOO BIOLOGY SERIES. 475

0317-3364 *See* FOOD IN CANADA BUYERS' DIRECTORY & SERVICES INDEX. 2337

0317-3399 *See* CHAMPS D'APPLICATION. 3373

0317-3429 *See* YOUR QUEBEC PENSION PLAN. 5314

0317-3437 *See* RAILWAY FREIGHT TRAFFIC (OTTAWA. QUARTERLY EDITION). 5435

0317-350X *See* SEASONAL FRUIT & VEGETABLE REPORT (ANNUAL SUMMARY). 2431

0317-3526 *See* ANNUAL REPORT - ENVIRONMENTAL CONTROL COUNCIL. 3109

0317-3585 *See* COMMUNITY EDUCATION SERIES. 3105

0317-3607 *See* CONFIDENCES (MONTREAL. 1972). 5187

0317-364X *See* CITADEL SCENE, THE. 5363

0317-381X *See* CONSUMER GUIDES (KAPUSKASING). 5782

0317-3828 *See* PROBATION & PAROLE STATISTICS (REGINA). 3082

0317-3917 *See* ALBERTA STATISTICAL REVIEW (ANNUAL ED.). 5320

0317-4018 *See* BULLETIN - SVETOVY KONGRES SLOVAKOV. 2681

0317-4026 *See* CANADIAN BUSINESS REVIEW, THE. 1467

0317-4077 *See* ANNUAL REPORT - DEFENCE CONSTRUCTION (1951) LIMITED. 4035

0317-4271 *See* DIRECTORY. ONTARIO POSTAL REGION. POSTAL CODE. 1144

0317-445X *See* ECONOMIC GEOLOGY REPORT (OTTAWA). 1374

0317-4697 *See* SUPPLY, DEMAND AND SALARIES; NEW GRADUATES OF UNIVERSITIES AND COMMUNITY COLLEGES. 1713

0317-4859 *See* REPORTS OF FAMILY LAW. 3122

0317-4956 *See* GERMANO-SLAVICA. 3391

0317-4964 *See* ELIZABETHAN THEATRE, THE. 5364

0317-4999 *See* PUBLIC ACCOUNTS: ALBERTA. 4743

0317-5065 *See* CAHIERS DES ETUDES ANCIENNES. 2612

0317-5227 *See* NBTA NEWS. 1766

0317-5243 *See* TEL QUE NOUS LE PENSONS ET AVONS ENVIE DE LE DIRE. 5369

0317-5340 *See* INTERNATIONAL BUSINESS NEWS MAGAZINE. 841

0317-5510 *See* REVUE MUNICIPALE. ANNUAIRE (MONTREAL). 4684

0317-5650 *See* AVICULTURAL JOURNAL, THE. 5615

0317-5782 *See* REGINA FRIENDSHIP CENTRE NEWSLETTER. 5304

0317-5804 *See* NEWSLETTER. SAFETY. CONSTRUCTION ASSOCIATION OF MONTREAL AND THE PROVINCE OF QUEBEC. 622

0317-5847 *See* REGIONAL TELEGRAPH, THE. 5794

0317-5855 *See* KEYNOTE (VANCOUVER). 4128

0317-588X *See* TORONTO LEGAL DIRECTORY. 3065

0317-5901 *See* ANALYSE DE L'INDUSTRIE DE LA CONSTRUCTION AU QUEBEC. 598

0317-5987 *See* PREVENTION AU CANADA, LA. 4796

0317-6029 *See* GEOSCOPE (MONTREAL). 2564

0317-6134 *See* CAPTAIN GEORGE'S YELLOW JOURNAL. 4858

0317-6142 *See* ANNUAIRE - UNIVERSITE D'OTTAWA. 1809

0317-6150 *See* INDEX COMMERCIAL, JUDICIAIRE, FINANCIER, L'. 2981

0317-6215 *See* SPELEO-QUEBEC. 1411

0317-6282 *See* PRAIRIE FORUM. 2754

ISSN Index

0317-6339 *See* PURCHASING PREFERENCE SURVEY : OFFICE EQUIPMENT AND SUPPLIES. **951**

0317-6347 *See* PURCHASING PREFERENCE SURVEY : TRAFFIC/TRANSPORTATION. **951**

0317-6363 *See* PURCHASING PREFERENCE SURVEY : MATERIALS HANDLING EQUIPMENT. **951**

0317-6401 *See* CANADIAN PLAINS PROCEEDINGS. **2726**

0317-641X *See* NATIONAL REPORTER (FREDERICTON, N.B. : BOUND CUMULATION). **3014**

0317-6460 *See* BULLETIN - UNITED NATIONS ASSOCIATION IN CANADA. **3125**

0317-6487 *See* MIGHT'S COBOURG, PORT HOPE, ONTARIO, CITY DIRECTORY. **2569**

0317-6495 *See* CANADIAN CURRENT TAX. **2947**

0317-6649 *See* CANADA BUSINESS CORPORATIONS ACT WITH REGULATIONS. **3097**

0317-669X *See* ANNUAL RECORD OF OPERATIONS - ATMOSPHERIC ENVIRONMENT SERVICE. **1420**

0317-6827 *See* ANNUAL REPORT - MINISTRY OF GOVERNMENT SERVICES. **4627**

0317-6878 *See* CA MAGAZINE. **740**

0317-6924 *See* WESTERN LABOUR ARBITRATION CASES. **3155**

0317-6983 *See* MALTESE DIRECTORY : CANADA, UNITED STATES. **2745**

0317-7017 *See* MEDIFACTS [SOUND RECORDING]. **3738**

0317-7033 *See* PALACHUV HLASATEL. **5792**

0317-7076 *See* DECKS AWASH. **2487**

0317-7114 *See* SM REPORT (BLUE SERIES). **2129**

0317-7130 *See* SM PAPER. **2129**

0317-7173 *See* CARTOGRAPHICA (1980). **2581**

0317-7203 *See* GUIDELINES FOR PASTORAL LITURGY. **5030**

0317-7254 *See* CARLETON GERMANIC PAPERS. **3373**

0317-7335 *See* SASKATCHEWAN LABOUR REPORT, THE. **1709**

0317-7645 See LEADERSHIP IN HEALTH SERVICES. **3787**

0317-7742 *See* RAPPORT D'ACTIVITIES - SERVICE DE L'HABITATION ET DE L'URBANISME. VILLE DE MONTREAL. **4678**

0317-7815 *See* AUTOMOBILE INSURANCE EXPERIENCE. **2874**

0317-7831 *See* MODEL AVIATION CANADA. **28**

0317-7904 *See* CANADIAN REVIEW OF STUDIES IN NATIONALISM. **2635**

0317-7947 *See* ANNUAL REPORT - INSURANCE CORPORATION OF BRITISH COLUMBIA. **2873**

0317-8021 *See* BULLETIN OF CANADIAN WELFARE LAW. **5275**

0317-8196 *See* ROAD SAFETY ANNUAL REPORT. **5443**

0317-8269 *See* B.C. LABOUR MARKET INFORMATION. **1654**

0317-8471 *See* VERS DEMAIN (EDITION FRANCAISE). **5225**

0317-8498 *See* MICHAEL (ROUGEMONT). **4481**

0317-851X *See* EGLISE, EN. **4955**

0317-8536 *See* DIRECTORY OF LIBRARIES IN MANITOBA. **3207**

0317-8641 *See* OCCASIONAL PAPER - FACULTY OF ENVIRONMENTAL STUDIES. UNIVERSITY OF WATERLOO. **2179**

0317-8765 *See* ANGLICAN YEAR BOOK. **4934**

0317-8803 *See* COMMUNIQUE - CONSEIL DE LA JEUNESSE SCIENTIFIQUE. **5095**

0317-8838 *See* NANAIMO DIRECTORY (BUSINESS EDITION). **2570**

0317-8854 *See* TABLEAU DES MEMBRES - ORDRE DES ARCHITECTES DU QUEBEC. **309**

0317-8951 *See* YOUR CANADA PENSION PLAN. **4759**

0317-9060 *See* INCOME TAX ACT. **4731**

0317-9087 *See* PROCEEDINGS OF THE ANNUAL CONFERENCE - CANADIAN COUNCIL ON INTERNATIONAL LAW. **3134**

0317-9095 *See* KINESIS (VANCOUVER). **5560**

0317-9222 *See* RETRAITE, LE. **3175**

0317-9257 *See* HOCKEY'S HERITAGE. **4899**

0317-9273 *See* BULLETIN DE LIAISON DU CONSEIL DE LA JEUNESSE SCIENTIFIQUE. **5090**

0317-9303 *See* MEMOIRE AUX GOUVERNEMENTS CANADIEN ET QUEBECOIS. **2792**

0317-9451 *See* CANADIAN SECURITIES COURSE, THE. **894**

0317-946X *See* PROVINCIAL AND MUNICIPAL FINANCES. **4742**

0317-9508 *See* MINING (TORONTO). **2146**

0317-9524 *See* MINES (TORONTO). **2145**

0317-9575 *See* NEWSLETTER - LONG POINT BIRD OBSERVATORY. **5618**

0317-9583 *See* MINUTES - ANNUAL CONVENTION OF THE EASTERN CANADA SYNOD, LUTHERAN CHURCH IN AMERICA. **5064**

0317-9656 *See* REVUE DE DROIT [FRENCH EDITION] (SHERBROOKE). **3043**

0317-9656 *See* REVUE DE DROIT (SHERBROOKE). **3043**

0317-9664 *See* CURRENT ESTIMATES - CITY OF WINNIPEG. **4719**

0317-9737 *See* DANCE IN CANADA. **1312**

0317-9885 *See* NEWS BURLINGTON. **5790**

0317-9893 *See* DISCUSSION PAPER - UNIVERSITY OF TORONTO, DEPARTMENT OF GEOGRAPHY. **2559**

0318-0042 *See* GOLOS INSTYTUTU. **2262**

0318-0069 *See* CABLE COMMUNICATIONS MAGAZINE. **1128**

0318-0123 *See* DONUM DEI (ENGLISH ED.). **4954**

0318-014X *See* SCANNER (TORONTO). **2759**

0318-0220 *See* COURIER (EDMONTON). **3275**

0318-0255 *See* TELEPHONE DIRECTORY. MANITOBA GOVERNMENT. **4690**

0318-0352 *See* CANADIAN INSURANCE CLAIMS DIRECTORY. **2877**

0318-0549 *See* NOUVELLES DE LA F M O Q (ENGLISH EDITION). **3623**

0318-0573 *See* TRINITE, LIBERTE. **5006**

0318-0581 *See* FAMILLE QUEBEC. **2279**

0318-059X *See* DELECTUS SEMINUM ET SPORARUM QUAE HORTUS BOTANICUS MONTIS-REGII PRO MUTUA COMMUTATIONE OFFERT. **508**

0318-0743 *See* MUNICIPAL DIRECTORY (TORONTO). **4667**

0318-0808 *See* ETUDES SLAVES (QUEBEC). **2687**

0318-0859 *See* CANADIAN PROCESS EQUIPMENT & CONTROL NEWS. **2101**

0318-1065 *See* WHETSTONE (LETHBRIDGE). **3453**

0318-1081 *See* APPROACHES TO ANSWERING THE UNIFORM FINAL EXAMINATIONS, PLUS EXAMINERS' COMMENTS. **738**

0318-1298 *See* MANITOBA GOVERNMENT PUBLICATIONS (MONTHLY ED.). **4664**

0318-1316 *See* EAST-WEST COMMERCIAL RELATIONS SERIES. **4520**

0318-1340 *See* LIAISON (CIMENTS CANADA LAFARGE). **1616**

0318-1391 *See* CANADIAN ECONOMIC COMMENT. **1468**

0318-1480 *See* LYSISTRATA (VICTORIA). **5560**

0318-1510 See STATISTICAL REPORT - CANADIAN ASSOCIATION FOR GRADUATE STUDIES. **1848**

0318-1529 *See* SERIALS LIST - UNIVERSITY OF REGINA, LIBRARY. **424**

0318-1634 *See* C R E S S SPECTROSCOPIC REPORT. **4399**

0318-1642 *See* ZA RIDNU CERKVU. **5038**

0318-1650 *See* GROVE EXAMINER, THE. **5785**

0318-1685 *See* SOCIALISME MONDIAL. **4546**

0318-1707 *See* PSYCHOLOGUE QUEBECOIS, LE. **4612**

0318-1766 *See* MINING EXPLORATION AND DEVELOPMENT REVIEW, BRITISH COLUMBIA AND YUKON TERRITORY. **2145**

0318-1839 *See* CANADIAN SOCIETY OF ANIMAL SCIENCE. PROCEEDINGS OF THE ANNUAL MEETING OF THE GENERAL SOCIETY AND THE WESTERN BRANCH. **5507**

0318-1863 *See* HERALD (MACKENZIE). **5786**

0318-1952 *See* YUKON NEWS (1972). **5798**

0318-207X *See* ISLAND STAR. **5786**

0318-2088 *See* MISTRAL. **3466**

0318-2118 *See* MANITOBA SPECTRA. **691**

0318-2134 *See* JOURNAL CHALEUR. **5787**

0318-2215 *See* C W C DATAFILE. **633**

0318-2339 *See* CITY OF COTE SAINT-LUC HOUSEHOLDER'S DIRECTORY. **2558**

0318-2452 *See* FEMME. **5556**

0318-2460 *See* WINDSOR THIS MONTH. **2550**

0318-2541 *See* LOGGING RESEARCH PROGRESS REPORT. **2402**

0318-2568 *See* CANADIAN FOLK MUSIC JOURNAL. **4107**

0318-2622 *See* ICI...ROSEMONT. **1829**

0318-2819 *See* SASKATCHEWAN PROVINCIAL HIGHWAYS ACCIDENT STATISTICS. **5402**

0318-2835 *See* NOUS JOURNAL. **3418**

0318-2843 *See* RENDEZ-VOUS 76 MONTREAL. **4914**

0318-2940 *See* PORT ALBERNI DIRECTORY (BUSINESS EDITION). **2573**

0318-2991 *See* TUITION AND LIVING ACCOMMODATION COSTS AT CANADIAN UNIVERSITIES. **1851**

0318-3017 *See* MARINE BUYERS' DIRECTORY. **5452**

0318-3114 *See* SIXTY CANADIAN MAGAZINES. **2546**

0318-3122 *See* S. M. STUDY. **2108**

0318-3238 *See* PERSPECTIVES (TORONTO). **1512**

0318-3378 *See* STRUCTURAL RESEARCH SERIES; REPORT. **2032**

0318-3521 *See* SCOUTING NEWS. **5236**

0318-3556 *See* ONTARIO ANNUAL PRACTICE (1973). **3142**

0318-3610 *See* MATRIX (LENNOXVILLE). **3410**

0318-3734 *See* REPORT ON SALARIES. **1707**

0318-3912 *See* ANNUAL REPORT OF THE MANITOBA WATER SERVICES BOARD. **5529**

0318-3955 *See* CO-OPERATIVE ASSOCIATIONS IN NOVA SCOTIA. **1541**

0318-4013 *See* WAGES, HOURS OF WORK AND OVERTIME PAY PROVISIONS IN SELECTED INDUSTRIES. ONTARIO. **1717**

0318-4064 See SOFTWARE DEVELOPMENT AND COMPUTER SERVICE INDUSTRY / STATISTICS CANADA, SERVICES, SCIENCE AND TECHNOLOGY DIVISION. **1203**

0318-4137 *See* RECHERCHES AMERINDIENNES AU QUEBEC. **2756**

0318-4137 *See* RECHERCHES AMERINDIENNES AU QUEBEC. **243**

0318-417X *See* PROCEEDINGS OF THE ANNUAL MEETING OF THE CANADIAN HYDROMETALLURGISTS. **4016**

0318-4196 *See* CONSTITUTION - ONTARIO FEDERATION OF LABOUR. **1661**

0318-4277 *See* CANADIAN FOREST INDUSTRIES. **2399**

0318-434X *See* ANNALS OF SAINT ANNE DE BEAUPRE (1974). **4934**

0318-4374 *See* COQUILLE, LA. **4950**

0318-4382 *See* ECHO D'AFRIQUE (QUEBEC). **2639**

0318-4412 *See* PHI ZERO. **4355**

0318-4447 *See* LOIS DU QUEBEC. **3004**

0318-4595 *See* REPERTOIRE DES ASSOCIATIONS. **707**

0318-479X *See* REVUE DES SCIENCES DE L'EDUCATION. **1780**

0318-4900 *See* PROCEEDINGS OF THE ... ANNUAL MEETING / UNIFORM LAW CONFERENCE OF CANADA. **3031**

0318-4935 See ... YEAR BOOK OF THE CANADIAN BAR ASSOCIATION AND THE MINUTES OF PROCEEDINGS OF THE ... ANNUAL MEETING, THE. 3077

0318-4935 See ... YEARBOOK OF THE CANADIAN BAR ASSOCIATION AND THE MINUTES OF PROCEEDINGS OF THE ... ANNUAL MEETING, THE. 3077

0318-4943 See ALBERTA FISHING GUIDE. 2294

0318-4951 See ANNUAL CONVENTION - CANADIAN NUMISMATIC ASSOCIATION. 2779

0318-4978 See ANNUAL EXHIBITION OF THE CANADIAN SOCIETY OF PAINTERS IN WATER COLOUR. 336

0318-5036 See PROCEEDINGS. ANNUAL CONFERENCE - CANADIAN ASSOCIATION OF ADMINISTRATIVE SCIENCES. 882

0318-5044 See ANNUAL REPORT - OFFICE OF THE FARMERS' ADVOCATE (ALBERTA). 2935

0318-5125 See EXPANSION DES CITES ET VILLES. 2822

0318-5133 See NEWSLETTER - CANADIAN SOCIETY OF ENVIRONMENTAL BIOLOGISTS. 2200

0318-5141 See CONTINUING EDUCATION (TORONTO). 4298

0318-5176 See ALBERTA MODERN LANGUAGE JOURNAL. 3263

0318-5184 See SURVEY OF CANADIAN NURSERY TRADES INDUSTRY. 2432

0318-5273 See HOUSEHOLD FACILITIES AND EQUIPMENT. 2811

0318-5338 See O A C E T T NEWSLETTER. 1989

0318-5362 See HORIZONS (ARMDALE). 2565

0318-5427 See MANUAL OF SOCIAL SERVICES IN MANITOBA. 5295

0318-5486 See BULLETIN - ASSOCIATION DES PROFESSEURS D'HISTOIRE LOCALE DU QUEBEC. 2724

0318-5494 See YESTERDAY'S NEWS. 2767

0318-5729 See AMIGO (MONTREAL). 4934

0318-5737 See AMISOL. 1060

0318-5753 See AMBER (DARTMOUTH). 3459

0318-5869 See REPORT SERIES (CANADA. INLAND WATERS DIRECTORATE). 5538

0318-5877 See HISTORICAL STREAMFLOW SUMMARY, ALBERTA. 1414

0318-5923 See HISTORICAL STREAMFLOW SUMMARY: SASKATCHEWAN. 1414

0318-6067 See REPERTOIRE DES ETABLISSEMENTS DE SANTE ET DE SERVICES SOCIAUX. 4798

0318-6075 See CROSS COUNTRY. 3462

0318-6229 See CAREERS FOR GRADUATES. 4202

0318-6288 See CARLETON MATHEMATICAL LECTURE NOTES. 3499

0318-6334 See COLLECTION DU DEPARTEMENT D'ECONOMIQUE. 75

0318-6377 See DI. DECISIONS INFORMATION. 1662

0318-6431 See CANADIAN JOURNAL OF SOCIOLOGY. 5241

0318-6725 See FABRERIES. 5608

0318-675X See CANADIAN GOVERNMENT PUBLICATIONS: CATALOGUE. 4697

0318-6784 See LYMAN ENTOMOLOGICAL MUSEUM AND RESEARCH LABORATORY MEMOIR. 4090

0318-6806 See S. L. A. N. T. : SAANEN, LAMANCHA, ALPINE, NUBIAN, TOGGENBURG. 221

0318-6814 See CANADA NORMANDIE. 2529

0318-6954 See ARCHIVARIA. 2479

0318-7020 See PARACHUTE. 361

0318-7063 See TECHNICAL REPORT (FOREST ENGINEERING RESEARCH INSTITUTE OF CANADA). 2396

0318-708X See NATIONAL INCOME AND EXPENDITURE ACCOUNTS. 1575

0318-7101 See SELECTED STATISTICS ON TECHNOLOGICAL INNOVATION IN INDUSTRY. 1538

0318-7225 See TRAINING IN INDUSTRY. 1715

0318-7306 See ACTION CANADA FRANCE. 817

0318-7349 See CAHIERS DE COURS DE L'HOLANTHROPE, LES. 4241

0318-7365 See GUIDING LIGHT, THE. 2534

0318-742X See CGA MAGAZINE. 740

0318-7489 See FINE (EDMONTON. 1974). 1746

0318-7527 See ONTARIO MUNICIPAL BOARD REPORTS. 3023

0318-7551 See ESKIMO; COUNTRY, INHABITANTS, CATHOLIC MISSIONS. 5029

0318-7705 See GARDEN CLIPPINGS. 2415

0318-7802 See HOMEMAKER'S MAGAZINE. 5558

0318-7942 See PRODUCTION, SHIPMENTS AND STOCKS ON HAND OF SAWMILLS IN BRITISH COLUMBIA. 1622

0318-8000 See REGLES DE CATALOGAGE ANGLO-AMERICAINE. VERSION FRANCAISE. BULLETIN. 3245

0318-806X See CANADIAN PEACE OFFICER. 3159

0318-8124 See REPORT OF THE AUDITOR GENERAL OF PRINCE EDWARD ISLAND TO THE LEGISLATIVE ASSEMBLY. 4745

0318-8205 See ICEA. INSTITUT CANADIEN D'EDUCATION DES ADULTES. 1800

0318-8280 See MONDES NOUVEAUX. 5209

0318-8418 See LIAISON (SHERBROOKE). 1093

0318-8442 See CANADIAN ISSUES (ASSOCIATION FOR CANADIAN STUDIES). 2726

0318-8450 See LABYRINTH (WATERLOO). 1078

0318-8477 See THUNDER COUNTRY OUTDOORS. 4879

0318-8531 See QUINCAILLERIE, MATERIAUX. 625

0318-8558 See JOURNAL OF EXPERIMENTAL AESTHETICS. 354

0318-8701 See FASHION TEXTILES MODE. 5350

0318-8752 See FRANCHISE ANNUAL (LEWISTON), THE. 677

0318-8809 See BUILDING PERMITS. 604

0318-8817 See CANADIAN BALANCE OF INTERNATIONAL PAYMENTS, THE. 4716

0318-9007 See ESTIMATES OF LABOUR INCOME (OTTAWA). 1532

0318-9090 See CANADIAN JOURNAL OF UNIVERSITY CONTINUING EDUCATION. 1800

0318-9104 See HOLIDAY NIAGARA. 5479

0318-9139 See ENTENDRE. 4387

0318-9147 See MARANATHA (ST-HYACINTHE). 4975

0318-918X See TECHNICAL PAPER SERIES - INSTITUTE FOR THE QUANTITATIVE ANALYSIS OF SOCIAL AND ECONOMIC POLICY, UNIVERSITY OF TORONTO. 1523

0318-9201 See VOIX ET IMAGES. 3451

0318-9236 See POUMONS. 3951

0318-9260 See PUMP & PRESS. 2370

0318-9279 See SEEKER (SARNIA). 4854

0318-9317 See PHENIX (ST-FULGENCE). 5792

0318-9325 See PRESTO. 4913

0318-9368 See BLACK BOOK USED SPECIALTY VEHICLE AND TRUCK GUIDE. 5407

0318-9392 See VIE OBLATE. 5038

0318-9414 See GUIDE DE ROUTE. 5478

0318-9422 See SANFORD EVANS GOLD BOOK, OFFICIAL SNOWMOBILE DATA AND USED PRICES. 5392

0318-9503 See EDUCATIONAL REQUIREMENTS AND SCHOOLS OF STUDY FOR HEALTH CAREERS. 3914

0318-9538 See CAMPBELL RIVER UPPER ISLANDER, THE. 5781

0318-9600 See BULLETIN - CANADIAN AURAL/ORAL HISTORY ASSOCIATION. 2724

0318-9651 See APARTMENT & BUILDING. 2815

0318-9678 See KONGRES UKRAJINCIV KANADY. 2743

0318-9686 See DIRECTORY OF SOCIAL SERVICES. OTTAWA-CARLETON. 5283

0319-0013 See KELOWNA CITY DIRECTORY. (1958. BUSINESS EDITION). 2567

0319-003X See ANNUAL CONFERENCE OF THE ATLANTIC CANADA ECONOMICS ASSOCIATION. 1462

0319-0080 See CANADIAN CHILDREN'S LITERATURE. 3372

0319-0110 See STRUCTURAL ENGINEERING REPORT. 2031

0319-0153 See ANNUAL CONVENTION - NEWFOUNDLAND AND LABRADOR FEDERATION OF LABOUR. 1644

0319-0161 See COMPUTING CANADA. 1257

0319-0196 See PEEL SENIORS REGIONAL NEWS. 5181

0319-0323 See INSIDE OXFAM. 4338

0319-0374 See INCOME AFTER TAX, DISTRIBUTIONS BY SIZE IN CANADA. 1566

0319-0439 See TOURIST GUIDE BOOK OF ONTARIO. 5494

0319-0463 See CAPE DORSET PRINTS. 377

0319-051X See CANADIAN REVIEW OF COMPARATIVE LITERATURE. 3372

0319-0560 See SWIM. 4924

0319-0617 See ANNUAL REVIEW, ALBERTA EDUCATION. 1725

0319-0714 See GLOBE AND MAIL, THE. 5785

0319-0714 See GLOBE AND MAIL. 5785

0319-0781 See TORONTO STAR. 5796

0319-0803 See CANADA'S FURNITURE MARKET. 2904

0319-0994 See WOMEN CAN. 5798

0319-1087 See REAL ESTATE DEVELOPMENT ANNUAL, THE. 4844

0319-1095 See BULLETIN - CENTRE INTERUNIVERSITAIRE D'ETUDES EUROPEENNES. 2680

0319-1249 See CHATEAUGUAY VALLEY HISTORICAL SOCIETY ANNUAL JOURNAL. 2727

0319-1303 See OTTAWA JEWISH BULLETIN & REVIEW. 2270

0319-1362 See BULL & BEAR. 893

0319-1656 See REGIONAL ECHO, THE. 5793

0319-1672 See MEAFORD CENTENNIAL, THE. 5789

0319-1710 See ECLOSION, L'. 5783

0319-1737 See ALBERTA ECHO. 2718

0319-1788 See ENTRE NOUS (OTTAWA). 1744

0319-180X See ORANGEVILLE CITIZEN, THE. 5792

0319-1818 See INFORMATION - L'ASSOCIATION QUEBECOISE DU TRANSPORT ET DES ROUTES. 5384

0319-1826 See FACTS OF THE GENERAL INSURANCE INDUSTRY IN CANADA. 2880

0319-1877 See ECOINDICATEUR DE LA BANQUE ROYALE. 1556

0319-1915 See ANNUAL - CANADIAN GLADIOLUS SOCIETY. 2409

0319-2113 See PACIFIC MOTORSPORT. 4911

0319-2318 See LIST OF EQUIPMENT AND MATERIALS. 619

0319-2385 See CONSTRUCTIVE CITIZEN PARTICIPATION. 5242

0319-2423 See FISCALITE AU CANADA, LA. 4726

0319-2431 See CANADIAN TAX NEWS. 2948

0319-2482 See CONGRES DES RELATIONS INDUSTRIELLES DE L'UNIVERSITE LAVAL. 1661

0319-2563 See DIRECTORY OF SPECIAL LIBRARIES IN THE MONTREAL AREA. 3208

0319-258X See REPERTOIRE DES SERVICES COMMUNAUTAIRES DU GRAND MONTREAL. BIEN-ETRE. SANTE. LOISIRS. 5304

0319-2644 See PROCEEDINGS OF THE ANNUAL MEETING OF THE CANADIAN PUBLIC HEALTH ASSOCIATION. 4796

0319-2709 See MART (MONTREAL). 2121

0319-2725 See QUEEN'S GAZETTE. 1843

0319-2792 See NILITE NEWS. 3237

0319-2822 See CYCLE CANADA. 4081

0319-2865 See MOTO JOURNAL. 4081

0319-2997 See CANADIAN EQUINE SPORTS. 4889

0319-3020 See VOTES AND PROCEEDINGS OF THE LEGISLATIVE ASSEMBLY OF MANITOBA. 4694

0319-3071 See PROGRESS AGAINST CANCER (TORONTO). 3822

0319-3098 See ANNUELLES ET LEGUMES. RESULTATS DES CULTURES D'ESSAI. 2409

0319-3187 See ELITE (MONTREAL). 2532

0319-3225 See CANADIAN FUNERAL DIRECTOR. 2406

0319-3284 See NEWS BULLETIN - DEVELOPMENT OFFICE, CARLETON UNIVERSITY. 1837

0319-3322 See CANADIAN BUSINESS LAW JOURNAL, THE. 3097

0319-3403 See CANADIAN ENERGY NEWS. 1934

0319-342X See T V THIS WEEK. 1140

0319-3438 See YARDSTICKS FOR COSTING. 631

0319-3446 See BIO-NOUVELLES. 444

0319-3454 See COMMUNICATOR (EDMONTON). 1732

0319-3535 See ANNUAL REPORT - ALBERTA HAIL AND CROP INSURANCE CORPORATION. 2873

0319-3667 See SUMMARY - ALBERTA SECURITIES COMMISSION. 3060

0319-3705 See MONTHLY STATISTICS. ALBERTA ELECTRIC ENERGY INDUSTRY. 1950

0319-3780 See ROUTES ET TRANSPORTS. 5392

0319-3829 See CALGARY Y F C FOCUS. 4942

0319-3837 See FOCUS ON YOUTH FOR CHRIST CALGARY. 4959

0319-3845 See TIRE A PART - ECOLE DE RELATIONS INDUSTRIELLES, UNIVERSITE DE MONTREAL. 947

0319-3926 See ACTUALITE JOLIETTAINE, L'. 2526

0319-3977 See MACHINERIE LOURDE. 2120

0319-4019 See MONARCHY CANADA. 4482

0319-406X See MANUAL & DIRECTORY - ONTARIO JOINT FICTION RESERVE. 3229

0319-4078 See PLEIN MONDE, EN. 4986

0319-4094 See PHILA-PRESSE. 2786

0319-4124 See ETOILE DE L'OUTAOUAIS-ST-LAURENT, L'. 5784

0319-4132 See HARMONIE SYNDICALE, L'. 1676

0319-4167 See MUNICIPALITY OF SHUNIAH. 4667

0319-4345 See NOUVEAU COSMOS-EXPRESS, LE. 30

0319-4442 See I P L O NEWS. 3214

0319-4523 See COMSERVANT, THE. 5280

0319-4558 See COMMUNIQUE - ASSOCIATION FOR PRESERVATION TECHNOLOGY. 295

0319-4566 See KINGSTON PUBLIC LIBRARY INQUIRER, THE. 3221

0319-4620 See MAJOR REPORT - CENTRE FOR URBAN AND COMMUNITY STUDIES, UNIVERSITY OF TORONTO. 2827

0319-4639 See CAPE BRETON'S MAGAZINE. 2726

0319-485X See RELIGIOUS STUDIES REVIEW. 4992

0319-4914 See CONSERVATIONIST (SUDBURY). 2191

0319-4973 See JOURNAL OF THE LEGISLATIVE ASSEMBLY OF THE PROVINCE OF PRINCE EDWARD ISLAND. 4659

0319-5031 See ALBERTA PHYSICIANS AND SURGEONS, PROVINCE OF ALBERTA. 3913

0319-5058 See CAMPBELL RIVER DIRECTORY (BUSINESS EDITION). 2558

0319-5082 See SUMMER IN CANADA. 1712

0319-5112 See ACTIVITES : LES BANQUES A CHARTE DU CANADA. 768

0319-5198 See CITES NOUVELLES. 5782

0319-5309 See MINI MOUTH MAGAZINE. 1066

0319-5414 See ALBERTAN'S NORTH SIDE MIRROR, THE. 5780

0319-5465 See SANAVIK COOPERATIVE BAKER LAKE PRINTS. 382

0319-5481 See CUMULATIF DES REFERENCES PEDAGOGIQUES. 1794

0319-5562 See MOUNTAINEER (VEDDER CROSSING). 4052

0319-5570 See SHELBURNE COUNTY TELECASTER. 1139

0319-5589 See ARROWSMITH STAR, THE. 5780

0319-5724 See CANADIAN JOURNAL OF STATISTICS, THE. 5325

0319-5759 See ENERGY PROCESSING CANADA. 1941

0319-5767 See AVENANT. 2875

0319-5805 See POINT (LASALLE). 5793

0319-5902 See C I E N, CANADIAN INDUSTRIAL EQUIPMENT NEWS. 3476

0319-5953 See INCORPORATION AND INCOME TAX IN CANADA. 4731

0319-5961 See FAMILY LIFE (TORONTO). 2279

0319-6038 See HURON SOIL AND CROP NEWS (1964). 173

0319-6143 See RESEARCH AND STUDIES - CARLETON UNIVERSITY. 1845

0319-616X See F C N, FLOOR COVERING NEWS. 2905

0319-6216 See COMPUTER STUDIES NEWSLETTER. 1257

0319-6224 See SOUTHERN GAZETTE. 5795

0319-6283 See CANADIAN MUSIC THERAPY JOURNAL. 4107

0319-6410 See LIST OF VISITING SCHOLARS IN CANADA. 1762

0319-6577 See CANADIAN SCENE (TORONTO. 1951). 2530

0319-6631 See ZINC. 4024

0319-664X See BULLETIN - CANADIAN TALENT LIBRARY. 3198

0319-6658 See NEWSLETTER - EXECUTIVE COMMITTEE, LEAGUE OF CANADIAN POETS. 3467

0319-6674 See BULLETIN - CANADIAN SOCIETY OF ZOOLOGISTS. 5579

0319-6739 See FRANCISCAN MISSIONARY. 5029

0319-6771 See ENVIRONMENTAL HEALTH REVIEW. 4774

0319-681X See CEGEPROPOS. 1814

0319-6887 See BHARATI (TORONTO). 2529

0319-6992 See NEWSLETTER - WORLD FEDERATION FOR MENTAL HEALTH. 3931

0319-7085 See CANNONS OF CONSTRUCTION, THE. 2948

0319-7115 See MOTS CROISES T V HEBDO. 4863

0319-7131 See RIDEAU. 388

0319-7166 See ANNEE SAINTE AVEC PAUL VI. 4935

0319-7190 See STRAFFORD FESTIVAL. 388

0319-7239 See JOINT VENTURES (OTTAWA). 1498

0319-7336 See HUME STUDIES. 4348

0319-7360 See CARIBOO CALLING. 2558

0319-7379 See CONTACT (TORONTO. 1972). 4386

0319-745X See COCHRANE TIMES. 5782

0319-7468 See COMMUNIQUE - CHILDREN'S AID SOCIETY OF OTTAWA. 5279

0319-7530 See EVERYWOMAN'S ALMANAC. 5555

0319-7549 See COMMON SENSE ECONOMICS. 1470

0319-762X See FORET ET PAPIER. 4233

0319-7808 See BULLETIN - CORPORATION PROFESSIONNELLE DES DIETETISTES DU QUEBEC. 4188

0319-7832 See CRAFTNEWS (TORONTO). 371

0319-7956 See TRUE NORTH. 5796

0319-7980 See ALBERTA DECISIONS, CIVIL AND CRIMINAL CASES. 2929

0319-7999 See SASKATCHEWAN DECISIONS, CIVIL AND CRIMINAL CASES. 3046

0319-8383 See COURIER (TORONTO). 3204

0319-8413 See DPN: DESIGN PRODUCT NEWS. 1971

0319-8421 See PALMARES LA QUEBECOISE. 4145

0319-843X See CROSS-CANADA COMMENT. 663

0319-8480 See DISCOVERY (VANCOUVER. 1972). 2191

0319-8510 See CROWN'S NEWSLETTER. 3106

0319-8626 See ENTERPRISE (VANCOUVER). 1542

0319-8715 See CANADIAN INDIA STAR, THE. 2648

0319-8774 See RAPPORT ANNUEL - CONSEIL DE LA PROTECTION DU CONSOMMATEUR. 1299

0319-891X See TEXTILE PRODUCTS INDUSTRIES. 5358

0319-9118 See FOREST RESEARCH INFORMATION PAPER. 2381

0319-9436 See STEELHEAD HARVEST ANALYSIS. 2314

0319-9495 See NATCON. 1692

0320-0027 See VOPROSY KINETIKI I KATALIZA. 1058

0320-0035 See GENETIKA I SELEKTSIIA V AZERBAIDZHANE. 546

0320-0094 See NEFTEPERERABOTKA I NEFTEHIMIJA (KAZAN). 987

0320-0108 See PISMA V ASTRONOMICESKIJ ZURNAL. 398

0320-0116 See PISMA V ZURNAL TEHNICESKOJ FIZIKI. 4417

0320-0132 See SBORNIK NAUCNYH TRUDOV - MAGNITOGORSKIJ GORNOMETALLURGICESKIJ INSTITUT IM. G. J. NOSOVA. 4018

0320-0167 See TRAVEL TO THE USSR. 5496

0320-023X See HIMICESKAJA TEHNOLOGIJA VOLOKNISTYH MATERIALOV. 1025

0320-0752 See VOENNYJ VESTNIK. 4060

0320-0825 See AVTOMATIZACIJA METALLURGICESKOGO PROIZVODSTVA. 3998

0320-0841 See ARKHITEKTURNOE NASLEDSTVO. 291

0320-0892 See TRUDY SAMARKANDSKOGO GOSUDARSTVENNOGO UNIVERSITETA. IM. ALISERA NAVOI. ISSLEDOVANIJA PO RUSSKOMU I SLAVANSKOMU AZYKOZNANIU. 3330

0320-1031 See ROSSIIANE. 3432

0320-104X See DIFFERENTSIALNYE URAVNENIJA (RJAZAN). 3503

0320-1074 See DVIGATELI VNUTRENNOGO SGORANIJA (OMSK). 5413

0320-1244 See KNIZHNAIA TORGOVLIA. OPYT, PROBLEMY, ISSLEDOVANIIA. 4829

0320-2372 See INOZEMNA FILOLOGIJA. 3287

0320-2887 See MAKTABDA UZBEK, RUS TILLARI VA ADABIETI. 3301

0320-2909 See REAKCIONNAJA SPOSOBNOST I MEHANIZMY REAKCIJ ORGANICESKIH SOEDINENIJ. 1057

0320-3077 See UKRAINS'KE MOVOZNAVSTVO. 3330

0320-4421 See ISTORIIA NARODNOHO HOSPODARSTVA TA EKONOMICHNOI DUMKY UKRAINSKOI RSR. 1497

0320-5452 See FILOSOFSKIE NAUKI (ALMA-ATA). 4347

0320-6386 See OCERKI FIZIKO-HIMICESKOJ PETROLOGII. 1443

0320-6432 See SKANDINAVSKIJ SBORNIK. 3321

0320-6572 See VISNIK LVIVSKOGO ORDENA LENINA DERZARNOGO UNIVERSITETU IM. IV. FRANKA. SERIJA MEHANIKO-MATEMATICNA. 3540

0320-6858 See AVRORA. 3365

0320-7102 See AVTOMETRIJA (NOVOSIBIRSK). 1218

0320-7218 See ADSORBCIJA I ADSORBENTY. 4396

0320-7390 See ALA TOO. 3359

0320-7838 See BIBLIOTEKOVEDENIE I BIBLIOGRAFIJA ZA RUBEZOM. 3194

0320-7919 See AKUSTICESKIJ ZURNAL. 4452

0320-8001 See VEK XX I MIR. 4537

0320-8117 See LRABER HASARAKAKAN GITUTYUNNERI. 5208

0320-8168 See VESTNIK STATISTIKI : ORGAN TSSU SSSR. 5346

0320-8370 See VSESVIT (KIIV). 2524

0320-8702 See VOPROSY GIDRODINAMIKI I TEPLOOBMENA V KRIOGENNYH SISTEMAH. 2096

0320-930X See ASTRONOMICESKIJ VESTNIK. 392

0320-9318 See ASTROFIZICESKIE ISSLEDOVANIJA. 391

0320-9326 See ATOMNAIA TEKHNIKA ZA RUBEZHOM. 1933

0320-9393 See ARHEOLOGICESKIJ SBORNIK. 259

0320-9466 See ARHIVI UKRAINI. 259

0320-9601 See ANTENNY (MOSKVA). 2035

0320-9695 See BIOLOGIA MORA (KIEV). 553

0320-9725 See BIOHIMIJA (MOSKVA). 483

0321-026X See BIULLETIN NAUCHNO-TEKHNICHESKOI INFORMATSII VSESOIUZNOGO NAUCHNO-ISSLEDOVATELSKOGO INSTITUTA ZERNOBOBOVYKH I KRUPIANYKH KULTUR. 200

0321-0391 See VESTNIK DREVNEJ ISTORII. 2632

0321-0502 See VETERINARIIA (UKRAINE. MINISTERSTVO SILSKOHO HOSPODARSTVA). 5524

0321-057X See VNESNJAJA TORGOVLJA. 857

0321-0596 See VODNYE RESURSY. 5541

0321-0642 See STUPENI. 1069

0321-0669 See VOKRUG SVIETA. 2579

0321-1363 See DONBAS : LITERATURNO-KHUDOZHNII TA HROMADS'KO-POLITYCHNYI ZHURNAL SPILKY PYSMENNYKIV UKRAINY. 2138

0321-1665 See IZVESTIIA AKADEMII NAUK GRUZII. SERIIA BIOLOGICHESKAIA. 459

0321-1665 See SAKARTVELOS SSR MECNIEREBATA AKADEMIIS MACNE. BIOLOGIIS SERIA. 472

0321-1703 See IZVESTIIA AKADEMII NAUK SSSR. SERIIA GEOLOGICHESKAIA. 1384

0321-172X See OBSHCHESTVO I EKONOMIKA. 1576

0321-1746 See IZVESTIIA AKADEMIIA NAUK TURKMENSKOI SSR. SERIIA BIOLOGICHESKIKH NAUK. 459

0321-1878 See ZVEZDA. 2525

0321-1975 See MEHANIKA TVERDOGO TELA (KIEV). 4429

0321-2068 See SSHA. 1595

0321-2092 See KOMMUNIST SOVETSKOJ LATVII. 4542

0321-2114 See KOMMUNIST. 4542

0321-2211 See VESTNIK KIEVSKOGO POLITEKHNICHESKOGO INSTITUTA. SERIIA PRIBOROSTROENIIA. 3489

0321-222X See RADIOELEKTRONIKA I ELEKTROSVIAZ. 1162

0321-2270 See LATVIJSKIJ MATEMATICESKIJ EZEGODNIK. 3516

0321-2653 See IZVESTIJA SEVERO-KAVKAZSKOGO NAUCNOGO CENTRA VYSSEJ SKOLY. TEHNICESKIE NAUKI. 5117

0321-2769 See VOPROSY KIBERNETIKI (TASKENT). 1252

0321-2858 See ISTOCNIKOVEDENIC OTECESTVENNOJ ISTORII. 2693

0321-2904 See LITERATURNOE OBOZRENIE. 3407

0321-2971 See TRUDY SEMINARA IMENI I. G. PETROVSKOGO. 3539

0321-3005 See IZVESTIJA SEVERO-KAVKAZSKOGO NAUCNOGO CENTRA VYSSEJ SKOLY. ESTESTVENNYE NAUKI. 1384

0321-3439 See UCENYE ZAPISKIE CAGI. 38

0321-3501 See PROBLEMY ZHURNALISTIKI. 2923

0321-382X See TEKHNOLOGIA I OBORUDOVANIE DEREVOOBRABATYVAIUSHCHIKH PROIZVODSTV. 635

0321-3900 See TEORIJA SLUCAINYH PROCESSOV. 3538

0321-3927 See VESTNIK KIEVSKOGO UNIVERSITETA. ASTRONOMIIA. 401

0321-4044 See VODOSNABZENIE I SANITARNAJA TEHNIKA. 2245

0321-4117 See VYCHISLITELNAIA I PRIKLADNAIA MATEMATIKA. 3541

0321-4249 See ZA RULEM. 5458

0321-4265 See ZAVODSKAJA LABORATORIJA. 1020

0321-4427 See TEORIJA FUNKCIJ, FUNKCIONALNYJ ANALIZ I IH PRILOZENIJA (HARKOV). 3538

0321-4729 See KOMBINATORNYI ANALIZ. 3516

0321-477X See AKUSTIKA I ULTRAZVUKOVAJA TEHNIKA (KIEV). 5082

0321-4885 See BJULLETEN INSTITUTA ASTROFIZIKI. 4398

0321-4966 See PROIZVODSTVO SPECIALNYH OGNEUPOROV. 4017

0322-8207 See PTT : REVUE. 1120

0322-8231 See VODNI HOSPODARSTVI. 5541

0322-8533 See TECHNICKE ZPRAVY (CKD PRAHA (FIRM) : 1978). 5162

0322-8657 See RADIOISOTOPY. 4419

0322-905X See NOVA MYSL. 4544

0322-9254 See LESNICKA PRACE. 2387

0322-9785 See ZVARACSKE SPRAVY. 4029

0323-0139 See FOLIA FACULTATIS SCIENTIARUM NATURALIUM UNIVERSITATIS PURKYNIANAE BRUNENSIS. GEOLOGIA. 5105

0323-0287 See FOLIA FACULTATIS SCIENTIARUM NATURALIUM UNIVERSITATIS PURKYNIANAE BRUNENSIS. PHYSICA. 4403

0323-0465 See ACTA PHYSICA SLOVACA. 4395

0323-052X See CASOPIS MATICE MORAVSKE (1968). 2683

0323-0570 See CASOPIS MORAVSKEHO MUZEA. VEDY SPOLECENSKE. 5194

0323-0627 See CASOPIS SLEZSKEHO MUZEA. SERIE A, VEDY PRIRODNI. 451

0323-0635 See GLASS REVIEW (PRAGUE, CZECHOSLOVAKIA). 2590

0323-0678 See CASOPIS SLEZSKEHO MUZEA. SERIE B, VEDY HISTORIKE. 4086

0323-1046 See LESNICKY CASOPIS. 2387

0323-1283 See HMM. 4121

0323-1569 See CESKE HUDEBNINY A GRAMOFONOVE DESKY. 4108

0323-2042 See MLADY SVET. 1066

0323-2220 See STUDIA COMENIANA ET HISTORICA. 1786

0323-2441 See NARODOPISNA REVUE. 242

0323-3057 See BAUSTOFFINDUSTRIE. AUSGABE B: BAUELEMENTE. 1599

0323-3162 See LANDSCHAFTSARCHITEKTUR. 2423

0323-3227 See FILM UND FERNSEHEN. 4070

0323-3286 See VERFUGUNGEN UND MITTEILUNGEN DES MINISTERIUMS FUR VOLKSBILDUNG. 1789

0323-3597 See DEUTSCHE NATIONALBIBLIOGRAPHIE UND BIBLIOGRAPHIE DES IM AUSLAND ERSCHIENENEN DEUTSCHSPRACHIGEN VEROFFENTLICHUNGEN. REIGE A. ESCHIENENE. 414

0323-3642 See DEUTSCHE NATIONALBIBLIOGRAPHIE UND BIBLIOGRAPHIE DER IM AUSLAND ERSCHIENENEN DEUTSCHSPRACHIGEN VEROFFENTLICHUNGEN. REIHE B, MONOGRAPHIEN UND PERIODIKA AUSSERHALB DES VERLAGSBUCHHANDELS. WOCHENTLICHES VERZEICHNIS / BEARBEITER UND HERAUSGEBER, DIE DEUTSCHE BIBLIOTHEK. 414

0323-3693 See JAHRESVERZEICHNIS DER MUSIKALIEN UND MUSIKSCHRIFTEN. 4124

0323-3847 See BIOMETRICAL JOURNAL. 3497

0323-4045 See ZEITSCHRIFT DER SAVIGNY-STIFTUNG FUER RECHTSGESCHICHTE. GERMANISTISCHE ABTEILUNG. 3077

0323-4088 See DRESDENER KUNSTBLATTER. 349

0323-4096 See ZEITSCHRIFT DER SAVIGNY-STIFTUNG FUER RECHTSGESCHICHTE. ROMANISTISCHE ABTEILUNG. 3456

0323-4126 See STUDIENMATERIAL ZUR WEITERBILDUNG MEDIZINISCH-TECHNISCHER LABORASSISTENTEN. 3643

0323-4134 See LEICHTATHLET BERLIN, DDR. 1953. 4903

0323-4142 See ZEITSCHRIFT DER SAVIGNY-STIFTUNG FUER RECHTSGESCHICHTE. KANONISTISCHE ABTEILUNG. 3077

0323-4207 See GOETHE-JAHRBUCH (WEIMAR). 3391

0323-4223 See WEIMARER BEITRAEGE. 3452

0323-4320 See ACTA HYDROCHIMICA ET HYDROBIOLOGICA. 1412

0323-4393 See MICROBIAL RESEARCH. 566

0323-4398 See ALLERGIE UND IMMUNOLOGIE. 3665

0323-4568 See ARBEIT UND ARBEITSRECHT. 1651

0323-4657 See NACHRICHTENTECHNIK - ELEKTRONIK. 1160

0323-4673 See BEITRAEGE FUER DIE FORSTWIRTSCHAFT. 2375

0323-4762 See GASTRONOMIE. 3746

0323-4886 See BAUSTOFFINDUSTRIE. AUSGABE A : PRIMARBAUSTOFFE. 600

0323-4916 See KOERPERERZIEHUNG. 2599

0323-4932 See FOLIA OPHTHALMOLOGICA. 3874

0323-4983 See ANAESTHESIOLOGIE UND REANIMATION. 3680

0323-5106 See MUSIKFORUM. 4138

0323-5211 See VOLLEYBALL. 4928

0323-5238 See FARBE UND RAUM. 614

0323-5386 See MEDIZIN AKTUELL. 3615

0323-5408 See ARCHIV FUER PHYTOPATHOLOGIE UND PFLANZENSCHUTZ. 500

0323-6129 See WISSENSCHAFTLICHE ZEITSCHRIFT DER TECHNISCHE HOCHSCHULE LEIPZIG. 5170

0323-6153 See MEDIZIN UND GESELLSCHAFT. 3615

0323-651X See AKTUELLE PROBLEME DER INTENSIVMEDIZIN (LEIPZIG). 3547

0323-6919 See JAHRBUCH DES ARBEITSKREISES THURINGER MUNZ- UND GELDGESCHICHTE. 2781

0323-7028 See FDGB REVIEW. 1669

0323-7648 See ACTA POLYMERICA. 5347

0323-8202 See GLAUBE UND HEIMAT. 5060

0323-8628 See DEUTSCHES SPORTECHO AUSGABE A. 4892

0323-8776 See ZFI-MITTEILUNGEN. 3947

0323-8946 See SCHRIFTENREIHE FUER GEOLOGISCHE WISSENSCHAFTEN. 1396

0323-9179 See PROBLEMI NA HIGIENATA. 4796

0323-9209 See PROBLEMI NA ONKOLOGIIATA. 3822

0323-9217 See BULGARIAN JOURNAL OF PHYSICS. 4398

0323-9438 See IZVESTIJA - DRZAVEN INSTITUT ZA KONTROL NA LEKARSTVENITE SREDSTVA. 3591

0323-9535 See IZVESTIA NA ARHEOLOGICESKIA INSTITUT. 270

0323-9780 See IZVESTIIA NA DURZHAVNITE ARKHIVI / MINISTERSTVO NA VUTRESHNITE RABOTI, OTDEL "DURZHAVEN ARKHIV". 2481

0323-9802 See MEDIKO-BIOLOGICNI PROBLEMI. 464

0323-9918 See BULGARSKO GEOFIZICHNO SPISANIE. 1403

0323-9950 See ACTA PHYSIOLOGICA ET PHARMACOLOGICA BULGARICA. 577

0323-9993 See KINO. 4073

0324-0207 See BULGARIAN HISTORICAL REVIEW. 2680

0324-0258 See SUVREMENNI PROBLEMI NA NEVROMORFOLOGIIATA. 3846

0324-0290 See FIZIOLOGIJA NA RASTENIJATA. 510

0324-0401 See BULGARIAN CHEMICAL COMMUNICATIONS. 963

0324-0495 See LITERATURNA MISL. 3407

0324-0509 See BULGARIAN ACADEMIC BOOKS. 4827

0324-0533 See IZVESTIA NA NARODNIA MUZEJ-VARNA. 4089

0324-0770 See ACTA ZOOLOGICA BULGARICA. 5573

0324-0894 See GEOLOGICA BALCANICA. 1377

0324-0959 See AKUSHERSTVO I GINEKOLOGIIA. 3756

0324-0967 See VEKOVE. 2714

0324-1068 See VETERINARNO-MEDICINSKI NAUKI. 5524

0324-1114 See VISSA GEODEZIJA. 2579

0324-1130 See BULGARIAN CHEMICAL COMMUNICATIONS. 963

0324-119X See MBI. MEDICO-BIOLOGIC INFORMATION. 3606

0324-1203 See ARHEOLOGIJA. 259

0324-1238 See IZKUSTVO. 2921

0324-1254 See ARHITEKTURA. 291

0324-1270 See EZIK I LITERATURA. 3281

0324-1440 See MEDITSINSKA TEKHNIKA / MA-TSENTR ZA NAUCHNA INFORMATSIIA PO MEDITSINA I ZDRAVEOPAZVANE S TSENTRALNA MEDITSINSKA BIBLIOTEKA. 3614

0324-1459 See ASTROFIZICHESKIE ISSLEDOVANIIA. 391

0324-1491 See PNEVMOLOGIIA I FTIZIATRIIA. 3950

0324-1521 See ENERGETIKA (SOFIJA). 2053

0324-1629 See RODOLIUBIE. 2707

0324-1645 See ETUDES BALKANIQUES. 2687

0324-1653 See BALKANSKO EZIKOZNANIE. 3267

0324-1661 See GEOTEKTONIKA, TEKTONOFIZIKA I GEODINAMIKA. 1381

0324-1718 See GEOKHIMIYA, MINERALOGIYA I PETROLOGIYA. 1440

0324-1793 See MUZEI I PAMETNITSI NA KULTURATA / KOMITET ZA KULTURA. 4093

0324-1947 See HELMINTOLOGIJA (SOFIJA). 5585

0324-1998 See OBSCA I SRAVNITELNA PATOLOGIJA. 3896

0324-2064 See OSZK HIRADO. 3240

0324-4652 See NEOHELICON (BUDAPEST). 3348

0324-4679 See PUBLICATIONS OF THE TECHNICAL UNIVERSITY FOR HEAVY INDUSTRY. SERIES B: METALLURGY. 4017

0324-5705 See MOSONMAGYAROVARI MEZOGAZDASAGTUDOMANYI KAR KOZLEMENYEI, A. 110

0324-5853 See PERIODICA POLYTECHNICA. CHEMICAL ENGINEERING. HIMIJA. 2015

0324-6051 See PERIODICA POLYTECHNICA : MECHANICAL ENGINEERING. MASHINOSTROENIE. 2124

0324-6221 See KARSZT ES BARLANG. 1408

0324-6523 See ACTA UNIVERSITATIS SZEGEDIENSIS. 2609

0324-6566 See SCRIPTA FACULTATIS SCIENTIARUM NATURALIUM UNIVERSITATIS PURKYNIANAE BRUNENSIS. GEOGRAPHIA. 2576

0324-6965 See ACTA UNIVERSITATIS SZEGEDIENSIS DE ATTILA JOZSEF NOMINATAE ACTA HISTORICA. 2672

0324-721X See ACTA CYBERNETICA. 1250

0324-8216 See ANESTEZJA, REANIMACJA, INTENSYWNA TERAPIA. 3681

0324-8232 See SZTUKA. 366

0324-8267 See ARCHIWUM MEDYCYNY SADOWEJ I KRJMINOLOGII. 3552

0324-8291 See STUDIES IN PHYSICAL ANTHROPOLOGY. 246

0324-8313 See JOURNAL OF TECHNICAL PHYSICS. 4410

0324-833X See POSTEPY BIOLOGII KOMORKI. 539

0324-8372 See JOURNAL OF HYDROLOGICAL SCIENCES. 1416

0324-8437 See PRACE INSTYTUTU SADOWNICTWA I KWIACIARSTWA W SKIERNIEWICACH. SERIA B, ROSLINY OZDOBNE. 2428

0324-8453 See FOTO (WARSAW, POLAND). 4369

0324-8461 See ARCHIWUM OCHRONY SRODOWISKA. 2161

0324-8496 See BIULETYN POLSKIEGO KOMITETU NORMALIZACJI I MIAR. 4029

0324-8526 See ZAGADNIENIA WYCHOWAWCZE A ZDROWIE PSYCHICZNE. 3912

0324-8534 See IMMUNOLOGIA POLSKA. 3670

0324-8542 See BULLETIN OF THE INSTITUTE OF MARITIME AND TROPICAL MEDICINE IN GDYNIA. 3985

0324-8569 See CONTROL AND CYBERNETICS. 1250

0324-864X See ECONOMIC PAPERS. 1484

0324-8666 See STUDIES IN HUMAN ECOLOGY. 246

0324-8674 See BUDOWNICTWO ROLNICZE. 602

0324-8712 See REPORTS ON PHILOSOPHY. 4358

0324-8747 See FOUNDATIONS OF CONTROL ENGINEERING. 1976

0324-8763 See POLISH ECOLOGICAL STUDIES. 2220

0324-8828 See ENVIRONMENT PROTECTION ENGINEERING. 2166

0324-9034 See CHEMIA. 967

0324-9174 See ZESZYTY NAUKOWE AKADEMII ROLNICZO-TECHNICZNEJ W OLSZTYNIE. GEODEZJA I URZADZENIA ROLNE. 2002

0324-9212 See TECHNOLOGIA ALIMENTORUM. 2359

0324-9603 See SERIA MONOGRAFIE - POLITECHNIKA WROCAWSKA, INSTYTUT MATEMATYKI. 3534

0324-9611 See SERIA STUDIA I MATERIAY - POLITECHNIKA WROCAWSKA, INSTYTUT MATEMATYKI. 3534

0324-9689 See PRACE NAUKOWE INSTYTUTU GORNICTWA POLITECHNIKI WROCAWSKIEJ. MONOGRAFIE. 2148

0325-0229 See CERAMICA Y CRISTAL. 2588

0325-0253 See REVISTA DE LA ASOCIACION ARGENTINA DE MINERALOGIA, PETROLOGIA Y SEDIMENTOLOGIA. 1395

0325-0288 See ANALES DE ARQUEOLOGIA Y ETNOLOGIA / UNIVERSIDAD NACIONAL DE CUYO, FACULTAD DE FILOSOFIA Y LETRAS. 254

0325-0326 See INDUSTRIA AZUCARERA, LA. 95

0325-0431 See DAVID Y GOLIATH : BOLETIN CLACSO. 2551

0325-0482 See BOLETIN DE LA ACADEMIA NACIONAL DE LA HISTORIA. 2723

0325-0520 See SIDERURGIA (BUENOS AIRES). 4019

0325-061X See REVISTA DEL INSTITUTO DE HISTORIA DEL DERECHO RICARDO LEVENE. 3041

0325-0679 See INDICE DE LA LITERATURA DENTAL PERIODICA EN CASTELLANO. 1324

0325-0687 See MERCADO. 1574

0325-0725 See REVISTA LATINOAMERICANA DE FILOSOFIA. 4359

0325-0741 See SALUD BUCAL. 1335

0325-0938 See REVISTA NEUROLOGICA ARGENTINA. 3845

0325-1179 See RSCA. 308

0325-1195 See CUADERNOS DE HISTORIA DE ESPANA. 2684

0325-1217 See RUNA. 245

0325-1403 See CNEA / REPUBLICA ARGENTINA, COMISION NACIONAL DE ENERGIA ATOMICA. 4446

0325-1594 See REVISTA DE CERAMICA EN LA CONSTRUCCION. 626

0325-1799 See INFORME TECNICO - ESTACION EXPERIMENTAL REGIONAL AGROPECUARIA PERGAMINO. 96

0325-1969 See BOLETIN ESTADISTICO TRIMESTRAL - INSTITUTO NACIONAL DE ESTADISTICA Y CENSOS. 5323

0325-2035 See GEOPOLITICA (INSTITUTO DE ESTUDIOS GEOPOLITICOS (BUENOS AIRES, ARGENTINA)). 2616

0325-2051 See BOLETIN DE LA ACADEMIA NACIONAL DE CIENCIAS. 5089

0325-2132 See PUBLICACION TECNICA (ESTACION EXPERIMENTAL REGIONAL AGROPECUARIAANGUIL). 123

0325-2167 See BOLETIN DE DIVULGACION TECNICA / SECRETARIA DE ESTADO DE AGRICULTURA Y GANADERIA DE LA NACION, INSTITUTO NACIONAL DE TECNOLOGIA AGROPECUARIA, ESTACION EXPERIMENTAL REGIONAL AGROPECUARIA ANGUIL. 67

0325-2280 See PATRISTICA ET MEDIAEVALIA. 4354

0325-2388 See ECONOMIC INFORMATION ON ARGENTINA. 1483

0325-2493 See SERIE DIDACTICA - FACULTAD DE AGRONOMIA Y ZOOTECNIA. UNIVERSIDAD NACIONAL TUCUMAN. 133

0325-2620 See ACTAS DEL CONGRESO GEOLOGICO ARGENTINO. 1365

0325-2787 See REVISTA ARGENTINA DE DERMATOLOGIA. 3722

0325-2957 See ACTA BIOQUIMICA CLINICA LATINOAMERICANA. 479

0325-3414 See INDUSTRIA CARNICA LATINOAMERICANA, LA. 213

0325-3899 See ANUARIO INTERAMERICANO DE ARCHIVOS. 2479

0325-3902 See ACAECER. 42

0325-3937 See ENSAYOS ECONOMICOS. 1591

0325-4186 See ANALES - CIDEPINT. 5082

0325-4437 See TEMAS DE PSICOLOGIA Y PSIQUIATRIA DE LA NINEZ Y ADOLESCENCIA. 3937

0325-4615 See SUMMA. 309

0325-4755 See REVISTA ARGENTINA DE MICOLOGIA : ORGANO DE DIFUSION DE LA SOCIEDAD ARGENTINA DE MICOLOGIA. 576

0325-4933 See ESCRITOS DE FILOSOFIA / C.ACADEMIA NACIONAL DE CIENCIAS, CENTRO DE ESTUDIOS FILOSOFICOS. 4346

0325-5298 See NOTICIERO - SOCIEDAD ARGENTINA DE INVESTIGACION OPERATIVA. 1989

0325-5476 See FIDE, COYUNTURA Y DESARROLLO. 1561

0325-5824 See DESARROLLO Y MODERNIZACION. 1555

0325-6081 See BOLETIN - ARCHIVO GENERAL DE LA PROVINCIA DE SANTA FE. 2723

0325-6251 See BIBLIOTECOLOGIA Y DOCUMENTACION. 3194

0325-6367 See CONTRIBUCIONES CIENTIFICAS DEL INSTITUTO ARGENTINO DE OCEANOGRAFIA. 1448

0325-6375 See REVISTA DE INVESTIGACION Y DESARROLLO PESQUERO. 2312

0325-6391 See REVISTA DE MEDICINA VETERINARIA. 5520

0325-6448 See SUMMARIOS. 309

0325-6901 See ATIPCA. ASOCIACION DE TECNICOS DE LA INDUSTRIA PAPELERA Y CELULOSICA ARGENTINA. 4232

0325-6928 See ESTUDIOS - INSTITUTO DE ESTUDIO ECONOMICOS SOBRE LA REALIDAD ARGENTINA Y LATINOAMERICANA. 1489

0325-6960 See NUEVAMERICA. 1769

0325-7487 See REVIEW OF THE RIVER PLATE, THE. 1581

0325-7541 See REVISTA ARGENTINA DE MICROBIOLOGIA. 569

0325-7592 See LIMNOBIOS. 555

0325-8106 See BOLETIN INFORMATIVO (ARGENTINA.) DEPARTAMENTO GENERAL DE IRRIGACION. 2087

0325-8203 See INTERDISCIPLINARIA. 4590

0325-8319 See BOLETIN GENETICO. ENGLISH EDITION. 543

0325-8483 See DOCUMENTO DE TRABAJO / INSTITUTO TORCUATO DI TELLA, CENTRO DE INVESTIGACIONES SOCIALES. **1663**

0325-8637 See LECTURA Y VIDA. **1900**

0325-8645 See BOLETIN INFORMATION - CEBIDE. **3558**

0325-8823 See ORIENTE-OCCIDENTE / INSTITUTO LATINOAMERICANO DE INVESTIGACIONES COMPARADAS SOBRE ORIENTE Y OCCIDENTE (ILICOD), UNIVERSIDAD DEL SALVADOR Y CONICET. **4984**

0325-8963 See NOTAS DE GEOMETRIA Y TOPOLOGIA / INMABB - CONICET. **3524**

0325-9161 See SITUACION COYUNTURAL DEL SECTOR AGROPECUARIO. **135**

0325-9226 See JOURNAL OF THE AMERICAN MEDICAL ASSOCIATION EN ARGENTINA. **3597**

0325-9250 See REVISTA DE LA FACULTAD DE AGRONOMIA / FACULTAD DE AGRONOMIA, UNIVERSIDAD DE BUENOS AIRES. **129**

0325-9471 See REVISTA DE LA FACULTAD DE DERECHO : PUBLICACION DE LA FACULTAD DE DERECHO DE LA UNIVERSIDAD NACIONAL DE ROSARIO. **3041**

0325-9587 See REVISTA DE LA UNIVERSIDAD NACIONAL DE RIO CUARTO. **5216**

0325-9684 See PARODIANA. **521**

0325-9757 See CUADERNOS DE ECONOMIA SOCIAL. **1478**

0325-9846 See REVISTA DE LOS CREA. **129**

0326-0550 See REVISTA ARGENTINA DE PRODUCCION ANIMAL. **5520**

0326-0674 See AMBIENTE MEDICO : REVISTA DEL HOSPITAL J.A. FERNANDEZ. **3775**

0326-0763 See REVISTA DEL DERECHO INDUSTRIAL. **3041**

0326-0941 See INCIPIT. **3395**

0326-1131 See AVANCE AGROINDUSTRIAL / EEAOC. **64**

0326-1301 See ANALISIS FILOSOFICO. **4340**

0326-1336 See NOTAS DE MATEMATICA DISCRETA. **3524**

0326-1352 See HISTORIA (BUENOS AIRES, ARGENTINA : 1981). **2736**

0326-1360 See AEROCOMERCIAL. **4**

0326-1441 See PHYSIS. SECCIONES A, B Y C. **5594**

0326-1484 See BOLETIN DEL MUSEO DE CIENCIAS NATURALES Y ANTROPOLOGICAS JUAN CORNELIO MOYANO. **262**

0326-1565 See PRECIO$ AGROPECUARIOS. **121**

0326-1638 See BIOLOGIA ACUATICA. **444**

0326-1956 See COMUNICACIONES BIOLOGICAS. **452**

0326-2383 See ACTA FARMACEUTICA BONAERENSE. **4288**

0326-2642 See INFORMACIONES (UNIVERSIDAD NACIONAL DE LA PLATA. BIBLIOTECA PUBLICA). **3215**

0326-2774 See PRUDENTIA IURIS. **3032**

0326-2928 See LETRAS DE BUENOS AIRES. **3404**

0326-3061 See PUNTO DE VISTA. **2552**

0326-3142 See MICROSCOPIA ELECTRONICA Y BIOLOGIA CELULAR : ORGANO OFICIAL DE LAS SOCIEDADES LATINOAMERICANA DE MICROSCOPIA ELECTRONICA E IBEROAMERICANA DE BIOLOGIA CELULAR. **573**

0326-3169 See CIENCIA DEL SUELO. **1353**

0326-3428 See REVISTA DE NEFROLOGIA, DIALISIS Y TRANSPLANTE : PUBLICACION CONJUNTA DE LA ASOCIACION REGIONAL DE DIALISIS Y TRASPLANTES RENALES DE CAPITAL FEDERAL Y PROVINCIA DE BUENOS AIRES Y LA SOCIEDAD ARGENTINA DE NEFROLOGIA. **3635**

0326-3789 See CIRPON, REVISTA DE INVESTIGACION. **5606**

0326-386X See IDEAS EN CIENCIAS SOCIALES / UNIVERSIDAD DE BELGRANO. **5202**

0326-3878 See IDEAS EN ARTE Y TECNOLOGIA / UNIVERSIDAD DE BELGRANO. **300**

0326-4068 See CONTRIBUCIONES : PUBLICACION TRIMESTRAL DEL CENTRO INTERDISCIPLINARIO DE ESTUDIOS SOBRE EL DESARROLLO LATINOAMERICANO. **1634**

0326-422X See AMBIENTE Y RECURSOS NATURALES : REVISTA DE DERECHO, POLITICA Y ADMINISTRACION. **3109**

0326-4629 See VETERINARIA ARGENTINA. **5523**

0326-4815 See ACTA ODONTOLOGICA LATINOAMERICANA. **1315**

0326-5412 See ANALES DE LA CATEDRA DE TISIONEUMONOLOGIA. **3948**

0326-5633 See CRISTIANISMO Y SOCIEDAD (BUENOS AIRES). **4951**

0326-6400 See REVISTA ARGENTINA DE LINGUISTICA. **3315**

0326-6427 See REVISTA ARGENTINA DE ESTUDIOS ESTRATEGICOS : R.A.E.E. **4055**

0326-6672 See ACTIVIDAD MINERA. **2132**

0326-6702 See SERVICIO DE INFORMACIONES RELIGIOSAS. **4996**

0326-7067 See REVISTA ORL. **3891**

0326-7458 See ESTUDIOS MIGRATORIOS LATINOAMERICANOS. **2732**

0326-7873 See REVISTA ARGENTINA NUCLEAR. **2158**

0326-7903 See MONOGRAFIAS - MUSEO ETNOGRAFICO MUNICIPAL "DAMASO ARCE". **241**

0326-8365 See INSTITUTO ARGENTINO DEL ENVASE. **4219**

0326-9671 See ANUARIO IEHS. **2721**

0327-0793 See LATIN AMERICAN APPLIED RESEARCH / PESQUISA APLICADA LATINO AMERICANA / INVESTIGACION APLICADA LATINOAMERICANA. **2014**

0327-0947 See CERAMICA MENDOZA. **2587**

0327-1676 See ANDES : ANTROPOLOGIA E HISTORIA. **2720**

0327-2265 See REVISTA DE DERECHO ADMINISTRATIVO. **3040**

0327-3210 See TERRITORIO PARA LA PRODUCCION Y CRITICA EN GEOGRAFIA Y CIENCIAS SOCIALES. **2577**

0327-4071 See FRENTE DE TORMENTA. **2734**

0327-4934 See ESTUDIOS SOCIALES SANTA FE. **5199**

0327-4950 See CUADERNO DE ACTUALIZACION TECNICA - ESTACION EXPERIMENTAL AGROPECUARIA MANFREDI. **77**

0327-5345 See COSTOS Y GESTION. **662**

0327-5426 See MONOGRAFIAS DE LA ACADEMIA NACIONAL DE CIENCIAS EXACTAS, FISICAS Y NATURALES. **5129**

0327-5477 See ECOLOGIA AUSTRAL. **2213**

0327-5752 See MEMORIA AMERICANA. **241**

0327-585X See ACTUALIDAD ECONOMICA : REVISTA BIMESTRAL DEL INSTITUTO DE ECONOMIA Y FINANZAS. **1460**

0327-6058 See ACTUALIZACION POLITICA. **4461**

0327-649X See ENTREPASADOS : REVISTA DE HISTORIA. **2732**

0327-6627 See PUBLICAR EN ANTROPOLOGIA Y CIENCIAS SOCIALES. **243**

0327-9022 See SUMMA+. **309**

0330-0005 See RESSOURCES EN EAU DE TUNISIE. **5539**

0330-2210 See CEDAC - CARTHAGE. **265**

0330-2601 See ECHANGES (FRANCE. AMBASSADE (TUNISIA). SERVICE CULTUREL). **2639**

0330-843X See REPPAL / CENTRE D'ETUDES PHENICIENNES-PUNIQUES ET DES ANTIQUITES LIBQUES. **280**

0330-8480 See REVUE TUNISIENNE DE COMMUNICATION. **1121**

0330-8596 See MUWASAFAT / AL-MAHAD AL-QAWMI LIL-MUWASAFAT WA-AL-MILKIYAH AL-SINAIYAH. **4031**

0330-9266 See MAGHREB, LE. **2641**

0331-0000 See NIGERBIBLIOS. **3236**

0331-0019 See NATIONAL BIBLIOGRAPHY OF NIGERIA, THE. **420**

0331-0086 See BARRISTER, THE. **2940**

0331-0094 See NIGERIAN JOURNAL OF ENTOMOLOGY. **5593**

0331-0124 See JOURNAL OF MEDICAL AND PHARMACEUTICAL MARKETING. **4311**

0331-0132 See LIBRARY SCIENTIST, THE. **3227**

0331-0175 See AFRICAN JOURNAL OF PSYCHIATRY, THE. **3919**

0331-0299 See DIRECTORY OF POST-PRIMARY INSTITUTIONS IN THE EAST-CENTRAL STATE OF NIGERIA. **1736**

0331-0353 See NIGERIA FORESTRY INFORMATION BULLETIN. **2389**

0331-0361 See PROCEEDINGS OF THE ANNUAL CONFERENCE OF THE NIGERIAN ECONOMIC SOCIETY. **1513**

0331-0434 See SUMMARY OF CURRENT INCOME TAX STATISTICS. **4701**

0331-0477 See STATISTICS OF EDUCATION IN LAGOS STATE. **1798**

0331-0485 See TOWN PLANNING MANUAL. **2837**

0331-0523 See SAVANNA. **1519**

0331-0531 See WEST AFRICAN JOURNAL OF MODERN LANGUAGES. **3333**

0331-054X See WEST AFRICAN JOURNAL OF SURGERY. **3977**

0331-0566 See OKIKE. **3420**

0331-0639 See DIRECTORIO INDUSTRIAL Y COMERCIAL DE HONDURAS. **1604**

0331-085X See CIVIL SERVANT, THE. **4702**

0331-0973 See NIGERIAN YELLOW PAGES : AN A TO Z TRADE DIRECTORY. **847**

0331-1422 See ODUMA. **327**

0331-1481 See NSUKKA LIBRARY NOTES. **3237**

0331-1619 See APPROVED ESTIMATES OF ANAMBRA STATE OF NIGERIA. **4711**

0331-2569 See SUNDAY TRIBUNE. **5807**

0331-3379 See SECOND ORDER. **4360**

0331-3468 See MUSE (NSUKKA). **3414**

0331-3646 See NIGERIAN JOURNAL OF INTERNATIONAL AFFAIRS. **4530**

0331-3751 See ANNUAL REPORT OF THE FORESTRY RESEARCH INSTITUTE OF NIGERIA FOR THE PERIOD **2375**

0331-4316 See NIGERIAN JOURNAL OF MEDICAL SCIENCES. **3622**

0331-4545 See KUKA. **3465**

0331-555X See BENDEL LIBRARY JOURNAL. **3194**

0331-670X See NIGERIAN JOURNAL OF PHARMACY. **4318**

0331-6742 See NOMA. **114**

0331-6793 See RESEARCH PAPER. FOREST SERIES. **2393**

0331-7285 See SAMARU: JOURNAL OF AGRICULTURE RESEARCH. **131**

0331-8168 See KIABARA. **2849**

0331-9113 See ABUH PHYSIO : THE JOURNAL OF THE PHYSIOTHERAPY DEPT. OF THE INSTITUTE OF HEALTH, AHMADU BELLO UNIVERSITY, ZARIA. **4378**

0332-0103 See IRELAND TODAY. **5481**

0332-0111 See IRISH BIRDS. **5617**

0332-0235 See GLASRA. **512**

0332-0251 See ECONOMICS AND RURAL WELFARE RESEARCH REPORT. **81**

0332-026X See BERKELEY NEWSLETTER. **4342**

0021-1249 See IRISH JOURNAL OF AGRICULTURAL AND FOOD RESEARCH. **97**

0332-0588 See JOURNAL - IRISH GRASSLAND AND ANIMAL PRODUCTION. **5512**

0332-0618 See SEARCH (DUBLIN). **4996**

0332-0707 See IRISH PHARMACY JOURNAL. **4309**

0332-0758 See ERIU. **3279**

0332-0782 See JOURNAL OF THE COUNTY KILDARE ARCHAEOLOGICAL SOCIETY. **272**

0332-0820 See NORTH MUNSTER ANTIQUARIAN JOURNAL. **1078**

0332-088X See OTHER CLARE. **2702**

0332-1118 See IBAR. **681**

0332-1126 See SCIENCE BUDGET. **5151**

0332-1150 See SCRIPTURE IN CHURCH. **4996**

0332-1169 *See* SAOTHAR. 1709

0332-1185 *See* BULLETIN - IRISH BIOGEOGRAPHICAL SOCIETY. 2557

0332-1428 *See* MILLTOWN STUDIES. 4977

0332-1460 *See* IRISH STUDIES IN INTERNATIONAL AFFAIRS. 4526

0332-1584 *See* BULLETIN / IRISH COUNCIL FOR CIVIL LIBERTIES. 4505

0332-1592 *See* PERITIA. 2702

0332-1649 *See* COMPEL. 2039

0332-1754 *See* MAGILL. 2519

0332-205X *See* TEANGA - IRISH ASSOCIATION FOR APPLIED LINGUISTICS. 3328

0332-2130 *See* IPU REVIEW. 4309

0332-2475 *See* AQUACULTURE TECHNICAL BULLETIN. 2296

0332-2483 *See* INSIDE IRELAND. 2518

0332-2653 *See* SINSEAR. 2324

0332-2688 *See* SEIRBHIS PHOIBLI : JOURNAL OF THE DEPARTMENT OF THE PUBLIC SERVICE. 4705

0332-270X *See* BEALOIDEAS. 2318

0332-284X *See* NEWSLETTER - IRISH MUSEUMS ASSOCIATION. 4094

0332-2947 *See* IRISH RUNNER. 4901

0332-298X *See* EIGSE CHEOL TIRE. 4160

0332-2998 *See* POETRY IRELAND REVIEW, THE. 3469

0332-3056 *See* WORLD OF IRISH NURSING. 3871

0332-3102 *See* IRISH MEDICAL JOURNAL. 3590

0332-3196 *See* ADVANCES IN NUMERICAL COMPUTATION SERIES. 3491

0332-3218 *See* PROFILES OF GENIUS SERIES. 5142

0332-3226 *See* PROCEEDINGS OF THE BAIL ... CONFERENCE. 5140

0332-3250 *See* DUBLIN UNIVERSITY LAW JOURNAL. 2964

0332-3285 *See* NEWSLETTER - SOCIETY OF IRISH PLANT PATHOLOGISTS. 520

0332-3315 *See* IRISH EDUCATIONAL STUDIES. 1755

0332-4095 *See* INTERNATIONAL CIVIL ENGINEERING ABSTRACTS. 2005

0332-4117 *See* CATHAIR NO MART. 2683

0332-415X *See* JOURNAL OF THE GALWAY ARCHAEOLOGICAL AND HISTORICAL SOCIETY. 272

0332-4214 *See* SCRIPTORES LATINI HIBERNIAE. 3434

0332-4273 *See* MOOREA : THE JOURNAL OF THE IRISH GARDEN PLANT SOCIETY. 2424

0332-4303 *See* IRISH ARCHIVES : JOURNAL OF THE IRISH SOCIETY FOR ARCHIVES. 2481

0332-4397 *See* OFFALY RESOURCES FOR ENVIRONMENTAL STUDIES / COUNTY OFFALY VOCATIONAL EDUCATION COMMITTEE. 2238

0332-4400 *See* HOTEL & CATERING REVIEW (BLACKROCK, DUBLIN). 2806

0332-4427 *See* PROCEEDINGS OF THE IRISH BIBLICAL ASSOCIATION. 5019

0332-4753 See IRISH JOURNAL OF EUROPEAN LAW. 2985

0332-4893 *See* IRISH ECONOMIC AND SOCIAL HISTORY. 2692

0332-5024 *See* STUDIA MUSICOLOGICA NORVEGICA. 4155

0332-5040 See VR & KLIMA. 1436

0332-5083 *See* FISKERIDIREKTORATETS SKRIFTER. SERIE ERNAERING. 2304

0332-5113 *See* RAPPORTER FRA GEOLOGISK INSTITUTT. 1393

0332-5148 *See* BALLADE : TIDSSKRIFT FOR NY MUSIKK. 4102

0332-5210 *See* EUROPEAN OFFSHORE PETROLEUM NEWSLETTER. 4256

0332-5334 *See* SCANDINAVIAN OIL-GAS MAGAZINE. 4277

0332-5415 *See* FOKUS PA FAMILIEN. 2280

0332-5423 *See* KAPITAL. 795

0332-5431 *See* LUTHERSK KIRKETIDENDE. 5063

0332-544X *See* NOROIL. 4266

0332-5482 *See* NORSK MUSIKKTIDSSKRIFT. 4142

0332-5490 *See* NORSK OLJEREVY. 4266

0332-5555 *See* OKONOMISK RAPPORT. 701

0332-5571 *See* REPORT SERIES / UNIVERSITY OF OSLO, DEPARTMENT OF PHYSICS. 4419

0332-5652 *See* NIPH ANNALS. 4794

0332-5709 See MEDDELELSER FRA SKOGFORSK / NORSK INSTITUTT FOR SKOGFORSKNING, INSTITUTT FOR SKOGFAG, NLH. 2387

0332-5741 *See* NORSK VETERINRTIDSSKIRFT 1970. 5517

0332-5768 *See* BULLETIN / NORGES GEOLOGISKE UNDERSKELSE. 1352

0332-5784 *See* DUGNAD. 235

0332-5865 *See* NORDIC JOURNAL OF LINGUISTICS. 3306

0332-5997 *See* TRADISJON. 2325

0332-6039 *See* SCANDINAVIAN JOURNAL OF MATERIALS ADMINISTRATION. 709

0332-608X *See* VIKING (OSLO). 2715

0332-6195 *See* TROMURA. NATURVITENSKAP. 4097

0332-6241 *See* AFRIKA INFORMASJON. 2637

0332-6330 *See* SOSIOLOGI I DAG. 5262

0332-6403 *See* MANEDSSTATISTIKK OVER UTENRIKSHANDELEN. 1536

0332-6470 *See* TIDSSKRIFT FOR NORSK PSYKOLOGFORENING. 4620

0332-7124 *See* ARBEIDERVERN. 2859

0332-7248 *See* JAZZNYTT. 4125

0332-7264 *See* NORSKLREREN. 3306

0332-7353 *See* MODELING, IDENTIFICATION AND CONTROL. 3523

0332-7531 *See* NORDLYD. 3306

0332-7647 *See* ARSBERETNING / TROMS MUSEUM. 4084

0332-768X *See* FAUNA NORVEGICA. SER. A., NORWEGIAN FAUNA EXCEPT ENTOMOLOGY AND ORNITHOLOGY. 5583

0332-7698 *See* FAUNA NORVEGICA. SER. B. 5608

0332-7701 *See* FAUNA NORVEGICA. SER. C., CINCLUS. 5583

0332-8422 *See* AKTUELLE SKATTETALL. 4708

0332-8988 *See* SAMFERDSEL (1979). 5392

0332-9666 *See* FRIIDRETT. 1091

0333-0370 *See* SPELEMANNSBLADET. 4154

0333-1024 *See* CEPHALALGIA. 3829

0333-1121 See FAGINFO. 83

0333-1342 *See* NORDISK SOSIALT ARBEID. 5299

0333-1504 *See* BANK- OG KREDITTSTATISTIKK: AKTUELLE TALL. 5323

0333-2241 See ICLAS NEWS. 5111

0333-256X *See* RANGIFER. 5596

0333-2802 *See* TROMURA. KULTURHISTOIRE : TROMS MUSEUMS RAPPORTSERIE. 2713

0333-2810 *See* SKATTERETT. 3055

0333-3280 *See* NORSK INSTITUTT FOR VANNFORSKNING. 5536

0333-3620 *See* IASP NEWSLETTER (INTERNATIONAL ASSOCIATION OF SCHOLARLY PUBLISHERS). 4815

0333-5275 *See* GEOGRAPHY RESEARCH FORUM. 2564

0333-533X *See* ENGLISH TEACHERS' JOURNAL (ISRAEL) / MINISTRY OF EDUCATION AND CULTURE, PEDAGOGICAL SECRETARIAT. 3279

0333-5372 *See* POETICS TODAY. 3424

0333-5925 *See* ISRAEL YEARBOOK OF HUMAN RIGHTS. 4510

0333-6298 *See* BWR TWRH. 5046

0333-6379 See KIBBUTZ TRENDS. 4542

0333-6425 *See* CURRENT RESEARCH (MAKHON HA-GEOLOGI (ISRAEL)). 1373

0333-6476 *See* ASSAPH. SECTION B. STUDIES IN ART HISTORY. 343

0333-693X *See* MEHKERE YERUSHALAYIM BE-SIFRUT IVRIT / HA-UNIVERSITAH HA-IVRIT BI-YERUSHALAYIM, HA-FAKULTAH LE-MADAE HA-RUAH, HA-MAKHON LE-MADAE HA-YAHADUT. 3410

0333-7030 *See* MEHKERE YERUSHALAYIM BE-FOLKLOR YEHUDI / HA-UNIVERSITAH HA-IVRIT BI-YERUSHALAYIM, HA-FAKULTAH LE-MADAE HA-RUAH, HA-MAKHON LE-MADAE HA-YAHADUT. 2322

0333-7081 *See* MEHKERE YERUSHALAYIM BE-MAHASHEVET YISRAEL / HA-UNIVERSITAH HA-IVRIT BI-YERUSHALAYIM, HA-FAKULTAH LE-MADAE HA-RUAH, HA-MAKHON LE-MADAE HA-YAHADUT. 5051

0333-7308 *See* ISRAEL JOURNAL OF PSYCHIATRY AND RELATED SCIENCES, THE. 3927

0333-7499 *See* ISRAEL MUSEUM JOURNAL, THE. 4089

0333-8347 *See* JEWISH LANGUAGE REVIEW. 3289

0333-838X *See* MAHUT. 3409

0333-8886 *See* ALON HA-NOTEA. 162

0333-9661 *See* STUDIES IN JEWISH EDUCATION / THE HEBREW UNIVERSITY OF JERUSALEM, THE MELTON CENTRE FOR JEWISH EDUCATION IN THE DIASPORA. 1786

0333-9858 *See* CURRENT CONTENTS OF PERIODICALS ON THE MIDDLE EAST. 2650

0334-0082 *See* INTERNATIONAL JOURNAL OF TURBO & JET-ENGINES. 24

0334-018X *See* JOURNAL OF PEDIATRIC ENDOCRINOLOGY, THE. 3905

0334-0236 *See* JOURNAL OF ORTHOPAEDIC SURGICAL TECHNIQUES, THE. 3882

0334-1046 *See* SPECTRUM (TEL AVIV, ISRAEL). 1711

0334-1607 *See* EXCAVATIONS AND SURVEYS IN ISRAEL. 268

0334-1763 *See* REVIEWS IN THE NEUROSCIENCES. 3845

0334-1771 *See* STUDIES IN ZIONISM. 5053

0334-1860 *See* JOURNAL OF INTELLIGENT SYSTEMS. 1214

0334-2123 *See* PHYTOPARASITICA. 522

0334-2212 *See* KIDMA. 1571

0334-2336 *See* DAAT. 5047

0334-2484 *See* SPECIAL PUBLICATION - AGRICULTURAL RESEARCH ORGANIZATION, THE VOLCANI CENTER. 137

0334-2484 *See* SPECIAL PUBLICATION - AGRICULTURAL RESEARCH ORGANIZATION. 137

0334-2603 *See* ISRAEL PHARMACEUTICAL JOURNAL. 4309

0334-2700 *See* JOURNAL OF THE AUSTRALIAN MATHEMATICAL SOCIETY. SERIES B : APPLIED MATHEMATICS, THE. 3515

0334-276X *See* SIFRUT YELADIM VA-NOAR. 1069

0334-2824 *See* DIRECTORY OF SCIENTIFIC & TECHNICAL ASSOCIATIONS IN ISRAEL. 5100

0334-3049 *See* INTERNATIONAL JOURNAL OF MEDICINE AND LAW. 3741

0334-309X *See* BIBLIOGRAPHY OF MODERN HEBREW LITERATURE IN TRANSLATION / BY ISAAC GOLDBERG. 3366

0334-3332 *See* YOMAN HA-PATENTIM VEHA-MIDGAMIN. 1310

0334-3650 *See* TARBIZS. 5053

0334-3804 *See* ISRAEL ENVIRONMENT BULLETIN. 2175

0334-3847 *See* INNOVATION. 5114

0334-3871 *See* ASSIA, JEWISH MEDICAL ETHICS. 3553

0334-4053 *See* YEDDA IAM. 2325

0334-4118 *See* JERUSALEM STUDIES IN ARABIC AND ISLAM. 2769

0334-4142 *See* COMMONWEALTH OF INDEPENDENT STATES AND THE MIDDLE EAST. 4518

0334-4258 *See* GALED. 2261

0334-4266 *See* MODERN HEBREW LITERATURE. 3412

0334-4355 *See* TEL AVIV (1974). 284

0334-441X See ECONOMIC REVIEW (JERUSALEM). 1485
0334-4436 See EVREI I EVREISKII NAROD. MATERIALY IZ SOVETSKOI PECHATI. 5047
0334-4509 See SCRIPTA CLASSICA ISRAELICA. 3320
0334-4525 See BRYNWT WSTYH HBRTYT. 5275
0334-472X See KIYWWNIYM. 5050
0334-4762 See RIV'ON LE-MEHKAR HEVRATI. 5217
0334-4916 See ARIEL : KETAV ET LI-YEDIAT ERETS-YISRAEL. 2611
0334-5114 See SYMBIOSIS (PHILADELPHIA, PA.). 474
0334-5734 See SOVIET ARMY : A DIGEST FROM THE SOVIET PRESS, THE. 4057
0334-5963 See ASSAPH. SECTION C. STUDIES IN THE THEATRE. 5361
0334-6056 See ICA INFORMATION. 4655
0334-6447 See JOURNAL OF POLYMER ENGINEERING. 2104
0334-6455 See HIGH TEMPERATURE MATERIALS AND PROCESSES. 4404
0334-6838 See MAZAL U'BRACHA. 1618
0334-6994 See KABBALAH. 4242
0334-701X See JEWISH HISTORY. 5049
0334-7311 See MICHMANIM / MIKHMANIM. 274
0334-7575 See MAIN GROUP METAL CHEMISTRY. 4008
0334-8938 See JOURNAL OF THE MECHANICAL BEHAVIOR OF MATERIALS. 2119
0334-9152 See ISRAEL JOURNAL OF VETERINARY MEDICINE. 5512
0334-973X See BE'EMET?!. 1060
0334-9977 See JOURNAL OF SOCIAL WORK AND POLICY IN ISRAEL. 5293
0335-0266 See BULLETIN BIBLIOGRAPHIQUE. 411
0335-1688 See CAHIERS DE LA TERRE CUITE, LES. 2587
0335-1793 See LIBERATION PARIS. 1973. 2849
0335-1971 See NUMISMATIQUE ET CHANGE REVIGNY-SUR-ORNAIN. 2782
0335-2013 See RELATIONS INTERNATIONALES. 4533
0335-2811 See PISCICULTEUR DE FRANCE. 2310
0335-2927 See THEATRE/PUBLIC. 5371
0335-3400 See ACTUALITES ECONOMIQUES DE LA REUNION. 1460
0335-3710 See BULLETIN TECHNIQUE APICOLE. 5580
0335-377X See PULP AND PAPER. 4237
0335-4024 See NOTES DE CONJONCTURE (FRANCE. DIRECTION DEPARTEMENTALE DE L'AGRICULTURE DE LA REUNION. SERVICE DE STATISTIQUE AGRICOLE). 115
0335-4997 See POINT VETERINAIRE, LE. 5518
0335-5004 See REVUE GENERAL NUCLEAIRE. 1956
0335-5047 See DROIT ET PRATIQUE DU COMMERCE INTERNATIONAL. 831
0335-508X See BULLETIN DES ETUDES VALERYENNES. 3369
0335-5233 See ARCHEOLOGIE ET BRETAGNE. 259
0335-5306 See COEUR ET SANTE PARIS. 3567
0335-5322 See ACTES DE LA RECHERCHE EN SCIENCES SOCIALES. 5189
0335-5330 See DOCUMENTS DE CARTOGRAPHIE ECOLOGIQUE. 2213
0335-5985 See ARCHIVES DE SCIENCES SOCIALES DES RELIGIONS. 4935
0335-6456 See CALAO. 1060
0335-6566 See MINERAUX ET FOSSILES, LE GUIDE DU COLLECTIONNEUR. 1358
0335-7198 See MIGRATIONS SANTE. 4791
0335-7414 See BULLETIN BIBLIOGRAPHIQUE. 4809
0335-7457 See REVUE FRANCAISE D'ALLERGOLOGIE ET D'IMMUNOLOGIE CLINIQUE. 3676
0335-7473 See COLLECTION D'ECOLOGIE. 2212

0335-752X See NOUVELLES DU LIVRE ANCIEN. 4831
0335-9255 See SCIENCES DE LA TERRE. INFORMATIQUE GEOLOGIQUE. 1396
0335-9581 See JOURNAL FRANCAIS D'HYDROLOGIE. 1415
0336-0067 See QUOTIDIEN DU MEDECIN. 5801
0336-1446 See ESPACES PARIS. 1970. 5469
0336-1454 See ECONOMIE ET STATISTIQUE. 1532
0336-1489 See DEFENSE NATIONALE. 4041
0336-1500 See COMMUNICATION ET LANGAGES PARIS. 3274
0336-1519 See BULLETIN DE L'ECOLE FRANCAISE D'EXTREME-ORIENT. 2647
0336-1551 See PENANT. 3025
0336-156X See REVUE DES ETUDES ISLAMIQUES. 5044
0336-1578 See REVUE DES SCIENCES SOCIALES DE LA FRANCE DE L'EST. 5217
0336-1837 See PETROLOGIE. 1459
0336-2086 See AGECOP LIAISON. 5238
0336-3791 See INFORMATIONS STATISTIQUES RAPIDES (INSTITUT NATIONAL DE LA STATISTIQUE ET DES ETUDES ECONOMIQUES (FRANCE)). 5329
0336-4410 See IVF, INGENIEURS DES VILLES DE FRANCE. 1981
0336-4933 See LITHOCLASTIA. 619
0336-5042 See CAHIERS DU C.R.E.S.M, LES. 2682
0336-5654 See LITTERATURE ORALE ARABO-BERBERE. 3408
0336-5913 See CAHIERS DE SEXOLOGIE CLINIQUE. 5187
0336-626X See AEROPORTS MAGAZINE. 5
0336-7274 See CREATIONS TISSUS. 1083
0336-7290 2630
0336-8106 See D.S (DICTIONNAIRE DE SPIRITUALITE). 5028
0336-9331 See FICHES DU CINEMA. 4069
0336-9730 See TRAVERSES. 367
0336-9811 See ENERGIE FLUIDE, L'AIR INDUSTRIEL. 1938
0337-0267 See BULLETIN DE LA SOCIETE DE BORDA. 2680
0337-1603 See ARTS D'AFRIQUE NOIRE. 314
0337-1891 See HIFI STEREO, VIDEO. 4121
0337-2693 See JOURNAL RPF. 2606
0337-2723 See INFORMATION SCIENTIFIQUE DU BIOLOGISTE, L'. 458
0337-3029 See PARFUMS, COSMETIQUES, AROMES. 405
0337-307X See FUTURIBLES (PARIS). 5246
0337-3126 See CONNEXIONS (PARIS). 4582
0337-4084 See DOSSIERS DE L'OUTRE-MER : BULLETIN D'INFORMATION DU CENADDOM, LES. 1556
0337-4971 See ANNUAIRE DU PAPIER, L'. 4232
0337-579X See BULLETIN DE LA SOCIETE ARCHEOLOGIQUE ET HISTORIQUE DE L'ORLEANAIS 1959. 263
0337-6176 See CAHIERS DU CENTRE UNIVERSITAIRE DE LA REUNION. 3272
0337-6338 See QUEL CORPS?. 1776
0337-6591 See PROVENCE GENEALOGIQUE PORT-DE-BOUC. 2468
0337-7091 See REGARDS SUR L'ACTUALITE. 4679
0337-7113 See BULLETIN DES AMIS DES MONUMENTS ROUENNAIS. 2681
0337-730X See REVUE FRANCAISE DU DOMMAGE CORPOREL. 2892
0337-8810 See CUISINE ET VINS DE FRANCE (1975). 2366
0337-9213 See MONDE DE L'EDUCATION, LE. 1900
0337-9515 See AFRIQUE AGRICULTURE. 45
0337-9566 See ACTUEL CIDJ. 2484
0337-9736 See REVUE D'ORTHOPEDIE DENTO-FACIALE. 1334

0338-0548 See BULLETIN D'INFORMATIONS PROUSTIENNES. 3339
0338-0599 See REVUE D'ETUDES COMPARATIVES EST-OUEST. 4546
0338-1439 See CAHIERS MEDICAUX. 3561
0338-1684 See DIABETE & METABOLISME. 3727
0338-1900 See OEUVRES ET CRITIQUES. 3349
0338-2052 See SIGNES D'AUJOURD'HUI PARIS. 5036
0338-2060 See REVUE FRANCAISE D'ETUDES POLITIQUES MEDITERRANEENNES. 2706
0338-2338 See PERSPECTIVES MEDIEVALES. 3423
0338-2389 See PRATIQUES. 3311
0338-2397 See PSYCHANALYSE A L'UNIVERSITE. 4609
0338-361X See ETUDES CORSES. 2846
0338-3849 See CAHIERS D'ENSEIGNEMENT DE LA SOFCOT. 3561
0338-4454 See DOCUMENTS D'ACTUALITE INTERNATIONALE. 1634
0338-4551 See REVUE FRANCAISE DE GESTION. 885
0338-4659 See PAYS SEDANAIS, LE. 2702
0338-487X See HERODOTE. 2565
0338-5019 See LIRE. 3405
0338-5256 See REVUE DE LA SOCIETE D'HISTOIRE ET D'ART DE LA BRIE ET DU PAYS DE MEAUX. 2706
0338-7208 See CAHIERS BLEUS. 3370
0338-8190 See INCONNU PARIS, L'. 5074
0338-8999 See ACTUALITES DE CHIMIE THERAPEUTIQUE. 4289
0338-9375 See ANNALES DE PSYCHOTHERAPIE. 3920
0338-9405 See BULLETIN D'AUDIOPHONOLOGIE BESANCON. 5316
0338-9987 See REVUE CHIBRET D'OPHTALMOLOGIE. 3879
0339-0055 See PRESENCE DE L'ENSEIGNEMENT AGRICOLE PRIVE. 121
0339-0195 See BULLETIN DE LA SOCIETE DES AMIS DU CHATEAU DE PAU. 2680
0339-3097 See CAHIERS DE L'ANALYSE DES DONNEES, LES. 5324
0339-3437 See CAHIERS D'ECONOMIE POLITIQUE. 4466
0339-4409 See AGRA ALIMENTATION. 45
0339-5456 See EDUCATION COMPAREE. 1739
0339-6045 See INFORMATIONS CHIMIE HEBDO. 978
0339-6517 See DOCUMENTS POUR LE MEDECIN DU TRAVAIL. 2861
0339-7041 See PUBLICATIONS ECONOMETRIQUES. 3529
0339-7203 See MONITOIRES DU CYMBALUM PATAPHYSICUM. 4353
0339-722X See S.T.A.L. 5521
0339-7513 See EDUCATION PERMANENTE. 1800
0339-7521 See REVUE DU PALAIS DE LA DECOUVERTE. 5148
0339-7858 See ACTUALITE POLICIERE 1975, L'. 3156
0339-7890 See ARCHEONUMIS. 259
0339-8854 See A.D.P.H.S.O. 3775
0339-9354 See CAHIERS D'HERALDIQUE. 2441
0339-9486 See TELECOM INFO. 1164
0339-9710 See BULLETIN DE L'ACADEMIE NATIONALE DE CHIRURGIE DENTAIRE. 3961
0340-000X See BIBLIOTHEKSFORUM BAYERN. 3195
0340-0034 See COMMUNICATION AND CYBERNETICS. 1250
0340-0050 See INTERNATIONAL CLASSIFICATION. 3218
0340-0107 See ZEITUNGS-INDEX. 5802
0340-0131 See INTERNATIONAL ARCHIVES OF OCCUPATIONAL AND ENVIRONMENTAL HEALTH. 2864
0340-014X See NORTH KOREA QUARTERLY. 4484

0340-0174 See ZEITSCHRIFT FUER HISTORISCHE FORSCHUNG. 2634
0340-0204 See JOURNAL OF NON-EQUILIBRIUM THERMODYNAMICS. 4431
0340-0220 See EXAKT. 5104
0340-0255 See FRIEDENSWARTE, DIE. 3128
0340-0271 See BAUANALYSIS. 600
0340-0301 See BUCH UND BIBLIOTHEK. 3197
0340-0352 See IFLA JOURNAL. 3214
0340-0409 See BIBLIOGRAPHIA CARTOGRAPHICA. 2580
0340-0425 See LEVIATHAN (DUSSELDORF). 5208
0340-0441 See SCALA DEUTSCHE AUSGABE. 2522
0340-0476 See MATERIALIEN ZUR POLITISCHEN BILDUNG. 4481
0340-0603 See EPITAPH. 3384
0340-0727 See PSYCHOLOGICAL RESEARCH. 4611
0340-0743 See IFF BULLETIN. 4428
0340-076X See EUROPEAN JOURNAL OF CLINICAL CHEMISTRY AND CLINICAL BIOCHEMISTRY. 487
0340-0778 See STEREO. 5319
0340-0824 See ZEITSCHRIFT FUER ARCHAEOLOGIE DES MITTELALTERS. 286
0340-0840 See FUNKTIONSANALYSE BIOLOGISCHER SYSTEME. 456
0340-0921 See FRONTAL (MARBURG). 1825
0340-0948 See INTERNATIONAL HOTEL TELEX. 2807
0340-1022 See TOPICS IN CURRENT CHEMISTRY. 994
0340-1073 See NEW CONCEPTS. 1056
0340-1162 See IMMUNITAT UND INFEKTION. 3670
0340-1200 See BIOLOGICAL CYBERNETICS. 1250
0340-1219 See RUNDSCHAU FUER FLEISCHBESCHAUER, TRICHINENSCHAUER UND GEFLUGELFLEISCHKONTROLLEURE. 4800
0340-1294 See BERGWELT. 4869
0340-1650 See WIST. WIRTSCHAFTSWISSENSCHAFTLICHES STUDIUM. 1596
0340-1707 See VIERTELJAHRSHEFTE ZUR WIRTSCHAFTSFORSCHUNG. 815
0340-174X See SUDOSTEUROPA-MITTEILUNGEN. 2712
0340-1758 See ZEITSCHRIFT FUER PARLAMENTSFRAGEN. 4695
0340-1766 See FREIE ZAHNARZT, DER. 1323
0340-1774 See INFORMATIONEN ZUR MODERNEN STADTGESCHICHTE : IMS. 2825
0340-1790 See AMTSBLATT DES BAYERISCHEN STAATSMINISTERIUMS FUER ARBEIT UND SOZIALORDNUNG. 3144
0340-1804 See ZEITSCHRIFT FUER SOZIOLOGIE. 5265
0340-1812 See MONATSSCHRIFT FUER DEUTSCHES RECHT. 3011
0340-1855 See ZEITSCHRIFT FUER RHEUMATOLOGIE. 3807
0340-1898 See DEUTSCHES TIERARZTEBLATT. 5508
0340-1960 See CURRENT TOPICS IN NUTRITIONAL SCIENCES. 4189
0340-2061 See ANATOMY AND EMBRYOLOGY. 3678
0340-2096 See ANATOMIA, HISTOLOGIA, EMBRYOLOGIA. 5502
0340-2207 See FREMDSPRACHLICHE UNTERRICHT, DER. 3282
0340-2215 See STUDIEN ZUR ALTAGYPTISCHEN KULTUR. 283
0340-2258 See DEUTSCHUNTERRICHT (STUTTGART). 3276
0340-2398 See ZEITSCHRIFT FUER BEVOELKERUNGSWISSENSCHAFT. 4561
0340-241X See VEROEFFENTLICHUNGEN AUS DER PATHOLOGIE. 3898
0340-2444 See ZEITSCHRIFT FUER ARBEITSWISSENSCHAFT. 1720

0340-2541 See AKTUELLE DERMATOLOGIE. 3717
0340-255X See PROGRESS IN COLLOID & POLYMER SCIENCE. 1056
0340-2592 See UROLOGE. AUSG. A, DER. 3993
0340-2649 See UNFALLCHIRURGIE. 3977
0340-269X See PHYTOCOENOLOGIA. 522
0340-2797 See NATURAL RESOURCES AND DEVELOPMENT. 2199
0340-2827 See AMERIKASTUDIEN. 2720
0340-2843 See PLANT RESEARCH AND DEVELOPMENT. 524
0340-2967 See F+I-BAU. 615
0340-3017 See ZAHNARZTEBLATT BADEN-WURTTEMBERG. 1337
0340-305X See PHLEBOLOGIE UND PROKTOLOGIE. 3800
0340-3068 See IBERO-AMERIKANISCHES ARCHIV. 2738
0340-3084 See WISU. DAS WIRTSCHAFTSSTUDIUM. 1854
0340-3130 See AKUPUNKTUR / DEUTSCHE ARZTEGESELLSCHAFT FUER AKUPUNKTUR E.V. ... [ET AL.]. 3547
0340-3157 See EUROPEAN JOURNAL OF PHARMACEUTICS AND BIOPHARMACEUTICS : OFFICIAL JOURNAL OF ARBEITSGEMEINSCHAFT FUER PHARMAZEUTISCHE VERFAHRENSTECHNIK E.V. 4303
0340-3165 See ANIMAL RESEARCH AND DEVELOPMENT. 5575
0340-3238 See DOKUMENTATION ARBEITSMEDIZIN. 3796
0340-3254 See MITTEILUNGEN AUS DER ARBEITSMARKT- UND BERUFSFORSCHUNG. 1691
0340-3297 See DOKUMENTATION OSTMITTELEUROPA. 2685
0340-3335 See CHED, CHEMIE EXPERIMENT + DIDAKTIK. 967
0340-3343 See CHEMIEFASERN, TEXTILINDUSTRIE. 5348
0340-3386 See 3 R, ROHRE, ROHRLEITUNGSBAU, ROHRLEITUNGSTRANSPORT. 2096
0340-3416 See DEUTSCHE NATIONALBIBLIOGRAPHIE UND BIBLIOGRAPHIE DER IM AUSLAND ERSCHIENENEN DEUTSCHSPRACHIGEN VEROFFENTLICHUNGEN. REIHE N, VORANKUNDIGUNGEN MONOGRAPHIEN UND PERIODIKA (CIP). WOCHENTLICHES VERZEICHNIS / BEARBEITER UND HERAUSGEBER, DIE DEUTSCHE BIBLIOTHEK. 414
0340-3505 See BADEN-WURTTEMBERGISCHE VERWALTUNGSPRAXIS. 4632
0340-3521 See ELEKTROWARME INTERNATIONAL. EDITION B : INDUSTRIELLE ELEKTROWARME. 2605
0340-3572 See FERNWAERME INTERNATIONAL. 2605
0340-3696 See ARCHIVES OF DERMATOLOGICAL RESEARCH. 3717
0340-3750 See BERICHT - NATURFORSCHENDE GESELLSCHAFT BAMBERG. 2188
0340-3858 See DGS, DEUTSCHE GEFLUGELWIRTSCHAFT UND SCHWEINEPRODUKTION. 210
0340-3955 See REGELUNGSTECHNIK (DUSSELDORF, GERMANY). 2127
0340-4099 See UNTERRICHTSWISSENSCHAFT. 1789
0340-4137 See MANAGEMENT-WISSEN. 878
0340-4277 See BEITRAEGE ZUR NATURKUNDE NIEDERSACHSENS. 4162
0340-4285 See TRANSITION METAL CHEMISTRY. 4022
0340-4358 See MITTEILUNGEN DER MATHEMATISCHEN GESELLSCHAFT IN HAMBURG. 3523
0340-4528 See INTERNATIONALES ARCHIV FUER SOZIALGESCHICHTE DER DEUTSCHEN LITERATUR. 3397
0340-4536 See V+T. VERKEHR UND TECHNIK. 5399

0340-4544 See WT. WERKSTATTSTECHNIK. 2132
0340-4560 See ZEITSCHRIFT FUER VERMESSUNGSWESEN. ZFV. 2034
0340-4641 See QUINTESSENZ DER ZAHNTECHNIK, DIE. 1334
0340-4749 See REFERATEORGAN SCHWEISSEN UND VERWANDTE VERFAHREN. 4027
0340-4773 See PROGRESS IN BOTANY. 525
0340-4803 See STAHL UND EISEN. 4020
0340-4838 See JAHRBUCH DER HAFENBAUTECHNISCHEN GESELLSCHAFT. 2091
0340-4900 See LITERATURBERICHTE UEBER WASSER, ABWASSER, LUFT UND FESTE ABFALLSTOFFE. 2235
0340-4927 See TELMA. 189
0340-4943 See MITTEILUNGEN DER MUNCHNER ENTOMOLOGISCHEN GESELLSCHAFT. 5591
0340-5060 See TECHNISCHE BERICHTE - THYSSEN. 4021
0340-5079 See TIEFBAU, INGENIEURBAU, STRASSENBAU. 2032
0340-5109 See ZENTRALBLATT FUER GEOLOGIE UND PALAEONTOLOGIE. TEIL 1: ALLGEMEINE, ANGEWANDTE, REGIONALE UND HISTORISCHE GEOLOGIE. 1401
0340-5141 See VR. VERMESSUNGSWESEN UND RAUMORDNUNG. 2579
0340-5214 See ZENTRALBLATT HALS- NASEN- OHRENHEILKUNDE, PLASTISCHE CHIRURGIE AN KOPF UND HALS. 3978
0340-529X See BESCHAFTIGUNGSTHERAPIE UND REHABILITATION. 1875
0340-5303 See SCHWESTER. DER PFLEGER, DIE. 3639
0340-5354 See JOURNAL OF NEUROLOGY. 3836
0340-5370 See BFUP. BETRIEBSWIRTSCHAFTLICHE FORSCHUNG UND PRAXIS. 861
0340-5389 See ELECTROMEDICA. DEUTSCHE AUSGABE. 3941
0340-5400 See RESEARCH IN MOLECULAR BIOLOGY. 471
0340-5435 See BUCHREIHE DER ANGLIA. 3369
0340-5443 See BEHAVIORAL ECOLOGY AND SOCIOBIOLOGY. 2212
0340-5478 See ZAHNARTZLICHER GESUNDHEITSDIENST. 1337
0340-5591 See ORTHOPAEDIE-TECHNIK. 3884
0340-5613 See ZEITSCHRIFT FUER PSYCHOSOMATISCHE MEDIZIN UND PSYCHOANALYSE. 3653
0340-5680 See DIAGNOSTIK. 3571
0340-5737 See MASCHINE, DIE. 2121
0340-5761 See ARCHIVES OF TOXICOLOGY. 3979
0340-5788 See AFRIKA. ENGLISH EDITION. 4515
0340-5877 See KINDERARZT, DER. 3602
0340-594X See STUDIEN ZUR GERMANISTIK, ANGLISTIK UND KOMPARATISTIK. 3325
0340-6067 See GAS AKTUELL. 4257
0340-6075 See VIRCHOWS ARCHIV. B, CELL PATHOLOGY. 3898
0340-6083 See GOTTINGER PREDIGTMEDITATIONEN. 4961
0340-6091 See FROHE BOTSCHAFT GOTTINGEN. 4960
0340-613X See GESCHICHTE UND GESELLSCHAFT (GOTTINGEN). 5201
0340-6199 See EUROPEAN JOURNAL OF PEDIATRICS. 3903
0340-6210 See LUTHER. 5062
0340-6245 See THROMBOSIS AND HAEMOSTASIS. 3801
0340-6253 See MATCH (MULHEIM). 985
0340-627X See ENCHORIA. 3278
0340-6318 See WOLFENBUTTELER BAROCK-NACHRICHTEN. 3454
0340-6369 See GIORGIO LEVI DELLA VIDA CONFERENCES. 2639
0340-6407 See ORIENS CHRISTIANUS. 5039

0340-644X See SAARLANDISCHES ARZTEBLATT. 3638

0340-6636 See GESCHAFTSBERICHT DER INDUSTRIEGEWERKSCHAFT BAU, STEINE, ERDEN FUER DIE BUNDESREPUBLIK DEUTSCHLAND. 1607

0340-6644 See FOTOWIRTSCHAFT, DIE. 4369

0340-6660 See FOTOMAGAZIN. 4369

0340-6660 See FOTO MAGAZIN. 4369

0340-6717 See HUMAN GENETICS. 547

0340-6849 See HOLDERLIN-JAHRBUCH. 3394

0340-6989 See KIELER STUDIEN. 1571

0340-6997 See EUROPEAN JOURNAL OF NUCLEAR MEDICINE. 3848

0340-7004 See CANCER IMMUNOLOGY AND IMMUNOTHERAPY. 3811

0340-7098 See MITTEILUNGEN DES SONDERFORSCHUNGSBEREICHS 79 FUER WASSERFORSCHUNG IM KUSTENBEREICH DER TECHNISCHEN UNIVERSITAT HANNOVER. 1452

0340-7268 See GESAMTSCHUL-INFORMATIONEN. 1748

0340-7330 See ANZEIGER FUER SCHADLINGSKUNDE, PFLANZENSCHUTZ, UMWELTSCHUTZ. 4244

0340-7349 See PUBLIC INTERNATIONAL LAW. 3134

0340-7403 See KRITISCHE BERICHTE. 355

0340-7551 See AMTS- UND MITTEILUNGSBLATT / BAM, BUNDESANSTALT FUER MATERIALFORSCHUNG UND -PRUFUNG. 1964

0340-7594 See JOURNAL OF COMPARATIVE PHYSIOLOGY. A, SENSORY, NEURAL, AND BEHAVIORAL PHYSIOLOGY. 582

0340-7608 See FORSCHUNGSBERICHT - BUNDESMINISTERIUM FUER FORSCHUNG UND TECHNOLOGIE. T, TECHNOLOGISCHE FORSCHUNG UND ENTWICKLUNG. 5105

0340-7705 See FORUM WARE. 2194

0340-7705 See FORUM WARE. 677

0340-7810 See VDL NACHRICHTEN. 144

0340-7918 See BETRIEBS-BERATER. 4713

0340-7926 See RECHT DER INTERNATIONALEN WIRTSCHAFT. 3035

0340-8019 See BRANDSCHUTZ (AUSGABE RHEINLAND-PFALZ). 4769

0340-8043 See FACHBERICHTE HUTTENPRAXIS METALLWEITERVERARBEITUNG. 4001

0340-8159 See ZEITSCHRIFT FUER PFLANZENKRANKHEITEN UND PFLANZENSCHUTZ (1970). 531

0340-8183 See MMG, MEDIZIN, MENSCH, GESELLSCHAFT. 3617

0340-8302 See FORTSCHRITTLICHE BETRIEBSEHRUNG UND INDUSTRIAL ENGINEERING. 2098

0340-8329 See ZEITSCHRIFT FUER LUFT- UND WELTRAUMRECHT. 3078

0340-8361 See ZEITSCHRIFTENINHALTSDIENST THEOLOGIE. 5011

0340-840X See AGRARRECHT. 2928

0340-8434 See ARBEIT UND SOZIALPOLITIK. 1651

0340-8485 See ZEITSCHRIFT FUER DAS GESAMTE KREDITWESEN. 817

0340-8515 See PHYSIK UND DIDAKTIK. 1902

0340-8590 See DEMOKRATIE UND RECHT (KOLN). 2959

0340-8655 See INSTRUMENT UND FORSCHUNG. 5114

0340-8779 See ENTSCHEIDUNGEN DER OBERVERWALTUNGSGERICHTE FUER DAS LAND NORDRHEIN-WESTFALEN IN MUENSTER SOWIE FUER DIE LANDER NIEDERSACHSEN UND SCHLESWIG-HOLSTEIN IN LUENEBURG. 2966

0340-8825 See MANUSCRIPTA GEODAETICA. 1408

0340-8914 See MAX-PLANCK-INSTITUT FUER PLASMAPHYSIK GARCHING BEI MUNCHEN. 4412

0340-9007 See FINANZ-RUNDSCHAU. 4726

0340-9023 See STUDIEN ZUR LITERATUR DER MODERNE. 3441

0340-918X See SOZIOLOGIE. 5263

0340-9341 See DEUTSCHE SPRACHE. 3276

0340-9422 See ZOR, ZEITSCHRIFT FUER OPERATIONS RESEARCH : METHODS AND MODELS OF OPERATIONS RESEARCH. 3542

0340-9422 See ZOR. ZEITSCHRIFT FUER OPERATIONS-RESEARCH. 5173

0340-9783 See HOHENHEIMER ARBEITEN. 92

0340-9937 See HERZ. 3705

0340-9961 See CHEMIE-TECHNIK. 2010

0341-0099 See BEITRAEGE ZUR GESCHICHTE DER PHARMAZIE. 4293

0341-0102 See UNIVERSITAS. 367

0341-0110 See APOTHEKER UND KUNST. 4292

0341-0129 See UNIVERSITAS. ENGLISH LANGUAGE EDITION (STUTTGART). 2856

0341-0137 See ZEITSCHRIFT DER DEUTSCHEN MORGENLANDISCHEN GESELLSCHAFT. 3335

0341-0145 See STUTTGARTER BEITRAEGE ZUR NATURKUNDE. SERIE A, BIOLOGIE. 474

0341-0153 See STUTTGARTER BEITRAEGE ZUR NATURKUNDE. SERIE B. GEOLOGIE UND PALAONTOLOGIE. 1399

0341-0161 See STUTTGARTER BEITRAEGE ZUR NATURKUNDE. SERIES C. ALLGEMEINVERSTAENDLICHE AUFSAETZE. 4172

0341-017X See ANGESTELLTEN MAGAZIN. 1643

0341-0218 See JAHRBUCH - MAX-PLANCK-GESELLSCHAFT. 5117

0341-0323 See NDZ. NEUE DELIWA-ZEITSCHRIFT. 1950

0341-0390 See NV; NEUE VERPACKUNG. 4220

0341-0439 See SPRECHSAAL. 2594

0341-0463 See ARCHIV FUER EISENBAHNTECHNIK; BEIHEFT ZU DER ZEITSCHRIFT EISENBAHN TECHNISCHE RUNDSCHAU. 5429

0341-0481 See GYNAKOLOGISCHE PRAXIS. 3761

0341-0501 See AKTUELLE ERNAHRUNGSMEDIZIN. 4186

0341-051X See AKTUELLE RHEUMATOLOGIE. 3802

0341-0552 See ZI INTERNATIONAL. 631

0341-0668 See RUNDSCHAU FUER FLEISCHUNTERSUCHUNG UND LEBENSMITTELUBERWACHUNG. 2356

0341-0676 See SPRECHSAAL 1976. 2594

0341-0781 See MELLIAND-TEXTILBERICHTE (1976). 5354

0341-082X See WELTMISSION (EVANGELISCHES MISSIONSWERK IN DER BUNDESREPUBLIK DEUTSCHLAND UND BERLIN WEST). 5008

0341-101X See HTM. HARTEREI-TECHNISCHE MITTEILUNGEN. 5111

0341-1044 See BETRIEB UND PERSONAL. 939

0341-1060 See BRAUNKOHLE (DUSSELDORF, 1972). 1934

0341-1281 See AEROKURIER. 4

0341-1370 See BTS BUEROTECHNISCHE SAMMLUNG, DAS RATIONELLE BUERO. 4210

0341-1540 See KORRESPONDENZ ABWASSER : KA. 2235

0341-1672 See FORTSCHRITT-BERICHTE DER VDI ZEITSCHRIFTEN. REIHE 8, MESS-, STEUERUNGS- UND REGELUNGSTECHNIK. 2055

0341-1850 See INDOGERMANISCHE FORSCHUNGEN. 3287

0341-1893 See MINERALOLTECHNIK. 1442

0341-1907 See NEUE JURISTISCHE WOCHENSCHRIFT. 3014

0341-1990 See SICHERE CHEMIEARBEIT. 992

0341-2040 See LUNG. 3950

0341-2059 See COMMUNICATIONS (SANKT AUGUSTIN). 1108

0341-2105 See GARTENPRAXIS. 2416

0341-2253 See WOLFENBUTTELER NOTIZEN ZUR BUCHGESCHICHTE. 4833

0341-2350 See KLINIKARZT, DER. 3602

0341-2377 See REACTIVITY AND STRUCTURE. 1047

0341-244X See FORSCHUNGEN ZUR RAUMENTWICKLUNG. 2823

0341-2512 See REFERATEBLATT ZUR RAUMENTWICKLUNG. 4679

0341-2601 See CCB : REVIEW FOR CHOCOLATE, CONFECTIONERY AND BAKERY. 2331

0341-2660 See O + I.E. UND P, OLHYDRAULIK UND PNEUMATIK. 2093

0341-2679 See WASSER, LUFT UND BODEN : WLB. 2245

0341-2687 See SCHMALENBACHS ZEITSCHRIFT FUER BETRIEBSWIRTSCHAFTLICHE FORSCHUNG. 850

0341-2695 See INTERNATIONAL ORTHOPAEDICS. 3882

0341-2733 See UMSATZSTEUER-RUNDSCHAU (COLOGNE, GERMANY : 1986). 3067

0341-2784 See ARCHITEKTUR WETTBEWERBE. 291

0341-2865 See JAHRBUCH DER HEIDELBERGER AKADEMIE DER WISSENSCHAFTEN. 5117

0341-2873 See ARCHAOLOGISCHE INFORMATIONEN. 258

0341-2881 See ARCHIV FUER HYDROBIOLOGIE. SUPPLEMENTBAND, MONOGRAPHISCHE BEITRAEGE. 553

0341-289X See ANNALEN DES HISTORISCHEN VEREINS FUER DEN NIEDERRHEIN, INSBESONDERE DAS ALTE ERZBISTUM KOLN. 2674

0341-2903 See NOTFALL-MEDIZIN (ERLANGEN). 3725

0341-2970 See EUROPAISCHER WETTERBERICHT. 1425

0341-3039 See ARGUMENT-SONDERBANDE. 5240

0341-3055 See ATEMWEGS- UND LUNGENKRANKHEITEN. 3948

0341-3063 See INTENSIVBEHANDLUNG. 3588

0341-3098 See MMW. MUNCHENER MEDIZINISCHE WOCHENSCHRIFT. 3617

0341-3195 See PAPIERE ZUR TEXTLINGUISTIK. 3309

0341-3659 See BM. BAU- + MOBELSCHREINER. 2904

0341-3683 See DIEBOLD-MANAGEMENT-REPORT. 665

0341-3780 See GOTTINGER GEOGRAPHISCHE ABHANDLUNGEN. 2565

0341-3810 See BAUWIRTSCHAFT (HAUPTVERBAND DER DEUTSCHEN BAUINDUSTRIE). 600

0341-3918 See BAYERISCHE VORGESCHICHTSBLATTER. 2677

0341-4027 See GEOLOGISCHES JAHRBUCH HESSEN. 1379

0341-4043 See GEOLOGISCHE ABHANDLUNGEN HESSEN. 1379

0341-4132 See BERGBAU-ROHSTOFFE-ENERGIE. 1438

0341-4159 See KUNST & ANTIQUITAETEN. 355

0341-4183 See BIBLIOTHEK. 3195

0341-4191 See STUDIEN ZUR INDOLOGIE UND IRANISTIK. 2665

0341-4213 See ATW NEWS. 4446

0341-4418 See MANAGER MAGAZIN. 878

0341-471X See SCHULBIBLIOTHEK AKTUELL. 3248

0341-4884 See SEXUALMEDIZIN. 3768

0341-4906 See BILD AM SONNTAG. 2485

0341-5023 See KLINISCHE ANASTHESIOLOGIE UND INTENSIVTHERAPIE. 3683

0341-5163 See NACHRICHTEN AUS CHEMIE, TECHNIK UND LABORATORIUM. 987

0341-5279 See PRAXIS DEUTSCH. 3311

0341-5589 See ELEKTRONIKPRAXIS. 2052

0341-5864 See ZIELSPRACHE DEUTSCH. 3336

0341-6151 See LAW AND STATE. 3132

0341-616X See ECONOMICS (TUBINGEN). 1487

0341-6178 See EDUCATION (TUBINGEN, GERMANY). 1741

0341-6321 See SYMPOSIA MEDICA HOECHST. 3644

0341-633X See LECTURE NOTES IN BIOMATHEMATICS. 463

0341-6356 See MONOGRAPH SERIES ON MINERAL DEPOSITS. 1442

0341-6364 See WEINWIRTSCHAFT, DIE. 2372

0341-6399 See GEOLOGISCHES JAHRBUCH, REIHE A : ALLGEMEINE UND REGIONALE GEOLOGIE BR DEUTSCHLAND UND NACHBARGEBIETE, TEKTONIK, STRATIGRAPHIE, PALAONTOLOGIE. 1379

0341-6402 See GEOLOGISCHES JAHRBUCH, REIHE B : REGIONALE GEOLOGIE, AUSLAND. 1379

0341-6410 See GEOLOGISCHES JAHRBUCH, REIHE C : HYDROGEOLOGIE, INGENIEURGEOLOGIE. 1413

0341-6429 See GEOLOGISCHES JAHRBUCH, REIHE D : MINERALOGIE, PETROGRAPHIE, GEOCHEMIE, LAGERSTATTENKUNDE. 1379

0341-6437 See GEOLOGISCHES JAHRBUCH, REIHE E : GEOPHYSIK. 1405

0341-6445 See GEOLOGISCHES JAHRBUCH, REIHE F : BODENKUNDE. 1379

0341-6593 See DTW. DEUTSCHE TIERAERZTLICHE WOCHENSCHRIFT. 5509

0341-6615 See KONSTRUIEREN + GIESSEN. 2119

0341-6631 See CHINA AKTUELL / INSTITUT FUER ASIENKUNDE. 4468

0341-6836 See MEERESFORSCHUNG. 1452

0341-6852 See COMPENDIUM - DEUTSCHE GESELLSCHAFT FUER MINERALOLWISSENSCHAFT UND KOHLECHEMIE E.V. 4253

0341-6860 See MEDIEN + ERZIEHUNG. 1117

0341-7050 See RECHT UND GESELLSCHAFT (MUNCHEN). 3036

0341-7093 See STAMM LEITFADEN DURCH PRESSE UND WERBUNG. 5802

0341-7115 See BRAUINDUSTRIE. 2365

0341-7131 See VR. VERPACKUNGS-RUNDSCHAU. 4222

0341-7166 See ZEITWENDE. 3356

0341-7344 See GRUPPENPRAXIS, DIE. 3579

0341-7387 See LEISTUNGSSPORT. 3954

0341-7638 See JOURNAL OF LITERARY SEMANTICS. 3290

0341-7727 See MPG SPIEGEL. 5130

0341-7816 See FINNISCH-UGRISCHE MITTEILUNGEN. 3281

0341-7840 See ARBEITS- UND SOZIALSTATISTIK. HAUPTERGEBNISSE / DER BUNDESMINISTER FUR ARBEIT UND SOZIALORDNUNG. 1651

0341-8162 See CATENA (GIESSEN). 166

0341-826X See DIAKONIE. 4953

0341-8294 See LEHREN UND LERNEN. 1761

0341-8308 See ARCHAOLOGISCHE BIBLIOGRAPHIE. 286

0341-8324 See ARCHIV FUER FRANKFUERTS GESCHICHTE UND KUNST. 2675

0341-8375 See ARCHIV FUER REFORMATIONSGESCHICHTE. BEIHEFT, LITERATURBERICHT. 2676

0341-8383 See ANZEIGER DES GERMANISCHEN NATIONALMUSEUMS. 337

0341-8391 See SPIXIANA. 5598

0341-8480 See ARS BAVARICA. 337

0341-8499 See AUSGRABUNGEN IN BERLIN. 2677

0341-8537 See BERLINER GEOGRAPHISCHE STUDIEN. 2556

0341-8561 See BERICHTE AUS DEM INSTITUT FUER MEERESKUNDE AN DER CHRISTIAN-ALBRECHTS-UNIVERSITAT KIEL. 553

0341-8634 See MUSEUM (BRAUNSCHWEIG). 4092

0341-8669 See UMSATZSTEUER-RUNDSCHAU (COLOGNE, GERMANY : 1986). 3067

0341-8685 See INTERNATIONAL JOURNAL OF PHYSICAL EDUCATION. 1856

0341-8693 See INTERNATIONALE KATHOLISCHE ZEITSCHRIFT. 5030

0341-9142 See ISTANBULER MITTEILUNGEN. 270

0341-924X See JAHRBUCH DER RHEINISCHEN DENKMALPFLEGE. 353

0341-9290 See MARBURGER GEOGRAPHISCHE SCHRIFTEN. 2568

0341-9339 See JAHRBUCH DES HISTORISCHEN VEREINS FUER MITTELFRANKEN. 2693

0341-9479 See BLATTER FUER WURTTEMBERGISCHE KIRCHENGESCHICHTE. 4939

0341-9592 See DIAKONIA (MAINZ, GERMANY : 1972). 4953

0341-9622 See BREMISCHES JAHRBUCH. 2679

0341-9657 See BERICHT DER STAATLICHEN DENKMALPFLEGE IM SAARLAND. ABTEILUNG KUNSTDENKMALPFLEGE. 261

0341-9673 See BERICHT DER STAATLICHEN DENKMALPFLEGE IM SAARLAND. ABTEILUNG BODENDENKMALPFLEGE. 261

0341-9762 See LIBERTAS. 4480

0341-9789 See RASEN. 2430

0341-9800 See EUROPAEISCHE GRUNDRECHTE - ZEITSCHRIFT. 4507

0341-9835 See ZFA. ZEITSCHRIFT FUER ALLGEMEINMEDIZIN. 3739

0341-9843 See ABHANDLUNGEN DER AKADEMIE DER WISSENSCHAFTEN IN GOTTINGEN. MATHEMATISCH-PHYSIKALISCHE KLASSE. 3490

0341-9851 See VMR; VETERINARY MEDICAL REVIEW. 5527

0341-9916 See JAHRBUCH DES VEREINS FUER AUGSBURGER BISTUMSGESCHICHTE E. V. 5031

0341-9975 See DIOZESE HILDESHEIM IN VERGANGENHEIT UND GEGENWART, DIE. 5028

0342-0124 See JAHRBUCH PREUSSISCHER KULTURBESITZ. 4089

0342-037X See DOKUMENTATIONSDIENST LATEINAMERIKA. AUSGEWAEHLTE NEUERE LITERATUR. 5198

0342-040X See DOKUMENTATIONSDIENST AFRIKA. AUSGEWAEHLTE NEUERE LITERATUR. 2496

0342-0426 See FUNK-TECHNIK. AUSGABE ZV (MUNCHEN). 1156

0342-0477 See SPRACHE-STIMME-GEHOR. 4394

0342-0671 See ERZIEHUNG UND WISSENSCHAFT. 1745

0342-068X See ZEITSCHRIFT FUER FLUGWISSENSCHAFTEN UND WELTRAUMFORSCHUNG. 40

0342-0752 See KORRESPONDENZBLATT DES VEREINS FUER NIEDERDEUTSCHE SPRACHFORSCHUNG. 3293

0342-0787 See KIELER ARBEITSPAPIERE. 1501

0342-0795 See DOKUMENTATION : MEDIZIN IM UMWELTSCHUTZ. 3573

0342-0809 See KOMPASS (BOCHUM), DER. 2886

0342-0884 See LINGUISTICA BIBLICA. 4974

0342-0914 See LUTHERJAHRBUCH. 4975

0342-104X See GIESSENER BEITRAEGE ZUR KUNSTGESCHICHTE. 351

0342-1120 See ARCHIV FUER HYDROBIOLOGIE. SUPPLEMENTBAND, ALGOLOGICAL STUDIES. 442

0342-1171 See MENNONITISCHE GESCHICHTSBLATTER. 5064

0342-118X See MITTEILUNGEN DER DEUTSCHEN ORIENT-GESELLSCHAFT ZU BERLIN. 2659

0342-1201 See MITTEILUNGEN DES KUNSTHISTORISCHES INSTITUTES FLORENZ. 358

0342-121X See MARBURGER JAHRBUCH FUER KUNSTWISSENSCHAFT. 357

0342-1279 See MITTEILUNGEN DES DEUTSCHEN ARCHAOLOGISCHEN INSTITUTS. 275

0342-1287 See MITTEILUNGEN DES DEUTSCHEN ARCHAOLOGISCHEN INSTITUTS, ROEMISCHE ABTEILUNG. 275

0342-1295 See MITTEILUNGEN DES DEUTSCHEN ARCHAOLOGISCHEN INSTITUTS, ATHENISCHE ABTEILUNG. 275

0342-1422 See NIETZSCHE-STUDIEN. 4353

0342-1430 See THEOLOGISCHE QUARTALSCHRIFT (MUNCHEN). 5004

0342-1465 See UNA SANCTA (METTINGEN). 5006

0342-1589 See DISKUSSION DEUTSCH. 3277

0342-1635 See DISTRIBUTION MAINZ. 923

0342-166X See DVZ DEUTSCHE VERKEHRS-ZEITUNG. 5381

0342-1686 See OBERBAYERISCHES ARCHIV. 2701

0342-1783 See ZEITSCHRIFT FUER WIRTSCHAFTS- UND SOZIALWISSENSCHAFTEN. 1528

0342-1791 See PHYSICS AND CHEMISTRY OF MINERALS. 1443

0342-183X See PSYCHOLOGIE IN ERZIEHUNG UND UNTERRICHT. 1903

0342-1864 See IBEROAMERICANA. 2738

0342-202X See FORUM, STADTE, HYGIENE. 2194

0342-2038 See SCHRIFTEN DES HISTORISCHEN MUSEUMS FRANKFURT AM MAIN. 364

0342-2046 See ROMISCHES JAHRBUCH DER BIBLIOTHECA HERTZIANA. 363

0342-2232 See ERFRISCHUNGSGETRANK, DAS. 2367

0342-2356 See UGARIT-FORSCHUNGEN. 3330

0342-2372 See THEOLOGISCHE BEITRAEGE. 5003

0342-2402 See SPORTUNTERRICHT. 1858

0342-2410 See VERKUNDIGUNG UND FORSCHUNG. 5007

0342-2518 See VERHANDLUNGEN DES HISTORISCHEN VEREINS FUER OBERPFALZ UND REGENSBURG. 2714

0342-2852 See ZEITSCHRIFT FUER UNTERNEHMENSGESCHICHTE. 725

0342-2895 See FRANZOSISCH HEUTE. 1895

0342-2933 See LAPIS (MUNCHEN). 1357

0342-300X See WSI MITTEILUNGEN. 1720

0342-3018 See TIERFREUND NURNBERG. 1070

0342-3026 See LABORATORIUMSMEDIZIN. 3603

0342-3131 See ZEITSCHRIFT DES HISTORISCHEN VEREINS FUER SCHWABEN. 2634

0342-3182 See BANK, DIE. 774

0342-3468 See ZEITSCHRIFT FUER ZIVILPROZESS. 3078

0342-3476 See ZLR, ZEITSCHRIFT FUER DAS GESAMTE LEBENSMITTELRECHT. 3078

0342-3573 See BINDEREPORT. 4824

0342-376X See GV-PRAXIS. 2343

0342-3816 See NEUEREN SPRACHEN, DIE. 3305

0342-393X See ZEITSCHRIFT FUER INDIVIDUALPSYCHOLOGIE. 4622

0342-3964 See BIBLIOGRAPHIE SOZIALISATION UND SOZIALPAEDAGOGIK. 5266

0342-4006 See NEW BUSINESS. 698

0342-4111 See SPRINGER SERIES IN OPTICAL SCIENCES. 4442

0342-4340 See WOLFENBUTTELER RENAISSANCE MITTEILUNGEN. 2716

0342-443X See KLINISCH-RADIOLOGISCHES SEMINAR. 3943

0342-4448 See SCHRIFTENREIHE INTENSIVMEDIZIN, NOTFALLMEDIZIN, ANASTHESIOLOGI. 3684

0342-4456 See BUCHEREI DES PNEUMOLOGEN. 3948

0342-4634 See ISBN REVIEW. 3218

0342-4642 See INTENSIVE CARE MEDICINE. 3588

0342-4731 See GB+GW; GARTNERBORSE UND GARTENWELT. 2416

0342-474X See VEROFFENTLICHUNGEN DES INSTITUTS FUER WASSERFORSCHUNG GMBH DORTMUND UND DER HYDROLOGISCHEN ABTEILUNG DER DORTMUNDER STADTWERKE AG. 5541

0342-4898 See HORGESCHADIGTEN PADAGOGIK. 4388

0342-4901 See LECTURE NOTES IN CHEMISTRY. 984

0342-5231 See GYMNASIUM (HEIDELBERG). 1077

0342-5258 See UNSERE JUGEND. 1789
0342-5282 See INTERNATIONAL JOURNAL OF REHABILITATION RESEARCH. 4389
0342-5592 See VERWALTUNGSRUNDSCHAU. 889
0342-5622 See OIL GAS. 4269
0342-5665 See ENERGY DEVELOPMENTS. 1940
0342-5681 See BERGBAU (HATTINGEN). 2135
0342-5703 See FISCHER UND TEICHWIRT. 4872
0342-572X See VEROFFENTLICHUNGEN DER ARBEITSGEMEINSCHAFT GETREIDEFORSCHUNG E.V., DETMOLD. 204
0342-5932 See WURZBURGER JAHRBUCHER FUR DIE ALTERTUMSWISSENSCHAFT. 1081
0342-5940 See WOLFENBUETTELER STUDIEN ZUR AUFKLAERUNG. 4365
0342-5991 See SITZUNGSBERICHTE DER BAYERISCHEN AKADEMIE DER WISSENSCHAFTEN. PHILOSOPHISCH-HISTORISCHE KLASSE. 1080
0342-6068 See GEWASSERSCHUTZ, WASSER, ABWASSER. 5533
0342-6173 See ZIELSPRACHE ENGLISCH. 3336
0342-6300 See JAHRBUCH DEUTSCH ALS FREMDSPRACHE. 3289
0342-6556 See ZB. ZIERPFLANZENBAU. 2434
0342-6580 See BRENNSTOFFSPIEGEL. 1600
0342-6696 See CHET, CHEMIE EXPERIMENT + I.E. UND TECHNOLOGIE. 1023
0342-6793 See TOPICS IN CURRENT PHYSICS. 4423
0342-684X See VEROFFENTLICHUNGEN FUER NATURSCHUTZ UND LANDSCHAFTSPFLEGE IN BADEN-WURTTEMBERG. 4173
0342-6947 See ANEP. ANNUAIRE EUROPEEN DE PETROLE. 4249
0342-6971 See WERTPAPIER-MITTLEILUNGEN. TEIL 4. ZEITSCHRIFT FUER WIRTSCHAFTS- UND BANKRECHT. 3088
0342-7013 See SIEBDRUCK, DER. 4569
0342-7064 See BETRIEBSWIRTSCHAFT STUTTGART, DIE. 643
0342-7145 See THEORIE UND PRAXIS DER SOZIALPADAGOGIK. 5004
0342-7188 See IRRIGATION SCIENCE. 175
0342-734X See ARCHAOLOGISCHES KORRESPONDENZBLATT. 258
0342-7536 See NOTA LEPIDOPTEROLOGICA. 467
0342-7560 See SURF. 4879
0342-7641 See LEDER UND HAUTEMARKT. 3185
0342-782X See FORSCHUNGSBERICHTE / INSTITUT FUER PHONETIK UND SPRACHLICHE KOMMUNIKATION DER UNIVERSITAT MUNCHEN. 3282
0342-7943 See ZDB FORDERUNGEN, ZIELVORSTELLUNGEN FUER DIE ... LEGISLATURPERIODE DES DEUTSCHEN BUNDESTAGES. 1720
0342-7951 See TW. TAGUNGS-WIRTSCHAFT TW, TAG.-WIRTSCH. 1525
0342-8176 See PROKLA. 1594
0342-8281 See RUDERSPORT. 595
0342-8311 See GEO. 4165
0342-8427 See SKANDINAVISTIK. 3437
0342-8702 See PR-MAGAZIN. 763
0342-8907 See KREBSBEKAMPFUNG. 3820
0342-9474 See SCHRIFTENREIHE DER LANDESANSTALT FUER IMMISSIONSSCHUTZ DES LANDES NORDRHEIN-WESTFALEN, ESSEN. 2242
0342-958X See MICROSCOPICA ACTA. SUPPLEMENT. 567
0342-9601 See MEDIZINISCHE MONATSSCHRIFT FUER PHARMAZEUTEN. 4315
0342-9857 See NEUE PRAXIS. 5298
0342-9873 See OBERPFALZ, DIE. 2701
0343-0103 See LOYAL. 4049
0343-0200 See MILCH PRAXIX UND RINDERMAST, DIE. 215
0343-0456 See KUNSTMAGAZIN. 356
0343-0642 See MD LEINFELDEN. 2902

0343-0758 See PAPERS ON FRENCH SEVENTEENTH CENTURY LITERATURE. 3422
0343-0987 See BEITRAEGE ZUR HYDROLOGIE. 1412
0343-107X See MITTEILUNGEN DER DEUTSCHEN BODENKUNDLICHE GESELLSCHAFT. 178
0343-1223 See MITTEILUNGEN - LEICHTWEISS-INSTITUT FUER WASSERBAU DER TECHNISCHEN UNIVERSITAT BRAUNSCHWEIG. 2093
0343-1258 See GRATIA. 3392
0343-1657 See LITERATUR FUER LESER. 3406
0343-2092 See GAS (MUNCHEN). 4257
0343-2203 See VEROFFENTLICHUNGEN DES INSTITUTS FUER KUSTEN- UND BINNENFISCHEREI HAMBURG. 2315
0343-2246 See KALTE UND KLIMATECHNIK. 2606
0343-2432 See DERMATOSEN IN BERUF UND UMWELT. 3720
0343-2521 See GEOJOURNAL. 2564
0343-3048 See ZENTRALBLATT HAUT- UND GESCHLECHTSKRANKHEITEN. 3723
0343-3110 See JAHRESTAGUNG - GESELLSCHAFT FUER INFORMATIK E.V. 1260
0343-3137 See DEUTSCHE ZEITSCHRIFT FUER MUND-, KIEFER- UND GESICHTS- CHIRURGIE. 3963
0343-3145 See DEUTSCHE SCHWARZBUNTE. 210
0343-3331 See INDEX RADIOLOGIAE. 3942
0343-334X See EUROPEAN PRODUCTION ENGINEERING : EPE. 1975
0343-3528 See PRIMATE REPORT. 5594
0343-3781 See LATEINAMERIKA STUDIEN. 2743
0343-379X See ROMANISTISCHE ZEITSCHRIFT FUER LITERATURGESCHICHTE. 3318
0343-3846 See DEUTSCH BAUERN-KORRESPOONDENZ. 78
0343-3862 See STAHL MARKT. 1627
0343-4109 See SOZIOLOGISCHE REVUE. 5263
0343-4117 See BIBLIOGRAPHIE ZUR GESCHICHTE DER DEUTSCHEN ARBEITERBEWEGUNG. 1530
0343-4125 See CONTRIBUTIONS TO SEDIMENTOLOGY. 1372
0343-4168 See POST UND SPORT. 4913
0343-4206 See HIFI & TV. 1132
0343-494X See INFORMATIONEN UND MATERIALIEN ZUR GEOGRAPHIE DER EUREGIO RHEIN-MAAS. 2566
0343-5202 See SPRACHE UND DATENVERARBEITUNG. 3323
0343-5377 See ZEITSCHRIFT FUER ENERGIEWIRTSCHAFT. 1961
0343-5520 See FORSCHUNGSBERICHTE AUS TECHNIK UND NATURWISSENSCHAFTEN. 5105
0343-5571 See FILM- UND TV-KAMERAMANN. 4070
0343-5725 See KLEINHEUBACHER BERICHTE. 396
0343-5733 See ARZTRECHT (1977). 3739
0343-5881 See EINKAUFS-1X1 DER DEUTSCHEN INDUSTRIE. 832
0343-5903 See BAUSTOFF UMSCHAU. 1599
0343-6237 See BIBLIOTHEQUE DE L'ECOLE DES CHARTES. 3195
0343-6462 See ENTWICKLUNG + LANDLICHER RAUM. 82
0343-6632 See LITERATURDIENST / HERAUSGEBER ; BUND FUER LEBENSMITTELRECHT UND LEBENSMITTELKUNDE. 2348
0343-6667 See EGMAGAZIN. 1634
0343-6705 See ERDOL-INFORMATIONSDIENST. 672
0343-6853 See HAUSTEX. 5351
0343-690X See VERFASSUNGSSCHUTZBERICHT. 1309
0343-706X See MUNCHENER GEOGRAPHISCHE ABHANDLUNGEN. 2569
0343-7256 See GEOGRAPHIE UND IHRE DIDAKTIK. 2564

0343-737X See SAMMLUNG GEOLOGISCHER FUHRER. 1396
0343-7442 See ALUMINIUM ENGLISH. 3997
0343-7493 See ERGEBNISSE DER BEOBACHTUNGEN AM ERDMAGNETISCHEN OBSERVATORIUM FURSTENFELDBRUCK IM JAHRE. 4443
0343-754X See ECONOMIC BULLETIN (BERLIN). 1556
0343-7655 See BERICHT DER NATURFORSCHENDEN GESELLSCHAFT AUGSBURG. 4163
0343-7728 See BORSEN-ZEITUNG 1972. 5801
0343-7965 See PROBLEME DER KUSTENFORSCHUNG IM SUDLICHEN NORDSEEGEBIET. 2573
0343-8147 See TATIGKEITSBERICHT - BUNDESANSTALT FUER GEOWISSENSCHAFTEN UND ROHSTOFFE. 1399
0343-8554 See ZEITSCHRIFT FUER LYMPHOLOGIE. 3653
0343-8651 See CURRENT MICROBIOLOGY. 561
0343-8694 See ARBEITSPAPIERE ZUR LINGUISTIK. 3266
0343-8732 See GOTTESDIENST. 4961
0343-9356 See SCHOTT-FORSCHUNGSBERICHTE. 1995
0343-9429 See KLINISCHE PSYCHOLOGIE UND PSYCHOPATHOLOGIE. 4602
0343-9712 See GEOWISSENSCHAFTEN (BOPPARD). 1381
0343-9771 See RECHT UND SCHADEN. 3036
0344-0338 See PATHOLOGY, RESEARCH AND PRACTICE. 3897
0344-1008 See FORSCHUNGSBERICHT. MATERIALBAND / UNIVERSITAT HAMBURG. 1824
0344-1369 See MARKETING MUNCHEN. 931
0344-1385 See FREIBURGER RUNDBRIEF. 4960
0344-1415 See FRAUENFRAGE IN DEUTSCHLAND, BIBLIOGRAPHIE / DEUTSCHER AKADEMIKERINNENBUND, DIE. 416
0344-1733 See LABORPRAXIS. 3603
0344-1822 See ALTE UND NEUE KUNST. 312
0344-1873 See ALT-HILDESHEIM. 2672
0344-2039 See EXPORT POLYGRAPH INTERNATIONAL. 378
0344-3086 See WAR AND SOCIETY NEWSLETTER. 4060
0344-3094 See GERMAN YEARBOOK OF INTERNATIONAL LAW. 3128
0344-3302 See MATHEMATICAL SYSTEMS IN ECONOMICS. 3520
0344-3736 See ZAHNARZT JOURNAL. 1337
0344-3752 See NUC COMPACT : COMPACT NEWS IN NUCLEAR MEDICINE. 3848
0344-3949 See KINDERGARTEN HEUTE. 1804
0344-4201 See INTERNISTISCHE WELT. 3798
0344-4325 See PERSPECTIVES IN MATHEMATICAL LOGIC. 3526
0344-4325 See SPRINGER SEMINARS IN IMMUNOPATHOLOGY. 3677
0344-4376 See KUCHE. 2348
0344-4422 See RESTAURANT- & HOTEL-MANAGEMENT. 2809
0344-4724 See TELCOM REPORT DEUTSCHE AUSGABE. 1164
0344-4880 See TELCOM REPORT (ENGLISH EDITION). 1164
0344-5038 See EXTRACTA UROLOGICA. 3990
0344-5046 See EXTRACTA ORTHOPAEDICA. 3881
0344-5062 See ALLERGOLOGIE. 3665
0344-5089 See BERLINER BEITRAEGE ZUR ARCHAOMETRIE. 261
0344-5224 See LINIE KOLN, DIE. 1085
0344-5607 See NEUROSURGICAL REVIEW. 3970
0344-5615 See MITTEILUNGEN AUS DEM INSTITUT FUER ALLGEMEINE BOTANIK HAMBURG. 518

0344-5666 See SCHRIFTEN AUS DER FORSTLICHEN FAKULTAT DER UNIVERSITAT GOTTINGEN UND DER NIEDERSACHSISCHEN FORSTLICHEN VERSUCHSANSTALT. 2395

0344-5690 See KULTUR & TECHNIK. 4090

0344-5704 See CANCER CHEMOTHERAPY AND PHARMACOLOGY. 3810

0344-5712 See ASG - MATERIALSAMMLUNG / AGRARSOZIALE GESELLSCHAFT. 63

0344-5879 See NACHRICHTEN AUS DEM KARTEN- UND VERMESSUNGSWESEN. SONDERHEFT. 2569

0344-5925 See DEUTSCHE ZEITSCHRIFT FUER SPORTMEDIZIN. 3954

0344-595X See KLINISCH-ONKOLOGISCHES SEMINAR. 3820

0344-5984 See KONTRASTE FREIBURG. 1992. 5031

0344-6166 See PRODUKTION 1978. 1622

0344-6204 See FORTSCHRITTE DER FERTILITATSFORSCHUNG. 3761

0344-6492 See SPORT-, BADER-, FREIZEIT-BAUTEN. 628

0344-6565 See SAMMLUNG GEOGRAPHISCHER FUHRER. 2575

0344-6727 See LINGUISTISCHE ARBEITEN TUBINGEN. 1688

0344-6735 See KONZEPTE DER SPRACH- UND LITERATURWISSENSCHAFT. 3293

0344-6786 See REIHE DER SCHRIFTEN - FREIES DEUTSCHES HOCHSTIFT. 3428

0344-7073 See KARLSRUHER MANUSKRIPTE ZUR MATHEMATISCHEN UND THEORETISCHEN WIRTSCHAFTS- UND SOZIALGEOGRAPHIE. 2567

0344-7103 See DEUTSCHE OPTIKERZEITUNG. 3874

0344-7154 See PHARMAKOTHERAPIE. 4324

0344-7634 See BUNDESANZEIGER. 4635

0344-7871 See RECHT UND POLITIK. 3036

0344-8010 See MIKRODOK (BADEN-BADEN, GERMANY). 1270

0344-810X See BOREAS (MUNSTER). 262

0344-8169 See SPRACHWISSENSCHAFT. 3323

0344-8231 See BLASMUSIK, DIE. 4104

0344-824X See STUDIEN UBER WIRTSCHAFTS- UND SYSTEMVERGLEICHE. 1595

0344-8266 See ANGLISTIK & ENGLISCHUNTERRICHT. 3264

0344-8401 See PHYSIK DATEN. 4416

0344-8622 See CURARE. 3924

0344-8657 See ZUCKERINDUSTRIE. 1031

0344-8746 See SICHERHEITS-BERATER. 947

0344-8754 See SPIELEN UND LERNEN. 1784

0344-8843 See MARKT & TECHNIK. 2071

0344-8967 See THERAPEUTISCHE KONZEPTE DER ANALYTISCHEN PSYCHOLOGIE C.G. JUNG. 4620

0344-9041 See TRIBUNE D'ALLEMAGNE, LA. 2524

0344-9084 See MITTEILUNGEN DER DEUTSCHEN GESELLSCHAFT FUER ALLGEMEINE UND ANGEWANDTE ENTOMOLOGIE. 5612

0344-9254 See UNITAS FRATRUM. 5068

0344-9327 See JOURNAL FUER BETRIEBSWIRTSCHAFT. 685

0344-9416 See MEDIZINTECHNIK (STUTTGART). 3615

0345-0015 See ARTES. 314

0345-0074 See STRIAE. 1399

0345-0147 See ACTA UNIVERSITATIS UMENSIS. 2841

0345-0295 See ANEKS. 2673

0345-0732 See ALKOHOL OCH NARKOTIKA. 1340

0345-0902 See ANTROPOLOGISKA STUDIER. 231

0345-0988 See ARBETSTERAPEUTEN. 3552

0345-1402 See NORDISK TIDSKRIFT FOR BETEENDETERAPI. 4606

0345-1410 See BETODLAREN. 2410

0345-1941 See BYGGREFERAT. 294

0345-2328 See DEVELOPMENT DIALOGUE. 1634

0345-2360 See DIDAKOMETRY AND SOCIOMETRY. 3277

0345-3057 See FILMHAFTET : TIDSKRIFT OM FILM OCH TV. 4070

0345-3626 See FOTO (STOCKHOLM, SWEDEN : 1983). 4369

0345-3766 See AFFARSVARLDEN (1974). 1544

0345-469X See HISTORISK TIDSKRIFT (STOCKHOLM). 2691

0345-4789 See HAFTEN FOR KRITISKA STUDIER. 4475

0345-4975 See INTERNATIONAL STUDIES IN THE NORDIC COUNTRIES NEWSLETTER. 4525

0345-4991 See INVANDRARTIDNINGEN PA LATT SVENSKA. 1919

0345-5068 See ICA-KURIREN. 2517

0345-5564 See JOURNAL OF TRAFFIC MEDICINE. 3600

0345-5653 See JEFFERSON. 4125

0345-7656 See ELEKTRONIKTIDNINGEN. 2052

0345-8768 See SPRAK OCH STIL. 3323

0345-8865 See OSSA. 3624

0346-1238 See SCANDINAVIAN ACTUARIAL JOURNAL. 2893

0346-217X See SVENSK MISSIONSTIDSKRIFT. 5001

0346-2250 See SVENSK VETERINARTIDNING. 5522

0346-251X See SYSTEM (LINKOPING). 3327

0346-2803 See TRO OCH LIV. 5006

0346-2846 See TRAINDUSTRIN (STOCKHOLM). 635

0346-4180 See VI. 2524

0346-4601 See WORLD POLLEN AND SPORE FLORA. 530

0346-4636 See VVS. 2608

0346-542X See MEDICINSK TEKNIK. 3614

0346-5632 See NARKOTIKAUTVECKLINGEN. 1347

0346-5748 See INDUSTRIVERKETS HOSTRAPPORT / STATENS INDUSTRIVERK. 1495

0346-6272 See STOCKHOLM STUDIES IN ENGLISH. 3324

0346-6302 4235

0346-6310 See ELTEKNIK MED AKTUELL ELEKTRONIK. 2053

0346-640X See DAGENS INDUSTRI. 664

0346-6582 See ASEA TIDNING. 2036

0346-6583 See QUARTERLY REVIEW / SVERIGES RIKSBANK. 805

0346-6728 See NORNA-RAPPORTER. 3306

0346-6787 See MEDDELANDEN FRAN LUNDS UNIVERSITETS GEOGRAFISKA INSTITUTION. AVHANDLINAR. 2569

0346-6868 See ECOLOGICAL BULLETINS. 2213

0346-6906 See CBI FORSKNING. 2020

0346-7090 See MEDDELANDEN / SVENSKA TRAASKYDDSINSTITUTET / REPORTS / THE SWEDISH WOOD PRESERVATION INSTITUTE. 2402

0346-7104 See NARINGSFORSKNING. SUPPLEMENT. 4194

0346-7287 See RURAL DEVELOPMENT STUDIES. 2834

0346-7775 See SCANORAMA. 709

0346-7856 See SKRIFTER UTGIVNA AV LITTERATURVETENSKAPLIGA INSTITUTIONEN VID UPPSALA UNIVERSITET. 3437

0346-8119 See SUMLEN. 4155

0346-8186 See EASTERN BUSINESS MAGAZINE. 670

0346-8240 See CBI RAPPORTER. 2020

0346-8313 See NOBEL SYMPOSIA. 5134

0346-8496 See STOCKHOLM STUDIES IN RUSSIAN LITERATURE. 3440

0346-8577 See SVETSAREN. 4028

0346-8720 See SCANDINAVIAN JOURNAL OF REHABILITATION MEDICINE. SUPPLEMENT. 3639

0346-8755 See SCANDINAVIAN JOURNAL OF HISTORY. 2708

0346-8852 See NORDIC JOURNAL OF PSYCHIATRY. SUPPLEMENT. 3932

0346-9212 See NYA ANTIK & AUKTION. 251

0346-9395 See CALIDRIS. 5580

0347-0520 See SCANDINAVIAN JOURNAL OF ECONOMICS, THE. 1520

0347-0911 See VARDFACKET. 4806

0347-0962 See DOCUMENT - SWEDISH COUNCIL FOR BUILDING RESEARCH. 2821

0347-0989 See MOTPOL. 3618

0347-1152 See SVERIGES FRIMARKEN OCH HELSAKER / SVERIGES FILATELIST-FORBUND. 2787

0347-1314 See ACTA UNIVERSITATIS UPSALIENSIS. 1722

0347-1837 See SVENSKA LANDSMAL OCH SVENSKT FOLKLIV. 3327

0347-2205 See SIPRI YEARBOOK : WORLD ARMAMENTS AND DISARMAMENT. 4057

0347-2965 See ARBETARRORELSENS ARSBOK. 1651

0347-3139 See QUARTERLY REVIEW - SKANDINAVISKA ENSKILDA BANKEN. 1580

0347-3236 See VAXTSKYDDSRAPPORTER. JORDBRUK. 529

0347-4240 See AICARC BULLETIN. 335

0347-4453 See KONSTPERSPEKTIV. 355

0347-5883 See NYTT - FORSKNINGSSTIFTELSEN SKOGSARBETEN. 2390

0347-6359 See TRAFIK-SKADOR. 5446

0347-7193 See ARBETSMILJO. 2859

0347-7290 See KOMMUNERNAS FINANSER. 4735

0347-772X See BARNBOKEN. 3365

0347-7835 See BULLETIN - NATIONALMUSEUM. 317

0347-8068 See MEDDELANDEN / SVENSKA FORSKNINGSINSTITUTET I ISTANBUL. 2623

0347-8262 See PLASTFORUM SCANDINAVIA. 4457

0347-8696 See IVL. B. 2233

0347-8742 See FLORA OF ECUADOR. 511

0347-9374 See ROHSSKA KONSTSLOJDMUSEETS ARSBOK. 375

0347-982X See RAPPORT - SVERIGES LANTBRUKSUNIVERSITET, INSTITUTIONEN FOR EKONOMI OCH STATISTIK. REPORT - DEPARTMENT OF ECONOMICS AND STATISTICS. 1537

0347-9838 See RAPPORT - SVERIGES LANTBRUKSUNIVERSITET, INSTITUTIONEN FOR HUSDJURS UTFODRING OCH VARD. 5519

0347-9994 See SWEDISH DENTAL JOURNAL. 1336

0348-0259 See RAPPORT - SVERIGES LANTBRUKSUNIVERSITET INSTITUTIONEN FOR BYGGNADSTEKNIK. 124

0348-0593 See SPECIALMEDDELANDE / SVERIGES LANTBRUKSUNIVERSITET, INSTITUTIONEN FOR LANTBRUKETS BYGGNADSTEKNIK. 628

0348-0976 See RAPPORTER FRAN JORDEBEARBETNINGSAVDELNINGEN, SVERIGES LANTBRUKSUNIVERSITET. 184

0348-1115 See FORESKRIFTER OM STATLIG TJANSTEPENSIONERING / STATENS ARBETSGIVARVERK. 1675

0348-1646 See NORDISK JUDAISTIK / SCANDINAVIAN JEWISH STUDIES. 5051

0348-1964 See STUDIES OF LAW IN SOCIAL CHANGE AND DEVELOPMENT. 3060

0348-2146 See LUNDER GERMANISTISCHE FORSCHUNGEN. 3300

0348-2650 See STFI-MEDDELANDE. SERIE A. 2404

0348-2863 See DALARNAS MUSEUMS SERIE AV RAPPORTER. 2820

0348-3339 See RAPPORTER OCH NOTISER - LUNDS UNIVERSITETS NATURGEOGRAFISKA INSTITUTION. 2574

0348-3568 See MEDDELANDEN FRAN INSTITUTIONEN FOR NORDISKA SPRAK VID STOCKHOLMS UNIVERSITET: MINS. 3301

0348-4041 See RAPPORT / SVERIGES LANTBRUKSUNIVERSITET. INSTITUTIONEN FOR MIKROBIOLOGI. 124
0348-4114 See GOTHENBURG STUDIES IN ART & ARCHITECTURE. 351
0348-4157 See RAPPORT / SVERIGES LANTBRUKSUNIVERSITE. INSTITUTIONEN FOR TRADGARDSVETENSKAP. 2429
0348-422X See RAPPORT / SVERIGES LANTBRUKSUNIVERSITET, INSTITUTIONEN FOR EKOLOGI OCH MILJOVARD. 2391
0348-4599 See RAPPORT - SVERIGES LANTBRUKSUNIVERSITET, INSTITUTION FOR VIRKESLARA. 2391
0348-503X See AKTUELLT OM HISTORIA. 2609
0348-5099 See UPPSALA STUDIES IN CULTURAL ANTHROPOLOGY. 247
0348-565X See RAPPORTER OCH UPPSATSER - SVERIGES LANTBRUKSUNIVERSITET INSTITUTIONEN FOR SKOGSGENETIK. 2392
0348-6133 See SAMLAREN (UPPSALA). 3433
0348-6613 See FOREDRAG VID PYROTEKNIKDAGEN. 975
0348-6672 See SWEDISH DENTAL JOURNAL. SUPPLEMENT. 1336
0348-6729 See ARETS TRYCK. 5322
0348-677X See UPPSALA UNIVERSITY, INSTITUTE OF PHYSICS. 4424
0348-6885 See BYGGNADSKULTUR. 606
0348-7180 See SYMPOSIUM ON CHEMICAL PROBLEMS CONNECTED WITH THE STABILITY OF EXPLOSIVES. 994
0348-7598 See NEWSLETTER - NATIONAL BOARD OF OCCUPATIONAL SAFETY AND HEALTH. 4794
0348-7636 See RAPPORT (SVERIGES LANTBRUKSUNIVERSITET. INSTITUTIONEN FOR SKOGSPRODUKTION). 2392
0348-7741 See MEIJERBERGS ARKIV FOR SVENSK ORDFORSKNING. 3302
0348-7954 See RAPPORT - SVERIGES LANTBRUKSUNIVERSITET. INSTITUTIONEN FOR SKOGLIG GENETIK OCH VAXTFYSIOLOGI. REPORT - SWEDISH UNIVERSITY OF AGRICULTURAL SCIENCES, DEPARTMENT OF FOREST GENETICS AND PLANT PHYSIOLOGY. 2392
0348-7962 See NY LITTERATUR OM KVINNOR : EN BIBLIOGRAFI / GOTEBORGS UNIVERSTIETSBIBLIOTEK, KVINNOHISTORISKA SAMLINGARNA. 5572
0348-7997 See TVARSNITT. 2856
0348-8365 See KVINNOVETENSKAPLIG TIDSKRIFT. 3764
0348-8799 See ANNUAL REPORT ON THE RESULTS OF TREATMENT IN GYNECOLOGICAL CANCER. 3809
0348-9329 See COSMIC AND SUBATOMIC PHYSICS REPORT. 4401
0348-9493 See ENERGIMAGASINET. 1938
0348-9507 See UPPSALA RESEARCH REPORTS IN CULTURAL ANTHROPOLOGY. 247
0348-9698 See ETHNOLOGIA SCANDINAVICA. 2319
0348-971X See FATABUREN. 236
0348-9833 See KAROLINSKA FORBUNDETS ARSBOK. 2518
0349-0068 See ANNUAL REPORT - INTERNATIONAL METEOROLOGICAL INSTITUTE IN STOCKHOLM. 1420
0349-0416 See ARSBOK / KUNGL. HUMANISTISKA VETENSKAPS-SAMFUNDET I UPPSALA. 2842
0349-053X See ARSBOK - VETENSKAPSSOCIETETEN I LUND. 1074
0349-1579 See HOTELL & PENSIONAT. 2806
0349-1773 See DROGMISSBRUK. 1343
0349-2176 See RAPPORTER OCH MEDDELANDEN - SVERIGES GEOLOGISKA UNDERSOKNING. 1393
0349-2834 See BEBYGGELSEHISTORISK TIDSKRIFT. 293
0349-3733 See TIDNINGEN BYGGINDUSTRIN. 630
0349-4225 See MANADSJOURNALEN. 3229

0349-6236 See ARSBOK FOR STATENS KONSTMUSEER. 337
0349-6244 See NORDICOM REVIEW OF NORDIC MASS COMMUNICATION RESEARCH, THE. 1118
0349-6279 See FOLKETS HISTORIA. 2616
0349-6287 See RAW MATERIALS REPORT. 2203
0349-7887 See RAPPORT / JONKOPINGS LANS MUSEUM. 243
0349-8913 See UPPSATSER - SVERIGESLANTBRUKSUNIVERSITET, INSTITUTIONEN FOR VIRKESLARA. 2397
0350-0020 See GODISNJAK - AKADEMIJA NAUKA I UMJETNOSTI BOSNE I HERCEGOVINE. CENTAR ZA BALKANOLOSKA ISPITIVANJA. 2847
0350-0039 See RADOVI ODJELJENJE DRUSTVENIH NAUKA. 1843
0350-0063 See ZDRAVSTVENI VESTNIK. 3652
0350-0179 See BALCANOSLAVICA. 2677
0350-0349 See BIBLIOGRAFIJA JUGOSLAVIJE SERIJSKE PUBLIKACIJE. 409
0350-0470 See ZBORNIK MATICE SRPSKE ZA SLAVISTIKU / MATICA SRPSKA, ODELJENJE ZA KNJIZEVNOST I JEZIK. 3335
0350-0705 See FOLIA MEDICA FACULTATIS MEDICINAE UNIVERSITATIS SARAEVIENSIS. 3577
0350-0802 See ISTORIJSKI CASOPIS. 2620
0350-0861 See GLASNIK ETNOGRAFSKOG INSTITUTA. 237
0350-1043 See BILTEN UDRUZENJA ORTODONATA JUGOSLAVIJE. 1317
0350-1221 See MEDICINSKI CASOPIS. 3614
0350-123X See GALAKSIJA. 5107
0350-1302 See PUBLICATIONS DE L'INSTITUT MATHEMATIQUE (BELGRADE). 3529
0350-1388 See NAUKA U PRAKSI BEOGRAD. 5132
0350-1418 See ANALI GAZI HASREV-BEGOVE BIBLIOTHEKE. 2673
0350-1531 See ORGANIZACIJA IN KADRI. 881
0350-154X See REVIJA ZA SOCIOLOGIJU. 5256
0350-1604 See BULLETIN SCIENTIFIQUE. SECTION B, SCIENCES HUMAINES. 2843
0350-1639 See MACEDONIAE ACTA ARCHAEOLOGICA. 273
0350-1728 See MAKEDONSKI ARHIVIST. 2482
0350-185X See JUZNOSLOVENSKI FILOLOG. 3293
0350-1892 See GODISEN ZBORNIK - FILOZOFSKI FAKULTET NA UNIVERZITETOT, SKOPJE. 4347
0350-1981 See GODISNJAK DRUSTVA ISTORICARA BOSNE I HERCEGOVINE. 2689
0350-2007 See MATHEMATICA BALKANICA. 3518
0350-2023 See BILTEN ZA HEMATOLOGIJU I TRANSFUZIJU. 3770
0350-2155 See JUGOSLOVENSKO VOCARSTVO. JOURNAL OF YUGOSLAV POMOLOGY. 177
0350-221X See SUVREMENA METODIKA NASTAVE HRVATSKOGA JEZIKA. 3327
0350-2252 See YUGOSLAV LAW. 3077
0350-2325 See INFORMATICA MUSEOLOGICA. 4089
0350-2457 See VETERINARSKI GLASNIK. 5524
0350-2538 See PSIHIJATRIJA DANAS. 3932
0350-2546 See SAMOUPRAVLJANJE (BELGRADE, SERBIA). 885
0350-2589 See GODISNJAK ZASTITE SPOMENIKA KULTURE HRVATSKE / REPUBLICKI ZAVOD ZA ZASTITU SPOMENIKA KULTURE ZAGREB. 351
0350-2708 See THEORETICAL AND APPLIED MECHANICS. 4430
0350-2856 See ARHIVIST. 2480
0350-2902 See JUGOSLOVENSKI ISTORIJSKI CASOPIS. 2695
0350-2953 See SAVREMENA POLJOPRIVREDNA TEHNIKA. 132
0350-3089 See MACEDONIAN REVIEW. 2849
0350-3607 See EMAJL-KERAMIKA-STAKLO. 2588
0350-3615 See FRAMENTA HERBOLOGICA JUGOSLAVICA. 88

0350-3623 See RADOVI - SVEUCILISTE U SPLITU, FILOZOFSKI FAKULTET, RAZDIO FILOLOS-KIH ZNANOSTI. 4358
0350-3631 See ACTA HISTORICO-OECONOMICA IUGOSLAVIAE. 1544
0350-3666 See ARHITEKTURA. 291
0350-3968 See GLAS SLAVONIJE. 5799
0350-4123 See KNJIZEVNA KRITIKA. 3402
0350-4301 See NOVI LIST. 5799
0350-4441 See PRAXIS VETERINARIA. 5518
0350-4557 See REVIJA RADA. 1708
0350-4662 See SLOBODNA DALMACIJA. 5799
0350-5006 See VECERNJI LIST. 5799
0350-5510 See ACTA ENTOMOLOGICA JUGOSLAVICA. 5573
0350-5774 See ZGODOVINSKI CASOPIS. 2634
0350-5901 See ACTA BIOLOGIAE ET MEDICINAE EXPERIMENTALIS. 439
0350-6134 See COLLEGIUM ANTROPOLOGICUM. 234
0350-6142 See COPPER (BOR, SERBIA). 4000
0350-6320 See HISTRIA ARCHAEOLOGICA. 269
0350-6428 See KNJIZEVNA ISTORIJA. 3402
0350-6525 See MOSTOVI (BELGRADE). 3304
0350-6673 See PRILOZI ZA KNJIZEVNOST, JEZIK, ISTORIJU I FOLKLOR. 3311
0350-6894 See SLAVISTICNA REVIJA. 3322
0350-7149 See VETERINARSKA STANICA. 5524
0350-7165 See VJESNIK ARHEOLOSKOG MUZEJA U ZAGREBU. 285
0350-7831 See CAKAVSKA RIC. 3272
0350-8005 See ZBORNIK RADOVA - POLJOPRIVREDNI FAKULTET. INSTITUT ZA STOCARSTVO, NOVI SAD. 224
0350-820X See SCIENCE OF SINTERING. 4018
0350-8447 See VJESNIK ZA ARHEOLOGIJU I HISTORIJU DALMATINSKU. 285
0350-848X See ZBORNIK FILOZOFSKE FAKULTETE / UNIVERZA V LJUBLJANI, FILOZOFSKA FAKULTETA. 3456
0350-8714 See GLASNIK CETINJSKIH MUZEJA. BULLETIN DES MUSEES DE CETIGNE. 237
0350-9494 See VARSTVO SPOMENIKOV. 332
0350-9559 See NEUROLOGIA CROATICA : GLASILO UDRUZENJA NEUROLOGA JUGOSLAVIJE, OFFICIAL JOURNAL OF YUGOSLAV NEUROLOGICAL ASSOCIATION. 3840
0351-0042 See DIABETOLOGIA CROATICA. 3728
0351-0093 See MEDICA JADERTINA. 3607
0351-0123 See IRCIHE BULLETIN / INTERNATIONAL REFERRAL CENTRE FOR INFORMATION HANDLING EQUIPMENT. 3218
0351-0840 See STRANI JEZICI. 3440
0351-0999 See ZITO HLEB. 5172
0351-1189 See PRIMERJALNA KNJIZEVNOST. 3425
0351-1375 See SAHOVSKI INFORMATOR. 4865
0351-1871 See POLIMERI (ZAGREB). 4459
0351-2193 See HISTORIJSKI ZBORNIK. 2691
0351-224X See ZBORNIK ZA UMETNOSTNO ZGODOVINO. ARCHIVES D'HISTOIRE DE L'ART. 2716
0351-2681 See ZBORNIK ZAVODA ZA POVIJESNE ZNANOSTI ISTRAZIVACKOG CENTRA JUGOSLAVENSKE AKADEMIJE ZNANOSTI I UMJETNOSTI. 2716
0351-272X See STARINE. 283
0351-2789 See ACTA ECCLESIASTICA SLOVENIAE. 2672
0351-286X See ECONOMIC ANALYSIS AND WORKERS' MANAGEMENT. 866
0351-2908 See GLASNIK SLOVENSKEGA ETNOLOSKEGA DRUSTVA. 237
0351-3238 See GEOGRAPHICA IUGOSLAVICA : BILTEN SAVEZA GEOGRAFSKIH DRUSTAVA JUGOSLAVIJE. 2562
0351-3564 See PUBLIC ENTERPRISE / INTERNATIONAL CENTER FOR PUBLIC ENTERPRISES IN DEVELOPING COUNTRIES. 2911
0351-4285 See CASOPIS ZA KRITIKO ZNANOSTI. 4540

0351-4323 *See* ETNOLOSKA ISTRAZIVANJA / ETNOGRAFSKI MUZEJ U ZAGREBU. **236**

0351-4331 *See* RAD DISPANZERA ZA PLUCNE BOLESTI I TUBERKULOZU. **3632**

0351-4501 *See* MEDITERRANEAN JOURNAL OF SOCIAL PSYCHIATRY / MEDITERRANEAN SOCIOPSYCHIATRIC ASSOCIATION. **3930**

0351-4536 *See* STAROHRVATSKA PROSVJETA. **2710**

0351-4552 *See* HERCEGOVINA (MOSTAR, BOSNIA AND HERCEGOVINA: 1981). **2690**

0351-4706 *See* FILOZOFSKA ISTRAZIVANJA. **4347**

0351-4749 *See* PUBLIKACIJE ELEKTROTEHNICKOG FAKULTETA. UNIVERZITET U BEOGRADU. SERIJA ELEKTROENERGETIKA. **2077**

0351-5796 *See* INTERNATIONAL REVIEW OF THE AESTHETICS AND SOCIOLOGY OF MUSIC. **4123**

0351-580X *See* ACTA STEREOLOGICA. **3491**

0351-6709 *See* RADOVI ZAVODA JUGOSLAVENSKE AKADEMIJE ZNANOSTI I UMJETNOSTI U ZADRU. **2704**

0351-7462 *See* NARODNA ZDRAVSTVENA KULTURA U SR SRBIJI. **3618**

0351-9112 *See* GODISEN ZBORNIK NA ZEMJODELSKIOT FAKULTET NA UNIVERZITETOT VO SKOPJE. **90**

0351-9120 *See* GODISNJAK JUGOSLOVENSKIH POZORISTA. **5364**

0351-9430 *See* BILTEN ZA HEMLJ, SIRAK I LEKOVITO BILJE. **502**

0352-0889 *See* ZBORNIK RADOVA PRIRODNO-MATEMATICKOG FAKULTETA. SERIJA ZA FIZIKU. **4425**

0352-1044 *See* BOOKS IN BOSNIA AND HERZEGOVINA. **3368**

0352-1311 *See* JUGOSLAVENSKA MEDICINSKA BIOKEMIJA. **3694**

0352-1346 *See* ZNANOST I PRAKSA U POLJOPRIVREDI I PREHRAMBENOJ TEHNOLOGIJI / OOUR POLJOPRIVREDNI INSTITUT. **531**

0352-1605 *See* REVIJA ZA PSIHOLOGIJU. **4615**

0352-1788 *See* ZBORNIK RADOVA PRIRODNO-MATEMATICKOG FAKULTETA. SERIJA ZA BIOLOGIJU. **476**

0352-1982 *See* AB, ARHITEKTOV BILTIN. **287**

0352-1990 *See* WISSENSCHAFTLICHE MITTEILUNGEN DES BOSNISCH-HERZEGOWINISCHEN LANDESMUSEUMS. HEFT A : ARCHAOLOGIE. **285**

0352-261X *See* VECERNJE NOVINE (1983). **5779**

0352-2695 *See* GODISNJAK / UNIVERZITET U SARAJEVU. **1825**

0352-3020 *See* FAGOPYRUM (LJUBLJANA). **83**

0352-3047 *See* SEMENARSTVO ZAGREB. **133**

0352-3160 *See* ISTORIJA 20. VEKA ; CASOPIS INSTITUTA ZA SAVREMENU ISTORIJU. **2620**

0352-3543 *See* YUGOSLAV ECONOMIC REVIEW. **1528**

0352-3659 *See* GEOFIZIKA ZAGREB. **1405**

0352-3837 *See* ICHTHYOS LJUBLJANA. **1356**

0352-3853 *See* POSEBNI IZDANIJA - MATEMATICKI FAKULTET NA UNIVERZITETOT "KIRIL I METODIJ", SKOPJE. **3527**

0352-3861 *See* GLASNIK ZA SUMSKE POKUSE. **2384**

0352-4728 *See* RAZVOJ. **2911**

0352-4906 *See* ZBORNIK MATICE SRPSKE ZA PRIRODNE NAUKE. **5172**

0352-5139 *See* JOURNAL OF THE SERBIAN CHEMICAL SOCIETY. **983**

0352-5562 *See* JUGOSLAVENSKA GINEKOLOGIJA I PERINATOLOGIJA. **3764**

0352-5600 *See* MIGRACIJSKE TEME. **1920**

0352-5686 *See* RAZISKAVE IN STUDIJE - KMETIJSKI INSTITUT SLOVENIJE. **125**

0352-5716 *See* ZBORNIK MATICE SRPSKE ZA ISTORIJU / MATICA SRPSKA, ODELJENJE ZA DRUSTVENE NAUKE. **2633**

0352-5740 *See* BULLETIN - ACADEMIE SERBE DES SCIENCES ET DES ARTS, CLASSE DES SCIENCES NATURELLES ET MATHEMATIQUES. SCIENCES NATURELLES. **5090**

0352-5759 *See* PUNIME MATEMATIKE. **3529**

0352-602X *See* MEDICINSKI ANALI. **3614**

0352-6100 *See* RADOVI MATEMATICKI / AKADEMIJA NAUKA I UMJETNOSTI BOSNE I HERCEGOVINE. **3530**

0352-664X *See* GODISNJAK VOJNOMEDICINSKE AKADEMIJE. **3579**

0352-6798 *See* RADOVI. RAZDIO FILOZOFIJE, PSIHOLOGIJE, SOCIOLOGIJE I PEDAGOGIJE / SVEUCILISTE U SPLITU, FILOZOFSKI FAKULTET--ZADAR. **4358**

0352-6844 *See* ZBORNIK MATICE SRPSKE ZA LIKOVNE UMETNOSTI / MATICA SRPSKA, ODELJENJE ZA LIKOVNE UMETNOSTI. **369**

0352-7115 *See* BILTEN SOKOJ. **4103**

0352-7220 *See* CATALOGUE OF YUGOSLAV PERIODICALS AND NEWSPAPERS. **5813**

0352-8553 *See* RAZVOJ, DEVELOPMENT INTERNATIONAL. **1639**

0352-8715 *See* SOL (ZAGREB). **3322**

0352-9193 *See* PREHRAMBENO-TEHNOLOSKA I BIOTEHNOLOSKA REVIJA. **2353**

0352-9444 *See* PREGLED NA MAGISTERSKI TRUDOVI ODBRANETI NA UNIVERZITETITE VO SR MAKEDONIJA VO PERIODOT ... / NARODNA I UNIVERAITETSKA BIBLIOTEKA KLIMENT OHRIDSKI--SKOPJE, REFERALEN CENTAR. **1842**

0352-9665 *See* FACTA UNIVERSITATIS. SERIES, MATHEMATICS AND INFORMATICS. **3505**

0353-0701 *See* DRAMA INFORMER, THE. **5363**

0353-4510 *See* FILOZOFSKI VESTNIK / SLOVENSKA AKADEMIJA ZNANOSTI IN UMETNOSTI, ZNANSTVENORAZISKOVALNI CENTER SAZU, FILOZOFSKI INSTITUT. **4347**

0353-5053 *See* PSYCHIATRIA DANUBINA. **3933**

0353-6386 *See* PRIZMA. **3312**

0353-7161 *See* EUROMASKE: THE EUROPEAN THEATRE QUARTERLY. **5364**

0353-7331 See SLOVENSKE NOVICE. **5810**

0353-8044 *See* ZBORNIK VETERINARSKE FAKULTETE, UNIVERZA LJUBLJANA. **5527**

0353-8052 *See* NOVA MATICA. **3349**

0353-8184 *See* NEODVISNI DNEVNIK. **5810**

0353-8249 *See* TEORIJSKA I PRIMENJENA MEHANIKA. **4429**

0353-8842 *See* NEUROLOGIA CROATICA : GLASILO UDRUZENJA NEUROLOGA JUGOSLAVIJE, OFFICIAL JOURNAL OF YUGOSLAV NEUROLOGICAL ASSOCIATION. **3840**

0353-8893 *See* PUBLIKACIJE ELEKTROTEHNICKOG FAKULTETA. SERIJA MATEMATIKA. **3529**

0353-9245 *See* EXPERIMENTAL AND CLINICAL GASTROENTEROLOGY. **3744**

0353-9504 *See* CROATIAN MEDICAL JOURNAL. **3569**

0353-9881 *See* OPHTHALMOLOGIA CROATICA. **3877**

0354-0243 *See* YUGOSLAV JOURNAL OF OPERATIONS RESEARCH. **1632**

0354-1088 *See* SLOVENSKE NOVICE. **5810**

0355-001X *See* SUOMEN KIRJALLISUUS. **3459**

0355-0036 *See* SIGNUM. **3249**

0355-0079 *See* YEARBOOK OF FINNISH FOREIGN POLICY. **4539**

0355-0087 *See* ANNALES ACADEMIAE SCIENTIARUM FENNICAE. SERIES A. I, MATHEMATICA DISSERTATIONS. **3493**

0355-0176 *See* KIRJALLISUUDENTUTKIJAIN SEURAN VUOSIKIRJA. **3402**

0355-0192 *See* MEMOIRES DE LA SOCIETE NEOPHILOLOGIQUE DE HELSINKI. **3302**

0355-0249 *See* ULKOMAANKAUPPA. **856**

0355-0303 *See* KANAVA (HELSINKI. 1973). **3345**

0355-0311 *See* KALEVALASEURAN VUOSIKIRJA. **3401**

0355-032X *See* SCANDINAVIAN FOREST ECONOMICS. **2394**

0355-0346 *See* BUSINESS CONTACTS IN FINLAND. **646**

0355-0567 *See* TEHO / TYOTEHOSEURA. **140**

0355-0648 *See* TIEDONANTOJA - RIISTA- JA KALATALOUDEN TUTKIMUSLAITOS KALANTUKIMUSOSASTO. **2315**

0355-0656 *See* SAMMANFATTNING AV ARTIKLARNA. **4916**

0355-0710 *See* TYOTEHOSEURAN JULKAISUJA. **143**

0355-1008 *See* BULLETIN OF THE INTERNATIONAL PEAT SOCIETY. **1934**

0355-1067 *See* PSYKOLOGIA. **4614**

0355-113X *See* ANNALES ACADEMIAE SCIENTIARUM FENNICAE. DISSERTATIONES HUMANARUM LITTERARUM. **2841**

0355-1253 *See* FINNISCH-UGRISCHE FORSCHUNGEN. **3281**

0355-1482 See TIEDONANTOJA / VALTION MAITOTALOUDEN TUTKIMUSLAITOS. **199**

0355-1628 *See* KEMIA. **1027**

0355-1725 *See* AJATUS; SUOMEN FILOSOFISEN YHDISTYKSEN VUOSIKIRJA. **4339**

0355-1776 *See* ETHNOLOGIA FENNICA. **235**

0355-1792 *See* ACTA PHILOSOPHICA FENNICA. **4339**

0355-1806 *See* SUOMEN MUSEO. **283**

0355-1822 *See* SUOMEN MUINAISMUISTOYHDISTYKSEN AIKAKAUSKIRJA. **283**

0355-1830 *See* KANSATIETEELLINEN ARKISTO **240**

0355-1938 *See* TAIDEHISTORIALLISIA TUTKIMUKSIA. **366**

0355-1962 *See* SUOMEN GEODEETTISEN LAITOKSEN TIEDONANTOJA. **1360**

0355-2047 *See* HELSINGIN SANOMAT. **5800**

0355-2160 *See* POLIISIN TIETOON TULLUT RIKOLLISUUS. **3082**

0355-2187 *See* TUOMIOISTUIMISSA KASITELLYT RIKOS- , SIVIILI- JA HALLINTOOIKEUDELLISET ASIAT. **3084**

0355-2268 *See* ENNAKKOTIEDOT KORKEAKOULUISSA SUORITETUISTA TUTKINNOISTA JA HYVAKSYTYISTA TOHTORINVAITOSKIRJOISTA. **1822**

0355-2276 *See* TILASTOTIEDOTUS. KT. **1587**

0355-2292 *See* KONKURSSITIEDOTE. **796**

0355-2314 *See* MYONNETYT RAKENNUSLUVAT. **621**

0355-2373 855

0355-256X *See* COMMENTATIONES SCIENTIARUM SOCIALIUM. **5196**

0355-2705 *See* ACTA POLYTECHNICA SCANDINAVICA. CIVIL ENGINEERING AND BUILDING CONSTRUCTION SERIES. CI. **2018**

0355-2713 *See* ACTA POLYTECHNICA SCANDINAVICA. MATHEMATICS AND COMPUTER SCIENCE SERIES. MA. **3490**

0355-2721 *See* ACTA POLYTECHNICA SCANDINAVICA. APPLIED PHYSICS SERIES PH. **4395**

0355-3140 *See* SCANDINAVIAN JOURNAL OF WORK, ENVIRONMENT & HEALTH. **2870**

0355-3213 *See* ARTES CONSTRUCTIONUM. **2018**

0355-3221 *See* ACTA UNIVERSITATIS OULUENSIS. SER. D, MEDICA. **3545**

0355-3728 *See* LOUNAIS-HAMEEN LUONTO. **2197**

0355-3779 *See* SIIRTOLAISUUS / SIIRTOLAISUUSINSTITUUTTI. **1921**

0355-4287 *See* TM. TEKNIIKAN MAAILMA. **5166**

0355-4317 *See* HYMY. **2774**

0355-4759 *See* HUOLTOAPU. **5288**

0355-4813 *See* KANSANELAKELAITOKSEN JULKAISUJA. AL. **3601**

0355-4821 *See* KANSANELAKELAITOKSEN JULKAISUJA. M. **2886**

0355-483X *See* KANSANELAKELAITOKSEN JULKAISUJA. ML. **5294**

0355-5100 *See* FINLAND HANDBOOK. **5470**

0355-533X *See* SUOMEN APTEEKKARILEHTI. **4330**

0355-550X *See* RAKENTAJAIN KALENTERI / SUOMEN RAKENNUSMESTARILIITTO. **625**

0355-578X *See* ACTA ACADEMIAE ABOENSIS. SER. A. HUMANIORA. **2841**

0355-7421 *See* TAITO. **376**

0355-8142 *See* BOTHNIAN BAY REPORTS. **1447**

0355-9521 *See* ANNALES CHIRURGIAE ET GYNAECOLOGIAE. **3756**

0355-9750 *See* ALKOHOLIPOLITIIKKA. **1340**

0355-9769 See NORDISK ALKOHOL TIDSKRIFT. **1347**

0355-9874 *See* ANNALES CHIRURGIAE ET GYNAECOLOGIAE. SUPPLEMENTUM. **3757**

0356-0376 *See* STUDIER I NORDISK FILOLOGI. **3325**

0356-0724 *See* HUFVUDSTADSBLADET. **5800**

0356-1437 *See* NORDIA. **2570**

0356-2654 *See* FINNISH FOUNDATION FOR ALCOHOL STUDIES (SERIES). **5105**

0356-3014 *See* MALLAS JA OLUT. **2369**

0356-3081 *See* SYOPA. **3824**

0356-3456 *See* ACTA PHARMACEUTICA FENNICA. **4288**

0356-3669 *See* KUNNALLISTIETEELLINEN AIKAKAUSKIRJA. **4660**

0356-5092 *See* HINNAT JA KILPAILU. **1608**

0356-5629 *See* FARAVID. **2616**

0356-7133 *See* AQUA FENNICA. **1412**

0356-7257 *See* METSATEHON TIEDOTUS. **2388**

0356-861X *See* KEVO NOTES. **462**

0356-9993 *See* INSURANCE IN FINLAND. **2883**

0357-1076 *See* FINNISH MARINE RESEARCH. **1449**

0357-1823 *See* TRANSACTIONS OF THE WESTERMARCK SOCIETY. **5264**

0357-1955 *See* NOSP-MIKRO. **421**

0357-2498 *See* LIIKUNNAN JA KANSANTERVEYDEN JULKAISUJA. **2599**

0357-2994 *See* BALTIC SEA ENVIRONMENT PROCEEDINGS. **1446**

0357-3346 *See* PUBLICATIONS OF THE UNIVERSITY OF KUOPIO. COMMUNITY HEALTH. SERIES ORIGINAL REPORTS. **4797**

0357-3370 *See* HELSINGIN VAESTO. **5328**

0357-3524 *See* LINTUMIES / SUOMEN LINTUTIETEELLINEN YHDISTYS. **5618**

0357-5527 *See* MAA- JA METSATALOUS. **105**

0357-5993 *See* REVIEWS - INSTITUTE OF OCCUPATIONAL HEALTH. **2869**

0357-6507 *See* MUISTIO (FINLAND. TILASTOKESKUS). **5333**

0357-6825 *See* ESPOON KAUPUNGIN TILASTOLLINEN VUOSIKIRJA. **5327**

0357-749X *See* VITRIINI. **2810**

0357-816X *See* SOTAHISTORIALLINEN AIKAKAUSKIRJA. **4057**

0357-9190 *See* TOIMINTAKERTOMUS / KORKEIN HALLINTO-OIKEUS. **3143**

0357-9387 *See* VTT SYMPOSIUM. **5169**

0357-9956 *See* OESTERBOTTEN. **2701**

0358-0202 *See* TIEDONANTOJA / VALTION MAITOTALOUDEN TUTKIMUSLAITOS. **199**

0358-3511 *See* MUOTO / TEOLLISUUSTAITEEN LIITTO ORNAMO. **304**

0358-4038 *See* TEHY. **3870**

0358-4283 *See* METSANTUTKIMUSLAITOKSEN TIEDONONTOJA. **2388**

0358-4828 *See* PHARMACOLOGICA ET PHYSIOLOGICA (OULU). **4322**

0358-4836 *See* ANAESTHESIOLOGICA (OULU). **3680**

0358-4844 *See* OBSTETRICA ET GYNECOLOGICA (OULU). **3766**

0358-4852 *See* OPHTHALMOLOGICA ET OTO-RHINO-LARYNGOLOGICA (OULU). **3877**

0358-4879 *See* CLINICAL CHEMICA (OULU). **3565**

0358-4887 *See* RADIOLOGICA (OULU). **3945**

0358-4895 *See* ANATOMICA, PATHOLOGICA, MICROBIOLOGICA. **3678**

0358-4917 *See* CHIRURGICA (OULU). **3962**

0358-5069 *See* PUBLICATIONS / TECHNICAL RESEARCH CENTRE OF FINLAND. **5143**

0358-5077 *See* TUTKIMUKSIA (VALTION TEKNILLINEN TUTKIMUSKESKUS). **5167**

0358-5522 *See* SCANDINAVIAN ECONOMIC HISTORY REVIEW, THE. **1583**

0358-5581 *See* OPUSCULUM. **3239**

0358-6243 *See* TILASTOTIEDOTUS. VL. **5345**

0358-6464 *See* JYVASKYLA CROSS-LANGUAGE STUDIES. **3293**

0358-7010 *See* LIIKUNTA JA TIEDE. **4903**

0358-710X *See* SCRIPTA HISTORICA. **2629**

0358-8017 *See* SEURA 1979. **2522**

0358-8904 *See* FORM FUNCTION FINLAND. **2098**

0358-9153 *See* SUOMEN AKATEMIAN JULKAISUJA. **138**

0358-9803 *See* KIRJASTOTIEDE JA INFORMATIIKKA. **3221**

0359-0607 *See* SUOMEN MATKAILU. **2523**

0359-1255 *See* TYOTERVEISET. **2871**

0359-2464 *See* GRAPHIC ARTS IN FINLAND. **379**

0359-5242 *See* SYNTEESI JYVASKYLA. **3444**

0359-7105 *See* DATUTOP, DEPARTMENT OF ARCHITECTURE, TAMPERE UNIVERSITY OF TECHNOLOGY OCCASIONAL PAPERS. **296**

0359-7431 *See* PORT OF HELSINKI HANDBOOK. **5454**

0360-0025 *See* SEX ROLES. **5257**

0360-0041 *See* PROFILES OF SCHEDULED AIR CARRIER PASSENGER TRAFFIC, TOP 100 U.S. AIRPORTS. **32**

0360-005X *See* MAINE FISH AND WILDLIFE. **2308**

0360-0076 *See* ANNUAL REPORT - COMMONWEALTH OF MASSACHUSETTS, OFFICE FOR CHILDREN. **4627**

0360-0114 *See* FLORIDA BAR NEWS. **2970**

0360-0149 *See* UNITED STATES COAST PILOT. 5, ATLANTIC COAST. GULF OF MEXICO, PUERTO RICO, AND VIRGIN ISLANDS. **4184**

0360-0157 *See* YOUNG SOCIALIST (NEW YORK. 1972). **3356**

0360-0181 *See* NEW CONVERSATIONS. **4980**

0360-019X *See* BIOPHYSICS (BOSTON). **494**

0360-0246 *See* ANNUAL REPORT - WEST VIRGINIA GOVERNOR'S HIGHWAY SAFETY ADMINISTRATION. **4630**

0360-0297 *See* POPULAR SCIENCE SERIES. **5139**

0360-0300 *See* ACM COMPUTING SURVEYS. **1170**

0360-0327 *See* SOVIET ASTRONOMY LETTERS. **400**

0360-0335 *See* SOVIET JOURNAL OF LOW TEMPERATURE PHYSICS. **4432**

0360-0343 *See* SOVIET JOURNAL OF PLASMA PHYSICS. **4421**

0360-036X *See* ITOGI, SUMMARIES OF SCIENTIFIC PROGRESS : DEVELOPMENT OF OIL AND GAS DEPOSITS. **4262**

0360-0394 *See* ITOGI, SUMMARIES OF SCIENTIFIC PROGRESS : HUMAN GENETICS. **548**

0360-0408 *See* ITOGI, SUMMARIES OF SCIENTIFIC PROGRESS : METEOROLOGY AND CLIMATOLOGY. **1426**

0360-0416 *See* ITOGI, SUMMARIES OF SCIENTIFIC PROGRESS : MICROBIOLOGY. **564**

0360-0424 *See* ITOGI, SUMMARIES OF SCIENTIFIC PROGRESS : OCEANOLOGY. **1450**

0360-0432 *See* ITOGI, SUMMARIES OF SCIENTIFIC PROGRESS: THEORETICAL PROBLEMS IN PHYSICAL AND ECONOMIC GEOGRAPHY. **2566**

0360-0440 *See* ITOGI, SUMMARIES OF SCIENTIFIC PROGRESS : VIROLOGY. **564**

0360-0459 See MEMBERSHIP DIRECTORY - AMERICAN SOCIETY FOR PUBLIC ADMINISTRATION, NATIONAL CAPITAL AREA CHAPTER. **4664**

0360-0467 *See* AREITO. **2255**

0360-0483 *See* ANNUAL REPORT - NEBRASKA COMMISSION ON LAW ENFORCEMENT AND CRIMINAL JUSTICE. **3157**

0360-0564 *See* ADVANCES IN CATALYSIS. **1049**

0360-0572 *See* ANNUAL REVIEW OF SOCIOLOGY. **5239**

0360-0629 *See* STATE OF NEW YORK COMPREHENSIVE CRIME CONTROL PLAN. **3177**

0360-0637 *See* EBSCO BULLETIN OF SERIALS CHANGES. **415**

0360-0661 *See* INDEX TO SCIENTIFIC REVIEWS. **5175**

0360-0718 *See* INDUSTRY WAGE SURVEY : METAL MINING. **1679**

0360-0726 *See* REHABILITATION WORLD. **4393**

0360-0750 *See* ANNUAL REPORT - ADVISORY COMMITTEE ON THE LAW OF THE SEA. **3180**

0360-0785 *See* PROFESSIONAL PERSONNEL CHARACTERISTICS. **1842**

0360-0793 *See* ACTIVITIES REPORT - U.S. NATIONAL COMMITTEE FOR THE INTERNATIONAL INSTITUTE OF REFRIGERATION. **2602**

0360-0807 *See* EDUCATIONAL FINANCE, CONNECTICUT. **1863**

0360-0815 *See* NATIONAL PANORAMA OF AMERICAN YOUTH, THE. **1766**

0360-084X *See* REPORT TO THE GOVERNOR - ARIZONA DEPARTMENT OF EDUCATION. **1778**

0360-0858 *See* GOLFGUIDE ANNUAL. **4897**

0360-0874 *See* LUSK'S CARROLL COUNTY REAL ESTATE DIRECTORY. **4840**

0360-0939 *See* ACA BULLETIN - ASSOCIATION FOR COMMUNICATION ADMINISTRATION. **1103**

0360-0939 *See* JACA : JOURNAL OF THE ASSOCIATION FOR COMMUNICATION ADMINISTRATION. **1114**

0360-0955 *See* CALIFORNIA COMMISSIONER OF CORPORATIONS CURRENT OFFICIAL OPINIONS ISSUED PURSUANT TO THE CORPORATE SECURITIES LAW OF 1968. **3097**

0360-0971 *See* INFORMATION REPORTS AND BIBLIOGRAPHIES. **3216**

0360-1013 *See* OHIO REVIEW (ATHENS), THE. **3420**

0360-1021 *See* ARCHAEOLOGY OF EASTERN NORTH AMERICA. **257**

0360-1048 *See* NEW MEXICO ALMANAC, THE. **4669**

0360-1056 *See* NORTH CAROLINA GENEALOGICAL SOCIETY JOURNAL, THE. **2464**

0360-1080 *See* LIBRARY CATALOG OF THE MARTIN P. CATHERWOOD LIBRARY OF THE NEW YORK STATE SCHOOL OF INDUSTRIAL AND LABOR RELATIONS, CORNELL UNIVERSITY. SUPPLEMENT. **1687**

0360-1099 *See* ANNUAL REPORT - MISSISSIPPI ARTS COMMISSION. **312**

0360-1188 *See* STATUS REPORT - PENNSYLVANIA TRANSPORTATION INSTITUTE. **5444**

0360-1196 *See* INTERNATIONAL BIBLIOGRAPHY ON BURNS. SUPPLEMENT. **3660**

0360-120X *See* SOVIET TECHNICAL PHYSICS LETTERS. **4422**

0360-1226 *See* JOURNAL OF ENVIRONMENTAL SCIENCE AND HEALTH. PART A, ENVIRONMENTAL SCIENCE AND ENGINEERING. **1982**

0360-1234 *See* JOURNAL OF ENVIRONMENTAL SCIENCE AND HEALTH. PART B, PESTICIDES, FOOD CONTAMINANTS, AND AGRICULTURAL WASTES. **2176**

0360-1277 *See* EDUCATIONAL GERONTOLOGY. **1800**

0360-1285 *See* PROGRESS IN ENERGY AND COMBUSTION SCIENCE. **1954**

0360-1293 *See* ACUPUNCTURE & ELECTRO-THERAPEUTICS RESEARCH. **3545**

0360-1315 *See* COMPUTERS & EDUCATION. **1222**

0360-1323 *See* BUILDING AND ENVIRONMENT. **602**

0360-1382 *See* HOME BUILDING & REMODELING. **616**

0360-1420 *See* JOURNAL OF CHRISTIAN RECONSTRUCTION, THE. **4968**

0360-1455 *See* NEW RIVER REVIEW. **3416**

0360-1463 *See* OFFICIAL COMPREHENSIVE DEVELOPMENT PLAN. **2830**

0360-1501 See SEMI-ANNUAL GEOGRAPHICAL INDEX OF SPECIALTY ADVERTISING DISTRIBUTORS. 765

0360-151X See BRIGHAM YOUNG UNIVERSITY LAW REVIEW. 2943

0360-1587 See CIVIL RIGHTS DIRECTORY. 4506

0360-1609 See ENERGY RESEARCH AND TECHNOLOGY. 1941

0360-1625 See PUBLICATIONS OF THE WEST VIRGINIA GEOLOGICAL SURVEY. 1392

0360-1730 See VETERINARY NEWS (ALBANY). 5526

0360-1757 See EIA ELECTRONICS MULTIMEDIA HANDBOOK. 2043

0360-1765 See LEVIATHAN & KINNIKINNIK. 2537

0360-1773 See MARKET CHRONICLE, THE. 906

0360-1781 See OBF, OF THE PEOPLE, BY THE PEOPLE, FOR THE PEOPLE. 4485

0360-1897 See PACIFIC THEOLOGICAL REVIEW. 4984

0360-1927 See JOURNAL OF LATIN AMERICAN LORE. 2321

0360-1935 See MAIN TITLE. 4129

0360-1943 See MUSIC BOOK GUIDE. 4133

0360-196X See CORRECTIONS COURT DIGEST, THE. 2957

0360-1978 See RICHMOND HISTORIAN, THE. 2759

0360-1986 See WOMEN'S WORK (WASHINGTON). 1718

0360-2001 See DISTRIBUTION OF STEEL CASTINGS SALES BY END USE OF PRODUCT. 923

0360-2060 See INDUSTRY WAGE SURVEY. DEPARTMENT STORES. 1679

0360-2079 See HOME PLANNING & DESIGN. 300

0360-2095 See DIRECTORY OF MEMBERS, LOT EXCHANGE, MAUSOLEUM CRYPT EXCHANGE, DOLLAR CREDIT PLANS. 2407

0360-2109 See PAUL'S RECORD MAGAZINE. 4145

0360-2125 See PRO BASKETBALL. 4913

0360-2133 See METALLURGICAL TRANSACTIONS. A. PHYSICAL METALLURGY AND MATERIALS SCIENCE. 4010

0360-2141 See METALLURGICAL TRANSACTIONS. B, PROCESS METALLURGY. 4010

0360-215X See DICTIONARY OF CONTEMPORARY QUOTATIONS. 3381

0360-2192 See MASKS (STANFORD). 2538

0360-2273 See POPULAR MECHANICS DO-IT-YOURSELF YEARBOOK. 5423

0360-2303 See SALE - SOTHEBY, PARKE-BERNET, LOS ANGELES. 364

0360-2311 See STATE PAYMENTS TO LOCAL GOVERNMENT. 4749

0360-232X See BANKS OF ARKANSAS, THE. 777

0360-2338 See BANKS OF MICHIGAN, THE. 777

0360-2346 See BANKS OF PENNSYLVANIA. 778

0360-2354 See BANKS OF OKLAHOMA. 778

0360-2362 See BANKS OF OHIO, THE. 778

0360-2370 See STUDIES IN EIGHTEENTH-CENTURY CULTURE. 2631

0360-2400 See MANAGEMENT CONTENTS. 731

0360-2419 See JACK DARR'S SERVICE CLINIC. 2067

0360-2435 See SURVEY OF LIBRARY MATERIAL EXPENDITURES AT STANFORD UNIVERSITY LIBRARIES. 3252

0360-2443 See CHORAL OVERTONES. 4109

0360-2508 See CHART BOOK OF GOVERNMENTAL DATA: ORGANIZATION, FINANCES AND EMPLOYMENT. 4717

0360-2516 See BILLBOARD INDEX. 5362

0360-2524 See CHORAL TONES. 4109

0360-2532 See DRUG METABOLISM REVIEWS (SOFTCOVER ED.). 4301

0360-2540 See SEPARATION AND PURIFICATION METHODS (SOFTCOVER ED.). 1029

0360-2559 See POLYMER-PLASTICS TECHNOLOGY AND ENGINEERING (SOFTCOVER ED.). 2015

0360-2575 See BULLETIN - GREATER ST. LOUIS DENTAL SOCIETY. 1318

0360-2583 See DRUGS AND THE PHARMACEUTICAL SCIENCES. 4302

0360-2613 See NEW DYNAMICS OF PREVENTIVE MEDICINE. 3620

0360-2672 See SCREE. 3352

0360-2699 See BIBLIOGRAPHIC GUIDE TO ART AND ARCHITECTURE. 334

0360-2702 See BIBLIOGRAPHIC GUIDE TO BUSINESS AND ECONOMICS. 726

0360-2710 See BIBLIOGRAPHIC GUIDE TO BLACK STUDIES. 2276

0360-2729 See BIBLIOGRAPHIC GUIDE TO CONFERENCE PUBLICATIONS. 409

0360-2737 See BIBLIOGRAPHIC GUIDE TO DANCE. 1314

0360-2745 See BIBLIOGRAPHIC GUIDE TO LAW. 2941

0360-2753 See BIBLIOGRAPHIC GUIDE TO MUSIC. 4160

0360-2761 See BIBLIOGRAPHIC GUIDE TO TECHNOLOGY. 5173

0360-277X See BIBLIOGRAPHIC GUIDE TO PSYCHOLOGY. 4622

0360-2788 See BIBLIOGRAPHIC GUIDE TO THEATRE ARTS. 5372

0360-280X See BIBLIOGRAPHIC GUIDE TO GOVERNMENT PUBLICATIONS - FOREIGN. 4696

0360-2834 See MARYLAND REGISTER. 3007

0360-2842 See NOAA DATA REPORT MESA. 2219

0360-2850 See OFFICIAL DIRECTORY OF REGISTERED NURSES AND LICENSED PRACTICAL NURSES. 3866

0360-2869 See PROGRAM DIRECTORY - ARKANSAS DEPARTMENT OF PLANNING. 4675

0360-2877 See CONCRETE PIPE INDUSTRY STATISTICS. 632

0360-2923 See WYOMING OIL AND GAS STATISTICS. 4285

0360-3016 See INTERNATIONAL JOURNAL OF RADIATION- ONCOLOGY, BIOLOGY, PHYSICS. 3818

0360-3024 See FAMILY MOTOR COACHING. 5382

0360-3032 See TRINITY JOURNAL. 2925

0360-3075 See ANNUAL PERFORMANCE STUDY - WINE AND SPIRITS WHOLESALERS OF AMERICA. 2363

0360-3156 See LGA BILL OF PARTICULARS. 3002

0360-3164 See PLATING AND SURFACE FINISHING. 4225

0360-3199 See INTERNATIONAL JOURNAL OF HYDROGEN ENERGY. 1948

0360-3245 See BOMB SUMMARY. 3158

0360-3261 See DICTIONARY CATALOG OF THE JEWISH COLLECTION. SUPPLEMENT. 415

0360-3296 See NATIONAL MEMBERSHIP DIRECTORY - WOMEN IN COMMUNICATIONS, INC. 1118

0360-3342 See LIBERTY, THEN AND NOW. 2537

0360-3350 See LADOC. 4972

0360-3385 See TRISTANIA. 3448

0360-3393 See AGRICULTURAL SITUATION IN THE PEOPLE'S REPUBLIC OF CHINA AND OTHER COMMUNIST ASIAN COUNTRIES, THE. 52

0360-3407 See GUIDE TO PROGRAMS - NATIONAL ENDOWMENT FOR THE ARTS. 321

0360-3431 See SOURCEBOOK OF CRIMINAL JUSTICE STATISTICS. 3083

0360-3512 See FEDERAL DIRECTORY, THE. 4648

0360-3520 See BODY FASHIONS/INTIMATE APPAREL. 1082

0360-3539 See CALLING THE WORLD. 1151

0360-3547 See ANNUAL REPORT - THE STATE OF OKLAHOMA, OFFICE OF COMMUNITY AFFAIRS AND PLANNING. 4629

0360-3687 See ANNUAL REPORT - AMERICAN INSTITUTE OF INDIAN STUDIES. 2255

0360-3695 See FILM & HISTORY (NEWARK, N.J.). 4069

0360-3709 See AMERICAN POETRY REVIEW, THE. 3460

0360-3717 See A.M.E. ZION QUARTERLY REVIEW, THE. 5054

0360-3725 See A.M.E. CHURCH REVIEW, THE. 4931

0360-3806 See ADCA, AMERICAN DIRECTORY OF COLLECTION AGENCIES AND ATTORNEYS. 768

0360-3814 See PERFORMING ARTS RESOURCES. 387

0360-3830 See VIRGINIA AGRICULTURAL STATISTICS. 157

0360-3857 See VIRGINIA BAR ASSOCIATION JOURNAL, THE. 3071

0360-3881 See SPECIAL REPORT - ALASKA. DIVISION OF GEOLOGICAL AND GEOPHYSICAL SURVEYS. 1398

0360-389X See ADVENTIST HERITAGE. 5054

0360-3911 See BROILER MARKETING FACTS. 922

0360-392X See BRIEFS OF ACCIDENTS INVOLVING MIDAIR COLLISIONS, U.S. GENERAL AVIATION. 14

0360-3946 See DEPARTMENT PUBLICATIONS - STATE OF CALIFORNIA, RESOURCES AGENCY, DEPARTMENT OF WATER RESOURCES. 5532

0360-3954 See LISTING OF AIRCRAFT ACCIDENTS-INCIDENTS BY MAKE AND MODEL, U.S. CIVIL AVIATION. 27

0360-3989 See HUMAN COMMUNICATION RESEARCH. 1112

0360-3997 See INFLAMMATION. 3587

0360-4012 See JOURNAL OF NEUROSCIENCE RESEARCH. 3837

0360-4020 See JOURNAL OF THE ASSOCIATION OF MILITARY DERMATOLOGISTS. 3721

0360-4039 See NURSING. 3863

0360-4063 See RESEARCH IN READING AND THE LANGUAGE ARTS. 3315

0360-4071 See QUALITY ROCK READER. 4148

0360-4098 See AGRICULTURAL SITUATION IN THE SOVIET UNION, THE. 52

0360-4128 See REPORT - COOPERATIVE ACCOUNTABILITY PROJECT. 1869

0360-4217 See NATIONAL JOURNAL (1975). 4483

0360-4225 See VISUAL DIALOG. 368

0360-425X See BANKS OF COLORADO, THE. 777

0360-4268 See BANKS OF ILLINOIS, THE. 777

0360-4276 See BANKS OF INDIANA, THE. 777

0360-4284 See BANKS OF IOWA, THE. 777

0360-4292 See BANKS OF LOUISIANA. 777

0360-4306 See BANKS OF MINNESOTA. 777

0360-4314 See BANKS OF MISSOURI, THE. 778

0360-4322 See BANKS OF WISCONSIN. 778

0360-4357 See DPI YELLOW PAGES. 5284

0360-4365 See IN THEORY ONLY. 4122

0360-4373 See OFFICIAL ABSTRACT OF VOTES : PRIMARY ELECTION. 4485

0360-4381 See RIVER CITY (WICHITA, KAN.). 4150

0360-4403 See URBAN AREAS OF WASHINGTON. 2578

0360-4446 See AEROSOL AND PRESSURIZED PRODUCTS SURVEY. 1020

0360-4497 See SOVIET JOURNAL OF BIOORGANIC CHEMISTRY. 1047

0360-4586 See CARLOAD WAYBILL STATISTICS. 5379

0360-4594 See FOOD AND NUTRITION PROGRAMS. 2909

0360-4608 See RECORD - TENNESSEE DEPARTMENT OF HUMAN SERVICES, THE. 5304

0360-4624 See ANNUAL REPORT - BOARD OF NURSE REGISTRATION AND NURSING EDUCATION. 3851

0360-4659 See ANNUAL REPORT OF THE JUDICIAL COUNCIL OF NEW MEXICO. 2934

0360-4667 See COUNTY RECREATION & PARK SERVICES STUDY (NORTH CAROLINA). 4706

0360-473X See DIRECTIONS (NEW YORK, N.Y. 1975). 3206

0360-4756 See JOURNAL - HONOLULU ACADEMY OF ARTS. 323

0360-4772 See SOUTH DAKOTA EDUCATIONAL STATISTICS DIGEST. 1797

0360-4780 See WOMEN'S PROGRAM. 5571

0360-4918 See PRESIDENTIAL STUDIES QUARTERLY. 4674

0360-4934 See WAGE CHRONOLOGY : BERKSHIRE HATHAWAY AND THE CLOTHING AND TEXTILE WORKERS. 1717

0360-4985 See INFORUM: ENVIRONMENTAL REPORT DATA SYSTEM. 2174

0360-5019 See INTERAGENCY TRAINING CATALOG OF COURSES. 4704

0360-5043 See SOVIET JOURNAL OF GLASS PHYSICS AND CHEMISTRY, THE. 1030

0360-5051 See PROJECT SUMMARIES OF THE CENTER FOR BUILDING TECHNOLOGY, NATIONAL BUREAU OF STANDARDS. 624

0360-506X See RETAILING TODAY. 957

0360-5078 See DIRECTORY OF THE TRANSPORTATION RESEARCH BOARD. 5381

0360-5094 See MIDWESTERN ADVOCATE. 3010

0360-5132 See OFFICIAL GAZETTE OF THE UNITED STATES PATENT AND TRADEMARK OFFICE. TRADEMARKS. 1307

0360-5175 See CONFERENCE SUMMARY REPORT - AVIATION REVIEW CONFERENCE. 17

0360-5191 See EAST CAROLINA MANUSCRIPT COLLECTION BULLETIN. 415

0360-5205 See ATA HANDBOOK. 2784

0360-5272 See RAIL TRANSIT DIRECTORY. 5435

0360-5280 See BYTE. 1273

0360-5302 See COMMUNICATIONS IN PARTIAL DIFFERENTIAL EQUATIONS. 3501

0360-5310 See JOURNAL OF MEDICINE AND PHILOSOPHY, THE. 3596

0360-5396 See TENNESSEE MOTOR VEHICLE TRAFFIC ACCIDENT FACTS. 5445

0360-5434 See OCCUPATIONAL EDUCATION. 1914

0360-5442 See ENERGY (OXFORD). 1941

0360-5469 See FINANCIAL STATEMENTS WITH SUPPLEMENTAL SCHEDULES. 1824

0360-5485 See AFFILIATE, THE. 2928

0360-5531 See OLD NORTHWEST, THE. 2752

0360-5582 See ROSTER OF DENTISTS AND DENTAL HYGIENISTS REGISTERED IN THE STATE OF MINNESOTA. 1335

0360-5647 See ANNUAL BUDGET TO CONTINUE CURRENT PROGRAMS. 4709

0360-5663 See REPORT ON KANSAS UNIFORM CONSUMER CREDIT CODE. 808

0360-5698 See CITIZEN PARTICIPATION AND VOLUNTARY ACTION ABSTRACTS. 5279

0360-571X See GAY LUTHERAN, THE. 2794

0360-5736 See DESCRIPTIVE REPORT OF PROGRAM ACTIVITIES FOR VOCATIONAL EDUCATION (OKLAHOMA CITY). 1912

0360-5744 See MASSACHUSETTS ECONOMIC ASSUMPTIONS. 1504

0360-5752 See MEMBERSHIP DIRECTORY AND AMERICAN CORRESPONDENTS OVERSEAS. 2922

0360-5817 See INFORMATION HOTLINE. 3216

0360-5841 See INVENTORY OF AGRICULTURAL RESEARCH. 97

0360-5876 See VIRGINIA GUARDPOST. 4060

0360-5914 See JOHNS HOPKINS UNIVERSITY SCHOOL OF MEDICINE POSTGRADUATE COURSE IN INTERNAL MEDICINE, THE. 3798

0360-5949 See TRANSACTIONS OF THE AMERICAN PHILOLOGICAL ASSOCIATION (1974). 3329

0360-6066 See NOAA PROFESSIONAL PAPER. 1453

0360-6074 See SMASH. 3437

0360-6082 See GEORGETOWN INTERNATIONAL REVIEW. 3128

0360-6090 See ACCELERATION AND PASSING ABILITY. 5375

0360-6112 See BUDDHIST TEXT INFORMATION. 5012

0360-6120 See ELDER CHURCHMAN, THE. 4955

0360-6171 See MONDAY MORNING (INDIANAPOLIS, IND.). 5065

0360-618X See NEWSLETTER OF THE CENTER FOR PROCESS STUDIES. 4982

0360-6236 See INACTIVE OIL AND GAS FIELDS. 4260

0360-6252 See KANSAS DIRECTORY. SUPPLEMENT. 4659

0360-6260 See IPA INTERGOVERNMENTAL ASSIGNMENT PROGRAM : REPORT, THE. 4658

0360-6279 See GOVERNMENT NATIONAL MORTGAGE ASSOCIATION EXAMINATION OF FINANCIAL STATEMENTS. 789

0360-6325 See LIGHTING DESIGN & APPLICATION. 2070

0360-6341 See BEHAVIOR THERAPY WITH CHILDREN. 4576

0360-6503 See PROCESS STUDIES. 4358

0360-652X See PATRISTICS. 4985

0360-6538 See ANNOTATED BIBLIOGRAPHY OF NEW PUBLICATIONS IN PERFORMING ARTS. 333

0360-6562 See ARCHITECTURE. NEW ENGLAND. 290

0360-6597 See MEMBERSHIP ROSTER - AMERICAN SOCIETY OF TRAVEL AGENTS INC. 5484

0360-6600 See PUBLIC WELFARE ACTIVITIES IN ARIZONA. 5303

0360-6627 See ANNUAL REPORT, BOND PAYMENT FUND. 4710

0360-6678 See BRIEFS OF FATAL ACCIDENTS INVOLVING WEATHER AS A CAUSE-FACTOR, U.S. GENERAL AVIATION. 15

0360-6716 See MUNICIPAL RECREATION & PARK SERVICES STUDY. 4707

0360-6813 See BRIEFS OF ACCIDENTS INVOLVING MISSING AND MISSING LATER RECOVERED AIRCRAFT, U.S. GENERAL AVIATION. 15

0360-6864 See COLUMBIA RIVER WATER MANAGEMENT REPORT. 2088

0360-6899 See DIRECTORY - AMERICAN PUBLIC WORKS ASSOCIATION. 4760

0360-6902 See STANDARD SPECIFICATIONS FOR TRANSPORTATION MATERIALS AND METHODS OF SAMPLING AND TESTING. 2031

0360-6929 See ANNUAL TECHNICAL CONFERENCE TRANSACTIONS - AMERICAN SOCIETY FOR QUALITY CONTROL. 860

0360-6945 See LUTHERAN JOURNAL, THE. 5063

0360-697X See AACSB NEWSLINE. 1806

0360-697X See NEWSLINE / AMERICAN ASSEMBLY OF COLLEGIATE SCHOOLS OF BUSINESS. 699

0360-7011 See AMMONIA PLANT SAFETY (AND RELATED FACILITIES). 2007

0360-7038 See WHO'S WHO IN ASSOCIATION MANAGEMENT. 436

0360-7119 See REPORTER. 946

0360-7127 See BRIEFS OF FATAL ACCIDENTS INVOLVING WEATHER AS A CAUSE-FACTOR, U.S. GENERAL AVIATION. 15

0360-7135 See CREATIVE WORLD. 4113

0360-7151 See LEGAL BIBLIOGRAPHIC DATA SERVICE : WEEKLY LISTING. 3081

0360-716X See NEWSLETTER - UNITED STATES. NAVY. SUPPLY CORPS. 4181

0360-7178 See AAMOA REPORTS. 4098

0360-7208 See BUSINESS, HEALTH AND EDUCATIONAL DISCIPLINES. 648

0360-7224 See I.D.A.A. COMMUNIQUE. 1324

0360-7232 See MENTALIS. 1330

0360-7259 See NUTRITION AND CLINICAL NUTRITION. 4195

0360-7275 See CHEMICAL ENGINEERING PROGRESS. 2010

0360-7283 See HEALTH & SOCIAL WORK. 5287

0360-7364 See SERGEANTS. 4057

0360-7372 See SURVEY OF LAW REVIEWS. 3061

0360-7399 See TRUCK WEIGHT SURVEY. 5398

0360-7437 See AAMC DIRECTORY OF AMERICAN MEDICAL EDUCATION. 1806

0360-7453 See VIOLATIONS OF HUMAN RIGHTS IN SOVIET OCCUPIED LITHUANIA, THE. 4514

0360-7488 See CUMULATIVE DOCUMENT ACCESSION LIST. 414

0360-7496 See CANOE (CAMDEN, ME.). 592

0360-750X See REPORT TO CONGRESS CONCERNING THE DEMONSTRATION OF FARE-FREE MASS TRANSPORTATION. 5391

0360-7518 See BIENNIAL REPORT - OKLAHOMA INDIAN AFFAIRS COMMISSION. 2256

0360-7526 See IOWA ELECTION HANDBOOK WITH ELECTION LAWS OF IOWA. 2984

0360-7534 See TRA DIGEST. 5494

0360-7542 See MANAGEMENT AWARENESS PROGRAM. 876

0360-7550 See NEMATOLOGY CIRCULAR. 466

0360-7569 See CURRENT CONCEPTS IN PSYCHIATRY. 3924

0360-7607 See HEMOSTASIS AND THROMBOSIS. 3772

0360-7623 See MEDICAL STUDENT (DARIEN). 3611

0360-7631 See RESEARCH ISSUES. 1348

0360-7666 See WARREN-TEED G.I. TRACT. 3748

0360-7674 See ENVIRONMENTAL GEOLOGY (COLORADO GEOLOGICAL SURVEY). 1375

0360-7690 See NUCLEAR REGULATION REPORTS. 3115

0360-7704 See PUBLIC AND SPECIAL ACTS. 3032

0360-7720 See ARIZONA TRAFFIC. 5439

0360-7763 See NATIONAL INSTITUTE OF DENTAL RESEARCH PROGRAMS. 1330

0360-7801 See U.S. MISSILE DATA BOOK. 4059

0360-7917 See REVISTA/REVIEW INTERAMERICANA. 5216

0360-7933 See RESOURCES FOR HEALTH R & D REPORT. 4799

0360-7941 See MODERN GOVERNMENT/NATIONAL DEVELOPMENT. 4666

0360-795X See JOURNAL OF CORPORATION LAW, THE. 3101

0360-7992 See ALABAMA LANDINGS, ANNUAL SUMMARY. 2293

0360-8034 See WILDFIRE STATISTICS. 2399

0360-8042 See FOUNDATIONS IN WISCONSIN. 4336

0360-8050 See REPORT TO THE GOVERNOR AND THE LEGISLATURE - STATE OF CALIFORNIA, DEPARTMENT OF CONSUMER AFFAIRS. 1299

0360-8069 See OHIO LIBRARIES. 3239

0360-8077 See MINNESOTA REAL ESTATE DIRECTORY. 4841

0360-8131 See COUNTRY MUSIC BOOKING GUIDE. 4112

0360-814X See PROCEEDINGS AWWA ANNUAL CONFERENCE. 4761

0360-8271 See BEST IN ENVIRONMENTAL GRAPHICS, THE. 377

0360-8298 See CUMBERLAND LAW REVIEW. 2957

0360-831X See SOCIAL REGISTER NEW ORLEANS. 2473

0360-8352 See COMPUTERS & INDUSTRIAL ENGINEERING. 2097

0360-8409 See ICARBS. 3214

0360-8476 See SEARCH AT THE STATE UNIVERSITY OF NEW YORK. 5156

0360-8484 See MATTHAY NEWS, THE. 4130

0360-8492 See GEOPUB REVIEW OF GEOGRAPHICAL LITERATURE. 2564

0360-8514 See COUNTRY DEMOGRAPHIC PROFILES. 4551

0360-8530 See BIENNIAL REPORT - TEXAS HISTORICAL COMMISSION. 2723

0360-8557 See ENGINEERING INDEX ANNUAL. 2004

0360-8581 See IEEE ENGINEERING MANAGEMENT REVIEW. 2059

0360-859X See SPECIAL REPORT - TRANSPORTATION RESEARCH BOARD, NATIONAL RESEARCH COUNCIL. 5393

0360-8654 See GUIDE TO MICROGRAPHIC EQUIPMENT. 4370

0360-8670 See AVIATION QUARTERLY. 13

0360-8689 See BEST IN PACKAGING, THE. 4218

0360-8697 See COUNTRY MUSIC EXPLORER. 4112

0360-8727 See RIDIM/RCMI NEWSLETTER. 363

0360-8743 See BEST IN ANNUAL REPORTS, THE. 642

0360-8794 See DIRECTORY OF MEMBERS, OFFICERS, COMMITTEES - AMERICAN VACUUM SOCIETY. 2113

0360-8808 See JOURNAL OF THE EVANGELICAL THEOLOGICAL SOCIETY. 4970

0360-8867 See MARINE GEOTECHNOLOGY. 1451

0360-8956 See IEEE STUDENT PRIZE PAPERS, THE. 2061

0360-8972 See PUBLICATION / OREGON STATE UNIVERSITY, SEA GRANT COLLEGE PROGRAM. 1455

0360-8999 See FOUNDRY MANAGEMENT & TECHNOLOGY. 4002

0360-9006 See RECENT ACTIVITIES - HASTINGS CENTER. 2253

0360-9022 See SOUTH DAKOTA COUNTY POOR RELIEF. 5310

0360-9030 See HISTORICAL FOOTNOTES (ST. LOUIS, MO.). 2618

0360-9049 See HEBREW UNION COLLEGE ANNUAL. 5048

0360-9057 See FAITHFUL WORD, THE. 4958

0360-9065 See FAITH-LIFE. 5060

0360-9073 See ECUMENICAL TRENDS. 4955

0360-9081 See AMERICAN ARCHIVIST, THE. 2478

0360-912X See SHOCKS. 3471

0360-9146 See UNIFORM CRIME REPORT FOR THE STATE OF MICHIGAN. 3084

0360-9170 See LANGUAGE ARTS. 1804

0360-9189 See WESCONN. 1853

0360-9219 See FINANCIAL INFORMATION, COLORADO SCHOOL DISTRICTS. 1864

0360-926X See REPORT OF THE SUPERINTENDENT OF BANKS AND SMALL LOAN COMPANIES. 808

0360-9278 See HEARING REHABILITATION QUARTERLY. 4388

0360-9340 See ILLINOIS STATE BUDGET IN BRIEF. 4731

0360-9405 See PERFORMANCE REPORT TO THE LEGISLATURE- LEGISLATIVE BUDGET BOARD. 4673

0360-9421 See POPE FAMILY REGISTER, THE. 2468

0360-9456 See EMPLOYERS' GUIDE TO WORKERS' COMPENSATION AND SAFE EMPLOYMENT LAWS OF OREGON. 3147

0360-9480 See HABARI - AFRICAN BIBLIOGRAPHIC CENTER. 2639

0360-9510 See DAILY REPORTER (SIOUX CITY), THE. 2958

0360-9553 See NON-FERROUS METAL DATA. 4013

0360-9626 See HONOLULU PRICES, WHOLESALE FRESH FRUITS AND VEGETABLES. 2343

0360-9669 See HORIZONS (VILLANOVA). 4963

0360-9685 See LUTHERAN SYNOD QUARTERLY, THE. 5063

0360-9693 See MILITARY CHAPLAINS' REVIEW. 4050

0360-974X See PETROLEUM ACTIVITY REPORT. 4272

0360-9774 See SHORT STORY INDEX. 3459

0360-9782 See PENSION BOARDS. 5065

0360-9804 See BULLETIN - ILLINOIS STATE WATER SURVEY. 5531

0360-9847 See ACCIDENT AND VIOLATION ANALYSIS FOR LICENSED OREGON DRIVERS. 5438

0360-991X See ZCLA JOURNAL. 5022

0360-9928 See MARATHON HANDBOOK. 4904

0360-9936 See QUALITY (WHEATON). 884

0360-9960 See ADVANCES IN BIOENGINEERING. 1963

0360-9987 See DIRECTORY OF DIESEL FUEL STATIONS COAST TO COAST, A. 4254

0361-0020 See RETAILING IN TENNESSEE. 957

0361-0128 See ECONOMIC GEOLOGY AND THE BULLETIN OF THE SOCIETY OF ECONOMIC GEOLOGISTS. 1374

0361-0144 See AMERICAN HUMANITIES INDEX, THE. 2857

0361-0160 See SIXTEENTH CENTURY JOURNAL, THE. 2629

0361-0225 See PERSPECTIVES IN NEUROENDOCRINE RESEARCH. 3732

0361-0241 See START OF MESSAGE. 3251

0361-0284 See CHECKLIST OF INDIANA STATE DOCUMENTS. 413

0361-0314 See REPORT ON FRINGE BENEFITS AND RELATED PRACTICES AFFECTING GENERAL EMPLOYEES OF CITIES. 4682

0361-0365 See RESEARCH IN HIGHER EDUCATION. 1845

0361-0470 See JOURNAL OF THE AMERICAN SOCIETY OF BREWING CHEMISTS. 982

0361-0497 See MIRD PAMPHLETS. 3944

0361-0519 See MISCELLANEOUS REPORT - STATE OF OHIO, DEPARTMENT OF NATURAL RESOURCES, DIVISION OF GEOLOGICAL SURVEY. 1388

0361-056X See CAMPAIGN PRACTICES REPORTS. 2947

0361-0578 See CITY OF ROCHESTER BUDGET. 4717

0361-0632 See RHODE ISLAND BASIC ECONOMIC STATISTICS. 1518

0361-0640 See RUBBER RED BOOK. 5078

0361-0691 See REGIONAL TOPICS. 2833

0361-0713 See IBRO NEWS. 3834

0361-073X See EXPERIMENTAL AGING RESEARCH. 3750

0361-0764 See STATISTICAL REFERENCE BOOK OF INTERNATIONAL ACTIVITIES. 1930

0361-0780 See ADMINISTRATION AND SUPPLEMENTARY INFORMATION : CATALOG - UNIVERSITY OF ALABAMA. 1859

0361-0802 See PILGRIMAGE. 4608

0361-0845 See COIN WORLD ALMANAC. 2780

0361-0853 See MANUFACTURING ENGINEERING. 1986

0361-0861 See SOUTHERN SCHOOL LAW DIGEST. 3057

0361-0888 See MEMBERSHIP DIRECTORY AND BUYERS' GUIDE - AMERICAN FROZEN FOOD INSTITUTE. 2350

0361-090X See CANCER DETECTION AND PREVENTION. 3811

0361-0918 See COMMUNICATIONS IN STATISTICS : SIMULATION AND COMPUTATION. 1282

0361-0926 See COMMUNICATIONS IN STATISTICS : THEORY AND METHODS. 3501

0361-0934 See COVENANT QUARTERLY, THE. 4951

0361-0942 See VIDEO SYSTEMS. 1142

0361-0985 See EDUCATIONAL OPPORTUNITIES OF GREATER BOSTON. 1800

0361-1019 See ANNUAL FINANCIAL REPORT OF THE DIRECTOR OF ADMINISTRATIVE SERVICES. 4709

0361-1116 See ABORTION RESEARCH NOTES. 587

0361-1213 See MICROSTRUCTURAL SCIENCE. 4012

0361-1256 See WILDLIFE RESEARCH. 2209

0361-1272 See UNIVERSITY OF ROCHESTER LIBRARY BULLETIN. 3255

0361-1299 See ROCKY MOUNTAIN REVIEW OF LANGUAGE AND LITERATURE. 3431

0361-1310 See SEMSCOPE, THE. 4685

0361-1329 See SURVEY OF BUYING POWER. 714

0361-1353 See ALASKA GEOGRAPHIC. 2553

0361-1434 See IEEE TRANSACTIONS ON PROFESSIONAL COMMUNICATION. 2063

0361-1442 See COMPUTERS AND PEOPLE. 1218

0361-1493 See DIRECTORY OF DRUG INFORMATION AND TREATMENT ORGANIZATIONS. 1343

0361-1507 See CAREER EDUCATION PROGRAM : PROGRAM PLAN. 1911

0361-1515 See GRASSROOTS (MADISON). 1344

0361-1531 See REVIEW OF EXISTENTIAL PSYCHOLOGY AND PSYCHIATRY (1972). 4615

0361-1574 See AREA WAGE SURVEY. GREENSBORO-WINSTON-SALEM-HIGH POINT, NORTH CAROLINA, METROPOLITAN AREA. 1652

0361-1582 See FEDERAL GRANT-IN-AID ACTIVITY IN FLORIDA : A SUMMARY REPORT. 4723

0361-1590 See INDIAN EDUCATION ACT OF 1972; REPORT OF PROGRESS, THE. 1752

0361-1612 See REPORT OF THE COUNCIL FOR TOBACCO RESEARCH--U.S.A., INC. 5373

0361-1639 See SOUTH CAROLINA HISTORIC PRESERVATION PLAN : ANNUAL PRESERVATION PROGRAM. 2761

0361-1663 See ABRAXAS (MADISON). 3459

0361-1817 See NURSE PRACTITIONER, THE. 3863

0361-185X See SELBYANA. 527

0361-1906 See JOURNAL OF THEOLOGY. 4971

0361-1930 See WHOLE EARTH NEWSLETTER. 5009

0361-1981 See TRANSPORTATION RESEARCH RECORD. 5397

0361-2007 See PROCEEDINGS, ANNUAL TECHNICAL MEETING - INSTITUTE OF ENVIRONMENTAL SCIENCES. 5140

0361-204X See NEW YORK FOLKLORE. 2323

0361-2112 See DRESS. 1083

0361-2120 See BIENNIAL REPORT - EDUCATIONAL COMMUNICATIONS BOARD. 1889

0361-2147 See ANTIQUE PHONOGRAPH MONTHLY, THE. 249

0361-2171 See WYOMING ADULT EDUCATION : ADULT EDUCATION PLAN. 1802

0361-221X See BATON TWIRLING RULES AND REGULATIONS. 383

0361-2236 See ECUMENICAL DIRECTORY OF RETREAT AND CONFERENCE CENTERS. 4955

0361-2260 See REPORT ON PARTICIPATION IN ASCS COUNTY PROGRAMS AND OPERATIONS BY RACIAL GROUPS. 126

0361-2287 See SCHOOL TRANSPORTATION SUMMARY. 1872

0361-2309 See CORPORATE EXAMINER, THE. 661

0361-2317 See COLOR RESEARCH AND APPLICATION. 5095

0361-2333 See PROSPECTS (NEW YORK). 2755

0361-2376 See CONGREGATIONAL JOURNAL. 5058

0361-2392 See LUTHERANS ALERT, NATIONAL. 5063

0361-2449 See RESEARCH NOTE NC. 2393

0361-2481 See WIND (PIKEVILLE, KY.). 3453

0361-2546 See REGISTRY OF TOXIC EFFECTS OF CHEMICAL SUBSTANCES [MICROFORM]. 3983

0361-2554 See REPORT OF INVESTIGATIONS - MISSOURI DEPARTMENT OF NATURAL RESOURCES, DIVISION OF RESEARCH AND TECHNICAL INFORMATION, GEOLOGICAL SURVEY. 1394

0361-2589 See VALUE LINE OTC SPECIAL SITUATIONS SERVICE, THE. 918

0361-2597 See TEXAS INDUSTRIAL COMMISSION ANNUAL REPORT. 1629

0361-2600 See ECOLOGY (HOUSTON). 2214

0361-2619 See SOUL & JAZZ RECORD, THE. 4153

0361-2635 See MICROPUBLISHERS' TRADE LIST ANNUAL, THE. 420

0361-2643 See QUALITY CONTROL : STATES' CORRECTIVE ACTION ACTIVITIES. 5303

0361-2651 See PROJECTS RECOMMENDED FOR DEAUTHORIZATION, ANNUAL REPORT. 2095

0361-266X See PTA HANDBOOK, THE. 1775

0361-2678 See VIEWPOINT (COLUMBUS). 332

0361-2686 See ELECTROCHEMICAL INDUSTRY. 1034

0361-2716 See SELECTIVE SERVICE NEWS. 4056

0361-2724 See PRESBYTERIAN KEY, THE. 5066

0361-2740 See SERIALS IN MICROFORM. 424

0361-2759 See HISTORY (WASHINGTON). 2619

0361-2783 See AUERBACH GUIDE TO COMPUTING EQUIPMENT SPECIFICATIONS. 1256

0361-2791 See CTA QUARTERLY. 5380

0361-2805 See COLLECTED REPRINTS - NATIONAL OCEAN SURVEY. 1448

0361-2813 See HOME IMPROVEMENT & REPAIR. 616

0361-2848 See WISCONSIN LIBRARY SERVICE RECORD. 3256

0361-2899 See OFFICIAL AAU TRAMPOLINE AND TUMBLING HANDBOOK. 4909

0361-2902 See HANDBOOK OF EMPLOYMENT SECURITY PROGRAM STATISTICS. 1533

0361-2929 See HEALTH FACILITIES DIRECTORY (SACRAMENTO). 3781

0361-2945 See APTD. 2224

0361-2953 See PROCEEDINGS OF THE ANNUAL GULF AND CARIBBEAN FISHERIES INSTITUTE AND THE ANNUAL INTERNATIONAL GAME FISH RESEARCH CONFERENCE. 2310

0361-2988 See COMPLETE HANDBOOK OF PRO FOOTBALL, THE. 4891

0361-3011 See FIELD & STREAM HUNTING ANNUAL. 4872

0361-3046 See SELECTED STUDIES IN MEDICAL CARE AND MEDICAL ECONOMICS. 3640

0361-3070 See INSTRUMENTATION IN THE MINING AND METALLURGY INDUSTRIES. 2140

0361-3097 See CBS REPORTS. 1130

0361-3135 See CBS NEWS SPECIAL REPORT. 1130

0361-3232 See SHOWCASE (NEW YORK). 3186

0361-3267 See COLLABORATIVE STUDY ON CEREBRAL PALSY, MENTAL RETARDATION, & OTHER NEUROLOGICAL & SENSORY DISORDERS OF INFANCY & CHILDHOOD. 3830

0361-3291 See SILENT PARTNER, THE. 4217

0361-3313 See ELECTRONICS AND COMMUNICATIONS ABSTRACTS JOURNAL (RIVERDALE, MD.). 2003

0361-3356 See OHIO SCHOOLS - OHIO. AUDITOR OF STATE. 1868

0361-3372 See PRACTICAL CARDIOLOGY. 3709

0361-3399 See NATIVE AERICAN TEXTS SERIES. 2268

0361-3437 See INCLUSIVE DIRECTORY OF INDEPENDENT OPERATING TELEPHONES. 1157

0361-3453 See FINE WOODWORKING. 634

0361-3461 See SOUTH DAKOTA HIGHWAY SAFETY WORK PROGRAM. 5444

0361-347X See OFFICIAL AAU TRACK AND FIELD HANDBOOK. 4908

0361-3569 See DAMMING THE SOLID WASTE STREAM : THE BEGINNING OF SOURCE REDUCTION IN MINNESOTA. 2227

0361-3577 See LOBLOLLY. 2744

0361-3593 See SOUTHWEST DIRECTORY OF ADVERTISING AND PUBLIC RELATIONS AGENCIES. 766

0361-3607 See STATISTICAL YEAR BOOK OF THE ELECTRIC UTILITY INDUSTRY. 4700

0361-3623 See STANDARD & POOR'S REGISTER OF CORPORATIONS, DIRECTORS AND EXECUTIVES. 713

0361-3666 See DISASTERS. 5284

0361-3682 See ACCOUNTING, ORGANIZATIONS AND SOCIETY. 737

0361-3712 See ARLINGTON CATHOLIC HERALD. 5024

0361-3771 See DIRECTORY OF PSYCHOSOCIAL INVESTIGATORS. 4585

0361-3801 See FINE PRINT (SAN FRANCISCO). 4565

0361-381X See BICYCLE DEALER SHOWCASE. 428

0361-3844 See ATTORNEYS AND AGENTS REGISTERED TO PRACTICE BEFORE THE U.S. PATENT AND TRADEMARK OFFICE. 2938

0361-3917 See SIE GUIDE TO BUSINESS & INVESTMENT BOOKS. 914

0361-3968 See ASIAN THOUGHT & SOCIETY. 4540

0361-3976 See PLAYING RULES. 4912

0361-3984 See ALASKA FISHING GUIDE. 2293

0361-4018 See ANNUAL REPORT - NEW YORK STATE MEDICAL CARE FACILITIES FINANCE AGENCY. 3776

0361-4034 See GROCERY DISTRIBUTION. 2342

0361-4050 See EMPLOYEE BENEFITS JOURNAL. 1665

0361-4069 See BENCHMARK PAPERS IN MICROBIOLOGY. 560

0361-4115 See DIRECTORY OF CERTIFIED PUBLIC ACCOUNTANTS AND PUBLIC ACCOUNTANTS OF OKLAHOMA. 743

0361-4131 See INTERNATIONAL FILM BUFF. 4072

0361-4158 See FAMILY SERVICES IN UTAH. 5285

0361-4166 See REHABILITATION GAZETTE. 4393

0361-4174 See MEDICAL ELECTRONICS & EQUIPMENT NEWS. 3609

0361-4190 See XEROX DISCLOSURE JOURNAL. 1310

0361-4220 See INTERNATIONAL GUILD GUIDE, THE. 5071

0361-4247 See BUYER'S DIRECTORY OF SUPPLIERS FOR GENERAL MERCHANDISE BUYERS. 949

0361-4298 See GAS FACTS. 4283

0361-4336 See CHILDREN TODAY. 5278

0361-4344 See FDA MEDICAL BULLETIN. 4305

0361-4360 See BELLE W. BARUCH LIBRARY IN MARINE SCIENCE, THE. 1446

0361-4387 See COSMETICS AND TOILETRIES. 403

0361-4425 See BULLETIN - YALE UNIVERSITY, SCHOOL OF FORESTRY AND ENVIRONMENTAL STUDIES. 2377

0361-4441 See CUBAN STUDIES. 2730

0361-4468 See HEALTH, UNITED STATES. 4781

0361-4476 See JOURNAL OF ENERGY AND DEVELOPMENT, THE. 1948

0361-4492 See ISSUES IN ARCHITECTURE. 301

0361-4522 See PESTICIDE-PCB IN FOODS PROGRAM. 4246

0361-4549 See SUMMARY OF SCHOOL REFERENDA IN DELAWARE. 1873

0361-4581 See FILMS BY AND/OR ABOUT WOMEN. 4071

0361-459X See MANUAL OF THE GENERAL ASSEMBLY OF THE STATE OF GEORGIA. 4664

0361-462X See ANNUAL REPORT - SOCIAL SCIENCE RESEARCH COUNCIL (NEW YORK). 5191

0361-4646 See BEHAVIORAL SCIENCES NEWSLETTER. 4577

0361-4662 See BOTTOMLINE. 1256

0361-4700 See WORKPAPERS OF THE SUMMER INSTITUTE OF LINGUISTICS, UNIVERSITY OF NORTH DAKOTA. 3333

0361-4719 See INSTRUMENTATION IN THE PULP AND PAPER INDUSTRY. 4234

0361-4727 See 1000 LARGEST U.S. BANKS. 768

0361-4743 See COMPETITIVE ANALYSIS : OHIO. 784

0361-4751 See AMERICAN FILM. 4063

0361-476X See CONTEMPORARY EDUCATIONAL PSYCHOLOGY. 4582

0361-4778 See COMPETITIVE ANALYSIS : VIRGINIA. 784

0361-4786 See COMPETITIVE ANALYSIS: PENNSYLVANIA. 784

0361-4794 See CURRENT MATHEMATICAL PUBLICATIONS. 3542

0361-4808 See BANKS OF GEORGIA, THE. 777

0361-4816 See BANKS OF KANSAS. 777

0361-4824 See BANKS OF KENTUCKY, THE. 777

0361-4832 See BANKS OF MISSISSIPPI, THE. 777

0361-4840 See BANKS OF NEBRASKA. 778

0361-4859 See BANKS OF NEW ENGLAND. 778

0361-4867 See BANKS OF TENNESSEE. 778

0361-4875 See BANKS OF THE CAROLINAS, THE. 778

0361-4883 See BANKS OF THE WEST. 778

0361-4891 See COMPETITIVE ANALYSIS : OKLAHOMA. 784

0361-4948 See TOUR BOOK : ALABAMA, LOUISIANA, MISSISSIPPI. 5492

0361-4956 See TOUR BOOK : GEORGIA, NORTH CAROLINA, SOUTH CAROLINA. 5492

0361-4964 See TOUR BOOK: KENTUCKY-TENNESSEE. 5492

0361-4980 See DIRECTORY OF LICENSED REAL ESTATE APPRAISERS. 4836

0361-4999 See ITHACAGUN HUNTING & SHOOTING ANNUAL. 4901

0361-5014 See SUMMARY OF BUDGET REQUESTS - STATE BOARD OF REGENTS. 1872

0361-5030 See FLIGHT OPERATIONS. 21

0361-5057 See COLLEGE RECRUITING REPORT. 1660

0361-5065 See BUOYANT FLIGHT. 15

0361-5103 See RHODE ISLAND DIRECTORY OF MANUFACTURERS. 3487

0361-5154 See JOURNAL OF THE HUMANITIES AND SOCIAL SCIENCES. 2849

0361-5162 See TRACE SUBSTANCES IN ENVIRONMENTAL HEALTH. 2221

0361-5170 See VICTIMOLOGY. 3178

0361-5219 See SOLID FUEL CHEMISTRY. 1030

0361-5227 See MODERN PSYCHOANALYSIS. 4604

0361-5235 See JOURNAL OF ELECTRONIC MATERIALS. 2068

0361-5243 See SUBJECT HEADINGS IN MICROFORM. 3251

0361-5251 See NATIONAL UNION CATALOG. REGISTER OF ADDITIONAL LOCATIONS. CUMULATIVE MICROFORM EDITION. 420

0361-526X See SERIALS LIBRARIAN, THE. 3249

0361-5294 See DOORS AND HARDWARE. 613

0361-5367 See CORNELL FOCUS. 77

0361-5413 See HISTORY IN AFRICA. 2640

0361-5472 See ORB (HARVARD), THE. 4984

0361-5499 See NATIONAL GEOGRAPHIC WORLD. 2570

0361-5537 See TRANSACTIONS - NORTH CAROLINA MEDICAL SOCIETY. 3647

0361-5553 See CLARINET (POCATELLO, IDAHO), THE. 4110

0361-5634 See ESSAYS IN ARTS AND SCIENCES. 2846

0361-5650 See AIR QUALITY IN MINNESOTA. 2223

0361-5669 See ARL ANNUAL SALARY SURVEY. 1654

0361-5731 See UNCOVER D.C. 2548

0361-574X See JOURNAL OF HISTORIC MADISON, INC. OF WISCONSIN, THE. 2741

0361-5774 See BLUEGRASS REFLECTIONS. 4104

0361-5804 See RESEARCH REPORT P. 128

0361-5812 See CAMPING AND TRAILERING GUIDE. 4870

0361-5839 See GIRLS BASKETBALL RULES BOOK. NATIONAL FEDERATION EDITION. 4896

0361-5847 See HOCKEY (NORWALK). 4899

0361-5855 See RECORDER REVIEW. 5318

0361-588X See BIG EIGHT, THE. 4887

0361-5901 See BUDGET REQUESTS - STATE BOARD OF REGENTS. 1728

0361-5928 See LESBIAN READER, THE. 2795

0361-5987 See PROCEEDINGS OF THE ANNUAL SOUTHWESTERN PETROLEUM SHORT COURSE. 4275

0361-5995 See SOIL SCIENCE SOCIETY OF AMERICA JOURNAL. **187**

0361-6029 See NEWSLETTER - AMERICAN SCHOOLS OF ORIENTAL RESEARCH. **1768**

0361-6045 See STUDIA SWEDENBORGIANA. **4362**

0361-6053 See ANNUAL ESTIMATE OF POPULATION FOR THE STATE OF GEORGIA. **4549**

0361-6061 See FACE TO FACE (NEW YORK). **4958**

0361-6126 See REPORT TO CONGRESS ON THE ECONOMIC IMPACT OF ENERGY ACTIONS. **1955**

0361-6169 See JAMES SPRUNT STUDIES IN HISTORY AND POLITICAL SCIENCE, THE. **2620**

0361-6207 See PROCEEDINGS OF THE SOUTH CAROLINA HISTORICAL ASSOCIATION, THE. **2755**

0361-6215 See PAPERS - WEST TENNESSEE HISTORICAL SOCIETY. **2753**

0361-6274 See HEALTH CARE MANAGEMENT REVIEW. **3781**

0361-6282 See DIRECTORY OF COMMUNITY CARE FACILITIES. **5282**

0361-6304 See WHO'S WHO IN P/M. **437**

0361-6320 See FLAME RETARDANCY OF POLYMERIC MATERIALS. **5351**

0361-6347 See NEW TITLES IN BIOETHICS. **3620**

0361-6371 See TRANSIT OPERATING REPORT. **5395**

0361-6398 See BOSTON BRUINS OFFICIAL YEARBOOK. **4887**

0361-6444 See SPUR REPORT. **2836**

0361-6452 See ANNUAL REPORT - SOUTHERN RESEARCH INSTITUTE. **5084**

0361-6495 See SAMUEL FRENCH'S BASIC CATALOGUE OF PLAYS. **424**

0361-6509 See ROAD ATLAS : UNITED STATES, CANADA, AND MEXICO. **1929**

0361-6525 See SOCIOBIOLOGY. **5597**

0361-655X See AREA WAGE SURVEY. GREENVILLE-SPARTANBURG, SOUTH CAROLINA, METROPOLITAN AREA. **1529**

0361-6568 See COLORADO INSURANCE INDUSTRY STATISTICAL REPORT. **2897**

0361-6576 See JOURNAL OF ECONOMICS. **1499**

0361-6584 See KRONOS. **2622**

0361-6614 See SEISMIC ENGINEERING PROGRAM REPORT. **1396**

0361-6622 See SELECTED REPORTS IN ETHNOMUSICOLOGY. **4152**

0361-6657 See COMPREHENSIVE DISSERTATION INDEX. SUPPLEMENT. **414**

0361-6665 See WAGE-PRICE LAW & ECONOMICS REVIEW. **1526**

0361-6673 See COLLECTION OF LEGAL OPINIONS, A. **3110**

0361-6843 See PSYCHOLOGY OF WOMEN QUARTERLY. **5565**

0361-6878 See JOURNAL OF HEALTH POLITICS, POLICY AND LAW. **2987**

0361-6886 See ACTA GEOLOGICA SINICA. **1364**

0361-6894 See BOSTON CELTICS. **4887**

0361-6924 See DIRECTORY OF MUNICIPAL AUTHORITIES IN PENNSYLVANIA. **4644**

0361-6932 See ILLINOIS REGIONAL PLANNING AGENCY DIRECTORY. **2825**

0361-7009 See SCIENCE FICTION REVIEW MONTHLY, THE. **3434**

0361-705X See SAN FRANCISCO MEDICINE. **3638**

0361-7130 See SOUTHERN CITY. **4686**

0361-7149 See SOVIET GEOLOGY AND GEOPHYSICS. **1397**

0361-7157 See ENGLISH GENEALOGICAL HELPER. **2446**

0361-7203 See COMPUTER LAW AND TAX REPORT. **2954**

0361-7254 See OREGON'S COMPREHENSIVE CRIMINAL JUSTICE PLAN. **3171**

0361-7378 See CRIMINAL JUSTICE IN SOUTH DAKOTA. **3162**

0361-7386 See AREA WAGE SURVEY. FRESNO, CALIFORNIA, METROPOLITAN AREA. **1652**

0361-7416 See HARVARD CLASS OF 1970 ANNIVERSARY REPORT. **1827**

0361-7459 See INTERNATIONAL A. A. DIRECTORY. **1345**

0361-7467 See PPF SURVEY. **946**

0361-7475 See STATISTICAL ABSTRACT - NEW YORK STATE DEPARTMENT OF STATE. **4699**

0361-7491 See ACTA - CENTER FOR MEDIEVAL AND EARLY RENAISSANCE STUDIES, STATE UNIVERSITY OF NEW YORK AT BINGHAMTON. **2672**

0361-7610 See GLASS AND CERAMICS. **2589**

0361-7637 See AREA WAGE SURVEY : WESTCHESTER COUNTY, NEW YORK. **1653**

0361-7661 See CHICAGO BANKS. **783**

0361-7688 See PROGRAMMING AND COMPUTER SOFTWARE. **1281**

0361-7734 See OPERATIVE DENTISTRY. **1332**

0361-7742 See PROGRESS IN CLINICAL AND BIOLOGICAL RESEARCH. **470**

0361-7858 See ANNUAL REPORT / THE POPULATION COUNCIL. **4549**

0361-7866 See SPARK (NEW YORK. 1971). **1997**

0361-7874 See AAAS HANDBOOK. **5079**

0361-7882 See INTERNATIONAL JOURNAL OF AFRICAN HISTORICAL STUDIES, THE. **2640**

0361-7904 See NATIONAL DIRECTORY OF SAFETY CONSULTANTS. **4792**

0361-7920 See CHECKLIST OF AMERICAN IMPRINTS, A. **413**

0361-7947 See THEATRE PROFILES. **5371**

0361-798X See ANNUAL REPORT - FEDERAL RESERVE BANK OF CLEVELAND. **771**

0361-803X See AMERICAN JOURNAL OF ROENTGENOLOGY (1976). **3938**

0361-8048 See ANNUAL - ASSOCIATION OF TRACK AND FIELD STATISTICIANS. **4856**

0361-8099 See NORTH DAKOTA HIGHWAY SAFETY IMPROVEMENT PROGRAM, ANNUAL REPORT. **5442**

0361-8102 See REGIONAL OCCUPATIONAL CENTERS AND PROGRAMS. **1915**

0361-8161 See ROSTER OF REGISTERED PROFESSIONAL ENGINEERS AND LAND SURVEYORS : ANNUAL REPORT. **2030**

0361-817X See WISCONSIN PHYSICIANS : DESCRIPTION AND DISTRIBUTION. **3917**

0361-8188 See LAKE MICHIGAN WATER QUALITY REPORT. **5535**

0361-820X See CREEL FAMILY QUARTERLY. **2278**

0361-8285 See BIENNIAL REPORT OF THE STATE GEOLOGIST (VERMILLION), THE. **1367**

0361-8307 See SURVEY OF STATE TRAVEL OFFICES. **5491**

0361-8331 See VECTOR (BURLINGTON). **5007**

0361-8374 See CABLE VISION. **1129**

0361-8455 See DIRECTORY OF MENTAL HEALTH SERVICES IN ILLINOIS. **4773**

0361-8528 See SCHOHARIE COUNTY HISTORICAL REVIEW. **2759**

0361-8552 See YELLOW BRICK ROAD (TEMPE, ARIZ.). **3455**

0361-8595 See RESEARCH MONOGRAPH SERIES - NATIONAL INSTITUTE ON DRUG ABUSE. **1348**

0361-8609 See AMERICAN JOURNAL OF HEMATOLOGY. **3770**

0361-8641 See THESAURUS LINGUAE GRAECAE; NEWSLETTER. **1080**

0361-8676 See SOUTH DAKOTA HISTORY. **2761**

0361-8684 See CHAIRMAN'S REPORT - THE ASIA SOCIETY--SEADAG. **1601**

0361-8706 See ANNUAL REPORT - FIRST NATIONAL STORES INC. **2327**

0361-8714 See CONFERENCE SERIES - FEDERAL RESERVE BANK OF BOSTON. **784**

0361-8757 See LUTHERAN COUNCIL IN THE U.S.A. NEWS BUREAU (NEWS RELEASE). **5063**

0361-8773 See JCT, JOURNAL OF COATINGS TECHNOLOGY. **4224**

0361-8854 See CONTEXT (CHICAGO. 1969). **4950**

0361-8862 See CONGREGATION, THE. **5058**

0361-8900 See BASIC DRUG LIST. **4293**

0361-8919 See DIRECTORY OF PUBLIC EDUCATION, STATE OF MARYLAND. **1862**

0361-8951 See SETON HALL LEGISLATIVE JOURNAL. **3048**

0361-896X See STATISTICS - STATE OF TENNESSEE, DEPARTMENT OF HUMAN SERVICES. **5267**

0361-8978 See TRANSPORTATION LINES ON THE GREAT LAKES SYSTEM. **5457**

0361-8986 See TRANSPORTATION LINES ON THE MISSISSIPPI RIVER SYSTEM AND THE GULF INTRACOASTAL WATERWAY. **5457**

0361-9001 See CHINESE SCIENCE. **5093**

0361-9036 See AFFIRMATIVE ACTION REPORT - TEXAS. EQUAL EMPLOYMENT OPPORTUNITY OFFICE. **4701**

0361-9052 See ANNUAL REPORT - NATIONAL PROFESSIONAL STANDARDS REVIEW COUNCIL. **3551**

0361-9060 See OPERATING FINANCE REPORT FOR ILLINOIS PUBLIC COMMUNITY COLLEGES. **1839**

0361-9079 See UNIFIED WORK PROGRAM. **5398**

0361-9087 See ANNUAL REPORT OF THE EASTERN ENVIRONMENTAL RADIATION FACILITY, U. S. ENVIRONMENTAL PROTECTION AGENCY. **2161**

0361-9117 See WOMEN ARTISTS NEWS. **333**

0361-9125 See TRANSPORTATION LINES ON THE ATLANTIC, GULF, AND PACIFIC COASTS. **5457**

0361-9133 See ANNUAL REPORT - PROJECT MODEL. **1910**

0361-9168 See BULLETIN - ASMP--THE SOCIETY OF PHOTOGRAPHERS IN COMMUNICATIONS. **4367**

0361-9176 See COMPREHENSIVE STATE PLAN FOR DRUG ABUSE CONTROL (VIRGINIA). **1342**

0361-9230 See BRAIN RESEARCH BULLETIN. **3829**

0361-9249 See CURRENT PRACTICE IN OBSTETRIC AND GYNECOLOGIC NURSING. **3760**

0361-9273 See GUIDEBOOK OF U.S. & CANADIAN POSTDOCTORAL DENTAL PROGRAMS. **1324**

0361-929X See MCN, THE AMERICAN JOURNAL OF MATERNAL CHILD NURSING. **3861**

0361-9311 See MENTAL HEALTH STATISTICAL NOTE. **4790**

0361-9400 See CONTINUOUS WAGE AND BENEFIT HISTORY. **1661**

0361-9419 See POOR RICHARD'S RECORD. **1841**

0361-9451 See WISCONSIN SPORTSMAN. **4880**

0361-946X See MEDIAEVALIA (BINGHAMTON). **2697**

0361-9508 See DISTRICT AND PRECINCT BOUNDARIES, STATE OF HAWAII. **4472**

0361-9516 See DIRECTORY OF MENTAL HEALTH AND ALCOHOLISM PROGRAMS IN MARYLAND. **4773**

0361-9524 See ERRL PUBLICATION. **82**

0361-9532 See NORTH CAROLINA MUNICIPAL EXPENDITURES FROM STATE STREET-AID ALLOCATIONS. **5442**

0361-9559 See PRO MUSICA SANA. **4147**

0361-9591 See MEANS CONSTRUCTION COST INDEXES. **620**

0361-9621 See EXPLICACION DE TEXTOS LITERARIOS. **3386**

0361-9648 See FODOR'S SPAIN. **5473**

0361-9729 See GIRLS & BOYS TOGETHER. **3458**

0361-9745 See DEVELOPMENTAL STUDIES AND LABORATORY INVESTIGATIONS CONDUCTED BY VETERINARY SERVICES DIAGNOSTIC LABORATORIES. **5508**

0361-9753 See ACTIVITIES - THE TENNESSEE STATE PLANNING OFFICE. **2813**

0361-9761 See FODOR'S HUNGARY. **5471**

0361-977X See FODOR'S ITALY. **5472**

0361-9788 See FLORIDA HANDBOOK, THE. **2733**

0361-9796 See FLORIDA ALMANAC. **2533**

0361-9974 See PLANT INVENTORY. 2427
0361-9990 See LEARNING (ROCKVILLE). 1761
0362-000X See HISTORICAL COLLECTIONS OF THE DANVERS HISTORICAL SOCIETY. 2737
0362-0018 See TREND IN ENGINEERING AT THE UNIVERSITY OF WASHINGTON, THE. 2000
0362-0026 See NUCLEUS (CAMBRIDGE), THE. 988
0362-0050 See NOTEBOOK OF EMPIRICAL PETROLOGY. 1459
0362-0085 See THEOLOGIA 21. 5003
0362-0131 See BUYER'S GUIDE TO MICROGRAPHIC EQUIPMENT, PRODUCTS AND SERVICES. 4367
0362-014X See CITRUS FRUIT INDUSTRY STATISTICAL BULLETIN. 2362
0362-0190 See FAMILY CREATIVE WORKSHOP, THE. 373
0362-0204 See FODOR'S EUROPE. 5471
0362-0220 See FODOR'S SOUTH AMERICA. 5473
0362-028X See JOURNAL OF FOOD PROTECTION. 2346
0362-0328 See CONSERVATION (SACRAMENTO). 2190
0362-0344 See TRAIL BREAKERS. 2475
0362-0360 See STATISTICS : CALENDAR YEAR REVIEW. 5267
0362-0476 See REFORMED LITURGY AND MUSIC. 4990
0362-0492 See UNITARIAN UNIVERSALIST CHRISTIAN, THE. 5068
0362-0506 See HIGHWAY & HEAVY CONSTRUCTION PRODUCTS. 5440
0362-0522 See SPRING. 4619
0362-0581 See BULLETIN - LUTHERAN THEOLOGICAL SEMINARY, GETTYSBURG. 5057
0362-0611 See REFLECTION (NEW HAVEN). 4990
0362-062X See JOURNAL OF REPRINTS OF DOCUMENTS AFFECTING WOMEN. 2989
0362-0670 See BARRON'S REGENTS EXAMS AND ANSWERS : BUSINESS MATHEMATICS. 642
0362-0697 See ECONOMIC CRIME DIGEST. 3163
0362-0727 See JOURNAL OF THE HOSPITAL FOR SPECIAL SURGERY, THE. 3968
0362-0743 See OHIO GENEALOGICAL HELPER, THE. 2465
0362-0751 See REVIEW / OAK RIDGE NATIONAL LABORATORY. 4451
0362-076X See ALMANAC OF AMERICAN POLITICS, THE. 4462
0362-0786 See FIRE PROTECTION GUIDE TO HAZARDOUS MATERIALS. 2289
0362-0808 See MASTER SERMON SERIES. 4976
0362-0816 See ASSOCIATE REFORMED PRESBYTERIAN, THE. 5055
0362-0859 See ETHICAL HUMANIST, THE. 2249
0362-0867 See EXPLOR (EVANSTON, ILL.). 4958
0362-0905 See FOCUS : CHICAGO. 4071
0362-0964 See THEATRE STUDIES. 5371
0362-0972 See INFORMATION DISPLAY (1975). 2064
0362-0999 See MICROFORM MARKET PLACE. 4822
0362-1103 See RULES AND REGULATIONS OF THE NEW YORK STATE THRUWAY AUTHORITY. 3045
0362-1162 See AUDIVIDEO INTERNATIONAL. 5315
0362-1197 See HUMAN PHYSIOLOGY. 581
0362-1243 See ANNUAL REPORT OF THE STATE OIL AND GAS SUPERVISOR. 4283
0362-1286 See INDUSTRIAL AND BUSINESS DIRECTORY OF TENNESSEE, ARKANSAS AND MISSISSIPPI. 1610
0362-1332 See FDA CONSUMER. 4647
0362-1367 See STATE SALES TAX COLLECTIONS REPORT. 4749
0362-1383 See ANNUAL REPORT - MASSACHUSETTS ADVOCACY CENTER. 2934
0362-1405 See FINANCIAL INDUSTRY NUMBER STANDARD DIRECTORY. 898

0362-1413 See BARRON'S REGENTS EXAMS AND ANSWERS, 9TH YEAR MATHEMATICS, ELEMENTARY ALGEBRA. 3496
0362-1529 See TRADITIO. 2713
0362-1537 See TRANSACTIONAL ANALYSIS JOURNAL. 4620
0362-1545 See USQR, UNION SEMINARY QUARTERLY REVIEW. 5007
0362-1553 See M.I.R.L. REPORT. 2143
0362-1561 See MICHIGAN FOUNDATION DIRECTORY. 4338
0362-157X See CONSUMER PROTECTION REPORT. 1295
0362-1588 See HOUSTON JOURNAL OF MATHEMATICS. 3507
0362-1596 See PARABOLA (MT. KISCO). 2323
0362-160X See SCREEN PRINTING TECHNIQUES. 4569
0362-1618 See NELB LINK. 3233
0362-1626 See ANNUAL REVIEW OF ENERGY AND THE ENVIRONMENT. 1932
0362-1634 See ADVANCES IN CEREAL SCIENCE AND TECHNOLOGY. 2326
0362-1642 See ANNUAL REVIEW OF PHARMACOLOGY AND TOXICOLOGY. 4291
0362-1650 See ATHEROSCLEROSIS REVIEWS. 3699
0362-1715 See MONOGRAPH - AMERICAN FISHERIES SOCIETY. 2308
0362-1731 See BULLETIN - SHAWNEE COUNTY HISTORICAL SOCIETY. 2725
0362-1804 See CALIFORNIA COMMISSIONER OF CORPORATIONS CURRENT OFFICIAL OPINIONS ISSUED PURSUANT TO THE FRANCHISE INVESTMENT LAW. 654
0362-1812 See NORTH DAKOTA JUDICIAL NEWS. 3018
0362-1952 See DEER SPORTSMAN. 4871
0362-1960 See DISNEY MAGAZINE. 1063
0362-1979 See J. PAUL GETTY MUSEUM JOURNAL, THE. 4089
0362-1995 See TERMINUS BUSINESS DIRECTORY. 715
0362-2428 See RESEARCH COMMUNICATIONS IN PSYCHOLOGY, PSYCHIATRY AND BEHAVIOR. 4615
0362-2436 See SPINE (PHILADELPHIA, PA. 1976). 3642
0362-2452 See BODY FASHIONS/INTIMATE APPAREL DIRECTORY. 1082
0362-2487 See ENJINE! ENJINE!. 2288
0362-2495 See GUN WORLD ANNUAL. 4897
0362-2517 See CERTIFICATION OF CONSTITUTIONAL LIMITATION ON THE BONDED DEBT OF THE STATE OF WASHINGTON. 4717
0362-2525 See JOURNAL OF MORPHOLOGY (1931). 583
0362-2576 See FINNISH AMERICAN ANNUAL. 2733
0362-2584 See BOX 1980. 1341
0362-2622 See OCCASIONAL PAPERS IN ENTOMOLOGY. 5612
0362-2711 See B & M BULLETIN. 5429
0362-272X See LEGISLATIVE MANUAL - GENERAL ASSEMBLY OF SOUTH CAROLINA. 4661
0362-2738 See SOUTH DAKOTA LEGISLATIVE MANUAL. 3057
0362-2770 See OPTIONS (WAYNE, N.J.). 2270
0362-2835 See THOREAU SOCIETY BOOKLET. 3446
0362-2886 See TECHNICAL REPORT - MARINE SCIENCES RESEARCH CENTER, STATE UNIVERSITY OF NEW YORK. 5162
0362-2959 See MUSICIAN'S GUIDE (BOSTON). 4137
0362-2967 See NEW JERSEY AREA LIBRARY DIRECTORY. 3234
0362-2991 See PROCEEDINGS OF THE ANNUAL SYMPOSIUM ON REDUCTION OF COSTS IN HAND-OPERATED GLASS PLANTS. 2593
0362-3017 See NUMERICAL SOLUTION OF PARTIAL DIFFERENTIAL EQUATIONS. 3525

0362-3106 See SANBORN MANHATTAN LAND BOOK OF THE CITY OF NEW YORK. 2575
0362-3157 See BENCHMARK PAPERS IN SYSTEMATIC AND EVOLUTIONARY BIOLOGY. 443
0362-3173 See LACTATION REVIEW, THE. 3764
0362-3181 See LUNG BIOLOGY IN HEALTH AND DISEASE. 3950
0362-3270 See OFFICIAL FIELD HOCKEY RULES FOR SCHOOL GIRLS. 4909
0362-3289 See ANNUAL REPORT OF THE IDAHO DEPARTMENT OF WATER RESOURCES. 5529
0362-3297 See FOCUS : MACROECONOMICS. 1592
0362-3300 See JOURNAL OF THE AMERICAN MUSICAL INSTRUMENT SOCIETY. 4126
0362-3319 See SOCIAL SCIENCE JOURNAL (FORT COLLINS), THE. 5220
0362-3351 See INFLUENZA SURVEILLANCE (1973). 3587
0362-3416 See EPRI JOURNAL. 2053
0362-3424 See RESIDENTIAL CONSTRUCTION IN SOUTHEAST MICHIGAN. 626
0362-3459 See GUIDE TO MINORITY BUSINESS DIRECTORIES. 678
0362-3556 See OFFICIAL JOURNAL OF THE PROCEEDINGS OF THE SENATE AND HOUSE OF REPRESENTATIVES OF THE STATE OF LOUISIANA AND THE LEGISLATIVE CALENDAR. 4485
0362-3564 See QUAERE (MINNEAPOLIS). 3033
0362-3572 See RECENT RESEARCHES IN THE MUSIC OF THE MIDDLE AGES AND EARLY RENAISSANCE. 4149
0362-3599 See TOUR BOOK : ARIZONA, NEW MEXICO. 5492
0362-3602 See TOUR BOOK : WESTERN CANADA AND ALASKA. 5493
0362-3610 See UNDERSTANDING FINANCIAL SUPPORT OF PUBLIC SCHOOLS. 1873
0362-3637 See AFROASIATIC LINGUISTICS. 3262
0362-3688 See NEW YORK TIMES FILM REVIEWS, THE. 4075
0362-3696 See JOURNAL - INTERNATIONAL UNION OF BRICKLAYERS AND ALLIED CRAFTSMEN. 1681
0362-3718 See REGIONAL PROFILES. 5255
0362-3769 See BULLETIN OF LAW, SCIENCE & TECHNOLOGY. 2944
0362-3785 See DIRECTORY OF CHEMICAL PRODUCERS OF ASIA AND AUSTRALASIA. 1023
0362-3793 See LABOR FORCE STATUS OF INDIANA RESIDENTS. 1683
0362-3807 See MEMBERSHIP DIRECTORY - METROPOLITAN WASHINGTON BOARD OF TRADE. 845
0362-3823 See WOODALL'S TRAILERING PARKS & CAMPGROUNDS. CANADIAN EDITION. 5499
0362-3858 See INCREMENTAL MOTION CONTROL SYSTEMS AND DEVICES NEWSLETTER. 2064
0362-3890 See FACTS AND FIGURES ON FOOTWEAR. 1084
0362-3904 See CITY POPULATION ESTIMATES - GEORGIA. STATE DATA CENTER. 4551
0362-3912 See ANNUAL REPORT OF THE IDAHO DEPARTMENT OF LABOR AND INDUSTRIAL SERVICES. 1649
0362-3955 See SOUND IMAGE. 331
0362-4013 See BULLETIN - PENNSYLVANIA STATE UNIVERSITY, COLLEGE OF AGRICULTURE, AGRICULTURAL EXPERIMENT STATION. 70
0362-4021 See GROUP (NEW YORK. 1977). 4588
0362-4048 See AMERICAN REHABILITATION. 5271
0362-4064 See OCCUPATIONAL HEALTH & SAFETY. 2866
0362-4145 See CHILDREN'S LITERATURE REVIEW. 3340
0362-4153 See FOREIGN ASSISTANCE PROGRAM. 2909
0362-417X See SMALL ENTERPRISE IN THE ECONOMY. 1521

0362-4188 See UNION CONTRACT EXPIRATIONS IN THE NORTH CENTRAL REGION 5. **1716**

0362-4196 See ALASKA LABOR FORCE ESTIMATES BY INDUSTRY & AREA. **1643**

0362-4218 See ANNUAL REPORT - STATE OF NEW JERSEY, DEPARTMENT OF INSTITUTIONS AND AGENCIES, DIVISION OF MEDICAL ASSISTANCE AND HEALTH SERVICES-MEDICAID. **2873**

0362-4226 See REPORT OF THE AGRICULTURE STUDY COMMITTEE OF SOUTH CAROLINA. **126**

0362-4234 See BLS FILE OF STATE, COUNTY, AND MUNICIPAL COLLECTIVE BARGAINING AGREEMENTS. **1655**

0362-4269 See CURRENT TREND REVIEW. **5326**

0362-4293 See LOST IN CANADA?. **2458**

0362-4307 See INTERNATIONAL TRADE & FINANCE REVIEW. **841**

0362-4315 See STATISTICAL SERVICES OF THE UNITED STATES GOVERNMENT. **4700**

0362-4323 See HYPERTENSION (NEW YORK). **3705**

0362-4331 See NEW YORK TIMES, THE. **5719**

0362-4358 See U.S. CHEMICAL PATENT INDEX. **1309**

0362-4366 See DIRECTORY : COMMUNITY DEVELOPMENT EDUCATION AND TRAINING PROGRAMS THROUGHOUT THE WORLD. **5244**

0362-4439 See PHARMACEUTICAL NEWS INDEX. **4334**

0362-4447 See BONSAI (PHOENIX). **2410**

0362-4455 See CODE & SYMBOL. **864**

0362-4463 See PROCEEDINGS, SOUTHERN WEED SCIENCE SOCIETY. **2429**

0362-4536 See IEEE STUDENT PAPERS. **2061**

0362-4579 See STATE LAWS GOVERNING BOXING AND WRESTLING IN CALIFORNIA, WITH RULES AND REGULATIONS. **3058**

0362-4587 See US MAGAZINE. **4060**

0362-4595 See CHICAGO. **2530**

0362-4668 See INTERDEPENDENCE. **4965**

0362-4676 See NEWSLETTER - WOMEN'S CAUCUS-RELIGIOUS STUDIES. **4982**

0362-4692 See STANDARD BEARER (GRAND RAPIDS), THE. **4999**

0362-4730 See EUROPEAN REVIEW (LEXINGTON, MASS.). **1560**

0362-4749 See GUN WORLD HUNTING GUIDE. **4897**

0362-4765 See POLITICAL SCIENCE UTILIZATION DIRECTORY, THE. **4490**

0362-4773 See PROBATE REPORTER. **3031**

0362-4781 See TEXAS REGISTER. **4690**

0362-4803 See JOURNAL OF LABELLED COMPOUNDS & RADIOPHARMACEUTICALS. **1054**

0362-4811 See ASIAN STUDIES NEWSLETTER. **2646**

0362-4846 See THREE RIVERS POETRY JOURNAL. **3472**

0362-4870 See JOURNAL OF THE AMERICAN ACADEMY OF PSYCHIATRY AND NEUROLOGY. **3930**

0362-4889 See LOW VISION ABSTRACTS. **4391**

0362-4994 See OPERATING SECTION PROCEEDINGS. **4271**

0362-5001 See AMJ, AIRPORT MANAGEMENT JOURNAL. **11**

0362-501X See CORPORATE SYSTEMS. **864**

0362-5028 See EARLY CHINA. **2650**

0362-5044 See FRENCH PERIODICAL INDEX. **416**

0362-5192 See FINANCIAL REPORT - ENERGY RESEARCH AND DEVELOPMENT ADMINISTRATION. **1944**

0362-5214 See PIG IRON. **3423**

0362-5397 See STANDARD METROPOLITAN STATISTICAL AREAS. **5339**

0362-5400 See ENVIRONMENTAL LEGISLATION REPORTER. **3112**

0362-5435 See QUARTERLY BUSINESS REVIEW. **706**

0362-5443 See APPLICATION OF OPTICAL INSTRUMENTATION IN MEDICINE. **3552**

0362-546X See NONLINEAR ANALYSIS. **3524**

0362-5524 See STATEWIDE SPACE SURVEY. **1848**

0362-5532 See COMPILATION OF LAW RELATING TO THE PRACTICE OF VETERINARY MEDICINE AND SURGERY. **2954**

0362-5575 See LOS ANGELES DAILY JOURNAL, THE. **3004**

0362-563X See NEWSLETTER - CENTER FOR REFORMATION RESEARCH. **4981**

0362-5648 See WISCONSIN LUTHERAN QUARTERLY. **5009**

0362-5664 See CLINICAL NEUROPHARMACOLOGY. **4296**

0362-5699 See REVIEWS IN PERINATAL MEDICINE. **3767**

0362-5729 See LOCAL GOVERNMENT LAW BULLETIN. **3004**

0362-5737 See TRUCK BROKER DIRECTORY. **5398**

0362-5745 See ARMY COMMUNICATOR, THE. **4036**

0362-5753 See WHO'S WHO AMONG BLACK AMERICANS. **436**

0362-5788 See EMPLOYMENT OF DISABLED AND VIETNAM ERA VETERANS IN THE FEDERAL GOVERNMENT. **4702**

0362-5826 See SUPERVISOR'S EEO REVIEW, THE. **1713**

0362-5850 See PLANTS & GARDENS. **2428**

0362-5907 See AGO TIMES, THE. **4099**

0362-5915 See ACM TRANSACTIONS ON DATABASE SYSTEMS. **1252**

0362-5923 See ACTIVITY PROGRAMMERS SOURCEBOOK. **1722**

0362-5931 See GEORGIA LEGISLATIVE REVIEW. **2974**

0362-5966 See OKLAHOMA STATE MINI-PLAN FOR THE ADMINISTRATION OF VOCATIONAL EDUCATION UNDER THE VOCATIONAL EDUCATION AMENDMENTS OF 1968. **1915**

0362-6008 See STATEWIDE SUMMARY OF FIRE PROTECTION DISTRICT FINANCE IN ILLINOIS. **2292**

0362-6016 See POLICY STUDIES DIRECTORY, THE. **5213**

0362-6040 See VACATION TRAVEL BY CANADIANS IN THE UNITED STATES. **5498**

0362-6075 See ANDOVER REVIEW, THE. **1888**

0362-6091 See TUNING BOARD, THE. **4157**

0362-6121 See RECORDER, THE. **3036**

0362-6148 See CHICAGO DAILY LAW BULLETIN. **2949**

0362-6180 See BUYERS' GUIDE FOR THE MASS ENTERTAINMENT INDUSTRY. **4849**

0362-6229 See ANNUAL REPORT OF SOUTH CAROLINA DEPARTMENT OF VETERANS AFFAIRS. **4035**

0362-6245 See U & LC. **4570**

0362-6288 See SURVEY NOTES / UTAH GEOLOGICAL SURVEY. **1399**

0362-630X See HIGH TIMES. **2488**

0362-6334 See TEXAS SCHOOL LAW BULLETIN. **3064**

0362-6350 See PROGRESS IN HEMOSTASIS AND THROMBOSIS. **3773**

0362-6377 See ANNUAL STATEMENT, CONCESSIONS IN THE CALIFORNIA STATE PARK SYSTEM. **4706**

0362-6385 See FIELD & STREAM FISHING ANNUAL. **2301**

0362-6415 See RED RIVER VALLEY HISTORICAL REVIEW. **2756**

0362-644X See A.I.D. BIBLIOGRAPHY SERIES : DEVELOPMENT ADMINISTRATION. **1528**

0362-6466 See FOOD & DRUG LETTER, THE. **2336**

0362-6482 See ANNUAL REPORT OF OPERATIONS AND FOREST PEST CONDITIONS. **2375**

0362-6563 See STEWARDSHIP REPORT, A. **4708**

0362-6652 See FAWCETT'S FISHING JOURNAL. **2301**

0362-6660 See KIDS FASHIONS MAGAZINE. **1085**

0362-6679 See SUMMARY OF KENTUCKY EDUCATION. **1798**

0362-6725 See YEARBOOK / TIRE AND RIM ASSOCIATION, INC. **5400**

0362-6784 See CURRICULUM INQUIRY. **1892**

0362-6792 See UNITED STATES GOVERNMENT GRANTS UNDER THE FULBRIGHT-HAYS ACT : UNIVERSITY LECTURING, ADVANCED RESEARCH. **4692**

0362-6830 See MONTHLY CATALOG OF UNITED STATES GOVERNMENT PUBLICATIONS. **4666**

0362-6849 See ANNUAL REPORT - ALASKA NATIVE MEDICAL CENTER. **3776**

0362-6881 See BENTLEY LIBRARY ANNUAL, THE. **3194**

0362-6903 See ELECTION RESULTS DATABOOK FOR CUYAHOGA COUNTY. **4645**

0362-6911 See FRONTIERS OF ECONOMICS. **1492**

0362-692X See HOURLY EARNINGS INDEX, THE. **1677**

0362-6962 See ANNUAL REPORT OF SURVEY-INVENTORY ACTIVITIES. **4869**

0362-6997 See ANNUAL REPORT - UNITED STATES DEPARTMENT OF THE INTERIOR, BUREAU OF SPORT FISHERIES AND WILDLIFE, FISH AND WILDLIFE SERVICE. **2187**

0362-7012 See US 1 WORKSH. **3449**

0362-7047 See LATVJU MAKSLA. **356**

0362-7055 See PROCEEDINGS OF THE ... MEETING OF THE FRENCH COLONIAL HISTORICAL SOCIETY. **2703**

0362-7063 See INNOVATIVE PROGRAMS FOR CHILD CARE : EVALUATION REPORT. **1804**

0362-7136 See CALIFORNIA LICENSED CONTRACTOR, THE. **606**

0362-7160 See DAISY SHOOTING ANNUAL. **4871**

0362-7179 See DIRECTORY OF SERVICES FOR MIGRANT FAMILIES. **5283**

0362-7187 See FINANCIAL REPORT - DEPARTMENT OF HEALTH & SOCIAL SERVICES, DIVISION OF HEALTH. **4775**

0362-7209 See REPORT TO THE VERMONT GENERAL ASSEMBLY. **1844**

0362-7217 See RESEARCH STUDY - DIVISION OF BUSINESS AND ECONOMIC RESEARCH, COLLEGE OF BUSINESS ADMINISTRATION, UNIVERSITY OF NEW ORLEANS. **1581**

0362-7233 See WAGE CHRONOLOGY : THE BOEING CO., WASHINGTON PLANTS, AND INTERNATIONAL ASSOCIATION OF MACHINISTS. **1717**

0362-725X See BUREAU OF MINES TECHNICAL PROGRESS REPORT. **2135**

0362-7322 See FISCAL YEAR SUMMARY REPORT OF POPULATION MOVEMENT. **3164**

0362-7330 See GOSPEL MUSIC ASSOCIATION ANNUAL DIRECTORY & YEARBOOK. **4119**

0362-7357 See NEW GOSPEL TREASURE SELECT-A-SONG. **4140**

0362-7403 See ANALOG ANNUAL. **3361**

0362-7438 See NEW MEXICO BOARD OF NURSING ANNUAL REPORT TO GOVERNOR. **3862**

0362-7446 See PROPOSED MICHIGAN ANNUAL SOCIAL SERVICES PLAN. **5302**

0362-7489 See REPORT OF PROBATION SUPERVISION WORKLOAD. **3174**

0362-7489 See REPORT OF PROBATION SUPERVISION WORKLOAD. **3174**

0362-7519 See TEXAS TRADE AND PROFESSIONAL ASSOCIATIONS AND OTHER SELECTED ORGANIZATIONS. **715**

0362-7535 See RESEARCH ABSTRACTS (ANN ARBOR). **423**

0362-7586 See CONSOLIDATED DEVELOPMENT DIRECTORY. **2819**

0362-7683 See RECORD-A-REF. SUPPLEMENT; COMMERCIAL RECORD REFERENCE. **1928**

0362-7713 See UNITED STATES COAST PILOT. 4, ATLANTIC COAST. CAPE HENRY TO KEY WEST. **4184**

0362-7721 See THOMAS REGISTER OF AMERICAN MANUFACTURERS AND THOMAS REGISTER CATALOG FILE. **3489**

0362-7772 See DEMOLITION AGE. **612**

0362-7799 See PETROLEUM MARKETER (NEW HAVEN). 4273

0362-7829 See NATIONAL TRAVEL EXPENDITURE STUDY. 5485

0362-7837 See RECREATION STATISTICS. 4856

0362-7888 See HARVEST (FARMINGTON). 3393

0362-7926 See TEXAS PHARMACY. 4330

0362-7969 See PAINTED BRIDE QUARTERLY, THE. 3467

0362-7977 See POST HIGH SCHOOL PLANS SURVEY. 1841

0362-7985 See REVIEW OF FINANCIAL ECONOMICS. 1518

0362-8019 See OFFICERS, COMMITTEES, CONSTITUTION AND BY-LAWS, MEMBERS / GROLIER CLUB. 5234

0362-8019 See OFFICERS, COMMITTEES, CONSTITUTION AND BY-LAWS, MEMBERS, REPORTS OF OFFICERS AND COMMITTEES. 5234

0362-8027 See HARVARD EDUCATIONAL REVIEW. REPRINT SERIES. 1750

0362-8140 See MODERN VETERINARY PRACTICE (1973). 5516

0362-8159 See TECHNICAL BULLETIN / OKLAHOMA AGRICULTURAL AND MECHANICAL COLLEGE, AGRICULTURAL EXPERIMENT STATION. 140

0362-8167 See STATION BULLETIN - AGRICULTURAL EXPERIMENT STATION. 137

0362-8175 See ENVIRONMENTAL GEOLOGY SERIES (NASHVILLE). 1375

0362-8183 See INDEX TO COMMONWEALTH LITTLE MAGAZINES. 2488

0362-8191 See HANDBOOK OF TABLES FOR MATHEMATICS. 3507

0362-8205 See SAE HANDBOOK. 5424

0362-8221 See RESEARCH, DEMONSTRATION AND EVALUATION STUDIES ON CHILD ABUSE AND NEGLECT. 5305

0362-823X See BUSINESS RESEARCH BULLETIN. 652

0362-8248 See REPORT ON DEPARTMENT OF HEALTH, OFFICE OF MENTAL RETARDATION, NORTH CENTRAL REGIONAL CENTER. 5305

0362-8264 See OREGON WILDLIFE COMMISSION FINANCIAL STATEMENT. 4876

0362-8337 See HEALTH CAREERS. 3581

0362-8388 See MISSOURI COMPREHENSIVE STATE PLAN FOR DRUG ABUSE PREVENTION AND TREATMENT. 1346

0362-8469 See PASSPORT OFFICE WORKLOADS AND ACCOMPLISHMENTS. 4673

0362-8493 See ACROSS THE TABLE. 3143

0362-8507 See INTERGOVERNMENTAL PERSPECTIVE. 4657

0362-8523 See POOR JOE'S PENNSYLVANIA FARM ALMANACK. 2543

0362-8531 See PROFESSIONAL RESPONSIBILITY. 3032

0362-8590 See BULLETIN OF THE HISTORICAL SOCIETY OF MONTGOMERY COUNTY, PENNSYLVANIA. 2725

0362-8647 See SELECCIONES DE AIR UNIVERSITY REVIEW. 35

0362-8701 See BEST'S INSURANCE SECURITIES RESEARCH SERVICE. 2876

0362-8779 See EXPERIMENTAL EDUCATION PROGRAMS FOR HANDICAPPED CHILDREN. 1879

0362-8787 See REPORT OF EDUCATION STATISTICS. 1796

0362-8833 See NRECA--APPA LEGAL REPORTING SERVICE. 3020

0362-8884 See BRIEFS OF ACCIDENTS INVOLVING AMATEUR-HOME BUILT AIRCRAFT, U.S. GENERAL AVIATION. 14

0362-8892 See WESTERN STATE UNIVERSITY LAW REVIEW. 3073

0362-8914 See AMERICAN JOURNAL OF ANCIENT HISTORY. 1073

0362-8930 See SCHOOL LIBRARY JOURNAL (NEW YORK, N.Y.). 3248

0362-9015 See NEWSLETTER - THE INTERNATIONAL COUNCIL ON THE FUTURE OF THE UNIVERSITY. 1837

0362-9066 See FPS. 1063

0362-9074 See HISTORY OF ANTHROPOLOGY NEWSLETTER. 237

0362-918X See JUVENILE COURT REPORT (LINCOLN). 3121

0362-9198 See REPORT - MARYLAND DIVISION OF CORRECTION. 3174

0362-9252 See ANNUAL REPORT - COMMISSION ON THE STATUS OF WOMEN OF SOUTH DAKOTA. 5550

0362-9317 See FINANCIAL AND OPERATING STATISTICS CLASS I MOTOR CARRIERS OF PASSENGERS. 5401

0362-9341 See MARRIAGE AND FAMILY NEWSLETTER. 2283

0362-9368 See PACKARD CORMORANT, THE. 5422

0362-9376 See PLASTICS DESIGN FORUM. 4458

0362-9562 See DIRECTORY OF RESOURCE ORGANIZATIONS AND MEDIA SERVING MINORITY COMMUNITIES IN CONNECTICUT. 1663

0362-9686 See GENERAL REPORT OF THE LEGISLATIVE COUNCIL TO THE LEGISLATURE. 4650

0362-9716 See OHIO INVENTORY OF BUSINESS AND INDUSTRIAL CHANGE. 700

0362-9724 See PRICE INDEX OF OPERATING COSTS FOR RENT STABILIZED APARTMENT HOUSES IN NEW YORK CITY. 1702

0362-9767 See AMERICAN INDIAN ARTIFACT PRICE GUIDE. 336

0362-9791 See JOURNAL OF EDUCATIONAL STATISTICS. 1795

0362-9805 See LEGISLATIVE STUDIES QUARTERLY. 4480

0362-9821 See TOURBOOK: COLORADO, UTAH. 5493

0362-9848 See CA SELECTS: PSYCHOBIOCHEMISTRY. 1008

0362-9856 See CA SELECTS: PHOTOCHEMISTRY. 1007

0362-9872 See CA SELECTS: MASS SPECTROMETRY. 1005

0362-9880 See CA SELECTS: FORENSIC CHEMISTRY. 1003

0362-9899 See CA SELECTS: ORGANOSILICON CHEMISTRY. 1006

0362-9902 See C.F.O. JOURNAL. 5616

0362-9910 See FORTITUDINE. 4176

0362-9929 See HEARINGS AND REPORTS OF COMMITTEES OF THE CALIFORNIA LEGISLATURE : A LISTING. 2978

0362-9953 See PROFESSIONAL, ADMINISTRATIVE, TECHNICAL AND CLERICAL PAY IN NEW YORK. 1703

0362-997X See VIKING COLLEGE CATALOG. 4820

0362-9996 See ANNUAL REPORT - GEORGIA ORGANIZED CRIME PREVENTION COUNCIL. 3157

0363-0013 See DIRECTORY : AREAWIDE PLANNING ORGANIZATIONS, STATE OF IOWA. 2821

0363-0021 See ECONOMIC REVIEW (SAN FRANCISCO). 1558

0363-003X See PENTHOUSE PHOTO WORLD. 4372

0363-0048 See PREVIEW OF UNITED STATES SUPREME COURT CASES. 3031

0363-0072 See STATISTICAL SUMMARY - COMMONWEALTH OF VIRGINIA, STATE MILK COMMISSION. 2362

0363-0102 See CALCULATOR LIB. 1173

0363-0129 See SIAM JOURNAL ON CONTROL AND OPTIMIZATION. 3534

0363-0137 See SOUTH DAKOTA EDUCATIONAL DIRECTORY. 1784

0363-0161 See BIBLIOGRAPHY OF BIOETHICS. 3555

0363-017X See CANCER BIOLOGY. 3810

0363-0188 See CURRENT PROBLEMS IN DIAGNOSTIC RADIOLOGY. 3940

0363-0226 See MCLEAN HOSPITAL JOURNAL. 3930

0363-0234 See SUICIDE & LIFE-THREATENING BEHAVIOR. 4619

0363-0242 See WOMEN & HEALTH. 3769

0363-0250 See ACTION FOR LIBRARIES. 3187

0363-0269 See HEMOGLOBIN. 3797

0363-0277 See LIBRARY JOURNAL (1976). 3225

0363-0307 See GOLDEN GATE UNIVERSITY LAW REVIEW. 2975

0363-0358 See PROCEEDINGS OF THE NATIONAL ASSOCIATION OF INSURANCE COMMISSIONERS. 2890

0363-0366 See MEDICAL AND HEALTH ANNUAL. 1927

0363-0404 See JOURNAL OF PRODUCTS LIABILITY. 2989

0363-0447 See FIRST PRINCIPLES. 4508

0363-0455 See GEODYNAMICS PROJECT : U.S. PROGRESS REPORT. 1376

0363-0463 See HAWAII PROSECUTOR-PUBLIC DEFENDER NEWSLETTER. 3107

0363-0471 See HISPAMERICA (COLLEGE PARK). 3394

0363-048X See HISPAMERICA. 3394

0363-0560 See FAMOUS PULP CLASSICS. 3387

0363-0625 See PROGRAMS AND PROGRESS. 5302

0363-0633 See REPORT OF RECIDIVISTS COMMITTED TO THE VIRGINIA STATE PENAL SYSTEM. 3174

0363-0668 See LUSK'S EAST SUFFOLK COUNTY REAL ESTATE DIRECTORY. 4840

0363-0692 See REPORT ON ADMINISTRATIVE ADJUDICATION OF TRAFFIC INFRACTIONS. 3038

0363-0722 See NATIONAL PARK SERVICE SCIENTIFIC MONOGRAPH SERIES. 1389

0363-0811 See DRINKING AND DRUG PRACTICES SURVEYOR, THE. 1343

0363-0870 See CAPITAL BUDGET AND SIX YEAR IMPROVEMENT PROGRAM. 4716

0363-0919 See EXPENSES AND APPROPRIATIONS OF THE MISSISSIPPI LEGISLATURE. 2968

0363-0927 See CHRONICLE GUIDE TO EXTERNAL & CONTINUING EDUCATION. 1800

0363-0951 See PROGRESS IN PSYCHOBIOLOGY AND PHYSIOLOGICAL PSYCHOLOGY. 585

0363-0978 See SHEPARD'S CRIMINAL JUSTICE CITATIONS. 3109

0363-1001 See VIDEOGRAPHY. 1143

0363-1036 See WHO WRITES WHAT IN LIFE AND HEALTH INSURANCE. 2896

0363-1109 See REPORT - INSTITUTE FOR THE FUTURE. 5215

0363-1168 See JOURNAL OF THE VIRGIN ISLANDS ARCHAEOLOGICAL SOCIETY. 272

0363-1184 See MANUAL OF THE SENATE AND HOUSE OF DELEGATES. 4664

0363-1214 See WASHINGTON NEWSLINES. 2549

0363-1230 See WEBSTER REVIEW. 3452

0363-1273 See BARRON'S MARKET LABORATORY. 892

0363-1281 See BIRTHS AND DEATHS BY JURISDICTION OF RESIDENCE. MARRIAGES AND DIVORCES BY COUNTY. 5323

0363-129X See CALIFORNIA WORKERS' COMPENSATION REPORTER. 3145

0363-1303 See FOODSERVICE EQUIPMENT DEALER. BUYERS GUIDE AND PRODUCT DIRECTORY. 2341

0363-1354 See NATIONAL BOAT BOOK. 594

0363-1362 See STATE JUDICIARY NEWS. 3058

0363-1370 See SUNSTONE. 5001

0363-1427 See HOSPITALITY SERIES. 2806

0363-1478 See SPORTING GOODS REGISTER, THE. 4921

0363-1486 See TOUR BOOK : ARKANSAS, KANSAS, MISSOURI, OKLAHOMA. 5492

0363-1494 See TOUR BOOK: CONNECTICUT, MASSACHUSETTS, RHODE ISLAND. 5492

0363-1508 See TOUR BOOK: ILLINOIS, INDIANA, OHIO. 5492

0363-1516 See TOUR BOOK: MAINE, NEW HAMPSHIRE, VERMONT. **5492**

0363-1524 See TOUR BOOK: MICHIGAN, WISCONSIN. **5493**

0363-1532 See TOUR BOOK: NEW JERSEY, PENNSYLVANIA. **5493**

0363-1540 See TOUR BOOK: NEW YORK. **5493**

0363-1567 See TOUR BOOK: OREGON, WASHINGTON. **5493**

0363-1575 See TOUR BOOK: TEXAS. **5493**

0363-1613 See COMMUNITY DEVELOPMENT BLOCK GRANT PROGRAM. DIRECTORY OF ALLOCATIONS FOR FISCAL YEARS **2818**

0363-1621 See CONTACT LENS FORUM. **4215**

0363-1656 See JOURNAL OF ROCKINGHAM COUNTY HISTORY AND GENEALOGY, THE. **2741**

0363-1672 See LITHUANIAN MATHEMATICAL JOURNAL. **3517**

0363-1702 See METALS WEEK PRICE HANDBOOK. **4011**

0363-1729 See MUNICIPAL SALARY SURVEY. **4667**

0363-1737 See NATIONAL METAL WORKING BLUE BOOK. **4013**

0363-1745 See OFF-ROAD (LOS ANGELES). **5422**

0363-1788 See TOUR BOOK: ATLANTIC PROVINCES AND QUEBEC. **5492**

0363-1796 See TRAVELCADE MAGAZINE. **5497**

0363-1826 See CAROLINAS GENEALOGICAL SOCIETY YEARBOOK. **2442**

0363-1834 See DEMOCRATIC REVIEW (WASHINGTON). **4471**

0363-1842 See DIRECTORY OF IOWA MUNICIPALITIES. **4643**

0363-1850 See EUREKA REVIEW. **3342**

0363-1885 See PC, PERSONAL COMMUNICATIONS SHOW DAILY. **2074**

0363-1893 See REASON PAPERS. **5215**

0363-1923 See ILLINOIS CLASSICAL STUDIES. **1077**

0363-1958 See SUMMARY OF HYDROLOGIC DATA COLLECTED IN DADE COUNTY, FLORIDA. **1418**

0363-1974 See WATER RESOURCES DATA. NEBRASKA. **5545**

0363-2091 See EASTERN CANADA CAMPING. **4871**

0363-2113 See FINANCIAL STATISTICS OF THE MAJOR PRIVATELY OWNED UTILITIES IN NEW YORK STATE. **4697**

0363-2121 See LEGISLATIVE FISCAL REPORT (CARSON CITY). **3001**

0363-2172 See BULLETIN OF THE GEORGIA HERPETOLOGICAL SOCIETY. **5579**

0363-2288 See FEDERAL-STATE MARKET NEWS REPORTS. **2335**

0363-2296 See ACI DIRECTORY. **2018**

0363-2318 See APPALACHIAN HERITAGE. **3362**

0363-2377 See ALLEGORICA. **3359**

0363-2415 See FISHERIES (BETHESDA). **2302**

0363-2423 See GLENDALE LAW REVIEW. **2975**

0363-2474 See TEXAS LIST, THE. **1714**

0363-2563 See DIRECTORY: LICENSED & CERTIFIED HEALTH CARE FACILITIES. **3779**

0363-2571 See ELECTIVE AND APPOINTIVE STATE OFFICERS, STATE OF MICHIGAN. **4645**

0363-2601 See INNOVATIVE GRADUATE PROGRAMS DIRECTORY. **1830**

0363-261X See INTERNATIONAL NAUTICAL INDEX. **4177**

0363-2679 See OKLAHOMA JOURNAL OF FORENSIC MEDICINE. **3742**

0363-2687 See SUMMARY OF ACTIVITIES - MENTAL HEALTH LAW PROJECT. **3060**

0363-2695 See TOUR BOOK: IDAHO, MONTANA, WYOMING. **5492**

0363-2717 See HISTORICAL ABSTRACTS. PART A, MODERN HISTORY ABSTRACTS. **2635**

0363-2725 See HISTORICAL ABSTRACTS. PART B, TWENTIETH CENTURY ABSTRACTS. **2635**

0363-2768 See JOURNAL OF INTER-AMERICAN MEDICINE, THE. **3595**

0363-2776 See HOMEOTHERAPY. **3774**

0363-2830 See DOWNTOWN PROMOTION REPORTER. **759**

0363-2845 See MEMBERSHIP DIRECTORY / INTERNATIONAL TRUMPET GUILD. **4130**

0363-2849 See ITG JOURNAL. **4124**

0363-2865 See JERUSALEM JOURNAL OF INTERNATIONAL RELATIONS, THE. **4526**

0363-2873 See JOURNAL OF LIBERTARIAN STUDIES, THE. **5206**

0363-289X See MINNESOTA ALMANAC, THE. **2746**

0363-2903 See ARETE (SAN FRANCISCO). **5273**

0363-292X See CRIMMER'S. **318**

0363-2938 See OFFICIAL ABSTRACT OF VOTES, GENERAL ELECTION. **4485**

0363-2946 See PROCEEDINGS OF THE ANNUAL MEETING OF THE BERKELEY LINGUISTICS SOCIETY. **3312**

0363-2954 See ROSTER - ARIZONA STATE BOARD OF ACCOUNTANCY. **751**

0363-2962 See TOLL FREE DIGEST. **1168**

0363-2997 See 1040 PREPARATION. **4708**

0363-3012 See FINANCIAL STATISTICS : VERMONT SCHOOL SYSTEMS. **1795**

0363-3047 See ANNUAL REPORT - TWENTIETH CENTURY FUND. **5228**

0363-3144 See TEACHING NOTES ON POPULATION. **4560**

0363-3152 See TRANSACTIONS OF THE HUGUENOT SOCIETY OF SOUTH CAROLINA. **5237**

0363-3209 See UNITED STATES COAST PILOT. 1, ATLANTIC COAST. EASTPORT TO CAPE COD. **4184**

0363-3217 See UNITED STATES COAST PILOT. 3, ATLANTIC COAST. SANDY HOOK TO CAPE HENRY. **4184**

0363-3225 See VERMONT LEGISLATIVE DIRECTORY AND STATE MANUAL. **4693**

0363-3268 See RESEARCH IN ECONOMIC HISTORY. **1581**

0363-3276 See WILSON QUARTERLY (WASHINGTON), THE. **2495**

0363-3284 See NEW COLLECTOR'S DIRECTORY, THE. **2775**

0363-3306 See ANNUAL REPORT - HUNTINGTON LIBRARY, ART GALLERY, BOTANICAL GARDENS. **3190**

0363-3330 See ANNUAL REPORT OF THE COMMISSIONER OF TRANSPORTATION TO THE GOVERNOR. **5376**

0363-3381 See STATE AGENCY EXPENDITURES BY COUNTY. **4748**

0363-3470 See PHILOLOGICAL PAPERS (1947). **3310**

0363-3500 See BIENNIAL REPORT OF THE VERMONT DEPARTMENT OF LIBRARIES. **3195**

0363-3519 See BULLETIN - VIRGINIA MUSEUM OF FINE ARTS. **4086**

0363-356X See WESTCHESTER PLANNING. **4694**

0363-3586 See BIOFEEDBACK AND SELF-REGULATION. **4577**

0363-3594 See BULLETIN INDEX-DIGEST SYSTEM, SERVICE ONE. INCOME TAX. **2944**

0363-3616 See MEMBERSHIP LIST - AMERICAN MENSA LIMITED. **5233**

0363-3624 See NURSE EDUCATOR. **3863**

0363-3640 See TU SHU KUAN HSUEH YU TZU HSUN KO HSUEH. **3254**

0363-3659 See MALEDICTA. **3301**

0363-3675 See WISCONSIN ASTROPHYSICS. **40**

0363-3683 See VOLUNTARY SUPPORT OF EDUCATION. **1853**

0363-3705 See TEQUESTA. **2762**

0363-3721 See DISARMAMENT NEWS & INTERNATIONAL VIEWS. **4520**

0363-373X See BETTER SCHOOLS (CHICAGO). **1727**

0363-3764 See BUS RIDE: BUS INDUSTRY DIRECTORY. **5378**

0363-3780 See EN PASSANT, POETRY. **3468**

0363-3837 See ABSTRACTS OF CONTRIBUTED PAPERS - MEDICAL CARE SECTION. **3543**

0363-387X See CARDIOVASCULAR PHYSIOLOGY (LONDON, ENGLAND). **3701**

0363-390X See HOSPITAL MANAGEMENT SERIES. **3784**

0363-3926 See MEDIQUIZ ANNUAL. **3614**

0363-3993 See NEW MEXICO ... HIGHWAY STATISTICS AND RELATED INFORMATION. **5401**

0363-4019 See ANNIVERSARY REPORT - HARVARD COLLEGE, CLASS OF 1971. **1808**

0363-4027 See SURVEY OF OUT-OF-STATE PASSENGER CARS AND OUT-OF-STATE CAMPER VEHICLES ON INTERSTATE, ARTERIAL AND PRIMARY HIGHWAYS IN VIRGINIA, A. **5445**

0363-4051 See LUTHERAN CHURCH DIRECTORY FOR THE UNITED STATES. **5063**

0363-4132 See GUIDEBOOK (UNIVERSITY OF TEXAS AT AUSTIN. BUREAU OF ECONOMIC GEOLOGY). **1382**

0363-4140 See ASTROLOGY ANNUAL REFERENCE BOOK, THE. **390**

0363-4167 See ALASKA MUNICIPAL OFFICIALS DIRECTORY. **4625**

0363-4183 See ANNUAL REPORT - DEPARTMENT OF HOUSING & COMMUNITY DEVELOPMENT. **2814**

0363-4205 See JOURNAL OF NEW JERSEY POETS. **3464**

0363-4248 See TEXAS ALMANAC AND STATE INDUSTRIAL GUIDE (1967). **2547**

0363-4310 See ASTROLOGY ANNUAL CALENDAR EPHEMERIS, THE. **390**

0363-4337 See ACTION (LITTLE ROCK), THE. **1544**

0363-440X See CAROLINAS GENEALOGICAL SOCIETY BULLETIN, THE. **2441**

0363-4485 See ANNUAL REPORT - DIVISION OF LABOR AND INDUSTRY (MARYLAND). **1649**

0363-4493 See CHESTNUT TREE, THE. **2443**

0363-4523 See COMMUNICATION EDUCATION. **1106**

0363-4531 See DIRECTORY OF ARCHITECTURAL FIRMS. **297**

0363-454X See BRASS RESEARCH SERIES. **4105**

0363-4566 See TEXAS SCHOOL DIRECTORY. **1787**

0363-4590 See SEEKER (PITTSBURG), THE. **2472**

0363-4655 See PHARMACOPEIAL FORUM. **4322**

0363-4671 See NEWSLETTER - INSTITUTE OF MEDICINE. **3621**

0363-471X See REFRESHER COURSES IN ANESTHESIOLOGY. **3684**

0363-4744 See HOUSING MARKET REPORT. **2824**

0363-4787 See T.U.B.A. JOURNAL. **4156**

0363-4795 See WORLD MILITARY AND SOCIAL EXPENDITURES. **4062**

0363-4817 See PACIFIC AREA DESTINATION HANDBOOK. **5488**

0363-4825 See DIVERSION (TITUSVILLE). **4850**

0363-4841 See ENCOMIA. **3342**

0363-4922 See SECURITY LETTER. **947**

0363-4930 See DIRECTORY OF THE OFFICERS, BOARD OF MANAGERS, COMMITTEES AND SECTIONS AFFILIATED AND COOPERATING ORGANIZATIONS. **2962**

0363-4965 See NASBO NEWSLETTER. **4738**

0363-499X See PHOTOCHEMICAL AND PHOTOBIOLOGICAL REVIEWS. **469**

0363-5015 See MERCURY IN WATER. **420**

0363-5023 See JOURNAL OF HAND SURGERY (ST. LOUIS, MO.), THE. **3967**

0363-504X See MODERN LITURGY. **4978**

0363-5074 See SEEDBED. **4996**

0363-5090 See SOUTH CAROLINA METALWORKING DIRECTORY. **4019**

0363-5104 See PRIMARY CARDIOLOGY. **3709**

0363-5155 See INVENTORY OF POPULATION PROJECTS IN DEVELOPING COUNTRIES AROUND THE WORLD. **4554**

0363-521X See IN VITRO. MONOGRAPH. **458**

0363-5236 See BYE CADMOS. **3370**

0363-5244 *See* PRO MUSICA MAGAZINE. 4147
0363-5252 *See* DAVISON'S "SALESMAN'S BOOK.". 5350
0363-5317 *See* BIENNIAL REPORT - TENNESSEE DEPARTMENT OF REVENUE. 4713
0363-535X *See* AMERICAN EXECUTIVE TRAVEL COMPANION. 5461
0363-5406 See BETTER HOMES AND GARDENS DECORATING IDEAS. WINDOW & WALL IDEAS. 2899
0363-5414 *See* DIKTA. 3206
0363-5422 *See* FEDERAL BUDGET; FOCUS AND PERSPECTIVES, THE. 4723
0363-5465 *See* AMERICAN JOURNAL OF SPORTS MEDICINE, THE. 3953
0363-5473 *See* AUDIT ACTION LETTER, THE. 3554
0363-5481 *See* LITERACY ADVANCE. 1881
0363-552X *See* FISHING IN THE MID ATLANTIC. 2303
0363-5570 *See* HARVARD UKRAINIAN STUDIES. 2690
0363-5597 *See* RADIO NAVIGATIONAL AIDS : ATLANTIC AND MEDITERRANEAN AREA. 4182
0363-566X *See* AMERICAN BUSINESS. 638
0363-5678 *See* PRANCING HORSE, THE. 5235
0363-5708 *See* INTERNATIONAL TROMBONE ASSOCIATION SERIES. 4123
0363-5732 *See* ABSTRACT JOURNAL IN EARTHQUAKE ENGINEERING. 2002
0363-5767 *See* CASTING & JEWELRY CRAFT. 2913
0363-5775 See QUARTERLY BULLETIN - DEPARTMENT OF REGIONAL PLANNING, COUNTY OF LOS ANGELES, CALIFORNIA. 2832
0363-5783 *See* GAVEL (SACRAMENTO), THE. 2973
0363-5899 *See* FEDERAL AID PLANNER. 1864
0363-5902 *See* FEDERAL-STATE PARTNERSHIP. 320
0363-5953 *See* READINGS IN EDUCATIONAL PSYCHOLOGY : CONTEMPORARY PERSPECTIVES. 1884
0363-5988 See RESEARCH PAPER PSW. 2393
0363-602X *See* UNIVERSITY OF MICHIGAN JOURNAL OF LAW REFORM. 3069
0363-6038 *See* DISCUSSION PAPER SERIES - DEPARTMENT OF GEOGRAPHY, SYRACUSE UNIVERSITY. 2559
0363-6046 *See* COMPLETE HANDBOOK OF SOCCER, THE. 4891
0363-6070 *See* BIENNIAL REPORT - STAFF SERVICES SECTION, DIVISION OF VOCATIONAL REHABILITATION. 1911
0363-6119 *See* AMERICAN JOURNAL OF PHYSIOLOGY : REGULATORY, INTEGRATIVE AND COMPARATIVE PHYSIOLOGY. 578
0363-6127 *See* AMERICAN JOURNAL OF PHYSIOLOGY RENAL, FLUID AND ELECTROLYTE PHYSIOLOGY. 578
0363-6135 *See* AMERICAN JOURNAL OF PHYSIOLOGY : HEART AND CIRCULATORY PHYSIOLOGY. 578
0363-6143 *See* AMERICAN JOURNAL OF PHYSIOLOGY : CELL PHYSIOLOGY. 577
0363-6283 *See* CRITICAL ISSUES (WASHINGTON DC). 5197
0363-6399 *See* DATA COMMUNICATIONS. 1241
0363-6410 *See* BIENNIAL REPORT OF THE OFFICE OF EMERGENCY ENERGY ASSISTANCE. 1933
0363-6429 *See* INSTRUCTIONAL EQUIPMENT GRANTS : TITLE VI-A HIGHER EDUCATION ACT OF 1975. 1830
0363-6437 *See* PAPERWORKER, THE. 1700
0363-6445 *See* SYSTEMATIC BOTANY. 528
0363-6453 *See* NAHRO ROSTER. 2829
0363-6488 *See* PHOTO REVIEW, THE. 4373
0363-650X *See* VOCATIONAL EDUCATION EVALUATION REPORT. 1917
0363-6526 *See* CURRENT CONCEPTS IN GASTROENTEROLOGY. 3743
0363-6542 *See* 1869 TIMES. 2784

0363-6550 *See* MIDWEST STUDIES IN PHILOSOPHY. 4353
0363-6569 *See* PASTORAL MUSIC. 4145
0363-6585 *See* MANUSCRIPTS FOR TUBA SERIES. 4130
0363-6666 *See* JOURNAL OF COMPARATIVE CULTURES, THE. 5249
0363-6682 *See* SUMMARY OF INSTITUTIONAL REQUESTS FOR OPERATING FUNDS. 1849
0363-6690 *See* WESTERN WILDLANDS. 2208
0363-6771 *See* GENERAL DENTISTRY. 1324
0363-678X See COMMERCIAL NEWS USA. 829
0363-6828 *See* DECISIONS ON GEOGRAPHIC NAMES IN THE UNITED STATES. 2559
0363-6836 *See* CURRENT POPULATION REPORTS. SERIES P-20, POPULATION CHARACTERISTICS. 4551
0363-6844 *See* TELEPHONE DIRECTORY - DEPARTMENT OF DEFENSE. 4059
0363-6917 *See* FAR EASTERN QUARTERLY, THE. 2651
0363-6941 *See* JOURNAL OF ENGLISH AND GERMANIC PHILOLOGY, THE. 3290
0363-695X See UNITED STATES COAST PILOT. 2, ATLANTIC COAST. CAPE COD TO SANDY HOOK. 4184
0363-6968 *See* NEW LIFE (DENVER). 5065
0363-6976 *See* NEW HORIZONS (COLUMBIA). 4981
0363-7034 *See* REGISTRY OF ENGINEERS AND LAND SURVEYORS AND REPORT OF THE STATE BOARD OF ENGINEERING EXAMINERS OF OREGON. 1993
0363-7050 *See* U.S.H.L. YEARBOOK. 4927
0363-7123 *See* INTERNATIONAL ORGANISATIONS IN WORLD POLITICS YEARBOOK. 4525
0363-7131 *See* NAFED DIRECTORY. 2291
0363-714X See GROUP STUDIES JOURNAL. 3926
0363-7174 *See* NATIONAL PHYSICIAN ASSISTANT PROGRAM PROFILE, THE. 3619
0363-7239 *See* CONGRESSIONAL RECORD (DAILY ED.). 2955
0363-731X See ACTION (CENTRAL ILLINOIS CONFERENCE EDITION). 4932
0363-7387 *See* AUDIT ACTION LETTER INFORMATION BONUS, THE. 738
0363-7425 *See* ACADEMY OF MANAGEMENT REVIEW, THE. 859
0363-745X See CU DIRECTORY. 384
0363-7492 *See* HISTORY NEWS (NASHVILLE, TENN.). 2737
0363-7514 *See* SURVEY OF MUNICIPAL PLANNING AND REGULATORY ACTIVITY, A. 2836
0363-7530 *See* TEXAS STATE DIRECTORY. 4690
0363-7549 *See* INTERNATIONAL SUBSCRIPTION AGENTS. 3218
0363-7565 *See* MONUMENTA ARCHAEOLOGICA (LOS ANGELES). 275
0363-7670 *See* SOUTH DAKOTA STATE PLAN FOR VOCATIONAL-TECHNICAL EDUCATION. 1915
0363-7689 *See* BLINDNESS, VISUAL IMPAIRMENT, DEAF-BLINDNESS. 4384
0363-7697 *See* RALLYE. 4914
0363-7751 *See* COMMUNICATION MONOGRAPHS. 1107
0363-7778 *See* MEDIA REVIEW DIGEST. 4080
0363-7832 *See* NATIONAL OBSERVER. NEWSPAPER INDEX, THE. 5693
0363-7867 *See* COLORADO LAWYER. 2952
0363-7875 See COMPILATION OF ABSTRACTS OF THESES SUBMITTED BY CANDIDATES FOR DEGREES. 5095
0363-7905 *See* WASHINGTON, D.C. MINI-MICRO COMPUTER REPORT, THE. 1273
0363-7913 See RHODE ISLAND MEDICINE. 3637
0363-7956 *See* ANNUAL REPORT / U.S. NUCLEAR REGULATORY COMMISSION. 2154
0363-7964 *See* MARKETING CALIFORNIA POTATOES FROM THE KERN DISTRICT AND STOCKTON DELTA DISTRICT. 2349
0363-7972 *See* DOLL CASTLE NEWS. 372

0363-7980 *See* CENTRAL SCHOOL LAW DIGEST. 2949
0363-8057 *See* GRADIVA. 3343
0363-8103 *See* ACTIVITIES AND PROGRAMS - OFFICE OF TELECOMMUNICATIONS POLICY. 1148
0363-8111 *See* PUBLIC RELATIONS REVIEW (RIVERDALE, N.Y.). 765
0363-8170 *See* COORDINATION DIRECTORY OF STATE AND FEDERAL AGENCY WATER AND LAND RESOURCES OFFICIALS. 2191
0363-8200 *See* DIPLOMATIC WORLD BULLETIN AND DELEGATES WORLD BULLETIN, THE. 4520
0363-8227 *See* HELICOPTER NEWS. 23
0363-8286 *See* MARKET ABSORPTION OF APARTMENTS. 2828
0363-8294 *See* CONSTRUCTION REPORTS: VALUE OF NEW CONSTRUCTION PUT IN PLACE. 610
0363-8332 *See* CURRENT TOPICS IN EARLY CHILDHOOD EDUCATION. 1803
0363-8340 *See* NATIONAL PROPERTY LAW DIGESTS. 3014
0363-8359 *See* MILITARY PERSONNEL AND DEPENDENTS IN HAWAII. 4062
0363-8367 *See* J & F RECORD SPECIAL. 4124
0363-8383 *See* ANNUAL REPORT. OPERATION OF THE COLORADO RIVER BASIN. PROJECTED OPERATIONS. 2087
0363-8456 *See* BULLETIN INDEX-DIGEST SYSTEM. SERVICE TWO. ESTATE AND GIFT TAX. 3117
0363-8464 *See* INDEX OF SPECIFICATIONS AND STANDARDS. 4045
0363-8472 *See* LARGE-PRINT SCORES AND BOOKS CATALOG. 4128
0363-8499 *See* BULLETIN INDEX-DIGEST SYSTEM. SERVICE FOUR. EXCISE TAX. 2944
0363-8502 *See* BULLETIN INDEX-DIGEST SYSTEM. SERVICE THREE. EMPLOYMENT TAXES. 3144
0363-8529 *See* SOVIET MICROELECTRONICS. 2082
0363-8537 *See* CONSTRUCTION REPORTS: NEW ONE-FAMILY HOMES SOLD AND FOR SALE. 2819
0363-8545 *See* FARM LABOR (WASHINGTON). 85
0363-8553 *See* CURRENT BUSINESS REPORTS. MONTHLY WHOLESALE TRADE, SALES, AND INVENTORIES. 663
0363-8561 *See* CROP PRODUCTION (WASHINGTON, D.C.). 169
0363-860X *See* RESERVE FORCES ALMANAC. 4055
0363-8618 *See* NATIONAL GUARD ALMANAC. 4052
0363-8626 *See* GENERAL HETEROCYCLIC CHEMISTRY SERIES. 976
0363-8642 *See* CEMENTS RESEARCH PROGRESS. 607
0363-8685 *See* EISENHOWER CONSORTIUM BULLETIN. 2378
0363-8693 *See* CORNELL INTERNATIONAL AGRICULTURE BULLETIN. 77
0363-8715 *See* JOURNAL OF COMPUTER ASSISTED TOMOGRAPHY. 3942
0363-874X See EDUCATIONAL DIRECTORY OF MISSISSIPPI SCHOOLS. 1741
0363-8758 *See* HOME PLANNING AND DECORATING. 2900
0363-8766 *See* RECORDS OF SELECTED PLAYERS. 4914
0363-8782 *See* TEXAS SPEECH COMMUNICATION JOURNAL. 1123
0363-8847 *See* BULLETIN - HUDSON FAMILY ASSOCIATION, SOUTH. 2440
0363-8855 *See* JOURNAL OF CLINICAL ENGINEERING. 3694
0363-8863 *See* LIBRARY EMPLOYEE RELATIONS NEWSLETTER, THE. 1688
0363-888X See ARCHIVAL ISSUES : JOURNAL OF THE MIDWEST ARCHIVES CONFERENCE. 2479
0363-8898 See FISHING IN MARYLAND. 2303

0363-891X *See* PSYCHOHISTORY REVIEW, THE. 2626

0363-8952 *See* PSYCHIATRY AND THE HUMANITIES. 3934

0363-8979 *See* NORTH AMERICAN BIRD BANDER. 5618

0363-8987 *See* FINANCIAL STUDIES OF THE SMALL BUSINESS. 675

0363-9029 *See* CASSETTE BOOKS. 4827

0363-9037 *See* MALEDICTA PRESS PUBLICATIONS. 3301

0363-9045 *See* DRUG DEVELOPMENT AND INDUSTRIAL PHARMACY. 4300

0363-9061 *See* INTERNATIONAL JOURNAL FOR NUMERICAL AND ANALYTICAL METHODS IN GEOMECHANICS. 2025

0363-907X *See* INTERNATIONAL JOURNAL OF ENERGY RESEARCH. 1947

0363-9185 *See* HELP (WASHINGTON). 1297

0363-9193 *See* BIENNIAL REPORT - STATE OF WISCONSIN ETHICS BOARD. 2249

0363-9274 *See* ACTUARIAL VALUATION, NEBRASKA STATE PATROLMEN'S RETIREMENT SYSTEM. 2872

0363-9290 *See* REPUBLICAN ALMANAC. 4493

0363-9312 *See* ANNUAL REPORTS - INDIANA STATE HIGHWAY COMMISSION, DIVISION OF ACCOUNTING & CONTROL. 5438

0363-9339 *See* WYOMING AGRICULTURAL STATISTICS. 157

0363-9371 *See* FED LETTER, THE. 4702

0363-9401 *See* SCA, STATE & COUNTY ADMINISTRATOR. 4685

0363-9444 *See* IMPACT (NEW YORK. 1970). 2367

0363-9460 *See* CONFRONTATION/CHANGE LITERARY REVIEW. 5196

0363-9517 *See* WARRANTY WATCH. 3072

0363-9568 *See* NURSING ADMINISTRATION QUARTERLY. 3863

0363-9606 See MARYLAND PUBLIC TV. 1134

0363-9614 *See* NATIONAL PRO-LIFE JOURNAL, THE. 589

0363-9665 *See* CINEMABOOK. 4066

0363-9673 *See* ANNUAL REPORT ON THE PROVISION OF CHILD WELFARE SERVICES IN NEW YORK STATE. 5273

0363-969X *See* AMATEUR ARCHAEOLOGIST. 253

0363-972X *See* DIRECTORY OF DANCE COMPANIES. 1313

0363-9762 *See* CLINICAL NUCLEAR MEDICINE. 3847

0363-9819 *See* RADIOLOGICAL QUALITY OF THE ENVIRONMENT. 2240

0363-9983 *See* CONTINENTAL DIRECTORY NMF. STANDARD POINT LOCATION CODES SPLC. 5400

0363-9991 *See* INTERSTATE. 3397

0364-0019 *See* MARCH FOR LIFE PROGRAM/JOURNAL. 2252

0364-0078 *See* COUNTRY STYLE MONTHLY. 4112

0364-0086 *See* TOURBOOK : MID-ATLANTIC. 5493

0364-0094 *See* AJS REVIEW. 5045

0364-0124 *See* ELECTRICITY SALES STATISTICS (MONTHLY). 2003

0364-0140 *See* FISH MEAL AND OIL. 2301

0364-0175 *See* RESEARCH REPORTS / SMITHSONIAN INSTITUTION. 5147

0364-0213 *See* COGNITIVE SCIENCE. 1212

0364-023X *See* FLEA MARKET TRADER. 836

0364-0337 *See* NEWSLETTER - DISASTER OPERATIONS OFFICE, STATE OF MISSOURI. 1073

0364-0396 *See* MONTHLY VITAL STATISTICS REPORT. 4562

0364-0418 *See* INTERNATIONAL FLIGHT INFORMATION MANUAL. 24

0364-0558 *See* CALENDARS OF THE UNITED STATES HOUSE OF REPRESENTATIVES AND HISTORY OF LEGISLATION. 4635

0364-0604 *See* FROZEN FISHERY PRODUCTS. 2304

0364-0620 *See* INTERNAL REVENUE CUMULATIVE BULLETIN. 4732

0364-0698 *See* NURSE TRAINING. 3863

0364-071X *See* COLT AMERICAN HANDGUNNING ANNUAL. 4891

0364-0736 *See* FARMER COOPERATIVES. 1542

0364-0752 *See* FINANCIAL STOCK GUIDE SERVICE. DIRECTORY OF ACTIVE STOCKS. 898

0364-0760 *See* CHARITIES USA. 5277

0364-0809 *See* CONSUMER GUIDE : CARS. 1295

0364-0817 *See* DIGEST OF OFFICIAL OPINIONS - ATTORNEY GENERAL (LITTLE ROCK). 3140

0364-0825 *See* HIGHWAY TRAFFIC STATISTICS. 5401

0364-0833 *See* AMERICAN BLACK DIRECTORY. 638

0364-0841 *See* INTERNATIONAL SERIES IN EXPERIMENTAL PSYCHOLOGY. 4592

0364-0973 *See* OFFICIAL REPORTS OF THE SUPREME COURT. 3021

0364-0981 *See* PROCEEDINGS OF THE MARINE SAFETY COUNCIL. 4182

0364-1007 *See* MONTHLY TREASURY STATEMENT OF RECEIPTS AND OUTLAYS OF THE UNITED STATES GOVERNMENT FOR PERIOD FROM 800

0364-1015 *See* MONTHLY STATEMENT OF THE PUBLIC DEBT OF THE UNITED STATES. 4737

0364-1074 *See* EIS. 2164

0364-1082 See GROUP & ORGANIZATION MANAGEMENT. 869

0364-1112 See STRESS AND EMOTION. 4619

0364-118X *See* ELC. 2965

0364-1228 *See* CURRENT INDEX TO STATISTICS. 3542

0364-1236 *See* LIBRARY RESOURCES FOR THE BLIND & PHYSICALLY HANDICAPPED. 3227

0364-1252 *See* PRODUCTION, PRICES, EMPLOYMENT, AND TRADE IN NORTHWEST FOREST INDUSTRIES. 1622

0364-1260 *See* GOVERNMENT PAPER SPECIFICATION STANDARDS. 4651

0364-1287 *See* ARMY LAWYER, THE. 3182

0364-1317 *See* ENVIRONMENT NEWS (BOSTON). 2166

0364-1376 *See* NEW PUBLICATIONS (UNITED STATES. BUREAU OF MINES). 2147

0364-1406 *See* FEDERAL REGISTER. 2970

0364-1465 *See* GREAT ISSUES. 1748

0364-152X *See* ENVIRONMENTAL MANAGEMENT (NEW YORK). 2168

0364-1546 *See* DIRT BIKE. 4081

0364-1619 *See* ANNUAL REPORT - SOUTH CAROLINA LAND RESOURCES CONSERVATION COMMISSION. 2187

0364-1708 *See* GLYPH. 3391

0364-1716 *See* CORRECTIONS, STATE OF RHODE ISLAND. 3161

0364-1724 *See* LAW ENFORCEMENT NEWS. 3169

0364-1783 *See* CONVERTED FLEXIBLE PACKAGING PRODUCTS. 4218

0364-1872 *See* GLASS CONTAINERS (WASHINGTON). 2589

0364-1880 *See* MANUFACTURERS' SHIPMENTS, INVENTORIES, AND ORDERS. 3483

0364-1910 *See* CHEMICAL INFORMATION BULLETIN. 968

0364-1953 *See* UPPER CERVICAL MONOGRAPH, THE. 4382

0364-202X *See* CATTLE ON FEED. 208

0364-2097 *See* SOJOURNERS. 4998

0364-216X *See* AESTHETIC PLASTIC SURGERY. 3958

0364-2186 *See* BIENNIAL REPORT OF OFFICE OF THE COMMISSIONER OF CREDIT UNIONS. 778

0364-2194 *See* BARBEQUE PLANET. 3365

0364-2208 *See* COLLEGE PLACEMENT AND CREDIT BY EXAMINATION. 1816

0364-2232 *See* VOICE FOR THE DEFENSE. 3109

0364-2267 *See* OFFICIAL SUMMARY OF SECURITY TRANSACTIONS AND HOLDINGS. 4739

0364-2313 *See* WORLD JOURNAL OF SURGERY. 3977

0364-2321 *See* SOVIET PHYSICS-LEBEDEV INSTITUTE REPORTS. 4422

0364-233X *See* NEBRASKA JUDICIAL NEWSLETTER. 3141

0364-2348 *See* SKELETAL RADIOLOGY. 3947

0364-2356 *See* GASTROINTESTINAL RADIOLOGY. 3941

0364-2372 *See* ANNUAL SUMMARY OF VITAL STATISTICS, KANSAS (1969). 5321

0364-2410 *See* MELA NOTES. 3230

0364-2429 *See* MONEY DIGEST. 799

0364-2437 *See* AFRO-AMERICANS IN NEW YORK LIFE AND HISTORY. 2254

0364-2453 *See* MANUAL OF PATENT EXAMINING PROCEDURE. 1306

0364-2461 *See* NEW PUBLICATIONS OF THE GEOLOGICAL SURVEY. 1389

0364-2488 *See* HEADQUARTERS TELEPHONE DIRECTORY. 22

0364-250X *See* MSA TAX CORRESPONDENT. 4737

0364-2518 *See* MERGE. 5441

0364-2577 *See* GUIDELINES TO METABOLIC THERAPY. 488

0364-2658 *See* DIGEST FOR REPORTERS. 170

0364-2682 *See* POULTRY SLAUGHTER. 218

0364-2763 *See* ALKALINE PULPING CONFERENCE. 4232

0364-2895 *See* CALIFORNIA ECONOMIC INDICATORS. 1550

0364-2909 *See* JOURNAL-BULLETIN RHODE ISLAND ALMANAC. 2536

0364-2925 *See* PROJECT REFERENCE FILE. 624

0364-2976 *See* JOURNAL OF THE HELLENIC DIASPORA. 2695

0364-2984 *See* OIL AND GAS REPORT (UNIVERSITY OF ALA.). 4269

0364-3107 *See* ADMINISTRATION IN SOCIAL WORK. 5270

0364-3166 *See* CHILD DEVELOPMENT PROGRAM EVALUATION REPORT (CALIFORNIA). 1731

0364-3190 *See* NEUROCHEMICAL RESEARCH. 3839

0364-3298 See INSURANCE SERVICE QUARTERLY REVIEW. 2884

0364-3301 *See* CORROSION PREVENTION/INHIBITION DIGEST. 2011

0364-331X *See* JEPPESEN SANDERSON AVIATION YEARBOOK. 25

0364-3344 *See* BOX 749. 3369

0364-3360 *See* WORLD TELECOMMUNICATIONS DIRECTORY. 1169

0364-3387 *See* VERMONT HISTORY NEWS. 2764

0364-3417 *See* ANNUAL REVIEW OF POPULATION LAW. 2935

0364-3425 *See* WEST VIRGINIA STATE BAR JOURNAL. 3073

0364-3441 *See* HELPING THE EXOFFENDER. 3165

0364-345X *See* PASSENGER TRANSPORT. 5389

0364-3468 *See* HIGHWAY & URBAN MASS TRANSPORTATION. 5383

0364-3484 *See* MASS TRANSIT (WASHINGTON, D.C.). 5386

0364-3557 *See* WATER RESOURCES DATA. WASHINGTON. 5546

0364-3565 *See* WATER RESOURCES DATA. WYOMING. 5546

0364-3581 *See* FEDERAL RULES OF EVIDENCE NEWS. 2970

0364-359X *See* DRAGONFLY (PORTLAND). 3382

0364-3603 *See* CLAIMS FORUM. 2951

0364-362X *See* NORTH CAROLINA ATTORNEY GENERAL REPORTS. 3142

0364-3646 *See* NAVY TECHNICAL DISCLOSURE BULLETIN / OFFICE OF NAVAL RESEARCH, DEPARTMENT OF THE NAVY. 4180

0364-3654 *See* SWEET'S SHOWROOM MARKET LIST. 630

0364-3670 ISSN Index

0364-3670 See INTERNATIONAL CODEN DIRECTORY. 5114

0364-3700 See NEW YORK TIMES CROSSWORD PUZZLES, THE. 4864

0364-3719 See NATIONAL LOCKSMITH, THE. 2812

0364-3824 See TASTE. 2792

0364-3840 See ECP REPORT. 1937

0364-3875 See OAG DESKTOP FLIGHT GUIDE (WORLDWIDE ED.). 5486

0364-3883 See WAGES IN NEW YORK CITY. 1717

0364-393X See ANTIQUE SHOP GUIDE. 249

0364-3964 See ANNUAL REPORT - INDUSTRIAL ENVIRONMENTAL RESEARCH LABORATORY. 2160

0364-3972 See MITRE TECHNICAL REPORT. 5129

0364-4014 See SPIRIT THAT MOVES US, THE. 3439

0364-4030 See PROCEEDINGS - REFINING DEPARTMENT. 4275

0364-4065 See WATER RESOURCES DATA FOR NEW MEXICO. 5544

0364-4073 See WATER RESOURCES DATA. MONTANA. 5545

0364-4081 See WATER RESOURCES DATA. KENTUCKY. 5545

0364-4200 See LEGISLATIVE CALENDAR / UNITED STATES HOUSE OF REPRESENTATIVES, COMMITTEE ON VETERAN AFFAIRS. 4661

0364-4308 See YIDDISH. 3455

0364-4324 See WATER RESOURCES DATA. IDAHO. 5545

0364-4332 See WATER RESOURCES DATA FOR ILLINOIS. 5544

0364-4340 See WATER RESOURCE DATA FOR INDIANA. 5543

0364-4359 See WATER RESOURCES DATA. IOWA. 5545

0364-4367 See WATER RESOURCES DATA. MARYLAND AND DELAWARE. 5545

0364-4375 See WATER RESOURCES DATA FOR MICHIGAN. 5544

0364-4383 See WATER RESOURCES DATA FOR MINNESOTA. 5544

0364-4421 See WATER RESOURCES DATA FOR WEST VIRGINIA. 5545

0364-443X See ULRF REPORTS. 2837

0364-4561 See CALIFORNIA ASSESSMENT PROGRAM RESULTS FOR EDUCATIONALLY HANDICAPPED PUPILS IN THE PRIMARY GRADES. 1876

0364-457X See STUDIO ONE. 331

0364-4626 See SOVIET JOURNAL OF COORDINATION CHEMISTRY. 1058

0364-4642 See TEXAS STATE PLAN FOR CONSTRUCTION OF COMMUNITY MENTAL HEALTH CENTERS. 4805

0364-4693 See ACCIDENT CONTROL REPORT. 2185

0364-4731 See AREA WAGE SURVEY: THE RALEIGH-DURHAM, NORTH CAROLINA, METROPOLITAN AREA. 1653

0364-474X See ELECTRIC PERSPECTIVES. 2043

0364-4766 See DIRECTORY OF HUMAN SERVICE ORGANIZATIONS. 5283

0364-4960 See CLIMATOLOGICAL DATA. OKLAHOMA. 1423

0364-5002 See CLIMATOLOGICAL DATA. WYOMING. 1424

0364-5010 See CLIMATOLOGICAL DATA. TENNESSEE. 1424

0364-5029 See CLIMATOLOGICAL DATA. NORTH DAKOTA. 1423

0364-5037 See CLIMATOLOGICAL DATA. SOUTH CAROLINA. 1424

0364-5045 See CLIMATOLOGICAL DATA. SOUTH DAKOTA. 1424

0364-510X See WATER RESOURCES DATA FOR MISSISSIPPI. 5544

0364-5134 See ANNALS OF NEUROLOGY. 3827

0364-5169 See MAGAZINE FOR EVERY US VETERAN, THE. 4049

0364-5177 See LIVE STEAM. 5432

0364-5215 See USBE NEWS. 3255

0364-5274 See ENERGY DAILY, THE. 1939

0364-5282 See LOCATION IDENTIFIERS. 27

0364-5304 See CLIMATOLOGICAL DATA. WISCONSIN. 1424

0364-5312 See CLIMATOLOGICAL DATA. NEVADA. 1423

0364-5320 See CLIMATOLOGICAL DATA. WASHINGTON. 1424

0364-5339 See CLIMATOLOGICAL DATA. NEW ENGLAND. 1423

0364-5371 See CLIMATOLOGICAL DATA. WEST VIRGINIA. 1424

0364-5401 See HOURLY PRECIPITATION DATA. KENTUCKY. 1425

0364-5444 See FARM BROADCASTERS LETTER. 84

0364-5487 See PETERS NOTES. 4146

0364-5495 See BIENNIAL REPORT - STATE OF WISCONSIN, INVESTMENT BOARD. 4713

0364-5525 See CONFERENCE PAPERS QUARTERLY INDEX. 414

0364-5584 See CLIMATOLOGICAL DATA. OHIO. 1423

0364-5592 See CLIMATOLOGICAL DATA. UTAH. 1424

0364-5606 See CLIMATOLOGICAL DATA. NEW YORK. 1423

0364-5614 See CLIMATOLOGICAL DATA. NEW JERSEY. 1423

0364-5622 See CLIMATOLOGICAL DATA. NEW MEXICO. 1423

0364-5630 See CLIMATOLOGICAL DATA. VIRGINIA. 1424

0364-5649 See LEGISLATIVE REPORT ON JUVENILE PROBATION SUBSIDY. 3169

0364-5673 See NEBRASKA NUMBERS. 1347

0364-5703 See DIRECTORY OF MEMBERS - CALIFORNIA SOCIETY, CERTIFIED PUBLIC ACCOUNTANTS. 743

0364-5711 See STANDARD & POOR'S INTERNATIONAL STOCK REPORT. 915

0364-5746 See TENNESSEE BLUE BOOK. 4690

0364-5754 See DOCUMENT RETRIEVAL INDEX. 3163

0364-5762 See CLIMATOLOGICAL DATA. ALASKA. 1422

0364-5843 See CLIMATOLOGICAL DATA. PENNSYLVANIA. 1423

0364-5851 See CLIMATOLOGICAL DATA. OREGON. 1423

0364-5916 See CALPHAD. 1050

0364-5924 See HAYES HISTORICAL JOURNAL: A JOURNAL OF THE GILDED AGE. 2736

0364-6041 See CLIMATOLOGICAL DATA. TEXAS. 1424

0364-605X See CLIMATOLOGICAL DATA. ARKANSAS. 1422

0364-6068 See CLIMATOLOGICAL DATA. MISSOURI. 1423

0364-6165 See HOURLY PRECIPITATION DATA. INDIANA. 1425

0364-619X See HOURLY PRECIPITATION DATA, PENNSYLVANIA. 1425

0364-6386 See HOURLY PRECIPITATION DATA. TENNESSEE. 1426

0364-6408 See LIBRARY ACQUISITIONS : PRACTICE AND THEORY. 3223

0364-6416 See SUMMARY OF SUPPLEMENTAL TYPE CERTIFICATES. 37

0364-6440 See NASA EARTH RESOURCES SURVEY PROGRAM. 1358

0364-6505 See EDEBIYAT (PHILADELPHIA, PA.). 3383

0364-653X See HOME PLANS & PROJECTS. 300

0364-6548 See HOMES FOR LEISURE LIVING. 300

0364-6572 See JOHN & MARY'S JOURNAL. 5232

0364-6580 See REPORT OF PERSONS DISCHARGED FROM PAROLE AND PERSONS VIOLATING PAROLE. 3174

0364-6645 See WORKING PAPERS IN BAKER LIBRARY. 723

0364-6661 See REPORT FROM THE CAPITAL. 4992

0364-667X See NEWSLETTER - MASSACHUSETTS BAY DISTRICT, UNITARIAN UNIVERSALIST CHURCHES. 4981

0364-6688 See INSIDE INTERIOR. 4657

0364-6742 See INTERNATIONAL NOTICES TO AIRMEN. 24

0364-6777 See NEW FOR CONSUMERS. 1298

0364-6793 See LATEST EDITIONS OF U.S. AIR FORCE AERONAUTICAL CHARTS. 4048

0364-6858 See FEDERAL MOTOR VEHICLE SAFETY STANDARDS AND REGULATIONS. 4648

0364-6858 See FEDERAL MOTOR VEHICLE SAFETY STANDARDS AND REGULATIONS. 5382

0364-6955 See DIRECTORY OF NATIONAL SOURCES OF DATA ON BLACKS IN HIGHER EDUCATION. 1821

0364-6963 See ANTIQUE MOTORCYCLE, THE. 4080

0364-698X See JOURNAL - AMERICAN WINE SOCIETY. 2368

0364-7005 See NEMATOLOGY LITERATURE LIST. 111

0364-7021 See SWEET'S SHOWROOM. 3488

0364-703X See TRUCK WEIGHT STUDY (JACKSON). 5398

0364-7056 See INDIAN SCHOOL JOURNAL. 1752

0364-7064 See NEWSLETTER / NATIONAL CARTOGRAPHIC INFORMATION CENTER. 2582

0364-7129 See MONTHLY BENEFIT STATISTICS (CHICAGO). 1536

0364-7153 See RECORDS OF EXOTICS. 4914

0364-7196 See WHO'S WHO IN FRESNO. 437

0364-7218 See ENTREPRENEUR. 672

0364-7234 See WORLD ECONOMIC CONDITIONS IN RELATION TO AGRICULTURAL TRADE. 1641

0364-7382 See VERMONT LIBRARY DIRECTORY. 3255

0364-7420 See TOBACCO MARKET REVIEW. SOUTHERN MARYLAND. 5374

0364-7501 See MUSICAL MAINSTREAM, THE. 4136

0364-7544 See CONGRESSIONAL RECORD INDEX. 2955

0364-7560 See LANDSAT U.S. STANDARD CATALOG. 27

0364-7587 See LANDSAT NON-U.S. STANDARD CATALOG. 27

0364-7609 See PRIMAVERA (CHICAGO). 3425

0364-7625 See ACCESS REPORTS. 4461

0364-765X See MATHEMATICS OF OPERATIONS RESEARCH. 3521

0364-7668 See RISING TIDE, THE. 4512

0364-7692 See HARVARD UNIVERSITY GAZETTE. 1092

0364-7714 See WATER SUPPLY & MANAGEMENT. 5548

0364-7781 See NUTMEG. 1838

0364-7803 See ANNUAL PROGRAM; LIBRARY SERVICES AND CONSTRUCTION ACT - SOUTH CAROLINA. STATE LIBRARY, COLUMBIA. 3190

0364-7919 See MERCURY (UNITED STATES. BUREAU OF MINES). 4026

0364-7935 See TIN (UNITED STATES. BUREAU OF MINES). 4022

0364-7978 700

0364-7986 See ADMINISTRATION & MANAGEMENT. 4624

0364-7994 See AGRICULTURE & FOOD. 53

0364-8028 See INDIAN LEADER, THE. 1752

0364-8044 See PANAMA CANAL SPILLWAY, THE. 5454

0364-8052 See MEMORANDUM OPINION AND ORDER. 1117

0364-8079 *See* NEWSLETTER (PRESIDENT'S COUNCIL ON PHYSICAL FITNESS AND SPORTS (U.S.)). **2600**

0364-8087 *See* RICE MARKET NEWS. **130**

0364-8095 *See* NATIONAL ELECTRIC RATE BOOK. **2073**

0364-8109 *See* WEEKLY SUMMARY OF NLRB CASES. **3155**

0364-8117 See RUSSIAN AERONAUTICS. **34**

0364-815X *See* MARQUEE (NORWALK), THE. **4130**

0364-8184 *See* NEW HORIZON (JERSEY CITY). **2269**

0364-8206 *See* SIKH DHARMA BROTHERHOOD. **4997**

0364-8214 *See* UNITED STATES TENNIS CLUB REGISTRY. **4927**

0364-8230 *See* CONEJO VALLEY BUSINESS. **659**

0364-8257 *See* ANNUAL REPORT - STATE OF OKLAHOMA, DEPARTMENT OF ECONOMIC AND COMMUNITY AFFAIRS. **1546**

0364-8281 *See* STATUS REPORT: CAPITAL IMPROVEMENT PROGRAM, BOND FUND SUMMARY. **4750**

0364-829X *See* BIBLIOGRAPHY OF AGRICULTURE : ANNUAL CUMULATION. **66**

0364-8370 *See* SELECTED INTEREST & EXCHANGE RATES. **811**

0364-8575 *See* WORLD THIS YEAR, THE. **4501**

0364-8591 *See* OLD TESTAMENT ABSTRACTS. **5013**

0364-863X *See* POSTAL BULLETIN. **1146**

0364-8753 *See* REGISTER OF OFFICERS - COAST GUARD. **4182**

0364-8761 *See* CABLE HANDBOOK. **1129**

0364-8788 *See* DIRECTORY FOR MEMBERS - SOCIETY OF MOTION PICTURE AND TELEVISION ENGINEERS, INC. **4067**

0364-8850 *See* TEXAS STATE PLAN FOR THE PREVENTION, TREATMENT, AND CONTROL OF ALCOHOL ABUSE AND ALCOHOLISM. **1349**

0364-8877 *See* FINANCIAL AIDS FOR HIGHER EDUCATION. **1824**

0364-8893 See RENTAL RATES COMPILATION. **626**

0364-9008 *See* DEFENSE BUSINESS. **4041**

0364-9008 *See* DEFENSE & ECONOMY : WORLD REPORT AND SURVEY. **4519**

0364-9024 *See* JOURNAL OF GRAPH THEORY. **3513**

0364-9059 *See* IEEE JOURNAL OF OCEANIC ENGINEERING. **2090**

0364-9105 *See* TECHNOLOGY ASSESSMENT & FORECAST. **5163**

0364-9156 *See* DIRECTORS & BOARDS. **865**

0364-9172 *See* SEA CHEST (BUXTON). **2760**

0364-9202 *See* STATISTICAL ABSTRACT OF COLORADO. **5339**

0364-9237 *See* SPEEDHORSE (MONTHLY), THE. **2802**

0364-927X *See* U.S. CIVIL AIRMEN STATISTICS. **42**

0364-9288 *See* ETHNOLOGUE. **3280**

0364-9296 *See* DIRECTORY OF WATER RESOURCES EXPERTISE. **5532**

0364-930X *See* ALFA OWNER. **5403**

0364-9334 *See* INFORMATION PRACTICES IN WYOMING STATE GOVERNMENT. **4656**

0364-9407 *See* VIETNAM QUARTERLY. **2667**

0364-9458 *See* OKLAHOMA CITY UNIVERSITY LAW REVIEW. **3022**

0364-9474 *See* FRIENDS OF WINE, THE. **2367**

0364-9490 *See* DELAWARE JOURNAL OF CORPORATE LAW, THE. **3099**

0364-9504 *See* AMERICAN ARACHNOLOGY. **5574**

0364-9512 *See* ANNUAL REPORT - BIOLOGICAL FIELD STATION, COOPERSTOWN, NEW YORK. **442**

0364-9539 See MCD WAREHOUSING DISTRIBUTION DIRECTORY. **845**

0364-9601 *See* STATE MEMBER BANKS OF THE FEDERAL RESERVE SYSTEM AND NONMEMBER BANKS THAT MAINTAIN CLEARING ACCOUNTS WITH FEDERAL RESERVE BANKS AND CORPORATIONS DOING FOREIGN BANKING OR FINANCING THAT MAINTAIN RESERVE ACCOUNTS WITH FEDERAL RESERVE BANKS. **812**

0365-0014 *See* ATTI E MEMORIE DELLA ACCADEMIA DI AGRICOLTURA, SCIENZE E LETTERE DI VERONA. **63**

0365-0081 *See* ATTI DELLA ACCADEMIA ROVERETANA DEGLI AGIATI. **1074**

0365-0138 *See* ASTRONOMY & ASTROPHYSICS. SUPPLEMENT SERIES. **392**

0365-0294 *See* ATTI DELLA ACCADEMIA PELORITANA DEI PERICOLANTI, CLASSE DI SCIENCE MEDICO-BIOLOGICHE. **443**

0365-0340 *See* ARCHIV FUER ACKER- UND PFLANZENBAU UND BODENKUNDE. **163**

0365-0375 *See* ANALES DE LA ASOCIACION QUIMICA ARGENTINA. **960**

0365-0588 *See* ACTA BOTANICA CROATICA. **496**

0365-0596 *See* ANAIS BRASILEIROS DE DERMATOLOGIA. **3717**

0365-0723 *See* ARQUIVOS BRASILEIROS DE MEDICINA. **3552**

0365-0871 *See* ARCHIVOS DE BIOQUIMICA, QUIMICA Y FARMACIA, TUCUMAN. **480**

0365-0979 *See* ARQUIVOS DE BIOLOGIA E TECNOLOGIA. **443**

0365-1029 *See* ANNALES UNIVERSITATIS MARIAE CURIE-SKODOWSKA. SECTIO A. MATHEMATICA. **3493**

0365-1118 *See* ANNALES UNIVERSITATIS MARIAE CURIE-SKODOWSKA. SECTIO E AGRICULTURA. **59**

0365-1185 *See* ANALES DE L'ACADEMIA NACIONAL DE CIENCIAS EXACTAS, FISICAS Y NATURALES, BUENOS AIRES. **5082**

0365-1398 *See* ACTA MONTANA. **2132**

0365-1541 *See* ACTA TROPICA. SUPPLEMENTUM. **3985**

0365-169X *See* ANNALI ITALIANI DI DERMATOLOGIA CLINICA E SPERIMENTALE. **3717**

0365-1797 See SUELO Y PLANTA. **188**

0365-1800 *See* ANALES DE LA ESTACION EXPERIMENTAL DE AULA DEI. **58**

0365-1932 *See* ANALES DE LA ESCUELA NACIONAL DE CIENCIAS BIOLOGICAS (MEXICO). **441**

0365-2017 *See* ANNALES DE L'EST. **2674**

0365-2459 *See* ARKIV FOR DET FYSISKE SEMINAR I TRONDHEIM. **4398**

0365-2467 *See* AGARDOGRAPH. **6**

0365-2777 *See* ANNALS OF THE GEOLOGICAL SURVEY OF EGYPT. **1365**

0365-2807 *See* AGRICULTURA TECNICA. **49**

0365-2998 *See* ARQUIVOS DO INSTITUTO BACTERIOLOGICO CAMARA PESTANA (LISBOA). **560**

0365-3498 *See* ANNALI DELL'ISTITUTO SPERIMENTALE PER LA ZOOTECNIA. **5575**

0365-3536 *See* ANALES DEL INSTITUTO DE INVESTIGACIONES VETERINARIAS. **5502**

0365-3803 *See* AKTUAL'NYE VOPROSY EPIDEMIOLOGII. **3733**

0365-4141 *See* APPARATURA I METODY RENTGENOVSKOGO ANALIZA. **3939**

0365-4389 *See* ANNALI DEL MUSEO CIVICO DI STORIA NATURALE GIACOMO DORIA. **4162**

0365-4508 *See* ARQUIVOS DO MUSEU NACIONAL. **4084**

0365-4710 *See* ATTI E MEMORIE / ACCADEMIA VIRGILIANA DI MANTOVA. **2842**

0365-4729 *See* ANNALI DELLA FACOLTA DI MEDICINA VETERINARIA DI PISA. **5503**

0365-4761 *See* ANNALES DE L'INSTITUT NATIONAL DE LA RECHERCHE AGRONOMIQUE DE TUNISIE. **59**

0365-4850 *See* ACTA NATURALIA ISLANDICA. **4161**

0365-4877 *See* ANALUSIS. **1012**

0365-5148 *See* ANALECTA VETERINARIA. **5502**

0365-5237 *See* ACTA OTO-LARYNGOLOGICA. SUPPLEMENT. **3885**

0365-5504 *See* ACTA PAEDIATRICA LATINA. **3899**

0365-5520 See ATTI DELLA ACCODEMIA PELORITANA DEI PERICOLANTI, CLASSE DI SCIENCE MEDICO-BIOLOGICHE. **443**

0365-5539 *See* ANNALES PHARMACEUTICI. **4291**

0365-575X *See* ANALELE - INSTITUTULUI DE CERCETARI PENTRU PROTECTIA PLANTELOR, ACADEMIA DE STIINTE AGRICOLE SI SILVICE. **498**

0365-5814 *See* ANNALES DE L'INSTITUT PHYTOPATHOLOGIQUE BENAKI. **499**

0365-5873 *See* AQEIC. BOLETIN TECNICO. **961**

0365-5954 *See* ACTA RADIOLOGICA. SUPPLEMENTUM. **3938**

0365-6187 *See* AROMATIKKUSU. **961**

0365-6233 *See* ARCHIV DER PHARMAZIE (WEINHEIM). **4292**

0365-6330 *See* ABSTRACTS OF ROMANIAN SCIENTIFIC AND TECHNICAL LITERATURE. **5079**

0365-6470 *See* ABHANDLUNGEN DER SACHSISCHEN AKADEMIE DER WISSENSCHAFTEN ZU LEIPZIG. MATHEMATISCH-NATURWISSENSCHAFTLICHE KLASSE. **5079**

0365-6527 *See* ANNALES DE LA SOCIETE BELGE DE MEDECINE TROPICALE. **3985**

0365-6861 *See* ACTUALITES SCIENTIFIQUES ET INDUSTRIELLES. **5080**

0365-7000 *See* ABHANDLUNGEN DER SENCKENBERGISCHEN NATURFORSCHENDEN GESELLSCHAFT. **4161**

0365-7043 *See* ANNALI DELL'ISTITUTO SPERIMENTALE PER LA NUTRIZIONE DELLE PIANTE. **59**

0365-7442 *See* AEROTECNICA MISSILI E SPAZIO, L'. **6**

0365-7779 *See* ANALES DE LA UNIVERSIDAD DE CHILE. **1724**

0365-7965 *See* ACTUALIDAD MEDICA. **3545**

0365-799X *See* ANNALI DELLA FACOLTA DI SCIENZE AGRARIE DELLA UNIVERSITA DEGLI STUDI DI NAPOLI, PORTICI. **59**

0365-8066 *See* ACTA MINERALOGICA-PETROGRAPHICA (SZEGED). **1437**

0365-8341 *See* ACTA DERMATO-VENEREOLOGICA. SUPPLEMENTUM. **3717**

0365-8406 *See* ARCHIV FUER ZUCHTUNGSFORSCHUNG. **5085**

0365-8414 *See* ATOMWIRTSCHAFT, ATOMTECHNIK. **2154**

0365-8554 *See* AZERBAJDZANSKOR NEFTJANOE HOZJAJSTVO. **3338**

0365-9402 *See* BOLETIN CHILENO DE PARASITOLOGIA. **449**

0365-9429 *See* BIOCHEMICAL REVIEWS. **481**

0365-9445 *See* BROMATOLOGIA I CHEMIA TOKSYKOLOGICZNA. **3979**

0365-9615 *See* BJULLETEN EKSPERIMENTALNOJ BIOLOGII I MEDICINY. **448**

0365-9798 *See* MATERIAUX POUR LA CARTE GEOLOGIQUE DE LA SUISSE. **1386**

0365-9844 *See* BERICHT DER NATURHISTORISCHEN GESELLSCHAFT HANNOVER. **4163**

0366-0176 *See* BOLETIN GEOLOGICO Y MINERO. **1367**

0366-0265 *See* BIBLIOGRAPHY ON THE HIGH TEMPERATURE CHEMISTRY AND PHYSICS OF MATERIALS LONDON. **962**

0366-0370 *See* BULLETIN OF THE INSTITUTE OF CHEMISTRY. ACADEMIA SINICA. **963**

0366-0486 *See* BIOLOGICKE LISTY. **446**

0366-0567 *See* BIOLOGICO, O. **446**

0366-0672 *See* BULLETIN - INDIAN SOCIETY OF SOIL SCIENCE. **165**

0366-077X *See* BRITISH JOURNAL OF DERMATOLOGY. SUPPLEMENT. **3718**

0366-0885 *See* BERICHTE DER KERNFORSCHUNGSANLAGE JULICH. **4446**

0366-1318 See BJULLETEN MOSKOVSKOGO OBSCESTVA ISPYTATELEJ PRIRODY. OTDEL GEOLOGICESKIJ. **1367**
0366-1326 See BULLETIN MENSUEL DE LA SOCIETE LINNEENNE DE LYON. **4164**
0366-1393 See BULLETIN OF THE NUTRITION INSTITUTE OF THE UNITED ARAB REPUBLIC. **4188**
0366-1644 See BOLETIN DE LA SOCIEDAD CHILENA DE QUIMICA. **962**
0366-1970 See BOLLETTINO E MEMORIE DELLA SOCIETA PIEMONTESE DI CHIRURGIA. **3961**
0366-2101 See BOLETIM DA SOCIEDADE GEOLOGICA DE PORTUGAL. **1367**
0366-2128 See BOLETIN DE LA SOCIEDAD BOTANICA DE MEXICO. **503**
0366-2241 See BOLLETTINO DEL SERVIZIO GEOLOGICO D'ITALIA. **1368**
0366-2284 See BIOS (PARIS). **2364**
0366-2330 See BOUW. **601**
0366-2403 See BOLLETTINO DI ZOOLOGIA AGRARIA E DI BACHICOLTURA. **68**
0366-242X See ATAC, ASOCIACION DE TECNICOS AZUCAREROS DE CUBA. **2328**
0366-3175 See BOLETIN DE LA SOCIEDAD ESPANOLA DE CERAMICA Y VIDRIO (1983). **2586**
0366-3353 See BULLETIN OF THE UNIVERSITY OF OSAKA PREFECTURE. SERIES B: AGRICULTURE AND BIOLOGY. **70**
0366-3477 See BULLETIN DE LA SOCIETE D'HISTOIRE NATURELLE DE TOULOUSE. **4163**
0366-3507 See BULLETIN DE LA SOCIETE DE PHARMACIE DE LILLE. **4294**
0366-3612 See KONGELIGE DANSKE VIDENSKABERNES SELSKAB. BIOLOGISKE SKRIFTER. **462**
0366-3876 See BULLETIN DE L'UNION DES PHYSICIENS. **4399**
0366-4104 See BULLETIN DU CERCLE D'ETUDES DES METAUX. **3999**
0366-4740 See BULLETIN OF THE FACULTY OF SCIENCE, ASSIUT UNIVERSITY. **5091**
0366-4848 See BULLETIN DER VEREINIGUNG SCHWEIZ. PETROLEUM-GEOLOGEN UND-INGENIEURE. **4252**
0366-4899 See BIULLETEN. **5506**
0366-502X See BIULLETEN GLAVNOGO BOTANICHESKOGO SADA. **502**
0366-5089 See BJULLETEN VULKANOLOGICESKIH STANCIJ. **1367**
0366-5232 See CALDASIA. **4164**
0366-5526 See CHEMIKA CHRONIKA. GENIKE EKDOSIS. **969**
0366-5607 See CHEMICAL COMMUNICATIONS / UNIVERSITY OF STOCKHOLM. **968**
0366-5887 See COLLOQUIUM DER GESELLSCHAFT FUER BIOLOGISCHE CHEMIE. **485**
0366-6298 See CHIRURGIA TORACICA, LA. **3962**
0366-6425 See CIRCULAR FARMACEUTICA. **4296**
0366-6611 See CHIKYU KAGAKU. **1371**
0366-6662 See CHOSON MINJUJUUI INMIN KONGHWAGUK KWAHAGWON TONGBO. **5094**
0366-6743 See CLINICAL JOURNAL (MANHASSET). **3565**
0366-676X See CLIO MEDICA. **3567**
0366-6913 See CERAMICA (SAO PAULO). **2587**
0366-693X See CHIMIKA CHRONIKA (INTERNATIONAL EDITION). **972**
0366-6999 See CHINESE MEDICAL JOURNAL. **3563**
0366-7022 See CHEMISTRY LETTERS. **1040**
0366-7073 See FOTOMAGAZIN. **4369**
0366-7154 See CHEMIE, MIKROBIOLOGIE, TECHNOLOGIE DER LEBENSMITTEL. **2331**
0366-757X See CODATA BULLETIN. **5095**
0366-7634 See COLLOQUES INTERNATIONAUX DU CENTRE NATIONAL DE LA RECHERCHE SCIENTIFIQUE. **234**
0366-8622 See DEUTSCHE APOTHEKER, DER. **4299**
0366-872X See DECHENIANA. **4165**

0366-8746 See DOKTORSAVHANDLINGAR VID CHALMERS TEKNISKA HOGSKOLA. **5101**
0366-9084 See DENSHI GIJUTSU SOGO KENKYUJO CHOSA HOKOKU. **2040**
0366-9092 See DENSHI GIJUTSU SOGO KENKYUJO IHO. **2041**
0366-9106 See DENSHI GIJUTSU SOGO KENKYUJO KENKYU HOKOKU. **2041**
0366-9297 See DENKI KAGAKU OYOBI KOGYO BUTSURI KAGAKU. **1034**
0366-9610 See DRAGER REVIEW. **1664**
0366-970X See DENKSCHRIFTEN DER SCHWEIZERISCHEN NATURFORSCHENDEN GESELLSCHAFT. **5099**
0367-0007 See DYNAMIC MASS SPECTROMETRY. **1014**
0367-021X See ENBI TO PORIMA. **4455**
0367-0236 See BULLETIN OF PHARMACY. **4295**
0367-0244 See ECOLOGY OF FOOD AND NUTRITION. **4190**
0367-0422 See EGYPTIAN JOURNAL OF CHEMISTRY. **975**
0367-0449 See ESTUDIOS GEOOGICOS (MADRID). **1375**
0367-052X See IGAKU KENSA. **3585**
0367-0597 See EKOLOGIJA. **2215**
0367-0643 See EKSPERIMENTALNA MEDITSINA I MORFOLOGIIA. **3574**
0367-0708 See ELEKTROTECHNIKA. **2052**
0367-0724 See EKSPERIMENTALNAIA VODNAIA TOKSIKOLOGIIA / AKADEMIIA NAUK LATVIISKOI SSR, INSTITUT BIOLOGII. **4244**
0367-1089 See EXCERPTA MEDICA. SECTION 2A. PHYSIOLOGY. **478**
0367-1119 See ENERGY DIGEST. **1940**
0367-1445 See ENTOMOLOGICESKOE OBOZRENIE. **5582**
0367-1526 See EXPLOSIFS. **1024**
0367-1631 See FIZIKA AERODISPERSNYH SISTEM (KIEV). **1425**
0367-1704 See FRODSKAPARRIT. **3283**
0367-1887 See SCIENTIFIC PUBLICATION - FRESHWATER BIOLOGICAL ASSOCIATION. **472**
0367-1933 See FACHHEFTE. CHEMIGRAPHIE, LITHOGRAPHIE UND TIEFDRUCK. **4565**
0367-2174 See DET FORSTLIGE FORSOEGSVAESEN I DANMARK : BERETNINGER UTGIVNE VED DEN FORSTLIGE FORSOEGSKOMMISSION. **2378**
0367-2409 See FIZIKO-KHIMICHESKAIA MEKHANIKA I LIOFILNOST DISPERSNYKH SISTEM. **455**
0367-2492 See FORSCHUNGSBERICHTE DES LANDES NORDRHEIN-WESTFALEN. **5105**
0367-2530 See FLORA. MORPHOLOGIE, GEOBOTANIK, OKOLOGIE. **2216**
0367-2743 See FONTILLES. **3720**
0367-3014 See FARMACIJA. **4304**
0367-3057 See FARMACEVTYCNYJ ZURNAL (KIIV. 1928). **4304**
0367-3073 See FERTILIZER SOCIETY OF SOUTH AFRICA JOURNAL. **87**
0367-326X See FITOTERAPIA. **510**
0367-3332 See FUJI JIHO. **2055**
0367-3685 See GEOLOGIE ALPINE. **1379**
0367-4061 See GUNMA DAIGAKU KYOYOBU KIYO. **2847**
0367-4134 See GEORGOFILI; ATTI DELLA ACCADEMIA DEI GEORGOFILI, I. **90**
0367-4150 See GEOLOGICA HUNGARICA. SERIES GEOLOGICA. **1377**
0367-4177 See GETREIDE, MEHL UND BROT (1972). **201**
0367-4223 See GESUNDE PFLANZEN. **2230**
0367-4231 See GEOPHYSICA. **1405**
0367-4290 See GEOLOGICESKIJ ZURNAL (KIEV. 1968). **1379**
0367-4665 See GIDROKHIMICHESKIE MATERIALY. **976**
0367-4762 See GACETA MEDICA DE CARACAS. **3578**
0367-4916 See GOSPODARKA MIESNA. **211**

0367-5041 See GRAELLSIA. **5585**
0367-5211 See BULLETIN OF THE GEOLOGICAL SOCIETY OF FINLAND. **1370**
0367-5335 See SPECIAL PUBLICATION - GEOLOGICAL SOCIETY OF SOUTH AFRICA. **1398**
0367-5610 See HARYANA AGRICULTURAL UNIVERSITY JOURNAL OF RESEARCH. **91**
0367-5726 See HOKKAIDO DAIGAKU NOGAKUBU HOBUN KIYO. **92**
0367-5807 See HAN'GUK CHUKSAN HAKHOE CHI. **5510**
0367-5866 See HI-HAKAI KENSA. **5109**
0367-5912 See HIROSHIMA DAIGAKU SEIBUTSU GAKKAI SHI. **457**
0367-5920 See HSIANG-KANG CH'IN HUI HSUEH YUAN HSUEH PAO. **1092**
0367-5939 See HOKKAIDO KYOIKU DAIGAKU KIYO. A SUGAKU-, BUTSURIGAKU-, KAGAKU-, KOGAKU-HEN. DAI 2-BU. **5110**
0367-5947 See HOKURIKU MASUIGAKU ZASSHI. **3683**
0367-5955 See HOKKAIDO NOGYO SHIKENJO KENKYU HOKOKU. **92**
0367-6048 See HOKKAIDORITSU NOGYO SHIKENJO HOKOKU. **92**
0367-6102 See HOKKAIDO IGAKU ZASSHI. **3584**
0367-6110 See HOKEN BUTSURI. **3584**
0367-6129 See HOKKAIDO DAIGAKU NOGAKUBU ENSHURIN KENKYU HOKOKU. **2384**
0367-6293 See HAN'GUK SIKPUM KWAHAKHOE CHI. **2343**
0367-6315 See HAN'GUK TOYANG PIRYO HAKHOE CHI. **173**
0367-6358 See HUA HSUEH SHIH CHIEH. **977**
0367-6439 See SCIENCE REPORTS OF THE HIROSAKI UNIVERSITY. **5153**
0367-648X See HYOMEN. **1025**
0367-6617 See REPORT - ISRAEL ATOMIC ENERGY COMMISSION. **4451**
0367-6722 See INDIAN JOURNAL OF ANIMAL RESEARCH. **212**
0367-6765 See IZVESTIJA AKADEMII NAUK SSSR. SERIJA FIZICESKAJA. **4407**
0367-6897 See PROCEEDINGS OF THE CONVENTION - INSTITUTE OF BREWING AUSTRALIAN AND NEW ZEALAND SECTION. **2370**
0367-7281 See INDIAN COCONUT JOURNAL (COCHIN). **174**
0367-729X See INTERNATIONAL CRIMINAL POLICE REVIEW. **3166**
0367-7389 See IBARAKI DAIGAKU KOGAKUBU KENKYU SHUHO. **1977**
0367-7435 See INDIAN ARCHIVES. **2481**
0367-7443 See IDOJARAS (BUDAPEST 1897). **1426**
0367-7524 See ISTANBUL UNIVERSITESI ECZACLK FAKULTESI MECMUAS. **4309**
0367-7788 See INDUSTRIEFEUERUNG. **2606**
0367-7850 See COMMUNICATION / THE INSTITUTION OF GAS ENGINEERS. **1968**
0367-7923 See BOLETIN GEOLOGICO - INSTITUTO GEOGRAFICO NACIONAL. **1367**
0367-7966 See IZVESTIIA GLAVNOI ASTRONOMICHESKOI OBSERVATORII V PULKOVE. **25**
0367-7974 See SBORNIK NAUCHNYKH TRUDOV / MINISTERVO RYBNOGO KHOZIAISTVA RSFSR, GOSUDARSTVENNYI NAUCHNO-ISSLEDOVATELSKII INSTITUT OZERNOGO I RECHNOGO RYBNOGO KHOZIAISTVA. **2312**
0367-8210 See TECNOLOGIA. **5165**
0367-8229 See INDIAN JOURNAL OF AGRICULTURAL CHEMISTRY. **94**
0367-8245 See INDIAN JOURNAL OF AGRICULTURAL RESEARCH. **95**
0367-827X See INDIAN JOURNAL OF ENVIRONMENTAL HEALTH. **2174**
0367-8288 See INDIAN JOURNAL OF ENTOMOLOGY, THE. **5609**
0367-8318 See INDIAN JOURNAL OF ANIMAL SCIENCES, THE. **5511**

0367-8326 See INDIAN JOURNAL OF MALARIOLOGY. 3797

0367-8350 See INDIAN JOURNAL OF PHYSIOLOGY AND ALLIED SCIENCES. 581

0367-8377 See INTERNATIONAL JOURNAL OF PEPTIDE AND PROTEIN RESEARCH. 1042

0367-8393 See INDIAN JOURNAL OF RADIO & SPACE PHYSICS. 4405

0367-8547 See INSATSU-KYOKU KENKYUJO HOKOKU. 4566

0367-939X See INDUSTRIELLE OBST- UND GEMUESEVERWERTUNG, DIE. 2344

0367-973X See INDIAN PHYTOPATHOLOGY. 513

0367-9993 See IRRIGATION AND POWER. 2091

0368-0029 See INDIAN SAFETY ENGINEER, THE. 1978

0368-0088 See INFORMACION SOBRE GRASAS Y ACEITES. 4192

0368-0762 See IRISH VETERINARY JOURNAL. 5512

0368-0770 See VERHANDLUNGEN - INTERNATIONALE VEREINIGUNG FUER THEORETISCHE UND ANGEWANDTE LIMNOLOGIE. 1418

0368-0789 See INVESTIGACION Y TECNICA DEL PAPEL. 4234

0368-0827 See INZYNIERIA I APARATURA CHEMICZNA. 978

0368-0983 See INDIAN ZOOLOGIST. 5586

0368-1025 See IZMERITELNAJA TEHNIKA. 4030

0368-1157 See JOURNAL OF AGRICULTURAL RESEARCH (LAHORE). 175

0368-1327 See JOURNAL OF THE AGRICULTURAL SOCIETY OF TRINIDAD & TOBAGO. 101

0368-1416 See JORNAL BRASILEIRO DE GINECOLOGIA. 3763

0368-1653 See JOURNAL OF THE CHINESE INSTITUTE OF CHEMICAL ENGINEERS. 2014

0368-1866 See JOURNAL OF DRUG RESEARCH. 4311

0368-2048 See JOURNAL OF ELECTRON SPECTROSCOPY AND RELATED PHENOMENA. 4435

0368-2145 See JOURNAL OF THE FACULTY OF SCIENCE, HOKKAIDO UNIVERSITY, SERIES 5, BOTANY. 516

0368-2196 See JOURNAL OF THE FACULTY OF SCIENCE, UNIVERSITY OF TOKYO. SECTION 3, BOTANY. 516

0368-2315 See JOURNAL DE GYNECOLOGIE, OBSTETRIQUE ET BIOLOGIE DE LA REPRODUCTION. 3763

0368-2498 See JOURNAL OF THE INSTITUTION OF ENGINEERS (INDIA). COMPUTER ENGINEERING DIVISION. 1230

0368-251X See JOURNAL OF THE INSTITUTE OF GEOLOGY, VIKRAM UNIVERSITY. 1385

0368-265X See JAPAN PESTICIDE INFORMATION. 4245

0368-2684 See JOURNAL OF THE INDIAN INSTITUTE OF SCIENCE. SECTION C: BIOLOGICAL SCIENCES. 5121

0368-2781 See JAPANESE JOURNAL OF ANTIBIOTICS, THE. 4309

0368-2811 See JAPANESE JOURNAL OF CLINICAL ONCOLOGY. 3819

0368-2897 See HAN'GUK NONGHWA HAKHOE CHI. 91

0368-3141 See PROCEEDINGS OF THE JAPAN CONGRESS ON MATERIALS RESEARCH. 1992

0368-3206 See JOURNAL OF THE MINE VENTILATION SOCIETY OF SOUTH AFRICA. 2142

0368-3303 See JOURNAL OF THE ASIATIC SOCIETY. 2505

0368-3419 See MEDDELANDE - JORDBRUKSTEKNISKA INSTITUTET. 107

0368-3826 See JOURNAL OF THE PHILIPPINE PHARMACEUTICAL ASSOCIATION. 4313

0368-4113 See JOURNAL OF SCIENCE OF THE HIROSHIMA UNIVERSITY. SERIES B. DIVISION 1. ZOOLOGY. 5588

0368-4172 See JOURNAL SUISSE DE HORLOGERIE ET DE BIJOUTERIE. 2915

0368-4466 See JOURNAL OF THERMAL ANALYSIS. 1055

0368-4636 See JOURNAL OF THE TEXTILE ASSOCIATION. 5353

0368-4644 See JOURNAL OF THE UNIVERSITY OF BOMBAY, SCIENCE: PHYSICAL SCIENCES, MATHEMATICS, BIOLOGICAL SCIENCES AND MEDICINE. 3515

0368-475X See KASEN GEPPO. 5353

0368-4814 See KAZANSKIJ MEDICINSKIJ ZURNAL. 3601

0368-4849 See KAGAKU SOCHI. 1026

0368-4881 See HAN'GUK SAENGHWAHAKOE CHI. 488

0368-492X See KYBERNETES. 1252

0368-511X See KYOTO DAIGAKU NOGAKUBU ENSHURIN HOKOKU. 2386

0368-5128 See KAGAWA DAIGAKU NOGAKUBU GAKUJUTSU HOKOKU. 101

0368-5128 See KAGAWA DAIGAKU NOGAKUBU GAKUZYUTU HOKOKU. 101

0368-5144 See KURUME DAIGAKU RONSO. 2506

0368-5179 See KEIO IGAKU. 3601

0368-5306 See KEIKINZOKU YOSETSU. 4027

0368-5330 See KFKI. 4411

0368-5365 See KOGYO GIJUTSUIN BISEIBUTSU KOGYO GIJUTSU KENKYUSHO KENKYU HOKOKU. 1027

0368-5373 See KENKYU HOKOKU - KANTO GAKUIN DAIGAKU KOGAKUBU. 1984

0368-5381 See KANAGAWA DAIGAKU KOGAKUBU KENKYU HOKOKU. 1984

0368-556X See HIMICESKAJA TEHNOLOGIJA (KIEV. 1971). 977

0368-5632 See KHIMIIA V SHKOLE. 983

0368-5829 See KYORIN IGAKKAI ZASSHI. 3603

0368-5837 See KUMAMOTO JOSHI DAIGAKU GAKUJUTSU KIYO. 1092

0368-6051 See BULLETIN OF NRLM. 4029

0368-6213 See KOSMOS (STOCKHOLM). 5124

0368-623X See KITA NIHON BYOGAICHU KENKYUKAIHO. 102

0368-6264 See KYUSHU DAIGAKU NOGAKUBU GAKUGEI ZASSHI. 5125

0368-6264 See KYUSHU DAIGAKU NOGAKUBU GAKUGEI ZASSHI. 103

0368-6272 See KOBUNKAZAI NO KAGAKU. 355

0368-6280 See KYOTO DAIGAKU NIHON KAGAKU SENI KENKYUJO KOENSHU. 5353

0368-6302 See FORHANDLINGER - DET KONGELIGE NORSKE VIDENSKABERS SELSKAB. 5105

0368-6310 See SKRIFTER (KONGELIGE NORSKE VIDENSKABERS SELSKAB). 5158

0368-6337 See KINZOKU. 4006

0368-6426 See KOBUNSHI KAKO. 4456

0368-6450 See KOGYO KAYAKU. 2143

0368-6485 See KOSMICHESKIE LUCHI. COSMIC RAYS. 4437

0368-654X See KOGYO REAMETARU. 4007

0368-6736 See KROVOOBRASCENIE. 3708

0368-6833 See KYUSHU SHIKA GAKKAI ZASSHI. 1329

0368-685X See KOGAI SHIGEN KENKYUJO HOKOKU. 2235

0368-7066 See KURORTOLOGIIA I FIZIOTERAPIIA. 2599

0368-7147 See KVANTOVAJA ELEKTRONIKA (MOSKVA). 2070

0368-7155 See KVANTOVAIA ELEKTRONIKA. 2070

0368-7163 See KIMYA VE SANAYI. 983

0368-7236 See KAWASAKI SEITETSU GIHO. 4006

0368-7368 See LAB-INSTRUMENTEN AMSTERDAM. 3603

0368-7430 See LABDEV. PART A, PHYSICAL SCIENCES. 5125

0368-7481 See LIBYAN JOURNAL OF SCIENCE, THE. 5126

0368-7546 See LOTTA CONTRO LA TUBERCOLOSI E LE MALATTIE POLMONARI SOCIALI. 3950

0368-7619 See LESNAIA PROMYSHLENNOST (MOSKVA). 2387

0368-7732 See LUCRARILE INSTITUTULUI DE CERCETARI VETERINARE SI BIOPREPARATE "PASTEUR". 5515

0368-8275 See MUNCHNER BEITRAEGE ZUR ABWASSER-, FISCHEREI- UND FLUSSBIOLOGIE. 556

0368-8283 See MEMORIAS. 5209

0368-8666 See MATEMATICESKIJ SBORNIK (MOSKVA). 3517

0368-8720 See ANALES DEL INSTITUTO DE BIOLOGIA, UNIVERSIDAD NACIONAL AUTONOMA DE MEXICO. SERIE ZOOLOGIA. 5575

0368-8798 See MITTEILUNGEN DER BUNDESFORSCHUNGSANSTALT FUER FORST- UND HOLZWIRTSCHAFT REINBEK BEI HAMBURG. 2388

0368-9123 See MONDO DEL LATTE, IL. 197

0368-9379 See MEMOIRS OF THE FACULTY OF ENGINEERING, HOKKAIDO UNIVERSITY. 1987

0368-9638 See MEMOIRS OF THE FACULTY OF ENGINEERING, KOBE UNIVERSITY. 1987

0368-9689 See MEMOIRS OF THE FACULTY OF SCIENCE, KYOTO UNIVERSITY. SERIES OF PHYSICS, ASTROPHYSICS, GEOPHYSICS AND CHEMISTRY. 4412

0368-9697 See MEDEDELINGEN VAN DE FACULTEIT LANDBOUWWETENSCHAPPEN, RIJKSUNIVERSITEIT, GENT. 3694

0368-9727 See MORFOGENEZ I REGENERATSIIA. 466

0369-0040 See MEMOIR - GEOLOGICAL SURVEY OF VICTORIA. 1387

0369-0369 See MEMOIRS OF THE INSTITUTE OF SCIENTIFIC AND INDUSTRIAL RESEARCH, OSAKA UNIVERSITY. 5128

0369-1055 See MITTEILUNGEN DES NATURWISSENSCHAFTLICHEN VEREINES FUER STEIERMARK. 5129

0369-1632 See MINE AND QUARRY. 2144

0369-1896 See MEMOIRES DE L'ACADEMIE DES SCIENCES, INSCRIPTIONS ET BELLES-LETTRES DE TOULOUSE. 2850

0369-1950 See MEMOIRS OF THE SCHOOL OF SCIENCE AND ENGINEERING. WASEDA UNIVERSITY. 1987

0369-2027 See MEMOIRES HORS SERIE DE LA SOCIETE GEOLOGIQUE DE FRANCE. 1387

0369-2086 See MINERALIA SLOVACA. 1441

0369-2302 See MITSUBISHI DENKI GIHO. 2073

0369-2507 See METEORITIKA. 397

0369-3171 See NAGOYA KOGYO DAIGAKU GAKUHO. 5130

0369-3333 See NAGOYA-SHI KOGYO KENKYUJO KENKYU HOKOKU. 1619

0369-3570 See KANKYO IGAKU KENKYUJO NENPO. 3601

0369-3651 See NEDERLANDS BOSBOUW TIJDSCHRIFT. 2389

0369-3783 See NENRYO OYOBI NENSHO. 1950

0369-3805 See NEPEGESZSEGUGY. 4793

0369-3902 See PROCEEDINGS OF THE NEW ZEALAND GRASSLAND ASSOCIATION. 122

0369-4097 See NUOVO CIMENTO DELLA SOCIETA ITALIANA DI FIZICA. SEZIONE A. 4449

0369-4100 See NUOVO CIMENTO DELLA SOCIETA ITALIANA DI FISICA. SEZIONE B. 4413

0369-4372 See KENKYU HOKOKU.--NIHON SEMBAI KOSHA CHUO KENKYUJO. 5373

0369-4550 See NIPPON KAISUI GAKKAI-SHI. 5536

0369-4577 See NIPPON KAGAKUKAI (1972). 987

0369-4585 See NIHON KESSHO GAKKAI SHI. 1033

0369-4658 See NOYAKU KENSAJO HOKOKU. 115

0369-4739 See NIHON KYOBU GEKA GAKKAI ZASSHI. 3970

0369-4747 See NIHON KINZOKU GAKKAI KAIHO. 4013

0369-5034 See NOVA ACTA LEOPOLDINA. 5135

0369-5247 See NOGYO OYOBI ENGEI. 113

0369-5417 *See* SKRIFTER - NORSK POLARINSTITUTT. 5158
0369-5611 *See* NAGOYA SHIRITSU DAIGAKU YAKUGAKUBU KENKYU NENPO. 4316
0369-5662 *See* NIHON SHASHIN GAKKAISHI. 4372
0369-5700 *See* NOSOKOMEIAKA HRONIKA. 3623
0369-5921 *See* NATTURUFRINGURINN. 4168
0369-6243 *See* NATURA (MILANO). 4168
0369-6464 *See* NUTRITION NEWS (ROSEMONT). 4196
0369-6715 *See* GEOLOGICAL SURVEY OF NEW SOUTH WALES, MINERAL INDUSTRY OF NEW SOUTH WALES. 2139
0369-674X *See* NIPPON YAKUZAISHIKAI ZASSHI. 4318
0369-707X *See* OCEANOGRAPHICAL MAGAZINE. 1454
0369-7290 *See* OGNEUPORY. 4014
0369-7436 *See* ONKOLOGIJA (KIEV). 3822
0369-7665 *See* ONSEN KOGAKKAI SHI. 2147
0369-769X *See* OILS AND OILSEEDS JOURNAL. 1044
0369-7827 *See* OSIRIS (BRUGES). 5136
0369-7843 *See* OSPEDALE MAGGIORE. 3790
0369-8009 *See* OYO BUTSURI. 4413
0369-8114 *See* PATHOLOGIE ET BIOLOGIE (PARIS). 3896
0369-8173 *See* PROGRES AGRICOLE ET VITICOLE, LE. 122
0369-8203 *See* PROCEEDINGS OF THE NATIONAL ACADEMY OF SCIENCES, INDIA. SECTION A : PHYSICAL SCIENCES. 4418
0369-8211 *See* PROCEEDINGS OF THE NATIONAL ACADEMY OF SCIENCES, INDIA. SECTION B : BIOLOGICAL SCIENCES. 5141
0369-8262 *See* APARTHEID NON. 4504
0369-8408 *See* PROBLEMI ATTUALI DI SCIENZA E DI CULTURA. 5139
0369-8629 *See* PCHELOVODSTVO. 119
0369-8963 *See* PERIODICO DI MINERALOGIA. 1443
0369-9277 *See* PROCEEDINGS - FERTILISER SOCIETY. 182
0369-9420 *See* PIGMENT & RESIN TECHNOLOGY. 4225
0369-951X *See* PHARMACOS CHANDIGARH. 4323
0369-9536 *See* PHILIPPINE ENTOMOLOGIST. 5594
0369-9560 *See* PHOTOGRAPHE, LE. 4324
0369-9579 *See* PHARMACIE HOSPITALIERE FRANCAISE, LA. 3791
0369-9714 *See* FARMACEUTISCH TIJDSCHRIFT VOOR BELGIE. 4304
0369-979X *See* PHARMAZIE HEUTE. 4324
0369-9986 *See* PROCEEDINGS OF THE LEEDS PHILOSOPHICAL AND LITERARY SOCIETY. SCIENTIFIC SECTION. 2852
0370-0046 *See* PROCEEDINGS OF THE INDIAN NATIONAL SCIENCE ACADEMY. PART A, PHYSICAL SCIENCES. 5140
0370-0291 *See* POLJOPRIVREDNA ZNANSTVENA SMOTRA. 120
0370-0305 *See* PROBLEMY KINETIKI I KATALIZA. 4417
0370-047X *See* PROCEEDINGS OF THE LINNEAN SOCIETY OF NEW SOUTH WALES. 4170
0370-0593 *See* POSTGRADUATE MEDICAL JOURNAL. SUPPLEMENT. 3628
0370-0704 *See* PARAMAGNITNYI REZONANS. 4445
0370-0747 *See* POLIMERY W MEDYCYNIE. 3628
0370-1093 *See* PROCEEDINGS OF THE OREGON ACADEMY OF SCIENCE. 5141
0370-1263 *See* PHYTOPHYLACTICA. 523
0370-1514 *See* PROGRESSO MEDICO (ROMA). 3972
0370-1573 *See* PHYSICS REPORTS. 4416
0370-1743 *See* PRZEGLAD SKORZANY. 3185
0370-1859 *See* PROCESS ENGINEERING. 2016
0370-1972 *See* PHYSICA STATUS SOLIDI. B : BASIC RESEARCH. 4415

0370-2057 *See* PROCEEDINGS OF THE ANNUAL CONVENTION OF THE SUGAR TECHNOLOGISTS' ASSOCIATION OF INDIA. 121
0370-2189 *See* PROBLEMY TEORII GRAVITATSII I ELEMENTARNYKH CHASTITS. 4450
0370-2219 *See* PROBLEMY TECHNIKI W MEDYCYNIE. 3629
0370-2561 *See* POLIMERIM VE-HOMARIM PLASTIYIM. 4459
0370-2677 *See* PROBLEMY ANALITICESKOJ HIMII. 1018
0370-2693 *See* PHYSICS LETTERS : PART B. 4450
0370-2715 *See* PRIKLADNAIA IADERNAIA SPEKTROSKOPIIA. 4440
0370-2723 *See* PHYTOMA. 522
0370-2731 *See* PROCEEDINGS OF THE NEW ZEALAND SOCIETY OF ANIMAL PRODUCTION. 219
0370-274X *See* PISMA V ZHURNAL EKSPERIMENTALNOI I TEORETICHESKOI FIZIKI. 4417
0370-2804 *See* PROCEEDINGS OF THE NEW ZEALAND PLANT PROTECTION CONFERENCE. 525
0370-3207 *See* REVISTA DE LA ACADEMIA DE CIENCIAS EXACTAS, FISICO-QUIMICAS Y NATURALES DE ZARAGOZA. 5148
0370-3576 *See* REVUE AGRICOLE ET SUCRIERE DE L'ILE MAURICE. 129
0370-3657 *See* RADEX RUNDSCHAU. 4445
0370-372X *See* REVISTA BRASILEIRA DE FARMACIA. 4328
0370-3797 *See* REVISTA BRASILEIRA DE QUIMICA. 991
0370-4106 *See* REVISTA CHILENA DE PEDIATRIA. 3911
0370-4246 *See* RYUKYU DAIGAKU NOGAKUBU GAKUJUTSU HOKOKU. 131
0370-4327 *See* REDIA. 5613
0370-4661 *See* REVISTA DE LA FACULTAD DE CIENCIAS AGRARIAS, UNIVERSIDAD NACIONAL DE CUYO. 129
0370-4726 *See* REVISTA DE FARMACIA E BIOQUIMICA DA UNIVERSIDADE DE SAO PAULO. 4328
0370-5226 *See* RECORDS OF THE GEOLOGICAL SURVEY OF INDIA. 1393
0370-5242 *See* RECORDS OF THE GEOLOGICAL SURVEY OF NEW SOUTH WALES. 1393
0370-5323 *See* REVUE HORTICOLE SUISSE. 2430
0370-5404 *See* REVISTA INDUSTRIAL Y AGRICOLA DE TUCUMAN. 129
0370-5463 *See* RIVISTA DEI COMBUSTIBILI. 4277
0370-5579 *See* RINSHO GANKA. 3879
0370-5633 *See* RINSHO KAGAKU. 991
0370-5943 *See* REVISTA LATINOAMERICANA DE QUIMICA. 1047
0370-6273 *See* ROMANIAN JOURNAL OF CHEMISTRY. 992
0370-629X *See* REVUE MEDICALE DE LIEGE. 3637
0370-6486 *See* REVISTA MEXICANA DE RADIOLOGIA. 3946
0370-6559 *See* BULLETIN - ROYAL SOCIETY OF NEW ZEALAND. 5091
0370-663X *See* ROSTLINNA VYROBA. 130
0370-6699 *See* REVUE PRATIQUE DU FROID ET DU CONDITIONNEMENT DE L'AIR. 2608
0370-6907 *See* REVISTA DE QUIMICA E FARMACIA RIO DE JANEIRO. 4328
0370-694X *See* REVISTA DE QUIMICA INDUSTRIAL. 1018
0370-7261 *See* RIVISTA SPERIMENTALE DI FRENIATRIA E MEDICINA LEGALE DELLE ALIENAZIONI MENTALI. 3936
0370-727X *See* RENDICONTI DEL SEMINARIO DELLA FACOLTA DI SCIENZE DELL'UNIVERSITA DI CAGLIARI. 5145
0370-7377 *See* RENDICONTI DEL SEMINARIO MATEMATICO E FISICO DI MILANO. 3531
0370-8047 *See* RYUSAN TO KOGYO. 1029
0370-8217 *See* SAIKO TO HOAN. 2870

0370-8241 *See* SAISHIN IGAKU. 3638
0370-8314 *See* SAMAB. 4096
0370-8691 *See* SOOBSCENIJA BJURAKANSKOJ OBSERVATORII. 400
0370-8799 *See* SIBIRSKII VESTNIK SELSKOKHOZIAISTVENNOI NAUKI. 134
0370-8918 *See* SCOTTISH BEEKEEPER. 132
0370-9361 *See* SUISAN DAIGAKKO KENKYU HOKOKU. 2314
0370-940X *See* SHIMANE DAIGAKU NOGAKUBU KENKYU HOKOKU. 134
0370-9531 *See* SEITAI NO KAGAKU. 473
0370-9574 *See* SENSHOKU KOGYO. 1029
0370-9612 *See* PHYSIOLOGY AND ECOLOGY JAPAN. 2220
0370-9671 *See* SENRYO TO YAKUHIN TOKYO. 1956. 1029
0370-9779 *See* SOILS AND FERTILIZERS IN TAIWAN. 187
0370-9841 *See* SEITO GIJUTSU KENKYUKAI SHI. 133
0370-985X *See* SHINDO GIJUTSU KENKYUKAI-SHI. 4019
0370-9868 *See* SEKIYU GIJUTSU KYOKAISHI. 4278
0370-9892 *See* MEMOIRES DE LA SOCIETE GEOLOGIQUE ET MINERALOGIQUE DE BRETAGNE. 1358
0370-9906 *See* SBORNIK TRUDOV - GOSUDARSTVENNYJ VSESOJUZNYJ NAUCNO--ISSLEDOVATELSKIJ STROITELNYH MATERIALOV I KONSTRUKCIJ IM. P.P. BUDNIKOVA. 627
0370-9957 *See* STUDIA GEOLOGICA SALMANTICENSIA. 1399
0370-999X *See* SHINDAN TO CHIRYO. 3641
0371-0025 *See* SHENG HSUEH HSUEH PAO. 4453
0371-005X *See* SHIMAZU HYORON. 5157
0371-0106 *See* SHASHIN KOGYO. 4376
0371-0165 *See* SITZUNGSBERICHTE DER HEIDELBERGER AKADEMIE DER WISSENSCHAFTEN, MATHEMATISCH-NATURWISSENSCHAFTLICHE KLASSE. 5158
0371-0459 *See* SCANDINAVIAN JOURNAL OF METALLURGY. 4018
0371-0548 *See* SEITAIGAKU KENKYU. 527
0371-0580 *See* SENI KIKAI GAKKAI SHI. 5355
0371-0718 *See* SEMENTO KONKURITO. 627
0371-0807 *See* SENI KOBUNSHI ZAIRYO KENKYUSHO KENKYU HOKOKU. 5355
0371-0874 *See* SHENG LI HSUEH PAO. 587
0371-0955 *See* SBORNIK RABOT / MINISTERSTVO SLSKOGO KHOZIAISTVA SSSR, LENINGRADSKII VETERINARNYI INSTITUT. 5521
0371-1722 *See* SBORNIK NAUCHNYKH TRUDOV / VSESOIUZNYI NAUCHNO-ISSLEDOVATELSKII INSTITUT LIUMINOFOROV I OSOBO CHISTYKH VESHCHESTV, VNIILIUMINOFOROV. 4441
0371-1927 *See* SOVETSKAIA TORGOVLIA. 851
0371-2192 *See* SOVREMENNYE PROBLEMY ORGANICESKOJ HIMII. 1047
0371-2222 *See* STUDIA PNEUMOLOGICA ET PHTISEOLOGICA CECHOSLOVACA. 3643
0371-2672 *See* SCIENCE REPORTS OF NIIGATA UNIVERSITY. SERIES D (BIOLOGY). 472
0371-2761 *See* SCIENCE REPORTS OF THE RESEARCH INSTITUTES. SERIES C, MEDICINE, THE. 3716
0371-2907 *See* SKOG & FORSKNING. 2395
0371-327X *See* SITZUNGSBERICHTE DER SACHSISCHEN AKADEMIE DER WISSENSCHAFTEN ZU LEIPZIG. MATHEMATISCH-NATURWISSENSCHAFTLICHE KLASSE. 3535
0371-3520 *See* SANTO TOMAS JOURNAL OF MEDICINE. 3638
0371-3733 *See* SBORNIK TRUDOV CENTRALNOGO NAUCNO-ISSLEDOVATELSKOGO INSTITUTA BUMAGI. 4238
0371-3768 *See* SODA TO ENSO. 2371

0371-3903 See SCIENCE REPORTS, TOHOKU UNIVERSITY, SERIES 3, MINERALOGY, PETROLOGY, ECONOMIC GEOLOGY. 1360

0371-3970 See PRIKLADNAIA GEOFIZIKA. 1443

0371-4020 See SUCRERIE FRANCAISE. 993

0371-408X See SUIYOKAI SHI. 2151

0371-411X See SUMITOMO KINZOKU. 4021

0371-4268 See SVJAZANNAJA VODA V DISPERSNYH SISTEMAH. 5540

0371-4616 See ZBORNIK VEDECKYCH PRAC VYSOKEJ SKOLY TECHNICKEJ V KOSICIACH. 5172

0371-4942 See SCHWEIZERISCHE ZEITSCHRIFT FUER OBST- UND WEINBAU. 2431

0371-5167 See TAKEDA KENKYUJO HO. 5161

0371-5264 See TECHNISCH-WISSENSFHAFTLICHE ABHANDLUNGEN DER OSRAM-GESELLSCHAFT. 5162

0371-5345 See TANSO. 994

0371-5965 See TOTTORI DAIGAKU KYOIKUGAKUBU KENKYU HOKOKU. SHINZEN KAGAKU. 1850

0371-6007 See TOKYO DAIGAKU NOGAKUBU ENSHURIN HOKOKU. 2397

0371-6562 See TRUDY EREVANSKOGO ZOOVETERINARNOGO INSTITUTA. 5599

0371-6619 See TRIBUNA FARMACEUTICA. 4331

0371-683X See TIJDSCHRIFT VOOR GENEESKUNDE. 3802

0371-7089 See TRUDY ORDENA LENINA GIDROMETEOROLOGICESKOGO NAUCNO-ISSLEDOVATELSKOGO CENTRA SSSR. 1436

0371-7119 See TRUDY GOSUDARSTVENNOGO OKEANOGRAFICESKOGO INSTITUTA. 1457

0371-7240 See GEOLOGICAL SURVEY REPORT. TASMANIA. 2139

0371-7453 See INSTITUTION OF MINING AND METALLURGY. TRANSACTIONS. SECTION B : APPLIED EARTH SCIENCES. 2140

0371-750X See TRANSACTIONS OF THE INDIAN CERAMIC SOCIETY. 2594

0371-7682 See JOURNAL OF THE FORMOSAN MEDICAL ASSOCIATION / TAI-WAN I CHIH. 3598

0371-7712 See JOURNAL OF THE FACULTY OF SCIENCE, UNIVERSITY OF TOKYO. SECTION III : BOTANY. 5120

0371-7844 See TRANSACTIONS. SECTION A, MINING INDUSTRY / INSTITUTION OF MINING & METALLURGY. 2152

0371-831X See TOKYO KASEI DAIGAKU KENKYU KIYO. 2793

0371-845X See TAI-WAN KO HSUEH. 5161

0371-8794 See TRUDY (INSTITUTUL AGRIKOL M.V. FRUNZE). 142

0371-9537 See TECNICA METALURGICA (BARCELONA). 4021

0371-9553 See INSTITUTION OF MINING AND METALLURGY. TRANSACTIONS. SECTION C : MINERAL PROCESSING AND EXTRACTIVE METALLURGY. 4004

0371-9685 See TRUDY ORDENA LENINA MATEMATICESKOGO INSTITUTA IM. V.A. STEKLOVA. 3539

0372-0187 See TRANSACTIONS - NEWCOMEN SOCIETY FOR THE STUDY OF THE HISTORY OF ENGINEERING AND TECHNOLOGY. 5166

0372-0322 See MEMOIRS OF THE TOKYO UNIVERSITY OF AGRICULTURE. 108

0372-0349 See TOTTORI DAIGAKU NOGAKUBU KENKYU HOKOKU. 142

0372-0586 See TRUDY PO PRIKLADNOJ BOTANIKE. GENETIKE I SELEKCII. 529

0372-1426 See TRANSACTIONS OF THE ROYAL SOCIETY OF SOUTH AUSTRALIA. 5167

0372-1566 See TAISHA. 3644

0372-1582 See TAEHAN SAENGNI HAKHOE CHI. 587

0372-2414 See YEN CHIU HUI PAO / TAI-WAN TANG YEH YEN CHIU SO. 191

0372-2864 See TRUDY - VSESOJUZNYJ NAUCNO-ISSLEDOVATELSKIJ INSTITUT MORSKOGO RYBNOGO HOZJAISTVA I OKEANOGRAFII. 2315

0372-2996 See TRUDY VSESOYUZNOGO INSTITUTA GELMINTOLOGII IM K. I. SKRYABINA. 1445

0372-3283 See TRUDY VSESOUZNOGO NAUCNO-ISSLEDOVATELSKOGO INSTITUTA ZERNOVOGO HOZAJSTVA. 143

0372-3305 See TRUDY VSESOJUZNOGO NAUCNO-ISSLEDOVATELSKOGO INSTITUTA ZELEZNODOROZNOGO TRANSPORTA. 5437

0372-333X See TAIWANIA. 529

0372-3666 See TRANSLATION - UNITED KINGDOM ATOMIC ENERGY AUTHORITY, RESEARCH GROUP, CULHAM LABORATORY. 4423

0372-4123 See UKRAINSKYI BOTANICHNYI ZHURNAL / AKADEMIIA NAUK UKRAINSKOI RSR, INSTYTUT BOTANIKY. 529

0372-4123 See UKRAINSKII BOTANICHNII ZHURNAL. 529

0372-4255 See SRD REPORT. UNITED KINGDOM ATOMIC ENERGY AUTHORITY, SAFETY AND RELIABILITY DIRECTORATE. 4422

0372-4638 See REVISTA DEL MUSEO DE LA PLATA. SECCION ZOOLOGIA. 4095

0372-5480 See VETERINARSKI ARHIV. 5524

0372-5715 See VGB-KRAFTWERKSTECHNIK. 2000

0372-5952 See VOPROSY INFEKCIONNOJ PATOLOGII I IMMUNOLOGII. 3716

0372-607X See VESTNIK KIEVSKOGO UNIVERSITETA. FIZIKA / MINISTERSTVO VYSSHEGO I SREDNEGO SPETSIALNOGO OBRAZOVANIIA USSR. 4424

0372-6088 See VISNIK KIIVSKOGO UNIVERSITETU. SERIJA HIMII. 995

0372-6223 See VERSLAGEN VAN LANDBOUWKUNDIGE ONDERZOEKINGEN DER RIJKSLANDBOUWPROEFSTATIONS. 144

0372-6827 See VETERINARIA (SARAJEVO). 5524

0372-6916 See VERHANDELINGEN VAN DE KONINKLIJKE ACADEMIE VOOR WETENSCHAPPEN, LETTEREN EN SCHONE KUNSTEN VAN BELGIE, KLASSE DER WETENSCHAPPEN. 5168

0372-7009 See VZRYVNOE DELO. 1030

0372-7025 See VOJENSKE ZDRAVOTNICKE LISTY. 3650

0372-7181 See WASEDA DAIGAKU RIKOGAKU KENKYUJO HOKOKU. 2001

0372-719X See WOOD RESEARCH. 2406

0372-7327 See JOURNAL OF THE KOREAN NUCLEAR SOCIETY. 4448

0372-7629 See YAKUZAIGAKU. 4333

0372-7661 See YAMAGUCHI DAIGAKU KOGAKUBU KENKYU HOKOKU. 2001

0372-7726 See YOKOHAMA IGAKU. 3652

0372-7777 See YALKUT LE-SIVIM, TEKHNOLOGYAH U-MINHAL SHEL TEKSTIL. 5360

0372-7785 See KAIHO. 102

0372-784X See YUAN I HSUEH PAO. 2434

0372-798X See ZASSO KENKYU. 148

0372-8277 See ZDRAVOOKHRANENIE KAZAKHSTANA. 4808

0372-8854 See ZEITSCHRIFT FUER GEOMORPHOLOGIE. 1401

0372-9311 See ZHURNAL MIKROBIOLOGII, EPIDEMIOLOGII I IMMUNOBIOLOGII. 3678

0372-9400 See ZESZYTY NAUKOWE AKADEMII GORNICZO-HUTNICZEJ IM. STANISAWA STASZICA. GORNICTWO. 1445

0372-9443 See ZESZYTY NAUKOWE AKADEMII GORNICZO-HUTNICZEJ IM. STANISAWA STASZICA. METALURGIA I ODLEWNICTWO. 4024

0372-9494 See ZESZYTY NAUKOWE POLITECHNIKI SLASKIEJ. CHEMIA. 996

0372-9508 See ZESZYTY NAUKOWE POLITECHNIKI SLASKIEJ. GORNICTWO. 2153

0372-9524 See ZESZYTY NAUKOWE POLITECHNIKI CZESTOCHOWSKIEJ. NAUKI TECHNICZNE. HUTNICTWO. 5172

0372-9796 See ZESZYTY NAUKOWE POLITECHNIKI SLASKIEJ. ENERGETYKA. 1961

0372-9893 See ZERNOVOE HOZAJSTVO. 191

0373-0204 See ZUCKER- UND SUSSWAREN WIRTSCHAFT. 2362

0373-0247 See ZHURNAL VSESOIUZNOGO KHIMICHESKOGO OBSHCHESTVA IM. D.I. MENDELEEVA. 996

0373-045X See PROCEEDINGS OF THE ANNUAL CONGRESS OF THE SOUTH AFRICAN SUGAR TECHNOLOGISTS' ASSOCIATION. 2353

0373-0468 See BONNER GEOGRAPHISCHE ABHANDLUNGEN. 2556

0373-0719 See TECHNIQUES ET ARCHITECTURE. 309

0373-0786 See PROCEEDINGS OF THE INDIAN SCIENCE CONGRESS. 5140

0373-0816 See ANNALES DE L'INSTITUT NATIONAL AGRONOMIQUE. 59

0373-0891 See ANNALES DES TRAVAUX PUBLICS DE BELGIQUE. 1964

0373-0956 See ANNALES DE L'INSTITUT FOURIER. 3493

0373-0972 See PALAEONTOGRAPHIA ITALICA. 1390

0373-1170 See ANALES DE LA FACULTAD DE VETERINARIA DE LEON. 5502

0373-1227 See STUDIA UNIVERSITATIS BABES-BOLYAI : MATHEMATICA. 3537

0373-1278 See TRUDY VSESOIUZNOGO ENTOMOLOGICHESKOGO OBSHCHESTVA. 5599

0373-1332 See SUMARSKI LIST. 138

0373-1391 See DELTION TES HELLENIKES MATHEMATIKES HETAIREIAS. 3503

0373-1537 See REVUE DES ETUDES GEORGIENNES ET CAUCASIENNES. 3316

0373-1545 See CERCETARI DE LINGVISTICA. 3273

0373-1677 See TIERZUCHT. 223

0373-1901 See MEMOIRES DE LA SOCIETE ARCHEOLOGIQUE DU MIDI DE LA FRANCE. 274

0373-191X See ASTRONOMICESKIJ CIRKULJAR, IZDAVAEMYJ BJURO ASTRONOMICESKIH SOOBSCENIJ AKADEMII NAUK SSSR. 392

0373-1928 See ETUDES CELTIQUES. 3336

0373-1944 See TRAVAIL & SECURITE. 2871

0373-1995 See JOURNAL OF THE INSTITUTION OF ENGINEERS (INDIA). CIVIL ENGINEERING DIVISION. 2026

0373-2002 See REVISTA DE PSICOLOGIA GENERAL Y APLICADA. 4616

0373-2029 See ARCHIVES OF MECHANICS. 2110

0373-2266 See ARDEA. 5614

0373-241X See GLASGOW NATURALIST. 4165

0373-2444 See IZVESTIIA AKADEMII NAUK SSSR. SERIIA GEOGRAFICHESKAIA. 2566

0373-2525 See SAUSSUREA. 527

0373-2568 See PIRINEOS. 2220

0373-2630 See REVUE D'ECONOMIE POLITIQUE. 1595

0373-2673 See ANNALI DELLA FACOLTA DI AGRARIA. UNIVERSITA DEGLI STUDI DI PERUGIA. 59

0373-2681 See GAZETA DE MATEMATICA. 3506

0373-2711 See MINERAL RESOURCES BULLETIN - GEOLOGICAL SURVEY OF WESTERN AUSTRALIA. 1388

0373-2908 See BULLETIN MATHEMATIQUE DE LA SOCIETE DES SCIENCES MATHEMATIQUES DE LA REPUBLIQUE SOCIALISTE DE ROUMANIE. 3498

0373-2959 See SCHWEIZERISCHE ZEITSCHRIFT FUER PILZKUNDE. 527

0373-2967 See CANDOLLEA. 506

0373-2975 See BOISSIERA. 502

0373-3009 See ARCHIVIO PER L'ANTROPOLOGIA E LA ETNOLOGIA. 231

0373-305X See COMPTE RENDU DES TRAVAUX EFFECTUES EN ... / INSTITUT TECHNIQUE DE LA BETTERAVE, ITB. 168

0373-3076 See BULLETIN DE LA SOCIETE NEUCHATELOISE DE GEOGRAPHIE. 2556

0373-3114 See ANNALI DI MATEMATICA PURA ED APPLICATA. 3494

0373-3149 *See* SERIE INTERNATIONALE D'ANALYSE NUMERIQUE. **3534**

0373-3165 *See* BUCHEREI DES PADIATERS. **3901**

0373-3173 *See* S.A.E. AUSTRALASIA. **5424**

0373-322X *See* ZEITSCHRIFT FUER EISENBAHNWESEN UND VERKEHRSTECHNIK. **5438**

0373-3297 *See* BULLETIN - SOCIETE LANGUEDOCIENNE DE GEOGRAPHIE. **2557**

0373-3343 *See* ASTRONOMICHESKII EZHEGODNIK SSSR. **392**

0373-3343 *See* ASTRONOMICHESKII EZHEGODNIK NA ... G. / INSTITUT TEORETICHESKOI ASTRONOMII ROSSIISKOI AKADEMII NAUK. **392**

0373-3475 *See* ATTI ERASSEGNA TECNICA - SOCIETA DEGLI INGEGNERI E DEGLI ARCHITETTI IN TORINO. **1966**

0373-3491 *See* BOLLETTINO DELLA SOCIETA ENTOMOLOGICA ITALIANA. **5606**

0373-353X *See* IZVESTIIA VSESOIUZNOGO GEOGRAFICHESKOGO OBSHCHESTVA. **2566**

0373-3629 *See* ANNALES HYDROGRAPHIQUES. **1412**

0373-367X *See* RIVISTA DEL CATASTO E DEI SERVIZI TECNICI ERARIALI. **2030**

0373-3742 *See* PUBLICATIONS DE L'OBSERVATOIRE ASTRONOMIQUE DE BEOGRAD. **398**

0373-3793 *See* INTERPERSONAL DEVELOPMENT. **3927**

0373-4064 *See* METAL BULLETIN MONTHLY. **4009**

0373-4137 *See* BOLLETTINO DI ZOOLOGIA. **5578**

0373-4250 *See* ANNUAL PROCEEDINGS / THE ASSOCIATED SCIENTIFIC AND TECHNICAL SOCIETIES OF SOUTH AFRICA, THE. **5083**

0373-4285 *See* RECHERCHE ET ARCHITECTURE. **307**

0373-4331 *See* BETONWERK + [I.E. UND] FERTIGTEIL-TECHNIK / CONCRETE PRECASTING PLANT AND TECHNOLOGY. **601**

0373-434X *See* RAPPORTS ET PROCES-VERBAUX DES REUNIONS COMMISSION INTERNATIONALE POUR L'EXPLORATION SCIENTIFIQUE DE LA MER MEDITERRANEE. **1455**

0373-4447 *See* LIBRARY AND INFORMATION SCIENCE. **3224**

0373-4498 *See* GEOGRAFSKI ZBORNIK. ACTA GEOGRAPHICA. **2562**

0373-4625 *See* ABEILLE DE FRANCE ET L'APICULTEUR, L'. **5573**

0373-4625 *See* ABEILLE DE FRANCE ET L'APICULTEUR, L'. **42**

0373-4633 *See* JOURNAL OF NAVIGATION, THE. **4177**

0373-4668 *See* VERHANDELINGEN DER KONINKLIJKE NEDERLANDSE AKADEMIE VAN WETENSCHAPPEN, AFDELING NATUURKUNDE. EERSTE SECTIE. **5168**

0373-4722 *See* JOURNAL OF THE FACULTY OF SCIENCE, UNIVERSITY OF TOKYO. SECTION V, ANTHROPOLOGY / TOKYO DAIGAKU RIGAKUBU KIYO. DAI 5-RUI, JINRUIGAKU. **239**

0373-4722 *See* JOURNAL OF THE FACULTY OF SCIENCE, UNIVERSITY OF TOKYO. SECTION V, ANTHROPOLOGY. **239**

0373-4870 *See* TRUDY SEMINARA PO VEKTORNOMU I TENZORNOMU ANALIZU. **3540**

0373-5001 *See* REVUE GENERALE DU GAZ. **4277**

0373-5133 *See* REVUE DU BOIS ET DE SES APPLICATIONS. **2404**

0373-5176 *See* BOLLETTINO DELL'INSTITUTO DI ENTOMOLOGIA DELL'UNIVERSITA DEGLI STUDI DI BOLOGNA. **5578**

0373-529X *See* SUPPLEMENTARY PAPERS - ROYAL INSTITUTION OF NAVAL ARCHITECTS. **4183**

0373-5303 *See* REVIEW OF THE NATIONAL RESEARCH COUNCIL (OTTAWA). **573**

0373-5338 *See* MEMOIRES DE L'INSTITUT FONDAMENTAL D'AFRIQUE NOIRE. **2499**

0373-5346 *See* RAILWAY GAZETTE INTERNATIONAL. **5436**

0373-5478 *See* ARCHIVES D'HISTOIRE DOCTRINALE ET LITTERAIRE DU MOYEN AGE. **4341**

0373-5524 *See* BOLETIM DO INSTITUTO OCEANOGRAFICO. **553**

0373-5605 *See* MEDDELELSER / NORSK PALARINSTITUTT. **5127**

0373-5680 *See* REVISTA DE LA SOCIEDAD ENTOMOLOGICA ARGENTINA. **5596**

0373-5729 *See* REVUE DES ETUDES BYZANTINES. **2706**

0373-5737 *See* REVUE DES ETUDES LATINES. **3316**

0373-580X *See* BOLETIN DE LA SOCIEDAD ARGENTINA DE BOTANICA. **502**

0373-5834 *See* CAHIERS D'OUTRE-MER. **2557**

0373-5893 *See* PROCEEDINGS OF THE ZOOLOGICAL SOCIETY. **5595**

0373-5982 *See* POSTEPY ASTRONAUTYKI. **398**

0373-6032 *See* REVUE D'ASSYRIOLOGIE ET D'ARCHEOLOGIE ORIENTALE. **281**

0373-6075 *See* REVUE D'HISTOIRE DES TEXTES. **3316**

0373-6121 *See* DENSHI JOHO TSUSHIN GAKKAI SHI. **1153**

0373-6156 *See* REVUE GENERALE DE DROIT INTERNATIONAL PUBLIC. **3135**

0373-6245 *See* SOUTH AFRICAN GEOGRAPHICAL JOURNAL. **2576**

0373-6261 *See* BULLETIN DE LA SOCIETE FRANCAISE DU RORSCHACH ET DES METHODES PROJECTIVES. **4578**

0373-630X *See* SEMITICA. **3320**

0373-6385 *See* MEMOIRS OF THE FACULTY OF SCIENCE, KYUSHU UNIVERSITY. SERIES A, MATHEMATICS. **3522**

0373-6482 *See* FOERDERN UND HEBEN. **2114**

0373-6512 *See* EXCERPTA MEDICA. SECTION 7. PEDIATRICS AND PEDIATRIC SURGERY. **3657**

0373-6547 *See* PRACE GEOGRAFICZNE - POLSKA AKADEMIA NAUK. **2573**

0373-658X *See* VOPROSY IAZYKOZNANIIA. **3332**

0373-6601 *See* R.F.M., REVUE FRANCAISE DE MECANIQUE. **2127**

0373-6687 *See* JOURNAL OF BRYOLOGY. **515**

0373-6725 *See* APPLICATIONS OF MATHEMATICS (PRAGUE). **3494**

0373-6725 *See* APPLICATIONS OF MATHEMATICS / CZECHOSLOVAK ACADEMY OF SCIENCES. **3494**

0373-6776 *See* MECHANIZACE ZEMEDELSTVI. **159**

0373-6873 *See* MEMORANDA SOCIETATIS PRO FAUNA ET FLORA FENNICA. **518**

0373-6938 *See* MEMOIR - GEOLOGICAL SURVEY. SOUTH AFRICA. **1387**

0373-7039 *See* ANNALES DE LA SOCIETE DES SCIENCES NATURELLES ET D'ARCHEOLOGIE DE TOULON ET DU VAR. **255**

0373-7063 *See* ACADEMIE ROYALE DES SCIENCES D'OUTRE-MER. CLASSE DES SCIENCES TECHNIQUES. **1722**

0373-7101 *See* BOLETIN ASTRONOMICO DEL OBSERVATORIO DE MADRID. **393**

0373-7349 *See* PROGRAMME DE PREVENTION CONTRE LA GRELE DE L'ASSOCIATION NATIONALE D'ETUDE ET DE LUTTE CONTRE LES FLEAUX ATMOSPHERIQUES. **1433**

0373-7462 *See* ANNALES DE L'EST; MEMOIRE. **2674**

0373-7527 *See* PROCEEDINGS - UNIVERSITY OF BRISTOL SPELAEOLOGICAL SOCIETY. **1409**

0373-7586 *See* ABHANDLUNGEN UND BERICHTE DES NATURKUNDEMUSEUMS GORLITZ. **4161**

0373-7640 *See* BERICHTE DER BAYERISCHEN BOTANISCHEN GESELLSCHAFT ZUR ERFORSCHUNG DER HEIMISCHEN FLORA. **501**

0373-7667 *See* MEMOIRES ET PUBLICATIONS DE LA SOCIETE DES SCIENCES, DES ARTS ET DES LETTRES DU HAINAUT. **325**

0373-7683 *See* PEREMENNYE ZVEZDY. **398**

0373-7748 *See* CONSTRUCTII. **608**

0373-7772 *See* CONDIZIONAMENTO DELL'ARIA, RISCALDAMENTO, REFRIGERAZIONE. **2604**

0373-7837 *See* BIULETYN. **66**

0373-7837 *See* BIULETYN INSTYTUTU HODOWLI I AKLIMATYZACJI ROSLIN. **66**

0373-7896 *See* BERICHTE DES GEOBOTANISCHEN INSTITUTES DER EIDG. TECHN. HOCHSCHULE, STIFTUNG RUBEL. **502**

0373-7934 *See* ACTA CARDIOLOGICA. SUPPLEMENTUM. **3697**

0373-8086 *See* JOURNAL OF CHILD PSYCHOLOGY AND PSYCHIATRY. **4594**

0373-8205 *See* ACTA FACULTATIS RERUM NATURALIUM UNIVERSITATIS COMENIANAE. PHYSIOLOGIA PLANTARUM. **497**

0373-8299 *See* ANNALES SOCIETATIS MATHEMATICAE POLONAE. COMMENTATIONES MATHEMATICAE. **3493**

0373-8302 *See* ROCZNIKI POLSKOGO TOWARZYSTWA MATEMATYCZNEGO, SERIA 2. WIADOMOSCI MATEMATYCZNE. **3532**

0373-8361 *See* NIHON JUI CHIKUSAN DAIGAKU KENKYU HOKOKU. **5517**

0373-840X *See* PESQUISAS. BOTANICA. **521**

0373-8493 *See* MITTEILUNGEN AUS DEM ZOOLOGISCHEN MUSEUM IN BERLIN. **5591**

0373-8701 *See* ANNALES DE LA SOCIETE D'HORTICULTURE ET D'HISTOIRE NATURELLE DE L'HERAULT. **2408**

0373-8825 *See* DFW, DOKUMENTATION, INFORMATION. **3206**

0373-8868 *See* RESEARCH AND DEVELOPMENT : R & D. **2108**

0373-8981 *See* ENTOMOLOGISCHE ABHANDLUNGEN. **5607**

0373-9023 *See* BULLETIN D'INFORMATION - BUREAU GRAVIMETRIQUE INTERNATIONAL. **4399**

0373-9139 *See* CIEL ET ESPACE REVUE. **394**

0373-9252 *See* ALGERBRA I LOGIKA. **3492**

0373-9465 *See* FOLIA ENTOMOLOGICA HUNGARICA. **5609**

0373-952x *See* BULLETIN DE LA SOCIETE D'AGRICULTURE, SCIENCES ET ARTS DE LA SARTHE. **316**

0373-9767 *See* JAHRBUCH DER AKADEMIE DER WISSENSCHAFTEN IN GOTTINGEN. **322**

0373-9805 *See* ACTUALITES DE CHIMIE ANALYTIQUE, ORGANIQUE, PHARMACEUTIQUE ET BROMATOLOGIQUE. **959**

0373-9821 *See* AVIACIJA I KOSMONAVTIKA. **12**

0373-9856 *See* PRZEMYS DRZEWNY. **635**

0373-9864 *See* POLIGRAFIKA. **4567**

0373-9953 *See* WISSENSCHAFTLICHE ZEITSCHRIFT DER ELEKTROTECHNIK. **2086**

0374-0056 *See* MITTEILUNGEN DER VERSUCHSANSTALT FUER WASSERBAU, HYDROLOGIE UND GLAZIOLOGIE. **1416**

0374-0315 *See* LETOPIS SLOVENSKE AKADEMIJE ZNANOSTI IN UMETNOSTI. **2849**

0374-0463 *See* ACTA LINGUISTICA HAFNIENSIA / PUBLISHED UNDER THE AUSPICES OF THE LINGUISTIC CIRCLE OF COPENHAGEN. **3261**

0374-0803 *See* SRPSKA AKADEMIJA NAUKA I UMETNOSTI. GLAS. ODELJENJE TEHNICKIH NAUKA. **5159**

0374-0994 *See* BULLETIN DE LA SOCIETE D'HISTOIRE NATURELLE DE L'AFRIQUE DU NORD. **4163**

0374-1001 *See* BULLETIN OF THE PERMANENT INTERNATIONAL ASSOCIATION OF NAVIGATION CONGRESSES. **2088**

0374-1222 *See* JAHRBUCH DER SCHIFFBAUTECHNISCHEN GESELLSCHAFT. **4177**

0374-1257 *See* MITTEILUNGEN AUS DEM MAX-PLANCK-INSTITUT FUER STROMUNGSFORSCHUNG UND DER AERODYNAMISCHEN VERSUCHSANSTALT. **28**

0374-1346 *See* BULLETIN D'INFORMATION DES GEOLOGUES DU BASSIN DE PARIS. **1369**

0374-1389 *See* VEDA A VYSKUM PRAXI. **1418**

0374-1443 See OLEOSCOPE PARIS. **117**

0374-1893 *See* GEOLOGICA HUNGARICA. SERIES PALAEONTOLOGICA. **4227**

0374-1958 See MITTEILUNGEN DER ASTRONOMISCHEN GESELLSCHAFT. 397

0374-1990 See FUNKCIONALNYJ ANALIZ I EGO PRILOZENIA. 3506

0374-2105 See OFTALMOLOGIJA. 3877

0374-2113 See CONFERENZE DEL SEMINARIO DI MATEMATICA DELL'UNIVERSITA DI BARI. 3502

0374-2261 See TREFILE, LE. 4022

0374-2466 See ASTRONOMICAL HERALD. 391

0374-2474 See ACTA POLYTECHNICA. III, PRACE CVUT V PRAZE / CESKE VYSOKE UCENI TECHNICKE V PRAZE. 2034

0374-2725 See BULLETIN OF MECHANICAL ENGINEERING LABORATORY. 2111

0374-2792 See CEGB DIGEST. 2038

0374-2806 See COMMENTS ON PLASMA PHYSICS AND CONTROLLED FUSION. 4400

0374-289X See DATA REPORT. 1257

0374-3063 See ELECTRONICS TODAY BOMBAY. 2050

0374-3098 See ELEKTRON INTERNATIONAL. 1110

0374-3144 See ELEKTRONIKINDUSTRIE. 2052

0374-3225 See FLUID APPARECCHIATURE IDRAULICHE E PNEUMATICHE. 2089

0374-3268 See GEOS. 2194

0374-3365 See INTERNATIONALES WISSENSCHAFTLICHES KOLLOQUIUM. 5116

0374-3519 See JOURNAL OF THE ROYAL SIGNALS INSTITUTION. 5232

0374-3535 See JOURNAL OF ELASTICITY. 4428

0374-4078 See POLISH ENGINEERING (1970). 1990

0374-4256 See REVUE POLYTECHNIQUE. 5148

0374-4272 See REVISTA ASTRONOMICA. 399

0374-4345 See NIIGATA DAIGAKU KOGAKUBU KENKYU HOKOKU. 1989

0374-4353 See RESEARCH DISCLOSURE. 5146

0374-4507 See SHISUTEMU, SEIGYO, JOHO. 886

0374-4663 See TAKENAKA GIJUTSU KENKYU HOKOKU. 2032

0374-468X See DENSHI JOHO TSUSHIN GAKKAI RONBUNSHI. D. 2041

0374-4795 See WORKS MANAGEMENT. 889

0374-4876 See JOURNAL OF THE KOREAN INSTITUTE OF ELECTRICAL ENGINEERS. 2070

0374-4884 See JOURNAL OF THE KOREAN PHYSICAL SOCIETY. 4410

0374-4914 See SAE MULLI. 4420

0374-4922 See REVISTA BRASILEIRA DE FISICA. 4420

0374-4957 See DIVISION OF APPLIED GEOMECHANICS TECHNICAL PAPER. 1971

0374-4965 See ACTA ANAESTHESIOLOGICA ITALICA. 3680

0374-4981 See ANNALI DELLA FACOLTA DI AGRARIA UNIVERSITA PERUGIA. 59

0374-5066 See ACTA BOTANICA ISLANDICA. 497

0374-5252 See AGRICULTURAL RESEARCH REVIEW. 51

0374-5449 See ARCHIV FUER METEOROLOGIE, GEOPHYSIK UND BIOKLIMATOLOGIE. SER. B: KLIMATOLOGIE, UMWELTMETEOROLOGIE, STRAHLUNGSFORSCHUNG. 1351

0374-5511 See ANALES DEL INSTITUTO DE BIOLOGIA, UNIVERSIDAD NACIONAL AUTONOMA DE MEXICO. SERIE BOTANICA. 498

0374-5546 See ANALES DEL MUSEO NACIONAL "DAVID J. GUZMAN.". 1724

0374-5600 See ACTA PAEDIATRICA JAPONICA. OVERSEAS EDITION. 3899

0374-5708 See AQUILA. 5614

0374-5759 See ANNUAL REPORT ON CACAO RESEARCH. 163

0374-6038 See BULLETIN & I.E. ET ANNALES DE LA SOCIETE ROYALE BELGE D'ENTOMOLOGIE. 5579

0374-6070 See BOLETIM CLINICO DES HOSPITAIS CIVIS DE LISBOA. 3558

0374-633X See BRITISH JOURNAL OF MENTAL SUBNORMALITY. 1876

0374-6569 See BIONIKA (KIEV). 1250

0374-6658 See BOLETIM TECNICO - DEPARTAMENTO NACIONAL DE OBRAS CONTRA AS SECAS. 2087

0374-6852 See CESKOSLOVENSKA GYNAEKOLOGIE. 3758

0374-7042 See CARIBBEAN MEDICAL JOURNAL. 3562

0374-7247 See DENDROFLORA. 2413

0374-7344 See DANISH REVIEW OF GAME BIOLOGY. 5581

0374-7387 See EANHS BULLETIN. 4165

0374-7565 See EPPO PUBLICATIONS. SERIES C. 509

0374-7646 See FRESHWATER FORUM. 456

0374-7778 See FLORA MALESIANA. SERIES I, SPERMATOPHYTA. 510

0374-7859 See GARDENS' BULLETIN, SINGAPORE, THE. 89

0374-8014 See HEALTH BULLETIN (EDINBURGH). 4778

0374-8049 See JOURNAL OF THE OCEANOLOGICAL SOCIETY OF KOREA. 1450

0374-8057 See ESSAYS AND STUDIES BY THE FACULTY OF HIROSHIMA JOGAKUIN COLLEGE. 1823

0374-8111 See HAN-GUK SUSAN HAKHOIJI. 2305

0374-826X See INDIAN JOURNAL OF HEREDITY. 548

0374-8405 See JOURNAL OF THE IRISH COLLEGES OF PHYSICIANS AND SURGEONS. 3598

0374-8537 See JOURNAL OF COFFEE RESEARCH. 176

0374-8898 See LUCRARI STIINTIFICE, INSTITUL AGRONOMIC "N. BALCESCU," BUCURESTI, SERIA D, ZOOTEHNIE. 5590

0374-9037 See MITTEILUNGEN DER FORSTLICHEN BUNDES-VERSUCHSANSTALT WIEN. 2388

0374-9061 See MITTEILUNGEN DER GEOGRAPHISCHEN GESELLSCHAFT IN HAMBURG. 2569

0374-9096 See MIKROBIYOLOJI BULTENI. 567

0374-9436 See MYKOLOGICKY SBORNIK. 519

0374-9525 See NAUCNO-TEHNICESKIJ BULLETEN' VSESOUZNOGO SELEKCIONNO-GENETICESKOGO INSTITUTA. 519

0374-9584 See NIGERIAN JOURNAL OF FORESTRY. 2389

0374-9797 See NOUVELLE REVUE D'ENTOMOLOGIE. 5612

0374-9851 See NIHON KONTAKUTO RENZU GAKKAI KAISHI. 3877

0374-9894 See NATURE CANADA. 2199

0375-0183 See ODONATOLOGICA. 467

0375-0299 See PALAEONTOGRAPHICA. ABTEILUNG B : PALAOPHYTOLOGIE. 4229

0375-0442 See PALAEONTOGRAPHICA. ABTEILUNG A : PALAOZOOLOGIE, STRATIGRAPHIE. 4229

0375-0728 See RECORDS OF THE BOTANICAL SURVEY OF INDIA. 526

0375-0736 See RICERCHE DI BIOLOGIA DELLA SELVAGGINA. 5596

0375-0760 See REVISTA CUBANA DE MEDICINA TROPICAL. 3986

0375-0906 See REVISTA DE GASTROENTEROLOGIA DE MEXICO. 3747

0375-1325 See REVUE SUISSE D'AGRICULTURE. 130

0375-1430 See REVUE SUISSE DE VITICULTURE, ARBORICULTURE, HORTICULTURE. 2430

0375-1465 See REVUE VERVIETOISE D'HISTOIRE NATURELLE. 4171

0375-1511 See RECORDS OF THE ZOOLOGICAL SURVEY OF INDIA. 5596

0375-1589 See SOUTH AFRICAN JOURNAL OF ANIMAL SCIENCE. 222

0375-1651 See SELLOWIA. 527

0375-2135 See FAUNISTISCHE ABHANDLUNGEN (LEIPZIG). 5608

0375-2232 See SBORNIK NAUCHNYKH TRUDOV (VSESOIUZNYI NAUCHNO-ISSLEDOVATELSKII INSTITUT SADOVODSTVA IM. I.V. MICHURINA). 2431

0375-2909 See STEENSTRUPIA. 5598

0375-2984 See SUDAN NOTES AND RECORDS. 2855

0375-3271 See TOKAI DAIGAKU KIYO : KAIYOGAKUBU. 474

0375-4561 See UMEA PSYCHOLOGICAL REPORTS. 4621

0375-4928 See VEDECKE PRACE VYSKUMNEHO USTAVU LUK A PASIENKOV V BANSKEJ BYSTRICI. 5523

0375-5010 See VEDECKE PRACE VYSKUMNEHO USTAVU ZIVOCISNEJ VYROBY V NITRE. 5168

0375-5193 See YEAR BOOK OF THE INDIAN NATIONAL SCIENCE ACADEMY, THE. 5171

0375-5207 See YONSEI REPORTS ON TROPICAL MEDICINE. 3987

0375-5231 See ZOOLOGISCHE ABHANDLUNGEN / STAATLICHES MUSEUM FUER TIERKUNDE IN DRESDEN. 5602

0375-5444 See ACTA GEOGRAPHICA SINICA. 2553

0375-5495 See AGRONOMY ABSTRACTS (MADISON, WIS.). 56

0375-5630 See GUIDEBOOK FOR THE ... ANNUAL FIELD CONFERENCE OF PENNSYLVANIA GEOLOGISTS. 1381

0375-5754 See SOILS AND LAND USE SERIES. 187

0375-5886 See BRITISH COLUMBIA SOIL SURVEY, REPORT. 165

0375-6122 See ZPRAVY GEOGRAFICKENO USTAVU CSAV. 2580

0375-6157 See BULLETIN (COLORADO GEOLOGICAL SURVEY). 1368

0375-6181 See COMMENTARI DELL'ATENEO DI BRESCIA. 2844

0375-6327 See FLUID INCLUSION RESEARCH. 1439

0375-6440 See GEOLOGICAL SOCIETY SPECIAL PUBLICATION. 1378

0375-6505 See GEOTHERMICS. 1413

0375-6572 See HEIDELBERGER GEOGRAPHISCHE ARBEITEN. 2565

0375-6653 See PUBLIC INFORMATION CIRCULAR - IOWA GEOLOGICAL SURVEY. 1392

0375-6742 See JOURNAL OF GEOCHEMICAL EXPLORATION. 2141

0375-684X See COASTAL STUDIES BULLETIN. LOUISIANA STATE UNIVERSITY. 1448

0375-7471 See QUARTAR. 1392

0375-7536 See REVISTA BRASILEIRA DE GEOCIENCIAS. 1360

0375-7587 See SCRIPTA GEOLOGICA. 1360

0375-7633 See BOLLETTINO DELLA SOCIETA PALEONTOLOGICA ITALIANA. 4226

0375-7854 See SCIENCE REPORTS OF THE TOHOKU UNIVERSITY. SERIES 7. GEOGRAPHY. 2576

0375-8087 See INFORMATION CIRCULAR - UNIVERSITY OF THE WITWATERSRAND, ECONOMIC GEOLOGY RESEARCH UNIT. 1383

0375-8265 See BULLETIN - WISCONSIN GEOLOGICAL AND NATURAL HISTORY SURVEY. 1371

0375-8338 See ACTA MEDICA CROATICA : CASOPIS HRVATSKE AKADEMIJE MEDICINSKIH ZNANOSTI. 3544

0375-8419 See TRUDY INSTITUTA OKEANOLOGII IM. P.P. SHIRSHOVA. 1458

0375-8427 See VETERINARNI MEDICINA. 5524

0375-8621 See BAYERISCHES LANDWIRTSCHAFTLICHES JAHRBUCH. 65

0375-8818 See WEIN-WISSENSCHAFT, DIE. 2361

0375-8842 See ENERGETIKA. 2113

0375-8990 See GIDROBIOLOGICESKIJ ZURNAL. 495

0375-9172 See TOKYO JIKEIKAI IKA DAIGAKU ZASSHI. 3646

0375-9202 See TOKYO NOGYO DAIGAKU NOGAKU SHUHO. 141

0375-9237 See AL-MAGALLA AL-MISRIYYA LI-N-NABAT. 498

0375-9253 See KAGAKU KOGAKU. 2014

0375-9393 See MINERVA ANESTESIOLOGICA. 3683

0375-9415 See MOLEKULIARNAIA BIOLOGIIA. 465

0375-9474 See NUCLEAR PHYSICS. A. 4449

0375-9504 See BANYASZATI ES KOHASZATI LAPOK. OENTOEDE. 2135

0375-9563 See PEDIATRIA (SANTIAGO). 3907

0375-9601 See PHYSICS LETTERS : PART A. 4416

0375-9660 See PROBLEMY ENDOKRINOLOGII. 3732

0375-9687 See PROGRESS OF THEORETICAL PHYSICS. SUPPLEMENT. 4418

0375-9709 See REVISTA DE LA REAL ACADEMIA DE FARMACIA DE BARCELONA. 4328

0375-9784 See RIVISTA ITALIANA DI PALEONTOLOGIA E STRATIGRAFIA. MEMORIA. 4230

0376-0030 See REVISTA DE LA FACULTAD DE AGRONOMIA DE LA UNIVERSIDAD CENTRAL DE VENEZUELA. ALCANCE. 129

0376-0308 See ADVANCES IN X-RAY ANALYSIS. 3938

0376-0421 See PROGRESS IN AEROSPACE SCIENCES. 32

0376-0685 See KYUSHU NOGYO SHIKENJO HOKOKU. 103

0376-0723 See LANDBAUFORSCHUNG VOLKENRODE, SONDERHEFT. 104

0376-0898 See CHEMIA STOSOWANA (1971). 2009

0376-1185 See TU. 5523

0376-1444 See TRUDY PALEONTOLOGICHESKOGO INSTITUTA. 4231

0376-1606 See ANZEIGER (OSTERREICHISCHE AKADEMIE DER WISSENSCHAFTEN). 5084

0376-1738 See GEOGRAPHISCHER JAHRESBERICHT AUS OSTERREICH. 2564

0376-2203 See SPELUNCA. 1411

0376-2491 See ZHONG HUA YI XUE ZA ZHI. 3653

0376-2556 See JAHRBUCH DES OBEROSTERREICHISCHEN MUSEALVEREINES. ABHANDLUNGEN. 4089

0376-2734 See PALAEONTOGRAPHICAL SOCIETY MONOGRAPHS. 4229

0376-2750 See RECORDS OF THE SOUTH AUSTRALIAN MUSEUM. 4095

0376-2793 See REVISTA DEL MUSEO ARGENTINO DE CIENCIAS NATURALES "BERNARDINO RIVADAVIA" E INSTITUTO NACIONAL DE INVESTIGACI,ON DE LAS CIENCIAS NATURALES. BOTANICA. 526

0376-401X See SPRACHE. 3323

0376-4079 See TAMKANG JOURNAL OF MATHEMATICS. 3538

0376-415X See INDIAN PHILOSOPHICAL QUARTERLY. 4349

0376-4230 See CONTRIBUTIONS TO VERTEBRATE EVOLUTION. 5581

0376-4265 See ESA BULLETIN. 18

0376-4516 See BULETINUL INSTITUTULUI DE PETROL SI GAZE. 4252

0376-4524 See IRANIAN JOURNAL OF AGRICULTURAL RESEARCH. 97

0376-4605 See ANNUAL SURVEY OF SOUTH AFRICAN LAW. 2935

0376-4672 See TAEHAN CHIKWA UISA HYOPHOE CHI. 1336

0376-4699 See INDIAN JOURNAL OF CHEMISTRY. SECTION B : ORGANIC INCLUDING MEDICINAL. 1042

0376-4710 See INDIAN JOURNAL OF CHEMISTRY. SECTION A, INORGANIC, BIO-INORGANIC, PHYSICAL, THEORETICAL & ANALYTICAL CHEMISTRY. 1015

0376-4745 See ELECTROTEHNICA, ELECTRONICA, AUTOMATICA. ELECTROTEHNICA. 2051

0376-4761 See PNEUMONOLOGIA POLSKA. 3950

0376-477X See CHUNG-HUA NUNG YEH YEN CHIU. 74

0376-480X See ADVANCES IN POLLEN-SPORE RESEARCH. 498

0376-4818 See JOURNAL OF THE UNIVERSITY OF KUWAIT, SCIENCE, THE. 5121

0376-4826 See STEIRISCHE BEITRAEGE ZUR HYDROGEOLOGIE. 1418

0376-4842 See CURRENT AWARENESS IN PARTICLE TECHNOLOGY / PUBLISHED AND COMPILED BY: PARTICLE SCIENCE AND TECHNOLOGY INFORMATION SERVICE, UNIVERSITY OF TECHNOLOGY, LOUGHBOROUGH, GREAT BRITAIN. 5098

0376-4907 See UNESCO ADULT EDUCATION INFORMATION NOTES. 1802

0376-5040 See CORE JOURNALS IN PEDIATRICS. 3902

0376-5059 See CORE JOURNALS IN OBSTETRICS/GYNECOLOGY. 3759

0376-5067 See TRENDS IN BIOCHEMICAL SCIENCES (AMSTERDAM. REFERENCE EDITION). 493

0376-5083 See IRRICAB. 175

0376-5156 See GEOPHYTOLOGY. 512

0376-5210 See GUIDE TO THE HOTELS IN SOUTH AFRICA. 2806

0376-5229 See GUIDE TO ELECTRONICS INDUSTRY IN INDIA. 2056

0376-5245 See GUIDE DE L'INDUSTRIE SENEGALAISE. 1608

0376-5253 See GRAZER BEITRAEGE. 3284

0376-5288 See REGISTRATION OF BIRTHS & DEATHS ACT. ANNUAL REPORT. 4559

0376-5296 See AVEGA. 3460

0376-544X See ANNUAL REPORT - ETHIOPIAN CHAMBER OF COMMERCE. 818

0376-5466 See ANNUAL REPORT - DEPARTMENT OF SPACE. GOVERNMENT OF INDIA. 11

0376-5520 See ANNUAL REPORT - ALIA. 11

0376-5563 See ANNUAL ADMINISTRATION REPORT - FOOD AND DRUG ADMINISTRATION, MAHARASHTRA STATE. 4626

0376-5687 See FORUM (SEMARANG). 5200

0376-5776 See CONGRESS MARCHES AHEAD. 4640

0376-5822 See CENSUS OF LIVESTOCK IN EUROPEAN AREAS. 209

0376-5954 See BULLETIN INTERIEUR - ASSOCIATION POUR LA PROTECTION CONTRE LES RAYONNEMENTS IONISANTS. 4434

0376-6039 See BOOKS IRELAND. 4812

0376-6187 See BULLETIN DE DOCUMENTATION INRS. 2860

0376-6276 See ACTUALITES CHIRURGICALES. 3957

0376-6322 See ANNUAL JOURNAL - SINGAPORE POLYTECHNIC BUILDING SOCIETY. 598

0376-6349 See SAFETY SCIENCE. 2869

0376-6357 See BEHAVIOURAL PROCESSES. 5577

0376-6403 See TRANSNATIONAL PERSPECTIVES. 3136

0376-6411 See TERRA ET AQUA. 2096

0376-6438 See OECD ECONOMIC SURVEYS. 1509

0376-6438 See OECD ECONOMIC SURVEYS: POLAND. 1510

0376-6454 See MYERS' FINANCE & ENERGY. 1950

0376-6535 See GONG FU. 4897

0376-656X See XINY IYAOXUE ZAZHI. 5171

0376-6578 See NAYA. 3414

0376-6616 See BANKER'S WORLD DIRECTORY, THE. 776

0376-6624 See BIBI. 5551

0376-6632 See BIOGRAPHICAL MEMOIRS OF FELLOWS OF THE INDIAN NATIONAL SCIENCE ACADEMY. 430

0376-6675 See BULLETIN OF THE BUREAU OF EDUCATIONAL AND PSYCHOLOGICAL RESEARCH, CALCUTTA. 4579

0376-6802 See NIVAG CONTOUR. 622

0376-6853 See SCHWEIZER BAUWIRTSCHAFT. 627

0376-7191 See QUARTERLY ECONOMIC COMMENTARY. 1514

0376-723X See IMME BOLETIN TECNICO. 2024

0376-7256 See INDIAN HIGHWAYS. 5441

0376-7361 See DEVELOPMENTS IN PETROLEUM SCIENCE. 4254

0376-7388 See JOURNAL OF MEMBRANE SCIENCE. 5119

0376-7396 See MEYLER'S SIDE EFFECTS OF DRUGS. 4315

0376-7418 See PHILOSOPHY AND MEDICINE. 4356

0376-7442 See TIJDSCHRIFT VOOR KINDERGENEESKUNDE. 3912

0376-7450 See COBALT + COBALT ABSTRACTS (ENGLISH ED.). 1023

0376-7493 See COAL & MINING REVIEW. 2137

0376-7531 See COMPTE RENDU ANALYTIQUE - REPUBLIQUE DU ZAIRE, CONSEIL LEGISLATIF NATIONAL. 4639

0376-7574 See CONTRIBUTIONS TO NEPALESE STUDIES. 2650

0376-7590 See COTECFLASH. 4368

0376-7612 See CAMEROUN 3E REPUBLIQUE. 1550

0376-7639 See CAHIERS DE MEDECINE DU TRAVAIL. 3561

0376-7647 See CAIRO. 2638

0376-7655 See CAJANUS. 4188

0376-7698 See CARIBBEAN ARCHIVES. 2481

0376-7701 See CARIBBEAN JOURNAL OF EDUCATION. 1730

0376-7744 See CATALOGUE OF GOVERNMENT PUBLICATIONS. GOVERNMENT OF TAMIL NADU. 412

0376-7779 See CAYMAN GAZETTE. 2949

0376-7787 See C.C.A.I. MONTHLY NEWSLETTER. 1294

0376-7795 See CDPRESS. 2683

0376-7833 See CERRAHPASA TIP FAKULTESI DERGISI. 3562

0376-7868 See CHARTERED SECRETARY (NEW DELHI). 863

0376-7884 See CIRCULARS - SOUTH AFRICAN ASTRONOMICAL OBSERVATORY. 394

0376-7892 See CIRUGIA PLASTICA IBERO-LATINOAMERICANA. 3962

0376-7914 See CLERICAL OFFICERS AND TYPISTS LISTS. 4638

0376-7965 See CONSERVATION OF CULTURAL PROPERTY IN INDIA. 2190

0376-8090 See DAMILICA. 2650

0376-8112 See DATOS - SOCIEDAD PRIVADA MUNICIPAL TRANSPORTES DE BARCELONA. 5380

0376-8120 See DEBATES : OFFICIAL REPORT - PROVINCIAL ASSEMBLY OF SIND. 4471

0376-8163 See DEGRES. 3276

0376-8201 See DEPTH NEWS INDONESIA. 1479

0376-821X See DETAILED CIVIL BUDGET ESTIMATES. GOVERNMENT OF WEST BENGAL. 4720

0376-8260 See DETAILED DEMAND FOR GRANTS OF HOUSING AND URBAN DEVELOPMENT DEPARTMENT. 2821

0376-8279 See DETAILED DEMAND FOR GRANTS OF LABOUR AND SOCIAL WELFARE DEPARTMENT. 1662

0376-8287 See DETAILED DEMAND FOR GRANTS OF LAW DEPARTMENT. 2960

0376-8295 See DETAILED DEMAND FOR GRANTS OF PLANNING DEPARTMENT. 1479

0376-8384 See DIPLOMATIC CORPS. MINISTRY OF EXTERNAL AFFAIRS (KINGSTON). 4520

0376-8422 See DIRECTORY. CLASSIFIED TRADE INDEX (NAIROBI). 831

0376-8430 See DIRECTORY - INTERNATIONAL ASSOCIATION OF LAW LIBRARIES. 2961

0376-8449 See DIRECTORY : KOREA ELECTRONICS MANUFACTURERS. 3477

0376-8473 See DIRECTORY OF ENGINEERING UNITS IN PAKISTAN. 2113

0376-8511 *See* DIRECTORY OF MEMBERS - PUNJAB HARYANA & DELHI CHAMBER OF COMMERCE AND INDUSTRY. **819**

0376-8546 *See* DIRECTORY OF PUBLIC ENTERPRISES IN INDIA. **1604**

0376-8570 *See* DIRECTORY OF SMALL SCALE INDUSTRIAL UNITS EMPLOYING FIVE OR MORE PERSONS IN THE UNORGANISED SECTOR IN HARYANA. **1663**

0376-8627 *See* DIRECTORY OF THE REPUBLIC OF SENEGAL. **4644**

0376-8635 *See* DIRECTORY - SINGAPORE INDIAN CHAMBER OF COMMERCE. **819**

0376-8651 *See* DOCUMENTATION SERVICE BULLETIN. **5198**

0376-8686 *See* DUTCH STUDIES. **2686**

0376-8716 *See* DRUG AND ALCOHOL DEPENDENCE. **1343**

0376-8724 *See* EGYPTIAN JOURNAL OF PHYSICS. **4402**

0376-8775 *See* EPISTEMONIKE EPETERIS TES ODONTIATRIKES SCHOLES TOU PANEPISTEMIOU ATHENON. **1323**

0376-8791 *See* ECONOMIC SURVEY OF SINGAPORE. **1558**

0376-8872 *See* ENGINEERING NEWS (CALCUTTA). **1973**

0376-8902 *See* ENGLISH IN AFRICA. **3384**

0376-8929 *See* ENVIRONMENTAL CONSERVATION. **2193**

0376-9097 *See* EXTERNAL TRADE OF LIBERIA : EXPORTS. **835**

0376-9100 *See* EVEREST REVIEW. **1561**

0376-9151 *See* EAST AFRICAN CERTIFICATE OF EDUCATION : REGULATIONS AND SYLLABUSES. **1862**

0376-9186 *See* EAST WEST TRADE INFORMATION BULLETIN. **832**

0376-9275 *See* ECONOMIC REPORT - TURKIYE IS BANKAS A.S. **1558**

0376-9429 *See* INTERNATIONAL JOURNAL OF FRACTURE. **2102**

0376-9526 *See* HANDBOOK FOR THE FACULTY OF ARTS AND FACULTY OF SOCIAL SCIENCES. **1827**

0376-9682 *See* ICHR NEWSLETTER. **2653**

0376-9690 *See* ILO CATALOGUE OF PUBLICATIONS IN PRINT. **1533**

0376-9771 *See* INDIA INTERNATIONAL CENTRE QUARTERLY. **2653**

0376-978X *See* INDIA LEATHER & LEATHER PRODUCTS DIRECTORY. **3184**

0376-981X *See* INDIAN CONSUMER COOPERATOR. **1542**

0376-9836 *See* INDIAN HISTORICAL REVIEW, THE. **2653**

0376-9844 *See* INDIAN JOURNAL OF CRIMINOLOGY. **3166**

0376-9879 *See* INDIAN JOURNAL OF SOCIAL SCIENCES. **5203**

0376-9887 *See* INDIAN MILLER. **202**

0376-9925 *See* INDICATORS OF SOCIO-ECONOMIC DEVELOPMENT OF GOA, DAMAN & DIU SINCE LIBERATION. **1567**

0376-9933 *See* INDICE DE TECNICOS PAPELEROS ESPANOLES. **4234**

0376-9941 *See* INDICE INDUSTRIAL. **1609**

0376-9968 *See* INDO-BURMA PETROLEUM COMPANY LIMITED ANNUAL REPORT. **4260**

0376-9984 *See* INDONESIA STATISTICS. **1534**

0377-0001 *See* INDONESIAN COMMERCIAL NEWSLETTERS. **1495**

0377-0028 *See* INDUSTRIAL AND TRADE DIRECTORY OF MALAWI. **840**

0377-015X *See* INTERNATIONAL JOURNAL OF ECOLOGY AND ENVIRONMENTAL SCIENCES. **2217**

0377-0168 *See* INTERNATIONAL JOURNAL OF ZOONOSES. **3589**

0377-0176 *See* INTERNATIONAL TRADE AND SINGAPORE. **841**

0377-0206 *See* INVESTIGACION MEDICA INTERNACIONAL. **3590**

0377-0257 *See* JOURNAL OF NON-NEWTONIAN FLUID MECHANICS. **2092**

0377-0265 *See* DYNAMICS OF ATMOSPHERES AND OCEANS. **1449**

0377-0273 *See* JOURNAL OF VOLCANOLOGY AND GEOTHERMAL RESEARCH. **1408**

0377-0311 *See* JAARLIKSE STRALINGSVERSLAG. **4435**

0377-0354 *See* JAHRBUCH DER WIENER GESELLSCHAFT FUER THEATERFORSCHUNG. **5365**

0377-0370 *See* JAPAN QUARTERLY (NEW DELHI). **2654**

0377-0400 *See* JOURNAL OF APPLIED MEDICINE. **3593**

0377-0419 *See* JOURNAL OF BUSINESS (SINGAPORE). **686**

0377-0427 *See* JOURNAL OF COMPUTATIONAL AND APPLIED MATHEMATICS. **3512**

0377-0435 *See* JOURNAL OF INDIAN EDUCATION. **1757**

0377-0443 *See* JOURNAL OF KERALA STUDIES. **2655**

0377-0451 *See* KOREAN JOURNAL OF INTERNATIONAL STUDIES, THE. **4528**

0377-0486 *See* JOURNAL OF RAMAN SPECTROSCOPY. **4436**

0377-0494 *See* JOURNAL OF SHIPPING, CUSTOMS & TRANSPORT LAWS. **3181**

0377-0508 *See* JOURNAL OF SOCIAL AND ECONOMIC STUDIES (NEW DELHI, INDIA). **5206**

0377-0524 *See* JOURNAL OF THE ALL INDIA INSTITUTE OF SPEECH AND HEARING, THE. **3889**

0377-0540 *See* JOURNAL OF THE ASIATIC SOCIETY OF BANGLADESH. **5232**

0377-0575 *See* JOURNAL OF THE GANGANATHA JHA KENDRIYA SANSKRIT VIDYAPEETHA. **3292**

0377-0621 *See* JOURNAL OF THE NATIONAL INTEGRATED MEDICAL ASSOCIATION. **3599**

0377-0648 *See* JSL, JOURNAL OF THE SCHOOL OF LANGUAGES. **3293**

0377-0729 *See* KOREAN JOURNAL OF COMPARATIVE LAW. **2993**

0377-0788 *See* LANDERBANK ECONOMIC BULLETIN. **1502**

0377-0869 *See* LAW AND SOCIETY QUARTERLY. **2994**

0377-0877 *See* LAWINENEREIGNISSE UND WITTERUNGSABLAUF IN OSTERREICH. **1386**

0377-0907 *See* LEGAL HISTORY. **2999**

0377-0915 *See* LEGAL ISSUES OF EUROPEAN INTEGRATION. **3132**

0377-0982 *See* LIPIKA. **386**

0377-0990 *See* LIST OF CULTURES. **566**

0377-1121 *See* MAJALAH KEDOKTERAN INDONESIA. **3606**

0377-113X *See* MAJI REVIEW. **2093**

0377-1148 *See* MALAYSIAN BUILDING & CONSTRUCTION. **619**

0377-1164 *See* MANA ANNUAL OF CREATIVE WRITING, THE. **3409**

0377-1172 *See* MANAGEMENT ABSTRACTS. **876**

0377-1202 See REVUE ROUMAINE DE MEDECINE INTERNE (1990). **3801**

0377-1237 *See* MEDICAL JOURNAL, ARMED FORCES INDIA. **3609**

0377-127X *See* MEGHALAYA YEAR BOOK, THE. **2658**

0377-1385 *See* MIGRATION AND TOURISM STATISTICS. **5500**

0377-1482 *See* MMTC NEWS. **1618**

0377-1490 *See* MODERN FIBRES. **5354**

0377-1555 *See* MONTHLY STATISTICAL BULLETIN OF BANGLADESH. **5333**

0377-1571 *See* M.R.S.O. REPORT. **2143**

0377-1636 *See* NATIONAL BIBLIOGRAPHY OF ZAMBIA, THE. **420**

0377-1717 *See* N.E.O.N., NATAL EDUCATION. ONDERWYS IN NATAL. **1765**

0377-1741 *See* NEW BOTANIST. **519**

0377-175X *See* NEW DIRECTIONS (SINGAPORE). **2660**

0377-1784 *See* NEWSLETTER - CENTRAL ARCHIVES FOR THE HISTORY OF THE JEWISH PEOPLE. **2482**

0377-1806 *See* NORWEGIAN OFFSHORE INDEX. **4267**

0377-192X *See* OLYMPIC REVIEW. **4910**

0377-1962 *See* ORDERS OF DAY. MINUTES OF PROCEEDINGS - COUNCIL OF EUROPE. PARLIAMENT ASSEMBLY. **4671**

0377-2063 *See* JOURNAL OF THE INSTITUTION OF ELECTRONICS AND TELECOMMUNICATION ENGINEERS. **1159**

0377-2071 See NATO ASI SERIES. SERIES C, MATHEMATICAL AND PHYSICAL SCIENCES. **3524**

0377-2152 *See* BOLETIM MENSAL DAS ESTATISTICAS DA AGRICULTURA E DA PESCA. **67**

0377-2217 *See* EUROPEAN JOURNAL OF OPERATIONAL RESEARCH. **5104**

0377-2292 *See* STATISTIQUES DES TRANSPORTS ET COMMUNICATIONS : CONTINENT, AZORES ET MADERE. **5402**

0377-2306 *See* ESTATISTICAS DO TURISMO. **5500**

0377-2543 *See* PACIFIC PERSPECTIVE. **2670**

0377-2586 *See* PAKISTAN PICTORIAL. **2770**

0377-2616 *See* PALESTINE (BEIRUT). **4531**

0377-2624 *See* PUBLICOTEC. **765**

0377-2632 *See* PANJI MASYARAKAT. **2662**

0377-2640 *See* PANORAMA AFRICAIN. **2642**

0377-2659 *See* PAPINEAU'S GUIDE TO JAKARTA. **5488**

0377-2667 *See* PARTY LIFE. **4544**

0377-2772 *See* PHILOSOPHY AND SOCIAL ACTION. **5253**

0377-2802 See PORTS AND DREDGING. **5454**

0377-2861 *See* PROCEEDINGS OF THE ... MEETING OF THE AGRICULTURAL CREDIT BOARD. **804**

0377-2969 *See* PROCEEDINGS OF THE PAKISTAN ACADEMY OF SCIENCES. **5141**

0377-2993 *See* PROGRAMME OF WORK AND BUDGET. **1579**

0377-3132 *See* PSYCHO-LINGUA. **3312**

0377-3167 *See* PUBLIC SECTOR ACCOUNTS OF LIBERIA. **4743**

0377-3310 *See* RAJASTHAN JOURNAL OF ENGLISH STUDIES, THE. **3314**

0377-3450 *See* RECSAM ANNUAL REPORT. **5145**

0377-3485 *See* REGISTERED TRADE UNIONS IN SOUTH AFRICA. **1705**

0377-3515 *See* RENDITIONS. **3429**

0377-3574 *See* CONTRIBUTIONS TO EPIDEMIOLOGY AND BIOSTATISTICS. **3734**

0377-368X *See* REPORT - INTERNATIONAL COMMISSION FOR THE CONSERVATION OF ATLANTIC TUNAS. ENGLISH VERSION. **2311**

0377-4724 *See* REVISTA DE CHIRURGIE ONCOLOGIE, RADIOLOGIE, O.R.L., OFTALMOLOGIE, STOMATOLOGIE. ONCOLOGIA. **3823**

0377-4732 *See* REVISTA ESPANOLA DE MEDICINA LEGAL. **3742**

0377-4929 *See* INDIAN JOURNAL OF PATHOLOGY & MICROBIOLOGY. **3895**

0377-4961 *See* REVISTA DE PEDIATRIE, OBSTETRICA SI GINECOLOGIE. OBSTETRICA SI GINECOLOGIE. **3768**

0377-497X *See* REVISTA DE MEDICINA-INTERNA, NEUROLOGIE, PSIHIATRIE, NEUROCHIRURGIE, DERMATO-VENEROLOGIE. NEUROLOGIE, PSIHIATRIE, NEUROCHIRURGIE. **3935**

0377-4988 *See* REVISTA DE MEDICINA INTERNA, NEUROLOGIE, PSIHIATRIE, NEUROCHIRURGIE, DERMATO-VENEROLOGIE. DERMATO-VENEROLOGIE. **3635**

0377-5135 *See* SCIENCES, TECHNIQUES, INFORMATIONS CRIAC. **5154**

0377-5232 *See* SEOUL NATIONAL UNIVERSITY FACULTY PAPERS : BIOLOGY AND AGRICULTURE SERIES. **473**

0377-5240 See SEOUL NATIONAL UNIVERSITY FACULTY PAPERS : HUMANITIES AND SOCIAL SCIENCE SERIES, A & B. **1847**

0377-5275 See SIERRA LEONE LIBRARY JOURNAL, THE. **3249**

0377-5305 See SINGAPORE FAMILY PHYSICIAN, THE. **3739**

0377-5380 See SOCIAL AND LABOUR BULLETIN. **1710**

0377-5429 See SOUTH AFRICAN LABOUR BULLETIN. **1711**

0377-5437 See SOUTHEAST ASIAN AFFAIRS. **4496**

0377-5739 See STATISTICAL YEARBOOK OF THE SOCIALIST REPUBLIC OF ROMANIA. **5341**

0377-5844 See SUMMARY OF STATISTICS. BUREAU OF STATISTICS, KONEDOBU. **5344**

0377-600X See TAX MONTHLY, THE. **4753**

0377-6026 See TEACHER EDUCATION AT MAKERERE. **1905**

0377-6093 See TEXTS ADOPTED BY THE ASSEMBLY - COUNCIL OF EUROPE. PARLIAMENTARY ASSEMBLY. **4690**

0377-631X See UNESCO LIST OF DOCUMENTS AND PUBLICATIONS. **426**

0377-6395 See VETERINER HEKIMLER DERNEGI DERGISI. **5527**

0377-6522 See WORKERS' COMPENSATION STATISTICS. **1540**

0377-6549 See WARTA KESEHATAN. **4807**

0377-6662 See YEARBOOK - IFA. **4759**

0377-6719 See YEARLY ALL INDIA CRIMINAL DIGEST. **3109**

0377-6727 See YOUNG MARCH, THE. **1071**

0377-6824 See CONSEQUENCE (COTONOU). **4344**

0377-6832 See DATA INDIA. **2650**

0377-6948 See DIRECTORY OF INSTITUTIONS OF ORIENTAL STUDIES IN OVERSEAS COUNTRIES. **2650**

0377-7081 See DOCUMENTATION IN PUBLIC ADMINISTRATION. **4645**

0377-7103 See EASTERN AFRICA JOURNAL OF RURAL DEVELOPMENT. **80**

0377-7154 See EGYPTIAN COMPUTER JOURNAL, THE. **1258**

0377-7162 See EKONOMI SUMATERA UTARA. **1559**

0377-7200 See GUIDE TO NORTH SUMATRA, INDONESIA. **5479**

0377-7227 See HANDBOOK - UNIVERSITI PERTANIAN MALAYSIA. **1827**

0377-7316 See ANUARIO DE ESTUDIOS CENTROAMERICANOS. **5191**

0377-7332 See EMPIRICAL ECONOMICS. **1488**

0377-7340 See INDIAN ELECTRONICS DIRECTORY. **2064**

0377-7359 See INDIAN FILMS (POONA). **4072**

0377-7383 See INDUSTRIAL VISTA. **1611**

0377-7391 See INDUSTRIAL WELDER. **4027**

0377-743X See JIJNASA. **2769**

0377-7464 See JOURNAL - THE INSTITUTION OF ENGINEERS, SINGAPORE. **1984**

0377-7472 See JOURNAL OF ENGINEERING EDUCATION IN SOUTHEAST ASIA. **1982**

0377-7480 See JOURNAL OF RURAL COOPERATION. **1542**

0377-7499 See KAILASH. **239**

0377-7537 See MAN-MADE TEXTILES IN INDIA. **5354**

0377-757X See MUNICIPALITIES AND CORPORATION CASES. **3012**

0377-7588 See NAMIBIA BULLETIN. **3133**

0377-7596 See OH CALCUTTA. **2507**

0377-7669 See PROCEEDINGS OF THE MEETING OF THE EXPERT PANEL ON AIR POLLUTION MODELING. **2239**

0377-7693 See PROGRESS REPORT - F.I.A.B. **3242**

0377-7723 See RAJASTHAN LAW WEEKLY, THE. **3034**

0377-7855 See REVIEWS IN LEUKAEMIA AND LYMPHOMA. **3823**

0377-7863 See REVISTA DE CHIRURGIE ONCOLOGIE, RADIOLOGIE, O.R.L., OFTALMOLOGIE, STOMATOLOGIE. OTO-RINO-LARINGOLOGIA. **3891**

0377-7871 See REVISTA DE CHIRURGIE, ONCOLOGIE, RADIOLOGIE, O.R.L. OFTALMOLOGIE, STOMATOLOGIE. SERIA : STOMATOLOGIE. **3635**

0377-7901 See SCIENCE AND TECHNOLOGY YEARBOOK. **5151**

0377-7928 See SINGAPORE PERIODICALS INDEX. **1929**

0377-7944 See SOUTH WEST AFRICA SERIES. **1397**

0377-8002 See TAMIL NADU JOURNAL OF CO-OPERATION, THE. **1543**

0377-8029 See UNIVERSITY AFFAIRS (DELHI). **1852**

0377-8053 See WATER RESOURCES JOURNAL. **5547**

0377-8088 See YOUNG BUDDHIST, THE. **5022**

0377-810X See ZAIRE BUSINESS. **1589**

0377-8134 See METROLOGIA APLICATA (1975). **4031**

0377-8142 See REVUE ROUMAINE DE BIOLOGIE. SERIE DE BIOLOGIE ANIMALE. **472**

0377-8150 See STUDII SI CERCETARI DE BIOLOGIE. SERIA BIOLOGIE ANIMALA. **474**

0377-8169 See STUDII SI CERCETARI DE BIOLOGIE. SERIA BIOLOGIE VEGETALA. **474**

0377-8207 See BOLETIN DE LA CATEDRA DE PEDIATRIA DE MADRID. **3901**

0377-8231 See BULLETIN ET MEMOIRES DE L'ACADEMIE ROYALE DE MEDECINE DE BELGIQUE. **3560**

0377-8282 See DRUGS OF THE FUTURE. **4302**

0377-8312 See LECTURE SERIES - VON KARMAN INSTITUTE FOR FLUID DYNAMICS. **2093**

0377-8320 See PSICODEIA. **4609**

0377-8347 See SCHWEIZERISCHE ZEITSCHRIFT FUER MILITAR- UND KATASTROPHENMEDIZIN. **3725**

0377-8398 See MARINE MICROPALEONTOLOGY. **4228**

0377-8401 See ANIMAL FEED SCIENCE AND TECHNOLOGY. **199**

0377-8444 See JOURNAL OF CHEMICAL SCIENCES. **980**

0377-8460 See RB. **625**

0377-8487 See VIGNANA BHARATHI. **5169**

0377-8592 See SAFETY MANAGEMENT. **2869**

0377-8711 See CORROSION & COATINGS SOUTH AFRICA. **2011**

0377-8967 See REVIEW OF POPULATION REVIEWS. **4559**

0377-8975 See BIBLIOGRAFIE VAN IN NEDERLAND VERSCHENEN KAARTEN. **2580**

0377-9017 See LETTERS IN MATHEMATICAL PHYSICS. **4411**

0377-9025 See METHODS AND PHENOMENA. **5128**

0377-905X See WASSER, ENERGIE, LUFT. **2096**

0377-9084 See FABRIMETAL. **3478**

0377-919X See JOURNAL OF PALESTINE STUDIES. **2655**

0377-9203 See ANNUAL REPORT - DEPARTMENT OF PUBLIC HEALTH. **4765**

0377-9211 See ARABIAN JOURNAL FOR SCIENCE AND ENGINEERING. **5085**

0377-9238 See BANGLADESH MEDICAL RESEARCH COUNCIL BULLETIN. **3555**

0377-9254 See JOURNAL OF ENGINEERING SCIENCES. **1982**

0377-9335 See ENTOMON. **5608**

0377-9343 See INDIAN JOURNAL OF CHEST DISEASES & ALLIED SCIENCES, THE. **3706**

0377-936X See JOURNAL - TIMBER DEVELOPMENT ASSOCIATION OF INDIA. **2402**

0377-9386 See PANTNAGAR JOURNAL OF RESEARCH. **5137**

0377-9408 See TOOL & ALLOY STEELS. **2130**

0377-9416 See TRANSACTIONS OF POWDER METALLURGY ASSOCIATION OF INDIA. **4022**

0377-9424 See AGRONOMIA COSTARRICENSE. **56**

0377-9483 See GATORRIG DAIHAG UIHAG-BU RONMUN-JIB. **3578**

0377-9505 See MANASAMANI. **5041**

0377-9556 See YAGHAG-HOI-JI. **4333**

0377-9572 See KOREAN JOURNAL OF BIOCHEMISTRY. **490**

0377-9610 See HIDUP. **5030**

0377-9653 See GANTAVYA. **2504**

0377-9661 See HIMALI SAUGATA. **3393**

0377-970X See REPORT OF THE COMPENSATION COMMISSIONER FOR OCCUPATIONAL DISEASES. **2868**

0377-9793 See AREA REPORT SERIES. **588**

0377-9920 See ASIAN WALL STREET JOURNAL. **640**

0377-9963 See MEDICAL PROGRESS (HONG KONG). **4315**

0378-0066 See GYERHAIG MIC HOHUBGI JIROHAN. **3949**

0378-0376 See ETUDES ECONOMIQUES DE L'O C D E: CANADA. **1489**

0378-0392 See MINERAL AND ELECTROLYTE METABOLISM. **3799**

0378-0430 See FERTILIZER TECHNOLOGY. **171**

0378-0449 See PLANT PROTECTION BULLETIN. **524**

0378-0473 See KANINA. **323**

0378-049X See HANDBOOK - INTERNATIONAL CHAMBER OF COMMERCE. **820**

0378-0546 See INSERM SYMPOSIUM. **3588**

0378-0600 See HONG KONG LAW JOURNAL. **2979**

0378-0619 See ACTA THERAPEUTICA. **4289**

0378-0643 See POESIE (BASEL, SWITZERLAND). **3424**

0378-0708 See BULLETIN DE L'ACADEMIE ROYALE DE LANGUE ET DE LITTERATURE FRANCAISES. **3270**

0378-0716 See BULLETIN DE LA CLASSE DE BEAUX-ARTS ACADEMIE ROYALE DE BELGIQUE. **316**

0378-0724 See MEMORIAS DE LA ACADEMIA MEXICANA DE LA HISTORIA. **2746**

0378-0759 See INDIAN LINGUISTICS. **3286**

0378-0864 See ABHANDLUNGEN DER GEOLOGISCHEN BUNDESANSTALT. **1364**

0378-0880 See COMMUNICATIONS & COGNITION. **1108**

0378-0953 See RAPPORT ANNUEL DU DEPARTEMENT DE GEOLOGIE ET DE MINERALOGIE DU MUSEE ROYAL DE L'AFRIQUE CENTRALE. **1393**

0378-1003 See INDIAN JOURNAL OF PSYCHOMETRY AND EDUCATION. **1752**

0378-1046 See JOURNAL OF THE EARTH AND SPACE PHYSICS. **4410**

0378-1070 See COMLA NEWSLETTER. **3203**

0378-1097 See FEMS MICROBIOLOGY LETTERS. **562**

0378-1100 See CRIME, LAW, AND SOCIAL CHANGE. **3161**

0378-1119 See GENE. **545**

0378-1127 See FOREST ECOLOGY AND MANAGEMENT. **2379**

0378-1135 See VETERINARY MICROBIOLOGY. **5526**

0378-1143 See ANNALS OF THE BHANDARKAR ORIENTAL RESEARCH INSTITUTE. **3265**

0378-116X See MEMORIAS DA ACADEMIA DAS CIENCIAS DE LISBOA. CLASSE DE LETRAS. **5233**

0378-1240 See GARCIA DE ORTA : SERIE DE GEOLOGIA. **1376**

0378-1267 See BULETINUL STIINTIFIC AL INSTITUTULUI POLITECHNIC CLUJ: SERIA CONSTRUCTII. **2019**

0378-178X See ECONOMIC AND FINANCIAL STATISTICS. **1531**

0378-1836 See INFORME - UNIVERSIDAD CENTRAL DE VENEZUELA, FACULTAD DE INGENIERIA, ESCUELA DE GEOLOGIA Y MINAS, LABORATORIO DE PETROGRAFIA Y GEOQUIMICA. 5113

0378-1844 See INTERCIENCIA. 5114

0378-1852 See REVISTA DE LA SOCIEDAD MEDICO-QUIRURGICA DEL HOSPITAL DE EMERGENCIA "PEREZ DE LEON.". 3973

0378-1887 See CHEMISCH WEEKBLAD. CHEMISCHE COURANT. 970

0378-1909 See ENVIRONMENTAL BIOLOGY OF FISHES. 2300

0378-1917 See PHYSICS AND CHEMISTRY OF MATERIALS WITH LAYERED STRUCTURES. 4415

0378-1984 See BHARATIYA VIDYA. 2647

0378-200X See CASTILLA (VALLADOLID). 3373

0378-2018 See MUSEO HISTORICO. 2747

0378-2158 See KENYA. 2641

0378-2166 See JOURNAL OF PRAGMATICS. 3291

0378-2220 See INFORMATION LETTER / UNITED NATIONS, DIVISION OF NARCOTIC DRUGS. 4307

0378-2239 See SPECIAL PAPER - JOINT FAO/WHO/OAU REGIONAL FOOD AND NUTRITION COMMISSION FOR AFRICA. 2358

0378-2255 See WHO REGIONAL PUBLICATIONS. EUROPEAN SERIES. 4807

0378-2271 See EUROPHYSICS CONFERENCE ABSTRACTS. 4402

0378-228X See PHARMACEUTICAL JOURNAL OF KENYA. 4320

0378-2352 See ISTANBUL UNIVERSITESI VETERINER FAKULTESI DERGISI. 5512

0378-2360 See JOURNAL OF CANCER. 3819

0378-2387 See CMFRI BULLETIN. 2299

0378-2395 See JOURNAL OF MAHARASHTRA AGRICULTURAL UNIVERSITIES. 176

0378-2409 See JOURNAL OF ROOT CROPS. 100

0378-2425 See APICULTURA IN ROMANIA. 5576

0378-2484 See IJDL. INTERNATIONAL JOURNAL OF DRAVIDIAN LINGUISTICS. 3286

0378-2506 See BYZANTION (BRUXELLES). 3370

0378-2654 See INDUSTRIAL DEVELOPMENT ABSTRACTS. 1610

0378-2697 See PLANT SYSTEMATICS AND EVOLUTION. 524

0378-2700 See EGYPTIAN JOURNAL OF DAIRY SCIENCE. 2334

0378-2735 See NOUVELLES - CICIAMS. 5033

0378-2778 See TIJDSCHRIFT VOOR ALCOHOL, DRUGS EN ANDERE PSYCHOTROPE STOFFEN. 1349

0378-2964 See INDIAN HORIZONS. 2848

0378-3006 See AFRICA DEVELOPMENT. 1544

0378-3073 See AUSTRIAN JOURNAL OF PUBLIC AND INTERNATIONAL LAW 1991. 3124

0378-3294 See REVISTA A.I.T. 5391

0378-3316 See ROCAS Y MINERALES. 2150

0378-3340 See REVISTA DEL PENSAMIENTO CENTROAMERICANO. 2512

0378-3375 See TLA NEWSLETTER (1983). 3253

0378-3480 See COURIER (BRUSSELS). 1554

0378-3588 See PFLANZLICHE ERZEUGUNG. 181

0378-3693 See BULLETIN OF THE EUROPEAN COMMUNITIES. 4634

0378-3758 See JOURNAL OF STATISTICAL PLANNING AND INFERENCE. 3514

0378-3766 See STUDIES IN THE MANAGEMENT SCIENCES. 5160

0378-3774 See AGRICULTURAL WATER MANAGEMENT. 52

0378-3790 See INORGANIC PERSPECTIVES IN BIOLOGY AND MEDICINE. 458

0378-3812 See FLUID PHASE EQUILIBRIA. 1052

0378-3820 See FUEL PROCESSING TECHNOLOGY. 1025

0378-3839 See COASTAL ENGINEERING (AMSTERDAM). 1968

0378-4037 See INTERNATIONAL BULLETIN OF SPORTS INFORMATION. 4900

0378-4045 See PROGRESS IN CLINICAL NEUROPHYSIOLOGY. 3844

0378-4150 See GERMAN LANGUAGE AND LITERATURE MONOGRAPHS. 3390

0378-4169 See LINGVISTICAE INVESTIGATIONES. 3299

0378-4177 See STUDIES IN LANGUAGE. 3326

0378-4177 See STUDIES IN LANGUAGE ORIGINS. 3326

0378-4207 See SIGMA : THE BULLETIN OF EUROPEAN STATISTICS. 5338

0378-4215 See ACTA IRANICA. DEUXIEME SERIE. HOMMAGES ET OPERA MINORA. 2767

0378-4266 See JOURNAL OF BANKING & FINANCE. 793

0378-4266 See JOURNAL OF BANKING & FINANCE MICROFORM. 793

0378-4274 See TOXICOLOGY LETTERS. 3984

0378-4290 See FIELD CROPS RESEARCH. 172

0378-4320 See ANIMAL REPRODUCTION SCIENCE. 5503

0378-4347 See JOURNAL OF CHROMATOGRAPHY. B, BIOMEDICAL APPLICATIONS. 1017

0378-4347 See JOURNAL OF CHROMATOGRAPHY. BIOMEDICAL APPLICATIONS. 980

0378-4371 See PHYSICA A. 4414

0378-4479 See RESULTATERNE AF KONJUNKTURUNDERSGELSEN HOS VIRKSOMHEDSLEDERE I FLLESSKABET. 1581

0378-4509 See AVANCES EN PRODUCCION ANIMAL. 5505

0378-4525 See BULLETIN - ZAMBIAN ORNITHOLOGICAL SOCIETY. 5616

0378-4533 See ZAMBIAN ORNITHOLOGICAL SOCIETY NEWSLETTER. 5621

0378-4606 See REVUE DE L'UNIVERSITE DE BRUXELLES. 5148

0378-4657 See GIDS OP MAATSCHAPPELIJK GEBIED. 5286

0378-4673 See BULLETIN DU MINISTERE DE LA SANTE PUBLIQUE ET DE LA FAMILLE. 4769

0378-469X See BALAFON. 2638

0378-4738 See WATER S. A. 5547

0378-4754 See MATHEMATICS AND COMPUTERS IN SIMULATION. 1282

0378-4835 See ONCOLOGIA (BARCELONA). 3821

0378-4843 See FCTL. FOLIA CHIMICA THEORETICA LATINA. 1052

0378-4851 See AFYA (NAIROBI). 3547

0378-486X See SRI LANKA JOURNAL OF THE HUMANITIES, THE. 2854

0378-5041 See OFFICIAL JOURNAL OF THE EUROPEAN COMMUNITIES: DEBATES OF THE EUROPEAN PARLIAMENT. 4670

0378-5068 See VOCATIONAL TRAINING. 1917

0378-5122 See MATURITAS. 3754

0378-5130 See WIRTSCHAFT UND GESELLSCHAFT. 1588

0378-5149 See OSTERREICHISCHE ZEITSCHRIFT FUER POLITIKWISSENSCHAFT. 4486

0378-5173 See INTERNATIONAL JOURNAL OF PHARMACEUTICS. 4308

0378-519X See DEVELOPMENTS IN CROP SCIENCE. 170

0378-5203 See JOURNAL OF ORGANOMETALLIC CHEMISTRY LIBRARY. 1043

0378-5378 See DOCPAL RESUMENES SOBRE POBLACION EN AMERICA LATINA. 4552

0378-5386 See BOLETIN DEMOGRAFICO - CENTRO LATINOAMERICANO DE DEMOGRAFIA. 4550

0378-5394 See BULLETIN D'INFORMATIONS SOCIALES. 1656

0378-5424 See TRAVAIL ET SOCIETE. 1715

0378-5467 See LABOUR EDUCATION. 1685

0378-5548 See REVISTA INTERNACIONAL DEL TRABAJO. 1708

0378-5564 See EDUCACION OBRERA. 1664

0378-5572 See EDUCATION OUVRIERE. 1664

0378-5599 See REVUE INTERNATIONALE DU TRAVAIL. 1708

0378-584X See ONKOLOGIE. 3822

0378-5866 See DEVELOPMENTAL NEUROSCIENCE. 3831

0378-5882 See OFFICIAL BULLETIN. SERIES A / INTERNATIONAL LABOUR OFFICE. 3152

0378-5890 See OFFICIAL BULLETIN. SERIES B / INTERNATIONAL LABOUR OFFICE. 1699

0378-5912 See TRENDS IN NEUROSCIENCES (REFERENCE ED.). 3847

0378-5920 See WORLD ECONOMY, THE. 1641

0378-5955 See HEARING RESEARCH. 3888

0378-6080 See SIDE EFFECTS OF DRUGS ANNUAL. 4329

0378-6099 See TOPICS IN PHOTOSYNTHESIS. 529

0378-6129 See RESEARCH MONOGRAPHS IN CELL AND TISSUE PHYSIOLOGY. 586

0378-620X See INTEGRAL EQUATIONS AND OPERATOR THEORY. 3509

0378-6218 See RESULTATE DER MATHEMATIK. 3531

0378-6277 See DIABETES (CARACAS). 3727

0378-6323 See INDIAN JOURNAL OF DERMATOLOGY, VENEREOLOGY AND LEPROLOGY. 3720

0378-6366 See MMR, MINERALS & METALS REVIEW. 4012

0378-6374 See NEDERLANDS TIJDSCHRIFT VOOR NATUURKUNDE (AMSTERDAM. 1991). 5132

0378-6501 See DRUGS UNDER EXPERIMENTAL AND CLINICAL RESEARCH. 4302

0378-651X See FINANCIAL MARKET TRENDS. 1491

0378-6617 See REVISTA GEOLOGICA DE CHILE. 1395

0378-6781 See NEWSLETTER ON DENGUE, YELLOW FEVER, AND AEDES AEGYPTI IN THE AMERICAS. 3621

0378-6862 See JAHRESBERICHT - LANDESMUSEUM JOANNEUM GRAZ. 4089

0378-6900 See ADVANCES IN CARDIOVASCULAR PHYSICS. 494

0378-6978 See OFFICIAL JOURNAL OF THE EUROPEAN COMMUNITIES : LEGISLATION. 3021

0378-6986 See OFFICIAL JOURNAL OF THE EUROPEAN COMMUNITIES : INFORMATION AND NOTICES. 3133

0378-7206 See INFORMATION & MANAGEMENT. 1254

0378-7346 See GYNECOLOGIC AND OBSTETRIC INVESTIGATION. 3761

0378-7354 See ADVANCES IN BIOLOGICAL PSYCHIATRY. 3919

0378-7362 See JUDGMENTS OF THE ADMINISTRATIVE TRIBUNAL OF THE INTERNATIONAL LABOUR ORGANISATION: ORDINARY SESSION. 3150

0378-7443 See RAHNAMAY-I MAJALLAH'HA-YI IRAN. 423

0378-7524 See HISTORY OF AGRICULTURE. 92

0378-7540 See CURRENT TRENDS IN LIFE SCIENCES. 507

0378-7559 See IRON AND STEEL (LUXEMBOURG, LUXEMBOURG : 1986). 4005

0378-7591 See REPORTS OF CASES BEFORE THE COURT OF JUSTICE AND THE COURT OF FIRST INSTANCE. 3038

0378-7656 See P-NOTES / FID, FEDERATION INTERNATIONALE DE DOCUMENTATION. 3240

0378-7699 See BOLETIN / INSTITUTO DEL MAR DEL PERU. 4163

0378-7753 See JOURNAL OF POWER SOURCES. 2118

0378-777X See ENVIRONMENTAL POLICY AND LAW. 3112

0378-7788 See ENERGY AND BUILDINGS. 614

0378-7796 See ELECTRIC POWER SYSTEMS RESEARCH. 2044

0378-7869 See BIBLIOGRAPHIE INTERNATIONALE D'HISTOIRE MILITAIRE / COMITE INTERNATIONAL DES SCIENCES HISTORIQUES, COMMISSION INTERNATIONALE D'HISTOIRE MILITAIRE COMPAREE, COMITE DE BIBLIOGRAPHIE. 4037

0378-7923 See MEMOIRES - ACADEMIE ROYALE DE BELGIQUE. CLASSE DES BEAUX-ARTS. COLLECTION IN 8. 325

0378-7931 See DEVIANCE ET SOCIETE. 4584

0378-7958 See PHARMA-FLASH. 4319

0378-7974 See REVISTA DE ESTUDIOS HISPANICOS (RIO PIEDRAS, P.R.). 3315

0378-7990 See AFRIBIBLIOS. 407

0378-8024 See JOURNAL OF TURKISH PHYTOPATHOLOGY, THE. 516

0378-8032 See GARCIA DE ORTA : SERIE DE ESTUDOS AGRONOMICOS. 89

0378-8113 See BANGLADESH VETERINARY JOURNAL. 5505

0378-8121 See JOURNAL OF BANGLADESH ACADEMY OF SCIENCES. 5118

0378-8148 See ATIRA TECHNICAL DIGEST. 5348

0378-8156 See INDIAN JOURNAL OF PHYSICAL ANTHROPOLOGY AND HUMAN GENETICS. 548

0378-8180 See JOURNAL OF OMAN STUDIES, THE. 2655

0378-8199 See MITTEILUNGEN DER OSTERREICHISCHEN GEOLOGISCHEN GESELLSCHAFT. 1388

0378-8202 See VEROFFENTLICHUNGEN AUS DEM NATURHISTORISCHEN MUSEUM WIEN. 4173

0378-8407 See TEMPO MEDICAL INTERNATIONAL. 3645

0378-8482 See REVISTA GEOGRAFICA DE CHILE TERRA AUSTRALIS. 2574

0378-8504 See AKTUELLE PROBLEME IN CHIRURGIE UND ORTHOPADIE. 3958

0378-8512 See KOREAN JOURNAL OF BIOCHEMISTRY. 490

0378-8601 See INFORME DE INVESTIGACION - CENTRO DE INVESTIGACIONES TECHNOGICAS. 5113

0378-8644 See ALMANACH - OSTERREICHISCHE AKADEMIE DER WISSENSCHAFTEN. 2513

0378-8652 See ANZEIGER / OSTERREICHISCHE AKADEMIE DER WISSENSCHAFTEN, PHILOSOPHISCH-HISTORISCHE KLASSE. 2675

0378-8660 See JAHRBUCH DER OSTERREICHISCHEN BYZANTINISTIK. 1078

0378-8733 See SOCIAL NETWORKS. 5259

0378-8741 See JOURNAL OF ETHNOPHARMACOLOGY. 4311

0378-8857 See ZAMBIA JOURNAL OF SCIENCE AND TECHNOLOGY. 5172

0378-8865 See HARVEST (PORT MORESBY). 91

0378-8911 See ASIAN CULTURE QUARTERLY. 2646

0378-8989 See ANALELE UNIVERSITATII BUCURESTI : BIOLOGIE. 441

0378-8997 See BULLETIN DE L'ACADEMIE DES SCIENCES AGRICOLES ET FORESTIERES. 69

0378-9004 See RESEARCH REPORTS - INTERNATIONAL INSTITUTE FOR APPLIED SYSTEMS ANALYSIS. 5147

0378-9292 See ORANJE VRYSTAAT EN NOORD-KAAPSE GIDS ORANGE FREE STATE AND NORTHERN CAPE DIRECTORY. 2500

0378-9411 See SOUTH AFRICAN OPTOMETRIST, SUID-AFRIKAANSE OOGKUNDIGE, THE. 4217

0378-9454 See VISTAS IN PLANT SCIENCES. 530

0378-9489 See BULLETIN D'INFORMATION - COMITE EURO-INTERNATIONAL DU BETON. 605

0378-9519 See JOURNAL OF ENTOMOLOGICAL RESEARCH. 5587

0378-9535 See URJA. 1960

0378-9551 See REVISTA SEGURIDAD. 1708

0378-9578 See ENERGIA E INDUSTRIA. 1972

0378-9608 See BOLETIM DA FACULDADE DE FARMACIA DE COIMBRA. 4294

0378-9675 See BULETINUL STIINTIFIC SI TEHNIC AL INSTITUTULUI POLITEHNIC "TRAIAN VUIA" TIMISOARA. SERIA CHIMIE. 2008

0378-9721 See BULLETIN OF ANIMAL HEALTH AND PRODUCTION IN AFRICA. 208

0378-9888 See NED. GEREF. TEOLOGIESE TYDSKRIF. 4980

0378-9896 See SUPLEMENTO ANTROPOLOGICO - UNIVERSIDAD CATOLICA. 246

0378-9993 See INDUSTRY AND ENVIRONMENT (ENGLISH EDITION). 2863

0379-0002 See REVIEWS ON POWDER METALLURGY AND PHYSICAL CERAMICS. 4018

0379-0037 See INDIAN JOURNAL OF APPLIED LINGUISTICS. 3286

0379-0207 See DENKSCHRIFTEN - OESTERREICHISCHE AKADEMIE DER WISSENSCHAFTEN, MATHEMATISCH-NATURWISSENSCHAFTLICHE KLASSE. 3503

0379-0231 See VEROFFENTLICHUNGEN DES TIROLER LANDESMUSEUM FERDINANDEUM. 2714

0379-0266 See ESTUDIOS DE LA SEGURIDAD SOCIAL / AISS. 1668

0379-0282 See INTERNATIONAL REVUE FUER SOZIALE SICHERHEIT. 1680

0379-0290 See CURRENT RESEARCH IN SOCIAL SECURITY. 5281

0379-0304 See SEGURIDAD SOCIAL. 1710

0379-0312 See REVUE INTERNATIONALE DE SECURITE SOCIALE. 5306

0379-0355 See METHODS AND FINDINGS IN EXPERIMENTAL AND CLINICAL PHARMACOLOGY. 4315

0379-0363 See AGENTS AND ACTIONS. SUPPLEMENTS. 3978

0379-038X See ANNALS OF THE NATIONAL ACADEMY OF MEDICAL SCIENCES (INDIA). 3550

0379-0401 See BULLETIN - BISMUTH INSTITUTE. 3999

0379-0436 See COMPARATIVE PHYSIOLOGY AND ECOLOGY. 579

0379-0444 See FORAGE RESEARCH. 88

0379-0452 See GEO-ECO-TROP. 2216

0379-0460 See GLASS UDYOG. 2590

0379-0479 See INDIAN JOURNAL OF CRYOGENICS. 4405

0379-0517 See MADRAS VETERINARY COLLEGE ANNUAL, THE. 5516

0379-055X See TOBACCO RESEARCH. 5374

0379-0622 See ZAMBEZIA. 5226

0379-0703 See JOURNAL OF OMAN STUDIES : SCIENTIFIC RESULTS OF THE ROYAL GEOGRAPHICAL SOCIETY. 2567

0379-0738 See FORENSIC SCIENCE INTERNATIONAL. 3740

0379-0762 See REVISTA INTERNACIONAL DE CIENCIAS SOCIALES. 5216

0379-0819 See JAHRBUCH DES OBEROSTERREICHISCHEN MUSEALVEREINES. BERICHTE. 354

0379-0827 See AGRICULTURAL ECONOMICS REPORT. AGRICULTURAL RESEARCH INSTITUTE (NICOSIA). 49

0379-0940 See AMERICAS (ENGLISH EDITION). 2551

0379-0991 See EUROPEAN ECONOMY. 1489

0379-1130 See JOURNAL - RUBBER RESEARCH INSTITUTE OF SRI LANKA. 177

0379-1173 See ISTANBUL TIP FAKULTESI MECMUASI. MONOGRAFI SERISINDEN. 3590

0379-1335 See OPERATIONAL HYDROLOGY REPORT. 1417

0379-1416 See BERICHTE DES NATURWISSENSCHAFTLICH-MEDIZINISCHEN VEREINS IN INNSBRUCK. 5088

0379-1432 See MITTEILUNGEN DER ABTEILUNG FUER GEOLOGIE, PALAONTOLOGIE UND BERGBAU AM LANDESMUSEUM JOANNEUM. SH. 1388

0379-1521 See HANGUK UIKWAHAK : THE OFFICIAL JOURNAL OF RESEARCH INSTITUTE OF MEDICAL SCIENCE OF KOREA. 3580

0379-153X See PORRIMER (SENUR). 1028

0379-1580 See BULLETIN - MINERAL RESOURCES DIVISION (SUVA). 1370

0379-1629 See REVISTA MEDICA DE PANAMA. 3636

0379-1645 See UNDP BUSINESS BULLETIN. 1525

0379-170X See MINERIA Y PETROLEO. 4264

0379-1718 See PROCEEDINGS OF THE INTERNATIONAL BIOMETRIC CONFERENCE. 469

0379-1726 See DIQIU HUAXUE. 1373

0379-1734 See ILO INFORMATION. U.S. EDITION. 1677

0379-1807 See BULLETIN DE LA SOCIETE BELGE DE GEOLOGIE. 1368

0379-184X See COMPTE RENDU DES RECHERCHES (STATION DAMELIORATION DES PLANTES, GEMBLOUX). 76

0379-2056 See EUROPEAN ECONOMY. SUPPLEMENT A, RECENT ECONOMIC TRENDS / COMMISSION OF THE ECONOMIC COMMUNITIES, DIRECTORATE-GENERAL FOR ECONOMIC AND FINANCIAL AFFAIRS. 1490

0379-2110 See EUROPEAN ECONOMY. SUPPLEMENT B, BUSINESS AND CONSUMER SURVEY RESULTS. 1490

0379-2218 See GENERAL INFORMATION PROGRAMME. UNISIST NEWSLETTER. 5107

0379-2269 See CHILDREN IN THE TROPICS. 3985

0379-2285 See ESA JOURNAL. 18

0379-2390 See REVISTA TRANSPORTURILOR SI TELECOMUNICATIILOR. 5391

0379-2455 See DESERTIFICATION CONTROL. 2227

0379-2595 See JAHRBUCH - STEIERMARKISCHE GEBIETSKRANKENKASSE FUR ARBEITER UND ANGESTELLTE. 3591

0379-2617 See MOTHER & CHILD (LAHORE). 2283

0379-2811 See BULLETIN (INTERNATIONAL ASSOCIATION OF LIGHTHOUSE AUTHORITIES). 4175

0379-2870 See PHILIPPINE LETTER, THE. 703

0379-2927 See JOURNAL FOR THE HISTORY OF ARABIC SCIENCE. 5118

0379-3044 See JOURNAL OF THE EGYPTIAN VETERINARY MEDICAL ASSOCIATION. 5513

0379-3109 See DOSSIER DE L'EUROPE. 1480

0379-3133 See EUROPEAN FILE. 2516

0379-3176 See JOURNAL OF THE SOCIETY OF COMMUNITY MEDICINE HONG KONG. 3599

0379-3419 See GUJARAT STATISTICAL REVIEW. 3542

0379-3435 See JOURNAL OF THE INLAND FISHERIES SOCIETY OF INDIA. 2307

0379-3478 See BULLETIN DE LIAISON DU COMITE INTERAFRICAIN D'ETUDES HYDRAULIQUES. 2088

0379-3494 See PUBLICATION - CENTRAL BOARD OF IRRIGATION AND POWER. 123

0379-3575 See AL-MAGALLA AL-MISRIYYA LI-L-MAHASIL. 162

0379-3664 See SCHWEIZERISCHE ZEITSCHRIFT FUER SOZIOLOGIE. 5257

0379-3680 See FID DIRECTORY. 4649

0379-3699 See ANNALES DE L'ECONOMIE PUBLIQUE, SOCIALE ET COOPERATIVE, LES. 1462

0379-3737 See SRI LANKA LABOUR GAZETTE. 1711

0379-3885 See JOURNAL OF INDIAN PSYCHOLOGY. 4597

0379-4024 See JOURNAL OF OPERATOR THEORY. 3514

0379-4032 See ISLAM AND THE MODERN WORLD. 5042

0379-4121 See ANNUAL DRUG DATA REPORT. 4291

0379-4172 See YICHUAN XUEBAO. 552

0379-4180 See TAIWAN SHUICHANXUE HUI KAN. 558

0379-4199 See TAIWAN SHENGYANJIU GONGMAIJU YONGYE SHIYAN-SUO YANJIU HUIBAO. 5373

0379-4229 See EUROPEAN APPLIED RESEARCH REPORTS. NUCLEAR SCIENCE AND TECHNOLOGY SECTION. 2155

0379-4288 See BANGLADESH HORTICULTURE. 2410

0379-4296 See BANGLADESH JOURNAL OF AGRICULTURAL SCIENCES. 64

0379-4318 See JOURNAL OF THE INSTITUTION OF ENGINEERS, BANGLADESH. 1983

0379-4350 See SOUTH AFRICAN JOURNAL OF CHEMISTRY. 992

0379-4369 See SOUTH AFRICAN JOURNAL OF WILDLIFE RESEARCH. 2205

0379-4377 See SOUTH AFRICAN JOURNAL OF PHYSICS. 4421

0379-4407 See OZW, OESTERREICHISCHE ZEITSCHRIFT FUER WIRTSCHAFTSRECHT. 3102

0379-4458 See ZEITSCHRIFT FUER MENSCHENKUNDE. 248

0379-4490 See HONG KONG PSYCHOLOGICAL SOCIETY BULLETIN. 4588

0379-4520 See ANNUAL REPORT / CHAMBER OF MINES OF SOUTH AFRICA. 2133

0379-4687 See CHEMSA. 2011

0379-4830 See CABO. 2638

0379-4857 See ACTA MEDICA DOMINICANA : REVISTA CIENTIFICA PARA MEDICOS. 3544

0379-4954 See BULLETIN DES ETUDES PORTUGAISES ET BRESILIENNES. 3270

0379-5071 See DEFENDER (NAIROBI). 4773

0379-508X See ACTA BOTANICA INDICA. 497

0379-5098 See BULLETIN - INDIAN GEOLOGISTS' ASSOCIATION. 1369

0379-511X See INDIAN GEOLOGICAL INDEX. 1382

0379-5136 See INDIAN JOURNAL OF MARINE SCIENCES. 1450

0379-5160 See JOURNAL - INDIAN ACADEMY OF GEOSCIENCE. 1384

0379-5179 See KAVAKA. 575

0379-5225 See PALAEONTOLOGIA INDICA. 4229

0379-5284 See SAUDI MEDICAL JOURNAL. 3638

0379-5349 See WIENER MITTEILUNGEN, WASSER, ABWASSER, GEWASSER. 5549

0379-5357 See MINERALIENFREUND. 1441

0379-542X See CHEIRON. 5507

0379-5446 See INDIAN FOUNDRY JOURNAL. 4003

0379-5462 See IPPTA. 4234

0379-5470 See JOURNAL OF ARMAMENT STUDIES. 4048

0379-5489 See JOURNAL OF NUCLEAR AGRICULTURE AND BIOLOGY. 100

0379-5497 See JOURNAL OF THE INDIAN ACADEMY OF WOOD SCIENCE. 2402

0379-5527 See MECHANICAL ENGINEERING BULLETIN. 2121

0379-556X See PHARMSTUDENT. 4324

0379-5594 See SEED RESEARCH. 186

0379-5608 See SOAPS, DETERGENTS & TOILETRIES REVIEW. 1030

0379-5640 See REUNION - COMITE INTERNATIONAL DES POIDS ET MESURES, COMITE CONSULTATIF POUR LES ETALONS DE MESURE DES RAYONNEMENTS IONISANTS, SECTION II. 4451

0379-5659 See REUNION - COMITE INTERNATIONAL DES POIDS ET MESURES, COMITE CONSULTATIF POUR LES ETALONS DE MESURE DES RAYONNEMENTS IONISANTS, SECTION III. 4032

0379-5721 See FOOD AND NUTRITION BULLETIN. 4191

0379-5829 See SACCHARUM. 185

0379-5837 See CERETARI AGRONOMICE IN MOLDOVA. 73

0379-587X See BOGAZICI UNIVERSITESI DERGISI : MUHENDISLIK. 1966

0379-5896 See CHIMICA ACTA TURCICA. 971

0379-5918 See HACETTEPE BULLETIN OF NATURAL SCIENCES AND ENGINEERING. 1356

0379-6000 See FOOD REVIEW. 2339

0379-6175 See SOUTH AFRICAN JOURNAL OF PHYSIOTHERAPY. 3642

0379-6205 See TYDSKRIF VIR STUDIES IN EKONOMIE EN EKONOMETRIE. 1525

0379-6264 See NOTE D'INFORMATION TECHNIQUE - CENTRE SCIENTIFIQUE ET TECHNIQUE DE LA CONSTRUCTION. 622

0379-6566 See ESA SP. 18

0379-6779 See SYNTHETIC METALS. 4021

0379-6787 See SOLAR ENERGY MATERIALS AND SOLAR CELLS : AN INTERNATIONAL JOURNAL DEVOTED TO PHOTOVOLTAIC, PHOTOTHERMAL, AND PHOTOCHEMICAL SOLAR ENERGY CONVERSION. 1957

0379-6914 See ABSTRACTS - SYMPOSIUM ON RECENT ADVANCES IN THE ANALYTICAL CHEMISTRY OF POLLUTANTS. 1012

0379-6922 See MUNDO NUEVO. 4529

0379-7015 See INFORMACIONES ESTADISTICAS. 3786

0379-7031 See WELEDA KORRESPONDENZBLATTER FUR ARZTE. 4332

0379-704X See SOCIAL SECURITY DOCUMENTATION. AFRICAN SERIES. 5308

0379-7074 See AFRICAN NEWS SHEET / INTERNATIONAL SOCIAL SECURITY ASSOCIATION. 5270

0379-7112 See FIRE SAFETY JOURNAL. 2290

0379-7309 See TUNG HSUEH PAO, TA. 5237

0379-7368 See JOURNAL OF THE CHINESE BIOCHEMICAL SOCIETY. 490

0379-7376 See NENG YUAN CHI KAN. 1950

0379-7449 See PSYCHOTRONIK. 4242

0379-7465 See HOKHMAH. 5061

0379-7481 See ACTA OCEANOGRAPHICA TAIWANICA. 1445

0379-7511 See DAIHAN GWANSANHAG HOI JI. 2138

0379-752X See DAIHAN JAIHWAR NUIHAG HOIJI. 4380

0379-7570 See CHINESE JOURNAL OF MATHEMATICS. 3500

0379-7627 See TECHNICAL BULLETIN - ASPAC, FOOD & FERTILIZER TECHNOLOGY CENTER. 2359

0379-7635 See RASAYANA SAMIKSHA. 990

0379-7678 See CHEMICAL ENGINEERING RESEARCH BULLETIN. 2010

0379-7724 See HIGHER EDUCATION IN EUROPE. 1828

0379-7759 See SIDERURGIA LATINOAMERICANA. 4019

0379-7791 See MESOPOTAMIA JOURNAL OF AGRICULTURE. 108

0379-7880 See ANALELE STIINTIFICE ALE UNIVERSITATII "AL. I. CUZA" DIN IASI. SERIE NOUA. SECTIUNEA III E, LINGVISTICA. 3264

0379-7899 See ANALELE STIINTIFICE ALE UNIVERSITATII "AL. I. CUZA" DIN IASI. SERIE NOUA. SECTIUNEA III F, LITERATURA. 3361

0379-7988 See BULLETIN OF THE HIGH INSTITUTE OF PUBLIC HEALTH, THE. 4769

0379-7996 See COMPENDIA RHEUMATOLOGICA. 3567

0379-8046 See SOUTH AFRICAN JOURNAL OF COMMUNICATION DISORDERS. 3846

0379-8070 See WORLD HEALTH STATISTICS QUARTERLY. 4811

0379-8097 See BIOLOGICAL MEMOIRS. 445

0379-8100 See CIOMS CALENDAR. 3564

0379-8127 See DOCUMENTS LIST. 4502

0379-8194 See JOURNAL OF SIKH STUDIES. 4970

0379-8267 See TREATY SERIES - UNITED NATIONS. 3137

0379-8275 See VETERINARIA TROPICAL. 5524

0379-8305 See DEVELOPMENTAL PHARMACOLOGY AND THERAPEUTICS. 4299

0379-8321 See MAGALLAT AL-GAMIYYAT AL-KIMYAWIYAAT AL-IRAQIWAT. 985

0379-8402 See PHILOSOPHICA. 4355

0379-8410 See OFFICIAL JOURNAL OF THE INSTITUTE OF LABOUR RELATIONS, UNIVERSITY OF SOUTH AFRICA. 1699

0379-8461 See DECISIONS AND REPORTS - EUROPEAN COMMISSION OF HUMAN RIGHTS. 4507

0379-8577 See CURATIONIS (PRETORIA). 3854

0379-8585 See ARCHITECTURE & COMPORTEMENT. 289

0379-864X See CHEMICAL SENSES. 485

0379-8658 See GREENHILL JOURNAL OF ADMINISTRATION. 4653

0379-8674 See MONTHLY OPERATIONAL SUMMARY. 1506

0379-8860 See SUID-AFRIKAANSE TYDSKRIF VIR ETNOLOGIE. 246

0379-8895 See SOUTH AFRICAN YEARBOOK OF INTERNATIONAL LAW. 3136

0379-8992 See SA - VERBRUIKER, DIE. 1299

0379-9069 See S.A. JOURNAL FOR RESEARCH IN SPORT PHYSICAL EDUCATION AND RECREATION. 1858

0379-9123 See REVISTA DE LA SOCIEDAD CIENTIFICA DEL PARAGUAY. 5148

0379-9468 See QUAESTIONES MATHEMATICAE : JOURNAL OF THE SOUTH AFRICAN MATHEMATICAL SOCIETY : TYDSKRIF VAN DIE SUID-AFRIKAANSE WISKUNDEVERENIGING. 3529

0379-9506 See GARCIA DE ORTA : SERIE DE BOTANICA. 511

0379-9522 See GEOTECNIA. 2024

0379-9557 See THEOLOGICAL REVIEW (BEIRUT, LEBANON). 5003

0379-9824 See CONCRETE JOHANNESBURG. 608

0379-9867 See CONTREE / RAAD VIR GEESTESWETENSKAPLIKE NAVORSING, INSTITUUT VIR GESKIEDENISNAVORSING, AFDELING STREEKGESKIEDENIS. 2638

0380-0008 See MANITOBA DECISIONS, CIVIL AND CRIMINAL CASES. 3006

0380-0121 See MENNONITE REPORTER. 5789

0380-0180 See MARKETING SOCIAL. 932

0380-0229 See ELECTRIC POWER STATISTICS (OTTAWA. MONTHLY ED.). 4697

0380-0334 See COMMUNICATIONS (OTTAWA). 1152

0380-0369 See VISTI - INSTYTUTU SV. VOLODYMYRA. 2275

0380-0547 See INFOMAT (ENGLISH ED.). 4698

0380-0601 See MOUTHPIECE (TORONTO). 4132

0380-0660 See SOVIET PANORAMA. 2710

0380-0768 See ANNUAL REPORT - COUNCIL OF MARITIME PREMIERS. 4515

0380-0822 See STEEL WIRE AND SPECIFIED WIRE PRODUCTS. 3488

0380-0830 See BIOGRAPHIES CANADIENNES-FRANCAISES. 430

0380-0857 See IF. INDUSTRIALIZATION FORUM. 616

0380-0881 See NORTHPOINT. 5134

0380-0903 See JOURNAL OF RHEUMATOLOGY. SUPPLEMENT, THE. 3805

0380-0946 See LETTRE DE L'ABBE GRAVEL, LA. 5062

0380-0954 See TRIP (MONTREAL). 2548

0380-0962 See KALENDAR SVITLA. 5031

0380-1306 See ALBERTA LEARNING RESOURCES JOURNAL. 1888

0380-1314 See CONSENSUS (OTTAWA). 4030

0380-1330 See JOURNAL OF GREAT LAKES RESEARCH. 1416

0380-1373 See METU KALENDORIUS - PRISIKELIMO PARAPIJA, EKONOMINE SEKCIJA. 2490

0380-1403 See UKRAJINSKYJ ZURNALIST. 2925

0380-1438 See CRDI EXPLORE, LE. 2908

0380-1470 See TRELLIS. 2432

0380-1489 See CANADIAN STUDIES IN POPULATION. 4550
0380-1616 See NEWSLEAF - ONTARIO GENEALOGICAL SOCIETY. 2462
0380-1624 See ONTARIO PIPELINE. 5537
0380-1667 See TUMBLEWEED. 5237
0380-1691 See NEWSLETTER - VANCOUVER ISLAND REGIONAL LIBRARY. 3236
0380-1705 See BULLETIN DES MEMBRES - SYNDICAT DES FONCTIONNAIRES PROVINCIAUX DU QUEBEC. 1656
0380-1721 See CAHIERS QUEBECOIS DE DEMOGRAPHIE. 4550
0380-1799 See ORCHESTRA CANADA. 4144
0380-1896 See CCTA NEWSLETTER. 1814
0380-1969 See ONTARIO TECHNOLOGIST, THE. 5136
0380-1977 See BULLETIN DU C. R. I. U. 2816
0380-2000 See QUEEN STREET MAGAZINE. 328
0380-2051 See JOURNAL DU NORD-OUEST, LE. 5787
0380-2159 See KREDYTOVA KOOPERATYVA BUDUCHNIST'. 1542
0380-223X See GENERAL INSURANCE REGISTER. 2881
0380-2299 See MODERN FINISHING METHODS. 4012
0380-2329 See GAS UTILITIES. 4258
0380-2361 See CANADIAN JOURNAL OF EDUCATION. 1730
0380-2736 See REVUE HIPPIQUE, LA. 2802
0380-2752 See PRINT ACTION. 4567
0380-2760 See MILIEU (SAINTE-FOY). 2198
0380-2779 See HORSE RACING MAGAZINE. 2799
0380-2795 See NEWSLETTER - ONTARIO CAMPUS CULTURE ASSOCIATION. 386
0380-285X See ONION. 361
0380-2949 See SANDESH (WINNIPEG). 2272
0380-2957 See INSIDE (NELSON). 3396
0380-299X See LINK (WINNIPEG. 1974). 2658
0380-3082 See SERVO LOISIR. 4917
0380-3120 See ANNUAL REPORT - ALBERTA AGRICULTURAL DEVELOPMENT CORPORATION. 60
0380-3147 See FORUM (DON MILLS). 2881
0380-3163 See FLEURISTE DU QUEBEC. 2435
0380-321X See FORET CONSERVATION. 2382
0380-3252 See UNIMA CANADA NOUVELLES. 389
0380-3279 See ALBERTA MUSEUMS REVIEW. 4083
0380-3333 See GREENMASTER. 4897
0380-335X See GAM ON YACHTING. 593
0380-352X See FEATHER FANCIER. 211
0380-3570 See CANADA, BELGIUM, LUXEMBOURG. 818
0380-3589 See TEACHING FORUM. 1850
0380-3651 See HOG MARKET PLACE QUARTERLY. 212
0380-3686 See KING TOWNSHIP WEEKLY, THE. 5788
0380-3694 See TOWN OF VAUGHAN WEEKLY, THE. 5796
0380-3775 See ANNUAIRE POLK DE SEPT-ILES. 2554
0380-3961 See ANNUAIRE POLK DE RIMOUSKI ET MONT-JOLI QUEBEC. 2554
0380-4127 See NOSTRADAMUS. EDITION QUEBECOISE. 4242
0380-4135 See PASS PROMOTER, THE. 5792
0380-4208 See LAND COMPENSATION REPORTS. 2993
0380-4275 See RESERVES OF COAL, PROVINCE OF ALBERTA. 1955
0380-4321 See ALBERTA COAL INDUSTRY ANNUAL STATISTICS. 1961
0380-4372 See MLLE-ACTUALITE. 2539
0380-4437 See MATTHEWS' LIST. 1116
0380-4542 See OAK BAY STAR. 5791
0380-4569 See TIMES OF NORTH AND WEST VANCOUVER, THE. 5796

0380-4585 See RAPPORT ANNUEL - REGIE DES RENTES DU QUEBEC. 2891
0380-4607 See LANGFORD TO COLWOOD TELEGRAM. 5788
0380-4615 See OIL PIPE LINE TRANSPORT (MONTHLY ED.). 4270
0380-4623 See MUSEOGRAMME. 4091
0380-464X See PRODUCTION, SHIPMENTS, AND STOCKS ON HAND OF SAWMILLS EAST OF THE ROCKIES. 2404
0380-4712 See WORLD OF ASP. 4808
0380-4720 See CENTRE STAGE MAGAZINE. 5362
0380-4771 See JOINT. 1832
0380-478X See NEWS LETTER - MCGILL UNIVERSITY COMPUTING CENTRE. 1197
0380-4941 See BULLETIN DE L'ASSOCIATION DE PARENTS DU COLLEGE VIEUX MONTREAL. 1812
0380-5042 See FRUIT AND VEGETABLE PRESERVATION. 2342
0380-5123 See EDMONTON CULTURE VULTURE, THE. 384
0380-5301 See ABBOTSFORD-CLEARBROOK DIRECTORY (BUSINESS EDITION). 2553
0380-5387 See RAPPORT ANNUEL, REGIME DES ALLOCATIONS FAMILIALES DU QUEBEC. 5303
0380-5522 See NORTHERN PERSPECTIVES. 2201
0380-5743 See VISUAL ARTS HANDBOOK. 367
0380-5751 See SPORTS DIRECTORY. 4922
0380-5786 See ASPHALT ROOFING. 633
0380-5832 See NEWFOUNDLAND QUARTERLY (1971). 2748
0380-5956 See TRAVELLER ACCOMMODATION STATISTICS. 5501
0380-5964 See RAILWAY OPERATING STATISTICS (MONTHLY ED.). 5436
0380-5980 See ON TARGET (CANADIAN EDITION). 4485
0380-6057 See ONTARIO GRAPE GROWER, THE. 2426
0380-6073 See TELESEMAINE. 1140
0380-6103 See QUOTIDIEN DE STATISTIQUE CANADA. 4699
0380-6146 See RETAIL TRADE (MONTHLY ED.). 957
0380-6197 See THUNDER BAY CAMPING GUIDE. 4879
0380-6251 See OTTAWA R & D REPORT. 5137
0380-6286 See CAMPUS BOOK STORES. 4821
0380-6294 See MOTION PICTURE THEATRES AND FILM DISTRIBUTORS. 4080
0380-6308 See RAILWAY CARLOADINGS (MONTHLY ED.). 5435
0380-6596 See EXILE (TORONTO). 3386
0380-6618 See PILOT (MONTREAL). 31
0380-6723 See PLANS. 2831
0380-6766 See PHOTO COMMERCE EXPRESS. 849
0380-6774 See GAZETTE DE L'UNIVERSITE DE MONCTON. 1091
0380-6804 See LABOUR FORCE (MONTHLY ED.). 1535
0380-6847 See COAL AND COKE STATISTICS. 2003
0380-6898 See CEMENT (OTTAWA). 606
0380-691X See CONSUMER PRICES AND PRICE INDEXES. 1471
0380-6936 See EMPLOYMENT, EARNINGS AND HOURS. 1666
0380-6936 See EMPLOYMENT, EARNINGS AND HOURS. 1532
0380-6987 See COMMUNIQUE - CANADIAN AUTOMOBILE ASSOCIATION. 5412
0380-6995 See STUDIES IN CANADIAN LITERATURE (FREDERICTON, N.B.). 3441
0380-7037 See CORRUGATED BOXES AND WRAPPERS. 4218
0380-7045 See DEPARTMENT STORE SALES AND STOCKS. 953
0380-7061 See FACTORY SALES OF ELECTRIC STORAGE BATTERIES. 2054
0380-707X See FOOTWEAR STATISTICS. 1088

0380-7150 See BULLETIN A B Q. 3197
0380-7223 See GYPSUM PRODUCTS. 632
0380-7762 See RACER (TORONTO). 4914
0380-7770 See PROCEEDINGS - CONVENTION, CANADIAN UNION OF PUBLIC EMPLOYEES. 1703
0380-7789 See CONVENTION REPORT - C U P E. 1661
0380-7797 See CANADA'S MINERAL PRODUCTION, PRELIMINARY ESTIMATES. 2136
0380-7843 See TELEPHONE STATISTICS. 1125
0380-7851 See PRIMARY IRON AND STEEL. 4016
0380-7894 See WHOLESALE TRADE. 857
0380-7916 See PROBE (LONDON). 2239
0380-8025 See PUBLISHER (OTTAWA). 4818
0380-8068 See DIRECTORY, MEMBER LIBRARIES, GEORGIAN BAY REGIONAL LIBRARY SYSTEM. 3206
0380-8076 See BULLETIN - GEORGIAN BAY REGIONAL LIBRARY SYSTEM. 3198
0380-8149 See RING, THE. 1846
0380-8181 See ST. JOHN NEWS. 5311
0380-8246 See LIVRE DE L'ANNEE. 1927
0380-8254 See VIE LITURGIQUE. 5038
0380-8297 See PUBLICATION - SASKATCHEWAN ADVISORY COUNCIL ON THE STATUS OF WOMEN. 5565
0380-8300 See STEWARDS' LEGISLATIVE HANDBOOK. 3154
0380-8378 See SUGAR SITUATION, THE. 2359
0380-8491 See NEWSLETTER - LEARNING RESOURCES COUNCIL OF THE ALBERTA TEACHERS' ASSOCIATION. 1867
0380-8572 See GREEN LEAVES. BRITISH COLUMBIA EDITION. 2384
0380-8629 See REFINED PETROLEUM PRODUCTS (MONTHLY ED.). 4276
0380-8718 See VISIBLE GRAIN SUPPLIES AND DISPOSITION. 204
0380-8815 See PRISMA (SASKATOON). 3311
0380-8831 See ONTARIO COUNCIL BULLETIN. 4671
0380-8866 See SHORE LINE, THE. 2783
0380-8874 See REPORTER (PORT ELGIN). 5794
0380-8912 See SUN (LEAMINGTON). 5795
0380-9102 See A T A MAGAZINE. 1887
0380-9129 See CALGARY CORD, THE. 4385
0380-917X See GRAPHIC ARTS PURCHASE PREFERENCE STUDY. 379
0380-9218 See CANADIAN JOURNAL OF INFORMATION SCIENCE. 3199
0380-9307 See DELIBERATIONS DE L'ASSOCIATION DENTAIRE CANADIENNE. 1320
0380-9455 See CANADA ON STAGE. 5362
0380-9463 See BRAND RECOGNITION STUDY : OFFICE EQUIPMENT & METHODS. 922
0380-9501 See COMPUTING STUDIES. 1257
0380-951X See ELECTRIC POWER STATISTICS. VOLUME 1. ANNUAL ELECTRIC POWER SURVEY OF CAPABILITY AND LOAD. 1962
0380-9552 See VANCOUVER (VANCOUVER, 1975). 5498
0380-9579 See LIAISON (OTTAWA). 3223
0380-9633 See MEGADRILOGICA. 5591
0380-9714 See COURRIER PEDAGOGIQUE, 1ER CYCLE DE L'ELEMENTAIRE. 1734
0380-9757 See COURRIER DE L'ENSEIGNEMENT INDIVIDUALISE A TOUTES LES ANIMATRICES ET A TOUS LES ANIMATEURS DU 2E CYCLE DE L'ELEMENTAIRE, LE. 3275
0380-9803 See ANNUAL REPORT - MANITOBA ENVIRONMENTAL COUNCIL. 2160
0380-9811 See REVUE COMMERCE (MONTREAL. 1975). 850
0380-982X See ARMS COLLECTING. 2771
0381-0003 See BULLETIN - SOCIETE DES JEUX DU QUEBEC. 4858
0381-0119 See NEWSLETTER - FRONTENAC HISTORIC FOUNDATION. 304
0381-0283 See HARRISTON REVIEW, THE. 5786

ISSN Index

0381-0402 *See* J. IIC-CG : JOURNAL OF THE INTERNATIONAL INSTITUTE FOR CONSERVATION, CANADIAN GROUP. **353**

0381-0410 *See* RESOURCES PAPER - UNIVERSITY OF BRITISH COLUMBIA, DEPARTMENT OF ECONOMICS. **1517**

0381-0720 See MCGILL MEDICAL JOURNAL. **3606**

0381-078X *See* SUPERFICIE DES PRINCIPALES GRANDES CULTURES. **189**

0381-0828 *See* ECONOMISTE (QUEBEC). **1559**

0381-0917 *See* INDICATOR (NANAIMO). **4848**

0381-0925 *See* CONTINUUM (DOWNSVIEW). **2956**

0381-095X *See* COMMUNICATOR (SPRINGHILL). **3160**

0381-0992 *See* RENOVATION BRICOLAGE. **626**

0381-1018 *See* FORUM (TORONTO. 1975). **1825**

0381-1050 *See* JR. RIDER, THE. **2800**

0381-1123 *See* QUEBEC NATURE. **4878**

0381-1158 *See* RUFANTHOLOGY. **3432**

0381-131X *See* INFORMATOR (MONTREAL). **2982**

0381-1352 *See* FCM FORUM (ENGLISH ED.). **4647**

0381-145X *See* 21ST GENERATION, THE. **2436**

0381-1476 *See* PROGRAM - CANADIAN LIBRARY ASSOCIATION, CONFERENCE. **3242**

0381-1522 *See* ORGANISATION POPULAIRE. **5300**

0381-1638 *See* UNIVERSITY OF TORONTO FACULTY OF LAW REVIEW. **3069**

0381-1751 *See* PROCEEDINGS OF THE MICROSCOPICAL SOCIETY OF CANADA. **573**

0381-1786 *See* FORESTRY TECHNICAL REPORT. **2382**

0381-1794 *See* SOCIETY (MONTREAL). **5260**

0381-1875 *See* DONT ACTE. **669**

0381-1913 *See* EXCELSIOR (QUEBEC). **1091**

0381-193X *See* ACTUA (MONTREAL). **1854**

0381-2332 *See* ONTARIO BUDGET. **4739**

0381-2510 *See* ANNUAL REPORT OF THE LAW REFORM COMMISSION OF BRITISH COLUMBIA. **2935**

0381-2650 *See* FOREST RESEARCH NOTE. **2381**

0381-2995 *See* NATIONAL AIR POLLUTION SURVEILLANCE. ANNUAL SUMMARY. **2237**

0381-3010 *See* GRAIN STATISTICS WEEKLY. **153**

0381-3398 *See* LIVRE DES FEUX, DES BOUEES ET DES SIGNAUX DE BRUME. EAUX INTERIEURES. **4178**

0381-3401 *See* LISTS OF LIGHTS, BUOYS AND FOG SIGNALS. INLAND WATERS. **4178**

0381-3649 *See* POULTRY MARKET REPORT. **218**

0381-3746 *See* THIS MAGAZINE. **2493**

0381-3789 *See* HORIZONS (TORONTO. 1966). **1829**

0381-3878 *See* REPORT OF THE MINISTRY OF COLLEGES AND UNIVERSITIES. **1844**

0381-4130 *See* CALENDAR OF EXPIRING COLLECTIVE AGREEMENTS. **1657**

0381-4327 *See* PUBLIC CONTRIBUTIONS ACT ... ANNUAL REPORT ..., THE. **5303**

0381-4580 *See* NATIVE STUDIES IN COLLEGES AND UNIVERSITIES. **2268**

0381-4610 *See* CONSERVATION COMMENT. **2190**

0381-4874 See PEACEKEEPING & INTERNATIONAL RELATIONS. **4531**

0381-4912 *See* NOVA SCOTIA DIRECTORY OF MANUFACTURERS. **3485**

0381-5005 *See* CATALYST (BRANTFORD). **3373**

0381-5021 *See* ARTISAN (OTTAWA. 1976). **370**

0381-5072 *See* BOOKS PURCHASED FOR DISPLAY PURPOSES. **411**

0381-5080 *See* METRO-SUD. **5789**

0381-5110 *See* KALENDAR HOLOSU SPASYTELJA. **5039**

0381-5129 *See* HOLOS SPASYTELIA. **4963**

0381-5145 *See* S P K W KANADZIE. **5236**

0381-5293 *See* MESSENGER (KITCHENER). **4976**

0381-5366 *See* TECHNIKAS APSKATS - LATVIESU INZENIERU APVIENIBA. **1998**

0381-5404 *See* TRANSPORT CANADIEN (1963). **5437**

0381-5447 *See* CANADIAN SPECTROSCOPIC NEWS (1972). **4434**

0381-548X *See* S S G M. SERVICE STATION & GARAGE MANAGEMENT. **5424**

0381-551X *See* TEXTILE MANUAL. **5358**

0381-5552 *See* LIMOUSIN LEADER, THE. **214**

0381-5609 *See* COGEODATA NEWSLETTER. **1372**

0381-5730 *See* LLOYD'S CANADIAN MUSIC DIRECTORY. **4129**

0381-5749 See LLOYD'S CANADIAN CHEMICAL, PHARMACEUTICAL, AND PRODUCT DIRECTORY. **4314**

0381-5838 *See* BULLETIN - CANADIAN SOCIETY OF LABORATORY TECHNOLOGISTS. **5090**

0381-5951 *See* ALBERTA COUNSELLETTER. **1723**

0381-6028 *See* BOOKMARK (VANCOUVER). **3197**

0381-6109 *See* THEM DAYS. **2763**

0381-6133 *See* NEWSLETTER - CANADIAN ASSOCIATION OF SLAVISTS. **2520**

0381-629X *See* DIRECTORY OF COMMUNITY SERVICES (NEW WESTMINSTER). **5282**

0381-6419 *See* NURSING QUEBEC. **3865**

0381-6443 *See* QUEBEC AU BOUT DES DOIGTS. **4865**

0381-6486 *See* C-C O R E NEWS. **1967**

0381-6591 *See* POETRY TORONTO. **3469**

0381-6605 *See* JOURNAL OF OTOLARYNGOLOGY, THE. **3889**

0381-6613 *See* ROCK FLUFF. **5794**

0381-6656 *See* AESTHETE, THE. **3358**

0381-6699 *See* SLAMMER. **3176**

0381-6729 *See* LABORATORY BUYERS GUIDE. **5125**

0381-6788 *See* M. B. E. T. A. NEWSLETTER. **691**

0381-6796 *See* AXIS (WATERLOO). **3193**

0381-6885 *See* HARROWSMITH (CANADIAN ED.). **2534**

0381-6931 *See* GAY MONTREAL. **2794**

0381-6982 *See* BARDY, LE. **5229**

0381-7032 *See* ARS COMBINATORIA. **3496**

0381-7075 *See* PEOPLE & PERSPECTIVES. **881**

0381-713X *See* ANNUAIRE GENERALE - COMMISSION SCOLAIRE REGIONALE DE L'ESTRIE. **1860**

0381-7229 *See* RED BOOK. NUMERICAL PHONE INDEX OF GREATER MONTREAL. **1928**

0381-7245 *See* BLUE BOOK OF CANADIAN BUSINESS, THE. **643**

0381-7253 *See* NEW HORIZONS. **242**

0381-7261 *See* BOOK NEWS FOR BOOKSELLERS AND LIBRARIANS. **4812**

0381-7318 *See* PERSPICACITE. **1840**

0381-7350 *See* LEFTWARD. **4543**

0381-7369 *See* CANADA QUILTS. **5183**

0381-7385 *See* CONSENSUS (TORONTO. 1975). **1552**

0381-7415 *See* LAPIN AU QUEBEC, LE. **2537**

0381-7423 *See* EYE SPY. **3164**

0381-7547 *See* PHILATELIE AU QUEBEC. **2786**

0381-7652 *See* CAHIERS D'ANIMATION MISSIONNAIRE. **4941**

0381-7687 *See* CANADIAN REALTY NEWS (EDITION FRANCAISE). **4835**

0381-7695 *See* HARNESS WORLD. **2799**

0381-7733 *See* SPECIAL REPORT (FOREST ENGINEERING RESEARCH INSTITUTE OF CANADA). **2395**

0381-7741 *See* TECHNICAL NOTE - FOREST ENGINEERING RESEARCH INSTITUTE OF CANADA. **2405**

0381-7741 *See* TECHNICAL NOTE - FOREST ENGINEERING RESEARCH INSTITUTE OF CANADA. **2396**

0381-8047 *See* CRUCIBLE (TORONTO). **5097**

0381-8098 *See* SCENE CHANGES. **5368**

0381-8144 *See* NEWSLETTER - SPECIAL EDUCATION ASSOCIATION. **1882**

0381-8152 *See* CENTRE (CHICOUTIMI). **5277**

0381-8179 *See* SANFORD EVANS GOLD BOOK OF USED CAR PRICES. **5425**

0381-8233 *See* ALMANACH DE KUYPER DE CHASSE ET PECHE, L'. **4868**

0381-8284 *See* TRANSPORTATION RESEARCH IN CANADA. **5446**

0381-8349 *See* EVASION. **5469**

0381-8365 *See* SMITHS FALLS STAR. **5794**

0381-8403 *See* SUMMER REVIEW SERVICE - CANADIAN UNIVERSITY PRESS. **1849**

0381-8411 *See* SUMMER NEWS SERVICE - CANADIAN UNIVERSITY PRESS. **1849**

0381-842X *See* FEATURE - CANADIAN UNIVERSITY PRESS. **1823**

0381-8454 *See* REVUE D'HISTOIRE DU BAS ST-LAURENT. **2758**

0381-856X *See* CALEDONIAN (PRINCE GEORGE). **3371**

0381-8578 *See* MIGHT'S OAKVILLE ONTARIO CITY DIRECTORY. **2569**

0381-8632 *See* O C S NOUVELLES. **1118**

0381-8667 *See* SHOP (DON MILLS). **2128**

0381-890X *See* PRELUDE (CALGARY). **4147**

0381-8950 *See* DEUTSCHE KATHOLIK IN KANADA, DER. **5028**

0381-8985 *See* WORKING PAPER - RETAILING AND INSTITUTIONAL RESEARCH PROGRAM, FACULTY OF MANAGEMENT STUDIES, UNIVERSITY OF TORONTO. **889**

0381-9132 *See* OLIFANT. **3420**

0381-9140 *See* NEW REVIEW OF EAST-EUROPEAN HISTORY. **2700**

0381-9167 *See* TORONTO TREE. **2475**

0381-9183 *See* FWTAO NEWSLETTER. **1747**

0381-9345 *See* TIPS & TOPICS. **5394**

0381-9396 *See* CANADIAN ELECTRONICS MARKET, THE. **2038**

0381-9469 *See* FOLIO (SASKATOON). **350**

0381-9477 *See* NEGRO DIRECTORY. **2269**

0381-9493 *See* RALLY REGULATIONS (WILLOWDALE). **4914**

0381-9507 *See* CANADIAN L P & TAPE CATALOGUE, THE. **5316**

0381-9531 *See* MAST. MANITOBA ASSOCIATION OF SCHOOL TRUSTEES. **4664**

0381-9566 *See* GEORGIAN (STEPHENVILLE). **5785**

0381-9582 *See* TEMA (SASKATOON). **1787**

0381-9590 *See* GRAF ITI (OTTAWA). **378**

0381-9604 *See* EASTERN STAR. **2732**

0381-9620 *See* PLASTICS IN CONSTRUCTION. **624**

0381-9841 *See* BULLETIN - A Q Q U A. **1368**

0381-9876 *See* UNIVERS (LIMOILOU). **5038**

0381-9906 *See* C. A. S. C. RACE REGULATIONS. **4889**

0381-9930 *See* TOYS & GAMES. **2585**

0382-0017 *See* HAVELOCK CITIZEN. **5786**

0382-0068 *See* VOICE OF UNITED SENIOR CITIZENS OF ONTARIO, INC. **5182**

0382-0181 *See* VIE CHRETIENNE, LA. **5007**

0382-0246 *See* WITCH AND THE CHAMELEON, THE. **3453**

0382-0254 *See* JEWISH TIMES (DOWNSVIEW). **5049**

0382-0262 *See* VIE FRANCAISE (QUEBEC). **2549**

0382-0289 *See* VISTA (SASKATOON). **1790**

0382-0335 *See* JEU. **5365**

0382-0424 *See* VISION (MONTREAL). **4461**

0382-0610 *See* UNDZER VEG (TORONTO). **2274**

0382-0653 *See* TEMISCAMIEN (1976). **5796**

0382-0718 *See* VECTOR (VANCOUVER). **3540**

0382-0734 *See* ANNUAL REPORT - HOLLINGER MINES LIMITED. **2133**

0382-0831 *See* NEWSLETTER - WESTMORLAND HISTORICAL SOCIETY. **2750**

0382-084X *See* LETTRES QUEBECOISES. **3405**

0382-1080 *See* LIST OF LIGHTS, BUOYS AND FOG SIGNALS. PACIFIC COAST. **4178**

0382-1110 *See* EDUCATION NOVA SCOTIA. **1740**

0382-1153 See S R F B NEWSLETTER. 34
0382-1161 See ANNUAL REPORT - COMMISSIONER OF OFFICIAL LANGUAGES. 3265
0382-1293 See STATUS REPORT - COUNTY RESTRUCTURING STUDIES PROGRAM. 4688
0382-1420 See REPORT OF THE AUDITOR GENERAL TO THE LEGISLATIVE ASSEMBLY (FREDERICTON). 4745
0382-1463 See ANNUAL REPORT - LAW REFORM COMMISSION OF CANADA. 2934
0382-1501 See ANNUAL REPORT - FARM CREDIT CORPORATION. 771
0382-1803 See ANNUAL REPORT - MINISTRY OF THE ATTORNEY GENERAL (TORONTO). 3139
0382-1846 See GOVERNMENT OF CANADA. TELEPHONE DIRECTORY. NATIONAL CAPITAL REGION. 1156
0382-2168 See MONTHLY STATISTICS. ALBERTA COAL INDUSTRY. 1963
0382-2192 See WOMEN IN THE LABOUR FORCE. FACTS AND FIGURES. 1718
0382-232X See CANADA COMMUNICABLE DISEASE REPORT. 4770
0382-232X See CANADA COMMUNICABLE DISEASE REPORT. 4770
0382-2486 See ANNUAL NORTHERN EXPENDITURE PLAN. 4709
0382-2494 See PROGRAMME ANNUEL DES DEPENSES DANS LE NORD. 4742
0382-2656 See HYDROLOGICAL EVENTS. 1414
0382-2826 See ANNUAL REPORT / ONTARIO HYDRO. 2035
0382-2834 See ONTARIO HYDRO STATISTICAL YEARBOOK (1973). 4699
0382-3229 See ANNUAL REPORT / THE CANADIAN DAIRY COMMISSION / RAPPORT ANNUEL / LA COMMISSION CANADIENNE DU LAIT. 192
0382-3482 See DIRECTORY OF ALBERTA GOVERNMENT LIBRARIES. 3206
0382-3547 See REPERTOIRE DES TAUX DE LOCATION. 2833
0382-4012 See MANUFACTURING INDUSTRIES OF CANADA. SUB-PROVINCIAL AREAS. 3483
0382-4055 See C C A RODEO NEWS. 4889
0382-408X See TEACHER (HALIFAX). 1906
0382-4144 See MANUFACTURING INDUSTRIES OF CANADA, NATIONAL AND PROVINCIAL AREAS. 3483
0382-4268 See C C A RODEO NEWS. 4889
0382-4284 See LIBRARY ACCESSIONS - ARCTIC INSTITUTE OF NORTH AMERICA. 3223
0382-4462 See BULLETIN AMI. 3559
0382-456X See ADVOCATE, THE. 2928
0382-4624 See CANADIAN LIVING. 5552
0382-4632 See ABEGWEIT REVIEW. 2253
0382-4713 See BULLETIN 78. 4888
0382-4780 See OUTLOOK (LETHBRIDGE). 3171
0382-490X See SUPPLEMENT (MONTREAL). 1885
0382-5027 See CURRENT INDEX TO COMMONWEALTH LEGAL PERIODICALS. 2957
0382-5191 See ALBERTA ENGLISH. 3262
0382-5256 See NEWS BULLETIN - ANIMAL DEFENCE LEAGUE OF CANADA. 226
0382-5272 See BRITISH COLUMBIA MONTHLY (VANCOUVER. 1972). 2529
0382-5280 See LUMERA, LA. 2489
0382-5744 See BACKGROUND PAPER - INSTITUTE OF LAW RESEARCH AND REFORM, UNIVERSITY OF ALBERTA. 2939
0382-5876 See CANADIAN FUNERAL NEWS. 2406
0382-6015 See GARBAGE COALITION. 2230
0382-6023 See GARBAGE COALITION BULLETIN. 2230
0382-6309 See POINT (DOLBEAU). 5793
0382-6384 See BEACON (TORONTO. 1970). 4938
0382-6627 See OWL (DON MILLS). 1067
0382-6996 See HEATING, PLUMBING, AIR CONDITIONING. BUYER'S GUIDE. 2605
0382-7038 See COMMENT (DON MILLS). 2878
0382-7194 See ECHO (OTTAWA). 5284

0382-7313 See NEW COMIC WORLD, THE. 4864
0382-7542 See PROMENADE (MONTREAL). 388
0382-7577 See BIG COUNTRY VOICE, THE. 5780
0382-7585 See CANADIAN POCKETAX (ENGLISH EDITION). 4716
0382-7658 See CANADIAN FRIEND, THE. 4942
0382-7682 See LEPROSY RELIEF CANADA INC. 4789
0382-7755 See INFO (SHERBROOKE). 1752
0382-7798 See COMMUNICATION ET INFORMATION. 1106
0382-781X See FARMSAFE. 86
0382-7852 See ORIENTATIONS ET POLITIQUES DE L'U P A. 117
0382-7879 See SCHOOL CALENDAR (TORONTO). 1871
0382-7933 See DIAKONIA MAS TES BASILEIAS (KANADE EKDOSIS). 4953
0382-7976 See REVUE ACEDA. 1884
0382-7992 See NOUVELLES DES PETITS FRERES. 5299
0382-8018 See C S S E NEWS. 1730
0382-8069 See CANADIAN MANUFACTURER (1908). 3476
0382-8085 See INUMMARIT (ESKIMO EDITION). 2264
0382-8174 See INSIDE CANADA. 2233
0382-8220 See ON S'PARLE. 4853
0382-8271 See NEWSLETTER - OTTAWA WOMEN'S CENTRE. 5562
0382-831X See NEWSLETTER - WRITERS' UNION OF CANADA. 3417
0382-8352 See BACKGROUNDER. 824
0382-8379 See WASCANA WITNESS. 5797
0382-8417 See NEWS FROM CANADA-JAPAN SOCIETY OF VANCOUVER. 5234
0382-8468 See ACTIVITES DU CQRI. 4514
0382-8476 See NURSCENE. 3862
0382-8530 See QUARTIER LATIN (MONTREAL. 1976). 1843
0382-8557 See CIAO (MONTREAL). 2258
0382-8565 See BRICK. 3338
0382-8662 See CANADIAN WORLD FEDERALIST (1975). 3125
0382-8700 See CANADIAN PUBLIC SERVICE WORKER'S BULLETIN. 1658
0382-8794 See COMUNIDADE (HULL). 5782
0382-8808 See MEDI-US. 3607
0382-8883 See NORD (HEARST). 5790
0382-9073 See DIRECTORY OF CANADIAN SCHOLARS AND UNIVERSITIES INTERESTED IN LATIN AMERICAN STUDIES. 2731
0382-909X See DESCANT (TORONTO). 3380
0382-912X See APPLICATION STATISTICS (TORONTO). 1793
0382-9197 See ADPA. AUTOMATIC DATA PROCESSING AND ARCHIVES. 2478
0382-9227 See VIBRATIONS (OTTAWA. 1975). 2839
0382-9251 See APAGAY (MONTREAL). 5780
0382-9286 See PIN UPS. 4375
0382-9472 See BULLETIN DE L'ENTRAIDE MISSIONNAIRE. 4941
0382-9804 See BULLETIN DU CENTRE DE QUEBEC DE LA S R A C. 394
0383-0047 See AU FIL DU BOIS. 2399
0383-008X See FRUIT AND VEGETABLE PRODUCTION. 172
0383-0098 See OPPORTUNITY (WINNIPEG). 1577
0383-0330 See COURIER (MONTREAL). 3989
0383-0462 See CAPTAIN CANUCK. 4858
0383-0535 See LINK (VICTORIA). 3228
0383-0802 See PEDAGOGIQUES. 1840
0383-0853 See SCOUT-JEUNESSE. 4878
0383-090X See M P & P, METAL-WORKING PRODUCTION & PURCHASING. 4007
0383-1086 See TROTTEUR DU MAQUIGNON. 2548
0383-1132 See REFLETS DE LA PHILATELIE AU QUEBEC. 2787

0383-1191 See CANADA GUNSPORT. 4889
0383-1213 See GOLDSTREAM GAZETTE. 5785
0383-1221 See NORTHERN PIONEER, THE. 5791
0383-1256 See NATIONAL THEATRE SCHOOL OF CANADA. 5366
0383-1272 See INFO LONGUEUIL. 4656
0383-1299 See NEWSLETTER / CANADIAN ASSOCIATION OF MUSIC LIBRARIES. 3235
0383-1353 See BOOWATT. 2529
0383-1515 See DECODEUR, LE. 1819
0383-1574 See CANADIAN POETRY ANNUAL, THE. 3461
0383-1620 See CATHOLIC REGISTER, THE. 5026
0383-1779 See DIRECTORY OF MINES PERSONNEL. 2138
0383-1825 See BULLETIN - MICROSCOPICAL SOCIETY OF CANADA. 572
0383-1833 See PRISME (MONTREAL). 4865
0383-1930 See VOLKS-CALENDAR FUR DIE DEUTSCHEN IN WEST-CANADA (MICROFICHE). 2495
0383-1949 See OR BLANC. 5791
0383-2015 See UTU NEWS CANADA. 1716
0383-2236 See PASTORALE-QUEBEC. 5034
0383-2392 See SELECTION OF RECENT ACQUISITIONS - CANADIAN IMPERIAL BANK OF COMMERCE, INFORMATION CENTRE, A. 1520
0383-2449 See CIGGT REPORT. 5430
0383-2457 See GUIDE TO ACCREDITATION OF CANADIAN MENTAL HEALTH SERVICES. 5287
0383-2554 See AUJOURD'HUI CREDO. 4937
0383-2635 See JESUS, MARIE ET NOTRE TEMPS. 4967
0383-2791 See BULLETIN OF OUTSTANDING ACQUISITIONS OF THE METROPOLITAN TORONTO CENTRAL LIBRARY. 3198
0383-283X See SQUATCHBERRY JOURNAL, THE. 3439
0383-2848 See BIBLIOGRAPHY SERIES - NORMAN PATERSON SCHOOL OF INTERNATIONAL AFFAIRS (CARLETON UNIVERSITY). 4501
0383-2910 See THESAURUS DE DESCRIPTEURS SUR L'EDUCATION. LISTE ROTATIVE ET ADDITIONS ET CORRECTIONS. 1929
0383-3445 See EVALUATION REPORT - PRAIRIE AGRICULTURAL MACHINERY INSTITUTE. 158
0383-3445 See EVALUATION REPORT - PRAIRIE AGRICULTURAL MACHINERY INSTITUTE. 2114
0383-3569 See WAGES, SALARIES AND HOURS OF LABOUR, NEW BRUNSWICK. 1717
0383-3593 See CLIMATE OF ALBERTA WITH DATA FOR YUKON AND NORTHWEST TERRITORIES, REPORT. 1422
0383-3623 See ALBERTA HANSARD. 4625
0383-3690 See ANNUAL REPORT - ALBERTA PUBLIC UTILITIES BOARD. 4626
0383-3739 See ANNUAL REPORT - ALBERTA ENVIRONMENT. 2160
0383-414X See ANNUAL REPORT - NATIONAL FARM PRODUCTS MARKETING COUNCIL. 61
0383-4301 See OECUMENISME (EDITION FRANCAISE). 4983
0383-431X See ECUMENISM. 4955
0383-4379 See ANNUAL REPORT OF THE CORRECTIONAL INVESTIGATOR. 3157
0383-4417 See GRAIN MATTERS. 201
0383-4638 See DEFENCE (OTTAWA. 1971). 4040
0383-4786 See ESTIMATES OF THE GOVERNMENT OF NOVA SCOTIA. 4722
0383-4808 See ANNUAL REPORT - DEPARTMENT OF SOCIAL SERVICES (HALIFAX). 5272
0383-4875 See FARM INPUT PRICE INDEX. 84
0383-5359 See BULLETIN / ALBERTA RESEARCH COUNCIL. 5090
0383-5456 See WATER RESOURCES BULLETIN : GROUND WATER SERIES. 5544
0383-574X See HOSPITAL STATISTICS. VOLUME 1. BEDS, SERVICES, PERSONNEL. 3660
0383-5766 See PASSENGER BUS AND URBAN TRANSIT STATISTICS. 5389

0383-5855 *See* PROVINCIAL FINANCIAL ASSISTANCE TO MUNICIPALITIES, BOARDS AND COMMISSIONS. **4742**

0383-5863 *See* ONTARIO FINANCES. **4739**

0383-5898 *See* STATISTICS - ONTARIO MINISTRY OF NATURAL RESOURCES. **2185**

0383-6061 *See* INTERCOM (WILLOWDALE). **5061**

0383-6118 *See* COURTENAY AND COMOX. **2559**

0383-6150 *See* RES BUREAUX BULLETIN. **4358**

0383-6185 *See* MON SEXE. **5188**

0383-6207 *See* DAIRY CONTACT. **193**

0383-6231 *See* DELIBERATIONS DU CONGRES - ASSOCIATION CANADIENNE DU PERSONNEL ADMINISTRATIF UNIVERSITAIRE. **1819**

0383-6274 *See* EVEIL, L'. **1746**

0383-6312 *See* SMALLHOLDER, THE. **135**

0383-6320 *See* SANTE MENTALE AU QUEBEC. **3936**

0383-6479 *See* ONTARIO CONSERVATION NEWS. **2201**

0383-6517 *See* KARATE KEBEC. **4902**

0383-669X *See* REVUE DU BARREAU, LA. **3043**

0383-669X *See* REVUE DU BARREAU. **3043**

0383-6711 *See* SOLIDARITES. **4998**

0383-672X *See* JALONS (REPENTIGNY). **5232**

0383-6738 *See* GOUT DE VIVRE, LE. **5246**

0383-6762 *See* DETAILLANT, LE. **4254**

0383-6894 *See* JOURNAL - CANADIAN ORAL HISTORY ASSOCIATION. **2740**

0383-6940 *See* STRENGTH. **5566**

0383-6967 *See* OTTAWA VALLEY PEOPLE'S YELLOW PAGES. **2572**

0383-7009 *See* ONTARIO SNOWMOBILER. **4911**

0383-719X *See* SMALL BUSINESS, A CANADIAN VIEWPOINT. **711**

0383-7262 *See* SCRIBE (VAL-DAVID). **4685**

0383-7297 *See* MAILLON, LE. **5295**

0383-7319 See INFO CANADA (DOWNSVIEW). **1188**

0383-7335 *See* GRIFFIN (HALIFAX). **299**

0383-7343 *See* TAHSIS INLET OUTLET, THE. **5795**

0383-7505 *See* BRANCH NOTES / WATERLOO-WELLINGTON BRANCH, ONTARIO GENEALOGICAL SOCIETY. **2439**

0383-7572 *See* PEUPLE-TRIBUNE. **5792**

0383-7653 *See* PRAIRIE HARVESTER. **4987**

0383-770X *See* CANADIAN BOOK REVIEW ANNUAL. **3339**

0383-7742 *See* NEWSLETTER - MANITOBA UNDERWATER COUNCIL. **4908**

0383-7777 *See* MAN UNDERWATER. **4904**

0383-7793 *See* CALENDAR / MCGILL UNIVERSITY. **1813**

0383-7866 *See* BONJOUR CHEZ-NOUS. **5780**

0383-7874 *See* MANAGEMENT COMPENSATION IN CANADIAN BANKING & FINANCE. **876**

0383-7890 *See* CIRCA 76. **250**

0383-7912 *See* FIREWEED : A FEMINIST QUARTERLY. **5557**

0383-7920 *See* CANADIAN RENTAL SERVICE. **1600**

0383-803X *See* EDITION SPECIALE. **5783**

0383-8080 *See* LAMBTON COUNTY GAZETTE, THE. **5788**

0383-8099 *See* LIFE SUPPORT. **3604**

0383-8102 *See* LOOKOUT (SIOUX LOOKOUT). **5789**

0383-8153 *See* ROSSLAND AND DISTRICT WEEKLY, THE. **5794**

0383-8161 *See* SHOESTRING PRESS. **5794**

0383-820X *See* WHISTLER QUESTION. **5797**

0383-8277 *See* PRIONS EN EGLISE (EDITION DOMINICALE). **4988**

0383-8307 *See* PRETRE ET PASTEUR. **4987**

0383-8358 *See* DIRECTORY OF LAW TEACHERS (MONTREAL). **2962**

0383-8498 *See* BRISEBOIS ET COMPAGNIE. **4858**

0383-8501 *See* I S A BULLETIN (1975). **5247**

0383-8528 *See* DIALECT. **5282**

0383-8536 *See* NUCLEAR CANADA YEARBOOK. **1951**

0383-8587 *See* SOIS PRET. **5236**

0383-8714 *See* ACTUALITE (MONTREAL. 1976). **2513**

0383-8927 *See* PARCOURS, LE. **1883**

0383-896X *See* ALERTE (STE-PETRONILLE. 1976). **4933**

0383-9028 *See* O R G A NEWS. **4267**

0383-9036 *See* B D K. BANDE DESSINEE KEBECOISE. **370**

0383-9184 *See* METRIC FACT SHEET. **4031**

0383-9192 *See* TALKING DRUMS. **2274**

0383-9249 *See* BRUCE TRAIL NEWS. **4869**

0383-9370 *See* SPEAK UP. **2762**

0383-9397 *See* BULLETIN DE L'UNION DES ARTISTES, LE. **1656**

0383-9494 *See* CRIMINAL REPORTS. **3106**

0383-9567 *See* NEWSLETTER - NOVA SCOTIA BIRD SOCIETY. **5592**

0383-9575 *See* DANDELION. **3380**

0383-9656 *See* OCCASIONAL REPORT - LAW SOCIETY OF UPPER CANADA. **3020**

0383-9664 *See* CYCLO NOUVELLES. **429**

0383-9699 *See* COMMERCE LEADING INDICATOR, THE. **828**

0383-9710 *See* IMAGE (VANCOUVER). **3586**

0383-9729 *See* COMMERCE CREDIT INDEX, THE. **828**

0383-9818 *See* JEWELLERY WORLD. **2914**

0383-9834 *See* ROYAL BANK TRENDICATOR REPORT. **1582**

0383-9893 *See* CANADIAN BUSINESS CONDITIONS. **655**

0383-9915 *See* KINGSTON WOMEN'S CENTRE NEWSLETTER. **5560**

0383-9958 *See* POLISH CANADIAN SCHOLARS, SCIENTISTS, WRITERS & ARTISTS. **328**

0383-9990 *See* STUDENT DISCUSSION PAPER. **2221**

0384-0077 *See* GUIDE DE LOCATION (MONTREAL). **2115**

0384-0123 *See* ROUND TABLE (BARRIE). **3247**

0384-0158 *See* BULLETIN DE LA SOCIETE HISTORIQUE DE SAINT-BONIFACE. **2681**

0384-0417 *See* PARAPET, THE. **4053**

0384-0441 *See* ETHNIC AND CULTURAL DIRECTORY. **2260**

0384-0530 *See* NOTRE SEMAINE COMMUNAUTAIRE. **4982**

0384-062X *See* EGALE, L'. **2965**

0384-0654 *See* WORKING WOMEN IN CANADA. **5572**

0384-0697 *See* REFLECTIONS (NORTH BATTLEFORD. 1976). **3244**

0384-0719 *See* INITIATIVE. **1567**

0384-0840 *See* NORTHERN MOSAIC (THUNDER BAY). **5791**

0384-0883 *See* REPORTS - BRITISH COLUMBIA ASSOCIATION OF HOSPITALS AND HEALTH ORGANIZATIONS. **3792**

0384-093X *See* MARSH & MAPLE. **3466**

0384-0972 *See* P D B, PROFESSIONAL DEVELOPMENT BULLETIN. **1771**

0384-0999 *See* CANADIAN YACHTING. **592**

0384-1162 *See* HIGHLIGHTS NEWSLETTER. **352**

0384-1294 *See* GAZETTE (MONTREAL). **5785**

0384-1413 **1803**

0384-1464 *See* CARIBBEAN DIALOGUE. **4467**

0384-1499 *See* NUTCRACKER, THE. **4544**

0384-1537 *See* DAY CARE (TORONTO). **5281**

0384-1588 *See* CANADIAN ART INVESTOR'S GUIDE, THE. **346**

0384-1642 *See* NEWSPACKET (ORILLIA). **3417**

0384-1820 *See* NEWSLETTER - CANADIAN MEDICAL AND BIOLOGICAL ENGINEERING SOCIETY. **3695**

0384-1863 See NEWSLETTER - ALBERTA HOME AND SCHOOL COUNCILS' ASSOCIATION. **1768**

0384-1871 *See* ORATORY, THE. **4984**

0384-2029 *See* REPORT OF THE PRESIDENT - MEDICAL RESEARCH COUNCIL (OTTAWA). **3633**

0384-2223 See VOTES AND PROCEEDINGS (OTTAWA). **4694**

0384-224X *See* VOTES AND PROCEEDINGS (OTTAWA). **4694**

0384-2479 *See* ANNUAL REPORT OF THE GOVERNMENT OF THE NORTHWEST TERRITORIES. **4628**

0384-2487 *See* BULLETIN OF PROCEEDINGS TAKEN IN THE SUPREME COURT OF CANADA. **2944**

0384-2568 *See* CANADA FEDERAL COURT REPORTS. **2947**

0384-3149 *See* FISHERIES RESEARCH BOARD OF CANADA REPORTS. **2302**

0384-3394 *See* HARDWARE, TOOL AND CUTLERY MANUFACTURERS (PRELIMINARY ED.). **2811**

0384-398X *See* OTHER MISCELLANEOUS MANUFACTURING INDUSTRIES. **3490**

0384-4781 *See* WIRE AND WIRE PRODUCTS MANUFACTURERS (PRELIMINARY ED.). **4023**

0384-5028 *See* MORNING WATCH (ST. JOHN'S). **1765**

0384-5052 *See* ONTARIO FOLKDANCER. **1314**

0384-5095 *See* REGLEMENTS - A S T E D. **3245**

0384-5176 *See* NOCTILUCA. **3418**

0384-5230 *See* OPTIMST, THE. **5563**

0384-5265 *See* ON HER MAJESTY'S SERVICE. **4485**

0384-5281 *See* COUPLE ET FAMILLE. **2278**

0384-5311 *See* C. A. U. T. G. NEWSLETTER. **3271**

0384-5486 See ECHOES (MEDICINE HAT). **4955**

0384-5648 *See* REPORTER - ONTARIO ENGLISH CATHOLIC TEACHERS' ASSOCIATION. **1903**

0384-5702 *See* C C N G REPORT. **1240**

0384-5710 *See* LANGUE ET LITTERATURE FRANCAISES AU CANADA (1970). **3296**

0384-5842 *See* NIGHTOUT. **4141**

0384-5915 *See* A C P D Q BULLETIN. **1314**

0384-5958 *See* FORESIGHT (MONTREAL). **2881**

0384-5990 *See* IMAGES (NELSON). **5558**

0384-6008 *See* DROIT POPULAIRE, LE. **5198**

0384-6016 *See* REALITE (QUEBEC). **4243**

0384-6032 *See* MONTHLY EX.-IM. OPPORTUNITIES. **846**

0384-6156 *See* CAVALIER (SAINT-GERMAIN-DE-GRANTHAM). **2798**

0384-6547 *See* BULLETIN - CANADIAN SOCIETY FOR ARCHAEOLOGY ABROAD, THE. **262**

0384-661X *See* COMMUNICATE (KAMLOOPS). **4949**

0384-6636 *See* OUR SCHOOLS. **1771**

0384-6679 *See* AMERICAN STAMP NEWS. **2784**

0384-6784 *See* JOURNAL L'ECLAIREUR ABITIBIEN. **2921**

0384-7225 *See* FELLOWS LECTURE. **4088**

0384-7322 *See* FRASER'S POTATO NEWSLETTER. **172**

0384-7349 *See* ISAKIMU. **2536**

0384-7357 *See* PROCES-VERBAL DU CONGRES GENERAL ANNUEL - SOCIETE SAINT-JEAN-BAPTISTE DE QUEBEC. **5235**

0384-7470 *See* NOUVELLES. SECURITE. ASSOCIATION DE LA CONSTRUCTION DE MONTREAL ET DU QUEBEC. **623**

0384-7632 *See* C P S NEWS LETTER (TORONTO). **2784**

0384-7691 *See* ALMANACH-GRAPHIQUE - CENTRE DE QUEBEC, SOCIETE ROYALE D'ASTRONOMIE DU CANADA. **391**

0384-7799 See BLUE BOOK OF C B S STOCK REPORTS. **892**

0384-7802 *See* BLUE BOOK OF C B S STOCK REPORTS. **892**

0384-7810 *See* PLEIN SOLEIL (MONTREAL). **3732**

0384-7845 *See* EVEIL (SAINT-EUSTACHE). **5784**

0384-7934 *See* SOUTH EAST LANCE. **5795**

0384-8159 *See* LIFE SCIENCES CONTRIBUTIONS / ROYAL ONTARIO MUSEUM. **4090**

0384-8167 See REVISTA CANADIENSE DE ESTUDIOS HISPANICOS. 3429
0384-8175 See ISLAND MAGAZINE, THE. 2739
0384-8191 See MOTS CROISES ECLAIR (EDITION SEMESTRIELLE). 4863
0384-8248 See SUNYATA (VICTORIA). 3443
0384-840X See MUNICIPAL HANDBOOK : THE CITY OF CALGARY. 4667
0384-8434 See CANADIAN BLACK BOOK. ONTARIO. 5408
0384-8469 See AJAKIRI. 2254
0384-8515 See DIRECTION (WINNIPEG). 4953
0384-8523 See ALCHEMIST (LASALLE). 3359
0384-8566 See KOORDINATOR VISTI UKRAJINSKOJ KREDYTOVOJ KOOPERACIJI. 796
0384-8639 See INSTITUTS DE COMPTABLES AGREES DU CANADA. EXAMENS FINAL. 745
0384-8701 See CONTACT C I L. 1602
0384-8779 See SOURD QUEBECOIS, LE. 5310
0384-8825 See PUBLICATIONS DE L'INSTITUT D'ETUDES MEDIEVALES. 2626
0384-8922 See PERSPECTIVE (TORONTO. 1967). 4986
0384-8965 See CANADIAN OIL AND GAS. 4253
0384-9058 See BRISE DE L'EST, I.A. 5275
0384-9066 See COMMUNIQUE - NATIONAL BOARD. ASSOCIATION OF ADMINISTRATIVE ASSISTANTS. 658
0384-9120 See REGARDS SUR ISRAEL (MONTREAL). 4493
0384-9147 See NEW DIRECTIONS (VANCOUVER). 2219
0384-9201 See TAXATION (DON MILLS). 4755
0384-9252 See CANADA REPORT. 826
0384-9260 See NOTE DE SERVICE - ASSOCIATION CANADIENNE DES PROFESSEURS D'UNIVERSITE. 1838
0384-9309 See CARGUIDE. 5409
0384-9325 See "30". 2917
0384-9333 See CONTEMPORARY AFFAIRS (TORONTO). 4519
0384-9465 See OFFICIAL DAILY BULLETIN - VANCOUVER STOCK EXCHANGE. 910
0384-9481 See MINUTES OF ANNUAL MEETING - BRITISH COLUMBIA ASSOCIATION OF HOSPITALS AND HEALTH ORGANIZATIONS. 3789
0384-9627 See CURRENTLY (TORONTO). 4087
0384-9694 See JOURNAL OF RELIGIOUS ETHICS, THE. 2251
0384-9724 See CATALOGUE DES MICROEDITIONS. 3200
0384-9856 See CAMPING CANADA. 4870
0384-9864 See CONGRESSUS NUMERANTIUM. 3502
0385-0005 See TOKAI JOURNAL OF EXPERIMENTAL AND CLINICAL MEDICINE. 3646
0385-0064 See FUKUOKA SHIKA DAIGAKU GAKKAI ZASSHI. 1324
0385-0072 See GIFU SHIKA GAKKAI ZASSHI. 1324
0385-0110 See NIHON SHISHUBYO GAKKAI KAISHI. 1331
0385-0129 See DE. JOURNAL OF DENTAL ENGINEERING. 1320
0385-0137 See SHIKA KISO IGAKKAI ZASSHI. 1335
0385-0196 See SOCHI SHIKENJO KENKYU HOKOKU. 136
0385-0218 See RAKUNO KAGAKU, SHOKUHIN NO KENKYU. 198
0385-0234 See KAWASAKI MEDICAL JOURNAL. 3601
0385-0307 See SHINSHIN IGAKU. 3641
0385-0447 See AEU : JOURNAL OF ASIA ELECTRONICS UNION. 2034
0385-0684 See GAN TO KAGAKU RYOHO. 3817
0385-0862 See HOKKAIDO KOGYO DAIGAKU KENKYU KIYO. 5110
0385-0900 See MIZUNAMI-SHI KASEKI HAKUBUTSUKAN KENKYU HOKOKU. 4228

0385-0919 See CHUGOKU BUNGAKU KENKYU (WASEDA DAIGAKU. CHUGOKU BUNGAKKAI). 3375
0385-096X See EBARA-INFIRUKO JIHO. 1971
0385-1001 See ZOSUI GIJUTSU. 5549
0385-1028 See ZENKOKU KOGAIKEN KAISHI. 2183
0385-1036 See MAKU. 463
0385-1109 See SHIMA MARINRANDO KENKYU HOKOKU. 5157
0385-1176 See SENPAKU KAIYO KOGAKU GIJUTSU BUNKEN SOKUHO. 4185
0385-132X See KUMAMOTO KOGYO DAIGAKU KENKYU HOKOKU. 5124
0385-1443 See BULLETIN OF THE KANAGAWA DENTAL COLLEGE. 1318
0385-1516 See DOJIN NYUSU. 1014
0385-1559 See JOURNAL OF PESTICIDE SCIENCE (TOKYO, 1975). 4245
0385-1575 See GIFU-KEN EISEI KENKYUJOHO. 4776
0385-1605 See NIHON SHIKA DAIGAKU KIYO. IPPAN KYOIKU KEI. 1331
0385-1613 See MATSUMOTO SHIGAKU. 1329
0385-1621 See SOILS AND FOUNDATIONS. 1996
0385-1664 See MASUI TO SOSEI. 3683
0385-1753 See KENKYU KIYO / TOKYO TORITSU JOHO SHORI KYOIKU SENTA. 1760
0385-1796 See BOEI IKA DAIGAKKO ZASSHI. 3558
0385-180X See KOKURITSU MINZOKUGAKU HAKUBUTSUKAN KENKYU HOKOKU. 240
0385-1907 See SEISO GIHO. 2243
0385-2105 See KAKURIKEN KEDKYU HOKOKU. 4448
0385-2318 See JAPAN FOUNDATION NEWSLETTER, THE. 5249
0385-2342 See ASIAN FOLKLORE STUDIES. 2318
0385-2369 See JAPANESE FINANCE AND INDUSTRY : QUARTERLY SURVEY. 793
0385-2385 See JAPANESE JOURNAL OF NEPHROLOGY, THE. 3990
0385-2393 See RINSHUO HINYUOKIKA. 3993
0385-2407 See JOURNAL OF DERMATOLOGY, THE. 3721
0385-2415 See UTSUNOMIYA DAIGAKU KYOIKUGAKUBU KIYO. 1873
0385-2423 See BULLETIN OF THE NATIONAL SCIENCE MUSEUM. SERIES A, ZOOLOGY. 5579
0385-2431 See BULLETIN OF THE NATIONAL SCIENCE MUSEUM. SERIES B, BOTANY. 505
0385-2520 See ROCK MAGNETISM AND PALEOGEOPHYSICS. 1410
0385-2563 See NIHON FUKUGO ZAIRYO GAKKAI SHI. 2107
0385-2571 See ADVANCED COMPOSITE MATERIALS : THE OFFICIAL JOURNAL OF THE JAPAN SOCIETY OF COMPOSITE MATERIALS. 2100
0385-2814 See NEMPO - TOKYO DAIGAKU OGATA KEISANKI SENTA. 1261
0385-3004 See EBARA JIHO. 1971
0385-3039 See BULLETIN OF THE NATIONAL SCIENCE MUSEUM. SERIES D, ANTHROPOLOGY. 233
0385-3152 See AKITA-KEN KAJU SHIKENJUO KENKYUU HUOKOKU. 2408
0385-3381 See MIE DAIGAKU KANKYO KAGAKU KENKYU KIYO. 2218
0385-3462 See DESIGN NEWS. 2097
0385-3667 See NIHON KYOBU RINSHO. 3800
0385-3675 See SAITAMA-KEN ENGEI SHIKENJO KENKYU HOKOKU. 2430
0385-3799 See REPORT OF THE RESEARCH LABORATORY OF ENGINEERING MATERIALS (TOKYO). 2108
0385-4000 See TOSHOKAN ZASSHI. 3253
0385-4035 See HOKKAIDO MATHEMATICAL JOURNAL. 3507
0385-406X See TOHOKU GAKUIN DAIGAKU RONSHU. EIGO, EIBUNGAKU. 3447

0385-4205 See DENKI GAKKAI RONBUNSHI. A, KISO ZAIRYO. 2040
0385-4213 See DENKI GAKKAI RONBUNSHI. B, ENERUGI, DENKI KIKI, DENRYOKU. 2040
0385-4221 See DENKI GAKKAI RONBUNSHI. C, EREKUTORONIKUSU, JOHO KOGAKU, SHISUTEMU. 2040
0385-437X See HONYURUI KAGAKU. 5585
0385-440X See IKA KIKAIGAKU. 3585
0385-4469 See TOYO IGAKU. 3646
0385-4507 See JOURNAL OF ELECTRONIC ENGINEERING : JEE. 2068
0385-4515 See JEI, JOURNAL OF THE ELECTRONICS INDUSTRY. 2068
0385-4655 See SENSHOKU-TAI. 551
0385-5015 See IYAKUHIN SOGO SAYO KENKYU. 4309
0385-5023 See DOKKYO JOURNAL OF MEDICAL SCIENCES. 3573
0385-5074 See SAITAMA IKA DAIGAKU ZASSHI. 3638
0385-5090 See HOSEKI GAKKAI SHI. 2914
0385-5201 See BOKIN BOBAI : NIHON BOKIN BOBAI GAKKAI SHI. 4294
0385-5392 See DOBOKU GAKKAI RONBUN HOKOKUSHU. 2022
0385-5414 See HETEROCYCLES. 1041
0385-5449 See KITASATO IGAKU. 3602
0385-549X See KANGO TENBO. 3860
0385-5600 See MICROBIOLOGY AND IMMUNOLOGY. 3674
0385-5643 See NETTAI IGAKU. 3986
0385-5694 See GEIJUTSU NENKAN (OSAKA, JAPAN). 321
0385-5759 See KANAZAWA IKA DAIGAKU ZASSHI. 3601
0385-5805 See NIHON BUKKYO SHIGAKU / NIHON BUKKYO SHIGAKUKAI. 5021
0385-602X See HOKKAIDO DAIGAKU KOGAKUBU KENKYU HOKOKU. BULLETIN OF THE FACULTY OF ENGINEERING, HOKKAIDO UNIVERSITY. 1977
0385-6046 See HOPPO BUNKA KENKYU. 321
0385-6054 See SCIENTIFIC PAPERS OF THE INSTITUTE OF ALGOLOGICAL RESEARCH, FACULTY OF SCIENCE, HOKKAIDO UNIVERSITY. 527
0385-6100 See STUDIES IN AMERICAN LITERATURE (NIHON AMERIKA BUNGAKKAI). 3441
0385-6151 See HAKKOKOGAKU KAISHI. 3693
0385-6186 See SAGA DAIGAKU RIKOGAKUBU SHUHO. 1995
0385-6275 See NIHON KESSHO SEICHO GAKKAI SHI. 1033
0385-6305 See SHONI NAIKA. 3911
0385-6313 See SHONI GEKA. 3911
0385-6321 See SOKA GAKKAI NEWS, THE. 5022
0385-6410 See KYUSHU BYOGAICHU KENKYUKAIHO. 517
0385-6445 See HOKKAIDO DAIGAKU NOGAKUBU NOJO KENKYU HOKOKU. 92
0385-6844 See ARIAKE KOGYO KOTO SEMMON GAKKO KIYO. 5086
0385-6860 See AICHI-KEN TOKONAME YOGYO GIJUTSU SENTA HOKOKU. 2585
0385-6909 See KOKUSAI KOGYO SHOYUKEN HOGO KYOKAI, NIHON BUKAI GEPPO. 1305
0385-7026 See CHIBA KOGYO DAIGAKU KENKYU HOKOKU. RIKO HEN. 5093
0385-7034 See CHINETSU. 1353
0385-7204 See GS NEWS TECHNICAL REPORT. 5108
0385-7255 See HOKKAI GAKUEN DAIGAKU HOGAKKAI HOGAKU KENKYU. 2978
0385-7271 See GAKUEN RONSHU. 1825
0385-7298 See JOURNAL OF THE SOCIETY OF AUTOMOTIVE ENGINEERS OF JAPAN. 5418
0385-7360 See DIAMOND INDUSTRIA. 5099
0385-7417 See BEHAVIORMETRIKA. 4577
0385-7832 See BULLETIN OF PRECISION AND INTELLIGENCE LABORATORY. 3476
0385-8146 See AURIS, NASUS, LARYNX. 3886

0385-8278 See KYUSHU DAIGAKU RIGAKUBU KENKYU HOKOKU. CHIKYU WAKUSEI KAGAKU. **1386**

0385-8367 See KINKI DAIGAKU IGAKU ZASSHI. **3602**

0385-8502 See JITCHUKEN ZENRINSHO KENKYUHO. **4309**

0385-8634 See NIIGATA DAIGAKU NOGAKUBU KENKYU HOKOKU. **113**

0385-8766 See YAMANASHI DAIGAKU KYOIKU GAKUBU KENKYU HOKOKU. DAI 2 BUNSATSU, SHIZEN KAGAKU KEI. **5171**

0385-8847 See PEPTIDE INFORMATION / PEPTIDE INSTITUTE, PROTEIN RESEARCH FOUNDATION. **1046**

0385-9088 See SHINRIN REKURIESHON KENKYU. **2395**

0385-9282 See TRANSACTIONS OF THE JAPAN WELDING SOCIETY. **4028**

0385-9290 See HYOGO-KEN KOGAI KENKYUJO KENKYU HOKOKU. **2232**

0385-9363 See NIPPON BYOINKAI ZASSHI. **3790**

0385-9843 See BUSSEIKEN DAYORI (TOKYO). **4427**

0385-9932 See KACHIKU HANSHOKUGAKU ZASSHI (TOKYO. 1977). **5589**

0386-037X See PROCESS, ARCHITECTURE. **306**

0386-0728 See HOMU SOGO KENKYUJO KENKYUBU KIYO. **3165**

0386-0752 See RESEARCH ACTIVITIES OF THE INSTITUTE OF ATOMIC ENERGY, KYOTO UNIVERSITY. **1955**

0386-1058 See SHINRIGAKU HYORON. **4618**

0386-1082 See DAITO BUNKA DAIGAKU KIYO. JINBUN KAGAKU. **2845**

0386-1112 See IATSS RESEARCH. **5441**

0386-118X See FUKUOKA DAIGAKU RIGAKU SHUHO. **5106**

0386-1597 See NIHON ZOSEN GAKKAISHI. **5453**

0386-2062 See YAKUGAKU TOSHOKAN. PHARMACEUTICAL LIBRARY BULLETIN. **3256**

0386-216X See KAGAKU KOGAKU RONBUNSHU. **2014**

0386-2178 See BUNSEKI. **1014**

0386-2186 See KOBUNSHI RONBUNSHU (TOKYO). **984**

0386-2194 See PROCEEDINGS OF THE JAPAN ACADEMY. SERIES A: MATHEMATICAL SCIENCES. **3528**

0386-2208 See PROCEEDINGS OF THE JAPAN ACADEMY. SERIES B: PHYSICAL AND BIOLOGICAL SCIENCES. **469**

0386-2240 See SURI KAGAKU. **3537**

0386-2550 See SEIDENKI GAKKAI SHI. **4445**

0386-2615 See NETSUSOKUTEI. **987**

0386-2682 See DOMYAKU KOKA. **3704**

0386-2763 See PETOROTEKKU. **4271**

0386-2895 See DENRYOKU DOBOKU. **2022**

0386-300X See ACTA MEDICA OKAYAMA. **3544**

0386-3034 See JOURNAL OF SCIENCE OF THE HIROSHIMA UNIVERSITY. SERIES A. PHYSICS AND CHEMISTRY (1971). **4410**

0386-3158 See HIROSHIMA FORUM FOR PSYCHOLOGY. **4588**

0386-3271 See TOKUSHU KYOIKU KENKYU SHISETSU HOKOKU. **1886**

0386-3425 See SNAKE. **5597**

0386-3433 See TECHNOLOGY REPORTS OF THE YAMAGUCHI UNIVERSITY. **5164**

0386-3530 See HOKURIKU KOSHU EISEI GAKKAISHI. **4783**

0386-3603 See YAKURI TO CHIRYO. **4333**

0386-3638 See NIKKEI MEKANIKARU. **2107**

0386-3816 See YAMAGUCHI-KEN GAIKAI SUISAN SHIKENJO KENKYU HOKOKU. **2316**

0386-3980 See NIHON RAIGAKKAI ZASSHI. **3622**

0386-4006 See SCIENCE REPORTS OF TOKYO WOMAN'S CHRISTIAN UNIVERSITY. **5153**

0386-4022 See SHIRON (TOKYO. 1953). **2629**

0386-4103 See OSAKA-SHI IGAKKAI ZASSHI. **3790**

0386-4286 See YOKOSUKA-SHI HAKUBUTSUKAN SHIRYOSHU. **4097**

0386-4294 See GUNMA DAIGAKU KYOIKU GAKUBU KIYO. JINBUN SHAKAI KAGAKU HEN. **1864**

0386-4391 See SASEBO KOGYO KOTO SENMON GAKKO KENKYU HOKOKU. **5149**

0386-4405 See KONAN JOSHI DAIGAKU KENKYU KIYO. **1092**

0386-4561 See KOTAIGUN SEITAI GAKKAI KAIHO. **4554**

0386-4634 See KYOSHOBA SOGO KENKYUJO HOKOKU. **2800**

0386-4715 See SHIKA JANARU. **1335**

0386-4766 See SAIBO. **472**

0386-491X See KINKI DAIGAKU KOGAKUBU KENKYU HOKOKU. **1984**

0386-4928 See KINKI DAIGAKU RIKOGAKUBU KENKYU HOKOKU. **5123**

0386-4952 See MEIJO DAIGAKU RIKO GAKUBU KENKYU HOKOKU. **5128**

0386-4987 See OSAKA DENKI TSUSHIN DAIGAKU KENKYU RONSHU. SHIZEN KAGAKU HEN. **5136**

0386-5096 See MITSUBISHI ELECTRIC ADVANCE. **2073**

0386-5444 See SOLAR TERRESTRIAL ENVIRONMENTAL RESEARCH IN JAPAN. **400**

0386-5495 See MOL. **2015**

0386-5576 See OHM. **2074**

0386-5924 See KAWASAKI IGAKKAISHI. **3601**

0386-5975 See TOYAMA DAIGAKU JINBUN GAKUBU KIYO. **2855**

0386-5991 See KODAI MATHEMATICAL JOURNAL. **3516**

0386-6092 See ACTA MEDICA KINKI UNIVERSITY. **3544**

0386-6106 See AKITA IGAKU. **3547**

0386-6157 See FUNTAI KOGAKKAISHI. **5106**

0386-6742 See CHIBA-KEN EISEI KENKYUJO KENKYU HOKOKU. **4771**

0386-6831 See TEREBIJON GAKKAISHI. **1998**

0386-6904 See TOOSHI KENKYU. **2712**

0386-7064 See TAIKI OSEN GAKKAI SHI. **2244**

0386-7129 See TSUKUBA DAIGAKU TAIIKU KAGAKUKEI KIYO. **1859**

0386-7137 See RIDERS CLUB TOKYO. 1978. **4854**

0386-7196 See CELL STRUCTURE AND FUNCTION. **534**

0386-720X See BULLETIN - NANZAN INSTITUTE FOR RELIGION AND CULTURE. **4941**

0386-7293 See CURRENT CONTENTS OF ACADEMIC JOURNALS IN JAPAN. THE HUMANITIES AND SOCIAL SCIENCES. **2845**

0386-7536 See SEIKATSU KAGAKU KENKYUJO KENKYU HOKOKU. **5156**

0386-765X See IBARAKI DAIGAKU KYOIKUGAKUBU KIYO. JIMBUN, SHAKAI KAGAKU, GEIJUTSU. **2504**

0386-8044 See SEKIGAISEN GIJUTSU. **4441**

0386-8109 See CHIRYOGAKU. **3563**

0386-8141 See SEITAI KAGAKU. **2221**

0386-8311 See JINKOGAKU KENKYU. **4554**

0386-8370 See MIYAGI-KEN NOGYO TANKI DAIGAKU KIYO. **109**

0386-846X See JOURNAL OF PHARMACOBIO-DYNAMICS. **4312**

0386-8710 See GEOGRAPHICAL REPORTS OF TOKYO METROPOLITAN UNIVERSITY. **1377**

0386-8729 See JIMBUN GAKUHO TOKYO. 1950. **2848**

0386-8893 See HOSEI SHIGAKU. **2620**

0386-8907 See REKISHI HYORON. **2627**

0386-8966 See RISSHO SHIGAKU. **2625**

0386-9032 See KENKYU KIYO / TOKUGAWA RINSEISHI KENKYUJO. **2386**

0386-9164 See NIHON REKISHI. **2660**

0386-9237 See REKISHIGAKU KENKYU. **2663**

0386-9253 See SEIYO SHIGAKU / NIHON SEIYOSHI GAKKAI. **2629**

0386-9318 See SHIEN (TOKYO. 1928). **2629**

0386-9342 See SHIGAKU KENKYU (HIROSHIMA. 1929). **2664**

0386-9350 See SHIKAN. **2629**

0386-9369 See SHIRIN (KYOTO. 1916). **2664**

0386-9539 See SEIBUTSUGAKUSHI KENKYU JAPANESE JOURNAL OF THE HISTORY OF BIOLOGY / NIHON KAGAKUSHU GAKKAI SEIBUTSUGAKUSHI BUNKAKAI HENSHU. **473**

0386-9555 See SUGAKUSHI KENKYU. **3537**

0386-9628 See HAIGAN. **3817**

0386-9687 See JIBI INKOKA TENBO. **3888**

0386-9709 See SHINKEI NAIKA. **3846**

0386-9717 See KETSUEKI TO MYAKUKAN. **3773**

0386-9784 See NISHI NIHON HIFUKA. **3722**

0386-9865 See RINSHO FUJINKA SANKA. **3768**

0386-9873 See SANFUJINKA NO SEKAI. **3768**

0387-0022 See IDEN. **547**

0387-0162 See BOIRA KENKYU. **1599**

0387-0200 See REZA KENKYU. **4441**

0387-0308 See JICHI IKA DAIGAKU KIYO. **3592**

0387-0324 See KANAGAWA DAIGAKU KOGAKU KOGAKU KENKYUJO SHOHO. **5122**

0387-0502 See CHUTANZO TO NETSUSHORI. **4000**

0387-0707 See SHOKUBUTSU BOEKIJO CHOSA KENKYU HOKOKU. **2431**

0387-0723 See UCHU KOKU KANKYO IGAKU. **3648**

0387-0758 See DENKI KYOKAI ZASSHI. **2040**

0387-0774 See DENSHI ZAIRYO. **2041**

0387-0790 See DOBOKU SEKO. **2022**

0387-0812 See AICHI KOGYO DAIGAKU KENKYU HOKOKU, B, SENMON KANKEI RONBUNSHU. **5081**

0387-0863 See FUNE NO KAGAKU. **1976**

0387-0936 See GOSEI JUSHI. **2102**

0387-0995 See KANAZAWA DAIGAKU KYOIKUGAKUBU KIYO : SHIZEN KAGAKU HEN. **1833**

0387-1002 See KANSAI BYOCHUGAI KENKYUKAI HO. **2422**

0387-1010 See KANSEN, ENSHO, MENEKI. **3674**

0387-1029 See KARYOKU GENSHIRYOKU HATSUDEN. **4448**

0387-1037 See KEMIKARU ENJINIYARINGU. **2014**

0387-1045 See KIKAI SEKKEI. **2119**

0387-1053 See KIKAI TO KOGU. **2119**

0387-1061 See KONKURITO KOGAKU. **619**

0387-1096 See KOON GAKKAISHI. **4007**

0387-1150 See NARA KOGYO KOTO SENMON GAKKO KENKYU KIYO. **5130**

0387-1304 See SUMITOMO JUKIKAI GIHO. **5160**

0387-1533 See NIHON REOROJI GAKKAI SHI. **5234**

0387-1789 See KIKAN KEIZAI KENKYU. **1571**

0387-1819 See SHO ENERUGI. **1956**

0387-1940 See ROBOT (TOKYO, 1971). **1216**

0387-1975 See SHOKUHIN SHOSHA. **2357**

0387-2025 See SUISHITSU ODAKU KENKYU (TOKYO. 1978). **2244**

0387-2203 See ZOSEN GIJUTSU. **4185**

0387-2254 See TAISEI KENSETSU GIJUTSU KENKYUJOHO. **5161**

0387-2289 See SEI MARIANNA IKA DAIGAKU ZASSHI. **3640**

0387-2327 See NISSHIN SEIKO GIHO. **4013**

0387-2335 See NOGYO DOBOKU GAKKAI RONBUNSHU. **179**

0387-2432 See MITSUBISHI JUKO GIHO. **5129**

0387-2513 See KEIKAKU GYOSEI / NIHON KEIKAKU GYOSEI GAKKAI. **2826**

0387-2645 See SHOKAKI GEKA. **3748**

0387-2688 See BIJUTSUSHIGAKU SENDAI. 1978. **344**

0387-2793 See JINKO MONDAI KENKYU. **4554**

0387-2815 See AMERIKA KENKYU (TOKYO. 1967). **3337**

0387-2866 See HOGAKU RONSO (KYOTO. 1919). **2978**

0387-2955 See KSU ECONOMIC AND BUSINESS REVIEW. **1571**

0387-3021 See KEIZAIGAKU RONSO KYOTO. 1949. **1501**

0387-3064 See KIKAN SHAKAI HOSHO KENKYU. **5294**

0387-3110 See KOKUGO TO KOKUBUNGAKU. **3293**

0387-3145 See KYOIKU SHAKAIGAKU KENKYU. **1760**

0387-3242 See NOGYO SOGO KENKYU. **113**

0387-3307 See SHAKAI KAGAKU KENKYU (TOKYO. 1948). **5218**

0387-3374 See TOKUSHU KYOKUGAKU KENKYU. **1886**

0387-3439 See STUDIES IN ENGLISH LITERATURE (TOKYO. 1960). **3442**

0387-3714 See FUKUSHIMA-KEN NOGYO SHIKENJO TOKUBETSU KENKYU HOKOKU. **89**

0387-382X See KAIYO KAGAKU GIJUTSU SENTA SHIKEN KENKYU HOKOKU. **1451**

0387-3870 See TOKYO JOURNAL OF MATHEMATICS. **3538**

0387-4141 See HISSU AMINOSAN KENKYU. **4191**

0387-4168 See NIHON GASU TABIN GAKKAI SHI. **2123**

0387-4185 See NEW VOICES (DIEGO MARTIN, TRINIDAD AND TOBAGO). **3416**

0387-4346 See NIPPON SHIKA IGAKKAI KAIHO. **1331**

0387-4508 See TRANSACTIONS OF JWRI. **4022**

0387-4818 See MACHIKANEYAMA RONSO : TETSUGAKUHEN. **2850**

0387-4982 See TSUKUBA JOURNAL OF MATHEMATICS. **3540**

0387-5008 See NIHON KIKAI GAKKAI RONBUNSHU. A. **2123**

0387-5016 See NIHON KIKAI GAKKAI RONBUNSHU. B. **2093**

0387-5024 See NIHON KIKAI GAKKAI RONBUNSHU. C. **2123**

0387-5245 See OEP : OFFICE EQUIPMENT & PRODUCTS. **4213**

0387-5253 See JOURNAL OF S C C J. **1026**

0387-5385 See MEIDEN REVIEW. INTERNATIONAL EDITION. **2072**

0387-5504 See NAVAL ARCHITECTURE AND OCEAN ENGINEERING. **4179**

0387-5512 See ZUGAKU KENKYU. **5173**

0387-5547 See TEIKYO IGAKU ZASSHI. **3645**

0387-5806 See JOHO SHORI GAKKAI RONBUN SHI / TRANSACTIONS OF INFORMATION PROCESSING SOCIETY OF JAPAN. **1260**

0387-5911 See KANSENSHOGAKU ZASSHI. **4788**

0387-6004 See SENRI ETHNOLOGICAL STUDIES. **245**

0387-6101 See JOURNAL OF INFORMATION PROCESSING. **1260**

0387-6144 See BULLETIN OF THE RESEARCH LABORATORY FOR NUCLEAR REACTORS. **2154**

0387-6896 See TOKYO FINANCIAL REVIEW. **814**

0387-6993 See TOTTORI-KEN YASAI SHIKENJO KENKYU HOKOKU. **189**

0387-7280 See KOKUSAI NIHON BUNGAKU KENKYU SHUKAI KAIGIROKU. **3402**

0387-737X See SEAMIC NEWS LETTER.B. **3640**

0387-7396 See JITENSHA GIJUTSU JOHO. **429**

0387-7604 See BRAIN & DEVELOPMENT (TOKYO. 1979). **3828**

0387-7647 See HIROSHIMA DAIGAKU SEIBUTSU SEISANGAKUBU KIYO. **457**

0387-7973 See JIKKEN SHAKAI SHINRIGAKU KENKYU. **4592**

0387-8082 See ACTA SUMEROLOGICA. **3261**

0387-8139 See NOGYO KIKAIKA KENKYUSHO HOKOKU. **160**

0387-821X See JOURNAL OF UOEH. **4788**

0387-8511 See BULLETIN OF THE NATIONAL SCIENCE MUSEUM. SERIES E, (PHYSICAL SCIENCES & ENGINEERING). **5091**

0387-8538 See REPORTS OF THE FACULTY OF SCIENCE AND ENGINEERING, SAGA UNIVERSITY MATHEMATICS. **3531**

0387-8783 See KANE : HITOTSUBASHI DAIGAKU FUZOKU TOSHOKAN HO. **3221**

0387-8805 See JOURNAL OF LIGHT & VISUAL ENVIRONMENT. **4436**

0387-9070 See NAGANO-KEN EISEI KOGAI KENKYUJO KENKYU HOKOKU. **4792**

0387-916X See DENSHI SHASHIN GAKKAISHI. **4368**

0387-9836 See SHOKURYO SEISAKU KENKYU. **2357**

0387-9925 See SHIMANE DAIGAKU RIGAKUBU KIYO. **5157**

0388-0001 See LANGUAGE SCIENCES (OXFORD). **3296**

0388-0036 See NIPPON GAKUSHIIN KIYO. **1769**

0388-0079 See BULLETIN OF THE MARINE ENGINEERING SOCIETY IN JAPAN. **1967**

0388-0125 See BULLETIN OF THE NIIGATA AIRGLOW OBSERVATORY. **1421**

0388-0168 See BULLETIN OF THE TOKYO METROPOLITAN REHABILITATION CENTER FOR THE PHYSICALLY AND MENTALLY HANDICAPPED. **1876**

0388-0176 See CHU-SHIKOKU STUDIES IN AMERICAN LITERATURE. **3375**

0388-0311 See FOCUS. JAPAN. **676**

0388-032X See FOCUS JAPAN. NOW IN JAPAN. **836**

0388-0435 See JAPAN ECHO. **2654**

0388-0508 See JOURNAL OF INTERCULTURAL STUDIES (HIRAKATA, OSAKA). **239**

0388-0796 See RENAISSANCE BULLETIN, THE. **3428**

0388-0923 See STEEL TODAY & TOMORROW (SEMIANNUAL EDITION). **4021**

0388-1008 See WASEDA BUSINESS & ECONOMIC STUDIES. **1588**

0388-1032 See WING NEWSLETTER. **39**

0388-130X See MEISEI DAIGAKU KENKYU KIYO. RIKO GAKUBU. **5128**

0388-1423 See AMJ NEWSLETTER. **1217**

0388-1458 See SHOKEN KEIZAIGAKKAI NEMPO. **913**

0388-1601 See RINSHO YAKURI. **4328**

0388-1709 See FUJIN KYOIKU JOHO. **1747**

0388-1717 See KYUSHU DAIGAKU DAIGAKUIN SOGO RIKOGAKU KENKYUKA HOKOKU. **1985**

0388-2217 See MITSUBACHI KAGAKU / HONEYBEE SCIENCE. **109**

0388-2241 See CHIBA REVIEW. **3374**

0388-2306 See HAM JOURNAL TOKYO. **1112**

0388-2330 See MEMOIRS OF THE COLLEGE OF AGRICULTURE, KYOTO UNIVERSITY. **108**

0388-2403 See NORIN SUISANSHO KACHIKU EISEI SHIKENJO KENKYU HOKOKU. **5517**

0388-2519 See EIGO EIBUNGAKU KENKYU (TOKYO. 1976). **3278**

0388-2810 See NAGASAKI DAIGAKU KYOIKU GAKUBU KYOKA KYOIKUGAKU KENKYU HOKOKU. **1901**

0388-2861 See JOURNAL OF THE ACOUSTICAL SOCIETY OF JAPAN (E), THE. **4453**

0388-3116 See KENKYU HOKOKU / HYOGO KENRITSU CHIKUSAN SHIKENJO. **102**

0388-3213 See KAGAKU GIJUTSU KENKYUJO HOKOKU / JOURNAL OF THE NATIONAL CHEMICAL LABORATORY FOR INDUSTRY. **983**

0388-337X See SANGYO IGAKU JANARU. **2870**

0388-3388 See SHOKUHIN SANGYO SENTA GIJUTSU KENKYU HOKOKU. **2357**

0388-3396 See MITSUBISHI GENSHIRYOKU GIHO. **5129**

0388-3612 See KYORITSU JOSHI DAIGAKU KASEI GAKUBU KIYO. **2791**

0388-3647 See KIYO - KYORITSU JOSHI TANKI DAIGAKU. BUNKA. **3402**

0388-3655 See KYORITSU JOSHI TANKI DAIGAKU SEIKATSU KAGAKUKA KIYO. **462**

0388-3698 See PEPTIDE CHEMISTRY : PROCEEDINGS OF THE ... SYMPOSIUM OF PEPTIDE CHEMISTRY. **988**

0388-3930 See ZAIRYO KAGAKU. **5172**

0388-4112 See MEMOIRS OF THE NATIONAL DEFENSE ACADEMY. MATHEMATICS, PHYSICS, CHEMISTRY, AND ENGINEERING. **3522**

0388-4171 See PEIN KURINIKKU. **3626**

0388-4252 See KIKAI GIJUTSU KENKYUJO SHOHO. **5123**

0388-4279 See KOKUSAI KANKEI GAKUBU KENKYU NENPO. **4527**

0388-4384 See NETSU KOKASEI JUSHI. **4457**

0388-4821 See KENKYU NENPO / NIHON DAIGAKU BUNRI GAKUBU (MISHIMA). **5123**

0388-5038 See JOHO SHORI KENKYU. **1213**

0388-5267 See ENERUGI FORAMU. **1943**

0388-5321 See HYOMEN KAGAKU. **1025**

0388-557X See ANNUAIRE. QUALITE DES EAUX. **5529**

0388-5585 See KURINIKARU SUTADI. **3861**

0388-5607 See SCIENCE REPORTS OF THE TOHOKU UNIVERSITY. EIGHTH SERIES. PHYSICS AND ASTRONOMY, THE. **4420**

0388-5623 See DAIGAKU TOSHOKAN KYORYOKU NYUSU. **3205**

0388-5631 See NAGAOKA GIJUTSU KAGAKU DAIGAKU KENKYU HOKOKU. **5130**

0388-6042 See KANAGAWA KENRITSU EISEI TANKI DAIGAKU KIYO. **3914**

0388-6107 See BIOMEDICAL RESEARCH (TOKYO). **3557**

0388-6115 See JAPAN PICTORIAL (NORTH AMERICAN EDITION). **2536**

0388-6166 See FUKUOKA-SHI EISEI SHIKENJO HO. **2230**

0388-6182 See SCIENCE REPORTS OF THE INSTITUTE OF GEOSCIENCE, UNIVERSITY OF TSUKUBA. SECTION B, GEOLOGICAL SCIENCES. **1396**

0388-6417 See JOCHI EIGO BUNGAKU KENKYU. **3289**

0388-6719 See GENDAI TOYO IGAKU. **3578**

0388-6735 See NIHON CHINETSU GAKKAI SHI. **1416**

0388-6913 See KORIGU : HIROSHIMA DAIGAKU KYOIKU KENKYU SENTA TSUSHIN. **1833**

0388-7081 See PATENTS & LICENSING. **1308**

0388-7367 See AICHI KYOIKU DAIGAKU KENKYU HOKOKU. GEIJUTSU, HOKEN TAIIKU, KASEI, GIJUTSU KAGAKU. **5081**

0388-7405 See NIHON KOKAI GAKKAI RONBUNSHU. **4181**

0388-7421 See DOBUTSU IYAKUHIN KENSAJO NEMPO. **5509**

0388-7448 See NEUROSCIENCES (KOBE. 1975). **3843**

0388-7588 See SHINKEI SEISHIN YAKURI. **3846**

0388-7596 See KEIO COMMUNICATION REVIEW. **1115**

0388-7723 See FUKUSHIMA-KEN NOGYO SHIKENJO KENKYU HOKOKU. **89**

0388-7790 See FUKUI-KEN NOGYO SHIKENJO HOKOKU. **89**

0388-788X See GYOBYO KENKYU. **2304**

0388-7995 See AICHI-KEN NOGYO SOGO SHIKENJO KEKNYU HOKOKU. **57**

0388-8177 See IKUSHUGAKU SAIKIN NO SHINPO. **548**

0388-8215 See KAGOSHIMA-KEN NOGYO SHIKENJO KENKYU HOKOKU. **102**

0388-8231 See KANAGAWA-KEN NOGYO SOGO KENKYUJO KENKYU HOKOKU. **102**

0388-8266 See KINJIN KENKYUJO KENKYU HOKOKU. **575**

0388-8371 See NARA-KEN NOGYO SHIKENJO KENKYU HOKOKU. **110**

0388-841X See NANSEI KAIKU SUISAN KENKYUJO KENKYU HOKOKU. **2309**

0388-8436 See NORIN SUISAN KENKYU KEISAN SENTA HOKOKU. A / BULLETIN OF THE COMPUTING CENTER FOR RESEARCH IN AGRICULTURE, FORESTRY, AND FISHERY. SERIES A. **114**

0388-8517 See NOGYO SHISETSU. **113**

0388-8614 See RINGYO KEIZAI. **2394**

0388-886X *See* KANSAI UNIVERSITY REVIEW OF LAW AND POLITICS. 2992

0388-905X *See* SHIMANE-KEN NOGYO SHIKENJO KENKYU HOKOKU. 134

0388-9130 *See* SHOKUBUTSU NO KAGAKU CHOSETSU. 527

0388-9335 *See* YAMAGUCHI JUIGAKU ZASSHI. 5527

0388-9386 *See* TROPICAL AGRICULTURE RESEARCH SERIES. 142

0388-9459 *See* KANKYO GIJUTSU. 2197

0388-9475 *See* KAWASAKI STEEL TECHNICAL REPORT (TOKYO. 1980). 4006

0388-9564 *See* TAIYO ENERUGI (TOKYO. 1975). 1959

0388-9718 *See* SUISAN KOGAKU KENKYUJO HOKOKU. 2314

0388-9734 *See* SHOJINKAI IGAKUSHI. 3641

0389-0007 *See* AJIKEN NYUSU. 1461

0389-0066 *See* GA DOCUMENT. 299

0389-0082 *See* HIROSHIMA-KEN KANKYO SENTA KENKYU HOKOKU. 2232

0389-0244 *See* KOCHI DAIGAKU GAKUJUTSU KENKYU HOKOKU. SHIZEN KAGAKU. 5124

0389-0252 *See* MEMOIRS OF THE FACULTY OF SCIENCE, KOCHI UNIVERSITY. SERIES A, MATHEMATICS. 3522

0389-0279 *See* KOCHI DAIGAKU RIGAKUBU KIYO. KAGAKU. 984

0389-0449 *See* KOCHI DAIGAKU KYOIKU GAKUBU KENKYU HOKOKU. DAI 3-BU. 5124

0389-0473 *See* KOCHI DAIGAKU GAKUJUTSU KENKYU HOKOKU. NOGAKU. 102

0389-0503 *See* ECONOMIC EYE. 1557

0389-0724 *See* GYOMU HOKOKU. 211

0389-0805 *See* NIHON KANKYO EISEI SENTA SHOHO. 2178

0389-0902 *See* IDEMITSU BIJUTSUKAN KANPO. 352

0389-1186 *See* JAPANESE SLAVIC AND EAST EUROPEAN STUDIES. 2694

0389-1623 *See* KENKYU KIYO / KAGOSHIMA JOSHI DAIGAKU. 1833

0389-1763 *See* NOSAGYO KENKYU. 2426

0389-1836 *See* AZABU DAIGAKU JUI GAKUBU KENKYU HOKOKU. 5505

0389-1844 *See* JUNKAN SEIGYO. 3601

0389-1887 *See* MEDICAL TECHNOLOGY (TOKYO. 1973). 3612

0389-1895 *See* SHIKA GIKO. 1335

0389-2263 *See* SHIKEN HOKOKU (NIHON SENBAI KOSHA. HIRATSUKA SEIZO SHIKENJO). 3488

0389-2328 *See* ASIA-OCEANIA JOURNAL OF OBSTETRICS AND GYNAECOLOGY. 3757

0389-2514 *See* NIHON KOGYO DAIGAKU KENKYU HOKOKU. 5134

0389-2603 *See* KOKUSAI KANKEI KENKYU (MISHIMA-SHI, JAPAN). 4528

0389-2859 *See* EHIME-KEN CHIKUSAN SHIKENJO KENKYU HOKOKU. 81

0389-3081 *See* TOKAI DAIGAKU KIYO. GAIKOKUGO KYOIKU SENTA. 3329

0389-3103 *See* NORIN SUISAN KENKYU KEISAN SENTA HOKOKU. B. 114

0389-3502 *See* JAPAN ... AN INTERNATIONAL COMPARISON. 1569

0389-3626 *See* SHOKA TO KYUSHU. 3748

0389-3693 *See* OBAYASHI REPOTO. 5135

0389-3898 *See* IGAKU TO YAKUGAKU. 3585

0389-3944 *See* SAPPORO IKA DAIGAKU JINBUN SHIZEN KAGAKU KIYO. 3638

0389-4002 *See* NIHON ZENKOKU SHOSHI / HENSHU, KOKURITSU KOKKAI TOSHOKAN SHUSHU SEIRIBU. 421

0389-4037 *See* NIHONGO KYOIKU. 3306

0389-4118 *See* ARUKORU KENKYU TO YAKUBUTSU IZON. 1341

0389-4274 *See* HAIKU BUNGAKUKAN KIYO. 3392

0389-4290 *See* ENSHO. 3574

0389-4304 *See* JSAE REVIEW. 5418

0389-4703 *See* NIHON KEISEI GEKA GAKKAI KAISHI. 3970

0389-5041 *See* KYOTO-FU EISEI KENKYUJO NENPO. 4788

0389-5351 *See* NANKAIKEN KIYO. 2670

0389-5564 *See* GEKA TO TAISHA, EIYO. 3965

0389-5602 *See* NIHON TOKEI GAKKAISHI (TOKYO. 1970). 5334

0389-5858 *See* YOSHOKU KENKYUJO KENKYU HOKOKU. 2316

0389-617X *See* TOKYO DENKI DAIGAKU KOGAKUBU KENKYU HOKOKU. 1999

0389-6277 *See* SENSHOKU KENKYU. 1029

0389-6498 *See* HOKEI RONSO (MORIOKA, 1980). 2978

0389-6609 *See* PUBLICATIONS OF THE SETO MARINE BIOLOGICAL LABORATORY. SPECIAL PUBLICATION SERIES. 557

0389-6625 *See* KOGAKU. 4437

0389-7079 *See* KETSUGO SOSHIKI. 3805

0389-7087 *See* KANTO SEIKEI SAIGAI GEKA GAKKAI ZASSHI. 3883

0389-8008 *See* TSURUMI DAIGAKU KIYO. DAI 1-BU, KOKUGO KOKUBUNGAKU HEN. 3330

0389-8016 *See* TSURUMI DAIGAKU KIYO. DAI 2-BU, GAIKOKUGO GAIKOKU BUNGAKU HEN. 3330

0389-8032 *See* TSURUMI DAIGAKU KIYO. DAI 4-BU, JINBUN SHAKAI HEN. 2855

0389-8040 *See* AKITA DAIGAKU KOZAN GAKUBU KENKYU HOKOKU. 2132

0389-9004 *See* NIHON TOKEI NENKAN. 5334

0389-9071 *See* TAIRYOKU KENKYU. 3644

0389-9098 *See* BYOIN YAKUGAKU. 4295

0389-9101 *See* KANSAI ZOSEN KYOKAI SHI / JOURNAL OF THE KANSAI SOCIETY OF NAVAL ARCHITECTS, JAPAN. 5450

0389-9160 *See* A + U. 286

0389-9268 *See* TAKAMATSU KOGYO KOTO SENMON GAKKO KENKYU KIYO. 5237

0389-9306 *See* ASAHIKAWA KOGYO KOTO SENMON GAKKO KENKYU HOBUN. 5086

0389-9330 *See* TOYAMA KENRITSU GIJUTSU TANKI DAIGAKU KENKYU HOKOKU. 5166

0389-9365 *See* KANAGAWA-KEN KOGAI SENTA KENKYU HOKOKU. 2176

0389-9535 *See* RISSHO DAIGAKU JINBUN KAGAKU KENKYUJO NENPO. BESSATSU. 2853

0390-0010 *See* ANNALI DELL'ISTITUTO SPERIMENTALE PER LA SELVICOLTURA. 2374

0390-0037 *See* CHRONOBIOLOGIA. 3795

0390-010X *See* RASSEGNA ECONOMICA. 1515

0390-0134 *See* GIORNALE ITALIANO DI ORTOPEDIA E TRAUMATOLOGIA. 3881

0390-0142 *See* CRITICA LETTERARIA. 3378

0390-0347 *See* MEDICO E PAZIENTE. 3614

0390-041X *See* INDUSTRIA, RIVISTA DI ECONOMIA E POLITICA INDUSTRIALE, L'. 1610

0390-0444 *See* COLTURE PROTETTE. 2412

0390-0460 *See* MICOLOGIA ITALIANA. 575

0390-0479 *See* VIGNEVINI. 2371

0390-0487 *See* ZOOTECNICA E NUTRIZIONE ANIMALE. 224

0390-0495 *See* RASSEGNA ITALIANA DI CHIRURGIA PEDIATRICA. 3973

0390-0541 *See* INDUSTRIE DELLE BEVANDE. 2367

0390-0576 *See* ANNALI DELL'ISTITUTO DI LINGUE E LETTERATURE GERMANICHE. 3362

0390-0584 *See* ANTICHITA PISANE. 2675

0390-0592 *See* ARCHEOLOGIA MEDIEVALE. 258

0390-0657 *See* CRITICA DEL DIRITTO. 2957

0390-0711 *See* MEDIOEVO ROMANZO. 3301

0390-0851 *See* SOCIOLOGIA DEL DIRITTO. 3056

0390-0975 *See* INFORMATICA E DIRITTO. 2982

0390-0991 *See* LAVORO E SINDACATO. 1687

0390-1009 *See* LIBRI E DOCUMENTI, ARCHIVO STORICO CIVICO E BIBLIOTECA TRIVULZIANA. 2622

0390-1025 *See* MODULO. 621

0390-105X *See* QUADERNI DI ECONOMIA DEL LAVORO. 1704

0390-1181 *See* AFFARI SOCIALI INTERNAZIONALI. 5189

0390-1319 *See* ARTE NAIVE. 341

0390-1378 *See* BANCHE E BANCHIERI. 774

0390-1513 *See* CASA STILE. 2583

0390-1572 *See* CIVILITA DEL BERE. 2366

0390-2102 *See* EUROPA DOMANI. 833

0390-2196 *See* GEO-ARCHEOLOGIA. 269

0390-2358 *See* ICP. 4260

0390-2412 *See* INCONTRI LINGUISTICI. 3286

0390-2420 *See* INFANZIA. 4590

0390-2439 *See* INFORMATION & I.E. E DOCUMENTAZIONE. 1260

0390-2447 *See* INFORMAZIONI AZIENDALI E PROFESSIONALI. 870

0390-2455 *See* INFORMAZIONE ELETTRONICA. 2064

0390-251X *See* LAVORO E PREVIDENZA OGGI. 3151

0390-2528 *See* LAVORO SICURO. 2865

0390-2692 *See* M & C. MEETING & CONGRESSI. 762

0390-2811 *See* MONDO CINESE. 2507

0390-3133 *See* PALLAVOLO. 4911

0390-3230 *See* PISCINE OGGI. 4912

0390-3311 *See* PRIMA COMUNICAZIONE. 1119

0390-346X *See* PSICOLOGIA CONTEMPORANEA. 4609

0390-3532 *See* STATO E PROSPETTIVE DELLA FORMAZIONE PROFESSIONALE IN ITALIA : RELAZIONE ANNUALE PRESENTATA DALL'ISFOL AL MINISTERO DEL LAVORO E DELLA PREVIDENZA SOCIALE IN ATTUAZIONE DELL'ART. 20 DELLA LEGGE-QUADRO SULLA FORMAZIONE PROFESSIONALE. 1712

0390-3842 *See* RIVISTA DI INFORMAZIONI MARITTIME. 3182

0390-4253 *See* STORIA ARCHITETTURA. 309

0390-492X *See* MEMORIE DI BIOLOGIA MARINA E DI OCEANOGRAFIA. 556

0390-5179 *See* SAGGI NEUROPSICOLOGIA INFANTILE PSICOPEDAGOGIA RIABILITAZIONE. 4617

0390-5187 *See* TRIBUNA POSTALE E DELLE TELECOMUNICAZIONI. 1147

0390-5330 *See* ECONOMIA E SOCIOLOGIA. 5198

0390-5349 *See* GIORNALE ITALIANO DI PSICOLOGIA. 4588

0390-5411 *See* CHRONICA DERMATOLOGICA. 3718

0390-5454 *See* ANNALI DELL'OSPEDALE MARIA VITTORIA DI TORINO. 3550

0390-5489 *See* ITALIAN JOURNAL OF ORTHOPAEDICS AND TRAUMATOLOGY. 3882

0390-5527 *See* ATTUALITA IN CHIRURGIA. 3960

0390-5551 *See* NUOVO CIMENTO DELLA SOCIETA ITALIANA DI FISICA [SEZIONE] C, IL. 4413

0390-5616 *See* JOURNAL OF NEUROSURGICAL SCIENCES. 3968

0390-5748 See INTERNATIONAL JOURNAL OF CLINICAL AND LABORATORY RESEARCH. 458

0390-5845 *See* GASLINI GENOVA. 3903

0390-587X *See* RASSEGNA PETROLIFERA. 4276

0390-590X *See* STATISTICA. 5339

0390-5942 *See* POSTE E TELECOMUNICAZIONI NELLO SVILUPPO DELLA SOCIETA. 1147

0390-6019 *See* RIVISTA DI TOSSICOLOGIA : SPERIMENTALE E CLINICA. 3983

0390-6078 *See* HAEMATOLOGICA (ROMA). 3772

0390-6132 *See* IMPIANTI. 1609

0390-6140 *See* ECONOMIA PUBBLICA. 1605

0390-6310 *See* COLLANA DI AGGIORNAMENTI IN ANESTESIA E RIANIMAZIONE. 3682

0390-6329 *See* QUADERNI - ISTITUTO DI RICERCA SULLE ACQUE. 5538

0390-6426 *See* STATISTICHE DELLA CACCIA, PESCA E COOPERAZIONE. 138

0390-6566 *See* STATISTICA ANNUALE DEL COMMERCIO CON L'ESTERO. TOMO 2. MERCI PER PAESI. 5339

0390-6604 *See* TOTUS HOMO. 4620

0390-6620 *See* INDICATORI MENSILI / ISTAT, ISTITUTO CENTRALE DI STATISTICA. 5328

0390-6655 *See* IDROTECNICA. L'ACQUA NELL'AGRICOLTURA NELL'IGIENE NELL'INDUSTRIA. **2090**
0390-6663 *See* CLINICAL AND EXPERIMENTAL OBSTETRICS & GYNECOLOGY. **3758**
0390-668X *See* RIVISTA DI INFORMATICA. **1202**
0390-6698 *See* TECNOLOGIA ELETTRICHE. INDUSTRIA ITALIANA ELETTROTECNICA ED ELETTRONICA. **2083**
0390-6736 *See* MB : MONTI E BOSCHI. **2387**
0390-6825 *See* OMNIA MEDICA ET THERAPEUTICA. ARCHIVIO. **3624**
0390-6841 *See* QUINTESSENZA, LA. **1334**
0390-7368 *See* ARCHIVIO DI ORTOPEDIA E REUMATOLOGIA. **3803**
0390-7740 *See* RAYS. **3946**
0390-8518 *See* BOLLETTINO UFFICIALE - MINISTERO DELLA PUBBLICA ISTRUZIONE. PARTE I. LEGI, DECRETI, REGOLAMENTI E ALTRE DISPOSIZIONI GENERALI. **1860**
0390-8798 *See* CORRIERE DEL MEDICO. **3569**
0390-9131 *See* BOLLETTINO LEGGI E DECRETI. **1656**
0390-9212 *See* IMPRESA E SOCIETA. **901**
0391-0970 *See* RIVISTA DI OSTETRICIA GINECOLOGIA PRATICA E MEDICINA PERINATALE. **3768**
0391-108X *See* ROCCA. **4994**
0391-1535 *See* CRONACHE ERCOLANESI. **3275**
0391-1551 *See* RIVISTA DI BIOLOGIA NORMALE E PATOLOGICA. **472**
0391-156X *See* NATURA BRESCIANA. **4168**
0391-1586 *See* INDUSTRIA MINERARIA (ROMA. 1957). **1382**
0391-1632 *See* MONITORE ZOOLOGICO ITALIANO. MONOGRAFIA. **5591**
0391-1675 *See* RAPPORTI ISTISAN. **3632**
0391-1683 *See* TECNOLOGIE MECCANICHE. **2130**
0391-173X *See* ANNALI DELLA SCUOLA NORMALE SUPERIORE DI PISA, CLASSE DI SCIENZE. **3493**
0391-1772 *See* MINERVA PSICHIATRICA. **3931**
0391-1780 *See* BOLLETTINO STORICO PISANO / SOCIETA STORICA PISANA. **2612**
0391-1845 *See* RIVISTA GIURUDICA DELLA SCUOLA. **1870**
0391-190X *See* RIVISTA TRIMESTRALE DI SCIENZA DELLA AMMINISTRAZIONE. **4684**
0391-1977 *See* MINERVA ENDOCRINOLOGICA. **3731**
0391-1985 *See* BOLLETTINO UFFICIALE - MINISTERO DELLA PUBBLICA ISTRUZIONE. PARTE IIE. ATTI DI AMMINISTRAZIONE. **1861**
0391-2000 *See* MONDO ORTODONTICO. **1330**
0391-2019 *See* HP ENERGIA TRASPORTI. **5383**
0391-2035 *See* CLINICA E LABORATORIO (ROMA). **3565**
0391-2051 *See* ATTI DELLA FONDAZIONE GIORGIO RONCHI (1976). **4433**
0391-2078 *See* ECONOMIA E POLITICA INDUSTRIALE. **1591**
0391-2108 *See* RIVISTA DI LETTERATURE MODERNE E COMPARATE. **3431**
0391-2159 *See* TRIBUNA STAMPA. **4570**
0391-2221 *See* RIVISTA ITALIANA DI CHIRURGIA PLASTICA. **3974**
0391-223X *See* SALUTE UMANA, LA. **4801**
0391-2493 *See* FILOLOGIA E CRITICA (SALERNO EDITRICE). **3387**
0391-2515 *See* GIORNALE STORICO DI PSICOLOGIA DINAMICA. **4588**
0391-2566 *See* MEDIOEVO. **4352**
0391-2612 *See* OFIOLITI. **1443**
0391-2825 *See* RIVISTA DI MEDICINA DEL LAVORO ED IGIENE INDUSTRIALE. **2869**
0391-2868 *See* TERAPIA FAMILIARE : RIVISTA INTERDISCIPLINARE DI RICERCA ED INTERVENTO RELAZIONALES. **4620**
0391-2876 *See* UOMO, L'. **247**
0391-3147 *See* LAVORO E MEDICINA. **3604**
0391-3155 *See* VUOTO, SCIENZA E TECNOLOGIA. **2131**

0391-3368 *See* ITALIANISTICA. **3397**
0391-3627 *See* MINERVA ANGIOLOGICA. **3799**
0391-3635 *See* MODO DESIGN MAGAZINE. **2902**
0391-3740 *See* NUOVE LEGGI CIVILI COMMENTATE. **3020**
0391-3813 *See* QUADERNI DELL ISTITUTO DI STORIA DELL ARTE MEDIEVALE E MODERNA, FACOLTA DI LETTERE E FILOSOFIA, UNIVERSITA DI MESSINA. **362**
0391-3910 *See* SEGNO PESCARA. **330**
0391-3929 *See* STORIA DELLA CITTA. **2836**
0391-3988 *See* INTERNATIONAL JOURNAL OF ARTIFICIAL ORGANS, THE. **3798**
0391-4089 *See* ITALIAN JOURNAL OF SPORTS TRAUMATOLOGY. **3954**
0391-4097 *See* JOURNAL OF ENDOCRINOLOGICAL INVESTIGATION. **3731**
0391-4119 *See* DIFESA DELLE PIANTE. **508**
0391-4127 *See* RICERCHE SLAVISTICHE. **3317**
0391-4135 *See* MESOPOTAMIA. **274**
0391-4186 *See* VERIFICHE. **4364**
0391-4216 *See* SPICILEGIO MODERNO. **3439**
0391-4240 *See* RIVISTA DI STORIA CONTEMPORANEA. **2522**
0391-4283 *See* RAGIONI CRITICHE, LE. **329**
0391-4364 *See* NOTIZIE DA PALAZZO ALBANI. **360**
0391-4380 *See* MUSICA DOMANI : ORGANO DELLA SOCIETA ITALIANA PER L'EDUCAZIONE MUSICALE. **4135**
0391-4399 *See* MUSEI FERRARESI. **325**
0391-481X *See* BULLETIN OF MOLECULAR BIOLOGY AND MEDICINE. **560**
0391-4836 *See* ANNALI DELL'ISTITUTO SPERIMENTALE PER IL TABACCO. **5372**
0391-4844 *See* MEDICINA GERIATRICA. **3754**
0391-4887 *See* RIVISTA DELLA SOCIETA ITALIANA DI SCIENZA DELL'ALIMENTAZIONE, LA. **2356**
0391-5115 *See* JOURNAL OF EUROPEAN ECONOMIC HISTORY, THE. **1570**
0391-5239 *See* DIRITTO FALLIMENTARE E DELLE SOCIETA COMMERCIALI. **2963**
0391-5271 *See* ECONOMIA MARCHE. **1556**
0391-5352 *See* MICROBIOLOGICA. **567**
0391-5360 *See* ENERGIE ALTERNATIVE HTE. **5103**
0391-5387 *See* PEDIATRIA MEDICA E CHIRURGICA, LA. **3907**
0391-5557 *See* ACQUA ARIA (1977). **2159**
0391-5603 *See* UROLOGIA. **3993**
0391-5611 *See* RIVISTA ITALIANA DEGLI ODONTOTECNICI. **1335**
0391-5654 *See* CULTURA NEOLATINA. **3276**
0391-5670 *See* GIORNALE DI ANESTESIA STOMATOLOGICA. **1324**
0391-5840 *See* VETRINA. **857**
0391-5859 *See* GORTANIA. **4165**
0391-5891 *See* LAMIERA. **4007**
0391-5913 *See* SOCIETA E SALUTE. **4803**
0391-5956 *See* ANNALI - INSTITUTO UNIVERSITARIO ORIENTALE, SEZIONE GERMANICA. ANGLISTICA. **3265**
0391-6081 *See* RICERCHE DI PSICOLOGIA. **4617**
0391-6111 *See* DIRITTO COMUNITARIO E DEGLI SCAMBI INTERNAZIONALI. **2962**
0391-6138 *See* GAZZETTA DELLA PICCOLA INDUSTRIA. **1492**
0391-6146 *See* QUALE IMPRESA. **1514**
0391-6170 *See* RIVISTA DI POLITICA ECONOMICA. **1595**
0391-6227 *See* ANTIFURTO. **5176**
0391-6391 *See* ELETTRONICA OGGI. **2052**
0391-6405 *See* FIORINO. **5804**
0391-6413 *See* GIORNALE DI MARKETING. **924**
0391-6685 *See* AVANTI. **5804**
0391-6715 *See* BOLLETTINO STORICO-BIBLIOGRAFICO SUBALPINO. **2679**
0391-6723 *See* BOZZE. **4517**
0391-674X *See* COOPERAZIONE. **2908**

0391-6855 *See* MONDO, IL. **2519**
0391-6863 *See* NAZIONE. **5804**
0391-6952 *See* ARCHIVIO DELLA SOCIETA ROMANA DI STORIA PATRIA (1947). **1074**
0391-7010 *See* ANNUARIO DELL'ISTITUTO STORICO ITALIANO PER L'ETA MODERNA E CONTEMPORANEA. **2675**
0391-7045 *See* SVILUPPO E ORGANIZZAZIONE. **887**
0391-7088 *See* BOLLETTINO DELL'ISTITUTO STORICO E DI CULTURA DELL'ARMA DEL GENIO. **4038**
0391-7231 *See* MEDICINA OSPEDALIERA ROMANA. **3613**
0391-724X *See* ALMA ROMA. **335**
0391-7282 *See* PRACTITIONER EDIZIONE ITALIANA. **3629**
0391-7304 *See* AQUILEIA NOSTRA. **256**
0391-7312 *See* QUADERNI DI TERZO MONDO. **4492**
0391-7320 *See* ARCHIVUM FRATRUM PRAEDICATORUM. **5024**
0391-7479 *See* CIVILTA MANTOVANA. **2683**
0391-7487 *See* OTTAGONO. **305**
0391-7487 *See* OTTAGONO. **3486**
0391-7487 *See* OTTAGONO. **2902**
0391-7495 *See* ITALIA MEDIEVALE E UMANISTICA. **3288**
0391-7509 *See* ITALIA FRANCESCANA. **3288**
0391-7517 *See* FELIX RAVENNA. **268**
0391-7525 *See* GIORNALE ITALIANO DI DIABETOLOGIA. **3730**
0391-7622 *See* PARMA NELL'ARTE. **327**
0391-7711 *See* LETTERA FINANZIARIA. **796**
0391-7738 *See* AVIAZIONE. **14**
0391-7762 *See* STUDI ETRUSCHI. **2711**
0391-7770 *See* ARCHIVIO STORICO ITALIANO. **2480**
0391-7789 *See* STUDI MUSICALI. **4155**
0391-7819 *See* SANTO, IL. **4995**
0391-7835 *See* STUDI DANTESCHI. **1080**
0391-786X *See* SOLE 24 ORE. **5805**
0391-8017 *See* ROMA COMUNE. **2492**
0391-8041 *See* CONTRIBUTI DEL CENTRO LINCEO INTERDISCIPLINARE DI SCIENZE E LORO APPLICAZIONI. **3502**
0391-8041 *See* SEMINARIO SULLA EVOLUZIONE BIOLOGICA E I GRANDI PROBLEMI DELLA BIOLOGIA : ATTI. **551**
0391-8084 *See* MONUMENTI ANTICHI. SERIE MISCELLANEA. **303**
0391-8092 *See* MONUMENTI ANTICHI. SERIE MONOGRAFICA / ACCADEMIA NAZIONALE DEI LINCEI. **303**
0391-8149 *See* ATTI DELLA ACCADEMIA NAZIONALE DEI LINCEI. MEMORIE CLASSE DI SCIENZE MORALI STORICHE E FILOLOGICHE. **2842**
0391-8165 *See* ARCHEOLOGIA CLASSICA. **258**
0391-8211 *See* BOLLETTINO DELL'ISTITUTO STORICO ARTISTICO ORVIETANO. **2612**
0391-8270 *See* BOLLETTINO DEI CLASSICI. **1074**
0391-8289 *See* NOTE ECONOMICHE - MONTE DEI PASCHI DI SIENA. **1593**
0391-8394 *See* QUADERNI SARDI DI ECONOMIA. **1579**
0391-8475 *See* NUOVI STUDI STORICI. **2624**
0391-8629 *See* INCONTRI DE ANESTESIA, RIANIMAZIONE E SCIENZE AFFINI. **3965**
0391-8645 *See* OLEODINAMICA PNEUMATICA LUBRIFICAZIONE. **5136**
0391-8696 *See* RIVISTA DI DIRITTO AGRARIO MILANO. **3044**
0391-8750 *See* STUDI ECONOMICI E SOCIALI. **1628**
0391-8866 *See* GIORNALE DEI CONGRESSI MEDICI : GCM : L'AGGIORNAMENTO IN DIRETTA DAI CONGRESSI, IL. **3578**
0391-8963 *See* REUMATOLOGO : PUBBLICA IL BOLLETTINO DELLA SOCIETA ITALIANA DI REUMATOLOGIA, IL. **3806**
0391-898X *See* PEDIATRIA OGGI MEDICA E CHIRURGICA. **3907**

0391-8998 *See* CLINICA OCULISTICA E PATOLOGIA OCULARE. **3893**

0391-9005 *See* GIORNALE DI CHIRURGIA, IL. **3965**

0391-9013 *See* GIORNALE ITALIANO DI OSTETRICIA E GINECOLOGIA. **3761**

0391-9048 *See* GIORNALE DI NEUROPSICOFARMACOLOGIN. **4306**

0391-9064 *See* ARTIBUS ET HISTORIAE. **4063**

0391-9099 *See* RICERCA FOLKLORICA, LA. **2324**

0391-9641 *See* REVISTA MINERALOGICA ITALIANA. **1444**

0391-9706 *See* ANIMAL BIOLOGY. **5502**

0391-9714 *See* HISTORY AND PHILOSOPHY OF THE LIFE SCIENCES. **457**

0391-9749 *See* NEMATOLOGIA MEDITERRANEA. **111**

0391-9757 *See* FISICA E TECNOLOGIA. **5105**

0391-9838 *See* GEOGRAFIA FISICA E DINAMICA QUATERNARIA. **1377**

0391-9854 *See* BOLLETTINO D'ARTE. **344**

0391-9889 *See* GIORNALE ITALIANO DI MEDICINA DEL LAVORO. **3578**

0391-9919 *See* PETROLIERE INTERNATIONAL (MILANO). **4274**

0391-9935 *See* QUADERNI DI CONTRACCEZIONE, FERTILITA, SESSUALITA. **5188**

0391-9994 *See* ACTUM LUCE. **2672**

0392-0054 *See* ARCHIVIO STORICO PUGLIESE. **2676**

0392-0062 *See* BOLLETTINO DEL MUSEO CIVICO DI STORIA NATURALE DI VERONA. **4085**

0392-0232 *See* ARCHIVIO STORICO LOMBARDO. **2676**

0392-0240 *See* ARCHIVIO STORICO MESSINESE. **2676**

0392-0259 *See* ARCHIVIO STORICO PRATESE. **2676**

0392-0283 *See* ARCHIVIO STORICO PER LE PROVINCE PARMENSI. **2676**

0392-0291 *See* ARCHIVIO VENETO. **2676**

0392-0305 *See* ARCHIVUM BOBIENSE : RIVISTA DEGLI ARCHIVI STORICI BOBIENSI. **2676**

0392-033X *See* ATTI E MEMORIE / SOCIETA SAVONESE DI STORIA PATRIA. **2677**

0392-0356 *See* BENEDICTINA. **4938**

0392-0445 *See* RIVISTA ITALIANA EPPOS. **405**

0392-0453 *See* VEDERE CONTACT INTERNATIONAL. **4217**

0392-0461 *See* ITALIAN JOURNAL OF NEUROLOGICAL SCIENCES. **3834**

0392-047X *See* FOLIA ONCOLOGICA. **3817**

0392-0488 *See* GIORNALE ITALIANO DI DERMATOLOGIA E VENEREOLOGIA. **3720**

0392-050X *See* ASSISTENZA SANITARIA, L'. **3777**

0392-0534 *See* STUDI TRENTINI DI SCIENZE NATURALI. ACTA GEOLOGICA. **1399**

0392-0542 *See* STUDI TRENTINI DI SCIENZE NATURALI. ACTA BIOLOGICA. **474**

0392-0593 *See* ZOOTECNIA INTERNATIONAL. **5603**

0392-0623 *See* ITALIAN JOURNAL OF GASTROENTEROLOGY, THE. **3746**

0392-064X *See* RIVISTA DI MERCEOLOGIA. **1625**

0392-0658 *See* ETA EVOLUTIVA (FIRENZE). **3903**

0392-0674 *See* ATTI DEL CONVEGNO NAZIONALE - SOCIETA ITALIANA DELLE SCIENZE VETERINARIE. **5505**

0392-0690 *See* STUDI TRENTINI DI SCIENZE STORICHE. **2855**

0392-0712 *See* ACTA THERMOGRAPHICA. SUPPLEMENT. **3938**

0392-0771 *See* CHIRURGIA DEL PIEDE. **3917**

0392-0836 *See* ATTI E MEMORIE DELL'ACCADEMIA TOSCANA DI SCIENZE E LETTERE LA COLOMBARIA. **2842**

0392-0895 *See* RIVISTA DI ARCHEOLOGIA. **281**

0392-095X *See* ANNALI DELLA SCUOLA NORMALE SUPERIORE DI PISA, CLASSE DI LETTERE E FILOSOFIA. **3362**

0392-100X *See* ACTA OTORHINO-LARYNGOLOGICA ITALICA. **3885**

0392-1026 *See* ASSISTENZA SOCIALE, L'. **5274**

0392-1042 *See* FEDERALISTA, IL. **4521**

0392-1050 *See* ARCHIVIO PER L'ALTO ADIGE. **2255**

0392-1107 *See* BOLLETTINO STORICO PER LA PROVINCIA DI NOVARA 1947. **2679**

0392-1158 *See* BRIXIA SACRA 1966. **2679**

0392-1255 *See* BOLLETTINO STORICO REGGIANO. **2679**

0392-128X *See* GIORNALE ITALIANO DI ONCOLOGIA. **3817**

0392-1336 *See* ATTI, ISTITUTO VENETO DI SCIENZE, LETTERE ED ARTI. CLASSE DI SCIENZE MORALI, LETTERE ED ARTI. **3364**

0392-1344 *See* CLINICA & TERAPIA CARDIOVASCOLARE. **3703**

0392-1360 *See* RIVISTA ITALIANA DI OTORINOLARINGOLOGIA, AUDIOLOGIA E FONIATRIA. **3891**

0392-1387 *See* GIORNALE ITALIANO DI ANGIOLOGIA. **3705**

0392-1395 *See* DERMATOLOGIA CLINICA. **3719**

0392-1417 *See* ORTOPEDIA E TRAUMATOLOGIA OGGI. **3884**

0392-1433 *See* NUOVA CLINICA OTORINOLARINGOIATRICA, LA. **3890**

0392-1496 *See* MEMORIE STORICHE FOROGIULIESI. **2698**

0392-1506 *See* CULTURA ATESINA. **318**

0392-1522 *See* RASSEGNA DEGLI ARCHIVI DI STATO. **2483**

0392-1670 *See* RIVISTA DI SESSUOLOGIA ROMA. **5188**

0392-1697 *See* SCRITTURA E CIVILTA. **3320**

0392-1727 *See* STUDI BITONTINI. **365**

0392-176X *See* ENOTECNICO, L'. **5103**

0392-1867 *See* QUADERNI FIORENTINI. **3350**

0392-1905 *See* CLINICAL ENZYMOLOGY SYMPOSIA. **451**

0392-1913 *See* OBIETTIVI E DOCUMENTI VETERINARI. **5517**

0392-1921 *See* DIOGENES (ENGLISH ED.). **4345**

0392-1948 *See* STUDI DI STORIA DELL'EDUCAZIONE. **1786**

0392-2065 *See* ARCHIVIO STORICO DI BELLUNO, FELTRE E CADORE. **2676**

0392-2219 *See* ATTI DELLA ACCADEMIA LIGURE DI SCIENZE E LETTERE. **5086**

0392-2227 *See* GIORNALE ITALIANO DI CHIMICA CLINICA. **976**

0392-2251 *See* ATLETICA LEGGERA. **2596**

0392-226X *See* ASTRA MILANO. **389**

0392-2278 *See* AUTONOMIE LOCALI E SERVIZI SOCIALI. **4631**

0392-2294 *See* AUTOMAZIONE NAVALE, L'. **591**

0392-2308 *See* ASTRONOMIA, L'. **391**

0392-2332 *See* NOUVELLES DE LA REPUBLIQUE DES LETTRES (NAPLES, ITALY). **3307**

0392-2391 *See* INDEX : QUADERNI CAMERTI DI STUDI ROMANISTICI. **2981**

0392-2545 *See* BIBLIOTECA E SOCIETA : RIVISTA DEL CONSORZIO PER LA GESTIONE DELLE BIBLIOTECHE COMUNALE DEGLI ARDENTI E PROVINCIALE "ANSELMO ANSELMI" DI VITERBO. **344**

0392-257X *See* BIBLIOGRAFIA IDG. A, DIRITTO COMMERCIALE. **3096**

0392-2588 *See* BIBLIOGRAFIA IDG. B, DIRITTO CANONICO ED ECCLESIASTICO. **4939**

0392-2596 *See* BIBLIOGRAFIA IDG. C, DIRITTO E PROCEDURA PENALE. **3105**

0392-2863 *See* AQUARIUM MILANO. **5576**

0392-291X *See* RIVISTA EUROPEA PER LE SCIENZE MEDICHE E FARMACOLOGICHE. **4328**

0392-2936 *See* EUROPEAN JOURNAL OF GYNAECOLOGICAL ONCOLOGY. **3817**

0392-2944 *See* GINECOLOGIA CLINICA. **3761**

0392-2952 *See* PSICOBIETTIVO ROMA. **4609**

0392-2990 *See* EUROPEAN JOURNAL OF EPIDEMIOLOGY. **3735**

0392-3002 *See* AGGIORNAMENTO DEL MEDICO. **3547**

0392-3010 *See* INFORMATORE FARMACEUTICO : ANNUARIO ITALIANO DEI MEDICAMENTI E DEI LABORATORI, L'. **4308**

0392-3037 *See* RENDICONTI DELLA SOCIETA GEOLOGICA ITALIANA. **1394**

0392-3088 *See* ACTA PHONIATRICA LATINA. **3885**

0392-3126 *See* BOLLETTINO PER LE FARMACODIPENDENZE E L'ALCOOLISMO. **1341**

0392-3452 *See* TECNOLOGIE CHIMICHE. **994**

0392-3495 *See* ESPERIENZE LETTERARIE. **3385**

0392-3525 *See* ITALIAN JOURNAL OF SURGICAL SCIENCES, THE. **3966**

0392-3568 *See* ITALIA CONTEMPORANEA. **2693**

0392-3584 *See* NOTIZIARIO CHIRURGICO. **3970**

0392-3622 *See* GIORNALE DELLA SUBFORNITURA, IL. **1607**

0392-3630 *See* GIORNALE DELL' INSTALLATORE ELETTRICO, IL. **2056**

0392-369X *See* NAUTICA. **4179**

0392-3789 *See* BOLLETTINO DI LEGISLAZIONE TECNICA. **5089**

0392-3797 *See* BOLLETTINO NAZIONALE PREVENZIONE INFORTUNI. **1656**

0392-3800 *See* INTERPLASTICS (MILANO). **4455**

0392-3894 *See* BRUTIUM. **2680**

0392-3967 *See* INTERNATIONAL PHYSICS SERIES. **4406**

0392-4033 *See* BOLLETTINO DELLA UNIONE MATEMATICA ITALIANA. A. **3497**

0392-4076 *See* MODELLISTICA. **2775**

0392-419X *See* ACTA NATURALIA DE L'ATENEO PARMENSE. **5080**

0392-4203 *See* ACTA BIO-MEDICA DE L'ATENEO PARMENSE. **3544**

0392-4270 *See* NOTIZIARIO DEL CENTRO DI DOCUMENTAZIONE. **421**

0392-4335 *See* NOTIZIARIO DI GIURISPRUDENZA DEL LAVORO. **3019**

0392-4416 *See* REVISTA DE PEDIATRIA PREVENTIVA E SOCIALE. NIPIOLOGIA. **3911**

0392-4424 *See* BOLLETTINO DELLA SOCIETA ITALIANA DI TOPOGRAFIA E FOTOGRAMMETRIA. **2556**

0392-4432 *See* BOLLETTINO DI STORIA DELLE SCIENZE MATEMATICHE. **3497**

0392-4483 *See* GIORNALE DI NEUROPSICHIATRIA DELL'ETA EVOLUTIVA : ORGANO UFFICIALE DELLA SOCIETA ITALIANA DI NEUROPSICHIATRIA INFANTILE. **3833**

0392-4505 *See* SALUTE E TERRITORIO. **3638**

0392-4513 *See* STORIA DELLARTE. **365**

0392-4548 *See* MEDICINA OGGI. **3613**

0392-4564 *See* MEMORIA (TURIN, ITALY). **2623**

0392-4599 *See* RECUPERARE. EDILIZIA DESIGN IMPIANTI. **307**

0392-4629 *See* NUA : INTERNATIONAL JOURNAL OF NEPHROLOGY, UROLOGY, ANDROLOGY. **3992**

0392-4718 *See* PASTICCERIA INTERNAZIONALE. **2352**

0392-4777 *See* RASSEGNA IBERISTICA. **3428**

0392-4815 *See* PASSATO E PRESENTE (FLORENCE, ITALY). **2625**

0392-4831 *See* TECNICA OSPEDALIERA MILANO. **3793**

0392-4866 *See* RIVISTA DEGLI STUDI ORIENTALI. **3317**

0392-4947 *See* SPAZIO E SOCIETA. **309**

0392-5005 *See* URBANISTICA INFORMAZIONI. **2838**

0392-5048 *See* SOCIOLOGIA DEL LAVORO. **5260**

0392-5110 *See* STUDI DI FILOLOGIA ITALIANA. **3324**

0392-5145 *See* ARCHIVIO DI MEDICINA LEGALE E DELLE ASSICURAZIONI. **3739**

0392-5153 *See* OPERATORE SANITARIO, L'. **3624**

0392-5234 *See* ARTE VENETA : RIVISTA DI STORIA DELL'ARTE. **341**

0392-5269 *See* CORSI DI CULTURA SULL'ARTE RAVENNATE E BIZANTINA. **318**

0392-5404 See SCHEDE MEDIEVALI. 2708
0392-5498 See MILLIMETRO, IL. 2922
0392-5528 See MUSEOLOGIA. 4091
0392-5609 See AGRICOLTURA RICERCA. 48
0392-5692 See ALTRIMEDIA. 1104
0392-5722 See ALTROCONSUMO. 2211
0392-5730 See AMBIENTE CUCINA, L'. 2898
0392-579X See AMMINISTRAZIONE E POLITICA. 4463
0392-5803 See CLINICAL CHEMISTRY NEWSLETTER. 972
0392-5870 See ANIMAZIONE SOCIALE. 5271
0392-6060 See LATTE 1976, IL. 196
0392-615X See ARCHIVIO DELLE LOCAZIONI E DEL CONDOMINIO. 2815
0392-6338 See MATERIALI E DISCUSSIONI PER L'ANALISI DEI TESTI CLASSICI. 1078
0392-6354 See MASSIMARIO PENALE COMPLETO DELLA CORTE SUPREMA DI CASSAZIONE. 3007
0392-6397 See MISURE CRITICHE. 3412
0392-6443 See MONDO LEGNO. 634
0392-6567 See UTENSIL. 2131
0392-6613 See OEBALIA. 556
0392-6621 See OTORINOLARINGOLOGIA. 3890
0392-6680 See ATTI - ISTITUTO VENETO DI SCIENZE, LETTERE ED ARTI. CLASSE DI SCIENZE FISICHE, MATEMATICHE E NATURALI. 5086
0392-6699 See EOS (ROMA). 3669
0392-6737 See NUOVO CIMENTO DELLA SOCIETA ITALIANA DI FISICA, [SEZIONE] D. 4449
0392-680X See PSICOLOGIA E SCUOLA. 1884
0392-6907 See LINGUISTICA COMPUTAZIONALE. 3299
0392-7032 See NOTIZIE E DOCUMENTI. 4484
0392-7059 See NUOVA RASSEGNA DI LEGISLAZIONE DOTTRINA E GIURISPRUDENZA. 3020
0392-7091 See NOTIZIARIO / SOCIETA ITALIANA DE BIOCHIMICA CLINICA. 988
0392-7113 See RASSEGNA DI DIRITTO E TECNICA DELLA ALIMENTAZIONE. 2355
0392-713X See SAGGI E MEMORIE DI STORIA DELL'ARTE. 364
0392-7164 See RASSEGNA DI STUDI TURISTICI. 5490
0392-7202 See RICERCHE DI STORIA DELL'ARTE. 363
0392-7229 See RIVISTA GIURIDICA DEL LAVORO. 1708
0392-7253 See SETTIMANA GIURIDICA, LA. 3048
0392-7296 See GIORNALE ITALIANO DI ENTOMOLOGIA. 5609
0392-7318 See CLINICA DIETOLOGICA, LA. 4188
0392-7334 See BOLLETTINO DEL CENTRO DI STUDI VICHIANI. 4342
0392-7512 See ALIMENTAZIONE, NUTRIZIONE, METABOLISMO (1979). 4187
0392-7601 See ITALICA ROMA. 2848
0392-7628 See BOLLETTINO DELL'ISTITUTO DI FILOLOGIA GRECA. 3270
0392-7679 See GIORNALE DI EMODINAMICA. 3704
0392-792X See IMBOTTIGLIAMENTO. 2367
0392-7946 See SCIENZASOCIETA. 5156
0392-8020 See TUTTOTURISMO. 5498
0392-8136 See TECNICA DELLA CONFEZIONE E DELLA MAGLIERIA. 5356
0392-8144 See TECNICA SANITARIA E MEDICINA DI COMUNITA : ORGANO UFFICIALE DELL'ASSOCIAZIONE NAZIONALE UFFICIALI SANITARI, MEDICI IGIENISTI. 4804
0392-8217 See PIXEL. 1234
0392-839X See CHIMICA OGGI. 3690
0392-8411 See ANNUARIO DELLE UNIVERSITA DEGLI STUDI IN ITALIA / ISTITUTO NAZIONALE DELL'INFORMAZIONE. 1810
0392-8438 See BOLLETINO DELL'ISTITUTO CENTRALE PER LA PATOLOGIA DEL LIBRO. QUADERNI. 3196

0392-8535 See DIALOGHI DI ARCHEOLOGIA. 266
0392-8543 See JOURNAL OF APPLIED COSMETOLOGY. 3721
0392-856X See CLINICAL AND EXPERIMENTAL RHEUMATOLOGY. 3565
0392-8586 See BIBLIOTECHE OGGI. 3194
0392-8608 See RASSEGNA DI ARCHITETTURA E URBANISTICA. 307
0392-8632 See CIVILTA CLASSICA E CRISTIANA. 3273
0392-8667 See COMUNICAZIONI SOCIALI. 1109
0392-873X See QUADERNI UTINENSI. 3427
0392-8764 See HEAT AND TECHNOLOGY. 4430
0392-8829 See AUTOMAZIONE OGGI. 2110
0392-8845 See COMPUTERWORLD ITALIA. 1180
0392-8888 See INFORMATICA OGGI. 1188
0392-890X See STRUMENTI MUSICALI. 4155
0392-8950 See D.A. DIFESA AMBIENTALE. 2213
0392-9000 See SICUREZZA E PREVENZIONE: ANTICRIMINE, ANTINCENDIO, ANTINFORTUNISTICA. 3176
0392-9078 See JOURNAL OF EXPERIMENTAL & CLINICAL CANCER RESEARCH : CR. 3819
0392-9086 See INDUSTRIA DEL LEGNO & DEL MOBILE, L'. 634
0392-9108 See INDICATORE CARTARIO : RASSEGNA BIBLIOGHAFICA MENSILE. 4234
0392-9221 See RIVISTA DEL CLUB ALPINO ITALIANO. 4915
0392-9264 See POLSO, IL. 3628
0392-9507 See JOURNAL OF FOETAL MEDICINE. 3763
0392-9515 See ACTA MEDITERRANEA DI PATOLOGIA INFETTIVA E TROPICALE. 3985
0392-9523 See RENDICONTI. A, SCIENZE MATEMATICHE E APPLICAZIONI / ISTITUTO LOMBARDO, ACCADEMIA DI SCIENZE E LETTERE. 3530
0392-9531 See RENDICONTI - ISTITUTO LOMBARDO, ACCADEMIA DI SCIENZE E LETTERE, B, SCIENZE CHEMICHE E FISICHE, GEOLOGICHE, BIOLOGICHE E MEDICHE. 1394
0392-9566 See MEZZOGIORNO D'EUROPA. 1574
0392-9590 See INTERNATIONAL ANGIOLOGY. 3966
0392-9620 See QUADERNI MARCHIGIANI DI MEDICINA. 3632
0392-9647 See SPORT & MEDICINA. 3956
0392-9663 See GERIATRICS ED. ITALIANA. 3751
0392-9698 See ACTA CARDIOLOGICA MEDITERRANEA. 3697
0392-9701 See STATO E MERCATO. 1522
0392-9752 See ESOPO, L'. 415
0392-9787 See RIVISTA DI PSICOLOGIA ANALITICA. 4617
0392-9876 See ARCHEOLOGIA VENETA. 258
0392-9981 See CINEMA D'OGGI. 4066
0393-0033 See FMR (ED. ITALIANA). 350
0393-0041 See FORUM IULII. 268
0393-005X See GARGANOSTUDI : RIVISTA DEL CENTRO STUDI GARGANICI. 2616
0393-0149 See PADUSA. 277
0393-0165 See PROSPETTIVE D'ARTE. 328
0393-0203 See RASSEGNA (BOLOGNA). 307
0393-022X See RIVISTA STORICA CALABRESE. 2707
0393-0327 See COMMUNICATIONES - PONTIFICIA COMMISSIO CODICI IURIS CANONICI RECOGNOSCENDO. 2954
0393-0394 See IMPEGNO OSPEDALIERO. 1677
0393-0440 See JOURNAL OF GEOMETRY AND PHYSICS. 4409
0393-0521 See AMBIENTE RISORSE SALUTE. 2160
0393-0564 See BIOCHIMICA CLINICA. 482
0393-0599 See MEDIA DUEMILA. 1195
0393-0637 See LANCET EDIZIONE ITALIANA, THE. 3603
0393-067X See DENTAL FLASH. 1320
0393-0750 See BOLLETTINO DEL MUSEO CIVICO DI PADOVA 4085

0393-0793 See INFORMATORE DEL RECUPERO, L'. 2217
0393-0807 See LABYRINTHOS. 356
0393-0890 See TENNIS ITALIANO, IL. 4925
0393-0971 See CH4 ENERGIA METANO. 1935
0393-098X See EDAV. EDUCAZIONE AUDIOVISIVA. 1737
0393-1099 See QUADERNI DI SCIENZE ANTROPOLOGICHE. 243
0393-1137 See RIVISTA ITALIANA DI BIOLOGIA E MEDICINA. 472
0393-1226 See QUADERNI DI SEMANTICA. 3313
0393-1315 See DIRITTO PROCESSUALE AMMINISTRATIVO. 2963
0393-1331 See INDUSTRIA MECCANICA, L'. 2115
0393-134X See LEGISLAZIONE PENALE. 3169
0393-1374 See ARCHIVIO GIURIDICO DELLE OPERE PUBBLICHE. 2936
0393-1420 See INGEGNERIA SISMICA. 2024
0393-1447 See SARCOIDOSIS. 3638
0393-1463 See CHIRURGIA OGGI : ORGANO UFFICIALE DELLA SOCIETA EMILIANO-ROMAGNOLA DI CHIRURGIA. 3962
0393-1471 See CHIRURGIA EPATOBILIARE. 3962
0393-1641 See GALLERIE E GRANDI OPERE SOTTERRANEE. 2023
0393-182X See RASSEGNA DI DIRITTO CIVILE. 3091
0393-1951 See BIELLESE, IL. 2485
0393-196X See BOLLETTINO DI OCEANOLOGIA TEORICA ED APPLICATA. 1447
0393-1978 See CARDIOLOGIA (ROMA). 3700
0393-2028 See RIVISTA DI CARDIOLOGIA PREVENTIVA E RIABILITATIVA : ORGANO DELL'ASSOCIAZIONE NAZIONALE DEI CENTRI PER LE MALATTIE CARDIOVASCOLARI. 3710
0393-2249 See MINERVA UROLOGICA E NEFROLOGICA. 3991
0393-2362 See ZETA (UDINE). 3473
0393-2397 See ATTI E MEMORIE DELLA ACCADEMIA PETRARCA DI LETTERE, ARTI E SCIENZE. 2842
0393-2400 See BOLLETTINO ECONOMICO (ROME, ITALY). 779
0393-246X See ISLAM, STORIS E CIVILTA. 5043
0393-24865 See QUADERNI PATAVINI DI LINGUISTICA. 3313
0393-2494 See RIVISTA ITALIANA DI DIRITTO DEL LAVORO. 3154
0393-2648 See CSELT TECHNICAL REPORTS. 1153
0393-2729 See INTERNATIONAL SPECTATOR, THE. 4525
0393-2915 See INFORMAZIONI E STUDI VIVALDIANI. 4122
0393-2931 See RENDICONTI DELLA ACCADEMIA DI ARCHEOLOGIA LETTERE E BELLE ARTI NAPOLI. 329
0393-2990 See EUROPEAN JOURNAL OF EPIDEMIOLOGY. 3735
0393-3059 See COOPERAZIONE. 2908
0393-3245 See QUADERNI PIGNONE. 2108
0393-3369 See AB (BRESCIA). 2159
0393-3415 See RIVISTA DI STORIA ECONOMICA. 1582
0393-3423 See BOLLETTINO S.I.A.M.E. 4379
0393-3512 See CERVIX AND THE LOWER FEMALE GENITAL TRACT, THE. 3758
0393-3598 See CRISTIANESIMO NELLA STORIA. 4951
0393-361X See PSICHIATRIA DELL'INFANZIA E DELL-ADOLESCENZA. 4609
0393-3660 See GAZZETTA MEDICA ITALIANA, ARCHIVIO PER LE SCIENZE MEDICHE. 3578
0393-3687 See STUDI ECUMENICI. 4999
0393-3695 See STUDI. FATTI. RICERCHE. 2493
0393-3725 See ITALY ITALY. 5481
0393-3741 See CALENDARIO DEL POPOLO, IL. 2613
0393-3857 See GRIFFITHIANA. 4071
0393-3865 See SEGNOCINEMA. 4077

0393-3873 *See* AGGIORNAMENTI IN CHIRURGIA GENERALE. **3958**

0393-3911 *See* AUTOMAZIONE INTEGRATA. **5087**

0393-3938 *See* ANCI RIVISTA. **4626**

0393-3954 *See* ANNALI - FONDAZIONE GIANGIACOMO FELTRINELLI. **4539**

0393-3962 *See* ANCI NOTIZIE. **4626**

0393-4012 *See* ORATORI DEL GIORNO, GLI. **3023**

0393-4101 *See* SANITA PUBBLICA. **4685**

0393-4241 *See* APICOLTURA : RIVISTA SCIENTIFICA DI APIDOLOGIA. **62**

0393-4292 *See* STORIA E MEDICINA POPOLARE. **3643**

0393-4462 *See* ARREDO. TESSILI-COMPLEMENTI. **5348**

0393-4586 *See* RASSEGNA AMMINISTRATIVA DELLA SCUOLA. **1869**

0393-4624 *See* RIVISTA DALMATICA, LA. **2707**

0393-4802 *See* ANNALI DELLA FACOLTA DI MEDICINA VETERINARIA. UNIVERSITA DI PARMA. **5503**

0393-4810 *See* RIVISTA DI POLITICA AGRARIA. RASSEGNA DELLA AGRICOLTURA ITALIANA. **130**

0393-4853 *See* BOLLETTINO DI PSICHIATRIA BIOLOGICA. **3922**

0393-4888 *See* CONFEZIONE. **5553**

0393-5108 *See* SINERGIE. **886**

0393-5183 *See* ENVIRONMENTAL DESIGN (ROME, ITALY). **298**

0393-5264 *See* FUNCTIONAL NEUROLOGY. **3833**

0393-5302 *See* NEW TRENDS IN ARRHYTHMIAS. **3708**

0393-5310 *See* NEW TRENDS IN EXPERIMENTAL AND CLINICAL PSYCHIATRY. **3931**

0393-5337 *See* GINECOLOGIA DELL'INFANZIA E DELL'ADOLESCENZA. **3761**

0393-5345 *See* NEW TRENDS IN CLINICAL NEUROPHARMACOLOGY : OFFICIAL JOURNAL OF THE EUROPEAN ASSOCIATION FOR CLINICAL NEUROPHARMACOLOGY. **3843**

0393-5523 *See* GESTIONESCUOLA. **869**

0393-5566 *See* ATTI E MEMORIE DELLA SOCIETA DALMATA DI STORIA PATRIA. **2677**

0393-5582 *See* RIVISTA ITALIANA DI NUTRIZIONE PARENTERALE ED ENTERALE : ORGANO UFFICIALE DELLA SOCIETA ITALIANA DI NUTRIZIONE PARENTERALE ED ENTERALE, SINPE - GASAPE. **4199**

0393-5590 *See* GIORNALE ITALIANO DI NEFROLOGIA. **3990**

0393-5620 *See* ISTISAN-CONGRESSI. **3591**

0393-585X *See* GARDENIA. **2415**

0393-5914 *See* RIVISTERIA. **2492**

0393-5930 *See* QUADERNI DI MEDICINA E CHIRURGIA : QMC. **3973**

0393-5949 *See* TATTI STUDIES, I. **2712**

0393-5957 *See* GIORNALE ITALIANO DI RICERCHE CLINICHE E TERAPEUTICHE. **3578**

0393-5965 *See* AEROBIOLOGIA. **441**

0393-604X *See* BOLLETTINO STATISTICO (ROME, ITALY). **779**

0393-6155 *See* INTERNATIONAL JOURNAL OF BIOLOGICAL MARKERS, THE. **3818**

0393-6163 *See* STUDI DI PSICOLOGIA DELL'EDUCAZIONE. **4619**

0393-635X *See* ACTA TOXICOLOGICA ET THERAPEUTICA. **3978**

0393-6384 *See* ARCHIVIO SICILIANO DE MEDICINA E CHIRURGIA. 4, ACTA MEDICA MEDITERRANEA. **3960**

0393-6392 *See* ARCHIVIO SICILIANO DI MEDICINA E CHIRURGIA. 5, ACTA PEDIATRICA MEDITERRANEA. **3900**

0393-6457 *See* LETTERA DALL'ITALIA. **324**

0393-6457 *See* STUDI DI PSICOLOGIA DELL EDUCAZIONE. **4619**

0393-6732 *See* CEMENTO 1945, IL. **607**

0393-6813 *See* LATIUM. **2849**

0393-6821 *See* QUADERNI DELL'ISTITUTO DI ARCHEOLOGIA E STORIA ANTICA / LIBERA UNIVERSITA ABRUZZESE DEGLI STUDI "G. D'ANNUNZIO", CHIETI. **279**

0393-6902 *See* PSICOANALISI CONTRO. **3932**

0393-7054 *See* AMBIENTE E SICUREZZA SUL LAVORO. **2858**

0393-7062 *See* BANCAMATICA. **774**

0393-7089 *See* ANTINCENDIO (1979). **2288**

0393-7240 *See* ATTI E MEMORIE - DEPUTAZIONE DI STORIA PATRIA PER LE PROVINCIE DI ROMAGNA. **2677**

0393-7267 *See* ARTE MEDIEVALE. **341**

0393-7380 *See* FOGLIO TORINO, IL. **4365**

0393-7437 *See* REGIONE E GOVERNO LOCALE. **4679**

0393-747X *See* ARTINUMBRIA. **341**

0393-7518 *See* RIABILITAZIONE E APPRENDIMENTO. **4382**

0393-7542 *See* ACTA ONCOLOGICA PADOVA. **3808**

0393-7593 *See* CLINICA ODONTOIATRICA DEL NORD AMERICA. **1319**

0393-764X *See* PROGRESSI CLINICI. CHIRUGIA. **3972**

0393-7798 *See* TUTELA. **5313**

0393-7801 *See* ULTRASONICA. **3769**

0393-7895 *See* GENTE VIAGGI. **5478**

0393-7917 *See* SCIENZA & VITA NUOVA. **4171**

0393-8018 *See* PROGETTO CARE ITALIA. **4796**

0393-8085 *See* MONDO UOMO. **3996**

0393-8131 *See* PHYTOPHAGA. **5612**

0393-8190 *See* MCM. **324**

0393-8212 *See* NUOVO GOVERNO LOCALE, IL. **4670**

0393-8220 *See* COSTRUZIONI STRADE CANTIERI. **2022**

0393-8255 *See* VERSUS (MILAN, ITALY). **3331**

0393-8379 *See* QUADERNI DI CINEMA. **4076**

0393-8387 *See* AUTO AND DESIGN. **5404**

0393-8476 *See* GIORNALE DEL FARMACISTA, IL. **4306**

0393-8492 *See* GIORNALE DEL MEDICO, IL. **3578**

0393-8522 *See* AESTHETICA. PRE-PRINT. **335**

0393-8859 *See* INSEGNARE ALL' HANDICAPPATO. **1880**

0393-9081 *See* ANTROPOLOGIA MEDICA : AM. **230**

0393-9154 *See* COENOSES. **2212**

0393-9162 *See* COSA VISTA, LA. **4067**

0393-9243 *See* ECONOMIA E BANCA. **1481**

0393-9340 *See* ANNALI ITALIANI DI MEDICINA INTERNA : ORGANO UFFICIALE DELLA SOCIETA ITALIANA DI MEDICINA INTERNA. **3794**

0393-9375 *See* HUMAN EVOLUTION. **237**

0393-9383 *See* INTERNATIONAL JOURNAL OF ANTHROPOLOGY. **238**

0393-9472 *See* SISTEMARICERCA. **5158**

0393-9510 *See* PROSPETTIVE SOCIALI E SANITARIE. **1704**

0393-9529 *See* QUADERNI DI SANITA PUBBLICA. **4797**

0393-9693 *See* FARMACI E TERAPIA. **4304**

0393-9707 *See* CULTURA & LIBRI. **2514**

0393-9723 *See* CORRIERE TERMO IDRO SANITARIO, IL. **2604**

0393-974X *See* JOURNAL OF BIOLOGICAL REGULATORS AND HOMEOSTATIC AGENTS. **460**

0393-9758 *See* ALMANACCO DI FOTOGRAFARE. **4366**

0393-9774 *See* PSICHIATRIA E PSICOTERAPIA ANALITICA. **3932**

0394-0055 *See* AREA (MILAN, ITALY). **291**

0394-0101 *See* MONOGRAFIE DE IL LAVORO NEUROPSICHIATRICO, LE. **3931**

0394-0136 *See* ANTOLOGIA DI BELLE ARTI. **337**

0394-0179 *See* ART E DOSSIER. **338**

0394-0209 *See* STORIA E DOSSIER. **2630**

0394-025X *See* THERAPY OF INFECTIOUS DISEASES. **4805**

0394-0276 *See* ETA VERDE, L'. **2215**

0394-0438 *See* AGRICOLTURA MEDITERRANEA (OSPEDALETTO). **48**

0394-0543 *See* GIORNALE DELL'ARTE (TURIN, ITALY). **321**

0394-0624 *See* ARX. **342**

0394-0691 *See* ATTI TICINENSI DI SCIENZE DALLA TERRA. **1366**

0394-0705 *See* CONTRIBUTI DEL CENTRO LINCEO INTERDISCIPLINAIRE BENIAMINO SEGRE. **3502**

0394-073X *See* CARDIOMYOLOGY. **450**

0394-0802 *See* PROSPETTIVA. **362**

0394-0810 *See* INDICIZZAZIONE, L'. **3215**

0394-0853 *See* GIARDINI. **2417**

0394-087X *See* INTERSCAMBIO. **1497**

0394-0926 *See* QUADERNI DI URBANISTICA E INFORMAZIONI. **2832**

0394-0942 *See* RIVISTA GIURIDICA SARDA. **3044**

0394-1027 *See* BOLLETTINO (CIVICI MUSEI VENEZIANI D'ARTE E DI STORIA). **4085**

0394-1132 *See* GB PROGETTI. **299**

0394-1248 *See* TEORIA POLITICA. **4498**

0394-1388 *See* NUOVO LABORATORIO ODONTOTECNICO, IL. **1331**

0394-1493 *See* FLASH ART (INTERNATIONAL EDITION). **350**

0394-1574 *See* ITALIAN CURRENT RADIOLOGY. **3942**

0394-1582 *See* IMPIANTISTICA ITALIANA. **617**

0394-1590 *See* COSTRUIRE IN LATERIZIO. **296**

0394-1663 *See* ATTI E MEMORIE DELLA SOCIETA TIBURTINA DI STORIA E D'ARTE GIA ACCADEMIA DEGLI AGEVOLI E COLONIA DEGLI ARCADI SIBILLINI. **2842**

0394-168X *See* MINERVA ORTOGNATODONTICA. **1330**

0394-1744 *See* ANNALI / FONDAZIONE DI STUDI DI STORIA DELL'ARTE ROBERTO LONGHI, FIRENZE. **336**

0394-1809 *See* ANNUARIO FILOSOFICO. **4341**

0394-1841 *See* BOLLETTINO STORICO DELLA BASILICATA / A CURA DELLA DEPUTAZIONE DI STORIA PATRIA DELLA LUCANIA. **2679**

0394-218X *See* ICOMOS INFORMATION. **300**

0394-2384 *See* VR VIDEOREGISTRARE. **4079**

0394-249X *See* GENE GEOGRAPHY : A COMPUTERIZED BULLETIN ON HUMAN GENE FREQUENCIES. **545**

0394-2503 *See* DERMATOLOGIA OGGI. **3719**

0394-2597 *See* MICOLOGIA E VEGETAZIONE MEDITERRANEA. **575**

0394-2694 *See* QUADERNI VENETI. **3427**

0394-2740 *See* FALLIMENTO E LE ALTRE PROCEDURE CONCORSUALI, IL. **2968**

0394-2791 *See* LACIO DROM : RIVISTA BIMESTRALE DI STUDI ZINGARI. **2321**

0394-2805 *See* AGRICOLTURA E INNOVAZIONE. **48**

0394-2813 *See* LINGUA E NUOVA DIDATTICA : LEND. **3298**

0394-283X *See* ORGANIZZAZIONE SANITARIA. **3790**

0394-2910 *See* EUROCARNI. **2334**

0394-2961 *See* COLLOQUI DEL SODALIZIO. **347**

0394-3127 *See* SPAZIO IMPRESA. **1711**

0394-3151 *See* VETERINARIA CREMONA. **5523**

0394-3275 *See* RIVISTA CISTERCENSE. **5035**

0394-3402 *See* DIABETES, NUTRITION & METABOLISM. **4189**

0394-3429 *See* PANORAMA DIFESA. **4053**

0394-3437 *See* J P 4. **25**

0394-3453 *See* MACPLAS. **4456**

0394-3518 *See* TAVERNA DE AUERBACH, LA. **3472**

0394-3569 *See* STUDI LINGUISTICI ITALIANI. **3324**

0394-3623 *See* NOTIZIARIO DEL LAVORO E PREVIDENZA. **1695**

0394-3631 *See* SOCIETA BILANCIO E CONTABILITA. **751**

0394-3666 *See* BIT FIRENZE. **3196**

0394-3682 See SPOSABELLA. 1087
0394-3690 See INCONTRI CEF. 942
0394-3704 See LINEA VERDE. 2424
0394-3933 See MEZZOGIORNO D'EUROPA. 1505
0394-4115 See MERIDIANA. 5209
0394-4247 See POPOLI. 2521
0394-428X See CONTEMPORANEA. 384
0394-4360 See SUBSIDIA AL CORPUS PHILOSOPHORUM MEDII AEVI. 4362
0394-4395 See QUADERNI DELLA RIVISTA ITALIANA DI MUSICOLOGIA / A CURA DELLA SOCIETA ITALIANA DI MUSICOLOGIA. 4148
0394-4719 See B.C.A. 316
0394-4727 See BOLLETTINO DELLA UNIONE STORIA ED ARTE. 344
0394-4808 See RASSEGNA DI STUDI E NOTIZIE. RACCOLTA DELLE STAMPE A. BERTARELLI. RACCOLTA DI ARTE APPLICATA. MUSEO DEGLI STRUMENTI MUSICALI. 329
0394-4816 See SPAZIO UMANO, LO. 331
0394-4859 See XENIA (ROMA). 285
0394-5006 See BULLETTINO DELLA DEPUTAZIONE ABRUZZESE DI STORIA PATRIA. 2681
0394-5065 See BIBLIOTECA DI STORIA DELLA SCIENZA. 4163
0394-5103 See EUROPEAN EARTHQUAKE ENGINEERING. 2023
0394-512X See TP. IL GIORNALE DELLA TRASMISSIONE DI POTENZA. 1999
0394-5219 See DAI CIVICI MUSEI D'ARTE E DI STORIA DI BRESCIA. STUDI E NOTIZIE. 348
0394-5243 See FORCE (ROME, ITALY). 3164
0394-5391 See RS. RIFIUTI SOLIDI. 2242
0394-5413 See RIVISTA DELLE TECNOLOGIE TESSILI. 5355
0394-5499 See STUDI MONTEFELTRANI. 2711
0394-5537 See AGRIGIORNALE DEL COMMERCIO. 54
0394-5596 See ANNALES TECTONIC : AT. 1365
0394-560X See BOLLETINO - LEGA ITALIANA CONTRO L'EPILESSIA. 3828
0394-5618 See ERBA D'ARNO. 2615
0394-5634 See IMPIANTO ELETTRICO, L'. 2064
0394-5871 See IA. INGEGNERIA AMBIENTALE. 2232
0394-588X See INGEGNERIA ALIMENTARE. LE CONSERVE ANIMALI. 2344
0394-5898 See QUATTRO ZAMPE. 5519
0394-6088 See CROCEVIA MERANO. 4641
0394-6134 See VISCOCHIRURGIA. 3977
0394-6169 See ADVANCES IN HORTICULTURAL SCIENCE. 2407
0394-6185 See ALI ANTICHE. 11
0394-6282 See RIVISTA INTERNAZIONALE DI MUSICA SACRA. 4150
0394-6320 See INTERNATIONAL JOURNAL OF IMMUNOPATHOLOGY AND PHARMACOLOGY. 3672
0394-6347 See REPERTORIO DEL FORO ITALIANO; LEGISLAZIONE, BIBLIOGRAFIA, GIURISPRUDENZA. 3037
0394-6444 See EUROPEAN JOURNAL OF INTERNATIONAL AFFAIRS, THE. 4473
0394-6460 See METODI & RICERCHE. 2698
0394-6479 See ASPE. AGENZIA DI STAMPA SUI PROBLEMI DELL' EMARGINAZIONE. 5240
0394-6592 See BOLLETTINO DEL LAVORO E DEI TRIBUTI. 3144
0394-6681 See EO NEWS. 2053
0394-6975 See TROPICAL ZOOLOGY. 5599
0394-7149 See BOLLETTINO MALACOLOGICO. 5578
0394-7157 See ATTI E MEMORIE / ACCADEMIA CLEMENTINA. 343
0394-7181 See TAVOLA, A. 2359
0394-7238 See DOCTOR PEDIATRIA. 3903
0394-7858 See MEDIOEVO E RINASCIMENTO : ANNUARIO DEL DIPARTIMENTO DI STUDI SUL MEDIOEVO E IL RINASCIMENTO DELL'UNIVERSITA DI FIRENZE. 2698
0394-7904 See PSICOLOGIA SOCIALE. 4609

0394-7912 See PSYCHOPATHOLOGIA. 4613
0394-817X See I CARE. 3585
0394-8196 See NATOM. FARMACIA NATURALE. 3619
0394-820X See AERONAUTICA & DIFESA. 4
0394-8226 See ANNALES THEOLOGICI. 4934
0394-8277 See COMUNI D'ITALIA. 4640
0394-8293 See UFFICIO TECNICO, L'. 5167
0394-8315 See DOSSIER. L'UFFICIO TECNICO. 298
0394-834X See RIVISTA GIURIDICA DI POLIZIA LOCALE. 3044
0394-8366 See DIRITTO ED ECONOMIA. 1479
0394-8382 See GEA. 2230
0394-8404 See ALIMENTARISTA, L'. 2326
0394-8412 See PUBBLICA AMMINISTRAZIONE OGGI. 4675
0394-8439 See RIVISTA DEL PERSONALE DELL'ENTE LOCALE. 4684
0394-8501 See ACHADEMIA LEONARDI VINCI. 4222
0394-8625 See ESSECOME. 3164
0394-882X See CASA TESSIL REPORTER. 5348
0394-8846 See NUOVO AREOPAGO, IL. 4983
0394-901X See DIABETE MILANO, IL. 4519
0394-9044 See ARCHIVI PER LA STORIA : RIVISTA DELL'ASSOCIAZIONE NAZIONALE ARCHIVISTICA ITALIANA. 2480
0394-9249 See ZODIAC (MILAN, ITALY : 1988). 311
0394-9257 See JOURNAL OF GENETICS & BREEDING. 548
0394-929X See SISTEMI & IMPRESA. 1627
0394-9338 See IRRIGAZIONE E DRENAGGIO. 175
0394-9362 See GIORNALE DI TECNICHE NEFROLOGICHE & DIALITICHE. 3990
0394-9370 See ETHOLOGY, ECOLOGY & EVOLUTION. 5583
0394-9427 See ALBA POMPEIA. 335
0394-9508 See CHIRURGIA. 3961
0394-9532 See AGING (MILAN, ITALY). 3749
0394-9540 See NEUROPSICOFARMACOLOGIA DEL COMPORTAMENTO. 4317
0394-9575 See MEDIA FORUM. 762
0394-9605 See U&C UNIFICAZIONE & CERTIFICAZIONE. 630
0394-980X See RICERCHE STORICO BIBLICHE : RSB. 5019
0394-9826 See ALCOLOGIA. 1340
0394-9869 See BIBLIOGRAPHIA MISSIONARIA / PONTIFICAL MISSIONARY LIBRARY OF THE CONGREGATION FOR THE EVANGELIZATION OF PEOPLES. 5012
0394-9877 See BML : BOLLETTINO DI MICROBIOLOGIA E INDAGINI DI LABORATORIO. 560
0394-9885 See INFORMATORE GIURIDICO DELLE ATTIVITA SPORTIVE, L'. 2982
0394-9982 See RIZA PSICOSOMATICA. 3637
0395-000X See ORDINAIRE DU PSYCHANALYSTE, L'. 4606
0395-0506 See SENOLOGIA. 3824
0395-1200 See CAHIERS DEBUSSY. 4106
0395-2037 See MONDE, LE. 5800
0395-2037 See MONDE, LE. 5800
0395-238X See ETUDES TOULOISES. 2687
0395-2649 See ANNALES (PARIS, FRANCE : 1946). 2513
0395-2681 See ASIE DU SUD-EST ET MONDE INSULINDIEN. 2646
0395-2916 See PAYSAGE ACTUALITES. 2427
0395-3556 See SEMANTIKOS. 3320
0395-3971 See CAHIERS D'OTO. RHINO. LARYNGOLOGIE, DE CHIRURGIE CERVICO FACIALE ET D'AUDIOPHONOLOGIE, LES. 3887
0395-4366 See AUTO HEBDO PARIS. 1976. 5439
0395-501X See ARCHIVES D'ANATOMIE ET DE CYTOLOGIE PATHOLOGIQUES. 3678
0395-5907 See CONNAISSANCE DES ARTS, PLAISIR DE FRANCE. 348

0395-6601 See TEXTES ET DOCUMENTS POUR LA CLASSE. 2523
0395-6989 See COMMONWEALTH. 3377
0395-7217 See BULLETIN D'ECOLOGIE. 2212
0395-7322 See BULLETIN BIBLIOGRAPHIQUE DE DOCUMENTATION TECHNIQUE / GROUPEMENT DE DOCUMENTATION DES INDUSTRIES EXTRACTIVES. 411
0395-7497 See BULLETIN TECHNIQUE - OFFICE NATIONAL DES FORETS. 2377
0395-7500 See BULLETIN MENSUEL DE LA SOCIETE VETERINAIRE PRATIQUE DE FRANCE. 5506
0395-7527 See BULLETIN TRIMESTRIEL DE LA SOCIETE MYCOLOGIQUE DE FRANCE. 574
0395-7632 See ETUDES PHILOSOPHIQUES. 4346
0395-7691 See EDUCATION RURALE. 1740
0395-773X See TRADUIRE / SOCIETE FRANCAISE DES TRADUCTEURS. 3329
0395-8175 See CAHIERS DU CREDIT MUTUEL. 781
0395-8191 See CHIFFRES POUR L'ALSACE. 1531
0395-8280 See DONNEES STATISTIQUES DU LIMOUSIN. 5326
0395-8418 See CAHIERS DE FONTENAY, LES. 2844
0395-8515 See FOURRAGES ACTUALITES. 88
0395-8531 See HORTICULTURE FRANCAISE. 2419
0395-8582 See ANTENNE MARSEILLE, L'. 5377
0395-8639 See PRATIQUE VETERINAIRE EQUINE. 5518
0395-8655 See PURPAN. 123
0395-8663 See GENIE RURAL. 89
0395-8671 See BULLETIN D'INFORMATION - CENTRE NATIONAL POUR L'EXPLOITATION DES OCEANS. 1447
0395-871X See TABLEAUX DE L'ECONOMIE BRETONNE. 1586
0395-8930 See SEMENCES ET PROGRES. 5156
0395-8973 See STATISTIQUES POUR L'ECONOMIE NORMANDE. 1539
0395-899X See REVUE FRANCAISE D'OENOLOGIE. 2370
0395-9007 See REVUE ECONOMIQUE DU SUD-OUEST. 1582
0395-9031 See REPERES (MONTPELLIER). 1538
0395-904X See REFLETS DE L'ECONOMIE FRANC-COMTOISE. 1516
0395-9112 See COURRIER DE L'A.C.I. 5028
0395-921X See REVUE DE L'INSTITUT NAPOLEON (1954). 2706
0395-9376 See BATIMENT, BATIR, LE. 600
0395-9473 See VUES SUR L'ECONOMIE D'AQUITAINE. 5346
0395-9740 See FORMATION FRANCE. 1747
0396-0064 See P.C.C. 4235
0396-0099 See STATISTIQUES & ETUDES : MIDI-PYRENEES. 5343
0396-2687 See BULLETIN DES CENTRES DE RECHERCHES EXPLORATION-PRODUCTION ELF-AQUITAINE. 1369
0396-3586 See INGENIEURS D'ENTRETIEN. 870
0396-4590 See AUSTRIACA. 2677
0396-4701 See CAHIERS ECONOMIQUES ET MONETAIRES. 781
0396-5015 See SEMAINE VETERINAIRE, LA. 5521
0396-518X See TRUITE OMBRE SAUMON. 2315
0396-5880 See INTERGEO BULLETIN. 2582
0396-5988 See DISCOURS ET DECLARATIONS DU PRESIDENT DE LA REPUBLIQUE FRANCAISE. 4644
0396-6046 See AFRIQUE EXPANSION. 2498
0396-6356 See TROUVAILLES PARIS. 1976. 367
0396-6666 See MAINTENANCE & ENTREPRISE PARIS. 1985
0396-7883 See CHAMBRES D'AGRICULTURE. 73
0396-8014 See DEVELOPPEMENT ET SANTE. 4773
0396-8235 See CHASSEUR D'IMAGES. 4368
0396-8669 See V.S.T. 3937

0396-8863 See BULLETIN D'INFORMATION ET DE LIAISON - ASSOCIATION DES SERVICES GEOLOGIQUES AFRICAINS. 1369

0396-891X See CAHIERS DE LITTERATURE ORALE. 2318

0396-8995 See ANTENNES. 860

0396-9371 See LIEN ECONOMIQUE : BULLETIN DE LA CHAMBRE DE COMMERCE ET D'INDUSTRIE DE BASSE-TERRE, LE. 1503

0396-9681 See HISTOIRE ET NATURE. 4166

0397-006X See CIMENTS, BETONS, PLATRES, CHAUX. 607

0397-0264 See TRAVAIL PROTEGE NIORT. 4209

0397-0329 See SANTE MAGAZINE. 4801

0397-1392 See INTEGREE, L'. 4566

0397-1635 See PARIS-MATCH 1976. 2521

0397-1643 See CAHIERS DE PROTHESE, LES. 1318

0397-2143 See CAHIERS D'INFORMATION DU DIRECTEUR DE PERSONNEL, LES. 939

0397-2844 See GEOLOGIE MEDITARRANEENNE. 1379

0397-3190 See NOUVELLE REVUE DU SON PARIS, LA. 2491

0397-3301 See INFFO FLASH. 1752

0397-4626 See REVUE HOSPITALIERE DE FRANCE. 3792

0397-4650 See CHANTIERS DE FRANCE. 607

0397-4820 See ENFANTS MAGAZINE PARIS. 1063

0397-5347 See JOURNAL DE RECHERCHE OCEANOGRAPHIQUE. 1450

0397-5495 See HARVARD, L'EXPANSION. 869

0397-569X See MIROIR DU CYCLISME 1960. 429

0397-579X See BULLETINS ET MEMOIRES (SOCIETE ARCHEOLOGIQUE ET HISTORIQUE DE LA CHARENTE : 1983). 2681

0397-6416 See CODE PERMANENT ENVIRONNEMENT ET NUISANCES. 2163

0397-6440 See INFORMATION DU VEHICULE, L'. 5384

0397-6513 See T.E.C. (PARIS). 2244

0397-6866 See REVUE CHIEN 2000. 4287

0397-7102 See BULLETIN MENSUEL D'INFORMATION DU CENTRE DE CREATION INDUSTRIELLE. 345

0397-7471 See PLOT POITIERS. 3527

0397-765X See HALIOTIS. 5585

0397-7730 See BULLETIN SIGNALETIQUE 780: POLYMERES, PEINTURES, BOIS, CUIRS. 1039

0397-7854 See SALUT!... PARIS. 1068

0397-7870 See REVUE FRANCAISE D'ETUDES AMERICAINES. 2759

0397-7897 See REVUE DE L'INFIRMIERE. INFORMATIONS. 3868

0397-7900 See REVUE DE L'INFIRMIERE ET DE L'ASSISTANTE SOCIALE. 4393

0397-7927 See REVUE DE GERIATRIE, LA. 3755

0397-8060 See PROGRES TECHNIQUE, LE. 5142

0397-8079 See EMBOUTEILLAGE, CONDITIONNEMENT. 4219

0397-829X See A.F.P. SCIENCES. 5079

0397-8389 See ECONOMIE FAMILIALE HOME ECONOMICS, L'. 2789

0397-8435 See INFORMATIONS CNC. 4072

0397-8435 See ACTIVITE CINEMATOGRAPHIQUE FRANCAISE . / CNC, CENTRE NATIONAL DE LA CINEMATOGRAPHIE, L'. 4062

0397-9148 See ALLERGIE ET IMMUNOLOGIE PARIS. 3665

0397-9180 See PEDIATRE, LE. 3907

0397-9210 See RAYONNEMENTS IONISANTS. 4441

0397-9296 See REVUE TECHNIQUE DE BATIMENT ET DES CONSTUCTIONS INDUSTRIELLES. 2030

0397-9520 See MEMOIRES DE L'INSTITUT DE GEOLOGIE DU BASSIN D'AQUITAINE. 1387

0397-9717 See BULLETIN - C.R.I.D.E.V. 4505

0397-9873 See REVUE TRIMESTRIELLE DE DROIT CIVIL (PARIS, FRANCE : 1980). 3091

0398-0022 See REVUE DROMOISE. 281

0398-0499 See JOURNAL DES MALADIES VASCULAIRES. 3706

0398-091X See BULLETIN DE L'ELEVAGE FRANCAIS. 208

0398-1185 See 01 INFORMATIQUE. 1169

0398-1657 See MANGANESE LITERATURE REVIEW. 1357

0398-2882 See ACTUALITES SOVIETIQUES PARIS. 4539

0398-3145 See CADRES CFDT. 1657

0398-3811 See SOURCES D'HISTOIRE MEDIEVALE. 2710

0398-4346 See REVUE ARACHNOLOGIQUE. 471

0398-494X See ANNALES DE RECHERCHES SYLVICOLES. 2374

0398-6659 See CAHIERS CELINE. 3370

0398-6772 See CENTRE DE RECHERCHES SUR LA RENAISSANCE (SERIES). 2683

0398-7604 See MEDECINE ET NUTRITON. 3607

0398-7620 See REVUE D'EPIDEMIOLOGIE ET DE SANTE PUBLIQUE. 3736

0398-7639 See EUROPEAN JOURNAL OF DRUG METABOLISM AND PHARMACOKINETICS. 4303

0398-8074 See CURIOSPRESS INTERNATIONAL. 4813

0398-8341 See SPORT BOWLING. 4920

0398-9011 See REVUE DE GEMMOLOGIE A.F.G. 2915

0398-9119 See COLLECTION DE MEDECINE LEGALE ET DE TOXICOLOGIE MEDICALE. 3740

0398-9275 See LISTE DES PUBLICATIONS DU COMMISSARIAT A L'ENERGIE ATOMIQUE / CENTRE D'ETUDES NUCLEAIRES DE SACLAY, SERVICE DE DOCUMENTATION. 1949

0398-9399 See VIGILANCE. 1790

0398-9518 See PUBLICATIONS DE L'INSTITUT D'ETUDES MEDIEVALES. 2626

0398-9771 See JOURNAL FRANCAIS D'OTO-RHINO-LARYNGOLOGIE. 3889

0398-9992 See LICORNE, LA. 3405

0399-0001 See CETIM INFORMATIONS. 2111

0399-0060 See BULLETIN DU MUSEE DE BEYROUTH. 4085

0399-0184 See REVUE DE LA SAINTONGE ET DE L'AUNIS. 363

0399-0206 See ANNALES DU TABAC. SECTION 1, RECHERCHE ET DEVELOPPEMENT. 5372

0399-0265 See REVUE S.A.M.U, LA. 1068

0399-029X See JOURNEES PARISIENNES DE PEDIATRIE. 3905

0399-0346 See JOURNAL DES AFRICANISTES. 238

0399-0354 See ANNALES DU TABAC. SECTION 2. 5372

0399-0370 See AFRIQUE ET L'ASIE MODERNES, L'. 2637

0399-0389 See ANNALES DU CENTRE UNIVERSITAIRE MEDITERRANEEN. 1089

0399-0443 See ANNALES DU CENTRE DE RECHERCHES SUR L'AMERIQUE ANGLOPHONE. 3362

0399-0508 See PROVINS ET SA REGION : BULLETIN DE LA SOCIETE D'HISTOIRE ET D'ARCHEOLOGIE DE PROVINS. 279

0399-0559 See RAIRO : RECHERCHE OPERATIONNELLE. 5144

0399-0648 See THESINDEX MEDICAL. 3645

0399-077X See MEDECINE ET MALADIES INFECTIEUSES. 3607

0399-0826 See ANNALES DE BRETAGNE ET DES PAYS DE L'OUEST. 2674

0399-0834 See TUNNELS ET OUVRAGES SOUTERRAINS VILLEURBANNE. 2033

0399-0974 See CYBIUM. 2299

0399-1075 See REVUE FRANCAISE D'AQUARIOLOGIE, HERPETOLOGIE. 557

0399-1237 See REVUE D'ARCHEOMETRIE. 281

0399-1245 See ANALYSES DE LA S.E.D.E.I.S. 1461

0399-1253 See PEUPLES MEDITERRANEENS. 2702

0399-1326 See CAHIERS IVAN TOURGUENIEV, PAULINE VIARDOT, MARIA MALIBRAN. 2613

0399-1350 See ANNUAIRE-BULLETIN DE LA SOCIETE DE L'HISTOIRE DE FRANCE. 2674

0399-1415 See CAHIERS LEOPOLD DELISLE. 2682

0399-1466 See TRAVAUX DE L'ASSOCIATION HENRI CAPITANT POUR LA CULTURE JURIDIQUE FRANCAISE. 1300

0399-1636 See NOUVELLES FISCALES (PARIS), LES. 801

0399-1784 See OCEANOLOGICA ACTA. 1454

0399-1989 See RECHERCHES GERMANIQUES. 2853

0399-2330 See ANNUAIRE DE LA SOCIETE D'HISTOIRE DU VAL DE VILLE. 2674

0399-2519 See BULLETIN DES G.T.V. 5506

0399-2535 See BUS ET CAR. 5378

0399-3558 See VITI. 190

0399-3698 See PREMIERE PARIS. 4853

0399-3914 See ANNEE DU MEDECIN, L'. 3550

0399-4112 See TECHNIQUES DE L'INGENIEUR. ELECTROTECHNIQUE. 2083

0399-4139 See TECHNIQUES DE L'INGENIEUR. METALLURGIE. 4021

0399-4147 See TECHNIQUES DE L'INGENIEUR. MESURES ET CONTROLE. 1998

0399-4198 See COLLECTION DE LA DIRECTION DES ETUDES ET RECHERCHES D'ELECTRICITE DE FRANCE. 2039

0399-449X See LETTRE D'INFORMATION - ANACT. 1687

0399-4708 See FORCE OUVRIERE HEBDO. 1675

0399-4988 See ENFANT D'ABORD, L'. 3903

0399-5461 See HEBDOCUIR. 3184

0399-6174 See BULLETIN DE L'I.N.A.O. 825

0399-6662 See DOSSIERS DU CENTRE REGIONAL ARCHEOLOGIQUE D'ALET, LES. 267

0399-6921 See COURRIER DES METIERS D'ART, LE. 348

0399-8320 See GASTROENTEROLOGIE CLINIQUE ET BIOLOGIQUE. 3745

0399-8533 See PERSPECTIVES AGRICOLES. 119

0399-8568 See PHOTO PARIS. 4373

0399-8606 See LETTRE DE L'EXPANSION, LA. 1503

0399-9874 See INSTALLATEUR EN CHAUFFAGE PLOMBERIE COUVERTURE GENIE CLIMATIQUE ELECTRICITE. 2606

0400-048X See ACOG NEWSLETTER. 3755

0400-4116 See ACTA PHARMACEUTICA INTERNATIONALIA. 4289

0400-776X See AGRICOLTURA DELL VENEZIE. 48

0400-8111 See AGRONOMIA SULRIOGRANDENSE. 56

0400-8456 See AIR ALMANAC (1953), THE. 6

0401-1457 See ALABAMA ENGINEER, THE. 1964

0401-1961 See ALASKA STATISTICAL QUARTERLY. 1528

0401-3174 See ALFOLD. 3359

0401-8680 See INVESTMENT BULLETIN. 902

0401-913X See NEWS CAST - AMERICAN IRIS SOCIETY. REGION 4. 2425

0402-0731 See NEWSLETTER - AMERICAN RESEARCH CENTER IN EGYPT. 276

0402-1142 See OFFICIAL REGISTER - AMERICAN SOCIETY OF CIVIL ENGINEERS. 2028

0402-1215 See PAPERS - AMERICAN SOCIETY OF MECHANICAL ENGINEERS. 2124

0402-1681 See SHORT COURSE IN AIRPORT MANAGEMENT. 35

0402-4249 See ANGOLITE. 3156

0402-4265 See ANGUS TOPICS. 205

0402-4621 See ANNALES DE READAPTATION ET DE MEDECINE PHYSIQUE : REVUE SCIENTIFIQUE DE LA SOCIETE FRANCAISE DE REEDUCATION FONCTIONNELLE DE READAPTATION ET DE MEDECINE PHYSIQUE. 4379

0402-4664 See ANNALES GEOLOGIQUES DES PAYS HELLENIQUES. 1365

0402-7493 See ARAB HORSE SOCIETY NEWS, THE. 2797

0402-7787 See ARBEITGEBER, DER. 1651

0402-7817 See ARBEITS- UND FORSCHUNGSBERICHTE ZUR SACHSISCHEN BODENDENKMALPFLEGE. 4084

0402-9054 See ARCHIVOS DE PEDIATRIA. 3900

0403-1911 See MINUTES OF THE MEETING - ARKANSAS-WHITE-RED BASINS INTER-AGENCY COMMITTEE. 5536

0403-4465 See ASIE NOUVELLE, L'. 1633

0404-3030 See AUTHORS GUILD BULLETIN. 3365

0404-5360 See KUO LI TAI-WAN TA HSUEH KUNG CHENG HSUEH KAN. 1985

0404-6307 See BADEN-WURTTEMBERG. 2677

0404-6749 See GREEN REVOLUTION (YORK, PA.). 4542

0404-6927 See BALLS AND BURLAPS. 2410

0404-6928 See TAP CHI VAN HOC. 3444

0404-7710 See BOLETIN CULTURAL Y BIBLIOGRAFICO. 3368

0404-8172 See BANDIERA ROSSA. 4540

0405-1203 See BEAUTY TRADE. 402

0405-2021 See BEITRAEGE ZUR GESCHICHTE DORTMUNDS UND DER GRAFSCHAFT MARK. 2678

0405-3923 See BELLMANSSTUDIER. 3366

0405-4474 See ARBOK - BERGEN, NORWAY. VESTLANDSKE KUNSTINDUSTRIMUSEUM. 370

0405-5497 See BAV RUNDBRIEF. 393

0405-5535 See BERLIN-BRANDENBURGISCHE BAUWIRTSCHAFT. 600

0405-668X See BETTER NUTRITION. 4187

0405-6701 See BETTERAVIER FRANCAIS. 164

0406-3597 See BITKI KORUMA BULTENI. 66

0406-3678 See BITUME ACTUALITES. 1599

0406-4224 See BLICK DURCH DIE WIRTSCHAFT. 5801

0406-6669 See BOLLETTINO UFFICIALE DEGLI IDROCARBURI E DELLA GEOTERMIA / MINISTERO DELL'INDUSTRIA, DEL COMMERCIO E DELL'ARTIGIANATO, DIREZIONE GENERALE DELLE MINIERE, UFFICIO NAZIONALE MINERARIO PER GLI IDROCARBURI E LA GEOTERMIA. 4252

0406-9595 See BRAVO MUNCHEN. 4064

0407-212X See DRILLING AND LAND REPORT. 1374

0407-4432 See TECHNICAL REPORT - DEPARTMENT OF OCEANOGRAPHY. 1457

0407-551X See REPORT - BUCYRUS-ERIE COMPANY. 707

0408-1560 See JAHRESHEFTE DES GEOLOGISCHEN LANDESAMTES IN BADEN-WURTTEMBERG. 1384

0408-1706 See JAHRBUCHER FUR STATISTIK UND LANDESKUNDE VON BADEN-WURTTEMBERG. 5329

0408-1749 See BADGER BIRDER, THE. 5577

0408-2206 See BAJAVAJA USKALOS'. 3365

0408-2621 See MATERIALY PO ISTORII AZERBAIDZHANA. 2658

0408-330X See BOLETIN ESTADISTICO. 779

0408-4748 See BANNER OF TRUTH, THE. 4937

0408-506X See BAPTIST DIGEST. 5056

0408-6007 See BARRISTER (UNIVERSITY OF MIAMI. SCHOOL OF LAW). 2940

0408-8220 See BEITRAEGE ZUR DEUTSCHEN VOLKS- UND ALTERTUMSKUNDE. 2318

0408-8298 See BEITRAEGE ZUR GESCHICHTE DER BIBLISCHEN EXEGESE. 5014

0408-8379 See BEITRAEGE ZUR GESCHICHTE DER UNIVERSITAT MAINZ. 1811

0408-9952 See POSEBNA IZDANJA INSTITUTA ZA ZASTITU BILJA. 525

0409-008X See SAOPSTENJA - REPUBLICKI ZAVOD ZA ZASTITU SPOMENIKA KULTURE SR SRBIJE. 308

0409-0179 See PUBLIKACIJE. SERIJA : ELEKTRONIKA, TELEKOMUNIKACIJE, AUTOMATIKA. 2077

0409-0829 See BENTON COUNTY PIONEER, THE. 2723

0409-1264 See BERKELEY-KOELNER RECHTSSTUDIEN. 2941

0409-1949 See BERLINER ABHANDLUNGEN ZUM PRESSERECHT. 2917

0409-2791 See BETRIEBSTECHNIK. 1966

0409-2805 See BETRIEBSWIRTSCHAFTLICHE FORSCHUNGEN. 861

0409-2945 See BEVERAGES. 2364

0409-2961 See BEZOPASNOST TRUDA V PROMYSHLENNOSTI. 2135

0409-347X See BIBLIOGRAFIA REGIONALNA WIELKOPOLSKI ZA R. ... / UNIWERSYTET IM. ADAMA MICKIEWICZA W POZNANIU. 409

0409-4093 See BIBLIOGRAPHY OF INDIAN ZOOLOGY. 5578

0409-5308 See BIBLIOTECA DE ESTUDIOS MADRILENOS. 2678

0409-5448 See ARCHIGINNASIO, L'. 3191

0409-6037 See BIBLIOTECA DELL'ARCHIVIO STORICO ITALIANO. 2480

0409-8536 See CAHIERS DES AMIS DE ROBERT BRASILLACH. 3371

0409-8846 See CAHIERS SAINT-SIMON. 2613

0410-3556 See CALIFORNIA TEACHER. 1890

0410-3882 See CALVINIST CONTACT. 5057

0410-5591 See OIL PIPE LINE TRANSPORT (ANNUAL ED.). 4270

0410-5907 See SPECIFIED DOMESTIC ELECTRICAL APPLIANCES. 2812

0410-7470 See GRAIN ELEVATORS IN CANADA. 201

0410-935X See KALENDAR KANADSKEJ SLOVENSKEJ LIGY. 2695

0411-0080 See CAPITAL CHEMIST, THE. 966

0411-0137 See CAPITAL SPOTLIGHT, THE. 5647

0411-2741 See CATHOLIC STANDARD (WASHINGTON, D.C.). 5026

0411-289X See CATTLE GUARD. 208

0411-3012 See CAVEAT. 2949

0411-4094 See REPORT - CENTRAL SOYA, INC., FORT WAYNE IND. 2627

0411-5384 See BOLLETINO DEL CENTRO ROSSINIANO DI STUDI. 4104

0411-7085 See DIRECTORY OF CHAIN RESTAURANT OPERATORS. 5070

0411-8421 See ZHEJIANG ZHONGYI ZAZHI. 3653

0411-8871 See CHEMICAL SPOTLIGHT. 969

0411-8987 See MITTEILUNGSBLATT / CHEMISCHE GESELLSCHAFT DER DEUTSCHEN DEMOKRATISCHEN REPUBLIK. 986

0411-9606 See CHIANG-SU CHIAO YU. 1731

0411-9630 See CHIAO HSUEH YU YEN CHIU. / JIAOXUE YU YANJIU. 1890

0412-0914 See CHIH WU PING LI HSUEH PAO. 506

0412-0914 See CHIH WU SHENG LI HSUEH TUNG HSUN. 506

0412-1058 See ANNUAL REPORT - CHILD WELFARE LEAGUE OF AMERICA, INC. 5272

0412-1961 See CHIN SHU HSUEH PAO. 4000

0412-264X See CHIRURGIA E PATOLOGIA SPERIMENTALE. SUPPLEMENTO. 3961

0412-2801 See CHORISTERS GUILD LETTERS. 4109

0412-3131 See CHRISTIAN LIBRARIAN (CEDARVILLE, OHIO), THE. 3202

0412-3417 See CHRISTOPHORUS STUTTGART. 5411

0412-4030 See CHUNG-HUA PI FU KO TSA CHIH. 3718

0412-4057 See CHUNG-HUA SHEN CHING CHING SHEN K'O TSA CHIH. 3829

0412-4081 See CHUNG-HUA YEN K'O TSA CHIH. 3873

0412-4154 See CHUNG-KUO ERH TUNG. 1062

0412-443X See CHUNG-SHAN TA HSUEH HSUEH PAO. CHE HSUEH SHE HUI KO HSUEH PAN. 5195

0412-4553 See CHURCH ADMINISTRATION. 4947

0412-4715 See CHUSHO KIGYO KEIEI BUNSEKI. 863

0412-6300 See TRANSACTIONS OF THE CITRUS ENGINEERING CONFERENCE. 189

0412-7994 See CLINICAL MEDICINE (WINNETKA. 1940). 3566

0412-8877 See ARQUIVOS. 4292

0413-4028 See COLLANA DI STUDI SULLA PUBBLICITA. 4813

0413-6869 See DENSHI TSUSHIN GAKKAI. DENSHI TSUSHIN GAKKAI ROMBUNSHI. 2041

0413-768X See RESEARCH PUBLICATION (COLORADO. GENERAL ASSEMBLY. LEGISLATIVE COUNCIL). 3039

0413-7949 See COLORADO CIVIL LIBERTIES. 4506

0413-8465 See REPORT - COLUMBIA UNIVERSITY. CONSERVATION OF HUMAN RESOURCES PROJECT. 1094

0414-0141 See FEDERAL EXCISE TAX REPORTS. 4723

0414-0494 See REPORTS. A - INTER-AFRICAN CONFERENCE. AGRICULTURE. 126

0414-0508 See REPORTS : E. 1516

0414-0516 See REPORTS : L. 1707

0414-0524 See REPORTS : SS. 5215

0414-0532 See REPORTS : ST. 5337

0414-0575 See BULLETIN - COMMISSION DE LA CARTE GEOLOGIQUE DU MONDE. 1368

0414-5798 See CONNECTICUT LABOR SITUATION / CONNECTICUT LABOR DEPARTMENT, EMPLOYMENT SECURITY DIVISION. 1661

0414-6883 See CONSTABLE. 3161

0414-8894 See DDR - REVUE; MAGAZINE AUS DER DEUTSCHEN DEMOKRATISCHEN REPUBLIK. 2515

0415-0368 See DARIEN HISTORICAL SOCIETY ANNUAL, THE. 2730

0415-1747 See DEFINIZIONI CRITICHE. 349

0415-505X See MRL BULLETIN. 3232

0415-6285 See WIRTSCHAFTSBERICHT UBER DIE LATEINAMERIKANISCHEN LAENDER SOWIE SPANIEN UND PORTUGAL. 1589

0415-8091 See DICTIONNAIRE DE BIOGRAPHIE FRANCAISE. 432

0415-8407 See DIGEST OF CHIROPRACTIC ECONOMICS, THE. 3572

0415-9659 See DIRECTORY OF MARYLAND MUNICIPAL OFFICIALS. 4702

0415-9675 See DIRECTORY OF MEMBERS, NEW YORK STATE LEGISLATURE, AND MEMBERS OF CONGRESS. 4643

0416-024X See DIRITTO SANITARIO MODERNO. 4773

0416-0274 See DISCERNER. 4954

0416-0525 See RETAIL OUTLETS FOR THE SALE OF DISTILLED SPIRITS. 957

0416-2773 See DONEGAL ANNUAL. 2685

0416-3184 See DOWN SOUTH. 2731

0416-5551 See DM. 4030

0416-6817 See DANISH HANDCRAFT GUILD. 5183

0416-6884 See DANSK AARBOG FOR MUSIKFORSKNING. 4113

0416-7066 See KULTURGEOGRAFISKE SKRIFTER. 2567

0416-7341 See ZESZYTY NAUKOWE POLITECHNIKI GDANSKIEJ. CHEMIA. 5172

0416-9565 See DEMOCRAZIA E DIRITTO. 2959

0416-9816 See DENKMALER RHEINISCHER MUSIK. 4114

0417- 1888 See BERICHT - DEUTSCHE GENOSSENSCHAFTSKASSE. 1464

0417-0164 See DETAILPRISER. 5326

0417-0792 See DERMATOLOGIJA I VENEROLOGIJA. 3719

0417-1152 See URBAN RENEWAL SERIES - DETROIT. CITY PLAN COMMISSION. 2838

0417-1225 See SHOPPING CENTERS IN THE DETROIT REGION. 2835

0417-1233 See URBAN ENVIRONMENT STUDY; PUBLICATION. 2183

0417-1411 See WISSENSCHAFTLICHE ABHANDLUNGEN. 146

0417-1489 See JAHRESBERICHT. 98

0417-1500 See SCHRIFTENREIHE. 2835

0417-2051 See MITTEILUNGEN DER DEUTSCHEN GESELLSCHAFT FUER MUSIK DES ORIENTS. 4131

0417-2256 See SONDERHEFT - DEUTSCHE KERAMISCHE GESELLSCHAFT. 2594

0417-2442 See ABHANDLUNGEN DER DEUTSCHEN ORIENT-GESELLSCHAFT. 253

0417-2957 See ZEITSCHRIFTENDIENST. 3257

0417-3341 See ABHANDLUNGEN. KOPTISCHE REIHE. 253

0417-3562 See DEUTSCHES METEOROLOGISCHES JAHRBUCH, BUNDESREPUBLIK. 1425

0417-4046 See DIADORA. 266

0417-4569 See DICTA / NEWSLETTER FOR ATTORNEYS OF SAN DIEGO COUNTY. 2960

0417-5131 See DIPLOMATIC PRESS DIRECTORY OF THE REPUBLIC OF CYPRUS INCLUDING TRADE INDEX AND BIOGRAPHICAL SECTION. 4520

0417-5433 See DIRECTORIO MEDICO PANAMENO. 3913

0417-5573 See DIRECTORY OF WASHINGTON BUSINESS ASSOCIATIONS. 667

0417-5751 See DIRECTORY OF CONVENTIONS. CENTRAL CONVENTION GUIDE. 758

0417-5751 See DIRECTORY OF CONVENTIONS. NORTHEAST & MID-ATLANTIC CONVENTION GUIDE. 758

0417-5751 See DIRECTORY OF CONVENTIONS. SOUTHEAST CONVENTION GUIDE. 758

0417-5751 See DIRECTORY OF CONVENTIONS. WEST CONVENTION GUIDE. 758

0417-612X See DIRECTORY OF MINE SUPPLY HOUSES, DISTRIBUTORS AND SALES AGENTS. 2138

0417-6480 See DIRECTORY OF SCIENTIFIC RESOURCES IN GEORGIA. 5100

0417-688X See TEACHER'S GUIDE TO CLASSROOM MANAGEMENT. 1906

0417-7371 See DIVULGACION TRIBUTARIA. 4720

0417-741X See DIXIE LUMBERMAN. 2400

0417-805X See DOCUMENTA MUSICOLOGICA. 2. REIHE: HANDSCHRIFTEN-FAKSIMILES. 4115

0417-8254 See DOCUMENTARIO DA VIDA RURAL. 79

0417-8300 See DOCUMENTATION MATHEMATIQUE. 3504

0417-870X See LIAISONS SOCIALES. DOCUMENTS. 5208

0417-9455 See BOLETIN DE DIVULGACIONES. 4163

0417-9994 See DORTMUNDER BEITRAGE ZUR ZEITUNGSFORSCHUNG. 2919

0418-0038 See GAKUJUTSU KENKYU NEMPO / DOSHISHA JOSHI DAIGAKU. 5231

0418-2472 See DAEHAN HWAHAK HWOEJEE. 974

0418-2693 See DAILY LABOR REPORT (WASHINGTON, D.C. : 1948). 1662

0418-2804 See DAIRY SCIENCE HANDBOOK. 194

0418-2898 See PUBLICATION - DAKAR. UNIVERSITE. CENTRE DE HAUTES ETUDES AFRO-IBERO-AMERICAINES. 1843

0418-2901 See COLLECTION - (DAKAR). 2638

0418-2952 See ANNALES DE LA FACULTE DES SCIENCES, UNIVERSITE DE DAKAR. 5083

0418-2960 See PUBLICATIONS - DAKAR. UNIVERSITE. SECTION DE LANGUES ET LITTERATURES. 3312

0418-3010 See DALHOUSIE DENTAL JOURNAL. 1320

0418-3290 See DANIEL BLUM'S OPERA WORLD. 4113

0418-3789 See DARE. 2487

0418-3827 See VEROFFENTLICHUNGEN DES INSTITUTS FUER NEUE MUSIK UND MUSIKERZIEHUNG DARMSTADT. 4158

0418-3878 See DARMSTADTER BEITRAEGE ZUR NEUEN MUSIK. 4113

0418-3886 See DARSTELLUNGEN UND QUELLEN ZUR GESCHICHTE DER DEUTSCHEN EINHEITSBEWEGUNG IM NEUNZEHNTEN UND ZWANZIGSTEN JAHRHUNDERT. 2685

0418-3894 See DARSTELLUNGEN ZUR AUSWARTIGEN POLITIK. 4519

0418-4025 See DARTNELL OFFICE ADMINISTRATION HANDBOOK, THE. 865

0418-4297 See DAUGAVAS VANAGU MENESRAKSTS. 2845

0418-4432 See MINIMIS, DE. 3010

0418-4513 See DEBRECENI DERI MUZEUM EVKONYVE, A. 4087

0418-4564 See STUDIA ROMANICA. SERIES LINGUISTICA. 3325

0418-4572 See STUDIA ROMANICA. SERIES LITTERARIA. 3441

0418-4580 See NEMET FILOLOGIAI TANULMANYOK. 3415

0418-4904 See DEEP SOUTH GENEALOGICAL QUARTERLY. 2445

0418-5129 See DEJINY A SOUCASNOST. 2614

0418-5420 See DELAWARE PHARMACIST. 4299

0418-5455 See ANNUAL REPORT / DELAWARE RIVER BASIN COMMISSION. 5529

0418-5633 See I.A.M.R. REPORT. 1677

0418-5730 See BULLETIN - NATIONAL MUSEUM, NEW DELHI. 4086

0418-5749 See REPORT - DELHI. PUBLIC LIBRARY. 3245

0418-5978 See DELTA PRIMATE REPORT. 5508

0418-6176 See DEN POEZII (LENINGRAD). 3462

0418-6559 See RAPPORT - GRONLANDS GEOLOGISKE UNDERSOGELSE. 1393

0418-6591 See ISFORHOLDENE I DE GRNLANDSKE FARVANDE. 1426

0418-6745 See DENMARK REVIEW. 665

0418-694X See DENTAL OUTLOOK, THE. 1321

0418-727X See COLLANA STORICA. 2684

0418-7296 See ATTI E MEMORIE - DEPUTAZIONE DI STORIA PATRIA PER LE ANTICHE PROVINCIE MODENESI. 2677

0418-7547 See DESARROLLO INDOAMERICANO. 2730

0418-7598 See TRANSACTIONS - DESERT BIGHORN COUNCIL. 2207

0418-7679 See DESIGN IN STEEL. 4001

0418-7717 See DESIGN IN FINLAND. 2899

0418-7946 See DETSKAIA LITERATURA. 3380

0418-8292 See MONTHLY REPORT OF THE DEUTSCHE BUNDESBANK. 1575

0418-8306 See REPORT OF THE DEUTSCHE BUNDESBANK FOR THE YEAR. 808

0418-8314 See STATISTISCHE BEIHEFTE ZU DEN MONATSBERICHTEN DER DEUTSCHEN BUNDESBANK. REIHE 2 : WERTPAPIERSTATISTIK. 1539

0418-8322 See STATISTISCHE BEIHEFTE ZU DEN MONATSBERICHTEN DER DEUTSCHEN BUNDESBANK. REIHE 3 : ZAHLUNGSBILANZSTATISTIK. 5343

0418-8330 See STATISTISCHE BEIHEFTE ZU DEN MONATSBERICHTEN DER DEUTSCHEN BUNDESBANK. REIHE 4 : SAISONBEREINIGTE WIRTSCHAFTSZAHLEN. 1539

0418-842X See MEXIKO-PROJEKT DER DEUTSCHEN FORSCHUNGSGEMEINSCHAFT, DAS. 2746

0418-8802 See DEUTSCHE LEHRER IM AUSLAND. 3276

0418-8896 See DEUTSCHES MOZARTFEST DER DEUTSCHEN MOZART-GESELLSCHAFT. 4114

0418-8926 See DEUTSCHE NEUDRUCKE. REIHE: BAROCK. 3380

0418-8950 See DEUTSCHE NEUDRUCKE. REIHE: TEXTE DES 19. JAHRHUNDERT. 3380

0418-8993 See DEUTSCHE REIHE FUR AUSLANDER. REIHE C : ERGANZUNGSHEFTE ZU GRAMMATISCHEN FRAGEN. 3276

0418-9426 See MITTEILUNGEN DES DEUTSCHEN GERMANISTENVERBANDES. 1764

0418-9469 See BERICHT - DEUTSCHER INDUSTRIE- UND HANDELSTAG. 1599

0418-9639 See DVS-BERICHTE. 4027

0418-9655 See BERICHT UBER DIE AUSGRABUNGEN IN OLYMPIA. 261

0418-968X See PERGAMENISCHE FORSCHUNGEN. 2572

0418-9698 See BAGHDADER MITTEILUNGEN. 261

0418-9728 See ABHANDLUNGEN. ISLAMISCHE REIHE. 253

0418-9744 See MADRIDER MITTEILUNGEN. 273

0418-9779 See GERMANISCHE DENKMALER DER VOLKERWANDERUNGSZEIT. SERIES B. DIE FRANKISCHEN ALTERTUMER DES RHEINLANDES. 269

0419-0041 See WISSENSCHAFTLICHE TAGUNG; VORTRAGE. 530

0419-005X See DEUTSCHSPRACHIGE ZEITSCHRIFTEN. 414

0419-0238 See DEVELOPMENTAL MEDICINE AND CHILD NEUROLOGY. SUPPLEMENT. 3831

0419-0254 See DEVELOPMENTS IN GEOTECTONICS. 1373

0419-0297 See DEVELOPMENTS IN SOLID EARTH GEOPHYSICS. 1404

0419-0955 See DIASTEMA. 1322

0419-1110 See DICTA. 1820

0419-1129 See DICTIONARIUM MUSICUM. 4114

0419-1153 See DICTIONNAIRE VIDAL. 4299

0419-1439 See DIJALEKTIKA. 5099

0419-1633 See DIOGENE (EDITION FRANCAISE). 2845

0419-1714 See DIPLOMATIC SERVICE LIST (GREAT BRITAIN), THE. 4471

0419-182X See DIRECT MAIL LIST RATES AND DATA. 758

0419-2052 See DIRECTORY OF MEMBERS - DIRECTORS GUILD OF AMERICA. 4068

0419-2273 See DIRECTORY OF BROADCAST EXECUTIVES (TORONTO). 1131

0419-2508 See DIRECTORY OF DEPARTMENT STORES. 953

0419-2559 See DIRECTORY OF EDUCATIONAL OPPORTUNITIES IN GEORGIA. 1912

0419-2699 See DIRECTORY OF GEORGIA MUNICIPAL OFFICIALS. 4702

0419-2745 See DIRECTORY OF INDIAN SCIENTIFIC PERIODICALS. 5174

0419-2915 See DIRECTORY OF LONDON PUBLIC LIBRARIES. 3207

0419-3350 See DIRECTORY OF PUBLISHED PROCEEDINGS. SERIES SEMT, SCIENCE/ENGINEERING/MEDICINE/TECHNOLOGY. ANNUAL CUMULATIVE VOLUME / INTERDOK. 5100

0419-3482 See DIRECTORY OF SCIENTIFIC RESEARCH INSTITUTIONS IN INDIA, THE. 5100

0419-3717 See DIRECTORY OF THE CANNING, FREEZING, PRESERVING INDUSTRIES, THE. 2333

0419-3776 See DIRECTORY OF THE MINERAL INDUSTRY IN VIRGINIA. 1439

0419-3903 See DIREKTOR. 866

0419-4071 See DISCOVER AMERICA SALES GUIDE. 5468

0419-4187 See DISPATCH (SPRINGFIELD, ILLINOIS). 2731

0419-4209 See DISSERTATION ABSTRACTS INTERNATIONAL. A, THE HUMANITIES AND SOCIAL SCIENCES. 2845

0419-4217 See DISSERTATION ABSTRACTS INTERNATIONAL. 415

0419-4225 See DISSERTATIONEN DER UNIVERSITAT WIEN. 5101

0419-4233 See DISSERTATIONES AD HISTORIAM RELIGIONUM PERTINENTES. 4954

0419-439X See DISTRICT OF COLUMBIA REGISTER. 4645

0419-4632 See DIZIONARIO BIBLIOGRAFICO DELLE RIVISTE GIURIDICHE ITALIANE. 3080

0419-4799 See DJEICH : REVUE DE L'ARMEE NATIONALE POPULAIRE, EL. 4043

0419-5205 See DOCUMENTA MUSICOLOGICA. 1. REIHE. DRUCKSCHRIFTEN-FAKSIMILES. 4115

0419-5361 See DOCUMENTATION PHOTOGRAPHIQUE, LA. 4368

0419-5671 See DOCUMENTS OF MODERN ARCHITECTURE. 298

0419-5779 See DOCUMENTS POUR SERVIR A L'HISTOIRE DE L'AFRIQUE EQUATORIALE FRANCAISE. DEUXIEME SERIE: BRAZZA ET LA FONDATION DU CONGO FRANCAIS. 2639

0419-5981 See DOKUMENTE DER MODERNEN ARCHITEKTUR. 298

0419-618X See BULLETIN - DOLMETSCH FOUNDATION. 4106

0419-683X See DOSSIERS DE L'HISTOIRE. 2615

0419-733X See JAHRBUCH DER STAATLICHEN KUNSTSAMMLUNGEN DRESDEN. 353

0419-7690 See DRUM. EAST AFRICAN EDITION. 2278

0419-8026 See DUISBURGER FORSCHUNGEN. 2685

0419-8069 See PUBLICATIONS OF THE FACULTY. 1869

0419-814X See DULUTH BUSINESS INDICATORS. 669

0419-8174 See BUILDING PERMITS. 604

0419-8824 See DZIEJE NAJNOWSZE. 2615

0419-9014 See STATISTISCHE BEIHEFTE ZU DEN MONATSBERICHTEN DER DEUTSCHEN BUNDESBANK. REIHE 1 : BANKENSTATISTIK NACH BANKENGRUPPEN. 734

0419-9855 See DELTA (PALMERSTON NORTH). 1735

0420-0063 See DESCENDER, THE. 2445

0420-0136 See GRUNDLAGEN ZUR PFLANZENQUARANTAENE. 173

0420-025X See ANTIKE MUNZEN UND GESCHNITTENE STEINE. 2779

0420-0446 See DICTIONNAIRE BIOGRAPHIQUE DU CANADA. 432

0420-0586 See DIRECTORY OF EDUCATIONAL INSTITUTIONS, RAJASTHAN. 1735

0420-0810 See DOCUMENTI DI ARCHITETTURA ARMENA. 298

0420-0918 See DOSHISHA AMERIKA KENKYU. 2615

0420-0942 See DRAFT FACTS FOR GRADUATES AND GRADUATE STUDENTS. 4043

0420-0985 See KLEINE PHILOSOPHISCHE BIBLIOGRAPHIEN. 4365

0420-1213 See DEMONSTRATIO MATHEMATICA. 3503

0420-9036 See EKOLOGIA POLSKA (1970). 2215

0421-3513 See EREKUTORONIKUSU. 2054

0421-4226 See ESOPE : BI-MENSUEL SOCIAL, POLITIQUE, ECONOMIQUE / PUBLIE AVEC LA COLLABORATION DE LA S.E.D.D.E.S. 1489

0421-7381 See REPORT ON THE SITUATION OF THE COMMUNITY. 1625

0421-8094 See EVANGELICAL MAGAZINE OF WALES. 4957

0422-0374 See EARLY GEORGIA. 267

0422-3586 See ECONOMIST. BRIEF, THE. 1559

0422-4108 See I.E. (CHICAGO). 4964

0422-5619 See EDILIZIA POPOLARE. 2821

0422-6399 See EDUCADORES; REVISTA LATINOAMERICANA DE EDUCACION. 1794

0422-7212 See EESTI POLLUMAJANDUSE AKADEEMIA TEADUSLIKE TOODE KOGUMIK. 81

0422-8707 See ELECTRICAL DISTRIBUTOR, THE. 2044

0422-888X See ELECTROACOUSTIQUE. 4452

0422-9053 See E.I.T.D. ELECTRONIC INDUSTRY TELEPHONE DIRECTORY. 1605

0422-9274 See ELEKTRICESKAJA I TEPLOVOZNAJA TJAGA. 5431

0422-9576 See ELELMISZERVIZSGALATI KOZLEMENYEK. 2334

0422-9622 See ELEMENTE DER MATHEMATIK VOM HOHEREN STANDPUNKT AUS. 3504

0422-9703 See ELEVAGE INSEMINATION. 210

0422-9894 See ELSEVIER OCEANOGRAPHY SERIES. 1449

0422-9967 See EMAKEELE SELTSI AASTARAAMAT. 3278

0423-1082 See ENERGETICA. 1937

0423-121X See ENFERMEDADES DEL TORAX. 3574

0423-183X See SELECTED PAPERS FROM THE ENGLISH INSTITUTE. 5218

0423-250X See ENTSCHEIDUNGEN DES BUNDESPATENTGERICHTS. 2966

0423-2607 See ENZYMES, THE. 487

0423-4243 See ESPRESSO, L'. 2487

0423-4456 See ESSEX RECUSANT. 5029

0423-4596 See ESTATE PLANNERS QUARTERLY. 3118

0423-4847 See ESTUDIOS DE DEUSTO. 2967

0423-5037 See ESTUDIOS TURISTICOS. 5469

0423-6378 See EUROPE BRIEF NOTES. 4647

0423-6394 See DAILY BULLETIN - EUROPE, AGENCE INTERNATIONAL D'INFORMATION POUR LA PRESSE. 2514

0423-6734 See EUR RAPPORT - COMMUNAUTE EUROPEENNE DE L'ENERGIE ATOMIQUE. 1944

0423-7846 See BULLETIN - EUROPEAN PARLIAMENT. 3125

0423-8699 See EVERLASTING NATION, THE. 4958

0423-8710 See EVERYBODY'S MONEY. 1296

0423-8990 See EXECUTIVE'S TAX REPORT. 4723

0423-9938 See ELECTRONIC ENGINEERS MASTER CATALOG. 2047

0424-0359 See EARLY ENGLISH CHURCH MUSIC. 4116

0424-107X See EAST KENTUCKIAN, THE. 2446

0424-1444 See EAST TEXAS HISTORICAL JOURNAL. 2732

0424-1932 See PROCEEDINGS OF THE ANNUAL EASTERN SNOW CONFERENCE. 1359

0424-2017 See SCIENTIFIC PUBLICATIONS FROM EASTMAN KODAK LABORATORIES. 4376

0424-2068 See ECCLESIASTICAL COURT DIGEST, THE. 2965

0424-2084 See STUDIES IN CHURCH HISTORY (LONDON, ENGLAND). 5000

0424-2238 See ECOLE DES PARENTS, L'. 2278

0424-2246 See ETUDES CHYPRIOTES. 2515

0424-2386 See ECONOMIA BRASILEIRA E SUAS PERSPECTIVAS, A. 1481

0424-2513 See ECONOMIC AFFAIRS (CALCUTTA). 1482

0424-267X See ECONOMIC COMPUTATION AND ECONOMIC CYBERNETICS STUDIES AND RESEARCH. 1251

0424-2769 See ECONOMIC EDUCATION BULLETIN (GREAT BARRINGTON). 789

0424-2904 See ECONOMIC RESEARCH JOURNAL. 1484

0424-3110 See ECONOMICS OF MARINE RESOURCES. 2192

0424-3218 See ECONOMIE ET POLITIQUE (PARIS. 1954). 1487

0424-3226 See ECONOMIE ET SOCIALISME. 1487

0424-3331 See WORLD OUTLOOK / EIU. 1527

0424-4923 See EDITOR & PUBLISHER INTERNATIONAL YEAR BOOK. 2919

0424-5059 See EDMUND'S USED CAR PRICES. 5414

0424-5318 See EDUCATION & SOCIAL SCIENCE. 1738

0424-5512 See EDUCATION IN THE NORTH. 1739

0424-6829 See EHIME DAIGAKU NOGAKUBU KIYO. 81

0424-6845 See EHIME DAIGAKU NOGAKUBU ENSHURIN HOKOKU. 2378

0424-6985 See EINHEIT DER GESELLSCHAFTSWISSENSCHAFTEN, DIE. 5199

0424-7086 See EISEI DOBUTSU. 5607

0424-7116 See EISZEITALTER UND GEGENWART. 1374

0424-7175 See EKLITRA / ASSOCIATION CULTURELLE PICARDE. 2515

0424-7388 See EKONOMIKA I MATEMATICHESKIE METODY. 1591

0424-7558 See EKONOMSKI PREGLED. 1591

0424-7701 See ELECTRA (PARIS. 1948). 2043

0424-7760 See ELECTRICAL ENGINEERING IN JAPAN. 2045

0424-8120 See ELECTRODIAGNOSTIC-THERAPIE. 3574

0424-8155 See ELECTROENCEPHALOGRAPHY AND CLINICAL NEUROPHYSIOLOGY. SUPPLEMENT. 3832

0424-8201 See PROCEEDINGS, ... ANNUAL MEETING, ELECTRON MICROSCOPY SOCIETY OF AMERICA. 573

0424-8562 See ELEKTROFACH, DAS. 2051

0424-8570 See ELEKTROHIMIA. 2051

0424-8848 See ELET ES IRODALOM. 2515

0424-9399 See EMPORIA STATE RESEARCH STUDIES, THE. 1744

0424-9879 See ENERGETIKA I ELEKTRIFIKACIA KIEV. 2053

0425-0435 See ENGLISH. A NEW LANGUAGE. 3278

0425-0494 See ENGLISH IN EDUCATION. 3279

0425-0575 See ENGLISH MISCELLANY. 3384

0425-0818 See MONOGRAPHIE ... DE L'ENSEIGNEMENT MATHEMATIQUE. 3523

0425-1016 See ENTOMOLOGICA. 5607

0425-1288 See ENTSCHEIDUNGEN DER OBERLANDESGERICHTE IN ZIVILSACHEN EINSCHLIESSLICH DER FREIWILLIGEN GERICHTSBARKEIT. 2966

0425-1466 See EPHEMERIDES MARIOLOGICAE. 4956

0425-1644 See EQUINE VETERINARY JOURNAL. 5509

0425-1687 See ERASME. 3384

0425-1695 See ERBE DEUTSCHER MUSIK. SONDERREIHE / HERAUSGEGEBEN IM AUFTRAGE DES STAATLICHEN INSTITUTS FUER MUSIKFORSCHUNG, DAS. 4116

0425-1768 See ERETRIA. 267

0425-2268 See ERLANGER BEITRAEGE ZUR SPRACH UND KUNSTWISSENSCHAFT. 1076

0425-2772 See ESPANOL ACTUAL. 3279

0425-3329 See YEARBOOK OF THE ESTONIAN LEARNED SOCIETY IN AMERICA. 1854

0425-3507 See ESTUDIOS DE ARQUEOLOGIA ALAVESA / DIPUTACION FORAL DE ALAVA, CONSEJO DE CULTURA. 267

0425-3698 See ESTUDIOS EMPRESARIALES. 866

0425-3906 See ESTUDOS DE ANTROPOLOGIA CULTURAL. 235

0425-4090 See ET AL. 5245

0425-4597 See ETHNOLOGIA EUROPAEA. 235

0425-4813 See ETUDES D'ARCHEOLOGIE CLASSIQUE. 267

0425-4929 See FURANSUGO FURANSU BUNGAKU KENKYU. 3283

0425-676X See FAMILY ECONOMICS REVIEW. 2790

0426-1216 See FILIPINKA WARSZAWA. 1063

0426-2700 See SHOBO KENKYUJO HOKOKU. 2292

0426-5688 See DIRECTORY OF MEMBERSHIP - FLORIDA COUNCIL OF TEACHERS OF ENGLISH. 3277

0426-570X See LEGISLATIVE BULLETIN - FLORIDA. 3001

0426-5750 See FLORIDA GARDENER, THE. 2414

0426-5912 See FLORIDA PLAYERS NEWSLETTER. 1824

0426-5920 See FLORIDA PRESS, THE. 2919

0426-6072 See FLORIDA VOTER, THE. 4474

0426-7680 See PURPOSE AND METHODS IN FISHERIES STATISTICS : DOCUMENT. 2317

0426-8261 See FOOTPRINTS (FORT WORTH). 2448

0427-0029 See FORSTTECHNISCHE INFORMATIONEN. 2383

0427-2129 See BULLETIN OFFICIEL DES DOUANES. 5378

0427-2161 See BULLETIN D'INFORMATION SUR L'ALCOOLISME. 1342

0427-6906 See FRUIT NOTES. 89

0427-7104 See FU TAN HSUEH PAO. TZU JAN KO HSUEH PAN. **5106**

0427-7945 See FYNSKE MINDER. **2689**

0427-8011 See FAA HORIZONS. **19**

0427-8038 See FAO FISHERIES BIOLOGY REPORT. **2300**

0427-8518 See F.S.U. REPORTS. **1823**

0427-8879 See FACTS (SEATTLE, WASH. : 1962). **5760**

0427-9026 See FACTS ON FILE FIVE-YEAR INDEX. **2616**

0428-0296 See FARMACIJA. **4304**

0428-0636 See FAUNA NA BULGARIIA / BULGARSKA AKADEMIIA NA NAUKITE, INSTITUT PO ZOOLOGIIA. **5583**

0428-0709 See FAUNE DE MADAGASCAR. **5583**

0428-111X See FEDERAL COURT CLERKS' NEWS, THE. **2969**

0428-1179 See FEDERAL PHARMACIST. **4305**

0428-1276 See ECONOMIC COMMENTARY (CLEVELAND). **1482**

0428-1365 See LIST OF MEMBER INSTITUTIONS - FEDERAL SAVINGS AND LOAN INSURANCE CORPORATION. **2887**

0428-1551 See PARIS ET ILE-DE-FRANCE / PUBLIES PAR LA FEDERATION DES SOCIETES ET ARCHEOLOGIQUES DE PARIS ET DE L'ILE DE FRANCE. **2702**

0428-1659 See BULLETIN / FEDERATION INTERNATIONALE DE GYMNASTIQUE. **4888**

0428-2094 See FELS MONOGRAPH SERIES. **580**

0428-2396 See PUBBLICAZIONI - FERRARA. CIVICO MUSEO DE STORIA NATURALE. **4171**

0428-2779 See FEUILLETS DE BIOLOGIE. **455**

0428-2957 See FICTION INDEX. **416**

0428-304X See FIELD STUDIES. **4165**

0428-4119 See MEMORIA - FINANCIERA NACIONAL DE CUBA. **798**

0428-4372 See KOETUSSELOSTUS - VAKOLA. **102**

0428-4836 See FIRST DAYS. **2785**

0428-4984 See FISCHEREI-FORSCHUNG. **2301**

0428-5573 See FLASHBACK (FAYETTEVILLE, ARK.). **2733**

0428-5670 See REPORT OF THE PROCEEDINGS : ANNUAL MEETING AND TECHNICAL FORUM. **4569**

0428-5735 See NEWSLETTER - FLIGHT SAFETY FOUNDATION. **30**

0428-6103 See MISCELLANEOUS PUBLICATIONS - FLORIDA. AGRICULTURAL EXPERIMENT, GAINESVILLE. LIBRARY. **109**

0428-6383 See REPORT - FLORIDA. LEGISLATURE. JOINT INTERIM COMMITTEE ON MENTAL HEALTH. **4680**

0428-6413 See FLORIDA AGRICULTURAL STATISTICS : CITRUS SUMMARY. **153**

0428-6456 See FLORIDA AGRICULTURAL STATISTICS: VEGETABLE SUMMARY. **87**

0428-6472 See MINUTES OF THE FLORIDA OUTDOOR RECREATIONAL DEVELOPMENT COUNCIL, FLORIDA OUTDOOR RECREATIONAL PLANNING COMMITTEE. **4874**

0428-6715 See ANALYSIS OF FACTORS RELATED TO THE OPERATION OF THE COLLEGES AND THE SCHOOLS AND THE INSTRUCTIONAL DEPARTMENTS OF THE FLORIDA STATE UNIVERSITY, AN. **1808**

0428-6782 See ECONOMICS SERIES- FLORIDA. UNIVERSITY, GAINESVILLE. AGRICULTURAL EXTENSION SERVICE. **81**

0428-707X See FLORIDA BUSINESS LEADER. **676**

0428-7088 See FLORIDA BUSINESS LETTER. SPECIAL MAPS AND GRAPHS OF FLORIDA. **676**

0428-7282 See YEAR BOOK - FLORIDA GENEALOGICAL SOCIETY, TAMPA, FLA. **2478**

0428-7703 See FLUGTECHNISCHE REIHE. **21**

0428-7738 See FLUID POWER HANDBOOK & DIRECTORY. **2089**

0428-8203 See FOLGER DOCUMENTS OF TUDOR AND STUART CIVILIZATION. **2688**

0429-0208 See FOOTWEAR NEWS FACT BOOK. **1084**

0429-1255 See TAI-WAN NUNG YEH NIEN PAO. **139**

0429-1530 See FORSCHUNGEN ZUR ETHNOLOGIE UND SOZIALPSYCHOLOGIE. **236**

0429-1565 See FORSCHUNGEN ZUR GESCHICHTE OBEROSTERREICHS. **2688**

0429-162X See FORSCHUNGEN ZUR SYSTEMATISCHEN UND OEKUMENISCHEN THEOLOGIE. **4959**

0429-288X See FRAGMENTA ENTOMOLOGICA. **5584**

0429-2944 See BULLETIN OFFICIEL DES ANNONCES DES MARCHES PUBLICS. **4635**

0429-3088 See JOURNAL OFFICIEL DE LA REPUBLIQUE FRANCAISE. DEBATS PARLEMENTAIRES, ASSEMBLEE NATIONALE (CUMULATIF). **4479**

0429-5714 See FRANKFURTER FORSCHUNGEN ZUR ARCHITEKTURGESCHICHTE. **299**

0429-6524 See FREIBURGER RECHTS- UND STAATSWISSENSCHAFTLICHE ABHANDLUNGEN. **4474**

0429-7164 See FRESNO PAST AND PRESENT. **2734**

0429-7326 See PYM NEWS: A PUBLICATION OF THE RELIGIOUS SOCIETY OF FRIENDS. **4988**

0429-7725 See FRONTIERS IN PHYSICS. **4403**

0429-7830 See FRUCHTHANDEL DUSSELDORF. **172**

0429-8284 See FUJI ELECTRIC REVIEW. **2055**

0429-8373 See FUKUI DAIGAKU KOGAKUBU KENKYU HOKOKU. **1976**

0429-8829 See PUBLICACIONES - FUNDACION VITORIA Y SUAREZ. **5235**

0429-9159 See FURUKAWA REVIEW. **2055**

0429-9310 See F A E M. **1746**

0429-9329 See FAO FISHERIES CIRCULAR. **2300**

0429-9337 See FAO FISHERIES REPORT. **2300**

0429-9345 See FAO FISHERIES TECHNICAL PAPER. **2301**

0429-9485 See FIW-SCHRIFTENREIHE. **1491**

0429-9639 See FABULOUS MEXICO - WHERE EVERYTHING COSTS LESS. **5469**

0429-9809 See FACSIMILE REPRINTS IN THE HISTORY OF SCIENCE. **5104**

0429-9949 See FACTS AND TRENDS (VANCOUVER). **1669**

0430-0009 See FACTS ON THE FUNDS. **898**

0430-0246 See FAKSIMILE-REIHE BACHSCHER WERKE UND SCHRIFTSTUCKE. **4117**

0430-0688 See FAR-WESTERNER, THE. **2733**

0430-0750 See FARM CHEMICALS HANDBOOK. **171**

0430-0785 See INCREASING UNDERSTANDING OF PUBLIC PROBLEMS AND POLICIES. **94**

0430-084X See FARM MANAGEMENT NOTES FOR ASIA AND THE FAR EAST. **85**

0430-0939 See FARMAKOLOGIJA I TOKSIKOLOGIJA (KIEV). **4305**

0430-0998 See FARMERS BULLETIN (WEST CUMBERLAND). **85**

0430-1188 See FAULKNER FACTS AND FIDDLINGS. **2733**

0430-1226 See FAUNA D'ITALIA. **5583**

0430-1420 See REVISTA - FEDERACION ARGENTINA DE COLEGIOS DE ABOGADOS. **3042**

0430-1692 See FEDERAL EMPLOYEES NEWS DIGEST. **4702**

0430-1862 See READINGS IN SOUTHERN FINANCE. **806**

0430-1897 See RESEARCH REPORT - FEDERAL RESERVE BANK OF BOSTON. **809**

0430-1978 See MONETARY TRENDS. **1505**

0430-1986 See NATIONAL ECONOMIC TRENDS. **1507**

0430-1994 See RATES OF CHANGE IN ECONOMIC DATA FOR TEN INDUSTRIAL COUNTRIES. **806**

0430-2222 See FATIPEC CONGRESS / ORGANISE PAR L'ASSOCIATION FRANCAISE DES TECHNICIENS DES PEINTURES ET VERNIS (A.F.T.P.V.). **4224**

0430-2761 See FEDNEWS, THE. **1669**

0430-2869 See FEELINGS & THEIR MEDICAL SIGNIFICANCE. **3576**

0430-2958 See FELL'S INTERNATIONAL COIN BOOK. **2781**

0430-3091 See FENWAY COURT. **350**

0430-3121 See FERGUSON FOUNDATION AGRICULTURAL ENGINEERING SERIES, THE. **87**

0430-3202 See ANNALI DELL'UNIVERSITA DI FERRARA. SEZIONE 7 : SCIENZE MATEMATICHE. **3494**

0430-327X See FERTILISER STATISTICS. **153**

0430-3288 See PRODUCTION AND CONSUMPTION OF FERTILISERS; ANNUAL REVIEW. **122**

0430-3393 See FESTKORPERPROBLEME. **4402**

0430-4055 See FIKR O NAZAR. **5042**

0430-4144 See FILIPINO METHODIST MAGAZINE, THE. **5060**

0430-4497 See BOLETIM DA FILMOTECA ULTRAMARINA PORTUGUESA. **2611**

0430-4578 See FILO METALLICO, IL. **4002**

0430-473X See FINANCES & DEVELOPPEMENT. **2909**

0430-4756 See MEMBERSHIP DIRECTORY - THE FINANCIAL ANALYSTS FEDERATION. **906**

0430-4845 See FINANCIAL STATISTICS OF PUBLIC UTILITIES. **4761**

0430-4977 See FINANZWISSENSCHAFTLICHE FORSCHUNGSARBEITEN. **1491**

0430-5094 See VALTION VIRALLISJULKAISUT. **4693**

0430-5574 See MERENKULKU. KAUPPALAIVASTO. **5453**

0430-5582 See MERENKULKU. MERILIIKENNE SUOMEN JA ULKOMAIDEN VALILLA. **5453**

0430-5817 See FINSK PALSTIDSKRIFT. **3183**

0430-6015 See FISH CONSERVATION HIGHLIGHTS. **2301**

0430-6155 See FITOPATOLOGIA. **510**

0430-6228 See FIZIKA GORENIIA I VZRYVA. **4403**

0430-6252 See FIZIKO-HIMICESKAJA MEHANIKA MATERIALOV. **1052**

0430-6465 See FLEISCHFORSCHUNG UND PRAXIS. **211**

0430-6651 See FLORE DE FRANCE. **511**

0430-7585 See STATISTICAL SUMMARY - FLORIDA CANNERS ASSOCIATION. **2362**

0430-7615 See PROCEEDINGS - FLORIDA CORRECTIONAL EDUCATION ASSOCIATION. **3173**

0430-7739 See FLORIDA J.O.H.P.E.R. **4776**

0430-778X See FLORIDA ORCHIDIST, THE. **2414**

0430-7887 See FLORIDA TURF GROWER. **87**

0430-7941 See ABSTRACTS - FLOUR MILLING AND BAKING RESEARCH ASSOCIATION. **2325**

0430-8301 See FOCUS ON INDONESIA. **2651**

0430-8417 See BIBLIS. **4824**

0430-8522 See FOI ET LE TEMPS. **4959**

0430-8603 See FOLIA ENTOMOLOGICA MEXICANA. **5609**

0430-8611 See FOLIA FACULTATIS MEDICAE UNIVERSITATIS COMENIANAE BRATISLAVIENSIS. **3577**

0430-876X See FOLK DIRECTORY, THE. **5231**

0430-8778 See FOLK LIFE. **2319**

0431-0233 See JOURNAL (GARDEN CLUB OF VIRGINIA). **2421**

0431-1213 See GENDAI YOGO NO KISO CHISHIKI. **3283**

0431-1930 See GEOCHILE. **2561**

0431-2155 See JOURNAL OF THE GEOLOGICAL SOCIETY OF CHINA. **1385**

0431-6045 See ECONOMIC SITUATION IN THE FEDERAL REPUBLIC OF GERMANY, THE. **1485**

0431-6983 See STATISTISCHER WOCHENDIENST. **5343**

0431-8722 See GINNASTICA MEDICA, LA. **3954**

0431-9168 See GLADIO GRAMS. **2417**

0432-0905 See GOODYEAR CHEMICAL REVIEW. **5075**

0432-658X See GREY MATTER. RETAIL EDITION. 759

0432-8884 See GUIA PRACTICA DEL EXPORTADOR E IMPORTADOR Y PARA TODO HOMBRE DE NEGOCIOS. 838

0432-9368 See GUIDE DU CONTRIBUABLE CANADIEN, LE. 678

0433-163X See GANNETTEER. 2920

0433-1818 See GARTEN UND KLEINTIERZUCHT. B : RASSEGEFLUGELZUCHTER. 211

0433-1834 See GARTEN UND KLEINTIERZUCHT. D : KLEINTIERZUCHTER. 211

0433-1931 See GAS COUNCIL RESEARCH COMMUNICATION. 4257

0433-194X See GAS DATA BOOK; BRIEF EXCERPTS FROM GAS FACTS. 4257

0433-2091 See GATOR GREEK, THE. 5231

0433-2644 See GEKA CHIRYO. 3965

0433-3209 See GENEALOGICAL RECORD (HOUSTON, TEX.), THE. 2450

0433-3233 See GENEALOGICAL TIPS. 2450

0433-342X See BULLETIN - GENERAL ELECTRIC COMPANY. RESEARCH LABORATORY. 2037

0433-3519 See STUDIES AND REVIEWS - GENERAL FISHERIES COUNCIL FOR THE MEDITERRANEAN. 2314

0433-3837 See BOLLETTINO DELL ISTITUTO DI LINGUE ESTERE / UNIVERSITA DEGLI STUDI DI GENOVA, FACOLTA DI ECONOMIA E COMMERCIO. 3270

0433-4035 See GENSHIRYOKU KOGYO. 2155

0433-5082 See GEORGE MACAULAY TREVELYN LECTURES. 2689

0433-5732 See UNIVERSITY OF GEORGIA LABORATORY OF ARCHAEOLOGY SERIES. 285

0433-6054 See GEORGIA OPERATOR, THE. 1492

0433-678X See BULLETIN / MUSIKRAT DER DEUTSCHEN DEMOKRATISCHEN REPUBLIK, SEKTION DDR DES INTERNATIONALEN MUSIKRATES. 4106

0433-7050 See ENTSCHEIDUNGEN DES BUNDESARBEITSGERICHTS. 3147

0433-7646 See ENTSCHEIDUNGEN DES BUNDESVERFASSUNGSGERICHTS. 2966

0433-7867 See AMTLICHE SCHRIFTTUM DER BUNDESREPUBLIK, DAS. 407

0433-8413 See GESCHICHTLICHE ARBEITEN ZUR WESTFAELISCHEN LANDESFORSCHUNG. 2689

0433-8731 See SITZUNGS-BERICHTE DER GESELLSCHAFT NATURFORSCHENDER FREUNDE ZU BERLIN. 4172

0433-9118 See GEWERKSCHAFTER, DER. 1676

0434-0078 See KYOIKUGAKUBU KENKYU HOKOKU. SHIZEN KAGAKU (GIFU). 5124

0434-0094 See GIFU YAKKA DAIGAKU KIYO. 4306

0434-0299 See GIORNALINO (NEW YORK, N.Y.), IL. 1748

0434-1473 See GOTTINGER HANDWERKSWIRTSCHAFTLICHE STUDIEN. 1607

0434-2593 See GOVERNMENT CONTRACTS CITATOR. 3100

0434-300X See GRAA ZA PROUCAVANJE SPOMENIKA KULTURE VOJVODINE. 351

0434-3336 See GRAND BATON, LE. 4119

0434-5797 See GREAT MASTERS OF THE PAST. 5231

0434-5835 See PROCEEDINGS OF THE GREAT PLAINS AGRICULTURAL COUNCIL. 122

0434-6238 See EIDIKAI MELETAI EPI TES GEOLOGIAS TES ELLADOS (ATHENAI). 1355

0434-6629 See ESSAIS ET TRAVAUX - GRENOBLE. UNIVERSITE. 1823

0434-6793 See RAPPORT / INSTITUUT VOOR BODEMVRUCHTBAARHEID. 184

0434-6971 See BULLETIN DU GROUPEMENT D'INFORMATIONS MUTUELLES AMPERE. 4399

0434-8877 See GUIDE TO GEORGIA. 5479

0434-9245 See GUILD OF BOOK WORKERS JOURNAL. 4828

0434-9342 See GUITAR NEWS. 4120

0434-9350 See GUITARRA MAGAZINE. 4120

0434-9474 See INFORMATIONAL SERIES - GULF STATES MARINE FISHERIES COMMISSION. 2305

0434-9490 See RESEARCH PROSPECTUS - GULF STATES MARINE FISHERIES COMMISSION. 2311

0434-9504 See TECHNICAL SUMMARY - GULF STATES MARINE FISHERIES COMMISSION. 2314

0435-0464 See GALAXY MAGAZINE. 3389

0435-1096 See GAMMA FIELD SYMPOSIA. 511

0435-1304 See GAS ENGINE MAGAZINE. 250

0435-1339 See GASTROENTEROLOGIA JAPONICA. 3745

0435-1363 See GASTROPODIA. 5584

0435-2033 See BULLETIN DES RECHERCHES AGRONOMIQUES DE GEMBLOUX. 69

0435-2459 See PRESS AND THE PEOPLE : THE ... ANNUAL REPORT OF THE GENERAL COUNCIL OF THE PRESS, THE. 2923

0435-284X See GENETIK. 546

0435-2866 See STUDIES ON VOLTAIRE AND THE EIGHTEENTH CENTURY. 3442

0435-3676 See GEOGRAFISKA ANNALER. SERIES A, PHYSICAL GEOGRAPHY. 2562

0435-3684 See GEOGRAFISKA ANNALER. SERIES B, HUMAN GEOGRAPHY. 2823

0435-3870 See GEOLOGIA APPLICATA E IDROGEOLOGIA. 1377

0435-3927 See GEOLOGICA ROMANA. 1377

0435-4001 See MEMOIR / GEOLOGICAL SOCIETY OF INDIA. 1387

0435-4036 See CHIJIL HAKHOE CHI. 1371

0435-4281 See GEOMORFOLOGIJA (MOSKVA). 2564

0435-4389 See GEORGE B. PEGRAM LECTURES. 1825

0435-4419 See MONOGRAPH. 5234

0435-4842 See ANNUAL REPORT - EMPLOYEES' RETIREMENT SYSTEM. 1649

0435-5377 See GEORGIA FOREST RESEARCH PAPER. 2383

0435-5393 See GEORGIA GENEALOGICAL SOCIETY QUARTERLY, THE. 2451

0435-5393 See GEORGIA GENEALOGICAL MAGAZINE. 2451

0435-5482 See GEORGIA MANUFACTURING DIRECTORY. 3479

0435-5806 See GERMAN PHOTOGRAPHIC ANNUAL, THE. 4370

0435-5903 See GERMANISTISCHE ABHANDLUNGEN (STUTTGART). 3284

0435-5911 See GERMANISTISCHE SCHRIFTENREIHE DER NORWEGISCHEN UNIVERSITATEN UND HOCHSCHULEN. 3284

0435-7523 See WISSENSCHAFTLICHE SCHRIFTENREIHE. 1527

0435-7965 See MONATLICHER WITTERUNGSBERICHT. 1431

0435-8112 See VEROFFENTLICHUNG - GESELLSCHAFT DER ORGELFREUNDE. 4158

0435-8287 See SCHRIFTEN - GESELLSCHAFT FUER SOZIALEN FORTSCHRITT. 5257

0435-8406 See GESHER (WORLD JEWISH CONGRESS. ISRAEL EXECUTIVE). 5047

0435-8600 See GEWERBLICHER RECHTSSCHUTZ UND URHEBERRECHT. INTERNATIONALER TEIL. 2974

0435-9380 See GHANA JOURNAL OF SOCIOLOGY. 5246

0435-9577 See WERKEN - GHENT. RIJKSUNIVERSITEIT. HOGERE SCHOOL VOOR HANDELS- EN ECONOMISCHE WETENSCHAPPEN. 1853

0435-9763 See GIESSENER BEITRAEGE ZUR ENTWICKLUNGSFORSCHUNG. REIHE 2 : MONOGRAPHIEN. 90

0435-978X See GIESSENER GEOGRAPHISCHE SCHRIFTEN. 2565

0435-9844 See RESEARCH BULLETIN OF THE FACULTY OF AGRICULTURE, GIFU UNIVERSITY. 127

0436-0222 See GIURISPRUDENZA COSTITUZIONALE. 3093

0436-0257 See GIVING USA. 4336

0436-029X See GLADIUS. 4044

0436-1105 See GODISNJAK GRADA BEOGRADA. 4088

0436-1180 See VEROFFENTLICHUNGEN - MAX-PLANCK-INSTITUT FUER GESCHICHTE. 2632

0436-1199 See BERICHT - MAX-PLANCK-INSTITUT FUER STROMUNGSFORSCHUNG. 2087

0436-1377 See GOLDEN EAGLE FILM AWARDS. 4071

0436-1539 See GOOD HOUSEKEEPING NEEDLECRAFT. 5184

0436-1563 See GOOD NEWS (WILMORE). 5060

0436-2020 See ARSTRYCK - GOTEBORGS ETNOGRAFISKA MUSEUM. 231

0436-2071 See SIK-RAPPORT. 4199

0436-2233 See GOVBANK TECHNICAL PAPERS. 789

0436-2438 See PROCEEDINGS, ANNUAL GOVERNOR'S CONFERENCE ON THE HANDICAPPED. 4392

0436-2829 See GRAMMATICA UNIVERSALIS. 3284

0436-2888 See COLECCION FILOLOGICA. 3274

0436-306X See GRANDS DOCUMENTS. LES EDITIONS DE MINUIT. 2847

0436-3574 See OVERSEAS TRADE STATISTICS OF THE UNITED KINGDOM. 732

0436-3779 See REPORT - GREAT BRITAIN. COMMITTEE ON SAFETY OF DRUGS. 4798

0436-399X See LAND RESOURCE STUDY. 1502

0436-4120 See REPORT ON FOREST RESEARCH. 2392

0436-5569 See LANDBOUWCIJFERS. 154

0436-6425 See MITTEILUNGEN AUS DEM INSTITUT FUER SEEFISCHEREI DER BUNDESFORSCHUNGSANSTALT FUER FISCHEREI. 2308

0437-2085 See DELTION TES HELLENIKES KTENIATRIKES HETAIREIAS. PERIODOS B. 5508

0437-3014 See HERBERGEN DER CHRISTENHEIT; JAHRBUCH FUER DEUTSCHE KIRCHENGESCHICHTE. 300

0437-6668 See HOKKAIDO DAIGAKU BUNGAKUBU KIYO. 321

0437-7168 See HOLZZUCHT, DIE. 2384

0438-0479 See HSIA-MEN TA HSUEH HSUEH PAO. TZU JAN KO HSUEH PAN. 5110

0438-0797 See XIN SHENG. 3455

0438-1629 See BULLETIN - HUMAN FACTORS SOCIETY. 1250

0438-1629 See BULLETIN / HUMAN FACTORS AND ERGONOMICS SOCIETY. 1250

0438-2242 See BUDAPEST STATISZTIKAI ZSEBKONYVE. 5323

0438-380X See HAIYANG KEXUE JIKAN. 554

0438-4679 See BEITRAEGE ZUR MITTELAMERIKANISCHEN VOLKERKUNDE. 2723

0438-4997 See HANDAI HOGAKU. 2976

0438-5047 See HANDBOOK FOR GEORGIA LEGISLATORS. 4654

0438-5403 See HANDEL WEWNETRZNY. 839

0438-6019 See HARCERSTWO WARSZAWA. 1064

0438-623X See PORT OF HOUSTON FOREIGN TRADE. 849

0438-6256 See CLUBS IN TOWN AND COUNTRY. 5230

0438-6566 See REPORT - HARVARD COLLEGE, CLASS OF 1959. 1844

0438-7473 See ANNUAL REPORT OF THE DEPARTMENT OF LABOR AND INDUSTRIAL RELATIONS, STATE OF HAWAII. 1649

0438-7619 See CIRCULAR - STATE OF HAWAII, DEPARTMENT OF LAND AND NATURAL RESOURCES, DIVISION OF WATER AND LAND DEVELOPMENT. 1413

0438-8399 See HAYNES EAGLE. 2452

0438-9573 See DELTION ELLENIKES MIKROBIOLOGIKES ETAIREIAS. 562

0439-0148 See HERALDO DE LA CIENCIA CRISTIANA, EL. 4962

0439-027X See HERITAGE (VAN BUREN), THE. 2736

0439-0377 See HERMSDORFER TECHNISCHE MITTEILUNGEN : HTM. 2590

0439-0687 See HESSISCHE FLORISTISCHE BRIEFE. 512

0439-0962 See HIDROTEHNICA. 2090

0439-1799 See HIROSHIMA KENRITSU NOGYO SHIKENJO HOKOKU. 92

0439-2027 See HISTORIA AGRICULTURAE. 92

0439-2132 See HISTORIA RELIGIONUM. 4963

0439-2248 See HISTORIC NANTUCKET. 2737

0439-2345 See HISTORICAL NEWS. 2618

0439-2434 See HISTORIELARARNAS FORENINGS ARSSKRIFT. 2618

0439-2620 See HISTORISKE MEDDELELSER OM KBENHAVN. ARBOG. 2691

0439-2965 See HOCHSCHUL-DIENST. 1750

0439-3503 See HOKKAIDO DAIGAKU CHIKYU BUTSURIGAKU KENKYU HOKOKU. 1406

0439-3600 See HOKURIKU NOGYO SHIKENJO HOKOKU. 93

0439-3678 See HOLIDAY TIME IN THAILAND. 5479

0439-4208 See HOMILETICA. 5030

0439-4216 See HOMME. 237

0439-5530 See HORISONT. 2847

0439-660X See HOUSTON LAWYER. 2979

0439-8017 See XUESHU JIKAN. 1528

0439-884X See HUMANISMUS UND TECHNIK. 2620

0440-0771 See TUINBOUWCIJFERS. 2434

0440-0852 See TO SHIN, HAI. 3646

0440-0917 See FACULTY PUBLICATION - TECHNION - ISRAEL INSTITUTE OF TECHNOLOGY, FACULTY OF CIVIL ENGINEERING. 2023

0440-1123 See HAKSURWON NONMUNJIP. CHAYON KWAHAK PYON. 5109

0440-1298 See FORSCHUNG UND ERGEBNISSE DES BEREICHES MEDIZIN. 3577

0440-1417 See JAHRBUCH - ALTONAER MUSEUM IN HAMBURG. 4089

0440-1522 See MONOGRAPHIEN ZUR VOLKERKUNDE. 241

0440-1697 See HAMBURGER GEOGRAPHISCHE STUDIEN. 2565

0440-1727 See HAMBURGER ROMANISTISCHE DISSERTATIONEN. 3285

0440-1905 See HANDBOOK OF ELECTRICITY SUPPLY STATISTICS. 2004

0440-2316 See HANGING LOOSE. 3463

0440-2332 See HANGUG JAMSA HAGNOI JI. 5585

0440-2413 See MISAENGMUL HAKHOE CHI. 567

0440-2588 See ECONOMIC STATISTICS YEARBOOK. 728

0440-2863 See MITTEILUNGEN DER HANS PFITZNER-GESELLSCHAFT. 4131

0440-2987 See HARAUI. 3463

0440-4106 See HARYANA REVIEW. 5479

0440-436X See REVISTA DEL HOSPITAL PSIQUIATRICO DE LA HABANA. 3936

0440-4866 See HIG (SERIES). 1406

0440-4904 See L.S.B. BULLETIN. 1386

0440-4947 See DIRECTORY OF STATE, COUNTY, AND FEDERAL OFFICIALS. 4644

0440-5056 See HAWAII BUSINESS. 679

0440-5145 See HAWAIIAN JOURNAL OF HISTORY, THE. 2669

0440-5234 See HAWKEYE HERITAGE. 2452

0440-5323 See HAYDN-STUDIEN. 4120

0440-5749 See HEAT TRANSFER RESEARCH. 2056

0440-5757 See YEARBOOK OF THE HEATHER SOCIETY. 5237

0440-5927 See HEGEL-STUDIEN. BEIHEFT,. 4348

0440-6044 See HEIDELBERGER FORSCHUNGEN. 3285

0440-6605 See HELMINTHOLOGIA. 5585

0440-6826 See HEMIJSKI PREGLED. 976

0440-7164 See HERMAEA. 3393

0440-7237 See HERNE, L'. 4348

0440-7296 See HERP. 5585

0440-7326 See HERPETON. 5585

0440-7334 See HERTIS OCCASIONAL PAPER. 3213

0440-7342 See HERTFORDSHIRE ARCHAEOLOGY. 269

0440-7563 See HESTIA. 4348

0440-8047 See HIKAKU BUNGAKU. 3393

0440-8411 See REPORT - PUBLIC ACCOUNTS COMMITTEE. 4746

0440-8772 See BULLETIN OF THE HIROSHIMA AGRICULTURAL COLLEGE. 69

0440-8888 See HISTOIRE DES SCIENCES MEDICALES. 3584

0440-8934 See HISTOIRE RELIGIEUSE DU CANADA. 4963

0440-8969 See HISTORIA. EINZELSCHRIFTEN. 2691

0440-9043 See HISTORIA HOSPITALIUM. 3783

0440-9094 See HISTORIA PARAGUAYA. 2736

0440-9191 See HISTORIC KINGSTON. 2737

0440-9205 See HISTORICA (CESKOSLOVENSKA AKADEMIE VED. SEKCE HISTORICKA). 2691

0440-9213 See HISTORICAL ARCHAEOLOGY. 269

0440-940X See HISTORICAL SOCIETY MIRROR. 2737

0440-9426 See CHRONICLE (ANN ARBOR). 2728

0440-971X See HISTORISCHE ZEITSCHRIFT. SONDERHEFT. 2619

0440-9736 See HISTORISCHES JAHRBUCH DER STADT LINZ. 2691

0440-9884 See HISTORY OF ECONOMIC THOUGHT NEWSLETTER. 1592

0441-0025 See ECONOMIC RESEARCH SERIES. 1484

0441-0351 See HOGAKU ZASSHI. 2978

0441-067X See JOURNAL OF THE FACULTY OF SCIENCE, HOKKAIDO UNIVERSITY. SERIES VII. GEOPHYSICS. 1408

0441-0734 See HOKKAIDO KOGYO KAIHATSU SHIKENJO HOKOKU. 5110

0441-0769 See SCIENTIFIC REPORTS OF THE HOKKAIDO SALMON HATCHERY. 2312

0441-0807 See SHUHO. BULLETIN OF THE HOKKAIDO PREFECTURAL AGRICULTURAL EXPERIMENT STATIONS. 134

0441-0807 See HOKKAIDO NOGYO SHIKENJO SHUHO. 92

0441-1196 See ALMANAKH GOMONU UKRAJINY. 2513

0441-2044 See HONOLULU. 2534

0441-2168 See HORISON. 3394

0441-2745 See HOSPITAL MEDICINE (NEW YORK, N.Y.). 3584

0441-3768 See HUA HSUEH. CHEMISTRY. 977

0441-3776 See HUA HSUEH TUNG PAO / CHUNG-KUO HUA HSUEH HUI. 977

0441-389X See HUDSON'S WASHINGTON NEWS MEDIA CONTACTS DIRECTORY. 2920

0441-4004 See MISCELLANEOUS SERIES - DEPARTMENT OF GEOGRAPHY, UNIVERSITY OF HULL. 2569

0441-4195 See HUMANISTIC JUDAISM. 5048

0441-4225 See JINBUN RONSHU / WASEDA DAIGAKU HOGAKKAI. 2986

0441-5590 See JAHRESBERICHT / KESTNER-MUSEUM. 4089

0441-6619 See HERALDRY IN CANADA. 2453

0441-6627 See HERBES ROUGES. 2534

0441-6651 See JOURNAL OF THE HERPETOLOGICAL ASSOCIATION OF AFRICA. 5589

0441-666X See HERPETOLOGY (PASADENA). 5585

0441-6813 See HOFMANNSTHAL BLATTER. 3394

0441-6910 See HUGUENOT TRAILS. 2454

0441-7119 See NEW EXPENDITURE. 4738

0441-747X See HOSHASEN SEIBUTSU KENKYU. 457

0442-0713 See ILLINOIS MUNICIPAL PROBLEMS; REPORT OF THE CITIES AND VILLAGES MUNICIPAL PROBLEMS COMMISSION TO THE GENERAL ASSEMBLY OF ILLINOIS. 4655

0442-2562 See ILLINOIS AGRICULTURAL STATISTICS. 154

0442-3844 See IN UNITY. 4964

0442-6851 See INDIAN INDUSTRIES. 681

0442-7637 See ANNUAL REPORT OF THE DIVISION OF FISH AND GAME, INDIANA DEPARTMENT OF CONSERVATION. 2186

0442-817X See INDIANA WEEKLY WEATHER CROP REPORT. 174

0443-5443 See TENTATIVE RECOMMENDED PRACTICE (INSTRUMENT SOCIETY OF AMERICA). 3488

0443-6976 See WISSENSCHAFTSRECHT, WISSENSCHAFTSVERWALTUNG, WISSENSCHAFTSFORDERUNG. 3076

0443-9058 See COLLECTED LETTERS OF THE INTERNATIONAL CORRESPONDENCE SOCIETY OF OBSTETRICIANS, GYNECOLOGISTS. 3759

0444-0013 See EDITED PROCEEDINGS ... INTERNATIONAL GALVANIZING CONFERENCE. 974

0444-4663 See IOWA ENGLISH BULLETIN. 3288

0444-9266 See BOLLETTINO DI INFORMAZIONI COSTITUZIONALI E PARLAMENTARI. NUOVA SERIE. 3092

0445-0108 See IZVESTIIA VYSSHIKH UCHEBNYKH ZAVEDENII. NEFT I GAZ / MINISTERSTVO VYSSHEGO I SREDNEGO SPETSIALNOGO OBRAZOVANIIA SSSR. 4262

0445-0736 See SCHRIFTENREIHE DES IFO-INSTITUT FUER WIRTSCHAFTSFORSCHUNG. 1396

0445-1694 See IBARAKI DAIGAKU NOGAKUBU GAKUJUTSU HOKOKU. 93

0445-1767 See ICARE. 23

0445-1953 See ANNUAL UPLAND GAME BIRD REPORT (BOISE). 5576

0445-2127 See IDAHO GENEALOGICAL SOCIETY QUARTERLY. 2454

0445-3034 See FISHERY PUBLICATION (SPRINGFIELD). 2303

0445-3042 See SPECIAL FISHERIES REPORT - STATE OF ILLINOIS. 2313

0445-3387 See HANDBOOK OF COLLECTIONS. 4088

0445-3395 See SCIENTIFIC PAPERS / ILLINOIS STATE MUSEUM. 1360

0445-3611 See ORGANIC SEMINAR ABSTRACTS. 1045

0445-4111 See ILLINOIS LAW ENFORCEMENT OFFICERS LAW BULLETIN. 3165

0445-5738 See REPORT - INDIA (REPUBLIC) COFFEE BOARD. 184

0445-5983 See BULLETIN OF AGRICULTURAL PRICES (INDIA). 69

0445-622X See BULLETINS OF THE GEOLOGICAL SURVEY OF INDIA. 1412

0445-6319 See ACTS OF PARLIAMENT. 4624

0445-6793 See LOK SABHA. PARLIAMENTARY COMMITTEES. SUMMARY OF WORK. 4663

0445-7722 See INDIAN JOURNAL OF SERICULTURE. 5586

0445-7897 See INDIAN MINERALS YEARBOOK. 2140

0445-7951 See INDIAN TOBACCO. 5373

0445-8370 See GEOLOGICAL SURVEY CIRCULAR (BLOOMINGTON). 1378

0445-8605 See INDIANA ARCHITECT. 301

0445-8664 See INDIANA DECISIONS AND LAW REPORTER. 2981

0445-8699 See INDIANA RURAL MANPOWER REPORT. 1678

0445-9474 See SERI STATISTIK PENGANGKUTAN KERETA API. RAILWAYS STATISTICS. 5402

0446-0138 See INDOOR COMFORT NEWS. 2901

0446-0243 See INDUSTRIA DEI FARMACI. 4307

0446-0375 See INDUSTRIAL DESIGN IN AMERICA. 2098

ISSN Index

0446-0995 See FACHSERI D. INDUSTRIE UND HANDWERK : REIHE 1. BESCHAFTIGUNG UND UMSATZ, BRENNSTOFF- UND ENERGIEVERSORGUNG DER INDUSTRIE. 1606

0446-1568 See INFORMACION SOBRE GRASAS Y ACEITES. 4192

0446-3013 See INSIDE PHOENIX. 1567

0446-3943 See JAHRBUCH FUER FRANKISCHE LANDESFORSCHUNG. 2694

0446-6241 See JAPAN LETTER. 2654

0446-6454 See NIPPON JUISHIKAI ZASSHI. 5517

0446-6586 See NIHON SHOKAKIBYO GAKKAI ZASSHI. 3800

0446-9283 See AL-MAGALLA AL-TIBBIYYA AL-URDUNIYYA. 3547

0447-2322 See JREA. 5432

0447-256X See JAHRBUCH DER LUFT- UND RAUMFAHRT. 25

0447-5291 See JAPAN COMMERCE AND INDUSTRY. 1613

0447-5321 See JAPAN COTTON STATISTICS AND RELATED DATA, THE. 154

0447-5763 See JAPAN TIMES (OVERSEAS ED.), THE. 5805

0447-5933 See NIHON SOCHI GAKKAI SHI. 203

0447-6425 See JELENKOR. 3399

0447-6441 See JEMNA MECHANIKA A OPTIKA. 4428

0447-7049 See JEWISH ACTION. 5048

0447-7227 See JIBI TO RINSHO. 3888

0447-8959 See TOKYO NOGYO DAIGAKU NOGAKU SHUHO. 141

0447-9408 See JOURNAL OF PARLIAMENTARY INFORMATION, THE. 4658

0447-953X See JOURNAL OF SPORTS PHILATELY. 2785

0448-0155 See ACTA GEOLOGICA. 1364

0448-0171 See JUGOSLAVENSKA PEDIJATRIJA. 3905

0448-116X See JADERNA ENERGIE. 1948

0448-133X See JAHRBUCH DER SAMMLUNG KIPPENBERG. 3398

0448-1488 See JAHRBUCH FUER ANTIKE UND CHRISTENTUM. ERGANZUNGSBAND. 4967

0448-1518 See JAHRBUCH FUER GEOLOGIE. 1384

0448-1607 See JAHRBUCH ZUR GESCHICHTE VON STADT UND LANDKREIS KAISERSLAUTERN. 2694

0448-1690 See RAJASTHAN UNIVERSITY STUDIES IN ENGLISH. 3427

0448-1933 See NATIONAL INCOME AND PRODUCT. 1536

0448-214X See JAMAICA ARCHITECT. 301

0448-2352 See BUDGET. 4714

0448-2433 See REPORT - JAMMU AND KASHMIR LEGISLATIVE COUNCIL, COMMITTEE ON PRIVILEGES. 4680

0448-8520 See JAPAN BANKING BRIEFS. 793

0448-861X See JAPAN ELECTRONICS BUYERS' GUIDE. 2068

0448-8679 See JAPAN PLASTICS INDUSTRY ANNUAL. 4455

0448-8806 See JAPANESE ANNUAL OF INTERNATIONAL LAW, THE. 3131

0448-8830 See JAPANESE FILMS. 4073

0448-8938 See JAPANESE RAILWAY ENGINEERING. 5432

0448-8954 See JAPANESE RELIGIONS. 4967

0448-9179 See JAUNA GAITA. 2848

0448-9241 See JAZYKOVEDNE STUDIE. 3289

0449-010X See JEWISH QUARTERLY, THE. 5049

0449-0339 See JINKO MONDAI KENKYUJO NENPO. 4554

0449-0576 See JOKULL. 1415

0449-0754 See JOHN BIRCH SOCIETY BULLETIN, THE. 4542

0449-0789 See JOHN COFFIN MEMORIAL LECTURE, THE. 2848

0449-1564 See ANNUAL OF THE DEPARTMENT OF ANTIQUITIES. 2645

0449-2153 See JOURNAL OF ALABAMA ARCHAEOLOGY. 271

0449-2544 See JOURNAL OF FOOT SURGERY, THE. 3918

0449-2757 See JOURNAL OF MATHEMATICAL SCIENCES. 3514

0449-3044 See JOURNAL OF PSYCHOPHARMACOLOGY. 4313

0449-3060 See JOURNAL OF RADIATION RESEARCH. 4436

0449-3087 See JOURNAL OF REPRODUCTION AND FERTILITY. SUPPLEMENT. 3597

0449-315X See JOURNAL OF SOCIAL RESEARCH (RANCHI). 239

0449-3354 See JOURNALISM SCHOLARSHIP GUIDE. 2921

0449-3370 See JOURNALISME. 2921

0449-363X See FILOLOGIJA. 3281

0449-4555 See JUVENTUD TECNICA. 5122

0449-4733 See JOURNAL DE L'ANNEE. 2621

0449-4873 See JEDNOTA ANNUAL FURDEK. 2740

0449-5063 See JOURNAL OF CALIFORNIA LAW ENFORCEMENT. 3167

0449-508X See JOURNAL OF PASTORAL COUNSELING, THE. 4969

0449-5128 See JOURNAL OF SYNAGOGUE MUSIC. 4126

0449-5152 See JOURNAL OFFICIEL DES COMMUNAUTES EUROPEENNES : COMMUNICATIONS ET INFORMATIONS. 26

0449-5225 See ECONOMIC SYSTEMS. 1558

0449-5233 See JAHRBUCH FUER INTERNATIONALE GERMANISTIK. 3289

0449-5314 See NEWS BULLETIN. 4699

0449-5519 See JUDICIAL HIGHLIGHTS BULLETIN. 2990

0449-5527 See PRILOZI I GRAA. 3311

0449-5713 See JOURNAL OF CERAMIC HISTORY. 2591

0449-5721 See JOURNAL OF PLANT AND MACHINERY. 2118

0449-7368 See KANADSKE LISTY (TORONTO. 1973). 5788

0449-749X See GANGTIE. 4002

0449-7732 See MONTHLY SUMMARY OF VITAL STATISTICS. 4810

0449-9042 See KASAI : NIHON KASAI GAKKAISHI. 2291

0450-0040 See KEIZAI SHINGO JITEN. 1593

0450-089X See KENTUCKY AND TENNESSEE LEGAL DIRECTORY, THE. 3141

0450-1489 See KERK EN THEOLOGIE. 4972

0450-2078 See KHIDROLOGIIA I METEOROLOGIIA. 1427

0450-2167 See HIRURGIJA (SOFIJA). 3965

0450-3171 See KIRKEHISTORISKE SAMLINGER. 2622

0450-609X See KOBE SHOSEN DAIGAKU KIYO. DAI 2-RUI, SHOSEN, RIKOGAKU HEN. 4178

0450-6413 See KOLNER DOMBLATT. 302

0450-7169 See KOMMUNALWIRTSCHAFT. 4660

0450-7886 See KONYVTAROS. 3222

0450-8955 See PRACE INSTYTUTU ODLEWNICTWA. 4015

0450-9250 See STUDIE. 5000

0451-0410 See KULTURELLES LEBEN. 1683

0451-0887 See KUNSTERZIEHUNG : ZEITSCHRIFT FUR LEHRER UND JUGENDERZIEHER. 324

0451-1964 See KAGAKU (KYOTO). 983

0451-2014 See KAGAKU KOGYO. 2014

0451-3665 See TEXTBOOKS SUITABLE FOR USE IN KANSAS SCHOOLS. 1787

0451-3991 See KANSAS CITY GENEALOGIST, THE. 2456

0451-4084 See KANSAS KIN. 2456

0451-4203 See KANZO (TOKYO, JAPAN : 1960). 3601

0451-5994 See KEIKINZOKU. 4006

0451-6281 See KEIZAIGAKU ZASSHI. 1501

0451-6915 See INFORMATION CIRCULAR / KENTUCKY GEOLOGICAL SURVEY. 1382

0451-7814 See FLORA OF TROPICAL EAST AFRICA. 511

0451-8306 See HIMICESKOE MASINOSTROENIE (KIEV). 2012

0451-9396 See KIKAI GIJUTSU. 2119

0451-9949 See KIRKWOOD HISTORICAL REVIEW. 2743

0452-2311 See KOATSU GASU. 1984

0452-2370 See KOBE DAIGAKU NOGAKU-BU KENKYU HOKOKU. SCIENCE REPORTS OF FACULTY OF AGRICULTURE, KOBE UNIVERSITY. 102

0452-2516 See KODAI. 272

0452-2591 See KODAK TECH BITS. 4371

0452-2834 See KOGYO ZAIRYO. 1984

0452-3458 See KOKYU TO JUNKAN. 3799

0452-3970 See KOMPAS. 5803

0452-4160 See MEMOIRS OF THE KONAN UNIVERSITY. SCIENCE SERIES. 5128

0452-599X See KOROSE A OCHRANA MATERIALU. 984

0452-6171 See SBORNIK VEDECKYCH PRAC. 1995

0452-7070 See MITTEILUNGEN DES KREMSER STADTARCHIVS. 2699

0452-7739 See KUESTE. 2093

0452-814X See KULTUUR JA ELU. 2536

0452-8255 See KUN CHUNG CHIH SHIH. 5611

0452-8514 See KUNST IN HESSEN UND AM MITTELRHEIN. 356

0452-9081 See KURTRIERISCHES JAHRBUCH. 2696

0452-9685 See KYOKA PURASUCHIKKUSU. 4456

0452-9731 See KYORITSU YAKKA DAIGAKU KENKYU NENPO. 4313

0453-0357 See KYUSHU KOGYO DAIGAKU KENKYU HOKOKU, KOGAKU. 5125

0453-0683 See KAGAKU KEIZAI. 1026

0453-073X See KAGAKU TO SEIBUTSU. 490

0453-0764 See KAGAWA DAIGAKU NOGAKUBU KIYO. 102

0453-0845 See KAGOSHIMA DAIGAKU NOGAKUBU GAKUJUTSU HOKOKU. 102

0453-0853 See MEMOIRS OF THE FACULTY OF AGRICULTURE, KAGOSHIMA UNIVERSITY. 108

0453-087X See KAGOSHIMA DAIGAKU SUISANGAKUBU KIYO. 102

0453-1507 See KAMI, PARUPU GIJUTSU TAIMUSU. 4234

0453-1906 See KANAGAWA KENRITSU HAKUBUTSUKAN KENKYU HOKOKU. SHIZEN KAGAKU. 4166

0453-2198 See TECHNOLOGY REPORTS OF KANSAI UNIVERSITY. 1998

0453-249X See REPORT - KANSAS STATE UNIVERSITY. INSTITUTE FOR SYSTEMS DESIGN AND OPTIMIZATION. 2017

0453-2600 See KANSAS STATISTICAL ABSTRACT. 5330

0453-2899 See KAO KU. 272

0453-2902 See KAOGU XUEBAO. 272

0453-3267 See VEROFFENTLICHUNGEN DES INSTITUTS FUER BODENMECHANIK UND FELSMECHANIK DER UNIVERSITAT FRIDERICIANA IN KARLSRUHE. 1400

0453-3283 See KARLSRUHER JURISTISCHE BIBLIOGRAPHIE. 3081

0453-3402 See KARSTENIA. 575

0453-3429 See KARTHAGO. 272

0453-3453 See KASETSART UNIVERSITY FISHERY RESEARCH BULLETIN. 2307

0453-3674 See KATALOG ROZPRAW DOKTORSKICH I HABILITACYJNYCH. 418

0453-4360 See KAZAN. 1408

0453-4387 See KEATS-SHELLEY JOURNAL. 3401

0453-4514 See JOURNAL OF THE OPERATIONS RESEARCH SOCIETY OF JAPAN. 5121

0453-4557 See KEIO BUSINESS REVIEW. 688

0453-4662 See KEISOKU TO SEIGYO. 1984

0453-4867 See KEMBLE OCCASIONAL, THE. 4566

0453-5669 *See* RESEARCH REPORT / UNIVERSITY OF KENTUCKY, WATER RESOURCES INSTITUTE. **5539**

0453-5677 *See* KENTUCKY CITY (1968), THE. **4660**

0453-5812 *See* KENTUCKY TRAVEL GUIDE. **5482**

0453-5855 *See* ESTIMATES OF RECURRENT EXPENDITURE OF THE GOVERNMENT OF KENYA. **4646**

0453-6460 *See* KENYA EXPORT NEWS (1976). **843**

0453-7580 *See* KERAMOS (BONN). **373**

0453-7637 *See* KERN-GEN, THE. **2456**

0453-7726 *See* KERYGMA UND DOGMA. BEIHEFT. **4972**

0453-7831 *See* REPORTS FROM THE KEVO SUBARCTIC RESEARCH STATION. **4171**

0453-8307 *See* HOLODILNAJA TEHNIKA I TEHNOLOGIJA. **5110**

0453-8315 *See* INFORMATSIONEN BIULETIN. KHRANITELNA PROMISHLENOST. **2344**

0453-8471 *See* KIELER HISTORISCHE STUDIEN. **2622**

0453-8501 *See* KIELER STUDIEN ZUR DEUTSCHEN LITERATURGESCHICHTE. **3401**

0453-8811 *See* KINETIKA I KATALIZ. **1055**

0453-8854 *See* KINGSTON LAW REVIEW, THE. **2992**

0453-8889 *See* KINKI DAIGAKU NOGAKUBU KIYO. **102**

0453-9249 *See* KIPLINGER CALIFORNIA LETTER, THE. **905**

0453-9273 *See* KIRCHE IM OSTEN. **5039**

0453-9281 *See* KIRCHE IM OSTEN. MONOGRAPHIENREIHE. **5062**

0453-929x *See* KIRCHE UND KONFESSION. **4972**

0453-9842 *See* JAHRESGABE - KLAUS-GROTH-GESELLSCHAFT. **3398**

0454-0158 *See* JAHRBUCH DES STIFTES KLOSTERNEUBURG. NEUE FOLGE. **5030**

0454-0689 *See* KNJIZEVNOST I JEZIK. **3293**

0454-1111 *See* KOBE UNIVERSITY ECONOMIC REVIEW. **1571**

0454-112X *See* KOBIJUTSU. **355**

0454-1138 *See* KOBUNSHI. **1044**

0454-1146 *See* KOBUTSUGAKU ZASSHI. **1440**

0454-1499 *See* KOGYO KANETSU. **2606**

0454-1545 *See* KOGYO YOSUI. **5535**

0454-1596 *See* KOKALOS : STUDI PUBBLICATI DALL'ISTITUTO DI STORIA ANTICA DELL'UNIVERSITA DI PALERMO. **1078**

0454-2010 *See* SEISHIN EISEI SHIRYO. **4802**

0454-3114 *See* KONGGAN. **323**

0454-3653 *See* ECONOMIC SURVEY OF THE ... KOREAN ECONOMY. **1558**

0454-4072 *See* KOREA TODAY (PYONGYANG). **2657**

0454-4102 *See* KOREAN BUSINESS DIRECTORY. **689**

0454-448X *See* KOSMOSOPHIE. **4351**

0454-482X *See* ROCZNIK MUZEUM ETNOGRAFICZNEGO W KRAKOWIE. **245**

0454-4862 *See* ZESZYT NAUKOWY - POLITECHNIKA KRAKOWSKA. BUDOWNICTWO LADOWE. **631**

0454-5354 *See* KRITIK (KBENHAVN). **3403**

0454-5419 *See* SPECIAL PUBLICATIONS - KROEBER ANTHROPOLOGICAL SOCIETY. **246**

0454-5524 *See* KRYSTALINIKUM. **1386**

0454-5648 *See* KUEI SUAN YEN HSUEH PAO. **1037**

0454-5915 *See* KULTUREN. **2622**

0454-5990 *See* KULTURNO-PROSVETITELNAIA RABOTA. **1881**

0454-6032 *See* KULTURPFLANZE : BEIHEFT. BERICHTE UND MITTEILUNGEN AUS DEM INSTITUT FUER KULTURPFLANZENFORSCHUNG DER DEUTSCHEN AKADEMIE DER WISSENSCHAFTEN ZU BERLIN IN GATERSLEBEN KRS. ASCHERLEBEN, DIE. **5251**

0454-6245 *See* KUML. **2696**

0454-6296 *See* K'UN CH'UNG HSUEH PAO. **5611**

0454-6520 *See* KUNST OG MUSEUM. **356**

0454-6601 *See* KUNSTJAHRBUCH DER STADT LINZ. **356**

0454-7306 *See* KWANSEI GAKUIN UNIVERSITY ANNUAL STUDIES. **1833**

0454-7675 *See* BULLETIN OF THE DISASTER PREVENTION RESEARCH INSTITUTE. **2019**

0454-7802 *See* MEMOIRS OF THE FACULTY OF SCIENCE, KYOTO UNIVERSITY. SERIES OF BIOLOGY. **464**

0454-8124 *See* KYUNGPOOK MATHEMATICAL JOURNAL. **3516**

0454-8132 *See* KYUSHU AMERICAN LITERATURE. **3403**

0454-8302 *See* KANAGAWA SHIGAKU : KANAGAWA SHIKA DAIGAKU GAKKAI ZASSHI. **1329**

0454-8833 *See* HIMIJA I TERMODINAMIKA RASTVOROV. **977**

0454-8973 *See* KNIGHT LETTER (FORT WORTH, TEX.). **2457**

0454-9015 *See* KOGAI. **2235**

0454-9244 *See* ANNUAL REPORTS OF THE RESEARCH REACTOR INSTITUTE, KYOTO UNIVERSITY. **4446**

0454-9910 *See* KIBERNETIKA I VYCISLITELNAJA TEHNIKA (KIEV). **1252**

0455-0315 *See* ATTORNEY GENERAL'S OPINIONS. **3139**

0455-0463 *See* KNJIZEVNA SMOTRA. **3402**

0455-0595 *See* KRATKIE SOOBSCENIA PO FIZIKE. **4411**

0455-2059 *See* LANZHOU DAXUE XUEBAO. ZIRAN ZIRAN KEXUE BAN. **5125**

0455-6000 *See* BAXTER SPRINGS CITIZEN. **5674**

0455-6550 *See* TRUDY LENINGRADSKOGO NAUCHNO-ISSLEDOVATELSKOGO PSIKHONEVROLOGICHESKOGO INSTITUTA IM. V. M. BEKHTEREVA. **3847**

0456-0434 *See* LIGHT (WASHINGTON), THE. **1688**

0456-3271 *See* LIVING WITH CHILDREN. **2282**

0456-3867 *See* LLOYD'S CANADIAN HARDWARE, ELECTRICAL AND BUILDING SUPPLY DIRECTORY. **619**

0456-5339 *See* LOOK JAPAN. **2506**

0456-5959 *See* REPORT OF PROJECTS / LOUISIANA AGRICULTURAL EXPERIMENT STATION. DEPT. OF AGRONOMY. **126**

0457-088X *See* LANDMAN (FT. WORTH). **4263**

0457-1231 *See* JAHRESBERICHT. **1681**

0457-2483 *See* LAW LIBRARY LIGHTS. **3222**

0457-3943 *See* WISSENSCHAFTLICHE ZEITSCHRIFT DER HOCHSCHULE FUER BAUWESEN LEIPZIG. **311**

0457-4184 *See* LEJEUNIA. **517**

0457-4214 *See* LEKARSKY OBZOR. **3604**

0457-6047 *See* LEVELTARI SZEMLE. **2482**

0457-7817 *See* TRANSACTIONS - SOUTH STAFFORDSHIRE ARCHAEOLOGICAL AND HISTORICAL SOCIETY. **284**

0457-9151 *See* MEMORIAS DEL MUSEO DE HISTORIA NATURAL JAVIER PRADO. **4167**

0458-0311 *See* LITERATURNAIA GRUZIIA. **3407**

0458-063X *See* LITURGY (WASHINGTON). **4974**

0458-1520 *See* PRACE I MATERIAY MUZEUM ARCHEOLOGICZNEGO I ETNOGRAFICZNEGO W LODZI. SERIA ARCHEOLOGICZNA. **278**

0458-1725 *See* LOGOS (COLUMBO, SRI LANKA). **2506**

0458-2039 *See* REPORT OF THE TROPICAL PRODUCTS INSTITUTE. **126**

0458-2241 *See* LONDON ORIENTAL BIBLIOGRAPHIES. **419**

0458-3035 *See* LOS ANGELES TIMES, THE. **5636**

0458-3108 *See* BULLETIN OF THE LOUDOUN COUNTY HISTORICAL SOCIETY, INC. **2725**

0458-3329 *See* FOLIO SERIES - LOUISIANA GEOLOGICAL SURVEY. **1376**

0458-4244 *See* LOZARSTVO I VINARSTVO. **2424**

0458-435X *See* LUCEAFARUL. **3409**

0458-4767 *See* MEDDELANDEN FRAN LUNDS UNIVERSITETS HISTORISKA MUSEUM. **274**

0458-497X *See* LUTHERAN DIGEST, THE. **5063**

0458-4988 *See* LUTHERAN EDUCATOR. **1762**

0458-5526 *See* L. RAY BUCKENDALE LECTURE. **2120**

0458-5682 *See* LSU FORESTRY NOTES. **105**

0458-5860 *See* BULLETIN DE LIAISON DES LABORATOIRES DES PONTS ET CHAUSSEES. **1967**

0458-5933 *See* LABORATORY ANIMAL HANDBOOKS. **3603**

0458-6123 *See* LADENBAU. **302**

0458-6506 *See* LALIT KALA. **324**

0458-6859 *See* LANDBAUFORSCHUNG VOLKENRODE. **104**

0458-7073 *See* SKRIFTER. **2709**

0458-7227 *See* LANE COUNTY HISTORIAN. **2743**

0458-7251 *See* LANGAGE ET L'HOMME, LE. **3294**

0458-726X *See* LANGAGES (PARIS). **3294**

0458-7294 *See* LANGUAGE AND LANGUAGE LEARNING. **3294**

0458-7774 *See* INFORME - INSTITUTO DEL MAR DEL PERU. **554**

0458-8428 *See* LAW ALUMNI JOURNAL, THE. **1102**

0458-8460 *See* LAW AND LEGISLATION IN THE GERMAN DEMOCRATIC REPUBLIC. **2994**

0458-8584 *See* LAW IN JAPAN. **2995**

0458-8630 *See* LAW OFFICE ECONOMICS AND MANAGEMENT. **875**

0458-8711 *See* JOURNAL OF THE LAW SOCIETY OF SCOTLAND, THE. **2989**

0458-9599 *See* LEGAL-LEGISLATIVE REPORTER NEWS BULLETIN. **3151**

0458-9971 *See* LEIDSE GERMANISTISCHE EN ANGLISTISCHE REEKS. **3404**

0459-021X *See* LEITFADEN DER ANGEWANDTEN MATHEMATIK UND MECHANIK. **3516**

0459-0864 *See* BIULLETEN VSESOIUZNOGO NAUCHNO-ISSLEDOVATELSKOGO INSTITUTA ZASHCHITY RASTENII. **502**

0459-1070 *See* LESKOVACKI ZBORNIK. **2696**

0459-1216 *See* LESOVODSTVO I AGROLESOMELIORATSIIA. **2387**

0459-1623 *See* LETTURE CLASSENSI. **3405**

0459-1801 *See* ZOOLOGISCHE BIJDRAGEN. **5602**

0459-2980 *See* LIBYA ANTIQUA / KINGDOM OF LIBYA, MINISTRY OF NATIONAL ECONOMY. **273**

0459-3383 *See* LIETUVOS TSR AUKSTUJU MOKYKLU MOKSLO DARBAI: BIOLOGIJA. **463**

0459-3391 *See* LIETUVOS TSR AUKSTUJU MOKYKLU MOKSLO DARBAI, CHEMIJA IR CHEMINIS TECHNOLOGIJA. **984**

0459-3456 *See* LIETUVOS TSR AUKSTUJU MOKYKLU MOKSLO DARBAI: ISTORIJA. **2697**

0459-3472 *See* LIETUVOS TSR AUKSTUJU MOKYKLU MOKSLO DARBAI: LITERATURA. **3405**

0459-410X *See* BOLETIN DEL INSTITUTO RIVA-AGUERO. **1074**

0459-4371 *See* LIMESFORSCHUNGEN. **273**

0459-4487 *See* LINCOLNSHIRE HISTORY AND ARCHAEOLOGY. **273**

0459-4541 *See* LINES REVIEW. **3346**

0459-469X *See* LINK. **2506**

0459-5009 *See* LIST OF CURRENT PERIODICAL PUBLICATIONS IN ETHIOPIA. **2635**

0459-5106 *See* LITERA. **3406**

0459-5351 *See* LITERATURA I ISKUSSTVO. **3406**

0459-5564 *See* LITERATUREN ARKHIV / BULGARSKA AKADEMIIA NA NAUKITE, INSTITUT ZA BULGARSKA LITERATURA. **3407**

0459-5637 *See* LITERATURNYI KIRGIZSTAN. **3346**

0459-5815 *See* LITTERATURE AFRICAINE. **3408**

0459-5866 *See* NEWSLETTER - LITTLE BIG HORN ASSOCIATES. **2749**

0459-5947 *See* LITUANISTIKOS DARBAI. **2697**

0459-6242 *See* LIVRE SLOVENE, LE. **3408**

0459-6730 *See* LOCK HAVEN REVIEW. **1834**

0459-6773 *See* LOCKHEED HORIZONS. **27**

0459-682X *See* ELEKTRYKA. **2052**

0459-7222 See MILITARY BALANCE, THE. 4050
0459-7230 See STRATEGIC SURVEY. 4058
0459-8113 See CONTRIBUTIONS IN SCIENCE (LOS ANGELES, CALIF.). 4165
0459-8768 See TECHNICAL REPORT - LOUISIANA WATER RESOURCES RESEARCH INSTITUTE. 5540
0459-8881 See LOUISIANA BAR JOURNAL. 3004
0459-9586 See ANNALES UNIVERSITATIS MARIAE CURIE-SKODOWSKA. SECTIO H OECONOMIA. 1462
0460-0029 See LUND ECONOMIC STUDIES. 1503
0460-0037 See LUND POLITICAL STUDIES. 4481
0460-0452 See VISNYK. SERIIA FILOLOHICHNA. 3332
0460-0509 See VISNYK L'VIVS'KOHO ORDENA LENINA DERZHAVNOHO UNIVERSYTETU IM IVANA FRANKA. SERIIA KHIMICHNA. 995
0460-0762 See LYRIKVANNEN. 3409
0460-1297 See LITTLE LAMP, THE. 4974
0460-1815 See FISHERIES BULLETIN (BATON ROUGE). 2302
0460-1955 See LATINO AMERICA. 2267
0460-2366 See BIULETYN LUBELSKIE TOWARZYSTWA NAUKOWEGO. MATEMATYKA, FIZYKA-CHEMIA. 3497
0460-2390 See M & B PHARMACEUTICAL BULLETIN. 4314
0460-332X See MCGILL UNIVERSITY. STORMY WEATHER GROUP. TECHNICAL REPORT. 1430
0460-5047 See MAGAZINE. 1617
0460-6590 See PAMPHLET - MAINE DEPARTMENT OF INLAND FISHERIES AND GAME, INFORMATION AND EDUCATION DIVISION. 2201
0460-6949 See MAINE EDUCATIONAL DIRECTORY. 1762
0460-7368 See MAJOR INDUSTRIES OF INDIA ANNUAL. 1617
0460-9581 See ANNUAL REPORT - THE MANITOBA HYDRO-ELECTRIC BOARD. 4759
0461-0636 See MARCH OF FAITH. 4975
0461-2981 See FINANCIAL REPORT - UNIVERSITY OF MASSACHUSETTS. 1824
0461-4593 See MATSUYAMA DAIGAKU RONSHU. 5209
0461-5220 See MECHANIZACJA ROLNICTWA. 160
0461-5905 See HUMAN PERFORMANCE REPORTS (1960). 4589
0461-6871 See MEIE ELU, TAHTRAAMAT. 2267
0461-9579 See METALURGIA (BUCURESTI). 4011
0462-372X See MICHIGANA. 2460
0462-8128 See BULLETIN - MISSISSIPPI BOARD OF WATER COMMISSIONERS. 5531
0462-8551 See MISSISSIPPI LAWYER, THE. 3011
0462-9760 See MODY TECHNIK. 5129
0463-9847 See ANALES DE CIENCIAS - UNIVERSIDAD DE MURCIA. 960
0464-1086 See MUZEALNICTWO. 4093
0464-2082 See MVA VIEWPOINTS. 1765
0464-2910 See MADERA COUNTY HISTORIAN, THE. 2745
0464-4387 See MAGNETISM. 4444
0464-5685 See ANNUAL REPORT - PINELAND HOSPITAL & TRAINING CENTER. 3776
0464-8005 See QUALITY PUBLICATION. 2355
0464-8072 See JOURNAL OF THE MAMMILLARIA SOCIETY, THE. 516
0464-8145 See MANA (ALEXANDRIA, VA.). 2519
0464-9680 See MARIAN STUDIES. 5032
0465-1057 See MARYLAND ECONOMY, THE. 1504
0465-1146 See PORT OF BALTIMORE HANDBOOK. 5454
0465-1499 See COMMERCE DIGEST (BOSTON). 828
0465-1588 See RESEARCH BULLETIN - COMMONWEALTH OF MASSACHUSETTS, DEPARTMENT OF EDUCATION, DIVISION OF RESEARCH AND STATISTICS. 1796

0465-2746 See MATERIALES DE CONSTRUCCION (MADRID). 620
0465-3238 See MATERIALY PO ARKHEOLOGII EVROPEISKOGO SEVERO-VOSTOKA. 274
0465-3696 See NEWS LETTER / MATHEMATICAL ASSOCIATION. 3524
0465-420X See HA-MAYAN. 2976
0465-4668 See MEDECINE D'AFRIQUE NOIRE. 3607
0465-546X See MEDICINA Y SEGURIDAD DEL TRABAJO. 2865
0465-5893 See MEDYCYNA PRACY. 3615
0466-2199 See NATIONAL DRAGSTER. 4906
0466-2865 See STATISTICAL YEAR BOOK - THE AUSTRALIAN GAS INDUSTRY. 4284
0466-6658 See NAVAJO YEARBOOK. 2268
0466-6992 See BIENNIAL REPORT OF THE DEPARTMENT OF WATER RESOURCES. 5531
0466-9959 See VERZAMELDE OVERDRUKKEN - PLANTENZIEKTENKUNDIGE DIENST. 2433
0467-5282 See FARMERS' NEWSLETTER, LARGE AREA. 86
0468-1835 See NIELSEN NEWSCAST, THE. 1135
0468-5725 See LIBRARY NOTES (CHAPEL HILL). 3226
0468-656X See STATISTISCHES JAHRBUCH NORDRHEIN-WESTFALEN. 5343
0468-6853 See NORTHEASTERN TOUR BOOK. 5486
0468-8678 See NOTES BIBLIOGRAPHIQUES. 3418
0468-9291 See NOTIZIARIO SULLE MALATTIE DELLE PIANTE. 520
0469-0281 See NOVA TRGOVINA. 848
0469-2608 See TWOS AND THREES TEACHER. 1908
0469-3922 See NSPA WASHINGTON REPORTER, THE. 749
0469-4244 See NACHRICHTEN AUS DEM KARTEN-UND VERMESSUNGSWESEN. REICHE II. 2582
0469-5097 See NANJING DAXUE XUEBAO. ZIRAN KEXUE. 5130
0469-5461 See ANNALI DELLA FACOLTA DI LETTERE E FILOSOFIA DELL'UNIVERSITA DI NAPOLI. 4341
0469-5550 See NARA IGAKU ZASSHI. 3618
0469-5941 See NARODNOE KHOZIAISTVO SSSR / TSENTRALNOE STATISTICHESKOE UPRAVLENIE PRI SOVETE MINISTROV SSSR. 1536
0469-6786 See ANNUAL NUMBER / NATIONAL ACADEMY OF SCIENCES, INDIA. 5083
0469-7405 See FROZEN FOOD PACK STATISTICS. 2362
0469-7928 See NASPO NEWSLETTER. 950
0469-9076 See BULLETIN. 1294
0470-0384 See FINGERTIP FACTS & FIGURES. 2379
0470-0929 See NATIONAL GEOGRAPHER. 2570
0470-3219 See NATIONAL STRIPPER WELL SURVEY. 2147
0470-3480 See NATIONAL WATERSHED CONGRESS; PROCEEDINGS. 5536
0470-3790 See NATURALEZA Y GRACIA. 4980
0470-3847 See INFORMATION BULLETIN - THE NATURE CONSERVANCY. 2195
0470-3855 See POLICY BULLETIN - THE NATURE CONSERVANCY. 2202
0470-3995 See UITGAVEN VAN DE NATUURWETENSCHAPPELIJKE WERKGROEP NEDERLANDSE ANTILLEN. 4173
0470-4606 See NAUCHNYE DOKLADY VYSSHEI SHKOLY. BIOLOGICHESKIE NAUKI. 466
0470-570X See NEBRASKA SPEECH AND HEARING JOURNAL. 4391
0470-6021 See NEDERLANDSE CHEMISCHE INDUSTRIE. 987
0470-6455 See NENDO KAGAKU. 1443
0470-6625 See NERVNAJA SISTEMA. 3839
0470-6684 See MAANDSTATISTIEK VAN DE INDUSTRIE. 3482

0470-7427 See SYNOPTIC AND UPPER AIR OBSERVATIONS IN THE NETHERLANDS. 1435
0470-8105 See NEUROLOGIA MEDICO-CHIRURGICA. 3840
0470-925X See OBIHIRO CHIKUSAN DAIGAKU GAKUJUTSU KENKYU HOKOKU DAI-1-BU. 116
0471-1688 See OFFICIAL MICHIGAN. 5693
0471-265x See INFORMATION CIRCULAR - STATE OF OHIO, DEPARTMENT OF NATURAL RESOURCES, DIVISION OF WATER. 5534
0471-3893 See OIL DIRECTORY OF TEXAS. 4269
0471-5640 See OLYMPISCHES FEUER. 4910
0471-6981 See ARCHEIA OPHTHALMOLOGIKES HETAIREIAS BOREIOU HELLADOS. 3872
0471-7309 See OPUSCULA ROMANA. 1078
0471-7376 See ORAFO ITALIANO. 2915
0471-8208 See EDUCATIONAL BULLETIN - FISH COMMISSION OF OREGON. 2300
0471-9506 See ORGANIZACIJA RADA. 1700
0472-0490 See ORIENT (MONTREAL). 4984
0472-142X See OSAKA KOGYO GIJUTSU SHIKENJO, KIHO. 5136
0472-1438 See OSAKA KOGYO GIJUTSU SHIKENJO HOKOKU. 1989
0472-3724 See ONU CRONICA MENSUAL. 4530
0472-4313 See OBROBKA PLASTYCZNA. 4014
0472-4674 See OCHANOMIZU IGAKU ZASSHI. 3623
0472-4682 See OCHANOMIZU JOSHI DAIGAKU JIMBUN KAGAKU KIYO. 327
0472-5158 See ODONTOLOGO (PANAMA), EL. 1331
0472-5182 See ODRA. 2520
0472-5522 See OSTERREICHISCHE KERAMISCHE RUNDSCHAU. 2593
0472-6049 See OFFICE AUTOMATION. 4213
0472-6243 See OFFICIAL MOTOR CARRIER DIRECTORY. 5388
0472-6340 See OFFSPRING. 1805
0472-7630 See OIL AND GAS REPORTER. 4269
0472-8602 See OLAJ, SZAPPAN, KOZMETIKA. 117
0472-8637 See OLAM HADASH. 2625
0472-8947 See ACTA UNIVERSITATIS PALACKIANAE OLOMUCENSIS. FACULTAS PHILOSOPHICA. HISTORICA. 2672
0472-8998 See ACTA UNIVERSITATIS PALACKIANAE OLOMUCENSIS FACULTATIS MEDICAE SUPPLEMENTUM. 3545
0472-9889 See GEOLOGICAL REPORT (TORONTO). 1378
0473-0496 See OPERATIONS RESEARCH/MANAGEMENT SCIENCE YEARBOOK. 881
0473-0992 See OPUSCULA ARCHAEOLOGICA (ZAGREB, CROATIA). 277
0473-1034 See OPUSCULA ZOOLOGICA - INSTITUTUM ZOOSYSTEMATICUM UNIVERSITATIS BUDAPESTINENSIS. 5593
0473-1425 See ORCHIDEE, DIE. 2426
0473-2014 See PROGRESS REPORT - OREGON STATE PARKS AND RECREATION DIVISION. 4707
0473-2170 See TECHNICAL REPORT - DEPARTMENT OF OCEANOGRAPHY. SCHOOL OF SCIENCE. OREGON STATE UNIVERSITY. 1457
0473-2456 See OREGON PHARMACIST. 4318
0473-2812 See BULLETIN DE L'ORGANISATION INTERNATIONALE DE METROLOGIE LEGALE. 4029
0473-3177 See COAL INDUSTRY IN EUROPE. 1602
0473-4351 See ORTNAMNSSALLSKAPETS I UPPSALA ARSSKRIFT. 3308
0473-4599 See JOURNAL OF OSAKA UNIVERSITY DENTAL SCHOOL, THE. 1327
0473-4882 See OSJECKI ZBORNIK. 4095
0473-5587 See OTOMESHON. 2124
0473-5609 See OTO-RINO-LARINGOLOGIIA. 3890
0473-7466 See OBZORNIK ZA MATEMATIKO IN FIZIKO. 3525

0473-7482 *See* OCCASIONAL PAPERS IN ARCHAEOLOGY. **277**

0473-7733 *See* OCHRONA PRZED KOROZJA. **2028**

0473-8675 *See* UVRES ET OPINIONS. **3450**

0473-8853 *See* OFFICIAL BASKETBALL RULES FOR MEN AND WOMEN. **4909**

0473-9434 *See* BURIED VALLEY INVESTIGATION. **1412**

0473-9507 *See* ABSTRACTS OF THESES AND DISSERTATIONS (BOWLING GREEN, OHIO). **1806**

0473-9604 *See* WORKING PAPERS IN LINGUISTICS (COLUMBUS, OHIO). **3333**

0473-9760 *See* OHIO ALMANAC. **2541**

0474-0076 *See* OIL AND GAS FEDERAL INCOME TAX MANUAL. **4268**

0474-0254 *See* OKAYAMA DAIGAKA NOGAKUBU GAKUJUTSU HOKUKU. **116**

0474-0742 *See* OKLAHOMA GENEALOGICAL SOCIETY QUARTERLY. **2465**

0474-0785 *See* OKLAHOMA VETERINARIAN, THE. **5517**

0474-1021 *See* PHILOSOPHICA, AESTHETICA. **4355**

0474-1242 *See* OLYMPISCHE FORSCHUNGEN. **2851**

0474-1528 *See* ONSEI NO KENKYU. THE STUDY OF SOUNDS. **4453**

0474-1560 *See* SEASONAL FRUIT AND VEGETABLE REPORT. **133**

0474-2559 *See* OPERA CORCONTICA. **4170**

0474-2885 *See* OPOLSKI ROCZNIK MUZEALNY. **2701**

0474-2974 *See* EKONOMIKA. **1559**

0474-3253 *See* NEWSLETTER - ORAL HISTORY ASSOCIATION. **2624**

0474-330X *See* ORBIS ACADEMICUS. **3239**

0474-3326 *See* ORBIT (NEW YORK). **3420**

0474-3342 *See* ORCHADIAN, THE. **2426**

0474-3369 *See* ORCRIST. **3420**

0474-3636 *See* VOCATIONAL EDUCATION IN OREGON. **1917**

0474-4535 *See* NEWS - OREGON HISTORICAL SOCIETY. **2749**

0474-4721 *See* OREGON'S AGRICULTURAL PROGRESS. **117**

0474-4772 *See* ORGANIC REACTION MECHANISMS. **1045**

0474-5124 *See* OECD ECONOMIC SURVEYS: AUSTRIA. **1509**

0474-5140 *See* OECD ECONOMIC SURVEYS: CANADA. **1510**

0474-5159 *See* OECD ECONOMIC SURVEYS: DENMARK. **1510**

0474-5191 *See* OECD ECONOMIC SURVEYS: ICELAND. **1510**

0474-5329 *See* OECD ECONOMIC SURVEYS : UNITED STATES. **1577**

0474-5442 *See* MAIN ECONOMIC INDICATORS. HISTORICAL STATISTICS / ORGANISATION FOR ECONOMIC CO-OPERATION AND DEVELOPMENT. **1573**

0474-5515 *See* LABOUR FORCE STATISTICS. **1686**

0474-5523 *See* MAIN ECONOMIC INDICATORS. **1573**

0474-5574 *See* OECD. ECONOMIC OUTLOOK. **1509**

0474-5884 *See* MARITIME TRANSPORT. **5452**

0474-6279 *See* OPEC BULLETIN. **4270**

0474-6546 *See* ORIENTAL MONOGRAPH SERIES. **2661**

0474-6589 *See* ORIENTAL STUDIES. **2661**

0474-6627 *See* ORIENTALIA GANDENSIA. **3308**

0474-7313 *See* ORNITOLOGIIA. **5593**

0474-7550 *See* ORTUNG UND NAVIGATION. **4181**

0474-7615 *See* ORYZA. **180**

0474-781X *See* SCIENCE REPORTS - OSAKA UNIVERSITY. COLLEGE OF GENERAL EDUCATION. **1858**

0474-7844 *See* BULLETIN OF UNIVERSITY OF OSAKA PREFECTURE. SERIES A : ENGINEERING AND NATURAL SCIENCES. **1967**

0474-795X *See* HOKEN TAIIKUGAKU KENKYU KIYO / OSAKA SHIRITSU DAIGAKU. **1855**

0474-8107 *See* OSMANIA JOURNAL OF ENGLISH STUDIES. **3421**

0474-8158 *See* OSNABRUCKER MITTEILUNGEN. **327**

0474-8476 *See* SBORNIK VEDECKYCH PRACI. VYSOKA SKOLA BANSKA, OSTRAVA. RADA HORNICKO-GEOLOGICKA. **1396**

0474-8484 *See* SBORNIK VEDECKYCH PRACI. RADA HUTNICKA. DOKLADY. SERIIA METALLURGICHESKAIA. TRANSACTIONS. METALLURGICAL SERIES. **4018**

0474-974X *See* OXFORD MEDIEVAL TEXTS. **2702**

0475-0071 *See* MEMOIRS OF THE FACULTY OF ENGINEERING. **1987**

0475-0209 *See* ONE WORLD (EDMONTON). **1770**

0475-025X *See* ONTARIO BIRD BANDING. **5619**

0475-042X *See* BULLETIN DE LA SOCIETE DE PATHOLOGIE EXOTIQUE. **3559**

0475-0934 *See* ONOMASTICA JUGOSLAVICA. **3308**

0475-1450 *See* ONTOGENEZ. **467**

0475-1876 *See* OLD CAR VALUE GUIDE. **5422**

0475-1906 *See* OPTIMUM (OTTAWA). **701**

0475-2058 *See* JOURNAL OF OSAKA DENTAL UNIVERSITY. **1327**

0475-2953 *See* PS (WASHINGTON, D.C.). **4054**

0475-3208 *See* MEMOIRS OF THE PACIFIC COAST ENTOMOLOGICAL SOCIETY. **5591**

0475-6126 *See* ANNUAL REPORT - PANAMA CANAL COMPANY, CANAL ZONE GOVERNMENT. **4629**

0475-9516 *See* PAYS DE BOURGOGNE. **362**

0476-9813 *See* PLANTES DE MONTAGNE / BULLETIN DE LA SOCIETE DES AMATEURS DE JARDINS ALPINS. **2428**

0477-0943 *See* POETRY FROM OXFORD. **3469**

0477-1826 *See* WYKAZ PATENTOW NA WYNALAZKI UDZIELONYCH PRZEZ URZAD PATENTOWY PRL W ROKU **1310**

0477-2008 *See* POLICE AND CONSTABULARY ALMANAC. **3171**

0477-4612 *See* BULLETIN OF THE POLONUS PHILATELIC SOCIETY. **2784**

0477-5449 *See* POODLE REVIEW, THE. **4287**

0477-6410 *See* PORT OF TORONTO NEWS. **5454**

0477-8626 *See* POWER PROTECTION. **1991**

0477-8685 *See* POZEMNI STAVBY. **624**

0478-0264 See WORSHIP AND PREACHING. **5010**

0478-1392 *See* PRESERVATION PROGRESS (CHARLESTON). **306**

0478-1546 *See* PRESSE. **2923**

0478-4049 *See* PRODUCTEUR D'AMIANTE, LE. **624**

0478-4251 *See* PRODUCTS FINISHING DIRECTORY. **4016**

0478-6378 *See* PROYECCION (GRANADA). **4988**

0478-6599 *See* PRZEGLAD MLECZARSKI. **198**

0478-7080 *See* PSZCZELARSTWO. **5595**

0478-8583 *See* INFORME ANUAL - ESTADO LIBRE ASOCIADO DE PUERTO RICO, COMISION DE SERVICIO PUBLICO. **4656**

0478-9997 *See* P-D NEWS. **944**

0479-0219 *See* PLI NEWS. **3029**

0479-480X *See* MAGYAR GRAFIKA. **380**

0479-7353 *See* PAYSANS. **119**

0479-7558 *See* PEANUT RESEARCH. **180**

0479-785X *See* PEDIATRIC WORLD. **3910**

0479-7876 *See* PEDIATRIJA (SOFIA). **3910**

0479-8007 *See* BEIJING NONGYE DAXUE XUEBAO. **65**

0479-9534 *See* JOURNAL OF THE PENNSYLVANIA OSTEOPATHIC MEDICAL ASSOCIATION, THE. **3599**

0480-2160 *See* PETROLEUM INTELLIGENCE WEEKLY. **4273**

0480-2853 *See* PHILANTHROPIC DIGEST. **4338**

0480-676X *See* QUALITY CROSSWORD PUZZLES. **4865**

0480-8029 *See* CONTRIBUCION - INSTITUTO ECUATORIANO DE CIENCIAS NATURALES. **5097**

0480-9068 *See* QUALITY CONTROL AND APPLIED STATISTICS YEARBOOK. **1992**

0480-9696 *See* ANNUAL REPORT - DEPARTMENT OF PRIMARY INDUSTRIES, QUEENSLAND. **60**

0480-970X *See* REPORT OF THE CO-ORDINATOR-GENERAL OF PUBLIC WORKS, QUEENSLAND. **4681**

0481-097X *See* QUADERNI DI CULTURA FRANCESE. **5254**

0481-1216 *See* QUAESTIONES DISPUTATAE. **4989**

0481-1275 *See* QUANTUM PHYSICS AND ITS APPLICATIONS. **4418**

0481-1356 *See* QUARTERLY BIBLIOGRAPHY ON CULTURAL DIFFERENCES, A. **2276**

0481-2085 *See* QUARTERLY JOURNAL OF ENGINEERING GEOLOGY, THE. **2029**

0481-2417 *See* FRUITS (QUEBEC). **1607**

0481-2468 *See* PORCS. **217**

0481-3545 *See* QUELLEN UND DARSTELLUNGEN ZUR ZEITGESCHICHTE. **2627**

0481-3553 *See* QUELLEN UND FORSCHUNGEN ZUR AGRARGESCHICHTE. **124**

0481-3596 *See* QUELLEN UND FORSCHUNGEN ZUR SPRACH- UND KULTURGESCHICHTE DER GERMANISCHEN VOLKER. **3313**

0481-8024 *See* RAT EN MUIS. **2241**

0481-9004 *See* REALTY. **4846**

0482-0819 *See* REFORM JUDAISM. **5052**

0482-430X *See* RETREADER'S JOURNAL. **707**

0482-5209 *See* REVISTA DE ADMINISTRACION PUBLICA. **4683**

0482-5276 *See* REVISTA DE CIENCIAS SOCIALES (SAN JOSE). **5216**

0482-5748 *See* REVISTA DE HISTORIA MILITAR. **4055**

0482-5985 *See* REVISTA DE ORTOPEDIA Y TRAUMATOLOGIA. **3884**

0482-6396 *See* REVISTA ESPANOLA DE ELECTRONICA. **2079**

0482-640X *See* REVISTA ESPANOLA ONCOLOGIA. **3823**

0482-6760 *See* REVISTA MEDICA (LA PAZ). **3636**

0482-9905 *See* RHODODENDRON UND IMMERGRUNE LAUBGEHOLZE JAHRBUCH. **2430**

0482-9905 *See* RHODODENDRON UND IMMERGRUNE LAUBGEHOLZE. **526**

0483-2140 *See* REPORT OF THE TREASURER (ROCHESTER). **750**

0483-4240 *See* ROUND QUARTER SERIES OF NEW POETS & ARTISTS. **3470**

0483-5093 *See* RUDY. **2150**

0483-7495 *See* TECHNICAL NOTES - RCA. **1140**

0483-786X *See* R.T.V.A. **5519**

0483-9005 *See* ANNUAL REPORT - THE RAILWAY & LOCOMOTIVE HISTORICAL SOCIETY, INC. **5429**

0483-9420 *See* RANDOM LENGTHS (EUGENE, OR.). **2404**

0484-0305 *See* READAPTATION PARIS. **5145**

0484-0828 *See* RECENT RESEARCHES IN THE MUSIC OF THE BAROQUE ERA. **4148**

0484-0887 *See* RECHERCHES AUGUSTINIENNES. **4989**

0484-1379 *See* RECONQUISTA. **4054**

0484-2685 *See* REFLECTOR (AMARILLO, TEX.), THE. **2469**

0484-3401 *See* REI CRETARIAE ROMANAE FAUTORUM ACTA. **2593**

0484-3916 *See* RENDEZVOUS (BUFFALO, N.Y.). **33**

0484-4041 *See* RENTAL RATE BLUE BOOK. **2128**

0484-4610 *See* REPORTER (PATERSON), THE. **3038**

0484-4823 *See* RERUM ECCLESIASTICARUM DOCUMENTA. SERIES MAIOR: FONTES. **5035**

0484-5412 See REPORT AND FINANCIAL STATEMENTS - RESERVE BANK OF AUSTRALIA. 1516

0484-5765 See RESTATEMENT, THE. 3039

0484-5854 See RESURRECTION PARIS. 5035

0484-7849 See REVISTA MEDICA (MEXICO). 3636

0484-8020 See REVISTA ODONTOLOGICA ECUATORIANA. 1334

0484-811X See REVISTA PORTUGUESA DE FARMACIA. 4328

0484-8268 See REVISTA URUGUAYA DE PSICOANALISIS. 4616

0484-8365 See REVOLUTION ET TRAVAIL. 1708

0484-8616 See REVUE DES ETUDES JUIVES. 5052

0484-8764 See REVUE FRANCAISE DE COMPTABILITE. 751

0484-8942 See REVUE NUMISMATIQUE. 2783

0484-9019 See RIT FISKIDEILDAR. 2312

0485-0637 See RHODODENDRON, THE. 2430

0485-1412 See RINSHO EIYO. 4198

0485-1420 See RINSHO KENSA. 3637

0485-1439 See RINSHO KETSUEKI. 3774

0485-2044 See JOURNAL OF THE RIO GRANDE VALLEY HORTICULTURAL SOCIETY. 2421

0485-294X See ROCKY MOUNTAIN BAPTIST. 5067

0485-3695 See DIRECTORY AND REGISTER / ROLLS-ROYCE OWNERS' CLUB. 5413

0485-4152 See QUADERNI DELL'ISTITUTO DI STORIA DELL'ARCHITETTURA. 307

0485-4802 See ROST KRISTALLOV / AKADEMIIA NAUK SSSR, INSTITUT KRISTALLOGRAFII IM. A.V. SHUBNIKOVA. 1033

0485-5140 See ROUNDUP (MINNEAPOLIS, MINN.), THE. 1314

0485-5167 See ROVESNIK. 1068

0485-6015 See RUMAH TANGGA DAN KESEHATAN. 4800

0485-764X See WILLIAM L. HUTCHESON MEMORIAL FOREST BULLETIN. 2398

0485-8255 See RSRI DISCUSSION PAPER SERIES. 5149

0485-8573 See RADIANSKE PRAVO. 3034

0485-893X See RADIOLOGIA IUGOSLAVICA. 3945

0485-8972 See RADIOTEHNIKA (HARKOV). 1138

0485-9383 See RULES COMPENDIUM UNDER CENTRAL ACTS. 3045

0485-9561 See RAJASTHAN MEDICAL JOURNAL, THE. 3632

0485-9758 See RAMSEY COUNTY HISTORY. 2756

0486-0373 See RASSEGNA PARLAMENTARE. 3093

0486-0837 See DEVELOPMENT STUDIES. 170

0486-0993 See REALES SITIOS. 363

0486-1140 See REBEL. 1705

0486-1205 See RECENT BOOKS IN MEXICO. 3244

0486-123X See RECENT RESEARCHES IN THE MUSIC OF THE RENAISSANCE. 4149

0486-1485 See RECHT IN OST UND WEST. 3036

0486-2236 See REFERATIVNYI ZHURNAL. N.51, ASTRONOMIIA. 399

0486-2325 See REFERATIVNYI ZHURNAL. KHIMIIA / AKADEMIIA NAUK SSSR, INSTITUT NAUCHNOI INFORMATSII. 991

0486-2902 See PAPERS IN REGIONAL SCIENCE : THE JOURNAL OF THE REGIONAL SCIENCE ASSOCIATION INTERNATIONAL. 2830

0486-3585 See RELIGIONEN DER MENSCHHEIT, DIE. 4991

0486-3658 See RELIGIOUS PERSPECTIVES. 4992

0486-3720 See RENAISSANCE AND MODERN STUDIES. 2853

0486-3739 See RENAISSANCE DRAMA. 5367

0486-400X See RENTGENOLOGIJA I RADIOLOGIJA. 3946

0486-4166 See REPERTORIEN ZUR DEUTSCHEN LITERATURGESCHICHTE. 3429

0486-4271 See REPERTORIUM PLANTARUM SUCCULENTARUM. 526

0486-4336 See REPORT ON MANAGEMENT SUCCESSION. 884

0486-4476 See REPORTS ON PROGRESS IN POLYMER PHYSICS IN JAPAN. 1057

0486-476X See RESEARCH AND DEVELOPMENT NEWS. 5538

0486-5553 See REPRINT - RESOURCES FOR THE FUTURE. 2203

0486-5561 See ANNUAL REPORT - RESOURCES FOR THE FUTURE. 2187

0486-5588 See RESPONSA MERIDIANA. 3039

0486-5642 See RESTORATION QUARTERLY. 4993

0486-6096 See REVIEW OF INTERNATIONAL AFFAIRS. 4534

0486-6134 See REVIEW OF RADICAL POLITICAL ECONOMICS, THE. 1594

0486-6398 See REVISTA BRASILEIRA DE MUSICA. 4149

0486-641X See REVISTA BRASILEIRA DE PSICANALISE. 4615

0486-6525 See REVISTA COLOMBIANA DE ANTROPOLOGIA. 244

0486-7890 See SAARLANDISCHE KREISZAHLEN. 5338

0486-8013 See SABRETACHE. 4056

0486-8161 See SACRAMENTO NEWSLETTER, THE. 3045

0487-3491 See SEMINARIO DE ARTE ARAGONES. 364

0487-6520 See SCHOCH LETTER, THE. 3722

0487-6776 See SCHOOL BUSINESS ADMINISTRATION PUBLICATION (SACRAMENTO). 1871

0487-8019 See SCHWEIZER MUNZBLATTER. 2783

0487-8965 See SCIENTIFIC MEETINGS. 5155

0487-9775 See SCREEN PROCESS PRINTING. 4569

0488-3896 See SERVICE STATION MANAGEMENT. 5425

0488-4965 See SETTLER (TOWANDA, PA. 1952), THE. 2760

0488-549X See SHARQ IULDUZI. 3436

0488-6097 See SHEPARD'S ALASKA CITATIONS. 3048

0488-6119 See SHEPARD'S MISSISSIPPI CITATIONS. 3052

0488-6186 See SHERIFF'S STAR (TALLAHASSEE, FLA.), THE. 3176

0488-6720 See SHIPMATE (ANNAPOLIS, MD.). 4183

0488-7484 See SHUKAN SHINCHO. 2508

0488-8812 See SIMPLICITY SCHOOL CATALOG. 5186

0489-0280 See SITES ET MONUMENTS. 2709

0489-1090 See SLAKT OCH HAVD. 2472

0489-2593 See SOCIAL DIRECTORY OF HOUSTON. 2546

0489-3824 See BOLETIN DE LA SOCIEDAD VALENCIANA DE PEDIATRIA. 3901

0489-555X See PROCEEDINGS ANNUAL MEETING / SOCIETY OF AMERICAN FORESTERS, NORTHERN CALIFORNIA SECTION. 2391

0489-5606 See ENGINEERING KNOW-HOW IN ENGINE DESIGN. 2113

0489-6211 See GODISNIK NA VISSIJA HIMIKO-TEHNOLOGICESKI INSTITUT--SOFIJA. 2012

0489-8850 See CIVIC CINEMA. 4638

0489-9563 See SOUTH OF THE MOUNTAINS. 2761

0490-1606 See SOZIALE ARBEIT. 5310

0490-1630 See SOZIALE SICHERHEIT (KOLN). 5310

0490-4788 See SPOLETIUM. 2710

0490-5474 See SPORTS TURF BULLETIN. 4923

0490-6756 See SSU-CHUAN TA HSUEH HSUEH PAO. TZU JAN KO HSUEH PAN. 4172

0491-0850 See STOCKHOLM STUDIES IN HISTORY OF ART. 365

0491-0869 See STOCKHOLM STUDIES IN HISTORY OF LITERATURE. 3440

0491-0893 See STOCKHOLMER GERMANISTISCHE FORSCHUNGEN. 2710

0491-0982 See STOMATOLOGIJA (SOFIJA). 1336

0491-6441 See SVAROCNOE PROIZVODSTVO. 4028

0491-8193 See SWIERSZCZYK. 3443

0492-1283 See TAG DES HERRN. 5037

0492-1712 See TAIWAN SUGAR. 189

0492-4134 See TEACHERS OF THE WORLD. 1906

0492-5882 See TEKSTIL. 5356

0492-6110 See TELETEKNIK (ENGLISH EDITION). 2084

0492-6749 See TEMPO E O MODO, O. 1586

0492-7079 See INFORMATION CIRCULAR - STATE OF TENNESSEE, DEPARTMENT OF CONSERVATION, DIVISION OF GEOLOGY. 1383

0492-746X See TENNESSEE MAGAZINE. 2547

0492-8539 See IF REPORT SERIES. 2305

0492-8717 See ANNUAL REPORT - LIQUEFIED PETROLEUM GAS DIVISION OF THE RAILROAD COMMISSION OF TEXAS. 4250

0492-973X See TEXAS SUPREME COURT JOURNAL, THE. 3064

0492-9829 See TEXAS WATER REPORT. 5541

0493-2137 See TIANJIN DAXUE XUEBAO. 5165

0493-4008 See SPECIAL PUBLICATIONS - TOKAI REGIONAL FISHERIES RESEARCH LABORATORY. 2313

0493-4253 See DENKI TSUSHIN DAIGAKU GAKUHO. 1109

0493-4326 See MISCELLANEOUS INFORMATION, THE TOKYO UNIVERSITY FORESTS. 2388

0494-3384 See 29ER, THE. 5632

0494-3880 See TAC ATTACK. 4058

0494-4445 See DALU ZAZHI TEKAN. 2650

0494-464X See TAGLICHE PRAXIS. 3644

0494-4739 See TAEHAN PIBU KWAHAKHOE CHI. 3723

0494-6367 See ANNUAL REPORT OF THE AIR SURVEY DIVISION. 2554

0494-6588 See ANNUAL REPORT OF THE LAND DIVISION. 2554

0494-6944 See TAP ROOTS (TUSKEGEE). 2474

0494-7061 See TAREAS. 5224

0494-8203 See SOURCE REFERENCES FOR FACTS AND FIGURES ON GOVERNMENT FINANCE. 4748

0494-8262 See ZEIHOGAKU. 4759

0494-8440 See TE REO. 3327

0494-9501 See TECNICA E METODOLOGIA ECONOMALE. 1629

0494-9846 See TEHNOLOGIJA MESA. 3488

0494-9900 See TEJIPAR. 199

0495-0127 See TELE ENGLISH EDITION. 1164

0495-0186 See TELECOMUNICAZIONI. 1166

0495-1026 See WATER RESOURCES SERIES (NASHVILLE, TENN.). 5547

0495-1492 See TENRI JOURNAL OF RELIGION. 5002

0495-1549 See TEOLOGIA ESPIRITUAL. 5002

0495-2340 See PROCEEDINGS OF THE ANNUAL CONFERENCE ON WATER FOR TEXAS. 5537

0495-2499 See LEGISLATIVE BUDGET ESTIMATES. 4736

0495-2928 See ANNUAL REPORT OF THE WILDLIFE DIVISION, PARKS AND WILDLIFE DEPARTMENT. 2186

0495-3789 See TEXTRACTS. 5359

0495-4025 See THALASSIA JUGOSLAVICA. 5598

0495-4548 See THEORIA. 4363

0495-5773 See TIERRAS DE LEON. 2712

0495-7199 See TOHOGAKU. 2666

0495-7318 See KENKYU HOKOKU TOHOKU NOGYO SHIKENJO. 102

0495-7490 See TOKAI-KU SUISAN KENKYUJO GYOSEKISHU. 2315

0495-7644 See TOKUSHUKO. 4022

0495-7725 See BULLETIN DE LA MAISON FRANCO-JAPONAISE. 2843

0495-775X See SENPAKU GIJUTSU KENKYUJO HOKOKU. 4183

0495-7792 See BULLETIN - JOURNAL OF THE TOKYO WOMEN'S MEDICAL COLLEGE. 3560

0495-8020 See BULLETIN OF THE TOKYO INSTITUTE OF TECHNOLOGY. 5091

0495-8306 See REPORT OF THE TOMATO GENETICS COOPERATIVE. 184

0495-8772 See TOR. 2712

0495-923X See ROCZNIK MUZEUM W TORUNIU. 4096

0495-9396 See CHRONIQUE / INSTITUT CATHOLIQUE DE TOULOUSE. 1732

0495-9701 See TOWER (HAMILTON). 3472

0495-9728 See PLANNING BULLETIN. 2831

0496-1803 See TRI-CITY GENEALOGICAL SOCIETY BULLETIN, THE. 2476

0496-3490 See TSO WU HSUEH PAO. 189

0496-4748 See ANNALI DELLA FACOLTA DI MEDICINA VETERINARIA DI TORINO. 5503

0496-6015 See TWAYNE'S UNITED STATES AUTHORS SERIES. 3448

0496-6058 See TWENTIETH CENTURY VIEWS. 3448

0496-6201 See TWO AND A BUD. 143

0496-6597 See SUT JOURNAL OF MATHEMATICS. 3537

0496-7046 See TAIWAN FINANCIAL STATISTICS MONTHLY. 1540

0496-7607 See TALES OF PARADISE RIDGE. 2631

0496-764X See MISCELLANEOUS PUBLICATION - TALL TIMBERS RESEARCH STATION. 465

0496-8026 See TANE. 4172

0496-831X See ANNUAL REPORT OF THE WATER DEVELOPMENT AND IRRIGATION DIVISION (DAR ES SALAAM). 2087

0496-8913 See TAR HEEL JUNIOR HISTORIAN. 2762

0496-9464 See STATISTICAL OUTLINE OF INDIA. 1538

0496-9685 See TAX FACTS ON LIFE INSURANCE. 2894

0496-9944 See TEACHER'S ARTS AND CRAFTS WORKSHOP. 376

0496-9960 See TEACHERS GUIDES TO TELEVISION. 1906

0497-0292 See BOLETIN INFORMATIVO TECHINT. 1599

0497-0489 See TECHNICAL TRANSLATION BULLETIN. 5162

0497-1140 See MONTHLY REPORT OF THE IRON & STEEL STATISTICS. 4026

0497-137X See TELECOMMUNICATION JOURNAL (ENGLISH EDITION). 1165

0497-1515 See TELEVISION DIGEST WITH CONSUMER ELECTRONICS (1984). 1140

0497-1817 See TEMENOS. 5002

0497-2074 See REPORT OF INVESTIGATIONS - TENNESSEE DIVISION OF GEOLOGY. 1395

0497-2317 See TENNESSEE AGRICULTURAL STATISTICS. 157

0497-2325 See TENNESSEE BAR JOURNAL. 3063

0497-2384 See TENNESSEE STUDIES IN LITERATURE. 3445

0497-2627 See TEORETICESKAJA I EKSPERIMENTALNAJA HIMIJA. 994

0497-2929 See U. B. C. REPORTS. 1851

0497-9478 See STEEL MARKET IN ..., THE. 1640

0497-9486 See MARCHE DE L'ACIER EN ..., LE. 1617

0498-0085 See UNITED NATIONS SPECIAL FUND, THE. 1587

0498-1308 See BULLETIN - UNITED PLANTERS' ASSOCIATION OF SOUTHERN INDIA, SCIENTIFIC DEPARTMENT. 165

0498-1367 See MUTUAL SECURITY PROGRAM FOR FISCAL YEAR 1952-, THE. 4052

0498-1987 See COTTONSEED VARIETIES PLANTED. 168

0498-2231 See ARS 41. 63

0498-224X See ARS 43 / AGRICULTURAL RESEARCH SERVICE, UNITED STATES DEPARTMENT OF AGRICULTURE. 63

0498-3564 See AFIP LETTER. 3892

0498-3637 See BOARD OF CONTRACT APPEALS DECISIONS. 3182

0498-6415 See GAZETTEER - UNITED STATES BOARD ON GEOGRAPHIC NAMES. 2561

0498-7284 See DEPARTMENT STORE INVENTORY PRICE INDEXES / U.S. DEPARTMENT OF LABOR, BUREAU OF LABOR STATISTICS. 953

0498-8485 See CURRENT POPULATION REPORTS. SERIES P-23, SPECIAL STUDIES. 4551

0498-935X See PERSONNEL MANAGEMENT SERIES (WASHINGTON). 4704

0498-9791 See FEDERAL REAL AND PERSONAL PROPERTY INVENTORY REPORT (CIVILIAN AND MILITARY) OF THE UNITED STATES GOVERNMENT COVERING ITS PROPERTIES LOCATED IN THE UNITED STATES, IN THE TERRITORIES, AND OVERSEAS. 4648

0499-0021 See CONFERENCE WITH THE DIRECTORS OF THE NATIONAL RECLAMATION ASSOCIATION. 2088

0499-0544 See LIVESTOCK SLAUGHTER (WASHINGTON, D.C.). 214

0499-0579 See PEANUT STOCKS AND PROCESSING. 180

0499-0587 See POTATOES AND SWEETPOTATOES. 182

0499-1583 See UNITED STATES CONTRIBUTIONS TO INTERNATIONAL ORGANIZATIONS. 1641

0499-4175 See WILDLIFE ABSTRACTS. 2209

0499-499X See QUARTERLY DIGEST OF UNPUBLISHED DECISIONS OF THE COMPTROLLER GENERAL OF THE UNITED STATES : CONTRACTS. 4677

0499-5198 See GROUND-WATER LEVELS IN THE UNITED STATES. NORTH-CENTRAL STATES. 5534

0499-6453 See CUMULATIVE LIST OF ORGANIZATIONS DESCRIBED IN SECTION 170 (C) OF THE INTERNAL REVENUE CODE OF 1954. 4719

0499-6909 See COST OF TRANSPORTING FREIGHT BY CLASS I AND CLASS II MOTOR COMMON CARRIERS OF GENERAL COMMODITIES. EASTERN-CENTRAL TERRITORY. 829

0499-9320 See NASA TECHNICAL MEMORANDUM. 29

0499-9355 See NASA TECHNICAL TRANSLATION. 30

0499-9797 See RESEARCH HIGHLIGHTS IN AGING. 3754

0500-2230 See RESEARCH AND DEVELOPMENT PROGRESS REPORT / OFFICE OF SALINE WATER. 2203

0500-3970 See ANNUAL REPORT / SUBVERSIVE ACTIVITIES CONTROL BOARD. 4464

0500-473X See TECHNICAL REPORT - U. S. WATERWAYS EXPERIMENT STATION, VICKSBURG, MISS. 2095

0500-4780 See CLIMATOLOGICAL DATA. PUERTO RICO AND VIRGIN ISLANDS. 1423

0500-490X See PAMPHLET - U.S. DEPARTMENT OF LABOR, EMPLOYMENT STANDARDS ADMINISTRATION, WOMEN'S BUREAU. 1700

0500-7194 See URODA WYD. POLSKIE. 5567

0500-7208 See UROLOGIA POLSKA. 3993

0500-7860 See UTAH ARCHAEOLOGY (NEWSLETTER). 285

0501-0918 See BULLETIN - UNDERHILL SOCIETY OF AMERICA. 2725

0501-1183 See UNIFORM COMMERCIAL CODE REPORTING SERVICE. 3067

0501-1213 See UNIFORM HOUSING CODE. 631

0501-2953 See WATER RESOURCES SERIES. 5547

0501-4603 See FRESH FRUIT AND VEGETABLE UNLOADS IN SOUTHERN CITIES BY COMMODITIES, STATES AND MONTHS. 837

0501-462X See FRESH FRUIT AND VEGETABLE UNLOADS IN MIDWESTERN CITIES BY COMMODITIES, STATES AND MONTHS. 837

0501-4670 See FEDERAL MILK ORDER MARKET STATISTICS. 153

0501-5782 See CRREL REPORT. 5097

0501-7467 See RESEARCH REPORT - UNITED STATES DEPARTMENT OF THE INTERIOR, BUREAU OF RECLAMATION. 2203

0501-798X See CLINICAL PROGRAMS FOR MENTALLY RETARDED CHILDREN. 3902

0501-8234 See TIDAL CURRENT TABLES. ATLANTIC COAST OF NORTH AMERICA. 4184

0501-9427 See SELECTED MANPOWER STATISTICS. 4062

0501-9877 See AMERICAN FOREIGN POLICY CURRENT DOCUMENTS (WASHINGTON, D.C. : 1984). 4515

0502-0166 See CAREERS IN THE UNITED STATES DEPARTMENT OF THE INTERIOR. 4202

0502-0395 See WATER POLLUTION SURVEILLANCE SYSTEM : ANNUAL COMPILATION OF DATA. 2247

0502-1456 See GROUND-WATER LEVELS IN THE UNITED STATES : NORTHEASTERN STATES. 2090

0502-1464 See GROUND-WATER LEVELS IN THE UNITED STATES. SOUTH-CENTRAL STATES. 5534

0502-2150 See SMALL BUSINESS ADMINISTRATION AND INVESTMENT ACT WITH AMENDMENTS. 711

0502-3262 See TECHNICAL REPORT - CIVIL ENGINEERING LABORATORY, NAVAL CONSTRUCTION BATTALION CENTER, PORT HUENEME, CALIFORNIA. 2032

0502-3343 See WORLD PORT INDEX. 5458

0502-3378 See NRL MEMORANDUM REPORT. 4181

0502-3548 See U. S. FOREST SERVICE RESEARCH NOTE NOR. 2397

0502-5001 See RESEARCH PAPER RM. 2393

0502-6679 See UNIVERSITY OF FLORIDA LAW CENTER NEWS, THE. 3068

0502-8450 See WATER CIRCULAR. 5542

0502-871X See UTAH MUSIC EDUCATOR. 4157

0502-9716 See U.S. HOUSING MARKETS. 2837

0502-9767 See U.S. OIL WEEK. 4281

0502-9988 See UCHENYE ZAPISKI KAFEDR MARKSISTSKO-LENINSKOI FILOSOFII VYSSHEI PARTIINOI SHKOLY PRI TSK KPSS I MESTNYKH VYSSHIKH PARTIINYKH SHKOL. 4364

0503-0021 See UCHENYE ZAPISKI PO STATISTIKE. 5345

0503-0455 See UFFICIOSTILE. 2903

0503-1001 See ANNALS OF THE UKRAINIAN ACADEMY OF ARTS AND SCIENCES IN THE UNITED STATES. 2842

0503-1036 See BJULETEN' - KOMITETU UKRAJINCIV KANADY. 2723

0503-1265 See UKRAINSKIJ FIZICESKIJ ZURNAL (KIEV, 1967). 4424

0503-1486 See UMBRAE CODICUM OCCIDENTALIUM. 2632

0503-1540 See MER (TOKYO, JAPAN). 1452

0503-1966 See UNIFORM COMMERCIAL CODE LAW LETTER, THE. 3067

0503-1982 See UNIFORMED SERVICES ALMANAC. 4059

0503-2636 See DIRECTORY (UNITARIAN UNIVERSALIST ASSOCIATION : 1965). 5059

0503-3551 See GENERAL MINUTES OF THE ANNUAL CONFERENCES OF THE UNITED METHODIST CHURCH. 5060

0503-3772 See HALF-YEARLY BULLETIN OF ELECTRIC ENERGY STATISTICS FOR EUROPE. BULLETIN SEMESTRIEL DE STATISTIQUES DE L'ENERGIE ELECTRIQUE POUR L'EUROPE. POLUGODOVOI BIULLETEN EVROPEISKOI STATISTIKI ELECTROENERGII. 1962

0503-4019 See SUPPLEMENT TO THE STATISTICAL YEARBOOK AND THE MONTHLY BULLETIN OF STATISTICS. 5344

0503-4221 See MONOGRAPHS ON EDUCATION. 1765

0503-4299 See UNESCO TECHNICAL PAPERS IN MARINE SCIENCE. 1458

0503-485X See REPORT ON THE HEALTH, POPULATION AND NUTRITION ACTIVITIES OF THE AGENCY FOR INTERNATIONAL DEVELOPMENT, DEPARTMENT OF STATE. 2911

0503-4922 See A.I.D. ECONOMIC DATA BOOK, NEAR EAST AND SOUTH ASIA. 2913

0503-5090 See NATIONAL TICK SURVEILLANCE PROGRAM. 5516

0503-5139 See HYDROLOGIC DATA FOR EXPERIMENTAL AGRICULTURAL WATERSHEDS IN THE UNITED STATES. 1414

0503-5368 See AIR UNIVERSITY ABSTRACTS OF RESEARCH REPORTS. 8

0503-5562 See RESEARCH REPORT - U. S. LAND LOCOMOTION RESEARCH LABORATORY, CENTER LINE, MICHIGAN. 1994

0503-6291 See VALIS-EESTLASE KALENDER. 1929

0503-8308 See SERIE DE CUENTOS PARA LA JUVENTUD. 1069

0503-8413 See ANTROPOLOGIA. 230

0503-8448 See LENGUAS MODERNAS. 3297

0503-9967 See BIENNIAL REPORT OF THE VERMONT RECREATION BOARD. 4849

0504-0523 See VESELYE KARTINKI. 1071

0504-0779 See VETERANS' VOICES. 3450

0504-3972 See UNIVERSITY OF VIRGINIA LAW SCHOOL FOUNDATION ANNUAL REPORT, THE. 3069

0504-4251 See VIRGINIA ENGINEER (1974), THE. 2000

0504-426X See VIRGINIA ENGLISH BULLETIN. 3332

0504-9806 See ESTUDIOS Y DOCUMENTOS. 4346

0504-9903 See ANALES DE LA UNIVERSIDAD CATOLICA DE VALPARAISO. 1808

0505-0146 See VANIDADES CONTINENTAL. 2793

0505-0332 See VASI SZEMLE SZOMBATHELY. 1958. 2714

0505-0448 See VECTOR (READING). 3450

0505-172X See COLECCION CIENCIAS SOCIALES. 5195

0505-1762 See COLECCION ESPACIO Y FORMA. 2818

0505-1827 See COLECCION TESIS DOCTORALES. 4344

0505-2009 See MEMORIE DI BIOGEOGRAFIA ADRIATICA. 2569

0505-205X See BOLLETTINO DEL MUSEO CIVICO DI STORIA NATURALE DI VENEZIA. 4163

0505-2793 See BERICHTE DES VEREINS NATUR UND HEIMAT UND DES NATURHISTORISCHEN MUSEUMS ZU LUBECK. 4163

0505-3668 See VERSAILLES PREGNY-CHAMBERY. 2714

0505-3862 See VESTNIK ISTORII MIROVOI KULTURY. 2632

0505-4176 See VIA PENSACOLA. 5458

0505-4435 See VICTORIAN REPORTS. 3071

0505-625X See VIRGIN ISLANDS GUIDANCE NEWSLETTER. 1917

0505-7043 See VIRGINIA AVIFAUNA. 5620

0505-8708 See VOICE M.A.N, THE. 2433

0505-8813 See VOICE OF THE TENNESSEE WALKING HORSE. 2803

0505-9372 See VOLKSWIRTSCHAFTLICHE SCHRIFTEN. 1526

0506-0044 See VOPROSY ISTORII RELIGII I ATEIZMA. 5008

0506-2160 See TRUDY ... SESSII VSESOIUZNOGO PALEONTOLOGICHESKOGO OBSHCHESTVA. 4231

0506-306X See VDGSA NEWS. 4158

0506-3159 See FORTSCHRITT-BERICHTE DER VDI ZEITSCHRIFTEN. REIHE 11, SCHWINGUNGS TECHNIK, LARMBEKAMPFUNG. 2230

0506-3590 See YEARBOOK OF POPULATION RESEARCH IN FINLAND. 4561

0506-4120 See VARAVIKSNE. 3450

0506-4155 See VARIA. 4928

0506-418X See VARIASARI. 2509

0506-4406 See VECKANS AFFARER. 717

0506-449X See VEGETACE CSSR. REIHE A. 529

0506-533X See BOLETIN - VENEZUELA. INSTITUTO AGRARIO NACIONAL. 68

0506-5798 See REVISTA DEL MINISTERIO DE JUSTICIA. 3041

0506-5992 See EDICIONES. 3208

0506-600X See BOLETIN DEL CENTRO DE INVESTIGACIONES HISTORICAS Y ESTETICAS. 293

0506-6034 See PUBLICACION - VENEZUELA. UNIVERSIDAD CENTRAL. CONSEJO DE DESARROLLO CIENTIFICO Y HUMANISTICO. 2852

0506-6115 See PUBLICACIONES. SERIE : SEMINARIOS. 1869

0506-6131 See CUADERNOS - VENEZUELA. UNIVERSIDAD CENTRAL, CARACAS. ESCUELA DE PERIODISMO. 3205

0506-6220 See FUENTES HISTORICAS. 2616

0506-631X See INFORME - DISTRITO FEDERAL (VENEZUELA). CONTRALORIA MUNICIPAL. 4732

0506-6913 See VERDE OLVO. 4060

0506-7049 See MITTEILUNGEN DES VEREINS FUER FORSTLICHE STANDORTSKUNDE UND FORSTPFLANZENZUCHTUNG. 2388

0506-7286 See VERFASSUNG UND RECHT IN UBERSEE. 3094

0506-7294 See VERGILIUS (1959). 1080

0506-7510 See BULLETIN - VERMONT FISH AND GAME DEPARTMENT. 2189

0506-7553 See SPECIAL BULLETIN - VERMONT GEOLOGICAL SURVEY. 1397

0506-7588 See STATE SERIES. 4688

0506-7715 See VERRI, IL. 3450

0506-7936 See VERZEICHNIS DER ORIENTALISCHEN HANDSCHRIFTEN IN DEUTSCHLAND. 2667

0506-7944 See VERZEICHNIS DER ORIENTALISCHEN HANDSCHRIFTEN IN DEUTSCHLAND. SUPPLEMENTBAND. 3336

0506-8010 See VESTIGIA. 2632

0506-8126 See VETERA CHRISTIANORUM. 5020

0506-8231 See VETERINARSTVI. 5524

0506-8347 See VIA (CAMB.). 310

0506-8894 See VIE DU TIERS-MONDE. 2912

0506-9408 See VIERTELJAHRSHEFTE FUER ZEITGESCHICHTE. SCHRIFTENREIHE. 2632

0506-9661 See VIETNAM BULLETIN. 2667

0506-9696 See VIETNAM COURIER. 2509

0506-9777 See VIETNAM MAGAZINE. 2667

0507-0252 See JOURNAL OF THE VIOLA DA GAMBA SOCIETY OF AMERICA. 4127

0507-0503 See BIENNIAL REPORT - VIRGINIA COMMISSION OF OUTDOOR RECREATION. 4869

0507-0619 See CHILDREN'S CASES DISPOSED OF BY THE JUVENILE COURTS. 3160

0507-066X See MARKET NEWS (RICHMOND). 107

0507-1305 See VIRGINIA SOCIAL SCIENCE JOURNAL. 5225

0507-1348 See VIRGINIAS, MARYLAND, DELAWARE AND DISTRICT OF COLUMBIA LEGAL DIRECTORY, THE. 3072

0507-1410 See VISHVESHVARANAND INDOLOGICAL JOURNAL. 3332

0507-1577 See VISTA/U.S.A. 5499

0507-1658 See VISUAL COMMUNICATIONS JOURNAL. 4570

0507-1690 See VITA EVANGELICA (ENGLISH EDITION). 5008

0507-1712 See VITA ITALIANA. 2524

0507-2298 See VOICE FOR EDUCATION, THE. 1790

0507-2379 See VOICE OF THE PHARMACIST. 4332

0507-2573 See VOLGA. 2524

0507-3367 See VOPROSY ISTORII ESTESTVOZNANIJA I TEHNIKI. 5169

0507-3529 See VOPROSY KLASSICHESKOI FILOLOGII. 3332

0507-3723 See VOPROSY MUZYKALNOI FORMY. 4158

0507-3758 See VOPROSY ONKOLOGIJ. 3825

0507-3871 See VOPROSY RUSSKOI LITERATURY. 3451

0507-4045 See VOPROSY TEORII PLAZMY. 4445

0507-4088 See VOPROSY VIRUSOLOGII. 571

0507-4150 See VORGANGE. 2524

0507-4428 See VRANJSKI GLASNIK. 2715

0507-5238 See VSPOMOGATELNYE ISTORICHESKIE DISTSIPLINY. 2633

0507-5386 See VYCHISLITELNYE METODY I PROGRAMMIROVANIE. 1281

0507-5475 See VYSOKOMOLEKULARNYE SOEDINENA. SERIA A. 995

0507-5548 See COMMUNICATIONES INSTITUTI FORESTALIS CECHOSLOVENIAE. 2377

0507-6528 See VABA EESTLASE TAHTRAAMAT. 2494

0507-6544 See VALLEY LEAVES. 2476

0507-6773 See PROCEEDINGS - VERTEBRATE PEST CONFERENCE. 4247

0507-6986 See VAJRA BODHI SEA. 5022

0507-7281 See VIOLONCELLO SOCIETY INC., NEWSLETTER. 4158

0508-1165 See WASHINGTON UNIVERSITY LIBRARY STUDIES. 3256

0508-122X See WASSER UND ABWASSER (VIENNA). 2245

0508-1976 See VLASTIVEDNY CASOPIS. 2715

0508-3052 See WEN SHIH CHE HSUEH PAO / KUO LI TAIWAN TA HSUEH. 2856

0508-4741 See REPORT / GEOLOGICAL SURVEY OF WESTERN AUSTRALIA. 1394

0508-4865 See WESTERN AUSTRALIAN NATURALIST, THE. 4173

0508-6191 See WESTWIND (LOS ANGELES, CALIF.). 333

0508-8410 See WINTERTHURER JAHRBUCH. 2716

0508-8550 See WIRTSCHAFT, DIE. 723

0508-9921 See WISCONSIN BUSINESS WOMAN, THE. 723

0509-089X See WOMEN'S CIRCLE. 5186

0509-1632 See WORLD AND PRESS. 3334

0509-6065 See VORTRAGE UND AUFSATZE. 1526

0509-6213 See WETTERAUER GESCHICHTSBLAETTER. 2715

0509-6677 See WIADOMOSCI INSTYTUTU MELORACJI I UZYTKOW ZIELONYCH. 2001

0509-6839 See BIULETYN WARZYWNICZY. BULLETIN OF VEGETABLE CROPS RESEARCH WORK. BIULLETEN PO OVOSHCHEVODSTVU. 2410

0509-6936 See ROCZNIK MUZEUM NARODOWEGO W WARSZAWIE. 4096

0509-7754 See BULLETIN - STATE OF WASHINGTON DIVISION OF POWER RESOURCES. 1934

0509-917X See WATERWAY GUIDE. MID-ATLANTIC EDITION. 597

0509-9528 See WEEKLY OF BUSINESS AVIATION, THE. 39

0509-9609 See WEGE DER FORSCHUNG. 3332

0509-9773 See WISSENSCHAFTLICHE ZEITSCHRIFT. 311

0510-002X See ANNUAL REPORT - NATIONAL VEGETABLE RESEARCH STATION. 163

0510-1387 See GUIDEBOOK - WEST TEXAS GEOLOGICAL SOCIETY. 1382

0510-2332 See WESTERN EXPRESS. 2788

0510-2626 See WESTERN RACING NEWS. 5428

0510-3517 See WHEAT INFORMATION SERVICE. 146

0510-372X See WHITE RIVER VALLEY HISTORICAL QUARTERLY. 2766

0510-3746 See ZAPISY BELARUSKAHA INSTYTUTU NAVUKI I MASTATSVA. 2716

0510-4262 See WIADOMOSCI MELIORACYJNE I LAKARSKIE. 3651

0510-6222 See EMPLOYMENT AND WAGES COVERED BY WISCONSIN'S U. C. LAW. 3147

0510-6966 See WISSENSCHAFT UND FORTSCHRITT. 5170

0510-7385 See WOMEN'S HOUSEHOLD. 5571

0510-8004 See PROCEEDINGS--SYMPOSIUM OF THE WORLD ASSOCIATION OF VETERINARY HYGIENISTS. 5519

0510-8675 See YELLOW-FEVER VACCINATING CENTRES FOR INTERNATIONAL TRAVEL. 4808

0510-9078 See ABRIDGED FINAL REPORT - WORLD METEOROLOGICAL ORGANIZATION. COMMISSION FOR AGRICULTURAL METEOROLOGY. 1419

0510-9221 See PROCEEDINGS - WORLD ORCHID CONFERENCE. 2429

0510-9671 See WRITERS AT WORK. 3454

0510-9833 See WURZBURGER GEOGRAPHISCHE ARBEITEN. 2579

0511-0289 See WYOMING DIRECTORY OF MANUFACTURING AND MINING. 3489

0511-0726 See A.A.G. BYDRAGEN. 42

0511-084X See WAKAYAMA MEDICAL REPORTS. 3650

0511-0939 See WALDHYGIENE. 2398

0511-1765 See STUDIA NAUK POLITYCZNYCH. 4497

0511-1943 See WASEDA ECONOMIC PAPERS. 1526

0511-3520 See WASSER-KALENDER (BERLIN). 5541

0511-3598 See WATER INFORMATION BULLETIN (BOISE). 5542

0511-3806 See WATERWAY GUIDE. SOUTHERN EDITION. 5458

0511-4187 See WEEKLY COMPILATION OF PRESIDENTIAL DOCUMENTS. 4701

0511-4225 See WEGWEISER ZUR VOLKERKUNDE. 2325

0511-4233 See WEHRMACHT IM KAMPF, DIE. 2633

0511-4365 See WELDING DATA BOOK. 4028

0511-4381 See WELDING RESEARCH NEWS. 4028

0511-4470 See CONTRIBUTION - NEW ZEALAND OCEANOGRAPHIC INSTITUTE. 1448

0511-4772 See WEN WU. 5269

0511-4772 See WENWU. 5225

0511-5272 See ECONOMIC REVIEW (WEST BENGAL, INDIA). 1558

0511-5280 See EXPLANATORY MEMORANDUM ON THE BUDGET OF THE GOVERNMENT OF WEST BENGAL. 4723

0511-5299 See STATEMENT SHOWING FINANCIAL RESULTS OF IMPORTANT SCHEMES OF GOVERNMENT INVOLVING TRANSACTIONS OF A COMMERCIAL OR SEMI-COMMERCIAL NATURE. 713

0511-5507 See STATISTICS OF EMPLOYMENT IN LOCAL BODIES IN WEST BENGAL. 1539

0511-5604 See WEST CANADIAN RESEARCH PUBLICATIONS OF GEOLOGY AND RELATED SCIENCES. SERIES 1. 1361

0511-6635 See PUBLIC AFFAIRS SERIES (MORGANTOWN). 1623

0511-7003 See REPORT OF THE GOVERNMENT CHEMICAL LABORATORIES. 1018

0511-7445 See WESTERN EXPLORER, THE. 2765

0511-7542 See OCCASIONAL PAPERS OF THE WESTERN FOUNDATION OF VERTEBRATE ZOOLOGY. 5593

0511-7550 See PROCEEDINGS OF THE WESTERN FOUNDATION OF VERTEBRATE ZOOLOGY. 5595

0511-7704 See WESTERN LUMBER FACTS. 2405

0511-8182 See ANNUAL REPORT - WESTERN STATES WATER COUNCIL. 5530

0511-8255 See BAROMETER (PORTLAND). 2399

0511-8484 See WESTPREUSSEN-JAHRBUCH. 2715

0511-8824 See WHITNEY REVIEW. 4097

0511-8832 See WHITTIER NEWSLETTER. 435

0511-8948 See WHO'S WHO IN CALIFORNIA (1956). 436

0511-8964 See WHO'S WHO IN FLORICULTURE. 437

0511-9049 See WHO'S WHO IN STEEL AND METALS. 438

0511-9162 See WIADOMOSCI HISTORYCZNE. 2633

0511-9294 See WIENER MUSIKWISSENSCHAFTLICHE BEITRAGE. 4159

0511-9375 See WIES WSPOCZESNA; PISMO RUCHU LUDOWEGO. 5265

0511-9456 See PROCEEDINGS - WILDERNESS CONFERENCE. 4171

0511-9480 See WILDLIFE PAMPHLET (PROVIDENCE). 2209

0511-9618 See WILLDENOWIA. 530

0512-0640 See INFORMATION CIRCULAR (WISCONSIN GEOLOGICAL AND NATURAL HISTORY SURVEY). 1383

0512-1175 See WISCONSIN ACADEMY REVIEW. 2856

0512-1329 See WISCONSIN AGRICULTURAL STATISTICS. 157

0512-1345 See BULLETIN - WISCONSIN VETERINARY MEDICAL ASSOCIATION. 5506

0512-1426 See WISSENSCHAFT UND GESELLSCHAFT. 2857

0512-1582 See WISSENSCHAFTLICHE MONOGRAPHIEN ZUM ALTEN UND NEUEN TESTAMENT. 5009

0512-1604 See WISSENSCHAFTLICHE UNTERSUCHUNGEN ZUM NEUEN TESTAMENT. 5020

0512-1817 See WOMEN OF KOREA. 5570

0512-2295 See WORLD (NEW YORK, N.Y. 1967). 753

0512-2716 See WORLD DIRECTORY OF AL-ANON FAMILY GROUPS AND ALATEENS. 1350

0512-2740 See WORLD DIRECTORY OF MATHEMATICIANS / PUBLISHED UNDER THE AUSPICES OF THE INTERNATIONAL MATHEMATICAL UNION. 3541

0512-2759 See WORLD DIRECTORY OF MEDICAL SCHOOLS. 3651

0512-3003 See BASIC DOCUMENTS. 4768

0512-3054 See WORLD HEALTH ORGANIZATION TECHNICAL REPORT SERIES. 4808

0512-3135 See WORLD HOSPITALS. 3793

0512-3739 See WORLD TRADE ANNUAL. 858

0512-4409 See WYOMING LABOR FORCE TRENDS. 1720

0512-4611 See WYOMING TRADE WINDS. 1528

0512-4727 See BULLETIN - WATER RESEARCH INSTITUTE (MORGANTOWN). 5531

0512-4743 See WEST VIRGINIA UNION LIST. 3256

0512-493X See MEMOIR - GEOLOGICAL SURVEY OF WYOMING. 1387

0512-5030 See WASSER UND ABWASSER IN FORSCHUNG UND PRAXIS. 5541

0512-5235 See WESTERN CATHOLIC REPORTER. 5038

0512-5421 See SPECIAL REPORT / CENTER FOR GREAT LAKES STUDIES, UNIVERSITY OF WISCONSIN-MILWAUKEE. 1847

0512-5804 See WHAT THEY SAID. 2633

0512-5847 See WHO'S WHO OF CONSUMER CREDIT MANAGEMENT, A. 439

0512-5901 See CHRISTMAS IDEAS FOR CHILDREN. 371

0512-610X See WASHINGTON NOTES ON AFRICA. 2500

0512-6320 See WIRTSCHAFTSRECHT. 3104

0512-6614 See XEROGRAMMATA; HOCHSCHULSCHRIFTEN ZUR PHILOSOPHIE. 4365

0512-9907 See YUGOSLAV REVIEW [A MONTHLY MAGAZINE OF THE SERBS, CROATS AND SLOVENES], THE. 2525

0513-0689 See INDEKS; MESECNI PREGLED PRIVREDNE STATISTIKE FNRJ. 5328

0513-1391 See YALE LAW REPORT. 3077

0513-1529 See CENTER PAPER (PRINCETON, N.J.). 4551

0513-1634 See BIULLETEN GOSUDARSTVENNOGO NIKITSKOGO BOTANICHESKOGO SADA. 502

0513-1715 See YAMAGUCHI DAIGAKU NOGAKUBU GAKUJUTSU HOKOKU. 148

0513-1731 See YAMAGUCHI IGAKU. 3652

0513-1812 See BULLETIN OF THE YAMAGUCHI MEDICAL SCHOOL. 3560

0513-2096 See YEARS AHEAD, THE. 5010

0513-2592 See BULLETIN OF THE FACULTY OF ENGINEERING, YOKOHAMA NATIONAL UNIVERSITY. 1967

0513-2673 See YONKERS HISTORICAL BULLETIN. 2767

0513-2711 See YORK PIONEER, THE. 2767

0513-3424 See YOUSE JINSHU. 4024

0513-3483 See JINGJI-BU GUOLI TAIWAN DAXUE HEBANYUVE SHENGWU SHIYAN-SUO YANJIU BAOGAO. 2306

0513-398X See YUKAGAKU. 1031

0513-417X See YADORIGA. 5600

0513-4617 See YALKUT MORESHET. 5054

0513-4676 See YAMAGATA DAIGAKU KIYO : NOGAKU. 147

0513-4692 See YAMAGATA DAIGAKU KIYO: SHIZEN KAGAKU. 5171

0513-4706 See YAMAGATA-KEN EISEI KENKYUJO HO. 4808

0513-4870 See YAO HSUEH HSUEH PAO. 4333

0513-5117 See YEAR BOOK OF NEUROLOGY AND NEUROSURGERY, THE. 3847

0513-5222 See YEAST (DAVIS, CALIF.). 571

0513-5230 See YEDI'OT GENAZIM. 5054

0513-5311 See YERMO. 5010

0513-5419 See IDISHE VORT, DOS. 5048

0513-5486 See YLLI. 2495

0513-5710 See YONAGO ACTA MEDICA. 3652

0513-5796 See YONSEI MEDICAL JOURNAL. 3652

0513-5907 See YOSUI TO HAISUI. 2248

0513-5974 See YOUNG EAST. 5022

0513-5982 See YOUNG FABIAN PAMPHLET. 4501

0513-6342 See YUASA JIHO / YUASA DENCHI KABUSHIKI KAISHA. 2087

0513-6776 See BULLETIN - YAKIMA VALLEY GENEALOGICAL SOCIETY. 2441

0513-8728 See ZDRAVOOHRANENIE (KISINEV). 4808

0513-8736 See ZDRAVOOKHRANENIE TURKMENISTANA / ORGAN MINISTERSTVA ZDRAVOOKHRANENIIA TSSR. 4809

0513-9058 See ZEITSCHRIFT FUER DIE GESCHICHTE DER SAARGEGEND. 2717

0513-9856 See ZINOCYY SVIT. 5572

0514-0188 See ZIVOT WARSAWA. 2275

0514-0994 See ZWIERCIADO. 5572

0514-1958 See ZAKONOMERNOSTI RAZMESENIA POLEZNYH ISKOPAEMYH. 1445

0514-2210 See ZARUBEZHNYE ZAPISKI. 2525

0514-2415 See ZDRAVOOHRANENIE TADZIKISTANA. 3652

0514-2431 See CSSR ZDRAVOTNICTVI. 4772

0514-2482 See ZEAL. 5011

0514-2563 See ZEITSCHRIFT FUER ANGEWANDTE ZOOLOGIE. BEIHEFTE. 5600

0514-2946 See ZEMENT UND BETON. 5172

0514-2989 See ZEMLIA I LIUDI. 2580

0514-4655 See ZWIASTUN. 5011

0514-4787 See ZWOLSE DRUKKEN EN HERDRUKKEN VOOR DER MAATSCHAPPIJ DER NEDERLANDSE LETTERKUNDE TE LEIDEN. 3456

0514-5090 See RADOVI ZAVODA ZA SLAVENSKU FILOLOGIJU. 3314

0514-5163 See ZAIRYO. 2001

0514-5562 See ANNUAL REPORT FOR THE YEAR ... / REPUBLIC OF ZAMBIA, MINISTRY OF HOME AFFAIRS. 4627

0514-5864 *See* ZASHCHITNYE POKRYTIIA NA METALLAKH / AKADEMIIA NAUK UKRAINSKOI SSR, INSTITUT PROBLEM MATERIALOVEDENIIA. **4024**

0514-5872 *See* ZASTITA BILJA. **530**

0514-6143 *See* ZBORNIK MATICE SRPSKE ZA FILOLOGIJU I LINGVISTIKU / MATICA SRPSKA, ODELJENJE ZA KNJIZEVNOST I JEZIK. **3335**

0514-616X *See* ZBORNIK ZASTITE SPOMENIKA KULTURE. RECUEIL DES TRAVAUX SUR LA PROTECTION DES MONUMENTS HISTORIQUES. **369**

0514-6364 *See* ZEITSCHRIFT FUER BIBLIOTHEKSWESEN UND BIBLIOGRAPHIE. SONDERHEFT. **3257**

0514-6496 *See* ZEITSCHRIFT FUER RECHTSPOLITIK. **4501**

0514-6658 *See* ZEMLJISTE I BILJKA. **149**

0514-7115 *See* ZENTRALBLATT FUER MINERALOGIE. TEIL I, KRISTALLOGRAPHIE UND MINERALOGIE. **1445**

0514-7123 *See* ZENTRALBLATT FUER MINERALOGIE. TEIL II. PETROGRAPHIE, TECHNISCHE MINERALOGIE, GEOCHEMIE UND LAGERSTATTENKUNDE. **1401**

0514-7158 *See* ZENTRALBLATT FUER VETERINARMEDIZIN. REIHE A. **5528**

0514-7336 *See* ZEPHYRUS. **286**

0514-7441 *See* ZHIVOTNOVUDNI NAUKI. **5528**

0514-7492 *See* ZURNAL ORGANICESKOJ HIMII. **1049**

0514-7506 *See* ZURNAL PRIKLADNOI SPEKTROSKOPII (MINSK). **4442**

0514-7727 *See* ZIVA ANTIKA. **1081**

0514-776X *See* ZIVOT (SARAJEVO). **3456**

0514-7867 *See* ZOGRAF : CASOPIS ZA SREDNJOVEKOVNU UMETNOST. **2717**

0514-7905 *See* ZONING BULL. (BOSTON, MASS.). **2839**

0514-7972 *See* ZOONOSES. **3654**

0514-8294 *See* ZUR POLITIK UND ZEITGESCHICHTE. **4501**

0514-8499 *See* NIHON ZOSEN GAKKAI RONBUNSHU. **4181**

0514-857X *See* ZENTRALASIATISCHE STUDIEN DES SEMINARS FUER SPRACH- UND KULTURWISSENSCHAFT ZENTRALASIENS DER UNIVERSITAT BONN. **2668**

0514-8782 *See* ZEITSCHRIFT FUER MILITARMEDIZIN. **3653**

0514-8790 *See* VEROFFENTLICHUNGEN DES ZENTRALINSTITUTS FUER PHYSIK DER ERDE. **1412**

0514-8863 *See* C A MONOGRAPHS, A. **1031**

0514-9193 *See* AF, ARTE FOTOGRAFICO. **4366**

0514-9738 *See* A.M.C. MAINE MOUNTAIN GUIDE, THE. **4868**

0515-0361 *See* ASTIN BULLETIN. **2874**

0515-0612 *See* AACHENER KUNSTBLATTER (DUMONT BUCHVERLAG). **335**

0515-1074 *See* BERICHTE DER ABWASSERTECHNISCHEN VEREINIGUNG. **2225**

0515-1147 *See* SESION INAUGURAL - REAL ACADEMIA DE FARMACIA DE BARCELONA. **4329**

0515-1694 *See* STUDII DE GRAMATICA. **3326**

0515-1864 *See* RECUEIL DES HISTORIENS DE LA FRANCE. DOCUMENTS FINANCIERS. **2705**

0515-2046 *See* JOURNAL OF THE ACADEMY OF FLORIDA TRIAL LAWYERS. **2989**

0515-2291 *See* ACCIAIO INOSSIDABILE, L'. **3996**

0515-2720 *See* ACTA ANAESTHESIOLOGICA SCANDINAVICA. SUPPLEMENT. **3680**

0515-3700 *See* ACTUALITES PHARMACEUTIQUES. **4289**

0515-4987 *See* ADVOCATE (BOISE, IDAHO), THE. **2928**

0515-5649 *See* AFKAR. **3358**

0515-6866 *See* AGRARWIRTSCHAFT. SONDERHEFT. **46**

0515-7803 *See* AICHI-KEN EISEI KENKYUSHOHO. **4764**

0515-9083 *See* FORSCHUNGS- UND SITZUNGSBERICHTE. **2823**

0515-9091 *See* JAHRESBERICHT (AKADEMIE FUR RAUMFORSCHUNG UND LANDESPLANUNG (GERMANY)). **2825**

0515-9628 *See* ARMJANSKIJ HIMICESKIJ ZURNAL. **961**

0516-2629 *See* IZVESTIA AKADEMII NAUK UZBEKSKIJ SSR. SERIA TEHNICESKIH NAUK. **1981**

0516-3145 *See* AKADEMISKA DZIVE. **1918**

0516-3854 *See* ALABAMA AGRIBUSINESS. **57**

0516-3870 *See* ALABAMA BIRDLIFE. **5614**

0516-3889 *See* ALABAMA CATTLEMAN. **204**

0516-396X *See* ALABAMA GENEALOGICAL REGISTER / BY BETTY WOOD THOMAS, THE. **2436**

0516-4842 *See* ALASKA EDUCATION NEWS. **1723**

0516-6551 *See* ALIGHIERI, L'. **3359**

0516-9011 *See* DIGEST OF COURT DECISIONS (NEW YORK, N.Y.). **2961**

0516-9216 *See* TECHNICAL LEAFLET / AMERICAN ASSOCIATION FOR STATE AND LOCAL HISTORY. **2631**

0516-9313 *See* AACTE DIRECTORY / AMERICAN ASSOCIATION OF COLLEGES FOR TEACHER EDUCATION. **1859**

0516-9518 *See* BULLETIN - THE AMERICAN ASSOCIATION OF VARIABLE STAR OBSERVERS. **394**

0516-9623 *See* AMERICAN ATHEIST, THE. **4933**

0516-9674 *See* FLORIDA TOUR BOOK. **5470**

0516-9968 *See* WASHINGTON LETTER (AMERICAN BAR ASSOCIATION). **3072**

0517-032X *See* AMERICAN BULLETIN, THE. **2718**

0517-1032 *See* SURVEY OF DENTAL PRACTICE. **1336**

0517-127X *See* COMPENDIUM. **1319**

0517-2160 *See* CUMULATIVE INDEX OF HOSPITAL LITERATURE. **3779**

0517-2292 *See* INFORMATION BULLETIN - AMERICAN INDONESIAN CHAMBER OF COMMERCE, INC. **820**

0517-404X *See* NUMISMATIC STUDIES. **2782**

0517-4856 *See* NEWSLETTER - AMERICAN SHORE AND BEACH PRESERVATION ASSOCIATION. **2200**

0517-5321 *See* ASME BOILER AND PRESSURE VESSEL CODE. **2110**

0517-564X *See* AMERICAN TRADE SCHOOLS DIRECTORY. **1910**

0517-5666 *See* TRUCK TAXES BY STATES. **5398**

0517-7731 *See* ANGLICAN, THE. **5055**

0517-8452 *See* ANNALES BOGORIENSES. **499**

0517-8606 *See* ANNALES NESTLE. **4187**

0518-018X *See* ANTIKE PLASTIK. **255**

0518-0333 *See* MONOGRAPH / ANTIQUARIAN HOROLOGICAL SOCIETY. **2916**

0518-066X *See* ANT. ANTRIEBSTECHNIK (1962). **5084**

0518-0678 *See* ANTROPOLOGIA FISICA CHILENA / UNIVERSIDAD DE CHILE, CENTRO DE ESTUDIOS ANTROPOLOGICOS. **230**

0518-1259 *See* APICOLTORE MODERNO, L'. **5605**

0518-1623 *See* APPROACH TO PHYSICAL SCIENCES. **4398**

0518-2107 *See* ARBEITEN ZUR KIRCHENGESCHICHTE HAMBURGS. **4935**

0518-2662 *See* ARBORETUM LEAVES. **500**

0518-2840 *See* ARCHE (1957). **5046**

0518-2867 *See* ARCHEION PONTOU. **2675**

0518-3499 *See* ARCHIVIO ECONOMICO DELL'UNIFICAZIONE ITALIANA. SERIE I. **1546**

0518-3766 *See* ARCHIWA BIBLIOTEKI I MUZEA KOSCIELNE. **5024**

0518-3839 *See* ARCTIC NEWS. **4936**

0518-4010 *See* ARENA TEKSTIL. **5347**

0518-4088 *See* ARGENSOLA. **1351**

0518-5289 *See* ARGUMENTY (WARSAW, POLAND). **4936**

0518-6129 *See* ARIZONA MUSIC NEWS. **4101**

0518-6374 *See* WATER RESOURCES SUMMARY (LITTLE ROCK). **5547**

0518-6617 *See* ARKANSAS AMATEUR, THE. **259**

0518-8172 *See* ARTS AND ACTIVITIES YEARBOOK. **342**

0518-8520 *See* ASCHEFFENBURGER JAHRBUCH FUER GESCHICHTE, LANDESKUNDE UND KUNST DES UNTERMAINGEBIETES. **342**

0518-8881 *See* ASIAN NEWS SHEET. **5274**

0519-1572 *See* BANK HOLDING COMPANY FACTS. **775**

0519-198X *See* ELENCO DEI QUOTIDIANI E PERIODICI ITALIANI. **415**

0519-3117 *See* YEARBOOK, WITH HISTORICAL AND GENEALOGICAL JOURNAL. **2767**

0519-3389 *See* ATOMIC ENERGY CLEARING HOUSE. **1933**

0519-3486 *See* ATOMIC INDUSTRY, THE. **1933**

0519-4334 *See* AUFSCHLUSS. SONDERHEFT. **1438**

0519-4555 *See* AUS DEM WALDE. **2375**

0519-5357 *See* CROPS AND PASTURES, TASMANIA / AUSTRALIAN BUREAU OF STATISTICS. **169**

0519-6124 *See* PARLIAMENTARY DEBATES, HOUSE OF REPRESENTATIVES, WEEKLY HANSARD. **4672**

0519-6140 *See* PARLIAMENTARY DEBATES, SENATE, WEEKLY HANSARD. **4672**

0519-6396 *See* BIBLIOTECA DI STUDI AMERICANI. **3338**

0519-7198 *See* BIBLIOTECA ROMANICA HISPANICA. I. TRATADOS Y MONOGRAFIAS. **3366**

0519-7201 *See* BIBLIOTECA ROMANICA HISPANICA. II. ESTUDIOS Y ENSAYOS. **3367**

0519-721x *See* BIBLIOTECA ROMANICA HISPANICA. III. MANUALES. **3269**

0519-7228 *See* BIBLIOTECA ROMANICA HISPANICA. IV. TEXTOS. **3367**

0519-7236 *See* BIBLIOTECA ROMANICA HISPANICA. V. DICCIONARIOS. **3269**

0519-7244 *See* BIBLIOTECA ROMANICA HISPANICA. VI. ANTOLOGIA HISPANICA. **3367**

0519-7252 *See* BIBLIOTECA ROMANICA HISPANICA. VII. CAMPO ABIERTO. **3367**

0519-7260 *See* BIBLIOTECA ROMANICA HISPANICA. VIII. DOCUMENTOS. **3367**

0519-7929 *See* BIBLIOTEKA ANALIZ LITERACKICH. **3367**

0519-8356 *See* BIBLIOTEKA MATEMATYCZNA. **3497**

0519-9700 *See* BIBLIOTHECA HISTORICA LUNDENSIS. **2611**

0520-0121 *See* ETUDES. **2687**

0520-0962 *See* BIGAKU / BIGAKKAI HEN. **4342**

0520-1969 *See* BIOLOSKI VESTNIK. **447**

0520-4100 *See* BOLETIN AMERICANISTA. **2611**

0520-4712 *See* COMERCIO EXTERIOR (LA PAZ). **828**

0520-5085 *See* JOURNAL OF J J GROUP OF HOSPITALS AND GRANT MEDICAL COLLEGE. **3787**

0520-5700 *See* BONNIERS SMA KONSTBOCKER. **344**

0520-6340 *See* BOSEI KANRI. **963**

0520-6790 *See* LOCAL HISTORY RECORDS - BOURNE SOCIETY. **2482**

0520-7568 *See* BRAUER-UND MAELZER-LEHRLING. **2329**

0520-9250 *See* SLASKIE SPRAWOZDANIA ARCHEOLOGICZNE. **282**

0520-9323 See ZESZYTY NAUKOWE AKADEMII ROLNICZEJ WE WROCAWIU. ZOOTECHNIKA. **149**

0520-9617 *See* BRIEF (BOSTON), THE. **2943**

0521-0011 *See* BULLETIN OF PHYSICAL EDUCATION. **1855**

0521-0097 *See* DIGEST - BRITISH CATTLE BREEDERS' CLUB. **210**

0521-0585 *See* BRITISH COLUMBIA LEGAL TELEPHONE DIRECTORY, THE. **3139**

0521-1573 *See* REPORT - BRITISH SCHOOLS EXPLORING SOCIETY. **5145**

0521-2359 *See* CASOPIS MORAVSKEHO MUZEA. VEDY PRIRODNI. **4086**

0521-2804 See JAHRESBERICHT - BIOLOGISCHE BUNDESANSTALT FUER LAND- UND FORSTWIRTWIRTSCHAFT IN BERLIN UND BRAUNSCHWEIG. 460

0521-3479 See STUDI ALIMENTARI CU APA. 5540

0521-3851 See ERDESZETI KUTATASOK. 82

0521-422X See MEZOGAZDASAGI GEPESITESI TANULMANYOK. 160

0521-4238 See MAGYAR MEZOGAZDASAGI MUZEUM KOZLEMENYEI, A. 106

0521-4785 See REGESZETI DOLGOZATOK. 280

0521-517X See REVISTA DEL HOSPITAL DE NINOS (BUENOS AIRES). 3911

0521-5722 See NEWSLETTER - BUFFALO AND ERIE COUNTY HISTORICAL SOCIETY. 2749

0521-6761 See BULLETIN APICOLE DE DOCUMENTATION SCIENTIFIQUE ET TECHNIQUE ET D'INFORMATION. 5579

0521-7032 See BULLETIN DES MUSEES ET MONUMENTS LYONNAIS. 4085

0521-7059 See BULLETIN DU JAPON (EDITION CANADIENNE). 825

0521-713X See BULLETIN HISTORIQUE ET ARTISTIQUE DU CALAISIS. 2681

0521-8098 See MEMORANDUM FROM TAX MANAGEMENT. 4737

0521-8136 See BURENIE (MOSKVA). 756

0521-8195 See BURGENSE. 4941

0521-9191 See BUTSURI TANKO / GEOPHYSICAL EXPLORATION. 1403

0521-9310 See PRACE. SERIA A. 2852

0521-9604 See BMI ORCHESTRAL PROGRAM SURVEY. 4104

0521-9744 See BABEL (FRANKFURT). 3267

0522- 7194 See BEITRAGE ZUR VERHALTUNGSFORSCHUNG. 4577

0522-0033 See BAR VON BERLIN, DER. 231

0522-0629 See BALL AND ROLLER BEARING ENGINEERING. 2111

0522-0653 See BALLET REVIEW. 1310

0522-0750 See ABSTRACTS OF THE THESES ACCEPTED FOR THE PH D. DEGREE OF BANARAS HINDU UNIVERSITY. 1806

0522-2133 See PROCEEDINGS - INSTITUT TEKNOLOGI BANDUNG. 5140

0522-246X See FOREIGN TRADE STATISTICAL DIGEST. 729

0522-2478 See BANK AUDITING AND ACCOUNTING REPORT. 774

0522-2494 See BANK DIRECTOR'S REPORT. 774

0522-2508 See BANK EXECUTIVES REPORT. 774

0522-2931 See BANKER, THE. 776

0522-3725 See ABSTRACT OF STATISTICS - BARBADOS. STATISTICAL SERVICE. 5320

0522-5337 See BAYERISCHE VERWALTUNGSBLATTER. 2940

0522-5949 See BEETHOVEN-JAHRBUCH. 4102

0522-6058 See BEHORDENVERZEICHNIS NORDRHEIN-WESTFALEN / LANDSAMT FUER DATENVERARBEITUNG UND STATISTIK NORDRHEIN-WESTFALEN. 4632

0522-6341 See BEITRAEGE ZUR DEUTSCHEN PHILOLOGIE. 3268

0522-6376 See BEITRAGE ZUR ERFORSCHUNG DER WIRTSCHAFTLICHEN ENTWICKLUNG. 1548

0522-6449 See BEITRAGE ZUR FREMDENVERKEHRSFORSCHUNG. 824

0522-6457 See BEITRAGE ZUR GANZHEITLICHEN WIRTSCHAFTS- UND GESELLSCHAFTSLEHRE. 2875

0522-6554 See BEITRAGE ZUR GESCHICHTE DER STADTE MITTELEUROPAS. 2611

0522-6570 See BEITRAEGE ZUR GESCHICHTE DER WISSENSCHAFT UND DER TECHNIK. 5087

0522-6643 See BEITRAEGE ZUR GESCHICHTE DES PARLAMENTARISMUS UND DER POLITISCHEN PARTEIEN / HERAUSGEGEBEN VON DER KOMMISSION FUER GESCHICHTE DES PARLAMENTARISMUS UND DER POLITISCHEN PARTEIEN. 4465

0522-6848 See BEITRAEGE ZUR KOLONIAL- UND UBERSEEGESCHICHTE. 2611

0522-7038 See BEITRAEGE ZUR REGIONALEN GEOLOGIE DER ERDE. 1366

0522-7232 See BEKESI ELET. 5087

0522-7291 See BOLETIM DO MUSEU PARAENSE EMILIO GOELDI. SERIE ANTROPOLOGIA. 232

0522-7496 See BULLETIN DE LA COMMISSION ROYALE DES MONUMENTS ET DES SITES (BELGIUM). 2680

0522-7585 See ETUDES STATISTIQUES (BRUSSELS, BELGIUM). 5327

0522-8352 See ZBORNIK NARODNOG MUZEJA U BEOGRADU. 286

0522-8530 See ZBORNIK RADOVA POLJOPRIVREDNOG FAKULTETA. 1854

0522-8670 See BELLMAN LECTURE, THE. 778

0522-8786 See PROCEEDINGS / BELTWIDE COTTON CONFERENCES. 182

0522-9014 See BENSHEIMER HEFTE. 4938

0522-9138 See PROTOKOLL. 849

0522-9189 See AARBOK FOR UNIVERSITETET I BERGEN., MATEMATISK-NATURVITENSKAPELIG SERIE. 5079

0522-9545 See SCHRIFTENREIHE. 1847

0522-9790 See BILDERHEFTE. 4084

0523-0160 See BERLINER GEOGRAPHISCHE ABHANDLUNGEN. 2556

0523-0209 See BERLINER JURISTISCHE ABHANDLUNGEN. 2941

0523-1035 See BETRIEBSWIRTSCHAFTLICHE SCHRIFTEN. 861

0523-1051 See BETTER BEEF BUSINESS. 643

0523-1159 See POPULATION ET FAMILLE. 4557

0523-1418 See BHASHA. 3268

0523-1760 See BIBLIOGRAFIA ESPANOLA (MADRID, SPAIN : 1958). 3457

0523-1795 See BIBLIOGRAFIA HISTORICA MEXICANA. 2723

0523-2201 See BIBLIOGRAFIJA JUGOSLAVIJE. KNJIGE, BROSURE I MUZIKALIJE. 4103

0523-2252 See BIBLIOGRAPHIA PATRISTICA. 4939

0523-2376 See BIBLIOGRAPHIE D'ETUDES BALKANIQUES. 2678

0523-2465 See BIBLIOGRAPHIE DER FRANZOSISCHEN LITERATURWISSENSCHAFT. 3457

0523-2767 See BIBLIOGRAPHIEN ZUR DEUTSCHEN LITERATUR DES MITTELALTERS. 3457

0523-2988 See BIBLIOGRAPHY OF SEISMOLOGY. 1362

0523-3456 See DISTRICT STATISTICAL HANDBOOK - (INDIA). 5326

0523-5057 See BIBLIOTHEQUE DES ARCHIVES DE PHILOSOPHIE. 4342

0523-5154 See BIBLISCHE UNTERSUCHUNGEN. 5015

0523-6207 See BINGO. 2498

0523-6827 See BIOPOLYMERS SYMPOSIA. 447

0523-7203 See BLACK HILLS NUGGETS. 2439

0523-7971 See BOCHUMER ARBEITEN ZUR SPRACH- UND LITERATURWISSENSCHAFT. 3368

0523-798X See BOCHUMER GEOGRAPHISCHE ARBEITEN. 2556

0523-8579 See BOHEMIA. 2485

0523-8587 See BOHEMIA (MUNCHEN). 2678

0523-9133 See BOLETIN INDIGENISTA VENEZOLANO. 232

0523-9141 See BOLETIN INDUSTRIAL. 1599

0523-9346 See BOLLETTINO DEI MUSEI COMUNALI DI ROMA. 4085

0523-9702 See BULLETIN OF THE PRINCE OF WALES MUSEUM OF WESTERN INDIA. 4086

0524-0344 See RHEINISCHE LANDESMUSEUM BONN, DAS. 4096

0524-0379 See KLEINE SCHRIFTEN. 3221

0524-045X See BONNER MATHEMATISCHE SCHRIFTEN. 3497

0524-0581 See BOOK REVIEW INDEX. 4821

0524-0654 See BOOKS AND ARTICLES ON ORIENTAL SUBJECTS PUBLISHED IN JAPAN. / TOHOGAKU KANKEI CHOSHO RONBUN MOKUROKU. 2634

0524-0832 See BULLETIN DE L'INSTITUT DE GEOLOGIE DU BASSIN D'AQUITAINE. 1369

0524-0913 See BORTHWICK PAPERS / UNIVERSITY OF YORK, BORTHWICK INSTITUTE OF HISTORICAL RESEARCH. 2679

0524-1111 See BOSTON BAR JOURNAL. 2943

0524-112X See BOSTON COLLEGE STUDIES IN PHILOSOPHY. 4342

0524-1170 See BOSTON ORGAN CLUB NEWSLETTER, THE. 4104

0524-1286 See RESEARCH REPORTS AND TECHNICAL NOTES - BOSTON UNIVERSITY. HUMAN RELATIONS CENTER. 1845

0524-1324 See FILM STUDIES. 4070

0524-1685 See BOVINE PRACTITIONER, THE. 5506

0524-2223 See ZBORNIK SLOVENSKEHO NARODNEHO MUZEA. 4097

0524-2304 See ANTHROPOLOGIA. 228

0524-2363 See ACTA FACULTATIS RERUM NATURALIUM UNIVERSITATIS COMENIANAE. ZOOLOGIA. 5573

0524-2371 See ACTA FACULTATIS RERUM NATURALIUM UNIVERSITATIS COMENIANAE. BOTANICA. 497

0524-2444 See BRAUNSCHWEIGER GEOGRAPHISCHE STUDIEN. 2556

0524-2932 See INFORMATIVO. 5203

0524-3130 See PUBLICACAO DO INSTITUTO DE PESQUISAS DA MARINHA. 470

0524-4994 See BULLETIN / BRITISH ARACHNOLOGICAL SOCIETY. 5579

0524-5354 See STATISTICS OF HOSPITAL CASES DISCHARGED. BRITISH COLUMBIA. 3662

0524-5451 See STATISTICS OF HOSPITALIZED ACCIDENTS : BRITISH COLUMBIA. 3662

0524-5613 See VARSITY OUTDOOR CLUB JOURNAL, THE. 4880

0524-627X See BRITISH INSTITUTE STUDIES IN INTERNATIONAL & COMPARATIVE LAW. 3125

0524-6431 See BULLETIN OF THE BRITISH MUSEUM (NATURAL HISTORY). ENTOMOLOGY SERIES. 5606

0524-6474 See REPORT ON THE BRITISH MUSEUM (NATURAL HISTORY). 4171

0524-6881 See BRNO STUDIES IN ENGLISH. 3270

0524-7349 See SOUPISY RUKOPISNYCH FONDU. 425

0524-7403 See ACTA UNIVERSITATIS AGRICULTURAE. FACULTAS AGRONOMICA. 44

0524-7438 See ACTA UNIVERSITATIS AGRICULTURAE FACULTAS SILVICULTURAE. 2373

0524-7802 See BULLETIN MENSUEL: POLLUTION ATMOSPHERIC, FUMEE ET SO2. MAANDBERICHT: LUCHTVERONTREINIGING, ROOK EN SO2. 2225

0524-7810 See OBSERVATIONS CLIMATOLOGIQUES. 1433

0524-7837 See BULLETIN DU JARDIN BOTANIQUE NATIONAL DE BELGIQUE. 504

0524-787X See BULLETIN D'OBSERVATIONS: MAREES TERRESTRES. WAARNEMINGSBERICHTEN: AARDGETIJDEN. 1352

0524-8140 See CERCETARI METALURGICE. INSTITUL DE CERCETARI METALURGICE (BUCURESTI). 4000

0524-8159 See BULETINUL STIINTIFIC / INSTITUTUL DE CONSTRUCTII BUCURESTI. 2019

0524-8414 See GERMANISTIK (BERLIN). 3284

0524-8906 See PETOFI IRODALMI MUZEUM EVKONYVE, A. 3423

0524-8965 See ANNALES UNIVERSITATIS SCIENTIARUM BUDAPESTINENSIS DE ROLANDO EOTVOS NOMINATAE. SECTIO GEOGRAPHICA. 2554

0524-8981 See ANNALES UNIVERSITATIS SCIENTIARUM BUDAPESTINENSIS DE ROLANDO EOTVOS NOMINATAE. SECTIO HISTORICA. 2841

0524-899X See ANNALES UNIVERSITATIS SCIENTIARUM BUDAPESTINENSIS DE ROLANDO EOTVOS NOMINATAE. SECTIO IURIDICA. 2933

0524-9007 See ANNALES UNIVERSITATIS SCIENTIARUM BUDAPESTINENSIS DE ROLANDO EOTVOS NOMINATAE. SECTIO MATHEMATICA. 3493

0524-9023 See ANNALES UNIVERSITATIS SCIENTIARUM BUDAPESTINENSIS DE ROLANDO EOTVOS NOMINATAE. SECTIO PHILOSOPHICA ET SOCIOLOGICA. 4341

0524-904X See BUDAPESTI EOETVOES LORAND TUDOMANYEGYETEM ALLAM ES JOGTUDOMANYI KARANAK ACTAI. 2944

0524-9767 See BOLETIN DEL INSTITUTO DE HISTORIA ARGENTINA Y AMERICANA DOCTOR EMILIO RAVIGNANI. 2612

0525-0811 See IZVESTIIA. 5535

0525-0870 See IZVESTIIA NA NAUCHNIIA ARKHIV / BULGARSKA AKADEMIIA NA NAUKITE, TSENTRALNA BIBLIOTEKA SUS SLUZHBA ZA NAUCHNA INFORMATSIIA I NAUCHEN ARKHIV. 2481

0525-1044 See BULLETIN ANALYTIQUE D'HISTOIRE ROMAINE / UNIVERSITE DE STRASBOURG, GROUPE DE RECHERCHE D'HISTOIRE ROMAINE. 2612

0525-1133 See BULLETIN D'ARCHEOLOGIE ALGERIENNE. 262

0525-1249 See BULLETIN DES SOCIETES D'HISTOIRE ET D'ARCHEOLOGIE DE LA MEUSE. 2681

0525-1516 See BULLETIN OF TIBETOLOGY. 2647

0525-1885 See BUNGEI (TOKYO, JAPAN : 1962). 2502

0525-1931 See BUNSEKI KAGAKU. 1014

0525-2156 See BULLETIN TO MANAGEMENT. 939

0525-3292 See BYZANTINA VINDOBONENSIA. 2682

0525-4507 See BYZANTINA NEERLANDICA. 2682

0525-4663 See BASKETBALL CASE BOOK. 4886

0525-4787 See GEWASSERKUNDLICHER JAHRESBERICHT DES LANDES BERLIN. 1413

0525-5090 See BOTSWANA NOTES AND RECORDS. 2498

0525-5201 See GEOLOGY STUDIES. SPECIAL PUBLICATIONS. 1380

0525-552X See FAIR EMPLOYMENT PRACTICE CASES. 3148

0525-5708 See BARROCO. 316

0525-5791 See BERICHTE UBER DIE AUSGRABUNGEN IN HAITHABU. 261

0525-6097 See COOLIA. 452

0525-6240 See BULLETIN D'INFORMATION. INFORMATION BULLETIN. 5372

0525-7951 See CAHIERS DE LA RECHERCHE AGRONOMIQUE, LES. 71

0525-9363 See TRANSPORTS EN EUROPE; BIBLIOGRAPHIE, LES. 5402

0526-6459 See C H P C PROGRESS. 2816

0526-6742 See C.O.A. BULLETIN. 4770

0526-6769 See CORE. 4506

0526-717X See CACTACEAS Y SUCULENTAS MEXICANAS. 505

0526-7196 See CACTUS AND SUCCULENT JOURNAL WOOLLAHRA. 2411

0526-7463 See CADRES. 781

0526-765X See CAHIERS BLEUS VETERINAIRES, LES. 5507

0526-8443 See CAHIERS PERCHERONS. 2514

0526-9938 See ARCHEOLOGICAL REPORT. 259

0527-0014 See SPECIAL REPORT / CALIFORNIA DIVISION OF MINES AND GEOLOGY. 1398

0527-0936 See ECONOMIC RESEARCH OF INTEREST TO AGRICULTURE / UNIVERSITY OF CALIFORNIA, DIVISION OF AGRICULTURAL SCIENCES, AGRICULTURAL EXPERIMENT STATION. 153

0527-1622 See CALIFORNIA TURFGRASS CULTURE. 2411

0527-2009 See CALIFORNIA BUILDER. 606

0527-2173 See CALIFORNIA COURTS COMMENTARY. 3139

0527-2181 See CALIFORNIA FRUIT & NUT ACREAGE. 166

0527-3277 See CALIFORNIA TOMATO GROWER, THE. 166

0527-4257 See CAMEROUN AGRICOLE, PASTORAL ET FORESTIER, LE. 71

0527-4664 See ANNUAL REPORT TO THE MINISTER OF AGRICULTURE (AGRICULTURAL STABILIZATION BOARD). 61

0527-4974 See CONSTRUCTION IN CANADA (ANNUAL ED.). 632

0527-5318 See GAS UTILITIES. TRANSPORT AND DISTRIBUTION SYSTEMS. 4258

0527-5369 See GREENHOUSE INDUSTRY. 2417

0527-575X See MONTHLY PRODUCTION OF SOFT DRINKS. 2369

0527-5911 See OILS AND FATS. 180

0527-6268 See STOCKS OF FOOD COMMODITIES IN COLD STORAGE AND OTHER WAREHOUSES. 199

0527-6411 See VENDING MACHINE OPERATORS. 958

0527-6497 See CANADIAN CIVIL AIRCRAFT REGISTER. 15

0527-6942 See STATISTICAL BASEBOOK SERIES - ECONOMICS SERVICE, DEPARTMENT OF FISHERIES OF CANADA. 2317

0527-7507 See LIST OF LICENCES UNDER THE EXCISE TAX ACT. 690

0527-7884 See INCOME TAX ACT ... ANNOTATED. 2981

0527-7892 See MARTIN'S ANNUAL CRIMINAL CODE. 3108

0527-8503 See REPORT - ROYAL COMMISSION ON ENERGY (OTTAWA). 1955

0527-8759 See CANADIAN ANALYST, THE. 2529

0527-9275 See DIRECTORY OF CANADIAN CHARTERED ACCOUNTANTS. 743

0527-9860 See CANADIAN UNITARIAN, THE. 4942

0528-0397 See INVESTIGATIONAL REPORT - DEPARTMENT OF NATURE CONSERVATION. 4166

0528-0559 See CAPITAL BAPTIST. 5057

0528-0761 See BOLETIN DE LA BIBLIOTECA DE LOS TRIBUNALES DEL DISTRITO FEDERAL FUNDACION ROJAS ASTUDILLO. 3196

0528-1725 See CAROLINA JOURNAL OF PHARMACY, THE. 4295

0528-2195 See MATHEMATICA BOHEMICA / CZECHOSLOVAK ACADEMY OF SCIENCES. 3518

0528-2276 See CASSELMAN CHRONICLE, THE. 2727

0528-2616 See CATALYST. (EVANSTON). 1731

0528-3280 See CAUCHO. 5075

0528-3647 See CELTIBERIA. 2613

0528-3701 See TECHNICAL REPORT - CEMENT AND CONCRETE ASSOCIATION. 2594

0528-4082 See REPORT AND ACCOUNTS - CENTRAL ELECTRICITY GENERATING BOARD (LONDON). 707

0528-4651 See CIRCULAIRES DU CENTRE DE RECHERCHES ET D'ETUDES OCEANOGRAPHIQUES. I.T. 1447

0528-5666 See SETTIMANE DI STUDIO DEL CENTRO ITALIANO DI STUDI SULL'ALTO MEDIOEVO. 2709

0528-7928 See CHALLENGE (HARRISBURG), THE. 5277

0528-9017 See CHEJIANG NONGYE KEXUE. 73

0528-9300 See REPORT - CHEMICAL BANK NEW YORK TRUST COMPANY. 807

0528-9432 See CHEMICHE VLAKNA. 5348

0528-9599 See CHEMUNG HISTORICAL JOURNAL, THE. 2727

0528-9688 See ZHENGLUN ZHOUKAN. 3356

0529-0279 See CHI-LIN TA HSUEH TZU JAN KO HSUEH HSUEH PAO. 5093

0529-0554 See JIAOYU YU WENHUA. 1755

0529-0740 See URBAN RENEWAL PROGRESS REPORT. 2838

0529-0937 See OCCASIONAL PAPERS - CHICAGO. UNIVERSITY. INDUSTRIAL RELATIONS CENTER. 1696

0529-097X See LAW SCHOOL RECORD. 2997

0529-1356 See CHIEH P'OU HSUEH PAO. 3679

0529-1399 See JIANZHU XUEBAO. 301

0529-1488 See CHIESA E QUARTIERE; QUADERNI DI ARCHITETTURA SACRA. 295

0529-1526 See CHIH WU FEN LEI HSUEH PAO. 506

0529-1542 See ZHIWU BAOHU. 531

0529-2263 See INFORME. 617

0529-3189 See CHINA LETTER. 657

0529-3294 See CHINE EN CONSTRUCTION, LA. 607

0529-472X See CHRISTIAN THEOLOGICAL SEMINARY BULLETIN. 4946

0529-5025 See CHRYSOSTOM : QUARTERLY BULLETIN OF THE SOCIETY OF ST JOHN CHRYSOSTOM. 4946

0529-5127 See HSU MU SHOU I HSUEH PAO / CHUNG-KUO HSU MU SHOU I HSUEH HUI. 5511

0529-5661 See CHUNG-HUA FANG SHE HSUEH TSA CHIH. 3939

0529-567X See CHUNG-HUA FU CHAN KO TSA CHIH. 3758

0529-5769 See ZHONGHUA MINGUO MAZUI XUEHUI ZAZHI. 3654

0529-5807 See CHUNG-HUA PING LI HSUEH TSA CHIH. 3893

0529-5815 See CHUNG-HUA WAI KAO TSA CHIH. 3962

0529-5858 See CHUNG I TSA CHIH. 3564

0529-5920 See CHUNG-KUO CHING CHI / THE CHINA ECONOMIST. 1470

0529-6005 See ZHONGGUO SHOUYI ZAZHI. 5528

0529-603X See CHUNG-KUO FU NU / ZHONGGUO FUNU. 5553

0529-6315 See CHUNG-KUO LIN YEH / ZHONGGUO LINYE / FORESTRY OF CHINA. 2377

0529-6463 See CHUNG-KUO SHU-HUA. 377

0529-6471 See CHUNG-KUO SHUI CHAN. 2299

0529-6676 See REPORT - CHUNG YANG YIN HANG. 807

0529-6838 See CHUOKORON. 5195

0529-7281 See CIENCIA AL DIA. 5094

0529-7451 See CINA. 2503

0529-777X See CINQUIEME SAISON. 3340

0529-7788 See CIRCE: CAHIERS DU CENTRE DE RECHERCHE SUR L'IMAGINAIRE. 4580

0529-8172 See REPORT. 2833

0529-9268 See CLEAN WATERS FOR OHIO. 2190

0529-9608 See CLINICA GINECOLOGICA, LA. 3758

0530-0371 See ANNUAL REPORT - SUGARCANE BREEDING INSTITUTE. 163

0530-0495 See COIR. 5349

0530-6442 See COLLANA DI STUDI DI STORIA E POLITICA AFRICANA. 2498

0530-7058 See COLLECTANEA HIBERNICA. 2684

0530-7678 See COLLECTION DES DICTIONNAIRES TECHNIQUES. 4253

0530-7848 See COLLECTION ESSAIS SUR L'HISTOIRE DU PROTESTANTISME FRANCAIS. 5058

0530-8089 See COLLECTION IDEES. 4344

0530-9190 See SITUATION. 3352

0530-9220 See COLLECTION STENDHALIENNE. 3376

0530-9581 See COLLEGE BOARD NEWS. 1816

0530-9751 See COLLEGIATE BASEBALL. 4890

0530-9778 See ATTI - COLLEGIO REGIONALE LOMBARDO DEGLI ARCHITETTI. 292

0530-9794 See VEROFFENTLICHUNGEN. 2714

0531-0059 See ACTES DU ... COLLOQUE INTERNATIONAL D'ETUDES GAULOISES, CELTIQUES ET PROTOCELTIQUES. 2609

0531-0067 See ACTES - COLLOQUE INTERNATIONAL D'HISTOIRE MARITIME. 4174

0531-0350 See ABHANDLUNGEN AUS DEM INDUSTRIESEMINAR DER UNIVERSITAT ZU KOLN. 1806

0531-1888 See ETUDES MUSULMANES. 5042

0531-1950 See ETUDES PRELIMINAIRES AUX RELIGIONS ORIENTALES DANS L'EMPIRE ROMAIN. 4956

0531-1969 See ETUDES REBELAISIENNES. 3386

0531-1985 See SPISY UNIVERZITY J. E. PURKYNE V BRNE, FILOZOFICKA FAKULTA. ETUDES ROMANES DE BRNO. 3323

0531-2051 See ETUDES TOGOLAISES. 2639

0531-2167 See EUPHORION. BEIHEFTE. 3386

0531-2450 See EUROPAISCHE SAGEN. 4957

0531-2485 See EUROPARECHT. 2967

0531-4119 See EFTA TRADE LES ECHANGES DE L'AELE. 832

0531-4127 See ANNUAL REPORT OF THE EUROPEAN FREE TRADE ASSOCIATION. 823

0531-4348 See LIST OF WORKING DOCUMENTS. 4662

0531-4577 See EUROPEAN TAXATION. SUPPLEMENTARY SERVICE. 4722

0531-4631 See EUROPEEN, L'. 2516

0531-495X See EVERYMAN'S SCIENCE. 5104

0531-5131 See INTERNATIONAL CONGRESS SERIES. 3588

0531-531X See EXERCISE EXCHANGE. 1894

0531-5344 See REPORT - AGRICULTURAL ECONOMICS UNIT. UNIVERSITY OF EXETER. 125

0531-5565 See EXPERIMENTAL GERONTOLOGY. 3751

0531-6243 See EXTRA VERSE. 3463

0531-7347 See EUROPAISCHE HOCHSCHULSCHRIFTEN. REIHE 6, PSYCHOLOGIE. 4586

0531-7479 See EUROPHYSICS NEWS. 4402

0531-8262 See ECONOMIC GEOLOGY (MONTPELIER, VT.). 1374

0531-8335 See REPORT - EDUCATION COMMISSION OF THE STATES. 1844

0531-8351 See EDUCATIONAL TRENDS, THE. 1743

0531-836X See EDUCATOR'S WORLD. 1743

0531-8874 See EARTH SCIENCE SERIES. 1354

0531-8955 See ECONOMIC REVIEW (KARACHI). 1558

0531-9110 See EKOLOGIJA. 2215

0531-9145 See EKSPRES. 2503

0531-9218 See ELEKTRONIKER. 2052

0531-9293 See EDRA; PROCEEDINGS OF THE ANNUAL ENVIRONMENTAL DESIGN RESEARCH ASSOCIATION CONFERENCE. 298

0531-9684 See FOLK MUSIC JOURNAL. 4118

0531-9811 See CATALOGHI DI MOSTRE. 347

0531-9870 See ANNALI DELLA FONDAZIONE LUIGI EINAUDI. 5190

0532-0488 See WORLD SOIL RESOURCES REPORTS. 191

0532-0984 See FOOD SCIENCE AND TECHNOLOGY: A SERIES OF MONOGRAPHS. 2340

0532-0992 See FOOD SERVICE RESEARCH ABSTRACTS. 2340

0532-1328 See FOREIGN REPORT. 4474

0532-1697 See FORM (CAMBRIDGE, ENGLAND). 350

0532-1700 See FORM (ALEXANDRIA). 4565

0532-2154 See FORSCHUNGEN ZUR KIRCHEN- UND DOGMENGESCHICHTE. 4959

0532-2189 See FORSCHUNGEN ZUR KUNSTGESCHICHTE UND CHRISTLICHEN ARCHAOLOGIE. 350

0532-2197 See FORSCHUNGEN ZUR OBERRHEINISCHEN LANDESGESCHICHTE. 2688

0532-2243 See FORSCHUNGEN ZUR VOR- UND FURGESCHICHTE (LEIPZIG, 1955-). 2616

0532-226X See FORSCHUNGSBEITRAGE ZUR MUSIKWISSENSCHAFT. 4118

0532-2499 See MEDDELANDE / FORSKNINGSSTIFTELSEN SKOGSARBETEN. 2387

0532-260X See BOLETIM DE ANTROPOLOGIA. 232

0532-2669 See FORTSCHRITT-BERICHTE DER VDI-ZEITSCHRIFTEN. REIHE 4, BAUINGENIEURWESEN. 2023

0532-3010 See FOTOMUVESZET. 4369

0532-3215 See FOUR SEASONS, THE. 511

0532-4092 See POLITIQUE ETRANGERE DE LA FRANCE, LA. 4491

0532-5692 See FODOR'S FRANCE. 5471

0532-579X See FRANCISCAN, THE. 4959

0532-582X See FRANK GERSTEIN LECTURES, THE. 211

0532-5838 See FRANK W. PIERCE MEMORIAL LECTURES, THE. 1675

0532-5854 See DEUTSCHE NATIONALBIBLIOGRAPHIE UND BIBLIOGRAPHIE DER IM AUSLAND ERSCHIENENEN DEUTSCHSPRACHIGEN VEROFFENTLICHUNGEN. REIHE D, MONOGRAPHIEN UND PERIODIKA -- HALBJAHRESVERZEICHNIS. 4813

0532-6028 See FRANKFURTER WIRTSCHAFTS- UND SOZIALWISSENSCHAFTLICHE STUDIEN. 5200

0532-6036 See BIBLIOGRAPHIC SERIES - FRANKLIN INSTITUTE, PHILADELPHIA, PA. 409

0532-6060 See FRANCUZSKIJ EZEGODNIK. 2688

0532-6109 See STATISTICS OF FRATERNAL BENEFIT SOCIETIES. 2898

0532-6656 See QUID?. 1928

0532-6729 See FRENCH FOREIGN POLICY. 4522

0532-6826 See FRENCH SCIENCE NEWS. 5106

0532-7091 See FCL NEWSLETTER. 4647

0532-7334 See FROM THE SOURDOUGH CROCK. 2320

0532-744X See FRONTIERS IN FUEL CELLS. 2055

0532-7679 See FRUSTULA ENTOMOLOGICA. 5584

0532-7865 See FUENTES E INVESTIGACIONES PARA LA HISTORIA DEL PERU. SERIE : TEXTOS CRITICOS. 2734

0532-8381 See MONOGRAFIA - FUNDACAO GETULIO VARGAS. 5233

0532-8500 See ANALES DE LA FUNDACION JUAN MARCH. 4334

0532-8721 See FUNKCIALAJ EKVACIOJ. 3506

0532-8799 See FUNTAI OYOBI FUMMATSU YAKIN. 4002

0532-9175 See A. A.'S FAR EAST BUSINESSMAN'S DIRECTORY. 821

0532-9329 See PRESIDENT'S REPORT - FLORIDA. ATLANTIC UNIVERSITY, BOCA RATON. 1842

0532-940X See EIFAC TECHNICAL PAPER. 2300

0533-005X See FOUNDRY CATALOG FILE. 4002

0533-0130 See FRANKLIN LECTURES IN THE SCIENCES AND HUMANITIES, THE. 5200

0533-0300 See FARMAKOTERAPEUTICKE ZPRAVY SPOFA. SUPPLEMENTUM. 4305

0533-070X See FORUM FOR EKONOMI OCH TEKNIK. 5106

0533-0866 See FRANCE PAYS ARABES. 2651

0533-0939 See FAMILY FINDINGS. 2447

0533-1153 See FIZIOLOGICHESKI AKTIVNYE VESHCHESTVA. 455

0533-1242 See FOCUS (ROCKVILLE). 455

0533-1250 See FOOTNOTE (WASHINGTON). 4649

0533-2052 See GREAT WESTERN SERIES, THE. 2488

0533-2117 See ANNUAL ABSTRACT OF GREATER LONDON STATISTICS. 5321

0533-2508 See GREEN SHEET. 4071

0533-2869 See GREYFRIAR (LOUDONVILLE N.Y.). 3392

0533-3067 See GROSSEN DARSTELLUNGEN DER MUSIKGESCHICHTE IN BAROCK UND AUFKLARUNG, DIE. 4119

0533-3164 See GROUP ANALYSIS. 3926

0533-3350 See GRUNDLAGEN DER GERMANISTIK. 3284

0533-5051 See GUIDE (TORONTO). 1676

0533-5248 See GUIDE TO AMERICAN DIRECTORIES. 1926

0533-5752 See ANNUAL ADMINISTRATION REPORT ON SCHEDULED AREAS IN GUJARAT STATE. 2814

0533-5884 See SOCIO-ECONOMIC REVIEW: GUJARAT STATE. 1584

0533-652X See THESES PUBLICATION SERIES. 1850

0533-6562 See TRANSACTIONS / GULF COAST ASSOCIATION OF GEOLOGICAL SOCIETIES. 1400

0533-6724 See GUNMA SYMPOSIA ON ENDOCRINOLOGY. 3730

0533-6961 See GUYANA YEAR BOOK. 2499

0533-7127 See GYPSY LOU SERIES. 2488

0533-7224 See GANDHI MEMORIAL LECTURE. 2651

0533-7275 See GENEALOGICAL REFERENCE BUILDERS NEWSLETTER. 2450

0533-7534 See GERMAN PATENTS GAZETTE: SECTION II, ELECTRICAL. 2056

0533-7542 See GERMAN PATENTS GAZETTE : SECTION III, MECHANICAL & GENERAL. 1304

0533-8301 See JOURNAL OF THE GEOLOGICAL SOCIETY OF IRAQ. 1385

0533-9480 See BERICHTE DER GESELLSCHAFT FUER MATHEMATIK UND DATENVERARBEITUNG. 3497

0533-9529 See KYOIKUGAKUBU KENKYU HOKOKU. SHIZEN KAGAKU (GIFU). 5124

0533-9855 See GUIDE TO STATIONARY PHASES FOR GAS CHROMATOGRAPHY. 4259

0534-0012 See GENETIKA. 546

0534-0020 See GENIE, THE. 2451

0534-0349 See GHANA JOURNAL OF EDUCATION. 1748

0534-0403 See GOTTINGER ARBEITEN ZUR GEOLOGIE UND PALAONTOLOGIE. 1381

0534-0489 See GRI NEWSLETTER. 4565

0534-0713 See RAPPORT D'ACTIVITE - INSTITUT D'EMISSION DES DEPARTEMENTS D'OUTRE-MER. 1580

0534-1299 See MONOGRAPHIE - INSTITUT INTERUNIVERSITAIRE DES SCIENCES NUCLEAIRES. 4448

0534-4255 See INSTRUMENTA PATRISTICA. 4965

0534-4352 See YEAR BOOK - INSURANCE ACCOUNTING AND STATISTICAL ASSOCIATION. 2896

0534-4638 See INTER ALIA. 2983

0534-6541 See INTERNATIONAL AFFAIRS REPORTS FROM QUAKER WORKERS. 4524

0534-669X See PROGRAM AND ABSTRACTS OF PAPERS - INTERNATIONAL ASSOCIATION FOR DENTAL RESEARCH. 1333

0534-7750 See INTERNATIONAL CAMELLIA SOCIETY JOURNAL, THE. 2420

0534-8145 See INTERNATIONAL COAL PREPARATION CONGRESS. 2140

0534-8706 See PROCEEDINGS. 4417

0534-9303 See HORMONAL STEROIDS : PROCEEDINGS. 3584

0534-9354 See PROCEEDINGS OF THE INTERNATIONAL CONGRESS ON MEDICAL RECORDS. 3630

0535-1219 See GENERAL REPORT / COMMITTEE ON WORK ON PLANTATIONS. 1675

0535-1219 See NOTE ON THE PROCEEDINGS / COMMITTEE ON WORK ON PLANTATIONS. 1695

0535-1588 See STATISTICAL YEARBOOK / INTERNATIONAL NORTH PACIFIC FISHERIES COMMISSION. 2317

0535-1634 See INTERNATIONAL OIL AND GAS DEVELOPMENT. 4283

0535-1634 See INTERNATIONAL OIL AND GAS DEVELOPMENT YEARBOOK. PART 1: EXPLORATION. 4261

0535-1774 See WORLD LIST OF FAMILY PLANNING ADDRESSES / INTERNATIONAL PLANNED PARENTHOOD FEDERATION. 591

0535-3378 See NOTES ON TIN. 4014

0535-4900 See INTISARI. 2505

0535-5133 See INVESTIGACION CLINICA. 3590

0535-5729 See JOURNAL OF THE IOWA ARCHEOLOGICAL SOCIETY. 272

0535-8361 See REVIEW OF THE GEOGRAPHICAL INSTITUTE OF THE UNIVERSITY OF ISTANBUL. 2574

0535-8418 See ISTANBUL UNIVERSITESI ORMAN FAKULTESI DERGISI. SERI A. 2385

0535-899X See ISTRUZIONE TECNICA E PROFESSIONALE 1959. 1831

0536-101X See IZVESTIJA VYSSIH UCEBNYH ZAVEDENIJ. GEODEZIAJA I AEROFOTOSEMKI. 2566

0536-1028 See IZVESTIJA VYSSIH UCEBNYH ZAVEDENIJ. GORNYJ ZURNAL. 2141

0536-1036 See IZVESTIIA VYSSHIKH UCHEBNYKH ZAVEDENII. LESNOI ZHURNAL. 2385

0536-1044 See IZVESTIJA VYSSIH UCEBNYH ZAVEDENIJ. MASINOSTROENIE. 2117

0536-1613 See SONDERSCHRIFT DES IFO-INSTITUTS FUR WIRTSCHAFTSFORSCHUNG. 1521

0536-1699 See IGY OCEANOGRAPHY REPORT. 1450

0536-1737 See IIC NEWS. 2195

0536-1761 See IIPA NEWSLETTER. 4655

0536-2067 See ISO MEMENTO. 4030

0536-2180 See TO CHO, I. 3748

0536-2288 See RESEARCH BULLETIN (CENTRE OF ARABIC DOCUMENTATION). 2770

0536-2326 See OCCASIONAL PUBLICATION / INSTITUTE OF AFRICAN STUDIES, UNIVERSITY OF IBADAN. 1093

0536-2520 See IBERO-AMERICANA PRAGENSIA. 2738

0536-3012 See JOURNAL OF THE IDAHO ACADEMY OF SCIENCE. 5120

0536-3683 See IKUSHUGAKU ZASSHI. 94

0536-3942 See DIRECTORY OF HEALTH CARE FACILITIES. 3779

0536-4132 See ILLINOIS NATURAL HISTORY SURVEY REPORTS, THE. 4166

0536-4604 See PAPERS PRESENTED AT THE ALLERTON PARK INSTITUTE. 3240

0536-5465 See IMAGE (ROCHESTER). 4370

0536-5708 See IMPARCIAL [MICROFORM], EL. 5802

0536-647X See INDEX OF ECONOMIC ARTICLES IN JOURNALS AND COLLECTIVE VOLUMES. 1533

0536-6712 See MEMOIR (ANTHROPOLOGICAL SURVEY OF INDIA). 241

0536-7093 See COFFEE STATISTICS. 152

0536-7832 See INDIAN ARCHAEOLOGY. 270

0536-8502 See BULLETIN ON FOOD STATISTICS. 2329

0536-8510 See INDIAN AGRICULTURE IN BRIEF. 94

0536-8782 See BULLETINS OF THE GEOLOGICAL SURVEY OF INDIA. SERIES A : ECONOMIC GEOLOGY. 1371

0536-9258 See FOREIGN AFFAIRS RECORD. 4522

0536-9290 See BUDGET / GOVERNMENT OF INDIA, MINISTRY OF FINANCE. 4714

0537-0078 See INDIAN TEXTILE BULLETIN. 5351

0537-0094 See BULLETIN OF THE OIL AND NATURAL GAS COMMISSION. 4252

0537-0280 See REPORT - JOINT COMMITTEE ON OFFICES OF PROFIT. 4680

0537-0507 See RUBBER BOARD BULLETIN. 5077

0537-0728 See UNIVERSITY DEVELOPMENT IN INDIA; BASIC FACTS AND FIGURES. 1852

0537-1309 See I.C.A.R. TECHNICAL BULLETIN (AGRIC). 93

0537-1643 See INDIAN FISHERIES BULLETIN. 2305

0537-1848 See MONTHLY PUBLIC OPINION SURVEYS. 2526

0537-197X See INDIAN JOURNAL OF AGRONOMY. 95

0537-1996 See INDIAN JOURNAL OF EXTENSION EDUCATION. 1752

0537-2003 See INDIAN JOURNAL OF FISHERIES. 2305

0537-2011 See INDIAN JOURNAL OF GEOGRAPHY, THE. 2566

0537-2038 See INDIAN JOURNAL OF MECHANICS AND MATHEMATICS. 3508

0537-2429 See INDIAN POLICE JOURNAL, THE. 3166

0537-2585 See JOURNAL OF THE INDIAN STATISTICAL ASSOCIATION. 5330

0537-2631 See INDIAN SUGAR YEAR BOOK. 2344

0537-2682 See INDIAN WORKER, THE. 1678

0537-2704 See INDIAN YEAR BOOK OF INTERNATIONAL AFFAIRS, THE. 4524

0537-2925 See GEOLOGICAL SURVEY MINERAL ECONOMICS SERIES. 1378

0537-2933 See GEOLOGICAL SURVEY SPECIAL REPORT. 1379

0537-3247 See PROCEEDINGS / INDIANA ACADEMY OF THE SOCIAL SCIENCES. 5213

0537-3468 See INDICADORES DE COYUNTURA. 1534

0537-3522 See INDICE HISTORICO ESPANOL. 2635

0537-5762 See INDUSTRIELLE WELT. 5203

0537-6041 See INFORMACIONES GEOGRAFICAS. 2566

0537-6554 See INDIAN JOURNAL OF ENGLISH STUDIES. 3396

0537-6998 See INGU MUNJE NONJIP. 4553

0537-7250 See INNSBRUCKER BEITRAEGE ZUR KULTURWISSENSCHAFT. 5247

0537-7560 See CONTRIBUTION - INSTITUT D'ASTRONOMIE ET DE GEOPHYSIQUE GEORGES LEMAITRE. MEDEDELINGEN VAN HET ASTRONOMISCH INSTITUUT VAN DE KATHOLIEKE UNIVERSITEIT LEUVEN. 394

0537-7919 See VEROFFENTLICHUNGEN. 5007

0537-7927 See VORTRAGE. 2715

0537-796X See IWL-FORUM. 5535

0537-9032 See SYMPOSIA OF THE INSTITUTE OF BIOLOGY. 474

0537-9342 See SELECTED LIST OF ACQUISITIONS CATALOGED. 3047

0537-9350 See LIST OF WORTHWHILE LIFE AND HEALTH INSURANCE BOOKS, A. 2887

0537-9741 See EXPLORATION AND ECONOMICS OF THE PETROLEUM INDUSTRY. 4256

0537-9989 See IEE CONFERENCE PUBLICATION. 2057

0538-1428 See REVISTA DEL INSTITUTO MEXICANO DEL PETROLEO. 4277

0538-1983 See ANALES TOLEDANOS. 2673

0538-2351 See INSTRUMENT MAINTENANCE MANAGEMENT. 2065

0538-2629 See INSURANCE MARKET PLACE, THE. 2883

0538-2793 See MEETING - INTER-AFRICAN CONFERENCE ON RURAL WELFARE. 5296

0538-446X See MEMBERSHIP DIRECTORY - INTERNATIONAL ASSOCIATION OF ASSESSING OFFICERS (1977). 4737

0538-4680 See MITTEILUNGEN - INTERNATIONALEN VEREINIGUNG FUER THEORETISCHE UND ANGEWANDTE LIMNOLOGIE. 1416

0538-4753 See INFORMATION BULLETIN / INTERNATIONAL ASTRONOMICAL UNION. 395

0538-4761 See INFORMATION BULLETIN ON VARIABLE STARS / COMMISSION 27 OF THE I.A.U. 395

0538-5318 See ICASALS PUBLICATION. 2565

0538-5865 See BULLETIN OF THE INTERNATIONAL COMMITTEE ON URGENT ANTHROPOLOGICAL AND ETHNOLOGICAL RESEARCH. 233

0538-6012 See TRANSACTIONS OF THE INTERNATIONAL CONFERENCE OF ORIENTALISTS IN JAPAN. 3329

0538-6349 See INTERNATIONAL CONGRESS CALENDAR. 4657

0538-6829 See INTERNATIONAL COTTON INDUSTRY STATISTICS. 5360

0538-6918 See CODATA NEWSLETTER. 5095

0538-7078 See ANNUAL MEMENTO / INTERNATIONAL DAIRY FEDERATION. 191

0538-7094 See INTERNATIONAL STANDARD FIL-IDF. 841

0538-8007 See INTERNATIONAL INVENTORY OF MUSICAL SOURCES. 4123

0538-8066 See INTERNATIONAL JOURNAL OF CHEMICAL KINETICS. 1053

0538-8228 See INTERNATIONAL JOURNAL OF SLAVIC LINGUISTICS AND POETICS. 3287

0538-8295 See COST OF SOCIAL SECURITY. LE COUT DE LA SECURITE SOCIALE. EL COSTO DE LA SEGURIDAD SOCIAL, THE. 5281

0538-8325 See LABOUR-MANAGEMENT RELATIONS SERIES. 1686

0538-8341 See SUMMARY OF INFORMATION RELATING TO THE SUBMISSION TO THE COMPETENT AUTHORITIES OF CONVENTIONS AND RECOMMENDATIONS ADOPTED BY THE INTERNATIONAL LABOR CONFERENCE (ARTICLE 19 OF THE CONSTITUTION). 1712

0538-8643 See DOCUMENTATION - INTERNATIONAL MARITIME COMMITTEE. 4176

0538-8759 See PAMPHLET SERIES - INTERNATIONAL MONETARY FUND. 1511

0538-8910 See REPORT OF THE ... SUMMER SESSION OF THE INTERNATIONAL OLYMPIC ACADEMY. 1857

0538-9089 See FAMILY PLANNING IN FIVE CONTINENTS. 588

0538-9143 See COMBINED PROCEEDINGS / INTERNATIONAL PLANT PROPAGATORS' SOCIETY. 2412

0538-9143 See COMBINED PROCEEDINGS - INTERNATIONAL PLANT PROPAGATORS' SOCIETY. 2412

0538-9992 See INTERNATIONAL SERIES OF MONOGRAPHS ON ELECTROMAGNETIC WAVES. 2067

0539-0184 See SOCIAL SCIENCE INFORMATION. 5220

0539-0281 See NEWS / INTERNATIONAL SOCIETY FOR ROCK MECHANICS. 1389

0539-1318 See REVIEW OF THE WORLD WHEAT SITUATION. 203

0539-1849 See INTERNATIONALES KUNST-ADRESSBUCH. 334

0539-242X See INVESTIGACIONES Y ENSAYOS. 2739

0539-2896 See MEMMINGER GESCHICHTSBLATTER. 2698

0539-4457 See METAL. 4009

0539-4511 See METAL/CENTER NEWS. 4009

0539-6115 See BOLETIN MEDICO DEL HOSPITAL INFANTIL DE MEXICO (SPANISH EDITION). 3901

0539-6476 See REPORT OF THE SENATE DELEGATION ON THE MEETING-MEXICO-UNITED STATES INTERPARLIAMENTARY GROUP. DELEGATION FROM THE UNITED STATES. 4533

0539-7413 See MICHIGAN HEALTH STATISTICS. 4810

0539-7545 See BULLETIN - MICHIGAN. GEOLOGICAL SURVEY DIVISION. 1369

0539-8908 See MICHIGAN SPORTSMAN (OSHKOSH WIS.). 4874

0540-0163 See MIKROELEMENTY V SSSR : BIULLETEN VSESOIUZNOI KOORDINATSONNOI KOMISSII PO MIKROELEMENTAM / AKADEMIIA NAUK LATVIISKOI SSR, INSTITUT BIOLOGII. 465

0540-049X See ANNALI DELLA FACOLTA DI AGRARIA UNIVERSITA CATTOLICA DEL SACRO CUORE MILANO. 59

0540-1259 See MINAMI OSAKA BYOIN IGAKU ZASSHI. 3617

0540-1437 See MINERALOGICA ET PETROGRAPHICA ACTA. 1441

0540-1887 See BIENNIAL REPORT - STATE OF MINNESOTA, DEPARTMENT OF CIVIL SERVICE. 4701

0540-2239 See UNIVERSITY OF MINNESOTA LAW SCHOOL NEWS. 3069

0540-2239 See MINNESOTA LAW ALUMNI NEWS. 1102

0540-3391 See MISKOLCI HERMAN OTTO MUZEUM KOZLEMENYEI, A. 4091

0540-3820 See DIRECTORY OF MISSISSIPPI ELECTIVE OFFICIALS. 4643

0540-3995 See MISSISSIPPI GENEALOGICAL EXCHANGE. 2461

0540-4568 See MISUL CHARYO. 374

0540-4894 See MIYAGI-KEN NOGYO TANKI DAIGAKU GAKUJUTSU HOKOKU. 109

0540-4932 See MIYAZAKI DAIGAKU KOGAKUBU KENKYU HOKOKU. 1988

0540-6021 See MOLKEREITECHNIK. 197

0540-7109 See REPORT - OFFICE OF THE STATE CO-ORDINATOR OF INDIAN AFFAIRS (MONTANA). 2272

0540-7575 See BULLETIN DU MUSEE INGRES. 4085

0540-8059 See MONTHLY LETTER ABOUT EVANGELISM. LETTRE MENSUELLE SUR L'EVANGELISATION, A. 4979

0540-8539 See MONUMENTS HISTORIQUES DE SEINE ET MARNE. 304

0540-8644 See BULLETIN - MORAVIAN THEOLOGICAL SEMINARY, THE. 4941

0540-889X See MORPHOLOGIAI ES IGAZSAGUGYI ORVOSI SZEMLE. 466

0540-9691 See NAUCHNYE TRUDY / MOSKOVSKII LESOTEKHNICHESKII INSTITUT. 2388

0541-1025 See TRUDY - VSESOJUZNYJ NAUCNO-ISSLEDOVATELSKIJ INSTITUT GIDROGEOLOGII INZENERNOJ GEOLOGII. 1400

0541-2331 See MITTEILUNGEN DER INTERNATIONALEN STIFTUNG MOZARTEUM. 4131

0541-2439 See MUEMLEKVEDELEM. 275

0541-3869 See MUSHROOM NEWS. 179

0541-4024 See MUSIC THEORY TRANSLATION SERIES. 4135

0541-4393 See PROCEEDINGS OF THE MUSKEG RESEARCH CONFERENCE. 2573

0541-4938 See INOCULUM (ITHACA, N.Y.). 5114

0541-5357 See MBI'S INDIAN INDUSTRIES ANNUAL. 1618

0541-5489 See MLA NEWS. 3232

0541-623X See KEITH CALLARD LECTURES. 3401

0541-6256 See CLIMATOLOGICAL BULLETIN (MONTREAL). 1422

0541-6329 See SOIL MECHANICS SERIES (MONTREAL, QUEBEC). 2031

0541-6388 See MACHINE BUILDING INDUSTRY. 2120

0541-6620 See MADAME AU FOYER. 5560

0541-721X See MAJALAH ILMU-ILMU SASTRA INDONESIA. 5251

0541-7406 See MAJALAH PERUSAHAAN GULA. 106

0541-7562 See BULLETIN OF THE INSTITUTE OF TRADITIONAL CULTURES. 5194

0541-8585 See REVISTA DEL INSTITUTO EGIPCIO DE ESTUDIOS ISLAMICOS EN MADRID. 2705

0541-8771 See MAESTRO, THE. 4129

0541-881X See MAGAZIN ISTORIC. 2697

0541-9298 See MAGYAR NYELVJARASOK. 3409

0542-092X See MAHARDDHIKA PRADIPTA. 240

0542-0938 See MAHASAGAR. 1451

0542-1098 See MAINE SCHOOL STATISTICS. 1795

0542-1292 See BULLETIN / MAINE ARCHAEOLOGICAL SOCIETY. 263

0542-2108 See MAKEDONSKI FOLKLOR. 2322

0542-3007 See GUIDE TO AGRICULTURAL PRODUCTION IN MALAWI. 91

0542-335X See SINGAPORE JOURNAL OF LEGAL STUDIES. 3055

0542-3937 See MALAYSIA INDUSTRIAL DIGEST. 1573

0542-5174 See MANIFEST : A NEWSLETTER TO THE ASSOCIATES OF THE JAMES FORD BELL LIBRARY, WILSON LIBRARY, UNIVERSITY OF MINNESOTA, THE. 419

0542-5395 See ANNUAL REPORT - MANITOBA CROP INSURANCE CORPORATION. 2873

0542-5492 See DEBATES AND PROCEEDINGS - LEGISLATIVE ASSEMBLY OF MANITOBA. 4641

0542-5778 See MANORAMA YEAR BOOK. 1927

0542-5808 See MANPOWER JOURNAL. 1689

0542-6502 See MARBURGER BEITRAGE ZUR MUSIKFORSCHUNG. 4130

0542-657X See MARBURGER THEOLOGISCHE STUDIEN. 4975

0542-6669 See MARCHE ROMANE. 3301

0542-6685 See MARCHES PUBLICS. 4664

0542-6758 See MARE BALTICUM. 4481

0542-6766 See MAREES TERRESTRES BULLETIN D'INFORMATIONS. 1357

0542-7762 See MARXIST REVIEW, THE. 4543

0542-7770 See MARXISTISCHE BLATTER. 4543

0542-8297 See MARYLAND AGRI-ECONOMICS. 107

0542-8386 See PROCEEDINGS - MARYLAND NUTRITION CONFERENCE FOR FEED MANUFACTURERS. 121

0542-8645 See SHITSURYO BUNSEKI. 1019

0542-9315 See PUBLICATION - WATER RESOURCES RESEARCH CENTER, UNIVERSITY OF MASSACHUSETTS AT AMHERST. 5538

0542-9560 See SERIALS M.I.T. LIBRARIES. 3249

0542-9676 See MUNICIPAL SALARY SURVEY : BENCH-MARK JOBS. 1692

0543-0119 See MATERIAUX ET ORGANISMES. 464

0543-0941 See MATHEMATICS AND ITS APPLICATIONS. 3520

0543-1905 See PRACE. 1702

0543-1972 See MEASUREMENT TECHNIQUES. 2121

0543-2243 See MEDECINE DE L'HOMME PARIS. 3607

0543-2480 See MEDICAL ALMANAC. 3607

0543-2774 See DIRECTORY. 3206

0543-3533 See MEDIUM AEVUM (MUNICH). 3347

0543-3665 See INTERNATIONAL PROBLEMS (BEOGRAD). 5204

0543-3754 See MEET THE PRESS : AMERICA'S PRESS CONFERENCE OF THE AIR. 2746

0543-5056 See MERCHANT EXPLORER, THE. 846

0543-5749 See METALLURGICSKAJA I GORNORUDNAJA PROMYSLENNOST. 4010

0543-5757 See METALLURGIE (MONS). 4010

0543-5846 See METALURGIJA : CASOPIS FAKULTETA, INSTITUTA I ZELJEZARE SISAK. 4011

0543-6095 See METHODOLOGY AND SCIENCE. 5209

0543-615X See METMENYS. 3411

0543-6222 See METODY I PRAKTIKA OPREDELENI EFFEKTIVNOSTI KAPITALNYH VLOZENIJ I NOVOJ TEHNIKI. 906

0543-7369 See BOLETIN SEMESTRAL - COLEGIO DE MEXICO. 1089

0543-7652 See PALEONTOLOGIA MEXICANA. 4229

0543-8233 See RESEARCH REPORT FROM THE MICHIGAN STATE UNIVERSITY AGRICULTURAL EXPERIMENT STATION, EAST LANSING. 127

0543-8330 See TECHNICAL REPORT - STATE RESOURCES PLANNING PROGRAM. 1586

0543-8470 See MICHIGAN'S OIL AND GAS FIELDS. 4264

0543-8497 See REPORT OF INVESTIGATION - GEOLOGICAL SURVEY (LANSING). 1394

0543-8926 See WATER BULLETIN (EAST LANSING). 1418

0543-9728 See MICHIGAN ARCHAEOLOGIST. 274

0543-9833 See MICHIGAN JEWISH HISTORY. 5051

0543-9930 See MICHIGAN SLAVIC MATERIALS. 3302

0544-0424 See MIDDLE EAST ECONOMIC SURVEY. 4264

0544-0440 See MIDDLE EAST JOURNAL OF ANESTHESIOLOGY. 3683

0544-0653 See MID-STREAM (INDIANAPOLIS). 4977

0544-070X See NEWSLETTER OF THE MIDWEST CHINESE STUDENT & ALUMNI SERVICES. 1102

0544-1188 See MIGRATION TODAY. 1920

0544-1269 See MIKROELEKTRONIKA. 2072

0544-1358 See ANNUARIO - ISTITUTO "AGOSTINO GEMELLI" PER LO STUDIO SPERIMENTALE DI PROBLEMI SOCIALI DELL'INFORMAZIONE VISIVA. 1104

0544-1706 See MILCHWIRTSCHAFTLICHE BERICHTE AUS DEN BUNDESANSTALTEN WOLFPASSING UND ROTHOLZ. 196

0544-2486 See MINERAL EXPLORATION, MINING, AND PROCESSING PATENTS. 2144

0544-2540 See MINERALOGICAL JOURNAL. 1441

0544-3105 See INFORMATION CIRCULAR - MINNESOTA GEOLOGICAL SURVEY. 1382

0544-3466 See WRRC BULLETIN. 5549

0544-3482 See WATER NEWSLETTER. 5543

0544-3571 See MINNESOTA HISTORIC SITES PAMPHLET SERIES. 2746

0544-358X See MEMBER NEWS / MINNESOTA HISTORICAL SOCIETY. 2746

0544-3733 See MINOS. 3302

0544-408X See MISCELANEA DE ESTUDIOS ARABES Y HERBAICOS. 3302

0544-4128 See MISCELLANEA MEDIAEVALIA. 2699

0544-4225 See HERMAN OTTO MUZEUM EVKONYVE, A. 4088

0544-4462 See REGULAR MEETING - BOARD OF MISSISSIPPI LEVEE COMMISSIONERS. 4679

0544-4802 See MISSISSIPPI BIBLE AND CEMETERY RECORDS. 2460

0544-4969 See MISSISSIPPI'S BUSINESS POPULATION. 695

0544-4993 See COURTS & CLE BULLETIN / THE MISSOURI BAR. 2957

0544-540X See TRANSACTIONS OF THE MISSOURI ACADEMY OF SCIENCE. 5166

0544-6066 See MIYAZAKI DAIGAKU NOGAKUBU KENKYU JIHO. 109

0544-6538 See MODERN DISTRIBUTION MANAGEMENT. 879

0544-7259 See MOSSBAUER EFFECT DATA INDEX. 2073

0544-7267 See MOGUCNOSTI. 3413

0544-7631 See BULLETIN DU MUSEE D'ANTHROPOLOGIE PREHISTORIQUE DE MONACO. 232

0544-8379 See MONOGRAPHIES TECHNIQUES SUR L'UTILISATION DES ACIERS SPECIAUX. 4013

0544-9987 See MONUMENTA MONODICA MEDII AEVI. HRSG. IM AUFTRAG DES INSTITUTS FUER MUSIKFORSCHUNG REGENSBURG MIT UNTERSTUTZUNG DER MUSIKGESCHICHTLICHEN KOMMISSION VON BRUNO STABLEIN. 4132

0545-0004 See MONUMENTA MUSICAE SACRAE. 4132

0545-008X See MONUMENTI ETRUSCHI. 2699

0545-0152 See MOODY'S BANK AND FINANCE MANUAL. 800

0545-0217 See MOODY'S INDUSTRIAL MANUAL. 907

0545-0233 See MOODY'S MUNICIPAL & GOVERNMENT MANUAL. 907

0545-0241 See MOODY'S PUBLIC UTILITY MANUAL. 908

0545-025X See MOODY'S TRANSPORTATION MANUAL. 5387

0545-0659 See MORTGAGE AND REAL ESTATE INVESTMENT GUIDE. 4841

0545-106X See NEW ENGLAND ECONOMIC ALMANAC. 1507

0545-1671 See NEW HAMPSHIRE REGISTER, STATE YEAR-BOOK AND LEGISLATIVE MANUAL. 4669

0545-171X See NEW HAMPSHIRE TOWN & CITY. 4669

0545-2376 See REPORT OF THE STATE FARMLAND EVALUATION ADVISORY COMMITTEE. 126

0545-3038 See TECHNICAL REPORT (NEW MEXICO. STATE ENGINEER OFFICE). 2095

0545-3151 See NEW MEXICO ARCHITECTURE. 304

0545-4158 See RESEARCH REPORT - NEW YORK CITY COMMISSION ON HUMAN RIGHTS. 4512

0545-4441 See A.E. RES. 42

0545-6339 See NEW YORK SCHOOL DISTRICT LAW LETTER, THE. 3016

0545-6371 See DIRECTORY - THE NEW YORK SOCIETY OF CLINICAL PSYCHOLOGISTS, INC. 4585

0545-6533 See ANNUAL REPORT - NEW YORK STATE HOUSING FINANCE AGENCY. 2814

0545-7564 See ANNUAL REPORT - NEW ZEALAND COUNCIL FOR EDUCATIONAL RESEARCH. 1725

0545-7572 See NEW ZEALAND CURRENT TAXATION. 4738

0545-7904 See NEW ZEALAND SOIL NEWS. 179

0545-803X See CONTRIBUTIONS - THE DOVE MARINE LABORATORY. 554

0545-8269 See "NEWS" FOR THE CANADIAN RABBIT BREEDER. 216

0545-8617 See NEWS ON INDONESIA. 4530

0545-9370 See NIEDERSACHSISCHE DENKMALPFLEGE. 360

0546-0352 See NIHON UNIVERSITY JOURNAL OF MEDICINE, THE. 3622

0546-0794 See NIHON KASAI GAKKAI RONBUNSHU. 1989

0546-0921 See TENKI. 1436

0546-1731 See NIPPON KOKAN TECHNICAL REPORT. OVERSEAS. 4013

0546-1766 See NIPPON KOSHU EISEI ZASSHI. 4794

0546-1960 See NIVA : ORHAN HALOUNAHA PRALENNIA BELARUSKAHA HRAMADSKA-KULTURNAHA TAVARYSTVA. 2270

0546-4714 See BAR NOTES. 2940

0546-8175 See PRIX NOBEL, LES. 2852

0546-8191 See NOVENYTERMELES. 179

0546-9414 See NUMISMATICKY SBORNIK. 2782

0546-9422 See NUMIZMATICKE VIJESTI / HRVATSKO NUMIZMATICKO DRUSTVO. 2782

0546-9600 See NUNG YEH CHING CHI. 116

0547-0196 See NYIREGYHAZI JOSA ANDRAS MUZEUM EVKONYVE, A. 2323

0547-0684 See LIMESTONE (WASHINGTON). 4007

0547-1729 See NAIKA. 3800

0547-2016 See ANNALES LITTERAIRES. 3362

0547-2121 See ANNALI - SEZIONE ROMANZA. 3265

0547-2407 See NARA KYOIKU DAIGAKU KIYO. SHIZEN KAGAKU. 5130

0547-3128 See NASE SNAHY, CASOPIS STALEJ KONFERENCIE SLOVENSKYCH DEMOKRATICKYCH EXULANTOV. 1920

0547-3136 See NASE STARINE. 304

0547-3578 See NAECON. 29

0547-3616 See JOURNAL OF THE NATIONAL AGRICULTURAL SOCIETY OF CEYLON. 101

0547-4175 See DIRECTORY - NATIONAL ASSOCIATION OF SCHOOLS OF MUSIC. 4114

0547-4205 See CURRICULUM REPORT. 1892

0547-4221 See NATIONAL ASSOCIATION OF SECRETARIES OF STATE HANDBOOK. 4668

0547-521X See YEARBOOK OF THE NATIONAL CONFERENCE OF STATE LEGISLATIVE LEADERS. 4695

0547-5511 See NATIONAL CONSTRUCTION ESTIMATOR / EDITED BY CAL PACIFIC ESTIMATORS. 622

0547-5554 See RESEARCH RESULTS DIGEST / NATIONAL COOPERATIVE HIGHWAY RESEARCH PROGRAM. 5443

0547-5562 See SUMMARY OF PROGRESS - NATIONAL COOPERATIVE HIGHWAY RESEARCH PROGRAM. 5445

0547-5570 See SYNTHESIS OF HIGHWAY PRACTICE. 5393

0547-6844 See BIRTH DEFECTS ORIGINAL ARTICLE SERIES. 3757

0547-7115 See BULLETIN OF THE NATIONAL GUILD OF CATHOLIC PSYCHIATRISTS, INC, THE. 3922

0547-7441 See PROCEEDINGS OF THE NATIONAL INSTITUTE FOR PETROLEUM LANDMEN. 4275

0547-7794 See LEGAL BULLETIN (WASHINGTON). 3087

0547-8154 See NATIONAL ECONOMIC PROJECTIONS SERIES. 1619

0547-8626 See ANIMALS FOR RESEARCH. 5503

0547-9193 See YEARBOOK - NATIONAL SOCIETY OF PUBLIC ACCOUNTANTS. 753

0548-0019 See NAUCNO-TEHNICESKAA INFORMACIA. SERIA 1, ORGANIZACIA I METODIKA INFORMACIONNOJ RABOTY. 3233

0548-0027 See NAUCNO-TEHNICESKAJA INFORMACIJA. VSESOJUZNYJ INSTITUT NAUCNOJ I TEHNICESKOJ INFORMACII. SERIJA 2. INFORMACIONNYE PROCESSY I SISTEMY. 1243

0548-0108 See NAUCHNOE UPRAVLENIE OBSHCHESTVOM. 4543

0548-0345 See NAUKA I CHELOVECHESTVO. 5131

0548-040X See NAUKA O ZEMI. GEOLOGICA. 1389

0548-0523 See NAUTOLOGIA. 4179

0548-0817 See REPORT OF INVESTIGATIONS / NEBRASKA GEOLOGICAL SURVEY. 1394

0548-0825 See RESOURCE REPORT / UNIVERSITY OF NEBRASKA CONSERVATION AND SURVEY DIVISION. 2204

0548-1228 See VERSLAGEN EN MEDEDELINGEN - COMMISSIE VOOR HYDROLOGISCH ONDERZOEK T.N.O. 1418

0548-1384 See NEED A LIFT?. 1837

0548-1457 See NEGRO EDUCATIONAL REVIEW, THE. 1767

0548-1546 See NELSON'S LAW OFFICE DIRECTORY. 3014

0548-1686 See NEOTROPICA. 5592

0548-1937 See MAANDSTATISTIEK POLITIE EN JUSTITIE. 3082

0548-2682 See NEUE AUSGRABUNGEN UND FORSCHUNGEN IN NIEDERSACHSEN. 2700

0548-2712 See NEUE BEITRAEGE ZUR LITERATURWISSENSCHAFT. 3415

0548-2739 See DBZ, NEUE DEUTSCHE BAUERNZEITUNG. 78

0548-2801 See NEUE HEIMAT. 4529

0548-2879 See NEUE MUSIK IN DER BUNDESREPUBLIK DEUTSCHLAND. 4140

0548-3441 See REPORT OF THE NEVADA INDIAN AFFAIRS COMMISSION. 2272

0548-3549 See INVENTORY SERIES - STATE OF NEVADA, DEPARTMENT OF CONSERVATION AND NATURAL RESOURCES. 2195

0548-3557 See WATER RESOURCES. INFORMATION SERIES. REPORT - NEVADA. 5546

0548-3646 See TECHNICAL REPORT - BUREAU OF GOVERNMENTAL RESEARCH, UNIVERSITY OF NEVADA. 4690

0548-3662 See PREPRINT SERIES - DESERT RESEARCH INSTITUTE. 1433

0548-3794 See NEVROLOGIJA, PSIHIATRIJA I NEVROHIRURGIJA. 3843

0548-4448 See NEW ENGLAND ECONOMIC INDICATORS. 1536

0548-4502 See JOURNAL OF THE NEW ENGLAND WATER POLLUTION CONTROL ASSOCIATION. 2234

0548-4901 See BULLETIN - WATER RESOURCES RESEARCH CENTER (DURHAM). 5531

0548-4928 See NEW HAMPSHIRE BAR JOURNAL. 3015

0548-4987 See JOURNAL OF THE NEW HAVEN COLONY HISTORICAL SOCIETY. 2742

0548-5851 See UNIFORM CRIME REPORTS, STATE OF NEW JERSEY. 3084

0548-5932 See NEW MATHEMATICAL LIBRARY. 3524

0548-5967 See RESEARCH REPORT - AGRICULTURAL EXPERIMENT STATION. 127

0548-5975 See MEMOIR - NEW MEXICO BUREAU OF MINES & MINERAL RESOURCES. 2143

0548-5983 See SCENIC TRIPS TO THE GEOLOGIC PAST. 1396

0548-6165 See GROUND-WATER LEVELS IN NEW MEXICO. BASIC DATA REPORT. 5533

0548-6327 See SPECIAL PUBLICATION - NEW MEXICO GEOLOGICAL SOCIETY. 1398

0548-6424 See NEW ORLEANS GENESIS, THE. 2462

0548-6505 See NEW POETRY. 3466

0548-6807 See TECHNICAL PAPER - FORESTRY COMMISSION OF NEW SOUTH WALES. 2396

0548-6882 See REPORT (UNIVERSITY OF NEW SOUTH WALES. WATER RESEARCH LABORATORY). 1417

0548-7366 See REAL ESTATE LAW AND PRACTICE COURSE HANDBOOK SERIES. 3034

0548-8729 See YEARBOOK - NEW YORK COUNTY LAWYERS' ASSOCIATION. 3077

0548-9415 See CANCER DATA. 3811

0548-9547 See TRIENNIAL REPORT - BOTANY DIVISION. 529

0548-9938 See HOSPITAL AND SELECTED MORBIDITY DATA. 4810

0549-0111 See RURAL REAL ESTATE MARKET IN NEW ZEALAND (WELLINGTON, N.Z. : 1981). 4847

0549-0146 See NEW ZEALAND AGRICULTURAL SCIENCE. 112

0549-0162 See ANNUAL REPORT OF THE NEW ZEALAND BIRD BANDING SCHEME. 5614

0549-0200 See NEW ZEALAND COMPANY REGISTER, THE. 699

0549-0219 See NEW ZEALAND CONCRETE CONSTRUCTION. 622

0549-026X See NEW ZEALAND ELECTRONICS REVIEW. 2073

0549-0510 See NEW ZEALAND MATHEMATICS MAGAZINE, THE. 3524

0549-0618 See NEW ZEALAND UNIVERSITIES LAW REVIEW. 3016

0549-0782 See PUBLICATIONS. 3243

0549-0898 See NEWFOUNDLAND CHURCHMAN. 4981

0549-1940 See HANDBOOK OF COMMERCE AND INDUSTRY IN NIGERIA. 838

0549-2513 See MONTHLY PETROLEUM INFORMATION. 4265

0549-317X See BALANCE OF PAYMENTS MONTHLY. 773

0549-3811 See TRANSACTIONS OF THE JAPAN SOCIETY FOR AERONAUTICAL AND SPACE SCIENCES. 38

0549-4540 See PUBLICATIONS OF THE MATHEMATICAL SOCIETY OF JAPAN. 3529

0549-4818 See NIIGATA DAIGAKU NOGAKUBU ENSHURIN HOKOKU. 2389

0549-4826 See NIIGATA DAIGAKU NOGAKUBU KIYO. MEMOIRS OF THE FACULTY OF AGRICULTURE, NIIGATA UNIVERSITY. 113

0549-4869 See NIIGATA-KEN NOGYO SHIKENJO KENKYU HOKOKU. 113

0549-494X See NIMROD : A MAGYAR VADASZOK ORSZAGOS SZOEVETSEGENEK LAPJA. 4876

0549-4974 See NINGEN KOGAKU. 2123

0549-6233 See NORDISK HANDELSKALENDER, SKANDINAVIASK ADRESSEBOG. 699

0549-7191 See AGARD CONFERENCE PROCEEDINGS. 6

0549-7213 See AGARD LECTURE SERIES. 6

0549-7434 See NORTH CAROLINA CENTRAL LAW JOURNAL. 3018

0549-7450 See NORTH CAROLINA COURT OF APPEALS REPORTS. 3018

0549-799X See NEWS - WATER RESOURCES RESEARCH INSTITUTE OF THE UNIVERSITY OF NORTH CAROLINA. 5536

0549-804X See HEALTH LAW BULLETIN. 2977

0549-8295 See AGRICULTURAL ECONOMICS REPORT (NORTH DAKOTA AGRICULTURAL EXPERIMENT STATIONS (FARGO). 49

0549-8449 See STATISTICS : CALENDAR YEAR REVIEW. 5267

0549-852X See NORTH DAKOTA TRAFFIC REPORT. 5442

0549-8880 See NORTHEAST. 3418

0549-8929 See PROCEEDINGS - NORTHEASTERN FOREST TREE IMPROVEMENT CONFERENCE. 2391

0549-9186 See NORTHERN NECK OF VIRGINIA HISTORICAL MAGAZINE. 2751

0549-9879 See ANNUAL REPORT OF THE COMMISSIONER OF THE NORTHWEST TERRITORIES. 4628

0550-032X See DOEDSARSAKER. HOVEDTABELLER. 4561

0550-0842 See NOTATKI ORNITOLOGICZNE. 5618

0550-0974 See NOTES FROM UNDERGROUND. 5388

0550-1156 See NOTIZIARIO CHIMICO E FARMACEUTICO. 988

0550-1326 See NOUVEAU COMMERCE, LE. 848

0550-1350 See NOUVEAUX CAHIERS, LES. 5051

0550-1717 See ANNUAL REPORT OF DEPARTMENT OF FISHERIES (HALIFAX). 2295

0550-2209 See RAD VOJVOANSKIH MUZEJA. 4095

0550-3175 See NUCLEAR-MEDIZIN. SUPPLEMENTUM. 3848

0550-3604 See NUIT DES TEMPS. 360

0550-371X See NUMIZMATIKA I SFRAGISTIKA / AKADEMIIA NAUK UKRAINSKOI SSR, INSTITUT ARKHEOLOGII. 2782

0550-3744 See NONG-LIN XUE BAO. 114

0550-3841 See NUOVI QUADERNI DEL MERIDIONE. 2520

0550-4082 See PUBLICATIONS OF THE NUTTALL ORNITHOLOGICAL CLUB. 5619

0550-4406 See NATIONAL ELECTRICAL CODE. 2292

0550-4554 See JAARVERSLAG - NEDERLANDSE HOUTBOND EN AANGESLOTEN VERENIGINGEN. 1613

0550-5089 See MOTOR ACCIDENTS IN NEW ZEALAND. 5387

0550-5666 See BULLETIN OF THE NATIONAL BRAILLE ASSOCIATION, INC. 1876

0550-5755 See CLASSROOM PRACTICES IN TEACHING ENGLISH. 3273

0550-6387 See PROCEEDINGS IN THE MUNICIPAL COURTS. 3082

0550-6557 See AMEX DATABOOK. 890

0550-6565 See NEWSLETTER - NEW YORK BOTANICAL GARDEN. 519

0550-6891 See NIGER. 2642

0550-7898 See ANNUAL NEVADA STREET AND HIGHWAY CONFERENCE. 5438

0550-7960 See DISTRIBUTION OF STATE FOUNDATION AID TO NEW HAMPSHIRE SCHOOL DISTRICTS. 1862

0550-8401 See NON-PROFIT ORGANIZATION TAX LETTER. 5299

0550-9246 See BULLETIN - NEPAL BANK LIMITED. 781

0551-0503 See PLASTICS AGE. 4457

0551-0678 See PLAYBILL. 5367

0551-1038 See PLZENSKY LEKARSKY SBORNIK. 3628

0551-1690 See POETRY BOOK SOCIETY BULLETIN. 3469

0551-326X See POLITICA ED ECONOMIA (ROME, ITALY : 1970). 1512

0551-3677 See POLNOHOSPODARSTVO. 120

0551-3855 See POLSKA BIBLIOGRAFIA PRAWNICZA / POLSKA AKADEMIA NAUK, INSTYTUT PANSTWA I PRAWA. 3082

0551-4932 See JOURNAL OF THE UNIVERSITY OF POONA, SCIENCE AND TECHNOLOGY. 5122

0551-5343 See PORADNIK JEZYKOWY. 3311

0551-6897 See POSTHORN, THE. 2786

0551-8393 See SBORNIK VYSOKE SKOLY CHEMICKO-TECHNOLOGICKE V PRAZE. B, ANORGANICKA CHEMIE A TECHNOLOGIE. 1037

0551-8407 See SBORNIK VYSOKE SKOLY CHEMICKO-TECHNOLOGICKE V PRAZE. G, MINERALOGIE. 1444

0551-9276 See PREDI-BRIEFS (CLEVELAND). 1621

0552-007X See PRESIDENT (NEW YORK), THE. 882

0552-1807 See PROBLEMI DEL SOCIALISMO. 4545

0552-2056 See PROBLEMY FIZIKI ATMOSFERY. 4417

0552-2234 See PROBLEMY RODZINY. 2285

0552-2668 See PROFESSOR DR. F. DE VRIES LECTURES. 5142

0552-4245 See PRZEGLAD ZACHODNIOPOMORSKI / INSTYTUT ZACHODNIOPOMORSKI. 2703

0552-430X See PRZYRODA POLSKA. 4171

0552-5829 See SOLNECHNYE DANNYE. 400

0552-7155 See PAAR SAMMUKEST EESTI KIRJANDUSE UURIMISE TEED. 3421

0552-7252 See PACIFIC COAST ARCHAEOLOGICAL SOCIETY QUARTERLY. 277

0552-7414 See PACIFIC JOURNAL OF THEOLOGY, THE. 4984

0552-7511 See PACIFIC PRINTERS PILOT. 4567

0552-8267 See MONTHLY FOREIGN TRADE STATISTICS OF PAKISTAN. 1536

0552-8968 See PAKISTAN HOTEL GUIDE. 2808

0552-9050 See PAKISTAN JOURNAL OF SCIENTIFIC RESEARCH. 5137

0552-9069 See PAKISTAN LABOUR GAZETTE. 3153

0552-9263 See PAKISTAN YEAR BOOK. 2507

0552-9344 See PALAEOHISTORIA (HAARLEM). 277

0552-9352 See PALAEONTOLOGIA JUGOSLAVICA. 4229

0552-9360 See JOURNAL OF THE PALAEONTOLOGICAL SOCIETY OF INDIA. 4227

0552-9395 See PALANTE. 3421

0553-0601 See NEW HORIZONS WORLD GUIDE. 5485

0553-0814 See ANUARIO DE DERECHO (PANAMA : 1981). 2935

0553-1098 See PANORAMA. 2521

0553-2124 See SBORNIK VEDECKYCH PRACI / VYSOKA SKOLA CHEMICKO-TECHNOLOGICKA PARDUBICE. 1029

0553-2159 See PARENTS (PARIS), LES. 2285

0553-2264 See SEMINAIRE SUR LES EQUATIONS AUX DERIVEES PARTIELLES. 3533

0553-2930 See PUBLICATIONS DE L'INSTITUT DE STATISTIQUE DE L'UNIVERSITE DE PARIS. 5336

0553-3139 See PARLAMENT, DAS. 4486

0553-4003 See PATRISTISCHE TEXTE UND STUDIEN. 4985

0553-4054 See PATTERSON'S SCHOOLS CLASSIFIED. 1839

0553-4283 See PEACE RESEARCH REVIEWS. 4487

0553-4429 See JANUS PANNONIUS MUZEUM EVKONYVE, A. 4089

0553-4755 See PELICAN HISTORY OF ART, THE. 362

0553-478X See PELOPONNESIAKA. 2702

0553-4968 See PENINJAU SEJARAH. 1902

0553-4992 See PENN AR BED BREST. 468

0553-5115 See PENNSYLVANIA'S INSURED UNEMPLOYED. 1701

0553-5719 See INFORMATION CIRCULAR - PENNSYLVANIA. BUREAU OF TOPOGRAPHIC AND GEOLOGIC SURVEY. 1382

0553-5980 See PENNSYLVANIA GEOGRAPHER, THE. 2572

0553-6502 See PERCUSSIVE NOTES. 4145

0553-6626 See PERIODICA POLYTECHNICA. CIVIL ENGINEERING. 2028

0553-6707 See PERISTIL (ZAGREB). 362

0553-6774 See PERMANENCE/DURABILITY OF THE BOOK. 4831

0553-6901 See PERMIAN HISTORICAL ANNUAL. 2754

0553-7150 See PERSONALITIES CARIBBEAN. 434

0553-8467 See PESQUISAS. ANTROPOLOGIA. 243

0553-8572 See PET DEALER. 4287

0553-8572 See PET DEALER ANNUAL GUIDE. 4287

0553-8882 See PETROLEUM GEOLOGY. 4272

0553-9536 See PHI THETA PAPERS. 1094

0553-9587 See BULLETIN OF THE PHILADELPHIA HERPETOLOGICAL SOCIETY. 5579

0554-0577 See PHILIPPINIANA SACRA. 2625

0554-0674 See PHILOLOGISCHE STUDIEN UND QUELLEN. 3310

0554-0739 See PHILOSOPHICAL STUDIES (DUBLIN, IRELAND). 4356

0554-0828 See PHILOSOPHISCHE RUNDSCHAU. BEIHEFT. 4356

0554-0992 See PHONAI. LAUTBIBLIOTHEK DER EUROPAEISCHEN SPRACHEN UND MUNDARTEN. DEUTSCHE REIHE. 3310

0554-1174 See PHYCOLOGICAL STUDIES. 469

0554-1182 See PHYKOS. 521

0554-2065 See PISATEL I ZHIZN / LITERATURNYI INSTITUT IMENI A. M. GORKOGO SOIUZA PISATELEI SSSR. 3423

0554-2081 See KHARCHOVA PROMYSLOVIST. 2347

0554-2324 See PIVOT (STATE COLLEGE, PA.). 3468

0554-2375 See PLAINS TALK. 2754

0554-288X See PLASTER JACKET, THE. 4230

0554-2901 See PLASTICHESKIE MASSY. 4457

0554-2952 See PLASTICS FOCUS. 4458

0554-3037 See PLAY INDEX. 5367

0554-3363 See PNEUMATIKE KYPROS. 3424

0554-3983 See POETRY PILOT. 3469

0554-4246 See POINTER, THE. 1883

0554-498X See POLISH YEARBOOK OF INTERNATIONAL LAW, THE. 3134

0554-5196 See POLITICAL SCIENCE REVIEW. 4490

0554-5455 See POLITISCHE BILDUNG (STUTTGART, GERMANY). 4491

0554-5579 See POLJOPRIVREDA I SUMARSTVO. 120

0554-7555 See PORTS AND HARBORS. 5454

0554-8004 See PRACE NAUKOWE INSTYTUT OCHRONY ROSLIN. 4247

0554-8144 See FILOLOGIA ANGIELSKA - UNIWERSYTET IM. ADAMA MICKIEWICZA W POZNANIU. 3281

0554-8195 See SERIA ARCHEOLOGIA / UNIWERSYTET IM. ADAMA MICKIEWICZA W POZNANIU, WYDZIA FILOZOFICZNO-HISTORYCZNY. 282

0554-8373 See POSTAL STATIONERY. 2786

0554-842X See POSTPRAXIS, DIE. 1147

0554-9701 See SBORNIK VYSOKE SKOLY CHEMICKO-TECHNOLOGICKE V PRAZE ... POTRAVINY. 2356

0554-9728 See SBORNIK VYSOKE SKOLY CHEMICKO-TECHNOLOGICKE V PRAZE. C, ORGANICKA CHEMIE A TECHNOLOGIE. 1047

0554-9736 See SBORNIK VYSOKE SKOLY CHEMICKO-TECHNOLOGICKE V PRAZE. D, TECHNOLOGIE PALIV. 4277

0555-0572 See PRESBYTERIAN LAYMAN, THE. 5066

ISSN Index

0555-0912 See PRETORIA ORIENTAL SERIES. 2662

0555-1099 See PRIKLADNAJA BIOHIMIJA I MIKROBIOLOGIJA. 492

0555-1137 See PRILOZI PROUCAVANJU JEZIKA. 3311

0555-1153 See PRILOZI ZA ORIJENTALNU FILOLOGIJU. 1079

0555-1633 See PRINT MEDIA PRODUCTION DATA. 764

0555-2648 See PROBLEMY ARKTIKI I ANTARKTIKI. 4170

0555-2656 See PROBLEMY BIONIKI. 1991

0555-2788 See PROBLEMY KOSMICESKOJ BIOLOGII. 469

0555-2818 See PROBLEMY MATEMATICESKOJ FIZIKI. 4417

0555-2923 See PROBLEMY PEREDACI INFORMACII. 5140

0555-3105 See PRODUCT DESIGN AND VALUE ENGINEERING. 1992

0555-3385 See PROFESSIONAL LIABILITY NEWSLETTER. 2890

0555-3482 See PROFIL : SOZIALDEMOKRATISCHE ZEITSCHRIFT FUR POLITIK, WIRTSCHAFT UND KULTUR. 4545

0555-3768 See PROGRESO (MEXICO). 2543

0555-4306 See PROGRESS IN THE ASTRONAUTICAL SCIENCES. 32

0555-4330 See PROGRESS OF MATHEMATICS. 3528

0555-4608 See PROMETEI. 434

0555-5299 See PSICHIATRIA GENERALE E DELL'ETA EVOLUTIVA. 3932

0555-5582 See PSYCHOLOGIA UNIVERSALIS. 4610

0555-5620 See PSYCHOLOGICAL RESEARCH BULLETIN. 4611

0555-5701 See PSYCHOLOGISCHES KOLLOQUIUM. 4612

0555-5914 See PUBLIC AFFAIRS (VERMILLION). 4676

0555-6392 See PUBLISHING, ENTERTAINMENT, ADVERTISING AND ALLIED FIELDS LAW QUARTERLY. 3033

0555-6406 See PUBLISISTIK. 3313

0555-6953 See PULSE (PICO RIVERA). 5519

0555-7631 See RESEARCH BULLETIN OF THE PANJAB UNIVERSITY. SCIENCE. 5146

0555-781X See PUNSOK HWAHAK. 1018

0555-7887 See PURASUCHIKKUSU. 4460

0555-8026 See TECHNICAL REPORT - PURDUE UNIVERSITY, WATER RESOURCES RESEARCH CENTER. 5540

0555-9456 See FARM ECONOMICS (UNIVERSITY PARK, PA.). 84

0555-9952 See PEUPLES DU MONDE. 4986

0556-0071 See PHILIPPINE JOURNAL OF INTERNAL MEDICINE. 3800

0556-0152 See PHYLLIS SCHLAFLY REPORT, THE. 4487

0556-0691 See POMORANIA ANTIQUA. 4230

0556-1094 See PRADALGE. 3424

0556-137X See PREPARONS L'AVENIR. 5139

0556-171X See PROBLEMY PROCNOSTI (KIEV). 1991

0556-2678 See PUBLICATIONS IN CONDUCT AND COMMUNICATION. 1094

0556-2813 See PHYSICAL REVIEW C : NUCLEAR PHYSICS. 4450

0556-2821 See PHYSICAL REVIEW D : PARTICLES AND FIELDS. 4415

0556-3321 See PAKISTAN JOURNAL OF BOTANY. 520

0556-3585 See EXPORT BY PENNSYLVANIA MANUFACTURERS. 834

0556-3860 See PHOTOCHEMISTRY (LONDON). 1056

0556-3968 See PLANNING AND RESOURCE DEVELOPMENT SERIES. 2202

0556-4409 See PAINTINDIA. 4224

0556-5189 See POP DIRECTORY. 4147

0556-5960 See REVISTA DE HISTORIA AMERICANA Y ARGENTINA. 2758

0556-5987 See REVISTA DE HISTORIA DE LAS IDEAS. 4359

0556-5995 See REVISTA DE HISTORIA DE ROSARIO. 2758

0556-6134 See REVISTA DE LITERATURAS MODERNAS. 3430

0556-6177 See REVISTA DE MEDICINA DE LA UNIVERSIDAD DE NAVARRA. 3973

0556-6428 See REVISTA DEL DERECHO COMERCIAL Y DE LAS OBLIGACIONES. 3102

0556-6533 See REVISTA ESPANOLA DE ANTROPOLOGIA AMERICANA. 244

0556-655X See REVISTA ESPANOLA DE MICROPALEONTOLOGIA. 4230

0556-6606 See REVISTA FORESTAL VENEZOLANA. 2394

0556-6940 See REVISTA PORTUGUESA DE FILOSOFIA. SUPLEMENTO BIBLIOGRAFICO. 4359

0556-705X See REVISTA VALENCIANA DE FILOLOGIA. 3316

0556-7165 See REVOLUTIONARY AGE. 4546

0556-7378 See REVUE DE DROIT CANONIQUE. 4993

0556-7394 See REVUE DE DROIT MILITAIRE ET DE DROIT DE LA GUERRE. 3183

0556-7432 See REVUE DE GEOMORPHOLOGIE DYNAMIQUE. 2575

0556-7440 See REVUE DE L'ARBITRAGE. 3043

0556-7734 See REVUE ENERGIE PRIMAIRE. 1956

0556-7963 See REVUE JURIDIQUE THEMIS (1970). 3044

0556-7963 See REVUE JURIDIQUE THEMIS (1970). 3044

0556-8072 See REVUE ROUMAINE D'HISTOIRE. 2706

0556-8471 See ANNUAL REPORT - RHODE ISLAND GOVERNOR'S COUNCIL ON MENTAL HEALTH. 4766

0556-8560 See OCCASIONAL PUBLICATION - NARRAGANSETT MARINE LABORATORY. 1453

0556-8595 See RHODE ISLAND BAR JOURNAL. 3044

0556-8609 See RHODE ISLAND JEWISH HISTORICAL NOTES. 2272

0556-8641 See PHILOSOPHICAL PAPERS (GRAHAMSTOWN). 4356

0556-9796 See KINFOLK. 2457

0556-9931 See RIDING LINE. 2628

0557-109X See KIKAN RIRON-KEIZAIGAKU. 1501

0557-1359 See RIVISTA DI STORIA DELL'AGRICOLTURA. 130

0557-1367 See RIVISTA DI STUDI BIZANTINI E NEOELLENICI. 2628

0557-1405 See RIVISTA ITALIANA DI GEOTECNICA. 1395

0557-1464 See RIVISTA TRIMESTRALE DI DIRITTO PUBBLICO. 3094

0557-1588 See PROCEEDINGS OF THE ROBERT A. WELCH FOUNDATION CONFERENCES ON CHEMICAL RESEARCH. 989

0557-1634 See SAMMELBANDE DER ROBERT-SCHUMANN-GESELLSCHAFT. 4151

0557-2231 See ROCZNIKI SZTUKI SLASKIEJ. 363

0557-2282 See RODNA GRUDA SLOVENIJA. 2272

0557-2614 See ROMANFUEHRER, DER. 424

0557-2630 See ROMANIAN FILM, THE. 4077

0557-272X See ROMANOSLAVICA / ASOCIATIA SLAVISTILOR DIN REPUBLICA POPULARA ROMINA. 3318

0557-2738 See ROMANTIC MOVEMENT. 3459

0557-3645 See QUARTERLY BULLETIN / ROSWELL MUSEUM AND ART CENTER. 4095

0557-384X See MONOGRAPHS - ROYAL ASIATIC SOCIETY OF GREAT BRITAIN AND FINLAND. MALAYSIAN BRANCH. 2659

0557-3912 See REPORTS FROM GENERAL PRACTICE. 3739

0557-4048 See REPORT OF THE COUNCIL - ROYAL INSTITUTE OF CHEMISTRY, LONDON. 991

0557-4129 See SELECTED LECTURES OF THE ROYAL SOCIETY. 570

0557-4161 See PROCEEDINGS OF THE ROYAL SOCIETY OF NEW ZEALAND. 5141

0557-4242 See ROYAL WESTERN AUSTRALIAN HISTORICAL SOCIETY'S NEWSLETTER. 2671

0557-4447 See LUSK'S MONTGOMERY COUNTY, MARYLAND, ASSESSMENT DIRECTORY. 4840

0557-465X See BULETINUL INSTITUTULUI AGRONOMIC CLUJ-NAPOCA. SERIA AGRICULTURA. 68

0557-4668 See BULETINUL INSTITUTUL AGRONOMIC CLUJ-NAPOCA. SERIA ZOOTEHNIE SI MEDICINA VETERINARA. 208

0557-5257 See BIULLETEN VERKHOVNOGO SUDA SSSR. 2942

0557-5583 See BULLETIN DE STATISTIQUE - DIRECTION DE LA STATISTIQUE ET DE LA DOCUMENTATION (RWANDA). 5324

0557-5737 See FER DE LANCE. 350

0557-6644 See RURAL RECONSTRUCTION (NEW DELHI). 2835

0557-6857 See RASSEGNA DI LETTERATURA TOMISTICA. 3427

0557-7705 See REVUE ARCHEOLOGIQUE DE NARBONNAISE. 281

0557-7721 See REVUE DE MEDECINE DE TOURS. 3636

0557-773X See REVUE DE MORET ET DE SA REGION, LA. 2706

0557-8620 See PROCEEDINGS OF THE ANNUAL CONFERENCE OF THE LAW OF THE SEA INSTITUTE. 3182

0557-9295 See RES GESTAE (INDIANAPOLIS, IND.). 3039

0557-9325 See REVIEW OF PROGRESS IN COLORATION AND RELATED TOPICS. 1029

0557-9430 See RIABILITAZIONE. 4393

0557-9783 See SZTANDAR MODYCH. 1070

0558-1265 See SAFYBI. 4329

0558-1931 See QUARTERLY - ST. LAWRENCE COUNTY HISTORICAL ASSOCIATION, THE. 2756

0558-194X See ANNUAL REPORT / SAINT LAWRENCE SEAWAY DEVELOPMENT CORPORATION. 5447

0558-3438 See JAHRESSCHRIFT / SALZBURGER MUSEUM CAROLINO AUGUSTEUM. 4089

0558-3667 See SAMMLUNG METZLER. 3433

0558-3764 See SAMSKRTAPRATIBHA. 3319

0558-4639 See SANANJALKA. 3319

0558-471X See SANFUJINKA CHIRYO. 3768

0558-6291 See ARCHIVOS DE LA FACULTAD DE MEDICINA DE ZARAGOZA. 3552

0558-6976 See SASKATCHEWAN ECONOMIC REVIEW. 1519

0558-8766 See SCHOLARS' CHOICE. 5013

0559-1414 See SCIENTIA ET PRAXIS. 5218

0559-2526 See BULLETIN - SEATTLE GENEALOGICAL SOCIETY. 2441

0559-331X See SEKKO TO SEKKAI. 1029

0559-3468 See SELECTED ARTICLES FROM LANGUAGE LEARNING. 3320

0559-4677 See SENIOR CITIZENS NEWS (WASHINGTON, D.C.). 5181

0559-4871 See SEQUENCES. 3471

0559-7102 See HITOTSUBASHI DAIGAKU KENKYU NENPO. SHAKAIGAKU KENKYU. 5201

0559-7765 See SHENG LI KO HSUEH CHIN CHAN. 587

0559-7781 See SHEPARD'S CALIFORNIA REPORTER CITATIONS. 3049

0559-779X See SHEPARD'S FEDERAL LABOR LAW CITATIONS. 3154

0559-8516 See SHINKU. 4429

0559-8672 See SHINYAKU TO RINSHO. 3641

0559-8680 See SHIONOGI KENKYUSHO NENPO. 5157

0559-8850 See SHIZUOKA DAIGAKU NOGAKUBU KENKYU HOKOKU. 134

0559-8958 See SHOKUBAI. 1058

0559-8974 See SHOKUHIN EISEI KENKYU. 4802

0559-8990 See SHOKUHIN KOGYO. THE FOOD INDUSTRY. 2357

0559-9202 See SHOSETSU GENDAI. 5074

0559-9296 See SHRIMP LANDINGS, ANNUAL SUMMARY. 2313

0559-9350 See SHUILI XUEBAO. 2095

0559-9385 See ACTA HYDROBIOLOGICA SINICA. 552

0559-9407 See SHUI WU HSUN KAN. 4748

0559-9628 See SIBRIUM. 282

0560-1894 See SKALK. 282

0560-222X See ZBORNIK - ARHEOLOSKI MUZEJ NA MAKEDONIJA. RECUEIL DES TRAVAUX. 286

0560-2416 See KUNGL. SKYTTEANSKA SAMFUNDETS HANDLINGAR. 2696

0560-3110 See VESTNIK SLOVENSKEGA KEMIJSKEGA DRUSTVA. 995

0560-3617 See SOCCER JOURNAL. 4919

0560-3870 See NEWSLETTER-SOCIAL WELFARE HISTORY GROUP. 5299

0560-6152 See JOURNAL OF THE SOCIETY OF ARCHER-ANTIQUARIES. 4902

0560-6225 See INDEX OF WELLS SHOT FOR VELOCITY. 4260

0560-642X See SPE : SOCIETY OF PETROLEUM ENGINEERS OF AIME. 4279

0560-6675 See SOCIJALIZAM. 4547

0560-8538 See SORIPAR. 2371

0560-9178 See MINERALS; A REPORT FOR THE REPUBLIC OF SOUTH AFRICA. 1442

0560-9208 See HANDBOOK (GEOLOGICAL SURVEY OF SOUTH AFRICA). 1382

0561-0095 See AE (SOUTH CAROLINA CROP AND LIVESTOCK REPORTING SERVICE). 44

0561-0214 See ROSTER OF LICENSED CONTRACTORS IN THE STATE OF SOUTH CAROLINA. 2030

0561-0478 See ARCHAEOLOGICAL STUDIES : CIRCULAR. 257

0561-0559 See SPECIAL REPORT - SOUTH DAKOTA STATE GEOLOGICAL SURVEY. 1398

0561-1245 See SOUTHERN DOG LOVERS DIGEST. 4288

0561-1784 See ANNUAL REPORT - THE SOUTHWESTERN LEGAL FOUNDATION. 2935

0561-3078 See SPACE VOLUME. 36

0561-4473 See ESTADISTICAS JUDICIALES DE ESPANA. 3080

0561-5445 See SPARKS QUARTERLY, THE. 2473

0561-6158 See SPICILEGIUM FRIBURGENSE. 4999

0561-6832 See JOURNAL OF THE SPORTS TURF RESEARCH INSTITUTE, THE. 4902

0561-7359 See BULLETIN - ACADEMIE SERBE DES SCIENCES ET DES ARTS. CLASSE DES SCIENCES SOCIALES. 5193

0561-7855 See STAHLBAU RUNDSCHAU. 2031

0561-9912 See JAHRESBERICHT - STEIERMARKISCHE GEBIETSKRANKENKASSE FUER ARBEITER UND ANGESTELLTE. 1681

0562-0694 See STIMME DER ORTHODOXIE. 5040

0562-083X See STOCK QUOTATIONS ON THE NEW YORK STOCK EXCHANGE. 916

0562-1372 See STORIES OF RESOURCE-FULL KANSAS. 1398

0562-1690 See STREAM OF HISTORY, THE. 2762

0562-1836 See STROITELI MATERIALI I SILIKATNA PROMISLENOST. 629

0562-1852 See STROITELSTVO. 629

0562-1887 See STROJARSTVO. 2244

0562-2174 See MONOGRAPH - STUDENT PERSONNEL ASSOCIATION FOR TEACHER EDUCATION. 1836

0562-2719 See STUDIA ANGLISTICA UPSALIENSIA. 3324

0562-2867 See STUDIA LITTERARIA. 3441

0562-3022 See STUDIA ROMANICA UPSALIENSIA. 3441

0562-3251 See STUDIEN ZUR BAYERISCHEN VERFASSUNGS- UND SOZIALGESCHICHTE. 2711

0562-3618 See STUDIES IN AUSTRALIAN BIBLIOGRAPHY. 425

0562-4231 See STUDIES OVER DE SOCIAAL-ECONOMISCHE GESCHIEDENIS VAN LIMBURG. 1585

0562-5084 See SUDAN JOURNAL OF VETERINARY SCIENCE AND ANIMAL HUSBANDRY, THE. 5522

0562-5122 See SUDAN SILVA. 2396

0562-5270 See BUCHREIHE DER SUDOSTDEUTSCHEN HISTORISCHEN KOMMISSION. 2680

0562-5297 See SUDOSTDEUTSCHE VIERTELJAHRESBLATTER. 2273

0562-6048 See SUNRISE (ALTADENA, CALIF.). 4362

0562-6579 See SURABU KENKYU. 2712

0562-7192 See SUVREMENNA MEDICINA. 3644

0563-0525 See MORA FERENC MUZEUM EVKONYVE, A. 4091

0563-0592 See ACTA BIOLOGICA (SZEGED. 1955). 440

0563-0746 See SZESZIPAR. 1628

0563-0991 See S D; SPACE DESIGN. 308

0563-1750 See ZOOLOGISCHE DOCUMENTATIE. 5603

0563-2013 See TESTMEVELES- ES SPORTEGESZSEGUGYI SZMELE. 3956

0563-2072 See TETRAHEDRON. SUPPLEMENT. 994

0563-2978 See TEXAS SCHOOL BUSINESS. 1787

0563-3079 See TEXTE DES SPATEN MITTELALTERS UND DER FRUHEN NEUZEIT. 3445

0563-3087 See TEXTE UND KOMMENTARE; EINE ALTERTUMSWISSENSCHAFTLICHE REIHE. 284

0563-3966 See THEATRE, LE. 5370

0563-4253 See THEOLOGIE HISTORIQUE. 5003

0563-430X See THEOLOGISCHE BUCHEREI. 5004

0563-4822 See THOMAS MANN STUDIEN. 3446

0563-4970 See THURN UND TAXIS-STUDIEN. 2631

0563-5020 See DIZHI KEXUE. 1373

0563-5578 See LUCRARI STIINTIFICE, INSTITUTUL AGRONOMIC TIMISOARA, SERIA AGRONOMIE. 105

0563-5586 See LUCRARI STIINTIFICE. INSTITUTUI AGRONOMIC TIMISOARA, SERIA MEDICINA VETERINARA. 5515

0563-573X See BULETINI I SHKENCAVE BUJQESORE. 68

0563-5780 See STUDIME FILOLOGJIKE. 3326

0563-5799 See STUDIME HISTORIKE. 2712

0563-6191 See TAX BURDEN ON TOBACCO, THE. 5373

0563-637X See TODAY'S MINISTRY (NEWTON CENTRE, MASS. : 1983). 5005

0563-6590 See REPORTS OF THE RESEARCH INSTITUTE FOR STRENGTH AND FRACTURE OF MATERIALS, TOHOKU UNIVERSITY. 1994

0563-6759 See PROCEEDINGS OF THE SCHOOL OF SCIENCE OF TOKAI UNIVERSITY. 5142

0563-6795 See PROCEEDINGS OF THE FACULTY OF SCIENCE OF TOKAI UNIVERSITY. 5140

0563-6981 See TOKUSHIMA DAIGAKU KYOYOBU KIYO. SHIZEN KAGAKU. 5166

0563-7546 See PAPERS OF SHIP RESEARCH INSTITUTE. 4181

0563-7937 See JOURNAL OF THE FACULTY OF ENGINEERING, UNIVERSITY OF TOKYO. SERIES B. 1983

0563-7945 See JOURNAL OF THE FACULTY OF ENGINEERING, UNIVERSITY OF TOKYO. SERIES A, ANNUAL REPORT. 1983

0563-8054 See ANNALS OF THE INSTITUTE OF SOCIAL SCIENCE. 5191

0563-8089 See TOYO BUNKA KENKYUJO KIYO. 2666

0563-8372 See REPORT OF THE TOKYO UNIVERSITY OF FISHERIES. 2311

0563-8887 See TOOLS & TILLAGE. 141

0563-9727 See ANNALES DE L'UNIVERSITE DES SCIENCES SOCIALES DE TOULOUSE. 5190

0563-9743 See HOMO (TOULOUSE). 5247

0563-9751 See LITTERATURES (TOULOUSE). 3408

0563-9786 See VIA DOMITIA. 2714

0564-0202 See TOYO BUNKA. 2666

0564-0482 See TRADE DIRECTORIES OF THE WORLD. 854

0564-0571 See TRADICIONES DE GUATEMALA. 2325

0564-0881 See TRAINING KEY. 3178

0564-1373 See TRANSPORTS. 5397

0564-1470 See TRAUMA (NEW YORK, N.Y.). 3742

0564-2108 See TRIAL AND TORT TRENDS. 3066

0564-2604 See ANNUAL STATISTICAL DIGEST - CENTRAL STATISTICAL OFFICE (PORT-OF-SPAIN). 5321

0564-2612 See CONTINUOUS SAMPLE SURVEY OF POPULATION. 4551

0564-2744 See TRINITY. 2632

0564-3295 See TROPICAL ECOLOGY. 2222

0564-3392 See TRUCK DATA BOOK. 5426

0564-3783 See CITOLOGIJA I GENETIKA (KIEV). 543

0564-3929 See TURANG XUEBAO. 190

0564-3945 See TU JANG TUNG PAO. 190

0564-4232 See TUBINGER GEOGRAPHISCHE STUDIEN. 2578

0564-4291 See TUBINGER WIRTSCHAFTSWISSENSCHAFTLICHE ABHANDLUNGEN. 1525

0564-4380 See TULANE STUDIES IN ROMANCE LANGUAGES AND LITERATURE. 3448

0564-4437 See TULSA ANNALS. 2476

0564-478X See CHISPA. 1062

0564-559X See TWAYNE'S ENGLISH AUTHOR SERIES. 435

0564-5603 See TWAYNE'S WORLD AUTHORS SERIES. 3448

0564-6162 See TEORETICESKAJA I MATEMATICESKAJA FIZIKA. 4423

0564-6197 See TEXAS TECH LAW REVIEW. 3064

0564-6898 See BULLETIN OF THE OCEAN RESEARCH INSTITUTE, UNIVERSITY OF TOKYO. 1447

0564-7207 See PROCEEDINGS - TALL TIMBERS CONFERENCE ON ECOLOGICAL ANIMAL CONTROL BY HABITAT MANAGEMENT. 4247

0564-7495 See TEXAS WATER DEVELOPMENT BOARD PUBLICATIONS CATALOG. 5541

0564-7630 See ANNUAL BULLETIN / RESEARCH INSTITUTE OF LOGOPEDICS AND PHONIATRICS, FACULTY OF MEDICINE, UNIVERSITY OF TOKYO. 3886

0564-7959 See TUBINGER BEITRAGE ZUR LINGUISTIK. 3330

0564-8742 See REPORT OF THE COMPUTER CENTRE, UNIVERSITY OF TOKYO. 1262

0564-9099 See NUCLEAR INDUSTRY, THE. 2157

0565-0127 See GAS SUPPLIES OF INTERSTATE NATURAL GAS PIPELINE COMPANIES / FEDERAL POWER COMMISSION, BUREAU OF NATURAL GAS, THE. 4258

0565-0585 See ANNUAL OPERATING PLAN, WESTERN DIVISION, MISSOURI RIVER BASIN. 2087

0565-0631 See PREAUTHORIZATION OF PLANNING ACTIVITIES OF THE BUREAU OF RECLAMATION, THE CORPS OF ENGINEERS, AND THE SOIL CONSERVATION SERVICE. 5537

0565-0674 See BUREAU OF RECLAMATION PROGRESS. 70

0565-0682 See PROJECT SKYWATER BIENNIAL REPORT. 5537

0565-0828 See CENSUS BUREAU METHODOLOGICAL RESEARCH. 4550

0565-0933 See GUIDE TO FOREIGN TRADE STATISTICS. 730

0565-1204 See U.S. TRADE WITH PUERTO RICO AND U.S. POSSESSIONS. 856

0565-1557 See LIGHT LIST. 4178

0565-1905 ISSN Index

0565-1905 See ACREAGE MARKETING GUIDES. SPRING VEGETABLES AND MELONS. 2407

0565-1921 See ACREAGE-MARKETING GUIDES, WINTER VEGETABLES AND POTATOES. 2325

0565-1980 See POULTRY MARKET STATISTICS. 156

0565-2014 See COTTONSEED QUALITY. 168

0565-2022 See LONG STAPLE COTTON REVIEW. 178

0565-2030 See SUMMARY OF COTTON FIBER AND PROCESSING TEST RESULTS. 5356

0565-2049 See DAIRY PLANTS SURVEYED AND APPROVED FOR USDA GRADING SERVICE. 193

0565-2065 See FRESH FRUIT AND VEGETABLE SHIPMENTS BY STATES, COMMODITIES, COUNTIES, STATIONS. 837

0565-2138 See LIST OF PLANTS OPERATING UNDER USDA POULTRY AND EGG GRADING AND EGG PRODUCTS INSPECTION PROGRAMS. 214

0565-2189 See HOGS AND PIGS (WASHINGTON, D.C.). 212

0565-2421 See CONSERVATION RESEARCH REPORT. 2190

0565-243X See PROGRESS REPORT ON PESTICIDES AND RELATED ACTIVITIES. 4247

0565-3061 See MANPOWER RESEARCH. 1689

0565-4408 See ANNUAL REPORT - UNITED STATES. ECONOMIC DEVELOPMENT ADMINISTRATION (1969). 1598

0565-4564 See CLIMATOGRAPHY OF THE UNITED STATES. 1422

0565-4866 See FLIGHT STANDARDS INFORMATION MANUAL. 21

0565-5560 See DAILY REPORT. SOVIET UNION / FOREIGN BROADCAST INFORMATION SERVICE. 1131

0565-596X See TECHNIQUES OF WATER-RESOURCES INVESTIGATIONS OF THE UNITED STATES GEOLOGICAL SURVEY. 5540

0565-6141 See TECHNICAL ABSTRACTS - U. S. GODDARD SPACE FLIGHT CENTER. 37

0565-6338 See FOREST SERVICE RESEARCH PAPER ITF. 2381

0565-7024 See ANNUAL REPORT TO THE PRESIDENT AND THE CONGRESS - NATIONAL ADVISORY COUNCIL ON THE EDUCATION OF DISADVANTAGED CHILDREN. 1875

0565-7059 See NASA CONTRACTOR REPORT. 29

0565-7458 See FINANCIAL STATISTICS OF INSTITUTIONS OF HIGHER EDUCATION: CURRENT FUNDS, REVENUES AND EXPENDITURES SUMMARY DATA. 1795

0565-775X See ANNUAL REPORT / NATIONAL INSTITUTE OF GENERAL MEDICAL SCIENCES. 442

0565-8066 See ACTA UNIVERSITATIS SZEGEDIENSIS. ACTA MINERALOGICA-PETROGRAPHICA. 1437

0565-811X See MEDICAL SUBJECT HEADINGS. 3230

0565-8136 See NUMERICAL WEATHER PREDICTION ACTIVITIES. 1432

0565-8284 See R & D ACTIVITIES IN STATE GOVERNMENT AGENCIES. 5144

0565-8306 See SCIENTIFIC MANPOWER. 5155

0565-856X See INFORMAL MANUSCRIPT - U.S. NAVAL OCEANOGRAPHIC OFFICE. 1450

0565-8802 See REVIEW AND ANALYSIS OF ARCHEOLOGY PROGRAM. 280

0565-9248 See FEDERAL PLAN FOR METEOROLOGICAL SERVICES AND SUPPORTING RESEARCH / U.S. DEPARTMENT OF COMMERCE, NATIONAL OCEANIC AND ATMOSPHERIC ADMINISTRATION, THE. 1425

0565-9310 See REGISTER OF REPORTING LABOR ORGANIZATIONS. 1705

0566-0009 See CASELOAD STATISTICS : STATE VOCATIONAL REHABILITATION AGENCIES. 5266

0566-0637 See REPORT OF THE VISA OFFICE. 1921

0566-0785 See UNITED STATES ATTORNEYS BULLETIN. 3067

0566-2036 See UNIVERSITEIT EN HOGESCHOOL. 1852

0566-2257 See UNIVERSITY NEWS. 1852

0566-2389 See UNIVERSITY OF RICHMOND LAW REVIEW. 3069

0566-263X See UNSERE KUNSTDENKMALER. 367

0566-2753 See UNTERSUCHUNGEN UBER GRUPPEN UND VERBANDE. 5269

0566-2761 See UNTERSUCHUNGEN ZUR GEGENWARTSKUNDE SUDOSTEUROPAS. 5225

0566-2818 See UNTERSUCHUNGEN ZUR ROMANISCHEN PHILOLOGIE. 3331

0566-330X See PAPERS FROM THE ANNUAL CONFERENCE. 2427

0566-392X See USPEKHI MIKROBIOLOGII. 570

0566-3946 See USPEHI SOVREMENNOJ GENETIKI. 552

0566-4632 See UTRECHTSE BIJDRAGEN TOT DE MUZIEKWETENSCHAP. 4157

0566-4640 See UTRECHTSE PUBLIKATIES VOOR ALGEMENE LITERATUURWETENSCHAP. 3450

0566-4683 See SPECIAL BULLETIN OF THE COLLEGE OF AGRICULTURE, UTSUNOMIYA UNIVERSITY. 136

0566-4691 See UTSUNOMIYA DAIGAKU NOGAKUBU GAKUJUTSU HOKOKU. 143

0566-5469 See COTTON FIBER AND PROCESSING TEST RESULTS. 5349

0566-6155 See UKRAINSKE MUZYKOZNAVSTVO. 4157

0566-6775 See NATIONAL AVIATION SYSTEM PLAN, THE. 30

0566-7186 See AERONAUTICS AND SPACE REPORT OF THE PRESIDENT. ACTIVITIES. 4

0566-764X See ESTIMATED WORLD REQUIREMENTS OF NARCOTIC DRUGS AND ESTIMATES OF WORLD PRODUCTION OF OPIUM. 1344

0566-7704 See CATALOGUE OF UNESCO PUBLICATIONS. 413

0566-7801 See DIRECTORY OF AREA WAGE SURVEYS. 1663

0566-8174 See ANNUAL PEAK DISCHARGES FROM SMALL DRAINAGE AREAS IN MONTANA THROUGH ... / UNITED STATES DEPARTMENT OF THE INTERIOR, GEOLOGICAL SURVEY. 1365

0566-8352 See BRIEFS OF ACCIDENTS INVOLVING MISSING AND MISSING LATER RECOVERED AIRCRAFT, U.S. GENERAL AVIATION. 15

0566-8794 See UOMO & CULTURA. 247

0566-8824 See URBAN LANGUAGE SERIES. 3331

0566-9618 See FAA STATISTICAL HANDBOOK OF AVIATION / FEDERAL AVIATION AGENCY. 19

0566-9847 See NASA'S UNIVERSITY PROGRAM. 30

0566-9995 See SCIENCE RESOURCES STUDIES HIGHLIGHTS. 5153

0567-0020 See EASTERN ARCTIC ICE, THE SEASONAL OUTLOOK. 1413

0567-0497 See ANNUAL REPORT ON THE UTAH STATE RETIREMENT SYSTEM, SCHOOL DIVISION TO THE UTAH STATE RETIREMENT BOARD. 1649

0567-1159 See AUSTRALIAN TOBACCO GROWERS' BULLETIN. 5372

0567-1248 See MONATSBERICHTE UBER DIE OSTERREICHISCHE LANDWIRTSCHAFT / AGRARWIRTSCHAFTLICHES INSTITUT DES BUNDESMINISTERIUMS FUER LAND- UND FORSTWIRTSCHAFT. 109

0567-1744 See AUTHOR SERIES. 2722

0567-2317 See AUTOMOTIVE REBUILDER. 5407

0567-2392 See AUTOPISTA. 5407

0567-2856 See AVICULTURAL BULLETIN. 5615

0567-2899 See AVIONICS NEWS. 14

0567-431X See AGRICULTURAL AND VETERINARY CHEMICALS. 960

0567-4840 See KANO STUDIES. 2499

0567-4921 See ABHANDLUNGEN AUS DEM GEBIETE DER AUGENHEILKUNDE. 3871

0567-4980 See ABHANDLUNGEN FUER DIE KUNDE DES MORGENLANDES / HRSG. VON DER DEUTSCHEN MORGENLANDISCHEN GESELLSCHAFT. 3260

0567-4999 See ABHANDLUNGEN ZUR KUNST-, MUSIK- UND LITERATURWISSENSCHAFT. 311

0567-5111 See ABOGADA INTERNACIONAL. THE INTERNATIONAL WOMAN LAWYER, LA. 3122

0567-5235 See ABSATZWIRTSCHAFT, DIE. 920

0567-560X See ACADEMIA (REAL ACADEMIA DE BELLAS ARTES DE SAN FERNANDO). 311

0567-5911 See ANALES DE LA ACADEMIA NACIONAL DE CIENCIAS. CUADERNO 2 : SERIE CIENCIAS DE LA NATURALEZA. 441

0567-6037 See BOLETIN DE LA ACADEMIA PUERTORRIQUENA DE LA HISTORIA. 2723

0567-6312 See STUDII SI MATERIALE DE ISTORIE MEDIE. 2712

0567-6320 See STUDII SI MATERIALE DE ISTORIE MODERNA. 2712

0567-638X See STUDII SI CERCETARI DE GEOLOGIE, GEOFIZICA, GEOGRAFIE. SERIA GEOLOGIE. 1399

0567-6487 See ACADEMIC REVIEWER, THE. 1807

0567-6509 See ANALES / ACADEMIA DE GEOGRAFIA E HISTORIA DE COSTA RICA. 2720

0567-672X See ACAROLOGIE. 439

0567-6738 See ANNUARIO DELLA ACCADEMIA DELLE SCIENZE DELL'INSTITUTO DI BOLOGNA : CLASSE DI SCIENZE FISICHE. 4397

0567-6746 See INDICI E SUSSIDI BIBLIOGRAFICI. 417

0567-7254 See ACTA ASIATICA. 2644

0567-7289 See ACTA BALTICA. 2672

0567-7351 See HUA HSUEH HSUEH PAO. 977

0567-7386 See ACTA CLINICA BELGICA. SUPPLEMENTUM. 3544

0567-7432 See ACTA FYTOTECHNICA. 2407

0567-7491 See ACTA GEOLOGICA ET GEOGRAPHICA UNIVERSITATIS COMENIANAE. GEOLOGICA. 1364

0567-7513 See ACTA GEOLOGICA LILLOANA. 1364

0567-7556 See ACTA HISTOCHEMICA. SUPPLEMENTBAND. 479

0567-7572 See ACTA HORTICULTURAE. 2407

0567-7580 See ACTA HUMBOLDTIANA. 2609

0567-7718 See ACTA MECHANICA SINICA. 4427

0567-7734 See ACTA MEDICA ET BIOLOGICA. 3544

0567-7785 See ACTA MEXICANA DE CIENCIA Y TECNOLOGIA. 5080

0567-784X See ACTA NEOPHILOLOGICA. 3357

0567-7874 See ACTA ORGANOLOGICA. 4098

0567-7920 See ACTA PALAEONTOLOGICA POLONICA. 4226

0567-7939 See ACTA PARASITOLOGICA LITUANICA. 5573

0567-7947 See ACTA PHYSICA ET CHIMICA DEBRECINA. 4395

0567-8099 See ACTA ROMANICA (SZEGED). 3261

0567-8242 See ACTA UNIVERSITATIS CAROLINAE. IURIDICA. MONOGRAPHIA. 2927

0567-8250 See ACTA UNIVERSITATIS CAROLINAE. MEDICA. MONOGRAPHIA. 3545

0567-8269 See ACTA UNIVERSITATIS CAROLINAE. PHILOLOGICA. 3261

0567-8293 See ACTA UNIVERSITATIS CAROLINAE. PHILOSOPHICA ET HISTORICA. 4339

0567-8307 See ACTA UNIVERSITATIS CAROLINAE. PHILOSOPHICA ET HISTORICA. MONOGRAPHIA. 2609

0567-8315 See ACTA VETERINARIA (BEOGRAD). 5501

0567-8331 See ACTA ZOOTECHNICA. 5574

0567-8757 See ACTUALITES HEMATOLOGIQUES. 3794

0567-8811 See ACTUALITES NEPHROLOGIQUES DE L'HOPITAL NECKER. 3988

0567-8854 See ACTUALITES PHARMACOLOGIQUES. 4289

0567-932X See ADELPHI PAPERS. **4514**

0567-9494 See ADMINISTRATIVE LAW NEWS (AMERICAN BAR ASSOCIATION. SECTION OF ADMINISTRATIVE LAW : 1974). **3091**

0567-9702 See ADULT TEACHER GUIDE. **4932**

0568-0425 See ADVOCATE (BOSTON, MASS.). **2928**

0568-0581 See AERONOMY REPORT. **5**

0568-062X See AEROSOL REVIEW. **4217**

0568-1057 See AFRICA; FOUILLES, MONUMENTS ET COLLECTIONS ARCHEOLOGIQUES EN TUNISIE. **2636**

0568-1715 See AFRIKA-STUDIEN. **2637**

0568-2339 See AGRA UNIVERSITY JOURNAL OF RESEARCH. LETTERS. **46**

0568-2517 See AGRICULTURA TECNICA EN MEXICO. **49**

0568-2606 See AGRICULTURAL DATA BOOK FOR THE FAR EAST AND OCEANIA, THE. **49**

0568-2800 See INDEX OF CURRENT RESEARCH ON PIGS / AGRICULTURAL RESEARCH COUNCIL. **94**

0568-2894 See AGRICULTURAL STATISTICS FOR ONTARIO. **150**

0568-3025 See AGROCIENCIA. **55**

0568-3106 See AGRONOMY NEWS. **162**

0568-3114 See AGROTECNIA DE CUBA. **57**

0568-3424 See ANNUAL REPORT - AIR CANADA. **11**

0568-3653 See AIR QUALITY MONOGRAPHS. **2223**

0568-3939 See AISTHESIS. **2841**

0568-4358 See VEROFFENTLICHUNGEN. **1080**

0568-465X See RASTENIEVDNI NAUKI. **2430**

0568-5222 See BIBLIOGRAFIIA IZDANII AKADEMII NAUK SSSR; EZHEGODNIK. BIBLIOGRAPHY OF PUBLICATIONS OF THE ACADEMY OF SCIENCES OF THE USSR; A YEAR-BOOK. **409**

0568-5230 See BULLETIN OF THE RUSSIAN ACADEMY OF SCIENCES, DIVISION OF CHEMICAL SCIENCE. **963**

0568-5524 See TRUDY GELMINTOLOGICHESKOI LABORATORII. **5599**

0568-5575 See TRUDY. **475**

0568-5656 See TRUDY - AKADEMIA NAUK SSSR, INSTITUT BIOLOGII VNUTRENNIH VOD. **475**

0568-5796 See DOKLADY I SOOBSCENIJA INSTITUTA ISTORII. **2615**

0568-6156 See TRUDY INSTITUTA GEOLOGII. **1400**

0568-6199 See KOMETY I METEORY. **396**

0568-6547 See IZVESTIIA SIBIRSKOGO OTDELENIIA AKADEMII NAUK SSSR. SERIIA BIOLOGICHESKIKH NAUK. **460**

0568-658X See TRUDY INSTITUTA GEOLOGII I GEOFIZIKI (NOVOSIBIRSK). **1400**

0568-7551 See AKTUELLE BEITRAGE DER STAATS- UND RECHTSWISSENSCHAFT. **2929**

0568-7632 See APOTHEKE HEUTE. **921**

0568-7683 See AKTUIL. **2501**

0568-7888 See GEOLOGICAL SURVEY OF ALABAMA INFORMATION SERIES. **1378**

0568-7896 See REPRINT SERIES - GEOLOGICAL SURVEY OF ALABAMA. **1395**

0568-806X See MAGAZINE - ALABAMA GENEALOGICAL SOCIETY, INC. **2459**

0568-8604 See BIOLOGICAL PAPERS OF THE UNIVERSITY OF ALASKA. **445**

0568-9163 See ALBERTA LIST. **4625**

0569-0242 See PROCEEDINGS OF THE ALL-INDIA CONGRESS OF ZOOLOGY. **5595**

0569-0803 See ALMAMATER. **57**

0569-1176 See ALOCANA. **3263**

0569-1338 See ALTALANOS NYELVESZETI TANULMANYOK. **3263**

0569-1346 See ALTAMURA. **335**

0569-1613 See ALZEYER GESCHICHTSBLATTER. **2673**

0569-1796 See AMATEUR WRESTLING NEWS. **4882**

0569-2032 See YEAR BOOK - AMERICAN ACADEMY OF ACTUARIES. **2896**

0569-2229 See NEWS-LETTER OF THE AMERICAN ANTIQUARIAN SOCIETY. **4831**

0569-2407 See AAAA ROSTER AND ORGANIZATION. **753**

0569-2423 See NEWSLETTER / AMERICAN ASSOCIATION OF BOTANICAL GARDENS AND ARBORETA. **519**

0569-2628 See OFFICIAL PROCEEDINGS, ANNUAL MEETING - AMERICAN ASSOCIATION OF FEED MICROSCOPISTS. **116**

0569-2857 See TOUR BOOK: ATLANTIC PROVINCES AND QUEBEC. **5492**

0569-2865 See MIDEASTERN TOUR BOOK. **5484**

0569-292X See AMERICAN BANK DIRECTORY. **769**

0569-308X See SECTION OF ADMINISTRATIVE LAW DIRECTORY. **3094**

0569-3314 See PUBLIC CONTRACT NEWSLETTER. **3033**

0569-3578 See ANNUAL REPORT / AMERICAN BUREAU OF SHIPPING. **5447**

0569-3772 See PREPRINTS OF PAPERS PRESENTED - AMERICAN CHEMICAL SOCIETY. DIVISION OF FUEL CHEMISTRY. **989**

0569-3799 See PREPRINTS - AMERICAN CHEMICAL SOCIETY. DIVISION OF PETROLEUM CHEMISTRY. **1028**

0569-3802 See PAPERS PRESENTED AT THE MEETING. **1045**

0569-3845 See AMERICAN CHRISTMAS TREE JOURNAL. **58**

0569-4027 See ACI STANDARDS / AMERICAN CONCRETE INSTITUTE. **2018**

0569-4345 See AMERICAN ECONOMIST (NEW YORK, N.Y. 1960), THE. **1461**

0569-4450 See CONTRIBUTIONS OF THE AMERICAN ENTOMOLOGICAL INSTITUTE. **5607**

0569-4515 See PROCEEDINGS OF THE ... CONSTITUTIONAL CONVENTION OF THE AFL-CIO. **1703**

0569-4515 See PROCEEDINGS OF THE CONSTITUTIONAL CONVENTION OF THE AFL-CIO. **1703**

0569-4523 See PUBLICATION - AMERICAN FEDERATION OF LABOR AND CONGRESS OF INDUSTRIAL ORGANIZATIONS. **1704**

0569-4612 See PROCEEDINGS, CONSTITUTIONAL CONVENTION OF THE INDUSTRIAL UNION DEPARTMENT, AFL-CIO. **1703**

0569-5058 See DIRECTORY - HOME ECONOMISTS IN BUSINESS, SECTION OF THE AMERICAN HOME ECONOMICS ASSOCIATION. **2789**

0569-5090 See PUBLICATIONS CATALOG - AMERICAN HOSPITAL ASSOCIATION. **3791**

0569-5457 See AICHE WORKSHOP. **2007**

0569-5473 See AICHE EQUIPMENT TESTING PROCEDURE. **2007**

0569-5503 See PROCEEDINGS / ELECTRONIC COMPONENTS & TECHNOLOGY CONFERENCE. **2076**

0569-5716 See PHYSICS MANPOWER, EDUCATION AND EMPLOYMENT STUDIES. **4427**

0569-5821 See DIRECTORY OF MEMBERS / THE INSTITUTE. **4836**

0569-5910 See CHARTING STEEL'S PROGRESS. **1601**

0569-6275 See FINANCIAL ASSISTANCE FOR LIBRARY EDUCATION. **3210**

0569-6356 See AMERICAN MOTOR CARRIER DIRECTORY (NORTH AMERICAN EDITION). **5375**

0569-6704 See CIRCULATION (WILMETTE, ILL.). **922**

0569-7344 See AMERICAN REVIEW OF ART AND SCIENCE. **336**

0569-7425 See EXCAVATIONS OF THE ATHENIAN AGORA: PICTURE BOOK. **268**

0569-8219 See SPECIAL PUBLICATION / AMERICAN SOCIETY OF MAMMALOGISTS. **5597**

0569-8243 See REPORT ON DIESEL AND GAS ENGINES POWER COSTS. **2128**

0569-8553 See ASHA REPORTS. **3886**

0569-8642 See AMERICAN STUDIES IN PAPYROLOGY. **1074**

0569-9789 See ANALECTA CALASANCTIANA. **5023**

0569-9797 See ANALECTA GEOLOGICA. **1365**

0569-9827 See ANALECTA MUSICOLOGICA. **4100**

0569-986X See ANALECTA ROMANICA. **3264**

0569-9878 See ANALES CERVANTINOS. **3361**

0569-9894 See ANALES DE ANATOMIA. **3678**

0569-9908 See ANALES DEL DESARROLLO. **441**

0569-9924 See ANALES GALDOSIANOS. **3337**

0570-006X See KENKYU KIYO / RESEARCH REPORTS OF THE ANAN TECHNICAL COLLEGE. ANAN KOGYO KOTO SENMON GAKKO. **5123**

0570-0329 See ANDHRA PRADESH BUDGET IN BRIEF. **4709**

0570-0345 See DETAILED IRRIGATION BUDGET. **4720**

0570-0388 See ECONOMIC & STATISTICAL BULLETIN. **1532**

0570-0760 See ANESTESIA E RIANIMAZIONE. **3681**

0570-0833 See ANGEWANDTE CHEMIE. INTERNATIONAL EDITION IN ENGLISH. **960**

0570-1244 See BIENNIAL SYMPOSIUM ON ANIMAL REPRODUCTION; [PROCEEDINGS]. **5505**

0570-1538 See AGRICULTURAL SCIENCE IN FINLAND. **52**

0570-1554 See ANNALES ARCHEOLOGIQUES ARABES SYRIENNES. **254**

0570-1783 See ANNALS OF AGRICULTURAL SCIENCE. **59**

0570-1791 See ANNALS OF ARID ZONE. **162**

0570-1791 See ANNALS OF AGRICULTURAL SCIENCE, MOSHTOHOR. **59**

0570-1864 See ANNALS OF REGIONAL SCIENCE, THE. **2814**

0570-1880 See ANNALS OF THE CAPE PROVINCIAL MUSEUMS. NATURAL HISTORY. **4162**

0570-1937 See ANNEE AFRICAINE. **2637**

0570-1953 See ANNEE CANONIQUE, L'. **2933**

0570-202X See ANNOTATIONES ZOOLOGICAE ET BOTANICAE. **5576**

0570-2259 See ANNUAIRE ROUMAIN D'ANTHROPOLOGIE. **228**

0570-2496 See ANNUAL INDEX OF THE REPORTS ON PLANT CHEMISTRY. **476**

0570-2666 See ANNUAL SURVEY OF INDIAN LAW. **2935**

0570-2844 See ANTARKTIKA. **5084**

0570-4065 See ANUARIO DE ESTUDIOS ATLANTICOS. **2675**

0570-4073 See ANUARIO DE GEOGRAFIA. **2554**

0570-4316 See ANUARIO HISPANO-LUSO-AMERICANO DE DERECHO INTERNACIONAL. **3124**

0570-4480 See ANZEN KOGAKU. **2096**

0570-4499 See TE AO HOU; THE MAORI MAGAZINE. **2671**

0570-4928 See APPLIED SPECTROSCOPY REVIEWS (SOFTCOVER ED.). **1013**

0570-4979 See APPROACH (NORFOLK). **4174**

0570-5118 See AQUATIC MICROBIOLOGY NEWSLETTER. **559**

0570-5169 See AQUILO. SER. BOTANICA. **500**

0570-5177 See AQUILO SER ZOOLOGICA. **5576**

0570-5274 See PAPERS AND DISCUSSIONS. **4271**

0570-5398 See ARABICA. **2767**

0570-622X See ARHAIOLOGIKON DELTION. **259**

0570-6270 See ARCHEOLOGIA. **258**

0570-6343 See ARHEOLOGIJA UN ETNOGRAFIJA. **259**

0570-6378 See ARCHETYPAL IMAGES IN GREEK RELIGION. **4935**

0570-6483 See ARCHITECTURAL INDEX, THE. **289**

0570-6602 See ARCHITEKTUR AKTUELL FACH-JOURNAL. **290**

0570-6629 See ARCHITETTURA; CRONACHE E STORIA, L'. 291

0570-720X See ARCHIVS. 2255

0570-7218 See ARCHIVUM (OVIEDO). 3266

0570-7242 See ARCHIVUM BIBLIOGRAPHICUM CARMELITANUM. 408

0570-7293 See ARCO. 2842

0570-7358 See ARDEOLA. 5615

0570-8869 See ARGO / NARODNI MUZEJ V LJUBLJANI. 4084

0570-8958 See ARHEOLOSKI RADOVI I RASPRAVE. 259

0570-8966 See ARHEOLOSKI VESTNIK. 259

0570-9008 See ARHIVSKI VJESNIK. 2480

0570-9326 See ANNUAL CHECKLIST OF PUBLICATIONS OF THE STATE OF ARIZONA. 3190

0570-9369 See LEAD AND ZINC INDUSTRY. 4007

0570-9652 See PUBLICATION - ARIZONA STATE UNIVERSITY. CENTER FOR METEORITE STUDIES. 398

0571-0189 See SPECIAL REPORT - AGRICULTURAL EXPERIMENT STATION, DIVISION OF AGRICULTURE, UNIVERSITY OF ARKANSAS, FAYETTEVILLE. 137

0571-0227 See SCHOOL CENSUS FOR THE STATE OF ARKANSAS. 1871

0571-026X See SPECIAL GROUND-WATER REPORT (LITTLE ROCK). 5539

0571-0472 See ARKANSAS FAMILY HISTORIAN, THE. 2438

0571-0502 See ARKANSAS LAWYER. 2937

0571-0626 See ARKHEOGRAFICHESKII EZHEGODNIK / AKADEMIIA NAUK SSSR, OTDELENIE ISTORICHESKIKH NAUK, ARKHEOGRAFICHESKAIA KOMISSIIA. 260

0571-1304 See ARRABONA. 337

0571-1371 See ARS ORIENTALIS. 337

0571-1509 See ART DE BASSE-NORMANDIE. 338

0571-2378 See ASAHI JANARU. 3192

0571-2726 See REPORT OF THE SESSION - ASIAN-AFRICAN LEGAL CONSULTATIVE COMMITTEE. 3180

0571-2742 See ASIAN AND AFRICAN STUDIES (BRATISLAVA, CZECHOSLOVAKIA). 2646

0571-3285 See BOLETIN / ASOCIACION ARGENTINA DE ASTRONOMIA. 393

0571-3692 See BOLETIN DE LA ASOCIACION ESPANOLA DE ORIENTALISTAS. 2647

0571-5350 See BULLETIN - ASSOCIATION DES AMIS DE RABELAIS ET DE LA DEVINIERE. 3369

0571-5865 See CAHIERS DE L'ASSOCIATION INTERNATIONALE DES ETUDES FRANCAISES. 3271

0571-625X See COMPENDIUM OF UNIVERSITY ENTRANCE REQUIREMENTS FOR FIRST DEGREE COURSES IN THE UNITED KINGDOM, A. 1818

0571-6489 See PROCEEDINGS OF THE ASSOCIATIONS OF ORTHODOX JEWISH SCIENTISTS. 5052

0571-7132 See ASTROFIZIKA. 391

0571-7256 See ASTROPHYSICS. 4398

0571-7868 See ATLANTIC SERIES : A COLLECTION OF STUDIES ON SUBJECTS RELATED TO THE NORTH ATLANTIC TREATY ORGANIZATION. 4516

0571-8236 See ATTAKAPAS GAZETTE. 2722

0571-8279 See ATTORNEY-CPA, THE. 2938

0571-8635 See AUDIO-DIGEST. OBSTETRICS AND GYNECOLOGY. 3757

0571-8805 See AUDUBON CONSERVATION REPORT. 2187

0571-8899 See AUGUSTA HISTORICAL BULLETIN. 2722

0571-9070 See VETUS LATINA. AUS DER GESCHICHTE DER LATEINISCHEN BIBEL. 5020

0572-0494 See ANNUAL REPORT ON THE TERRITORY OF NORFOLK ISLAND. 4629

0572-1431 See PROCEEDINGS [OF THE CONFERENCE]. 5442

0572-144X See SPECIAL REPORT - AUSTRALIAN ROAD RESEARCH BOARD. 5444

0572-2691 See AVTOMATIKA (KIEV). 1218

0572-2721 See AL AWAMIA. 57

0572-3000 See ABACO (MADRID, SPAIN). 3357

0572-3159 See AERONOMICA ACTA. A. 5

0572-3299 See IZVESTIIA : MEKHANIKA TVERDOGO TELA. 2117

0572-4082 See ARION (BUDAPEST, HUNGARY). 3460

0572-4252 See ACM MONOGRAPH SERIES. 1170

0572-4953 See AMERICAN ASSOCIATION OF LAW LIBRARIES NEWSLETTER. 3189

0572-502X See AGMA DIRECTORY. 2109

0572-5801 See MITTEILUNGSBLATT DER BUNDESANSTALT FUER WASSERBAU. 2093

0572-5933 See BANK AUTOMATION NEWSLETTER. 774

0572-6034 See BANYASZATI ES KOHASZATI LOPOK. KOOLAJ ES FOLDGAZ. 2135

0572-6239 See JAHRBUCH DES STAATLICHEN INSTITUTS FUER MUSIKFORSCHUNG PREUSSISCHER KULTURBESITZ. 4124

0572-6263 See BERLINER BEITRAEGE ZUR NAMENFORSCHUNG. 3268

0572-6301 See BEST'S MARKET GUIDE. 2876

0572-6565 See BIOTECHNOLOGY AND BIOENGINEERING SYMPOSIUM. 3688

0572-6972 See MONOGRAPH SERIES - FACULTY OF COMMERCE AND BUSINESS ADMINISTRATION, UNIVERSITY OF BRITISH COLUMBIA. 696

0572-7022 See OCCASIONAL SYMPOSIUM. 5517

0572-709X See IRON AND STEEL INDUSTRY. ANNUAL STATISTICS FOR THE UNITED KINGDOM. 1612

0572-7251 See ANNALES UNIVERSITATIS SCIENTIARUM BUDAPESTINENSIS DE ROLANDO EOTVOS NOMINATAE. SECTIO LINGUISTICA. 3265

0572-7545 See BUSINESS ASIA. 646

0572-807X See BIBLIOGRAPHY : PUBLICATIONS RESULTING FROM COUNCIL SUPPORT. 5227

0572-8258 See TECHNICAL REPORT - LAMONT-DOHERTY GEOLOGICAL OBSERVATORY. 1399

0572-8274 See CONSTITUTIONS OF THE UNITED STATES, NATIONAL AND STATE. 3092

0572-8312 See NOTES ON SELECTED ACQUISITIONS. 3237

0573-0791 See REPORT OF WORK CARRIED OUT. 471

0573-2018 See COMPOSTELLANUM. 5028

0573-2107 See COMPUTERS IN BIOMEDICAL RESEARCH. 3568

0573-2697 See COLLANA DI STUDI E DOCUMENTAZIONE. 1602

0573-2913 See PROCEEDINGS OF THE ANNUAL CONFERENCE FOR MUNICIPAL CLERKS. 4675

0573-665X See CONNECTICUT MARKET DATA. 1531

0573-7419 See CONSTRUCTIA DE MASINI. 2112

0573-777X See CONTACT. 4950

0573-7796 See CONTACT - NATIONAL ASSOCIATION OF FREE WILL BAPTISTS. 5058

0573-8164 See CONTINENTAL COMMENTS. 5412

0573-8547 See CONTRIBUTIONS TO CALIFORNIA ARCHAEOLOGY. 266

0573-8555 See CONTRIBUTIONS TO ECONOMIC ANALYSIS. 1471

0574-1831 See COST OF DOING BUSINESS, PARTNERSHIPS & PROPRIETORSHIPS. 662

0574-1831 See COST OF DOING BUSINESS : CORPORATIONS. 662

0574-203X See BOLETIN TECNICO / INTER-AMERICAN INSTITUTE OF AGRICULTURAL SCIENCES. 68

0574-3680 See COVERED WAGON, THE. 2730

0574-377X See CRAIGHEAD COUNTY HISTORICAL QUARTERLY, THE. 2730

0574-3869 See CRAWFORD COUNTY LEGAL JOURNAL. 2957

0574-4741 See CRONACHE DI CHIMICA. 973

0574-6086 See BIBLIOGRAFIA CUBANA. 408

0574-8070 See CUU QUOC (MICROFICHE). 5813

0574-8259 See MEMOIR (CYPRUS. GEOLOGICAL SURVEY DEPT.). 1387

0574-8526 See VESTNIK. 1921

0574-9549 See CIS : CHROMOSOME INFORMATION SERVICE. 451

0574-9549 See C I S; CHROMOSOMES INFORMATION SERVICE. 543

0575-0385 See CAHIERS ALSACIENS D'ARCHEOLOGIE, D'ART ET D'HISTOIRE. 265

0575-0512 See CAHIERS D'ETUDES COMTOISES. 2682

0575-0598 See CAHIERS DE CLIO. 5241

0575-0717 See CAHIERS DE LA HAUTE-LOIRE LE PUY. 2682

0575-0865 See CAHIERS DES INGENIEURS AGRONOMES. 1967

0575-089X See CAHIERS DES DIX. 2725

0575-1144 See CAHIERS PAUL CLAUDEL. 3371

0575-1276 See CAHIERS STAELIENS. 3339

0575-1330 See MELANGES - INSTITUT DOMINICAIN D'ETUDES ORIENTALES DU CAIRE. 3302

0575-1373 See BULLETIN OF THE FACULTY OF PHARMACY. 4295

0575-1454 See MAJALLAT MAHAD AL-MAKHTUTAT AL-ARABIYAH / JAMIAT. 3301

0575-1772 See BULLETIN OF THE INSTITUTE OF POST GRADUATE MEDICAL EDUCATION AND RESEARCH. 3560

0575-2124 See CALIBAN (TOULOUSE, FRANCE). 3371

0575-3104 See COUNTY REPORT - CALIFORNIA. DIVISION OF MINES AND GEOLOGY. 1372

0575-3317 See REPORTS - CALIFORNIA COOPERATIVE OCEANIC FISHERIES INVESTIGATIONS. 2311

0575-4550 See CSE REPORT. 1819

0575-4577 See EVALUATION COMMENT. 1746

0575-4941 See CONTRIBUTION (CALIFORNIA WATER RESOURCES CENTER). 1413

0575-4968 See REPORT - CALIFORNIA WATER RESOURCES CENTER. 5538

0575-5298 See CALIFORNIA AGRICULTURAL DIRECTORY (BERKELEY, CALIF.). 71

0575-5700 See CALIFORNIA GEOGRAPHER, THE. 2557

0575-5751 See CALIFORNIA HISTORIAN. 2725

0575-5964 See SOCIOECONOMIC REPORT. 3642

0575-6200 See CALIFORNIA STATISTICAL ABSTRACT. 5325

0575-6316 See JOURNAL / CALIFORNIA TRIAL LAWYERS ASSOCIATION. 2986

0575-6383 See CALL OF THE PLATEAU. 2726

0575-6863 See CAMBRIDGE SOUTH ASIAN STUDIES. 2648

0575-786X See ADVANCE STATISTICS OF EDUCATION. 1793

0575-7975 See BUILDING PERMITS, ANNUAL SUMMARY. 632

0575-805X See CANADIAN FORESTRY STATISTICS. 2399

0575-8521 See FEDERAL GOVERNMENT FINANCE. 4723

0575-8548 See FIELD CROP REPORTING SERIES. 171

0575-8629 See FUNERAL DIRECTORS. 2407

0575-8645 See GENERAL REVIEW OF THE MINERAL INDUSTRIES. MINES, QUARRIES AND OIL WELLS. 1362

0575-8750 See INCOME DISTRIBUTIONS BY SIZE IN CANADA. 1533

0575-8823 See INTER-CORPORATE OWNERSHIP. 1612

0575-9412 See PRINTING, PUBLISHING AND ALLIED INDUSTRIES. 4568

0575-9455 See PRODUCTS SHIPPED BY CANADIAN MANUFACTURERS. 3486

0575-9463 See PROVINCIAL GOVERNMENT ENTERPRISE FINANCE. 4675

0575-9536 See PULPWOOD AND WOOD RESIDUE STATISTICS. 2404

0575-9560 *See* RADIO AND TELEVISION BROADCASTING. 1137

0575-9587 *See* REFINED PETROLEUM PRODUCTS. VOLUME 2. CONSUMPTION OF PETROLEUM PRODUCTS. 4276

0576-0119 *See* CORPORATION TAXATION STATISTICS (OTTAWA). 4697

0576-0186 *See* CONSUMPTION OF CONTAINERS AND OTHER PACKAGING SUPPLIES BY THE MANUFACTURING INDUSTRIES. 4218

0576-0917 *See* NEWFOUNDLAND FISHERIES. 2309

0576-1123 *See* LABOUR STANDARDS IN CANADA. 1686

0576-1409 *See* ADMINISTRATION FEDERALE DU CANADA, L'. 4624

0576-2243 *See* CANADIAN TIDE AND CURRENT TABLES. PACIFIC COAST. 1447

0576-2367 *See* SURFACE WATER DATA. BRITISH COLUMBIA. 5540

0576-2383 *See* SURFACE WATER DATA. ONTARIO. 1418

0576-2405 *See* SURFACE WATER DATA : SASKATCHEWAN. 1418

0576-2944 *See* MDRP. 2828

0576-3819 *See* PROCEEDINGS OF THE STANDING SENATE COMMITTEE ON FOREIGN AFFAIRS. 4532

0576-3835 *See* PROCEEDINGS OF THE STANDING SENATE COMMITTEE ON LEGAL AND CONSTITUTIONAL AFFAIRS. 3093

0576-3851 *See* PROCEEDINGS OF THE STANDING SENATE COMMITTEE ON NATIONAL FINANCE. 4675

0576-4076 *See* ANNUAL REPORT / SOLICITOR GENERAL CANADA. 3157

0576-4688 *See* CANADIAN BEEKEEPING. 72

0576-5161 *See* TRANSACTIONS - ENGINEERING AND OPERATING DIVISION. CANADIAN ELECTRICAL ASSOCIATION. 2084

0576-5277 *See* CANADIAN-GERMAN FOLKLORE. 2318

0576-5501 *See* CANADIAN INTELLIGENCE SERVICE. 4636

0576-5986 *See* MEMBERSHIP DIRECTORY - CANADIAN PSYCHIATRIC ASSOCIATION. REPERTOIRE DES MEMBRES - ASSOCIATION DES PSYCHIATRES DU CANADA. 3930

0576-6370 *See* OCCASIONAL PAPER - CANADIAN WILDLIFE SERVICE. 2201

0576-6478 *See* CANADO-AMERICAIN, LE. 2530

0576-6842 *See* NEW SERIES. 1837

0576-6850 *See* BULLETIN - CAPE TOWN. UNIVERSITY OF CAPE TOWN. DEPARTMENT OF GEOLOGY. 1368

0576-7172 *See* CARBOHYDRATE CHEMISTRY. 1040

0576-7334 *See* CAREERS IN BUSINESS. 4202

0576-7423 *See* CARETAS : ILUSTRACION PERUANA. 346

0576-7954 *See* CARNEGIE QUARTERLY. 1814

0576-808X *See* CAROLINA COMMENTS. 2481

0576-8233 *See* CARTA DE ESPANA. 2514

0576-8896 *See* CATALOGO BOLAFFI DELL'ARCHITETTURA ITALIANA. 294

0576-9515 *See* PUBLICATIONS. (MONOGRAPH SERIES). 5035

0576-9736 *See* CEDAR COUNTY HISTORICAL SOCIETY REVIEW, THE. 2727

0576-9760 *See* CELJSKI ZBORNIK. 2683

0576-9787 *See* CELLULOSE CHEMISTRY AND TECHNOLOGY. 1021

0577-0394 *See* CENTRAL AFRICAN AIRWAYS GUIDE TO THE FEDERATION OF RHODESIA AND NYASALAND. 16

0577-0807 *See* CENTRAL ILLINOIS GENEALOGICAL QUARTERLY. 2442

0577-0963 *See* BULLETIN - CENTRAL STATES ANTHROPOLOGICAL SOCIETY (U.S.). 232

0577-098X *See* DIRECTORY OF MEMBERSHIP - CENTRAL STATES SPEECH ASSOCIATION. 1110

0577-1099 *See* CENTRE COUNTY HERITAGE. 2727

0577-1145 *See* SERIE : ETUDES SYNDICALES. 1710

0577-148X *See* COURRIER HEBDOMADAIRE DU C.R.I.S.P. 5196

0577-1757 *See* COURRIER DU CENTRE INTERNATIONAL D'ETUDES POETIQUES. 3461

0577-2168 *See* BOLLETTINO DEL CENTRO CAMUNO DI STUDI PREISTORICI. 344

0577-2567 *See* DOCUMENTOS - CENTRO DE INFORMACION Y DOCUMENTACION PARA AMERICA LATINA. 5326

0577-277X *See* BOLLETINO - CENTRO DI STUDI FILOLOGICI E LINGUISTICI SICILIANI. 3269

0577-3199 *See* REPORTS AND MEMOIRS. 280

0577-3334 *See* CERAMICA DE CULTURA MAYA ET AL. 265

0577-3644 *See* HYDROBIOLOGICAL STUDIES. 1414

0577-3725 *See* SBORNIK HISTORICKY. 2628

0577-4179 *See* C'EST-A-DIRE (MONTREAL). 3273

0577-5132 *See* CHALLENGE (WHITE PLAINS). 1469

0577-5574 *See* CHARIOTEER, THE. 3374

0577-6066 *See* CHEMICAL ECONOMICS NEWSLETTER. 968

0577-6392 *See* CRIB : CHEMOTHERAPY RESEARCH BULLETIN. 4298

0577-6406 *See* CHEMSPHERE. 1022

0577-6619 *See* CHI HSIANG HSUEH PAO. 1421

0577-6686 *See* CHI HSIEH KUNG CHENG HSUEH PAO. 2111

0577-6848 *See* CHIBA DAIGAKU KOGAKUBU KENKYU HOKOKU. 5093

0577-6880 *See* CHIBA-KEN NOGYO SHIKENJO KENKYU HOKOKU. 73

0577-7127 *See* RESEARCH SERIES. 2663

0577-7135 *See* TRANSCRIPT. 2667

0577-7496 *See* CHIH WU HSUEH PAO. 506

0577-750X *See* CHIH WU PAO HU HSUEH HUI HUI K'AN. 506

0577-7518 *See* CHIH WU PAO HU HSUEH PAO. 506

0577-7658 *See* CHIKUSAN SHIKENJO KENKYU HOKOKU. 73

0577-781X *See* CHILDREN'S BOOKS IN PRINT (LONDON, ENGLAND). 4827

0577-7925 *See* BOLETIN TECNICO - CHILE. DIRECCION DE AGRICULTURA Y PESCA. 67

0577-7933 *See* BOLETIN DE ESTADISTICA MINERA. 2002

0577-7976 *See* INDUSTRIAS MANUFACTURERAS. 3481

0577-8042 *See* CARTA GEOLOGICA DE CHILE. 1371

0577-8174 *See* ESTADISTICAS (CHILE. SERVICIO DE SEGURO SOCIAL). 2897

0577-8298 *See* PUBLICACIONES. 5595

0577-8425 *See* PUBLICACIONES EN CIENCIAS AGRICOLAS. 123

0577-8468 *See* PUBLICACIONES. 1514

0577-8484 *See* ANO PEDAGOGICO. 1725

0577-8514 *See* INFORMATIVO ESTADISTICO. 5329

0577-8557 *See* ARCHIVOS. 4575

0577-8573 *See* PUBLICACIONES - CHILE. UNIVERSIDAD, SANTIAGO. SEMINARIO DE DERECHO PUBLICO. 3033

0577-893X *See* CHUNG-JUO YIN MU. 4065

0577-9065 *See* BULLETIN - CHINESE HISTORICAL SOCIETY OF AMERICA. 2724

0577-9073 *See* CHINESE JOURNAL OF PHYSICS (TAIPEI). 4399

0577-9103 *See* CHINESE TRADE UNIONS, THE. 1659

0577-9170 *See* QINGHUA XUEBAO. 2770

0577-9294 *See* CHIP CHATS. 633

0577-9316 *See* CHIRIBOTAN. 5094

0577-9391 *See* CHITANIUMU, JIRUKONIUMU. 4000

0577-943X *See* CHMELARSTVI. 166

0577-9766 *See* CHOSEN GAKUHO. 2649

0577-991X *See* UNIVERSITY OF CANTERBURY PUBLICATIONS. 1852

0578-0039 *See* RELIGION AND SOCIETY REPORT. 4991

0578-0144 *See* CHRISTIAN SCIENCE MONITOR (INDEXES). 4946

0578-0225 *See* POLITISCHES JAHRBUCH DER CHRISTLICH - DEMOKRATISCHEN UNION DEUTSCHLANDS. 4491

0578-039X *See* CHRONICA HORTICULTURAE. 2412

0578-0462 *See* CHRONICLES OF SMITH COUNTY, TEXAS. 2728

0578-0578 *See* CHRONOSTRATIGRAPHIE UND NEOSTRATOTYPEN. 1353

0578-0705 *See* CHUAN CHI WEN HSUEH. 431

0578-073X *See* CHUAN KUO HSIN SHU MU. 4821

0578-0780 *See* CHUBUN KENKYU. 3375

0578-0918 *See* CHUGOKU. 2649

0578-0934 *See* CHUGOKU BUNGAKUHO. 3375

0578-1175 *See* CHUN CHIU. 2502

0578-1310 *See* CHUNG-HUA ERH KO TSA CHI. / ZHONGHUA ERKE ZAZHI / CHINESE JOURNAL OF PEDIATRICS. 3902

0578-1345 *See* ZHONGHUA LINXUE JIKAN. 2398

0578-1426 *See* CHUNG-HUA NEI KO TSA CHIH. 3564

0578-154X *See* JOURNAL OF THE CHINA SOCIETY. 5232

0578-1736 *See* CHUNG-KUO NUNG YEH HUA HSUEH. HUI CHIH. 972

0578-1752 *See* CHUNG-KUO NUNG YEH KO HSUEH. 74

0578-1825 *See* ZHONGGUO DIZHI XUEHUI ZHUANKAN. 1402

0578-1930 *See* CHUNG-KYO YU WEN (TAIPEI, TAIWAN). 3273

0578-1949 *See* CHUNG-KUO YU EN (JEN MIN CHIAO YU CHU PAN SHE). 3273

0578-2228 *See* BULLETIN - CHUO DAIGAKU, TOKYO. FACULTY OF SCIENCE AND ENGINEERING. 1967

0578-2724 *See* CIMBEBASIA. MEMOIR. 2638

0578-2775 *See* LECTURES IN MEMORY OF LOUISE TAFT SEMPLE. 3404

0578-2988 *See* CINEMA ONE. 4066

0578-3097 *See* CIRCLE K. 1090

0578-3208 *See* CISLA PRO KAZDEHO. 5325

0578-3224 *See* CISTERCIAN STUDIES QUARTERLY. 5027

0578-3461 *See* STUDY - CITIZENS' RESEARCH FOUNDATION. 5160

0578-3747 *See* CIVIL ENGINEERING IN JAPAN. 2020

0578-4034 *See* CIVILITA VENEZIANA. FONTI E TESTI. SERIE TERZA : LETTERE, MUSICA E TEATRO. 2683

0578-459X *See* CLASSIQUES AFRICAINS. 3376

0578-4875 *See* DAIRY SCIENCE EXTENSION LEAFLET. 194

0578-5391 *See* ACTA MUSEI NAPOCENSIS. 2672

0578-5634 *See* COASTAL ENGINEERING IN JAPAN. 2088

0578-6533 *See* IOWA ADVOCATE. 2984

0578-655X *See* NEWSLETTER - IOWA ARCHEOLOGICAL SOCIETY. 276

0578-6967 *See* IRAN (LONDON). 2505

0578-736X *See* ANNUAL REPORT - IRISH SEA FISHERIES BOARD. 2294

0578-7483 *See* IRISH JOURNAL OF AGRICULTURAL RESEARCH. 97

0578-7661 *See* IRON & STEEL REVIEW. 4005

0578-7904 *See* ISHIKAWAJIMA-HARIMA GIHO. 1981

0578-8072 *See* ISLAMIC STUDIES. 5043

0578-9230 *See* PROCEEDINGS (AKADEMYAH HA-LEUMIT HA-YISREELIT LE-MADAIM). 2852

0578-932X *See* BOOKS FROM ISRAEL. 4825

0578-9583 *See* ISSLEDOVANIIA PO UPRUGOSTI I PLASTICHNOSTI. 4428

0578-9850 *See* BOLLETTINO DELL'ISTITUTO DI STORIA E DI ARTE DEL LAZIO MERIDIONALE. 2612

ISSN Index

0578-9923 See ANNALI / ISTITUTO ITALIANO DI NUMISMATICA. 2779

0579-0263 See ISTORIJA (SKOPJE). 2693

0579-1316 See QUADERNI DELLA RASSEGNA DEGLI ARCHIVI DI STATO. 2483

0579-2746 See HOKOKU. JOURNAL OF THE FACULTY OF AGRICULTURE, IWATE UNIVERSITY. 92

0579-2975 See IZVESTIJA VYSSIH UCEBNYH ZAVEDNIJ. AVIACIONNAJA TEHNIKA. 25

0579-2983 See IZVESTIJA VYSSIH UCEBNYH ZAVEDENIJ, ENERGETIKA. 1948

0579-2991 See IZVESTIJA VYSSIH UCEBNYH ZAVEDENIJ. HIMIJA I HIMICESKAJA TEHNOLOGIJA. 979

0579-2991 See IZVESTIJA VYSSIH UCEBNYH ZAVEDENIJ. HIMIJA I HIMICESKAJA TEHNOLOGIJA. 979

0579-3009 See IZVESTIA VYSSIH UCEBNYH ZAVEDENIJ. PISEVAA TEHNOLOGIA. 2345

0579-3149 See INCOMES DATA PANORAMA. 1677

0579-3920 See TECHNICAL REPORT - INTERNATIONAL PACIFIC HALIBUT COMMISSION. 2314

0579-3998 See INTERNATIONALE BIBLIOTHEK FUER ALLGEMEINE LINGUISTIK. 3288

0579-4005 See INTRODUKTSIIA I AKKLIMATIZATSIIA RASTENII (KIEV, UKRAINE). 2420

0579-4005 See INTRODUKTSIIA TA AKLIMATYZATSII ROSLIN NA UKRAINI. 97

0579-4374 See IMMIGRATION HISTORY NEWSLETTER, THE. 1919

0579-4706 See GEOLOGICAL SURVEY OF INDIA MISCELLANEOUS PUBLICATION. 1378

0579-4749 See JOURNAL OF THE INDIAN ACADEMY OF FORENSIC SCIENCES. 3741

0579-5125 See INSTITUTE FOR WORKERS' CONTROL PAMPHLET. 943

0579-5435 See ICRU REPORT. 3941

0579-5613 See ISO INFORMATION. 4124

0579-7152 See ICHTHYOLOGIA. 5586

0579-7780 See STUDIEN UND ARBEITEN DER THEOLOGISCHEN FAKULTAT. 5000

0579-7926 See BULLETIN DE L'INSTITUT NATIONAL SCIENTIFIQUE ET TECHNIQUE D'OCEANOGRAPHIE ET DE PECHE. 553

0579-8620 See NAUCHNYE TRUDY. 4013

0579-9368 See VESTNIK MOSKOVSKOGO UNIVERSITETA SERIIA I, MATEMATIKA, MEKHANIKA. 3540

0579-9384 See VESTNIK MOSKOVSKOGO UNIVERSITETA. SERIIA II. KHIMIIA. 995

0579-9392 See VESTNIK MOSKOVSKOGO UNIVERSITETA. SERIIA III, FIZIKA, ASTRONOMIIA. 4424

0579-9406 See VESTNIK MOSKOVSKOGO UNIVERSITETA. SERIJA 4: GEOLOGIJA. 1400

0579-9414 See VESTNIK MOSKOVSKOGO UNIVERSITETA. SERIIA V, GEOGRAFIIA. 2579

0580-0943 See MAGAZYN HISTORYCZNY. 2697

0580-1362 See MUENCHENER TEXTE UND UNTERSUCHUNGEN ZUR DEUTSCHEN LITERATUR DES MITTELALTERS. 3413

0580-1400 See MUENCHENER THEOLOGISCHE ZEITSCHRIFT. 5032

0580-2008 See VEROFFENTLICHUNGEN DES OSTEUROPA-INSTITUTES MUNCHEN. REIHE: WIRTSCHAFT UND GESELLSCHAFT. 1588

0580-261X See MUSEUM JOURNAL (LUBBOCK), THE. 4092

0580-2954 See MUSICA BRITANNICA. 4135

0580-3225 See MUSIK DES OSTENS. 4137

0580-3713 See MUZICA. 4139

0580-373X See MUZIKOLOSKI ZBORNIK. 4139

0580-3772 See MY COUNTRY. 2747

0580-3829 See MYCOLOGIA MEMOIR. 575

0580-3896 See MYOTIS. 5592

0580-4105 See STRATEGY PAPERS (NATIONAL STRATEGY INFORMATION CENTER). 4535

0580-4485 See MINOSEG ES MEGBIZHATOSAG. 4220

0580-4736 See MAGYAR MUEEMLE KVEDELEM. 303

0580-4760 See A MAGYAR TALALKOZO KRONIKAJA. 2671

0580-5120 See ANNUAL REPORT - MALAYAN AGRICULTURAL PRODUCERS ASSOCIATION. 60

0580-5287 See MAN IN SOUTHEAST ASIA. 240

0580-6062 See DISCUSSION PAPER - CENTER FOR RESEARCH ON ECONOMIC DEVELOPMENT, THE UNIVERSITY OF MICHIGAN. 1480

0580-6143 See MICHIGAN MINERAL PRODUCERS : ANNUAL DIRECTORY. 1441

0580-6976 See MUSEUM BRIEFS. 4092

0580-7247 See MLO, MEDICAL LABORATORY OBSERVER. 3617

0580-8162 See MODERN PHOTOGRAPHY ANNUAL. 4371

0580-8650 See ANALES DEL SEMINARIO DE METAFISICA. 4340

0580-9029 See MARYLAND STATISTICAL ABSTRACT. 5332

0580-9029 See MARYLAND STATISTICAL ABSTRACT. 1504

0580-9320 See MEDICINA TERMALE E CLIMATOLOGIA. 3613

0580-9517 See METHODS IN MICROBIOLOGY. 566

0580-9746 See TECHNICAL REPORT - INSTITUTE OF WATER RESEARCH (EAST LANSING). 5540

0581-0086 See MINNESOTA GENEALOGIST. 2460

0581-0124 See MISCELLANEA BAVARICA MONACENSIA. 2699

0581-0280 See PUBLICATIONS. 2852

0581-0353 See MONOGRAPHIEN ZUR SCHWEIZER GESCHICHTE. 2699

0581-1538 See MIKROBIOLOGIJA. 567

0581-1856 See FUENTES PARA LA HISTORIA SOCIAL Y ECONOMICA DEL RIO DE LA PLATA. 2734

0581-2801 See SAGA DAIGAKU NOGAKUBU IHO. 131

0581-2917 See SAGGI E RICERCHE DI LETTERATURA FRANCESE. 3432

0581-295X See SAGUENAYENSIA. 2759

0581-2976 See SAHARIEN, LE. 2500

0581-300X See MONTHLY NEWS BULLETIN. 3413

0581-3344 See ST. LOUIS BAR JOURNAL. 3058

0581-3441 See ST. MARY'S LAW JOURNAL. 3058

0581-4693 See SAMS PHOTOFACT CB RADIO SERIES. 1138

0581-4766 See ANNUAL REPORT - SAMUEL H. KRESS FOUNDATION. 5273

0581-5029 See SAN FRANCISCO KEEPER'S VOICE, THE. 2545

0581-572X See SANKHYA. SERIES A. 5338

0581-5738 See SANKHYA. SERIES B. 5338

0581-5916 See NOTICIAS - SANTA BARBARA HISTORICAL SOCIETY. 2751

0581-6165 See PAPERS IN ANTHROPOLOGY (MUSEUM OF NEW MEXICO). 243

0581-6378 See INFORME TECNICO (INSTITUTO FORESTAL (SANTIAGO, CHILE)). 2385

0581-6386 See MANUAL - INSTITUTO FORESTAL, CHILE. 2387

0581-734X See SAPTAHIKA HINDUSTANA. 2508

0581-748X See RADOVI SUMARSKOG FAKULTETA I INSTITUTA ZA SUMARSTVO U SARAJEVU. 2391

0581-7897 See SARAWAK MUSEUM JOURNAL, THE. 4096

0581-8028 See CROP AND WEATHER REPORT. 168

0581-8435 See SASKATCHEWAN MUNICIPAL DIRECTORY. 4685

0581-8575 See SATYAKATHA. 424

0581-8893 See SAWADDI. 2663

0581-9180 See SBORNIK GEOLOGICKYCH VED. LOZISKOVA GEOLOGIE, MINERALOGIE. 1444

0581-9385 See SCALA INTERNATIONAL. 2522

0582-0170 See SCHRIFTEN ZU REGIONAL- UND VERKEHRSPROBLEMEN IN INDUSTRIE- UND ENTWICKLUNGSLANDERN. 1583

0582-0243 See SCHRIFTEN ZUM VERGLEICH VON WIRTSCHAFTSORDNUNGEN. 1595

0582-0367 See SCHRIFTEN ZUR KIRCHEN- UND RECHTSGESCHICHTE. 2708

0582-0421 See BEITRAEGE ZUR POLITISCHEN WISSENSCHAFT. 4465

0582-0553 See SCHRIFTEN ZUR VERFASSUNGSGESCHICHTE. 4495

0582-0588 See SCHRIFTEN ZUR WIRTSCHAFTS- UND SOZIALGESCHICHTE. 5218

0582-1150 See STADEN-JAHRBUCH. 2762

0582-1592 See BULLETIN / SOCIETE SUISSE DES AMERICANISTES. 233

0582-2300 See SCIENCES DE LA TERRE. MEMOIRES. 1396

0582-2343 See SCIENTIA AGRICULTURAE BOHEMOSLOVACA. 132

0582-2351 See SCIENTIA PAEDAGOGICA EXPERIMENTALIS. 1783

0582-303X See PROCEEDINGS OF THE ANNUAL CONFERENCE. 3242

0582-3234 See SCRIPTA ISLANDICA. 2709

0582-3250 See SCRIPTA SCIENTIFICA MEDICA. 3639

0582-3471 See SEA CHEST, THE. 2760

0582-3668 See SEAWAY MARITIME DIRECTORY. 5456

0582-3730 See SECULAR DEMOCRACY. 4685

0582-3951 See SEGES (FRIBOURG). 3320

0582-4052 See SEIBUTSU BUTSURI. 4420

0582-4176 See SEIKATSU EISEI. 4802

0582-4184 See SEIKEI DAIGAKU KOGAKUBU KOGAKU HOKOKU. 5156

0582-4532 See SEKAI. 2629

0582-4664 See SEKIYU GAKKAI SHI. 4278

0582-4818 See SELECCIONES AVICOLAS. 221

0582-4877 See SELECTA PLANEGG. 3640

0582-5075 See SELEKTSIIA I SEMENOVODSTVO (KIEV). 186

0582-5083 See BULLETIN OF SELENIUM-TELLURIUM, THE. 2135

0582-6314 See SEMINARIUM. 5036

0582-7906 See SERIE ORIENTALE ROMA. 2664

0582-8872 See SEVENTY SIX. 4278

0582-8902 See SEVERO-ZAPAD EVROPEISKOI CHASTI SSSR. 134

0582-9348 See SHAKER QUARTERLY, THE. 4997

0582-9402 See SHAKESPEARE STUDIES. 3435

0582-9615 See SHARQ (CAIRO, EGYPT). 2664

0582-9860 See SHENG LI CHIH KUANG. 2664

0582-9887 See SHEPARD'S LAW REVIEW CITATIONS. 3051

0582-9909 See SHEPARD'S UNITED STATES ADMINISTRATIVE CITATIONS. 3054

0582-9917 See SHEPARD'S UNITED STATES PATENTS AND TRADEMARKS CITATIONS. 3054

0583-0230 See SHIH KAN. 3471

0583-0419 See SHIN KINZOKU KOGYO. 4019

0583-0516 See SHINKIN TO SHINKINSHO. 576

0583-0621 See SHINSHU DAIGAKU NOGAKUBU KIYO. 134

0583-0915 See SHIZUOKA DAIGAKU KOGAKUBU KENKYU HOHOKU. 1996

0583-094X See SHIZUOKA-KEN NOGYO SHIKENJO KENKYU HOKOKU. 134

0583-1024 See SHOCK AND VIBRATION DIGEST, THE. 2006

0583-1032 See SHOCK AND VIBRATION MONOGRAPH SERIES. 2128

0583-1121 See SHOKUHIN KAIHATSU. 2357

0583-1431 See SHU HSUEH HSUEH PAO. 3534

0583-1776 See NEWSLETTER - SIBERIAN HUSKY CLUB OF AMERICA. 4287

0583-1938 See SIEBENBURGISCHES ARCHIV. 2709

0583-3655 See YEARBOOK OF STATISTICS: SINGAPORE. 5347

0583-421X *See* SINGMUL HAKHOE CHI. **528**

0583-4465 *See* SISSONS STAMP AUCTION. **2787**

0583-4554 *See* SITULA. **2709**

0583-4597 *See* AL-SIYASAH AL-DAWLIYAH. **4462**

0583-4961 *See* GLASNIK - INSTITUT ZA NACIONALNA ISTORIJA SKOPJE. **2689**

0583-5380 *See* SLAVICA PRAGENSIA. **3321**

0583-5437 *See* SLAVISTISCHE FORSCHUNGEN. **2709**

0583-5623 *See* SLOVAKIA (WEST PATERSON, N.J.). **2709**

0583-564X *See* SLOVANSKE STUDIE. **2709**

0583-5759 *See* PRACE INSTYTUTU SADOWNICTWA I KWIACIARSTWA W SKIERNIEWICACH. SERIA B, ROSLINY OZDOBNE. **2428**

0583-6123 *See* SLOVENSKA ARCHIVISTIKA. **2483**

0583-6255 *See* SLOVO (ZAGREB). **3322**

0583-6573 *See* SMOKE SIGNAL (TUCSON), THE. **2629**

0583-6824 *See* SOCIAL LIST OF WASHINGTON, D.C. AND SOCIAL PRECEDENCE IN WASHINGTON, THE. **4686**

0583-7057 *See* SOCIAL WORK (MANILA). **5309**

0583-7138 *See* SOCIALISM, THEORY AND PRACTICE. **4546**

0583-7316 *See* BOLETIN DE LA SOCIEDAD BOLIVARIANA DEL PARAGUAY. **2724**

0583-7472 *See* BOLETIN DE LA SOCIEDAD ESPANOLA DE HISTORIA DE LA FARMACIA. **4294**

0583-7693 *See* REVISTA DE LA SOCIEDAD QUIMICA DE MEXICO. **991**

0583-7952 *See* ATTI E MEMORIE DELLA SOCIETA MAGNA GRECIA. **2611**

0583-8002 *See* BOLLETTINO DELLA SOCIETA STORICA MAREMMANA. **2679**

0583-8142 *See* ANNALES DE LA SOCIETE BELGE D'HISTOIRE DES HOPITAUX. **3776**

0583-8193 *See* REVUE DE LA MANCHE. **281**

0583-8282 *See* RECUEIL DE MEMOIRES ET TRAVAUX PUBLIE PAR LE SOCIETE D'HISTOIRE DU DROIT ET DES INSTITUTIONS DES ANCIENS PAYS DE DROIT ECRIT. **3036**

0583-8363 *See* ANNALES MUSICOLOGIQUES, MOYEN-AGE ET RENAISSANCE. **4100**

0583-8517 *See* BULLETIN. **3777**

0583-8797 *See* BULLETIN BIBLIOGRAPHIQUE DE LA SOCIETE RENCESVALS. **3369**

0583-9009 *See* ... SYMPOSIUM OF THE SOCIETY FOR DEVELOPMENTAL BIOLOGY, THE. **474**

0583-9181 *See* NEWSLETTER - SOCIETY FOR THE PRESERVATION OF LONG ISLAND ANTIQUITIES. **251**

0583-936X *See* PROGRESS IN TECHNOLOGY. **5142**

0584-0554 *See* SOIL SURVEY HORIZONS. **187**

0584-0821 *See* O SOLO. **180**

0584-1259 *See* SOPHIA. **5040**

0584-1321 *See* SORGHUM NEWSLETTER. **136**

0584-1380 *See* SOSHIOROJI. **5262**

0584-164X *See* SOULE NEWSLETTER. **2473**

0584-2360 *See* BIBLIOGRAPHY AND SUBJECT INDEX OF SOUTH AFRICAN GEOLOGY. **1361**

0584-2840 *See* CSIR RESEARCH REPORT. **611**

0584-3103 *See* SOUTH AMERICA TRAVEL DIGEST. **5491**

0584-3219 *See* QUARTERLY GEOLOGICAL NOTES - GEOLOGICAL SURVEY OF SOUTH AUSTRALIA. **1392**

0584-3448 *See* MINERALS REPORT. **1442**

0584-4029 *See* SOUTHAMPTON RECORDS SERIES. **5236**

0584-4150 *See* MEDIEVAL AND RENAISSANCE STUDIES (DURHAM). **2698**

0584-4207 *See* RENAISSANCE PAPERS. **3428**

0584-4266 *See* NEWSLETTER - SOUTHEASTERN WISCONSIN REGIONAL PLANNING COMMISSION. **2829**

0584-4290 *See* TECHNICAL REPORT - SOUTHEASTERN WISCONSIN REGIONAL PLANNING COMMISSION. **2836**

0584-4487 *See* SOUTHERN GENEALOGIST'S EXCHANGE QUARTERLY, THE. **2473**

0584-4568 *See* SOUTHERN PACIFIC MOTIVE POWER ANNUAL. **5437**

0584-4738 *See* SOUTHERN THEATRE. **5368**

0584-5025 *See* SMRC-NEWSLETTER. **2760**

0584-5041 *See* PROCEEDINGS OF THE ANNUAL MEETING - SOUTHWESTERN PHILOSOPHY OF EDUCATION SOCIETY. **1774**

0584-522X *See* SOVETSKAIA ESTRADA I TSIRK. **388**

0584-5335 *See* SOVETSKII EZHEGODNIK MEZHDUNARODNOGO PRAVA / SOVETSKAIA ASSOTSIATSIIA MEZHDUNARODNOGO PRAVA. **3136**

0584-5750 *See* SOVREMENNAIA LITERATURA ZA RUBEZHOM. **3438**

0584-5998 *See* SOZIALPOLITISCHE SCHRIFTEN. **5223**

0584-6048 *See* SOZIOLOGISCHE ABHANDLUNGEN. **5263**

0584-6099 *See* PROCEEDINGS / SPACE CONGRESS. **32**

0584-6374 *See* ANALES DEL INSTITUTO DE ESTUDIOS MADRILENOS. **2673**

0584-8016 *See* SPAN (CHICAGO, ILL.). **914**

0584-8164 *See* SPEAKER AND GAVEL. **3322**

0584-8539 *See* SPECTROCHIMICA ACTA. PART A : MOLECULAR SPECTROSCOPY. **4441**

0584-8547 *See* SPECTROCHIMICA ACTA. PART B : ATOMIC SPECTROSCOPY. **4422**

0584-8555 *See* SPECTROSCOPIC PROPERTIES OF INORGANIC AND ORGANOMETALLIC COMPOUNDS. **1019**

0584-8717 *See* SPELEO DIGEST. **1411**

0584-9209 *See* SPORTS IN THE GDR. **4923**

0584-9365 *See* SPOTLIGHT ON AFRICA. **4496**

0584-9888 *See* ZBORNIK RADOVA VIZANTOLOSKOG INSTITUTA. **2634**

0584-9993 *See* SCHRIFTENREIHE DES STAATSARCHIVS DRESDEN. **2483**

0585-0096 *See* STADTBAUWELT. **2836**

0585-0118 *See* STAEDEL-JAHRBUCH. **365**

0585-0444 *See* STANDARD TRADE INDEX OF JAPAN. **1595**

0585-0576 *See* STANFORD LAWYER. **3058**

0585-0738 *See* TECHNICAL REPORT (STANFORD UNIVERSITY. DEPT. OF CIVIL ENGINEERING). **2032**

0585-0886 *See* STARINE CRNE GORE. **2710**

0585-1173 *See* STATE DIRECTORY OF KENTUCKY. **4687**

0585-1661 *See* STATISTIKEN UBER DEN AUSSENHANDEL. ANALYTISCHE UBERSICHTEN: AUSFUHR. **852**

0585-1777 *See* STATISTICAL POCKET BOOK OF THE DEMOCRATIC SOCIALIST REPUBLIC OF SRI LANKA. **5340**

0585-1815 *See* STATISTICAL POCKET-BOOK OF YUGOSLAVIA. **5340**

0585-1858 *See* STATISTICAL YEARBOOK OF THE SOCIALIST FEDERAL REPUBLIC OF YUGOSLAVIA / SOCIALIST FEDERAL REPUBLIC OF YUGOSLAVIA, FEDERAL STATISTICAL OFFICE. **5341**

0585-1920 *See* STATISTICKI GODISNJAK JUGOSLAVIJE. **5341**

0585-198X *See* STATISTICS SOURCES. **5342**

0585-2013 *See* STATISTIKA. **5342**

0585-2382 *See* STEEL RESEARCH FOR CONSTRUCTION; BULLETIN. **628**

0585-2544 *See* STEREOPHILE. **5319**

0585-3044 *See* BERICHT (VOLKSWAGENSTIFTUNG). **2485**

0585-3214 *See* BULLETIN - MEDELHAVSMUSEET. **263**

0585-3532 *See* STOCKHOLM CONTRIBUTIONS IN GEOLOGY. **1398**

0585-3575 *See* ACTA UNIVERSITATIS STOCKHOLMIENSIS. STOCKHOLM SLAVIC STUDIES. **3357**

0585-3583 *See* STUDIER I MODERN SPRAKVETENSKAP. **3325**

0585-3699 *See* STONES & BONES NEWSLETTER. **246**

0585-427X *See* STROMUNGSMECHANIK UND STROMUNGSMASCHINEN. **2108**

0585-430X *See* STROITELNYE MATERIALY. **629**

0585-4733 *See* STUDI DI ESTETICA : BOLLETTINO SEMESTRALE DELLA SEZIONE DI ESTETICA DEL DIPARTIMENTO DI FILOSOFIA DELL'UNIVERSITA DI BOLOGNA. **331**

0585-4768 *See* STUDI DI LETTERATURA FRANCESE. **3440**

0585-4776 *See* STUDI DI LETTERATURA ISPANO-AMERICANA. **3440**

0585-4954 *See* STUDI MAGREBINI. **2643**

0585-4962 *See* STUDI MEDIOLATINI E VOLGARI. **3441**

0585-4997 *See* STUDI SUL BOCCACCIO. **435**

0585-5047 *See* STUDIA ALBANICA. **2711**

0585-511X *See* STVDIA ET ACTA ORIENTALIA. **2665**

0585-5160 *See* STUDIA GERMANISTICA UPSALIENSIA. **3324**

0585-5276 *See* STUDIA I MATERIAY LUBELSKIE / MUZEUM OKREGOWE W LUBLINIE. **4096**

0585-5292 *See* STUDIA ISLAMICA. **5045**

0585-5306 *See* STUDIA JUDAICA; FORSCHUNGEN ZUR WISSENSCHAFT DES JUDENTUMS. **5053**

0585-5349 *See* STUDIA MARINA. **1457**

0585-5373 *See* STUDIA MISSIONALIA UPSALIENSIA. **5000**

0585-5470 *See* STUDIA PHILOSOPHIAE CHRISTIANAE. **4362**

0585-5500 *See* STUDIA POST-BIBLICA. **5000**

0585-5594 *See* STUDIA THEOLOGICA VARSAVIENSIA. **5000**

0585-5616 *See* STUDI TRENTINI DI SCIENZE NATURALI. SEZIONE B. BIOLOGICA. **5160**

0585-5675 *See* STUDIE A PRACE LINGUISTICKE. **3325**

0585-5810 *See* STUDIEN UND QUELLEN ZUR VERSGESCHICHTE. **3354**

0585-5837 *See* STUDIEN UND TEXTE ZUR GEISTESGESCHICHTE DES MITTELALTERS. **2711**

0585-5853 *See* STUDIEN ZU DEN BOGAZKOY-TEXTEN. **3325**

0585-6272 *See* STUDIEN ZUR UMWELT DES NEUEN TESTAMENTS. **5000**

0585-6892 *See* STUDIES IN MATHEMATICS (NEW HAVEN). **3537**

0585-6906 *See* STUDIES IN MEDICAL GEOGRAPHY. **3643**

0585-6914 *See* STUDIES IN MEDIEVAL AND REFORMATION THOUGHT. **5000**

0585-6965 *See* STUDIES IN PHILOSOPHY AND THE HISTORY OF PHILOSOPHY. **4362**

0585-7023 *See* STUDIES IN PRE-COLUMBIAN ART AND ARCHAEOLOGY. **283**

0585-718X *See* STUDIES IN SPELEOLOGY. **1399**

0585-7457 *See* STUDIES ON THE TEXTS OF THE DESERT OF JUDAH. **5053**

0585-749X *See* STUDII SI ARTICOLE DE ISTORIE. **2711**

0585-766X *See* STUDIUM (MADRID). **3443**

0585-7945 *See* STUTTGARTER BEITRAGE ZUR GESCHICHTE UND POLITIK. **4497**

0585-7953 *See* STUTTGARTER BERICHTE ZUR SIEDLUNGSWASSERWIRTSCHAFT. **5540**

0585-7961 *See* STUTTGARTER BIBELSTUDIEN. **5020**

0585-8364 *See* SUCHASNIST. **3443**

0585-8658 *See* BOLETIM DE RECURSOS NATURAIS. **2188**

0585-8682 *See* SUDETENLAND. **2712**

0585-878X *See* SUFFOLK RECORDS SOCIETY (SERIES). **2712**

0585-881X *See* SUGAR CLUB ANNUAL, THE. **2358**

0585-9131 *See* SUMITOMO SEARCH, THE. **4021**

0585-9158 *See* SUMMA MUSICAE MEDII AEVI. **4155**

0585-9840 *See* SURFACES. **4021**

0586-0709 See BULLETIN - SVENSKT MUSIKHISTORISKT ARKIV. 4106

0586-3716 See NEPRAJZ ES NYELVTUDOMANY. 242

0586-3791 See SZILIKATTECHNIKA. 1030

0586-4291 See SCRIPTA LIMNOLOGICA UPSALIENSIA. COLLECTIO. 1418

0586-5360 See SAGA OCH SED. 1094

0586-5719 See SCIENTIFIC AMERICAN RESOURCE LIBRARY. READINGS IN PSYCHOLOGY. 4618

0586-5964 See SETON HALL LAW REVIEW. 3048

0586-6235 See SOCIAL STUDIES PROFESSIONAL, THE. 5222

0586-6391 See COMMENTARI; RIVISTA DI CRITICA E STORIA DELL'ARTE. 348

0586-660X See SPRACHHEILPADAGOGE, DER. 4394

0586-6928 See STUDIES IN LANGUAGE AND LINGUISTICS. 3326

0586-7614 See SCHIZOPHRENIA BULLETIN. 3936

0586-7703 See SCHRIFTTUM UND PRAXIS. 3722

0586-7924 See SERAPIS. 2643

0586-9412 See SANTAJIWA. 2508

0586-9587 See SCANDINAVIAN JOURNAL OF THORACIC AND CARDIOVASCULAR SURGERY. SUPPLEMENTUM. 3710

0587-0674 See SOUTHERN UTE DRUM, THE. 2273

0587-1719 See PAPERS OF THE ARCHAEOLOGICAL SOCIETY OF NEW MEXICO. 278

0587-1921 See JOURNAL OF THE ASSAM SCIENCE SOCIETY. 5120

0587-1964 See ASAO MONOGRAPH. 231

0587-2200 See BERICHT UBER DIE SOZIALE LAGE. SOZIALBERICHT, TATIGKEITSBERICHT DES BUNDESMINISTERIUMS FUER SOZIALE VERWALTUNG. 5274

0587-2243 See AUTOKOZLEKEDES (BUDAPEST. 1964). 5405

0587-2421 See ACTA EUROPAEA FERTILITATIS. 3544

0587-2650 See DOKLADY. 80

0587-2871 See JOURNAL OF THE AMERICAN ANIMAL HOSPITAL ASSOCIATION, THE. 5513

0587-2936 See COMMITTEE REPORTS - LOCAL GOVERNMENT LAW SECTION OF THE AMERICAN BAR ASSOCIATION. 2953

0587-341X See AQUARIUS (LOGAN). 5530

0587-3452 See ARCH +. 288

0587-3576 See ART DIRECTORS' INDEX TO PHOTOGRAPHERS. 4366

0587-3835 See AUSSENPOLITIK (ENGLISH EDITION). 4516

0587-4149 See ANNALES DE L'UNIVERSITE D'ABIDJAN. SERIE F: ETHNOSOCIOLOGIE. 228

0587-4246 See ACTA PHYSICA POLONICA, A. 4395

0587-4254 See ACTA PHYSICA POLONICA, B. 4445

0587-4815 See ALLAMI GAZDASAG. 57

0587-4971 See POLICY RESOLUTIONS ADOPTED BY THE CONSTITUTIONAL CONVENTION. 1702

0587-5064 See JOURNAL OF THE AMERICAN STUDIES ASSOCIATION OF TEXAS. 2742

0587-5161 See ANTHROPOS (LJUBLJANA). 4574

0587-5277 See JAHRBUCH DES ARCHIVS DER DEUTSCHEN JUGENDBEWEGUNG. 5249

0587-5404 See ARGUMENTA PALAEOBOTANICA. 4226

0587-5455 See ARTI MUSICES. 4101

0587-5994 See CO-EXISTENCE (DORDRECHT). 4518

0587-6060 See BOLETIM - COIMBRA. UNIVERSIDADE. CENTRO DE ESTUDOS GEOGRAFICOS. 1074

0587-8160 See COLECCION DE DOCUMENTOS PARA LA HISTORIA DEL COMERCIO EXTERIOR DE MEXICO. 1551

0587-9914 See COLECCION TAMESIS. SERIA A : MONOGRAFIAS. 2514

0587-9957 See COLECCION TEATRO. 5363

0588-0750 See COLLANA DI STUDI CICERONIANI. 2684

0588-0777 See COLLANA DI STUDI CLASSICI. 1076

0588-1757 See COLLECTION D'ESTHETIQUE. 2844

0588-1773 See COLLECTION DE DOCUMENTS INEDITS SUR L'HISTOIRE DE FRANCE. SERIE IN-8. 2684

0588-2206 See COLLECTION "LES GRANDS PROBLEMES DE LA BIOLOGIE.". 451

0588-2478 See COLLECTION "SCIENCES SOCIALES DU TRAVAIL.". 5196

0588-2699 See COLLEGE CHEMISTRY FACULTIES. 973

0588-277X See ANNUAL MEETING PROCEEDINGS - COLLEGE ENTRANCE EXAMINATION BOARD. 1809

0588-3237 See COLLOQUIUM. 4948

0588-3253 See COLLOQUIUM GEOGRAPHICUM. 2558

0588-3377 See FORSCHUNGSBERICHTE DES INSTITUTS FUR VERKEHRSWISSENSCHAFT AN DER UNIVERSITAT ZU KOLN. 1824

0588-3431 See KATALOGE. 355

0588-344X See KLEINE SCHRIFTEN. 4090

0588-3954 See SERIE DE PLANEAMIENTO. 1583

0588-3970 See SERIE INSTRUMENTOS DE POLITICA AGRARIA. 133

0588-4225 See BULLETIN - COLOMBO, CEYLON. FISHERIES RESEARCH STATION. 2297

0588-4241 See PROGRESS OF THE COLOMBO PLAN. 2911

0588-4349 See COLORADO EDUCATION DIRECTORY. 1732

0588-4462 See RESEARCH REVIEW - COLORADO. DIVISION OF WILDLIFE. 4878

0588-4519 See ANNUAL REPORT - LEGISLATIVE AUDIT COMMITTEE. (COLORADO). 4710

0588-4705 See UNIVERSITY OF COLORADO STUDIES. SERIES IN BIBLIOGRAPHY. 427

0588-490X See SERIES A. MASTERWORKS OF YESTERDAY. 4152

0588-4934 See COLORADO COLLEGE STUDIES (1958), THE. 1817

0588-5035 See NEWSLETTER - COLORADO RIVER ASSOCIATION. 4876

0588-5108 See COLOURAGE ANNUAL. 5349

0588-5132 See MONOGRAPH SERIES - COLT ARCHAEOLOGICAL INSTITUTE. 275

0588-618X See BULLETIN DU COMITE FRANCAIS DE CARTOGRAPHIE. 2581

0588-6562 See CANADIAN INSURANCE LAW REPORTER. 2948

0588-6589 See PREPARING YOUR INCOME TAX RETURNS : CANADA AND PROVINCES. 4741

0588-6902 See BULLETIN DES COMMUNAUTES EUROPEENNES. 1466

0588-7127 See BULLETIN. COMMISSION ON INSURANCE TERMINOLOGY. 2876

0588-7194 See PROBLEMS OF UNITED STATES ECONOMIC DEVELOPMENT. 1513

0588-7445 See COMMON MARKET LAW REPORTS. 2953

0588-7739 See NEWSLETTER (COMMONWEALTH SCIENCE COUNCIL (GREAT BRITAIN). EARTH SCIENCES PROGRAMME). 1358

0588-778X See DISTRIBUTION MAPS OF PESTS. SERIES A (AGRICULTURAL). 79

0588-8018 See COMMUNICATIONS (PARIS. 1962). 1108

0588-8387 See COMMUNITY: EAST AFRICAN COMMUNITY MONTHLY MAGAZINE, THE. 2498

0588-8700 See NOTES ET MEMOIRES - COMPAGNIE FRANCAISE DES PETROLES. 1390

0588-9278 See COMPREHENSIVE EDUCATION. 1733

0588-9448 See COMPUTERS (CROYDON). 1236

0588-9715 See CONCEPTS FOR TRAFFIC SAFETY. 5439

0589-090X See MAIN RECOMMENDATIONS, PROCEEDINGS AND AGENDA NOTES. 2827

0589-1469 See PLASMA PHYSICS AND CONTROLLED NUCLEAR FUSION RESEARCH. 4417

0589-2813 See MEMORIA TECNICA - CONGRESO LATINAMERICANO DE SIDERURGIA. 4008

0589-3127 See TRANSACTIONS - CONGRESS ON IRRIGATION AND DRAINAGE. 2096

0589-3143 See PROCEEDINGS OF THE INDIAN SOCIETY OF THEORETICAL AND APPLIED MECHANICS. 2125

0589-3178 See CONGRESSIONAL STAFF DIRECTORY. 4640

0589-3577 See CONNECTICUT CIRCUIT COURT REPORTS. CASES ARGUED AND DETERMINED IN THE APPELLATE DIVISION OF THE CIRCUIT COURT, AND MEMORANDA FILED IN THE CIRCUIT COURT OF THE STATE OF CONNECTICUT. 3140

0589-3720 See QUADRANGLE REPORT. 1392

0589-3739 See REPORT OF INVESTIGATIONS - STATE GEOLOGICAL AND NATURAL HISTORY SURVEY OF CONNECTICUT. 1394

0589-3747 See VEGETATION OF CONNECTICUT NATURAL AREAS, THE. 529

0589-400X See CONNECTICUT WATER RESOURCES BULLETIN. 5532

0589-4468 See CONSERVATION COURT DIGEST, THE. 2190

0589-4476 See EDUCATION : KEY TO CONSERVATION. 2192

0589-5014 See CONTACT. 939

0589-5413 See CONTINENTAL HANDBOOK & GUIDE TO WESTERN EUROPE. 5412

0589-5634 See GATT BIBLIOGRAPHY, 1947-1953; THE TEXT OF THE GATT, SELECTED GATT PUBLICATIONS, A CHRONOLOGICAL LIST OF REFERENCES TO THE GATT. SUPPLEMENT. 729

0589-5669 See INTERNATIONAL TRADE - GENERAL AGREEMENT ON TARIFFS AND TRADE. 841

0589-5820 See CONTRIBUTIONS A L'ETUDE DES SCIENCES DE L'HOMME. 5097

0589-6355 See COOPERATIVE HOUSING JOURNAL. 2819

0589-6681 See COPENHAGEN WORKING PAPERS IN LINGUISTICS. 3275

0589-6924 See ANUARIO DEL DEPARTAMENTO DE HISTORIA. 2610

0589-7432 See CORNELL VETERINARIAN. SUPPLEMENT. 5508

0589-7483 See CORNING RESEARCH. 2588

0589-784X See CORPORATE COUNSEL'S ANNUAL. 3098

0589-7904 See CORPORATE PLANNING IDEAS. 661

0589-7920 See CORPORATE REPORT FACT BOOK. 895

0589-8021 See CORPUS DER MINOISCHEN UND MYKENISCHEN SIEGEL. 266

0589-8048 See CORPUS FONTIUM HISTORIAE BYZANTINAE. 2684

0589-8056 See CORPUS HISPANORUM DE PACE. 2729

0589-8080 See CORPUS PHILOSOPHORUM DANICORUM MEDII AEVI. 4344

0589-8447 See COSMETIC WORLD. 403

0589-8765 See COSTRUTTORI ITALIANI NEL MONDO. 2021

0589-9036 See RESEARCH REPORT / COUNCIL FOR BRITISH ARCHAEOLOGY. 280

0589-9208 See REPORT - COUNCIL FOR BRITISH ARCHAEOLOGY. 280

0589-9427 See EDUCATION IN EUROPE. SECTION 2. GENERAL AND TECHNICAL EDUCATION. 1739

0589-9443 See EDUCATION IN EUROPE. SECTION IV, GENERAL / COUNCIL FOR CULTURAL CO-OPERATION OF THE COUNCIL OF EUROPE. 1739

0590-0107 See COUNTY COURIER. 2729

0590-0123 See PROCEEDINGS - COUNTY JUDGES' AND COMMISSIONERS' CONFERENCE. 4675

0590-0158 See CALIFORNIA COUNTY FACT BOOK. 2557

0590-0239 See COURRIER DES PAYS DE L'EST. 1478

0590-0301 See COURTROOM MEDICINE. 2957

0590-0441 See CRACKNELL'S LAW STUDENT'S COMPANION. 2957

0590-0727 1467

0590-0875 See MONOGRAPH SERIES - CRIMINAL LAW EDUCATION AND RESEARCH CENTER. 3108

0590-0980 See CRITERION (CHICAGO). 4951

0590-1154 See CRONICA DE LA GUERRA ESPANOLA. 2730

0590-160X See CUADERNOS DE ANTROPOLOGIA (CIUDAD DE GUATEMALA). 234

0590-1626 See CUADERNOS DE ARAGON. 2684

0590-1871 See CUADERNOS DE ETNOLOGIA Y ETNOGRAFIA DE NAVARRA. 234

0590-2916 See CUBA AZUCAR. 2332

0590-3351 See CUADERNOS OCEANOGRAFICOS. 1448

0590-3378 See CUMBERLAND LAWYER, THE. 2957

0590-3386 See CUMBERLAND SEMINARIAN, THE. 4952

0590-3394 See CUMBRIA. 2514

0590-3890 See CURRENT SOVIET POLICIES. 4541

0590-4102 See CURRENT PRIMATE REFERENCES. 5174

0590-451X See MITTEILUNGEN UND FORSCHUNGSBEITRAGE DER CUSANUS-GESELLSCHAFT. 4353

0590-4609 See REVISTA DEL ARCHIVO HISTORICO DEL CUZCO. 2758

0590-4641 See CYCLE GUIDE ROAD TEST ANNUAL. 4081

0590-4862 See STATISTICAL ABSTRACT - STATISTICS AND RESEARCH DEPARTMENT (NICOSIA). 5340

0590-4935 See ANNUAL REPORT - CYPRUS ORNITHOLOGICAL SOCIETY. 5614

0590-5001 See CZECHOSLOVAK ECONOMIC PAPERS. 1479

0590-5702 See DIRECT SELLING IN CANADA. 923

0590-580X See NORTH OF 60. MINES AND MINERALS ACTIVITIES. 2147

0590-5850 See PROCEEDINGS OF THE ANNUAL MEETING OF THE CANADIAN MINERAL PROCESSORS. 4016

0590-5966 See CASOPIS ZA ZGODOVINO IN NARODOPISJE. 2613

0590-6334 See CICINDELA. 5580

0590-6598 See PUBLICATIONS - COMMITTEE ON TAXATION, RESOURCES AND ECONOMIC DEVELOPMENT. 4743

0590-711X See CPDA NEWS. 1303

0590-7748 See INSECT LIBERATIONS IN CANADA. 5609

0590-8450 See COATING. 2011

0590-8817 See CORD SPORTFACTS FISHERMAN ANNUAL. 2299

0590-8876 See COSTUME. 1083

0590-9120 See REVISTA - CALI, COLOMBIA. UNIVERSIDAD DEL VALLE. DIVISION DE INGENIERIA. 1994

0590-9325 See MARKET RESEARCH HANDBOOK. 930

0590-9384 See LIST OF LIGHTS, BUOYS AND FOG SIGNALS. ATLANTIC COAST. 4178

0590-966X See ARQUIVOS DO CENTRO CULTURAL PORTUGUES. 2676

0590-9783 See CHARITIES DIGEST. 5277

0590-983X See CHICOREL INDEX SERIES. 2844

0591-0137 See SUPPLEMENTARY PAPER - COMMITTEE FOR ECONOMIC DEVELOPMENT OF AUSTRALIA. 1523

0591-017X See CONCERN LONDON. 2278

0591-0218 See CODASYL COBOL JOURNAL OF DEVELOPMENT. 1278

0591-0307 See CONTACT LENS MEDICAL SEMINAR. 3873

0591-0358 See CAHIERS DE L'INSTITUT DU MOYENAGE GREC ET LATIN / UNIVERSITE DE COPENHAGUE. 3271

0591-0374 See CORD SPORTFACTS HOCKEY GUIDE. 4891

0591-0722 See DAMS WITHIN JURISDICTION OF THE STATE OF CALIFORNIA. 2088

0591-1230 See CHEMICAL INDUSTRIAL UNDERTAKINGS LICENSED. 968

0591-1281 See CHIPS & SHIPS. 2727

0591-1745 See DIRECTORY OF THE COMMISSION OF THE EUROPEAN COMMUNITIES. 3127

0591-2083 See COOS GENEALOGICAL BULLETIN. 2444

0591-2237 See COUNTRY MUSIC PEOPLE. 4112

0591-2296 See CRUX OF THE NEWS. 4952

0591-2334 See CUSTOM CAR. 5412

0591-2377 See ZYCIE SZKOY WYZSZEJ. 1792

0591-2385 See ZYGON. 5012

0591-2741 See IUCN PUBLICATIONS NEW SERIES. SUPPLEMENTARY PAPER. 2196

0626-2238 See ECOLE DES PARENTS. 1737

0700-0774 See MANUFACTURERS OF ELECTRIC WIRE AND CABLE (PRELIMINARY ED.). 3483

0700-0847 See EMPLOYMENT AND IMMIGRATION REVIEW : ONTARIO. 1666

0700-1207 See NATIONAL BUILDING CODE OF CANADA. 622

0700-1223 See CANADIAN PLUMBING CODE. 2604

0700-124X See NATIONAL FIRE CODE OF CANADA. 2292

0700-1320 See CANADIAN FARM BUILDING CODE. 606

0700-1584 See T. E. S. L. TALK. 1786

0700-1665 See TAXATION STATISTICS (OTTAWA). 4701

0700-1789 See NOTICE TO MARINERS (ANNUAL EDITION 1976). 4181

0700-2033 See INDUSTRY PRICE INDEXES. 1534

0700-205X See QUARTERLY ESTIMATES OF TRUSTEED PENSION FUNDS. 1705

0700-2092 See PUBLIC SECTOR, THE. 4677

0700-2254 See ANNUAL REPORT OF THE PARLIAMENTARY LIBRARIAN. 3191

0700-2408 See METRIC MONITOR. 4031

0700-2971 See MANITOBA STATISTICAL REVIEW. 1504

0700-3021 See PHOTO LIFE. 4373

0700-303X See 7/15, LE JOURNAL DES JEUNES. 5779

0700-3099 See TAYLOR'S INDUSTRY DIGEST. 1628

0700-3129 See WINNIPEG FOLK FESTIVAL NEWSLETTER. 4159

0700-3234 See ITALIANA VITA. 2693

0700-3277 See TALKING BOOKS AVAILABLE IN THE PUBLIC LIBRARIES OF METROPOLITAN TORONTO. 4832

0700-3315 See SNOWMOBILE ANNUAL. 4919

0700-3420 See NORTH PEACE PICTORIAL. 2541

0700-3447 See PONTIAC SHOP MANUAL SUPPLEMENT. 5423

0700-3471 See MONTHLY DIRECTORY OF S. ASIAN ASSOCIATIONS & BUSINESSES, THE. 696

0700-3528 See MONDAY REPORT ON RETAILERS. 955

0700-3536 See GAY RISING. 2794

0700-3579 See A C P NEWSLETTER. 4811

0700-3617 See OVERVIEW (TORONTO). 4486

0700-3641 See BREEZE. 3197

0700-365X See ESTUAIRE. 3462

0700-3668 See COLLEGE COMMENT (THUNDER BAY). 1816

0700-3692 See U W GUIDELINES. 1851

0700-3838 See MUSIC RESEARCH NEWS. 4134

0700-3854 See IN REVIEW (TORONTO. 1975). 5247

0700-3862 See LABOUR (HALIFAX). 1686

0700-3862 See LABOUR (HALIFAX). 1686

0700-3897 See RURAL GLEANINGS. 4994

0700-3900 See L'ECOUTE, A. 4128

0700-3994 See DIVER DOWN. 4893

0700-4176 See OUTLOOK (VANCOUVER). 5234

0700-4192 See MISSIONS DES FRANCISCAINS. 5032

0700-4222 See MONTREAL PEOPLE'S YELLOW PAGES. 2569

0700-4249 See POVUNGNITUK. 2271

0700-432X See EQUIPEMENT ET METHODES. 614

0700-4389 See COMMUNIQUE - SOCIETE D'ARCHITECTURE DE MONTREAL. 295

0700-4427 See NEWS AND VIEWS - SIMCOE COUNTY HISTORICAL ASSOCIATION. 2749

0700-480X See SOURCES (TORONTO). 2924

0700-4834 See SKY LETTERS. 3471

0700-4869 See IMPACT (MONTREAL. ENGLISH EDITION). 839

0700-4966 See CORDULIA. 5581

0700-5008 See MARQUEE (TORONTO). 4074

0700-5040 See HABITABEC. 2823

0700-5067 See ACTION (WINDSOR). 4240

0700-5075 See PREVENIR (QUEBEC). 2403

0700-5083 See BULLETIN D'INFORMATION - FOIRE INTERNATIONALE DU LIVRE DE MONTREAL. 4827

0700-5105 See LAURIER CAMPUS. 1834

0700-5121 See COLLECTIVE BARGAINING : STATISTICS IN EDUCATION. 1793

0700-513X See DANS LA MELEE. 1662

0700-5172 See ZVAZAJ. 2767

0700-5199 See SZAMADAS. 2762

0700-5202 See SLAVNA NADEJE. 5067

0700-5229 See SPOKESMAN (EDMONTON). 4394

0700-5237 See RESOURCE (OTTAWA). 227

0700-5245 See RESSOURCE (OTTAWA). 227

0700-5261 See COMMUNICATEUR, LE. 1106

0700-527X See NORTHERN LIFE (SUDBURY). 5791

0700-5318 See OPUS (LONDON, ONT.). 4144

0700-5369 See LITERACY (TORONTO). 1881

0700-5385 See RURAL VOICE (BLYTH). 131

0700-5431 See BULLETIN - SOCIETE DES DIPLOMES DE L'ECOLE DE BIBLIOTHECONOMIE DE L'UNIVERSITE DE MONTREAL. 3198

0700-5474 See C H L A/A B S C NEWSLETTER. 3199

0700-5539 See INVESTMENT REPORTER. 903

0700-5555 See STANDARD CANADIAN PLATE BLOCK CATALOGUE, THE. 2787

0700-5741 See PROCEEDINGS - COMMONWEALTH MINING AND METALLURGICAL CONGRESS. 2148

0700-6004 See RESEAU. 5147

0700-6039 See DOCUMENTS HISTORIQUES - SOCIETE HISTORIQUE DU NOUVEL-ONTARIO. 2731

0700-6500 See NOTRE-DAME DU CAP. 5033

0700-6543 See PRIORITIES (VANCOUVER). 5564

0700-6659 See CONGRES ANNUEL - CONSEIL CANADIEN DA LA SECURITE. 4772

0700-6691 See ANNUAL REPORT AND MINUTES OF THE ANNUAL MEETING - CANADIAN SEED GROWERS' ASSOCIATION. 162

0700-6802 See SCARBORO MISSIONS. 4995

0700-6896 See PUBLICATIONS OF THE MCMASTER UNIVERSITY ASSOCIATION FOR 18TH CENTURY STUDIES. 2626

0700-7167 See GUARDIAN (WINDSOR). 5785

0700-7272 See ANNUAIRE POLK DE SOREL TRACY ET ST-JOSEPH. 2554

0700-7388 See BOATING NEWS (VANCOUVER). 592

0700-7949 See EXCHANGE (TORONTO). 5060

0700-8058 See MANOTICK NEWS, THE. 5789

0700-8066 See MENNONITE HISTORIAN. 5064

0700-8082 See MALTON PILOT, THE. 5789

0700-8090 See BULLETIN - I C S S. 4888

0700-8139 See GLAS K O H T-A. 3578
0700-8147 See LOK AWAZ (PANJABI EDITION). 2744
0700-8163 See WATNO DUR, THE. 2765
0700-8171 See VESTNIK CESKOSLOVENSKYCH SPOLKU V MONTREALE. 2764
0700-8198 See BJULETEN SUSPILNOJI SLUZLY KANADY. 5275
0700-8279 See SPOKESWOMAN FOR ABORTION LAW REPEAL. 3058
0700-8392 See ANIMALS' VOICE. 225
0700-8732 See CANADIAN BOATING. 592
0700-8791 See SPORT QUEBEC. 4921
0700-9011 See PLAN CANADA NEWS. 5301
0700-9046 See SPORT ALBERTA NEWS. 4920
0700-9054 See KEBEK KOMIK. 4862
0700-9062 See INFORMATION (SAINTE-JULIE). 5786
0700-9127 See PENNY PRESS, THE. 4864
0700-916X See JERAGEH. 2740
0700-9178 See CONSTRUCTION ALBERTA NEWS. 608
0700-9194 See PETIT ALMANACH DES LETTRES, LE. 3423
0700-9275 See SEA PEN. 557
0700-9283 See RECORDS OF EARLY ENGLISH DRAMA. 5367
0700-9313 See VOIX DU SANCTUAIRE. 5008
0700-933X See UP THE GATINEAU. 2764
0700-9380 See GIFTS & TABLEWARES. 2584
0700-9410 See FT. GARRY PIONEER. 5785
0700-9429 See INTERCOM (MONTREAL. ENGLISH EDITION). 3287
0700-9445 See NAME GLEANER. 3304
0700-947X See PAROIKIAKA NEA. 5792
0700-9496 See KHAOUA. 5031
0700-950X See NORTH FRONTENAC NEWS. 5790
0700-9518 See ST. VITAL LEADER. 5795
0700-9534 See WHO? (SHERBROOKE). 2766
0700-9623 See U L C NEWS (EDITION FRANCAISE). 4033
0700-9666 See S O S GARDERIES. 1805
0700-9798 See NEWSLETTER OF THE C A F. 5252
0700-9801 See JOURNAL OF PSYCHOLOGY AND JUDAISM. 4600
0700-9860 See NEWSLETTER - ONTARIO CULTURAL OLYMPIC PROGRAM. 326
0700-9909 See OUTDOOR CREST (1975). 4876
0700-9917 See GUARD THE NORTH. 3392
0700-995X See OTTAWA NEWSLETTER. 5300
0701-0001 See SHOW RING. 4288
0701-0028 See GESTION (LAVAL). 868
0701-0079 See REDCLIFF REVIEW. 5793
0701-0109 See ZPRAVODAJ - CESKOSLOVENSKE NARODNI SDRUZENI V KANADE, ODBOCKA VANCOUVER. 2550
0701-0176 See STELCO TENDANCES. 629
0701-0184 See CULTURE & TRADITION. 2319
0701-0192 See POSOL. 5034
0701-0214 See DRAUDZES VESTIS. 4954
0701-0222 See EFFLUENT. 2088
0701-0230 See PALABRE, LA. 1543
0701-0281 See CAIRN, THE. 4086
0701-0303 See BULLETIN JURIDIQUE. 2944
0701-0400 See CONNECTIONS (EDMONTON). 2190
0701-0451 See CHRISTIAN OUTREACH. 4945
0701-0508 See PANJAB. URDU. 2753
0701-0516 See ACTUALITE IMMOBILIERE. 4833
0701-0524 See ACQUISITIONS LIST - CENTRE OF CRIMINOLOGY LIBRARY, UNIVERSITY OF TORONTO. 3078
0701-0532 See LIAISON (MONTREAL. 1975). 4662
0701-0575 See BULLETIN - C P A A C M P A. 1144
0701-0605 See BLACK DIAL DIRECTORY. 2723
0701-0648 See BONNE NOUVELLE DE L'ALLIANCE. 5057

0701-0656 See ALPHA (WOLFEVILLE). 3359
0701-0702 See PROMOTION (TORONTO). 764
0701-0710 See C I M REPORTER. 2136
0701-0729 See CALEDONIA TIMES. 4942
0701-0745 See GRAND SLAM (OTTAWA). 4897
0701-0761 See NORTH SHORE TIMES (STE-THERESE). 5791
0701-077X See PREMIERE, EN. 4076
0701-0788 See CATHOLIC NEW TIMES. 5026
0701-0796 See DOWNTOWN ACTION. 1556
0701-080X See ENGINEERING FORUM (TORONTO). 1973
0701-0818 See CONTACT (MONTREAL. 1976). 5187
0701-0842 See CENTRAL BUTTE STAR, THE. 5781
0701-0869 See TOWN OF VAUGHAN VANGUARD, THE. 2548
0701-0877 See PLAIN DEALER (FREDERICTON). 5793
0701-094X See B P L BEEP, THE. 3193
0701-0974 See DURHAM TODAY. 832
0701-1008 See ETUDES INUIT. 236
0701-1024 See ALBERTA SCIENCE EDUCATION JOURNAL. 5082
0701-1083 See JANE CORRIDOR, THE. 2536
0701-113X See NOUVELLE DU HAUT ST-FRANCOIS. 2541
0701-1199 See MUSKOKA FREE PRESS. 5790
0701-1210 See HEALTH CAREERS NEWS. 4204
0701-1229 See BULLETIN - AGENCE DE PRESSE LIBRE DU QUEBEC. 2917
0701-1288 See B C TODAY. 2722
0701-1326 See PHOTOGRAPHER (VANCOUVER). 4374
0701-1334 See LEISURE NEWSLETTER. 5251
0701-1342 See LOISIR. INFORMATION. 4852
0701-1350 See DIETETIQUE (MONTREAL). 4190
0701-1369 See WINGS (CALGARY). 39
0701-1377 See NEWSLETTER - MEMORIAL SOCIETY ASSOCIATION OF CANADA. 2407
0701-1385 See BULLETIN DE LA SOCIETE DE PHILOSOPHIE DU QUEBEC. 4343
0701-1423 See SOUTHSIDE MIRROR, THE. 2546
0701-1490 See HORIZON D'OR. 5288
0701-1512 See TRIANGLE D'OR, LE. 1524
0701-1547 See ACTION (WINNIPEG). 5550
0701-1571 See WESTERN WHEEL. 2550
0701-158X See ANNALS OF AIR AND SPACE LAW. 3123
0701-1598 See BULLETIN DE L'AIDE JURIDIQUE. 3179
0701-1601 See BULLETIN DE LA FEDERATION DE MONTREAL DES CAISSES DESJARDINS. 825
0701-1636 See ANNUAIRE - ASSOCIATION DES ROUTES ET TRANSPORTS DU CANADA. 5376
0701-1687 See P I Q PRODUITS POUR L'INDUSTRIE QUEBECOISE. 3486
0701-1709 See ELAN (HAUTERIVE). 1091
0701-1725 See PLEINS FEUX SUR LE TAXI. 5389
0701-1725 See BULLETIN - MANITOBA DENTAL ASSOCIATION. 1318
0701-1733 See CANADIAN CASES ON THE LAW OF TORTS. 3089
0701-1741 See TIAC NEWSLETTER. 5492
0701-1776 See ALBERTA ARCHAEOLOGICAL REVIEW, THE. 253
0701-1784 See CANADIAN WATER RESOURCES JOURNAL. 5531
0701-1792 See JOURNAL OF UKRAINIAN GRADUATE STUDIES. 2695
0701-1814 See DIRECTORY OF PROFESSIONAL ENGINEERS OF ONTARIO. 1971
0701-1865 See ANTENNE (MONTREAL). 3265
0701-1997 See NUTRIGUIDE. 4195
0701-2101 See PROCEEDINGS OF THE ... ANNUAL MEETING / ACADIAN ENTOMOLOGICAL SOCIETY. 5595
0701-2586 See MULTICULTURALISM. 5252

0701-2837 See BUZZ (THUNDER BAY). 4941
0701-2861 See ADMINISTRATEUR SCOLAIRE PROFESSIONNEL, L'. 1859
0701-3086 See WORKING PAPER - FACULTY OF ADMINISTRATION, UNIVERSITY OF OTTAWA. 723
0701-3299 See MESSENGER (STEINBACK). 4976
0701-3418 See FOSTERLETTER. 2280
0701-3558 See CRAG AND CANYON. 4871
0701-4031 See CAHIERS D'HISTOIRE DE L'UNIVERSITE LAVAL, LES. 2725
0701-4262 See SELON SA PAROLE. 4996
0701-4686 See EVOLUTION (MONTREAL). 2487
0701-4724 See FINANCIAL POST GOVERNMENT & MUNICIPAL SURVEY. 4649
0701-4945 See PHENOMENA (TORONTO). 4242
0701-5151 See ANNUAL REPORT / ALBERTA RESEARCH COUNCIL. 2096
0701-5216 See BUILDING PRACTICE NOTE. 604
0701-5224 See NOTE D'INFORMATION SUR LA CONSTRUCTION. 622
0701-5267 See DIGEST DE LA CONSTRUCTION AU CANADA. 612
0701-5542 See BIBLIO-JEUNES; NIVEAUX PRESCOLAIRE ET ELEMENTAIRE: SUPPLEMENT. 408
0701-5666 See RAPPORT ANNUEL - REGIE DE L'ASSURANCE-DEPOTS DU QUEBEC. 806
0701-6336 See SASK RIGHTS. 4512
0701-6433 See ANNUAL REPORT - SASKATCHEWAN CENTRE OF THE ARTS. 313
0701-6441 See REPORT ON TRAVEL ON SASKATCHEWAN HIGHWAYS. 5443
0701-6557 See RAPPORT ANNUEL. MERITE AGRICOLE. 124
0701-7065 See CROP AND WEATHER REPORT. 168
0701-7502 See AGRICULTURAL REAL ESTATE VALUES IN ALBERTA. 4833
0701-7510 See TELEPHONE DIRECTORY. GOVERNMENT OF ALBERTA AND THE LEGISLATIVE ASSEMBLY OF ALBERTA. 4690
0701-760X See INDEX OF CURRENT B.C. REGULATIONS. 2981
0701-7898 See QUARTERLY SHIPMENTS OF OFFICE FURNITURE PRODUCTS. 4214
0701-7928 See AIR CARRIER TRAFFIC AT CANADIAN AIRPORTS (QUARTERLY EDITION). 7
0701-7936 See PERIODICALS PUBLISHING RECORD. 422
0701-8002 See NATURAL LIFE (UNIONVILLE. 1991). 2600
0701-8347 See SUMMARY OF TECHNICAL REPORT - FOREST ENGINEERING RESEARCH INSTITUTE OF CANADA. 2396
0701-8517 See PROTEGEZ-VOUS. 1299
0701-8568 See HIGHWAY TRANSPORT BOARD BULLETIN. 5383
0701-8665 See VERNON'S BURLINGTON AND HAMILTON SUBURBAN DIRECTORY. 2578
0701-8746 See LUTTE OUVRIERE (MONTREAL). 4543
0701-8878 See RELATIVELY SPEAKING (EDMONTON). 2469
0701-8894 See YA HOTLINE. 1071
0701-8967 See CRSSS 09. 5281
0701-9009 See PRIVE, LE. 1774
0701-9033 See FICHIER BIOLOGIQUE. 455
0701-9491 See RAPPORT ANNUEL / REGIE DES LOTERIES DU QUEBEC. 4678
0701-9599 See GOVERNMENT OF ONTARIO TELEPHONE DIRECTORY. 1156
0701-9637 See ENVIRONMENT VIEWS. 2166
0701-9890 See NEWSLETTER / SOCIETY OF THE SEVEN SAGES. 3417
0701-9971 See ANNUAL REPORT OF THE ONTARIO HIGHWAY TRANSPORT BOARD. 5376
0702-0007 See MEMORIAL UNIVERSITY OF NEWFOUNDLAND OCCASIONAL PAPERS IN BIOLOGY. 464

0702-0031 See DEMOGRAPHIC BULLETIN (TORONTO). 4551

0702-0147 See PROCEEDINGS OF THE NORTHERN LIBRARIES COLLOQUY. 3242

0702-0260 See PERIODICALS AND NEWSPAPERS IN THE COLLECTIONS OF THE LIBRARY OF PARLIAMENT. 3259

0702-0376 See COURRIER DES FAMILLES, LE. 5412

0702-0465 See QUARTERLY REPORT ON ENERGY SUPPLY-DEMAND IN CANADA. 1954

0702-0481 See INTERNATIONAL JOURNAL OF MINI & MICROCOMPUTERS. 1274

0702-0538 See ANNUAL REPORT OF THE ONTARIO HUMAN RIGHTS COMMISSION. 4504

0702-0643 See DISCUSSION PAPER SERIES - ONTARIO ECONOMIC COUNCIL. 1480

0702-0724 See ANNUAL REPORT - SECURITIES COMMISSION (EDMONTON). 4629

0702-0945 See BAKERS JOURNAL. 2328

0702-0961 See ESTIMATES OF EMPLOYEES BY PROVINCE AND INDUSTRY (CUMULATED EDITION). 1532

0702-0988 See STATISTICS RELATING TO REGIONAL AND MUNICIPAL GOVERNMENTS IN BRITISH COLUMBIA. 4700

0702-0996 See RAPPORT ANNUEL - COMMISSION DES TRANSPORTS DU QUEBEC. 5390

0702-1755 See YOUNG. 1096

0702-3154 See CANADIAN STAMP NEWS. 2784

0702-3162 See CANADIAN COIN NEWS. 2780

0702-3286 See ALBERTA FIELD/POOL PRODUCTION AND INJECTION MONTHLY SUPPLEMENT. 4249

0702-3316 See ANNUAL REPORT OF THE SASKATCHEWAN DEVELOPMENT FUND CORPORATION OF THE PROVINCE OF SASKATCHEWAN. 772

0702-3839 See LIAISON II. 3223

0702-455X See ENTREPRISE (MONTREAL). 672

0702-4894 See WEE GIANT. 3452

0702-5068 See JOURNAL DE CLAVIS, LE. 2536

0702-5084 See CANADIAN ADVENTIST MESSENGER. 5057

0702-5300 See ACCOUNTER (CALGARY). 736

0702-5459 See ON-SITE (EDMONTON). 2830

0702-5777 See FLEET SAFETY & HEALTH. 2862

0702-5785 See IN THE DRIVER'S SEAT. 5417

0702-6005 See FOREIGN INVESTMENT REVIEW. 899

0702-6528 See CANNED AND FROZEN FRUITS AND VEGETABLES. 2330

0702-6609 See ELECTRIC POWER STATISTICS. VOLUME 3. INVENTORY OF PRIME MOVER AND ELECTRIC GENERATING EQUIPMENT. 1962

0702-6803 See MAGOOK. 3409

0702-6846 See CRUDE PETROLEUM AND NATURAL GAS PRODUCTION. 4254

0702-696X See FROM THE ROOFTOPS. 1542

0702-701X See SKI CANADA. 4918

0702-7125 See PAST & PRESENT (WATERLOO). 2852

0702-7133 See T H E S A NEWSLETTER. 2792

0702-7206 See MUNICIPAL AND PLANNING LAW REPORTS. 3012

0702-729X See DIRECTORY OF MEMBERS - QUEBEC ASSOCIATION OF SCHOOL ADMINISTRATORS. 1862

0702-7303 See ROTHNIUM MAGAZINE. 3432

0702-732X See CONSERVATION. 2190

0702-7338 See WHAT'S COOKING. 2793

0702-7435 See EDMONTON COMMERCE AND INDUSTRY. 832

0702-7532 See NEW LITERATURE & IDEOLOGY. 3416

0702-7559 See AT THE LIBRARY. 3192

0702-763X See OAK LAKE TOWN AND COUNTRY NEWS. 5791

0702-7656 See BULLETIN - ASSOCIATION DES MEDECINS DE LANGUE FRANCAISE DU CANADA (1977). 3559

0702-7737 See ANNUAIRE - CONFERENCE DES EVEQUES CATHOLIQUES DU CANADA. 5023

0702-7745 See S. A. L. T. NEWSLETTER. 3247

0702-7796 See GLEBE REPORT. 5785

0702-7818 See ATLANTIS (WOLFVILLE). 5551

0702-7826 See MEDICAL DIRECTORY - COLLEGE OF PHYSICIANS AND SURGEONS OF ALBERTA. 3915

0702-7877 See DIALOGUE (CANADIAN CHAMBER OF COMMERCE. EDITION FRANCAISE). 819

0702-7885 See ROAD & MOTOR SPORT. 4915

0702-7893 See STANDARD (SWAN RIVER). 5795

0702-7915 See NUNATSIAQ NEWS. 5791

0702-7966 See CANADIAN FISH FANCIERS. 2298

0702-7974 See OTTAWA ARCHAEOLOGIST, THE. 277

0702-7982 See CHATSWORTH RECORD AND THE QUEEN'S BUSH QUILL, THE. 5781

0702-7990 See COMMUNICATOR (VANCOUVER). 2918

0702-8008 See ADDICTION THERAPIST, THE. 1338

0702-8024 See OEIL DE FEU. 5300

0702-8032 See PROJECT: PROGRESS NEWSLETTER. 3242

0702-8040 See ONTARIO TRAFFIC SAFETY. 5442

0702-8202 See OIL AND GAS PRODUCTION REPORT. 4268

0702-8210 See OTTAWA LETTER. 4671

0702-8245 See NEWSLETTER FOR UGARITIC STUDIES. 3417

0702-8296 See BULLETIN - MARO PROGRESSIVE LEARNING SYSTEMS. 1803

0702-8318 See AUTOMOTIVE MARKETER. 5406

0702-8334 See CARLETON INTERNATIONAL STUDIES. 4517

0702-8350 See DIRECTORY - CENTRAL ONTARIO REGIONAL LIBRARY SYSTEM. 3206

0702-8369 See CENTRE LINE (TORONTO). 5409

0702-8385 See IMPORTWEEK. 839

0702-8393 See FUGUE. 4118

0702-8415 See META (TORONTO). 4543

0702-8466 See JOURNAL OF PSYCHIATRY & NEUROSCIENCE. 3929

0702-8474 See NEWSLETTER - CANADIAN INSTITUTE OF UKRAINIAN STUDIES. 2700

0702-8504 See NUDISTES DU QUEBEC. 4794

0702-8547 See VIEWPOINT (TORONTO. 1961). 1588

0702-8571 See ESPOIR (LASALLE). 4473

0702-8679 See TRIINU. 2763

0702-8733 See CANADIAN HIGHWAY CARRIERS GUIDE. 5378

0702-875X See INFORMATION - A R C A D. 3166

0702-8814 See GRADUATES' GAZETTE, THE. 1826

0702-8830 See DERIVE URBAINE, LA. 384

0702-8865 See ALTERNATE ROUTES. 5238

0702-8881 See SHEEP CANADA MAGAZINE. 221

0702-892X See DISC JOKIES. 1131

0702-8970 See MEDICAMENTS D'AUJOURD'HUI. 4315

0702-8989 See WELDON TIMES, THE. 3073

0702-8997 See ANTHROPOLOGIE ET SOCIETES. 229

0702-9004 See TIGHTWIRE. 3178

0702-9012 See MUSIC MCGILL. 4134

0702-9020 See EAR FALLS ECHO, THE. 5783

0702-9160 See MUSIQUE PERIODIQUE. 4139

0702-9225 See MOVING TO MONTREAL. 4841

0702-9241 See CALGARY WOMEN'S NEWSPAPER. 5552

0702-9268 See CANADA SPECIALIZED POSTAGE STAMP CATALOGUE. 2784

0702-9292 See NEWSLETTER / NOVA SCOTIA SCHOOL BOARDS ASSOCIATION. 1867

0702-9306 See ANNUAL REPORT - DIVISION OF TUBERCULOSIS CONTROL (LEDGERS). 3948

0702-9578 See DECISIONS DISCIPLINAIRES CONCERNANT LES CORPORATIONS PROFESSIONNELLES. 665

0702-9667 See ANNUAL REPORT - ALBERTA LABOUR. 1648

0702-9683 See DECISIONS DE LA COMMISSION DES AFFAIRES SOCIALES. 4642

0702-9853 See ORGANIZATION OF THE GOVERNMENT OF ALBERTA. 4671

0702-9861 See LAND MANAGEMENT REPORT. 2386

0703-0037 See NATIONAL INCOME AND EXPENDITURE ACCOUNTS : THE ANNUAL ESTIMATES. 1575

0703-0312 See ENROUTE. 2533

0703-0428 See URBAN HISTORY REVIEW. 2764

0703-0606 See JOURNAL OF THE NEW BRUNSWICK MUSEUM. 4090

0703-0665 See NEGOTIATED WORKING CONDITIONS (VICTORIA). 1693

0703-0762 See RAPPORT ANNUEL - COMMISSION DES SERVICES JURIDIQUES. 3034

0703-0770 See RAPPORT D'ACTIVITES - OFFICE DES PROFESSIONS DU QUEBEC. 4678

0703-0967 See CAHIERS DE BIOLOGIE (OTTAWA. 1973). 450

0703-1130 See MEMOIR (CANADIAN SOCIETY OF PETROLEUM GEOLOGISTS). 1387

0703-1157 See CHEM 13 NEWS. CHEM 12 NEWS. 967

0703-119X See CONTACT (DON MILLS). 4836

0703-1246 See ORGAN (WINNIPEG). 3420

0703-1254 See ORGAN (ABBOTSFORD). 3420

0703-1297 See TRAVAUX ET RECHERCHES GRIC / GROUPE DE RECHERCHE EN INFORMATION ET COMMUNICATION. 3253

0703-1319 See WEEKLY CRIMINAL BULLETIN. 3109

0703-1378 See CANADIAN NEWSLETTER FOR OPEN GOVERNMENT, THE. 4636

0703-1408 See SIGHT & SOUND (MISSISSAUGA). 4078

0703-1440 See BIG COUNTRY CARIBOO MAGAZINE. 2723

0703-1459 See CANADIAN JOURNAL OF IRISH STUDIES, THE. 3372

0703-1491 See DROCHAID. 2259

0703-1513 See MONITOR (CHARLOTTETOWN). 5790

0703-1521 See CATHOLIC TIMES (MONTREAL). 5026

0703-1556 See GLENGARRY LIFE. 2734

0703-1580 See SCOTTISH TRADITION. 2545

0703-1599 See CANADIANA GERMANICA. 2683

0703-1688 See D O R L S TECHNICAL SERVICES COMMITTEE'S INFORMATION EXCHANGE. 3205

0703-1742 See DIRECTORY - CANADIAN TESTING ASSOCIATION. 865

0703-1785 See JACKPOT. 4862

0703-1793 See NOVA SCOTIA LIBERAL, THE. 4484

0703-1866 See PLOUGHSHARES MONITOR. 4532

0703-1939 See BUSINESS VALUATOR. 740

0703-1947 See JOURNAL OF BUSINESS VALUATION, THE. 746

0703-1963 See BULLETIN DE NOUVELLES - SOCIETE CANADIENNE DE DROIT CANONIQUE. 5025

0703-1998 See PHILIPPINE-CANADIAN TRADE GUIDE. 849

0703-2056 See SKI QUEBEC (SAINT-LAURENT). 4918

0703-2072 See STUDENT ADVOCATE (OTTAWA). 1848

0703-2102 See BEACON TIMES. 5780

0703-2129 See CANADIAN LAWYER. 2948

0703-2153 See ANNUAIRE TELEPHONIQUE - CENTRE DE CULTURE DIALOGUE ORIENTAL. 5239

0703-217X See NEWSLETTER - CANADIAN SCIENCE WRITER'S ASSOCIATION. 2922

0703-2412 See MUNICIPAL COUNSELLOR. **4667**

0703-2501 See INDEXES TO ONTARIO MUNICIPAL BOARD APPLICATIONS DISPOSED OF... AND TO LAND COMPENSATION BOARD APPLICATIONS DISPOSED OF **2981**

0703-2595 See GRANTS AND AWARDS GUIDE - MEDICAL RESEARCH COUNCIL. **3579**

0703-2625 See ANNUAL REPORT. SUPERINTENDENT OF BANKRUPTCY (OTTAWA). **3084**

0703-2633 See ANNUAL REPORT - STATISTICS CANADA. **5321**

0703-2692 See AIR PASSENGER ORIGIN AND DESTINATION. DOMESTIC REPORT. **8**

0703-2749 See LOCAL GOVERNMENT FINANCE REVENUE AND EXPENDITURE ASSETS AND LIABILITIES ACTUAL. **4736**

0703-2757 See JOSEMARIA ESCRIVA DE BALAGUER (EDITION FRANCAISE). **4967**

0703-2765 See MATHEWS' C A T V. **1134**

0703-3052 See STUDIES IN MUSIC FROM THE UNIVERSITY OF WESTERN ONTARIO. **4155**

0703-3060 See BRITISH COLUMBIA LAW REPORTS (CALGARY). **2943**

0703-3109 See ALBERTA REPORTS (FREDERICTON, N.B. : BOUND CUMULATION). **3180**

0703-3117 See ALBERTA LAW REPORTS. **2929**

0703-4512 See NOR SEROUNT. **4982**

0703-4520 See FORGE (MONTREAL). **4541**

0703-4539 See FORGE (MONTREAL. EDITION FRANCAISE). **4541**

0703-458X See DOWN HOME. **4115**

0703-4687 See CRIMINAL REPORTS FOURTH SERIES. **3106**

0703-4687 See REAL PROPERTY REPORTS. **3035**

0703-4709 See ZOUNDS. **4160**

0703-4725 See FLUTE, LA. **3164**

0703-4733 See NATOTAWIN. **2748**

0703-4768 **3263**

0703-4784 See QUEBECOIS DU COMTE DE VANIER, LE. **4493**

0703-4849 See ANNUAL REPORT OF THE SASKATCHEWAN COMPUTER UTILITY CORPORATION OF THE PROVINCE OF SASKATCHEWAN. **1235**

0703-489X See MATERIAL HISTORY REVIEW. **2745**

0703-5276 See AALT TECHNICIAN. **3186**

0703-5292 See WINNIPEG GUIDE, THE. **5798**

0703-5314 See CAREER CANDIDATES. **4201**

0703-5357 See ATLANTIC CO-OPERATOR, THE. **1541**

0703-5551 See BUSINESS LAW REPORTS. **3096**

0703-5578 See TEMPS DE L'UNION NATIONALE, LE. **4498**

0703-5624 See C P H A HEALTH DIGEST. **4770**

0703-5640 See SPECIAL BULLETIN - THEATRE CANADA. **5368**

0703-5667 See CANADA GREEN. **2412**

0703-5675 See QUARTERLY JOURNAL - JOHN HOWARD SOCIETY OF QUEBEC. **3174**

0703-5721 See GAZETTE OFFICIELLE DU QUEBEC, PARTIE 2; LOIS ET REGLEMENTS. **2973**

0703-5756 See GAZETTE OFFICIELLE DU QUEBEC. PARTIE 1. AVIS JURIDIQUE. **2533**

0703-5764 See DIABETES DIALOGUE. **3727**

0703-5780 See CONTACT (MONTREAL. 1977). **1661**

0703-5810 See SALMO SALAR. **2312**

0703-5837 See CHARLTON NUMISMATIC BULLETIN, THE. **2780**

0703-5861 See NEWSLETTER - CANADIANS FOR A DEMOCRATIC WORKPLACE. **1694**

0703-5888 See NIAGARA ANGLICAN, THE. **5065**

0703-5926 See WHITE LIST OF CUSTOMS OFFICERS IN CANADA, THE. **4695**

0703-5977 See ANNUAL REPORT OF THE DEPARTMENT OF AGRICULTURE AND MARKETING (HALIFAX). **61**

0703-6078 See BULLETIN - TOURING OFFICE OF THE CANADA COUNCIL. **384**

0703-6248 See MANITOBA VACATION GUIDE. **5483**

0703-6256 See MANITOBA VACATION GUIDE. **5483**

0703-6337 See REVUE D'INTEGRATION EUROPEENNE. **4494**

0703-6426 See DIRECTORY, OCCUPATIONAL SAFETY AND HEALTH LEGISLATION IN CANADA. **2961**

0703-6485 See DAVANTAGE. **4952**

0703-6507 See DAWSON AND HIND. **4087**

0703-654X See ROAD MOTOR VEHICLES. FUEL SALES. **5391**

0703-6752 See LIVING WITH CHRIST. COMPLETE EDITION. **4974**

0703-6760 See LIVING WITH CHRIST. SUNDAY EDITION. **4974**

0703-6825 See NIAGARA GUILD OF CRAFTS. **374**

0703-6906 See T 'N T, TRUCK 'N TRAILER. **5394**

0703-6922 See IMPACT. **4655**

0703-699X See JOUR (MONTREAL. 1977). **5787**

0703-7007 See LINK (MISSISSAUGA. 1977). **3228**

0703-7058 See PAPERS AND RECORDS - THUNDER BAY HISTORICAL MUSEUM SOCIETY. **4095**

0703-7074 See CANADIAN HORSESHOE PITCHERS YEAR BOOK. **4889**

0703-7139 See POSSIBLES. **5213**

0703-7163 See MONEYLETTER. **907**

0703-7198 See GAZETTE DE MALARTIC, LA. **5785**

0703-7244 See CABLE TELEVISION. **1129**

0703-7252 See TELECOMMUNICATIONS STATISTICS. **1125**

0703-7333 See STOCKS OF FROZEN MEAT PRODUCTS. **2358**

0703-7368 See FAMILY INCOMES. CENSUS FAMILIES. **2287**

0703-7384 See CORPUS ADMINISTRATIVE INDEX. **4640**

0703-7392 See LOCAL GOVERNMENT EMPLOYMENT. **1688**

0703-7481 See HINTERLAND WHO'S WHO. **4166**

0703-7643 See PEST MANAGEMENT PAPERS. **2238**

0703-7716 See TORONTO STOCK EXCHANGE '300' STOCK PRICE INDEX SYSTEM, THE. **917**

0703-7724 See RURAL DELIVERY. **2544**

0703-7732 See BENEFITS CANADA. **938**

0703-7821 See GREENBORO. **2735**

0703-783X See NEWS - ONTARIO COUNCIL OF RABBIT CLUBS. **5234**

0703-7864 See HAND-MADE. **373**

0703-7945 See FARM CASH RECEIPTS (QUARTERLY ED.). **84**

0703-8011 See NOUVELLE LITTERATURE ET IDEOLOGIE. **3418**

0703-8178 See T V B. **4866**

0703-8348 See ETHNIC DIRECTORY OF WINDSOR & ESSEX COUNTY. **2260**

0703-8356 See GELBVIEH EYEOPENER. **211**

0703-8364 See NORTHERN BREED, THE. **2751**

0703-8380 See CADENZA (SASKATOON). **4106**

0703-8437 See FIRST PEOPLE, THE. **2733**

0703-8623 See ROYAL GAZETTE. NEW BRUNSWICK. **4684**

0703-8674 See ROLLIN' HOMES. **5490**

0703-8704 See NEWSART (TORONTO). **360**

0703-8712 See PARALLELOGRAMME (VANCOUVER). **361**

0703-8720 See ARTS & SCIENCE MONOGRAPHS. **314**

0703-8747 See VICTORIA COUNTY RECORD. **5797**

0703-8763 See EDMONTON AREA SERIES REPORT. **4552**

0703-8852 See VOICE OF THE ESSEX FARMER, THE. **145**

0703-8917 See INFO DE L'A U C C. **1830**

0703-895X See CANADIAN TOKEN, THE. **2772**

0703-8968 See BRIAR PATCH. **5193**

0703-8976 See INTERNATIONAL PROJECT BOOKLET. **2910**

0703-8992 See CANADIAN JOURNAL OF REMOTE SENSING. **16**

0703-9034 See NORTH-EAST REGION COMMUNITY BOOSTER, THE. **5790**

0703-9042 See NEW EDINBURGH NEWS. **5790**

0703-9093 See JOSEMARIA ESCRIVA DE BALAGUER (ENGLISH EDITION). **4967**

0703-9107 See PECHEUR ET CHASSEUR QUEBECOIS. **4912**

0703-9166 See EXTENSION INFORMATION BULLETIN. **83**

0703-9190 See NATIVE SISTERHOOD. **2268**

0703-9220 See COWICHAN NEWS. **5783**

0703-9263 See NEW FOUNDATIONS. **1694**

0703-9352 See CONSUMER PRICE INDEX (OTTAWA). **1471**

0703-9360 See THIS IS THE VOICE OF CASA. **767**

0703-9387 See WAWATAY NEWS. **2275**

0703-9433 See SASKATCHEWAN ANGLICAN. **4995**

0703-9476 See BEST CANADIAN STORIES. **3366**

0703-9581 See LEBRETON. **2827**

0703-959X See NEWSLETTER - CARIBBEAN ASSOCIATION OF NOVA SCOTIA. **2749**

0703-9743 See ALL ABOUT HOMES. **4834**

0703-9824 See FESTIVAL INTERNATIONAL DU FILM DE LA CRITIQUE QUEBECOISE. **4069**

0703-9875 See VIE DE FEMME. **5567**

0703-9883 See VIBRATIONS (MONTREAL). **4158**

0703-9999 See BULLETIN - NATIONAL SHEVCHENKO MUSICAL ENSEMBLE GUILD OF CANADA. **4106**

0704-0024 See PHOTOGRAPHIC CANADIANA. **4374**

0704-0083 See ACORN, THE ARCHITECTURAL CONSERVANCY OF ONTARIO R NEWSLETTER. **287**

0704-0148 See PUBLICATION OF THE HANNAH INSTITUTE FOR THE HISTORY OF MEDICINE. **3631**

0704-0156 See NOUVEAU CARABIN. **1838**

0704-0202 See GLOBAL NEWS. **5785**

0704-0210 See BRACEBRIDGE EXAMINER. **5781**

0704-0229 See ELK ISLAND TRIANGLE, THE. **5784**

0704-0237 See OWEN SOUND LIFE. **5792**

0704-0245 See NORFOLK GAZETTE, THE. **5790**

0704-0261 See REGIONAL NEWS (CAYUGA). **5794**

0704-0288 See ADVOCATES' QUARTERLY. **3088**

0704-0296 See NEWSLETTER - VISUAL ARTS & CRAFTS COMMUNICATION COUNCIL OF ALBERTA. **374**

0704-0318 See LIMOI. **5233**

0704-0334 See ICI QUEBEC (REPENTIGNY). **417**

0704-0377 See MPS IN THE NEWS. **3012**

0704-0385 See GO FOR SPORTS. **4896**

0704-0393 See C L I C 'S LEGAL MATERIALS LETTER. **2945**

0704-0407 See HOSPITAL TRUSTEE. **3785**

0704-0431 See SEVERN-WASHAGO MIRROR. **5794**

0704-0458 See HIGHWAY 43 LEADER. **5786**

0704-0474 See COURRIER FRONTENAC. **5782**

0704-0490 See BOWDEN EYE OPENER. **5781**

0704-0512 See VISUAL ARTS NEWS. **368**

0704-0539 See RESEAU (MONTREAL). **4992**

0704-058X See MARIE-EVE. **2538**

0704-0628 See PLUG IN. **3241**

0704-0652 See MARITIMER (AMHERST). **4391**

0704-0660 See JOURNAL DE CORNWALL, LE. **5787**

0704-0717 See CANADIAN WORKSHOP. **633**

0704-0733 See TROT. **2803**

0704-0792 See CARIBOU, LE. **5781**

0704-0822 See ARGO NEWS. **4884**

0704-0873 See BULLETIN SUR LES RELATIONS DU TRAVAIL (EDITION ANGLAISE). 1657

0704-0881 See MA CAISSE D'ECONOMIE. 1542

0704-1217 See LARU STUDIES. 4661

0704-1225 See CANADIAN JOURNAL OF FAMILY LAW. 3120

0704-1497 See DIRECTORY OF CANADIAN ENVIRONMENTAL EXPERTS. 2163

0704-1500 See "MOVIN". 5433

0704-1616 See RAPPORT ANNUEL - MUSEE NATIONAL DES SCIENCES ET DE LA TECHNOLOGIE (OTTAWA). 5144

0704-1616 See ANNUAL REPORT - NATIONAL MUSEUM OF SCIENCE AND TECHNOLOGY (OTTAWA). 4083

0704-1748 See MAIN ESTIMATES OF CURRENT EXPENDITURE OF THE PROVINCE OF MANITOBA. 4736

0704-1969 See LIGNE DE MASSE, LA. 4543

0704-1993 See TRAVAUX DES CAMPEUSES D'ETE AU CAMP ROLLAND-GERMAIN (1976). 4173

0704-2035 See RECUEIL DE DROIT FISCAL QUEBECOIS. 3036

0704-2426 See PROCEEDINGS OF THE CANADIAN AGRICULTURAL OUTLOOK CONFERENCE. 122

0704-2493 See ANNUAL REPORT TO THE LEGISLATURE OF THE ALCOHOL AND DRUG COMMISSION (VICTORIA). 1341

0704-2663 See ANNUAL REPORT - ONTARIO ADVISORY COUNCIL ON SENIOR CITIZENS. 5178

0704-2752 See ONTARIO GEOLOGICAL SURVEY MISCELLANEOUS PAPER. 1390

0704-2809 See FOREST RESEARCH (TORONTO). 2381

0704-2884 See CURRENT RESEARCH - GEOLOGICAL SURVEY OF CANADA. 1372

0704-2930 See INCOME TAX RULING. 4731

0704-3694 See CANADIAN INDUSTRY REPORT OF FISHERIES AND AQUATIC SCIENCES. 2298

0704-3708 See RAPPORT CANADIEN A L'INDUSTRIE SUR LES SCIENCES HALIEUTIQUES ET AQUATIQUES. 2311

0704-3899 See REFERENCE LIST OF HEALTH SCIENCE RESEARCH IN CANADA. 3633

0704-4062 See ECO/LOG. CANADIAN POLLUTION LEGISLATION. 2227

0704-4380 See KRONIKA (TORONTO). 2536

0704-4488 See ALBERTA FACT SHEET. 5178

0704-4550 See GAZETTE DES FEMMES, LA. 5557

0704-4666 See BULLETIN D'INVENTAIRE DES INSECTES DU QUEBEC. 5606

0704-4739 See SAFETY UPDATE. 4801

0704-478X See TRANS F M. 1141

0704-4798 See ANNUAL REPORT / NORTHWEST ATLANTIC FISHERIES ORGANIZATION. 2294

0704-481X See PENDULUM (KINGSTON). 3171

0704-4895 See WASAGA BEACH NEWS (1979). 5797

0704-4909 See CHIMO (TORONTO). 5021

0704-4917 See ADRENAL MEDULLA, THE. 3546

0704-500X See SCHEDULE-INDUCED BEHAVIOR. RESEARCH & THEORY. 4617

0704-5174 See CARLETON INTERNATIONAL. 1731

0704-5263 See PERCEPTION (OTTAWA). 5301

0704-5352 See VOIX SEFARAD. 2275

0704-5387 See PUBLIC WAREHOUSING. 705

0704-5417 See LIVRE DES FEUX, DES BOUEES ET DES SIGNAUX DU BRUME. COTE DU PACIFIQUE. 4178

0704-5506 See THURSDAY REPORT, THE. 1850

0704-5522 See CONCERNED CANADIAN. 2531

0704-5603 See HOUSE OF COMMONS DEBATES (OTTAWA. DAILY ED.). 4654

0704-5646 See CANADIAN POETRY (LONDON, ONT.). 3461

0704-5689 See LAVALIN. 1985

0704-5700 See YEATS ELIOT REVIEW. 3455

0704-5719 See MESSIEURS, MES AMOURS. 3466

0704-576X See SYLLOGEUS - NATIONAL MUSEUM OF NATURAL SCIENCES. 4097

0704-5808 See LAND COMPENSATION BOARD INDEX TO APPLICATIONS DISPOSED OF. 2993

0704-5816 See TORONTO FILMMAKERS' CO-OP. 4079

0704-5824 See OCCASIONAL - NOVA SCOTIA MUSEUM. 4094

0704-5859 See SONG NEWS. 187

0704-5883 See NEW RELIGIONS NEWSLETTER. 4981

0704-5905 See NEWSLETTER FOR TARGUMIC & COGNATE STUDIES. 3306

0704-5980 See GULF DEALER. 4259

0704-5999 See EDITION QUEBECOISE. 5070

0704-6146 See ENTRE-GENS, L'. 1542

0704-6189 See M A A E BULLETIN. 357

0704-6278 See BRITISH COLUMBIA. 3476

0704-6286 See GERMINATION. 3463

0704-6324 See SOURCE (MONTREAL, QUEBEC). 4998

0704-6340 See REVUE ALERTE. 4800

0704-6359 See HOSPITALITE (TORONTO). 5071

0704-6391 See CANADIAN FIREFIGHTER, THE. 2288

0704-6421 See TRACES. TEACHERS OF RELIGION AND CHRISTIAN ETHICS IN SASKATCHEWAN. 5005

0704-643X See LEISURE FORUM. 4851

0704-6472 See ROBINSON'S FORTNIGHTLY. 2544

0704-6561 See PROFESSOR DIVINSKY'S SELECT RESTAURANT GUIDE. 5072

0704-6588 See CROSSCURRENTS (SASKATOON). 318

0704-6596 See ELEMENTARY-SECONDARY SCHOOL ENROLMENT. 1794

0704-6618 See ANCESTOR INDEX. 2437

0704-6685 See REGINA MAGAZINE. 5490

0704-6723 See LIAISON ST-LOUIS. 2537

0704-6766 See CONSTRUCTION SAFETY JOURNAL. 610

0704-6804 See AIRFORCE. 9

0704-6936 See ISSUES, EVENTS & IDEAS. 1804

0704-6952 See CAHIERS D'HISTOIRE (QUEBEC). 2725

0704-7002 See POLYPHONY (TORONTO). 2754

0704-7029 See JOURNAL DE L'AGE D'OR, LE. 5291

0704-7037 See PUBLICATION B / CENTRE INTERNATIONAL DE RECERCHES SUR LE BILINGUISME. 3312

0704-7037 See PUBLICATION B. CENTRE INTERNATIONAL DE RECHERCHES SUR LE BILINGUISME. 3312

0704-7053 See REGENT PARK COMMUNITY NEWS. 5793

0704-707X See ALGONQUIN IMPACT. 5780

0704-7142 See CULOT, LE. 1734

0704-7150 See IMPRESSION (MONTREAL). 380

0704-7177 See FORUM (FEDERATION CANADIENNE DES MUNICIPALITES). 4649

0704-7231 See RECORDER (TORONTO). 4149

0704-7282 See CISILUTE. 5782

0704-7290 See INTRINSIC. 3464

0704-7355 See WEB. 1790

0704-7363 See SUBURBAN MIRROR, THE. 5795

0704-7371 See GLOUCESTER GUIDE. 385

0704-7428 See IMAGE DE LA MAURICIE. 5480

0704-7452 See RESEARCH DIRECTORY - MEMORIAL UNIVERSITY OF NEWFOUNDLAND. OFFICE OF RESEARCH. 1845

0704-7495 See NEWSLETTER - UNIVERSITY OF ALBERTA, WESTERN CANADIANA PUBLICATIONS PROJECT. 421

0704-7509 See B. C. JOURNAL OF SPECIAL EDUCATION. 1875

0704-7592 See RESEARCH REPORT SERIES. GENERAL / BROCK UNIVERSITY, DEPARTMENT OF GEOLOGICAL SCIENCES. 1395

0704-7614 See REPRINT SERIES - CANADIAN SOCIETY OF PETROLEUM GEOLOGISTS. 1395

0704-7622 See SPECIAL PUBLICATION - SASKATCHEWAN GEOLOGICAL SOCIETY. 1398

0704-7630 See RECUEIL DES SENTENCES DE L'EDUCATION. 1869

0704-772X See REPORT - FOREST PEST MANAGEMENT INSTITUTE. 2392

0704-7770 See VOIX DE L'A.M.S.A, LA. 4694

0704-7878 See DIRECTORY - AMERICAN WATER WORKS ASSOCIATION, ONTARIO SECTION. 5532

0704-7886 See LUNDI, LE. 5560

0704-7908 See PRESTIGE BEAUTE. 405

0704-7916 See ARTSATLANTIC. 315

0704-7932 See CANADA'S DATA PROCESSING MARKET. 1256

0704-7983 See HOCKEY (MONTREAL). 4899

0704-7991 See CANADA NOW. 2726

0704-8017 See COMMERCE NEWS. 819

0704-8343 See ANNUAL REPORT - GEORGETOWN SHIPYARD INC. 4174

0704-8815 See NOTRE HOPITAL. 3790

0704-9153 See OVO MAGAZINE (1978). 4372

0704-9226 See HALTON FARM NEWS. 91

0704-9412 See CANADIAN FARM & HOME ALMANAC (1978). 2530

0704-948X See LIAISON - AMIS DU JARDIN BOTANIQUE DE MONTREAL. 2423

0704-9722 See CANADIAN JOURNAL OF CRIMINOLOGY. 3159

0704-9730 See REPERTOIRE LEGISLATIF DE L'ASSEMBLEE DU QUEBEC. 3037

0704-9765 See ADMINISTRATION ET GESTION. 4624

0704-9811 See TAR PAPER (EDMONTON). 4280

0705-0003 See JOURNAL DE L'A. I. H. P. Q, LE. 4786

0705-0038 See CHILDREN'S BOOK NEWS (TORONTO). 1061

0705-0216 See NEWSLETTER. 2200

0705-0348 See CRUX MATHEMATICORUM. 3502

0705-0410 See MATHNEWS. 3522

0705-0437 See MILLE PLUMES. 358

0705-0453 See THEATRE (QUEBEC). 5371

0705-0542 See ENTREPRISE (QUEBEC). 866

0705-0569 See JARGON (HULL). 1092

0705-0577 See OBJECTIF PREVENTION (MONTREAL). 4794

0705-0615 See MASSE (MONTREAL). 1690

0705-0623 See BULLETIN - LE MONDE BICYCLETTE. 428

0705-0631 See ENTRE NOUS (TROIS-RIVIERES). 5199

0705-0666 See DIMENSIONS (HULL). 1820

0705-0674 See P M E : REVUE DE LA PETITE ET MOYENNE ENTREPRISE. 702

0705-0690 See ARDOISE, L'. 1810

0705-0704 See EASTWORD (HALIFAX). 3383

0705-081X See HAMILTON EXPRESS, LE. 5786

0705-0828 See INTERBLOCS. 3786

0705-0879 See PALAN, LE. 4985

0705-0917 See PROVIDENCE DES PAUVRES, MERE GAMELIN, LA. 5066

0705-0925 See PROVIDENCE OF THE POOR, MOTHER EMILIE GAMELIN. 4988

0705-1034 See NEWSLETTER. 2829

0705-1085 See DIONYSIUS. 1076

0705-1093 See DECORATION CHEZ-SOI. 2899

0705-1115 See BULLETIN OF THE FOLKLORE STUDIES ASSOCIATION OF CANADA. 2318

0705-1158 See FOLKLORE (OTTAWA). 2320

0705-1166 See INDEC COMMUNICATOR, THE. 1751

0705-1328 See JOURNAL OF CANADIAN POETRY. 3464

0705-1336 See HELLENOKANADIKI HEBDOMADA. 5786

0705-1360 See ALL-CANADA WEEKLY SUMMARIES. 3088

0705-1379 See FREELANCE (REGINA). 3389

0705-1433 See CANADIAN FOOTWEAR JOURNAL. 1082

0705-1506 See SEMINAR PAPERS - ASSOCIATION OF ONTARIO HOUSING AUTHORITIES. 2835

0705-1611 See NEWSLETTER - THE JOHN MACMURRAY SOCIETY. 5234

0705-1697 See GREEN LEAVES. WESTERN CANADA ED, THE. 2384

0705-1751 See FLAMBEE, LA. 4256

0705-1786 See SHOPPERS' GUIDE TO CANADIAN LIFE INSURANCE PRICES (SUDBURY, ONT. : 1980). 2893

0705-1824 See FLAGSHIP. 593

0705-1840 See SANFORD EVANS GOLD BOOK OF MOTORCYCLE DATA AND USED PRICES. 4083

0705-1867 See VANI. 2274

0705-1875 See DIRECTORY AND NEWSLETTER - FORESTRY ALUMNI ASSOCIATION, UNIVERSITY OF TORONTO. 1101

0705-1891 See NEWSLETTER - CANADIAN GEOTHERMAL RESOURCES ASSOCIATION. 1389

0705-1913 See REVIEW OF ARCHITECTURE AND LANDSCAPE ARCHITECTURE. 308

0705-1972 See INTERVENTION (QUEBEC). 2535

0705-2006 See CANADIAN JOURNAL OF ARCHAEOLOGY. 265

0705-2022 See WORKING TEACHER. 1791

0705-2030 See M D T, MOTORCYCLE DEALER & TRADE. 4081

0705-2065 See SANFORD EVANS GOLD BOOK OF OUTBOARD MOTOR DATA AND USED PRICES. 596

0705-2081 See METRIC STEEL. BULLETIN. 4012

0705-212X See LAWN & GARDEN TRADE. 2423

0705-2197 See CANADIAN GRAPHIC COLLECTOR. 377

0705-2332 See DIVISION OF SOILS DIVISIONAL REPORT. 170

0705-2332 See BOOKS IN DANISH. 4825

0705-2480 See CHINOOK REGIONAL LIBRARY DIRECTORY. 3201

0705-2499 See CURRENT & CHOICE. 414

0705-2553 See STANDARDBRED, THE. 2802

0705-2669 See MANITOBA ARCHAEOLOGICAL QUARTERLY. 273

0705-2731 See CARIBBEAN YEAR BOOK, THE. 2727

0705-2820 See OTTAWA-HULL : THE KEY. 2572

0705-2855 See ARCHIVIST, THE. 2480

0705-291X See DRUGS AND THERAPEUTICS FOR MARITIME PRACTITIONERS. 4302

0705-2944 See CAHIER HISTORIQUE. 2725

0705-3002 See CANADIAN JOURNAL OF ITALIAN STUDIES. 3372

0705-3010 1081

0705-3029 See BULLETIN - INTERNATIONAL ASSOCIATION FOR MOBILIZATION OF CREATIVITY. 3560

0705-3037 See YOU (VANCOUVER). 406

0705-3061 See JURISPRUDENCE EXPRESS. 2991

0705-307X See INFORMATION C B. 1133

0705-3096 See QUEBEC ETUDIANT (STE-FOY). 1843

0705-310X See WESTERN CANADIAN ANTIQUE & ART DEALERS YEARBOOK. 252

0705-3118 See DIRECTORY - CANADIAN RELIGIOUS CONFERENCE. 4953

0705-3126 See PCEC. PRIVATE CAREER EDUCATION COUNCIL. 4208

0705-3150 See WILDERNESS ARTS AND RECREATION (1977). 4880

0705-3177 See ETHNIC DIRECTORY. 2260

0705-3215 See C'EST POUR QUAND. 3758

0705-324X See INFORMATION REPORT DPC-X. 2384

0705-3274 See BC-X - PACIFIC FOREST RESEARCH CENTRE. 2375

0705-3401 See BUDGET: ESTIMATES (QUEBEC). 4714

0705-3436 See LOISIR ET SOCIETE. 4852

0705-3444 See RUDE. 2544

0705-3452 See TWO THIRDS. 2912

0705-3606 See ZONE LIBRE. 2550

0705-3657 See CANADIAN JOURNAL OF COMMUNICATION. 1105

0705-3673 See TERMINOLOGIE COMPTABLE. 752

0705-3681 See NAN'S KNIT-KNACKS. 5354

0705-369X See INJURED ATHLETE, THE. 3587

0705-3711 See GUIDE TO U.S. CITIES. 5479

0705-3754 See CRESCENT INTERNATIONAL. 4470

0705-3762 See R A I F. RESEAU D'ACTION ET D'INFORMATION POUR LES FEMMES. 5565

0705-3797 See EPISODES. 1375

0705-3819 See CHILDRENS' MYSTERY WORD. 4859

0705-3843 See JOURNAL - CANADIAN FEDERATION OF UNIVERSITY WOMEN. 5559

0705-3851 See FEMMES D'ICI. 5556

0705-3878 See AGRI-BOOK MAGAZINE. 47

0705-3908 See PEN-VISTA. BILINGUAL EDITION. 3171

0705-3940 See NOMAD (WILLOWDALE). 5486

0705-3983 See AGRICULTURE AND FORESTRY BULLETIN. 53

0705-4009 See CLASSICAL MUSIC MAGAZINE (MISSISSAUGA). 4110

0705-4033 See SUN (FREDERICTON). 5795

0705-4041 See MENNONITISCHE POST. 5064

0705-405X See EDMONTON SUN, THE. 5783

0705-4084 See NEWSLETTER - COMPARATIVE AND INTERNATIONAL EDUCATION SOCIETY OF CANADA (1975). 1768

0705-4130 See PROGRES FORESTIER, LE. 2391

0705-4149 See MONDE AQUATIQUE. 2308

0705-4157 See ALUMI-NEWS. 598

0705-4289 See STOCKS OF FRUIT AND VEGETABLES. 2358

0705-4319 See CONTROL AND SALE OF ALCOHOLIC BEVERAGES IN CANADA, THE. 2366

0705-4343 See AIR PASSENGER ORIGIN AND DESTINATION. CANADA-UNITED STATES. 7

0705-4580 See CANADIAN JOURNAL OF REGIONAL SCIENCE, THE. 2817

0705-4718 See LITHIUM AND ANIMAL BEHAVIOR. 5515

0705-4769 See BACKGROUND STUDY / SCIENCE COUNCIL OF CANADA. 5087

0705-4831 See N. S. TRAPPER'S NEWSLETTER. 2388

0705-4890 See LETTER OF THE LAA, THE. 3223

0705-5005 See ENSEMBLE (LACHINE). 3780

0705-5153 See OFFICE EQUIPMENT AND SUPPLIES MARKET IN CANADA, THE. 4213

0705-5188 See JOURNAL DU JEUNE CINEMA QUEBECOIS, LE. 4073

0705-5196 See CANMET REPORT. 1438

0705-5269 See INTERNATIONAL TRAVEL, ADVANCE INFORMATION. 5481

0705-5455 See REPERTOIRE DE VEDETTES-MATIERE. 1929

0705-5463 See CANADIAN FUTURES. 1468

0705-551X See PRODUCTION AND INVENTORIES OF PROCESS CHEESE AND INSTANT MILK POWDER. 198

0705-5560 See ACADIAN LETTERS. 958

0705-5587 See DIRECTORY. OCCUPATIONAL PROGRAMS - CANADIAN ADDICTIONS FOUNDATION. 1343

0705-5595 See NEW MOTOR VEHICLE SALES (MONTHLY ED.). 5401

0705-5765 See TERTIARY EDUCATION, TASMANIA / AUSTRALIAN BUREAU OF STATISTICS. 1850

0705-579X See STATISTIQUES FINANCIERES DU GOUVERNEMENT DU QUEBEC. 4700

0705-5870 See GERMAN JOURNAL OF PSYCHOLOGY, THE. 4587

0705-5900 See ATMOSPHERE-OCEAN. 1420

0705-6087 See ALBERTA LIBRARY NEWS. 3189

0705-6249 See DIRECTORY OF CANADIAN ORCHESTRAS AND YOUTH ORCHESTRAS / ANNUAIRE CANADIEN DES ORCHESTRES ET ORCHESTRES DES JEUNES. 4114

0705-6257 See BULLETIN DE LIAISON - SECTEUR PUBLIC. 1656

0705-6281 See AUTOMOTIVE SERVICE DATA BOOK. 5407

0705-6311 See PHYSICIAN'S MANAGEMENT MANUALS. 3916

0705-6338 See SERVANT, THE. 4996

0705-6346 See LUMIERE ET PAIX. 2252

0705-6370 See NOUVELLES ACQUISITIONS - UNIVERSITE DE MONTREAL, BIBLIOTHEQUE DE MEDECINE VETERINAIRE. 3237

0705-6389 See ADE. ALCOHOL AND DRUG EDUCATION. 1338

0705-6397 See ARC (OTTAWA). 3460

0705-6486 See BOOKS IN JAPANESE. 4826

0705-6532 See MOUVEMENT (OTTAWA). 1542

0705-6567 See LURELU. 1066

0705-6621 See A C P NOTEBOOK. 4811

0705-6656 See CONTINUO. 4111

0705-6710 See CANADIAN PAPER ANALYST. 4233

0705-6761 See EMBOUTEILLEUR QUEBECOIS, L'. 2366

0705-677X See ANNUAL CONFERENCE PROCEEDINGS - INSTITUTE OF TRANSPORTATION ENGINEERS, CANADA. 5376

0705-6834 See MEMBERSHIP DIRECTORY - CANADIAN ASSOCIATION FOR INFORMATION SCIENCE. 3230

0705-6842 See CENTRE LETTER (BANFF). 317

0705-6869 See MAGAZINE STOP. 2538

0705-6885 See CONGRESSO (TORONTO). 2729

0705-6907 See INPRINT (PETERBOROUGH). 353

0705-6923 See QUEBEC VERT. 2202

0705-6931 See LEADLINE, THE. 2592

0705-694X See TEMPS FOU, LE. 2547

0705-6966 See CANADIAN BLACK BOOK. 5408

0705-7032 See DAVANTAGE (POINTE-CLAIRE). 5244

0705-7040 See ECHO DU TRANSPORT, L'. 5381

0705-7075 See DIRECTORY OF COMMUNITY SERVICES, OTTAWA-CARLETON. 5282

0705-7113 See AUSTRALASIAN JOURNAL OF AMERICAN STUDIES : AJAS. 2722

0705-713X See PARENTS D'AUJOURD'HUI. 2284

0705-7199 See GEOGRAPHIE PHYSIQUE ET QUATERNAIRE. 2563

0705-7210 See GREAT CANADIAN HOMESTEADER, THE. 90

0705-7334 See PROGRAMME DU ... EXERCICE - CHAMBRE DE COMMERCE DU DISTRICT DE MONTREAL. 821

0705-7423 See NATIONAL 5-PIN BOWLERS NEWS. 4906

0705-7490 See ABITIBI-PRICE. 5779

0705-7504 See TECHNICAL MANUAL - CANADIAN SOCCER ASSOCIATION. 4925

0705-7520 See GITE (ST-JOSEPH). 2805

0705-7571 See GRAPHIC ARTS MARKET IN CANADA (1978). 379

0705-7814 See WISE OWL NEWS (TORONTO). 2871

0705-7830 See JOURNAL OF HOME ECONOMICS EDUCATION. 2791

0705-7989 See NEWSLETTER / ASSOCIATION FOR CANADIAN THEATRE RESEARCH. 5366

0705-8063 See VANDANCE (VANCOUVER). 1314

0705-8101 See AGRICULTURAL TRENDS (BRISBANE, QLD.). 52

0705-8101 See INFORMATION - FEDERATION DES C. L. S. C. DU QUEBEC. SUPPLEMENT, L'. 5290

0705-8209 See BOOKS IN ARMENIAN. 4825

0705-8225 See BOOKS IN LITHUANIAN. 4826

0705-8268 See BOOKS IN YIDDISH. 4826

0705-8322 See SERVICE DE LA BIBLIOTHEQUE : SUPPLEMENT AU GUIDE DE L'USAGER. 3661

0705-8330 See CANADIAN BUSINESS ECONOMICS. 1467

0705-8365 See CUVANTUL ROMANESC. 2259

0705-839X See ACHIMOWIN. 5779

0705-8454 See A S T I S CURRENT AWARENESS BULLETIN. 406

0705-856X See FACTS (OTTAWA). 1669

0705-8578 See EMBOUTEILLEUR QUEBECOIS (EDITION ANGLAISE). 2366

0705-8586 See A T E N S CONFERENCE REPORT. 3357

0705-8594 See MIDDLE EAST FOCUS. 4528

0705-8748 See FARM GATE, THE. 84

0705-8780 See POURQUOI CHANTER?. 4147

0705-8810 See CANADIAN POLICE COLLEGE JOURNAL. 3159

0705-8942 See CAHIERS DE SPIRITUALITE IGNATIENNE. 4941

0705-8993 See MARINE TRADES (1978). 845

0705-9019 See B.C. MUSIC EDUCATOR. 4101

0705-9027 See THYME. 2763

0705-906X See WESTERN GROCER MAGAZINE (1977). 2361

0705-9078 See ATLANTIC MATHEMATICS BULLETIN. 3496

0705-9108 See BULLISIANA. 394

0705-9124 See CELTA SOCIAL. 5781

0705-9175 See MOVIE WORKS WEEKLY, THE. 4075

0705-9213 See PANORAMA (HULL). 387

0705-923X See IMAGE LACHINE. 2535

0705-9272 See ENVIRONMENT SYSTEMS & INDUSTRIES. 614

0705-9418 See ESPECIALLY FOR SENIORS. 5179

0705-9485 See CANADA GAZETTE. PART 3. 2529

0705-9515 See HOUSE PRICE TRENDS AND RESIDENTIAL CONSTRUCTION COSTS IN THE TORONTO REAL ESTATE BOARD MARKET AREA AND IN CANADA. 4838

0705-9590 See APPEL DU SACRE-COEUR, L'. 5055

0706-0084 See MANUFACTURING + MARKETING OPPORTUNITIES; BULLETIN. 3484

0706-0106 See ANNUAL REPORT--ONTARIO HERITAGE FOUNDATION. 2721

0706-0335 See BUDGET. ADDITIONAL INFORMATION : ESTIMATES. 4714

0706-0424 See CHARLTON'S STANDARD CATALOGUE OF CANADIAN COINS. 2780

0706-0475 See PAPERS IN MANITOBA ARCHAEOLOGY. FINAL REPORT. 278

0706-0491 See PAPERS IN MANITOBA ARCHAEOLOGY. PRELIMINARY REPORT. 278

0706-0505 See PAPERS IN MANITOBA ARCHAEOLOGY. POPULAR SERIES. 278

0706-0556 See ESPLUMOIR, L'. 3462

0706-0564 See BULLETIN - PUBLIC SERVICE COMMISSION OF CANADA. 4635

0706-0661 See CANADIAN JOURNAL OF PLANT PATHOLOGY. 505

0706-067X See ROAD MOTOR VEHICLES. REGISTRATIONS. 5443

0706-0793 See SCIENCE STATISTICS. 5176

0706-0882 See MANITOBA PHYSICAL EDUCATION TEACHERS' ASSOCIATION. 1857

0706-0890 See REPORT OF THE STANDING COMMISSION ON REFORM OF THE ELECTORAL DISTRICTS. 4681

0706-0955 See NORTHWARD JOURNAL. 360

0706-098X See MUSEES. 4091

0706-1005 See CONCORDIA UNIVERSITY MAGAZINE. 1090

0706-1048 See VRAC, EN. 4538

0706-1056 See BRITEQ PRESSE. 1934

0706-1072 See ENVIRONMENTAL STUDIES. 2170

0706-120X See BULLETIN PSILOG, LE. 4241

0706-1226 See STUDIES IN WEST PATRICIA ARCHAEOLOGY. 283

0706-1226 See ARCHAEOLOGICAL RESEARCH REPORT (TORONTO). 257

0706-1250 See CARREFOUR. 4343

0706-1293 See ANNUAL INTERNATIONAL CONFERENCE / CANADIAN NUCLEAR ASSOCIATION. 2154

0706-1307 See PEAT NEWS. 119

0706-1382 See C A F C DIALOGUE. 2288

0706-1412 See ALBERTA'S ENERGY RESOURCES. 1931

0706-1420 See ALBERTA ELECTRIC INDUSTRY. ANNUAL STATISTICS. 1961

0706-1498 See BULLETIN DE STATISTIQUES - COMMISSION DES VALEURS MOBILIERES DU QUEBEC. 893

0706-151X See INPUT. 3217

0706-1684 See COMMERCIAL PRICE LIST - N.F.B. PHOTOTHEQUE. 4067

0706-1706 See LABOUR CAPITAL AND SOCIETY. 1685

0706-1757 See TEMISCOUATA, LE. 2762

0706-1773 See INFORMATIQUE QUEBEC. 1260

0706-1811 See COURTAGE IMMOBILIER, LE. 2191

0706-182X See CEGEP-PRESSE. 4637

0706-1854 See INFORMATION REPORT / PETAWAWA NATIONAL FORESTRY INSTITUTE. 2385

0706-1889 See WRITING (NELSON). 3473

0706-196X See LOTO-LIAISON. 4663

0706-1994 See COMPTES RENDUS MATHEMATIQUES DE L'ACADEMIE DES SCIENCES. 3501

0706-215X See BULLETIN VOYAGES. 5465

0706-2168 See CANADIAN GEOGRAPHIC. 2558

0706-2192 3853

0706-2249 See CHOIX : DOCUMENTATION IMPRIMEE. 3201

0706-2257 See CHOIX: DOCUMENTATION AUDIOVISUELLE. 1891

0706-2265 See CHOIX JEUNESSE : DOCUMENTATION IMPRIMEE. 3201

0706-2338 See DIRECTORY OF CANADIAN UNIVERSITIES. 1820

0706-2508 See RAPPORT ANNUEL - CENTRE DE RECHERCHE INDUSTRIELLE DU QUEBEC. 1623

0706-2575 See ANNUAL REPORT - CANADIAN GRAIN COMMISSION. 60

0706-2613 See AGENDA (OTTAWA). 5081

0706-2710 See PUBLIC ACCOUNTS (REGINA). 4743

0706-2893 See BRITISH COLUMBIA POLICE JOURNAL. 3158

0706-2907 See SCHOOL LIBRARY NEWSLETTER. 3248

0706-2915 See SCHOOL LIBRARY NEWSLETTER. 3248

0706-3083 See PROVINCIAL ECONOMIC ACCOUNTS. 4742

0706-3180 See LIVRET DES REGLEMENTS DE LA FEDERATION CANADIENNE DES ARCHERS (1974). 4903

0706-3296 See ARCHAEOLOGICAL RESEARCH REPORT (TORONTO). 257

0706-3318 See JOURNAL REGIONAL (QUEBEC). 5787

0706-3350 See MANITOBA GAZETTE, THE. 4481

0706-3431 See CHRONIQUE (QUEBEC). 2481

0706-3644 See COMMUNICANTES. 4949

0706-3652 See UNIVERSITIES. ENROLLMENT AND DEGREES. 1852

0706-3679 See EDUCATION IN CANADA. 1794

0706-3717 See MINORITY AND SECOND LANGUAGE EDUCATION. ELEMENTARY AND SECONDARY LEVELS. 1764

0706-3806 See ANNUAL REPORT - JUSTICE DEVELOPMENT COMMISSION (BRITISH COLUMBIA). 2934

0706-3857 See FIREWEED. 5556

0706-3954 See TRANSPO. 5395

0706-4152 See TECHNICAL BULLETIN - CANADIAN CONSERVATION INSTITUTE. 2206

0706-425X See REPORT OF THE AGRICULTURAL RESEARCH INSTITUTE OF ONTARIO. 126

0706-4624 See NOUVELLES FISCALES DU QUEBEC. 4739

0706-4659 See WEEKLY CHECKLIST OF CANADIAN GOVERNMENT PUBLICATIONS. 4694

0706-4667 See C. O. E. Q. JOURNAL, THE. 1729

0706-4713 See U-CHOOSE. 1095

0706-4810 See ANNUAL REPORT - MINISTRY OF HEALTH (VICTORIA). 4766

0706-4926 See WAGES AND WORKING CONDITIONS BY OCCUPATION. 1717

0706-5019 See OCCUPATIONAL HEALTH AND SAFETY LAW. 3020

0706-5035 See VERNON'S CITY OF TIMMINS, ONTARIO, DIRECTORY. 2578

0706-5094 See WILD ROSE CHRONICLE. 5798

0706-5116 See BENCHMARK (CHARLOTTETOWN). 1811

0706-5132 See DIVER MAGAZINE. 4893

0706-5205 See ECHANGE (NORANDA). 3208

0706-5280 See GASOLINE RAINBOW. 3390

0706-5361 See BULLETIN - CONSEIL DES AFFAIRES FRANCO-ONTARIENNES. 4634

0706-5388 See CARSWELL'S PRACTICE CASES. 3089

0706-5493 See ALERT : MEDICAL DEVICES. 3547

0706-554X See NEWS IN BRIEF (TORONTO). 1508

0706-5574 See WITHOUT PREJUDICE (EDMONTON). 2896

0706-5582 See CANADIAN JOURNAL OF LIFE INSURANCE. 2877

0706-5604 See THALIA (OTTAWA). 3445

0706-5655 See ESTATES & TRUSTS REPORTS. 3118

0706-5698 See ANNUAL REPORT / VIA RAIL CANADA INC. 5429

0706-6333 See RAPPORT DU MINISTRE DE L'EDUCATION (TORONTO). 1776

0706-635X See ASSURVIE. 2874

0706-6449 See DAZZLE. 403

0706-6449 See JOURNAL OF STUDIES IN THE BHAGAVADGITA, THE. 5041

0706-6457 See CANADIAN TECHNICAL REPORT OF FISHERIES AND AQUATIC SCIENCES. 2299

0706-6465 See CANADIAN DATA REPORT OF FISHERIES AND AQUATIC SCIENCES. 2298

0706-6473 See CANADIAN MANUSCRIPT REPORT OF FISHERIES AND AQUATIC SCIENCES. 2298

0706-6481 See CANADIAN SPECIAL PUBLICATION OF FISHERIES AND AQUATIC SCIENCES. 2299

0706-6503 See CANADIAN BULLETIN OF FISHERIES AND AQUATIC SCIENCES. 2298

0706-652X See CANADIAN JOURNAL OF FISHERIES AND AQUATIC SCIENCES. 2298

0706-6589 See RAPPORT MANUSCRIT CANADIEN DES SCIENCES HALIETIQUES ET AQUATIQUES. 5538

0706-6724 See FACULTY & ADMINISTRATIVE DIRECTORY - THE UNIVERSITY OF BRITISH COLUMBIA. 1864

0706-6775 See BRIEF TO THE ONTARIO COUNCIL ON UNIVERSITY AFFAIRS (YORK UNIVERSITY). 1812

0706-683X See MILTON WEEKLY TRIBUNE. 5789

0706-6899 See CANCELLED LEAVES. 3372

0706-6902 See INVENTORS DIGEST. 1305

0706-6937 See RAFIKI. 2911

0706-697X See DIRECTORY - CANADIAN INTERUNIVERSITY ATHLETIC UNION. 4892

0706-7003 See FAITH TODAY (TORONTO). 4958

0706-7011 See MADOC NEWS, THE. 5789

0706-7046 See LOCAL EXCHANGE, THE. 2537
0706-7178 See COURT JUDGEMENT REPORT (NEW BRUNSWICK ED.). 2957
0706-7224 See FREELANCER (MAYERTHORPE). 5784
0706-7240 See MACKLIN MIRROR. 5789
0706-7380 See IMPRINT (WATERLOO). 1829
0706-7399 See APPRENTICE (OTTAWA). 4857
0706-7402 See ECHO DES CANTONS. 2732
0706-7410 See SONECRAN. 331
0706-7429 See NIAGARA BRUCE TRAIL CLUB. 4876
0706-7437 See CANADIAN JOURNAL OF PSYCHIATRY. 3923
0706-7534 See FOOTWEAR FORUM. 1084
0706-7550 See VAUXHALL ADVANCE, THE. 5797
0706-7682 See GREAT EXPEDITIONS. 5478
0706-7747 See FOREST TIMES. 2381
0706-7763 See DISCO FEVER. 4115
0706-7798 See PUBLIC LIBRARY SERVICES NEWSLETTER. 3243
0706-795X See DES LIVRES ET DES JEUNES. 3380
0706-7984 See NEW MUSIC. 4140
0706-7992 See SUBJECT TO CHANGE. 3937
0706-8085 See REACHING THE MANITOBA MARKET. 765
0706-8107 See CANADIAN REVIEW OF ART EDUCATION, RESEARCH AND ISSUES. 346
0706-8115 See REVUE DE L'UNIVERSITE SAINTE-ANNE. 1846
0706-8166 See CAVING INTERNATIONAL. 4871
0706-8328 See ANNUAIRE DE L'EGLISE DU QUEBEC. 5023
0706-8387 See SCHMAGG. 2545
0706-8409 See NEW INDIA BULLETIN. 4484
0706-8549 See BULLETIN - UNIVERSITY RELATIONS AND INFORMATION OFFICE, UNIVERSITY OF MANITOBA. 1813
0706-8581 See AFRICA (LEVIS). 4932
0706-8662 See WHAT'S NEW IN PUBLICATIONS (EDMONTON). 427
0706-8808 See QUAD (PAISLEY). 4054
0706-8964 See DUNHILL LIABILITY LOSS REPORT. 2964
0706-9006 See STONEY MONDAY. 3440
0706-9022 See NEWSLETTER - BRITISH COLUMBIA COUNCIL FOR THE FAMILY. 2284
0706-9286 See PRESS REVIEW (TORONTO). 2923
0706-9294 See OPERATION LIBERTE. 4511
0706-9502 See ANNUAL REPORT - COUNCIL OF MINISTERS OF EDUCATION, CANADA. 1725
0706-9596 See FISHERIES MANUSCRIPT REPORT. 2302
0706-9731 See ARTS B. C. 314
0706-9774 See ANNUAIRE - ARCHIDIOCESE DE SHERBROOKE (1977). 5023
0706-9782 See C A S A S NEWS. 70
0706-9812 See ACUPUNCTURE TODAY. 3546
0706-9839 See MEMBERS' HANDBOOK - THE ALBERTA TEACHERS' ASSOCIATION. 1866
0706-9944 See REPORTS LIST - EDUCATIONAL RESEARCH INSTITUTE OF BRITISH COLUMBIA. 1778
0706-9987 See T A Q JOURNAL, A. 3327
0706-9995 See GUIDE DU TRANSPORT PAR CAMION INC. 5383
0707-0063 See UNION WOMAN. 1716
0707-0195 See NEWSLETTER - PROVINCIAL COUNCIL OF WOMEN OF BRITISH COLUMBIA. 5562
0707-0306 See ALBERTA GOVERNMENT LIBRARIES' NEWSLETTER. 3189
0707-073X See SCOTTISH BANNER, THE. 2272
0707-0780 See HERITAGE SEEKERS. 2453
0707-087X See NOVA SCOTIA HOSTELLER. 2808
0707-0926 See OPEN INTEREST. 910
0707-0934 See M S ONTARIO. 3837

0707-1035 See COMMON USAGE DRUG SCHEDULE. 4297
0707-1078 See SIMERA (QUEBEC). 2545
0707-1248 See MULTI-YEAR PLAN - HUMBER COLLEGE OF APPLIED ARTS AND TECHNOLOGY. 1836
0707-1434 See ANNUAL REPORT - ALBERTA HEALTH AND SOCIAL SERVICES DISCIPLINES COMMITTEE. 3913
0707-1906 See SPORT ONTARIO NEWS. 4921
0707-1957 See UNB FORESTRY FOCUS. 2397
0707-1973 See REPORT OF THE SASKATCHEWAN SAFETY COUNCIL PUBLIC OPINION POLL, A. 4798
0707-204X See HEBDO A H P Q. 3783
0707-2147 See LTA CONFERENCE. 3300
0707-2228 See P. A. L., PREVENT, AVOID LOSSES. 3171
0707-2279 See WORLDWIND. 1071
0707-2287 See EDIOS. 4345
0707-2295 See SOUTH CENTRAL BANNER. 5795
0707-2325 See COASTER, THE. 5782
0707-2333 See SCRATCHING RIVER POST, THE. 5794
0707-2406 See EN-TROPHY INSTITUTE REVIEW. 4190
0707-2422 See GEOSCIENCES IN CANADA (1976). 1356
0707-2457 See NSSLA BULLETIN. 3237
0707-2481 See PORTFOLIO (HAMILTON). 5454
0707-2511 See VIE PEDAGOGIQUE. 1790
0707-2554 See HIGHLAND HERITAGE. 2453
0707-2562 See RESERVOIR ANNUAL (1977). 4276
0707-2716 See EN-TROPHY INSTITUTE REVIEW. 4190
0707-2767 See STATISTICAL REVIEW OF COAL IN CANADA. 2006
0707-2775 See JURISPRUDENCE EN DROIT DU TRAVAIL. DECISIONS DES COMMISSAIRES DU TRAVAIL. 3150
0707-2783 See FISHERIES POLLUTION REPORT (LETHBRIDGE). 2302
0707-2902 See CANADIAN BOOK OF CORPORATE MANAGEMENT. 863
0707-2910 See SANTE MENTALE AU CANADA. 4801
0707-2937 See MONTHLY COLLECTOR (SUDBURY). 2786
0707-2945 See CANADIAN MUSLIM, THE. 5042
0707-3054 See JOURNAL OF CORPORATE MANAGEMENT, THE. 3101
0707-3062 See NEWSLETTER - COMMUNICATION EFFECTIVENESS CENTRE. 1118
0707-3178 See ONTARIO OUT OF DOORS. 4876
0707-3186 See RUNNER (EDMONTON). 1858
0707-3216 See MINUTES OF PROCEEDINGS AND EVIDENCE OF THE SPECIAL COMMITTEE ON A NORTHERN GAS PIPELINE. 4264
0707-3283 See INCOME SECURITY PROGRAMS. 5289
0707-3364 See NORTHLAND TODAY MAGAZINE. 5486
0707-3542 See ROLLCALL. 3917
0707-3623 See MINERAL INDUSTRY REPORT. NORTHWEST TERRITORIES. 1618
0707-3674 See BIBLIOTHECA MEDICA CANADIANA. 3195
0707-3747 See CONSER MICROFICHE. 3204
0707-3836 See HILBORN FAMILY JOURNAL. 2453
0707-3844 See DIRECTORY - CANADIAN ASSOCIATION OF GEOGRAPHERS. 2559
0707-3860 See CHINOOK REPORTER. 5782
0707-3879 See CHIEF EXECUTIVES COMPENSATION IN CANADA. 1659
0707-3941 See HALTON CONSUMER. 1297
0707-3968 See THOROUGH. 1999
0707-3976 See ZYCIE OTTAWY. 5266
0707-4360 See MY PET. 4287
0707-4395 See BIOESTHETIQUE. 402
0707-4611 See CHICKADEE. 1061

0707-4794 See THAMESFORD TOWN CRIER. 5796
0707-4808 See PROCEEDINGS OF THE WORKSHOP OF THE CANADIAN AGRICULTURAL ECONOMICS SOCIETY. 122
0707-4905 See COURIER WEEKEND. 5782
0707-493X See BUSINESS PRESS. 651
0707-4956 See CASTOR REVIEW. 5781
0707-4964 See SLAVE RIVER JOURNAL. 5794
0707-5022 See ONTARIO LABOUR. 1700
0707-5081 See JOUETS (MONTREAL. 1976). 2584
0707-509X See WEST EDMONTON EXAMINER. 5797
0707-5316 See MONTREAL WRITERS' FORUM. 3413
0707-5324 See LUSITANO (CAMBRIDGE). 5789
0707-5332 See INTERNATIONAL HISTORY REVIEW, THE. 2620
0707-543X See FRIDAY TIMES. 5785
0707-5448 See OPASQUIA TIMES. 5791
0707-5472 See SOCIALIST FULCRUM. 4547
0707-5510 See DEMARCHE, LA. 384
0707-5529 See REFLET D'AMOS, LE. 5793
0707-5588 See ASCENT. 1933
0707-5650 See NEW CANADIAN SLOVENE DIARY, THE. 2269
0707-574X See HANDBOOK FOR INDIANS IN OTTAWA-HULL, A. 2262
0707-5995 See COMMUNIQUE - MANITOBA DIVISION, CANADIAN CANCER SOCIETY. 3815
0707-6185 See WINNIPEG MAGAZINE. 2550
0707-6908 See EASTERN SHORE ECHO. 5783
0707-6916 See COASTAL COURIER. 5782
0707-6924 See BOOKS NOW. 3368
0707-6932 See LINK FOR MCMASTER PART-TIME STUDENTS, THE. 1761
0707-7017 See TRAVAILLEUR (QUEBEC). 1715
0707-7106 See SWAMP GAS JOURNAL, THE. 37
0707-7130 See CONNECTIONS (POINTE CLAIRE). 2444
0707-7157 See KAMOURASKA (LA POCATIERE). 5787
0707-7165 See ENVOL (MONTREAL. 1978). 5617
0707-7203 See ECHOS PHILATELIQUES. 2785
0707-7211 See NOUVELLES ET DOCUMENTS - LA PROVINCE CANADIENNE DES PERES DE SAINTE-CROIX. 4982
0707-7270 See JOURNAL OF OTOLARYNGOLOGY. SUPPLEMENT, THE. 3889
0707-7300 See CANADIAN MULTICULTURAL SCENE. 2258
0707-7548 See VITAL STATISTICS ANNUAL REVIEW. 4807
0707-7572 See QUEBEC SUD-OUEST. 5793
0707-7629 See CANADIAN LOCATIONS OF JOURNALS INDEXED FOR MEDLINE. 3200
0707-7653 See STUDY BINDER - CHARTERED ACCOUNTANTS STUDENTS' ASSOCIATION OF ONTARIO. 751
0707-7696 See UNITE PROLETARIENNE. 4548
0707-7726 See LIAISONS (MONTREAL). 3297
0707-7807 See JOURNAL OF PRACTICAL APPROACHES TO DEVELOPMENTAL HANDICAP. 4390
0707-7815 See THOUGHTS ON INTERNATIONAL DEVELOPMENT. 1640
0707-7858 See JOURNAL DES TRAVAILLEURS D'HOPITAUX. 5787
0707-7874 See CANADIAN ENVIRONMENTAL LAW REPORTS. 3110
0707-7939 See LIGHT TRUCK EQUIPMENT NEWS. 5788
0707-7998 See BRANT NEWS. 5781
0707-8048 See BULLETIN - CANADIAN FEDERATION FOR THE HUMANITIES. 2843
0707-8056 See WARRIOR (SHEARWATER. 1978). 4060
0707-8064 See CALGARY COMMERCE. 826
0707-8102 See ONTARIO/CANADA ACCOMMODATIONS. 2808

0707-8137 See OUTAOUAIS GENEALOGIQUE. 2466

0707-8315 See DEBATES AND PROCEEDINGS - NOVA SCOTIA HOUSE OF ASSEMBLY. 4641

0707-8412 See RESOURCES FOR FEMINIST RESEARCH : RFR. 5565

0707-848X See MICROEDITIONS DE LA BIBLIOTHEQUE. CATALOGUE. 420

0707-8498 See FISHERIES MANAGEMENT REPORT (ALBERTA. FISH AND WILDLIFE DIVISION). 2302

0707-8501 See JUSTICE (QUEBEC). 2991

0707-8544 See 25-1-1. 2671

0707-8552 See STUDIES IN POLITICAL ECONOMY. 4497

0707-8617 See PATH FINDER (VANCOUVER). 3626

0707-8633 See TRAIT D'UNION (QUEBEC). 1850

0707-8919 See RULES OF THOROUGHBRED RACING. 2802

0707-8927 See LAMBI, LE. 2266

0707-8935 See CORRESPONDANCES (SILLERY). 2213

0707-8951 See PRETIRES, CONFERENCE TECHNOLOGIQUE ESTIVALE. 4237

0707-8978 See MINUTES OF PROCEEDINGS AND EVIDENCE OF THE STANDING COMMITTEE ON NORTHERN PIPELINES. 4264

0707-8994 See PROCEEDINGS OF THE SPECIAL COMMITTEE OF THE SENATE ON A NORTHERN GAS PIPELINE. 4275

0707-9001 See PROCEEDINGS OF THE SPECIAL COMMITTEE OF THE SENATE ON THE NORTHERN PIPELINE. 4275

0707-9036 See FEMININ PLURIEL. 5555

0707-9044 See PROCEEDINGS OF THE SUBCOMMITTEE ON CHILDHOOD EXPERIENCES AS CAUSES OF CRIMINAL BEHAVIOUR. 3173

0707-9079 See REPORT - ALBERTA ENVIRONMENT. RESEARCH SECRETARIAT. 2181

0707-9109 See ANNALES DES SCIENCES MATHEMATIQUES DU QUEBEC. 3493

0707-9133 See COMMUNICATOR (ST. JOHN'S). 4639

0707-9141 See DEUS LOCI. 3380

0707-9230 See BUDGET. RENSEIGNEMENTS SUPPLEMENTAIRES : REFORME DE LA FISCALITE MUNICIPALE. 4715

0707-9389 See 24 IMAGES. 4062

0707-9516 See REVUE QUEBECOISE DE SEXOLOGIE. 5188

0707-9524 See CANADIAN BRIDGE DIGEST (1977). 4858

0707-9532 See ARTS BULLETIN OF THE CANADIAN CONFERENCE OF THE ARTS. 314

0707-963X See ANNUAL REPORT - SASKATCHEWAN HEALTH, HEARING AID PLAN. 4383

0707-9656 See MONTREAL REVIEW. 2747

0707-9672 See BALOUNE. 4857

0707-9699 See REVUE INTERNATIONALE D'ACTION COMMUNAUTAIRE (MONTREAL). 2834

0707-9737 See TEACHERS IN UNIVERSITIES (OTTAWA. 1976). 1849

0707-9753 See TELEPHONE STATISTICS (MONTHLY ED.). 1125

0707-9796 See SURVEILLANCE REPORT. 2182

0707-9818 See ALBERTA RURAL DEVELOPMENT STUDIES. 57

0708-000X See OMINECA ADVERTISER, THE. 5791

0708-0239 See CRANBROOK'S RESPONSE. 5783

0708-0263 See AT A GLANCE. 3192

0708-028X See NEWS BULLETIN - SASKATCHEWAN RAIL COMMITTEE. 5433

0708-0646 See BULLETIN - CANADA POST. 1144

0708-0735 See MEMO FROM PROBE. 5252

0708-0859 See B. C. PEACE NEWS. 4516

0708-1006 See PHYSIOQUEBEC. 4381

0708-1073 See CONSTRUCTION SIGHTLINES. 610

0708-109X See STANDOUT MAGAZINE. 2796

0708-1332 See EXPORT CANADA. 834

0708-1421 See PROCEEDINGS OF THE SPECIAL SENATE COMMITTEE ON RETIREMENT AGE POLICIES. 1703

0708-1502 See BULLETIN CAN/OLE. 5090

0708-1510 See REPERTOIRE DE LA VIE FRANCAISE EN AMERIQUE. 2544

0708-1545 See STATISTIQUES - UNIVERSITE LAVAL. 1798

0708-1553 See KEY BUSINESS RATIOS. 731

0708-1561 See SUPER MAGAZINE. 2547

0708-157X See ANNUAL MEETING - NATIONAL UNION OF STUDENTS. 1809

0708-1596 See NEWSPAPERS AND PERIODICALS CURRENTLY RECEIVED BY THE LIBRARY OF PARLIAMENT INCLUDING THE READING ROOM OF THE HOUSE OF COMMONS. 4699

0708-1715 See REVUE DU NOUVEL ONTARIO. 2759

0708-1936 See BIO-JOULE. 1933

0708-1952 See NEWSLETTER - WATERLOO POTTERS' WORKSHOP. 374

0708-1960 See SAFRICAN NEWS. 4495

0708-1979 See NEWSLETTER OF THE YELLOWHEAD REGIONAL LIBRARY. 3235

0708-1995 See U N B ENGINEERING NEWSLETTER. 2000

0708-2002 See CANADIAN DENTAL FACULTY AND STAFF REGISTER. 1318

0708-207X See PLACOTEUX. 2543

0708-2169 See HIBALLER FOREST MAGAZINE. 2384

0708-2215 See INSTALLATION DES SYSTEMES DE GICLEURS, L'. 1979

0708-2398 See ETUDES CREOLES. 3280

0708-2479 See VOCE EVANGELICA. 5008

0708-2568 See METRO TELECASTER (1977). 1134

0708-2827 See WORKING PAPER (LAW REFORM COMMISSION OF CANADA). 3076

0708-3157 See LABOUR FORCE INFORMATION. 1535

0708-3173 See OPTOMETRISTE. 4216

0708-3181 See ATLANTIC NUMISMATIST, THE. 2779

0708-319X See ETIENNE GILSON SERIES, THE. 4346

0708-3300 See FERRIES, BRIDGES, CRUISES. 5382

0708-3319 See TRAVERSIERS, PONTS ET CROISIERES. 855

0708-336X See PRODUCTION AND DISPOSITION OF TOBACCO PRODUCTS. 5373

0708-3599 See NEWSLETTER / U.N.B. TEMPERANCE UNION. 5299

0708-3823 See URBAN AND REGIONAL RESEARCH IN CANADA. 2837

0708-3912 See BULLETIN - OFFICE DE LA CONSTRUCTION DU QUEBEC. 4635

0708-3998 See REPORT OF THE CHIEF ELECTORAL OFFICER ON THE ... GENERAL ENUMERATION. 4680

0708-4048 See ANNUAL REPORT - PROVINCIAL AGRICULTURAL LAND COMMISSION (BRITISH COLUMBIA). 61

0708-4285 See CANADA WATER YEAR BOOK. 5531

0708-4331 See HIGH FLIGHT. 23

0708-4366 See ELECTRONIC PRODUCTS AND TECHNOLOGY. 2048

0708-4382 See UNIVERSITY OF TORONTO REVIEW. 3449

0708-4897 See PRODUCTION AND STOCKS OF EGGS AND POULTRY. 219

0708-4927 See FLARE (TORONTO). 5557

0708-4978 See PROCEEDINGS OF THE SUBCOMMITTEE ON OFF-TRACK BETTING. 2801

0708-4986 See JOURNAL DU TRAVAIL (QUEBEC. 1979). 1681

0708-5079 See REVUE DE PLANIFICATION FISCALE ET SUCCESSORALE. 3119

0708-5125 See RULES OF STANDARDBRED RACING. 2802

0708-515X See SIGNATURE (VANCOUVER). 4819

0708-5249 See NACOI FORUM. 2268

0708-5303 See CHATELAINE'S NEW MOTHER. 2277

0708-5354 See ART EDUCATION (SASKATOON). 338

0708-5389 See ATROPOS. 3364

0708-5400 See ATLANTIC INSIGHT. 2485

0708-5427 See GOALGETTER. 4896

0708-5435 See PHOTO COMMUNIQUE. 4373

0708-5516 See ANNUAL REPORT - CANADIAN HUMAN RIGHTS COMMISSION. 4504

0708-5583 See OTTAWA BRANCH NEWS - ONTARIO GENEALOGICAL SOCIETY. 2466

0708-5591 See CANADIAN PSYCHOLOGY. 4579

0708-5702 See BULLETIN AGRICOLE, DISTRICT DE TIMISKAMING. 68

0708-5710 See PROJECT INFORMATION EXCHANGE (SELECTED DOCUMENTS). 5302

0708-5745 See UNIMA CANADA. 389

0708-580X See HORIZON (MONTREAL. 1979). 2263

0708-5842 See BUSINESS (TORONTO). 5552

0708-594X See CANSCAIP NEWS. 1061

0708-5974 See EYE (DOWNSVIEW. 1979). 2616

0708-6008 See ON TRACK. 31

0708-6059 See RAPPORT ANNUEL - SOCIETE QUEBECOISE D'INITIATIVES AGRO-ALIMENTAIRES. 124

0708-6113 See SPORT ONTARIO DIRECTORY OF SPORTS, RECREATION AND PHYSICAL EDUCATION. 4920

0708-613X See VOTRE AFFAIRE, C'EST NOTRE AFFAIRE. 815

0708-6148 See NOUVELLES DE LA PETITE ENTREPRISE. 700

0708-6164 See DAIRY GOAT GAZETTE (1977). 193

0708-6199 See CONCRETE PRODUCTS MANUFACTURERS (PRELIMINARY ED.). 3477

0708-6229 See CONSTRUCTION TYPE PLYWOOD. 2400

0708-6350 See NEWS & VIEWS - ONTARIO GENEALOGICAL SOCIETY, LEEDS & GRENVILLE BRANCH. 2462

0708-6377 See VIGNE A A, LA. 1350

0708-6474 See CONA JOURNAL. 3854

0708-711X See ORDO (1977). 5033

0708-7152 See "CRISS-CROSS" MONTREAL METROPOLITAIN. 5467

0708-7152 See "CRISS-CROSS" MONTREAL METROPOLITAIN. 5467

0708-7217 See ANNUAL REPORT OF THE PARLIAMENTARY COMMISSIONER. OMBUDSMAN. 4628

0708-7233 See ANNUAL STATISTICS / MANITOBA HEALTH SERVICES COMMISSION. 4809

0708-7241 See CANADIAN DIRECTORY OF INDUSTRIAL DISTRIBUTORS. 826

0708-7292 See E A UPDATE SUMMARY. 2164

0708-7624 See PROCEEDINGS OF THE CANADIAN ASSOCIATION FOR LABORATORY ANIMAL SCIENCE. 5519

0708-7632 See TEMPS DE VIVRE (MONTREAL). 5182

0708-790X See MICROLOG NEWSLETTER. 4816

0708-8132 See NICOLA VALLEY HISTORICAL QUARTERLY. 2750

0708-9031 See EXCISE NEWS. 2968

0708-918X See NEWSLETTER - PLANETARY ASSOCIATION FOR CLEAN ENERGY. 1951

0708-9392 See ANNUAL REPORT - CANADIAN BROADCASTING CORPORATION. 1126

0708-9457 See MANITOBA CHINESE POST. 5789

0708-9465 See HEALTH SCIENCES INFORMATION IN CANADA. LIBRARIES. 3213

0708-949X See INDO-CANADIAN TIMES. 5786

0708-9503 See PERDESI PANJAB. 5792

0708-9562 See POETIC LICENCE (CALGARY). 3468

0708-9570 See QUARTERLY - CANADIAN GOAT SOCIETY. **220**

0708-9597 See NEWSLETTER - ASSOCIATION OF BRITISH COLUMBIA DRAMA EDUCATORS. **5366**

0708-9627 See MILIEU DE VIE. **4852**

0708-9635 See CANADIAN MUSICIAN. **4107**

0708-9813 See MISSION (QUEBEC). **5032**

0708-9821 See SOUTH WEST NOVA. **5491**

0708-983X See GUIDE CASTELRIAND. **2735**

0708-9864 See REPORT - ASSOCIATION FOR REPORT ON CONFEDERATION. **4680**

0708-9945 See MONOGRAPHIE - ECOLE DE RELATIONS INDUSTRIELLES, UNIVERSITE DE MONTREAL. **944**

0708-9961 See RAINCOAST. **1068**

0708-997X See CHILD FOCUS. **2277**

0709-0013 See LAKES LETTER. **1416**

0709-003X See METROPOLITAN TORONTO BUSINESS JOURNAL, THE. **693**

0709-0056 See PARABOLE. **5018**

0709-0102 See BRITISH COLUMBIA GROWER. **68**

0709-0188 See P. D. DIGEST. **1796**

0709-020X See LINK (OTTAWA). **1761**

0709-0269 See CANADIAN MARATHON ANNUAL. **4889**

0709-0285 See BOARD OF DIRECTORS, COMMITTEE CHAIRMEN - CANADIAN CHAMBER OF COMMERCE. **818**

0709-0358 See BALITA. **5780**

0709-0366 See CAREER NEWS (WATERLOO). **4202**

0709-0412 See GOVERNMENT OF CANADA PUBLICATIONS. QUARTERLY CATALOGUE. **4698**

0709-0439 See RESOURCEBOOK. **1625**

0709-0455 See WESTERN SIKH SAMACHAR. **2766**

0709-0501 See ISSUES IN THE CANADIAN ECONOMY. **1568**

0709-0528 See NEWS 'N' NOTES - INDUSTRIAL EDUCATION COUNCIL OF THE ALBERTA TEACHERS' ASSOCIATION. **1867**

0709-0536 See SERIAL HOLDINGS IN NEWFOUNDLAND LIBRARIES. **3249**

0709-0595 See DRUMHELLER SUN, THE. **5783**

0709-0641 See NEW BOOK NEWS FROM QUEBEC. **4817**

0709-065X See MONTREAL SCOP. **386**

0709-0676 See BULLETIN - ASSOCIATION FOR THE STUDY OF CANADIAN RADIO AND TELEVISION. **1128**

0709-0692 See QUART DE ROND. **625**

0709-0749 See DIRECTORY OF COMMUNITY SERVICES (SUDBURY). **5282**

0709-0757 See CANADIAN PROFESSIONAL REAL ESTATE DIRECTORY FOR THE PROVINCE OF BRITISH COLUMBIA. **4835**

0709-082X See BIRCH BARK ALLIANCE, THE. **4446**

0709-0846 See TOBIQUER. **2763**

0709-0854 See SASKATCHEWAN BUSINESS. **709**

0709-0862 See LABOUR SCENE, THE. **1686**

0709-0870 See DISCUSSION PAPER SERIES (UNIVERSITY OF CALGARY. DEPT. OF ECONOMICS). **1480**

0709-1222 See TECHNICAL REPORT (UNIVERSITY OF NEW BRUNSWICK. DEPT. OF SURVEYING ENGINEERING). **2032**

0709-1230 See JOURNAL OF COMMERCE (VANCOUVER). **842**

0709-1370 See NATIONAL (OTTAWA. 1978). **1882**

0709-1532 See WESTERN SPORTSMAN. **4929**

0709-1605 See ANNUAL REPORT - EXPORT DEVELOPMENT CORPORATION. **822**

0709-1915 See VOICE OF THE MIDDLESEX FARMER, THE. **145**

0709-2121 See CALENDAR OF EVENTS (VICTORIA. 1979). **2486**

0709-2148 See DEFI. **4386**

0709-2172 See BULLETIN A L'USAGE DES TRAPPEURS. **4888**

0709-2180 See FORUM (VICTORIA). **3140**

0709-2253 See STATISTICAL BULLETIN - CANADIAN PULP AND PAPER ASSOCIATION. **4239**

0709-2334 See DIMENSIONS (MONTREAL). **1735**

0709-2415 See AMUSEMENT JEUNESSE. **4856**

0709-2423 See MANITOBA BUSINESS. **691**

0709-2431 See ALBERTA CONSTRUCTION. **598**

0709-2482 See PROFESSIONAL SCHOOLS FACTSHEETS. **1842**

0709-2490 See U C P A JOURNAL. **1851**

0709-2504 See JOURNAL DE L'APUC (EDITION FRANCAISE). **1832**

0709-2563 See PULP & PAPER CANADA ANNUAL AND DIRECTORY. **4238**

0709-258X See ANNUAL REPORT OF THE LAND VALUE APPRAISAL COMMISSION. **4834**

0709-2598 See B. C. CROWN COUNSEL NEWSLETTER. **3105**

0709-2628 See BULLETIN - MUSEUM OF INDIAN ARCHAEOLOGY. UNIVERSITY OF WESTERN ONTARIO. **4085**

0709-2725 See MUSEUM NOTES (LONDON). **4092**

0709-2768 See PRODUCTION AND STOCKS OF TEA, COFFEE, AND COCOA. **2370**

0709-2830 See FRONT (KINGSTON. 1978). **3389**

0709-2938 See RESEARCH SUMMARIES IN CANADIAN BUSINESS EDUCATION. **707**

0709-2946 See CANADIAN BUSINESS EDUCATION INDEX. **655**

0709-3225 See FINE CUISINE D'HENRI BERNARD, LA. **2790**

0709-3365 See HERITAGE (TROIS-RIVIERES). **2453**

0709-3373 See POETRY CANADA REVIEW. **3350**

0709-3403 See CANADIAN SECURITY. **5176**

0709-3438 See DIRECTORY OF CHEMICAL ENGINEERING RESEARCH IN CANADIAN UNIVERSITIES (1979). **2012**

0709-3497 See PETIT INTELLECTUEL, LE. **4864**

0709-3616 See DEBATS DE L'ASSEMBLEE LEGISLATIVE DU QUEBEC. **4642**

0709-3632 See JOURNAL DES DEBATS (QUEBEC). **4478**

0709-3713 See SUMMARY OF ORDERS AND APPROVALS - ENERGY RESOURCES CONSERVATION BOARD. **1958**

0709-3845 See COMMUNISTE (MONTREAL). **4541**

0709-3896 See INVENTAIRE DE LA RECHERCHE SUBVENTIONNEE ET COMMANDITEE. **1831**

0709-4027 See SCOPE NOTES (EDMONTON). **2483**

0709-4043 See SOLAR TECHNICAL SERIES (OTTAWA). **1957**

0709-4116 See ANIMAG. **4285**

0709-4132 See NEWSLINE - UNIVERSITY OF WINDSOR. **1837**

0709-4140 See URBAN CANADA (SELECTED PUBLICATIONS). **2837**

0709-4191 See COMMON SENSE (GALENDA BAY). **2226**

0709-4256 See ENTREMISE, L'. **1744**

0709-4426 See NEWFOUNDLAND JOURNAL OF GEOLOGICAL EDUCATION, THE. **1389**

0709-4469 See HORIZONS PHILOSOPHIQUES. **4348**

0709-4523 See TECHNICAL REPORT - FORINTEK CANADA CORP., EASTERN LABORATORY. **2396**

0709-4531 See FINANCIAL STATEMENTS / BRITISH COLUMBIA LIQUOR DISTRIBUTION BRANCH. **2367**

0709-4582 See PARLIAMENTARY GOVERNMENT. **4486**

0709-4590 See LRIS NEWSLETTER. **2387**

0709-4604 See ACA BULLETIN. **2478**

0709-4647 See SHARE (TORONTO). **5794**

0709-4663 See METRO MATIN. **5789**

0709-4698 See VICTORIAN PERIODICALS REVIEW. **3355**

0709-4744 See SAILING CANADA. **596**

0709-4787 See REPERTOIRE - ASSOCIATION DES INGENIEURS-CONSEILS DU QUEBEC. **1993**

0709-4795 See ONTARIO ELEMENTARY AND SECONDARY SCHOOL ENROLMENT PROJECTIONS. **1770**

0709-4949 See ANNUAL REPORT / PUBLIC AND PRIVATE RIGHTS BOARD. **2935**

0709-4981 See FINANCIAL PROCEDURES BULLETIN. **4649**

0709-5031 See SOLNOTE. **2608**

0709-504X See SOL (WINNIPEG). **1957**

0709-5139 See PROVINCIAL JUDGES JOURNAL. **3142**

0709-5201 See FLORILEGIUM. **2616**

0709-5228 See OE&M. OFFICE EQUIPMENT & METHODS (1979). **4213**

0709-5252 See CANADIAN OCCUPATIONAL HEALTH & SAFETY NEWS. **2860**

0709-5333 See LEGISLATIVE REPORT (EDMONTON). **3002**

0709-5341 See MOTOR VEHICLE REPORTS. **3012**

0709-5384 See CANADIAN MANAGEMENT CENTRE PRESENTS MANAGEMENT DEVELOPMENT PROGRAMMES. **863**

0709-549X See ULTIMATE REALITY AND MEANING. **4364**

0709-552X See RADIO (MONTREAL). **1137**

0709-5562 See HISTORIC GUELPH. **2736**

0709-5600 See SUPREME COURT OF CANADA DECISIONS. CIVIL AND CRIMINAL CASES. **3061**

0709-5635 See CINEMAG. **4066**

0709-5643 See QUEBEC CANADA (MONTREAL). **4493**

0709-5775 See MAGAZINE ILLUSTRE. **2538**

0709-5856 See REVUE DU MARCHE ALIMENTAIRE. **129**

0709-5864 See FOOD MARKET COMMENTARY. **2338**

0709-6003 See JOURNAL DU R C M, LE. **4478**

0709-602X See MONTHLY NEWSPRINT STATISTICS / CANADIAN PULP AND PAPER ASSOCIATION. **4240**

0709-6119 See NEWS, SOUTHERN AFRICA. **5790**

0709-616X See SALT (EDMONTON). **4995**

0709-6178 See INDIA TODAY. NORTH AMERICAN EDITION. **2535**

0709-6216 See FARM MACHINERY COSTS AS A GUIDE TO CUSTOM RATES. **159**

0709-6259 See FRIENDSHIP FORUM. **5286**

0709-6313 See MONOGRAPHS IN EDUCATION (WINNIPEG). **1765**

0709-6402 See RECOUP. **2241**

0709-6461 See CONSIDERATIONS. **4344**

0709-6488 See FAUT LIRE, IL. **3210**

0709-6569 See NSRSA. NOVA SCOTIA READING SPECIALISTS ASSOCIATION. **1769**

0709-6771 See COMMERCIAL PRICE LIST FOR STILL PHOTOGRAPHS. **4368**

0709-678X See COMMERCIAL PRICE LIST - N.F.B. PHOTOTHEQUE. **4067**

0709-681X See NICKLE'S DAILY OIL BULLETIN. **4266**

0709-6828 See ENTERPRISER OTTAWA. **1606**

0709-6836 See INDUSTRIE DE L'HABITATION MANUFACTUREE, L'. **2825**

0709-6844 See WINNEPEG WOMAN. **5568**

0709-6895 See ABSTRACTS OF PAPERS PRESENTED AT THE ... WORLD CONGRESS OF THE INTERNATIONAL POLITICAL SCIENCE ASSOCIATION. **4514**

0709-6941 See PARTICIPATION (OTTAWA). **4487**

0709-7069 See PROCEEDINGS - SPORT B. C., ANNUAL GENERAL MEETING. **4913**

0709-7085 See RIDEAU TRAIL NEWSLETTER, THE. **4878**

0709-7093 See LEISURE WHEELS. **5385**

0709-7158 See COUNTERPOINT'S BASIC CLASSICAL RECORD LIBRARY GUIDE. **4112**

0709-7166 See COUNTERPOINT CLASSICAL RECORD REVIEW. **4112**

0709-7174 See MUSICAL NEWS (TORONTO). 4136

0709-7751 See LANGUAGE AND SOCIETY. 3295

0709-7778 See B. C. FRESH WATER FISHING GUIDE. 2297

0709-7794 See NEWSLETTER - INUIT CULTURAL INSTITUTE. 2749

0709-7999 See SPACE TRAVEL MAGAZINE. 36

0709-8006 See NOUVELLES UNIVERSITAIRES (MONTREAL). 1695

0709-8030 See LULU REVU. 3409

0709-8065 See GUIDE TO SERIAL PUBLICATIONS - MANAGEMENT STUDIES LIBRARY, UNIVERSITY OF TORONTO. 730

0709-8138 See ENTERPRISE WEST. 866

0709-8146 See SASKATCHEWAN EDUCATIONAL ADMINISTRATOR, THE. 1870

0709-8219 See COMPOSERS WEST. 4111

0709-8421 See DIRECTORY OF CANADIAN THEATRE SCHOOLS, A. 5363

0709-8448 See DIRECTORY / SPECTROSCOPY SOCIETY OF CANADA. 4401

0709-8456 See KIRON, LE. 4903

0709-8502 See ANNALES DE BIOCHIMIE CLINIQUE DU QUEBEC. 480

0709-8510 See ENTRE-NOUS - SOCIETE DES ELEVEURS DE BOVINS CANADIENS. 210

0709-860X See INFORMATION BULLETIN - CORPORATIONS TAX BRANCH. 4732

0709-8634 See OPEN DOOR (BRITISH COLUMBIA LIBRARY TRUSTEES ASSOCIATION). 3239

0709-8677 See NATIONAL LIFELINER, THE. 5297

0709-8812 See VIE SERVITE. 5007

0709-8820 See UNIWORLD (OTTAWA). 1789

0709-8847 See ENVIRONNEMENT (MONTREAL). 2184

0709-8855 See IMAGINE (MONTREAL). 3395

0709-8863 See SOLARIS. 3437

0709-8936 See JOURNAL - CANADIAN DENTAL ASSOCIATION. 1325

0709-8936 See JOURNAL - CANADIAN DENTAL ASSOCIATION (FRENCH EDITION). 1325

0709-9045 See RESEARCH NEWSLETTER - FACULTY OF HOME ECONOMICS, UNIVERSITY OF ALBERTA. 2792

0709-9118 See UNION DES ECRIVAINS QUEBECOIS. 1716

0709-9142 See GOVERNMENT REPORT FOR NONPROFITS. ONTARIO. 5286

0709-9177 See HIBOU (ST-LAMBERT). 1064

0709-9185 See AFTER 8?. 1723

0709-9207 See REVUE DE L'ACLA. 3316

0709-9231 See CAHIER (UNIVERSITE DE MONTREAL. DEPARTEMENT DE SCIENCES ECONOMIQUES). 1467

0709-9347 See CONNAISSANCE ET VIE. 2614

0709-9363 See B C S T A REPORTS. 1860

0709-9444 See URBA. 4692

0709-9487 See RENCONTRE (QUEBEC. EDITION FRANCAISE). 4679

0709-9495 See RENCONTRE (QUEBEC. EDITION ANGLAISE). 4679

0709-9541 See ABS NEWSTATS. 5320

0709-9592 See ATHANOR (WESTMOUNT). 3460

0709-9797 See BROADCAST + TECHNOLOGY. 1128

0709-9851 See PUBLICATION / UNIVERSITE DE MONTREAL, CENTRE DE RECHERCHE SUR LES TRANSPORTS. 5390

0709-986X See RAPPORT DE RECHERCHE - ECOLE DES HAUTES ETUDES COMMERCIALES (MONTREAL). 706

0709-9916 See TECHNICAL REPORT (SASKATCHEWAN. SASKATCHEWAN HIGHWAYS AND TRANSPORTATION). 2032

0709-9983 See ANNUAL REPORT - JUSTICE INSTITUTE OF BRITISH COLUMBIA. 2934

0710-0019 See SUN (GRAND CENTRE). 5795

0710-0027 See INFO-MATHS. 3509

0710-0051 See BADMINTON CHALLENGE. 4886

0710-0078 See COLLINGWOOD TIMES, THE. 5782

0710-0086 See COMMUNITY REFLECTION. 5782

0710-0116 See NEWCASTLE INDEPENDENT (1977). 5790

0710-0132 See ACCESS (LONDON, ONT.). 3186

0710-0140 See PHYS 13 NEWS. 4414

0710-0159 See MONTAGE (TORONTO. 1981). 5234

0710-0175 See WEEKLY REVIEW (VIKING). 5797

0710-0191 See VAUGHAN COURIER, THE. 5797

0710-0213 See SOUTH SHORE NEWS. 5795

0710-0221 See TRI-LAKE RECORDER, THE. 5796

0710-023X See SALAM (MONTREAL). 5036

0710-0248 See BETA RELEASE. 3726

0710-0272 See EGATIKA NEA. 5784

0710-0299 See PUBLICATION SERIES. WORKING PAPERS ON SOCIAL WELFARE IN CANADA. 5303

0710-0310 See PUBLICATION SERIES. BIBLIOGRAPHIC SERIES (UNIVERSITY OF TORONTO. FACULTY OF SOCIAL WORK). 1796

0710-0329 See PUBLICATION SERIES. MONOGRAPH SERIES (UNIVERSITY OF TORONTO. FACULTY OF SOCIAL WORK). 5303

0710-0353 See CANADIAN UNIVERSITY MUSIC REVIEW. 4107

0710-0361 See PLAYBOAR MAGAZINE. 4287

0710-040X See PASSEPORT GASTRONOMIQUE. QUEBEC ET ALENTOURS. 5072

0710-0418 See CONGRES JUIF CANADIEN RAPPORT INTERIMAIRE. 2258

0710-0469 See PAPPUS. 521

0710-0493 See DIG (TORONTO). 2249

0710-0507 See INDUSTRIAL DIRECTORY FOR THE RESTIGOUCHE REGION. 1610

0710-0523 See SKI TRAILS (VANCOUVER, B.C. : CA. 1978). 4918

0710-0531 See INDEPENDENT BUSINESS FORUM. 681

0710-0566 See QUARTERLY NEWSLETTER / CANADIAN FORESTRY ASSOCIATION OF BRITISH COLUMBIA. 2391

0710-0590 See CANADIAN MOTORCYCLE RIDER. 4081

0710-0612 See ANGELOS (HALIFAX). 4934

0710-0663 See FORESIGHT (TORONTO). 4776

0710-0671 See PREVOYANCE. 4796

0710-068X See CROSS-CULTURAL PSYCHOLOGY BULLETIN. 4583

0710-0701 See CPRS NATIONAL NEWSLETTER. 758

0710-071X See COMMUNIQUE NATIONAL DE LA SCRP. 757

0710-0728 See SUBURBAN TORONTO CRISS-CROSS DIRECTORY. 5491

0710-0744 See BCATA JOURNAL FOR ART TEACHERS (1979). 343

0710-0809 See REPORTS / EDUCATIONAL RESEARCH INSTITUTE OF BRITISH COLUMBIA. 1778

0710-0825 See PROCEEDINGS OF THE ... BIENNIAL CONFERENCE OF THE CANADIAN SOCIETY FOR COMPUTATIONAL STUDIES OF INTELLIGENCE. 1216

0710-0841 See WINDSOR YEARBOOK OF ACCESS TO JUSTICE, THE. 3075

0710-085X See PETIT RAPPORTEUR DE STONEHAM, TEWKESBURY ET ST-ADOLPHE, LE. 4673

0710-0868 See BULLETIN DE RECHERCHE - UNIVERSITE DE SHERBROOKE. DEPARTEMENT DE GEOGRAPHIE. 2557

0710-0884 See ALMANACH DE LA FEMME. 5550

0710-0914 See DANGEROUS GOODS : NEWSLETTER. 5380

0710-0922 See NOUVELLES (CANADA. DIVISION DU TRANSPORT DES MARCHANDISES DANGEREUSES). 2866

0710-0949 See REPORTER (ALLISTON). 5794

0710-0973 See CASE HISTORY OF AN ACCIDENT OR INCIDENT. 2860

0710-099X See CLAIRON (MONTREAL). 5016

0710-1082 See GRAVENHURST LEADER, THE. 5785

0710-1090 See FACE A LA JUSTICE. 3164

0710-1112 See TAMARAW TIMES. 5795

0710-1120 See ARCADIAN RECORDER. 5780

0710-1139 See ANGLICAN NEWS (COBOURG). 5023

0710-1163 See ARQ : ARCHITECTURE/QUEBEC. 292

0710-1228 See MUSEUM NEWS - UKRAINIAN MUSEUM OF CANADA. 4092

0710-1236 See BANKUBA SHINPO. 5780

0710-1279 See EAST GEORGIAN BAY HISTORICAL JOURNAL. 2731

0710-1287 See RESSOURCES CULTURELLES DES FRANCOPHONES HORS QUEBEC. 2757

0710-1309 See HOLSTEIN JOURNAL. 195

0710-1368 See AMIS DE LA BANQUE D'YEUX DU QUEBEC. 3872

0710-1414 See INFO BASKET. 4900

0710-1422 See DELTA OPTIMIST, THE. 5783

0710-1457 See PHOENIX RISING (TORONTO, ONT.). 3932

0710-1481 See CANADIAN JOURNAL OF NATIVE EDUCATION. 1730

0710-1562 See CVPOP. CENTRE VIDEO POPULAIRE DE LA RIVE-SUD. 1130

0710-1619 See DOWNTOWNER (TORONTO). 5783

0710-1627 See SYNAXIS. 5002

0710-1643 See TIGER-CAT FACT BOOK / TIGER-CATS FOOTBALL. 4926

0710-166X See NUTRITION QUARTERLY. 4196

0710-1686 See GAZETTE DE QUEBEC. 4650

0710-1694 See ABOYEUR, L'. 2788

0710-1708 See ECLUSE, L'. 5783

0710-1740 See NOTTAWASAGA/SUNNIDALE NEWS, THE. 5791

0710-1767 See NOTES ET DOCUMENTS - DEPARTEMENT DE GEOGRAPHIE. UNIVERSITE DE MONTREAL. 2571

0710-1805 See MARTIN'S RELATED CRIMINAL STATUTES. 3108

0710-1821 See REGINA. ROSS INDUSTRIAL PARK. 2833

0710-1856 See DELTA REPORT, THE. 1153

0710-1945 See INITIATIVE (ST. JOHN). 5114

0710-197X See CELAT-INFORMATION. 2318

0710-1988 See MYSTIQUE (TORONTO). 5188

0710-1996 See ESSA BULLETIN. 1668

0710-2011 See YORK REGIONAL TOPIC, THE. 5798

0710-2038 See AUDIBLE (TORONTO). 4884

0710-2089 See HEBDO COLLEGE. 1827

0710-2135 See TOPIC (VANCOUVER). 5068

0710-2143 See JOURNAL OPTION GLOBALE. 323

0710-2151 See ORIENTATIONS (TORONTO). 1839

0710-2186 See JOURNAL ST-LOUIS. 5787

0710-2216 See SNIPS (FREDERICTON, N.B.). 5158

0710-2224 See SPECTRUM (TORONTO. 1979). 812

0710-2232 See HOTLINE (VANCOUVER). 1677

0710-2240 See CABLE COMMUNIQUE (BIWEEKLY. ENGLISH EDITION). 1128

0710-2259 See CABLE COMMUNIQUE (BI-HEBDOMADAIRE. EDITION FRANCAISE). 1128

0710-2267 See TECHNICAL COMMUNIQUE - CANADIAN CABLE TELEVISION ASSOCIATION. 1122

0710-2291 See INTERPLAN. 1981

0710-2305 See RAPPORT ANNUEL - CONSEIL REGIONAL DE LA SANTE ET DES SERVICES SOCIAUX DE QUEBEC. 5303

0710-2313 See DIALOGUE - MANITOBA TELEPHONE SYSTEM. 1153

0710-2364 See POINT COMMUN, LE. 5793

0710-2429 See DIRECTORY - CANADIAN LIFE AND HEALTH INSURANCE ASSOCIATION. 2878

0710-2437 See PERIODICAL HOLDINGS / HELEN K. MUSSALLEM LIBRARY, CANADIAN NURSES ASSOCIATION. 3866
0710-2534 See TRAVAUX DE LINGUISTIQUE QUEBECOISE. 3329
0710-2577 See SOCCER ILLUSTRATED (TORONTO). 4919
0710-2658 See NIMBUS TWO. 3417
0710-2666 See CANADIAN OPERA COMPANY. 4107
0710-2674 See RAMA ANNUAL. 912
0710-2712 See JOURNAL / MANITOBA ELEMENTARY TEACHERS' ASSOCIATION. 1804
0710-2720 See EQUIPMENT JOURNAL. 2114
0710-2755 See NORTHERN ONTARIO BUSINESS. 700
0710-2801 See ONTARIO GOLF NEWS. 4911
0710-281X See LONDON TRIBUNE. 5789
0710-2895 See PERFORMANCE (MONTREAL, QUEBEC). 945
0710-2976 See ENTRANCE REQUIREMENTS FOR DIPLOMA SCHOOLS OF NURSING AND SCHOOLS OF PRACTICAL NURSING. 3855
0710-3034 See PIG PAPER, THE. 4146
0710-3417 See MALT NEWSLETTER. 3229
0710-3425 See GUELPH MAGAZINE. 5478
0710-345X See ONTARIO BRANCH NEWS. 4795
0710-3468 See CCR FUTURES TRADING GUIDE. 894
0710-3476 See TWIST & SHOUT. 4157
0710-3492 See WHY? MAGAZINE. 1806
0710-3522 See POLYSCOPE (MONTREAL). 1094
0710-362X See PEM : PLANT ENGINEERING AND MAINTENANCE. 2124
0710-3638 See REFLEXION (MONTREAL). 1094
0710-3670 See PEMMICAN JOURNAL, THE. 2753
0710-3689 See BULLETIN / VILLE DE MONT-LAURIER. 4635
0710-3697 See GLENBOW (EXHIBITIONS AND EVENTS). 4088
0710-376X See RAPPORT ANNUEL / REGIE DES PERMIS D'ALCOOL DU QUEBEC. 4678
0710-3786 See COUP D'OEIL (NAPIERVILLE). 5782
0710-3794 See MERCREDI SOIR, LE. 5789
0710-3905 See BONNYVILLE NOUVELLE. 4887
0710-4278 See INITIALES (HALIFAX). 3396
0710-4340 See CANADIAN JOURNAL OF EDUCATIONAL COMMUNICATION. 1105
0710-4375 See TREELINE. 3447
0710-4383 See RULES AND BY-LAWS / CANADIAN TRACK AND FIELD ASSOCIATION. 4915
0710-4391 See REGLEMENTS OFFICIELS / ASSOCIATION CANADIENNE D'ATHLETISME. 4914
0710-4405 See CANADIAN RECREATIONAL VEHICLE GUIDE. 5379
0710-4537 See STRAND. 5795
0710-4561 See COURRIER DU SURVENANT, LE. 5782
0710-457X See MCIC NEWS. 4528
0710-4588 See GUIDES OF UNDERWRITERS' LABORATORIES OF CANADA. 2881
0710-4669 See PERSPECTIVES CANADA (ENGLISH EDITION). 5253
0710-4707 See YEARBOOK. 5069
0710-4804 See PROFESSIONAL MANAGER'S DIGEST, THE. 883
0710-4820 See JEWELLERY JOURNAL. 2914
0710-4847 See OSPREY. 4170
0710-5002 See COLLECTIF PAROLES. 2728
0710-5061 See TICKER TAPE (TORONTO). 5005
0710-507X See NOTICE TO MEMBERS - TORONTO STOCK EXCHANGE. 910
0710-5088 See NOTICE TO MEMBERS. FUTURES MEMORANDUM (TORONTO STOCK EXCHANGE). 910
0710-5096 See NOTICE TO MEMBERS. OPTIONS MEMORANDUM (TORONTO STOCK EXCHANGE). 910

0710-510X See FRATERNITY NEWS - FRATERNITY FOR CANADIAN ASTROLOGERS. 390
0710-5134 See SUMMARY PROCEEDINGS OF THE ANNUAL CONFERENCE - FEDERATION OF CANADIAN MUNICIPALITIES. 4689
0710-5142 See EASTERN OFFSHORE NEWS. 4255
0710-5185 See PASQUIN, LE. 2466
0710-5193 See COLLECTIVE BARGAINING HANDBOOK. 939
0710-5207 See NEDERLANDSE BOEKEN. 4830
0710-5215 See SUOMENKIELISIA KIRJOJA. 4832
0710-5231 See LIVROS EM PORTUGUES. 4830
0710-5290 See POLSKIE KSIAZKI (TORONTO). 4831
0710-5304 See NIHONGO-NO-TOSHO. 4831
0710-5339 See FLAMBOROUGH NEWS. 5784
0710-5363 See MID-TOWN/MT. PLEASANT REVUE. 5789
0710-5398 See ANNUAIRE (CANADIAN UNIVERSITY MUSIC SOCIETY). 4100
0710-5401 See AYLMER BULLETIN. 5780
0710-541X See TOWN CRIER (COCHRANE). 5796
0710-5428 See PIONEER (COCHRANE). 5793
0710-5460 See OROMOCTO POST, THE. 5792
0710-5479 See VOIE LACTEE. 3769
0710-5487 See LANTZVILLE LOG, THE. 5788
0710-5495 See DEVON DISPATCH, THE. 5783
0710-5541 See 2 RIVES, LES. 5779
0710-555X See CIRA NEWSLETTER. 1659
0710-5568 See NOUVELLES (CENTRALE DE L'ENSEIGNEMENT DU QUEBEC. 1695
0710-5614 See COMMUNIQUE / CANADIAN DENTAL ASSOCIATION. 1319
0710-5630 See SERVICES AUX MEMBRES - ASSOCIATION DE LA CONSTRUCTION DE MONTREAL ET DU QUEBEC. 1710
0710-5649 See GRIFFON (DRUMMONDVILLE). 5785
0710-5665 See FIL DES PHIL- ANTHROPES, LE. 385
0710-569X See LANCE K. LERAY'S BAKERY WORLD OF CANADA. 2348
0710-5703 See BCGEU NEWS & VIEWS. 1655
0710-572X See COLLOQUES SCIENTIFIQUES / LES FLORALIES INTERNATIONALES DE MONTREAL. 75
0710-5746 See NOTICE TO MEMBERS - TRANS CANADA OPTIONS INC. 801
0710-5754 See ROSTER OF DEPARTMENTS OF GEOGRAPHY, CANADIAN UNIVERSITIES AND COLLEGES. 2575
0710-5770 See NEWS-GRAM - CHRISTIAN BUSINESS MEN OF CANADA. 4981
0710-5789 See RAPPEL (MONTREAL). 4878
0710-5797 See QUEBECOIS LIBRE D'OUTREMONT, LE. 5793
0710-5843 See GUT (TORONTO). 2534
0710-5851 See CENTREFOLD (BRANDON). 2817
0710-586X See INFORMATION MONT-ROLLAND. 4656
0710-5878 See FACS SHEET. 2790
0710-5924 See NEWSLETTER AND INTERIM REPORT / ROYAL BANK OF CANADA. 801
0710-5932 See JET (CALGARY). 25
0710-5940 See INDUSTRIAL RELATIONS BULLETIN (VANCOUVER). 1678
0710-5975 See OF COMPOUND INTEREST. 1067
0710-6025 See RECREACTION (VANIER). 4708
0710-6092 See FACTS & FEATURES / ONTARIO RESEARCH FOUNDATION. 5104
0710-6106 See OTTAWA-CARLETON HEADLINER. 118
0710-6122 See ORDONNANCE (MONTREAL). 4318
0710-6130 See ORDONNANCE. DOSSIER. 4318
0710-6157 See NURSING MONTREAL. 3864
0710-6211 See ENTREFILETS. 4646
0710-622X See CANADIAN OIL & GAS HANDBOOK. 4253

0710-6238 See EGLISE DE CHICOUTIMI ... ANNUAIRE DIOCESAIN. 5029
0710-6297 See CONTEST AND LOTTERY NEWS. 4640
0710-6319 See BIBLIO SERVICE. 1727
0710-6327 See MINUTES OF PROCEEDINGS AND EVIDENCE OF THE SPECIAL COMMITTEE ON REGULATORY REFORM. 3010
0710-6335 See ACCENTS (NEW BRUNSWICK TEACHERS' ASSOCIATION. MUSIC EDUCATION COUNCIL). 4098
0710-6343 See PLANNED PARENTHOOD OF TORONTO. 590
0710-6386 See INN MAGAZINE. 2807
0710-6394 See RAPPORT ANNUEL / SOCIETE QUEBECOISE D'INFORMATION JURIDIQUE. 3243
0710-6416 See WEST PRINCE GRAPHIC. 5797
0710-6491 See POINT D'INTERROGATION (CHICOUTIMI). 1702
0710-6521 See POINT D'INTERROGATION ?. ENGLISH SECTION. 1702
0710-6564 See SHELF LISTING - MIDWESTERN REGIONAL LIBRARY SYSTEM. 5794
0710-6572 See TITLE LISTING - MIDWESTERN REGIONAL LIBRARY SYSTEM. 426
0710-6580 See AUTHOR LISTING - MIDWESTERN REGIONAL LIBRARY SYSTEM. 408
0710-667X See MANUSCRIPT REPORT SERIES - MARINE SCIENCES AND INFORMATION DIRECTORATE. 1451
0710-6874 See ALBERTA ENERGY RESOURCE INDUSTRIES, MONTHLY STATISTICS. 1961
0710-6920 See LAST GASP. 2177
0710-7307 See INTER URBA. 4657
0710-7323 See HOUSING NEWSLETTER (OTTAWA). 2825
0710-7331 See NEWSLETTER (ASSOCIATION OF ANCIENT HISTORIANS). 1078
0710-7412 See ANNUAL REPORT - BRITISH COLUMBIA BOARD OF PAROLE. 3157
0710-7641 See CANADIAN FISHERIES AND OCEAN INDUSTRIES DIRECTORY, THE. 2298
0710-7676 See BRANDON DIRECTORY, THE. 2529
0710-7692 See FOCUS (NEW BRUNSWICK TEACHERS' ASSOCIATION. SOCIAL STUDIES COUNCIL). 5200
0710-7714 See BUSINESS EDUCATION NEWS (FREDERICTON). 647
0710-7722 See 3 R'S (FREDERICTON, N.B.). 1720
0710-7773 See PATHWAYS (FREDERICTON). 1883
0710-779X See SOLUTIONS (FREDERICTON). 5158
0710-7935 See PEST MANAGEMENT REPORT 4246
0710-815X See REPORTER (SUPPLY AND SERVICES CANADA). 4682
0710-8265 See TELEPHONE DIRECTORY (GREATER VANCOUVER AND AREA EDITION). 4690
0710-8435 See FINANCIAL REPORT - MANITOBA DEPARTMENT OF FINANCE. 4725
0710-8559 See CULTURES CANADA : NEWSLETTER OF THE CANADIAN CONSULTATIVE COUNCIL ON MULTICULTURALISM. 5243
0710-8915 See GUIDE D'IMPOT SUR LE REVENU DES AGRICULTEURS. 4730
0710-8990 See ANNUAL REPORT / ONTARIO ADVISORY COUNCIL ON MULTICULTURALISM AND CITIZENSHIP. 2720
0710-9148 See ANIMAL MAGAZINE, L'. 4285
0710-9350 See DOCUMENTS DE PRESSE MENSUELS : ARTS PLASTIQUES. 319
0710-9466 See TECH. MEMO. - UNIVERSITY OF GUELPH. DEPARTMENT OF LAND RESOURCE SCIENCE. 189
0710-958X See NEWS FOR SENIORS. 5180
0710-9679 See MIS INTERRUPT. 879
0710-9695 See MONTHLY NEWS - MULTICULTURAL COUNCIL OF WINDSOR AND ESSEX COUNTY. 2268

ISSN Index

0710-9733 *See* MINUTES OF PROCEEDINGS AND EVIDENCE OF THE SPECIAL COMMITTEE ON THE FEDERAL- PROVINCIAL FISCAL ARRANGEMENTS. **4665**

0710-9857 *See* BULLETIN REGIONAL SUR LE MARCHE DU TRAVAIL (REGION DES CANTONS DE L'EST). **1657**

0710-9865 *See* BULLETIN REGIONAL SUR LE MARCHE DU TRAVAIL (REGION LAURENTIDES-LANAUDIERE). **1657**

0710-9911 *See* EQUINOX (CAMDEN EAST). **2560**

0710-992X *See* INNSIDE NEWS. **2807**

0710-9938 *See* COURRIER EXPRESS DE VAUDREUIL-SOULANGES, LE. **5782**

0711-0081 *See* UPPER CANADIAN, THE. **252**

0711-0103 *See* PRINCIPAL ISSUE. **1868**

0711-0170 *See* QUARTER NOTES (TORONTO). **4148**

0711-0235 *See* PROCEEDINGS OF INNOVATION CANADA INC. **704**

0711-026X *See* JONATHAN (MONTREAL). **5049**

0711-0316 *See* PROFITS / FEDERAL BUSINESS DEVELOPMENT BANK. **804**

0711-0340 *See* CLIN D'OEIL (VILLE MONT-ROYAL). **402**

0711-0359 *See* CHRONIQUES DE LA DROUINERIE, LES. **2443**

0711-0413 *See* DIRECTORY OF CANADIAN ARCHIVES. **2481**

0711-0480 *See* NEWSBOARD (MONTREAL, QUEBEC). **2403**

0711-0502 *See* MAXI-LOISIR. **386**

0711-0510 *See* SEMAINE INTERNATIONALE, LA. **2629**

0711-0529 *See* CAHIER - SOCIETE HISTORIQUE DU MARIGOT, LONGUEUIL (1980). **2725**

0711-0537 *See* OFFICIAL RULES / RINGETTE CANADA. **4910**

0711-0561 *See* DIRECTIONS (TORONTO. 1981). **1820**

0711-0758 *See* PAR-DELA LE RIDEAU. **2753**

0711-0774 *See* SEXTANT (SEPT-ILES). **5794**

0711-0782 *See* ANNUAL REPORT / DEPARTMENT OF FISHERIES AND OCEANS. **2294**

0711-0901 *See* RIG LOCATOR. **4277**

0711-0944 *See* APERITIF. **2327**

0711-1053 *See* CPU JOURNAL (1981). **1661**

0711-1126 *See* INSIDE EDGE. **4900**

0711-1177 *See* RENDEZVOUS (FREDERICTON). **3315**

0711-1231 *See* YOUR DAILY CYCLE GUIDE. **401**

0711-1258 *See* REZO. **330**

0711-1304 *See* NOS LUTTES (1981). **1695**

0711-1312 *See* ART LINE. **370**

0711-1320 *See* ANNUAL REPORT - ENVIRONMENT CANADA (1980). **2160**

0711-1355 *See* CIRCUIT (TORONTO. 1977). **1541**

0711-1509 *See* LEARN ENGLISH IN CANADA. **3297**

0711-1533 *See* MANITOBA PSYCHOLOGIST. **4603**

0711-1681 *See* PREVENTION PREVIEW. **4796**

0711-169X *See* ACTUALITES PREVENTION. **4763**

0711-1703 *See* DIRECTORY OF LABOUR ORGANIZATIONS IN CANADA. **1663**

0711-1754 *See* MEDWAY VALLEY NEWS (1978). **2198**

0711-1762 *See* NEWSFILE (TORONTO). **5790**

0711-1770 *See* SPECIAL LIBRARIES IN THE EDMONTON AREA (1981). **3250**

0711-1789 *See* ENTRE NOUS, LES MARTIN. **2446**

0711-1797 *See* BLONDE COUNTRY / ANNUAL HEARD REFERENCE ED. **207**

0711-1827 *See* SAMPLINGS. **3433**

0711-1835 *See* RAPPORT DE L'OFFICE DU CREDIT AGRICOLE DU QUEBEC CONCERNANT L'ADMINISTRATION DE LA LOI SUR LE CREDIT FORESTIER. **806**

0711-1843 *See* MUSTARD SEED. **5065**

0711-1967 *See* CANADIAN COMMUNICATIONS REGULATION & POLICY. **1151**

0711-1975 *See* ASSU NEWS. **5780**

0711-2009 *See* INTERLOCUTEUR. **1865**

0711-2092 *See* ACTUALITE JUIVE. **5045**

0711-2122 *See* HUMAN RIGHTS (MONTREAL). **4509**

0711-2122 *See* HUMAN RIGHTS (MONTREAL). **4509**

0711-2130 *See* INSEPARABLES. **2281**

0711-2149 *See* SUNDAY GAZETTE. **5795**

0711-2157 *See* INFORMATION PROCHE-ORIENT. **2654**

0711-2173 *See* CANADIAN C.S. LEWIS JOURNAL, THE. **3372**

0711-2181 *See* COLDWATER JOURNAL, THE. **5782**

0711-2211 *See* FRAGMENTS (SCARBOROUGH, ONT.). **4959**

0711-222X *See* JOURNAL OF LEISURABILITY (1980). **4389**

0711-2238 *See* DIRECTORY / MANITOBA DENTAL ASSOCIATION. **1322**

0711-2254 *See* UQAR-INFORMATION. **1853**

0711-2270 *See* RED MENACE. **4546**

0711-2335 *See* FREELANCE (VANCOUVER). **677**

0711-2416 *See* BULLETIN - CANADIAN ASSOCIATION OF COLLEGE AND UNIVERSITY STUDENT SERVICES. **1812**

0711-2440 *See* CAHIERS DU GERAD. **1467**

0711-2467 *See* SASKATCHEWAN VETERINARY MEDICAL ASSOCIATION NEWSLETTER. **5521**

0711-2475 *See* CAHIER DE RECHERCHE - FACULTE DE L'AMENAGEMENT, UNIVERSITE DE MONTREAL. **2816**

0711-2564 *See* LECTURE NOTES SERIES (UNIVERSITY OF WATERLOO. CONSTRUCTION MANAGEMENT GROUP). **619**

0711-2572 *See* RESEAU PLEIN-AIR. **4878**

0711-270X *See* NRC SOLAR INFORMATION SERIES. **1951**

0711-2769 *See* ALDERSGATE NEWS. **4933**

0711-2807 *See* ANNUAL REPORT. JUDGES OF THE PROVINCIAL COURT SUPERANNUATION FUND. **3139**

0711-2815 *See* ANNUAL REPORT / RECREATION, PARKS AND WILDLIFE FOUNDATION. **4706**

0711-2947 *See* GREY/CLARK TRADE NEWS. **838**

0711-2963 *See* PRESSE-LIBRE. **2543**

0711-2971 *See* IN PROCESS (OTTAWA). **4655**

0711-2998 *See* POOL & SPA MARKETING. **934**

0711-3005 *See* POOL & SPA MARKETING. SUPPLEMENT. **934**

0711-3021 *See* SASKATCHEWAN COUNCIL OF SOCIAL STUDIES TEACHER. **5217**

0711-303X *See* SHIP-BY-TRUCK OFFICIAL ONTARIO DIRECTORY AND BUYER'S GUIDE. **5392**

0711-3056 *See* DIRECTORY OF MEMBERS / ASSOCIATION OF CANADIAN UNIVERSITY PRESSES. **4814**

0711-3064 *See* CANADIAN MOTORSPORT ANNUAL ..., THE. **5408**

0711-3102 *See* SMC NATIONAL REPORT. **2835**

0711-3196 *See* SALARY SURVEY. ADMINISTRATIVE, FINANCE, AND DATA PROCESSING REPORT. **1709**

0711-3226 *See* SCORE (TORONTO). **4917**

0711-3250 *See* INVENTORY OF PHYSICAL FACILITIES OF ONTARIO UNIVERSITIES / PREPARED BY THE RESEARCH DIVISION OF THE COUNCIL OF ONTARIO UNIVERSITIES. **1831**

0711-3269 *See* HUMBER MAGAZINE WORLD. **4815**

0711-3277 *See* MINING REVIEW (NORTH VANCOUVER). **2146**

0711-3285 *See* LUCARNE. **302**

0711-3293 *See* LOISIR LONGUEUIL. **4852**

0711-3307 *See* MINI-JEUX, LES. **4863**

0711-3315 *See* FORMAT CINEMA. **4071**

0711-3331 *See* DESK-REFERENCE DIRECTORY. **4892**

0711-3358 *See* KINGSTON COMMERCE. **843**

0711-3420 *See* BEAUCE MEDIA. **5780**

0711-3439 *See* VILLAGEOIS, LE. **5797**

0711-3447 *See* CHEM TRENDS. **967**

0711-3455 *See* REVUE JEUNESSE. **4865**

0711-3463 *See* HEBDO SCIENCE. **5109**

0711-3471 *See* ACADEMY NEWS!. **4098**

0711-3501 *See* ONTARIO ELECTRICAL CONTRACTOR, THE. **2074**

0711-3528 *See* GAZETTE DE LA BUTTE, LA. **5286**

0711-3617 *See* ON CAMPUS (SASKATOON). **1839**

0711-3676 *See* LIST OF ACCEPTED ADHESIVE-TYPE NAMEPLATES. **1616**

0711-3684 *See* CALGARY CITY SCENE. **5781**

0711-3692 *See* MAGAZINE (NORTH VANCOUVER). **2538**

0711-3730 *See* PROCEEDINGS. ANNUAL CONFERENCE - CANADIAN ACADEMIC ACCOUNTING ASSOCIATION. **750**

0711-3773 *See* WINNIPEG SUN (1980). **5798**

0711-3781 *See* MIRABEL (SAINT-EUSTACHE). **5790**

0711-379X *See* SEAFARER (HAWKESBURY, ONT.). **596**

0711-3803 *See* NEWSLETTER (HISTORICAL SOCIETY OF OTTAWA). **2749**

0711-3811 *See* MORINVILLE MIRROR. **5790**

0711-382X *See* ALGONQUIAN AND IROQUOIAN LINGUISTICS. **3263**

0711-3838 *See* NEWSLETTER - FEDERATION OF ONTARIO MEMORIAL SOCIETIES. **2407**

0711-3862 *See* BRITISH COLUMBIA SPORT SALMON FISHING NEWS. **2297**

0711-3889 *See* LABOUR ADVOCATE (ST. CATHARINES). **1685**

0711-3897 *See* FOURTHOUGHT NEWSLETTER. **4347**

0711-3900 *See* AVA-YI IRAN. **5780**

0711-3919 *See* WORLD SOCCER NEWS. **4930**

0711-3927 *See* FORESIGHT (EDMONTON). **5179**

0711-3943 *See* PROVINCIAL MEMBERS OF PARLIAMENT (METRO). **4675**

0711-396X *See* FEUILLET D'INFORMATION DE LA VILLE DE SAINT-LEONARD, LE. **4649**

0711-3986 *See* N.S.U.C. UNDERWATER NEWS. **4905**

0711-4044 *See* RED CROSS TODAY / BRITISH COLUMBIA-YUKON DIVISION. **5304**

0711-4222 *See* PAKIZAH INTIRNASHINAL. **5564**

0711-4257 *See* LIFELINES SASKATCHEWAN (1981). **4789**

0711-4397 *See* GRAND BABILLARD, LE. **4652**

0711-4427 *See* VALLEY REVIEW (PEMBROKE). **5796**

0711-4435 *See* WOMEN TODAY (BEETON). **5570**

0711-4451 *See* FRIDAY CITIZEN, THE. **5784**

0711-4478 *See* NEWSLETTER - WOMEN'S EQUAL RIGHTS ASSOCIATION. **5563**

0711-4567 *See* ENTRAIDE SOCIALE, L'. **5784**

0711-4613 *See* TECHNICAL REPORT - UNIVERSITY OF WATERLOO. DEPARTMENT OF ELECTRICAL ENGINEERING. **2083**

0711-463X *See* WOMEN'S RIGHTS BULLETIN. **5571**

0711-4648 *See* INSTANT (THEATRE DU GANOUE). **3464**

0711-4680 *See* KOSOY'S TRAVEL GUIDE TO EUROPE. **5482**

0711-4702 *See* KOSOY'S TRAVEL GUIDE TO FLORIDA AND THE SOUTH. **5482**

0711-4710 *See* TRAVEL GUIDE TO MEXICO, CENTRAL AMERICA AND SOUTH AMERICA, A. **5495**

0711-4737 *See* HERITAGE BOOK, THE. **4962**

0711-4745 *See* JOURNAL MASKOUTAIN, LE. **5787**

0711-4753 *See* PIERRE-BRILLANT. **5793**

0711-4761 *See* ETCHEMIN DE ST-ROMUALD, L'. **5784**

0711-480X *See* COMMUNIQUE - CANADIAN ASSOCIATION OF HOUSING AND RENEWAL OFFICIALS. **2818**

0711-4826 *See* SPINDRIFTER, THE. **3439**

0711-4834 *See* REGIONAL DE DRUMMONDVILLE. **5793**

0711-4877 See CONSTITUTION, BY-LAWS AND REGULATIONS - INVESTMENT DEALERS' ASSOCIATION OF CANADA. 895

0711-4915 See PROCEEDINGS OF THE RED DEER SURGICAL SOCIETY. 3972

0711-4931 See PERSPECTIVES / THE NIAGARA INSTITUTE. 5212

0711-494X See AGENDA / THE NIAGARA INSTITUTE. 859

0711-4966 See PRETEXTES (TROIS-RIVIERES). 3425

0711-4974 See B.C. SCIENCE TEACHERS NEWS UPDATE. 5087

0711-4982 See ANNUAIRE DE HULL, GATINEAU, AYLMER, QUEBEC. 2554

0711-5075 See JOURNAL OF STRATEGIC AND SYSTEMIC THERAPIES, THE. 3929

0711-5288 See QUEBEC TECHNOLOGIE. 5144

0711-5318 See ENQUETE-SALAIRES (1981). 1667

0711-5326 See WORKING PAPER - DEPARTMENT OF ECONOMICS. UNIVERSITY OF NEW BRUNSWICK. 1527

0711-5342 See NEXUS (HAMILTON, ONT.). 242

0711-5350 See PHILIGRAM (1980). 2075

0711-5377 See LEADER (OTTAWA. 1976). 4851

0711-5431 See INFORMATION CIRCULAR / ALBERTA TREASURY, CORPORATE TAX ADMINISTRATION. 4656

0711-5474 See ECRIRE (MONTREAL). 3383

0711-5504 See MAFIA 67. 4663

0711-5571 See RAPPORT ANNUEL / BUREAU D'AUDIENCES PUBLIQUES SUR L'ENVIRONNEMENT. 1580

0711-5598 See QUEBEC EN REVUE(S). 328

0711-5628 See LIGHTHOUSE (BURLINGTON). 1357

0711-5644 See INTERNATIONAL MONEY MARKETS (TORONTO). 792

0711-5660 See FORESTERIE ATOUT. 2381

0711-5806 See ENVIRONNEMENT PLUS. 2171

0711-5830 See BULLETIN DU TRIMESTRE / ASSOCIATION INTERNATIONALE DES SECRETAIRES PROFESSIONNELLES, SECTION DE L'OUTAOUAIS. 862

0711-5903 See STUDIES IN CHRISTIANITY AND JUDAISM. 5000

0711-5911 See MIRROR (LONDON, ONT.). 1093

0711-6012 See BULLETIN / (UNIVERSITY OF WESTERN ONTARIO, DEPT. OF PSYCHIATRY). 3922

0711-6039 See PROCEEDINGS (QUEEN'S UNIVERSITY (KINGSTON, ONT.). CENTRE FOR RESOURCE STUDIES). 2148

0711-6136 See VOYAGE EN GROUPE. 5499

0711-6179 See CIRCUL'ART. 384

0711-6187 See PROGRAMMES - SOCIETE QUEBECOISE DE SPELEOLOGIE. 1409

0711-6225 See CHILE BUSINESS UPDATE. 656

0711-6233 See LONDON MAGAZINE (LONDON, ONT.). 2537

0711-6322 See CAFES ET RESTAURANTS CHOUETTES. 5070

0711-6330 See NWT DATA BOOK. 2571

0711-6349 See OCCASIONAL PAPER (INTERNATIONAL OMBUDSMAN INSTITUTE). 4670

0711-639X See KNIT & CHAT. 5184

0711-6411 See MANITOBA LABOUR MARKET INFORMATION BULLETIN. 1689

0711-6446 See BULLETIN - SOCIETE DES AMIS DU JARDIN VAN DEN HENDE INC. 2411

0711-6454 See SNOW-GOER. 4919

0711-6470 See CANADIAN POOL & PATIO CONSUMERS HANDBOOK. 4849

0711-6497 See BANK FACTS. 774

0711-6659 See CANADIAN ACOUSTICS. 2162

0711-6659 See CANADIAN ACOUSTICS. 4107

0711-6683 See SIM NOW. 4997

0711-6705 See JIAJING HUABAO. 5787

0711-6721 See CANADIAN DATA REPORT OF HYDROGRAPHY AND OCEAN SCIENCES. 2298

0711-6748 See CANADIAN CONTRACTOR REPORT OF HYDROGRAPHY AND OCEAN SCIENCES. 1447

0711-6764 See CANADIAN TECHNICAL REPORT OF HYDROGRAPHY AND OCEAN SCIENCES. 1447

0711-6780 See ENVIRONMENTS. 2822

0711-6829 See ALLIANCE (MONTREAL. 1969). 1860

0711-6926 See RESEARCH BULLETIN - ST. THOMAS PSYCHIATRIC HOSPITAL. 3935

0711-7000 See ANNUAL REPORT - TASKFORCE ON THE CHURCHES AND CORPORATE RESPONSIBILITY. 5239

0711-7027 See CANAL-ISEP. 4636

0711-7075 See JOURNAL OF SYSTEMIC THERAPIES. 3597

0711-7078 See HIGHLIGHTS OF THE COLLECTIONS / THE MONTREAL MUSEUM OF FINE ARTS. 4088

0711-7086 See AU FIL DES COLLECTIONS. 4084

0711-7094 See KULLSHOT. 4862

0711-7108 See GLOBEHOPPER. 5478

0711-7132 See RAPPORT ANNUEL - REGIE DE L'ELECTRICITE ET DU GAZ. 4678

0711-7140 See HAZARDOUS WASTE MANAGEMENT HANDBOOK. 2231

0711-7159 See OPPORTUNITIES (SCARBOROUGH). 1700

0711-723X See NEWSLETTER (UNIVERSITY OF TORONTO. FACULTY OF SOCIAL WORK. ALUMNI ASSOCIATION). 5252

0711-7248 See NEWS / CONSUMER ACTION LEAGUE. 1298

0711-7256 See CAL NEWS. 1294

0711-7299 See CANADA BOOK AUCTIONS RECORDS. 4827

0711-7388 See HUMAN, THE. 589

0711-7418 See LIEN (HULL). 3861

0711-7426 See TW (TORONTO, ONT.). 5567

0711-7450 See LANGLEY TIMES. 5788

0711-7485 See HERIZONS. 5558

0711-7515 See PHAT : PRESENTATION HOUSE ARTS TABLOID. 381

0711-7590 See BROADWATER MARKET LETTER. 68

0711-7639 See OBJECTION. 3020

0711-7647 See RAMPIKE (TORONTO). 3427

0711-7671 See JSW. JOURNAL OF STUDENT WRITING. 3400

0711-7744 See BULLETIN MUNICIPAL - CONSEIL MUNICIPAL DE SAINT-LOUIS-DE-TERREBONNE. 4634

0711-7760 See OFFICIAL BULLETIN / RECREATION ASSOCIATION OF NOVA SCOTIA. 4853

0711-7884 See DP MARKET FACTS. 1258

0711-7906 See VALLEE DES FORTS. 5498

0711-7914 See VIDEOMANIA. 4867

0711-7922 See MART JOURNAL. 1763

0711-7930 See DAY CARE CENTRES AND NURSERY SCHOOLS HAMILTON-WENTWORTH. 5281

0711-7957 See SENTIER CHASSE-PECHE. 4878

0711-7965 See POLYMETRIC REPORT (N.Y.S.E. ED.). 803

0711-7973 See GOURMET BOUTIQUE. 2811

0711-8015 See METRIC CONSTRUCTION PRODUCTS FILE. 621

0711-8031 See ASBESTOS MA VILLE. 4630

0711-8066 See SELECTED NEW TITLES / LEGISLATIVE LIBRARY OF MANITOBA. 424

0711-8074 See HEBDO DE LA ROUGE, L'. 5786

0711-8112 See COMMUNIQUE - CDA. 4189

0711-8163 See AVIATION BUSINESS REPORT. 13

0711-8198 See ANNUAL REPORT OF THE MINISTER UNDER THE CROP INSURANCE ACT. 61

0711-8287 See NOTRE ECONOMIE. 1508

0711-849X See ANNUAL REPORT / ONTARIO LABOUR RELATIONS BOARD. 3144

0711-852X See GROSS DOMESTIC PRODUCT BY INDUSTRY (MONTHLY EDITION). 1533

0711-8651 See BUDGET. RENSEIGNEMENTS SUPPLEMENTAIRES : IMPOTS. 4715

0711-8813 See DALHOUSIE FRENCH STUDIES. 3379

0711-8929 See SEXUALLY TRANSMITTED DISEASES IN CANADA. 4802

0711-9178 See SASKATCHEWAN TRAFFIC ACCIDENT FACTS. 5444

0711-9453 See ANALYSIS OF BICYCLE/MOTOR VEHICLE COLLISIONS REPORTED IN MANITOBA, JANUARY 1,-DECEMBER 31 ..., AN. 5376

0711-9674 See ACQUISITIONS - CANADIAN HOUSING INFORMATION CENTRE. 2813

0711-9682 See LEGISLATURE OF ONTARIO DEBATES. OFFICIAL REPORT (HANSARD). STANDING COMMITTEE ON REGULATIONS AND OTHER STATUTORY INSTRUMENTS. 3002

0711-9917 See PUBLICATIONS CATALOGUE - ATOMIC ENERGY CONTROL BOARD. 1954

0712-0370 See CAHIER TECHNIQUE - DIRECTION GENERALE DE LA PLANIFICATION. OFFICE OF PLANIFICATION ET DE DEVELOPPEMENT DU QUEBEC. 2816

0712-0451 See DOCUMENTATION TECHNIQUE - COMMISSION DE LA FONCTION PUBLIQUE DU QUEBEC. 4645

0712-0613 See CAHIER D'INFORMATION - MINISTERE DE L'AGRICULTURE DES PECHES ET DE L'ALIMENTATION. DIRECTION GENERALE DES PECHES MARITIMES. DIRECTION DE LA RECHERCHE SCIENTIFIQUE ET TECHNIQUE. 2298

0712-0680 See NOTE - SERVICE DE LA RECHERCHE FORESTIERE. 2390

0712-0745 See OFFSHORE INDUSTRIAL DIRECTORY. 4267

0712-0761 See STATEMENTS AND SPEECHES / EXTERNAL AFFAIRS, CANADA. 4535

0712-1016 See CALUMET JOURNAL. 2257

0712-1067 See OCCASIONAL PAPER (UNIVERSITY OF BRITISH COLUMBIA. CENTRE FOR TRANSPORTATION STUDIES). 5388

0712-1075 See CITIZEN. CAPITAL IDEAS, THE. 5782

0712-1083 See REGIONAL NEWSPAPER, THE. 5794

0712-1105 See MIRROR (DAWSON CREEK). 5790

0712-1113 See SURREY/NORTH DELTA TODAY. 5795

0712-1148 See MCGILL JOURNAL OF POLITICAL ECONOMY, THE. 1504

0712-1180 See ETAT DU MONDE. 4520

0712-127X See BLAIN FAMILY NEWSLETTER, THE. 2439

0712-1288 See NEWSLETTER / VIETNAMESE ASSOCIATION, TORONTO. 2269

0712-1296 See SIGNAL (RYCROFT). 5794

0712-1318 See PUNDIT. 3426

0712-1326 See NOW (TORONTO. 1981). 4853

0712-1334 See CENTRE THIRD. 4889

0712-1342 See NURSING HOMES (TORONTO). 3790

0712-1350 See REVUE ET BULLETIN DE L'ASSOCIATION CANADIENNE DES ENSEIGNANTS NOIRS. 1780

0712-1385 See WRITING (TORONTO). 3455

0712-1490 See WORKING PAPER ... / CO-OPERATIVE FUTURE DIRECTIONS PROJECT. 1543

0712-1571 See INTERCULTURE (MONTREAL. ED. FRANCAISE). 4965

0712-1636 See ONTARIO VACATION FARMS. 5487

0712-1695 See RM MARIANNHILL. 4994

0712-1709 See RESEARCH (TORONTO BOARD OF EDUCATION. RESEARCH DEPT.). 1779

0712-1733 See KOREA TIMES. TORONTO EDITION. 5788

0712-1768 See YOUTH (FREDERICTON, N.B.). 1072

ISSN Index

0712-1806 See WELLAND NEWS MAGAZINE. 5797

0712-1822 See GREENSCAPE. 2417

0712-1865 See WANGAR. 5797

0712-1873 See ARCHTYPE (TORONTO). 4383

0712-1881 See VANCOUVER CITY DIRECTORY (1992). 2578

0712-1954 See ATTITUDE (MONTREAL). 2793

0712-1997 See DIRECTORY - CANADIAN ASSOCIATION OF PATHOLOGISTS. 3894

0712-2012 See ECONOSCOPE. 1487

0712-2055 See CARIBOU NEWS. 2189

0712-2063 See INDORAIR. 4784

0712-2101 See NEW DIRECTIONS (WINNIPEG). 5298

0712-2179 See GUELPH HISTORICAL SOCIETY NEWSLETTER. 2735

0712-2187 See BULLETIN DE L'INSTITUT D'HISTOIRE DE L'AMERIQUE FRANCAISE. 2724

0712-2195 See ONTARIO CHESS NEWS. 4864

0712-2284 See MORTGAGE BROKER. 908

0712-2292 See CROITRE. 4951

0712-2330 See CAHIERS D'HISTOIRE (MONTREAL). 2613

0712-2438 See SONANCES. 4153

0712-2446 See BEYOND SIGHT. 4887

0712-2462 See LIFELINE (SORRENTO). 4789

0712-2470 See PROCEEDINGS OF THE ANNUAL CONFERENCE OF CANADIAN TECHNICAL ASPHALT ASSOCIATION. 2029

0712-2489 See NOUVEAU JOURNAL DE ST-MICHEL, LE. 5791

0712-2519 See CUE (VANCOUVER). 1222

0712-2535 See ACQ INFORME. 43

0712-2594 See MANITOBA CONSTRUCTION & RESOURCE INDUSTRIES. 619

0712-2624 See ETHELBERT ECHO. 5784

0712-2632 See JIM RENNIE'S SPORTS LETTER. 4901

0712-2640 See PRESENT (MATANE). 5793

0712-2659 See CRAFT SCHOOL. 371

0712-2667 See ETOILE DU MATIN. 5016

0712-2683 See TRUCK NEWS (TORONTO). 5398

0712-2691 See FOCUS (RED DEER). 2823

0712-2705 See PETITE CAISSE. 5792

0712-2713 See METOIKOS. 2267

0712-2748 See COOPERATIVES ET DEVELOPPEMENT. 1542

0712-2756 See CHRONIQUE HYPOTHECAIRE / COMPAGNIE D'ASSURANCE D'HYPOTHEQUES DU CANADA. 783

0712-2772 See NOTATION (ENGLISH EDITION). 386

0712-2780 See HUMANITE (MONTREAL). 5288

0712-2799 See BYTOWN TIMES. 2916

0712-2810 See RACONTEUR (TIMMINS). 5793

0712-2829 See NGOMA (ENGLISH EDITION). 1883

0712-2837 See NGOMA (EDITION FRANCAISE). 1883

0712-2861 See FILON. 1439

0712-2888 See CITADIN DE LA GARDEUR. 4638

0712-290X See PAR SI PAR LA. 4145

0712-2918 See CMI EXPRESS. 827

0712-2934 See FOOD FOR THOUGHT (VANCOUVER). 88

0712-2942 See TARGET (TORONTO). 5002

0712-2950 See NEWSLETTER (HUMANE SOCIETY OF OTTAWA-CARLETON). 5298

0712-2977 See PAPERASSE. 5792

0712-2993 See ROSEMERE-NOUVELLES. 4684

0712-3019 See PERIODICITE. 4673

0712-3027 See BEACONSFIELD REPORTER. 5780

0712-3035 See NEWSLETTER (NATIONAL COUNCIL OF WOMEN OF CANADA). 5562

0712-3043 See WEEKLY NEWS (STRATFORD). 5797

0712-3086 See COURANT, LE. 3830

0712-3094 See TALLYBOARD. 2396

0712-3108 See CENTRES HOSPITALIERS. GUIDE BUDGETAIRE. 3778

0712-3132 See NEWSLETTER (OPEN DOOR SOCIETY OF OTTAWA). 5299

0712-3205 See SOCIAL ACTIVITIES FOR ADULTS. 4854

0712-3221 See GENOS (WINNIPEG, MAN.). 2794

0712-3248 See VIE MUNICIPALE A JONQUIERE, LA. 4693

0712-3272 See CAYO PUBLICATION. 4108

0712-3299 See TOULADI. 5796

0712-3302 See DATACOMMUNICATOR. 1153

0712-3310 See ARC-EN-CIEL (ROUYN). 313

0712-3345 See OMELLETTE, L'. 5791

0712-3361 See SOURCE (RIMOUSKI, QUEBEC). 2221

0712-337X See GLOBULE ROUGE. 1091

0712-3388 See OLD AGE SECURITY, GUARANTEED INCOME SUPPLEMENT, SPOUSE'S ALLOWANCE. 2889

0712-340X See INDEX DE LA LEGISLATION OUVRIERE. 3149

0712-3418 See INDEX OF LABOUR LEGISLATION. 3149

0712-3566 See FENAISON. 3387

0712-3620 See INFORMATION FOR COLLECTORS. 1383

0712-3663 See TELECOM MARKET LETTER, THE. 1164

0712-3760 See BRITISH COLUMBIA TEACHERS' FEDERATION : SALARY AGREEMENT. 1861

0712-3817 See MOUSQUETON, LE. 4875

0712-3914 See MATRICULE ZERO. 1835

0712-3949 See INFO-POINTELIERE. 4656

0712-4228 See CITOYEN (CAP-SANTE). 4638

0712-4236 See REFERENCE (COMMUNAUTE URBAINE DE MONTREAL. OFFICE DE L'EXPANSION ECONOMIQUE). 1515

0712-4244 See REFERENCE (COMMUNAUTE URBAINE DE MONTREAL. OFFICE D'EXPANSION ECONOMIQUE. ENGLISH EDITION). 1516

0712-4260 See PUBLICATIONS IN ARCHAEOLOGY (OTTAWA). 279

0712-4279 See WILDE TIMES. 2796

0712-4295 See POLITICAL ALERTS. 4488

0712-4376 See READER'S CHOICE (TORONTO). 3428

0712-4546 See EDMONTON AND ALBERTA BUSINESS. 671

0712-4570 See COURANT (MONTREAL). 4871

0712-4589 See ALPHA DELTA PHI LITERARY JOURNAL, THE. 1089

0712-4597 See ESTIMATES - PROVINCE OF BRITISH COLUMBIA. 4722

0712-4600 See RAPPORT ANNUEL / COMMISSION DE PROTECTION DU TERRITOIRE AGRICOLE DU QUEBEC. 2203

0712-4627 See TECHNOSTYLE. 3444

0712-4635 See EDUQ : BIBLIOGRAPHIE ANALYTIQUE SUR L'EDUCATION AU QUEBEC. 1794

0712-4767 See RENAISSANCE UNIVERSAL JOURNAL. 4533

0712-4775 See BULLETIN / HEALTH SCIENCES ASSOCIATION OF ALBERTA. 1657

0712-4791 See MONTHLY ECONOMIC REVIEW (OTTAWA). 1506

0712-4813 See SPECTROSCOPY (OTTAWA, ONT.). 993

0712-4848 See CANADIAN SCIENCE (DOWNSVIEW, ONT.). 5092

0712-4910 See MADOC REVIEW. 2537

0712-4929 See OGGI CANADA. 5791

0712-4945 See WASAGA BEACH TIMES. 2549

0712-4953 See INDEPENDENT (PORT HOPE). 5786

0712-4961 See SCARBOROUGH HISTORICAL NOTES & COMMENTS. 2759

0712-497X See INTERNATIONAL THOROUGHBRED DIGEST. 2800

0712-4988 See BEACON (GLACE BAY). 5780

0712-4996 See GREENHOUSE CANADA. 2417

0712-5038 See GOOD BEGINNINGS NEWSLETTER. 1748

0712-5054 See NIEN GIAM VIET-NAM, MONTREAL. 2750

0712-5062 See PASSING TONES. 4145

0712-5070 See COMUNITA (MONTREAL). 2729

0712-5089 See NORTHWEST EXPLORER (SIOUX LOOKOUT). 5791

0712-5135 See CANADIAN AQUATICS. 4889

0712-5151 See SPECIALISTE (GATINEAU, QUEBEC). 5319

0712-5275 See NEWSLETTER / COMMITTEE ON SOCIALIST STUDIES. 4544

0712-5291 See BREEDER AND FEEDER. 207

0712-5321 See BANK OF BRITISH COLUMBIA'S PIONEER NEWS. 775

0712-5348 See NORTH SHORE NEWS. 5791

0712-5364 See REACH (VANCOUVER). 3632

0712-5550 See PHILIPPINE NEWS BULLETIN. 2662

0712-5569 See SIMCOE MIRROR, THE. 5794

0712-5585 See F.I.B.A. RULES CASEBOOK. 4894

0712-5631 See MOTS CROISES POUR TOUT L'MONDE. 4863

0712-5704 See SHAMA (TORONTO). 2273

0712-5747 See LEISUREWAYS. 4852

0712-5801 See SHUTTLE. 4917

0712-5828 See HIGHLIGHTS (LONDON, ONT.). 5328

0712-5836 See SOUNDS ABOUT SUNDAY (1981). 3056

0712-5844 See CCPE NEWS. 1967

0712-5879 See HIGHLIGHTS (CALGARY. 1978). 352

0712-5887 See IBAO NEWS. 2882

0712-5895 See TORONTO CONSTRUCTION NEWS. 630

0712-5976 See RE/MAX INTER. 4843

0712-5984 See SUPER SEXE. 5188

0712-6018 See ORGASME. 5188

0712-6026 See SCANDALE (MONTREAL). 5188

0712-6034 See SEXE PLUS. 5188

0712-6042 See COEUR ATOUT. 5187

0712-6069 See INFLUX (MONTREAL, QUEBEC). 3464

0712-6077 See HORIZONS (OAKVILLE). 4963

0712-6107 See OBJECTIF - A.L.P.A. 4372

0712-6115 See LIBSAT. 3228

0712-6239 See NEWSLETTER / MONTREAL POETS' INFORMATION EXCHANGE. 3467

0712-6263 See MARIPOSA FOLK FESTIVAL. 4130

0712-6298 See NSIAA NEWS. 5135

0712-631X See ENCORE (EDMONTON). 4116

0712-6336 See IROQUOIAN, THE. 4874

0712-6360 See LIVING IN NORTH YORK. 2568

0712-6387 See FOUR-TOWN JOURNAL. 5784

0712-6417 See WINDMILL HERALD. 5798

0712-645X See BORGO. 4104

0712-6468 See RESIDENTIAL LAND AND HOUSING SURVEY / THE CITY OF CALGARY, PLANNING DEPARTMENT. 2834

0712-6476 See HOMESTEAD (KENTVILLE). 5786

0712-6522 See NOTES AND NEWS / DURHAM EAST SOIL & CROP IMPROVEMENT ASSOCIATION. 179

0712-6530 See REPERTOIRE (UNIVERSITY OF CALGARY. FACULTY OF FINE ARTS). 329

0712-6565 See RECUEIL FISCAL. PROBLEMES ET SOLUTIONS. 4744

0712-6573 See RECUEIL FISCAL. COURS D'IMPOT. 750

0712-6689 See ONTARIO MEDICINE. 3916

0712-6700 See L'ESTAMPE, DE. 380

0712-676X See NEWSLETTER - CANADIAN ASSOCIATION ON GERONTOLOGY. 5180

0712-6778 See CANADIAN OPERATING ROOM NURSING JOURNAL. 3853

0712-6794 See COURRIER SAINT-HUBERT. 5783
0712-6808 See BULLETIN DE CHATEAUGUAY, LE. 4634
0712-6824 See VEILLEUR, LE. 5313
0712-6867 See SOCIAL INFOPAC (TORONTO). 2761
0712-6891 See TELESPECTATEUR, LE. 1140
0712-6921 See TAX MEMO (PRICE WATERHOUSE (FIRM)). 4753
0712-7170 See VISPAC NEWSLETTER. 2085
0712-7227 See SESSIONS DE FORMATION... / COSE. 886
0712-7243 See RESOURCE-MAG. 2924
0712-7308 See SAINT-HUBERT, NOTRE VILLE. 4684
0712-7375 See AGRICULTURE NORTH. 54
0712-7391 See TRAFICS. 332
0712-7464 See CHRONIQUE (LAC BEAUPORT). 5782
0712-7499 See DIRECTORY OF CERTIFICATES OF AUTHORIZATION HOLDERS AUTHORIZED TO PRACTISE PROFESSIONAL ENGINEERING IN THE PROVINCE OF ONTARIO. 1970
0712-757X See VOTRE BOTTIN DE CROSSE. 4928
0712-7588 See RENDEZVOUS (BRANTFORD). 3174
0712-7626 See INDUSTRY OUTLOOK UPDATE 159
0712-7642 See SERVICE CLUBS IN HAMILTON-WENTWORTH. 5307
0712-7774 See CEREBUS. 4858
0712-7871 See RAIN FOREST (PORT ALBERNI, B.C.). 3427
0712-788X See INSTITUTE OF URBAN STUDIES PUBLICATION. 2825
0712-7944 See STUDENT TIMES (MONTREAL). 5795
0712-8045 See INFORM ACTION - ACTION LIBAN. 2654
0712-8088 See PROGRAMME DE LOISIR. 387
0712-8096 See NEW DIRECTION (TORONTO). 5018
0712-810X See EDUCO. 1863
0712-8177 See JOHN KETTLE'S FUTURELETTER. 685
0712-8193 See PUBLI-NORMES. 764
0712-8223 See PERSPECTIVES STATISTIQUES (QUEBEC). 5301
0712-8290 See RECORD (TORONTO). 4149
0712-8320 See FUTURE IS TODAY, THE. 4960
0712-8339 See INTERDIT. 5187
0712-8355 See TRANSIT NEWS CANADA. 5395
0712-838X See RENCONTRES GAIES. 2796
0712-8398 See LESBO (MONTREAL). 2795
0712-841X See LEGAL ALERT. 3101
0712-8428 See HOCKEY PROFESSIONNEL. 4899
0712-8533 See GUIDE DE LA BIBLIOTHEQUE DU CENTRE AUDIO-VISUEL - COLLEGE JEAN-DE-BREBEUF. 3212
0712-8576 See PETIT A PETIT. 5301
0712-8592 See INDUSTRIAL CHEMICALS AND SYNTHETIC RESINS. 1025
0712-8606 See ABOUT. 2526
0712-8614 See CAR (MONTREAL, QUEBEC). 5409
0712-8657 See TEOROS. 5492
0712-8762 See PROVINCIAL GROSS DOMESTIC PRODUCT BY INDUSTRY. 4742
0712-8770 See CERAMISTE. 2588
0712-8789 See NOUVELLES CSN. 1695
0712-8835 See BULLETIN - INSTITUT DES AGRONOMES DU N.-B. INSTITUT AGRICOLE DU CANADA. 69
0712-8878 See KANADA KURIER (ALBERTA AUSG.). 5787
0712-8886 See KANADA KURIER (AUSGABE FUER BRITISH COLUMBIA). 5787
0712-8894 See KANADA KURIER (MANITOBA AUSG.). 5787
0712-8908 See KANADA KURIER (MONTREAL AUSG.). 5787

0712-8916 See KANADA KURIER (ONTARIO AUSGABE). 5787
0712-8924 See KANADA KURIER (OTTAWA AUSG.). 5787
0712-8932 See KANADA KURIER (SASKATCHEWAN AUSG.). 5787
0712-8940 See KANADA KURIER (TORONTO AUSGABE). 5788
0712-8991 See WHITE WALL REVIEW. 3453
0712-9041 See ADNEWS (OCT. 13, 1981). 754
0712-9068 See KINGSTON THIS WEEK. 5788
0712-9084 See ALGONQUIN PERIODICALS, UNION LISTING / ALGONQUIN RESOURCE CENTRE, STUDENT SERVICES DIVISION. 3189
0712-9092 See STEEL DESIGN. 2031
0712-9122 See BACK TO BACK (TORONTO, ONT.). 3803
0712-9130 See STRATEGIE +. 713
0712-9173 See PETAWAWA POST. 4054
0712-9203 See BIENNIAL REPORT / INSTITUTE OF OCEANOGRAPHY, MCGILL UNIVERSITY. 1446
0712-9262 See JOURNAL / Q.F.M.A. 2906
0712-9297 See WHSTC LIBRARY CATALOG. 3256
0712-9300 See DROIT DU TRAVAIL EXPRESS. 3146
0712-9319 See BIOME (ENGLISH ED.). 4085
0712-9343 See ALBERTA INSURANCE DIRECTORY. 2873
0712-936X See COMMUNIQUE / HUMAN FACTORS ASSOCIATION OF CANADA. 2860
0712-9467 See TECHNOLOGY TODAY (MISSISSAUGA). 5164
0712-9564 See CORPIQ VOUS INFORME. 4836
0712-9599 See LIBEREZ LES VACANCES. 5295
0712-9661 See BULLETIN - CITE DE COTE SAINT-LUC. 4634
0712-967X See ENTRE NOUS GENS DE BERNIERES. 4646
0712-9688 See EDUCATION MILLE-ILES. 1863
0712-9726 See PRAPFALLS. 3241
0712-9750 See SOUTHWINDS. 1784
0712-9769 See MORGUARD REPORT. 4841
0712-9777 See DIRECTORY, NON-OPERATING LIBRARY BOARDS / GEORGIAN BAY REGIONAL LIBRARY SYSTEMS. 3206
0712-9785 See DIRECTORY OF OPERATING LIBRARIES / GEORGIAN BAY REGIONAL LIBRARY SYSTEM. 3207
0712-9793 See BULLETIN - ASSOCIATION D'EDUCATION DU QUEBEC. 1729
0712-9815 See CANADIAN JOURNAL OF HISTORY OF SPORT. 4889
0712-9890 See CONSULTANT (MONTREAL. 1974). 1969
0712-9904 See INVESTORS' BULLETIN (MILTON). 4966
0712-9912 See JOURNAL OF CONTINUING MEDICAL EDUCATION. 3594
0712-9947 See PARLONS PEDAGOGIE. 1839
0712-9955 See NEWSLETTER / ACADEMY OF CANADIAN WRITERS. 3416
0712-9963 See PRESCOLAIRE. 1805
0712-9971 See ONTARIO NURSING HOMES. 3790
0713-0082 See HANSARD : OFFICIAL REPORT / LEGISLATIVE ASSEMBLY OF THE NORTHWEST TERRITORIES. 4654
0713-0139 See CANTONS. 5781
0713-0163 See FATIMA CRUSADER. 4958
0713-0171 See AUTHOR'S NEWS. 4812
0713-021X See LIBERTARIAN VOICE. 4480
0713-0236 See NATIONAL FACTORY & EQUIPMENT NEWS. 160
0713-0287 See REVIEW - SASKATCHEWAN ASSOCIATION ON HUMAN RIGHTS. 4512
0713-0317 See MEDIA FIVE BULLETIN, THE. 325
0713-0333 See VOICE (OTTAWA). 3178
0713-0341 See EXPORT NEWS (OTTAWA). 834
0713-0368 See EXPORTATIONS NOUVELLES. 835

0713-0465 See AGRICULTURAL AID TO DEVELOPING COUNTRIES. 2907
0713-049X See ENTRE GENS D'ICI. 1744
0713-0511 See NATIONAL NEWS LETTER - FEDERATION OF MILITARY AND UNITED SERVICES INSTITUTES OF CANADA. 4052
0713-052X See CLASS / CANADIAN LADIES ASSOCIATION OF SHOOTING SPORTS. 4890
0713-0546 See WAPITI. 3256
0713-0562 See TIDE (LEWISPORTE). 5796
0713-0597 See NUCLEAR NOTES (TORONTO). 2157
0713-0627 See FORNERI, IL. 3282
0713-0872 See ESTIMATES OF EXPENDITURE. SUPPLEMENTARY INFORMATION. RECONCILIATION OF HISTORICAL DATA. 4722
0713-1224 See ALBERTA'S RECLAMATION RESEARCH PROGRAM. 162
0713-1283 See CBC CLASSICAL CATALOGUE. 4108
0713-1291 See CBC JAZZ AND POPULAR RECORD CATALOGUE. 4108
0713-1313 See INSECT AND DISEASE CONTROL IN THE HOME GARDEN. 4245
0713-1348 See CANADIAN FISHERIES, LANDINGS. 2298
0713-1445 See INFOR-MER. MINES. 2004
0713-1631 See AGRICULTURAL LAND RESERVE STATISTICS. 150
0713-1674 See QUARTERLY JOURNAL - CANADIAN GENERAL STANDARDS BOARD. 4677
0713-1682 See INFORMATION REPORT - DEPARTMENT OF CONSUMER AFFAIRS AND ENVIRONMENT, RESEARCH AND ASSESSMENT BRANCH. 1297
0713-1755 See CANADA PENSION PLAN CONTRIBUTION AND UNEMPLOYMENT INSURANCE PREMIUM TABLES. 1658
0713-1763 See SUPPLEMENTARY CANADA PENSION PLAN CONTRIBUTION AND UNEMPLOYMENT INSURANCE PREMIUM TABLES. 1713
0713-1771 See UNEMPLOYMENT INSURANCE PREMIUM TABLES ... PROVINCE OF QUEBEC. 2895
0713-178X See SUPPLEMENTARY UNEMPLOYMENT INSURANCE PREMIUM TABLES ... PROVINCE OF QUEBEC. 2894
0713-1887 See ANNUAL REPORT ... OF ALBERTA HEALTH FACILITIES REVIEW COMMITTEE. 3776
0713-2050 See HOLSTEIN SIRE CATALOGUE. 195
0713-2123 See NORTHWEST TERRITORIES GAZETTE; PART II. 4670
0713-214X See NEOLOGIE EN MARCHE. 3305
0713-2158 See CANADIAN FISHERIES ANNUAL STATISTICAL REVIEW. 2317
0713-2565 See PACIFIC MARINE SCIENCE REPORT. 1455
0713-2727 See NEWSLETTER (MARIGOLD LIBRARY SYSTEM). 3235
0713-2840 See TRAVEL-LOG. 5496
0713-3030 See COMMUNIQUE - SASKATCHEWAN POWER CORPORATION. 1602
0713-3111 See CONNAISSONS NOS VOISINS. 5467
0713-3162 See GIGUERERIE (EDITION FRANCAISE). 2451
0713-3219 See REVIEW - NORTH-SOUTH INSTITUTE (OTTAWA). 1625
0713-3219 See REVUE : UN BULLETIN DE L'INSTITUT NORD-SUD. 1625
0713-3235 See CANADIAN WOMEN'S STUDIES. 5553
0713-3286 See CANADIAN MONEYSAVER. 894
0713-3332 See WOMEN IN THE UNIVERSITY GRADUATING POPULATION. 1854
0713-3359 See MANITOBA AGRICULTURE STATISTICS. 154
0713-3383 See PASTORAL SCIENCES. 4985
0713-3391 See WORLD VIEW (TORONTO). 5010

0713-3413 *See* ROYAUME (LIMOILOU, QUEBEC). **4994**

0713-3421 *See* CSSE CONTACT. **2861**

0713-343X *See* INSIDE QUEBEC (QUEBEC, QUEBEC). **2739**

0713-3448 *See* LETTRE DE QUEBEC, LA. **2744**

0713-3529 *See* LISTE DES FILMS VISES PAR CATEGORIES DE SPECTATEURS. **4074**

0713-3545 *See* GAMUT (TORONTO). **321**

0713-357X *See* UNIFORM FINAL EXAMINATION REPORT / THE INSTITUTES OF CHARTERED ACCOUNTANTS IN CANADA AND BERMUDA. **752**

0713-3634 *See* YOUTH & ADULTS TOGETHER. **5011**

0713-3677 *See* GOOD-NEWS-LETTER. **4961**

0713-3804 *See* INFORMATION FINANCIERE ET LES FLUCTUATIONS DES PRIX, L'. **745**

0713-3898 *See* NURTURING. **2284**

0713-3901 *See* TALES OF THE TWELVE. **4097**

0713-391X *See* GAZETTE - CANADIAN FORCES BASE GAGETOWN (1981). **4044**

0713-3928 *See* RACONTE. **5423**

0713-3936 *See* CANADIAN JOURNAL OF COMMUNITY MENTAL HEALTH. **5276**

0713-3960 *See* NEWSLETTER / CENTRE FOR EDITING EARLY CANADIAN TEXTS. **3417**

0713-4002 *See* CHO'N-TRO'I. **5195**

0713-4010 *See* SCHOOL DISTRICT, COLLEGE AND INSTITUTE CONTINUING EDUCATION DATA. **1802**

0713-4029 *See* COLLECTIVE BARGAINING IN NEW BRUNSWICK. **1660**

0713-4045 *See* ALBERTA CONSTRUCTION & RESOURCE INDUSTRIES DIRECTORY/PURCHASING GUIDE. **598**

0713-4150 *See* FORECAST (LONDON, ONT.). **1425**

0713-4169 *See* PINARDIERE. **2467**

0713-4207 *See* P5. PERSONAL PARTICIPATION IN PURSUIT OF PHYSICAL PROFICIENCY. **2600**

0713-4231 *See* HEBDO-COOP. **1542**

0713-424X *See* HEBDO-COOP. ENGLISH EDITION. **1542**

0713-4258 *See* CAHIERS PAUL LEAUTAUD. **3371**

0713-4266 *See* BREAKING THE SILENCE (OTTAWA, ONT.). **5552**

0713-4282 *See* TREMBLAIE. **2476**

0713-4290 *See* BULLETIN DE NOUVELLES - CORPORATION PROFESSIONNELLE DES TRAVAILLEURS SOCIAUX DU QUEBEC. **5275**

0713-4290 *See* MAGAZINE DES ARTS MARTIAUX DU QUEBEC, LE. **4903**

0713-4355 *See* TRANSFERT. **1886**

0713-4436 *See* ARBRE DE VIE (LOUISEVILLE). **4379**

0713-4460 *See* BOOKS IN ARABIC (1980). **4825**

0713-4479 *See* NEWSLETTER / ATLANTIC CANADA INSTITUTE. **2541**

0713-4495 *See* BOOKS IN CHINESE (1980). **4825**

0713-4517 *See* CANADIAN POLICE CHIEF NEWSLETTER. **3159**

0713-4533 *See* BOOKS IN DUTCH (1980). **4825**

0713-4568 *See* BOOKS IN CROATIAN. **4825**

0713-4681 *See* DIRECTORY OF COMMUNITY SERVICES FOR WATERLOO REGION. **5282**

0713-4711 *See* RAPPORT ANNUEL - SERVICE DE RECHERCHE EN DEFENSE DES CULTURES. **4678**

0713-472X *See* BOURSES D'ETUDES ET DE PERFECTIONNEMENT DE L'ENSEIGNEMENT SUPERIEUR. **1812**

0713-4789 *See* NEW MARITIMES. **5790**

0713-4800 *See* MUNICIPALITE (1982). **4667**

0713-4916 *See* PROGRESS REPORT - SOCIETE D'ENERGIE DE LA BAIE JAMES. **705**

0713-4991 *See* LIVE (LAVAL). **4129**

0713-5009 *See* CONTACT (SOCIETE DE RELATIONS D'AFFAIRES, ECOLE DES HAUTES ETUDES COMMERCIALES. 1981). **659**

0713-5335 *See* BOOKS IN BENGALI (1980). **4825**

0713-536X *See* NEWS UPDATE / CANADIAN AIR TRAFFIC CONTROL, ASSOCIATION. **30**

0713-5386 *See* LIBRARY POCKETFUL, A. **3226**

0713-5424 *See* PROCEEDINGS - GRAPHICS INTERFACE. **1243**

0713-5459 *See* TOBACCO IN CANADA. **5374**

0713-5467 *See* TABAC AU CANADA. **5373**

0713-5483 *See* EXPRESS (DRUMMONDVILLE). **5784**

0713-5521 *See* PRISME (QUEBEC. 1964). **5793**

0713-553X *See* LOISIRS-PRESSE. **4903**

0713-5688 *See* ECHO : JOURNAL DU SYNDICAT PROFESSIONNEL DES INGENIEURS DE L'HYDRO-QUEBEC, L'. **1664**

0713-5726 *See* TRACT (CHICOUTIMI). **5796**

0713-5734 *See* PHARE (ROUYN). **2754**

0713-5750 *See* PSYCHOLOGISTS REGISTERED IN ONTARIO. **4612**

0713-5777 *See* REGINA THIS MONTH. **2574**

0713-5807 *See* PULP & PAPER JOURNAL. **4238**

0713-5815 *See* NYAME AKUMA. **277**

0713-5858 *See* HANDBOOK / CANADIAN ASSOCIATION FOR UNIVERSITY CONTINUING EDUCATION. **1827**

0713-5866 *See* SAVE THE BULKLEY NEWSLETTER. **2204**

0713-5904 *See* DAVID DUNLAP DOINGS, THE. **395**

0713-5998 *See* BOOKS IN SPANISH (1980). **4826**

0713-6048 *See* SEJOURS A LA FERME. **1626**

0713-6099 *See* FILM LIBRARY CATALOGUE / NATIONAL HEALTH AND WELFARE. **3210**

0713-6196 *See* SHIPMENTS OF SOLID FUEL BURNING HEATING PRODUCTS. **1956**

0713-620X *See* BROSSARD ECLAIR. **5781**

0713-6242 *See* MACE DIALOGUE. **1801**

0713-6285 *See* NEWSLETTER - KITCHENER WATERLOO REGIONAL FOLK ARTS MULTICULTURAL CENTRE. **2749**

0713-6315 *See* ANTIQUE SHOWCASE. **249**

0713-634X *See* TRADE CONNECTIONS. **854**

0713-6358 *See* DIRECTORY OF NEW BRUNSWICK LIBRARIES. **3207**

0713-6420 *See* JOURNAL L'INFORMATION DU NORD. **5787**

0713-648X *See* NOVA SCOTIA SCHOOL TELEVISION. ELEMENTARY. **1769**

0713-651X *See* MINUTES OF PROCEEDINGS AND EVIDENCE OF THE SUB-COMMITTEE ON DREE PROGRAMMES (QUEBEC) OF THE STANDING COMMITTEE ON REGIONAL DEVELOPMENT. **4665**

0713-6668 *See* BULLETIN - PUBLIC SERVICE ALLIANCE OF CANADA (1978). **1657**

0713-6714 *See* VOS AFFAIRES MUNICIPALES. **4694**

0713-6722 *See* MIRIAD. **3412**

0713-6781 *See* DIRECTORY / ONTARIO AMATEUR FOOTBALL ASSOCIATION. **4892**

0713-679X *See* PEUPLE/COURRIER DE LA COTE-DU-SUD. **5792**

0713-6803 *See* ANJOU (ANJOU, QUEBEC). **4626**

0713-682X *See* SILLERY VOUS INFORME. **4686**

0713-6862 *See* MESSAGER DE LA MINGANIE, LE. **5789**

0713-6919 *See* IC. INFORMATION CONSTRUCTION. **616**

0713-6986 *See* PUBLICATIONS LIST - MANITOBA. DEPARTMENT OF NATURAL RESOURCES. **2202**

0713-6994 *See* RENSEIGNEMENTS AUX PARENTS / COMMISSION SCOLAIRE SAINT-EXUPERY. **1869**

0713-7044 *See* MINERAL POLICY SECTOR INTERNAL REPORT. **2144**

0713-7060 *See* PROCEEDINGS - CANADIAN SYMPOSIUM ON REMOTE SENSING. **31**

0713-7095 *See* SASKATCHEWAN REPORTS. **3046**

0713-7109 *See* MANITOBA REPORTS (FREDERICTON, N.B. : BOUND CUMULATION). **3006**

0713-715X *See* ANNUAL REPORT - NOVA SCOTIA DEPARTMENT OF CONSUMER AFFAIRS. **1293**

0713-7192 *See* TAX INFORMATION BULLETIN. **4753**

0713-7257 *See* FEDERAL CORPORATE TAX RETURN, THE. **4723**

0713-7508 *See* SUB-COMMITTEE OF THE STANDING COMMITTEE ON EXTERNAL AFFAIRS AND NATIONAL DEFENCE ON ARMED FORCES RESERVES. **4058**

0713-7591 *See* UNIVERSITY OF ALBERTA DATA LIBRARY CATALOGUE. **3255**

0713-7613 *See* VISITORS & CONVENTION SERVICES NEWSLETTER. **5499**

0713-7621 *See* LIEN (ORDRE DES TECHNICIENS EN RADIOLOGIE DU QUEBEC). **3943**

0713-7745 *See* NEWFOUNDLAND AND LABRADOR : CAMPGROUND GUIDE. **4852**

0713-7753 *See* ONE SKY REPORT. **1638**

0713-7761 *See* LEADER (GLOUCESTER). **4851**

0713-780X *See* SURNAME EXCHANGE / SASKATCHEWAN GENEALOGICAL SOCIETY. **2474**

0713-7826 *See* WORK PROGRAM / FERIC. **2398**

0713-7907 *See* WEEKLY DIGEST OF FAMILY LAW. **3122**

0713-7958 *See* REVUE D'HISTOIRE LITTERAIRE DU QUEBEC ET DU CANADA FRANCAIS. **3430**

0713-7974 *See* LIFELINE - CANADIAN MEMORIAL CHIROPRACTIC COLLEGE. **5788**

0713-7982 *See* PUBLICATIONS SERIES (JOINT CENTRE ON MODERN EAST ASIA). **2662**

0713-8024 *See* ECHO MUNICIPAL. **4645**

0713-8040 *See* VOIX FRANCO-ONTARIENNE, LA. **2765**

0713-8059 *See* HARMONIE-QUEBEC : BULLETIN OFFICIEL, FEDERATION DES HARMONIES DU QUEBEC. **4120**

0713-8067 *See* ALBERTA PERSPECTIVE. **5271**

0713-8083 *See* HUNGARIAN STUDIES REVIEW. **2692**

0713-8091 *See* OTTAWA QUARTERLY. **1620**

0713-8113 *See* TROUBADOUR (FREDERICTON). **4157**

0713-8121 *See* POP ROCK. **4147**

0713-813X *See* CTD POCKET GUIDE, THE. **2781**

0713-8172 *See* UBC DATA LIBRARY CATALOGUE. MICROFORM. **3254**

0713-8180 *See* DISCUSSION PAPER (JOINT CENTRE ON MODERN EAST ASIA). **2650**

0713-8199 *See* NOTES DE RECHERCHE (UNIVERSITY OF OTTAWA. DEPT. OF POLITICAL SCIENCE). **4484**

0713-8369 *See* MOVING TO & AROUND ALBERTA. **4841**

0713-8377 *See* MOVING TO & AROUND TORONTO & AREA. **4841**

0713-8385 *See* MOVING TO & AROUND SASKATCHEWAN. **4841**

0713-8407 *See* MOVING TO & AROUND VANCOUVER & B.C. **4841**

0713-8431 *See* BULLETIN SSQ SUR LES LOIS SOCIALES. FRANCAIS. **5276**

0713-8466 *See* WORKING PAPER - SCHOOL OF URBAN & REGIONAL PLANNING. UNIVERSITY OF WATERLOO. **2839**

0713-8474 *See* INFORMATION UPDATE - HUB, INFORMATION SERVICES. **4389**

0713-8539 *See* E AKROPOLIS. **5783**

0713-8547 *See* FOCUS WOMEN. **5557**

0713-8555 *See* ANNUAL BRIEF SUBMITTED BY THE QUEBEC ASSOCIATION FOR THE MENTALLY RETARDED TO THE GOVERNMENT OF QUEBEC. **5271**

0713-8776 *See* OFFICIAL MANITOBA SHIP-BY-TRUCK DIRECTORY (1983). **5388**

0713-8806 *See* NEWSLETTER / INNISFIL HISTORICAL SOCIETY. **2749**

0713-8865 *See* BRITISH COLUMBIA WEEKLY LAW DIGEST. **2943**

0713-892X *See* ALBERTA WEEKLY LAW DIGEST. **2930**

0713-8946 See PREPARING YOUR CORPORATE TAX RETURNS. **4741**
0713-8954 See SUBJECT MATTER INDEX TO PUBLIC AND PRIVATE STATUTES OF NEW BRUNSWICK. **3060**
0713-8962 See SAINT JOHN CITY DIRECTORY (1992). **2575**
0713-8970 See ATLANTIC PROVINCES REPORTS. **2937**
0713-8989 See NEW BRUNSWICK REPORTS (1969). **3015**
0713-9098 See PRODUCTION AND SHIPMENTS OF BLOW-MOULDED PLASTIC BOTTLES. **4460**
0713-9144 See ENERGY UPDATE (ENERGY, MINES AND RESOURCES CANADA). **1942**
0713-9330 See AIR QUALITY, NORTHWESTERN ONTARIO : ANNUAL REPORT **2223**
0714-0045 See SURVEY METHODOLOGY. **5224**
0714-0053 See PUBLICATIONS PRICE LIST / ONTARIO GEOLOGICAL SURVEY AND MINERAL RESOURCES BRANCH. **1392**
0714-0169 See STUDY - ROYAL COMMISSION ON MATTERS OF HEALTH AND SAFETY ARISING FROM THE USE OF ASBESTOS IN ONTARIO. **4804**
0714-0207 See RESEARCH REPORT / ATOMIC ENERGY CONTROL BOARD. **1955**
0714-1017 See DEVELOPMENTS (EDMONTON). **1342**
0714-2056 See WHAT'S BREWING. **2372**
0714-2080 See BULLETIN DE LIAISON / ASSOCIATION DES RELATIONNISTES DU QUEBEC. **756**
0714-2099 See INFO-DETAIL (1991 ENGLISH ED.). **840**
0714-2099 See INFO-DETAIL / LE CONSEIL QUEBECOIS DU COMMERCE DE DETAIL. **840**
0714-2129 See BOOKS IN ESTONIAN (1980). **4825**
0714-2153 See DISTANCES ROUTIERES. **5440**
0714-2188 See DIRECTORY OF CANADIAN MUSEUMS AND RELATED INSTITUTIONS. **4087**
0714-2382 See BOOKS IN FINNISH (1980). **4825**
0714-2420 See BOOKS IN FRISIAN (1980). **4826**
0714-2455 See BOOKS IN GERMAN (1980). **4826**
0714-2471 See BOOKS IN GREEK (1980). **4826**
0714-2501 See BOOKS IN GUJARATI. **4826**
0714-2528 See BOOKS IN HINDI (1980). **4826**
0714-2544 See BOOKS IN HUNGARIAN (1980). **4826**
0714-2579 See ACS NEWSLETTER / ASSOCIATION FOR CANADIAN STUDIES. **2526**
0714-2609 See BOOKS IN ITALIAN. **4826**
0714-2773 See BOOKS IN POLISH (1980). **4826**
0714-279X See BOOKS IN PORTUGUESE (1980). **4826**
0714-282X See BOOKS IN PANJABI (1980). **4826**
0714-2862 See LIBRARY WORKER. **1688**
0714-2870 See INKSTONE. **3464**
0714-2927 See BOOKS IN UKRAINIAN (1980). **4826**
0714-296X See BOOKS IN URDU (1980). **4826**
0714-3044 See NEWSLETTER / CANADIAN SOCIETY OF AGRICULTURAL ENGINEERING. **160**
0714-3117 See J'INVESTRIE. **793**
0714-3133 See CONSTRUCTION ATLANTIC. **608**
0714-315X See ROSTER / RESTAURANTS & FOODSERVICES ASSOCIATION OF BRITISH COLUMBIA. **5073**
0714-3192 See CONTACT - UNIVERSITE SIMON FRASER. FACULTE D'EDUCATION. **3275**
0714-3206 See PROVINCIAL BUILDING & CONSTRUCTION TRADES COUNCIL OF ONTARIO. **625**
0714-3222 See MANITOBA WINNIPEG BUILDING AND CONSTRUCTION TRADES COUNCIL YEARBOOK. **1689**
0714-3230 See VISITANDIN, LE. **5797**
0714-3257 See WORD LOOM. **3454**
0714-3281 See CO-OP UPDATE (ST. JOHN'S). **1541**
0714-3303 See S'ORGANISER. **5794**

0714-3338 See SEEDS. **1885**
0714-3370 See BULLETIN D'INFORMATION - CONSEIL DES UNIVERSITES (SAINTE-FOY). **1812**
0714-346X See SPI CANADA ... PROGRAM, ... ACCOMPLISHMENTS. **4460**
0714-3494 See PSYCHOLOGIE PREVENTIVE. **4612**
0714-3508 See TORONTO SOUTH ASIAN REVIEW, THE. **3447**
0714-3559 See REVUE DE PRESSE / FEDERATION DES CAISSES POPULAIRES DESJARDINS DE MONTREAL ET DE L'OUEST-DU-QUEBEC. **810**
0714-3621 See CHEVRE QUEBEC. **209**
0714-363X See LOGGING & SAWMILLING JOURNAL. **2402**
0714-3672 See NOVA SCOTIA GENEALOGIST, THE. **2465**
0714-3680 See LAMAZE IN ONTARIO. **3764**
0714-3761 See MAIGRIR MEDECINE BEAUTE. **4194**
0714-3788 See TIPPS. **2778**
0714-3869 See DEAR COLLEAGUE (ST. CATHARINES, ONT.). **1862**
0714-3877 See OVALTA / ASSOCIATION TOURISTIQUE REGIONALE DE L'ABITIBI-TEMISCAMINGUE. **1620**
0714-3885 See INFO-SAINT-BRUNO. **4656**
0714-4032 See DEFI-SCIENCE. **1091**
0714-4067 See JE ME PETITDERBROUILLE. **5117**
0714-4091 See TERRAVUE. **2032**
0714-413X See WRITING IN PEEL. **3455**
0714-4172 See FREE-FALL (BANFF, ALTA.). **3389**
0714-4202 See NIAGARA'S SEASONS. **5486**
0714-4237 See REVUE DE L'ACTIVITE DANS L'INDUSTRIE DE LA CONSTRUCTION / OFFICE DE LA CONSTRUCTION DU QUEBEC, SERVICE RECHERCHE ET DEVELOPPEMENT. **626**
0714-4261 See REGISTRE-ANNUAIRE - MENSA CANADA. **5236**
0714-427X See AVENIR DU NORD (SAINT-JEROME, QUEBEC : 1981). **5780**
0714-4288 See RESSOURCES ET VOUS. **3175**
0714-430X See ASSURANCE I.A.R.D. AU CANADA. **2874**
0714-444X See ONTARIO COLLEGE NEWSLETTER. **1094**
0714-4458 See MEMBERSHIP LIST / THE QUINTE BRANCH, O.G.S. **2460**
0714-4520 See MEDIATEUR, LE. **325**
0714-4555 See STATISTIQUES CORRECTIONNELLES QUEBECOISES. **3177**
0714-4601 See BETWEEN US. **1811**
0714-4644 See SUBMISSION TO THE GOVERNMENT OF NEW BRUNSWICK / NATIONAL FARMERS UNION, REGION 1. **138**
0714-4733 See MANITOBA HOME AND SCHOOL NEWS. **1762**
0714-475X See NORTHLINE. **1838**
0714-4776 See METRO GUIDE (MONTREAL, QUEBEC). **5386**
0714-4784 See HEBDO DE BELLECHASSE (DORCHESTER), L'. **5786**
0714-4857 See RESEARCH NOTE - MINERAL EXPLORATION RESEARCH INSTITUTE (1977). **2150**
0714-4865 See DOSSIER - INSTITUTE DE RECHERCHE EN EXPLORATION MINERALE. **2138**
0714-4873 See HUMAN AFFAIRS. **5202**
0714-489X See MINI RECREATION. **4863**
0714-508X See INFORMATION SAINT-CONSTANT. **4656**
0714-556X See LIEN, LE. **1542**
0714-5578 See BREF (OTTAWA), EN. **1889**
0714-5624 See SENIOR SCENE. **5182**
0714-5659 See CAHIER - DEPARTEMENT D'ECONOMIQUE, FACULTE DES SCIENCES SOCIALES, UNIVERSITE LAVAL. **1467**
0714-5705 See ARN MESSAGER. **5780**
0714-5721 See CANADIAN QUILL. **3272**

0714-5756 See SENIOR CITIZENS' CONSULTANTS OF ST. CATHARINES INC. **5181**
0714-5780 See GUIDE PRATIQUE DES ETUDES COLLEGIALES. **1826**
0714-5810 See HUB (HAY RIVER). **2535**
0714-5861 See LEMON-AID NEW CAR GUIDE. **5418**
0714-5896 See LIVING SAFETY FOR THE CANADIAN FAMILY. **4789**
0714-5918 See RESOURCES - CANADIAN INSTITUTE OF RESOURCES LAW. **3116**
0714-5926 See ARCADE (MONTREAL). **3363**
0714-6116 See SEL & POIVRE. **5073**
0714-6124 See CURRICULUM RESOURCES. **3379**
0714-6132 See OMBUDSMAN OFFICE PROFILES / INTERNATIONAL OMBUDSMAN OFFICE PROFILES. **3022**
0714-6221 See CCI NOTES. **2189**
0714-637X See DRUMHELLER MAIL. **5783**
0714-6647 See NEWSLETTER - SOCIAL SCIENCE COMPUTING LABORATORY. **5211**
0714-6736 See OHS BULLETIN. **2541**
0714-6795 See WOMEN IN BUSINESS. **723**
0714-6892 See YELLOW PAPERS, THE. **1792**
0714-6906 See 10.5155.20 : ART CONTEMPORAIN. **335**
0714-6914 See MERCER BULLETIN, THE. **1690**
0714-6981 See BRAVO (TORONTO). **383**
0714-7058 See AURORA (GRAND CENTRE). **3193**
0714-7066 See HACTION. **5287**
0714-7074 See BULLETIN - CANADIAN NUCLEAR SOCIETY. **4446**
0714-7082 See JOURNAL / SASKATCHEWAN MATHEMATICS TEACHERS' SOCIETY. **3516**
0714-7104 See AUTO SPORT. **4885**
0714-7198 See INQUIRY (KINGSTON). **682**
0714-7228 See WORKING PAPER SERIES - DEPARTMENT OF BUSINESS, SCHOOL OF BUSINESS AND ECONOMICS, WILFRID LAURIER UNIVERSITY. **723**
0714-735X See PLEINE FORME / SOCIETE CANADIENNE DU CANCER. **3822**
0714-7376 See SORTIE (MONTREAL). **2796**
0714-7422 See MARKETNEWS. **5317**
0714-7430 See SPECIAL NEGO. **1711**
0714-7503 See WORK ABROAD. **4210**
0714-7546 See BIC (MONTREAL, QUEBEC : 1981). **5229**
0714-7570 See SPGQ EN NEGOTIATION. **1711**
0714-7619 See DENTURO +. **1322**
0714-7635 See CONJONCTURE DES AFFAIRES. **1470**
0714-7686 See RESURRECTION BULLETIN, THE. **4993**
0714-7805 See RAPPORT ANNUEL / BUREAU DE LA PROTECTION CIVILE DU QUEBEC. **4054**
0714-7864 See SYSTEMLETTER. **1262**
0714-7880 See LOAVES & FISHES (TORONTO, ONT.). **4974**
0714-7910 See ISSUES IN THE CANADIAN ECONOMY. TEACHER'S NOTES. **1497**
0714-8003 See SAT SANDESH (MONTREAL). **4995**
0714-8038 See LIEN HOA. **2658**
0714-8070 See CANADIAN RECORD CATALOGUE. **4107**
0714-8100 See TRANSACTION. **5068**
0714-8135 See FERGUS-ELORA PHOENIX. **5784**
0714-8143 See CANADIAN PARLIAMENTARY HANDBOOK. **4467**
0714-8151 See HOME RENOVATIONS. **2811**
0714-816X See EXPLORE (CALGARY). **4871**
0714-8208 See REFORMED PERSPECTIVE. **4990**
0714-8216 See LECTURE FAITE. **2999**
0714-8232 See OTTAWA-HULL GASTRONOMIC. **5072**
0714-8240 See CSAS NEWSLETTER. **209**
0714-8267 See SKI NAUTIQUE NEWS. **4918**
0714-8275 See HOUALLET. **2454**

0714-8283 *See* GUILLEMOT, LE. **5585**

0714-8305 *See* PHSC JOURNAL. **1146**

0714-8356 *See* COUNTRY MUSIC NEWS (OTTAWA). **4112**

0714-8402 *See* INSURANCE T.R.A.C. REPORT, CANADA. **2884**

0714-8453 *See* CONSEIL DU PATRONAT DU QUEBEC ET SES MEMBRES AFFILEES, LE. **1661**

0714-8461 *See* REPERTOIRE DES ASSOCIATIONS PATRONALES QUEBECOISES. **1706**

0714-850X *See* PREUVES (MONTREAL). **405**

0714-8534 *See* PRINCE ALBERT SUN. **5793**

0714-8550 *See* CONNECTIONS JOURNAL. **2190**

0714-8569 *See* MEMBERS & CARS. **5418**

0714-8585 *See* BUSINESS LIFE (1980). **650**

0714-8607 *See* SASKATOON BUSINESS DIRECTORY. **709**

0714-8615 *See* RENEWABLE ENERGY NEWS NORTHEAST. **1955**

0714-864X *See* HOT WACKS. **4121**

0714-8658 *See* DIRECTORY - BRITISH COLUMBIA MOTOR TRANSPORT ASSOCIATION. **5381**

0714-8674 *See* ENTRE PARENTHESES. **1744**

0714-878X *See* CANADIAN ORTHO-PROS, THE. **3881**

0714-8798 *See* SENIOR WORLD QUARTERLY. **5182**

0714-8801 *See* AT ISSUE (REGINA, SASK.). **2722**

0714-8828 *See* ACTUALITE VIE. **2248**

0714-8844 *See* HAMPSTEAD JOURNAL. **5786**

0714-8879 *See* RENAL FAMILY. **3993**

0714-8887 *See* MIMEOGRAPHED BIBLIOGRAPHY SERIES - INDUSTRIAL RELATIONS CENTRE. QUEEN'S UNIVERSITY. **420**

0714-8941 *See* PUBLIC STAMP AUCTION. **2787**

0714-895X *See* MARIGOLD LIBRARY SYSTEM DIRECTORY. **3230**

0714-9050 *See* SASKATCHEWAN MULTICULTURAL MAGAZINE. **2272**

0714-9093 *See* FOUR BY FOUR (MONTREAL, QUEBEC). **3463**

0714-9107 *See* BABILLARD DE R.D.P. **5780**

0714-9263 *See* ENVIRONMENT UPDATE (CANADA. ENVIRONMENT CANADA). **2228**

0714-9298 *See* HAI WAI SHU LIN. **2735**

0714-9301 *See* ANNUAL FORECAST OF ALBERTA SCHOOL ENROLMENTS, ... **1860**

0714-931X *See* DOCUMENTS JURIDIQUES INTERNATIONAUX. **3127**

0714-9476 *See* CONTINUITE. **348**

0714-9786 *See* WOMEN'S EDUCATION. **1791**

0714-9808 *See* CANADIAN JOURNAL ON AGING. **3750**

0714-9948 *See* LIVRE D'ICI (MENSUEL). **4830**

0714-9956 *See* CFBS NEWSLETTER / CANADIAN FEDERATION OF BIOLOGICAL SOCIETIES. **451**

0715-0237 *See* OWMC EXCHANGE, THE. **2238**

0715-0830 *See* PEST LEAFLET (VICTORIA). **4246**

0715-1055 *See* DONNEES SUR LA POPULATION ACTIVE : QUEBEC, ONTARIO ET CANADA. **5326**

0715-1438 *See* AGRICULTURAL STATISTICS AND REVIEW OF AGRICULTURE. **150**

0715-1519 *See* REPERTOIRE DES PRIX LITTERAIRES. **3429**

0715-1608 *See* GOVERNMENT RELATIONS. **1826**

0715-1624 *See* DIRECTORY OF LIBRARIES AND ARCHIVAL INSTITUTIONS IN PRINCE EDWARD ISLAND. **3207**

0715-1640 *See* ALBERTA LIBRARY BOARD REPORT. **3189**

0715-1942 *See* STAFF AND CLASS DATA FOR COLLEGES AND INSTITUTES. **1848**

0715-1977 See AFFIRMATIVE ACTION FORUM (SASKATOON). **1642**

0715-2086 *See* ARCHAEOLOGY IN NEWFOUNDLAND & LABRADOR. **257**

0715-2361 *See* LOOK AT LEISURE, A. **4852**

0715-2396 *See* NEWSLETTER / ALBERTA HERITAGE FOUNDATION FOR MEDICAL RESEARCH. **3621**

0715-240X *See* ANNUAL REVIEW / ALBERTA AGENCY FOR INTERNATIONAL DEVELOPMENT. **2907**

0715-2612 *See* NOTABLE CANADIAN CHILDREN'S BOOKS. SUPPLEMENT. **3237**

0715-2647 *See* ANNUAL REPORT - TERRITORIAL HOSPITAL INSURANCE SERVICES AND MEDICARE. **2874**

0715-271X *See* JURISTAT. **3081**

0715-2965 *See* ANNUAL REPORT ... SASKATCHEWAN AGRICULTURAL RETURNS STABILIZATION FUND. **61**

0715-2973 *See* ADULT CORRECTIONAL SERVICES IN CANADA. **3078**

0715-3007 *See* SIDETREKKED. **3436**

0715-3015 *See* LIVYERE, THE. **2744**

0715-3023 *See* LAND AND HUMAN SETTLEMENTS. **2910**

0715-3139 *See* ALS NEWS. **3802**

0715-3155 *See* ALBERTA SASKATCHEWAN MANITOBA CRIMINAL DECISIONS. **3104**

0715-321X *See* VALLEY REPORTER. **5796**

0715-3236 *See* NEWSLETTER / NORTHWESTERN SOCIETY OF INTESTINAL RESEARCH. **3800**

0715-3244 *See* CANADIAN JOURNAL OF NATIVE STUDIES, THE. **2726**

0715-3325 *See* OTTAWA REPORTER, THE. **5792**

0715-3341 *See* NEWS WAVE. **326**

0715-3368 *See* NEWSLETTER / NATIONAL SURVIVAL INSTITUTE. **2219**

0715-3392 *See* UPDATE / INTERPRETATION CANADA. **1789**

0715-3465 *See* NEWSLETTER - LAW SOCIETY OF ALBERTA. **3017**

0715-3481 *See* MANITOBA SOCIAL WORKER. **5295**

0715-3570 *See* INTERVENTIONS ECONOMIQUES POUR UNE ALTERNATIVE SOCIALE. **1497**

0715-3627 *See* HALIFAX FIELD NATURALISTS NEWSLETTER. **4166**

0715-3651 *See* CANOLA DIGEST. **72**

0715-366X *See* BULLETIN - ONTARIO DIVISION. CANADIAN RED CROSS SOCIETY. **4769**

0715-3732 See UPDATE, MARKET FORECAST, ELECTRIC ENERGY REQUIREMENTS IN THE NORTHWEST TERRITORIES. **1959**

0715-3740 *See* UPDATE, MARKET FORECAST, ELECTRIC ENERGY REQUIREMENTS IN THE NORTHWEST TERRITORIES. **1959**

0715-3759 *See* BRIEFLY SPEAKING. **2943**

0715-3775 *See* CANADIAN IRIS SOCIETY NEWSLETTER. **5229**

0715-3783 *See* GRENVILLE SENTINEL. **2735**

0715-3902 *See* EKATA. **2532**

0715-3910 *See* RANJIT. **5793**

0715-4011 *See* INTERIOR VOICE. **3396**

0715-4046 *See* SENIORS TODAY. **5182**

0715-4054 *See* ARAB DAWN (1977). **4515**

0715-4100 *See* NEWS, VIEWS AND REVIEWS - ARCHITECTURAL INSTITUTE OF BRITISH COLUMBIA. **304**

0715-4127 See GRANDE PRAIRIE CITY DIRECTORY. **4652**

0715-4135 *See* AWAZ (TORONTO). **5780**

0715-4143 *See* HA-SHILTH-SA. **5785**

0715-4186 *See* NEWSLETTER - NATIONAL LEGAL AID RESEARCH CENTRE. **3180**

0715-4224 *See* PLEA. PUBLIC LEGAL EDUCATION ASSOCIATION OF SASKATCHEWAN. **3029**

0715-4259 *See* BETWEEN THE ISSUES. **2212**

0715-4267 *See* BULLETIN (INTER PARES (ORGANIZATION)). **2908**

0715-4275 *See* NEWSLETTER / WEST COAST ENVIRONMENTAL LAW RESEARCH FOUNDATION. **3115**

0715-4283 *See* NEWSLETTER - TASK FORCE ON WOMEN'S ISSUES. **5563**

0715-4321 *See* DAILY NEWS HALIFAX-DARTMOUTH EDITION. **5783**

0715-433X *See* NEWSLETTER / THE CALGARY INSTITUTE FOR THE HUMANITIES. **2851**

0715-4356 *See* PRO-LIFE NEWS. **3767**

0715-4372 *See* VOICE OF THE HURON FARMER, THE. **145**

0715-4410 *See* NEA TOY HAMILTON. **5790**

0715-4437 *See* KINATUINAMOT ILLENGAJUK / LABRADOR INUIT ASSOCIATION. **2536**

0715-4445 *See* NEW PERSPECTIVE (HAMILTON). **2269**

0715-4461 *See* MARKHAM MONTH. **2538**

0715-4488 *See* GRAVELBOURG GAZETTE. **5785**

0715-450X *See* TIMES OF DOWNTOWN LONDON, THE. **2547**

0715-4518 *See* FLETCHER-O'LEARY PERIODICAL, THE. **2448**

0715-4526 *See* NEWSLETTER / B.C.A.I. CENTRE. **216**

0715-4534 *See* PAPERS PRESENTED AT THE MID-WINTER MEETING OF THE ALBERTA BRANCH OF THE CANADIAN BAR ASSOCIATION. **3024**

0715-4542 *See* CANADIAN QUARTERLY ECONOMIC REVIEW. **1550**

0715-4569 *See* LUMBY REVIEW. **5789**

0715-4593 *See* KOOTENAY GRAPEVINE, THE. **5788**

0715-4631 *See* LEASIDE VILLAGER, THE. **5788**

0715-464X *See* FOREST HILL VILLAGER. **5784**

0715-4674 *See* NORTHERN ALBERTA FARMER (FORT SASKATCHEWAN). **115**

0715-4690 *See* AU NATUREL (MONTREAL). **4768**

0715-4720 *See* WAYZGOOSE. **4570**

0715-4739 *See* LANARK, LEEDS AND GRENVILLE COMMUNITY INFORMATION DIRECTORY. **5294**

0715-4747 *See* CASSIOPEIA (VICTORIA). **394**

0715-4755 *See* NEWFOUNDLAND & PRINCE EDWARD ISLAND REPORTS (BOUND CUMULATION). **3017**

0715-4771 *See* INTER-AMERICAN ARBITRATION. **2983**

0715-478X *See* COMMON GROUND (CHARLOTTETOWN). **5553**

0715-4798 *See* BRITISH COLUMBIA DECISIONS, STATUTE CITATOR. **2943**

0715-4801 *See* PANJABI ESHEEA TAEEMZ (MARCH, 1975). **5792**

0715-4828 *See* CIRCUIT (FREDERICTON). **3691**

0715-4844 *See* ACTUALITE-SEMENCE. **161**

0715-4860 *See* CANADIAN RIGHTS REPORTER. SECOND SERIES. **4505**

0715-4887 *See* VALLEY NEWS (MONTEBELLO). **5796**

0715-4895 *See* VANCOUVER NEWS (VANCOUVER, 1977). **5797**

0715-4925 *See* FORT MCMURRAY EXPRESS. **5784**

0715-4941 *See* LABRADORIAN, THE. **5788**

0715-495X *See* HUSKY FEVER. **4899**

0715-4976 *See* SAINT JOHN FOLK CLUB RAG, THE. **4151**

0715-4992 *See* ROCKY VIEW TIMES, THE. **5794**

0715-5034 *See* S & L MUSEUM NEWSLETTER. **4096**

0715-5042 *See* FARM PAPER. **85**

0715-5050 *See* REGIONAL REFLECTIONS. **4679**

0715-5077 See CRAFT CONNECTION, THE. **371**

0715-5093 *See* ATUAGATSANGA / LABRADOR CRAFT PRODUCERS ASSOCIATION. **370**

0715-5131 *See* FREE PRESS (SPARWOOD). **5784**

0715-514X *See* NORTHERN JOURNAL, THE. **5791**

0715-5166 *See* INTERCULTURAL STUDIES (MONTREAL, QUEBEC). **1753**

0715-5182 *See* BACKYARDS. **1060**

0715-5212 *See* SOCIETY NEWS - SOCIETY OF ONTARIO HYDRO MANAGEMENT AND PROFESSIONAL STAFF. **1627**

0715-5271 *See* RURAL ROUTE (WALLACEBURG, ONT.). **5794**

0715-5301 See FORUM - CANADIAN COUNCIL ON 4-H CLUBS. **5231**

0715-5328 See PEEL MULTICULTURAL SCENE. **2270**

0715-5352 See IGNACE COURIER. **5786**

0715-5360 See KETTLE RIVER ECHO, THE. **5788**

0715-5379 See NEWS / BRITISH COLUMBIA MEDICAL ASSOCIATION. **3621**

0715-545X See COUNTY NEIGHBOURS. **5782**

0715-5468 See MADISON'S CANADIAN LUMBER REPORTER. **2402**

0715-5476 See OSCAR : OTTAWA SOUTH COMMUNITY ASSOCIATION REVIEW. **5792**

0715-5484 See NEWSFLASH / NEW BRUNSWICK TEACHERS' ASSOCIATION. **1768**

0715-5514 See PERSONNEL (OTTAWA). **4673**

0715-5522 See SNAFU (LOW). **4866**

0715-5549 See NIGHTWINDS. **3417**

0715-5646 See PUBLIC LETTER (MISSISSAUGA). **2543**

0715-5654 See CMHA FOCUS. **5279**

0715-5689 See CITY & COUNTRY HOME. **2904**

0715-5719 See PLASTIZINE. **381**

0715-5735 See PENSE PROGRESS. **5792**

0715-5778 See CALENDAR (WINFIELD). **5781**

0715-5786 See NORTH SHORE SENTINEL. **5791**

0715-5808 See BRITISH COLUMBIA LABOUR RELATIONS BOARD DECISIONS. **3144**

0715-5840 See NYUGATI MAGYARSAG (CALGARY). **2751**

0715-5867 See RAPPORT - NORTH CENTRAL REGIONAL LIBRARY SYSTEM (NEWSLETTER). **3244**

0715-5891 See FUR-BEARERS, THE. **226**

0715-5913 See PATRIS (VANCOUVER). **5792**

0715-5921 See SRBIJA (WINONA). **5795**

0715-5948 See HI-RISE. **2534**

0715-5956 See CBAC NEWS. **347**

0715-5980 See NEWSLETTER (CRIMINAL LAWYERS' ASSOCIATION (TORONTO, ONT.)). **3108**

0715-5999 See CANADIAN SPEECH COMMUNICATION JOURNAL. **1105**

0715-6065 See INFOSEVEC. **1752**

0715-6219 See RAPPORT ANNUEL / MINISTERE DE L'AGRICULTURE, DES PECHERIES ET DE LA'ALIMENTATION. **4678**

0715-6359 See UNION EXPRESS, L'. **1716**

0715-6448 See MAJOR CAPITAL PROJECTS INVENTORY. **797**

0715-6510 See REPORT OF THE COUNCIL FOR FRANCO-ONTARIAN EDUCATION. **1778**

0715-6618 See REPERTOIRE DES VINS ET DES SPIRITUEUX, QUEBEC. **2370**

0715-6626 See STUDIO MAGAZINE, THE. **382**

0715-6669 See REVUE CREDIT. **885**

0715-6758 See ANNUAL REPORT / MANITOBA DATA SERVICES. **1235**

0715-6804 See MUNICIPAL OFFICIALS OF MANITOBA. **4667**

0715-7037 See DIALOGUE - COUNCIL OF MINISTERS OF EDUCATION. **3277**

0715-7045 See CURRENTS (TORONTO). **5244**

0715-7053 See MOVING TO & AROUND WINNIPEG & MANITOBA. **4841**

0715-7118 See CANADIAN LEGISLATURES. **4636**

0715-741X See BORDURES. **3922**

0715-7533 See LTBC : LIBRARY TECHNICIANS ASSOCIATION OF BRITISH COLUMBIA. **3229**

0715-7541 See NOUVELLES D'ICITTE. **2751**

0715-7592 See INFO-BOURG. **4656**

0715-7649 See ANALYSTE (MONTREAL, QUEBEC). **2527**

0715-7657 See STATISTICS ON ALCOHOL AND DRUG USE IN CANADA AND OTHER COUNTRIES. **1350**

0715-7746 See BULLETIN DE L'ASSOCIATION QUEBECOISE DE TELEDETECTION. **2037**

0715-7770 See RAPPORT ANNUEL / OFFICE DE LA SECURITE DU REVENU DES CHASSEURS ET PIEGEURS CRIS. **5303**

0715-7908 See STATISTIQUES SUR LA RECHERCHE ET LE DEVELOPPEMENT INDUSTRIELS AU QUEBEC. **5160**

0715-7975 See PROFIL (LONGUEUIL). **849**

0715-7983 See NORTHERN DECISIONS. **3115**

0715-8130 See REPERTOIRE (UNIVERSITE DU QUEBEC A MONTREAL). **4832**

0715-8238 See COUP D'OEIL (VICTORIAVILLE). **1818**

0715-8556 See TAX NOTES (EDMONTON). **4753**

0715-8564 See ASSUREUR VIE A L'ECOUTE. **2874**

0715-8599 See LORRAIN, LE. **4663**

0715-8602 See JOURNAL - CANADIAN RED CROSS SOCIETY. BLOOD PROGRAMME. **5291**

0715-8629 See TECHNICAL REPORT - UNIVERSITY OF GUELPH, SCHOOL OF ENGINEERING. **1998**

0715-8645 See RESEARCH REPORT / ATOMIC ENERGY CONTROL BOARD. **1955**

0715-8661 See CISTI NEWS. **3202**

0715-8726 See VOX BENEDICTINA. **5038**

0715-8777 See COMPASS (TORONTO). **4949**

0715-8904 See NATIONAL NEWSLETTER (CANADIAN PARENTS FOR FRENCH). **3305**

0715-8912 See RAYON (SAINTE-AGATHE-DES-MONTS). **3244**

0715-8920 See TEXTE (TORONTO). **3354**

0715-9048 See COMPUTER PROCESSING OF CHINESE & ORIENTAL LANGUAGES. **3274**

0715-9293 See REPORT ON THE DEMOGRAPHIC SITUATION IN CANADA. **4562**

0715-9366 See WHO'S WHO IN CANADIAN LITERATURE. **3453**

0715-9471 See CANADIAN PALLIATIVE CARE DIRECTORY, THE. **3778**

0715-9609 See DIDASCO. **1735**

0715-9684 See PSYCHOTROPES (MONTREAL). **1348**

0715-9714 See ANNUAL REPORT / SASKATCHEWAN HEALTH RESEARCH BOARD. **4766**

0715-9781 See SECTION A - REVUE D'ARCHITECTURE. **308**

0715-9862 See PERFORATIONS. **4076**

0715-9897 See CLIMAT (MONTREAL). **1421**

0715-9900 See APOSTROPHE (SILLERY). **5551**

0715-9994 See REVUE FRONTENAC. **3431**

0716-0046 See CUADERNOS DE ECONOMIA (SANTIAGO). **1478**

0716-0054 See NUCLEOTECNICA. **2157**

0716-0095 See CARTA MAGNETICA DE CHILE. **1353**

0716-0127 See AREA GEOCIENCIAS. **1366**

0716-0151 See RESUMENES ANALITICOS EN EDUCACION. **1797**

0716-0240 See ESTUDIOS INTERNACIONALES. **4473**

0716-0321 See ESTUDIOS SOCIALES (SANTIAGO, CHILE). **5199**

0716-0348 See APUNTES DE INGENIERIA. **1965**

0716-0518 See EDUCACION FISICA, CHILE / UNIVERSIDAD DE CHILE, FACULTAD DE EDUCACION, DEPARTAMENTO DE EDUCACION FISCA, DEPORTES Y RECREATION. **1855**

0716-0542 See LENGUAS MODERNAS (SANTIAGO). **3297**

0716-0631 See COLECCION ESTUDIOS CIEPLAN. **1552**

0716-0720 See PARASITOLOGIA AL DIA : REVISTA DE LA SOCIEDAD CHILENA DE PARASITOLOGIA. **3626**

0716-0763 See BOLETIN ANTARTICO CHILENO. **2551**

0716-078X See REVISTA CHILENA DE HISTORIA NATURAL (VALPARAISO, CHILE : 1983). **4171**

0716-0852 See ARQ. **292**

0716-0909 See ACTA LITERARIA. **3337**

0716-114X See BOLETIN MICOLOGICO. **5506**

0716-1174 See INGENIERIA DE SISTEMAS. **1978**

0716-1182 See CHUNGARA. **266**

0716-1190 See CHILE FORESTAL. **2377**

0716-1220 See REVISTA DE PSIQUIATRIA CLINICA DEL DEPARTAMENTO DE PSIQUIATRIA Y SALUD MENTAL, DIVISION DE CIENCIAS MEDICAS NORTE, FACULTAD DE MEDICINA, UNIVERSIDAD DE CHILE. **3936**

0716-1417 See REVISTA DE CIENCIA POLITICA (SANTIAGO). **4494**

0716-1468 See ESTUDIOS NORTEAMERICANOS. **2732**

0716-1530 See BOLETIN DEL MUSEO CHILENO DE ARTE PRECOLOMBINO. **232**

0716-1549 See REVISTA CHILENA DE NUTRICION : ORGANO OFICIAL DE LA SOCIEDAD CHILENA DE NUTRICION, BROMATOLOGIA Y TOXICOLOGIA. **4198**

0716-1689 See AGRO-CIENCIA / FACULTAD DE CIENCIAS AGROPECUARIAS Y FORESTALES, UNIVERSIDAD DE CONCEPCION. **55**

0716-2006 See CIENCIA Y TECNOLOGIA DEL MAR / COMITE OCEANOGRAFICO NACIONAL. **1447**

0716-2138 See BIZANTION NEA HELLAS. **3367**

0716-2308 See CELULOSA Y PAPEL. **4233**

0716-2367 See BOLETIN MENSUAL - BANCO CENTRAL DE CHILE. **779**

0716-2405 See INDICADORES DE COMERCIO EXTERIOR. **840**

0716-260X See AVANCES EN CIENCIAS VETERINARIAS. **5505**

0716-2774 See ENFOQUES EN ATENCION PRIMARIA. **3574**

0716-2790 See REVISTA MUSICAL CHILENA. **4150**

0716-2812 See REVISTA CHILENA DE HISTORIA Y GEOGRAFIA. **2757**

0716-3428 See EDUCACION FISICA, CHILE / UNIVERSIDAD DE CHILE, FACULTAD DE EDUCACION, DEPARTAMENTO DE EDUCACION FISCA, DEPORTES Y RECREATION. **1855**

0716-3460 See HOY. **3344**

0716-3630 See REVISTA CHILENA DE PSICOLOGIA. **4616**

0716-5072 See ACTA ENTOMOLOGICA CHILENA. **5604**

0716-534X See REVISTA FRUTICOLA. **129**

0716-5439 See BOLETIN DE LA ACADEMIA CHILENA DE LA HISTORIA. **2723**

0716-5447 See REVISTA CHILENA DE HISTORIA DEL DERECHO. **3040**

0716-5455 See REVISTA DE ESTUDIOS HISTORICO-JURIDICOS. **3041**

0716-5463 See BOLETIN DE LA ACADEMIA CHILENA CORRESPONDIENTE DE LA REAL ACADEMIA ESPANOLA. **3368**

0716-5803 See REVISTA DE MATEMATICAS APLICADAS. **3531**

0716-5927 See REVISTA DE ANALISIS ECONOMICO / PROGRAMA DE POSTGRADO EN ECONOMIA, ILADES / GEORGETOWN UNIVERSITY. **1595**

0716-5994 See CIENCIA E INVESTIGACION FORESTAL. **2377**

0716-6478 See ANALES DEL INSTITUTO DE LA PATAGONIA. SERIE CIENCIAS SOCIALES. **5190**

0716-6486 See ANALES DEL INSTITUTO DE LA PATAGONIA. SERIE CIENCIAS NATURALES. **4161**

0716-7865 See DERECHO A LA INFANCIA. **5281**

0716-8446 See SCIENTIA. SERIES A. MATHEMATICAL SCIENCES. **3533**

0716-9760 See BIOLOGICAL RESEARCH. **445**

0720-0056 See BRUCKMANNS PANTHEON. **345**

0720-0447 See FORUM KRITISCHE PSYCHOLOGIE. **4587**

0720-048X See EUROPEAN JOURNAL OF RADIOLOGY. **3941**

0720-0536 See MIKROOEKOLOGIE UND THERAPIE. **3617**

0720-0587 See ZEITSCHRIFT FUER BADER- UND KLIMAHEILKUNDE. **3652**

0720-0706 See LUNGE + ATMUNG. A. **3950**

0720-0730 See HERZ + GEFASSE. **3583**

0720-0773 *See* SEAWATER AND DESALTING. 2243

0720-1206 *See* DEUTSCHE LEBENSMITTEL-EINZELHANDEL IM SPIEGEL DER STATISTIK, DER. 2333

0720-1214 *See* QZ. QUALITAT UND ZUVERLASSIGKEIT. 1623

0720-1370 *See* SICHERHEIT IN CHEMIE UND UMWELT. 992

0720-1605 *See* STRAFVERTEIDIGER. 3109

0720-1842 *See* ZOOPHYSIOLOGY. 5603

0720-1877 *See* SCHRIFTENREIHE DER GDMB GESELLSCHAFT DEUTSCHER METALLHUTTEN- UND BERGLEUTE. 4018

0720-1893 *See* ARCHIV FUER TIERARZTLICHE FORTBILDUNG. 5504

0720-213X *See* ZOOMORPHOLOGY. 5603

0720-2156 *See* ARCHAEOLOGIA ATLANTICA. 256

0720-2563 *See* NUMBER THEORY. 3525

0720-2571 *See* TOPOLOGY (BERLIN, WEST). 3539

0720-258X *See* NUMERICAL ANALYSIS. 3525

0720-2598 *See* GEOMETRY. 3507

0720-2601 *See* REAL ANALYSIS. 3530

0720-261X *See* PARTIAL DIFFERENTIAL EQUATIONS. 3526

0720-2628 *See* PROBABILITY AND STOCHASTIC PROCESSES. 3527

0720-2946 *See* DRUCKSACHE - BUNDESRAT. 4472

0720-3098 *See* ALLMENDE. 3359

0720-3322 *See* RADIOLOGIE. 3945

0720-3373 *See* KRANKENHAUS-HYGIENE + INFEKTIONSVERHUTUNG. 4788

0720-3438 *See* WARMETECHNIK. 2608

0720-3462 *See* ERGEBNISSE DER CHIRURGISCHEN ONKOLOGIE. 3816

0720-3659 *See* GESCHICHTE IN KOLN. 2689

0720-3772 *See* NEUERWERBUNGEN THEOLOGIE UND ALLGEMEINE RELIGIONSWISSENSCHAFT. 4980

0720-3896 *See* BALLETT-JOURNAL/DAS TANZARCHIV. 1311

0720-3977 *See* KRANKENHAUSTECHNIK. 3787

0720-423X *See* PAN (OFFENBURG). 361

0720-4299 *See* FORTSCHRITTE DER NEUROLOGIE, PSYCHIATRIE. 3833

0720-4361 *See* ZEITSCHRIFT FUER SOZIALISATIONSFORSCHUNG UND ERZIEHUNGSSOZIOLOGIE. 5265

0720-4442 *See* MC : DIE MIKROCOMPUTER-ZEITSCHRIFT. 1269

0720-454X *See* GEOOKODYNAMIK. 1355

0720-485X *See* DIFFERENTIAL GEOMETRICAL METHODS IN MATHEMATICAL PHYSICS. 4401

0720-5007 *See* BEHINDERTENPADAGOGIK IN THEORIE UND PRAXIS. 1875

0720-5104 *See* REITEN UND FAHREN. 4914

0720-5139 *See* AKTUELLER INFORMATIONSDIENST AFRIKA. BEIHEFT / INSTITUT FUER AFRIKA-KUNDE, DOKUMENTATIONS-LEITSTELLE AFRIKA. 2498

0720-5260 *See* FOTOGESCHICHTE. 4369

0720-5775 *See* RHETORIK. 3317

0720-5953 *See* KONSTRUKTION (1981). 2120

0720-5988 *See* MEXICON. 2746

0720-6003 *See* ARZTEZEITSCHRIFT FUER NATURHEILVERFAHREN : ORGAN DES ZENTRALVERBANDES DER ARZTE FUER NATURHEILVERFAHREN E. V. 3553

0720-6240 *See* ET. ENERGIEWIRTSCHAFTLICHE TAGESFRAGEN. 1944

0720-6763 *See* ABI-TECHNIK. 3186

0720-678X *See* SPRINGER SERIES IN INFORMATION SCIENCES. 4619

0720-7123 *See* AUSKUNFT. 3193

0720-728X *See* MATHEMATISCHE SEMESTERBERICHTE. 3522

0720-8006 *See* BAYERISCHE BLATTER FUER VOLKSKUNDE. 231

0720-8073 *See* WIND KRAFT JOURNAL. 1960

0720-8227 *See* ANGEWANDTE STATISTIK UND OKONOMETRIE. 1528

0720-8715 *See* PROCEEDINGS OF THE INTERNATIONAL WORKSHOP ON GROSS PROPERTIES OF NUCLEI AND NUCLEAR EXCITATIONS. 4450

0720-8731 *See* FETT IN DER PARENTERALEN ERNAHRUNG. 4191

0720-9207 *See* JAHRESTAGUNG KERNTECHNIK. 2156

0720-9339 See AUSZUGE AUS DEN EUROPAISCHEN PATENTSCHRIFTEN. TEIL III, UBRIGE VERARBEITUNGSINDUSTRIE UND ARBEITSVERFAHREN, MASCHINEN- UND FAHRZEUGBAU, ERNAHRUNG, LANDWIRTSCHAFT. 1301

0720-9339 See AUSZUGE AUS DEN EUROPAISCHEN PATENTSCHRIFTEN. TEIL II, ELEKTROTECHNIK, PHYSIK, FEINMECHANIK UND OPTIK, AKUSTIK. 1301

0720-9339 See AUSZUGE AUS DEN EUROPAISCHEN PATENTSCHRIFTEN. TEIL I, GRUND- UND ROHSTOFFINDUSTRIE, CHEMIE UND HUTTENWESEN, BAUWESEN, BERGBAU. 1301

0720-9355 *See* HAEMOSTASEOLOGIE. 3580

0720-9428 *See* HENKEL-REFERATE : EXCERPTS OF HENKEL RESEARCH PAPERS. 976

0720-9525 *See* THEMEN DER PRAKTISCHEN THEOLOGIE, THEOLOGIA PRACTICA. 5003

0720-9762 *See* ZEITSCHRIFT FUER PHYSIKALISCHE MEDIZIN, BALNEOLOGIE, MED. KLIMATOLOGIE. 3653

0720-9878 *See* INFORMATIONSDIENST - VEREIN DEUTSCHER INGENIEURE. NEUE FERTIGUNGSVERFAHREN. 1978

0720-9886 *See* INFORMATIONSDIENST - VEREIN DEUTSCHER INGENIEURE. MECHANISCHE VERBINDUNGSTECHNIK. 1978

0720-9940 *See* VERFAHRENSRICHTLINIEN FUER DIE MIKROBIOLOGISCHE DIAGNOSTIK. 570

0721-0078 *See* REVUE INTERNATIONALE DE PARODONTIE & DENTISTERIE RESTAURATRICE. 1335

0721-099X *See* MITTEILUNGSBLATT DER BUNDESANSTALT FUER FLEISCHFORSCHUNG, KULMBACH. 216

0721-1244 *See* FREIZEITPADAGOGIK. 1747

0721-1392 *See* AMERICAN UNIVERSITY STUDIES. SERIES I, GERMANIC LANGUAGES AND LITERATURES. 3263

0721-1457 *See* SCHRIFTENREIHE DER BUNDESAPOTHEKERKAMMER ZUR WISSENSCHAFTLICHEN FORTBILDUNG. GRUNE REIHE. 4329

0721-1694 *See* GSF-BERICHT. 2173

0721-183X *See* BUNTE HUND, DER. 1060

0721-1902 *See* DB. DEUTSCHE BAUZEITUNG (1981). 296

0721-1937 *See* ANZEIGER FUER DIE SEELSORGE. 4935

0721-2178 *See* E+Z, ENTWICKLUNG UND ZUSAMMENARBEIT. 1490

0721-2399 *See* ARCHAOLOGISCHE JAHR IN BAYERN, DAS. 258

0721-2585 *See* HK, HOLZ- UND MOBELINDUSTRIE. 634

0721-2631 *See* STATISTICS & DECISIONS. 5342

0721-2887 *See* MIGRATION (BERLIN, WEST). 1920

0721-3107 *See* AFRIKA UND DIE DEUTSCHEN : JAHRBUCH DER DEUTSCHEN AFRIKA-STIFTUNG. 2637

0721-3115 *See* PROPELLANTS, EXPLOSIVES, PYROTECHNICS. 1028

0721-3220 *See* SHIPPING STATISTICS YEARBOOK. 5456

0721-3719 *See* JAPANISCHE STUDIEN ZUR DEUTSCHEN SPRACHE UND LITERATUR. 3289

0721-3727 *See* GERMANIC STUDIES IN AMERICA. 3390

0721-3735 *See* LUBECKER SCHRIFTEN ZUR ARCHAOLOGIE UND KULTURGESCHICHTE / AMT FUER VOR- UND FRUHGESCHICHTE (BODENDENKMALPFLEGE) DER HANSESTADT LUBECK. 273

0721-3743 *See* BLOCH-ALMANACH. 4342

0721-3751 *See* SHIPPING STATISTICS (ZEITSCHRIFT). 5456

0721-3808 *See* ZEITSCHRIFT FUER WIRTSCHAFTSPOLITIK. 1528

0721-4030 *See* NEW YORKER STUDIEN ZUR NEUEREN DEUTSCHEN LITERATURGESCHICHTE. 3416

0721-4049 *See* PROGRESS IN CLINICAL PHARMACOLOGY. 4326

0721-4235 *See* DAIDALOS. 296

0721-4294 *See* TRIERER STUDIEN ZUR LITERATUR. 3447

0721-4499 *See* GC. GRUNER MARKT, GARTENCENTER +. 2416

0721-4502 *See* STUDIEN ZUR KRITISCHEN PSYCHOLOGIE. 4619

0721-4588 *See* RENO. 706

0721-474X *See* FORUM - KIELER WISSENSCHAFTSVERLAG VAUK. 88

0721-4979 *See* KARLSRUHER BEITRAEGE. 2695

0721-5088 *See* INFORMATIONSDIENST SUDLICHES AFRIKA. 4477

0721-5185 *See* TJI : TOBACCO JOURNAL INTERNATIONAL. 5373

0721-5207 *See* CURRENT CONTENTS AFRICA. 2496

0721-5231 *See* ASIEN. 2501

0721-5665 *See* PHARMA-MARKETING-JOURNAL. 1512

0721-6173 *See* BAUWIRTSCHAFTLICHE INFORMATIONEN / BETRIEBSWIRTSCHAFTLICHES INSTITUT DER WESTDEUTSCHEN BAUINDUSTRIE. 600

0721-6858 See EUROPEAN RESEARCH LIBRARIES COOPERATION : THE LIBER QUARTERLY. 3209

0721-6890 *See* WISTRA. 3109

0721-6912 *See* FOOD COMPOSITION AND NUTRITION TABLES / DIE ZUSAMMENSETZUNG DER LEBENSMITTEL, NAEHRWERT-TABELLEN. 4191

0721-7110 *See* VITAMIN D. 4200

0721-7153 *See* BIELEFELDER KATALOG KLASSIK. 5320

0721-7242 *See* INFORMATIONSDIENST - VEREIN DEUTSCHER INGENIEURE. STRANGPRESSEN VON METALLEN. 1978

0721-7250 *See* APPLIED PHYSICS. A, SOLIDS AND SURFACES. 4397

0721-7269 *See* APPLIED PHYSICS. B, PHOTOPHYSICS AND LASER CHEMISTRY. 4433

0721-7595 *See* JOURNAL OF PLANT GROWTH REGULATION. 515

0721-7714 *See* PLANT CELL REPORTS. 539

0721-7730 *See* FOTO CREATIV. 4369

0721-8184 *See* SELECTA (PLANEGG, GERMANY). 3640

0721-8222 *See* RHEUMA, SCHMERZ & ENTZUNDUNG. 3637

0721-832X *See* GRAEFE'S ARCHIVE FOR CLINICAL AND EXPERIMENTAL OPHTHALMOLOGY. 3875

0721-8400 *See* GEOGRAPHIE HEUTE. 2563

0721-8672 *See* STUDENT UND PRAKTIKANT. 4330

0721-9067 *See* ZEITSCHRIFT FUER SPRACHWISSENSCHAFT : ORGAN DER DEUTSCHEN GESELLSCHAFT FUER SPRACHWISSENSCHAFT. 3335

0721-9245 *See* BPT-BERICHT. 3558

0721-930X *See* JAHRESBERICHT - GESELLSCHAFT FUER STRAHLEN- UND UMWELTFORSCHUNG MHB MUNCHEN. 460

0721-9318 *See* ANGIO : ZEITSCHRIFT DER DEUTSCHEN GESELLSCHAFT FUER GEFASSCHIRURGIE. 3698

0721-9776 *See* ESSEN & TRINKEN. 2334

0722-0057 *See* REFERATEORGAN MESSEN MECHANISCHER GROSSEN. 1993

0722-0189 *See* BEITRAEGE ZUR FEMINISTISCHEN THEORIE UND PRAXIS. 5551

0722-0723 *See* CATENA SUPPLEMENT. 1353

0722-0839 See DEUTSCHER FORSCHUNGSDIENST. GERMAN RESEARCH SERVICE. 5099

0722-0987 See COMPUTER PERSONLICH. 1177

0722-1029 See PTA IN DER APOTHEKE. 4326

0722-1541 See NERVENHEILKUNDE. 3839

0722-1819 See HANDCHIRURGIE, MIKROCHIRURGIE, PLASTISCHE CHIRURGIE. 3965

0722-219X See TUMORDIAGNOSTIK & THERAPIE. 3824

0722-2416 See GERMAN YEARBOOK ON BUSINESS HISTORY. 1564

0722-2432 See ARBEITSKOSTEN IM PRODUZIERENDEN GEWERBE UND IM DIENSTLEISTUNGSBEREICH. 1529

0722-2572 See OFFICE-MANAGEMENT (BADEN-BADEN). 880

0722-2858 See RUNDSCHAU FUER INTERNATIONALE DAMENMODE MIT DOB- + HAKA-PRAXIS. 1087

0722-2866 See RUNDSCHAU FUER INTERNATIONALE HERRENMODE MIT DOB- + HAKA-PRAXIS. 1087

0722-2904 See TECNOLOGIA MILITAR. 4059

0722-2912 See DIN-MITTEILUNGEN + ELEKTRONORM. 4030

0722-3056 See ZENTRALBLATT RECHTSMEDIZIN. 3743

0722-3064 See ZENTRALBLATT NEUROLOGIE, PSYCHIATRIE. 3847

0722-3072 See ZENTRALBLATT RADIOLOGIE. 3947

0722-3218 See PACKAGING SCIENCE AND TECHNOLOGY ABSTRACTS. 5175

0722-3226 See MILITARY TECHNOLOGY. 4051

0722-3250 See DEUTSCHE-BANK-BULLETIN ENGLISCHE AUSGABE. 787

0722-3269 See ADVANCES IN PHYSICAL GEOCHEMISTRY. 960

0722-3277 See ZEITSCHRIFT FUER PHYSIK. B, CONDENSED MATTER. 4425

0722-3285 See ARBEITSMARKT IN HESSEN. JAHRESBERICHT, DER. 1651

0722-348X See ZEITSCHRIFT FUER PHYTOTHERAPIE. 531

0722-3587 See ASSISTENZ. 2255

0722-3625 See SCHWERPUNKT MEDIZIN. 3639

0722-3684 See FUNKTIONELLE BIOLOGIE & MEDIZIN. 456

0722-3773 See NEUE ENTOMOLOGISCHE NACHRICHTEN. 5592

0722-382X See BERICHTE DES INSTITUTES FUER METEOROLOGIE UND GEOPHYSIK DER UNIVERSITAT FRANKFUERT/MAIN. 1420

0722-3951 See VGB-TB. 1960

0722-4028 See CORAL REEFS. 1448

0722-4060 See POLAR BIOLOGY. 5594

0722-4087 See INTERNATIONALE JAHRESTAGUNG / FRAUNHOFER-INSTITUT FUER TREIB-UND EXPLOSIVSTOFFE. 2013

0722-4397 See ZKG INTERNATIONAL. 632

0722-4400 See ZKG INTERNATIONAL. EDITION B. 632

0722-477X See PRAXIS MEDIZINISCHER DOKUMENTATION / DEUTSCHER VERBAND MEDIZINISCHER DOKUMENTARE E.V. 3629

0722-480X See SUDOST EUROPA : [MONATSSCHRIFT DER ABTEILUNG GEGENWARTSFORSCHUNG DES SUDOST-INSTITUTS]. 5224

0722-5091 See CLINICAL NEUROPATHOLOGY. 3894

0722-5369 See JAHRBUCH FUER NEUE POLITISCHE OKONOMIE. 1497

0722-5733 See ZFL : INTERN. ZEITSCHRIFT FUER LEBENSMITTEL-TECHNOLOGIE UND -VERFAHRENSTECHNIK. 2361

0722-6268 See BALLETT INTERNATIONAL. 1310

0722-6349 See RESEARCH (GOTTINGEN, GERMANY). 244

0722-6764 See CHEMIE IN LABOR UND BIOTECHNIK : CLB. 969

0722-6950 See DYNAMIK IM HANDEL 1982. 2334

0722-6985 See ZENTRALORGAN CHIRURGIE. 3978

0722-706X See FISCHWAID (1982). 2301

0722-7485 See ZEITSCHRIFT FUHRUNG + ORGANISATION : ZFO. 725

0722-7566 See FAC, FORTSCHRITTE DER ANTIMIKROBIELLEN UND ANTINEOPLASTISCHEN CHEMOTHERAPIE. 3817

0722-7728 See BERICHTE AUS WASSERGUTEWIRTSCHAFT UND GESUNDHEITSINGENIEURWESEN. 5087

0722-7736 See MITTEILUNGEN AUS DEM AUSSCHUSS FUER PULVERMETALLURGIE. 4012

0722-7833 See SIEGENER PERIODICUM ZUR INTERNATIONALEN EMPIRISCHEN LITERATURWISSENSCHAFT. 3436

0722-7906 See INTEGER PROGRAMMING AND RELATED AREAS. 3509

0722-8287 See NAHVERKEHR, DER. 5442

0722-8333 See UNFALLVERHUTUNGSBERICHT STRASSENVERKEHR : BERICHT DES BUNDESMINISTERS FUER VERKEHR UBER MASSNAHMEN AUF DEM GEBIET DER UNFALLVERHUTUNG IM STRASSENVERKEHR. 5398

0722-8821 See SUDOSTASIEN AKTUELL. 2665

0722-8880 See NAVAL FORCES. 4180

0722-8953 See ZENTRALBLATT KINDERHEILKUNDE. 3912

0722-9003 See LASER UND OPTOELEKTRONIK. 4411

0722-9313 See DIN-KATALOG FUER TECHNISCHE REGELN. 5099

0722-9488 See TIZ. 2152

0722-9674 See BERICHTE PATHOLOGIE. 3893

0722-9852 See BERICHTE GYNAKOLOGIE, GEBURTSHILFE. 3757

0722-9933 See ZENTRALBLATT OPHTHALMOLOGIE. 3880

0723-0036 See ZAHLEN ZUR KOHLENWIRTSCHAFT. 1632

0723-0311 See PSP : PFLANZENSCHUTZ-PRAXIS. 525

0723-0338 See REAL (BERLIN, WEST). 3428

0723-0516 See JAHRBUCH / THOMAS-MORUS-GESELLSCHAFT. 3398

0723-0664 See TECHNIK UND GESELLSCHAFT (FRANKFURT AM MAIN, GERMANY). 5162

0723-0745 See MITTEILUNGEN FU BERLIN : AMTSBLATT DER FREIEN UNIVERSITAT BERLIN. 1093

0723-0869 See EXPOSITIONES MATHEMATICAE. 3505

0723-0893 See NUKLEARE ENTSORGUNG. 1952

0723-0931 See NEUROPSYCHIATRIA CLINICA. 3931

0723-1172 See THEATERZEITSCHRIFT. 389

0723-1180 See RECHTSHISTORISCHES JOURNAL. 3036

0723-1229 See CURRENT TOPICS IN NEUROENDOCRINOLOGY. 3727

0723-1350 See WEINWIRTSCHAFT. MARKT, DIE. 2372

0723-1369 See WEINWIRTSCHAFT. TECHNIK, DIE. 2372

0723-1393 See MEDICINE AND LAW. 3742

0723-1520 See MONATSSCHRIFT FUER BRAUWISSENSCHAFT. 2369

0723-2020 See SYSTEMATIC AND APPLIED MICROBIOLOGY. 570

0723-2128 See MEDIEN-BULLETIN. 1134

0723-2225 See GATE ESCHBORN. 5107

0723-2276 See KINDERKRANKENSCHWESTER. 3906

0723-2454 See NEUES GLAS. 2592

0723-2470 See BRYOLOGISCHE BEITRAEGE. 504

0723-2632 See ROCK MECHANICS AND ROCK ENGINEERING. 2150

0723-2659 See BERICHT DES PRASIDENTEN, ZAHLENSPIEGEL. 1811

0723-3353 See INTERNATIONAL JOURNAL OF MYCOLOGY AND LICHENOLOGY. 575

0723-3361 See M-+-A-REPORT 1982. 820

0723-3590 See BIBLIOGRAPHIE DER BUCH- UND BIBLIOTHEKSGESCHICHTE : BBB. 4821

0723-3655 See SYNFORM. 1048

0723-3868 See PERSONALFEUHRUNG. 945

0723-4066 See DATZ : AQUARIEN TERRARIEN. 2773

0723-4074 See TASCHENBUCH INFORMATION & DOKUMENTATION. 3252

0723-4775 See INSTALLATION, DKZ. 2065

0723-4864 See EXPERIMENTS IN FLUIDS. 2089

0723-4880 See SCHRIFTEN ZUR EUROPAISCHEN SOZIAL- UND VERFASSUNGSGESCHICHTE. 5218

0723-5003 See MEDIZINISCHE KLINIK (MUNCHEN. 1983). 3615

0723-5054 See TK REPORT. 2360

0723-5100 See ARAB MEDICO. 3552

0723-5364 See KOPFSCHMERZ. 3602

0723-6204 See WELTMISSION, DIE. 5008

0723-6271 See CHEMISTRY OF PEPTIDES AND PROTEINS. 1040

0723-6557 See ZEITSCHRIFT FUER KLINISCHE PSYCHOLOGIE, PSYCHOPATHOLOGIE UND PSYCHOTHERAPIE. 4622

0723-6875 See TI. GESCHAFTSREISE. 5492

0723-6913 See ARZNEIMITTELTHERAPIE. 4293

0723-6980 See D+C. DEVELOPMENT AND COOPERATION (ENGLISH EDITION). 1555

0723-7065 See NUKLEARMEDIZINER, DER. 3848

0723-7537 See DRUCKLUFTTECHNIK (MAINZ). 5102

0723-7561 See BG, DIE. 2876

0723-7685 See DIN-ANZEIGER FUER TECHNISCHE REGELN. 4030

0723-7774 See PRODUZIERENDES GEWERBE (HAMBURG, GERMANY). 1622

0723-7812 See VORTRAGE FUER PFLANZENZUCHTUNG. 530

0723-7839 See MODELLHUT 1975. 1086

0723-7847 See SCHRIFTENREIHE DES BUNDESMINISTERS FOR ERNAHRUNG, LANDWIRTSCHAFT UND FORSTEN. REIHE A, ANGEWANDTE WISSENSCHAFT. 132

0723-7871 See JAHRBUCH DES MUSEUMS FUER KUNST UND GEWERBE HAMBURG. 354

0723-7901 See DHF. DEUTSCHE HEBE- UND FORDERTECHNIK. 2102

0723-791X See SITZUNGSBERICHTE. ABT. 1, BIOLOGISCHE WISSENSCHAFTEN UND ERDWISSENSCHAFTEN. 5158

0723-8045 See GERMAN JOURNAL OF OPHTHALMOLOGY. 3875

0723-8045 See OPHTHALMOLOGE : ZEITSCHRIFT DER DEUTSCHEN OPHTHALMOLOGISCHEN GESELLSCHAFT, DER. 3877

0723-8207 See ALLGEMEINBILDENDE SCHULEN IN NORDRHEIN-WESTFALEN. 1723

0723-8398 See EAST ASIA (FRANKFURT AM MAIN, GERMANY). 1556

0723-8630 See FUNDE UND AUSGRABUNGEN IM BEZIRK TRIER. 268

0723-8800 See INTERDISZIPLINARE GERONTOLOGIE. 3752

0723-8835 See SPECIAL PUBLICATION ... OF THE SOCIETY FOR GEOLOGY APPLIED TO MINERAL DEPOSITS. 1398

0723-886X See MITTEILUNGEN DES VEREINS DEUTSCHER EMAILFACHLEUTE E.V. UND DES DEUTSCHEN EMAIL ZENTRUMS E.V. 2592

0723-8878 See LECTINS, BIOLOGY, BIOCHEMISTRY, CLINICAL BIOCHEMISTRY. 463

0723-8886 See MEDIZINRECHT. 3742

0723-8991 See JUGENDBUCH HEUTE / ARBEITSGEMEINSCHAFT VON JUGENDBUCHVERLEGERN. 1065

0723-9416 See ZEITSCHRIFT FUER WIRTSCHAFTSRECHT. 3088

0723-9432 See EUROPAISCHE SICHERHEIT. 4043

0723-9459 See WISSENSCHAFTLICHE BERICHTE AUS DER HOCHMAGNETFELDANLAGE DER TECHNISCHEN UNIVERSITAT BRAUNSCHWEIG. 1854

0723-953X See LISTE DER DIPLOMATISCHEN MISSIONEN UND ANDEREN VERTRETUNGEN IN BONN. 4662

0723-9629 See BETRIEBSWIRTSCHAFTLICHE BLATTER. 861

0724-0856 See BMFT-JOURNAL. 5089

0724-147X See DUZ, UNIVERSITATS-ZEITUNG : DAS DEUTSCHE HOCHSCHULMAGAZIN. 1822

0724-1712 See ROBOTER. 1216

0724-1976 See INFORMATIONSDIENST VDI : INSTANDHALTUNG. 1978

0724-2247 See RECHT & PSYCHIATRIE. 3935

0724-3332 See GRUPPE & SPIEL. 1895

0724-343X See KULTUR CHRONIK. 323

0724-3472 See TRIBOLOGIE UND SCHMIERUNGSTECHNIK. 1048

0724-410X See ZEITSCHRIFT FUER PHYSIKALISCHE CHEMIE. SUPPLEMENTHEFT (NEUE FOLGE). 1059

0724-4452 See ELEMENTA THEOLOGIAE. 4955

0724-4606 See RAPS : FACHZEITSCHRIFT FUER OL- UND EIWEISSPFLANZEN. 125

0724-4762 See JAHRBUCH DRITTE WELT. 2620

0724-4983 See WORLD JOURNAL OF UROLOGY. 3994

0724-4991 See ORAL-PROPHYLAXE / HERAUSGEBER, VEREIN FUER ZAHNHYGIENE E.V. 1332

0724-5130 See EUROPEAN JOURNAL OF CELL BIOLOGY. SUPPLEMENT. 536

0724-5246 See ORIENTIERUNGEN ZUR WIRTSCHAFTS- UND GESELLSCHAFTSPOLITIK. 5212

0724-5297 See BAD INTERN. 3555

0724-5548 See IRB-LITERATURAUSLESE. 3397

0724-5637 See DEUTSCHE STEUER-ZEITUNG. 4720

0724-567X See NEUE ARZNEIMITTEL. 4317

0724-5823 See SOWJETUNION (MUNCHEN). 2710

0724-6137 See BERLINER THEOLOGISCHE ZEITSCHRIFT : THEOLOGIA VIATORUM NEUE FOLGE : HALBJAHRESSCHRIFT FUER THEOLOGIE IN DER KIRCHE. 4938

0724-6145 See ADVANCES IN BIOCHEMICAL ENGINEERING/BIOTECHNOLOGY. 2007

0724-6226 See CONTACTOLOGIA-BUECHEREI. 4215

0724-6234 See TRIALOG. 630

0724-6331 See PALAEO ICHTHYOLOGICA. 4228

0724-6528 See HAEUSER. 299

0724-6706 See EINSTEIN QUARTERLY, THE. 3574

0724-6765 See VERHANDLUNGSBERICHT DER DEUTSCHEN GESELLSCHAFT FUR LASERMEDIZIN E.V. / ... TAGUNG. 3649

0724-6811 See M.D. COMPUTING. 1268

0724-6870 See ENTSORGUNGSPRAXIS. 2165

0724-696X See BRAUWELT (1978). 2329

0724-7028 See NEWSLETTER - IEA HEAT PUMP CENTER. 2607

0724-7117 See DOKUMENTATION. WETTBEWERB, PANORAMA, KINDERFILMFEST / INTERNATIONALE FILMFESTSPIELE BERLIN. 4068

0724-7125 See DEUTSCHES METEOROLOGISCHES JAHRBUCH, BUNDESREPUBLIK DEUTSCHLAND. 1425

0724-7141 See CALCIUM ANTAGONISMUS AKTUELL. 3561

0724-7265 See THYSSEN EDELSTAHL TECHNISCHE BERICHTE. 4021

0724-7567 See MEDITERRANEAN LANGUAGE REVIEW. 3301

0724-7591 See DIGITALE BILDDIAGNOSTIK. 3941

0724-7605 See DVGW-NACHRICHTEN. 4255

0724-7656 See ZELLULOID. 4080

0724-7907 See EUROPEAN ARCHIVES OF OTO-RHINO-LARYNGOLOGY. SUPPLEMENT. 3888

0724-8156 See JAHRBUCH FUER OPERNFORSCHUNG. 4124

0724-8172 See MEDICAL FOCUS (WURZBURG, GERMANY). 3609

0724-8482 See JAHRBUCH STAHL / HERAUSGEBEN VOM VEREIN DEUTSCHER EISENHUTTENLEUTE. 1613

0724-8490 See PACKUNG & TRANSPORT. 5389

0724-8679 See C'T. 1181

0724-8717 See WORLD GUIDE TO SPECIAL LIBRARIES. 3260

0724-8741 See PHARMACEUTICAL RESEARCH. 4321

0724-8784 See SCHRIFTENREIHE LEBENSMITTELCHEMIE, LEBENSMITTELQUALITAT. 2356

0724-8822 See ARCHIVUM EURASIAE MEDII AEIVI. 2676

0724-8954 See ARCHAOLOGISCHE AUSGRABUNGEN IN BADEN-WURTTEMBERG. 258

0724-9004 See ZAC, ZEITSCHRIFT FUER ANTIMIKROBIELLE, ANTINEOPLASTISCHE CHEMOTHERAPIE. 3652

0724-956X See WOLFENBUTTELER ABHANDLUNGEN ZUR RENAISSANCEFORSCHUNG. 2716

0724-9616 See INFO DAF. INFORMATIONEN DEUTSCH ALS FREMDSPRACHE. 1830

0724-9713 See SPRACHE UND LITERATUR IN WISSENSCHAFT UND UNTERRICHT. 3323

0725-0037 See ACQUISITION, BIBLIOGRAPHY, CATALOGUING NEWS / NATIONAL LIBRARY OF AUSTRALIA. 3187

0725-0096 See SCRIPSI. 3434

0725-0177 See PAPERS OF THE JAPANESE STUDIES CENTRE. 2662

0725-0312 See WETLANDS. 1361

0725-0320 See BULLETIN / RESERVE BANK OF AUSTRALIA. 781

0725-0509 See COPYRIGHT REPORTER. 1303

0725-0827 See ANNUAL REPORT - NATIONAL ENERGY ADVISORY COMMITTEE CANBERRA. 1932

0725-086X See AUSTRALASIAN TEXTILES. 5348

0725-1009 2101

0725-1092 See SQUARE ONE SYDNEY. 3536

0725-1130 See ANNUAL CATALOGUE OF COMMONWEALTH PUBLICATIONS. 407

0725-2390 See APSA NEWSLETTER. 4464

0725-2455 See DIARY OF SOCIAL LEGISLATION AND POLICY. 5282

0725-2919 See TECHNICAL AID TO THE DISABLED JOURNAL. 4394

0725-2986 See JOURNAL OF ELECTRICAL AND ELECTRONICS ENGINEERING, AUSTRALIA. 2068

0725-3109 See AUSTRALIAN BUSINESS INDEX. 5274

0725-3125 See ELECTRICITY SUPPLY INDUSTRY IN QUEENSLAND, FINANCIAL REPORT, THE. 2046

0725-3249 See ACTIVITIES DIGEST. 3748

0725-3338 See AUSTRALIAN FARM JOURNAL. 64

0725-3362 See FOOTWEAR NEWS AUSTRALIA. 1084

0725-3931 See YOUR COMPUTER MOSMAN. 1207

0725-430X See DISCUSSION PAPERS - AUSTRALIAN NATIONAL UNIVERSITY, CENTRE FOR ECONOMIC POLICY RESEARCH. 1480

0725-4415 See AUSTRALIAN PERSONAL COMPUTER. 1265

0725-4598 See REPORT - CSIRO MARINE LABORATORIES. 2311

0725-4695 See CONFERENCE SERIES / AUSTRALIAN WATER RESOURCES COUNCIL. 5532

0725-4709 See MIMS ANNUAL, AUSTRALIAN EDITION. 4315

0725-4873 See SET HAWTHORN. 1783

0725-4938 See AUSTRALIAN COAL GEOLOGY : JOURNAL OF THE COAL GEOLOGY GROUP OF THE GEOLOGICAL SOCIETY OF AUSTRALIA. 1366

0725-4946 See THIS AUSTRALIA. 2511

0725-5136 See THESIS ELEVEN. 5264

0725-6221 See MINERAL INFORMATION SERIES ADELAIDE. 2144

0725-6272 See AES WORKING PAPER. 2159

0725-654X See SENTENCING STATISTICS, HIGHER CRIMINAL COURTS, VICTORIA. 3083

0725-6558 See INFORMATION BULLETIN. P & R. 2174

0725-6868 See JOURNAL OF INTERCULTURAL STUDIES. 1919

0725-7015 See LU REES ARCHIVES. 3229

0725-7392 See SEDIMENTOLOGICAL NEWSLETTER. 1396

0725-7759 See AGFACTS / DEPARTMENT OF AGRICULTURE, NEW SOUTH WALES. 45

0725-783X See FLINDERS UNIVERSITY OF SOUTH AUSTRALIA. INSTITUTE FOR ATOMIC STUDIES, FIAS-R. 2155

0725-847X See MISCELLANEOUS PUBLICATION - WESTERN AUSTRALIA DEPARTMENT OF AGRICULTURE. 109

0725-8488 See CURRICULUM DIGEST - CURRICULUM DEVELOPMENT CENTRE. 1892

0725-8526 See DIVISION OF SOILS DIVISIONAL REPORT. 170

0725-8739 See MERIGAL. 226

0725-914X See PROGENITOR. 2468

0725-9379 See RETAIL ESTABLISHMENTS AND SELECTED SERVICE ESTABLISHMENTS, HOTELS AND ACCOMMODATION, TASMANIA / AUSTRALIAN BUREAU OF STATISTICS. 2809

0725-9492 See RESEARCH REPORT (TROPICAL FRUIT RESEARCH STATION (N.S.W.)). 185

0725-9727 See ANNUAL REPORT - DEPARTMENT OF MINES AND ENERGY, NORTHERN TERRITORY. 2133

0726-0075 See WESTIR'S WESTERN SYDNEY LETTER. 2511

0726-0288 See KEY BUSINESS DIRECTORY OF AUSTRALIA : KBD. 688

0726-0644 See ABN NEWS / NATIONAL LIBRARY OF AUSTRALIA, AUSTRALIAN BIBLIOGRAPHIC NETWORK. 3186

0726-0784 See QUEENSLAND LAW REPORTER. 3034

0726-0822 See PROCEEDINGS OF THE ... CONFERENCE OF THE AUSTRALIAN SOCIETY OF SUGAR CANE TECHNOLOGISTS. 183

0726-0865 See STEEL PROFILE. 4020

0726-1195 See SOCIAL SECURITY JOURNAL. 5308

0726-1470 See RARE FRUIT COUNCIL OF AUSTRALIA INC. NEWSLETTER. 2430

0726-1519 See HANDBOOK (SOUTH AUSTRALIA. DEPT. OF MINES AND ENERGY). 2140

0726-1527 See SPECIAL PUBLICATION / DEPARTMENT OF MINES AND ENERGY. 2151

0726-2132 See CLASSROOM COMPUTING. 1222

0726-2183 See NEWSLETTER - SUZUKI TALENT EDUCATION ASSOCIATION OF AUSTRALIA (VICTORIA). 4141

0726-2256 See AUSTRALIAN HORTICULTURE. 2409

0726-2566 See AUSTRALIAN BEAUTY COUNTER. 402

0726-2655 See EDUCATION AND SOCIETY (MELBOURNE). 1738

0726-3139 See AUSTRALIAN CLINICAL REVIEW. 3554

0726-3252 See AUSTRALIAN COMMUNICATION REVIEW. 1104

0726-3406 See BASIC PAPER - PARLIAMENT OF THE COMMONWEALTH OF AUSTRALIA, LEGISLATIVE RESEARCH SERVICE, DEPARTMENT OF THE PARLIAMENTARY LIBRARY. 4632

0726-352X See MICROCOMPUTER NEWS. 1195

0726-3589 See CREATIVE SOURCE AUSTRALIA. 4368

0726-3716 See NEWSLETTER OF THE AUSTRALIAN ROBOT ASSOCIATION. 1220

0726-3864 See AUSTRALIA AND NEW ZEALAND JOURNAL OF DEVELOPMENTAL DISABILITIES. 4384

0726-4127 See SCAN (NORTH SYDNEY). 1904

0726-416X See CURRICULUM AND TEACHING. 1734

0726-4178 See INTERNATIONAL REVIEW OF SOCIOLOGY OF EDUCATION. 5248

0726-4240 See AUSTRALIAN JOURNAL ON AGEING. 3749

0726-4623 See PLANTLINE. 3486

0726-5115 See AUSTRALIAN JOURNAL OF REMEDIAL EDUCATION. 1727

0726-5239 See BULLETIN OF THE AUSTRALIAN SOCIETY OF LEGAL PHILOSOPHY. 2945

0726-5646 See AUSTRALIAN SAILING. 591

0726-5816 See ADMINISTRATIVE LAW DECISIONS. 2927

0726-5859 See AUSTRALIAN TAX CASES. 4712

0726-5883 See AUSTRALIAN INDUSTRIAL LAW REVIEW. 2938

0726-5956 See AUSTRALIAN CONSUMER SALES AND CREDIT LAW REPORTER. 2938

0726-6103 See VIVA MT. LAWLEY. 2275

0726-6553 See A.C.T. PAPERS ON EDUCATION. 1720

0726-6588 See CSIRO DIVISION OF ENTOMOLOGY REPORT. 5581

0726-6685 See WESTERN AUSTRALIAN ECONOMIC REVIEW. 1631

0726-6715 See HISTORIC ENVIRONMENT. 2669

0726-6847 See PRAXIS DARLING HEIGHTS. 1902

0726-7126 See PARENT AND CITIZEN. 1771

0726-7215 See FLINDERS JOURNAL OF HISTORY AND POLITICS. 4474

0726-8602 See AUSTRALIAN JOURNAL OF LINGUISTICS. 3267

0726-9072 See MASK BLACKBURN. 386

0726-9943 See ANNUAL REPORT ... ON ACTIVITIES TO 30 JUNE ... / THE AUSTRALIAN BICENTENNIAL AUTHORITY. 4629

0727-0046 See ALTRO POLO. 2673

0727-0062 See N.S.W. REALTY AUCTIONEER. 4841

0727-095X See QUEENSLAND PLANNING LAW REPORTS. 3034

0727-1182 See ART & TEXT. 338

0727-1239 See ARTLINK. 342

0727-1255 See CLASSROOM. 1891

0727-1301 See COMMUNICATIONS LAW BULLETIN. 1108

0727-1476 See AUSTRALIAN NATIONAL ACCOUNTS, INPUT-OUTPUT TABLES, COMMODITY DETAILS. 1530

0727-1611 See HEALTH INSURANCE SURVEY, AUSTRALIA. 2897

0727-2022 See WESTERN AUSTRALIA IN BRIEF. 3073

0727-2545 See CURRENT AUSTRALIAN HEALTH SERIALS. 3656

0727-2596 See AUSTRALIAN ENERGY STATISTICS / DEPARTMENT OF NATIONAL DEVELOPMENT AND ENERGY. 1961

0727-2774 See AIR TRANSPORT STATISTICS. FLIGHT CREW LICENCES. 41

0727-3061 See HISTORICAL RECORDS OF AUSTRALIAN SCIENCE. 5110

0727-3096 See ATS FOCUS. 5086

0727-3126 See AUSTRALIAN ROWING. 4885

0727-3134 See NEWSLETTER - AUSTRALIAN ANTHROPOLOGICAL SOCIETY. 242

0727-3215 See AUSTRALASIAN CATHOLIC RECORD, THE. 5024

0727-3304 See HEALTH AND SAFETY BULLETIN. 2862

0727-3525 See AUSTRALIAN GAS INDUSTRY DIRECTORY, THE. 4251

0727-3606 See AUSTRALIAN GRAPEGROWER AND WINEMAKER. 2363

0727-3738 See REPORT OF THE AUSTRALIA AND NEW ZEALAND COMBINED DIALYSIS AND TRANSPLANT REGISTRY. 3633

0727-3800 See MINERALS INDUSTRY SURVEY. 4012

0727-3924 See LIST OF HOLDINGS - AUSTRALIAN NATIONAL UNIVERSITY, RESEARCH SCHOOL OF SOCIAL SCIENCES, ARCHIVES OF BUSINESS AND LABOUR. 690

0727-4025 See AUSTRALIAN MUSIC STUDIES. 4101

0727-4076 See ANNUAL SURVEY OF AUSTRALIAN LAW, AN. 2935

0727-419X See AUSTRALIAN JOURNAL OF COAL MINING TECHNOLOGY AND RESEARCH, THE. 2134

0727-5366 See ENVIRONMENT VICTORIA. 2192

0727-5757 See NEW SOUTH WALES MINERAL INDUSTRY REVIEW. 2147

0727-5994 See POLITICAL AND SOCIAL CHANGE MONOGRAPH. 4488

0727-601X See TECHNICAL REPORT / DEPARTMENT OF AGRICULTURE, SOUTH AUSTRALIA. 140

0727-615X See FREESAIL. 4895

0727-6273 See INFORMATION SERIES - QUEENSLAND DEPARTMENT OF PRIMARY INDUSTRIES. 458

0727-6753 See DIRECTORY OF CSIRO RESEARCH PROGRAMS / COMPILED BY THE SCIENCE COMMUNICATION UNIT, BUREAU OF SCIENTIFIC SERVICES. 5100

0727-6796 See ACE NEWS. 1722

0727-6826 See CURRICULUM EXCHANGE. 1892

0727-6842 See OIL & GAS AUSTRALIA. 4268

0727-6850 See AUSTRALIAN SOCCER WEEKLY. 4885

0727-730X See AUSTRALIAN HOSPITAL ENGINEER. 3777

0727-7369 See TRANSACTIONS OF THE INSTITUTION OF ENGINEERS, AUSTRALIA. MECHANICAL ENGINEERING. 2131

0727-758X See BUSINESS REVIEW WEEKLY : BRW. 652

0727-8349 See AUSTRALIAN MARKETING RESEARCHER. 921

0727-8926 See APAIS. AUSTRALIAN PUBLIC AFFAIRS INFORMATION SERVICE. 4696

0727-9078 See SOIL SURVEY BULLETIN (NEW SOUTH WALES). 187

0727-9272 See MINERAL PRODUCTION, NEW SOUTH WALES. 2144

0727-9620 See CUNNINGHAMIA : ECOLOGICAL CONTRIBUTIONS FROM THE NATIONAL HERBARIUM OF NEW SOUTH WALES. 507

0727-971X See DO IT. 2615

0728-0645 See REPORT OF THE DIRECTOR - DEPARTMENT OF CHILDREN'S SERVICES. 5305

0728-067X See CONFERENCE AND WORKSHOP SERIES - QUEENSLAND DEPARTMENT OF PRIMARY INDUSTRIES. 1602

0728-0912 See VOX REFORMATA. 5008

0728-1188 See JOURNAL OF THE ROYAL UNITED SERVICES INSTITUTE OF AUSTRALIA. 4048

0728-1226 See AUSTRALIAN HORSE AND RIDER. 2797

0728-2311 See RECORD - GEOLOGICAL SURVEY OF WESTERN AUSTRALIA. 1393

0728-3008 See CONSUMING INTEREST. CHIPPENDALE. 1296

0728-3717 See NEWSLETTER - AUSTRALIAN ASSOCIATION OF FILM AND VIDEO LIBRARIES. 3235

0728-4586 See AZIMUTH. 599

0728-4632 See AUSTRALIAN PHARMACIST / PHARMACEUTICAL SOCIETY OF AUSTRALIA. 4293

0728-4837 See CLINICAL MICROBIOLOGY UPDATE PROGRAMME. 561

0728-487X See TTUV NEWS. 1908

0728-4896 See ARCHAEOLOGY IN OCEANIA. 257

0728-5256 See CATALOGUE OF SCRIPTS HELD AT THE SALAMANCA SCRIPT RESOURCE CENTRE. 317

0728-5639 See LIGHTING IN AUSTRALIA. 2071

0728-5736 See AUSTRALIAN & NEW ZEALAND INSURANCE CASES. 2874

0728-5914 See MERIDIAN (BUNDOORA, VIC.). 3347

0728-6082 See FEDERAL COURT REPORTER. 2969

0728-6155 See AUSTRALIAN JOURNAL OF PSYCHOTHERAPY. 4575

0728-6309 See AUSTRALIAN PLANNING APPEAL DECISIONS. 2939

0728-6481 See DIXSON LIBRARY REPORT. 3208

0728-7178 See CONFERENCE SERIES - AUSTRALASIAN INSTITUTE OF MINING AND METALLURGY. 2138

0728-7186 See BULLETIN OF PROCEEDINGS IN ... - NSW INSTITUTE FOR EDUCATIONAL RESEARCH. 1729

0728-7224 See ENGINEERING GEOLOGY SPECIALIST GROUP PAPERS. 1375

0728-7275 See OWNER BUILDER MAGAZINE. 623

0728-7879 See ANNUAL REPORT - ENGINEERING AND WATER SUPPLY DEPARTMENT ADELAIDE. 2087

0728-8069 See ANNUAL REPORT - ELECTRICITY TRUST OF SOUTH AUSTRALIA. 2035

0728-8093 See REPORT AND STATEMENT OF THE PIPELINES AUTHORITY OF SOUTH AUSTRALIA. 4276

0728-8433 See AUSTRALIAN CULTURAL HISTORY. 2668

0728-859X See AIAS OCCASIONAL PUBLICATION. 57

0728-8727 See NATIONAL DOG. 5516

0728-8883 See ANNUAL REPORT - AUSTRALIAN BROADCASTING TRIBUNAL. 1126

0728-9502 See AUSTRALIAN WATER RESOURCES COUNCIL WATER MANAGEMENT SERIES. 5530

0728-9820 See BUILDING SURVEYOR MELBOURNE. 605

0729-0799 See MOTOR INDUSTRY JOURNAL. 5420

0729-1345 See PRACTICAL GUIDES FOR SUCCESSFUL DENTISTRY / PREPARED BY THE AUSTRALIAN DENTAL STANDARDS LABORATORY FOR THE AUSTRALIAN DENTAL ASSOCIATION. 1333

0729-1485 See JOURNAL OF LAW AND INFORMATION SCIENCE. 2988

0729-154X See HISTORY TEACHER BRISBANE. 1896

0729-1809 See EQUALS ADELAIDE. 1744

0729-199X See STATISTICAL BULLETIN FOR PUBLIC LIBRARIES IN WESTERN AUSTRALIA. 3260

0729-2104 See WA EDUCATION NEWS. 1790

0729-218X See ANTIBIOTIC GUIDELINES. 3551

0729-2341 See CONFERENCE - AUSTRALASIAN CORROSION ASSOCIATION. 2011

0729-2473 See WAR & SOCIETY. 2633

0729-2546 See VSTA NEWSDATA. 1790

0729-2716 See HUMAN RIGHTS CANBERRA. 4508

0729-2775 See COMPANY AND SECURITIES LAW JOURNAL. 3098

0729-3356 See AUSTRALIAN JOURNAL OF LAW AND SOCIETY. 2938

0729-3682 See AUSTRALIAN PLANNER : JOURNAL OF THE ROYAL AUSTRALIAN PLANNING INSTITUTE. 2815

0729-3739 See ENERGY INFORMATION ADELAIDE. 1940

0729-3828 See SUPERFUNDS. 4751

0729-4042 See CHRISTIANS WRITING. 3375

0729-4069 See PESA JOURNAL. 4271

0729-4271 See DIRECTORY OF AUSTRALIAN PUBLIC LIBRARIES. 3206

0729-4352 See AUSTRALIAN ABORIGINAL STUDIES (CANBERRA, A.C.T. : 1983). 2668

0729-4360 See HIGHER EDUCATION RESEARCH AND DEVELOPMENT. 1828

0729-5081 See MODE FOR BRIDES. 2283

0729-5162 See KTAV NEWSPAPER. 1804

0729-5529 See SCUBA DIVER. 4917

0729-5898 See LEMEL. 2915

0729-6010 See IANUA. 1804

0729-6274 See JOURNAL OF THE AUSTRALIAN WAR MEMORIAL. 4048

0729-6436 See SOLAR PROGRESS. 1957

0729-6533 See ANARE RESEARCH NOTES. 1365

0729-7904 See ARBITRATOR BARTON. 2936

0729-7963 See RADIATION PROTECTION IN AUSTRALIA. 4798

0729-8226 See NATIONAL CONSERVATION STRATEGY FOR AUSTRALIA. NCSA NEWSLETTER. 2198

0729-8463 See ACROD NEWSLETTER. 4383

0729-8579 See JOURNAL OF INTEGRATIVE AND ECLECTIC PSYCHOTHERAPY. 3929

0729-8595 See AUSTRALIAN SOCIETY. 2510

0729-9397 See ATRI TURF NOTES. 2797

0729-9435 See W.A. PRIMARY PRINCIPAL. 1806

0729-9885 See ANNUAL REPORT / THE UNIVERSITY OF ADELAIDE. 1809

0729-9990 See TECHNICAL REPORT (CONSERVATION COMMISSION OF THE NORTHERN TERRITORY). 2206

0730-0018 See MAVERICK GUIDE TO AUSTRALIA, THE. 5484

0730-0034 See MINORITY EDUCATION. 1764

0730-0050 See JOURNAL OF ACOUSTIC EMISSION. 1981

0730-0077 See CLINICAL AND EXPERIMENTAL HYPERTENSION. PART A, THEORY AND PRACTICE. 3703

0730-0085 See CLINICAL AND EXPERIMENTAL HYPERTENSION. PART B, HYPERTENSION IN PREGNANCY. 3758

0730-0107 See OCCASIONAL PAPERS / REPRINTS SERIES IN CONTEMPORARY ASIAN STUDIES. 2661

0730-0123 See NATIONAL DEVELOPMENT (WESTPORT, CONN.). 1507

0730-014X See NARA NEWS. 1135

0730-0158 See KEYBOARD (CUPERTINO, CALIF.). 4128

0730-0212 See MORTGAGE BANKING. 800

0730-0247 See EVOLUTIONARY BLUES. 4521

0730-0271 See FIDELITY (MARSHFIELD, WIS.). 4959

0730-028X See SWEDISH-AMERICAN HISTORICAL QUARTERLY. 2762

0730-0301 See ACM TRANSACTIONS ON GRAPHICS. 1231

0730-031X See BIOTECHNOLOGY LAW REPORT. 3689

0730-0360 See CHASE FINANCIAL QUARTERLY. 783

0730-0743 See STATISTICS OF INCOME. SOI BULLETIN. 4700

0730-0808 See MIRROR. 1330

0730-0832 See NEONATAL NETWORK. 3906

0730-0883 See JOURNAL OF OCULAR THERAPY & SURGERY. 3876

0730-0891 See ROCKY MOUNTAIN ENERGY DIRECTORY. 1956

0730-0905 See BROADWOVEN GRAY FABRIC PRODUCTION. SEASONAL ADJUSTMENT SUPPLEMENT. 5348

0730-0913 See JOURNAL OF THE AMERICAN COLLEGE OF TOXICOLOGY. 3982

0730-093X See CAMLS NEWS. 3199

0730-0972 See BRIDE GUIDE (SAN DIEGO, CALIF.), THE. 2277

0730-1006 See BRIDE GUIDE (LOS ANGELES, CALIF.), THE. 2277

0730-1014 See SEMICONDUCTOR INDUSTRY AND BUSINESS SURVEY. 2080

0730-1049 See T'AI CHI. 2601

0730-1138 See GEORGIA GAZETTE (SAVANNAH, GA.: 1978), THE. 5653

0730-1154 See SOURCE BOOK OF AMERICAN STATE LEGISLATION, THE. 3056

0730-1189 See ELECTRONIC RETAILING (NEW YORK, N.Y.). 2048

0730-1197 See MODULAR HI-FI COMPONENTS SERVICE DATA. 2073

0730-1227 See JOURNAL OF ACADEMIC SKILLS. 1832

0730-1235 See RHODE ISLAND ROOTS. 2470

0730-1251 See COALITION CLOSE-UP. 4518

0730-1278 See PHARMASOURCES. 4324

0730-1286 See ANNUAL REPORT / MARCH OF DIMES BIRTH DEFECTS FOUNDATION. 3551

0730-1308 See ENDODONTIC BIBLIOGRAPHY. 1338

0730-1316 See BIOGRAPHY AND GENEALOGY MASTER INDEX. 430

0730-1324 See USP DI/UPDATE. 4332

0730-1332 See UNITED STATES DIRECTORY OF FEDERAL REGIONAL STRUCTURE. 4692

0730-1359 See NEUE GERMANISTIK. 3415

0730-1367 See CALIFORNIA PERIODICALS INDEX. 412

0730-1383 See TEACHING HISTORY (EMPORIA, KAN.). 2631

0730-1391 See APPLESOURCE. 1284

0730-1405 See BURLESON FAMILY BULLETIN. 2441

0730-1413 See FOOD ENGINEERING'S ... DIRECTORY OF U.S. FOOD & BEVERAGE PLANTS. 2337

0730-143X See MEDICARE, HEALTH INSURANCE FOR THE AGED AND DISABLED. SUMMARY-UTILIZATION AND REIMBURSEMENT BY PERSON. 5295

0730-1448 See MEDICAL STAFF DIRECTORY. 1330

0730-1537 See WORLD PRODUCTIVITY NEWS. 724

0730-1553 See ANNUAL CONFERENCE / NATIONAL ASSOCIATION OF CHURCH BUSINESS ADMINISTRATORS. 4935

0730-1561 See ANNUAL CONFERENCE / NATIONAL ASSOCIATION OF CHURCH BUSINESS ADMINISTRATORS. 4935

0730-1588 See MENTAL HEALTH SERVICE SYSTEM REPORTS. SERIES DN. HEALTH / MENTAL HEALTH RESEARCH. 4604

0730-1685 See GENTRY FAMILY GAZETTE AND GENEALOGY EXCHANGE. 2451

0730-1693 See PANOLA STORY, THE. 2466

0730-174X See INTERNATIONAL UFO REPORTER. 24

0730-1766 See ALTERNATIVE MEDIA. 4463

0730-1812 See RADICAL HISTORIANS NEWSLETTER. 2627

0730-1863 See PUBLIC EXECUTIVE PROJECT BULLETIN. 4676

0730-1901 See PRECIOUS METALS (BROOKLYN, N.Y.). 4015

0730-1928 See PSYCSCAN. LD/MR. 4623

0730-1936 See SHEPARD'S BANKRUPTCY CITATIONS. 3048

0730-1944 See SHEPARD'S SOUTHERN REPORTER CITATIONS. 3054

0730-1952 See SHEPARD'S SOUTHWESTERN REPORTER CITATIONS. 3054

0730-1979 See SHEPARD'S NORTHEASTERN REPORTER CITATIONS. 3053

0730-2010 See ICIASF RECORD. 23

0730-2029 See AMS NEWSLETTER (BOSTON, MASS.). 1419

0730-2045 See INVESTIGATOR (EL PASO, TEX.), THE. 1297

0730-2061 See SHEPARD'S UNITED STATES CITATIONS. CASES. 3054

0730-2096 See SHEPARD'S COLORADO CITATIONS. 3049

0730-2126 See SHEPARD'S NORTH CAROLINA CITATIONS. 3053

0730-2142 See PERKINS JOURNAL. 4986

0730-2177 See SOUTHEASTERN POLITICAL REVIEW. 4496

0730-2207 See PLANT BREEDING REVIEWS. 2427

0730-2231 See TORCH (WASHINGTON, D.C. : 1980), THE. 2548

0730-224X See NEWSREAL. 4817

0730-2274 See HOTLINE. 3213

0730-2290 See INTEGRATED CIRCUIT DISCONTINUED DEVICES. 2065

0730-2304 See CRITICAL TEXTS. 3341

0730-2312 See JOURNAL OF CELLULAR BIOCHEMISTRY. 489

0730-2339 See PROGRESS IN MEDICAL RADIATION PHYSICS. 3944

0730-2347 See TEXAS HEART INSTITUTE JOURNAL. 3710

0730-2355 See INTELLECTUAL ACTIVIST, THE. 4477

0730-2363 See RELIGION AND LIFE LETTERS. 4990

0730-2436 See COST FORECASTING SERVICE APPLICATIONS BULLETIN. 611

0730-2444 See DEAN AND DIRECTOR. 1862

0730-2460 See GROUP INSURANCE PLANS. HEALTH, DENTAL, PRESCRIPTION, OPTICAL. 2881

0730-2487 See KITCHEN & BATH BUSINESS. 2901

0730-2495 See FRETZLETTER. 2449

0730-255X See UNIX TOPICS FOR USERS. 1206

0730-2568 See DRINKING/DRIVING LAW LETTER. 2964

0730-2584 See MEXICAN FORUM, THE. 2538

0730-2606 See MARKETING (GUILFORD, CONN.). 931

0730-2614 See JOURNAL OF HALACHA AND CONTEMPORARY SOCIETY. 5050

0730-2649 See LEGISLATIVE REVIEW ACTIVITY - UNITED STATES. CONGRESS. SENATE. COMMITTEE ON LABOR AND HUMAN RESOURCES. 3002

0730-2657 See SPINNER (NEW BEDFORD, MASS.). 2762

0730-2665 See FORMS OF BUSINESS AGREEMENTS & RESOLUTIONS. 676

0730-2681 See SURGICAL GASTROENTEROLOGY. 3748

0730-2711 See ANNUAL REVIEW ... U.S. ZINC AND CADMIUM INDUSTRY, INCLUDING STATEMENTS FROM OTHER COUNTRIES. 1598

0730-2746 See SUPPLEMENTAL CLIMATOLOGICAL DATA, LATE REPORTS AND CORRECTIONS. CALIFORNIA. 1435

0730-2762 See SUPPLEMENTAL CLIMATOLOGICAL DATA, LATE REPORTS AND CORRECTIONS. NEW JERSEY. 1435

0730-2797 See SUPPLEMENTAL CLIMATOLOGICAL DATA, LATE REPORTS AND CORRECTIONS. NEW ENGLAND. 1435

0730-2827 See LIMNOLOGICAL CONTRIBUTION. 1416

0730-2835 See SUPPLEMENTAL CLIMATOLOGICAL DATA, LATE REPORTS AND CORRECTIONS. NEBRASKA. 1435

0730-2843 See SUPPLEMENTAL CLIMATOLOGICAL DATA, LATE REPORTS AND CORRECTIONS. KANSAS. 1435

0730-2851 See SUPPLEMENTAL CLIMATOLOGICAL DATA, LATE REPORTS AND CORRECTIONS. KENTUCKY. 1435

0730-286X See SUPPLEMENTAL CLIMATOLOGICAL DATA, LATE REPORTS AND CORRECTIONS. LOUISIANA. 1435

0730-2878 See SUPPLEMENTAL CLIMATOLOGICAL DATA, LATE REPORTS AND CORRECTIONS. MARYLAND & DELAWARE. 1435

0730-2886 See JOURNAL OF CLASSICAL PHYSICS, THE. 4408

0730-2908 See INSIDERS, THE. 901

0730-2924 See COMPLETE GUIDE TO AMERICAN POCKET WATCHES, THE. 2916

0730-2975 See AMERICAN TRAKEHNER, THE. 2796

0730-2983 See RECORD - SOCIETY OF ACTUARIES. MEETING. 2891

0730-3009 See PROCEEDINGS OF THE INSTITUTE ON PLANNING, ZONING, AND EMINENT DOMAIN. 3031

0730-3025 See DOE STATE & LOCAL ASSISTANCE PROGRAMS. 1936

0730-3033 See WHO, WHAT, & WHERE IN COMMUNICATIONS SECURITY. 1169
0730-305X See SULFUR (PASADENA, CALIF.). 3443
0730-3068 See WORKSHOPS FOR LEGAL ASSISTANTS. BANKRUPTCY. 3076
0730-3068 See WORKSHOPS FOR LEGAL ASSISTANTS. LITIGATION, LEGAL RESEARCH AND WRITING, ENVIRONMENTAL LAW AND TOXIC TORT LITIGATION. 3769
0730-3068 See WORKSHOPS FOR LEGAL ASSISTANTS. EMPLOYEE BENEFITS. 3076
0730-3084 See JOURNAL OF PHYSICAL EDUCATION, RECREATION & DANCE. 1856
0730-3084 See JOPERD. 1856
0730-3157 See PROCEEDINGS - INTERNATIONAL COMPUTER SOFTWARE & APPLICATIONS CONFERENCE. 1289
0730-3181 See FOLKLORE PAPERS OF THE UNIVERSITY FOLKLORE ASSOCIATION. 2320
0730-3238 See DISPATCH - COLUMBIA UNIVERSITY. CENTER FOR AMERICAN CULTURE STUDIES, THE. 2731
0730-3254 See MONTHLY COFFEE STATISTICS. 2362
0730-3297 See GAY/LESBIAN MEDIA DIRECTORY WORLDWIDE. 2794
0730-3300 See TEXTURES AND MICROSTRUCTURES. 1033
0730-3327 See TRANSLATOR REFERRAL, TRANSLATION SERVICES DIRECTORY. 3329
0730-3335 See REFERENCE SOURCES FOR THE SOCIAL SCIENCES AND HUMANITIES. 5215
0730-3394 See MARINE FISHERIES MANAGEMENT REPORTER. 2308
0730-3440 See STATUS, PROGRESS, AND PROBLEMS IN FEDERAL AGENCY ACCOUNTING. 4701
0730-3475 See ORO MADRE. 3421
0730-3491 See PRACTICAL DIABETOLOGY. 3732
0730-3521 See INSTA-MATCH DIRECTORY OF MINORITY OWNED BUSINESSES IN TEXAS. 683
0730-3556 See CHANNELS (CINCINNATI, OHIO). 1413
0730-3564 See AAS HISTORY SERIES. 3
0730-3572 See SHEPARD'S ALABAMA CITATIONS. 3048
0730-3580 See PETERSEN'S BIG BOOK OF AUTO REPAIR. 5423
0730-3629 See SHEPARD'S ARIZONA CITATIONS. 3048
0730-3637 See SHEPARD'S ARKANSAS CITATIONS. 3048
0730-3661 See SHEPARD'S CALIFORNIA CITATIONS (1919). 3049
0730-3688 See SHEPARD'S CONNECTICUT CITATIONS. 3049
0730-3718 See SHEPARD'S FLORIDA CITATIONS. 3050
0730-3742 See SHEPARD'S GEORGIA CITATIONS. 3050
0730-3785 See LIBRARY COMPENSATION REVIEW. 3225
0730-3815 See OF COUNSEL (NEW YORK, N.Y.). 3021
0730-3823 See NATIONAL TELEPHONE DIRECTORY FOR BROKERS, DEALERS, BANKS, MUTUAL FUNDS. 801
0730-3831 See SHEPARD'S INDIANA CITATIONS. 3051
0730-3866 See SHEPARD'S IOWA CITATIONS. 3051
0730-3904 See SHEPARD'S ILLINOIS CITATIONS. 3050
0730-3947 See SHEPARD'S KANSAS CITATIONS. 3051
0730-3971 See SHEPARD'S KENTUCKY CITATIONS. 3051
0730-4005 See SHEPARD'S LOUISIANA CITATIONS. 3051
0730-403X See SHEPARD'S MARYLAND CITATIONS. 3051
0730-4064 See SHEPARD'S MASSACHUSETTS CITATIONS. 3051
0730-4102 See SHEPARD'S MICHIGAN CITATIONS. 3051
0730-4145 See SHEPARD'S MINNESOTA CITATIONS. 3052
0730-417X See SHEPARD'S MISSOURI CITATIONS. 3052
0730-420X See SHEPARD'S NEW JERSEY CITATIONS. 3052
0730-4234 See SHEPARD'S NEW YORK SUPPLEMENT CITATIONS. 3053
0730-4242 See SHEPARD'S NEW YORK STATUTE CITATIONS. 3052
0730-4269 See SHEPARD'S NEW YORK MISCELLANEOUS CITATIONS. 3052
0730-4277 See SHEPARD'S NEW YORK COURT OF APPEALS CITATIONS. 3052
0730-4293 See SHEPARD'S OHIO CITATIONS. 3053
0730-4323 See SHEPARD'S OKLAHOMA CITATIONS. 3053
0730-4358 See SHEPARD'S OREGON CITATIONS. 3053
0730-4382 See SHEPARD'S PENNSYLVANIA CITATIONS. 3053
0730-4439 See SHEPARD'S TENNESSEE CITATIONS. 3054
0730-4463 See SHEPARD'S TEXAS CITATIONS. 3054
0730-4498 See SHEPARD'S VIRGINIA CITATIONS. 3055
0730-4528 See SHEPARD'S WASHINGTON CITATIONS. 3055
0730-4579 See SHEPARD'S WEST VIRGINIA CITATIONS. 3055
0730-4625 See DIMENSIONS OF CRITICAL CARE NURSING. 3855
0730-4633 See SHEPARD'S FEDERAL CITATIONS. 3050
0730-4641 See SHEPARD'S RESTATEMENT OF THE LAW CITATIONS. 3054
0730-465X See SHEPARD'S CODE OF FEDERAL REGULATIONS CITATIONS. 3049
0730-4692 See SHEPARD'S SOUTHEASTERN REPORTER CITATIONS. 3054
0730-4706 See SHEPARD'S NORTHWESTERN REPORTER CITATIONS. 3053
0730-4714 See SHEPARD'S FEDERAL TAX LOCATOR. 3050
0730-4722 See ALI-ABA COURSE OF STUDY. REAL ESTATE SYNDICATIONS. MATERIALS. 2931
0730-479X See TOCQUEVILLE REVIEW, THE. 5224
0730-4803 See CURRENT POPULATION REPORTS. SERIES P-60, CONSUMER INCOME. 1478
0730-4811 See HOT ROD MAGAZINE ENGINES. 5416
0730-4838 See THYRISTOR DISCONTINUED DEVICES D.A.T.A BOOK. 2084
0730-4846 See TRANSISTOR DISCONTINUED DEVICES D.A.T.A. BOOK. 2085
0730-4919 See JOURNAL / CALIFORNIA TRIAL LAWYERS ASSOCIATION. 2986
0730-4927 See SUPPLEMENTAL CLIMATOLOGICAL DATA, LATE REPORTS AND CORRECTIONS. NEW MEXICO. 1435
0730-4978 See BURNETT FAMILY NEWSLETTER. 2441
0730-5001 See CARILLON NEWS. 4107
0730-5028 See FEDERAL FINANCIAL REGULATORY DIGEST. 2969
0730-5036 See GILCREASE MAGAZINE OF AMERICAN HISTORY AND ART, THE. 4088
0730-5044 See HOT ROD MAGAZINE PICKUPS & MINI-TRUCKS. 5416
0730-5117 See STUDENT GUIDE TO MASS MEDIA INTERNSHIPS, THE. 1122
0730-5141 See MINORITY/ETHNIC MEDIA GUIDE, USA. 1117
0730-515X See NEW SOUTHERN LITERARY MESSENGER, THE. 3416
0730-5168 See ROTA-GENE. 2471
0730-5176 See EXPORT REPORT - WESTERN WOOD PRODUCTS ASSOCIATION. 2400
0730-5184 See BEACON REVIEW. 3365
0730-5192 See CORPORATE PUBLIC ISSUES AND THEIR MANAGEMENT. 662
0730-5206 See GALLERY WORKS. 3463
0730-5214 See MENNONITE FAMILY HISTORY. 2460
0730-5222 See DIRECTORY OF DELAWARE LIBRARIES, A. 3207
0730-5257 See INTERNATIONAL MEDIA GUIDE. CONSUMER MAGAZINES WORLDWIDE : IMG. 761
0730-5257 See INTERNATIONAL MEDIA GUIDE. BUSINESS/PROFESSIONAL, EUROPE. 760
0730-5273 See INTERNATIONAL MEDIA GUIDE. EDITION, BUSINESS/PROFESSIONAL PUBLICATIONS, EUROPE. 761
0730-5354 See INTERNATIONAL DIRECTORY (ALEXANDRIA, VA.). 5290
0730-5400 See TRACTION YEARBOOK. 5394
0730-5427 See HAZARD ASSESSMENT OF CHEMICALS. 2173
0730-5443 See PUPIL TRANSPORTATION NEWS. 5390
0730-5478 See JOURNAL OF UFO STUDIES, THE. 26
0730-5486 See LABOR-MANAGEMENT RELATIONS IN THE PUBLIC SERVICE. 1683
0730-5524 See PATIENT CARE LAW. 3025
0730-5540 See NATIONAL REGISTER OF HEALTH SERVICE PROVIDERS IN PSYCHOLOGY. SUPPLEMENT. 4605
0730-5621 See BASIC PETROLEUM DATA BOOK (WASHINGTON, D.C. : 1981). 4252
0730-5672 See LABDATA. 1615
0730-5796 See SECURITIES INDUSTRY YEARBOOK. 913
0730-5869 See SHEPARD'S DELAWARE CITATIONS. 3049
0730-5885 See SHEPARD'S HAWAII CITATIONS. 3050
0730-5893 See SHEPARD'S IDAHO CITATIONS. 3050
0730-5923 See SHEPARD'S MAINE CITATIONS. 3051
0730-5931 See SHEPARD'S MONTANA CITATIONS. 3052
0730-594X See SHEPARD'S NEBRASKA CITATIONS. 3052
0730-5974 See SHEPARD'S NEVADA CITATIONS. 3052
0730-5982 See SHEPARD'S NEW HAMPSHIRE CITATIONS. 3052
0730-6008 See SHEPARD'S NEW MEXICO CITATIONS. 3052
0730-6016 See SHEPARD'S NORTH DAKOTA CITATIONS. 3053
0730-6024 See SHEPARD'S RHODE ISLAND CITATIONS. 3054
0730-6032 See SHEPARD'S SOUTH DAKOTA CITATIONS. 3054
0730-6059 See SHEPARD'S SOUTH CAROLINA CITATIONS. 3054
0730-6091 See SHEPARD'S VERMONT CITATIONS. 3055
0730-6105 See SHEPARD'S WYOMING CITATIONS. 3055
0730-613X See ISLAMIC REVOLUTION. 5043
0730-6148 See JOURNAL OF AMERICAN INDIAN FAMILY RESEARCH, THE. 2455
0730-6156 See TELEMARKETING. 1167
0730-6164 See SOURCEBOOK (WASHINGTON, D.C.), THE. 309
0730-6172 See PLAINS POETRY JOURNAL. 3468
0730-6180 See VIDEO INDUSTRY DIRECTORY. 1142
0730-6199 See COMPUMATH CITATION INDEX : CMCI. 3542
0730-6202 See CABLE TV TAX LETTER. 1129
0730-6210 See NEW HAMPSHIRE LAW DIRECTORY & DAYBOOK. 3015
0730-6229 See SHEPARD'S PROFESSIONAL AND JUDICIAL CONDUCT CITATIONS. 3143
0730-6237 See FOUNDATION REPORTER (1990). 5286

0730-6237 See FOUNDATION REPORTER (1990). 4727

0730-6245 See SECOL REVIEW, THE. 3320

0730-6261 See SHEPARD'S PUERTO RICO CITATIONS. 3054

0730-6334 See NATIONAL MINORITY BUSINESS INFORMATION SYSTEM. 697

0730-6350 See RELIGION INDEXES. THESAURUS. 3245

0730-6369 See NEW JERSEY/USEPA REGION II WATER RESOURCES MANAGEMENT AGREEMENT. 5536

0730-6377 See QDP REPORTS. 705

0730-6474 See MINERALS EXPLORATION ALERT. 1442

0730-6482 See ULTRASTRUCTURAL PATHOLOGY PUBLICATION SERIES, AN. 3898

0730-6490 See PROCEEDINGS OF THE ... SUGAR PROCESSING RESEARCH CONFERENCE. 989

0730-6504 See TECHNIQUES AND COMMENTS. 630

0730-6520 See HERALD (CONROE, TEX.), THE. 2453

0730-6555 See DIVORCE TAXATION. 3120

0730-6563 See REED-DUNN'S BUSINESS REVIEW. 706

0730-6601 See SUPPLEMENTAL CLIMATOLOGICAL DATA, LATE REPORTS AND CORRECTIONS. FLORIDA. 1435

0730-661X See SUPPLEMENTAL CLIMATOLOGICAL DATA, LATE REPORTS AND CORRECTIONS. COLORADO. 1435

0730-6628 See INFORMED. BLUE BANNER EDITION. 4308

0730-6679 See ADVANCES IN POLYMER TECHNOLOGY. 4453

0730-6695 See INTERNATIONAL JOURNAL OF BEHAVIORAL GERIATRICS. 3752

0730-6725 See PEDIATRICS FOR PARENTS. 3910

0730-6784 See AIR FORCE MAGAZINE. 4034

0730-6792 See ANIMAL RIGHTS LAW REPORTER. 2933

0730-6806 See DP DIRECTORY. 1258

0730-6814 See ANNUAL SUMMARY - IOWA. STATE DEPT. OF HEALTH. DIVISION OF DISEASE PREVENTION. 3712

0730-6849 See SUPPORT SERVICES SALARIES SURVEY. 1713

0730-6857 See STANFORD ITALIAN REVIEW. 3353

0730-6865 See STANDARDS FOR BLOOD BANKS AND TRANSFUSION SERVICES. 3774

0730-689X See BANKING POLICY REPORT. 3085

0730-6911 See ANNUAL REPORT - NATIONAL CANCER INSTITUTE (U.S.). FIELD STUDIES AND STATISTICS PROGRAM. 3808

0730-692X See YOUR MONEY (CHICAGO, ILL.). 920

0730-6938 See JOURNAL OF THE ANNUAL CONVENTION - EPISCOPAL CHURCH. DIOCESE OF BETHLEHEM. 5062

0730-6954 See FY ANNUAL REPORT ON IN-HOUSE ENERGY MANAGEMENT. 1945

0730-6962 See SOCIAL PSYCHOLOGY (GUILFORD, CONN.). 4618

0730-6970 See COMMUNIS SCRIPTURA. 2954

0730-7004 See AMERICAN HEALTH (NEW YORK, N.Y.). 2596

0730-7039 See SHEPARD'S FEDERAL CIRCUIT TABLE. 3050

0730-7055 See DATAPRO REPORTS ON MINICOMPUTERS. INTERNATIONAL EDITION. 1274

0730-711X See CATALYST (DES MOINES, IOWA : 1971), THE. 3201

0730-7152 See NONDESTRUCTIVE TESTING MONOGRAPHS AND TRACTS. 1989

0730-7160 See OCCASIONAL PAPERS - ART LIBRARIES SOCIETY OF NORTH AMERICA. 3238

0730-7187 See ART DOCUMENTATION. 3192

0730-7209 See ILLINOIS ENERGY CONSUMPTION. 1946

0730-7217 See COMMODITY PERSPECTIVE. 895

0730-7225 See WHO'S WHO IN LANDSCAPE CONTRACTING (1979). 2433

0730-7241 See BODYSHOP BUSINESS. 5408

0730-725X See MAGNETIC RESONANCE IMAGING. 3943

0730-7268 See ENVIRONMENTAL TOXICOLOGY AND CHEMISTRY. 2229

0730-7322 See PROGRESS (MUSCLE SHOALS, ALA.). 123

0730-7330 See 201. 3357

0730-7349 See CHRONICLE OF THE CATHOLIC CHURCH IN LITHUANIA (CHICAGO, ILL.), THE. 5027

0730-7357 See DIRECTORY, LICENSED REAL ESTATE BROKERS AND SALES ASSOCIATES. 4836

0730-7365 See SAEOPP JOURNAL. 1870

0730-7381 See DATAPRO SOFTWARE NEWS. 1258

0730-7497 See DATAPRO BANKNEWS. 787

0730-7500 See DATAPRO MININEWS. INTERNATIONAL EDITION. 1258

0730-7519 See DATAPRO NEWSCOM. INTERNATIONAL EDITION. 1258

0730-7578 See CLINICAL INSTRUMENT SYSTEMS : CIS. 3691

0730-7608 See PEST CONTROL TECHNOLOGY. 4246

0730-7624 See HIGHLIGHTS OF STATE UNEMPLOYMENT COMPENSATION LAWS. 3149

0730-7632 See PETROLEUM INFORMATION INTERNATIONAL. 4273

0730-7640 See YARNCRAFT. 5186

0730-7659 See BIRTH (BERKELEY, CALIF.). 3757

0730-7675 See MEMBERSHIP DIRECTORY - NATIONAL SOCIETY FOR PERFORMANCE AND INSTRUCTION. 1224

0730-7721 See ACCOUNTING FOR LAWYERS. 737

0730-7756 See MEMBERSHIP DIRECTORY / SOCIETY OF COSMETIC CHEMISTS. 1027

0730-7764 See NICKEL TOPICS (1966). 4013

0730-7780 See AMERICAN JOURNAL OF PHARMACY AND THE SCIENCES SUPPORTING PUBLIC HEALTH (1981). 4290

0730-7799 See COMMUNICATION BRIEFINGS. 757

0730-7810 See MEDICAL ABSTRACTS NEWSLETTER. 3660

0730-7829 See MUSIC PERCEPTION. 4134

0730-7845 See PROCEEDINGS OF THE ARAB SCHOOL ON SCIENCE AND TECHNOLOGY. 5140

0730-7918 See BIOLOGY OF CARBOHYDRATES. 4188

0730-7942 See MEDICARE, USE OF SKILLED NURSING FACILITIES. 2888

0730-7950 See PERSONS ENROLLED FOR MEDICARE. 2890

0730-7985 See PROCEEDINGS / FRONTIERS OF POWER CONFERENCE. 1953

0730-8000 See JOURNAL OF SHELLFISH RESEARCH. 2307

0730-8019 See RECENT ADVANCES IN CLINICAL THERAPEUTICS. 3632

0730-8027 See BIOMEDICAL LABORATORY TECHNICAL REPORT. 3556

0730-8086 See NTIAC NEWSLETTER. 1989

0730-8116 See GEOREF NEWSLETTER, THE. 1380

0730-8124 See GIDROLIZNAIA I LESOKHIMICHESKAIA PROMYSHLENNOST. 4233

0730-8132 See SILVER INSTITUTE LETTER. 4019

0730-8140 See STAINLESS STEELS DIGEST. 4020

0730-823X See ELECTRO- AND MAGNETOBIOLOGY. 454

0730-8256 See WEATHER & CLIMATE REPORT. 1436

0730-837X See AMERICAN LAW REPORTS. ALR 5TH, ANNOTATIONS AND CASES. 2932

0730-8388 See STEEL (WASHINGTON, D.C. : 1976). 4021

0730-840X See CLINICAL SOCIOLOGY REVIEW. 5242

0730-8469 See BULLETIN - UNITED STEELWORKERS OF AMERICA. LOCAL 7896 (FITCHBURG, MASS.), THE. 1657

0730-8485 See JOURNAL OF EXPERIMENTAL PATHOLOGY. 3895

0730-8531 See OHIO VALLEY CAVER. 1409

0730-8566 See CONFERENCE RECORD OF THE ... ANNUAL ACM SYMPOSIUM ON PRINCIPLES OF PROGRAMMING LANGUAGES. 1279

0730-8574 See ASCATOPICS. 2496

0730-8612 See BIBLIOPHILOS (UNION CITY, PA.). 2529

0730-8639 See MATHEMATICS AND COMPUTER EDUCATION. 3520

0730-8647 See RUNZHEIMER ON CARS & LIVING COSTS. 1299

0730-8655 See RUNZHEIMER REPORTS ON TRANSPORTATION. 5392

0730-8663 See RUNZHEIMER REPORTS ON TRAVEL MANAGEMENT. 5490

0730-8701 See ASAE DISTINGUISHED LECTURE SERIES; TRACTOR DESIGN. 158

0730-8728 See IMPORTED WINE MARKET IN AMERICA, THE. 2367

0730-8736 See WORLD OF BANKING, THE. 817

0730-8779 See DATAPRO DIRECTORY OF SOFTWARE. 1285

0730-8795 See DATAPRO DIRECTORY OF MICROCOMPUTER SOFTWARE. 1237

0730-8809 See DATAPRO REPORTS ON BANKING AUTOMATION. 787

0730-8817 See DATAPRO REPORTS ON RETAIL AUTOMATION. 1258

0730-8868 See POETRY MAG, A. 3469

0730-8876 See TRANSAFRICA FORUM. 4536

0730-8884 See WORK AND OCCUPATIONS. 4210

0730-8906 See ACCENT ON MUSIC. 4098

0730-8914 See ANNUAL REPORT OF ACTIVITIES. 4035

0730-8922 See FEDERAL STUDENT FINANCIAL AID HANDBOOK. 1823

0730-8949 See NOVOE RUSSKOE SLOVO. 5719

0730-9023 See ARTSEARCH. 383

0730-9031 See PERFORMING ARTS IDEABOOKS. 387

0730-904X See EXPLORATIONS IN ETHNIC STUDIES. 2261

0730-9058 See CW/PS SPECIAL STUDY. 4040

0730-9082 See GEORGETOWNER, THE. 2534

0730-9120 See MAQUINARIA PARA PLASTICOS. 930

0730-9139 See STUDIES IN LATIN AMERICAN POPULAR CULTURE. 331

0730-9147 See SEMINARS IN UROLOGY. 3993

0730-9155 See MOLY CORROSION INHIBITORS. 2015

0730-9171 See MULTI-LEVEL MARKETING TAX AND FINANCIAL NEWSLETTER / MLM. 933

0730-9198 See IFT BASIC SYMPOSIUM SERIES. 4192

0730-9244 See IEEE CONFERENCE RECORD-ABSTRACTS. 2024

0730-9295 See INFORMATION TECHNOLOGY AND LIBRARIES. 3217

0730-9317 See PROCEEDINGS, VERY LARGE DATA BASES. 1254

0730-9325 See TESOL MEMBERSHIP DIRECTORY. 3328

0730-935X See TECHNICAL PAPERS PRESENTED AT GENERAL SESSIONS AND COMMITTEE WORKSHOPS. ANNUAL MEETING. 5437

0730-9368 See J. CROSS EXECUTIVE ALERT. 685

0730-9376 See BAY AREA CONSUMERS' CHECKBOOK. 1293

0730-9384 See POLITICS AND THE LIFE SCIENCES. 4490

0730-9481 See ARTS + ARCHITECTURE. 314

0730-949X *See* MONEY MARKET FUND SURVEY'S COMPLETE DIRECTORY OF MONEY MARKET FUNDS. **907**

0730-9511 *See* GUIDE TO THE FEDERAL BUDGET, THE. **4730**

0730-952X *See* LEGAL BRIEFS FOR THE CONSTRUCTION INDUSTRY. **2999**

0730-9538 *See* CONTROL AND COMPUTERS. **1219**

0730-9546 *See* ADVANCES IN CERAMICS. **2585**

0730-9562 *See* PARASITIC DISEASES. **568**

0730-9597 *See* MYCOLOGY SERIES. **576**

0730-9600 *See* NATO CHALLENGES OF MODERN SOCIETY. **2237**

0730-9619 *See* WATER RESEARCH TOPICS. **5543**

0730-9678 *See* HYDRAULICS AND HYDROLOGY SERIES. **2090**

0730-9694 *See* TECHNICAL REPORT / WOODS HOLE OCEANOGRAPHIC INSTITUTION. **1457**

0730-9708 *See* VERANO, UN. **3450**

0730-9724 *See* QUEENS COLLEGE LAW JOURNAL. **3033**

0730-9775 *See* MINUTES OF THE ... ANNUAL INTERNATIONAL CONFERENCE OF DOBLE CLIENTS. **2073**

0730-9783 *See* INDEX TO THE LONG ISLANDER, THE. **5717**

0730-9791 *See* JAZZ EDUCATORS JOURNAL. **4124**

0730-9813 *See* IMPACT OF TRAVEL ON STATE ECONOMIES, THE. **5480**

0730-9821 *See* NEBRASKA MINERAL OPERATIONS REVIEW. **1443**

0730-983X *See* SUPPLEMENT TO ORGANIZATION OF FEDERAL EXECUTIVE DEPARTMENTS AND AGENCIES. **4689**

0730-9848 *See* U.S. DIRECT INVESTMENT ABROAD. **918**

0730-9864 *See* STATE WATER PROJECT ANNUAL REPORT OF OPERATIONS. **5539**

0730-9872 *See* TELECOMMUNICATIONS SOURCEBOOK. **1166**

0730-9937 *See* CATALOG MARKETER, THE. **4813**

0730-9988 *See* COMMITTEE REPORT / LAWYERS' COMMITTEE FOR CIVIL RIGHTS UNDER LAW. **4506**

0731-003X *See* WORLD BUSINESS DIGEST. **723**

0731-0102 *See* BUSINESS ELECTRONICS NETWORKS. **647**

0731-0153 *See* REDBOOK / TAA, TEXAS APARTMENT ASSOCIATION. **2832**

0731-017X *See* NEW MEXICO ... HIGHWAY STATISTICS AND RELATED INFORMATION. **5401**

0731-0226 *See* ANNUAL FINANCIAL REPORT OF THE TEXAS PARKS & WILDLIFE DEPARTMENT. **2186**

0731-0234 *See* SOCIAL QUESTIONS BULLETIN (1981). **4997**

0731-0250 *See* CABLE TV INVESTOR. **1129**

0731-0269 *See* CABLE TV FRANCHISING. **1129**

0731-0277 *See* ASSESSMENT DIGEST. **4711**

0731-0285 *See* PROPERTY TAX JOURNAL. **4742**

0731-0331 *See* DIRECTORY OF RELIGION BROADCASTING (1982/83), THE. **4953**

0731-034X *See* NEW SOCIALIST (DENVER, COLO.), THE. **4544**

0731-0366 *See* PURRRRR!. **4287**

0731-0382 *See* EMBERS (GUILFORD, CONN.). **3462**

0731-0390 *See* AAZPA ... ANNUAL CONFERENCE PROCEEDINGS. **5572**

0731-0439 *See* AAZPA REGIONAL CONFERENCE PROCEEDINGS. **5572**

0731-0455 *See* PLACES (CAMBRIDGE, MASS.). **306**

0731-0463 *See* EVANGELICAL SUNDAY SCHOOL TEACHER'S GUIDE, THE. **4957**

0731-0536 *See* DEBITS AND DEPOSIT TURNOVER AT COMMERCIAL BANKS. **787**

0731-0560 *See* ANNUAL REPORT - NEW YORK STATE DEPARTMENT OF COMMERCE. **823**

0731-0625 *See* NATIONAL DIRECTORY OF CERTIFIED PUBLIC ACCOUNTANTS, THE. **748**

0731-0633 *See* EFOC, FIBER OPTICS & COMMUNICATIONS PROCEEDINGS. **5102**

0731-0641 *See* ANNUAL REVIEW OF JAZZ STUDIES. **4100**

0731-0692 *See* STATISTICAL REPORT ON MERGERS AND ACQUISITIONS. **1539**

0731-0714 *See* PRE/TEXT. **3311**

0731-0722 *See* TIME-SENSITIVE DELIVERY GUIDE. **5394**

0731-0730 *See* GOVERNMENTAL AFFAIRS REVIEW. **4388**

0731-0781 *See* GLORY SONGS. **4119**

0731-079X *See* CACHE REGISTER, THE. **1236**

0731-082X *See* CRIMINAL DEFENSE NEWSLETTER. **3105**

0731-0846 See VIDEO TEST ANNUAL AND BUYER'S GUIDE. **2085**

0731-0854 *See* CHINESE YEARBOOK OF INTERNATIONAL LAW AND AFFAIRS. **3126**

0731-0897 *See* SHIH TAXNG. **3436**

0731-0927 *See* ENERGY STATUS REPORT. **1942**

0731-096X *See* PLACES OF INTEREST. **2796**

0731-096x See FERRARI'S PLACES OF INTEREST. **2794**

0731-0978 *See* INVESTIGATIVE REPORTER, THE. **2921**

0731-0986 See CONTRACTING INTELLIGENCE. **4640**

0731-1001 *See* ASTERISK (NEW YORK, N.Y.). **1255**

0731-101X See DA UPDATE. **1319**

0731-1036 *See* CONFERENCE PROCEEDINGS / CANADIAN MATHEMATICAL SOCIETY. **3502**

0731-1109 *See* YOU & THE LAW. **3077**

0731-1125 *See* GLOBAL CHURCH GROWTH. **4960**

0731-1141 *See* EDUCATIONAL PSYCHOLOGY GUILFORD, CONN. **4586**

0731-1168 *See* REPORT FOR ... / UNITED STATES ATTORNEY, NORTHERN DISTRICT OF ILLINOIS. **3038**

0731-1206 *See* ANNUAL SURVEY - NATIONAL ASSOCIATION OF STATE SCHOLARSHIP AND GRANT PROGRAMS. **1809**

0731-1214 *See* SOCIOLOGICAL PERSPECTIVES. **5261**

0731-1230 *See* PHOTONICS SPECTRA (PITTSFIELD, MASS. 1982). **4440**

0731-1265 *See* INTERNATIONAL JOURNAL OF LEGAL INFORMATION. **3218**

0731-1273 *See* JOURNAL OF GROUP PSYCHOTHERAPY, PSYCHODRAMA AND SOCIOMETRY. **3929**

0731-1281 *See* JOURNAL OF CASH MANAGEMENT. **873**

0731-129X *See* CRIMINAL JUSTICE ETHICS. **2249**

0731-1303 *See* RETAIL TECHNOLOGY. **957**

0731-1370 *See* BEST OF ACLD, THE. **1875**

0731-1400 *See* ADVANCES IN PERINATAL MEDICINE. **3756**

0731-1435 *See* NEWSLETTER - LEAGUE OF OREGON CITIES (1980). **4669**

0731-1443 *See* INFORMATION UPDATE / LEAGUE OF OREGON CITIES. **2535**

0731-1494 *See* MISSISSIPPI FRINGE BENEFIT SURVEY. **1691**

0731-1524 *See* FOLKLORE AND MYTHOLOGY STUDIES (LOS ANGELES, CALIF. : 1980). **2320**

0731-1613 *See* JOURNAL OF KOREAN STUDIES (SEATTLE, WASH. : 1979), THE. **2655**

0731-1664 *See* PROCEEDINGS OF THE PLANT GROWTH REGULATOR SOCIETY OF AMERICA. **525**

0731-1672 *See* BASIC AND CLINICAL CARDIOLOGY. **3699**

0731-1680 *See* SCIENCE AND PRACTICE OF SURGERY. **3974**

0731-1737 *See* ROCKY MOUNTAIN MAGAZINE ... MEETING AND CONVENTION GUIDE TO THE ROCKY MOUNTAIN REGION. **5490**

0731-1745 *See* EDUCATIONAL MEASUREMENT, ISSUES AND PRACTICE. **1893**

0731-1753 *See* PEPTIDE AND PROTEIN REVIEWS. **492**

0731-1788 *See* LAUGHING MATTERS. **4863**

0731-1885 *See* GUTMANN PUMA/EXPLORER KNIFE ANNUAL. **4873**

0731-1923 *See* ... BOSTON RESTAURANT GUIDE, THE. **5070**

0731-1974 *See* STANDARD & POOR'S CREDITWEEK. **915**

0731-2008 *See* STOCK CAR CLASSIFICATION GUIDE. **5426**

0731-2016 *See* SIMPLY STATED. **3437**

0731-2040 *See* FOCUS (MATHEMATICAL ASSOCIATION OF AMERICA). **3505**

0731-2059 *See* PACIFIC COAST STUDIO DIRECTORY. **4075**

0731-2148 *See* JOURNAL OF RELIGION AND PSYCHICAL RESEARCH, THE. **4969**

0731-2164 *See* COUNTRY DECORATING IDEAS. **2899**

0731-2180 *See* SEXTANT (WASHINGTON, D.C.). **1272**

0731-2199 *See* ADVANCES IN HEALTH ECONOMICS AND HEALTH SERVICES RESEARCH. **4763**

0731-2261 *See* SOLZHENITSYN STUDIES. **156**

0731-2326 *See* PROBLEM BEHAVIOR MANAGEMENT. **4608**

0731-2334 *See* INNOVATION (MCLEAN, VA.). **2099**

0731-2342 *See* AMS STUDIES IN THE SEVENTEENTH CENTURY. **2673**

0731-2350 *See* ASK (BETHESDA, MD.). **5086**

0731-2385 *See* NOTES - NEW YORK (N.Y.) DEPT. OF RECORDS AND INFORMATION SERVICES. **4670**

0731-2393 *See* BLOOD ALCOHOL TESTING FOR MOTOR VEHICLE DEATHS, WISCONSIN. **3158**

0731-2415 *See* DIRECTORY OF LICENSEES / TEXAS STATE BOARD OF PUBLIC ACCOUNTANCY. **743**

0731-244X *See* ANNUAL REPORT - RHODE ISLAND. DEPT. OF HEALTH (1979). **4766**

0731-2458 *See* NATIONAL INSTITUTE ON DRUG ABUSE STATISTICAL SERIES. SERIES. **1350**

0731-2466 *See* NEW SPEAKERS AND LECTURERS. **3306**

0731-2547 *See* ORTHODOX OBSERVER. **4984**

0731-2571 *See* WALDEN'S ABC GUIDE AND PAPER PRODUCTION YEARBOOK. **4239**

0731-2636 *See* FLUE. **320**

0731-2679 *See* AHORA (EL PASO, TEX.). **5054**

0731-2687 *See* ACCION (EL PASO, TEX.). **5054**

0731-2717 *See* CONQUISTADORES. ALUMNOS. **5058**

0731-2725 *See* CONQUISTADORES. MAESTROS. **5058**

0731-2733 *See* ADELANTE (EL PASO, TX.). **5054**

0731-2741 *See* MARCHEMOS (EL PASO, TEX.). **3230**

0731-2776 *See* MONEY TRENDS (SKANEATELES, N.Y.). **799**

0731-2830 *See* INTERNATIONAL LICHENOLOGICAL NEWSLETTER. **514**

0731-2849 *See* PROGRESS IN MUTATION RESEARCH. **551**

0731-2857 *See* UNIVERSITY PRESS BOOKS FOR PUBLIC LIBRARIES. **3255**

0731-2865 *See* UNITED STATES AIR FORCE ACADEMY JOURNAL OF PROFESSIONAL MILITARY ETHICS. **4059**

0731-289X *See* DIRECTORY OF SPECIAL PURPOSE FACILITIES FOR THE EDUCATION OF THE HANDICAPPED. **1878**

0731-2911 *See* INTER-SOCIETY COLOR COUNCIL NEWS. **5114**

0731-2938 *See* MICHIGAN CETA ACTIVITY REPORT FOR **1690**

0731-2946 *See* MISSOURI FOLKLORE SOCIETY JOURNAL. **2322**

0731-2954 *See* REPORTS OF CASES ARGUED AND DETERMINED IN THE TAX COURT OF NEW JERSEY. **3038**

0731-3004 *See* NTIS TITLE INDEX ON MICROFICHE. **5135**

0731-3012 *See* MESSENGER OF THE CHESTERFIELD HISTORICAL SOCIETY OF VIRGINIA, THE. **2746**

0731-3020 *See* JOURNAL OF THE CHESTERFIELD HISTORICAL SOCIETY OF VIRGINIA. **2742**

0731-3047 *See* ART OF MEDICATION, THE. **4292**

0731-3063 *See* LOMA LINDA UNIVERSITY SURGEON. **3969**

0731-3071 *See* DIGEST OF PAPERS - INTERNATIONAL SYMPOSIUM ON FAULT-TOLERANT COMPUTING (1979). **1182**

0731-308X *See* CONFERENCE PROCEEDINGS / LOS ALAMOS SCIENTIFIC LABORATORY. **5096**

0731-311X *See* SUBSURFACE GEOLOGY SERIES. **1399**

0731-3144 *See* ARMY TRAINER. **4037**

0731-3152 *See* ALA WHERE TO STAY BOOK, EAST. **2803**

0731-3179 *See* GUILFORD GENEALOGIST, THE. **2452**

0731-3195 *See* ANNUAL REPORT OF THE COLORADO JUDICIARY. **3139**

0731-3225 *See* UPDATE (ATLANTA, GA.). **2159**

0731-325X *See* OUR FAMILY LEGACY. **2466**

0731-3268 *See* ADULT BASIC AND SECONDARY EDUCATION. **1799**

0731-3276 See DAILY REPORT. CENTRAL EURASIA. INDEX. **1130**

0731-3284 *See* OHIO ARTS COUNCIL BIENNIAL REPORT. **327**

0731-3292 *See* GEOGRAPHICAL BULLETIN (YPSILANTI, MICH.), THE. **2563**

0731-3306 *See* OREGON SALMON AND STEELHEAD SPORT CATCH STATISTICS. **2317**

0731-3314 *See* HOT ROD MAGAZINE KIT CAR. **5416**

0731-3365 *See* JOB OPPORTUNITIES BULLETIN. **1681**

0731-3373 *See* NEWSLETTER - WISCONSIN LABOR HISTORY SOCIETY. **1695**

0731-3381 *See* HEALTH CARE SUPERVISOR, THE. **3781**

0731-339X *See* ANNUAL GUIDE TO PUBLIC POLICY EXPERTS, THE. **5191**

0731-3403 *See* MEDIEVAL & RENAISSANCE DRAMA IN ENGLAND. **5366**

0731-3446 *See* AFFIRMATIVE ACTION PLAN - MAINE. DEPT. OF MENTAL HEALTH AND CORRECTIONS. **4763**

0731-3470 *See* MOTORCYCLE INDUSTRY BUSINESS JOURNAL, THE. **4082**

0731-3497 *See* SUMMER MINING INDUSTRY SURVEY. **2152**

0731-3500 *See* LINGUISTICS OF THE TIBETO-BURMAN AREA. **3299**

0731-3527 *See* NEWS FROM THE LIBRARY OF CONGRESS. **3234**

0731-3551 *See* CURRENCY COMPETITION. **786**

0731-356X *See* ELECTRIC MACHINES AND POWER SYSTEMS. **2043**

0731-3594 *See* DIRECTORY OF FEDERAL STATISTICAL DATA FILES. **3258**

0731-3632 *See* MAGNETIC SEPARATION NEWS. **4444**

0731-3675 *See* MEDIA SPECTRUM. **3230**

0731-3721 *See* ARBITRON TELEVISION POPULATION BOOK. **4549**

0731-3748 *See* FINANCIAL DIRECTORY OF PENSION FUNDS. ILLINOIS, NO. SUBURBAN CHICAGO (OAK PARK, SKOKIE, EVANSTON & OTHERS). **1670**

0731-3756 *See* FINANCIAL DIRECTORY OF PENSION FUNDS. ILLINOIS, SO. SUBURBAN CHICAGO (EVERGREEN PARK, CHICAGO HEIGHTS, JOLIET & OTHERS). **1671**

0731-3764 *See* JOURNAL OF UNDERGRADUATE RESEARCH IN PHYSICS, THE. **4410**

0731-3772 *See* LIMERENCE FORUM. **4603**

0731-3799 *See* FOOD & BEVERAGE MARKETING. **2336**

0731-3802 *See* APPAREL SALES/MARKETING COMPENSATION SURVEY. **921**

0731-3810 *See* JOURNAL OF TOXICOLOGY. CLINICAL TOXICOLOGY. **3982**

0731-3837 *See* JOURNAL OF TOXICOLOGY. TOXIN REVIEWS. **3982**

0731-3845 *See* CLAN CHATTER. **2443**

0731-3896 *See* DELAWARE GENEALOGICAL SOCIETY JOURNAL. **2445**

0731-3993 *See* SVET (BROOKLYN, NEW YORK, N.Y.). **5053**

0731-4027 *See* D-J-M ENZYME REPORT. **453**

0731-4035 *See* TEXAS BUILDERS AND CONTRACTORS DIRECTORY. **630**

0731-4051 *See* CHAPTER NEWSLETTER - BIG BAND SOCIETY. ED WALKER CHAPTER. **4109**

0731-4078 *See* PROCEEDINGS OF THE UNITARIAN UNIVERSALIST HISTORICAL SOCIETY, THE. **5066**

0731-4094 *See* GRANITE & MARBLE DIRECTORY ... / AMERICAN MONUMENT ASSOCIATION. **2140**

0731-4108 *See* PROCEEDINGS OF THE AMERICAN ETHNOLOGICAL SOCIETY. **243**

0731-4116 *See* DAILY REPORT, EASTERN EUROPE. INDEX. **1131**

0731-4140 *See* ALUMNAE DIRECTORY - BENNETT COLLEGE (GREENSBORO, N.C.). **1096**

0731-4159 *See* ALUMNI DIRECTORY - BETHEL COLLEGE (MCKENZIE, TENN.). **1097**

0731-4183 *See* AOCS MONOGRAPH. **961**

0731-4191 *See* PROCEEDINGS OF THE ... ANNUAL CONVENTION OF THE WIRE ASSOCIATION INTERNATIONAL, INC. **4016**

0731-4213 *See* COLLEGIATE MICROCOMPUTER. **1266**

0731-4388 *See* BOOK REPORT (COLUMBUS, OHIO). **3196**

0731-440X *See* INDEX TO COURSE HANDBOOKS. **2981**

0731-4426 See DIRECTORY OF PUBLICATIONS RESOURCES. **4814**

0731-4450 *See* DECISIONS OF THE UNITED STATES MERIT SYSTEMS PROTECTION BOARD. **4702**

0731-4469 *See* TWIN FIDDLE TREASURY, THE. **4157**

0731-4493 *See* ANNUAL FALL MEETING / SECTION OF LITIGATION, AMERICAN BAR ASSOCIATION. **2934**

0731-4507 *See* CASH MANAGEMENT ANALYST, THE. **1468**

0731-4515 *See* ACCESSIONS LIST, BRAZIL. CUMULATIVE LIST OF SERIALS / LIBRARY OF CONGRESS. **406**

0731-4604 *See* CORPORATE CAPITAL TRANSACTIONS ALERT. **4719**

0731-4612 *See* FARMERS FEDERAL TAX ALERT. **86**

0731-4620 *See* OIL & GAS TAX ALERT / THE RESEARCH INSTITUTE OF AMERICA. **4739**

0731-4655 *See* MIDEAST PRESS REPORT. **4528**

0731-4663 *See* PASSAIC REVIEW. **3349**

0731-4671 *See* PHOTOVOLTAIC INSIDER'S REPORT. **1953**

0731-468X *See* PET ANIMAL HEALTH LETTER, THE. **5518**

0731-4698 *See* TRACTOR DIGEST. **161**

0731-471X *See* SERVICE BULLETIN (SAN JOSE, CALIF.). **5425**

0731-4728 *See* WORLD AFFAIRS JOURNAL. **4538**

0731-4787 *See* NEW CAR COST GUIDE. **5421**

0731-4795 *See* MODEL BUILDER (1981). **2775**

0731-4809 *See* UPDATE (WILMINGTON, N.C.). **5038**

0731-4817 *See* RACKHAM JOURNAL OF THE ARTS AND HUMANITIES, THE. **2852**

0731-4833 *See* DISPUTE RESOLUTION PROGRAM DIRECTORY. **2963**

0731-4841 See NEWSLETTER OF THE GYPSY LORE SOCIETY. **2323**

0731-4930 *See* EARTH ENERGY. **1937**

0731-4957 *See* ERS SPECIAL REPORT. **1745**

0731-4981 *See* RESEARCH & CREATIVE ACTIVITY. **5146**

0731-5066 *See* OPEN FILE REPORT (SOCORRO, N.M.). **2147**

0731-5082 *See* STANFORD JOURNAL OF INTERNATIONAL LAW. **3136**

0731-5090 *See* JOURNAL OF GUIDANCE, CONTROL, AND DYNAMICS. **26**

0731-5112 *See* CAMPBOOK. SOUTHEASTERN. **4870**

0731-5120 *See* ANNUAL WATER-RESOURCES REVIEW, WHITE SANDS MISSILE RANGE. **5530**

0731-5163 *See* DRUG NEWSLETTER (ST. LOUIS, MO.). **4301**

0731-5171 *See* FERROELECTRICS. LETTERS SECTION. **2054**

0731-518X *See* ID HANDBOOK OF FOODSERVICE DISTRIBUTION. **2343**

0731-5198 *See* INDEPENDENT (NEW YORK, N.Y. : 1978). **4072**

0731-5236 *See* POETICS JOURNAL. **3350**

0731-5341 *See* INTERNATIONAL ENERGY ANNUAL. **1947**

0731-535X *See* CAMPBOOK. SOUTH CENTRAL. **4870**

0731-5368 *See* AMERICAN MACHINIST MANUFACTURING COST ESTIMATING GUIDE. **3475**

0731-5376 *See* COUNTRY CRAFTS. **371**

0731-5384 *See* CORNELL JOURNAL OF ARCHITECTURE, THE. **296**

0731-5392 *See* YEARBOOK & DIRECTORY OF THE CHRISTIAN CHURCH (DISCIPLES OF CHRIST). **5010**

0731-5406 *See* SCHUMPERT MEDICAL QUARTERLY. **3639**

0731-5449 *See* BYLINE (EVANSTON, ILL.). **2917**

0731-5465 *See* OCCASIONAL PAPERS ON RELIGION IN EASTERN EUROPE. **4983**

0731-5473 *See* GETTING THERE BY TRAIN, TRANSIT, BOAT & BUS. **5383**

0731-549X *See* FREELANCE WRITER'S REPORT. **2920**

0731-5589 *See* TRENDS UPDATE (NEW YORK, N.Y.). **4833**

0731-5600 *See* KITCHEN AND BATH IDEAS. **2902**

0731-5619 *See* PENSION FUND DIRECTORY. **911**

0731-5627 *See* WEATHER ALMANAC, THE. **1436**

0731-5643 *See* UNITED STATES DIRECTORIES OF MINORITY CONTRACTORS, YELLOW PAGES, THE. **717**

0731-5651 *See* INTERSTATE TAX REPORT. **4733**

0731-566X *See* PEOPLE WITH SPECIAL NEEDS. **1883**

0731-5694 *See* HEALTH SCIENCE REVIEW (NEW YORK, N.Y.). **3582**

0731-5708 See CMJ NEW MUSIC REPORT. **4110**

0731-5716 *See* FILM FILE ... , THE. **4069**

0731-5724 *See* JOURNAL OF THE AMERICAN COLLEGE OF NUTRITION. **4194**

0731-5732 *See* ENVIRONMENTAL FORUM (WASHINGTON, D.C.), THE. **3111**

0731-5767 *See* IMMIGRATION LAW REPORT. **2980**

0731-5791 *See* ZONING AND PLANNING LAW HANDBOOK. **3078**

0731-5805 *See* SECURITIES LAW HANDBOOK / BY HAROLD S. BLOOMENTHAL. **3103**

0731-5813 *See* TRADEMARK LAW HANDBOOK. **1309**

0731-5880 *See* AITIA. **4339**

0731-5899 *See* PSYCHONEPHROLOGY. **3992**

0731-5902 *See* PEDIATRIC HABILITATION. **3908**

0731-5910 *See* CURRENT TRENDS IN UROLOGY. **3989**

0731-5945 *See* HEALTH SCIENCES VIDEOLOG, THE. **4781**

0731-5961 *See* NURSING DIMENSIONS EDUCATION SERIES. **3864**

0731-6097 *See* REPORTER - CHICAGO REGIONAL MARKETING AREA. **935**

0731-6194 *See* REPORT OF THE JOINT LEGISLATIVE COMMITTEE ON MOTOR VEHICLES, HIGHWAY AND TRAFFIC SAFETY TO THE LEGISLATURE OF THE STATE OF NEW YORK. **5391**

0731-6240 *See* TENNESSEE NURSERY DIGEST. **140**

0731-6291 See ENERGYGRAMS (OAK RIDGE, TENN.). 1943

0731-6305 See MIDDLE EAST BUSINESS INTELLIGENCE. 933

0731-6321 See POLICY PAPERS IN INTERNATIONAL AFFAIRS. 4532

0731-633X See DIRECTORY OF SPECIAL LIBRARIES AND INFORMATION CENTERS. 3208

0731-6445 See HYDRO-ABSTRACTS. 5534

0731-6496 See DIRECTORY / THE YOUNG LAWYERS DIVISION OF THE AMERICAN BAR ASSOCIATION. 2962

0731-650X See CORPORATE CAPITAL TRANSACTIONS COORDINATOR. 742

0731-6518 See SUNSTONE REVIEW (SALT LAKE CITY, UTAH). 5068

0731-6526 See WOODALL'S ... RETIREMENT DIRECTORY. 5182

0731-6607 See HEALTH SERVICES DIRECTORY. 3781

0731-6615 See INTERNATIONAL HEALTH PLANNING SERIES. 4785

0731-6755 See JOURNAL OF ADVANCED COMPOSITION. 3289

0731-6763 See AMERICAN-ARAB AFFAIRS. 4515

0731-6844 See JOURNAL OF REINFORCED PLASTICS AND COMPOSITES. 2104

0731-6941 See ECONOMIC DEVELOPMENT AND LAW CENTER REPORT. 1556

0731-6968 See HARBOUR, HARBOR, HARBER, AND WITT, WHITT, WHIT FAMILY ASSOCIATION BULLETIN. 2452

0731-6992 See STATISTICAL SUMMARY OF THE COLORADO JUDICIARY. 3083

0731-700X See FINANCIAL DIRECTORY OF PENSION FUNDS. OHIO, SOUTHERN, CINCINNATI AREA. 1673

0731-7018 See FINANCIAL DIRECTORY OF PENSION FUNDS. OHIO, SOUTHERN, EXCLUDING CINCINNATI AREA (COLUMBUS, DAYTON, ATHENS & OTHERS). 1673

0731-7026 See FINANCIAL DIRECTORY OF PENSION FUNDS. OHIO, NORTHERN, CLEVELAND AREA. 1673

0731-7050 See PROGRESS REPORT - HEALTH AND SAFETY RESEARCH DIVISION. 4797

0731-7085 See JOURNAL OF PHARMACEUTICAL AND BIOMEDICAL ANALYSIS. 4311

0731-7107 See CHILD & FAMILY BEHAVIOR THERAPY. 4580

0731-7115 See CLINICAL GERONTOLOGIST. 3750

0731-7131 See TECHNICAL SERVICES QUARTERLY. 3252

0731-7158 See PSYCHOTHERAPY IN PRIVATE PRACTICE. 4614

0731-7190 See FEDERAL LANDS. 1944

0731-7220 See INTERNATIONAL HEALTH NEWS. 4785

0731-7263 See DIRECTORY, CALIFORNIA CAMPAIGN CONTRIBUTORS. 4472

0731-728X See THOMAS COOK BUSINESS TRAVELER. 5492

0731-7301 See FINANCIAL DIRECTORY OF PENSION FUNDS. MINNESOTA (EXCLUDING MINNEAPOLIS-ST. PAUL AREA). 1671

0731-7328 See FINANCIAL DIRECTORY OF PENSION FUNDS. GEORGIA, EXCLUDING ATLANTA AREA. 1670

0731-7379 See FINANCIAL DIRECTORY OF PENSION FUNDS. MICHIGAN, DETROIT CITY PROPER. 1671

0731-7395 See FINANCIAL DIRECTORY OF PENSION FUNDS. KENTUCKY. 1671

0731-7409 See REMODELING IDEAS. 626

0731-7417 See METRO NEW YORK DIRECTORY OF MANUFACTURERS. 3484

0731-7433 See CAUSE & FUNCTION. 5276

0731-7484 See FINANCIAL DIRECTORY OF PENSION FUNDS. MICHIGAN, SOUTHERN, EXCLUDING DETROIT & SUBURBS (FLINT, GRAND RAPIDS, KALAMAZOO & OTHERS). 1671

0731-7484 See FINANCIAL DIRECTORY OF PENSION FUNDS. TEXAS, SOUTHERN (AUSTIN, SAN ANTONIO, VICTORIA, CORPUS CHRISTI). 1674

0731-7557 See WRRI REPORT. 5549

0731-759X See SEPM REPRINT SERIES. 4230

0731-762X See SPECIAL PUBLICATION - UNITED STATES. BUREAU OF MINES. 2151

0731-7638 See WATER RESOURCES BASIC RECORDS REPORT. 5544

0731-7689 See MOLECULAR CRYSTALS AND LIQUID CRYSTALS. SUPPLEMENT SERIES. 1033

0731-7700 See CHINA BUSINESS & TRADE. 827

0731-7727 See SOVIET BUSINESS & TRADE (1982). 851

0731-7824 See HERBARIUM NEWS. 512

0731-7840 See ENCYCLOPEDIA OF OCCULTISM & PARAPSYCHOLOGY. 4241

0731-7867 See DICTIONARY OF LITERARY BIOGRAPHY YEARBOOK. 432

0731-7905 See INTRODUCTION TO FEDERAL TAXATION (ENGLEWOOD CLIFFS, N.J.). 4733

0731-7972 See COURT COMMENTARIES. 3140

0731-7980 See CUMBERLAND POETRY REVIEW. 3462

0731-7999 See RESEARCH IN REAL ESTATE : A RESEARCH ANNUAL. 4846

0731-8014 See HEISEY NEWS. 2590

0731-8022 See POLITICAL SCIENCE ABSTRACTS. ANNUAL SUPPLEMENT. 4490

0731-8049 See ALCOHOL RESEARCH REVIEW SERIES. 1339

0731-8065 See LITHIUM RESEARCH REVIEW SERIES. 4007

0731-8073 See PROGRAM EVALUATION IN THE HEALTH FIELDS. 4796

0731-809X See CENTER FOR POLICY RESEARCH MONOGRAPH SERIES. 5195

0731-8103 See CAMPBOOK. SOUTHWESTERN. 4870

0731-8111 See BOLETIN ANGLOHISPANO. 2942

0731-8146 See INSIDERS BASEBALL FACT-BOOK EXTRA. 4900

0731-8162 See INSIDERS BASEBALL FACT-BOOK. 4900

0731-8189 See CURRENT TREATY INDEX. 3080

0731-8197 See MRQ. 2775

0731-8235 See CLINICAL REVIEWS IN ALLERGY. 3668

0731-8251 See STATISTICAL REPORT. RURAL TELEPHONE BORROWERS. 1125

0731-8278 See INVESTMENT COMPANIES REREGULATION AND THE CHANGING ROLE OF OUTSIDE DIRECTORS. 3101

0731-8316 See REPORT - NORTHEASTERN FOREST EXPERIMENT STATION (BROOMALL, PA.) (1977/78). 2392

0731-8332 See JOURNAL OF PRISON & JAIL HEALTH. 3167

0731-8359 See BULLETIN - AMERICAN ACADEMY OF OTOLARYNGOLOGY-HEAD AND NECK SURGERY, THE. 3887

0731-8367 See ON-LINE (DURHAM, N.H.). 1243

0731-8375 See CORNSILK. 2444

0731-8405 See AIRCRAFT REMOTE SENSING OF SOIL MOISTURE AND HYDROLOGIC PARAMETERS, TAYLOR CREEK, FLA., AND LITTLE RIVER, GA. DATA REPORT. 1412

0731-8413 See SPECIAL ASPECTS OF EDUCATION. 1885

0731-843X See DIS COLLECTOR (CHESWOLD, DEL. : 1981). 4115

0731-8464 See STATISTICS OF VIRGINIA PUBLIC LIBRARIES AND INSTITUTIONAL LIBRARIES. 3260

0731-8529 See DALLAS OPERA MAGAZINE, THE. 4113

0731-8553 See DIRECTORY OF MEMBERS / THE NATIONAL ASSOCIATION OF REAL ESTATE INVESTMENT TRUSTS, INC. 4836

0731-857X See ARTHUR FROMMER'S DOLLARWISE GUIDE TO THE SOUTHEAST AND NEW ORLEANS. 5461

0731-8596 See DRUG TOPICS REDBOOK UPDATE. 4301

0731-8618 See ADVANCES IN SOLAR ENERGY. 1931

0731-8634 See COOK'S INDEX. 2789

0731-8650 See OCCUPATIONAL PROGRAMS IN CALIFORNIA PUBLIC COMMUNITY COLLEGES. 4207

0731-8693 See NATIONAL REAL ESTATE INVESTOR. DIRECTORY ISSUE. 4842

0731-8723 See AAA WORLD. HAWAII. 5459

0731-874X See ANNUAL PROCEEDINGS. WATER SYMPOSIUM / ARIZONA WATER SYMPOSIUM. 5529

0731-8766 See DIRECTORY / FORUM COMMITTEE ON COMMUNICATIONS LAW. 2961

0731-8774 See CHEMICAL BUSINESS. 968

0731-8863 See STATISTICS OF PAPER, PAPERBOARD AND WOOD PULP. 4240

0731-8898 See JOURNAL OF ENVIRONMENTAL PATHOLOGY, TOXICOLOGY AND ONCOLOGY. 3819

0731-891X See ALUMNI DIRECTORY - CORNELL COLLEGE (MOUNT VERNON, IOWA). 1098

0731-8928 See ALUMNI DIRECTORY - CALIFORNIA COLLEGE OF ARTS AND CRAFTS (OAKLAND, CALIF.). 1097

0731-8944 See MIDEAST DIRECTIONS. 2769

0731-8960 See LEON COUNTY HISTORICAL COLLECTIONS. 2744

0731-8979 See JOHNSON REPORTER (LINCOLN, NEB.), THE. 2455

0731-9010 See ALUMNAE DIRECTORY - QUEENS COLLEGE (CHARLOTTE, N.C.). 1096

0731-9029 See ATLANTA JOURNAL, THE ATLANTA CONSTITUTION INDEX (ANNUAL). 2528

0731-9045 See CHICAGO TRIBUNE INDEX. 5814

0731-9053 See ADVANCES IN ECONOMETRICS. 1460

0731-9088 See TEXAS LAWYER'S CIVIL DIGEST. 3064

0731-9096 See OREGON INTERNATIONAL TRADE DIRECTORY. 848

0731-9134 See TALK SHOW DIRECTORY. 1140

0731-9150 See RUNZHEIMER REPORTS ON RELOCATION. 4847

0731-9185 See NATIONAL FIVE DIGIT ZIP CODE AND POST OFFICE DIRECTORY. 1145

0731-9193 See TOXICOLOGIST, THE. 3984

0731-9207 See S. KLEIN NEWSLETTER ON COMPUTER GRAPHICS, THE. 1235

0731-924X See U.S. CRUDE OIL, NATURAL GAS, AND NATURAL GAS LIQUIDS RESERVES, ANNUAL REPORT. 4281

0731-9258 See JOURNAL OF COMPUTERS IN MATHEMATICS AND SCIENCE TEACHING, THE. 1224

0731-9266 See REVIEWS OF CLINICAL INFECTIOUS DISEASES. 3716

0731-9290 See WORDWATCHING. 1791

0731-9304 See AUERBACH REPORTER. 1235

0731-9312 See INSIDE RADIO. 1133

0731-9320 See GRADUATE AND UNDERGRADUATE PROGRAMS AND COURSES IN MIDDLE EAST STUDIES IN THE UNITED STATES, CANADA, AND ABROAD (1982). 1826

0731-9371 See MIDDLE EAST INSIGHT. 4482

0731-938X See VERIDIAN. 3355

0731-941X See EDUCATION UPDATE (CHICAGO, ILL.). 1323

0731-9460 See BILLBOARD EN ESPANOL. 4103

0731-9487 See LEARNING DISABILITY QUARTERLY. 1881

0731-9509 See DIRECTORY, UNITED WAY AFFILIATED INFORMATION AND REFERRAL SERVICES. 5284

0731-9525 See DIRECTORY - SOUTH DAKOTA REAL ESTATE BOARD. 4837

0731-9541 See SOCCER RULE BOOK. 4919

0731-955X *See* JOURNAL OF THE CLAN CAMPBELL SOCIETY (UNITED STATES OF AMERICA). **2455**

0731-9576 *See* STATISTICAL ANNUAL / COFFEE, SUGAR & COCOA EXCHANGE INC. **733**

0731-9584 *See* ALUMNAE DIRECTORY - COLUMBIA COLLEGE (COLUMBIA, S.C.). **1096**

0731-9592 *See* NOUVEAU. **623**

0731-9606 *See* GENEALOGICAL JOURNAL (LEXINGTON, N.C.), THE. **2450**

0731-9649 *See* RESEARCH (BLACKSBURG, VA.). **1845**

0731-9711 *See* LRE REPORT. **3005**

0731-9770 *See* SPORTS MEDICINE DIGEST. **3956**

0731-9770 *See* SPORTSMEDICINE DIGEST. **3956**

0731-9800 *See* ANNUAL MEETING - INTERNATIONAL OIL SCOUTS ASSOCIATION. **4249**

0731-9819 *See* GREEN GUIDE FOR ELECTRIC LIFT TRUCKS. **5383**

0731-9827 *See* GREEN GUIDE FOR LIFT TRUCKS. **5383**

0731-9835 *See* GREEN GUIDE FOR OFF-HIGHWAY TRUCKS & TRAILERS. **5383**

0731-986X *See* SIR PRESENTS 2 BY 2. **2493**

0731-9916 *See* LADY'S CIRCLE PATCHWORK QUILTS. **5184**

0731-9959 *See* LADY'S CIRCLE 1,001 CHRISTMAS IDEAS. **374**

0731-9983 *See* LADY'S CIRCLE HOME MAKING CRAFT IDEAS. **374**

0731-9991 *See* TEEN BAG. **1070**

0732-0043 *See* SPORTS QUARTERLY PRESENTS INSIDE HOCKEY. **4923**

0732-0124 *See* BILLBOARD INTERNATIONAL TALENT & TOURING DIRECTORY. **4103**

0732-0167 *See* NUTRITION & THE M.D. **4196**

0732-0175 *See* PROCEEDINGS OF THE INTERNATIONAL SYMPOSIUM ON COMPUTER AIDED SEISMIC ANALYSIS AND DISCRIMINATION. **5140**

0732-0183 *See* MEDICAL UPDATE (CHICAGO, ILL.). **3612**

0732-0205 *See* MCCARVILLE REPORT, THE. **4481**

0732-0213 *See* FAMILY-IN-TOUCH. **2279**

0732-0264 *See* PUBLIC LAND LAW REVIEW, THE. **3033**

0732-0280 *See* LUPUS NEWS. **3721**

0732-0299 *See* DALLAS OBSERVER. **384**

0732-0329 *See* TREE PLANTER, THE. **2397**

0732-0345 *See* FLRA REPORT OF CASE DECISIONS AND FSIP RELEASES. **4649**

0732-0388 *See* ALUMNI DIRECTORY - NICHOLS SCHOOL (BUFFALO, N.Y.). **1099**

0732-0396 *See* HARPETH GLEANINGS. **2735**

0732-040X *See* ALUMNI DIRECTORY / GLENVILLE STATE COLLEGE. **1098**

0732-0418 *See* FOREIGN DIRECT INVESTMENT IN THE UNITED STATES ... TRANSACTIONS. **899**

0732-0434 *See* TRAVEL GUIDE, MEXICO AND CENTRAL AMERICA. **5495**

0732-0450 *See* ALUMNI DIRECTORY / WEST LIBRARY STATE COLLEGE. **1100**

0732-0469 *See* BOND BUYER (NEW YORK, N.Y. 1982), THE. **892**

0732-0493 *See* OPERATING BUDGET - TEXAS. STATE PURCHASING AND GENERAL SERVICES COMMISSION. **4671**

0732-0531 *See* PAPERS OF THE EAST-WEST POPULATION INSTITUTE. **4556**

0732-054X *See* WOMAN'S DAY CROSSWORDS. **4867**

0732-0558 *See* GEOSCITECH CITATION INDEX. **1356**

0732-0574 *See* ACTINOMYCETES (1982), THE. **558**

0732-0582 *See* ANNUAL REVIEW OF IMMUNOLOGY. **3666**

0732-0590 *See* CANADIAN COUNTY CONNECTIONS. **2441**

0732-0604 *See* CHICAGO CONTRACTORS REGISTER. **607**

0732-0620 *See* LATEST SCOOP, THE. **2348**

0732-0655 *See* INDEX TO THE SCIENCE FICTION MAGAZINES (1979). **3396**

0732-0671 *See* ADVANCES IN LIBRARY ADMINISTRATION AND ORGANIZATION. **3187**

0732-0701 *See* REAL ESTATE AND PUBLIC UTILITY PROPERTY TAXES. **4843**

0732-071X *See* COLORADO CITY RETAIL SALES BY STANDARD INDUSTRIAL CLASSIFICATION. **952**

0732-0736 *See* REPORT - CINCINNATI BAR ASSOCIATION. **3037**

0732-0779 *See* PERSONAL GROWTH AND BEHAVIOR. **4607**

0732-0787 *See* RESIDENTS IN WISCONSIN JUVENILE CORRECTIONAL INSTITUTIONS (1979). **3175**

0732-0795 *See* RESIDENTS IN WISCONSIN JUVENILE CORRECTIONAL INSTITUTIONS (1979). **3175**

0732-0825 *See* MASSACHUSETTS APPELLATE TAX BOARD REPORTER. **4736**

0732-0833 *See* CONNECTICUT WORKER'S COMPENSATION REVIEW OPINIONS. **3145**

0732-085X *See* CONTRIBUTIONS TO THE STUDY OF AGING. **3750**

0732-0876 *See* ORION (NEW YORK, N.Y.). **4170**

0732-0892 *See* NEW YORK TIMES FILE, CRITICAL ISSUES. RESEARCH GUIDE AND INDEX, THE. **2922**

0732-0906 *See* HUMAN RIGHTS DIRECTORY WESTERN EUROPE. **4508**

0732-0922 *See* LAWYER'S MICROCOMPUTER, THE. **2998**

0732-0930 *See* CRIMINAL TRIAL MANUAL, CALIFORNIA. SUPPLEMENT. **3106**

0732-0965 *See* PROBATION AND PAROLE DIRECTORY (COLLEGE PARK, MD.). **3173**

0732-0973 *See* DESIGN FOR ARTS IN EDUCATION. **318**

0732-0981 *See* ORIGIN TO DESTINATION. SHIPMENTS OF WESTERN LUMBER BY STATE AND MODE OF TRANSPORTATION. **2403**

0732-099X *See* SALARIES (CAMBRIDGE, MASS.). **1709**

0732-1007 *See* EAGLET, THE. **2446**

0732-1015 *See* COLORADO STATE AND COUNTY RETAIL SALES BY STANDARD INDUSTRIAL CLASSIFICATION (ANNUAL). **953**

0732-1023 *See* COMMERCIAL FINANCE, FACTORING, AND OTHER ASSET-BASED LENDING. **3086**

0732-104X *See* SERVICEMEN'S AND VETERAN'S GROUP LIFE INSURANCE PROGRAMS, ANNUAL REPORT. **4057**

0732-1074 *See* KAR INTERNATIONAL. **4480**

0732-1082 *See* PAPERS IN THE SOCIAL SCIENCES. **5212**

0732-1120 *See* SYNFUELS HANDBOOK. **4280**

0732-118X *See* NEW IDEAS IN PSYCHOLOGY. **4605**

0732-1236 *See* CAB FARE. **5378**

0732-1252 *See* DIRECTORY, CERTIFIED APPLIANCES AND ACCESSORIES. **2811**

0732-1260 *See* PRIMARY CARE FOCUS. **3738**

0732-1279 *See* REPRODUCTIVE MEDICINE. **3767**

0732-1317 *See* RESEARCH IN PUBLIC POLICY ANALYSIS AND MANAGEMENT. **5215**

0732-1333 *See* DIRECTORY OF PSYCHOLOGISTS AND PSYCHOLOGICAL EXAMINERS LICENSED AND REGISTERED IN TENNESSEE. **4585**

0732-1368 *See* HYBRIDOMA PROFILES. **547**

0732-1384 *See* FOREIGN FORUM YEARBOOK INTERNATIONAL. **836**

0732-1503 *See* NEBRASKA MUSIC EDUCATOR, THE. **4139**

0732-1511 *See* PICTURE (SANTA FE SPRINGS, CALIF.). **4375**

0732-1562 *See* WOMEN'S STUDIES QUARTERLY. **5571**

0732-1597 *See* NUMBERS NEWS, THE. **4555**

0732-1619 *See* ATHANOR (TALLAHASSEE, FLA.). **343**

0732-1635 *See* OLD WORLD ARCHAEOLOGY NEWSLETTER. **277**

0732-166X *See* HI-LITES OF NATIVE BUSINESS. **679**

0732-1732 *See* BANKING REVIEW (LEXINGTON, MASS.). **777**

0732-1767 *See* DIRECTORY OF INSURANCE COMPANIES (SANTA FE, N.M.). **2878**

0732-1791 *See* JOURNAL OF SECONDARY AND ADULT READING. **1898**

0732-1813 *See* ECONOMIC REVIEW (ATLANTA, GA.). **789**

0732-183X *See* JOURNAL OF CLINICAL ONCOLOGY. **3819**

0732-1848 *See* NEW TREND (BALTIMORE, MD.). **4530**

0732-1864 *See* NINETEENTH-CENTURY LITERATURE CRITICISM. **3349**

0732-1872 *See* HOMILY SERVICE. **4963**

0732-1880 *See* ENTERTAINMENT AND SPORTS LAWYER : PUBLICATION OF THE FORUM COMMITTEE ON THE ENTERTAINMENT AND SPORTS INDUSTRIES, THE. **2966**

0732-1899 *See* NORTHERN BUSINESS AND ECONOMIC REVIEW. **1593**

0732-1902 *See* PRO FOOTBALL GUIDE. **4913**

0732-1929 *See* LITERATURE AND BELIEF. **3407**

0732-1953 *See* ILRU INSIGHTS. **4389**

0732-1988 *See* NEWS - NEW YORK STATE PUBLIC EMPLOYMENT RELATIONS BOARD. **1694**

0732-2119 *See* PROFESSIONAL SERVICES MANAGEMENT JOURNAL. **883**

0732-2186 *See* BULLETIN OF ASIAN GEOGRAPHY. **2557**

0732-2224 *See* BECKETT CIRCLE, THE. **3365**

0732-2267 *See* MIMBAR PERMIAS. ENGLISH EDITION. **1764**

0732-2305 *See* ELECTRIC POWER MONTHLY. **2043**

0732-2313 *See* TRAVEL GUIDE, MEXICO. **5495**

0732-2321 *See* HANDBOOK TO THE SEASON / CINCINNATI SYMPHONY ORCHESTRA. **4120**

0732-233X *See* FACTS ABOUT STORE DEVELOPMENT. **2334**

0732-2399 *See* MARKETING SCIENCE (PROVIDENCE, R.I.). **932**

0732-2445 *See* EIS ... DIRECTORY. **3734**

0732-2569 *See* COUNTRY LIVING (NEW YORK, N.Y.). **2789**

0732-2577 *See* CAMPBOOK. NORTHWESTERN. **4870**

0732-2585 *See* CAMPBOOK. NORTH CENTRAL. **4870**

0732-2607 *See* PROCEEDINGS - INTERNATIONAL SYMPOSIUM ON URBAN HYDROLOGY, HYDRAULICS, AND SEDIMENT CONTROL (1981). **2094**

0732-2623 *See* REHAB BRIEF. **1884**

0732-264X *See* CONSOLIDATED PLAN / MISSOURI DEPARTMENT OF MENTAL HEALTH. **4772**

0732-2658 *See* CONSOLIDATED PLAN. APPENDICES / MISSOURI DEPARTMENT OF MENTAL HEALTH. **4772**

0732-2666 *See* RISK MANAGEMENT FOR EXECUTIVE WOMEN. **2892**

0732-2674 *See* WORKING PAPERS IN IRISH STUDIES. **2716**

0732-2763 *See* E/MJ LIBRARY OF OPERATING HANDBOOKS. **2138**

0732-2771 *See* NEWSLETTER - ASSOCIATION OF AMERICAN LAW SCHOOLS. SECTION ON WOMEN IN LEGAL EDUCATION. **3017**

0732-2798 *See* OFFICIAL GUIDE - TIME FINANCE ADJUSTERS (FIRM). **802**

0732-2801 *See* MONTANA AIR QUALITY DATA AND INFORMATION SUMMARY FOR **2236**

0732-281X *See* NORTH CAROLINA RULES OF COURT, WITH AMENDMENTS RECEIVED TO **3142**

0732-2860 *See* UPSTATE NEW YORK DIRECTORY OF MANUFACTURERS. **3489**

0732-2879 *See* SEARCHERS & RESEARCHERS OF ELLIS COUNTY, TEXAS. **2472**

0732-2933 *See* RESPONSE (SOLANA BEACH, CALIF.). 4799

0732-2992 *See* MUQARNAS. 304

0732-300X *See* THEATRE TIMES. 5371

0732-3026 *See* NATIONAL GUIDE. SUPPLEMENT, THE. 1766

0732-3034 *See* GUIDE TO THE EVALUATION OF EDUCATIONAL EXPERIENCES IN THE ARMED SERVICES. 1827

0732-3115 *See* UPPER MIDWEST REPORT. 717

0732-3123 *See* JOURNAL OF MATHEMATICAL BEHAVIOR, THE. 3513

0732-3395 *See* MEYER'S DIRECTORY OF GENEALOGICAL SOCIETIES IN THE U.S.A. AND CANADA. 2460

0732-345X *See* ALUMNI DIRECTORY / CATAWBA COLLEGE. 1097

0732-3484 *See* BIOMEDICAL FOUNDATIONS OF OPHTHALMOLOGY. 3872

0732-3506 See ADVANCES IN STRAWBERRY RESEARCH. 44

0732-3530 *See* CATALOG OF NEW YORK STATE VISUAL ARTISTS SELECTED FOR THE CREATIVE ARTISTS PUBLIC SERVICE PROGRAM, A. 347

0732-3565 *See* ADVANCES IN LAW AND CHILD DEVELOPMENT. 3119

0732-3573 *See* ADULT LIFE AND WORK LESSON ANNUAL. 4932

0732-3670 *See* UTD PHILATELIC BULLETIN, THE. 2788

0732-3697 *See* MINIATURE PATTERNS & PRODUCTS MAGAZINE. 374

0732-3808 *See* INSERVICE (SYRACUSE, N.Y.). 1864

0732-3867 *See* SOUTH ASIA BULLETIN. 2665

0732-4049 *See* TOWN HALL JOURNAL. 4691

0732-4235 *See* OPTOELECTRONICS DISCONTINUED DEVICES. 2074

0732-4286 *See* GEOLOGOS. 1380

0732-4324 *See* TEXAS BAPTIST HISTORY. 5068

0732-4340 *See* ANCHOR (LOMITA, CALIF.). 4934

0732-4383 *See* CURRENT TOPICS IN CHINESE SCIENCE. SECTION A, PHYSICS. 4401

0732-4391 *See* CURRENT TOPICS IN CHINESE SCIENCE. SECTION B, CHEMISTRY. 974

0732-4413 *See* CURRENT TOPICS IN CHINESE SCIENCE. SECTION D, BIOLOGY. 453

0732-4421 *See* CURRENT TOPICS IN CHINESE SCIENCE. SECTION E, ASTRONOMY. 395

0732-443X *See* CURRENT TOPICS IN CHINESE SCIENCE. SECTION F, EARTH SCIENCE. 1354

0732-4448 *See* CURRENT TOPICS IN CHINESE SCIENCE. SECTION G, MEDICAL SCIENCE. 3570

0732-4456 *See* CONTRIBUTIONS TO THE STUDY OF MASS MEDIA AND COMMUNICATIONS. 1109

0732-4464 *See* CONTRIBUTIONS IN CRIMINOLOGY AND PENOLOGY. 3161

0732-4529 *See* LEGAL WRITING JOURNAL. 3001

0732-4537 *See* LEGAL NEWSLETTER (SPRINGFIELD, ILL.). 4704

0732-4545 *See* ANNOTATED STUDENT AFFAIRS BIBLIOGRAPHY. 3654

0732-4561 *See* FUNDAMENTALS OF SECURED TRANSACTIONS. 2972

0732-457X *See* DELLBOOK OF SUPERWINNERS, THE. 4892

0732-460X *See* PROFESSIONALS IN CHEMISTRY. 990

0732-4618 *See* ANNUAL FINANCIAL REPORT AND REPORT OF OPERATIONS / PUBLIC EMPLOYEES' RETIREMENT SYSTEM, STATE OF CALIFORNIA. 4626

0732-4650 *See* A (BROOKLYN, N.Y.). 3357

0732-4677 *See* AGRICULTURAL EDUCATION MAGAZINE, THE. 50

0732-4685 *See* BERGER BUILDING & DESIGN COST FILE. UNIT PRICES. SOUTHERN EDITION, THE. 600

0732-4715 *See* GEORGE WRIGHT FORUM, THE. 2194

0732-4723 *See* DIRECTORY OF HUMAN RESOURCE SERVICES & PRODUCTS, THE. 666

0732-4758 *See* DIMENSIONS (EXXON CORPORATION). 1604

0732-4766 *See* RESEARCH PERSPECTIVES (RALEIGH, N.C.). 127

0732-4782 *See* NEW BODY. 2600

0732-4820 *See* NEW ENGLAND FOLK DIRECTORY, THE. 4140

0732-4855 *See* JEWISH LIFE IN GREATER WASHINGTON. 5049

0732-488X *See* REFLECTIONS (CORPUS CHRISTI, TEX.). 2469

0732-4898 *See* PIT & QUARRY DIRECTORY OF THE U.S. NONMETALLIC MINING INDUSTRIES. 2148

0732-4901 *See* LAWYERS WEEKLY GUIDEBOOK. 2998

0732-491X *See* ARNOLD G. RUDOFF'S TAX SHELTER DIRECTORY. 891

0732-4928 *See* ANNUAL OF THE SOCIETY OF CHRISTIAN ETHICS, THE. 4935

0732-4944 *See* CONTEMPORARY PHILOSOPHY (BOULDER, COLO.). 4344

0732-5045 *See* WASHINGTON STATE MONTHLY ELECTRICAL STATUS REPORT. 2085

0732-5061 See TUBERCULOSIS BEDS IN HOSPITALS. 3952

0732-507X *See* OCCASIONAL PAPER - MAXWELL GRADUATE SCHOOL OF CITIZENSHIP AND PUBLIC AFFAIRS. METROPOLITAN STUDIES PROGRAM. 4670

0732-5215 *See* DIRECTORY OF FINANCIAL AIDS FOR WOMEN. 1821

0732-5223 *See* CLINICAL SUPERVISOR, THE. 4581

0732-5258 *See* PIP COLLEGE "HELPS" NEWSLETTER. 1883

0732-5266 *See* SHORT STORY INTERNATIONAL. SEEDLING SERIES. 1069

0732-5274 *See* SHORT STORY INTERNATIONAL. STUDENT SERIES. 1069

0732-5282 *See* COMPENSATION (WASHINGTON, D.C. : 1982). 1660

0732-5304 *See* BIBLIOGRAPHY OF PUBLICATIONS OF THE COASTAL ENGINEERING RESEARCH CENTER AND THE BEACH EROSION BOARD. 410

0732-5312 *See* WATER SUPPLY OUTLOOK ... FOR THE NORTHEASTERN UNITED STATES. 1419

0732-5347 *See* CAMPBOOK. WESTERN CANADA AND ALASKA. 4870

0732-5398 *See* NITTANY GROTTO NEWS. 1358

0732-541X *See* NATIONAL ADVERTISING INVESTMENTS IN NEWSPAPERS. 762

0732-5428 *See* ACTUARIAL RESEARCH CLEARING HOUSE. 2872

0732-5452 *See* KENTUCKY LIBRARIES. 3221

0732-5495 *See* CRYPTOGRAPHY MAGAZINE. 2773

0732-5517 *See* FROM THE DRAGON'S DEN. 2785

0732-5525 *See* SMALL BUSINESS TAX SAVER. 4748

0732-5533 *See* TECHNOLOGY UPDATE. 5164

0732-555X *See* MARKETING UPDATE (CLEVELAND, OHIO). 932

0732-5568 *See* CHEMICAL INDUSTRY UPDATE. NORTH AMERICA. 968

0732-5576 *See* CHEMICAL INDUSTRY UPDATE. OVERSEAS. 1601

0732-5606 *See* RESEARCH FRONTS IN ISI/BIOMED. 5146

0732-5649 *See* ZANY WORD SEARCH & FIND PUZZLES. 4868

0732-5657 *See* SUPER MAZE CRAZE PUZZLE PICTURES. 4866

0732-5665 *See* ELECTRICAL ACCIDENT INVESTIGATION HANDBOOK. 2861

0732-5673 *See* WHO'S WHO IN WASHINGTON. 438

0732-5789 *See* BUILDING COST MANUAL. 603

0732-5819 *See* EFL GAZETTE, THE. 3278

0732-5835 *See* EDMUND'S ECONOMY CAR BUYING GUIDE. 5413

0732-586X *See* REGION (WASHINGTON, D.C.), THE. 2833

0732-5886 *See* ISLE SONANTE, L'. 3464

0732-5959 *See* TRIAL BAR NEWS (SAN DIEGO, CALIF.). 3066

0732-5967 *See* DIRECTORY OF WOMEN IN THE MATHEMATICAL SCIENCES. 3503

0732-5975 *See* DIRECTORY OF SOUTH CAROLINA PORT SERVICES. 5448

0732-5983 *See* DIRECTORY OF MAJOR MALLS. 954

0732-6041 *See* AASP NEWSLETTER. 1364

0732-6084 *See* OREGON LABOR MARKET INFORMATION DIRECTORY. 1700

0732-6173 *See* ANNUAL CONFERENCE PROCEEDINGS - STANDARDS ENGINEERING SOCIETY. CONFERENCE. 1965

0732-6181 *See* PROCEEDINGS - ALLERTON CONFERENCE ON COMMUNICATION, CONTROL AND COMPUTING. 2076

0732-619X *See* PROCEEDINGS OF THE CONFERENCE ON EXPLOSIVES AND BLASTING TECHNIQUES. 1991

0732-6262 *See* ENDOCRINE PHYSIOLOGY. 3729

0732-6270 *See* LATIN AMERICAN REVIEW (LEXINGTON, MASS.). 1572

0732-6297 *See* KENTUCKY ALUMNUS. 1102

0732-6319 *See* OPEN DOOR (LEXINGTON, KY.), THE. 1102

0732-6378 *See* FEMINIST FORUM. 5556

0732-6394 *See* LEGISLATIVE HISTORY OF TITLES I-XX OF THE SOCIAL SECURITY ACT. 3002

0732-6408 *See* WATER RESOURCES DEVELOPMENT IN IOWA. 5546

0732-6416 *See* AFROASIATIC DIALECTS. 3262

0732-6424 *See* SOURCES FROM THE ANCIENT NEAR EAST. 2664

0732-6440 *See* BIBLIOTHECA MESOPOTAMICA. 261

0732-6467 *See* BIBLIOTHECA AEGYPTIA. 2638

0732-6475 *See* OCCASIONAL PAPERS ON THE NEAR EAST. 2661

0732-6483 *See* SYRO-MESOPOTAMIAN STUDIES. 2665

0732-6491 *See* MONOGRAPHS ON THE ANCIENT NEAR EAST. 2659

0732-6505 *See* AIDS AND RESEARCH TOOLS IN ANCIENT NEAR EASTERN STUDIES. 2767

0732-6556 *See* MISSOURI RULES OF COURT, STATE AND FEDERAL. 3141

0732-6564 *See* BENDER'S ... PAYROLL TAX GUIDE. 2941

0732-6572 *See* DIRECTORY OF INCENTIVE TRAVEL INTERNATIONAL. 5468

0732-6580 See JOURNAL OF IMMUNOTHERAPY. 3674

0732-6599 *See* BUY BOOKS WHERE, SELL BOOKS WHERE. 4812

0732-6610 *See* FREEDOM IN THE WORLD. 4508

0732-6637 *See* LITERARY MAGAZINE REVIEW. 3346

0732-6645 *See* TOURNAMENTS ILLUMINATED. 2713

0732-6653 *See* PRODUCER'S MASTERGUIDE, THE. 1136

0732-6661 *See* FAYETTE ANCESTORS SURNAME INDEX. 2448

0732-667X *See* GLITCHES (BEND, ORE.). 1233

0732-6688 *See* U.S. IDENTIFICATION MANUAL. 3178

0732-6696 *See* CATALOG SOURCES FOR CREATIVE PEOPLE, NEWS & UPDATES. 1924

0732-6718 *See* MACHINE-MEDIATED LEARNING. 1224

0732-6734 *See* COMMONWEALTH NOVEL IN ENGLISH. 3340

0732-6742 *See* RAVE REVIEW, THE. 3185

0732-6750 *See* INTI (PROVIDENCE, R.I.). 3397

0732-6823 *See* DECISION LINE. 664

0732-684X *See* EARTHCARE NORTHWEST. 2192

0732-6890 See WARP AND WEFT (MCMINNVILLE, OR.). 5359

0732-6971 See STATISTICAL SERVICES DIRECTORY. 5340

0732-7013 See ANNUAL REPORT OF THE NATIONAL INSTITUTES OF HEALTH. PROGRAM BEHAVIORAL NUTRITION RESEARCH AND TRAINING. 4187

0732-7099 See ALTERNATE ENERGY SOURCES. 1931

0732-7110 See GEOTECHNOLOGY. 1356

0732-7137 See MARINE SCIENCES (NEW YORK, N.Y. : 1982). 1452

0732-7145 See FINANCIAL DIRECTORY OF PENSION FUNDS. ILLINOIS, SOUTHERN DOWNSTATE (CHAMPAIGN, SPRINGFIELD, EAST ST. LOUIS & OTHERS). 1671

0732-7188 See ENVIRONMENTAL ENGINEERING & POLLUTION CONTROL. 2228

0732-7218 See MODERN METHODS IN PHARMACOLOGY. 4316

0732-7226 See COLORADO AGRIBUSINESS ROUNDUP. 75

0732-7250 See KORIAN-OMERIKAN. 2743

0732-7269 See BLACK CAUCUS. 5275

0732-7277 See URBAN RESEARCH REVIEW. 2838

0732-7285 See CRIMINAL TRIAL MANUAL. NEW JERSEY. 3106

0732-7293 See CRIMINAL TRIAL MANUAL. MARYLAND. 3106

0732-7315 See CAMPBOOK. NORTHEASTERN. 4870

0732-7331 See MARKETING INFORMATION. 931

0732-734X See WORLD BUSINESS (MENLO PARK, CALIF.). 858

0732-7358 See DIRECTORY OF INDUSTRY DATA SOURCES. WESTERN EUROPE. 1604

0732-7366 See GUIDE TO THE ENERGY INDUSTRIES. 1945

0732-7374 See ACCESSIONS LIST, SOUTHEAST ASIA. CUMULATIVE LIST OF SERIALS, BURMA, THAILAND AND LAOS. 406

0732-7439 See HEALTH POLICY WEEK. 4780

0732-7447 See SMITHSONIAN INSTITUTION LIBRARIES RESEARCH GUIDE. 3250

0732-7498 See DIRECTIONS (KANSAS CITY, MO.). 3572

0732-7501 See PORTABLE COMPANION, THE. 1272

0732-751X See CREATIVE TAX PLANNING FOR REAL ESTATE TRANSACTIONS. 4836

0732-7536 See LEGAL TIMES. 3001

0732-7552 See ATTORNEY FEE AWARDS REPORTER. 2938

0732-7579 See ADVANCED WILL DRAFTING. 3117

0732-7587 See OFFICER AND WARRANT OFFICER DIRECTORY. 4053

0732-7595 See LOGSDON CONNECTIONS. 2458

0732-7625 See MARKETING LETTUCE FROM SALINAS-WATSONVILLE, OTHER CENTRAL CALIFORNIA DISTRICTS AND COLORADO. 2349

0732-7668 See SATELLITE ORBIT. 1163

0732-7676 See WORLD FUTURE SOCIETY. 5237

0732-7706 See BASE (BERKELEY, CALIF.). 5087

0732-7714 See SHEPARD'S FEDERAL TAX CITATIONS. 3050

0732-7722 See SHEPARD'S FEDERAL OCCUPATIONAL SAFETY AND HEALTH CITATIONS. 3050

0732-7730 See TULSA STUDIES IN WOMEN'S LITERATURE. 3448

0732-7749 See WORKING PAPER SERIES - UNIVERSITY OF ARIZONA. MEXICAN AMERICAN STUDIES AND RESEARCH CENTER. 5226

0732-7757 See CABLE TV INVESTOR CHARTS. 1129

0732-7773 See SCHOLASTIC DYNAMATH. 3532

0732-7781 See GIST (CAMPO, CALIF.). 4347

0732-782X See DIRECTORY OF REGISTERED PROFESSIONAL ARCHITECTS, ENGINEERS, AND LAND SURVEYORS. 298

0732-7862 See ISS DIRECTORY OF OVERSEAS SCHOOLS. 1755

0732-7889 See DAY CARE JOURNAL. 5281

0732-7900 See UNITED STATES COURTS (PICTORIAL SUMMARY), THE. 3143

0732-7935 See REPORT (JOINT INSTITUTE FOR LABORATORY ASTROPHYSICS). 4419

0732-7943 See A/E MARKETING JOURNAL. 920

0732-7986 See PSYCHOTHERAPY RESEARCH REVIEW SERIES. 3631

0732-8001 See LECTOR (BERKELEY, CALIF.). 3346

0732-801X See METRO MISCELLANEOUS PUBLICATION. 3231

0732-8028 See PROCEEDINGS OF THE ... ANNUAL CONFERENCE AND EXPOSITION OF THE NATIONAL COMPUTER GRAPHICS ASSOCIATION, INC. 1234

0732-8044 See FEAT MAGAZINE, THE. 2230

0732-8052 See BAKER & TAYLOR'S SCHOOL SELECTION GUIDE. 1727

0732-8079 See GENETIC AND CELLULAR TECHNOLOGY. 545

0732-8087 See JOURNAL OF COAL QUALITY, THE. 1948

0732-8125 See MARYLAND PUBLIC TV. 1134

0732-8141 See ADVANCES IN PROSTAGLANDIN, THROMBOXANE, AND LEUKOTRIENE RESEARCH. 3726

0732-815X See MEANS SQUARE FOOT COSTS : RESIDENTIAL, COMMERCIAL, INDUSTRIAL, INSTITUTIONAL. 621

0732-8176 See AMERICAN POOL PLAYER. 4883

0732-8184 See ABA SECTION OF TAXATION ANNUAL ADVANCED STUDY SESSIONS. SELECTED PROBLEMS AND TECHNIQUES IN ESTATE PLANNING. 3117

0732-8222 See BIENNIAL REPORT - ILLINOIS COMMISSION ON ATOMIC ENERGY. 4632

0732-8230 See HIGHWAY TAXES AND FEES. 5441

0732-8257 See EPA PROGRAM STATUS REPORT, OIL SHALE. 2229

0732-8265 See URBAN OUTLOOK. 2838

0732-8281 See CFANEWS (WASHINGTON, D.C.). 1294

0732-829X See BIENNIAL REPORT - ILLINOIS COMMISSION ON ATOMIC ENERGY. 4632

0732-8303 See JOURNAL OF CARBOHYDRATE CHEMISTRY. 1042

0732-8311 See NUCLEOSIDES & NUCLEOTIDES. 491

0732-8346 See COMPUTER BUSINESS (LOS ANGELES, CALIF.). 1208

0732-8354 See HICKSON MONEY REPORT. 790

0732-8362 See WHAT'S HAPPENING IN WASHINGTON. 1874

0732-8389 See FLOWER ESSENCE JOURNAL, THE. 4776

0732-8397 See COAL TRANSPORTATION REPORT. 5379

0732-8419 See PHARMACEUTICAL PREPARATIONS, EXCEPT BIOLOGICALS. 4320

0732-8435 See CPA JOURNAL (1975), THE. 742

0732-8478 See US-CHINA TRADE STATISTICS. 735

0732-8494 See WASHINGTON TIMES (WASHINGTON, D.C. : 1982), THE. 5648

0732-8524 See DIRECTORY OF PROFESSIONAL WORKERS IN STATE AGRICULTURAL EXPERIMENT STATIONS AND OTHER COOPERATING STATE INSTITUTIONS. 79

0732-8540 See WESTERN MACHINERY AND STEEL WORLD. BUYERS GUIDE. 2132

0732-8567 See REPORT OF INVESTIGATIONS - MISSISSIPPI MINERAL RESOURCES INSTITUTE. 1444

0732-8621 See IRON AND STEEL FOUNDRIES AND STEEL INGOT PRODUCERS. 4005

0732-863X See CONSUMER DEBTORS AND THE BANKRUPTCY CODE. 3086

0732-8648 See TELEVISION & CABLE FACTBOOK. 1140

0732-8702 See PROCEEDINGS ANNUAL MEETING / SOCIETY OF AMERICAN FORESTERS, NORTHERN CALIFORNIA SECTION. 2391

0732-8818 See EXPERIMENTAL TECHNIQUES (WESTPORT, CONN.). 2114

0732-8826 See ANNUAL REPORT / INTERNATIONAL CENTER FOR THE DISABLED. 4383

0732-8850 See ANNUAL NOTRE DAME ESTATE PLANNING INSTITUTE. 3117

0732-8877 See AMERICAN EXPORT MARKETER, THE. 822

0732-8893 See DIAGNOSTIC MICROBIOLOGY AND INFECTIOUS DISEASE. 562

0732-8907 See SENTENCES. 3176

0732-8923 See ANTITHESIS (MARIETTA, PA.). 5074

0732-894X See HCL CATALOGING BULLETIN. 3213

0732-8966 See NEWSLETTER - UNIVERSITY OF SOUTHERN CALIFORNIA. ARMENIAN MUSICAL STUDIES. 4141

0732-8982 See DIRECTORY OF DIPLOMATES / AMERICAN BOARD OF FAMILY PRACTICE. 3737

0732-9016 See ELECTRONIC ENGINEERS MASTER CATALOG. 2047

0732-9075 See INFORMATION CIRCULAR - ARKANSAS GEOLOGICAL COMMISSION. 1382

0732-9113 See JOURNAL OF LEGAL PLURALISM AND UNOFFICIAL LAW. 2988

0732-913X See MID-AMERICAN REVIEW OF SOCIOLOGY. 5252

0732-9148 See ANNUAL REPORT - MONTANA. FIRE MARSHAL BUREAU. 5272

0732-9156 See VIRGINIA REVIEW. 4693

0732-9199 See S. KLEIN DIRECTORY OF COMPUTER GRAPHICS SUPPLIERS, THE. 1235

0732-9202 See ARKANSAS DOCUMENTS. 408

0732-9210 See LIVING BIRD (1991). 5618

0732-9237 See LEASING OPPORTUNITIES (1983). 690

0732-9245 See CAREE COMMUNICATOR. 5057

0732-9253 See NEWSLETTER FROM C.A.R.E.E.'S CHRISTIAN-MARXIST ENCOUNTER TASK GROUP. 4981

0732-927X See SUBJECT DIRECTORY OF SPECIAL LIBRARIES AND INFORMATION CENTERS. 3251

0732-9326 See NORTH CAROLINA ECONOMIC ANNUAL REVIEW. 1576

0732-9334 See MID-ATLANTIC JOURNAL OF BUSINESS, THE. 694

0732-9342 See HOUSING REPORT FOR KENTUCKY. 2825

0732-9350 See AUTOMOTIVE LITERATURE INDEX. 5406

0732-9385 See GREEN SHEET - UNITED STATES. DEPT. OF HEALTH AND HUMAN SERVICES, THE. 4777

0732-9393 See BULLETIN - SOCIETY OF WETLAND SCIENTISTS (U.S.). 450

0732-9407 See FIBER OPTICS WEEKLY UPDATE. 1155

0732-9504 See LADY'S CIRCLE KNITTING & CROCHET CREATIVE IDEAS. 5184

0732-9512 See MICRO DISCOVERY. 1269

0732-9598 See ADVANCES IN INFANCY RESEARCH. 4571

0732-9636 See MEDICAL LIABILITY MONITOR. 3008

0732-9644 See FLESCHNER SERIES IN CRITICAL CARE NURSING, THE. 3856

0732-9768 See MARKETING FLORIDA TROPICAL FRUITS & VEGETABLES. 2349

0732-9776 See INDUSTRIAL ENERGY EFFICIENCY IMPROVEMENT PROGRAM, THE. 1946

0732-9792 See FATAL ACCIDENT REPORTING SYSTEM. 5440

0732-9806 See ISSUES (DALLAS, TEX.). 2536

0732-9814 See RUTGERS UNIVERSITY STUDIES IN CLASSICAL HUMANITIES. HUMANITIES. 1079
0732-9830 See DETAILED MORTALITY STATISTICS, ALABAMA. 4552
0732-9849 See ILLINOIS UNIFORM CRIME REPORTS USER'S GUIDE UPDATE. 3081
0732-9857 See DIRECTORY / SECTION OF TORT AND INSURANCE PRACTICE. 2962
0732-9873 See DIRECTORY / TOY TRAIN OPERATING SOCIETY. 2584
0732-9881 See DISCIPLIANA (1960). 4954
0732-989X See GEOPHYSICS, THE LEADING EDGE OF EXPLORATION. 1406
0732-9911 See INTERNATIONAL LAND RIG DRILLING REPORT, THE. 2141
0732-992X See WOMEN ORGANIZING. 5570
0732-9962 See FAMILY LIFE EDUCATOR. 2279
0732-9997 See WATER RESOURCES DATA. SOUTH CAROLINA. 5545
0733-0030 See TRAVEL AND ENTERTAINMENT, BUSINESS OR PLEASURE?. 4756
0733-0049 See LENDING TRANSACTIONS AND THE BANKRUPTCY REFORM ACT. 3087
0733-0057 See FUNDAMENTAL CONCEPTS OF ESTATE PLANNING. 3118
0733-0073 See BLACK WILLOW. 3460
0733-009X See INTERNATIONAL PETROCHEMICAL REPORT, THE. 978
0733-0103 See BUYING STRATEGY FORECAST FOR PURCHASING MANAGERS. 949
0733-0138 See EARLY WARNING FORECAST. 1480
0733-0170 See TRADESHOW WEEK. 767
0733-0197 See TRANSPORT (DE)REGULATION REPORT. 5395
0733-0200 See OLIPHANT WASHINGTON SERVICE. 1952
0733-0219 See OLIPHANT WASHINGTON SERVICE. ENERGY SUMMARY. 1952
0733-0227 See OLIPHANT WASHINGTON SERVICE. DIGEST AND CALENDAR OF ACTIVITIES OF THE...CONGRESS ... SESSION OF POSSIBLE INTEREST. 4270
0733-0243 See CURRENT DEVELOPMENTS IN COPYRIGHT LAW. 1303
0733-0251 See REGISTRY OF MEMBERS - CLINICAL SOCIOLOGY ASSOCIATION. 5255
0733-026X See OTC HANDBOOK. 910
0733-0286 See CLEMENTS' ENCYCLOPEDIA OF WORLD GOVERNMENTS. BIANNUAL SUPPLEMENT. 4468
0733-0294 See TAYLOR'S ENCYCLOPEDIA OF GOVERNMENT OFFICIALS, FEDERAL AND STATE. SUPPLEMENT. 4498
0733-0308 See BAMBOO RIDGE. 3365
0733-0324 See FORDYCE LETTER, THE. 1675
0733-0332 See HRPLANNING NEWSLETTER, THE. 941
0733-0340 See GARDEN IDEAS & OUTDOOR LIVING. 2415
0733-0367 See SIEGRUNEN. 2709
0733-0375 See SYLLABUS / UNIVERSITY OF HEALING. 1849
0733-0383 See SAIL INDEX. 595
0733-043X See ACE (NEW YORK, N.Y.). 4881
0733-0448 See ACC BASKETBALL HANDBOOK. 4881
0733-0545 See WEEKLY COAL PRODUCTION. 2153
0733-0553 See PETROLEUM SUPPLY MONTHLY. 4274
0733-0642 See LA FILE. 2422
0733-0669 See SPORTS AND THE COURTS. 3058
0733-0677 See WATERFRONT WORLD. 2839
0733-0707 See RESTORATION & MANAGEMENT NOTES. 2204
0733-0898 See PROCEEDINGS OF THE ... SPRING MEETING (INDUSTRIAL RELATIONS RESEARCH ASSOCIATION : 1979). 1703
0733-0928 See OFFSHORE RIG LOCATION REPORT, THE. 4267

0733-0979 See ANNUAL STATISTICAL BULLETIN. PUBLIC UNIVERSITY LIBRARY STATISTICS. 5321
0733-1207 See PANDORA. 5564
0733-1223 See FLORIDA RELATIVE VALUE STUDIES. 3576
0733-1231 See ALL ABOUT ISSUES. 4933
0733-124X See PROCEEDINGS OF THE GREENWOOD GENETIC CENTER. 550
0733-1266 See OFFICE GUIDE TO ORLANDO. 4213
0733-1274 See SOFTWARE PROTECTION. 1227
0733-1282 See PROCEEDINGS OF THE SECTION ON STATISTICAL EDUCATION - AMERICAN STATISTICAL ASSOCIATION. SECTION ON STATISTICAL EDUCATION. 5336
0733-1290 See AMERICAN JOURNAL OF FORENSIC PSYCHOLOGY, THE. 3739
0733-1304 See HGS INTERNATIONAL'S REAS LETTER. 4838
0733-1398 See IN VIVO (NEW YORK, N.Y.). 681
0733-1436 See REFEREE (FRANKSVILLE, WIS.). 4914
0733-1460 See VISION (SAN ANTONIO, TEX.). 5755
0733-1517 See AGRICULTURE REVIEW (LEXINGTON, MASS.). 54
0733-1533 See AFRICUS. 821
0733-1541 See ALUMNI DIRECTORY / STATE UNIVERSITY OF NEW YORK AT ALBANY. 1099
0733-1606 See DRAMATISTS SOURCEBOOK. 5364
0733-1614 See ELECTRONICS INSIGHT. 2049
0733-1630 See SUPER BOWL FACT BOOK. 4924
0733-172X See NOISE POLLUTION PUBLICATIONS ABSTRACTS. 2179
0733-1738 See POLICY ANALYSES IN INTERNATIONAL ECONOMICS. 1639
0733-1754 See WATER FLYING. 39
0733-1770 See AGRICULTURAL ENGINEERING INDEX. 150
0733-1843 See FABRICNEWS. 5350
0733-1851 See NCBL NOTES. 3014
0733-1916 See USBE. 427
0733-1924 See TRENIE I IZNOS. 2108
0733-1932 See INTERNATIONAL SERIES IN MODERN APPLIED MATHEMATICS AND COMPUTER SCIENCE. 3510
0733-1940 See INTERNATIONAL SERIES ON SYSTEMS AND CONTROL. 2067
0733-1959 See JOURNAL OF CELLULAR BIOCHEMISTRY. SUPPLEMENT. 489
0733-2017 See ANNUAL REPORT - MISSISSIPPI. DEPT. OF WILDLIFE CONSERVATION. 2186
0733-2033 See THEATRE HISTORY STUDIES. 5370
0733-2041 See STATISTICS OF PUBLIC SCHOOL LIBRARIES / MEDIA CENTERS. 3260
0733-205X See STANDARD & POOR'S OTC PROFILES. 915
0733-2068 See CROP PROTECTION RESEARCH. 4244
0733-2076 See JOURNAL OF AQUACULTURE & AQUATIC SCIENCES. 460
0733-2084 See AUTOMOTIVE MARKET REPORT. 921
0733-2130 See COLLECTOR EDITIONS. 2772
0733-2165 See LITERARY CRITICISM REGISTER. 3357
0733-222X See BIO/TECHNOLOGY (NEW YORK, N.Y. 1983). 5088
0733-2238 See DOLLS. 372
0733-2254 See TAX AVOIDANCE DIGEST. 4752
0733-2262 See DOCTOR'S OFFICE, THE. 3914
0733-2297 See SAN BERNARDINO STREET ATLAS. ZIP CODE EDITION. 1147
0733-2335 See UNIFORM PLUMBING CODE. 2608
0733-2351 See MANUFACTURED HOUSING INDUSTRY ... BUYER'S MANUAL. 2828
0733-236X See ALASKA EDUCATION DIRECTORY. 1723
0733-2386 See DISPLAY AND IMAGING TECHNOLOGY. 1971

0733-2394 See MEMORY AND MICROCOMPUTERS. 1269
0733-2408 See BUSINESS FORUM (LOS ANGELES, CALIF.). 648
0733-2424 See MORALITY. 2252
0733-2440 See WHO'S WHO IN INTERIOR LANDSCAPING. 437
0733-2459 See JOURNAL OF CLINICAL APHERESIS. 3819
0733-2467 See NEUROUROL. URODYN. 3843
0733-2475 See OREGON BARS. 3023
0733-2491 See JOURNAL OF LAW AND COMMERCE, THE. 2988
0733-2548 See OSSC REPORT. 1771
0733-2564 See OFFICEMATION PRODUCT REPORTS. 4213
0733-2572 See BLACK'S GUIDE TO THE METRO DENVER OFFICE SPACE MARKET. 4210
0733-2599 See ABSTRACTS OF RESEARCH IN PASTORAL CARE AND COUNSELING. 5012
0733-2610 See ... BUSINESS ONE IRWIN BUSINESS AND INVESTMENT ALMANAC, THE. 651
0733-2661 See BIOLOGICAL THERAPY. 3774
0733-2726 See SEED CROPS. ANNUAL SUMMARY. 186
0733-2734 See MOVIE MIRROR. 4075
0733-2823 See SPORTING NEWS ... COLLEGE FOOTBALL YEARBOOK, THE. 4921
0733-2831 See KHIMICHESKAIA FIZIKA. 1055
0733-2858 See DIRECTORY OF EDUCATIONAL INSTITUTIONS ACCREDITED BY THE ACCREDITING COMMISSION OF THE ASSOCIATION OF INDEPENDENT COLLEGES AND SCHOOLS. 1820
0733-2912 See ALASKA BUDGET IN BRIEF. 4709
0733-2920 See DIRECTORY / AMERICAN GROUP PSYCHOTHERAPY ASSOCIATION. 3924
0733-2998 See LEFT INDEX. 4502
0733-3013 See MOTHERING. 2283
0733-3048 See NEWSLETTER / AMERICAN SOCIETY OF INDEXERS. 3234
0733-3056 See EQUIPMENT MANAGEMENT. 1975
0733-317X See NURSINGWORLD JOURNAL. 3866
0733-3188 See ZOO BIOLOGY. 5601
0733-3196 See FOOTLOOSE LIBRARIAN, THE. 5474
0733-3285 See NATIONAL AND FEDERAL LEGAL EMPLOYMENT REPORT, THE. 3013
0733-3293 See ASCD UPDATE. 1888
0733-3315 See POPULAR COMMUNICATIONS. 1119
0733-3323 See EXPLORATIONS IN SIGHTS AND SOUNDS. 2261
0733-3390 See IRISH LITERARY SUPPLEMENT. 3397
0733-3412 See EXECUTIVE COMPENSATION. 674
0733-351X See INVESTING COMMON CENTS. 902
0733-3536 See COMPUTER-AIDED ENGINEERING. 1228
0733-3544 See CLARINETWORK. 4110
0733-3560 See AMERICAN HISTORY. 2719
0733-3609 See ANNUAL REPORT - OKLAHOMA. STATE BOARD OF EXAMINERS OF PSYCHOLOGISTS. 4574
0733-3633 See REPORT TO THE COLORADO WATER QUALITY CONTROL COMMISSION. 5538
0733-3927 See SWS CONTRACT REPORT. 1418
0733-401X See UCLA JOURNAL OF ENVIRONMENTAL LAW & POLICY. 3117
0733-4044 See NOAA DATA REPORT ERL GLERL. 1416
0733-4060 See ONGOING CURRENT BIBLIOGRAPHY OF PLASTIC AND RECONSTRUCTIVE SURGERY (1980). 3661
0733-4184 See NEWS FROM DRAFTING WILLS AND TUST AREEMENTS. 3118
0733-4249 See ANNUAL FORUM PROCEEDINGS - AMERICAN HELICOPTER SOCIETY. 11

0733-4265 *See* MASSON MONOGRAPHS IN DIAGNOSTIC PATHOLOGY. **3896**

0733-4273 *See* JOURNAL OF PSYCHOLOGY AND CHRISTIANITY. **4969**

0733-429X *See* PIERCE PIANO ATLAS. **4146**

0733-4303 *See* LEADER'S EQUIPMENT LEASING NEWSLETTER. **2998**

0733-4311 *See* AUSLEGUNG. **4342**

0733-4354 *See* CLINICS IN EMERGENCY MEDICINE. **3723**

0733-4397 *See* SCHEDULE OF NIH CONFERENCES. **3639**

0733-4443 *See* CURRENT AWARENESS IN BIOLOGICAL SCIENCES. **478**

0733-4478 *See* GOOD HOUSEKEEPING'S MOMS WHO WORK. **2280**

0733-4486 *See* MICHIGAN JOURNAL OF POLITICAL SCIENCE. **4481**

0733-4540 *See* COMPARATIVE CIVILIZATIONS REVIEW. **5196**

0733-4559 *See* OUR HERITAGE (WILLS POINT, TEX.). **2466**

0733-4605 *See* SOUND ADVICE. **4847**

0733-4613 *See* BUSINESS REORGANIZATIONS UNDER THE BANKRUPTCY CODE. **3086**

0733-463X *See* NEWSLETTER / TRAVELING EXHIBITION INFORMATION SERVICE. **360**

0733-4648 *See* JOURNAL OF APPLIED GERONTOLOGY. **3753**

0733-4672 *See* MEDICARE EXPLAINED. **2888**

0733-4680 *See* JOURNAL OF TRACE AND MICROPROBE TECHNIQUES. **1017**

0733-4710 *See* ANIMAL PEOPLE'S DIRECTORY, THE. **225**

0733-4737 *See* OHIO FOLKLORE. **2323**

0733-4745 *See* RECREATIONAL VEHICLE BLUE BOOK. **5391**

0733-477X *See* OREGON DIRECTORY OF AMERICAN INDIAN RESOURCES. **2270**

0733-4796 *See* IN-STORE BAKERY PRODUCTION AND MARKETING. **2344**

0733-480X *See* STATUS OF EQUAL EMPLOYMENT OPPORTUNITY PROGRAM (WASHINGTON, D.C. : 1970). **4705**

0733-4826 *See* WORKING TOGETHER FOR YESTERDAY, TODAY, AND TOMORROW (LINCOLN, NEB.). **5572**

0733-4869 *See* ARTSCENE (LOS ANGELES, CALIF.). **342**

0733-4915 *See* P.U.R. ANALYSIS OF INVESTOR-OWNED ELECTRIC AND GAS UTILITIES, THE. **4761**

0733-4923 *See* GARDEN DESIGN. **2415**

0733-5032 *See* BLACK'S REVIEW (WASHINGTON ED.). **4210**

0733-5059 *See* BLACK'S GUIDE. HOUSTON OFFICE SPACE MARKET. **4210**

0733-5067 *See* BLACK'S GUIDE. SUBURBAN MANHATTAN OFFICE SPACE MARKET. **4210**

0733-5113 *See* JOURNAL OF ARTS MANAGEMENT AND LAW, THE. **386**

0733-513X *See* LEADER'S PRODUCT LIABILITY LAW AND STRATEGY. **2999**

0733-5156 *See* GOVERNMENT SALES STRATEGIST. **4652**

0733-5164 *See* OFFICE TECHNOLOGY MANAGEMENT. **4213**

0733-5210 *See* JOURNAL OF CEREAL SCIENCE. **176**

0733-5229 *See* ANNUAL WHO'S IN CHARGE HERE YEARBOOK. **2721**

0733-5237 *See* PENNSYLVANIA DIRECTORY OF MANUFACTURERS (HOHOKUS, N.J.). **3486**

0733-5253 *See* MUSICIAN (GLOUCESTER, MASS.). **4137**

0733-5288 *See* ELAN (NEW YORK, N.Y.). **2532**

0733-5296 *See* SOO, THE. **5436**

0733-530X *See* RECREATION VEHICLE FINANCING. **4744**

0733-5326 *See* CALIFORNIA PARKS & RECREATION. **4706**

0733-5377 *See* LEISURE LINES (SACRAMENTO, CALIF.). **4706**

0733-5407 *See* AIRFARE DISCOUNT BULLETIN. **9**

0733-5423 *See* C.S.P.G. SEMINAR. **1371**

0733-5504 *See* CABLE PRODUCT NEWS. **1129**

0733-5555 *See* FOCUS (MENLO PARK, CALIF.). **1824**

0733-558X *See* RESEARCH IN THE SOCIOLOGY OF ORGANIZATIONS. **5255**

0733-5687 *See* IAFP FINANCIAL PLANNING UPDATE. **4731**

0733-5695 *See* PLAYGUY. **3996**

0733-5709 *See* BIOTECHNOLOGY RESEARCH ABSTRACTS. **3655**

0733-5733 *See* REPORT / MARKETING SCIENCE INSTITUTE. **935**

0733-5768 *See* NEWSLETTER / MARKETING SCIENCE INSTITUTE. **934**

0733-5784 *See* YEARBOOK / INDIANA DENTAL ASSOCIATION. **1337**

0733-5792 *See* COMPUTATIONAL SEISMOLOGY. **1404**

0733-5806 *See* CALIFORNIA THEATRE ANNUAL. **5362**

0733-5830 *See* PROCEEDINGS OF THE SECTION ON SURVEY RESEARCH METHODS. **3542**

0733-5903 *See* LONG TERM ENERGY PLAN. **1949**

0733-5911 *See* LONG TERM ENERGY PLAN. EXECUTIVE SUMMARY. **1949**

0733-592X *See* LONG TERM ENERGY PLAN. APPENDICES. **1949**

0733-5989 *See* ECOTASS (ENGLISH EDITION). **1487**

0733-5997 *See* EKOTASS (DEUTSCHE AUSGABE). **1488**

0733-6012 *See* MCD. MIDDLE ATLANTIC EDITION. **5386**

0733-6020 *See* INDEPENDENT STUDY CATALOG (PRINCETON, N.J.), THE. **1830**

0733-6063 *See* TECHNICAL PAPERS - SOCIETY OF EXPLORATION GEOPHYSICISTS. INTERNATIONAL MEETING AND EXPOSITION. **1411**

0733-6098 *See* PROCEEDINGS OF THE ANNUAL INSTITUTE - EASTERN MINERAL LAW FOUNDATION (U.S.). ANNUAL INSTITUTE. **3031**

0733-6152 *See* JOHN A. PUGSLEY'S COMMON SENSE VIEWPOINT. **904**

0733-6160 *See* ARBITRATION & THE LAW. **2936**

0733-6217 *See* PERSPECTIVES ON DEATH AND DYING SERIES. **4355**

0733-6233 *See* LAW OF THE HANDICAPPED : REPORTER AND COMMENTATOR, THE. **2996**

0733-6241 *See* PETROLEUM TAXATION, PETROLEUM LEGISLATION REPORT. **4274**

0733-6314 *See* SKY CALENDAR. **399**

0733-6349 *See* PHILADELPHIA CITY PAPER. **5738**

0733-6357 *See* FAULKNER NEWSLETTER AND YOKNAPATAWPHA REVIEW, THE. **432**

0733-6373 *See* PROGRAM AND ABSTRACTS / INTERSCIENCE CONFERENCE ON ANTIMICROBIAL AGENTS AND CHEMOTHERAPY. **568**

0733-6381 *See* OUSLEY NEWSLETTER. **2466**

0733-639X *See* ONE ON ONE (ALBANY, N.Y.). **3022**

0733-642X *See* ECONOMIC REVIEW OF TRAVEL IN AMERICA, THE. **5469**

0733-6438 *See* QUANTUS, COMPENDIUM OF DIRECTORS. **884**

0733-6470 *See* CHRONOS (WALTHAM, MASS.). **5242**

0733-6497 *See* MOBILE/MANUFACTURED HOME BLUE BOOK. **3484**

0733-6500 *See* RACING, FARM, CORPORATE, AND STABLE NAMES. **2802**

0733-6535 *See* JOURNAL OF VOLUNTEER ADMINISTRATION, THE. **5293**

0733-6551 *See* TODAY'S DELINQUENT. **3178**

0733-6586 *See* NEWS TALK. **1927**

0733-6608 *See* GRASSROOTS DEVELOPMENT. **2910**

0733-6616 *See* HAMBONE (STANFORD, CALIF.). **3392**

0733-6691 *See* ELECTROCHEMISTRY & ELECTROCHEMICAL ENGINEERING. **1034**

0733-6764 *See* BORGO FAMILY HISTORIES. **2612**

0733-6845 *See* CONTRA COSTA COUNTY POPULAR STREET ATLAS (CENSUS TRACT ED.). **2559**

0733-6918 *See* LOS ANGELES COUNTY POPULAR STREET ATLAS (CENSUS TRACT ED.). **2568**

0733-7272 *See* PHYSICAL EDUCATION GOLD BOOK. **1857**

0733-740X *See* SANTA CLARA COUNTY POPULAR STREET ATLAS (ZIP CODE ED.). **2575**

0733-7574 *See* PHOENIX AND VICINITY POPULAR STREET ATLAS, INCLUDING MARICOPA COUNTY (CENSUS TRACT EDITION). **2572**

0733-7663 *See* PIERCE COUNTY POPULAR STREET ATLAS (CENSUS TRACT ED.). **2572**

0733-7760 *See* COLLECTIONS / GEORGIA HISTORICAL SOCIETY. **2728**

0733-7809 *See* NEW YORK FINE PRINT. **2269**

0733-804X *See* FLORIDA CRIME AND DELINQUENCY. **3164**

0733-8058 *See* CATASTROPHISM AND ANCIENT HISTORY. **2613**

0733-8074 *See* ACCESS (RESEARCH TRIANGLE PARK, N.C.). **1265**

0733-8082 *See* DEFENSE/AEROSPACE COMPANY CONTRACT QUARTERLY. **17**

0733-8104 *See* WASHINGTON REPORT ON AFRICA. **4499**

0733-8228 *See* TEXTBOOK NEWS. **1787**

0733-8244 *See* INSIDE TEXTILES. **5352**

0733-8252 *See* NEW PRODUCT DEVELOPMENT. **934**

0733-8309 *See* RAND MCNALLY CAMPGROUND & TRAILER PARK GUIDE, EASTERN. **4708**

0733-8368 *See* TOURBOOK. NORTH CENTRAL. **5493**

0733-8384 *See* CHARACTERISTICS OF WORK-RELATED INJURIES AND ILLNESSES IN MAINE. **2860**

0733-8392 *See* STRICKLAND SCENE. **2474**

0733-8503 *See* LINK (CLEVELAND, OHIO). **357**

0733-8511 *See* INTERIOR DECORATORS' HANDBOOK. **2901**

0733-8538 *See* VALUATION CONSULTANT, THE. **717**

0733-8554 *See* CABOT MARKET LETTER, THE. **893**

0733-8562 *See* V.M.E.A. NOTES. **4157**

0733-8600 *See* CABLE COMMUNICATIONS IN MINNESOTA. **1128**

0733-8619 *See* NEUROLOGIC CLINICS. **3840**

0733-8627 *See* EMERGENCY MEDICINE CLINICS OF NORTH AMERICA. **3724**

0733-8635 *See* DERMATOLOGIC CLINICS. **3719**

0733-8643 *See* CURRENT LITERATURE REVIEW IN OBSTETRICS & GYNECOLOGY. **3759**

0733-8651 *See* CARDIOLOGY CLINICS. **3700**

0733-866X *See* REGISTER OF THE SPENCER MUSEUM OF ART, THE. **4095**

0733-8678 *See* SPACE PRESS. **36**

0733-8686 *See* ULSTER-AMERICAN NEWSLETTER. **2764**

0733-8708 *See* SPORTSTYLE (CONSUMER EDITION). **4923**

0733-8716 *See* IEEE JOURNAL ON SELECTED AREAS IN COMMUNICATIONS. **1157**

0733-8724 *See* JOURNAL OF LIGHTWAVE TECHNOLOGY. **4436**

0733-8740 *See* SPORTS HIGH. **4922**

0733-8759 *See* COUNTRY HERITAGE. **4112**

0733-8856 *See* SPECIAL PUBLICATIONS : GULF COAST ASSOCIATION OF GEOLOGICAL SOCIETIES. **1398**

0733-8864 *See* PHOLEOS. **1409**

0733-8899 *See* VANITY FAIR (NEW YORK, N.Y.). **2549**

0733-8902 *See* CLAO JOURNAL, THE. **3873**

0733-8937 *See* KINDEX. **3081**

0733-8961 *See* INFORMATION REPORT (WASHINGTON, D.C.), THE. **682**

0733-9003 See PROGRESS AND TOPICS IN CYTOGENETICS. **539**

0733-9062 See SAFRA. **5052**

0733-9089 See MONDAY REPORT (TALLAHASSEE, FLA.), THE. **1866**

0733-9100 See GEOTHERMAL REPORT. **1945**

0733-9135 See POPULATION REPORTS. SERIES M, SPECIAL TOPICS (ENGLISH ED.). **4558**

0733-9143 See HEALTH POLICY (NEW YORK, N.Y.). **4780**

0733-9283 See RESULTS FROM THE COOPERATIVE COORDINATED OAT BREEDING NURSERIES, AND THE UNIFORM WINTER-HARDINESS NURSERIES. **1543**

0733-9291 See EXECUTIVE EDGE. **674**

0733-9305 See INFOPERSPECTIVES. **1238**

0733-9321 See SYMPOSIA ON FRONTIERS OF PHARMACOLOGY. **4330**

0733-933X See CLINICAL DISORDERS ON PEDIATRIC NUTRITION. **4188**

0733-9348 See ALPINE SKIING COMPETITION GUIDE. WESTERN/ROCKY EDITION. **4882**

0733-9356 See ALPINE SKIING COMPETITION GUIDE. EASTERN/CENTRAL EDITION. **4882**

0733-9364 See JOURNAL OF CONSTRUCTION ENGINEERING AND MANAGEMENT. **2025**

0733-9372 See JOURNAL OF ENVIRONMENTAL ENGINEERING (NEW YORK N.Y.). **2233**

0733-9380 See JOURNAL OF PROFESSIONAL ISSUES IN ENGINEERING EDUCATION AND PRACTICE. **2026**

0733-9399 See JOURNAL OF ENGINEERING MECHANICS. **2118**

0733-9402 See JOURNAL OF ENERGY ENGINEERING. **2118**

0733-9410 See JOURNAL OF GEOTECHNICAL ENGINEERING. **1385**

0733-9429 See JOURNAL OF HYDRAULIC ENGINEERING (NEW YORK, N.Y.). **2092**

0733-9437 See JOURNAL OF IRRIGATION AND DRAINAGE ENGINEERING. **2092**

0733-9445 See JOURNAL OF STRUCTURAL ENGINEERING (NEW YORK, N.Y.). **2026**

0733-9453 See JOURNAL OF SURVEYING ENGINEERING. **2026**

0733-947X See JOURNAL OF TRANSPORTATION ENGINEERING. **2026**

0733-9488 See JOURNAL OF URBAN PLANNING AND DEVELOPMENT. **2026**

0733-9496 See JOURNAL OF WATER RESOURCES PLANNING AND MANAGEMENT. **5535**

0733-950X See JOURNAL OF WATERWAY, PORT, COASTAL, AND OCEAN ENGINEERING. **2092**

0733-9526 See ILLINOIS WRITERS REVIEW. **3344**

0733-9534 See ORANGE COUNTY BUSINESS TO BUSINESS. **701**

0733-9542 See NEW VICO STUDIES. **4353**

0733-9569 See COASTAL AND ESTUARINE SCIENCES. **2212**

0733-9615 See DEVIL'S MILLHOPPER, THE. **3462**

0733-964X See FLORIDA BUSINESS GUIDE, THE. **676**

0733-9658 See FLORIDA, IN REVIEW. **1344**

0733-9674 See LET'S CHEER. **4903**

0733-9712 See UGAZINE. **1095**

0733-9720 See VISTAS (MIAMI, FLA.). **2549**

0733-9739 See DBS NEWS. **1153**

0733-9771 See CAMPAIGN PEOPLE. **4467**

0733-9836 See DENTAL ASEPSIS REVIEW. **1320**

0733-9844 See NATIONAL JOURNAL OF MEDICINE & MEDICAL RESEARCH. **3619**

0733-9852 See MENTAL HEALTH SERVICE SYSTEM REPORTS. SERIES EN, MENTAL HEALTH ECONOMICS. **4790**

0734-0028 See HOSPITAL CONTRACTS MANUAL. **2979**

0734-0044 See CURRICULUM UPDATE (ALEXANDRIA, VA.). **1892**

0734-0052 See MARRIAGE (SAINT PAUL, MINN.). **2283**

0734-0133 See SYNTAX QUARTERLY. **1204**

0734-0141 See ON CAMPUS WITH WOMEN. **5563**

0734-0168 See CRIMINAL JUSTICE REVIEW (ATLANTA, GA.). **3162**

0734-0176 See CRAFTS 'N THINGS. **371**

0734-0192 See DIRECTORY OF CHEMICAL DEPENDENCY PROGRAMS IN MINNESOTA. **1343**

0734-0206 See BASS PLAYER QUARTERLY. **4102**

0734-0214 See BENSON TRACE, THE. **2439**

0734-0222 See NEW CRITERION (NEW YORK, N.Y.), THE. **326**

0734-0230 See PENNSYLVANIA HIGH SCHOOL ATHLETIC YEARBOOK. **4912**

0734-0273 See INDEX TO RESEARCH FRONTS IN ISI/GEOSCITECH. **1382**

0734-0281 See ON KEY. **4143**

0734-029X See PERFORMANCE MANAGEMENT MAGAZINE. **882**

0734-0311 See VOPROSY VIRUSOLOGII. **571**

0734-032X See MISSOURI POPULATION ESTIMATES, BY COUNTY, BY AGE, BY SEX. **4554**

0734-0346 See INDUSTRIAL SAFETY AND APPLIED HEALTH PHYSICS ANNUAL REPORT FOR **2863**

0734-0451 See SEMINARS IN HEARING. **3891**

0734-0478 See SEMINARS IN SPEECH AND LANGUAGE. **3320**

0734-0486 See MONOGRAPH / COMMITTEE FOR MONETARY RESEARCH AND EDUCATION. **799**

0734-0508 See NCAA MEN'S WATER POLO RULES. **4907**

0734-0524 See LONG RANGE JUDICIAL FACILITY PLAN. **3141**

0734-0559 See MCCUTCHEON'S FUNCTIONAL MATERIALS. NORTH AMERICAN EDITION. **1027**

0734-0567 See MCCUTCHEON'S EMULSIFIERS & DETERGENTS (INTERNATIONAL EDITION). **1027**

0734-0575 See JAPAN ECONOMIC DAILY. **1498**

0734-0583 See COMPUTER DIRECTORY AND BUYERS' GUIDE, THE. **1244**

0734-0591 See DISPOSITIO. **3382**

0734-0605 See DIRECTORY OF AMERICAN POETS AND FICTION WRITERS, A. **3381**

0734-0648 See TRANSIT RESEARCH ABSTRACTS (1992). **5395**

0734-0656 See INTERNATIONAL INVESTMENT LETTER. **902**

0734-0664 See GERODONTOLOGY. **3751**

0734-0699 See LOONFEATHER. **3346**

0734-0702 See FIRE PREVENTION NOTES. **2289**

0734-0710 See CONJOINT DIRECTORY OF AMERICAN ACADEMY OF OTOLARYNGOLOGY-HEAD AND NECK SURGERY, AND AMERICAN ACADEMY OF FACIAL PLASTIC AND RECONSTRUCTIVE SURGERY, AND AMERICAN NEUROTOLOGY SOCIETY, AND AMERICAN RHINOLOGIC SOCIETY, AND AMERICAN SOCIETY OF OPHTHALMOLOGIC AND OTOLARYNGOLOGIC ALLERGY. **3887**

0734-0788 See NOTES ON TRANSLATION. **5018**

0734-080X See FUTRAL, FUTRELL, FUTRELLE AND RELATED FAMILIES, WATKINS, CLIFFORD, WOOD. **2449**

0734-0842 See FROM THE STATE CAPITALS. ALCOHOLIC BEVERAGE CONTROL. **3164**

0749-2790 See FROM THE STATE CAPITALS. PUBLIC SAFETY & JUSTICE POLICIES. **3165**

0734-0931 See FROM THE STATE CAPITALS. WORKERS' COMPENSATION. **1675**

0734-0966 See ... OREGON STATE BAR ECONOMIC SURVEY, THE. **3023**

0734-0982 See WISCONSIN ALMANAC, THE. **2766**

0734-0990 See LRE PROJECT EXCHANGE. **3005**

0734-1008 See DIRECTIONARY OF THE DEFENSE INDUSTRY INCLUDING NATO AND WARSAW PACT COUNTRIES. **4042**

0734-1008 See DICTIONARY OF THE DEFENSE INDUSTRY. **4042**

0734-1016 See OFFICIAL STEAMSHIP SERVICE DIRECTORY, THE. **5453**

0734-1032 See JOURNAL OF THE CONDUCTORS' GUILD. **4127**

0734-1067 See FROM THE STATE CAPITALS. PARKS AND RECREATION TRENDS, (NEW HAVEN, CONN.). **4706**

0734-1105 See FROM THE STATE CAPITALS. LABOR RELATIONS. **3148**

0734-1121 See FROM THE STATE CAPITALS. TAXES-PROPERTY (NEW HAVEN, CONN.). **4727**

0734-1156 See FROM THE STATE CAPITALS. PUBLIC HEALTH (1982). **4776**

0734-1199 See FROM THE STATE CAPITALS. TOURIST BUSINESS PROMOTION (NEW HAVEN, CONN.). **5474**

0734-1202 See FROM THE STATE CAPITALS. FEDERAL ACTION AFFECTING THE STATES (NEW HAVEN, CONN.). **4650**

0734-1237 See FROM THE STATE CAPITALS. ENVIRONMENTAL REGULATION. **2230**

0734-1407 See CRC HANDBOOK OF CLINICAL ENGINEERING. **3691**

0734-1415 See TAPPI JOURNAL. **4239**

0734-1431 See PROGRAM PLANS. NURSING BASIC SERIES. **3867**

0734-1458 See OPERATIONS MANAGEMENT REVIEW. **881**

0734-1482 See PROTOTYPE MODELER. **2777**

0734-1490 See NORTHERN ILLINOIS UNIVERSITY LAW REVIEW. **3018**

0734-1504 See ZHURNAL NAUCHNOI I PRIKLADNOI FOTOGRAFII I KINEMATOGRAFII. **4378**

0734-1512 See HISTORY AND TECHNOLOGY. **5110**

0734-1520 See POVERKHNOST. **4417**

0734-1539 See FACULTY STUDIES - CARSON-NEWMAN COLLEGE. **4958**

0734-1571 See FLOTATION SLEEP INDUSTRY. BUYERS GUIDE. **2905**

0734-1601 See FROM THE STATE CAPITALS. PUBLIC ASSISTANCE & WELFARE TRENDS (NEW HAVEN, CONN.). **5286**

0734-1644 See CHEMICAL ENGINEERING, CONCEPTS AND REVIEWS. **2009**

0734-1660 See PREVENTIVE LAW REPORTER. **3030**

0734-1679 See KHIMIIA I TEKHNOLOGIIA VODY. **2235**

0734-1687 See AQUATIC TOXICOLOGY SERIES. **2211**

0734-1695 See CONTROL AND SYSTEMS THEORY. **2039**

0734-1709 See STATISTICS OF INCOME. PARTNERSHIP RETURNS (1977). **4700**

0734-1741 See NORTH & CENTRAL AMERICAN DIRECTORY. **4142**

0734-1768 See JOURNAL OF THE SOCIETY FOR INFORMATION DISPLAY. **3221**

0734-1784 See PLASTICS BUSINESS NEWS. **4458**

0734-1822 See BALANCING THE SCALES. **3179**

0734-1865 See BIBLIOTHECA AMERICANA (CORAL GABLES, FLA.). **3195**

0734-1873 See CANCER NURSING NEWS. **3853**

0734-189X See CVGIP. IMAGE UNDERSTANDING. **1233**

0734-189X See CVGIP. GRAPHICAL MODELS AND IMAGE PROCESSING. **1233**

0734-1903 See BOOK OF SEMI STANDARDS. **2037**

0734-1938 See LAW REVIEW JOURNAL. **2996**

0734-1962 See ASCE PUBLICATIONS INFORMATION. **2002**

0734-1970 See MCGRAW-HILL'S MEDICAL UTILIZATION REVIEW. **3606**

0734-1989 See NEW DRUG COMMENTARY. **4317**

0734-2012 See BULLETIN OF THE FRIENDS OF THE OWEN D. YOUNG LIBRARY. **3198**

0734-2020 See HISTORICAL GENEALOGICAL MAGAZINE SPECIALIZING IN CLINTON AND BOONE COUNTIES. **2453**

0734-2055 See RAINEY TIMES. **2469**

0734-2071 See ACM TRANSACTIONS ON COMPUTER SYSTEMS. **1246**

0734-208X See WHO'S WHO IN TOBACCO / CONFECTIONERY DISTRIBUTION. **438**

0734-2101 See JOURNAL OF VACUUM SCIENCE & TECHNOLOGY. A: VACUUM, SURFACES, AND FILMS. **4410**

0734-211X See JOURNAL OF VACUUM SCIENCE & TECHNOLOGY. B, MICROELECTRONICS AND NANOMETER STRUCTURES PROCESSING, MEASUREMENT AND PHENOMENA. **4410**

0734-2306 See BOSTON REVIEW (CAMBRIDGE, MASS. : 1982). **3368**

0734-2349 See TAXWISE GIVING. **4755**

0734-242X See WASTE MANAGEMENT & RESEARCH. **2246**

0734-2454 See FEDERAL CIVIL RIGHTS ENFORCEMENT BUDGET, THE. **4508**

0734-2497 See BOSTON SYMPHONY ORCHESTRA. **4104**

0734-2659 See FALL COLLEGE ENROLLMENTS BY RACIAL/ETHNIC CATEGORY. **1823**

0734-2705 See CAMPBOOK. MIDEASTERN. **4870**

0734-2721 See PRINTWORLD DIRECTORY OF CONTEMPORARY PRINTS AND PRICES. **381**

0734-2748 See KANSAS CITY BUSINESS JOURNAL. **688**

0734-2802 See NEW CANAAN HISTORICAL SOCIETY ANNUAL, THE. **2748**

0734-2829 See JOURNAL OF PSYCHOEDUCATIONAL ASSESSMENT. **4599**

0734-2837 See ALLIANCE (NORWOOD, N.J.). **637**

0734-2845 See DUN'S BUSINESS RANKINGS. **669**

0734-2853 See JAPAN MARKET, THE. **842**

0734-287X See ROBOTICS TODAY (ANNUAL ED.). **1216**

0734-2888 See ATHLON'S PRO FOOTBALL. **4884**

0734-2896 See SONIDO (NEW YORK, N.Y.). **4153**

0734-2918 See OUTDOOR LIFE DEER HUNTER'S YEARBOOK. **4877**

0734-2934 See BELLINGHAM REVIEW, THE. **3366**

0734-2942 See REGIONAL INFORMATION SERVICE. **1580**

0734-2950 See REGIONAL INFORMATION SERVICE. SOUTHERN REGION. **1580**

0734-2969 See REGIONAL INFORMATION SERVICE. WESTERN REGION. **1580**

0734-2977 See REGIONAL INFORMATION SERVICE. NORTHEAST REGION. **1580**

0734-2985 See REGIONAL INFORMATION SERVICE. NORTH CENTRAL REGION. **1580**

0734-3027 See PROPHETIC VOICES (NOVATO, CALIF.). **3425**

0734-3035 See LIBRARY ISSUES. **3225**

0734-306X See JOURNAL OF LABOR ECONOMICS. **1500**

0734-3078 See SHELTER SENSE. **5307**

0734-3086 See MEMORANDUM - AMERICAN LIBRARY ASSOCIATION. OFFICE FOR INTELLECTUAL FREEDOM. **1306**

0734-3108 See MOBIUS (ALEXANDRIA, VA.). **695**

0734-3124 See BIRTH PSYCHOLOGY BULLETIN. **3758**

0734-3140 See PITTSBURGH UNDERGRADUATE REVIEW, THE. **2852**

0734-3159 See H & E COMPUTRONICS INC. **1185**

0734-3213 See DEVELOPMENT IN AGING. **5178**

0734-3256 See HARRIS ILLINOIS INDUSTRIAL DIRECTORY. **1608**

0734-3264 See INTERSERVICE JOURNAL OF MILITARY & POLICE SCIENCE AND THE INTELLIGENCE PROFESSION, THE. **4046**

0734-3299 See YEAR BOOK OF CRITICAL CARE MEDICINE, THE. **3652**

0734-3302 See TODAY'S SUPERVISOR. **2871**

0734-3310 See RESEARCH STRATEGIES. **3245**

0734-3329 See GOETHE YEARBOOK. **432**

0734-3361 See CREATIVE COMPUTING SOFTWARE BUYER'S GUIDE. **1237**

0734-337X See ANNUAL REPORT OF BOARD OF MEDICAL EXAMINERS. **3913**

0734-3434 See DESERT PLANTS. **508**

0734-3469 See CONGRESS & THE PRESIDENCY. **4469**

0734-3531 See ENTEROVIRUS SURVEILLANCE. **3574**

0734-354X See NATIONAL TRADE AND PROFESSIONAL ASSOCIATIONS OF THE UNITED STATES (WASHINGTON, D.C. : 1982). **5234**

0734-3558 See MELLON ECONOMIC BRIEFING. **1504**

0734-3671 See CONFEDERATE HISTORICAL INSTITUTE JOURNAL. **2614**

0734-3698 See OCCASIONAL MISCELLANY OF THE LIBRARY COMPANY OF PHILADELPHIA. **3238**

0734-3701 See JOURNAL-GAZETTE (FORT WAYNE, IND.), THE. **5665**

0734-371X See REVIEW OF PUBLIC PERSONNEL ADMINISTRATION. **4705**

0734-3795 See NIBBLE. **1280**

0734-3809 See JOURNAL OF THE SAN JUAN ISLANDS. **5761**

0734-3817 See COMMUTER (COLLEGE PARK, MD.), THE. **5380**

0734-3884 See REVIEW / SOCIETY OF ARCHITECTURAL HISTORIANS, SOUTHERN CALIFORNIA CHAPTER. **308**

0734-3914 See SPECIAL SCIENTIFIC REPORT - NORTH CAROLINA. DIVISION OF MARINE FISHERIES. **2313**

0734-3949 See SOLAR WASHINGTON. **1957**

0734-4007 See LANDMARKS (SEATTLE, WASH.). **2743**

0734-4015 See REVIEW OF LITIGATION, THE. **3040**

0734-404X See OKLAHOMA ECONOMIC OUTLOOK. **1511**

0734-4058 See KENTUCKY JOURNAL OF ECONOMICS AND BUSINESS, THE. **1501**

0734-4066 See ORIGINAL NEW ENGLAND GUIDE, THE. **5487**

0734-4155 See ALASKA OCSEAP NEWSLETTER. **2185**

0734-4260 See CONTEMPORARY POETS OF AMERICA. **3461**

0734-4295 See LEG SHOW. **3995**

0734-4317 See PAINTERS & ALLIED TRADES DISTRICT COUNCIL 9 SPOTLITE NEWS. **1700**

0734-4341 See CONSUMER MARKETS SERVICE. **1295**

0734-4368 See JOURNAL OF COMMUNICATION THERAPY. **4595**

0734-4392 See AMERICAN MUSIC (CHAMPAIGN, ILL.). **4099**

0734-4406 See POST MORTEM ESTATE PLANNING. **3118**

0734-4422 See DOING BUSINESS IN CANADA. **667**

0734-4430 See U.S. LONG-TERM REVIEW. **1540**

0734-4449 See U.S. LONG-TERM REVIEW. **1540**

0734-4473 See TOTLINE. **1908**

0734-449X See CORMOSEA BULLETIN. **3204**

0734-4503 See WESTERN EUROPEAN SPECIALISTS SECTION NEWSLETTER. **3333**

0734-4546 See ACSUS. CANADIAN STUDIES UPDATE. **2717**

0734-4570 See PNCC STUDIES. **4987**

0734-4597 See COMPUTERIZED INVESTING. **895**

0734-4627 See INFECTIOUS DISEASES AND ANTIMICROBIAL AGENTS. **3714**

0734-466X See ICP SOFTWARE JOURNAL. **1286**

0734-4694 See CONNECTICUT FOUNDATION DIRECTORY. **4335**

0734-4708 See DAVISON'S TEXTILE BUYERS GUIDE (1980). **5350**

0734-4759 See FACT BOOK (STATE COUNCIL OF HIGHER EDUCATION IN VIRGINIA). **1823**

0734-4791 See INTERNATIONAL POPULAR CULTURE. **5204**

0734-4805 See P/M TECHNOLOGY NEWSLETTER. **4014**

0734-4856 See CORD NEWSLETTER. **1311**

0734-4880 See MONTHLY STOCK REVIEW. **907**

0734-4937 See STUDIES OF ISRAELI SOCIETY. **5263**

0734-4961 See LAWRENCE REVIEW OF NATURAL PRODUCTS, THE. **4313**

0734-497X See RIVER CITY REVIEW (LOUISVILLE, KY.). **3431**

0734-4988 See ANCESTORS WEST. **2437**

0734-5003 See HEALTH & MEDICAL YEAR BOOK. **3581**

0734-502X See MARKET TECHNICIANS ASSOCIATION JOURNAL. **906**

0734-5089 See VIRGINIA HISTORICAL ABSTRACTS. **2765**

0734-5119 See CBASSE NEWSLETTER. **5195**

0734-5151 See ARIES' BIOTECHNOLOGY CHEMONOMIES REPORT. **3685**

0734-5178 See MODULES/HYBRIDS. **2073**

0734-5399 See SMATV NEWS. **1139**

0734-547X See AUTOMOBILE INSURANCE LOSSES, INJURY COVERAGES. CLAIM FREQUENCY RESULTS FOR ... MODELS. **2875**

0734-5496 See GRAND STREET. **3391**

0734-5518 See WILDLIFE POPULATIONS AND RESEARCH UNIT PROJECT DESCRIPTIONS. **2209**

0734-5526 See ANNUAL SCIENCE AND TECHNOLOGY REPORT TO THE CONGRESS. **5084**

0734-5534 See JOURNAL - INTERNATIONAL CHINESE SNUFF BOTTLE SOCIETY. **251**

0734-5550 See ON TARGET (TRENTON, N.J.). **1868**

0734-5585 See TV CROSSWORDS. **4867**

0734-5615 See JOIDES JOURNAL. **1450**

0734-5631 See GEOPHYSICS REPRINT SERIES. **1406**

0734-5666 See WASHINGTON NURSE, THE. **3871**

0734-5682 See CARROLL COUNTY GENEALOGICAL QUARTERLY. **2442**

0734-5712 See VALLEY FORGE JOURNAL, THE. **2764**

0734-5720 See WHO'S WHO AMONG BLACK WOMEN IN CALIFORNIA. **436**

0734-5747 See WATER RESOURCES DATA. NORTH CAROLINA. **5545**

0734-578X See SOUTHEASTERN ARCHAEOLOGY. **282**

0734-5836 See NUCLEAR TIMES (NEW YORK, N.Y.). **4485**

0734-5879 See SANDIA TECHNOLOGY. **5149**

0734-5895 See SPELEONEWS. **4878**

0734-5984 See FIRE PROTECTION HANDBOOK. **2289**

0734-5992 See BIKE TECH. **428**

0734-6018 See REPRESENTATIONS (BERKELEY, CALIF.). **2853**

0734-6026 See AMERICAN ASSOCIATION FOR GERIATRIC PSYCHIATRY NEWSLETTER. **3919**

0734-6158 See EMMANATIONS. **1744**

0734-6166 See DRUG LAW REPORT. **2964**

0734-6182 See WILEY SEARCH UPDATE USER NETWORK. **1244**

0734-6247 See SPECIAL BULLETIN - PENNSYLVANIA. BUREAU OF TOPOGRAPHIC AND GEOLOGIC SURVEY. **1397**

0734-6468 See CHARACTERISTICS OF DOCTORAL SCIENTISTS AND ENGINEERS IN THE UNITED STATES. DETAILED STATISTICAL TABLES. **5174**

0734-6506 See FDC REPORTS. PRESCRIPTION AND OTC PHARMACEUTICALS. MID-WEEK REPORT. **4305**

0734-6514 See FDC REPORTS. PRESCRIPTION AND OTC PHARMACEUTICALS. **4305**

0734-6530 See PC/SFA ... SNACK FOOD MANAGEMENT REPORT. **2353**

0734-6557 See INTERINDUSTRY REVIEW. **1567**

0734-6565 See ANNUAL REPORT - PENNSYLVANIA. BUREAU OF FORESTRY. **2375**

0734-6573 See U.S. AUTOMOTIVE SERVICES BULLETIN. **5427**

0734-659X See PROCEEDINGS / ELECTRONICS TEST AND MEASUREMENT CONFERENCE. **2076**

0734-6603 See VIRGINIA COUNTRY. **2549**

0734-6611 See POLIOMYELITIS SURVEILLANCE (1978). **4795**

0734-6638 See PROFILE OF STATE-CHARTERED BANKING, A. 804
0734-6662 See CHICAGO TALENT SOURCEBOOK. 757
0734-6670 See JOURNAL OF COLLEGE ADMISSIONS, THE. 1832
0734-6727 See SAN DIEGO MAGAZINE (1968). 2545
0734-6786 See DIRECTORY OF U.S. LABOR ORGANIZATIONS. 1663
0734-6832 See DIRECTORY OF BUSINESS CAPITAL SOURCES. 896
0734-6840 See DIRECTORY OF LENDING & LEASING INSTITUTIONS. 788
0734-6875 See MUSIC THERAPY PERSPECTIVES. 4135
0734-6891 See BASEBALL RESEARCH JOURNAL. 4886
0734-6905 See NATIONAL PASTIME, THE. 4906
0734-7073 See CULINARY & FINE ARTS NEWS. 318
0734-7146 See ADVANCED MATERIALS (METUCHEN, N.J.). 2100
0734-7219 See NEA TODAY. 1767
0734-7243 See COAL PLANNER. 2137
0734-7251 See COLEMAN GUIDE TO CAMPING & THE GREAT OUTDOORS. 4871
0734-726X See PUBLIC SECTOR LABOR RELATIONS. 3153
0734-7278 See TEXAS COMMERCIAL HARVEST STATISTICS. 2318
0734-7294 See WASHINGTON STATE ENERGY USE PROFILE. 1960
0734-7308 See FEDERAL REGISTER DIGEST SERVICE. 1746
0734-7324 See ALCOHOLISM TREATMENT QUARTERLY. 1340
0734-7332 See JOURNAL OF PSYCHOSOCIAL ONCOLOGY. 3819
0734-7340 See STOCK CAR RACING. 4924
0734-7367 See MUSIC THERAPY (NEW YORK, N.Y.). 4135
0734-7421 See OFFICE POLICY SURVEY, TWIN CITY AREA. 1699
0734-743X See INTERNATIONAL JOURNAL OF IMPACT ENGINEERING. 2103
0734-7456 See USA TODAY (ARLINGTON, VA.). 5687
0734-7464 See PAPERS PRESENTED AT THE ... ANNUAL CONFERENCE / RURAL ELECTRIC POWER CONFERENCE. 2074
0734-7499 See PROCEEDINGS OF THE INTERNATIONAL CONFERENCE ON THERMAL INSULATION. 1992
0734-7537 See MINNESOTA TAX JOURNAL. 4737
0734-7545 See AMERICAN LANGUAGE JOURNAL, THE. 3263
0734-7588 See HOME HEALTH JOURNAL. 3584
0734-7618 See AMS ARS POETICA. 3360
0734-7634 See NUC. CARTOGRAPHIC MATERIALS. 2571
0734-7650 See NUC. BOOKS. 3237
0734-7669 See NUC. AUDIOVISUAL MATERIALS. 4080
0734-7685 See MANUALS AND REPORTS ON ENGINEERING PRACTICE. 2027
0734-7707 See MINNESOTA TAX COURT DECISIONS. 4737
0734-7723 See FLORIDA POWER & LIGHT COMPANY TEN YEAR POWER PLANT SITE REPORT. 2055
0734-7812 See SOUTHERN BANKERS DIRECTORY. 812
0734-7839 See REAL ESTATE BULLETIN (SACRAMENTO, CALIF.). 4844
0734-7960 See NATIONAL PARK GUIDE (NEW YORK, N.Y.). 4707
0734-8010 See FODOR'S EASTERN EUROPE. 5471
0734-8037 See BANK INCOME TAX RETURN MANUAL, THE. 775
0734-8142 See NEW BOOKS IN THE COMMUNICATIONS LIBRARY. 1118

0734-8169 See CHILDREN'S MEDIA MARKET PLACE. 1106
0734-8185 See SCHWENDEMAN'S DIRECTORY OF COLLEGE GEOGRAPHY OF THE UNITED STATES. 2576
0734-8274 See NATIONAL STUDY OF SUPERMARKET SHOPPERS. CENSUS PROFILE, THE. 1298
0734-8355 See MILLER'S COMPREHENSIVE GAAP GUIDE / MARTIN A. MILLER. 748
0734-8401 See U TURN. 367
0734-8452 See CIRCULAR - UNIVERSITY OF FLORIDA. AGRICULTURAL EXPERIMENT STATIONS. 74
0734-8479 See MEANS SITE WORK & LANDSCAPE COST DATA. 621
0734-8495 See TOPEKA GENEALOGICAL SOCIETY QUARTERLY, THE. 2475
0734-8517 See GREAT LAKES CAMPBOOK. 4873
0734-8525 See GUIDE TO ACCOUNTING CONTROLS. SUPPLEMENT. 744
0734-8541 See HARRIS PENNSYLVANIA INDUSTRIAL DIRECTORY. 1608
0734-8584 See RHETORICA. 3317
0734-8606 See ABINGDON CLERGY TAX RECORD BOOK. 4708
0734-8630 See SEMINARS IN REPRODUCTIVE ENDOCRINOLOGY. 3733
0734-8657 See SUPPLEMENT TO BOOKS ON DEMAND. 426
0734-8665 See BRECHT YEARBOOK, THE. 3369
0734-8673 See CA SELECTS: NEW PLASTICS. 1005
0734-8681 See CA SELECTS: PLASTICS ADDITIVES. 1007
0734-869X See CA SELECTS: FIBER-REINFORCED PLASTICS. 1002
0734-8703 See CA SELECTS: POLYESTERS. 1008
0734-8711 See CA SELECTS: PAPER ADDITIVES. 1007
0734-872X See CA SELECTS: NOVEL NATURAL PRODUCTS. 1005
0734-8738 See CA SELECTS: LUBRICANTS, GREASES & LUBRICATION. 1004
0734-8746 See CA SELECTS: ENHANCED PETROLEUM RECOVERY. 1002
0734-8754 See CA SELECTS: EMULSIFIERS & DEMULSIFIERS. 1001
0734-8762 See CA SELECTS: PAINT ADDITIVES. 1007
0734-8770 See CA SELECTS: ELECTROCHEMICAL ORGANIC SYNTHESIS. 1001
0734-8789 See CA SELECTS: COLORANTS & DYES. 1000
0734-8797 See CA SELECTS: CHELATING AGENTS. 999
0734-8800 See CA SELECTS: CATALYST REGENERATION. 999
0734-8819 See CA SELECTS: NOVEL POLYMERS FROM PATENTS. 1005
0734-8827 See CA SELECTS: POLYMER BLENDS. 1008
0734-8835 See CA SELECTS: POLYMER DEGRADATION. 1008
0734-8843 See CA SELECTS: INITIATION OF POLYMERIZATION. 1004
0734-8851 See CA SELECTS: BLOCK & GRAFT POLYMERS. 998
0734-8894 See AATCC TECHNICAL MANUAL. 5347
0734-8924 See WEEKLY BANK CLEARINGS. 816
0734-8967 See SKY (NEW YORK, N.Y. : 1971). 35
0734-8991 See ALTA NEWSLETTER. 3189
0734-9033 See WHOLE AGAIN RESOURCE GUIDE, THE. 5265
0734-9041 See JOURNAL OF FIRE SCIENCES. 2291
0734-9068 See INFORMATION INDUSTRY DIRECTORY. 3216
0734-9076 See MYSTERY NEWS. 3348
0734-9084 See INTERNATIONAL DRUG REVIEW. 4308

0734-9114 See CERTIFIED PROTECTION PROFESSIONAL DIRECTORY. 3160
0734-9149 See PUBLIC ADMINISTRATION QUARTERLY. 4676
0734-9165 See IMPACT ASSESSMENT BULLETIN. 2173
0734-9211 See UNITED STATES INVESTOR. 918
0734-9262 See CORPORATE COMMUNICATIONS TECHNOLOGY. 661
0734-9343 See COAL PREPARATION (NEW YORK, N.Y.). 2137
0734-9351 See SOVIET SCIENTIFIC REVIEWS. SECTION D, PHYSICOCHEMICAL BIOLOGY REVIEWS. 5159
0734-9386 See OFFSHORE SERVICE VESSELS. A GUIDE TO THE FOREIGN FLEET. 4267
0734-9505 See GMP AWARENESS REPORT. 4306
0734-9513 See FEDERAL COURT PROCUREMENT DECISIONS. 2969
0734-953X See WILSON WAREHOUSE. 2477
0734-9548 See EXPERIMENT STATION BULLETIN / MAINE AGRICULTURAL EXPERIMENT STATION, UNIVERSITY OF MAINE AT ORONO. 82
0734-9556 See TECHNICAL BULLETIN - MAINE AGRICULTURAL EXPERIMENT STATION. 139
0734-9599 See CHINA: INTERNATIONAL TRADE (WASHINGTON, D.C. : 1980). 827
0734-9629 See PROCEEDINGS - ABRASIVE ENGINEERING SOCIETY (U.S). CONFERENCE/EXHIBITION. 4016
0734-9637 See INFORMATION SOURCES. 3216
0734-9653 See REAL ESTATE: DEBTORS' AND CREDITOR'S RIGHTS. 806
0734-9661 See CURRENT ISSUE OUTLINE. 1448
0734-967X See FINANCIAL INDUSTRY SALARY SURVEY (DENVER, COLO. : 1982). 1674
0734-9750 See BIOTECHNOLOGY ADVANCES. 3688
0734-9777 See BACK STAGE. TV FILM & TAPE PRODUCTION DIRECTORY. 1126
0734-9831 See HISTORY OF PSYCHOANALYSIS MONOGRAPH. 3926
0734-9882 See MID-AMERICA THEOLOGICAL JOURNAL. 4977
0734-9890 See EMOTIONS AND BEHAVIOR MONOGRAPHS. 4586
0734-9904 See WESTERN TAX. 3074
0734-9920 See NATIONAL HISPANIC JOURNAL. 2268
0734-9939 See CURRENT MEDICINE. 3570
0734-9963 See CUTBANK. 3379
0734-9971 See CIVIL ENGINEERING STUDIES. GEOTECHNICAL RESEARCH SERIES. 2021
0734-9998 See MUTUAL AID. 4792
0735-0007 See CONTEMPORARY POLICY ISSUES. 1471
0735-0015 See JOURNAL OF BUSINESS & ECONOMIC STATISTICS. 1534
0735-0023 See STREAMLINED SEMINAR. 1872
0735-0031 See HERE'S HOW (RESTON, VA.). 1864
0735-004X See ADVANCES IN LEARNING AND BEHAVIORAL DISABILITIES. 1874
0735-0058 See NATIONAL OPERATIONS/AUTOMATION SURVEY. 801
0735-0066 See SERVICE MANUAL. CAMARO. 5425
0735-0082 See SUPERINTENDENT'S DIGEST. 1873
0735-0104 See ADVANCES IN VIRAL ONCOLOGY. 3808
0735-0112 See INTERNATIONAL DIRECTORY OF ACCESS GUIDES, THE. 4389
0735-0120 See INTERNATIONAL JOURNAL OF OROFACIAL MYOLOGY, THE. 1325
0735-0171 See ADVANCES IN READING/LANGUAGE RESEARCH. 1887
0735-018X See TIMBER TRAILS. 2475
0735-0198 See RHETORIC REVIEW. 3317
0735-0201 See GOVERNANCE DIRECTORY. 1825
0735-021X See INDEX TO 35MM EDUCATIONAL FILMSTRIPS. 1896

0735-0287 See GENEALOGICAL COMPUTER PIONEER. 2449

0735-0295 See BOOKMARK (MOSCOW, IDAHO), THE. 3197

0735-0309 See HYDRO-INDEX. 1414

0735-0333 See DOMESTIC AND IMPORTED VEHICLES TOWING MANUAL. 5413

0735-0341 See CLASSICS IN PSYCHOANALYSIS. 4581

0735-035X See NATIONAL DIRECTORY OF INVESTMENT NEWSLETTERS, THE. 909

0735-0368 See NCAA MEN'S AND WOMEN'S SOCCER RULES. 4907

0735-0376 See SURVEY AND ANALYSIS OF BUSINESS TRAVEL POLICIES & COSTS. 5491

0735-0392 See WESTERN CIVILIZATION. 2633

0735-0414 See ALCOHOL AND ALCOHOLISM (OXFORD). 1339

0735-0503 See GEOTHERMAL HOT LINE. 1945

0735-0511 See GEO2. 1376

0735-0600 See GEOLOGIC MAP - MONTANA BUREAU OF MINES AND GEOLOGY. 1377

0735-0643 See JOURNAL OF MINORITY BUSINESS FINANCE. 795

0735-066X See PNW COAST LUMBER PRICE INDEX. 2403

0735-0678 See REAL ESTATE FINANCING REPORT. 4844

0735-0716 See LOUISIANA ANNUAL OIL AND GAS REPORT. 4263

0735-0732 See HEALTHCARE FINANCIAL MANAGEMENT. 3782

0735-0783 See TENNESSEE PHILOLOGICAL BULLETIN. 3328

0735-0791 See RELIABILITY PHYSICS. 2079

0735-0805 See PROCEEDINGS - SOUTHEASTERN ASSOCIATION OF STATE HIGHWAY AND TRANSPORTATION OFFICIALS (U.S.). MEETING. 5390

0735-0813 See LINCOLN LIBRARY OF ESSENTIAL INFORMATION (COLUMBUS, OHIO : 1982), THE. 3228

0735-0821 See JOURNAL OF THE NATIONAL ASSOCIATION OF ADMINISTRATIVE LAW JUDGES. 3093

0735-083X See HOT ROD ... ANNUAL. 5416

0735-0848 See HEALTH DATA INVENTORY. 4779

0735-0872 See R&D REVIEW (JACKSON, MISS.). 5144

0735-0880 See STATE HEALTH PLAN (LITTLE ROCK, ARK.). 4804

0735-1097 See JOURNAL OF THE AMERICAN COLLEGE OF CARDIOLOGY. 3707

0735-1135 See TENNESSEE'S BUSINESS (MURFREESBORO, TENN.). 715

0735-1216 See READINGS IN GULF COAST GEOLOGY. 1393

0735-1259 See JOURNAL OF TEACHING WRITING. 3292

0735-1283 See AMERICAN REVIEW OF DIAGNOSTICS. 3698

0735-1348 See ANCIENT TL. 254

0735-1399 See NEWS JOURNAL - SOCIETY FOR COMMERCIAL ARCHEOLOGY (U.S.). 304

0735-1437 See STATE OF SMALL BUSINESS, THE. 713

0735-1488 See A.I.D. EVALUATION SPECIAL STUDY. 5079

0735-1534 See REFERENCE REPORT : A PUBLICATION OF EDUCATIONAL MATERIALS DISTRIBUTORS. 1903

0735-1542 See TEXAS AGRICULTURAL EXPORT DIRECTORY. 141

0735-1550 See SAUL BELLOW JOURNAL. 434

0735-1585 See JOSLIN'S JAZZ JOURNAL. 4125

0735-1631 See AMERICAN JOURNAL OF PERINATOLOGY. 3756

0735-1690 See PSYCHOANALYTIC INQUIRY. 3934

0735-178X See CONSUMER ANALYSIS (MILWAUKEE, WIS.). 1552

0735-1798 See MICHIGAN LIVING. 5484

0735-1844 See ISDN (BROOKLINE, MASS.). 1191

0735-1895 See THEATERWORK MAGAZINE. 5370

0735-1909 See VITAE SCHOLASTICAE. 1790

0735-1917 See WATER SUPPLY. 5548

0735-1933 See INTERNATIONAL COMMUNICATIONS IN HEAT AND MASS TRANSFER. 4431

0735-1968 See JOURNAL OF PARK AND RECREATION ADMINISTRATION. 4706

0735-1992 See ANNUAL REPORT - NATIONAL INSTITUTE OF HEALTH (U.S.). DIVISION OF RESEARCH SERVICES. 3551

0735-2034 See ANNUAL REPORT / GROUP OF THIRTY. 771

0735-2077 See CATFISH (WASHINGTON, D.C.). 2299

0735-214X See AFL-CIO INTERNAL DISPUTES PLAN, THE. 1642

0735-2166 See JOURNAL OF URBAN AFFAIRS. 2826

0735-231X See OVERSEAS ASSIGNMENT DIRECTORY SERVICE. 5488

0735-2336 See RECENT ADDITIONS TO BAKER LIBRARY. 3244

0735-2379 See ELECTRONIC MAIL EXECUTIVES DIRECTORY. 1144

0735-2387 See HILLSDALE REVIEW. 2534

0735-2395 See PROGRAM PLAN - UNITED STATES. FOOD SAFETY AND INSPECTION SERVICE. 4198

0735-2417 See INDIANA MANUFACTURERS DIRECTORY. 3481

0735-2425 See URBAN SOCIETY. 5265

0735-2492 See NUCLEAR REACTOR SAFETY. 2157

0735-2506 See NUCLEAR FUEL CYCLE. 1952

0735-2514 See MEDICAL STAFF FORUM. 3788

0735-2530 See CLINICAL INFANT REPORTS. 4581

0735-2565 See EDUCATIONAL MICRO REVIEW. 1223

0735-2611 See ELECTRIC POWER SUPPLY AND DEMAND. 2043

0735-2689 See CRITICAL REVIEWS IN PLANT SCIENCES. 507

0735-2700 See SOVIET AGRICULTURAL SCIENCES. 136

0735-2719 See JOURNAL OF CONTEMPORARY MATHEMATICAL ANALYSIS. 3512

0735-2727 See IZVESTIIA VYSSHIKH UCHEBMYKH ZAVEDENII. RADIOELEKTRONIKA. 2067

0735-2751 See SOCIOLOGICAL THEORY. 5261

0735-2794 See TERREBONNE LIFE LINES. 2474

0735-2832 See BRIDGEPORT LAW REVIEW. 2943

0735-2840 See FOR FORMULATION CHEMISTS ONLY. 975

0735-2883 See ALL ABOUT MEDICAID. 2873

0735-2891 See ALL ABOUT MEDICARE. 2873

0735-3073 See DEEP SKY. 395

0735-3081 See RESOURCE RECOVERY REPORT. 2242

0735-309X See PIONEER WAGON, THE. 2467

0735-3154 See VITO (SEATTLE, WASH.), LA. 2275

0735-3170 See JOURNAL OF CHILDHOOD COMMUNICATION DISORDERS. 1880

0735-3243 See ANNUAL REPORT. PLANNING AND DEVELOPMENT. 61

0735-3278 See FREESTONE FRONTIERS. 2449

0735-3286 See EMPLOYMENT SECURITY STATISTICAL BULLETIN. 1532

0735-3316 See ELECTRONIC INDUSTRY MANUFACTURERS REPRESENTATIVES LOCATOR. 3478

0735-3324 See FEDERAL STAFF DIRECTORY. 4648

0735-3421 See WOMEN IN DESIGN INTERNATIONAL COMPENDIUM. 376

0735-3650 See CHARACTERISTICS OF PROFESSIONAL STAFF IN CALIFORNIA PUBLIC SCHOOLS. 1861

0735-3669 See CONTRIBUTIONS FROM THE UNIVERSITY OF KANSAS HERBARIUM. 507

0735-3677 See DATA BASE NEWSLETTER (PRINCETON, N.J.). 1253

0735-3707 See DIRECTORY OF OUTPLACEMENT FIRMS. 940

0735-3766 See JOURNAL OF BUSINESS LOGISTICS. 5385

0735-3812 See SOCIAL SECURITY FORUM. 5308

0735-3847 See INTEGRATIVE PSYCHIATRY. 3926

0735-3855 See VIETNAM FORUM, THE. 2667

0735-3863 See DATA PROCESSING AUDITING REPORT. 3571

0735-388X See TELECOMMUNICATIONS COUNSELOR. 1165

0735-3936 See BEHAVIORAL SCIENCES & THE LAW. 2940

0735-3944 See INSURANCE AND EMPLOYEE BENEFITS LITERATURE. 2883

0735-4010 See NEW JERSEY MUNICIPAL LAW NEWS. 3015

0735-4037 See PERSPECTIVES IN PSYCHOTHERAPY. 4607

0735-4134 See PEACE NEWSLETTER (SYRACUSE, N.Y.). 4531

0735-4355 See DIRT RIDER. 4081

0735-4371 See JOURNAL OF GUITAR ACOUSTICS. 4126

0735-4436 See MD/PC. 3007

0735-4576 See HYST'RY MYST'RY MAGAZINE. 2620

0735-4584 See NEW VOICES IN AMERICAN POETRY. 3467

0735-4606 See ANNUAL REPORT / SYRACUSE (N.Y.) DEPT. OF AVIATION. 11

0735-4665 See SAGETRIEB. 3470

0735-4703 See PUBLIC ADMINISTRATOR AND THE COURTS, THE. 4676

0735-4711 See BAND & FESTIVAL GUIDE. 4102

0735-4738 See EMPLOYEE RELATIONS REPORT (RICHMOND, VA.). 1665

0735-4746 See EXECUTIVE MANAGEMENT AND MOTIVATION. 867

0735-4754 See MASON MEMORIES. 2745

0735-4762 See NUTRITION UPDATE (NEW YORK, N.Y.). 4197

0735-4770 See PRECIOUS METALS MONTHLY REVIEW. 4015

0735-4797 See BULLETIN - AMERICAN FEDERATION OF ASTROLOGERS. 390

0735-4819 See PREFERRED STOCK HANDBOOK. 911

0735-4843 See LAW OFFICE MANAGEMENT & ADMINISTRATION REPORT. 2996

0735-5068 See RESIDENTIAL BUILDERS COMPENSATION SURVEY. 1708

0735-519X See ALASKA PHARMACIST. 4290

0735-5394 See ENVIRONMENTAL FINANCE. 4721

0735-5424 See WESTERN WATER. 5548

0735-5467 See SPECIAL PUBLICATIONS - MISSOURI ARCHAEOLOGICAL SOCIETY. 283

0735-5483 See MOTORYACHT. 594

0735-5505 See NORTHERNTIER LEGAL JOURNAL. 3019

0735-5513 See OFFICIAL INTERNATIONAL BUSINESS DIRECTORY OF THE SPANISH SPEAKING WORLD. 700

0735-5548 See CAMERON'S FOODSERVICE PROMOTIONS REPORTER. 757

0735-5572 See ARCHIVE (TUCSON, ARIZ.), THE. 4366

0735-567X See TELEVISION EQUIPMENT SPECIFICATION SERVICE. 2084

0735-5815 See BAPTIST PEACEMAKER. 5056

0735-5912 See MARINE POLICY REPORTS. 3181

0735-5920 See QUARTERLY REVIEW ON DOUBLESPEAK. 1120

0735-5939 See REFERENCE / TEXAS A & M UNIVERSITY, DEPARTMENT OF OCEANOGRAPHY. 1455

0735-5963 See STUDENT FINANCIAL AID BULLETIN (ATHENS, GA.). 1872

0735-6021 See U.S. CONGRESSMAN JACK BRINKLEY REPORTS FROM WASHINGTON. 4692

0735-6064 See MIAMI NEWSPAPERS INDEX. 5650

0735-6145 See ECONOMIC RESEARCH REPORT (SAN FRANCISCO, CALIF.). 2366

0735-6161 See WOOD AND FIBER SCIENCE. 2406

0735-617X See DIRECTORY OF INDEPENDENT IBM PERSONAL COMPUTER HARDWARE AND SOFTWARE, THE. 1182

0735-6188 See COST EFFECTIVENESS RESOURCE PERSONNEL DIRECTORY. 3569

0735-6196 See CROSSROAD TRAILS. 2444

0735-6218 See FORGE (JONESVILLE, MICH.). 2448

0735-6242 See DUTCHESS, THE. 2446

0735-6331 See JOURNAL OF EDUCATIONAL COMPUTING RESEARCH. 1224

0735-6358 See CHOICES (EVANSTON, ILL.). 1062

0735-6420 See JOURNAL - FLORIDA GENEALOGICAL SOCIETY (1978). 2455

0735-6455 See ARCHIE (NEW YORK, N.Y.). 4857

0735-648X See JOURNAL OF CRIME & JUSTICE. 3167

0735-6498 See REFERENCE BOOK OF CORPORATE MANAGEMENTS. 884

0735-651X See OFFICIAL HIGH SCHOOL ICE HOCKEY RULES. 4909

0735-6595 See DELAWARE LAWYER. 2959

0735-6609 See JAPANESE REVIEW. 1498

0735-6625 See SCHOOL STAFFING RATIOS. 1872

0735-665X See PUBLISHERS' CATALOGS ANNUAL. 4818

0735-6668 See CREATIVE COMPUTING BUYER'S GUIDE TO PERSONAL COMPUTERS, PERIPHERALS, AND ELECTRONIC GAMES. 1266

0735-6676 See OFFICIAL GUIDE, OUTDOOR POWER EQUIPMENT. 160

0735-6722 See JOURNAL OF HEALTH ADMINISTRATION EDUCATION, THE. 4786

0735-6730 See QUARTERLY / BOULDER GENEALOGICAL SOCIETY. 2469

0735-6757 See AMERICAN JOURNAL OF EMERGENCY MEDICINE, THE. 3723

0735-6811 See OHIO CROP AND WEATHER. 116

0735-682X See FAMILY BACKTRACKING. 2447

0735-6846 See JOURNAL OF HUMANISTIC EDUCATION AND DEVELOPMENT, THE. 1898

0735-6854 See QUALIS. 4819

0735-6862 See SOLAR INDEX. 1957

0735-6870 See SOUTHERN ECHOES. 2473

0735-6889 See SPRING (NEW YORK, N.Y. : 1982). 3472

0735-6897 See THEORY AND RESEARCH IN BEHAVIORAL PEDIATRICS. 3912

0735-6927 See WOMEN'S POLITICAL REPORTER / GEORGIA WOMEN'S POLITICAL CAUCUS. 4500

0735-696X See GEORGIA FARM BUREAU NEWS. 90

0735-6986 See TEEN TIMES (WASHINGTON, D.C.). 2792

0735-7028 See PROFESSIONAL PSYCHOLOGY, RESEARCH AND PRACTICE. 4609

0735-7036 See JOURNAL OF COMPARATIVE PSYCHOLOGY (1983). 4595

0735-7044 See BEHAVIORAL NEUROSCIENCE. 4576

0735-7079 See NEWSBRIEF / AMERICAN CONSERVATORY OF MUSIC. 4140

0735-7087 See RETAIL AD WEEK. 765

0735-7133 See SUN DOG. 3443

0735-7389 See CHERRY UTILIZATION. 166

0735-7427 See RED TAPE (DETROIT, MICH.). 3244

0735-7443 See SCLC (ATLANTA, GA.). 4995

0735-7486 See MARINE BRIEFS. 1451

0735-7494 See ECHINODERMS NEWSLETTER, THE. 5582

0735-7583 See OIL & GAS REPORT (TALLAHASSEE, FLA.). 4269

0735-7613 See TRAFFIC TOPICS. 5394

0735-7788 See MUSICAL AMERICA. INTERNATIONAL DIRECTORY OF THE PERFORMING ARTS. 386

0735-7818 See MONTANA LIBRARY DIRECTORY, WITH STATISTICS OF MONTANA PUBLIC LIBRARIES. 3259

0735-7826 See COLLISION ESTIMATING GUIDE, IMPORTED OLDER MODELS. 5412

0735-7850 See PROFESSIONAL INCOME OF ENGINEERS (1981). 1992

0735-7885 See KALLIOPE. 323

0735-7893 See PUERTO RICO TAXES. 4743

0735-7907 See CANCER INVESTIGATION. 3811

0735-7915 See CLINICAL RESEARCH AND REGULATORY AFFAIRS. 4297

0735-7923 See JOURNAL OF INDUSTRIAL IRRADIATION TECHNOLOGY. 981

0735-7931 See POLYMER-PLASTICS TECHNOLOGY AND ENGINEERING (SOFTCOVER ED.). 2015

0735-794X See RESEARCH FRONTS IN ISI. COMPUMATH. 3531

0735-7966 See TECHNICAL NOTES - UNITED STATES. DEPT. OF HEALTH AND HUMAN SERVICES. DIVISION OF CHILDREN, YOUTH, AND FAMILY POLICY. 5312

0735-7982 See REPORT OF AIB CHAPTER PROGRAMS & ... ACTIVITIES. 807

0735-8016 See SHIAWASSEE STEPPIN' STONES. 2472

0735-8032 See ALLERTONIA. 498

0735-8172 See PRODUCTIVITY REPORT FOR ALL PRODUCERS BY STATE, COUNTY, & TYPE MINING. 2148

0735-8237 See ZHONGGUO ZHI CHUN. 2668

0735-8253 See STEAM COAL WATCH. 2151

0735-8261 See MARMAC GUIDE TO HOUSTON AND GALVESTON, A. 5483

0735-827X See MARMAC GUIDE TO ATLANTA, A. 5483

0735-8318 See U.S. CATHOLIC HISTORIAN. 5037

0735-8326 See ROCK STAR BAZAAR. 4151

0735-8334 See REFUGEE RESETTLEMENT PROGRAM. 5304

0735-8342 See SOUTHERN STUDIES. 2761

0735-8350 See WASHINGTON BUSINESS LAW REPORTER. 3104

0735-8393 See PERFORMING ARTS JOURNAL. 387

0735-8407 See LINK LINE. 1761

0735-8466 See MAGNESIUM MILL PRODUCTS. 1617

0735-8490 See EDITORS ONLY. 2919

0735-8504 See ITALIAN GREYHOUND, THE. 4286

0735-8520 See RETAIL SECURITY DIGEST. 3039

0735-8539 See REPORT ON TRAFFIC ACCIDENTS AND INJURIES. 5443

0735-8547 See AMERICAN JOURNAL OF POLICE. 3156

0735-8563 See REVIEW OF INSTITUTIONAL THOUGHT, THE. 1594

0735-8571 See NEW LIBRARY SCENE, THE. 3234

0735-858X See COLLISION ESTIMATING GUIDE IMPORTED. 5412

0735-861X See CAD/CAM, CAE, SURVEY, REVIEW, AND BUYERS' GUIDE. 1173

0735-8628 See COCK-A-DOODLE WAKE UP WORLD. 4948

0735-8660 See KERAULOPHON, THE. 4127

0735-8679 See INDEX OF CURRENT REGULATIONS OF THE MARITIME ADMINISTRATION, MARITIME SUBSIDY BOARD, NATIONAL SHIPPING AUTHORITY. 3181

0735-8687 See DIRECTORY OF MEMBERS - ELECTROCHEMICAL SOCIETY. 1051

0735-8695 See BARNER FAMILY NEWSLETTER, THE. 2438

0735-8733 See STATE LEGISLATIVE REPORT. 4688

0735-8830 See FELLOWSHIPS, SCHOLARSHIPS, AND RELATED OPPORTUNITIES IN INTERNATIONAL EDUCATION. 1823

0735-8938 See RUTGERS COMPUTER & TECHNOLOGY LAW JOURNAL. 1202

0735-8946 See HIGH SCHOOL WRESTLING RULES. 4898

0735-8962 See DRI MONTHLY FINANCIAL FORECASTS AND ANALYSES FIXED INCOME INVESTMENT SERVICE. 788

0735-9004 See VIRGINIA TAX REVIEW. 3072

0735-9020 See YACHTSMAN'S GUIDE TO THE VIRGIN ISLANDS & PUERTO RICO. 5500

0735-9063 See YOUNG EXECUTIVE. 889

0735-9071 See FLORIDA REAL ESTATE BROKER & THE LAW, THE. 4837

0735-9144 See TAYLOR QUARTERLY, THE. 2474

0735-9187 See EQUAL EMPLOYMENT OPPORTUNITY IN THE FEDERAL COURTS. 3147

0735-9195 See NCAA MEN'S ICE HOCKEY RULES AND INTERPRETATIONS. 4907

0735-9209 See POLISH HERITAGE. 2754

0735-9225 See INVESTING & TRADING WITH SPANISH SPEAKING COUNTRIES. 902

0735-9233 See ART OF HOTEL ADVERTISING, THE. 756

0735-9276 See SIMULATION SERIES. 1283

0735-9306 See CLINICAL ECOLOGY. 3565

0735-9330 See CODE NEWS (CLEVELAND, OHIO). 608

0735-9349 See POLISH GENEALOGICAL SOCIETY NEWSLETTER. 2468

0735-9349 See RODZINY : THE JOURNAL OF THE POLISH GENEALOGICAL SOCIETY OF AMERICA. 2470

0735-9357 See COLLECTORS' MARKETPLACE DIRECTORY. NEW YORK CITY DESIGN. 2772

0735-9365 See PROJECTS IN PROGRESS (COLUMBUS, OHIO). 1915

0735-9381 See PROCESSED WORLD. 3425

0735-939X See JOURNAL OF AGRICULTURAL ENTOMOLOGY. 5610

0735-9446 See ELECTRIC POWER SUPPLY AND DEMAND FOR THE CONTIGUOUS UNITED STATES. 2043

0735-9462 See PARK SCIENCE. 2202

0735-9551 See MEDICAL MALPRACTICE - OB/GYN LITIGATION REPORTER. 3741

0735-956X See CURRENT AWARENESS IN BIOTECHNOLOGY. 3691

0735-9608 See HANDBOOK / NATIONAL ASSOCIATION OF SCHOOLS OF DANCE. 1313

0735-9640 See PLANT MOLECULAR BIOLOGY REPORTER. 523

0735-9683 See HEALTH MARKETING QUARTERLY. 3582

0735-9691 See NATAT'S REPORTER. 4668

0735-9713 See PAINTING & WALLCOVERING CONTRACTOR. 4224

0735-9721 See LITERATURE ANALYSIS OF MICROCOMPUTER PUBLICATIONS : LAMP. 1209

0735-973X See BUC USED BOAT PRICE GUIDE. 592

0735-9764 See ANNUAL REPORT / INDIANA STATE ADVISORY COUNCIL ON VOCATIONAL EDUCATION. 1910

0735-9810 See GEOLOGY SERIES (LAWRENCE, KAN.). 1380

0735-9918 See FEDERAL TAX COMPLIANCE PLANNING. 4724

0735-9926 See VIRGIN ISLANDS OF THE UNITED STATES. GOVERNOR. BUDGET. 4758

0735-9942 See ... SURVEY OF BUYING POWER FORECASTING SERVICE, THE. 1523

0735-9977 See AUERBACH DATA BASE MANAGEMENT. 1253

0735-9985 See AUERBACH SYSTEMS DEVELOPMENT MANAGEMENT. 1246

0736-0002 See AUERBACH DATA COMMUNICATIONS MANAGEMENT. 1256

0736-0010 See FOODLINES. 5286

0736-0037 See NUTRITION RESEARCH NEWSLETTER. 4201

0736-0045 See CLIC QUARTERLY. 3202

0736-0053 See OPERA QUARTERLY, THE. 4144

0736-0088 See MASSON MONOGRAPHS IN PEDIATRIC HEMATOLOGY/ONCOLOGY. 3906

0736-0096 See NUTRITION WEEK. 4197

0736-010X See CONSUMER HEALTH. 4772

0736-0118 See MEDICAL ONCOLOGY AND TUMOR PHARMACOTHERAPY. 3821

0736-0126 See INSURANCE AND FINANCIAL REVIEW, THE. 2883

0736-0134 See REGISTER OF THE AMERICAN SADDLEBRED HORSE ASSOCIATION (INCORPORATED), THE. 2802

0736-0142 See QUARTERLY / CHRISTIAN LEGAL SOCIETY. 3033

0736-0150 See INSIDE (ALBANY, N.Y.). 3100

0736-0177 See INDEPENDENT SCHOOLS (PRINCETON, N.J.). 1752

0736-0185 See ORANGE COUNTY GENEALOGICAL SOCIETY. 2465

0736-0258 See JOURNAL OF CLINICAL NEUROPHYSIOLOGY. 3834

0736-0266 See JOURNAL OF ORTHOPAEDIC RESEARCH. 3882

0736-0339 See CRITTENDEN REPORT REAL ESTATE FINANCING. 4836

0736-0401 See SECURITY LETTER SOURCE BOOK. 5177

0736-0436 See ADVISOR (CHAMPAIGN, ILL.), THE. 1722

0736-0444 See AMERICAN LEAGUE REDBOOK. 4882

0736-0452 See DIRECTORY OF AUTO AFTERMARKET SUPPLIERS. 5413

0736-0460 See INDO-PACIFIC FISHES. 5586

0736-0509 See CONTRIBUTIONS FROM THE NEW YORK BOTANICAL GARDEN. 507

0736-0517 See COMMERCIAL LEASE LAW INSIDER. 2953

0736-0533 See SCHOLASTIC NEWS (PILOT EDITION). 1094

0736-055X See SCHOLASTIC NEWS (RANGER EDITION). 1781

0736-0592 See SCHOLASTIC NEWS (EXPLORER EDITION). 1781

0736-0614 See SCHOLASTIC NEWS (CITIZEN ED.). 1781

0736-0657 See SELECTED ATOMIC ENERGY PRODUCTS. 1956

0736-0673 See NOTES ON LINGUISTICS. 3306

0736-0681 See TECHNICAL INFORMATION BULLETIN - PARENTERAL DRUG ASSOCIATION. 4330

0736-0711 See PLAYS IN PROCESS. 5367

0736-0770 See VISUAL ARTS RESEARCH. 368

0736-0797 See HEP HIGHER EDUCATION DIRECTORY, THE. 1827

0736-0800 See APPLELAND BULLETIN, THE. 2437

0736-0851 See POWDER DIFFRACTION FILE ORGANIC PHASES SEARCH MANUAL. HANAWALT, ALPHABETICAL, FORMULAE. 1046

0736-0878 See CO-OP SOURCE DIRECTORY. 757

0736-0886 See KERSHNER KINFOLK. 2456

0736-0932 See FORUM FOR SOCIAL ECONOMICS, THE. 1491

0736-0959 See DIPLOMATIC REGISTER AND DESK REFERENCE. 3127

0736-0975 See FIDUCIARY TAX RETURN GUIDE. 4724

0736-0983 See PLANNING FOR HIGHER EDUCATION. 1841

0736-1084 See LINDEN LANE MAGAZINE. 324

0736-1092 See STATISTICAL ANNUAL - MINNEAPOLIS GRAIN EXCHANGE. 156

0736-1122 See BARNHART DICTIONARY COMPANION, THE. 1923

0736-1149 See THRESHOLD (CHICAGO, ILL.). 310

0736-122X See SN DISTRIBUTION STUDY OF GROCERY STORE SALES. 2357

0736-1238 See REPRODUCTION BULLETIN. 4238

0736-1386 See NOTIFICATIONS / HCRS INFORMATION EXCHANGE. 2201

0736-1394 See NOTIFICATIONS / HCRS INFORMATION EXCHANGE. 2201

0736-1459 See NEWS - ASSISTANCE LEAGUE OF SOUTHERN CALIFORNIA. 5298

0736-167X See TELEMARKETING UPDATE. 767

0736-1688 See REFUNDING UPDATE. 1299

0736-170X See ALMOST FREE RECIPES AND COOKBOOKS UPDATES. 2788

0736-1718 See FAMILY SYSTEMS MEDICINE. 3737

0736-1750 See MEDIA LAW NOTES. 3008

0736-1769 See COMPILATION OF ABSTRACTS OF THESES SUBMITTED BY CANDIDATES FOR DEGREES. 5095

0736-1777 See GOLD STATISTICS AND ANALYSIS. 730

0736-1785 See EDITORIAL EXCELLENCE. 2919

0736-1807 See COMMERCIAL ACTIVITIES INVENTORY REPORT AND FIVE-YEAR REVIEW SCHEDULE / DEPARTMENT OF DEFENSE. 4039

0736-1858 See FAMILY RECORDS TODAY. 2447

0736-1882 See SELF PUBLISHING UPDATE. 710

0736-1890 See RECYCLING UPDATE. 2220

0736-1912 See SELF EMPLOYMENT UPDATE. 710

0736-1920 See CAREER PLANNING AND ADULT DEVELOPMENT JOURNAL. 4202

0736-1939 See CAMPING TRAILER & TRAVEL TRAILER TRADE-IN-GUIDE. 5378

0736-1971 See LOS ANGELES COMMERCIAL DIRECTORY. 844

0736-198X See W.W. 1 AERO. 39

0736-2099 See COMMUNITY (ALEXANDRIA, VA. : 1982). 5279

0736-2110 See MOTORS AND GENERATORS. 2073

0736-2129 See DIRECTORY OF OPERATING SMALL BUSINESS INVESTMENT COMPANIES. 896

0736-217X See REPORTING FROM THE RUSSELL SAGE FOUNDATION. 5236

0736-220X See BEVERAGE ALCOHOL MARKET REPORT. 2364

0736-2269 See FACTS AND FINDINGS. 2446

0736-2293 See ADVANCES IN BIOTECHNOLOGICAL PROCESSES. 3685

0736-2358 See FIELDING'S CARIBBEAN. 5470

0736-2390 See CHAMBERS HELPING CHAMBERS. 2442

0736-2404 See COWETA COUNTY GENEALOGICAL SOCIETY MAGAZINE. 2444

0736-2412 See DOHNER FAMILY NEWSLETTER. 2445

0736-2420 See MCKINNEY MAZE, THE. 2460

0736-2439 See TRINITY PAPERS, THE. 1095

0736-2447 See ULTRALIGHT PILOT. 38

0736-2455 See ANNUAL SILVER REVIEW AND OUTLOOK. 3998

0736-2463 See BUFFALO CHIPS. 2440

0736-248X See JOURNAL OF INSURANCE REGULATION. 2885

0736-2498 See MARS EXCHANGE. 2459

0736-2501 See NOISE CONTROL ENGINEERING JOURNAL. 2178

0736-251X See VIRGINIA WOOLF MISCELLANY. 3355

0736-2528 See MARS EXCHANGE. 2459

0736-2536 See AEROSPACE ENGINEERING (WARRENDALE, PA.). 5

0736-2587 See VIDEO TEST ANNUAL AND BUYER'S GUIDE. 2085

0736-2595 See NEWSLETTER - AMERICAN ASSOCIATION OF BIBLE COLLEGES. 4981

0736-2609 See NATIONAL WATER CONDITIONS. 5536

0736-2625 See BYELORUSSIAN YOUTH. 2682

0736-2633 See DAVENPORT NEWSLETTER, THE. 2444

0736-265X See INDIAN-ARTIFACT MAGAZINE. 270

0736-2692 See BOOK OF APPLE SOFTWARE, THE. 1284

0736-2706 See BOOK OF ATARI SOFTWARE, THE. 1284

0736-2714 See CONTRIBUTIONS IN PSYCHOLOGY. 4582

0736-2765 See INFORMATION BULLETIN - AMERICAN BAR ASSOCIATION. STANDING COMMITTEE ON SPECIALIZATION. 2982

0736-2838 See GEURIN GAZETTE. 2451

0736-2846 See QUINLAN PRIVATE TRUCK LAW REPORT, THE. 3034

0736-2854 See DODD DIGGINGS. 2445

0736-2889 See MICHIGAN MANUFACTURERS DIRECTORY. 3484

0736-2935 See NOISE-CON PROCEEDINGS. 2178

0736-296X See LCPA BROADSIDE. 3223

0736-2986 See TV EXECUTIVE, THE. 1141

0736-2994 See STOCHASTIC ANALYSIS AND APPLICATIONS. 3536

0736-3001 See JOURNAL OF ENVIRONMENTAL SCIENCE AND HEALTH. PART C, ENVIRONMENTAL CARCINOGENESIS & ECOTOXICOLOGY REVIEWS. 2234

0736-3044 See CENTER FOR SELF SUFFICIENCY UPDATE. 1876

0736-3397 See U.S. TRADE SHIFTS IN SELECTED COMMODITY AREAS. 1525

0736-3443 See HEALTH LAWYER, THE. 2978

0736-3559 See ALMANAC OF SEAPOWER, THE. 4174

0736-3605 See FOCUS ON CRITICAL CARE. 3856

0736-3613 See ALTERNATIVES TO THE HIGH COST OF LITIGATION. 3095

0736-3648 See AUERBACH DATA CENTER OPERATIONS MANAGEMENT. 1255

0736-3680 See PLANETARY REPORT, THE. 398

0736-3737 See AUTOMATION NEWS (NEW YORK, N.Y.). 1218

0736-3745 See FACETS FEATURES. 4068

0736-3761 See JOURNAL OF CONSUMER MARKETING, THE. 927

0736-3796 See AUTOHARPOHOLIC, THE. 4101

0736-3850 See WASHINGTON STATE YEARBOOK. 4694

0736-3893 See COMPUTERTALK FOR THE PHARMACIST. 4297

0736-3907 See MOSASAUR, THE. 4228

0736-3923 See ANNUAL REPORT - VIRGINIA WATER RESOURCES RESEARCH CENTER. 5530

0736-3931 See DES MOINES COUNTY GENEALOGICAL SOCIETY. 2445

0736-394X See DES MOINES COUNTY GENEALOGICAL SOCIETY. 2445

0736-3958 See VAN ZANDT RECORD, THE. 2476

0736-3966 See POETRY INDEX ANNUAL. 3469

0736-3974 See TEXT (NEW YORK, N.Y. : 1985). 3354

0736-4024 See AREA FOOTPRINTS. 2438

0736-4040 See BURBANK FAMILY NEWS. 2441

0736-4059 See LAKE COUNTY (IL) GENEALOGICAL SOCIETY QUARTERLY. 2457

0736-4083 See UNIQUE (EAST HANOVER, N.J.). 1244

0736-413X See ELECTRIC UTILITY WEEK. 2044

0736-4156 See TELECOMMUNICATIONS PRODUCT REVIEW. 1166

0736-4172 See SIBBALD GUIDE. PROFILES OF THE TOP COMPANIES & FINANCIAL INSTITUTIONS IN: OKLAHOMA, LOUISIANA, ARKANSAS, THE. 811

0736-4229 See METROPOLITAN OPERA BOX. 4131

0736-4237 See NRBA RADIONEWTECH. 1135

0736-4261 See JOURNAL / FORT SMITH HISTORICAL SOCIETY, THE. 2740

0736-427X See HIGH TECH INVESTOR. 900

0736-4288 See PRESCHOOL CHILDREN'S CHURCH TEACHER GUIDE. 4987

0736-4318 See WISCONSIN PUBLICATIONS IN THE HISTORY OF SCIENCE AND MEDICINE. 3651

0736-4326 ISSN Index

0736-4326 *See* PHYSIOLOGIC AND PHARMACOLOGIC BASES OF DRUG THERAPY. **4325**

0736-4342 *See* GERONTOLOGICAL ABSTRACTS. **3659**

0736-4350 *See* CURRENT CONCEPTS IN ALLERGY AND CLINICAL IMMUNOLOGY. **3668**

0736-4369 *See* CONTEMPORARY ISSUES IN CLINICAL NUTRITION. **4189**

0736-4377 *See* CHIROPRACTIC HISTORY. **4379**

0736-4385 *See* MEMBERSHIP ROSTER - AMERICAN ACADEMY OF PSYCHOANALYSIS. **4603**

0736-4393 *See* JOURNAL OF CLINICAL IMMUNOASSAY. **3673**

0736-4415 *See* BUSINESS CURRENTS. TECHNICAL REPORT. **939**

0736-4482 *See* EXEMPT SALARY SURVEY. **1668**

0736-4504 *See* COAL PRODUCTION. **2137**

0736-4539 *See* ADVANCES IN PLANT PATHOLOGY. **498**

0736-4547 *See* PROTEIN ABNORMALITIES. **586**

0736-4563 *See* NEUROLOGY AND NEUROBIOLOGY. **3841**

0736-4598 *See* QUARTERLY COAL REPORT (WASHINGTON, D.C.). **1954**

0736-4628 *See* QUARRY WEST. **3427**

0736-4644 *See* BACON'S MEDIA ALERTS. **756**

0736-4652 *See* TAMPA BAY SUNCOAST BUSINESS DIRECTORY, THE. **715**

0736-4660 *See* NAFSA DIRECTORY OF INSTITUTIONS AND INDIVIDUALS IN INTERNATIONAL EDUCATIONAL EXCHANGE. **1836**

0736-4679 *See* JOURNAL OF EMERGENCY MEDICINE, THE. **3725**

0736-4687 *See* CHEMMATTERS. **971**

0736-4709 *See* PROCEEDINGS - CORPORATE AVIATION SAFETY SEMINAR. **32**

0736-4733 *See* CREATIVE WOMAN (PARK FOREST SOUTH, ILL.), THE. **5554**

0736-4784 *See* WOMEN'S DIRECTORY FOR THE CEDAR RAPIDS AND IOWA CITY AREA, A. **5570**

0736-4792 *See* PARTICIPATION IN ADULT EDUCATION. **1802**

0736-4849 *See* REVIEW - NAVAL RESEARCH LABORATORY (U.S.). **4182**

0736-4865 *See* YOU AND YOUR BUSINESS. **724**

0736-4873 *See* NEWSLETTER - PEOPLE'S MEDICAL SOCIETY (U.S.). **3621**

0736-4881 *See* MATRIMONIAL STRATEGIST, THE. **3121**

0736-4903 *See* LC FOLK ARCHIVE FINDING AID. **5269**

0736-4911 *See* LC FOLK ARCHIVE REFERENCE AID. **2325**

0736-4962 *See* DAIRY WORLD (MILLBURY, MASS.). **194**

0736-4970 *See* ADRIFT. **3358**

0736-4997 *See* ANNUAL ENERGY SUMMARY. **1932**

0736-5004 *See* MICHIANA SEARCHER. **2460**

0736-5055 *See* REVIEW OF BIOLOGICAL RESEARCH IN AGING. **3754**

0736-5128 *See* NCAA MEN'S AND WOMEN'S SWIMMING AND DIVING RULES. **4907**

0736-5144 *See* NCAA MEN'S AND WOMEN'S RIFLE RULES. **4907**

0736-5160 *See* NCAA FOOTBALL RULES AND INTERPRETATIONS. **4906**

0736-5195 See READ-EASY MEN'S AND WOMEN'S BASKETBALL RULES. **4914**

0736-5209 *See* NCAA BASEBALL RULES. **4906**

0736-5225 *See* MANAGEMENT TECHNOLOGY (NEW YORK, N.Y. : 1983). **5127**

0736-5276 *See* INTERNATIONAL EDUCATION JOURNAL. **1753**

0736-5292 *See* GENEALOGY AND LOCAL HISTORY TITLES ON MICROFICHE. **2450**

0736-5322 *See* AIGA JOURNAL OF GRAPHIC DESIGN. **376**

0736-5330 *See* ACARI INDEX, THE. **4461**

0736-5357 *See* APALACHEE. **2721**

0736-5365 *See* APELLES. **313**

0736-5470 *See* EYAS, THE. **2193**

0736-5497 *See* HAMPSHIRE REVIEW AND THE SOUTH BRANCH INTELLIGENCER, THE. **5763**

0736-5586 *See* LAKE POWELL FISHERIES INVESTIGATIONS. **2307**

0736-5594 *See* PELLISSIPPIAN (CLINTON, TENN.). **2467**

0736-5616 *See* ANALYSES OF THE ... ILLINOIS PUBLIC LIBRARY STATISTICS. **3257**

0736-5632 *See* CLASSICAL RAG (SILVER SPRING, MD.). **2531**

0736-5659 *See* AMERICAN BANKERS ASSOCIATION BANKING LITERATURE INDEX. **3084**

0736-5667 *See* NORTH CENTRAL NORTH DAKOTA GENEALOGICAL RECORD. **2464**

0736-5675 *See* SOFTWARE RETAILING. **1245**

0736-5683 *See* SOUTHSIDE VIRGINIAN, THE. **2473**

0736-5705 *See* ELECTRONIC BUSINESS FORECAST. **2046**

0736-5713 *See* GUIDE TO THE UNITED STATES TREATIES IN FORCE, A. **3128**

0736-5721 *See* PROCEEDINGS OF THE INTERNATIONAL GAS RESEARCH CONFERENCE. **4275**

0736-573X *See* ENVIRONMENTAL STATUTES. **3112**

0736-5748 *See* INTERNATIONAL JOURNAL OF DEVELOPMENTAL NEUROSCIENCE. **3834**

0736-5764 *See* SERVICE BUSINESS. **710**

0736-5829 *See* ADAPTED PHYSICAL ACTIVITY QUARTERLY. **1854**

0736-5845 *See* ROBOTICS AND COMPUTER-INTEGRATED MANUFACTURING. **1216**

0736-5853 *See* TELEMATICS AND INFORMATICS. **1167**

0736-587X *See* PROCEEDINGS OF THE CONFERENCE - ASSOCIATION FOR COMPUTATIONAL LINGUISTICS. MEETING. **3312**

0736-590X *See* IEEE CONFERENCE RECORD OF ... POWER MODULATOR SYMPOSIUM. **2059**

0736-5926 *See* SUCCESSFUL CASH FLOW STRATEGIES. **813**

0736-5934 *See* RESTORATION (TUCSON, ARIZ.). **252**

0736-5969 *See* INSURANCE BENEFITS SURVEY. TWIN CITY AREA. **2883**

0736-6019 *See* CHEMCYCLOPEDIA. **1021**

0736-6051 *See* DIRECTORY OF PENSION FUNDS AND THEIR INVESTMENT MANAGERS. **896**

0736-606X *See* CURRENT ANALYSIS. **830**

0736-6086 *See* ETHNIC RACIAL BROTHERHOOD (1982). **2260**

0736-6094 *See* WILDLIFE DISEASE REVIEW. **5527**

0736-6116 *See* MOTORCYCLE RED BOOK. **4082**

0736-6132 *See* COME-ALL-YE (HATBORO, PA.). **2319**

0736-6140 *See* ASTE NEWSLETTER. **1965**

0736-6159 *See* ANNUAL REPORT / BATTELLE MEMORIAL INSTITUTE. **5084**

0736-6175 *See* YALE POLITICAL MONTHLY. **4501**

0736-6183 *See* DIRECTORY OF GOVERNMENT OFFICIALS. FEDERAL, STATE, COUNTY, CITY, TOWNSHIP AND SPECIAL DISTRICT OFFICIALS IN NORTH DAKOTA. **4643**

0736-6205 *See* BIOTECHNIQUES. **3557**

0736-623X *See* EARTH SCIENCES HISTORY. **1355**

0736-6256 *See* NO-LOAD FUND INVESTOR, THE. **910**

0736-6264 *See* HANDBOOK FOR NO-LOAD FUND INVESTORS, THE. **900**

0736-6280 *See* SOUTHERN BODYBUILDER. **2601**

0736-6299 *See* SOLVENT EXTRACTION AND ION EXCHANGE. **1019**

0736-637X *See* DIRECTORY OF CLUB OFFICERS. **1101**

0736-6426 *See* ALUMNI DIRECTORY / CALIFORNIA STATE UNIVERSITY, NORTHRIDGE. **1097**

0736-6442 *See* PECOS TRAILS. **2467**

0736-6450 *See* NATIONAL SURVEY OF FISHING, HUNTING, AND WILDLIFE-ASSOCIATED RECREATION. **4875**

0736-6469 *See* TAX FOUNDATION'S LIBRARY BULLETIN. **3252**

0736-6477 *See* WILDERNESS (WASHINGTON, D.C.). **2209**

0736-6515 *See* STEREO REVIEW'S STEREO ... BUYERS GUIDE. **5319**

0736-654X *See* STRATEGY & TACTICS MAGAZINE (SPECIAL ED.). **4058**

0736-6574 *See* JOURNAL OF MACROMOLECULAR SCIENCE. REVIEWS IN MACROMOLECULAR CHEMISTRY AND PHYSICS. **981**

0736-6639 *See* REPORT - BROWN UNIVERSITY. DIVISION OF ENGINEERING. **1993**

0736-6647 *See* VIRUSES IN WASTE, RENOVATED, AND OTHER WATERS. **2245**

0736-6655 *See* CAVING IN THE ROCKIES. **1404**

0736-6671 *See* ALUMNI DIRECTORY - UNIVERSITY OF ROCHESTER. SCHOOL OF MEDICINE AND DENTISTRY. **1100**

0736-6701 See STATE OF AMERICA'S CHILDREN. **5311**

0736-671X *See* PHOTO RESOURCES. **4373**

0736-6736 *See* HONEYMOON HIDEAWAYS. **5480**

0736-6760 *See* AFRICAN URBAN STUDIES (EAST LANSING, MICH.). **2813**

0736-6787 *See* ANNUAL PLANNING INFORMATION. HUMBOLDT COUNTY. **1646**

0736-6809 *See* ART ECONOMIST, THE. **338**

0736-6817 *See* POLICIES AND METHODOLOGIES. DATA PROCESSING SECURITY AND CONTROL. **1261**

0736-6825 *See* FACIAL PLASTIC SURGERY. **3964**

0736-6876 *See* NEWSLETTER / OPERA ORCHESTRA OF NEW YORK. **4141**

0736-6884 *See* MINOR PLANET CIRCULARS/MINOR PLANETS AND COMETS. **397**

0736-6892 *See* SIGUCCS NEWSLETTER. **1244**

0736-6906 *See* SIGCHI BULLETIN. **1249**

0736-6914 *See* MICROELECTRONICS AND SIGNAL PROCESSING. **1195**

0736-6922 *See* INTERNATIONAL COMET QUARTERLY, THE. **395**

0736-6949 *See* MUSELETTER (WASHINGTON, D.C.). **4132**

0736-6957 *See* SMALL BUSINESS COMPUTER NEWS. **1272**

0736-6965 *See* TECHNICAL NEWS - PERKIN-ELMER CORPORATION. **5162**

0736-6981 *See* EDPACS. **1226**

0736-7015 *See* KAGAN CENSUS OF CABLE AND PAY TV. UPDATE, THE. **1134**

0736-7023 *See* CRYPTOZOOLOGY. **5581**

0736-704X *See* ... MAGIC DIRECTORY, THE. **4863**

0736-7066 *See* BROOKS FAMILY QUERY EXCHANGE, THE. **2440**

0736-7074 *See* BIG BEND REGISTER. **2439**

0736-7082 *See* ARCHIBALD CLAN NEWSLETTER. **2437**

0736-7090 *See* RECENT AWARDS IN ENGINEERING. **1993**

0736-7112 *See* BUYERS GUIDE - NATIONAL TOOLING & MACHINING ASSOCIATION. **949**

0736-7120 *See* BIBLIOGRAPHY OF DIARRHOEAL DISEASES. **3743**

0736-7139 *See* LIST OF SERIALS INDEXED FOR ONLINE USERS. **3660**

0736-7147 *See* COMMUNITY RELATIONS REPORT (BARTLESVILLE, OKLA.), THE. **757**

0736-7163 *See* SIGNIFICANT ISSUES SERIES. **4535**

0736-7171 *See* BETTER REP MANAGEMENT. **861**

0736-718X *See* MINERVA (ARLINGTON, VA.). **4051**

0736-721X *See* ADA LETTERS. **1278**

0736-7236 *See* JOURNAL OF SOCIAL AND CLINICAL PSYCHOLOGY. **4601**

0736-7252 *See* APPA NEWSLETTER. **1810**

0736-7260 *See* SEYBOLD REPORT ON DESKTOP PUBLISHING, THE. **1263**

0736-7317 *See* OFFICER REVIEW. **4053**

0736-7333 *See* BERKS COUNTY MEDICAL RECORD, THE. **3555**

0736-7341 *See* NATIONAL NETWORK DIRECTORY. **359**

0736-7392 *See* METHOD (LOS ANGELES, CALIF.). **4353**

0736-7406 *See* UNIVERSITY OF CHICAGO SICKLE CELL CENTER HEMOGLOBIN SYMPOSIA, THE. **3648**

0736-7414 *See* BIOLOGICAL RESPONSES IN CANCER. **3809**

0736-7511 *See* STATE EDUCATION LEADER. **1785**

0736-7562 *See* DENVER DOWNTOWN DIRECTORY, THE. **665**

0736-7600 *See* CHRISTIAN WRITER'S SERVICE GUIDE. **4946**

0736-7619 *See* ART IN AMERICA. ANNUAL GUIDE TO GALLERIES, MUSEUMS, ARTISTS. **339**

0736-7627 *See* JOURNAL OF STAFF, PROGRAM & ORGANIZATION DEVELOPMENT, THE. **1898**

0736-7643 *See* ASTUTE INVESTOR (KINGSTON, TENN.), THE. **891**

0736-766X *See* STATE OF ILLINOIS PLAN FOR THE TREATMENT AND PREVENTION OF ALCOHOL ABUSE AND ALCOHOLISM. **1349**

0736-7678 *See* TREE TALK (JACKSONVILLE, TEX.). **2475**

0736-7686 *See* VISIONS (KINGSTON, N.Y.). **332**

0736-7694 *See* CARDOZO ARTS & ENTERTAINMENT LAW JOURNAL. **2948**

0736-7716 *See* POPULATION TRENDS AND PUBLIC POLICY. **4559**

0736-7724 *See* JOURNAL OF THE AMERICAN SPORTING BOOK COLLECTOR, THE. **2774**

0736-7740 *See* MUSIC REFERENCE COLLECTION, THE. **4134**

0736-7759 *See* DIRECTORY OF FREE PROGRAMS, PERFORMING TALENT AND ATTRACTIONS, THE. **384**

0736-7805 *See* PAPERS PRESENTED AT THE PICA CONFERENCE. **2074**

0736-7821 *See* OFFICIAL HIGH SCHOOL BASEBALL RULES. **4909**

0736-7848 *See* PUBLIC FUND DIGEST. **4743**

0736-7880 *See* AMERICAN JOURNAL OF PRIMATOLOGY. SUPPLEMENT. **441**

0736-7899 *See* ARTHROPOD-BORNE VIRUS INFORMATION EXCHANGE. **443**

0736-7910 *See* MASTERS THESES IN THE PURE AND APPLIED SCIENCES ACCEPTED BY COLLEGES AND UNIVERSITIES OF THE UNITED STATES AND CANADA. **5127**

0736-7929 *See* HEALTHLINE (SAN MATEO, CALIF.). **2598**

0736-7953 *See* AUTOMOBILE RED BOOK. **5406**

0736-7988 *See* OFFICIAL WISCONSIN AUTOMOBILE VALUATION GUIDE. **5422**

0736-8003 *See* SPECIAL CIRCULAR - OHIO AGRICULTURAL RESEARCH AND DEVELOPMENT CENTER. **136**

0736-802X *See* ROOTS TRACER. **2471**

0736-8038 *See* ZERO TO THREE. **3912**

0736-8046 *See* PEDIATRIC DERMATOLOGY. **3908**

0736-8070 *See* DISASTER MEDICINE (PHILADELPHIA, PA.). **3724**

0736-8119 *See* MARMAC GUIDE TO LOS ANGELES, A. **2568**

0736-8127 *See* MARMAC GUIDE TO PHILADELPHIA, A. **5483**

0736-8135 *See* MARMAC GUIDE TO NEW ORLEANS, A. **5483**

0736-8151 *See* FEDERALIST (WASHINGTON, D.C. : 1980), THE. **2733**

0736-8208 *See* PIONEER PATHFINDER. **2467**

0736-8232 *See* PTC NEWSLETTER. **1308**

0736-8240 *See* CASE COMMENTARIES AND BRIEFS. **3105**

0736-8259 *See* MASTER PRODUCTION SCHEDULING. **1617**

0736-8267 *See* PASSENGER AND IMMIGRATION LISTS INDEX. SUPPLEMENT. **2466**

0736-8305 *See* EXECUTION AND CONTROL SYSTEMS. **1228**

0736-8313 *See* MANUFACTURING RESOURCE PLANNING. **1617**

0736-8321 *See* MATERIAL REQUIREMENTS PLANNING. **1618**

0736-8348 *See* SMART'S INSURANCE BULLETIN. **2893**

0736-8364 *See* FEDERAL RECREATION FEE REPORT. **4850**

0736-8372 *See* OIL & GAS STOCKS HANDBOOK / STANDARD & POOR'S CORPORATION. **910**

0736-8380 *See* INA PROFESSIONAL LIABILITY BULLETIN, SCHOOLS. **2980**

0736-8399 *See* INA PROFESSIONAL LIABILITY BULLETIN, ATTORNEYS. **2980**

0736-8410 *See* BIENNIAL REPORT UNDER THE GREAT LAKES WATER QUALITY AGREEMENT OF 1978. **5531**

0736-8437 *See* MOTOR VEHICLE IDENTIFICATION. **5420**

0736-8445 *See* MACLAREN STANDARD, THE. **2459**

0736-8518 *See* ALEF. **2254**

0736-8542 *See* MILLER'S SOLUTIONS TO THE UNIFORM CPA EXAM. **748**

0736-8577 *See* MILLER'S COMPREHENSIVE GAAP GUIDE. STUDENT EDITION. **748**

0736-8593 *See* COMPUTERS IN NURSING. **3854**

0736-8666 *See* INFOBRAZIL / CENTER OF BRAZILIAN STUDIES. **1567**

0736-8674 *See* HANDBOOK OF CANCER IMMUNOLOGY, THE. **3817**

0736-881X *See* ELBERT ROGERS' WASHINGTON STATE SCORE. **2532**

0736-8828 See DIRECTORY OF CLUB OFFICERS. **1101**

0736-8887 *See* NEWSLETTER (CHINESE AMERICAN LIBRARIANS ASSOCIATION). **3235**

0736-8968 *See* UNIVERSITY RESEARCH IN BUSINESS AND ECONOMICS. **1540**

0736-9026 *See* ANNUAL CONTRACTOR EVALUATION REPORT FOR BLUE CROSS/BLUE SHIELD OF MICHIGAN. PART B CARRIER. **1644**

0736-9034 *See* BOOKS ON DEMAND: AUTHOR GUIDE. INTERNATIONAL ED. **4826**

0736-9050 *See* BU$INESS OF HERBS, THE. **2411**

0736-9069 *See* BROADCAST INVESTOR CHARTS. **893**

0736-9077 *See* CAPELL'S CIRCULATION REPORT. **4813**

0736-9115 *See* ANCESTOR HUNT. **2437**

0736-9123 *See* PAPERS IN COMPARATIVE STUDIES. **2851**

0736-9158 *See* VITAMIN E ... ABSTRACTS. **4200**

0736-9166 *See* WORK TIMES. **723**

0736-9174 *See* SUNDAY SCHOOL YOUTH TEACHER. **5001**

0736-9182 *See* FREE INQUIRY IN CREATIVE SOCIOLOGY. **5246**

0736-9212 *See* YELLOW SILK. **3455**

0736-9220 *See* HOOK (BONITA, CALIF.), THE. **4177**

0736-9239 *See* EXPORTER (NEW YORK, N.Y.), THE. **835**

0736-9255 *See* ATOMIC VETERANS' NEWSLETTER. **4037**

0736-9263 *See* NEUROLOGIC ILLNESS: DIAGNOSIS & TREATMENT. **3840**

0736-928X *See* TRIVIA. **3355**

0736-9352 *See* ELECTRIC POWER ANNUAL. **2003**

0736-9360 *See* PROFILE SURVEY - ASSOCIATION OF COLLEGE, UNIVERSITY AND COMMUNITY ART ADMINISTRATORS. **328**

0736-9379 *See* ADVENTURE. MEDIA KIT. **1103**

0736-9387 *See* ANNALS OF DYSLEXIA. **1874**

0736-9433 *See* WOMEN'S LEGAL DEFENSE FUND NEWSLETTER, THE. **3076**

0736-945X *See* EGYPT THEN AND NOW. **2768**

0736-9468 *See* HAYES OF AMERICA HERALD. **2452**

0736-9476 *See* NATIONAL DIRECTORY OF CATHOLIC HIGHER EDUCATION. **1836**

0736-9506 *See* CSIS AFRICA NOTES. **2499**

0736-9514 *See* GALLUP REPORT INTERNATIONAL. **5327**

0736-9522 *See* NATIONAL WILDLIFE FEDERATION'S CONSERVATION. **3114**

0736-9549 *See* BULLETIN OF THE REED ORGAN SOCIETY, INC. **4106**

0736-9603 *See* ENVIRONMENTAL OPPORTUNITIES. **2193**

0736-9662 *See* JUBILEE INTERNATIONAL. **4971**

0736-9700 *See* LATIN AMERICA AND CARIBBEAN CONTEMPORARY RECORD. **2743**

0736-9735 *See* PSYCHOANALYTIC PSYCHOLOGY. **4610**

0736-9743 *See* BETTER BEAGLING MAGAZINE. **4285**

0736-9794 *See* AMERICAN ELM, THE. **2436**

0736-9808 *See* NATURAL GAS ANNUAL. **4265**

0736-9824 *See* OHIO REGIONAL ART DIRECTORY, THE. **381**

0736-9867 *See* STUDIES IN LANGUAGE LEARNING. **3326**

0736-9883 *See* FAMILY TIES (HOLLAND GENEALOGICAL SOCIETY). **2447**

0736-9921 *See* SUPREME COURT ECONOMIC REVIEW. **1523**

0736-9948 *See* AMERICAN EXAMINER (EAST LANSING, MICH.). **2718**

0736-9956 *See* FODOR'S JAPAN. **5472**

0737-0008 *See* COGNITION AND INSTRUCTION. **1891**

0737-0016 *See* JOURNAL OF COMMUNITY HEALTH NURSING. **3858**

0737-0024 *See* HUMAN-COMPUTER INTERACTION. **1186**

0737-0032 *See* MUSICAL WOMAN, THE. **4137**

0737-0105 *See* DIXIE GUN WORKS BLACKPOWDER ANNUAL. **3478**

0737-0113 *See* EVERGREEN STATE FILM & VIDEO INDEX, THE. **1132**

0737-013X *See* STATUS OF SCIENCE REVIEWS. **5160**

0737-0164 *See* SEG ABSTRACTS. **1396**

0737-016X **1085**

0737-0172 *See* THEATRE DIRECTORY OF THE SAN FRANCISCO BAY AREA. **5370**

0737-0318 *See* GROWING CHILD RESEARCH REVIEW. **1748**

0737-0334 *See* COMPUTER BOOK REVIEW. **1176**

0737-0350 *See* SIPISCOPE. **5158**

0737-0369 See IBC/DONOGHUE'S MUTUAL FUNDS ALMANAC. **900**

0737-0377 See IBC/DONOGHUE'S MONEY FUND DIRECTORY. **900**

0737-0393 *See* MISSISSIPPI KITE, THE. **5591**

0737-0407 *See* ARISTOS. **313**

0737-0415 *See* INDUSTRIAL COMMUNICATIONS. **1113**

0737-044X *See* WATER LAW NEWSLETTER (BOULDER, COLO. : 1976). **3182**

0737-0458 *See* LIST OF MEMBERS / BIBLIOGRAPHICAL SOCIETY OF AMERICA. **419**

0737-0466 *See* COYOTE (TUCSON, ARIZ.). **2332**

0737-0547 *See* REVIEW OF CURRENT DHHS, DOE, AND EPA RESEARCH RELATED TO TOXICOLOGY. **3983**

0737-0555 *See* LANGSTON HUGHES REVIEW, THE. **3345**

0737-0601 *See* ANNUAL REPORT AND FINANCIAL STATEMENTS / ALASKA MEDICAL FACILITY AUTHORITY. **3776**

0737-061X *See* NATIONWIDE DIRECTORY. MAJOR MASS MARKET MERCHANDISERS. **1086**

0737-0652 *See* JOURNAL OF ENERGETIC MATERIALS (JOEM). **4431**

0737-0679 *See* WALT WHITMAN QUARTERLY REVIEW. **3452**

0737-0709 See VALUE LINE OPTIONS. **918**
0737-0717 See VALUE LINE CONVERTIBLES. **918**
0737-0733 See ANNUAL REPORT - NEW JERSEY NETWORK (FIRM). **1149**
0737-0741 See SCOTT STAMP MONTHLY. **2787**
0737-0768 See BRAVEAR. **2529**
0737-0776 See PROPAGANDA (NEW HYDE PARK, N.Y.). **4147**
0737-0806 See JOURNAL OF EQUINE VETERINARY SCIENCE. **2800**
0737-0822 See READINGS AND PERSPECTIVES IN MEDICINE. **3632**
0737-0873 See GRIOT (HOUSTON, TEX.), THE. **2735**
0737-089X See LAW & INEQUALITY. **2994**
0737-0903 See DISTRIBUTION MANAGEMENT. **923**
0737-0970 See SOUTHERN MICHIGAN REGIONAL INDUSTRIAL PURCHASING GUIDE. **951**
0737-1004 See LIST OF NURSERYMEN, FLORISTS & DEALERS AND PLANT INSPECTION AND QUARANTINE OFFICIALS. **2435**
0737-1012 See FAYETTE FACTS. **2448**
0737-1020 See HIGH VOLUME PRINTING. **4565**
0737-1071 See RESEARCH ON TECHNOLOGICAL INNOVATION MANAGEMENT AND POLICY. **884**
0737-108X See ELEPHANT (DETROIT, MICH.). **5582**
0737-1152 See LAW SCHOOL TRANSCRIPT, THE. **2997**
0737-1195 See JOURNAL OF POLYMORPHOUS PERVERSITY. **4599**
0737-1209 See PUBLIC HEALTH NURSING (BOSTON, MASS.). **3867**
0737-1217 See DEFENSE (ARLINGTON, VA.). **4041**
0737-1233 See CELL ANALYSIS. **533**
0737-125X See INNOVATIONS IN CLINICAL PRACTICE : A SOURCE BOOK. **4590**
0737-1268 See OCCUPATIONAL SAFETY AND HEALTH LAW. **3020**
0737-1276 See UNIVERSITY OF MINNESOTA CONTINUING MEDICAL EDUCATION. **3649**
0737-1306 See STARMONT STUDIES IN LITERARY CRITICISM (MERCER ISLAND, WASH.). **3353**
0737-1314 See NEW YORK STATE DIRECTORY, THE. **4669**
0737-1373 See BARGAIN BOOK, THE. **2788**
0737-1381 See AFTERMATH. **4856**
0737-139X See CUYAHOGA REVIEW. **3379**
0737-142X See LUDWIG SYMPOSIA. **3820**
0737-1446 See APA MEMBERSHIP REGISTER. **4574**
0737-1454 See INTERNATIONAL JOURNAL OF CELL CLONING. **537**
0737-1535 See SMALL POND MAGAZINE OF LITERATURE, THE. **3437**
0737-1543 See STATE AND REGIONAL ECONOMIC ILLINOIS DATA BOOK. **1538**
0737-1578 See EDUCATIONAL RESOURCES INFORMATION CENTER CLEARINGHOUSE. **1893**
0737-1586 See MOODY'S HANDBOOK OF DIVIDEND ACHIEVERS. **907**
0737-1624 See NORTH DAKOTA AGRICULTURAL STATISTICS (FARGO, N.D.). **155**
0737-1632 See LANDSCAPING HOMES & GARDENS GARDEN PLANS. **2423**
0737-1659 See DX NEWS. **2773**
0737-1705 See SING OUT BULLETIN, THE. **4153**
0737-1713 See NATURAL GAS MONTHLY (WASHINGTON, D.C.). **4265**
0737-1748 See COASTAL PLAINS FARMER NORTH CAROLINA, VIRGINIA ED. **75**
0737-1756 See COASTAL PLAINS FARMER. ALABAMA, FLORIDA ED. **75**
0737-1845 See ELECTRIC POWER SUPPLY AND DEMAND. **2043**
0737-1896 See VITAL STATISTICS (CONCORD, N.H.). **5346**

0737-1918 See CREEM CLOSEUP. **4113**
0737-1926 See PACE SYNTHETIC FUELS REPORT. **1952**
0737-1969 See SEASONALLY ADJUSTED TRAFFIC AND CAPACITY. MAJORS, SCHEDULED SERVICE, SYSTEM, DOMESTIC AND INTERNATIONAL OPERATIONS. **5444**
0737-2094 See CHAPTER 1 HANDBOOK. **4717**
0737-2159 See BANKING LAW ANTHOLOGY. **3085**
0737-2183 See OPERATIVE (NEW YORK, N.Y.). **2542**
0737-2329 See ROSTER - TENNESSEE STATE BOARD OF ARCHITECTURAL AND ENGINEERING EXAMINERS. **308**
0737-2477 See DIAGNOSTIQUE. **1735**
0737-2590 See LAW SCHOOL JOURNAL. **2996**
0737-2612 See BEST OF NEWSPAPER DESIGN (MEMBER ED.), THE. **2917**
0737-2620 See TRAVEL MARKET REPORT : NATIONAL TRAVEL SURVEY TABULATIONS AND ANALYSIS. **5496**
0737-2655 See CHART AND QUILL. **2442**
0737-2663 See CHILTON'S MOTOR/AGE ... PROFESSIONAL MECHANIC'S REFERENCE GUIDE. **5411**
0737-268X See ALASKA QUARTERLY REVIEW. **3359**
0737-2698 See HISTORY OF HIGHER EDUCATION ANNUAL. **1829**
0737-2701 See ELECTRIC UTILITY FORECASTING IN NEW JERSEY. **2044**
0737-2795 See WILLIAM MITCHELL ENVIRONMENTAL LAW JOURNAL. **3117**
0737-2817 See INSULATION GUIDE. **1947**
0737-285X See NEW YOUTH CONNECTIONS. **1067**
0737-2868 See KEYSTONE SEEKERS GENEALOGICAL QUARTERLY. **2456**
0737-2876 See NOTES ON SCRIPTURE IN USE. **5018**
0737-2884 See INTERNATIONAL JOURNAL OF SATELLITE COMMUNICATIONS. **1158**
0737-2906 See PERSONAL COMPUTER AGE. **1272**
0737-2957 See MANAGING SOLID WASTE IN OREGON. **2236**
0737-2973 See SOUTH BEND AREA GENEALOGICAL SOCIETY. **2473**
0737-2981 See NATIONAL URBAN MASS TRANSPORTATION STATISTICS. **5401**
0737-299X See STANDARD & POOR'S SEMI-WEEKLY CALLED BOND RECORD. **915**
0737-3007 See CEA CONGRESSIONAL LEDGER. **4637**
0737-3112 See PROBATE LAW JOURNAL. **3031**
0737-3120 See BROADCASTING AND GOVERNMENT. **1128**
0737-3147 See WASHINGTON BUSINESS JOURNAL. **719**
0737-3244 See COMMUNICATOR'S JOURNAL. **1108**
0737-3252 See JOURNAL OF HEALTH CARE MARKETING. **927**
0737-3279 See BULLETIN / CAPE COD GENEALOGICAL SOCIETY. **2440**
0737-3325 See ACCOUNTING AND AUDITING DISCLOSURE MANUAL. **736**
0737-3392 See COMPARATIVE REPORT OF LOCAL GOVERNMENT REVENUES AND EXPENDITURES, YEAR ENDED JUNE 30, ... **4718**
0737-3430 See PHELON'S WOMEN'S APPAREL SHOPS. **1086**
0737-3449 See EPSCC NEWSLETTER. **4894**
0737-3457 See ABRIDGED CATHOLIC PERIODICAL AND LITERATURE INDEX, THE. **5012**
0737-349X See EEI WASHINGTON LETTER. **1937**
0737-3503 See WASHINGTON REPORT (INTERSTATE CONFERENCE ON WATER PROBLEMS). **4694**
0737-3600 See REAL ESTATE REVIEW'S WHO'S WHO IN REAL ESTATE. **434**

0737-3678 See LOCAL 2 NEWS. **2291**
0737-3708 See CURRENT COMMUNICATIONS IN MOLECULAR BIOLOGY. **452**
0737-3724 See NEW INTERNATIONAL (NEW YORK, N.Y. : 1983). **4543**
0737-3732 See OUTLOOK (SEATTLE, WASH. : 1983). **590**
0737-3740 See COUNTRY HOME. **2899**
0737-3759 See QUEBEC STUDIES. **2756**
0737-3767 See INTERNATIONAL AFFAIRS AND DEFENSE. **4524**
0737-3937 See DRYING TECHNOLOGY. **1024**
0737-3961 See ALASKA REGION REPORT. **2374**
0737-397X See NAMES IN THE NEWS. **434**
0737-402X See ALTERNATIVE METHODS IN TOXICOLOGY. **3978**
0737-4038 See MOLECULAR BIOLOGY AND EVOLUTION. **465**
0737-4046 See CORPORATE ACQUISITIONS, MERGERS, AND DIVESTITURES. **3098**
0737-4100 See DAILY STOCK PRICE RECORD. OVER-THE-COUNTER. **896**
0737-4119 See DAILY STOCK PRICE RECORD. NEW YORK STOCK EXCHANGE. **896**
0737-4127 See DAILY STOCK PRICE RECORD. AMERICAN STOCK EXCHANGE. **896**
0737-4135 See STOCK GUIDE. **916**
0737-4143 See SOUTHWEST JOURNAL OF LINGUISTICS. **3322**
0737-4178 See FEDLINK TECHNICAL NOTES. **3210**
0737-4186 See BENCH SHEET, THE. **1013**
0737-4216 See NEW YORK PEDIATRICIAN. **3906**
0737-4267 See MEMBERSHIP DIRECTORY - INTERNATIONAL ASSOCIATION OF ASSESSING OFFICERS. PERSONAL PROPERTY SECTION. **4737**
0737-4275 See ANNUAL PLANNING INFORMATION. COLUMBUS, GEORGIA, STANDARD METROPOLITAN STATISTICAL AREAS, COLUMBUS CONSORTIUM. **1645**
0737-4291 See PAINTING ANNUAL. **361**
0737-4313 See COMPUTERS (GREENWICH, CONN.). **1273**
0737-4321 See NEWSLETTER / JOHNSTON COUNTY GENEALOGICAL SOCIETY. **2463**
0737-433X See NEWSLETTER / JOHNSTON COUNTY GENEALOGICAL SOCIETY. **2463**
0737-4356 See MATHEMATICAL SCIENCES PROFESSIONAL DIRECTORY. **3520**
0737-4429 See OUTLOOK / EDUCATIONAL COMMISSION FOR FOREIGN MEDICAL GRADUATES. **3625**
0737-4461 See INDEX TO INTERNATIONAL STATISTICS. **5328**
0737-4607 See JOURNAL OF ACCOUNTING LITERATURE. **746**
0737-4674 See CONSENSUS DEVELOPMENT CONFERENCE SUMMARIES. **3568**
0737-4682 See BETHESDA MESSENGER. **4938**
0737-4704 See FINE MADNESS. **3388**
0737-4720 See LINGUISTIC NOTES FROM LA JOLLA. **3298**
0737-4747 See POETRY FLASH. **3469**
0737-478X See HARRIS FAMILY NEWSLETTER, THE. **2452**
0737-4798 See HARGROVE NEWSLETTER, THE. **2452**
0737-481X See ESTES TRAILS. **2446**
0737-4828 See JOURNAL OF EVOLUTIONARY PSYCHOLOGY. **3399**
0737-4836 See TRANSLATION REVIEW. **3329**
0737-4852 See FINAL STATISTICAL REPORT - CALIFORNIA. PRUNE MARKETING COMMITTEE. **729**
0737-4860 See SURVEY OF OFFICE SALARIES, PERSONNEL PRACTICES, AND BENEFITS. **1713**
0737-4879 See SURVEY OF SUPERVISORY PERSONNEL SALARIES. **1713**
0737-4887 See SURVEY OF DATA PROCESSING SALARIES. **1713**

0737-4941 See WACO FARM AND LABOR JOURNAL (1986). 145

0737-5034 See TANG STUDIES. 334

0737-5077 See MOBILE PHONE NEWS. 1160

0737-5123 See PARENTING STUDIES. 2284

0737-5131 See PAEDOVITA. 5300

0737-5166 See ACTA PAEDOLOGICA. 4570

0737-5204 See NATIONAL FEDERATION HANDBOOK. 4906

0737-5212 See BASKETBALL RULES SIMPLIFIED AND ILLUSTRATED ... FOR OFFICIALS, COACHES, PLAYERS, SPECTATORS. 4887

0737-5239 See ILL. IA. MO. SEARCHER, THE. 2454

0737-5255 See GOVERNMENT PROGRAMS AND PROJECTS DIRECTORY. 4652

0737-5328 See TEACHER EDUCATION QUARTERLY (CLAREMONT, CALIF.). 1906

0737-5344 See DESIGN BOOK REVIEW. 296

0737-5352 See CIRA PAPER. 1421

0737-5387 See NEW OBSERVATIONS. 3416

0737-5425 See PROGRAM ON ENVIRONMENT AND BEHAVIOR MONOGRAPH. 5213

0737-545X See SURVEYS, POLLS, CENSUSES, AND FORECASTS DIRECTORY. 5344

0737-5468 See JOURNAL RECORD (OKLAHOMA CITY, OKLA.), THE. 688

0737-5522 See BLACK MESSIAH. 3367

0737-5530 See NORTHWEST PLAYER. 4908

0737-5549 See PALESTINE HUMAN RIGHTS BULLETIN. 4511

0737-5557 See THUNDERBIRD (PULLMAN, WASH.), THE. 284

0737-5573 See DIRECTORY OF CHAMBERS OF COMMERCE IN TEXAS. 819

0737-5581 See UNITED METHODIST REPORTER (DALLAS, TEX.), THE. 5068

0737-5700 See ROBOTICS UPDATE. 1216

0737-5727 See VALVE BUYERS HANDBOOK. 2131

0737-5743 See TRANSMISSION/DISTRIBUTION HEALTH & SAFETY REPORT. 2085

0737-5778 See SOCIAL WORK AND CHRISTIANITY. 5309

0737-5867 See HIGH TIDINGS. 4088

0737-5883 See CREATIVE. 758

0737-5891 See NEW YORK STATE TAX MONITOR. 3016

0737-5913 See PROSPECTIVE REIMBURSEMENT SYSTEM BASED ON PATIENT CASE-MIX FOR NEW JERSEY HOSPITALS, A. 3791

0737-5921 See PROCEEDINGS OF THE ANNUAL TECHNICAL CONFERENCE. 3486

0737-5956 See QUARTERLY EXECUTIVE TREND REPORT. 1348

0737-5972 See IN THE GROVE. 3214

0737-6022 See PROFESSIONAL REPORT - ALASKA. DIVISION OF GEOLOGICAL AND GEOPHYSICAL SURVEYS. 1392

0737-6030 See MEDIGUIDE TO INFECTIOUS DISEASES. 3715

0737-6065 See WILEY SERIES ON DEVELOPMENTS IN NURSING RESEARCH. 3871

0737-6073 See MEDIGUIDE TO ORTHOPAEDICS. 3883

0737-6081 See MEDIGUIDE TO SKIN CONDITIONS. 3722

0737-609X See CRITICAL REVIEWS IN TROPICAL MEDICINE. 3985

0737-6146 See ADVANCES IN ANESTHESIA. 3680

0737-6197 See TAIWAN YU SHIJIE. 2666

0737-6219 See HEALTHCARE MICROCOMPUTING NETWORK. 1267

0737-6227 See HUNTER SAFETY INSTRUCTOR. 4899

0737-6235 See DBPH NEWSLETTER. 3205

0737-626X See BUREAU OF MINES RESEARCH. 2135

0737-6278 See BRIDGE (WASHINGTON, D.C. : 1969), THE. 1966

0737-6316 See HUTTON CONSTRUCTION CATALOG : MECHANICAL PRODUCTS. 2115

0737-6324 See COST OF PRODUCING MILK ON N.C. GRADE A DAIRY FARMS, THE. 192

0737-6332 See FATAL MOTOR VEHICLE ACCIDENT COMPARATIVE DATA REPORT. 5440

0737-6340 See BRONTE NEWSLETTER. 3369

0737-6383 See AUDIT REPORT. TEXAS COMMISSION ON ALCOHOLISM. 1341

0737-6413 See BANKING WORLD. 777

0737-6421 See ASTRONOMICAL ALMANAC, THE. 391

0737-6448 See CONTRIBUTIONS IN ANTHROPOLOGY AND HISTORY. 234

0737-6499 See COAL SITUATION, THE. 1935

0737-6529 See MEDALS YEARBOOK. 4049

0737-6545 See ARES. SPECIAL ED. 5074

0737-657X See PALMETTO AVIATION. 31

0737-6596 See NATIONAL ALUMNI DIRECTORY - ITHACA COLLEGE. 1102

0737-6626 See VINTAGE BUYERS GUIDE. 2372

0737-6634 See AUCTION PRICES REALIZED. U.S. COINS. 2779

0737-6650 See AMERICAN ASIAN REVIEW, THE. 2645

0737-6707 See NOTES ON LITERACY. 3307

0737-6758 See RIDDELL, RIDDLE, RUDDELL TRAIL, THE. 2470

0737-6766 See OCCULTATION NEWSLETTER. 398

0737-6782 See JOURNAL OF PRODUCT INNOVATION MANAGEMENT, THE. 687

0737-6812 See ANS NEWS. 2154

0737-6855 See MUPPET MAGAZINE. 1066

0737-6863 See NIH PUBLICATION. 4794

0737-6871 See SOCIAL PROCESS IN HAWAII (1979). 5220

0737-6928 See MIKE BRUNO'S WHAT'S NEW(S) IN GRAPHIC COMMUNICATIONS. 381

0737-6960 See RADWASTE NEWS. 2241

0737-6987 See KIN IN LINN. 2457

0737-7002 See SLAVIC AND EAST EUROPEAN ARTS. 330

0737-7010 See CENTER RESEARCH REPORTS AND RECORD OF ACTIVITIES. 347

0737-7029 See HISPANIC FOCUS. 2276

0737-7037 See JOURNAL OF FOLKLORE RESEARCH. 2321

0737-7150 See RESEARCH NOTE PNW. 2393

0737-7185 See AMATEUR RADIO CALL DIRECTORY. UNITED STATES LISTINGS. GEOGRAPHICAL INDEX. 1126

0737-7215 See INSIGHT & HINDSIGHT. 4590

0737-7290 See WILEY SERIES ON NEW HORIZONS IN ONCOLOGY. 3825

0737-7355 See INDIANA JOURNAL OF POLITICAL SCIENCE. 4477

0737-7363 See JOURNAL OF CONTINUING HIGHER EDUCATION, THE. 1832

0737-738X See PATRISTIC AND BYZANTINE REVIEW, THE. 4985

0737-738X See ORTHODOX THOUGHT AND LIFE : A JOURNAL DEVOTED TO POPULAR ORTHODOX ENLIGHTENMENT AND EASTERN CHRISTIAN SPIRITUALITY. 4984

0737-7428 See SHIPYARD CHRONICLE. 4183

0737-7436 See JOURNAL OF THE PRINT WORLD. 4566

0737-7444 See FEDERAL EXPENDITURE BY STATE FOR FISCAL YEAR. 1561

0737-7452 See ADVANCES IN DEVELOPMENTAL AND BEHAVIORAL PEDIATRICS. 3899

0737-7460 See BSCS JOURNAL, THE. 449

0737-7495 See OHIO MANUFACTURERS DIRECTORY. 3485

0737-7568 See HEALTH SPECTRUM. 4781

0737-7622 See COMMUNICATIONS LAWYER : PUBLICATION OF THE FORUM COMMITTEE ON COMMUNICATIONS LAW, AMERICAN BAR ASSOCIATION. 2954

0737-7630 See PASSPORT TO LEGAL UNDERSTANDING. 3025

0737-7649 See RULES AND REGULATIONS. PART 99, DISASTER COMMUNICATIONS SERVICE. 1121

0737-7665 See MUSEUMS / NATIONAL ENDOWMENT FOR THE ARTS. 4093

0737-7673 See LEUKEMIA REVIEWS INTERNATIONAL. 3820

0737-7681 See HYDROLOGIC DATA - CALIFORNIA. DEPT. OF WATER RESOURCES. SAN JOAQUIN DISTRICT. 1414

0737-769X See JOURNAL OF CHINESE RELIGIONS. 4968

0737-7703 See DIGEST - UNIVERSITY OF PENNSYLVANIA. DEPT. OF FOLKLORE AND FOLKLIFE, THE. 2333

0737-7711 See RATHBUN, RATHBONE, RATHBURN FAMILY HISTORIAN. 2469

0737-7746 See AVIATION LITIGATION REPORTER. 2939

0737-7762 See SOCIAL CONCEPT. 5219

0737-7770 See INFORMATION INTELLIGENCE, ONLINE LIBRARIES, AND MICROCOMPUTERS. 3216

0737-7789 See WINDSTORM. 4159

0737-7797 See RESOURCE SHARING & INFORMATION NETWORKS. 3245

0737-7843 See PERIODICAL TITLE ABBREVIATIONS. 3240

0737-7908 See ROBOTICS WORLD. 1216

0737-7932 See ITAWAMBA SETTLERS. 2455

0737-7940 See IOWA MANUFACTURERS REGISTER. 3481

0737-7959 See HITMEN. 4121

0737-7967 See NERIM AND ALLIED FAMILIES NEWS. 2462

0737-7975 See PIERRE-FORT - PIERRE GENEALOGICAL SOCIETY, THE. 2467

0737-7983 See CATALOG OF CELL LINES. 3893

0737-8009 See CITY OPERA SPOTLIGHT. 4110

0737-8017 See PROCEEDINGS OF THE ... ANNUAL ACM SYMPOSIUM ON THEORY OF COMPUTING. 1200

0737-8025 See CHEMICAL INDUSTRIES (NEW YORK, N.Y. : 1979). 968

0737-8033 See CHEMISTRY AND PHARMACOLOGY OF DRUGS. 970

0737-8076 See HOT OFF THE COMPUTER. 3213

0737-8092 See NEWSLETTER - CENTER FOR HOLOCAUST STUDIES (BROOKLYN, NEW YORK, N.Y.). 2700

0737-8122 See OFFICE MANAGEMENT. 700

0737-8130 See LDRC BULLETIN. 2998

0737-8181 See INTERNATIONAL DREDGING REVIEW. 1979

0737-8211 See SYSTEMATIC BOTANY MONOGRAPHS. 529

0737-8246 See QUAKER YEOMEN, THE. 2468

0737-8254 See NORTH CAROLINA INDEPENDENT, THE. 5724

0737-8459 See FLUTE WORKER, THE. 4118

0737-8483 See MEMBRANE & SEPARATION TECHNOLOGY NEWS. 985

0737-8505 See PERSONAL ROBOTICS NEWS. 1215

0737-8513 See TOXIC CHEMICALS LITIGATION REPORTER. 3116

0737-8548 See WORLD SPACEFLIGHT NEWS. 40

0737-8556 See COMPUTING PHYSICIAN. 3568

0737-8580 See BEST WORLD SHORT STORIES. 3366

0737-8602 See INDIANA PRESERVATIONIST, THE. 5480

0737-8688 See MALINI. 2267

0737-8718 See FEDERAL TAX COURSE (STUDENTS ED.). 2970

0737-8726 See EXPERT AND THE LAW, THE. 2968

0737-8742 See DISCURSO LITERARIO. 3382

0737-8742 See DISCURSO. 3381

0737-8815 See OUTLOOK FOR TRAVEL AND TOURISM. 5488

0737-8823 See EUPHORBIA JOURNAL, THE. 2414

0737-8831 See LIBRARY HI TECH. 3225

0737-884X See CALIFORNIA ROAD ATLAS AND TRAVEL GUIDE. ZIP CODE EDITION. 2557
0737-8858 See OUTLOOK FOR THE MEDIA. 3309
0737-8882 See PHARMACOLOGY IN NURSING. 3867
0737-8904 See THERIAULT'S BOOK OF DOLLS. 376
0737-8912 See GRINNELL REVIEW, THE. 1826
0737-8939 See PC WORLD. 1271
0737-8947 See BOSTON UNIVERSITY INTERNATIONAL LAW JOURNAL. 3125
0737-8971 See LAWMARK. 2997
0737-8998 See OFFICE SYSTEMS RESEARCH JOURNAL. 700
0737-9005 See ZOOBOOKS (SAN DIEGO, CALIF.). 5601
0737-9021 See EMIE BULLETIN. 3209
0737-903X See HOSPITAL MANAGEMENT REVIEW. 3659
0737-9080 See FILM REVIEW ANNUAL. 4070
0737-9153 See MOBIL TRAVEL GUIDE. FREQUENT TRAVELERS' GUIDE TO MAJOR CITIES. 5484
0737-917X See LOGISTICS OUTLOOK FOR SHIPPERS. 844
0737-920X See CONNECTICUT FAMILY LAW JOURNAL, THE. 3120
0737-9218 See WHITE HOUSE WEEKLY. 2766
0737-9226 See TREE CLIMBER (SALINA, KAN.). 2475
0737-9242 See ROOTS & BRANCHES. 5338
0737-9250 See SATELLITE SERVICES SOURCEBOOK, THE. 1163
0737-9269 See BLIND ALLEYS. 3460
0737-9277 See UTAH STATE BAR DIRECTORY. 3070
0737-9285 See NEWSLETTER - NATIONAL CENTER FOR THE STUDY OF COLLECTIVE BARGAINING IN HIGHER EDUCATION AND THE PROFESSIONS (U.S.). 1837
0737-9412 See CARTE ITALIANE. 3373
0737-9447 See IWAA NEWS. 353
0737-948X See AGRICULTURAL CREDIT CONDITIONS SURVEY. 49
0737-9498 See BEST EDITORIAL CARTOONS OF THE YEAR. 377
0737-951X See DATA BASE ALERT. 1253
0737-9544 See CONTEMPORARY PSYCHOTHERAPY REVIEW. 3924
0737-9595 See PREREFUNDED BOND SERVICE. 803
0737-9889 See SEAFORD HISTORICAL SOCIETY QUARTERLY. 2760
0737-9935 See GROWER ADVISOR. 2418
0738-0070 See WISCONSIN MANUFACTURERS REGISTER. 3489
0738-0127 See STARMONT REFERENCE GUIDE. 3439
0738-0143 See WINNING SWEEPSTAKES NEWSLETTER. 2779
0738-0151 See CHILD & ADOLESCENT SOCIAL WORK JOURNAL. 5277
0738-0186 See LEADER'S LEGAL TECH NEWSLETTER. 2998
0738-0208 See JOBLESS NEWSLETTER. 1681
0738-0232 See HAZARDOUS WASTE CONSULTANT, THE. 2231
0738-0305 See BIBLIOGRAPHY OF SOVIET LASER DEVELOPMENTS. 2036
0738-033X See RUBBER, PRODUCTION, SHIPMENTS, AND STOCKS. 5078
0738-0348 See WAREHOUSES LICENSED UNDER U.S. WAREHOUSE ACT. 718
0738-0372 See ANNUAL REPORT - NATIONAL CANCER INSTITUTE (U.S.). DIVISION OF EXTRAMURAL ACTIVITIES. 3808
0738-0380 See WESTWARD INTO NEBRASKA. 2477
0738-0399 See ELECTRONIC DESIGN'S GOLD BOOK. 2047
0738-0429 See MODERN MASTERS SERIES. 358
0738-0496 See RESMEDICA. 3634
0738-0518 See CONSUMER SOURCEBOOK. 1295

0738-0534 See HOMILETIC. 4963
0738-0550 See FEDERATION NEWS (LOS ANGELES, CALIF.), THE. 1669
0738-0569 See COMPUTERS IN THE SCHOOLS. 1222
0738-0577 See OCCUPATIONAL THERAPY IN HEALTH CARE. 1883
0738-0593 See INTERNATIONAL JOURNAL OF EDUCATIONAL DEVELOPMENT. 1754
0738-0615 See CONSUMER PHARMACIST, THE. 4298
0738-0623 See POLICE MISCONDUCT AND CIVIL RIGHTS LAW REPORT. 4511
0738-064X See AMS STUDIES IN ANTHROPOLOGY. 228
0738-0658 See PUERTO RICO HEALTH SCIENCES JOURNAL. 3631
0738-0690 See PREVIEW (NORTHBROOK, ILL.). 704
0738-0720 See CURRENT METHODS IN CELLULAR NEUROBIOLOGY. 452
0738-0739 See HOLOCAUST STUDIES ANNUAL. 2691
0738-0763 See ESSAYS IN GRAHAM GREENE. 3385
0738-078X See ALUMNI DIRECTORY / UNIVERSITY OF EVANSVILLE. 1100
0738-0798 See ANNUAL REVIEW, NORTH CAROLINA. 2935
0738-081X See CLINICS IN DERMATOLOGY. 3718
0738-0852 See ALUMNI DIRECTORY / THE ALUMNI ASSOCIATION OF THE UNIVERSITY OF VIRGINIA. 1099
0738-0860 See WILEY SERIES IN PSYCHOLOGY AND PRODUCTIVITY AT WORK. 4621
0738-0887 See DIRECTORY OF INDUSTRIAL HEAT PROCESSING AND COMBUSTION EQUIPMENT. UNITED STATES MANUFACTURERS, THE. 613
0738-0895 See JOURNAL OF ARCHITECTURAL AND PLANNING RESEARCH. 301
0738-0917 See PULP & PAPER WEEK. 4238
0738-0925 See RECENT PUBLICATIONS IN NATURAL HISTORY. 4174
0738-0968 See SPACE AGE TIMES. 35
0738-0984 See HOSPITAL LAW NEWSLETTER. 3741
0738-0992 See COMMERCIAL NEWS USA. ANNUAL DIRECTORY. 829
0738-100X See PROCEEDINGS / ACM IEEE DESIGN AUTOMATION CONFERENCE. 1234
0738-1018 See MALPRACTICE REPORTER. ANESTHESIOLOGY, THE. 3005
0738-1026 See MALPRACTICE REPORTER, THE. 3005
0738-1034 See COMPENSATION & BENEFITS REPORT. 1660
0738-1069 See JOURNAL OF COGNITIVE REHABILITATION, THE. 3835
0738-1085 See MICROSURGERY. 3970
0738-1093 See OVERLAND JOURNAL. 2752
0738-1123 See SAVINGS BANK AND SAVINGS AND LOAN ASSOCIATION SURVEY OF SALARIES AND PERSONNEL PRACTICES. 1709
0738-1131 See ARCHITECTURE CALIFORNIA. 290
0738-114X See PLANNING & ZONING NEWS. 2831
0738-1158 See ALUMNI DIRECTORY / BRYANT COLLEGE. 1097
0738-1174 See ALUMNI DIRECTORY / SOUTHERN METHODIST UNIVERSITY. 1099
0738-1182 See ALUMNI DIRECTORY - UNIVERSITY OF CALIFORNIA, LOS ANGELES. GRADUATE SCHOOL OF MANAGEMENT. 1100
0738-1204 See GROUNDWATER QUALITY MONITORING PROGRAM. 5534
0738-1212 See SPORT AMERICANA BASEBALL MEMORABILIA AND AUTOGRAPH PRICE GUIDE, THE. 4920
0738-1220 See PORTABLE COMPUTER. 1272
0738-1247 See PARASCOPE. 3142

0738-128X See MONOGRAPH / [WORLD REHABILITATION FUND]. 4381
0738-1328 See VECTOR (HARVARD, MASS.), THE. 815
0738-1360 See MARINE RESOURCE ECONOMICS. 2308
0738-1379 See LATIN AMERICAN JEWISH STUDIES NEWSLETTER (1983). 5050
0738-1395 See COA REVIEW. 1342
0738-1409 See ENGLISH LEADERSHIP QUARTERLY. 1863
0738-1417 See SUPPORT FOR THE LEARNING AND TEACHING OF ENGLISH. 3327
0738-1425 See INTERNATIONAL DEVELOPMENT RESOURCE BOOKS. 2910
0738-1433 See WOMEN'S REVIEW OF BOOKS, THE. 3356
0738-145X See AGRICELL REPORT. 48
0738-1492 See LEADER / NATIONAL WILDLIFE FEDERATION, THE. 2197
0738-1514 See MINNESOTA MANUFACTURERS REGISTER. 3484
0738-1522 See INFORMATION AMERICA. 3215
0738-1549 See MASSOG. 2459
0738-1557 See ALUMNI DIRECTORY - CULINARY INSTITUTE OF AMERICA. 1098
0738-159X See FLOWER OF THE FOREST BLACK GENEALOGICAL JOURNAL. 2448
0738-1670 See NATIONAL DEVELOPMENT. MIDDLE EAST/AFRICA. 622
0738-1697 See NEW YORK JURY VERDICT REPORTER (METROPOLITAN ED.), THE. 3016
0738-1719 See ETHNIC INFORMATION SOURCES OF THE UNITED STATES. 2260
0738-1727 See JOURNAL OF MODERN GREEK STUDIES. 2695
0738-1743 See POLYMER YEARBOOK. 1046
0738-1751 See ANTIMICROBIC NEWSLETTER, THE. 559
0738-176X See UNITED STATES ACHIEVEMENT ACADEMY NATIONAL AWARDS. 435
0738-1778 See RAIL HOBBYIST. 5434
0738-1786 See FRESH FRUIT AND VEGETABLE ARRIVALS IN EASTERN CITIES BY COMMODITIES, STATES, AND MONTHS. 1607
0738-1808 See TOMBSTONE TRAILS. 2475
0738-1824 See COMPETITIVE MATERIALS SERVICE. 829
0738-1832 See SURVEY OF LABORATORY TECHNICIAN SALARIES. 1713
0738-1867 See PACIFIC MOUNTAIN QUARTERLY. 2830
0738-1891 See QUARTERLY / OREGON GENEALOGICAL SOCIETY. 2469
0738-1905 See CEDAR TREE, THE. 2442
0738-1913 See COLLECTIVE BARGAINING IN HIGHER EDUCATION AND THE PROFESSIONS. 1815
0738-1921 See SUMMER LEGAL EMPLOYMENT GUIDE. 3061
0738-193X See REPUBLICANS ABROAD. 4683
0738-1948 See MALPRACTICE REPORTER. OB/GYN, THE. 3005
0738-1956 See MALPRACTICE REPORTER. HOSPITALS, THE. 3005
0738-1972 See SUMMARY JUDGEMENT. 3060
0738-1999 See ALUMNI DIRECTORY / DICKINSON COLLEGE. 1098
0738-2006 See ALUMNI DIRECTORY / JOHNSON C. SMITH UNIVERSITY. 1098
0738-2014 See ANALYTICAL ELECTRON MICROSCOPY. 572
0738-2022 See JOURNAL OF FORTH APPLICATION AND RESEARCH, THE. 1279
0738-2030 See JOURNAL OF INTERMOUNTAIN ARCHEOLOGY. 271
0738-2146 See QUARTERLY JOURNAL / OFFICE OF THE COMPTROLLER OF THE CURRENCY. 805
0738-2154 See BULLETIN SOLIDARNOSC. 1657
0738-2170 See BOMA EXPERIENCE EXCHANGE REPORT. 4834
0738-2200 See MBA EMPLOYMENT GUIDE. 692

0738-2219 See ALUMNI DIRECTORY / TEXAS A & I UNIVERSITY. 1099

0738-2235 See MISSISSIPPI LEGAL DIRECTORY, THE. 3011

0738-2243 See FRESH FRUIT AND VEGETABLE ARRIVALS IN WESTERN CITIES BY COMMODITIES, STATES, AND MONTHS. 1607

0738-2278 See ADVANCES IN ORTHOPAEDIC SURGERY. 3958

0738-2294 See GESAR. 5021

0738-2324 See GUIDE TO THE HIGH TECHNOLOGY INDUSTRIES. 5108

0738-2332 See CLEARING UP. 4760

0738-2340 See WHERE TO WRITE FOR VITAL RECORDS. 2477

0738-2359 See FLAMING GORGE RESERVOIR FISHERIES INVESTIGATIONS. 2304

0738-2375 See AAOMS DIRECTORY / AMERICAN ASSOCIATION OF ORAL AND MAXILLOFACIAL SURGEONS. 1314

0738-2391 See ROOTS & SHOOTS QUARTERLY. 2471

0738-2405 See KOVELS' ANTIQUES & COLLECTIBLES PRICE LIST, THE. 251

0738-2421 See HOLLY SOCIETY JOURNAL. 5231

0738-2480 See LAW AND HISTORY REVIEW. 2994

0738-2510 See ALUMNAE/I DIRECTORY / LAKE ERIE COLLEGE. 1097

0738-2529 See SPRINGER'S HANDBOOK OF NORTH AMERICAN CINDERELLA STAMPS, INCLUDING TAXPAID REVENUES. 1147

0738-2650 See NEWS. PRODUCTIVITY AND COSTS. 1619

0738-2677 See INTERNATIONAL ULTRAVIOLET EXPLORER (IUE) NASA NEWSLETTER. 24

0738-2707 See ABSTRACTS OF SOVIET AND EAST EUROPEAN EMIGRE PERIODICAL LITERATURE. 2513

0738-2715 See IDEAS (YOUTH SPECIALTIES (ORGANIZATIONS)). 1064

0738-2812 See NEW HAVEN STUDIES IN INTERNATIONAL LAW AND WORLD PUBLIC ORDER, THE. 3133

0738-2820 See SIRIUS (LOS ANGELES, CALIF.). 2500

0738-2898 See JOURNAL OF ENVIRONMENTAL HORTICULTURE. 2421

0738-2901 See DEADLINE (CHICAGO, ILL.). 2918

0738-2936 See LAPEL PIN POTPOURRI. 5184

0738-2944 See JOURNAL OF CHRISTIAN HEALING, THE. 4968

0738-2979 See MEDIGUIDE TO CARDIOLOGY. 3708

0738-2987 See MEDIGUIDE TO OB/GYN. 3765

0738-2995 See MEDIGUIDE TO PAIN. 3614

0738-3002 See MEDIGUIDE TO RHEUMATOLOGY. 3806

0738-3029 See OBG DIAGNOSIS. 3766

0738-3037 See NATIONAL DEVELOPMENT. ASIA. 1507

0738-3045 See TELECOMMUNICATIONS DIRECTORY (DETROIT, MICH.). 1165

0738-3053 See MAGNOLIA (HAMMOND, LA.). 5233

0738-3096 See GOVERNMENT TENDER REPORT. 4652

0738-3207 See MONOGRAPH (MAXWELL GRADUATE SCHOOL OF CITIZENSHIP AND PUBLIC AFFAIRS. METROPOLITAN STUDIES PROGRAM). 4666

0738-3231 See PROCEEDINGS - SYMPOSIUM ON INSTRUMENTATION FOR THE PROCESS INDUSTRIES (TEXAS A & M UNIVERSITY). 1028

0738-3258 See EXECUTIVE BUDGET - DISTRICT OF COLUMBIA. 4722

0738-3266 See FEDERAL SOFTWARE EXCHANGE CATALOG. 1279

0738-3312 See GOVERNMENT UNION CRITIQUE, THE. 1676

0738-3355 See TECHNICAL ANALYSIS OF STOCKS AND COMMODITIES (JOURNAL). 917

0738-3398 See IBCD. 1566

0738-3436 See OUT SOCIALISM. 4544

0738-3460 See NOTES : NEWSLETTER OF THE ASSOCIATION OF GOVERNING BOARDS OF UNIVERSITIES AND COLLEGES. 1838

0738-3517 See ALUMNI DIRECTORY / WILLIAMS COLLEGE. 1100

0738-3614 See COMPUTERS IN PSYCHIATRY/PSYCHOLOGY. 3923

0738-3630 See ALUMNI DIRECTORY / UNIVERSITY OF DENVER. 1100

0738-3657 See TRAFFIC ACCIDENT FACTS (DOVER, DEL.). 5446

0738-3681 See RESOURCE DIRECTORY. TOURING PERFORMING COMPANIES. 388

0738-369X See MASSACHUSETTS LAWYERS DIARY AND MANUAL : INCLUDING BAR DIRECTORY. 3007

0738-3738 See ALUMNI DIRECTORY / EMORY & HENRY COLLEGE. 1098

0738-3746 See ENVIRONMENT, SAFETY, HEALTH AT DOE FACILITIES. 2861

0738-3762 See ALUMNI DIRECTORY - UNIVERSITY OF VIRGINIA. ALUMNI ASSOCIATION. 1100

0738-3770 See GENEALOGICAL GOLDMINE. 2450

0738-3800 See FLYING BUYERS' GUIDE. 21

0738-3819 See ISS MATCHBOOK. 4212

0738-386X See INDIANA REVIEW. 3344

0738-3886 See NFPC NEWS NOTES / NATIONAL FEDERATION OF PRIESTS' COUNCILS. 4982

0738-3940 See FIRE & EMERGENCY WORLD. 2288

0738-3967 See MS QUARTERLY REPORT. 3838

0738-3983 See PENNSYLVANIA EDUCATION DIRECTORY. 1772

0738-4009 See UBU REPERTORY THEATER PUBLICATIONS. 5372

0738-4017 See PERSONAL INVESTING (WOODLAND HILLS, CALIF.). 911

0738-4076 See BIOTECHNOLOGY MONTHLY UPDATE. 3689

0738-4114 See BIOMASS ENERGY INCL. ALCOHOL FUELS MONTHLY UPDATE. 1934

0738-4122 See DIRECTORY OF FINANCIAL AIDS FOR MINORITIES. 1821

0738-4130 See TRACINGS. 3253

0738-419X See ANNEX COMPUTER REPORT. 1170

0738-4203 See F.Y.E.O. 4044

0738-422X See RECENT DEVELOPMENTS IN ALCOHOLISM. 1348

0738-4262 See COMPUTER SECURITY, AUDITING AND CONTROLS. 1226

0738-4270 See COM-AND, COMPUTER AUDIT NEWS DEVELOPMENTS. 741

0738-4297 See EXECUTIVE'S HANDBOOK ON POLITICAL CONTRIBUTIONS. 4473

0738-4300 See GOVERNMENT COMPUTER NEWS. 4651

0738-4319 See COGNOTES. 3202

0738-4343 See WALL STREET COMPUTER REVIEW. 919

0738-4351 See SECUTITIES TRADERS' MONTHLY. 913

0738-4394 See PERSPECTIVES IN ETHOLOGY. 5518

0738-4467 See SAMPAN. 4684

0738-453X See CURRENT POPULATION REPORTS. SER. P-25, POPULATION ESTIMATES AND PROJECTIONS. 4551

0738-4602 See AI MAGAZINE. 1211

0738-4637 See WHO'S WHO, CHICANO OFFICEHOLDERS. 436

0738-4688 See PERSPECTIVES IN ASTHMA. 3950

0738-470X See SPECTRUM (ROCKVILLE, MD.). 3642

0738-4726 See CHILD NURTURANCE. 2277

0738-4750 See TRANSLATION SERVICES DIRECTORY. 3329

0738-4858 See INSTITUTE REPORT (KALAMAZOO, MICH.), THE. 1680

0738-4866 See GUNN SALUTE, THE. 2452

0738-4882 See ACTIVE SOLAR INSTALLATIONS SURVEY. 1930

0738-4947 See ALABAMA MEDICINE. 3547

0738-4955 See PINEAL RESEARCH REVIEWS. 585

0738-498X See BRANDING IRON OF THE BILL RICE RANCH, THE. 4384

0738-5099 See CM BULLETIN. 4638

0738-5102 See SOUTHERN HISTORIAN, THE. 2761

0738-5110 See ALEXANDER CITY OUTLOOK, THE. 5625

0738-5137 See EVENING TELEGRAM (ROCKY MOUNT, N.C.). 5723

0738-5153 See TALLAHASSEE DEMOCRAT. 5651

0738-5161 See BOYCOTT REPORT. 2257

0738-517X See PUERTO DEL SOL. 3426

0738-5196 See ALUMNI DIRECTORY - QUEENS COLLEGE (NEW YORK, N.Y.). 1099

0738-520X See DIRECTORY, MEMBERS AND ASSOCIATE MEMBERS - AMERICAN APPAREL MANUFACTURERS ASSOCIATION (1983). 1083

0738-5218 See AMERICAN MENSA REGISTER. 5228

0738-5226 See GENEALOGICAL AIDS BULLETIN (1978). 2449

0738-5234 See EWGS BULLETIN. 2446

0738-5242 See SAILBOAT & SAILING JOURNAL. 596

0738-5250 See ALUMNI DIRECTORY / VIRGINIA INTERMONT COLLEGE. 1100

0738-5269 See GENETIC MAPS. 546

0738-5277 See HIGHWAY SAFETY LITERATURE (1973). 5440

0738-5285 See TAX MANAGEMENT, PRIMARY SOURCES. 4753

0738-5579 See BOND FUND SURVEY. 779

0738-5587 See FORTUNE INTERNATIONAL. 677

0738-5595 See BUSINESS ENVIRONMENT RISK INFORMATION. 893

0738-5625 See HISPANIC AMERICAN ARTS. 321

0738-565X See WHEELS OF TIME. 5399

0738-5676 See POWER LINE (WASHINGTON, D.C.), THE. 1953

0738-5714 See F.C.C. WEEK. 1111

0738-5803 See REPORT - UNIVERSITY OF TEXAS AT AUSTIN. ATMOSPHERIC SCIENCE GROUP. 1434

0738-5854 See BOSTON HERALD (1982), THE. 5688

0738-5870 See ANNUAL REPORT OF THE ARCHITECT OF THE CAPITOL FOR THE PERIOD 287

0738-5889 See REMAINS TO BE FOUND. 2469

0738-5897 See ALUMNI DIRECTORY - LOOMIS CHAFFEE SCHOOL. 1098

0738-5900 See COMPUTER NEWS OF SAN DIEGO. 1177

0738-5919 See ANTITRUST LAW HANDBOOK. 3095

0738-5927 See PUBLIC CITIZEN. 1299

0738-5943 See RICE WORLD & SOYBEAN NEWS, THE. 185

0738-596X See NUT KERNEL, THE. 2426

0738-6001 See CREATION/EVOLUTION. 543

0738-6028 See COLONIAL WATERBIRDS. 5617

0883-1416 See GRASSROOTS ECONOMIC ORGANIZING NEWSLETTER. 1592

0738-6060 See MEDICAL SCHOOL ADMISSION REQUIREMENTS, UNITED STATES AND CANADA. 1835

0738-6095 See BLACK'S GUIDE. ORANGE COUNTY OFFICE SPACE MARKET. 4210

0738-6176 See PSYCHOTHERAPY PATIENT, THE. 3935

0738-6206 See PACE ENVIRONMENTAL LAW REVIEW. 3115

0738-6230 See ANNUAL STATISTICAL REPORT / AMERICAN ASSOCIATION OF COLLEGES OF OSTEOPATHIC MEDICINE. 3654

0738-6311 See TOUCHING. 2912

0738-632X See JOURNAL OF COMMUNITY GARDENING. 2421
0738-6354 See MICRO SOFTWARE MARKETING. 1288
0738-6362 See SALESMAN'S INSIDER. 709
0738-6400 See POLIS (BOSTON, MASS.). 3470
0738-6419 See GOOD NEWS LETTER (WASHINGTON, D.C.), THE. 5030
0738-6427 See FRANKLIN OFFSET CATALOG. 4565
0738-646X See CSI FEDERAL REGISTER ABSTRACTS (MASTER EDITION). 4641
0738-6494 See JUST COMPENSATION. 2991
0738-6508 See INTERNATIONAL POLICY REPORT. 4525
0738-6516 See SIZZLE SHEET, THE. 936
0738-6524 See SHROUD SPECTRUM INTERNATIONAL. 5157
0738-6532 See RENEWABLE RESOURCES JOURNAL. 2203
0738-6583 See EXECUTIVE HOUSEKEEPING TODAY. 2790
0738-6591 See AIRCRAFT BLUEBOOK-PRICE DIGEST. 9
0738-6613 See PRINTOUT (NEWTONVILLE, MASS.). 4569
0738-6648 See JACKSONIANA. 2455
0738-6656 See RANGER RICK. 1068
0738-6664 See ALUMNI DIRECTORY / CUSHING ACADEMY. 1098
0738-6672 See ALUMNAE/I DIRECTORY - RUTGERS LAW SCHOOL (NEWARK, N.J.). 1097
0738-6699 See TOP LINE. 888
0738-6729 See BEHAVIOR ANALYST, THE. 4576
0738-6745 See URNER BARRY'S MEAT & POULTRY DIRECTORY. 223
0738-6753 See MIDWEST AGRICULTURAL LAW JOURNAL. 3010
0738-6796 See ALUMNI AND ALUMNAE DIRECTORY / HOBART AND WILLIAM SMITH COLLEGES. 1097
0738-680X See ALUMNI DIRECTORY / CHOATE ROSEMARY HALL. 1097
0738-6818 See ALUMNI DIRECTORY / GRAMBLING STATE UNIVERSITY. 1098
0738-6826 See TR NEWS. 5394
0738-6842 See ALUMNAE DIRECTORY / STEPHENS COLLEGE. 1096
0738-6869 See BUSINESS NEWS, SAN DIEGO. 651
0738-6877 See CREDIT CODE LETTER, THE. 1296
0738-6885 See CHURCH SECRETARY'S SWAP SHOP, THE. 4948
0738-6931 See DISTRICT OF COLUMBIA REAL ESTATE REPORTER. 4837
0738-694X See CALIFORNIA IN PRINT. 4636
0738-6958 See PRIVATE SECURITY CASE LAW REPORTER. 3031
0738-6974 See ADMINISTRATIVE RADIOLOGY. 3938
0738-6982 See EXECUTIVE COMPENSATION REPORTS (ALEXANDRIA, VA.). 940
0738-7008 See CRAB CREEK REVIEW. 2532
0738-7024 See BUSINESS IDEAS NEWSLETTER. 649
0738-7032 See UNLIMITED TIMES, THE. 717
0738-7040 See INSIDE WOMEN'S TENNIS. 4900
0738-7067 See BIG BANDS, THE. 4103
0738-7091 See VIP NEWSLETTER. 4394
0738-713X See MICROCONTAMINATION. 2072
0738-7156 See MICROBANKER. 798
0738-7164 See STUDIES IN MEDIEVALISM. 2711
0738-7199 See VENTURE PRODUCT NEWS. 5168
0738-7210 See ECONOMIC REPORT (ALBUQUERQUE, N.M.), THE. 1484
0738-7229 See KEEPING SCORE. 1501
0738-7237 See MIRROR, THE. 4977
0738-7245 See NAUTICAL RESEARCH JOURNAL. 4179

0738-7253 See BUSINESS & ACQUISITION NEWSLETTER. 645
0738-727X See MISSISSIPPI SUPERVISOR AND CHANCERY CLERK, CIRCUIT CLERK, TAX ASSESSOR & COLLECTOR. 4666
0738-7288 See BOWSER REPORT, THE. 893
0738-7296 See KANSAS CITY GRAIN MARKET REVIEW. 1501
0738-730X See LANCASTER LIVESTOCK REPORTER. 214
0738-7318 See RELIGIOUS HERALD, THE. 4992
0738-7350 See JOURNAL OF UROLOGICAL NURSING. 3991
0738-7520 See CITIZEN (AUBURN, N.Y.), THE. 5715
0738-7555 See GPN NEWSLETTER. 1132
0738-7563 See VIDEO NETWORKS. 1142
0738-7571 See MARSHALL COUNTY HISTORICAL QUARTERLY. 2745
0738-758X See ON GUARD (CLEVELAND, TENN.). 4983
0738-7601 See JOBS AVAILABLE. 1681
0738-7628 See VEA (HATO REY, P.R.). 2494
0738-7644 See TEXAS OPTOMETRY. 4217
0738-7687 See LIVING OFF THE LAND. 2424
0738-7709 See COURIER-STANDARD-ENTERPRISE. 5715
0738-7717 See ROCKIN' 50'S. 4151
0738-7741 See ALABAMA BAPTIST, THE. 5625
0738-775X See MISSISSIPPI ARCHAEOLOGY. 275
0738-7776 See CHEMECOLOGY. 2162
0738-7784 See INTERCHANGE - ERIC PROCESSING AND REFERENCE FACILITY. 3217
0738-7792 See AIM REPORT. 2917
0738-7806 See GENERATIONS (SAN FRANCISCO, CALIF.). 5179
0738-7911 See TALKIN' UNION (TAKOMA PARK MD.). 1713
0738-7938 See IIC DOCUMENT SERVICE. 1113
0738-7946 See HOSPITAL GIFT SHOP MANAGEMENT. 869
0738-7962 See PARISH TEACHER. 4985
0738-7970 See JOURNAL / SOUTHERN CALIFORNIA DENTAL ASSISTANTS ASSOCIATION. 1329
0738-7989 See JOURNAL OF MATERIALS EDUCATION, THE. 2103
0738-7997 See JOURNAL OF NORTHEAST ASIAN STUDIES. 4479
0738-8004 See WRITTEN WORD, THE. 1792
0738-8012 See WORD FROM WASHINGTON. 5314
0738-8020 See POTTERY SOUTHWEST. 2593
0738-8039 See WESTERN PHOTOGRAPHER. 4378
0738-8047 See GALVESTON DAILY NEWS (HOUSTON, TEX.: 1865). 5750
0738-8055 See WEEKLY WESTPORT REPORTER, THE. 5704
0738-8071 See DISCOVER SOUTHWEST WISCONSIN'S HIDDEN VALLEYS. 5468
0738-8098 See LOUISIANA OUT-OF-DOORS. 4874
0738-8101 See YOUNG AND ALIVE. 4395
0738-811X See HEALTH FACTS. 4779
0738-8144 See CORRECTIONS COMPENDIUM. 5281
0738-8152 See ALPHABETICAL DIRECTORY OF ATTORNEYS IN NEW YORK STATE. 2932
0738-8160 See ALUMNI DIRECTORY / NEW MEXICO MILITARY INSTITUTE. 1099
0738-8179 See ALUMNI DIRECTORY / SIENA COLLEGE. 1099
0738-8187 See FIRE AND CASUALTY, LIFE AND DISABILITY INSURANCE MANUAL. 2880
0738-8209 See QUARTERLY / CENTRAL GEORGIA GENEALOGICAL SOCIETY, INC. 2469
0738-8217 See INTERNATIONAL FORUM FOR PSYCHOANALYSIS. 4590

0738-8268 See GOODLET FAMILY NEWSLETTER, THE. 2451
0738-8276 See MOON FAMILY NEWSLETTER, THE. 2461
0738-8292 See NURSING JOURNALS INDEX, THE. 3864
0738-8306 See OUR NAME'S THE GAME. 2466
0738-8322 See BLUE BOOK OF PHOTOGRAPHY PRICES. 4367
0738-8349 See DEMING HEADLIGHT (1956). 5712
0738-8357 See FOLK ART FINDER. 350
0738-8365 See NEW YORK ANTIQUE ALMANAC OF ART, ANTIQUES, INVESTMENTS & YESTERYEAR, THE. 251
0738-8373 See POCAHONTAS TIMES. 5764
0738-8381 See ROCKY MOUNTAIN QUARTER HORSE. 2802
0738-839X See DIRECTORY OF COMPUTER & SOFTWARE STOREFRONT DEALERS. 1182
0738-8411 See FORUM INDEX, THE. 5814
0738-842X See REVIEW OF THE UNITED STATES SYNTHETIC FUELS CORPORATIONS FINANCIAL STATEMENTS. 4683
0738-8438 See REPORT OF ... COMMISSIONER OF AGRICULTURE, FOOD AND RURAL RESOURCES TO THE ... REGULAR SESSION OF THE ... MAINE STATE LEGISLATURE. 126
0738-8470 See FTP-NEA ADVOCATE. 1747
0738-8489 See EVANGELIST (ALBANY, N.Y.), THE. 5029
0738-8497 See ROUNDUP (WASHINGTON, D.C.), THE. 2759
0738-8527 See REPORTER (LONG BEACH, CALIF.). 1707
0738-8543 See LIST (VERO BEACH, FLA.). 1268
0738-8551 See CRITICAL REVIEWS IN BIOTECHNOLOGY. 3691
0738-856X See METHOTREXATE UPDATE. 3616
0738-8586 See VICTOR VALLEY MAGAZINE. 2549
0738-8594 See PERSONAL SELLING POWER. 934
0738-8624 See NOTES PLUS. 1901
0738-8632 See FEDERAL TAX COORDINATOR 2D. 4724
0738-8640 See KNOWLEDGE (FORT WORTH, TEX.). 3345
0738-8675 See AMERICAN RADIO REPORT. 1126
0738-8691 See PEDIATRIC NOTES. 3909
0738-8705 See PANHANDLER, THE. 3467
0738-8799 See BEER PAPER, THE. 2364
0738-8802 See SECOND OPINIONS ON HEALTH CARE ISSUES. 3640
0738-8810 See TRACKS (LANSING, MICH.). 2207
0738-8829 See HERITAGE WEST (SACRAMENTO, CALIF.). 251
0738-8837 See TEJAS JOURNAL OF AUDIOLOGY AND SPEECH PATHOLOGY. 3891
0738-8845 See CMC NEWS. 1174
0738-8853 See JESSE MEYER'S BEVERAGE DIGEST. 2368
0738-8861 See PROGRESSIVE PLATTER. 4147
0738-887X See YOUNG PEOPLE TODAY. 2495
0738-8888 See INTERNATIONAL CURRENCY REPORT. 1636
0738-890X See FURNITURE WORLD (NEW YORK, N.Y.). 2906
0738-8942 See CONFLICT MANAGEMENT AND PEACE SCIENCE. 4518
0738-8950 See JOURNAL OF AGRIBUSINESS. 99
0738-8977 See BUSINESS WORCESTER. 654
0738-8993 See SPOON RIVER QUARTERLY, THE. 3353
0738-9000 See CREATIVE BLACK BOOK, THE. 758
0738-9051 See SPECTRUM NEWSLETTER. 1122
0738-9094 See TRAVELWRITER MARKETLETTER. 2925
0738-9108 See SOUTH END NEWS (BOSTON, MASS.). 5690
0738-9116 See IMPARTIAL CITIZEN (SYRACUSE, N.Y. : 1980), THE. 2263
0738-9140 See WARREN REPORT, THE. 889

0738-9159 See NATIONAL COUNCIL NEWS (ROCKVILLE, MD.). 5297

0738-9167 See LEVINSON LETTER, THE. 875

0738-9183 See PRENSA SAN DIEGO, LA. 2271

0738-9213 See COMPUTER BUYER'S GUIDE AND HANDBOOK. 1266

0738-923X See MAGNETIC MEDIA INTERNATIONAL NEWSLETTER. 2071

0738-9264 See FUTURIFIC. 2487

0738-9299 See FRANK. 3343

0738-9310 See SCIENCE OF FOOD AND AGRICULTURE. 2356

0738-9345 See CONTRIBUTIONS TO THE STUDY OF WORLD LITERATURE. 3378

0738-9396 See MID-ATLANTIC ARCHIVIST, THE. 2623

0738-9418 See CHANGING SCHOOLS (MUNCIE, IND. 1731

0738-9477 See NECNP NEWSLETTER. 2237

0738-9485 See NEWSLETTER / CALIFORNIA COUNCIL FOR INTERNATIONAL TRADE. 847

0738-9507 See TECHNOLOGY WATCH FOR THE GRAPHIC ARTS AND INFORMATION INDUSTRIES. 382

0738-9515 See TRAVEL INDUSTRY WORLD YEARBOOK. 5496

0738-9523 See FORUM FOR READING. 1824

0738-9566 See COLLEGE ADMISSIONS DATA HANDBOOK. NORTHEAST REGION. 1815

0738-9574 See COLLEGE ADMISSIONS DATA HANDBOOK. MID-WEST REGION. 1815

0738-9582 See COLLEGE ADMISSIONS DATA HANDBOOK. WEST REGION. 1816

0738-9590 See COLLEGE ADMISSIONS DATA HANDBOOK. SOUTHEAST REGION. 1815

0738-9604 See CAREFREE ENTERPRISE. 2530

0738-9612 See TECHNIQUES FOR SUCCESS IN FUND-RAISING, MARKETING, AND PUBLIC RELATIONS FOR NONPROFIT ORGANIZATIONS. 767

0738-9620 See TEXTILE FLAMMABILITY DIGEST. 5357

0738-9639 See OLDER AMERICAN (BOSTON, MASS.), THE. 3754

0738-9655 See JOHN DONNE JOURNAL. 3345

0738-9663 See ILLINOIS ISSUES. 4476

0738-9671 See NEW MEXICO HUMANITIES REVIEW. 2851

0738-968X See IPM PRACTITIONER, THE. 4245

0738-971X See NORTHEAST SUN. 1951

0738-9728 See INTERNATIONAL LAWYERS' NEWSLETTER. 3130

0738-9736 See KANHISTIQUE. 2743

0738-9744 See DENTAL COMPUTER NEWSLETTER. 1320

0738-9752 See QUARTERLY JOURNAL OF IDEOLOGY. 5254

0738-9760 See JOURNAL OF APPLIED RABBIT RESEARCH, THE. 460

0738-9779 See TRIBUNE - INTERNATIONAL WOMEN'S TRIBUNE CENTRE, THE. 5567

0738-9795 See AMERICAN COWBOY. 4882

0738-9809 See OIL AND GAS FIELD CODE MASTER LIST. 4268

0738-9817 See ALUMNI DIRECTORY - COLUMBIA COLLEGE (COLUMBIA UNIVERSITY). 1098

0738-9833 See OCEAN REALM. 1453

0738-9841 See PORTUGUESE STUDIES REVIEW. 2703

0738-985X See NATCHEZ TRACE TRAVELER. 2461

0738-9868 See MINNEAPOLIS STAR AND TRIBUNE INDEX (MINNEAPOLIS, MINN.). 5697

0738-9884 See SPACE BUSINESS NEWS. 35

0738-9892 See SANTA FE ROUTE, THE. 5436

0738-9906 See PREDICASTS' BASEBOOK. 1513

0738-9930 See TYLERTOWN TIMES, THE. 5702

0738-9949 See US ARCHER, THE. 4927

0738-9973 See WALDENBOOKS BESTSELLERS. 4833

0738-9981 See COLLECTRIX. 250

0738-999X See FLORIDA FIELD NATURALIST. 5584

0739-0017 See SABINE INDEX (MANY, LA. : 1879). 5684

0739-0033 See FILLERS FOR PUBLICATIONS. 2919

0739-0041 See FLORIDA GEOGRAPHER, THE. 2560

0739-005X See JOURNAL / NORTH LA. HIST. ASSOC. 2740

0739-0068 See NEAR EAST ARCHAEOLOGICAL SOCIETY BULLETIN. 275

0739-0076 See ADAMS ADDENDA. 2436

0739-0084 See TEACHERS & WRITERS. 3444

0739-0092 See TODAY'S FARMER. 141

0739-0106 See GAZETTE, GOOCHLAND, THE. 5758

0739-0122 See QUA'TOQTI. 5630

0739-0130 See LEGISLATIVE BULLETIN / OHIO CITIZENS' COUNCIL. 3001

0739-0157 See KANSAS ENGLISH. 1899

0739-0181 See DIXON TRIBUNE, THE. 5634

0739-019X See ANGLERS' NEWS. 2294

0739-0203 See PONTIAC-OAKLAND COUNTY LEGAL NEWS. 3029

0739-0238 See POTATO STATISTICAL YEARBOOK. 156

0739-0246 See CHOWAN HERALD, THE. 5723

0739-0262 See NORTHWEST OIL REPORT. 4267

0739-0270 See AAMI NEWS. 3543

0739-0289 See MORTICIANS OF THE SOUTHWEST. 2407

0739-0297 See LIBRARIAN'S WORLD. 3223

0739-0319 See MIAMI TIMES, THE. 5650

0739-0327 See WATERFOWLER'S WORLD. 2208

0739-036X See CLOSED LOOP (MINNEAPOLIS, MINN.). 2111

0739-0386 See LOEX NEWS. 3228

0739-0394 See CAMPUS LAW ENFORCEMENT JOURNAL. 3159

0739-0408 See TENNESSEE EDUCATION. 1787

0739-0424 See MISSISSIPPI MUD, THE. 325

0739-0440 See WESLEYAN WORLD. 5009

0739-0459 See BULLETIN / INSTITUTE FOR ANTIQUITY AND CHRISTIANITY. 4941

0739-0475 See GALLERIES (WASHINGTON, D.C.). 4088

0739-0483 See CALIFORNIA PHARMACIST. 4295

0739-0491 See TEXTILE BUSINESS OUTLOOK. 5357

0739-0564 See STANDARDS MONITOR. 3642

0739-0572 See JOURNAL OF ATMOSPHERIC AND OCEANIC TECHNOLOGY. 1426

0739-0580 See RECORD IN EDUCATIONAL ADMINISTRATION AND SUPERVISION. 1869

0739-0602 See OUTDOOR PRESS, THE. 4877

0739-0645 See SEARCH (FAIRFIELD, CONN.). 710

0739-0653 See PEEK (65). 1264

0739-070X See QUEBEC BOOKS. 4831

0739-0750 See FIELDING'S ECONOMY CARIBBEAN. 2560

0739-0769 See FIELDING'S BERMUDA AND THE BAHAMAS. 5470

0739-0793 See FIELDING'S MEXICO. 5470

0739-0807 See FIELDING'S HAVENS AND HIDEAWAYS USA. 2805

0739-0823 See FUTUREVIEWS. 1185

0739-084X See GRAND RIVER VALLEY REVIEW, THE. 2735

0739-0874 See COMPUTER ECONOMIC$ REPORT. 1256

0739-0882 See FAMILY THERAPY NETWORKER, THE. 2280

0739-0904 See CORNERSTONE CLUES. 2444

0739-0939 See AIRPOST JOURNAL, THE. 1144

0739-0955 See NORTHWEST STAR. 5686

0739-0963 See MITTELMAN LETTER, THE. 1330

0739-0971 See TRANET. 2207

0739-098X See INTERNATIONAL JOURNAL OF APPLIED PHILOSOPHY, THE. 2251

0739-0998 See JAIL & PRISONER LAW BULLETIN. 3166

0739-1013 See DATA-TEK SEMICONDUCTOR PRICE GUIDE. 2040

0739-1056 See COLLEGE MEDIA REVIEW. 2918

0739-1072 See BAYLOR BUSINESS REVIEW. 642

0739-1080 See WESTERN PREHISTORIC RESEARCH ARCHEOLOGICAL MONOGRAPH. 285

0739-1102 See JOURNAL OF BIOMOLECULAR STRUCTURE & DYNAMICS. 461

0739-1110 See INDUSTRIAL ORGANIZATIONAL PSYCHOLOGIST, THE. 4590

0739-1137 See IASSIST QUARTERLY. 3258

0739-1145 See CURRENT EVENTS SWEEPSTAKES. 2730

0739-1161 See PERFORMING ARTS FORUM. 387

0739-117X See MOTOR COACH AGE. 5387

0739-1196 See LAKE CHARLES AMERICAN-PRESS. 5684

0739-120X See HOLOSPHERE. 4370

0739-1226 See NATIONAL DIRECTORY OF COLLEGE ATHLETICS (WOMEN'S EDITION), THE. 4906

0739-1234 See BALDWIN'S OHIO TAX SERVICE. 2939

0739-1250 See COMMUNAL SOCIETIES. 5242

0739-1277 See WILLOW SPRINGS. 3356

0739-1307 See ATHENS LC NEWS COURIER. 5625

0739-1323 See ANNUAL FORUM - AMERICAN BAR ASSOCIATION. FORUM COMMITTEE ON FRANCHISING. ANNUAL FORUM. 3095

0739-1331 See DIRECTORY OF ALUMNI / PENNSYLVANIA STATE UNIVERSITY, COLLEGE OF EARTH AND MINERAL SCIENCES. 1101

0739-1366 See ALUMNI DIRECTORY / UNIVERSITY OF REDLANDS. 1100

0739-1374 See ORGANIZATIONS EXEMPT FROM LIMITED SALES AND USE TAX. 4740

0739-1390 See BULLETIN OF THE INTERNATIONAL COUNCIL FOR TRADITIONAL MUSIC. 4106

0739-1404 See OCCUPATIONS OF FEDERAL WHITE-COLLAR AND BLUE-COLLAR WORKERS. 4207

0739-1412 See NATCHEZ TRACE NEWSLETTER. 2461

0739-1420 See TOLL-FREE TRAVEL/VACATION PHONE DIRECTORY. 5492

0739-1447 See GENEALOGICAL RECORD OF STRAFFORD COUNTY, THE. 2450

0739-1463 See TEXAS FORESTRY (LUFKIN, TEX.). 2396

0739-1471 See PROCEEDINGS - NATIONAL ONLINE MEETING. 1275

0739-1544 See NCECA JOURNAL. 2592

0739-1552 See NCECA NEWSLETTER. 2592

0739-1560 See METROPOLITAN AREA GUIDE TO SERIALS. 420

0739-1587 See CORPORATE & INCENTIVE TRAVEL. 661

0739-1595 See INTERNATIONAL ROBOTICS YEARBOOK, THE. 1213

0739-1609 See NEWSLETTER - NATIONAL COUNCIL FOR THERAPY AND REHABILITATION THROUGH HORTICULTURE (U.S.). 2425

0739-1617 See NATIONAL EDUCATOR, THE. 5637

0739-1641 See ALBUM NETWORK, THE. 4099

0739-1684 See FEDERAL JOBS DIGEST. 4204

0739-1706 See LAWYER HIRING & TRAINING REPORT. 2997

0739-1714 See SOUTHERN PARTISAN, THE. 4496

0739-1722 See CAR PRICES. 5409

0739-1730 See CAROLINA INDIAN VOICE, THE. 2258

0739-1749 See DAUGHTERS OF SARAH. 4952

0739-1773 See BULLETIN OF THE INSTITUTE FOR CONTINUING DENTAL EDUCATION OF THE QUEENS COUNTY DENTAL SOCIETY. 1318

0739-1781 *See* JOURNAL OF WEATHER MODIFICATION, THE. **1427**

0739-1803 *See* LESBIAN NEWS (CANOGA PARK, CALIF.), THE. **2795**

0739-1811 *See* NATURAL GAS INTELLIGENCE. **4265**

0739-1824 *See* BULLETIN - SOCIETY FOR SPANISH AND PORTUGUESE HISTORICAL STUDIES (U.S.) **2681**

0739-1838 *See* RED RIVER VALLEY HERITAGE PRESS, THE. **2756**

0739-1854 *See* HARVARD INTERNATIONAL REVIEW. **4523**

0739-1862 *See* COMPANY THESAURUS / PREDICASTS, INC. **1602**

0739-1889 *See* LIMITED OFFERING EXEMPTIONS: REGULATION D. **3101**

0739-1897 *See* ENTERTAINMENT, PUBLISHING AND THE ARTS HANDBOOK. **385**

0739-1943 *See* JOURNAL OF SOUTHWEST GEORGIA HISTORY, THE. **2742**

0739-196X *See* REAL LIFE MAGAZINE. **363**

0739-1978 *See* PANEL DISCUSSION SERIES. **3024**

0739-1994 *See* CHARLES FARRELL'S DANCE BUSINESS NEWSLETTER. **1311**

0739-2001 *See* GRAY PANTHER NETWORK. **5286**

0739-2036 *See* HUMAN ETHOLOGY NEWSLETTER. **237**

0739-2052 *See* HABITAT (FALMOUTH, ME.). **2194**

0739-2079 *See* QUARTERLY - PHI LAMBDA KAPPA MEDICAL FRATERNITY. **3917**

0739-2095 *See* BLUE BOOK FOR THE APPLE COMPUTER, THE. **1172**

0739-2125 *See* MINERAL INDUSTRY SURVEYS. GRAPHITE, NATURAL IN **2144**

0739-2133 *See* PIMA CATALOG. **4237**

0739-2141 *See* MAGILL'S CINEMA ANNUAL. **4074**

0739-2168 *See* IRA REPORTER, THE. **904**

0739-2184 *See* SMITH FUNDING REPORT. **1847**

0739-2214 *See* NPTA MANAGEMENT NEWS. **4235**

0739-2222 *See* SITUATIONS WANTED; JOBS WANTED. **4209**

0739-2257 *See* BOATS & HARBORS. **592**

0739-2281 *See* SEARCHING TOGETHER. **5067**

0739-229X *See* SONUS. **4153**

0739-2303 *See* TEILHARD STUDIES. **4363**

0739-2311 *See* UTAH HOLIDAY. **5498**

0739-232X *See* WIND RIVER RENDEZVOUS, THE. **2766**

0739-2338 *See* EXPERIENTIAL EDUCATION. **1746**

0739-2346 *See* PANEL RESOURCE PAPER. **1902**

0739-2354 *See* CROSSCURRENTS (WESTLAKE VILLAGE, CALIF.) **3379**

0739-2419 *See* SUPPLIERS DIRECTORY (COLORADO SPRINGS, COLO.). **5001**

0739-2443 *See* NICHI BEI TIMES. **5637**

0739-2451 *See* ANNUAL REVIEW OF BANKING LAW. **3084**

0739-246X *See* ANNUAL REPORT FROM THE SECRETARY OF THE DEPARTMENT OF HEALTH AND HUMAN SERVICES TO THE PRESIDENT AND CONGRESS OF THE UNITED STATES : DRUG ABUSE PREVENTION, TREATMENT, AND REHABILITATION. **1341**

0739-2478 *See* POWELL PATHS. **2468**

0739-2494 *See* BARRISTER (PHILADELPHIA, PA.), THE. **2940**

0739-2532 *See* CATALYST FOR CHANGE. **1861**

0739-2540 *See* RECORDER (AMSTERDAM, N.Y.). **5720**

0739-2559 *See* SPECTRUM (ST. PAUL, MINN.). **1921**

0739-2567 *See* FINANCIAL DIRECTORY OF PENSION FUNDS. NEW JERSEY, SOUTHERN. TRENTON, CAMDEN, ATLANTIC CITY & OTHERS. **1672**

0739-2575 *See* FINANCIAL DIRECTORY OF PENSION FUNDS. PENNSYLVANIA, EASTERN, EXCLUDING PHILADELPHIA AREA. HARRISBURG, WILKESBARRE & OTHERS. **1673**

0739-2583 *See* FINANCIAL DIRECTORY OF PENSION FUNDS. INDIANA, NORTHERN. SOUTH BEND, FT. WAYNE, MUNCIE & OTHERS. **1671**

0739-2591 *See* FINANCIAL DIRECTORY OF PENSION FUNDS. CALIFORNIA, SOUTHERN. LOS ANGELES CITY PROPER. **1670**

0739-2605 *See* FINANCIAL DIRECTORY OF PENSION FUNDS. NEW YORK, MANHATTAN-DOWNTOWN. WALL ST. TO 40 ST. **1672**

0739-2613 *See* FINANCIAL DIRECTORY OF PENSION FUNDS. VIRGINIA, NORTHERN. (ARLINGTON, WINCHESTER, HARRISONBURG & OTHERS). **1674**

0739-2621 *See* FINANCIAL DIRECTORY OF PENSION FUNDS. CONNECTICUT, SOUTHERN. STAMFORD, NEW HAVEN, NEW LONDON & OTHERS. **1670**

0739-263X *See* FINANCIAL DIRECTORY OF PENSION FUNDS. NORTH CAROLINA, WESTERN. WINSTON-SALEM, LEXINGTON, GREENSBORO, CHARLOTTE & OTHERS. **1673**

0739-2648 *See* FINANCIAL DIRECTORY OF PENSION FUNDS. MASSACHUSETTS, EXCLUDING BOSTON & SUBURBS. WORCESTER, SPRINGFIELD, PITTSFIELD & OTHERS. **1671**

0739-2656 *See* FINANCIAL DIRECTORY OF PENSION FUNDS. FLORIDA, NORTHERN. JACKSONVILLE, TALLAHASSEE, GAINESVILLE & OTHERS. **1670**

0739-2664 *See* FINANCIAL DIRECTORY OF PENSION FUNDS. FLORIDA, SOUTHERN. WEST PALM BEACH, MIAMI, FT. MYER & OTHERS. **1670**

0739-2672 *See* FINANCIAL DIRECTORY OF PENSION FUNDS. CALIFORNIA, SOUTHERN, SO. SUBURBAN LOS ANGELES. INGLEWOOD, WHITTIER, LONG BEACH & OTHERS. **1670**

0739-2680 *See* FINANCIAL DIRECTORY OF PENSION FUNDS. NEW YORK. BROOKLYN, S.I., BRONX, QUEENS. **1672**

0739-2710 *See* FINANCIAL DIRECTORY OF PENSION FUNDS. PENNSYLVANIA, WESTERN, EXCLUDING PITTSBURGH AREA. ERIE, NEW CASTLE, GREENSBURG & OTHERS. **1673**

0739-2729 *See* FINANCIAL DIRECTORY OF PENSION FUNDS. CALIFORNIA, SOUTHERN, NO. SUBURBAN LOS ANGELES. VENTURA, PASADENA, ALHAMBRA & OTHERS. **1670**

0739-2737 *See* FINANCIAL DIRECTORY OF PENSION FUNDS. CALIFORNIA, NORTHERN, EXCLUDING SAN FRANCISCO. OAKLAND, SAN JOSE, FRESNO & OTHERS. **1670**

0739-2745 *See* FINANCIAL DIRECTORY OF PENSION FUNDS. NEW YORK, MANHATTAN-MIDTOWN, 41 ST. TO 50 ST. **1672**

0739-2753 *See* FINANCIAL DIRECTORY OF PENSION FUNDS. WISCONSIN, SOUTHERN, EXCLUDING MILWAUKEE AREA. MADISON, LACROSSE, OSHKOSH & OTHERS. **1674**

0739-2761 *See* FINANCIAL DIRECTORY OF PENSION FUNDS. NEW YORK, EASTERN UPSTATE. POUGHKEEPSIE, ALBANY, GLENS FALLS & OTHERS. **1672**

0739-277X *See* FINANCIAL DIRECTORY OF PENSION FUNDS. WISCONSIN, MILWAUKEE CITY PROPER. **1674**

0739-2788 *See* FINANCIAL DIRECTORY OF PENSION FUNDS. TEXAS, SOUTHERN, HOUSTON & EAST COAST (PASADENA & BEAUMONT). **1674**

0739-2796 *See* FINANCIAL DIRECTORY OF PENSION FUNDS. NORTH CAROLINA, EASTERN. RALEIGH, FAYETTEVILLE, WILMINGTON & OTHERS. **1673**

0739-280X *See* FINANCIAL DIRECTORY OF PENSION FUNDS. CONNECTICUT, NORTHERN. HARTFORD, WILLIMANTIC, WATERBURY & OTHERS. **1670**

0739-2818 *See* FINANCIAL DIRECTORY OF PENSION FUNDS. ILLINOIS, NORTHERN, EXCLUDING CHICAGO AREA. KANKAKEE, ROCKFORD, PEORIA & OTHERS. **1671**

0739-2826 *See* FINANCIAL DIRECTORY OF PENSION FUNDS. MISSOURI, WESTERN. KANSAS CITY, ST. JOSEPH, SPRINGFIELD & OTHERS. **1672**

0739-2834 *See* FINANCIAL DIRECTORY OF PENSION FUNDS. ILLINOIS, CHICAGO CITY PROPER. **1670**

0739-2842 *See* FINANCIAL DIRECTORY OF PENSION FUNDS. NEW YORK, MANHATTAN-UPTOWN. 51 ST. TO HARLEM RIVER. **1672**

0739-2850 *See* FINANCIAL DIRECTORY OF PENSION FUNDS. NEW YORK, WESTERN UPSTATE. ROCHESTER, BUFFALO, ELMIRA & OTHERS. **1672**

0739-2869 *See* FINANCIAL DIRECTORY OF PENSION FUNDS. INDIANA, SOUTHERN (INDIANAPOLIS, TERRE HAUTE, EVANSVILLE & OTHERS). **1671**

0739-2877 *See* FINANCIAL DIRECTORY OF PENSION FUNDS. MISSOURI, EASTERN. ST. LOUIS, JEFFERSON CITY & OTHERS. **1672**

0739-2907 See WORLD PUBLISHING MONITOR. **4822**

0739-2931 *See* NATIONAL NEWSLETTER - ASSOCIATION OF PART-TIME PROFESSIONALS (U.S.). **4206**

0739-294X *See* BUNKERFUELS REPORT. **4252**

0739-3024 *See* DIRECTORY / ASSOCIATION OF AMERICAN UNIVERSITY PRESSES. **4813**

0739-3059 *See* ANALYSIS OF MARYLAND SALES AND USE TAX ... REVENUES COLLECTED IN MONTGOMERY COUNTY / MONTGOMERY COUNTY GOVERNMENT, DEPARTMENT OF FINANCE. **4709**

0739-3067 *See* NBA REGISTER. **4906**

0739-3075 *See* ENERGY STATISTICS (CHICAGO, ILL.). **1962**

0739-3113 *See* CARE CASSETTES. **4942**

0739-3121 *See* REPORTER (LOS ANGELES, CALIF.). **2924**

0739-313X *See* INTERCONTINENTAL ADVANCED MANAGEMENT REPORT, THE. **871**

0739-3148 *See* NEW POLITICAL SCIENCE. **4484**

0739-3156 *See* OFFICE PROFESSIONAL, THE. **1118**

0739-3172 *See* ISSUES IN ACCOUNTING EDUCATION. **745**

0739-3180 *See* CRITICAL STUDIES IN MASS COMMUNICATION. **1109**

0739-3199 *See* HIGDON FAMILY NEWSLETTER. **2453**

0739-3202 *See* TEXAS BOOKS IN REVIEW. **4833**

0739-3210 *See* DOCKET (ST. PAUL, MINN.). **2963**

0739-3229 *See* FACT BOOK - NAVAL RESEARCH LABORATORY (U.S.). **4176**

0739-3237 *See* FINANCIAL DIRECTORY OF PENSION FUNDS. TEXAS, NORTHERN (DALLAS, DENTON, SHERMAN). **1673**

0739-3245 *See* FINANCIAL DIRECTORY OF PENSION FUNDS. GEORGIA, ATLANTA AREA. **1670**

0739-327X *See* NATIONAL AUCTION BULLETIN. **2775**

0739-3288 *See* ACTIVITIES OF THE HOUSE COMMITTEE ON GOVERNMENT OPERATIONS. **4623**

0739-3350 *See* SUPERCONDUCTIVE TECHNOLOGY IN REVIEW. **5161**

0739-3369 *See* JOURNAL OF VOCATIONAL EDUCATION RESEARCH, THE. **1914**

0739-3385 *See* FINANCIAL DIRECTORY OF PENSION FUNDS. CALIFORNIA, SOUTHERN, EXCLUDING LOS ANGELES AREA (SAN DIEGO, SANTA ANA, SAN BERNARDINO & OTHERS). **1670**

0739-3393 *See* CATALOGING SERVICE BULLETIN INDEX. **3200**

0739-3431 *See* HANSON'S GUIDELINES. **4212**

0739-344X *See* TRADESWOMEN. **5567**

0739-3466 *See* HOSPITAL GRAPHICS. **379**

0739-3474 *See* CARRIER PIDGIN, THE. **3273**

0739-3482 *See* VIRGINIA APPALACHIAN NOTES. **2476**

0739-3504 *See* DAILY HAMPSHIRE GAZETTE. **5688**

0739-3512 *See* CHINA : INTERNATIONAL TRADE. ANNUAL STATISTICAL SUPPLEMENT. **727**

0739-3547 *See* GULF COAST OIL DIRECTORY. **4259**

0739-3555 *See* HOUSTON OIL DIRECTORY. **4260**

0739-3563 *See* KENNETH COLEMAN'S REALITY THEORY NEWSLETTER. **4602**

0739-3601 *See* PARALEGAL, THE. **3025**

0739-361X *See* PROCEEDINGS, DIRECTORY AND HANDBOOK OF THE NATIONAL ASSOCIATION OF ACADEMIES OF SCIENCE, THE. **5140**

0739-3679 *See* ENERGY INFORMATION ABSTRACTS ANNUAL. **1962**

0739-3695 *See* COUNTERMAN. **5412**

0739-3709 *See* AMERICAN FIRE JOURNAL. **2287**

0739-3725 *See* MODERN SALES TECHNOLOGY. **933**

0739-3784 *See* ROAD RACE MANAGEMENT. **4915**

0739-3792 *See* ALASKA (EL CAJON, CALIF.). **5460**

0739-3806 *See* SPECULUM (COLUMBUS, OHIO), THE. **5522**

0739-3830 *See* NORTH CAROLINA PLUMBING-HEATING-COOLING FORUM. **2607**

0739-3849 *See* NEWTON GRAPHIC, THE. **5689**

0739-3857 *See* ARIZONA CONSUMER, THE. **1293**

0739-3865 *See* POINT OF BEGINNING- POB. **2028**

0739-3873 *See* BUSINESS MAILERS REVIEW. **650**

0739-3881 *See* AFFAIRE DE COEUR. **5073**

0739-389X *See* INTERNATIONAL RISK CONTROL REVIEW. **2872**

0739-3938 *See* SOUTHERN POLITICAL REPORT. **4496**

0739-3989 *See* REPORT TO CONGRESS, ADMINISTRATION OF THE WILD FREE-ROAMING HORSE AND BURRO ACT. **4682**

0739-4004 *See* UPDATE ON STATE LEGISLATION. **3070**

0739-4012 *See* BENCHMARK PAPERS IN TOXICOLOGY. **3979**

0739-4071 See REPORT TO CONGRESS, ADMINISTRATION OF THE WILD FREE-ROAMING HORSE AND BURRO ACT. **4682**

0739-408X *See* ROCK MAGAZINE (BEVERLY HILLS, CALIF.). **4150**

0739-4098 *See* MEDIATION QUARTERLY. **3121**

0739-4101 *See* PIONEER (LAWRENCE, KAN.), THE. **2467**

0739-4144 *See* TEXTILE PRICING OUTLOOK. **5358**

0739-4179 *See* WASHINGTON MEMO. **3122**

0739-4195 *See* EDUCATIONAL LEAFLET. **1374**

0739-4217 *See* HEALTH LETTER (SAN ANTONIO, TEX.), THE. **4780**

0739-4233 *See* E-LAB. **1936**

0739-4241 *See* PROVENANCE. **2483**

0739-425X *See* CHILDREN'S ADVOCATE, THE. **5279**

0739-4276 *See* HAMSTER INFORMATION SERVICE. **5510**

0739-4284 *See* POST HARVEST SCIENCE AND TECHNOLOGY RESEARCH. **120**

0739-4292 *See* NOAA TECHNICAL REPORT NWS. **1432**

0739-4306 *See* HEAVY METAL TIMES. **4121**

0739-4314 *See* DIGITAL REVIEW (NEW YORK, N.Y.). **1267**

0739-4330 *See* COUNTY AGENTS. **77**

0739-4349 *See* GEORGIA FIREFIGHTER. **2290**

0739-439X *See* MONOGRAPH AND RESEARCH SERIES (UNIVERSITY OF CALIFORNIA, LOS ANGELES. INSTITUTE OF INDUSTRIAL RELATIONS). **5209**

0739-4411 *See* WELLNESS JOURNAL, THE. **4807**

0739-442X *See* FAMILY (ROCHESTER, N.Y.), THE. **2280**

0739-4438 *See* CALIFORNIA INTERMOUNTAIN NEWS. **5633**

0739-4446 *See* PRIMARILY NURSING. **3867**

0739-4462 *See* ARCHIVES OF INSECT BIOCHEMISTRY AND PHYSIOLOGY. **5605**

0739-4489 *See* PRECIS (DENVILLE, N.J.). **2075**

0739-4519 *See* DATEK PRINTER DATABASE SERVICE. **1258**

0739-456X *See* JOURNAL OF PLANNING EDUCATION AND RESEARCH. **2826**

0739-4586 *See* VIRGINIA JOURNAL, THE. **1859**

0739-4616 *See* TITLE INDEX OF CURRENT REVIEWS. **426**

0739-4640 *See* GLOBAL RISK ASSESSMENTS: ISSUES, CONCEPTS, AND APPLICATIONS. **900**

0739-4667 *See* BOOK ON STARTING PITCHERS. **4887**

0739-4683 *See* D.I.N. NEWSERVICE. **1342**

0739-4691 *See* TEXAS BLUE BOOK OF LIFE INSURANCE STATISTICS (1982), THE. **2898**

0739-473X *See* COMMUNITY COLLEGE HUMANIST, THE. **2844**

0739-4748 *See* INFORME INTERCONTINENTAL SOBRE GERENCIA AVANZADA. **870**

0739-4772 *See* HERITAGE OF THE GREAT PLAINS. **2736**

0739-4780 *See* EASTERN TRAVEL SALES GUIDE. **5468**

0739-4799 *See* FIXED INCOME JOURNAL, THE. **899**

0739-4802 *See* FILIPINO DIRECTORY OF CALIFORNIA, THE. **2733**

0739-4810 *See* CURRENT HEMATOLOGY AND ONCOLOGY. **3771**

0739-4829 *See* PV NEWS. **1954**

0739-4845 *See* BIBLIOGRAPHY SERIES / CENTER FOR CREATIVE PHOTOGRAPHY, UNIVERSITY OF ARIZONA. **4367**

0739-4853 *See* AGAINST THE CURRENT. **4462**

0739-4918 *See* MUNICIPAL INSTRUCTORS' SECTION NEWS. **4667**

0739-4926 *See* NEWS-RECORD (GILLETTE, WYO.), THE. **5772**

0739-4934 *See* NEWSLETTER / HISTORY OF SCIENCE SOCIETY. **5133**

0739-4969 *See* OUTERBRIDGE. **3421**

0739-4977 *See* OFFICIAL PROCEEDINGS - INTERNATIONAL WATER CONFERENCE. **5536**

0739-5043 *See* CAREER OPPORTUNITIES NEWS. **4202**

0739-506X *See* LIBRARY AND INFORMATION SCIENCE EDUCATION STATISTICAL REPORT. **3258**

0739-5078 *See* DAILY ASTORIAN, THE. **5733**

0739-5086 *See* JUDAICA LIBRARIANSHIP. **3221**

0739-5124 *See* CHICAGO THEOLOGICAL SEMINARY REGISTER, THE. **4943**

0739-5132 *See* LAW OFFICE GUIDE IN COMPUTERS. **2996**

0739-5159 *See* ELECTRICAL OVERSTRESS/ELECTROSTATIC DISCHARGE SYMPOSIUM PROCEEDINGS. **2154**

0739-5175 *See* IEEE ENGINEERING IN MEDICINE AND BIOLOGY MAGAZINE. **3693**

0739-5183 *See* LEGAL NEWSLETTER (WASHINGTON, D.C.). **3000**

0739-5205 *See* STANGER'S DRILLING FUND YEARBOOK. **4279**

0739-523X *See* CULLMAN TRIBUNE, THE. **5626**

0739-5272 *See* MOTHEROOT JOURNAL. **4830**

0739-5302 *See* PIC (DOYLESTOWN, PA.). **1883**

0739-5329 *See* NEWSPAPER RESEARCH JOURNAL. **4817**

0739-5353 *See* ANNUAL REPORT - UNITED STATES. FOREIGN CLAIMS SETTLEMENT COMMISSION. **3123**

0739-5361 *See* CURRENT BUSINESS REPORTS. BR, MONTHLY RETAIL TRADE, SALES AND INVENTORIES. **953**

0739-537X *See* WORLD ART TRENDS. **369**

0739-5396 *See* INTERNATIONAL OLYMPIC LIFTER. **4901**

0739-540X *See* CURRENT REFERENCES IN FISH RESEARCH. **2317**

0739-5418 *See* FRIENDLY LETTER, A. **5060**

0739-5434 *See* HOME WINEMAKER, THE. **2367**

0739-5442 *See* ONE TO ONE. **1135**

0739-5450 *See* NEWSLETTER - LEARNING STYLES NETWORK (NATIONAL ASSOCIATION OF SECONDARY SCHOOL PRINCIPALS). **1901**

0739-5485 *See* ADDISON-WESLEY BOOK OF ATARI SOFTWARE, THE. **1283**

0739-5507 *See* STATESMAN JOURNAL. **5734**

0739-5523 *See* SELECTED READINGS IN PLASTIC SURGERY. **3974**

0739-554X *See* E-Z TELEPHONE DIRECTORY OF BROKERS AND BANKS, THE. **788**

0739-5558 *See* CHILDREN'S FOLKLORE REVIEW, THE. **2318**

0739-5566 *See* ECONOMIC NEWS FROM ITALY. **1557**

0739-5612 *See* BULLETIN OF THE ARCHAEOLOGICAL SOCIETY OF CONNECTICUT. **264**

0739-5620 *See* BULLETIN - CORPUS CHRISTI GEOLOGICAL SOCIETY. **1368**

0739-5639 *See* BULLETIN OF HISTORICAL RESEARCH IN MUSIC EDUCATION, THE. **4106**

0739-5647 *See* NATIONAL MONTHLY CONDOMINIUM EXECUTIVE REPORT. **4841**

0739-568X *See* SCUBA TIMES. **4917**

0739-5698 *See* TRAVEL WEEKLY'S WORLD TRAVEL DIRECTORY. **5497**

0739-5728 *See* HELICOPTER ANNUAL. **22**

0739-5779 *See* FINANCIAL DIRECTORY OF PENSION FUNDS. PENNSYLVANIA, EASTERN, PHILADELPHIA CITY PROPER. **1673**

0739-5787 *See* FINANCIAL DIRECTORY OF PENSION FUNDS. MINNESOTA, MINNEAPOLIS-ST. PAUL AREA. **1672**

0739-5795 *See* GOUCHER. **1091**

0739-5809 *See* THOROUGHBRED STALLION RECORDS OF **2803**

0739-5825 *See* PROCEEDINGS OF THE INTERNATIONAL TECHNICAL CONFERENCE ON SLURRY TRANSPORTATION. **2094**

0739-5868 *See* MEDICAL MICROBIOLOGY. **566**

0739-5876 *See* RADIOACTIVE WASTE MANAGEMENT AND THE NUCLEAR FUEL CYCLE. **2240**

0739-5892 *See* INDEX OF SOVIET AND CHINESE MILITARY AFFAIRS IN ANNUAL US DEFENSE DEPARTMENT REPORTS. **4045**

0739-5914 *See* MIND, THE MEETINGS INDEX. SERIES SEMT, SCIENCE, ENGINEERING, MEDICINE, TECHNOLOGY. **5175**

0739-5922 *See* UNIX/WORLD. **1265**

0739-5930 *See* YEAR BOOK OF DIGESTIVE DISEASES, THE. **3802**

0739-5949 *See* YEAR BOOK OF HAND SURGERY, THE. **3977**

0739-5957 *See* BULLETIN / WEST TEXAS GEOLOGICAL SOCIETY. **1371**

0739-6007 *See* NEWSLETTER - FLORIDA GENEALOGICAL SOCIETY. **2463**

0739-6023 *See* PROGRESS (SEATTLE, WASH.), THE. **5034**

0739-6031 *See* MALPRACTICE PREVENTION REPORTER. **3005**

0739-604X *See* GOSPEL MUSIC OFFICIAL DIRECTORY. **4119**

0739-6058 *See* ANNUAL REPORT - UNITED STATES. DEPT. OF THE TREASURY. OFFICE OF THE INSPECTOR GENERAL. **4711**

0739-6082 *See* HEIR-LINES (LAKE ORION, MICH.). **2452**

0739-6090 *See* GENIE BUG. **2451**

0739-6120 *See* NEW ENGLAND DIRECTORY FOR COMPUTER PROFESSIONALS. **1238**

0739-6147 *See* ALUMNI DIRECTORY / MICHIGAN STATE UNIVERSITY, COLLEGE OF AGRICULTURE AND NATURAL RESOURCES. **1098**

0739-6155 *See* PIONEER TIMES. **2467**

0739-618X *See* BUSINESS PUBLICATIONS INDEX AND ABSTRACTS. **727**

0739-6236 *See* SERVICE DEALER'S NEWSLETTER. SDN. **5739**

0739-6260 *See* MICRON AND MICROSCOPICA ACTA. **573**

0739-6279 *See* BASELINE DATA REPORT. **4632**

0739-6341 *See* HENCKEL GENEALOGICAL BULLETIN. **2453**

0739-635X *See* AIR FORCE OFFICER'S GUIDE, THE. **4034**

0739-6368 *See* DIGEST OF STATE LAND SALES REGULATIONS, THE. **4836**

0739-6376 See LAND TRENDS (NEW YORK, N.Y.). 4840

0739-6406 See AMERICAN UNIVERSITY STUDIES. SERIES VI, FOREIGN LANGUAGE INSTRUCTION. 3263

0739-6422 See CHRISTIAN LIFE COMMUNITIES HARVEST. 4945

0739-6457 See WARMAN'S AMERICANA & COLLECTIBLES. 2779

0739-6481 See MAGNETIC NORTH. 4444

0739-652X See BROKEN BENCH REVIEW. 3085

0739-6538 See WASHINGTON REMOTE SENSING LETTER. 1361

0739-6546 See AMERICAN CLAY EXCHANGE. 2586

0739-6562 See DRUG ABUSE UPDATE. 1343

0739-6570 See SHAKESPEARE ON FILM NEWSLETTER. 3435

0739-6619 See TAX FACTS ON INVESTMENTS. 917

0739-6627 See ANNUAL REPORTS - OREGON STATE BAR. 2935

0739-6643 See TRAIL SEEKERS. 2475

0739-6651 See SAVAGE FAMILY DEPOSITORY NEWSLETTER. 2471

0739-666X See WOMEN AND MINORITIES IN SCIENCE AND ENGINEERING. 5170

0739-6686 See ANNUAL REVIEW OF NURSING RESEARCH. 3851

0739-6694 See BEGINNING (IOWA CITY, IOWA). 4812

0739-6724 See NATIONAL DIRECTORY OF HOLISTIC HEALTH PROFESSIONALS, THE. 3618

0739-6732 See QUALITY CONTROL SCANNER, THE. 4569

0887-7521 See WEBSTER AGRICULTURAL LETTER, THE. 145

0739-6791 See FOOD & FIBER LETTER, THE. 2336

0712-3663 See NORTHERN BUSINESS INFORMATION'S TELECOM PERSPECTIVES. 1161

0739-6848 See OPEN ENTRIES. 1915

0739-6899 See ALUMNI DIRECTORY / UNIVERSITY OF MINNESOTA MEDICAL SCHOOL. 1100

0739-6961 See ALMANAC FOR FARMERS & CITY FOLK, THE. 2527

0739-697X See NEAS. NEWSLETTER OF ENGINEERING ANALYSIS SOFTWARE. 1988

0739-7003 See TINTA (SANTA BARBARA, CALIF.). 3446

0739-7046 See FAITH AND PHILOSOPHY : JOURNAL OF THE SOCIETY OF CHRISTIAN PHILOSOPHERS. 4346

0739-7062 See NEW YORK STATE PHARMACIST, CENTURY II. 4318

0739-7089 See MULTIMEDIA & VIDEODISC MONITOR. 1619

0739-7100 See UMTRI RESEARCH REVIEW, THE. 5398

0739-7119 See PROBLEMY VOSTOCHNOI EVROPY. 4492

0739-7127 See ANNUAL REPORT - TUSKEGEE INSTITUTE. HUMAN RESOURCES DEVELOPMENT CENTER. 5239

0739-7143 See FROMMER'S ... GUIDE TO PHILADELPHIA & ATLANTIC CITY. 5477

0739-7186 See JOHN HANCOCK COMPANIES ... ANNUAL REPORT. 2885

0739-7208 See TELE CONFERENCE. 715

0739-7240 See DOMESTIC ANIMAL ENDOCRINOLOGY. 3728

0739-7283 See SAGE ANNUAL REVIEWS OF COMMUNITY MENTAL HEALTH. 4801

0739-7313 See ADVANCES IN CHILD BEHAVIORAL ANALYSIS AND THERAPY. 4571

0739-7321 See SEXUAL BEHAVIOR (NEW YORK, N.Y. : 1982). 5188

0739-733X See EAR CLINICS INTERNATIONAL. 3887

0739-7348 See INFECTIOUS DISEASE ALERT. 3672

0739-7356 See REFLECTOR (UNIVERSITY PARK, MD.), THE. 3315

0739-7364 See FUNDAMENTALS OF CANCER MANAGEMENT. 3817

0739-7437 See COLLISION. 5411

0739-7453 See GLAD NEWS, THE. 4388

0739-747X See NOR'WESTING. 594

0739-7526 See LIBRARY OF CONGRESS ACQUISITIONS. RARE BOOK AND SPECIAL COLLECTIONS DIVISION. 3226

0739-7569 See AMERICAN JOURNAL OF TAX POLICY, THE. 4709

0739-7577 See PRISON LAW & ADVOCACY. 3173

0739-7690 See LEGISLATIVE STATUS REPORT (NATIONAL ASSOCIATION OF COMMUNITY HEALTH CENTERS). 3002

0739-7712 See SCHOOL LIBRARY MEDIA ANNUAL. 3248

0739-7720 See DALLASFED DISTRICT HIGHLIGHTS. 787

0739-7747 See AVISO (WASHINGTON, D.C.). 4084

0739-7771 See COMPUTER LAW REPORTER. 2954

0739-7798 See DARTNELL'S ... SALES FORCE COMPENSATION SURVEY. 1662

0739-7852 See JOHN WHITMER HISTORICAL ASSOCIATION JOURNAL, THE. 5061

0739-7860 See CALIFORNIA REGULATORY LAW REPORTER, THE. 2946

0739-7917 See CENTRAL ISSUES IN ANTHROPOLOGY. 233

0739-8018 See POWER PLAY. 1199

0739-8026 See INVESTOR, U.S.A. 903

0739-8034 See HEALTH CARE COSTS. 4778

0739-8042 See CALIFORNIA TODAY. 2162

0739-8050 See TEXAS ENERGY REPORTER. 1959

0739-8069 See JOURNAL - MIDDLE STATES COUNCIL FOR THE SOCIAL STUDIES (U.S.). 5205

0739-8093 See FAYETTE CONNECTION, THE. 2448

0739-8131 See FILIPINO PHYSICIANS IN AMERICA. 3576

0739-814X See ASFA AQUACULTURE ABSTRACTS. 2296

0739-8158 See FRAM (BANGOR, ME.). 5474

0739-8190 See FINDER BINDER, (NEW ORLEANS, LA.). 759

0739-8212 See MARKETING ORC INDEX. 931

0739-8239 See FRANCHISE LEGAL DIGEST. 3100

0739-8247 See ANNUAL REPORT ON THE WORK OF THE GEORGIA COURTS. 2935

0739-8271 See PENS, PENCILS, AND MARKING DEVICES. 1621

0739-828X See EMOTIONAL FIRST AID. 4586

0739-831X See HUAFU YOUBAO. 5686

0739-8328 See PROBLEMS IN GENERAL SURGERY. 3972

0739-8360 See PACIFIC REVIEW (SAN DIEGO, CALIF.). 3421

0739-8395 See BUSINESS WEEK (INDUSTRIAL ED.). 653

0739-8409 See INTERNATIONAL BUSINESS WEEK. 683

0739-8417 See KIBERNETIKA I VYCHISLITELNAIA TEKHNIKA. ENGLISH. 1251

0739-8425 See JOURNAL OF SUPERHARD MATERIALS. 4006

0739-8476 See MACRAE'S INDUSTRIAL DIRECTORY ARIZONA, NEW MEXICO. 1616

0739-8514 See INSTITUTE OF CRIMINOLOGY & FORENSIC SCIENCES BULLETIN. 3166

0739-8549 See OLD ENGLISH NEWSLETTER. SUBSIDIA. 3420

0739-8557 See REGISTER-GUARD, THE. 5734

0739-8565 See YEAR BOOK / DUTCHESS COUNTY HISTORICAL SOCIETY. 2766

0739-8573 See CURRENT EMERGENCY THERAPY. 3724

0739-8603 See MUNDO HISPANO (AUSTIN, TEX.), EL. 2268

0739-862X See NARF LEGAL REVIEW, THE. 3013

0739-8638 See LIFLINE. 3228

0739-8646 See ARTPAPER. 342

0739-8662 See ARTS JOURNAL (ASHEVILLE, N.C.), THE. 315

0739-8700 See MINNESOTA MONTHLY (COLLEGEVILLE, MINN.). 2539

0739-8719 See SINGLE DAD'S LIFESTYLE. 2286

0739-8727 See BRYAN-COLLEGE STATION EAGLE. 5747

0739-8743 See AUTOMATED OFFICE SYSTEMS. 4210

0739-8778 See THESAURUS, MANUFACTURING ENGINEERING TERMS. 3253

0739-8824 See DRUGS IN RESEARCH. 4302

0739-8840 See QUARTERLY REVIEW OF THE EASTERN NORTH CAROLINA GENEALOGICAL SOCIETY, THE. 2469

0739-8867 See MASSACHUSETTS AGRICULTURE. 107

0739-8891 See OUTLOOK FOR U.S. AGRICULTURAL EXPORTS (1982). 118

0739-8913 See CHRISTIAN EDUCATION JOURNAL. 4944

0739-8921 See CANDY INDUSTRY BUYING GUIDE. 2330

0739-893X See MISSOURI FOREST PEST REPORT. 2388

0739-9014 See INFORMATION SYSTEMS MANAGEMENT. 870

0739-9065 See EQUINE VETERINARY DATA. 2798

0739-909X See ACLD NEWSBRIEFS. 1874

0739-9103 See S.E.M. NEWSLETTER (1981). 4151

0739-9111 See NLADA CORNERSTONE. 3180

0739-9138 See INVESTMENT GUIDE (GREAT BARRINGTON, MASS.). 902

0739-9146 See STATUS NEWS. 2924

0739-9154 See CHFC REPORT. 3778

0739-9189 See CALC REPORT. 4942

0739-9200 See CHINOOK OBSERVER. 5760

0739-9219 See COMMUNITY PRESS (MILLBROOK, ALA.). 5626

0739-9227 See COMMUNITY SERVICES CATALYST. 1800

0739-9235 See FARMER STOCKMAN OF THE MIDWEST. 85

0739-9251 See GEORGIA VOTER. 4474

0739-9278 See NATIONAL TECHNICAL INSTITUTIE FOR THE DEAF FOCUS. 4391

0739-9308 See SOUTH CAROLINA STATISTICAL ABSTRACT. 5338

0739-9324 See VOICE OF THE TURTLE (SAN DIEGO, CALIF.). 5237

0739-9332 See HEALTH CARE FOR WOMEN INTERNATIONAL. 3762

0739-9340 See PRO-MOTION. 935

0739-9391 See INDIANA ALWAYS. 2738

0739-9413 See BUSINESS AND HEALTH. 645

0739-9448 See REFLECTIONS (CHAMPAIGN, ILL.). 307

0739-9480 See DETROIT LEGAL NEWS (DAILY ED.). 2960

0739-9499 See GEOGRAPHICAL INDEX SUPPLEMENT. 2563

0739-9502 See GALLUP MONTHLY REPORT ON EATING OUT, THE. 5071

0739-9529 See SEMINARS IN INTERVENTIONAL RADIOLOGY. 3946

0739-9561 See HOSPITAL PHARMACY SERVICE "INSTANT UP-DATE". 4307

0739-957X See HOSPITAL PHARMACY DIRECTOR'S MONTHLY MANAGEMENT SERIES. 4306

0739-9588 See VITAL SIGNS PHARMACY SERVICES NEWSLETTER. 4332

0739-9596 See PHARMACY HEALTH-LINE. 4323

0739-9618 See DURHAM RECORD, THE. 2731

0739-9677 See DADEVILLE RECORD, THE. 5626

0739-9693 See WHERE TO GO IN MINNEAPOLIS & ST. PAUL. 5499

0739-9723 See MERCHANT MAGAZINE, THE. 2402

0739-9731 See STETSON LAW REVIEW. 3059

0739-9758 See CHRONICLE (CRESWELL, OR.). 5733

0739-9766 See PAHA NEWSLETTER. 2270

0739-9774 See INSIDE MS. 3834

0739-9790 See RIVER CIRCULAR, THE. 2759

0739-9804 See HIGH SCHOOL GIRLS GYMNASTICS RULES AND MANUAL. 4898

0739-9839 See HANDBOOK - NATIONAL ASSOCIATION OF SCHOOLS OF THEATRE (U.S.). 5364

0739-9863 See HISPANIC JOURNAL OF BEHAVIORAL SCIENCES. 2262

0739-988X See LINK-UP (MINNEAPOLIS, MINN. 1983). 1242

0739-9898 See INTERNATIONAL NETWORKS. 1158

0739-991X See CURRENT (WASHINGTON, D.C. : 1980). 1153

0739-9936 See BANK ACQUISITION REPORT. 774

0739-9944 See SURVEY OF ARCHITECTURAL SALARIES. 309

0739-9987 See REPORT OF THE CHAIRMAN - UNITED STATES. PRESIDENT'S CANCER PANEL. 3823

0740-0020 See FOOD MICROBIOLOGY. 563

0740-0071 See INTERPRETE ALUMNOS, EL. 1102

0740-008X See JOURNAL OF EQUIPMENT LEASE FINANCING, THE. 873

0740-011X See VIRGINIA FORESTS (1974). 2398

0740-0152 See JOURNAL OF THE NORTH AMERICAN WOLF SOCIETY. 5589

0740-0195 See FOCUS - JOINT CENTER FOR POLITICAL STUDIES. 2261

0740-0225 See NASE ZITTJA. 5562

0740-0233 See YALE WEEKLY BULLETIN AND CALENDAR. 1096

0740-0241 See TAARS NEWS & NOTES. 284

0740-0276 See FRASER OPINION LETTER, THE. 1492

0740-0306 See CONTRARY INVESTOR FOLLOW-UP, THE. 895

0740-0330 See COMMENTS ON ETYMOLOGY. 3274

0740-0357 See EDCAL. 1737

0740-0403 See MUSEUM YEAR, THE. 4092

0740-0411 See SUPERVISOR'S NEWSLETTER, THE. 947

0740-0446 See AMERICAN UNIVERSITY STUDIES. SERIES VII, THEOLOGY AND RELIGION. 4934

0740-0497 See AMERICAN UNIVERSITY STUDIES. SERIES XII, SLAVIC LANGUAGES AND LITERATURE. 3360

0740-0500 See STARS (SEATTLE, WASH.). 1905

0740-0519 See LAWYERS LETTER / JUDICIAL ADMINISTRATION DIVISION, AMERICAN BAR ASSOCIATION, LAWYERS CONFERENCE. 3141

0740-0527 See CALIFORNIA CABLETTER. 1150

0740-0535 See WASHINGTON FEDERAL SCIENCE NEWSLETTER. 5169

0740-0586 See CANADIAN VETERINARY PHARMACEUTICALS & BIOLOGICALS. 5507

0740-0624 See PERSPECTIVES ON LOCAL PUBLIC FINANCE AND PUBLIC POLICY. 4741

0740-0632 See CUADERNOS DE ALDEEU. 3205

0740-0640 See RADIATION PROTECTION MANAGEMENT. 2868

0740-0659 See FAITH AND MISSION. 4958

0740-0667 See PREPRINT EXTENDED ABSTRACT - AMERICAN CHEMICAL SOCIETY. DIVISION OF ENVIRONMENTAL CHEMISTRY. 989

0740-0675 See HISTORY OF PHILOSOPHY QUARTERLY. 4348

0740-0683 See CA SELECTS: AUTOMATED CHEMICAL ANALYSIS. 998

0740-0691 See CA SELECTS: NATURAL PRODUCT SYNTHESIS. 1005

0740-0705 See CA SELECTS: POLYURETHANES. 1008

0740-0713 See CA SELECTS: FERMENTATION CHEMICALS. 1002

0740-0721 See CA SELECTS: CROSSLINKING REACTIONS. 1000

0740-073X See CA SELECTS: WATER TREATMENT. 1010

0740-0748 See CA SELECTS: CONTROLLED RELEASE TECHNOLOGY. 1000

0740-0756 See CA SELECTS: CARBOHYDRATES (CHEMICAL ASPECTS). 998

0740-0780 See CARROUSEL ART. 250

0740-0802 See SPOTLIGHT ON YOUTH SPORTS. 4923

0740-0837 See GARDNER NEWS (1983), THE. 5688

0740-0845 See MONOGRAPHS IN EPIDEMIOLOGY AND BIOSTATISTICS. 3736

0740-0853 See SAYBROOK REVIEW. 4617

0740-090X See LAW AND LEGAL INFORMATION DIRECTORY. 2994

0740-0926 See JOURNAL OF THE AMERICAN OSTEOPATHIC ACADEMY ORTHOPEDICS. 3883

0740-0942 See LAWYER'S PC, THE. 2998

0740-0985 See BELLEVILLE TELESCOPE (BELLEVILLE, KAN. : 1923). 5674

0740-1027 See TRENDS DATA. 4059

0740-1043 See CANADIAN LEGAL & LEGISLATIVE BENEFITS REPORTER. 3145

0740-1078 See POWELL TRIBUNE, THE. 5772

0740-1086 See HEALTHWISE. 2598

0740-1116 See HUNGER NOTES. 2910

0740-1159 See ON LOCATION, THE NATIONAL FILM & VIDEOTAPE PRODUCTION DIRECTORY. 4075

0740-1183 See COUNCIL SPOTLIGHT BOOKNOTES. 4502

0740-1191 See MINNESOTA VOTER, THE. 4482

0740-1205 See MR. COGITO. 3466

0740-1221 See BIOTECH MARKET NEWS & STRATEGIES. 448

0740-1248 See QUARTERLY REVIEW OF WINES. 2370

0740-1329 See SPENCER'S RETIREMENT PLAN SERVICE. 2894

0740-1361 See OHIO BEVERAGE JOURNAL. 2370

0740-137X See PROTECTION OF ASSETS BULLETIN. 804

0740-1388 See EXCESS EXPRESS. 2879

0740-1396 See RISK MANAGEMENT NEWSLETTER. 2892

0740-1418 See OSHANEWS. 2868

0740-1426 See SAFETY MANAGEMENT NEWSLETTER. 4801

0740-1434 See AG PILOT INTERNATIONAL. 6

0740-1469 See COMPUTER INDUSTRY LITIGATION REPORTER. 1303

0740-1477 See ELLIS COUSINS NEWSLETTER, THE. 2446

0740-1531 See M.C.G.S. REPORTER. 2459

0740-154X See SAGA OF SOUTHERN ILLINOIS. 2471

0740-1558 See YEARBOOK FOR TRADITIONAL MUSIC. 4159

0740-1566 See FILM (DENVER, COLO.). 4069

0740-1604 See PC WEEK (U.S. ED.). 1271

0740-1620 See ALUMNI DIRECTORY - ALBANY STATE COLLEGE. 1097

0740-1671 See ALUMNI DIRECTORY - TRINITY COLLEGE (HARTFORD, CONN.). 1099

0740-168X See SEMIANNUAL REPORT - UNITED STATES. DEPT. OF AGRICULTURE. OFFICE OF THE INSPECTOR GENERAL. 133

0740-1698 See ELECTRIC LIGHTING FIXTURES. 2043

0740-1701 See HEALTH MANPOWER STATISTICS. 4062

0740-1728 See POST CARD COLLECTORS' BULLETIN. 2776

0740-1736 See PRICES OF AMERICA, THE. 2468

0740-1744 See D.C. CODE UPDATER. 2958

0740-1752 See ALUMNI DIRECTORY / BELMONT ABBEY COLLEGE. 1097

0740-1760 See BUTADIENE ANNUAL. 1600

0740-1779 See ALUMNI DIRECTORY - CHRISTIAN BROTHERS COLLEGE (MEMPHIS, TENN.). 1098

0740-1787 See ALUMNI DIRECTORY / CREIGHTON PREPARATORY SCHOOL. 1098

0740-1795 See ALUMNI DIRECTORY - VIRGINIA UNION UNIVERSITY (RICHMOND, VA.). 1100

0740-1809 See WIRE ROPE NEWS & SLING TECHNOLOGY. 3489

0740-1817 See PETROLEUM FRONTIERS. 4272

0740-1833 See JOURNAL OF MULTI-CULTURAL AND CROSS-CULTURAL RESEARCH IN ART EDUCATION. 354

0740-185X See SCHOOLTECHNEWS. 1782

0740-1868 See KRAUS CURRICULUM DEVELOPMENT LIBRARY. 1899

0740-1876 See CHRISTIAN EDUCATION INFORMER, THE. 4944

0740-1892 See MEDIA PROFILES. THE HEALTH SCIENCES EDITION. 4790

0740-1906 See MEDIA PROFILES. THE CAREER DEVELOPMENT EDITION. 944

0740-1914 See ANESTHESIAFILE. 3681

0740-1922 See ELECTRON (WILLOUGHBY, OHIO), THE. 5728

0740-1930 See UNDERSEA JOURNAL, THE. 4855

0740-1949 See DAILY COURT REVIEW. 2958

0740-1965 See SCHATZKAMMER DER DEUTSCHEN SPRACHE, DICHTUNG UND GESCHICHTE. 3433

0740-1981 See BIG TIMBER PIONEER (1983), THE. 5705

0740-2007 See ANCIENT PHILOSOPHY (PITTSBURGH, PA.). 4340

0740-2015 See COMPUTER BOOKBASE. 1256

0740-2023 See DELAWARE COAST PRESS. 5647

0740-204X See EEO TRENDS AND ISSUES. 1664

0740-2082 See INTERNATIONAL JOURNAL OF SPORT BIOMECHANICS. 495

0740-2090 See GAZETTE (HAVERHILL, MASS.). 5688

0740-2104 See BAPTIST MESSAGE. 5056

0740-2112 See KODIAK DAILY MIRROR, THE. 5629

0740-2120 See ADVOCATE (NEWARK, OHIO), THE. 5726

0740-2163 See BLACK MALE/FEMALE RELATIONSHIPS. 5240

0740-2171 See COLUMBUS MAGAZINE. 2729

0740-218X See ON THE BEAM. 4392

0740-2198 See ART MARKETING LETTER, THE. 339

0740-2201 See EQUAL PLAY. 5555

0740-2252 See ACID PRECIPITATION DIGEST. 2223

0740-2260 See BROOKLYN GRAPHIC, THE. 5714

0740-2279 See JOURNAL OF LATIN COMMUNITY HEALTH, THE. 4787

0740-2325 See FLORIDA TIMES-UNION (JACKSONVILLE, FLA. : 1910). 5649

0740-2341 See RADIO IN THE UNITED STATES. 1137

0740-2384 See NEW YORK SPORTS. 4907

0740-2392 See AGADA. 5045

0740-2406 See HEALTH COST MANAGEMENT. 3581

0740-2546 See CORPORATE FINANCE BLUEBOOK, THE. 784

0740-2554 See LRB SUMMARIES (KEW GARDENS, QUEENS, NEW YORK, N.Y.). 3005

0740-2562 See PEANUT INDUSTRY GUIDE. 119

0740-2570 See SEMINARS IN DIAGNOSTIC PATHOLOGY. 3898

0740-2589 See INDIA-WEST GUIDE AND BUSINESS DIRECTORY. 1609

0740-2600 See BIG HORN COUNTY NEW. 5705

0740-2643 See BROOKLYN RECORD. 5714

0740-2651 See MOOREFIELD EXAMINER AND HARDY COUNTY NEWS, THE. 5764

0740-2708 See JOURNAL OF CORRECTIONAL EDUCATION (1974). 3167

0740-2716 See ADVERTISING SPECIALTY REGISTER (1983). 754
0740-2740 See SELLERS LETTERS. 2472
0740-2775 See WORLD POLICY JOURNAL. 4538
0740-2783 See AMERICAN MALACOLOGICAL BULLETIN. 5574
0740-2805 See PRICES OF AMERICA, THE. 2468
0740-2813 See NATIONAL DIRECTORY OF WOMEN ELECTED OFFICIALS. 4483
0740-283X See CREATIVE BLACK BOOK (PORTFOLIO ED.), THE. 758
0740-2848 See PUBLICATIONS AND PATENTS - UNITED STATES. AGRICULTURAL RESEARCH SERVICE. EASTERN REGIONAL RESEARCH CENTER (1981). 1308
0740-2856 See BOCA RATON. 2529
0740-2880 See LITERATURE CRITICISM FROM 1400 TO 1800. 3346
0740-2899 See BUSINESS JOURNAL (MILWAUKEE, WIS.), THE. 649
0740-2929 See MACRAE'S STATE INDUSTRIAL DIRECTORY. MARYLAND, DISTRICT OF COLUMBIA, DELAWARE. 3483
0740-2929 See MACRAE'S INDUSTRIAL DIRECTORY. MARYLAND, D.C., DELAWARE. 3483
0740-2961 See STANDARDS INFOBRIEFS. 2108
0740-2996 See SEED REPORT. 133
0740-3003 See FREEWAY/L.A. 5440
0740-3038 See ANNUAL REPORT - FEDERAL ENFORCEMENT TRAINING CENTER. 3157
0740-3046 See COUSINS ET COUSINES. 2444
0740-3119 See CATALOG AGE. 757
0740-3127 See SOCIAL ISSUES RESOURCES SERIES. 5308
0740-3135 See DAILY WORLD (ABERDEEN, WASH.). 5760
0740-3178 See FERTILITY ASSISTANCE. 3576
0740-3186 See HOT COCO. 1267
0740-3194 See MAGNETIC RESONANCE IN MEDICINE. 3943
0740-3208 See MIDWEST REVIEW (WAYNE, NEB. : 1975). 2746
0740-3216 See BUMPER STICKERS FOR SALE. 922
0740-3224 See JOURNAL OF THE OPTICAL SOCIETY OF AMERICA. B, OPTICAL PHYSICS. 4437
0740-3232 See JOURNAL OF THE OPTICAL SOCIETY OF AMERICA. A, OPTICS AND IMAGE SCIENCE. 4437
0740-3283 See NEW ORDER (LINCOLN, NEB.), THE. 4544
0740-3291 See CULTURAL SURVIVAL QUARTERLY. 4507
0740-3321 See BIG CROSSWORDS. 4857
0740-3348 See PRIEST RIVER TIMES. 5657
0740-3399 See CREATION SOCIAL SCIENCE AND HUMANITIES QUARTERLY. 5196
0740-3410 See CITY PAPER (BALTIMORE, MD.). 5686
0740-3437 See L.A. PARENT. 1066
0740-3445 See IMPACT (GREAT FALLS, MONT.). 4045
0740-3453 See PROCEEDINGS OF THE ... ANNUAL FINANCIAL MANAGEMENT CONFERENCE, THE. 4675
0740-3461 See CONSENSUS (CHICAGO, ILL.). 4040
0740-347X See FAXON INTERNATIONAL NEWSLETTER. 675
0740-3488 See OPERATION AND EFFECT OF THE DOMESTIC INTERNATIONAL SALES CORPORATION LEGISLATION ... ANNUAL REPORT, THE. 848
0740-3496 See ENERGY-RELATED MANPOWER. 1941
0740-3526 See MICROPRO USERS' MONTHLY. 1269
0740-3569 See NEW FROM EUROPE. 5132
0740-3577 See NEW FROM U.S. 2540
0740-3593 See SEX OVER FORTY. 5188

0740-3607 See AMERICAN BUILDING CONTRACTOR, THE. 598
0740-3615 See INFECTION CONTROL & UROLOGICAL CARE. 3990
0740-3666 See INVESTING IN CRISIS. 902
0740-3674 See HOSPITAL/COMMUNITY RELATIONS PROFESSIONAL. 3783
0740-3690 See FEDERAL PARKS & RECREATION. 4850
0740-3704 See CAPITAL PRESS. 5733
0740-3712 See LOCATOR OF USED MACHINERY & EQUIPMENT. 2120
0740-3755 See MUSIC INDUSTRY PRODUCTS. 4134
0740-3771 See BULLETIN / PACIFIC SEABIRD GROUP. 5616
0740-3801 See PRODUCT ALERT. 2354
0740-3852 See LOOKOUT. NON-FOODS. 2348
0740-3860 See LOOKOUT. FOODS. 2348
0740-3909 See ANNUAL ENERGY REVIEW (WASHINGTON, D.C.). 1932
0740-3925 See CHECKBOOK'S GUIDE TO HEALTH INSURANCE PLANS FOR FEDERAL EMPLOYEES. 2878
0740-3992 See NURSING AND HEALTH CARE (SHERMAN OAKS, CALIF.). 3863
0740-4018 See AMERICA'S CORPORATE FAMILIES AND INTERNATIONAL AFFILIATES. 638
0740-4034 See LOUDOUN TIMES-MIRROR. 5759
0740-4050 See ABA/BNA LAWYERS' MANUAL ON PROFESSIONAL CONDUCT. CURRENT REPORTS. 2926
0740-4069 See PRECIOUS METALS DIGEST. 911
0740-4077 See WORKAMERICA. 1718
0740-4085 See COMPUTER PUBLISHERS & PUBLICATIONS. 1236
0740-4093 See QUILT DIGEST, THE. 5185
0740-4107 See BRIGHAM YOUNG UNIVERSITY ... FIRESIDE AND DEVOTIONAL SPEECHES. 4940
0740-4131 See CAMPING MAGAZINE, THE. 4870
0740-4158 See PHOTOGRAPHS (NEW YORK, N.Y. : 1982). 4374
0740-4166 See REPORTER. ROCKLEDGE EDITION, THE. 5651
0740-4174 See USP DI. DRUG INFORMATION FOR THE HEALTH CARE PROVIDER. 4332
0740-4190 See ANNUAL ENERGY OUTLOOK. 1931
0740-4204 See LEGISLATIVE BULLETIN - ASSOCIATION OF WASHINGTON CITIES. 3001
0740-4212 See SPRINGER SERIES ON PSYCHIATRY. 3937
0740-4247 See VIDEO MARKETING SURVEYS AND FORECASTS. 2085
0740-4271 See SECONDARY MORTGAGE MARKETS. 810
0740-428X See MACRAE'S INDUSTRIAL DIRECTORY. IOWA, NEBRASKA. 1616
0740-4298 See MACRAE'S STATE INDUSTRIAL DIRECTORY. PENNSYLVANIA. 1617
0740-4379 See PERSONALITY ASSESSMENT SYSTEM FOUNDATION JOURNAL. 4607
0740-4387 See FISHERIES MANAGEMENT ANNUAL PROGRESS REPORT ON PROJECTS IN THE ... WORK SCHEDULE. 2302
0740-4395 See NEWSLETTER / ROSS COUNTY GENEALOGICAL SOCIETY. 2464
0740-4409 See UNDER CONSTRUCTION. 2476
0740-4417 See SAN DIEGO LEAVES & SAPLINGS. 2471
0740-445X See COMPUTERS IN HUMAN SERVICES. 1179
0740-4492 See BIOLOGICAL EXTINCTION. 445
0740-4549 See SOURCE BOOK (NEW YORK, N.Y. 1983), THE. 5310
0740-4557 See AMERICAN UNIVERSITY STUDIES. SERIES XIII, LINGUISTICS. 3263
0740-4565 See AMERICAN UNIVERSITY STUDIES. SERIES XIV, EDUCATION. 1808
0740-4573 See SCOTT COUNTY JOURNAL (SCOTTSBURG, IND.), THE. 5667

0740-4581 See AUSTIN CHRONICLE (SCOTTSBURG, IND.), THE. 5746
0740-4603 See UNITY IN A MULTICULTURAL U.S.A. 4513
0740-4611 See REGIONAL DIRECTORY - CAPITAL AREA PLANNING COUNCIL. 4679
0740-462X See COLLEGE OF SCIENCE ALUMNI DIRECTORY, THE PENNSYLVANIA STATE UNIVERSITY. 1101
0740-4689 See MACRAE'S STATE INDUSTRIAL DIRECTORY. MASSACHUSETTS, RHODE ISLAND. 1616
0740-4700 See WISCONSIN WATER QUALITY ... REPORT TO CONGRESS. 5549
0740-4727 See VALLEY JOURNAL, THE. 2764
0740-4735 See FRESH FRUIT AND VEGETABLE PRICES. 89
0740-4743 See SPARTANBURG HERALD-JOURNAL. 5743
0740-4794 See CLASSIC CAR BIMONTHLY. 5411
0740-4824 See BROOKLYN JOURNAL OF INTERNATIONAL LAW. 3125
0740-4832 See GRASSROOTS FUNDRAISING JOURNAL. 4337
0740-4921 See DETAILS (NEW YORK, N.Y.). 3995
0740-4948 See SARATOGA SUN (SARATOGA, WYO.), THE. 5772
0740-4956 See FOCUS, LIBRARY SERVICE TO OLDER ADULTS, PEOPLE WITH DISABILITIES. 3211
0740-4964 See CONSUMER ALERT COMMENTS. 1294
0740-4980 See FT SYSTEMS. 1254
0740-4999 See NORTHWEST TRAIL TRACER. 2464
0740-5006 See GENEALOGICAL SOCIETY OF IREDELL COUNTY, N.C, THE. 2450
0740-5030 See SELECTED MFRS. INDEX SURVEY. 1710
0740-5065 See MILITARY LIVING. 4051
0740-5073 See MILITARY LIVING'S R & R REPORT. 4051
0740-5111 See AMERICAN UNIVERSITY STUDIES. SERIES XV, COMMUNICATIONS. 1104
0740-5154 See KEEPSAKE MAGAZINE FOR BRIDES. 2282
0740-5162 See PROCEEDINGS OF THE ... CONFERENCE / INTERNATIONAL COAL TESTING CONFERENCE. 1028
0740-5170 See FREE CASH FLOW. 1492
0740-5197 See BASH MAGAZINE, THE. 3979
0740-5200 See DATA BASED ADVISOR. 1253
0740-5227 See LAREDO MORNING TIMES. 5751
0740-5235 See LOUISIANA EDUCATION RESEARCH JOURNAL. 1762
0740-526X See NEIGHBORHOOD IDEAS. 2829
0740-5278 See GAS PROCESSORS REPORT. 4258
0740-5286 See CHASE'S ANNUAL EVENTS. 5268
0740-5367 See TIMBERTOWN LOG. 2475
0740-5375 See INTERNATIONAL JOURNAL OF ISLAMIC AND ARABIC STUDIES. 2768
0740-5383 See GRANT ADVISOR, THE. 1826
0740-5405 See CYRANO'S JOURNAL. 1109
0740-5413 See STUDENT GUIDE (NEW YORK, N.Y.), THE. 1848
0740-5464 See BOTTOMLINE (WASHINGTON, D.C. : 1983). 779
0740-5472 See JOURNAL OF SUBSTANCE ABUSE TREATMENT. 1346
0740-5502 See INFORMATION AND BEHAVIOR. 1113
0740-5510 See NEWSLETTER / SOCIETY FOR ARMENIAN STUDIES. 2660
0740-5529 See PELICAN GUIDE TO THE BAHAMAS. 5488
0740-5537 See JOURNAL OF CIVIL DEFENSE. 1073
0740-557X See UNITED MUTUAL FUND SELECTOR. 918

0740-5596 See INSIGHTS INTO OPEN EDUCATION/ UNIVERSITY OF NORTH DAKOTA. 1896

0740-5618 See FRIENDLY WOMAN, THE. 5557

0740-5650 See NATIONAL CLIMATE PROGRAM : ANNUAL REPORT. 1432

0740-5715 See JOURNAL OF LEARNING SKILLS, THE. 1757

0740-5790 See STATISTICAL YEARBOOK OF MUNICIPAL FINANCE. 4700

0740-5804 See AMPERSAND (SAN FRANCISCO, CALIF.), THE. 4563

0740-5812 See MADAMINA. 4129

0740-5820 See LATHAM LETTER, THE. 2177

0740-5847 See ENVIRONMENTAL NOTICE BULLETIN. 2229

0740-5936 See FREEDOM IN EDUCATION. 1747

0740-5944 See GWIAZDA POLARNA. 5767

0740-5960 See ACADEMIC JOURNAL (NEWTOWN, CONN.), THE. 1721

0740-5979 See HERBARIST, THE. 2418

0740-5987 See CLEBURNE COUNTY HISTORICAL SOCIETY JOURNAL. 2728

0740-5995 See NAIA NEWS. 4905

0740-6002 See PLANT VARIETY PROTECTION OFFICE OFFICIAL JOURNAL. 2428

0740-6029 See COMMAND HISTORY - UNITED STATES. NAVAL FACILITIES ENGINEERING COMMAND. 4175

0740-6053 See MACRAE'S INDUSTRIAL DIRECTORY. WISCONSIN. 1616

0740-607X See MACRAE'S INDUSTRIAL DIRECTORY. MISSOURI. 1616

0740-6096 See MACRAE'S INDUSTRIAL DIRECTORY. MICHIGAN. 1616

0740-610X See MACRAE'S INDUSTRIAL DIRECTORY. OREGON. 1616

0740-6126 See MACRAE'S INDUSTRIAL DIRECTORY. COLORADO, UTAH, NEVADA. 1616

0740-6134 See MACRAE'S INDUSTRIAL DIRECTORY. WASHINGTON STATE. 1616

0740-6150 See MIDLIFE WELLNESS. 3765

0740-6169 See NEWSLETTER - SOCIETY FOR HISTORIANS OF AMERICAN FOREIGN RELATIONS. 4530

0740-6185 See KENTUCKY CLUBWOMAN, THE. 5232

0740-6231 See COMPUTER PUBLISHING & ADVERTISING REPORT. 1177

0740-624X See GOVERNMENT INFORMATION QUARTERLY. 3212

0740-6258 See BUSINESS OF FUR, THE. 3183

0740-6266 See ISLANDWIDE RUNNER. 4901

0740-6401 See ANNUAL REPORT OF THE AMERICAN BIBLE SOCIETY. 5014

0740-6428 See DIRECTORY : NORTH DAKOTA CITY OFFICIALS. 4643

0740-6460 See NEWSLETTER - MISSIONS ADVANCED RESEARCH AND COMMUNICATIONS CENTER. 4982

0740-6673 See CARPENTER AND RELATED FAMILY HISTORICAL JOURNAL, THE. 2442

0740-669X See INTERNATIONAL REPORT (IRVINE, CALIF.). 4477

0740-672X See MUTUAL MAGAZINE (PHILADELPHIA, PA. : 1980), THE. 5433

0740-6738 See ASTRO-TALK. 1284

0740-6746 See INTERNATIONAL OLD LACERS INC., BULLETIN. 5352

0740-6762 See EXHIBIT BUILDER QUARTERLY. 867

0740-6789 See WILLAMETTE JOURNAL OF THE LIBERAL ARTS, THE. 333

0740-6797 See TRANSACTIONS OF THE SOCIETY FOR COMPUTER SIMULATION. 1283

0740-6800 See DATA BASE PRODUCT REPORTS / MIC. 1253

0740-6819 See AUTOMATED LAW OFFICE CONSULTANT, THE. 2939

0740-6835 See CONSCIENCE (WASHINGTON, D.C.). 588

0740-6851 See LONG-DISTANCE LETTER, THE. 1159

0740-6886 See EDUCATIONAL AND BUSINESS SOFTWARE, RELATED PRODUCTS, HOME, SCHOOL, AND OFFICE FOR ATARI. 1285

0740-6894 See EDUCATIONAL AND BUSINESS SOFTWARE, RELATED PRODUCTS-HOME, SCHOOL, AND OFFICE FOR, TRS-80. 1285

0740-6916 See USP DI. ADVICE FOR THE PATIENT. 4331

0740-6924 See DUN'S PROSPECT FINDER. ARKANSAS, LOUISIANA, OKLAHOMA, TEXAS. 1556

0740-6940 See PACIFIC FLYWAY WATERFOWL REPORT. 5593

0740-6959 See PROFESSION. 3312

0740-6967 See CATARACT (NEW YORK, N.Y.). 3873

0740-6991 See MESSENGER (FORT DODGE, IOWA), THE. 5671

0740-7025 See GAP CONFERENCE REPORT / RESEARCH PROGRAM, CYSTIC FIBROSIS FOUNDATION. 3578

0740-7122 See SENIOR ADVOCATE (SACRAMENTO, CALIF.), THE. 5181

0740-7181 See DIRECTORY OF MEMBERS - AMERICAN STATISTICAL ASSOCIATION; BIOMETRIC SOCIETY. EASTERN NORTH AMERICAN REGION. BIOMETRIC SOCIETY. WESTERN NORTH AMERICAN REGION. 5326

0740-719X See CONTEMPORARY GERMAN PHILOSOPHY. 4344

0740-7203 See NATIONAL DIRECTORY OF ADDRESSES AND TELEPHONE NUMBERS (NEW YORK, N.Y.), THE. 697

0740-7211 See HOMES INTERNATIONAL. 2824

0740-722X See AEROSPACE AMERICA. 5

0740-7238 See CLINICAL UPDATE. SPORTS MEDICINE. 3953

0740-7262 See HEALTH LITERATURE REVIEW. 4780

0740-7297 See RULES FOR CERTIFICATION OF CARGO CONTAINERS. 4221

0740-7335 See SOUTHWEST VIRGINIAN, THE. 2473

0740-7343 See OKLAHOMA TRIENNIAL STATE HEALTH PLAN. 4794

0740-736X See LIBRARY HOTLINE. 3225

0740-7386 See AUA UPDATE SERIES. 3988

0740-7394 See LINSCOTT'S DIRECTORY OF IMMUNOLOGICAL AND BIOLOGICAL REAGENTS. 3674

0740-7459 See IEEE SOFTWARE. 1286

0740-7467 See IEEE SIGNAL PROCESSING MAGAZINE. 2060

0740-7475 See IEEE DESIGN & TEST OF COMPUTERS. 1229

0740-7483 See YACHTING'S BOAT BUYERS GUIDE. 597

0740-7548 See SELF-HELP GROUP DIRECTORY. 5307

0740-7564 See TOTH-MAATIAN REVIEW, THE. 2494

0740-7602 See CRYPTOLOG. 4176

0740-7610 See ZOOLOGICAL PARKS AND AQUARIUMS IN THE AMERICAS. 5601

0740-7653 See FLASHMAPS INSTANT GUIDE TO BOSTON. 5470

0740-7688 See CALIFORNIA LIBRARY DIRECTORY. 3199

0740-770X See WOMEN & PERFORMANCE. 5372

0740-7750 See SOMATIC CELL AND MOLECULAR GENETICS. 551

0740-7769 See JOURNAL OF ASSISTED REPRODUCTION AND GENETICS. 3763

0740-7823 See EXQUISITE CORPSE. 3463

0740-784X See CELL MEMBRANES, METHODS AND REVIEWS. 533

0740-7858 See CIRCUS ROCK IMMORTALS. 4110

0740-7866 See RESOURCE DIRECTORY FOR THE APPLE COMPUTER, THE. 1239

0740-7890 See PERMAFROST. 3350

0740-7939 See FINANCIAL PREDICTIONS. 675

0740-7947 See CPI NATIONAL REPORT. 4583

0740-7955 See BROADSIDE (NEW YORK, N.Y. 1962). 4105

0740-7971 See NUTSHELL (SNOWMASS VILLAGE, COLO.). 944

0740-798X See FLORIDA STAR (JACKSONVILLE, FLA. : 1951), THE. 2616

0740-7998 See BIBLICAL EVANGELIST, THE. 4938

0740-8013 See OAK LEAVES (BAY CITY, TEX.). 2465

0740-8021 See TENNESSEE LINGUISTICS. 3328

0740-803X See AIR DEFENSE ARTILLERY. 4033

0740-8048 See YALE LAW & POLICY REVIEW. 3077

0740-8102 See GUIDE TO GRADUATE DEGREE PROGRAMS IN ARCHITECTURAL HISTORY. 299

0740-8161 See MUSHROOM (MOSCOW, IDAHO). 575

0740-817X See IIE TRANSACTIONS. 2098

0740-8188 See LIBRARY & INFORMATION SCIENCE RESEARCH. 3224

0740-8226 See MEDICAL AND PEDIATRIC ONCOLOGY. SUPPLEMENT. 3906

0740-8242 See ISSUES AND REVIEWS IN TERATOLOGY. 581

0740-8250 See DIRECTORY OF PSYCHIATRY RESIDENCY TRAINING PROGRAMS. 3924

0740-8277 See STATISTICAL REPORT - EXECUTIVE OFFICE FOR U.S. ATTORNEYS. 3083

0740-8285 See CASUAL LIVING. 2904

0740-8331 See SOUTH CAROLINA JOURNAL OF HEALTH, PHYSICAL EDUCATION, RECREATION AND DANCE. 1784

0740-8358 See AMERICAN ARCHEOLOGY. 254

0740-8366 See MINNESOTA INSURANCE. 2888

0740-8374 See GUIDE TO SOFTWARE PRODUCTIVITY AIDS. 1238

0740-8404 See AMATYC REVIEW, THE. 3492

0740-8439 See BOOK - AMERICAN ANTIQUARIAN SOCIETY, THE. 4824

0740-848X See 4-H SOUNDER. 1059

0740-8498 See WELLNESS NEWSLETTER, THE. 2602

0740-8501 See WASHINGTON COUNSELETTER. 1790

0740-851X See UCLA BUSINESS FORECAST FOR CALIFORNIA, THE. 1525

0740-8528 See SPECIAL INTEREST REPORT / THE AMERICAN COUNCIL FOR JUDAISM. 5053

0740-8536 See ANNALS OF THE CHINESE HISTORICAL SOCIETY OF THE PACIFIC NORTHWEST / MEI-KUO HSI PEI HUA JEN LI SHIH HSUEH HUI, THE. 2255

0740-8609 See MEAT AND POULTRY INSPECTION DIRECTORY. 215

0740-8625 See STUDIES IN CONTEMPORARY JEWRY. 5053

0740-865X See GOSHEN COLLEGE RECORD, THE. 1825

0740-8676 See AFTERMARKET STATISTICAL YEARBOOK. 5400

0740-8684 See NUTRITION REPORT, THE. 4196

0740-8722 See MLA INTERNATIONAL BIBLIOGRAPHY OF BOOKS AND ARTICLES ON THE MODERN LANGUAGES AND LITERATURES (OPTION C). 3303

0740-8730 See MLA INTERNATIONAL BIBLIOGRAPHY OF BOOKS AND ARTICLES ON THE MODERN LANGUAGES AND LITERATURES (OPTION B). 3412

0740-8781 See NEWSLETTER / MONMOUTH COUNTY HISTORICAL ASSOCIATION. 2750

0740-8803 See WATER RESOURCES DATA. WISCONSIN. 5546

0740-882X See DENUNCIA (WASHINGTON, D.C.). 4471

0740-8889 See GLASS ART SOCIETY PHOTOGRAPHIC DIRECTORY. 2589

0740-8897 See PROCEEDINGS OF THE SPI ANNUAL TECHNICAL/MARKETING CONFERENCE. 989

0740-8900 See MECHANISMS OF INORGANIC AND ORGANOMETALLIC REACTIONS. 1037

0740-8919 See WALL STREET MICRO INVESTOR. 919

0740-8943 See COMMUNICATIONS FROM THE INTERNATIONAL BRECHT SOCIETY. 3377

0740-896X See TRI-STATE PACKET OF THE TRI-STATE GENEALOGICAL SOCIETY, THE. 2476

0740-8978 See AMERICAN PUBLIC OPINION INDEX. 5238

0740-8986 See TOUCHSTONE (MARSHALL, TEX.). 2763

0740-8994 See NEW ENGLAND JOURNAL ON CRIMINAL AND CIVIL CONFINEMENT. 3170

0740-9001 See HARRISON HERITAGE. 2452

0740-901X See VANDERBILT MEDICAL ALUMNI DIRECTORY. 1103

0740-9028 See ADVANCES IN CLADISTICS : PROCEEDINGS OF THE ... MEETING OF THE WILLI HENNIG SOCIETY. 440

0740-9079 See DIGGER'S DIGEST (YUBA CITY, CALIF. : 1980), THE. 2445

0740-9087 See EMPLOYERS' HEALTH COSTS SAVINGS LETTER. 3574

0740-9095 See WORKING PAPER - FLORIDA STATE UNIVERSITY. CENTER FOR THE STUDY OF POPULATION. 4561

0740-9109 See COLORADO FEVER. 5466

0740-9117 See NORTH AMERICAN RETAIL FURRIERS DIRECTORY. 3185

0740-9125 See PLOUGH, THE. 4986

0740-9133 See NORTHEAST AFRICAN STUDIES. 2500

0740-9141 See TAR RIVER POETRY. 3472

0740-9214 See ARTS QUARTERLY (NEW ORLEANS, LA. 1978). 342

0740-9222 See MILK FACTS. 196

0740-9230 See HIGHER EDUCATION DIRECTORY. 1828

0740-9257 See AMERICAN UNIVERSITY STUDIES. SERIES II, ROMANCE LANGUAGES AND LITERATURE. 3263

0740-9281 See RAND RESEARCH REVIEW. 1515

0740-929X See BLACK NATION, THE. 2256

0740-9303 See OPHTHALMIC PLASTIC AND RECONSTRUCTIVE SURGERY. 3877

0740-9311 See CLOCKWATCH REVIEW. 317

0740-9354 See TELECONNECT. 1166

0740-9362 See ALUMNI DIRECTORY / SHAW UNIVERSITY. 1099

0740-9370 See LOYOLA ENTERTAINMENT LAW JOURNAL. 3004

0740-9389 See LOTT FAMILY NEWSLETTER, THE. 2458

0740-9427 See SUMMARY OF LEGISLATIVE ACTIVITIES - UNITED STATES. CONGRESS. HOUSE. COMMITTEE ON PUBLIC WORKS AND TRANSPORTATION. 3061

0740-9443 See RESEARCH AND TECHNOLOGY PROGRAM. 2833

0740-9451 See MICROCIRCULATION, ENDOTHELIUM, AND LYMPHATICS. 3616

0740-946X See SIGLO XX (LINCOLN, NEB.). 3436

0740-9508 See NATIONAL SOCIALIST (ARLINGTON, VA.), THE. 4543

0740-9516 See WORDENS PAST. 2478

0740-9532 See OFFICIAL HIGH SCHOOL BOYS GYMNASTICS RULES. 4909

0740-9540 See UNITED STATES COURT OF INTERNATIONAL TRADE REPORTS. 3137

0740-9583 See GENETIC EPISTEMOLOGIST, THE. 546

0740-9613 See LET'S PRAY TOGETHER. 5031

0740-963X See COPPER VALLEY VIEWS. 5629

0740-9648 See ESCAPE TO THE MINNESOTA GOOD TIMES. 2533

0740-9664 See INDIANA DAILY STUDENT, THE. 1092

0740-9699 See MOHAWK, THE. 2461

0740-9702 See SARATOGA (RHINEBECK, N.Y.), THE. 2471

0740-9710 See FOOD & FOODWAYS. 5245

0740-9729 See MONOGRAPHS IN PRIMATOLOGY. 5591

0740-9737 See GENEWATCH. 3692

0740-9753 See BULLETIN (SPECIAL LIBRARIES ASSOCIATION. FLORIDA CHAPTER). 3198

0740-9788 See DRIVER LICENSING LAWS ANNOTATED. SUPPLEMENT. 2964

0740-9834 See SENATE ELECTION LAW GUIDEBOOK. 3047

0740-9877 See TIMBER UPDATE, TIMBER MARKETS THROUGH 1990. 2405

0740-9893 See EXCELLENCE IN TEACHING. 1894

0740-9915 See DIRECTORY OF SOUTHERN BAPTIST CHURCHES. 5059

0740-9923 See 305(B) TECHNICAL REPORT FOR OKLAHOMA. 2222

0740-9931 See CONSUMER PROTECTION REPORT. 1295

0740-9966 See U.S. CRUDE OIL DISTILLATION REFINING CAPACITY SURVEY FOR 4281

0741-000X See WEYER'S FLOTTENBUCH (NORTH AMERICAN ED.). 4185

0741-0034 See TECOLOTE, EL. 2493

0741-0042 See CAD/CAM MANAGEMENT STRATEGIES. 1218

0741-0050 See EXECUTIVE COMPUTING. 1237

0741-0069 See COMMUNICATIONS CONCEPTS. 1108

0741-0077 See ONLINE DATABASE SEARCH SERVICES DIRECTORY. 3239

0741-0107 See LICENSING BOOK, THE. 4830

0741-0115 See NATIONAL BAR ASSOCIATION MAGAZINE. 3013

0741-0123 See REVIEWS IN ECONOMIC GEOLOGY. 1395

0741-0158 See IMPORTED CARS & TRUCKS, TRANSMISSION SERVICE & REPAIR. 5416

0741-0166 See DIRECTORY OF HELICOPTER OPERATORS IN THE UNITED STATES, CANADA, MEXICO, AND PUERTO RICO. 17

0741-0212 See YEAR'S BEST MYSTERY & SUSPENSE STORIES, THE. 3455

0741-0239 See INSTITUTIONAL EQUITY SERVICES. 901

0741-0263 See DYNAMIC (NEW YORK, N.Y.). 4472

0741-0271 See WESTMINSTER REVIEW (NEW WILMINGTON, PA.), THE. 3453

0741-028X See TAE KWON DO TIMES. 4925

0741-0298 See BRASILIANS, THE. 2724

0741-031X See CALIFORNIA LIBRARY STATISTICS. 3257

0741-0336 See ASIAN AMERICAN JOURNEY, THE. 4936

0741-0379 See M.A.C. 2482

0741-0387 See WITHIN ASAE. 2001

0741-0395 See GENETIC EPIDEMIOLOGY. 3735

0741-0492 See FILM NEWS INTERNATIONAL. 4070

0741-0506 See NEW BREWER, THE. 2369

0741-0565 See MEMBERS' COMPUTERIZED DATA EXCHANGE. 2460

0741-0573 See STATE MEDICAL FACILITIES PLAN (RALEIGH, N.C.). 4804

0741-0581 See MICROSCOPY RESEARCH AND TECHNIQUE. 573

0741-0603 See APPLICATION OF COMPUTERS AND OPERATIONS RESEARCH IN THE MINERAL INDUSTRY / SPONSORED BY COLORADO SCHOOL OF MINES. 1171

0741-0611 See GEOGRAPHIC DISTRIBUTION OF VA EXPENDITURES. 4044

0741-0689 See WATER RESOURCES DATA. ALASKA. 5544

0741-0697 See WATER RESOURCES DATA. COLORADO. 5544

0741-0700 See AMERICAN UNIVERSITY STUDIES. SERIES IV, ENGLISH LANGUAGE AND LITERATURE. 3263

0741-0727 See NAIC NEWS, THE. 2888

0741-0735 See WOMEN'S & CHILDREN'S WEAR AND FASHION ACCESSORIES BUYERS. 1088

0741-076X See ALA ... WORLDWIDE DIRECTORY & FACT BOOK. 4034

0741-0808 See HIGH-TECH MATERIALS ALERT. 1977

0741-0832 See REPORT OF INVESTIGATIONS - ALASKA. DIVISION OF GEOLOGICAL AND GEOPHYSICAL SURVEYS. 1394

0741-0859 See FACTS & FIGURES OF THE U.S. PLASTICS INDUSTRY. 4455

0741-0867 See LOUISIANA DIRECTORY OF CITIES, TOWNS, AND VILLAGES. 2745

0741-0883 See WRITTEN COMMUNICATION. 1124

0741-1014 See MHFA UPDATE. 2828

0741-1111 See AMERICAN POLITICS (WASHINGTON, D.C. : 1983). 4463

0741-112X See MEMBERSHIP AND STATISTICAL DIRECTORY - NEW ENGLAND GAS ASSOCIATION. 4284

0741-1138 See ISLA (OAKLAND, CALIF.). 2739

0741-1162 See PRE-LAW JOURNAL. 3030

0741-1170 See LAW SCHOOL ADMINISTRATOR'S JOURNAL. 2996

0741-1189 See LEGAL BIBLIOGRAPHY JOURNAL. 3081

0741-1197 See LAW TEACHER'S JOURNAL. 2997

0741-1200 See BRIDGE (SALEM, OR.), THE. 2724

0741-1219 See PATENT, TRADEMARK, AND COPYRIGHT LAWS. 1307

0741-1235 See SOCIOLOGY OF SPORT JOURNAL. 4919

0741-1243 See MILWAUKEE MAGAZINE. 2538

0741-1251 See GEORGIA FARMER (BALTIMORE, MD.). 90

0741-126X See GUOJI RIBAO. 5635

0741-1278 See MUTUAL FUND SPECIALIST, THE. 908

0741-1286 See HERMES AMERICANUS. 3285

0741-1294 See MASONRY SOCIETY JOURNAL, THE. 620

0741-1340 See MILITARY MANPOWER STATISTICS. 4062

0741-1359 See POWER REACTOR EVENTS. 2158

0741-1413 See INTERNATIONAL ELECTROCHEMICAL PROGRESS. 978

0741-1421 See PLUMBLINE. 1841

0741-1448 See FLORIDA FOLIAGE. 511

0741-1464 See NATIONAL PETROLEUM COUNCIL. 4265

0741-1537 See FOLIO (LOUISVILLE, KY.). 5060

0741-1588 See POOR KONRAD. 4987

0741-160X See RADIOLOGY & IMAGING LETTER. 3849

0741-1618 See CURRENT ADVANCES IN PROTEIN BIOCHEMISTRY. 478

0741-1618 See CURRENT ADVANCES IN PROTEIN CHEMISTRY. 478

0741-1626 See CURRENT ADVANCES IN CELL AND DEVELOPMENTAL BIOLOGY. 477

0741-1642 See CURRENT ADVANCES IN GENETICS & MOLECULAR BIOLOGY. 477

0741-1650 See CURRENT ADVANCES IN IMMUNOLOGY & INFECTIOUS DISEASES. 3656

0741-1669 See CURRENT ADVANCES IN APPLIED MICROBIOLOGY & BIOTECHNOLOGY. 477

0741-1677 See CURRENT ADVANCES IN NEUROSCIENCE. 3656

0741-1685 See CURRENT ADVANCES IN TOXICOLOGY. 3656

0741-1693 See CURRENT ADVANCES IN ENDOCRINOLOGY AND METABOLISM. 3656

0741-1715 See SOUND & VIDEO CONTRACTOR. 5319

0741-1723 See NATIONAL ACCIDENT SAMPLING SYSTEM. 5401

0741-1731 See SPACE CALENDAR. 35

0741-1758 See EVANGELICAL JOURNAL. 4957

0741-1766 See KAITE, EL. 380

0741-1782 See NOAA'S OFFICE OF UNDERSEA RESEARCH ... REPORT. 1453

0741-1790 See AVALON TO CAMELOT. 3365

0741-1812 See INCOME STOCKS HANDBOOK. 901

0741-1979 See PRINTING AND GRAPHIC ARTS BUYERS : PGAB. 4568

0741-2029 *See* TECHNICAL LITERATURE ABSTRACTS (WARRENDALE, PA. : 1987). **1998**

0741-2029 *See* SAE TECHNICAL LITERATURE ABSTRACTS. **1995**

0741-2037 *See* CROSSROADS (DE KALB, ILL.). **2503**

0741-2045 *See* KATES KIN. **2456**

0741-2193 *See* JOURNAL OF BUDDHIST PHILOSOPHY. **5021**

0741-2207 *See* BLUE & GRAY MAGAZINE. **2723**

0741-2223 *See* JOURNAL OF ROBOTIC SYSTEMS. **1214**

0741-224X *See* STATE ADVISORY COMMITTEE HANDBOOK / UNITED STATES COMMISSION ON CIVIL RIGHTS. **4513**

0741-2266 *See* ... TRANSPORTATION SYSTEM MANAGEMENT REPORT FOR NORTHEASTERN ILLINOIS, THE. **5397**

0741-2274 See EQUAL EMPLOYMENT OPPORTUNITY REPORT. MINORITIES AND WOMEN IN APPRENTICESHIP PROGRAMS AND REFERRAL UNIONS. **1667**

0741-2282 *See* PEER FACILITATOR QUARTERLY. **1772**

0741-2312 *See* CHILD AND FAMILY POLICY. **5277**

0741-2320 *See* TODAY'S THERAPEUTIC TRENDS. **3646**

0741-2347 *See* APPLE INDEX, THE. **1264**

0741-2355 *See* IBM PC INDEX, THE. **1186**

0741-2363 *See* BUSINESS COMPUTER INDEX, THE. **1172**

0741-2371 *See* CALIFORNIA'S THE GREEN BOOK. **4636**

0741-238X *See* ADVANCES IN THERAPY. **3546**

0741-2398 *See* CHILD CARE WORK. **5278**

0741-241X *See* FOLIO'S MEDICAL DIRECTORY OF MASSACHUSETTS. **3914**

0741-2460 *See* WAVELENGTH (NEW ORLEANS, LA.). **4158**

0741-2479 *See* EQUAL EMPLOYMENT OPPORTUNITY REPORT. MINORITIES AND WOMEN IN APPRENTICESHIP PROGRAMS AND REFERRAL UNIONS. **1667**

0741-2487 *See* GRANTSMANSHIP NEWS. **4337**

0741-2533 *See* HEAT EXCHANGER DESIGN HANDBOOK : HEDH. **4430**

0741-2541 *See* DATAPRO REPORTS ON MICROCOMPUTERS. **1267**

0741-2568 *See* ANNUAL REPORT / AGRICULTURAL COOPERATIVE DEVELOPMENT INTERNATIONAL. **1541**

0741-2576 *See* TEXAS LINGUISTIC FORUM. **3328**

0741-2592 *See* AFRIQUE HISTOIRE U.S. **2637**

0741-2827 *See* YEARBOOK OF GERMAN-AMERICAN STUDIES. **2766**

0741-2851 *See* OPEN SYSTEMS COMMUNICATION. **1243**

0741-286X *See* OPEN SYSTEMS DATA TRANSFER. **1243**

0741-2878 *See* CIS FEDERAL REGISTER INDEX. **4697**

0741-2894 *See* SENIOR VOICE (ANCHORAGE, ALASKA). **2545**

0741-2924 *See* IOWA REVIEW QUARTERLY. **4658**

0741-2940 *See* I.S.C.A. QUARTERLY, THE. **380**

0741-2983 *See* MEDIA WATCH. LOS ANGELES/ORANGE COUNTY. **1117**

0741-3092 *See* MANAGEMENT CONSULTING (BOSTON, MASS.). **4206**

0741-3106 *See* IEEE ELECTRON DEVICE LETTERS. **2059**

0741-3173 *See* LOCAL/STATE FUNDING REPORT / GIS, GOVERNMENT INFORMATION SERVICES. **4663**

0741-322X *See* ANNUAL REPORT / PRESIDENTIAL ADVISORY COMMITTEE ON SMALL AND MINORITY BUSINESS OWNERSHIP. **639**

0741-3238 *See* NOPA MANUFACTURER SELLING COSTS SURVEY. **4212**

0741-3246 See CHILTON'S MOTORCYCLE AND ATV REPAIR MANUAL. **4081**

0741-3254 *See* PIB MAGAZINE ADVERTISING ANALYSIS. CURRENT QUARTER BRAND-MAGAZINE DETAIL. **763**

0741-3270 *See* CORPORATE AUTHOR AUTHORITY LIST. **3204**

0741-3319 *See* BUTLER COUNTY NEWS (GEORGIANA, ALA.). **5625**

0741-3335 *See* PLASMA PHYSICS AND CONTROLLED FUSION. **4450**

0741-3351 *See* ARTIST'S MAGAZINE, THE. **314**

0741-336X *See* STANDARD FOR AUDITING COMPUTER APPLICATIONS, A. **812**

0741-3378 *See* LATIN AMERICAN ISSUES. **2743**

0741-3386 *See* STATE OF TEXAS WATER QUALITY MANAGEMENT, ANNUAL WORK PROGRAM, THE. **5539**

0741-3408 *See* CHAMPIONS OF FREEDOM. **1590**

0741-3424 *See* EXECUTIVE COMPENSATION SURVEY (PRINCETON, N.J.). **1668**

0741-3440 *See* LIVING (SOUTH FLORIDA ED.). **4840**

0741-3475 See FROM THE STATE CAPITALS. THE OUTLOOK FROM THE STATE CAPITALS. **2972**

0741-3483 *See* FROM THE STATE CAPITALS. URBAN DEVELOPMENT. **2823**

0741-3505 *See* FROM THE STATE CAPITALS. FAMILY RELATIONS. **2280**

0741-3521 *See* FROM THE STATE CAPITALS. PUBLIC EMPLOYEE POLICY. **940**

0741-353X *See* FROM THE STATE CAPITALS. CIVIL RIGHTS. **4508**

0741-3602 *See* DEFENSE COMMUNICATION STUDY, THE. **4041**

0741-3610 *See* CPA DIGEST. **742**

0741-3629 *See* ENERGY DESIGN UPDATE. **1939**

0741-3653 *See* JOURNAL OF EDUCATIONAL PUBLIC RELATIONS. **1757**

0741-3661 *See* TECHNICAL INSIGHTS ANNUAL REPORT ON GENETIC TECHNOLOGY. **3696**

0741-367X *See* TECHNICAL INSIGHTS ANNUAL REPORT ON INDUSTRIAL ROBOTS. **1217**

0741-3750 *See* OPPORTUNITY (CHICAGO, ILL. : 1983). **701**

0741-3785 *See* IFC'S FINANCIAL NEWS REVIEW. **790**

0741-3793 *See* DISPUTE RESOLUTION PAPERS SERIES. **2963**

0741-3866 *See* FINS AND FEATHERS (CONNECTICUT ED.). **5583**

0741-3874 *See* FINS AND FEATHERS (KANSAS, ED.). **5583**

0741-4005 *See* FINS AND FEATHERS (SOUTH DAKOTA ED.). **5583**

0741-4102 *See* WOMEN & THE LAW REPORT. **3076**

0741-4129 *See* PAPERBOARD PACKAGING'S INTERNATIONAL CONTAINER DIRECTORY. **4221**

0741-4161 *See* COMMUNITY LEADERS OF AMERICA (1981). **431**

0741-417X *See* LEGAL INVESTIGATOR, THE. **3000**

0741-4188 *See* LIBRARY CURRENTS. **3225**

0741-4218 *See* CLINICAL CARDIOLOGY ALERT. **3703**

0741-4226 *See* LINEAR CIRCUITS DATA BOOK. **2071**

0741-4234 *See* NEUROLOGY ALERT. **3841**

0741-4242 *See* LONG STORY, THE. **3408**

0741-4269 *See* INTERNATIONAL TAX & BUSINESS LAWYER. **3131**

0741-4285 *See* RUN. **1272**

0741-4307 *See* ADVENT CHRISTIAN WITNESS (1983), THE. **5054**

0741-4331 *See* SUMMARY OF MOTOR VEHICLE TRAFFIC ACCIDENTS. URBAN. **5445**

0741-4358 *See* SUMMARY OF MOTOR VEHICLE TRAFFIC ACCIDENTS. STATEWIDE. **5445**

0741-4366 *See* SUMMARY OF MOTOR VEHICLE TRAFFIC ACCIDENTS INVESTIGATED / REPORTED BY STATE POLICE. **5445**

0741-4374 *See* SUMMARY OF MOTOR VEHICLE TRAFFIC ACCIDENTS. NEW ORLEANS. **5445**

0741-4390 *See* SUMMARY OF MOTOR VEHICLE TRAFFIC ACCIDENTS. NEW IBERIA. **5445**

0741-4404 *See* SUMMARY OF MOTOR VEHICLE TRAFFIC ACCIDENTS. MONROE. **5445**

0741-4439 *See* SUMMARY OF MOTOR VEHICLE TRAFFIC ACCIDENTS. KENNER. **5445**

0741-4455 *See* SUMMARY OF MOTOR VEHICLE TRAFFIC ACCIDENTS. GRETNA. **5445**

0741-4471 *See* SUMMARY OF MOTOR VEHICLE TRAFFIC ACCIDENTS. BATON ROUGE. **5445**

0741-448X *See* SUMMARY OF MOTOR VEHICLE TRAFFIC ACCIDENTS. ALEXANDRIA. **5445**

0741-4498 *See* GROWING EDGE (LOS ANGELES, CALIF.), THE. **1748**

0741-4501 *See* SOFTWARE MAINTENANCE NEWS. **1291**

0741-451X *See* WATER RESOURCES DATA. SOUTH DAKOTA. **5545**

0741-4528 *See* STATUS OF NATIONAL DIRECT STUDENT LOAN DEFAULTS. **1848**

0741-4536 *See* DIRECTORY OF SPECIAL LIBRARIES AND INFORMATION CENTERS IN TEXAS. **3208**

0741-4587 *See* UPDATE (ELIZABETHTOWN, PA.). **39**

0741-4595 *See* PRACTICAL TAX GUIDE FOR THE HORSE OWNER, A. **2801**

0741-4633 *See* AMERICAN ACADEMY OF PHYSICAL EDUCATION PAPERS. **1854**

0741-465X *See* ISSUES OF THE AMERICAN COUNCIL FOR JUDAISM. **5048**

0741-4676 *See* REVIEW OF THE FEDERAL CROP INSURANCE CORPORATION'S FINANCIAL STATEMENTS. **809**

0741-4684 *See* NICHD ANNUAL REPORT. **3907**

0741-4706 *See* FINANCIAL DIRECTORY OF PENSION FUNDS. NEW HAMPSHIRE. **1672**

0741-4714 *See* FINANCIAL DIRECTORY OF PENSION FUNDS. COLORADO. **1670**

0741-4749 *See* PROFESSIONAL REGULATION NEWS. **3916**

0741-4773 *See* HIDDEN VALLEY JOURNAL. **2453**

0741-479X *See* FINANCIAL DIRECTORY OF PENSION FUNDS. NORTH DAKOTA. **1673**

0741-4803 *See* WATER RESOURCES DATA. KANSAS. **5545**

0741-4811 *See* SMALL BUSINESS SUBCONTRACTING DIRECTORY. **711**

0741-482X *See* SECURITY AND SPECIAL POLICE LEGAL UPDATE. **3176**

0741-4838 *See* SCHOOL FOOD SERVICE DIRECTOR. **2356**

0741-4870 *See* BETTER BOAT. **591**

0741-4900 *See* BK SPECIAL REPORT. **4713**

0741-496X *See* ART-TALK. **340**

0741-4978 *See* PAC-FINDER SYSTEM 34/36 SOFTWARE DIRECTORY. **1289**

0741-4994 *See* BIBLIOGRAPHIC SERIES / PROFESSIONAL SERVICES DEPARTMENT, INTERNATIONAL ASSOCIATION OF ASSESSING OFFICERS. **4696**

0741-5028 *See* BLUEFISH. **3460**

0741-5036 *See* LEGAL DIRECTORY OF WASHINGTON STATE. **2999**

0741-5109 *See* FEDERAL ORGANIZATION SERVICE. **4648**

0741-5117 *See* FINANCIAL DIRECTORY OF PENSION FUNDS. NEBRASKA. **1672**

0741-5125 *See* VIDEO LAW MONTHLY. **1123**

0741-5141 *See* MENTAL HEALTH LAW REPORTER. **3009**

0741-515X *See* CARDIOLOGISTS' LEGAL LETTER. **2948**

0741-5168 *See* ALASKA'S MINERAL INDUSTRY. **1437**

0741-5206 *See* PLASTIC SURGICAL NURSING. **3867**

0741-5214 *See* JOURNAL OF VASCULAR SURGERY. **3969**

0741-5230 *See* ACID PRECIPITATION. **2223**

0741-5249 *See* SOLAR THERMAL ENERGY TECHNOLOGY. **1957**

0741-529X See REVIEW OF THE AUDIT OF THE NATIONAL CONSUMER COOPERATIVE BANK'S FINANCIAL STATEMENTS. 809

0741-532X See WEST'S FEDERAL TAXATION. FEDERAL TAX FORMS. 4758

0741-5338 See KEY FINDER. 2456

0741-5346 See WEST'S EDUCATION LAW DIGEST. 3074

0741-5400 See JOURNAL OF LEUKOCYTE BIOLOGY. 3799

0741-5419 See SOLAR ENERGY AND NONFOSSIL FUEL RESEARCH. 136

0741-5427 See FINANCIAL DIRECTORY OF PENSION FUNDS. PENNSYLVANIA, WESTERN (PITTSBURGH AREA). 1673

0741-5435 See TOMAHAWK (ELLWOOD CITY, PA.), THE. 1850

0741-5443 See MIDDLE MANAGEMENT PERSONNEL. 944

0741-5451 See MICROCOMPUTERS IN TRANSPORTATION. SOFTWARE AND SOURCE BOOK. 5387

0741-546X See LIVING (FLORIDA GULF COAST ED.). 2537

0741-5486 See LIVING (HOUSTON, ED.). 4840

0741-5508 See LIVING (DENVER ED.). 2537

0741-5540 See PENNSYLVANIA LAW FINDER. 3025

0741-5567 See NEBULA AWARDS, THE. 3414

0741-5575 See MAJOR PROBLEMS IN VETERINARY MEDICINE. 5516

0741-5656 See GEOTHERMAL TECHNOLOGY PUBLICATIONS AND RELATED REPORTS, A BIBLIOGRAPHY. 1962

0741-5672 See BULLETIN OF THE SOCIETY FOR AMERICAN ARCHAEOLOGY. 264

0741-5699 See BIOSCIENCE RESEARCH REPORTS. RESEARCH NOTES IN ANIMAL BEHAVIOUR. 5578

0741-5729 See BARBARA BRABEC'S NATIONAL HOME BUSINESS REPORT. 642

0741-5737 See AMERICAN SALON: OFFICIAL PUBLICATION OF THE NHCA. 402

0741-5753 See SOCIETY FOR GERMAN-AMERICAN STUDIES NEWSLETTER. 2273

0741-5761 See SOCIAL IMPACT ASSESSMENT. 5259

0741-577X See F.A.R.O.G. FORUM JOURNAL BILINGUE. 5200

0741-5788 See BULWARK (CHICAGO, ILL.), THE. 4505

0741-580X See MODEM NOTES. 1264

0741-5818 See TRAVEL SMART FOR BUSINESS. 5496

0741-5826 See TRAVEL SMART. 5496

0741-5834 See LIGHTWAVE. 4438

0741-5842 See SHAW. 3352

0741-5869 See OPTICAL MEMORY NEWS. 1277

0741-5885 See JAZZIZ (GAINESVILLE, FLA.). 4125

0741-5893 See COMPUTERS-R-DIGITAL. 1179

0741-5958 See THIRD RAIL (LOS ANGELES, CALIF.). 3446

0741-5966 See PUBLISHERS IDEA EXCHANGE. 4818

0741-5974 See AEROSTATION (ALEXANDRIA, VA.). 6

0741-6016 See MICROCOMPUTER INDUSTRY UPDATE. 1209

0741-6075 See JOURNAL OF CHRISTIAN JURISPRUDENCE. 2987

0741-6083 See CALIFORNIA HOUSING PLAN, THE. 2817

0741-6091 See KOVELS ON ANTIQUES AND COLLECTIBLES. 251

0741-6105 See TEXARKANA USA GENEALOGIST'S QUARTERLY, THE. 2474

0741-6148 See PUBLISHING RESEARCH QUARTERLY. 4819

0741-6156 See THEORY AND PRACTICE : JOURNAL OF THE MUSIC THEORY SOCIETY OF NEW YORK STATE. 4156

0741-6164 See PHONETICIAN, THE. 3310

0741-6180 See IN CONTEXT (SEQUIM, WASH.). 4349

0741-6210 See CROTON REVIEW. 3379

0741-6229 See ZETETIC SCHOLAR. 4243

0741-6245 See MAYO CLINIC HEALTH LETTER (ENGLISH ED.). 4789

0741-6253 See DIABETES SELF-MANAGEMENT. 3728

0741-6261 See RAND JOURNAL OF ECONOMICS, THE. 1594

0741-627X See JOURNAL - SOCIETY FOR THE STUDY OF BLACK PHILOSOPHY (U.S.), THE. 4351

0741-6288 See SALES OF DISTILLED SPIRITS. 2370

0741-6296 See WATER RESOURCES DATA. MISSOURI. 5545

0741-6326 See U.S. MEDICAL LICENSURE STATISTICS ... AND LICENSURE REQUIREMENTS 3662

0741-6334 See ELECTRONIC FUEL INJECTION, DIAGNOSIS & TESTING. 5414

0741-6423 See CASE STUDY - AMERICAN PRODUCTIVITY CENTER. 1601

0741-6504 See CREATIVE OHIO. 372

0741-6512 See DRG MONITOR. 3573

0741-6520 See CELLULAR BUSINESS. 1151

0741-6547 See DUNN REPORT, ELECTRONIC PUBLISHING & PREPRESS SYSTEMS NEWS & VIEWS. 4814

0741-6555 See FEMINIST BOOKSTORE NEWS. 5556

0741-6563 See PRIMARY SOURCE (JACKSON, MISS.). 2482

0741-6571 See SURVEY OF JEWISH AFFAIRS. 2274

0741-6849 See MONTANA STATE ARCHITECTURAL REVIEW. 303

0741-6881 See WOODSON WATCHER PLUS ALLIED LINES. 2477

0741-689X See LAMBERT'S COMMUNICATIONS DIRECTORY, WASHINGTON-BALTIMORE. 1115

0741-6903 See DIRECTORY OF GENERAL MERCHANDISE VARIETY CHAINS & SPECIALTY STORES. 954

0741-692X See FEDERAL COURT MANAGEMENT STATISTICS. 3080

0741-6954 See DOUGLAS TRAILS AND TRACES. 2446

0741-6997 See HR REPORTER. 941

0741-7004 See FOUNDATION GIVING WATCH. 4336

0741-7047 See TEEN LEADER SYNDICATED STUDY. 1300

0741-7101 See FINS AND FEATHERS (VIRGINIA, ED.). 5584

0741-7136 See ADULT EDUCATION QUARTERLY (AMERICAN ASSOCIATION FOR ADULT AND CONTINUING EDUCATION). 1799

0741-7160 See EXPORT GRAFICAS USA. 378

0741-7225 See NEW ENGLAND TALK SHOW DIRECTORY. 1135

0741-7233 See COMPARATIVE POLITICS (GUILFORD, CONN.). 4469

0741-725X See RESIDENTIAL ENERGY CONSUMPTION SURVEY. HOUSING CHARACTERISTICS. 2834

0741-7268 See CURRENT BUSINESS REPORTS. REVISED MONTHLY WHOLESALE TRADE, SALES AND INVENTORIES. 830

0741-7284 See KNOX COUNTY, ILLINOIS GENEALOGICAL SOCIETY QUARTERLY. 2457

0741-7403 See FAMILIA LATINA. 2278

0741-7454 See CARDIOLOGIC CONSULTATION. 3700

0741-7462 See INFECTIOUS DISEASES CAPSULE & COMMENT. 4784

0741-7470 See ORTHOPEDIC SURGEONS' LEGAL LETTER. 3742

0741-7489 See DERMATOLOGIC CAPSULE & COMMENT. 3719

0741-7527 See ANNALI D'ITALIANISTICA. 3362

0741-7543 See PALLADIAN STUDIES IN AMERICA. 305

0741-7586 See PACIFIC MARITIME MAGAZINE. 5453

0741-7594 See YOUNG AUTHOR'S MAGAZINE. 2926

0741-7624 See SIDE STREETS OF THE WORLD. 5491

0741-7632 See BATEMAN DATUM. 2438

0741-7659 See DOUBLE REED, THE. 4115

0741-7667 See LSI JOURNAL. 1280

0741-7748 See CONSUMING PASSIONS. 4189

0741-7780 See SHEET MUSIC EXCHANGE, THE. 4152

0741-7802 See HARFORD HISTORICAL BULLETIN. 2452

0741-7896 See PUBLICATIONS OF THE AMERICAN FOLKLIFE CENTER. 2323

0741-7950 See PROCEEDINGS, ANNUAL CONVENTION - NEWSPAPER GUILD. CONVENTION. 1703

0741-8035 See MSC/NASTRAN APPLICATION MANUAL. IBM EDITION. 1195

0741-8132 See BUSINESS BOOK REVIEW. 646

0741-8140 See DIRECTORY OF INTERPRETERS FOR THE DEAF IN TEXAS. 5283

0741-8159 See FORSYTH COUNTY GENEALOGICAL SOCIETY JOURNAL, THE. 2448

0741-8167 See HONDURAS UPDATE. 2512

0741-8191 See HIMA DIRECTORY. 4783

0741-8205 See BUYER'S GUIDE OF PRODUCTS AND SERVICES IN THE ST. LOUIS REGION. 826

0741-8213 See THREE-YEAR REPORT / FUND FOR THE CITY OF NEW YORK. 5312

0741-8221 See WIRING DEVICES AND SUPPLIES. 2086

0741-823X See U.S. SECONDARY FIBRE STUDY. 4239

0741-8248 See NORTHWEST MISSOURI GENEALOGY SOCIETY JOURNAL. 2464

0741-8264 See CIRCUIT RIDER (SPRINGFIELD, ILL.), THE. 2443

0741-8280 See ADVANCES IN ECONOMIC BOTANY. 498

0741-8329 See ALCOHOL (FAYETTEVILLE, N.Y.). 1339

0741-8345 See BLUE CHIP FINANCIAL FORECASTS. 779

0741-8361 See REPORT ON AT & T, THE. 1162

0741-8388 See STATE TELEPHONE REGULATION REPORT. 1164

0741-8442 See DISPUTE RESOLUTION RESOURCE DIRECTORY. 2963

0741-8450 See SIMON WIESENTHAL CENTER ANNUAL. 2709

0741-8469 See RADIO BUSINESS REPORT. 1137

0741-8477 See BOSTON UNIVERSITY JOURNAL OF TAX LAW. 2943

0741-8485 See POLICY AND RESEARCH REPORT. 5213

0741-8493 See EXPLORE (LAWRENCE, KAN.). 1823

0741-8507 See GROUND WATER MODELING NEWSLETTER. 5534

0741-8523 See WRAP UP (NORWOOD, N.J.). 3652

0741-8531 See WRAP UP ON LATIN AMERICAN AGRICULTURE, FOOD, FISHING & LIVESTOCK. 1589

0741-8612 See OKLAHOMA REGISTER, THE. 3022

0741-8639 See SAGE (ATLANTA, GA.). 5565

0741-8647 See MACWORLD (SAN FRANCISCO, CALIF.). 1268

0741-8655 See AUTHOR BIOGRAPHIES MASTER INDEX. 430

0741-8663 See FINANCIAL DIRECTORY OF PENSION FUNDS. MAINE. 1671

0741-8671 See FINANCIAL DIRECTORY OF PENSION FUNDS. NEVADA. 1672

0741-868X See FINANCIAL DIRECTORY OF PENSION FUNDS. MISSISSIPPI. 1672

0741-8701 See FINANCIAL DIRECTORY OF PENSION FUNDS. SOUTH DAKOTA. 1673

ISSN Index

0741-871X *See* FINANCIAL DIRECTORY OF PENSION FUNDS. RHODE ISLAND. 1673

0741-8736 *See* GEORGE MASON UNIVERSITY LAW REVIEW. 2973

0741-8760 *See* LOCOMOTIVE (HARTFORD, CONN.), THE. 5432

0741-8809 *See* COMPUTER LAW MONITOR, THE. 2954

0741-8825 *See* JUSTICE QUARTERLY. 3168

0741-8876 *See* WASHINGTON JOURNALISM REVIEW (1983). 2925

0741-8892 *See* FIFTY BILLION DOLLAR DIRECTORY, THE. 954

0741-8957 *See* ADVANCES IN NEUROPSYCHOLOGY AND BEHAVIORAL NEUROLOGY. 3826

0741-8981 *See* NEWSWEEK ON CAMPUS. 1838

0741-9015 *See* FOOD & WINE (NEW YORK, N.Y.). 2790

0741-9023 *See* PRESERVATION TECH NOTES. 306

0741-9031 *See* KENTUCKY MANUFACTURERS REGISTER. 3482

0741-9058 *See* LIBRARY HI TECH NEWS. 3225

0741-9066 *See* COMPLEAT LAWYER, THE. 2954

0741-9090 *See* ANNUAL REVIEW OF MILITARY RESEARCH AND DEVELOPMENT. 4035

0741-9112 *See* BERRY ALUMNI DIRECTORY. 1101

0741-9120 *See* GENERAL TEEN SYNDICATED STUDY. 1492

0741-9147 *See* NATIONAL WOMEN'S HEALTH REPORT. 4792

0741-9155 *See* CHATTAHOOCHEE REVIEW, THE. 3339

0741-9163 *See* SACRED ART JOURNAL. 364

0741-9228 *See* BIENNIAL REPORT - AMERICAN INSTITUTE OF INDIAN STUDIES. 2647

0741-9236 *See* STANDARD ... U.S. COIN CATALOGUE. 2783

0741-9244 *See* UPDATE - UNITED STATES. OFFICE OF CONVERTER REACTOR DEVELOPMENT. 2159

0741-9260 *See* COMPILATION OF GAO'S WORK ON TAX ADMINISTRATION ACTIVITIES. 741

0741-9279 *See* NCAA MEN'S AND WOMEN'S SKIING RULES. 4907

0741-9287 *See* COST SURVEY (1992). 3778

0741-9295 *See* WASHINGTON LOBBYISTS & LAWYERS DIRECTORY, THE. 3072

0741-9317 *See* NEWARK PRESS. 2922

0741-9325 *See* REMEDIAL AND SPECIAL EDUCATION. 1884

0741-9341 *See* ADVANCES IN COMPUTING RESEARCH. 1170

0741-9368 *See* HEALTHCARE MARKETING REPORT. 3782

0741-9384 *See* HORA (NEW YORK, N.Y.). 1313

0741-9414 *See* WASHINGTON INFORMER, THE. 2275

0741-9449 *See* MINNESOTA JOURNAL. 4665

0741-9457 *See* YALE JOURNAL ON REGULATION. 3076

0741-9473 *See* RIA ROBOTICS GLOSSARY. 1216

0741-9481 *See* JOURNAL OF CHILD AND YOUTH CARE WORK. 5291

0741-9627 *See* NOW L.A. / OFFICIAL PUBLICATION OF THE LOS ANGELES CHAPTER, NATIONAL ORGANIZATION FOR WOMEN (NOW). 5563

0741-9635 *See* QUARTERLY NEWS JOURNAL OF THE CROSBY ARBORETUM, A. 5235

0741-9643 *See* PETROLEUM MARKETING MONTHLY. 934

0741-9686 *See* SEX EDUCATION COALITION NEWS. 1783

0741-9708 *See* UTAH BIG GAME RANGE TREND STUDIES. 4928

0741-9724 *See* CURRENT ISSUES IN CLINICAL PSYCHOLOGY. 4584

0741-9767 *See* STATISTICAL BULLETIN - METROPOLITAN LIFE INSURANCE COMPANY (1984). 2897

0741-9783 *See* ADVANCES. 3546

0741-9813 *See* INVESTOR'S YEARBOOK. 903

0741-983X *See* RENEWABLE ENERGY. 1954

0741-9848 *See* AMERICAN VEGETABLE GROWER (1983). 162

0741-9856 *See* WEED CONTROL MANUAL. 2433

0741-9880 *See* BRANDYWINE MAGAZINE. 2485

0741-9899 *See* ANNOTATED GUIDE TO WOMEN'S PERIODICALS IN THE U.S. & CANADA, THE. 5550

0741-9910 *See* LILY YEARBOOK OF THE NORTH AMERICAN LILY SOCIETY, INC, THE. 2424

0741-9929 *See* OCEAN STATE BUSINESS. 700

0741-9937 *See* ALGEBRAS, GROUPS, AND GEOMETRIES. 3492

0741-9953 *See* INTERNATIONAL BOOK COLLECTORS ALMANAC/NEWSLETTER. 4829

0741-997X *See* ABSOLUTE REFERENCE. 1283

0742-0021 *See* REAL ESTATE FINANCE TODAY. 4844

0742-0072 *See* FINANCIAL DIRECTORY OF PENSION FUNDS. ALABAMA. 1669

0742-0080 *See* FINANCIAL DIRECTORY OF PENSION FUNDS. DISTRICT OF COLUMBIA. 1670

0742-0099 *See* FINANCIAL DIRECTORY OF PENSION FUNDS. ALASKA. 1669

0742-0102 *See* FINANCIAL DIRECTORY OF PENSION FUNDS. ARKANSAS. 1669

0742-0110 *See* FINANCIAL DIRECTORY OF PENSION FUNDS. ARIZONA. 1669

0742-0129 *See* FINANCIAL DIRECTORY OF PENSION FUNDS. IOWA. 1671

0742-0137 *See* FINANCIAL DIRECTORY OF PENSION FUNDS. LOUISIANA. 1671

0742-0153 *See* FINANCIAL DIRECTORY OF PENSION FUNDS. MONTANA. 1672

0742-0161 *See* FINANCIAL DIRECTORY OF PENSION FUNDS. OREGON. 1673

0742-017X *See* FINANCIAL DIRECTORY OF PENSION FUNDS. TENNESSEE. 1673

0742-0188 *See* FINANCIAL DIRECTORY OF PENSION FUNDS. UTAH. 1674

0742-0196 *See* FINANCIAL DIRECTORY OF PENSION FUNDS. VERMONT. 1674

0742-020X *See* WHO'S WHO IN PIPELINING. 437

0742-0218 *See* ALUMNAE REGISTER / MOUNT HOLYOKE COLLEGE. 1097

0742-0226 *See* ARIZONA STATE UNIVERSITY LAW FORUM. 2937

0742-0242 *See* SPONSORED RESEARCH IN THE HISTORY OF ART. 365

0742-0277 *See* BLACK ISSUES IN HIGHER EDUCATION. 1812

0742-0323 *See* CHILTON'S IMPORT LABOR GUIDE AND PARTS MANUAL. 5411

0742-034X *See* TRENDS (SCOTTSDALE, ARIZ.). 332

0742-0366 *See* ABMD DIRECTORY OF CERTIFIED EMERGENCY PHYSICIANS. 3723

0742-0374 *See* ABMS DIRECTORY OF CERTIFIED UROLOGISTS. 3987

0742-0390 *See* ANNUAL REPORT / NATIONAL SOFT DRINK ASSOCIATION. 2363

0742-0420 *See* ANTIQUE TOY WORLD. 2583

0742-0447 *See* SAILBOAT TRADE-IN GUIDE, BLUE BOOK. 596

0742-0463 *See* VULKANOLOGIIA I SEISMOLOGIA. 1412

0742-0501 *See* PUBLISHERS DIRECTORY. 4818

0742-051X *See* TEACHING AND TEACHER EDUCATION. 1906

0742-0528 *See* CHRONOBIOLOGY INTERNATIONAL. 451

0742-0552 *See* BLUEPRINTS - NATIONAL BUILDING MUSEUM (U.S.). 293

0742-0587 *See* FISHING (NEW YORK, N.Y.). 2303

0742-0595 *See* FISHING SECRETS. 2303

0742-0609 *See* BASS (NEW YORK, N.Y.). 2297

0742-0633 *See* COMPUTER SECURITY ALERT. 1226

0742-0684 *See* RATINGS BOOK, THE. 1292

0742-0722 *See* FASTFACTS HOTEL MOTEL LOCATOR, UNITED STATES & CANADA. 2805

0742-0757 *See* TENNESSEE TAX GUIDE. 4756

0742-0803 *See* HIGHER EDUCATION LAW REPORT. 2978

0742-082X *See* FRINGE BENEFITS FOR TEACHERS IN PUBLIC SCHOOLS. 1864

0742-0846 *See* DORSEY DREAMS. 2445

0742-0862 *See* SCHEDULED SALARIES FOR PROFESSIONAL PERSONNEL IN PUBLIC SCHOOLS. 1710

0742-0870 *See* WAGES AND SALARIES PAID SUPPORT PERSONNEL IN PUBLIC SCHOOLS. 1874

0742-0889 *See* CONSTRUCTION CLAIMS CITATOR, THE. 609

0742-0927 *See* CALIFORNIA POLICY CHOICES. 4636

0742-0935 *See* MATURE OUTLOOK. 5180

0742-096X *See* ALLEGHENY REVIEW, THE. 1089

0742-0978 *See* AUERBACH DA TAGRAM. DATA SECURITY MANAGEMENT. 860

0742-0994 *See* GENTRY FAMILY GAZETTE AND GENEALOGY EXCHANGE. 2451

0742-101X *See* VOCEADOR, EL. 1790

0742-1036 *See* PROFESSIONAL COMPUTING. 1272

0742-1052 *See* WN TRENDS, HEALTH CARE AND MANAGEMENT. 4808

0742-1087 *See* U.S. DISTRICT COURT FEDERAL FILINGS ALERT. 3067

0742-1095 *See* WANT'S FEDERAL-STATE COURT DIRECTORY. 3143

0742-1117 *See* BIBLIOTHECA AFROASIATICA. 3367

0742-1141 *See* BYZANTINA KAI METABYZANTINA. 2647

0742-115X *See* HUMANA CIVILITAS. 2847

0742-1192 *See* COMPUTER LAWYER, THE. 2955

0742-1222 *See* JOURNAL OF MANAGEMENT INFORMATION SYSTEMS. 3220

0742-1230 *See* GREAT LAKES WASTE & POLLUTION REVIEW MAGAZINE. 2230

0742-129X *See* CHARITON COLLECTOR, THE. 2727

0742-1354 *See* MISSOURI STATE PLAN FOR HIGH BLOOD PRESSURE CONTROL. 3708

0742-1389 *See* BLUE BOOK (BALTIMORE, MD.). 2439

0742-1419 *See* FAMILY HISTORY CAPERS. 2447

0742-1435 *See* PRACTICE LIFE. 3629

0742-1478 *See* HEALTH CARE STRATEGIC MANAGEMENT. 3781

0742-1494 *See* VINTAGE '45. 5568

0742-1508 *See* COCKPIT (LANCASTER, CALIF.). 16

0742-1524 *See* TOGETHER (MONROVIA, CALIF.). 2912

0742-1532 *See* ELECTRON DISPLAY WORLD. 2046

0742-1567 *See* ACUTE CARE MEDICINE. 3546

0742-1575 *See* WATER RESOURCES DATA. TEXAS. 5546

0742-1591 *See* GAYLORD HUB, THE. 5696

0742-1605 *See* PEDIATRIC NETWORK. 3909

0742-1648 *See* INTERIOR LANDSCAPE INDUSTRY. 2420

0742-1656 *See* ART THERAPY : JOURNAL OF THE AMERICAN ART THERAPY ASSOCIATION. 4575

0742-1664 *See* FRINGE BENEFITS FOR ADMINISTRATORS IN PUBLIC SCHOOLS. 1864

0742-1702 *See* COUNTY EXECUTIVE DIRECTORY. 4641

0742-1710 *See* MUNICIPAL EXECUTIVE DIRECTORY. 4667

0742-1729 *See* FEDERAL REGIONAL EXECUTIVE DIRECTORY. 4648

0742-1753 *See* ASCE ANNUAL COMBINED INDEX. 2002

0742-1796 *See* BIOMEDICAL ETHICS REVIEWS. 3556

0742-1818 *See* VENTANA (NEW YORK, N.Y.), LA. 2764

0742-1850 See RAILROAD FACTS (WASHINGTON, D.C.). 5435

0742-1869 See TOBACCO MARKET REVIEW. BURLEY. 5374

0742-1893 See FAMILY PLANNING GRANTEES, DELEGATES & CLINICS. 588

0742-1915 See JOURNAL OF CLINICAL PSYCHIATRY ADVANCES IN PSYCHIATRIC TREATMENT MONOGRAPH SERIES, THE. 3928

0742-1923 See AMERICAN UNIVERSITY STUDIES. SERIES XVIII, AFRICAN LITERATURE. 3360

0742-1931 See INTERNATIONAL JOURNAL OF ADULT ORTHODONTICS AND ORTHOGNATHIC SURGERY, THE. 1325

0742-194X See YEAR BOOK OF PODIATRIC MEDICINE AND SURGERY (CHICAGO, ILL.), THE. 3918

0742-1974 See ENGINEERING INDEX MONTHLY. 2004

0742-2008 See WASHINGTON CREDIT LETTER. 816

0742-2024 See SPORTS INDUSTRY NEWS. 4923

0742-2075 See HUDSON VALLEY REGIONAL REVIEW, THE. 2847

0742-2091 See CELL BIOLOGY AND TOXICOLOGY (PRINCETON SCIENTIFIC PUBLISHERS). 533

0742-2113 See STORIES (BOSTON, MASS.). 3440

0742-2318 See BIO-BASE. 430

0742-2342 See MICROCOMPUTERS FOR INFORMATION MANAGEMENT. 1269

0742-2350 See CUMULATIVE INDEX OF SAE TECHNICAL PAPERS. 5412

0742-2466 See FLORIDA REVIEW (ORLANDO, FLA.), THE. 3463

0742-2695 See NEW JERSEY AND NEW YORK PORT HANDBOOK. 5453

0742-2709 See SOCIOECONOMIC CHARACTERISTICS OF MEDICAL PRACTICE. 3917

0742-2725 See CURRENT THEMES IN TROPICAL SCIENCE. 5098

0742-2733 See PHILOSOPHY IN CONTEXT. 4357

0742-275X See PATENT NEWSLETTER. LASERS/ELECTRO-OPTICS, THE. 1307

0742-2768 See RAG MAG (GOODHUE, MINN.). 3427

0742-2784 See COMPILER, THE. 1175

0742-2806 See NESTLE NUTRITION WORKSHOP SERIES. 4195

0742-2822 See ECHOCARDIOGRAPHY (MOUNT KISCO, N.Y.). 3704

0742-2830 See DIRECTORY OF SOVIET OFFICIALS. NATIONAL ORGANIZATIONS. 4644

0742-3012 See CONGRESSIONAL PRESENTATION / UNITED STATES TRADE AND DEVELOPMENT PROGRAM. 1552

0742-3071 See DIABETIC MEDICINE. 3728

0742-308X See GENERICS MAGAZINE. 4306

0742-3098 See JOURNAL OF PINEAL RESEARCH. 583

0742-3136 See UNIX REVIEW. 1239

0742-3187 See MONOGRAPH SERIES / AMERICAN GROUP PSYCHOTHERAPY ASSOCIATION. 3931

0742-3195 See ANTIMICROBIAL CHEMOTHERAPY SERIES. 3551

0742-3217 See DERMATOLOGY (NEW YORK, N.Y.). 3719

0742-3225 See FAMILY MEDICINE. 3737

0742-3233 See COMPUTERS IN LIFE SCIENCE EDUCATION. 1222

0742-3284 See MICHIGAN SPEECH-LANGUAGE-HEARING ASSOCIATION JOURNAL / MSHA. 4391

0742-3306 See DIRECTORY OF HOSPITALITY EDUCATORS. 2805

0742-3322 See ADVANCES IN STRATEGIC MANAGEMENT. 859

0742-3330 See SERBIAN STUDIES. 2709

0742-3349 See DIRECTORY OF DISTINGUISHED AMERICANS, THE. 432

0742-3381 See DIRECTORY & GUIDE - FLORIDA INSTITUTE OF CONSULTING ENGINEERS. 1970

0742-3438 See AGING NETWORK NEWS. 5178

0742-3497 See NONPROFIT COUNSEL, THE. 4338

0742-3519 See COLUMBUS COMPUTER XCHANGE. 1175

0742-3543 See AUSTIN BUSINESS EXECUTIVE. 641

0742-3616 See CURRENT TOPICS IN REPRODUCTIVE ENDOCRINOLOGY. 3727

0742-3624 See ALOFT. 2527

0742-3632 See CINCOM. 1106

0742-3640 See INTERNATIONAL JOURNAL ON WORLD PEACE. 4524

0742-3667 See PROCEEDINGS, ANNUAL CONFERENCE - NATIONAL CENTER FOR THE STUDY OF COLLECTIVE BARGAINING IN HIGHER EDUCATION AND THE PROFESSIONS (U.S.). CONFERENCE. 1842

0742-3675 See UNITED STATES TRADE FAIR. 952

0742-3705 See SYMPOSIUM PROCEEDINGS - SOCIETY OF EXPERIMENTAL TEST PILOTS. SYMPOSIUM. 37

0742-3713 See ECONOMIC DEVELOPMENT REVIEW (SCHILLER PARK, ILL.). 1483

0742-373X See DIRECTORY OF MEMBERS / THE MANUSCRIPT SOCIETY. 2773

0742-3748 See FREE PHILOSOPHER QUARTERLY, THE. 4347

0742-3799 See INSIDE NUTRITION. 4192

0742-3802 See SEMI-ANNUAL REPORT OF THE INSPECTOR GENERAL, U.S. SMALL BUSINESS ADMINISTRATION. 3103

0742-3888 See STATISTICS OF PUBLIC SCHOOL SYSTEMS IN THE TWENTY LARGEST U.S. CITIES. 1798

0742-3896 See L.E.R.S. MONOGRAPH SERIES. 3708

0742-390X See CURRENT ORNITHOLOGY. 5617

0742-3918 See TRACK TECHNIQUE. 4927

0742-3942 See BANKING LAW REPORT. 3085

0742-3950 See WOODALL'S ... TENT CAMPING GUIDE. WESTERN REGION. 5499

0742-3969 See WOODALL'S ... TENT CAMPING GUIDE. EASTERN EDITION. 4881

0742-3977 See WOODALL'S THE TENTING DIRECTORY. CENTRAL REGION. 4881

0742-3985 See INTERNATIONAL GUIDE TO PERIODICALS & REFERENCE WORKS. 5115

0742-4019 See ORTHODOX TRADITION. 4984

0742-4027 See BEST MEDIA. 1105

0742-4035 See CATALOG SHOPPER. 952

0742-4043 See NATIONAL WINTER STORMS OPERATIONS PLAN. 1432

0742-4051 See FOOD, DRUG, COSMETIC, AND MEDICAL DEVICE LAW DIGEST. 2971

0742-4094 See GENEALOGISTS IN THE UNITED STATES AND CANADA. 2450

0742-4108 See RECEPTORS AND LIGANDS IN INTERCELLULAR COMMUNICATION. 540

0742-4116 See MOVIES (NEW YORK, N.Y.), THE. 4075

0742-4124 See PRIME SOURCE MINI REFERENCE DIRECTORY. MOST WANTED NAMES AND ADDRESSES OF : MAIL ORDER COMPANIES. 704

0742-4132 See PRIME SOURCE MINI REFERENCE DIRECTORY. MOST WANTED NAMES AND ADDRESSES OF : MAILING LIST COMPANIES. 704

0742-4140 See PRIME SOURCE MINI REFERENCE DIRECTORY. MOST WANTED NAMES AND ADDRESSES OF : MANUFACTURERS' REPRESENTATIVES. 704

0742-4159 See PRIME SOURCE MINI REFERENCE DIRECTORY. MOST WANTED NAMES AND ADDRESSES OF : VENTURE CAPITAL COMPANY. 704

0742-4175 See PRIME SOURCE MINI REFERENCE DIRECTORY. MOST WANTED NAMES AND ADDRESSES OF : IMPORTER REGISTER. 704

0742-4183 See PRIME SOURCE MINI REFERENCE DIRECTORY. MOST WANTED NAMES AND ADDRESSES OF : CHAIN STORES AND DEPARTMENT STORES. 956

0742-4191 See PRIME SOURCE MINI REFERENCE DIRECTORY. MOST WANTED NAMES AND ADDRESSES OF--FOREIGN CONSULATE [I.E. CONSULATES] IN U.S.A. 4532

0742-4221 See DIABETES/METABOLISM REVIEWS. 3728

0742-4248 See CLUES (BOWLING GREEN, OHIO). 5074

0742-4256 See SOVIET SCIENTIFIC REVIEWS SUPPLEMENT SERIES. PHYSICOCHEMICAL BIOLOGY. 496

0742-4299 See OFFICIAL USFL GUIDE AND REGISTER. 4910

0742-4302 See VOICE (ORLAND PARK, ILL), THE. 145

0742-4329 See TENNESSEE ATTORNEYS DIRECTORY. 3063

0742-4345 See ALUMNI DIRECTORY / UNIVERSITY OF CALIFORNIA, DAVIS. 1100

0742-4353 See ALUMNI DIRECTORY - UNIVERSITY OF CALIFORNIA, BERKELEY. GRADUATE SCHOOL OF BUSINESS ADMINISTRATION. 1099

0742-4361 See NCAA MEN'S LACROSSE RULES. 4907

0742-4388 See NATIONAL TORT LAW DIGESTS. 3014

0742-4426 See RIVER QUALITY REPORT. 2242

0742-4442 See POCKET PRICE GUIDE. 2812

0742-4477 See AGRIBUSINESS (NEW YORK, N.Y.). 48

0742-4485 See GOLF DIGEST ALMANAC, THE. 4896

0742-4493 See CALIFORNIA BRIDE. LOS ANGELES EDITION. 2277

0742-4523 See U.S. MOPED, 3 & 4 WHEELER, MOTOR SCOOTERS, ETC. IMPORTS. 5375

0742-454X See RED FOX REVIEW. 3428

0742-4566 See COUNTRY CHRONICLE, THE. 5766

0742-4574 See BOXES AND ARROWS. 1253

0742-4582 See MONTHLY REPORT ON THE NUCLEAR FUEL MARKET. 2156

0742-4612 See MISSISSIPPI RAG, THE. 4131

0742-4639 See WORD AMONG US, THE. 5038

0742-4647 See MEALEY'S LITIGATION REPORTS. ASBESTOS. 3007

0742-4655 See MEALEY'S LITIGATION REPORTS. IRANIAN CLAIMS. 3132

0742-4671 See JOURNAL OF FILM AND VIDEO. 4073

0742-4698 See INTERNATIONAL JOURNAL OF WORLD STUDIES, THE. 4524

0742-4701 See ADVOCATE MEN. 5186

0742-471X See AWARE (DARBY, PA.). 4768

0742-4728 See E NEW YORKE. 2532

0742-4744 See LIVINGSTON FAMILY NEWSLETTER. 2458

0742-4779 See HEIR LINES (LEBANON, OHIO). 2452

0742-4787 See JOURNAL OF TRIBOLOGY. 2119

0742-4795 See JOURNAL OF ENGINEERING FOR GAS TURBINES AND POWER. 2118

0742-4817 See LOS ANGELES TIMES INDEX. 5692

0742-4825 See INTERNATIONAL TECHNOLOGY DISCLOSURES. 1305

0742-4914 See BIBLIOGRAPHY ON CABLE TELEVISION : BCTV. 1124

0742-4930 See TEACHING, LEARNING, COMPUTING : TLC. 1225

0742-4949 See PETERSON'S GUIDE TO COLLEGES IN THE MIDWEST. 1841

0742-4957 See PETERSON'S GUIDE TO COLLEGES IN THE MIDDLE ATLANTIC STATES. 1841

0742-4965 See PETERSON'S GUIDE TO COLLEGES IN NEW YORK. 1840

0742-4973 See PETERSON'S GUIDE TO COLLEGES IN NEW ENGLAND. 1840

0742-4981 See PAGES (NORTHEAST ED.). 5488

0742-499X See MISSISSIPPI BIBLE AND CEMETERY RECORDS. 2460

0742-5007 See ALUMNAE DIRECTORY / THE BREARLEY SCHOOL. 1096

0742-5015 See TRI-COUNTY SEARCHER, THE. 2476

0742-504X See IBRO HANDBOOK SERIES. 3833

0742-5058 See SOFTWARE EXPRESS. 1272

0742-5066 See ANNUAL REPORT - CHESAPEAKE BAY FOUNDATION. 4162

0742-5074 See PROFILE OF REAL ESTATE FIRMS. 4843

0742-5120 See LICENSING, COUNTERSIGNING, AND SURPLUS LINE LAWS FOR THE 50 STATES, DISTRICT OF COLUMBIA, PUERTO RICO, AND THE VIRGIN ISLANDS. 3003

0742-5139 See FINANCIAL DIRECTORY OF PENSION FUNDS. IDAHO. 1670

0742-5244 See INSIGHT (BOSTON, MASS.). 3396

0742-5252 See ELLIOTT WAVE THEORIST, THE. 897

0742-5287 See HISPANIC LINGUISTICS. 3285

0742-5317 See REPORT - FEDERAL BAR ASSOCIATION. SECTION OF TAXATION. 3037

0742-5325 See PUBLIC JUSTICE REPORT. 4676

0742-5333 See INTERNATIONAL DOCUMENTARY. 4072

0742-5341 See REPORT ON IBM, THE. 1201

0742-5368 See PANTHEIST VISION. 4354

0742-5376 See TIMELINES (EUGENE, OR). 2253

0742-5384 See TELECOMMUNICATIONS ALERT. 1165

0742-5430 See LIAISON BULLETIN (WASHINGTON, D.C.). 1881

0742-5457 See ASIAN THEATRE JOURNAL. 383

0742-5465 See CALIFORNIAN (CUPERTINO, CALIF.), THE. 2726

0742-5473 See DICKENS QUARTERLY. 3381

0742-5503 See MYSTICS QUARTERLY (IOWA CITY, IOWA). 3414

0742-5511 See GROUNDS MANAGEMENT FORUM. 2418

0742-552X See DETENTION REPORTER. 3163

0742-5538 See HISTORICAL GUIDES TO THE WORLD'S PERIODICALS AND NEWSPAPERS. 2920

0742-5546 See PROCEEDINGS - DISTILLERS FEED CONFERENCE (1980). 2353

0742-5562 See JOURNAL OF THE MIDWEST MODERN LANGUAGE ASSOCIATION, THE. 3292

0742-5589 See BUY BLACK. 952

0742-5600 See REAL ESTATE COMPUTER REVIEW. 4844

0742-5627 See INNOVATIVE HIGHER EDUCATION. 1830

0742-5678 See CAROLINA REAL ESTATE JOURNAL. 4835

0742-5686 See COMPUT-A-CAL. 5174

0742-5694 See BUILDING PRODUCTS DIGEST. 2399

0742-5716 See COMPUTER-AIDED DESIGN, ENGINEERING, AND DRAFTING. 1231

0742-5759 See LIBRARY SOFTWARE REVIEW. 1288

0742-5783 See RADIO PC REPORT. 1137

0742-5805 See OFFICIAL PRICE GUIDE TO ANTIQUE JEWELRY, THE. 2915

0742-5821 See INTERNATIONAL DIRECTORY OF NUCLEAR UTILITIES. 2156

0742-583X See NORTHEAST ALABAMA SETTLERS. 2464

0742-5848 See CONVENIENCE STORE INDUSTRY'S COMPENSATION SURVEY REPORT FOR ..., THE. 1661

0742-5872 See NATCHITOCHES GENEALOGIST, THE. 2461

0742-5910 See ALL-IRELAND HERITAGE, THE. 2436

0742-5929 See JOURNAL OF CHINESE STUDIES (ALBUQUERQUE, N.M.). 2505

0742-5937 See COMPENSATION REPORT, MANAGEMENT EMPLOYEES IN HOSPITAL & NURSING HOME MANAGEMENT COMPANIES. 939

0742-5953 See IFAC PROCEEDINGS SERIES. 1219

0742-597X See JOURNAL OF MANAGEMENT IN ENGINEERING. 1983

0742-5996 See RING SYSTEMS HANDBOOK. 1047

0742-6003 See 1199 NEWS. 1642

0742-602X See MERGER AND ACQUISITION SOURCEBOOK. 693

0742-6038 See WHO'S WHO IN NORTH DAKOTA. 437

0742-6046 See PSYCHOLOGY & MARKETING. 935

0742-6062 See ENVIRONMENTAL AUDIT ADVISER. 2192

0742-6089 See USED COMPUTER GUIDE. 1239

0742-6100 See AMERICAN ILLUSTRATION SHOWCASE. 376

0742-6143 See SALARIES OF ENGINEERS IN EDUCATION. 1995

0742-6151 See GTE NETWORK SYSTEMS WORLD-WIDE COMMUNICATIONS JOURNAL. 1112

0742-616X See ADMINISTRATION LAW JUDGE DECISIONS REPORT. 3143

0742-6178 See HOUSING PRODUCTION (BALTIMORE, MD.). 2825

0742-6186 See ADVANCES IN INDUSTRIAL AND LABOR RELATIONS. 1642

0742-6208 See RV BUYERS GUIDE. 5392

0742-6216 See UNIFORM CPA EXAMINATION. QUESTIONS AND UNOFFICIAL ANSWERS. 752

0742-6224 See YEATS. 3455

0742-6240 See HIGH ROADS FOLIO. 2534

0742-6283 See ANNUAL LABOR MARKET REVIEW. HACKENSACK LABOR AREA #5600, NEW JERSEY. 1645

0742-6291 See JOURNAL OF MINORITY AGING, THE. 5180

0742-6313 See ADVANCES IN MENTAL RETARDATION AND DEVELOPMENTAL DISABILITIES. 3919

0742-6321 See WHO'S WHO IN STAINED GLASS. 437

0742-633X See INFOPRENEUR. 1157

0742-6348 See NORTHERN JOURNAL OF APPLIED FORESTRY. 2389

0742-6356 See WINEGAR TREE, THE. 2477

0742-6410 See HAZARD MONTHLY. 2230

0742-6445 See TELECOM INSIDER. 1164

0742-650X See FERNBANK QUARTERLY. 5105

0742-6534 See CATALYST (MONTPELIER, VT.). 1468

0742-6550 See BUSINESS JOURNAL (PORTLAND, OR.), THE. 650

0742-6607 See JR. (PETERBOROUGH, N.H.). 1268

0742-6615 See DZIENNIK ZWIAZKOWY. 5660

0742-6631 See GERMANTOWN CRIER. 2734

0742-6739 See FILM INDUSTRY GAZETTE. 4070

0742-6755 See DIRECTORY OF INFORMATION AGE NEWSLETTERS. 1237

0742-6771 See IRISH AMERICAN WHO'S WHO, THE. 433

0742-678X See DIRECTIONS (AUSTIN, TEX.). 1237

0742-6801 See BIBLIOGRAPHIES AND INDEXES IN WORLD LITERATURE. 3366

0742-681X See BIBLIOGRAPHIES AND INDEXES IN PSYCHOLOGY. 4577

0742-6828 See BIBLIOGRAPHIES AND INDEXES IN AMERICAN HISTORY. 2634

0742-6836 See BIBLIOGRAPHIES AND INDEXES IN RELIGIOUS STUDIES. 4939

0742-6844 See BIBLIOGRAPHIES AND INDEXES IN ANTHROPOLOGY. 248

0742-6852 See BIBLIOGRAPHIES AND INDEXES IN WORLD HISTORY. 2634

0742-6860 See BIBLIOGRAPHIES AND INDEXES IN AMERICAN LITERATURE. 3457

0742-6895 See BIBLIOGRAPHIES AND INDEXES IN SOCIOLOGY. 5266

0742-6909 See BIBLIOGRAPHIES AND INDEXES IN LAW AND POLITICAL SCIENCE. 4501

0742-6917 See BIBLIOGRAPHIES AND INDEXES IN EDUCATION. 1793

0742-695X See BIO-BIBLIOGRAPHIES IN AMERICAN LITERATURE. 3367

0742-6968 See BIO-BIBLIOGRAPHIES IN MUSIC. 4103

0742-6984 See RELIGION & SOCIETY REPORT, THE. 4991

0742-700X See INTERNATIONAL PLAYERS CHESS NEWS, THE. 4862

0742-7077 See SATELLITE DIRECTORY AND BUYERS GUIDE. 1163

0742-7085 See PENSION AND PROFIT SHARING PLANS FOR SMALL & MEDIUM SIZE BUSINESS. 703

0742-7107 See MODELTEC. 5129

0742-7115 See CONSTITUTIONAL COMMENTARY. 3092

0742-7123 See NEW BOOKS ON WOMEN AND FEMINISM. 5562

0742-714X See NATIONAL SURVEY OF FISHING, HUNTING, AND WILDLIFE-ASSOCIATED RECREATION. LOUISIANA. 4875

0742-7158 See NATIONAL SURVEY OF FISHING, HUNTING, AND WILDLIFE-ASSOCIATED RECREATION. ILLINOIS. 4875

0742-7166 See NATIONAL SURVEY OF FISHING, HUNTING, AND WILDLIFE-ASSOCIATED RECREATION. CONNECTICUT. 4875

0742-7174 See NATIONAL SURVEY OF FISHING, HUNTING, AND WILDLIFE-ASSOCIATED RECREATION. ARKANSAS. 4875

0742-7190 See NATIONAL SURVEY OF FISHING, HUNTING, AND WILDLIFE-ASSOCIATED RECREATION. NEW YORK. 4875

0742-7204 See DIRECTORY OF NEW MEXICO MANUFACTURERS (1991). 1604

0742-7212 See ANCESTOR CHARTS. 2437

0742-7263 See OIL SCOUTS DIRECTORY. 4270

0742-7271 See BULLETIN (UNITED STATES. BUREAU OF JUSTICE STATISTICS). 3079

0742-728X See ARMY MORALE, WELFARE, AND RECREATION. 4036

0742-7298 See ANAHEIM ... BUSINESS AND INDUSTRIAL DIRECTORY. 638

0742-7301 See RESEARCH IN PERSONNEL AND HUMAN RESOURCES MANAGEMENT. 946

0742-731X See RETROFIT OF BUILDING ENERGY SYSTEMS AND PROCESSES. 2608

0742-7328 See SUPPLEMENT TO THE ANNUAL ENERGY OUTLOOK. 1958

0742-7352 See TALLASU HANIN CHUSO MIT OPSOROK. 714

0742-7379 See AIRPORT EXECUTIVES. 10

0742-7387 See INTERNATIONAL ART MATERIAL DIRECTORY AND BUYERS' GUIDE. 353

0742-7417 See AUTOMOBILES CLASSIQUES (ENGLISH EDITION). 5406

0742-7425 See INFORMATION SERIES - VIRGINIA POLYTECHNIC INSTITUTE AND STATE UNIVERSITY. COLLEGE OF AGRICULTURE AND LIFE SCIENCES. 96

0742-7433 See FEMINIST PERIODICALS (MADISON, WIS.). 5556

0742-7441 See FEMINIST COLLECTIONS (MADISON, WIS.). 5556

0742-745X See PROGRESS IN CLINICAL RHEUMATOLOGY. 3806

0742-7476 See COMPARATIVE COSTS AND STAFFING REPORT FOR COLLEGE AND UNIVERSITY FACILITIES. 1862

0742-7522 See GRADUATE STUDIES JOURNAL. 1800

0742-7603 See NIOSH REPORT ON OCCUPATIONAL SAFETY AND HEALTH. 2866

0742-7611 See SEMIOTICS. 3320

0742-762X See MLA REPORT, THE. 3182

0742-7638 See YALOBUSHA PIONEER. 2766

0742-7654 See KINFOLKS (LAKE CHARLES, LA.). 2457

0742-7700 See GRAPPA. 2367

0742-7719 See INTERNATIONAL BLOOD/PLASMA NEWS. 3772

0742-7727 See HOOFPRINTS FROM THE YELLOWSTONE CORRAL OF THE WESTERNERS. 2738

0742-7735 See ALASKAN EPIPHANY. 5054

0742-7751 See ACT NEWSLETTER (SIMSBURY, CONN.). 1887

0742-7778 See CALICO JOURNAL. 1222

0742-7808 See UNITED STATES SWIMMING RULES AND REGULATIONS. 4927

0742-7816 See FEDERAL TAXATION (HOUSTON, TEX.). 4724

0742-7824 See CORPORATE, PARTNERSHIP, ESTATE AND GIFT TAXATION. 4719

0742-7832 See INDIVIDUAL TAXATION. 4732

0742-7859 See PRACTICAL SUPERVISION. 882

0742-7921 See CATALOG - FORESTRY SUPPLIERS, INC. 2377

0742-793X See PENNSYLVANIA RECREATION & PARKS. 4707

0742-7972 See LAPIDUS LETTER, THE. 2537

0742-7999 See HORSETRADER, THE. 2800

0742-8014 See RAHAVARD : NASHRIYAH-I ANJUMAN-I DUSTDARAN-I FARHANG-I FARSI. 2662

0742-8022 See ANNUAL EVALUATION - NEW MEXICO. ENVIRONMENTAL IMPROVEMENT DIVISION. 2160

0742-8057 See COLLEGE REVIEW (DENVER, COLO.), THE. 3567

0742-8065 See HOSIERY NEWS / NATIONAL ASSOCIATION OF HOSIERY MANUFACTURERS. 5351

0742-8073 See MOTOR HOME TRADE-IN GUIDE. 2828

0742-8111 See VIDEO TIMES (SKOKIE, ILL.). 4378

0742-812X See COLLECTIBLE AUTOMOBILE. 5411

0742-8146 See MICHIGAN FINANCIAL JOURNAL. 798

0742-8162 See REMARK. 1201

0742-8170 See N.Y. JOURNAL JAPAN. 4529

0742-8189 See BRUCE DAVID COHEN'S THE GOOD LIFE. 2529

0742-8197 See AMERICAN EAGLE (ESTERO, FLA.), THE. 2609

0742-8219 See HORTIDEAS. 2419

0742-8227 See CURRENT STUDIES IN LIBRARIANSHIP. 3205

0742-826X See JOURNAL OF DIETETIC SOFTWARE. 4193

0742-8278 See NEW MEXICO MUSICIAN, THE. 4140

0742-8286 See COMMERCIAL-NEWS (DANVILLE, ILL.), THE. 5659

0742-8308 See BICYCLE PAPER, THE. 428

0742-8316 See PRENTISS HEADLIGHT, THE. 5701

0742-8367 See KENTUCKY NURSE. 3860

0742-8383 See DIAGNOSTIC RADIOLOGY SERIES (NEW YORK, N.Y.). 3940

0742-8413 See COMPARATIVE BIOCHEMISTRY AND PHYSIOLOGY. C, COMPARATIVE PHARMACOLOGY AND TOXICOLOGY. 4297

0742-843X See STATES AND SMALL BUSINESS, THE. 713

0742-8464 See GUIDE TO PETROLEUM STATISTICAL INFORMATION. 4283

0742-8472 See BULLETIN / OVERHOLSER FAMILY ASSOCIATION. 2441

0742-8480 See COLLEGE BAND DIRECTORS NATIONAL ASSOCIATION JOURNAL. 4110

0742-8502 See URANIUM MILL TAILINGS MANAGEMENT. 2152

0742-8510 See WHO'S WHO IN WEST VIRGINIA (CLARKSBURG, W. VA.). 438

0742-8695 See NUEXCO REVIEW. 2157

0742-8820 See WHITE LIGHT, THE. 4243

0742-8839 See MOTION PICTURE INVESTOR. 908

0742-8871 See STATUS REPORT - UNITED STATES. HEALTH CARE FINANCING ADMINISTRATION. OFFICE OF RESEARCH AND DEMONSTRATIONS. 3643

0742-888X See TAX SHELTER ANALYST. 3062

0742-8898 See MAGICK CIRCLE DIRECTORY OF OCCULT GOODS AND SERVICES, THE. 4242

0742-8901 See GOVERNMENT CONTRACTS SECTION NEWSLETTER. 2975

0742-891X See ELLIOTT WAVE COMMODITY LETTER, THE. 897

0742-8928 See COMPASS ROSE. 658

0742-8936 See SOUTH DAKOTA AUTHORS' CATALOG. 4832

0742-8987 See CAMPBELL'S LIST. 2947

0742-8995 See BULLETIN - COSMOS CLUB (WASHINGTON, D.C.). 5229

0742-9045 See NATIONAL DIRECTORY OF LOCAL RESEARCHERS. 2462

0742-9061 See ANNUAL REPORT - MAINE. DEPT. OF MARINE RESOURCES. 442

0742-907X See INDOCHINA JOURNAL. 2653

0742-9088 See REPRODUCER, THE. 2777

0742-910X See AQUA-FIELD SPORTSMAN. 3475

0742-9118 See DIRECTORY OF USSR FOREIGN TRADE ORGANIZATIONS AND OFFICIALS. 831

0742-9223 See JOB SEARCH. A GUIDE FOR UNIVERSITY OF VERMONT STUDENTS. 4205

0742-924X See CONNECTICUT INSURANCE LAW REVIEW, THE. 2955

0742-9258 See NEWSLETTER (GENEALOGICAL SOCIETY OF ORIGINAL MUSCOGEE COUNTY). 2463

0742-9266 See OHIO BAR REPORTS. 3021

0742-9274 See N.A.D.A. MOBILE HOME MANUFACTURED HOUSING APPRAISAL GUIDE. 3485

0742-9282 See ADVANCE FORECAST REPORT TO THE MINNESOTA ENVIRONMENTAL QUALITY BOARD 2034

0742-9347 See NEW HAMPSHIRE COLLEGE JOURNAL. 1093

0742-9363 See BUILDING A MARRIAGE. 2277

0742-938X See VDT NEWS. 4806

0742-9398 See MICRO MONEY. 1269

0742-9428 See DIARIO, LA PRENSA, EL. 5716

0742-9436 See INTERFEM. 5559

0742-9487 See COOPERATIVE INFORMATION REPORT. 76

0742-9495 See FARMER COOPERATIVE STATISTICS. 1532

0742-9533 See CALDWELL COUNTY GENEALOGICAL SOCIETY, INC. 2441

0742-9576 See ARAB AMERICAN ALMANAC. 2721

0742-9622 See CARDIO. 3700

0742-9649 See DUN'S LATIN AMERICA'S TOP 25,000. 669

0742-9657 See MUTUAL FUND LETTER, THE. 908

0742-9665 See LEBANON NEWS (WASHINGTON, D.C. 1978). 2489

0742-9673 See ADMINISTRATIVE LAW NOTES / SECTION ON ADMINISTRATIVE LAW, FEDERAL BAR ASSOCIATION. 3091

0742-9681 See READER (HOUGHTON, MICH.). 1777

0742-969X See HOSPICE JOURNAL, THE. 5288

0742-9738 See MAWA REVIEW. 3410

0742-9746 See PET LOVERS' GAZETTE. 4287

0742-9770 See PRYOR REPORT, THE. 4209

0742-9797 See MEXICAN STUDIES. 1505

0742-9800 See CODING CLINIC FOR ICD-9-CM. 3778

0742-9819 See FOCUS ON SURGICAL EDUCATION. 3965

0742-9851 See BRANCHES & TWIGS : NEWSLETTER OF GENEALOGICAL SOCIETY OF VERMONT. 2440

0742-986X See MEMBER'S YEAR BOOK - AMERICAN SOCIETY OF CORPORATE SECRETARIES. 879

0742-9908 See RENAISSANCE TOO MAGAZINE. 2544

0742-9916 See OUTLOOK ON IBM. 1238

0742-9940 See PRACTICE (NEW YORK, N.Y.). 4545

0742-9967 See IOWA RULES OF COURT. 3141

0742-9975 See CORPORATE SHOWCASE. 377

0743-0019 See JOURNAL OF TURKISH STUDIES. 5207

0743-0043 See BRICK IN ARCHITECTURE. 293

0743-0159 See FINANCIAL COMPUTING. 1185

0743-0167 See JOURNAL OF RURAL STUDIES. 5250

0743-0175 See DEFENSE ANALYSIS. 4040

0743-0183 See AICHE APPLICATIONS SOFTWARE SURVEY FOR PERSONAL COMPUTERS. 1284

0743-023X See MANUFACTURING OPERATIONS. 3484

0743-0248 See IAFC COMMITTEE LIST. 616

0743-0264 See LIVING ANEW. 4603

0743-0272 See CORPORATE CONTROL ALERT. 895

0743-0299 See ASBESTOS PROPERTY LITIGATION REPORTER. 599

0743-0302 See MICROCOMPUTERS FOR LIBRARIES. 1269

0743-0310 See BENCHMARK (WASHINGTON, D.C.). 3092

0743-0345 See SURVEYS AND REFERENCE WORKS IN MATHEMATICS. 3537

0743-037X See NEW IN COMPUTING MAGAZINE AND BUYER'S GUIDE. 1238

0743-0388 See PERSPECTIVES (ARLINGTON, VA.). 4673

0743-0396 See COUNTERTRADE OUTLOOK. 830

0743-040X See ARLIS/NA UPDATE. 3192

0743-0450 See PROCEEDINGS OF THE ANNUAL CONVENTION - AMERICAN ASSOCIATION OF BOVINE PRACTITIONERS. CONVENTION. 5519

0743-0493 See JOURNAL OF REALITY THERAPY. 4600

0743-0515 See POLYMERIC MATERIALS SCIENCE AND ENGINEERING. 4459

0743-0531 See METHODS IN EXPLORATION SERIES. 4264

0743-0604 See SHORT-TERM ENERGY OUTLOOK. QUARTERLY PROJECTIONS. 1956

0743-0620 See SHORT-TERM ENERGY OUTLOOK. VOLUME II, METHODOLOGY. 1956

0743-0663 See AAA WORLD (MISSISSIPPI EDITION). 5459

0743-0701 See ROBOT INSIDER. 1221

0743-071X See EMPIRICAL STUDIES OF PSYCHOANALYTICAL THEORIES. 3925

0743-0728 See HANDBOOK OF STATE LEGISLATIVE LEADERS, THE. 4475

0743-0736 See AAA WORLD (LOUISIANA ED.). 5459

0743-0744 See FLORIDA TOURISM HOTLINE. 5470

0743-0752 See REVIEWS OF INFRARED AND MILLIMETER WAVES. 4441

0743-0760 See REVIEW OF PROGRESS IN QUANTITATIVE NONDESTRUCTIVE EVALUATION. 1994

0743-0779 See GROWTH AND MATURATION FACTORS. 580

0743-0809 See PRUDENT SPECULATOR, THE. 912

0743-0841 See ANIMAL WELFARE INSTITUTE QUARTERLY, THE. 225

0743-0868 See CALIFORNIA COUNTY. 2529

0743-0876 See OCEAN AIR INTERACTIONS. 1359

0743-0892 See OVERSEAS JOB-PERSONALQUARTER. 1700

0743-0914 See JACKSONVILLE JOURNAL. 5650

0743-0922 See CAPEARTS. 370

0743-0957 See BONNET-T-E'S & KIN, THE. 2439

0743-0973 See FODOR'S SCOTLAND. 5473

0743-0981 *See* ANNUAL REPORT / KANSAS ADVISORY COUNCIL ON AGING. **3749**

0743-1007 *See* CONTACTS INFLUENTIAL. DENVER. **660**

0743-1031 *See* MOTOR EMISSION CONTROL MANUAL. **5419**

0743-1066 *See* JOURNAL OF LOGIC PROGRAMMING, THE. **1280**

0743-1082 *See* POLITICS AND POLICY. **4490**

0743-1090 *See* WILEY/RONALD-NATIONAL ASSOCIATION OF ACCOUNTANTS PROFESSIONAL BOOK SERIES. **753**

0743-1112 *See* LEXUS USA. **1288**

0743-1155 *See* SPORTSWEAR INTERNATIONAL (U.S.A. ED.). **1087**

0743-1163 *See* TEXAS MANUFACTURERS REGISTER. **3488**

0743-1171 *See* SALES AIDS HOTLINE, THE. **708**

0743-1236 *See* INDEPENDENT SECTOR. **4655**

0743-1244 *See* RETURN TO THE SOURCE. **4993**

0743-1279 *See* MB NEWS (NEW YORK, N.Y.). **1134**

0743-1287 *See* ANNUAL REPORT / THE AMERICAN COMMITTEE ON AFRICA. **4464**

0743-1309 *See* SCOUTING REPORT, THE. **4917**

0743-1333 *See* WEST VIRGINIA DOCTORS OF MEDICINE. **3917**

0743-1341 *See* NEWSLETTER OF THE NORTH SUBURBAN GENEALOGICAL SOCIETY. **2463**

0743-1384 *See* TALK OF THE MONTH. **3444**

0743-1406 *See* SOUTHERN CALIFORNIA ANTHOLOGY, THE. **3438**

0743-1422 *See* LONG TERM CARE MANAGEMENT. **3605**

0743-1430 *See* PAC-NEWS. **3240**

0743-1449 *See* REGISTER OF FORMER CADETS. SUPPLEMENT. **4055**

0743-1481 *See* RBMS NEWSLETTER. **4832**

0743-1503 *See* IN JOPLIN METROPOLITAN. **5480**

0743-1511 *See* TIMESDAILY (SHOALS EDITION). **5628**

0743-152X *See* TIMESDAILY (REGIONAL ED.). **5628**

0743-1546 *See* PROCEEDINGS OF THE ... IEEE CONFERENCE ON DECISION & CONTROL. **2077**

0743-1562 *See* DIGEST OF TECHNICAL PAPERS / SYMPOSIUM ON VLSI TECHNOLOGY. **2041**

0743-1570 *See* COMPENDIUM OF TECHNICAL PAPERS : INSTITUTE OF TRANSPORTATION ENGINEERS ... ANNUAL MEETING. **5439**

0743-1589 *See* WORKSHOP SUMMARIES : A PUBLICATION OF THE AMERICAN SOCIETY OF PLANT PHYSIOLOGISTS. **587**

0743-1597 *See* PROGRESS IN COMPUTER SCIENCE. **1201**

0743-1619 *See* PROCEEDINGS OF THE AMERICAN CONTROL CONFERENCE. **1991**

0743-1635 *See* CPL BIBLIOGRAPHY. **2840**

0743-1643 *See* PROGRESS IN MATHEMATICS (BOSTON, MASS.). **3528**

0743-1651 *See* PROGRESS REPORTS (WELDING RESEARCH COUNCIL (US)). **4027**

0743-166X *See* PROCEEDINGS / IEEE INFOCOM. **1200**

0743-1694 *See* URPE. **1525**

0743-1732 *See* CASE 1. **2020**

0743-1740 *See* YEAR'S BEST SCIENCE FICTION (NEW YORK, N.Y.), THE. **3455**

0743-1759 *See* NORTH CAROLINA JOURNAL OF INTERNATIONAL LAW AND COMMERCIAL REGULATION. **3133**

0743-1767 *See* ANNUAL REPORT / HAWAII COASTAL ZONE MANAGEMENT PROGRAM. **2814**

0743-1791 *See* BOSTON GLOBE, THE. **5687**

0743-1813 *See* CONTACTS INFLUENTIAL. PHOENIX, ARIZONA. **660**

0743-183X *See* BLUE MOUNTAIN HERITAGE. **2439**

0743-1848 *See* VOIX DES PRAIRIES, LA. **2476**

0743-1856 *See* MISSISSIPPI ARMCHAIR RESEARCHER, THE. **2460**

0743-1864 *See* COMMUNITY AFFAIRS QUARTERLY. **2818**

0743-1872 *See* CRIME LABORATORY DIGEST. **3080**

0743-2097 *See* PAPERS OF LEVERETT SALTONSTALL, THE. **2625**

0743-2135 *See* INTERFACES IN PSYCHOLOGY. **4590**

0743-216X *See* DAY RESEARCHER. **2445**

0743-2224 *See* COMPLETE BOOK OF TAX DEDUCTIONS. **4718**

0743-2259 *See* FOOTWORK. **2846**

0743-2267 *See* STEAMBOAT SPRINGS MAGAZINE. **2493**

0743-2283 *See* TELESPAN. **1167**

0743-2291 *See* CHINESE FOR AFFIRMATIVE ACTION NEWSLETTER. **4468**

0743-2348 *See* AMERICAN BUSINESS REVIEW. **859**

0743-2356 *See* WOMAN OF POWER. **5569**

0743-2399 *See* WORLD CHRISTIAN : TODAY'S MISSION MAGAZINE. **5010**

0743-2402 *See* CVC VIDEO REPORT. **2040**

0743-2410 *See* ANDREJ BELYJ SOCIETY NEWSLETTER, THE. **3457**

0743-2429 *See* INTERNATIONAL JOURNAL OF FRONTIER MISSIONS. **4965**

0743-2453 *See* SOUTH CAROLINA APPELLATE DIGEST, THE. **3057**

0743-2461 *See* BEST-SELLING HOME PLANS FROM HOME MAGAZINE. **2899**

0743-247X *See* EQUITABLE DISTRIBUTION JOURNAL. **2967**

0743-2496 *See* VIETNAM WAR NEWSLETTER. **4060**

0743-250X *See* COUNTERTRADE & BARTER INTERNATIONAL. **830**

0743-2534 *See* PC ABSTRACTS. **1270**

0743-2550 *See* JOURNAL OF CHRISTIAN NURSING. **3858**

0743-2569 *See* COST OF LIVING NEWS. **1552**

0743-2577 *See* KORION PIPUL. **2266**

0743-2623 *See* CONTACTS INFLUENTIAL. DALLAS, DALLAS COUNTY, TEXAS. **660**

0743-264X *See* CONTACTS INFLUENTIAL. WASHINGTON, D.C. **660**

0743-2674 *See* CONTACTS INFLUENTIAL. PORTLAND, OREGON. **660**

0743-2682 *See* CONTACTS INFLUENTIAL. EAST BAY. **660**

0743-2690 *See* CONTACTS INFLUENTIAL. SAN FRANCISCO, CALIFORNIA. **660**

0743-2712 *See* CONTACTS INFLUENTIAL. SOUTH SAN DIEGO COUNTY. **660**

0743-2755 *See* AMELIA. **3360**

0743-2763 *See* KRIEGBAUM HERITAGE, THE. **2457**

0743-2801 *See* AMONG THE COLES. **2437**

0743-281X *See* LOG TRAIN, THE. **5432**

0743-2828 *See* GREEN COUNTRY QUARTERLY, THE. **2452**

0743-2844 *See* INTERIOR BUDGET IN BRIEF, THE. **4657**

0743-2860 *See* DORM. **1091**

0743-2895 *See* INSIDE THE LEADING MAIL ORDER HOUSES. **760**

0743-2917 *See* BLUE MOON. **3367**

0743-2925 *See* ILLINOIS SMALL PRESS DIRECTORY. **4815**

0743-3069 *See* SPACE ENTERPRISE TODAY. **35**

0743-3085 *See* OF SUBSTANCE. **3021**

0743-3107 *See* CONTINENTAL DRIFTER. **3378**

0743-3115 *See* PIZZA TODAY. **2353**

0743-3174 See NORTHEAST ALABAMA SETTLERS. **2464**

0743-3182 *See* CAR CRAFT ANNUAL. **5409**

0743-3204 *See* BOMB (NEW YORK, N.Y.). **316**

0743-3271 *See* INDUSTRIAL WEST (EL MONTE, CALIF.). **1611**

0743-3328 *See* FODOR'S TEXAS. **5473**

0743-3336 *See* FODOR'S LOS ANGELES AND NEARBY ATTRACTIONS. **5472**

0743-3433 *See* NEW ISSUES ALERT. **909**

0743-3441 *See* FLORIDA UNDERWRITER. **2881**

0743-3492 *See* INDEX TO ELECTRIC UTILITY WEEK. **4761**

0743-3522 *See* NEWS / ART DECO SOCIETY OF NEW YORK. **359**

0743-3530 *See* MAXIMUM ROCKNROLL. **4130**

0743-3778 *See* WHOLESALE DRUGS MAGAZINE. **4332**

0743-3794 *See* CPA EXAMINATION REVIEW. THEORY AND PRACTICE. **742**

0743-3808 *See* BEHAVIOR RESEARCH METHODS, INSTRUMENTS, & COMPUTERS : A JOURNAL OF THE PSYCHONOMIC SOCIETY, INC. **4576**

0743-3816 *See* SOCIETY FOR ORGANIC PETROLOGY NEWSLETTER, THE. **1459**

0743-3832 *See* MEETING PLANNERS ALERT. **944**

0743-3840 *See* CLAIMS ADMINISTRATION, INSURANCE, TORT COURT DECISIONS DIGEST. **2878**

0743-3859 *See* CLAIMS ADMINISTRATION, WORKERS' COMPENSATION COURT DECISIONS DIGEST. **2878**

0743-3875 See CLAIMS ADMINISTRATION, INSURANCE, TORT COURT DECISIONS DIGEST. **2878**

0743-3883 *See* CHALLENGE GRANTS / NATIONAL ENDOWMENT FOR THE ARTS. **317**

0743-3913 *See* JAGUAR JOURNAL. **5417**

0743-3921 *See* PERSONAL TAX & FINANCIAL PLANNING GUIDE. **4740**

0743-3956 *See* NATIONAL MEAT PACKER REFERENCE GUIDE. **216**

0743-3972 *See* WOMEN'S LARGE & HALF SIZE SPECIALTY STORES. **1088**

0743-4081 *See* NATIONAL DIRECTORY OF BLIND TEACHERS. **1766**

0743-409X *See* PROCEEDINGS / SYMPOSIUM AND EXHIBITION ON THE ART OF GLASSBLOWING. **2593**

0743-4103 *See* INDEX TO THE SEMI-PROFESSIONAL FANTASY MAGAZINES. **3396**

0743-4111 *See* MCCLURE CENTER MAGAZINE. **1195**

0743-412X *See* TRIAL ADVOCATE QUARTERLY. **3066**

0743-4146 *See* ANNUAL INSTITUTE OF EMPLOYMENT LAW. **3144**

0743-4154 *See* RESEARCH IN THE HISTORY OF ECONOMIC THOUGHT AND METHODOLOGY. **1594**

0743-4189 *See* SHAA. **4393**

0743-4197 *See* COUNTY INFORMATION SERVICE. **4641**

0743-4227 *See* ASTRO-NEWS (BATON ROUGE, LA.). **390**

0743-4243 *See* VIRGINIAN (STAUNTON, VA.), THE. **2549**

0743-4251 *See* ABSTRACTS IN MARYLAND ARCHEOLOGY. **253**

0743-4324 *See* SURVEY OF PRESS FREEDOM IN LATIN AMERICA, A. **4497**

0743-4405 *See* ALUMNI DIRECTORY / GROVE CITY COLLEGE. **1098**

0743-4448 *See* PINE TREE FLYER. **5434**

0743-4499 *See* SURVEY OF STATE INVOLVEMENT IN PUBLIC TRANSPORTATION. **5393**

0743-4502 *See* GEORGE D. HALL'S CONNECTICUT SERVICE DIRECTORY. **1607**

0743-4510 *See* ENCYCLOPEDIA OF MEDICAL ORGANIZATIONS AND AGENCIES. **3574**

0743-4529 *See* NCPC QUARTERLY. **2829**

0743-4537 *See* INTERACTIVE VIDEO. **1133**

0743-457X *See* COMPUTER GUIDE. **1273**

0743-460X *See* WEEKLY BULLET, THE. **4929**

0743-4618 *See* AUGMENTATIVE AND ALTERNATIVE COMMUNICATION. **1104**

0743-4626 *See* CRIMINAL PROCEDURE HANDBOOK. **3106**

0743-4634 *See* ANNUAL REVIEW OF CELL BIOLOGY. **532**

0743-4707 See TOBACCO REPRINT SERIES. 5374

0743-4804 See BIOENERGETIC ANALYSIS. 3921

0743-4812 See COMMON CARRIER WEEK. 1151

0743-4839 See LIBRARY TIMES INTERNATIONAL. 3227

0743-4863 See CRITICAL REVIEWS IN THERAPEUTIC DRUG CARRIER SYSTEMS. 4298

0743-4898 See BARBIE (NEW YORK, N.Y. 1984). 1060

0743-4979 See CELLE NEWSLETTER. 2442

0743-4995 See DIRECTORY OF LIBRARY AND INFORMATION CONSULTANTS IN METROPOLITAN WASHINGTON. 3207

0743-5010 See TOP FIVE CONTRACTORS RECEIVING THE LARGEST DOLLAR VOLUME OF PRIME CONTRACT AWARDS IN EACH STATE. 1629

0743-5037 See COLORADO MEDICINE. DIRECTORY OF PHYSICIANS. 2878

0743-507X See P & S / THE COLLEGE OF PHYSICIANS AND SURGEONS OF COLUMBIA UNIVERSITY. 3625

0743-5088 See PRIDE INSTITUTE JOURNAL OF LONG TERM HOME HEALTH CARE. 4796

0743-5096 See DIRECTORY OF BILINGUAL SPEECH-LANGUAGE PATHOLOGISTS AND AUDIOLOGISTS. 4386

0743-5118 See ANNUAL REPORT - FIELD FOUNDATION OF ILLINOIS. 5239

0743-5134 See ANNUAL REPORT / ARIZONA DEPARTMENT OF WATER RESOURCES. 5529

0743-5150 See IMAGE--THE JOURNAL OF NURSING SCHOLARSHIP. 3857

0743-5185 See GOURGUES REPORT, THE. 900

0743-5207 See SECURITY FACTS. 885

0743-5223 See ITINERARY (BAYONNE, N.J.), THE. 5481

0743-5231 See WOOD MACHINING NEWS. 2406

0743-524X See EUCHARISTIC MINISTER. 5029

0743-5258 See MASS MARKET RETAILERS. 955

0743-5274 See PETROLEUM FEEDSTOCKS IN 4272

0743-5282 See WEST VIRGINIA MINING DIRECTORY. 2153

0743-5312 See BEST'S EXECUTIVE DATA SERVICE. LIFE-HEALTH INDUSTRY MARKETING RESULTS. LIFE LINES-EXPERIENCE BY STATE. 2875

0743-5320 See BEST'S EXECUTIVE DATA SERVICE. LIFE-HEALTH INDUSTRY MARKETING RESULTS. ACCIDENT & HEALTH LINES-EXPERIENCE BY STATE. 2875

0743-5355 See TAIWAN GONGLUNBAO. 5640

0743-5363 See WORLD CURRENCY YEARBOOK. 816

0743-5371 See DIRECTORY OF SOVIET OFFICIALS. REPUBLIC ORGANIZATIONS. 4644

0743-5401 See PROFITABLE LAWYER, THE. 3032

0743-541X See TELEFOCUS. 1166

0743-5452 See THEATRE SOUTHWEST. 5371

0743-5460 See ANNUAL SECURITY AND SHRINKAGE STUDY. 860

0743-5479 See AIRCRAFT REMOTE SENSING OF SOIL MOISTURE AND HYDROLOGIC PARAMETERS, CHICKASHA, OKLA., ... DATA REPORT. 162

0743-5487 See BUDGET HIGHLIGHTS - UNITED STATES. DEPT. OF ENERGY. OFFICE OF THE CONTROLLER. 4634

0743-5495 See BICYCLE SPORT. 428

0743-5517 See ARCHITECTURAL DIGEST. THE ... ART AND ANTIQUES ANNUAL. 289

0743-5525 See TRUCKER'S ALMANAC. 5398

0743-5533 See ALUMNI DIRECTORY - BOSTON UNIVERSITY. SCHOOL OF MEDICINE. ALUMNI ASSOCIATION. 3548

0743-555X See ACCOMPLISHMENTS FOR RESEARCH, EXTENSION, AND HIGHER EDUCATION / JOINT COUNCIL ON FOOD AND AGRICULTURAL SCIENCES. 42

0743-5584 See JOURNAL OF ADOLESCENT RESEARCH. 4593

0743-5592 See ADVANCES IN THE BIOLOGY OF DISEASE. 3892

0743-5630 See CIT REAL ESTATE REPORT. 4835

0743-5649 See RECREATION AND PARKS LAW REPORTER. 3036

0743-5657 See ARIZONA LABOR MARKET NEWSLETTER. 1653

0743-5665 See NATURAL GAS (NEW YORK, N.Y.). 4265

0743-572X See TESTAMENT. 5003

0743-5789 See SWEET'S CATALOG FILE. PRODUCTS FOR HOME BUILDING AND REMODELING. 629

0743-5797 See ANALYTICAL INSTRUMENTATION. 3549

0743-5800 See ENDOCRINE RESEARCH. 3729

0743-5843 See GENEALOGICAL AND HISTORICAL MAGAZINE OF THE SOUTH, THE. 2449

0743-586X See ERANOS LECTURES. 4586

0743-5878 See TIME-LIFE ACCESS. APPLE. 1273

0743-5886 See TIME-LIFE ACCESS. IBM. 1273

0743-5916 See STATE PLAN FOR DEVELOPMENTAL DISABILITIES (HARRISBURG, PA.). 4688

0743-5959 See MEDICARE AND MEDICAID DATA BOOK, THE. 5295

0743-5991 See ISTF NOTICIAS. 2385

0743-6017 See PUBLICATIONS IN INDIANA MEDICAL HISTORY. 3631

0743-6025 See POSTHYPE. 2491

0743-605X See CATO POLICY REPORT. 1468

0743-6076 See ELECTRICAL COMPONENT LOCATOR. DOMESTIC CARS, LIGHT TRUCKS & VANS, IMPORTED CARS & TRUCKS. 5414

0743-6084 See CAR SERVICE MANUAL. 5409

0743-6122 See WHO'S WHO IN AMERICA'S RESTAURANTS. 436

0743-6130 See EXECUTIVE COMPENSATION ... SURVEY RESULTS. 1668

0743-6149 See EVALUATING YOUR FIRM'S INJURY & ILLNESS RECORD. CONSTRUCTION INDUSTRIES. 1668

0743-6173 See SURGICAL STERILIZATION SURVEILLANCE. TUBAL STERILIZATION AND HYSTERECTOMY IN WOMEN AGED 15-44. 3768

0743-6211 See MUNICIPAL/COUNTY EXECUTIVE DIRECTORY ANNUAL. 4667

0743-6211 See MUNICIPAL/COUNTY EXECUTIVE DIRECTORY. 4667

0743-6246 See SEAPORT. 2760

0743-6289 See OIL INDUSTRY NEWS. 4269

0743-6343 See MICROSYSTEMS COMPETITIVE REVIEW. 1270

0743-6378 See OPHTHALMIC OBSERVER. 3877

0743-6394 See SALON TODAY. 405

0743-6408 See LLEWELLYN'S ... DAILY PLANETARY GUIDE. 390

0743-6416 See HUNGER PROJECT PAPERS, THE. 5288

0743-6467 See EXXON TRAVEL CLUB TRAVEL GUIDE. CENTRAL USA. 5469

0743-6475 See PERSPECTIVE (ALBANY, N.Y. 1983). 3029

0743-6483 See WAHKAW, THE. 2477

0743-6505 See PRECEPTROL. 568

0743-6521 See RECOMBINANT DNA, VECTORS & HOSTS. 569

0743-653X See STATE PLAN FOR VOCATIONAL EDUCATION IN NORTH DAKOTA / STATE BOARD FOR VOCATIONAL EDUCATION. 1916

0743-6572 See CROP AND LIVESTOCK ANNUAL SUMMARY. 77

0743-6580 See MEDALIST FLASHBACK NOTEBOOK. 4904

0743-6599 See SELECTED COMPUTER ARTICLES / NATIONAL DEFENSE UNIVERSITY, DEPARTMENT OF DEFENSE COMPUTER INSTITUTE. 1262

0743-6610 See PASADENA JOURNAL OF BUSINESS. 702

0743-6637 See TRAUMA QUARTERLY. 3977

0743-6645 See AMERICAN UNIVERSITY STUDIES. SERIES XIX, .GENERAL LITERATURE. 3360

0743-6661 See JOURNAL OF INSURANCE MEDICINE (NEW YORK, N.Y.). 2885

0743-670X See NEA ... ALMANAC OF HIGHER EDUCATION, THE. 1837

0743-6785 See VIRGINIA CLIMATE ADVISORY. 1436

0743-6815 See COST AND QUALITY OF FUELS FOR ELECTRIC UTILITY PLANTS (ANNUAL). 2039

0743-6831 See SOUTH CENTRAL REVIEW. 3322

0743-684X See JOURNAL OF RECONSTRUCTIVE MICROSURGERY. 3968

0743-6858 See GEAR TECHNOLOGY. 2114

0743-6874 See OHIO GOLFER MAGAZINE. 4910

0743-6890 See DIRECTORY OF MANAGEMENT CONSULTANTS. 865

0743-6904 See GREATER NEW YORK DIRECTORY, THE. 2881

0743-6963 See ARIZONA JOURNAL OF INTERNATIONAL AND COMPARATIVE LAW. 3124

0743-6998 See SUMMARY OF RESEARCH AWARDS. 714

0743-7005 See CROSSWORDS GALORE. 4859

0743-7021 See PERSPECTIVES (WASHINGTON, D.C. 1984). 2754

0743-7056 See CHOSON ILBO (MIJU PAN). 5715

0743-7072 See NATIONAL DIRECTORY OF COMMUNICATION CUSTOMER PREMISE EQUIPMENT WIRING & EQUIPMENT INSTALLERS, WITH RATE INFORMATION BY CITY, STATE & REGION, THE. 2073

0743-7099 See WOMACK COURIER. 2477

0743-7102 See WINN PARISH COURIER. 2477

0743-7129 See AUTO RACING MEMORIES & MEMORABILIA. 4885

0743-7161 See NEWPORT BEACH. 2541

0743-7218 See WISCONSIN BALTIC STUDIES. 2766

0743-7242 See GROLIER POETRY PRIZE. 3463

0743-7269 See DISPATCH (ROCKVILLE, MD.). 5381

0743-7307 See GAMC NEWS. 868

0743-7315 See JOURNAL OF PARALLEL AND DISTRIBUTED COMPUTING. 1260

0743-7323 See REVIEW OF THE U.S. ECONOMY. 1518

0743-7331 See HAZARDOUS WASTE MANAGEMENT IN MASSACHUSETTS. 2231

0743-7366 See MINORITY/WOMEN'S BUSINESS ENTERPRISES DIRECTORY. 1618

0743-7390 See FRINGE BENEFITS FOR SUPERINTENDENTS IN PUBLIC SCHOOLS. 1864

0743-7404 See EXAMINATION OF THE PANAMA CANAL COMMISSION'S FINANCIAL STATEMENTS. 5449

0743-7439 See SOUTHERN FRIEND, THE. 5067

0743-7447 See STATE OF MUNICIPAL SERVICES, THE. 4688

0743-7463 See LANGMUIR. 1055

0743-7471 See GRAYWOLF ANNUAL, THE. 3392

0743-748X See TWINS LETTER, THE. 4621

0743-7498 See DUNCAN'S RADIO MARKET GUIDE. 1131

0743-7528 See MATERIAL CULTURE DIRECTORIES. 5251

0743-7560 See BIBLIOGRAPHIES AND INDEXES IN GERONTOLOGY. 3750

0743-7579 See IROQUOIS STALKER, THE. 2454

0743-7609 See SHOWCASE. 382

0743-7641 See MISSOURI ARCHAEOLOGICAL SOCIETY QUARTERLY. 275

0743-7668 See OPINIONS OF THE NEW YORK STATE COMPTROLLER. 3023

0743-7676 See STATE MENTAL RETARDATION FACILITY DATA. 5311

0743-7692 See COMPARISON OF COMPENSATION PAID SCIENTISTS AND ENGINEERS IN RESEARCH AND DEVELOPMENT. 1660

0743-7730 See HOT LINE FARM EQUIPMENT GUIDE'S QUICK REFERENCE GUIDE FOR FARM TRACTORS AND COMBINES. **159**

0743-7749 See JOURNAL OF MODERN HELLENISM. **2266**

0743-779X See SOUTHERN BUSINESS & ECONOMIC JOURNAL, THE. **712**

0743-782X See PROVERBIUM (COLUMBUS, OHIO). **2323**

0743-7889 See STUDIES IN ROMANTIC AND MODERN LITERATURE. **3442**

0743-7897 See MILITARY SPACE. **28**

0743-7919 See COMPUTERIZED SURNAME MAGAZINE. **2443**

0743-7927 See NATIONAL INSURANCE LAW REVIEW. **3013**

0743-7943 See SEAT MARKET, THE. **810**

0743-7951 See WISCONSIN INTERNATIONAL LAW JOURNAL. **3138**

0743-7986 See OEA FOCUS. **1770**

0743-7994 See U.S. RAIL NEWS. **5437**

0743-8036 See CURRENT LITERATURE IN NEPHROLOGY. **3989**

0743-8044 See VIEWS (BOSTON, MASS.). **4378**

0743-8052 See WASHINGTON MISSOURIAN. **5704**

0743-8079 See MEDICAL BENEFITS. **2887**

0743-8095 See MAGAZINE OF VIRGINIA GENEALOGY. **2459**

0743-8125 See BOW WAVE'S BOATING. **592**

0743-8141 See LAKE AND RESERVOIR MANAGEMENT. **2235**

0743-815X See CPA EXAMINATION REVIEW. **742**

0743-8176 See PRIMARY CARE & CANCER. **3822**

0743-8184 See CIC'S SCHOOL DIRECTORY. IDAHO. **1891**

0743-8249 See OAG POCKET FLIGHT GUIDE (NORTH AMERICAN EDITION). **5486**

0743-829X See ENERGY STUDIES (AUSTIN, TEX.). **1942**

0743-8303 See PRUDHOE BAY JOURNAL. **5629**

0743-8346 See JOURNAL OF PERINATOLOGY. **3764**

0743-8354 See OB/GYN CLINICAL ALERT. **3766**

0743-8362 See NIE NOTES. **1901**

0743-8389 See CINEMA BLUE. **2486**

0743-8397 See DAILY TERRITORIAL, THE. **5630**

0743-8400 See AGRICHEMICAL BRIEFING. **48**

0743-846X See PROCEEDINGS OF THE ANNUAL SYMPOSIUM, SAFE ASSOCIATION. **32**

0743-8478 See KETTERING REPORT. **5207**

0743-8508 See PENNY MINING STOCK REPORT. **910**

0743-8532 See JOURNAL OF THE INSTITUTE FOR THE NEW MAN. **5250**

0743-8591 See EDWARDS JOURNAL, THE. **2446**

0743-8613 See INFORMATION STRATEGY. **870**

0743-8621 See PERCUSSIONER INTERNATIONAL AUDIO MAGAZINE. **5318**

0743-8656 See SMALL COMPUTERS IN BIOMEDICAL RESEARCH. **3696**

0743-8672 See OFFICIAL PRICE GUIDE TO KITCHEN COLLECTIBLES, THE. **2776**

0743-8680 See OFFICIAL PRICE GUIDE TO COLLECTIBLE TOYS, THE. **2584**

0743-8699 See OFFICIAL PRICE GUIDE TO GLASSWARE, THE. **2592**

0743-8702 See OFFICIAL GUIDE TO BUYING & SELLING ANTIQUES AND COLLECTIBLES, THE. **252**

0743-8710 See OFFICIAL PRICE GUIDE TO COLLECTOR PLATES, THE. **2776**

0743-8729 See OFFICIAL ENCYCLOPEDIA OF ANTIQUES AND COLLECTIBLES, THE. **252**

0743-8737 See OFFICIAL PRICE GUIDE TO WICKER, THE. **2906**

0743-8826 See HAZARD PREVENTION. **2862**

0743-8834 See ACOA ACTION NEWS. **4503**

0743-894X See BETTER HOMES AND GARDENS WOOD. **2904**

0743-8958 See BRIDGE BUILDER (SCHENECTADY, N.Y.), THE. **2440**

0743-8982 See SPACE R & D ALERT. **36**

0743-9008 See GMRMLN UPDATE. **3212**

0743-9032 See OZARK SOCIETY JOURNAL. **2753**

0743-9040 See GALLEY (HARRISONBURG, VA.), THE. **2449**

0743-9075 See RAIL CLASSICS & RAILWAY QUARTERLY. **5434**

0743-9113 See MENTAL HEALTH PLAN (AUGUSTA, ME.). **4790**

0743-913X See LIGHT YEAR (CLEVELAND, OHIO). **3465**

0743-9156 See JOURNAL OF PUBLIC POLICY & MARKETING. **929**

0743-9180 See REPORT OF THE ... UNITED NATIONS ISSUES CONFERENCE. **4533**

0743-9202 See HIGHLIGHTS FROM INFECTIONS IN SURGERY. **3965**

0743-9237 See NEW CONCEPTS IN CARDIAC IMAGING. **3708**

0743-9253 See POWER AND ELITES. **5213**

0743-9261 See YEAR BOOK OF INFECTIOUS DISEASES, THE. **3716**

0743-927X See VOX MEDIAEVALIS. **1080**

0743-930X See CURRENT ONCOLOGY. **3815**

0743-9326 See FODOR'S CHICAGO. **5471**

0743-9342 See TEXAS FAMILY LAW REPORTER. **3122**

0743-9350 See U.S. COINS, CURRENCY & STAMPS. **2783**

0743-9385 See FODOR'S NEW ORLEANS. **5472**

0743-9423 See INVESTOR'S BUSINESS DAILY. **903**

0743-9458 See RISK LINE. **2892**

0743-9520 See LEVISON LETTER, THE. **875**

0743-9539 See ANNUAL REVIEW OF CHRONOPHARMACOLOGY. **4291**

0743-9547 See JOURNAL OF SOUTHEAST ASIAN EARTH SCIENCES. **1357**

0743-9571 See OFFICIAL PRICE GUIDE TO ANTIQUE CLOCKS, THE. **2916**

0743-961X See NORTH CENTRAL ILLINOIS GENEALOGICAL SOCIETY. **2464**

0743-9628 See BORGO BIOVIEWS. **431**

0743-9652 See UPDATE, GCLC. **3255**

0743-9695 See INTERNATIONAL REGISTER OF MARKETERS AND SUPPORTERS OF IBM PRODUCTS. **1245**

0743-9709 See TRADE SHOW & CONVENTION GUIDE. **767**

0743-9725 See DIRECTORY OF VOLUNTARY AGENCIES. **5284**

0743-9741 See FODOR'S WASHINGTON, D.C. **5474**

0743-9776 See OFFICIAL PRICE GUIDE TO ANTIQUE & MODERN FIREARMS, THE. **4053**

0743-9784 See OFFICIAL PRICE GUIDE TO AMERICAN SILVER AND SILVER PLATE, THE. **4014**

0743-9792 See OFFICIAL PRICE GUIDE TO PAPERBACKS & MAGAZINES, THE. **2776**

0743-9806 See CHEMUNITY. **971**

0743-9822 See STUDIES IN THE HISTORY OF MUSIC. **4155**

0743-9849 See EXILE (PASADENA, CALIF.). **4474**

0743-9873 See CHILDREN'S MAGAZINE GUIDE. **3258**

0743-9962 See RURAL LIVING (LANSING, MICH.). **131**

0743-9989 See SMALL FARMER'S JOURNAL. **135**

0743-9997 See ARIZONA BUSINESS REPORTS. **639**

0744-0006 See YANKEES MAGAZINE. **4931**

0744-0022 **5074**

0744-0030 See STATISTICS OF INCOME. SOLE PROPRIETORSHIP RETURNS. **4700**

0744-0049 See NATIONAL STRENGTH & CONDITIONING ASSOCIATION JOURNAL. **1857**

0744-0081 See COMPUTER INDUSTRY UPDATE. **1208**

0744-0103 See USCTA NEWS. **2803**

0744-0170 See COMPUTERS AND OFFICE AND ACCOUNTING MACHINES. **1602**

0744-0219 See DAYLILY JOURNAL, THE. **2413**

0744-0251 See RESPUESTA. **4993**

0744-0278 See NORTH STAR BAPTIST. **4982**

0744-0340 See ASPHALT AND TAR ROOFING AND SIDING PRODUCTS. **599**

0744-0375 See ACTION (GREENWOOD, IND.). **4623**

0744-0448 See EXEGETICAL RESOURCE. **5016**

0744-0456 See CITY PAGES. **317**

0744-0480 See WATER RESOURCES DEVELOPMENT BY THE US ARMY CORPS OF ENGINEERS IN OKLAHOMA. **5546**

0744-0499 See DAY (NEW LONDON, CONN.), THE. **5645**

0744-0596 See GENESIS (WASHINGTON, D.C.). **3761**

0744-060X See NEW YORK NATIVE. **2795**

0744-0618 See RADIO COMMUNICATIONS REPORT. **1137**

0744-0650 See TRANSFORMERS. **2085**

0744-0677 See LIFE LINES (LINCOLN, NEB.). **5180**

0744-0731 See COLLIE REVIEW. **4286**

0744-074X See MOTORHOME. **5387**

0744-0766 See SMYTH COUNTY NEWS. **5759**

0744-0804 See DIRECTORY OF FEDERAL HEALTH/MEDICINE GRANTS AND CONTRACTS PROGRAMS. **3572**

0744-0898 See EPIDEMIOLOGY MONITOR, THE. **4775**

0744-0901 See DOLL READER. **2584**

0744-091X See AMERICAN EXPRESS SKY GUIDE. **11**

0744-0960 See BASIC GRANTS. **1811**

0744-0987 See TEXAS GARDENER (WACO, TX.). **2432**

0744-0995 See GATOR BAIT. **4896**

0744-1002 See CAREER WORLD (HIGHLAND PARK, ILL. 1981). **4202**

0744-1010 See ADDRESS LIST / NATIONAL CLEARINGHOUSE FOR CENSUS DATA SERVICES. **5320**

0744-1029 See ACUHO INTERNATIONAL NEWS. **1807**

0744-1045 See INSURANCE LITIGATION REPORTER. **2983**

0744-1061 See HAMPTON ROADS SHIPPING NEWS, THE. **5450**

0744-1088 See ASSOCIATIONS REPORT. **860**

0744-1118 See SOUTHERN POST, THE. **5724**

0744-1193 See BUILDER (WASHINGTON, D.C. : 1981). **602**

0744-1266 See WALLEYE. **4880**

0744-1282 See DAIRY MARKET NEWS. **193**

0744-1320 See TEXAS WATER RESOURCES. **5541**

0744-1355 See SPEECH TECHNOLOGY. **1122**

0744-1363 See AMERICAN SKATING WORLD. **4883**

0744-1398 See ANADARKO DAILY NEWS, THE. **5731**

0744-1401 See RICHLAND COUNTY NEWS-MONITOR. **5726**

0744-141X See NEWS PROGRESS (SULLIVAN, ILL.). **5661**

0744-1452 See AG. MARKET CHARTS. **45**

0744-1495 See ORTHODOX HERALD, THE. **5039**

0744-1509 See ARIZONA JEWISH POST. **5629**

0744-1517 See HAY MARKET NEWS (BELL, CALIF.). **925**

0744-1533 See GRAIN MARKET NEWS (BELL, CALIF.). **90**

0744-155X See STAR (LAKEWOOD, COLO.), THE. **5425**

0744-1576 See HOME & AWAY. IOWA. **5479**

0744-1606 See TRAVELAGE MIDAMERICA. **5497**

0744-1630 See APPEARANCES OF LEADING CHINESE OFFICIALS. **4630**

0744-1649 See STITCH 'N SEW QUILTS. **5186**

0744-1657 See TEST & MEASUREMENT WORLD. **2084**

0744-1673 See DATA SOURCES. **1237**

0744-169X *See* MULTI-HOUSING MAINSTREAM. **2828**

0744-1711 *See* INDEPENDENT HERALD (ONEIDA, TENN.). **5745**

0744-172X *See* BUSINESS TIMES (EAST HARTFORD, CONN.), THE. **653**

0744-1738 *See* HOBBY MERCHANDISER (NEW YORK, N.Y.). **2774**

0744-1754 *See* PACIFIC MAGAZINE (HONOLULU, HAWAII). **2511**

0744-1770 *See* NEW GENERATING PLANTS. **2073**

0744-1797 *See* BULLDOG (LOS ANGELES, CALIF.). **4201**

0744-1843 *See* CONNECTICUT BEVERAGE JOURNAL. **2366**

0744-1851 *See* TIMES-UNION (ROCHESTER, N.Y.). **5721**

0744-186X *See* DEFENDER (DES MOINES, IOWA), THE. **4507**

0744-1983 *See* PORAC LAW ENFORCEMENT NEWS. **3173**

0744-2017 *See* PARABLES, ETC. **4985**

0744-2033 *See* CAROLINA FARMER (NORTH CAROLINA ED.). **72**

0744-2106 *See* SOUTHERN LOGGIN' TIMES. **2404**

0744-2114 *See* ENTERPRISE (BROCKTON, MASS.). **5688**

0744-2130 *See* MAJOR HOUSEHOLD APPLIANCES. **2812**

0744-2203 *See* GOSPEL EVANGEL, THE. **4961**

0744-2238 *See* LAKOTA TIMES, THE. **5744**

0744-2254 *See* KANSAS REGISTER. **4659**

0744-2270 *See* ANTIFRICTION BEARINGS. **3475**

0744-2289 *See* BYZANTINE CATHOLIC WORLD, THE. **5735**

0744-2297 *See* VIRGINIA POSTMASTER, THE. **1148**

0744-2327 *See* CABLE WEEK. ORANGE-SEMINOLE-OSEOLA ED. **1129**

0744-2343 *See* SNE COMMUNICATOR. **4199**

0744-2351 *See* CENTRAL CALIFORNIA VEGETABLE REPORT. **2331**

0744-236X *See* CALIFORNIA NOTARY BULLETIN. **4636**

0744-2394 *See* VALLEY HORSE NEWS, THE. **5704**

0744-2440 *See* SELECTED INSTRUMENTS AND RELATED PRODUCTS. **1626**

0744-2467 *See* WINNING (TULSA, OKLA.). **4867**

0744-2475 *See* PEELINGS II : THE MAGAZINE OF APPLE SOFTWARE EVALUATION. **1271**

0744-2483 *See* CAROLINA FOOD DEALER, THE. **2330**

0744-2505 *See* MIT REPORT (CAMBRIDGE, MASS. : 1981), THE. **5129**

0744-2513 *See* MODERN JEWELER (1981). **2915**

0744-253X *See* BEEF BUSINESS BULLETIN. **207**

0744-2548 *See* RURAL TELECOMMUNICATIONS. **1163**

0744-2572 *See* MUSTANG TIMES. **5421**

0744-2580 *See* SUMMARY OF PROCEEDINGS / AMERICAN NURSES' ASSOCIATION ... CONVENTION. **3870**

0744-2653 *See* CALIFORNIA ORNAMENTAL CROPS REPORT. **2435**

0744-267X *See* CATHOLIC SUN (SYRACUSE, N.Y.), THE. **5026**

0744-2785 *See* PREDICASTS F & S INDEX OF CORPORATE CHANGE. **1621**

0744-2807 *See* SERTOMAN. **5307**

0744-2815 *See* OFFICE TECHNOLOGY MANAGEMENT (GARDEN CITY, N.Y.). **880**

0744-2823 *See* DRUGS AND DRUG ABUSE EDUCATION NEWSLETTER, (1982). **1344**

0744-2866 *See* BASKETBALL TIMES. **4887**

0744-2939 *See* COLLEGIATE QUARTERLY. **5058**

0744-2947 *See* INTERNAL AUDITING ALERT. **745**

0744-298X *See* POULTRY MARKET NEWS REPORT (CHICAGO, ILL.). **218**

0744-2998 *See* MONTHLY COLDS STORAGE REPORT (CHICAGO, ILL.). **216**

0744-303X *See* EGG MARKET NEWS REPORT (CHICAGO, ILL.). **210**

0744-3056 *See* SIDE-SADDLE NEWS. **2802**

0744-3072 *See* SAN FRANCISCO BARRISTER. **3046**

0744-3102 *See* MAGAZINE & BOOKSELLER. **4816**

0744-3110 *See* JASPER JOURNAL, THE. **5696**

0744-3129 *See* ENSIGN (SAN MATEO, CALIF.), THE. **593**

0744-3161 *See* PRESS MAGAZINE, THE. **1086**

0744-317X *See* NEW YORK CITY FRUIT AND VEGETABLE REPORT. **112**

0744-3196 *See* MARYLAND WHOLESALE FRUIT & VEGETABLE REPORT. **178**

0744-3226 *See* DOLPHIN DIGEST. **4893**

0744-3234 *See* DIARIO LAS AMERICAS. **5649**

0744-3242 *See* DANVILLE REGISTER, THE. **5758**

0744-3269 *See* COMTEC CABLE TELEVISION VIEWERS GUIDE. **1130**

0744-3277 *See* BONSAI CLUBS INTERNATIONAL. **2410**

0744-3285 *See* JOURNAL (CAMP VERDE, ARIZ.), THE. **5630**

0744-3366 *See* NEWS - FLORIDA ASSOCIATION OF SOIL AND WATER CONSERVATION DISTRICT SUPERVISORS. **2200**

0744-3447 *See* BUFFALO FRUIT AND VEGETABLE REPORT. **68**

0744-3471 *See* PROFESSIONALS. **3725**

0744-3528 *See* PODIATRY MANAGEMENT. **3918**

0744-3587 *See* PHILADELPHIA BUSINESS JOURNAL. **703**

0744-3609 *See* ULTRARUNNING. **4927**

0744-3625 *See* SUPERVISOR'S BULLETIN FOR ADMINISTRATION AND OFFICE SUPPORT GROUPS. **887**

0744-3676 *See* EMPLOYEE SERVICES MANAGEMENT. **940**

0744-3692 *See* LOUISIANA GAME & FISH. **4874**

0744-3714 *See* FLORIDA CUT FLOWER AND FERN REPORT. **2435**

0744-3722 *See* LIP (LANCASTER, PA.). **3346**

0744-3730 *See* SOUTH CAROLINA FIREMAN MAGAZINE, THE. **2292**

0744-3773 *See* SHOTGUN SPORTS. **4917**

0744-3781 *See* OLD STURBRIDGE VISITOR. **4094**

0744-3846 *See* LONG TERM VALUES. **905**

0744-3862 *See* DARIEN NEWS-REVIEW. **5645**

0744-3870 *See* FORT COLLINS REVIEW. **5642**

0744-3889 *See* NATIONAL JOURNAL (ALLENTOWN, PA.). **2592**

0744-3900 *See* PLANT SYSTEMS & EQUIPMENT. **3486**

0744-3927 *See* MORTGAGE MARKETPLACE, THE. **800**

0744-3943 *See* JONQUIL. **5232**

0744-3951 *See* INTERNATIONAL LIMOUSIN JOURNAL. **213**

0744-396X *See* KENTUCKY DENTAL JOURNAL. **1329**

0744-4001 *See* ATHENS OBSERVER, THE. **5652**

0744-401X *See* BUTLER EAGLE (BUTLER, PA. : DAILY). **5735**

0744-4028 *See* GARDEN ISLAND, THE. **5655**

0744-4036 *See* KEYSTONE (PITTSBURGH, PA. 1968), THE. **5432**

0744-4044 *See* TENNESSEE PROFESSIONAL ENGINEER, THE. **1998**

0744-4052 *See* CHRISTIAN MISSIONS IN MANY LANDS. **4945**

0744-4060 *See* CHRISTIAN INDEX (MEMPHIS, TENN.), THE. **5058**

0744-4079 *See* CHANNELS (NEWBURY PARK, CALIF.). **4943**

0744-4087 *See* INDEPENDENT METHODIST BULLETIN, THE. **5061**

0744-4095 *See* CINCINNATI FRESH FRUIT AND VEGETABLE REPORT. **167**

0744-4117 *See* INDIVIDUAL WITH DISABILITIES EDUCATION LAW REPORT. **2982**

0744-415X *See* VICTORIAN HOMES. **310**

0744-4184 *See* ARKANSAS SPORTSMAN. **4869**

0744-4192 *See* MISSISSIPPI GAME & FISH (MARIETTA, GA.). **4874**

0744-4206 *See* MEDICAL ECONOMICS FOR SURGEONS. **3969**

0744-4230 *See* PENNSYLVANIA MAGAZINE (CAMP HILL, PA.). **5488**

0744-4249 *See* BYLINE (OKLAHOMA CITY, OKLA.). **2918**

0744-4257 *See* HORSE TIMES. **2799**

0744-432X *See* RAYS FROM THE ROSE CROSS. **4243**

0744-4400 *See* TALLAHASSEE ADVERTISER, THE. **5651**

0744-4451 *See* GEORGIA CATTLEMAN. **211**

0744-4508 *See* WESTERN AND CENTRAL NEW YORK FRUIT AND VEGETABLE REPORT. **190**

0744-4516 *See* REAL ESTATE PROFESSIONAL, THE. **4845**

0744-4524 *See* WEEKLY INDIA TRIBUNE. **5662**

0744-4532 *See* GREATER PHILADELPHIA ECONOMIST, THE. **1493**

0744-4540 *See* BARR'S POST CARD NEWS. **1144**

0744-4583 *See* VOICE OF NORTH CAROLINA SCHOOL BOARDS ASSOCIATION. **1874**

0744-4591 *See* WEST HAWAII TODAY. **5656**

0744-4664 *See* SEAFOOD LEADER. **2313**

0744-4672 *See* OPTIMIST MAGAZINE, THE. **5234**

0744-4680 *See* NORTHWEST ARTS. **326**

0744-4710 *See* RESOURCE RECYCLING / NORTH AMERICA'S RECYCLING JOURNAL. **2242**

0744-4761 *See* TEXAS HEREFORD. **222**

0744-477X *See* SANTA FE REPORTER, THE. **5713**

0744-4834 *See* CALIFORNIA POTATO & ONION REPORT. **2330**

0744-4958 *See* BEVERAGE RETAILER WEEKLY. **2364**

0744-4966 *See* MANHATTAN MEDICINE. **3606**

0744-4990 *See* FARM BUREAU PERSPECTIVE. **84**

0744-5008 *See* GREAT AMERICAN COW TRADER, THE. **211**

0744-5059 *See* MODEL AVIATION. **2775**

0744-5083 *See* SALVATION ARMY YOUTH. **5306**

0744-5105 *See* JOE WEIDER'S MUSCLE & FITNESS. **2599**

0744-5121 *See* SHAPE (WOODLAND HILLS, CALIF.). **2601**

0744-5148 *See* NORTH DAKOTA PEACE OFFICER. **3170**

0744-5172 *See* IN THE CREASE. **4899**

0744-5199 *See* SANTA BARBARA MAGAZINE. **2545**

0744-5253 *See* LABOR ARBITRATION INFORMATION SYSTEM. **3150**

0744-527X *See* ALGONQUIN COUNTRYSIDE. **5658**

0744-5288 *See* MACKINAC, THE. **2177**

0744-530X *See* BETTER BUILDINGS. **601**

0744-5318 *See* AZALEA CITY NEWS & REVIEW. **5625**

0744-5326 *See* INTERNATIONAL RAILWAY JOURNAL AND RAPID TRANSIT REVIEW. **5432**

0744-5369 *See* RIVER GROVE MESSENGER. **5662**

0744-5377 *See* SCHILLER PARK INDEPENDENT. **5662**

0744-5385 *See* PARK RIDGE ADVOCATE. **5661**

0744-5393 *See* NILES SPECTATOR. **5661**

0744-5407 *See* ROSEMONT PROGRESS. **5662**

0744-5431 *See* NORTHEAST MISSISSIPPI DAILY JOURNAL. **5701**

0744-544X *See* GRAND RAPIDS HERALD-REVIEW. **5696**

0744-5474 *See* ARIZONA LAND & PEOPLE. **62**

0744-5504 *See* TV LINK. **1141**

0744-5512 *See* HARDWICK GAZETTE, THE. **5757**

0744-5520 *See* HANGUK ILBO (HOUSTON, TEX.). **5750**

0744-5555 *See* ROUND UP (UNIVERSITY PARK, N.M.). **5713**

0744-5601 *See* BLUE BERET. **2485**

0744-5636 See PENNSYLVANIA HOSPITALS. **3790**

0744-5644 See SOONER POSTMASTER. **1147**

0744-5660 See INTERNATIONAL TRADE ALERT (NEW YORK, N.Y.). **841**

0744-5679 See NTDRA MEMBERGRAM. **5076**

0744-5741 See TV 2 (SAINT PAUL, MINN.). **1141**

0744-5792 See HAWAII ISLAND GUIDE. **5479**

0744-5806 See ILLINOIS BENEDICTINE MAGAZINE, THE. **1092**

0744-5814 See GOSPEL MESSAGE, THE. **4961**

0744-5830 See ANTELOPE VALLEY PRESS. **5633**

0744-5881 See OIL & GAS INVESTOR. **4268**

0744-589X See FMG, THE. **3576**

0744-5938 See SOUTHWEST WOMAN. **5566**

0744-5962 See KART SPORT. **5418**

0744-5989 See COLLECTORS' SHOWCASE (SAN DIEGO, CALIF.). **250**

0744-5997 See FLORIDA WATERMELON REPORT. **172**

0744-6004 See CRUISING AROUND THE WORLD. **5467**

0744-6020 See ORTHOPEDIC NURSING / NATIONAL ASSOCIATION OF ORTHOPEDIC NURSES. **3884**

0744-6055 See ORLANDO SENTINEL, THE. **5650**

0744-608X See IOWA DAIRY MARKETING NEWS. **195**

0744-6101 See SPRINGFIELD NEWS-SUN. **5730**

0744-6128 See TRAI TIM DU'C ME. **5005**

0744-6152 See FLORIDA REAL ESTATE COMMISSION NEWS & REPORTS. **4838**

0744-6160 See CALIFORNIA POULTRY REPORT. **208**

0744-6179 See BLADE MAGAZINE, THE. **2771**

0744-6233 See TRAVEL PRINTOUT. **5496**

0744-625X See ALIMENTOS PROCESADOS. **2326**

0744-6268 See INDIVIDUAL RETIREMENT PLANS GUIDE : IRA, SEP, KEOGH. **790**

0744-6306 See NATIONAL CLOTHESLINE (MIDWEST ED.), THE. **5354**

0744-6314 See NURSING MANAGEMENT. **3864**

0744-6349 See FIRST HAND. **2794**

0744-6357 See PEST MANAGEMENT. **4246**

0744-6373 See WASHINGTON LIVING. **2549**

0744-6381 See PACIFIC UNION RECORDER. **4984**

0744-6403 See APPAREL NEWS SOUTH. **1081**

0744-642X See REAL ESTATE BUSINESS. **4844**

0744-6454 See AMERICAN LABOR BEACON. **1643**

0744-6462 See CHANNEL GUIDE. **1130**

0744-6470 See HOSPITAL EMPLOYEE HEALTH. **3784**

0744-6489 See JEI REPORT. **1498**

0744-6500 See NATURAL GAS HANDBOOK. **4265**

0744-6535 See AAA TRAVELER. MUSKINGUM AAA EDITION, THE. **5403**

0744-6586 See DENNI HLASATEL. **5659**

0744-6608 See SHELTIE PACESETTER. **4288**

0744-6616 See AMERICAN PRINTER (1982). **4563**

0744-6624 See WARBIRDS. **39**

0744-6632 See JEWISH NEWS (RICHMOND, VA.), THE. **5049**

0744-6640 See HOME SHOP MACHINIST, THE. **2115**

0744-6667 See COMPUTER GAMING WORLD. **1230**

0744-6683 See ILLINOIS ECONOMIC REPORT. **1494**

0744-6705 See LITCHFIELD COUNTY TIMES, THE. **5645**

0744-6713 See JOURNAL OF STATE TAXATION. **4735**

0744-6721 See PROFESSIONAL EMPLOYEES IN STATE GOVERNMENT. **4675**

0744-6748 See 1ST READING (SACRAMENTO, CALIF.). **2926**

0744-6756 See CALIFORNIA TORT REPORTER. **2947**

0744-6780 See SPREADING THE FAME OF CHRIST. **4999**

0744-6829 See RACKING REVIEW, THE. **2802**

0744-6837 See DAILY INDEPENDENT (ASHLAND, KY), THE. **5680**

0744-6861 See NEW ENGLAND BRIDE. **2283**

0744-690X See EASTERN ARKANSAS WEEKLY SHOPPING GUIDE. **1296**

0744-6918 See FLUTE TALK. **4118**

0744-6926 See PROPERTY TAX REPORT. **4742**

0744-6934 See OUTREACH (STILLWATER, OKLA.). **1094**

0744-6942 See NAPA COUNTY RECORD AND NAPA VALLEY NEWS. **5637**

0744-6969 See OCTAGONIAN OF SIGMA ALPHA MU, THE. **1093**

0744-6985 See BAPTIST COURIER. **5056**

0744-7035 See CD SUMMARY. **3712**

0744-7043 See READING-BERKS AUTO CLUB MAGAZINE. **5423**

0744-7078 See ADMINISTRATOR (MADISON, WIS.). **1859**

0744-7086 See TULARE COUNTY FARM BUREAU NEWS. **143**

0744-7116 See TIDEWATER ADVANTAGE. NEWPORT NEWS EDITION, THE. **5759**

0744-7132 See JOURNAL OF OPHTHALMIC NURSING & TECHNOLOGY. **3859**

0744-7140 See NATIONAL AD SEARCH, THE. **4206**

0744-7167 See CONSTRUCTION SUPERVISION & SAFETY LETTER. **610**

0744-7183 See ECU REPORT, THE. **1822**

0744-7191 See FLYFISHING. **2304**

0744-7205 See GROWTH INDEX, THE. **820**

0744-7213 See JOHN WESLEY COLLEGE CRUSADER. **1092**

0744-7221 See BARNSTABLE PATRIOT. **5687**

0744-723X See BIG REEL, THE. **4064**

0744-7248 See THAILAND BIBLE LITERATURE. **5020**

0744-7302 See HERALD (SHARON, PA.), THE. **5736**

0744-7345 See BROADLY GRADED TEACHER'S RESOURCE GUIDE. **1889**

0744-737X See NAS GOLOS. **2268**

0744-7388 See TENNESSEE FARM FACTS. **140**

0744-7418 See RIVER CITIES. **1299**

0744-7434 See FIRST TEACHER. **1895**

0744-7450 See RIPON COLLEGE UPDATE. **1846**

0744-7477 See ARIZONA CAPITOL TIMES. **4630**

0744-7493 See QUARTERLY - INTERNATIONAL PLASTIC MODELERS' SOCIETY. UNITED STATES BRANCH. **4460**

0744-7515 See PRINCETON MAGAZINE (PRINCETON, N.J. : 1982). **1094**

0744-7531 See NEWSLINE - NATIONAL RURAL ELECTRIC WOMEN'S ASSOCIATION (U.S.). **2073**

0744-7582 See WILLIAMS NORTHERN LIGHT. **5699**

0744-7590 See LONG ISLAND'S NIGHTLIFE MAGAZINE. **4852**

0744-7604 See TIGER RAG. **4926**

0744-7612 See COMMUNICATION WORLD (SAN FRANCISCO, CALIF.). **1107**

0744-7620 See TWOS AND THREES TEACHER. **1908**

0744-7671 See BANKRUPTCY LAW LETTER. **3085**

0744-768X See BULLETIN DIGEST. **4941**

0744-7701 See FUR RANCHER. **3184**

0744-771X See STEUBENVILLE REGISTER, THE. **5730**

0744-7728 See BROOKLYN COURIER. **5714**

0744-7736 See RX ET CETERA. **4328**

0744-7779 See EMPLOYEE RELATIONS BULLETIN (NEW YORK, N.Y.). **1665**

0744-7787 See FARM INDUSTRY NEWS SUNBELT. **84**

0744-7809 See ATV NEWS. **4080**

0744-7817 See PROFESSIONAL MONITOR / MICHIGAN ASSOCIATION OF THE PROFESSIONS, THE. **3032**

0744-7841 See SATELLITE TV WEEK. NORTH AMERICAN EDITION. **1163**

0744-785X See SOUTH COAST WEEK. **5734**

0744-7930 See BEACON (ACTON, MASS.), THE. **5687**

0744-7949 See LITTLETON INDEPENDENT, THE. **5689**

0744-7957 See WESTFORD EAGLE. **5690**

0744-7973 See LAKE FORESTER. **5661**

0744-7981 See TEXAS PUBLIC UTILITY NEWS. **4762**

0744-8007 See PETROLEUM INFORMATION'S NATIONAL WILDCAT MONTHLY. **4273**

0744-8066 See STEEL YACHT, THE. **596**

0744-8074 See LIONS MAGAZINE. **1093**

0744-8139 See SUN-SENTINEL (FORT LAUDERDALE, FLA.). **5651**

0744-8147 See FORT LAUDERDALE NEWS. **5649**

0744-8155 See PACIFIC AUTOMOTIVE NEWS. **5422**

0744-8163 See DIVERSITY. **508**

0744-818X See MASSACHUSETTS DECISIONS REPORTED IN NORTH EASTERN REPORTER, SECOND SERIES. **3007**

0744-8295 See BREAKOUT. **4888**

0744-8317 See OREGON COAST. **5487**

0744-8376 See OHIO STATE BAR ASSOCIATION REPORT (1981). **3022**

0744-8384 See N.J. VASA HOME FAMILY. **2283**

0744-8392 See PA. JAYCEES FUTURE. **5235**

0744-8457 See BEDFORD GAZETTE (BEDFORD, PA.). **5734**

0744-8481 See JOURNAL OF AMERICAN COLLEGE HEALTH. **3593**

0744-8503 See YOUR CHICAGO EXPRESS. **2897**

0744-8511 See TIMBERTALK. **2405**

0744-852X See LIBERTYVILLE REVIEW. **5661**

0744-8538 See MUNDELEIN REVIEW. **5661**

0744-8546 See POMERANIAN REVIEW. **4287**

0744-8554 See QRZ DX. **1162**

0744-8562 See PREACHER'S PERIODICAL, THE. **4987**

0744-8589 See NEW COVENANT (ANN ARBOR, MICH.). **5033**

0744-8600 See CALIFORNIAI MAGYARSAG. **2257**

0744-8627 See COUNTRY TIMES. **5695**

0744-8635 See INTERIORSCAPE. **2420**

0744-8643 See WORLD OF PUMPS. **2132**

0744-8651 See U.S. MARITIME MONTHLY. **4184**

0744-866X See SILHOUETTE (IDAHO FALLS, IDAHO), THE. **5657**

0744-8716 See WEST'S EDUCATION LAW REPORTER. **3074**

0744-8759 See LA MESA COURIER. **5636**

0744-8767 See BANK WAGE-HOUR AND PERSONNEL REPORT. **1654**

0744-8813 See JUNIOR HIGH TEACHER. **1899**

0744-8821 See NEWSLETTER-UNIVERSITY OF WASHINGTON. **1197**

0744-883X See SUNDAY INDEPENDENT, THE. **5682**

0744-8864 See WAREHOUSING SUPERVISOR'S BULLETIN. **719**

0744-8872 See SUN/COAST ARCHITECT/BUILDER. **629**

0744-8902 See NEVADA LEGAL NEWS. **3015**

0744-8910 See KURYER ZJEDNOCZENIA. **5729**

0744-8988 See GREENHOUSE MANAGER. **2417**

0744-8996 See TECHNICAL SOARING. **37**

0744-9046 See INDIANA CASES REPORTED IN NORTH EASTERN REPORTER, SECOND SERIES. **2981**

0744-9143 See APARTMENT MANAGEMENT NEWSLETTER. **4834**

0744-9178 See VISIONS (MORAINE, OHIO). **5038**

0744-9194 See LAKELAND BOATING (1982). **594**

0744-9208 See MONTHLY NEWS LETTER / MAINE MERCHANTS ASSOCIATION. **696**

0744-9216 See DEC PROFESSIONAL, THE. **1246**

0744-9240 See RICHARDSON CONSTRUCTION COST TREND REPORTER, THE. 626
0744-933X See PILOT (BOSTON, MASS.), THE. 31
0744-9348 See SAN FRANCISCO ATTORNEY, THE. 3046
0744-9372 See THIRD COAST. 2547
0744-947X See JOURNAL-AMERICAN. 5761
0744-9488 See CHAMPION (HOUSTON, TEX.), THE. 3105
0744-9518 See BAPTIST MESSENGER (OKLAHOMA CITY, OKLA.). 5056
0744-9526 See CLARION-LEDGER, THE. 5700
0744-9550 See NORTHBROOK STAR. 5661
0744-9569 See RVBUSINESS / FROM THE EDITORS OF TL ENTERPRISES. 5392
0744-9593 See NORTH CAROLINA FARM BUREAU NEWS. 115
0744-9631 See ACFA BULLETIN. 4285
0744-964X See SOCCER MATCH. 4919
0744-9658 See UNION REPORTER (DIAMOND BAR, CALIF.). 1716
0744-9666 See SUN (CHAPEL HILL, N.C.). 3443
0744-9682 See JOURNAL : MACOMB COUNTY DENTAL SOCIETY. 1326
0744-9690 See FAMILY LIFE TODAY. 2279
0744-9755 See OPTIMIST HOTLINE. 5234
0744-981X See FLORIDA CASES REPORTED IN SOUTHERN REPORTER, SECOND SERIES. 2970
0744-9828 See COLORADO REPORTER COLORADO CASES REPORTED IN PACIFIC REPORTER, SECOND SERIES. 2952
0744-9879 See COLLECTORS MART. 250
0744-9895 See CALIFORNIA ACCOUNTANT, THE. 740
0744-9909 See BENTON HARBOR FRUIT MARKET (1982). 164
0744-9941 See IAWCM BULLETIN. 3480
0744-9976 See NSPI NEWSLETTER. 4853
0744-9984 See JOURNAL OF CHIROPRACTIC. 3594
0745- See DIRECTORY OF GERIATRIC PUBLICATIONS, THE. 3750
0745-001X See AMERICAN AGRICULTURE NEWS. 58
0745-0044 See WILMETTE LIFE. 5662
0745-0052 See UIW NEWSLETTER. 1715
0745-0079 See GULFSHORE LIFE. 2534
0745-0109 See IOWA CROP REPORT. 175
0745-0117 See NEBRASKA WEATHER & CROPS. 179
0745-0192 See DIRT WHEELS MAGAZINE. 4893
0745-0206 See DELAWARE COUNTY TIMES. 5715
0745-0214 See AVIATION EQUIPMENT MAINTENANCE. 13
0745-0257 See SOUTHERN CROSS (SAN DIEGO, CALIF.). 5036
0745-0265 See CHALLENGES (MIDDLETOWN, CONN.). 1061
0745-0273 See MAINE UNITED METHODIST, THE. 5063
0745-029X See HELPING HAND (JANESVILLE, WIS.), THE. 4962
0745-0311 See ELECTRONIC MEDIA. 1131
0745-0346 See EXPLORING 1 FOR LEADERS. 5060
0745-0362 See WESTERN NEWS (LIBBY, MONT.), THE. 5706
0745-0370 See DALLAS COWBOYS OFFICIAL WEEKLY. 4892
0745-0389 See RV TRADE DIGEST (CHICAGO, ILL. 1981). 5392
0745-0486 See EVANGELICAL VISITOR. 4957
0745-0494 See EAST WEST. 2532
0745-0540 See PHILADELPHIA HOME VIEWER, THE. 2543
0745-0567 See CUSTOM BIKE CHOPPERS. 4081
0745-0575 See WOMEN'S HOUSEHOLD CROCHET. 5186
0745-0583 See MISSOURI ALUMNUS. 1102

0745-0621 See HUMAN RESOURCES MANAGEMENT. PERSONNEL PRACTICES/COMMUNICATIONS. 942
0745-0664 See NORTHERN CALIFORNIA JEWISH BULLETIN. 5051
0745-0702 See BIG SANDY & HAWKINS JOURNAL AND TRI-AREA NEWS, THE. 5747
0745-0729 See WINDOWS (COLLEGE STATION, TEX.). 5169
0745-077X See COMMERCE (HACKENSACK, N.Y.). 658
0745-0788 See GODS REVIVALIST AND BIBLE ADVOCATE. 5016
0745-0796 See NEWINGTON TOWN CRIER. 5646
0745-0818 See JEWISH JOURNAL (BROOKLYN, N.Y.). 5717
0745-0834 See ARIZONA WILDLIFE NEWS. 2187
0745-0842 See LIVESTOCK (TOPEKA, KAN.). 215
0745-0850 See SYSTEMS & SOFTWARE. 1249
0745-0877 See CPA PERSONNEL REPORT. 939
0745-0893 See N.Y. HABITAT. 4841
0745-0907 See MEDICAL ADVERTISING NEWS. 762
0745-0923 See SCAN MAGAZINE. 1139
0745-0958 See DELTA EPSILON SIGMA JOURNAL. 5230
0745-1032 See CANDY INDUSTRY (1982). 2330
0745-1059 See TEACHERAID. 1873
0745-1067 See KANSAS CITY STAR, THE. 5703
0745-1075 See COMPUTERS IN HEALTHCARE. 1179
0745-1083 See BULL GATOR. 1089
0745-1148 See HOSPITAL SECURITY AND SAFETY MANAGEMENT. 3785
0745-1164 See RESOURCE (KANSAS CITY, MO.). 5067
0745-1202 See GERIATRIC CONSULTANT. 3751
0745-1237 See MISSOURI SCHOOLS. 1764
0745-1245 See SHARING THE VICTORY. 4917
0745-1253 See BROOKINGS REVIEW, THE. 5193
0745-127X See SALINA JOURNAL, THE. 5678
0745-1334 See MOUNTAIN STATESMAN (GRAFTON, W. VA.). 5764
0745-1342 See CPA COMPUTER REPORT. 742
0745-1350 See LAKE ELSINORE VALLEY SUN-TRIBUNE. 5636
0745-1369 See ATTORNEYS MARKETING REPORT. 2938
0745-1377 See WEBSTER HERALD, THE. 5722
0745-1415 See RENO GAZETTE-JOURNAL. 5708
0745-1466 See HOSPITAL ADMITTING MONTHLY. 3783
0745-1474 See TENNESSEE BUSINESS (NASHVILLE, TENN.). 715
0745-1512 See WATER QUALITY ASSOCIATION NEWSLETTER. 2247
0745-1520 See WASSAJA (1982). 2765
0745-1547 See TENNIS TALK & SPORTS REVIEW. 4926
0745-1555 See A TO Z. 2185
0745-1628 See HOBIE HOT LINE. 593
0745-1636 See CORPORATE MEETINGS AND INCENTIVES. 5467
0745-1717 See HEALTH CARE SYSTEMS (NEW YORK, N.Y.). 3581
0745-1733 See MID ATLANTIC PURCHASING. 950
0745-1776 See PORT CHALLENGER. 218
0745-1784 See GROWER (SHAWNEE MISSION, KAN.), THE. 173
0745-1903 See WATAUGA DEMOCRAT. 5724
0745-192X See PRESENT TRUTH OF THE APOKALYPSIS, THE. 4987
0745-1962 See CIRCLE K. 1090
0745-1989 See TOLEDO UNION JOURNAL. 5731
0745-2012 See SHELTIE INTERNATIONAL. 4288
0745-2039 See KENNEBEC JOURNAL (AUGUSTA, ME. : 1975). 5685
0745-2047 See NEWTON TAB, THE. 5689
0745-2055 See BOSTON TAB, THE. 5688
0745-2063 See CAMBRIDGE TAB, THE. 5688

0745-2071 See BROOKLINE TAB, THE. 5688
0745-211X See FARMERS' ADVANCE, THE. 5692
0745-2128 See SENTINEL-STANDARD. 5693
0745-2195 See NORTHWEST BAPTIST WITNESS. 5065
0745-2209 See GFWC CLUBWOMAN. 5557
0745-2233 See COMMUNICATOR (ARLINGTON, VA. 1981). 1861
0745-2268 See OKLAHOMA OIL REPORTER, THE. 4270
0745-2276 See NATIONAL SHUFFLER. 4864
0745-2306 See FEDERAL LOCAL COURT RULES. 3089
0745-2322 See YIHUA BAO. 5763
0745-2330 See PENTECOSTAL FREE-WILL BAPTIST MESSENGER. 5066
0745-2365 See TRADITIONAL TAEKWON-DO. 4927
0745-239X See NASE DEJINY. 2461
0745-2454 See MIDDLEBURY COLLEGE MAGAZINE. 1093
0745-2462 See PALOS VERDES REVIEW. 2542
0745-2489 See SUCCESS (CHICAGO, ILL.). 714
0745-2535 See MISSISSIPPI MORBIDITY REPORT. 5333
0745-256X See BOLLETINO : OFFICIAL PUBLICATION OF THE ITALIAN CATHOLIC FEDERATION. 5024
0745-2586 See PENNSYLVANIA BEACON, THE. 5738
0745-2608 See CARIBBEAN CONNECTIONS. 2486
0745-2616 See HUMAN SERVICES (WOODHAVEN, N.Y.). 5288
0745-2624 See JOURNAL - AMERICAN ASSOCIATION FOR MEDICAL TRANSCRIPTION. 3592
0745-2667 See SEC TODAY, THE. 913
0745-2683 See DAILY NEWS JOURNAL (MURFREESBORO, TENN.), THE. 5745
0745-2691 See BUFFALO NEWS, THE. 5714
0745-2705 See NEBRASKA LUTHERAN. 5065
0745-273X See WING WORLD. 4083
0745-2748 See MANTECA BULLETIN. 5637
0745-2810 See COLLAGE (WHEELING, ILL.). 2531
0745-2829 See BULLETIN - SIOUX FALLS COLLEGE (SIOUX FALLS, S.D.). 1813
0745-2896 See MAKAI. 1451
0745-2918 See CHALLENGE OF CONSERVATIVE BAPTIST HOME MISSIONS, THE. 5057
0745-2969 See CABLETIME. 1150
0745-2993 See MICROWAVES & RF. 4438
0745-3000 See MODERN CELL BIOLOGY. 538
0745-3019 See GEM (FINDLAY, OHIO), THE. 4960
0745-3027 See PERSPECTIVE (COLUMBUS, OHIO). 5235
0745-3086 See FORWARD (MADISON, WIS.). 5557
0745-3116 See COUNTRY HANDCRAFTS. 371
0745-3167 See ADOPTED CHILD. 2276
0745-3191 See POLK COUNTY ELEGANCE. 2543
0745-3205 See NABE NEWS (CLEVELAND, OHIO). 1506
0745-3213 See UC CLIP SHEET. 1851
0745-323X See ALABAMA JOURNAL, THE. 5625
0745-3302 See CUTW VOICE. 1662
0745-3450 See AGRI NEWS. 5694
0745-3469 See NUT GROWER. 180
0745-3485 See PERSPECTIVES (RIDGEFIELD, CONN.). 1990
0745-3515 See NOTRE DAME LAW REVIEW, THE. 3019
0745-3523 See CESSNA OWNER MAGAZINE, THE. 16
0745-3531 See NEWSLETTER - NATIONAL ASSOCIATION OF SOCIAL WORKERS. WASHINGTON STATE CHAPTER. 5299
0745-354X See SUN BELT BUILDINGS JOURNAL. 4847
0745-3558 See SUNDAY SERMONS. 5001

0745-3574 *See* STANDARD-TIMES (NEW BEDFORD, MASS.), THE. **5690**

0745-3612 *See* TODAY'S CATHOLIC (SAN ANTONIO, TEX.). **5037**

0745-3655 *See* CADILAC EVENING NEWS. **5691**

0745-3663 *See* WEBSTER POST, THE. **5722**

0745-3671 *See* COMMUNICATOR. **1108**

0745-3698 *See* AMERICAN BAPTIST QUARTERLY. **5055**

0745-3744 *See* MELROSE PARK HERALD WITH NEWS OF STONE PARK. **5661**

0745-3787 *See* PORK. **217**

0745-3795 *See* LANDSCAPE & IRRIGATION. **2422**

0745-3841 See OAKLAND TRIBUNE (OAKLAND, CALIF. 1991). **5638**

0745-385X *See* OKLAHOMA EAGLE, THE. **5732**

0745-3884 *See* ROCKY MOUNTAIN AMERICAN BAPTIST. **5067**

0745-3906 *See* MINNEAPOLIS REALTOR. **4841**

0745-3930 *See* CORONA-NORCO INDEPENDENT. **5634**

0745-3949 *See* DANCSCENE. **1313**

0745-3981 *See* STANFORD MAGAZINE, THE. **1095**

0745-399X *See* CATHOLIC ACCENT, THE. **5025**

0745-4023 *See* NORWALK REFLECTOR (NORWALK, OHIO : DAILY). **5729**

0745-4074 *See* EVANGELIZE (MINNEAPOLIS, MINN.). **5060**

0745-4104 *See* GROCERS JOURNAL OF CALIFORNIA. **2342**

0745-4120 *See* GLADES COUNTY DEMOCRAT. **5649**

0745-4147 *See* SUNY GENESCO COMPASS. **1095**

0745-4163 *See* UNITED TEACHER (LOS ANGELES, CALIF.). **1788**

0745-418X *See* NETWORK NEWS (BLUFFTON, OHIO). **5065**

0745-4201 *See* FTD FAMILY. **2435**

0745-421X *See* ATTORNEYS COMPUTER REPORT. **2938**

0745-4260 *See* LEXINGTON HERALD-LEADER. **5681**

0745-4279 *See* RANCHLAND NEWS. **2544**

0745-4295 *See* VISUAL MERCHANDISING & STORE DESIGN. **958**

0745-4317 *See* MARYLAND AGRI-VIEWS. **107**

0745-4341 *See* CAM REPORT. **4201**

0745-4368 *See* SPURS & FEATHERS. **4923**

0745-4406 *See* NEW YORK LAW JOURNAL DIGEST-ANNOTATOR. **3082**

0745-4430 *See* SHORE LINES. **5019**

0745-4449 *See* LATAX REPORT. **4736**

0745-4473 *See* SOUTH CAROLINA BUSINESS JOURNAL. **712**

0745-449X *See* DIE CASTING MANAGEMENT. **3477**

0745-4503 *See* FOOD INSTITUTE REPORT, THE. **2337**

0745-452X *See* AGRI-PRACTICE. **47**

0745-4538 *See* HEALTHMARKETING. **4782**

0745-4554 *See* PHYSICIANS' TRAVEL & MEETING GUIDE. **5488**

0745-4570 *See* COMICS BUYER'S GUIDE, THE. **4859**

0745-4589 *See* LOUISIANA CASES REPORTED IN SOUTHERN REPORTER, SECOND SERIES. **3004**

0745-4619 See GOLD COAST. **2534**

0745-4651 *See* ELECTRIC CONSUMER. **1937**

0745-4678 *See* HEALTH INDUSTRY TODAY. **3581**

0745-4724 *See* DESERET NEWS (SALT LAKE CITY, UTAH : 1964). **5756**

0745-4813 *See* BI-STATE REPORTER. **5658**

0745-4821 *See* EQUAL OPPORTUNITY IN HOUSING. **2822**

0745-483X *See* CENTRE DAILY TIMES. **5735**

0745-4848 *See* ONONDAGA VALLEY NEWS. **5719**

0745-4856 *See* COMMERCIAL APPEAL, THE. **5744**

0745-4864 *See* AGRICULTURAL AVIATION (WASHINGTON, D.C.). **6**

0745-4880 *See* MANAGEMENT REPORT (NEW YORK, N.Y.). **944**

0745-4910 *See* MEDICAL CENTER. **3788**

0745-5011 *See* LEISURE WORLD NEWS. **2537**

0745-5046 *See* OKLAHOMA REALTOR. **4842**

0745-5054 *See* MUSIC ROW. **4135**

0745-5100 *See* AIR CARGO WORLD. **5375**

0745-5127 *See* NATIONAL CATHOLIC FORESTER. **5032**

0745-5178 *See* AMERICAN FOLKLORE SOCIETY NEWSLETTER, THE. **2318**

0745-5194 *See* MEDICAL ANTHROPOLOGY QUARTERLY. **241**

0745-5267 *See* RAILPACE NEWSMAGAZINE. **5435**

0745-5275 *See* OAG PACIFIC AREA POCKET FLIGHT GUIDE. **5486**

0745-5291 *See* COMPUTER + SOFTWARE NEWS. **1245**

0745-5305 *See* GROWING WITHOUT SCHOOLING. **1895**

0745-5321 *See* VALLEY-FOOTHILLS NEWS, THE. **5630**

0745-5356 *See* NEW YORK JEWISH WEEK, THE. **2269**

0745-5364 *See* DAILY MIDWAY DRILLER. **5634**

0745-5402 *See* RUIDOSO NEWS. **5713**

0745-5429 *See* MONTANA MORBIDITY REPORT. **4554**

0745-5445 *See* NAUJIENOS. **5661**

0745-5453 *See* AMERIKANSKI SLOVENEC (CHICAGO, ILL.). **5658**

0745-547X *See* EVENING JOURNAL (LUBBOCK, TEX.). **5749**

0745-5518 *See* SEMINARY NEWS (ENID, OKLA.). **4996**

0745-5526 *See* ST. TAMMANY NEWS-BANNER, THE. **5684**

0745-5534 *See* DAILY MESSENGER (UNION CITY, TENN.). **5745**

0745-5542 *See* TIMES-PRESS (STREATOR, ILL.). **5662**

0745-5550 *See* EVENING LEADER (SAINT MARYS, OHIO). **5728**

0745-5585 *See* DESERT POST. **5634**

0745-5607 *See* LONG ISLAND JEWISH WEEK, THE. **5051**

0745-5615 *See* ACTION AND REACTION. **4514**

0745-5631 *See* PINELLAS PARK NEWS. **5650**

0745-5747 *See* TULSA BUSINESS CHRONICLE. **5733**

0745-5828 *See* CHARIOT (CRAWFORDSVILLE, IND.). **3374**

0745-5836 *See* BAPTIST BIBLE TRIBUNE. **5056**

0745-5860 *See* NEW KIT CAR MONTHLY, THE. **5421**

0745-5895 *See* CALIFORNIANS (SAN FRANCISCO, CALIF.), THE. **2726**

0745-5909 *See* COLLIN COUNTY COMMERCIAL RECORD. **5748**

0745-5925 *See* SHEPARD'S UNIFORM COMMERCIAL CODE CITATIONS. **3054**

0745-5933 *See* BUSINESS MARKETING. **922**

0745-5941 *See* HIGH-PERFORMANCE PONTIAC. **5416**

0745-5968 *See* MORNING GLORY. **4979**

0745-5976 *See* MACON COUNTY TIMES. **5745**

0745-5992 *See* BLACK RADIO EXCLUSIVE. **1127**

0745-600X *See* BETTER LIVING TODAY. **2485**

0745-6050 *See* CATHOLIC TIMES (COLUMBUS, OHIO), THE. **5026**

0745-6093 *See* SECURITY MANAGEMENT, PROTECTING PROPERTY, PEOPLE ASSETS. **710**

0745-6131 *See* FERC PRACTICE AND PROCEDURE MANUAL. **1944**

0745-6166 *See* SANTA MARIA TIMES. **5640**

0745-6174 *See* LEWISVILLE DAILY LEADER. **5751**

0745-6182 *See* ESCAPE (SALT LAKE CITY, UTAH). **5469**

0745-6212 *See* MILPITAS POST. **5637**

0745-6220 *See* MOUNTAIN COURIER-NEWS. **5637**

0745-6247 *See* OSCEOLA SENTINEL-TRIBUNE. **5672**

0745-6255 *See* SARATOGA NEWS. **5640**

0745-6263 *See* VENICE GONDOLIER, THE. **5651**

0745-628X *See* NORTH COUNTRY GAZETTE. **5719**

0745-6298 *See* CHALLENGE (CARTHAGE, ILL.). **1877**

0745-6336 *See* VALLEY NEWS (APPLE VALLEY, CALIF.). **5641**

0745-6344 *See* GOLD PROSPECTOR. **2140**

0745-6360 *See* ANNIE'S CROCHET NEWSLETTER. **5183**

0745-6379 *See* OREGON PUBLISHER. **4818**

0745-6425 *See* SULPHUR SPRINGS NEWS-TELEGRAM. **5755**

0745-6441 *See* ADVENTIST REVIEW (WEEKLY, SOUTHWESTERN EDITION). **5054**

0745-6468 *See* GARTH ANALYSIS, THE. **5246**

0745-6484 *See* SOUTHAMPTON PRESS, THE. **5721**

0745-6506 *See* AMAZING HEROES. **1059**

0745-6557 *See* AMERIKA WOCHE. **5658**

0745-6565 *See* HAWAII TV DIGEST. **1132**

0745-6603 *See* GULF COAST LUMBERMAN AND BUILDING MATERIAL DISTRIBUTOR (HOUSTON, TEX. : 1982). **2401**

0745-6611 *See* DAILY SPECTRUM (SAINT GEORGE, UTAH), THE. **5756**

0745-6646 *See* COMMUNITY HERALD (MONONA, WIS.), THE. **5766**

0745-6654 *See* DINUBA SENTINEL. **5634**

0745-6751 *See* SECURITY SYSTEMS ADMINISTRATION. **5177**

0745-6786 *See* ALABAMA ECHOES. **4933**

0745-6794 *See* COLDWATER DAILY REPORTER. **5691**

0745-6816 *See* LEADER (POINT PLEASANT BEACH, N.J.). **5710**

0745-6824 *See* FINE TOOL JOURNAL, THE. **250**

0745-6859 *See* JOURNAL MESSENGER, THE. **5759**

0745-6875 *See* KEN-TON BEE. **5717**

0745-6891 *See* CABLE VIEWER MAGAZINE. **1129**

0745-6905 *See* RUG HOOKER NEWS & VIEWS, THE. **5185**

0745-6921 See WORLD WASTES. **2248**

0745-6956 *See* COURIER DEMOCRAT. **5631**

0745-6972 *See* BEAGLE BUGLE. **1060**

0745-6999 *See* JOURNAL OF RESOURCE MANAGEMENT AND TECHNOLOGY, THE. **2234**

0745-7006 *See* BUTLER COUNTY BANNER. **5679**

0745-7014 *See* CHICAGO DEFENDER (1973). **5659**

0745-7030 *See* CENTRAL RECORD (MEDFORD, N.J.). **5709**

0745-7049 *See* NATIONAL OTC STOCK JOURNAL, THE. **909**

0745-7065 *See* SCHOLASTIC UPDATE. **1782**

0745-7073 *See* HAWAII INVESTOR. **4838**

0745-7103 *See* INDIANA AGRI-NEWS. **95**

0745-7111 *See* COAL VALLEY NEWS. **5763**

0745-7138 *See* JOURNAL OF MICROCOMPUTER APPLICATIONS. **1268**

0745-7146 *See* MONEYTALK. **2490**

0745-7170 *See* $ELF-RELIANT. **833**

0745-7189 *See* TEDDY BEAR AND FRIENDS, THE. **2778**

0745-7200 *See* VIRGINIA EXTENSION. **1543**

0745-7227 *See* EVENING WORLD (SPENCER, IND.). **5664**

0745-7251 *See* CANBY NEWS. **5695**

0745-7278 See HEALTH NEWS & REVIEW. **4191**

0745-7324 *See* GREENHOUSE GROWER. **2417**

0745-7332 *See* ADIRONDACK ECHO. **5713**

0745-7367 *See* LEAF-CHRONICLE, THE. **5745**

0745-7383 *See* MONTESANO GRAYS HARBOR COUNTY VIDETTE, THE. **5761**

0745-7405 See TITONKA TOPIC. 5673
0745-7413 See WASHINGTON PHARMACIST, THE. 4332
0745-7421 See LANCASTER NEWS, THE. 5742
0745-743X See DAILY UNION (JUNCTION CITY, KAN.). 5675
0745-7472 See HEARING JOURNAL, THE. 3888
0745-7499 See CRESSON & GALLITZIN MAINLINER, THE. 5735
0745-7502 See GOLF REPORTER, THE. 4897
0745-7545 See REPOSITORY (CANTON, OHIO), THE. 5730
0745-7561 See CITIZEN (JAY, OKLA.). 5731
0745-7588 See UMPQUA FREE PRESS. 5734
0745-7618 See GOSPEL TIDINGS (OMAHA, NEB.). 5060
0745-7626 See MOBILE RADIO TECHNOLOGY. 1135
0745-7642 See MISSOURI CASES REPORTED IN SOUTH WESTERN REPORTER, SECOND SERIES. 3011
0745-7685 See WAYNE COUNTY MAIL. 5722
0745-7707 See BAXTER BULLETIN. 5631
0745-774X See EDGEWATER TRIBUNE. 5642
0745-7766 See EVERYTHING'S ARCHIE. 4860
0745-7774 See ARCHIE'S PALS 'N GALS. 4857
0745-7790 See EMPLOYMENT RELATIONS TODAY. 1667
0745-7804 See STATESVILLE RECORD & LANDMARK. 5724
0745-7839 See JOURNAL / AMERICAN RHODODENDRON SOCIETY. 2421
0745-7847 See ISLANDS (SANTA BARBARA, CALIF.). 5481
0745-7863 See PEKIN DAILY TIMES. 5661
0745-7898 See ALMA TIMES-STATESMAN. 5652
0745-791X See MINERAL COUNTY MINER, THE. 5643
0745-8037 See PENNSYLVANIA REPORTER. 3025
0745-8096 See DELAWARE STATE NEWS AND MARYLAND STATE NEWS. 5647
0745-810X See GURNEE PRESS. 5660
0745-8118 See WARREN-NEWPORT PRESS. 5662
0745-8126 See BICYCLE BUSINESS JOURNAL. 428
0745-8150 See COMMUNITY NEWS (BROWNS MILLS, N.J.), THE. 5709
0745-8177 See WASECA COUNTY NEWS. 5699
0745-8215 See FE Y VIDA. 5060
0745-8258 See KINDERGARTEN TEACHER. 4972
0745-8355 See FOCUS ON FARMING. 88
0745-8371 See MOTHERS TODAY. 3765
0745-838X See COFFEY COUNTY TODAY. 5675
0745-8398 See OVID GAZETTE, THE. 5720
0745-8452 See CFTC ADMINISTRATIVE REPORTER. 826
0745-8495 See EVANGELICAL METHODIST, THE. 5060
0745-8509 See STAR (NEW YORK, N.Y.), THE. 2273
0745-8517 See SKEETER, THE. 4918
0745-8525 See ILLINOIS GRAIN & LIVESTOCK MARKET NEWS. 202
0745-8533 See COIN SLOT (LUZERNE, PA.), THE. 250
0745-855X See DOTHAN EAGLE. 5626
0745-8584 See MYRTLE BEACH JOURNAL, THE. 5637
0745-8606 See TWIN CITIES CHRISTIAN, THE. 5006
0745-8614 See GAZETTE, POWHATAN, THE. 5758
0745-8630 See NURSINGWORLD JOURNAL. 3866
0745-8649 See BLACK BEAT. 4103
0745-8657 See TODAY NEWS. 5630
0745-8673 See BLACKSTONE VALLEY TRIBUNE. 5687
0745-8681 See DES PLAINES EDITION OF THE TIMES. 5659

0745-8711 See PRIVATE CABLE. 1136
0745-872X See SKAGWAY NEWS, THE. 5629
0745-8738 See MIDWEST POETRY REVIEW. 3466
0745-8800 See QUADERNI SARDI DI ECONOMIA PODPORUJICI JEDMPTA STATU TEXAS. 2755
0745-8835 See NEW YORK STATE CONSERVATION COUNCIL COMMENTS. 2200
0745-886X See ACCOUNTING STANDARDS. CURRENT TEXT. 737
0745-886X See ACCOUNTING STANDARDS. CURRENT TEXT AS OF JUNE 1 ... / FINANCIAL ACCOUNTING STANDARDS BOARD. 737
0745-8878 See LUSK'S NORTHERN VIRGINIA REAL ESTATE GUIDE. 4840
0745-8908 See NORTH JERSEY PROSPECTOR, THE. 5711
0745-8916 See SOUTHWEST DAILY TIMES, THE. 5678
0745-8959 See MARIN COUNTY COURT REPORTER. 3006
0745-8991 See WORLD GRAIN. 204
0745-9017 See LAKE EUFAULA WORLD. 5732
0745-9033 See DAIRYMEN'S DIGEST. NORTH CENTRAL REGION EDITION. 194
0745-905X See FILIPINO AMERICAN, THE. 2261
0745-9092 See DOLLARS & SENSE (WASHINGTON, D.C. 1979). 4720
0745-9106 See NOME NUGGET (NOME, ALASKA : 1938). 5629
0745-9173 See VICTORY (SAN DIEGO, CALIF.). 5007
0745-9181 See JOURNAL OF AGRICULTURAL TAXATION & LAW. 2986
0745-9203 See WINTER PARK OUTLOOK. 5651
0745-9254 See JAMAICA PLAIN CITIZEN ROXBURY CITIZEN. 5689
0745-9262 See HYDE PARK TRIBUNE, THE MATTAPAN TRIBUNE. 5689
0745-9297 See TOLEDO TECHNICAL TOPICS. 5166
0745-9300 See LAMAR DEMOCRAT. 5703
0745-9327 See SHOFAR (WASHINGTON, D.C.), THE. 5052
0745-9335 See BALDWIN LEDGER, THE. 5674
0745-9351 See BUSINESS REVIEW (WASHINGTON ED.), THE. 652
0745-936X See BIG RED NEWS. 5714
0745-9432 See INSIDE UVA. 1864
0745-9467 See SUSSEX-SURRY DISPATCH. 5759
0745-9483 See PARK RECORD (1964), THE. 5757
0745-9599 See TRIBUNE-STAR, THE. 5667
0745-9602 See OFFICERS MANAGER'S LETTER. 880
0745-9610 See ENGLEWOOD HERALD, THE. 5642
0745-9653 See EMPLOYMENT-AT-WILL REPORTER. 3147
0745-9661 See GRAND FORKS HERALD. 5725
0745-967X See MICHIGAN DAILY, THE. 5693
0745-9688 See PARAGLIDE. 4053
0745-9696 See SEATTLE TIMES, THE. 5762
0745-970X See SEATTLE POST-INTELLIGENCER (1921). 5762
0745-9742 See WINNETKA NEWS/VOICE. 5662
0745-9750 See WILMETTE NEWS/VOICE. 5662
0745-9777 See NORTHBROOK NEWS/VOICE. 5661
0745-9793 See LA CROSSE TRIBUNE. 5768
0745-9815 See GLENVIEW NEWS/VOICE. 5660
0745-9823 See CORTLAND DEMOCRAT (1877), THE. 5715
0745-9831 See EAGLE (CAMBRIDGE, N.Y.), THE. 5716
0745-984X See ENERGY MANAGEMENT TECHNOLOGY. 5103
0745-9858 See MONEYPAPER, THE. 696
0745-9874 See NTSB REPORTER. 5388
0745-9920 See COUNTRY PRESS. 5642
0745-9971 See AMERIKAN UUTISET. 5647
0746-0015 See SPECTRUM (WHEATON, ILL.). 4999

0746-0023 See BUSINESS FACILITIES. 648
0746-004X See CANAL ZONE STUDY GROUP. 2784
0746-0082 See MIAMI CHIEF (CANADIAN, TEX.). 5752
0746-0104 See BIBLE ADVOCATE (BROOMFIELD, COLO.). 5014
0746-0201 See N.Y. CIVIL LIBERTIES. 4511
0746-0228 See UTAH-IDAHO SOUTHERN BAPTIST WITNESS. 5068
0746-0260 See CLACKAMAS COUNTY REVIEW, THE. 5733
0746-0279 See VOZ DE PORTUGAL. 2549
0746-0309 See CROCKETT CO. SENTINEL, TRI-CO. NEWS, CROCKETT TIMES, THE. 5745
0746-035X See FEDERAL MERIT SYSTEMS REPORTER. 4702
0746-0368 See MICHIGAN HEALTH & SAFETY DIGEST. 4791
0746-0384 See TAX UPDATE FOR BUSINESS OWNERS. 4754
0746-0392 See TIMES OF TI. 5721
0746-0414 See CHAUTAUQUAN DAILY, THE. 5714
0746-0430 See DAILY PROGRESS (CHARLOTTESVILLE, VA.), THE. 5758
0746-0511 See CATHOLIC COMMENTATOR, THE. 5025
0746-052X See SUBURBAN NEWS (FRANKLIN LAKES, N.J. : 1981). 5711
0746-0538 See DELTA WEEKLY. 5700
0746-0554 See ARCHITECTURE (WASHINGTON, D.C.). 290
0746-0570 See LOGAN BANNER (LOGAN, W. VA. : DAILY). 5764
0746-0619 See TIPTON COUNTY TRIBUNE. 5667
0746-0627 See VASA STAR, THE. 2274
0746-066X See SHELTER ISLAND REPORTER. 5721
0746-0678 See BROOKSHIRE BANNER. 5747
0746-0716 See ADEL NEWS TRIBUNE. 5651
0746-0724 See PRESS-ENTERPRISE (BLOOMSBURG, PA.). 5739
0746-0813 See HIGHLAND PARK NEWS (HIGHLAND PARK, ILL.). 5660
0746-083X See CROSS COUNTRY JOURNAL. 4892
0746-0872 See DAILY REPORTER (SPENCER, IOWA), THE. 5669
0746-0880 See GOSPEL HERALD AND THE SUNDAY SCHOOL TIMES. 4961
0746-0910 See POST AND COURIER, THE. 5743
0746-0961 See LOUISVILLE MESSENGER, THE. 5706
0746-0988 See VOZ (DENVER, COLO.). 5644
0746-0996 See STUDIO PHOTOGRAPHY. 4377
0746-102X See ARCADE HERALD. 5713
0746-1046 See HIGH SPRINGS HERALD. 5649
0746-1062 See PENNSYLVANIA CPA JOURNAL. 749
0746-1070 See OPHTHALMOLOGY MANAGEMENT. 3878
0746-1100 See THIS WEEK MAGAZINE (PORTLAND, ORE.). 5734
0746-1119 See AD-EXPRESS AND DAILY IOWEGIAN AND CITIZEN. 5656
0746-1127 See CINCINNATI BENGALS REPORT, THE. 4890
0746-1151 See ARIZONA BEVERAGE GUIDE. 2363
0746-1186 See VIRGINIA FARMER (BALTIMORE, MD.). 144
0746-1259 See CAMPNEWS (PHILADELPHIA, PA.). 4870
0746-1291 See MISSOURI JEWISH POST & OPINION. 2268
0746-1305 See WESTERN COLLEGE READING & LEARNING ASSOCIATION NEWSLETTER. 1853
0746-1321 See SAVINGS INSTITUTIONS. 810
0746-133X See AHEPAN. 1723
0746-1399 See GUADALUPE COUNTY COMMUNICATOR. 5712

0746-1402 *See* CENTERVIEWS (HONOLULU, HAWAII). **1814**
0746-1410 *See* CANINE CHRONICLE. **4286**
0746-1429 *See* CHRONICLE (CHARLESTON, S.C.), THE. **5742**
0746-1437 *See* DOUGLAS COUNTY POST-GAZETTE. **5706**
0746-1461 *See* MICHIGAN WORKERS' COMP DIGEST. **3152**
0746-150X *See* WISCONSIN REPORTER. **3075**
0746-1526 *See* WEST'S PERSONAL INJURY NEWS. **3074**
0746-1569 *See* BATES COUNTY NEWS-HEADLINER, THE. **5702**
0746-1585 *See* SACRAMENTO SPORTS. **4916**
0746-1623 *See* ARGUS-TIMES, THE. **5731**
0746-1658 *See* CAROLINE COUNTY TIMES-RECORD, THE. **5685**
0746-1666 *See* HOME PRESS, THE. **5703**
0746-1674 *See* JOURNAL-OPINION. **5757**
0746-1682 *See* SIERRA NORTH STAR. **2545**
0746-1712 *See* TRI-COUNTY JOURNAL. **5704**
0746-1739 *See* NURSING ECONOMIC$. **3864**
0746-1747 *See* PENFIELD POST-REPUBLICAN. **5720**
0746-1771 *See* LAWRENCE LEDGER, THE. **5710**
0746-178X *See* PRINCETON PACKET, THE. **5711**
0746-1798 *See* AMELIA BULLETIN MONITOR, THE. **5758**
0746-1844 *See* WESTCHESTER BAR JOURNAL. **3073**
0746-1968 *See* ATMORE ADVANCE, THE. **5625**
0746-2018 *See* FRANK SCHAFFER'S SCHOOLDAYS. **1895**
0746-2034 *See* KOKOMO TRIBUNE (KOKOMO, IND. : 1966). **5665**
0746-2042 *See* HERALD-TRIBUNE, THE. **5664**
0746-2077 *See* AUTOMOTIVE CHAIN STORE (NEW YORK, N.Y.). **5406**
0746-2093 *See* EAST ROCKAWAY LYNNBROOK OBSERVER. **5716**
0746-2115 *See* ANDALUSIA STAR-NEWS, THE. **5625**
0746-2131 *See* GRANBURY TABLET, THE. **5750**
0746-2182 *See* SUNDAY NEWS SUN. **5651**
0746-2204 *See* IOWA STATER, THE. **1831**
0746-2255 *See* KENTUCKY ENGINEER. **1984**
0746-2271 *See* SOUTH FLORIDA BUSINESS JOURNAL. **712**
0746-2298 *See* MICHIGAN SNOWMOBILER. **5386**
0746-2301 *See* HI-DESERT STAR. **5635**
0746-2328 *See* CAMPUS ACTIVITIES PROGRAMMING. **1813**
0746-2336 *See* WINDSOR CHRONICLE, THE. **5758**
0746-2395 *See* CHILTON'S I&CS. **1968**
0746-2417 *See* NURSERY TEACHERS' GUIDE (CHURCH OF GOD OF PROPHECY ED.). **1901**
0746-2425 *See* HIGH SCHOOL NEWS AND GRAPHICS. **2920**
0746-2441 *See* FASTENER TECHNOLOGY INTERNATIONAL. **2114**
0746-2468 *See* FUTURES (CEDAR FALLS, IOWA). **899**
0746-2506 *See* EMERGENCY MEDICINE REPORTS. **3724**
0746-2522 *See* CONSUMER MAGAZINE AND AGRI-MEDIA RATES AND DATA / SRDS. **758**
0746-2557 *See* BLUE & GOLD ILLUSTRATED. **1089**
0746-2565 *See* MICHIGAN ALUMNUS. **1102**
0746-2611 *See* GARFIELD-MAPLE HEIGHTS SUN. **5728**
0746-262X *See* BEDFORD SUN BANNER. **5727**
0746-2638 *See* QUAIL UNLIMITED MAGAZINE. **5619**
0746-2654 *See* THERMAL BELT NEWS JOURNAL. **5724**
0746-2735 See TRAVERSE (TRAVERSE CITY, MICH.). **2494**

0746-2751 *See* ACCREDITED RESIDENT MANAGER NEWS / INSTITUTE OF REAL ESTATE MANAGEMENT OF THE NATIONAL ASSOCIATION OF REALTORS. **859**
0746-2824 *See* JASPER NEWS-BOY, THE. **5751**
0746-2867 *See* JOURNAL TIMES, THE. **5768**
0746-2875 *See* BORZOI QUARTERLY (WHEAT RIDGE, COLO.), THE. **4286**
0746-2921 *See* SECURITY CLINIC. **710**
0746-293X *See* CREDIT & COLLECTION CLINIC. **785**
0746-2964 *See* DENVER BUSINESS. **665**
0746-2980 *See* MOOSE LAKE STAR GAZETTE (1983). **5697**
0746-2999 *See* ELECTRONIC ENTERTAINMENT. **4850**
0746-3014 *See* EDITOR'S FORUM (KANSAS CITY, MO.). **2919**
0746-3057 *See* TEEN TEACHER'S MANUAL. **1907**
0746-309X *See* EDUCATION FORWARD. **1863**
0746-312X *See* SHEPARD'S FEDERAL ENERGY LAW CITATIONS (QUARTERLY). **3050**
0746-3197 *See* COMMANDER (TACOMA, WASH.). **1175**
0746-3235 *See* LAWTON MORNING PRESS. **5732**
0746-3251 *See* COUNTRY NEWS. **2531**
0746-3294 *See* CAPITOL REVIEW, THE. **5748**
0746-3324 *See* GRIFFIN DAILY NEWS. **5653**
0746-3340 See GLENDALE NEWS-PRESS (1993). **5635**
0746-3359 *See* HIGH COUNTRY INDEPENDENT PRESS. **5705**
0746-3405 *See* COMPUTERIZED MANUFACTURING. **1236**
0746-3413 *See* LUTHERAN AMBASSADOR, THE. **5062**
0746-3421 *See* CLARION-LEDGER, JACKSON DAILY NEWS, THE. **5700**
0746-3472 *See* QUEEN CITY HERITAGE. **2756**
0746-3499 *See* AVE MARIA (LEMONT, ILL.). **5024**
0746-3502 *See* SALT LAKE TRIBUNE (SALT LAKE CITY, UTAH : 1890). **5757**
0746-3510 *See* CARBONDALE NEWS (CARBONDALE, PA. : 1961). **5735**
0746-3537 *See* TECHNOLOGY TEACHER, THE. **5164**
0746-360X *See* EL PASO HERALD-POST. **5749**
0746-3618 *See* NEW AGE JOURNAL (1983). **4186**
0746-3626 *See* GRAPHICOMMUNICATOR. **1112**
0746-3634 *See* BLACKPOWDER REPORT, THE. **3476**
0746-3669 *See* BUSINESS ADVOCATE (WASHINGTON, D.C. : 1983), THE. **3096**
0746-3677 *See* GSD NEWS (1983). **299**
0746-3693 *See* LONGMEADOW NEWS. **5645**
0746-3766 *See* JOJOBA HAPPENINGS. **98**
0746-3774 *See* AUTO INDUSTRY MAGAZINE. **5404**
0746-3790 See MILWAUKEE MAGAZINE. **2538**
0746-3812 *See* C-SPAN UPDATE. **5647**
0746-3820 *See* PACKAGING (BOSTON, MASS.). **4220**
0746-3839 *See* MODERN OFFICE TECHNOLOGY. **4212**
0746-3847 *See* MANSFIELD NEWS-MIRROR. **5752**
0746-3863 *See* HUNTERDON REVIEW AND THE HIGH BRIDGE GAZETTE. **5710**
0746-3871 *See* COLUSA COUNTY FARMER, THE. **5634**
0746-3901 *See* TIMES-POST. **5702**
0746-391X *See* NATIONAL MARINER, THE. **1453**
0746-3928 *See* PORTUGUESE TIMES (NEW BEDFORD, MASS.). **5689**
0746-3944 *See* SEE THE TREASURE COAST. **5490**
0746-3979 *See* COMMUNICATOR OF PHI DELTA CHI FRATERNITY, THE. **5230**
0746-3987 *See* CHEROKEE SCOUT. **5723**
0746-3995 *See* CORVALLIS GAZETTE-TIMES. **5733**

0746-4029 *See* WATER CONDITIONING & PURIFICATION. **5542**
0746-4037 *See* NANTY-GLO JOURNAL, THE. **5737**
0746-4045 *See* METRO TIMES (DETROIT, MICH.), THE. **5692**
0746-4061 *See* BETHEL JOURNAL, THE. **5727**
0746-410X *See* BUSINESS RECORD (DES MOINES, IOWA). **652**
0746-4126 *See* MESQUITE NEWS, THE. **5752**
0746-4142 *See* LIGHT CHAMPION. **5752**
0746-4169 *See* HARALSON GATEWAY-BEACON, THE. **5653**
0746-4177 *See* ATLA ADVOCATE. **2937**
0746-4185 *See* CATHOLIC HERALD (SACRAMENTO, CALIF.). **5026**
0746-4193 *See* REPORTER (VACAVILLE, CALIF.). **5639**
0746-4258 *See* PRESS-ENTERPRISE (RIVERSIDE, CALIF.). **5638**
0746-4266 *See* FORT MADISON DAILY DEMOCRAT. **5670**
0746-4274 *See* LAKELAND TIMES. **5768**
0746-4304 *See* LAKE COUNTY RECORD-BEE. **5636**
0746-4312 *See* HANGUK ILBO, ROSUENJELSU. **5635**
0746-4320 *See* MARINA NEWS (LONG BEACH, CALIF.). **5637**
0746-4339 *See* WELEETKAN, THE. **5733**
0746-438X *See* CHRONICLE (BARTON, VT.). **5757**
0746-4398 *See* OPINION-TRIBUNE, THE. **5672**
0746-4452 *See* SOUTHEAST MISSOURIAN. **5704**
0746-4460 *See* DEPEW BEE. **5716**
0746-4479 *See* KYRIAKATIKA NEA. **5689**
0746-4487 *See* LANCASTER BEE. **5717**
0746-4495 *See* MISSOULIAN (MISSOULA, MONT. 1961). **5693**
0746-4509 See DIRECCION (KANSAS CITY, MO.). **4953**
0746-4525 *See* BIBLICAL RESEARCH MONTHLY. **5015**
0746-4533 *See* CLARK COUNTY FARM BUREAU NEWS (MARTINSVILLE, ILL.). **75**
0746-4584 *See* FLORIDA CATHOLIC, THE. **5029**
0746-4592 *See* WILLOW GROVE GUIDE. **5741**
0746-4606 *See* TIMES-CHRONICLE. **5740**
0746-4657 *See* AUGUSTA FOCUS. **5652**
0746-4665 *See* STATESBORO HERALD. **5655**
0746-469X *See* CLINICAL LASER MONTHLY. **3566**
0746-4703 See HOSPITAL'S MEDICARE POLICY & PAYMENT REPORT, THE. **3786**
0746-4754 *See* INDEPENDANT PROFESSIONAL AND FLORIDA BUSINESS JOURNAL, THE. **681**
0746-4789 *See* COUNTRY CONNECTION, THE. **5731**
0746-4797 *See* RAINBOW (PROSPECT, KY.). **1272**
0746-4843 *See* EVENING TIMES (SAYRE, PA.). **5736**
0746-4886 *See* ISLAND PACKET, THE. **5742**
0746-4894 *See* THOMASVILLE TIMES-ENTERPRISE. **5655**
0746-4932 *See* DAILY FREEMAN (KINGSTON, N.Y. 1969), THE. **5715**
0746-4967 *See* UNIVERSITY DAILY KANSAN. **5679**
0746-4975 *See* BOSTON BUSINESS JOURNAL, THE. **644**
0746-5114 *See* COMMON GROUND (DES MOINES, IOWA). **5028**
0746-5122 *See* OFFICE TOPICS. **944**
0746-5130 *See* P. E. O. RECORD. **5235**
0746-5149 *See* UNIVERSITY OF VIRGINIA RECORD. **1096**
0746-5157 *See* STAR (TINLEY PARK ED.), THE. **5662**
0746-5173 *See* STAR (HARVEY-MARKHAM AREA ED.), THE. **5662**
0746-5181 *See* STAR (CHICAGO HEIGHTS AREA [ED.]), THE. **5662**
0746-5254 *See* SECOND CIRCUIT DIGEST. **3047**

0746-5270 See OHIO RESTAURANT JOURNAL. 5072
0746-5289 See NEWFIELD NEWS. 5719
0746-5297 See MONTICELLO NEWS (MONTICELLO, FLA.). 5650
0746-536X See WOLFE CITY MIRROR, THE. 5756
0746-5394 See SEATTLE MEDIUM, THE. 5762
0746-5416 See OCEAN COUNTY OBSERVER. 5711
0746-5432 See JINSHAN SHIBAO. 5636
0746-5467 See NOPA INDUSTRY REPORT. 4212
0746-5483 See GORDON QUARTERLY, THE. 4286
0746-5548 See CHICO ENTERPRISE-RECORD. 5633
0746-5564 See BULLETIN OF THE MICHIGAN DENTAL HYGIENISTS' ASSOCIATION, THE. 1318
0746-5580 See WYOMING CATHOLIC REGISTER, THE. 5038
0746-5599 See DESERT TRAIL, THE. 5634
0746-5645 See CEDAR VALLEY TIMES (VINTON, IOWA : 1971). 5669
0746-5653 See FEDERAL REGULATION OF EMPLOYMENT NEWSLETTER. 3148
0746-5688 See REPORTER (LONG BEACH, CALIF.), THE. 5639
0746-5726 See SYNCHRO. 4925
0746-5734 See GEORGETOWN TIMES, THE. 5742
0746-5742 See STAR (FRANKFORT, ILL.), THE. 5662
0746-5769 See MICHIGAN'S OIL & GAS NEWS (1983). 4264
0746-5823 See HOOD RIVER NEWS. 5733
0746-584X See DICKENSON STAR, THE. 5758
0746-5858 See DAILY REPUBLIC (FAIRFIELD, CALIF.). 5634
0746-5866 See DAILY NEWS (RHINELANDER, WIS. : 1968), THE. 5766
0746-5874 See GLEANER (PORTLAND, OR.). 4960
0746-5882 See GLENVILLE PATHFINDER, THE. 5763
0746-5890 See GLENVILLE DEMOCRAT, THE. 5763
0746-5963 See GEORGIA JOURNAL (ATHENS, GA.). 2534
0746-5971 See JEANNETTE SPIRIT, THE. 5737
0746-598X See BARON'S MICROCOMPUTING REPORTS. 1265
0746-6021 See PORTAGE LAKES HERALD, THE. 5730
0746-603X See DRIPPING SPRINGS DISPATCH, THE. 5749
0746-6056 See PEMBROKE REPORTER. 5689
0746-6080 See EXPRESS (MECHANICVILLE, N.Y.). 5716
0746-6102 See POSTCARD COLLECTOR. 2777
0746-6110 See D & B REPORTS. 664
0746-6129 See LIBRARY ADMINISTRATOR'S DIGEST. 3224
0746-617X See GRAND MARAIS PILOT & PICTURED ROCKS REVIEW, THE. 5692
0746-6188 See DAILY NEWS (WHITTIER, CALIF.), THE. 5634
0746-6196 See GLIDDEN GRAPHIC, THE. 5670
0746-620X See AAOHN NEWS / AMERICAN ASSOCIATION OF OCCUPATIONAL HEALTH NURSES, INC. 3850
0746-6218 See PORTSMOUTH HERALD, THE. 5709
0746-6250 See NORTH AMERICAN WHITETAIL. 4876
0746-6315 See WILTON-DURANT ADVOCATE NEWS. 5674
0746-6323 See WEST COUNTY TIMES. 5641
0746-6358 See QUINCY HERALD-WHIG, THE. 5661
0746-6382 See GOLDEN TRANSCRIPT, THE. 5643
0746-6404 See FOODDAY UPDATE. 5733
0746-6412 See BROWNSVILLE TIMES, THE. 5747
0746-6439 See AINSWORTH STAR-JOURNAL. 5726

0746-6447 See ANDOVER ADVOCATE, THE. 5674
0746-6498 See INNKEEPING WORLD. 2807
0746-6579 See IOWA IIA AUDIT UPDATE. 745
0746-6641 See CERTIFIED ENGINEERING TECHNICIAN. 1968
0746-665X See CHEBOYGAN DAILY TRIBUNE. 5691
0746-6668 See MILES MESSENGER. 5752
0746-6676 See SOUTH HILL ENTERPRISE, THE. 5759
0746-6692 See NEW ENGLAND COUNTRY FOLKS. 2540
0746-6730 See RICHFIELD REAPER, THE. 5757
0746-6749 See INDUSTRY ENGINEER. 1978
0746-6773 See PC RETAILING. 1245
0746-6811 See BIG SPRING HERALD. 5747
0746-6838 See VINDICATOR (LIBERTY, TEX.). 5755
0746-6846 See SHENANDOAH HERALD, SHENANDOAH VALLEY, THE. 5759
0746-6889 See KINGDOM BUILDER / BAPTIST TRAINING UNION, THE. 5062
0746-7036 See EGG HARBOR NEWS, THE. 5710
0746-7060 See WESTERN BOWLER. 4929
0746-7079 See GARNET AND WHITE, THE. 5231
0746-7087 See ELY ECHO. 5695
0746-7125 See CLEVELAND ADVOCATE (CLEVELAND, TEX.), THE. 5748
0746-7141 See CONVERTING MAGAZINE. 1602
0746-7168 See CLASS ACTION REPORTS. 2951
0746-7184 See ECHO (HUMBLE, TEX.). 5749
0746-7222 See PERRY CHIEF (PERRY, IOWA : 1983). 5672
0746-7265 See AUERBACH EDP AUDITING. 739
0746-7273 See AUERBACH COMPUTER PROGRAMMING MANAGEMENT. 1278
0746-7281 See AUERBACH DATA SECURITY MANAGEMENT. 1225
0746-729X See WORLD MINING EQUIPMENT. 2153
0746-7303 See DALLAS POST TRIBUNE, THE. 5749
0746-7370 See DAILY LEDGER (ANTIOCH, CALIF.). 5634
0746-7389 See PITTSBURG POSTDISPATCH, THE. 5638
0746-7397 See G.I. JOE. 4861
0746-7419 See DEATH VALLEY GATEWAY GAZETTE. 5707
0746-746X See PINELLAS COUNTY REVIEW. 803
0746-7478 See OUACHITA CITIZEN, THE. 5684
0746-7486 See STATEMENT OF FINANCIAL ACCOUNTING STANDARDS. 751
0746-7494 See CARROLL COUNTY TIMES. 5685
0746-7508 See COMMACK NEWS. 5715
0746-7516 See ELKHART TRUTH, THE. 5663
0746-7540 See MITCHELL COUNTY PRESS-NEWS, THE. 5671
0746-7559 See PERRY DAILY JOURNAL, THE. 5732
0746-7567 See RAYNE INDEPENDENT, THE. 5684
0746-7575 See OLYMPIAN (OLYMPIA, WASH.). 5761
0746-7605 See ADVERTISER (NEW MILFORD, CONN.). 5644
0746-763X See LECTERN RESOURCE. 4973
0746-7664 See MARVEL FANFARE (NEW YORK, N.Y.). 4863
0746-7672 See RUBBERSTAMPMADNESS. 2777
0746-7699 See VIDEOLOG. 4079
0746-7702 See NEW DISCIPLES TEACHER, THE. 5065
0746-7745 See CITIZEN-STATESMAN. 5744
0746-7761 See CHIEF CIVIL SERVICE LEADER, THE. 5715
0746-777X See HUMBOLDT BEACON AND FORTUNA ADVANCE, THE. 5635
0746-7834 See IEEE OCEANIC ENGINEERING SOCIETY. NEWSLETTER. 2060

0746-7869 See VORWARTS (NEW YORK, N.Y.). 5722
0746-7885 See HFD. 2906
0746-7893 See NORTHEAST RIDING. 4082
0746-794X See INDEPENDENT-MESSENGER. 5758
0746-7966 See BASEBALL CARD NEWS. 2771
0746-8016 See HARTVILLE NEWS, THE. 5728
0746-8075 See ADIRONDACK MOUNTAIN TIMES. 2527
0746-8121 See COMMUNICATIONSWEEK (MANHASSET, N.Y.). 1152
0746-8156 See SAN MARCOS NEWS. 5754
0746-8172 See ALCONA COUNTY REVIEW. 5690
0746-8180 See REGISTER CITIZEN. 5646
0746-8202 See COFFEYVILLE JOURNAL (COFFEYVILLE, KAN. : 1964). 5675
0746-8210 See CINCINNATI MAGAZINE. 5466
0746-8237 See CONAN THE KING. 4859
0746-8253 See CHRISTADELPHIAN ADVOCATE, THE. 4944
0746-8261 See BRANDON VALLEY CHALLENGER. 5743
0746-827X See MISSOURI NEWS. 4978
0746-8288 See INDIANA MEDICINE. 3587
0746-8334 See LEVELLAND LEADER. 5751
0746-8342 See COLLEGE MATHEMATICS JOURNAL, THE. 3500
0746-8350 See MONITOR (TRENTON, N.J.), THE. 5710
0746-8377 See CONSTRUCTION PROJECT NEWS. GREATER DETROIT EDITION. 610
0746-8385 See COTTON FARMING. 168
0746-8423 See PACIFIC GROVE, PEBBLE BEACH TRIBUNE. 5638
0746-8431 See CD RATELINE. 782
0746-8474 See RECORD (LOUISVILLE, KY.), THE. 5682
0746-8504 See AUTO CLUB NEWS (LOS, ANGELES CALIF.). 5404
0746-8512 See CALHOUN COUNTY ADVOCATE. 5669
0746-8539 See GREENWICH NEWS. 5645
0746-8563 See DAILY NEWS (LEBANON, PA.), THE. 5736
0746-8601 See SEA (LOS ANGELES, CALIF.). 596
0746-861X See YOUNG SALVATIONIST. 5010
0746-8636 See CONNECTICUT TRAVELER. 5467
0746-8652 See CORPORATE BOARD, THE. 661
0746-8660 See ARCHIE AT RIVERDALE HIGH. 4857
0746-8679 See WISE COUNTY MESSENGER. 5756
0746-8709 See IOWA MEDICINE. 3590
0746-8725 See MASSACHUSETTS AUXILIARE, THE. 5233
0746-8768 See VERNON NEWS/VOICE. 5662
0746-8806 See PIONEER NEWS (SHEPHERDSVILLE, KY.), THE. 5682
0746-8822 See ORACLE (SANTA ANA, CALIF.), THE. 4606
0746-8830 See COUNTDOWN (ATHENS, OHIO). 17
0746-8865 See DAILY CHALLENGE. 5715
0746-8873 See JOURNAL (LEWIS AND CLARK COLLEGE, PORTLAND, OR.). 1832
0746-8903 See ST. LOUIS MANAGER. 886
0746-8911 See BUSINESS RADIO. 1150
0746-892X See ADWEEK (SOUTHWEST ED.). 755
0746-8938 See MUNDELEIN NEWS. 5661
0746-8962 See TRENDS & TECHNIQUES IN THE CONTEMPORARY DENTAL LABORATORY. 1337
0746-8997 See GEYER'S OFFICE DEALER. 4211
0746-9012 See CPI PURCHASING. 1023
0746-9055 See SHIAWASSEE COUNTY JOURNAL. 5693
0746-9071 See CRAIN'S TIRE BUSINESS. 663
0746-9101 See PICKERINGTON TIMES-SUN, THE. 5730

0746-9179 See RESEARCH & DEVELOPMENT (BARRINGTON, ILL.). 5146
0746-9233 See CONNECTION (ATLANTA, GA. 1983), THE. 784
0746-9241 See WORLDWIDE CHALLENGE (SAN BERNARDINO, CALIF.). 5010
0746-9276 See SOUTH DAKOTA EPISCOPAL CHURCH NEWS. 4998
0746-9292 See INTERCONNECTION JOURNAL, THE. 5559
0746-9330 See BLACKSHEAR TIMES, THE. 5652
0746-9373 See WASHINGTON JEWISH WEEK. 5053
0746-9381 See SOAP OPERA WORLD. 2546
0746-9438 See NEMO. 359
0746-9446 See EXECUTIVE AIR GUIDE. 18
0746-9454 See BICYCLES TODAY. 428
0746-9462 See SENSORS (PETERSBOROUGH, N.H.). 1996
0746-9497 See BUSINESS TRAVEL REVIEW. 5465
0746-9500 See BACK PAIN MONITOR. 3554
0746-9527 See COURIER NEWS. 5631
0746-956X See PHILADELPHIA TRIBUNE (1884). 5738
0746-9586 See NFPA JOURNAL. 2292
0746-9624 See DOLL CRAFTER. 372
0746-9632 See BLOOMFIELD JOURNAL, THE. 5645
0746-9640 See WILDLIFE ART NEWS. 368
0746-9683 See EMPLOYMENT RELATIONS BULLETIN. 3147
0746-9756 See TEXAS CHURCH WOMAN. 5003
0746-9764 See MOHAVE DAILY MINER AND KINGMAN DAILY MINER, THE. 5630
0746-9772 See PERFORMANCE (FORT WORTH, TEX.). 387
0746-9802 See WESTLAKER TIMES, THE. 5731
0746-9837 See 4SIGHT. 4366
0746-9888 See BAKER VALLEY NEWS. 5633
0746-9896 See MONTANA WILDLIFE (BOZEMAN, MONT.). 2198
0746-990X See BACKSTREETS. 2485
0746-9918 See VENTURA COUNTY. 2549
0746-9926 See CANYON CRIER NEWS. 5633
0746-9934 See DEMOCRAT-LEADER (FAYETTE, MO.). 5703
0746-9942 See FAYETTE ADVERTISER, THE. 5703
0746-9969 See CUBA PATRIOT AND FREE PRESS. 5715
0746-9985 See HSMAI MARKETING REVIEW. 2807
0747-0010 See DAILY SPECTRUM (CEDAR CITY, UTAH), THE. 5756
0747-0029 See PROGRESS (WELLS, NEV.). 5734
0747-007X See INSIGHTS (WASHINGTON, D.C.). 4900
0747-0088 See ABA JOURNAL. 2926
0747-010X See BEEFALO NICKEL. 207
0747-0126 See FARO (NEW WILMINGTON, PA.), IL. 5200
0747-0134 See COMMERCIAL RENOVATION. 608
0747-0142 See ENTERPRISE (FALMOUTH, MASS.), THE. 5688
0747-0150 See NCOA JOURNAL (SAN ANTONIO, TEX.). 4052
0747-0185 See SPECIAL RECREATION DIGEST. 4854
0747-0193 See COMPUTER CONTENTS. 1208
0747-0207 See SCRIPTURE COMES ALIVE. 5019
0747-0223 See CALIFORNIA SPORTSCAR CLUB NEWS. 5408
0747-0231 See INDEX-JOURNAL, THE. 5742
0747-024X See FAMILY GUIDE, THE. 2279
0747-0282 See BOURBON COUNTY CITIZEN, THE. 5679
0747-0304 See SUMTER JOURNAL, THE. 5651
0747-0320 See MARYLAND BUSINESS & LIVING. 692

0747-0355 See EVENING SUN (NORWICH, N.Y.). 5716
0747-0363 See AMERICAN (BLACKDUCK, MINN.), THE. 5694
0747-0371 See BICYCLE USA. 428
0747-041X See DICKSON HERALD, THE. 5745
0747-0428 See DESOTO NEWS-ADVERTISER. 5749
0747-0460 See PCM. 1271
0747-0622 See GARDEN RAILWAYS. 5431
0747-0649 See OFFICE OF INSTRUCTIONAL TECHNOLOGY NEWSLETTER. 5136
0747-0711 See EMPIRE STATE REPORT (1982). 4645
0747-0738 See SALISBURY POST, THE. 5724
0747-0746 See TCM GROWER, THE. 139
0747-0754 See ESTHERVILLE DAILY NEWS. 5670
0747-0819 See CLUB INTERNATIONAL (NEWTOWN, CONN.). 3994
0747-0827 See CLUB (NEWTOWN, CONN.). 5230
0747-0843 See AMERICAN TRAVELER. 5461
0747-086X See QUEENSWEEK. 5720
0747-0878 See NOTICIAS - NATIONAL FOREIGN TRADE COUNCIL. 848
0747-0894 See INDY CAR RACING MAGAZINE. 4900
0747-0908 See MEDIA MEMO (ENGLEWOOD, COLO.). 1116
0747-0932 See NATIONAL GEOGRAPHIC TRAVELER. 5485
0747-0940 See HAPPY HANDS NEEDLECRAFT NEWS. 5184
0747-0959 See TEXAS SHORES. 1457
0747-0967 See PERRY NEWS-HERALD. 5650
0747-0975 See HARRINGTON JOURNAL, THE. 5647
0747-0991 See OSCEOLA (TALLAHASSEE, FLA.), THE. 4911
0747-1025 See ST. CLOUD STATE UNIVERSITY CHRONICLE. 1095
0747-1041 See PICKUPS 'N PANELS IN PRINT. 5389
0747-1130 See SOUTH CAROLINA NEWS (CLEVELAND, TENN.). 4998
0747-1149 See HAVELOCK PROGRESS, THE. 5723
0747-1165 See TRIBUNE-TIMES. 5743
0747-1173 See HOTLINE (WILLISTON, N.D.). 4260
0747-1181 See RECORD (GRAFTON, N.D.). 5726
0747-119X See MARFA INDEPENDENT AND THE BIG BEND SENTINEL, THE. 5752
0747-1262 See TEXAS PROFESSIONAL ENGINEER (1981). 1998
0747-1270 See GATEWAY ENGINEER. 1976
0747-1289 See AIPE FACILITIES. 1964
0747-1300 See TIMES RECORD (BRUNSWICK, ME), THE. 5685
0747-1335 See AVIDEO. 1104
0747-1343 See AUGUSTA CHRONICLE (1885), THE. 5652
0747-136X See NEWS WEEKLY, THE. 2490
0747-1378 See TRIAL TALK. 3066
0747-1416 See LEADER (TREMONTON, UTAH), THE. 5756
0747-1432 See SUNDAY SUN-JOURNAL. 5685
0747-1440 See UPPER PENINSULA CATHOLIC, THE. 5038
0747-1467 See CAPE COD TIMES. 5688
0747-1491 See HIGH POINT ENTERPRISE, THE. 5723
0747-1513 See MENA STAR, THE. 5632
0747-1521 See RECORD-GAZETTE. 5638
0747-1556 See TEXAS LONGHORN JOURNAL. 222
0747-1564 See ADULT SABBATH SCHOOL LESSONS (EASY ENGLISH ED.). 5054
0747-1599 See HYBRID CIRCUIT TECHNOLOGY. 5111
0747-1602 See MISSISSIPPI (JACKSON, MISS. 1982). 2539

0747-1610 See SENTINEL (SHILLINGTON, PA.), THE. 5739
0747-1629 See BUSINESS DIGEST (PORTSMOUTH, N.H.). 647
0747-1653 See SWIFT COUNTY MONITOR-NEWS. 5699
0747-167X See MEMPHIS BUSINESS JOURNAL. 693
0747-170X See EDWARD WILLIAMS WEEKLY, THE. 5716
0747-1718 See FLUSHING OBSERVER, THE. 5692
0747-1726 See WEST VALLEY NEWS, THE. 5694
0747-1734 See MILAN STANDARD WATSON JOURNAL, THE. 5697
0747-1742 See GRAND BLANC NEWS, THE. 5692
0747-1750 See NEWS (LAREDO, TEX.), THE. 5752
0747-1769 See AGRICULTURAL NEWS (HAMDEN, N.Y.). 50
0747-1793 See FRANCESVILLE TRIBUNE. 5664
0747-1815 See ROCKFORD SQUIRE, THE. 5693
0747-1823 See BALTIMORE BUSINESS JOURNAL. 641
0747-1831 See BILLINGS COMMERCE. 825
0747-1858 See GREENSBORO NEWS & RECORD. 5723
0747-1874 See COLUMBIA MISSOURIAN. 5703
0747-1890 See DAILY DEMOCRAT (WOODLAND, CALIF.). 5634
0747-1904 See PEARL PRESS, THE. 5701
0747-1912 See LOUISIANA HORSE. 2800
0747-1947 See MOORE AMERICAN, THE. 5732
0747-1955 See RIVER PARISHES GUIDE. 5684
0747-2021 See WHEAT RIDGE JEFFERSON SENTINEL, THE. 5644
0747-2080 See CHECKPOINT (IRVING, TEX.). 5410
0747-2099 See SAN JOSE MERCURY NEWS. 5639
0747-2102 See ICP ADMINISTRATIVE & ACCOUNTING SOFTWARE. 681
0747-2129 See EMERY COUNTY PROGRESS (1977). 5756
0747-2161 See RECORD-OUTLOOK, THE. 5739
0747-217X See PLUS (PAWLING, N.Y.). 4986
0747-2188 See NEWS CHRONICLE (PAWLING, N.Y.), THE. 5719
0747-2196 See SOUNDVIEW EXECUTIVE BOOK SUMMARIES. 712
0747-220X See PRESS DEMOCRAT (SANTA ROSA, CALIF.). 5638
0747-2218 See CLEARWATER NAVIGATOR. 2226
0747-2242 See FORSYTH COUNTY NEWS, THE. 5653
0747-2250 See FISHING GAZETTE (MARGATE, N.J.). 2303
0747-2315 See DAN CHUA. 5028
0747-2358 See TACO TIMES. 5651
0747-2374 See REGISTER STAR. 5720
0747-2390 See METUCHEN, EDISON REVIEW. 5710
0747-2412 See MEADVILLE TRIBUNE (1955). 5737
0747-2420 See BLOOD BANK WEEK. 3770
0747-248X See CENTRAL IDAHO STAR-NEWS, THE. 5656
0747-2498 See CODY ENTERPRISE, THE. 5772
0747-2501 See DAILY NEWS LEADER, THE. 5758
0747-2528 See PETROLEUM INDEPENDENT. 4272
0747-2536 See PREPARED FOODS. 2353
0747-2544 See FLEET EQUIPMENT. 5382
0747-2552 See BMX ACTION. 428
0747-2560 See FINE DINING. 5071
0747-2579 See POLICE CHRONICLE, THE. 3172
0747-2595 See MOUNT PROSPECT TIMES. 5661
0747-2706 See LANCASTER CONFERENCE NEWS. 5062
0747-2757 See FRANCE AMERIQUE (NEW YORK, N.Y.). 5716
0747-282X See GALVA NEWS, THE. 5660
0747-2838 See WROVA REPORTER, THE. 5662

0747-2862 See NEWS & RECORD. 5759

0747-2889 See COLUMBUS GAZETTE (COLUMBUS JUNCTION, IOWA), THE. 5669

0747-2900 See TIMES (WEBSTER, MASS.), THE. 5690

0747-2927 See DAILY REGISTER (PORTAGE, WIS.). 5766

0747-2943 See MILLCREEK SUN, THE. 5737

0747-2986 See OKLAHOMA DECISIONS REPORTED IN PACIFIC REPORTER, SECOND SERIES. 3022

0747-301X See MARYLAND AGRI-FACTS. 178

0747-3028 See UNIVERSITY OF HARTFORD OBSERVER. 1096

0747-3079 See PERFUSION LIFE. 3773

0747-3109 See AWARDS QUARTERLY. 501

0747-3117 See FLORIDA SECURITY & INVESTIGATORS JOURNAL. 3164

0747-315X See ATHLETIC BUSINESS. 640

0747-3176 See HOMEOWNER, THE. 616

0747-3184 See SINGLE (TAMPA, FLA.). 5258

0747-3206 See SPIRITS, WINE & BEER MARKETING IN MINNESOTA, NORTH AND SOUTH DAKOTA. 2371

0747-3214 See SPIRITS, WINE & BEVERAGE MARKETING IN IOWA. 2371

0747-3222 See MERCER MESSENGER. 5710

0747-3230 See STURGIS JOURNAL (MICHIGAN EDITION). 5694

0747-3265 See NATIONAL BILLIARD NEWS, THE. 4906

0747-3273 See BELLEFONTAINE EXAMINER. 5727

0747-3303 See PARSONS ADVOCATE. 5764

0747-3311 See GLENCOE NEWS/VOICE. 5660

0747-3338 See ADVANCE REPORTER, THE. 5722

0747-3362 See CNC WEST. 3477

0747-3370 See ROMANTIC TIMES. 5074

0747-3397 See FISH SNIFFER (NORTHERN CALIFORNIA-NEVADA ED.), THE. 5635

0747-3435 See ORANGE COUNTY APARTMENT NEWS. 2830

0747-3443 See DALLES CHRONICLE, THE. 5733

0747-3486 See YOUTHWORKER JOURNAL. 5011

0747-3532 See SCOTTISH TERRIER QUARTERLY, THE. 4288

0747-3575 See COMIC READER, THE. 1062

0747-3583 See JOURNAL OF IMAGING SCIENCE AND TECHNOLOGY, THE. 5118

0747-3591 See MEDIAPOLIS NEWS (MEDIAPOLIS, IOWA : 1984). 5671

0747-3613 See PUBLIC POWER WEEKLY. 4762

0747-3648 See MIDWEST OUTDOORS. 4874

0747-3656 See COUGAR REPORT, THE. 1091

0747-3672 See VALLEY : LEBANON VALLEY COLLEGE MAGAZINE, THE. 1096

0747-3680 See LAW ENFORCEMENT TECHNOLOGY. 3169

0747-3699 See CAPITAL DISTRICT BUSINESS REVIEW. 655

0747-3710 See SANDERSVILLE PROGRESS, THE. 5655

0747-3729 See PIONEER, ALL-ALASKA WEEKLY, THE. 5629

0747-3737 See WRIGHTSVILLE HEADLIGHT, THE. 5655

0747-3753 See SANDY PARKER'S FUR WORLD. 3185

0747-3761 See ELK VALLEY TIMES OBSERVER AND NEWS, THE. 5745

0747-3788 See UNION-SUN AND JOURNAL. 5721

0747-3796 See PHARMACEUTICAL MANUFACTURING. 4320

0747-380X See INTIMACY. 5074

0747-3826 See CLASS (NEW YORK, N.Y.). 2486

0747-3869 See DANSKE PIONEER, DEN. 5659

0747-3885 See HOUSEWARES MERCHANDISING. 2812

0747-3893 See BIBLE JOURNEYS FOR CHRISTIANS. 5014

0747-3931 See EASY HOME COMPUTER. 1267

0747-4008 See TELEGRAPH (NORTH PLATTE, NEB.). 5707

0747-4024 See WEST MIFFLIN AREA RECORD. 5740

0747-4040 See HANSON REPORTER. 5688

0747-4059 See ONSAT. 1136

0747-4067 See ENTERPRISE (BOARDMAN, OR.), THE. 5733

0747-4075 See INDEPENDENT PRESS (BLOOMFIELD, N.J.). 5710

0747-4105 See TUFTS UNIVERSITY DIET & NUTRITION LETTER. 4199

0747-4113 See EXPRESS (BANGOR, MICH.), THE. 5692

0747-4121 See MARKET REPORT & NEWSLETTER. 215

0747-4148 See DRAG RACING WORLD / AMERICAN HOT ROD ASSOCIATION, AHRA. 4893

0747-4156 See EATON COUNTY NEWSCHRONICLE. 5692

0747-4172 See BULLETIN OF THE AMERICAN IRIS SOCIETY. 2411

0747-4180 See NEWS-PILOT. 5637

0747-4237 See SOCIALIST ACTION (SAN FRANCISCO, CALIF.). 4496

0747-4253 See POTTSBORO PRESS. 5753

0747-4261 See GLASS MAGAZINE. 2590

0747-4296 See NATIONAL JOB MARKET. 4206

0747-430X See NEVADA JOURNAL (NEVADA, IOWA). 5672

0747-4377 See LACEY BEACON. 5710

0747-4393 See BLACK BOOK. OLD CAR ... MARKET GUIDE. 5407

0747-4415 See FOND DU LAC CLARION, THE. 5767

0747-444X See GREATER PHOENIX JEWISH NEWS. 5047

0747-4482 See SILVER (WHITTIER, CALIF.). 4019

0747-4512 See NEWS HERALD (SARALAND, ALA.), THE. 5627

0747-458X See MOUNT OLIVE HERALD, THE. 5661

0747-4598 See BUREAU NEWS / BUREAU OF WHOLESALE SALES REPRESENTATIVES. 644

0747-461X See CARDIOVASCULAR NEWS. 3701

0747-4628 See CORNELL CHRONICLE. 1091

0747-4644 See DISNEY CHANNEL MAGAZINE, THE. 1131

0747-4652 See GREATER BATON ROUGE BUSINESS REPORT, THE. 678

0747-4660 See WHOOT. 2550

0747-4679 See ANESTHESIOLOGY NEWS. 3958

0747-4695 See TEEN MACHINE. 1070

0747-4733 See BOSSIER PRESS-TRIBUNE. 5683

0747-4741 See MID-ISLAND TIMES & LEVITTOWN TIMES. 5718

0747-475X See TRAVELWARE. 1630

0747-4776 See CHEROKEE DAILY TIMES. 5669

0747-4784 See RURAL ELECTRIC NEWS LETTER. 4684

0747-4814 See NORTH CENTRAL ILLINOIS GENEALOGICAL SOCIETY. 2464

0747-4849 See CALDWELL COUNTY GENEALOGICAL SOCIETY, INC. 2441

0747-4857 See DATA BOOK OF SOCIAL STUDIES MATERIALS AND RESOURCES. 5197

0747-4873 See CARROLL COUSINS. 2442

0747-4881 See ELECTRIC UTILITY INDUSTRY REVIEW. 1605

0747-489X See IMAGINE (BOSTON, MASS.). 3464

0747-4911 See ILLINOIS RUNNER. 4899

0747-4938 See ECONOMETRIC REVIEWS. 1481

0747-4946 See SEQUENTIAL ANALYSIS. 3533

0747-4954 See NEW TRADE NAMES IN THE RUBBER AND PLASTICS INDUSTRIES. 5076

0747-4970 See NEW ENGLAND JOURNAL OF BLACK STUDIES. 2269

0747-4989 See VERY BEGINNING (LYNN-MAR COMMUNITY SCHOOL DISTRICT ED.), THE. 1789

0747-4997 See DIRECTORY AND LISTING OF PAINTINGS AS SHOWN IN THE MAGAZINE "ANTIQUES", A. 349

0747-5047 See OFFICIAL PRICE GUIDE TO OLD BOOKS & AUTOGRAPHS, THE. 2776

0747-5055 See OFFICIAL PRICE GUIDE TO SCOUTING COLLECTIBLES, THE. 5234

0747-5063 See VACUUM CIRCUITS. 5399

0747-5071 See SHIJIE RIBAO (SAN FRANCISCO, CALIF.). 5640

0747-508X See GIRL SCOUTS AROUND NEW YORK. 5231

0747-511X See MICROCOMPUTER VENDOR DIRECTORY. 1269

0747-5128 See ANIMAL WELFARE. LIST OF LICENSED EXHIBITORS. 225

0747-5136 See ANIMAL WELFARE. LIST OF REGISTERED CARRIERS AND INTERMEDIATE HANDLERS. 225

0747-5144 See ANIMAL WELFARE. LIST OF REGISTERED RESEARCH FACILITIES. 225

0747-5160 See PAPERS AND PROCEEDINGS OF APPLIED GEOGRAPHY CONFERENCES. 2572

0747-5179 See ARCHITECTURAL DESIGNS. 289

0747-5187 See ANALYSIS OF THE PRESIDENT'S BUDGETARY PROPOSALS, AN. 4709

0747-5225 See COMIC BOOKS, PAPERBACKS, MAGAZINES. 413

0747-5233 See CONSTRUCTION BRIEFINGS COLLECTION, THE. 609

0747-5241 See ANNALS OF THEORETICAL PSYCHOLOGY. 4574

0747-525X See LOOKING AHEAD (WASHINGTON, D.C. : 1982). 1638

0747-5276 See REINSURANCE DIRECTORY. 2891

0747-5284 See SCULPTURE REVIEW. 364

0747-5306 See OIL AND GAS (URBANA, ILL.). 4269

0747-5314 See ANNUAL REPORT ON TOBACCO STATISTICS (1980). 5375

0747-5357 See OFFICIAL PRICE GUIDE TO COLLECTOR KNIVES, THE. 2776

0747-5365 See OFFICIAL PRICE GUIDE TO ORIENTAL COLLECTIBLES, THE. 2776

0747-5373 See OFFICIAL PRICE GUIDE TO PAPER COLLECTIBLES, THE. 2776

0747-5403 See SPEEDWAY SCENE. 4920

0747-5411 See SERIALS PERSPECTIVE. 424

0747-5438 See BNA ONLINE. 1274

0747-5454 See CURRENT TOPICS IN RESEARCH ON SYNAPSES. 580

0747-5500 See AMERICAN WIND ENERGY ASSOCIATION WIND ENERGY WEEKLY, THE. 1931

0747-5527 See NATIONAL STAMPAGRAPHIC. 381

0747-5535 See QUARTERLY JOURNAL OF BUSINESS AND ECONOMICS. 706

0747-5543 See CROSS SECTIONS (RICHMOND, VA.). 786

0747-5586 See AIRCRAFT CERTIFICATION DIRECTORY. 9

0747-5594 See ANNUAL PETROLEUM REVIEW. 4250

0747-5624 See RELATIVELY SEEKING. 2469

0747-5632 See COMPUTERS IN HUMAN BEHAVIOR. 4582

0747-5659 See POLITICAL ANIMAL (1993), THE. 4488

0747-5667 See MISSOURI STATE GENEALOGICAL ASSOCIATION JOURNAL. 2461

0747-5675 See HUGHES FAMILY LETTER. 2454

0747-5683 See OFFICIAL GUIDE TO COIN COLLECTING, THE. 2782

0747-5691 See OFFICIAL PRICE GUIDE TO MILITARY COLLECTIBLES, THE. 2776

0747-5705 See OFFICIAL PRICE GUIDE TO POTTERY & PORCELAIN, THE. 2592

0747-5713 See UNIT INVESTMENT TRUSTS DISTRIBUTIONS. 918

0747-5721 See PETROLEUM MARKETERS' HANDBOOK. 4273

0747-573X See RECRUITER JOURNAL. 4054

0747-5748 See PRAYER GROUP DIRECTORY. 5034

0747-5756 See OFFICIAL PRICE GUIDE TO TOYS, THE. 2584

0747-5764 See CONSOLIDATED FEDERAL FUNDS REPORT. VOLUME II, SUBCOUNTY AREAS. 4640

0747-5810 See ESWAU HUPPEDAY. 2446

0747-5837 See NAB CLEARINGHOUSE QUARTERLY. 1692

0747-5853 See AMERICAN SWIMMING COACHES ASSOCIATION WORLD CLINIC YEARBOOK. 4883

0747-5853 See WORLD CLINIC YEARBOOK / AMERICAN SWIMMING COACHES ASSOCIATION. 4930

0747-5888 See DELL CHAMPION VARIETY PUZZLES. 4859

0747-5896 See DELL CROSSWORD SPECIAL. 4859

0747-590X See DELL CHAMPION CROSSWORD PUZZLES. 4859

0747-5926 See DELL OFFICIAL WORD SEARCH PUZZLES. 4860

0747-5934 See DELL CROSSWORDS AND VARIETY PUZZLES. 4859

0747-5993 See JOURNAL OF SWIMMING RESEARCH, THE. 4902

0747-6000 See ASCA NEWSLETTER (FORT LAUDERDALE, FLA.). 4884

0747-6000 See AMERICAN SWIMMING : A PUBLICATION OF THE AMERICAN SWIMMING COACHES ASSOCIATION. 4883

0747-6019 See MEAT PRICE OUTLOOK. 215

0747-6027 See SOFTWARE JOURNAL, THE. 1290

0747-6035 See NEWS FROM C.U.N.Y. LIBRARIES. 3234

0747-6043 See ISSUES IN EDUCATION. 1755

0747-606X See AMERICAN HOMEOPATHY (1984). 3774

0747-6078 See SHELLS AND SEA LIFE. 5597

0747-6086 See COMMUNITY SERVICE BUSINESS. 5196

0747-6108 See AFRICAN URBAN QUARTERLY. 2813

0747-6116 See HOST/PATHOGEN NEWS. 3585

0747-6124 See DATELINE HYPERTENSION. 3704

0747-6132 See NEONATOLOGY LETTER. 3765

0747-6140 See WORKING PARENTS. 2287

0747-6159 See TENNESSEE SCHOOL BOARDS JOURNAL. 1873

0747-6175 See AJL NEWSLETTER. 3188

0747-6205 See SECURITY, ANTI-TERRORISM AND LOSS PREVENTION EQUIPMENT AND DEVICES BUYERS GUIDE. 5177

0747-623X See SOLETTER. 1997

0747-6256 See JOURNAL OF BASQUE STUDIES. 2694

0747-6264 See U.S. GELATIN-GLUE-BONES. IMPORTS. 855

0747-6302 See MODERN MATURITY (NRTA ED.). 5180

0747-6345 See ILLINOIS ARCHITECTURE REFERENCE DIRECTORY, THE. 300

0747-6353 See ADVANCES IN FORENSIC PSYCHOLOGY AND PSYCHIATRY. 4571

0747-6388 See FMR (ENGLISH ED.). 350

0747-6418 See TITLE MASTER. 426

0747-6434 See DIRECTORY - COUNCIL OF SCOTTISH CLAN ASSOCIATIONS. 2731

0747-6469 See LAW AND THE WORKPLACE. 3151

0747-6485 See LEXINGTON GENEALOGICAL EXCHANGE. 2458

0747-6493 See UP-LAND FISHING. 2315

0747-6531 See ANNUAL REPORT - NATIONAL INSTITUTE OF MENTAL HEALTH (U.S.). DIVISION OF INTRAMURAL RESEARCH PROGRAMS. 3920

0747-6558 See POMMERSCHEN LEUTE, DIE. 2468

0747-6566 See LEONARD'S ANNUAL PRICE INDEX OF ART AUCTIONS. 357

0747-6574 See INFORMATIVO JURIDICO (WASHINGTON D.C.). 3129

0747-6582 See FIDELITY & SURETY NEWS : FSN. 2970

0747-6612 See ADVANCE ANNOTATION SERVICE TO THE CODE OF ALABAMA 1975. 2928

0747-6620 See ALABAMA RULES ANNOTATED. 2929

0747-6655 See MUSIC BUSINESS DIRECTORY. 4133

0747-6663 See LATAH COUNTY GENEALOGICAL SOCIETY. 2458

0747-668X See DIGEST OF TECHNICAL PAPERS / IEEE INTERNATIONAL CONFERENCE ON CONSUMER ELECTRONICS. 2041

0747-6698 See PUBLICATIONS OF THE NATIONAL GEODETIC SURVEY. 399

0747-6701 See CORPORATE VIEW, MINNESOTA, A. 662

0747-6728 See NEWSLETTER / ROSE FAMILY ASSOCIATION. 2464

0747-6736 See ANTIQUES (ORLANDO, FLA.). 249

0747-6744 See STONE LION REVIEW. 3440

0747-6795 See ANNUAL REPORT TO CONGRESS ON THE POST-VIETNAM ERA VETERANS' EDUCATIONAL ASSISTANCE PROGRAM. 4035

0747-6817 See CENTER FOR SPORTS SPONSORSHIP'S SPONSOR QUEST, THE. 4889

0747-6876 See JOHNSON COUNTY HISTORICAL SOCIETY JOURNAL. 2740

0747-6949 See DISTRICT OF COLUMBIA COURT RULES ANNOTATED. 3140

0747-6965 See OFFICIAL CODE OF GEORGIA ANNOTATED. ADVANCE INFORMATION SERVICE. 3021

0747-7074 See TENNESSEE CODE ANNOTATED ADVANCE ANNOTATION SERVICE. 3063

0747-7171 See JOURNAL OF SYMBOLIC COMPUTATION. 3514

0747-7201 See ALA SURVEY OF LIBRARIAN SALARIES. 1643

0747-7236 See CHEAP INVESTOR, THE. 894

0747-7287 See STRELEC (JERSEY CITY, N.J.). 3440

0747-735X See MICHIGAN ENVIRONMENTAL REPORT:. 2177

0747-7368 See JOURNAL OF GASTRONOMY, THE. 2347

0747-7376 See HOSPITAL FOOD & NUTRITION FOCUS. 4192

0747-7384 See QRC ADVISOR. 3791

0747-7392 See OFFICIAL PRICE GUIDE TO RECORDS, THE. 4143

0747-7406 See MODERN CHLOR-ALKALI TECHNOLOGY. 986

0747-7449 See AIR AND SPACE LAWYER: FORUM COMMITTEE ON AIR AND SPACE LAW. AMERICAN BAR ASSOCIATION, THE. 2929

0747-7465 See UNIQUE HOMES. 310

0747-7503 See COMMUNITY DEVELOPMENT EXECUTIVE, THE. 819

0747-752X See PROFESSIONAL AUDIO BUYERS REFERENCE GUIDE. 5318

0747-7538 See WHO'S WHO IN INDIAN RELICS. 437

0747-7570 See OFFICIAL PRICE GUIDE TO COLLECTOR HANDGUNS, THE. 2776

0747-7589 See OFFICIAL PRICE GUIDE TO COLLECTOR GUNS, THE. 2776

0747-7600 See PULP VOICES, OR, SCIENCE FICTION VOICES. 3426

0747-7686 See GREAT RIVERS. 2565

0747-7708 See BENELUX REPORT. 1599

0747-7716 See NATIONAL CULINARY REVIEW, THE. 2350

0747-7775 See SPECTRA (STONY BROOK, N.Y.). 331

0747-7791 See CHRISTMAS WITH SOUTHERN LIVING. 371

0747-7805 See WESTERN MARYLAND GENEALOGY. 2477

0747-7813 See ALEXANDER PARIS REPORT, THE. 890

0747-7872 See MCKINNEY'S NEW YORK RULES OF COURT. 3141

0747-7902 See ANNALS OF CHILD DEVELOPMENT. 4573

0747-7929 See ADVANCES IN INTERNATIONAL COMPARATIVE MANAGEMENT. 859

0747-7937 See BUSINESS INSURANCE. DIRECTORY OF CORPORATE BUYERS OF INSURANCE, BENEFIT PLANS AND RISK MANAGEMENT SERVICES. 649

0747-7961 See LAW ENFORCEMENT OFFICERS KILLED AND ASSAULTED. 3169

0747-7988 See GAS TURBINE WORLD (1984). 2114

0747-7996 See VRA ECONOMIC DIGEST. 5073

0747-8003 See CORPORATE GIVING WATCH. 5280

0747-8011 See ULULA. 3449

0747-8038 See NEWSLETTER - ASSOCIATION OF FAMILY AND CONCILIATION COURTS. CALIFORNIA CHAPTER, THE. 2889

0747-8135 See ANNUAL CONVENTION REFERENCE MATERIALS. 2934

0747-8151 See AEROSPACE CONSULTANTS DIRECTORY. 5

0747-8178 See OFFICIAL PRICE GUIDE TO COLLECTOR PRINTS, THE. 2776

0747-8186 See EMPLOYMENT OPPORTUNITIES / UNITED STATES ENVIRONMENTAL PROTECTION AGENCY, PERSONNEL MANAGEMENT DIVISION. 940

0747-8283 See CLUB INDUSTRY. 2596

0747-8291 See ULTRAPURE WATER. 5541

0747-8356 See HANGUK ILBO, SAEN PURANSISUKO. 5635

0747-8372 See MEMBERSHIP DIRECTORY / AMERICAN CHIROPRACTIC ASSOCIATION. 3615

0747-8399 See YEARBOOK OF CONSTRUCTION ARTICLES. 631

0747-8445 See MAGAZINE / HUXFORD GENEALOGICAL SOCIETY, INC. 2459

0747-8453 See SOUTHERN INDIANA GENEALOGICAL SOCIETY QUARTERLY. 2473

0747-8461 See MEN'S HEALTH (EMMAUS, PA. 1985). 3616

0747-847X See BOOKNOTES (PORTLAND, ORE.). 4825

0747-8526 See OFFICIAL INVESTORS GUIDE, BUYING, SELLING SILVER COINS, THE. 910

0747-8542 See CRIMINAL DIVISION. 3162

0747-8607 See TAX MANAGEMENT COMPENSATION PLANNING JOURNAL. 917

0747-8631 See PULSE (1984). 4988

0747-864X See SEABURY JOURNAL, THE. 4996

0747-8674 See OFFICIAL INVESTORS GUIDE, BUYING, SELLING SILVER DOLLARS, THE. 910

0747-8682 See OFFICIAL INVESTORS GUIDE, BUYING, SELLING GOLD COINS, THE. 910

0747-8712 See SACRAMENTO (JONSSON COMMUNICATIONS CORPORATION). 2544

0747-8739 See NEWS FROM THE NORTHWEST. 2462

0747-8747 See OFFICIAL PRICE GUIDE TO BOTTLES, OLD & NEW, THE. 2776

0747-8763 See OUTSIDE PLANT. 1119

0747-8771 See WYOMING'S COMPREHENSIVE REPORT ON TRAFFIC ACCIDENTS. 5446

0747-878X See PRELAW ADVISER'S KIT. 3030

0747-8798 See POPULAR PHOTOGRAPHY'S SLR PHOTOGRAPHY. 4375

0747-8801 See HISTORIC CLAY TOBACCO PIPE STUDIES. 269

0747-8879 See AFRICAN WORLD NEWS, THE. 2498

0747-8887 See HOT WIRE. 5558

0747-8895 See MID-AMERICAN REVIEW. 3411

0747-8909 See AEJMC NEWS. 2917

0747-8917 See BANKRUPTCY STRATEGIST, THE. 3085

0747-8925 See MEDICAL MALPRACTICE LAW & STRATEGY. 3008

0747-8933 See COMPUTER LAW STRATEGIST. 2954
0747-8976 See ARS ROSACEAE. 2409
0747-900X See AMERICAN BUDDHIST NEWSLETTER, THE. 5020
0747-9026 See KNITTERS. 5184
0747-9034 See KITABNAMAH-I RAHAVARD. 3402
0747-9050 See CPE STRATEGIES. 1153
0747-9069 See BADMINTON MAGAZINE, THE. 4886
0747-9085 See EMERGENCY MANAGEMENT TODAY : AN INFORMATION SERVICE OF EMERGENCY MANAGEMENT INFORMATION SERVICES. 1073
0747-9093 See JD/MBA QUARTERLY. 2986
0747-9107 See ALMANAC OF BUSINESS AND INDUSTRIAL FINANCIAL RATIOS. 637
0747-9115 See JOURNAL OF TAXATION OF INVESTMENTS. 904
0747-9131 See BENEFITS TODAY. 2941
0747-9182 See MINERALS & METALLURGICAL PROCESSING. 4012
0747-9239 See SEISMIC INSTRUMENTS. 1410
0747-9263 See ALTERNATIVE DESIGNS. 4764
0747-9298 See LEGAL INFORMATION MANAGEMENT INDEX. 3082
0747-9301 See JOURNAL OF THE SOCIETY FOR ARMENIAN STUDIES. 2656
0747-931X See UNVEILING. 3449
0747-9360 See DESIGN ISSUES. 297
0747-9387 See SEVENTH CIRCUIT DIGEST. 3048
0747-9395 See FORDHAM INTERNATIONAL LAW JOURNAL. 3128
0747-9409 See SITES (NEW YORK, N.Y.). 330
0747-9417 See ACSM BULLETIN. 2580
0747-9441 See FAMILY TREE TALK. 2447
0747-9484 See INVESTMENT COMPANIES (NEW YORK, N.Y. 1983). 3100
0747-9492 See ECONOMIC INDICATORS OF THE FARM SECTOR. PRODUCTION AND EFFICIENCY STATISTICS. 153
0747-9565 See MIDWEST MESSENGER (SOUTH EDITION). 1160
0747-9573 See PACKAGED SOFTWARE REPORTS / MIC. 1289
0747-959X See FOCUS ON SPECIAL EDUCATION LEGAL PRACTICES. 2971
0747-962X See IDENTIFICATION JOURNAL. 870
0747-9638 See ENERGY CONSERVATION BULLETIN (WASHINGTON, D.C.). 1939
0747-9662 See JOURNAL OF ECONOMIC AND SOCIAL MEASUREMENT. 5206
0747-9700 See FEDERAL CONTRACT DISPUTES. 2969
0747-9727 See THIRTEEN (PORTLANDVILLE, N.Y.). 3446
0747-9735 See WATERWORLD NEWS. 2248
0747-9743 See ... HIGHER EDUCATION PUBLIC ADMINISTRATION DIRECTORY, THE. 4654
0747-976X See NATIONAL AIRSPACE SYSTEM PLAN. ENGINEERING AND DEVELOPMENT. 30
0747-9786 See ANTIQUE & CLASSIC CARS, TRUCKS, MOTORCYCLES. 5404
0747-9794 See ILLINOIS MAGAZINE. 2738
0747-9808 See OFFICIAL HIGH SCHOOL FOOTBALL RULES. 4909
0747-9832 See UNITED FLY TYERS' ROUNDTABLE. 2315
0747-9840 See CHAMP CHANNELS. 5580
0747-9859 See EVANSIA. 509
0747-9891 See NEHGS NEXUS. 2462
0747-9921 See ARIS FUNDING REPORT. SOCIAL AND NATURAL SCIENCES REPORT. 5191
0747-9948 See CECON RECORD (1983). 2038
0747-9956 See DISC SPORTS. 4893
0747-9964 See JOURNAL OF ENGINEERING TECHNOLOGY. 1982
0748-0008 See TEXAS ECONOMIC FORECAST. 1524
0748-0016 See PERSONAL ENGINEERING & INSTRUMENTATION NEWS. 1230

0748-0032 See SPECIAL PUBLICATION / THE UNIVERSITY OF GEORGIA, COLLEGE OF AGRICULTURE, EXPERIMENT STATION. 137
0748-0059 See IMAGE UNDERSTANDING. 1219
0748-0067 See ADVANCES IN TEACHER EDUCATION. 1887
0748-0075 See CHEMICAL AND PHYSICAL CHARACTERISTICS OF WATER IN ESTUARIES OF TEXAS. 5532
0748-0083 See ZONING REPORT (MARGATE, FL.), THE. 2839
0748-0113 See FLORIDA ARMCHAIR RESEARCHER, THE. 2448
0748-0121 See OFFICIAL PRICE GUIDE TO ROYAL DOULTON, THE. 2592
0748-0148 See NEWSLETTER (ROYAL SCHOOL OF CHURCH MUSIC (WARREN, CONN.). 4141
0748-0156 See PARAPSYCHOLOGY IN THE USSR. 4242
0748-0164 See CROSS CURRENTS (ANN ARBOR, MICH.). 3275
0748-0172 See INTERNATIONAL TRADE REPORTER. CURRENT REPORTS. 841
0748-0237 See IDAHO BROADCASTING GUIDE. 1133
0748-0245 See TOPS IDEAS. 2601
0748-0318 See MEAT ANIMALS, PRODUCTION, DISPOSITION, AND INCOME. 215
0748-0423 See YEAR IN REVIEW (RICHMOND, VA.), THE. 2361
0748-0458 See SORKINS' DIRECTORY OF BUSINESS & GOVERNMENT (ST. LOUIS ED.). 712
0748-0466 See CAROLINA CHEMTIPS. 966
0748-0482 See ISLAMIC AFFAIRS. 5043
0748-0539 See SPECIAL PUBLICATION (AMERICAN SOCIETY OF ICHTHYOLOGISTS AND HERPETOLOGISTS). 5597
0748-0571 See REPORT OF A VANTAGE CONFERENCE. 4533
0748-0601 See WHO'S WHO OF CALIFORNIA EXECUTIVE WOMEN. 438
0748-061X See COMPENSATION & BENEFITS MANAGEMENT. 864
0748-0636 See CONTEMPORARY AUTHORS AUTOBIOGRAPHY SERIES. 431
0748-0644 See RDI MONOGRAPHS ON FOREIGN AID AND DEVELOPMENT. 4533
0748-0679 See CURRENT RESEARCH UPDATES IN HUMAN SEXUALITY. 5187
0748-0695 842
0748-0709 See INTERNATIONAL TRADE REPORTER. DECISIONS (1984). 842
0748-0725 See PEACEWORK (CAMBRIDGE, MASS.). 4487
0748-0733 See FIBER WORLD. 5351
0748-0741 See COMMUNITY COLLEGE HUMANITIES REVIEW, THE. 2844
0748-0806 See EDUCATIONAL CHANGE. 1741
0748-0814 See JOURNAL OF LAW AND RELIGION, THE. 2988
0748-0830 See OUTLOOK FOR SUMMER TRAVEL. 5488
0748-0881 See VIDEO SOURCE BOOK, THE. 4377
0748-089X See RESEARCH SERVICE DIRECTORY (NEW YORK, N.Y.). 935
0748-0903 See TURBOMACHINERY INTERNATIONAL HANDBOOK. 2131
0748-1012 See LICKING LANTERN, THE. 2458
0748-1063 See NATIONAL OCEANOGRAPHIC FLEET OPERATING SCHEDULES FOR 1453
0748-1071 See LANCASTER COUNTY CONNECTIONS. 2457
0748-108X See EMC TECHNOLOGY ... ANTHOLOGY. 2053
0748-1101 See ELLERY QUEEN'S PRIME CRIMES. 5074
0748-111X See OFFICIAL PRICE GUIDE TO MUSIC COLLECTIBLES (ORLANDO, FLA. : 1984), THE. 4143
0748-1152 See OFFICIAL PRICE GUIDE TO POCKET KNIVES, THE. 4014
0748-1160 See OFFICIAL PRICE GUIDE TO SPORTS COLLECTIBLES, THE. 4910

0748-1179 See DISTRICT COUNCIL JOURNAL. 4645
0748-1187 See DEATH STUDIES. 4584
0748-1195 See DECEMBER ROSE. 5178
0748-1209 See GENERAL TECHNICAL REPORT INT. 2383
0748-1217 See RESEARCH NOTE SE. 2393
0748-1225 See RESEARCH PAPER SO. 2393
0748-1241 See RESOURCE BULLETIN INT. 2393
0748-125X See EXTENSION BULLETIN - WASHINGTON STATE UNIVERSITY. COOPERATIVE EXTENSION. 83
0748-1268 See BULLETIN / WEST VIRGINIA UNIVERSITY AGRICULTURAL AND FORESTRY EXPERIMENT STATION. 70
0748-1276 See DIVIDENDS FROM WOOD RESEARCH. 2378
0748-1284 See RESOURCE BULLETIN PNW. 2393
0748-1314 See GENERAL TECHNICAL REPORT NE. 2383
0748-1357 See RESOURCE BULLETIN NE. 2393
0748-1365 See OFFICIAL PRICE GUIDE TO FOOTBALL CARDS (1984), THE. 2776
0748-1403 See SAFETY ALERT. 2869
0748-142X See PULPWOOD HIGHLIGHTS. 4238
0748-1489 See OCEANIC ABSTRACTS (BETHESDA, MD.). 1363
0748-1527 See ENVIRONMENTAL ASSESSMENT OF THE ALASKAN CONTINENTAL SHELF. ANNUAL REPORTS OF PRINCIPAL INVESTIGATORS FOR THE YEAR ENDING 2166
0748-1543 See DIRECTORY OF COMPUTER SOFTWARE, A. 1285
0748-1578 See FUTURES (EAST LANSING, MICH.). 89
0748-1586 See FOREST RESEARCH IN THE SOUTHEAST. 2381
0748-1608 See PULP & PAPER PROJECT REPORT. 4238
0748-1616 See CURRENT PUBLICATIONS FROM THE FOREST, WILDLIFE AND RANGE EXPERIMENT STATION. 2378
0748-1675 See MASS ENTERTAINMENT BUYERS GUIDE. 4863
0748-1683 See WAY OF THE ZEPHYR, THE. 5428
0748-1721 See CFRU PROGRESS REPORT. 2377
0748-1748 See CFRU RESEARCH NOTE. 2377
0748-1756 See MEASUREMENT AND EVALUATION IN COUNSELING AND DEVELOPMENT. 1763
0748-1764 See WELLNESS PERSPECTIVES. 4807
0748-1780 See IMAGE (ST. LOUIS, MO.). 3395
0748-1810 See FOCUS ON DENTAL COMPUTERS. 1323
0748-1837 See CONSULTANT PRACTICE. 864
0748-1845 See FINANCIAL ADVERTISING REVIEW. 759
0748-1853 See BRICKMAN LETTER, THE. 893
0748-1861 See TRANSPLANTATION AND IMMUNOLOGY LETTER. 3976
0748-1888 See HARDIN FAMILY COURIER. 2452
0748-1896 See FUSION TECHNOLOGY. 2155
0748-1934 See NC ARTS. 325
0748-1942 See SURGERY ALERT. 3975
0748-1977 See JOURNAL OF CLINICAL MONITORING. 3594
0748-1993 See COAL MINING TECHNOLOGY, ECONOMICS, AND POLICY. 2137
0748-2019 See COASTAL BEND APARTMENT & RENTAL GUIDE. 4835
0748-2027 See MINING AND PUBLIC LANDS REPORT. 2145
0748-2035 See LIBRARIES (TULSA, OKLA.). 3223
0748-2043 See SMALL COMPUTERS IN THE ARTS NEWS. 330
0748-2051 See MICROPSYCH NETWORK. 4604
0748-206X See INTERNATIONAL INDUSTRY DOSSIER. 1612
0748-2086 See YEAR IN BRIEF, THE. 4061
0748-2108 See OFFICIAL PRICE GUIDE TO MINT ERRORS AND VARIETIES, THE. 2783

0748-2116 See LOGOS (ARGONNE, ILL.). 5126

0748-2140 See BUSINESS ONE IRWIN INVESTOR'S HANDBOOK, THE. 893

0748-223X See WORLDWIDE DIRECTORY OF EAST INDIANS QUARTERLY. 2495

0748-2256 See TODAY'S TRIVIA. 2494

0748-2264 See COMIC TALE EASY READER. 1062

0748-2280 See ISKCON WORLD REVIEW, THE. 4966

0748-2310 See PORTER'S GUIDE TO CONGRESSIONAL ROLL CALL VOTES. HOUSE. 4674

0748-2329 See PORTER'S GUIDE TO CONGRESSIONAL ROLL CALL VOTES. SENATE. 4491

0748-2337 See TOXICOLOGY AND INDUSTRIAL HEALTH. 3984

0748-2345 See ON LINE (GAINESVILLE, FLA.). 117

0748-2353 See IMPACT (GAINESVILLE, FLA.). 94

0748-237X See CLIPPER STUDIES IN THE AMERICAN THEATER. 5363

0748-2396 See CAMP RESORT LAW REPORT. 2947

0748-2469 See OFFICIAL DIRECTORY OF NEW JERSEY LIBRARIES AND MEDIA CENTERS. 3238

0748-2485 See ROOTS AND LEAVES. 2471

0748-2493 See RUTLAND HISTORICAL SOCIETY QUARTERLY. 2759

0748-2507 See BULLETIN OF THE WHATCOM GENEALOGICAL SOCIETY. 2440

0748-2515 See WESTERN MONTANA GENEALOGICAL SOCIETY BULLETIN. 2477

0748-2558 See SHAKESPEARE BULLETIN. 5368

0748-2590 See TEXAS KIN. 2475

0748-2612 See WATER & WASTEWATER DIGEST. 2247

0748-2639 See IRAQ VIEWS & NEWS. 2768

0748-2655 See JOURNAL - AMERICAN CIVIL LIBERTIES UNION FOUNDATION. NATIONAL PRISON PROJECT. 3167

0748-2663 See EMPLOYEE BENEFITS IN MEDIUM AND LARGE FIRMS. 1665

0748-2671 See U.S. INDUSTRIAL OUTLOOK (1984). 1630

0748-268X See STORM DATA FOR THE UNITED STATES. 1435

0748-2698 See MEANS MECHANICAL COST DATA. 620

0748-2701 See PROJECT SUMMARIES - NATIONAL SCIENCE FOUNDATION (U.S.). DIVISION OF SCIENCE RESOURCES STUDIES. 5142

0748-2728 See BANJO SOUNDSHEET. 4102

0748-2736 See HOUSER HUNTERS NEWSLETTER. 2454

0748-2744 See NEBRASKA LEGAL DIRECTORY, THE. 3014

0748-2752 See NORTH DAKOTA AND SOUTH DAKOTA LEGAL DIRECTORY, THE. 3018

0748-2760 See CONTEMPORARY GERIATRIC MEDICINE. 3750

0748-2795 See MARION COUNTY, ALABAMA TRACKS. 2459

0748-2892 See OCULAR REVIEW. 3971

0748-2914 See HORROR SHOW, THE. 3394

0748-2922 See ECONOMIC TRENDS (CLEVELAND, OHIO). 1485

0748-2930 See ROMANIAN PHILATELIC STUDIES. 2787

0748-2949 See SUMMARY OF SAFETY MANAGEMENT AUDITS. 4804

0748-2957 See MARYLAND PROSECUTOR, THE. 3108

0748-3007 See CLADISTICS. 451

0748-304X See CERAMIC WORLD. 2587

0748-3082 See LIST OF PROPRIETARY SUBSTANCES AND NONFOOD COMPOUNDS AUTHORIZED FOR USE UNDER USDA INSPECTION AND GRADING PROGRAMS. 2348

0748-3090 See LAUGH FACTORY. 2537

0748-3104 See COMUNICACIONES (CORAL GABLES, FLA.). 1152

0748-3120 See MAINE BUSINESS AND EMPLOYMENT LAW. 3101

0748-3155 See EXERCISE PHYSIOLOGY (NEW YORK, N.Y.). 3954

0748-3163 See REAL ESTATE LEASING REPORT. 4844

0748-318X See REAL ESTATE FINANCE. 4844

0748-321X See JOURNAL OF VETERINARY MEDICAL EDUCATION. 5514

0748-3236 See FADUM REPORT, THE. 4233

0748-3295 See CONTACTS INFLUENTIAL. COLORADO FRONT RANGE. 660

0748-3309 See CORYELL KIN. 2444

0748-3317 See OFFICIAL PRICE GUIDE TO BASEBALL CARDS (1984), THE. 2775

0748-3325 See HIVELY'S CHOICE. 1750

0748-3333 See HEALTH PHYSICS/RADIATION PROTECTION ENROLLMENTS AND DEGREES. 3941

0748-3341 See DUQUETTE'S SHOW CAR QUARTERLY. 5413

0748-3406 See VENTURE INWARD / THE MAGAZINE OF THE ASSOCIATION FOR RESEARCH AND ENLIGHTENMENT. 5007

0748-383X See HEALTH MATRIX. 3740

0748-3872 See PACER (QUINLAN, TEX.), THE. 2542

0748-3899 See SAN FRANCISCO BAY ARCHITECTS' REVIEW. 308

0748-4003 See MATURE OUTLOOK NEWSLETTER. 5180

0748-4054 See PRESCHOOL PERSPECTIVES. 1805

0748-4062 See POET (SHREVEPORT, LA.), THE. 3468

0748-4089 See ASIA-PACIFIC AFRICA-MIDDLE EAST PETROLEUM DIRECTORY. 4251

0748-4119 See TENNESSEE DAIRY STATISTICS. 157

0748-4127 See PASCAL & MODULA2. 1280

0748-4135 See WORKERS' COMPENSATION LAWS OF CALIFORNIA, THE. 3155

0748-4151 See REPORT TO CONGRESS ON ABNORMAL OCCURRENCES. 2158

0748-4240 See BURRELLE'S WOMEN'S MEDIA DIRECTORY. 1105

0748-4259 See BURRELLE'S BLACK MEDIA DIRECTORY. 1105

0748-4305 See GEORGE WASHINGTON JOURNAL OF INTERNATIONAL LAW AND ECONOMICS, THE. 3128

0748-4321 See LEGACY (AMHERST, MASS.). 3404

0748-433X See REPORT OF THE ... UNITED NATIONS OF THE NEXT DECADE CONFERENCE. 4533

0748-4356 See AFRICA INSIDER. 4462

0748-4364 See HIGHER EDUCATION ABSTRACTS. 1795

0748-4380 See HOOVER ESSAYS. 4476

0748-4399 See COLOR XEROX ANNUAL. 377

0748-4402 See CALIFORNIA ALMANAC. 5324

0748-4410 See ADVANCES IN CLINICAL NEUROPSYCHOLOGY. 3826

0748-4429 See CONTACTS INFLUENTIAL. LOS ANGELES COUNTY, SOUTH BAY. 660

0748-4437 See CONTACTS INFLUENTIAL. TAMPA BAY. 660

0748-4461 See COMPUTER GAMES. 1230

0748-4518 See JOURNAL OF QUANTITATIVE CRIMINOLOGY. 3167

0748-4526 See NEGOTIATION JOURNAL. 4483

0748-4577 See PINTURA : AMERICAN ROCK ART RESEARCH ASSOCIATION NEWSLETTER, LA. 362

0748-4585 See LANGE'S HANDBOOK OF CHEMISTRY. 984

0748-4593 See TRIBUNE - INTERNATIONAL WOMEN'S TRIBUNE CENTRE (FEB. FRANCAISE), LA. 5567

0748-4615 See FOREIGN LANGUAGE BOOKS. 4388

0748-4623 See JOURNAL OF PROFESSIONAL SERVICES MARKETING. 929

0748-4631 See INTERFLO. 841

0748-464X See ZORYAN BULLETIN, THE. 2668

0748-4658 See JOURNAL OF PROPULSION AND POWER. 26

0748-4666 See DENTAL ADVISOR. 1320

0748-4682 See DOXOLOGY. 4954

0748-4690 See JOURNAL OF FERTILIZER ISSUES. 176

0748-4704 See LOS GATOS WEEKLY. 5636

0748-4747 See ENVIRONMENTAL ISSUES REPORT. 2168

0748-4755 See PRICING ADVISOR, THE. 1513

0748-478X See CURRENTS (WASHINGTON, D.C. 1983). 1819

0748-481X See NATURAL RESOURCES INFORMATION DIRECTORY FOR THE STATE OF CONNECTICUT AND LIST OF PUBLICATIONS FOR THE CONNECTICUT GEOLOGICAL AND NATURAL HISTORY SURVEY. 2199

0748-4836 See SELECTED AUDIOVISUAL MATERIALS PRODUCED BY THE UNITED STATES GOVERNMENT. 1139

0748-4852 See MEDICAL DEVICES REPORT. 3608

0748-4895 See STRATEGIC PLANNING MANAGEMENT. 887

0748-4925 See VERMONT BAR JOURNAL & LAW DIGEST, THE. 3071

0748-5034 See SMOKE SIGNALS FROM THE ASSINIBOINE GENEALOGICAL SOCIETY. 2472

0748-5069 See ANIMAL ORGANIZATIONS & SERVICES DIRECTORY. 225

0748-5077 See ANNUAL REPORT TO THE OKLAHOMA TURNPIKE AUTHORITY. 4629

0748-5093 See CATALOG OF UNIVERSITY PRESENTATIONS. 4771

0748-5166 See SHINTAFFER NEWSLETTER, THE. 2472

0748-5212 See ADVANCES IN PLASTIC AND RECONSTRUCTIVE SURGERY. 3958

0748-5255 See KANSAS COURT RULES AND PROCEDURE. 3141

0748-5263 See CATONSVILLE TIMES. 5686

0748-5271 See ARBUTUS TIMES. 2485

0748-528X See LAUREL LEADER. 5686

0748-5298 See HOWARD COUNTY TIMES (COLUMBIA, MD.). 5686

0748-5344 See ETHICS RESOURCE CENTER REPORT. 2250

0748-5352 See SLEEP WATCHERS. 3641

0748-5379 See GRAND ISLAND INDEPENDENT. 5706

0748-5387 See GRAND ISLAND INDEPENDENT. 5706

0748-5484 See TEXT TECHNOLOGY. 1205

0748-5492 See ISSUES IN SCIENCE AND TECHNOLOGY. 5116

0748-5522 See OFFICIAL PRICE GUIDE TO HUMMEL FIGURINES & PLATES, THE. 2776

0748-5530 See ANNUAL REPORT / PUERTO RICO INDUSTRIAL DEVELOPMENT COMPANY. 891

0748-5549 See BUDGET-WISE HOUSE PLANS. 293

0748-5565 See KENTUCKY PIONEER GENEALOGY AND RECORDS. 2456

0748-559X See PERMANENT COLLECTION ILLUSTRATED CHECKLIST. 362

0748-562X See CHAPTER 11 REPORTER. 3086

0748-5727 See CALIFORNIA SENIOR CITIZEN. 5633

0748-5743 See INTERACTIVE LEARNING INTERNATIONAL. 1223

0748-5751 See JOURNAL OF ACCOUNTING EDUCATION. 746

0748-5786 See JOURNAL OF EDUCATION FOR LIBRARY AND INFORMATION SCIENCE. 3220

0748-5816 See UTILIZATION OF SHORT-TERM GENERAL AND SPECIALTY HOSPITALS IN METROPOLITAN CHICAGO FOR THE ... QUARTER OF 3793

0748-5824 See I.D.B.I. GUIDE, INTERNATIONAL DRIVE BELT INTERCHANGE. 2115

0748-5840 See OFFICIAL PRICE GUIDE TO COMIC BOOKS & COLLECTIBLES, THE. 2776

0748-5875 See ANNUAL REPORT / INTERNATIONAL FERTILIZER DEVELOPMENT CENTER. 163

0748-5891 See OHIO APPELLATE DECISIONS INDEX. CRIMINAL CASES. 3108

0748-5905 See AMERICAN FOLK MUSIC AND FOLKLORE RECORDINGS. 4099

0748-5913 See MEN'S NEWS MAGAZINE. 3996

0748-5972 See ENERGY ANALYST. 1938

0748-5999 See TECHNIQUE (INDIANAPOLIS, IND.). 4925

0748-6006 See USA GYMNASTICS. 4928

0748-6014 See ASIA CABLE. 1126

0748-6022 See FARMER'S MARKET (GALESBURG, ILL.). 3387

0748-6030 See CREDIT DECISIONS. 785

0748-6073 See COAL PEOPLE. 2728

0748-6081 See SILICON MOUNTAIN REPORT. 1626

0748-6111 See RADIOPHARMACY AND RADIOPHARMACOLOGY YEARBOOK. 3849

0748-6138 See BUSINESS FIRST (LOUISVILLE, KY.). 648

0748-6146 See BUSINESS FIRST (COLUMBUS, OHIO). 648

0748-6170 See OPINIONS OF THE ATTORNEY GENERAL OF OHIO. 3142

0748-6189 See XALMAN; ALMA CHICANA DE AZTLAN. 3455

0748-6219 See DE PERE JOURNAL. 5766

0748-6235 See GUIDE TO FREE COMPUTER MATERIALS. 1895

0748-6251 See ROOT CELLAR PRESERVES. 2470

0748-6278 See ANNUAL PROCUREMENT AND FEDERAL ASSISTANCE REPORT. 4626

0748-6294 See BLOSSOM MUSIC CENTER. 4104

0748-6316 See MANAGEMENT SUMMARY. 2887

0748-6332 See STEVENS POINT JOURNAL (STEVENS POINT, WIS. : 1981 : DAILY). 5771

0748-6359 See WASHINGTON PACIFIC REPORT, THE. 4499

0748-6367 See CHEVRON FOCUS. 4253

0748-6405 See SPRINGS MAGAZINE (COLORADO SPRINGS, COLO.). 2546

0748-6456 See SCRIPTWRITERS MARKET. 4077

0748-6464 See CENTER (LOUISVILLE, KY.), THE. 384

0748-6499 See CULTIC STUDIES JOURNAL. 5243

0748-6502 See INFORMATION BULLETIN (ROMANIAN-AMERICAN HERITAGE CENTER (U.S.). 2739

0748-6510 See POMONA : NORTH AMERICAN FRUIT EXPLORERS' QUARTERLY. 2428

0748-657X See COMMUNICATION BOOKNOTES. 1125

0748-660X See COMPUTERIZED DRAFTING AND DESIGN NEWSLETTER. 1232

0748-6642 See PHYSIOLOGICAL CHEMISTRY AND PHYSICS AND MEDICAL NMR. 469

0748-6677 See AGLOW. 4933

0748-6693 See PHYTOPHTHORA NEWSLETTER. 523

0748-6715 See METHODOLOGICAL SURVEYS IN BIOCHEMISTRY AND ANALYSIS. 490

0748-6731 See AMERICAN HISTORY (WESTPORT, CONN.). 2719

0748-6782 See GILMORE SUGAR MANUAL, THE. 173

0748-6804 See NEW FOUNDATION PAPERS. 4981

0748-6812 See WOODVILLE LEADER AND DUNN COUNTY PICTORIAL MESSENGER, THE. 5772

0748-6839 See UNION WRITES NEWSLETTER. 1716

0748-6855 See HOLISTIC MASSAGE. 2598

0748-6863 See RIPON COMMONWEALTH-PRESS, THE. 5770

0748-6898 See AMERY FREE PRESS. 5765

0748-6928 See JUNIOR (HAGERSTOWN, MD.). 4971

0748-7002 See MEANS ELECTRICAL COST DATA. 620

0748-7142 See TRSA ORGANIZATION. 5359

0748-7169 See BERKELEY NEWSLETTER (BERKELEY, CALIF.). 962

0748-7231 See RESOURCE DIRECTORY OF DOE INFORMATION ORGANIZATIONS. 1955

0748-7304 See JOURNAL OF BIOLOGICAL RHYTHMS. 460

0748-7312 See RAINBOW HERALD, THE. 4989

0748-7320 See KOI USA. 2422

0748-7339 See OCCASIONAL PAPER - BOSTON UNIVERSITY. CENTER FOR ARCHAEOLOGICAL STUDIES. 277

0748-7347 See TRANSIT PULSE. 5395

0748-7355 See TODAY'S SINGLE. 5567

0748-738X See CHIME NEWSLETTER, THE. 1731

0748-7398 See TRAVEL & LEARNING ABROAD. 5495

0748-7401 See TRANSWORLD SKATEBOARDING. 4927

0748-7533 See PROCEEDINGS OF THE ... ANNUAL DREDGING SEMINAR. 2094

0748-7541 See REPORT TO EXECUTIVES ON MIDDLE MARKET FINANCIAL MANAGEMENT. 808

0748-7568 See HEJNA. 2262

0748-7576 See PROCEEDINGS OF THE ANNUAL NACD CONVENTION. 2202

0748-7592 See CURRENT PROBLEMS IN FEDERAL CIVIL PRACTICE. 3089

0748-7606 See OFFICIAL PRICE GUIDE TO RADIO, TV & MOVIE MEMORABILIA, THE. 1135

0748-7630 See READING & WRITING QUARTERLY. 1884

0748-7657 See CIVIL LAW OPINIONS OF THE JUDGE ADVOCATE GENERAL, UNITED STATES AIR FORCE. 3089

0748-7665 See I.S.I. GUIDE, INTERNATIONAL SEAL INTERCHANGE. 2115

0748-7711 See JOURNAL OF REHABILITATION RESEARCH AND DEVELOPMENT. 4380

0748-772X See CULTURAL FUTURES RESEARCH. 234

0748-7746 See TEXAS CITRUS TREE INVENTORY SURVEY. 189

0748-7754 See FOURTH QUARTER AND ANNUAL REPORT ON THE TEXAS BOVINE BRUCELLOSIS PROGRAM / TEXAS ANIMAL HEALTH COMMISSION, AUSTIN TEXAS. 211

0748-7819 See CURRENT DEVELOPMENTS IN ANTHROPOLOGICAL GENETICS. 544

0748-7827 See ROSE FAMILY BULLETIN. 2471

0748-7835 See VENDOR SELECTOR SERVICE. 1631

0748-7851 See INVENTORS' VOICE. 5116

0748-7878 See WORKER'S COMPENSATION LAW BULLETIN. 3155

0748-7886 See VS NEWS. 1273

0748-7975 See ACCOUNTING AND TAX INDEX. 725

0748-7983 See EUROPEAN JOURNAL OF SURGICAL ONCOLOGY. 3817

0748-7991 See ADVANCED MATERIALS FOR OPTICS AND ELECTRONICS. 5080

0748-8009 See MEDICINE AND WAR. 3613

0748-8017 See QUALITY AND RELIABILITY ENGINEERING INTERNATIONAL. 1992

0748-8025 See COMMUNICATIONS IN APPLIED NUMERICAL METHODS. 3500

0748-8033 See MEDICAL DEVICES REPORT. 3608

0748-8068 See AMERICAN JOURNAL OF COSMETIC SURGERY, THE. 3958

0748-8106 See CHRISTMAS IDEAS. 371

0748-8114 See WHITE HOUSE HISTORY. 2633

0748-8149 See ILLINOIS HISTORICAL JOURNAL. 2738

0748-8157 See FRONTIERS OF HEALTH SERVICES MANAGEMENT. 5286

0748-8165 See NUTRITION FORUM (PHILADELPHIA, PA.). 4196

0748-8173 See MONTHLY REPORT - ASSOCIATION OF AMERICAN PUBLISHERS. 4817

0748-8211 See PHYSICIANS DRG NEWSLETTER. 5301

0748-8238 See JOURNAL OF ST. LUKE'S HEART INSTITUTE. 3707

0748-8246 See CALIFORNIA ENERGY PRICES. 1934

0748-8270 See LITIGATION UNDER THE FEDERAL OPEN GOVERNMENT LAWS. 4481

0748-8297 See MOSINEE TIMES, THE. 5769

0748-8319 See AMERICAN HAWKWATCHER. 5614

0748-8327 See NRMA AD/PRO. 763

0748-8335 See PROFITMAKER, THE. 849

0748-8343 See AMERICAN BREWERIANA JOURNAL. 2363

0748-8378 See SAVING AND PRESERVING ARTS AND CULTURAL ENVIRONMENTS. 330

0748-8386 See STRESS MEDICINE. 3643

0748-8394 See OUTPOST EXCHANGE. 1298

0748-8424 See GRANT'S INTEREST RATE OBSERVER. 1493

0748-8475 See THOUGHT & ACTION (WASHINGTON, D.C.). 1850

0748-8483 See MICRO MAINFRAME CONNECTION. 1269

0748-8491 See EDUCATION & TREATMENT OF CHILDREN. 1893

0748-8505 See POWER TECHNOLOGY NEWS. 1991

0748-8521 See MEYSSEL, MIKESELL, MIXSELL FAMILY NEWSLETTER. 2460

0748-853X See CDC LIBRARY SERIAL HOLDINGS. 413

0748-8556 See MITCHELL GUIDE. NEW YORK CITY, THE. 5296

0748-8580 See CURRENT RESEARCH IN FILM. 4067

0748-8599 See ANNUAL REVIEW OF POLITICAL SCIENCE. 4464

0748-8602 See ADVANCES IN HUMAN-COMPUTER INTERACTION. 1217

0748-8610 See COMPUTER RETAILERS' GUIDE. 1266

0748-8637 See TIMEPIECE (NAPLES, FLA.). 2763

0748-8653 See BIOLOGICAL MEMBRANES (NEW YORK, N.Y. : 1985). 445

0748-8726 See OFFICIAL PRICE GUIDE TO COLLECTIBLES OF THE THIRD REICH, THE. 4053

0748-8742 See KALEIDOSCOPE (AKRON, OHIO), THE. 3401

0748-8750 See ANNUAL REPORT / NORFOLK SOUTHERN. 5429

0748-8769 See ENVIRONMENTAL LAW (WASHINGTON D.C.). 3112

0748-8777 See NEW MEDICAL SCIENCE. 3620

0748-8793 See JOURNAL OF CHILD AND ADOLESCENT PSYCHOTHERAPY. 4594

0748-8815 See KETTERING REVIEW. 4660

0748-8831 See ONE-PERSON LIBRARY, THE. 3239

0748-884X See GNOSIS ANTHOLOGY. 4347

0748-8858 See CATALOG OF GOVERNMENT PATENTS. 1302

0748-8890 See INTERNATIONAL EMPLOYMENT HOTLINE. 4205

0748-8904 See SCIENCE WEEKLY. LEVEL A. 1904

0748-8947 See EMERGENCY MEDICINE (GLENDALE, CALIF.). 3574

0748-8971 See VASCULAR REPORTS. 3977

0748-898X See CURRENT INDEX OF COMPUTER LITERATURE. 1181

0748-9080 See OPINIONS OF THE ATTORNEY GENERAL OF KENTUCKY. 3142

0748-9099 See PRO REVIEW, THE. 4375

0748-9102 See PRICE MOMENTUM CHARTS AND REPORT / QUANTITATIVE ANALYSIS SERVICE. 911

0748-9110 *See* NORTHEAST MONITORING PROGRAM ... ANNUAL REPORT. **2237**

0748-9129 *See* TIMBER REVIEW. **2405**

0748-9145 *See* ENERGY PERFORMANCE REVIEW. **1605**

0748-9153 *See* OFF-PRICE NEWS. THE BOOK ON OUTLET & OFF-PRICE LEASING, THE. **956**

0748-917X *See* OFF-PRICE NEWS OF ..., THE. **956**

0748-9196 *See* IEEE ELECTRO TECHNOLOGY REVIEW. **2059**

0748-9234 *See* UNIVERSITY OF CALIFORNIA, BERKELEY, WELLNESS LETTER. **4806**

0748-9250 *See* CIM STRATEGIES. **3476**

0748-9285 *See* MLA NEWS LETTER - MINNESOTA LIBRARY ASSOCIATION. **3232**

0748-9293 *See* MUSICAL NEWS (SAN FRANCISCO, CALIF.). **4136**

0748-9307 *See* HOLISTIC OPTOMETRIST, THE. **4215**

0748-9315 *See* PERSONAL ROBOTICS MAGAZINE. **1215**

0748-9331 *See* COMPUTER JOURNAL (KALISPELL, MONT.). **1177**

0748-934X *See* GAFFNEY LEDGER, THE. **5742**

0748-9358 *See* MARKETING INTELLIGENCE. FIBEROPTIC. **1159**

0748-9366 See INTERNATIONAL BANKING FOCUS. **792**

0748-948X *See* MANUFACTURING SYSTEMS. **1617**

0748-9501 *See* CHIBRET INTERNATIONAL JOURNAL OF OPHTHALMOLOGY (ENGLISH ED.). **3873**

0748-951X *See* CGL REPORTER. **2877**

0748-9528 *See* SECOND OPINION (SAN FRANCISCO, CALIF.). **4802**

0748-9544 *See* GREAT LAKES REPORTER, THE. **2172**

0748-9560 *See* ZA NETWORK NEWS REPORTS. **1143**

0748-9579 *See* TIMELINE. **2763**

0748-9633 *See* JOURNAL OF COUNSELING AND DEVELOPMENT. **1913**

0748-9641 *See* REPORT OF THE ... STRATEGY FOR PEACE US FOREIGN POLICY CONFERENCE. **4533**

0748-965X *See* CUMBERLAND ADVOCATE. **5766**

0748-9668 *See* COLLEGIATE SPORTS REPORT. **4890**

0748-9676 *See* INTERNATIONAL UNIVERSITY POETRY QUARTERLY, THE. **3464**

0748-9684 *See* NEWSLETTER - INTERNATIONAL UNIVERSITY (INDEPENDENCE, MO.). **1837**

0748-9692 *See* WORLDLAW. **3138**

0748-9706 *See* SHOFAR (MELVILLE, N.Y.). **1069**

0748-9781 *See* LUNAR SAMPLE NEWSLETTER. **396**

0748-9854 *See* TEXAS HUNTER'S DIRECTORY. **4879**

0748-9889 See COMPUTERCRAFT (HICKSVILLE, N.Y.). **1266**

0748-9897 *See* EASTERN COMPUTING FARMER. **80**

0748-9919 *See* ORIGINS RESEARCH. **4354**

0748-996X *See* LINN'S U.S. STAMP YEARBOOK. **2785**

0749-0003 *See* EMPLOYEE ASSISTANCE QUARTERLY. **2861**

0749-0062 *See* ASIAN STUDIES CENTER BACKGROUNDER. **4516**

0749-0100 *See* BULLETIN - EASTERN STATES ARCHEOLOGICAL FEDERATION (U.S.). MEETING. **263**

0749-0143 *See* KURISUCHYON HEROLDU. **5636**

0749-016X *See* NEW ENGLAND JOURNAL OF PUBLIC POLICY. **4668**

0749-0186 *See* VIEWTRON MAGAZINE & GUIDE. **2549**

0749-0208 *See* JOURNAL OF COASTAL RESEARCH. **1357**

0749-0224 *See* MINNESOTA LEGAL DIRECTORY, THE. **3010**

0749-0232 *See* JOURNAL OF APPLIED SOCIOLOGY - SOCIETY FOR APPLIED SOCIOLOGY (U.S.). **5249**

0749-0291 *See* JAMES DICKEY NEWSLETTER. **3464**

0749-0313 *See* NEW HAMPSHIRE LIBRARY STATISTICS. **3259**

0749-033X *See* WINE SPECTATOR'S GUIDE TO SELECTED WINES, THE. **2372**

0749-0372 *See* BIOTECHNOLOGY SOFTWARE. **3689**

0749-0399 *See* FACIAL ORTHOPEDICS AND TEMPOROMANDIBULAR ARTHROLOGY. **3881**

0749-050X *See* DIRECTORY OF INFORMATION AND REFERRAL SERVICES IN THE UNITED STATES AND CANADA. **5283**

0749-0526 *See* GREAT LAKES TROLLING ANNUAL. **2304**

0749-0534 *See* ICC REGISTER. **2979**

0749-0569 See LET'S GO. THE BUDGET GUIDE TO GREECE & TURKEY. **5483**

0749-0593 *See* ... RETREAT DIRECTORY, THE. **4993**

0749-0607 *See* PARKER'S BUSINESS STATUTES AND SECURITIES RULES OF TEXAS. **3102**

0749-0615 *See* BAR BRIEF (BEVERLY HILLS, CALIF.). **2939**

0749-0631 *See* NEWSLETTER / CLERMONT COUNTY GENEALOGICAL SOCIETY. **2463**

0749-064X *See* CONTEMPORARY THEATRE, FILM, AND TELEVISION. **384**

0749-0674 *See* NATO-WARSAW AND STRATEGIES. **4483**

0749-0682 *See* INTERNATIONAL ANNUAL JOURNAL OF ARTS, SCIENCES, ENGINEERING, AGRICULTURE, AND TECHNOLOGY. **5114**

0749-0690 *See* CLINICS IN GERIATRIC MEDICINE. **3750**

0749-0704 *See* CRITICAL CARE CLINICS. **3779**

0749-0712 *See* HAND CLINICS. **3881**

0749-0720 *See* VETERINARY CLINICS OF NORTH AMERICA. FOOD ANIMAL PRACTICE, THE. **5525**

0749-0739 *See* VETERINARY CLINICS OF NORTH AMERICA. EQUINE PRACTICE, THE. **5525**

0749-0755 *See* SOUND POST (GRANITE FALLS, MINN.). **4154**

0749-0763 *See* KLANSMAN, THE. **2266**

0749-0771 *See* SLIPSTREAM (NIAGARA FALLS, N.Y.). **3471**

0749-0992 *See* PIB MAGAZINE ADVERTISING ANALYSIS. ADVERTISING PAGE INDEX. **763**

0749-1018 *See* BODY TALK. **5551**

0749-1034 *See* WEST'S FEDERAL TAX MANUAL WITH WESTLAW. **3074**

0749-1042 *See* NATIONAL FORENSIC JOURNAL. **3742**

0749-1050 *See* WASHINGTON INQUIRER. **4538**

0749-1093 *See* MACRAE'S DIRECTORY OF FIRMS MARKETING THROUGH MANUFACTURERS' REPRESENTATIVES. **3482**

0749-1158 *See* NEW YORK STATE MUSEUM MEMOIR. **4169**

0749-1190 *See* MONOGRAPHS IN PSYCHOBIOLOGY. **466**

0749-1255 *See* HOTLINE - NEWSLETTER ASSOCIATION OF AMERICA. **2920**

0749-1298 *See* CORAPORTER. **1918**

0749-131X *See* CONNECTICUT SCHOOL OF LAW ANNUAL. **2955**

0749-1328 *See* PRIORITIES FOR RESEARCH, EXTENSION, AND HIGHER EDUCATION : A REPORT TO THE SECRETARY OF AGRICULTURE. **121**

0749-1352 *See* TRAIL WALKER. **2548**

0749-1379 *See* DAILY CITIZEN (BEAVER DAM, WIS. : 1971). **5766**

0749-1387 *See* FACES (PETERBOROUGH, N.H.). **1063**

0749-1409 *See* WOMEN'S STUDIES IN COMMUNICATION. **1124**

0749-1425 *See* JOURNAL OF THE ASSOCIATION FOR PERSONS WITH SEVERE HANDICAPS, THE. **1881**

0749-145X *See* INDUSTRIAL VEGETATION MANAGEMENT (1982). **95**

0749-1476 See WEST'S FEDERAL TAXATION. INDIVIDUAL PRACTICE SETS. **4758**

0749-1484 *See* COMPUTING AND COMMUNICATIONS PROTECTION. **1226**

0749-1484 *See* DATA PROCESSING & COMMUNICATIONS SECURITY. **1257**

0749-1522 *See* JONES JOURNEYS. **2455**

0749-1530 *See* FAMILY VINES. **2447**

0749-1549 *See* ON-STAGE STUDIES. **5367**

0749-1581 *See* MAGNETIC RESONANCE IN CHEMISTRY : MRC. **1044**

0749-159X *See* NUMERICAL METHODS FOR PARTIAL DIFFERENTIAL EQUATIONS. **3525**

0749-1603 *See* ADVANCES IN ROBOTICS. **1210**

0749-1646 *See* THURGOOD MARSHALL LAW REVIEW. **3064**

0749-1670 *See* SRRT NEWSLETTER (CHICAGO, ILL.). **3251**

0749-1697 *See* KING'S SOUTHERN COAL. **1614**

0749-1700 *See* KING'S WESTERN COAL. **1614**

0749-1719 *See* KING'S NORTHERN COAL. **1614**

0749-1735 *See* ARIZONA DEPARTMENT OF WATER RESOURCES BULLETIN. **5530**

0749-1743 *See* MEMOIRS OF THE NATURAL HISTORY FOUNDATION OF ORANGE COUNTY. **4167**

0749-1751 *See* ANTHROQUEST. **230**

0749-1786 *See* BIBLIOGRAPHIES AND INDEXES IN ECONOMICS AND ECONOMIC HISTORY. **1530**

0749-1794 *See* UNDERWATER USA. **4927**

0749-1816 *See* AWANYU. **260**

0749-1824 *See* CAKE DECORATING. **2330**

0749-1832 *See* VOLLEYBALL CASE BOOK AND OFFICIALS MANUAL. **4928**

0749-1840 *See* INSURANCE SERVICE. COMMERCIAL INSURANCE MARKET STUDY / DATA RESOURCES, INC. **2884**

0749-1867 *See* ROYCE QUARTERLY, THE. **2471**

0749-1980 *See* U.S. WATER NEWS. **5541**

0749-2006 *See* MARLIN. **2308**

0749-2081 *See* SEMINARS IN ONCOLOGY NURSING. **3869**

0749-2111 *See* CONFERENCE PROCEEDINGS - WESTERN FORESTRY COUNCIL (U.S.) CONFERENCE. **2378**

0749-2138 *See* GREEN THUMB NEWS. **2417**

0749-2162 *See* INDUSTRIAL RELATIONS RESEARCH ASSOCIATION SERIES NEWSLETTER. **1678**

0749-2170 *See* LECTURE NOTES-MONOGRAPH SERIES. **5332**

0749-2197 *See* AGRICULTURAL RESEARCH IN KANSAS. **51**

0749-2227 *See* JOURNAL OF LAW & POLITICS. **2988**

0749-2243 *See* HANDBOOK OF ADVERTISING & MARKETING SERVICES. **759**

0749-2286 *See* HOMICIDE SURVEILLANCE. **3165**

0749-2308 *See* AFRICAN SPECIAL BIBLIOGRAPHIC SERIES. **407**

0749-2316 *See* EFFECTIVE ADVERTISING. **759**

0749-2332 *See* AGENCY SALES. **921**

0749-2375 *See* CALIFORNIA MUNICIPAL BOND ADVISOR. **893**

0749-2391 *See* MAINSTREAM AMERICA. **4481**

0749-2421 *See* OCCASIONAL PAPERS (UNIVERSITY OF NEW MEXICO. MUSEUM OF SOUTHWESTERN BIOLOGY). **2219**

0749-2448 *See* POPULATION TODAY. **4558**

0749-2472 *See* RESOUND. **4149**

0749-2529 *See* EVALUATING TAX SHELTER OFFERINGS. **4722**

0749-2537 *See* CREATIVE WORD PROCESSING IN THE CLASSROOM : CWP. **1292**

0749-2553 *See* BIRNBAUM'S FRANCE. **5464**

0749-2561 *See* STEPHEN BIRNBAUM TRAVEL GUIDE, A. **5491**

0749-260X *See* DOG RIVER REVIEW. **3382**

0749-2642 *See* ADC TIMES. **2254**

0749-2650 See AMERICAN COMMUNITY, TECHNICAL, AND JUNIOR COLLEGES. 1910
0749-2685 See INTERNATIONAL REGISTRY OF ORGANIZATION DEVELOPMENT PROFESSIONALS AND ORGANIZATION DEVELOPMENT HANDBOOK, THE. 433
0749-2715 See FAX/NET, PUBLIC ACCESS FACSIMILE STATION DIRECTORY. 1155
0749-2758 See FROM THE STATE CAPITALS. ENVIRONMENTAL REGULATION. 2230
0749-2766 See FROM THE STATE CAPITALS. CONSTRUCTION POLICIES. 615
0749-2774 See FROM THE STATE CAPITALS. TRANSPORTATION POLICIES. 5383
0749-2790 See FROM THE STATE CAPITALS. JUSTICE POLICIES. 3165
0749-2804 See FROM THE STATE CAPITALS. PARKS AND RECREATION TRENDS, (NEW HAVEN, CONN.). 4706
0749-2820 See FROM THE STATE CAPITALS. TAXATION AND REVENUE POLICIES. 4727
0749-2839 See COMPUTER LANGUAGE. 1218
0749-2847 See INSURANCE COMPANY RATINGS REPORTER. 2883
0749-2871 See CRESCENT REVIEW, THE. 2532
0749-2898 See PSI RESEARCH. 4242
0749-2928 See ACCOUNTING OFFICE MANAGEMENT & ADMINISTRATION REPORT. 737
0749-2936 See BROADCAST STATS. 1124
0749-2952 See SHOWBOATS INTERNATIONAL. 596
0749-3002 See ANATOMICAL RECORD. SUPPLEMENT, THE. 3678
0749-3061 See CIVIL LIBERTIES IN TEXAS. 4506
0749-3096 See CHILDREN'S LITERATURE AWARDS AND WINNERS. 3374
0749-310X See FAMILY SAFETY AND HEALTH (U.S. ED.). 4775
0749-3118 See FAMILY SAFETY AND HEALTH (CANADIAN ED.). 4775
0749-3126 See PROINE, HE. 5720
0749-3177 See CRD NEWS / COMMITTEE FOR THE RIGHTS OF THE DISABLED. 4506
0749-3185 See TEXAS PSYCHOLOGIST. 4620
0749-3193 See ABSTRACTS OF STAFF REPORTS. 42
0749-3207 See SELECTED ACQUISITIONS BULLETIN - UNIVERSITY OF KENTUCKY. LIBRARIES. MAP DEPT. 2576
0749-3223 See AMERICAN BIOTECHNOLOGY LABORATORY. 3685
0749-3312 See ECONOMIC POISONS ... REPORT (BISMARCK, N.D.). 2413
0749-3347 See CHARACTERISTICS OF PERSONS ENTERING PAROLE. 3160
0749-338X See NEWSLETTER / MAP ONLINE USERS GROUP. 3235
0749-3401 See O'NEIL DATABASE. 802
0749-3495 See MALPRACTICE REPORTER. PODIATRY, THE. 3005
0749-3509 See VIBRANT LIFE. 2601
0749-3533 See ORGANIST'S COMPANION, THE. 4144
0749-3541 See FUGATE FAMILY NEWSLETTER, THE. 2449
0749-3584 See BIBLE OF WEATHER FORECASTING, THE. 1420
0749-3746 See REPORT - VIRGINIA. STATE BOARD OF NURSING. 3868
0749-3770 See PROJECT CONCERN INTERNATIONAL ... ANNUAL REPORT. 2911
0749-3789 See PROJECT CONCERN INTERNATIONAL ... ANNUAL REPORT. 2911
0749-3797 See AMERICAN JOURNAL OF PREVENTIVE MEDICINE. 3549
0749-3851 See 2600. 1225
0749-3878 See MAPPING SCIENCES AND REMOTE SENSING. 2582
0749-3924 See TRANSITIONS IN MENTAL RETARDATION. 4620
0749-3932 See OFFICE SYSTEMS ERGONOMICS REPORT. 1989
0749-3940 See EVERYONE'S BACKYARD. 2171

0749-4009 See OHIO GRANGER. 116
0749-4017 See YEAR-END REGULATORY REVIEW. 724
0749-4025 See JOURNAL OF CLASSROOM INTERACTION, THE. 1756
0749-4033 See ETHNOMUSICOLOGY AT UCLA. 4117
0749-4041 See YEAR BOOK OF VASCULAR SURGERY, THE. 3978
0749-405X See WISCONSIN STATE JOURNAL (MADISON, WIS. : 1862). 5772
0749-4068 See CAPITAL TIMES, THE. 5766
0749-4092 See FRIENDS OF THE LILLY LIBRARY NEWSLETTER, THE. 3211
0749-4106 See SOUTHERN CALIFORNIA EARLY MUSIC SOCIETY NEWSLETTER. 4154
0749-4114 See NEW YORK CLIMATE. 1432
0749-4122 See MULTIHULLS. 4905
0749-4149 See UNIVERSITY STUDIES IN MEDIEVAL AND RENAISSANCE LITERATURE. 3449
0749-4300 See NEIROKHIMIIA. 3839
0749-4319 See COVENANTER WITNESS. 4951
0749-4327 See PROCEEDINGS OF THE ANNUAL MEETING / ARKANSAS STATE HORTICULTURAL SOCIETY. 2429
0749-4351 See JOKESMITH, THE. 1114
0749-436X See BELTWAY NATURALIST, THE. 5462
0749-4394 See COSSA WASHINGTON UPDATE. 5196
0749-4408 See CP3SI NEWS. 4038
0749-4416 See POLITICS & MARKETS. 4490
0749-4459 See OUTWARD BOUND. 4877
0749-4467 See CONTEMPORARY MUSIC REVIEW. 4111
0749-4475 See CITRUS DIGEST. 1601
0749-4505 See FAMILY ASSOCIATION NEWSLETTER, DRODDY, DRODY, DRAWDY & VARIANTS, THE. 2447
0749-4513 See JOURNAL OF PARTNERSHIP TAXATION. 4734
0749-453X See WORK, STUDY, TRAVEL ABROAD. 1791
0749-4548 See TRUCK CAMPER TRADE-IN GUIDE. 5398
0749-4556 See DIRECTOIRE. NEW YORK METROPOLITAN ED., INCLUDING SUBURBAN DESIGNER RESOURCES, LE. 2905
0749-4564 See JAZZ WORLD (NEW YORK, N.Y. 1984). 4125
0749-4637 See MSPB/FLRA CASE DECISIONS. 3152
0749-4653 See BURPEE GARDENS. 2411
0749-4696 See PARTNERSHIPS. 1621
0749-470X See BIBLIOGRAPHIES OF MODERN AUTHORS (SAN BERNARDINO, CALIF.). 3457
0749-4742 See HEALTH FREEDOM NEWS (MONROVIA, CALIF.). 4779
0749-4793 See WORLD FEDERALIST (ARLINGTON, VA.). 4501
0749-4815 See BIRNBAUM'S EUROPE FOR BUSINESS TRAVELERS. 5464
0749-4823 See GENERAL PHYSICS ADVANCE ABSTRACTS. 4403
0749-4874 See ADVANCED TECHNOLOGY IN WASHINGTON STATE. 5081
0749-4882 See HARBUS NEWS, THE. 869
0749-4890 See CARTMEL, CARTMELL, CARTMILL FAMILY QUARTERLY, THE. 2442
0749-4920 See PULSE (YANKEE GROUP). 1239
0749-4971 See ANTIQUE MAPS, SEA CHARTS, CITY VIEWS, CELESTIAL CHARTS & BATTLE PLANS. 2554
0749-5005 See U.S. REGULATORY REPORTER. 5313
0749-503X See YEAST CHICHESTER (WEST SUSSEX). 1048
0749-5056 See WHOLE EARTH REVIEW. 2495
0749-5102 See INDUSTRY WAGE SURVEY. NURSING AND PERSONAL CARE FACILITIES. 1679
0749-5145 See NIGERIAN NEWS, THE. 2500

0749-5153 See STRATEGIC HEALTH CARE MARKETING. 3793
0749-5161 See PEDIATRIC EMERGENCY CARE. 3725
0749-517X See AROUND THE BEND (RICHMOND, TEX.). 2438
0749-5250 See LASER DISC NEWSLETTER, THE. 5317
0749-5277 See APPLE ACCESS. 1264
0749-5285 See HOOP/NBA TODAY. 4899
0749-5315 See INDONESIA REPORTS. 2654
0749-5323 See BOOKS ON TRIAL (NEW YORK, N.Y.). 2943
0749-5331 See BIOCHEMICAL ARCHIVES. 481
0749-5390 See FRESH FRUIT AND VEGETABLE ARRIVAL TOTALS FOR 23 CITIES / UNITED STATES DEPARTMENT OF AGRICULTURE, AGRICULTURAL MARKETING SERVICE, FRUIT AND VEGETABLE DIVISION. 837
0749-5404 See MEDIUM-TERM CORPORATE TOTAL RATE-OF-RETURN INDEXES. 797
0749-5471 See WESTERN STATES JEWISH HISTORY. 2275
0749-5498 See TRAVIS COUNTY BUSINESS GUIDE. 716
0749-551X See GROCERY DISTRIBUTION ANALYSIS AND GUIDE (1983). 2342
0749-5528 See SOUTHERN CALIFORNIA WOMEN'S CAUCUS FOR ART. 365
0749-5536 See TECHNICAL PUBLICATION R8-TP / UNITED STATES DEPARTMENT OF AGRICULTURE, FOREST SERVICE, SOUTHERN REGION. 2396
0749-5579 See CHILTON'S LABOR GUIDE AND PARTS MANUAL (1980). 5411
0749-5595 See POLICE LABOR MONTHLY. 3172
0749-5617 See COGENERATION LETTER, THE. 1935
0749-5633 See DESPENCER, LE. 2445
0749-5684 See CERTIFIED COPY, THE. 2442
0749-5692 See ON & OFF ROAD MAINTENANCE AND FUEL COST INDEX. 5422
0749-5706 See BIBLIOGRAPHY SERIES - UNITED STATES. DEPT. OF JUSTICE. 3079
0749-5714 See BAHAMAS DATELINE. 891
0749-5749 See EC UPDATE. 670
0749-579X See WHARTON INTERNATIONAL AGRICULTURE SERVICE. LONG-TERM FORECAST. 146
0749-5803 See WHARTON INTERNATIONAL AGRICULTURE SERVICE. MEDIUM TERM FORECAST. 146
0749-5811 See WORLD SERVICE DATA BANKS. 1641
0749-582X See WORLD SERVICE DATA BANKS. 1641
0749-5838 See WORLD LONG-TERM ECONOMIC OUTLOOK. 1527
0749-5846 See WORLD MODEL HISTORICAL DATA. 1589
0749-5854 See WHARTON AGRICULTURE SERVICE. 146
0749-5870 See INDUSTRY PLANNING SERVICE. 1567
0749-5897 See TRULY PORTABLE. 1273
0749-5900 See PEACE & DEMOCRACY NEWS. 4531
0749-5927 See ANCESTRY NEWSLETTER. 2437
0749-5935 See WILEY SERIES ON CANCER INVESTIGATION AND MANAGEMENT. 3825
0749-5943 See EAST TROY NEWS, THE. 5767
0749-5951 See IMMIGRANT COMMUNITIES & ETHNIC MINORITIES IN THE UNITED STATES & CANADA. 2263
0749-596X See JOURNAL OF MEMORY AND LANGUAGE. 4598
0749-5978 See ORGANIZATIONAL BEHAVIOR AND HUMAN DECISION PROCESSES. 4606
0749-5994 See TALISMAN (COLUMBUS, OHIO). 3472
0749-6001 See CENSORSHIP NEWS. 1106
0749-601X See NORDIC WEST. 4908
0749-6028 See MONEYWI$E. 799

0749-6036 See SUPERLATTICES AND MICROSTRUCTURES. 5161
0749-6125 See WORLD ECONOMIC OUTLOOK (PHILADELPHIA, PA.). 1527
0749-6133 See BUILDING STONE MAGAZINE. 604
0749-615X See BUCKLEY-LITTLE CATALOGUE OF BOOKS AVAILABLE FROM AUTHORS, THE. 411
0749-6168 See BELL FAMILY NEWSLETTER, THE. 2439
0749-6176 See HOYT'S ISSUE. 2454
0749-6192 See PEDIGREE POINTERS / STEVENS POINT AREA GENEALOGICAL SOCIETY. 2467
0749-6311 See NEW YORK MODEL. 1507
0749-6362 See ENERGY REVIEW (ALBANY, N.Y.). 1942
0749-6400 See NORTH LIGHT. 360
0749-6419 See INTERNATIONAL JOURNAL OF PLASTICITY. 2103
0749-6427 See WICAZO SA REVIEW. 2766
0749-6435 See SALOME (CHICAGO, ILL.). 1314
0749-6478 See TENNIS BUYER'S GUIDE (NORWALK, CONN.). 4925
0749-6494 See WHARTON LONG-TERM FORECAST EXTENSION TO THE YEAR 1526
0749-6508 See CENTRALLY PLANNED ECONOMIES OUTLOOK. 1469
0749-6524 See INFECTIONS IN MEDICINE. 3735
0749-6540 See HASAD AL-SHAHR. 2488
0749-6591 See PERSONAL INJURY VERDICT REVIEWS. 3026
0749-6567 See PERSONAL INJURY VERDICT REVIEWS. MEDIA AND GOVERNMENT. 3026
0749-6583 See PERSONAL INJURY VERDICT REVIEWS. RETAILING, BANKING, AND OTHER SERVICE ESTABLISHMENTS. 3026
0749-6591 See PERSONAL INJURY VERDICT REVIEWS. TRUCKING, RAILROAD & MARINE LINES. 3026
0749-6613 See SECTION OF ADMINISTRATIVE LAW DIRECTORY. 3094
0749-6664 See VEALER, THE. 2360
0749-6672 See HOSPITAL MATERIALS MANAGEMENT NEWS. 3784
0749-6680 See DATA BASE DIRECTORY. 1253
0749-6737 See INSECTA MUNDI. 5609
0749-6753 See INTERNATIONAL JOURNAL OF HEALTH PLANNING & MANAGEMENT, THE. 4785
0749-6818 See WISCONSIN COUNTIES. 4695
0749-6826 See ADVANCES IN APPLIED BUSINESS STRATEGY. 859
0749-6834 See CHAGRIN VALLEY DIRECTORY. 2727
0749-6850 See JOHNSON COUNTY GENEALOGIST, THE. 2455
0749-6877 See PROCEEDINGS - UNIVERSITY/GOVERNMENT/INDUSTRY MICROELECTRONICS SYMPOSIUM. 2077
0749-6885 See ALTERNATIVE LIBRARY LITERATURE. 3189
0749-6931 See FOOTNOTES (WASHINGTON, D.C.). 5245
0749-6982 See NEW HOLSTEIN REPORTER. 5769
0749-6990 See WESTINE REPORT. 5772
0749-7008 See HUDSON STAR-OBSERVER. 5768
0749-7016 See HILLSBORO SENTRY-ENTERPRISE. 5768
0749-7024 See CLINTONVILLE TRIBUNE-GAZETTE. 5766
0749-7040 See TRI-COUNTY NEWS (OSSEO, WIS.), THE. 5771
0749-7059 See LADYSMITH NEWS (LADYSMITH, WIS. : 1927). 5768
0749-7075 See S.A.M. ADVANCED MANAGEMENT JOURNAL (1984). 885
0749-7083 See AUGUSTA AREA TIMES. 5765
0749-7091 See MOUNT HOREB MAIL. 5769
0749-7105 See MAYVILLE NEWS, THE. 5769
0749-7121 See SHEBOYGAN PRESS (SHEBOYGAN, WIS. : 1924). 5770
0749-713X See KENOSHA NEWS. 5768

0749-7148 See SHAWANO EVENING LEADER. 5770
0749-7156 See SHORELINE LEADER, THE. 5770
0749-7164 See OZAUKEE PRESS (PORT WASHINGTON, WIS. : 1969). 5770
0749-7172 See REPORTER (FOND DU LAC, WIS.), THE. 5770
0749-7180 See DOOR COUNTY ADVOCATE. 5767
0749-7199 See OZAUKEE COUNTY NEWS GRAPHIC. 5770
0749-7202 See CAMBRIDGE NEWS (CAMBRIDGE, WIS.). 5766
0749-7210 See BRILLION NEWS, THE. 5765
0749-7237 See COUNTY LEDGER-PRESS, THE. 5766
0749-7253 See NIAGARA JOURNAL, THE. 5769
0749-7261 See BURLINGTON STANDARD-PRESS. 5765
0749-7296 See CA SELECTS: CORROSION-INHIBITING COATINGS. 1000
0749-730X See CA SELECTS: DRILLING MUDS. 1001
0749-7318 See CA SELECTS: NOVEL PESTICIDES & HERBICIDES. 1005
0749-7326 See CA SELECTS: PHOTOSENSITIVE POLYMERS. 1007
0749-7334 See CA SELECTS: PLASMA & REACTIVE ION ETCHING. 1007
0749-7342 See CA SELECTS: RADIATION CURING. 1009
0749-7350 See CA SELECTS: SELENIUM & TELLURIUM CHEMISTRY. 1009
0749-7369 See CA SELECTS: WATER-BASED COATINGS. 1010
0749-7377 See FOSTER BULLETIN ON DEREGULATED GAS. 4256
0749-7415 See AL-NAZEER. 4462
0749-7423 See ADVANCES IN MOTIVATION AND ACHIEVEMENT: A RESEARCH ANNAUL. 1807
0749-7431 See ADVANCES IN ANALYTICAL TOXICOLOGY. 3978
0749-7474 See CPC ANNUAL, THE. 4203
0749-7512 See WYOMING ANNUAL PLANNING REPORT. 1720
0749-758X See COFFEY COUSINS' CLEARINGHOUSE. 2443
0749-7644 See GESTUS. 3391
0749-7652 See CABLE TV LAW REPORTER. 2945
0749-7679 See SHAONIEN ZHONGGUO (SAN FRANCISCO, CALIF.). 5640
0749-7709 See CASE UPDATE. 2949
0749-7741 See PTERIDOLOGIA. 525
0749-7768 See WORD PLAYS. 5372
0749-7857 See ANNUAL PLANNING INFORMATION REPORT. COLORADO. 1647
0749-7911 See BANK NEWS. 775
0749-7946 See IMPACT YEARBOOK. 2367
0749-7962 See NORTHWEST ENVIRONMENTAL JOURNAL, THE. 2179
0749-7970 See KOREAN AND KOREAN-AMERICAN STUDIES BULLETIN. 2657
0749-8004 See JOURNAL OF ENTOMOLOGICAL SCIENCE. 5610
0749-8012 See PROFESSIONAL REAL ESTATE REPORTS. 4843
0749-8047 See CLINICAL JOURNAL OF PAIN, THE. 3565
0749-8055 See CONVULSIVE THERAPY. 3568
0749-8063 See ARTHROSCOPY. 3880
0749-8071 See WEALTH FORMULA, THE. 4758
0749-8217 See LEVERNET. 690
0749-8233 See TERMINATION OF EMPLOYMENT. 3154
0749-8284 See OHIO CPA JOURNAL, THE. 749
0749-8314 See JASPER COUNTY GLEANER, THE. 2455
0749-8365 See CONTACTS INFLUENTIAL. LOS ANGELES COUNTY, LAX. 660
0749-8373 See KANSAS CITY METRO BUSINESS DIRECTORY. 5766
0749-8381 See FORT INDUSTRY REFLECTIONS. 2448

0749-839X See ABMS DIRECTORY OF CERTIFIED PLASTIC SURGEONS. 3957
0749-8470 See INTERNATIONAL JOURNAL OF CLINICAL NEUROPSYCHOLOGY, THE. 4591
0749-8519 See MID-COUNTY TIMES, THE. 5769
0749-8527 See STATE ACTION REPORTER, NATURAL GAS AND ELECTRIC POWER. ABSTRACTS/INDEX. 4279
0749-8543 See INCOME PER SHARE BEFORE SECURITIES GAINS OR LOSSES. 790
0749-856X See VITAL SIGNS (STORRS, CONN.). 4621
0749-8586 See DISABILITY RAG, THE. 4387
0749-8608 See NEWSLETTER - AUTOMATED OFFICE CO. 4212
0749-8616 See HERALD OF REPRESSION IN UKRAINE. 4508
0749-8624 See VISNYK REPRESIJ V UKRAINI. 4499
0749-8632 See CHILD'S PLAY (CHICAGO, ILL.). 1803
0749-8640 See REAL ESTATE NEWSLINE. 4844
0749-8659 See CHILDREN'S ALBUM, THE. 1061
0749-8683 See MINK. 1618
0749-890X See INDUSTRIAL FIRE WORLD. 2291
0749-9043 See KING'S INTERNATIONAL COAL TRADE & WORLD COAL STATISTICS. 2142
0749-906X See CHE VUOI?. 3563
0749-9078 See LEX COLLEGII. 1834
0749-9108 See BETHEL COURIER (BETHEL, ME 1976), THE. 2723
0749-9116 See ARCHEOLOGICAL AND HISTORICAL DATA RECOVERY PROGRAM. 258
0749-9132 See FOREIGN INTELLIGENCE LITERARY SCENE. 4522
0749-9175 See PROGRESS IN PROBABILITY. 3542
0749-9183 See QUARTERLY STATISTICAL REPORT - EDISON ELECTRIC INSTITUTE. STATISTICAL DEPT. 4699
0749-9191 See CONCRETE ... SOURCEBOOK. 1969
0749-9213 See CARPATHO-RUSYN AMERICAN. 2258
0749-923X See LONG-TERM SERVICE DATA BANKS. 1573
0749-9248 See COMPLETE HANDBOOK OF THE OLYMPIC GAMES, THE. 4891
0749-9272 See WINES & VINES. BUYER'S GUIDE ISSUE. 2373
0749-9280 See BIBLICAL BULLETIN. 5015
0749-9302 See DIGEST OF SOFTWARE REVIEWS : EDUCATION, THE. 1285
0749-9310 See TEXAS LONE STAR. 1873
0749-9337 See ANNUAL REPORT ON THE STATUS OF POVERTY IN CALIFORNIA, AN. 5273
0749-9345 See NOA NEWSLETTER. 4141
0749-940X See DUST (BIG COVE TANNERY, PA.). 432
0749-9418 See BUSINESS FIRST (BUFFALO, N.Y.). 648
0749-9442 See SPECIAL PUBLICATION - UNIVERSITY OF COLORADO, BOULDER. NATURAL HAZARDS RESEARCH AND APPLICATIONS INFORMATION CENTER. 5310
0749-9477 See TECHNICAL REPORT CERC. 1998
0749-9485 See CPA EXAMINATION REVIEW. AUDITING. 742
0749-9531 See URISA NEWS (1982). 3255
0749-954X See CALLIGRAPH. 377
0749-9574 See EPISCOPAL WOMEN'S HISTORY PROJECT, THE. 5059
0749-9671 See PUBLICATION / ALASKA GEOLOGICAL SOCIETY. 1392
0749-9701 See REPORT ON ACTIVITIES / JOHN D. AND CATHERINE T. MACARTHUR FOUNDATION. 4339
0749-971X See BABY TALK (1977). 3900
0749-9728 See RMCLAS REVIEW. 2552
0749-9736 See NATIONAL DIRECTORY OF CORPORATE PUBLIC AFFAIRS. 762

0749-985X ISSN Index

0749-985X *See* NEWSLINE - TRAVEL INDUSTRY ASSOCIATION OF AMERICA. **5486**

0749-9868 *See* MEDIA AUDIT. CORPUS CHRISTI, TEXAS. QUARTERLY REPORT, THE. **4554**

0749-9876 *See* MINERAL INFORMATION SOURCES. **1358**

0749-9884 *See* NATIONAL REPORT FOR TRAINING AND DEVELOPMENT. **880**

0749-9930 *See* TENNESSEE LABOR MARKET INFORMATION DIRECTORY. **1714**

0749-9949 *See* TEXAS MEDIA GUIDE, THE. **1123**

0749-9973 *See* MEDICAL AND HEALTH INFORMATION DIRECTORY. **3608**

0749-999X *See* TECHNOLOGY STOCK MONITOR. **917**

0750-0181 *See* I.N. REVUE DES TECHNIQUES NOUVELLES EN SERRURERIE MENUISERIE MIROITERIE. **634**

0750-0416 *See* BULLETIN OFFICIEL DU MINISTERE DE LA JUSTICE (FRANCE). **2945**

0750-0424 *See* COTE DESFOSSES. **5800**

0750-1080 *See* INFORMATIQUE PROFESSIONNELLE, L'. **1260**

0750-1269 *See* ASSEMBLAGES 1981. **1021**

0750-1331 *See* BULLETIN DE LA COMMISSION DEPARTEMENTALE D'HISTOIRE ET D'ARCHEOLOGIE DU PAS-DE-CALAIS. **263**

0750-1412 *See* BULLETIN ET MEMOIRES DE LA SOCIETE ARCHEOLOGIQUE DU DEPARTEMENT D'ILLE-ET-VILAINE. **263**

0750-1420 *See* MEMOIRES DE LA SOCIETE D'HISTOIRE ET D'ARCHEOLOGIE DE BRETAGNE. **274**

0750-1455 *See* SUPPLEMENT, LE. **2253**

0750-1552 *See* C.F.P. CHAUD FROID PLOMBERIE. **2604**

0750-1978 *See* SOURCES CHRETIENNES. **5040**

0750-2079 *See* MUSIQUE ET CULTURE STRASBOURG. **4138**

0750-2087 *See* CHRIST SEUL. **4943**

0750-2524 *See* QUESTIONS D'ODONTO-STOMATOLOGIE, LES. **1334**

0750-3253 *See* PRESENT PARIS. **2521**

0750-3288 *See* JOURNAL DE LA MAISON, LE. **2906**

0750-3520 *See* LUI PARIS. **3995**

0750-3547 *See* ETUDES INDO-EUROPEENNES. **2515**

0750-3555 *See* UNION PARIS. 1972. **717**

0750-3563 *See* COIFFURE ET STYLES PARIS. **403**

0750-3628 *See* VOGUE HOMMES. **1088**

0750-6112 *See* TRAVAUX DE L'INSTITUT DE PHONETIQUE D'AIX. **3329**

0750-6155 *See* PRATIQUE MEDICALE, LA. **3629**

0750-6570 *See* BULLETIN DE LA SOCIETE MERIDIONALE DE SPELEOLOGIE ET DE PREHISTOIRE 1976. **263**

0750-6635 *See* DOCUMENTS DES LABORATOIRES DE GEOLOGIE, LYON. **1374**

0750-7046 *See* CATALOGUE AFNOR. **4030**

0750-7313 *See* RAPPORT D'ACTIVITE / BUREAU NATIONAL DE METROLOGIE (FRANCE). **4032**

0750-7321 *See* BIOLOGIA GALLO-HELLENICA. **444**

0750-7364 *See* STATISTIQUE ET ANALYSE DES DONNEES. **5343**

0750-7658 *See* ANNALES FRANCAISES D'ANESTHESIE ET DE REANIMATION. **3682**

0750-7674 *See* BULLETIN OFFICIEL DE LA PROPRIETE INDUSTRIELLE BREVETS D'INVENTION ABREGES ET LISTES. **1310**

0750-7682 *See* SCIENCES VETERINAIRES, MEDECINE COMPAREE. **5521**

0750-8131 *See* CARROSSERIE. **5379**

0750-8239 *See* JURIS-CLASSEUR DE DROIT INTERNATIONAL. **3131**

0750-8387 *See* JURIS-CLASSEUR DE LA SECURITE SOCIALE. **2990**

0750-8662 *See* FISCALITE IMMOBILIERE. **4727**

0750-8964 *See* TRAVAIL ET MAITRISE. **948**

0750-9278 *See* REVUE DES DEUX MONDES (1982). **3430**

0751-0772 *See* BULLETIN OFFICIEL (FRANCE. MINISTERE DES RELATIONS EXTERIEURES). **4517**

0751-2163 *See* ITALIQUES / UNIVERSITE DE LA SORBONNE NOUVELLE (PARIS III), U.E.R. D'ITALIEN ET ROUMAIN, CENTRE DE RECHERCHES SUR L'ITALIE MODERNE ET CONTEMPORAINE. **3397**

0751-2325 *See* RHODANIE. **2628**

0751-2708 *See* MEDIEVALES. **2623**

0751-3496 *See* COMMUNISME (PARIS, FRANCE : 1982). **4540**

0751-4239 *See* CAHIERS D'ETUDES GERMANIQUES. **3371**

0751-5294 *See* BULLETIN DE LA SOCIETE HISTORIQUE ET SCIENTIFIQUE DES DEUX-SEVRES. **2681**

0751-5405 *See* VOILES ET VOILIERS PARIS. **596**

0751-5464 *See* PUBLI 10. **764**

0751-5774 *See* SUFFRAGES. **405**

0751-5804 *See* REVUE DES SCIENCES MORALES & POLITIQUES. **4494**

0751-6002 *See* OKAPI. **5593**

0751-6037 *See* CIRCUITS CULTURE PARIS. **167**

0751-6320 *See* COURRIER DU MEUBLE PARIS, LE. **2904**

0751-6614 *See* OBSERVATIONS ET DIAGNOSTICS ECONOMIQUES. **1509**

0751-6681 *See* SEDES SAPIENTIAE. **5036**

0751-7033 *See* IRIS. **4073**

0751-7149 *See* HYGIE. **4783**

0751-7149 *See* PROMOTION AND EDUCATION. **4797**

0751-7378 *See* AGRISCOPE : REGARDS SUR L'AGRICULTURE. **54**

0751-7580 *See* ANTARES LA VALETTE. **3362**

0751-7696 *See* ADOLESCENCE (PARIS, FRANCE). **4571**

0751-9478 *See* LEGIPRESSE. **3001**

0751-9532 *See* EQUIVALENCES. **3279**

0751-994X *See* OFFICIEL DU CYCLE ET DU MOTOCYCLE, L'. **4082**

0752-1693 *See* GEOPOLITIQUE. **4522**

0752-2452 *See* ARIES / ASSOCIATION POUR LA RECHERCHE ET L'INFORMATION SUR L'ESOTERISME. **4240**

0752-272X *See* POESIE (PARIS, FRANCE : 1984). **3468**

0752-3408 *See* HISTORAMA (PARIS, FRANCE : 1984). **2690**

0752-4072 *See* TECHNIQUE ET SCIENCE INFORMATIQUES : TSI. **1262**

0752-4080 *See* BIBLIOGRAPHIE LATINOAMERICAINE D'ARTICLES / INSTITUT DES HAUTES ETUDES DE L'AMERIQUE LATINE, CENTRE DE DOCUMENTATION. **410**

0752-4412 *See* EGYPTE/MONDE ARABE. **4472**

0752-4757 *See* T.V. VIDEO JAQUETTES. **1122**

0752-4978 *See* ROBOTS CERGY. **1217**

0752-501X *See* JOURNAL DES PSYCHOLOGUES, LE. **4592**

0752-5168 *See* LETTRE DE LA CONCURRENCE, LA. **690**

0752-5370 *See* NOUVELLES DERMATOLOGIQUES, LES. **3722**

0752-5656 *See* REVUE ARCHEOLOGIQUE DE PICARDIE. **281**

0752-5729 *See* RECHERCHE EN DANSE, LA. **1314**

0752-6180 *See* FINANCE (PARIS). **4725**

0753-0759 *See* RECUEIL DES ACTES ADMINISTRATIFS DE LA PREFECTURE DE LA REUNION. **3093**

0753-2601 *See* BULLETIN DE DROIT COMPARE DU TRAVAIL ET DE LA SECURITE SOCIALE. **3144**

0753-2830 *See* JOURNAL DE TOXICOLOGIE CLINIQUE ET EXPERIMENTALE. **3981**

0753-311X *See* ECONOMIE DU TOURISME, L'. **5469**

0753-3322 *See* BIOMEDICINE & PHARMACOTHERAPY. **3557**

0753-3918 *See* ACTUALITES BIOLOGIQUES. **440**

0753-3969 *See* ANNALES DE PALEONTOLOGIE (1982). **4226**

0753-4000 *See* NOUVEAU DETECTIVE, LE. **3171**

0753-4418 *See* CAHIERS DE LA FONCTION PUBLIQUE ET DE L'ADMINISTRATION. **4635**

0753-4973 *See* ALYTES. **5574**

0753-5015 *See* GAZETTE DU LIVRE MEDIEVAL. **4828**

0753-5058 *See* ANIMATEUR D'ENTRAINEMENT PHYSIQUE DANS LE MONDE MODERNE, L'. **2596**

0753-6019 *See* OSTEOPATHIE : THERAPIES MANUELLES. **4795**

0753-7417 *See* BULLETIN DE LA SOCIETE FRANCAISE DE CANCEROLOGIE PRIVEE. **3810**

0753-8413 *See* BULLETIN - SOCIETE D'HISTOIRE DU CANTON DE LAPOUTROIE VAL D'ORBEY. **2681**

0753-874X *See* ACTUALITE LEGISLATIVE DALLOZ. **2927**

0753-9711 *See* TRAVAIL SOCIAL ACTUALITES PARIS. **5313**

0754-023X *See* INFINI, L'. **2517**

0754-0590 *See* EMBALLAGES MAGAZINE. **4233**

0754-068X *See* JEUX & JOUETS MAGAZINE. **2584**

0754-0698 *See* FRUITS & LEGUMES. **2342**

0754-0876 *See* COMPOSITES PARIS. **4454**

0754-121X *See* TRACTEURS & MACHINES AGRICOLES PARIS. **161**

0754-1619 *See* TENDANCES DE LA CONJONCTURE. CAHIER 2, GRAPHIQUES SUR 20 ANS. **5345**

0754-1627 *See* TENDANCES DE LA CONJONCTURE. CAHIER 1, GRAPHIQUES SUR 10 ANS. **5344**

0754-1996 *See* INDUSTRIE DE L'INFORMATION. **3215**

0754-4618 *See* J.T.R. INFORMATIONS. **5385**

0754-5215 *See* L.A.E. LA LETTRE AFRIQUE ENERGIES. **1949**

0754-9245 *See* RESPIRER. **3951**

0755-0863 *See* HORS CADRE. **4072**

0755-0871 *See* IMMUNOLOGIE MEDICALE. **3671**

0755-0960 *See* FABULA (LILLE, FRANCE). **3387**

0755-1460 *See* OFFICIEL DES CONGRES ET DU TOURISME D'AFFAIRES, L'. **700**

0755-1908 *See* GRAPH AGRI REGIONS. **90**

0755-1916 *See* SOINS. CARDIOLOGIE. **3710**

0755-1940 *See* AGENCE ECONOMIQUE ET FINANCIERE. **768**

0755-1959 *See* CLASSIQUES FRANCAIS DU MOYEN-AGE. **1076**

0755-2076 *See* POSITIONS DES THESES. **1841**

0755-2181 *See* INFORMATIONS TECHNIQUES - CEMAGREF. **96**

0755-219X *See* MESURES (PARIS, FRANCE : 1983). **1987**

0755-2238 *See* BILANS POLITIQUES ECONOMIQUES ET SOCIAUX HEBDOMADAIRES. **643**

0755-2386 *See* SECURITE ET MEDECINE DU TRAVAIL. **2870**

0755-2483 *See* BULLETIN DE LA SOCIETE DES ETUDES LITTERAIRES, SCIENTIFIQUES ET ARTISTIQUES DU LOT. **2843**

0755-2793 *See* BULLETIN - FRANCE. PARLEMENT (1946-). ASSEMBLEE NATIONALE. **4634**

0755-3412 *See* OCEANOGRAPHIE. NOTES ET DOCUMENTS. **1454**

0755-3579 *See* SOFT & MICRO. **1272**

0755-3617 *See* MEMOIRES DE L'ACADEMIE DES SCIENCES, ARTS ET BELLES LETTRES DE DIJON. **178**

0755-365X *See* MARINE MARCHANDE EN ..., LA. **5452**

0755-4796 *See* LIVRET DE LA RECHERCHE / INSTITUT NATIONAL DES LANGUES ET CIVILISATIONS ORIENTALES. **2658**

0755-4982 *See* PRESSE MEDICALE (1983), LA. **3629**

0755-5016 *See* EAU, L'INDUSTRIE, LES NUISANCES, L'. **2227**

0755-6225 *See* OPTION QUALITE. **1620**

0755-6365 See RESEAUX ET CHALEUR (ORLEANS). **1955**

0755-7000 *See* SOMMAIRES DE SECURITE SOCIALE. **5310**

0755-7256 *See* DIALOGUES D'HISTOIRE ANCIENNE. **2614**

0755-7272 *See* BULLETIN - HOT CLUB DE FRANCE. **4106**

0755-7272 *See* BULLETIN DU HOT-CLUB DE FRANCE. **4106**

0755-7337 *See* BASKET-BALL. **4886**

0755-7639 *See* DANSER. **1313**

0755-7752 *See* NOUVELLE REVUE D'ONOMASTIQUE. **421**

0755-7809 *See* ESPACE POPULATIONS SOCIETES. **4552**

0755-7876 *See* LETTRE DE LA F.I.D.H. / FEDERATION INTERNATIONALE DES DROITS DE L'HOMME, LA. **4510**

0755-7981 *See* PETROLE ET ENTERPRISE. **4271**

0755-8074 *See* HOMMES ET FONCTIONS. **4476**

0755-883X *See* AR FALZ. **3363**

0755-8848 *See* SKOL VREIZH. **1784**

0755-8902 *See* REVUE DE L'ECONOMIE SOCIALE, LA. **1518**

0755-9208 *See* CAHIERS D'ECONOMIE ET SOCIOLOGIE RURALES. **5194**

0755-9593 *See* SCIENCES DE L'EDUCATION POUR L'ERE NOUVELLE, LES. **1783**

0756-368X *See* HYPER G.A.P. **680**

0756-4643 See TRANSPORT MAGAZINE PARIS. **5395**

0756-564X *See* JE BOUQUINE. **1065**

0756-7138 *See* LEXIQUE (LILLE). **3297**

0756-9750 *See* CAHIERS SAVOYARDS DE GENEALOGIE. **2441**

0757-0112 *See* TELE K7. **1140**

0757-0171 *See* JEUN. LIB. **1065**

0757-1631 *See* AXES SCHILTIGHEIM. **2111**

0757-1984 *See* NINETEEN. **1067**

0757-2271 *See* BEAUX ARTS MAGAZINE. **343**

0757-2859 *See* BULLETIN DE L'ACHETEUR, LE. **294**

0757-3065 *See* TRAVAIL (PARIS, FRANCE). **1715**

0757-3529 *See* ACTUALITE RELIGIEUSE DANS LE MONDE (1983). **4932**

0757-4223 *See* EXPO NEWS. **834**

0757-648X *See* ARAB NEWS & REPORTS. **2501**

0757-8768 *See* COURRIER DE LA MONETIQUE ET DE LA CARTE A MEMOIRE, LE. **830**

0757-9314 *See* CHANTIERS AMERINDIA. **3273**

0758-1475 *See* ACTES DE LECTURE, LES. **1722**

0758-170X *See* NOUVEAUX CAHIERS D'ALLEMAND. **3418**

0758-1726 *See* POLITIQUES ET MANAGEMENT PUBLIC. **4491**

0758-1858 *See* BREF BULLETIN DE RECHERCHES SUR L'EMPLOI ET LA FORMATION. **1656**

0758-1882 *See* PRATIQUE MEDICALE & CHIRURGICALE DE L'ANIMAL DE COMPAGNIE. **5518**

0758-2714 *See* CAHIERS D'ANTHROPOLOGIE ET BIOMETRIE HUMAINE. **233**

0758-3168 See ACTION AUTOMOBILE ET TOURISTIQUE, L'. **5403**

0758-3826 *See* J3E L JOURNAL DE L EQUIPMENT ELECTRIQUE ET ELECTRONIQUE. **2067**

0758-4083 *See* TERRE INFORMATION. **2577**

0758-4180 *See* MIKADO. **1764**

0758-489X *See* EPURE. **2053**

0758-4938 *See* LOU PROUVENCAU A L'ESCOLO. **3300**

0758-5373 *See* INFOS PARIS. **96**

0758-5683 *See* ANTHROPOLOGIE MARITIME. **229**

0758-590X *See* EPI / REVUE TRIMESTRIELLE DE L'ASSOCIATION ENSEIGNMENT PUBLIC ET INFORMATIQUE. **1744**

0758-6531 *See* DONNEES SOCIALES. **5244**

0758-671X *See* JURIS-CLASSEUR COLLECTIVITES LOCALES. **2990**

0758-6760 *See* CAHIERS LORRAINS, LES. **2682**

0758-6868 *See* POPULATION ET SANTE TROPICALES. **3986**

0758-7708 *See* ARCHEOLOGIE DU MIDI MEDIEVAL. **259**

0758-802X *See* P.J.R. PRAXIS JURIDIQUE ET RELIGION. **4984**

0758-816X *See* REPERTOIRE DES BANQUES DE DONNEES EN CONVERSATIONNEL. **3245**

0758-833X *See* ORSTOM ACTUALITES. **5136**

0758-8623 *See* POSIDONIA NEWSLETTER. **1455**

0758-8703 See S.T.P. PHARMA PRATIQUES : TECHNIQUES REGLEMENTATIONS. **4329**

0758-881X *See* REVUE DE LA SOCIETE DES AMIS DU MUSEE DE L'ARMEE. **4056**

0758-9670 *See* AQUITANIA. **2675**

0759-0385 *See* FILM FRANCAIS 1983, LE. **4070**

0759-0644 *See* MICROBIOLOGIE, ALIMENTS, NUTRITION. **108**

0759-1063 *See* BMS. BULLETIN DE METHODOLOGIE SOCIOLOGIQUE. **5240**

0759-125X *See* CAHIERS / COMEDIE-FRANCAISE, LES. **5362**

0759-1586 *See* CAHIERS DU CENTRE INTERDISCIPLINAIRE DES SCIENCES DU LANGAGE. **3271**

0759-1594 *See* LETTRE DU GYNECOLOGUE, LA. **3764**

0759-2167 *See* ALPIRANDO. **4882**

0759-2280 *See* MEDECINE ET CHIRURGIE DU PIED. **3918**

0759-2310 *See* CAHIERS - ASSOCIATION INTERNATIONALE DES ENTRETIENS ECOLOGIQUES. **2212**

0759-2345 *See* AUTRE EUROPE, L'. **2677**

0759-2736 *See* CABINETS MINISTERIELS. **4466**

0759-2744 *See* PRESIDENCE DE LA REPUBLIQUE. **4674**

0759-6065 *See* AUTOMOBILES CLASSIQUES. **5406**

0759-6677 *See* LETTRE DE BOURBON, LA. **2641**

0759-6898 *See* BREF (PARIS). **384**

0759-7673 *See* INVESTIR (PARIS). **792**

0759-9048 *See* DOSSIERS ET DOCUMENTS - INSTITUT FRANCAIS D'ARCHITECTURE. **298**

0760-1751 *See* PANGEA : BULLETIN D'INFORMATION SUR LA COOPERATION GEOLOGIQUE INTERNATIONALE / CENTRE INTERNATIONAL POUR LA FORMATION ET LES ECHANGES GEOLOGIQUES. **1390**

0760-1999 *See* BOISSONS DE FRANCE, JEAN PRIMUS. **2365**

0760-2626 *See* MISSION (DEPARTEMENT EVANGELIQUE FRANCAIS D'ACTION APOSTOLIQUE). **5064**

0760-4211 *See* LETTRE DU GROUPEMENT NATIONAL DE LA COOPERATION, LA. **1638**

0760-5099 *See* FEU ET LUMIERE SAINT-BROLADRE. **5029**

0760-548X *See* REVUE DE L ASSOCIATION FRANCAISE DES AMIS DES CHEMINS DE FER. **5436**

0760-5641 *See* LEZ VALENCIENNES / UNIVERSITE DE VALENCIENNES. **3405**

0760-5668 *See* TERRAIN (PARIS, 1983). **246**

0760-579X *See* CAHIERS DE LA RECHERCHE DEVELOPPEMENT, LES. **71**

0760-6443 *See* FAIM DEVELOPPEMENT MAGAZINE PARIS. **4958**

0760-6516 *See* SCIENCE & VIE. MICRO. **5151**

0760-7237 *See* FRUITS. **3389**

0760-7245 *See* FORUM DES AUDIOPHILES PARIS. **4118**

0760-758X *See* GAZETTE MEDICALE. **3578**

0760-9736 *See* ADULIS. **2636**

0760-9868 *See* REVUE DES OENOLOGUES ET DES TECHNIQUES VITIVINICOLES ET OENOLOGIQUES. **185**

0761-1285 *See* INFORMATION AND LIAISON BULLETIN / INSTITUT KURDE DE PARIS. **2768**

0761-1749 *See* PASCAL FOLIO. F16, CHIMIE ANALYTIQUE, MINERALE ET ORGANIQUE. **1018**

0761-182X *See* PASCAL FOLIO. F41, GISEMENTS METALLIQUES ET NON METALLIQUES, ECONOMIE MINIERE. **2147**

0761-1897 *See* PASCAL FOLIO. F52, BIOCHIMIE, BIOPHYSIQUE MOLECULAIRE, BIOLOGIE MOLECULAIRE ET CELLULAIRE. **468**

0761-1900 *See* PASCAL FOLIO. F53, ANATOMIE ET PHYSIOLOGIE DES VERTEBRES. **3679**

0761-1927 *See* PASCAL FOLIO. F55, BIOLOGIE VEGETALE. **468**

0761-1943 *See* PASCAL FOLIO. F70, PHARMACOLOGIE, TRAITEMENTS MEDICAMENTEUX. **4319**

0761-2192 *See* PASCAL EXPLORE. E72, OTORHINOLARYNGOLOGIE, STOMATOLOGIE, PATHOLOGIE CERVICOFACIALE. **3890**

0761-2214 *See* PASCAL EXPLORE. E74, PNEUMOLOGIE. **3950**

0761-2265 *See* PASCAL EXPLORE. E79, PATHOLOGIE ET PHYSIOLOGIE OSTEOARTICULAIRES. **3884**

0761-229X *See* PASCAL EXPLORE. E82, GYNECOLOGIE, OBSTETRIQUE, ANDROLOGIE. **3766**

0761-2303 *See* PASCAL EXPLORE. E83, ANESTHESIE ET REANIMATION. **3683**

0761-2311 *See* PASCAL EXPLORE. E84, GENIE BIOMEDICALE, INFORMATIQUE BIOMEDICALE. **3695**

0761-2494 *See* ADVANCES IN MODELLING & SIMULATION. **2109**

0761-2516 *See* MODELLING, SIMULATION & CONTROL. B. **2122**

0761-2591 *See* TROPISMES / CENTRE DE RECHERCHES ANGLO-AMERICAINES. **3448**

0761-2818 See ECHOS DE L'EXPORTATION PARIS, LES. **832**

0761-3032 *See* ANTHROPOZOOLOGICA PARIS. **5576**

0761-3423 *See* REPERES ET REFERENCES STATISTIQUES SUR LES ENSEIGNEMENTS ET LA FORMATION. **1796**

0761-3857 *See* SITUATIONS. **1710**

0761-3962 *See* ACTES DE COLLOQUES (BREST). **1445**

0761-3970 *See* RAPPORTS SCIENTIFIQUE ET TECHNIQUES DE L'IFREMER. **1455**

0761-3989 *See* CAMPAGNES OCEANOGRAPHIQUES FRANCAISES. **1447**

0761-5035 *See* LETTRE DU CARDIOLOGUE, LA. **3708**

0761-5779 *See* CONFORT MENAGER. **758**

0761-7232 *See* CAHIERS DE L'ECOLE SAINT-JEAN. **2612**

0761-7267 *See* DOSSIERS DE LA BIBLE, LES. **4954**

0761-7305 *See* ARCHITECTURE VERNACULAIRE, L'. **290**

0761-7909 *See* ARCHITECTURE MEDITERRANEENNE. **290**

0761-8239 *See* T.E.M. TEXTE EN MAIN. **3444**

0761-8328 *See* BULLETIN DE LA SOCIETE FRANCAISE DE PARASITOLOGIE. **449**

0761-8417 *See* REVUE DE PNEUMOLOGIE CLINIQUE : LE POUMON ET LE COEUR. **3951**

0761-8425 *See* REVUE DES MALADIES RESPIRATOIRES. **3951**

0761-8654 *See* ANNUAIRE DE LA SOCIETE D'HISTOIRE DES QUATRE CANTONS. **2674**

0761-9243 *See* GIBIER, FAUNE SAUVAGE. **2216**

0761-9529 *See* MARIONNETTES PARIS. **4852**

0761-9553 *See* CLARINETTE MAGAZINE. **4110**

0761-9863 *See* JOURNAL DE LA FORMATION CONTINUE & DE L'E.A.O, LE. **1832**

0761-9871 *See* CAHIERS DE SOCIOLOGIE ECONOMIQUE ET CULTURELLE, ETHNOPSYCHOLOGIE. **5241**

0762-0195 See GUIDE DES RATIOS DES REGIONS / MINISTERE DE L'INTERIEUR, LE SECRETAIRE D'ETAT AUPRES DU MINISTRE DE L'INTERIEUR CHARGE DES COLLECTIVITES TERRITORIALES, DIRECTION GENERALE DES COLLECTIVITES LOCALES, MISSION D'ETUDES ET DE STATISTIQUES. 5328

0762-0616 See S.I.T.R.A.M., TRAFIC INTERNATIONAL / MINISTERE DE L'EQUIPEMENT, DU LOGEMENT, DE L'AMENAGEMENT DU TERRITOIRE ET DES TRANSPORTS, DEPARTEMENT DES SYNTHESES STATISTIQUES ET ECONOMIQUES. 5392

0762-0969 See COMPTES RENDUS DE L'ACADEMIE DES SCIENCES. 5096

0762-2929 See CARNETS STATISTIQUES - CAISSE NATIONALE DE L'ASSURANCE MALADIE DES TRAVAILLEURS SALARIES. 5325

0762-3267 See RENCONTRES PEDAGOGIQUES PARIS. 1777

0762-3291 See 303. 335

0762-3690 See LETTRE INTERNATIONALE. 3405

0762-4476 See PROCOF MEDICAL. 3630

0762-5642 See MEDIASPOUVOIRS. 1117

0762-5731 See ARCHITECTES, ARCHITECTURE. 288

0762-6193 See CAHIERS DU CRIC. 3371

0762-6819 See NOUVELLE REVUE D'ETHNOPSYCHIATRIE. 242

0762-7475 See SYNAPSE. 3846

0762-8129 See BULLETIN DE LA SOCIETE DES FOUILLES ARCHEOLOGIQUES ET DES MONUMENTS HISTORIQUES DE L'YONNE. 263

0762-915X See JOURNAL DE TRAUMATOLOGIE DU SPORT. 3954

0763-0018 See COMPOSITES ET NOUVEAUX MATERIAUX. 4454

0763-0387 See INFORMATIONS HOSPITALIERES. 3786

0763-1219 See REVUE FRANCAISE DE DROIT ADMINISTRATIF. 3094

0763-1901 See ARACHNOLOGIA : BULLETIN D'INFORMATION ET DE LIAISON DU CENTRE INTERNATIONAL DE DOCUMENTATION ARACHNOLOGIQUE. 5576

0763-6776 See AFRICAN SMALL MAMMAL NEWSLETTER. 5574

0763-7063 See BEAUX LIVRES. 4824

0763-7446 See ABSTRACT CARDIO PARIS. 3697

0763-7454 See ABSTRACT DERMATO PARIS. 3717

0763-8515 See LETTRE DU MANAGER. 875

0763-8922 See MAGASIN AGRICOLE (PARIS). 106

0763-9686 See VOCABLE (ENGLISH ED.). 2856

0764-0021 See FEMME ACTUELLE. 5556

0764-3470 See MAPPEMONDE. 2582

0764-3578 See BANCS D'ESSAI DU TOURISME, LES. 5462

0764-4442 See COMPTES RENDUS DE L'ACADEMIE DES SCIENCES. SERIE I, MATHEMATIQUE. 3501

0764-4450 See COMPTES RENDUS DE L'ACADEMIE DES SCIENCES. SERIE II, MECANIQUE, PHYSIQUE, CHIMIE, SCIENCES DE L'UNIVERS, SCIENCES DE LA TERRE. 5096

0764-4469 See COMPTES RENDUS DE L'ACADEMIE DES SCIENCES. SERIE III, SCIENCES DE LA VIE. 5096

0764-4523 See FEMME PARIS, 1984. 5556

0764-4663 See PELERIN MAGAZINE. 4986

0764-5104 See QUOTIDIEN DU PHARMACIEN, LE. 4327

0764-5562 See MOYEN ORIENT & OCEAN INDIEN, XVIE-XIXE. 2642

0764-583X See RAIRO. MATHEMATICAL MODELLING AND NUMERICAL ANALYSIS. 3530

0764-6232 See REVUE D'ETUDES. 1780

0764-7565 See NOUVELLE ALTERNATIVE, LA. 4511

0764-7573 See AWAL. 2256

0764-7611 See CRISOL NANTERRE. 663

0764-809X See TRANSPAC ACTUALITES. 5395

0764-8103 See BULLETIN D'AUDIOPHONOLOGIE, ANNALES SCIENTIFIQUES DE L'UNIVERSITE DE FRANCHE-COMTE. MEDECINE & PHARMACIE. 3559

0764-8111 See ARGUS DU LIVRE DE COLLECTION. REPERTOIRE BIBLIOGRAPHIQUE, L'. 408

0764-8499 See CAHIERS DE LA CINEMATHEQUE, LES. 4064

0764-8650 See ACTUALITES SCIENTIFIQUES ET TECHNIQUES DANS LES INDUSTRIES AGRO-ALIMENTAIRES. 44

0764-8928 See GRADHIVA. 237

0764-9673 See ART ET ARCHEOLOGIE EN RHONE ALPES. 338

0764-9878 See CEMOTI. CAHIERS D'ETUDES SUR LA MEDITERRANEE ORIENTALE ET LE MONDE TURCO-IRANIEN. 2648

0765-0019 See TRAITEMENT DU SIGNAL. 2159

0765-006X See ENTRAINEMENTS & SYSTEMES. 2113

0765-0094 See LETTRE EUROPEENNE DU PROGRES TECHNIQUE, LA. 5126

0765-0124 See SOURCES (PARIS). 2630

0765-0418 See SFT. SMARTER FINANCIAL TECHNOLOGIES ENGLISH ED. 811

0765-0574 See EUROPEAN SPACE DIRECTORY. 18

0765-0752 See REVUE EUROPEENNE DES MIGRATIONS INTERNATIONALES. 1921

0765-0779 See RECHERCHE TECHNOLOGIE 1985. 1623

0765-0787 See BULLETIN AGRONOMIQUE PETIT-BOURG. 68

0765-104X See CAHIERS DE LA DAFI. 265

0765-1074 See DIRASAT KURDIYAH. 2768

0765-1155 See RECHERCHES SUR L'IMAGINAIRE. 3428

0765-121X See NOISE (PARIS, FRANCE). 360

0765-1252 See ANNUAIRE - 4 SOCIETES D'HISTOIRE DE LA VALLEE DE LA WEISS. 2674

0765-1325 See BASES PARIS. 1274

0765-1333 See PROBLEMES D'AMERIQUE LATINE. 2512

0765-1465 See FRANCIS BULLETIN SIGNALETIQUE. 521, SOCIOLOGIE. 5245

0765-1473 See FRANCIS BULLETIN SIGNALETIQUE. 529, ETHNOLOGIE. 236

0765-1597 See SCIENCE & SPORTS. 3956

0765-1635 See TRAVAUX DE DIDACTIQUE DU FRANCAIS LANGUE ETRANGERE. 3329

0765-1937 See BULLETIN BIBLIOGRAPHIQUE - CENTRE DE RECHERCHE ET D'ETUDE POUR LA DIFFUSION DU FRANCAIS. 411

0765-2046 See EUROPEAN BIOTECHNOLOGY NEWSLETTER (PARIS). 3692

0765-3069 See TECHNOLOGIES BANCAIRES. 813

0765-3530 See SON, VIDEO MAGAZINE. 5319

0765-3697 See SOCIETIES (PARIS, FRANCE). 5259

0765-412X See EVENEMENT DU JEUDI, L'. 2733

0765-5290 See REANIMATION, SOINS INTENSIFS, MEDECINE D'URGENCE. 3632

0765-5320 See EQUINOXE (NANTES). 455

0765-5428 See CONSERVATION RESTAURATION. 348

0765-5762 See ENTREPRISES FORMATION. 4204

0765-5983 See DIAPASON HARMONIE. 4114

0765-7579 See ENSEIGNEMENT ET GESTION (PARIS). 866

0765-7846 See CANCER JOURNAL (VILLEJUIF), THE. 3811

0765-913X See SAFETY RESEARCH NEWS. 2869

0765-9261 See BULLETIN D'ESTHETIQUE DERMATOLOGIQUE ET COSMETOLOGIE. 402

0765-9326 See CAHIER DES ARTS ET DES ARTISTES. 346

0765-9547 See MEDECINE SCOLAIRE ET UNIVERSITAIRE. 4790

0765-9849 See CAMERA INTERNATIONAL. 4368

0765-9911 See CREATION MAGAZINE. 758

0766-1991 1172

0766-3633 See CARDIOLOGIE PRATIQUE PARIS. 3700

0766-3897 See ACTUALITES MEDICALES INTERNATIONALES PSYCHIATRIE. 3919

0766-4214 See ETUDES ET TRAVAUX SUR CENDRARS. 3575

0766-4257 See CHRONIQUES ITALIENNES. 3273

0766-4516 See BULLETIN D'HISTOIRE DE LA REVOLUTION FRANCAISE. 2681

0766-5075 See ETUDES MONGOLES ET SIBERIENNES. 2687

0766-5105 See GEODYNAMIQUE. 1377

0766-5210 See REVUE PRATIQUE DE CONTROLE INDUSTRIEL 1984. 3487

0766-5385 See LETTRE DE TELETEL, LA. 1115

0766-5466 See LYON MEDITERRANEE MEDICAL. MEDECINE DU SUD-EST. 3605

0766-5687 See PREVENTIQUE. 2868

0766-5725 See TECHN. BIOL. - 1985. 3644

0766-5911 See ANNUAIRE - SOCIETE D'HISTOIRE ET D'ARCHEOLOGIE DE COLMAR. 2675

0766-6047 See POLITIQUE INDUSTRIELLE. 1621

0766-6268 See NOTE DE CONJONCTURE DE L'I.N.S.E.E. 1576

0766-6500 See REMISIS. 1921

0766-6934 See BIJOUTIER : REVUE FRANCAISE DES BIJOUTIERS HORLOGERS, LE. 2916

0766-7159 See PUBLICATIONS TECHNIQUES DES CHARBONNAGES DE FRANCE. 2149

0766-8007 See TRANS RURAL EXPRESS. 5395

0766-821X See BANCATIQUE. 774

0766-883X See LETTRE - C.A.F. 1503

0766-9208 See PROFESSION COMPTABLE, LA. 750

0766-9968 See TRAVAUX EN COURS. 3539

0767-0273 See RECHERCHE ET INDUSTRIE. 5145

0767-0303 See LIEUX DE L'ENFANCE. 1066

0767-0508 See VOGUE DECORATION. 2903

0767-094X See REVUE DE LA NAVIGATION, PORTS & INDUSTRIES. 5455

0767-0974 See MEDECINE SCIENCES : M/S. 464

0767-1121 See MANAGEMENT ET CONJONCTURE SOCIALE PARIS. 877

0767-1288 See BULLETIN OFFICIEL DU MINISTERE DELEGUE CHARGE DE LA MER. 3180

0767-1407 See DOCUMENTS DE RECHERCHES EN MEDECINE GENERALE. 3737

0767-1822 See TRAITE DE LA SECURITE SOCIALE. 5313

0767-1830 See GUIDE DES CONVENTIONS INTERNATIONALES DE SECURITE SOCIALE. 2811

0767-2004 See REVUE MEDICALE DE L'ASSURANCE MALADIE. 3637

0767-2055 See ANTIGONE. 4366

0767-2853 See SCIENCE DU SOL (1984). 185

0767-2861 See BULLETIN FRANCAIS DE LA PECHE ET DE LA PISCICULTURE. 2298

0767-337X See ARBORESCENCES (PARIS). 2375

0767-3701 See RECHERCHE ET APPLICATIONS EN MARKETING. 935

0767-3744 See FRENESIE. 3925

0767-3981 See FUNDAMENTAL & CLINICAL PHARMACOLOGY. 4305

0767-399X See EUROPEAN PSYCHIATRY. 3925

0767-4538 See RAPPORT ANNUEL AU PRESIDENT DE LA REPUBLIQUE ET AU PARLEMENT / COMMISSION DE LA SECURITE DES CONSOMMATEURS. 849

0767-4538 See RAPPORT AU PRESIDENT DE LA REPUBLIQUE ET AU PARLEMENT. 4493

0767-4635 See D.E.R. ... PANORAMA. 2040

0767-4775 See DOSSIERS DE L'AUDIOVISUEL. 3278

0767-5259 See AUTREMENT DIRE. 3267

0767-6468 See CAHIERS DE L'ORIENT, LES. 2612

0767-709X See REVUE ARCHEOLOGIQUE DE L'OUEST. 281

ISSN Index

0767-7138 *See* PARADE SAUVAGE. BULLETIN. **3422**

0767-7189 *See* REVUE D'ELEVAGE ET DE MEDECINE VETERINAIRE DE NOUVELLE CALEDONIE. **5520**

0767-7243 *See* MUSEE CONDE. **4091**

0767-7294 *See* VESTNIK, LE MESSAGER. **2524**

0767-7367 *See* ANNALES DE LA SOCIETE GEOLOGIQUE DU NORD. **1365**

0767-7375 *See* MEMOIRES DE LA SOCIETE GEOLOGIQUE DU NORD. **1358**

0767-807X *See* PICSOU MAGAZINE. **1068**

0767-8177 *See* GUIDE CUISINE PARIS. **2790**

0767-9203 *See* SOCIETE D'EMULATION DE LA VENDEE 1971. **364**

0767-9432 *See* QUALITIQUE PARIS. **2852**

0767-9513 *See* HERMES (PARIS, FRANCE : 1988). **4476**

0767-9866 *See* BSP BAREME SOCIAL PERIODIQUE. **5193**

0767-9874 *See* JOURNEES DE LA RECHERCHE PORCINE EN FRANCE. **5515**

0768-0341 *See* COLLECTION ENSEIGNEMENT DES SCIENCES. **5095**

0768-1305 *See* CENTRE INTERUNIVERSITAIRE DE RECHERCHE SUR LA RENAISSANCE ITALIENNE. **3373**

0768-2050 *See* INSTITUT / INSTITUT DE FRANCE. **4089**

0768-3650 *See* ETUDES QUATERNAIRES. MEMOIRE. **1375**

0768-6625 *See* JUSQU'A LA MORT ACCOMPAGNER LA VIE. **3601**

0768-7559 *See* ANNALES DE PSYCHIATRIE. **3920**

0768-8172 *See* MBI MUSIC BUSINESS INFORMATIONS. **4130**

0768-9284 See QUALITE EN MOUVEMENT PARIS LA DEFENSE. **4032**

0768-9098 *See* INFORMATIONS CANADIENNES 1969. **820**

0768-9179 *See* PHARMACIEN HOSPITALIER, LE. **4321**

0768-9284 *See* PUBLICATIONS MATHEMATIQUES DE LA FACULTE DES SCIENCES DE BESANCON. THEORIE DES NOMBRES. **3529**

0768-9403 *See* MUNTU. **3304**

0768-956X *See* SONOVISION PARIS. **1121**

0768-9829 *See* CAHIERS DES SCIENCES HUMAINES. **5194**

0769-0088 *See* HOR YEZH. **3286**

0769-0541 *See* PUBLICATION OCCASIONNELLE - CENTRE INTERNATIONAL POUR LA FORMATION ET LES ECHANGES GEOLOGIQUES. **1392**

0769-0886 *See* RECHERCHES SUR DIDEROT ET SUR L'ENCYCLOPEDIE. **3428**

0769-0975 *See* ARCHIMAG VINCENNES. **2479**

0769-1432 *See* FLASH ... SUR LA RECHERCHE SCIENTIFIQUE ET MEDICALE A L'UNIVERSITE PIERRE ET MARIE CURIE. **3576**

0769-1696 *See* CATALOGUE DE LIVRES AU FORMAT DE POCHE. **412**

0769-1734 *See* SOUVENANCE ANABAPTISTE. **4999**

0769-1793 *See* DIETETIQUE ET MEDICINE. **4189**

0769-1912 *See* CAHIERS DE LA PEINTURE, LES. **346**

0769-2412 *See* LOCALDOC / GROUPEMENT DE RECHERCHES COORDONNEES SUR L'ADMINISTRATION LOCALE; CENTRE D'ETUDE ET DE RECHERCHE SUR LA VIE LOCALE. **4663**

0769-3206 *See* MATERIAUX POUR L'HISTOIRE DE NOTRE TEMPS. **2623**

0769-3362 *See* DROIT ET SOCIETE. **2964**

0769-3656 *See* ETUDES DANUBIENNES. **2687**

0769-3710 *See* INTRAMUROS. **301**

0769-4504 *See* CAHIERS DE L'I.H.T.P, LES. **2612**

0769-489X *See* ANNALES D'ECONOMIE ET DE STATISTIQUE. **1462**

0769-5918 *See* DOSSIERS DU MARKETING DIRECT, LES. **923**

0769-6027 *See* ATOUT CHAT. **5577**

0769-6094 *See* SAVOIRS ET FORMATION. **2792**

0769-7996 *See* COMPORTEMENTS. **580**

0769-8933 *See* AUTO-MOTO MONTLHERY. **5439**

0770-0075 *See* CRITIQUE REGIONALE. **5243**

0770-0512 *See* BELGIAN JOURNAL OF OPERATIONS RESEARCH, STATISTICS AND COMPUTER SCIENCE. **1208**

0770-0822 *See* HANDELINGEN VAN HET GENOOTSCHAP VOOR GESCHIEDENIS. **2690**

0770-111X *See* COURRIER DU BOIS, LE. **633**

0770-1276 *See* HYPERTENSIE IN DE HUISARTSENPRAKTIJK. **3705**

0770-1470 *See* FREE LABOUR WORLD. **1675**

0770-1683 *See* OIEC BIMESTRIEL BULLETIN. **1883**

0770-1713 See CEREVISIA AND BIOTECHNOLOGY. **2366**

0770-1748 *See* NATUURWETENSCHAPPELIJK TIJDSCHRIFT. **4169**

0770-1772 *See* TARIF DES SPECIALITES PHARMACEUTIQUES. **4330**

0770-237X *See* ACCIDENTS DE LA CIRCULATION SUR LA VOIE PUBLIQUE AVEC TUES OU BLESSES. **5438**

0770-2515 *See* LAIT ET NOUS, LE. **196**

0770-2817 *See* ANTIQUITE CLASSIQUE, L'. **1074**

0770-285X *See* AGRICONTACT ED. FRANCAISE. **48**

0770-2965 *See* STUDIA DIPLOMATICA. **4497**

0770-3198 *See* CLINICAL RHEUMATOLOGY. **3804**

0770-321X *See* FOOT MAGAZINE. **4850**

0770-3724 *See* BULLETIN OF COMPARATIVE LABOUR RELATIONS. **3145**

0770-3767 *See* CAHIER D'ETHOLOGIE APPLIQUEE. **5580**

0770-4224 *See* PATIENT CARE NEDERLAND. **3626**

0770-450X *See* LIAISONS INTERNATIONALES / CENTRE OECUMENIQUE DE LIAISONS INTERNATIONALES. **4528**

0770-4518 *See* RECHERCHES ECONOMIQUES DE LOUVAIN. **1515**

0770-4569 *See* ANNUAIRE - INSTITUT ROYAL METEOROLOGIQUE DE BELGIQUE. MAGNETISME TERRESTRE. **1365**

0770-4585 *See* BULLETIN DE L'IRES. **1466**

0770-4720 *See* INTERFACE OPPREBOIS. **5778**

0770-4984 *See* MONUMENTEN EN LANDSCHAPPEN : M & L. **303**

0770-6472 *See* ANNALES DE DROIT DE LOUVAIN. **2933**

0770-7193 *See* WATER (BRUSSEL). **5542**

0770-7274 *See* CENTRE SCIENTIFIQUE ET TECHNIQUE DE LA CONSTRUCTION. **607**

0770-8521 *See* CONTRADICTIONS BRUXELLES. **1471**

0770-8548 *See* ANNALS OF PUBLIC AND CO-OPERATIVE ECONOMY. **1545**

0770-8602 *See* REVUE GENERALE (1985). **2492**

0770-9021 *See* COURRIER DE GAND, LE. **5778**

0770-920X *See* GIFAP BULLETIN. **1025**

0770-9471 *See* JOURNAL OF HEAD & NECK PATHOLOGY. **3595**

0770-996X *See* SWISS NEWS. **852**

0771-0313 *See* CAHIERS DU G.E.R.M, LES. **3561**

0771-0364 *See* COMMUNIQUE HEBDOMADAIRE (INSTITUT NATIONAL DE STATISTIQUE (BELGIUM) : 1982). **5325**

0771-0410 *See* COMMUNIQUE HEBROMADAIRE (INSTITUT NATIONAL DE STATISTIQUE (BELGIUM) : 1982). **5325**

0771-0461 *See* MINUTES / OCIC. **4074**

0771-0607 *See* NOTE TECHNIQUE DU CENTRE DE RECHERCHES AGRONOMIQUE DE LETAT. **115**

0771-0704 *See* TIJDSCHRIFT RECHTSDOCUMENTATIE. **3064**

0771-095X *See* RESTANT. **3315**

0771-1034 *See* ENGLISH PAGES. **3209**

0771-1107 *See* JOURNAL A. **1981**

0771-1158 *See* BULLETIN DE LA SOCIETE MATHEMATIQUE DE BELGIQUE. SERIE B. **3497**

0771-1182 *See* BULLETIN MENSUEL DE L'OFFICE NATIONAL DE L'EMPLOI. **1657**

0771-1204 *See* BULLETIN DE LA SOCIETE MATHEMATIQUE DE BELGIQUE. SERIE A. **3497**

0771-1522 *See* KNIPSELKRANT ECONOMIE. **1502**

0771-1530 *See* REVUE BELGE DE SECURITE SOCIALE. **5306**

0771-2022 *See* NEWSLETTER / INTERNATIONAL UNION FOR THE SCIENTIFIC STUDY OF POPULATION. **4555**

0771-2367 *See* FARMACEUTISCH TIJDSCHRIFT VOOR BELGIE 1971. **4304**

0771-2510 *See* ARGUS BELGE, L'. **5778**

0771-2723 *See* ANNALES D'HISTOIRE DE L'ART ET D'ARCHEOLOGIE. **336**

0771-2839 *See* PROMOSAFE (NEDERLANDSE ED.). **2868**

0771-2871 *See* STEEL STATISTICAL YEARBOOK / INTERNATIONAL IRON AND STEEL INSTITUTE, COMMITTEE ON STATISTICS. **1628**

0771-3312 *See* TROPICULTURA. **142**

0771-3398 *See* CENTRE DE DOCUMENTATION PAYSANNE DU PARAGUAY. **1551**

0771-341X *See* CHIMIE. **971**

0771-3703 *See* GERMANISTISCHE MITTEILUNGEN. **3284**

0771-4033 *See* REVUE BELGE DU FEU. **2292**

0771-4181 *See* BESWA REVUE. **2225**

0771-4602 *See* JANSSEN CHIMICA ACTA. **979**

0771-4653 *See* CAHIERS THEATRE LOUVAIN. **5362**

0771-4874 *See* MONITEUR DU FILM EN BELGIQUE, LE. **4074**

0771-5080 *See* NEDERLANDS VAN NU. **3305**

0771-5102 *See* LEX-INTERDOC. **3002**

0771-5676 *See* BELGIAN MEDICAL YEAR-BOOK. **3555**

0771-5684 See EUROPEAN JOURNAL OF PHYSICAL MEDICINE & REHABILITATION. **4380**

0771-5692 *See* ETUDES ET DOCUMENTS DU CERCLE ROYAL D'HISTOIRE ET D'ARCHEOLOGIE D'ATH ET DE LA REGION. **2687**

0771-6273 *See* BULLETIN FINANCIER - BANQUE BRUXELLES LAMBERT. **780**

0771-6303 *See* SOUNDTRACK. **5319**

0771-6435 *See* CAHIERS. **2612**

0771-6494 *See* MUSEON, LE. **420**

0771-6524 *See* CAHIERS DE L'INSTITUT DE LINGUISTIQUE DE LOUVAIN. **3271**

0771-6532 *See* ENJEUX NAMUR. **1894**

0771-6680 *See* CAHIERS DE LA WALLONIE ET DE BRUXELLES / GROUPE DE SOCIOLOGIE WALLONNE, LES. **5241**

0771-6788 *See* REVUE BELGE DE MUSICOLOGIE. **4150**

0771-6796 *See* REVUE DE L'INSTITUT DE SOCIOLOGIE. **5217**

0771-7016 *See* MUSICA ANTIQUA : ACTUELE INFORMATIE OVER OUDE MUZIEK. **4135**

0771-7172 *See* KOEPEL VIJF. **1760**

0771-730X *See* CHIMIE NOUVELLE. **972**

0771-7342 *See* COMMUNICATIE. **1106**

0771-7369 *See* NOUVELLES DE LA SCIENCE ET DES TECHNOLOGIES. **5135**

0771-761X *See* ARTE FACTUM (ANTWERPEN). **340**

0771-7776 *See* SACRIS ERUDIRI. **4995**

0771-7784 *See* COMPUTERRECHT. **1178**

0771-7962 *See* ANNUAIRE DES COMMUNAUTES EUROPEENNES ET DES AUTRES ORGANISATIONS EUROPEENNES. **4515**

0771-8020 *See* BONNE SOIREE. **4849**

0771-8071 *See* SPIROU. **5075**

0771-839X *See* JAARBOEK / STAD BRUGGE, STEDELIJKE MUSEA. **4089**

0771-9833 *See* MANAGER GENT. **878**

0772-0033 *See* TRAVEL JOURNALIST, THE. **5496**

0772-0831 See LETTRE DE CONJONCTURE (BRUSSELS, BELGIUM). 1572

0772-084X See AFRIKA FOCUS : TIJDSCHRIFT VAN DE AVRUG. 2498

0772-0890 See FINANCIEEL EKONOMISCHE TIJD, DE. 1491

0772-1404 See PROCEEDINGS - BELGIAN CONGRESS OF ANESTHESIOLOGY. 3972

0772-1668 See CURRENT LEGAL THEORY : INTERNATIONAL JOURNAL FOR DOCUMENTATION ON LEGAL THEORY. 2958

0772-2125 See BINDTEKEN. 5268

0772-2257 See SEMINAIRE DE MATHEMATIQUE. 3533

0772-2621 See TIJDSCHRIFT VAN DE NATIONALE BANK VAN BELGIE. 814

0772-3326 See ONDERNEMEN. 5065

0772-3784 See IDES ... ET AUTRES. 3395

0772-4837 See FISKOLOOG. 1491

0772-494X See TUEXEMIA. 2222

0772-5183 See NIEUWSBRIEF - LIGA VOOR MENSENRECHTEN. 3017

0772-5310 See ENTREPRISE ET LE DROIT, L'. 2966

0772-585X See BESTE KEUS VOOR KANTOOR EN BEDRIJF. 1875

0772-6287 See MEUBELECHO. 2906

0772-6694 See STATISTIQUES DU COMMERCE EXTERIEUR DE L'UNION ECONOMIQUE BELGO-LUXEMBURGEOISE. 734

0772-6856 See PRAKTISCH MANAGEMENT. 882

0772-6961 See BULLETIN TRIMESTRIEL DE LA FONDATION AUSCHWITZ. 2681

0772-7240 See LANDBOUWLEVEN. 104

0772-7488 See ARCHEOLOGIE IN VLAANDEREN. 259

0772-764X See BEVOLKING EN GEZIN. 4550

0772-7674 See TIJDSCHRIFT VOOR ECONOMIE EN MANAGEMENT. 1524

0772-7704 See STATISTIQUES INDUSTRIELLES. 1539

0772-7712 See STATISTIQUES DE LA CONSTRUCTION ET DU LOGEMENT. 633

0772-7852 See STUDIA IRANICA. 2665

0772-8425 See VLAAMSE TOERISTISCHE BIBLIOTHEEK. 5499

0772-876X See AVIASTRO (1984). 12

0772-8867 See CREW REPORTS. 5554

0772-9219 See PSYCHOANALYSE. 4610

0772-9405 See TEST ACHATS MAGAZINE. 1300

0773-0292 See DAUPHIN. 1062

0773-0306 See BONJOUR AVERBODE. 1060

0773-0357 See COMM - EUROPEAN REGIONAL CLEARING HOUSE FOR COMMUNITY WORK. 5279

0773-0543 See GESTION 2000. 868

0773-1922 See HINTERLAND ENGLISH ED. 5110

0773-2279 See CINE-FICHES DE GRAND ANGLE, LES. 4065

0773-3577 See NIEUW WERELDTIJDSCHRIFT : NWT. 2520

0773-3666 See KWARTAALOVERZICHT VAN DE ECONOMIE. 905

0773-4123 See ANNALEN - KONINKLIJKE MUSEUM VOOR MIDDEN-AFRIKA ECONOMISCHE WETENSCHAPPEN. 1462

0773-4182 See CC AI. 1212

0773-4239 See RONDOM GEZIN. 2285

0773-4980 See ENQUETES DU MUSEE DE LA VIE WALLONNE. 2615

0773-5251 See APEX (BRUSSELS). 5576

0773-5618 See BAREEL. 1918

0773-5855 See ANDERE SINEMA. 4063

0773-591X See GRAFISCH NIEUWS. 4815

0773-6177 See CEREVISIA AND BIOTECHNOLOGY. 2366

0773-6215 See STATISTIQUES DU COMMERCE EXTERIEUR DE L'UNION ECONOMIQUE BELGO-LUXEMBURGEOISE. ETATS DEVELOPPES / ROYAUME DE BELGIQUE, MINISTERE DES AFFAIRES ECONOMIQUES, INSTITUT NATIONAL DE STATISTIQUE. 734

0773-6231 See DOE HET VEILIG. 2861

0773-6401 See TIJDSCHRIFT VOOR BESTUURSWETENSCHAPPEN EN PUBLEKRECHT. 3064

0773-7394 See EDUCATION-TRIBUNE LIBRE. 1741

0773-7467 See BULLETIN USUEL DES LOIS ET ARRETES (BRUXELLES). 4635

0773-7688 See DIALECTES DE WALLONIE, LES. 3277

0773-8439 See REVUE BURKINABE DE DROIT. 3042

0773-9532 See PART DE L'IL, LA. 361

0773-9664 See APERCU ECONOMIQUE TRIMESTRIEL. 1546

0773-9796 See NOUVELLES DU PATRIMOINE. 305

0774-0115 See REVUE BELGE DU CINEMA. 4077

0774-0689 See SPECIAL PUBLICATION / EUROPEAN AQUACULTURE SOCIETY. 2313

0774-1286 See MUSEUMSTRIP. 4093

0774-1863 See ART & FACT. 313

0774-2827 See ONS GEESTEILJK ERF. 4983

0774-2851 See JAARBOEK - ARCA LOVANIENSIS ARTES ATQUE HISTORIAE RESERANS DOCUMENTA. 322

0774-286X See HANDELINGEN DER MAATSCHAPPIJ VOOR GESCHIEDENIS EN OUDHEIDKUNDE TE GENT. 2617

0774-2908 See HUMANISTICA LOVANIENSIA. 3286

0774-3254 See HANDELINGEN / KONINKLIJKE ZUIDNEDERLANDSE MAATSCHAPPIJ VOOR TAAL- EN LETTERKUNDE EN GESCHIEDENIS. 3285

0774-3297 See ETHNOLOGIA FLANDRICA. 2319

0774-4323 See INFOR MARECHALERIE. 3396

0774-4919 See CITEAUX, COMMENTARII CISTERCIENSES. 5027

0774-5141 See BELGIAN JOURNAL OF LINGUISTICS. 3268

0774-5230 See BONNE NOUVELLE. 4939

0774-5435 See JAARBOEK VAN DE GESCHIED- EN OUDHEIDKUNDIGE KRING VOOR LEUVEN EN OMGEVING. 2693

0774-5885 See REVUE BELGE DE NUMISMATIQUE ET DE SIGILLOGRAPHIE. 2783

0774-6180 See BEP. 3555

0774-6318 See DODONAEUS. 2846

0775-0234 See BELGISCH TIJDSCHRIFT VOOR SOCIALE ZEKERHEID. 5274

0775-0285 See BELGISCH TIJDSCHRIFT VOOR TANDHEELKUNDE. 1317

0775-0293 See REVUE BELGE DE MEDECINE DENTAIRE 1984. 1334

0775-0501 See HUISARTS NU : MAANDBLAD VAN DE WETENSCHAPPELIJKE VERENIGING DER VLAAMSE HUISARTSEN : HANU. 3738

0775-051X See ADVANCES IN PROTEIN PHOSPHATASES. 577

0775-0803 See JUS MEDICUM. 3741

0775-1443 See BELGIUM, ECONOMIC AND COMMERCIAL INFORMATION. 1464

0775-2814 See TIJDSCHRIFT VOOR BELGISCH BURGERLIJK RECHT : TBBR. 3091

0775-2903 See EUROTECH FORUM JOURNAL. 5104

0775-2911 See TRADE FLASH BRUXELLES. 888

0775-311X See STATISTIQUES JUDICIAIRES. 3083

0775-3128 See VOLKSKUNDE (1940). 2325

0775-3209 See REVUE EUROPEENNE DE DROIT DE LA CONSOMMATION. 3043

0775-3381 See TYPOLOGIE DES SOURCES DU MOYEN AGE OCCIDENTAL. 2713

0775-454X See ARTEMIA NEWSLETTER. 2296

0775-4663 See REVUE DE DROIT INTERNATIONAL ET DE DROIT COMPARE. 3135

0775-5694 See SYSTEEMTEORETISCH BULLETIN - INTERAKTIE AKADEMIE. 1886

0775-602X See LAB PRODUCTS INTERNATIONAL. BRUSSELS. 463

0775-6992 See ANIMALIS FAMILIARIS BRUSSEL. 5503

0775-7239 See ENTREPRENEUR MAGAZINE (BERTRIX). 672

0775-7506 See ANNALEN VAN DE KONINKLIJKE OUDHEIDKUNDIGE KRING VAN HET LAND VAN WAAS. 2674

0775-8251 See DIGO KAPELLEN. 1892

0775-9479 See CAHIERS DU SCENARIO BRUXELLES, LES. 4064

0775-9592 See OPERA BOTANICA BELGICA. 520

0776-0086 See BULLETIN DE LA SOCIETE ROYALE BELGE D'ETUDES GEOLOGIQUES ET ARCHEOLOGIQUES LES CHERCHEURS DE WALLONIE. 1368

0776-0256 See DROITS DE L'HOMME SANS FRONTIERES. 4507

0776-068X See BIB-KRANT LEUVEN. 3194

0776-0698 See STARS MARIEMBOURG. 425

0776-1244 See ANNALES DE L'INSTITUT ARCHEOLOGIQUE DU LUXEMBOURG. 255

0776-1252 See ANNALES DU CERCLE ARCHEOLOGIQUE D'ENGHIEN. 255

0776-1260 See BULLETIN DE L'INSTITUT ARCHEOLOGIQUE LIEGEOIS. 263

0776-1295 See BULLETIN DE LA SOCIETE D'ART ET D'HISTOIRE DU DIOCESE DE LIEGE. 2843

0776-1309 See BULLETIN DE LA SOCIETE ROYALE LE VIEUX-LIEGE. 2681

0776-1317 See CAHIERS DE MARIEMONT, LES. 4086

0776-1325 See LIMBURG. 2519

0776-135X See ANNALES DU CERCLE ARCHEOLOGIQUE DE MONS. 255

0776-2143 See LANDBOUWTIJDSCHRIFT (1988). 104

0776-2976 See HANDELINGEN VAN DE KONINKLIJKE KRING VOOR OUDHEIDKUNDE, LETTEREN EN KUNST VAN MECHELEN. 321

0776-2984 See ACTA ARCHAEOLOGICA LOVANIENSIA. 253

0776-3093 See RECORDER WEVELGEM. 990

0776-3395 See TRENDS-TENDANCES (BRUXELLES). 1587

0776-3670 See ARTES TEXTILES. 5348

0776-3689 See PAYS GAUMAIS, LE. 327

0776-4111 See GEZELLIANA. 3284

0776-4472 See TUINBOUW VISIE. 2432

0776-4677 See ACTUALQUARTO GERPINNES. 2276

0776-5533 See HANDELINGEN VAN DEN GESCHIED- EN OUDHEIDKUNDIGE KRING VAN KORTRIJK. 321

0776-7943 See JOURNAL OF AFRICAN ZOOLOGY. 5587

0776-8508 See TARGET 92 / COMMISSION OF THE EUROPEAN COMMUNITIES, DIRECTORATE-GENERAL INFORMATION, COMMUNICATIONS, CULTURE. 1586

0777-0553 See EUROPEAN ARCHIVES OF BIOLOGY. 455

0777-0626 See ANTWERP FACETS. 2913

0777-0707 See CAHIERS INTERNATIONAUX DE PSYCHOLOGIE SOCIALE, LES. 4579

0777-2173 See ETUDES ET RECHERCHES ARCHEOLOGIQUES DE L'UNIVERSITE DE LIEGE. 268

0777-2181 See REVUE E 1989. 2079

0777-2238 See BULLETIN DE DOCUMENTATION - MINISTERE DES FINANCES, SERVICE D'ETUDES ET DE DOCUMENTATION. 4715

0777-2572 See BULLETIN CRR. 5439

0777-2734 See EUROPEAN JOURNAL OF MECHANICAL ENGINEERING. 2114

0777-3455 See LEJOTIEK BRUSSEL. 5251

0777-3579 See REVUE TRIMESTRIELLE DES DROITS DE L'HOMME. 4512

0777-5466 See BULLETIN DU CENTRE GENEVOIS D'ANTHROPOLOGIE / MUSEE D'ETHNOGRAPHIE, DEPARTEMENT D'ANTHROPOLOGIE. 232

0777-6268 See AGENDA DES FESTIVALS AUDIOVISUELS EN EUROPE, L'. 5315

0777-6276 See BELGIAN JOURNAL OF ZOOLOGY. 5577

0777-6349 See ONDERNEMING, DE. 2607

0777-6357 See ENTREPRISE 1951, L'. 2605

0777-8309 See PRO VETERINARIO ENGLISH ED. 5518

0777-8805 See LOUVAIN BREWING LETTERS. 2369

0777-9216 See BMB BURO INFORMATIKA. 643

0778-0893 See PEDAGOGIES BRUXELLES. 1772

0778-2624 See AMCHAM : THE MAGAZINE OF THE AMERICAN CHAMBER OF COMMERCE IN BELGIUM. 818

0778-2640 See CEREVISIA AND BIOTECHNOLOGY. 2366

0778-2837 See ARCHEOLOGIE IN VLAANDEREN. 259

0778-3124 See ARCHIVES INTERNATIONALES DE PHYSIOLOGIE, DE BIOCHIMIE ET DE BIOPHYSIQUE. 578

0778-4031 See BELGIAN JOURNAL OF BOTANY. 501

0778-4287 See AMPHORA BRAINE-L'ALLEUD. 254

0778-4910 See BIOMEDICAL & HEALTH RESEARCH. 3686

0778-5097 See BRANDSTOFFEN BRUSSEL. 1021

0778-5607 See JAARBOEK / KONINKLIJKE BELGISCHE COMMISSIE VOOR VOLKSKUNDE, VLAAMSE AFDELING. 2321

0778-7065 See FOOD POLICY INTERNATIONAL. 88

0778-7383 See ANPI MAGAZINE. 2288

0778-7588 See BUSINESS & TELECOM (NEDERLANDSE ED.). 645

0778-7928 See EUROPE ENVIRONMENT. 2171

0778-8304 See TRAJECTA. 5037

0778-9750 See JOURNAL OF MEDIEVAL LATIN : A PUBLICATION OF THE NORTH AMERICAN ASSOCIATION OF MEDIEVAL LATIN, THE. 3291

0779-1119 See LARVICULTURE & ARTEMIA NEWSLETTER. 2307

0780-1785 See LAAKARIT. 1329

0780-1807 See HAMMASLAAKARIT. 1324

0780-2285 See TRIBOLOGIA. 2000

0780-3281 See SLAVICA HELSINGIENSIA. 3321

0780-5292 See TYOTERVEYSPAIVAT. 1587

0780-6655 See FOUNDATION FOR BIOTECHNICAL AND INDUSTRIAL FERMENTATION RESEARCH. 2367

0780-7554 See STATISTIK OVER PENSIONSTAGARNA I FINLAND. 5267

0780-9212 See DOCUMENT OF MINISTRY FOR FOREIGN AFFAIRS, FINNISH INTERNATIONAL DEVELOPMENT AGENCY. 2909

0780-9859 See ARSIS. 313

0781-0032 See MUSEO HELSINKI. 4091

0781-1705 See STUK-A. 3643

0781-2698 See ACTA POLYTECHNICA SCANDINAVICA. CHEMICAL TECHNOLOGY AND METALLURGY SERIES. 2007

0781-3333 See STUDIA SLAVICA FINLANDENSIA. 3325

0781-3619 See JAHRBUCH FUER FINNISCH-DEUTSCHE LITERATURBEZIEHUNGEN. 3398

0781-7789 See FINNPAP WORLD. 4233

0782-0011 See GLIMTAR UR ALANDS FOLKKULTUR. 2320

0782-050X See LUTUKKA. 2697

0782-1069 See FINNISH MUSIC QUARTERLY. 4117

0782-1875 See SUOMALAISTEN ANITTEIDEN LUETTELO. CATALOGUE OF FINNISH RECORDINGS. 4155

0782-226X See ARCTIC MEDICAL RESEARCH. 3552

0782-2790 See HELSINGIN YLIOPISTON YMPARISTONSUOJELUN LAITOKSEN JULKAISUJA. 2195

0782-2979 See SCIMP SELECTIVE CO-OPERATIVE INDEX OF MANAGEMENT PERIODICALS. 733

0782-4386 See AGRICULTURAL SCIENCE IN FINLAND. 52

0782-5315 See KOTIMAAN VESILIIKENNE. 5385

0782-7342 See CONTENTA RELIGIONUM. 4950

0782-7423 See SIKSI : THE NORDIC ART REVIEW. 330

0782-7784 See INTERNATIONAL PEAT JOURNAL. 1948

0782-7873 See HALLITUKSEN KEHITYSYHTEISTYOKERTOMUS EDUSKUNNALLE VUODELTA. 1565

0782-7881 See REGERINGENS BERATTELSE TILL RIKSDAGEN OM UTVECKLINGSSAMARBETET. 1516

0782-8233 See WIDER WORKING PAPERS. 1588

0782-825X See TIETOPALVELU. 3253

0782-9671 See NORDISK ALKOHOL TIDSKRIFT. 1347

0783-1374 See ALKOHOLITILASTOLLINEN VUOSIKIRJA / ALKOHOLSTATISTISK AARSBOK / ALCOHOL STATISTICAL YEARBOOK. 1340

0783-4365 See FINNISH GAME RESEARCH. 2216

0783-5892 See SPHINX (HELSINKI, FINLAND). 5159

0783-6201 See EAST AFRICAN NEWSLETTER ON OCCUPATIONAL HEALTH AND SAFETY. 4774

0783-6899 See WORK HEALTH SAFETY. 2871

0783-8069 See RESEARCH REPORT - LAPPEENRANTA UNIVERSITY OF TECHNOLOGY. DEPARTMENT OF INFORMATION TECHNOLOGY. 5147

0783-9472 See PUBLICATIONS OF THE WATER AND ENVIRONMENT RESEARCH INSTITUTE. 1417

0784-1469 See TUTKIMAS JA TEKNIIKKA. 5176

0784-235X See ARKEOLOGIA SUOMESSA. 260

0784-5073 See NORDIC PULP & PAPER. 4235

0784-5197 See FINNISH ECONOMIC PAPERS. 1491

0784-638X See UNIVERSITY OF OULU. DEPARTMENT OF INFORMATION PROCESSING SCIENCE. SERIES A, RESEARCH PAPERS. 5168

0784-6509 See BULLETIN (SUOMEN PANKKI). 781

0784-722X See VALMET PAPER NEWS. 4239

0784-7289 See INTERNATIONAL PULP & PAPER MARKETS. 4234

0784-7726 See BN. 4104

0784-8242 See KOULUTUS. 1760

0784-8323 See SVT. JULKINEN TALOUS. 5344

0784-8404 See MAA- JA METSATALOUS HELSINKI. 1988. 154

0784-8412 See TUPAKKATILASTO. 5374

0784-8463 See LIIKENTEEN TILINPAATOSTILASTO. 5385

0784-9044 See TALONRAKENNUSYRITYSTEN TILINPAATOSTILASTO. 3488

0784-9079 See TEOLLISUUSYRITYSTEN TILINPAEAETOESTILASTO / BOKSLUTSSTATISTIK OEVER INDUSTRIFOERETAG / FINANCIAL STATEMENTS STATISTICS OF INDUSTRIAL ENTERPRISES. 1540

0784-9095 See TUKKUKAUPAN TILINPAATOSTILASTO. 855

0784-9109 See VAHITTAISKAUPAN TILINPAATOSTILASTO. 815

0784-929X See METSATYONTEKIJOIDEN VUOSIANSIOT / TILASTOKESKUS. 5333

0784-9370 See KUNTASEKTORIN KUUKAUSIPALKAT / TILASTOKESKUS. 4660

0784-9656 See PANOS-TUOTOS. 1577

0784-9745 See VALTION MENOT LAANEITTAIN. 4757

0785-0522 See GRAAFINEN TEOLLISUUS. 4565

0785-0522 See ELINTARVIKETEOLLISUUS. 2334

0785-0530 See METALLITEOLLISUUS. 4009

0785-0549 See TEKSTIILI- JA VAATETUSTEOLLISUUS. 5356

0785-3165 See ENERGIATILASTOT / KAUPPA- JA TEOLLISUUSMINISTERIO, ENERGIAOSASTO. 1938

0785-3890 See ANNALS OF MEDICINE (HELSINKI). 3550

0785-4218 See ENNAKKOTIETOJA TEOLLISUUDESTA / TILASTOKESKUS. 5326

0785-546X See ALOITTANEET JA LOPETTANEET YRITYKSET. 637

0785-5540 See BUSINESS FINLAND. 648

0785-7500 See MAATILAREKISTERI. 106

0785-7527 See SAIRAANHOITAJA / SUOMEN SAIRAANHOITAJALIITTO RY. 3869

0785-8760 See ENTOMOLOGICA FENNICA. 5607

0785-9015 See ELAVAN KUVAN VUOSIKIRJA. 4068

0786-0021 See ENERGIAN TUOTANTO JA VESIHUOLTO. 1938

0786-003X See HUONEKALU- JA MUU TEOLLISUUS. 2906

0786-0048 See KEMIAN TEOLLISUUS (FINLAND. TILASTOKESKUS). 1570

0786-2180 See SUOMEN LAAKETILASTO / LAAKEINFORMAATION JA -TILASTOINNIN YHTEISTYOTOIMIKUNTA. 3662

0786-3624 See KUNNALLINEN VIRKALUETTELO. 4660

0786-5686 See HOITOTIEDE. 3856

0786-8170 See TROPICAL FORESTRY REPORTS. 2397

0786-8413 See UNIVERSITY OF OULU. DEPARTMENT OF INFORMATION PROCESSING SCIENCE. SERIES A, RESEARCH PAPERS. 5168

0786-9916 See IACEE NEWSLETTER. 1977

0787-0396 See ARCHIVES OF COMPLEX ENVIRONMENTAL STUDIES : ACES. 2161

0788-2211 See LEIF : LIFE AND EDUCATION IN FINLAND. 1801

0788-3080 See PUHELINYRITYSTEN TILINPAATOSTILASTO. 1162

0788-5199 See TIEDONANTOJA - MAATALOUDEN TALOUDELLINEN TUTKIMUSLAITOS. 141

0788-5318 See TYOPAPEREITA - TAITEEN KESKUSTOIMIKUNTA. 332

0788-5695 See STUDY IN FINLAND: ENGLISH LANGUAGE PROGRAMMES AND STUDIES IN FINNISH UNIVERSITIES / MINISTRY OF EDUCATION. 3326

0788-5717 See COMMENTATIONES PHYSICO-MATHEMATICAE ET CHEMICO-MEDICAE. 4400

0789-2764 See SLAVICA TAMPERENSIA. 3322

0789-600X See AGRICULTURAL SCIENCE IN FINLAND. 52

0789-9343 See ATENEUM HELSINKI. 343

0790-004X See TREOIR. 4157

0790-0090 See JOURNAL / ARKLOW HISTORICAL SOCIETY. 2694

0790-0260 See GUIDE SERIES - GEOLOGICAL SURVEY OF IRELAND. 1381

0790-0430 See FOOD IRELAND. 2337

0790-0473 See JOURNAL OF THE IRISH SOCIETY FOR LABOUR LAW. 3150

0790-0619 See RENEWABLE SOURCES OF ENERGY. 1955

0790-0627 See INTERNATIONAL JOURNAL OF WATER RESOURCES DEVELOPMENT. 5534

0790-0929 See AQUACULTURE IRELAND. 2295

0790-1186 See IRISH JOURNAL OF PSYCHIATRY. 3927

0790-150X See SOFTWARE ABSTRACTS FOR ENGINEERS : SAFE. 1210

0790-1690 See BULLETIN / IRISH MATHEMATICAL SOCIETY. 3498

0790-1747 See IRISH BIOTECH NEWS. 459

0790-1763 See IRISH JOURNAL OF EARTH SCIENCES. 1356

0790-2239 See BAKERY WORLD. 2328

0790-3642 See FRIENDLY WORD, THE. 5060

0790-4304 See BANDON HISTORICAL JOURNAL. 2611

0790-486X See CONSUMER CHOICE. 1294

0790-5122 See TRADE STATISTICS OF IRELAND. 734

0790-567X See GENERAL REGISTER OF MEDICAL PRACTITIONERS. PART 1, FULLY REGISTERED MEDICAL PRACTITIONERS AS AT ... / THE MEDICAL COUNCIL. 3914

0790-5750 See INTERNATIONAL STRUCTURAL ENGINEERING ABSTRACTS. 2025

0790-5769 See INTERNATIONAL BUILDING SCIENCE & CONSTRUCTION ABSTRACTS. 2024

0790-6056 See VISITOR DUBLIN. 5498

0790-696X See MEDIUM-TERM REVIEW / THE ECONOMIC AND SOCIAL RESEARCH INSTITUTE. 1574

0790-7060 See JOURNAL OF THE IRISH FAMILY HISTORY SOCIETY. 2455

0790-7362 See IRISH MARKETING REVIEW. 927

0790-7850 See IRISH REVIEW (CORK, IRELAND). 2518

0790-8318 See LANGUAGE, CULTURE, AND CURRICULUM. 3295

0790-8334 See STATISTICAL BULLETIN. 5340

0790-8342 See IRISH ARCHITECT. 301

0790-892X See ARCHAEOLOGY IRELAND. 257

0790-8970 See STATISTICAL ABSTRACT DUBLIN. 1986. 5339

0790-9470 See MEDIUM-TERM REVIEW / THE ECONOMIC AND SOCIAL RESEARCH INSTITUTE. 1574

0790-9667 See IRISH JOURNAL OF PSYCHOLOGICAL MEDICINE. 3927

0790-9969 See POPULATION AND LABOUR FORCE PROJECTIONS / CENTRAL STATISTICS OFFICE. 4556

0791-0177 See ANNUAL REPORT OF THE MINISTER FOR AGRICULTURE AND FOOD. 61

0791-038X See GPA IRISH ARTS REVIEW YEARBOOK, THE. 351

0791-0797 See AUTHENTIK AUTHENTIK IN ENGLISH. 3267

0791-105X See IRISH STAGE & SCREEN. 5365

0791-1084 See ANNUAL REVIEW OF IRISH LAW. 2935

0791-1386 See BANKING IRELAND. 777

0791-1513 See HALLEL CAPPOQUIN. 5030

0791-2137 See IRISH SKIPPER, THE. 4177

0791-2471 See CORPORATE ACCOUNTING INTERNATIONAL. 742

0791-248X See RED TIDE NEWSLETTER. 1455

0791-2617 See SUNDAY BUSINESS POST, THE. 5803

0791-2641 See CHILDREN'S BOOKS IN IRELAND. 4827

0791-2765 See BANK MARKETING INTERNATIONAL DUBLIN. 921

0791-2927 See INDUSTRIAL EMPLOYMENT, EARNINGS AND HOURS WORKED, DETAILS FOR SUPPLEMENTARY NACE SUB-SECTORS. 1610

0791-3036 See PRODUCTION OF MILK AND MILK PRODUCTS. 198

0791-3044 See PIG STATISTICS, NUMBER AND WEIGHT OF PIGS SLAUGHTERED AT BACON FACTORIES. 120

0791-3095 See PIG SURVEY. 217

0791-3206 See LIVE REGISTER, MONTHLY AREA ANALYSIS DUBLIN. 1503

0791-329X See INDUSTRIAL DISPUTES DUBLIN. 1495

0791-3346 See AGRICULTURAL INPUT PRICE INDEX DUBLIN. 50

0791-3354 See AGRICULTURAL OUTPUT PRICE INDEX DUBLIN. 51

0791-3443 See TOURISM AND TRAVEL DUBLIN. 5493

0791-3524 See AGRICULTURAL STATISTICS, JUNE ..., LAND UTILISATION AND NUMBERS OF LIVESTOCK, REGIONAL ANALYSIS. 52

0791-3664 See EUROPEAN ACCOUNTANT DUBLIN. 743

0791-3931 See EAST EUROPEAN BANKER. 788

0791-4326 See INTERNATIONAL DIRECTORY OF CIVIL ENGINEERING/CONSTRUCTION SOFTWARE. 1287

0791-492X See INTERNATIONAL BUILDING SCIENCE & STRUCTURAL ABSTRACTS. 617

0791-539X See IISH CIMINAL LW JURNAL. 3107

0791-5403 See IRISH JOURNAL OF EUROPEAN LAW. 2985

0791-6833 See IRISH JOURNAL OF AGRICULTURAL AND FOOD RESEARCH. 97

0791-7201 See INSURANCE INDUSTRY INTERNATIONAL. 2883

0791-7481 See LAWYER INTERNATIONAL. 2997

0791-7945 See BIOLOGY AND ENVIRONMENT : PROCEEDINGS OF THE ROYAL IRISH ACADEMY. 446

0791-847X See HUMAN RESOURCES INTERNATIONAL. 942

0792-0032 See ENVIRONMENTAL POLICY REVIEW. 2168

0792-0318 See NOAH. 3418

0792-0393 See HEBREW UNIVERSITY STUDIES IN LITERATURE AND THE ARTS. 3393

0792-044X See YIDDISHKEIT. 5054

0792-0660 See JEWISH ART (JERUSALEM. 1986). 354

0792-0970 See MASABEY 'ENWS. 1690

0792-1233 See SCIENCE AND ENGINEERING OF COMPOSITE MATERIALS. 2108

0792-156X See ISRAELI JOURNAL OF AQUACULTURE, BAMIDGEH. 2306

0792-3252 See BALSANWT 'IBRIYT. 3267

0792-3910 See JEWISH BIBLE QUARTERLY, THE. 5017

0792-4259 See INVERTEBRATE REPRODUCTION & DEVELOPMENT. 5586

0792-4615 See OTHER ISRAEL : NEWSLETTER OF THE ISRAELI COUNCIL FOR ISRAELI-PALESTINIAN PEACE, THE. 2270

0792-4739 See BIBLICAL POLEMICS. 4939

0792-5077 See DRUG METABOLISM AND DRUG INTERACTIONS. 3796

0792-5891 See TARBUT (NEW YORK, N.Y. : 1989). 331

0792-6049 See JERUSALEM REPORT, THE. 2526

0792-6855 See JOURNAL OF BASIC AND CLINICAL PHYSIOLOGY AND PHARMACOLOGY. 582

0792-7797 See HUMAN RIGHTS UPDATE (CHICAGO, ILL.). 4509

0792-8483 See JOURNAL OF NEURAL TRANSPLANTATION & PLASTICITY. 3835

0792-9765 See LINK. 690

0792-9978 See ISRAEL JOURNAL OF PLANT SCIENCES. 514

0793-0283 See HETEROCYCLIC COMMUNICATIONS. 976

0793-0291 See METAL-BASED DRUGS. 986

0794-0831 See NIGERIAN JOURNAL OF GUIDANCE AND COUNSELLING, THE. 4606

0794-1293 See NIGERIAN JOURNAL OF MICROBIOLOGY. 568

0794-4373 See NEW ERA NURSING IMAGE INTERNATIONAL. 3862

0794-4845 See TROPICAL VETERINARIAN IBADAN. 3987

0794-7046 See TCNN RESEARCH BULLETIN. 5002

0794-7194 See JOURNAL OF FOOD & AGRICULTURE. 2346

0794-7348 See AFRICAN DENTAL JOURNAL : OFFICIAL PUBLICATION OF THE FEDERATION OF AFRICAN DENTAL ASSOCIATIONS. 1315

0794-7968 See INSIGHT LAGOS. 1987. 4965

0794-859X See NIGERIAN JOURNAL OF PHYSIOLOGICAL SCIENCES : OFFICIAL PUBLICATION OF THE PHYSIOLOGICAL SOCIETY OF NIGERIA. 584

0794-8883 See NIGERIAN JOURNAL OF INDUSTRIAL RELATIONS. 1619

0795-0101 See TROPICAL FRESHWATER BIOLOGY. 475

0795-1477 See CORPORATE DIRECTORY OF NIGERIA'S BESTSELLERS. 661

0795-3097 See JOURNAL OF AFRICAN PSYCHOLOGY (SOUTH OF THE SAHARA, THE CARIBBEAN, AND AFRO-LATIN AMERICA). 4593

0795-4123 See OCCASIONAL PAPERS - NATIONAL HORTICULTURAL RESEARCH INSTITUTE. 2426

0795-4131 See TECHNICAL BULLETIN - NATIONAL HORTICULTURAL RESEARCH INSTITUTE. 2432

0795-414X See RESEARCH BULLETIN - NATIONAL HORTICULTURAL RESEARCH INSTITUTE. 2430

0795-4778 See AFRICAN JOURNAL OF LIBRARY, ARCHIVES & INFORMATION SCIENCE. 3188

0795-8692 See NIGERIAN JOURNAL OF PALMS AND OIL SEEDS. 112

0797-0315 See BOLETIN DE INVESTIGACION - FACULTAD DE AGRONOMIA (MONTEVIDEO). 67

0797-0323 See NOTAS TECNICAS - FACULTAD DE AGRONOMIA (MONTEVIDEO). 115

0797-6275 See REVISTA DE LA DIRECCION DE EDUCACION. 1780

0797-6402 See DESLINDES : REVISTA DE LA BIBLIOTECA NACIONAL. 3380

0797-6488 See TEMAS DE COMUNICACION. 1123

0798-0019 See REVISTA DE LA SOCIEDAD BOLIVARIANA. 2758

0798-0035 See FITOPATOLOGIA VENEZOLANA. 510

0798-0841 See CUADERNOS DE ACTUALIDAD INTERNACIONAL. 5197

0798-1147 See POLITICA INTERNACIONAL CARACAS. 4488

0798-1171 See REVISTA DE FILOSOFIA MARACAIBO. 4359

0798-1945 See LATINAMERICAN FORESTRY BIBLIOGRAPHY / INSTITUTO FORESTAL LATINOAMERICANO. 2386

0798-4618 See BOLETIN DERMATOLOGIA SANITARIO. 3718

0800-0638 See EUROPE'S 15,000 LARGEST COMPANIES DIE 15,000 GROSSTEN UNTERNEHMEN EUROPAS LES 15,000 PLUS GRANDES SOCIETES DE L'EUROPE. 673

0800-0735 See MENNESKER OG RETTIGHETER. 4510

0800-0980 See FAGINFO. 83

0800-1235 See ELSKAPER. 5449

0800-1464 See Z (OSLO, NORWAY). 4080

0800-2045 See DERAP WORKING PAPERS. 2821

0800-2355 See DNC OIL NOW. 4254

0800-2843 See LNNSSTATISTIKK FOR ANSATTE I SKOLEVERKET. 1866

0800-3076 See NORSK LINGVISTISK TIDSSKRIFT : NLT. 3306

0800-3173 See KAPITAL DATA. 688

0800-336X See NYTT NORSK TIDSSKRIFT. 4485

0800-3831 See ACTA BOREALIA. 1351

0800-4072 See LUFTFARTSSTATISTIKK / CIVIL AVIATION STATISTICS NORWAY. 41

0800-4072 See ARSRAPPORT. 12

0800-532X See TEKNISK UKEBLAD. 5165

0800-5419 See HERBA. 2343

0800-5818 See INDUSTRISTATISTIKK. HEFTE 2, VARETALL. 1534

0800-5974 See LANDBRUKS KONOMISK FORUM. 104

0800-6733 See EKSPORT AKTUELT / FRA NORGES EKSPORTRAD. 833

0800-6865 See SOMMERFELTIA. 528

0800-7683 See FACT SHEET (NORWAY. OLJE OG ENERGIDEPARTEMENTET). 4256

0800-8582 See SKOG INDUSTRI. 4239

0800-9805 See NORSK BOKFORTEGNELSE. MUSIKKTRYKK. THE NORWEGIAN NATIONAL BIBLIOGRAPHY / UTARBEIDET VED NORSK MUSIKKSAMLING, UNIVERSITETSBIBLIOTEKET I OSLO. 4142

0801-0056 See FORSIKRINGSSELSKAPER. 2881
0801-1745 See NORSK STATSVITENSKAPELIG TIDSSKRIFT. 4484
0801-1834 See LIVSTEGN. 3300
0801-3128 See THEORETIC PAPERS / INSTITUTE OF MATHEMATICS, UNIVERSITY OF OSLO. 3538
0801-3322 See BETA. 861
0801-3500 See NORMAT. 3524
0801-4914 See INTERNATIONAL CHALLENGES / FROM THE FRIDTJOF NANSEN INSTITUTE. 1450
0801-5236 See PC WORLD NORGE 1987. 1271
0801-5333 See NORSK LANDBRUKSFORSKING. 115
0801-5341 See NORWEGIAN JOURNAL OF AGRICULTURAL SCIENCES. 115
0801-5775 See ICAME JOURNAL / INTERNATIONAL COMPUTER ARCHIVE OF MODERN ENGLISH. 3286
0801-5988 See IT BERGEN. 943
0801-7220 See NORDISK ST-FORUM. 5211
0801-7778 See ARBEIDERHISTORIE. 1651
0801-8324 See ECONOMIC SURVEY / CENTRAL BUREAU OF STATISTICS OF NORWAY. 1485
0801-9282 See COLLEGIUM MEDIEVALE. 2613
0801-9533 See ARSMELDING - NORGES VETERINRHGSKOLE. 5504
0801-9991 See ALDRING OG ELDRE. 5178
0802-0914 See NORSK LANDBRUKSFORSKING. SUPPLEMENT. 115
0802-0957 See NORAGRIC OCCASIONAL PAPERS. SERIES C : DEVELOPMENT AND ENVIRONMENT. 114
0802-1473 See REGIONAL DELIGHET. 3661
0802-3956 See WORKING PAPERS IN LINGUISTICS / UNIVERSITY OF TRONDHEIM. 3333
0802-4618 See N & M. NATUR OG MILJ. 2198
0802-5428 See GLASS & PORSELEN. 2589
0802-6106 See INTERNATIONAL JOURNAL OF APPLIED LINGUISTICS. 3287
0802-7285 See NORSK ANTHROPOLOGISK TIDSSKRIFT. 242
0802-7323 See TERSKEL / MUSEET FOR SAMTIDSKUNST. 366
0802-7870 See LAST OG BUSS. 5418
0802-8532 See ITF RAPPORT / NORGES LANDBRUKSHGSKOLE, INSTITUTT FOR TEKNISKE FAG. 98
0802-8818 See NORD REVY : TIDSSKRIFT FOR REGIONAL UDVIKLING, NAERINGSLIV, MILJOE. 2829
0802-9210 See MELDING / NORGES LANDBRUKSHGSKOLE, INSTITUTT FOR KONOMI OG SAMFUNNSFAG. 107
0802-9474 See EUROIL. 4255
0802-9768 See FAG TIDSSKRIFTET SYKEPLEIEN. 3856
0803-0030 See RAPPORT - CHR. MICHELSENS INSTITUTT, AVDELING FOR SAMFUNNSVITENSKAP OG UTVIKLING. 5214
0803-0103 See STAT & STYRING. 4687
0803-0685 See SUDANIC AFRICA. 2643
0803-2173 See FAGINFO. 83
0803-2866 See MEDDELELSER FRA SKOGFORSK / NORSK INSTITUTT FOR SKOGFORSKNING, INSTITUTT FOR SKOGFAG, NLH. 2387
0803-3293 See VR & KLIMA. 1436
0803-5253 See ACTA PAEDIATRICA (OSLO). 3899
0803-5288 See EUROPEAN JOURNAL OF EXPERIMENTAL MUSCULOSKELETAL RESEARCH. 3804
0803-5326 See ACTA PAEDIATRICA. SUPPLEMENT. 3899
0803-6160 See KUNSTARBOK ART YEARBOOK, NORWAY. 356
0803-7051 See BLOOD PRESSURE. 3699
0803-706X See INTERNATIONAL FORUM OF PSYCHOANALYSIS. 4590
0803-8740 See NORA: NORDIC JOURNAL OF WOMEN'S STUDIES. 5563

0803-9488 See NORDIC JOURNAL OF PSYCHIATRY. 3931
0803-9496 See NORDIC JOURNAL OF PSYCHIATRY. SUPPLEMENT. 3932
0804-4643 See EUROPEAN JOURNAL OF ENDOCRINOLOGY / EUROPEAN FEDERATION OF ENDOCRINE SOCIETIES. 3730
0810-0039 See ESTIMATED RESIDENT POPULATION BY SEX AND AGE, STATES AND TERRITORIES OF AUSTRALIA. 4552
0810-0187 See STREET MACHINE SYDNEY. 5393
0810-042X See NEWS LETTER - LIBRARIANS' CHRISTIAN FELLOWSHIP OF AUSTRALIA. 3234
0810-056X See VICTORIAN TEACHER. 1908
0810-0713 See AUSTRALIAN JOURNAL OF CLINICAL HYPNOTHERAPY AND HYPNOSIS, THE. 2857
0810-0926 See NEWSLETTER - SOUTH AUSTRALIAN ADVISORY COMMITTEE ON LIBRARY SERVICES TO THE DISABLED. 3236
0810-1434 See SOFT TECHNOLOGY. 1957
0810-1868 See AUSTRALIAN JOURNAL OF HISTORICAL ARCHAEOLOGY, THE. 260
0810-1906 See AUSTRALIAN-CANADIAN STUDIES. 2722
0810-2465 See DAWSONS LOCAL PINK PAGES. RYDE, HUNTERS HILL. 1925
0810-249X See TV WEEK MELBOURNE. 1142
0810-2627 See CATEGORY B. 1731
0810-2643 See DAWSONS LOCAL PINK PAGES. HILLS DISTRICT. 1924
0810-2686 See AUSTRALIAN JOURNALISM REVIEW : AJR. 2917
0810-3011 See UPDATED ECONOMICS. 1525
0810-3240 See BSES BULLETIN. 165
0810-4123 See AUSTRALASIAN DRAMA STUDIES. 5361
0810-4670 See DAWSON'S LOCAL PINK PAGES. EASTERN SUBURBS. 1924
0810-4689 See DAWSON'S LOCAL PINK PAGES. NORTHERN DISTRICTS. 1924
0810-5200 See SINATRA INTERNATIONAL. 435
0810-5343 See AUSTRALIAN HISTORICAL BIBLIOGRAPHY. BROADSHEET. 2668
0810-5391 See ACCOUNTING AND FINANCE PARKVILLE. 736
0810-5499 See AUSTRALIAN INCOME TAX LEGISLATION IN 2 VOLUMES. 2. REGULATIONS, RATING ACTS, INTERNATIONAL AGREEMENTS, OTHER LEGISLATION. 4712
0810-5669 See LOCAL GOVERNMENT ENGINEERS ASSOCIATION OF NEW SOUTH WALES JOURNAL. 1985
0810-574X See TEXTILE & APPAREL MANUFACTURER. 1087
0810-5766 See OCCASIONAL PAPER SERIES - FISHERIES AND WILDLIFE DIVISION, MINISTRY FOR CONSERVATION. 2201
0810-5774 See TECHNICAL REPORT SERIES / ARTHUR RYLAH INSTITUTE FOR ENVIRONMENTAL RESEARCH. 2206
0810-588X See FIELD GUIDE - GEOLOGICAL SOCIETY OF AUSTRALIA (INC.), SPECIALIST GROUP IN TECTONICS AND STRUCTURAL GEOLOGY. 1375
0810-5928 See AUSTRALASIAN SPORTING SHOOTER. 4884
0810-6029 See DESIGN WORLD. 297
0810-6118 See ABTEE. 1125
0810-6185 See GEOLOGICARTOGRAPHY. 2582
0810-6649 See TESOL NEWS. 1907
0810-7211 See QUARTERLY MAGAZINE - MUSIC TEACHERS' ASSOCIATION OF NEW SOUTH WALES. 4148
0810-7440 See NEWS BULLETIN OF THE AUSTRALIAN DENTAL ASSOCIATION. 1331
0810-7491 See AUSTRALIAN HEALTH CARE SYSTEM, THE. 4768
0810-8056 See AMDEL NEWS. 3997
0810-8064 See RAWLINSON'S AUSTRALIAN CONSTRUCTION HANDBOOK. 625

0810-8404 See GROUNDWATER RESEARCH / CSIRO, [DIVISION OF GROUNDWATER RESEARCH]. 5534
0810-8633 See YEAR BOOK, AUSTRALIA. 5346
0810-8749 See TAFE MAGAZINE. 1916
0810-8862 See REPORT / DIVISION OF MINERAL ENGINEERING. 2017
0810-8889 See MEMOIR ... OF THE ASSOCIATION OF AUSTRALASIAN PALAEONTOLOGISTS. 4228
0810-9028 See PROMETHEUS. 3242
0810-9265 See ALISA. AUSTRALIAN LIBRARY AND INFORMATION SCIENCE ABSTRACTS. 3257
0810-9532 See TECHNICAL MEMORANDUM - SUPERVISING SCIENTIST FOR THE ALLIGATOR RIVERS REGION. 5162
0810-9567 See BLAIR'S GUIDE VICTORIA. 5465
0810-9729 See JOURNAL OF PROFESSIONAL LEGAL EDUCATION, THE. 2989
0810-9966 See RESEARCH REPORT - SUPERVISING SCIENTIST FOR THE ALLIGATOR RIVERS REGION. 5147
0811-0026 See PAPERS IN PIDGIN AND CREOLE LINGUISTICS. 3309
0811-0174 See BIBLIOGRAPHY OF EDUCATION THESES IN AUSTRALIA. 1793
0811-0336 See TRANSITION NEWS. 1908
0811-0360 See DAWSON'S LOCAL PINK PAGES. LOWER NORTH SHORE. 1924
0811-0433 See QUATERNARY AUSTRALASIA. 1393
0811-0697 See MODERN BOATING 1980. 594
0811-0727 See ELECTRONICS TODAY INTERNATIONAL. 2050
0811-0913 See BUILDING AND RELATED STATISTICS, TASMANIA. 632
0811-1057 See RURAL EDUCATION REVIEW. 1781
0811-1146 See URBAN POLICY AND RESEARCH. 2838
0811-1359 See LIBRARY BULLETIN - AUSTRALIAN BROADCASTING TRIBUNAL. 3224
0811-2541 See AUSTRALIAN BASKETBALLER. 4885
0811-2622 See SOIL NOTE. 187
0811-2711 See SANA UPDATE NEWSLETTER. 4056
0811-2908 See AUSTRALIAN ABORIGINES IN THE NEWS. GEOGRAPHIC GUIDE TO HEADINGS AND INDEX TO THE CLIPPINGS. 2256
0811-3130 See AURISA NEWS. 2815
0811-3149 See SOUNDS AUSTRALIAN : AUSTRALIAN MUSIC CENTRE JOURNAL. 4154
0811-3165 See AUSTRALIAN EDUCATION DIRECTORY / DEPT. OF EDUCATION AND YOUTH AFFAIRS. 1726
0811-3394 See QUEENSLAND FAMILY HISTORIAN : JOURNAL OF THE QUEENSLAND FAMILY HISTORY SOCIETY, INC. 2469
0811-3653 See BEAGLE : OCCASIONAL PAPERS OF THE TERRITORY MUSEUM OF ARTS AND SCIENCES, THE. 2843
0811-3661 See AUSTRALIAN FAMILY MELBOURNE. 2276
0811-4447 See AGRICULTURAL ECONOMICS BULLETIN (SYDNEY). 49
0811-4498 See ANNUAL REPORT BY THE INSPECTOR-GENERAL IN BANKRUPTCY ON THE OPERATION OF THE BANKRUPTCY ACT 1966. 3138
0811-4536 See SCIENCE POLICY IN THE NETHERLANDS. 5152
0811-4692 See ACFOA NEWS. 4514
0811-479X See DAWSON'S LOCAL PINK PAGES. KU-RING-GAI. 1924
0811-4927 See AUSTRALIAN DATABASE DEVELOPMENT ASSOCIATION NEWSLETTER. 1253
0811-5559 See IBIS LINKS. 2454
0811-5796 See LAW IN CONTEXT (BUNDOORA, VIC.). 2995
0811-5842 See EC NEWS. 1481

0811-5931 See AUSTRALIAN DRILLING. **1966**

0811-6202 *See* AUSTRALIAN JOURNAL OF COMMUNICATION. **1104**

0811-6253 *See* DIRECTORY OF ARTS LIBRARIES AND RESOURCE COLLECTIONS IN AUSTRALIA. **3206**

0811-6318 *See* CANBERRA BULLETIN OF PUBLIC ADMINISTRATION. **4636**

0811-6407 *See* DEFENDER NORTH MELBOURNE. **3179**

0811-6458 *See* FACTS AND FIGURES - NATIONAL COUNCIL OF INDEPENDENT SCHOOLS. **1863**

0811-6636 *See* GUIDE TO ETHNIC MEDIA IN VICTORIA / VICTORIAN ETHNIC AFFAIRS COMMISSION. **2262**

0811-6997 *See* AVA NEWS. **5505**

0811-7179 *See* DOLLY. **1063**

0811-7195 *See* NORTHERN TERRITORY PARENT. **1867**

0811-7225 *See* COMPUTERS AND LAW SYDNEY. **1178**

0811-7276 *See* DAWSON'S LOCAL PINK PAGES. LIVERPOOL. **1924**

0811-8698 *See* HOOFBEATS. **2799**

0811-9023 *See* WORKFORCE. **1719**

0811-9260 *See* AUSTRALIAN INTERNATIONAL LAW NEWS. **3124**

0811-9392 *See* ADDLIS NEWS. **1338**

0811-9511 *See* NEWSLETTER / AUSTRALIAN MAP CIRCLE. **2570**

0812-0056 *See* FIREMAN MELBOURNE, THE. **2290**

0812-0099 *See* AUSTRALIAN JOURNAL OF EARTH SCIENCES. **1351**

0812-0102 *See* DIVERSITY EAST MELBOURNE. **5244**

0812-0293 *See* MINFO. **2145**

0812-0676 *See* ATF BACKGROUND NOTES. **1888**

0812-0803 *See* NEWSLETTER - AUSTRALIAN COMPARATIVE AND INTERNATIONAL EDUCATION SOCIETY. **1768**

0812-1176 *See* DAWSON'S LOCAL PINK PAGES. BLACKTOWN. **1924**

0812-129X *See* AUSTRALIAN INVESTOR. **641**

0812-1435 *See* ITATE JOURNAL. **1897**

0812-1494 *See* CAPITAL NEWS. **4107**

0812-1567 *See* REVIEW BULLETIN. **3246**

0812-1664 *See* RESEARCH REPORT OR OCCASIONAL PAPER / THE UNIVERSITY OF NEWCASTLE, DEPARTMENT OF ECONOMICS. **1517**

0812-1710 *See* READING AROUND SERIES. **1777**

0812-2016 *See* RADIO AND TELEVISION BROADCASTING STATIONS. **1137**

0812-2024 *See* INTELLECTUAL PROPERTY REPORTS. **1305**

0812-2237 *See* DIVISION OF WILDLIFE AND RANGELANDS RESEARCH TECHNICAL PAPER. **2191**

0812-2253 *See* GEOTECTURE. **1381**

0812-2598 *See* LIVESTOCK AND LIVESTOCK PRODUCTS, AUSTRALIA. **154**

0812-2660 *See* RESEARCH REPORT ... / DIVISION OF MANUFACTURING TECHNOLOGY, COMMONWEALTH SCIENTIFIC AND INDUSTRIAL RESEARCH ORGANIZATION. **3487**

0812-2792 *See* AUSTRALIAN FOREST INDUSTRIES JOURNAL (1982). **2375**

0812-3314 *See* TRANSACTIONS OF THE INSTITUTION OF ENGINEERS, AUSTRALIA. MULTI-DISCIPLINARY ENGINEERING. **1999**

0812-339X *See* BIENNIAL REPORT / CSIRO, DIVISION OF RADIOPHYSICS. **4398**

0812-3837 *See* AUSTRALIAN ADVERSE DRUG REACTIONS BULLETIN. **1341**

0812-3896 *See* AUSTRALASIAN HEALTH AND HEALING. **2596**

0812-3985 *See* EXPLORATION GEOPHYSICS (MELBOURNE). **4402**

0812-4086 *See* CRUISING HELMSMAN. **593**

0812-4353 *See* AUSTRALIAN EVANGEL. **4937**

0812-4930 *See* RANGE MANAGEMENT NEWSLETTER. **124**

0812-5074 See CONSUMER ACTION CANBERRA. **1294**

0812-5643 *See* DAWSON'S LOCAL PINK PAGES. FAIRFIELD. **1924**

0812-566X *See* ANNUAL REPORT / VICTORIAN ETHNIC AFFAIRS COMMISSION. **4630**

0812-6119 *See* TECH TEACHER. **1907**

0812-6755 *See* ARCHEION : THE NEWSLETTER OF THE STATE ARCHIVES. **2479**

0812-695X *See* AUSTRALIAN TAX FORUM. **4712**

0812-7050 *See* DAWSON'S LOCAL PINK PAGES. MANLY-WARRINGAH. **1924**

0812-7158 *See* ARTISAN MELBOURNE. **5192**

0812-7301 *See* SALAC SIGNAL. **3247**

0812-7352 *See* RIVERINA LIBRARY REVIEW. **3247**

0812-7387 *See* RECORDS OF THE AUSTRALIAN MUSEUM. SUPPLEMENT. **5596**

0812-7735 *See* STREAMLINE UPDATE / DEPARTMENT OF RESOURCES AND ENERGY. **5540**

0812-8308 *See* SPORT HEALTH. **3956**

0812-8383 *See* AGORA NORWOOD. **3188**

0812-8405 *See* BLACK VOICES. **232**

0812-857X *See* AUSTRALIAN MINING AND PETROLEUM LAW ASSOCIATION YEARBOOK. **2939**

0812-8901 *See* RISK MEASUREMENT SERVICE KENSINGTON. **885**

0812-9126 *See* BREAK THROUGH CAMPSIE. **3197**

0812-9258 *See* NUCOS [MICROFORM] : NATIONAL UNION CATALOGUE OF SERIALS HELD IN AUSTRALIAN LIBRARIES. **3237**

0812-9304 *See* INFORUM. **3857**

0812-9495 *See* AUSTRALIAN GARDEN JOURNAL, THE. **2409**

0812-9746 *See* EDUCATIONAL ADMINISTRATION REVIEW. **1863**

0813-006X *See* BADMINTON SIDELINES. **4886**

0813-0183 *See* INTERNATIONAL JOURNAL OF MANAGEMENT. **871**

0813-0272 *See* QUALITY AUSTRALIA. **883**

0813-0426 *See* ROCK ART RESEARCH. **281**

0813-0523 *See* AUSTRALIAN SEA HERITAGE. **2611**

0813-0531 *See* AUSTRALIAN JOURNAL OF ADVANCED NURSING. **3852**

0813-0876 *See* AUSTRALIAN AVIATION. **12**

0813-1139 *See* CASH MANAGEMENT TRUSTS, AUSTRALIA. **727**

0813-1600 *See* CINEDOSSIER. **4066**

0813-1643 *See* IMVS NEWSLETTER / PREPARED BY THE STAFF OF THE INSTITUTE OF MEDICAL AND VETERINARY SCIENCE. **5511**

0813-1767 *See* NEWSLETTER - AUSTRALIAN COAL ASSOCIATION. **2147**

0813-1988 *See* SPUMS JOURNAL. **3642**

0813-2127 *See* ANNUAL REPORT - SOUTH AUSTRALIAN CHAMBER OF MINES INCORPORATED. **2134**

0813-2283 *See* ACHPER NATIONAL JOURNAL [MICROFORM], THE. **2595**

0813-2364 *See* AUSTRALIAN PRISONERS. **3078**

0813-2577 *See* SPORTING TRADITIONS. **4922**

0813-2844 *See* ASIA TODAY. **640**

0813-300X *See* ENVIRONMENTAL AND PLANNING LAW JOURNAL. **3111**

0813-3107 *See* BIBLIOGRAPHY (AUSTRALIA. PARLIAMENT). **4696**

0813-3425 *See* ARTS AND EDUCATION. **1726**

0813-3514 *See* AUSTRALIAN PETROLEUM SERVICES INDEX. **4283**

0813-4030 *See* DAWSON'S LOCAL PINK PAGES. PARRAMATTA AND HOLROYD. **1925**

0813-4049 *See* DAWSON'S LOCAL PINK PAGES. CRONULLA-SUTHERLAND. **1924**

0813-4057 *See* DAWSON'S LOCAL PINK PAGES. BANKSTOWN. **1924**

0813-4472 *See* WORKING PAPER - UNIVERSITY OF NEWCASTLE, FACULTY OF MEDICINE. **3651**

0813-4537 *See* AUSTRALIAN DISABILITY REVIEW. **4384**

0813-4758 See INFORMATION TECHNOLOGY INDEX. **1188**

0813-4820 *See* INDONESIAN STUDIES. **5203**

0813-4839 *See* BEHAVIOUR CHANGE. **4577**

0813-5215 *See* ENERGY ALTERNATIVES. **1938**

0813-5363 *See* EQUAL OPPORTUNITY NEWSLETTER. **1744**

0813-5444 *See* VIRUS INFORMATION EXCHANGE NEWSLETTER FOR SOUTH-EAST ASIA AND THE WESTERN PACIFIC. **571**

0813-5452 See ASIA-PACIFIC DEFENCE REPORTER ANNUAL REFERENCE EDITION. **4037**

0813-5886 *See* OUTRIDER (INDOOROOPILLY, QLD.). **3421**

0813-6270 *See* ACT NEWSLETTER - SOCIETY FOR COMPUTERS AND THE LAW, A.C.T. **2927**

0813-6394 *See* VICTORIAN BRANCH NEWS. **3650**

0813-6580 *See* TEACHER HOBART. **1786**

0813-6939 *See* IMPART. **3214**

0813-7099 See INFORMATION MANAGEMENT & COMPUTER SECURITY. **1188**

0813-7455 *See* JOBSON'S QUARTERLY. **685**

0813-7471 *See* HOSPITAL & HEALTHCARE AUSTRALIA. **3783**

0813-751X *See* BMR RESEARCH NEWSLETTER. **1352**

0813-779X *See* ADMINISTRATIVE APPEALS REPORTS. **4624**

0813-7846 *See* PIED PIPER. **1068**

0813-7978 *See* HOUSING QUEENSLAND. **2825**

0813-8095 *See* AUSTRALIAN ARTIST. **343**

0813-8206 *See* QUEENSLAND TEACHERS PROFESSIONAL MAGAZINE. **1903**

0813-8230 *See* PROCEEDINGS OF THE NEW SOUTH WALES SOCIETY FOR COMPUTERS AND THE LAW. **3031**

0813-8389 *See* COMMONWEALTH OF AUSTRALIA GAZETTE. TARIFF CONCESSIONS. **829**

0813-8990 *See* LILITH (FITZROY, VIC.). **5560**

0813-9008 *See* INTERNATIONAL CLINICAL NUTRITION REVIEW. **4192**

0813-9423 *See* ECTACOM. **1487**

0813-9474 *See* NATIONAL ECONOMIC REVIEW. **1507**

0813-9733 *See* WORKING PAPERS OF THE JAPANESE STUDIES CENTRE. **2668**

0813-9741 *See* NATIONAL LEGAL EAGLE. **3013**

0814-0626 *See* AUSTRALIAN JOURNAL OF ENVIRONMENTAL EDUCATION. **1726**

0814-0936 *See* AUSTRALIAN ORTHOPTIC JOURNAL. **3872**

0814-0960 *See* NSW JOURNAL OF SPECIAL EDUCATION. **1883**

0814-1185 *See* INSIDE INDONESIA. **2505**

0814-1231 *See* ADMIN REVIEW. **4624**

0814-1770 *See* DAWSON'S LOCAL PINK PAGES. PENRITH AND LOWER BLUE MOUNTAINS. **1925**

0814-1819 *See* OCCASIONAL PAPERS FROM THE MUSEUM OF VICTORIA. **4169**

0814-2025 *See* SAM. SUBSTANCE ABUSE MONTHLY. **1348**

0814-2262 *See* BOARD OF THE SOUTH AUSTRALIAN MUSEUM ANNUAL REPORT. **4085**

0814-2513 *See* CLASS RACEHORSES OF AUSTRALIA AND NEW ZEALAND. **2798**

0814-2912 *See* AUSTRALIAN BANKER. **773**

0814-3021 *See* QUEENSLAND ARCHAEOLOGICAL RESEARCH. **280**

0814-303X *See* ISSUES BRISBANE. **1755**

0814-334X *See* SCHOOL LIBRARY FORUM. **3248**

0814-3595 *See* BIENNIAL REPORT / GLEN INNES AGRICULTURAL RESEARCH AND ADVISORY STATION. **66**

0814-3641 See CURRICULUM CONCERNS : NEWSLETTER OF ACSA. 1734

0814-3668 See AUSTRALIAN TABLE TENNIS. 4885

0814-3757 See MELBOURNE PSYCHOLOGY MONOGRAPHS. 4603

0814-3811 See ASPBAE COURIER. 1799

0814-401X See COMMUNITY QUARTERLY. 2818

0814-4133 See ACIAR FOOD LEGUME NEWSLETTER. 42

0814-4273 See BUSINESS COUNCIL BULLETIN. 646

0814-4370 See AUSTRALIA'S POPULATION TRENDS AND PROSPECTS. 4549

0814-4540 See TOWN AND COUNTRY FARMER. 142

0814-4680 See TREES AND NATURAL RESOURCES. 2207

0814-4788 See LAW HANDBOOK - REDFERN LEGAL CENTRE. 2995

0814-4834 See INTERCHANGE SYDNEY. 1801

0814-5105 See POVERTY LINES AUSTRALIA. 5213

0814-5180 See ABLATIVE. 636

0814-5539 See LIB TEC. 3223

0814-5571 See SCHOOL MANAGEMENT SYSTEMS NEWSLETTER. 1871

0814-5628 See AUSTRALIAN JOURNAL OF ASTRONOMY. 393

0814-5725 See JOURNAL OF THE AUSTRALIAN POPULATION ASSOCIATION. 4554

0814-5806 See INSIDE DINING. 5071

0814-5857 See MUSICOLOGY AUSTRALIA. 4137

0814-6039 See ACOUSTICS AUSTRALIA / AUSTRALIAN ACOUSTICAL SOCIETY. 4452

0814-673X See AUSTRALIAN JOURNAL OF EDUCATIONAL TECHNOLOGY. 1810

0814-6764 See EX NIHILO TECHNICAL JOURNAL. 4958

0814-6802 See EDUCATION LINKS. 1740

0814-6942 See AD NEWS SURRY HILLS. 753

0814-7094 See PROSPECT ADELAIDE. 1802

0814-723X See AUSTRALIAN AND NEW ZEALAND JOURNAL OF FAMILY THERAPY, THE. 2276

0814-7477 See REPORT - NORTHERN TERRITORY GEOLOGICAL SURVEY, DEPARTMENT OF MINES AND ENERGY. 1394

0814-7752 See COACHING DIRECTOR. 4890

0814-7973 See OCCASIONAL PAPER - SOUTH PACIFIC SMALLHOLDER PROJECT, UNIVERSITY OF NEW ENGLAND. 1509

0814-8074 See CHARTAC ACCOUNTANCY NEWS. 740

0814-8120 See CHARTAC TAX PLANNING NEWS. 740

0814-8155 See DEATHS, TASMANIA. 4561

0814-8392 See SCHOOL LIBRARY NEWS. 3248

0814-8589 See AUSTRALIAN BAR REVIEW. 2938

0814-8805 See METAPHYSICAL REVIEW, THE. 3411

0814-9046 See AUSTRALIAN INTELLECTUAL PROPERTY CASES. 2938

0814-9054 See AUSTRALIAN TORTS REPORTS. 2939

0814-9127 See CHILDREN IN HOSPITAL. 4580

0814-9267 See WHEAT AUSTRALIA INTERNATIONAL. 191

0814-9283 See HANDBOOK / THE DEPARTMENT OF TECHNICAL AND FURTHER EDUCATION OF SOUTH AUSTRALIA. 1749

0814-9763 See AUSTRALIAN AND NEW ZEALAND JOURNAL OF OPHTHALMOLOGY. 3872

0814-9879 See NATIONAL DIRECTORY OF TRANSLATORS, INTERPRETERS AND LANGUAGE AIDES. 3305

0814-9992 See RESEARCH REVIEW / DIVISION OF CHEMICAL AND WOOD TECHNOLOGY. 991

0815-0249 See NUCLEAR SPECTRUM. 2157

0815-032X See FEDERAL GOVERNMENT, THE. 2669

0815-0494 See ACQUISITIONS ULTIMO. 3187

0815-0575 See AUSTRALIAN ENERGY RESEARCH. 1933

0815-0753 See WISENET. 5568

0815-0796 See METASCIENCE. 5128

0815-1318 See TOURISTICS. 5494

0815-2063 See ENCORE MANLY. 4068

0815-208X See AUSTRALIAN DRIED FRUITS NEWS. 2328

0815-2195 See PLANT PROTECTION QUARTERLY. 120

0815-2276 See INDEPENDENT LIVING. 4389

0815-2357 See TECHNICAL REPORT SERIES (VICTORIA. DEPT. OF AGRICULTURE AND RURAL AFFAIRS). 140

0815-3094 See RELIGIOUS EDUCATION JOURNAL OF AUSTRALIA. 1777

0815-3132 See VICTORIAN REAL ESTATE JOURNAL. 4848

0815-3191 See AUSTRALASIAN PLANT PATHOLOGY. 500

0815-3701 See AUSTRALIAN TAFE TEACHER. 1911

0815-3922 See FAMILY HISTORY FOR BEGINNERS. 2447

0815-4112 See FLOWER LINK. 2448

0815-4384 See MARKETING LETTER MILSONS POINT. 931

0815-4465 See LANDSCOPE. 2197

0815-4473 See INDEPENDENT REPORTER JOLIMONT. 1751

0815-4902 See FOCUS AUSTRALIA. 2669

0815-5232 See DIRECTORY OF AUSTRALIAN COMPOSERS. 4114

0815-5615 See MEDIA PEOPLE (N.S.W./A.C.T. ED.). 1125

0815-5992 See ADELAIDE REVIEW. 312

0815-6050 See BUILDING AND CONSTRUCTION LAW. 602

0815-6409 See JOURNAL OF OCCUPATIONAL HEALTH AND SAFETY, AUSTRALIA AND NEW ZEALAND, THE. 2864

0815-6514 See POTATO GROWER. 182

0815-676X See MEAT RESEARCH NEWSLETTER. 215

0815-6816 See PELANGI TOOWOOMBA. 5212

0815-6883 See COAL JOURNAL. 2137

0815-6905 See INFOCUS NEWS MAGAZINE. 2264

0815-7006 See NATURE AND HEALTH. 2600

0815-709X See SURFACE COATINGS AUSTRALIA. 1030

0815-7162 See MISCELLANEOUS BULLETIN (NEW SOUTH WALES. DIVISION OF AGRICULTURAL SERVICES). 108

0815-7235 See NEWSLETTER - EARTH SCIENCES HISTORY GROUP. 1358

0815-7251 See REVIEW OF INDONESIAN AND MALAYSIAN AFFAIRS. 4494

0815-7383 See HYBRID GRAIN SORGHUM YIELD RESULTS. 173

0815-7596 See WORKING PAPER / NATIONAL CENTRE FOR DEVELOPMENT STUDIES, AUSTRALIAN NATIONAL UNIVERSITY. 146

0815-7650 See RESEARCH BULLETIN - DEPARTMENT OF TECHNICAL AND FURTHER EDUCATION SOUTH AUSTRALIA. 1778

0815-8150 See TALENTED. 1849

0815-8398 See BIENNIAL CONFERENCE - AUSTRALIAN & NEW ZEALAND ASSOCIATION OF EDUCATORS OF THE VISUALLY HANDICAPPED. 1889

0815-841X See PLD NEWSLETTER. 3241

0815-8428 See LIBTECH NEWS. 3228

0815-9017 See COMMONWEALTH OF AUSTRALIA GAZETTE. PURCHASING AND DISPOSALS. 949

0815-9068 See HANDBOOK AND CALENDAR - MURDOCH UNIVERSITY 1986. 1827

0815-9319 See JOURNAL OF GASTROENTEROLOGY AND HEPATOLOGY. 3747

0815-936X See QUEENSLAND NURSE, THE. 3867

0815-9424 See DEVELOPMENT DOSSIER. 1918

0815-953X See MEANJIN (PARKVILLE, VIC.). 3410

0815-9564 See FREE TO BE. 1804

0815-9602 See INVESTIGATING. 5116

0816-0376 See NEWSLETTER - AUSTRALIAN PHOTOGRAMMETRIC AND REMOTE SENSING SOCIETY. 1358

0816-0430 See NATIONAL LIQUOR NEWS. 2369

0816-0465 See DEATHS, QUEENSLAND. 4561

0816-0694 See NEWSLETTER - INSTITUTE OF BREWING, AUSTRALIA AND NEW ZEALAND SECTION. 2370

0816-1089 See AUSTRALIAN JOURNAL OF EXPERIMENTAL AGRICULTURE. 64

0816-1224 See INTERDATA FINANCIAL HANDBOOK. 791

0816-1623 See AVPI. AGRICULTURAL AND VETERINARY PRODUCT INDEX. 64

0816-1658 See AUSTRALIAN GEOGRAPHIC : THE JOURNAL OF THE AUSTRALIAN GEOGRAPHIC SOCIETY. 2555

0816-1909 See PHOTO & VIDEO RETAILER. 4372

0816-200X See INFORMAA QUARTERLY. 3215

0816-2018 See AUSTRALIAN JOURNAL OF TAFE RESEARCH AND DEVELOPMENT. 1810

0816-2107 See WORKERS COMPENSATION REPORT. 1719

0816-2735 See SIR ROBERT MADGWICK LECTURE. 1847

0816-2816 See ANNUAL REPORT / THE LIVESTOCK AND MEAT AUTHORITY OF QUEENSLAND. 206

0816-3030 See AUSTRALIAN ADMINISTRATIVE LAW BULLETIN, THE. 2938

0816-3073 See ANNUAL REPORT / DEPARTMENT OF INDUSTRY, TECHNOLOGY AND COMMERCE. 4627

0816-3103 See SA BUILDING WORKER. 1709

0816-3294 See AUSTRALIAN DOLL DIRECTORY. 2771

0816-3391 See PROJECTIONS OF THE POPULATIONS OF AUSTRALIA, STATES AND TERRITORIES. 4559

0816-3405 See LANDFORM. 1386

0816-3596 See AUSTRALASIAN PAINT AND PANEL. 4222

0816-3634 See FOOD MANUFACTURING NEWS. 2338

0816-3669 See AUSTRALIAN PHOTOGRAPHY DIRECTORY. 4367

0816-455X See GOLD GAZETTE. 4003

0816-4622 See CLINICAL AND EXPERIMENTAL OPTOMETRY. 4215

0816-4649 See AUSTRALIAN FEMINIST STUDIES. 5551

0816-4800 See LAW JOURNAL / QUEENSLAND INSTITUTE OF TECHNOLOGY. 2995

0816-486X See ANIMAL LIBERATION ACTION. 225

0816-4991 See COUNCIL PAPER - ECONOMIC PLANNING ADVISORY COUNCIL. 1472

0816-5122 See AUSTRALIAN EDUCATIONAL AND DEVELOPMENTAL PSYCHOLOGIST. 4575

0816-5165 See ISLANDS/AUSTRALIA WORKING PAPERS. 2910

0816-5173 See RURAL DEVELOPMENT WORKING PAPER / NATIONAL CENTRE FOR DEVELOPMENT STUDIES, THE AUSTRALIAN NATIONAL UNIVERSITY. 1582

0816-5181 See WORKING PAPERS IN TRADE AND DEVELOPMENT. 2913

0816-5432 See SPUNTI E RICERCHE. 3439

0816-5947 See FURNISHING FLOORS. DOMESTIC AND CONTRACT. 2905

0816-6048 See PERSONAL FINANCE, AUSTRALIA. 732

0816-6234 See OCCASIONAL PAPER - AUSTRALIAN GEOSCIENCE INFORMATION ASSOCIATION. 1359

0816-6617 See BULLETIN OF THE CENTRE FOR TASMANIAN HISTORICAL STUDIES. 2612

0816-6757 See TECHNICAL REPORT (WESTERN AUSTRALIA. DEPT. OF CONSERVATION AND LAND MANAGEMENT). 2207

0816-6919 See FREMANTLE ARTS REVIEW. 320

ISSN Index

0816-7095 See SRI LANKA HUMAN RIGHTS BULLETIN. 4513

0816-7249 See TAFE NSW HANDBOOK. 1916

0816-780X See CONTRIBUTIONS OF THE ECONOMIC GEOLOGY RESEARCH UNIT. 1372

0816-7923 See ACIAR TECHNICAL REPORTS SERIES. 43

0816-8059 See NEWSLETTER - SCHOOL OF MEDICAL EDUCATION, UNIVERSITY OF NEW SOUTH WALES. 3621

0816-8741 See NUDE PACIFIC TRAVEL GUIDE. 5486

0816-8792 See CORDELL'S BUILDING COST GUIDE. HOUSING, NEW CONSTRUCTION. QUEENSLAND. 611

0816-8806 See CORDELL'S BUILDING COST GUIDE. HOUSING, NEW CONSTRUCTION. VICTORIA. 611

0816-8822 See CORDELL'S BUILDING COST GUIDE. HOUSING, NEW CONSTRUCTION. NEW SOUTH WALES. 611

0816-8830 See CORDELL'S BUILDING COST GUIDE. COMMERCIAL AND INDUSTRIAL. VICTORIA. 611

0816-8865 See CORDELL'S BUILDING COST GUIDE. COMMERCIAL AND INDUSTRIAL. QUEENSLAND. 611

0816-8903 See CORDELL'S BUILDING COST GUIDE. COMMERCIAL AND INDUSTRIAL. NEW SOUTH WALES. 611

0816-9020 See AUSTRALIAN EDUCATIONAL COMPUTING. 1222

0816-9128 See SURVEY OF MANUFACTURING CONDITIONS AND FUTURE PROSPECTS IN N.S.W. 3488

0816-9330 See AUDIOVISION AND PROSOUND. 5315

0816-9349 See PRIME NUMBER. 3527

0816-9411 See REPORT - COAL CORPORATION OF VICTORIA. 2149

0816-956X See ONLINE CURRENTS. 3239

0816-9837 See TRIPLE A. 815

0816-990X See RENAL EDUCATOR. 3992

0817-0088 See MAGPIES. 3409

0817-0576 See CSIRO DIVISION OF ATMOSPHERIC RESEARCH RESEARCH REPORT. 1424

0817-072X See TECHNICAL COMPUTING (ALEXANDRIA). 1204

0817-1440 See DATASPORT. 4892

0817-1866 See AUSTRALIAN ANTARCTIC AND SUB-ANTARCTIC RESEARCH PROGRAMMES ... COMMENTS ON CURRENT ACTIVITIES AND ... PROPOSED PROGRAMMES / AUSTRALIAN ACADEMY OF SCIENCE, NATIONAL COMMITTEE FOR ANTARCTIC RESEARCH. 1402

0817-1947 See BIENNIAL REPORT / CSIRO DIVISION OF GEOMECHANICS. 1367

0817-2048 See AUSTRALIAN SOCIETY FOR SPORTS HISTORY BULLETIN. 4885

0817-2455 See YOUR PHARMACY. 4333

0817-2773 See SAILBOARD EXTRA. 4916

0817-2935 See TRAVEL AUSTRALIA SYDNEY. 5495

0817-3192 See AUSTRALIA'S TOP 500 COMPANIES. 726

0817-3532 See FREEDOM OF INFORMATION REVIEW. 3179

0817-3907 See AUSTRALIAN MEDICAL RECORD JOURNAL / MEDICAL RECORD ASSOCIATION OF AUSTRALIA. 3777

0817-4113 See AUSTRALIAN ENERGY MANAGEMENT NEWS. 1933

0817-4148 See GIPPSLAND WRITER. 3463

0817-4210 See CORDELL'S BUILDING COST GUIDE. COMMERCIAL, INDUSTRIAL AND HOUSING. WESTERN AUSTRALIA. 611

0817-4245 See ANNUAL REPORT / SOIL CONSERVATION SERVICE OF NSW. 163

0817-4474 See AMBULANCE WORLD (1986). 3723

0817-4792 See EXCEL. 3954

0817-4997 See BIENNIAL RESEARCH REPORT (INSTITUTE OF ENERGY AND EARTH RESOURCES (AUSTRALIA). DIVISION OF MINERAL CHEMISTRY). 1352

0817-5748 See WING SPAN (MOONEE PONDS). 5621

0817-5764 See SMALL BUSINESS IN WESTERN AUSTRALIA. 711

0817-5810 See STAFF DEVELOPMENT IN AUSTRALIAN LIBRARIES. 3251

0817-5837 See COMCISE. 1470

0817-6043 See POWER EQUIPMENT AUSTRALASIA. 2124

0817-6191 See LIPSCOMBE REPORT. 1949

0817-6213 See PACIFIC COMPUTER WEEKLY. 1198

0817-623X See AUSTRALIAN JOURNAL OF FAMILY LAW. 3119

0817-6337 See AUSTRALIAN PLUMBING INDUSTRY MAGAZINE. 2603

0817-6353 See WHO'S PEGGING. 4282

0817-637X See COSMETICS AEROSOLS & TOILETRIES IN AUSTRALIA. 403

0817-654X See AUSTRALIAN GOLD, GEM AND TREASURE MAGAZINE. 3998

0817-6604 See AUSTRALIAN CROQUET GAZETTE. 4885

0817-685X See COMMODITY STATISTICAL BULLETIN. 75

0817-6922 See NEUE HEIMAT UND WELT. 5777

0817-7066 See GAZETTE - LAW SOCIETY OF THE AUSTRALIAN CAPITAL TERRITORY. 2973

0817-7686 See HORSE MAGAZINE. 2799

0817-8038 See PACIFIC ECONOMIC BULLETIN. 1511

0817-8542 See TRENDS AND ISSUES IN CRIME AND CRIMINAL JUSTICE. 3178

0817-8550 See AUSTRALIAN STOCK HORSE JOURNAL. 2797

0817-8798 See LABOUR STUDIES BRIEFING. 4528

0817-9263 See AUSTRALIAN PETROLEUM ACCUMULATIONS REPORT / DEPARTMENT OF RESOURCES AND ENERGY, BUREAU OF MINERAL RESOURCES, GEOLOGY AND GEOPHYSICS. 4251

0817-9344 See INFORMATION PAPER - AUSTRALIAN BUREAU OF STATISTICS. 1926

0817-9573 See AUSTRALIAN PRIMATOLOGY. 5577

0817-9646 See AUSTRALIAN JOURNAL OF MINING. 2134

0817-9751 See UNITED NATIONS REVIEW. 4537

0818-0032 See MONASH PUBLICATIONS IN HISTORY. 2623

0818-0148 See GAZETTE OF LAW AND JOURNALISM. 2973

0818-0164 See INVERTEBRATE TAXONOMY. 5587

0818-0210 See PADDLE POWER. 4877

0818-0261 See AUSTRALIAN WOODWORKER. 633

0818-027X See FARM SURVEYS REPORT. 85

0818-044X See TRADE PRACTICES COMMISSION BULLETIN. 3065

0818-0555 See SING OUT EAST DONCASTER. 4153

0818-0563 See INTERNATIONAL JOURNAL OF EDUCOLOGY. 1754

0818-0628 See TIME AUSTRALIA. 2511

0818-0687 See DIRECTORY OF TERTIARY EXTERNAL COURSES IN AUSTRALIA. 1736

0818-1128 See POWDERHOUND SKI MAGAZINE'S NEW ZEALAND SKI GUIDE. 4913

0818-1624 See PACIFIC NEWS BULLETIN. 2511

0818-1713 See RURAL UPDATE. 131

0818-1748 See COMPUTER DOWNLOAD. 1222

0818-2019 See ACT SCIENCE TEACHER. 1887

0818-206X See PROFESSIONAL NEWS. 1805

0818-2507 See AV UPDATE. 3193

0818-304X See NOTES ON PURE MATHEMATICS. 3525

0818-3236 See S.A. LAW LIBRARIANS BULLETIN. 3247

0818-3279 See QUEENSLAND STUDIES IN GERMAN LANGUAGE AND LITERATURE. 3313

0818-3317 See SCAN : SUMMARISING CONTEXTS, ACTION AND NETWORKS. 1710

0818-3473 See FINE LINE. 3388

0818-3597 See MATERIALS AUSTRALIA. 4008

0818-3856 See REGISTER OF COMMONWEALTH STATISTICAL COLLECTIONS. 423

0818-4445 See PRESCRIPTION PRODUCTS GUIDE. 4325

0818-4968 See MINERAL POLICY ISSUES OCCASIONAL PAPER. 4012

0818-5077 See GOLF AUSTRALIA. 4896

0818-5204 See TRANSIT AUSTRALIA. 5395

0818-5522 See AUSTASIA AQUACULTURE MAGAZINE. 2296

0818-5670 See ENVIRONMENTAL HEALTH REVIEW, AUSTRALIA : THE OFFICIAL JOURNAL OF THE AUSTRALIAN INSTITUTE OF ENVIRONMENTAL HEALTH. 2167

0818-6286 See INTERACTION (CANBERRA, A.C.T.). 1880

0818-6510 See AUSTRALIAN ORIENTEER JAMISON. 4885

0818-6561 See PASTRYCOOKS AND BAKERS NEWS MONTHLY. 2353

0818-710X See PERIOD HOME RENOVATOR BUYER'S GUIDE. 2907

0818-7339 See CORNSTALK GAZETTE. 384

0818-8114 See PARENT'S SAY. 1772

0818-8149 See AUSTRALIAN SLAVONIC AND EAST EUROPEAN STUDIES : JOURNAL OF THE AUSTRALIAN AND NEW ZEALAND SLAVISTS' ASSOCIATION AND OF THE AUSTRALASIAN ASSOCIATION FOR STUDY OF THE SOCIALIST COUNTRIES. 3267

0818-8203 See AUSTRALIAN GOAT FARMER. 206

0818-8238 See MULGA RESEARCH CENTRE JOURNAL. 41

0818-8491 See ELECTRIC VEHICLE NEWS MELBOURNE. 5414

0818-8653 See BRIEFS/ BREAD RESEARCH INSTITUTE OF AUSTRALIA. 2329

0818-8726 See BIENNIAL REPORT / AGRICULTURAL RESEARCH AND ADVISORY STATION, CONDOBOLIN. 66

0818-8823 See MULTICULTURALISM IN EDUCATION NEWSLETTER. 1765

0818-9056 See DANDENONG VALLEY LIBRARIES REPORTER. 3205

0818-9110 See AUSTRALIAN GEOMECHANICS. 2101

0818-9307 See AUSTRALIAN SKIING SURRY HILLS. 4885

0818-9382 See BULLETIN - UNIVERSITY OF MELBOURNE GALLERY SOCIETY AND THE DEPARTMENT OF FINE ARTS. 346

0818-9641 See IMMUNOLOGY AND CELL BIOLOGY. 3671

0818-9757 See ASPESA PAPERS. 1726

0818-9935 See ASIAN-PACIFIC ECONOMIC LITERATURE. 1530

0819-0283 See RSI STUDENT NEWSLETTER. 1709

0819-0615 See JOURNAL / AUSTRALIAN JEWISH HISTORICAL SOCIETY. 2265

0819-0739 See BLAST MANUKA. 2510

0819-0852 See AUSTRALIAN FOLKLORE. 2318

0819-0887 See AUSTRALIAN PROSTHODONTIC JOURNAL. 1317

0819-0933 See FOREIGN TRADE, AUSTRALIA. MERCHANDISE EXPORTS / AUSTRALIAN BUREAU OF STATISTICS. 729

0819-1212 See LOCAL GOVERNMENT MANAGEMENT. 4662

0819-1530 See CREATION EX NIHILO. 4951

0819-1816 See NEWSLETTER - STATE LIBRARY OF TASMANIA 1986. 3236

0819-1824 See N.S.W. MASTER PLUMBER. 2607

0819-2642 See RESEARCH PAPER - UNIVERSITY OF MELBOURNE, DEPARTMENT OF ECONOMICS. 1517

0819-2839 See FOREIGN TRADE, AUSTRALIA. MERCHANDISE IMPORTS / AUSTRALIAN BUREAU OF STATISTICS. 729

ISSN Index

0819-3363 *See* AUSTRALASIAN CYCLING AND TRIATHLON NEWS. 4884

0819-341X *See* AUSTRALIAN SUPER REVIEW. 773

0819-3592 *See* MONTHLY RAINFALL REVIEW. AUSTRALIA. 1431

0819-3606 *See* PHOENIX REVIEW. 3423

0819-4262 *See* COMMERCIAL LAW QUARTERLY. 2953

0819-4688 729

0819-470X *See* LOCAL GOVERNMENT FOCUS. 4662

0819-4920 *See* PHRONEMA. 1094

0819-5358 *See* FICTION FOCUS. 3387

0819-5404 *See* RESEARCH STUDY - EXECUTIVE SUPPORT SERVICE, EDUCATION DEPARTMENT OF TASMANIA. 1845

0819-5633 *See* RECORD WARBURTON. 4990

0819-5668 *See* GOOD HEALTH WARBURTON. 2597

0819-6001 *See* BALANCE OF PAYMENTS, AUSTRALIA. REGIONAL SERIES ON MICROFICHE. 4696

0819-6508 *See* AUSTRALIAN MINERALOGIST. 2134

0819-6648 *See* ADBRIEF REGISTER. 754

0819-7091 *See* COMMONWEALTH OF AUSTRALIA GAZETTE. BUSINESS. 658

0819-7105 *See* COMMONWEALTH OF AUSTRALIA GAZETTE. GOVERNMENT NOTICES. 4639

0819-7288 *See* OTIS RUSH. 327

0819-7849 *See* AUSTRALIAN NUTGROWER. 164

0819-7857 *See* ACIAR WORKING PAPER. 43

0819-8632 *See* TURF CRAFT AUST. 4927

0819-8691 *See* HISTORY OF EDUCATION REVIEW. 1750

0819-8756 *See* ANNUAL REPORT FOR THE PERIOD ... / CANCER FOUNDATION OF WESTERN AUSTRALIA INC. 3808

0819-9000 *See* M.O.C.A. BULLETIN. 357

0819-9183 *See* BEHAVIOUR PROBLEMS BULLETIN. 1875

0819-9558 *See* IAAH NEWSLETTER. 4783

0819-9752 *See* QUEENSLAND WRITER. 3427

0819-9817 *See* COMMUNICATION NEWS. 1107

0819-9868 *See* FOREIGN TRADE, AUSTRALIA. MERCHANDISE IMPORTS. DETAILED COMMODITY TABLES. 729

0819-9957 See AUSTRALIAN JOURNAL OF JEWISH STUDIES. 2256

0820-0025 *See* COMMERCE INTERNATIONAL DU QUEBEC. 1633

0820-0084 *See* CONTACT (ST-ANACLET DE LESSARD). 4640

0820-0165 *See* MUSE (OTTAWA). 4091

0820-0165 *See* MUSE (OTTAWA). 4091

0820-0211 *See* WATDOC NEWSLETTER. 5541

0820-0270 *See* ROULEZ SANS VOUS FAIRE ROULER. GUIDE DES VOITURES D'OCCASION. 5424

0820-0386 *See* ANNALES DE L'EXAMEN FINAL UNIFORME / ORDRES DES COMPTABLES AGREES DU CANADA ET DES BERMUDES. 738

0820-0416 *See* MUSIC DIRECTORY CANADA. 4133

0820-0424 *See* SIGNE DE PISTE. 5236

0820-0521 *See* LIBRARY AND INFORMATION SCIENCE UPDATE. 3224

0820-0645 *See* GUIDE MEDIA - CONCORDES. 4897

0820-0653 *See* TAX & TARIFF BULLETIN. 4752

0820-070X *See* PASSE-SPORTS. 4911

0820-0726 *See* LETTRE AFRICAINE, LA. 4528

0820-0750 *See* MICROCOMPUTER APPLICATIONS (ANAHEIM). 1269

0820-0777 *See* PROGRAMME D'ASSOCIE / INSTITUT D'ASSURANCE DU CANADA. 2891

0820-0793 *See* REVUE DE LA SOCIETE HISTORIQUE DU MADAWASKA (1982). 2758

0820-0858 *See* OFFSHORE RESOURCES. 4267

0820-0890 *See* DIRES. 5198

0820-2737 *See* NOVA SCOTIA BUSINESS JOURNAL. 700

0820-2893 *See* HERITAGE LINK. 2690

0820-2931 *See* PARKLAND REGIONAL LIBRARY NEWSLETTER. 3240

0820-3296 *See* CURRENTS / CANADA-ASIA WORKING GROUP. 4507

0820-3334 *See* TELE DES ENFANTS, LA. 1140

0820-3431 *See* NEWS (CANADIAN SOCIETY OF CINEMATOGRAPHERS). 4075

0820-3458 *See* INTERVENOR : NEWSLETTER OF THE CANADIAN ENVIRONMENTAL LAW ASSOCIATION. 3113

0820-3911 *See* NEWSLETTER (MEMORIAL UNIVERSITY OF NEWFOUNDLAND. MARITIME HISTORY GROUP). 5453

0820-3946 *See* CMAJ. CANADIAN MEDICAL ASSOCIATION JOURNAL. 3567

0820-3997 *See* ANNUAL REPORT - LAND RESOURCE SCIENCE. UNIVERSITY OF GUELPH. 163

0820-4217 *See* MC. MENSA CANADA COMMUNICATIONS. 5233

0820-4446 *See* MUNICIPAL & INDUSTRIAL WATER & POLLUTION CONTROL. 2236

0820-4683 *See* STOCKGROWER DIGEST, THE. 222

0820-4799 See HAMILTON LAWYER. 2976

0820-4896 *See* CANADIAN OPERA COMPANY NEWS (1986). 4107

0820-4942 See VIVRE A PIERREFONDS. 2765

0820-4942 See VIVRE A PIERREFONDS. 2549

0820-4969 *See* REVUE VOILE QUEBEC, LA. 595

0820-5000 *See* CARRIEROLOGIE. 1658

0820-5027 See ICI BOUCHERVILLE. 4655

0820-5043 *See* SASK. REPORT. 2545

0820-5086 *See* PLAISANCIERS. 595

0820-5167 *See* GLOBAL ECONOMIC OUTLOOK (TORONTO). 1492

0820-5280 *See* FREIGHTER, THE. 5784

0820-537X *See* ONTARIO LIBRARY SERVICE ESCARPMENT : DIRECTORY. 3239

0820-5450 *See* CADALYST. 1231

0820-5515 *See* QUATRE-TEMPS. 525

0820-5515 *See* QUATRE-TEMPS (MONTREAL). 526

0820-5523 *See* ARDOISE (QUEBEC). 2815

0820-5582 *See* SOUTHERN AFRICA REPORT (TORONTO). 2643

0820-5655 *See* TRUXBOOK. 855

0820-5698 *See* LONDON BUSINESS MONTHLY MAGAZINE. 690

0820-571X *See* WESTERN RIDER (1987). 2803

0820-5728 *See* ACTION - NATIONAL ACTION COMMITTEE ON THE STATUS OF WOMEN. 5550

0820-5752 *See* B. ALLAN MACKIE SCHOOL OF LOG BUILDING. 633

0820-5930 *See* CANADIAN JOURNAL OF MEDICAL RADIATION TECHNOLOGY. 3939

0820-5949 *See* FORUM / THE ASSOCIATION OF CANADIAN FACULTIES OF DENTISTRY. 1323

0820-6066 *See* MANITOBA MODERN LANGUAGE JOURNAL. 3301

0820-6120 *See* PROGRAMME F.I.A.C. 2891

0820-6163 *See* FITNESS BULLETIN, THE. 2597

0820-6260 *See* PC YOUTH TODAY. 4487

0820-6295 *See* ECHO-X. 3941

0820-6309 *See* MISE A JOUR DE LA LISTE DES MEMBRES DU CIEE AU 2699

0820-6333 *See* JE NE VEUX PAS MOURIR A L'ACADEMIE FRANCAISE. 3399

0820-6449 *See* ZUPNI VJESNIK NASE GOSPE KRALJICE HRVATA, TORONTO, HRVATSKIH MUCENIKA, MISSISSAUGA. 5038

0820-6457 *See* SPORTS (COACHING ASSOCIATION OF CANADA : 1980). 1858

0820-6465 *See* MATERNAL HEALTH NEWS. 3764

0820-6503 *See* AVIS MUNICIPAL - VILLE DE CHARNY. 4631

0820-6643 *See* SURETE. 5312

0820-6686 *See* WORLDLIT. 1887

0820-6724 *See* NORTHWEST EXPLORER (YELLOWKNIFE). 2541

0820-6759 *See* INDUSTRIAL PRODUCT IDEAS!. 3481

0820-6813 *See* CANADIAN REINER, THE. 2798

0820-6848 *See* PRAIRIE LANDSCAPE MAGAZINE. 2428

0820-6880 *See* INTERNATIONAL HAIR ROUTE. 3720

0820-6937 *See* MANUSCRIPT LETTERS OR COMMUNIQUES PUBLISHED IN THE ARCHDIOCESE OF OTTAWA. 5032

0820-6945 *See* LETTRES MANUSCRITES OU COMMUNIQUES PUBLIES DANS L'ARCHIDIOCESE D'OTTAWA. 5031

0820-7216 *See* QUEBEC DIMANCHE. 5793

0820-7224 *See* STREET & DIRT. 4083

0820-7240 *See* LAND ECONOMIST. 1502

0820-7283 *See* RENAL FAMILY (ED. FRANCAISE). 3993

0820-7305 *See* INTERNATIONAL PROGRAMS, GENERAL REPORT / CANADIAN TEACHERS' FEDERATION AND ITS MEMBERS. 1897

0820-7313 *See* PHILOCRITIQUE. 4355

0820-7364 *See* NAPO NEWS. 5297

0820-7399 *See* ASSOCIATION MONDIALE DES MEDECINS FRANCOPHONES (1982). 3553

0820-7402 *See* CASAULT FOL. 5781

0820-7429 *See* INFO-R.A.A.Q. 5289

0820-747X *See* COLLECTION ANALYSE DES NOUVEAUX PROGRAMMES. 1891

0820-7488 *See* CESKOSLOVENSKA CESTA 2683

0820-7518 *See* GOELAND (MONTREAL). 5286

0820-7526 *See* NOTRE PAIN QUOTIDIEN (CAP-DE-LA-MADELEINE, QUEBEC). 4982

0820-7577 *See* VOICE OF THE VALLEY (WARDSVILLE). 1790

0820-7593 *See* CHRISTIAN RENEWAL. 4945

0820-7658 *See* COMMUNICATIONS - INSTITUT PROFESSIONNEL DE LA FONCTION PUBLIQUE DU CANADA. 1108

0820-7720 *See* TRAIT D'UNION (ROUYN). 4691

0820-7763 *See* INTERPROVINCIAL COMPARISONS OF UNIVERSITY FINANCING. 1831

0820-778X *See* DES CHANTIERS ET DES HOMMES. 612

0820-7801 *See* ELLENOKANADIKA CHRONIKA. 5784

0820-781X *See* CHAMBRE BLANCHE. 347

0820-7836 *See* ASSOCIATION DE MESSES DES MISSIONNAIRES DES SAINTS-APOTRES, L'. 4936

0820-7860 *See* COLLECTION ORGANISATION PEDAGOGIQUE. 1861

0820-7879 *See* LOST/STOLEN SECURITIES. 797

0820-7887 *See* SCANDALOUS INTERNATIONAL NEWS. 4535

0820-7909 *See* CREATIVE ARTS (HAMILTON). 318

0820-7933 *See* INDEX CHRONOLOGIQUE / INDEX CHRONOLOGIQUE - CONSEIL DU PATRONAT DU QUEBEC. 1678

0820-7941 *See* BULLETIN (ALBERTA TEACHERS' ASSOCIATION. SCIENCE COUNCIL). 5090

0820-795X *See* ENTRAIDE COOP. 1542

0820-7976 *See* MOREHA LE-MOREH. 2659

0820-7984 *See* MCMASTER COURIER, THE. 5789

0820-8018 *See* TELECOM (SAINTE-FOY). 1165

0820-8026 *See* THAT WAS THE WEEK THAT WAS. 917

0820-8174 *See* PERLY'S BLUEMAP ATLAS, METROPOLITAN TORONTO AND VICINITY. 2572

0820-8190 *See* ENGINEERING DIMENSIONS. 1972

0820-8212 *See* CANADIAN PODIATRY ASSOCIATION NEWSLETTER. 3917

0820-8247 *See* CRSCL NEWSLETTER. 3341

0820-8255 *See* NIGOG +, LE. 4818

0820-8301 *See* CONTACT-ACADIE. 2729

0820-8328 See FACT BOOK / ATHABASCA UNIVERSITY. **1823**

0820-8344 See CANADIAN BIKER MAGAZINE, THE. **4080**

0820-8352 See BLUE BUFFALO. **3367**

0820-8379 See NEWSLETTER OF THE ALBERTA FAMILY HISTORIES SOCIETY. **2463**

0820-8417 See KALFOU. **2743**

0820-8425 See REPERTOIRE DES MEMBRES DE L'UNION DES ARTISTES. **388**

0820-8522 See REPERTOIRE COMMERCIAL DE LA REGION DU SUD-EST. **849**

0820-8530 See SERVICES FOR SENIORS. **5307**

0820-8700 See LASSALETTER. **1761**

0820-8778 See 4E JOUR. **4931**

0820-8794 See LANSDOWNE'S CONSTRUCTION COSTS HANDBOOK. **619**

0820-8816 See ECONOMIQUE (MONTREAL). **1487**

0820-8832 See JOURNEY (KITCHENER). **380**

0820-8859 See FIRST CHOICE CANADA. **5382**

0820-8891 See VOTRE HOROSCOPE (MONTREAL. 1982). **391**

0820-8921 See CINE BULLES. **4065**

0820-8964 See GUIDE D'ACHAT DE LA VOITURE USAGEE. **5415**

0820-9006 See ARTHRITIS NEWS (TORONTO). **3803**

0820-9030 See CEREALS AND OILSEEDS REVIEW. **200**

0820-9057 See DECISION (CANADIAN ED.). **4952**

0820-909X See CANADIAN SOCIAL WORK REVIEW. **5276**

0820-9189 See PHENOMENOLOGY AND PEDAGOGY. **4355**

0820-9200 See INFO-RESEAU - MINISTERE DE L'EDUCATION. **1752**

0820-9219 See SCIENCE COUNCIL OF CANADA REPORT (1979). **5151**

0820-926X See CODA MAGAZINE. **4110**

0820-9278 See BULLETIN MUNICIPAL / OUTREMONT. **4634**

0820-9545 See 16 MM FILM CATALOGUE - RED RIVER COMMUNITY COLLEGE, LEARNING RESOURCES CENTRE. **4062**

0820-9626 See RHYTHM (SASKATOON). **4150**

0820-9669 See SUPPLEMENT / DIOCESE DE SAINTE-ANNE-DE-LA-POCATIERE. **5037**

0820-9863 See BECOIS-VOLANT. **4887**

0820-9979 See ANNUAL REPORT - DEPARTMENT OF HEALTH AND SOCIAL SERVICES (CHARLOTTETOWN). **4765**

0820-9995 See ASSOCIATION DES STOMISES DES BASSES LAURENTIDES. **3777**

0821-0012 See INSOLVENCY BULLETIN. **3087**

0821-0098 See BOOK OF RECORDS, NATIONALS - SOFTBALL CANADA. **4887**

0821-0101 See COURRIER P.R.H. MONTREAL. **4583**

0821-0128 See CARP NEWS. **5276**

0821-0160 See TAKE FIVE (SASKATOON, SASK.). **2547**

0821-0187 See SOUTH VANCOUVER REVUE. **5795**

0821-0209 See ACCENT ON ARTS. **5054**

0821-0225 See STOUFFVILLE SUN. **5795**

0821-0233 See WATER NEWS (CAMBRIDGE). **5543**

0821-025X See SQUASH LIFE. **4923**

0821-0314 See PERSUASIONS (VICTORIA). **3423**

0821-0357 See BULLDOZER. **3158**

0821-0373 See NEWSLETTER - HERITAGE ST. CATHARINES. **2749**

0821-0381 See NOUS TOUTES. **5299**

0821-039X See NEWSLETTER / CANADIAN ASSOCIATION OF RHODES SCHOLARS. **1837**

0821-0403 See ESQUIMALT STAR, THE. **5784**

0821-0551 See UPDATE, MARKET FORECAST, ELECTRIC ENERGY REQUIREMENTS IN YUKON. **4762**

0821-056X See UPDATE, MARKET FORECAST, ELECTRIC ENERGY REQUIREMENTS IN YUKON. **4762**

0821-0594 See BASIC FACTS ABOUT CORRECTIONS IN CANADA. **3158**

0821-0675 See TECHNICAL PAPER - CENTRE FOR RESOURCE STUDIES, QUEEN'S UNIVERSITY. **1445**

0821-0683 See ALBERTA PROVINCIAL PARKS USER STATISTICS. **4856**

0821-0756 See INDEPENDENCE NEWS. **901**

0821-0764 See TAX PLANNING CHECKLIST. **3062**

0821-0772 See LISTE TEMOIN SUR LA PLANIFICATION FISCALE. **4736**

0821-0780 See TAX FACTS AND FIGURES (MONTREAL). **4752**

0821-0799 See MINI-RECUEIL DE RENSEIGNEMENTS FISCAUX. **3010**

0821-0810 See JIM. JOURNAL INFORMATION MUNICIPALE. **4658**

0821-1043 See TUTORIAL (UNIVERSITY OF ALBERTA. COMPUTING SERVICES). **1262**

0821-1094 See INFORMATION U.M.R.C. **4656**

0821-1108 See CHORUS (HALIFAX). **4109**

0821-1116 See 16MM FILM ADDENDUM - MIDWESTERN REGIONAL LIBRARY SYSTEM. **4062**

0821-1124 See PRAIRIE FIRE (WINNIPEG). **3424**

0821-1248 See WRF COMMENT. **1527**

0821-1264 See PROPOS DE CUISINE. **624**

0821-1299 See RESEARCH PAPER - RESEARCH GROUP ON LEISURE AND CULTURAL DEVELOPMENT, UNIVERSITY OF WATERLOO. **5269**

0821-1329 See MAGAZINE CONTRE-JOUR. **4903**

0821-1388 See REPERES, ESSAIS EN EDUCATION. **1778**

0821-1442 See SII VOUS INFORME. **4997**

0821-1450 See CM : CANADIAN MATERIALS FOR SCHOOLS AND LIBRARIES. **3376**

0821-1469 See HISTORIGRAM. **2737**

0821-1477 See AVIRON (ED QUEBECOISE). **5780**

0821-1485 See LYNN RIVER REVIEW. **3346**

0821-1493 See GROUP INSURANCE SURVEY. **2881**

0821-1507 See PERSPECTIVES - AMERICAN PROBATION AND PAROLE ASSOCIATION. **3171**

0821-1582 See SUGGESTED LIST OF MEDICAL BOOKS & JOURNALS. **3662**

0821-1590 See SUPPLEMENT ONE, HEALTH SCIENCES BOOKS & JOURNALS. **4832**

0821-168X See BREAD OF LIFE (ANCASTER). **4940**

0821-1728 See REFLET DE TADOUSSAC. **2544**

0821-1752 See CONGRES - ENTRAIDE MISSIONNAIRE. **4950**

0821-1817 See CAHIERS DE L'ARMUQ, LES. **4106**

0821-1876 See CIRCUIT (MONTREAL). **3273**

0821-2023 See POCKET PRO GOLF MAGAZINE. **4912**

0821-2120 See WARNOCK HERSEY APPRAISAL COMPANY. **4848**

0821-2171 See EAGLEVIEW POST, THE. **5783**

0821-218X See JONCTION (ASTON JONCTION). **4658**

0821-221X See SERVICE CIRCULAR - LEARN. **1783**

0821-2228 See NEWSLETTER - LEARN. **1768**

0821-2236 See CANADIAN HOSPITAL ENGINEERING JOURNAL. **3778**

0821-2252 See CLIN D'OEIL - CENTRE HOSPITALIER DES BOIS-FRANCS. **5279**

0821-2287 See SLATE (TORONTO). **4096**

0821-2295 See CARIBBEAN FOCUS. **2726**

0821-2333 See THIS WEEK (HARROW). **5796**

0821-2341 See CONTACT (TEMISCAMING). **2531**

0821-235X See CALEDON COMMENT. **4870**

0821-2368 See INFO / NORTH YORK. **4656**

0821-2376 See NORTH LANCE. **5791**

0821-2422 See MAA NEWS. **357**

0821-2430 See NEWSLETTER - COLCHESTER HISTORICAL SOCIETY. **2749**

0821-2465 See HUMBER HIGHLIGHTS. **3786**

0821-2473 See TIMES (WINNIPEG). **5796**

0821-249X See KILLAM WORLD. **1833**

0821-2503 See STOPWATCH. **1858**

0821-2538 See MINES AND MINERAL RESOURCES. **1358**

0821-2589 See COMMUNIQUE / THE INSTITUTE FOR THE STUDY OF WOMEN. **5553**

0821-2600 See ATLANTIC ENERGY NEWS. **1933**

0821-2619 See PROFESSIONAL AND SERVICE DIRECTORY, METRO TORONTO. **1622**

0821-2635 See LABOUR ARBITRATION (VANCOUVER, B.C.). **3151**

0821-2643 See CAPITALISM (LONDON, ONT.). **4467**

0821-2651 See CANADIAN AFTERMARKET, THE. **5408**

0821-2686 See OBRA (MONTREAL). **4983**

0821-2708 See FUNCTIONS. **3506**

0821-2724 See FARMING FOR THE FUTURE. **86**

0821-2732 See AGRICULTURE DE L'AVENIR, L'. **53**

0821-2740 See TORONTO IRISH NEWS. **2763**

0821-2791 See CALGARY FOLK CLUB. **4106**

0821-2937 See B.C. WORKER'S HEALTH NEWSLETTER. **2859**

0821-2996 See URBAN TRANSIT FACTS IN CANADA. **5399**

0821-3003 See PARLONS RAISON (1983). **3422**

0821-3038 See GREENFIELD PARK JOURNAL. **5785**

0821-3186 See HAQQ (ST-LEONARD). **5246**

0821-3216 See RIVISTA DI STUDI ITALIANI. **3431**

0821-3275 See MARKWICK MIDDEN. **2459**

0821-3283 See NSMEA NOTES. **4142**

0821-3305 See MENTAL HEALTH (TORONTO. 1979). **3930**

0821-3305 See MENTAL HEALTH (TORONTO. 1979). **5296**

0821-3356 See EXTRA TO THE ONTARIO WELFARE REPORTER. **5285**

0821-3372 See LAKESIDE LEADER. **5788**

0821-3488 See FRANCOIS AUJOURD'HUI. **4959**

0821-3615 See SUNRISE EXPRESS. **1070**

0821-3623 See LEARNING WITH COMPUTERS (SCARBOROUGH, ONT.). **1224**

0821-3674 See NEWSLETTER - MANITOBA ASSOCIATION FOR EDUCATIONAL DATA SYSTEMS. **1224**

0821-3690 See MEREDITH MEMORIAL LECTURES (1975). **3009**

0821-3704 See TAXLETTER. **917**

0821-3801 See COLLECTION PALEO-QUEBEC. **266**

0821-381X See GEOSCIENCE CANADA REPRINT SERIES. **1355**

0821-3917 See BIULETYN ZWIAAZKU NAUCZYCIELSTWA POLSKIEGO W KANADZIE. **3269**

0821-3925 See HEALTH NEWS (TORONTO). **3582**

0821-4034 See ALMANACH POPULAIRE CATHOLIQUE. **5023**

0821-4050 See BRIEF TO THE ONTARIO COUNCIL ON UNIVERSITY AFFAIRS / RYERSON POLYTECHNICAL INSTITUTE. **1812**

0821-4069 See WORKING PAPER (UNIVERSITY OF WATERLOO. ACCOUNTING GROUP). **753**

0821-4077 See LITIR NEWSLETTER OF VICTORIAN STUDIES. **3407**

0821-4107 See CENTRAL THEMES. **4943**

0821-4123 See BASEBALL (MONTREAL). **4886**

0821-414X See JOURNAL REGIONAL (SAINT-JEAN). **5787**

0821-4166 See INGENIEURS-CONSEILS CANADA (1981). **1978**

0821-4174 See MESSAGER DORVAL, LE. **5789**

0821-4182 See ELEGANT (MONTREAL). **1084**

0821-4247 See SEW IT BEGINS. **5186**

ISSN Index

0821-4360 See DAY CARE FOR CHILDREN (KITCHENER). 5281
0821-4379 See COMMUNIQUE / CANADIAN COMMUNICATION ASSOCIATION. 1108
0821-4425 See ESSAYS IN THEATRE. 5364
0821-4433 See DOSSIERS CSN (1980 OCT.). 1664
0821-4476 See NEWS / THEATRE ONTARIO. 5366
0821-4484 See PACIFIC PROGRESS. 1839
0821-4549 See NOUVELLES - ASSOCIATION DES PROFESSEURS DE FRANCAIS DES UNIVERSITES ET COLLEGES CANADIENS. 3307
0821-4573 See MONTREALITES. 4666
0821-4603 See LIVRE DE REGLEMENTS ADMINISTRATIFS / FEDERATION QUEBECOISE DE HOCKEY SUR GLACE INC. 4903
0821-4638 See DIRECTORY / CANADIAN ASSOCIATION OF LAW LIBRARIES. 3206
0821-4670 See SAILING LIFE. 596
0821-4689 See EGG PRODUCER, THE. 210
0821-4697 See POCKETAX QUEBECOIS. 4741
0821-4700 See HOCKEY ONTARIO MAGAZINE. 4899
0821-4735 See BENRI CHO / BANKUBA IJUSHA NO KAI. 2723
0821-4743 See SOLSTICE NEWS. 4153
0821-4778 See SPOTLIGHT (VANCOUVER). 388
0821-4794 See WOMEN LIKE ME. 723
0821-4808 See FUTURE PLANNER. 5200
0821-4816 See LAKEFIELD, THE CHRONICLE. 5788
0821-4824 See HIGHWAY 12 WEEKENDER. 5786
0821-4891 See PRAIRIE ARTS. 328
0821-4905 See TOMORROW'S OFFICE. 888
0821-4913 See ENERGY MANAGEMENT (OTTAWA, ONT.). 1940
0821-4964 See NASHARA AL-GHADA'ID AL-ALAMIYYAH (ARABIC ED.). 4482
0821-4980 See SOCIALIST CHALLENGE (MONTREAL). 4547
0821-5049 See ACSI-ON. 3187
0821-5081 See JOURNAL DE VILLERAY, LE. 5787
0821-509X See GA PLAINSONG NOTES. 4119
0821-5111 See ABEILLE. 5572
0821-512X See EDUCATED CONSUMER. 1296
0821-5154 See PARLIAMENTARY ALERT. 4672
0821-5197 See WEST TORONTO NEWS-EXPRESS, THE. 5797
0821-5235 See UPDATE (UKRAINIAN MUSEUM OF CANADA (SASKATOON, SASK.)). 4097
0821-5251 See PEACE ARCH NEWS WEEKENDER, THE. 5792
0821-5278 See LETHBRIDGE MAGAZINE. 2537
0821-5286 See RIGHTS AND LIBERTIES. 4512
0821-5294 See FREE SPACE. 5557
0821-5340 See INTRODUCTION TO FEDERAL INCOME TAXATION IN CANADA. 4733
0821-5359 See GENERATIONS (FREDERICTON). 2450
0821-5383 See SOLICITORS' LIABILITY INDEX. 3056
0821-543X See ILLISIBLE. 5786
0821-5472 See HAMBROOK HERALD, THE. 2452
0821-5499 See AURORA (GREENWOOD). 4037
0821-5510 See PERSONAL PROPERTY SECURITY ACT. 3028
0821-5529 See AUDIO-VISUAL PRESENTATIONS / CANADIAN JEWISH CONGRESS, AUDIO-VISUAL DEPARTMENT. 5315
0821-5553 See WHITECOURT FREE PRESS, THE. 5798
0821-5561 See CRITIQUE (CLANDEBOYE). 4067
0821-5588 See GRAPHICS EXCHANGE. 379
0821-5596 See WOMEN'S INVESTMENT NETWORK NEWSLETTER. 920
0821-5693 See GLABC DIRECTORY. 3212
0821-5758 See DOCTOR'S REVIEW. 4850
0821-5782 See RINGETTE REVIEW. 4865
0821-5790 See POETRY 'N' PROSE. 3469

0821-5839 See BRIERCREST ECHO. 4940
0821-5847 See DURHAM SPECTRUM AND RECREATION. 5783
0821-5855 See GARDENERS DIGEST. 2415
0821-5944 See CANADIAN SAILINGS. 5448
0821-5979 See OJIBWAY CREE RESOURCE CENTRE CATALOGUE. 2270
0821-5987 See REVUE PHARMACOCINETIQUE. 4328
0821-5995 See NAPJAINK (WEST-HILL). 4979
0821-607X See PROGRAMS REGULATIONS - INSTITUTE OF CANADIAN BANKERS. 804
0821-6088 See REGLEMENTS RELATIFS AUX PROGRAMMES - INSTITUT DES BANQUIERS CANADIENS. 807
0821-6177 See BORDERLAND REPORTER. 5781
0821-6258 See OUTFRONT (OTTAWA). 4392
0821-6290 See MAC-TALLA - CLAN MACQUARRIE OF ATLANTIC CANADA. 2459
0821-6312 See TORONTO CHRONICLE, THE. 2548
0821-638X See FRIENDS (HALIFAX). 5286
0821-6398 See INTERCOM / CO-OPERATIVE COLLEGE OF CANADA. 1542
0821-6428 See SAWT AL-URUBAH (TURANTU). 5794
0821-6479 See ATLANTIC CHARISMATIC. 5024
0821-6509 See NEWSLETTER - NATIONAL ASSOCIATION OF FRIENDSHIP CENTRES. 5298
0821-6525 See NUOVO MONDO (EDMONTON). 5791
0821-6576 See BULLETIN / EASTERN FISHERMEN'S FEDERATION. 2297
0821-6649 See LANSDOWNE LETTER, THE. 619
0821-6657 See NEWSLETTER - CHANGE. 3235
0821-6673 See CANADIAN ULTRALIGHT NEWS. 16
0821-6681 See FRAME BY FRAME (TORONTO, ONT.). 1132
0821-6819 See TODAY'S HEALTH (TORONTO). 4805
0821-6886 See BULLETIN BAKHTINE, LE. 3338
0821-6924 See QUOI DE N'OEUF. 220
0821-7033 See OEIL OUVERT. 5300
0821-7068 See COAL FOCUS / THE COAL ASSOCIATION OF CANADA. 2137
0821-7114 See THUMPER (ST. ALBERT, ALTA.). 4926
0821-7157 See ANLA BULLETIN / ASSOCIATION OF NEWFOUNDLAND AND LABRADOR ARCHIVISTS. 2479
0821-719X See CHARTER OF RIGHTS DECISIONS. 4505
0821-7246 See SCIENCE LINK. 2924
0821-7254 See INDEX COMMERCIAL DE MONTREAL. 839
0821-7262 See ROCKY VIEW FIVE VILLAGE WEEKLY. 5794
0821-7270 See ELLENIKA NEA (LONDON, ONT.). 5784
0821-7300 See BUILDING COST GUIDE. MOBILE HOME. 603
0821-7319 See BUILDING COST GUIDE. YARD IMPROVEMENTS. 603
0821-7327 See BUILDING COST GUIDE. AGRICULTURAL. 603
0821-7335 See REVIEW - COLE HARBOUR RURAL HERITAGE SOCIETY. 2757
0821-7343 See AUTO-QUEBEC. 5405
0821-736X See NEWSCAP. 1867
0821-7378 See NOUVEL-EST. 5791
0821-7394 See EASY LIVING GUIDE : THE ORIGINAL GUIDE FOR THE COMMUNITIES OF NEW WESTMINSTER, COQUITLAM, PORT MOODY, BURNABY. 2487
0821-7440 See DAIRY CATTLE. 210
0821-7491 See DELANEY REPORT ON R.R.S.P.'S, THE. 1662
0821-7505 See ALMANACH DE L'AUTO (MONTREAL). 5403
0821-7513 See BULLETIN - CANADIAN FARM AND INDUSTRIAL EQUIPMENT INSTITUTE. 158

0821-7556 See PALAEONTOGRAPHICA CANADIANA. 4229
0821-7572 See BIBLIOFANTASIAC, THE. 3366
0821-7610 See INN BUSINESS (ESSEX, ONT.). 2807
0821-7629 See PROJET EDUCATIF (SAINT-JEROME). 1842
0821-7688 See CHAN LY. 5058
0821-7696 See CHIEFTAIN (IROQUOIS). 5782
0821-770X See REVUE HOLSTEIN QUEBEC, LA. 198
0821-7718 See ALBERTA TRANSPORTATION (CALGARY). 5375
0821-7769 See REGINA - CITY OF REGINA. 2756
0821-7785 See ECHO (OTTAWA. 1977). 4302
0821-7815 See HABILITES LOISIRS. 4388
0821-7882 See ON RECORD (TORONTO). 5300
0821-7912 See ANNUAL REVIEW OF CRIMINAL LAW. 3105
0821-7947 See REEL WEST DIGEST. 4077
0821-7955 See TORONTO LIFE FASHION. 406
0821-7971 See COUNTRY TIMES (THORNHILL). 4112
0821-8129 See RAPPORT DU VERIFICATEUR GENERAL DU CANADA A LA CHAMBRE DES COMMUNES (1979). 4678
0821-820X See FIRE LOSSES IN BRITISH COLUMBIA IN 2289
0821-8234 See MONOGRAPH - CANMET. 2146
0821-8544 See PETROLEUM PROCESSING IN CANADA. 4273
0821-9222 See ESPACE (MONTREAL). 349
0821-9869 See ECHO DE MONNOIR. 2732
0821-9885 See ANNUAIRE DE L'EGLISE CATHOLIQUE AU CANADA. 5023
0821-9885 See ANNUAIRE DE L'EGLISE CATHOLIQUE AU CANADA. 5023
0822-028X See NEWSLETTER / TORONTO OCCUPATIONAL HEALTH RESOURCE COMMITTEE. 2865
0822-0395 See BULLETIN MUNICIPAL / VILLE DE MONTREAL-NORD. 4634
0822-0409 See INFO MEP. 1752
0822-0581 See CHAN NHU / VIETNAMESE-CANADIAN BUDDHIST ASSOCIATION. 5021
0822-0638 See COMMUNICATING TOGETHER. 1106
0822-0794 See JOURNAL COTE-DES-NEIGES. 5787
0822-0808 See NORTHERN LIGHTS (CHELMSFORD). 3467
0822-0956 See REGISTERED PRIVATE VOCATIONAL SCHOOLS. 1915
0822-1006 See AUTO MODIFIEE, L'. 4885
0822-1014 See OPINIONS. 4671
0822-1081 See NATIONAL BANKING LAW REVIEW. 3087
0822-109X See CANADIAN JOURNAL OF INSURANCE LAW. 2948
0822-126X See HANSARD, OFFICIAL REPORT OF DEBATES / LEGISLATIVE ASSEMBLY OF ONTARIO, STANDING COMMITTEE ON SOCIAL DEVELOPMENT. 4654
0822-1561 See PALMARES - ALL CANADA POETRY CONTESTS. 3467
0822-1596 See DENTALETTER, THE. 1322
0822-1685 See UNION LIST OF PERIODICALS / CASLIS, CALGARY CHAPTER. 3254
0822-1723 See PEUPLES (MONTREAL). 2271
0822-1790 See PUBLIC SERVICE STAFF RELATIONS BOARD DECISIONS. 3033
0822-1839 See SERVICE COMMERCIAL DU CANADA A L'ETRANGER. 851
0822-2061 See NEWSLETTER - WOMEN'S INTER-CHURCH COUNCIL OF CANADA. 4982
0822-2142 See FUELSAVER. 5383
0822-2193 See HANSARD OFFICIAL REPORT OF DEBATES / LEGISLATIVE ASSEMBLY OF ONTARIO, STANDING COMMITTEE ON RESOURCES DEVELOPMENT. 4654
0822-2320 See CANADIAN WILDLIFE ADMINISTRATION. 2189

0822-2363 See WINDSCRIPT. 3453
0822-2401 See NEWS LETTER OF THE ST. ANDREW'S SOCIETY OF TORONTO. 5234
0822-2460 See PHOENIX (OTTAWA. 1983). 1543
0822-2479 See RESOURCE DIRECTORY (TORONTO). 2903
0822-2517 See YORKVIEW. 2767
0822-2525 See ANNUAL REVIEW OF THE ROYAL INSCRIPTIONS OF MESOPOTAMIA PROJECT. 3265
0822-2576 See CANADIAN UNION CATALOGUE OF LIBRARY MATERIALS FOR THE HANDICAPPED [MICROFORM] / CATALOGUE COLLECTIF CANADIEN DES DOCUMENTS DE BIBLIOTHEQUE POUR LES PERSONNES HANDICAPEES. 3200
0822-2584 See NATIONAL INSOLVENCY REVIEW. 3087
0822-2592 See CONTACT / COMITE NATIONAL MIXTE DE L'ACCP & SCF. 3161
0822-2711 See WORK DIGEST. 1718
0822-2754 See IRSST / IRSST, INSTITUT DE RECHERCHE EN SANTE ET EN SECURITE DU TRAVAIL DU QUEBEC, L'. 2864
0822-2762 See TAMIL EELAM DOCUMENTATION BULLETIN. 4513
0822-2908 See SABORD, LE. 330
0822-2983 See REGARD SUR LA BIBLIOTHEQUE DU COLLEGE DE L'ASSOMPTION. 3244
0822-3033 See COUP DE POUCE (MONTREAL). 5554
0822-3394 See TERMINUS (MONTREAL). 3445
0822-3521 See TRAIT D'UNION - FEDERATION DES CAISSES POPULAIRES ACADIENNES. 1543
0822-3637 See FOCUS ON AGING. 5200
0822-367X See DECISION OF THE UMPIRE. 3146
0822-3726 See INTERPRETATION REVENU QUEBEC. 4733
0822-3890 See ONTARIO BIRDS. 5619
0822-3998 See MARKETING OPTIONS. 931
0822-4048 See R.P.N.A.M. UPDATE. 3867
0822-4056 See ESCALE (QUEBEC). 4176
0822-4080 See SHELBURNE HISTORICAL SOCIETY (NEWSLETTER). 2760
0822-4137 See CONFERENCIER (MONTREAL). 4640
0822-4145 See MOTS CACHES SUPERMAGAZINE. 4863
0822-417X See AT THE DUNLOP. 4084
0822-4226 See SONG (TORONTO). 3471
0822-4250 See REGION 1 SUBMISSION TO THE GOVERNMENT OF PRINCE EDWARD ISLAND. 125
0822-4269 See IDEES DE MA MAISON, LES. 2901
0822-4331 See 596. 4366
0822-4382 See ANNUAL REPORT - ALBERTA DEPARTMENT OF HOUSING. 2814
0822-451X See TELE-C.L.E.F. 3063
0822-4706 See PWACONTACT. 1928
0822-4749 See CHOIRS ONTARIO. 4109
0822-4811 See LISTES - ASSOCIATION CANADIENNE DES PRODUCTEURS DE PATES ET PAPIERS, SECTION TECHNIQUE. 4235
0822-482X See CHARLTON CANADA STAMP ALBUM & STORYBOOK, THE. 2784
0822-4838 See OPERATIONAL GEOGRAPHER, THE. 2571
0822-4889 See COLLECTABLES AUCTION / CHARLTON AUCTIONS. 2772
0822-4897 See JEWELLERY AUCTION / CHARLTON AUCTIONS. 2914
0822-4900 See NUMISMATIC AUCTION / CHARLTON AUCTIONS. 2782
0822-4919 See PHILATELIC AUCTION / CHARLTON AUCTIONS. 2786
0822-4927 See COLLECTABLES AUCTION. 2772
0822-4935 See JEWELLERY AUCTION - TOREX. 2914
0822-4943 See MILITARIA AUCTION - TOREX. 2781

0822-496X See PHILATELIC AUCTION - TOREX. 2786
0822-4978 See FESTIVAL OF FRIENDS. 4117
0822-4986 See RAPPORT DU SERVICE DE LA BIBLIOTHEQUE DE L'UNIVERSITE DU QUEBEC A CHICOUTIMI. 3243
0822-5028 See RAPPORTS DE CONSTRUCTION SOUTHAM. 625
0822-5044 See SUBVENTIONS. 2836
0822-5109 See INFORM-ACTION - EDUCATEURS FRANCO-MANITOBAINS. 1752
0822-5117 See REVUE DE DROIT JUDICIAIRE. 3091
0822-5133 See BOISBRIAND (1983). 4633
0822-5141 See PROSPECTUS - CONCORDES. 4913
0822-5168 See AUTONOMOUS LIVING. 2788
0822-5176 See CANADIAN BLACK BOOK, USED TRUCK AND VAN GUIDE. 5408
0822-5192 See CCI NOUVELLES. 1967
0822-5206 See PREPRINTS A / TECHNICAL SECTION, CANADIAN PULP AND PAPER ASSOCIATION. 4237
0822-5214 See PREPRINTS B / TECHNICAL SECTION, CANADIAN PULP AND PAPER ASSOCIATION. 4237
0822-5222 See GRAND PRIX LABATT DU CANADA. REGLEMENTS. 5415
0822-5257 See SUR MESURE. 1802
0822-529X See RALLYE : REGLEMENTS. 4914
0822-5389 See REPERTOIRE / LA CHAMBRE DE COMMERCE DE LA PROVINCE DE QUEBEC. 821
0822-5443 See SALON DU LIVRE DE MONTREAL. 4832
0822-5451 See PLAN TRIENNAL DE DEVELOPPEMENT / UNIVERSITE DU QUEBEC A CHICOUTIMI. 1841
0822-546X See CONCOURS LITTERAIRE. 3377
0822-5478 See CHRONOLOGICAL INDEX / CONSEIL DU PATRONAT DU QUEBEC. 413
0822-5508 See BULLETIN SPECIAL - INSTITUT TECCART. 2037
0822-5516 See CIRCUIT FERME (INSTITUT TECCART). 4400
0822-5524 See TOUT A LOISIR. 4855
0822-5559 See JEUNESSE FRANCOIS D'ASSISE. 4967
0822-5591 See INFO-SARDEC. 1679
0822-5613 See COMMUNICATION-PARENTS. 1861
0822-5621 See CHAMPIONS DU SPORT AMATEUR, LES. 4889
0822-563X See PROGRES DU NORD, AHUNTSIC. 5793
0822-5672 See PASSANT, EN. 4864
0822-5699 See BULLETIN SSQ RESPECTING SOCIAL LAWS. 2945
0822-5702 See SP QUEBEC. 3846
0822-5710 See ACAATO HANDBOOK. 1806
0822-5729 See ON TARGET WEEKLY. 5487
0822-5788 See BANK CREDIT ANALYST. INVESTMENT AND BUSINESS FORECAST, THE. 892
0822-5796 See DISCOVERY (VICTORIA). 4087
0822-580X See TRANSPORT OF THUNDER BAY. 5395
0822-5818 See PAPERBACKS BY MAIL. 4831
0822-5842 See RPNABC PROFILE. 3869
0822-5877 See DOSSIER POELES A BOIS. 2604
0822-5915 See PROCEEDINGS OF THE ... ANNUAL MEETING / ACADIAN ENTOMOLOGICAL SOCIETY. 5595
0822-5931 See ONTARIO MUSEUM ANNUAL. 4095
0822-5974 See HEMOPHILIA ONTARIO. 3772
0822-6016 See CULTURE SERVICE BULLETIN. 318
0822-6261 See D.O.T.C. NEWS (1983). 5783
0822-6342 See CHESNAIE. 4637
0822-6350 See ECRITS SUR LE CINEMA (SUPPLEMENT). 4068

0822-6369 See DIRECTORY / CANADIAN SOCIETY FOR RENAISSANCE STUDIES. 2685
0822-6377 See OUR TIMES (TORONTO). 1700
0822-644X See NUMERO (MONTREAL). 326
0822-6474 See CAMPING CLUES. 4870
0822-6482 See HOW OTTAWA SPENDS. 4655
0822-6512 See MAGAZINES / HALIFAX CITY REGIONAL LIBRARY. 419
0822-658X See NEWSLETTER (FRIENDS OF THE OTTAWA PUBLIC LIBRARY). 3235
0822-6598 See COOPRIX INFORMATION (1983). 1296
0822-6601 See ONTARIO EDUCATION REVIEW (TORONTO. 1982). 1839
0822-6644 See BULLETIN OAQ. 294
0822-6687 See IMPORT FILE (1982). 839
0822-6709 See CANADIAN COMPUTER LAW REPORTER. 2947
0822-6733 See DEPARTMENTAL WORKING PAPER - CARLETON UNIVERSITY. DEPARTMENT OF SOCIOLOGY AND ANTHROPOLOGY. 235
0822-6768 See BULLETIN DE LIAISON / FEDERATION DES ASSOCIATIONS DE FAMILLES MONOPARENTALES DU QUEBEC. 2277
0822-6776 See INFO PREVENTION. 5384
0822-6784 See BADMINTON REVIEW (ST. ALBERT). 4886
0822-6792 See SCIENCE DU SPORT. 1858
0822-6806 See ONTARIO AMATEUR WRESTLING ASSOCIATION RESULTS BOOK. 4911
0822-6830 See CANADIAN BANKER (1983). 782
0822-6849 See BANQUIER (MONTREAL). 778
0822-6911 See Q.A.G.T. NEWSLETTER. 2574
0822-6938 See JOURNAL DE ST-DOMINIQUE. 5787
0822-6970 See POLYMETRIC REPORT (T.S.E. ED.). 911
0822-7098 See COULICOU. 1062
0822-711X See SOCIAL DEVELOPMENT OVERVIEW. 5308
0822-7128 See DEVELOPPEMENT SOCIAL EN PERSPECTIVES. 5282
0822-7144 See COURRIER AGRIROYAL. 77
0822-7152 See DIRECTORY - CANADIAN PAYMENTS ASSOCIATION. 787
0822-7187 See ICBA. INDEPENDENT CANADIAN BUSINESS ASSOCIATION OF BRITISH COLUMBIA. 1609
0822-7225 See WESTCOAST READER, THE. 2550
0822-7268 See MICROSPIRIT. 1764
0822-7284 See FRANC-NORD. 2194
0822-7292 See QUOI DE NEUF? (STE-FOY). 1776
0822-7314 See INFO-RURAL. 95
0822-7330 See EXPRESS EQUESTRE. 2799
0822-7373 See TOPONYME, LE. 2577
0822-742X See LIST OF ELECTRODES CERTIFIED TO CSA W48 SERIES OF STANDARDS AND APPLICABLE AWS A5. SPECIFICATIONS. 4027
0822-7438 See CO-OP NORTH. 1541
0822-7500 See PRAIRIE SOUNDS. 4147
0822-7527 See NOUVELLES - ASSOCIATION DES BIBLIOTHEQUES DE L'ONTARIO. GUILDE DES SERVICES EN FRANCAIS. 3237
0822-7535 See HEBDO DE LAVAL, L'. 5786
0822-7543 See LIT-POT-HEC. 876
0822-7551 See SASKATCHEWAN WATER NEWS. 5539
0822-7578 See NEWSLETTER - CANADIAN ATHLETIC THERAPISTS ASSOCIATION. 3955
0822-7594 See PERIODICA MUSICA. 4145
0822-7616 See RESUMES DE JURISPRUDENCE PENALE DU QUEBEC. 3083
0822-7632 See CONTACT - ASSOCIATION OF REGISTRARS OF THE UNIVERSITIES AND COLLEGES OF CANADA. 1818
0822-7683 See ENCAN - FRASER BROS. LTD. 349
0822-7713 See COLLECTABLES AUCTION / CHARLTON AUCTIONS. 2772

ISSN Index

0822-7713 See NUMISMATIC AUCTION / CHARLTON AUCTIONS. 2782

0822-7713 See JEWELLERY AUCTION / CHARLTON AUCTIONS. 2914

0822-7713 See PHILATELIC AUCTION / CHARLTON AUCTIONS. 2786

0822-773X See BULLETIN / FONDS DE RECHERCHES ET DE DEVELOPPEMENT FORESTIER. 2376

0822-7748 See TORONTO & AREA AIRPORT BUSINESS DIRECTORY. 37

0822-7799 See CANADIAN DIRECTORY OF SHOPPING CENTRES. 952

0822-7810 See GRIEVANCE AND ADJUDICATION SECTION REPORTS / PUBLIC SERVICE ALLIANCE OF CANADA. 2975

0822-7829 See RAPPORTS DE LA SECTION DES GRIEFS ET DE L'ARBITRAGE. 3034

0822-7853 See SECURITAIRE. 4917

0822-7896 See VOICE (VANCOUVER. 1983). 5797

0822-790X See CITY MAGAZINE (WINNIPEG). 4638

0822-7918 See BUDGETING FOR BASIC NEEDS AND BUDGETING FOR MINIMUM ADEQUATE STANDARD OF LIVING. 2789

0822-7926 See RADIO ATIVITE INC. 4148

0822-7942 See NOMADIC PEOPLES. 2270

0822-7969 See NATIONAL FARMERS UNION, REGION 8, SUBMISSION TO THE GOVERNMENT OF BRITISH COLUMBIA 110

0822-8027 See CANADIAN MEETING PLANNER. 655

0822-8035 See NOVO MUNDO (TORONTO). 5791

0822-8043 See TALK OF THE THAMES. 5540

0822-8086 See OTTAWA, HULL (NEPEAN). 2572

0822-8108 See EDMONTON BULLET, THE. 319

0822-8116 See JOURNAL L'ACTION. 1092

0822-8132 See PERSPECTIVES - ST. BONIFACE GENERAL HOSPITAL. 3791

0822-8140 See KW MAGAZINE. 2536

0822-8167 See INFO-COMPTOIR MUSICAL. 4122

0822-8175 See NEWSLETTER / BRITISH COLUMBIA CHORAL FEDERATION. 4140

0822-8183 See WFCD COMMUNICATOR. 146

0822-8205 See CYCLES ET TENDANCES. 1590

0822-8213 See EXPRESSION (OTTAWA). 5285

0822-823X See AUDIO VISUAL CATALOGUE - PACIFIC VOCATIONAL INSTITUTE. 1888

0822-8248 See DIRECTORY / COLLEGE OF VETERINARIANS OF ONTARIO. [DISKETTE]. 5509

0822-8256 See OUR LITTLE YELLOW BOOK. 2902

0822-8280 See AMATEUR SPORT NEWS (SOUTHERN ALBERTA ED.). 4882

0822-8299 See CROSSFIELD CHRONICLE. 5783

0822-8329 See REVUE DES ECHANGES DE L'ASSOCIATION FRANCOPHONE INTERNATIONALE DES DIRECTEURS D'ETABLISSEMENTS SCOLAIRES, LA. 1780

0822-8353 See NEWSLETTER / SCARBOROUGH HISTORICAL SOCIETY. 5234

0822-837X See MISSION (ST-LAMBERT, QUEBEC), EN. 4978

0822-8396 See COMMUNICATEUR (OTTAWA). 1151

0822-8418 See CIRCA. CONFLITS INTERNATIONAUX, LES REGIONS ET LE CANADA. 4518

0822-8426 See CHAC INFO. 4771

0822-8434 See NOUVELLES D'OGILVIE. 1620

0822-8450 See GETTING THERE (BURLINGTON, ONT.). 1072

0822-8469 See HORIZON JEUNESSE. 1072

0822-8493 See INFORMATION COULEUR (MONTREAL). 4435

0822-8531 See TETE, EN. 1850

0822-854X See BULLETIN DE NOUVELLES / FEDERATION QUEBECOISE DES SPORTS AERIENS, SECTEUR VOL LIBRE. 4888

0822-8620 See GOVERNMENT DIRECTORY FOR BRITISH COLUMBIA WITH SELECTED FEDERAL CONTACTS. 4651

0822-8671 See BOUNDARY CREEK TIMES, THE. 5781

0822-8698 See CANADA OFFSHORE BUYERS GUIDE. 4252

0822-8701 See REVUE DE PRESSE DU ... FESTIVAL D'ETE DE QUEBEC, LA. 5269

0822-8728 See MOTS CROISES FRANCAIS ANGLAIS. 4863

0822-8736 See ONTARIO FISHERMAN. 2309

0822-8833 See POINT DE REPERE (MONTREAL). 422

0822-8949 See BOTTIN / UNION CANADIENNE DES RELIGIEUSES CONTEMPLATIVES. 4940

0822-8957 See CITOYEN (COWANSVILLE). 5782

0822-8965 See BOTTIN DU MOUVEMENT ETUDIANT / PRESSE ETUDIANTE DU QUEBEC. 1812

0822-9058 See PHYSIOLOGY CANADA (1983). 585

0822-9066 See STRATFORD FOR STUDENTS. 5369

0822-9104 See HANDBOOK : CONSTITUTION, DIRECTORY, BYLAWS, POLICIES, BUDGET, LEGISLATION / ONTARIO PUBLIC SCHOOL FEDERATION. 1864

0822-9163 See PEOPLE'S CLASSIFIEDS, THE. 848

0822-918X See CAPITAL REGION CREATIVE SERVICES DIRECTORY, THE. 317

0822-9201 See KIN MAGAZINE. 2457

0822-9228 See TRAVEL SCOOP. 5496

0822-9236 See INFO SID TELIDON II. 1133

0822-9252 See SPIRALE (SHERBROOKE). 4619

0822-9279 See R.A.P.H.A.T. REGROUPEMENT DES ASSOCIATIONS DE PERSONNES HANDICAPEES DE L'ABITIBI-TEMISCAMINGUE. 5303

0822-9309 See BULLETIN NATIONAL DU CCA. 5275

0822-935X See DIRECTORY OF O.C.U.L. LIBRARIES. 3207

0822-9368 See ANNUAIRE (CONSEIL DE LA COOPERATION DE LA SASKATCHEWAN). 822

0822-9376 See BULLETIN - FEDERATION DES ETUDIANTS DE L'U. DE O. 1089

0822-9406 See HOME SUPPORT SERVICES IN METROPOLITAN TORONTO. 5288

0822-9430 See REPERTOIRE DES MEMBRES / ORDRE DES AGRONOMES DU QUEBEC. 125

0822-9430 See REPERTOIRES DES MEMBRES. 125

0822-9481 See CAPT. LILLIE'S BRITISH COLUMBIA COAST GUIDE AND RADIOTELEPHONE DIRECTORY. 4175

0822-9503 See HURON HISTORICAL NOTES. 2738

0822-9538 See NEWSLETTER (CANADIAN BOOKBINDERS AND BOOK ARTISTS GUILD). 4831

0822-9546 See RESEARCH REPORT / CANADIAN STUDIES COMMITTEE; FACULTY OF ARTS, FACULTY OF GRADUATE STUDIES AND RESEARCH, MCGILL UNIVERSITY. 423

0822-9589 See SIX, CINQ ET APRES : INNOVATIONS DANS L'ECONOMIE MUNICIPALE. 4748

0822-9597 See SIX, FIVE AND COUNTING : INNOVATIONS IN MUNICIPAL ECONOMY. 4748

0822-9600 See RUPTURE (TORONTO). 3432

0822-9619 See MISSION IMPOSSIBLE. 5296

0822-9678 See WARDAIR WORLD (1983). 5499

0822-9694 See STRATEGIE (TORONTO). 916

0822-9724 See HAMILTON CUE MAGAZINE. 2534

0822-9740 See REVIEW / UKRAINIAN CANADIAN PROFESSIONAL AND BUSINESS FEDERATION. 708

0822-9759 See BC ATHLETICS RECORD. 4887

0822-9783 See TAPES BY MAIL CATALOGUE. 4160

0822-9902 See QUEBEC-URSS INFORMATION. 2704

0822-9937 See POETRY MONTREAL. 3469

0822-997X See REFERENCE - COMPUTING SERVICES. UNIVERSITY OF ALBERTA. 1262

0822-9988 See BLUE JAY NEWS. 4163

0823-0080 See DECIMA QUARTERLY REPORT. 2730

0823-0145 See CANSPA COMMUNICATOR. 4849

0823-0153 See VANIEROIS, LE. 1525

0823-0161 See NEWSLETTER - VANCOUVER HISTORICAL SOCIETY (1980). 2750

0823-0188 See ANNUAIRE DES FEMMES DE MONTREAL, L'. 5271

0823-0196 See FINANCIAL REPORTING DEVELOPMENTS (TORONTO, ONT.). 744

0823-020X See CANADIAN HOUSING. MONTHLY ANALYSIS. 2817

0823-0218 See ALBERTA RURAL MONTH. 57

0823-0226 See CANADIAN SOLAR DIRECTORY (1983). 1934

0823-0234 See MICROMONTH. 1269

0823-0315 See AGLOW NEWSLETTER (MELVILLE). 5054

0823-0382 See FORUM / CANADIAN SOCIETY FOR INDUSTRIAL SECURITY. 5177

0823-0498 See MONDE DU ROCK. 4132

0823-0552 See FUNGI CANADENSES. 575

0823-0579 See CALGARY WORKING PAPERS IN LINGUISTICS. 3272

0823-065X See PRIVATE AND PUBLIC INVESTMENT IN CANADA. INTENTIONS. 911

0823-0668 See PRIVATE AND PUBLIC INVESTMENT IN CANADA. REVISED INTENTIONS. 911

0823-0773 See MINTEC : MINING TECHNOLOGY ABSTRACTS. 2006

0823-0900 See SHIPMENTS OF PLASTIC FILM AND BAGS MANUFACTURED FROM RESIN. 4460

0823-1117 See MATHEMATICS COUNCIL NEWSLETTER (1983). 3520

0823-1133 See CORPUS ALMANAC & CANADIAN SOURCEBOOK. 1924

0823-1168 See BULLETIN - CANADIAN ASSOCIATION FOR UNIVERSITY CONTINUING EDUCATION. 1812

0823-1184 See NEWSLETTER / MANITOBA LIBRARY TRUSTEES ASSOCIATION. 3235

0823-1214 See WHOLESALE TRADE STATISTICS. WHOLESALE MERCHANTS, AGENTS AND BROKERS. 857

0823-129X See AUTHOR INDEX - CARLETON UNIVERSITY. 408

0823-132X See NEWSPAPER GEOG. LIST - CARLETON UNIVERSITY. 5790

0823-1338 See MUSIC SCORE CATALOGUE - CARLETON UNIVERSITY. 4160

0823-1346 See JW PLUS. 2915

0823-1354 See CHIMO MAGAZINE. 2530

0823-1362 See INTERNATIONAL DIRECTORY - ROYAL BANK OF CANADA. 792

0823-1435 See SYNAPSE (REGINA). 4363

0823-1478 See ENERGY NEWS (OTTAWA. 1982). 1941

0823-1486 See BULLETIN SUR L'ENERGIE (OTTAWA, ONT.). 1934

0823-1494 See LABOUR TIMES. 3151

0823-1508 See TRUE NORTH / DOWN UNDER. 3448

0823-1605 See MJP. MONTREAL JOURNAL OF POETICS. 3466

0823-1664 See TECHNICAL REPORT SERIES OF THE LABORATORY FOR RESEARCH IN STATISTICS AND PROBABILITY. 3538

0823-1672 See JOURNALIST (EDMONTON). 1092

0823-1729 See LISTE DES PERIODIQUES / CENTRE D'INFORMATION SUR LE DEVELOPPEMENT. 2911

0823-1737 See NEWFOUNDLAND STUDIES. 2749

0823-1745 See PEGG. ASSOCIATION OF PROFESSIONAL ENGINEERS, GEOLOGISTS AND GEOPHYSICISTS OF ALBERTA (MONTHLY ED.). 1990

0823-1788 See EAST COAST OFFSHORE. 4255

0823-1796 See SCANDINAVIAN-CANADIAN STUDIES. 2759

0823-1834 See ENVOI (MONTREAL). 4894

0823-1869 See GATHERING. 4960

0823-1915 See EXCALIBUR (DOWNSVIEW, ONT.). 5784

0823-2040 See SDC INFORMATIONS. 1543

0823-2059 See EXPLORATION IN BRITISH COLUMBIA. 2139

0823-2105 See BULLETIN CANADIEN D'HISTOIRE DE LA MEDECINE. 3559

0823-2113 See MICROLOG, MICROFICHE COLLECTIONS. 420

0823-213X See INTERVENANT. 1345

0823-2148 See CRAFT CONTACTS (1983). 371

0823-2164 See POST-SECONDARY ENROLMENT STATISTICS. 1796

0823-2180 See DREAMWEAVER MAGAZINE. 4585

0823-2350 See ALBERTA LEGAL TELEPHONE DIRECTORY. 3138

0823-2393 See HORIZONS (SAINT JOHN. 1982). 4088

0823-2458 See SYMPOSIUM / DEUTSCHKANADISCHE STUDIEN. 3443

0823-2490 See NUIT BLANCHE. 3419

0823-2504 See CANADA CHINCHILLA. 5507

0823-2547 See OUR KINGDOM MINISTRY. FOR CANADA. 4984

0823-2555 See MINISTERE DU ROYAUME POUR LE CANADA, LE. 5064

0823-2571 See MINISTERO DEL REGNO PER IL CANADA, IL. 5064

0823-258X See NUESTRO MINISTERIO DEL REINO PARA EL CANADA. 5065

0823-2598 See NOSSO MINISTERIO DO REINO PARA O CANADA. 5065

0823-261X See HALTE JEUNESSE ET FOI (1982). 4962

0823-2660 See RESEARCH REPORT / CANADIAN ELECTRICAL ASSOCIATION. 2079

0823-2679 See BOREAL INTERNATIONAL. 3460

0823-2717 See NATIONAL DIRECTORY / CANADIAN INSTITUTE OF FOOD SCIENCE AND TECHNOLOGY. 2350

0823-2725 See CMBC ALUMNI BULLETIN. 1101

0823-2768 See REPERTOIRE ANNOTE DES PUBLICATIONS DES COMMISSIONS SCOLAIRES. NIVEAUX PRESCOLAIRE ET PRIMAIRE. 1869

0823-2776 See REPERTOIRE ANNOTE DES PUBLICATIONS DES COMMISSIONS SCOLAIRES. NIVEAU SECONDAIRE. 1869

0823-2784 See TERRE DE CHEZ NOUS. DOSSIER D'INFORMATION TECHNIQUE ET PROFESSIONNELLE, LA. 141

0823-2857 See MONTREAL CUISINE. 5072

0823-2873 See CANADIAN PULP AND PAPER CAPACITY. 4233

0823-289X See BULLETIN DU MOUVEMENT TRI-ACTION, LE. 825

0823-2903 See OCEAN RESOURCES. 1453

0823-2911 See BULLETIN / MANITOBA NATURALISTS SOCIETY. 4164

0823-3039 See DISCUSSION PAPER - SIMON FRASER UNIVERSITY, DEPARTMENT OF GEOGRAPHY. 2559

0823-311X See REVUE STATISTIQUE DU CANADA. SUPPLEMENT. 5337

0823-3276 See THERE IS. 3472

0823-3306 See PROVINCIAL FILM LIBRARY RESOURCE CATALOGUE. 3242

0823-3322 See SENTENCES ARBITRALES DE LA FONCTION PUBLIQUE. 1710

0823-3330 See CANADEXPORT (ENGLISH ED.). 826

0823-3403 See PORTE A PORTE. 1543

0823-3454 See STATISTICAL REVIEW - EXPORT DEVELOPMENT CORPORATION. 852

0823-3489 See STATUTES OF ALBERTA. 3059

0823-3594 See CALOTTE, LA. 3922

0823-3799 See SAILING DIRECTIONS, LABRADOR AND HUDSON BAY. 596

0823-3837 See KINDRED SPIRITS. 2457

0823-3918 See CUSSCO NEWSLETTER. 4773

0823-3926 See LETTRE DES COMMUNICATIONS - CLAUDE PICHE COMMUNICATIONS. 1115

0823-3934 See NEW BRUNSWICK COURIER. 5790

0823-3993 See MESURE ET EVALUATION EN EDUCATION. 1764

0823-406X See ECOLOGICAL LAND CLASSIFICATION SERIES. 2214

0823-4124 See ARTERE (MONTREAL). 3777

0823-4159 See LANGUAGE IN FOCUS (MISSISSAUGA, ONT.). 3295

0823-4450 See ALBERTA MANUFACTURERS INDEX. 3475

0823-4531 See CAMPUS DIGEST. 1090

0823-4590 See FREE METHODIST HERALD. 5060

0823-4604 See MAINE-ANJOU INTERNATIONAL. 215

0823-4639 See ROSTER DE L'ACTL. 3637

0823-4760 See AGRI-FOOD PERSPECTIVES. 47

0823-4949 See STATUTES OF THE YUKON TERRITORY. 3059

0823-5015 See WHO'S WHO OF CANADIAN WOMEN. 439

0823-5023 See JOHNSON'S INDEX TO CANADIAN ART AUCTIONS. 354

0823-5112 See LEVRES URBAINES. 3465

0823-518X See HEBDO CARRIERES (MONTREAL). 1677

0823-5198 See MAITRE FRIGORISTE. 2071

0823-5228 See CANADIAN CHEMICAL NEWS. 1021

0823-5392 See BULLETIN - SOTRAC. 2189

0823-5406 See SERIALS HOLDINGS MICROFORM / WILFRID LAURIER UNIVERSITY. 424

0823-5414 See INFO COMMERCE. 840

0823-5430 See MICROBITS. 2072

0823-5503 See ECHO DES FRONTIERES, L'. 5783

0823-552X See ACTUALITE DIOCESAINE. 4932

0823-5570 See MONDE A BICYCLETTE, LE. 429

0823-5635 See LOOK (MONTREAL). 1085

0823-5651 See MOUVEMENTS. 1691

0823-566X See ANNUAIRE / COMMISSION SCOLAIRE REGIONALE LOIS-FRECHETTE. 1724

0823-5686 See GUIDE DE L'USAGER / UNIVERSITE DU QUEBEC A TROIS-RIVIERES, SERVICE DE LA BIBLIOTHEQUE, LE. 3212

0823-5708 See TEMPS LIBRE (MONTREAL). 5492

0823-5716 See CANADIAN MINES, PERSPECTIVE. 2136

0823-5724 See IDEES ET PRATIQUES ALTERNATIVES. 2217

0823-5740 See CUSO FORUM (OTTAWA, ONT. : 1980). 1634

0823-5864 See ANNUAL REPORT INCLUDING ... OBJECTIVES AND ACTION PLANS - EQUAL OPPORTUNITIES FOR WOMEN. 5551

0823-6011 See WEEK-END NATIONAL, LE. 2550

0823-6046 See DIRECTORY OF COMMUNITY SERVICES IN REGIONAL NIAGARA. 5282

0823-6062 See COMMUNITY DEVELOPMENT (GUELPH). 2818

0823-6089 See CANADIAN FARMTAX. 4716

0823-6097 See CHRONIQUEUR DE L'ILE, LE. 2728

0823-6100 See GENS D'AFFAIRES. 1607

0823-6119 See HORS D'ORDRE. 5202

0823-6127 See VIREO. 4820

0823-6135 See P'TIT ROBERT, LE. 5302

0823-6143 See ONTARIO RECYCLING UPDATE. 2238

0823-616X See CITEPHILE. 5279

0823-6178 See AMIS DE JESUS, LES. 4934

0823-6186 See CHAINON (OTTAWA. 1983). 2727

0823-6216 See CONNOLLY REPORT, THE. 895

0823-6240 See NOUVEL ESSOR MARCELLE MALLET. 4982

0823-6275 See NEWSLETTER / UNITED NATIVE FRIENDSHIP CENTRE. 2750

0823-6283 See MULTICULTURAL EDUCATION JOURNAL. 1765

0823-6305 See INFO-VOLLEY. 4900

0823-6313 See LEXICOM. 747

0823-6321 See QUEBECOIS VAUDREUIL-SOULANGES, LE. 4493

0823-6348 See HERMINE. 2882

0823-6356 See MARIE-PIER. 5561

0823-6380 See GREEN. 4897

0823-6399 See TICKLEACE. 3472

0823-6410 See HOME QUARTER. 212

0823-6429 See CANADIAN AUCTIONEER, THE. 862

0823-6437 See COMPUTING NOW!. 1273

0823-6453 See ONTARIO OUTDOORSMAN. 4876

0823-6488 See INTERNATIONAL MINERALS SCENE, THE. 1440

0823-650X See GEOTECHNICAL NEWS. 1381

0823-6526 See KICK IT OVER. 4542

0823-6542 See THUNDER BAY MAGAZINE. 2547

0823-6577 See FRATERNALLY YOURS. 2261

0823-6593 See VISITOR GUIDE TO WOODLAND PARK TRAVEL REGION. 5499

0823-6607 See VISITOR GUIDE TO PRAIRIE VALLEYS TRAVEL REGION. 5499

0823-6615 See VISITOR GUIDE TO FRONTIER VISTA TRAVEL REGION. 5498

0823-6631 See REGARD NOUVEAU. 5793

0823-6658 See COMMERCE RIVE-SUD. 828

0823-6674 See CANADIAN AMPUTEE SPORTS ASSOCIATION. 4889

0823-6682 See GUIDE DU VIN, LE. 2367

0823-6712 See CAMROSE REVIEW, THE. 3372

0823-6720 See ALBERTA FARM & RANCH. 57

0823-6763 See ORILLIA SUN. 5792

0823-678X See TRIBUTE MAGAZINE. 4079

0823-6798 See HOSPITAL PRODUCTS AND TECHNOLOGY. 3584

0823-6801 See EQUITY (VANCOUVER). 672

0823-6828 See LIBRARY SERVICES BULLETIN (CO-OPERATIVE COLLEGE OF CANADA). 1542

0823-6844 See ETAIT DEUX FOIS, IL. 2278

0823-6860 See GUIDES FOR FAMILY BUDGETING. 2790

0823-6879 See INFORMATION BELLECOMBE. 2535

0823-6887 See COUNTY GROWER. 77

0823-6909 See LIST OF MEDICAL PRACTITIONERS CURRENTLY LICENSED TO PRACTISE IN THE PROVINCE / THE COLLEGE OF PHYSICIANS AND SURGEONS OF MANITOBA. 3914

0823-6925 See TRIANGLE NEWS (CORONACH). 5796

0823-6933 See ATLANTIC CANADA RESEARCH LETTER. 2722

0823-6941 See MENSUEL DE STE-DOROTHEE, LE. 5789

0823-695X See IN THE MIDDLE. 1751

0823-6976 See INTERNATIONAL FUR FASHION REVIEW. 3184

0823-6984 See PLANTE-A-TOUT. 2428

0823-7034 See VORTEX (TORONTO). 4867

0823-7042 See KEN-CUR REPORT, THE. 905

0823-7069 See OUR DIOCESE (GRAND FALLS). 5033

0823-7107 See ETHNIC CLOUT. 759

0823-7123 See MOTS A TROUVER RG. 4863

0823-7131 See ONOWAY TRIBUNE. 5791

0823-7352 See HEALTHY HORIZONS. 2343

0823-7387 See NORTH KAWARTHA TIMES. 5791

0823-7425 See NORTH THOMPSON JOURNAL. 2541

0823-7468 See ICCSASW SOLIDARITY BULLETIN. 1609

0823-7492 See PAGIDEX. 4319

0823-7557 See CARSTAIRS COURIER, THE. 5781

0823-7573 See RIVERVIEW GAZETTE, THE. 5794

0823-7646 See STARTER COLLECTION FOR JUNIOR HIGH SCHOOLS, A. 3251

0823-7662 See BEAU LIEU (SAINTE-PETRONILLE, QUEBEC). 4632
0823-7689 See CENTRAL AMERICA UPDATE. 4467
0823-7697 See POINTS A POINTS. 5185
0823-7735 See ISLAND FARMER. 98
0823-7743 See BRITANNIA (TORONTO). 2514
0823-7751 See ESSO NORTH. 4255
0823-776X See JUMELLO, LE. 2282
0823-7786 See DRUGS & DEVICES. 4302
0823-7794 See C'EST MOI. 402
0823-7859 See AUDIO-FILE. 3192
0823-7875 See GUILD GAZETTE. 4119
0823-7883 See BULLETIN OZANAM / SOCIETE DE SAINT-VINCENT DE PAUL, HULL ET GATINEAU. 4941
0823-7891 See DIRECTORY OF SURNAMES - ONTARIO GENEALOGICAL SOCIETY. 2445
0823-793X See ESQUIVE (MONTREAL, QUEBEC). 4894
0823-7948 See NEWSLETTER (CANADIAN MODERN PENTATHLON ASSOCIATION). 4908
0823-7956 See ILLUSTRATED CATALOG OF FREE CATALOGS AND SOURCES FOR EVERYTHING IMAGINABLE. 2488
0823-7980 See CALGARY INDUSTRIAL LAND SURVEY. 2816
0823-7999 See NEWSLETTER (S.U.C.C.E.S.S.). 5299
0823-8006 See FRAPPE. 1675
0823-8014 See APPUI. 2721
0823-8138 See PROSPECTIVE (MONTREAL. 1984). 2891
0823-8162 See OCSM NEWSLETTER. 4142
0823-8197 See CANADIAN REAL ESTATE (DON MILLS. 1983). 4835
0823-8200 See EDMONTON & AREA AVIATION BUSINESS DIRECTORY. 5381
0823-8219 See CALGARY & AREA AVIATION BUSINESS DIRECTORY. 5378
0823-8243 See OKANAGAN SEASONS. 2542
0823-8278 See CONSORT (HALIFAX). 4111
0823-8308 See ANGLICAN MESSENGER (EDMONTON). 5055
0823-8324 See NEWSLETTER / PRINCE EDWARD ISLAND MUSEUM AND HERITAGE FOUNDATION. 4094
0823-8332 See UP-DATE - B.C. NUTRITION COUNCIL. 4199
0823-8448 See MANITOBA CURLING REVIEW. 4904
0823-8464 See HOME MISSIONS (TORONTO). 4963
0823-8472 See HORTICULTURE REVIEW. 2419
0823-8499 See GUIDE DE LA MOTO (MONTREAL, 1984). 4081
0823-8502 See TOWN & COUNTRY BED & BREAKFAST IN B.C., CANADA. 5494
0823-8561 See NEWSLETTER - ALBERTA SURFACE RIGHTS FEDERATION. 112
0823-8588 See MANITOBA CAMPING DIRECTORY. 4874
0823-8596 See OFFICIAL HELLENIC YEAR BOOK (1984). 2752
0823-8669 See CONSCIENCE CANADA NEWSLETTER. 4718
0823-8693 See ENGANCE NEWSLETTER. 5555
0823-8707 See BOOKS FROM BRITISH COLUMBIA. 411
0823-8715 See JOURNAL (INSTITUTE FOR SASKATCHEWAN STUDIES). 1498
0823-874X See CANADIAN SPORTS AWARDS, ATHLETE OF THE MONTH. 4889
0823-8804 See OSAP ANNOUNCEMENT, SUMMARY AND ANALYSIS. 1839
0823-8812 See IMSS NEWSLETTER. 4964
0823-8839 See TAPE RECORDER (NOVA SCOTIA TEACHERS UNION. TEACHERS ASSOCIATION FOR PHYSICAL EDUCATION). 1858
0823-891X See REPERTOIRE DES SERVICES COMMUNAUTAIRES (SUDBURY). 5305
0823-8944 See MONTREAL NOW!. 3466

0823-9096 See ACTUALITE CANADA. 2526
0823-9118 See NEWS CANADA (TORONTO). 2541
0823-9142 See WOMEN'S ORGANIZATIONS IN HAMILTON-WENTWORTH. 5571
0823-9150 See CONTEMPORARY ACCOUNTING RESEARCH. 742
0823-9177 See GAUCHE SOCIALISTE. 4542
0823-9231 See AWASIS (JOURNAL). 2256
0823-9258 See TODAY'S PARENT. 2286
0823-9266 See GREAT EXPECTATIONS. 3579
0823-9274 See TRANSMARGE. 5264
0823-9339 See CANADIAN ARTIFICIAL INTELLIGENCE NEWSLETTER. 1212
0823-9355 See ALIMENTOLOGUE. 2326
0823-9363 See BETA NEWSLETTER. 642
0823-9398 See GOODLIFE (TORONTO). 2534
0823-9428 See CARREFOUR SALESIEN. 1814
0823-9436 See JUSTICE REPORT. 3168
0823-9436 See JUSTICE REPORT. 3168
0823-9452 See TO (TORONTO, ONT.). 2547
0823-9487 See BULLETIN - ASSOCIATION CANADIENNE POUR L'AVANCEMENT DES ETUDES NEERLANDAISES. 2680
0823-9533 See S.C.A.N. : SIMCOE COUNTY ANCESTORS' NEWS. 2471
0823-955X See MEMBERSHIP LIST / CAPAC. 4130
0823-9576 See NORTHERN POLITICS REVIEW. 4502
0823-9584 See DATA RESOURCES MODEL OF CANADIAN ENERGY MARKETS, THE. 1936
0823-9592 See RETRIEVAL CODE INDEX - DATA RESOURCES OF CANADA. 3246
0823-9606 See NEWSLETTER - BILL PRANKARD EVANGELISTIC ASSOCIATION. 4981
0823-9614 See CLINS D'OEIL DE DIEU. 4948
0823-9665 See BUSINESS ADVISORY REVIEW. 645
0823-9681 See CALEDON CITIZEN. 5781
0823-969X See REPERTOIRE DE LA LECTURE FRANCOPHONE, LE. 4819
0823-9703 See OPTION PAIX. 4530
0823-9746 See ARTSBOARD (TORONTO). 383
0823-9827 See KEYS TO HEALTH. 3602
0823-9843 See THAMES RIVER REVIEW. 2207
0823-9851 See INTERCHANGE - SCHOOL OF BUSINESS AND ECONOMICS. WILFRID LAURIER UNIVERSITY. 683
0823-9940 See COMPUTERS IN EDUCATION (TORONTO, ONT.). 1222
0824-0310 See FEDERAL SCIENTIFIC ACTIVITIES. 5174
0824-0337 See CANADIAN CRIME STATISTICS. 3079
0824-0353 See TECHNOLOGY NOTEBOOK (TECHNICAL UNIVERSITY OF NOVA SCOTIA). 5164
0824-0388 See VAN (RIVIERE BEAUDETTE). 5007
0824-0442 See SUBSCRIBERS DIRECTORY - TELEFLORA CANADA. 2436
0824-0469 See MARINE MAMMAL SCIENCE. 1452
0824-0493 See PROCEEDINGS OF THE ... ANNUAL CONFERENCE / INSTITUT DE READAPTATION DE MONTREAL. 4392
0824-0507 See REPERTOIRE DES ETABLISSEMENTS / SERVICE DES RECHERCHES ET DE LA STATISTIQUE, VILLE DE LAVAL. 707
0824-0574 See REBEL YOUTH. 5255
0824-0604 See WESTERN LIVING (VANCOUVER ED.). 2904
0824-0612 See WESTERN LIVING (EDMONTON ED.). 2550
0824-0639 See INUIT ART ENTHUSIASTS NEWSLETTER, THE. 353
0824-0655 See REPERTOIRE DES ECOLES - CONSEIL SCOLAIRE DE L'ILE DE MONTREAL. 1778
0824-0663 See CHOOSE LIFE (WEYBURN, SASK.). 2249
0824-0671 See NOUVELLE FEMME (MONTREAL, QUEBEC). 5563

0824-068X See PUCE A L'ORIELLE (MONTREAL). 1776
0824-0698 See COMMON GROUND (VANCOUVER). 3774
0824-0736 See CAHIERS DU LABRAPS. 1813
0824-0868 See 2 X 4. 633
0824-0906 See BULLETIN SKI NAUTIQUE. 4888
0824-0965 See QUEBEC G. 2796
0824-1309 See REVUE VOYAGEUR, LA. 5490
0824-1317 See JOURNAL D'OUTREMONT, LE. 2536
0824-1333 See ALLERGY ALERT. 3665
0824-1341 See PAPER - PACIFIC GROUP FOR POLICY ALTERNATIVES. 5300
0824-135X See SERIES - PACIFIC GROUP FOR POLICY ALTERNATIVES. 5307
0824-1368 See ISSUE (VANCOUVER). 353
0824-1384 See CONTINUING CARE RESOURCES. 3778
0824-1406 See WILLS FOR ALBERTA. 3119
0824-1414 See CANADIAN ARABIAN RACING REFERENCE. 2797
0824-1422 See TON AMI. 5005
0824-1430 See ANNUAIRE / CORPORATION PROFESSIONNELLE DES URBANISTES DU QUEBEC. 2814
0824-1457 See YAYA. 3257
0824-1465 See TRAVERS LES VIGNES, A. 2371
0824-1481 See A LA PAGE (STE-MARIE). 5779
0824-149X See INTERLAKE'S REGIONAL NEWS, THE. 5786
0824-1503 See MAIN DE L'AGE D'OR, LA. 5180
0824-152X See PALLISER PAGES. 3240
0824-1546 See FEUILLET SPIRITUEL DE L'OEUVRE DU PELERINAGE DES MALADES. 4959
0824-1554 See CANADIAN ORCHID JOURNAL, THE. 2412
0824-1600 See BIOSPHERE (OTTAWA). 2188
0824-1724 See PSYCHOLOGIE QUEBEC. 4612
0824-1732 See NEWSLETTER OF THE KINGS COUNTY HISTORICAL AND ARCHIVAL SOCIETY, INC. 2750
0824-1767 See CHAROLAIS BANNER. 209
0824-1813 See NEW EDITION. 5210
0824-1821 See PARTAGE (MONTREAL). 5018
0824-1848 See VOLUNTEERS IN ACTION. 5313
0824-1856 See CANADIAN LACEMAKER GAZETTE. 5183
0824-1902 See PERSONNES C.L.E.F. 3028
0824-197X See FIRST READING. 5245
0824-1996 See DIRECTORY OF THE CANADIAN BOTANICAL ASSOCIATION & CANADIAN SOCIETY OF PLANT PHYSIOLOGISTS. 508
0824-2062 See CATALYST / CITIZENS FOR PUBLIC JUSTICE. 4467
0824-2062 See CATALYST (TORONTO. 1982). 2727
0824-2089 See RAPPORT - FORINTEK CANADA CORP., LABORATOIRE DE L'EST. 2391
0824-2100 See ANGLES (VANCOUVER). 2793
0824-2119 See SPECIAL PUBLICATION - FORINTEK CANADA CORP. EASTERN LABORATORY. 2404
0824-2135 See REVIEW REPORT - FORINTEK CANADA CORP., EASTERN LABORATORY. 2394
0824-2178 See X-IT. 3455
0824-2186 See COMMUNIQUE (LAW SOCIETY OF MANITOBA). 2954
0824-2194 See NEWSVIEWS / CANADIAN JEWELLERS INSTITUTE. 2915
0824-2224 See OTA VIEWPOINT. 5389
0824-233X See BRANCHLINE (OTTAWA). 5429
0824-2348 See QUEBECER, THE. 4493
0824-2402 See KINEDIT. 5788
0824-2429 See CLAYTON HOUSING FORECAST. 2818
0824-2445 See Z'HUITRES. 2634
0824-2453 See MACHINIST CANADA, THE. 1689

0824-247X See VOIX DU PEUPLE (TORONTO). 4548

0824-2526 See YOGA LIFE (1982). 4365

0824-2577 See INFORMAL LOGIC (WINDSOR, ONT.). 4349

0824-2585 See CANADIAN CASES ON THE LAW OF INSURANCE. 2947

0824-2593 See CONSTRUCTION LAW REPORTS. 2956

0824-2607 See CANADIAN CASES ON EMPLOYMENT LAW. 3145

0824-2615 See ADMINISTRATIVE LAW REPORTS (TORONTO). 3091

0824-2623 See CANADIAN INTELLECTUAL PROPERTY REPORTS. 1302

0824-2666 See CANADIAN DRUG IDENTIFICATION CODE. 4295

0824-2674 See FIRE PROTECTION VIDEO, FILM AND SLIDE CATALOGUE. 2289

0824-2682 See DARTMOUTH BUSINESS NEWS. 664

0824-2712 See LELIRE ET L'ECRIRE. 5788

0824-278X See DOUBLE FEATURE (LETHBRIDGE). 2278

0824-2801 See TOUTE JUSTICE (OTTAWA, ONT.), EN. 3065

0824-281X See JUST CAUSE. 2991

0824-2828 See ECONOMIC REVIEW (REGINA. 1980). 1485

0824-2917 See NEWSLETTER - CANADIAN PHYSIOTHERAPY ASSOCIATION. SPORTS PHYSIOTHERAPY DIVISION. 3955

0824-295X See NOTES DE RECHERCHES - GEOGRAPHIE. UNIVERSITE D'OTTAWA. 2571

0824-2976 See RAPPORT ANNUEL / CORPORATION PROFESSIONNELLE DES COMPTABLES EN ADMINISTRATION INDUSTRIELLE DU QUEBEC. 750

0824-2992 See GREEN'S MAGAZINE. 3392

0824-300X See ACCOUNTING PRINCIPLES AND PRACTICES IN CANADA AND THE UNITED STATES OF AMERICA. 737

0824-3042 See CCB NATIONAL NEWSLETTER. 4385

0824-3050 See AKADEMIAJ STUDOJ. 3262

0824-3069 See AU POINT. 1810

0824-3077 See CULTURAMA. 318

0824-3085 See FOLKLORE (MOOSE JAW). 2320

0824-3093 See MENNONITE MEDICAL MESSENGER (WINNIPEG, MAN.). 3616

0824-3131 See EXPENSES OF SALES REPRESENTATIVES, TAX TREATMENT. 674

0824-314X See CORPORATE TAX RETURN HANDBOOK. 4719

0824-3158 See MANUEL POUR LA PREPARATION DES DECLARATIONS D'IMPOT DES CORPORATIONS. 4736

0824-3166 See AFRICA INLAND MISSION, CANADA. 4932

0824-3190 See B.C. REGIONAL FISHING GUIDE. CARIBOO, CHILCOTIN. 2297

0824-3220 See RESEARCH REPORT SERIES - BROCK GEOLOGICAL SCIENCES. STUDIES IN ENVIRONMENTAL EARTH SCIENCES. 1360

0824-3239 See RESEARCH REPORT SERIES - BROCK UNIVERSITY. DEPARTMENT OF GEOLOGICAL SCIENCES. STUDIES IN SEDIMENTARY PROCESSES. 1459

0824-3247 See RESEARCH REPORT SERIES - BROCK UNIVERSITY. DEPARTMENT OF GEOLOGICAL SCIENCES. STUDIES IN PALEOZOIC STRATIGRAPHIC INVESTIGATIONS. 1395

0824-3271 See RESEARCH REPORT SERIES - BROCK UNIVERSITY. DEPARTMENT OF GEOLOGICAL SCIENCES. STUDIES IN PALEOECOLOGY. 1395

0824-328X See RESEARCH REPORT SERIES - BROCK UNIVERSITY. DEPARTMENT OF GEOLOGICAL SCIENCES. STUDIES IN LANDSCAPE GEOCHEMISTRY. 1395

0824-3298 See MAN AND NATURE. 2622

0824-3328 See WEST INDIAN (TORONTO). 4500

0824-3336 See RISK ABSTRACTS. 4811

0824-3344 See ADVOCATES' SOCIETY JOURNAL, THE. 2928

0824-3352 See ALPHABETICAL LIST OF ENGLISH LANGUAGE BOOK TITLES AVAILABLE FROM CANADIAN SOURCES MICROFORM. 407

0824-3425 See ECONOMIC UPDATE - DOMINION SECURITIES AMES. ECONOMICS. 1558

0824-3433 See NORTHWEST TERRITORIES REPORTS. 3019

0824-3433 See NORTHWEST TERRITORIES REPORTS. 3019

0824-3441 See OPTICAL PRISM. 4216

0824-3468 See ACTION (REGINA). 2526

0824-3484 See NORTHERN MOSIAC (LLOYDMINSTER). 326

0824-3492 See ZEST (NELSON). 3456

0824-3514 See INFORMATION SOLUTIONS/ INFORMATION PLUS. 926

0824-3522 See NASE ZAJEDNISTVO. 4979

0824-3573 See 204 REPORTER. 1642

0824-3581 See NEWFOUNDLAND HERALD, THE. 2490

0824-359X See PATRIDES (TORONTO). 2270

0824-362X See REVIEW OF MAJOR INVESTMENT PROJECTS IN CANADA. 913

0824-3646 See CANMORE LEADER. 5781

0824-3654 See ORCHESTRA RESOURCE GUIDE. 4144

0824-3689 See DOCUMENTATION DU MINISTERE DE L'ENERGIE ET DES RESSOURCES, REPERTOIRE. 1555

0824-3719 See SMALL BUSINESS REPORT (OTTAWA). 711

0824-3727 See CANADA'S HOUSING CRISIS. 2817

0824-3735 See BULLETIN SUR LA PME. 1600

0824-3794 See PHOTOVOLTAICS TECHNIQUE. 4414

0824-3816 See BOLIVIA (MONTREAL). 2724

0824-3824 See FORESTRY REPORT (OTTAWA). 2382

0824-3832 See RAPPORT SUR L'INDUSTRIE FORESTIERE. 2391

0824-3883 See RAPPORT SUR LES FEMMES. 5214

0824-3972 See NEW FARMER'S FINDER. 160

0824-3980 See ECONOMIC ANALYSIS OF BRITISH COLUMBIA. 1482

0824-3999 See AMATEUR SPORT NEWS (SOUTHERN BRITISH COLUMBIA ED.). 4882

0824-4006 See AMATEUR SPORT NEWS (NORTHERN BRITISH COLUMBIA ED.). 4882

0824-4014 See AMATEUR SPORT NEWS (BRITISH COLUMBIA ED.). 4882

0824-4022 See AMATEUR SPORT NEWS (SOUTHERN SASKATCHEWAN ED.). 4882

0824-4030 See AMATEUR SPORT NEWS (NORTHERN SASKATCHEWAN ED.). 4882

0824-4049 See AMATEUR SPORT NEWS. 4882

0824-4057 See AMATEUR SPORT NEWS (EDMONTON ED.). 4882

0824-4065 See AMATEUR SPORT NEWS (CENTRAL ALBERTA ED.). 4882

0824-4073 See OFFICE CONNECTIONS. 4213

0824-4081 See NORTHERN WOMAN JOURNAL. 5563

0824-409X See EDMONTON REPORT ON ECONOMIC DEVELOPMENT, THE. 1559

0824-4146 See DISCUSSION PAPER SERIES - FACULTY OF BUSINESS ADMINISTRATION. SIMON FRASER UNIVERSITY. 1480

0824-4154 See COMMUNIQUE - SOCIETE D'ARTHRITE. 3804

0824-4170 See POUR LA SUITE DES JEUX. 4913

0824-4189 See DIALOGUE IMMERSION. 3277

0824-4219 See SPORTMEDINFO FROM THE SPORT MEDICINE COUNCIL OF CANADA. 3956

0824-4251 See ATRIA. 4084

0824-4286 See IMPACT (VAL-BELAIR (QUEBEC)). 2535

0824-4316 See DOCUMENT DE TRAVAIL - UNIVERSITE D'OTTAWA. FACULTE D'ADMINISTRATION. 667

0824-4421 See LAW UNION NEWS (TORONTO). 2997

0824-4448 See BULLETIN / CIVIL LIBERTIES ACTION SECURITY PROJECT. 4505

0824-4456 See NDP ANTI-WAR NEWSLETTER. 4529

0824-4472 See VICTORIA BUSINESS REVIEW. 1631

0824-4480 See MUSCLE WEST. 2600

0824-4529 See LONDON'S WHO & WHY MAGAZINE. 433

0824-4561 See 1441. 5779

0824-457X See EXCHANGE (KITCHENER). 833

0824-4596 See LONDON METROBULLETIN. 4663

0824-4650 See KONGRES POLONII KANADYJSKIEJ. 2743

0824-4669 See ONTARIO ANNOTATED FAMILY LAW SERVICE (BOUND EDITION). 3122

0824-4715 See AISPICH CHAKWAN. 5271

0824-4731 See EXPRESSION (WINNIPEG. ENGLISH ED.). 4958

0824-474X See EXPRESSION (WINNIPEG, DEUTSCHE AUSG.). 4958

0824-4766 See CANADA A-Z. 4252

0824-4774 See BRITISH COLUMBIA HOLSTEIN NEWS. 192

0824-4782 See WIP FUN. 3256

0824-4790 See COMPUTER LAW (TORONTO). 2955

0824-4812 See RIGHT TRACK (TORONTO). 2802

0824-4820 See NCSA NEWSLETTER. 5297

0824-4839 See UPDATE - ALCOHOL-DRUG EDUCATION SERVICE. 1350

0824-4863 See HEALTH & PHYSICAL EDUCATION NEWSLETTER. 1855

0824-4871 See PANORAMA - NORANDA (ED. FRANCAISE). 1621

0824-4936 See ESTUAIRE GENEALOGIQUE, L'. 2446

0824-4944 See REPORT FROM THE DEPARTMENT OF MATHEMATICS AND STATISTICS. 3531

0824-4960 See BRIDGES (TORONTO). 1728

0824-5045 See NATIONAL NEWSLETTER - CANADIAN ASSOCIATION OF SEXUAL ASSAULT CENTRES. 5297

0824-5053 See JOURNAL OF MENNONITE STUDIES. 4969

0824-507X See TOT TALK. 4805

0824-5096 See ACID RAIN NOTES. 2223

0824-510X See TRANSMISSION (MONTREAL). 3329

0824-5150 See KITCHENER-WATERLOO RECORD. 5788

0824-5177 See TOWARZYSTWO D/S UCHOCZCOW W NANAIMO. 5312

0824-5193 See BAN THONG TIN (NANAIMO REFUGEE CO-ORDINATION SOCIETY). 5274

0824-5266 See CANADIAN HUMAN RIGHTS YEARBOOK. 4505

0824-5282 See MCGILL WORKING PAPERS IN LINGUISTICS. 3301

0824-5304 See LONDON LEAF. 2458

0824-5347 See JUBILEE (MISSISSAUGA). 3168

0824-5355 See BY APPOINTMENT ONLY. 5552

0824-5398 See DIRECTORY OF RESOURCES FOR SENIOR CITIZENS OF OTTAWA-CARLETON. 5283

0824-5401 See INTERIM (TORONTO). 3762

0824-5444 See CALGARY COMMUNITY SERVICES DIRECTORY. 5276

0824-5452 See CANADIAN COPYRIGHT INSTITUTE. 1302

0824-5479 See PRIME TIME MAGAZINE. 5181

0824-5487 See WORLD OF WHEELS. 5428

0824-5495 See ARTS IN GUELPH, THE. 315

0824-5517 See REFLECTIONS (LONDON, ONT.). 1843

0824-5533 See WORLD OIL MARKET ANALYSIS. 4282

0824-555X See BORN-AGAIN CHRISTIAN DIRECTORY-CATALOG, THE. 4939

0824-5568 See APNA WATAN (MONTREAL, QUEBEC). 5780

0824-5576 See A3. 287

0824-5592 See BOOKS IN TAGALOG (1980). 4826

0824-5614 See NEWSLETTER / LONDON AND MIDDLESEX COUNTY HISTORICAL SOCIETY. 2749

0824-5622 See ETHICS IN-SERVICE. 2250

0824-5665 See RMS NEWS. 2272

0824-5673 See MENNOGESPRACH (WATERLOO). 5063

0824-5681 See HEALTH, LABOR & SAFETY REPORT. 2863

0824-5800 See COMERCIO (TORONTO. 1982). 5782

0824-5851 See HUA HSIEH HUEI T'UNG HSIN. 2535

0824-586X See RESISTANCE (VANCOUVER). 4493

0824-5894 See OVERVIEW (UNIVERSITY OF ALBERTA. COMPUTING SERVICES). 1261

0824-5908 See AL'MANAKH VYDAVNYTSTVA "TRYZUB". 4812

0824-5991 See VISTI / (OSEREDOK UKRAINSKOI KULTURY I OSVITY. 2765

0824-6009 See SCINTILLA (TORONTO). 3434

0824-6017 See ZHUJI. 5798

0824-6076 See NEW LINK. 2748

0824-6114 See TOURIST COUNCIL NEWS. 5494

0824-6181 See GPMC NEWSLETTER. 2342

0824-6238 See UKRAINSKE VIDRODZHENNJA. 2714

0824-6254 See SUPERMAGAZINE D'ARTISANAT LES MOUSTARTS. 376

0824-6297 See MACKENZIE OUTREACH. 357

0824-6300 See MAGYAR HIRMONDO (CALGARY). 2745

0824-6378 See HENRY B. ZIMMER'S PROBLEMS & QUESTIONS IN CANADIAN TAXATION. 2978

0824-6394 See JOURNAL (ASHCROFT). 5787

0824-6459 See CENTRAL LIBRARY SELECTED ACQUISITIONS RELATING TO URBAN AFFAIRS. 413

0824-6505 See AISPLAYBACK. 3188

0824-6521 See QUAKER COMMITTEE ON JAILS & JUSTICE (1981). 3174

0824-653X See OBSERVATEUR ORTHODOXE, L'. 4983

0824-6556 See REGIONAL REVIEW NEWSLETTER. 2833

0824-6572 See ST. CATHARINES. 5491

0824-6602 See CAHIERS DE L'ACADEMIE (MONTREAL). 2784

0824-6610 See ADVANCE (ZURICH). 5779

0824-6629 See ON COURT. 4911

0824-6637 See CANADIAN ROSE ROOTS. 2441

0824-6653 See BREAK-THROUGH (HARTNEY). 4105

0824-667X See HENRY B. ZIMMER'S INCOME TAX PROBLEMS WITH DETAILED SOLUTIONS. 4730

0824-6696 See GUARDIAN CAPITAL'S VIEWPOINT. 1493

0824-6718 See NIGHTMOVES. 4141

0824-6726 See SOUTH VOICE, THE. 5795

0824-6769 See OPERATING SURVEY OF CANADIAN RETAILING. 956

0824-6823 See SALE - D & J RITCHIE. 364

0824-6882 See REFERENCE SERIES. HEMATOLOGY. 3773

0824-6890 See CLAYTON CONSUMER REPORT. 1294

0824-6904 See CANADIAN PRINT & PORTFOLIO. 377

0824-6912 See ELECTRONIC AGE (TORONTO). 2046

0824-6947 See SCRIBE (VANCOUVER). 2760

0824-6998 See INSTITUT DE RADIOTELEVISION POUR ENFANTS. 1133

0824-7005 See CHILDREN'S BROADCAST INSTITUTE. 1130

0824-703X See DRUGS IN PEDIATRICS. 3903

0824-7056 See METAL K.O. 4131

0824-7064 See INTELLECTUAL PROPERTY JOURNAL. 1305

0824-7102 See DRUGS IN PSYCHIATRY (POINTE-CLAIRE). 4302

0824-7226 See CPA FREEWHEELER. 4386

0824-7315 See PARKINSON NETWORK. 3626

0824-7323 See RECREATION PRACTITIONERS BULLETIN. 4854

0824-7331 See SEMINAR ANNUAL - ONTARIO GENEALOGICAL SOCIETY. 2472

0824-734X See MARINE ENGINEERING DIGEST. 1986

0824-7358 See MANITOBA COMPOSERS' ASSOCIATION. 4129

0824-7404 See OBSTETRICS AND GYNAECOLOGY (OTTAWA). 3766

0824-7412 See ANAESTHESIOLOGY. 3680

0824-7420 See WORLD OF LUBAVITCH. 5053

0824-7471 See METAL TRENDS. 1618

0824-7501 See STAR (VICTORIA). 5795

0824-7536 See LIST OF CERTIFIED HEALTH CARE PRODUCTS AND SERVICES. 3605

0824-7544 See CRIMINAL LAW DIGEST. SUPPLEMENT (TORONTO 1982). 3106

0824-7552 See CIVIL RIGHTS (VANCOUVER). 4506

0824-7579 See TIDEPOOL (HAMILTON). 3446

0824-7706 See GLUT. 2735

0824-7714 See CARLETON PAPERS IN APPLIED LANGUAGE STUDIES. 3272

0824-7730 See DADSWELL FAMILY BULLETIN. 2444

0824-7749 See BULLETIN - SPECIAL LIBRARIES ASSOCIATION, EASTERN CANADA CHAPTER. 3198

0824-7773 See HAGALO USTED MISMO - BRACE RESEARCH INSTITUTE. 4404

0824-782X See EMC. EDUCATIONAL MEDIA SPECIAL INTEREST COUNCIL. 3209

0824-7900 See SPORT ADMINISTRATOR, THE. 4920

0824-7935 See COMPUTATIONAL INTELLIGENCE. 1212

0824-796X See CAHIERS D'HISTOIRE DE LA RIVIERE DU NORD, LES. 2725

0824-7986 See BRITISH COLUMBIA GAZETTE. PART II, REGULATIONS, THE. 2943

0824-8095 See GUIDE DES USAGERS / UNIVERSITE DE SHERBROOKE-BIBLIOTHEQUE GENERALE. 3212

0824-8125 See NEW TRAIL (1982). 1102

0824-8133 See INDUSTRIAL RESEARCH AND DEVELOPMENT STATISTICS ... WITH ... FORECASTS. 5175

0824-8214 See VIVA VIRUS. 389

0824-8230 See A L'AUTRE, UNE. 3755

0824-8265 See ANNUAL REPORT / CANADIAN NATIONAL. 5376

0824-8281 See INHALO-SCOPE. 4308

0824-8427 See CHALLENGER (NORTH VANCOUVER). 1731

0824-8451 See SASKATCHEWAN HEALTH MANPOWER REPORT. 3917

0824-8494 See AMI DES BETES, L'. 4285

0824-8567 See RAPPORT ANNUEL DU CURATEUR PUBLIC (1977). 4798

0824-8583 See GREAT LAKES NAVIGATION. 5449

0824-8605 See PROCEEDINGS - CANADIAN CONFERENCE ON COAL. 1443

0824-8613 See GUIDE GENERAL DES COMITES - ASTED. 3212

0824-8621 See ETUDES HELLENIQUES. 2687

0824-8729 See MARINE EQUIPMENT DIRECTORY. 4179

0824-880X See ACIDIC PRECIPITATION IN ONTARIO STUDY. 2223

0824-8826 See REALISATIONS RECENTES A PETAWAWA. 2392

0824-8907 See NATIONAL ARCHIVES NEWSLETTER. 2482

0824-8915 See ANNUAL REPORT - MINISTRY OF TOURISM AND RECREATION (TORONTO). 5461

0824-9040 See MENSUEL DE LACHUTE, LE. 5789

0824-9091 See ARS TEXTRINA. 5348

0824-9180 See BULLETIN DE LIAISON / PRESSE ETUDIANTE DU QUEBEC. 1812

0824-9210 See GENERAL INDEX TO PUBLISHED REPORTS, MINERAL RESOURCES GROUP. 2139

0824-9415 See QUARTERLY / ROYAL CANADIAN MOUNTED POLICE, THE. 3174

0824-9547 See CAHIERS DU GRIDEQ. 1541

0824-9709 See CHIROPRACTIC RESEARCH ARCHIVES COLLECTION. 3563

0824-9849 See SPORTING SCENE (SCARBOROUGH, ONT.). 4922

0824-9873 See ANNUAL REPORT / PRINCE EDWARD ISLAND LENDING AUTHORITY. 772

0824-989X See ANNUAL REPORT / COLLEGE RELATIONS COMMISSION. 1809

0824-9946 See PROVINCIAL NEWSJOURNAL - INFANT DEVELOPMENT PROGRAMMES OF B.C. 5302

0824-9970 See BALLET CANADA INTERNATIONAL. 1310

0825-0014 See HANDBOOK FOR MEMBERS OF THE NORTHWEST TERRITORIES TEACHERS' ASSOCIATION, A. 1895

0825-0049 See ECHEC +. 4860

0825-0103 See B.C. DIGEST (VICTORIA). 2722

0825-012X See MINUTES OF PROCEEDINGS AND EVIDENCE OF THE SUB-COMMITTEE ON INDIAN WOMEN AND THE INDIAN ACT OF THE STANDING COMMITTEE ON INDIAN AFFAIRS AND NORTHERN DEVELOPMENT. 2267

0825-0138 See MINUTES OF PROCEEDINGS AND EVIDENCE OF THE SPECIAL COMMITTEE ON PENSION REFORM. 1691

0825-0146 See MINUTES OF PROCEEDINGS AND EVIDENCE OF THE SUB-COMMITTEE OF THE STANDING COMMITTEE ON AGRICULTURE ON FARM CREDIT ARRANGEMENTS. 108

0825-0162 See RESEARCH REPORT / ATOMIC ENERGY CONTROL BOARD. 1955

0825-0197 See PS. 1843

0825-0251 See MINUTES OF PROCEEDINGS AND EVIDENCE OF THE SPECIAL JOINT COMMITTEE OF THE SENATE AND OF THE HOUSE OF COMMONS ON SENATE REFORM. 4665

0825-0324 See NETWORK (TORONTO. 1984). 2600

0825-0332 See RESEAU (TORONTO). 2601

0825-0367 See TPUG MAGAZINE. 1205

0825-0383 See CANADIAN JOURNAL OF ADMINISTRATIVE SCIENCES. 863

0825-0391 See PMC. PRACTICE OF MINISTRY IN CANADA. 4986

0825-0456 See INTERNATIONAL SEMIOTIC SPECTRUM. 2848

0825-0464 See MODULE D'AUTOFORMATION. 3618

0825-0596 See NOVATEUR, LE. 1620

0825-0677 See MINUTES OF PROCEEDINGS AND EVIDENCE OF SUB-COMMITTEE B OF THE SPECIAL COMMITTEE ON EMPLOYMENT OPPORTUNITIES FOR THE '80S. 1691

0825-0707 See REVUE ECONOMIQUE - CHAMBRE DE COMMERCE DE LAVAL. 1518

0825-107X See INFO SOURCE (ENGLISH ED.). 4656

0825-124X See INCOME ESTIMATES FOR SUBPROVINCIAL AREAS. 1494

0825-1339 See PRODUCTION, SALES, AND STOCKS OF MAJOR APPLIANCES. 2812

0825-1711 See CARING FOR ANIMALS (OTTAWA, ONT.). 226

0825-1770 See FORESTRY NEWSLETTER (SAULT STE. MARIE). 2382

0825-186X See APLIC BULLETIN. 3191

0825-1886 See SWEETGRASS. 2274

0825-2084 See TECHNICAL BULLETIN - AGRICULTURE CANADA. RESEARCH BRANCH. 139

0825-219X ISSN Index

0825-219X *See* MINING AND MINERAL PROCESSING OPERATIONS IN CANADA. **2145**

0825-2483 *See* ATLAS OF ALBERTA'S CRUDE BITUMEN RESERVES. **4251**

0825-2556 *See* CHILDREN'S BULLETIN FOR NURSERY AND KINDERGARTEN TEACHERS AND LEADERS. **1890**

0825-2696 *See* CONNECTIONS (WILLOWDALE). **1602**

0825-2777 *See* CULTURES DU CANADA FRANCAIS. **2730**

0825-2815 *See* ANNUAL SALARIES, NURSES, MAJOR HOSPITAL AGREEMENTS, CANADA. **3851**

0825-2823 *See* BULLETIN / ASSOCIATION CANADIENNE DE LINGUISTIQUE. **3270**

0825-3005 *See* CLINIMED. **3567**

0825-3021 *See* CANADIAN COMMUNICATIONS NETWORK LETTER. **1151**

0825-3498 *See* MAN TO MAN (OTTAWA). **5251**

0825-3854 *See* CANADIAN ART (TORONTO, 1984). **346**

0825-3927 *See* ANNUAIRE DES BIBLIOTHECAIRES-CONSEILS DU QUEBEC. **3190**

0825-4044 *See* WINTER RECREATION DIRECTORY. **4855**

0825-4494 *See* THEATRE QUEBEC. **5371**

0825-477X *See* WHISTLE PUNK. **2398**

0825-4850 *See* HIGHLIGHT QUEBEC. **4963**

0825-4982 *See* BUSINESS & THE LAW. **3096**

0825-4990 *See* AUTO PREVENTION. **5405**

0825-513X *See* ACTES DU CONGRES / ASSOCIATION CANADIENNE DES PROFESSEURS D'IMMERSION. **1722**

0825-5172 *See* TECHNOLOGUE. **5163**

0825-5229 *See* A.I.P. CANADA (ENGLISH ED.). **3**

0825-5318 *See* HEARTWOOD. **4588**

0825-5326 *See* CARFAX (HULL, QUEBEC). **3372**

0825-5687 See FORAGE SEED UPDATE. **88**

0825-5709 *See* ALBERTA TRAFFIC COLLISION FACTS. **5438**

0825-5784 *See* HYPERION PC. **1186**

0825-5822 *See* CAHIERS DU CETAI / CENTRE D'ETUDES EN ADMINISTRATION INTERNATIONALE, LES. **1633**

0825-608X *See* CANADIAN OCCUPATIONAL SAFETY AND HEALTH LAW MONTHLY REPORT. **2948**

0825-6667 *See* SUMMARY OF ECONOMIC AND LOAD FORECASTS. **4762**

0825-6683 *See* DIPLOMATIC, CONSULAR, AND OTHER REPRESENTATIVES IN CANADA. **4642**

0825-6764 *See* GUIDE GRIMALDI DE MONTREAL, LE. **5479**

0825-6896 *See* SUMMARY OF OPERATIONS / MINERAL RESOURCES DIVISION. **2151**

0825-6926 *See* BULLETIN DU CONSEIL DE LA LANGUE FRANCAISE. **3271**

0825-7019 *See* FARM CREDIT STATISTICS. **729**

0825-7043 *See* FINANCIAL STATEMENTS & FINANCIAL STATISTICS / CAISSE DE DEPOT ET PLACEMENT DU QUEBEC. **4649**

0825-7159 *See* PROVINCIAL GEOLOGISTS JOURNAL. **1392**

0825-7256 *See* CANADIAN INTELLECTUAL PROPERTY REVIEW. **1302**

0825-7345 *See* CARILLON (CANADA. DEPT. OF VETERANS AFFAIRS). **4637**

0825-7361 *See* ANNUAL REPORT OF THE PRIVACY COMMISSIONER. **2935**

0825-7507 *See* REACH TH' PEOPLE. **5367**

0825-7515 *See* CANADIAN CIVIL ENGINEER. **2020**

0825-7531 *See* EMPATHIC PARENTING. **5284**

0825-754X *See* CANADIAN VET SUPPLIES. **5507**

0825-7752 *See* NEWSLETTER / CANADIAN TELEBOOK AGENCY. **4817**

0825-7868 *See* LIAISON - COUNCIL OF MINISTERS OF EDUCATION, CANADA. **1761**

0825-7914 *See* PISCES. **2310**

0825-8031 *See* PROTEXTILE. **5355**

0825-8260 *See* NATIONAL DIRECTORY, HOME HEATING PRODUCTS. **2607**

0825-8449 *See* CHUCHOTERIES. **1861**

0825-8597 *See* JOURNAL OF PALLIATIVE CARE. **5292**

0825-8708 *See* INTER (HAUTE-VILLE, QUEBEC). **385**

0825-9178 *See* BOUSSOLE. **3922**

0825-9216 *See* NATIONAL BALANCE SHEET ACCOUNTS. **4738**

0825-9879 *See* SCIENCE ET FRANCOPHONIE. **5151**

0825-9895 *See* CHANTIERS (ANJOU). **607**

0825-9984 *See* ANNUAIRE ASTRONOMIQUE (MONTREAL, QUEBEC). **391**

0826-0001 See NEWS - ONTARIO FEDERATION OF INDEPENDENT SCHOOLS. **1768**

0826-0095 *See* HALIFAX AND DARTMOUTH CLUBS AND ORGANIZATIONS (1983). **5231**

0826-0125 *See* HLABC FORUM. **3213**

0826-0133 *See* HEJIRA (MONTREAL, QUEBEC). **3463**

0826-0206 *See* CIE NATIONAL NEWS. **1935**

0826-0273 *See* PUBLICATION (UNIVERSITY OF GUELPH. UNIVERSITY SCHOOL OF RURAL PLANNING AND DEVELOPMENT). **2832**

0826-032X *See* FLIGHT SAFETY BULLETIN. **21**

0826-0338 *See* ANNUAIRE : L'EGLISE DE MONTREAL. **5023**

0826-0508 *See* BODY POLITIC XTRA. **2793**

0826-0613 *See* INFORMATION LISTING / REGIONAL CLERK'S DEPT. **4656**

0826-0621 *See* CONVENING CIRCULAR AND SYNOD JOURNAL FOR THE ... SESSION OF SYNOD. **4950**

0826-0648 *See* IN TOUCH (OTTAWA). **5112**

0826-094X *See* WHAT'S NEW IN ACCOUNTING CANADA. **753**

0826-0974 *See* RELEVE DES NOUVEAUX INSCRITS. **1844**

0826-1024 *See* CSCC NEWS. **973**

0826-1067 *See* JOURNAL OF RARE OLD BOOKS, THE. **4829**

0826-1083 *See* SECURITY & PROTECTION. **5177**

0826-1113 *See* OTTAWA GREENS NEWSLETTER. **4486**

0826-1121 *See* GALLERY (LETHBRIDGE). **351**

0826-113X *See* VERDIGRIS MAGAZINE. **2549**

0826-1164 *See* PROVENANCE (LONDON). **4095**

0826-1210 *See* TRIBUTE GOES TO THE MOVIES. **4079**

0826-1326 *See* BULLETIN DE NOUVELLES / FEDERATION QUEBECOISE DES SPORTS AERIENS, SECTEUR PARACHUTISME. **4888**

0826-1334 *See* LISTE DES NOUVEAUTES - COLLEGE DE L'ASSOMPTION. BIBLIOTHEQUE DU COLLEGIAL. **3228**

0826-1458 *See* FORUM - FORUM FOR YOUNG CANADIANS. **4474**

0826-1547 *See* COMPUTERWORLD CANADA. **1236**

0826-1725 *See* ANNUAL REPORT - FOREST RESEARCH COUNCIL OF BRITISH COLUMBIA. **2374**

0826-192X *See* ELECTROSOURCE : PRODUCT REFERENCE GUIDE AND TELEPHONE DIRECTORY. **2050**

0826-1946 *See* INFORMATION FOR MEMBERS / NOVA SCOTIA LIBRARY ASSOCIATION. **3215**

0826-1954 *See* CANALS CANADA. **5379**

0826-1997 *See* NEWSLETTER / CANADIAN OWNERS & PILOTS ASSOCIATION. **30**

0826-2004 *See* STATISTICAL REPORT - ALBERTA ADVANCED EDUCATION AND MANPOWER. **1797**

0826-2098 *See* WILLOW TRANSFER QUARTERLY. **2595**

0826-2179 *See* ELECTRONICS PRODUCT NEWS. **2050**

0826-2187 *See* DIALOGO. **2731**

0826-2233 *See* ANNUAIRE DENTAIRE / ORDRE DES DENTISTES DU QUEBEC. **1316**

0826-2241 *See* SNOW LAKE NEWS. **5794**

0826-2276 *See* PENSEE DE BAGOT. **5792**

0826-2314 *See* A.H.M.H. INC. : ASSOCIATION DU HOCKEY MINEUR DE HULL INC. **4881**

0826-2322 *See* JOURNAL PERIODIQUE. **396**

0826-2349 *See* WESTIN. **2550**

0826-2527 *See* OTTAWA-HULL (OTTAWA, ONT.). **386**

0826-256X *See* FLAMING CARROT COMICS. **4861**

0826-2586 *See* MS. TREE. **5074**

0826-2594 *See* FEELING FINE. **4191**

0826-2616 *See* INFO JEUNES PC. **4477**

0826-2667 *See* ARMENIAN CAUSE, THE. **2645**

0826-2705 *See* MICROINFO (TORONTO). **1269**

0826-273X *See* DEFI (OTTAWA). **5783**

0826-2748 *See* MOUTON NOIR. **5790**

0826-2756 *See* VITA SANA. **4806**

0826-2764 *See* PAIX D'URGENCE. **4530**

0826-2799 *See* NOUVELLES DE L'A.Q.T. **4413**

0826-2802 *See* BOAT GUIDE. **592**

0826-2861 *See* CATALOGUE - FUNNEL. **4065**

0826-2896 *See* ATLANTIC LEGAL TELEPHONE DIRECTORY. **3139**

0826-2918 *See* TROUBADOUR : BULLETIN BIMESTRIEL. **332**

0826-2926 *See* STUDY PAPER SERIES / CANADIAN CERTIFIED GENERAL ACCOUNTANTS' RESEARCH FOUNDATION. **752**

0826-2942 *See* C.S.A. NEWSLETTER - CANADIAN SOCIETY OF AGRONOMY (1983). **165**

0826-2969 *See* NEWSLETTER - FIGURE SKATING COACHES OF CANADA. **4908**

0826-2985 *See* FARM BULLETIN (ST. PIERRE, MAN.). **84**

0826-2993 See REVIEW - NORTH-SOUTH INSTITUTE (OTTAWA). **1625**

0826-3000 See REVUE : UN BULLETIN DE L'INSTITUT NORD-SUD. **1625**

0826-3019 *See* ORC REPORT. **4876**

0826-3035 *See* COUNTY MAGAZINE (BLOOMFIELD. 1983). **2729**

0826-3116 *See* REPERTOIRE DES ACTIVITES DE FORMATION ET D'INFORMATION. **2868**

0826-3140 *See* COAST TO COAST COUNTRY. **4110**

0826-3205 *See* JOURNAL OF THE ... GENERAL SYNOD / ANGLICAN CHURCH OF CANADA. **5062**

0826-3310 *See* SELECTIONS - MODERN LANGUAGES SERVICES BRANCH (RICHMOND). **3459**

0826-337X *See* LIST OF SCHOOLS IN MANITOBA. **1762**

0826-3663 *See* CANADIAN JOURNAL OF LATIN AMERICAN AND CARIBBEAN STUDIES. **2726**

0826-3671 *See* FIVE LIBRARY REGIONS ..., PROVINCE OF NEW BRUNSWICK, THE. **3211**

0826-3922 *See* BLACKFLASH. **4367**

0826-4139 See MISSISSAUGA BUSINESS TIMES. **695**

0826-4198 *See* WORKERS' COMPENSATION REPORTER. **1719**

0826-421X *See* REFERENCE SERIES. MICROBIOLOGY. **569**

0826-4260 *See* COMMUNITY DIGEST (VANCOUVER). **2531**

0826-4279 *See* JUNIOR HOCKEY ACTION. **4902**

0826-4295 *See* ST. LAMBERT JOURNAL. **5795**

0826-435X *See* TESL CANADA JOURNAL. **3328**

0826-4376 *See* ANNUAL WILD WEST SHOW. **337**

0826-4392 *See* PLANS DE MAISONS DU QUEBEC. **624**

0826-4503 *See* VOIR DIRE (MONTREAL). **4395**

0826-4511 *See* VOILE LIBRE (MONTREAL, QUEBEC). **4928**

0826-452X *See* BULLETIN TECHNIQUE / INSTIUT CANADIEN DE TOLE D'ACIER EN BATIMENT. **2019**

0826-4538 *See* PUB. - INSTITUT CANADIEN DE TOLE D'ACIER EN BATIMENT. **2029**

0826-4546 *See* ENTREFILET (POINTE CLAIRE). **2334**

0826-4554 *See* MEAT PROBE. **2349**

ISSN Index

0826-4686 See RED DEER CITY DIRECTORY (1992). 2574

0826-4694 See CENTRE ON AGING NEWS. 5178

0826-4740 See MOTS CACHES J'AIME, LES. 4863

0826-4775 See THROUGH THE YEARS. 2763

0826-4805 See INTERCHANGE (TORONTO. 1984). 1753

0826-4805 See INTERCHANGE (TORONTO. 1984). 1753

0826-4864 See INTERFACE (MONTREAL. 1984). 5114

0826-4899 See CANADIAN MOONLIGHTER'S DIGEST. 1658

0826-4929 See NETWORK OF SASKATCHEWAN WOMEN (1983). 5562

0826-497X See ACA NEWS (EDMONTON). 5177

0826-4996 See QUIRES. 4148

0826-5003 See WINDSPORT. 4929

0826-5046 See REGIONAL NIAGARA INDUSTRIAL DIRECTORY. 1624

0826-5054 See BOOKMARK (VANCOUVER). 3197

0826-5119 See ANNUAIRE / FRERES PRECHEURS, PROVINCE SAINT-DOMINIQUE DU CANADA. 4935

0826-516X See CONFERENCE REPORT - PRIMARY ELEMENTARY TEACHERS ASSOCIATION. 1862

0826-5216 See SEE THE MUSIC. 4152

0826-5224 See TOUR DE SUTTON, LE. 4855

0826-5240 See BARBIZON. 2788

0826-5283 See HISTORIEN MUNICIPAL, L'. 2737

0826-5305 See SPORTS-LOISIRS (MONTREAL). 4923

0826-5313 See HOCKEY AMATEUR. 4898

0826-5321 See ATOSSEMENT VOTRE. 2296

0826-533X See PROMISE (REGINA). 5066

0826-5356 See SITE. 627

0826-5631 See REPERTOIRE DES EDITEURS ET DE LEURS DISTRIBUTEURS. 4819

0826-5682 See MAGAZINE EQUESTRE (1984). 2800

0826-5712 See PHOTO PIPELINE. 4373

0826-581X See NEWS BRIEF - ENVIRONMENTAL LAW CENTRE (EDMONTON). 3115

0826-5828 See INDUSTRIAL ASSISTANCE PROGRAMS IN CANADA. 1610

0826-5887 See JOURNAL - CANADIAN OLDTIMERS' HOCKEY ASSOCIATION. 4901

0826-5909 See RADDLE MOON. 3427

0826-5984 See FREE MUSIC MAGAZINE. 4118

0826-5992 See SPORTING LIFE (WESTMOUNT, QUEBEC). 4921

0826-6026 See CANADIAN CIVIL AVIATION. 15

0826-6131 See SUPPLEMENT TO THE NATIONAL BUILDING CODE OF CANADA, THE. 629

0826-6166 See SPECIAL VOLUME (CANADIAN INSTITUTE OF MINING AND METALLURGY : 1982). 2151

0826-6204 See CANADIAN FURNITURE AND FURNISHINGS DIRECTORY. 2904

0826-6220 See JOURNAL OF PULP AND PAPER SCIENCE. 4234

0826-6425 See APC (SASKATCHEWAN. AIR POLLUTION CONTROL BRANCH). 2224

0826-6433 See MANUSCRIPT REPORTS - INTERNATIONAL DEVELOPMENT RESEARCH CENTRE. 107

0826-6778 See CANADIAN CRITICAL CARE NURSING JOURNAL. 3852

0826-6808 See ONTARIO HOSPITALS DIRECTORY. 3790

0826-6905 See ODA SUGGESTED FEE GUIDE FOR GENERAL PRACTITIONERS. 1331

0826-7243 See PROCESS INDUSTRIES CANADA. 2016

0826-7278 See CANADIAN HOUSING. 2817

0826-7294 See ANNUAL REPORT - OMBUDSMAN. ONTARIO (1984). 4629

0826-7391 See DIRECTORY OF COMMUNITY SERVICES FOR HAMILTON-WENTWORTH. 5282

0826-7413 See MANUFACTURERS DIRECTORY, WINDSOR-ESSEX COUNTY, ONTARIO, CANADA. 3483

0826-743X See CANADIAN ROSE ANNUAL (1983). 2412

0826-7464 See ANACRUSIS. 4100

0826-7499 See CONSOLATA MISSIONARIES. 4950

0826-7642 See CANADIAN HOUSE AND HOME. 2904

0826-7731 See VILLE (MONTREAL), EN. 5498

0826-7758 See MONTHLY INDICATORS - WOOD GUNDY LIMITED. 1506

0826-7766 See DROITS DE LA PERSONNE. BULLETIN D'INFORMATION SUR LA RECHERCHE ET L'ENSEIGNEMENT. 4507

0826-8045 See INFO-COOP. 1495

0826-8142 See IDENTIFICATION CANADA. 5289

0826-8185 See INTERNATIONAL JOURNAL OF ROBOTICS & AUTOMATION. 1213

0826-8258 See EDUCATION STATISTICS BULLETIN. 1740

0826-8355 See CANADIAN FEDERAL GOVERNMENT HANDBOOK. 4636

0826-8428 See BOTTIN QUEBECOIS DES CHERCHEURS EN GENEALOGIE. 2439

0826-8541 See DIRECTORY OF MEMBERS / THE BIBLIOGRAPHICAL SOCIETY OF CANADA. 415

0826-8673 See GUIA SOCIAL DEL TRABAJADOR. 3148

0826-8681 See GUIDA SOCIAL DO TRABALHADOR. 3148

0826-869X See GUIDA SOCIALE DEL LAVORATORE. 3148

0826-9335 See BRAUCH REPORT ON ELECTRONIC PUBLISHING, THE. 4812

0826-9343 See C.S.N.D.T. JOURNAL. 4427

0826-9475 See P.E.I. LABOUR MARK. BULL. 1700

0826-9505 See INTERPRETATION BULLETIN / ALBERTA TREASURY, CORPORATE TAX ADMINISTRATION. 3100

0826-9521 See PEACE MAGAZINE. 4531

0826-953X See ANNUAL REPORT / SASKATCHEWAN HUMAN RIGHTS COMMISSION. 4504

0826-9661 See YEARBOOK OF ITALIAN STUDIES. 3455

0826-967X See BORDER/LINES. 4185

0826-9696 See KIDS TORONTO. 4851

0826-9726 See CANADIAN ART. CATALOGUE OF THE NATIONAL GALLERY OF CANADA. 346

0826-9726 See EUROPEAN AND AMERICAN PAINTING, SCULPTURE AND DECORATIVE ARTS. 320

0826-9831 See TORONTO JOURNAL OF THEOLOGY. 5005

0826-9866 See CINEACTION!. 4065

0826-9874 See QUEBEC PHARMACIE (MONTREAL, 1981). 4327

0826-9904 See ANNUAL REPORT, INFORMATION COMMISSIONER. 4627

0826-9971 See PALISADE POST. 278

0827-0074 See AMA NEWSLETTER. 2478

0827-0090 See DECADE OF EDUCATION FINANCE. 1794

0827-0139 See BULLETIN AEF. 5552

0827-018X See ARCHIVES CANADA MICROFICHES. 2479

0827-0198 See ANNUAIRE THEATRAL, L'. 5361

0827-0317 See BRITISH COLUMBIA ENERGY SUPPLY AND REQUIREMENTS FORECAST. TECHNICAL REPORT. 1934

0827-0325 See BRITISH COLUMBIA ENERGY SUPPLY AND REQUIREMENTS FORECAST. TECHNICAL REPORT. 1934

0827-0333 See BRITISH COLUMBIA ENERGY SUPPLY AND REQUIREMENTS FORECAST. SUMMARY REPORT. 1934

0827-0465 See DAILY / STATISTICS CANADA, THE. 4697

0827-0708 See CANADA: THE STATE OF THE FEDERATION. 4636

0827-0732 See CAYENNE. 5553

0827-0864 See GUIDE TO THE CANADIAN FINANCIAL SERVICES INDUSTRY. 789

0827-0899 See CANADIAN JOURNAL OF RESEARCH IN EARLY CHILDHOOD EDUCATION, THE. 1803

0827-1038 See CLINICAL BIOFEEDBACK AND HEALTH. 4581

0827-1224 See CANADIAN UNIVERSITY DISTANCE EDUCATION DIRECTORY / REPERTOIRE DE L'ENSEIGNEMENT A DISTANCE DANS LES UNIVERSITES CANADIENNES. 1814

0827-1305 See DENTAL PRACTICE MANAGEMENT (DON MILLS, ONT.). 1321

0827-150X See FLEUR DESIGN. 2435

0827-1550 See INTERCULTURAL HORIZONS. 5247

0827-1690 See APPROCHES (MONTREAL, QUEBEC). 4935

0827-1844 See APPRENTISSAGE ET SOCIALISATION (1991). 1875

0827-1887 See PHILOSOPHER (MONTREAL, QUEBEC). 4355

0827-2034 See DIRECTORY - CANADIAN STAMP DEALERS' ASSOCIATION. 2785

0827-2042 See BRITISH COLUMBIA SPORT FISHING. 2297

0827-2077 See KAHTOU. 2536

0827-2085 See NOUVELLE (BEAUMONT). 5791

0827-2093 See RENEWABLE ENERGY NEWS (CANADIAN ED.). 1955

0827-2131 See TRACE NEWSLETTER - TORONTO REGION AGGREGATION OF COMPUTER ENTHUSIASTS. 1205

0827-2247 See ONTARIO DEMOCRAT, THE. 4485

0827-2255 See CALABRIA MIA (DOWNSVIEW, ONT.). 2682

0827-2263 See WOMEN'S CONCERNS. 5009

0827-2298 See OTTAWA BANDING GROUP. 5619

0827-2352 See ONTARIO OUTDOOR GUIDE & CALENDAR. 4876

0827-2387 See MOLE. 4131

0827-2395 See DOMINION (TORONTO). 5059

0827-2409 See WILDLIFE COLLECTABLES JOURNAL, THE. 2209

0827-2417 See NETWORK (NIAGARA FALLS). 5298

0827-2425 See NEW POET'S HANDBOOK / THE LEAGUE OF CANADIAN POETS. 3466

0827-245X See V.I.T.A. NEWSLETTER (WINNIPEG. 1992). 1917

0827-2484 See HOME ENTERTAINMENT GUIDE (FM GUIDE ED.). 4851

0827-2514 See NOTES - CANADIAN FEDERATION OF STUDENTS, ONTARIO. 1838

0827-2530 See TRANSACTOR, THE. 1273

0827-2557 See FREE FLIGHT (OTTAWA ONT.). 4895

0827-2603 See ALBERTA BUSINESS (CALGARY). 637

0827-2611 See REGIONAL (KENORA). 2544

0827-262X See COMPUTEK. 1266

0827-2638 See BOWBENDER MAGAZINE. 4888

0827-2654 See VIEWPOINT - INSURANCE BUREAU OF CANADA. 2896

0827-2697 See CANADIAN APPRAISER, THE. 4835

0827-2700 See MENTAL HEALTH NEWS BULLETIN. 4790

0827-2735 See ASPLO NEWSLETTER. 3192

0827-2743 See NEWSLETTER / INSTITUTE OF VICTORIA LIBRARIANS. 3235

0827-2786 See DARTMOUTH BUSINESS DIRECTORY. 664

0827-2794 See BRIAN COSTELLO ON MONEY MANAGEMENT. 4713

0827-2816 See TALBOT TIMES. 2474

0827-2824 See ISLAND GROWER, THE. 2420

0827-2921 See PRAIRIE JOURNAL OF CANADIAN LITERATURE, THE. 3424

0827-293X See CANADIAN WRITER'S JOURNAL. 3372

0827-2956 See SASKATOON THE BEAUTIFUL. 5490

0827-2964 See OUTDOOR ALBERTA. 4876

0827-3022 See FOCUS ON NIGERIA. 2639

0827-3049 See TEACHING TODAY (EDMONTON). 1907

0827-3081 See VANCOUVER ARTS DIRECTORY. 332

0827-3103 See FIT THIRD AGE. 3751

0827-312X See SUNDIAL (TORONTO). 5001

0827-3146 See NEWSLETTER - COACH HOUSE PRESS. 2922

0827-3154 See LUMO. 3300

0827-3162 See ALDEN'S CONCISE TORONTO GUIDE. 5460

0827-3200 See TOUCHSTONE (WINNIPEG). 5005

0827-3308 See ONTARIO APPEAL CASES (BOUND CUMULATION). 3022

0827-3383 See INTERNATIONAL JOURNAL OF SPECIAL EDUCATION. 1880

0827-3391 See CANADIAN JOURNAL OF SPECIAL EDUCATION. 1876

0827-3472 See SALAR. 2312

0827-3480 See CONSTRUCTION LAW LETTER. 2956

0827-3502 See CHEF DE FORME - RESEAU PARTICIPACTION. 2596

0827-357X See CARO BULLETIN. 347

0827-3669 See CARLETON-OTTAWA MATHEMATICAL LECTURE NOTE SERIES. 3499

0827-3677 See TAX PROFILE (DON MILLS, ONT.). 4754

0827-3766 See CRANE LIBRARY NEWS SUBSTITUTE. 3204

0827-3774 See EPILOGES (MONTREAL). 2487

0827-3812 See MISTER X. 4863

0827-3944 See NATIVE WOMEN'S NEWS. 2268

0827-3960 See NEWFOUNDLAND LIFESTYLE. 2748

0827-4045 See COURRIER ROUMAIN (MONTREAL). 5196

0827-4053 See RAM'S HORN (SCOTSBURN). 124

0827-407X See TORONTO CONSTRUCTION TRENDS. 630

0827-4207 See TORONTO TONIGHT. 4855

0827-4266 See WEEKLY DIGEST OF CIVIL PROCEDURE, THE. 3091

0827-4290 See DOIG'S DIGEST. 4254

0827-4312 See CANADIAN CREDIT REVIEW. 782

0827-4339 See RESUME DES RECHERCHES - STATION DE RECHERCHES. SAINT-JEAN, QUEBEC. 128

0827-441X See ISAAC PITBLADO LECTURES 2985

0827-4576 See OH&S CANADA. 2867

0827-4614 See CONSTRUCTION INDUSTRY EMPLOYMENT LAW. 3145

0827-4673 See WRONGFUL DISMISSAL EMPLOYMENT LAW. 3155

0827-4681 See JOURNAL / THE CANADIAN FOUNDATION FOR ILEITIS AND COLITIS. 3747

0827-4703 See THOSE ANNOYING POST BROS. 4867

0827-4711 See INFO PRESSE COMMUNICATIONS. 1113

0827-4789 See INITIATIVE. 5290

0827-4851 See NEW BRUNSWICK EDUCATIONAL ADMINISTRATOR. 1867

0827-4932 See ON LINE/ON WARD. 1275

0827-4940 See READER (VANCOUVER). 4832

0827-5556 See PUBLIC WORKS (LONDON, ONT.). 3350

0827-5564 See SERVICIO MENSUAL DE INFORMACION Y DOCUMENTACION - AGENCIA LATINOAMERICANA DE INFORMACION. 2760

0827-5637 See MAINTAINER (VANCOUVER). 876

0827-5726 See SPORTING GOODS REVIEW. 4921

0827-5750 See ALBERTA BUSINESS WHO'S WHO & DIRECTORY. 429

0827-5785 See PROVINCIAL OUTLOOK. ECONOMIC FORECAST. 1579

0827-5955 See BULLETIN OF THE GUILD OF CARILLONNEURS IN NORTH AMERICA. 4106

0827-6056 See NATURAL GAS MARKET REPORT. 4265

0827-6129 See ITALIAN CANADIANA. 3397

0827-6153 See NEW DIRECTIONS (VANCOUVER. 1985). 4483

0827-6331 See JOURNAL OF SMALL BUSINESS AND ENTREPRENEURSHIP. 687

0827-6609 See STANDARD (ELLIOT LAKE). 5795

0827-6854 See TODAY'S SENIORS. 5182

0827-6978 See LINK. 2568

0827-7389 See ONTARIO LUPUS ASSOCIATION NEWSLETTER (1985). 3806

0827-7680 See REPORT ON BUSINESS MAGAZINE. 707

0827-7893 See FRASER FORUM. 1491

0827-7958 See OVTA NEWS. 5488

0827-8040 See AFRICAN LETTER, THE. 2254

0827-8156 See RELEVE DES INSCRIPTIONS. 1796

0827-8687 See ETHIOPIAN JEWRY REPORT. 5047

0827-8717 See ON YOUR OWN, A DIRECTORY FOR WOMEN. 5300

0827-8725 See ON YOUR OWN, A DIRECTORY FOR YOUNG MEN. 5300

0827-8911 See EASTERN WOODS & WATERS. 4871

0827-9012 See KANADAN SUOMALAINEN. 2536

0827-9624 See POSTCENSAL ANNUAL ESTIMATES OF POPULATION BY MARITAL STATUS, AGE, SEX AND COMPONENTS OF GROWTH FOR CANADA, PROVINCES AND TERRITORIES. 4562

0827-9713 See PRESBYTERIAN HISTORY. 4987

0827-9772 See SOUS-TERRE. 1411

0827-987X See ANNUAL REPORT OF THE PRINCE EDWARD ISLAND DEPARTMENT OF COMMUNITY AND CULTURAL AFFAIRS. 4628

0828-0061 See PRINCE EDWARD ISLAND MUNICIPAL DIRECTORY. 4674

0828-0150 See CANADIAN INTERCONNECT DIRECTORY, THE. 1151

0828-0584 See DEVELOPMENT / CANADIAN INTERNATIONAL DEVELOPMENT AGENCY. 1555

0828-0622 See CANADIAN CAPITAL PROJECTS. 893

0828-0827 See CANADIAN JOURNAL OF REHABILITATION. 4379

0828-0967 See CERTIFIED PUBLIC HOSPITAL LIST. 3778

0828-1289 See IDLER (TORONTO). 2535

0828-1327 See NASTAWGAN. 594

0828-1432 See LENS : LENTIL EXPERIMENTAL NEWS SERVICE. 178

0828-1513 See OCCASIONAL PAPERS IN ETHNIC AND IMMIGRATION STUDIES. 2270

0828-1521 See NEWS/NORTH. 5790

0828-1602 See CHINA AND OURSELVES. 4943

0828-170X See CANADIAN BOND PRICES. 654

0828-1742 See TRAINING IDEAS. 1916

0828-1769 See GOSPEL WITNESS (TORONTO. 196?). 4961

0828-1777 See ELECTRIC LAMPS, LIGHT BULBS, AND TUBES. 3478

0828-1785 See WINNIPEG FREE PRESS. 5798

0828-1807 See CHRONICLE-HERALD, THE. 5782

0828-1815 See CALGARY HERALD. 5781

0828-184X See LONERGAN STUDIES NEWSLETTER. 4974

0828-1858 See ALASKA HISTORY. 2718

0828-1939 See ANNUAL REPORT - DEPARTMENT OF OCEANOGRAPHY. UNIVERSITY OF BRITISH COLUMBIA. 1446

0828-1998 See PRELIMINARY STATEMENT OF CANADIAN INTERNATIONAL TRADE. 849

0828-2056 See NEWSLETTER - BULGARIAN STUDIES ASSOCIATION. 2624

0828-2161 See CANADIAN AUTOMOTIVE FLEET. 5378

0828-2390 See U.B.C. PLANNING PAPERS. CANADIAN PLANNING ISSUES. 2837

0828-2404 See U.B.C. PLANNING PAPERS. COMPARATIVE URBAN & REGIONAL STUDIES. 1587

0828-2412 See U.B.C. PLANNING PAPERS. DISCUSSION PAPERS. 1587

0828-2501 See STATISTIQUES DE L'AGRICULTURE, DES PECHES ET DE L'ALIMENTATION. 157

0828-2536 See REPORT AND MINUTES - ECONOMIC COMMISSION. INTERNATIONAL CIVIL AVIATION ORGANIZATION. 33

0828-2544 See UPDATE ..., ENERGY ACTIVITIES, PROVINCE OF PRINCE EDWARD ISLAND. 1959

0828-2773 See MUSEUMNEWS (HALIFAX). 4093

0828-282X See CANADIAN JOURNAL OF CARDIOLOGY. 3700

0828-2870 See PUBLICATION - AGRICULTURE CANADA (ENGLISH ED.). 123

0828-2897 See SURFACE AND MARINE TRANSPORT. 5393

0828-3095 See LIVESTOCK REPORT (1985). 214

0828-3117 See ANNUAL REPORT / BRITISH COLUMBIA PLACE LTD. 4834

0828-3176 See UNEMPLOYMENT INSURANCE STATISTICS. ANNUAL SUPPLEMENT (OTTAWA). 2895

0828-3192 See ARCHIVY (WINDSOR). 2480

0828-3575 See MEDICAL WORLD MAGAZINE. 3612

0828-3699 See STUDIO FILE. 366

0828-3893 See CANADIAN JOURNAL OF COUNSELLING. 1876

0828-3907 See SASKATCHEWAN INDIAN FEDERATED COLLEGE JOURNAL. 2759

0828-4083 See GRAIL (WATERLOO). 4961

0828-4121 See RESEARCH BULLETIN - CITY OF TORONTO PLANNING AND DEVELOPMENT. RESEARCH AND INFORMATION SECTION. 2833

0828-4334 See MEDIUM-TERM PLANNING GUIDELINES. 1950

0828-4474 See CANADA TOMORROW (TORONTO, ONT.). 654

0828-4504 See VANCOUVER & AREA AIRPORT BUSINESS DIRECTORY. 39

0828-4539 See TABLE TENNIS TECHNICAL. 4925

0828-4601 See MOVING TO THE SAN FRANCISCO BAY AREA AND GREATER SACRAMENTO. 4841

0828-4660 See NURSING PRACTICE. 3865

0828-4679 See HORSE INDUSTRY DIRECTORY OF CANADA. 2799

0828-4695 See APPELES A LA LIBERTE (LEGARDEUR, QUEBEC). 4935

0828-4725 See RENDEZVOUS & LONGRIFLES. 4914

0828-4733 See GENERAL STAFF JOURNAL, THE. 4861

0828-4849 See VIKING TOURIST GUIDE. 5498

0828-4865 See QUARTERLY - CANADIAN CAT ASSOCIATION. 4287

0828-4938 See BULLETIN D'INFORMATION UFOLOGIQUE. 15

0828-4946 See DECORATION JET SET AMBIANCE. 2899

0828-4954 See ENTRAINEUR, L'. 4894

0828-4989 See MONDE JURIDIQUE, LE. 3011

0828-5012 See REVUE QUEBECOISE DE BRIDGE, LA. 4865

0828-5020 See MALCOLM LOWRY REVIEW, THE. 3347

0828-5268 See CANQUA NEWSLETTER. 1353

0828-5292 See DIVIDENDE. 831

0828-5365 See BRUNSWICK TAX REPORT, THE. 4714

0828-542X See JOURNAL - ONTARIO OCCUPATIONAL HEALTH NURSES ASSOCIATION. 3860

0828-5462 See ANNUAIRE ... DE L'ASSOCIATION CANADIENNE DES PERIODIQUES CATHOLIQUES. 407

0828-5543 See KENT DIRECTORY. 2567

0828-5608 See XYZ (MONTREAL, QUEBEC). 3455

0828-5624 See WATCOM NEWS. 1282

0828-5683 See HELICOM FROM MIRABEL. 1608

0828-5705 See PROGRAMME DES ACTIVITES CULTURELLES ET SPORTIVES. 4913

0828-5713 See OTTAWA ON THE RECORD. 4486

0828-5721 See INVEST CANADA (TORONTO, ONT. : 1984). 902

0828-5772 See CMM : CANADIAN MEDIA MAG. 4443

0828-5780 See Q.T.C. TODAY. 4989

0828-5799 See UPDATE - NATIONAL ASSOCIATION OF CANADIANS OF ORIGIN IN INDIA. 2764

0828-5810 See CANADIAN PLASTICS STATISTICAL YEAR BOOK. 4461

0828-5942 See K.V.P. MANITOBA NEWS. 3896

0828-5993 See ROLLING EAST. 4083

0828-6035 See NOUVELLES DE CAMMAC MONTREAL. 4142

0828-6132 See S.P.E.A. BULLETIN / THE SASK. PHYSICAL EDUCATION ASSOC. 1858

0828-6140 See QUI FAIT QUOI. 388

0828-6183 See VILLE DE JONQUIERE, VILLE A CONGRES ET TOURISTIQUE. 2765

0828-6213 See ATTRACTION. 823

0828-6248 See REPORTER (LONDON). 5794

0828-6256 See PROVINCIAL REPORT - CANADIAN FORESTRY ASSOCIATION OF BRITISH COLUMBIA. 2391

0828-6280 See CITY OF TORONTO INDUSTRIAL DIRECTORY. 1601

0828-6299 See FORESTRY ON THE HILL. 2382

0828-6345 See COURIER NETWORK. 830

0828-6396 See PERSPECTIVES IN CARDIOLOGY. 3709

0828-654X See DEMOCRATIC WOMEN. 5554

0828-6558 See FEMMES DEMOCRATIQUES. 4474

0828-6566 See VOLUNTEER OPPORTUNITIES. 5313

0828-6574 See SOLPLAN REVIEW. 2835

0828-6604 See SCREAM (OTTAWA, ONT.). 4535

0828-6647 See OFFICIAL GUIDE & RECORD BOOK / THE NATIONAL HOCKEY LEAGUE. 4909

0828-6760 See TESL MANITOBA. 1907

0828-6841 See VERDURE (VALLEYFIELD). 2222

0828-6914 See CPJ : CANADIAN PHARMACEUTICAL JOURNAL. 4298

0828-6930 See CANADIAN CHALLENGE. 4942

0828-6949 See ATACC NEWSLETTER. 1222

0828-6965 See NEWSLETTER - CROSS-CULTURAL COMMUNICATION CENTRE. 2269

0828-7007 See MEMBERSHIP LIST - CANADIAN ASSOCIATION OF MUSIC LIBRARIES (1984). 3231

0828-7090 See HUMANE MEDICINE. 3585

0828-7201 See INDICATEUR (OTTAWA). 1978

0828-7236 See NEWSLETTER (GOLDEN RODS & REELS, VICTORIA, B.C.). 2309

0828-7341 See ANGLER & HUNTER (PETERBOROUGH, ONT.). 4869

0828-7449 See CAHIER DES JOURNEES HORTICOLES ORNEMENTALES. 2411

0828-7465 See AXES (RIMOUSKI). 4101

0828-7503 See LOTTERY & GAMING REVIEW. 4863

0828-7511 See ASIFA. ASSOCIATION INTERNATIONALE DU FILM D'ANIMATION, CANADA. 4063

0828-7597 See COLLECTION OF TALKS OF HISTORICAL INTEREST, A. 2728

0828-7600 See CHAROLAIS CONNECTION. 209

0828-7619 See CANADIAN GARDEN NEWS. 2412

0828-7643 See CANADIAN JOURNAL OF MEDICAL TECHNOLOGY (ED. FRANCAISE). 3562

0828-7651 See COLCHESTER COUNTY, NOVA SCOTIA, TRAVEL GUIDE. 5466

0828-7686 See ERINDALE REVIEW. 3385

0828-7694 See UPDATE - CHINOOK REGIONAL LIBRARY. 3255

0828-7759 See ELK POINT LAKELAND REVIEW. 5784

0828-7821 See NEW BRUNSWICK BRANCH NEWS. 1507

0828-7899 See BIG FISH COUNTRY FISHING GUIDE. 2297

0828-7902 See CURRENT (RICHMOND). 2299

0828-797X See INTERCULTURE. 4965

0828-8046 See CFB GANDER GAZETTE. 4039

0828-8070 See WORKING HOLIDAYS. SUPPLEMENT FOR NORTH AMERICAN READERS. 5499

0828-8089 See PME (LAVAL). 703

0828-8151 See ECHOS GENEALOGIQUES. 2446

0828-8178 See MONTHLY STOCK CHARTS. 907

0828-8208 See AIR CHARTER STATISTICS / STATISTICS CANADA, TRANSPORTATION DIVISION, AVIATION STATISTICS CENTRE. 7

0828-8259 See CANADIAN HORTICULTURAL HISTORY. 2412

0828-8461 See MINPROC : MINERAL PROCESSING ABSTRACTS. 2006

0828-864X See EQUINEWS. 2799

0828-8666 See HUMANOMICS. 1608

0828-8690 See OTTAWA MOSAIC, THE. 5253

0828-8739 See RANGER RICK (OTTAWA). 4171

0828-9034 See CURLING CANADA. 4892

0828-9131 See SWORD. SIKH WORLD ORGANIZATION'S REVIEW AND DIGEST. 5001

0828-9239 See PROJECT MAGAZINE. 1992

0828-9247 See PEGBAR. 381

0828-9468 See REVUE D'HISTOIRE DE LA COTE-NORD. 2758

0828-9522 See RESOURCE (DON MILLS, ONT.). 4846

0828-9654 See WILDERNESS TRAILS 'N' TALES. 4880

0828-9662 See JIM TAYLOR'S CURRENTS. 4967

0828-9735 See PERTH COUNTY PROFILES. 2467

0828-9859 See LEATHER AND ALLIED PRODUCTS INDUSTRIES. 3184

0828-9891 See FURNITURE AND FIXTURE INDUSTRIES. 2905

0828-9980 See SENEY NEWSLETTER. 2472

0828-9999 See REVUE QUEBECOISE DE DROIT INTERNATIONAL. 3135

0829-0369 See TRAVAIL ET SANTE. 2871

0829-044X See CONRAD GREBEL REVIEW, THE. 4950

0829-0474 See OFFICIAL DIRECTORY OF CANADIAN MUSEUMS AND RELATED INSTITUTIONS, THE. 4094

0829-0547 See WESTERN CANADIAN ANTHROPOLOGIST, THE. 247

0829-0652 See YUKON DATA BOOK. 2550

0829-075X See CANADIAN CO-OPERATIVE WOOLGROWERS MAGAZINE, THE. 1541

0829-0784 See ART POST, THE. 340

0829-0814 See CANADA JOURNAL (DEUTSCHE AUSG.). 654

0829-0954 See LIBERATION (MILTON. 1984). 4973

0829-1020 See CPF IMMERSION REGISTRY, THE. 3275

0829-1098 See UNEMPLOYMENT INSURANCE STATISTICS (OTTAWA). 2895

0829-1152 See CHANNEL (ONTARIO LIBRARY SERVICE, TRENT). 3201

0829-1373 See HAMILTON THIS MONTH. 678

0829-1489 See PROJECT NORTH JOURNAL. 2271

0829-1756 See PASSENGER BUS AND URBAN TRANSIT STATISTICS (MONTHLY ED.). 5389

0829-1772 See ANNUAL REPORT - PRAIRIE FARM REHABILITATION ADMINISTRATION. 61

0829-1802 See BULLETIN DE DROIT IMMOBILIER. 2944

0829-1888 See CANADIAN MEDIA DIRECTORS COUNCIL MEDIA DIGEST. 5194

0829-2019 See NATIONAL CREDITOR/DEBTOR REVIEW. 3087

0829-2078 See ANNUAL SURVEY OF COMMUNITY PHARMACY OPERATIONS. 4291

0829-2094 See LAW PRACTICE MANAGEMENT. 2996

0829-2132 See CANADIAN AVIATION NEWS (1984). 15

0829-2167 See STUDIA PHONETICA. 3325

0829-2175 See CREDIT UNION WAY. 786

0829-2221 See SCOTT'S REPERTOIRES, FABRICANTS DU QUEBEC. 3487

0829-2248 See SCOTT'S DIRECTORIES, WESTERN MANUFACTURERS. 3487

0829-2299 See VICE VERSA (MONTREAL, QUEBEC). 2549

0829-240X See CONTRETEMPS (MONTREAL). 2212

0829-2442 See COURRIER LAURENTIDES (EDITION EST). 5782

0829-2507 See SCIENTIA CANADENSIS. 5154

0829-254X See CAAT TRACKS. 3199

0829-2612 See NOUVELLES / LA FEDERATION DES SOCIETES D'HISTOIRE DU QUEBEC. 2751

0829-2809 See PHARMACY PRACTICE (MISSISSAUGA). 4323

0829-2922 See RELIGIOUS STUDIES AND THEOLOGY. 4992

0829-2930 See CORINTHIAN HORSE SPORT. 2798

0829-3023 See CANADIAN TRACKSIDE GUIDE. 5430

0829-3139 See WEEKLY STOCK CHARTS. ... CANADIAN RESOURCE COMPANIES. 919

0829-318X See TREE PHYSIOLOGY. 2397

0829-3201 See CANADIAN JOURNAL OF LAW AND SOCIETY. 2948

0829-321X See INTERNATIONAL INSIGHTS. 4524

0829-3279 See SEA KAYAKER. 596

0829-3309 See CAMPUS CANADA (TORONTO, ONT.). 1090

0829-3473 See ENTERPRISE (REGINA, SASK.). 1488

0829-3627 See CANPLAY. 5362

0829-3678 See SOUND & VISION (TORONTO). 1627

0829-3724 See REPORT TO THE PEOPLE / YOUTH FOR CHRIST KINGSTON. 4992

0829-383X See PREFERRED SHARES & WARRANTS. 911

0829-3848 See MANIE DES JEUX, LA. 4863

0829-3856 See NORTHERN CURLING REVIEW. 4908

0829-3864 See OUTPUT (RICHMOND HILL). 1224

0829-4003 See CANADIAN TREASURY MANAGEMENT REVIEW. 782

0829-4038 See WESTERN LIVING (VICTORIA ED.). 2550

0829-4046 See WESTERN LIVING (CALGARY ED.). 2550

0829-4135 See ALBERTA NATIVE NEWS. 2254

0829-4216 See UNITY / ASSOCIATION OF IROQUOIS AND ALLIED INDIANS. 2274

0829-4275 See TROIS. 3448

0829-4291 See NEWSLETTER (ROYAL CANADIAN COLLEGE OF ORGANISTS). 4141

0829-4321 See NEWSLETTER / ALBERTA ASSOCIATION OF COLLEGE LIBRARIANS. 3234

0829-4437 See AGO NEWS. 335

0829-4666 See GOSPEL HERALD BEAMSVILLE. 4961

0829-4763 See WHEATGROWER (REGINA). 191

0829-481X See BC BUSINESS. 642

0829-4836 See CANADIAN JOURNAL OF MARKETING RESEARCH. 922

0829-4941 See SAINT-LAURENT JOURNAL. 4684

0829-4976 See BOOKS--NOTED FOR YOU. 4821

0829-5026 See CANADIAN WEST (1985). 2726

0829-5131 See OSMOSE (MONTREAL). 3866

0829-5239 See BRUNSWICK BUSINESS JOURNAL, THE. 644

0829-5263 See QUEBEC CONSTRUCTION (ED. MENSUELLE). **625**

0829-5344 See CANADIAN FOLK MUSIC BULLETIN. **4107**

0829-545X See MARINER (VANCOUVER, B.C.). **5452**

0829-5476 See JURISTE (MONCTON). **1092**

0829-5557 See BULLETIN D'INFORMATION TOXICOLOGIQUE. **3979**

0829-5735 See CANADIAN JOURNAL OF SCHOOL PSYCHOLOGY. **1730**

0829-576X See WORKER CO-OPS (TORONTO. 1980). **1543**

0829-6014 See VITALITY. **2602**

0829-6030 See DIRECTORY OF FEDERAL GOVERNMENT SCIENTIFIC & TECHNOLOGICAL ESTABLISHMENTS. **5100**

0829-6146 See MVP. **4905**

0829-6154 See ATV CANADA. **1966**

0829-6200 See RESEARCH REPORT - EXPERT COMMITTEE ON WEEDS. EASTERN CANADA SECTION. **127**

0829-6235 See EARNINGS OF MEN AND WOMEN. **1531**

0829-6340 See ONTARIO NURSING HOME JOURNAL. **3790**

0829-643X See FOOD (TORONTO). **2340**

0829-6650 See TRIBUNE (GRAVELBOURG). **5796**

0829-7142 See NEWSLETTER / COUNCIL OF NOVA SCOTIA ARCHIVES. **2482**

0829-7177 See UNIVERSITY FINANCE, TREND ANALYSIS. **1852**

0829-7401 See OPERATING RESULTS. MEN'S RETAIL CLOTHING STORES. **1088**

0829-741X See OPERATING RESULTS. RETAIL DRUG STORES. **4334**

0829-7460 See PROCEEDINGS OF THE STANDING SENATE COMMITTEE ON BANKING, TRADE AND COMMERCE. **849**

0829-7584 See RESEARCH REPORT - EXPERT COMMITTEE ON WEEDS. WESTERN CANADA SECTION. **127**

0829-7622 See GEOGRAPHICAL MONOGRAPHS. **2563**

0829-7681 See ELS MONOGRAPH SERIES. **3342**

0829-772X See CIVIC PUBLIC WORKS. **4760**

0829-7800 See COLLECTIVE BARGAINING SETTLEMENTS IN ONTARIO 1985. **1660**

0829-7908 See PUBLICS (MONTREAL). **765**

0829-7983 See CAP-AUX-DIAMANTS. **2726**

0829-8157 See TRADEASIA MAGAZINE. **854**

0829-8211 See BIOCHEMISTRY AND CELL BIOLOGY. **481**

0829-8319 See ... BRITISH COLUMBIA COLLECTIVE BARGAINING REVIEW AND OUTLOOK, THE. **1656**

0829-8351 See NICKEL (TORONTO). **4013**

0829-8564 See COMPLEAT MOTHER, THE. **3759**

0829-8653 See RIGID INSULATING BOARD, WOOD FIBRE AND MINERAL PRODUCTS. **2404**

0829-8777 See CANADIAN MAGAZINE INDEX. **2496**

0829-8815 See ENTOURAGE (DOWNSVIEW, ONT.). **5284**

0829-8947 See TRUCKING IN CANADA. **5398**

0829-8998 See PROFESSIONAL MUSICIAN (DOWNSVIEW). **4147**

0829-9013 See INCITE (TORONTO). **352**

0829-9021 See QUEBEC MARINE FISHERIES, MONTHLY LANDING STATISTICS BY SPECIES. **2311**

0829-9137 See MULTICULTURAL EDUCATION COUNCIL NEWSLETTER OF THE ALBERTA TEACHERS' ASSOCIATION. **1765**

0829-9153 See METRO PLANNING REVIEW. **2828**

0829-917X See TEACHERS' MONEY MATTERS. **1713**

0829-9269 See CITIZEN (SAINT JOHN, N.B.). **5782**

0829-9277 See WORKING PAPER / UNIVERSITY OF TORONTO, DEVELOPMENT STUDIES PROGRAMME. **1527**

0829-982X See AZURE (TORONTO). **2898**

0829-9889 See HOUSEWARES CANADA. **2811**

0829-9935 See INTERNATIONAL ABSTRACTS IN DERMATOLOGY. **3720**

0830-0011 See AVISO (HALIFAX). **1889**

0830-0089 See ANNUAL REPORT / NATIONAL LIBRARY OF CANADA / RAPPORT ANNUEL / BIBLIOTHEQUE NATIONALE DU CANADA. **3190**

0830-0097 See CANADIAN IMPORTS BY DOMESTIC AND FOREIGN CONTROLLED ENTERPRISES. **826**

0830-0143 See SASK-TRENDS MONITOR. **1519**

0830-0151 See LAWYERS WEEKLY (SCARBOROUGH). **2998**

0830-0380 See JURISPRUDENCE LOGEMENT. **2991**

0830-0402 See RECUEILS DE JURISPRUDENCE DU QUEBEC. COUR PROVINCIALE, COUR DES SESSIONS DE LA PAIX, TRIBUNAL DE LA JEUNESSE. **3037**

0830-0445 See JOURNAL OF DISTANCE EDUCATION / REVUE DE L'ENSEIGNEMENT A DISTANCE. **1756**

0830-0593 See CANADIAN THOROUGHBRED. **2798**

0830-0739 See OKANAGAN HISTORY. **2752**

0830-0763 See NON-WAGE PROVISIONS IN SASKATCHEWAN COLLECTIVE AGREEMENTS. **1695**

0830-0887 See NATURAL LIFE MAGAZINE. **4194**

0830-1093 See R&D - ALBERTA RESEARCH COUNCIL. **5144**

0830-1808 See ATLANTIC TRUCKING. **5377**

0830-1913 See RECREATION BRITISH COLUMBIA (1985). **4853**

0830-1921 See SPORTS BUSINESS. **958**

0830-1972 See WEEKLY STOCK CHARTS. CANADIAN AND U.S. INDUSTRIAL COMPANIES. **919**

0830-6729 See EFFECTIF ETUDIANT - UNIVERSITE DE MONCTON. **1822**

0830-8284 See WILDERNESS ALBERTA. **2209**

0830-8411 See NOTES - CANADIAN ASSOCIATION OF YOUTH ORCHESTRAS. **4142**

0830-8535 See GREATER WINNIPEG BUSINESS. **678**

0830-8586 See AMI (MISSISSAUGA, ONT.). **383**

0830-8705 See PORT HOLE (SCARBOROUGH). **595**

0830-8721 See GUITAR CANADA. **4120**

0830-8802 See SUCCESS, PROMOTION & PROFITS. **937**

0830-887X See JOURNAL DES PATES ET PAPIERS. **4234**

0830-9000 See CANADIAN JOURNAL OF VETERINARY RESEARCH. **5507**

0830-9221 See YOUTH UPDATE (REXDALE, ONT.). **3179**

0830-9272 See SCOTT'S DIRECTORIES. ONTARIO MANUFACTURERS. **3487**

0830-9396 See NORTHERN MINER MAGAZINE, THE. **2147**

0830-9590 See REVUE INTERNATIONALE DES SCIENCES DE L'EAU. **1417**

0830-9760 See ALBERTA PARLIAMENTARY DIGEST. **2929**

0830-9825 See SUMMARY REPORT ... CANADIAN REGIONAL CONFERENCE. COMMONWEALTH PARLIAMENTARY ASSOCIATION. **4497**

0830-9868 See ANNUAL SALARY SURVEYS. PRODUCTION & DISTRIBUTION REPORT. **1650**

0831-0076 See ONTARIO BLUEWATER VISITOR GUIDE. **5487**

0831-0203 See CANADIAN BAND JOURNAL. **4107**

0831-0319 See STOP (MONTREAL). **3440**

0831-0467 See DEPECHE. **1662**

0831-0513 See ANNUAIRE DU TRAVAIL. **1644**

0831-0777 See REVUE SAINTE ANNE, LA. **5035**

0831-0785 See SON HI-FI VIDEO. **5319**

0831-0807 See HARDWARE MERCHANDISING, BUILDING SUPPLY DEALER. **2811**

0831-0866 See VERITABLE AMIE. **5567**

0831-0998 See PRACTICAL ALLERGY & IMMUNOLOGY. **3675**

0831-1048 See CAHIERS DE RECHERCHE SOCIOLOGIQUE. **5241**

0831-148X See ROYAL LEPAGE SURVEY OF CANADIAN HOUSE PRICES. **2834**

0831-1846 See PEACE & SECURITY. **4531**

0831-1854 See SCOTT'S DIRECTORIES, ATLANTIC MANUFACTURERS. **3487**

0831-1994 See SPECIAL DELIVERY (WINNIPEG). **3250**

0831-2052 See INFODEX, INDEX DE LA PRESSE. **2488**

0831-2060 See CANADIAN YOUNG ASTRONAUT, THE. **16**

0831-2133 See ART IMPRESSIONS. **339**

0831-2184 See TORONTO'S WEDDING BELLS. **2286**

0831-2249 See MHLA BULLETIN. **3231**

0831-229X See CANADIAN WRESTLER (1985). **4889**

0831-2478 See RRT. **3952**

0831-2516 See DISMISSAL AND EMPLOYMENT LAW DIGEST. **3146**

0831-2559 See BORDER CROSSINGS (WINNIPEG, MAN.). **316**

0831-2591 See GARGOUILLE MAGAZINE. **4861**

0831-2621 See PETS MAGAZINE (1985). **4287**

0831-2788 See TOURIST GUIDE, GREATER QUEBEC AREA. **5494**

0831-2796 See GENOME. **546**

0831-2885 See NEWSLETTER / NATIVE ART STUDIES ASSOCIATION OF CANADA. **2269**

0831-2907 See CARRIAGE TRADE (SARNIA, ONT.). **5348**

0831-2966 See MAGAZINE CARGUIDE. **5418**

0831-2974 See CANADIAN CERAMICS QUARTERLY. **2587**

0831-3008 See CANADIAN GUERNSEY JOURNAL. **192**

0831-3016 See FORUM (REGINA, SASK.). **3211**

0831-3040 See MSOS JOURNAL. **5180**

0831-3067 See VACANCES POUR TOUS. **5498**

0831-3091 See CIEL VARIABLE :LE MANIFESTE DU TEMPS. **347**

0831-3148 See DIRECTORY / ONTARIO LIBRARY SERVICE, RIDEAU. **3208**

0831-3180 See ABSTRACTS OF NATIVE STUDIES. **2276**

0831-3210 See PERIODICALS / OTTAWA PUBLIC LIBRARY. **3240**

0831-3210 See PERIODICALS - OTTAWA PUBLIC LIBRARY (1991). **3240**

0831-3245 See MANITOBA JOURNAL OF COUNSELLING : MJC. **1882**

0831-3318 See EAF JOURNAL. **1862**

0831-3377 See FEMINIST ACTION. **5556**

0831-3571 See PERSPECTIVES ECONOMIQUES (TORONTO). **1512**

0831-375X See RG. **2796**

0831-3865 See ONTARIO FARMER (WESTERN ED.). **117**

0831-3881 See CMA : THE MANAGEMENT ACCOUNTING MAGAZINE. **741**

0831-411X See INTER-MECANIQUE DU BATIMENT. **617**

0831-4411 See JASMU : JOURNAL POUR L'AVANCEMENT DES SOINS MEDICAUX D'URGENCE. **3786**

0831-4527 See CANADIAN FREE TRADER. **826**

0831-4535 See FOCUS ON CANADIAN EMPLOYMENT AND EQUALITY RIGHTS. **1675**

0831-4640 See DEFI. **3205**

0831-4667 See MAITRISE DE L'ENERGIE (MONTREAL). **1950**

0831-4799 See OIL & GAS REPORT (NORTH VANCOUVER, B.C.). **4268**

0831-4888 See FOCUS - CANADIAN STANDARDS ASSOCIATION. **4030**

0831-4985 See COLLECTION FORUM (OTTAWA). **4165**

0831-5213 See MONTREAL MAGAZINE. **4863**

0831-540X See INFO CDAME. **1223**

0831-5477 See BOTTOM LINE (MARKHAM). **739**

0831-5493 See GUIDANCE & COUNSELLING. 1748

0831-5698 See CANADIAN SOCIAL TRENDS. 5241

0831-5701 See TENDANCES SOCIALES CANADIENNES. 5264

0831-5825 See ECHANGE (EDMONTON). 3278

0831-585X See NATIVE STUDIES REVIEW. 2268

0831-5930 See ROOTS, BRANCHES AND TWIGS (ONTARIO GENEALOGICAL SOCIETY. KENT COUNTY BRANCH). 2471

0831-6031 See PERSPECTIVES / ALBERTA ASSOCIATION OF REGISTERED OCCUPATIONAL THERAPISTS. 3932

0831-6074 See MCCAUSLAND'S ORDER OF DIVINE SERVICE. 4976

0831-6465 See OMNI. 3624

0831-6473 See RAPPORT D'ACTIVITE - SURETE DU QUEBEC. 3174

0831-6503 See BLUE CHART REPORT, THE. 2876

0831-6570 See TECHNOLOGIE ET THERAPIE DU COMPORTEMENT. 3937

0831-6708 See INUIT ART QUARTERLY. 353

0831-6899 See ELECTRIC PROPULSION. 2044

0831-7291 See BUSINESS DYNAMICS (100 MILE HOUSE). 647

0831-7348 See CANADIAN LABOUR ARBITRATION SUMMARIES. 3145

0831-7445 See PERSPECTIVES - GERONTOLOGICAL NURSING ASSOCIATION. 3866

0831-8212 See OPERATING COSTS OF TRUCKS IN CANADA. 5389

0831-8247 See INFORMATION REPORT - NORTHERN FORESTRY CENTRE. 2385

0831-8255 See INFORMATION REPORT - NEWFOUNDLAND FORESTRY CENTRE. 2385

0831-8530 See HEALTH & NUTRITION UPDATE. 4191

0831-859X See ESSE. 349

0831-8603 See MACHINERY & EQUIPMENT MRO. 2120

0831-8670 See CURRENT THERAPY IN SPORTS MEDICINE. 3954

0831-8891 See WESTERN REPORT. 2766

0831-9057 See SASKATCHEWAN TRADE DIRECTORY (1986). 3487

0831-9103 See INTERCOMM - INTERPRETATION CANADA. ONTARIO SECTION. 4706

0831-9138 See CANADIAN TRAVEL PRESS WEEKLY. 5465

0831-9197 See NEWSLETTER - INTERNATIONAL BOARD ON BOOKS FOR YOUNG PEOPLE. CANADIAN SECTION (1980). 1067

0831-9197 See NEWSLETTER - INTERNATIONAL BOARD ON BOOKS FOR YOUNG PEOPLE. CANADIAN SECTION (1980). 1067

0831-9227 See BULLETIN (AMNESTY INTERNATIONAL. CANADIAN SECTION-ENGLISH-SPEAKING). 4504

0831-9286 See REPERTOIRE DES ORGANISMES CULTURELS DE L'ABITIBI-TEMISCAMINGUE. 329

0831-9502 See CONTEMPORARY VERSE TWO. 3461

0831-9510 See NEWSLETTER OF THE CPA/SCP SECTION ON WOMEN & PSYCHOLOGY. 4605

0831-9774 See CORPORATE BOND RECORD, THE. 661

0831-9782 See PREMIERE (MISSISSAUGA). 4076

0831-9871 See NEWSLETTER OF THE GANANOQUE HISTORICAL SOCIETY. 2750

0832-008X See BULLETIN - CANADIAN POLITICAL SCIENCE ASSOCIATION (1979). 4466

0832-0128 See COA BULLETIN. 3881

0832-0160 See MEMBERSHIP DIRECTORY, PLANT SOURCE LIST. 2424

0832-0179 See CANADA LUTHERAN (NATIONAL ED.). 5057

0832-0322 See RECORDER. 2149

0832-0500 See CANADIAN OUTLOOK, EXECUTIVE SUMMARY. 1590

0832-0543 See PARATRACKS / CANADIAN PARAPLEGIC ASSOCIATION-MANITOBA DIVISION. 4392

0832-0683 See CANADA AMONG NATIONS. 4517

0832-0705 See FEDERAL SALES TAX. 4724

0832-0748 See RECORD OF NEW ISSUES. 912

0832-0772 See SURVEY OF PREDECESSOR AND DEFUNCT COMPANIES (1985). 734

0832-0780 See REAL ESTATE JOURNAL, THE. 4844

0832-1132 See MOTOCYCLISTE (MONTREAL). 4082

0832-1191 See FAITH TODAY (WILLOWDALE). 4958

0832-1213 See PERFORMANCE (OTTAWA). 1146

0832-1299 See VANCOUVER SUN (1986). 5797

0832-1310 See CPF ONTARIO. 3275

0832-1329 See NASA GAZETA. 2922

0832-140X See CONTACT - CANADIAN COUNCIL FOR INTERNATIONAL COOPERATION. 4519

0832-1469 See AVIRON CANADIEN. 591

0832-1647 See YOUR BUSINESS (SMITHS FALLS). 724

0832-1655 See FOREST PLANNING-CANADA. 2380

0832-1922 See LANG VAN. 2489

0832-2007 See IRANIYAN (TORONTO). 5786

0832-235X See COMMERCIAL LAW DIGEST. 3097

0832-2414 See CHAPLEAU SENTINEL. 5781

0832-2503 See CANADIAN MARKETS (1986). 727

0832-2562 See ON TAP (ENGLISH ED.). 2370

0832-2589 See FUT / BREWERS ASSOCIATION OF CANADA / L'ASSOCIATION DES BRASSEURS DU CANADA, EN. 2367

0832-2937 See BENGOUGH BULLETIN. 5780

0832-3542 See PROVINCIAL OUTLOOK. EXECUTIVE SUMMARY. 1513

0832-4174 See STAR-PHOENIX (SASKATOON, SASK.). 5795

0832-4298 See DAILY GRAPHIC (PORTAGE LA PRAIRIE. 1954). 5783

0832-4719 See MONDAY MAGAZINE (1983). 696

0832-4867 See ALBERTA FARM & RANCH, FARM DIRECTORY. 57

0832-512X See MASTHEAD (MISSISSAUGA). 4816

0832-5340 See FEMINISME EN REVUE, LE. 5556

0832-5359 See BIO FAX. 1464

0832-543X See FOCUS AFRICA. 2639

0832-5502 See ATLANTIC FORESTRY JOURNAL. 2375

0832-5618 See O.S.E.A. NEWSLETTER. 360

0832-5804 See CONSTRUCTION MANITOBA. 610

0832-6096 See MANITOBA MEDICINE. 3606

0832-610X See CANADIAN JOURNAL OF ANAESTHESIA. 3682

0832-6193 See TRUMPETER (VICTORIA). 2222

0832-6215 See EXPORTS OF CANADIAN GRAIN AND WHEAT FLOUR. 200

0832-6223 See LABOUR NEWS & GRAPHICS. 1686

0832-6533 See CANADIAN HEAVY EQUIPMENT GUIDE. 606

0832-655X See DIRECTORY OF STATISTICS IN CANADA. 5326

0832-6770 See SANTE. 5566

0832-6916 See ANNUAL REPORT / ALBERTA FORESTRY, LANDS AND WILDLIFE. 2374

0832-6983 See CANADIAN FAMILY LAW QUARTERLY. 3119

0832-7122 See INFORMATION REPORT - GREAT LAKES FORESTRY CENTRE. 2384

0832-7130 See MISCELLANEOUS REPORT - GREAT LAKES FORESTRY CENTRE. 2388

0832-722X See NORTHERN AQUACULTURE. 2309

0832-7238 See VIE EN ESTRIE. 2549

0832-7688 See COMMERCIAL INSOLVENCY REPORTER. 3086

0832-7823 See JOURNAL OF MICROWAVE POWER AND ELECTROMAGNETIC ENERGY, THE. 2069

0832-7858 See CAHIER SPECIAL D'INFORMATION - DIRECTION GENERAL DES PECHES MARITIMES. DIRECTION DE LA RECHERCHE SCIENTIFIQUE ET TECHNIQUE. 2298

0832-7890 See ABILITY AND ENTERPRISE. 5269

0832-8048 See SANTE SOCIETE. 5306

0832-8196 See PERFORMANCE (VANIER). 4912

0832-8293 See NOVA SCOTIA CHRISTMAS TREE JOURNAL. 2390

0832-8315 See VOICES (EDMONTON). 3332

0832-8587 See PORTUS (OTTAWA). 5454

0832-8595 See HOME BUSINESS ADVOCATE, THE. 680

0832-8609 See CONTRIBUTIONS TO HUMAN HISTORY. 234

0832-865X See DIRECTORY OF THE ARTS (OTTAWA). 319

0832-8684 See ARGENT ET VOUS, L'. 772

0832-8692 See SURVEY OF DRUG STORE TRENDS, A. 4330

0832-8722 See BANKING & FINANCE LAW REVIEW. 3085

0832-8773 See AEB, AGRICULTURAL ECONOMICS AND BUSINESS. 44

0832-8781 See CANADIAN JOURNAL OF WOMEN AND THE LAW. 2948

0832-8811 See COMMERCE (RED DEER). 828

0832-8900 See AUTO SPORT (MONTREAL. 1992). 4885

0832-8927 See RECUEIL DE DROIT DE LA FAMILLE. 3122

0832-8935 See RECUEIL EN RESPONSABILITE ET ASSURANCE. 3037

0832-8943 See RECUEIL DE DROIT IMMOBILIER. 3036

0832-9117 See CA MAGAZINE. 740

0832-9176 See CANADIAN SOURCES OF ENVIRONMENTAL INFORMATION. 2226

0832-9184 See CLINICIEN. 3566

0832-9249 See NEWFOUNDLAND LIBRARY ASSOCIATION BULLETIN. 3234

0832-9257 See INDEX TO CANADIAN LEGAL LITERATURE (LIBRARY ED.). 3081

0832-9257 See CANADIAN LEGAL LITERATURE. 3079

0832-929X See COMPORTEMENT HUMAIN. 4582

0832-932X See NEW CANADIAN REVIEW. 3415

0832-9354 See RESOURCE. 4992

0832-9370 See EQUITY (TORONTO. 1986). 4507

0832-9605 See INSIDE OLA. 3217

0832-9656 See FUSION MAGAZINE. 2589

0832-9842 See APPLYING RESEARCH TO THE CLASSROOM. 1888

0832-9869 See OPHTHALMIC PRACTICE. 3877

0832-9958 See INFO-DIABETE : BULLETIN D'INFORMATION DE LA SECTION PROFESSIONNELLE DE L'ASSOCIATION DU DIABETE DU QUEBEC. 3731

0832-9966 See BEFFROI. 3365

0832-9990 See CANADIAN ATV DEALERS BLUE BOOK. 826

0833-0018 See JOURNAL OF WILD CULTURE, THE. 2196

0833-0026 See MTL. MONTREAL. 2539

0833-0034 See EXPLORATION, DEVELOPMENT AND CAPITAL EXPENDITURES FOR MINING AND PETROLEUM AND NATURAL GAS WELLS, INTENTIONS. 4256

0833-0050 See NOUVEAUTES DE LA BIBLIOTHEQUE ADMINISTRATIVE. 4670

0833-0239 See CONSTRUIRE (QUEBEC). 611

0833-0476 See HANSARD OFFICIAL REPORT OF DEBATES. 4654

0833-0530 See ORIENTATION (MONTREAL. 1986). 1700

0833-0603 See AGATE. ALBERTA GIFTED AND TALENTED EDUCATION. 1874

0833-0611 See GTEC NEWS. 1879

0833-062X See BUSINESS REPORT. 652

0833-0689 See TIMBERLINES. 2397

0833-076X See CANADIAN JOURNAL OF INFECTION CONTROL : THE OFFICIAL JOURNAL OF THE COMMUNITY & HOSPITAL INFECTION CONTROL ASSOCIATION-CANADA, THE. 4770

0833-0867 See ALBERTA'S FISHING & HUNTING MAGAZINE. 2294

0833-0875 See SCHOOL LAW COMMENTARY. 3046

0833-0883 See MAGYAR ELET. 5789

0833-0891 See FINE ART & AUCTION REVIEW. 350

0833-0948 See CANADIAN CAVER, THE. 4870

0833-0980 See COLLNET. 3203

0833-1014 See GRAND FALLS ADVERTISER. 5785

0833-1065 See GULF NEWS. 5785

0833-1235 See CANADIAN JOURNAL OF SPORT SCIENCES. 3953

0833-1510 See FLAGSCAN. 2448

0833-1677 See RESEARCH MONEY. 4339

0833-1685 See ASSOCIATION DES FAMILLES KIROUAC : BULLETIN, L'. 2438

0833-1731 See ANNUAL REPORT. 4626

0833-1782 See REVUE CURLING QUEBEC, LA. 4915

0833-1812 See JOURNAL DE L'IMMERSION, LE. 3289

0833-1871 See PAPERS IN CANADIAN ECONOMIC DEVELOPMENT. 2830

0833-2010 See SNOWMAN NEWS. 4919

0833-2045 See CATALOGUE / MAPS ALBERTA. 2581

0833-2193 See MEDICAL JOURNAL - UNIVERSITY OF TORONTO. 3610

0833-2207 See MEDICAL JOURNAL - UNIVERSITY OF TORONTO. 3610

0833-2274 See OPERATING RESULTS. RETAIL FLORISTS. 2435

0833-2282 See OPERATING RESULTS. RETAIL JEWELLERY STORES. 2915

0833-238X See CONSTRUCTION PRICE STATISTICS (QUARTERLY ED.). 632

0833-2614 See CONTRIBUTIONS TO THE GEOLOGY OF THE NORTHWEST TERRITORIES. 1372

0833-2878 See ADMINISTRATIVE ASSISTANT'S UPDATE. 859

0833-2908 See YOUR NEWS. 5798

0833-305X See DIRECTORY / CONSULTING ENGINEERS OF ONTARIO. 1970

0833-3424 See FLYER (EDMONTON, ALTA.). 21

0833-3432 See MONEY DIGEST (BATH). 907

0833-3505 See ENERGY ALBERTA. 1938

0833-3831 See DAN SHA. 5783

0833-384X See HALTON BUSINESS JOURNAL (1986). 678

0833-3858 See LISAN AL-ARAB. 5788

0833-4390 See AAROGRAM. 4248

0833-448X See ECO ALERT / CONSERVATION COUNCIL. 2192

0833-451X See ACE. ASSOCIATION OF CULTURAL EXECUTIVES. 312

0833-4641 See GVRD NEWS. 4653

0833-5176 See ANNUAL STATISTICAL REVIEW - PROVINCE OF PRINCE EDWARD ISLAND. PLANNING & STATISTICS DIVISION. DEPARTMENT OF FINANCE. 1529

0833-5192 See PROCEEDINGS OF THE ... ANNUAL CONVENTION, INCLUDING THE ... ANNUAL CONVENTION OF THE WESTERN CANADA SECTION, AMERICAN WATER WORKS ASSOCIATION, AND THE ... ANNUAL CONVENTION OF THE WESTERN CANADA POLLUTION CONTROL ASSOCIATION, WATER POLLUTION CONTROL FEDERATION. 5537

0833-532X See CANADIAN GLOBAL ALMANAC, THE. 1924

0833-5672 See LIST OF SHIPS. 5451

0833-5737 See CRIMINAL INJURIES COMPENSATION. 3080

0833-6210 See AGRICULTURE ECONOMIC STATISTICS. 53

0833-7012 See COLLECTIVE BARGAINING IN NEW BRUNSWICK. 1660

0833-7195 See JOB FUTURES. 4205

0833-7209 See EMPLOI-AVENIR. 4204

0833-7322 See FEDERAL REGULATORY PLAN. 4648

0833-7519 See CANADIAN CHILDREN. 1803

0833-7594 See HEALTH PROMOTION (OTTAWA). 4781

0833-7608 See PROMOTION DE LA SANTE (OTTAWA). 2240

0833-7659 See ANNUAL REPORT - PUBLIC SAFETY SERVICES (ALBERTA). 4766

0833-7926 See SURVEILLANCE. 3644

0833-8000 See ENJEU - ENJEU ET ENVIRONNEMENT JEUNESSE. 2215

0833-8019 See INDEPENDENT (ELMIRA). 5786

0833-8116 See REFLET (EMBRUN, ONT.). 2544

0833-823X See EARTHKEEPING ONTARIO. 80

0833-8264 See CANADIAN DENTAL ASSISTANTS' ASSOCIATION : JOURNAL. 1318

0833-8337 See CRAFTS PLUS. 371

0833-8477 See ALBERTA DOCTORS' DIGEST, THE. 3547

0833-8493 See FILTER (BRANTFORD). 3941

0833-8590 See SANTE CULTURE. 245

0833-8590 See SANTE CULTURE. 3936

0833-8868 See MEMBERSHIP ROSTER - AUTOMOTIVE RETAILERS ASSOCIATION (WINNIPEG). 955

0833-8973 See LIST OF CERTIFIED PLUMBING PRODUCTS (1983). 2606

0833-899X See LIST OF CERTIFIED OCCUPATIONAL HEALTH AND SAFETY PRODUCTS. 2865

0833-9090 See PEST CONTROL CANADA. 4246

0833-918X See QUEBEC YACHTIING, VOILE & MOTEUR. 595

0833-921X See JOURNAL BARREAU, LE. 2986

0833-9228 See INFORMATEUR CATHOLIQUE (1985). 4964

0833-9414 See PEN AND INK. 362

0833-9422 See OIL & GAS EXPLORATION JOURNAL (CALGARY, ALTA.). 4268

0833-9430 See GOVERNMENT BOND RECORD. 789

0833-9457 See HEALTH CAREER PATHS. 3914

0833-9503 See NEWSLETTER (CANADIAN BAND ASSOCIATION. ONTARIO CHAPTER). 4141

0833-9597 See SURVEY OF INDUSTRIALS (TORONTO. 1985). 734

0833-9600 See SURVEY OF MINES AND ENERGY RESOURCES. 2152

0833-966X See VACANT URBAN RESIDENTIAL LAND SURVEY, ... UPDATE. 2838

0833-9791 See RECREATIONAL VEHICLE LIFE (1984). 4854

0833-9821 See DIRECTORY OF MEMBERS - PERIODICAL WRITERS ASSOCIATION OF CANADA. 2919

0833-9864 See BOUT DE PAPIER. 2485

0833-9864 See BOUT DE PAPIER. 4517

0833-9880 See ENTRE LE POUCE ET L'INDEX. 3574

0834-0064 See MW : MEN'S WEAR OF CANADA. 1086

0834-0102 See ALL POINTS BULLETIN. 5375

0834-0188 See COMMUNICATION - INSTITUTE OF CHARTERED ACCOUNTANTS OF BRITISH COLUMBIA. 741

0834-020X See BUSINESS NEWS (ST. JOHN'S, NFLD.). 651

0834-0242 See OUTLOOK - CANADIAN JEWISH OUTLOOK SOCIETY. 5051

0834-0366 See REVOLTES (MONTREAL, QUEBEC). 4494

0834-0420 See SURVEY OF FUNDS (TORONTO. 1985). 916

0834-0471 See AGENT CANADA. 5460

0834-0536 See HAMILTON REPORT. 678

0834-0552 See BUSINESS TRAVELLER AND LEISURE TIME PLANNER. 5465

0834-065X See PHARMACTUEL. 4323

0834-0676 See HALIFAX METROPOLITAN AREA BUSINESS DIRECTORY. 678

0834-0862 See PORT OF HALIFAX (HALIFAX-DARTMOUTH PORT COMMISSION). 5454

0834-0889 See IDECO BULLETIN. 1751

0834-1443 See AQUILON (YELLOWKNIFE). 3266

0834-1451 See BULLETIN DE LA F.A.A.F., N.-B, LE. 69

0834-1486 See LISTEN (ENGLISH EDITION, OTTAWA). 4390

0834-1494 See PROBE. 1333

0834-1508 See C.H.W. LETTER. 893

0834-1516 See CANADIAN JOURNAL OF PROGRAM EVALUATION, THE. 4636

0834-1656 See GUILD NEWS (TORONTO. 1979). 4120

0834-1729 See NEWSLETTER (YORK UNIVERSITY (TORONTO, ONT.). INSTITUTE FOR SOCIAL RESEARCH). 5211

0834-1737 See GEMS OF POETRY AND PROSE. 3390

0834-177X See WINDSPEAKER. 5798

0834-1788 See NEWSLETTER / APPLIED SCIENCE TECHNOLOGISTS AND TECHNICIANS OF BRITISH COLUMBIA. 5133

0834-1915 See JOURNAL / THE CANADIAN ASSOCIATION FOR HEALTH, PHYSICAL EDUCATION AND RECREATION. 1856

0834-194X See ASIA PACIFIC REPORT. 2501

0834-2008 See NEWSLETTER / ONTARIO FORESTRY ASSOCIATION. 2389

0834-2105 See ONTARIO JUDO NEWSLETTER. 4911

0834-2121 See COFAQ'TUALITE : BULLETIN DE LIAISON DE LA CONFEDERATION DES ORGANISMES FAMILIAUX DU QUEBEC. 5279

0834-2202 See CANADIAN TOY & DECORATION FAIR : DIRECTORY. 2583

0834-2245 See CJO : CANADIAN JOURNAL OF OPTOMETRY. 4215

0834-227X See PHOTOVIDEO. 4375

0834-230X See ALLO POLICE (1986). 3156

0834-2423 See LEMON-AID (1985). 5418

0834-2431 See ALIMENTATION (MONTREAL). 2326

0834-2466 See CATALYST (VANCOUVER. 1986). 5092

0834-258X See TRAVEL CHINA NEWSLETTER. 5495

0834-2709 See ARCTIC PETROLEUM REVIEW. 4251

0834-2903 See BROWSE (WEST HILL. 1991). 5579

0834-292X See WORKLIFE REPORT, THE. 1719

0834-2946 See RULE BOOK / CANADIAN VOLLEYBALL ASSOCIATION. 4915

0834-3055 See CONSTITUTION, BY-LAWS, REGULATIONS, HISTORY / CANADIAN AMATEUR HOCKEY ASSOCIATION. 4891

0834-311X See RACER WEST, THE. 4914

0834-3152 See CONJONCTURE CANADIENNE. 784

0834-3160 See DIETETIQUE EN ACTION. 4189

0834-3187 See INFOCUS. 4072

0834-3241 See FUTURES CANADA (1984). 5200

0834-3365 See FOODSTORE MAGAZINE. 2341

0834-3829 See NOVA SCOTIA CRAFT NEWS / NSDCC. 374

0834-3845 See CONTACT - CANADIAN PROFESSIONAL SALES ASSOCIATION. 659

0834-3845 See CONTACT - ASSOCIATION CANADIENNE DES PROFESSIONNELS DE LA VENTE. 659

0834-3888 See ESPIAL CANADIAN DATA BASE DIRECTORY, THE. 1259

0834-3950 See ITINERAIRE DE LA MONTEREGIE, L'. 5481

0834-3977 See CANADIAN AMATEUR (1987). 2037

0834-4302 See FRESHWATER. 4176

ISSN Index

0834-440X *See* LOGGING INDUSTRY. **2399**

0834-4620 See WASAGA STAR TIMES. **5797**

0834-4825 *See* JOURNAL OF ORTHOMOLECULAR MEDICINE. **3929**

0834-5414 *See* BEALE'S INDUSTRY LETTER, VANCOUVER. **2375**

0834-5643 *See* BELLE RIVER NORTH ESSEX NEWS. **5780**

0834-5686 *See* BOTHWELL TIMES. **5781**

0834-5783 *See* AGINCOURT NEWS. **5779**

0834-5899 *See* BRIGHTON INDEPENDENT, THE. **5781**

0834-6151 *See* CLINTON NEWS-RECORD. MICROFORM. **5782**

0834-616X *See* GRAND VALLEY STAR AND VIDETTE. **5785**

0834-6275 *See* GERALDTON-LONGLAC TIMES STAR. **5785**

0834-6518 *See* GEORGETOWN INDEPENDENT. **5785**

0834-6623 *See* GRIMSBY INDEPENDENT. **5785**

0834-6666 *See* LEADER (MORRISBURG). **5788**

0834-6674 *See* KINCARDINE INDEPENDENT, THE. **5788**

0834-6682 *See* MANITOULIN EXPOSITOR. **5789**

0834-6720 See ELMIRA INDEPENDENT. **5784**

0834-6828 *See* MATTAWA RECORDER [MICROFORM], THE. **5789**

0834-6925 *See* CANADIAN CHAMPION. **5781**

0834-700X *See* TOWN OF MOUNT ROYAL WEEKLY POST. **5796**

0834-7042 *See* PELHAM HERALD. **5792**

0834-7131 *See* SCARBOROUGH NEWS. **5794**

0834-7166 *See* PORT DOVER MAPLE LEAF. **5793**

0834-7336 *See* UXBRIDGE TIMES-JOURNAL. **5796**

0834-7344 *See* TILBURY TIMES. **5796**

0834-7425 *See* STAYNER SUN [MICROFORM], THE. **5795**

0834-745X *See* VILLAGER (TORONTO. 1982). **5797**

0834-7824 *See* AXONE (DARTMOUTH). **3852**

0834-910X *See* ALBERTA CRAFT MAGAZINE. **369**

0834-938X *See* SELECTED FORESTRY STATISTICS, CANADA. **2395**

0834-9614 *See* CAUT BULLETIN. **1814**

0834-969X *See* NEW CATALYST. **2540**

0834-9789 *See* ICAE NEWS. **1800**

0834-9797 *See* CARGO EXPRESS. **16**

0834-9908 *See* REPERTOIRE DES BIENS A STATUT PARTICULIER. **4846**

0835-0000 *See* FOOD INDUSTRIES (OTTAWA). **2337**

0835-0019 *See* BEVERAGE AND TOBACCO PRODUCTS INDUSTRIES. **2364**

0835-0027 *See* RUBBER AND PLASTIC PRODUCTS INDUSTRIES. **5077**

0835-0043 *See* PRIMARY TEXTILE INDUSTRIES. **5355**

0835-006X *See* CLOTHING INDUSTRIES. **1083**

0835-0078 *See* WOOD INDUSTRIES. **2406**

0835-0094 *See* PAPER AND ALLIED PRODUCTS (OTTAWA). **4235**

0835-0116 *See* PRIMARY METAL INDUSTRIES (1985). **4016**

0835-0124 *See* FABRICATED METAL PRODUCTS INDUSTRIES. **4001**

0835-0132 *See* MACHINERY INDUSTRIES, EXCEPT ELECTRICAL MACHINERY (1986). **2121**

0835-0140 *See* TRANSPORTATION EQUIPMENT INDUSTRIES (1986). **5396**

0835-0159 *See* ELECTRICAL AND ELECTRONIC PRODUCTS INDUSTRIES. **2044**

0835-0167 *See* NON-METALLIC MINERAL PRODUCTS INDUSTRIES (OTTAWA). **1443**

0835-0167 *See* NON-METALLIC MINERAL PRODUCTS INDUSTRIES (OTTAWA). **1443**

0835-0175 *See* REFINED PETROLEUM AND COAL PRODUCTS INDUSTRIES. **4276**

0835-0183 *See* CHEMICAL AND CHEMICAL PRODUCTS INDUSTRIES (1986). **1021**

0835-0191 *See* OTHER MANUFACTUREING INDUSTRIES. **3486**

0835-0213 *See* ANNUAL REPORT - MINISTRY OF HOUSING (TORONTO. 1986). **2814**

0835-0280 *See* BUS (ST-LAURENT). **1729**

0835-0310 *See* PADDLER. **595**

0835-0337 *See* DEFI-A.C.L. **318**

0835-0728 See DIRECTORY OF MEMBERS / CANADIAN LIBRARY ASSOCIATION. **3207**

0835-0752 *See* FRDA REPORT. **2383**

0835-085X *See* LISTING OF SUPPLEMENTARY DOCUMENTS, SUPPLEMENT / STATISTICS CANADA, LIBRARY. **3259**

0835-0868 *See* REVUE DE L'ATEQ, LA. **1870**

0835-0892 *See* JURISFEMME (OTTAWA). **2990**

0835-0906 *See* FARM PRODUCT PRICE INDEX. **153**

0835-1031 *See* MECHANICAL TRADE CONTRACTORS. **621**

0835-104X *See* ELECTRICAL TRADE CONTRACTORS. **613**

0835-1058 *See* HIGHWAY, ROAD, STREET AND BRIDGE CONTRACTORS. **616**

0835-1074 *See* RESIDENTIAL GENERAL CONTRACTORS AND DEVELOPERS. **626**

0835-1090 *See* SPECIAL TRADE CONTRACTORS. **628**

0835-1384 *See* BULLETIN (COMMISSION DES VALEURS MOBILIERES DU QUEBEC). **893**

0835-1457 *See* MILIEU (OTTAWA). **2236**

0835-1732 *See* INFO-CREPUQ. **1830**

0835-1740 *See* OCTANE. **4267**

0835-1791 *See* GLOBAL PLASTICS REPORT. **4455**

0835-1813 *See* RESEARCH ON LANGUAGE AND SOCIAL INTERACTION. **3315**

0835-1937 *See* ACQUISITIONS - ARCHIVES PUBLIQUES CANADA. **407**

0835-1945 *See* ACCESSIONS - PUBLIC ARCHIVES CANADA. **406**

0835-1996 *See* NICKLE'S CANADIAN ENERGY INDEX. **1951**

0835-2305 *See* ADF NEWS. **44**

0835-233X *See* WORK INJURIES. **2871**

0835-2453 *See* SKILLS LETTER. **1710**

0835-2925 *See* BRITISH COLUMBIA POLITICS & POLICY. **4466**

0835-2933 *See* LIFE INSURANCE TABLES. **2887**

0835-3026 *See* JCMCC : THE JOURNAL OF COMBINATORIAL MATHEMATICS AND COMBINATORIAL COMPUTING. **3511**

0835-3069 *See* MEDICAL PSYCHOTHERAPY. **3611**

0835-3220 *See* MUSELETTER (ST. ALBERT, ALTA.). **4091**

0835-3271 *See* TLC -- FOR PLANTS. **2432**

0835-3360 *See* ANNUAIRE DES RESSOURCES COMMUNAUTAIRES DE LILE DE MONTREAL. **5271**

0835-3581 *See* REVUE QUEBECOISE DE LINGUISTIQUE THEORIQUE ET APPLIQUEE. **3317**

0835-3638 *See* ANCIENT HISTORY BULLETIN. **1074**

0835-3689 *See* CURRENT SURGICAL THERAPY. **3963**

0835-3778 *See* ENVIRONMENTAL & WASTE MANAGEMENT WORLD. **2228**

0835-3808 *See* IMMIGRATION LAW REPORTER (DON MILLS). **2980**

0835-3921 *See* OPTIONS CARRIERES. **4208**

0835-4014 *See* PLAY AND PARENTING CONNECTIONS. **3241**

0835-4057 *See* QUARTERLY DEMOGRAPHIC STATISTICS. **4562**

0835-412X *See* CHRISTIAN WEEK. **4946**

0835-4251 *See* SMALL BUSINESS WORLD MAGAZINE. **711**

0835-426X *See* ATLANTIC CHAMBER JOURNAL. **818**

0835-4588 *See* MEMO'ART. **358**

0835-4634 *See* TRUSTED PENSION FUNDS FINANCIAL STATISTICS. **918**

0835-4650 See IVANOUVELLES (MONTREAL). **872**

0835-4650 See IVANOUVELLES (MONTREAL). **872**

0835-4669 *See* MUTUAL FUND SOURCEBOOK (TORONTO). **908**

0835-4693 *See* DIRECTORY. POSTAL CODE. **1144**

0835-4790 *See* LUMIERES (MONTREAL). **4074**

0835-4944 *See* CANADIAN JOURNAL FOR THE STUDY OF ADULT EDUCATION. **1800**

0835-5134 *See* INDUSTRIAL SPECIALTIES NEWS. **4455**

0835-5169 *See* VIVRE LE PRIMAIRE. **1806**

0835-5223 See MAGAZINE ENFANTS, LE. **1066**

0835-5266 *See* ENERGY ALERT (TORONTO). **1938**

0835-5428 *See* ANNUAL REPORT TO THE LEGISLATIVE ASSEMBLY - PROVINCE OF BRITISH COLUMBIA. OMBUDSMAN. **4629**

0835-5509 *See* NEWSLETTER / EQUINE RESEARCH CENTRE AT GUELPH. **2801**

0835-5533 *See* SHIPPING IN CANADA. **5456**

0835-5681 *See* INTERCHANGE - CITIZENSHIP DEVELOPMENT BRANCH (TORONTO). **5290**

0835-5754 *See* PARENT'S DIGEST (CHILLIWACK). **2284**

0835-5770 *See* OKAMI : JOURNAL DE LA SOCIETE D'HISTOIRE D'OKA. **2752**

0835-5797 *See* PRODUCTION AND SHIPMENTS OF STEEL PIPE AND TUBING. **4016**

0835-5819 *See* INTERACTION - CANADIAN CHILD DAY CARE FEDERATION. **5290**

0835-5851 *See* ALCES. **2186**

0835-6009 *See* LEGAL RESEARCH UPDATE. **3000**

0835-605X *See* ENVIRONMENTAL SCIENCE & ENGINEERING (AURORA). **1975**

0835-6246 *See* FARMING FACTS. **86**

0835-636X *See* ONTARIO FAMILY LAW REPORTER. **3122**

0835-6742 *See* CANADIAN JOURNAL OF ADMINISTRATIVE LAW & PRACTICE. **3092**

0835-6785 See GREATER QUEBEC AREA TOUR OPERATOR MANUAL. **5478**

0835-7099 See JOURNAL OF PRE-RAPHAELITE STUDIES (1992), THE. **2848**

0835-7129 See AVIATION, AEROSPACE & DEFENCE UPDATE. **12**

0835-7366 *See* RESPONSE TO THE ... REPORT OF THE AUDITOR GENERAL - PROVINCE OF BRITISH COLUMBIA. FINANCE AND CORPORATE RELATIONS. **809**

0835-7560 *See* AMERICAN & WORLD INTELLECTUAL PROPERTY REPORT. **1301**

0835-7641 *See* ETC (MONTREAL). **350**

0835-7714 *See* J'AIME LIRE (SAINT-LAMBERT). **1065**

0835-7900 *See* CANADIAN JOURNAL OF GASTROENTEROLOGY, THE. **3743**

0835-8044 *See* HOCKEY COACHING JOURNAL. **4899**

0835-8087 *See* NATIONAL LABOUR REVIEW. **3152**

0835-8095 *See* PIXEL (TORONTO). **1234**

0835-8184 *See* SAFETY INFOGRAM. **2869**

0835-8443 *See* TTR : TRADUCTION, TERMINOLOGIE, REDACTION. **3330**

0835-8451 *See* EC NEWSLETTER - DELEGATION OF THE COMMISSION OF THE EUROPEAN COMMUNITIES. **1634**

0835-846X *See* CANADA'S WOMEN. **1531**

0835-8478 *See* CANADA'S MEN. **1530**

0835-8486 *See* CANADA'S YOUTH. **1531**

0835-8494 *See* CANADA'S OLDER WORKERS. **1530**

0835-8559 *See* CANADA'S UNIONIZED WORKERS. **1531**

0835-8583 *See* PENSION PLAN COVERAGE IN CANADA. **1537**

0835-8672 *See* A RAYONS OUVERTS. **3186**

0835-8702 *See* BEL AGE, LE. **5178**

0835-8710 See BREF DE L'ACAQ, EN. 5178
0835-8974 See PEDAGOGIE COLLEGIALE. 1840
0835-9148 See CANADIAN ECONOMIC OBSERVER. 1468
0835-9245 See CANADIAN CORPORATE LAW REPORTER. 3097
0835-9296 See SOCIAL RESOURCES INVENTORY. CALGARY REGION. 5308
0835-9369 See MAGAZINE DE LA COMMUNICATION GRAPHIQUE, LE. 380
0835-9407 See BUSINESS TODAY, CONSTRUCTION NEWS. 606
0835-9628 See PERSUASIONS. OCCASIONAL PAPERS (VICTORIA). 3423
0835-9636 See DROIT DISCIPLINAIRE EXPRESS. 2964
0835-9733 See FREEDOM OF INFORMATION AND PROTECTION OF INDIVIDUAL PRIVACY. DIRECTORY OF GENERAL RECORDS. 4650
0835-9768 See CANADIAN LEGAL LITERATURE. 3079
0835-9768 See LEGISLATION (SCARBOROUGH). 3001
0835-9776 See CANADIAN CASE AND STATUTE CITATIONS / REFERENCES JURISPRUDENTIELLES ET LEGISLATIVES CANADIENNES. 2947
0835-9806 See INSIDE HOCKEY (DON MILLS, ONT.). 4900
0835-9962 See AUDIO VISUAL CATALOGUE / LIBRARY, JUSTICE INSTITUTE OF BRITISH COLUMBIA. 408
0835-9989 See NEWS EXTRA. 2541
0836-0014 See QUEBEC A VOTRE PORTEE, LE. 2756
0836-0073 See FREE MATERIALS FOR SCHOOLS AND LIBRARIES. 1895
0836-0081 See MATURITE. 5295
0836-0197 See NETWORK (TORONTO. 1987). 386
0836-0278 See BULLETIN / CANADIAN WATER AND WASTEWATER ASSOCIATION. 5531
0836-0421 See GRAMMATEION (TORONTO). 321
0836-0456 See CANADIAN INSURANCE LAW REVIEW. 2948
0836-0464 See BIBLIO-EXPRESS. 3194
0836-0650 See INNOVATIONS. 2791
0836-088X See EPILOGUE (HALIFAX, N.S.). 3209
0836-0960 See CANADIAN SHAREOWNER. 894
0836-0987 See BULLETIN - INSTITUT NATIONAL DE RECHERCHE SUR LES EAUX. 5531
0836-1002 See FILM/VIDEO CANADIANA. 4070
0836-1126 See ANNUAL REPORT - MINISTRY OF LABOUR AND CONSUMER SERVICES (VICTORIA). 1649
0836-1371 See R AND D OUTLOOK. 1623
0836-1398 See PHYSICS ESSAYS. 4415
0836-1444 See CHIROPRACTIC REPORT, THE. 4380
0836-1509 See ANNUAL REPORT - ALBERTA TRANSPORTATION AND UTILITIES. 5376
0836-155X See T-L NETWORK. 3252
0836-1576 See PROFIL (TROIS-RIVIERES). 4796
0836-1630 See AUTOPINION (OTTAWA). 5407
0836-205X See TOURISME+, LE JOURNAL DES VOYAGES. 5493
0836-2114 See PLAYBACK (TORONTO). 1136
0836-2149 See SCANDINAVIAN FORUM. 2272
0836-2394 See EMPLOYMENT BULLETIN - CANADA LAW BOOK INC. 3147
0836-2807 See PHOENIX (WATERLOO). 3468
0836-298X See KIDS CAN READ (LONDON, ONT.). 3221
0836-3021 See CANADIAN BANKING REVIEW / CANADIAN BOND RATING SERVICE. 727
0836-303X See CANADIAN REVIEW OF SOCIAL POLICY (1987). 5276
0836-3102 See AU "PAYS" DE MATANE. 2722
0836-3196 See CANADIAN (VERNON, B.C.). 655
0836-3218 See INRS NOUVELLES. 5114
0836-3374 See FAITS SUR LES ASSURANCES DE PERSONNES AU CANADA. 2880

0836-3463 See FORUM / ASSOCIATION OF CANADIAN MEDICAL COLLEGES. 3577
0836-3536 See COURRIER FRANCAIS (1991). 3275
0836-3749 See FLOWER SHOP. 2435
0836-3838 See INVIVO. 459
0836-3935 See CODE DU TRAVAIL DU QUEBEC ET REGLEMENTS. 1659
0836-3951 See INTERNATIONAL GUIDE, EDMONTON. 5481
0836-4001 See CANADIAN LIFE AND HEALTH INSURANCE FACTS. 2877
0836-4192 See DIRECTORY / WESTCOASTS WOMEN'S NETWORK. 5554
0836-4214 See OMCA RESOURCE GUIDE. 1620
0836-4362 See OSLA. ONTARIO ASSOCIATION OF SPEECH-LANGUAGE PATHOLOGISTS AND AUDIOLOGISTS. 3896
0836-4397 See WEST VANCOUVER REPORT. 2839
0836-4400 See THIS WEEK AT CARLETON (1987). 1850
0836-4443 See METROPOLITAN TORONTO ... ANNUAL VISITORS GUIDE. 5484
0836-4451 See WESTERN CANADA OUTDOORS (SASKATCHEWAN EDITION). 2208
0836-446X See WESTERN CANADA OUTDOORS (ALBERTA EDITION). 2208
0836-4486 See REPORT OF PROCEEDINGS. ANNUAL GENERAL MEETING - BRITISH COLUMBIA SCHOOL TRUSTEES ASSOCIATION. 1778
0836-4664 See FREDERICTON, NEW BRUNSWICK, ATLANTIC CANADA TOUR PLANNING MANUAL. 5474
0836-4702 See NATURE NORTHWEST. 4169
0836-4796 See BC WOMAN TO WOMAN MAGAZINE. 5551
0836-4915 See COTEAU REVIEW. 5782
0836-4974 See GARDENS WEST. 2416
0836-5040 See GREENPEACE (CANADA ED.). 2194
0836-5059 See DIMENSIONS. 4241
0836-5148 See HOCKEY SCOUTING REPORT. 4899
0836-5164 See CANADIAN SHIPBUILDING, OFFSHORE AND MARINE INDUSTRIES. 5448
0836-5369 See DIFFUSION BECANCOUR. 974
0836-5482 See MICROVIEW (TORONTO). 1195
0836-5709 See REPERTOIRE DES MEMBRES - ORDRE DES INGENIEURS FORESTIERS DU QUEBEC. 2392
0836-5768 See DOMINION LAW REPORTS. FOURTH SERIES, INDEX, ANNOTATIONS, TABLE OF CASES. 2964
0836-5814 See TAX TIPS - DOANE, RAYMOND, PANNELL. 4754
0836-5857 See RENOVATOR, THE. 626
0836-5873 See INSIGHT ON COLLECTABLES (1987). 251
0836-6063 See JEWISH POST & NEWS, THE. 5786
0836-6098 See WOUND & SKIN CARE. 3723
0836-6160 See DIRECTIONS - ONTARIO ASSOCIATION FOR COMMUNITY LIVING. 4386
0836-6233 See PLANNED PARENTHOOD NEWFOUNDLAND/LABRADOR. 590
0836-6314 See DRUG PROTOCOL. 4301
0836-6616 See LIAISON - CANADIAN ASSOCIATION OF LEGAL ASSISTANTS. 3003
0836-6616 See LIAISON - CANADIAN ASSOCIATION OF LEGAL ASSISTANTS. 3003
0836-6632 See UNB LAW JOURNAL. 3067
0836-6667 See HONG KONG MONITOR. 1635
0836-6756 See CANADIAN MARKET PULP STATISTICS. 4232
0836-6845 See BULLETIN / THE NATIONAL EATING DISORDER INFORMATION CENTRE. 3829
0836-690X See OCTO-GRAPHE. 1868
0836-6918 See FILET (MONTREAL, QUEBEC). 4959
0836-6926 See FETES ET FESTIVALS. 4850

0836-6942 See MAGAZINE AFFAIRES PLUS. 797
0836-7078 See LIVRES DISPONIBLES CANADIENS DE LANGUE FRANCAISE. 4816
0836-7094 See SOCIALIST WORKER (TORONTO). 4547
0836-7124 See GLASNIK (NORTH BURNABY). 2689
0836-7221 See PRO-CHOICE NEWS. 590
0836-7248 See TRAPPEUR QUEBECOIS, LE. 4879
0836-7264 See MOTONEIGE QUEBEC. 4905
0836-7272 See EMERGENCY PREHOSPITAL MEDICINE. 3724
0836-7310 See CONCERN (REGINA). 3854
0836-7353 See TRAVEL A LA CARTE. 5494
0836-7655 See TOURBILLON DE LA SQTRP, LE. 3646
0836-768X See NIAGARA BUSINESS DIRECTORY. 699
0836-7884 See INTERNATIONAL ABSTRACTS IN HYPERTENSION. 3706
0836-799X See CANADIAN AGGREGATES. 606
0836-8619 See BOOK TRADE IN CANADA, WITH WHO'S WHERE, THE. 4812
0836-866X See INITIATIVES (TORONTO). 1896
0836-9410 See ALBERTA TRANSFER GUIDE. 1808
0837-0222 See COMPAGNIES, SOCIETES PAR ACTIONS ET FAILLITE. 3089
0837-0346 See ALBERTA DEMOCRAT, THE. 4462
0837-0672 See VABA EESTLANE. 2476
0837-1059 See ANNUAL REPORT / THE ATLANTIC SALMON FEDERATION. 2295
0837-1342 See HOLLANDSE KRANT. 2263
0837-1512 See TODAY'S TRUCKING. 5394
0837-2446 See ANNUAL REPORT / TELEFILM CANADA. 4063
0837-2470 See EMPLOI AU QUEBEC. 1664
0837-2535 See ANNUAL REPORT OF OPERATIONS UNDER THE MEAT IMPORT ACT. 206
0837-3175 See TORONTO SUN. MICROFORM, THE. 5796
0837-3299 See WINDMILL HERALD (CENTRAL-EASTERN CANADA ED.). 5798
0837-3752 See EV CIRCUIT - ELECTRIC VEHICLE CLUB OF OTTAWA. 2054
0837-4171 See ANNUAL REPORT / DEPARTMENT OF TOURISM. 5461
0837-5496 See RAPPORT ANNUEL - CONSEIL REGIONAL DE LA SANTE ET DES SERVICES SOCIAUX DE L'OUTAOUAIS. 4798
0837-5771 See EMERGENCY PREPAREDNESS DIGEST. 1073
0837-5771 See REVUE DE LA PROTECTION CIVILE, LA. 5256
0837-5836 See REVUE ECONOMIQUE TRIMESTRIELLE (OTTAWA). 1518
0837-6425 See ANNUAL REPORT / MANITOBA RESEARCH COUNCIL. 4464
0837-645X See RAPPORT ANNUEL / FONDS FCAR, FONDS POUR LA FORMATION DE CHERCHEURS ET L'AIDE A LA RECHERCHE. 5144
0837-6786 See ANNUAL REPORT - MANITOBA NATURAL RESOURCES. 2133
0837-6816 See ANNUAL REPORT / AMHC, ALBERTA MORTGAGE AND HOUSING CORPORATION. 2814
0837-6840 See ANNUAL REPORT / MANITOBA LOTTERIES FOUNDATION. 4627
0837-6875 See ANNUAL REPORT OF THE SASKATCHEWAN PORK PRODUCERS MARKETING BOARD. 2327
0837-7111 See INTER-MISSION (QUEBEC). 4657
0837-7138 See RAPPORT ANNUEL / CONSEIL CONSULTATIF DE L'ENVIRONNEMENT. 4678
0837-7251 See HEALTH PERSONNEL IN CANADA. 4780
0837-7375 See LIST OF ALBERTA PUBLICATIONS AND LEGISLATION. 4662
0837-757X See RAPPORTS D'ACTIVITE / DIRECTION DE LA RECHERCHE GEOLOGIQUE. 1393

ISSN Index

0837-8649 *See* MONTHLY STATISTICAL REVIEW - SASKATCHEWAN. BUREAU OF STATISTICS (1978). **5333**

0837-9750 *See* ALBERTA'S RESERVES OF CRUDE OIL, OIL SANDS, GAS, NATURAL GAS LIQUIDS, AND SULPHUR. **4249**

0837-9823 *See* ANNUAL REPORT / SASKATCHEWAN LEGISLATIVE LIBRARY. **4629**

0837-9831 *See* PORTRAIT DE LA FISCALITE DES PARTICULIERS AU QUEBEC, STATISTIQUES / REDIGE PAR LE MINISTERE DU REVENU DU QUEBEC. **3029**

0837-9971 *See* SUBVENTIONS A LA RECHERCHE, BOURSES D'EXCELLENCE ET SUBVENTIONS POUR ETUDESET ANALYSES. **5223**

0838-0015 *See* GUIDE DE LA ROUTE, FLORIDE. **5478**

0838-0058 *See* PAY EQUITY GUIDE. **702**

0838-0139 See CANADIAN FACILITY MANAGEMENT & DESIGN. **863**

0838-0392 *See* C (TORONTO. 1987). **346**

0838-0430 *See* JOURNAL OF BAHA'I STUDIES. **4968**

0838-0449 *See* INDEX DE L'ACTUALITE, L'. **5786**

0838-0457 *See* INDEX DES AFFAIRES, L'. **870**

0838-049X *See* NEWFOUNDLAND ANCESTOR. **2462**

0838-0651 *See* RYERSON REVIEW OF JOURNALISM. **2924**

0838-0872 *See* POWER BOATING CANADA. **595**

0838-0899 *See* ANNUAL REPORT / BRITISH COLUMBIA, INDUSTRIAL RELATIONS COUNCIL. **1597**

0838-0961 *See* CANADIAN PETROLEUM TAX JOURNAL. **4716**

0838-1313 *See* DANCE CONNECTION. **1311**

0838-1380 *See* BULLETIN, UNIVERSITY-INDUSTRY PROGRAMS. **3561**

0838-1453 *See* LITTERATURES (MONTREAL). **3408**

0838-1488 See LUMIERE D'ENCRE. **3409**

0838-1542 *See* JOHN TWIGG'S REPORT ON B.C. **1498**

0838-1550 *See* PAGANS FOR PEACE. **4242**

0838-164X *See* JOURNAL OF PRISONERS ON PRISONS. **3167**

0838-1658 *See* GALLERIE (NORTH VANCOUVER, B.C.). **321**

0838-1674 *See* OPTION SERRE. **2426**

0838-1690 *See* BULLETIN / CANADIAN EQUESTRIAN FEDERATION. **2797**

0838-1925 *See* ALLERGY & CLINICAL IMMUNOLOGY NEWS. **3665**

0838-2026 *See* FONTANUS FROM THE COLLECTIONS OF MCGILL UNIVERSITY. **3211**

0838-2174 *See* LEISURE AND PERSONAL SERVICES. **1616**

0838-2182 *See* BUSINESS SERVICES. **1600**

0838-2239 *See* IMPOSTURE (MONTREAL). **352**

0838-228X *See* CANADIAN HR REPORTER. **939**

0838-2395 *See* COTTAGE LIFE. **4849**

0838-2433 *See* MEDECINES NOUVELLES (QUEBEC). **4314**

0838-2638 *See* NOVA SCOTIA MEDICAL JOURNAL, THE. **3623**

0838-2875 *See* EDUCATION LAW JOURNAL. **2965**

0838-2948 *See* CANADIAN JOURNAL OF NURSING ADMINISTRATION. **3852**

0838-3200 See DISCOVERING ALBERTA. **5468**

0838-3340 *See* CONTACT - CANADIAN ELECTROACOUSTIC COMMUNITY. **2039**

0838-3596 *See* WINDSOR REVIEW OF LEGAL AND SOCIAL ISSUES. **3075**

0838-360X *See* LIBRARY FOOTNOTES. **3225**

0838-3693 *See* ANNUAL REPORT - HEALTH AND COMMUNITY SERVICES. NEW BRUNSWICK. **4765**

0838-3715 *See* FAMILY EXPENDITURE IN CANADA (1978). **1490**

0838-3863 *See* TOURISM IN CANADA. **5493**

0838-3871 *See* NUCLEAR SECTOR FOCUS. **1952**

0838-3898 *See* FAMILY FOOD EXPENDITURE IN CANADA (1982). **1490**

0838-391X *See* ALPHA BEAT SOUP. **3359**

0838-4061 *See* SPORT & LEISURE. **4854**

0838-4134 See CHASSE AU QUEBEC, PRINCIPALES REGLES, LA. **4871**

0838-4185 *See* WOODWORKING (MARKHAM). **2406**

0838-4223 *See* STATISTICS CANADA CATALOGUE (1988). **4700**

0838-4274 See VISTA (EDMONTON). **1790**

0838-4347 *See* CLSC EXPRESS. **5279**

0838-438X *See* BUSINESS COMPUTER NEWS. **646**

0838-4452 *See* PERFORMING ARTS / STATISTICS CANADA, EDUCATION, CULTURE AND TOURISM DIVISION. **334**

0838-4479 *See* RECHERCHES FEMINISTES. **5565**

0838-4525 *See* SCRUTINY (SASKATOON, SASK.). **1783**

0838-4711 *See* JOURNAL OF INDIGENOUS STUDIES, THE. **2741**

0838-4843 *See* CHARTER OF RIGHTS NEWSLETTER. **4505**

0838-4967 *See* NORTH WEST COURANT. **3185**

0838-5009 *See* A PRIORI (OTTAWA). **1859**

0838-5041 *See* CANADIAN PEACE REPORT. **4517**

0838-5106 See CHRONIQUES DU PROTECTEUR DU CITOYEN. **4637**

0838-5459 *See* BULLETIN - ASSOCIATION QUEBECOISE POUR L'ETUDE DE L'IMPRIME. **431**

0838-5505 *See* ISLAND PARENT MAGAZINE. **2281**

0838-5513 *See* MASCOUCHOIS. **4852**

0838-5696 *See* THEATRUM (TORONTO). **5371**

0838-5777 See CANADIAN BIOTECH NEWS. **3690**

0838-5998 *See* B.C. MINERAL STATISTICS ANNUAL SUMMARY TABLES. **2134**

0838-603X *See* FUSE MAGAZINE. **320**

0838-6226 *See* EGLISE DE NICOLET, ANNUAIRE. **5029**

0838-6366 *See* OIL PATCH MAGAZINE. **4269**

0838-6463 See THUNDER BAY METRO TRADE INDEX. **853**

0838-6498 *See* NEXUS II. **5563**

0838-6579 *See* ALLIANCE REPORT. **2527**

0838-6595 *See* FOCUS ON EQUALITY. **4508**

0838-6609 *See* QUEEN'S PAPERS IN INDUSTRIAL RELATIONS. **1705**

0838-6730 *See* BULLETIN / SASKATCHEWAN CHORAL FEDERATION. **4106**

0838-679X *See* ATLANTIC FIREFIGHTER. **2288**

0838-6811 *See* OFFICIAL FAX DIRECTORY (CANADIAN ED.). **1161**

0838-6854 *See* HOSPITALITE, HOTELLERIE, RESTAURATION, L'. **2806**

0838-7052 *See* MISSIONNAIRES ENSEMBLE. **4978**

0838-7176 *See* VOICES (TORONTO, ONT.). **4705**

0838-7249 *See* NEWSLETTER / LETHBRIDGE HISTORICAL SOCIETY. **2749**

0838-7397 *See* SALLY ANN. **4995**

0838-7605 *See* SPECTRUM (ALBERTA SCHOOL TRUSTEES ASSOCIATION). **1872**

0838-7818 See MS TORONTO (1991). **4391**

0838-7990 *See* ALLIANCE (OTTAWA. ENGLISH ED.). **1643**

0838-8032 *See* COMMON GROUND (REGINA). **1660**

0838-8083 *See* MOMENT (TORONTO). **5252**

0838-8164 *See* INTERNATIONAL CENTRE NEWS (WINNIPEG). **1919**

0838-8334 *See* CHALLENGE FUND JOURNAL. **1090**

0838-8512 *See* FARMING TODAY (WELLINGTON-WATERLOO-PERTH ED.). **86**

0838-8539 *See* LIST OF CERTIFIED ELECTRICAL EQUIPMENT (1988). **2071**

0838-8881 *See* CONJONCTURES (MONTREAL). **5242**

0838-9268 See PERFORMER (TORONTO). **1314**

0838-9330 *See* CENTURY HOME (1988). **294**

0838-9349 *See* JOURNAL DE MUSIQUE ANCIENNE. **4125**

0838-9365 *See* DAILIES. **895**

0838-9446 *See* FEMME PLUS (MONTREAL). **5556**

0838-9535 *See* ELECTRONIC COMPOSITION & IMAGING. **1263**

0838-9586 *See* VIDEO SCENE. **4079**

0838-9683 *See* CHILD CARE. **3901**

0838-9772 See TRAVEL NEWS AMERICAS. **5496**

0838-9845 *See* ... CANADIAN MEDICAL DEVICE DIRECTORY, THE. **3562**

0838-990X See CARP. CANADIAN ASSOCIATION OF RETIRED PERSONS. **5178**

0839-0088 *See* ACCC COMMUNITY. **1807**

0839-0185 *See* HAMILTON SPECTATOR (DAILY : 1984). **5786**

0839-0452 *See* METROPOLITAN TORONTO CITY DIRECTORY (1988). **2538**

0839-0681 *See* LONDON FREE PRESS (MORNING : 1907). **5788**

0839-086X See PETERBOROUGH EXAMINER (DAILY ED.). **5792**

0839-0878 *See* PETERBOROUGH EXAMINER (DAILY ED.). **5792**

0839-0959 See BOTTIN DE L'INDUSTRIE DE LA MUSIQUE AU QUEBEC. **4104**

0839-105X *See* JIB GEMS. **4089**

0839-1300 *See* DIMENSIONS. **865**

0839-1335 *See* VISITOR (KITCHENER, ONT.). **5499**

0839-1483 *See* WELCOME BACK STUDENT GUIDE. **1791**

0839-1572 *See* NIAGARA FALLS REVIEW. **5790**

0839-1629 *See* DIRECTEUR D'ASSOCIATION. **665**

0839-1866 *See* CANADIAN JOURNAL OF DIAGNOSIS. **3561**

0839-2277 *See* WINDSOR STAR MICROFORM, THE. **5798**

0839-2676 *See* DEUTSCHE PRESSE (TORONTO. GERMAN ED.). **5783**

0839-3222 *See* OTTAWA CITIZEN. MICROFORM, THE. **5792**

0839-3311 *See* PROVINCE. **5793**

0839-4164 *See* EXAMINER (BARRIE). **5784**

0839-427X *See* TIMES COLONIST (VICTORIA). **5796**

0839-4377 *See* SSHRC NEWS. **5223**

0839-4555 *See* CAHIERS DU CENTRE D'ETUDES DE L'ASIE DE L'EST. **2844**

0839-458X *See* REVUE ANDRE MALRAUX. **3351**

0839-4938 *See* LETHBRIDGE HERALD MICROFORM, THE. **5788**

0839-6361 *See* MONTHLY MLS STATISTICAL SURVEY. **4841**

0839-640X *See* QUARTERLY MLS STATISTICAL SURVEY. **4843**

0839-6523 *See* NEW BRUNSWICK SOIL SURVEY, REPORT. **111**

0839-7309 See ANNUAIRE TELEPHONIQUE DES ORGANISMES SCOLAIRES DE LA MONTEREGIE. **1724**

0839-7465 See PROGRAMME DE PERFECTIONNEMENT, PERFECTIONNEMENT COLLECTIF. **1775**

0839-7481 See PROGRAMME DE PERFECTIONNEMENT, PERFECTIONNEMENT COLLECTIF POUR LE PERSONNEL DES SERVICES DE L'EDUCATION DES ADULTES. **1802**

0839-7805 See ECOLES SECONDAIRES DE LA CECM, LES. **1737**

0839-7813 See SOCIAL ISSUES NEWS. **4997**

0839-8429 *See* BUDGET. BUDGET SPEECH AND ADDITIONAL INFORMATION. **4714**

0839-8445 *See* BUDGET. DISCOURS SUR LE BUDGET ET RENSEIGNEMENTS SUPPLEMENTAIRES. **4714**

0839-8585 *See* COMPREHENSIVE PUBLICATION LIST - MINISTRY OF FORESTS AND LANDS (VICTORIA). **2378**

0839-8631 *See* INFOCUS (EDMONTON). **1752**

ISSN Index

0839-8658 See ANNUAL REPORT / SASKATCHEWAN ENVIRONMENT AND PUBLIC SAFETY. **4766**

0839-945X See THEATRE, DANSE, MUSIQUE, ARTS MULTIDISCIPLINAIRES ET MULTIMEDIAS. **332**

0839-9476 See THEATRE, DANSE, MUSIQUE, ARTS MULTIDISCIPLINAIRES ET MULTIMEDIAS. **332**

0839-9484 See PROGRAMME D'AIDE ... DU MINISTERE DES AFFAIRES CULTURELLES AIDE AUX ARTISTES PROFESSIONNELS. **328**

0839-9492 See THEATRE, DANSE, MUSIQUE, ARTS MULTIDISCIPLINAIRES ET MULTIMEDIAS. **332**

0839-9506 See ANNUAL REPORT / INVESTMENT CANADA. **891**

0839-9549 See EDC TODAY. **832**

0840-1705 See PROCEEDINGS OF THE SPECIAL COMMITTEE OF THE SENATE ON NATIONAL DEFENCE. **4054**

0840-190X See LEGAL PERSPECTIVES. **3000**

0840-2035 See PUBLICATIONS CATALOGUE / INSTITUTE FOR RESEARCH IN CONSTRUCTION. **625**

0840-2035 See PUBLICATIONS CATALOGUE - INSTITUTE FOR RESEARCH IN CONSTRUCTION (OTTAWA). **633**

0840-2043 See STATUTES OF SASKATCHEWAN. **3059**

0840-3503 See UNITRADE SPECIALIZED CATALOGUE OF CANADIAN STAMPS. **2788**

0840-3651 See DIRECTORY OF LABOUR ORGANIZATIONS IN NEW BRUNSWICK. **1663**

0840-3813 See DOLL & TOY COLLECTOR (LONDON). **2773**

0840-3902 See NEWSLETTER - DALHOUSIE UNIVERSITY. SCHOOL OF LIBRARY AND INFORMATION STUDIES. **3235**

0840-3929 See COMPUTER PAPER (BRITISH COLUMBIA ED.). **1177**

0840-3945 See INDEPENDENT TRUCKER. **5384**

0840-4003 See VOICES (SURREY). **3451**

0840-4011 See BULLETIN - INSTITUT SIMONE DE BEAUVOIR. **5552**

0840-4313 See VISUAL MEDIA. **4079**

0840-4348 See HOME BUILDER MAGAZINE. **616**

0840-4496 See FIFTY-FIVE PLUS (BATTERSEA). **5179**

0840-4631 See TESSERA (BURNABY). **3445**

0840-464X See BRITISH COLUMBIA'S WEDDING BELLS. **2277**

0840-4666 See SUSTAINABLE DEVELOPMENT. **2206**

0840-4704 See HEALTHCARE MANAGEMENT FORUM. **3782**

0840-478X See ARGUS PROMOTIONNEL OFICHIER D'ORDINATEUR. **1104**

0840-4798 See ARGUS SECTORIEL. **3266**

0840-4821 See JOICE. JOURNAL OF INTERNATIONAL AND COMPARATIVE ECONOMICS. **1637**

0840-4836 See TECHNOLOGIES DE L'INFORMATION ET SOCIETE. **5163**

0840-4917 See CANADIAN INVESTOR (TORONTO. 1984). **894**

0840-4968 See FIRE RESEARCH NEWS. **2289**

0840-4976 See ALBERTA GOVERNMENT PUBLICATIONS. **407**

0840-5395 See 50 PLUS (DURHAM, ONT.). **5177**

0840-5417 See BULLETIN - AQUACULTURE ASSOCIATION OF CANADA. **449**

0840-5417 See BULLETIN - AQUACULTURE ASSOCIATION OF CANADA. **449**

0840-5476 See TELEMANAGEMENT (PICKERING). **1167**

0840-5492 See OKANAGAN LIFE (KELOWNA. 1988). **2541**

0840-562X See UNIVERSITY OF TORONTO MAGAZINE. **1853**

0840-5735 See TAXATION TODAY (WINNIPEG). **4755**

0840-5778 See THY KINGDOM COME (BURNABY, B.C.). **5005**

0840-5832 See ULCN. UNION LIST OF CANADIAN NEWSPAPERS. **3254**

0840-5891 See ESCENA LATINOAMERICANA, LA. **5364**

0840-5905 See INTERNATIONAL DIRECTORY OF COMPUTER ANIMATION PRODUCERS. **1234**

0840-6014 See CANADA, A PORTRAIT. **1550**

0840-612X See ON BALANCE (VANCOUVER). **1119**

0840-6146 See ALBERTA OIL & FORESTRY REVIEW QUARTERLY. **4249**

0840-6170 See QST CANADA. **1992**

0840-6189 See BOREALIS (TORONTO). **4706**

0840-6200 See CANADIAN HORSEMAN (GUELPH). **2797**

0840-6286 See EIGHTEENTH-CENTURY FICTION (DOWNSVIEW, ONT.). **3383**

0840-6529 See HEALTH REPORTS / RAPPORT SUR LA SANTE / STATISTIQUE CANADA, DIVISION DE LA SANTE. STATISTICS CANADA, HEALTH DIVISION. **4781**

0840-6693 See ATLANTIC MINING JOURNAL. **2134**

0840-6715 See HORSEPOWER (AURORA). **2800**

0840-6723 See MINING SOURCE BOOK. **2146**

0840-6839 See VECTOR PUBLIC OPINION REPORT. **5265**

0840-6863 See CANADIAN INVESTMENT REVIEW. **894**

0840-707X See PLOWMAN (BROOKLIN). **3468**

0840-7150 See INTERNATIONAL STUDENT PARTICIPATION IN CANADIAN EDUCATION. **1754**

0840-7185 See ANNUAL REPORT / MINISTRY OF CITIZENSHIP. **4627**

0840-7193 See ANNUAL REPORT - MINISTRY OF CULTURE AND COMMUNICATIONS (TORONTO). **1149**

0840-7231 See REVIEW OF PROFESSIONAL EMPLOYMENT. **1708**

0840-7266 See CAHIERS DE PROPRIETE INTELLECTUELLE. **1302**

0840-7312 See CANADIAN COMPUTER RESELLER. **1173**

0840-7339 See OUR SCHOOLS, OUR SELVES. **1771**

0840-769X See NEWSLETTER / THIRD WORLD LIBRARIES INTEREST GROUP. **3236**

0840-7738 See BRIDGING THE GAP (LANCASTER). **2440**

0840-7754 See JOURNAL OF MOTOR VEHICLE LAW. **2989**

0840-7797 See DATABASE CANADA. **1253**

0840-7827 See LIAISON ENERGIE FRANCOPHONIE. **1949**

0840-7886 See ESTATES & TRUSTS JOURNAL. **3118**

0840-7908 See LISTE BIMESTRIELLE DES PUBLICATIONS DU GOUVERNEMENT DU QUEBEC. **4698**

0840-8041 See PERSPECTIVES / COMMISSAIRE A L'INFORMATION ET A LA PROTECTION DE LA VIE PRIVEE/ONTARIO. **4673**

0840-8068 See NURSERY CROP PRODUCTION GUIDE FOR COMMERCIAL GROWERS. **180**

0840-8106 See HOMEOWNER REPAIR AND RENOVATION EXPENDITURE IN CANADA. **634**

0840-8114 See PATHWAYS (HAMILTON). **2179**

0840-819X See MEMBERSHIP DIRECTORY AND HANDBOOK. **3230**

0840-822X See OPHEA JOURNAL. **1857**

0840-8238 See MONTHLY SURVEY OF MANUFACTURING. **3485**

0840-8289 See AGRISCIENCE (OTTAWA). **54**

0840-8386 See SMDI INTERNATIONAL NEWSLETTER. **3807**

0840-8491 See DEMOGRAPHIC AND INCOME STATISTICS FOR POSTAL AREAS, CANADA. **5326**

0840-8548 See BIOLOGUE (WATERLOO). **446**

0840-8610 See AMERICAN MINES HANDBOOK. **2133**

0840-8688 See CANADIAN JOURNAL OF ELECTRICAL AND COMPUTER ENGINEERING. **1227**

0840-870X See GOVERNMENT BUSINESS OPPORTUNITIES. **950**

0840-8750 See PERSPECTIVES ON LABOUR AND INCOME. **1537**

0840-8785 See QUEBEC FRANCE. **5214**

0840-8831 See REGISTERED NURSE (TORONTO). **3868**

0840-9137 See IE, INVESTMENT EXECUTIVE. **900**

0840-9145 See CLUB REGIONAL DE L'ENTREPRENEURSHIP, LE. **864**

0840-9153 See CABLECASTER (TORONTO). **1129**

0840-9269 See EDUCATION FORUM (TORONTO. 1988). **1893**

0840-9331 See BULLETIN / ASSOCIATION OF CANADIAN MAP LIBRARIES AND ARCHIVES. **2581**

0840-9455 See DIRECTORY OF NATURAL GAS COMPANY OPERATIONS. **4760**

0840-9536 See COURRIER (SOCIETE D'HISTOIRE DES FRANCO-COLOMBIENS). **2730**

0840-9633 See BULLETIN / REGROUPEMENT DES PROFESSIONNELS DE LA DANSE DU QUEBEC. **1311**

0840-9668 See EDUCATION ET FORMATION AU QUEBEC. **1739**

0840-982X See JOURNAL OF CHILD AND YOUTH CARE. **5291**

0840-9935 See ETHICA (RIMOUSKI). **2249**

0841-0798 See ONTARIO PUBLIC SECTOR. **4671**

0841-1883 See HOME HEALTH CARE. **4783**

0841-1956 See CORPORATE ETHICS MONITOR, THE. **661**

0841-2014 See SNOW GOER'S WATER GOER. **596**

0841-2200 See HRVATSKI GODNISNJAK ZA GODINU. **1926**

0841-2227 See SOURCES-ENAP. **4686**

0841-2472 See UPDATE - ONTARIO TRUCKING ASSOCIATION. **5399**

0841-2537 See MANITOBA LEGAL SERVICES DIRECTORY. **3180**

0841-2588 See WEST HILL NEWS. **5797**

0841-2626 See LAW NOW. **2995**

0841-2642 See TREE TRACER. **2475**

0841-2650 See STREETSOUND (TORONTO). **4155**

0841-2707 See NORTH YORK NEWS (1970?). **5791**

0841-2898 See CANADIAN MINING LIFE & EXPLORATION NEWS. **2136**

0841-6001 See WEBB'S POSTAL STATIONERY CATALOGUE OF CANADA AND NEWFOUNDLAND. **1148**

0841-6036 See BADMINTON TODAY. **4886**

0841-6060 See CANADAWORKS! : THE SERVICE EMPLOYEES INTERNATIONAL UNION MAGAZINE. **1658**

0841-6109 See PERSPECTIVES PHARMACEUTIQUES. **4319**

0841-6141 See INCOME TAX BULLETINS, CIRCULARS, RULINGS. **4731**

0841-615X See PURCHASING MANAGEMENT. **951**

0841-6397 See TRACES (MONTREAL). **1908**

0841-6419 See VALLEY COURIER (PORT ALBERNI, B.C. : 1988). **5796**

0841-6621 See TAX PLANNING GUIDE. **4754**

0841-6982 See HOCKEY AUJOURD'HUI. **4898**

0841-7563 See TIDES OF CHANGE. **2207**

0841-758X See RAYON JEUNESSE. **1068**

0841-7741 See SCIENCE ET COMPORTEMENT. **4618**

0841-7997 See PARTENAIRE (SAINT-HUBERT). **5564**

0841-8012 See TABLEAU (WINNIPEG, MAN.). **366**

0841-8195 See TALL NEWSLETTER (1984). **3252**

0841-8209 See CANADIAN JOURNAL OF LAW AND JURISPRUDENCE, THE. **2948**

0841-8233 See CISM JOURNAL. **2581**

0841-9116 See DEAF CANADIAN ADVOCATE. 4386

0841-9191 See MLD CANADIAN TRAVELLER. 5484

0841-923X See HERITAGE HEARTH. 4088

0841-9507 See REACH. 4393

0841-9574 See TEACHER (VANCOUVER). 1787

0841-9663 See MEETINGS MONTHLY, NEWS BULLETIN. 5484

0841-9787 See JAVELIER (LA POCATI'ERE). 2740

0842-0408 See PROGRAMME WITH ABSTRACTS - CANADIAN METEOROLOGICAL AND OCEANOGRAPHIC SOCIETY. 1455

0842-084X See WOLSLEY BULLETIN, THE. 5798

0842-0866 See ARGONAUTA (POINTE-CLAIRE. 1986). 4174

0842-0947 See SCHEDULE & RULE BOOK - NATIONAL HOCKEY LEAGUE. 4916

0842-1048 See REPERTOIRE - ASSOCIATION CANADIENNE DE DEVELOPPEMENT INDUSTRIEL (1987). 1624

0842-1110 See BULLETIN SUR LES COMPOSITES. 4454

0842-1129 See COMPOSITES REPORT / FIBERGLAS CANADA INC. 4454

0842-1420 See DISCOURS SOCIAL (MONTREAL). 3381

0842-1765 See MOOSEHEAD ANTHOLOGY. 3413

0842-1838 See VIES-A-VIES (MONTREAL. 1988). 4621

0842-1854 See ACTUALITES SDM. 1103

0842-1935 See SECRETAIRE MODERNE (1988). 710

0842-1951 See DIRECTION INFORMATIQUE. 1182

0842-1986 See GARDAVUE (LONGUEUIL). 5286

0842-2192 See ENQUETE SUR L'EMPLOI ET LA REMUNERATION. 1667

0842-2958 See VOLLEYBALL COACHES JOURNAL. 4928

0842-2966 See REGISTER AND FIRM INDEX / THE ALBERTA ASSOCIATION OF ARCHITECTS. 307

0842-2982 See OWNERSHIP STRUCTURE OF PRINCIPAL PETROLEUM COMPANIES IN CANADA. 4271

0842-2990 See PROCEEDINGS OF THE STANDING SENATE COMMITTEE ON FISHERIES. 2311

0842-3008 See PROCEEDINGS OF THE STANDING SENATE COMMITTEE ON AGRICULTURE AND FORESTRY. 122

0842-3024 See NEW FEDERATION, THE. 2540

0842-3148 See REFORMER (EDMONTON). 4493

0842-3202 See CANADA HEALTH ACT ANNUAL REPORT. 5276

0842-3210 See INFO - NURSES ASSOCIATION OF NEW BRUNSWICK. 3857

0842-3733 See ANNUAL PROGRESS REPORT TO THE INTERNATIONAL JOINT COMMISSION FROM THE INTERNATIONAL REFERENCE GROUP ON GREAT LAKES POLLUTION FROM LAND USE ACTIVITIES (PLUARG). 2224

0842-3946 See ZIMMER'S QUICK & EASY COMPUTER TAX PROGRAM. 4759

0842-4136 See OCLA-LINK. 3238

0842-4241 See KIDS VANCOUVER DIRECTORY, THE. 1065

0842-4500 See DISCOVERY NEWS. 3478

0842-4624 See ESSENTIEL (SAINT-LAURENT). 5555

0842-4632 See ANNUAL REPORT / THE MANITOBA FARM LANDS OWNERSHIP BOARD. 61

0842-4810 See GOVERNMENT ESTIMATES. 4728

0842-5116 See TALKING BOOKS (THUNDER BAY). 4833

0842-5132 See WILDFLOWER. 2209

0842-5159 See BULLETIN: KAWARTHA BRANCH, ONTARIO GENEALOGICAL SOCIETY, THE. 2440

0842-5205 See CROSS-COUNTRY CONNECTION, THE. 5783

0842-5280 See ANNUAL SALARY SURVEYS. EXECUTIVE COMPENSATION REPORT. 1650

0842-5353 See HEALTHCARE COMPUTING & COMMUNICATIONS CANADA. 3782

0842-5361 See ANNUAIRE - CEGEP DE LA GASPESIE ET DES ILES. 1809

0842-537X See CARDIOVASCULAR RISK FACTORS. 3702

0842-5477 See SAFETY SMARTS. 2869

0842-5531 See COMPUTER DEALER NEWS SOURCE GUIDE. 1236

0842-5698 See CODE MUNICIPAL FD DU QUEBEC. 4638

0842-5914 See AQUACULTURE TODAY. 442

0842-6023 See KIDS TORONTO DIRECTORY, THE. 1065

0842-6546 See TRANSPORT CANADA CORPORATE PRIORITIES. 854

0842-6686 See REPORT ON THE ADVISORY COMMITTEE TO THE PRIME MINISTER ON THE BUSINESS/GOVERNMENT EXECUTIVE EXCHANGE PROGRAM. 707

0842-7259 See PUBLIC SERVICE MANAGEMENT PENSION PLAN, ANNUAL REPORT. 4677

0842-8336 See DIALOG (EDMONTON). 4386

0842-8409 See ENSEMBLE. 4956

0842-8417 See JOURNAL OF THE ONTARIO SOCIETY FOR EDUCATION THROUGH ART. 354

0842-8425 See FWTAO GUIDEBOOK. 1879

0842-9375 See BULLETIN / PLANNED PARENTHOOD FEDERATION OF CANADA. 588

0842-957X See REVUE QUEBECOISE DURBANISME. 2834

0842-9588 See ATLANTIC CONSTRUCTION JOURNAL. 599

0842-9596 See ATLANTIC TRANSPORTATION JOURNAL. 5377

0842-960X See VANCOUVER SUBURBAN DIRECTORY. 5498

0842-9693 See ZONE HEATING NEWS. 2609

0842-9707 See NEWS / METROPOLITAN TORONTO REFERENCE LIBRARY. 3234

0842-9715 See VOCE DEGLI ITALO CANADESI. 5797

0842-9855 See WESTERN AUTOBODY. 5428

0842-9960 See MAITRES (MONTREAL). 3005

0843-0217 See NEWSLETTER / MCGILL UNIVERSITY GRADUATE SCHOOL OF LIBRARY AND INFORMATION STUDIES. 1837

0843-0284 See KID PROOF. 1065

0843-0403 See 100 MILE HOUSE FREE PRESS. 5779

0843-0578 See CLAIRVOYANT (MONTREAL). 4385

0843-0586 See ALTERNATIVE (MONTREAL, QUEBEC). 1643

0843-0764 See NEWSLETTER / BRITISH COLUMBIA SOCIAL STUDIES TEACHERS' ASSOCIATION OF THE BRITISH COLUMBIA TEACHERS' FEDERATION. 1901

0843-0861 See MEMBERSHIP DIRECTORY, PLANT SOURCE LIST. 2424

0843-090X See CANADIAN EMPLOYMENT LAW TODAY. 3145

0843-0942 See CFCM REPORT. 4943

0843-0985 See PERSPECTIVES - INSTITUT D'ASSURANCE DU CANADA. 2890

0843-140X See CORPO CLIP. 3204

0843-1507 See SCN : THE SHOPPING CENTRE NEWSLETTER. 957

0843-1566 See OUTBOUND (WILLOWDALE). 31

0843-168X See BC PHARMACIST. 4293

0843-1779 See EDUCATION LEADER (VANCOUVER). 1740

0843-1981 See CONTACT MAGAZINE (CALGARY). 2588

0843-218X See CANADIAN DANCERS NEWS (1988). 1311

0843-2198 See ARTS DIRECTORY (HAMILTON). 314

0843-221X See TORONTO FINANCIAL INSTITUTIONS TELEPHONE DIRECTORY, METRO TORONTO AND VICINITY. 814

0843-2236 See COMMUNIQUE - LEARNING DISABILITIES ASSOCIATION OF ONTARIO. 1877

0843-2260 See ARTS BEAT (HAMILTON). 342

0843-2287 See POETRY MARKETS FOR CANADIANS. 3469

0843-2295 See WORLD ENERGY NEWS (CALGARY). 4282

0843-2309 See BUDGET - ALBERTA WHEAT POOL. 165

0843-2392 See CANADIAN PLASTICS AUTOMOTIVE DIRECTORY. 5408

0843-2457 See LIST OF ACCREDITED HEALTH CARE FACILITIES. 3788

0843-2511 See DIRECTORY OF PRODUCTS AND MANUFACTURERS (SAINT JOHN, N.B.). 3478

0843-2538 See CELEBRATE! (OTTAWA). 4943

0843-2570 See OTTAWA SUN, THE. 5792

0843-2635 See PHYSICAL EDUCATION DIGEST. 4912

0843-2651 See CIRCUIT INDUSTRIEL. 3476

0843-2716 See DPWT TIMES, THE. 4387

0843-2902 See COMPUTING & COMMUNICATIONS NEWSLETTER. 1180

0843-3097 See SURVEY OF PENSION PLANS IN CANADA. 1713

0843-3151 See JAZZ REPORT (TORONTO). 4125

0843-3356 See WESTWORLD MAGAZINE (BRITISH COLUMBIA ED.). 2495

0843-3461 See VAN DUSEN BOTANICAL GARDEN BULLETIN. 529

0843-3607 See COLOURIST (OTTAWA). 4400

0843-3690 See BULLETIN / COLLEGE OF DENTAL SURGEONS OF BRITISH COLUMBIA, THE. 1317

0843-3704 See UNITED WAY RESEARCH SERVICES BULLETIN. 5313

0843-3747 See ARIA NEWS. 5315

0843-4042 See ANNUAL REPORT / ONTARIO, MINISTRY OF TRANSPORTATION. 5376

0843-4174 See WORLD TRADE NEWSPAPER. 858

0843-4182 See LITTEREALITE. 3408

0843-4247 See CANADIAN JOURNAL OF DERMATOLOGY, THE. 3718

0843-4255 See CANADIAN JOURNAL OF OB/GYN & WOMEN'S HEALTH CARE, THE. 3758

0843-4263 See CANADIAN JOURNAL OF PEDIATRICS, THE. 3901

0843-4379 See ENERGY STUDIES REVIEW. 1942

0843-4387 See FAX BY TWIGG. 835

0843-4395 See VICTORIA INSIDER. 2765

0843-4441 See HEUREUX QUI COMMUNIQUE. 1112

0843-445X See DREAMS & VISIONS. 3382

0843-4468 See NOUVELLES PRATIQUES SOCIALES. 5299

0843-4530 See RAIL IN CANADA. 5434

0843-4557 See TEEN GENERATION. 1070

0843-459X See LANDMARK (CALGARY). 2422

0843-4611 See ANNALS OF SEX RESEARCH. 5186

0843-4700 See AGENCY INSIGHT. 4764

0843-493X See AVIATION (OTTAWA). 13

0843-4964 See INTERNATIONAL BULLETIN OF LAW & MENTAL HEALTH. 2983

0843-4972 See CURRENT RESEARCH - NEWFOUNDLAND. GEOLOGICAL SURVEY BRANCH. 1439

0843-5030 See GEO INFO. 4650

0843-5049 See AUSTRALIAN & NEW ZEALAND STUDIES IN CANADA. 3364

0843-5057 See HISTORICAL STUDIES IN EDUCATION. 1750

0843-5081 See EDUCATION TODAY (TORONTO). 1740

0843-5197 See SEEDS & SOWERS. 1905

0843-5243 See JOURNAL OF FOREST ENGINEERING. 2385

0843-5278 See LIAISON - INTERGOVERNMENTAL COMMITTEE ON URBAN AND REGIONAL RESEARCH. 2827

0843-5340 *See* HUNTSMAN MARINE SCIENCE NEWS. 1449

0843-5405 *See* MENTORING INTERNATIONAL. 4604

0843-5421 *See* MERGERS AND ACQUISITIONS IN CANADA (RICHMOND HILL, ONT.). 693

0843-5561 *See* ATLANTIC GEOLOGY. 1366

0843-557X *See* ANNUAL RETAIL TRADE. 952

0843-5812 *See* UNIVERSITY OF TORONTO DENTAL JOURNAL. 1337

0843-5901 *See* OHLA NEWSLINE. 3239

0843-5952 *See* REVUE TIRES A PART. 4617

0843-5979 *See* DIRECT ACCESS (CALGARY). 4386

0843-6002 *See* SASKATOON HISTORY REVIEW. 2759

0843-6096 *See* CANADIAN JOURNAL OF CARDIOVASCULAR NURSING. 3700

0843-6142 *See* INDEX TO STATISTICS CANADA SURVEYS AND QUESTIONNAIRES. 4698

0843-6150 *See* JOURNAL OF CEPHALOPOD BIOLOGY. 461

0843-6290 *See* SIGNATURE : A JOURNAL OF THEORY AND CANADIAN LITERATURE. 3437

0843-6363 *See* ELLE QUEBEC. 404

0843-638X See NORTHERN VOICE. 2201

0843-6584 *See* TRACE MINERALS, FOOD AND HEALTH. 4199

0843-6657 *See* IICCG BULLETIN. 322

0843-6665 *See* VOTRE SUCCES. 718

0843-672X See EMPLOYERS' HUMAN RIGHTS & EQUITY REPORT. 1665

0843-6819 *See* PROSPECT (VANCOUVER). 2148

0843-6827 *See* REVUE DE LA CINEMATHEQUE, LA. 4077

0843-6894 *See* CROP REPORT / SASKATCHEWAN WHEAT POOL. 169

0843-6924 *See* SHEM TOV. 2472

0843-6940 *See* CANADIAN STRATEGIC FORECAST, THE. 4467

0843-7041 *See* GLASS CANADA. 2589

0843-7076 *See* LAW OFFICE MANAGEMENT JOURNAL. 2996

0843-7084 *See* CANADIAN LEGAL FAX DIRECTORY. 3140

0843-7114 *See* IMPACT, LABOUR LAW & MANAGEMENT PRACTICES. 3149

0843-7173 See CATALOGUE DES FOURNITURES ET DU MOBILIER. 4211

0843-7289 *See* SPECIAL ISSUES. 3250

0843-7343 *See* ELECTRICITY TODAY (PICKERING). 2046

0843-7378 *See* DEPARTMENT OF GEOGRAPHY PUBLICATION SERIES. 2559

0843-7521 *See* UTLAS INFO TRACK. 427

0843-753X *See* INDICATORS OF SCIENCE AND TECHNOLOGY (OTTAWA). 5112

0843-7548 *See* FOCUS ON CULTURE. 4553

0843-7564 *See* CANADA'S IMMIGRATION & CITIZENSHIP BULLETIN. 1918

0843-7602 *See* CHRISTIAN VISION. 3375

0843-7769 See MARCHE (MONTREAL). 4904

0843-7815 *See* ABOVE & BEYOND. 2553

0843-7823 *See* MANITOBA JOURNAL OF TECHNOLOGY EDUCATION. 5127

0843-7904 *See* VENTURE (EDMONTON). 1525

0843-7920 *See* AQUELARRE (VANCOUVER). 5551

0843-798X *See* INFO-AEF : FEUILLET D'INFORMATION DU RESEAU D'ACTION-EDUCATION-FEMMES. 5559

0843-8064 *See* ELEUTHERIA (OTTAWA). 4345

0843-8145 *See* INDO-CANADIAN NATIONAL NEWS. 2739

0843-8552 See GEO PLEIN-AIR. 4896

0843-865X *See* QUEBEC SCEPTIQUE. 4243

0843-8706 *See* INTERNATIONAL NEWSLETTER OF MARITIME HISTORY. 5450

0843-8714 *See* INTERNATIONAL JOURNAL OF MARITIME HISTORY. 4177

0843-9117 *See* JOURNAL OF APPLIED RECREATION RESEARCH. 4851

0843-9184 *See* ART GALLERY OF NOVA SCOTIA JOURNAL. 313

0843-9214 *See* MOVING TO & AROUND HAMILTON, C.T.T., BRANTFORD, BURLINGTON & NIAGARA. 4841

0843-9532 *See* CD PLUS COMPACT DISC CATALOGUE. 4108

0843-9559 *See* CAHIERS FRANCO-CANADIENS DE LOUEST. 3272

0843-9656 *See* QUEBECOISEAUX (MONTREAL). 5619

0843-9753 *See* ALGORITHM, THE PERSONAL PROGRAMMING NEWSLETTER. 1265

0843-9931 *See* ALBERTA (EDMONTON). 312

0843-994X *See* CANADIAN JOURNAL OF CME. 3561

0843-9966 *See* CARE CONNECTION, THE. 3853

0844-0069 See MMC : MEDIAS MAGNETIQUES CANADA. 4444

0844-0506 *See* ASSOCIATION NEWS - INDUSTRIAL FIRST AID ATTENDANTS ASSOCIATION OF BRITISH COLUMBIA. 3795

0844-0883 *See* ACTION INFORMATIQUE. 1235

0844-0905 *See* ECHO ABITIBIEN. 5783

0844-1707 *See* MAGAZIN'ART (WESTMOUNT). 324

0844-1804 *See* VIE EN PLEIN AIR. 5427

0844-1871 *See* GUIDE DU PORT DE MONTREAL & REPERTOIRE DU TRANSPORT. 5383

0844-1901 *See* ICAM NEWS. 300

0844-2487 *See* HABITABEC QUEBEC. 616

0844-2665 *See* BEAUCE NOUVELLE. 5780

0844-2959 *See* NETWORK NEWS / NATIONAL DAY CARE RESEARCH NETWORK. 5297

0844-3238 See DIRECT MARKETING NEWS (MARKHAM). 923

0844-3416 *See* BULLETIN / CANADIAN SOCIETY FOR MESOPOTAMIAN STUDIES. 262

0844-3459 *See* MUIR'S ORIGINAL LOG HOME GUIDE FOR BUILDERS AND BUYERS. 621

0844-3637 *See* METROPOLIS. 325

0844-3718 See CANADIAN JOURNAL OF HUMAN SEXUALITY, THE. 5187

0844-3750 *See* YOUR UNION MATTERS. 1720

0844-3955 *See* STAT (VANCOUVER). 852

0844-398X *See* WHITBY FREE PRESS. 5797

0844-398X *See* WHITBY FREE PRESS. 5797

0844-4552 *See* CALGARY ECONOMIC DEVELOPMENT NEWS. 1467

0844-4587 *See* HINDU-CHRISTIAN STUDIES BULLETIN. 5041

0844-465X *See* ANNUAIRE DES EDITEURS. 4812

0844-4749 See PATRONS PICK TORONTO'S FAVOURITE RESTAURANTS. 5072

0844-5303 *See* ONT. SHEEP NEWS. 217

0844-5559 *See* EASTER SEALER. 5284

0844-5567 *See* WESTCOAST MARINER. 5458

0844-5621 *See* CANADIAN JOURNAL OF NURSING RESEARCH, THE. 3852

0844-5753 *See* HAPPENINGS. 3213

0844-5761 *See* AMETHYST MATTERS : NEWSLETTER OF AMETHYST WOMEN'S ADDICTION CENTRE. 5271

0844-5818 *See* TORONTO CHILDREN'S CHORUS. 4157

0844-5842 See INFOOD (EDMONTON). 2344

0844-5869 *See* NIKKEI VOICE. 2750

0844-5923 *See* RECHERCHE EN EDUCATION MUSICALE AU QUEBEC. 1777

0844-5982 *See* RETIREMENT LIFESTYLE. 5181

0844-6237 *See* ETAPE EN ETAPE. 2481

0844-6334 *See* FORESTERIE SANS DETOUR, LA. 2381

0844-6377 *See* ANNUAIRE DES ORGANISMES DENSEIGNEMENT PRIMAIRE ET SECONDAIRE PUBLIC. 1724

0844-6695 *See* MAIN ESTIMATES - BUDGET BUREAU. 4736

0844-6725 *See* MAIN ESTIMATES - FINANCIAL MANAGEMENT SECRETARIAT (YELLOWKNIFE. 1987). 4663

0844-6962 See SUPPORT FOR PROFESSIONAL ARTISTS. 331

0844-7020 *See* SASKATCHEWAN TELECOMMUNICATIONS / SASKATCHEWAN PUBLIC UTILITIES REVIEW COMMISSION. 1163

0844-7152 *See* ENERGIE AU QUEBEC EN PRIMEUR, L'. 1938

0844-7357 *See* ECHANGES, BOURSES, VOYAGES. 1737

0844-7535 *See* NOVA SCOTIA DEPARTMENT OF COMMUNITY SERVICES, THE. 4670

0844-7586 See ORIENTATIONS STRATEGIQUES DES ARCHIVES NATIONALES DU CANADA. 2482

0844-7586 See STRATEGIC APPROACHES OF THE NATIONAL ARCHIVES OF CANADA. 2484

0844-7594 *See* ORIENTATIONS STRATEGIQUES DES ARCHIVES NATIONALES DU CANADA. 2482

0844-7594 *See* STRATEGIC APPROACHES OF THE NATIONAL ARCHIVES OF CANADA. 2484

0844-8353 *See* IMPORTS, MERCHANDISE TRADE, H.S. BASED. 839

0844-8361 *See* EXPORTS, MERCHANDISE TRADE, H.S. BASED. 835

0844-837X *See* IMPORTS BY COUNTRY, H.S. BASED. 839

0844-8671 *See* STATUS REPORT / THE PREMIER'S COUNCIL ON THE STATUS OF PERSONS WITH DISABILITIES, ALBERTA, THE. 4394

0844-8698 *See* ESSENCE EXPRESS. 833

0844-8701 See IRC PERSPECTIVES. 4658

0844-9031 *See* ALIMENTATION QUEBEC, FISHERIES. 2294

0844-9082 *See* STOCK GUIDE (WILLIAMSTOWN). 813

0844-9228 *See* CANMET BUSINESS PLAN. 4636

0844-9430 *See* ANNUAL REPORT - MANITOBA HEALTH RESEARCH COUNCIL. 3550

0845-0056 *See* MANITOBA PRODUCTION STATISTICS REPORT. 1536

0845-0382 *See* ORIENTATIONS TRIENNALES ET PLAN ANNUEL / GOUVERNEMENT DU QUEBEC, CONSEIL DU STATUT DE LA FEMME. 5212

0845-0722 *See* AUDITOR'S REPORT AND FINANCIAL STATEMENTS FOR THE YEAR ENDED DECEMBER 31 4712

0845-0919 *See* REPORT ON GREAT LAKES WATER QUALITY : REPORT TO THE INTERNATIONAL JOINT COMMISSION / GREAT LAKES WATER QUALITY BOARD. 5538

0845-096X *See* DIRECTORY OF INSTITUTIONS - ONTARIO. FREEDOM OF INFORMATION AND PRIVACY BRANCH. 4643

0845-1109 *See* ... ANNUAL REVIEW OF THE NATIONAL TRANSPORTATION AGENCY OF CANADA, THE. 5377

0845-1214 *See* REPORT / GREAT LAKES SCIENCE ADVISORY BOARD. 5538

0845-1338 *See* UPDATE (EASTER SEAL SOCIETY (ONTARIO). 4394

0845-1664 *See* REPERTOIRE DU SERVICE DES DELEGUES COMMERCIAUX DU CANADA. 850

0845-2512 See RECRUITING & SUPERVISION TODAY. 946

0845-2555 *See* MICMAC NEWS. 5789

0845-2563 See HOCKEY NEWS ... YEARBOOK, THE. 4899

0845-2784 See WHO'S WHO (PQ/ATLANTIC ED.). 1263

0845-2792 See WHO'S WHO (WESTERN CANADA ED.). 1263

0845-2970 *See* CANADIAN JOURNAL OF GERIATRICS, THE. 3750

0845-3020 *See* FLIS NEWSLETTER. 3211

0845-3039 *See* DIRECTORY OF OCEAN SHIPPING SERVICES. 5448

0845-308X *See* CSSS NEWSLETTER. 170

0845-311X See REPERTOIRE / CORPORATION DES TRADUCTEURS, TRADUCTRICES, TERMINOLOGUES ET INTERPRETES DU NOUVEAU-BRUNSWICK. **3315**

0845-4078 *See* QUINQUENNIAL REVIEW. **2832**

0845-4183 *See* VALLEY SENTINEL (VALEMOUNT). **5797**

0845-4213 *See* PLANT (WILLOWDALE). **882**

0845-437X See IPAC QUARTERLY. **4261**

0845-4450 *See* PUBLIC (TORONTO). **328**

0845-4469 *See* ABILITIES (CALGARY). **4382**

0845-4485 *See* RESEARCH BULLETIN (PEEL (ONT. : REGIONAL MUNICIPALITY). BOARD OF EDUCATION). **1779**

0845-4493 *See* BULLETIN / UKRAINIAN CANADIAN COMMITTEE, SASKATCHEWAN PROVINCIAL COUNCIL, THE. **2725**

0845-4507 *See* LISTE DES RELIGIEUX ET CATALOGUE DES MAISONS ET OEUVRES / CONGREGATION DE SAINTE-CROIX, SOCIETE DES PERES, LA PROVINCE CANADIENNE. **4974**

0845-4531 See RADIOCOMM MAGAZINE. **1138**

0845-4639 *See* NATIONAL BALLET MAGAZINE. **386**

0845-4795 *See* CROSSTALK AND ANGLICAN JOURNAL EPISCOPAL. **5058**

0845-4817 *See* BAN VIET (1987). **2256**

0845-4825 *See* ONTARIO LAWYER'S PHONE BOOK, THE. **3023**

0845-5007 *See* AF&R, ALBERTA FARM & RANCH MAGAZINE. **44**

0845-5066 *See* PROGRAMME, PROCEEDINGS / CANADIAN FEDERATION OF BIOLOGICAL SOCIETIES. **585**

0845-5341 *See* RE-NEW (PORT HOPE). **2832**

0845-5376 *See* NEWSLETTER / CANADIAN ASSOCIATION FOR GRADUATE EDUCATION IN LIBRARY, ARCHIVAL, AND INFORMATION STUDIES. **1837**

0845-6208 *See* DIRECTORY OF PRODUCTS AND MANUFACTURERS, NEW BRUNSWICK, CANADA. **3478**

0845-6534 See EXPLORATEUR (MONTREAL). **1323**

0845-6798 *See* FUR TRADE JOURNAL OF CANADA (1987). **3184**

0845-7301 See ECONOMIC REFORM (TORONTO). **1484**

0845-7328 *See* CANADIAN TREASURER. **655**

0845-7611 See WHAT'S HAPPENING MAGAZINE (BELLEVILLE. 1991). **389**

0845-812X See WHAT'S NEW IN WELDING. **4023**

0845-8251 *See* HEALTH WATCH (TORONTO). **4782**

0845-8391 *See* RECREATIONAL FLYER, THE. **33**

0845-8448 *See* SHOWS & EXHIBITIONS. **766**

0845-8464 *See* ALLIANCE (NATIVE ALLIANCE OF QUEBEC). **5780**

0845-8618 *See* MEMBERSHIP DIRECTORY - INDUSTRIAL DEVELOPERS ASSOCIATION OF CANADA. **1618**

0845-8677 *See* DALHOUSIE NEWS (HALIFAX). **1091**

0845-874X See CONNEXIONS DIGEST, THE. **5242**

0845-8847 *See* NEWSLETTER - UPPER CANADA RAILWAY SOCIETY (1980). **5433**

0845-8987 *See* CANADIAN TOURIST TRAVEL GUIDE. **5465**

0845-8995 *See* MEMBERSHIP DIRECTORY / OSLA. **3889**

0845-924X See RAPPORT ANNUEL - SOCIETE DES ALCOOLS DU QUEBEC (1986?). **4678**

0845-9258 See VARIETES DE POMMES DE TERRE AU CANADA. **144**

0845-9401 *See* REVUE JURIDIQUE DES ETUDIANTS ET ETUDIANTES DE L'UNIVERSITE LAVAL, LA. **3043**

0845-9606 *See* ANNUAL REPORT - MANITOBA ENVIRONMENT AND WORKPLACE SAFETY AND HEALTH. **2160**

0845-9630 *See* RESEARCH BRANCH REPORT - RESEARCH STATION, SUMMERLAND, BRITISH COLUMBIA. **184**

0846-0019 *See* CANADIAN OBITUARY RECORD. **2406**

0846-0051 *See* BRITISH COLUMBIA MINERAL EXPLORATION REVIEW. **2135**

0846-0140 *See* DES MOTS ET DES GENS (SAINT-LAURENT). **4642**

0846-0140 *See* DES MOTS ET DES GENS (SAINT-LAURENT). **4642**

0846-0159 See B.C. EXPORTER. **824**

0846-0353 *See* FAMILY CONNECTION (REGINA). **2279**

0846-0361 *See* JOURNAL DES DEBATS - QUEBEC (PROVINCE). ASSEMBLEE NATIONALE. COMMISSION PARLEMENTAIRE SUR L'AVENIR POLITIQUE ET CONSTITUTIONNEL DU QUEBEC. **4658**

0846-0396 *See* BARRHAVEN INDEPENDENT. **5780**

0846-0469 *See* TRADING TRENDS. **917**

0846-0477 *See* DIVERS FREE PRESS. **4893**

0846-0620 *See* BUSINESS PLAN (VICTORIA). **4715**

0846-0663 *See* HEALTHY EATING. **4191**

0846-0671 *See* GUIDE DU PASSAGE A LA RETRAITE. **5179**

0846-068X See PREDICTIONS / JOJO SAVARD. **390**

0846-0698 *See* REPERTOIRE DES OUTILS DE REFERENCE. **423**

0846-0701 *See* NWT HELP DIRECTORY. **5299**

0846-0795 *See* NOUVELLES HYDRO, PROJETS D'EQUIPEMENT EN BASSE-COTE-NORD. **2093**

0846-085X See CURRENT STATUS OF LEGISLATION IN THE HOUSE OF COMMONS AND SENATE OF CANADA. **4471**

0846-1015 *See* IMAGINARY TALES. **3395**

0846-1023 *See* MEMBERSHIP ROSTER / CANADIAN PETROLEUM TAX SOCIETY. **4737**

0846-1031 *See* VSE BUSINESS REPORT. **919**

0846-104X See HUNTER EDUCATION NEWS (PETERBOROUGH). **4873**

0846-1058 *See* BUSINESS NORTHWEST. **651**

0846-1074 *See* OTTAWA CITIZEN SKI GUIDE, THE. **4911**

0846-1112 *See* TAX BREAKS. **4752**

0846-1155 *See* VALUE ADVISOR. **918**

0846-121X See BC HEALTH AND DISEASE SURVEILLANCE. **4768**

0846-1309 *See* MEDICAL NETWORKS. **3610**

0846-1333 *See* SPORTING CLASSICS (OTTAWA). **5425**

0846-1414 *See* AVIATEUR AUJOURDHUI. **12**

0846-1953 See SOCIETAIRE (MONTREAL). **2893**

0846-1961 See SOCIETAIRE (MONTREAL). **2893**

0846-2038 *See* DIRECTORY OF MEMBERS / CANADIAN LIBRARY ASSOCIATION. **3207**

0846-264X See HANDBOOK FOR NON-CLASSROOM STUDENTS / ALBERTA DISTANCE LEARNING CENTRE. **1749**

0846-2658 *See* HANDBOOK FOR CLASSROOM STUDENTS/ ALBERTA DISTANCE LEARNING CENTRE. **1749**

0846-2682 See BULLETIN / ROYAL ASTRONOMICAL SOCIETY OF CANADA. **394**

0846-2895 *See* COMPENSATION FOCUS. **4639**

0846-2895 *See* COMPENSATION FOCUS. **4639**

0846-2917 *See* INFO CLUB. **1542**

0846-2917 *See* INFO CLUB (OTTAWA ED.). **1495**

0846-2976 See LITT RESTAURANT GUIDE, THE. **5071**

0846-2984 *See* LITT RESTAURANT GUIDE (NATIONAL ED.). **5071**

0846-2992 *See* LITT RESTAURANT GUIDE, THE. **5071**

0846-300X See LITT RESTAURANT GUIDE (QUEBEC ED.). **5071**

0846-3018 *See* LITT RESTAURANT GUIDE (WESTERN ED.). **5071**

0846-3042 *See* CANADIAN HUNTING & SHOOTING MAGAZINE, THE. **4870**

0846-3093 *See* R.E.P.P.: RESERVE EXECUTIVE PRACTICE POINTS / FIRST NATIONS RESOURCE COUNCIL. **2271**

0846-3174 *See* CANADIAN BOWHUNTING. **4870**

0846-3182 *See* CANADIAN BOWHUNTING. **4870**

0846-3190 *See* HISTORICAL PORT HOPE. **2737**

0846-3204 *See* PULSE CROP NEWS. **183**

0846-3212 *See* WORLD GRAIN LIST. **147**

0846-3247 *See* ALASKA CONTRACTOR : A PUBLICATION OF THE ASSOCIATED GENERAL CONTRACTORS OF ALASKA, THE. **598**

0846-3255 *See* BYTOWN FIRE BRIGADE NEWSLETTER, THE. **2288**

0846-3298 *See* EMBER (MARKHAM). **2260**

0846-3301 *See* DIOCESAN POST. **5059**

0846-3336 *See* REPORT OF THE STEERING COMMITTEE TO THE STANDING COMMMITTEE ON PUBLIC ACCOUNTS. **4746**

0846-3409 *See* APPRENTI SORCIER (GATINEAU). **4857**

0846-3492 *See* CITADELS NEWS. **4890**

0846-3514 *See* CAREER DIRECTORY (TORONTO. 1992). **4201**

0846-3530 *See* PACIFIC MUSIC. **4145**

0846-3654 *See* HALIBURTON FISHING GUIDE. **2305**

0846-3905 *See* CHRISTIAN RESOURCE DIRECTORY. **4946**

0846-3913 *See* KEY (CALGARY). **5788**

0846-3948 *See* ROUGE VALLEY, PARK FORUM. **4708**

0846-3980 *See* ACTIVITY REPORT - PUBLIC LEGAL EDUCATION AND INFORMATION SERVICE OF NEW BRUNSWICK. **4623**

0846-3980 *See* ACTIVITY REPORT - PUBLIC LEGAL EDUCATION AND INFORMATION SERVICE OF NEW BRUNSWICK. **4624**

0846-4243 *See* CHRISTIAN WORLD REPORT, THE. **4946**

0846-426X See MUSICOLOGY AND ETHNOMUSICOLOGY AT YORK. **4137**

0846-4618 *See* FQSE EN ACTION, LA. **4895**

0846-4715 *See* NEWS - ONTARIO PUBLIC SCHOOL TEACHERS' FEDERATION (1989). **1768**

0846-4782 *See* HEALTH OF ANIMALS. **5511**

0846-5029 *See* ANNUAL REPORT / CANMET. **1437**

0846-5274 See AVENIR MONTREAL. 1991. **1464**

0846-5312 *See* CAHIER - SOCIETE D'HISTOIRE DES PAYS-D'EN-HAUT (1989). **2612**

0846-5320 *See* PIONEER CHRISTIAN MONTHLY. **4986**

0846-5339 *See* ESPACES VERTS. **2414**

0846-5347 *See* COMMUNIC-ACTION (VICTORIAVILLE). **1106**

0846-5371 *See* CANADIAN ASSOCIATION OF RADIOLOGISTS JOURNAL. **3939**

0846-5495 *See* INTERNATIONAL DIRECTORY TO CANADIAN STUDIES. **2739**

0846-5495 *See* INTERNATIONAL DIRECTORY TO CANADIAN STUDIES. **2739**

0846-5843 See MANAGER NEWSLETTER. **1145**

0846-5843 See MANAGER NEWSLETTER. **878**

0846-6327 *See* INDEX TO MUSEOLOGICAL LITERATURE. **4089**

0846-6351 *See* REPORT OF THE CHIEF ELECTORAL OFFICER OF CANADA. **4493**

0846-6610 *See* REPORTS AND PUBLICATIONS - PACIFIC FORESTRY CENTRE. **2392**

0846-7145 *See* SUMMER VISITATION AND OUTDOOR RECREATION STATISTICAL REPORT. **4879**

0846-7390 *See* AESE BLUELINE. **1351**

0846-7951 *See* ANNUAL REPORT OF THE BOARD OF TRUSTEES FOR THE YEAR - PUBLIC ARCHIVES OF NOVA SCOTIA. **2479**

0846-8001 *See* STATISTIQUES FINANCIERES EN ..., LES. **1539**

0846-8583 *See* ARCHITECTURAL, ENGINEERING AND SCIENTIFIC SERVICES. **5085**

0846-8648 *See* CVA REVIEW. **4067**

0846-8877 See BULLETIN / ROYAL ASTRONOMICAL SOCIETY OF CANADA. **394**

ISSN Index

0846-9105 See FABRICANTS DE PRODUITS ELECTRIQUES ET ELECTRONIQUES AU QUEBEC, REPERTOIRE, LES. **2054**

0846-9121 See SCIENCE REVIEW (DARTMOUTH). **1456**

0846-9229 See OCCUPATIONAL HEALTH & SAFETY MAGAZINE. **2866**

0846-9253 See REPORT OF THE CANADIAN MULTICULTURALISM COUNCIL. **2757**

0846-9415 See SELECTIVE ACQUISITIONS. **3248**

0846-9423 See MINUTES OF PROCEEDINGS AND EVIDENCE OF THE STANDING COMMITTEE ON MULTICULTURALISM AND CITIZENSHIP. **2539**

0846-9709 See REPERTOIRE ... DES FICHIERS DES MINISTERES ET ORGANISMES DU GOUVERNEMENT DU QUEBEC. **4679**

0846-9717 See TOURIST RECEPTION CENTRE SURVEY. **5494**

0846-9962 See BC TOURISM ROOM REVENUES. **5462**

0847-0065 See THEOLOGICAL DIGEST & OUTLOOK. **5003**

0847-0146 See HERITAGE INSTITUTIONS. **4088**

0847-0197 See METALS ECONOMICS GROUP STRATEGIC REPORT. **2144**

0847-0316 See CANADIAN NATURAL GAS FOCUS. **4253**

0847-0456 See INTERNATIONAL CD-ROM REPORT, THE. **1189**

0847-0464 See FORUM ON CORRECTIONS RESEARCH. **3164**

0847-0553 See SURFACING (TORONTO). **5356**

0847-0561 See PAWN TO INFINITY. **3462**

0847-0588 See AVIATION & AEROSPACE. **13**

0847-0685 See GREAT LAKES FISHERMAN. **2304**

0847-1061 See CANADIAN POWER ILLUSTRATED. **592**

0847-1126 See GOOD TIMES (TORONTO). **5179**

0847-1223 See SOUND RECORDING. **5319**

0847-1231 See PERIODICAL PUBLISHING. **4818**

0847-1266 See DIDASKALIA (OTTERBURNE). **4953**

0847-1304 See CHRONIQUE DES RELATIONS EXTERIEURES DU CANADA. **4518**

0847-1304 See CHRONIQUE DES RELATIONS EXTERIEURES DU CANADA. **4518**

0847-1398 See RRM REPORT. **3792**

0847-1444 See BC AGRICULTURE. **65**

0847-1495 See AGENDA - ONTARIO HOSPITAL ASSOCIATION. **719**

0847-1525 See BRITISH COLUMBIA ECONOMIC AND STATISTICAL REVIEW. **1465**

0847-1568 See ELITE CMA. **743**

0847-1622 See SEMIOTIC REVIEW OF BOOKS. **1121**

0847-1711 See CHAMPAGNE HORROR. **3373**

0847-1851 See UHF. ULTRA HIGH FIDELITY. **5319**

0847-2068 See ENVIRONMENTAL LAW ALERT. **3111**

0847-2130 See THOMPSON-OKANAGAN DEVELOPMENT REGION MANUFACTURERS DIRECTORY. **3489**

0847-2378 See HOME CARE TODAY. **5288**

0847-2645 See PAPETIERES DU QUEBEC, LES. **4236**

0847-2785 See IN YOUR INTEREST. **790**

0847-2831 See REPORT ON BUSINESS, CANADA COMPANY HANDBOOK. **707**

0847-2882 See CANADIAN WOMEN'S PERIODICALS INDEX. **5552**

0847-2890 See ADVOCATE (EDMONTON). **5270**

0847-2939 See COMMUNION, EN. **5028**

0847-2971 See JOURNAL OF HUMAN JUSTICE, THE. **2987**

0847-2998 See BRITISH COLUMBIA REPORT (VANCOUVER). **2724**

0847-3080 See OALA NEWS. **2426**

0847-3269 See INTERNATIONAL JOURNAL OF DYNAMIC ASSESSMENT AND INSTRUCTION. **1753**

0847-3277 See ARTICHOKE (CALGARY). **341**

0847-3463 See CANADIAN GARDENING. **2412**

0847-351X See INCOME TAX ACT AND REGULATIONS, DEPARTMENT OF FINANCE TECHNICAL NOTES. **4731**

0847-3536 See UNIVERSITIES TELEPHONE DIRECTORY. **1852**

0847-3587 See RAPPORT ANNUEL / CONSEIL DE LA FAMILLE. **2285**

0847-382X See FOLLOWING CHAIN AND COMPASS : NEWSLETTER OF THE ARCHIVAL AND HISTORY COMMITTEE OF SMITH TOWNSHIP. **2733**

0847-3846 See GREATER QUEBEC AREA TOUR OPERATOR MANUAL. **5478**

0847-3889 See CONSTITUTIONAL FORUM. **3092**

0847-3900 See BUSINESS GUIDE, THE. **648**

0847-3994 See INTERNATIONAL VIDEOVUE. **4073**

0847-4109 See UNISCOPE (HULL). **1851**

0847-415X See INTERNATIONAL BULLETIN OF MORITA THERAPY. **4590**

0847-432X See RECREATION QUEBEC. **4865**

0847-4478 See JOURNAL OF THE CANADIAN HISTORICAL ASSOCIATION. **2742**

0847-4516 See ANNUAL REPORT - MINISTRY OF PARKS (VICTORIA). **4705**

0847-4524 See ENVIROLINE (CALGARY). **2165**

0847-4583 See CATALOGUE DE PUBLICATIONS EUROPEENNES. **606**

0847-4583 See EUROPEAN PUBLICATIONS CATALOGUE. **614**

0847-4834 See GUIDE PLEIN AIR DU QUEBEC. **4873**

0847-4915 See INFO-LOG MAGAZINE. **1245**

0847-4958 See ART ET CULTURE AU QUEBEC. **313**

0847-4966 See SCIENCE ET TECHNOLOGIE AU QUEBEC. **5151**

0847-4974 See ECONOMIE ET AFFAIRES AU QUEBEC. **671**

0847-5253 See WOMEN AND THE LAW (FREDERICTON). **3076**

0847-5261 See FEMME ET LA LOI, LA. **2970**

0847-5288 See INDEPENDENT SENIOR, THE. **5179**

0847-5407 See HRD TREND REPORT. **941**

0847-5520 See CANADIAN NURSING HOME. **3778**

0847-5547 See CAD SYSTEMS. **1231**

0847-5636 See MINORITE INVISIBLE. **4391**

0847-5644 See ATARISTE. **1265**

0847-5717 See BRITISH COLUMBIA & ALBERTA HOME BUSINESS REPORT. **644**

0847-5733 See REVUE FRANCOPHONE DE LA DEFICIENCE INTELLECTUELLE. **3845**

0847-5741 See WEANS NEWSLETTER. **1917**

0847-5857 See WORKERS' COMPENSATION MANAGING CLAIMS. **2896**

0847-5911 See REVUE CANADIENNE D'ETUDES CINEMATOGRAPHIQUES. **4077**

0847-7795 See SABIAN NEWS BEAT CATALOG. **4151**

0847-8090 See PATIENT UPDATE. **3790**

0847-8538 See BLUE LINE MAGAZINE. **3158**

0847-8597 See WHITECOURT STAR. **5798**

0847-8988 See HANOVER POST POSTSCRIPTS, THE. **5786**

0847-9097 See ADBUSTERS (VANCOUVER). **754**

0847-9119 See TRAMES (MONTREAL). **2837**

0847-9348 See TOURS ON MOTORCOACH. **5494**

0847-9356 See INNKEEPER. **2807**

0847-9364 See UPDATE. **1908**

0847-9380 See MAGAZINE PAIN DE VIE. **3605**

0847-9437 See JOURNAL - CANADIAN FUSION FUELS TECHNOLOGY PROJECT. **4262**

0847-9445 See CANADIAN JOURNAL OF QUALITY IN HEALTH CARE, THE. **4770**

0847-9453 See HUMAN RESOURCES PROFESSIONAL. **942**

0847-947X See CANADIAN EMERGENCY NEWS. **4770**

0847-9488 See LIBRARY NEWS - GEAC LIBRARY INFORMATION SYSTEM. **3226**

0847-9607 See PITCH-IN NEWS. **2202**

0847-9720 See DIRECTORY OF CORPORATE MEMBER FIRMS AND MEMBER-ASSOCIATIONS / CANADIAN CONSTRUCTION ASSOCIATION. **613**

0847-978X See ANGLICAN JOURNAL. **4934**

0847-9798 See AGIR (MONTREAL). **3123**

0847-9933 See EARTH WORDS (OTTAWA). **2227**

0847-9968 See HARDWARE & HOME CENTRE MAGAZINE. **2811**

0848-0435 See CANADIAN FINANCE LETTER. **893**

0848-0877 See MEMO (QUEBEC). **693**

0848-0893 See KALEIDOSCOPE REGINA. **5122**

0848-1008 See IN BUSINESS WINDSOR. **681**

0848-1059 See CHANGING FACES, CHANGING TIMES. **3201**

0848-1253 See LITT RESTAURANT GUIDE (NATIONAL ED.). **5071**

0848-1393 See TABLES CHAMPETRES ET PROMENADES A LA FERME AU QUEBEC. **5073**

0848-1431 See NATIONAL REPORT ON INTERNATIONAL STUDENTS IN CANADA, THE. **1766**

0848-144X See UNIVERSELLES (QUEBEC). **5567**

0848-1482 See IMPACT - PROFESSIONAL ASSOCIATION OF CANADIAN THEATRES. **5365**

0848-1512 See VICTORIAN REVIEW. **3450**

0848-1563 See HISTORICAL PAPERS / CANADIAN SOCIETY OF CHURCH HISTORY. **4963**

0848-158X See CANADIAN TRAVELLER (TORONTO, ONT.). **1061**

0848-1660 See INTEGRITY. **2251**

0848-1679 See LAWG REPORT. **4510**

0848-1741 See SERVANT (THREE HILLS). **4996**

0848-1970 See JOURNAL OF SPEECH-LANGUAGE PATHOLOGY AND AUDIOLOGY. **4390**

0848-1989 See MANITOBA CONSUMER (1985). **1298**

0848-2128 See ANNUAL REPORT / ALBERTA CULTURE AND MULTICULTURALISM. **2528**

0848-2489 See CONGRES - ASSOCIATION DE PLANIFICATION FISCALE ET FINANCIERE. **3118**

0848-2497 See ACTA DIRECTORY. **5460**

0848-2659 See ORDER PAPER AND NOTICE PAPER. **4671**

0848-2845 See ALBERTA POPULATION GROWTH. **4549**

0848-2969 See REPERTOIRE TOPONYMIQUE DU QUEBEC (1988). **2574**

0848-3663 See ETATS FINANCIERS DES ENTREPRISES DU GOUVERNEMENT DU QUEBEC (1988). **1489**

0848-3701 See PRODUCT CATALOGUE - ONTARIO. ADDICTION RESEARCH FOUNDATION. **422**

0848-3809 See VISION, TERRE ET FORET. **2398**

0848-3876 See DEPARTMENT OF INDUSTRY, TRADE AND TOURISM AND LOTTERIES FUNDED PROGRAMS, FITNESS AND SPORT DIRECTORATES, SUPPLEMENTARY INFORMATION FOR LEGISLATIVE REVIEW, ... EXPENDITURE ESTIMATES. **4720**

0848-399X See ALBERTA HEALTH AND SOCIAL SERVICE EDUCATION PROGRAMS INVENTORY. **5271**

0848-4244 See ALBERTA TRANSFER GUIDE. **1808**

0848-4317 See ANNUAL REPORT / CANADIAN CENTRE FOR MANAGEMENT DEVELOPMENT. **4627**

0848-4317 See ANNUAL REPORT-CANADIAN CENTRE FOR MANAGEMENT DEVELOPMENT. **860**

0848-4449 See YEAR BOOK AND DIRECTORY - UNITED CHURCH OF CANADA. **5010**

0848-4457 See STRATEGY (TORONTO. 1991). **937**

0848-4554 See ANNUAL REPORT / EXTERNAL AFFAIRS AND INTERNATIONAL TRADE CANADA. **4515**

0848-4597 *See* GUIDE TO FEDERAL PROGRAMS AND SERVICES. **4653**

0848-4686 *See* CANADA CORPORATIONS BULLETIN. **3097**

0848-4740 *See* NATIONAL DRUG INTELLIGENCE ESTIMATE. **1347**

0848-4805 See INFO SOURCE (ENGLISH ED.). **4656**

0848-4813 See INFO SOURCE (ED. FRANCAISE). **4656**

0848-4856 *See* ACCESSIONS LIST - EXTERNAL AFFAIRS AND INTERNATIONAL TRADE CANADA. LIBRARY. **3186**

0848-4880 See INFO SOURCE (ED. FRANCAISE). **4656**

0848-4910 See UPDATE - SOCIAL SCIENCE FEDERATION OF CANADA. **5225**

0848-4910 See UPDATE / SOCIAL SCIENCE FEDERATION OF CANADA. **5225**

0848-502X *See* HOUSEHOLD FACILITIES BY INCOME AND OTHER CHARACTERISTICS, REVISED ESTIMATES. **2812**

0848-5194 *See* FINANCIAL RESULTS - GOVERNMENT OF CANADA. **4725**

0848-5313 *See* SASKATCHEWAN FOOD PROCESSORS DIRECTORY. **2356**

0848-5607 *See* FEDERAL-PROVINCIAL PROGRAMS AND ACTIVITIES, A DESCRIPTIVE INVENTORY. **4648**

0848-5704 *See* SECURITE ET CONTROLE DES EXPLOSIFS AU CANADA. **2150**

0848-5712 *See* EXPLOSIVE SAFETY AND CONTROL IN CANADA. **2012**

0848-5771 *See* SUMMARY OF THE ACTIVITY REPORT - CENTRE DE RECHERCHES MINERALES SAINTE-FOY. **4394**

0848-5844 *See* ANNUAL REPORT - PRINCE EDWARD ISLAND. DEPT. OF THE ENVIRONMENT (1989). **2187**

0848-5909 *See* GOVERNMENT OF CANADA. TELEPHONE DIRECTORY. CENTRAL REGION. **1156**

0848-5917 *See* LABOUR LAW UPDATE. **3151**

0848-5925 *See* LEGISLATION DU TRAVAIL. **1615**

0848-5933 *See* MAIN ESTIMATES, HIGHLIGHTS BY MINISTRY. **4663**

0848-600X *See* NBC/NFC NEWS. **622**

0848-6220 *See* BUDGET DES DEPENSES PRINCIPAL DE LA PROVINCE DU MANITOBA. **4714**

0848-631X *See* ALBERTA RESTAURANT NEWS. **5070**

0848-6433 *See* MAJOR WAGE SETTLEMENTS. **1689**

0848-659X *See* ABSTRACTS - ALBERTA. BUREAU OF STATISTICS. **5320**

0848-6697 *See* ANNUAIRE TELEPHONIQUE DES ORGANISMES SCOLAIRES DE LA MONTEREGIE. **1724**

0848-6719 *See* ANNUAL REVIEW - ATLANTIC LOTTERY, CANADA. **4630**

0848-6727 *See* REVUE ANNUELLE - LOTO ATLANTIQUE, CANADA. **4683**

0848-6743 *See* FACTSHEET - BRITISH COLUMBIA. AQUACULTURE AND COMMERCIAL FISHERIES BRANCH. **83**

0848-6751 *See* GREENHOUSE VEGETABLE PRODUCTION GUIDE (EDMONTON). **173**

0848-676X *See* PHYSICIAN'S NEWSLETTER (1990). **3916**

0848-6778 *See* FACT SHEET / SENIORS ADVISORY COUNCIL FOR ALBERTA. **5179**

0848-6786 *See* PEACE RIVER NEWSLETTER. **119**

0848-6794 *See* ALBERTA FIRE NEWS (1990). **2287**

0848-6832 *See* SCIENCE UPDATE (YELLOWKNIFE). **5154**

0848-6840 *See* SUNATUINNARNIK QAUJISAQTULIRINIRMUT TUSAGAKSAIT. **5161**

0848-6859 *See* DIRECTIONS - PUBLIC SERVICE COMMISSION OF CANADA. **4643**

0848-6859 *See* DIRECTIONS - PUBLIC SERVICE COMMISSION OF CANADA. **4643**

0848-6913 *See* FISHING INCOME TAX GUIDE. **4727**

0848-7049 *See* ONTARIO WAGE DEVELOPMENTS, COLLECTIVE BARGAINING SETTLEMENTS. **1700**

0848-7138 *See* ZOOM ON THE NFB. **4080**

0848-7162 *See* NATIONAL GRAINS UPDATE (EASTERN ED.). **203**

0848-7170 *See* NATIONAL GRAINS UPDATE (WESTERN ED.). **203**

0848-7189 *See* POINT, SECTEUR DES GRAINS (ED. DE L'EST). **203**

0848-7197 *See* POINT, SECTEUR DES GRAINS (ED. DE L'OUEST). **203**

0848-7243 See BERRY & VEGETABLE INFORMER. **65**

0848-7251 See INFORMATION AND APPLICATION GUIDE / CANADIAN STUDIES AND SPECIAL PROJECTS DIRECTORATE. **2739**

0848-726X *See* FINE ART PUBLICATIONS ... / NATIONAL GALLERY OF CANADA. **320**

0848-7316 *See* BULLETIN DE FRANCAIS 30. **3270**

0848-7324 *See* VISIONS (VICTORIA). **4708**

0848-7340 *See* STAFF DEVELOPMENT CALENDAR - ALBERTA. ALBERTA FAMILY AND SOCIAL SERVICES. STAFF DEVELOPMENT. **5311**

0848-7413 *See* RELAIS LOISIR. **388**

0848-7421 *See* RESPIROLOGIE (POINTE-CLAIRE). **3951**

0848-7448 *See* CLC TODAY. **1659**

0848-7456 *See* MAILBOX LIBRARY SERVICE. **3229**

0848-7464 *See* BIBLIOTHEQUE POSTALE (1989). **3195**

0848-7499 *See* MATHEMATICS AND SCIENCES BULLETIN. **3520**

0848-7510 *See* BULLETIN DE MATHEMATIQUES ET SCIENCES. **3498**

0848-7537 *See* SOCIAL STUDIES 30 BULLETIN. **5221**

0848-757X *See* INFORM (WINNIPEG). **1188**

0848-7642 *See* DRH COMMUNICATIONS QUARTERLY, THE. **1110**

0848-7677 *See* SIDING & WINDOW CONTRACTOR. **627**

0848-7804 *See* HIGHLIGHT (VICTORIA). **4782**

0848-7839 *See* PRIMARY PLANNER. **1805**

0848-7855 *See* GUIDE TO PREPARING FINANCIAL STATEMENTS. **789**

0848-791X *See* MINUTES OF PROCEEDINGS AND EVIDENCE OF THE SPECIAL COMMITTEE ON CANADA-UNITED STATES AIR TRANSPORT SERVICES. **28**

0848-7928 *See* MINUTES OF PROCEEDINGS AND EVIDENCE OF THE SPECIAL COMMITTEE ON SUBJECT MATTER OF BILL C-80 (FIREARMS). **4665**

0848-7936 *See* MINUTES OF PROCEEDINGS AND EVIDENCE OF THE SUB-COMMITTEE ON NORAD OF THE STANDING COMMITTEE ON EXTERNAL AFFAIRS AND INTERNATIONAL TRADE. **846**

0848-7952 *See* CONTOURS (OTTAWA). **2559**

0848-8061 *See* RAPPORT DU PRESIDENT GENERAL - SYNDICAT DES FONCTIONNAIRES PROVINCIAUX DU QUEBEC. **1705**

0848-8134 *See* DIRECTORY OF BARRIER-FREE BUILDING PRODUCTS. **297**

0848-8142 See ALBERTA BEEF (1991). **205**

0848-8258 *See* SELECT HOMES & FOOD. **2792**

0848-8312 *See* HOME GOODS RETAILING. **2906**

0848-8339 *See* FLOOR COVERING PLUS. **615**

0848-838X *See* ALBERTA & BRITISH COLUMBIA GOLF GUIDE. **4882**

0848-841X *See* BRANTCHES - ONTARIO GENEALOGICAL SOCIETY. BRANT COUNTY BRANCH. **2440**

0848-8436 *See* MCGILL REPORTER. **1835**

0848-8452 *See* RADIO AMATEUR DU QUEBEC. **1137**

0848-8460 *See* PITA JOURNAL. **1805**

0848-8479 *See* MELANIE KLEIN AND OBJECT RELATIONS. **4603**

0848-8495 *See* B.C. SCHOOL COUNSELLORS' NEWSLETTER : A PUBLICATION OF THE BRITISH COLUMBIA SCHOOL COUNSELLORS' ASSOCIATION. **1860**

0848-8525 *See* APT BULLETIN (1986). **288**

0848-8533 *See* REPORT - TRINITY WESTERN UNIVERSITY. **1094**

0848-8541 *See* HEMSON TORONTO LAND USE REPORT. **4654**

0848-8622 *See* HEMSON PLANNING & DEVELOPMENT REPORT. **2824**

0848-8649 *See* CANADIAN CD-ROM NEWS. **1173**

0848-8754 *See* LINKS - ENVIRONMENTAL EDUCATORS' PROVINCIAL SPECIALIST ASSOCIATION. **2177**

0848-8770 *See* NOUVEAU PARAQUAD. **4392**

0848-8835 *See* REVUE DE LIMPERIALE. **4277**

0848-8843 *See* IMPERIAL OIL REVIEW (1989). **4260**

0848-8851 *See* N.B.I.A. NEWSLETTER (1989). **110**

0848-8886 *See* FORUM / CONFERENCE OF DEFENCE ASSOCIATIONS. **4044**

0848-8975 *See* CANADIAN VENDING MAGAZINE (L989). **1600**

0848-9009 *See* MHLA NEWS. **3231**

0848-9025 *See* JOURNAL - PROVINCIAL ASSOCIATION OF CATHOLIC TEACHERS. **1759**

0848-9033 *See* ABORIGINAL VOICE, THE. **2609**

0848-9068 *See* DEFI-SANTE. **2596**

0848-9106 **1934**

0848-9114 *See* ENERGYTRENDS. **1943**

0848-9149 See BCOQ DIRECTORY. **5056**

0848-9203 *See* VERNON'S ... BRANTFORD CITY DIRECTORY. **2578**

0848-9386 *See* HARVEST FIELD MINISTRIES : NEWSLETTER. **4962**

0848-9610 *See* JEFFREY HOARE NUMISMATIC AUCTION IN CONJUNCTION WITH TOREX. **2781**

0848-9629 *See* CANADIAN JOURNAL OF HERBALISM. **2412**

0848-9645 *See* ME. MUSIC EXPRESS MAGAZINE. **4130**

0848-9807 See PHOTO SELECTION (1991). **4373**

0848-9815 *See* TOURISME OUTAOUAIS BONJOUR. **5493**

0848-984X *See* CONNEXIONS (ASSOCIATION CANADIENNE DE L'ELECTRICITE). **1936**

0848-9947 *See* NATIONAL NETWORK. **3862**

0849-0015 See CHANTIERS JEUNESSE. **5277**

0849-0082 See CAMPING, CARAVANING (MONTREAL). **4870**

0849-0252 *See* SASKATCHEWAN CHINESE TELEPHONE DIRECTORY. **1163**

0849-035X *See* VO. VIE OUVRIERE. **1716**

0849-0465 *See* VENTES AUX ENCHERES PUBLIQUES. **367**

0849-0538 *See* RESTAURANTS (QUEBEC). **5073**

0849-0619 *See* MANITOBA, WINNIPEG AND VICINITY CHINESE TELEPHONE DIRECTORIES. **1159**

0849-0635 *See* COUNTRY SIDE MAGAZINE. **2789**

0849-0643 *See* BULLETIN DE L'ASSOCIATION PROFESSIONNELLE DES GEOLOGUES ET DES GEOPHYSICIENS DU QUEBEC. **1368**

0849-0694 *See* REPERTOIRE DES INDUSTRIES MANUFACTURIERES DU NORD-OOUEST. **707**

0849-0724 *See* BULLETIN - FONDATION DE L'UQAM. **1813**

0849-0759 *See* ACTION - CANADIAN ASSOCIATION FOR THE ADVANCEMENT OF WOMEN IN SPORT AND PHYSICAL ACTIVITY. **4881**

0849-0767 *See* CANADIAN PRINTER. **4564**

0849-0805 *See* VERNON'S ... BELLEVILLE CITY DIRECTORY. **1123**

0849-0813 *See* VERNON'S ... NORTH BAY CITY DIRECTORY. **2578**

0849-0848 *See* BRUCE & GREY BRANCH OF O.G.S. **2440**

0849-0872 *See* OKANAGAN LIFE PROGRESS. **701**

0849-0899 *See* MCMASTER JOURNAL OF THEOLOGY. **4976**

0849-0902 *See* NEW DRUG INFORMATION DIGEST. **1347**

0849-097X *See* HANDBOOK - ALBERTA BADMINTON ASSOCIATION. **4898**

0849-1054 See 2ND TIER, THE. **3543**

0849-1070 *See* TRANSPLANTATION, IMPLANTATION TODAY. **540**

0849-1089 *See* EDUCATION ET FRANCOPHONIE. **1739**

0849-1127 *See* TRIFLUVIEN (TROIS-RIVIERES. 1990). **4691**

0849-1259 *See* C-FAR NEWSLETTER. **2908**

0849-133X *See* INTENTION MISSIONNAIRE. **4965**

0849-1364 *See* BCA INTEREST RATE FORECAST. **778**

0849-1410 *See* ARK (TORONTO). **2187**

0849-1577 *See* LIEN, LE. **2282**

0849-1593 *See* NOUVEAU DIALOGUE EN BREF. **3862**

0849-1615 See SCCUQ-INFO. **1710**

0849-1623 *See* JOURNAL QUEBEC QUILLES, LE. **4902**

0849-1801 *See* SI BUSINESS. **1239**

0849-181X *See* CAVELTI'S MARKET REPORT. **894**

0849-1836 *See* OTTAWA BUSINESS MAGAZINE. **702**

0849-1887 See MONTREAL & AREA AVIATION BUSINESS DIRECTORY (FRENCH EDITION). **29**

0849-1887 See MONTREAL & AREA AVIATION BUSINESS DIRECTORY. **29**

0849-1992 *See* GUIDE TOURISTIQUE, CHAUDIERE-APPALACHES. **5479**

0849-2093 *See* OTTAWA-HULL, CANADA'S CAPITAL. **5487**

0849-2115 *See* NATIONAL NEWS - NATIONAL PENSIONERS AND SENIOR CITIZENS FEDERATION. **5180**

0849-2212 *See* NOTE TO CAPCO. **4245**

0849-2271 *See* NEOLEX (FREDERICTON). **3141**

0849-2352 *See* PROJET BIO-ALIMENTAIRE. **123**

0849-2360 *See* AGRI-FOOD AND FISHERIES PROJECT, THE. **47**

0849-2387 *See* HALIFAX METRO PROFILE. **1493**

0849-2395 *See* CVO UPDATE. **5508**

0849-2409 *See* RESOURCE GUIDE AND DIRECTORY - ALBERTA CHAMBER OF RESOURCES. **4277**

0849-262X *See* HARD ACT TO FOLLOW. **2976**

0849-2646 *See* NIGHTINGALE (OTTAWA). **3622**

0849-2867 *See* NEWS & VIEWS - CANADIAN FEDERATION OF INDEPENDENT BUSINESS. **699**

0849-2875 See MANDAT (WILLOWDALE. 1991). **691**

0849-2883 *See* CANADIAN MEDIA LIST, THE. **1105**

0849-2913 *See* ENGINEER (HALIFAX). **1972**

0849-2921 *See* REGULATION UPDATE & OPERATING AUTHORITY BULLETIN. **5391**

0849-2964 *See* CANADIAN RAILWAY MODELLER. **5430**

0849-309X *See* WHERE ROCKY MOUNTAINS. **2579**

0849-3103 *See* BCOQ DIRECTORY. **5056**

0849-3111 *See* HEARTBEAT (VANCOUVER). **3583**

0849-3138 *See* QUARTERLY / THE ALLERGY AND ENVIRONMENTAL HEALTH ASSOCIATION. **3676**

0849-3154 *See* BULLETIN - PATENT AND TRADE INSTITUTE OF CANADA (1990). **1302**

0849-3308 *See* EMO OUTLOOK. **4645**

0849-3383 *See* NURSE TO NURSE. **3863**

0849-3391 *See* ECONOMIC JUSTICE REPORT. **1557**

0849-3405 *See* FANCIERS DIGEST, THE. **4286**

0849-3588 *See* JOURNAL L'ARISTOCRATE. **4593**

0849-3596 *See* QUARTERLY STATEMENTS OF FINANCIAL OPERATIONS ENDING **4743**

0849-3650 *See* PROGRAM OVERVIEW - WASTEWATER TECHNOLOGY CENTRE, CANADA. **2240**

0849-3685 *See* MEMBERSHIP DIRECTORY & BUYERS' GUIDE / ONTARIO HOTEL AND MOTEL ASSOCIATION. **2807**

0849-3839 See MODIFICATION AU TARIF. **846**

0849-3901 *See* BUSINESS PEOPLE MAGAZINE (WINNIPEG. 1990). **651**

0849-391X *See* DIRECTORY OF OMBUDSMEN AND INTERNATIONAL OMBUDSMAN OFFICES. **4644**

0849-3928 *See* ANNUAIRE - UNION DES ECRIVAINES ET ECRIVAINS QUEBECOIS. **2917**

0849-3952 *See* NATIONAL RADIO GUIDE. **1135**

0849-4800 *See* EDULAW SCHOOL NEWSLETTER. **2965**

0849-4975 *See* WOMANIST (OTTAWA). **5569**

0849-4983 See MID-CANADA OUTDOORS. **4874**

0849-5009 *See* VETERINARIAN MAGAZINE. **5524**

0849-5017 *See* BUSINESS IN VANCOUVER. **649**

0849-5416 See AREAS SERVED BY NATURAL GAS. **4759**

0849-567X *See* RICH VIVONE'S INSIGHT INTO GOVERNMENT. **4684**

0849-5718 *See* JUST BETWEEN FRIENDS. **2489**

0849-5726 *See* ANNUAIRE DU CINEMA QUEBECOIS. **4063**

0849-5734 *See* JOURNAL DES JEUNES (SAINT-BONIFACE). **1065**

0849-5793 *See* COTE 100. **895**

0849-5866 *See* ADA NEWSLETTER (EDMONTON). **1315**

0849-6013 *See* B C LAWYERS' TELEPHONE, FAX AND SERVICES DIRECTORY. **2939**

0849-6056 *See* ISLANDSIDE MAGAZINE. **2739**

0849-6188 *See* ANGUS TIMES. **205**

0849-6692 *See* FURNITURE MAGAZINE. **2905**

0849-6714 *See* CONDOMINIUM (TORONTO. 1989). **4836**

0849-6854 *See* PREVENTION NETWORK. **1348**

0849-6900 See CHRYSALIS CONNECTION. **5279**

0849-7508 See CUSTOMER INFORMATION - BRITISH COLUMBIA. PURCHASING COMMISSION. **949**

0849-8288 *See* GOLDBELT GAZETTE. **5785**

0849-830X *See* ... HEALTH & WELL-BEING RESOURCES DIRECTORY, THE. **3581**

0849-8334 *See* REPERTOIRE DES PRODUITS ET SERVICES HORTICOLES DE LAVAL. **2430**

0849-987X *See* AFFIRMATIVE ACTION/STATUS OF WOMEN. **4503**

0849-9888 *See* BRITISH COLUMBIA ASSOCIATION FOR COMMUNITY LIVING NEWS. **3922**

0849-9918 See CANADIAN SPEECHES, ISSUES OF THE DAY. **1105**

0850-2005 *See* ETHIOPIQUES. **2639**

0850-8712 *See* CODESRIA BULLETIN. **5195**

0851-0202 *See* MONTHLY INFORMATION REVIEW - BANQUE MAROCAINE DU COMMERCE EXTERIEUR. **846**

0851-0466 *See* ACTES DE L'INSTITUT AGRONOMIQUE ET VETERINAIRE HASSAN II. **44**

0851-2582 *See* SUCRERIE MAGHREBINE. **188**

0852-0070 *See* GFG REPORT. **2383**

0852-4877 *See* SELECTA / DAS WOCHENMAGAZIN DES ARZTES. **3640**

0852-8225 *See* HUMOR. **3395**

0853-0262 *See* POPULASI. **4556**

0853-0785 *See* PROSPEK. **1513**

0853-4454 *See* JURNAL FILSAFAT. **4351**

0854-1566 *See* TROPICAL BIODIVERSITY. **2207**

0855-000X *See* ASEMKA. **3364**

0855-0484 *See* GHANA JOURNAL OF CHEMISTRY. **976**

0856-003X *See* TANZANIA NATIONAL BIBLIOGRAPHY (MONTHLY). **426**

0856-0269 *See* JOURNAL OF THE TANZANIA ASSOCIATION OF FORESTERS. **2386**

0856-048X *See* KISWAHILI. **3293**

0856-0838 *See* UKULIMA WA KISASA. **143**

0856-2105 *See* TANZANIA TRADE CURRENTS : A JOURNAL OF THE BOARD OF EXTERNAL TRADE. **853**

0856-2369 *See* ANNUAL REPORT / INSTITUTE OF RESOURCE ASSESSMENT. **1597**

0857-0361 *See* SEAMEO QUARTERLY / SOUTHEAST ASIAN MINISTERS OF EDUCATION ORGANIZATION. **1783**

0857-0817 *See* MOSQUITO BORNE DISEASES BULLETIN. **4792**

0857-1554 *See* BUFFALO JOURNAL. **5090**

0857-2062 *See* ASIA-PACIFIC NEWSLETTER. **2646**

0857-491X *See* CONTOURS BANGKOK. **4506**

0857-6181 *See* ABSTRACTS OF AIT REPORTS AND PUBLICATIONS ON ENERGY. **1961**

0857-7749 *See* PTIT FOCUS. **4276**

0858-0375 *See* TROPMED NEWSLETTER. **3987**

0858-1088 *See* PHUKET MARINE BIOLOGICAL CENTER. **557**

0860-0007 *See* FASCICULI ARCHAEOLOGIAE HISTORICAE. **268**

0860-021X *See* BIOLOGY OF SPORT. **3953**

0860-0295 *See* ZESZYTY NAUKOWE UNIWERSYTETU JAGIELLONSKIEGO. PRACE INFORMATYCZNE. **1207**

0860-097X *See* MONOGRAFIA - POLITECHNIKA KRAKOWSKA IM. TADEUSZA KOSCIUSZKI. **5129**

0860-102X *See* STUDIA I MATERIAY Z DZIEJOW NAUKI POLSKIEJ. SERIA II, HISTORIA NAUK SCISYCH, PRZYRODNICZYCH I TECHNICZNYCH. **5223**

0860-1089 *See* POLSKI PRZEGLAD RADIOLOGII. **3849**

0860-1100 *See* ZESZYTY NAUKOWE AKADEMII GORNICZO-HUTNICZEJ IM. STANISAWA STASZICA. CHEMIA. **996**

0860-1674 *See* BAJTEK. **1171**

0860-1844 *See* ARCHIWUM HISTORII I FILOZOFII MEDYCYNY. **3552**

0860-2212 *See* SZCZECINSKIE ROCZNIKI NAUKOWE. NAUKI SPOECZNE. **5224**

0860-2581 *See* ROZPRAWY MATEMATYCZNE. **3532**

0860-2603 *See* ACTA ACADEMIAE AGRICULTURAE AC TECHNICAE OLSTENENSIS. ZOOTECHNICA. **5573**

0860-2611 *See* ACTA ACADEMIAE AGRICULTURAE AC TECHNICAE OLSTENENSIS. PROTECTIO AQUARUM ET PISCATORIA. **43**

0860-2832 *See* ACTA ACADEMIAE AGRICULTURAE AC TECHNICAE OLSTENENSIS. AGRICULTURA. **43**

0860-2840 *See* ACTA ACADEMIAE AGRICULTURAE AC TECHNICAE OLSTENENSIS. VETERINARIA. **5501**

0860-2859 *See* ACTA ACADEMIAE AGRICULTURAE AC TECHNICAE OLSTENENSIS. TECHNOLOGIA ALIMENTORUM. **43**

0860-2948 *See* ACTA ACADEMIAE AGRICULTURAE AC TECHNICAE OLSTENENSIS. OECONOMICA. **43**

0860-2956 *See* ACTA ACADEMIAE AGRICULTURAE AC TECHNICAE OLSTENENSIS. AEDIFICATIO ET MECHANICA. **43**

0860-3081 *See* GOSPODARKA, ADMINISTRACJA PANSTWOWA. **4650**

0860-3464 *See* SZTUKA DLA DZIECKA. **366**

0860-3723 *See* EUROCRIMINOLOGY / INSTITUTE OF CRIME PROBLEMS. **3164**

0860-4037 *See* ANIMAL SCIENCE PAPERS AND REPORTS / POLISH ACADEMY OF SCIENCES INSTITUTE OF GENETICS AND ANIMAL BREEDING, JASTRZEBIEC. **59**

0860-4436 *See* DETEKTYW. **4860**

0860-4592 *See* RES PUBLICA. **2492**

0860-5769 *See* IKONOTHEKA : PRACE INSTYTUTU HISTORII SZTUKI UNIWERSYTETU WARSZAWSKIEGO. **322**

0860-5882 *See* POLISH-ANGLOSAXON STUDIES / UNIWERSYTET IM. ADAMA MICKIEWICZA W POZNANIU. **2271**

0860-6161 *See* POSTEPY REHABILITACJI / AKADEMIA WYCHOWANIA FIZYCZNEGO. **4382**

0860-6811 *See* POLSKA, DANE STATYSTYCZNE. **5336**

0860-6846 *See* EKONOMIKA I ORGANIZACJA PRZEDSIEBIORSTWA. **1605**

0860-7001 *See* ARCHIVES OF MINING SCIENCES. **2134**

0860-7222 *See* TURBULENCE / [INITIATED BY THERMAL MACHINERY INSTITUTE, TECHNICAL UNIVERSITY OF CZESTOCHOWA, POLAND]. **2856**

0860-7427 *See* PROBLEMS IN TEXTILE GEOGRAPHY / INTERNATIONAL STANDING WORKING GROUP ON TEXTILE GEOGRAPHY. **5355**

0860-7583 *See* METALOZNAWSTWO, OBROBKA CIEPLNA, INZYNIERIA POWIERZCHNI. **4011**

0860-7591 *See* WARSAW VOICE, THE. **5808**

0860-8156 *See* REVIEW OF COMPARATIVE LAW, THE. **3040**

0860-908X *See* GAZETA WYBORCZA. **5808**

0860-9357 *See* KWARTALNIK HISTORII I TEORII RUCHU ZAWODOWEGO. **1683**

0860-9519 *See* NARTY KRAKOW. **4905**

0860-9594 *See* STUDIA SOCIETATIS SCIENTIARUM TORUNENSIS. SECTIO H, MEDICINA. **3643**

0861-007X *See* NAUKA ZA GORATA. **2388**

0861-0509 *See* ACTA CYTOBIOLOGICA ET MORPHOLOGICA. **531**

0861-0762 *See* BULGARIAN JOURNAL OF METEOROLOGY & HYDROLOGY. **1421**

0861-1033 *See* DAIDZHEST. **2514**

0861-2085 *See* STUDIA PHONETICA POSNANIENSIA. **3325**

0861-2153 *See* LITERATUREN FORUM. **5779**

0861-3117 *See* INSIDER, THE. **2518**

0861-4393 *See* KINO. **4073**

0861-4830 *See* POLITICHESKI IZSLEDVANIIA. **4490**

0861-5047 *See* BALKANMEDIA. **1104**

0861-556X *See* BULGARIAN QUARTERLY. **316**

0861-6701 *See* BANKOV PREGLED / BULGARSKA NARODNA BANKA. **777**

0861-7899 *See* FILOSOFSKI ALTERNATIVI. **4346**

0861-8259 *See* INFEKTOLOGIA. **3714**

0862-0407 *See* SLOVAK MUSIC. **4153**

0862-1195 *See* FOLIA NUMISMATICA. **2781**

0862-2930 *See* VYZKUMY V CECHACH. **2715**

0862-3562 *See* VEDECKOTECHNICKY ROZVOJ V ZEMEDELSTVI. **144**

0862-5158 *See* NOVITATES BOTANICAE UNIVERSITATIS CAROLINAE. **520**

0862-5247 *See* ACTA SOCIETATIS ZOOLOGICAE BOHEMOSLOVACAE. **5573**

0862-5468 *See* CERAMICS (PRAHA). **2588**

0862-5921 *See* LIDOVE NOVINY. **5799**

0862-6111 *See* CESKY CASOPIS HISTORICKY / CESKOSLOVENSKA AKADEMIE VED. **2613**

0862-7487 *See* NARODNI KNIHOVNA. **3232**

0862-7584 *See* VECKO : B.V. **4060**

0862-7932 *See* MAGAZIN CSN. **1617**

0862-7940 *See* APPLICATIONS OF MATHEMATICS (PRAGUE). **3494**

0862-7940 *See* APPLICATIONS OF MATHEMATICS / CZECHOSLOVAK ACADEMY OF SCIENCES. **3494**

0862-7959 *See* MATHEMATICA BOHEMICA / CZECHOSLOVAK ACADEMY OF SCIENCES. **3518**

0862-8351 *See* NARODOPISNA REVUE. **242**

0862-8416 *See* FUNCTIONAL AND DEVELOPMENTAL MORPHOLOGY. **456**

0862-8424 *See* LITTERARIA PRAGENSIA. **3408**

0862-8440 *See* SVET LITERATURY. **3443**

0862-8459 *See* CASOPIS PRO MODERNI FILOLOGII / CESKOSLOVENSKA AKADEMIE VED. **3273**

0862-8726 *See* PRUMYSLOVE VLASTNICTVI / VYDAVA FEDERALNI URAD PRO VYNALEZY. **1308**

0862-8912 *See* BULLETIN OF THE NATIONAL GALLERY IN PRAGUE. **345**

0862-9021 *See* BIBLIOTHECA MUSICA - NARODNI KNIHOVNA CR. **4103**

0862-9129 *See* EKOLOGIA CSFR / ECOLOGY CSFR. **2215**

0862-9382 *See* : CASOPIS INFORMACNICH PRACOVNIKU, KNIHOVNIKU A UZIVATELU INFORMACI, I. **3200**

0862-9773 *See* ROCENKA OBECNYCH DEJIN. **2628**

0862-979X *See* MEDIAEVALIA HISTORICA BOHEMICA. **2698**

0863-0445 *See* JOURNAL OF NEW GENERATION COMPUTER SYSTEMS. **1192**

0863-0453 *See* JOURNAL OF INFORMATION RECORDING MATERIALS (1985). **4371**

0863-0593 *See* JOURNAL OF INFORMATION PROCESSING AND CYBERNETICS. **1251**

0863-0631 *See* WISSENSCHAFTLICHE ZEITSCHRIFT DER HUMBOLDT-UNIVERSITAT ZU BERLIN. REIHE MATHEMATIK/NATURWISSENSCHAFTEN. **5170**

0863-0658 *See* WISSENSCHAFTLICHE ZEITSCHRIFT DER HUMBOLDT-UNIVERSITAT ZU BERLIN REIHE AGRARWISSENSCHAFTEN. **146**

0863-0682 *See* SLB BURIER : NACHRICHTEN AUS DER SACHSISCHEN LANDESBIBLIOTHEK DRESDEN. **3437**

0863-0712 *See* WISSENSCHAFTLICHE ZEITSCHRIFT DER HOCHSCHULE FUER ARCHITEKTUR UND BAUWESEN WEIMAR AUSGABE A. **311**

0863-0720 *See* WISSENSCHAFTLICHE ZEITSCHRIFT DER HOCHSCHULE FUER ARCHITEKTUR UND BAUWESEN WEIMAR AUSGABE B. **311**

0863-0925 *See* WISSENSCHAFTLICHE ZEITSCHRIFT DER TECHNISCHEN UNIVERSITAT OTTO VON GUERICKE MAGDEBURG. **2033**

0863-1042 *See* CONTRIBUTIONS TO PLASMA PHYSICS (1988). **4401**

0863-1204 *See* WISSENSCHAFTLICHE ZEITSCHRIFT DER UNIVERSITAT ROSTOCK. NATURWISSENSCHAFTLICHE REIHE. **5170**

0863-1840 *See* INTERNATIONALE AGRAR-INDUSTRIE-ZEITSCHRIFT. **97**

0863-2332 *See* ERKRANKUNGEN DER ZOOTIERE : VERHANDLUNGSBERICHT DES INTERNATIONALEN SYMPOSIUMS UEBER DIE ERKRANKUNGEN DER ZOOTIERE. **5509**

0863-2693 *See* FUER DIE MEDIZINISCHE PRAXIS. **3577**

0863-2790 *See* INNOVATION & MANAGEMENT. **1304**

0863-3592 *See* DEUTSCHES BIENEN JOURNAL. **78**

0863-4106 *See* ZENTRALBLATT FUER PATHOLOGIE : GENERAL PATHOLOGY/PATHOLOGICAL ANATOMY. **3899**

0863-4564 *See* BERLINER DEBATTE INITIAL : ZEITSCHRIFT FUER SOCIALWISSENSCHAFTLICHEN DISKURS. **5192**

0863-4904 *See* DEUTSCHE STOMATOLOGIE. **1322**

0863-5412 *See* AERZTEBLATT THUERINGEN. **3547**

0863-5544 *See* WISSENSCHAFTLICHE TAGUNGEN DER TECHNISCHEN UNIVERSITAT KARL-MARX-STADT. **5170**

0864-0122 *See* INFORMACION LABORAL (HAVANA, CUBA). **5289**

0864-0300 *See* REVISTA CUBANA DE INVESTIGACIONES BIOMEDICAS. **3635**

0864-0327 *See* MUCHACHA. **5561**

0864-0564 *See* SOMOS JOVENES. **1069**

0864-0831 *See* REVISTA JURIDICA (CUBA. MINISTERIO DE JUSTICIA. DEPTO. DE DIVULGACION). **3042**

0864-1420 *See* CUBA, ECONOMIA PLANIFICADA. **1478**

0864-2133 *See* REVISTA CUBANA ALIMENTACION Y NUTRICION. **4198**

0864-2621 *See* REVISTA CUBANA DE CONSTRUCCION NAVAL; REVISTA CIENTIFICO TECNICA. **5455**

0864-3466 *See* REVISTA CUBANA DE SALUD PUBLICA. **4799**

0864-4403 *See* REVISTA DE AFRICA Y MEDIO ORIENTE. **4494**

0864-4551 *See* BIOTECNOLOGIA APLICADA : REVISTA DE LA SOCIEDAD IBEROLATINOAMERICANA PARA INVESTIGACIONES SOBRE INTERFERON Y BIOTECNOLOGIA EN SALUD. **3690**

0864-4616 *See* GRANMA INTERNACIONAL. **5799**

0864-4624 *See* GRANMA INTERNATIONAL. **5799**

0864-4659 *See* CIENCIAS DE LA INFORMACION. **3202**

0864-7410 *See* HUNGARIAN AGRICULTURAL ENGINEERING. **93**

0864-8921 *See* MAGYAR UROLOGIA. **3991**

0864-991X *See* HEALTH INFORMATION AND LIBRARIES. **3213**

0865-0497 *See* ITD. IZOTOPTECHNIKA, DIAGNOSZTIKA. **3591**

0865-1329 *See* KONYVTARI LEVELEZO/LAP. **3222**

0865-2090 *See* MATHEMATICA PANNONICA. **3518**

0865-3763 *See* VENGERSKII MERIDIAN. **5225**

0865-5464 *See* WOSINSKY MOR MUZEUM EVKONYVE, A. **4097**

0865-7580 *See* AUTOMATIZALAS ES ROBOTTECHNIKA. **2036**

0865-8579 *See* HUNGARIAN MARKET REPORT. **1494**

0865-8943 *See* ECONOMIC TRENDS IN EASTERN EUROPE. **1558**

0865-9109 *See* HEVES MEGYEI HIRLAP. **5802**

0865-9222 *See* BALNEOLOGIA, GYOGYFURDOUGY, GYOGYIDEGENFORGALOM. **4849**

0865-9435 *See* UJ ERDEKES UJSAG. **4855**

0866-4013 *See* MAGYAR RESTAURALAS. **357**

0866-4323 *See* GEOGRAPHIA MEDICA. SUPPLEMENT / GEOGRAPHIA MEDICA. SONDERBAND. **3735**

0866-4749 *See* UJ MAGYAR HIREK. **2524**

0866-482X *See* FEHERJE ES BIOTERMEK. **86**

0866-5192 *See* KUTATASSZERVEZESI TAJEKOZTATO. **5124**

0866-6865 *See* AULA : TARSADALOM ES GAZDASAG : A BUDAPESTI KOZGAZDASAGTUDOMANYI EGYETEM FOLYOIRATA. **1464**

0866-7497 *See* NGHIEN CUU LICH SU. **2660**

0866-9619 *See* KOMPUTER W SZKOLE. **1224**

0866-9902 *See* BAZAR KATOWICE. **4857**

0867-0005 *See* GOSPODARKA NARODOWA (WARSAW, POLAND : 1990). **1564**

0867-0064 *See* MAOPOLSKA KRAKOW. **2519**

0867-0072 *See* MYSL NARODOWA POLSKA. **4482**

0867-0218 *See* BESTSELLER BODZ. **4824**

0867-0374 *See* CZAS KRAKOWSKI. **5807**

0867-0390 *See* GAZETA POLICYJNA. **3165**

0867-0404 *See* MAGAZYN KRYMINALNY 997. **4863**

0867-0633 *See* TEKSTY DRUGIE. **3444**

0867-082X *See* ROCZNIKI STATYSTYCZNE. **5338**

0867-0846 *See* MATERIALY I OPRACOWANIA STATYSTYCZNE. **5332**

0867-1095 *See* ZESZYTY NAUKOWE UNIWERSYTETU JAGIELLONSKIEGE. UNIVERSITATIS IAGELLONICAE ACTA CHIMICA. **996**

0867-1427 *See* ZESZYTY NAUKOWE AKADEMII ROLNICZEJ WE WROCAWIU. ROZPRAWA HABILITACYJNA. **149**

0867-1486 *See* TENIS STOOWY. **4925**

0867-1761 *See* FOLIA HORTICULTURAE. **2415**

0867-1966 *See* ROCZNIK MUZEUM GORNOSLASKIEGO W BYTOMIU. ENTOMOLOGIA. **5613**

0867-2105 *See* DOM I WNETRZE. **2900**

0867-2237 *See* NIE WARSZAWA. **4484**

0867-2288 *See* PREMIERA KATOWICE. **4076**

0867-2490 See UFO BIAYSTOK. 4186
0867-2806 See BOKSER WARSZAWA. 4824
0867-2814 See SYBIRACY WARSZAWA. 2274
0867-3055 See MEDYK WARSZAWA. 3615
0867-3195 See WEDKARZ POLSKI. 2315
0867-3357 See ZESZYTY NAUKOWE. BIOLOGIA / UNIWERSYTET GDANSKI. 476
0867-3608 See DZIS WARSZAWA. 2515
0867-3772 See PRZEGLAD NARODOWY. 2521
0867-3993 See CZARNY PAS. 4892
0867-4248 See KUJAWY I POMORZE. 2518
0867-4310 See SAM NA SAM. 4865
0867-4329 See MOJE LEKTURY. 1066
0867-4337 See JACHTING WARSZAWA. 593
0867-4493 See INTERNATIONAL AFFAIRS STUDIES. 4524
0867-4507 See TRYBUNA SLASKA 1990. 5808
0867-4590 See GOS PORANNY. 5808
0867-4663 See WEDKARSTWO I TY. 4880
0867-4787 See NASTOLATKI WARSZAWA. 1067
0867-5090 See DZIENNIK LUBELSKI. 5807
0867-5244 See KRYTYKA. 2696
0867-5864 See SEKRETY HISTORII. 2629
0867-5961 See TYGODNIK POPULARNY ZWIAZKOWIEC. 1715
0867-6410 See SWIAT KARATE. 4924
0867-6550 See PARKI NARODOWE. 2220
0867-6704 See CHAMPION KATOWICE. 2798
0867-700X See BIULETYN INSTYTUTU LEKOW 1990. 1089
0867-7204 See BUCHALTER SZCZECIN. 740
0867-7514 See PRZEGLAD PODATKOWY. 4742
0867-7905 See POLISH POPULATION REVIEW / POLISH DEMOGRAPHIC SOCIETY [AND] CENTRAL STATISTICAL OFFICE. 4556
0867-8383 See POLISH JOURNAL OF OCCUPATIONAL MEDICINE AND ENVIRONMENTAL HEALTH. 3628
0867-8715 See QUMRAN CHRONICLE. 5019
0867-8723 See SUPER EXPRESS. 5808
0868-4790 See DZVIN : CHASOPYS SPILKY PYSMENNYKIV UKRAINY. 3383
0868-4855 See SLOVO. 3437
0868-5045 See ETYKA, ESTETYKA I TEORIIA KULTURY / MINISTERSTVO VYSHCHOI I SEREDNOI SPETSIALNOI OSVITY URSR, KYIVSKYI ORDENA LENINA I ORDENA ZHOVTNEVOI REVOLIUTSII DERZHAVNYI UNIVERSYTET IM. T.H. SHEVCHENKA. 2250
0868-5169 See IZVESTIIA SIBIRSKOGO OTDELENIIA AKADEMII NAUK SSSR. SERIIA REGION. EKONOMIDA I SOTSIOLOGIIA. 1568
0868-5797 See SOTSIALNO-POLITICHESKIE NAUKI. 4547
0868-5827 See MEGAPOLIS EXPRESS. 5809
0868-5894 See EESTI TEADUSTE AKADEEMIA TOIMETISED. OKOLOOGIA. 2215
0868-6009 See BIZNES : ZHURNAL SOIUZA MENEDZHEROV SSSR. 643
0868-6556 See LATVIJAS ZINATNU AKADEMIJAS VESTIS. 5125
0868-6718 See FILOSOFIIA I SOVREMENNYI MIR / MINISTERSTVO NARODNOGO OBRAZOVANIIA BSSR [I] BELORUSSKII ORDENA TRUDOVOGO KRASNOGO ZNAMENI GOSUDARSTVENNYI UNIVERSITET IMENI V.I. LENINA. 4541
0868-7110 See MOSKOVSKII ZHURNAL. 304
0868-7188 See KHOZIAIN. 102
0868-8249 See LATVIJAS KIMIJAS ZURNALS. 984
0868-8257 See LATVIAN JOURNAL OF PHYSICS AND TECHNICAL SCIENCES. 4411
0868-8273 See POLITYKA I CHAS : ZHURNAL T SK KOMPARTII UKRAINY. 4545
0868-8710 See SOGLASIE. 3437
0868-9024 See EKRAN. 4068
0868-9644 See UKRAINSKA KULTURA. 2524
0868-9679 See MOLDOVA SI LUMEA. 4543
0869-0022 See STUPENI. 1069
0869-0499 See OBSHCHESTVENNYE NAUKI I SOVREMENNOST : ONS. 5211

0869-0685 See NAROD I DEMOKRATIIA. 4482
0869-1177 See RUSSKOE PROSHLOE. 2708
0869-1479 See KHOZIAIN. 102
0869-1487 See ZEMLIA I LIUDY UKRAINY. 148
0869-1908 See VOSTOK / AKADEMIIA NAUK SSSR, INSTITUT VOSTOKOVEDENIIA [I] INSTITUT AFRIKI. 2667
0869-2084 See KLINICHESKAIA LABORATORNAIA DIAGNOSTIKA. 3896
0869-2092 See EKSPERIMENTALNAIA I KLINICHESKAIA FARMAKOLOGIIA. 4303
0869-2106 See ROSSISKII MEDITSINSKII ZHURNAL : ORGAN MINISTERSTVA ZDRAVOOKHRANENIIA RSFSR. 3637
0869-2114 See MATERINSTVO I DETSTVO / MINISTERSTVO ZDRAVOOKHRANENIIA ROSSIISKOI FEDERATSII. 3906
0869-3102 See GLAS. 3391
0869-3382 See ZEMLIA SIBIR. 2580
0869-3595 See KYIVSKA STAROVYNA. 3403
0869-4095 See REFERATIVNYI ZHURNAL. 04, 04D, BIOLOGIIA. FIZIKO-KHIMICHESKAIA BIOLOGIIA / VSESOIUZNYI INSTITUT NAUCHNOI I TEKHNICHESKOI INFORMATSII. 493
0869-4400 See ZAKON : ZHURNAL DLIA DELOVYKH LIUDEI. 3077
0869-4915 See BIBLIOTEKA. 3194
0869-494X See MIR ZHENSHCHINY. 5561
0869-544X See SLAVIANOVEDENIE. 2709
0869-5652 See DOKLADY AKADEMII NAUK / ROSSIISKAIA AKADEMIIA NAUK. 5101
0869-5911 See PETROLOGY. 1459
0869-6055 See ZAPISKI VSEROSSIISKOGO MINERALOGICHESKOGO OBSHCHESTVA / ROSSIISKAIA AKADEMIIA NAUK. 1445
0869-608X See BIBLIOTEKOVEDENIE. 3194
0869-7760 See MEDITSINSKAIA POMOSHCH / MEDICAL CARE / MINISTERSTVO ZDRAVOOKHRANENIA RF. 3614
0869-7809 See GEOEKOLOGIIA, INZHENERNAIA GEOLOGIIA, GIDROGEOLOGIIA, GEOKRIOLOGIIA / ROSSIISKAIA AKADEMIIA NAUK. 1377
0869-8171 See MIR MUZEIA. 4091
0869-866X See PROBLEMY SOTSIALNOI GIGIENY I ISTORIIA MEDITSINY / NII SOTSIALNOI GIGIENY, EKONOMIKI I UPRAVLENIIA ZDRAVOOKHRANENIEM IM N.A. SEMASHKO RAMN, AO ASSOTSIATSIIA 'MEDITSINSKAIA LITERATURA.'. 4796
0869-8902 See GARMONIIA. 4776
0870-001X See ESTUDOS, ENSAIOS E DOCUMENTOS (PORTUGAL. JUNTA DE INVESTIGACOES CIENTIFICAS DO ULTRAMAR). 5103
0870-0028 See STUDIA. 2630
0870-0036 See MEMORIAS DO INSTITUTO DE INVESTIGACAO CIENTIFICA TROPICAL. 5128
0870-0095 See BOLETIM TRIMESTRAL - BANCO DE PORTUGAL. 1548
0870-0230 See FARMACIA PORTUGUESA. 4304
0870-0249 See ALMANSOR. 2672
0870-0478 See BOLETIM CULTURAL / CAMARA MUNICIPAL DO PORTO. 5268
0870-0761 See BOLETIM CULTURAL - ASSEMBLEIA DISTRITAL DE LISBOA. 5268
0870-077X See ANAIS - ACADEMIA PORTUGUESA DA HISTORIA. 2673
0870-0990 See ANTROPOLOGIA PORTUGUESA. 230
0870-1008 See BOLETIM DE LEGISLACAO ECONOMICA. 779
0870-1059 See CORTICA. 1602
0870-1067 See REPOSITORIO DE TRABALHOS DO L.N.I.V. 5520
0870-1164 See CORROSAO E PROTECCAO DE MATERIALS. 2101
0870-1180 See BOLETIM / SOCIEDADE PORTUGUESA DE QUIMICA. 962
0870-1466 See BOLETIM DA DIRECCAO GERAL DOS EDIFICIOS E MONUMENTOS NACIONAIS. 293
0870-1504 See JORNAL ARQUITECTOS. 301

0870-1695 See CIENCIA BIOLOGICA. B, ECOLOGIA E SISTEMATICA. 2212
0870-2306 See ARQUEOLOGIA (PORTO). 260
0870-2551 See REVISTA PORTUGUESA DE CARDIOLOGIA. 3710
0870-287X See AIP INFORMACAO. 637
0870-3043 See PLANEAMENTO (LISBOA). 1512
0870-3205 See STATISTIQUES DES SOCIETES. ESTATISTICAS DAS SOCIEDADES. 5343
0870-3531 See ECONOMIA (LISBOA). 1481
0870-3841 See COLOQUIO : ARTES. 317
0870-4112 See BIBLOS. 3195
0870-4139 See REVISTA PORTUGUESA DE FILOLOGIA. 3316
0870-4287 See STOMA. 1336
0870-4457 See ESTUDOS DE ANTROPOLOGIA CULTURAL E SOCIAL. 235
0870-4600 See BOLETIM DE FILOLOGIA. 3269
0870-4619 See BOLETIM DO ARQUIVO HISTORICO MILITAR. 4038
0870-466X See BOLETIM / INSTITUTO HISTORICO DA ILHA TERCEIRA. 2611
0870-4783 See JORNAL DE PSICOLOGIA. 4592
0870-5283 See REVISTA PORTUGUESA DE FILOSOFIA. 4359
0870-5364 See ELECTRICIDADE. 2045
0870-5879 See ESTUDOS DE HISTORIA E CARTOGRAFIA ANTIGA. MEMORIAS. 2615
0870-6190 See MUNDO DA ARTE. 359
0870-6344 See ESTUDOS DE CASTELO BRANCO. 2615
0870-6457 See CADERNOS DE ARQUEOLOGIA (BRAGA, PORTUGAL). 265
0870-6581 See ARQUIPELAGO. CIENCIAS DA NATUREZA. 4162
0870-6735 See SERIE SEPARATAS / CENTRO DE ESTUDOS DE HISTORIA E CARTOGRAFIA ANTIGA. 2709
0870-7227 See BOLETIM DA SOCIEDADE PORTUGUESA DE ENTOMOLOGIA. 5606
0870-7618 See BROTERIA 1925. 2843
0870-7650 See COLOQUIO/CIENCIAS. 5095
0870-8231 See ANALISE PSICOLOGICA. 4573
0870-8339 See BRIGANTIA. 2679
0870-8584 See ESTUDOS ITALIANOS EM PORTUGAL. 2687
0870-9025 See REVISTA PORTUGUESA DE SAUDE PUBLICA / ESCOLA NACIONAL DE SAUDE PUBLICA. 4800
0870-9351 See REVISTA (INSTITUTO GEOGRAFICO E CADASTRAL (PORTUGAL)). 2583
0871-0430 See PRELO : REVISTA DA IMPRENSA NACIONAL/CASA DA MOEDA. 3425
0871-0635 See ANAIS DA UTAD. 58
0871-0759 See REVISTA DE GUIMARAES. 2705
0871-0783 See MONTHLY BULLETIN / BANCO DE PORTUGAL, RESEARCH AND STATISTICS DEPARTMENT. 799
0871-0996 See MUNDA : REVISTA DO GRUPO DE ARQUEOLOGIA E ARTE DO CENTRO. 275
0871-1747 See COMUNICACOES - INSTITUTO DE INVESTIGACAO CIENTIFICA TROPICAL. SERIE DE CIENCIAS DE ENGENHARIA GEOGRAFICA. 2559
0871-1755 See COMUNICACOES DO INSTITUTO DE INVESTIGACAO CIENTIFICA TROPICAL, SERIE DE CIENCIAS BIOLOGICAS. 452
0871-1771 See COMUNICACOES DO INSTITUTO DE INVESTIGACAO CIENTIFICA TROPICAL, SERIE DE CIENCIAS HISTORICAS, ECONOMICAS E SOCIOLOGICAS. 1470
0871-178X See COMUNICACOES DO INSTITUTO DE INVESTIGACAO CIENTIFICA TROPICAL, SERIE DE CIENCIAS ETNOLOGICAS E ETNOMUSEOLOGICAS. 2258
0871-1798 See COMUNICACOES - INSTITUTO DE INVESTIGACAO CIENTIFICA TROPICAL. SERIE DE CIENCIAS DA TERRA. 1354
0871-1992 See CIDADE DE EVORA, A. 2844
0871-2221 See REVISTA INOVACAO. 1780

0871-2352 *See* REVISTA DE CIENCIAS HISTORICAS : [PUBLICACAO DO DEPARTAMENTO DE CIENCIAS HISTORICAS DA UNIVERSIDADE PORTUCALENSE]. **2705**

0871-2549 *See* SKIN CANCER LISBOA. **3824**

0871-3413 *See* ARQUIVOS DE MEDICINA : REVISTA DE CIENCIA E ARTE MEDICAS. **3552**

0871-3643 *See* BOLETIM DO CENTRO DE DOCUMENTACAO 25 DE ABRIL. **5193**

0871-4304 *See* ARQUIVOS DE REUMATOLOGIA E DOENCAS OSTEO-ARTICU-LARES. **3803**

0871-4592 *See* ARQUIVOS DA MATERNIDADE DR. ALFREDO DA COSTA. **3757**

0871-4649 *See* REVISTA PORTUGUESA DE HEMORREOLOGIA : ORGAO OFICIAL DA SOCIEDADE PORTUGUESA DE HEMORREOLOGIA / SOCIEDADE PORTUGUESA DE HEMORREOLOGIA. **3773**

0871-4843 *See* ARQUIVOS DO MUSEU BOCAGE. NOVA SERIE. **4162**

0871-5440 *See* DGF INFORMACAO. **508**

0871-5718 *See* ONCOLOGIA PORTO. **3821**

0871-6102 *See* ARQUIVO COIMBRAO (BOLETIM DA BIBLIOTECA MUNICIPAL). **3192**

0871-7486 *See* PENELOPE (LISBON, PORTUGAL). **2625**

0871-7516 *See* CADERNOS DE CONSULTA PSICOLOGICA. **4579**

0871-8148 *See* SINTRIA / GABINETE DE ESTUDOS DE ARQUEOLOGIA, ARTE E ETNOGRAFIA, MUSEU REGIONAL DE SINTRA OE MUSEU ARQUEOLOGICO DE SAO MIGUEL DE ODRINHAS. **282**

0871-9276 *See* ARTES PLASTICAS LISBOA. **341**

0871-9497 *See* LEGISLACAO LISBOA. (1991). **4480**

0872-1696 *See* DIARIO ECONOMICO. **1479**

0882-004X *See* COLORADO WHO'S WHO. **431**

0882-0074 *See* FODOR'S BOSTON. **5471**

0882-0139 *See* IMMUNOLOGICAL INVESTIGATIONS. **3671**

0882-0171 *See* ARDELL WELLNESS REPORT, THE. **4767**

0882-0198 *See* OFFICE AUTOMATION NEWS : THE PUBLICATION OF THE OFFICE AUTOMATION SOCIETY INTERNATIONAL. **4213**

0882-0201 *See* EARLY KEYBOARD STUDIES NEWSLETTER. **4116**

0882-021X *See* TEXAS SCHOOL ADMINISTRATOR'S LEGAL DIGEST. **3064**

0882-0228 *See* SELECTIONS (GRADUATE MANAGEMENT ADMISSION COUNCIL). **886**

0882-0244 *See* CJ INTERNATIONAL. **3160**

0882-0252 *See* HEALTH PROMOTION NEWSLETTER. **4781**

0882-0260 *See* WHO'S WHO IN FEDERAL GOVERNMENT PRIME CONTRACTORS. **437**

0882-0279 *See* LABOR SURPLUS AREAS. **1685**

0882-0287 *See* COMMUNICATIONS IN STATISTICS : STOCHASTIC MODELS. **5325**

0882-0295 *See* VAR (CAMDEN, ME.). **1168**

0882-0341 *See* ANNUAL REPORT - CONGRESSIONAL AWARD FOUNDATION (U.S.) **4627**

0882-035X *See* ANNUAL REPORT - HISTORICAL SOCIETY OF YORK COUNTY (PA.). **2720**

0882-0368 *See* JAZZ FESTIVALS INTERNATIONAL DIRECTORY. **4124**

0882-0376 *See* EGON RONAY'S TWA GUIDE ... TO GOOD RESTAURANTS IN 35 EUROPEAN BUSINESS CITIES. **5070**

0882-0384 *See* TEXAS LEAGUE SAVINGS ACCOUNT. **813**

0882-0406 *See* APPLE BITS. **1171**

0882-0422 *See* GENEALOGICAL CLEARINGHOUSE QUARTERLY, THE. **2449**

0882-0481 *See* FITNESS MANAGEMENT (SOLANA BEACH, CALIF.). **2597**

0882-049X *See* MAGAZINE DESIGN & PRODUCTION. **2922**

0882-0511 *See* SEMINARS IN VETERINARY MEDICINE AND SURGERY (SMALL ANIMALS). **5522**

0882-052X *See* SEMINARS IN ORTHOPAEDICS. **3884**

0882-0538 *See* SEMINARS IN OPHTHALMOLOGY. **3879**

0882-0546 *See* SEMINARS IN RESPIRATORY INFECTIONS. **3952**

0882-0589 *See* MARTIN BROWER'S ORANGE COUNTY REPORT. **692**

0882-0627 *See* JOURNAL OF NURSING STAFF DEVELOPMENT : JNSD. **3859**

0882-0635 *See* TENNESSEE ANCESTORS. **2474**

0882-0643 *See* BLACK RESOURCE GUIDE, THE. **2257**

0882-0651 *See* BROWN BOOK (OAKLAND, CALIF.), THE. **1265**

0882-0708 *See* BEST BOOKS FOR YOUNG ADULTS. **4824**

0882-0783 *See* JOURNAL OF POLICE AND CRIMINAL PSYCHOLOGY. **3167**

0882-0791 *See* BARTON BULLETIN OF THE BARTON HISTORICAL SOCIETY, INC, THE. **2438**

0882-0813 *See* VAJRADHATU SUN, THE. **5022**

0882-0821 *See* FINANCIAL DIRECTORY OF PENSION FUNDS. WEST VIRGINIA, THE. **1674**

0882-083X *See* FINANCIAL DIRECTORY OF PENSION FUNDS. KANSAS, THE. **1671**

0882-0856 *See* GATHERINGS FROM THE ADIRONDACK FOOTHILLS. **2734**

0882-0880 *See* ADVANCES IN DERMATOLOGY. **3717**

0882-0910 *See* WOMEN AND WORK (BEVERLY HILLS, CALIF.). **1718**

0882-0929 *See* ALERT (SACRAMENTO, CALIF.). **817**

0882-0945 *See* BUDDHIST-CHRISTIAN STUDIES. **5020**

0882-0953 *See* RESPIRATORY PROTECTION NEWSLETTER. **2869**

0882-0961 *See* CHRISTIAN COMPUTER NEWS. **1174**

0882-1038 *See* AMERICAN DEFENSE ANNUAL. **4034**

0882-1046 *See* JOURNAL OF CONTEMPORARY HEALTH LAW AND POLICY, THE. **2987**

0882-1100 *See* SPE MONOGRAPH SERIES. **1847**

0882-1127 *See* AMERICAN JOURNALISM. **2917**

0882-1135 *See* WOMEN'S QUARTERLY REVIEW. **5571**

0882-1143 *See* DIGEST OF TECHNICAL INFORMATION. **1153**

0882-1178 *See* TREASURE CHEST NEWS. **2475**

0882-1208 *See* CHESAPEAKE COUSINS. **2443**

0882-1232 *See* JOURNAL OF CURRICULUM AND SUPERVISION. **1897**

0882-1240 *See* DIMENSIONS (NEW YORK, N.Y.). **2685**

0882-1267 *See* FRENCH POLITICS AND SOCIETY. **4474**

0882-1275 *See* NATIONAL SPIRITUALIST (INDIANAPOLIS, IND.), THE. **4980**

0882-1305 *See* LBL RESEARCH REVIEW. **4448**

0882-1348 *See* SCIFANT. **5074**

0882-1372 *See* VOLLEYBALL RULE BOOK. **4928**

0882-1410 *See* ARTIFICIAL INTELLIGENCE ABSTRACTS. **1208**

0882-1437 *See* CAD/CAM ABSTRACTS. **1231**

0882-1445 *See* PUBLIC TECHNOLOGY. **5143**

0882-1453 *See* COMPUTER SECURITY DIGEST. **1226**

0882-1461 *See* TELEPHONE SELLING REPORT. **937**

0882-147X *See* MORNING COFFEE CHAPBOOK SERIES. **3466**

0882-1496 *See* MARKET MOVES. **1238**

0882-1518 *See* PROFESSIONAL UPHOLSTERER, THE. **2903**

0882-1577 *See* HEALTH PROGRESS (SAINT LOUIS, MO.). **3781**

0882-1593 *See* BLACK ELECTED OFFICIALS. **4465**

0882-1623 *See* GENEALOGICAL GEMS. **2450**

0882-1631 *See* CARROLLTONIAN. **2442**

0882-1666 *See* SYSTEMS AND COMPUTERS IN JAPAN. **1249**

0882-1674 *See* TRIDENT (WASHINGTON, D.C.). **2788**

0882-178X *See* OPTION (LOS ANGELES, CALIF.). **4144**

0882-181X *See* SIMON GREENLEAF LAW REVIEW : A PUBLICATION OF THE SIMON GREENLEAF SCHOOL OF LAW, THE. **4513**

0882-1828 *See* LADDER (WASHINGTON, D.C.), THE. **3294**

0882-1852 *See* BIOLOGICAL THERAPIES IN DENTISTRY. **1317**

0882-1860 *See* DIRECTORY OF DENTAL EDUCATORS (WASHINGTON, D.C. : 1983). **1322**

0882-1879 *See* ISLAND PROPERTIES REPORT. **4839**

0882-1887 *See* ISLAND PROPERTIES REPORT. QUARTERLY REPORT. **4839**

0882-1895 *See* LONG ISLAND RECREATION & VISITORS GUIDE. **5483**

0882-1909 *See* SCROGGINS NATIONAL LAW ENFORCEMENT DIRECTORY. **3176**

0882-1933 *See* OLSCHWANGER JOURNAL. **2465**

0882-1941 *See* DIRECTORY - NATIONAL COUNCIL OF SAVINGS INSTITUTIONS (U.S.). **788**

0882-1968 *See* NORTH AMERICAN CULTURE. **5253**

0882-1976 *See* HMTC UPDATE. **4783**

0882-1984 *See* MARINE EQUIPMENT CATALOG. **4179**

0882-1992 *See* CRAIN'S DETROIT BUSINESS. **663**

0882-200X *See* COMPUTER & ELECTRONICS GRADUATE, THE. **4203**

0882-2026 *See* ANNUAL REPORT ON THE FOOD AND AGRICULTURAL SCIENCES, FROM THE SECRETARY OF AGRICULTURE TO THE PRESIDENT AND THE CONGRESS OF THE UNITED STATES. **61**

0882-2034 *See* SCIENTIFIC AWAKENING IN THE RESTORATION. **5155**

0882-2042 *See* RESEARCH SERIES. **280**

0882-2050 *See* MERLYN'S PEN. **1066**

0882-2085 *See* ORGAN HANDBOOK. **4144**

0882-2093 *See* INTERNATIONAL DIATOMIST DIRECTORY. **514**

0882-2115 *See* ICES JOURNAL. **2024**

0882-2123 *See* AMBASSADOR REPORT. **4933**

0882-214X *See* PITCH PIPE, THE. **4146**

0882-2158 *See* TRACES OF SOUTH CENTRAL KENTUCKY. **2475**

0882-2166 *See* GAELIC GLEANINGS. **2449**

0882-2204 *See* INDEX TO INFORMATION (WASHINGTON, D.C.). **942**

0882-2239 *See* ANNUAL REPORT OF INTRAMURAL ACTIVITIES - NATIONAL INSTITUTE OF ALLERGY AND INFECTIOUS DISEASES (U.S.). **3712**

0882-2247 *See* WASHINGTON MEMO - NATIONAL COUNCIL OF SAVINGS INSTITUTIONS (U.S.). **816**

0882-2255 *See* SOCIAL MARKETING UPDATE. **936**

0882-228X *See* MAGAZINE OF HISTORY. **2622**

0882-2301 *See* CHILD'S DOCTOR, THE. **3902**

0882-2328 *See* YEARBOOK / GENERAL SOCIETY OF COLONIAL WARS. **2766**

0882-2336 *See* PUBLICATIONS OF THE GENERAL SOCIETY OF COLONIAL WARS. **5235**

0882-2395 *See* DAVIESS COUNTY HISTORICAL QUARTERLY, THE. **2730**

0882-2409 *See* REMOTE SENSING QUARTERLY LITERATURE REVIEW. **2574**

0882-2417 *See* ANNUAL REPORT - NAVY PERSONNEL RESEARCH AND DEVELOPMENT CENTER (U.S.). **4035**

0882-2425 *See* LOT OF BUNKUM. YEARBOOK, A. **2458**

0882-2433 *See* DATA-ACQUISITION DATABOOK. **2040**

0882-2441 See CURRENT RESEARCH UPDATES. OBSTETRICS & GYNECOLOGY. 3657

0882-245X See ANNUAL REPORT - NATIONAL FOUNDATION FOR ADVANCEMENT IN THE ARTS (U.S.). 313

0882-2492 See ARCHITECTURES. 290

0882-2506 See BIOGRAPHICAL DIRECTORY - AMERICAN PSYCHIATRIC ASSOCIATION. 430

0882-2522 See AMERICAN NATIVE PRESS. 5631

0882-2549 See DUPLEX PLANET, THE. 3382

0882-2573 See KANE'S BEVERAGE WEEK. 2368

0882-2689 See JOURNAL OF PSYCHOPATHOLOGY AND BEHAVIORAL ASSESSMENT. 4600

0882-2697 See CALIFORNIA ASSOCIATION OF MACHINE EMBROIDERY. 5183

0882-2700 See HOMECARE (LOS ANGELES, CALIF.). 5288

0882-2786 See INTERNATIONAL JOURNAL OF ORAL AND MAXILLOFACIAL IMPLANTS, THE. 1325

0882-2816 See POODLE VARIETY. 4287

0882-2832 See ABMS DIRECTORY OF CERTIFIED NEUROLOGICAL SURGEONS. 3957

0882-2840 See ALAN REVIEW, THE. 3359

0882-2859 See BUFFALO BUSINESS JOURNAL. 644

0882-2883 See INSCRIPTIONS (STEVENS POINT, WIS.). 2454

0882-2913 See GUIDE FOR THE SELECTION OF TANKERS. 4176

0882-2921 See FACES ROCKS. 4117

0882-293X See FINANCIAL DIRECTORY OF PENSION FUNDS. SOUTH CAROLINA, THE. 1673

0882-2948 See FINANCIAL DIRECTORY OF PENSION FUNDS. WYOMING, THE. 1674

0882-2956 See FINANCIAL DIRECTORY OF PENSION FUNDS. HAWAII, THE. 1670

0882-2964 See FINANCIAL DIRECTORY OF PENSION FUNDS. NEW MEXICO, THE. 1672

0882-2972 See FINANCIAL DIRECTORY OF PENSION FUNDS. PUERTO RICO, THE. 1673

0882-2980 See FINANCIAL DIRECTORY OF PENSION FUNDS. DELAWARE, THE. 1670

0882-2999 See OFFICIAL PRICE GUIDE TO COLLECTIBLE CAMERAS, THE. 2776

0882-3006 See OSTERREICH IN AMERIKANISCHE SICHT. 3421

0882-3014 See SYSTEMS RESEARCH AND INFORMATION SCIENCE. 3252

0882-3022 See FACT SHEET - FOOD ANIMAL CONCERNS TRUST. 226

0882-3030 See FOLIO (BROCKPORT, N.Y.). 3388

0882-3049 See CULTURA LUDENS. 5197

0882-3065 See MEAT PRICE RELATIONSHIPS. 1618

0882-3073 See CORPORATE FINANCE LETTER. 785

0882-309X See PETERSON'S GUIDE TO COLLEGES IN THE SOUTHEAST. 1841

0882-3103 See PETERSON'S GUIDE TO COLLEGES IN THE SOUTHWEST. 1841

0882-312X See RANGEL'S REPORTS. 2627

0882-3138 See RESEARCH IN FINANCE. SUPPLEMENT. 808

0882-3154 See NEWS / WESTERN RESERVE HISTORICAL SOCIETY. 2749

0882-3170 See NCAA MEN'S AND WOMEN'S CROSS COUNTRY AND TRACK AND FIELD RULES. 4907

0882-3219 See VIRGINIA INDUSTRIAL DIRECTORY. 1631

0882-3251 See GLOBAL DEVELOPMENT REPORT. 2910

0882-3294 See MICROGRAPHICS AND OPTICAL STORAGE EQUIPMENT REVIEW. 1277

0882-3316 See EMERGING PATTERNS OF WORK AND COMMUNICATIONS IN AN INFORMATION AGE. 5244

0882-3340 See ATARI EXPLORER. 1264

0882-3367 See AIA DIRECTORY OF HELIPORTS & HELISTOPS IN THE UNITED STATES, CANADA, PUERTO RICO, AND DIRECTORY OF HOSPITAL HELIPORTS & HELISTOPS. 6

0882-3375 See JOURNAL OF TECHNOLOGY IN ADDICTION & RECOVERY. 1346

0882-3383 See SANTA CLARA COMPUTER AND HIGH-TECHNOLOGY LAW JOURNAL. 3046

0882-3391 See JOURNAL OF FAMILY AND ECONOMIC ISSUES. 2281

0882-3421 See CALIFORNIA PEDIATRICIAN. 3901

0882-3448 See SHOESTRING MARKETER, THE. 936

0882-3456 See QUORUM REPORT. 4678

0882-3464 See SPECULATOR (BUTTE, MONT.), THE. 2762

0882-3472 See ATTITUDE (BROOKLYN (NEW YORK, N.Y.)). 1310

0882-3480 See PERFORMANCE REVIEW (RESTON, VA.), THE. 1199

0882-3499 See SOFT-LETTER. 1290

0882-3502 See SUCCESSFUL ADVERTISING STRATEGIES. 767

0882-3510 See SOCIAL MARKETING UPDATE. 936

0882-3529 See SOCIAL MARKETING UPDATE. 5219

0882-3537 See ENERGY POLICY STUDIES (NEWARK, DEL.). 1941

0882-3545 See PASTOR'S STORY FILE, THE. 4985

0882-3553 See INTERNATIONAL HIGH TECHNOLOGY REPORT. 5115

0882-3561 See COOKSTOVE NEWS. 5097

0882-357X See CALIFORNIA HISTORY ACTION. 2725

0882-3618 See LONG ISLAND DIRECTORY OF MANUFACTURERS. 3482

0882-3626 See LONG ISLAND ASSOCIATION DIRECTORY OF DIVERSIFIED SERVICES. 690

0882-3634 See MARKER (NEW YORK, N.Y.), THE. 3606

0882-3669 See BULLETIN - NATIONAL FOUNDATION FOR UNEMPLOYMENT COMPENSATION & WORKERS' COMPENSATION (U.S.). 1657

0882-3677 See CURRENT AWARENESS SERVICE (CAMBRIDGE, MASS.). 3205

0882-3685 See PENNSYLVANIA GENEALOGICAL MAGAZINE, THE. 2467

0882-3693 See CENTRAL TEXAS ARCHEOLOGIST. 265

0882-3707 See ECOS CRISTOFOROS. 4955

0882-3715 See FINEST HOUR. 2688

0882-3723 See FOURTH WORLD JOURNAL. 1491

0882-3731 See RIGHT OF AESTHETIC REALISM TO BE KNOWN, THE. 4360

0882-374X See SNAKE RIVER ECHOES. 2760

0882-3758 See THERMOLOGY. 3645

0882-3766 See GOVERNMENT RESEARCH DIRECTORY. 5108

0882-3774 See NEWSLETTER / FREMONT-CUSTER HISTORICAL SOCIETY. 2749

0882-3790 See FLORA-LINE, THE. 2435

0882-3804 See LETTER EXCHANGE, THE. 3404

0882-3812 See NATURAL RESOURCES & ENVIRONMENT. 3114

0882-3820 See CLEAN YIELD, THE. 895

0882-3863 See EQUITY AND CHOICE. 1744

0882-3871 See JOURNAL OF COST ANALYSIS, THE. 747

0882-3901 See INFORME COLOMBIANO. 2739

0882-3979 See MCGRAW-HILL'S COMPUTER CAREERS. 4206

0882-4002 See SOVIET JOURNAL OF COMPUTER AND SYSTEMS SCIENCES. 1221

0882-4010 See MICROBIAL PATHOGENESIS. 3715

0882-4029 See UNITARIAN UNIVERSALISM. 5068

0882-4045 See LIST OF CLASSES OF UNITED STATES GOVERNMENT PUBLICATIONS AVAILABLE FOR SELECTION BY DEPOSITORY LIBRARIES. 419

0882-4096 See COMMUNICATION RESEARCH REPORTS. 1107

0882-4126 See HIGHER EDUCATION (NEW YORK, N.Y. : 1985). 1828

0882-4142 See IVY JOURNAL. 514

0882-4150 See HAMERSKY & ALLIED FAMILIES NEWSLETTER. 2452

0882-4193 See BEST FESTIVALS OF NORTH AMERICA. 383

0882-4207 See WASHINGTON RETAIL REPORT. 958

0882-4223 See NEWSLETTER / MAINE HISTORICAL SOCIETY. 2749

0882-4231 See MEMBERSHIP SURNAME LIST. 2460

0882-4258 See EXCELLENCE IN HIGHWAY DESIGN. 2023

0882-4266 See MOUNTAIN EMPIRE GENEALOGICAL QUARTERLY, THE. 2461

0882-4274 See ACGIH TRANSACTIONS. 2858

0882-4290 See METRO (SAN JOSE, CALIF.). 2538

0882-4312 See BERKELEY WOMEN'S LAW JOURNAL. 2941

0882-4339 See NATIONAL PRESERVATION NEWS. 3233

0882-4355 See BETWEEN OUR SELVES. 5192

0882-4371 See CULTURAL CRITIQUE. 5197

0882-438X See AMS STUDIES IN EDUCATION. 1724

0882-4398 See SOCIAL ONCOLOGY NETWORK ... NEWSLETTER. 5259

0882-4428 See BEAN HOME NEWSLETTER, THE. 1060

0882-4436 See BUSINFO. 654

0882-4452 See LIFE SKILLS NEWS. 2791

0882-4460 See CHOCOLATE SINGLES. 2258

0882-4479 See CONTEMPORARY HEALTH JOURNAL. 4772

0882-4487 See AMERICAN INDIAN REGISTRY FOR THE PERFORMING ARTS, THE. 383

0882-4495 See AMERICAN INDIAN TALENT DIRECTORY. 383

0882-4509 See CUNY-INDUSTRY FORUM SERIES, THE. 1819

0882-4517 See JOURNAL OF RESEARCH OF THE AMERICAN FEDERATION OF ASTROLOGERS. 390

0882-4568 See GREEN BOOK (MEMPHIS, TENN.). 1607

0882-4584 See TECHNOLOGY ASSESSMENT AND RESEARCH PROGRAM FOR OFFSHORE MINERALS OPERATIONS. 2244

0882-4614 See GERIATRIC MEDICINE ANNUAL. 3751

0882-4630 See NASFAA NEWSLETTER. 1866

0882-4657 See EXERCISE FOR MEN ONLY. 2597

0882-4681 See CORPORATE TIMES. 1602

0882-469X See VIEWS & VISIONS. 3879

0882-4711 See EXPORT TODAY. 834

0882-472X See WHAT'S LINE. 3256

0882-4738 See UTAH STATE BULLETIN. 3070

0882-4762 See MARKETING TRENDS (ED. FRANCAISE). 932

0882-4770 See MARKETING TRENDS (DEUTSCHE AUSG.). 932

0882-4789 See MARKETING TRENDS (ED. ESPANOLA). 932

0882-4797 See MARKETING TRENDS (ED. ITALIANA). 932

0882-4843 See FEMINIST TEACHER. 1894

0882-486X See DORIS LESSING NEWSLETTER. 3382

0882-4894 See HIGH PLAINS APPLIED ANTHROPOLOGIST. 237

0882-4908 See JUKEBOX COLLECTOR. 4127

0882-4924 See BANKRUPTCY LAW HANDBOOK. 3085

0882-4932 See ARIZONA PORTFOLIO, THE. 337

ISSN Index

0882-4940 See ROCKWALL TEXAS SUCCESS, THE. 5754

0882-4959 See IEEE TRANSLATION JOURNAL ON MAGNETICS IN JAPAN. 4444

0882-4983 See GEOTECHNICAL FABRICS REPORT. 5351

0882-4991 See USDF DRESSAGE INSTRUCTORS, CLINICIANS, TRAINERS, JUDGES, TECHNICAL DELEGATES DIRECTORY. 2803

0882-5009 See USDF CALENDAR OF COMPETITIONS. 2803

0882-5025 See CLASS OF ... EMPLOYMENT REPORT AND SALARY SURVEY. 1659

0882-5033 See DIRECTORY OF LEGAL EMPLOYERS (1985). 2962

0882-5041 See FEDERAL AND STATE JUDICIAL CLERKSHIP DIRECTORY. 2968

0882-5106 See GENEALOGY GLEANINGS. 2450

0882-5130 See USDF BULLETIN. 2803

0882-5149 See NATIONAL CATTLE FEEDLOT, MEAT PACKER AND GRAIN DEALERS DIRECTORY. 216

0882-5203 See ANNUAL REPORT OF THE U.S. DEPARTMENT OF HEALTH AND HUMAN SERVICES TO THE CONGRESS OF THE UNITED STATES ON SERVICES PROVIDED TO HANDICAPPED CHILDREN IN PROJECT HEAD START. 5272

0882-522X See TO YOUR GOOD HEALTH. 4805

0882-5270 See PRODUCER PRICE INDEXES (EXPANDED VERSION). 1622

0882-5297 See AFRO-AMERICAN CULTURE SOCIETY MONOGRAPH SERIES. 2717

0882-5319 See CONVENTION REPORTER. 3568

0882-5335 See TEXAS NATURAL HISTORY. 4173

0882-5343 See BOOKS FOR CHILDREN WASHINGTON, D.C.). 4825

0882-5351 See AMERICAN MAGAZINE AND HISTORICAL CHRONICLE, THE. 2719

0882-536X See DIRECTORY OF HARDLINES DISTRIBUTORS. 2811

0882-5394 See HADRONIC JOURNAL SUPPLEMENT. 4404

0882-5408 See PLANETARY ENCOUNTER. 398

0882-5424 See TAPORI. 1070

0882-5432 See BILL DANIELS' ILLUSTRATED TRADE REFERENCES. PROFESSIONAL AUDIO AND COMMERCIAL/INDUSTRIAL SOUND EQUIPMENT BUYERS' GUIDE. 4452

0882-5440 See STANDARD & POOR'S EMERGING & SPECIAL SITUATIONS. 915

0882-5467 See STOCK MARKET ENCYCLOPEDIA (1985). 916

0882-5475 See HUMANITIES EDUCATION. 2847

0882-5483 See ARKANSAS ARCHEOLOGICAL SURVEY TECHNICAL PAPER. 259

0882-5491 See ARKANSAS ARCHEOLOGICAL SURVEY RESEARCH SERIES. 259

0882-5505 See FRANCHISE HANDBOOK, THE. 1297

0882-5513 See PREVENTION UPDATE NEWSLETTER. 5301

0882-5521 See TAFT NONPROFIT EXECUTIVE, THE. 887

0882-553X See SPORTSEARCH. 4856

0882-5572 See ARIZONA WILDLIFE VIEWS. 2187

0882-5580 See EMPLOYEE BENEFIT PLANS UNDER ERISA. 3146

0882-5602 See BIENNIAL SURVEY OF UNIVERSITIES OFFERING AN ORGANIZED CURRICULUM IN COMMERCE AND BUSINESS ADMINISTRATION. 1811

0882-5610 See WORLD WARSHIPS FORECAST. 4185

0882-5629 See COMPUTER SOFTWARE/HARDWARE INDEX. 1284

0882-5645 See TOPICS IN PAIN MANAGEMENT. 3646

0882-5653 See BURIED TREASURES. 2441

0882-5688 See BROADCAST EQUIPMENT BUYERS GUIDE (SHAWNEE MISSION, KAN.). 1127

0882-5696 See HAZARDOUS WASTE & HAZARDOUS MATERIALS. 2231

0882-570X See JOURNAL OF AUTOMATION AND INFORMATION SCIENCES. 1220

0882-5726 See DATA BROADCASTING REPORT. 1131

0882-5734 See FLAVOUR AND FRAGRANCE JOURNAL. 2335

0882-5750 See STUDIES IN PHILANTHROPY (WASHINGTON, D.C.). 4339

0882-5769 See ORGANIZATION TRENDS. 4338

0882-5777 See ADVANCING CONVERTING AND PACKAGING TECHNOLOGIES. 4217

0882-584X See URBAN WILDLIFE MANAGER'S NOTEBOOK. 2208

0882-5858 See URBAN WILDLIFE NEWS. 2222

0882-5866 See ACADEMIC TALENT. 1721

0882-5890 See SCHARTZER-SCHERTZER CONNECTION, THE. 2471

0882-5904 See SCHNEIDER CONNECTIONS. 2471

0882-5912 See PATENTS (HADLEY, N.Y.), THE. 2466

0882-5920 See GIRLS' AND WOMEN'S TAEKWONDO NEWSLETTER, THE. 4896

0882-5939 See SLOANE REPORT, THE. 1203

0882-5947 See INDEX TO SCIENCE FICTION ORIGINAL ANTHOLOGIES. 3396

0882-5963 See JOURNAL OF PEDIATRIC NURSING. 3859

0882-5971 See GEORGIA TREND. 1492

0882-598X See HEALTH LETTER (WASHINGTON, D.C.). 3582

0882-5998 See YEAR BOOK OF HEMATOLOGY, THE. 3774

0882-6005 See DIRECTORY OF CONSULTANTS IN BIOTECHNOLOGY, THE. 3691

0882-6021 See DIRECTORY OF CONSULTANTS IN PLASTICS AND CHEMICALS, THE. 4454

0882-6048 See DIRECTORY OF CONSULTANTS IN ENVIRONMENTAL SCIENCE, THE. 2163

0882-6056 See DIRECTORY OF CONSULTANTS IN LASERS AND PHYSICS, THE. 4401

0882-6064 See DIRECTORY OF CONSULTANTS IN ELECTRONICS, THE. 2042

0882-6072 See HYPNOSIS REPORTS. 2858

0882-6110 See ADVANCES IN ACCOUNTING. 738

0882-6129 See ADVANCES IN GEOPHYSICAL DATA PROCESSING. 1402

0882-6137 See ADVANCES IN MAN-MACHINE SYSTEMS RESEARCH. 2034

0882-6145 See ADVANCES IN GROUP PROCESSES. 5238

0882-6188 See GROUNDWATER MONITOR. 1414

0882-6196 See READING PLUS (NEW YORK, N.Y.). 3428

0882-6218 See BARNARD'S RETAIL MARKETING REPORT. 861

0882-6234 See SOCIAL SECURITY ALERT (1985). 2893

0882-6242 See OWNER AND MANAGER. 881

0882-6250 See EMPLOYMENT ALERT. 3147

0882-6269 See GEMSTONE REGISTRY BULLETIN, THE. 2914

0882-6277 See IMPACT BEVERAGE TRENDS IN AMERICA REVIEW AND FORECAST, THE. 2367

0882-6307 See VIRGINIA SAGE'S MANAGEMENT TECHNOLOGY. 889

0882-6323 See OBER INCOME LETTER. 910

0882-6331 See NETWORK NEWS (WASHINGTON, D.C. 1982). 4529

0882-6366 See WORKERS' ADVOCATE SUPPLEMENT, THE. 4500

0882-6374 See LCPA'S INDEX TO LIBRARY OF CONGRESS INFORMATION BULLETIN. 3223

0882-6382 See NEW & EMERGING TECHNOLOGY. 5132

0882-6390 See CHILDSCOPE. 3902

0882-6404 See JOURNAL OF INDUSTRIAL TECHNOLOGY / THE NATIONAL ASSOCIATION OF INDUSTRIAL TECHNOLOGY. 5118

0882-6447 See CADUCEUS (SPRINGFIELD, ILL.). 3561

0882-6463 See EXECUTIVE PC LETTER, THE. 867

0882-648X See BOGG (ARLINGTON, VA.). 3368

0882-6501 See AVOTAYNU. 2438

0882-6528 See ST. CLAIR COUNTY GENEALOGICAL SOCIETY QUARTERLY. 2473

0882-6536 See NFF UPDATE. 4484

0882-6587 See GOVERNMENT MICROCOMPUTER LETTER. 1267

0882-6595 See BLACFAX. 2256

0882-6609 See VISION (PASADENA, CALIF.). 5008

0882-6617 See CLINICAL UPDATE. 3566

0882-665X See SMART CARDS AND COMMENTS. 1227

0882-6676 See WHEEL-O-RAMA. 5428

0882-6684 See DRUG THERAPY TOPICS. 4301

0882-6714 See JOURNAL OF THE AMERICAN ACADEMY OF MATRIMONIAL LAWYERS, THE. 3121

0882-6730 See INTERNATIONAL AEROSPACE DIRECTORY. 24

0882-6765 See HOFSTRA ENVIRONMENTAL LAW DIGEST. 3113

0882-6773 See NEWKIRK NOTES. 2462

0882-6781 See PROFESSIONAL OFFICE DESIGN. 2902

0882-679X See REPORT TO THE GOVERNORS. 4682

0882-6811 See KILT AND HARP, THE. 4128

0882-6838 See ART TO ZOO. 1888

0882-6846 See NEWSLETTER - CONSORTIUM OF RHODE ISLAND ACADEMIC AND RESEARCH LIBRARIES. 3235

0882-6862 See ST. GAME. 1230

0882-6870 See DIRECTORY OF ACCREDITED INSTITUTIONS, CANDIDATES FOR ACCREDITATION. 1820

0882-6897 See ANTIQUE TRADER ANTIQUES & COLLECTIBLES PRICE GUIDE, THE. 249

0882-6935 See QUADRENNIAL REVIEW OF MILITARY COMPENSATION. 4054

0882-6943 See UTILIZATION OF SHORT-TERM GENERAL AND SPECIALTY HOSPITALS IN METROPOLITAN CHICAGO FOR THE YEAR ENDING DECEMBER 31 3793

0882-696X See GUTHRIE JOURNAL OF THE DONALD GUTHRIE FOUNDATION FOR MEDICAL RESEARCH, THE. 3579

0882-6994 See SOVIET ECONOMY (SILVER SPRING, MD.). 1640

0882-7001 See INSIDE DIRECT MARKETING. 926

0882-701X See DIRECT RESPONSE MARKETING TO SCHOOLS NEWSLETTER. 923

0882-7028 See WAVE (ROCKAWAY BEACH, N.Y.), THE. 5722

0882-7036 See PREACHING (JACKSONVILLE, FLA.). 4987

0882-7087 See OPUS INCERTUM. 305

0882-7095 See DDR-STUDIEN. 2685

0882-7133 See ANNUAL DEGARMO LECTURE. 1724

0882-715X See PRESERVATION LAW REPORTER. 3030

0882-7176 See CORPORATE GIVING DIRECTORY. 4335

0882-7214 See UNITED CHURCH NEWS (NATIONAL EDITION). 5731

0882-7230 See PUBLIC WORKS PRO-VIEWS. 883

0882-7249 See FACILITIES MANAGER : THE OFFICIAL PUBLICATION OF THE ASSOCIATION OF PHYSICAL PLANT ADMINISTRATORS OF UNIVERSITIES AND COLLEGES. 867

0882-729X See BEST BUYS & DISCOUNT PRICES. 1293

0882-7311 See STALKER. 2473

0882-732X See TIMBER MART-SOUTH ... YEARBOOK. 2405

0882-7362 See KIT GUNS & HOBBY GUNSMITHING. 2774

0882-7370 See THREADS MAGAZINE. 5359

0882-7400 See PUBLISHED. 3426

0882-7419 See POWERTECHNICS MAGAZINE. 4417

0882-7427 See SPECIAL REPORT IN APPLIED MARINE SCIENCE AND OCEAN ENGINEERING. 2095

0882-7443 See SOFTWHERE. MANUFACTURING. 1291

0882-7451 See BRIDAL GUIDE. 2277

0882-7478 See NEWS LETTER / PRESERVATION LEAGUE OF NEW YORK STATE. 304

0882-7486 See CRAFT SHOW DIGEST. 371

0882-7508 See MINERAL PROCESSING AND EXTRACTIVE METALLURGY REVIEW. 2144

0882-7516 See ACTIVE AND PASSIVE ELECTRONIC COMPONENTS. 2034

0882-7524 See TOPICS IN GERIATRIC REHABILITATION. 3755

0882-7532 See BLACK VIDEO GUIDE, THE. 4064

0882-7559 See GOFFS/GOUGHS, THEIR ANCESTORS & DESCENDANTS. 2451

0882-7583 See ANNUAL REPORT - UTAH. DEPT. OF NATURAL RESOURCES. 4630

0882-7591 See CORPORATE FINANCE (NEW YORK, N.Y. 1991). 785

0882-7613 See DACS ANNOTATED BIBLIOGRAPHY. ANNUAL SUPPLEMENT, THE. 1362

0882-7621 See CODE NAME DIRECTORY. US. 4039

0882-763X See CURRENT FEDERAL AID RESEARCH REPORT. FISH. 2299

0882-7664 See COMMERCIAL REAL ESTATE BROKERS DIRECTORY, THE. 4835

0882-7699 See SOFTWHERE. EDUCATION COURSEWARE. 1291

0882-7702 See SOFTWARE. EDUCATION ADMINISTRATION. 1290

0882-7729 See CHRISTIAN SCIENCE MONITOR (1983), THE. 5688

0882-7737 See EUROPEAN TRAVEL & LIFE. 5469

0882-7745 See DIRECTORY OF UNITED STATES TRADITIONAL AND ALTERNATIVE COLLEGES AND UNIVERSITIES. 1821

0882-7753 See REHABILITATION R&D PROGRESS REPORTS. 4382

0882-7761 See COLUMBUS AND CENTRAL OHIO HISTORIAN. 2729

0882-7788 See SOUTHERN SHIPPER. 5457

0882-7818 See COMPUTER BUYING GUIDE. 1266

0882-7842 See CALIFORNIA FAMILY LAW MONTHLY. 3119

0882-7877 See JOHN HORAN'S SPORTS INK. 4901

0882-7893 See JOURNAL OF INTERPRETATION (SILVER SPRING, MD.). 5292

0882-7907 See HURRICANE ALICE. 5558

0882-7915 See CURRENTS (CHAPEL HILL, N.C.). 4189

0882-7958 See ADVANCED MATERIALS & PROCESSES. 2100

0882-7966 See INTERNATIONAL BAROMETER. 5204

0882-7974 See PSYCHOLOGY AND AGING. 4612

0882-7982 See YARN MARKET NEWS. 5360

0882-8059 See INTERMODAL REPORTER. 5384

0882-8067 See NEW ACCOUNTANT. 749

0882-8075 See NODE, THE. 5211

0882-8083 See HEMATOLOGY REVIEWS AND COMMUNICATIONS. 3772

0882-8091 See SPEEDX. 1122

0882-8121 See MATHEMATICAL GEOLOGY. 1386

0882-8156 See WEATHER AND FORECASTING. 1436

0882-8164 See ENVIRONMENTAL CARCINOGENESIS REVIEWS. 3816

0882-8180 See KICK (NEW YORK, N.Y. 1983). 4903

0882-8199 See SPEEDXGRAM. 1122

0882-8202 See BARRON FAMILY NEWSLETTER, THE. 2438

0882-8229 See MUSIC REVELATION. 4134

0882-8245 See VIRAL IMMUNOLOGY. 3677

0882-8253 See ADVERTISING CAREER DIRECTORY. 754

0882-8261 See BOOK PUBLISHING CAREER DIRECTORY. 4825

0882-8288 See PUBLIC RELATIONS CAREER DIRECTORY. 764

0882-8296 See PETERSON DIRECTORY. 1161

0882-8318 See INDEX TO CHIROPRACTIC LITERATURE. 3804

0882-8326 See ANNUAL REPORT - CALIFORNIA. DEPT. OF FORESTRY. 2374

0882-8334 See LONG-TERM BENTHIC MONITORING PROGRAMS NEAR THE MORGANTOWN AND CALBERT CLIFFS POWER PLANTS. 1949

0882-8377 See G.A.S. LITES. 2449

0882-8458 See WOMEN'S TRAVEL CONNECTIONS. 5499

0882-8474 See NEWSLETTER (AFRO-AMERICAN HISTORICAL AND GENEALOGICAL SOCIETY (WASHINGTON, D.C.) : 1983). 2749

0882-8482 See LIFELONG LEARNING (BERKELEY, CALIF.). 1761

0882-8490 See FILMS/VIDEO. 1132

0882-8504 See JOURNAL OF THE ARTISTS' CHOICE MUSEUM, THE. 4090

0882-8512 See FREETHOUGHT TODAY. 4960

0882-8520 See YOUTH LAW NEWS. 3122

0882-8539 See SHOFAR (WEST LAFAYETTE, IND.). 5052

0882-8547 See BUSINESS UNIV. JOURNAL, THE. 1172

0882-8555 See MEDICAL MALPRACTICE LITIGATION REPORTER. 3008

0882-8571 See ARTS CALENDAR QUARTERLY, THE. 314

0882-858X See SAFETY MANUAL / HELICOPTER ASSOCIATION INTERNATIONAL. 34

0882-861X See ENGINEERING LITERATURE GUIDES. 1973

0882-8628 See PRESCRIPTION DRUG NEWS. 4325

0882-8652 See HYPNOTHERAPY TODAY. 2858

0882-8660 See TECHNOLOGY ASSESSMENT (COMPUTER/ELECTRONICS ED.). 5163

0882-8679 See QUARTERLY REPORT (MERCER ISLAND, WASH.), THE. 706

0882-8687 See POPHAM FAMILY NEWSLETTER. 2468

0882-8695 See ATHENS NEWS (ATHENS, OHIO). 5726

0882-8709 See CORPORATE TRAVEL. 5467

0882-8725 See COLORADO WHEAT GROWER. 167

0882-8733 See REAL ESTATE DIGEST, THE. 4844

0882-8741 See ST. GEORGE MAGAZINE. 5491

0882-8768 See PLAY IT SAFE. 703

0882-8776 See QUALITY AND PRODUCTIVITY PLUS. 706

0882-8792 See CENTRAL NEVADA'S GLORIOUS PAST. 2727

0882-8806 See COURTNEY CHRONICLE. 2444

0882-8849 See TEXAS A & M BUSINESS FORUM. 715

0882-8857 See CIVILIAN MANPOWER STATISTICS. 4061

0882-8881 See CINCINNATI BUSINESS COURIER. 657

0882-889X See METABOLIC, PEDIATRIC AND SYSTEMIC OPHTHALMOLOGY (1985). 3876

0882-8938 See OVERSEAS LIVING. 2542

0882-8962 See WASHINGTON-AREA MICROCOMPUTER DIRECTORY, THE. 1273

0882-8970 See COMPETITORS AND COMPETITION OF THE U.S. POSTAL SERVICE. 1144

0882-8989 See BIBLIOGRAPHY OF PUBLICATIONS RESULTING FROM NCHSR EXTRAMURAL RESEARCH. 4809

0882-8997 See ANNUAL REPORT / MARYLAND COMMISSION ON HEREDITARY DISORDERS. 542

0882-9012 See TOWARD CLOSER TIES. 1850

0882-9055 See CARPENTER (NEW YORK, N.Y.), THE. 633

0882-9071 See ONCE UPON A TIME (ARLINGTON, TEX.). 2786

0882-908X See FLICC NEWSLETTER. 3211

0882-9098 See JOURNAL OF THE PATENT AND TRADEMARK OFFICE SOCIETY. 1305

0882-9136 See COMPILATION OF STATE AND FEDERAL PRIVACY LAWS. 2954

0882-9144 See REAL ESTATE ANALYSIS AND PLANNING SERVICE. 4843

0882-9152 See ... HOMECARE MARKET REPORT, THE. 3584

0882-9187 See MINIATURES DEALER (CLIFTON, VA. : 1985). 2774

0882-9209 See GEORGIA ARMCHAIR RESEARCHER, THE. 2451

0882-9217 See RECOMMENDATIONS AND REPORTS / ADMINISTRATIVE CONFERENCE OF THE UNITED STATES. 4678

0882-9225 See PEDIATRIC REVIEWS AND COMMUNICATION. 3909

0882-9233 See SURGICAL RESEARCH COMMUNICATIONS. 3976

0882-9276 See ISSUE PAPER / U.S. COMMITTEE FOR REFUGEES. 1919

0882-9292 See AGRI-NATURALIST. 47

0882-9314 See PERFORMANCE (FORT WORTH, TEX.). 387

0882-9322 See CHARLOTTESVILLE ALBEMARLE OBSERVER. 5758

0882-9365 See AAHS JOURNAL. 3

0882-9403 See SENIOR CITIZENS ADVOCATE AND ASPECTS OF AGING. 5181

0882-9411 See JASA SHARE. 5205

0882-942X See CHILDREN & TEENS TODAY. 5278

0882-9438 See FLORIDA MANUFACTURERS REGISTER. 3479

0882-9446 See INTERNATIONAL BIBLIOGRAPHY OF THEATRE. 5372

0882-9462 See NEW MOTON GUIDE TO AMERICAN COLLEGES WITH A BLACK HERITAGE, THE. 1837

0882-9470 See NEW MOTON GUIDE TO AMERICAN COLLEGES WITH A BLACK HERITAGE, THE. 1837

0882-9489 See GOING PUBLIC. 789

0882-9527 See NEWSLETTER / STANISLAUS COUNTY GENEALOGICAL SOCIETY. 2464

0882-9543 See DENTAL HYGIENE NEWS (ROCHESTER, N.Y.). 1321

0882-956X See ACCOUNTING EDUCATION NEWS. 736

0882-9616 See TUCKERTON BEACON (TUCKERTON, N.J. : 1985). 5712

0882-9624 See POA (1985). 2801

0882-9632 See SOCCER TEXAS. 4919

0882-9640 See WISCONSIN SILENT SPORTS. 4930

0882-9683 See EMBASSY REPORT (LATIN AMERICA & CARIBBEAN ED.). 4520

0882-9691 See WHEAT GROWER (WASHINGTON, D.C.), THE. 146

0882-9748 See PREPARING PERSONAL INJURY CASES FOR TRIAL. 3030

0882-9756 See MAJALLAT AL-SALAM. 5039

0882-9802 See KINSHIP KRONICLE. 2457

0882-9837 See DATA ON VIETNAM ERA VETERANS. 4062

0882-9845 See ANNUAL REPORT - LOUISIANA STATE BAR ASSOCIATION. 2934

0882-9853 See CUYAHOGA CRIMINAL DEFENSE LAWYERS ASSOCIATION NEWSLETTER. 3106

0882-987X See CHAMBERLAIN ASSOCIATION NEWS. 2442

0882-9950 See LEVERAGED LEASING. 3002

0883-0029 See AEGIS (WASHINGTON, D.C.). 4503

0883-0053 See EX AUDITU. 4958

0883-0061 See KEEPER'S LOG. 2026

0883-007X See DAIRY (SAINT PAUL, MINN.). 194

0883-0088 See AGRICULTURAL ECONOMICS TECHNICAL PUBLICATION. 50

0883-0096 See AEROSPACE INFORMATION REPORT. 5

ISSN Index

0883-0118 *See* SAN BERNARDINO, RIVERSIDE COUNTIES STREET ATLAS AND DIRECTORY (ZIP CODE ED.). **2575**

0883-0126 *See* RED BASS. **329**

0883-0142 *See* AMARANTH TODAY. **162**

0883-0185 *See* INTERNATIONAL REVIEWS OF IMMUNOLOGY. **3672**

0883-0215 *See* NEW MENORAH. **4981**

0883-0223 *See* FRANKIE CROCKER'S MUSIC TRACK. **4118**

0883-024X *See* ANTHROPOLOGY OF WORK REVIEW. **230**

0883-0258 *See* DIMENSIONAL STONE. **613**

0883-0266 *See* MONTHLY PRESCRIBING REFERENCE. **3618**

0883-0290 *See* CLINICAL UPDATE IN PEDIATRICS. **3902**

0883-0304 *See* TRAUMA (PRINCETON, N.J.). **3977**

0883-0312 *See* DIRECTIONS IN ONCOLOGY. **3816**

0883-0320 *See* CLINICAL OPHTHALMOLOGY UPDATE. **3873**

0883-0339 *See* CLINICAL UPDATE IN NEPHROLOGY. **3796**

0883-0347 *See* US SWIMMING NEWS. **4927**

0883-0355 *See* INTERNATIONAL JOURNAL OF EDUCATIONAL RESEARCH. **1897**

0883-0436 *See* HOME CENTER PRODUCTS REPORT. **839**

0883-0444 *See* JOURNAL OF REFRACTIVE AND CORNEAL SURGERY. **3597**

0883-0452 *See* HEALTHSPAN. **3740**

0883-0487 *See* LETTER OF CREDIT UPDATE. **796**

0883-0495 *See* MMD 1,000, THE. **933**

0883-0517 *See* CURRENT ISSUES IN INTERNATIONAL SHIP FINANCE. **2957**

0883-0525 *See* LAW OFFICE MANAGEMENT (1981). **2996**

0883-055X *See* CURRENT DEVELOPMENTS IN BANKRUPTCY AND REORGANIZATION. **3086**

0883-0568 *See* ALASKA LAW REVIEW. **2929**

0883-0576 *See* TOXIC SUBSTANCES CONTROL ACT. **3116**

0883-0606 *See* DRIS CATALOG OF SUPPORT SERVICES. **4043**

0883-0622 *See* CANADIAN TREASURY SERVICES. **4716**

0883-072X *See* AMERICAN INTELLIGENCE JOURNAL. **4034**

0883-0738 *See* JOURNAL OF CHILD NEUROLOGY. **3904**

0883-0746 *See* LANDLORD VS. TENANT/NYC. **2993**

0883-0754 *See* EXPERIMENTAL MUSICAL INSTRUMENTS. **4117**

0883-0797 *See* JUST CROSSSTITCH. **5184**

0883-0827 *See* AAEL NEWS BULLETIN. **768**

0883-0835 *See* HOMEHEALTH MAGAZINE. **4783**

0883-0843 *See* GUARDMOUNT. **3182**

0883-0851 *See* HUMAN RESOURCES NEWSLETTER. **942**

0883-086X *See* ITALIANO (NEW YORK, N.Y.), L'. **2693**

0883-0878 *See* BIOPROCESS ENGINEERING. **1966**

0883-0908 *See* STRESS AND COPING. **4619**

0883-0916 *See* ACCESS (MILWAUKEE, WIS.). **636**

0883-0924 *See* LEGAL ASPECTS OF PSYCHIATRIC PRACTICE. **2999**

0883-0932 *See* TRANSPORTING PERSONAL FIREARMS. **5397**

0883-0940 *See* CLOUD FAMILY JOURNAL. **2443**

0883-0959 *See* LAW LETTER & JOURNAL. **2995**

0883-0967 *See* ANNUAL REPORT / VIRGINIA AGRICULTURAL DEVELOPMENT AUTHORITY. **61**

0883-0975 *See* DIRECTORY OF AMERICAN FULBRIGHT SCHOLARS : UNIVERSITY LECTURING & ADVANCED RESEARCH ABROAD. **1820**

0883-0991 *See* AMERICAN SPACEMODELLING. **2771**

0883-1009 *See* CROSS COUNTY GENEALOGICAL PUBLICATION. **2444**

0883-1017 *See* ANNUAL REPORT / VIRGINIA AGRICULTURAL FOUNDATION. **61**

0883-105X *See* AMERICAN STUDIES INTERNATIONAL. **2719**

0883-1068 *See* AMERICAN STUDIES INTERNATIONAL NEWSLETTER. **2719**

0883-1106 *See* WXXI PROGRAM GUIDE (1985). **1143**

0883-1122 *See* DANCE MUSIC REPORT. **4113**

0883-1157 *See* ROMANCE QUARTERLY. **3318**

0883-1173 *See* ABOUT ALFORDS. **2436**

0883-1181 *See* CHAPMAN CHATTER. **2442**

0883-119X *See* WISE WOMAN, THE. **5568**

0883-1203 *See* ABMS DIRECTORY OF CERTIFIED PATHOLOGISTS. **3892**

0883-1211 *See* ABMS DIRECTORY OF CERTIFIED ORTHOPAEDIC SURGEONS. **3880**

0883-122X *See* ABMS DIRECTORY OF CERTIFIED ANESTHESIOLOGISTS. **3680**

0883-1262 *See* ADVANCED MICRO DEVICES ... ANNUAL PROCEEDINGS. **1265**

0883-1297 *See* LEGAL INFORMATION ALERT. **3081**

0883-1300 *See* SCP JOURNAL. **4995**

0883-1319 *See* SCP NEWSLETTER. **4996**

0883-1327 *See* EDUTECH REPORT, THE. **1223**

0883-1335 *See* TAX FOUNDATION'S TAX FEATURES. **4752**

0883-1343 *See* ICMM NEWS. **4089**

0883-1351 *See* PALAIOS. **4229**

0883-136X *See* JOHN NAISBITT'S TREND LETTER. **1569**

0883-1378 *See* JOURNAL OF INFERENTIAL AND DEDUCTIVE BIOLOGY. **461**

0883-1394 *See* PAPILLION TIMES. **5707**

0883-1416 *See* CHANGING WORK (NEW HAVEN, CONN.). **1659**

0883-1467 *See* SESAME (MEDFORD, OR.). **4819**

0883-1475 *See* SIDA, BOTANICAL MISCELLANY. **527**

0883-1483 *See* GOVERNMENT ACCOUNTANTS JOURNAL, THE. **744**

0883-1513 *See* HERITAGE. THE YORKER SCENE. **2736**

0883-153X *See* POLYMER CONTENTS. **4461**

0883-1548 *See* BIENNIAL REPORT OF THE NEW YORK STATE SCIENCE SERVICE. **5088**

0883-1556 *See* WORLD DEVELOPMENT FORUM. **1527**

0883-1580 *See* SPORTS PERIODICALS INDEX, THE. **4923**

0883-1602 *See* WILLIAMSON DAILY NEWS. **5765**

0883-1637 *See* GREENBURGH ENQUIRER, THE. **5716**

0883-1645 *See* CALDWELL INFORMER. **5722**

0883-1661 *See* INVESTMENT PORTFOLIO GUIDE. **903**

0883-1688 *See* SHHH. **4393**

0883-170X *See* GREENFIELD QUARTERLY. **2452**

0883-1726 *See* NEWSLETTER - COMMON SHORES. **4842**

0883-1750 *See* MED DEV. **3607**

0883-1777 *See* BARRETT TRANSPORTATION NEWSLETTER. **5377**

0883-1793 *See* EMBASSY REPORT (MIDDLE EAST ED.). **4520**

0883-1807 *See* EMBASSY REPORT (ED. : AUSTRALIA, CANADA, JAPAN NEW ZEALAND, SCANDINAVIA & WESTERN EUROPE). **4520**

0883-1815 *See* EMBASSY REPORT (AFRICA ED.). **4520**

0883-1823 *See* EMBASSY REPORT (ASIA & OCEANIA ED.). **4520**

0883-1831 *See* DSI-RAIL ROUTING SUPPLEMENT, THE. **5431**

0883-1866 *See* COMPUTERS IN ACCOUNTING. **741**

0883-1874 *See* PEDIATRIC ASTHMA, ALLERGY & IMMUNOLOGY. **3908**

0883-1890 *See* ENTERTAINMENT MAGAZINE, THE. **4850**

0883-1904 *See* JEWISH VEGETARIANS OF NORTH AMERICA : NEWSLETTER. **4192**

0883-1912 *See* FOODSERVICE DIRECTORY. **2341**

0883-1920 *See* GALLATIN TRAILS. **2449**

0883-1939 *See* SENIOR CITIZENS WORLD. **5181**

0883-1947 *See* CONGRESSIONAL RECORD (PERMANENT ED.). **2955**

0883-1963 *See* CONSUMER HEALTH & NUTRITION INDEX. **4200**

0883-2013 *See* APHASIA, APRAXIA, AGNOSIA. **3827**

0883-2099 *See* NEWSLETTER OF THE SOUTHWEST VIRGINIA COPENHAVER FAMILY. **2463**

0883-2102 *See* API ACCOUNT, THE. **738**

0883-2188 *See* FARM FINANCIAL CONDITIONS REVIEW. **84**

0883-2234 *See* RETAIL SECURITY MANAGEMENT LETTER. **3175**

0883-2293 *See* PERSON-CENTERED REVIEW. **4607**

0883-2323 *See* JOURNAL OF EDUCATION FOR BUSINESS. **687**

0883-2374 *See* NASSAU LITERARY REVIEW, THE. **1093**

0883-2382 *See* PLEASURE HUNT MAGAZINE. **5489**

0883-2390 *See* AMIGA WORLD. **1264**

0883-2404 *See* PROCEEDINGS OF THE CONFERENCE OF THE AMERICAN ACADEMY OF ADVERTISING (1985). **764**

0883-2447 *See* FINANCIAL SERVICES LAW REPORT. **3086**

0883-2455 *See* ENTERTAINMENT LAW & FINANCE. **2966**

0883-2463 *See* BIRNBAUM'S SOUTH AMERICA. **5464**

0883-2471 *See* BIRNBAUM'S HAWAII. **5464**

0883-248X See BIRNBAUM'S BAHAMAS, TURKS & CAICOS. **5463**

0883-248X See BIRNBAUM'S BERMUDA. **5463**

0883-2498 *See* BIRNBAUM'S EUROPE. **5464**

0883-2501 *See* BIRNBAUM'S UNITED STATES. **5464**

0883-251X *See* BIRNBAUM'S USA FOR BUSINESS TRAVELERS. **5464**

0883-2536 *See* NEWNAN TIMES-HERALD, THE. **5654**

0883-2552 See LMA BUSINESSLETTER, THE. **215**

0883-2560 *See* SPEC-COM. **1139**

0883-2579 *See* PTA BULLETIN. **1869**

0883-2587 *See* SALT (CHICAGO, ILL.). **4995**

0883-2617 *See* FRANCE (NEW YORK, N.Y. 1983). **5474**

0883-2625 *See* MEXICO (NEW YORK, N.Y. 1983). **5484**

0883-2633 *See* ITALY (NEW YORK, N.Y. 1984). **5481**

0883-2641 *See* CANADA (NEW YORK, N.Y. 1983). **5465**

0883-265X *See* STANFORD BUSINESS SCHOOL MAGAZINE. **713**

0883-2692 *See* CLARK CLARION, THE. **2443**

0883-2706 *See* MYERS OF AMERICA. **2461**

0883-2730 *See* OUA/DATA'S ... GUIDE TO CORPORATE GIVING IN MAINE. **4338**

0883-2749 *See* COLONIAL WILLIAMSBURG INTERPRETER, THE. **2729**

0883-2757 *See* UNIVERSITY MONOGRAPHS. **4281**

0883-2765 *See* GLEANINGS (BEAVER FALLS, PA.) **2451**

0883-2773 *See* VENTURE CAPITAL JOURNAL. **919**

0883-2781 *See* COLLAGE (CAMP HILL, PA.). **4760**

0883-2803 *See* CODE NAME DIRECTORY. INTERNATIONAL. **4039**

0883-282X *See* SPECTRUM (WINTER HAVEN, FLA.). **4503**

0883-2846 *See* BROOKLYN LITERARY REVIEW. **1101**

0883-2862 See ANNUAL REPORT - CENTER FOR MATERIALS SCIENCE (NATIONAL MEASUREMENT LABORATORY). 4029

0883-2870 See CITRUS FRUITS (1976). 167

0883-2889 See INTERNATIONAL JOURNAL OF RADIATION APPLICATIONS AND INSTRUMENTATION. PART A, APPLIED RADIATION AND ISOTOPES. 4406

0883-2897 See INTERNATIONAL JOURNAL OF RADIATION APPLICATIONS AND INSTRUMENTATION. PART B, NUCLEAR MEDICINE AND BIOLOGY. 3848

0883-2900 See MATERIALS FORUM. 1986

0883-2919 See WORLD ENGLISHES. 3334

0883-2927 See APPLIED GEOCHEMISTRY. 1366

0883-2943 See CURRENT ALTERNATIVE ENERGY RESEARCH AND DEVELOPMENT IN ILLINOIS. 1936

0883-2951 See TROPHY BIG GAME INVESTIGATIONS AND HUNTING SEASON RECOMMENDATIONS / STATE OF NEVADA, DEPARTMENT OF WILDLIFE, DIVISION OF GAME. 4927

0883-296X See MODERN BLACK MEN. 3996

0883-2978 See ABMS DIRECTORY OF CERTIFIED PREVENTIVE MEDICINE PHYSICIANS. 3543

0883-2986 See ABMS DIRECTORY OF CERTIFIED PHYSICAL MEDICINE AND REHABILITATION PHYSICIANS. 3543

0883-2994 See ABMS DIRECTORY OF CERTIFIED ALLERGY AND IMMUNOLOGY PHYSICIANS. 3662

0883-3001 See ABMS DIRECTORY OF CERTIFIED OTOLARYNGOLOGISTS. 3912

0883-301X See ANNUAL PLANNING INFORMATION. MERCED COUNTY. 1647

0883-3036 See PRACTICE BUILDER, THE. 704

0883-3044 See MINNEAPOLIS/ST. PAUL CITYBUSINESS. 695

0883-3052 See ERISA CITATOR. 1667

0883-3087 See GDG REPORT, THE. 3165

0883-3095 See PRE- AND PERI-NATAL PSYCHOLOGY JOURNAL. 3767

0883-3117 See COLLISION ESTIMATING GUIDE, DOMESTIC OLDER MODELS. 5411

0883-3125 See STAR TREK III. 4078

0883-3133 See Y WEEKLY, THE. 5756

0883-3141 See STEELABOR. 1712

0883-3176 See ANNUAL REPORT - NATIONAL CANCER INSTITUTE (U.S.). DIVISION OF CANCER PREVENTION AND CONTROL. 3808

0883-3222 See ANNUAL REPORT - OREGON. SOLID WASTE DIVISION. 2224

0883-3249 See ANNUAL REPORT - MARYLAND. ADVISORY COUNCIL ON ALCOHOLISM CONTROL. 1341

0883-329X See ANNUAL REPORT OF THE FARM CREDIT ADMINISTRATION. 61

0883-3303 See ANNUAL REPORT - ARIZONA. OFFICE OF THE STATE CLIMATOLOGIST. 1420

0883-3311 See NRC TLD DIRECT RADIATION MONITORING NETWORK. 4438

0883-3338 See ILLINOIS LABOR MARKET REVIEW. 1677

0883-3370 See FEDERAL BENEFITS FOR VETERANS AND DEPENDENTS. 4044

0883-3389 See RENATO ROSALDO LECTURE SERIES MONOGRAPH. 2272

0883-3397 See SMALL BUSINESS SOURCEBOOK. 711

0883-3400 See SCHOMBURG CENTER JOURNAL, THE. 2272

0883-3419 See FUTURE REFLECTIONS. 4388

0883-3427 See MILITARY BUSINESS REVIEW. 950

0883-3435 See ACID RAIN ESSENTIALS. 2223

0883-3443 See MENTAL HEALTH SYSTEMS SOFTWARE DIRECTORY. 3616

0883-3508 See ANNUAL REPORT / ONONDAGA COUNTY PUBLIC LIBRARY. 3191

0883-3532 See EDITING HISTORY. 4814

0883-3559 See HISTORIANS OF EARLY MODERN EUROPE. 2691

0883-3575 See FOREIGN EXCHANGE LONG-TERM OUTLOOK. 1635

0883-3583 See NORTH AMERICAN DIRECTORY & REFERENCE GUIDE OF ASIAN INDIAN BUSINESSES AND INDEPENDENT PROFESSIONAL PRACTITIONERS ALONG WITH COMMUNITY REFERENCE GUIDE & TRAVEL INFORMATION. 699

0883-363X See GOVERNOR'S OFFICE OF ENERGY RESOURCES ANNUAL REPORT. 1945

0883-3648 See NOTRE DAME JOURNAL OF LAW, ETHICS & PUBLIC POLICY. 3019

0883-3656 See ADVANCES IN APPLIED SOCIAL PSYCHOLOGY. 4571

0883-3664 See ODYSSEUS (FLUSHING, N.Y.). 5487

0883-3680 See MATERIAL CULTURE. 241

0883-3699 See HEALTH CARE EXPENDITURES IN KANSAS. 4810

0883-3710 See SOMETHING SPECIAL PATTERN CLUB. 5186

0883-3753 See GOVERNMENTS OF ALABAMA. 4728

0883-3761 See GOVERNMENTS OF ARKANSAS. 4728

0883-377X See GOVERNMENTS OF CALIFORNIA. 4728

0883-3788 See GOVERNMENTS OF COLORADO. 4728

0883-3796 See GOVERNMENTS OF CONNECTICUT. 4728

0883-380X See GOVERNMENTS OF FLORIDA. 4728

0883-3818 See GOVERNMENTS OF GEORGIA. 4728

0883-3826 See GOVERNMENTS OF ILLINOIS. 4728

0883-3834 See GOVERNMENTS OF INDIANA. 4728

0883-3842 See GOVERNMENTS OF IOWA. 4728

0883-3850 See GOVERNMENTS OF KANSAS. 4728

0883-3869 See GOVERNMENTS OF KENTUCKY. 4728

0883-3877 See GOVERNMENTS OF LOUISIANA. 4728

0883-3885 See GOVERNMENTS OF MAINE. 4728

0883-3893 See GOVERNMENTS OF MASSACHUSETTS. 4728

0883-3907 See GOVERNMENTS OF MICHIGAN. 4728

0883-3915 See GOVERNMENTS OF MINNESOTA. 4728

0883-3923 See GOVERNMENTS OF MISSISSIPPI. 4728

0883-3931 See GOVERNMENTS OF MISSOURI. 4728

0883-394X See GOVERNMENTS OF NEBRASKA. 1493

0883-3958 See GOVERNMENTS OF NEW JERSEY. 4729

0883-3966 See GOVERNMENTS OF NEW YORK. 4729

0883-3974 See GOVERNMENTS OF NORTH DAKOTA. 4729

0883-3982 See GOVERNMENTS OF OHIO. 4729

0883-3990 See GOVERNMENTS OF OKLAHOMA. 4729

0883-4008 See GOVERNMENTS OF PENNSYLVANIA. 4729

0883-4016 See GOVERNMENTS OF SOUTH DAKOTA. 4729

0883-4024 See GOVERNMENTS OF TENNESSEE. 4729

0883-4032 See GOVERNMENTS OF TEXAS. 4729

0883-4040 See GOVERNMENTS OF VERMONT. 4729

0883-4059 See GOVERNMENTS OF VIRGINIA. 4729

0883-4067 See GOVERNMENTS OF WASHINGTON. 4729

0883-4075 See GOVERNMENTS OF WEST VIRGINIA. 4729

0883-4083 See GOVERNMENTS OF WISCONSIN. 4729

0883-4091 See GOVERNMENTS OF THE CAROLINAS. 4729

0883-4105 See GOVERNMENTS OF THE NORTHWEST. 4729

0883-4113 See GOVERNMENTS OF THE WEST. 4729

0883-4121 See GOVERNMENTS OF THE NORTHEAST. 4729

0883-413X See 1,000 LARGEST GOVERNMENTS, THE. 4623

0883-4172 See AAMI MEMBERSHIP DIRECTORY. 3543

0883-4199 See OFFICIAL ... NATIONAL FOOTBALL LEAGUE RECORD & FACT BOOK. 4909

0883-4202 See CYBERNETIC (FAIRFAX, VA.). 1250

0883-4210 See CHRISTIAN ACTIVITIES CALENDAR (MIDDLE ATLANTIC ED.). 4944

0883-4237 See STATISTICAL SCIENCE. 5340

0883-4245 See GAAP. 744

0883-4261 See TEXT ON MICROFORM. 3253

0883-4296 See MICRO ECONOMICS / THE BOSTON COMPUTER SOCIETY. 694

0883-4318 See CONOCO (WILMINGTON, DEL.). 1602

0883-4334 See BAY WINDOWS. 2793

0883-4377 See MINNELLA'S POCKET-GUIDE TO COPIERS. 4212

0883-4385 See MINNESOTA AG MANUAL, THE. 108

0883-4407 See ACQUISITIONS AND MERGERS IN A TROUBLED ENVIRONMENT. 3094

0883-4423 See CALIFORNIA WINE WINNERS. 2366

0883-4431 See GUN TRADER'S GUIDE, THE. 2774

0883-4458 See MONTANA ... NETWORK REVIEW. 2236

0883-4474 See TAX, SEC, AND ACCOUNTING ASPECTS OF CORPORATE ACQUISITIONS. 3104

0883-4482 See SNOW COVER SURVEYS. 1418

0883-4490 See CURRENT EUROPEAN ANAESTHESIOLOGY. 3682

0883-4504 See POLITICAL ISSUES IN NURSING. 3867

0883-4555 See CONSUMER FINANCE LAW QUARTERLY REPORT. 3086

0883-458X See GAS TURBINE WORLD HANDBOOK. 2114

0883-4601 See INTERNATIONAL TREASURY SERVICES. 4733

0883-4628 See NORTH AMERICAN MULTINATIONAL BANKING. 801

0883-4636 See FINANCIAL REPORT / OLD DOMINION UNIVERSITY. 1824

0883-4644 See REPORT TO EXECUTIVES ON LARGE COMPANIES' BANKING PRACTICES. 808

0883-4660 See TRADITIONAL HOME. 2903

0883-4687 See FOREIGN TRADE FAIRS NEW PRODUCTS NEWSLETTER. 836

0883-4695 See ABA SOFTWARE REVIEW. 2926

0883-4709 See JOINT MEMBERSHIP DIRECTORY - AMERICAN SOCIETY OF HUMAN GENETICS. 548

0883-475X See SCHOLASTIC CHOICES. 2792

0883-4792 See WALL STREET JOURNAL ADVERTISING REPORT. 767

0883-4857 See COOPERATIVE ADVERTISING PLANS FOR YELLOW PAGES. 758

0883-4881 See COMPUTER (DURANGO, COLO.). 1236

0883-489X See CAMERA (DURANGO, COLO.). 4368

0883-4903 See ONCOLOGY UPDATE. 3822

0883-4911 See PHYSICIAN'S GUIDE TO MONEY MANAGEMENT. 803

0883-492X See OB/GYN TRENDS AT MOUNT SINAI SCHOOL OF MEDICINE. 3766

0883-4938 See PHYSICIAN'S SPORTSLIFE. 2600

0883-4946 See CARDIOLOGY WORLD NEWS. 3701

0883-4954 See INNOVATIONS IN SURGERY AT THE LAHEY CLINIC MEDICAL CENTER. 3966

0883-4962 See INNOVATIONS IN UROLOGY. 3990

0883-4970 See FORUM (BONNER, MONT.). 5016

0883-4989 See ELECTRONICS (1985). 2048

0883-5136 See LOS ANGELES, ORANGE COUNTIES STREET ATLAS AND DIRECTORY (ZIP CODE EDITION). 2568

0883-5225 See RIVERSIDE COUNTY STREET ATLAS AND DIRECTORY. 2575

0883-5322 See TICKER TAPE PARADE. 814

0883-5330 See DIRECTORY OF BIOMEDICAL AND HEALTH CARE GRANTS. 3572

0883-5349 See ALLURE (NEW YORK, N.Y. 1985). 402

0883-5365 See ORAL TRADITION. 2323

0883-5381 See HEALTHCARE EXECUTIVE. 3782

0883-5403 See JOURNAL OF ARTHROPLASTY, THE. 3966

0883-542X See PROCEEDINGS OF THE ANNUAL TECHNICAL SYMPOSIUM - WILD GOOSE ASSOCIATION. TECHNICAL SYMPOSIUM. 2202

0883-5438 See MONTAGE (ROCKVILLE, MD.). 2539

0883-5462 See GREEN MAGAZINE. 2173

0883-5470 See POET'S MARKET. 3470

0883-5500 See PROCEEDINGS OF NELS. 3312

0883-5519 See COMBUSTION SCIENCE AND TECHNOLOGY BOOK SERIES. 1051

0883-556X See MADDEN FAMILY NEWSLETTER. 2459

0883-5608 See PERSONAL IDENTIFICATION NEWS. 1227

0883-5616 See MAKING WAVES (PASADENA, CALIF.). 5233

0883-5640 See FORUM OF PHI SIGMA IOTA, THE. 3282

0883-5659 See ADVENTURES IN TOTAL DEVELOPMENT. 4572

0883-5667 See CHURCH (NEW YORK, N.Y.). 4947

0883-5683 See COMPUTER PICTURES. 1232

0883-5691 See TOPICS IN CLINICAL NUTRITION. 4199

0883-5705 See PETERSEN'S KIT CAR. 5423

0883-5721 See VA PRACTITIONER. 3793

0883-573X See VOICE (EAST LANSING, MICH.). 1790

0883-5748 See DAILY NEWS (PULLMAN, WASH.). 5760

0883-5772 See SOFTWARE INDUSTRY BULLETIN. 1290

0883-5810 See ATHA. 343

0883-5837 See REFLECTIONS ON SPACE. 33

0883-5896 See IMPORTANT ADVANCES IN ONCOLOGY. 3818

0883-5926 See ALLEE'S ALL AROUND. 2436

0883-5985 See COGENERATION JOURNAL, THE. 4400

0883-5993 See JOURNAL OF THORACIC IMAGING. 3600

0883-6000 See EMORY VICO STUDIES. 4345

0883-6019 See COMPUTER LAW ANNUAL. 2954

0883-6035 See ANNUAL PROCEEDINGS, PRE-CONVENTION REPORT - LOCOMOTIVE MAINTENANCE OFFICERS ASSOCIATION (U.S.). 5429

0883-6043 See FODOR'S AMSTERDAM. 5470

0883-6078 See AIPLA QUARTERLY JOURNAL. 1301

0883-6086 See PERSPECTIVES (TOLEDO, OHIO). 3350

0883-6094 See STEVEN SPIELBERG FILM SOCIETY NEWSLETTER, THE. 4078

0883-6108 See CORNERSTONE (SAN ANTONIO, TEX.), THE. 4950

0883-6116 See CALIFORNIA LOCAL PROBATE RULES. 2946

0883-6124 See ANZA VALLEY OUTLOOK. 5633

0883-6183 See IN FASHION. 1085

0883-6221 See AMERICAN SERIES IN MATHEMATICAL AND MANAGEMENT SCIENCES. 3492

0883-623X See VESTNIK LENINGRADSKOGO UNIVERSITETA. MATEMATIKA, MEKHANIKA, ASTRONOMIIA. 2131

0883-6248 See NEW SCHOOL OBSERVER, THE. 1093

0883-6256 See DMA MATTERS. 923

0883-6272 See SPACE POWER. 1958

0883-6353 See GEOARCHAEOLOGY. 269

0883-6361 See CRACKED. 2532

0883-640X See RADIO/TV HIGHLIGHTS. 1137

0883-6442 See OLDE TIMES. 2752

0883-6469 See ROCKAMERICA GUIDE TO VIDEO/MUSIC, THE. 4151

0883-6523 See POLAND LEADER. 5730

0883-6531 See LAWRENCE COUNTY ADVOCATE. 5745

0883-6566 See MCFARLAND COMMUNITY LIFE. 5769

0883-6574 See COLLINSVILLE HERALD (COLLINSVILLE, ILL.), THE. 5659

0883-6612 See ANNALS OF BEHAVIORAL MEDICINE. 3654

0883-6620 See IPADE ALAGBARA. 5268

0883-6655 See SHIBAO ZHOU KAN (MEIZHOU-BAN). 5721

0883-668X See AIRBRUSH TECHNIQUES. 369

0883-6698 See DNI JOURNAL. 4773

0883-671X See WALLACE MINER, THE. 5658

0883-6728 See COLORADO EPISCOPALIAN, THE. 5058

0883-6752 See PAGES (CHICAGO, ILL.). 2923

0883-6760 See STATE REVENUE NEWSLETTER, THE. 2787

0883-6795 See AATF NATIONAL BULLETIN. 3260

0883-6809 See OUT OF DOORS (PIERRE, S.D.). 4876

0883-6817 See SCWDC. 4917

0883-6825 See SHOW-ME UNDERWRITER, THE. 2893

0883-6833 See BUCKEYE SPORTS BULLETIN. 4888

0883-6841 See USA OUTDOORS. 4880

0883-685X See LEWIS LIVING. 105

0883-6876 See GRIT (CAYUGA, IND.). 5286

0883-6884 See CONTRIBUTIONS IN MILITARY STUDIES. 4040

0883-6922 See CHILDREN'S VIDEO REPORT. 1062

0883-6930 See SOAP OPERA NOW. 2546

0883-6949 See MANNLICHER COLLECTOR, THE. 251

0883-6973 See IN HOUSE GRAPHICS. 380

0883-7007 See CITIZEN GEORGIAN, THE. 5652

0883-7015 See BARTLESVILLE EXAMINER-ENTERPRISE. 5731

0883-7066 See SYSTEM DYNAMICS REVIEW. 3537

0883-7090 See ADULT VIDEO NEWS. 4366

0883-7104 See RANDALLSTOWN NEWS. 5687

0883-7112 See CENTRAL MISSOURI NEWS. 5703

0883-7155 See INTERNATIONAL DESIGN YEARBOOK, THE. 2906

0883-7198 See CLINICAL PEDIATRICS (NEW YORK. 1985). 3902

0883-7201 See INSTRUMENTATION-RESEARCH. 978

0883-721X See INDIA-WEST. 5636

0883-7228 See MOTORCYCLE DRAG RACING. 4082

0883-7236 See LIVING THE WORD. LEVEL 8, GRADES TEN-TWELVE STUDENT'S RESOURCE. 4974

0883-7252 See JOURNAL OF APPLIED ECONOMETRICS (CHICHESTER, ENGLAND). 1592

0883-7279 See PRATT JOURNAL OF ARCHITECTURE. 306

0883-7317 See WHO'S WHO IN CONSUMER ELECTRONICS. 436

0883-7325 See MIDCONTINENT OIL WORLD. 4264

0883-7333 See KITCHEN GARDEN (NEWARK, DEL.), THE. 2422

0883-735X See ROTKIN REVIEW, THE. 4376

0883-7368 See ALMANAKH UKRAINSKOHO NARODNOHO SOIUZU. 1923

0883-7376 See A.P.L.I.C. SPECIAL PUBLICATION. 3186

0883-7384 See ASSET (ST. LOUIS, MO.), THE. 738

0883-7406 See LENT (VAN LENT) NEWSLETTER. 2458

0883-7449 See TENTATIVE ... OIL AND GAS UNIT OF PRODUCTION VALUES. 4280

0883-7457 See NIOSH CERTIFIED EQUIPMENT LIST AS OF 2866

0883-7473 See EXECUTIVE AND OWNERSHIP REPORT. CLASS I & II MOTOR CARRIERS OF PROPERTY. 673

0883-7503 See FICTION (NOVATO, CALIF.). 3387

0883-752X See HAZARD TIMES, THE. 5681

0883-7554 See IEEE ELECTRICAL INSULATION MAGAZINE. 2059

0883-7562 See JOURNAL OF ANALYTIC SOCIAL WORK. 5291

0883-7570 See JOURNAL OF HOSPITAL MARKETING. 3787

0883-7589 See JOURNAL OF MARKETING FOR MENTAL HEALTH. 4787

0883-7597 See JOURNAL OF PHARMACEUTICAL MARKETING & MANAGEMENT. 4311

0883-7600 See CORYELL NEWSLETTER. 2444

0883-7619 See IMPACT VALVES. 2115

0883-7643 See MONOGRAPH - UNIVERSITY OF WASHINGTON. CENTER FOR SOCIAL WORK RESEARCH. 5296

0883-7678 See STORY (SAINT PAUL, MINN.). 4999

0883-7686 See YORKIE TALES. 4288

0883-7694 See MRS BULLETIN. 2107

0883-7708 See LAMB'S PASTURES. 2457

0883-7716 See CLEARY NEWS. 2443

0883-7775 See BOATMAN NEWSLETTER. 2439

0883-7783 See NORTH CAROLINA LAW MONITOR, THE. 3018

0883-7791 See WEEDMAN NEWSLETTER. 2477

0883-7805 See MANLEY FAMILY NEWSLETTER. 2459

0883-7813 See WATERSKI (WINTER PARK, FLA.). 4929

0883-7821 See VENTURE ROAD. 5498

0883-7856 See GOVERNMENT FINANCE REVIEW. 4728

0883-7864 See BAPTIST TRUE UNION. 5056

0883-7880 See CAM MAGAZINE. 606

0883-7899 See MONTANA CATHOLIC, THE. 5032

0883-7902 See MENTAL AND PHYSICAL DISABILITY LAW REPORTER. 3009

0883-7910 See PITTSBURGH BUSINESS TIMES-JOURNAL. 703

0883-7929 See JEWELRY AD REVIEW. 761

0883-7937 See GLIDER RIDER'S ULTRALIGHT FLYING. 22

0883-7945 See NORTHWEST RUNNER. 4908

0883-7953 See AMERICA'S FASTEST GROWING COMPANIES (1985). 638

0883-7961 See KREFELD IMMIGRANTS AND THEIR DESCENDANTS. 2457

0883-8038 See THOROUGHBRED BUSINESS. 2803

0883-8046 See ROCKY MOUNTAIN HIGH TECHNOLOGY DIRECTORY. 5148

0883-8100 See JOURNAL / WORLD RESOURCES INSTITUTE. 5293

0883-8135 See CANADA (WASHINGTON, D.C. 1985). 2726

0883-8143 See HISTORY LIVES HERE. 2737

0883-8151 See JOURNAL OF BROADCASTING & ELECTRONIC MEDIA. 1134

0883-816X See MUSLIM JOURNAL. 5044

0883-8194 See FOCUS (AUSTIN, TEX. 1985). 1247

0883-8208 See COLORADO HIGH TECHNOLOGY DIRECTORY. 5095
0883-8216 See HEALTH SCIENCE (1985). 4781
0883-8240 See PROFESSIONAL INSURANCE AGENTS OF NEW YORK. 2890
0883-8275 See AFL-CIO LEGISLATIVE ALERT!. 1642
0883-8283 See FERROELECTRICS AND POLAR MATERIAL. 4402
0883-8291 See REVIEWS OF MAGNETIC RESONANCE IN MEDICINE. 3849
0883-8305 See PALEOCEANOGRAPHY. 1455
0883-8313 See NATIONAL GREENHOUSE GARDENER. 2425
0883-833X See ANTIQUE REVIEW. 249
0883-8348 See GASTROENTEROLOGY & ENDOSCOPY NEWS. 3745
0883-8364 See IN VITRO CELLULAR & DEVELOPMENTAL BIOLOGY. PLANT. 513
0883-8364 See IN VITRO CELLULAR & DEVELOPMENTAL BIOLOGY. ANIMAL. 537
0883-8380 See BEEHIVE HISTORY. 2722
0883-8402 See UTILITY SUPERVISION (1985). 948
0883-8410 See LITERATURE SCAN. TRANSPLANTATION. 3969
0883-8429 See RACQUET (NEW YORK, N.Y. : 1985). 4914
0883-8437 See AUDIO (DURANGO, COLO.). 5315
0883-8526 See ALASKA NATIVE LANGUAGE CENTER RESEARCH PAPERS. 3262
0883-8534 See JOURNAL OF MULTICULTURAL COUNSELING AND DEVELOPMENT. 4598
0883-8542 See APPLIED ENGINEERING IN AGRICULTURE. 1965
0883-8569 See EDITOR'S WORKSHOP NEWSLETTER. 2919
0883-8577 See PALESTINE FOCUS. 2625
0883-8607 See SPEAKER'S DIGEST. 1122
0883-8631 See AGROTECHNOLOGY TRANSFER. 57
0883-8682 See BARRISTERS NEWSLETTER. 2940
0883-8690 See GOVERNMENT ASSISTANCE ALMANAC. 4651
0883-8720 See SAVVY MANAGEMENT MONTHLY. 885
0883-8755 See WOODWARD NEWS. 5733
0883-8798 See PENTHOUSE LETTERS. 3996
0883-8828 See TECHLETTER. 4248
0883-8852 See ENDLESS VACATION - RESORT CONDOMINIUMS INTERNATIONAL, THE. 5469
0883-8909 See ANNALS - ASSOCIATION FOR ASIAN STUDIES. SOUTHEAST CONFERENCE. 2645
0883-8933 See ACCORD (NEW YORK, N.Y.). 5054
0883-8941 See SECRETS OF WINNERS. 4618
0883-895X See GEOSCIENCE CONTENTS. 1380
0883-8984 See ARKANSAS JOURNAL (LITTLE ROCK, ARK. : 1985). 1598
0883-900X See HEALTH CARE RESOURCES IN PENNSYLVANIA, LONG TERM CARE FACILITIES. 3581
0883-9026 See JOURNAL OF BUSINESS VENTURING. 686
0883-9077 See CHRISTMAS IS COMING! (HARDCOVER). 371
0883-9115 See JOURNAL OF BIOACTIVE AND COMPATIBLE POLYMERS. 980
0883-9123 See SHAKESPEAREAN CRITICISM (DETROIT, MICH.). 3352
0883-9131 See BELOIT FICTION JOURNAL. 3366
0883-9182 See ANNUAL REVIEW OF BIOPHYSICS AND BIOMOLECULAR STRUCTURE. 494
0883-9204 See BIBLE COLLECTORS' WORLD. 5014
0883-9212 See JOURNAL OF CARDIOPULMONARY REHABILITATION. 3706
0883-9239 See BULLETIN / THE DAYTON ART INSTITUTE. 346
0883-9336 See APPRISE. 2721
0883-9344 See BULLETIN / HOSPITAL FOR JOINT DISEASES. 3804

0883-9360 See CONTRACT FURNITURE BUYER'S GUIDE. 4211
0883-9395 See SOCIAL RESPONSIBILITY, BUSINESS, JOURNALISM, LAW, MEDICINE. 3103
0883-9409 See DENVER UNIVERSITY LAW REVIEW. 2959
0883-9417 See ARCHIVES OF PSYCHIATRIC NURSING. 3851
0883-9433 See JOURNAL OF POST ANESTHESIA NURSING. 3859
0883-9441 See JOURNAL OF CRITICAL CARE. 3594
0883-9468 See GUNS & AMMO ACTION SERIES. 4897
0883-9514 See APPLIED ARTIFICIAL INTELLIGENCE. 1211
0883-9549 See NEWSLETTER - AMERICAN ASSOCIATION FOR THE ADVANCEMENT OF SLAVIC STUDIES. 2700
0883-9549 See AAASS NEWSLETTER. 2671
0883-9565 See SEMI-ANNUAL BOOKLIST. 3470
0883-9581 See STATE CLIMATOLOGIST, THE. 1434
0883-9603 See CENTRAL MONTANA WAGON TRAILS. 2442
0883-9611 See BROOMSTICK. 5552
0883-962X See BROWNSTONER, THE. 293
0883-9689 See WORKING PAPER - JOINT CENTER FOR HOUSING STUDIES OF MIT AND HARVARD UNIVERSITY. 2839
0883-9697 See JOURNAL OF MIDDLE ATLANTIC ARCHAEOLOGY. 271
0883-9700 See RESEARCH AND APPLICATIONS IN MUSIC EDUCATION. 4149
0883-9719 See ENVIRON (FORT COLLINS, COLO.). 5199
0883-9727 See DIRECTIONS (NEW YORK, N.Y. : 1985). 923
0883-9735 See COAL & SYNFUELS TECHNOLOGY. 1023
0883-9743 See ASPEN'S ADVISOR FOR NURSE EXECUTIVES. 3851
0883-9778 See BURRELLE'S NEW JERSEY MEDIA DIRECTORY. 1105
0883-9808 See MICROGRAPHICS NEWSLETTER. 1195
0883-9816 See CINCINNATI ROMANCE REVIEW. 3376
0883-9832 See ISRAELI FOREIGN AFFAIRS. 4526
0883-9859 See INVENTORS' DIGEST (COLORADO SPRINGS, COLO.). 5116
0883-9867 See CALIFORNIA WORKERS' COMPENSATION ENQUIRER. 2877
0883-9905 See POTOMAC CHILDREN. 1068
0883-9956 See IN DANCE. 1313
0883-9980 See CSL (NEW YORK, N.Y.). 3379
0883-9999 See BURRELLE'S NEW ENGLAND MEDIA DIRECTORY. 1105
0884-0016 See ADVANCED STUDIES IN CONTEMPORARY MATHEMATICS. 3491
0884-0032 See CIVIL RICO REPORT. 3089
0884-0075 See CALIFORNIA PRISONER, THE. 3159
0884-0091 See BOLETIN - ACADEMIA NORTEAMERICANA DE LA LENGUA ESPANOLA. 3269
0884-0105 See FOAL REGISTRATIONS OF ILLINOIS CONCEIVED AND FOALED, AND ILLINOIS FOALED THOROUGHBREDS. 2799
0884-0156 See MECHANICAL PARTS/LABOR ESTIMATING GUIDE. DOMESTIC GLASS. 5418
0884-0172 See POMOST. 2703
0884-0180 See HAY DRAMAGITAKAN HANDES. 2781
0884-0229 See WHO'S WHO IN THE STONE BUSINESS. 631
0884-0237 See OFFICIAL PRICE GUIDE TO BEER CANS & COLLECTIBLES, THE. 2775
0884-030X See INSIDE ALABAMA POLITICS. 4477
0884-0385 See HYDRO REVIEW. 2090
0884-0393 See FODOR'S MADRID. 5472

0884-0431 See JOURNAL OF BONE AND MINERAL RESEARCH. 3805
0884-044X See MARQUIS WHO'S WHO DIRECTORY OF ONLINE PROFESSIONALS. 1275
0884-0458 See WORKING PAPERS IN LINGUISTICS (HONOLULU, HAWAII). 3333
0884-0482 See ILLINOIS APPELLATE REPORTS. 2980
0884-0490 See ASHRAE TECHNICAL DATA BULLETIN. 2603
0884-0504 See GROUP'S JR. HIGH MINISTRY. 1064
0884-0628 See HOUSTON CITY MAGAZINE. 2738
0884-0636 See CAVITATION AND MULTIPHASE FLOW FORUM. 1967
0884-0687 See TRAVEL BUSINESS REPORT. 5495
0884-0717 See HEALTH IS WEALTH. 4780
0884-0741 See RESEARCH IN GOVERNMENTAL AND NONPROFIT ACCOUNTING. 4746
0884-0768 See UCLA PACIFIC BASIN LAW JOURNAL. 3067
0884-0806 See FOOD PROTECTION REPORT. 2339
0884-0822 See FORTH DIMENSIONS. 1286
0884-0830 See MONITOR (ROCKVILLE, MD.). 1270
0884-0881 See DIGITAL PUBLISHING. 4813
0884-0911 See DIRECTORY OF PERIODICALS ONLINE. SCIENCE & TECHNOLOGY : INDEXED, ABSTRACTED & FULL TEXT. 3258
0884-092X See ANIMAL HEALTH NEWSLETTER. 5502
0884-0997 See MACUSER (NEW YORK, N.Y.). 1268
0884-1012 See ROBOT EXPERIMENTER. 1216
0884-1039 See BIRNBAUM'S CANADA. 5464
0884-1063 See UNITED STATES GOVERNMENT ANNUAL REPORT. 4692
0884-1101 See MEMBERSHIP/COMMITTEE DIRECTORY - NATIONAL ASSOCIATION OF MEAT PURVEYORS (U.S.). 2350
0884-1128 See GOLD BOOK OF NAVAL AVIATION, THE. 22
0884-1136 See ENSIGN (SALT LAKE CITY, UTAH). 5059
0884-1152 See SELECTED MEDICAL CARE STATISTICS. 4062
0884-1179 See GEORGIA ECONOMIC OUTLOOK. 1492
0884-1209 See BIRNBAUM'S MEXICO. 5464
0884-1217 See GEORGIA LAW LETTER. 2974
0884-1225 See JOURNAL OF HYPERBARIC MEDICINE. 3595
0884-1233 See JOURNAL OF TEACHING IN SOCIAL WORK. 5293
0884-1241 See JOURNAL OF MARKETING FOR HIGHER EDUCATION. 1833
0884-1276 See ANNUAL REPORT / LOS ANGELES OLYMPIC ORGANIZING COMMITTEE. 4883
0884-1284 See LIST OF TATTOOED REGISTERED HARNESS HORSES. 2800
0884-1292 See GOLD REVIEW AND OUTLOOK. 1607
0884-1306 See COPYRIGHT MANAGEMENT CIRCLE. 1303
0884-1314 See 500 CONTRACTORS RECEIVING THE LARGEST DOLLAR VOLUME OF PRIME CONTRACT AWARDS FOR RESEARCH, DEVELOPMENT, TEST, AND EVALUATION. 4033
0884-1322 See FOAL REGISTRATIONS, ILLINOIS CONCEIVED & FOALED STANDARDBREDS. 2799
0884-1357 See VMEBUS SYSTEMS. 1273
0884-1373 See SOUTHERN BUSINESS REVIEW. 886
0884-1381 See ANNUAL REPORT - CAMP FIRE, INC. 5228
0884-139X See DEFENSE NEWS (SPRINGFIELD, VA.). 4041

0884-1454 See OFFICIAL AMERICAN BOARD OF MEDICAL SPECIALTIES (ABMS) DIRECTORY OF BOARD CERTIFIED NUCLEAR MEDICINE SPECIALISTS, THE. 3849

0884-1462 See ABMS DIRECTORY OF CERTIFIED THORACIC SURGEONS. 3957

0884-1470 See ABMS DIRECTORY OF CERTIFIED COLON AND RECTAL SURGEONS. 3957

0884-1489 See ABMS DIRECTORY OF CERTIFIED DERMATOLOGISTS. 3717

0884-1497 See ABMS DIRECTORY OF CERTIFIED PEDIATRICIANS. 3899

0884-1500 See ABMS DIRECTORY OF CERTIFIED NEUROLOGISTS. 3825

0884-1519 See ABMS DIRECTORY OF CERTIFIED PSYCHIATRISTS. 3918

0884-1527 See ABMS DIRECTORY OF CERTIFIED SURGEONS. 3957

0884-1535 See ABMS DIRECTORY OF CERTIFIED OBSTETRICIANS AND GYNECOLOGISTS. 3755

0884-1543 See OFFICIAL AMERICAN BOARD OF MEDICAL SPECIALTIES (ABMS) DIRECTORY OF BOARD CERTIFIED MEDICAL SPECIALISTS, THE. 3623

0884-1586 See STANGER'S PARTNERSHIP SPONSOR DIRECTORY DIRECTORIES BUSINESS. 916

0884-1616 See PRATT'S GUIDE TO VENTURE CAPITAL SOURCES. 911

0884-1624 See AIRLINE SEATING GUIDE (POCKET ED.). 10

0884-1632 See GEORGIA CRIMINAL TRIAL PRACTICE / BY WILLIAM W. DANIEL. 3107

0884-1667 See MSBA IN BRIEF. 3012

0884-1683 See DELAWARE CORPORATION LAW UPDATE (EXECUTIVE EDITION). 3099

0884-173X See OHIO REGISTER OF MANUFACTURERS. 3485

0884-1748 See HIGHLIGHTS - HENRY LUCE FOUNDATION. 1750

0884-1756 See UNIVERSITY OF MIAMI INTER-AMERICAN LAW REVIEW, THE. 3137

0884-1780 See TERA ANALYSIS. 1959

0884-1802 See EXXON TRAVEL CLUB TRAVEL GUIDE. CANADA. 5469

0884-1810 See STATUS REPORT ON THE ENERGY-RELATED INVENTIONS PROGRAM. 1958

0884-1829 See MINORITY ENGINEER : ME, THE. 1988

0884-1926 See CIVIL ENGINEERING EDUCATION. 2020

0884-1977 See BUSINESS LAWYER UPDATE, THE. 3097

0884-1985 See PERFORMANCE & INSTRUCTION (1985). 1773

0884-2027 See COMPUTER SCIENCE AND APPLIED MATHEMATICS. 3502

0884-2043 See CLIO (FORT WAYNE, IND.). 3376

0884-2078 See DIAL. WNET/THIRTEEN (COMPOSITE ED.). 1131

0884-2094 See HEALTHY PEOPLE. 4782

0884-2108 See TERRELL TRAILS. 2474

0884-2124 See DIRECTORY OF VIDEO, COMPUTER, AND AUDIO-VISUAL PRODUCTS, THE. 1893

0884-2132 See DATA FROM THE DRUG ABUSE WARNING NETWORK. SEMIANNUAL REPORT. 1342

0884-2140 See PHELPS COUNTY GENEALOGICAL SOCIETY QUARTERLY. 2467

0884-2175 See JOURNAL OF OBSTETRIC, GYNECOLOGIC, AND NEONATAL NURSING : JOGNN. 3859

0884-2205 See MO INFO. 3232

0884-2213 See APPEARANCES. 313

0884-2221 See ARREARAGE TABLES OF AMOUNTS DUE AND UNPAID 90 DAYS OR MORE ON FOREIGN CREDITS OF THE UNITED STATES GOVERNMENT (1979). 4711

0884-2264 See IMPACT COMPRESSORS. 2115

0884-2272 See COMMUNICATIONS TECHNOLOGY. 1130

0884-2280 See CHILDREN'S BUSINESS. 1083

0884-2299 See PETERSON'S COLLEGE SELECTION SERVICE. TWO-YEAR COLLEGES. 1840

0884-2329 See CROP VALUES (WASHINGTON, D.C.). 169

0884-2337 See SPACE ENTREPRENEURS DIRECTORY. 1627

0884-2426 See REVIEW OF SECURITIES & COMMODITIES REGULATION, THE. 3040

0884-2604 See DATA TRAINING. 1257

0884-2744 See NEW YORK FILM ANNEX. 4075

0884-2795 See REIMBURSEMENT ADVISOR. 3792

0884-2817 See CONNECTICUT CPA QUARTERLY. 741

0884-2884 See DRUG DESIGN AND DISCOVERY. 4300

0884-2914 See JOURNAL OF MATERIALS RESEARCH. 2103

0884-2930 See WYOMING, THE HUB OF THE WHEEL. 2857

0884-2949 See FAULKNER JOURNAL, THE. 3387

0884-2957 See BELLES LETTRES (ARLINGTON, VA.). 3366

0884-2981 See EUTHANASIA REVIEW, THE. 2250

0884-3007 See HART'S PETROLEUM PROFESSIONALS (ROCKY MOUNTAIN ED.). 4259

0884-3031 See RICHARD C. YOUNG'S INTELLIGENCE REPORT. 810

0884-3120 See HANGUK ILBO, TENBO. 5643

0884-3139 See HANGUK ILBO, HAWAI. 5655

0884-3198 See UCLA JOURNAL OF DANCE ETHNOLOGY. 1314

0884-3236 See LATE IMPERIAL CHINA. 2658

0884-3309 See TRANSACTIONS - PIONEER AMERICA SOCIETY. 2763

0884-3368 See DIRECTORY. HOSPITAL EQUIPMENT & SUPPLIES. 3779

0884-3457 See CREAM CITY REVIEW. 3340

0884-3481 See DIRECTORY. SWIMMING POOL DEALERS & CONTRACTORS. 613

0884-3554 See REFUGEE REPORTS. 1921

0884-3562 See AMERICAN FLY FISHER, THE. 2294

0884-3643 See COMMUNIQUE / NATIONAL ASSOCIATION FOR GIFTED CHILDREN. 1877

0884-3716 See RESEARCH NEWS - FAMILY HISTORY WORLD. 2470

0884-3724 See DUN'S CONSULTANTS DIRECTORY. 866

0884-3759 See FUEL SCIENCE & TECHNOLOGY INTERNATIONAL. 2139

0884-3775 See HAZARDOUS WASTE AND TOXIC TORTS. 3112

0884-3791 See WARREN'S MOVIE POSTER PRICE GUIDE. 4079

0884-3848 See PAINT & COATINGS INDUSTRY. 4224

0884-3910 See NEWS FOR YOU (SYRACUSE, N.Y.). 5719

0884-3996 See JOURNAL OF BIOLUMINESCENCE AND CHEMILUMINESCENCE. 495

0884-4011 See DECORATIVE ARTS SOCIETY NEWSLETTER, THE. 372

0884-4038 See QUALITY & PRODUCTIVITY IMPROVEMENT NEWSLETTER, THE. 1623

0884-4054 See DEFENSE & FOREIGN AFFAIRS WEEKLY. 4041

0884-4119 See PETERSON'S FINANCIAL AID SERVICE. 1840

0884-4135 See TIMES (CANAL WINCHESTER, OHIO). 5730

0884-4240 See IRISH AMERICA. 2739

0884-4291 See CREATIVE CHILD AND ADULT QUARTERLY, THE. 1877

0884-4356 See AMERICAN VOICE (LOUISVILLE, KY.), THE. 3360

0884-4372 See SEXUAL COERCION & ASSAULT. 5257

0884-4429 See WILLIAM AND MARY BILL OF RIGHTS JOURNAL, THE. 3075

0884-4437 See COPYRIGHT LAW JOURNAL, THE. 1303

0884-4461 See DOLCIANI MATHEMATICAL EXPOSITIONS, THE. 3504

0884-4488 See CHILE ECOMOMIC REPORT. 1551

0884-450X See RARE BOOKS AND MANUSCRIPTS LIBRARIANSHIP. 3244

0884-4526 See RECOUP'S MATERIALS RECYCLING MARKETS. 2241

0884-4550 See PETROLEUM MANAGEMENT (HOUSTON, TEX.). 4273

0884-4615 See YOUR COMPUTER CAREER. 4210

0884-4704 See REGISTER (SHREWSBURY, N.J.), THE. 5711

0884-4720 See ELECTRONIC MUSICIAN. 4116

0884-4739 See BASSIN'. 2297

0884-4747 See ARTILLERYMAN, THE. 4037

0884-4755 See AVIATION DIGEST. 13

0884-4771 See NORTHEAST OIL WORLD. 4267

0884-478X See EMPLOYEE BENEFITS REPORT. 1665

0884-4828 See ELECTRONIC WARFARE DIGEST. 4043

0884-4836 See EMERGENCY MEDICAL TECHNICIAN LEGAL BULLETIN. 3724

0884-4852 See ECONOMIC POLICY ISSUES. 4721

0884-4879 See EBONY MAN. 3995

0884-4976 See SMART LIVING. 2546

0884-4992 See TV GAME SHOW MAGAZINE. 4867

0884-5050 See ENERGY AND TECHNOLOGY REVIEW. 1939

0884-5107 See WASHINGTON CRIMINAL JUSTICE REPORT'S CRIME VICTIMS DIGEST. 3179

0884-5123 See PROCEEDINGS - INTERNATIONAL TELEMETERING CONFERENCE. 2076

0884-5131 See IN THE WIND (ANGOURA HILLS, CALIF.). 4081

0884-5166 See NEW ENGLAND LIVING. 2540

0884-5336 See NUTRITION IN CLINICAL PRACTICE. 4196

0884-5352 See JOURNAL OF CAREER PLANNING & EMPLOYMENT. 4206

0884-5379 See FIDES ET HISTORIA. 4959

0884-5409 See PROCEEDINGS / CARNAHAN CONFERENCE ON SECURITY TECHNOLOGY. 3173

0884-5506 See CHRISTIAN EDUCATION TODAY. 4944

0884-5514 See SHINING STAR (CARTHAGE, ILL.). 1905

0884-5557 See MORNING CALL (ALLENTOWN, PA.), THE. 5737

0884-5581 See BEHAVIORAL RESIDENTIAL TREATMENT. 3921

0884-5611 See DOLLARS & SENSE (CHICAGO, ILL.). 669

0884-5646 See UPTIME (APPLE II). 1206

0884-5670 See AMERICAN GUIDE TO U.S. COINS. 2779

0884-5735 See PALATINE IMMIGRANT, THE. 2466

0884-5816 See AGE OF JOHNSON, THE. 3358

0884-5840 See SUMMER THEATRE DIRECTORY (DORSET, VT.). 5369

0884-5859 See DIRECTORY OF UNDERGRADUATE POLITICAL SCIENCE FACULTY. 4472

0884-5883 See PROCEEDINGS OF THE OCEAN DRILLING PROGRAM. PART A, INITIAL REPORT. 1391

0884-5913 See KINEMATIKA I FIZIKA NEBESNYKH TEL. 396

0884-593X See WIRED LIBRARIAN'S NEWSLETTER. 3256

0884-5956 See OHIO LEPIDOPTERIST. 5593

0884-6006 See DIRECTORY OF LITERARY MAGAZINES. 3381

0884-6049 See WRITE TO FAME. 3454

0884-6057 See TAX MANAGEMENT WEEKLY REPORT. 4753

0884-6081 *See* BIENNIAL REPORT ON THE SPECIAL SUPPLEMENTAL FOOD PROGRAM FOR WOMEN, INFANTS, AND CHILDREN, AND ON THE COMMODITY SUPPLEMENTAL FOOD PROGRAM. **2328**

0884-6111 *See* SMOKY MOUNTAIN HISTORICAL SOCIETY NEWSLETTER. **2760**

0884-612X *See* TRANSAFETY REPORTER. **4805**

0884-6154 *See* SOCIALIST (LOS ANGELES, CALIF.). **4547**

0884-6162 *See* AGWEEK. **57**

0884-6170 *See* RANCHO MIRAGE POST. **5638**

0884-6189 *See* CATHEDRAL CITY POST. **5633**

0884-6197 *See* CHURCH MEDIA LIBRARY MAGAZINE. **3202**

0884-6219 *See* SOUTHWEST OIL WORLD. **4278**

0884-6227 *See* UPDATE USSR. **4499**

0884-626X *See* MOTORCYCLE INDUSTRY MAGAZINE : MI. **4082**

0884-6294 *See* ANTIQUES & COLLECTING HOBBIES. **249**

0884-6316 *See* AIM INTERNATIONAL. **4933**

0884-6324 *See* DES (NORWALK, CONN. 1984). **2112**

0884-643X *See* ABMS DIRECTORY OF CERTIFIED FAMILY PHYSICIANS. **3736**

0884-6448 *See* ABMS DIRECTORY OF CERTIFIED INTERNISTS. **3794**

0884-6510 *See* BENNETT EXCHANGE, THE. **2439**

0884-6537 *See* COMMON CAUSE MAGAZINE. **4469**

0884-6545 *See* PAPER, PAPERBOARD & WOOD PULP. **4240**

0884-660X *See* LEATHER TODAY. **3185**

0884-6669 *See* AGE. **2436**

0884-6677 *See* Y.E.S. QUARTERLY. **5600**

0884-6685 *See* VOICE PROCESSING. **1168**

0884-6774 *See* HOME BUILDER'S JOURNAL, THE. **616**

0884-6782 *See* FINANCIAL TIMES (NORTH AMERICAN EDITION). **675**

0884-6804 *See* JOURNAL OF COMPOSITES TECHNOLOGY & RESEARCH. **2103**

0884-6812 *See* ANALYTICAL AND QUANTITATIVE CYTOLOGY AND HISTOLOGY. **531**

0884-688X *See* GOOD APPLE NEWSPAPER, THE. **1895**

0884-6898 *See* GMDA BULLETIN. **1324**

0884-6901 *See* GRAPHIC COMMUNICATIONS WORLD. **4565**

0884-691X *See* PREPARATION OF ANNUAL DISCLOSURE DOCUMENTS. **3030**

0884-6936 *See* ANALYST'S HANDBOOK. **890**

0884-6944 *See* MALCOLM HULKE STUDIES IN CINEMA AND TELEVISION. **4074**

0884-6952 *See* STUDIES IN JUDAICA AND THE HOLOCAUST. **5053**

0884-7010 *See* CONSECRATED LIFE (ENGLISH ED.). **4950**

0884-7045 *See* CONOCO. **4253**

0884-7053 *See* CONNECTICUT PRESERVATION. **295**

0884-7118 *See* MARQUIS WHO'S WHO INDEX TO WHO'S WHO BOOKS. **433**

0884-7126 *See* 3 & 4 WHEEL ACTION. **4881**

0884-7142 *See* ELECTED LEADER. **866**

0884-7169 *See* COMMUNITY, TECHNICAL, AND JUNIOR COLLEGE JOURNAL. **1818**

0884-7185 *See* FOOD BROKER QUARTERLY. **2336**

0884-7193 *See* CHURCH BYTES. **4947**

0884-7231 *See* VAN CONVERSION BLUE BOOK OFFICIAL MARKET REPORT. **5427**

0884-724X *See* INTERNATIONAL JOURNAL OF SHORT-TERM PSYCHOTHERAPY. **4591**

0884-7274 *See* BILL ATKINSON'S NEWS REPORT. **1599**

0884-7339 *See* COGENERATION. **2112**

0884-7347 *See* GUIDE TO GRADUATE EDUCATION IN SPEECH-LANGUAGE PATHOLOGY AND AUDIOLOGY. **1826**

0884-7398 *See* ADMISSIONS MARKETING REPORT. **1807**

0884-741X *See* HOME HEALTHCARE NURSE. **3856**

0884-7452 *See* CAS BIOTECH UPDATES. ENVIRONMENTAL BIOTECHNOLOGY. **3690**

0884-7460 *See* CAS BIOTECH UPDATES. GENETIC ENGINEERING. **966**

0884-7479 *See* CAS BIOTECH UPDATES. BIOSENSORS. **3690**

0884-7487 *See* CAS BIOTECH UPDATES. PHARMACEUTICAL APPLICATIONS. **4295**

0884-7517 *See* GUITAR PLAYER LEGENDS OF GUITAR. **4120**

0884-7525 *See* KAUFMAN KOUNTY KONNECTIONS. **2456**

0884-7568 *See* FORUM (ROSSLYN, VA.). **1747**

0884-7592 *See* WESTERN OIL WORLD. **4282**

0884-7606 *See* AGRI-PULSE. **47**

0884-7630 *See* YOUNG FASHIONS MAGAZINE. **1088**

0884-7657 *See* 401 (K) REPORTER, THE. **890**

0884-7819 *See* DESCRIPTOR FREQUENCY LIST. **3205**

0884-7894 *See* GREEN BOOK'S HARDWOOD LUMBER MARKETING DIRECTORY. **2401**

0884-7967 *See* GULF COAST OIL WORLD. **4259**

0884-7983 *See* CROWN JEWELS OF THE WIRE. **1153**

0884-8009 *See* VOCATIONAL EDUCATION JOURNAL. **1917**

0884-8025 *See* CABLEPLUS MAGAZINE. **1129**

0884-8068 *See* MEDINA COUNTY STORY. **2460**

0884-8076 *See* CHILD SUPPORT REPORT. **3120**

0884-8092 *See* COMBINED CUMULATIVE INDEX TO OBSTETRICS AND GYNECOLOGY. **3655**

0884-8106 *See* NATS JOURNAL / NATIONAL ASSOCIATION OF TEACHERS OF SINGING JOURNAL, THE. **4139**

0884-8114 *See* CHAMBEREXECUTIVE. **819**

0884-8173 *See* INTERNATIONAL JOURNAL OF INTELLIGENT SYSTEMS. **1213**

0884-8181 *See* ENVIRONMENTAL TOXICOLOGY AND WATER QUALITY. **3980**

0884-819X *See* IMAGES (DAYTON, OHIO). **3464**

0884-8238 *See* INDUSTRY FACT SHEET. **4234**

0884-8246 *See* INFORMATION CIRCULAR - MISSOURI. DIVISION OF GEOLOGICAL SURVEY AND WATER RESOURCES. **1382**

0884-8297 *See* INTERNATIONAL JOURNAL OF PSYCHOSOMATICS. **3589**

0884-8300 *See* ... DIRECTORY OF VARS, THE. **1245**

0884-8319 *See* SCIENTIFIC SERIALS REVIEW. BIOMEDICINE. **472**

0884-8351 *See* CAMPAIGN FINANCE LAW. **2947**

0884-8378 *See* NEW BOAT AND MOTOR PRICE GUIDE BLUE BOOK. **594**

0884-8394 *See* INTERSTATE INFORMATION REPORT. **2984**

0884-8416 *See* PETERSON'S COLLEGE SELECTION SERVICE. FOUR-YEAR COLLEGES. **1840**

0884-8424 *See* JOURNAL OF THE ASSOCIATION OF CHILDREN'S PROSTHETIC-ORTHOTIC CLINICS. **3883**

0884-8432 *See* MODERN GREEK STUDIES YEARBOOK. **2699**

0884-8440 *See* INDEX TO SCIENTIFIC BOOK CONTENTS. **5112**

0884-8475 *See* SRC GREEN BOOK OF 5-TREND 35-YEAR CHARTS, THE. **914**

0884-8521 *See* DRUG UTILIZATION REVIEW. **4302**

0884-8548 *See* FLORIDA SHIPPER, THE. **5449**

0884-8629 *See* STATE BANKING, CREDIT UNION, AND SAVINGS, AND LOAN ASSOCIATION LEGISLATION. **3088**

0884-8696 *See* GEORGIA STATE LITERARY STUDIES. **3390**

0884-870X *See* STRESS IN MODERN SOCIETY. **4619**

0884-8734 *See* JOURNAL OF GENERAL INTERNAL MEDICINE. **3798**

0884-8750 *See* MONROE JOURNAL, THE. **5627**

0884-8785 *See* PALM BEACH REVIEW. **3024**

0884-8815 *See* BROOKGREEN JOURNAL. **345**

0884-8823 *See* POPULAR WOODWORKING. **2403**

0884-8912 *See* VICKSBURG EVENING POST. **5702**

0884-8947 *See* TRUCKS. **5398**

0884-8971 *See* SOCIOLOGICAL FORUM (RANDOLPH, N.J.). **5260**

0884-8998 *See* HOSPITAL HOME HEALTH. **3584**

0884-9013 *See* WORKS (LOS ANGELES, CALIF.). **2550**

0884-903X *See* AIDS WEEKLY. **3665**

0884-9056 *See* DIRECTORY OF FOUNDATIONS OF THE GREATER WASHINGTON AREA. **4335**

0884-9080 *See* ITALIAN GENEALOGIST. **2455**

0884-9110 *See* PROFILES OF REGULATORY COMPLIANCE. **5302**

0884-9129 *See* HR/PC. **941**

0884-9137 *See* FRED TROST'S OUTDOORS DIGEST. **4872**

0884-9153 *See* JOURNAL OF STUDENT FINANCIAL AID, THE. **1758**

0884-917X *See* DIRECTORY OF MINING PROGRAMS. **2138**

0884-9196 *See* PEACE CORPS TIMES. **2911**

0884-920X *See* OVERTONES (LINCOLN, NEB.). **3240**

0884-9331 *See* MARYLAND JOURNAL OF INTERNATIONAL LAW AND TRADE. **3132**

0884-934X *See* COMMITMENT PLUS. **864**

0884-9382 *See* NATIONAL INTEREST, THE. **4529**

0884-9390 *See* AMERICAN VISIONS. **2720**

0884-9404 *See* ADVANCES IN PEDIATRIC INFECTIOUS DISEASES. **3899**

0884-9471 *See* ADVANCED MILITARY COMPUTING. **1210**

0884-951X *See* BUSINESS PUBLISHING (CAROL STREAM, ILL.). **4812**

0884-9528 *See* PHOTO-LAB-INDEX. **4373**

0884-9536 *See* NATIONAL DIRECTORY OF BULLETIN BOARD SYSTEMS. **1196**

0884-9641 *See* FREE VENICE BEACHHEAD. **5635**

0884-9722 *See* CONTACTS INFLUENTIAL. FORT WORTH, TEXAS, TARRANT COUNTY. **660**

0884-9889 *See* FRIENDS (WARREN, MICH.). **5415**

0884-9919 *See* MICHIGAN LIBRARIAN (1985). **3231**

0884-9951 *See* ANNUAL REPORT / U.S. NAVY'S MILITARY SEALIFT COMMAND. **4174**

0884-996X *See* OUA/DATA'S ... GUIDE TO CORPORATE & FOUNDATION GIVING IN VERMONT. **4338**

0885-0003 *See* WASTE TREATMENT TECHNOLOGY NEWS. **2246**

0885-0046 *See* ISSUES (CHICAGO, ILL.). **3857**

0885-0062 *See* JOHNS HOPKINS SERIES IN THE MATHEMATICAL SCIENCES. **3511**

0885-0097 *See* CA SELECTS: ACID RAIN & ACID AIR. **997**

0885-0100 *See* CA SELECTS: CERAMIC MATERIALS (PATENTS). **999**

0885-0119 *See* CA SELECTS: CHEMICAL VAPOR DEPOSITION. **999**

0885-0127 *See* CA SELECTS: COLOR SCIENCE. **1000**

0885-0135 *See* CA SELECTS: CONDUCTIVE POLYMERS. **1000**

0885-0143 *See* CA SELECTS: ELECTRICALLY CONDUCTIVE ORGANICS. **1001**

0885-0151 *See* CA SELECTS: ELECTRONIC CHEMICALS & MATERIALS. **1001**

0885-0178 *See* CA SELECTS: LASER-INDUCED CHEMICAL REACTIONS. **1004**

0885-0186 *See* CA SELECTS: ORGANIC OPTICAL MATERIALS. **1006**

0885-0194 *See* CA SELECTS: PHASE TRANSFER CATALYSIS. **1007**

0885-0208 *See* CA SELECTS: PHOTOCHEMICAL ORGANIC SYNTHESIS. **1007**

ISSN Index

0885-0216 See CA SELECTS: PHOTORESISTS. 1007

0885-0224 See CA SELECTS: POLYMERIZATION KINETICS & PROCESS CONTROL. 1008

0885-0232 See CA SELECTS: SPECTROCHEMICAL ANALYSIS. 1009

0885-0259 See POWERCONVERSION & INTELLIGENT MOTION. 1991

0885-0291 See SPIRIT (SISTERS, OR.). 4999

0885-0305 See EASY COMPUTING. 1183

0885-033X See MACRAE'S STATE INDUSTRIAL DIRECTORY. NEW YORK STATE. 1616

0885-0372 See RELIGIOUS STUDIES NEWS. 4992

0885-0429 See CHILDREN'S LITERATURE ASSOCIATION QUARTERLY. 3340

0885-0445 See EDP AUDITOR JOURNAL, THE. 1258

0885-0496 See SELECCIONES DEL READER'S DIGEST (UNITED STATES ED.). 2492

0885-0607 See INTERNATIONAL JOURNAL OF INTELLIGENCE AND COUNTER INTELLIGENCE. 4046

0885-0615 See HUMAN RESEARCH REPORT. 3585

0885-0631 See QUICK & EASY CROCHET. 5185

0885-064X See JOURNAL OF COMPLEXITY. 3512

0885-0658 See STARMONT PULP AND DIME NOVEL STUDIES. 3439

0885-0666 See JOURNAL OF INTENSIVE CARE MEDICINE. 3595

0885-0674 See MEXICAN SPORTFISHING NEWS. 4874

0885-0690 See GOOD FOOD MAGAZINE. 2342

0885-0704 See FOOD AND JUSTICE. 172

0885-0720 See SOUTH FLORIDA POETRY REVIEW. 3471

0885-0747 See FRONT ROW. 385

0885-0771 See BULL'S-EYE NEWS. 4888

0885-078X See CORNELL AND LAKE HOLCOMBE COURIER, THE. 5766

0885-0798 See CADOTT SENTINEL, THE. 5766

0885-081X See WITTENBERG ENTERPRISE AND BIRNAMWOOD NEWS (WITTENBERG, WIS. : 1982). 5772

0885-0836 See ADVANCES IN BEHAVIORAL MEDICINE. 4571

0885-1034 See BUSINESS ACCOUNTING FOR LAWYERS NEWSLETTER / PRACTISING LAW INSTITUTE. 3096

0885-1131 See OFFICE PROCEDURES. 3738

0885-114X See OCCUPATIONAL MEDICINE (PHILADELPHIA, PA.). 2867

0885-1158 See MEDICAL PROBLEMS OF PERFORMING ARTISTS. 3611

0885-1166 See OUTPATIENT SURGERY. 3971

0885-1174 See HUMAN STRESS. 4589

0885-1255 See DIEN AN TH O. 5758

0885-1271 See DALLAS WEEKLY, THE. 5749

0885-1328 See HUDSON'S STATE CAPITALS NEWS MEDIA CONTACTS DIRECTORY. 1133

0885-1360 See CORPORATE DIRECTORS' COMPENSATION. 661

0885-1468 See SOCIALIST WORKER (CHICAGO, ILL.), THE. 4547

0885-1476 See PINHOLE JOURNAL. 4375

0885-1522 See TANNING TRENDS. 1628

0885-159X See DICKINSON'S FDA. 4642

0885-1603 See PRIVATE SCHOOLS OF THE UNITED STATES. 1774

0885-1611 See WORLD SATELLITE ALMANAC. 1169

0885-1638 See REPAIR CAR/NEW CAR DIRECTORY, THE. 5424

0885-1662 See NEW TIMES (MOBILE, ALA.), THE. 5627

0885-1735 See EI ENVIRONMENTAL SERVICES DIRECTORY. 2227

0885-1808 See PROFESSIONAL STAINED GLASS. 2593

0885-1980 See CURRENT ADVANCES IN CLINICAL CHEMISTRY. 1011

0885-1999 See FAIRFAX. 2533

0885-2006 See EARLY CHILDHOOD RESEARCH QUARTERLY. 1803

0885-2014 See COGNITIVE DEVELOPMENT. 4581

0885-2030 See OUTLAW BIKER MAGAZINE. 4082

0885-209X See SHOPPING CENTER DIGEST. 957

0885-2111 See RESEARCH IN CONSUMER BEHAVIOR. 935

0885-212X See RESEARCH IN POLITICS AND SOCIETY. 4493

0885-2200 See THIRD WORLD IN PERSPECTIVE. 5224

0885-2308 See COMPUTER SPEECH & LANGUAGE. 3274

0885-2316 See PROCEEDINGS / ... ANNUAL THIRD WORLD CONFERENCE. 1639

0885-2324 See RESEARCH INTO PRACTICE DIGEST, THE. 1904

0885-2340 See TV PROGRAM INVESTOR. 1141

0885-2375 See THORP COURIER, THE. 5771

0885-2421 See SOUTHERN TIDINGS. 4998

0885-2502 See AIR PROGRESS WARBIRDS INTERNATIONAL. 8

0885-2545 See JOURNAL OF CULTURAL ECONOMICS. 323

0885-2626 See VIRGINIA SETTLERS (QUARTERLY). 2476

0885-2685 See TEXAS REVIEW (HUNTSVILLE, TEX.), THE. 3354

0885-2693 See SECURITY TRADERS HANDBOOK. 1520

0885-2715 See HIGH TECHNOLOGY LAW JOURNAL. 2978

0885-2987 See TEMPLE ENVIRONMENTAL LAW & TECHNOLOGY JOURNAL. 3116

0885-2995 See COLLECTORS' JOURNAL OF ANCIENT ART. 347

0885-3010 See IEEE TRANSACTIONS ON ULTRASONICS, FERROELECTRICS, AND FREQUENCY CONTROL. 4452

0885-3053 See MINOT DAILY NEWS, THE. 5726

0885-3061 See FEDERAL LABOR-MANAGEMENT AND EMPLOYEE RELATIONS CONSULTANT, THE. 1669

0885-3134 See JOURNAL OF PERSONAL SELLING & SALES MANAGEMENT, THE. 928

0885-3177 See PANCREAS. 3800

0885-3185 See MOVEMENT DISORDERS. 3838

0885-3274 See LITERATURE AND CONTEMPORARY REVOLUTIONARY CULTURE. 3407

0885-3282 See JOURNAL OF BIOMATERIALS APPLICATIONS. 3694

0885-3339 See ADVANCES IN THE ECONOMIC ANALYSIS OF PARTICIPATORY AND LABOR-MANAGED FIRMS. 1642

0885-3363 See INTERNATIONAL ADVERTISER (NEW YORK, N.Y. 1985). 760

0885-3371 See POULTRY TIMES (NATIONAL ED.). 218

0885-3398 See CAMPUS SAFETY REPORT NEWSLETTER. 4770

0885-3436 See SOUTHERN RURAL SOCIOLOGY. 5263

0885-3517 See JOURNAL OF THE CHARLES H. TWEED INTERNATIONAL FOUNDATION. 1328

0885-355X See GULF OF MEXICO REPORT. NEWSLETTER EDITION. 4259

0885-3827 See METALWORKING MACHINERY. 4012

0885-3827 See METALWORKING MACHINERY. 4012

0885-386X See KURDISH STUDIES. 2769

0885-3886 See PHENOMENOLOGICAL INQUIRY. 4355

0885-3894 See PUBLIC GARDEN, THE. 2429

0885-3908 See INTERNATIONAL TRADE JOURNAL, THE. 841

0885-3916 See ANNALS (SOCIETY OF LOGISTICS ENGINEERS). 1964

0885-3924 See JOURNAL OF PAIN AND SYMPTOM MANAGEMENT. 3596

0885-3940 See ANNUAL - THEATRE HISTORICAL SOCIETY (U.S.). 5361

0885-3959 See SISAC NEWS. 3249

0885-3975 See GUILD (NEW YORK, N.Y.). 373

0885-3991 See TOY BOOK, THE. 2585

0885-4017 See A2-CENTRAL. 1170

0885-4025 See EAST TENNESSEE ROOTS. 2446

0885-4122 See JOURNAL OF PLANNING LITERATURE. 2840

0885-4149 See MANUFACTURERS HANOVER ECONOMIC REPORT, THE. 1504

0885-4238 See LABOR RESEARCH REVIEW. 1685

0885-4300 See SOCIALISM AND DEMOCRACY. 4546

0885-4327 See MINERAL NEWS (COEUR D'ALENE, IDAHO). 1441

0885-4335 See DIRECTIONS IN FAITH. 4953

0885-4378 See LUCHA STRUGGLE. 5208

0885-4408 See LIST OF RECENT PERIODICAL ARTICLES. 1503

0885-4416 See ON THE RISK. 2889

0885-4459 See MASON COUNTY GENEALOGICAL SOCIETY NEWSLETTER, THE. 2459

0885-4483 See COMMENTS ON MODERN PHYSICS. PART B, COMMENTS ON CONDENSED MATTER PHYSICS. 4400

0885-4505 See BIOCHEMICAL MEDICINE AND METABOLIC BIOLOGY. 3556

0885-4513 See BIOTECHNOLOGY AND APPLIED BIOCHEMISTRY. 3688

0885-453X See JACKSONVILLE BUSINESS JOURNAL. 685

0885-4572 See ADULT DAY CARE LETTER. 5270

0885-4580 See HEIDEGGER STUDIES. 4348

0885-4610 See MEDIAFILE. 2922

0885-4653 See MATHEMATICAL SURVEYS AND MONOGRAPHS. 3520

0885-467X See MCNEESE REVIEW, THE. 3347

0885-470X See M/R. 2537

0885-4718 See CAPITAL (RHINEBECK, N.Y.), THE. 2441

0885-4726 See JOURNAL OF HEALTH CARE CHAPLAINCY. 4969

0885-4734 See JOURNAL OF CHEMICAL DEPENDENCY TREATMENT. 1345

0885-4742 See MIDWESTERN MISCELLANY. 3411

0885-4750 See FABULOUS MUSTANGS & EXOTIC FORDS. 5414

0885-4769 See JACKSONVILLE TODAY. 2536

0885-4777 See 100 HIGHEST YIELDS. 768

0885-4831 See CONNECTICUT HISTORICAL SOCIETY BULLETIN, THE. 2729

0885-4874 See MINNESOTA AGRICULTURAL ECONOMIST. 108

0885-4947 See PILGRIM JOURNAL, THE. 5235

0885-5005 See SCREEN IMAGING TECHNOLOGY FOR ELECTRONICS. 2080

0885-5013 See SAGUARO. 3432

0885-503X See MUSIC FORUM, THE. 4133

0885-5056 See MOBIL WORLD. 4264

0885-5099 See NATIONAL RAILWAY BULLETIN. 5433

0885-5102 See MARTIN COUNTY NEWS. 5752

0885-5110 See NORTH HOLLAND SERIES IN SYSTEM SCIENCE AND ENGINEERING. 5134

0885-5625 See INDUSTRIAL BIOPROCESSING. 1946

0885-565X See NEWSLETTER / FEDERATION OF SCHOOLS OF ACCOUNTANCY. 749

0885-5684 See ADVANCED MANUFACTURING TECHNOLOGY. 1217

0885-5722 See ROCK & ICE. 4878

0885-5765 See PHYSIOLOGICAL AND MOLECULAR PLANT PATHOLOGY. 521

0885-5773 See OCCASIONAL PAPERS ON LINGUISTICS. 3307

0885-5781 See METAL ARCHITECTURE. 303

0885-579X See JOURNAL OF PERSONALITY DISORDERS. 4599

0885-5862 See NOTRE DAME MATHEMATICAL LECTURES. 3525

0885-5870 See NORTHWEST ENERGY NEWS. 2201
0885-5919 See OCCASIONAL REVIEW (SAN JOSE, CALIF.), THE. 3467
0885-5927 See OCULUS (NEW YORK, N. Y.). 305
0885-5935 See GAS DAILY. 4257
0885-5951 See SOVIET BIOLOGICAL RESEARCH ABSTRACTS. 473
0885-6001 See NORTH CAROLINA STUDIES IN THE ROMANCE LANGUAGES AND LITERATURES. 3306
0885-6028 See JOURNAL OF NATIONAL BLACK NURSES' ASSOCIATION : JNBNA. 3859
0885-6036 See ORGANIZER (WASHINGTON, D.C.). 5253
0885-6060 See MICHIGAN DRY BEAN DIGEST. 178
0885-6079 See ATENEA (MAYAGUEZ, P.R.). 343
0885-6087 See HYDROLOGICAL PROCESSES. 1414
0885-6095 See WESTERN JOURNAL OF APPLIED FORESTRY. 2398
0885-6125 See MACHINE LEARNING. 1215
0885-6133 See COMMON GROUND (ARLINGTON, VA.). 4639
0885-615X See BEAR NEWS. 2188
0885-6168 See EXECUTIVE AIDS WATCH. 673
0885-6176 See OUTLOOK ON AT&T. 1161
0885-6222 See HUMAN PSYCHOPHARMACOLOGY. 4307
0885-6230 See INTERNATIONAL JOURNAL OF GERIATRIC PSYCHIATRY. 3752
0885-6249 See JOURNAL OF COMMUNITY AND APPLIED SOCIAL PSYCHOLOGY. 5249
0885-6257 See EUROPEAN JOURNAL OF SPECIAL NEEDS EDUCATION. 1878
0885-6265 See INTERNATIONAL PEDIATRICS. 3904
0885-6311 See PANORAMA (HOUSTON, TEX.). 749
0885-6362 See GEOBYTE. 2139
0885-6370 See PUBLICATION DESIGN ANNUAL. 381
0885-6389 See SUN (BOLINBROOK EDITION). 5662
0885-6400 See DAV MAGAZINE (1985). 5281
0885-6435 See SEACOAST LIFE. 2545
0885-6540 See NEW AMERICAN (BELMONT, MASS.), THE. 4483
0885-6567 See TALBOTTON NEW ERA. 5655
0885-6583 See OHIO CHESS BULLETIN. 4864
0885-6613 See PHILADELPHIA INQUIRER (1969), THE. 5738
0885-6621 See DISTRICT HEATING AND COOLING. 2604
0885-663X See CHRYSLER POWER. 1968
0885-6680 See PLAZA (CAMBRIDGE, MASS.). 3424
0885-6702 See ACT (NEW YORK, N.Y.), THE. 335
0885-6729 See SOCIAL INDICATORS NETWORK NEWS. 5219
0885-6737 See PLANNING NEWS (ALBANY, N.Y.). 2831
0885-680X See WATERTOWN DAILY TIMES (WATERTOWN, WIS.). 5771
0885-6834 See STATISTICAL REFERENCE INDEX. 5340
0885-6842 See SOMETHING ABOUT THE AUTHOR. AUTOBIOGRAPHY SERIES. 3438
0885-6869 See ST. LOUIS/SOUTHERN ILLINOIS LABOR TRIBUNE. 1711
0885-6877 See FOOD-SERVICE EAST. 2340
0885-6885 See INSIDE TRACK (MIAMI, FLA.). 870
0885-6893 See AMERICAN PUBLIC OPINION DATA. 5238
0885-6907 See TEXAS BANKING. 813
0885-6931 See PRACTICING CPA, THE. 750
0885-6966 See NEWSLETTER NEWSLETTER, THE. 2922
0885-7016 See PRESERVATION BRIEFS. 2755
0885-7024 See CIVIL ENGINEERING (NEW YORK, N.Y. 1983). 2021

0885-7032 See FMG NEWSLETTER / CIVIC RESEARCH CENTER. 3576
0885-7083 See CATALOGUE OF FORAMINIFERA. SUPPL. 4164
0885-7091 See NURSING BUSINESS NEWS. 700
0885-7113 See BALUNGAN. 4102
0885-7121 See PORTLAND REV. (1981). 3424
0885-713X See QUALITY ASSURANCE AND UTILIZATION REVIEW : OFFICIAL JOURNAL OF THE AMERICAN COLLEGE OF UTILIZATION REVIEW PHYSICIANS. 3632
0885-7148 See ASTROLOGY & PARAPSYCHOLOGY TODAY. 390
0885-7156 See POWDER DIFFRACTION. 4015
0885-7172 See FAIR EMPLOYMENT COMPLIANCE. 3148
0885-7202 See EMPLOYEE COMMUNICATION. 1110
0885-7237 See ECONEWS (ARCATA, CALIF.). 2192
0885-7253 See METAPHOR AND SYMBOLIC ACTIVITY. 3411
0885-7288 See CAREER DEVELOPMENT FOR EXCEPTIONAL INDIVIDUALS. 1911
0885-7377 See L. A. ARCHITECT. 302
0885-7385 See POSTA (LAKE OSWEGO, OR.), LA. 2786
0885-7393 See TRACS JOURNAL. 1886
0885-7423 See PSYCHOLOGY AND SOCIOLOGY OF SPORT. 4612
0885-744X See MEDICAL MALPRACTICE PREVENTION. 3008
0885-7458 See INTERNATIONAL JOURNAL OF PARALLEL PROGRAMMING. 1279
0885-7466 See SOCIAL JUSTICE RESEARCH (NEW YORK, N.Y.). 5219
0885-7474 See JOURNAL OF SCIENTIFIC COMPUTING. 5120
0885-7482 See JOURNAL OF FAMILY VIOLENCE. 2282
0885-7490 See METABOLIC BRAIN DISEASE. 3838
0885-7512 See MONOGRAPHIC REVIEW. 3413
0885-7547 See CAREER PATHFINDER, THE. 4202
0885-761X See MONOGRAPH SERIES - UNIVERSITY OF TULSA. 3348
0885-7628 See NORTHWEST PASSAGES HISTORICAL NEWSLETTER. 2751
0885-7636 #y 0883-1165 See VEGETARIAN JOURNAL. 4200
0885-7660 See INFORMATION INDUSTRY BULLETIN. 3216
0885-7679 See NATIONAL CATTLEMEN. 216
0885-7717 See PSYCHIATRIC HOSPITAL, THE. 3791
0885-7733 See PROGRESS IN SCIENTIFIC COMPUTING. 1201
0885-7741 See RECORDER (NEW YORK, N.Y. 1985), THE. 2627
0885-775X See PROFESSIONAL PAPER - INDIANA STATE UNIVERSITY. DEPT. OF GEOGRAPHY AND GEOLOGY. 2573
0885-7776 See MEMOS (SPRINGFIELD, MO.). 4976
0885-7792 See NUTRITION ACTION HEALTH LETTER. 4195
0885-7814 See NORRIDGE NEWS. 5661
0885-7822 See HEAVY METAL. 3393
0885-7849 See ANNUAL REPORT ... ANNUAL MEETING / OREGON HORTICULTURAL SOCIETY. 2409
0885-7881 See PUBLICATIONS IN OPERATIONS RESEARCH SERIES. 1201
0885-7954 See PUBLICATIONS / AUGUSTAN REPRINT SOCIETY. 3426
0885-7970 See I AIN'T LYING. 2318
0885-7989 See COMMERCIAL NEWS INTERNATIONAL. 5634
0885-8004 See JOYFUL WOMAN MAGAZINE, THE. 5559
0885-8039 See REMODELING (WASHINGTON, D.C.). 626

0885-8047 See ORANGE LEADER (ORANGE, TEX.). 5753
0885-8055 See BUSINESS SOFTWARE REVIEW. 1172
0885-8063 See ITC COMMUNICATOR. 1114
0885-8144 See REFLECTIONS (INDIANAPOLIS, IND.). 3868
0885-8152 See COUNTRYMARK. 168
0885-8195 See JOURNAL OF CANCER EDUCATION, THE. 3819
0885-8276 See AMERICAN JOURNAL OF PHYSIOLOGIC IMAGING. 577
0885-8292 See AUTO ADVERTISING REPORT. 756
0885-8306 See REPORTS OF THE STATE BIOLOGICAL SURVEY OF KANSAS. 471
0885-8314 See MCHENRY COUNTY ILLINOIS CONNECTION QUARTERLY. 2460
0885-8330 See TRANSPORTATION ENERGY RESEARCH. 5396
0885-8365 See CORPORATE PHILANTHROPY REPORT. 4335
0885-8373 See REPORTS OF INVESTIGATIONS - SOUTHERN METHODIST UNIVERSITY. INSTITUTE FOR THE STUDY OF EARTH AND MAN. 5146
0885-8381 See RESOURCE BULLETIN SE. 2393
0885-839X See BROOKLYN PAPER, THE. 5714
0885-8403 See MILITARY LIFESTYLE (UNITED STATES EDITION). 4051
0885-842X See NEW JERSEY MEDICINE. 3620
0885-8454 See ROWAN COUNTY REGISTER. 2471
0885-8462 See CONTEMPORARY GRAPHIC ARTISTS. 377
0885-8500 See COMMON BOUNDARY, THE. 4582
0885-8527 See LAS CRUCES BULLETIN. 5814
0885-8551 See WRESTLING ALL STARS, HEROES & VILLAINS. 4931
0885-856X See TORT & INSURANCE LAW JOURNAL. 3065
0885-8578 See BREAKTHROUGH (ATLANTA, GA.). 2771
0885-8608 See NATURAL AREAS JOURNAL. 2199
0885-8624 See JOURNAL OF BUSINESS & INDUSTRIAL MARKETING, THE. 927
0885-8659 See SHMATE. 2629
0885-8691 See SERIE LINGUISTICA PERUANA. 3321
0885-8837 See FIRE APPARATUS JOURNAL. 2289
0885-8950 See IEEE TRANSACTIONS ON POWER SYSTEMS. 2063
0885-8969 See IEEE TRANSACTIONS ON ENERGY CONVERSION. 2062
0885-8977 See IEEE TRANSACTIONS ON POWER DELIVERY. 2063
0885-8985 See IEEE AEROSPACE AND ELECTRONIC SYSTEMS MAGAZINE. 23
0885-8993 See IEEE TRANSACTIONS ON POWER ELECTRONICS. 2063
0885-9000 See IEEE EXPERT. 1229
0885-9043 See CONFIDENTIAL, REPORT FROM ZURICH. 1470
0885-906X See TIMBER PROCESSING. 2405
0885-9078 See SEC REPORT. 4917
0885-9086 See PRESS ARGUS-COURIER. 5632
0885-9116 See EXPOSURE DRAFT (STAMFORD, CONN. 1974). 743
0885-9132 See BULLETIN / AMERICAN ASSOCIATION OF UNIVERSITY WOMEN. 1812
0885-9140 See SOUTH DAKOTA MUSEUM, THE. 4096
0885-9167 See EYECARE BUSINESS. 4215
0885-9175 See CONTACT LENS SPECTRUM. 4215
0885-9183 See COMPLETE BASEBALL RECORD BOOK, THE. 4891
0885-9191 See TMJ UPDATE. 1336
0885-9205 See MANHATTAN POETRY REVIEW. 3465
0885-9221 See SPE PRODUCTION ENGINEERING. 4279

0885-923X See SPE FORMATION EVALUATION. 4279

0885-9248 See SPE RESERVOIR ENGINEERING. 4279

0885-9264 See CONTACT LENS UPDATE. 3873

0885-9299 See BUILDING ECONOMICS. 603

0885-9302 See SIXTEENTH CENTURY BIBLIOGRAPHY. 2636

0885-9310 See SOUTHWEST PHILOSOPHICAL STUDIES. 4361

0885-9337 See BOULEVARD (NEW YORK, N.Y.). 3368

0885-937X See COLLEGE WOMAN (BURBANK, CALIF.). 1817

0885-940X See CITY & STATE (CHICAGO, ILL.). 4717

0885-9418 See MATHEMATICAL CONCEPTS AND METHODS IN SCIENCE AND ENGINEERING. 3518

0885-9434 See MIT PRESS SERIES IN SIGNAL PROCESSING, OPTIMIZATION, AND CONTROL, THE. 4412

0885-9477 See SPARROW. 3471

0885-9507 See MICROCOMPUTERS IN CIVIL ENGINEERING. 2027

0885-9531 See WEST SIDE SPIRIT (CITY EDITION). 5722

0885-9574 See SELECTED PAPERS FROM THE WEST VIRGINIA SHAKESPEARE AND RENAISSANCE ASSOCIATION. 3435

0885-9612 See SHELTERFORCE. 2835

0885-9647 See BLACK ELEGANCE. 2529

0885-9671 See DIRECTORY OF HOSPITAL PERSONNEL, THE. 3779

0885-968X See EMBLEMATICA. 3384

0885-9698 See TECHNIQUES IN ORTHOPAEDICS (ROCKVILLE, MD.). 3885

0885-9701 See JOURNAL OF HEAD TRAUMA REHABILITATION, THE. 4380

0885-971X See TOPICS IN ACUTE CARE AND TRAUMA REHABILITATION. 3646

0885-9744 See SPE DRILLING ENGINEERING. 4278

0885-9787 See ARETE. 5273

0885-9795 See AGAIN MAGAZINE. 4933

0885-9841 See SHOPPING CENTERS TODAY. 957

0885-985X See JOURNAL OF SOCIAL STUDIES RESEARCH. 5207

0885-9868 See GONZAGA SPECIAL REPORT. 2975

0885-9876 See GEOLOGICAL SURVEY REPORT OF PROGRESS. 1378

0885-9884 See JOURNAL OF THE ASSOCIATION OF TEACHERS OF JAPANESE, THE. 3292

0885-9922 See LUTHERAN PARTNERS. 5063

0885-9930 See BUILDING ECONOMIC ALTERNATIVES. 1465

0885-9949 See MARINE TEXTILES. 5354

0885-9965 See AOR OBSERVER, THE. 4210

0885-9973 See MAINE BAR JOURNAL. 3005

0885-999X See CUTTING EDGE (NEW ROCHELLE, N.Y.). 1734

0886-005X See CHAMPS-ELYSEES (NASHVILLE, TENN.). 3273

0886-005X See CHAMPS-ELYSEES. 2514

0886-0076 See DIRECTORY OF AMERICAN RESEARCH AND TECHNOLOGY. 5174

0886-0092 See READERS' GUIDE ABSTRACTS (MICROFORM). 423

0886-0106 See INDUSTRIAL LASER HANDBOOK, THE. 4435

0886-0114 See INTERNATIONAL ARBITRATION REPORT. 3129

0886-0122 See MEALEY'S LITIGATION REPORT. TOBACCO. 3007

0886-0130 See NUCLEAR GEOPHYSICS. 1409

0886-0130 See INTERNATIONAL JOURNAL OF RADIATION APPLICATIONS AND INSTRUMENTATION. PART E, NUCLEAR GEOPHYSICS, THE. 1407

0886-0149 See OCEAN NAVIGATOR. 1453

0886-0165 See NON-CREDIT LEARNING NEWS. 1801

0886-0181 See PC COMPANION. 1198

0886-022X See RENAL FAILURE. 3992

0886-0238 See HEMATOLOGIC PATHOLOGY. 3894

0886-0246 See READING RESEARCH AND INSTRUCTION. 3314

0886-0254 See BOATBUILDER (RIVERSIDE, CONN.). 592

0886-0262 See HERITAGE QUEST. 2453

0886-0408 See LAW BOOKS IN REVIEW. 2995

0886-0424 See STUDIES IN THE HISTORY OF ART (WILLIAMSTOWN, MASS.). 366

0886-0432 See STUDIA LINGUISTICA ET PHILOLOGICA. 3324

0886-0440 See JOURNAL OF CARDIAC SURGERY. 3966

0886-0459 See LETTERS OF CREDIT REPORT. 796

0886-0467 See LASERS IN THE LIFE SCIENCES. 4438

0886-0475 See CORPORATE PRACTICE SERIES. BNA'S CORPORATE COUNSEL WEEKLY. 3099

0886-0483 See HOW (BETHESDA, MD.). 380

0886-0556 See COMPUTER SHOPPER. 1244

0886-0564 See MINERAL INDUSTRY SURVEYS. 2144

0886-0572 See MARYLAND MEDICAL JOURNAL (1985). 3606

0886-0599 See BECKETT BASEBALL CARD MONTHLY. 2771

0886-0637 See WILDFOWL (ADEL, IOWA). 4880

0886-0653 See MEDICAL ETHICS ADVISOR. 2252

0886-0661 See TESL REPORTER. 1787

0886-070X See STATISTICAL ECOLOGY SERIES. 2221

0886-0750 See STANFORD FRENCH AND ITALIAN STUDIES. 3439

0886-0793 See GOURMET FOOD & WINE FESTIVALS OF NORTH AMERICA. 5268

0886-0882 See TECHNICAL BULLETIN - NATIONAL COUNCIL OF THE PAPER INDUSTRY FOR AIR AND STREAM IMPROVEMENT (U.S.). (1981). 4239

0886-0890 See TECHNOLOGY FORECASTS AND TECHNOLOGY SURVEYS. 5163

0886-0912 See ROCKY MOUNTAIN PAY DIRT. 2150

0886-0920 See SOUTHWESTERN PAY DIRT. 2151

0886-0955 See NEW JERSEY BOATER. 594

0886-1013 See ART LAW AND ACCOUNTING REPORTER. 2937

0886-103X See TECHNOLOGY MANAGEMENT ACTION. 5164

0886-1064 See JOURNAL (AMERICAN ACADEMY OF GNATHOLOGIC ORTHOPEDICS). 1325

0886-1080 See ORIENTEERING NORTH AMERICA. 4911

0886-1099 See AFFILIA. 5270

0886-117X See WORLD HISTORY BULLETIN. 2633

0886-1188 See MACKNIT. 5184

0886-1234 See AMERICAN LEGION, THE. 4034

0886-1242 See TIMBER PRODUCER, THE. 2405

0886-1269 See TENNESSEE WILDLIFE (NASHVILLE, TENN. 1977). 2207

0886-1293 See COMPANY (CHICAGO, ILL.). 4949

0886-1315 See INFANT SCREENING. 3904

0886-1331 See TIN (WASHINGTON, D.C. ANNUAL). 2152

0886-134X See BETTY AND VERONICA COMICS DIGEST MAGAZINE. 4857

0886-1447 See WRI PAPER. 1527

0886-1498 See SUCCESSFUL SALESWOMAN. 714

0886-1501 See SHARING IDEAS. 2545

0886-1528 See INTERNATIONAL REVIEW OF INDUSTRIAL AND ORGANIZATIONAL PSYCHOLOGY. 4591

0886-1544 See CELL MOTILITY AND THE CYTOSKELETON. 533

0886-1560 See SEARCH (SANTA CLARA, CALIF.). 3248

0886-1587 See ADVANCES IN CRYOGENIC ENGINEERING MATERIALS. 1964

0886-1609 See RADIO CONTROL CAR ACTION. 2777

0886-1633 See EVALUATION PRACTICE. 5200

0886-1641 See JOURNAL OF SOCIAL BEHAVIOR AND PERSONALITY. 4601

0886-165X See LAS VEGAS INTERNATIONALE. 2537

0886-1668 See GRIO' (BLACK HISTORY ED.). 2735

0886-1714 See NEWS IN PHYSIOLOGICAL SCIENCES. 584

0886-1730 See TRANSACTIONS OF THE MORAVIAN HISTORICAL SOCIETY. 5068

0886-179X See LUZ (CLAYTON, MO.), LA. 3300

0886-1803 See DEBATE ISSUES. 1734

0886-182X See OSIA NEWS. 2491

0886-1846 See VIE (CLAYTON, MO.), LA. 3332

0886-1862 See HOGAKU. 4121

0886-1897 See PODIUM (CHICAGO, ILL.), THE. 4146

0886-1935 See CLOSING THE GAP. 1877

0886-1994 See COMPETITIVE ADVANTAGE, THE. 757

0886-2052 See SPECIALTY NEWS. 851

0886-2060 See WORKS AND DAYS. 333

0886-2079 See SOUTH FLORIDA MEDICAL REVIEW. 3642

0886-2087 See VOICE NEWS. 1168

0886-2095 See HEALTH CARE COMPETITION WEEK. 4778

0886-2125 See PERSONNEL POSTSCRIPT. 3626

0886-2141 See RELIGION WATCH. 4991

0886-2168 See UPSTART CROW, THE. 3449

0886-2230 See NETMANAGER. 880

0886-2257 See AIR & SPACE SMITHSONIAN. 6

0886-229X See ANNUAL REVIEW OF COMMUNICATIONS. 1149

0886-2362 See TOKEN PERSPECTIVES NEWSLETTER. 1205

0886-2397 See LOCALNETTER NEWSLETTER, THE. 1193

0886-2400 See DATACOM READER SERVICE. 1237

0886-2435 See CHANGE EXCHANGE. 3140

0886-246X See HIGHLIGHTS OF FEDERAL UNEMPLOYMENT COMPENSATION LAWS. 3148

0886-2478 See FRANCE MAGAZINE. 2517

0886-2508 See SCHOOL LAW BULLETIN (CHAPEL HILL, N.C.). 1871

0886-2516 See REVISTA JURIDICA DE LA UNIVERSIDAD DE PUERTO RICO. 3042

0886-2540 See NEW ENGLAND JURY VERDICT REVIEW AND ANALYSIS. 3090

0886-2567 See ALMANAC OF FEDERAL PACS. 4462

0886-2575 See UNIX PRODUCTS DIRECTORY. 1206

0886-2605 See JOURNAL OF INTERPERSONAL VIOLENCE. 5292

0886-2648 See SUFFOLK TRANSNATIONAL LAW JOURNAL. 3136

0886-2648 See SUFFOLK TRANSNATIONAL LAW REVIEW. 3136

0886-2680 See SOUTH DAKOTA MAGAZINE (YANKTON, S.D.). 2546

0886-2729 See FLORIDA MARKET UPDATE. 1561

0886-2737 See MANHATTAN OFFICE BUILDINGS. DOWNTOWN. 4840

0886-277X See REGISTER OF NATIONAL CERTIFIED COUNSELORS. 5304

0886-2796 See DOROT. 2445

0886-2818 See WIND ENERGY NEWS. 1960

0886-2826 See SACRAMENTO MEDICINE. 3638

0886-3008 See FISHING & HUNTING JOURNAL. 4872

0886-3032 See SPIN (NEW YORK, N.Y.). 4154

0886-3121 See IN-PLANT REPRODUCTIONS & ELECTRONIC PUBLISHING. 4815

0886-3148 See ASH AT WORK. 2134

0886-3210 See CALIFORNIA WESTERN INTERNATIONAL LAW JOURNAL. 3125

0886-3261 See CITIZEN NEWS-RECORD (ROBBINS ED.), THE. 5723

0886-327X See CORPORATE COUNSEL REVIEW. 3098

0886-3296 See SOUTHWESTERN UNIVERSITY LAW REVIEW. 3057

0886-330X See INDIANA FACTBOOK (BLOOMINGTON, IND.). 2535

0886-3342 See OFFICIAL GUIDE TO U.S. LAW SCHOOLS, THE. 1838

0886-3407 See WILDFOWL CARVING AND COLLECTING. 376

0886-344X See AMPHIBIOUS WARFARE REVIEW. 4034

0886-3458 See WILDLIFE HARVEST. 4880

0886-3490 See ARMS CONTROL REPORTER, THE. 4516

0886-3504 See GREAT TASTE. 2342

0886-3520 See JOURNAL OF THE COPYRIGHT SOCIETY OF THE U.S.A. 1305

0886-3547 See TAX MANAGEMENT ESTATES, GIFTS, AND TRUSTS JOURNAL. 3119

0886-3628 See SOFTWARE LAW JOURNAL. 3056

0886-3687 See COMPENSATION AND BENEFITS REVIEW. 1660

0886-3717 See U.S.-ARAB COMMERCE. 855

0886-3725 See MANHATTAN OFFICE BUILDINGS. MIDTOWN. 4840

0886-3733 See ROWLETT RECORD AMERICAN. 5754

0886-3741 See CANDY MARKETER (1985). 2330

0886-3784 See READINGS - AMERICAN ORTHOPSYCHIATRIC ASSOCIATION. 3935

0886-3792 See CHILDREN FOR TODAY'S PARENT. 2278

0886-3806 See CYPRIS. 4226

0886-3830 See BETTER WORLD. 4577

0886-3857 See AIR PROGRESS MILITARY AIRPOWER. 4034

0886-3865 See VICTORIANS INSTITUTE JOURNAL. 5237

0886-3881 See NATIONAL DIRECTORY OF MINORITY-OWNED BUSINESS FIRMS. 697

0886-389X See NATIONAL DIRECTORY OF WOMEN-OWNED BUSINESS FIRMS. 697

0886-3946 See REGIONAL DIRECTORY OF MINORITY & WOMEN-OWNED BUSINESS FIRMS. (WESTERN EDITION). 706

0886-3962 See EXETER NEWS-LETTER (1867), THE. 5708

0886-3970 See CARD REPORT (AMES, IOWA. 1986). 72

0886-4063 See KNOWLEDGE MATTERS. 4351

0886-4144 See LOADSTAR. 1288

0886-4152 See SOFTDISK. 1203

0886-4179 See SERIALS DIRECTORY (BIRMINGHAM, ALA. PRINT ED.), THE. 3249

0886-4209 See OTTUMWA COURIER. 5672

0886-4225 See COMPUTERWHAT?. 1179

0886-4241 See NEW MEXICO QUARTER HORSE, THE. 2801

0886-4268 See PRECIOUS FIBERS. 5355

0886-4284 See CHILDREN'S FUN PUZZLES (1985). 4858

0886-4306 See OBSERVER (NEW YORK, N.Y. : 1985). 3020

0886-4330 See ZIONSVILLE TIMES SENTINEL. 5668

0886-4357 See AMERICAN RED ANGUS. 205

0886-4365 See ALMOND FACTS. 2408

0886-4373 See AGRONOMY RESEARCH REPORT AG. 56

0886-4381 See AGRONOMY DEPARTMENT SERIES. 56

0886-4403 See AGRONOMY RESEARCH REPORT. 56

0886-4411 See POWER AND MOTORYACHT. 595

0886-442X See POPULAR MUSIC : AN ANNOTATED INDEX OF AMERICAN POPULAR SONGS. 4147

0886-4446 See COOKING LIGHT (SOUTHERN LIVING, INC.). 4189

0886-4454 See BIOCATALYSIS. 480

0886-4470 See ARCHIVES OF OTOLARYNGOLOGY-HEAD & NECK SURGERY. 3886

0886-4489 See BIG SKY ECONOMICS. 66

0886-4500 See ANNUAL RESEARCH REPORT - RED RIVER VALLEY AGRICULTURAL EXPERIMENT STATION (BOSSIER CITY, LA.). 163

0886-4527 See PAR EXCELLANCE MAGAZINE. 4911

0886-4535 See FASB TECHNICAL BULLETIN. 744

0886-4551 See SCHOLASTIC UPDATE (TEACHERS' ED.). 2545

0886-4594 See CALENDAR FOR NEW MUSIC, THE. 4106

0886-4691 See VITAL & HEALTH STATISTICS. SERIES 3, ANALYTICAL AND EPIDEMIOLOGICAL STUDIES. 4811

0886-473X See BULLETIN B - OKLAHOMA STATE UNIVERSITY. AGRICULTURAL EXPERIMENT STATION. 68

0886-4748 See KATY KEENE. 4862

0886-4780 See POTATO COUNTRY. 182

0886-4845 See ECONOMIC INFORMATION REPORT (GAINESVILLE, FLA.). 81

0886-4861 See D.A.E. RESEARCH REPORT. 78

0886-4934 See ORANGE COUNTY REGISTER, THE. 5638

0886-5124 See CALIFORNIA POULTRY LETTER. 208

0886-5140 See COMMENTS ON TOXICOLOGY. 3980

0886-5159 See AMERICAN PRESBYTERIANS. 5055

0886-5175 See WARD'S AUTOMOTIVE REPORTS. 5402

0886-5183 See AKRON BUSINESS REPORTER. 637

0886-5213 See WASHINGTON STATE BAR NEWS. 3073

0886-5256 See NORTHWEST REVIEW OF BOOKS, THE. 4831

0886-5272 See HISTORICAL FOOTNOTES (STONINGTON, CONN.). 2737

0886-5299 See YOUR BIG BACKYARD. 1072

0886-5345 See ECONOMIC AND SOCIAL ISSUES. 81

0886-537X See TELEPHONE BYPASS NEWS. 1167

0886-5477 See JOURNAL OF PASTORAL PSYCHOTHERAPY. 4599

0886-5507 See PPURI. 2507

0886-5558 See CHOICES (AMES, IOWA). 73

0886-5604 See CRUISE DIGEST. 5467

0886-5612 See COPYCAT MAGAZINE. 1891

0886-5639 See MICHIGAN BUSINESS (SOUTHFIELD, MICH. : 1984). 694

0886-5647 See NATIONWIDE OVERNIGHT STABLING DIRECTORY. 2801

0886-5655 See JOURNAL OF BORDERLANDS STUDIES. 2740

0886-5663 See PRODUCE BUSINESS. 2354

0886-5671 See ELECTRONIC CHEMICALS NEWS. 2047

0886-5698 See CURRENT POPULATION REPORTS. SERIES P-70, HOUSEHOLD ECONOMIC STUDIES. 4551

0886-5701 See JOURNAL OF READING EDUCATION. 1758

0886-571X See RESIDENTIAL TREATMENT FOR CHILDREN & YOUTH. 5306

0886-5760 See GEORGIA VETERINARIAN, THE. 5510

0886-5779 See HORTICULTURAL NEWS (NEW BRUNSWICK, N.J.). 2419

0886-5787 See INFORMATION SHEET - MISSISSIPPI STATE UNIVERSITY. COOPERATIVE EXTENSION SERVICE. 1542

0886-5809 See DOCUMENT IMAGE AUTOMATION. 1277

0886-5833 See FLOWER AND NURSERY REPORT FOR COMMERCIAL GROWERS. 2414

0886-5841 See FOREST FIRE NEWS. 2379

0886-5884 See FEED & FEEDING DIGEST. 200

0886-5906 See FARM ECONOMICS : FACTS AND OPINIONS. 84

0886-5949 See EXTERIORS. 614

0886-5965 See GEORGETOWN GRAPHIC. 5680

0886-6007 See JOURNAL (CROSBY, N.D.), THE. 5725

0886-6015 See CIVILIAN-BASED DEFENSE. 4039

0886-6147 See TRAVEL BUSINESS MANAGER, THE. 5495

0886-6155 See WEST TEXAS HISTORICAL ASSOCIATION YEAR BOOK, THE. 2765

0886-6163 See WHAT TO BUY FOR BUSINESS (U.S. ED.). 4214

0886-618X See SURFACE MOUNT TECHNOLOGY TODAY. 4423

0886-6198 See GLOBAL AFFAIRS. 4522

0886-621X See FEDERAL LITIGATOR. 3089

0886-6236 See GLOBAL BIOGEOCHEMICAL CYCLES. 1041

0886-635X See ISSUE BRIEFING PAPER / UNITED STATES DEPARTMENT OF AGRICULTURE. 98

0886-6457 See PACS & LOBBIES. 4511

0886-6481 See THOUGHTS FOR ALL SEASONS. 3446

0886-6503 See SIERRA HERITAGE. 5491

0886-6554 See VIM & VIGOR. 2601

0886-6570 See CINEMATOGRAPH. 317

0886-6600 See CROSS STITCH & COUNTRY CRAFTS. 5183

0886-6619 See NJ AUDUBON. 2200

0886-6643 See ELECTRONIC HOUSE. 1267

0886-666X See STANFORD LITERATURE REVIEW. 3353

0886-6694 See PREVENTING SEXUAL ABUSE. 5301

0886-6708 See VIOLENCE AND VICTIMS. 3178

0886-6716 See CHEMICAL DESIGN AUTOMATION NEWS. 968

0886-6767 See OFFICE AUTOMATION REPORT, THE. 4213

0886-6813 See AD VANTAGE (CANOGA PARK, CALIF.). 753

0886-683X See PLANT BIBLIOGRAPHY. 2427

0886-6864 See OTAN NEWSLETTER. 5593

0886-6880 See YEARBOOK / CLAREMONT READING CONFERENCE. 3334

0886-6899 See PROCEEDINGS OF THE ... FORAGE AND GRASSLAND CONFERENCE. 122

0886-697X See HYDROWIRE. 2056

0886-702X See PROGRAM - AMERICAN DAIRY SCIENCE ASSOCIATION. MEETING. 198

0886-7038 See PROGRESS REPORT - IDAHO. AGRICULTURAL EXPERIMENT STATION. 123

0886-7062 See CONNEXIONS (OAKLAND, CALIF.). 5553

0886-7097 See STUDIES IN AMERICAN DRAMA, 1945-PRESENT. 5369

0886-7143 See EMPHASIS, NURSING. 3855

0886-7151 See NOTICIAS DEL PUERTO DE MONTEREY. 326

0886-7178 See PURPA LINES. 1954

0886-7186 See CLINICAL ONCOLOGY ALERT. 3815

0886-7194 See COMPUTER MARKETING NEWSLETTER, THE. 1244

0886-7208 See ANTIQUES & FINE ART. 249

0886-7283 See PROCEEDINGS OF THE ANNUAL MEETING OF THE FLORIDA STATE HORTICULTURAL SOCIETY. 2429

0886-733X See PROCEEDINGS OF THE MICHIANA AREA HISTORIANS. 2626

0886-7348 See BOISE STATE UNIVERSITY WESTERN WRITERS SERIES. 431

0886-7356 See CULTURAL ANTHROPOLOGY. 234

0886-7372 See RESEARCH REPORT / INTERNATIONAL FOOD POLICY RESEARCH INSTITUTE. 2355

0886-7380 See RESEARCH PAPER INT. 2393

0886-7461 See BIOINVENTION. 3686

0886-747X See PROCEEDINGS OF THE ANNUAL INSTITUTE - ROCKY MOUNTAIN MINERAL LAW INSTITUTE. 3115

0886-7526 See MONOGRAPH - GEOLOGICAL SURVEY OF ALABAMA. 1388

0886-7585 See RURAL DEVELOPMENT RESEARCH REPORT. 131

0886-7607 See SDI MONITOR. 4056

0886-7623 See SPECIAL REPORT - NEW YORK STATE AGRICULTURAL EXPERIMENT STATION. 137

0886-764X See GREAT ACTIVITIES. 1855

0886-7682 See STEP-BY-STEP GRAPHICS. 382

0886-7690 See YEARBOOK OF AGRICULTURE (1980), THE. 148

0886-7747 See INTER-AMERICAN LEGAL MATERIALS / AMERICAN BAR ASSOCIATION, SECTION OF INTERNATIONAL LAW AND PRACTICE, INTER-AMERICAN LAW COMMITTEE. 2983

0886-7771 See RADIUS (MENDOCINO, CALIF.). 328

0886-778X See ADVANCE (WASHINGTON, D.C. 1986). 1460

0886-7798 See TUNNELLING AND UNDERGROUND SPACE TECHNOLOGY. 2033

0886-8018 See KEY NEUROLOGY AND NEUROSURGERY. 3837

0886-8026 See KEY OPTHALMOLOGY. 3876

0886-8042 See IMAGE PROCESSING TECHNOLOGY. 5112

0886-8085 See ECONOMIC IMPACT (WASHINGTON, D.C.). 1557

0886-8115 See NEW ART EXAMINER. 359

0886-8123 See LEADERSHIP WITH A HUMAN TOUCH. 875

0886-8131 See GLASS ART MAGAZINE (BROOMFIELD, COLO.). 2589

0886-8174 See PUGET SOUND COMPUTER USER. 1201

0886-8190 See CATHOLIC SINGLES. 5242

0886-8204 See COMMERCIAL LENDING REVIEW. 783

0886-8212 See PAPER CLIPP. 4235

0886-8220 See CONTRIBUTIONS IN MEDICAL STUDIES. 3568

0886-828X See ALTERNATIVE ENERGY (BEVERLY HILLS, CALIF.). 1931

0886-8360 See IOLA HERALD, THE. 5768

0886-845X See ENTRY (ANN ARBOR, MICH.). 4369

0886-8506 See ELECTRONIC MARKET TRENDS. 2047

0886-8514 See ENERGY BUSINESS. 1939

0886-8557 See TENNESSEE EMPLOYMENT LAW UPDATE, THE. 3154

0886-8611 See RURAL DEVELOPMENT NEWS. 4847

0886-8697 See OZ COLLECTOR, THE. 3421

0886-8719 See MIDNIGHT MARQUEE. 386

0886-8751 See BEAUTY CLASSIC. 402

0886-8778 See MOTOR FREIGHT CONTROLLER. 5387

0886-8794 See REALTOR (LANSING, MICH.). 4845

0886-8808 See OBSERVER (DE WITT, IOWA. NATIONAL ED.). 5672

0886-8816 See PRESS & SUN-BULLETIN. 5720

0886-8832 See MILITARY CLUB & HOSPITALITY. 2350

0886-8840 See FORT BRAGG ADVOCATE-NEWS. 5635

0886-8913 See BIOETHICS LITERATURE REVIEW. 2249

0886-9014 See RESEARCH REPORT - UNIVERSITY OF MICHIGAN. POPULATION STUDIES CENTER. 4559

0886-9022 See PLASTICS INDUSTRY NEWS (DENVER, COLO.). 4458

0886-9049 See OUR RIGHT TO KNOW. 4486

0886-9138 See PORTABLE PAPER, THE. 1199

0886-9162 See WORKERS' COMPENSATION JOURNAL OF OHIO. 1719

0886-9189 See MACRAE'S BLUE BOOK (1986). 1616

0886-9197 See PADDLER (FALLBROOK, CALIF.). 4877

0886-9227 See PUBLICATION - COASTAL PLAINS CENTER FOR MARINE DEVELOPMENT SERVICES. 1455

0886-9235 See PROCEEDINGS OF THE NATIONAL GROUND WATER QUALITY SYMPOSIUM. 5537

0886-9278 See SOCIETY FOR NURSING HISTORY GAZETTE, THE. 3869

0886-9286 See SOCIAL STUDIES JOURNAL (PENNSYLVANIA COUNCIL FOR THE SOCIAL STUDIES). 5221

0886-9308 See U.S. GEOLOGICAL SURVEY WATER-SUPPLY PAPER. 1400

0886-9324 See TECHNICAL REPORT - U. S. ARMY RESEARCH INSTITUTE FOR THE BEHAVIORAL AND SOCIAL SCIENCES. 4059

0886-9359 See DONOR BRIEFING. 5284

0886-9367 See INTERNATIONAL JOURNAL OF ANALYTICAL AND EXPERIMENTAL MODAL ANALYSIS, THE. 2116

0886-9375 See REGULATED RIVERS. 1359

0886-9383 See JOURNAL OF CHEMOMETRICS. 980

0886-9456 See UNIVERSITY OF DETROIT MERCY LAW REVIEW. 3068

0886-9480 See AMAZING COMPUTING. 1264

0886-9596 See FRESH!. 4118

0886-9626 See SAIL BOARDER INTERNATIONAL. 4916

0886-9634 See CRANIO. 3569

0886-9642 See TELEPROFESSIONAL. 937

0886-9669 See WINDOW FASHIONS. 2904

0886-9685 See CIVIL ENGINEERING PRACTICE. 2021

0886-9693 See EMPIRE STATE FARMER. 81

0886-9707 See AMERICAN PRAYER. 638

0886-9723 See JOURNAL OF AMBULATORY CARE MARKETING. 3725

0886-9766 See RX BEING WELL. 4328

0886-9782 See OVER-55 FINANCIAL MANAGEMENT LETTER. 802

0886-9812 See EXCELLENCE (LOUISVILLE, KY.). 1286

0886-9839 See TELEPHONE MANAGEMENT STRATEGIST. 1167

0886-9863 See RESORT & HOTEL MANAGEMENT. 884

0886-9871 See OLATHE DAILY NEWS, THE. 5678

0886-988X See PHARMACY PRACTICE NEWS. 4323

0886-9901 See CLEANING AND RESTORATION. 5349

0886-9936 See NEW YORK HERALD TIMES CROSSWORD PUZZLES ONLY. 4864

0886-9995 See NEW JERSEY SUCCESS. 698

0887-008X See INTERNATIONAL DIRECTORY OF DISCONTINUED ICS AND DISCRETE SEMICONDUCTORS. 2066

0887-0152 See PETERSON'S COMPETITIVE COLLEGES. 1840

0887-0187 See ABA BANK COMPLIANCE. 768

0887-0209 See ALALITCOM, THE. 3359

0887-0217 See TEACHING THINKING & PROBLEM SOLVING. 4620

0887-0241 See POPULATION REPORTS (BALTIMORE, MD.). 4557

0887-0284 See HYDROCARBON PROCESSING (U.S. ED.). 4260

0887-0292 See AIDS ALERT. 3663

0887-0365 See PARENT AND PRESCHOOLER : PP. 1771

0887-0373 See PUBLIC AFFAIRS QUARTERLY. 4676

0887-0403 See WORLD RESOURCES. 2210

0887-042X See CREATIVE CLASSROOM. 1892

0887-0446 See PSYCHOLOGY & HEALTH. 4797

0887-0470 See RETAIL TENANT DIRECTORY. 957

0887-0519 See ALMANAC OF THE 50 STATES. 1923

0887-0535 See FOOD AND NUTRITION QUARTERLY INDEX. 4191

0887-0551 See DIRECTORY OF GRANTS IN THE HUMANITIES. 2845

0887-0586 See JOURNAL OF WAVE-MATERIAL INTERACTION. 2104

0887-0594 See CENTRAL AMERICA NEWSPAK. 4467

0887-0624 See ENERGY & FUELS. 1939

0887-0632 See SENIOR ADULT STUDENT GUIDE. 4996

0887-0675 See MEDICASSETTE. RADIOLOGY. 3943

0887-0691 See MEDICAL REMARKETER, THE. 1618

0887-0713 See BERKSHIRE GENEALOGIST, THE. 2439

0887-0764 See CONGRESS MONTHLY (1985). 2258

0887-0802 See SENTINEL (CARLISLE, PA.), THE. 5739

0887-0837 See NEWS (TELL CITY, IND.). 5666

0887-0934 See SOUTHEASTERN OUTLOOK. 4998

0887-0942 See FEDERATION OF INSURANCE & CORPORATE COUNSEL QUARTERLY. 2880

0887-1000 See TELEVISION TRENDS. 1141

0887-1035 See SUPERSTAR WRESTLER. 4866

0887-1078 See HISTORY MICROCOMPUTER REVIEW. 2619

0887-1086 See INDUSTRY AND HEALTH CARE (CAMBRIDGE, MASS.). 2863

0887-1094 See CELEBRATION (HAGERSTOWN, MD.). 5057

0887-1116 See CENTENNIAL STATE LIBRARIES. 3201

0887-1167 See SINGLE ADULT MINISTRY INFORMATION. 4997

0887-1175 See COMPUTING INFORMATION DIRECTORY. 727

0887-1183 See LEGAL HANDBOOK FOR ARCHITECTS, ENGINEERS AND CONTRACTORS. 2999

0887-1191 See CIVIL RIGHTS LITIGATION AND ATTORNEY FEES ANNUAL HANDBOOK. 4506

0887-1205 See IMMIGRATION PROCEDURES HANDBOOK. 1919

0887-1264 See COLE CHRONICLE. 2443

0887-1310 See FLORIDA PARENT. 2280

0887-1337 See ANALYSIS OF KEY SEC NO-ACTION LETTERS. 3095

0731-2857 See UNIVERSITY PRESS BOOKS FOR PUBLIC AND SECONDARY SCHOOL LIBRARIES. 3255

0887-137X See EBRI ISSUE BRIEF. 1664

0887-1388 See EMPLOYEE BENEFIT NOTES. 1665

0887-140X See NEWSLETTER - THE ASSOCIATION FOR THE ANTHROPOLOGICAL STUDY OF PLAY. 4853

0887-1418 See HAND PAPERMAKING. 4234

0887-1426 See VICTORY LANE. 4928

0887-1450 See TRAINING SOLUTIONS / DIGITAL CONTROLS. 1205

0887-1493 See AIDS POLICY & LAW. 2928

0887-1507 See PLAYWRIGHT'S COMPANION, THE. 5367

0887-154X See BLUE SKY PRACTICE FOR PUBLIC AND PRIVATE OFFERINGS. 2942

0887-1566 See FOCUS ON AUTISTIC BEHAVIOR. 3577

0887-1574 See INDEX TO BOOK REVIEWS IN RELIGION. 5012

0887-1647 See TELECOMMUNICATORS DISPATCH, THE. 1166

0887-1701 See TV TECHNOLOGY. 1168

0887-171X See POLLING REPORT, THE. 5254

0887-1736 See COMPLICATIONS IN ORTHOPEDICS. 3881
0887-1752 See RESOURCE (ATLANTA, GA.). 2892
0887-1779 See HEAD INJURY UPDATE. 3965
0887-1825 See KEY NOTES (YPSILANTI, MICH.). 1760
0887-1922 See JOHN T. REED'S REAL ESTATE INVESTOR'S MONTHLY. 4839
0887-1930 See CORPORATE TECHNOLOGY DIRECTORY. 3477
0887-1949 See MATERIALS AND PROCESSING REPORT. 2104
0887-1973 See METRO HANDBOOK AND DIRECTORY OF MEMBERS. 3231
0887-2007 See HIGH SCOPE RESOURCE. 1750
0887-204X See UNIVERSITY OF FLORIDA HUMANITIES MONOGRAPHS. 2856
0887-2058 See JOURNAL OF BUSINESS STRATEGIES. 686
0887-2074 See SOUTH COAST POETRY JOURNAL. 3471
0887-2082 See JOURNAL OF BIOCHEMICAL TOXICOLOGY. 3981
0887-2104 See OPERATIONS FORUM. 2238
0887-2120 See WOMAN ENGINEER. (GREENLAWN, N.Y.), THE. 2001
0887-2155 See DUCKBURG TIMES, THE. 2532
0887-2171 See SEMINARS IN ULTRASOUND, CT, AND MR. 3946
0887-2236 See BIOLOGICAL AND CULTURAL TESTS FOR CONTROL OF PLANT DISEASES. 66
0887-2244 See THOROUGHBRED TIMES. 2803
0887-2287 See INSTALLATION NEWS. 1612
0887-2333 See TOXICOLOGY IN VITRO. 3984
0887-2376 See SCIENCE SCOPE (WASHINGTON, D.C.). 5153
0887-2384 See CREATIVE NEEDLE. 5183
0887-2392 See SOVIET MEDICAL REVIEWS. SECTION B, PHYSICOCHEMICAL ASPECTS OF MEDICINE REVIEWS. 3898
0887-2414 See PRIMARY CARE CASE MANAGEMENT NEWSLETTER. 3738
0887-2430 See ADVANCES IN MASS SPECTROMETRY (1985). 4432
0887-2449 See INVESTMENT MANAGEMENT WORLD. 903
0887-2481 See SMALL LAW OFFICE MANAGEMENT REPORT. 3055
0887-2546 See COMBAT WEAPONS. 4039
0887-2554 See LAMP OF DELTA ZETA, THE. 1834
0887-2562 See TAX MANAGEMENT WASHINGTON TAX REVIEW. 4753
0887-2570 See JOURNAL OF HEART AND LUNG TRANSPLANTATION, THE. 3967
0887-2597 See HEARTLAND JOURNAL. 3393
0887-2627 See WASHINGTON WOMAN (ARLINGTON, VA.). 5568
0887-2716 See APPLE LIBRARY USERS GROUP NEWSLETTER. 1171
0887-2783 See SOCIAL HISTORY OF ALCOHOL REVIEW, THE. 1349
0887-283X See DICKINSON JOURNAL OF INTERNATIONAL LAW. 3127
0887-2899 See NATIONAL JURY VERDICT REVIEW AND ANALYSIS, THE. 3090
0887-2910 See AGRI-TIMES NORTHWEST. 48
0887-2937 See CLOTHING AND TEXTILE ARTS INDEX, THE. 1083
0887-3003 See RTW REVIEW. 1087
0887-302X See CLOTHING AND TEXTILES RESEARCH JOURNAL. 5349
0887-3038 See FLORIDA FUNDING. 868
0887-3100 See EURO-AMERICAN QUARTERLY. 4473
0887-3119 See SUNCOAST THEATRE GRAPEVINE, THE. 5369
0887-3127 See ASIAN MEDICAL & BIOTECHNOLOGY NEWS. 3685
0887-3135 See HOLSTON PASTFINDER. 2453
0887-316X See PUBLISHER'S MULTINATIONAL DIRECT. 4818

0887-3208 See FLORIDA REAL ESTATE & DEVELOPMENT UPDATE. 4837
0887-3224 See BIOLOGY OF EXTRACELLULAR MATRIX. 447
0887-3267 See HUMANISTIC PSYCHOLOGIST, THE. 4589
0887-3488 See SOVIET MEDICAL REVIEWS. SECTION D, IMMUNOLOGY REVIEWS. 3677
0887-3496 See SOVIET MEDICAL REVIEWS. SECTION E, VIROLOGY REVIEWS. 570
0887-350X See KIDDIE KARE MAGAZINE. 1760
0887-3526 See TENNESSEE TRUCKER, THE. 5394
0887-3569 See CONTEMPORARY SOCIAL ISSUES (SANTA CRUZ, CALIF.). 5227
0887-3577 See SOCIAL THEORY. 5228
0887-3585 See PROTEINS. 470
0887-3593 See JOURNAL OF THE NORTH AMERICAN BENTHOLOGICAL SOCIETY. 2218
0887-3631 See JOURNAL OF CULTURAL GEOGRAPHY. 2567
0887-364X See STATE OF THE WORLD. 1585
0887-3658 See FRONTIERS OF CLINICAL NEUROSCIENCE. 3833
0887-3674 See NOTICIECC. 1769
0887-3690 See CREATIVE QUILTING. 5183
0887-3712 See HLB NEWSLETTER, THE. 3797
0887-3739 See LILRC NEWSLETTER AND CALENDAR. 3228
0887-3747 See HUNTSVILLE LETTER, THE. 1494
0887-3763 See REFERENCE AND RESEARCH BOOK NEWS. 3244
0887-378X See MILBANK QUARTERLY, THE. 4791
0887-3798 See PRODUCTIVE AGING NEWS. 5302
0887-3801 See JOURNAL OF COMPUTING IN CIVIL ENGINEERING. 2025
0887-381X See JOURNAL OF COLD REGIONS ENGINEERING. 2025
0887-3828 See JOURNAL OF PERFORMANCE OF CONSTRUCTED FACILITIES. 2025
0887-3836 See VIDEO REGISTER AND TELECONFERENCING RESOURCES DIRECTORY, THE. 2085
0887-3844 See NEW DIRECTIONS IN INFORMATION MANAGEMENT. 3233
0887-3852 See AIDS & PUBLIC POLICY JOURNAL. 3663
0887-3895 See FOOD PLANT EQUIPMENT. 2339
0887-4026 See VARIA AEGYPTIACA. 2632
0887-4034 See CRIMINAL JUSTICE POLICY REVIEW. 3162
0887-4050 See SMALL BUSINESS PREFERENTIAL SUBCONTRACT OPPORTUNITIES MONTHLY. 711
0887-4085 See GOVERNMENT PRIME CONTRACTS MONTHLY. 4651
0887-4093 See MULTI-INDUSTRY DEVELOPMENTS. 1619
0887-4107 See GOVERNMENT PRODUCTION PRIME CONTRACTORS DIRECTORY. 4652
0887-4115 See BELLOWING ARK. 3366
0887-4131 See PRIVILEGED TRAVELER, THE. 5489
0887-414X See BEAUTY AGE. 402
0887-4158 See INDEX TO THE CATALOGING SERVICE BULLETIN. 3215
0887-4174 See TEXAS FISH & GAME. 4879
0887-4182 See WORLD MEDIA REPORT (WASHINGTON, D.C.) 1124
0887-4212 See TRIAL TACTICS AND TECHNIQUES. 3066
0887-4247 See HARRIS WEST VIRGINIA MANUFACTURING DIRECTORY. 3480
0887-4255 See HARRIS KENTUCKY INDUSTRIAL DIRECTORY. 1608
0887-4271 See WAUSAU DAILY HERALD. 5771
0887-428X See WASHINGTON SPECTATOR (1985), THE. 2549
0887-4298 See ADVANCES IN FAMILY PSYCHIATRY. 3919
0887-4301 See NORTHROP UNIV. LAW J. AEROSP., BUS. TAX. 3019

0887-431X See COLLEGE UNION & ON-CAMPUS HOSPITALITY. 1090
0887-4336 See ELECTRONIC REPRESENTATIVES DIRECTORY. 2048
0887-4395 See BULLETIN - PORTLAND ART ASSOCIATION (OR.). 345
0887-4409 See BULLETIN OF THE WEST VIRGINIA ASSOCIATION OF COLLEGE ENGLISH TEACHERS, THE. 3370
0887-4417 See JOURNAL OF COMPUTER INFORMATION SYSTEMS, THE. 1260
0887-445X See HVAC PRODUCT NEWS. 2605
0887-4468 See PUBLIC INNOVATION ABROAD. 2832
0887-4476 See SYNAPSE (NEW YORK, N.Y.). 3801
0887-4492 See LAKE EFFECT. 3403
0887-4514 See ADLA. 335
0887-4557 See COMMUNIQUE (MILWAUKEE, WIS.), THE. 3854
0887-4646 See MISSOURI DENTAL JOURNAL (JEFFERSON CITY, MO.). 1330
0887-4700 See U.S. OIL WEEK. 4281
0887-4727 See STATE EXECUTIVE DIRECTORY ANNUAL. 4687
0887-4727 See FEDERAL EXECUTIVE DIRECTORY ANNUAL. 4648
0887-4751 See BROWARD REVIEW. 3096
0887-476X See HEIGHTS HERALD. 5664
0887-4778 See COMMERCIAL INVESTMENT REAL ESTATE JOURNAL. 4835
0887-4808 See FINANCIAL MANAGERS' STATEMENT. 868
0887-4832 See RESOURCE BULLETIN SO. 2394
0887-4840 See GENERAL TECHNICAL REPORT PNW. 2383
0887-4859 See GENERAL TECHNICAL REPORT SE (1981). 2383
0887-4875 See GENERAL TECHNICAL REPORT SO. 2383
0887-4913 See PROCEEDINGS OF THE CENTER FOR JEWISH-CHRISTIAN LEARNING. 4988
0887-4921 See INTERNATIONAL DIRECTORY OF SYSTEMS HOUSES AND COMPUTER OEM'S. 1238
0887-493X See ALABAMA HERITAGE. 2717
0887-4999 See ALMANAC OF THE CANNING, FREEZING, PRESERVING INDUSTRIES, THE. 2362
0887-5006 See FLORIDA NURSING REVIEW. 3856
0887-5049 See PRISM (SAINT PAUL, MINN.). 4988
0887-5081 See IMPACT PUMP NEWS. 2115
0887-5103 See DUN'S HEALTHCARE REFERENCE BOOK. 3780
0887-5162 See DOCUMENT IMAGE AUTOMATION UPDATE. 1277
0887-5170 See HAYDEN'S FERRY REVIEW. 3344
0887-5200 See TODAY'S EXECUTIVE. 888
0887-5219 See MEN'S GUIDE TO FASHION. 1086
0887-5235 See FLORISSANT VALLEY QUARTERLY. 2733
0887-5316 See HUMAN RESOURCES YEARBOOK. 942
0887-5324 See TECH WRITING TIPS. 3328
0887-5332 See TOM PETERS ON ACHIEVING EXCELLENCE. 888
0887-5340 See PORTLAND MONTHLY. 2573
0887-5367 See HYPATIA (EDWARDSVILLE, ILL.). 5558
0887-5413 See BULLETIN OF THE GLOUCESTER COUNTY HISTORICAL SOCIETY. 2725
0887-543X See JOURNAL OF THE LYCOMING COUNTY HISTORICAL SOCIETY, THE. 2742
0887-5448 See HARLOW'S WOODEN MAN. 2617
0887-5456 See WAX DATA. 1631
0887-5499 See HUNGRY MIND REVIEW. 4829
0887-5502 See JOURNAL OF COUNSELING AND HUMAN SERVICE PROFESSIONS. 4595
0887-5510 See BOARD (CHULA VISTA, CALIF.), THE. 1728
0887-5553 See COMPUTER SYSTEMS JOURNAL. 1178

0887-5561 See INFORMATION SYSTEMS JOURNAL. 3217

0887-5588 See BUSINESS JOURNAL (CHARLOTTE, N.C.). 649

0887-5596 See NORTH CAROLINA ENGLISH TEACHER. 1901

0887-5634 See SHIJIE RIBAO (HOUSTON, TEX.). 5754

0887-5669 See DENTIST (WACO, TEX.). 1322

0887-5707 See MAGNETS IN YOUR FUTURE. 3943

0887-5715 See REDNECK REVIEW OF LITERATURE, THE. 3428

0887-5723 See BLACK FILM REVIEW. 4064

0887-5731 See CHRONICLES (ROCKFORD, ILL.). 2844

0887-5855 See NUEVA LUZ. 4372

0887-5863 See NEW YORK METS INSIDE PITCH. 4907

0887-588X See NORTHWEST GEORGIA HISTORICAL & GENEALOGICAL QUARTERLY. 2464

0887-5898 See GOLDEN BALL GRAPEVINE, THE. 2735

0887-591X See CHOCOLATIER. 2331

0887-5952 See SERGIO ARAGONES GROO THE WANDERER (NEW YORK, N.Y.). 4866

0887-6045 See JOURNAL OF SERVICES MARKETING, THE. 929

0887-6053 See BIBELOT (DAYTON, OHIO). 4938

0887-6061 See BALLOON LIFE. 4886

0887-607X See BULLETIN / SOCIETE DES PROFESSEURS FRANCAIS EN AMERIQUE. 1861

0887-610X See ENERGY WATCH (SACRAMENTO, CALIF.). 1942

0887-6134 See BIOLOGICAL MASS SPECTROMETRY. 1013

0887-6142 See PROGRESS IN PESTICIDE BIOCHEMISTRY AND TOXICOLOGY. 4247

0887-6169 See CLINICAL VISION SCIENCES. 3566

0887-6177 See ARCHIVES OF CLINICAL NEUROPSYCHOLOGY. 3827

0887-6185 See JOURNAL OF ANXIETY DISORDERS. 4593

0887-6193 See ADVANCES IN LOW-TEMPERATURE PLASMA CHEMISTRY, TECHNOLOGY, APPLICATIONS. 3770

0887-6207 See BIOSCAN. 3687

0887-6215 See ONLINE COMMUNICATIONS. 1197

0887-6223 See GREAT LAKES TRAVEL & LIVING. 5478

0887-6231 See OLD SPARTANBURG DISTRICT GENEALOGY. 2465

0887-624X See JOURNAL OF POLYMER SCIENCE. PART A, POLYMER CHEMISTRY. 1043

0887-6266 See JOURNAL OF POLYMER SCIENCE. PART B, POLYMER PHYSICS. 1043

0887-6274 See CLINICAL NURSE SPECIALIST. 3853

0887-6290 See GEORGIST JOURNAL, THE. 677

0887-6339 See TALON (MILWAUKEE, WIS.), THE. 4498

0887-6398 See COUNTER-TERRORISM. 5196

0887-6495 See BIOCHEMISTRY OF THE ELEMENTS. 482

0887-6541 See COSMETIC SCIENCE AND TECHNOLOGY SERIES. 403

0887-6622 See CONDENSED MATTER NEWS. 4401

0887-6681 See XAVIER REVIEW. 3356

0887-6703 See SPECTROSCOPY. 4453

0887-672X See HOSPITAL TECHNOLOGY ALERTS. 3785

0002-9866 4049

0887-6746 See PROCEEDINGS OF THE LAURANCE REID GAS CONDITIONING CONFERENCE. 4275

0887-6827 See OFFSHORE SERVICE VESSELS. A GUIDE TO THE AMERICAN FLEET. 5453

0887-6835 See OFFSHORE TUGS. A GUIDE TO THE AMERICAN FLEET. 4268

0887-6851 See VIDEO LIBRARIAN, THE. 4377

0887-686X See HYDROLOGICAL SCIENCE AND TECHNOLOGY. 1415

0887-6878 See EXHIBIT BUILDER. 1606

0887-6916 See ADVANCES IN OTOLARYNGOLOGY--HEAD AND NECK SURGERY. 3958

0887-6924 See LEUKEMIA. 3820

0887-6959 See NEWSLETTER / WHITMAN COUNTY GENEALOGICAL SOCIETY. 2464

0887-7033 See RUNNING RESEARCH NEWS. 4916

0887-705X See AIC NEWS : NEWSLETTER OF THE AMERICAN INSTITUTE FOR CONSERVATION OF HISTORIC AND ARTISTIC WORKS. 335

0887-7106 See ALERT! (NEW YORK, N.Y. 1984). 2718

0887-7114 See TALES OF THE TEEN TITANS. 4866

0887-7130 See RESOURCE BULLETIN NC. 2204

0887-7335 See NEW YORK REGGAE TIMES. 4140

0887-7343 See EMERGENCY MEDICINE OBSERVER. 3724

0887-736X See FOR FORMULATION CHEMISTS ONLY. 975

0887-7386 See APIS, THE. 226

0887-7394 See TOXICS LAW REPORTER. 3116

0887-7408 See RATE%GRAM. 1515

0887-7491 See CAPACITOR AND RESISTOR TECHNOLOGY SYMPOSIUM. 1967

0887-7505 See BED & BREAKFAST UPDATE. 5462

0887-7521 See AGRICULTURAL CREDIT LETTER, THE. 1460

0887-753X See RICE PLUS. 1625

0887-7580 See BLACK MASKS. 5362

0887-7629 See POLITICAL RISK SERVICES LETTER. 1512

0887-7653 See AMERICAN JOURNAL OF ISLAMIC SOCIAL SCIENCES, THE. 5190

0887-7661 See NETWORK WORLD. 1243

0887-7750 See IMMUNE INTERVENTION. 3670

0887-7785 See CRIMINAL JUSTICE (CHICAGO, ILL. 1986). 3162

0887-7793 See CORPORATE OFFICERS & DIRECTORS LIABILITY LITIGATION REPORTER. 3099

0887-7807 See FAILED BANK AND THRIFT LITIGATION REPORTER. 3086

0887-7815 See PHARMACEUTICAL LITIGATION REPORTER. 3029

0887-7823 See GENERAL AVIATION ACCIDENT REPORT. 2973

0887-7831 See TOBACCO INDUSTRY LITIGATION REPORTER. 3065

0887-784X See COMMODITIES LITIGATION REPORTER. 895

0887-7858 See INSURANCE INDUSTRY LITIGATION REPORTER : THE NATIONAL JOURNAL OF RECORD OF INSURANCE LITIGATION. 2983

0887-7866 See ANDREWS SCHOOL ASBESTOS ALERT. 598

0887-7912 See SHORE LINE TIMES. 5646

0887-7939 See EVENING NEWS (HARRISBURG, PA.), THE. 5736

0887-7963 See TRANSFUSION MEDICINE REVIEWS. 3647

0887-7971 See AMERICAN JOURNAL OF CARDIAC IMAGING. 3698

0887-798X See WORKFORCE (WASHINGTON, D.C.). 1719

0887-8005 See AMERICAN JOURNAL OF CARDIOVASCULAR PATHOLOGY, THE. 3698

0887-8013 See JOURNAL OF CLINICAL LABORATORY ANALYSIS, THE. 3594

0887-803X See HAIR INTERNATIONAL NEWS. 404

0887-8048 See NEW JERSEY FOLKLIFE. 2322

0887-8064 See WASHINGTON INFORMATION DIRECTORY. 4694

0887-8161 See FUNDS, AGENTS, CUSTODIANS, SUPPLIERS. 899

0887-8218 See FORUM FOR APPLIED RESEARCH AND PUBLIC POLICY. 1944

0887-8226 See PROVIDENCE BUSINESS NEWS. 5741

0887-8242 See ANNUAL REVIEW PULMONARY AND CRITICAL CARE MEDICINE. 3948

0887-8250 See JOURNAL OF SENSORY STUDIES. 2347

0887-8285 See POLICE OFFICER GRIEVANCES BULLETIN. 3172

0887-8331 See REGISTRY OF WOMEN IN RELIGIOUS STUDIES, A. 4990

0887-8420 See PRIVATE CLUBS. 5235

0887-8439 See CONSUMER REPORTS TRAVEL LETTER. 1295

0887-8463 See WINE ADVOCATE, THE. 2372

0887-851X See MARGIN (COLORADO SPRINGS, COLO.), THE. 1504

0887-8528 See METROWEST BUSINESS REVIEW, THE. 693

0887-8625 See INTERNATIONAL JOURNAL OF CHILDBIRTH EDUCATION, THE. 3762

0887-8692 See AI ALERT. 1210

0887-8706 See SOUTHERN AFRICA PROJECT ANNUAL REPORT. 4496

0887-8722 See JOURNAL OF THERMOPHYSICS AND HEAT TRANSFER. 4431

0887-8730 See TEACHER EDUCATOR, THE. 1906

0887-8781 See PRECIS (NEW YORK, N.Y.). 306

0887-882X See LATIN AMERICA FINANCE. 796

0887-8854 See JOURNEY (LYNCHBURG, VA.). 4971

0887-8897 See SHAMAN'S DRUM. 4997

0887-8919 See PATHWAYS & PASSAGES. 2467

0887-8927 See WISCONSIN ARBORIST, THE. 2183

0887-896X See ABA JUVENILE & CHILD WELFARE LAW REPORTER. 3119

0887-8978 See BOOK & PAPER GROUP ANNUAL, THE. 344

0887-8994 See PEDIATRIC NEUROLOGY. 3909

0887-9036 See BANDWORLD. 4102

0887-9044 See IDOC MIDDLE EAST QUARTERLY. 2768

0887-9060 See CASTING WORLD. 3999

0887-9095 See LEADING EDGE LIGHTHOUSE. 689

0887-9117 See YEARBOOK ON SOCIALIST LEGAL SYSTEMS. 3138

0887-9133 See AGVENTURE. 57

0887-9141 See CADENCE (AUSTIN, TEX.). 1173

0887-915X See SEMINAR LECTURE NOTES / SID, SOCIETY FOR INFORMATION DISPLAY. 1202

0887-9168 See CEO INTERVIEWS. 1601

0887-9214 See MEAT SOURCE. 2350

0887-9222 See KRESGE ART MUSEUM BULLETIN. 355

0887-9249 See SOUTH CAROLINA OUT-OF-DOORS. 2205

0887-9257 See TAPROOT. 3444

0887-9281 See ANNUAL REPORT, SECTION OF PUBLIC UTILITY, COMMUNICATIONS AND TRANSPORTATION LAW. 4759

0887-9303 See CRITICAL CARE NURSING QUARTERLY. 3854

0887-9311 See HOLISTIC NURSING PRACTICE. 3856

0887-932X See PUBLIC COMMUNICATION AND BEHAVIOR. 1120

0887-9338 See SCOPE/36. 1202

0887-9346 See WORLD & I, THE. 2495

0887-9362 See JAPAN LASER REPORT. 4435

0887-9397 See SHOOTING SPORTS RETAILER. 957

0887-9400 See INTOWNER, THE. 5647

0887-9427 See COW IN THE ROAD. 318

0887-9451 See NEW VIDEO. 4075

0887-9478 See BUSINESS SOFTWARE DIRECTORY. 1284
0887-9486 See TEACHING & LEARNING : THE JOURNAL OF NATURAL INQUIRY. 1906
0887-9532 See JOURNAL OF EPSILON PI TAU, THE. 1757
0887-9559 See WORLD STATUS MAP. 5499
0887-9567 See ON BEYOND WAR. 4485
0887-963X See INTERCOM (LIVINGSTON, N.J.). 1157
0887-9648 See MACINTOUCH. 1194
0887-9672 See PCI JOURNAL. 2028
0887-9680 See CITIZEN AIRMAN. 4039
0887-9702 See WEB OF SPIDER-MAN. 4867
0887-9745 See ELFQUEST. 4860
0887-9753 See ENVIRONMENTAL MANAGER'S COMPLIANCE ADVISOR, THE. 3112
0887-977X See OUTLOOK (LINCOLN, NEB.). 4984
0887-9788 See IOWA STYLE. 404
0887-9818 See CRAFT & NEEDLEWORK AGE. 5183
0887-9850 See CARDIAC SURGERY. 3961
0887-9869 See SPINE (PHILADELPHIA, PA. 1986). 3975
0887-9877 See AVIATION INTERNATIONAL NEWS. 13
0887-9893 See NONPROFIT ALMANAC. 5299
0887-9923 See LLAMAS. 5590
0887-9958 See LINGUISTICA EXTRANEA. STUDIA. 3299
0887-9982 See TIKKUN. 2274
0888-0018 See PEDIATRIC HEMATOLOGY AND ONCOLOGY. 3773
0888-0050 See DAIRY FOODS. 193
0888-0077 See CHATTANOOGA LIFE & LEISURE. 2486
0888-0085 See FACILITY MANAGER. 868
0888-0107 See POST-GAZETTE (BOSTON, MASS.). 5689
0888-0131 See PORTABLE 100 (1986). 1199
0888-014X See ABC TODAY. 597
0888-0158 See DIRECTORY OF HOME FURNISHINGS RETAILERS. 2905
0888-0166 See DIRECTORY OF HIGH-VOLUME INDEPENDENT RESTAURANTS. 5070
0888-0204 See COUNTRYSIDE (BARRINGTON, ILL.). 5659
0888-0212 See ENTERPRISE NEWS (PIXLEY, CALIF.). 5635
0888-0220 See LEADER-NEWS (WASHBURN, N.D.), THE. 5725
0888-0255 See CHURCH MINISTRIES WORKER. 4947
0888-0263 See MIAMI REVIEW. 5718
0888-0271 See SCOTTSDALE PROGRESS. 5630
0888-0301 See FABRICATOR (ROCKFORD, ILL.). 3478
0888-031X See KARATE, KUNG-FU ILLUSTRATED. 4902
0888-0336 See PORCELAIN ARTIST. 2593
0888-0352 See PROVIDER (WASHINGTON, D.C.). 5302
0888-0360 See GROCERY MARKETING. 2343
0888-0379 See NATIONAL JEWISH POST & OPINION (INDIANAPOLIS, INC. : 1984). 5665
0888-0387 See INTERIOR CONSTRUCTION. 617
0888-0395 See JOURNAL OF NEUROSCIENCE NURSING, THE. 3859
0888-0409 See WEST VIRGINIA HILLBILLY (RICHWOOD, W.VA. : 1986). 5765
0888-045X See BOTTOM LINE (NEW YORK, N.Y.), THE. 3197
0888-0468 See JEWISH JOURNAL OF GREATER LOS ANGELES, THE. 5049
0888-0476 See U.S.-CHINA ECONOMIC JOURNAL. 1525
0888-0492 See VIDEO EXTRA. 1168
0888-0522 See FEDERAL TAX MANUAL. 4724
0888-0530 See NURSING & ALLIED HEALTH (CINAHL) ... SUBJECT HEADING LIST. 3863
0888-062X See NASHVILLE CABLEGUIDE. 1135

0888-0646 See JURY VERDICTS WEEKLY. 2991
0888-0670 See WEEKLY COMMERCIAL NEWS (LOS ANGELES, CALIF.). 719
0888-0689 See VARIA (MONTCHANIN, DEL.). 2549
0888-0697 See SOVIET MEDICAL REVIEWS. SECTION A, CARDIOLOGY REVIEWS. 3710
0888-0700 See SOVIET MEDICAL REVIEWS. SECTION F, ONCOLOGY REVIEWS. 3824
0888-0743 See EWOKS. 4860
0888-0751 See HEATHCLIFF. 4862
0888-076X See DECORATIVE ARTS DIGEST. 372
0888-0786 See SERODIAGNOSIS AND IMMUNOTHERAPY IN INFECTIOUS DISEASE. 570
0888-0808 See ELLE (NEW YORK, N.Y.). 5555
0888-0832 See WINDHAM PHOENIX. 2550
0888-0840 See ADWEEK (NEW ENGLAND ED.). 755
0888-0859 See QUARTER RUNNING HORSE CHART BOOK, THE. 2802
0888-0867 See DETROIT MONTHLY. 2532
0888-1014 See GRADUATE RESEARCH IN URBAN EDUCATION AND RELATED DISCIPLINES. 1826
0888-1022 See MID-ATLANTIC COUNTRY. 2538
0888-1057 See ST WORLD. 1265
0888-1065 See CARIB BASIN TRADE UPDATE. 1601
0888-1081 See AVALON HILL GENERAL. 4857
0888-1103 See WHEEL (SAN FRANCISCO, CALIF.). 5428
0888-1111 See DISCIPLES THEOLOGICAL DIGEST, THE. 4954
0888-1154 See AMERICAN ROWING. 4883
0888-1189 See TILLER AND TOILER (1986), THE. 5678
0888-1227 See COMPOSITES & ADHESIVES NEWSLETTER, THE. 1023
0888-1243 See TAX DIRECTORY, THE. 4752
0888-1286 See LANGUAGE OF DANCE SERIES. 1313
0888-1316 See WORD ON WORSHIP. 5010
0888-1332 See FNP NEWSLETTER. FOOD INDUSTRY REPORT. 2335
0888-1340 See VIRGINIA BUSINESS. 718
0888-1375 See EASTWEST NATURAL HEALTH. 2596
0888-1413 See BUSINESS ORGANIZATIONS, AGENCIES, AND PUBLICATIONS DIRECTORY. 651
0888-143X See NOTICIAS DEL MUNDO. 5719
0888-1502 See CALIFORNIA LANDSCAPE MAGAZINE. 2411
0888-1537 See BIFOCAL. 3179
0888-1561 See BOAT PENNSYLVANIA. 592
0888-157X See WORLD (ASHEVILLE, N.C.). 2550
0888-1715 See CALIFORNIA GROWER (VISTA, CALIF.). 71
0888-1723 See INFORMATION BULLETIN / ERIC CLEARINGHOUSE FOR SCIENCE, MATHEMATICS AND ENVIRONMENTAL EDUCATION. 5113
0888-1804 See AGRIDATA NETWORK REVIEW. 54
0888-1901 See BRANFORD REVIEW, THE. 5645
0888-191X See NA'AMAT WOMAN. 2770
0888-1944 See COLLECTOR CAR NEWS. 2772
0888-1960 See DUNCANVILLE SUBURBAN. 5749
0888-1979 See NEW NONWOVENS WORLD, THE. 5354
0888-1987 See COMPUTER PERIODICALS INDEX. 1266
0888-2010 See NEWS TIMES (NEWPORT, OR.). 5733
0888-2053 See FOOTWEAR NEWS MAGAZINE. 1084
0888-2061 See WHOLE LIFE. 4807
0888-2088 See COMPUTER SOFTWARE ENGINEERING SERIES. 1178
0888-2096 See PRINCIPLES OF COMPUTER SCIENCE SERIES. 1200

0888-210X See COLLEGE STUDENT AFFAIRS JOURNAL, THE. 1817
0888-2118 See DIGITAL SYSTEM DESIGN SERIES. 1182
0888-2134 See ELECTRICAL ENGINEERING COMMUNICATIONS AND SIGNAL PROCESSING. 2045
0888-2142 See JOURNAL OF THE SUFFOLK ACADEMY OF LAW. 2990
0888-2177 See COMPUTERS IN EDUCATION SERIES. 1179
0888-2193 See COMPUTERS AND MATH SERIES. 1179
0888-2231 See APPLICATIONS OF COMPUTER SCIENCE SERIES. 1171
0888-224X See ADVANCES IN VLSI AND COMPUTER SYSTEM SERIES. 1246
0888-2258 See REVOLUTIONARY WAR MAGAZINE. 2758
0888-2266 See TRUSST TIMES. 5398
0888-2274 See AUGUSTINIAN HERITAGE. 4937
0888-2290 See HANGUK ILBO, SOBUNGMI. 5761
0888-238X See SERICHAI. 5640
0888-2398 See FEMALE PATIENT. PRACTICAL ADVICE FOR PRIMARY CARE, THE. 3760
0888-2401 See FEMALE PATIENT. PRACTICAL OB/GYN MEDICINE, THE. 3760
0888-2428 See HOSPITAL PHYSICIAN (SURGERY/EMERGENCY/SPECIALTIES ED.). 3584
0888-2436 See LEMKIVSCINA. 2696
0888-2452 See INTERIM (LAS VEGAS, NEV.). 3464
0888-2460 See MIDEAST MONITOR. 2770
0888-2517 See HEARING HEALTH. 1297
0888-2517 See VOICE (DALLAS, TEX.), THE. 4395
0888-2525 See FRESH START, THE. 1607
0888-255X See SECURED LENDER, THE. 811
0888-2681 See REPORT OF THE INTERAGENCY TOXIC SUBSTANCES DATA COMMITTEE. 3983
0888-269X See FEDERAL PAY AND BENEFITS REPORTER. 4702
0888-2746 See HOUSING AND SOCIETY. 2824
0888-2770 See CAREER CHOICES NEWSLETTER, THE. 4201
0888-2851 See COUNTY LINE (PANAMA CITY, FLA.), THE. 2444
0888-2851 See COUNTY LINE. 2444
0888-286X See DIRECTIONS IN APPLIED NUTRITION. 4190
0888-3009 See SCHOLASTIC PRE-K TODAY. 1781
0888-3017 See LEDGER (RIDGEFIELD, CONN.), THE. 5645
0888-3025 See RURAL BUILDER. 627
0888-3033 See REAL-TIME INTERFACE. 1201
0888-3068 See HOSPITAL MATERIALS MANAGEMENT. 3784
0888-3106 See STRINGS (SAN ANSELMO, CALIF.). 4155
0888-3122 See CORNELL WORKING PAPERS IN LINGUISTICS. 3275
0888-3149 See BANK MARKETING. 775
0888-3165 See ANNUAL PROCEEDINGS / DUBLIN SEMINAR FOR NEW ENGLAND FOLKLIFE. 255
0888-3173 See EDITORS' NOTES. 2919
0888-3181 See ALBA DE AMERICA. 3359
0888-319X See IN VITRO TOXICOLOGY. 3981
0888-3203 See JOURNAL OF DRAMATIC THEORY AND CRITICISM. 5365
0888-3270 See MECHANICAL SYSTEMS AND SIGNAL PROCESSING. 2122
0888-3297 See VIDEO VISION. 1142
0888-3319 See SPRINGHOUSE, THE. 2324
0888-3327 See MARKETERS FORUM MAGAZINE. 930
0888-3394 See REPORT - GROUP FOR THE ADVANCEMENT OF PSYCHIATRY (1984). 3935
0888-3408 See GREEN LANDS. 2173
0888-3424 See PRACTICING ARCHITECT. 306
0888-3440 See ULTIMATE ISSUES. 5053
0888-3459 See WESTCHESTER COMMERCE. 857

0888-3467 See PERFORMANCE MATERIALS. 1621

0888-3483 See NUTRITION CLINICS. 4196

0888-3491 See WALKER'S WORLD NEWSLETTER. 4928

0888-3513 See KERUX. 4972

0888-3521 See HOWLING DOG. 3394

0888-353X See TELEPHONE MARKETING COUNCIL NEWSLETTER. 937

0888-3548 See CARTA-LEON DESDE WASHINGTON SOBRE ADMINISTRACION DE RECURSOS HUMANOS. 939

0888-3556 See IRISH PEOPLE (NEW YORK, N.Y. : 1972). 2518

0888-367X See EXTRA !NCOME. 674

0888-3696 See HOOSIER UNITED METHODIST NEWS. 5061

0888-3742 See BEST AMERICAN ESSAYS, THE. 3366

0888-3769 See RELIGION & LITERATURE. 4990

0888-3785 See AI EXPERT. 1210

0888-3793 See MACRAE'S STATE INDUSTRIAL DIRECTORY. NORTH CAROLINA, SOUTH CAROLINA, VIRGINIA. 1616

0888-3807 See ROBESON COUNTY REGISTER, THE. 2470

0888-3882 See UNIVERSITY OF CINCINNATI STUDIES IN HISTORICAL AND CONTEMPORARY EUROPE. 2714

0888-3904 See STUDIES IN MODERN GERMAN LITERATURE. 3442

0888-3920 See SOVIET MEDICAL REVIEWS. SECTION C, HEMATOLOGY REVIEWS. 3774

0888-3955 See FOLLOWUP FILE. 2919

0888-3963 See ORO VALLEY TERRITORIAL. 5630

0888-3971 See STATUS REPORT ON SPEECH RESEARCH. 3324

0888-4013 See HOUSTONIAN MAGAZINE. 2535

0888-4048 See SOLAR TIMES (MADISON, CONN.). 1957

0888-4064 See TEACHER EDUCATION AND SPECIAL EDUCATION. 1886

0888-4072 See SOUNDINGS (MILWAUKEE, WIS.). 5457

0888-4080 See APPLIED COGNITIVE PSYCHOLOGY. 4574

0888-4102 See FEMALE BODYBUILDING AND WEIGHT TRAINING. 2597

0888-4110 See EXECUTIVE SPEECHES (DAYTON, OHIO). 674

0888-4129 See DISTRIBUTED PROCESSING PRODUCT REPORTS. 1183

0888-4145 See HUNTSVILLE ITEM, THE. 5751

0888-4153 See HIGH PLAINS LITERARY REVIEW. 3344

0888-4226 See COLUMBIA-VLA JOURNAL OF LAW & THE ARTS. 2953

0888-4277 See FLORIDA ARCHAEOLOGY. 268

0888-4315 See JUSTICE PROFESSIONAL, THE. 2991

0888-4323 See TECHNICAL COMMUNICATION QUARTERLY. 1122

0888-4331 See UTAH PRESERVATION/RESTORATION. 2764

0888-4390 See JOURNAL OF NEUROLOGIC REHABILITATION. 3836

0888-4404 See BIOCHROMATOGRAPHY. 483

0888-4412 See OBSIDIAN II. 3419

0888-4463 See LIBRARY ADMINISTRATION & MANAGEMENT. 3224

0888-448X See RADIATION EFFECTS BULLETIN. 990

0888-4501 See DEALERSCOPE MERCHANDISING. 953

0888-451X See CHILTON COUNTY NEWS (CLANTON, ALA. : 1986). 5625

0888-4552 See PRACTICING ANTHROPOLOGY. 243

0888-4595 See INDIVIDUAL PSYCHOLOGY REPORTER. 4590

0888-4609 See WOMEN'S RECORD, THE. 5571

0888-4633 See HOME EDUCATION MAGAZINE. 1751

0888-4730 See CRUCIBLE (WILSON, N.C.). 3379

0888-4757 See RECTANGLE, THE. 3428

0888-4773 See JOURNAL OF SPORT MANAGEMENT. 4902

0888-4781 See SPORT PSYCHOLOGIST, THE. 4619

0888-479X See APPLIED MATHEMATICS. 3495

0888-4803 See SOVIET SCIENTIFIC REVIEWS. SECTION F, PHYSIOLOGY AND GENERAL BIOLOGY REVIEWS. 473

0888-4811 See KOSHER GOURMET MAGAZINE, THE. 2791

0888-4846 See PENINSULA (REDWOOD CITY, CALIF.). 2543

0888-4862 See NATURE FRIEND MAGAZINE. 2200

0888-4870 See ATHLETICS EMPLOYMENT WEEKLY. 4201

0888-5109 See CONSULTANT PHARMACIST, THE. 4298

0888-5168 See GENERAL SERIES - UTAH WATER RESEARCH LABORATORY. 5533

0888-5184 See OUTCROP (DENVER, COLO.). 1390

0888-5230 See THIRD DECADE, THE. 2763

0888-5257 See VSTRECI (PHILADELPHIA, PA.). 3473

0888-5265 See WORLD AIRSHOW NEWS. 40

0888-5273 See ANCESTORS UNLIMITED (MCCOOK, NEB.). 2437

0888-5281 See PERSPECTIVES (GRAND RAPIDS, MICH.). 4986

0888-5303 See NUC URBAN EXCHANGE. 2829

0888-5311 See MID-ATLANTIC FOODSERVICE NEWS. 2350

0888-532X See JIM HENSON'S MUPPET BABIES. 4862

0888-5346 See NORTHWEST LIVING. 2541

0888-5397 See QUALITATIVE RESEARCH METHODS. 5214

0888-5400 See ADMINISTRATIVE AND ACCOUNTING GUIDE FOR GOVERNMENT CONTRACTS. 738

0888-5443 See TRADITIONAL ARCHERY. 4927

0888-5451 See ANTIQUEWEEK. 249

0888-546X See ARIZONA DAILY STAR. 5629

0888-5478 See TUCSON CITIZEN (1977). 5630

0888-5508 See OSERS NEWS IN PRINT. 5300

0888-5567 See ACA JOURNAL, THE. 1338

0888-5613 See LATIN AMERICAN INDIAN LITERATURES JOURNAL. 3403

0888-5621 See JOURNAL OF WOMEN AND RELIGION. 4971

0888-5648 See EXCHANGE (FORT WORTH, TEX.). 3914

0888-5656 See FSMB HANDBOOK. 4204

0888-5664 See FSMBNEWSLINE (FORT WORTH, TEX.). 3577

0888-5672 See GOURD, THE. 90

0888-5680 See PHOTO/DESIGN. 4373

0888-5702 See JAPAN-U.S. BUSINESS REPORT. 685

0888-5710 See JAPAN ECONOMIC SURVEY. 1636

0888-5729 See NUCLEUS (CAMBRIDGE, MASS.). 4053

0888-5745 See YELLOW BRICK ROAD (ROCHESTER, N.Y.). 1071

0888-5753 See STUDIES IN POPULAR CULTURE. 2855

0888-577X See SEW IT SEAMS. 5186

0888-580X See EAST ASIAN BUSINESS INTELLIGENCE. 923

0888-5842 See YM. 1071

0888-5885 See INDUSTRIAL & ENGINEERING CHEMISTRY RESEARCH. 2013

0888-5893 See TRAINER'S WORKSHOP. 947

0888-6008 See BREAST DISEASE. 3558

0888-6016 See BAYRUT TAYMZ. 5633

0888-6032 See TOPICS IN TOTAL COMPENSATION. 888

0888-6075 See LASER NURSING. 3861

0888-6083 See MASSACHUSETTS MUNICIPAL PROFILES. 5332

0888-6091 See CONFLUENCIA (GREELEY, COLO.). 5196

0888-6113 See NOTES ON MATHEMATICS AND ITS APPLICATIONS. 3525

0888-6121 See NEWSLETTER OF THE NORTH CAROLINA FOLKLORE SOCIETY. 2323

0888-613X See INTERNATIONAL JOURNAL OF APPROXIMATE REASONING. 1213

0888-6199 See FARMINGTON OBSERVER. 5692

0888-627X See AMERICAN KENNEL CLUB AWARDS. 4285

0888-6296 See JOURNAL OF CARDIOTHORACIC AND VASCULAR ANESTHESIA. 3683

0888-630X See AMERICAN UNIVERSITY JOURNAL OF INTERNATIONAL LAW AND POLICY, THE. 3123

0888-6342 See FRANKLIN HISTORICAL REVIEW. 2734

0888-6393 See INTERNATIONAL DRUG & DEVICE REGULATORY MONITOR. 4308

0888-6504 See JOURNAL OF RESEARCH ON COMPUTING IN EDUCATION. 1224

0888-6512 See ASTROPHYSICAL LETTERS AND COMMUNICATIONS. 393

0888-6547 See NATURALIST REVIEW. 2199

0888-6555 See AUDUBON NATURALIST NEWS : A PUBLICATION OF THE AUDUBON NATURALIST SOCIETY OF THE CENTRAL ATLANTIC STATES. 4162

0888-658X See MEDICAL MALPRACTICE VERDICTS, SETTLEMENTS & EXPERTS. 3008

0888-6601 See JOURNAL OF PAN AFRICAN STUDIES, THE. 5206

0888-661X See HUDSON VALLEY GREEN TIMES. 2173

0888-6709 See MEANS FACILITIES COST DATA. 303

0888-6725 See REPORT OF INVESTIGATIONS - UNIVERSITY OF TEXAS AT AUSTIN. BUREAU OF ECONOMIC GEOLOGY. 1395

0888-6814 See APPALACHIAN ROOTS. 2437

0888-6822 See WISCONSIN HOME GALLERY MAGAZINE. 2904

0888-6830 See AGING RESEARCH & TRAINING NEWS. 3749

0888-6849 See HAZ-MAT TECHNOLOGY. 4777

0888-689X See SOVIET MATERIALS SCIENCE REVIEWS. 2129

0888-6903 See PROPERTY DATA UPDATE. 4418

0888-6911 See BULLETIN OF THE INTERNATIONAL CENTRE FOR HEAT AND MASS TRANSFER. 2111

0888-692X See FORENSIC REPORTS. 3740

0888-6938 See HAIR (NEW YORK, N.Y.). 5268

0888-6970 See LOGO EXCHANGE. 1280

0888-6989 See MAPNETTER NEWSLETTER, THE. 1194

0888-6997 See OSINETTER NEWSLETTER, THE. 1198

0888-7012 See CRIMINAL LAW NEWSLETTER (SAN JOSE, CALIF.). 3106

0888-7063 See JOURNAL OF THE KANSAS DENTAL ASSOCIATION. 1328

0888-711X See HOSPITAL TECHNOLOGY SERIES. 3785

0888-7136 See MEDICAL DEVICES BULLETIN. 3608

0888-7225 See INTERNATIONAL BIOTECHNOLOGY LABORATORY. 3693

0888-7233 See COMPARATIVE ECONOMIC STUDIES. 1470

0888-7292 See TELECOM/EYE BEE EM. 1164

0888-7314 See JOURNAL OF DECORATIVE AND PROPAGANDA ARTS, THE. 373

0888-7330 See HEALTH WORLD. 4782

0888-7357 See PHYSICAL MEDICINE AND REHABILITATION. 3884

0888-7381 See CMRR REPORT. 5316

0888-7403 See CONSERVATIVE CHRONICLE. 2531

0888-742X ISSN Index

0888-742X *See* NUCLEAR MEDICINE LITERATURE UPDATING AND INDEXING SERVICE, THE. **4670**

0888-7462 *See* INTERNATIONAL JOURNAL OF POWDER METALLURGY (PRINCETON, N.J.). **4004**

0888-7470 *See* BIOPROCESS TECHNOLOGY. **3687**

0888-7500 *See* RECEPTOR BIOCHEMISTRY AND METHODOLOGY. **471**

0888-7543 *See* GENOMICS (SAN DIEGO, CALIF.). **546**

0888-7551 *See* BIBLIOGRAPHIES AND INDEXES IN SCIENCE AND TECHNOLOGY. **5088**

0888-756X *See* PRENSA (ORLANDO, FLA.), LA. **5650**

0888-7586 *See* CONTRABAND. **5683**

0888-7624 *See* DIRECTORY OF NURSING HOMES (PHOENIX, ARIZ.). **5178**

0888-7640 *See* EDUCATIONAL SERIES ON CHINESE MEDICINE. **3573**

0888-7675 *See* JOHNS HOPKINS STUDIES IN HEALTH CARE FINANCE AND ADMINISTRATION. **3786**

0888-7691 *See* CONTEMPORARY ISSUES IN OPHTHALMOLOGY. **3873**

0888-7713 *See* ANNUAL REPORT OF CANCER INCIDENCE IN MASSACHUSETTS. **3808**

0888-7721 *See* BIBLIO-PROFILE. **3803**

0888-773X *See* CONTROLLED DRUG BIOAVAILABILITY. **4298**

0888-7748 *See* CLINICAL AND EXPERIMENTAL NUTRITION. **4188**

0888-7756 *See* CONTEMPORARY ISSUES IN INFECTIOUS DISEASES. **3712**

0888-7799 *See* QUARTERLY OIL COMPANY PERFORMANCE. **4276**

0888-7802 *See* OZ (MANHATTAN, KAN.). **305**

0888-7829 *See* MODERN FOOD SERVICE NEWS. **5072**

0888-7861 *See* KALAMAZOO VALLEY FAMILY NEWSLETTER, THE. **2456**

0888-787X *See* QUARTERLY DOMESTIC & GLOBAL FORECASTS OF KEY ECONOMIC INDICATORS. **1514**

0888-787X *See* QUARTERLY CONSENSUS FORECAST OF KEY ECONOMIC INDICATORS. **1579**

0888-7926 *See* U.S. STATISTICS. **5345**

0888-7950 *See* CLINICAL LABORATORY MANAGEMENT REVIEW. **4771**

0888-7985 *See* JOURNAL OF INFORMATION SYSTEMS, THE. **747**

0888-7993 *See* ACCOUNTING HORIZONS. **737**

0888-8000 *See* COMMERCIAL LAW BULLETIN (CHICAGO, ILL.). **3097**

0888-8027 *See* LINGUISTICS AND LANGUAGE BEHAVIOR ABSTRACTS. **3336**

0888-8035 *See* NINCDS RESEARCH PROGRAM. MULTIPLE SCLEROSIS, THE. **3843**

0888-8051 *See* NATIONAL TOXICOLOGY PROGRAM TECHNICAL REPORT SERIES. **3983**

0888-8086 *See* RADIOLOGICAL HEALTH BULLETIN. **3945**

0888-8132 *See* NATIONAL FORUM OF EDUCATIONAL ADMINISTRATION AND SUPERVISION JOURNAL. **1766**

0888-8140 *See* HARRIS OHIO INDUSTRIAL DIRECTORY. **1608**

0888-8159 *See* PETERSON'S GUIDE TO COLLEGES IN THE WEST. **1841**

0888-8167 *See* HARRIS MICHIGAN INDUSTRIAL DIRECTORY (TWINSBURG, OHIO: 1984). **1608**

0888-8175 *See* HARRIS INDIANA INDUSTRIAL DIRECTORY. **1608**

0888-8183 *See* ENERGY REPORT (ARLINGTON, VA.). **1941**

0888-8191 *See* CIRCULATION MANAGEMENT (SPRINGFIELD, OR.). **2918**

0888-8299 *See* SCI NURSING. **3869**

0888-8337 *See* DRUG AND CHEMICAL TOXICOLOGY (NEW YORK, N.Y. 1984). **3980**

0888-8353 *See* ASTRONOMICAL DATA CENTER BULLETIN. **391**

0888-8396 *See* ALBUQUERQUE BI-WEEKLY REPORT, THE. **921**

0888-840X *See* ARIZONA HUNTER & ANGLER. **4884**

0888-8418 *See* CARDIOLOGY BOARD REVIEW. **3700**

0888-8442 *See* COMPUTE!'S ATARI ST DISK & MAGAZINE. **1180**

0888-8485 *See* ARKANSAS CITY TRAVELER (ARKANSAS CITY, KAN. : 1970). **5674**

0888-8493 *See* THOMAS REGISTER'S INBOUND LOGISTICS. **853**

0888-8507 *See* PC MAGAZINE. **1270**

0888-8507 *See* PC MAGAZINE (NEW YORK, N.Y.). **1271**

0888-8507 *See* PC MAGAZINE (NEW YORK, N.Y.). **1271**

0888-8515 *See* FOODSERVICE EQUIPMENT & SUPPLIES SPECIALIST. **2341**

0888-8582 *See* RIGHT TO KNOW COMPLIANCE ADVISOR. **2869**

0888-8612 *See* WINDS OF CHANGE (BOULDER, COLO.). **5169**

0888-8639 *See* JOURNAL OF VOCATIONAL AND TECHNICAL EDUCATION. **1914**

0888-8698 *See* NEWSNET ACTION LETTER. **3236**

0888-8701 *See* NEWSLETTER OF THE AMERICAN HANDEL SOCIETY. **4141**

0888-871X *See* INDUSTRIAL POLICY NEWS. **1611**

0888-8744 *See* NATCHEZ DEMOCRAT (1916), THE. **5701**

0888-8752 *See* MIDDLEBURY STUDIES IN RUSSIAN LANGUAGE AND LITERATURE. **3302**

0888-8779 *See* CULTURE, ETHNICITY, AND NATION. **5197**

0888-8809 *See* MOLECULAR ENDOCRINOLOGY (BALTIMORE, MD.). **3732**

0888-8833 *See* OPEN HANDS. **2795**

0888-8868 *See* KAPPA ALPHA JOURNAL, THE. **5232**

0888-8892 *See* CONSERVATION BIOLOGY. **2190**

0888-8981 *See* LEASING AND FINANCIAL SERVICES MONITOR, THE. **690**

0888-899X *See* AMERICAN RIVERS. **2186**

0888-9007 *See* JUSER (LOS ANGELES, CALIF.). **2769**

0888-9015 *See* CUE SHEET, THE. **4113**

0888-9066 *See* PRACTICE PERSONNEL BULLETIN. **946**

0888-9074 *See* BAPTIST TRUMPET (LITTLE ROCK, ARK.). **5056**

0888-9090 *See* LC GC. **984**

0888-9104 *See* HARDWOOD MARKET REPORT (MEMPHIS, TENN.). **2401**

0888-9112 *See* CUED SPEECH NEWS. **4386**

0888-9120 *See* JUSTICE FOR CHILDREN. **3121**

0888-9139 *See* CRITTENDEN REAL ESTATE BUYERS. **4836**

0888-9147 *See* CRITTENDEN INCOME PROPERTY DEALS. **4836**

0888-9163 *See* PASTFINDER. **2466**

0888-9201 *See* ISSUES (SAINT LOUIS, MO.). **2251**

0888-9287 *See* ADVANCES IN MOTOR DEVELOPMENT RESEARCH. **4572**

0888-9325 *See* SPIDR NEWS. **1711**

0888-935X *See* INDUSTRIAL LASER REVIEW. **4435**

0888-9368 *See* NIGHT LIGHT, THE. **4606**

0888-9384 *See* CHRYSALIS (NEW YORK, N.Y.). **4343**

0888-9406 *See* IN-STAT ELECTRONICS REPORT. **2064**

0888-9465 *See* HEALTH PROFESSIONS REPORT. **3582**

0888-9473 *See* RECORDER (MONTEREY, VA.). **5759**

0888-949X *See* NBER DIGEST, THE. **1507**

0888-9538 *See* VIDEO MONITOR (SILVER SPRING, MD.). **1168**

0888-9546 *See* ILLINOIS NATURAL HISTORY SURVEY SPECIAL PUBLICATION. **4166**

0888-9600 *See* FLORIDA LIVING. **2533**

0888-9651 *See* AAEA NEWSLETTER (AMES, IOWA). **42**

0888-9678 *See* RESEARCH PAPER SE. **2393**

0888-9686 *See* RESEARCH PAPER NC. **2393**

0888-9708 *See* RESOURCE BULLETIN RM. **2393**

0888-9724 *See* IN THE MAINSTREAM (WASHINGTON, D.C.). **4389**

0888-9732 *See* PERSPECTIVE (MADISON, WIS.). **3029**

0888-9740 *See* PERSONALITY, PSYCHOPATHOLOGY, AND PSYCHOTHERAPY. **4607**

0888-9775 *See* NEWYORK WOMAN. **5563**

0888-9805 *See* MCGRAW-HILL'S HEALTH BUSINESS. **4790**

0888-9996 *See* TOWN AND COUNTRY (LANSDALE, PA.). **5740**

0889-0005 *See* DAILY NEWS (LONGVIEW, WASH.), THE. **5760**

0889-0013 *See* FORT WORTH STAR-TELEGRAM. **5750**

0889-003X *See* NATIONAL CALENDAR OF OPEN COMPETITIVE ART EXHIBITIONS. **374**

0889-0056 *See* ADVOCATE-MESSENGER, THE. **5679**

0889-0064 *See* MUTUAL FUND CHARTIST. **800**

0889-0072 *See* WASTE RECOVERY REPORT. **2246**

0889-0080 *See* WESTERN STAR (BESSEMER, ALA.), THE. **5628**

0889-0099 *See* FLORIDA TOURISM INDUSTRY REPORT. **5470**

0889-0102 *See* CALIFORNIA FORESTRY NOTE. **2377**

0889-0145 *See* NEW GERMAN REVIEW. **3415**

0889-0153 *See* DREW. **1822**

0889-017X *See* MENTAL HEALTH LAW NEWS. **3009**

0889-0196 *See* ELECTRONICS PURCHASING. **2050**

0889-0234 *See* DWI JOURNAL. **2965**

0889-0242 *See* PRESSURE (BETHESDA, MD.). **3629**

0889-0250 *See* TECHNOLOGY TRANSFER ABSTRACTS. **5164**

0889-0277 *See* JOURNAL OF THE SHAW HISTORICAL LIBRARY, THE. **3221**

0889-0293 *See* INTERNATIONAL JOURNAL OF SOCIAL EDUCATION, THE. **5204**

0889-0382 *See* DIRECTORY OF NEW ENGLAND MANUFACTURERS. **3478**

0889-0390 *See* GEORGE D. HALL'S DIRECTORY OF CENTRAL ATLANTIC STATES MANUFACTURERS. **3479**

0889-0404 *See* DEFENSE DAILY. **4041**

0889-0412 *See* CANADA NEWS (AUBURNDALE, FLA.). **5649**

0889-0439 *See* MICHIGAN RETAILER, THE. **879**

0889-0471 *See* STOCKS OF GRAIN AT SELECTED TERMINAL & ELEVATOR SITES. WEEKLY ED. **203**

0889-048X *See* AGRICULTURE AND HUMAN VALUES. **53**

0889-0501 *See* ORIGINS (GRAND RAPIDS, MICH.). **2752**

0889-051X *See* GUIDE TO FLORIDA RETIREMENT LIVING. **5179**

0889-0528 *See* EDITOR'S CHOICE CLIP ART QUARTERLY. **378**

0889-0536 *See* ONE, TWO, THREE, FOUR. **4143**

0889-0544 *See* SOUTHEASTERN VISUAL RESOURCES NEWSLETTER. **331**

0889-0552 *See* FINANCIAL PLANNING FOCUS [SOUND RECORDING]. **2880**

0889-0560 *See* KEEPING CURRENT. **2886**

0889-0579 *See* NAACOG NEWSLETTER. **3862**

0889-0609 *See* AMERICAN LABOR (WASHINGTON, D.C.). **1643**

0889-0617 *See* CHERAW CHRONICLE. **5741**

0889-0625 *See* SECURITY LAW NEWSLETTER. **3176**

0889-0633 *See* CHEMICAL WASTE LITIGATION REPORTER. **3110**

0889-0641 See RICO LAW REPORTER. 3103

0889-065X See PERSONALIST FORUM, THE. 4355

0889-0668 See JOURNAL OF EXPLOSIVES ENGINEERING, THE. 1982

0889-0676 See TRI-CITY LEDGER (FLOMATON), THE. 5628

0889-0684 See ENTERPRISE (PONCHATOULA, LA.). 5683

0889-0692 See THRASHER (SAN FRANCISCO, CALIF.). 4926

0889-0714 See FAIR TIMES. 4860

0889-0730 See ALMANAKH PANORAMA. 5632

0889-0749 See NATIONAL SCHOOL BUS REPORT. 5388

0889-0765 See CENTER FOCUS. 4943

0889-0773 See MEDIUM (BOTHELL, WASH.). 3230

0889-0781 See WHEREVER IN THE WORLD, FOR JESUS' SAKE. 5009

0889-082X See COMPUTER INDUSTRY REPORT. 1256

0889-0838 See MADDUX REPORT, THE. 691

0889-0854 See EEPA NEWS BULLETIN. 2043

0889-0889 See TRANSPORTATION IN AMERICA. 5402

0889-0897 See PROFESSIONAL INVESTOR, THE. 912

0889-0951 See MEDIA SPORTS BUSINESS. 1134

0889-0986 See LIMRA'S MARKETFACTS. 2887

0889-1273 See QED STATE-BY-STATE SCHOOL GUIDE [MASSACHUSETTS]. 1776

0889-1575 See JOURNAL OF FOOD COMPOSITION AND ANALYSIS. 1026

0889-1583 See JOURNAL OF THE JAPANESE AND INTERNATIONAL ECONOMIES. 1637

0889-1591 See BRAIN, BEHAVIOR, AND IMMUNITY. 3828

0889-1648 See CALIFORNIA, FOLKS & LORE. 2318

0889-1664 See RAMBUNCTIOUS REVIEW. 3427

0889-1699 See TURNAROUNDS & WORKOUTS. 815

0889-1729 See SCIENTIFIC AND TECHNICAL ORGANIZATIONS AND AGENCIES DIRECTORY. 5155

0889-1761 See BRAZIL SERVICE. 1465

0889-177X See ANVIL'S RING, THE. 3998

0889-1834 See SOUTH CAROLINA FARMER : THE SOUTH CAROLINA FARM BUREAU FEDERATION NEWS. 136

0889-1842 See RODDY REPORT. DALLAS COUNTY, THE. 4847

0889-1893 See AMERICAN JOURNAL OF ALTERNATIVE AGRICULTURE. 58

0889-1915 See TEMPLE INTERNATIONAL AND COMPARATIVE LAW JOURNAL. 3136

0889-1931 See DEADLINES (HAWLEY, MASS.). 296

0889-1990 See VOLLEYBALL MONTHLY. 4928

0889-2113 See REFERENCE POINT. CUMULATIVE INDEX : FOOD INDUSTRY ABSTRACTS. 2355

0889-2113 See REFERENCE POINT. 2355

0889-2121 See AMERICAN FITNESS QUARTERLY. 2596

0889-2148 See AFGHANISTAN FORUM. 2484

0889-2156 See MENNONITE WEEKLY REVIEW. 5677

0889-2172 See ARTS EDUCATION REVIEW OF BOOKS, THE. 315

0889-2202 See PROGRESSIVE REVIEW (WASHINGTON, D.C.), THE. 4675

0889-2210 See DECORATING DIGEST CRAFT AND HOME PROJECTS. 372

0889-2229 See AIDS RESEARCH AND HUMAN RETROVIRUSES. 3664

0889-2237 See BIRMINGHAM BUSINESS JOURNAL. 643

0889-2245 See TWIN CITY NEWS (CHATTAHOOCHEE, FLA.). 5651

0889-2288 See CARLSONREPORT. 952

0889-2296 See MIAMI TODAY. 5650

0889-230X See BOSTON ROCK. 4104

0889-2326 See RIVERSIDE QUARTERLY. 3431

0889-2334 See CHESTERFIELD ADVERTISER, THE. 5742

0889-2342 See COLUMBIA MAGAZINE (COLUMBIA, MD.). 2531

0889-2369 See LAKE OSWEGO REVIEW. 5733

0889-2393 See PHOTOFINISHING NEWS LETTER. 4374

0889-2407 See OHIO FISHERMAN. 4876

0889-2415 See SOCM SENTINEL, THE. 2205

0889-2423 See INDEPENDENT FLORIDA ALLIGATOR, THE. 1092

0889-2431 See DAILY COMMERCIAL RECORD. 5748

0889-2482 See JOURNAL OF HEALTHCARE MATERIAL MANAGEMENT. 3787

0889-258X See LINDLEYANA : THE SCIENTIFIC JOURNAL OF THE AMERICAN ORCHID SOCIETY. 517

0889-2644 See BROADCAST BANKER/BROKER. 780

0889-2695 See HUNGARIAN HERITAGE REVIEW. 2263

0889-2717 See ALL TV PUBLICITY OUTLETS, NATIONWIDE. 755

0889-2725 See ... POLITICAL RISK YEARBOOK. SUB-SAHARAN AFRICA, THE. 4489

0889-2741 See CITIES OF THE WORLD. 5466

0889-2776 See METRO CALIFORNIA MEDIA. 1117

0889-2784 See NATIONAL RADIO PUBLICITY OUTLETS. 1135

0889-2830 See ENTERPRISE (SPRING CITY, TN). 5745

0889-2873 See NASHVILLE BUSINESS JOURNAL. 696

0889-289X See BICYCLE GUIDE. 428

0889-2911 See PARADOX USER'S JOURNAL. 1289

0889-2938 See GUAM & MICRONESIA GLIMPSES. 2669

0889-2970 See RURAL HERITAGE. 252

0889-2989 See DO-IT-YOURSELF RETAILING. 2811

0889-3012 See ASSEMBLAGE. 292

0889-3039 See ANCESTOR UPDATE. 2437

0889-3047 See REVIEW OF AUSTRIAN ECONOMICS, THE. 1517

0889-3055 See TAX ANALYSTS' DAILY TAX HIGHLIGHTS & DOCUMENTS. 4751

0889-308X See INFORM LETTER (WICHITA, KAN.), THE. 5676

0889-3098 See STAR DATE : THE ASTRONOMY NEWS REPORT / THE UNIVERSITY OF TEXAS AT AUSTIN MCDONALD OBSERVATORY. 400

0889-3101 See HERALD (MONTEREY, CALIF.), THE. 5635

0889-311X See CRYSTALLOGRAPHY REVIEWS. 1031

0889-3136 See BEST OF LONG RANGE PLANNING, THE. 642

0889-3144 See RAPRA REVIEW REPORTS. 2108

0889-3152 See CAT MEWS FOR A HEALTHIER CAT. 5507

0889-3209 See SALES UPBEAT. 709

0889-3217 See SEAFOOD BUSINESS (CAMDEN, ME.). 2357

0889-3225 See ROUNDEL. 5424

0889-3233 See WACO FARM AND LABOR JOURNAL (1986). 145

0889-3241 See ACI STRUCTURAL JOURNAL. 2018

0889-325X See ACI MATERIALS JOURNAL. 2018

0889-3268 See JOURNAL OF BUSINESS AND PSYCHOLOGY. 4594

0889-3276 See STACCATO (TERRE HAUTE, IND.). 4154

0889-3292 See ACADEMIC FINANCIER. 1806

0889-3322 See FLORIDA GAME & FISH (MARIETTA, GA.). 4872

0889-3330 See COALFIELD PROGRESS, THE. 5758

0889-3349 See TOUR & TRAVEL NEWS. 5492

0889-3357 See RICHMOND BUSINESS JOURNAL, THE. 708

0889-3365 See NBER MACROECONOMICS ANNUAL. 1593

0889-3381 See MICROBIOLOGICAL UPDATE, THE. 567

0889-339X See STUMPAGE PRICE REPORT (EUGENE, OR.). 2404

0889-3403 See BUSINESS JOURNAL OF NEW JERSEY (JAMESBURG, N.J : 1985). 649

0889-3411 See NUCLEAR MONITOR, THE. 4449

0889-342X See NAOS (ENGLISH ED.). 3304

0889-3438 See PROFESSIONAL REPORT (BOSTON, MASS.). 1201

0889-3454 See HAZARDOUS MATERIALS NEWSLETTER (BARRE, VT.). 2231

0889-3489 See DODGE CITY DAILY GLOBE, THE. 5675

0889-3497 See SUN MAGAZINE. 4280

0889-3519 See ALCOHOLIC BEVERAGE EXECUTIVES' NEWSLETTER INTERNATIONAL. 2363

0889-3535 See JOURNAL / THE WISCONSIN ASSOCIATION FOR HEALTH, PHYSICAL EDUCATION, RECREATION, AND DANCE, WAHPERD. 1856

0889-3543 See VOICE (FRANKLIN, WIS.), THE. 3793

0889-3551 See WASHINGTON JOURNAL OF HEALTH, PHYSICAL EDUCATION, RECREATION AND DANCE. 1859

0889-356X See SIXTH CIRCUIT REVIEW. 3055

0889-3578 See FOURTH CIRCUIT REVIEW (LOUISVILLE, KY.). 2972

0889-3608 See MEAT SHEET, THE. 2350

0889-3640 See MIAMI MEANDERINGS. 2746

0889-3667 See INTERNATIONAL JOURNAL OF COMPARATIVE PSYCHOLOGY. 4591

0889-3675 See JOURNAL OF POETRY THERAPY. 4599

0889-3799 See MISSOURI GAME & FISH. 4875

0889-3802 See KENTUCKY GAME & FISH. 4874

0889-3810 See NEWS-SUN (NEWPORT, PA.), THE. 5738

0889-3829 See AT THE MUSEUM. 343

0889-3888 See TRUCK IDENTIFICATION BOOK. 5427

0889-3918 See AUTOMOTIVE WEEK. 5407

0889-3926 See MICAP RECAP. 1346

0889-3942 See BREAKTHROUGH (EAST ORANGE, N.J.). 1728

0889-3969 See ADVANCES IN PATHOLOGY AND LABORATORY MEDICINE. 3892

0889-4000 See IBFAN NEWS. 5289

0889-4019 See CAREER DEVELOPMENT QUARTERLY, THE. 4201

0889-4027 See CARIBUS. 2727

0889-4094 See SAILING WORLD. 596

0889-4140 See INTELLIGENCER JOURNAL. 5737

0889-4167 See GAUGE RAIL-ROADING, O. 2773

0889-4175 See TALENT EDUCATION JOURNAL. 4156

0889-4183 See HALES REPORT, INSURANCE BROKERAGE, THE. 2881

0889-4191 See BIOELECTROMAGNETICS SOCIETY NEWSLETTER. 4398

0889-4205 See MADISON COUNTY RECORD. 5627

0889-4248 See UTILITY COMMUNICATOR'S EXCHANGE. 4762

0889-4256 See WINE INVESTOR. EXECUTIVE EDITION, THE. 2372

0889-4337 See TODAY'S CPA. 752

0889-4353 See ZENAIR NEWS. 40

0889-4361 See LUSCOMBE ASSOCIATION NEWS. 28

0889-437X See CUB CLUES. 17

0889-4388 See BUCKER NEWS LETTER, THE. 15

0889-4396 See EBRI QUARTERLY PENSION INVESTMENT REPORT. 897

0889-4434 See POULTRY SCIENCE REVIEWS. 218

0889-4442 See MONTGOMERY BUSINESS. 696

0889-4493 See MANAGER'S LEGAL BULLETIN. 3151

0889-4507 See VERBUM (SAN DIEGO, CALIF.). 382

0889-4558 See CHILD CARE CENTER. 5278

0889-4566 See LATEST COMPOSITE FEATURE RELEASE SCHEDULE. 324

0889-4574 See LEGISLATIVE NEWS ALERT. 4661

0889-4590 See NEWSPAPER FINANCIAL EXECUTIVE JOURNAL. 2922

0889-4604 See NEW MEXICO JOURNAL OF READING, THE. 1767

0889-4612 See DIXON TELEGRAPH (DIXON, ILL. : 1985). 5659

0889-4647 See JOURNAL OF NURSING CARE QUALITY. 3859

0889-4655 See JOURNAL OF CARDIOVASCULAR NURSING, THE. 3858

0889-4671 See DIRECTORY OF ALABAMA HEALTH SCIENCE LIBRARIES AND HANDBOOK OF THE ALABAMA HEALTH LIBRARIES ASSOCIATION. 3206

0889-468X See CONTINUING THE CONVERSATION. 4344

0889-4698 See PROBLEMS IN ANESTHESIA. 3684

0889-4701 See PROBLEMS IN CRITICAL CARE. 3629

0889-471X See PROBLEMS IN UROLOGY. 3992

0889-4728 See C3I REPORT. 4038

0889-4744 See MONTHLY MINI-LESSONS IN CARE OF THE AGING. 5180

0889-4779 See SALES LEADS (RIVIERA BEACH, FLA.). 708

0889-4787 See VALLEY POTATO GROWER. 143

0889-4795 See LET'S PLAY HOCKEY. 4903

0889-4809 See MINNESOTA FLYER. 28

0889-4841 See CAPITOL UPDATE. 4637

0889-485X See JONESREPORT. 927

0889-4876 See SECURITY AFFAIRS. 4535

0889-4884 See MAILBOX NEWS. 2791

0889-4906 See ENGLISH FOR SPECIFIC PURPOSES (NEW YORK, N.Y.). 3278

0889-4922 See INTERNATIONAL RECORDING EQUIPMENT & STUDIO DIRECTORY. 5317

0889-4973 See VIDEOMAKER. 1168

0889-5007 See COUNTRY FACTS. 1472

0889-504X See JOURNAL OF TURBOMACHINERY. 2119

0889-5058 See YOUTHWORKER UPDATE. 1720

0889-5074 See ADVANCES IN CARDIAC SURGERY. 3957

0889-5090 See REPORTER (O'FALLON, ILL.), THE. 3038

0889-5104 See BREVARD BUSINESS NEWS. 644

0889-5147 See TELECONFERENCING DIRECTORY. 1166

0889-5155 See DOLORES STAR. 5642

0889-518X See GREENE COUNTY DEMOCRAT (EUTAW, ALA.), THE. 5626

0889-5198 See GRASSROOTS FOR HIGH RISQUE LIBRARIANS. 3212

0889-5236 See PSYCSCAN: PSYCHOANALYSIS. 4623

0889-5244 See PILIPINAS. 2662

0889-5260 See ENERGY STATISTICS SOURCEBOOK. 1962

0889-5279 See MIDGETS & MINI-SPRINTS RACING NEWS. 4904

0889-5333 See TARGET MARKETING. 937

0889-5341 See MONITORING TIMES. 1135

0889-5406 See AMERICAN JOURNAL OF ORTHODONTICS AND DENTOFACIAL ORTHOPEDICS. 1315

0889-5414 See HOSPITALITY LAW. 2979

0889-5422 See EMPLOYEE TESTING & THE LAW. 3147

0889-5465 See HEALTH CARE COMPENSATION & BENEFITS ADVISOR. 4778

0889-549X See WOMEN'S LETTER, THE. 5571

0889-552X See AMERICAN MIDDLE SCHOOL EDUCATION. 1860

0889-5538 See MEDICAL BUSINESS JOURNAL, THE. 3608

0889-5570 See PENNSYLVANIA SPEECH COMMUNICATION ANNUAL, THE. 1119

0889-5597 See CREDIT UNION NEWSWATCH. 786

0889-5600 See MENNONITE LIBRARIAN AND ARCHIVIST, THE. 3231

0889-5619 See FARMERS & CONSUMERS MARKET BULLETIN. 85

0889-5627 See TIMES CLARION (HARLOWTON, MONT.), THE. 5706

0889-5635 See BLITZ (LOS ANGELES, CALIF.). 4104

0889-5643 See MONTESSORI OBSERVER / IMS, THE. 1765

0889-566X See LAWTON CONSTITUTION, THE. 5732

0889-5678 See NEW HORIZONS (MILWAUKEE, WIS.). 1767

0889-5708 See WASHINGTON CRIME NEWS SERVICES' NARCOTICS CONTROL DIGEST. 3178

0889-5716 See WASHINGTON CRIME NEWS SERVICES' ORGANIZED CRIME DIGEST. 3178

0889-5724 See WASHINGTON CRIME NEWS SERVICES' CRIMINAL JUSTICE DIGEST. 3072

0889-5732 See WASHINGTON CRIME NEWS SERVICES' TRAINING AIDS DIGEST. 3179

0889-5740 See FIRE CONTROL DIGEST. 2289

0889-5759 See ROBOTICS REPORT, THE. 1216

0889-5767 See COMMUNITY CRIME PREVENTION DIGEST. 3160

0889-5775 See AQUASPHERE (BOSTON, MASS. : 1985). 442

0889-5783 See AMIGA USER, THE. 1264

0889-5791 See RIP (LOS ANGELES, CALIF.). 4150

0889-5848 See JOURNAL FOR CHRISTIAN STUDIES, A. 4967

0889-5856 See SCAG TELECOMMUNITY. 1163

0889-5864 See PASADENA HERITAGE. 2753

0889-5880 See CMN OFFICE MACHINE NEWS. 4211

0889-5899 See OSTOMY/WOUND MANAGEMENT. 3624

0889-5902 See FROZEN FOOD DIGEST. 2341

0889-5910 See COMPUTER REPORT & THE PC STREET PRICE INDEX. 1246

0889-5929 See PENNSTATE AGRICULTURE. 119

0889-5937 See NEW MEXICO BUSINESS CURRENT ECONOMIC REPORT. 1536

0889-5953 See DICKINSON'S PSAO. 665

0889-597X See DIRECTORY OF OIL REFINERIES. 4254

0889-5988 See BIGGER, FASTER, STRONGER JOURNAL. 4887

0889-5996 See CIRCUS REPORT, THE. 4849

0889-6003 See JURY TRIALS AND TRIBULATIONS, INC. 2991

0889-6011 See TEXAS COLLEGE ENGLISH. 1850

0889-602X See LOOKING OUT FOR YOUR LEGAL RIGHTS. 3004

0889-6038 See US FIRE SPRINKLER REPORTER. 2293

0889-6054 See SPACE TODAY. 400

0889-6070 See FRESNO BEE, THE. 5635

0889-6089 See AMATEUR SATELLITE REPORT. 1148

0889-6127 See VIRGINIAN-PILOT, THE. 5760

0889-6135 See LEDGER-STAR. 5759

0889-6151 See ECONOCAST. 2164

0889-616X See OLSEN'S BIOTECHNOLOGY REPORT. 3695

0889-6178 See NEWSLETTER OF THE AFRO-AMERICAN RELIGIOUS HISTORY GROUP OF THE AMERICAN ACADEMY OF RELIGION. 2750

0889-6186 See HISTORY TRAILS. 2737

0889-6194 See COMPUTER USE IN SOCIAL SERVICES NETWORK : NEWSLETTER. 1178

0889-6208 See IN MOTION FILM & VIDEO PRODUCTION MAGAZINE. 4370

0889-6216 See START (SAN FRANCISCO, CALIF.). 1204

0889-6224 See PUBLICATION / ARKANSAS WATER RESOURCES RESEARCH CENTER. 5537

0889-6259 See MASTER TEACHER, THE. 1900

0889-6283 See UROLOGY ANNUAL. 3994

0889-6291 See IRAN TODAY. 4510

0889-6313 See PSYCHOBIOLOGY (AUSTIN, TEX.). 4610

0889-6348 See PROTEUS (SHIPPENSBURG, PA.). 3426

0889-6356 See OCCASIONAL PAPERS IN LANGUAGE, LITERATURE AND LINGUISTICS. SERIES A. 3307

0889-6372 See CREATIVE BLACK BOOK (PRODUCER'S ED.), THE. 758

0889-6380 See OWYHEE OUTPOST. 2753

0889-6402 See ORGANIZATION DEVELOPMENT JOURNAL. 881

0889-6410 See LAKE STREET REVIEW, THE. 3403

0889-6445 See BUGLE. 2189

0889-6461 See TECH STREET JOURNAL. 5162

0889-647X See KENTUCKY POETRY REVIEW. 3345

0889-6569 See SOAP OPERA PHOTOROMANCE. 2546

0889-6607 See INVENTORY OF MUSIC ICONOGRAPHY. 4124

0889-6712 See ANIMALS' VOICE (CHICO, CALIF.), THE. 225

0889-6720 See MONTESSORI NEWS / IMS. 1765

0889-6747 See WINFIELD DAILY COURIER (1931), THE. 5679

0889-6836 See INFOCUS (PHILADELPHIA, PA.). 1188

0889-6917 See LANGUAGE ASSOCIATION BULLETIN. 1899

0889-6925 See MINERAL MATTERS. 2144

0889-6941 See INDIANA MATHEMATICS TEACHER. 3509

0889-6976 See CHIROPRACTIC SPORTS MEDICINE. 3953

0889-6992 See TOPEKA BUSINESS REPORT, THE. 716

0889-7018 See REHABILITATION EDUCATION (ELMSFORD, N.Y.). 1884

0889-7034 See NUTRITION SAVVY. 4197

0889-7077 See SUBSTANCE ABUSE. 1349

0889-7085 See SPECIALTY TRAVEL INDEX: THE DIRECTORY TO SPECIAL INTEREST TRAVEL. 5491

0889-7123 See WATER TREATMENT INSTITUTE NEWSLETTER. 2248

0889-7158 See CALLIOPE (BRISTOL, R.I.). 3371

0889-7166 See WAVES (SPRING VALLEY, CALIF.). 2096

0889-7174 See CHANGING MEN (MADISON, WIS.). 3994

0889-7182 See SCHOLARLY INQUIRY FOR NURSING PRACTICE. 3869

0889-7190 See ASAIO JOURNAL (1992). 3960

0889-7204 See PROGRESS IN CARDIOVASCULAR NURSING. 3709

0889-7247 See MORRELL, MORRILL FAMILIES ASSOCIATION NEWSLETTER. 2461

0889-728X See SCULPTURE (WASHINGTON, D.C.). 364

0889-7328 See MILITARY HISTORY (HERNDON, VA.). 4050

0889-7344 See CAMPUS ECOLOGIST, THE. 2212

0889-7352 See ALASKA OIL & INDUSTRY NEWS. 4249

0889-7395 See CRA REVIEW, THE. 1590

0889-7417 See INTERNATIONAL QUARTERLY (PRINCETON, N.J.). 1754

0889-7425 See SYMBOLS. 246

0889-7433 See AURA (BIRMINGHAM, ALA.). 3364

0889-745X *See* OKLAHOMA BAPTIST CHRONICLE, THE. **4983**

0889-7468 *See* ALABAMA DEVELOPMENT NEWS. **1545**

0889-7506 *See* CIRCULAR - LOUISIANA AGRICULTURAL EXPERIMENT STATION. **74**

0889-7514 *See* QCPE BULLETIN. **1057**

0889-7565 *See* MONTHLY NEWSPRINT STATISTICAL REPORT. **4566**

0889-7581 *See* PAN PIPES. **4145**

0889-759X *See* JEAN RHYS REVIEW. **3399**

0889-7662 *See* ABA BANKERS WEEKLY. **768**

0889-7670 *See* CONNECTICUT MAGAZINE (FAIRFIELD, CONN.). **2531**

0889-7735 *See* IOWA PHARMACIST. **4309**

0889-7743 *See* YALE JOURNAL OF INTERNATIONAL LAW, THE. **3138**

0889-7794 *See* NARC OFFICER, THE. **3170**

0889-7816 *See* HANDBOOK OF NON-PRESCRIPTION DRUGS. **4306**

0889-7840 *See* BULLISH CONSENSUS, THE. **1466**

0889-7891 *See* SOUTH AMERICAN EXPLORER. **4878**

0889-793X *See* NEWSDAY (NEW YORK ED.). **5719**

0889-7956 *See* W.K. KELLOGG FOUNDATION ANNUAL REPORT. **4339**

0889-7972 *See* FANATIC READER, THE. **2533**

0889-8065 *See* CIRCULAR / WEST VIRGINIA UNIVERSITY AGRICULTURAL AND FORESTRY EXPERIMENT STATION. **75**

0889-8138 *See* MIDWEST LIVING. **2538**

0889-8154 *See* UNIVERSITY CITY LIGHT. **5641**

0889-8162 *See* WASHINGTON REPORTS. 2D SERIES. **3072**

0889-8170 *See* ADVANCE (DES MOINES, IOWA). **1125**

0889-8189 *See* CHINA PAINTER, THE. **371**

0889-8197 *See* EXPLORATORIUM QUARTERLY. **4087**

0889-8200 *See* BYTE BUYER, THE. **1172**

0889-8227 *See* APPLIED MANAGEMENT NEWSLETTER. **938**

0889-8235 *See* GUILFOYLE REPORT, THE. **925**

0889-8243 *See* CTNS BULLETIN. **5098**

0889-8308 *See* INTELLIGENT INSTRUMENTS & COMPUTERS. **1220**

0889-8391 *See* JOURNAL OF COGNITIVE PSYCHOTHERAPY, THE. **4595**

0889-8405 *See* NCEOA JOURNAL. **1766**

0889-8413 *See* PERSPECTIVES ON PREVENTION. **3626**

0889-8421 *See* EVERYTHING NATURAL. **2790**

0889-843X *See* KIDS COOKING NEWSLETTER. **2791**

0889-8448 *See* PERSPECTIVES IN MEXICAN AMERICAN STUDIES. **2625**

0889-8480 *See* MATHEMATICAL POPULATION STUDIES. **4554**

0889-8499 *See* NEWSPAPERS CAREER DIRECTORY. **2922**

0889-8502 *See* MAGAZINES CAREER DIRECTORY. **4816**

0889-8510 *See* MARKETING & SALES CAREER DIRECTORY. **930**

0889-8529 *See* ENDOCRINOLOGY AND METABOLISM CLINICS OF NORTH AMERICA. **3729**

0889-8537 *See* ANESTHESIOLOGY CLINICS OF NORTH AMERICA. **3681**

0889-8545 *See* OBSTETRICS AND GYNECOLOGY CLINICS OF NORTH AMERICA. **3766**

0889-8553 *See* GASTROENTEROLOGY CLINICS OF NORTH AMERICA. **3745**

0889-8561 *See* IMMUNOLOGY AND ALLERGY CLINICS OF NORTH AMERICA. **3671**

0889-857X *See* RHEUMATIC DISEASE CLINICS OF NORTH AMERICA. **3807**

0889-8588 *See* HEMATOLOGY/ONCOLOGY CLINICS OF NORTH AMERICA. **3772**

0889-8618 *See* BEEVILLE BEE-PICAYUNE. **5747**

0889-8650 *See* SOUTH ASIA IN REVIEW. **2665**

0889-8677 *See* VILLAGE TIMES, THE. **5722**

0889-8685 *See* CREATIVE LOAFING (1978). **5653**

0889-8693 *See* EXPLORATIONS (DAYTON, OHIO). **4958**

0889-8707 *See* CONNECTICUT HEALTH CARE. **3778**

0889-8715 *See* CARTHAGE REPUBLICAN TRIBUNE. **5714**

0889-8723 *See* IJS JAZZ REGISTER. **4122**

0889-8731 *See* AL-ARABIYYA. **3262**

0889-8790 *See* REMEMBER THAT SONG. **4149**

0889-8804 *See* DOUBLE TALK. **2789**

0889-8812 *See* STORYTELLERS OF SAN DIEGO NEWSLETTER. **3440**

0889-8847 *See* ATTITUDES & ARABESQUES. **1310**

0889-8863 *See* PARENTS' PRESS. **2285**

0889-8871 *See* GRANTS ADMINISTRATION NEWS. **4652**

0889-8898 *See* FARIBAULT DAILY NEWS. **5695**

0889-8936 *See* EMERGING TRENDS. **4955**

0889-8979 *See* AT&T TECHNOLOGY. **1149**

0889-907X *See* TELECOMMUNICATIONS DEVELOPMENT REPORT. **1165**

0889-9134 *See* II COMPUTING. **1187**

0889-9142 *See* IMAGING UPDATE. **4565**

0889-9193 *See* SEMICONDUCTOR PACKAGING UPDATE. **4222**

0889-9274 *See* FORECLOSURE LAW BULLETIN. **3086**

0889-9312 *See* BNA CRIMINAL PRACTICE MANUAL. CURRENT REPORTS. **2942**

0889-9320 *See* LICENSING INTERNATIONAL. **3003**

0889-9347 *See* INDONESIA MIRROR. **2654**

0889-9355 *See* INDONESIA ISSUES. **2654**

0889-9363 *See* NAFSA GOVERNMENT AFFAIRS BULLETIN. **1920**

0889-9371 *See* SCHOOL LIBRARY MEDIA ACTIVITIES MONTHLY. **3248**

0889-938X *See* REVIEW OF INDUSTRIAL ORGANIZATION. **1625**

0889-9398 *See* OPERA COMPANION, THE. **4143**

0889-9401 *See* ANALYSIS OF VERBAL BEHAVIOR, THE. **4573**

0889-941X *See* CORPORATE MONTHLY. **661**

0889-9436 *See* MISSION FRONTIERS. **4978**

0889-9444 *See* MANAGEMENT STRATEGY. **4707**

0889-9487 *See* DIRECTORY OF PROGRAMS IN SOVIET & EAST EUROPEAN STUDIES. **2685**

0889-9495 *See* RADIANCE (OAKLAND, CALIF.). **405**

0889-9525 *See* TECHNICAL TRENDS. **917**

0889-9533 *See* MICROPUBLISHING REPORT. **4816**

0889-9606 *See* HI-TECH AD PLACEMENT REPORT. **760**

0889-9614 *See* SKYWATCHER'S ALMANAC. **399**

0889-9711 *See* HERALD-NEWS (EDMONTON, KY.), THE. **5681**

0889-9746 *See* JOURNAL OF FLUIDS AND STRUCTURES. **2092**

0889-9762 *See* SEYBOLD REPORT ON PUBLISHING SYSTEMS, THE. **4819**

0889-9797 *See* CASINO CHRONICLE. **2804**

0889-9819 *See* NORTH AMERICAN COPIER & COPYBOARD GUIDE. **4567**

0889-9827 *See* NORTH AMERICAN ELECTRONIC TYPEWRITER GUIDE. **4213**

0889-9851 *See* TETON VALLEY NEWS. **5657**

0889-9886 *See* AUTHORIZED OA DEALER REPORT, THE. **824**

0889-9894 *See* PRICING STRATEGY. **803**

0889-9908 *See* JOB HUNTER, THE. **4205**

0889-9924 *See* PROFESSIONAL FLORAL DESIGNER, THE. **2436**

0889-9932 *See* MICROSOFT SYSTEMS JOURNAL. **1288**

0889-9967 *See* PROFIT-BUILDING STRATEGIES FOR BUSINESS OWNERS. **804**

0890-0000 *See* WESTERN WEATHER. **1437**

0890-0019 *See* RAISED DOT COMPUTING NEWSLETTER. **1201**

0890-0027 *See* COMMERCIAL CARPET DIGEST. **5349**

0890-0035 *See* GREEKAMERICAN, THE. **2262**

0890-0086 *See* COLD-DRILL MAGAZINE. **3376**

0890-0132 *See* JOURNAL OF INTERDISCIPLINARY STUDIES. **4969**

0890-0159 *See* ADVANCES IN BEHAVIORAL ECONOMICS. **1460**

0890-023X *See* MARKET MONTH. **906**

0890-0256 *See* THUNDERCATS MAGAZINE. **1070**

0890-0264 *See* SPECTRUM (TAKOMA PARK, MD.). **4999**

0890-0272 **4938**

0890-0280 *See* GUANGARA LIBERTARIA. **2617**

0890-0299 *See* WINE & SPIRITS (BERKELEY, CALIF.). **2372**

0890-0302 *See* CALIFORNIA PSYCHOLOGIST, THE. **4579**

0890-0329 *See* OBSERVER-DISPATCH (UTICA ED.), THE. **5719**

0890-0337 *See* SAN FRANCISCO BUSINESS TIMES. **709**

0890-0353 *See* FAMILIES OF WYOMING CO., WV. **2447**

0890-0361 *See* FAMILIES OF YANCEY COUNTY, NC. **2447**

0890-037X *See* WEED TECHNOLOGY. **145**

0890-0388 *See* SCIENCE WEEKLY. LEVEL PRE-A. **1904**

0890-0396 *See* AIR & WATER POLLUTION CONTROL. **2223**

0890-040X *See* UAW FACTS. **1715**

0890-0434 *See* MASSACHUSETTS DAILY COLLEGIAN, THE. **5689**

0890-0450 *See* OLD HICKORY REVIEW. **3420**

0890-0477 *See* LOUISIANA LITERATURE. **3408**

0890-0485 *See* NINNAU : THE NORTH AMERICAN WELSH NEWSLETTER. **2270**

0890-0493 *See* JOURNAL OF HUMANISTIC EDUCATION. **1898**

0890-0523 *See* JOURNAL OF MASS MEDIA ETHICS. **2251**

0890-0566 *See* MINNESOTA LITERATURE NEWSLETTER. **3412**

0890-0574 *See* AUSTIN MAGAZINE. **2528**

0890-0604 *See* ARTIFICIAL INTELLIGENCE FOR ENGINEERING DESIGN, ANALYSIS AND MANUFACTURING. **1211**

0890-0655 *See* PUBLIC PROGRAMS NEWSLETTER. **2323**

0890-068X *See* NATIONAL TOMBSTONE EPITAPH, THE. **2747**

0890-0698 *See* INTERNATIONAL GAME WARDEN, THE. **2195**

0890-0795 *See* CMJ NEW MUSIC REPORT. **4110**

0890-0809 *See* BEE (DANVILLE, VA.). **5758**

0890-0841 *See* BOOKS & RELIGION. **4939**

0890-0876 *See* WESTERN & EASTERN TREASURES. **4880**

0890-0884 *See* ADHESIVES & SEALANTS NEWSLETTER. **1049**

0890-0906 *See* GENETIC ENGINEERING AND BIOTECHNOLOGY RELATED FIRMS WORLDWIDE DIRECTORY. **3692**

0890-0914 *See* GEORGE ODIORNE LETTER, THE. **868**

0890-0930 *See* SUN-REPORTER, THE. **5640**

0890-0949 *See* LOS ANGELES OBSERVER. **2537**

0890-0957 *See* DICK DAVIS DIGEST. **896**

0890-0981 *See* WYSIWYG. **4820**

0890-1007 *See* OKLAHOMA CONSTITUTION, THE. **4671**

0890-1112 *See* JOURNAL OF RITUAL STUDIES. **4970**

0890-1120 *See* ARTHRITIS TODAY. **3803**

0890-1139 *See* BIRNBAUM'S ITALY. **5464**

0890-1147 *See* PUTNAM COUNTY COURIER (CARMEL, N.Y. : 1852). **5646**

0890-1163 *See* JOURNAL OF MINORITY EMPLOYMENT. **1682**

0890-1171 See AMERICAN JOURNAL OF HEALTH PROMOTION. 4764

0890-1198 See TELCOM HIGHLIGHTS. 1164

0890-1201 See EARTHWATCH OREGON. 2164

0890-121X See PRIVATE EDUCATION LAW REPORT. 3031

0890-1236 See SCHOOLS ADVOCATE, THE. 3046

0890-1244 See DIRECTORY - AMERICAN ELECTRONICS ASSOCIATION. 2042

0890-1252 See SATELLITE RETAILER. 957

0890-1260 See SATELLITE TIMES. 1626

0890-1287 See SLVGS NEWS, THE. 2472

0890-1309 See FINANCIAL FUTURES. 1490

0890-1333 See ARIZONA ARCHAEOLOGICAL COUNCIL NEWSLETTER. 259

0890-1341 See ARAB BOOK WORLD. 4823

0890-1422 See KEEPING UP. 5207

0890-1449 See CURRENT TOPICS IN PULMONARY PHARMACOLOGY AND TOXICOLOGY. 3980

0890-1473 See CALIFORNIA STAATS-ZEITUNG. 5633

0890-1481 See FAMILY CIRCLE COOKBOOK. 2790

0890-149X See GALVES AUTO PRICE LIST (AMERICAN USED CARS ED.). 5415

0890-1511 See ARCO ADVERTISER, THE. 5656

0890-1538 See INTERP CENTRAL CLEARINGHOUSE NEWSLETTER. 4205

0890-1554 See ALABAMA LITERARY REVIEW. 3359

0890-1562 See TRANSWORLD IDENTITY SERIES. 246

0890-1570 See SECOND OPINION (PARK RIDGE, ILL.). 3640

0890-1597 See TENNESSEE JOURNAL OF HEALTH, PHYSICAL EDUCATION, RECREATION, AND DANCE / TENNESSEE ASSOCIATION OF HEALTH, PHYSICAL EDUCATION, RECREATION, AND DANCE. 1859

0890-1619 See NEW OPTIONS. 4529

0890-1651 See DIRECTORY OF MINNESOTA CITY OFFICIALS. 4643

0890-166X See ECONOCLAST (HOUSTON, TEX.), THE. 1481

0890-1678 See HAWAIIAN ARCHAEOLOGY. 269

0890-1686 See MICHIGAN HISTORICAL REVIEW, THE. 2746

0890-1724 See SAND MOUNTAIN REPORTER. 5628

0890-1759 See SPY (NEW YORK, N.Y.). 2546

0890-1767 See MAINTENANCE : THE NEWSLETTER FOR PROFESSIONAL TRUCK EQUIPMENT EXECUTIVES. 5386

0890-1775 See MAINTENANCE (NEWSLETTER FOR PROFESSIONAL TRUCK EQUIPMENT MANAGERS). 5386

0890-1783 See MAINTENANCE (NEWSLETTER FOR PROFESSIONAL TRUCK EQUIPMENT SUPERVISORS). 5386

0890-1791 See MAINTENANCE (NEWSLETTER FOR PROFESSIONAL TRUCK DRIVER/OWNERS). 5386

0890-1813 See CA SELECTS: ARTIFICIAL SWEETENERS. 997

0890-1821 See CA SELECTS: MEMORY & RECORDING DEVICES & MATERIALS. 1005

0890-183X See CA SELECTS: ASYMMETRIC SYNTHESIS & INDUCTION. 998

0890-1856 See CA SELECTS: CARBON & GRAPHITE FIBERS. 998

0890-1864 See CA SELECTS: CATALYTIC & KINETIC ANALYSIS. 999

0890-1872 See CA SELECTS: FIBER OPTICS & OPTICAL COMMUNICATION. 1002

0890-1880 See CA SELECTS: FORMULATION CHEMISTRY. 1003

0890-1899 See CA SELECTS: ION CHROMATOGRAPHY. 1004

0890-1902 See CA SELECTS: PHARMACEUTICAL ANALYSIS. 1007

0890-1910 See CA SELECTS: PHARMACEUTICAL CHEMISTRY (JOURNALS). 1007

0890-1929 See CA SELECTS: PHARMACEUTICAL CHEMISTRY (PATENTS). 1007

0890-1937 See CA SELECTS: PLATINUM & PALLADIUM CHEMISTRY. 1008

0890-1945 See CA SELECTS: POLYACRYLATES (JOURNALS). 1008

0890-1953 See CA SELECTS: QUATERNARY AMMONIUM COMPOUNDS. 1009

0890-1961 See CA SELECTS: SILICAS & SILICATES. 1009

0890-2038 See ANNUAL REPORT - FLORIDA COOPERATIVE EXTENSION SERVICE. 60

0890-2070 See EUROPEAN JOURNAL OF PERSONALITY. 4587

0890-2100 See OHIO INSTRUCTIONAL GRANTS ANNUAL REPORT. 1838

0890-2143 See COMPUTER ENTERTAINER. 1230

0890-2178 See BUSINESS BRIEFS (DETROIT, MICH.). 646

0890-2194 See RECREATION EXECUTIVE REPORT. 4853

0890-2208 See NOLO NEWS. 3017

0890-2216 See CONFEDERATE VETERAN (MURFREESBORO, TENN.). 2729

0890-2224 See ON OUR BACKS. 2795

0890-2240 See YALE DAILY NEWS. 5647

0890-2259 See HEALTHWEEK. 4782

0890-2291 See USED CARS TODAY. 5427

0890-2313 See OREGON BIRDS. 5593

0890-233X See HORSE INDUSTRY DIRECTORY. 2799

0890-2402 See CELLULAR MARKETING. 922

0890-2461 See PHILOSOPHY, THEOLOGY. 4357

0890-247X See PARENTING (SAN FRANCISCO, CALIF.). 2284

0890-2496 See PETER BERLIN REPORT ON SHRINKAGE CONTROL (STORE MANAGERS ED.), THE. 1621

0890-250X See PETER BERLIN REPORT ON SHRINKAGE CONTROL (EXECUTIVE ED.), THE. 1621

0890-2534 See ANVIL MAGAZINE. 2797

0890-2577 See INTERNATIONAL JOURNAL OF PRODUCTION ECONOMICS. 1612

0890-2658 See VIEWPOINT / ASSOCIATION OF REHABILITATION PROGRAMS IN DATA PROCESSING. 5313

0890-2666 See PROGRESS TIMES. 5753

0890-2682 See FOCUS ON THE NEWS. 5660

0890-2690 See OZARK VISITOR. 5704

0890-2720 See INTERNATIONAL JOURNAL OF SUPERCOMPUTER APPLICATIONS, THE. 1287

0890-2739 See JOURNAL OF CARNIOMANDIBULAR DISORDERS, THE. 3834

0890-2747 See JOURNAL OF ENERGETICS AND FLUIDS ENGINEERING. 2091

0890-2763 See ADVANCES IN R&D. 5081

0890-2771 See ADVANCES IN HIGH-TECH MATERIALS. 5081

0890-278X See AGHE EXCHANGE. 3748

0890-2801 See BISBEE MAGAZINE. 2723

0890-281X See SPECIAL EVENTS. 2809

0890-2828 See NSFRE NEWS. 763

0890-2852 See TOURS & RESORTS. 5494

0890-2879 See MONROE MONITOR/VALLEY NEWS. 5761

0890-2917 See YEARBOOK OF LANGLAND STUDIES, THE. 3473

0890-2925 See AIR CHARTER GUIDE, THE. 5375

0890-2933 See BROOM, BRUSH & MOP. 1600

0890-2968 See REDWOOD RESEARCHER. 2469

0890-2976 See WORLD TRADE IN LIQUIFIED PETROLEUM GASES. 4282

0890-2984 See UTILITY REPORTER (SCHENECTADY, N.Y.). 4762

0890-2992 See FOR YOUR INFORMATION (NEW YORK, N. Y.). 320

0890-300X See INNOVATOR'S DIGEST. 5114

0890-3018 See INDUSTRIAL HEALTH & HAZARDS UPDATE. 2863

0890-3034 See CONFIDENTIAL REPORT FOR ATTORNEYS. 2955

0890-3050 See LAKE SUPERIOR MAGAZINE. 2537

0890-3069 See ARID SOIL RESEARCH & REHABILITATION. 163

0890-3077 See TWINS. 2286

0890-3107 See TARTAN, THE. 1095

0890-3131 See SHAPE (SEATTLE, WASH.). 4802

0890-3166 See WEEKLY READER. EDITION K. 1791

0890-3174 See WEEKLY READER. PRE-K EDITION. 1791

0890-3182 See WEEKLY READER. EDITION 5. 1791

0890-3190 See WEEKLY READER. EDITION 4. 1791

0890-3204 See WEEKLY READER. EDITION 3. 1790

0890-3212 See WEEKLY READER. EDITION 2. 1790

0890-3220 See WEEKLY READER. EDITION 1. 1790

0890-3239 See WEEKLY READER. SENIOR EDITION. 1791

0890-3255 See BIRTH GAZETTE, THE. 3757

0890-3344 See JOURNAL OF HUMAN LACTATION. 3763

0890-3352 See TENSO. 3445

0890-3379 See FOCUSING FOLIO, THE. 4347

0890-3395 See WOMEN ALIVE. 5009

0890-3417 See NCAHF NEWSLETTER. 1298

0890-3433 See PUCKERBRUSH REVIEW. 3350

0890-345X See ABILENE REFLECTOR-CHRONICLE. 5668

0890-3514 See GOLFWEEK. 4897

0890-3530 See NETWORK (SALT LAKE CITY, UTAH). 5562

0890-3557 See LOLLIPOPS. 1900

0890-3565 See ARRL HANDBOOK FOR THE RADIO AMATEUR, THE. 1126

0890-3573 See SURPRISES. 1070

0890-3603 See STA PHANTOM, THE. 1627

0890-362X See DU PONT REGISTRY. 1971

0890-3654 See CRITICAL MASS (BERKELEY, CA). 4951

0890-3670 See SCIENTIST (PHILADELPHIA, PA.), THE. 5156

0890-3700 See QUARTERLY OF THE NATIONAL ASSOCIATION FOR OUTLAW AND LAWMAN HISTORY, INC. 2756

0890-3719 See ILLINOIS HERITAGE ASSOCIATION NEWSLETTER. 2454

0890-3727 See NORDEN NEWS. 5517

0890-3735 See NATURE SOCIETY NEWS. 5592

0890-3743 See GLASS NEWS. 2590

0890-3751 See ARMADA TIMES. 5691

0890-3786 See WILD BLUEBERRY GROWER. 2433

0890-3816 See QUARTERLY - ASSOCIATION OF PROFESSIONAL GENEALOGISTS (U.S.). 2468

0890-3832 See MANUAL OF THE LEGISLATURE OF NEW JERSEY. 4664

0890-3840 See PORTLAND FAMILY CALENDAR. 2543

0890-3859 See PARENTING FOR PEACE AND JUSTICE NETWORK : [NEWSLETTER]. 5300

0890-3972 See PODIATRIC PRODUCTS. 3918

0890-4006 See TEENQUEST. 1070

0890-4049 See MICHIGAN DISTRIBUTORS DIRECTORY. 694

0890-4065 See JOURNAL OF AGING STUDIES. 5249

0890-4073 See ADVANCES IN HEALTH EDUCATION. 4763

0890-4081 See INTERNATIONAL CHRISTIAN DIGEST : ICD. 4965

0890-409X See CLINICAL CONNECTION, THE. 4385

0890-4111 See AMERICAN TRANSLATORS ASSOCIATION SCHOLARLY MONOGRAPH SERIES. 3263

0890-412X See AMERICAN UNIVERSITY STUDIES. SERIES XX, FINE ARTS. **312**

0890-4146 See 1949-50-51 FORD/MERCURY OWNERS MAGAZINE. **5403**

0890-4154 See CHANGING HOMES. **4835**

0890-4162 See TEDDY BEAR REVIEW. **376**

0890-4170 See SPOTLIGHT (WAYNE, N.J.). **1103**

0890-4189 See LOOKINGFIT. **2599**

0890-4197 See NATHANIEL HAWTHORNE REVIEW : THE OFFICIAL PUBLICATION OF THE NATHANIEL HAWTHORNE SOCIETY, THE. **3348**

0890-4200 See SENIOR TIMES (WELLESLEY, MASS.), THE. **2545**

0890-4227 See CURRENT PACKAGING ABSTRACTS (PISCATAWAY, N.J.). **4218**

0890-4235 See TERRITORIAL, THE. **2547**

0890-4278 See CORPORATE REPORT WISCONSIN. **662**

0890-4294 See DIFFERENTIA (FLUSHING, N.Y.). **4345**

0890-4308 See COMPUTER ECONOMICS SOURCEBOOK. **1256**

0890-4316 See DP BUDGET. **1258**

0890-4332 See HEAT RECOVERY SYSTEMS & CHP. **4430**

0890-4340 See LOS ANGELES SENTINEL. **5636**

0890-4383 See CONOMIKES REPORTS ON MEDICAL PRACTICE MANAGEMENT : AN INFORMATION SERVICE OF CONOMIKES ASSOCIATES, INC. **3568**

0890-4391 See WEST MICHIGAN PROFILE. **2550**

0890-4421 See PERSPECTIVES ON STAFFING & SCHEDULING. **3790**

0890-4448 See CHEROKEE ONE FEATHER, THE. **2258**

0890-4456 See DEWITT COUNTY GENEALOGICAL QUARTERLY. **2445**

0890-4464 See BULLETIN OF THE ASIA INSTITUTE. **2647**

0890-4480 See WORLD BOOK HEALTH & MEDICAL ANNUAL, THE. **3651**

0890-4537 See ACCESS (NEW YORK, N.Y. : 1983). **1722**

0890-4553 See WATER POLLUTION CONTROL ASSOCIATION OF PENNSYLVANIA MAGAZINE. **2247**

0890-457X See BIBLE TEACHING FOR CONFIDENT LIVING. **5015**

0890-460X See ROCKBILL. **4151**

0890-4626 See TRI-COUNTY NEWS (ZEARING, IOWA. 1986), THE. **5673**

0890-4634 See CENTER QUARTERLY. **4368**

0890-4642 See ISSUE WATCH. **4658**

0890-4715 See CHILD CARE MANAGEMENT. **2277**

0890-4723 See NEW HOMES. **4842**

0890-4758 See TRANSLATION PERSPECTIVES. **3329**

0890-4766 See WORLDWIDE TRAVEL PLANNER. **5500**

0890-4782 See STUFFED. **1069**

0890-4790 See EFFECTIVE SPECIAL SERVICES MANAGEMENT. **866**

0890-4847 See STUDIES IN AFRICAN AND AFRO-AMERICAN CULTURE. **2643**

0890-4863 See PC LIFE. **1198**

0890-4871 See CALIFORNIA INSURANCE LAW REPORT. **2946**

0890-4898 See PRACTICAL TAX LAWYER, THE. **3030**

0890-4928 See POLITICAL RISK DATABASE. **4489**

8755-3627 See QUONDAM ET FUTURUS (BIRMINGHAM, ALA.). **3351**

0890-4952 See COUNTRY DATABASE. **4470**

0890-4960 See INTERNATIONAL PRESERVATION NEWS. **3218**

0890-4987 See GLOBAL STUDIES PROGRAM NOTES. **2488**

0890-5029 See TROLLEY COACH NEWS. **5397**

0890-5037 See LAW AND MENTAL HEALTH. **2994**

0890-5096 See ANNALS OF VASCULAR SURGERY. **3959**

0890-510X See WORLD AND UNITED STATES AVIATION AND SPACE RECORDS AS OF **40**

0890-5118 See ANALYTIC TEACHING. **4340**

0890-5134 See TRA FOODSERVICE DIGEST. **2360**

0890-5142 See INTERNATIONAL TRADE REPORT. **2401**

0890-5207 See LODE STAR, THE. **2308**

0890-5215 See ONS NEWS. **3866**

0890-5231 See RELEASE PRINT. **4077**

0890-524X See SCROLL (MALVERNE, N.Y.). **1292**

0890-5258 See ARKANSAS EPISCOPALIAN, THE. **5055**

0890-5266 See SCREEN ACTOR HOLLYWOOD. **4077**

0890-5282 See MOODY'S OTC UNLISTED MANUAL. **908**

0890-5304 See OUTDOOR PHOTOGRAPHER. **4372**

0890-5312 See CROSSSTITCH SAMPLER. **5183**

0890-5339 See JOURNAL OF ORTHOPAEDIC TRAUMA. **3882**

0890-5355 See TENNESSEE FAMILY LAW LETTER. **3122**

0890-5363 See GEOTHERMAL SCIENCE AND TECHNOLOGY. **1406**

0890-5401 See INFORMATION AND COMPUTATION. **1219**

0890-5428 See HUMAN SERVICE EDUCATION. **1751**

0890-5436 See FOOD BIOTECHNOLOGY. **3692**

0890-5444 See MEMBRANCE SEPARATION ENGINEERING. **2027**

0890-5452 See MECHANICS OF STRUCTURES AND MACHINES. **2106**

0890-5460 See OCEAN PHYSICS AND ENGINEERING. **1453**

0890-5487 See CHINA OCEAN ENGINEERING. **2088**

0890-5495 See NINETEENTH CENTURY CONTEXTS. **3417**

0890-5509 See HAZARDOUS & SOLID WASTE MINIMIZATION & RECYCLING REPORT. **2231**

0890-5517 See QUICK FROZEN FOODS ANNUAL PROCESSORS' DIRECTORY AND BUYERS' GUIDE. **2355**

0890-5533 See BIOMATERIALS, ARTIFICIAL CELLS, AND IMMOBILIZATION BIOTECHNOLOGY. **3686**

0890-5541 See AVALOKA. **4937**

0890-5568 See LIVING PRAYER. **4974**

0890-5584 See RESTAURANTS USA. **5073**

0890-5592 See PROCEEDINGS OF THE ... SEMINAR OF CATASTROPHISM AND ANCIENT HISTORY. **2626**

0890-5657 See AFRICA TELECOMMUNICATIONS REPORT. **1148**

0890-5673 See NATURAL RESOURCES COMPUTER NEWSLETTER. **2199**

0890-5681 See EQUATOR (SAN FRANCISCO, CALIF.). **2533**

0890-5738 See SACRAMENTO BEE, THE. **5639**

0890-5746 See CHILDREN'S BOOK REVIEW (PROVO, UTAH). **3201**

0890-5754 See WORSHIP AND ARTS. **5010**

0890-5819 See GRAPE VINE NEWSLETTER, THE. **2617**

0890-5878 See CAREER RESOURCE GUIDE. **1658**

0890-5908 See CAC NEWS - CHICAGO ARTISTS' COALITION. **346**

0890-5924 See SAM KINCH'S TEXAS WEEKLY. **5754**

0890-5932 See MIDLAND REPORTER-TELEGRAM, THE. **5752**

0890-5959 See U.S. EMPLOYMENT OPPORTUNITIES. **4209**

0890-6009 See OAK RIDGER, THE. **5746**

0890-6017 See PIEDMONT JOURNAL-INDEPENDENT, THE. **5627**

0890-6025 See ALTAMONT ENTERPRISE (1983), THE. **5713**

0890-6041 See LABOR UNITY (U.S. ED.). **1685**

0890-6076 See SKI PATROL MAGAZINE. **4803**

0890-6130 See NATURE, SOCIETY, AND THOUGHT. **5210**

0890-6149 See ALASKA HISTORY (ANCHORAGE, ALASKA). **2718**

0890-6157 See MINER'S NEWS. **2145**

0890-6165 See BULLETIN OF THE DEPARTMENT OF INTERNATIONAL AFFAIRS, AFL-CIO, THE. **4517**

0890-6238 See REPRODUCTIVE TOXICOLOGY (ELMSFORD, N.Y.). **3983**

0890-6270 See STARMONT POPULAR CULTURE STUDIES. **5223**

0890-6327 See INTERNATIONAL JOURNAL OF ADAPTIVE CONTROL AND SIGNAL PROCESSING. **1979**

0890-6386 See LEISURE ARTS. **324**

0890-6408 See APALACHEE QUARTERLY, THE. **3362**

0890-6416 See BAG OF TRICKS. **1727**

0890-6432 See ORBUS. **701**

0890-6440 See JAZZLETTER. **4125**

0890-6459 See TEACHER EDUCATION & PRACTICE. **1905**

0890-6467 See ONCOGENE RESEARCH. **3821**

0890-6491 See WEAVINGS. **5008**

0890-653X See FIBEROPTIC PRODUCT NEWS. **1155**

0890-6548 See IMAGEN (SAN JUAN, P.R.). **2488**

0890-6599 See JOURNAL OF NEUROLOGICAL & ORTHOPAEDIC MEDICINE & SURGERY, THE. **3967**

0890-6610 See NDA PIPELINE, THE. **4317**

0890-6645 See AMERICA'S CORPORATE FAMILIES. **638**

0890-6653 See HERBS, SPICES, AND MEDICINAL PLANTS : RECENT ADVANCES IN BOTANY, HORTICULTURE, AND PHARMACOLOGY. **173**

0890-6661 See JOURNAL OF CRANIOFACIAL GENETICS AND DEVELOPMENTAL BIOLOGY. SUPPLEMENT. **582**

0890-667X See EVANGELISM (MEQUON, WIS.). **4957**

0890-6688 See STARTEXT INK. **1122**

0890-6785 See PAYPHONE EXCHANGE. **702**

0890-6793 See CHRISTIAN CHALLENGE, THE. **5058**

0890-6823 See FACTSHEET FIVE. **385**

0890-6858 See JOURNAL - WESTERN NEW YORK GENEALOGICAL SOCIETY. **2456**

0890-6866 See UNIVERSE IN THE CLASSROOM, THE. **401**

0890-6874 See JOURNAL OF HEALTH OCCUPATIONS EDUCATION. **3595**

0890-6890 See MAGAZINE (ABINGTON, PA.). **3409**

0890-6939 See PARKER'S GAZETTE. **2753**

0890-6947 See FEDERAL SERVICE LABOR RELATIONS REVIEW. **1669**

0890-6955 See INTERNATIONAL JOURNAL OF MACHINE TOOLS & MANUFACTURE. **2116**

0890-698X See GEORGIA JOURNAL OF READING. **1748**

0890-6998 See REVUE CELFAN. **3430**

0890-7021 See SIALIA. **5597**

0890-703X See EVANGELICAL STUDIES BULLETIN. **4957**

0890-7048 See PROGRESS IN ENDOCRINE RESEARCH AND THERAPY. **3732**

0890-7064 See JOURNAL OF PSYCHOLOGY & HUMAN SEXUALITY. **4600**

0890-7080 See OPTOMETRY TIMES. **4217**

0890-7102 See DUNGEON (LAKE GENEVA, WISC.). **4860**

0890-7110 See SCIENCE/HEALTH ABSTRACTS. **5152**

0890-7129 See TOWPATHS. **5394**

0890-7153 See MORNINGSTAR MUTUAL FUNDS. **908**

0890-7188 See NURSING DIAGNOSIS NEWSLETTER. **3864**

0890-7196 See OUTDOOR JOURNAL. **4877**

0890-720X *See* FOOD INDUSTRY NEWSLETTER (FAIRFAX, VA.), THE. **2337**

0890-7218 *See* LASA FORUM / LATIN AMERICAN STUDIES ASSOCIATION. **2743**

0890-7226 *See* DESKTOP PUBLISHING AND OFFICE AUTOMATION BUYER'S GUIDE AND HANDBOOK. **1263**

0890-7234 *See* PRINTERS BUYER'S GUIDE AND HANDBOOK. **1265**

0890-7242 *See* GUAYULERO, EL. **3480**

0890-7269 *See* CALIBAN (ANN ARBOR, MICH.). **3461**

0890-7277 *See* FIRST THINGS (RUSH CITY, MINN.). **5060**

0890-7315 *See* INSIDE LITIGATION. **3090**

0890-7331 *See* STRATEGIC DEFENSE. **4058**

0890-734X *See* BIOTEKHNOLOGIIA. **3690**

0890-7498 *See* OFFICIAL HELICOPTER BLUE BOOK, THE. **30**

0890-7528 *See* CAS BIOTECH UPDATES. AGRICULTURE. **72**

0890-7587 *See* MDR WATCH. **3606**

0890-7595 *See* MEDALLION (AUSTIN, TEX.). **2745**

0890-7609 *See* CARN (CHICAGO, ILL.). **655**

0890-7625 *See* LAND LETTER (WASHINGTON, D.C.). **2197**

0890-7641 *See* MANA MEMBERS DIRECTORY OF MANUFACTURERS' SALES AGENCIES. **3483**

0890-765X *See* JOURNAL OF RURAL HEALTH, THE. **4787**

0890-7668 *See* AEROBICS NEWS, THE. **2595**

0890-7722 *See* MAGILL BOOK REVIEW. **4830**

0890-7749 See JOURNAL OF TRANSLATION AND TEXTLINGUISTICS. **3292**

0890-7757 See RETIREMENT HOUSING BUSINESS REPORT. **2834**

0890-7765 *See* LAWYER REFERRAL NETWORK. **2997**

0890-7803 *See* DIETETIC CURRENTS. **4189**

0890-7811 *See* GERIATRIC MEDICINE CURRENTS. **3751**

0890-782X *See* OFFICIAL VIDEO DIRECTORY & BUYER'S GUIDE, THE. **5318**

0890-7854 *See* ASSERT. **4575**

0890-7862 *See* BANKRUPTCY DEVELOPMENTS JOURNAL. **3085**

0890-7889 *See* TECHNOLOGY AND LEARNING. **5163**

0890-7900 *See* SMT TRENDS. **2081**

0890-7986 *See* PROGRESSIVE GROCER'S ... DIRECTORY OF MASS MERCHANDISERS. **956**

0890-801X See COMPASS (SYRACUSE, N.Y.). **5412**

0890-8044 *See* IEEE NETWORK. **1241**

0890-8060 *See* WASHINGTON BEVERAGE INSIGHT. **2372**

0890-8079 *See* LALOGGIA'S SPECIAL SITUATION REPORT AND STOCK MARKET FORECAST. **796**

0890-8087 *See* KENTWOOD LEDGER, THE. **5684**

0890-8117 *See* ECLECTIC THEOSOPHIST, THE. **4955**

0890-8125 *See* DALLAS QUARTERLY, THE. **2444**

0890-8133 *See* ORIGINS (CHICAGO, ILL. 1984). **5018**

0890-815X *See* PRIVATIZATION REPORT, THE. **1622**

0890-8168 *See* SOUTH ALABAMIAN (JACKSON, ALA.), THE. **5628**

0890-8176 *See* FRIEND OF THE FAMILY FARM, THE. **89**

0890-8265 *See* ACCESS TO ENERGY. **1930**

0890-8273 *See* COUNCIL ON UNDERGRADUATE RESEARCH NEWSLETTER. **1818**

0890-8281 *See* SCRAPBOOK PAGES. **2760**

0890-829X *See* PRINCE WILLIAM NEWSLETTER. **624**

0890-832X *See* VITAL CONNECTIONS. **5269**

0890-8338 *See* INTERCHANGE (ALLIANCE FOR ARTS EDUCATION (U.S.)). **322**

0890-8346 *See* NEW JERSEY STATE LIBRARY IMPRESSIONS. **2748**

0890-8362 *See* KENTUCKY EXPLORER, THE. **2743**

0890-8389 *See* BRITISH ACCOUNTING REVIEW, THE. **740**

0890-8400 *See* CASE DIGEST (SACRAMENTO, CALIF.). **3105**

0890-8419 *See* SCHOOL SLATE. **1871**

0890-8427 *See* OCCUPATIONAL EDUCATION FORUM. **1914**

0890-8435 *See* PHILADELPHIA NEW OBSERVER, THE. **5738**

0890-8443 *See* REPORTER (LANSDALE, PA.), THE. **5739**

0890-8451 *See* RECALL/REGULATORY ANALYSIS. **3035**

0890-8494 *See* FIRE SERVICE LABOR MONTHLY. **1674**

0890-8508 *See* MOLECULAR AND CELLULAR PROBES. **465**

0890-8524 *See* JOURNAL OF PRODUCTION AGRICULTURE. **176**

0890-8540 *See* DISCOVERY CHANNEL, THE. **1153**

0890-8567 *See* JOURNAL OF THE AMERICAN ACADEMY OF CHILD AND ADOLESCENT PSYCHIATRY. **3929**

0890-8575 *See* NATURAL RESOURCE MODELING. **2199**

0890-8583 *See* REFORMED WORSHIP. **4990**

0890-8591 *See* BARBERTON HERALD. **5727**

0890-8605 *See* LOUISVILLE LAW EXAMINER. **3004**

0890-863X *See* LATINOGRAMA. **2267**

0890-8648 *See* UNITED STATES OF ACORN. **5313**

0890-8656 *See* HERALD-STAR, THE. **5728**

0890-8664 *See* BUSINESS AVIATION SAFETY. **15**

0890-8672 *See* JALEO. **4124**

0890-8699 *See* ELECTRONIC DISPLAY NEWS. **2047**

0890-8710 *See* YOMIURI SHIMBUN (NEW YORK, N.Y.). **5641**

0890-8745 *See* SPORTS TREND. **958**

0890-8753 *See* PHOTO BUSINESS. **4372**

0890-8761 *See* WASHINGTON LAWYER, THE. **3072**

0890-877X *See* BIOLOGY BULLETIN MONTHLY. **446**

0890-8826 *See* SECURITY (NEWTON, MASS.). **3176**

0890-8842 *See* NEWSLETTER / TENNESSEE CITIZENS FOR WILDERNESS PLANNING. **2200**

0890-8850 *See* CALENDAR / UNIVERSITY ART MUSEUM BERKELEY. **4086**

0890-8885 *See* CROSS TIMBERS REVIEW. **2845**

0890-8893 *See* LANCASTER COUNTY HERITAGE. **2457**

0890-8923 *See* BLOODLINES :. **4286**

0890-9008 *See* BUILDING SUPPLY & HOME CENTERS. **604**

0890-9016 *See* CLINICAL TRANSPLANTS. **3962**

0890-9024 *See* WEST HILLS REVIEW. **3452**

0890-9032 *See* CHURCH PIANIST, THE. **4110**

0890-9059 *See* TECHNOLOGY FOR NURSING. **3870**

0890-9075 *See* PREPARATIVE CHROMATOGRAPHY. **989**

0890-9091 *See* ONCOLOGY (WILLISTON PARK, N.Y.). **3822**

0890-9113 *See* JEWISH FOLKLORE AND ETHNOLOGY REVIEW. **2321**

0890-9121 *See* AUTO GALLERY. **2110**

0890-913X *See* JOURNAL OF PRIVATE ENTERPRISE, THE. **687**

0890-9164 *See* INSURANCE TAX REVIEW, THE. **2884**

0890-9172 *See* CONTRIBUTIONS OF THE GREAT BASIN FOUNDATION. **5532**

0890-9202 *See* BOATRACING. **592**

0890-9237 *See* VOGUE KNITTING INTERNATIONAL. **5186**

0890-9245 *See* HEALTH EMPLOYMENT LAW UPDATE. **3148**

0890-9253 *See* EMPLOYMENT LAW UPDATE (EVANSVILLE, IND.). **3147**

0890-927X *See* FRB SF WEEKLY LETTER. **1492**

0890-9369 *See* GENES & DEVELOPMENT. **545**

0890-9377 *See* CONTRIBUTIONS TO THE STUDY OF ANTHROPOLOGY. **234**

0890-9423 *See* VIRGINIA/WEST VIRGINIA QUERIES. **2476**

0890-9512 *See* MORGAN REPORT ON DIRECTORY PUBLISHING. **4817**

0890-9520 *See* JOURNAL OF RURAL AND SMALL SCHOOLS. **1758**

0890-9547 *See* CHARTERING MAGAZINE'S YACHT VACATIONS. **5466**

0890-9555 *See* REVUE FRANCOPHONE DE LOUISIANE. **3431**

0890-9563 *See* EDGE (MORRISTOWN, N.J.). **1154**

0890-9598 *See* HARPER'S BAZAAR EN ESPANOL. **1085**

0890-9660 *See* ROUNDUP RECORD-TRIBUNE & WINNETT TIMES. **5706**

0890-9687 *See* SYNTHESIS (MINNEAPOLIS, MINN.). **4156**

0890-9695 *See* WOMENWISE. **4808**

0890-9709 *See* ASSOCIATION MARKETING. **921**

0890-9717 *See* FRIENDS OF KEBYAR. **299**

0890-9741 See MASCULINITIES : OFFICIAL PUBLICATION OF THE MEN'S STUDIES ASSOCIATION, NATIONAL ORGANIZATION FOR MEN AGAINST SEXISM. **3995**

0890-9768 *See* AUTOMATIC I.D. NEWS. **1217**

0890-9776 *See* STEVE FORRESTER'S NORTHWEST LETTER FROM WASHINGTON, D.C. **4497**

0890-9792 *See* PERSPECTIVES (RENSSELAER, IND.). **1840**

0890-9814 See DESIGN FIRM MANAGEMENT & ADMINISTRATION REPORT. **865**

0890-9830 *See* TODAY'S SUNBEAM. **5711**

0890-9857 *See* VINDICATOR (YOUNGSTOWN, OHIO). **5731**

0890-9881 *See* STATEN ISLAND REGISTER. **5721**

0890-9903 *See* CHINESE JOURNAL OF INFRARED AND MILLIMETER WAVES. **4399**

0890-9911 *See* EXCHANGE BOOK (YOUNGSTOWN, ARIZ.). **5469**

0890-9938 *See* JACKSON SUN (JACKSON, TENN. 1895), THE. **5745**

0890-9954 *See* REEDER'S ECONOMIC DIGEST. **1515**

0890-9970 *See* AMERICA'S TEXTILES INTERNATIONAL. **5347**

0890-9997 *See* HISTORICAL STUDIES IN THE PHYSICAL AND BIOLOGICAL SCIENCES. **4404**

0891-0006 *See* CURRENT SEPARATIONS. **1051**

0891-0022 *See* TRIANGLE BUSINESS. **5724**

0891-0030 *See* POPULATION REPORTS. SERIES C, FEMALE STERILIZATION (ENGLISH ED.). **4557**

0891-0049 *See* POPULATION REPORTS. SERIES D, MALE STERILIZATION (ENGLISH ED.). **4558**

0891-009X *See* WATERTOWN DAILY TIMES (WATERTOWN, N.Y. : 1929). **5722**

0891-0103 *See* BACON'S RADIO/TV DIRECTORY. **1126**

0891-0111 *See* PROGRESS IN BEHAVIORAL STUDIES. **4609**

0891-012X *See* RECRUITMENT AND RETENTION IN HIGHER EDUCATION. **1843**

0891-0138 *See* INTERNATIONAL SAMPE SYMPOSIUM AND EXHIBITION. **2103**

0891-0154 *See* FOOD & SERVICE / TEXAS RESTAURANT ASSOCIATION. **2336**

0891-0162 *See* AAOHN JOURNAL. **3849**

0891-0200 See HEALTH SYSTEMS REVIEW. **3782**

0891-0219 See WASHINGTON RETAIL WEEKLY. **958**

0891-0227 *See* LEADER-TELEGRAM. **5768**

0891-0235 *See* JOURNAL OF STEWARDSHIP. **4970**

0891-0243 *See* MAC TITLES IN PRINT. **1194**

0891-0278 *See* EXERCISE STANDARDS & MALPRACTICE REPORTER, THE. **2968**

0891-0316 See SOVIET CASTINGS TECHNOLOGY. 4019

0891-0324 See RUSSIAN FOREST SCIENCES. 2394

0891-0537 See INSIDE BLUEGRASS. 4122

0891-0545 See RAFT (CLEVELAND, OHIO). 3314

0891-0588 See CRAFTWORKS FOR THE HOME. 372

0891-0596 See CAREER GUIDE (PARSIPPANY, N.J.), THE. 4211

0891-060X See MICROBIAL ECOLOGY IN HEALTH AND DISEASE. 3616

0891-0618 See JOURNAL OF CHEMICAL NEUROANATOMY. 3834

0891-0634 See BNA'S BANKING REPORT. 3085

0891-0650 See LAS AMERICAS JOURNAL. 4480

0891-0685 See PSYCSCAN: APPLIED EXPERIMENTAL AND ENGINEERING PSYCHOLOGY. 4623

0891-0693 See OBSERVER-REPORTER. 5738

0891-0707 See WRESTLING (VERNON CENTER, MINN.). 4931

0891-0723 See CO-WORKER. 1659

0891-0731 See ECM POST-REVIEW, THE. 5695

0891-074X See FAVORITE WESTERNS, SERIAL WORLD. 4068

0891-0766 See CANCER VICTORS JOURNAL. 3813

0891-0774 See FINIGAN WINE LETTER, THE. 2367

0891-0847 See APLICOMMUNICATOR. 4549

0891-0855 See CAREER PILOT JOB REPORT. 16

0891-088X See MAINSTREAM (SACRAMENTO, CALIF.). 226

0891-0952 See SERVICES MARKETING NEWSLETTER. 886

0891-0960 See DOWNEAST ANCESTRY. 2446

0891-0979 See ENERGY & EDUCATION. 1939

0891-1010 See ELEMENTARY ECONOMIST, THE. 1488

0891-1029 See CENTER CITY REPORT. 2817

0891-1037 See NEWTON-EVANS RESEARCH COMPANY'S MARKET TRENDS DIGEST FOR THE COMPUTER, COMMUNICATIONS, AND CONTROLS INDUSTRIES. 1197

0891-1053 See ENVIRONMENTAL ASSESSMENT OF THE ALASKAN CONTINENTAL SHELF. FINAL REPORTS OF PRINCIPAL INVESTIGATORS. PHYSICAL SCIENCE STUDIES. 2166

0891-1118 See BANNER PRESS NEWSPAPER, THE. 5747

0891-1150 See CLEVELAND CLINIC JOURNAL OF MEDICINE. 3564

0891-1177 See JOURNAL OF THE ORDER OF BUDDHIST CONTEMPLATIVES, THE. 5021

0891-1207 See PROFESSIONAL COMMUNICATOR, THE. 1120

0891-1223 See PEDIATRIC LENGTH OF STAY BY DIAGNOSIS AND OPERATION, UNITED STATES. 3908

0891-1258 See WELLINGTON'S WORRY-FREE INVESTING. 919

0891-1304 See TO YOUR HEALTH. 4805

0891-1371 See WITNESS (FARMINGTON HILLS, MICH.). 3453

0891-1398 See HOMER INDEX, THE. 5692

0891-141X See EQUIPMENT TODAY. 614

0891-1428 See JACKSONVILLE MAGAZINE. 2536

0891-1436 See LIAN HE RI BAO. 5718

0891-1444 See LUA MI. 3409

0891-1452 See GUIDELINES FOR TODAY. 4961

0891-1509 See CHEESE MARKET NEWS. 192

0891-1525 See CAP TODAY. 3893

0891-1622 See SALES PROMOTION MONITOR. 709

0891-1649 See WORLDLETTER. 5265

0891-1657 See GETTING MARRIED. 2280

0891-1665 See ALABAMA SHPA MONTHLY REVIEW. 4764

0891-1673 See MCGUFFEY WRITER, THE. 1066

0891-169X See HARTSVILLE VIDETTE, THE. 5745

0891-1762 See JOURNAL OF GLOBAL MARKETING. 927

0891-1770 See 20/20'S VISIONMONDAY. 1596

0891-1797 See SAFETY & HEALTH. 2869

0891-1800 See SURGICAL ROUNDS FOR ORTHOPAEDICS. 3885

0891-1827 See WOMEN IN THE ARTS / THE NATIONAL MUSEUM OF WOMEN IN THE ARTS. 369

0891-1851 See KITPLANES. 27

0891-1886 See CPI DIGEST. 973

0891-1908 See PAPERS GIVEN AT THE ... ANNUAL CONFERENCE ON EDITORIAL PROBLEMS, UNIVERSITY OF TORONTO. 3422

0891-1916 See INTERNATIONAL JOURNAL OF POLITICAL ECONOMY. 4477

0891-1975 See CAUSA INTERNATIONAL SEMINAR SERIES (NEW YORK, N.Y. : 1986). 4517

0891-2017 See COMPUTATIONAL LINGUISTICS (ASSOCIATION FOR COMPUTATIONAL LINGUISTICS). 1175

0891-2041 See HANDBOOK OF GYNECOLOGY & OBSTETRICS. 3762

0891-2076 See BASIC & CLINICAL IMMUNOLOGY. 3667

0891-2084 See GENERAL OPHTHALMOLOGY. 3875

0891-2092 See CLINICAL CARDIOLOGY (LOS ALTOS , CALIF.). 3703

0891-2106 See BASIC HISTOLOGY. 532

0891-2173 See GERIATRIC LENGTH OF STAY BY DIAGNOSIS AND OPERATION, UNITED STATES. 3751

0891-2238 See CLINICAL ANATOMY (NORWALK, CONN.). 3565

0891-2254 See HANDY APPRAISAL CHART. 616

0891-2262 See MADISON MESSENGER. 5729

0891-2270 See GROVE CITY SOUTHWEST MESSENGER. 5728

0891-2289 See SOUTHEAST MESSENGER. 5730

0891-2297 See WESTSIDE MESSENGER. 5731

0891-2300 See EASTSIDE MESSENGER. 5728

0891-2319 See SEATRADE WEEK. 5455

0891-2327 See BIG SANDY NEWS (LOUISA, KY. : 1974). 5679

0891-2378 See SPSM&H. 3439

0891-2416 See JOURNAL OF CONTEMPORARY ETHNOGRAPHY. 5249

0891-2424 See ECONOMIC DEVELOPMENT QUARTERLY. 1483

0891-2432 See GENDER & SOCIETY. 5200

0891-2513 See COMPLEX SYSTEMS. 3501

0891-2556 See CARBONATES AND EVAPORITES. 1371

0891-2572 See KENNEDY'S CAREER STRATEGIST. 4206

0891-2599 See PROFESSIONAL APARTMENT MANAGEMENT. 4843

0891-2629 See MACRAE'S STATE INDUSTRIAL DIRECTORY. NEW JERSEY. 1616

0891-2653 See FOR THE RECORD. 2481

0891-267X See TECHTRENDS INTERNATIONAL. 5165

0891-2718 See CALIFORNIA, CITIES, TOWNS & COUNTIES. 4636

0891-2726 See SOVIET JOURNAL OF PSYCHOLOGY. 4619

0891-2734 See WILDLIFE CONSERVATION REPORT. 2209

0891-2742 See LIBRARY PERSONNEL NEWS. 943

0891-2777 See DAILY HERALD (PROVO, UTAH. 1939), THE. 5756

0891-2785 See FACT SHEET - ACADEMIC COLLECTIVE BARGAINING INFORMATION SERVICE. 1669

0891-2793 See PHARMACEUTICAL NEWS CAPSULE, THE. 4320

0891-2807 See DISTRENDS. 1605

0891-2823 See ASIAN AND PACIFIC POPULATION FORUM. 4549

0891-2904 See VALUES. 1630

0891-2912 See INTERFACE. 1157

0891-2920 See ARCHEOMATERIALS. 259

0891-2947 See SECONDARY MARKETING EXECUTIVE. 936

0891-2955 See BITS & BYTES REVIEW. 1172

0891-2963 See HISTORICAL BIOLOGY. 457

0891-298X See SINK. 3437

0891-3013 See RADIOACTIVE EXCHANGE, THE. 2240

0891-303X See TECHNICAL COMPUTING. 1204

0891-3064 See NATIONAL NEWSPATCH, THE. 1882

0891-3072 See HAZCHEM ALERT. 4777

0891-3129 See INDEX TO COLORADO STATE PUBLICATIONS. 4656

0891-3137 See NEW ENGLAND BAPTIST (NORTHBOROUGH, MASS.), THE. 5065

0891-3145 See COLORADO OUTDOOR JOURNAL. 4871

0891-3161 See BIOTECH INVESTOR. 892

0891-3196 See EMPLOYEE ASSISTANCE PROGRAM UPDATE. 866

0891-320X See MONOGRAPH / AMERICAN HEART ASSOCIATION. 3708

0891-3218 See SELECTED ACQUISITIONS - ENGINEERING SOCIETIES LIBRARY. ACQUISITIONS DEPT. 1996

0891-3250 See HEALTH MANAGEMENT QUARTERLY. 3781

0891-3277 See ACLA NEWSLETTER. 3357

0891-3293 See AGORA (RALEIGH, N.C.). 1089

0891-3331 See AMERICAN DELI-BAKERY NEWS. 2326

0891-3358 See CURRENT CONTENTS. CLINICAL MEDICINE. 3656

0891-3374 See HOPE HEALTH LETTER. 4783

0891-3382 See INTERNATIONAL TRENDS IN THORACIC SURGERY. 3966

0891-3390 See AMERICAN GOVERNMENT. 4463

0891-3420 See VOICES (DEERFIELD, ILL.). 5008

0891-3447 See OPEN SQUARES, THE. 1314

0891-3463 See COLORADO ENVIRONMENTAL REPORT, THE. 2190

0891-3498 See NEWS FROM RILA. 360

0891-3501 See NEW DOMINION (ALEXANDRIA, VA.). 2540

0891-351X See CHINA REPORT. POLITICAL, SOCIOLOGICAL AND MILITARY AFFAIRS. 4468

0891-3641 See BIRTH-ORIGIN STUDY OF TEXAS NEWBORNS, A. 4550

0891-365X See MACTIMES. 1194

0891-3668 See PEDIATRIC INFECTIOUS DISEASE JOURNAL, THE. 3908

0891-3676 See MODERN CONCEPTS IN IMMUNOLOGY. 3675

0891-3706 See TWIGS MAGAZINE. 2476

0891-3722 See BEST OF ARIZONA, THE. 5463

0891-3730 See BUILDINGS ENERGY TECHNOLOGY. 1934

0891-3749 See BIBLIOGRAPHIC GUIDE TO MICROFORM PUBLICATIONS. 409

0891-3757 See OPERA FANATIC. 4143

0891-3781 See HOSPICE FORUM. 5288

0891-3811 See CRITICAL REVIEW (NEW YORK, N.Y.). 4470

0891-382X See CALIFORNIA PLANNING & DEVELOPMENT REPORT. 2817

0891-3846 See EVANGELIZING TODAY'S CHILD. 4958

0891-3862 See CHI KO HSUEH, TA. 5093

0891-3870 See DIRECTIONS IN PSYCHIATRY. 3924

0891-3889 See PERIODICALS SCANNED AND ABSTRACTED. LIFE SCIENCES COLLECTION. 5175

0891-3897 See ADAMHA DATA BOOK. 1338

0891-3927 See LET THE PEOPLE WORSHIP. 4973

0891-3978 See IDEA FACTORY, THE. 3286

0891-3994 See MEDICAL SUBJECT HEADINGS. SUPPLEMENTARY CHEMICAL RECORDS. 3230

0891-4044 See CIO LETTER, THE. 657

0891-4087 See LANG CLASSICAL STUDIES. 1078
0891-4125 See WORLD ECONOMIC DATA. 1527
0891-4141 See LABOR RELATIONS WEEK. 1685
0891-4168 See MOLECULAR GENETICS, MICROBIOLOGY AND VIROLOGY. 568
0891-4176 See EARTHQUAKE RESEARCH IN CHINA. 1374
0891-4214 See READ, AMERICA!. 1776
0891-4222 See RESEARCH IN DEVELOPMENTAL DISABILITIES. 4615
0891-4230 See NATURAL GAS PRODUCER PRICES. 4265
0891-4249 See ASHRAE INSIGHTS. 2603
0891-4370 See GEORGETOWN IMMIGRATION LAW JOURNAL. 2974
0891-4435 See WORLD NUCLEAR PERFORMANCE. 1961
0891-4443 See PLANNED GIFTS COUNSELOR, THE. 882
0891-446X See AMERICAN PURPOSE. 4515
0891-4478 See INTERNATIONAL JOURNAL OF TECHNOLOGY & AGING. 3752
0891-4486 See INTERNATIONAL JOURNAL OF POLITICS, CULTURE, AND SOCIETY. 5248
0891-4494 See JOURNAL OF NEAR-DEATH STUDIES. 4241
0891-4508 See TEACHING PRE-K-8. 1805
0891-4591 See CURRENT ESTIMATES FROM THE NATIONAL HEALTH INTERVIEW SURVEY, UNITED STATES. 4772
0891-4605 See MACRAE'S STATE INDUSTRIAL DIRECTORY: MAINE, NEW HAMPSHIRE, VERMONT. 1616
0891-4621 See ROBOTICS AND EXPERT SYSTEMS. 1216
0891-463X See OUTSTANDING INVESTOR DIGEST. 910
0891-4648 See OFFICIAL NASCAR YEARBOOK AND PRESS GUIDE, THE. 4909
0891-4664 See LUNAR & PLANETARY INFORMATION BULLETIN. 396
0891-4672 See ONLINE TODAY. 3239
0891-4702 See MIT PRESS SERIES IN INFORMATION SYSTEMS. 1195
0891-4729 See INSIGHTS FOR SUCCESS. 871
0891-4796 See MUSCLE CAR REVIEW. 5421
0891-4834 See HIMALAYAN RESEARCH BULLETIN. 2652
0891-4850 See WORLD DEFENSE FORCES. 4061
0891-5016 See HEALTHCARE MARKETING ABSTRACTS. 925
0891-5059 See CONTRACT HEALTHCARE. 3568
0891-5083 See INTERNATIONAL JOURNAL OF SCIENCE AND TECHNOLOGY. 5115
0891-5121 See 123 USER'S JOURNAL. 1283
0891-5148 See AVIATION GROUND EQUIPMENT MARKET. 13
0891-5164 See MARIN INDEPENDENT JOURNAL. 5637
0891-5172 See VIOLENCE, AGGRESSION TERRORISM. 5265
0891-5180 See SOCIAL PHARMACOLOGY. 4329
0891-5202 See CAREERS & THE DISABLED. 4202
0891-5237 See PROFESSIONAL QUILTER MAGAZINE, THE. 5185
0891-5245 See JOURNAL OF PEDIATRIC HEALTH CARE. 3905
0891-5296 See COCKRELL CONNECTION, THE. 2443
0891-5318 See MERIDIAN SOFTWARE ANALYSIS BULLETIN. 2490
0891-5326 See RE:VIEW - FRIENDS OF PHOTOGRAPHY. 4376
0891-5385 See WATER & WASTEWATER INTERNATIONAL. 5542
0891-5393 See JAMES WHITE REVIEW, THE. 3345
0891-5415 See CONTEMPORARY MUSIC STUDIES. 4111
0891-5466 See TEXAS JOURNAL OF AGRICULTURE AND NATURAL RESOURCES. 141

0891-5474 See SCHOOL LAW NEWSLETTER (VERNON, TEX.), THE. 3046
0891-5490 See STOPPING AND RANGES OF IONS IN MATTER, THE. 4422
0891-5520 See INFECTIOUS DISEASE CLINICS OF NORTH AMERICA. 3714
0891-5539 See BAYSTATE REALTOR. 4834
0891-5547 See RUFF TIMES (1986), THE. 913
0891-5571 See TRANSACTIONS (DOKLADY) OF THE USSR ACADEMY OF SCIENCES. EARTH SCIENCE SECTIONS. 1361
0891-558X See CONSUMER LENDING REPORT. 1295
0891-5598 See VIRGINIA UNITED METHODIST ADVOCATE. 5069
0891-5601 See JACKSONVILLE NEWS. 5631
0891-561X See HUAYU KUAIBAO. 5717
0891-5628 See POST (CARLE PLACE, N.Y.). 1162
0891-5709 See NATIONAL REPORT ON SUBSTANCE ABUSE, THE. 1347
0891-5725 See MINISTRIES TODAY. 4977
0891-5741 See DOSSIER (WASHINGTON, D.C.). 2532
0891-5784 See PROGRESS IN ANESTHESIOLOGY (SAN ANTONIO, TEX.). 3684
0891-5849 See FREE RADICAL BIOLOGY & MEDICINE. 487
0891-5865 See JOURNAL OF DOCUMENTATION PROJECT MANAGEMENT. 1192
0891-5881 See DIALOGUE & ALLIANCE. 4953
0891-589X See MARKETLETTER (MARKET ED.). 2435
0891-5946 See HAY & FORAGE GROWER. 202
0891-5989 See MODERN SCIENCE AND VEDIC SCIENCE. 4186
0891-5997 See DESIGN FIRM DIRECTORY (ENVIRONMENTAL AND INTERIOR DESIGN ED.). 2899
0891-6004 See INFODB. 1254
0891-6055 See INDEX CHEMICUS (1987). 1011
0891-608X See SPSC LETTER. 4496
0891-611X See GARLAND'S BANKRUPTCY BULLETIN. 3086
0891-6136 See POETS & WRITERS. 3470
0891-6144 See HIMALAYAN INSTITUTE QUARTERLY GUIDE TO PROGRAMS AND OTHER OFFERINGS. 4348
0891-6152 See EXPERIMENTAL HEAT TRANSFER. 4430
0891-6187 See MODEL T TIMES. 5387
0891-6209 See AMC JOURNAL. 2133
0891-6225 See ELECTRICAL ENGINEERING AND ELECTRONICS. 2045
0891-625X See JOURNAL OF SPECULATIVE PHILOSOPHY, THE. 4351
0891-6322 See NORWAY TIMES. 5719
0891-6330 See AMERICAN JOURNAL OF FAMILY LAW. 3119
0891-6357 See SOFTWARE SERIES - NEW YORK STATE GEOLOGICAL SURVEY. 1397
0891-6365 See LITERARY RESEARCH. 3406
0891-6373 See WASHINGTON'S LAND & PEOPLE. 145
0891-6381 See CHOREOGRAPHY AND DANCE. 1311
0891-6446 See RHODES TODAY. 1094
0891-6608 See AHA NEWS (CHICAGO, ILL.). 3775
0891-6616 See INTERNATIONAL GYMNAST (1986). 4900
0891-6624 See HMO PRACTICE. 5287
0891-6632 See JOURNAL OF DIABETES AND ITS COMPLICATIONS. 3731
0891-6640 See JOURNAL OF VETERINARY INTERNAL MEDICINE. 5514
0891-6683 See ASIA-PACIFIC POPULATION & POLICY. 4549
0891-6713 See DATABASE SEARCHER. 1253
0891-6721 See WHITE-COLLAR CRIME REPORTER, THE. 3179
0891-6780 See EAST-WEST FILM JOURNAL. 4068
0891-6829 See CHINA LAW REPORTER. 2950

0891-6845 See UNITED STATES REPORTS. 3068
0891-6918 See MILLER COMPREHENSIVE GOVERNMENTAL GAAP GUIDE. 748
0891-6934 See AUTOIMMUNITY (CHUR, SWITZERLAND). 3667
0891-6950 See BOTTOM LINE ON ALCOHOL IN SOCIETY, THE. 1341
0891-6969 See COMMON LIVES, LESBIAN LIVES. 2794
0891-6977 See EATING DISORDERS DIGEST. 4774
0891-7000 See ECONOMIC DEVELOPMENT BRIEFS. 1557
0891-7035 See SCANNING MICROSCOPY. 574
0891-7078 See GREAT BEND TRIBUNE (1972). 5676
0891-7086 See ALCOHOL, DRUGS AND DRIVING. 1339
0891-7116 See MELTON JOURNAL, THE. 1763
0891-7124 See JOURNAL FOR THE ANTHROPOLOGICAL STUDY OF HUMAN MOVEMENT AT NEW YORK UNIVERSITY. 238
0891-7140 See JOURNAL OF GAY & LESBIAN PSYCHOTHERAPY. 2794
0891-7159 See DUPAGE. 2731
0891-7167 See PRODUCTIVITY VIEWS. 883
0891-7183 See PUBLIC RISK. 1514
0891-7213 See AEGEAN REVIEW. 3358
0891-7256 See ILLINOIS PUBLIC PENSIONS. 901
0891-7272 See COURIER (MIDDLETOWN, N.J.), THE. 5709
0891-7329 See EDELSTEIN PRO FOOTBALL LETTER, THE. 4894
0891-7337 See LAND INVESTMENT NEWS. 905
0891-7396 See ADVANCES IN HUMAN NUTRITION. 4186
0891-7426 See AIDS INFORMATION EXCHANGE. 4764
0891-7450 See AFB ACTION. 4763
0891-7515 See FEDERAL TRADE COMMISSION DECISIONS. 3100
0891-7523 See FISHERIES AND WILDLIFE RESEARCH AND DEVELOPMENT. 2301
0891-7604 See OLD PRINT SHOP PORTFOLIO, THE. 4567
0891-7612 See PROCEEDINGS OF THE SOCIETY OF MAGNETIC RESONANCE IN MEDICINE. 4445
0891-7639 See JOURNAL OF MUSIC THEORY PEDAGOGY, THE. 4126
0891-7647 See LOCOMOTIVE & RAILWAY PRESERVATION. 5432
0891-7655 See INTERNATIONAL RAILWAY TRAVELER, THE. 5432
0891-7701 See MIDWIFERY TODAY. 3765
0891-771X See BIRD TALK. 4285
0891-7736 See PROCEEDINGS - WINTER SIMULATION CONFERENCE. 1283
0891-7760 See ADHESIVES ABSTRACTS. 1049
0891-7779 See ANXIETY, STRESS AND COPING. 4574
0891-7795 See HEALTH, SOCIETY, AND CULTURE. 5246
0891-7833 See RANDOM LENGTHS BUYERS' & SELLERS' GUIDE. 2404
0891-7884 See SCHOLARSHIPS AND LOANS FOR NURSING EDUCATION. 3869
0891-7930 See JOURNAL OF HEALTHCARE PROTECTION MANAGEMENT. 3787
0891-7957 See COAL ASH MARKET REPORT. 1602
0891-7965 See PARAGLIDE (FORT BRAGG, N.C.). 5724
0891-7973 See MAPICS THE MAGAZINE. 879
0891-7981 See SILVER CITY DAILY PRESS (1963). 5713
0891-8023 2548
0891-8066 See ANNUAL REPORT - RAILROAD RETIREMENT BOARD. 1650
0891-8104 See LONG-TERM CARE QUARTERLY. 3788
0891-8147 See ONCOLOGY DATA BASE FOCUS. 3822

ISSN Index

0891-8163 See PHYSICIANS & COMPUTERS. 1261

0891-8171 See JOURNAL OF GNATHOLOGY, THE. 1327

0891-818X See SOL (HOUSTON, TEX.), EL. 5754

0891-8198 See CD-ROMS IN PRINT. 1276

0891-8244 See HOWARD WAY LETTER, THE. 869

0891-8252 See SEMINOLE TRIBUNE, THE. 5651

0891-8260 See FOCAL POINTS. 3874

0891-8295 See TRANSACTIONS - AMERICAN BRONCHO-ESOPHAGOLOGICAL ASSOCIATION. MEETING. 3952

0891-8309 See MONTHLY SUMMARY - UNITED STATES. AGRICULTURAL MARKETING SERVICE. POULTRY DIVISION. MARKET NEWS BRANCH. 110

0891-8333 See DIRECTORY OF FEDERAL LABORATORY & TECHNOLOGY RESOURCES. 5100

0891-8341 See STATE NURSING LEGISLATION QUARTERLY. 3059

0891-8414 See ANNUAL U.S. ECONOMIC DATA. 1463

0891-8422 See CLINICS IN PODIATRIC MEDICINE AND SURGERY. 3917

0891-8465 See ANNUAL REPORT OF THE DIGESTIVE DISEASES COORDINATING COMMITTEE TO THE SECRETARY, U.S. DEPARTMENT OF HEALTH AND HUMAN SERVICES. 3795

0891-849X See STUDIES IN HEALTH AND HUMAN SERVICES. 4804

0891-8511 See IDIS. 4307

0891-8546 See ANTITRUST FREEDOM OF INFORMATION LOG. 3095

0891-8619 See SOUTHWEST STORYTELLER'S GAZETTE. 3438

0891-8627 See RANDOM LENGTHS (SAN PEDRO, CALIF.). 5638

0891-8651 See MONDAY MORNING REPORT. 5296

0891-866X See S.O.S. 5306

0891-8686 See INQUIRER AND MIRROR. 5689

0891-8694 See FALMOUTH OUTLOOK, THE. 5680

0891-8708 See RUSTON DAILY LEADER, THE. 5684

0891-8716 See REVIEW, THE. 5647

0891-8759 See WRITERS' JOURNAL (SAINT PAUL, MINN.). 3454

0891-8767 See ALIVE NOW!. 4933

0891-8775 See ABC NEWS INDEX. 1125

0891-8791 See POSITIVE APPROACH, A. 4392

0891-8813 See BOOK MARKETING UPDATE. 4824

0891-8821 See MAKING CITIES LIVABLE NEWSLETTER. 2827

0891-8872 See OFFICIAL OVERSTREET COMIC BOOK PRICE GUIDE, THE. 4864

0891-8880 See REFORMA NEWSLETTER. 3244

0891-8899 See WEBER STUDIES. 2856

0891-8910 See PRACTICAL COMMUNICATIONS. 1347

0891-8929 See CLINICAL DIABETES. 3726

0891-8961 See FOOD SCIENCE AND TECHNOLOGY (NEW YORK, N.Y. 1984). 2340

0891-8988 See MILES CITY STAR. 5705

0891-8996 See IN-PLANT PRINTER & ELECTRONIC PUBLISHER. 4565

0891-9003 See SCIENTIFIC COMPUTING & AUTOMATION. 1221

0891-9011 See NSEA VOICE. 1769

0891-9070 See ART TIMES (SAUGERTIES, N.Y.). 340

0891-9089 See OREGON MATHEMATICS TEACHER, THE. 3526

0891-9100 See CROSSOSOMA. 507

0891-9119 See SAMNA WARQ. 2643

0891-9127 See PC REF. 1271

0891-9186 See SOUTHWESTERN MASS COMMUNICATION JOURNAL. 1122

0891-9194 See MAINE ORGANIC FARMER & GARDENER, THE. 106

0891-9208 See OUR TIMES. 3932

0891-9224 See JUSTICE WATCH / COMMITTEE FOR PUBLIC JUSTICE, INC. 2992

0891-9232 See MATURE HEALTH. 4789

0891-9240 See WEST VIRGINIA ADVOCATE, THE. 5765

0891-9267 See HEALTHCARE MANAGEMENT TEAM LETTER. 3583

0891-9275 See ELDERLY HEALTH SERVICES LETTER. 5284

0891-9283 See BIOTECHNOLOGY IN JAPAN NEWSSERVICE. 3689

0891-9291 See NASH & CIBINIC REPORT, THE. 4668

0891-9313 See VIDEO JOURNAL OF ECHOCARDIOGRAPHY. 3711

0891-9313 See VIDEO JOURNAL OF COLOR FLOW IMAGING. 3947

0891-9356 See NINETEENTH-CENTURY LITERATURE. 3417

0891-9364 See HOME CARE ECONOMICS. 5287

0891-9372 See ROCK & ROLL CONFIDENTIAL. 4150

0891-9461 See PHARMACEUTICAL PRODUCTION TECHSOURCE. 4321

0891-9526 See ENR. 1975

0891-9534 See FLOWER AND GARDEN (KANSAS CITY, MO. : 1982). 2414

0891-9542 See SIMSBURY NEWS, THE. 5646

0891-9585 See WOODSTOCK SERIES, THE. 4159

0891-9593 See ESSAYS ON FANTASTIC LITERATURE. 3385

0891-9607 See BORGO REFERENCE GUIDES. 1923

0891-9615 See BORGO CATALOGING GUIDES. 3197

0891-9623 See BORGO LITERARY GUIDES. 3368

0891-9631 See BLACK POLITICAL STUDIES. 4465

0891-9666 See CHRISTIAN HISTORY (WORCESTER, PA.). 4945

0891-9674 See TEA NEWSLETTER. 1786

0891-9704 See DELTA COUNTY INDEPENDENT. 5642

0891-9720 See SPRINGER SERIES ON SOCIAL WORK. 5311

0891-9747 See CONTEMPORARY ISSUES IN SMALL ANIMAL PRACTICE. 5508

0891-9763 See HEMATOLOGY (NEW YORK, N.Y.). 3772

0891-978X See BIORHEOLOGY. SUPPLEMENT. 448

0891-9801 See MAGNETOHYDRODYNAMICS (NEW YORK, N.Y. 1989). 2071

0891-9828 See DRUG STORE NEWS, INSIDE PHARMACY. 4301

0891-9836 See CAPITAL JOURNAL (ALBANY, N.Y.). 1468

0891-9852 See REAL ESTATE FINANCING UPDATE. 4844

0891-9860 See DIGITAL NEWS (BOSTON, MASS.). 1182

0891-9879 See ADVANCES IN ADOLESCENT MENTAL HEALTH. 4571

0891-9887 See JOURNAL OF GERIATRIC PSYCHIATRY AND NEUROLOGY. 3753

0891-9895 See UNIVERSITY OF PENNSYLVANIA JOURNAL OF INTERNATIONAL BUSINESS LAW. 3104

0891-9917 See CURRENT REVIEWS IN CLINICAL ANESTHESIA. 3682

0891-9933 See HAWAII DENTAL JOURNAL. 1324

0891-995X See SAE GROUND VEHICLE STANDARDS INDEX. 5424

0891-9976 See ENGINEERED SYSTEMS. 2113

0892-001X See CLINICAL PHARMACOLOGY (NEW YORK, N.Y.). 4297

0892-0036 See HEALTH TECHNOLOGY CASE STUDY. 3582

0892-0052 See CROSSWORDS TO RELAX WITH. 4859

0892-0060 See MASTER LECTURE SERIES, THE. 4603

0892-0079 See CONTEMPORARY ISSUES IN CLINICAL ONCOLOGY. 3815

0892-0109 See DIRECTORY OF GRADUATE MEDICAL EDUCATION PROGRAMS. 3572

0892-0125 See AIDS TARGETED INFORMATION NEWSLETTER. 3664

0892-015X See DAILY REPORT. CHINA. 2650

0892-0168 See NEW YORK HERALD TRIBUNE LARGE PRINT CROSSWORDS. 4864

0892-0176 See CD-ROM APPLICATIONS FORUM. 1173

0892-0206 See MANAGEMENT IN EDUCATION. 1762

0892-0249 See JOURNAL OF THE N.J. ASSOCIATION OF OSTEOPATHIC PHYSICIANS AND SURGEONS, THE. 3599

0892-0281 See CHRISTIAN RETAILING. 952

0892-029X See JOURNAL OF PACKAGING TECHNOLOGY. 4219

0892-0354 See ELECTRON MICROSCOPY REVIEWS. 572

0892-0362 See NEUROTOXICOLOGY AND TERATOLOGY. 3843

0892-0435 See TOPICS IN PEDIATRICS. / MINNEAPOLIS CHILDREN'S HEALTH CENTER. 3912

0892-0443 See TOWNSFOLK. 2494

0892-0524 See FLORIDA REAL ESTATE JOURNAL. 4838

0892-0532 See INTERNATIONAL SOCIETY OF BASSISTS. 4123

0892-0559 See MINARET (LOS ANGELES, CALIF.), THE. 5044

0892-0591 See JOURNAL OF DIRECT MARKETING. 927

0892-0605 See CLR REPORTS. 3202

0892-0664 See MENTAL HEALTH, UNITED STATES. 4604

0892-0753 See COASTAL MANAGEMENT. 2190

0892-0796 See THEATRE JOBLIST. 389

0892-080X See HISTORIC DOCUMENTS. 4476

0892-0818 See RESOURCES IN AGING. 5306

0892-0850 See ANDREWSREPORT (INDIANAPOLIS, IND.). 4834

0892-0915 See CRITICAL REVIEWS IN NEUROBIOLOGY. 3569

0892-0923 See ADMINISTRATIVE ACTION. 1807

0892-094X See ISI ONLINE NEWS. 3219

0892-0990 See HAWAII (SAN JUAN CAPISTRANO, CALIF.). 5479

0892-1008 See RPCVOICE. 5256

0892-1016 See JOURNAL OF RAPTOR RESEARCH, THE. 5588

0892-1024 See ART CULINAIRE (ATLANTA, GA.). 2788

0892-1059 See JOURNAL OF ELECTROPHYSIOLOGY. 2069

0892-1091 See VERNAL EXPRESS. 5757

0892-1113 See GUNNISON COUNTRY TIMES, THE. 5643

0892-1121 See AFTERMARKET BUSINESS. 637

0892-1148 See CAPPER'S. 5674

0892-1180 See INSIDER GUN NEWS, THE. 4873

0892-1202 See ART LOVERS' ART & CRAFT FAIR BULLETIN. 370

0892-1245 See GENERAL UROLOGY. 3990

0892-1253 See REVIEW OF MEDICAL PHYSIOLOGY. 586

0892-1261 See PIONEER HERALD, THE. 5672

0892-1318 See IHPS REPORT. 4784

0892-1326 See WHITE BEAR PRESS, THE. 5699

0892-1334 See ST. LOUIS METROPOLITAN MEDICINE. 3642

0892-1350 See KENTUCKY PARKS. 2197

0892-1369 See HISPANIC TIMES MAGAZINE. 4204

0892-1377 See BANKING REGULATOR. 3085

0892-1407 See SHOOTING STAR REVIEW. 3436

0892-1415 See QUALITY LIVING. 2491

0892-1423 See GOODWIN NEWS, THE. 2451

0892-1458 See LINER'S INSURANCE MARKETING INSIDER. 2887

0892-1474 See NUTRITION FUNDING REPORT, THE. 4196
0892-1504 See CHANGES (DEERFIELD BEACH, FLA.). 5277
0892-1571 See MARTYRDOM AND RESISTANCE. 2267
0892-1598 See COMMUNITY STORYTELLERS QUARTERLY NEWSLETTER, THE. 5268
0892-1601 See GASTROENTEROLOGY (NEW YORK, N.Y. : 1983). 3745
0892-161X See WORLD OPERA SCHEDULE. 4159
0892-1652 See STEEL EMPLOYMENT NEWS. 1712
0892-1660 See DIRECTORY OF EXPERTS AND CONSULTANTS IN SCIENCE AND ENGINEERING. 5100
0892-1733 See NASIG NEWSLETTER, THE. 3232
0892-1768 See ACTION UPDATE. 1596
0892-1776 See GILDEA REVIEW. 2194
0892-1784 See ST. CROIX VALLEY PRESS. 5698
0892-1792 See NORTH SUBURBAN PRESS. 5697
0892-1806 See QUAD COMMUNITY PRESS. 5698
0892-1814 See MESSENGER (MADISON, N.C.). 5723
0892-1822 See CBA RECORD. 2949
0892-1830 See LEFSETZ LETTER, THE. 4128
0892-1849 See WING & SHOT. 4880
0892-1857 See PRAEGER MONOGRAPHS IN INFECTIOUS DISEASE. 4795
0892-1865 See CONTEMPORARY WRITINGS ON LONG TERM CARE PHARMACY. 4298
0892-1873 See MONOGRAPHS IN CONTEMPORARY AUDIOLOGY. 3889
0892-1881 See DIRECTORY OF TOXICOLOGY TESTING INSTITUTIONS IN THE UNITED STATES. 3980
0892-189X See PRING MARKET REVIEW. 804
0892-1903 See BIOVENTURE VIEW. 448
0892-1911 See IMPROVISOR. 4122
0892-192X See OUR REGION. 2830
0892-1938 See SOUTHEAST ASIA HIGH TECH REVIEW. 1627
0892-1962 See TRANSACTIONS OF THE AMERICAN GYNECOLOGICAL AND OBSTETRICAL SOCIETY. 3769
0892-1989 See MARGARETOLOGIST, THE. 2915
0892-1997 See JOURNAL OF VOICE. 3600
0892-2012 See PINE CITY PIONEER. 5698
0892-2020 See TRANSACTIONS OF THE ... ANNUAL MEETING OF THE BIOELECTRICAL REPAIR AND GROWTH SOCIETY. 475
0892-2047 See CONSTRUCTION INDEX. 632
0892-2055 See NUCLEAR PLANT JOURNAL. 1952
0892-2098 See MARSHALL ISLANDS JOURNAL (1980). 5806
0892-2101 See COMMENTS ON MODERN CHEMISTRY. PART B, COMMENTS ON AGRICULTURAL AND FOOD CHEMISTRY. 1041
0892-211X See WATER QUALITY INTERNATIONAL. 2247
0892-2144 See EWING EXCHANGE. 2446
0892-2152 See CARROLL CABLES. 2442
0892-2187 See CLINICAL CHEMISTRY AND ENZYMOLOGY COMMUNICATIONS. 972
0892-2209 See TEACHING PROFESSOR, THE. 1850
0892-225X See BOX ELDER NEWS JOURNAL (1986). 5756
0892-2284 See AMERICAN FISHERIES SOCIETY SYMPOSIUM. 2294
0892-2330 See THESIS. 1850
0892-2349 See CALIFORNIA BUSINESS LAW PRACTITIONER. 3097
0892-2365 See INTELLECTUAL PROPERTY LAW (CHUR, SWITZERLAND). 1305
0892-2373 See DRUG FILES, THE. 4300
0892-239X See HART BEAT, THE. 5750
0892-2438 See LITERATURE SCAN. ANESTHESIOLOGY. 3683
0892-2454 See OHIO MEDICINE. 3624

0892-2462 See WORLD (BOSTON, MASS.), THE. 5010
0892-2497 See ISLAND DISPATCH. 5717
0892-2500 See FRIENDS OF FLORIDA FOLK. 2320
0892-2527 See EDUCATIONAL SOFTWARE PC COMPATIBILITY GUIDE, THE. 1285
0892-256X See COENZYMES AND COFACTORS. 1041
0892-2586 See LEWISTON MORNING TRIBUNE. 5657
0892-2624 See INTERNATIONAL SAMPE TECHNICAL CONFERENCE SERIES. 2103
0892-2640 See WORLD RADIO REPORT. 1143
0892-2659 See WINGSPAN. 1791
0892-2675 See PERSPECTIVES ON SCIENCE AND CHRISTIAN FAITH. 4986
0892-2683 See CELLULAR SALES & MARKETING. 1151
0892-2691 See FAMILY IN AMERICA, THE. 2279
0892-2713 See BOOK OF PAPERS - AMERICAN ASSOCIATION OF TEXTILE CHEMISTS AND COLORISTS. INTERNATIONAL CONFERENCE & EXHIBITION. 5348
0892-2721 See MUSIC OF THE SPHERES. 4186
0892-2756 See DIRECTORY OF ONLINE HEALTHCARE DATABASES, THE. 3572
0892-2764 See CONTEMPORARY FAMILY THERAPY. 2278
0892-2772 See MEDICAL HUMANITIES REVIEW. 3609
0892-2780 See MODEL SHOPPER. 2775
0892-2802 See UNISYS WORLD OPEN SYSTEMS NEWS. 1206
0892-2829 See HP CHRONICLE, THE. 1186
0892-2845 See UNISYS WORLD. 1206
0892-2853 See EDUCATIONAL OASIS. 1893
0892-2888 See ADVANCES IN SPECTROSCOPY (1986). 4433
0892-2896 See PREVIEW. 362
0892-290X See MOVING FORWARD : THE NATIONAL NEWSPAPER FOR PEOPLE WITH DISABILITIES. 4391
0892-2969 See LOG (DESTIN, FLA.). 5650
0892-2985 See SUPERFUND. 2244
0892-3094 See COLUMBIA (TACOMA, WASH.). 2729
0892-3108 See MEDICAL LASER INDUSTRY REPORT. 1618
0892-3116 See WREE-VIEW OF WOMEN FOR RACIAL AND ECONOMIC EQUALITY, THE. 4514
0892-3124 See MICHIGAN REGISTER. 3010
0892-3175 See INTERNATIONAL SERIES IN EXPERIMENTAL SOCIAL PSYCHOLOGY. 4592
0892-3183 See ATV SPORTS. 4884
0892-3280 See TRADING CYCLES. 917
0892-3299 See EXECUTIVE COMMUNICATIONS. 1111
0892-3310 See JOURNAL OF SCIENTIFIC EXPLORATION. 5120
0892-3329 See SATELLITE DIRECT. 1626
0892-3337 See CONSTRUCTION NEWS WEST. 610
0892-3345 See ATLANTA JEWISH TIMES, THE. 5652
0892-3353 See LINCOLN COUNTY LEADER. 5733
0892-337X See RAINBOW NEWS. 1201
0892-340X See CULT OBSERVER, THE. 5268
0892-3515 See CANAL HISTORY AND TECHNOLOGY PROCEEDINGS. 2088
0892-354X See OPTICAL ENGINEERING (NEW YORK, N.Y.). 1989
0892-3582 See A.S.A. ARTISAN. 335
0892-3647 See AMERICAN JOURNAL OF DISTANCE EDUCATION, THE. 1724
0892-3736 See MEDICAL ROUNDS. 3611
0892-3752 See FUNWORLD. 4861
0892-3787 See MORBIDITY AND MORTALITY WEEKLY REPORT. CDC SURVEILLANCE SUMMARIES. 4792
0892-3809 See PAPER (NEW YORK, N.Y.). 327

0892-3817 See NCR CONNECTION. 697
0892-385X See APPALOOSA JOURNAL. 2797
0892-3876 See INFORM (SILVER SPRING, MD.). 4370
0892-3884 See CHINA DIGEST, THE. 1551
0892-3892 See ADVISOR (NOROTON, CONN.). 754
0892-3922 See TRAIL RIDER MAGAZINE. 4855
0892-3930 See CRITICAL CARE OUTLOOK. 3569
0892-3957 See PERSPECTIVES IN PLASTIC SURGERY. 3972
0892-3965 See PLASTIC SURGERY OUTLOOK. 3972
0892-3973 See IMMUNOPHARMACOLOGY AND IMMUNOTOXICOLOGY. 3672
0892-3981 See CONTEMPORARY ECONOMIC PROBLEMS (1987). 1552
0892-399X See TRANSNATIONAL DATA AND COMMUNICATIONS REPORT. 1168
0892-4015 See WHAT EVERY ENGINEER SHOULD KNOW. 2001
0892-4023 See UNMANNED SYSTEMS. 2085
0892-4082 See CARDIAC IMPULSE. 3700
0892-4147 See IRAN NAMEH. BUNYAD-I MUTALAAT-I IRAN. 2654
0892-4163 See HARRISON INDEPENDENT. 5717
0892-4171 See QUALITY CITIES. 4677
0892-418X See LYNN/LINN LINEAGE QUARTERLY. 2459
0892-4198 See DISTRESSED REAL ESTATE LAW ALERT. 3086
0892-4201 See AMS STUDIES IN THE EMBLEM. 4563
0892-4228 See CORROSION ENGINEERING (NEW YORK, N.Y.). 2011
0892-4236 See AIRLINE, SHIP & CATERING ONBOARD SERVICES MAGAZINE. 2326
0892-4244 See AAVSO MONOGRAPH. 391
0892-4260 See ADVANCES IN COMPUTER-AIDED ENGINEERING DESIGN. 1231
0892-4287 See NATIONAL JOURNAL OF SOCIOLOGY. 5252
0892-4341 See CHAMPIONS. 4858
0892-435X See SPANISH FORK PRESS, THE. 5757
0892-4406 See CALIFORNIA DAIRY INFORMATION BULLETIN. 192
0892-4422 See INSURANCE LAW ANTHOLOGY. 2983
0892-4430 See TAX LAW ANTHOLOGY. 3062
0892-4449 See LABOR LAW ANTHOLOGY. 3150
0892-4457 See MONTGOMERY ADVERTISER (1987), THE. 5627
0892-4465 See KWOC LIST OF PETROLEUM ABSTRACTS' EXPLORATION & PRODUCTION THESAURUS, AND NEW E & P TERMS. 4263
0892-4473 See BIOLOGICAL TECHNIQUES SERIES. 445
0892-4481 See COUNTRY INNS GAZETTE. 2805
0892-4546 See INTERNATIONAL LEADS. 3218
0892-4562 See STRATEGIES (RESTON, VA.). 1858
0892-4600 See BULLETIN (ASSOCIATION FOR THE BIBLIOGRAPHY OF HISTORY (U.S.)). 2635
0892-4635 See LISP AND SYMBOLIC COMPUTATION. 1280
0892-466X See GORGET ET SASH : JOURNAL OF THE EARLY MODERN WARFARE SOCIETY. 4044
0892-4678 See MULTISTATE TAX ANALYST. 4738
0892-4686 See CHRISTIAN PSYCHOLOGY FOR TODAY. 4580
0892-4805 See PARTNER'S REPORT. 3025
0892-4821 See CAD WORLD. 1173
0892-4848 See CORPORATE CRIMINAL LIABILITY REPORTER. 3098
0892-4856 See GREGORY'S A-SERIES TECHNICAL JOURNAL. 1238
0892-4872 See INSTRUCTION DELIVERY SYSTEMS. 1189
0892-4880 See JOURNAL OF LAND USE & ENVIRONMENTAL LAW. 3113

0892-4899 See KENTUCKY MARQUEE. 5365

0892-4902 See LABOR MILITANT. 1684

0892-4910 See MOVEMENT THEATRE QUARTERLY. 5366

0892-4937 See NEW BRASS KEY. 2462

0892-4945 See NOAH'S ARK. 1067

0892-4961 See TUG LINES. 1281

0892-497X See USSR TECHNOLOGY UPDATE. 5168

0892-4996 See VISITOR BEHAVIOR. 4621

0892-5003 See NOVASCOPE. 2491

0892-5011 See LEARNING DISABILITIES RESEARCH AND PRACTICE. 1881

0892-502X See LEARNING DISABILITIES RESEARCH AND PRACTICE. 1881

0892-5038 See RUNNING JOURNAL. 4916

0892-5046 See CONSULTING-SPECIFYING ENGINEER. 2097

0892-5070 See JOURNAL OF CLINICAL ELECTROPHYSIOLOGY. 582

0892-5089 See SPLICE (NEW YORK, N.Y.). 331

0892-5135 See EXTENSIONS (YPSILANTI, MICH.). 1746

0892-5143 See HOME SATELLITE NEWSLETTER, THE. 1156

0892-516X See LIMITED PARTNERSHIP INVESTMENT REVIEW. 690

0892-5186 See TEXAS TELLER QUARTERLY NEWSLETTER. 3445

0892-5216 See FASHIONEWS (BURLINGAME, CALIF.). 1084

0892-5224 See WISCONSIN GEOGRAPHER. 2579

0892-5232 See CORPORATE JOBS OUTLOOK!. 4203

0892-5364 See FULL-COURT PRESS, THE. 5696

0892-5372 See AGING ALERT. 5178

0892-5380 See TENNESSEE PUBLIC WORKS. 4690

0892-5399 See BILL OF FARE. 5070

0892-5410 See GREAT LAKES SAILOR (AKRON, OHIO). 593

0892-5429 See MUTABLE DILEMMA, THE. 4242

0892-5437 See VIOLEXCHANGE, THE. 4158

0892-5445 See MONEY MACHINE. 1195

0892-5453 See COMMUNITY COLLEGE CAPSULES. 1817

0892-5461 See ENERGY BOOKS QUARTERLY. 1962

0892-547X See IMMIGRATION POLICY & LAW. 2980

0892-5488 See WORK IN AMERICA. 948

0892-5496 See ENABLE EXCHANGE NEWSLETTER. 1184

0892-5534 See WILDBIRD. 5621

0892-5542 See TRADING SYSTEMS TECHNOLOGY. 1249

0892-5569 See COMPARATIVE URBAN AND COMMUNITY RESEARCH. 5196

0892-5585 See LPTV REPORT, THE. 1134

0892-5593 See UNIVERSITY OF CHICAGO LEGAL FORUM. 3068

0892-5631 See SERVICE BUREAU NEWSLETTER. 1626

0892-564X See GARDEN CENTER BULLETIN, THE. 2415

0892-5674 See HIGH FRONTIER NEWSWATCH. 4045

0892-5712 See CRISWELL THEOLOGICAL REVIEW. 4951

0892-5739 See SOUTHERN WASTE INFORMATION EXCHANGE CATALOG, THE. 2243

0892-5763 See PEGBOARD (MENLO PARK, CALIF.). 1230

0892-5771 See HDTV NEWSLETTER. 1132

0892-578X See ONION WORLD. 2426

0892-5812 See RIGHTING WORDS. 2924

0892-5828 See LIAN HE TONG XUN. 2658

0892-5836 See NORMAL (NEW YORK, N.Y.). 326

0892-5879 See SUPPORT LINE (CHICAGO, ILL.). 4199

0892-5887 See INSURANCE AND RISK MANAGEMENT--FOR BUSINESS AND GOVERNMENT. 2883

0892-5895 See BULLETIN - YELL COUNTY HISTORICAL & GENEALOGICAL ASSOCIATION (ARK.). 2441

0892-5917 See SITUATION REPORT - SECURITY AND INTELLIGENCE FOUNDATION (WASHINGTON, D.C.). 4686

0892-5925 See TENNESSEE ENVIRONMENTAL REPORT. 2182

0892-5933 See PUBLIC EMPLOYMENT RECRUITER BULLETIN : PERB. 1704

0892-5941 See POMPEIIANA NEWSLETTER. 3311

0892-595X See POMPEIIANA NEWSLETTER. 3311

0892-5984 See OF A LIKE MIND. 4186

0892-5992 See SMALL BUSINESS EXCHANGE. 711

0892-6026 See FOSTER'S DAILY DEMOCRAT. 5708

0892-6034 See BUSINESS INFORMATION FROM YOUR PUBLIC LIBRARY. 649

0892-6042 See NUTRITION NOW. 4196

0892-6077 See MEAT & POULTRY. 2349

0892-6085 See FARM & POWER EQUIPMENT DEALER. 158

0892-6107 See ORANGE COUNTY BUSINESSWEEK. 701

0892-6115 See HARVARD JOURNAL OF HISPANIC POLICY. 2262

0892-6123 See SECRETARIAL CONSULTANT, THE. 710

0892-6131 See PRAIRIELAND PIONEER. 2468

0892-614X See WORLD MEDICAL REVIEWS IN PERINATOLOGY. 3912

0892-6158 See REPORT ON INDUSTRIAL COMMUNICATIONS, THE. 884

0892-6166 See ATHLETE, THE. 4884

0892-6174 See QUALITY CARE ADVOCATE. 5303

0892-6182 See NEWSLETTER (LINCOLN-LANCASTER COUNTY GENEALOGICAL SOCIETY). 2463

0892-6204 See NUTRITION UPDATE (SAN CLEMENTE, CALIF.). 3623

0892-6212 See REVIEW OF TEXAS BOOKS. 4832

0892-6220 See BRANCHES (BERKELEY, CALIF.). 2257

0892-6239 See NEWPORT MINER, THE. 5761

0892-6247 See WORLD OF PERSONNEL. 1720

0892-6255 See RING OF FIRE. 244

0892-6263 See QUARTERLY NEWSLETTER - WOMEN'S THEOLOGICAL CENTER (BOSTON, MASS.). 4989

0892-6271 See LONE STAR HORSE REPORT. 2800

0892-628X See HERS NEWSLETTER. 3762

0892-6298 See JOURNAL OF THE INTERNATIONAL SOCIETY FOR RESPIRATORY PROTECTION. 1983

0892-631X See NEWSLETTER - COLUMBIA UNIVERSITY. CENTER FOR SOCIAL POLICY AND PRACTICE IN THE WORKPLACE. 1695

0892-6328 See COLUMBUS ART. 348

0892-6336 See HISTORIC SCHAEFFERSTOWN RECORD. 2737

0892-6344 See NEW CONSTRUCTION (INTERNATIONAL ED.). 622

0892-6352 See PLASMA NEWS REPORT. 1028

0892-6360 See RADIO AGE (AUGUSTA, GA.). 1137

0892-6379 See SVOBODNYJ MIR. 426

0892-6395 See CALIFORNIA JOB JOURNAL. 1658

0892-6409 See INDIAN MARKET. 2264

0892-6417 See SWAIA UPDATE. 2274

0892-6433 See VANGUARD. 2838

0892-6441 See TUSTIN NEWS, THE. 5641

0892-645X See BEVERLY HILLS COURIER, THE. 5633

0892-6468 See PREVIEW (RICHARDSON, TEX.). 387

0892-6476 See TALON (AURORA, COLO.). 5598

0892-6492 See AMERICAN COUNTRY. 2788

0892-6506 See MALACOLOGY DATA NET. 5590

0892-6514 See CAT FANCY (SAN JUAN CAPISTRANO, CALIF.). 4286

0892-6522 See DOG FANCY (LOS ANGELES, CALIF.). 4286

0892-6530 See U.S. RAG. 3449

0892-6573 See POLICE LAW JOURNAL. 3172

0892-6581 See SUCCESSFUL MAGAZINE PUBLISHING. 4820

0892-6603 See SHORTHORN, THE. 1095

0892-6611 See GRAPEVINE (DOWNERS GROVE, ILL.), THE. 2488

0892-662X See WINE EAST. 2372

0892-6638 See FASEB JOURNAL, THE. 455

0892-6646 See CALIFORNIA-NEVADA UNITED METHODIST REPORTER, THE. 5057

0892-6654 See INDIAN HIGHWAYS (TEMPE, ARIZ.). 2263

0892-6662 See MESSENGER OF TRUTH (MOUNDRIDGE, KAN.). 4976

0892-6719 See INTERFAITH WOMEN'S NEWS & NETWORK. 5559

0892-6727 See PRIVATE LABEL PRODUCT NEWS. 3486

0892-6735 See FIVE OWLS, THE. 1063

0892-676X See ID SYSTEMS. 5111

0892-6778 See BANKING SOFTWARE REVIEW. 777

0892-6794 See ETHICS & INTERNATIONAL AFFAIRS. 4520

0892-6808 See SOVIET TECHNOLOGY REVIEWS. SECTION B, THERMAL PHYSICS REVIEWS. 4432

0892-6875 See MINERALS ENGINEERING. 2144

0892-6913 See HAZARD'S PAVILION. 4121

0892-6921 See LATER YEARS (LAFAYETTE, IND.), THE. 5294

0892-6956 See ROHWEDDER. 3470

0892-6964 See CALIFORNIA READER, THE. 3272

0892-6972 See NATIONAL DIRECTORY OF HEAD INJURY REHABILITATION SERVICES. 3618

0892-6980 See PDS UPDATE. 4319

0892-6999 See SOVIET AGRICULTURAL BIOLOGY. PART 1, PLANT BIOLOGY. 136

0892-7014 See BIOFOULING (CHUR, SWITZERLAND). 444

0892-7022 See MOLECULAR SIMULATION. 4429

0892-7049 See ANTIBODY, IMMUNOCONJUGATES, AND RADIOPHARMACEUTICALS. 3809

0892-7057 See JOURNAL OF THERMOPLASTIC COMPOSITE MATERIALS. 1026

0892-7073 See LAW SEMINAR JOURNAL. 2997

0892-7081 See CLINICAL DECISIONS IN OBSTETRICS AND GYNECOLOGY. 3758

0892-709X See HOSPITAL PUBLIC RELATIONS ADVISOR. 760

0892-7103 See FOCUS ON GERIATRIC CARE & REHABILITATION. 3751

0892-7111 See ACSUS MEMBERSHIP DIRECTORY. 2717

0892-7138 See STANFORD ENVIRONMENTAL LAW JOURNAL. 3116

0892-7146 See TECHPAK. 4222

0731-0277 See ASSESSMENT JOURNAL. 4711

0892-7189 See SAN FRANCISCO OPERA. 4151

0892-7219 See JOURNAL OF OFFSHORE MECHANICS AND ARCTIC ENGINEERING. 2092

0892-7227 See BIRTH TRAUMA. 2942

0892-7243 See WARFIELD'S BUSINESS RECORD. 719

0892-726X See ADVANCES IN EPILEPTOLOGY. 3826

0892-7278 See TWICE. 2085

0892-7286 See EUROPEAN MONOGRAPHS IN SOCIAL PSYCHOLOGY. 4587

0892-7294 See LOSE WEIGHT NATURALLY NEWSLETTER. 4194

0892-7308 See 11TH CIRCUIT LAW LETTER. 2926

0892-7332 See TECHNOLOGY FOR LABORATORY MEDICINE. 3644

0892-7340 See TECHNOLOGY FOR IMAGING AND RADIOLOGY. 3947

0892-7367 See FINDING. 3210

0892-7375 See VISIBILITIES. 2796

0892-7413 See SOLUTIONS (BOCA RATON, FLA.). 886

0892-7421 See VOICE OF THE HAWKEYES, THE. 4928

0892-743X See LDB INTERIOR TEXTILES. 5354

0892-7456 See ZHONG XI LIAO WANG TAI. 2668

0892-7537 See JOURNAL OF WORLD PREHISTORY. 272

0892-7545 See EMPLOYEE RESPONSIBILITIES AND RIGHTS JOURNAL. 3147

0892-7553 See JOURNAL OF INSECT BEHAVIOR. 5610

0892-7561 See JOURNAL OF DEVELOPMENTAL AND PHYSICAL DISABILITIES. 4389

0892-7626 See JOURNAL OF APPLIED BUSINESS RESEARCH. 685

0892-7669 See NURSING ASSISTANT : OFFICIAL PUBLICATION OF THE AMERICAN ASSOCIATION OF NURSING ASSISTANTS. 3863

0892-7677 See HEALTH SYSTEMS PLAN (HOUSTON, TEX.). 2978

0892-7685 See ORTHOPAEDIC KNOWLEDGE UPDATE ... HOME STUDY SYLLABUS. 3883

0892-7731 See HEALTH INDUSTRY BUYERS GUIDE : HIBG. 3581

0892-774X See TREE TRIMMER, THE. 3647

0892-7790 See JOURNAL OF ENDOUROLOGY. 3990

0892-7812 See FINANCIAL SOURCEBOOKS' SOURCES. 924

0892-7820 See MARIEL (MIAMI, FLA. : 1986). 2745

0892-7839 See ALUMNEWS (NORFOLK, VA.). 1097

0892-7847 See SKYLINES (WASHINGTON, D.C.). 4847

0892-7855 See CUPA NEWS (WASHINGTON D.C. : 1987). 1819

0892-7901 See ADVANCES IN PSYCHOPHYSIOLOGY. 577

0892-7936 See ANTHROZOOS. 5576

0892-7960 See FRENCH ICE. 373

0892-7979 See TENNESSEE ANTHROPOLOGIST. 246

0892-7987 See BIOTECHNOLOGY BUSINESS REPORT. 3688

0892-8002 See RADIO AMATEUR CALLBOOK. INTERNATIONAL LISTINGS, EXCLUSIVE OF NORTH AMERICA & HAWAII. 1137

0892-807X See MARYLAND POETRY REVIEW (BROOKLANDVILLE, MD.). 3466

0892-8088 See UNIX SYSTEM SUPPORT & UPDATE NEWS. 1206

0892-810X See SUPREME COURT RECORD. 3061

0892-8118 See MACWEEK. 1238

0892-8150 See DEVELOPMENTAL CLINICAL PSYCHOLOGY AND PSYCHIATRY. 4584

0892-8193 See SALES MOTIVATION (SANTA MONICA, CALIF.). 709

0892-8215 See DAILY RECORD (WOOSTER, OHIO), THE. 5728

0892-8231 See MICHIGAN RESTAURATEUR (1987). 5072

0892-824X See BUILDER/DEALER. 602

0892-8274 See ADWEEK'S MARKETING WEEK. 755

0892-8282 See GEORGE D. HALL'S DIRECTORY OF NORTH CAROLINA MANUFACTURERS. 3479

0892-8312 See FARM INDUSTRY NEWS (1984). 159

0892-8320 See HOT BOAT. 593

0892-8339 See MUSEUM ANTHROPOLOGY. 242

0892-8355 See OUTDOOR SPORTS & RECREATION. 4877

0892-8363 See NORTHWEST PALATE, THE. 2351

0892-8436 See SOURCE SAMPLING NEWS. 2243

0892-8525 See COUNTRY WOMAN. 5554

0892-8533 See INSURANCE SOFTWARE REVIEW. 2884

0892-8606 See BELLE GLADE EREC RESEARCH REPORT. 65

0892-8649 See TAX POLICY AND THE ECONOMY. 1595

0892-8657 See ARMY RD & A BULLETIN. 4036

0892-8665 See JASNA NEWS. 3398

0892-8673 See BRIGHT. 2529

0892-869X See AUSTIN BUSINESS JOURNAL. 641

0892-8703 See NEW HAMPSHIRE SUNDAY NEWS. 5708

0892-8711 See ARIZONA REPUBLIC. 5629

0892-8738 See BANGOR DAILY NEWS. 5687

0892-8762 See AGING, IMMUNOLOGY AND INFECTIOUS DISEASE. 3662

0892-8789 See SOUTHERN VERMONT. 2546

0892-8797 See CHROMATOGRAPHY. 1014

0892-8819 See ANIMALS AGENDA. 225

0892-8835 See SOUTHERN NEW JERSEY BUSINESS DIGEST. 712

0892-8886 See WORKING PAPERS IN LINGUISTICS (SEATTLE, WASH.). 3333

0892-8959 See VITAL & HEALTH STATISTICS. SERIES 5, COMPARATIVE INTERNATIONAL VITAL AND HEALTH STATISTICS REPORTS. 4806

0892-8967 See INTERNATIONAL CONTACT LENS CLINIC (1987). 4216

0892-8991 See KIDSART NEWS. 1065

0892-9017 See JOURNAL OF MINERAL LAW & POLICY. 2989

0892-9025 See GULF COAST HISTORICAL REVIEW. 2735

0892-9033 See CALIFORNIA DUI REPORT. 3105

0892-9076 See PACIFIC FISHERIES REVIEW. 2310

0892-9084 See ALABAMA COUNTY DATA BOOK. 4625

0892-9092 See YOUTH THEATRE JOURNAL. 5372

0892-9106 See FLORA ONLINE. 511

0892-9130 See ILLINOIS INTERSCHOLASTIC, THE. 4899

0892-9165 See KHRONIKA ZASHCHITY PRAV V SSSR. 4510

0892-9203 See BLACK SWAMP HERITAGE. 2529

0892-922X See ELLIS ISLAND SERIES. 1918

0892-9262 See DIRECTORY OF MICROCOMPUTER SOFTWARE IN THE HUMAN SERVICES, A. 1285

0892-9270 See SPACE TECHNOLOGY (OXFORD). 36

0892-9300 See CHRISTIAN CONQUEST. 4944

0892-9327 See CARDIOLOGY MANAGEMENT. 3701

0892-9343 See PR ACTIVITY REPORT. 3241

0892-9351 See HEALTH AND SAFETY SCIENCE ABSTRACTS. 4810

0892-9378 See REPORT WRITING UPDATE. 3174

0892-9386 See GASTROENTEROLOGY (GLENDALE, CALIF.). 3745

0892-9408 See WITHOUT PREJUDICE. 4514

0892-9424 See WORLDWIDE BUSINESS CONNECTION. 724

0892-9459 See SPECTRUM. 1122

0892-9467 See NETLINE. 1196

0892-9548 See WATER JOURNAL. 5543

0892-9556 See ADVANCES IN NONPROFIT MARKETING. 920

0892-9580 See GIFTED CHILD TODAY, THE. 1063

0892-9599 See CREATIVE KIDS. 1062

0892-9661 See JPL PUBLICATION. 26

0892-9696 See Z MISCELLANEOUS. 3456

0892-9718 See MEDIEVAL AND RENAISSANCE MONOGRAPH SERIES. 2698

0892-9726 See VISION AND VISUAL HEALTH CARE. 3879

0892-9769 See CAROUSEL NEWS & TRADER, THE. 250

0892-9807 See WITTYWORLD. 376

0892-9831 See MBEA TODAY. 1763

0892-9882 See SCIENCE & GLOBAL SECURITY. 4535

0892-9912 See JOURNAL OF TECHNOLOGY TRANSFER, THE. 5120

0892-9947 See LASERS & OPTRONICS. 4438

0893-0031 See JAYCEES MAGAZINE (GREENSBORO, N.C.). 5232

0893-0120 See ETHNOARTS INDEX. 334

0893-0139 See INDEX TO REPRODUCTIONS IN ART PERIODICALS : IRAP. 352

0893-0198 See CURA ANIMARUM. 3569

0893-021X See BANK/FINANCIAL SERVICES MARKETING. 774

0893-0244 See PALATE PLEASERS. 2352

0893-0252 See DROOD REVIEW OF MYSTERY, THE. 5074

0893-0260 See LURZER'S INT'L ARCHIVE. 762

0893-0279 See MOMA (NEW YORK, N.Y.). 358

0893-0333 See ELECTRONIC SHOPPING NEWS. 1154

0893-035X See CLINTON CHRONICLE (CLINTON, S.C.), THE. 5742

0893-0376 See CONNECTICUT ENGLISH JOURNAL. 1891

0893-0384 See CONTINUING HIGHER EDUCATION REVIEW. 1818

0893-0406 See SNA MONTHLY REVIEW. 1203

0893-0457 See APEC JOURNAL. 1965

0893-0465 See CITY & SOCIETY. 2818

0893-0473 See CIVIL RIGHTS UPDATE. 4506

0893-052X See FEDERAL COMPUTER WEEK. 1247

0893-0538 See ACTIVITIES OF DAILY LIVING UPDATE. 2526

0893-0562 See GOODLAND DAILY NEWS, THE. 5676

0893-0570 See ADA STRATEGIES. 1255

0893-0589 See OCCASIONAL PAPERS - BOWDOIN COLLEGE. MUSEUM OF ART. 4094

0893-0619 See DEFENSE MEDIA REVIEW. 4041

0893-0643 See GO. 5478

0893-0694 See CALIFORNIA CONNECTIONS PUBLICATIONS. 1658

0893-0724 See AAICJ NEWSLETTER. 4503

0893-0759 See DAILY MOUNTAIN EAGLE. 5626

0893-0767 See PICKENS COUNTY HERALD. 5627

0893-0775 See METRO CHICAGO REAL ESTATE. 4841

0893-0791 See COMPUTER INDUSTRY ALMANAC. 1176

0893-0805 See RICHMOND AFRO-AMERICAN AND RICHMOND PLANET (RICHMOND, VA. : 1941). 5687

0893-0848 See CHILD AND YOUTH CARE FORUM. 5278

0893-1011 See MEALEY'S LITIGATION REPORTS. BAD FAITH. 3007

0893-102X 3956

0893-1054 See RADIOLOGY TODAY. 3946

0893-1097 See DECORATIVE ARTIST'S WORKBOOK. 372

0893-1186 See COUNTRY INNS AND BACKROADS. BRITAIN AND IRELAND. 2804

0893-1194 See BED & BREAKFAST AMERICAN STYLE. 5462

0893-1208 See CAR BOOK, THE. 5409

0893-1232 See WASHINGTON REPORT ON LATIN AMERICA & THE CARIBBEAN. 857

0893-1240 See CRUISE INDUSTRY NEWS QUARTERLY, THE. 5467

0893-1240 See CRUISE INDUSTRY NEWS (NEWSLETTER). 5467

0893-1259 See TMS-LETTER, THE. 937

0893-1291 See COUNTRY INNS AND BACK ROADS (CONTINENTAL EUROPE ED.). 2804

0893-1305 See ABSTRACTS OF PAPERS READ AT THE ... ANNUAL MEETING OF THE AMERICAN MUSICOLOGICAL SOCIETY. 4098

0893-1321 See JOURNAL OF AEROSPACE ENGINEERING. 25

0893-133X *See* NEUROPSYCHOPHARMACOLOGY (NEW YORK, N.Y.). **3842**

0893-1348 *See* BISHOP MUSEUM OCCASIONAL PAPERS. **5088**

0893-1356 *See* NURSING EDUCATORS MICROWORLD. **3864**

0893-1364 *See* INVESTMENT LIMITED PARTNERSHIPS LAW REPORT. **903**

0893-1526 *See* AIDS LITERATURE & NEWS REVIEW. **3664**

0893-1550 *See* CARIBBEAN WRITER, THE. **3373**

0893-1585 *See* NEUROCOMPUTERS. **1197**

0893-164X *See* PSYCHOLOGY OF ADDICTIVE BEHAVIORS. **4613**

0893-1674 *See* ANNUAL REPORT ... - MSU-DOE PLANT RESEARCH LABORATORY. **499**

0893-1712 *See* OT WEEK. **1883**

0893-181X *See* RHODE ISLAND QUERIES. **2470**

0893-1828 *See* RESOURCE MANAGEMENT. **4055**

0893-1879 *See* HOOKED ON CROCHET!. **5184**

0893-1895 *See* NEW WORLD OF TRAVEL, THE. **5485**

0893-1976 *See* TRENDS THROUGH **1587**

0893-2034 *See* JOURNAL OF CURRENT PODIATRIC MEDICINE, THE. **3918**

0893-2069 *See* TREE SHAKER / EASTERN KENTUCKY GENEALOGICAL SOCIETY. **2475**

0893-2123 *See* PERSPECTIVES ON TECHNOLOGY. **882**

0893-2131 *See* CABLE TV BANKER/BROKER. **1600**

0893-214X *See* TRANSACTIONS OF THE WESTERN SECTION OF THE WILDLIFE SOCIETY. **2207**

0893-2174 *See* INTERNATIONAL JOURNAL OF PROSTHODONTICS, THE. **1325**

0893-2190 *See* JOURNAL OF PERINATAL & NEONATAL NURSING, THE. **3859**

0893-2212 *See* BIG BLUE DISK. **1284**

0893-2220 *See* FORTE (MILWAUKEE, WIS.). **4118**

0893-2247 *See* QUICK 'N EASY COOKIN'. **2792**

0893-2255 *See* MINNESOTA REAL ESTATE JOURNAL. **4841**

0893-2271 *See* IDAHO ARCHAEOLOGIST. **270**

0893-228X *See* CHEMICAL RESEARCH IN TOXICOLOGY. **3979**

0893-2298 *See* INDIANA FACTS. **2535**

0893-2301 *See* CENTRAL & INNER ASIAN STUDIES. **2648**

0893-2336 *See* NEUROMETHODS. **3841**

0893-2344 *See* REPUBLICAN CHINA. **2663**

0893-2395 *See* HISPANIC ISSUES. **3394**

0893-2425 *See* SAN FRANCISCO CHRONICLE INDEX. **5814**

0893-2433 *See* DETROIT NEWS INDEX, THE. **5814**

0893-2441 *See* DENVER POST INDEX (1987), THE. **5691**

0893-2468 *See* AMERICAN BANKER INDEX (ANN ARBOR, MICH.). **769**

0893-2476 *See* HOUSTON POST INDEX, THE. **5692**

0893-2492 *See* BARCLAYS UNITED STATES NINTH CIRCUIT SERVICE. **2940**

0893-2506 *See* BARCLAYS CALIFORNIA SUPREME COURT SERVICE. **2940**

0893-2522 *See* DEALERNEWS (1987). **4081**

0893-2549 *See* PERSONAL REPORT FOR THE PROFESSIONAL SECRETARY. **4208**

0893-2557 *See* AIKEN STANDARD. **5741**

0893-2573 *See* PUBLIC AND LOCAL ACTS OF THE LEGISLATURE OF THE STATE OF MICHIGAN. **3032**

0893-2654 *See* RISK & BENEFITS MANAGEMENT. **2892**

0893-2662 *See* TRADESHOW & EXHIBIT MANAGER. **767**

0893-2700 *See* KAGAN MEDIA INDEX, THE. **1614**

0893-2719 *See* MIDWEST REAL ESTATE NEWS. **4841**

0893-2727 *See* BOSTON GLOBE INDEX (1987), THE. **5814**

0893-276X *See* COLUMBIANA. **2531**

0893-2816 *See* MISSOURI MANUFACTURERS REGISTER. **3484**

0893-2824 *See* WEST VIRGINIA MANUFACTURERS REGISTER. **3489**

0893-2859 *See* INTERNATIONAL COMPUTER LAW ADVISER. **1189**

0893-2875 *See* SIGSMALL/PC NOTES. **1272**

0893-2891 *See* TENNESSEE GROWER. **189**

0893-2905 *See* PSYCHIATRIC TIMES, THE. **3933**

0893-2913 *See* INDIANA UNIVERSITY URALIC AND ALTAIC SERIES. **3287**

0893-2921 *See* CHRONICLES (PHILADELPHIA, PA.). **2443**

0893-2948 *See* NORTH TEXAS TRAIL TRACERS. **2464**

0893-2956 *See* NEWSLETTER - NEW MEXICO LIBRARY ASSOCIATION. **3235**

0893-2980 *See* PROCEEDINGS OF THE CASUALTY ACTUARIAL SOCIETY. **2890**

0893-2999 *See* SIGCUE OUTLOOK. **1225**

0893-3022 *See* CREATIVE LIVING (MILWAUKEE, WIS.). **2532**

0893-3030 *See* TRAFFIC LAW REPORTS. **3065**

0893-3049 *See* CAPITAL COMPUTER DIGEST. **1173**

0893-3057 *See* SALINE, THE. **2471**

0893-3065 *See* DIRECTORY OF TRADITIONAL MUSIC. **4115**

0893-3073 *See* BUSINESS FLYER, THE. **648**

0893-3081 See AIRPORT BUSINESS. **637**

0893-309X *See* TATE TRAILS. **2474**

0893-3103 *See* QUARTERLY (NEW YORK, N.Y. : 1987). **3427**

0893-3111 *See* BISHOP MUSEUM BULLETIN IN ANTHROPOLOGY. **232**

0893-312X *See* BISHOP MUSEUM BULLETIN IN ZOOLOGY. **5578**

0893-3138 *See* BISHOP MUSEUM BULLETINS IN BOTANY. **502**

0893-3146 *See* BISHOP MUSEUM BULLETIN IN ENTOMOLOGY. **5606**

0893-3162 *See* GATHERING GIBSONS. **2449**

0893-3189 *See* MANAGEMENT COMMUNICATION QUARTERLY. **1115**

0893-3200 *See* JOURNAL OF FAMILY PSYCHOLOGY. **4597**

0893-3286 *See* REFLECTOR (1983), THE. **5701**

0893-3308 *See* UPDATE - WOMEN IN COMMUNICATIONS, INC. BOSTON PROFESSIONAL CHAPTER. **1123**

0893-3316 *See* KAHPERD JOURNAL (PITTSBURG, KAN.). **1857**

0893-3332 *See* REAL ESTATE CENTER JOURNAL. **4844**

0893-3340 *See* LOCAL HISTORIAN (COLUMBUS, OHIO). **2744**

0893-3359 *See* STANLY COUNTY GENEALOGICAL SOCIETY JOURNAL, THE. **2473**

0893-3367 *See* MIDWEST VOLLEYBALL MAGAZINE. **4905**

0893-3391 See NCBA COOPERATIVE BUSINESS JOURNAL. **697**

0893-3413 *See* ENVIRONMENTAL MANAGEMENT NEWS. **2168**

0893-3448 *See* NEWS-LEADER (SPRINGFIELD, MO.). **5704**

0893-3456 *See* LOS ALAMOS MONITOR. **5712**

0893-3464 *See* VISTA PRESS, THE. **5641**

0893-3472 *See* N (MINNEAPOLIS, MINN.). **2922**

0893-3480 *See* MACNEWS. **691**

0893-3502 *See* EL CHICANO (COLTON, CALIF.). **5634**

0893-3510 *See* DAVIS REVIEW. **1603**

0893-3529 *See* HUFACT QUARTERLY. **1977**

0893-3537 *See* VERSATILITY. **4424**

0893-3545 See AMERICAN PAPERMAKER (1991). **4232**

0893-357X *See* JOURNAL OF PESTICIDE REFORM. **4245**

0893-3588 *See* SURFACE MOUNT TECHNOLOGY. **2083**

0893-3596 *See* CLERGY MALPRACTICE ALERT. **2951**

0893-360X *See* QUALITY BY DESIGN. **625**

0893-3618 *See* INTERNATIONAL HALLEY WATCH : IHW. **396**

0893-3642 *See* SANFORD HERALD (SANFORD, FLA.). **5651**

0893-3650 *See* ROCK SPRINGS DAILY ROCKET-MINER. **5772**

0893-3669 *See* PARIS POST-INTELLIGENCER, THE. **5746**

0893-3677 *See* NEW JERSEY HERALD (1960), THE. **5711**

0893-3693 *See* JEFFERSON COUNTY CHRONICLE. **5701**

0893-3707 *See* HERALD-CHRONICLE (WINCHESTER, TENN.), THE. **5745**

0893-3758 *See* DEMPSEY CANADIAN LETTER, THE. **2532**

0893-3766 *See* NINETEENTH CENTURY THEATRE. **5367**

0893-3774 *See* NUCLEAR LICENSING REPORTS. **2157**

0893-3782 *See* WESTBOROUGH NEWS, THE. **5690**

0893-3790 *See* SOUTHERN HERALD (LIBERTY, MISS.), THE. **5701**

0893-3812 *See* MORNING NEWS (BLACKFOOT, IDAHO), THE. **5657**

0893-3820 *See* INDIAN TIME (ROOSEVELTOWN, N.Y.). **5717**

0893-3839 *See* BROWNSVILLE STATES-GRAPHIC. **5744**

0893-3863 *See* MILITARY VEHICLES. **4051**

0893-3871 *See* JOURNAL OF OSTEOPATHIC SPORTS MEDICINE : JOSM. **3954**

0893-388X *See* PHYSICAL ACOUSTICS. **4453**

0893-3898 *See* "LOOKING UP" TIMES, THE. **3408**

0893-3901 *See* ART CALENDAR (GREAT FALLS, VA.). **338**

0893-391X *See* BRIDGES (NEW YORK, N.Y. : 1986). **2529**

0893-3936 *See* IAFC ON SCENE. **2291**

0893-3944 *See* INVESTMENTS LIMITED PARTNERSHIPS HANDBOOK. **903**

0893-3952 *See* MODERN PATHOLOGY. **3896**

0893-3960 *See* INTERNATIONAL JOURNAL OF ENGINEERING FLUID MECHANICS. **2091**

0893-4088 *See* ARTS & LETTERS (DAYTON, TENN.). **314**

0893-410X *See* WALTON TRIBUNE, THE. **5655**

0893-4118 *See* APPLE-WORKS FORUM. **1171**

0893-4142 *See* MINNESOTA UNITED METHODIST REPORTER. **5697**

0893-4150 *See* ROOTS & BRANCHES. **2471**

0893-4215 *See* COMMUNICATION REPORTS (PULLMAN, WASH.). **1107**

0893-4231 *See* PROTECTING CHILDREN. **5302**

0893-424X *See* FARMING SYSTEMS RESEARCH PAPER SERIES. **86**

0893-4266 *See* CONFERENCE PROCEEDINGS - IEEE PACIFIC RIM CONFERENCE ON COMMUNICATIONS, COMPUTERS AND SIGNAL PROCESSING. **1152**

0893-4282 See JOURNAL OF AGRICULTURAL & ENVIRONMENTAL ETHICS. **2251**

0893-4290 *See* NEWSLETTER - AFRICAN-AMERICAN FAMILY HISTORY ASSOCIATION. **2463**

0893-4304 *See* PORT JEFFERSON RECORD (1969). **5720**

0893-4347 *See* RESEARCH RECOMMENDATIONS. **707**

0893-4401 *See* RYE CHRONICLE, THE. **5720**

0893-4428 *See* ADVENTURES OF SUPERMAN, THE. **4856**

0893-4452 *See* ENVIRONMENTAL NUTRITION. **4190**

0893-4460 *See* JOE WEIDER'S MEN'S FITNESS. **2599**

0893-4509 *See* PHOENIX (MINNEAPOLIS, MINN.), THE. **4608**

0893-4525 *See* RACONTEUR (BATON ROUGE, LA. ANNUAL ED.), LE. **2469**

0893-4533 *See* ASBESTOS CONTROL REPORT. **2224**

0893-4592 *See* SIGNAL (LISBON, OHIO). **5730**

0893-4606 *See* ON ONE WHEEL. **429**

0893-4630 *See* BIRD OBSERVER (BELMONT, MASS.). **5615**

0893-4665 *See* ROV REVIEW. **2095**

0893-4738 *See* NURSE SEARCH. **3863**

0893-4746 *See* PREFERRED TRAVELLER. **5489**

0893-4827 *See* JOURNAL OF POLYGRAPH SCIENCE, THE. **3167**

0893-4843 *See* CD COMPUTING NEWS. **1276**

0893-4851 *See* VERA LEX. **2253**

0893-486X *See* CHILDREN'S FOCUS. **1061**

0893-4940 *See* NIOSH CURRENT INTELLIGENCE BULLETIN. **2866**

0893-4975 *See* NAPL SPECIAL REPORT. **4566**

0893-4983 *See* DIFFERENTIAL AND INTEGRAL EQUATIONS. **3503**

0893-5017 *See* EXCEL (SAN FRANCISCO, CALIF.). **5200**

0893-5025 *See* ALTERNATIVES (INGRAM, TEX.). **2595**

0893-5068 *See* AIDS PATIENT CARE. **3664**

0893-5084 *See* AIDS REPORT (WESTPORT, CONN.). **3664**

0893-5106 *See* OAPSE/AFSCME ADVOCATE. **1868**

0893-5149 *See* JOURNAL (OGDENSBURG, N.Y.), THE. **5717**

0893-5165 *See* CURRENT CONTENTS. HEALTH SERVICES ADMINISTRATION. **4772**

0893-5203 *See* STARMONT HARDCOVER COLLECTION. **3439**

0893-5211 *See* STARMONT FACSIMILE FICTION. **3439**

0893-5238 *See* AMERICAN FITNESS. **2595**

0893-5246 *See* ROYAL AMBASSADOR LEADERSHIP. **4994**

0893-5254 *See* PIONEER (MEMPHIS, TENN.). **4986**

0893-5262 *See* LAD (MEMPHIS, TENN.). **5062**

0893-5289 *See* JOURNAL / OHIO SCHOOL BOARDS ASSOCIATION. **1865**

0893-5297 *See* SUPERCONDUCTORS UPDATE. **2082**

0893-5300 *See* IMMUNODEFICIENCY REVIEWS. **3670**

0893-5335 *See* SHOWPAGE. **1202**

0893-536X *See* HEARTS AFLAME. **5030**

0893-5378 *See* YALE JOURNAL OF CRITICISM, THE. **3356**

0893-5386 *See* JOURNAL HOLDINGS IN THE NATIONAL CAPITAL AREA. **2921**

0893-5394 *See* AMERICAN INDIAN AND ALASKA NATIVE MENTAL HEALTH RESEARCH. **5271**

0893-5408 *See* DAWSON COUNTY GENEALOGICAL NEWSLETTER. **2445**

0893-5416 *See* JOURNAL OF THE MAGOFFIN COUNTY HISTORICAL SOCIETY, THE. **2456**

0893-5424 *See* HIGH-TECHNOLOGY BUSINESSTRENDS. **679**

0893-5483 *See* PROGRESS IN SELF PSYCHOLOGY. **4609**

0893-5556 *See* BED TIMES. **2904**

0893-5564 *See* CAPITAL JOURNAL (PIERRE, S.D.). **5743**

0893-5572 *See* BOSTON WOMAN. **5552**

0893-5580 *See* ANTIPODES (BROOKLYN, NEW YORK, N.Y.). **3362**

0893-5602 *See* MEANS HEAVY CONSTRUCTION COST DATA. **620**

0893-5696 *See* RETHINKING MARXISM. **1594**

0893-5718 *See* MONROE COUNTY GENEALOGICAL SOCIETY NEWS. **2461**

0893-5769 *See* WISCONSIN OUTDOOR JOURNAL. **4880**

0893-5777 *See* SHIPWRECKS & TREASURE MAGAZINE. **5456**

0893-5793 *See* SLUDGE MANAGEMENT SERIES. **2243**

0893-5939 *See* DIABETES IN THE NEWS (1987). **3728**

0893-5947 *See* CYCON COMMUNICATIONS' COMPUTER PR UPDATE. **758**

0893-5963 *See* CURRENTS IN COMPARATIVE ROMANCE LANGUAGES AND LITERATURES. **3379**

0893-5998 *See* NORC REPORTER, THE. **5252**

0893-6005 *See* NEW STUDIES IN AESTHETICS. **359**

0893-603X *See* INTERNATIONAL JOURNAL OF PERSONAL CONSTRUCT PSYCHOLOGY. **4591**

0893-6048 *See* WEEKLY AMERICAN (POPLAR BLUFF, MO.). **5704**

0893-6080 *See* NEURAL NETWORKS. **1215**

0893-6099 *See* HEALTH CARE LAW NEWSLETTER. **2977**

0893-6110 *See* ADVANCES IN BEHAVIORAL ASSESSMENT OF CHILDREN AND FAMILIES. **4571**

0893-6129 *See* FRONTIERS IN IMMUNOASSAY AND BIOTECHNOLOGY. **3692**

0893-6188 *See* JNMM : JOURNAL OF THE INSTITUTE OF NUCLEAR MATERIALS MANAGEMENT. **2156**

0893-620X *See* LIP SERVICE. **4129**

0893-6218 *See* PEDIATRIC THERAPEUTICS AND TOXICOLOGY. **3909**

0893-6226 *See* KALEIDOSCOPE (MADISON, WIS.). **1759**

0893-6242 *See* HEALTH & ENVIRONMENT DIGEST. **4777**

0893-6250 *See* MEDICAL PRODUCT MANUFACTURING NEWS. **3611**

0893-6293 *See* PERINATAL PRACTICE. **3766**

0893-6331 *See* INVITATION. BIBLE STUDIES FOR AGES 3-4. TEACHER. **4966**

0893-6366 *See* INVITATION. BIBLE STUDIES FOR AGES 5-6 (LEAFLETS). **4966**

0893-6382 *See* INVITATION. BIBLE STUDIES FOR AGES 5-6. TEACHER. **4966**

0893-6390 *See* INVITATION. BIBLE STUDIES FOR ELEMENTARY A (LEAFLETS). **4966**

0893-6439 *See* WINNING HOOPS. **4929**

0893-6447 *See* HARLEY WOMEN. **4851**

0893-6455 *See* SOFTWARE DIGEST RATINGS REPORT. **1290**

0893-651X *See* LEADSOURCE. CLEVELAND METRO EAST. **689**

0893-6528 *See* LEADSOURCE. CLEVELAND METRO WEST. **689**

0893-6552 *See* AI TODAY. **1211**

0893-6560 *See* WILDLIFE JOURNAL. **2209**

0893-6587 *See* AEROMED WEEK. **5270**

0893-6595 *See* OFFICE NURSE, THE. **3866**

0893-6609 *See* NEUROSCIENCE RESEARCH COMMUNICATIONS. **3843**

0893-6617 *See* GENESIS (MITCHELLVILLE, MD.). **4960**

0893-6633 *See* DYSMORPHOLOGY AND CLINICAL GENETICS. **4387**

0893-665X See CLINICAL DENTAL BRIEFING. **1319**

0893-6684 *See* POLYMER BLENDS, ALLOYS, AND INTERPENETRATING POLYMER NETWORKS ABSTRACTS. **988**

0893-6692 *See* ENVIRONMENTAL AND MOLECULAR MUTAGENESIS. **544**

0893-6773 *See* TRENDS IN LAW LIBRARY MANAGEMENT AND TECHNOLOGY. **3254**

0893-679X See INVITATION. BIBLE STUDIES FOR ELEMENTARY C (LEAFLETS). **4966**

0893-6862 *See* EUROPAISCHE STADTKULTUR. **5200**

0893-6889 *See* SEXUALITY AND LITERATURE. **3435**

0893-6935 *See* BERKELEY INSIGHTS IN LINGUISTICS AND SEMIOTICS. **3268**

0893-6943 *See* UNDERCAR DIGEST. **5427**

0893-7044 *See* SUSPECT CHEMICALS SOURCEBOOK. UPDATE SERVICE. **1030**

0893-7060 *See* FINANCIAL PLANNING NEWS. **898**

0893-7109 *See* ITC NEWS - UNITED STATES. DEPT. OF AGRICULTURE. INFORMATION TECHNOLOGY CENTER. **3219**

0893-7133 *See* NEW DEVELOPMENTS IN EMPLOYMENT DISCRIMINATION. **3152**

0893-7265 *See* LOS ANGELES (LAPORTE, PA.). **2537**

0893-7362 *See* ETHNIC REPORTER (CLAREMONT, CALIF.), THE. **2260**

0893-7400 *See* JOURNAL OF THE AMERICAN ACADEMY OF PHYSICIAN ASSISTANTS. **3597**

0893-7443 *See* LEBEN (CLAYTON, MO.), DAS. **3297**

0893-7451 *See* QUIRK'S MARKETING RESEARCH REVIEW. **765**

0893-746X *See* ROCKY MOUNTAIN SPORTSMAN (COLORADO SPRINGS, COLO.). **4878**

0893-7524 *See* ARTHRITIS CARE AND RESEARCH. **3803**

0893-7613 *See* AIDS CRISIS, THE. **3663**

0893-7621 *See* HOME BUSINESS ADVISOR. **680**

0893-763X *See* CURRENT THERAPY NEWSLETTER. **3570**

0893-7648 *See* MOLECULAR NEUROBIOLOGY. **3838**

0893-7664 *See* TOMBSTONE, THE. **2475**

0893-7702 *See* AQUAPHYTE. **500**

0893-7745 *See* DENVER BUSINESS JOURNAL, THE. **665**

0893-7753 *See* GILA HERITAGE. **2451**

0893-7788 *See* MARKETING FOR LAWYERS. **3006**

0893-7796 *See* CANADIAN ORTHODOX MISSIONARY, THE. **5039**

0893-780X *See* JOURNAL OF COMPENSATION AND BENEFITS. **1682**

0893-7842 *See* NEW AMERICAN WRITING. **3415**

0893-7850 *See* NEW PERSPECTIVES QUARTERLY. **4484**

0893-7877 *See* TEXAS INSTRUMENTS TECHNICAL JOURNAL. **1230**

0893-7915 *See* DAILY TRIBUNE (AMES, IOWA), THE. **5669**

0893-7931 *See* NINETEENTH-CENTURY STUDIES (CHARLESTON, S.C.). **3417**

0893-7958 *See* AMETHYST (ATLANTA, GA.). **2793**

0893-8067 *See* LIVING PHYSICS. **4411**

0893-8075 *See* PCNETTER NEWSLETTER, THE. **1199**

0893-8083 *See* LISTEN REAL LOUD. **5560**

0893-8091 *See* CHEER NEWS TODAY. **4889**

0893-8121 *See* PART B NEWS. **2889**

0893-8172 *See* MUNICIPAL WORKER LAW BULLETIN. **3152**

0893-8199 *See* DEFENSE & INDUSTRY WORLD REPORT. **4041**

0893-8202 *See* NATIONAL UNDERWRITER (LIFE, HEALTH / FINANCIAL SERVICES ED.). **2889**

0893-8210 *See* SPORTS, PARKS & RECREATION LAW REPORTER, THE. **3058**

0893-8229 *See* MEDICAL MALPRACTICE DEFENSE REPORTER, THE. **3008**

0893-8245 *See* RISK MANAGEMENT REPORTER FOR THE HEALTH CARE PROFESSIONAL, THE. **3044**

0893-8261 *See* COMPUTE!S PC MAGAZINE. **1180**

0893-8288 *See* MOUNT OLIVE REVIEW. **3413**

0893-8342 See MEDIA STUDIES JOURNAL. **1117**

0893-8377 *See* COMPUTER RESELLER NEWS. **1244**

0893-8415 *See* FEDERAL MANAGERS QUARTERLY. **868**

0893-844X *See* SYRACUSE NEW TIMES. **2493**

0893-8474 *See* AUTISM RESEARCH REVIEW INTERNATIONAL, THE. **4575**

0893-8482 See PACIFIC RIM ENTREPRENEUR. ASIAN MARKET UPDATE. **848**

0893-8490 *See* METROPOLITAN REVIEW (CHICAGO, ILL.). 2828

0893-8512 *See* CLINICAL MICROBIOLOGY REVIEWS. 561

0893-8520 *See* AARCTIMES. 3947

0893-8547 *See* VETERAN (WASHINGTON, D.C.). 4060

0893-858X *See* ASBESTOS ABATEMENT REPORT. 4767

0893-8598 *See* JAPANESE AMERICAN VERNACULAR NEWSPAPERS, ABSTRACT-INDEX. 3219

0893-8601 *See* BULLETIN / THE JAPANESE AMERICAN LIBRARY. 2257

0893-861X *See* CONDENSED MATTER THEORIES. 4401

0893-8652 *See* JOURNAL OF THE AMERICAN BOARD OF FAMILY PRACTICE, THE. 3738

0893-8660 *See* GLASS COLLECTOR'S DIGEST. 2589

0893-8717 *See* PROCEEDINGS OF THE INTERNATIONAL CONFERENCE / ... COASTAL ENGINEERING CONFERENCE. 2029

0893-8725 *See* CARDIOTHORACIC SURGERY. 3701

0893-8776 *See* INTERNATIONAL WATER REPORT. 2233

0893-8822 *See* CONTEMPORARY ISSUES IN FETAL AND NEONATAL MEDICINE. 3759

0893-8849 *See* JOURNAL OF THE WORLD AQUACULTURE SOCIETY. 2307

0893-8873 *See* BANKING WEEK. 777

0893-8911 *See* MANHATTAN LAWYER. 3006

0893-8946 *See* SITUATION AND OUTLOOK REPORT. TOBACCO. 5373

0893-8962 *See* KASHU MAINICHI. 5636

0893-8970 *See* CHAR-KOOSTA NEWS. 4505

0893-8989 *See* POLICE (CARLSBAD, CALIF.). 3171

0893-8997 *See* TEXAS FFA MAGAZINE. 141

0893-9004 *See* NEWS-REVIEW (INYOKERN, CALIF.), THE. 5637

0893-9055 *See* PANTOGRAPH OF POSTAL STATIONERY, THE. 2786

0893-9063 *See* NEW YORK BAPTIST, THE. 4981

0893-908X *See* ANDERSON HERALD-BULLETIN. 5662

0893-9128 *See* GRANT PROPOSAL NEWS. 4729

0893-9136 *See* COMMONWEALTH LETTERS. 1470

0893-9349 *See* INSIDE WORD (MACINTOSH ED.). 1287

0893-9373 *See* TODAY'S BEST NONFICTION. 3447

0893-9403 See HISTORIC PRESERVATION FORUM. 2618

0893-9454 *See* REVIEW OF FINANCIAL STUDIES, THE. 809

0893-9462 *See* SMART CARD MONTHLY. 1203

0893-9489 *See* ACTION PURSUIT GAMES. 4856

0893-9500 *See* EAR (NEW YORK, N.Y.). 4115

0893-9519 *See* BERNARD ZICK'S REAL ESTATE FINANCING & MORTGAGE REPORT. 778

0893-9535 See HUMANE INNOVATIONS AND ALTERNATIVES. 226

0893-9543 *See* VILLAGE VIEWS. 310

0893-9586 *See* SYSTEMTALK. 1204

0893-9640 *See* SUPREME COURT LAW JOURNAL. 3061

0893-9659 *See* APPLIED MATHEMATICS LETTERS. 3495

0893-9675 *See* CRITICAL REVIEWS IN ONCOGENESIS. 3815

0893-9683 *See* CONDE NAST'S TRAVELER. 5466

0893-9691 *See* PENNSYLVANIA EDUCATION LAW REPORT. 3025

0893-9780 *See* ANNUAL REPORT OF THE CONNECTICUT HISTORICAL SOCIETY, THE. 2720

0893-9810 See APPLICATIONS OF ARTIFICIAL INTELLIGENCE: KNOWLEDGE-BASED SYSTEMS. 1211

0893-9888 *See* SIGN BUSINESS. 710

0893-9934 *See* CD-ROM LIBRARIAN. 1174

0894-0061 *See* JOURNAL OF CUTANEOUS AGING & COSMETIC DERMATOLOGY. 3721

0894-0207 *See* CONTEST NEWS-LETTER. 758

0894-0223 *See* CARIBBEAN NEWSLETTER (NEW YORK, N.Y.). 2727

0894-0258 *See* HOMEBUYER'S GUIDE. DALLAS/FT. WORTH. 4838

0894-0282 *See* MOLECULAR PLANT-MICROBE INTERACTIONS. 518

0894-0304 *See* LUTHERAN COMMENTATOR. 4975

0894-0347 *See* JOURNAL OF THE AMERICAN MATHEMATICAL SOCIETY. 3515

0894-041X *See* POWER PACK. 1068

0894-0436 *See* ARCHITECTURAL LIGHTING. 289

0894-0479 *See* INK & GALL. 353

0894-0487 *See* FAMILY FOOTSTEPS QUARTERLY. 2447

0894-0525 *See* CHI HSIANG HSUEH PAO (CHUNG-KUO CHI HSIANG HSUEH HUI). 1421

0894-0533 *See* INDOOR POLLUTION LAW REPORT. 3113

0894-0584 *See* MID-ISLAND HERALD (PLAINVIEW-OLD BETHPAGE EDITION). 5718

0894-0649 See IEG DIRECTORY OF SPONSORSHIP MARKETING. 926

0894-0657 *See* NOTRE DAME STUDIES IN LAW AND CONTEMPORARY ISSUES. 3019

0894-0681 *See* EQUITY & EXCELLENCE. 1744

0894-069X *See* NAVAL RESEARCH LOGISTICS. 4180

0894-0711 *See* PC AI. 1215

0894-0762 *See* AFRO SCHOLAR NEWSLETTER. 5189

0894-0789 *See* NEW TECHNOLOGY WEEK. 5133

0894-0797 *See* CARD NEWS. 782

0894-0800 *See* NORTHWESTERNER (LARKSPUR, CALIF.). 5433

0894-0819 *See* SIGOIS BULLETIN. 1249

0894-0886 *See* SYNCHROTRON RADIATION NEWS. 4442

0894-0959 *See* SEMINARS IN DIALYSIS. 3640

0894-0975 *See* CINCINNATI DENTAL SOCIETY BULLETIN (1979). 1319

0894-0983 *See* RESEARCH SAFETY MONOGRAPH SERIES. 3823

0894-1009 *See* COMPENDIUM (NEWTOWN, PA.). 1319

0894-1025 *See* CLINICAL HEMOSTASIS REVIEW. 3565

0894-1033 *See* SORKIN'S DIRECTORY OF BUSINESS & GOVERNMENT (KANSAS CITY ED.). 712

0894-1041 *See* WATKINS REPORT ON CONSULTANTS' MARKETING STRATEGIES, THE. 889

0894-105X *See* TAMPA BAY (CLEARWATER, FLA.). 2762

0894-1076 *See* PERSPECTIVES IN NURSING. 3866

0894-1084 *See* PROCEEDINGS OF THE AMERICAN ACADEMY OF CARDIOVASCULAR PERFUSION, THE. 3709

0894-1106 *See* AFRRI REPORTS. 441

0894-1114 *See* DIRECTORY OF MEDICAL FACILITIES. REGION VIII, DENVER. 3779

0894-1122 See PEDIATRIC EMERGENCY & CRITICAL CARE. 3908

0894-1130 *See* JOURNAL OF HAND THERAPY. 4380

0894-1149 *See* JAPAN MATERIALS NEWS (METALS PARK, OHIO). 4005

0894-1181 *See* BUREAU COUNTY REPUBLICAN, THE. 5658

0894-1211 *See* OFFICIAL DETECTIVE. 5074

0894-1238 *See* MUSIC & SOUND RETAILER, THE. 4133

0894-1254 *See* LANDSCAPE MANAGEMENT. 2423

0894-1270 *See* AUTO AGE (VAN NUYS, CALIF.). 5404

0894-1289 *See* EAA EXPERIMENTER. 18

0894-1300 *See* DRUG ENFORCEMENT REPORT (NEW YORK, N.Y.). 1343

0894-1319 *See* THIRD WORLD WEEK. 2912

0894-1335 *See* YOUR WORLD (WASHINGTON, D.C.). 2495

0894-1408 *See* LIBERTY (PORT TOWNSEND, WASH.). 4481

0894-1491 *See* GLIA (NEW YORK, N.Y.). 3833

0894-1513 *See* AIRPORT POCKET GUIDE (DOMESTIC ED.). 5460

0894-1521 *See* WORLDWIDE GOVERNMENT DIRECTORY, WITH INTERNATIONAL ORGANIZATIONS. 4695

0894-153X *See* WALKER'S MANUAL OF WESTERN CORPORATIONS. 718

0894-1599 *See* DAILY EASTERN NEWS, THE. 1091

0894-1653 *See* DAIRYMEN'S DIGEST (MORNING GLORY FARMS ED.). 194

0894-170X *See* CONNECTIONS (FULLERTON, CALIF.). 1180

0894-1718 *See* OAG TRAVEL PLANNER. (EUROPEAN EDITION). 5487

0894-1734 See OAG TRAVEL PLANNER (PACIFIC ASIA ED.). 5487

0894-1742 *See* DTEXPERT. 4721

0894-1769 *See* NEWSLETTER / NATIONAL ALOPECIA AREATA FOUNDATION, NAAF. 3715

0894-1777 *See* EXPERIMENTAL THERMAL AND FLUID SCIENCE. 4427

0894-1793 *See* ITALIAN JOURNAL. 2693

0894-1815 *See* CPA MANAGING PARTNER REPORT. 742

0894-184X *See* THOMAS GROCERY REGISTER. FOOD MARKETERS' HANDBOOK. 2360

0894-1858 *See* COMPUTER LAW FORMS HANDBOOK. 2954

0894-1866 *See* COMPUTERS IN PHYSICS. 4401

0894-1882 *See* DON LARSON'S BUSINESS NEWSLETTER. 669

0894-1904 *See* CLAMOR (LAREDO, TEX.). 2531

0894-1912 *See* JOURNAL OF CONTINUING EDUCATION IN THE HEALTH PROFESSIONS, THE. 3594

0894-1920 *See* SOCIETY & NATURAL RESOURCES. 2205

0894-1939 *See* JOURNAL OF INVESTIGATIVE SURGERY. 3967

0894-2005 *See* JOB SHOP TECHNOLOGY (MIDWEST EDITION). 1613

0894-203X *See* IMMUNOHEMATOLOGY. 3772

0894-2064 *See* BROWNSVILLE HERALD (BROWNSVILLE, TEX. : 1910). 5747

0894-2080 *See* EMPLOYEE SECURITY CONNECTION. 940

0894-2188 *See* HOLLYWOOD STUDIO MAGAZINE. 4072

0894-2218 *See* MOUNTAIN PRESS (SEVIERVILLE, TENN.), THE. 5745

0894-2226 *See* SERLIN REPORT ON PARALLEL PROCESSING, THE. 1202

0894-2277 *See* CURRENT SURGICAL DIAGNOSIS & TREATMENT. 3963

0894-2285 *See* PRINCIPLES OF CLINICAL ELECTROCARDIOGRAPHY. 3709

0894-2293 *See* CURRENT EMERGENCY DIAGNOSIS & TREATMENT. 3724

0894-2307 *See* DECATUR DAILY DEMOCRAT. 5663

0894-234X *See* ASIAN ART. 343

0894-2358 *See* HISPANIC BOOKS BULLETIN. 4828

0894-2366 *See* ADVANCES IN CRIMINOLOGICAL THEORY. 3156

0894-2374 *See* MCGRAW-HILL HAZARDOUS WASTE MONITOR. 2236

0894-2498 *See* JOURNAL OF YOUTH SERVICES IN LIBRARIES. 3221

0894-2528 *See* THEORETICAL PARAPSYCHOLOGY. 4243

0894-2536 *See* CHINA CENTER OF ADVANCED SCIENCE AND TECHNOLOGY (WORLD LABORATORY) SYMPOSIUM/WORKSHOP PROCEEDINGS. 5093

0894-2552 See WASHINGTON EVENING JOURNAL, THE. 5673

0894-2560 See CANTON HERALD (CANTON, TEX.). 5748

0894-2595 See CARTOMANIA. 2558

0894-2609 See MATURE MARKET REPORT. 933

0894-2684 See JOURNAL OF AEROSOL MEDICINE. 3949

0894-2692 See MLM NEWS. 762

0894-2706 See AMERICAN GOLD NEWS & WESTERN PROSPECTOR. 1437

0894-2714 See CUBAN HERITAGE. 5197

0894-2757 See YEAR BOOK OF GERIATRICS AND GERONTOLOGY. 3755

0894-2803 See SECURITIES INTERNATIONAL. 1520

0894-2811 See OCCUPATIONAL AND ENVIRONMENTAL MEDICINE REPORT, THE. 5300

0894-282X See PUBLISHING NOTES. 4819

0894-2838 See JOURNAL OF COMMUNICATION AND RELIGION, THE. 4968

0894-2846 See ENCYCLOPEDIA OF ASSOCIATIONS. REGIONAL, STATE, AND LOCAL ORGANIZATIONS. 5231

0894-296X See HARRIS OHIO SERVICES DIRECTORY. 1608

0894-301X See BUGLE (COTTONWOOD, ARIZ.), THE. 5629

0894-3036 See LINKS (NEW YORK, N.Y.). 4789

0894-3079 See WORLD FOOTWEAR. 1088

0894-3087 See WORLD LEATHER. 3186

0894-3109 See NORTHWEST ETHNIC NEWS. 2270

0894-3117 See REFERENCECLIPPER. 1201

0894-3184 See NURSING SCIENCE QUARTERLY. 3865

0894-3214 See PACKAGING TECHNOLOGY AND SCIENCE. 4221

0894-3230 See JOURNAL OF PHYSICAL ORGANIC CHEMISTRY. 1043

0894-3257 See JOURNAL OF BEHAVIORAL DECISION MAKING. 4594

0894-3265 See FORUM. 2449

0894-3273 See SAN JUAN RECORD (1953), THE. 5757

0894-3311 See OSTEOPOROSIS UPDATE. 3624

0894-3346 See FOCUS ON THE FAMILY (ARCADIA, CALIF. 1982). 2280

0894-3354 See TEXAS JOURNAL OF IDEAS, HISTORY, AND CULTURE. 2855

0894-3362 See NORTHERN REVIEW, THE. 326

0894-3370 See INTERNATIONAL JOURNAL OF NUMERICAL MODELLING. 2067

0894-3389 See CARE BEARS. 1061

0894-3397 See ALIEN LEGION, THE. 4856

0894-3427 See MASSACHUSETTS FACTS. 2538

0894-3443 See CAR STEREO REVIEW (LOS ANGELES, CALIF.). 5316

0894-346X See DIRECTORY MARKETPLACE. 415

0894-3478 See INSIGHTS (MANHATTAN BEACH, CALIF.). 760

0894-3494 See ISLAND (OAKLAND, CALIF.). 2693

0894-3524 See INSIGHTS (CLIFTON, N.J.). 3100

0894-3532 See PERSONAL COMPUTER REPORT (MINEOLA, N.Y.). 1199

0894-3605 See LOCOMOTIVE ENGINEERS JOURNAL (1987). 1688

0894-3656 See NURSING DATA REVIEW. 3863

0894-3672 See AMBULATORY CARE. 3775

0894-3699 See ERIC (DUBLIN, OHIO). 1745

0894-3710 See SMALL ANIMAL PRACTICE. 5522

0894-3737 See RICOCHET (NEW YORK, N.Y.). 330

0894-3745 See ISI ATLAS OF SCIENCE. IMMUNOLOGY. 3672

0894-3753 See ISI ATLAS OF SCIENCE. BIOCHEMISTRY. 488

0894-3788 See ELECTRIC UTILITY BUSINESS. 4760

0894-3796 See JOURNAL OF ORGANIZATIONAL BEHAVIOR. 4598

0894-3826 See WASHINGTON CRIME NEWS SERVICES' CORPORATE SECURITY DIGEST. 3178

0894-3842 See GOVERNING (WASHINGTON, D.C.). 4475

0894-3850 See PENNSYLVANIA FACTS. 2543

0894-3907 See REVIEW OF RESEARCH IN DEVELOPMENTAL EDUCATION. 1780

0894-3907 See JOURNAL OF DEVELOPMENTAL EDUCATION. 1756

0894-3923 See SELECTIVE ELECTRODE REVIEWS. 1035

0894-3958 See BANK ACCOUNTING & FINANCE. 774

0894-3982 See ELECTRONIC PUBLISHING. 4814

0894-3990 See BABY CONNECTION, THE. 1727

0894-4024 See BOSTON BULLETIN ON CHEMICALS AND DISEASE. 4294

0894-4032 See WICHITA BUSINESS JOURNAL. 720

0894-4040 See AMERICAN INDIAN REPORT. 2719

0894-4059 See MIDWESTERN FOLKLORE. 2322

0894-4083 See COUNTRY ACCENTS. 2899

0894-4105 See NEUROPSYCHOLOGY. 4605

0894-4113 See GIFT REPORTER. 2584

0894-4172 See HEALTH CONFIDENTIAL. 4779

0894-4180 See ENERGY WEST (SAN CLEMENTE, CALIF.). 1942

0894-4202 See GUIDE TO STATE AND FEDERAL RESOURCES FOR ECONOMIC DEVELOPMENT, THE. 1493

0894-4237 See COACHING VOLLEYBALL. 4890

0894-4245 See COACHING WOMEN'S BASKETBALL. 4890

0894-4253 See PLAY & CULTURE. 5213

0894-4288 See THOMAS REGISTER'S MID-YEAR GUIDE TO FACTORY AUTOMATION PRODUCTS, SYSTEMS, SERVICES. 1235

0894-4342 See MEANS ASSEMBLIES COST DATA. 620

0894-4377 See YOUTH SPORTS. 4931

0894-4385 See ADVANCES IN UROLOGY. 3988

0894-4393 See SOCIAL SCIENCE COMPUTER REVIEW. 1272

0894-4431 See KANSAS SPORTS. 4902

0894-444X See NORTHWEST LABOR PRESS. 5733

0894-4458 See PACIFIC COAST JOURNAL. 2801

0894-4520 See SENSORY SYSTEMS. 587

0894-4547 See GUIDE TO THE AMERICAN LEFT (KANSAS CITY, MO. 1984). 4502

0894-4563 See PLANT BIOLOGY. 523

0894-4652 See MEXICO MAGAZINE (CARBONDALE, COLO.). 2538

0894-4679 See HEALTH MANAGER'S UPDATE. 4780

0894-4806 See LONG ISLAND BUSINESS NEWS. 690

0894-4822 See CFO ALERT. 740

0894-4849 See DANCE (NEW YORK, N.Y. 1988). 1312

0894-4857 See MERTON ANNUAL, THE. 4976

0894-4865 See FAMILY BUSINESS REVIEW. 674

0894-4873 See PSYCHIATRY DRUG ALERTS. 3934

0894-4903 See NEW YORK REAL ESTATE LAW REPORTER. 4842

0894-4946 See GRAVURE (NEW YORK, N.Y. 1987). 4565

0894-4954 See GATESVILLE MESSENGER AND STAR-FORUM. 5750

0894-4997 See ... DIRECTORY OF U.S. CORPORATIONS, THE. 667

0894-5004 See SURVEY OF WORLD ADVERTISING EXPENDITURES. 767

0894-5020 See ADVANCE RELEASE OF DATA FOR THE ... STATISTICAL YEARBOOK OF THE ELECTRIC UTILITY INDUSTRY. 4759

0894-5055 See TOY FARMER, THE. 2778

0894-5098 See MEDICAL HYPNOANALYSIS JOURNAL. 4603

0894-5128 See LODGING AND RESTAURANT INDEX. 5483

0894-5136 See INDIA BRIEFING. 2653

0894-5152 See SCHOOL INTERVENTION REPORT. 1782

0894-5179 See MUSTANG (LOS ANGELES, CALIF.). 5421

0894-5217 See REMOTE SENSING NEWSLETTER IN ANTHROPOLOGY AND ARCHAEOLOGY. 4419

0894-5225 See TELEVISION MARKET INSIGHT. 1167

0894-5233 See KRISIS (INTERNATIONAL CIRCLE FOR RESEARCH IN PHILOSOPHY). 4351

0894-525X See WALT DISNEY'S MICKEY MOUSE. 1071

0894-5268 See WALT DISNEY UNCLE SCROOGE. 4867

0894-5284 See WALT DISNEY'S COMICS AND STORIES. 4867

0894-5322 See OIL & GAS RESERVE DISCLOSURES. 4269

0894-5365 See CORPUS CHRISTI CALLER-TIMES. 5748

0894-5373 See ID (NEW YORK, N.Y. : 1984). 2098

0894-5373 See I.D. 2098

0894-5403 See WOODSHOP NEWS. NORTHEAST. 2406

0894-5446 See CAROLINA PIEDMONT. 5466

0894-5489 See MINIATURE BOOK SOCIETY NEWSLETTER, THE. 4830

0894-5535 See CHALLENGE (BLOOMINGTON, ILL.). 4858

0894-5632 See MINNESOTA THOROUGHBRED JOURNAL. 2801

0894-5640 See CHICAGO TIMES MAGAZINE. 2530

0894-5659 See CROCHET PATTERNS BY HERRSCHNERS. 5183

0894-5748 See EXEC-U-TARY, THE. 673

0894-5764 See INDUSTRIAL ENERGY BULLETIN. 1610

0894-5772 See SOUTHWESTERN ARCHIVIST. 3250

0894-5802 See VARBUSINESS. 1239

0894-5810 See HIGH PERFORMANCE OPTOMETRY. 4215

0894-5837 See WRITING TEACHER (SAN ANTONIO, TEX.). 1908

0894-5853 See CHOICES IN CARDIOLOGY. 3702

0894-587X See ADMINISTRATION AND POLICY IN MENTAL HEALTH. 5270

0894-5888 See JOURNAL OF ADVANCEMENT IN MEDICINE. 3593

0894-5926 See CONNEXIONS (CUPERTINO, CALIF.). 1241

0894-5942 See WATERWORKER. 1401

0894-5950 See COMPOSER NEWS. 4111

0894-5969 See ADVANCES IN BUSINESS MARKETING AND PURCHASING. 920

0894-5985 See NRAO NEWSLETTER. 397

0894-5993 See LEGAL STUDIES FORUM, THE. 3000

0894-6019 See URBAN ANTHROPOLOGY AND STUDIES OF CULTURAL SYSTEMS AND WORLD ECONOMIC DEVELOPMENT. 247

0894-6027 See WORLDWIDE HOTEL INDUSTRY. 2810

0894-6043 See CASE RESEARCH JOURNAL. 863

0894-606X See SHIRIM. 3471

0894-6078 See NEW PRESS (QUEENS, N.Y.), THE. 3416

0894-6108 See ULI MARKET PROFILES. 4848

0894-6116 See PODIATRY TRACTS. 3918

0894-6140 See READING RAINBOW GAZETTE. 5720

0894-6159 See GNOSIS (SAN FRANCISCO, CALIF.). 4960

0894-6175 See ASSET SALES REPORT. 773

0894-6183 See SPICE. 4999

ISSN Index

0894-6213 See COMPUTER INDUSTRY FORECASTS (1987). **1236**

0894-6337 See EUROPEAN STUDIES JOURNAL, THE. **2687**

0894-6361 See STUDIES IN THE BIBLE AND EARLY CHRISTIANITY. **5019**

0894-6388 See JOURNAL OF THE KAFKA SOCIETY OF AMERICA. **3345**

0894-6396 See CHAMINADE LITERARY REVIEW. **3339**

0894-6418 See CSR HOTLINE. **1153**

0894-6434 See HERE IS YOUR INDIANA GOVERNMENT. **4654**

0894-6442 See MYTHS AND FACTS. **4529**

0894-6469 See SUPERB CROSSWORDS. **4866**

0894-6507 See IEEE TRANSACTIONS ON SEMICONDUCTOR MANUFACTURING. **2063**

0894-6523 See MONGOLIA SOCIETY NEWSLETTER (1985), THE. **2659**

0894-6566 See JOURNAL OF ELDER ABUSE & NEGLECT. **5291**

0894-6574 See IBD NETWORK PROFILE. **681**

0894-6582 See BUSINESS ETHICS (MADISON, WIS.). **2249**

0894-6590 See EPILEPSY ADVANCES IN CLINICAL EXPERIMENTAL RESEARCH. **3832**

0894-6604 See X-FACTOR. **4868**

0894-6620 See IFR. **23**

0894-6655 See INSIDE EPA'S ENVIRONMENTAL POLICY ALERT. **3113**

0894-6663 See GOLD BOOK OF PHOTOGRAPHY PRICES. **4370**

0894-668X See MARITIME ADVISOR. COURT CASE DIGEST, THE. **3181**

0894-6728 See ATJ NEWSLETTER. **3267**

0894-6779 See PLASMAPHERESIS. **3627**

0894-6809 See IC MASTER. **2057**

0894-6817 See CORPORATE FINANCE. **784**

0894-6825 See BUSINESS AND ECONOMIC HISTORY. **645**

0894-7031 See DIRECTORY OF LIBRARY & INFORMATION PROFESSIONALS. **3207**

0894-7058 See ESSENTIAL GUIDE TO PRESCRIPTION DRUGS, THE. **4303**

0894-7074 See UPTIME FOR THE PC. **1206**

0894-7120 See NABOKOVIAN, THE. **3414**

0894-7155 See AG CONSULTANT. **45**

0894-7163 See EARTHQUAKES & VOLCANOES. **1404**

0894-7317 See JOURNAL OF THE AMERICAN SOCIETY OF ECHOCARDIOGRAPHY. **3707**

0894-7376 See BACKLETTER, THE. **3554**

0894-7414 See SPECIALTY AUTOMOTIVE PARTS AND ACCESSORIES. **5425**

0894-7465 See ROCKTON-ROSCOE HERALD. **5662**

0894-7473 See M & S TIMES. **5386**

0894-7481 See WOODWORKER, THE. **5734**

0894-752X See CREDIT UNION REPORT. **786**

0894-7589 See PLIMOTH PLANTATION JOURNAL : THE NEWSLETTER OF PLIMOTH PLANTATION. **2754**

0894-7597 See RESPONSE TO THE VICTIMIZATION OF WOMEN AND CHILDREN. **5306**

0894-7635 See SUPERCONDUCTOR WEEK. **1997**

0894-7651 See DISTRIBUTION CENTER MANAGEMENT. **866**

0894-7708 See PROCEEDINGS OF THE ANNUAL VETERINARY MEDICAL FORUM. **5519**

0894-7767 See MID-SOUTH HUNTING & FISHING NEWS. **4874**

0894-7775 See UNION LABOR JOURNAL. **1716**

0894-7821 See TEACHERS INTERACTION. **5002**

0894-783X See SANTA ROSA NEWS (1987). **5713**

0894-7856 See BOW & ARROW HUNTING. **4869**

0894-7872 See NATIONAL NOTARY, THE. **4668**

0894-7899 See OAK SQUARE. **3419**

0894-7929 See EXPLORER (FALLS CHURCH, VA.), THE. **1323**

0894-7945 See NEWSLETTER OF THE AMERICAN ASSOCIATION OF AUSTRALIAN LITERARY STUDIES. **3349**

0894-7953 See MODERN DENTAL PRACTICE. **1330**

0894-7961 See HEALTHCARE TRENDS REPORT. **3782**

0894-7988 See CHILD (NEW YORK, N.Y.). **2277**

0894-802X See COMPASS, THE. **1353**

0894-8038 See VASCULAR SURGERY OUTLOOK. **3977**

0894-8046 See PERSPECTIVES IN VASCULAR SURGERY. **3972**

0894-8054 See PERSPECTIVES IN COLON AND RECTAL SURGERY. **3971**

0894-8062 See COLON AND RECTAL SURGERY OUTLOOK. **3962**

0894-8100 See NEW VOICE (LOUISVILLE, KY.). **5681**

0894-8119 See GUN LIST. **4873**

0894-8135 See GREENE COUNTY HISTORICAL JOURNAL. **2735**

0894-8186 See CAMERON'S READYART BULLETIN. **346**

0894-8194 See USAE. **5687**

0894-8216 See SPECULATORS MAGAZINE. **914**

0894-8267 See TEXTILE ANALYSIS BULLETIN SERVICE. **5357**

0894-8275 See AMERICAN JOURNAL OF DENTISTRY. **1315**

0894-8313 See STEPPING BACK IN TIME. **2473**

0894-833X See TALKING LEAVES (WARRENVILLE, ILL.). **2206**

0894-8348 See FURNITURE & CABINET MANUFACTURING. **2905**

0894-8356 See ALABAMA WILDLIFE. **4868**

0894-8410 See JOURNAL OF THE SOUTHWEST. **2742**

0894-8429 See HORTICULTURAL PRODUCTS REVIEW. **2419**

0894-8437 See ANIMAL HEALTH (WEST LAFAYETTE, IND.). **205**

0894-8445 See JOURNAL / CALIFORNIA RARE FRUIT GROWERS. **98**

0894-8453 See JOURNAL OF CAREER DEVELOPMENT. **4206**

0894-847X See AWRA MONOGRAPH SERIES. **5531**

0894-8488 See WILLIWAW. **3473**

0894-8542 See STARS AND STRIPES, THE NATIONAL TRIBUNE, THE. **4057**

0894-8550 See COMMENTS ON THEORETICAL BIOLOGY. **452**

0894-8569 See HPB SURGERY. **3965**

0894-8577 See JOURNAL OF CONTEMPLATIVE PSYCHOTHERAPY. **3928**

0894-8631 See LIBRARIES & CULTURE. **4829**

0894-864X See FILM WRITERS GUIDE. **4070**

0894-8658 See TELEVISION WRITERS GUIDE. **1141**

0894-8720 See KID CARE MAGAZINE. **5294**

0894-8755 See JOURNAL OF CLIMATE. **1426**

0894-8763 See JOURNAL OF APPLIED METEOROLOGY (1988). **1426**

0894-8771 See ULTRASOUND QUARTERLY. **3648**

0894-878X See NEUROPSYCHIATRY, NEUROPSYCHOLOGY, BEHAVIORAL NEUROLOGY. **3841**

0894-8801 See WHO KNOWS, A GUIDE TO WASHINGTON EXPERTS. **4695**

0894-8844 See BURLINGTON FREE PRESS (1923), THE. **5760**

0894-8860 See CRITICAL REVIEW OF BOOKS IN RELIGION. **3340**

0894-8879 See JOURNAL OF LAW AND ETHICS IN DENTISTRY. **1327**

0894-8895 See ANCESTRAL PURSUIT. **2437**

0894-8917 See BETWEEN THE LAKES. **2723**

0894-8925 See HARLAN FOOTPRINTS. **2452**

0894-8941 See COMPUTERS AND COMPUTING INFORMATION RESOURCES DIRECTORY. **1241**

0894-8968 See STRANGE MAGAZINE. **2493**

0894-900X See NATURAL GAS MARKETING ... INDUSTRY DIRECTORY. **4265**

0894-9018 See NATURAL GAS MARKETING. END USER DIRECTORY. **4265**

0894-9026 See ATCC QUARTERLY NEWSLETTER. **443**

0894-9034 See JOURNAL OF THE ACADEMY FOR EVANGELISM IN THEOLOGICAL EDUCATION. **4970**

0894-9042 See ACCESS (CHICAGO, ILL.). **1315**

0894-9077 See INTERNATIONAL JOURNAL OF EXPERT SYSTEMS. **1213**

0894-9085 See JOURNAL OF RATIONAL-EMOTIVE AND COGNITIVE-BEHAVIOR THERAPY. **4600**

0894-9093 See VACATIONS (HOUSTON, TEX.). **5498**

0894-9115 See AMERICAN JOURNAL OF PHYSICAL MEDICINE & REHABILITATION. **4379**

0894-9166 See ACTA MECHANICA SOLIDA SINICA. **5080**

0894-9190 See GEOGRAPHIC THESAURUS. **2562**

0894-9204 See EXPLORATION AND PRODUCTION THESAURUS. **3210**

0894-9212 See EDI NEWS. **1183**

0894-9239 See SMALL STREET JOURNAL (COLORADO SPRINGS, COLO.). **2924**

0894-9255 See JOURNAL OF ACQUIRED IMMUNE DEFICIENCY SYNDROMES. **3673**

0894-9263 See PREMIERE (NEW YORK, N.Y. 1987). **4076**

0894-928X See ISIE. **5290**

0894-9301 See CIO (FRAMINGHAM, MASS.). **863**

0894-931X See AIDS. **3663**

0894-9328 See PETERSON'S GUIDE TO TWO-YEAR COLLEGES. **1841**

0894-9336 See PETERSON'S GUIDE TO FOUR-YEAR COLLEGES. **1841**

0894-9344 See PETERSON'S ANNUAL GUIDES TO GRADUATE STUDY. BOOK 1, PETERSON'S GUIDE TO GRADUATE AND PROFESSIONAL PROGRAMS. **1840**

0894-9352 See PETERSON'S GUIDE TO GRADUATE PROGRAMS IN THE HUMANITIES AND SOCIAL SCIENCES. **1841**

0894-9360 See PETERSON'S ANNUAL GUIDES TO GRADUATE STUDY. BOOK 3, PETERSON'S GUIDE TO GRADUATE PROGRAMS IN THE BIOLOGICAL AND AGRICULTURAL SCIENCES. **1840**

0894-9379 See PETERSON'S ANNUAL GUIDES TO GRADUATE STUDY. BOOK 4, PETERSON'S GUIDE TO GRADUATE PROGRAMS IN THE PHYSICAL SCIENCES AND MATHEMATICS. **1840**

0894-9387 See PETERSON'S GUIDE TO GRADUATE PROGRAMS IN ENGINEERING AND APPLIED SCIENCES. **1841**

0894-9395 See PETERSON'S COLLEGE MONEY HANDBOOK. **1840**

0894-9409 See PETERSON'S GUIDE TO INDEPENDENT SECONDARY SCHOOLS. **1773**

0894-9417 See PETERSON'S SUMMER OPPORTUNITIES FOR KIDS AND TEENAGERS. **4853**

0894-9425 See PETERSON'S JOB OPPORTUNITIES FOR ENGINEERING, SCIENCE, AND COMPUTER GRADUATES. **4208**

0894-9433 See PETERSON'S JOB OPPORTUNITIES FOR BUSINESS AND LIBERAL ARTS GRADUATES. **703**

0894-9468 See VISUAL ANTHROPOLOGY (JOURNAL). **247**

0894-9581 See TELEPUBLISHING REPORT. **4820**

0894-959X See CLINICAL LABORATORY SCIENCE. **3566**

0894-9603 See MACINTOSH BUSINESS LETTER, THE. **1194**

0894-962X See TRUCKSTOP WORLD. **5398**

0894-9697 See BILL SHIPP'S GEORGIA. **4633**

0894-9743 See FLORIDA ENVIRONMENTS. **2172**

0894-9816 See LAM-MISPAHA. **5050**

0894-9832 See GENDERS (AUSTIN, TEX.). **2846**

0894-9840 See JOURNAL OF THEORETICAL PROBABILITY. 3515

0894-9859 See SYSTEMS PRACTICE. 1249

0894-9867 See JOURNAL OF TRAUMATIC STRESS. 4602

0894-9875 See FOUNDATIONS OF PHYSICS LETTERS. 4403

0894-9891 See MANAGED HEALTH CARE DIRECTORY. 3788

0894-9905 See MANAGED HEALTH CARE DIRECTORY. 3788

0894-9921 See PATRICIA SEYBOLD'S OFFICE COMPUTING REPORT. 1292

0894-993X See ACADEMIC LIBRARY BOOK REVIEW. 4822

0894-9948 See ARIZONA ONLINE USER GROUP. 1274

0894-9980 See HEALTHCARE COMMUNITY RELATIONS & MARKETING LETTER. 3583

0895-0008 See KNOWLEDGE CENTER COURSEWARE LIBRARY. 1193

0895-0016 See DEFENSE COUNSEL JOURNAL. 3089

0895-0032 See KATIPUNAN (OAKLAND, CALIF. : 1987). 2656

0895-0067 See BTA JOURNAL. 644

0895-0083 See COLORADO HISTORY NEWS. 2729

0895-0091 See EDISON-NORWOOD EDITION OF THE TIMES REVIEW. 5660

0895-0105 See EDGEBROOK EDITION OF THE TIMES REVIEW. 5660

0895-0113 See ROSEMONT EDITION OF THE TIMES. 5662

0895-013X See PARK RIDGE EDITION OF THE TIMES HERALD. 5661

0895-0148 See DES PLAINES EDITION OF THE TIMES. 5659

0895-0156 See IEEE COMPUTER APPLICATIONS IN POWER. 2059

0895-0164 See CHICAGO FED LETTER. 783

0895-0172 See JOURNAL OF NEUROPSYCHIATRY AND CLINICAL NEUROSCIENCES, THE. 3929

0895-0326 See BULLETIN (AUSTIN, TEX.), THE. 1172

0895-0334 See UNISYS WORLD. EUROPE. 1239

0895-0342 See HP CHRONICLE. EUROPE, THE. 1186

0895-0350 See SPORTS HERITAGE. 4922

0895-0377 See COUNTRY (GREENDALE, WIS.). 2531

0895-0385 See JOURNAL OF SPINAL DISORDERS. 3805

0895-0393 See FILMFAX. 4070

0895-0407 See ADVANCED COMPOSITES. 2100

0895-0482 See AMERICAN UNIVERSITY STUDIES. SERIES XXI, REGIONAL STUDIES. 2609

0895-0490 See AMERICAN UNIVERSITY STUDIES. SERIES XXII, LATIN AMERICAN STUDIES. 2719

0895-0512 See AMERICAN UNIVERSITY STUDIES. SERIES XXIV, AMERICAN LITERATURE. 3360

0895-0539 See CONCORD REVIEW, THE. 2614

0895-0563 See GEOTECHNICAL SPECIAL PUBLICATION. 2023

0895-0598 See SPORTING NEWS COLLEGE BASKETBALL, THE. 4921

0895-0601 See SPORTING NEWS ... PRO BASKETBALL YEARBOOK, THE. 4922

0895-0628 See WORD PROCESSING, QUALITY CLINIC. 1292

0895-0644 See DIABETES PATIENT. 3728

0895-0652 See JOURNAL OF DIABETES MANAGEMENT. 3731

0895-0660 See PRIMARY DIABETOLOGY. 3732

0895-0695 See SEISMOLOGICAL RESEARCH LETTERS. 1397

0895-075X See BICYCLE RIDER. 428

0895-0792 See HERITAGE (CARSON, CALIF.). 2262

0895-0822 See NEWSLETTER / THE CROW WING COUNTY HISTORICAL SOCIETY. 2750

0895-0830 See EPISCOPAL TEACHER. 5059

0895-0857 See PAST, PRESENT & FUTURE. 2543

0895-0865 See POTTER COUNTY HISTORICAL SOCIETY QUARTERLY BULLETIN. 2625

0895-0970 See TRADEWINDS (SAINT JOHN, V.I.). 5813

0895-0997 See CLASSIC TOY TRAINS. 2772

0895-1039 See TELLER VISION. 813

0895-1047 See CONVENIENT AUTOMOTIVE SERVICES RETAILER. 5412

0895-108X See HEALTHACTION MANAGERS. 4782

0895-1101 See ADVISING QUARTERLY, THE. 1722

0895-1136 See FOCUS ON THE FAMILY CLUBHOUSE. 1063

0895-1152 See QUARTERLY BULLETIN - ASHTABULA COUNTY HISTORICAL SOCIETY. 2755

0895-1179 See LIBRARY OUTREACH REPORTER. 3226

0895-1217 See ASSETS AND LIABILITIES OF INSURED DOMESTICALLY CHARTERED AND FOREIGN RELATED BANKING INSTITUTIONS. 773

0895-125X See ARTIFEX (MINNEAPOLIS, MINN.). 4575

0895-1268 See ARCHAEUS. 4575

0895-1292 See FORUM (FARGO, N.D.), THE. 5725

0895-1306 See RICHARD C YOUNG'S INTERNATIONAL GOLD REPORT. 1518

0895-1381 See NEW ADVOCATE (BOSTON, MASS.), THE. 3415

0895-139X See DIRECTORY OF BOOK, CATALOG, AND MAGAZINE PRINTERS. 4564

0895-1403 See LEADER IN THE CHURCH SCHOOL TODAY. 4973

0895-1454 See SITUATION AND OUTLOOK REPORT. WHEAT. 135

0895-1489 See MONTANA AGRESEARCH. 110

0895-1500 See SHEEP AND GOAT, WOOL AND MOHAIR. 221

0895-1543 See MUSI*KEY. 4138

0895-1551 See SAN ANTONIO BUSINESS JOURNAL. 709

0895-156X See CHARISMA AND CHRISTIAN LIFE. 4943

0895-1578 See PROCEEDINGS OF THE ... ANNUAL INSTITUTE OF OIL AND GAS LAW AND TAXATION. 3031

0895-1586 See OKLAHOMA HOME & LIFE STYLE. 2542

0895-1594 See MORGAN MESSENGER (BERKELEY SPRINGS, W. VA.). 5764

0895-1608 See PACKAGE PRINTING AND CONVERTING. 4220

0895-1624 See GEORGETOWN (WASHINGTON, D.C. : 1987). 1091

0895-1632 See BUSINESS JOURNAL (PHOENIX, ARIZ.), THE. 650

0895-1659 See DOCKET, THE. 2963

0895-1683 See HARVARD ALUMNI DIRECTORY. 1102

0895-1713 See ANNUAL DIGEST OF PUBLIC UTILITIES REPORTS. 4760

0895-173X See JOURNAL OF FORENSIC IDENTIFICATION. 3741

0895-1748 See TRAINING AND DEVELOPMENT LITERATURE INDEX. 947

0895-1772 See MID-AMERICAN JOURNAL OF BUSINESS. 694

0895-1780 See BLACK CONGRESSIONAL MONITOR. 2256

0895-1799 See MARKETING TREASURES. 932

0895-1853 See ELECTRIC RD&D. 2044

0895-187X See OMNI ONLINE DATABASE DIRECTORY. 3239

0895-1926 See BIOLOGICAL REPORT (WASHINGTON, D.C.). 445

0895-1942 See FUNGAL GENETICS NEWSLETTER. 563

0895-2000 See SCIENCE AND TECHNOLOGY DATA BOOK. 5150

0895-2051 See ECONOMIC INDICATORS OF THE FARM SECTOR. NATIONAL FINANCIAL SUMMARY. 81

0895-2078 See NEWSLETTER - FAIRFAX GENEALOGICAL SOCIETY (FAIRFAX COUNTY, VA.). 2463

0895-2094 See CHILDREN'S VIDEO REVIEW NEWSLETTER. 4065

0895-2108 See C/A/S/E OUTLOOK. 1172

0895-2116 See ELECTRIC LINES. 2043

0895-2124 See MAGAZINEWEEK (FRAMINGHAM, MASS.). 4816

0895-2132 See JEFFERSON PARISH TIMES & DEMOCRAT / KENNER CITY NEWS. 5684

0895-2191 See WARD'S AUTOMOTIVE INTERNATIONAL. 5428

0895-2213 See INTERNATIONAL TELEVISION & VIDEO ALMANAC. 1133

0895-2221 See CHILDREN'S WORLD (BOSTON, MASS.). 1877

0895-2248 See LIBRARY VIDEO MAGAZINE. VIDEORECORDING. 3228

0895-2256 See FREE SPIRIT (MINNEAPOLIS, MINN.). 1063

0895-2272 See QUALITY AND PRODUCTIVITY MANAGEMENT. 883

0895-2299 See CALIFORNIA ENVIRONMENTAL INSIDER. 2162

0895-2310 See EXTRA! (NEW YORK, N.Y. 1987). 2919

0895-2361 See COALDAT MARKETING REPORT. UTILITY FORMAT. 1935

0895-2442 See AGRICULTURE TODAY. 54

0895-2450 See BISBEE OBSERVER, THE. 5629

0895-2469 See MISSOURI DIRECTORY OF MANUFACTURERS (1988). 3484

0895-2477 See MICROWAVE AND OPTICAL TECHNOLOGY LETTERS. 2072

0895-2485 See CDS CONNECTION. 3201

0895-2493 See CUSTOM BUILDER. 612

0895-2523 See INTERIM CASE CITATIONS TO THE RESTATEMENTS OF THE LAW. 2983

0895-254X See SPECIALTY BOOKSELLERS DIRECTORY. 4820

0895-2590 See BOURNE COURIER. 5688

0895-2612 See NORDEN (NEW YORK, N.Y.). 5719

0895-2620 See NORDSTJERNAN (1991). 5719

0895-2639 See STANDARD & POOR'S RATINGS HANDBOOK. 915

0895-2671 See NATIONAL MEDICAL CARE UTILIZATION AND EXPENDITURE SURVEY. SERIES C, ANALYTICAL REPORT. 3789

0895-2698 See TRAVEL & LEISURE'S WORLD TRAVEL OVERVIEW. 5495

0895-2728 See NATIONAL MEDICAL CARE UTILIZATION AND EXPENDITURE SURVEY. SERIES B, DESCRIPTIVE REPORT. 3789

0895-2736 See TEXAS BANKRUPTCY COURT REPORTER, THE. 3088

0895-2760 See COMPUTER GRAPHICS WORLD BUYERS GUIDE. 1232

0895-2779 See JOURNAL OF SPORT & EXERCISE PSYCHOLOGY. 4901

0895-2787 See CONTROLLER'S REPORT (NEW YORK, N.Y.). 864

0895-2795 See PHARMACEUTICAL PROCESSING. 4321

0895-2809 See NURSINGCONNECTIONS (WASHINGTON, D.C.). 3866

0895-2817 See BAY VIEWER, THE. 5765

0895-2825 See STAR TRIBUNE (MINNEAPOLIS, MINN.). 5699

0895-2833 See JOURNAL OF FEMINIST FAMILY THERAPY. 2282

0895-2841 See JOURNAL OF WOMEN & AGING. 5559

0895-285X See WALT DISNEY'S MICKEY MOUSE MAGAZINE. 1071

0895-2876 See SOUTHERN ROOTS AND SHOOTS. 2473

0895-2930 See AMERICAN DENTAL ASSOCIATION NEWS. 1315

0895-2965 See INN GUIDE, THE. 2807
0895-299X See INTERNATIONAL BOND AND MONEY MARKET PERFORMANCE. 792
0895-3023 See OFFSHORE DRILLING MONTHLY. 4267
0895-3058 See HISTORICAL NEWSLETTER (O'NEILL, NEB.). 2618
0895-3090 See FOOD FIRST DEVELOPMENT REPORT. 5285
0895-3139 See RIGHT HERE. 2492
0895-3147 See J.K. LASSER'S MONTHLY TAX LETTER. 4734
0895-3155 See AIMS NEWSLETTER. 5081
0895-3171 See HOTLINE - CHILDREN'S RIGHTS OF NEW YORK (ORGANIZATION). 5288
0895-318X See DENTAL TEAMWORK. 1321
0895-3198 See ABORIGINAL SCIENCE FICTION. 3357
0895-321X See SHUTTERBUG. 4376
0895-3260 See HAZARDOUS MATERIALS CONTROL. 2231
0895-3287 See RECORD-HERALD AND INDIANOLA TRIBUNE, THE. 5672
0895-3295 See GEORGIA OUTDOOR NEWS. 4872
0895-3309 See JOURNAL OF ECONOMIC PERSPECTIVES, THE. 1499
0895-3317 See PLANECON REPORT. 1638
0895-3376 See MAGAZINE ARTICLE SUMMARIES (PRINT ED.). 2497
0895-3384 See CHAPTER ONE. 1814
0895-3457 See PACIFIC BEACH LIGHT. 5638
0895-3465 See L.A. STYLE. 1085
0895-3562 See YEARBOOK OF THE AMERICAN READING FORUM. 3334
0895-3570 See PLANNER, THE. 803
0895-3635 See MONEY MANAGER PREVIEWS. 799
0895-3643 See AMERICAN JOURNAL OF GYNECOLOGIC HEALTH, THE. 3756
0895-3651 See FRANCE TODAY (SAN FRANCISCO, CALIF. 1987). 2688
0895-366X See ANCHOR POINT. 3264
0895-3678 See WORKAMPER NEW$. 1718
0895-3716 See ELECTRICAL MANUFACTURING (LIBERTYVILLE, ILL.). 3478
0895-3740 See RAISING KIDS. 2285
0895-3767 See HACHETTE GUIDE TO GREAT BRITAIN, THE. 5479
0895-3791 See BUSINESS DIGEST (HYANNIS, MASS.). 647
0895-3805 See MANAGING AUTOMATION. 1234
0895-3848 See ADWEEK SPECIAL REPORT. 755
0895-3880 See NATIONAL FORUM OF APPLIED EDUCATIONAL RESEARCH JOURNAL. 1867
0895-3899 See USED CAR BOOK (NEW YORK, N.Y.), THE. 5427
0895-3902 See COMPACT DISC NEWS. 1175
0895-3910 See GASTRONOME (NEW YORK, N.Y.). 5071
0895-3945 See LAW ENFORCEMENT INTELLIGENCE ANALYSIS DIGEST. 3168
0895-3961 See DAZE INC, THE. 2588
0895-397X See LIVING WELL WITH DIABETES. 3731
0895-3988 See BIOMEDICAL AND ENVIRONMENTAL SCIENCES. 447
0895-3996 See JOURNAL OF X-RAY SCIENCE AND TECHNOLOGY. 3943
0895-4046 See HONEY HOLE. 4899
0895-4097 See PROCEEDINGS OF THE ANNUAL NORTH AMERICAN POWER SYMPOSIUM. 2076
0895-4127 See LIFELINE (SEATTLE, WASH.). 1346
0895-4135 See TRAVEL TIDINGS. 5496
0895-4143 See PERFECT VISION, THE. 1136
0895-4151 See DESIGNNET (AUSTIN, TEX.). 1233
0895-4186 See FINANCIAL EXECUTIVE (1987). 675
0895-4194 See BETTY AND VERONICA. 4857
0895-4208 See MILITARY POLICE (1987). 3169

0895-4275 See SCHULENBURG STICKER, THE. 5754
0895-4283 See INDIA WORLDWIDE. 2653
0895-4291 See ABERNATHY WEEKLY REVIEW, THE. 5746
0895-4305 See PLANO STAR COURIER (1986). 5753
0895-4313 See MEDICAL OFFICE REPORT. 3610
0895-4321 See NATIONAL DIRECTORY OF MAGAZINES, THE. 2539
0895-433X See HANG GLIDING. 4898
0895-4356 See JOURNAL OF CLINICAL EPIDEMIOLOGY. 3735
0895-4364 See SERIES ON NURSING ADMINISTRATION. 3869
0895-4372 See WORKSHOP (LOUISVILLE, KY.). 1292
0895-4437 See COMMUNITY TRANSPORTATION REPORTER : CTR. 5380
0895-4445 See CHEMTRACTS. ORGANIC CHEMISTRY. 1041
0895-4496 See MASON FAMILY NEWSLETTER. 2459
0895-450X See FENESTRATION (RIVERTON, N.J.). 614
0895-4518 See DATABASE PROGRAMMING & DESIGN. 1253
0895-4534 See IRISH VOICE (NEW YORK, N.Y.). 5717
0895-4550 See MEDIA MERGERS & ACQUISITIONS. 692
0895-4623 See THOMSON BANK DIRECTORY. 814
0895-4690 See CHINESE AMERICAN FORUM. 1731
0895-4712 See POLITICAL PIX. 2923
0895-4720 See JOURNAL OF BANK TAXATION, THE. 793
0895-4755 See QUARTERLY - OLDE MECKLENBURG GENEALOGICAL SOCIETY (N.C.). 2469
0895-4798 See SIAM JOURNAL ON MATRIX ANALYSIS AND APPLICATIONS. 3534
0895-4801 See SIAM JOURNAL ON DISCRETE MATHEMATICS. 3534
0895-481X See BUCKMASTERS WHITETAIL MAGAZINE. 4869
0895-4852 See ACADEMIC QUESTIONS. 1807
0895-4925 See VITAL & HEALTH STATISTICS. SERIES 15, DATA FROM THE NATIONAL HEALTH SURVEY. 4807
0895-495X See BIRDER'S WORLD. 5616
0895-4968 See PRAYING (KANSAS CITY, MO.). 5034
0895-500X See JOURNAL - LEWIS COUNTY HISTORICAL SOCIETY. 2740
0895-5018 See THIRD WORLD LEGAL STUDIES. 3136
0895-5026 See ETHIKOS. 2250
0895-5034 See ORTHODONTIC REVIEW. 1332
0895-5042 See PROP. 65 NEWS. 3115
0895-5069 See PC CAD DIGEST. 1198
0895-5077 See NETWORKS IN-DEPTH. 1160
0895-5093 See NEW RESEARCH REPORTS. 1619
0895-5182 See CLAFLIN REVIEW, THE. 1090
0895-5220 See LRA'S ECONOMIC NOTES. 1688
0895-531X See LIBRARY COMPUTER SYSTEMS AND EQUIPMENT REVIEW. 3225
0895-5336 See AMERICAN JOURNAL OF ALZHEIMER'S CARE AND RELATED DISORDERS & RESEARCH. 3827
0895-5344 See NELSON COUNTY ARENA (MICHIGAN, N.D. : 1919). 5726
0895-5352 See SOUTH FLORIDA. 2546
0895-5360 See GUFFEY'S JOURNAL. 4838
0895-5387 See WEST MICHIGAN BOWLER. 4929
0895-5441 See LC GC INTERNATIONAL. 984
0895-545X See U.S. AGRICULTURAL POLICY GUIDE. 4691
0895-5476 See HICKSVILLE ILLUSTRATED NEWS. 5717
0895-5492 See SECURED LENDING ALERT. 811

0895-5506 See AGRICULTURE MATERIALS IN LIBRARIES. 3188
0895-5514 See EDUCATION MATERIALS IN LIBRARIES. 3209
0895-5549 See NEW YORKIN UUTISET. 5719
0895-5573 See SOUTHERN REGISTER : THE NEWSLETTER OF THE CENTER FOR THE STUDY OF SOUTHERN CULTURE, THE UNIVERSITY OF MISSISSIPPI, THE. 2761
0895-5603 See FOR QUATTRO. 1286
0895-562X See JOURNAL OF PRODUCTIVITY ANALYSIS. 1614
0895-5638 See JOURNAL OF REAL ESTATE FINANCE AND ECONOMICS, THE. 4839
0895-5646 See JOURNAL OF RISK AND UNCERTAINTY. 1500
0895-5689 See UNITED & BABSON INVESTMENT REPORT. 918
0895-5697 See MARKETING COMPUTERS. 1194
0895-5700 See RE NEWS DIGEST. 1954
0895-5727 See PSYCHOTROPICS (RENO, NEV.). 3986
0895-5778 See NATIONAL EMPLOYMENT OPPORTUNITIES NEWSLETTER. COMPUTER/ELECTRONIC FIELD ENGINEERING. 1692
0895-5786 See BLUEPRINT FOR SOCIAL JUSTICE. 5193
0895-5808 See CA SELECTS: ENZYME ASSAYS. 1002
0895-5816 See CA SELECTS: STRUCTURE-ACTIVITY RELATIONSHIPS. 1010
0895-5824 See CA SELECTS: SOLID STATE NMR. 1009
0895-5832 See CA SELECTS: SILOXANES & SILICONES. 1009
0895-5840 See CA SELECTS: POLYIMIDES. 1008
0895-5859 See CA SELECTS: ORGANOMETALLICS IN ORGANIC SYNTHESIS. 1006
0895-5867 See CA SELECTS: NONLINEAR OPTICAL MATERIALS. 1005
0895-5875 See CA SELECTS: NEW ANTIBIOTICS. 1005
0895-5883 See CA SELECTS: ISOMERIZATION & CATALYSTS. 1004
0895-5891 See CA SELECTS: HOT-MELT ADHESIVES. 1003
0895-5905 See CA SELECTS: FREE RADICALS (BIOCHEMICAL ASPECTS). 1003
0895-5913 See CA SELECTS: FOOD & FEED ANALYSIS. 1002
0895-5921 See CA SELECTS: FLUOROPOLYMERS. 1002
0895-593X See CA SELECTS: ENZYME APPLICATIONS. 1002
0895-5948 See CA SELECTS: CERAMIC MATERIALS (JOURNALS). 999
0895-5956 See CA SELECTS: CARBON FIBER COMPOSITES. 998
0895-5964 See CA SELECTS: ALKYLATION & CATALYSTS. 997
0895-5972 See CA SELECTS: FREE RADICALS (ORGANIC ASPECTS). 1003
0895-5980 See CA SELECTS: AIR POLLUTION (BOOKS & REVIEWS). 997
0895-5999 See REPORT ON SCIENCE AND HUMAN RIGHTS. 4512
0895-6006 See CONTINUOUS IMPROVEMENT. 3477
0895-6014 See ON THE ISSUES. 5563
0895-6022 See YEARBOOK - CASUALTY ACTUARIAL SOCIETY. 2897
0895-6030 See FRAME/WORK (LOS ANGELES, CALIF.). 4369
0895-6049 See SOUTHWEST PROFILE. 2546
0895-6065 See TAOS MAGAZINE. 2547
0895-6073 See CALIFORNIA SCHOOL BOARDS JOURNAL. 1861
0895-6103 See SANTA CLARA COUNTY CONNECTIONS. 2471
0895-6111 See COMPUTERIZED MEDICAL IMAGING AND GRAPHICS. 3940
0895-6138 See TIMES RECORD NEWS. 5755

ISSN Index

0895-6154 See FLYFAIRE VACATIONS. 5470

0895-6162 See MANAGING WITH COMPUTERS. 1194

0895-6200 See ART OF EATING, THE. 2327

0895-6219 See JOURNAL OF PARALEGAL EDUCATION AND PRACTICE. 2989

0895-6235 See AFRICAN-AMERICAN TRAVELER, THE. 2553

0895-6286 See SURVIVING TOGETHER. 4536

0895-6308 See RESEARCH TECHNOLOGY MANAGEMENT. 5147

0895-6340 See COMPUTING SYSTEMS. 1279

0895-6391 See WAUKESHA COUNTY FREEMAN, THE. 5771

0895-6405 See CONNECTION (BOSTON, MASS.). 1818

0895-6464 See VISTA DE MEXICO, LA. 5499

0895-6499 See CAS BIOTECH UPDATES. ANTIBODY CONJUGATES. 484

0895-6545 See JOURNALISM & MASS COMMUNICATION DIRECTORY. 2921

0895-6588 See COMPUTER INFORMATION REVIEW. 1176

0895-6618 See CAS BIOTECH UPDATES. DNA FORMATION & REPAIR. 543

0895-6626 See CAS BIOTECH UPDATES. BIOCHEMICAL IMMOBILIZATION & BIOCATALYTIC REACTORS. 484

0895-6782 See GUIDE TO MUSCLE CARS. 5415

0895-6790 See DESIGN SYSTEMS STRATEGIES. 1233

0895-6820 See 21ST CENTURY SCIENCE & TECHNOLOGY. 5078

0895-6839 See POTTER LEADER-ENTERPRISE. 5738

0895-6855 See RETHINKING SCHOOLS. 1779

0895-6871 See BUTTERICK HOME CATALOG (1985). 5183

0895-6898 See SAN ANTONIO PERSPECTIVE. 1519

0895-6901 See AUSTIN PERSPECTIVE. 1598

0895-6928 See ECB NEWSLETTER. 2192

0895-7061 See AMERICAN JOURNAL OF HYPERTENSION. 3698

0895-7118 See COMPACT (CHICAGO, ILL.). 5280

0895-7126 See SWENSON CENTER NEWS. 2474

0895-7142 See ACCIDENT AND SAFETY ADVISORY : ASA. 4763

0895-7177 See MATHEMATICAL AND COMPUTER MODELLING. 3518

0895-7258 See JOURNAL OF INDO-EUROPEAN STUDIES : MONOGRAPH SERIES. 5206

0895-7266 See TAX SHOP 1040. 4754

0895-7274 See FRANCHISING (PITTSBURGH, PA.). 677

0895-7312 See VILLA RICAN, THE. 5655

0895-7347 See APPLIED MEASUREMENT IN EDUCATION. 1726

0895-7371 See ASTC NEWSLETTER. 5086

0895-7398 See COMPUTER SHOPPER'S PC CLONES. 1177

0895-7444 See DOUGLAS COUNTY PIONEER. 2446

0895-7460 See NEW MERCERSBURG REVIEW, THE. 4981

0895-7479 See SECOND MESSENGER AND PHOSPHOPROTEINS. 586

0895-7533 See LABORATORY ROBOTICS AND AUTOMATION. 1214

0895-7541 See EW DESIGN ENGINEERS' HANDBOOK. 1975

0895-755X See SPOTLIGHT ON AIDS. 3677

0895-7592 See STORIES (LOS ANGELES, CALIF.). 3440

0895-7606 See NATIVE PEOPLES. 2747

0895-7622 See HENCEFORTH. 4962

0895-7657 See BODY, MIND, SPIRIT. 4185

0895-7673 See JOURNAL OF TRAINING & PRACTICE IN PROFESSIONAL PSYCHOLOGY, THE. 4602

0895-7681 See NATICK BULLETIN (1982). 5689

0895-769X See ANQ (LEXINGTON, KY.). 3362

0895-7703 See VETERINARY MEDICINE REPORT. 5526

0895-772X See GREEN MARKETS DEALER REPORT. 2417

0895-7738 See MELTS. 4412

0895-7746 See SSELECT. 1204

0895-7789 See NACS WEEKLY BULLETIN. 879

0895-7819 See CALLIGRAPHY REVIEW (NORMAN, OKLA.). 377

0895-7851 See GREAT BARRINGTON HISTORICAL SOCIETY NEWSLETTER. 2617

0895-7894 See PAPERS IN APPLIED LINGUISTICS--MICHIGAN. 3309

0895-7916 See CHAPLAINCY TODAY. 4943

0895-7959 See HIGH PRESSURE RESEARCH. 4404

0895-7967 See SEMINARS IN VASCULAR SURGERY. 3974

0895-7975 See PAYROLL MANAGER'S LETTER. 1512

0895-7983 See HARRIS POLL, THE. 5246

0895-7991 See CLAIMS (SEATTLE, WASH.). 2878

0895-8009 See MONOGRAPHS OF THE AMERICAN ASSOCIATION ON MENTAL RETARDATION. 1882

0895-8017 See AMERICAN JOURNAL OF MENTAL RETARDATION. 4383

0895-8033 See NEWS & NOTES - AMERICAN ASSOCIATION ON MENTAL RETARDATION. 1882

0895-805X See CINEVUE. 4368

0895-8076 See URBAN DESIGN UPDATE: NEWSLETTER OF THE INSTITUTE FOR URBAN DESIGN. 2837

0895-8084 See FLORIDA FACTS (DALLAS, TEX.). 2533

0895-8092 See IOWA FACTS (DALLAS, TEX.). 2536

0895-8106 See NORTH CAROLINA FACTS (DALLAS, TEX.). 2541

0895-8114 See NEW HAMPSHIRE FACTS. 2540

0895-8157 See PUBLIC HEALTH COMMENTS. 4797

0895-8165 See PENINSULA HERITAGE. 5034

0895-819X See NATIONAL ASSOCIATION FOR OLMSTED PARKS. 4707

0895-8211 See NAVY MEDICINE. 3619

0895-822X See ORDNANCE (ABERDEEN PROVING GROUND, MD.). 4053

0895-8246 See MORFOGEN ASSOCIATES NEWS. 325

0895-8254 See LONGEVITY (NEW YORK, N.Y. : 1988). 3754

0895-8351 See SHIFT (SAN FRANCISCO, CALIF.). 330

0895-8378 See INHALATION TOXICOLOGY. 3981

0895-8416 See THREADS OF LIFE. 2475

0895-8467 See MOUNTAIN BIKE ACTION. 4905

0895-8505 See LARKSPUR REPORT, THE. 4480

0895-8521 See EXPLORER NEWS. 2560

0895-853X See JOURNAL OF BANK ACCOUNTING & AUDITING, THE. 793

0895-8548 See TRANSPORTATION & DISTRIBUTION. 5457

0895-8580 See PENASEE GLOBE. 5693

0895-867X See UPTIME (MACINTOSH). 1206

0895-8688 See UPTIME (COMMODORE C64 AND 128). 1206

0895-8696 See JOURNAL OF MOLECULAR NEUROSCIENCE. 3835

0895-8726 See INFONETICS ANALYST, THE. 1188

0895-8742 See ELECTRONIC SYSTEMS INFORMATION BULLETIN. 2048

0895-8750 See JOURNAL OF PSYCHOLOGICAL TYPE. 4600

0895-8777 See MONITOR (CLEARWATER, FLA.). 933

0895-8785 See COURIER-NEWS (BRIDGEWATER, N.J.). 5709

0895-8793 See BERKSHIRE EAGLE, THE. 5687

0895-8807 See NORTH JERSEY HERALD & NEWS, THE. 5711

0895-8815 See INTERNATIONAL JOURNAL OF VALUE BASED MANAGEMENT. 684

0895-8815 See INTERNATIONAL JOURNAL OF VALUE-BASED MANAGEMENT. 1190

0895-8831 See JOURNAL OF CLINICAL DENTISTRY, THE. 1326

0895-8858 See DOMESTIC VIOLENCE LAW BULLETIN. 3120

0895-8874 See SUBSTANCE ABUSE IN SCHOOLS. 1349

0895-8882 See AIDS EDUCATION. 3663

0895-8920 See ARIEL (LEXINGTON, KY.). 3363

0895-8939 See CALVERT CO. MARYLAND GENEALOGY NEWSLETTER. 2441

0895-8947 See SPACE STATION NEWS. 36

0895-9005 See AMERICAN WOODTURNER. 822

0895-903X See TECHNOLOGY BUSINESS. 5163

0895-9048 See EDUCATIONAL POLICY (LOS ALTOS, CALIF.). 1742

0895-9056 See MINISTRY DEVELOPMENT JOURNAL. 5064

0895-9064 See CHICAGO CONSUMER (CHICAGO, ILL. : 1987). 1294

0895-9080 See HOLOGRAPHY NEWS. 1608

0895-9099 See WORLD PLASTICS MONITOR. 4461

0895-9145 See ETHICAL INVESTOR. 897

0895-9234 See INTERNATIONAL CREATIVITY NETWORK NEWSLETTER : ICN. 1753

0895-9269 See LITERATI CHICAGO. 3406

0895-9285 See HUMAN PERFORMANCE. 4589

0895-9293 See BANK TECHNOLOGY NEWS. 776

0895-9307 See GREEN MOUNTAINS REVIEW. 3392

0895-9323 See STARMONT POPULAR FICTION. 3439

0895-934X See SUN BELT FLOOR COVERING. 2907

0895-9374 See ADVANCES IN DENTAL RESEARCH. 1315

0895-9382 See KAUAI. 5482

0895-9390 See MAUI UPDATE, THE. 5484

0895-9412 See LAW FIRM PROFIT REPORT. 2995

0895-9420 See JOURNAL OF AGING & SOCIAL POLICY. 5179

0895-9439 See SHORT STORY CRITICISM. 3436

0895-9455 See CONFEDERATE CHRONICLES OF TENNESSEE. 2729

0895-9471 See U.S. KIDS. 1071

0895-948X See KEYS (NORTHFIELD, ILL.). 4128

0895-9498 See PUNTOS CARDINALES. 4988

0895-9544 See ACCA DOCKET. 3094

0895-9579 See STAYING WELL SCHOOL NEWS. 1785

0895-9595 See COMPUTE'S APPLE APPLICATIONS. 1180

0895-9609 See MAUI. 5484

0895-965X See WHO'S WHO OF EMERGING LEADERS IN AMERICA. 439

0895-9668 See MUSHING (ESTER, ALASKA). 4905

0895-9706 See PINTER REVIEW, THE. 3423

0895-9714 See PEACEMAKERS. 4487

0895-9722 See NATIONAL DIPPER, THE. 2350

0895-9730 See ORNAMENT COLLECTOR, THE. 2776

0895-9765 See AIDS CABISCO NEWS. 3663

0895-9781 See AGRICULTURAL POLICY AND ECONOMIC ISSUES. 51

0895-979X See FUTURE RESOURCES. 1607

0895-9803 See CURRENT ADVANCES IN CANCER RESEARCH. 3656

0895-9811 See JOURNAL OF SOUTH AMERICAN EARTH SCIENCES. 1357

0895-982X See LENGTH OF STAY BY DIAGNOSIS AND OPERATION, UNITED STATES. 3787

0895-9838 See LENGTH OF STAY BY DIAGNOSIS AND OPERATION, NORTHEASTERN REGION. 3787

0895-9846 See LENGTH OF STAY BY DIAGNOSIS AND OPERATION, NORTH CENTRAL REGION. 3787

0895-9854 *See* LENGTH OF STAY BY DIAGNOSIS AND OPERATION, SOUTHERN REGION. **3787**

0895-9862 *See* LENGTH OF STAY BY DIAGNOSIS AND OPERATION, WESTERN REGION. **3788**

0895-9900 *See* PROCEEDINGS OF THE ... STEELMAKING CONFERENCE. **4016**

0895-9927 *See* INFORMATION BROKER (HOUSTON, TEX.). **3215**

0895-9935 *See* RESEARCH IN POLITICAL SOCIOLOGY. **5255**

0895-9951 *See* VERDICT (FALLBROOK, CALIF. : 1987). **5007**

0895-996X *See* CONTEMPORARY ISSUES IN NUCLEAR IMAGING. **3847**

0895-9978 *See* CSSA SPECIAL PUBLICATION - CROP SCIENCE SOCIETY OF AMERICA. **169**

0895-9986 *See* HEALTH CONSCIOUSNESS (OVIEDO, FLA.). **4779**

0895-9994 *See* MONOGRAPHS IN ECONOMIC ANTHROPOLOGY. **241**

0896-0011 *See* CLASSICAL AND MEDIEVAL LITERATURE CRITICISM. **3376**

0896-0054 *See* GREAT PLAINS SOCIOLOGIST, THE. **5246**

0896-0135 *See* NELSON'S DIRECTORY OF INVESTMENT RESEARCH. **909**

0896-0143 *See* NELSON'S DIRECTORY OF INVESTMENT MANAGERS. **909**

0896-0194 *See* NATIONAL BLACK LAW JOURNAL. **3013**

0896-0216 *See* EXPORT MARKETS FOR U.S. GRAIN AND PRODUCTS. **83**

0896-0240 *See* SITUATION AND OUTLOOK REPORT. SUGAR AND SWEETENER. **135**

0896-0267 *See* BRAIN TOPOGRAPHY. **3829**

0896-0275 *See* MEDICAL LASER BUYERS' GUIDE. **1618**

0896-0283 *See* COURIER JOURNAL (JUPITER, FLA.), THE. **5649**

0896-0291 *See* WAXAHACHIE DAILY LIGHT, THE. **5755**

0896-0313 *See* FILEMAKER REPORT, THE. **1286**

0896-033X *See* 1 SOFT DECISION NEWS. **1283**

0896-0348 *See* MILITARY ROBOTICS. **1215**

0896-0364 *See* ARIZONA FILM, THEATRE & TELEVISION : AFT & T. **383**

0896-0380 See MIND MATTERS. **4604**

0896-0402 *See* COMPUTERIZED DIRECTORY OF NEW BUSINESSES. **659**

0896-0437 *See* SUPER AUTOMOTIVE SERVICE. **5426**

0896-0453 *See* TEXAS ECONOMIC INDICATORS (AUSTIN, TEX.: 1987). **1586**

0896-0488 *See* NACS CAMPUS FOCUS. **1836**

0896-050X *See* NEW IMAGE, THE. **4216**

0896-0569 *See* THROMBOSIS RESEARCH. SUPPLEMENT. **3774**

0896-0577 *See* AIR CARRIER INDUSTRY SCHEDULED SERVICE TRAFFIC STATISTICS QUARTERLY. **6**

0896-0607 *See* NUCLEAR MEDICINE (NEW YORK, N.Y.). **3623**

0896-0615 *See* WORLD WATCH (WASHINGTON, D.C.). **1596**

0896-0623 *See* REGIONAL IMMUNOLOGY. **3676**

0896-064X *See* TAMPA REVIEW. **2547**

0896-0666 *See* CONNECT (SUISUN, CALIF.). **3203**

0896-0674 *See* GOVERNMENT PRODUCTIVITY NEWS. **4652**

0896-0682 *See* EXPORT CONTROL NEWS. **834**

0896-0704 *See* MRI DECISIONS. **3944**

0896-0712 *See* ROUGE (BATON ROUGE, LA.). **2492**

0896-0720 *See* VLA NEWSLETTER. **3255**

0896-0798 *See* EXCELLENCE (ROSS, CALIF.). **5414**

0896-0801 *See* HINDUISM TODAY. **5041**

0896-0925 *See* MONGOLIA SOCIETY SPECIAL PAPERS, THE. **2659**

0896-0941 *See* EMPLOYEE ASSISTANCE PROGRAM MANAGEMENT LETTER. **866**

0896-095X *See* INDIA CURRENTS. **2488**

0896-0968 *See* INTERNATIONAL CHORAL BULLETIN. **4123**

0896-0976 *See* ELECTRONIC PHOTOGRAPHY NEWS. **4369**

0896-100X *See* IMAGING ABSTRACTS. **4378**

0896-1018 *See* JOURNAL OF THE AMERICAN ROMANIAN ACADEMY OF ARTS AND SCIENCES. **2518**

0896-1042 *See* DAILY COMMERCIAL (LEESBURG LAKE/SUMTER EDITION). **5649**

0896-1069 *See* PIPELINE & UTILITIES CONSTRUCTION. **2124**

0896-1077 *See* OFFICIAL OPINIONS FROM THE SUPREME JUDICIAL COURT OF MASSACHUSETTS EDITION. **3021**

0896-1093 *See* RATON RANGE (1985). **5713**

0896-1107 *See* JOURNAL OF SUPERCONDUCTIVITY. **2069**

0896-114X *See* HARRIMAN INSTITUTE FORUM, THE. **2690**

0896-1182 *See* CURRENT REVIEWS FOR POST ANESTHESIA CARE NURSES. **3855**

0896-1190 *See* NATIONAL INSTITUTE ON DRUG ABUSE STATISTICAL SERIES. SERIES H. **1350**

0896-1255 *See* ADVANCES IN HEALTH EDUCATION AND PROMOTION. **4763**

0896-1263 *See* NEPHROLOGY NEWS & ISSUES. **3992**

0896-1301 *See* IRIS (CHARLOTTESVILLE, VA.). **5204**

0896-1336 *See* KINDERBOOK NEWSLETTER, THE. **3401**

0896-1352 *See* MUSIC PERFORMANCE RESOURCES. **4134**

0896-1360 *See* ECCSSA JOURNAL, THE. **5198**

0896-1409 *See* ARGONAUT (MOSCOW, IDAHO). **5656**

0896-1433 *See* AMERICAN VIET PRESS. **2484**

0896-1441 *See* IDEAS (RESTON, VA.). **925**

0896-145X *See* HP PROFESSIONAL. **1186**

0896-1468 *See* PARENTGUIDE NEWS. **2284**

0896-1506 *See* NEW ENGLAND ENTERTAINMENT DIGEST. **5366**

0896-1530 *See* JOURNAL OF INTERNATIONAL CONSUMER MARKETING. **928**

0896-1557 *See* BONANZA BUGLE, THE. **2724**

0896-1611 *See* MANUFACTURING REVIEW. **3484**

0896-1638 *See* SEWANEE MEDIAEVAL STUDIES. **2709**

0896-1646 *See* SEA HISTORY GAZETTE. **5455**

0896-1654 *See* AACG NEWSLETTER. **1031**

0896-1670 *See* SNACK WORLD. **2358**

0896-1697 *See* WRAP. **1124**

0896-1735 *See* ENGINEERING INTERNATIONAL. **2023**

0896-1786 *See* TURKEY HUNTER, THE. **4880**

0896-1794 *See* FLORIDA WATER RESOURCES JOURNAL. **5533**

0896-1840 *See* PAYPERVIEWS (HARTSDALE, N.Y.). **1136**

0896-1905 *See* STUDIES IN TECHNOLOGY AND SOCIAL CHANGE SERIES. **5160**

0896-1913 *See* FOR THE RECORD. **3140**

0896-193X *See* NAILS. **2792**

0896-1956 *See* THEATER WEEK. **5370**

0896-1972 *See* INDIAN AWARENESS CENTER NEWS LETTER. **2263**

0896-1980 *See* FULTON COUNTY FOLK FINDER. **2449**

0896-1999 See POST AND COURIER, THE. **5743**

0896-2022 *See* TURTLE QUARTERLY. **2274**

0896-209X *See* LUTHERAN WOMAN TODAY. **5063**

0896-2111 *See* WANG IN THE NEWS. **1239**

0896-212X See WORKSTATION (AUSTIN, TEX.). **1207**

0896-2154 *See* LIVING WORLD (LOS ANGELES, CALIF.). **2252**

0896-2162 *See* DIRECTORY OF SINGLE-UNIT SUPERMARKET OPERATORS. **2333**

0896-2189 *See* WESTERN LEGAL HISTORY. **3073**

0896-2197 *See* PULITZER PRIZES, THE. **3426**

0896-2251 *See* GULF COAST. **3392**

0896-226X *See* ESSAYS IN ECONOMIC AND BUSINESS HISTORY : SELECTED PAPERS FROM THE ECONOMIC AND BUSINESS HISTORICAL SOCIETY. **1560**

0896-2294 *See* INTERNATIONAL JOURNAL ON THE UNITY OF THE SCIENCES. **5115**

0896-2359 *See* CIVIC HEALTH OCCASIONAL PAPER. **3667**

0896-2367 *See* PROCEEDINGS, NOBCCHE. **989**

0896-2383 *See* BYU JOURNAL OF PUBLIC LAW, THE. **2945**

0896-2391 *See* RECOVERING (SAN FRANCISCO, CALIF.). **1348**

0896-2413 *See* GOD'S SPECIAL PEOPLE. **4960**

0896-2472 *See* REPORT (OHIO STATE UNIVERSITY. BYRD POLAR RESEARCH CENTER). **5146**

0896-2537 *See* REGIONAL ECONOMIES AND MARKETS. **1516**

0896-2642 *See* BUENA SALUD. **4769**

0896-2669 *See* UPDATE - NATIONAL INSTITUTE OF DYSLEXIA (U.S.). **1886**

0896-2685 *See* SPRINKLER AGE. **2292**

0896-2693 *See* NOW AND THEN (JOHNSON CITY, TENN.). **2751**

0896-2715 *See* CATHOLIC SPIRIT (AUSTIN, TEX.). **5026**

0896-2766 *See* CALIFORNIA HOSPITALS. **3777**

0896-2774 *See* BIT DROPPER, THE. **1172**

0896-2790 *See* JASONVILLE LEADER, THE. **5665**

0896-2804 *See* EGG INDUSTRY (MOUNT MORRIS, ILL. : 1987). **210**

0896-2863 *See* DISSOCIATION (SMYRNA, GA.). **4585**

0896-2871 *See* VIDEO CHOICE. **4079**

0896-2898 *See* PAN-EROTIC REVIEW. **5188**

0896-2960 *See* CRITICAL REVIEWS IN PHYSICAL AND REHABILITATION MEDICINE. **507**

0896-2979 See CHINESE ENVIRONMENT & DEVELOPMENT. **2558**

0896-2987 *See* TREASURY MANAGER, THE. **888**

0896-3002 *See* NATIONAL REPORT ON WORK & FAMILY. **5297**

0896-3010 *See* INTERNATIONAL SECURITIES REGULATION REPORT. **3130**

0896-3045 *See* BROWNING NEWSLETTER (BURLINGTON, VT.), THE. **5090**

0896-3053 *See* O-BLEK (STOCKBRIDGE, MASS.). **3419**

0896-307X *See* BULLETIN / ASSOCIATION OF CHRISTIAN ECONOMISTS. **1465**

0896-3096 *See* FOLIO (SAINT LOUIS, MO.). **2733**

0896-3134 *See* ADA TODAY. **4461**

0896-3150 *See* NEW HEAVEN, NEW EARTH. **5665**

0896-3169 *See* ECA MAGAZINE. **1971**

0896-3177 *See* COLORADO CONNOISSEUR, THE. **2331**

0896-3207 *See* TUGBOAT (PROVIDENCE, R.I.). **1249**

0896-3231 *See* I/S ANALYZER. **4212**

0896-3266 *See* CAD EVOLUTION. **1967**

0896-3274 *See* ROCHESTER BUSINESS JOURNAL (ROCHESTER, N.Y. : 1987). **708**

0896-3282 *See* JUSTICE LEAGUE INTERNATIONAL. **4862**

0896-3312 *See* BEAVER COUNTY NEWS (MILFORD, UTAH : 1956). **5756**

0896-3401 *See* SUPERCONDUCTIVITY FLASH REPORT. **2082**

0896-341X *See* THYMUS UPDATE. **3645**

0896-3444 *See* CIMLINC TECHNICAL UPDATE. **5095**

0896-355X *See* HOMEWORDS (WASHINGTON, D.C.). **5288**

0896-3568 *See* JOURNAL OF BUSINESS & FINANCE LIBRARIANSHIP. **3219**

0896-3576 *See* ACQUISITIONS LIBRARIAN, THE. **3187**

0896-3592 *See* QUARTERLY OF THE NATIONAL WRITING PROJECT AND THE CENTER FOR THE STUDY OF WRITING, THE. **1776**

0896-3614 See AUTOMOTIVE PARTS INTERNATIONAL. 5407
0896-3673 See SATELLITE TV PRE-VUE. 1138
0896-3703 See BUSINESS PERSPECTIVES (MEMPHIS, TENN.). 651
0896-3746 See INFANTS AND YOUNG CHILDREN. 3904
0896-3835 See OCCUPATIONAL HEALTH & SAFETY NEWS DIGEST. 2866
0896-386X See TEMPO. 752
0896-3878 See TIMBUKTU. 3446
0896-3908 See MARKETING LIBRARY SERVICES. 3230
0896-3916 See GAMES (BASIC ED.). 4861
0896-3924 See GAMES (BASIC ED.). 4861
0896-3932 See NCRTL SPECIAL REPORT. 1901
0896-3940 See TEACHING, COACHING, SUPERVISING NEWSLETTER. 1906
0896-3975 See ATLANTA HISTORY. 2722
0896-3991 See BOBBIN (1987). 1082
0896-4009 See GEORGIA MANUFACTURERS REGISTER. 3479
0896-4017 See CHICAGO & COOK COUNTY MARKETING DIRECTORY. 922
0896-4068 See SILVERPLATTER EXCHANGE, THE. 1203
0896-4084 See TIMES LEADER (WILKES-BARRE, PA.). 5740
0896-4092 See GIFT & STATIONERY BUSINESS. 2584
0896-4106 See SYLVIA PORTER'S PERSONAL FINANCE. 917
0896-4114 See ASTA AGENCY MANAGEMENT. 5462
0896-4122 See NEW YORK EDUCATION LAW REPORT. 3016
0896-4130 See LINCOLN LABORATORY JOURNAL, THE. 5126
0896-4165 See INVESTECH MUTUAL FUND ADVISOR. 902
0896-419X See TRI-COUNTY GENEALOGY. 2476
0896-4203 See FOOD MARKETING BRIEFS. 2338
0896-422X See ADVANCED COATINGS & SURFACE TECHNOLOGY. 1020
0896-4246 See MICHIGAN WASTE REPORT. 2236
0896-4289 See BEHAVIORAL MEDICINE (WASHINGTON, D.C.). 3555
0896-4297 See NEW THEOLOGY REVIEW. 4981
0896-4327 See JOURNAL OF INTERVENTIONAL CARDIOLOGY. 3707
0896-4386 See DAVID H. BOWEN'S SOFTWARE SUCCESS. 1181
0896-4394 See ASSEMBLIES OF GOD HERITAGE. 4936
0896-4432 See FIRST STRIKE. 2781
0896-4467 See KEY OBSTETRICS AND GYNECOLOGY. 3764
0896-4475 See YEAR BOOK OF INFERTILITY, THE. 3652
0896-4505 See FOODSERVICE DISTRIBUTOR, THE. 2341
0896-4521 See BOOKWATCH (SAN FRANCISCO, CALIF.), THE. 4827
0896-4556 See INCENTIVE TAXATION. 4731
0896-4572 See BREASTFEEDING ABSTRACTS. 3655
0896-4599 See THIS MONTH ON LONG ISLAND. 5492
0896-4602 See LUTHER FAMILY NEWSLETTER, THE. 2458
0896-4653 See BALTIMORE MENU DIRECTORY. 2328
0896-4661 See LOGAN COUNTY NEWS (CRESCENT, OKLA.). 5732
0896-467X See TAMPA BAY BUSINESS JOURNAL. 714
0896-4696 See WEIGHT WATCHERS WOMEN'S HEALTH AND FITNESS NEWS. 4807
0896-470X See ADVANCES IN DISCOURSE PROCESSES. 3261
0896-4750 See MUSIC, COMPUTERS & SOFTWARE. 1240

0896-4815 See MEDICARE-MEMORANDUM (OUTPATIENT CLINIC ED.). 5296
0896-4831 See MEDICAL INTERFACE. 3609
0896-4858 See WILDFLOWER (AUSTIN, TEX. 1988). 530
0896-4874 See MOTORIST (ALLENTOWN, PA.). 5420
0896-4920 See BEING SINGLE. 2485
0896-4998 See BNA ADMINISTRATIVE PRACTICE MANUAL. CURRENT REPORTS. 4633
0896-5005 See SOMA (SAN FRANCISCO, CALIF.). 2546
0896-5021 See INTERNIST'S CLINICAL UPDATE. 3590
0896-5048 See NONPROFIT TIMES, THE. 880
0896-5080 See CANCER THERAPY AND CONTROL. 3812
0896-5099 See COMMENTS ON DEVELOPMENTAL NEUROBIOLOGY. 3830
0896-5102 See WIND ENERGY TECHNOLOGY. 1960
0896-5145 See ENERGY STORAGE SYSTEMS. 1942
0896-5153 See NUCLEAR REACTORS AND TECHNOLOGY. 2157
0896-5161 See INDUSTRIAL ENERGY TECHNOLOGY. 1946
0896-517X See CLEAN COAL TECHNOLOGIES. 1935
0896-5188 See ADVANCED OIL AND GAS RECOVERY TECHNOLOGIES. 1930
0896-5196 See ELECTRIC ENERGY SYSTEMS. 1937
0896-520X See ADVANCED FOSSIL ENERGY TECHNOLOGIES. 1930
0896-5269 See MULTICULTURAL LEADER. 1765
0896-5307 See PRACTICAL REVIEWS IN CANCER MANAGEMENT. 3822
0896-5315 See PRACTICAL REVIEWS IN ANESTHESIOLOGY. 3684
0896-5323 See PRACTICAL REVIEWS IN INTERNAL MEDICINE (1984). 3800
0896-5331 See PRACTICAL REVIEWS IN NUCLEAR MEDICINE. 3849
0896-534X See PRACTICAL REVIEWS IN PATHOLOGY. 3897
0896-5358 See PRACTICAL REVIEWS IN PSYCHIATRY (BIRMINGHAM, ALA.). 3932
0896-5374 See PRACTICAL REVIEWS IN RADIOLOGY. 3944
0896-5382 See PRACTICAL REVIEWS IN EMERGENCY MEDICINE. 3725
0896-5390 See PRACTICAL REVIEWS IN OB/GYN. 3767
0896-5404 See PRACTICAL REVIEWS IN SURGERY. 3972
0896-5412 See PRACTICAL REVIEWS IN FAMILY PRACTICE. 3738
0896-5420 See PRACTICAL REVIEWS IN UROLOGY. 3992
0896-5439 See PRACTICAL REVIEWS IN GASTROENTEROLOGY. 3747
0896-5447 See PRACTICAL REVIEWS IN ORAL MAXILLOFACIAL SURGERY. 3972
0896-5455 See PRACTICAL REVIEWS IN PEDIATRICS. 3910
0896-5463 See PRACTICAL REVIEWS IN CARDIOLOGY. 3709
0896-548X See JOURNAL OF TRACE ELEMENTS IN EXPERIMENTAL MEDICINE, THE. 3600
0896-5552 See PROFESSIONAL ROOFING. 624
0896-5579 See FARMER (MINNESOTA ED.). 85
0896-5595 See JOURNAL OF CONTEMPORARY LEGAL ISSUES. 2987
0896-5633 See NEWSLETTER (AMERICAN ACADEMY OF PSYCHIATRY AND THE LAW). 3931
0896-565X See INTERNATIONAL WORKCAMP DIRECTORY / VOLUNTEERS FOR PEACE. 5290
0896-5706 See CAMPING AND RV MAGAZINE. 4849
0896-5722 See IMPORT SERVICE. 5416
0896-5730 See OHIO WRITER. 2923

0896-5765 See CLINICAL RC MANAGER. 3778
0896-5781 See INTERNATIONAL PERMACULTURE SPECIES YEARBOOK, THE. 2217
0896-5803 See JOURNAL OF REAL ESTATE RESEARCH, THE. 4839
0896-5811 See JOURNAL OF LEGAL STUDIES EDUCATION, THE. 2988
0896-5846 See JOURNAL OF INTRAVENOUS NURSING. 3858
0896-5900 See SOLID STATE AND SUPERCONDUCTIVITY ABSTRACTS. 4427
0896-5919 See VIROLOGY & AIDS ABSTRACTS. 3662
0896-5927 See PUC BULLETIN. 4762
0896-5935 See UPHOLSTERY MANUFACTURING. 2907
0896-5951 See TURNSTILE (NEW YORK, N.Y.). 3448
0896-596X See BIOGERON RESEARCH INDEX. AGING, LONGEVITY, & LIFE EXTENSION. 3556
0896-6001 See GUN SHOW CALENDAR. 4850
0896-601X See SOVIET MEDICAL REVIEWS SUPPLEMENT SERIES. SECTION D, IMMUNOLOGY. 3677
0896-6052 See PENTON'S CONTROLS & SYSTEMS. 3486
0896-6095 See STARLIGHT (WILSON, N.C.). 4999
0896-6141 See KWOC LIST OF PETROLEUM ABSTRACTS' GEOGRAPHIC THESAURUS AND GEOGRAPHIC THESAURUS. SUPPLEMENTAL DESCRIPTORS. 1386
0896-615X See SHADES VALLEY SUN, THE. 5628
0896-6206 See LOUISIANA ALMANAC. 1927
0896-6230 See BANK ASSET/LIABILITY MANAGEMENT. 774
0896-6249 See EVANSVILLE PRESS. 5664
0896-6257 See GEOTHERMAL ENERGY (OAK RIDGE, TENN.). 1945
0896-6273 See NEURON (CAMBRIDGE, MASS.). 466
0896-6281 See FINE GARDENING. 2414
0896-629X See NATIONAL POLITICAL SCIENCE REVIEW. 4483
0896-6346 See NEW PERSPECTIVES ON TURKEY. 5210
0896-6362 See DREISER STUDIES. 3382
0896-6370 See AIDS LAW REPORTER, THE. 2928
0896-6389 See FILM THREAT. 4070
0896-6389 See FILM THREAT. 4070
0896-6400 See NATIONAL LEAGUE GREEN BOOK. 4906
0896-6435 See CAIN AND SCOTT COMMERCIAL INVESTMENT STUDY, THE. 4835
0896-6443 See NCCLS DOCUMENT. 466
0896-646X See MICHIGAN COUNTIES. 4665
0896-6478 See NEW MEXICO PROGRESS, THE. 5298
0896-6494 See EXECUTIVE INVESTMENT LETTER, THE. 897
0896-6559 See VACATIONS UNLIMITED. 5498
0896-6567 See MANAGED CARE OUTLOOK. 3788
0896-6575 See AIRLINERS (MIAMI, FLA.). 5460
0896-6591 See BIBLIOGRAPHIES AND INDEXES IN MEDICAL STUDIES. 3555
0896-6605 See VOICE FOR EDUCATION, THE. 1790
0896-6613 See EDELL HEALTH LETTER, THE. 3573
0896-6621 See JOURNAL OF RESEARCH IN PHARMACEUTICAL ECONOMICS. 4313
0896-6664 See AI APPLICATIONS. 1210
0896-6672 See OREGON FOCUS (PORTLAND, OR.). 1136
0896-6680 See POCKET GUIDE FOR THE MOVIES ON VIDEO. 4076
0896-6702 See CURRENT CONSTRUCTION REPORTS. C22, HOUSING COMPLETIONS. 612
0896-6737 See CURRENT CONSTRUCTION REPORTS. C21, NEW RESIDENTIAL CONSTRUCTION IN SELECTED METROPOLITAN STATISTICAL AREAS. 2819

ISSN Index

0896-6761 *See* CURRENT CONSTRUCTION REPORTS. C20, HOUSING STARTS. **2819**

0896-6834 *See* YARD & GARDEN. **2434**

0896-6877 *See* AAFP REPORTER. **3736**

0896-6915 *See* NURSING HOMES (1991). **3790**

0896-6966 *See* JOURNAL OF PHARMACOEPIDEMIOLOGY. **3596**

0896-6974 *See* JOURNAL OF EPILEPSY. **3835**

0896-7032 *See* LOOKING FORWARD (SEATTLE, WASH.). **4789**

0896-7067 *See* TODAY'S CHEMIST AT WORK. **994**

0896-7075 *See* LAWYERS' LIABILITY REVIEW. **2998**

0896-7083 *See* EOSAT LANDSAT APPLICATION NOTES. **1110**

0896-7091 *See* EOSAT LANDSAT DATA USER NOTES. **1355**

0896-7113 *See* ISMEC, MECHANICAL ENGINEERING ABSTRACTS. **2005**

0896-7148 *See* AMERICAN LITERARY HISTORY. **3360**

0896-7156 *See* MARKETING HIGHER EDUCATION. **931**

0896-7172 *See* HOME & STUDIO RECORDING. **5317**

0896-7180 *See* RADON NEWS DIGEST. **2241**

0896-7210 *See* JOURNAL WATCH. **3660**

0896-7229 *See* PROCOMM ENTERPRISES MAGAZINE. **1162**

0896-7237 *See* REMINERALIZE THE EARTH. **184**

0896-7253 *See* PESTICIDES AND YOU. **4247**

0896-7261 *See* ROLLERCOASTER! MAGAZINE. **4865**

0896-7288 *See* MINIATURES SHOWCASE. **2775**

0896-7296 *See* HUDSPETH REPORT, THE. **5480**

0896-730X *See* AUSTIN DAILY RECORD. **2938**

0896-7326 *See* CTA ACTION (1986). **1862**

0896-7350 *See* REFUND EXPRESS. **2492**

0896-7377 *See* VALLEJO BUSINESS. **717**

0896-7385 *See* CANCERWEEKLY (ATLANTA, GA.). **3814**

0896-7415 *See* BREMER COUNTY BROWSINGS. **2440**

0896-7423 *See* CATALYST (ATLANTA, GA.). **3373**

0896-744X *See* TECHNOLOGY FUTURES NEWSLETTER. **5163**

0896-7563 *See* BASEBALL CARD PRICE GUIDE MONTHLY. **2771**

0896-7571 *See* SOVIET SCIENTIFIC REVIEWS. SECTION G, GEOLOGY REVIEWS. **1397**

0896-758X *See* SNOW COUNTRY. **4919**

0896-7601 *See* MEANS LIGHT COMMERCIAL COST DATA. **620**

0896-7660 *See* CHINESE THEOLOGICAL REVIEW. **4943**

0896-7695 *See* REFEREE (ARLINGTON, VA.), THE. **1018**

0896-7709 *See* WHO'S WHO IN THE WEST (1971). **438**

0896-7717 *See* WORD FOR WORD. **1273**

0896-7725 *See* EXPERT (LOUISVILLE, KY.). **1267**

0896-7733 *See* OUT/LOOK (SAN FRANCISCO, CALIF.). **2795**

0896-7768 *See* JOURNAL OF ADOLESCENT CHEMICAL DEPENDENCY. **1345**

0896-7776 *See* TOTAL EMPLOYEE INVOLVEMENT. **888**

0896-7784 *See* SPECIAL EDUCATION LEADERSHIP. **1885**

0896-7792 *See* FINANCIAL AID FOR VETERANS, MILITARY PERSONNEL, AND THEIR DEPENDENTS. **5285**

0896-7911 *See* BEST PAPERS PROCEEDINGS / ACADEMY OF MANAGEMENT. **861**

0898-2201 *See* PAIS INTERNATIONAL IN PRINT. **5227**

0896-7938 *See* PSYCHOANALYTIC PERSPECTIVES ON ART : PPA. **362**

0896-7946 *See* WRITER'S NORTHWEST HANDBOOK. **4820**

0896-7962 *See* HOME FASHIONS MAGAZINE. **2900**

0896-7970 *See* DIEHARD (BOSTON, MASS.). **2773**

0896-7997 *See* CAHHS INSIGHT. **3777**

0896-8039 *See* ANGLICAN AND EPISCOPAL HISTORY. **5055**

0896-8047 *See* NOTES ON NURSING SCIENCE. **3862**

0896-8063 *See* TATTOO ADVOCATE. **5269**

0896-8071 *See* CLARION CALL (SAN FRANCISCO, CALIF.), THE. **4948**

0896-8101 *See* BIBLIOGRAPHIC GUIDE TO ANTHROPOLOGY AND ARCHAEOLOGY. **261**

0896-8152 *See* JEWISH STORYTELLING NEWSLETTER. **3399**

0896-8160 *See* NEW ENGLAND GARDENER. **2425**

0896-8179 *See* HISTORIC PRESERVATION FORUM. **2618**

0896-8187 *See* RELIGIOUS FUNDING MONITOR. **4992**

0896-8209 *See* PC PUBLISHING. **4818**

0896-8233 *See* EASTERN COLLEGE FOOTBALL MAGAZINE. **4893**

0896-8276 *See* ST. PAUL'S FAMILY MAGAZINE. **365**

0896-8292 *See* KANSAS CITY MAGAZINE & THE TOWN SQUIRE. **2743**

0896-8306 *See* SOVIET MEDICAL REVIEWS. SECTION G, NEUROPHARMACOLOGY REVIEWS. **4330**

0896-8314 *See* FIREHOUSE LAWYER MONTHLY NEWSLETTER. **2970**

0896-8322 *See* DISCOVERIES (PORT TOWNSEND, WASH.). **2773**

0896-8373 *See* GARDEN CLUB OF AMERICA NEWSLETTER, THE. **2415**

0896-8381 *See* JOURNAL OF THE IOWA ACADEMY OF SCIENCE, THE. **5121**

0896-8403 *See* ADOBE NEWS (1988). **598**

0896-8411 *See* JOURNAL OF AUTOIMMUNITY. **3673**

0896-8438 *See* JOURNAL OF OBJECT-ORIENTED PROGRAMMING. **1280**

0896-8446 *See* JOURNAL OF SUPERCRITICAL FLUIDS, THE. **1017**

0896-8462 *See* PROCEEDINGS OF THE LEBEDEV PHYSICS INSTITUTE OF THE ACADEMY OF SCIENCES OF RUSSIA. **4418**

0896-8500 *See* INVESTMENT MANAGEMENT WEEKLY. **903**

0896-8527 *See* MINING BUSINESS DIGEST. **2145**

0896-8535 *See* IRELAND REPORT, WOMEN'S HEALTH MARKETING, THE. **2599**

0896-8586 *See* TECHNOLOGY UPDATE (PALO ALTO, CALIF.). **4394**

0896-8594 *See* INDOOR POLLUTION NEWS. **2232**

0896-8608 *See* PERITONEAL DIALYSIS INTERNATIONAL. **3800**

0896-8624 *See* MEANS RESIDENTIAL COST DATA. **621**

0896-8659 *See* PROCESSING (CHICAGO ILL.). **1028**

0896-8683 *See* BIRNBAUM'S GREAT BRITAIN. **5464**

0896-8691 *See* BIRNBAUM'S IRELAND. **5464**

0896-8705 *See* LACTUCA (SUFFERN, N.Y.). **3403**

0896-8748 *See* RADIOLOGY OUTLOOK. **3946**

0896-8802 *See* GOREZONE (NEW YORK, N.Y.). **385**

0896-8942 *See* MOUNTAIN RECORD. **5021**

0896-8985 *See* CIRCUIT CELLAR INK. **1227**

0896-8993 *See* AMERICAN SONGWRITER. **4099**

0896-9043 *See* COLLECTORS PHOTOGRAPHY. **4368**

0896-9051 *See* SAFE WORKER. **2869**

0896-906X *See* BOWNE DIGEST FOR CORPORATE & SECURITIES LAWYERS. **3079**

0896-9159 *See* COMMUNITY CHANGE. **2818**

0896-9205 *See* CRITICAL SOCIOLOGY. **5243**

0896-9221 *See* CURRENT CONSTRUCTION REPORTS. C40, HOUSING UNITS AUTHORIZED BY BUILDING PERMITS. **612**

0896-9299 *See* UCI JOURNAL. **1095**

0896-9329 *See* CREDIT CARD MANAGEMENT. **785**

0896-9337 *See* ORIGINAL NINJA, THE. **4864**

0896-9345 *See* ALWAYS JUKIN'. **4099**

0896-9418 *See* DULUTH NEWS-TRIBUNE (1987), THE. **5695**

0896-9426 *See* COOPERATIVE PARTNERS. **192**

0896-9442 *See* HOME ENERGY (BERKELEY, CALIF.). **1946**

0896-9469 *See* VITAL STATISTICS ON CONGRESS. **4693**

0896-9523 *See* BOOK PEDDLER, THE. **3368**

0896-9531 *See* BAD ATTITUDE. **2793**

0896-9566 *See* CANCER EN PUERTO RICO / ESTADO LIBRE ASOCIADO DE PUERTO RICO, DEPARTAMENTO DE SALUD, PROGRAMA CONTROL DEL CANCER, REGISTRO CENTRAL DEL CANCER. **3811**

0896-9574 *See* EDUCATING ABLE LEARNERS, DISCOVERING & NURTURING TALENT. **1878**

0896-9590 *See* COLTON CLARION. **2443**

0896-9620 *See* CLINICAL KINESIOLOGY. **4380**

0896-9647 *See* INFECTIONS IN UROLOGY. **3990**

0896-9655 *See* UNIFORM SIGN CODE. **631**

0896-9655 *See* UNIFORM BUILDING CODE STANDARDS. **630**

0896-9663 *See* UNIFORM BUILDING CODE STANDARDS. **630**

0896-9671 *See* UNIFORM MECHANICAL CODE. **631**

0896-9701 *See* UNIFORM SIGN CODE. **631**

0896-9736 *See* UNIFORM FIRE CODE. **2293**

0896-9744 *See* UNIFORM FIRE CODE STANDARDS. **2293**

0896-9752 *See* ANALYSIS OF REVISIONS OF THE UNIFORM BUILDING CODE, U.B.C. STANDARDS **2933**

0896-9779 *See* TEXAS HIGH TECHNOLOGY DIRECTORY. **5165**

0896-9795 *See* QUARTERMASTER PROFESSIONAL BULLETIN. **4545**

0896-9825 *See* NEWSLETTER / CONFERENCE GROUP ON ITALIAN POLITICS & SOCIETY. **4530**

0896-9841 *See* OPTICAL PUBLISHING DIRECTORY, THE. **4818**

0896-985X *See* PERSONNEL PRACTICE IDEAS. **945**

0896-9868 *See* IFR REFRESHER. **23**

0896-9884 *See* MONI TALK. **1619**

0896-9922 *See* C.J. THE AMERICAS. **3159**

0896-9949 *See* OSHA COMPLIANCE ADVISOR. **2867**

0896-9957 *See* OSHA TRAINING BULLETIN FOR SUPERVISORS. **2868**

0896-9965 *See* HORNS OF PLENTY, MALCOLM COWLEY AND HIS GENERATION. **3394**

0897-0068 *See* BOCA NATIONAL BUILDING CODE, THE. **601**

0897-0084 *See* BOCA NATIONAL FIRE PREVENTION CODE, THE. **2288**

0897-0092 *See* BOCA NATIONAL MECHANICAL CODE, THE. **2603**

0897-0106 *See* ETHICS, EASIER SAID THAN DONE. **2250**

0897-0122 *See* MINERAL LAW SERIES. **3010**

0897-0130 *See* LABORATORY PC USER. **1268**

0897-0149 *See* LEAR'S (NEW YORK, N.Y.). **5560**

0897-0157 *See* PASSPORT TO WORLD BAND RADIO. **1136**

0897-0181 *See* BUSINESS CREDIT. **781**

0897-022X *See* HARDWOOD FLOORS. **2401**

0897-0262 *See* REAL ESTATE ACCOUNTING & TAXATION. **4843**

0897-0270 *See* MULTIPLE SCLEROSIS RESEARCH REPORTS. **3838**

0897-0289 *See* IBM DIRECTIONS. **1186**

0897-0297 *See* EMS LEADER, THE. **3724**

0897-0319 *See* NEW HAMPSHIRE SPIRIT. **4907**

0897-0335 *See* TIDINGS (WESTERLY, R.I.). **2763**

0897-0378 *See* INTERNAL AUDITING (BOSTON, MASS.). **745**

0897-0386 *See* BEST RECIPES. 2328

0897-0394 *See* JOURNAL OF BORDERLAND RESEARCH, THE. 4241

0897-0408 *See* TRIAD BUSINESS. 716

0897-0432 *See* DIRECTORY OF INDUSTRIAL DESIGNERS. 2098

0897-0459 *See* CHRISTIAN SOCIAL ACTION (WASHINGTON, D.C.). 4946

0897-0483 *See* GEORGE SAND STUDIES. 3343

0897-0491 *See* MARINE LOG (NEW YORK, N.Y.). 5452

0897-0505 *See* POST-STAR (GLENS FALLS, N.Y. : 1974). 5720

0897-0521 *See* JOURNAL OF THE FANTASTIC IN THE ARTS. 3400

0897-0599 *See* BULLETIN OF AMERICAN GARDEN HISTORY, A. 2411

0897-0645 *See* BOARDING SCHOOLS DIRECTORY. 1728

0897-0653 *See* FIVE-YEAR FORECAST OF BUSINESS CLIMATE TRENDS IN 85 COUNTRIES. 1491

0897-067X *See* CFTC REPORT. 826

0897-0696 *See* ISSUES IN WRITING. 2921

0897-070X *See* PROJECTS IN METAL. 4017

0897-0769 *See* MOVING IMAGE REVIEW. 4075

0897-0785 *See* BROOKGREEN GARDENS NEWSLETTER. 2410

0897-0807 *See* AMERICAN MOTOR CARRIER DIRECTORY (NORTH AMERICAN EDITION). 5375

0897-0823 *See* AIRPOWER JOURNAL. 4034

0897-0920 *See* DAYTON DAILY NEWS (DAYTON, OHIO : 1987). 5728

0897-0939 *See* UPDATE (HACKENSACK, N.J.). 4214

0897-0947 *See* PROCEEDINGS OF THE SOCIETY FOR CALIFORNIA ARCHAEOLOGY. 279

0897-0963 *See* MUSCLECARS (HACKENSACK, N.J.). 5421

0897-1005 *See* NOETIC SCIENCES REVIEW. 4606

0897-1013 *See* NOETIC SCIENCES BULLETIN. 4606

0897-103X *See* REFERENCE (SAINT LOUIS, MO.). 3951

0897-1072 *See* SCIENCE FICTION & FANTASY FORUM. 3434

0897-1129 *See* R:VIEW (TACOMA, WASH.). 1202

0897-1137 *See* NEW TECH NEWS. 3234

0897-1153 *See* MONITOR (ATLANTA, GA.), THE. 4482

0897-120X *See* CSIA NEWS. 4519

0897-1218 *See* CONNECTICUT JOURNAL OF INTERNATIONAL LAW. 3126

0897-1234 *See* CONNECTICUT PROBATE LAW JOURNAL, THE. 2955

0897-1277 *See* JURIMETRICS (CHICAGO, ILL.). 2990

0897-1323 *See* FLORA LEVY LECTURE IN THE HUMANITIES, THE. 2846

0897-1331 *See* IN THE PUBLIC INTEREST (AMHERST, N.Y.). 2980

0897-1358 *See* BULLETIN / LAWYERS COMMITTEE FOR HUMAN RIGHTS. 4505

0897-1439 *See* U.S. UNION SOURCEBOOK. 1715

0897-1471 *See* ACOG CURRENT JOURNAL REVIEW. 3755

0897-148X *See* MI GLOBO. 1804

0897-1498 *See* AMERICAN HORSES IN SPORT. 2796

0897-151X *See* INDEX TO PROCEEDINGS OF THE IEEE. 2064

0897-1609 *See* CUSTOMS TODAY. 4719

0897-1617 *See* CORPORATE COUNSEL'S QUARTERLY. 3098

0897-1676 *See* INSIDE U.S. TRADE. 840

0897-1722 See NAACOG'S WOMEN'S HEALTH NURSING SCAN. 3862

0897-1757 *See* DRUG UTILIZATION IN THE U.S. 4302

0897-182X *See* DIRECTORY OF FAMILY PRACTICE RESIDENCY PROGRAMS. 3737

0897-1862 *See* JOURNAL OF ECONOMIC GROWTH. 1499

0897-1870 *See* ENDOMETRIOSIS ASSOCIATION NEWSLETTER. 3760

0897-1889 *See* JOURNAL OF DIGITAL IMAGING. 3942

0897-1897 *See* APPLIED NURSING RESEARCH : ANR. 3851

0897-1900 *See* JOURNAL OF PHARMACY PRACTICE. 4312

0897-196X *See* GAMES JUNIOR. 4861

0897-1986 *See* KNOWLEDGE AND POLICY. 1115

0897-2001 *See* PETROLEUM TERMINAL ENCYCLOPEDIA. 4274

0897-2028 *See* STALSBY/ WILSON'S WHO'S WHO IN NATURAL GAS SUPPLY. 4279

0897-2044 *See* QUARTERLY REPORT ON MONEY FUND EXPENSE RATIOS. 805

0897-2052 *See* BUSINESS FAX. 1150

0897-2109 *See* AMERICAN IRISH NEWSLETTER, THE. 2609

0897-2222 *See* NATIONAL JEWISH LAW REVIEW. 3013

0897-2249 *See* SEA FRONTIERS (1988). 1456

0897-2281 *See* METROPOLITAN NEWS-ENTERPRISE. 5637

0897-229X *See* INNER HORIZONS. 5030

0897-2346 *See* SOUTHWEST PHILOSOPHY REVIEW. 4361

0897-2400 *See* JOURNAL OF CONTEMPORARY ART. 354

0897-2451 *See* BULLETIN OF PALEOMALACOLOGY. 4226

0897-2524 *See* ALKALINE PAPER ADVOCATE. 4232

0897-2559 *See* MAIN STREET NEWS. 2827

0897-2613 *See* RESIST (SOMERVILLE, MASS.). 4493

0897-2621 *See* FLORIDA SCUBA NEWS. 4895

0897-263X *See* COMPOSITION CHRONICLE. 3377

0897-2680 *See* SOFTWARE LAW BULLETIN, THE. 3056

0897-2699 *See* HAZARDOUS WASTE BUSINESS. 2231

0897-2737 *See* CATTLE BUSINESS IN MISSISSIPPI. 72

0897-2761 *See* HARVARD BLACKLETTER JOURNAL, THE. 4508

0897-280X *See* GARDEN TALK. 2415

0897-2826 *See* IBEW JOURNAL. 1677

0897-2915 1113

0897-2931 *See* PRACTICAL ASPECTS OF DIABETES MANAGEMENT. 3732

0897-2982 *See* WILKIE COLLINS SOCIETY JOURNAL. 3453

0897-3016 *See* RESEARCH IN ORGANIZATIONAL CHANGE AND DEVELOPMENT. 884

0897-3059 *See* GHAA'S NATIONAL DIRECTORY OF HMOS. 4776

0897-3067 *See* BRAZIL WATCH (WASHINGTON, D.C. 1987). 1549

0897-3075 *See* JOURNAL OF POPULAR LITERATURE. 3400

0897-313X *See* CRUISER (1985), THE. 2378

0897-3156 *See* GUIDE TO BACKGROUND INVESTIGATIONS, THE. 1676

0897-3199 *See* INFORMATION MANAGEMENT SOURCEBOOK. 3216

0897-3210 See LOCAL AREA NETWORKS. 1193

0897-3237 *See* AGRICOLA ; CRIS. 48

0897-3261 *See* ICE CREAM REPORTER. 2343

0897-327X *See* TOUCHSTONE (CHICAGO, ILL. 1986). 5005

0897-3296 *See* CDROM DATABASES. 1174

0897-3318 *See* CATALYST (MENLO PARK, CALIF.), THE. 1876

0897-3350 *See* DOUGHTY TREE, THE. 2446

0897-3393 *See* HARVARD JOURNAL OF LAW & TECHNOLOGY. 2976

0897-3407 *See* MEALEY'S LITIGATION REPORTS. SUPERFUND. 3114

0897-3423 *See* CANYON LEGACY. 2613

0897-3458 *See* BASKETMAKER (WESTLAND, MICH.). 370

0897-3474 *See* NTIS (DUBLIN, OHIO). 421

0897-3482 *See* BOWMAN'S ACCOUNTING REPORT. 739

0897-3598 *See* HEALTH ADVOCATE (MADISON, WIS.). 3581

0897-3660 *See* ADVANCES IN INTERNATIONAL ACCOUNTING. 738

0897-3695 *See* SOUTHEAST LOUISIANA HISTORICAL PAPERS. 2761

0897-3792 *See* ORGANIC GARDENING (1988). 2426

0897-3806 *See* CLINICAL ANATOMY (NEW YORK, N.Y.). 3679

0897-3849 *See* POPULATION & DEVELOPMENT. 4556

0897-3873 *See* PENNINGTON COUNTY NEWS. 5744

0897-3881 *See* COMPETITIVE EDGE (BEVERLY HILLS, CALIF.). 659

0897-389X *See* TRAVEL & TOURISM LAW BIBLIOGRAPHY. 3083

0897-3903 *See* HAIR & BEAUTY NEWS. 404

0897-3938 *See* DALLAS PERSPECTIVE. 1479

0897-3946 *See* TOPICS IN THE NEUROSCIENCES. 3846

0897-3962 *See* JOURNAL OF INTEGRAL EQUATIONS AND APPLICATIONS, THE. 3513

0897-3989 *See* DIRECTORY OF ART AND DESIGN FACULTIES IN COLLEGES AND UNIVERSITIES, U.S. AND CANADA. 349

0897-4012 *See* NATIONAL VANGUARD. 5252

0897-4020 *See* POSTCARD CLASSICS. 375

0897-408X *See* CHRISTIAN COUNTY GENEALOGICAL SOCIETY. 2443

0897-411X *See* INTERNATIONAL COMPUTER UPDATE. 1189

0897-4128 *See* SOURCE FILE. 1203

0897-4179 *See* CORVETTE QUARTERLY. 5412

0897-4195 *See* GUIDE TO WRITERS CONFERENCES, THE. 3392

0897-4217 *See* KEPNER TREGOE BUSINESS REVIEW. 875

0897-4268 *See* GLOBAL CLIMATE CHANGE DIGEST. 1425

0897-4349 *See* SPEAKER REPORT, THE. 3439

0897-4357 *See* UTOPIA 2. 5225

0897-4365 *See* IRON AGE (NEW YORK, N.Y. 1987). 4004

0897-4403 *See* HIGH-PURITY SUBSTANCES. 977

0897-4438 *See* JOURNAL OF INTERNATIONAL FOOD & AGRIBUSINESS MARKETING. 2347

0897-4446 *See* JOURNAL OF COUPLES THERAPY. 2281

0897-4454 *See* WOMEN & CRIMINAL JUSTICE. 3179

0897-4462 *See* DIRECTORY OF STATE EDUCATION AGENCIES. 1736

0897-4497 *See* HORSE WORLD USA. 2800

0897-4519 *See* INDOCHINA CHRONOLOGY. 2653

0897-4527 *See* INSTITUTE TODAY. 791

0897-4543 *See* SHEBOYGAN FALLS NEWS, THE. 5770

0897-4551 *See* CALDWELL MESSENGER (CALDWELL, KAN. 1942), THE. 5674

0897-456X *See* TELEGRAPH (ALTON, ILL.), THE. 5662

0897-4608 *See* ATLANTA SINGLES. 2485

0897-4616 *See* FLORIDA PHARMACY TODAY. 4305

0897-4624 *See* FLORIDA JOURNAL OF ENVIRONMENTAL HEALTH. 2172

0897-4640 *See* COAST & COUNTRY. 2531

0897-4667 *See* WORLD MILITARY EXPENDITURES AND ARMS TRANSFERS. 4061

0897-4683 *See* ETHNIC WOMAN, THE. 2260

0897-4705 *See* CISA WORKING PAPER (LOS ANGELES, CALIF. : 1985). 4518

0897-4713 See COLLEGE HOCKEY. 4890

ISSN Index

0897-4721 See WOW! (NEW YORK, N.Y. 1987). 389

0897-4756 See CHEMISTRY OF MATERIALS. 971

0897-4764 See NATIONAL ASSOCIATION OF DESKTOP PUBLISHERS FORUM, THE. 4817

0897-4810 See FEDERAL DATA BASE FINDER, THE. 1254

0897-4845 See PRIVATE LABEL (EXECUTIVE EDITION). 882

0897-4888 See ENVOI (NEW YORK, N.Y.). 3384

0897-490X See INSIDER TRADING REGULATION. 901

0897-4926 See CITY & COUNTRY CLUB LIFE. 2530

0897-4977 See OJIBWE TIMES, THE. 5697

0897-5027 See ID MAGAZINE. 5202

0897-5035 See HARD TIMES (MERIDEN, CONN.). 2452

0897-5051 See OREGON WHEAT. 1620

0897-506X See TERRA NOVA (WASHINGTON, D.C.). 4536

0897-5078 See CRUISE MAGAZINE. 5467

0897-5086 See INTERNATIONAL FREEDOM FOUNDATION. 1636

0897-5094 See NEW WAVES. 5536

0897-5108 See STANDARD & POOR'S/ LIPPER MUTUAL FUND PROFILES. 915

0897-5116 See WISCONSIN SMALL BUSINESS COUNSELOR. 889

0897-5132 See WOLFMAN REPORT ON THE PHOTOGRAPHIC & IMAGING INDUSTRY IN THE UNITED STATES. 4378

0897-5167 See BNA'S REVIEW OF WHAT'S NEW. 3196

0897-5213 See MOUNTAIN BIKE. 4905

0897-5221 See BUSINESS INSIGHT. 649

0897-5256 See WRIGHT/CHAMBERS REPORT, THE. 4570

0897-5264 See JOURNAL OF COLLEGE STUDENT DEVELOPMENT. 1832

0897-5280 See LECTURA DANTIS (CHARLOTTESVILLE, VA.). 3404

0897-5345 See H.A.N.D.S. ON GUIDE. 373

0897-5353 See JOURNAL OF FAMILY PSYCHOTHERAPY. 2282

0897-5418 See MEDICAL LETTER HANDBOOK OF ADVERSE DRUG INTERACTIONS, THE. 4314

0897-5442 See DIRECTORY OF DISCOUNT DEPARTMENT STORES (NEW YORK, N.Y. : 1988). 953

0897-5469 See MARRIAGE PARTNERSHIP. 4975

0897-5507 See GIS WORLD. 2565

0897-5523 See ACADEMY NEWSLETTER, THE. 5079

0897-5531 See PROCEEDINGS / BELTWIDE COTTON CONFERENCES. 182

0897-554X See AMBULATORY MEDICINE LETTER, THE. 3548

0897-5566 See FERMILAB REPORT. 4447

0897-5574 See TEMPDIGEST (HOUSTON, TEX.). 4209

0897-5639 See ONCODISC (PHILADELPHIA, PA.). 3821

0897-5647 See NURSING SCAN IN RESEARCH. 3865

0897-5698 See ORANGE COUNTY LAWYER. 3023

0897-5728 See BERNAN ASSOCIATES' GOVERNMENT PUBLICATIONS NEWS. 4632

0897-5736 See 501(C)(3) MONTHLY LETTER. 636

0897-5760 See STRIKEFORCE MORITURI. 4866

0897-5795 See NEW ENGLAND ANTIQUES JOURNAL. 251

0897-5833 See RESORTS & GREAT HOTELS. 2809

0897-5914 See WHO'S WHO IN INTERIOR DESIGN. 2904

0897-5922 See NATIONAL OFFICE DIRECTORY. 697

0897-5930 See JOURNAL OF TEACHING IN INTERNATIONAL BUSINESS. 688

0897-5949 See HEART HEALTH DIGEST. 4782

0897-5957 See CARDIOVASCULAR DRUG REVIEWS. 3701

0897-5973 See CONFETTI (ELK GROVE VILLAGE, ILL.). 1109

0897-6007 See PUBLISH! (SAN FRANCISCO, CALIF.). 1263

0897-6015 See CIVIL WAR (BERRYVILLE, VA.). 2728

0897-6023 See PETERSON'S GUIDE TO GRADUATE PROGRAMS IN BUSINESS, EDUCATION, HEALTH, AND LAW. 4208

0897-6031 See OPPORTUNITY NOCS. 881

0897-6058 See CHIROPRACTIC (FORT WAYNE, IND.). 4379

0897-6074 See JOURNAL OF THE ANCIENT NEAR EASTERN SOCIETY, THE. 2621

0897-6104 See MINERVA'S BULLETIN BOARD. 4051

0897-6112 See DRUGS IN PREGNANCY AND LACTATION. 4302

0897-6139 See FAXON GUIDE TO CD-ROM. 1185

0897-6171 See KELLEY BLUE BOOK NEW CAR PRICE MANUAL. 5418

0897-6201 See MODERN BAKING. 2350

0897-621X See HOMESTYLES HOME PLANS. 300

0897-6228 See DESIGNERS' COLLECTION HOME PLANS. 297

0897-6236 See DISTINGUISHED HOME PLANS. HOMES FOR SLOPING SITES. 298

0897-6287 See STOCK PHOTO DESKBOOK, THE. 4377

0897-6295 See NEONATOLOGY (NORWALK, CONN.). 3765

0897-6309 See INTERNAL MEDICINE. 3797

0897-6317 See PSYCHIATRY (NORWALK, CONN.). 3934

0897-6422 See ENVIRONMENTAL HEALTH BULLETIN (WASHINGTON, D.C.). 4774

0897-6473 See JOURNAL SEAMUS : THE JOURNAL OF THE SOCIETY FOR ELECTRO-ACOUSTIC MUSIC IN THE UNITED STATES. 4127

0897-6481 See LUCIDITY. 3465

0897-6538 See NELSON'S DIRECTORY OF 'NEGLECTED STOCK' OPPORTUNITIES. 909

0897-6546 See LAW & SOCIAL INQUIRY. 2994

0897-6554 See OPERA MONTHLY. 4143

0897-6619 See SMITH COLLEGE STUDIES IN HISTORY. 2629

0897-6627 See POWDER AND BULK ENGINEERING. 1991

0897-6694 See MINERAL LAW NEWSLETTER. 3010

0897-6708 See IMMIGRATION BRIEFINGS. 2980

0897-6716 See LYRA (GUTTENBERG, N.J.). 3409

0897-6724 See WORLD EDUCATION NEWS & REVIEWS. 1791

0897-6740 See CORPORATE ANTI-TAKEOVER DEFENSES. 661

0897-6775 See HERITAGE EDUCATION QUARTERLY. 2481

0897-6813 See IEEE 802.3 REPORT. 2058

0897-6821 See BERLITZ TRAVELLER'S GUIDE TO THE CARIBBEAN, THE. 5463

0897-683X See BERLITZ TRAVELLER'S GUIDE TO FRANCE, THE. 5462

0897-6856 See BERLITZ TRAVELLER'S GUIDE TO IRELAND, THE. 5463

0897-6864 See BERLITZ TRAVELLER'S GUIDE TO ENGLAND & WALES, THE. 5462

0897-697X See HAN'GUK KYONGJE SINMUN. 2920

0897-7127 See BUSINESS-TO-BUSINESS DIRECT MARKETER, THE. 922

0897-7135 See CONTRACTOR (NEWTON, MASS.). 2604

0897-7151 See JOURNAL OF NEUROTRAUMA. 3837

0897-7186 See JOURNAL OF HEALTH & SOCIAL POLICY. 5292

0897-7194 See GROWTH FACTORS (CHUR, SWITZERLAND). 456

0897-7208 See FOODSERVICE DIRECTOR. 2341

0897-7224 See CHINA STATISTICS MONTHLY. 5325

0897-7283 See UTAH FISHING. 4880

0897-7313 See WINSTON'S TRAVEL DELUXE. 5499

0897-7348 See PERMACULTURE ACTIVIST, THE. 119

0897-7380 See YALE PUBLICATIONS IN THE HISTORY OF ART. 369

0897-7410 See ITALIAN QUERIES. 2455

0897-7429 See BATCHELDER REVIEW. 2438

0897-7437 See NURSE ANESTHESIA. 3683

0897-750X See COASTAL CRUISING. 4890

0897-7534 See HARTFORD MONTHLY. 2534

0897-7542 See LETRAS PENINSULARES. 3404

0897-7550 See BIOLOGICAL MONITORING. 445

0897-7607 See MANAGING FOR HEALTH. 4789

0897-7615 See HEALTHY COMPANIES. 679

0897-7631 See ELECTRONICS HANDBOOK. 2049

0897-7704 See YO YO TIMES. 1071

0897-7739 See MASSACHUSETTS QUERIES. 2459

0897-7747 See OHIO QUERIES. 2465

0897-7755 See NORTH CAROLINA QUERIES. 2464

0897-7763 See PAGE PEDIGREE. 2466

0897-7771 See OAKES ACORNS. 2465

0897-778X See FARR FOOTNOTES. 2448

0897-7798 See GATES GAZETTE. 2449

0897-7828 See STUDIES IN CLASSICAL GREEK. 1080

0897-7836 See RENAISSANCE AND BAROQUE. 2627

0897-7844 See TWENTIETH CENTURY AMERICAN JEWISH WRITERS. 3448

0897-7852 See COMPREHENSIVE INDEX, CALIFORNIA CODE OF REGULATIONS. 3079

0897-7860 See SMALL SIBLINGS. 2472

0897-7879 See BRICKER BRANCHES. 2440

0897-7925 See VERMONT BUSINESS MAGAZINE. 718

0897-7992 See BENEFITS LAW JOURNAL. 3144

0897-8018 See JOURNAL OF HOME HEALTH CARE PRACTICE. 5292

0897-8026 See INTERNATIONAL NEWS ON FATS, OILS AND RELATED MATERIALS. 1025

0897-8085 See SOFTWARE MAGAZINE (WESTBOROUGH, MASS.). 1290

0897-8107 See SLOVAK CATHOLIC FALCON. 5036

0897-8115 See BUILDING TIMES MAGAZINE. 4940

0897-814X See TREASURE CHEST (NEW YORK, N.Y.). 252

0897-8174 See NEW ORLEANS MAGAZINE (1988). 2540

0897-8263 See ZOOSCAPE (LOS ANGELES, CALIF.). 5603

0897-8298 See NORTHERN CALIFORNIA MONTHLY. 2541

0897-831X See ROTOR (ALEXANDRIA, VA.). 34

0897-8328 See WASHINGTON EXECUTIVE TRAVEL REPORT. 5499

0897-8336 See PRODUCTION AND INVENTORY MANAGEMENT JOURNAL. 883

0897-8352 See PUBLICATIONS IN ANTHROPOLOGY AND HISTORY. 243

0897-8360 See AUTOMOBILE (NEW YORK, N.Y. : 1988). 5406

0897-8395 See LITTLETON TIMES. 5643

0897-8484 See STAFF LEADER. 887

0897-8492 See WINE SPECTATOR'S WINE COUNTRY GUIDE TO CALIFORNIA, THE. 2372

0897-8514 See POLITICAL RISK YEARBOOK. VOL. 7, EUROPE. OUTSIDE THE EUROPEAN COMMUNITY. 4490

0897-8522 See POLITICAL RISK YEARBOOK. VOL. 6, EUROPE. COUNTRIES OF THE EUROPEAN COMMUNITY. 4532

0897-8530 See ... POLITICAL RISK YEARBOOK. MIDDLE EAST & NORTH AFRICA, THE. 4489

0897-8549 See ... POLITICAL RISK YEARBOOK. SOUTH AMERICA, THE. **4489**

0897-8557 See ... POLITICAL RISK YEARBOOK. NORTH & CENTRAL AMERICA, THE. **4489**

0897-8565 See POLITICAL RISK YEARBOOK. VOL. 5, ASIA & THE PACIFIC. **4489**

0897-8573 See IOWA STUDIES IN AFRICAN ART. **353**

0897-859X See ARTS INDIANA. **315**

0897-8697 See PARENTS & TEENAGERS. **2284**

0897-8735 See BIG HORN COUNTY NEW. **5705**

0897-8743 See COLUSA COUNTY SUN HERALD. **5634**

0897-8751 See CPI (BALTIMORE, MD.). **5412**

0897-876X See UPDATE IN PEDIATRIC DENTISTRY. **1337**

0897-8778 See GAS BUYERS GUIDE. **4257**

0897-8786 See HUMAN QUEST. **4963**

0897-8794 See VIRGINIA GAME & FISH. **4880**

0897-8808 See PENNSYLVANIA GAME & FISH. **4877**

0897-8816 See NORTH CAROLINA GAME & FISH. **4876**

0897-8875 See SHOWPLACE (GRAND RAPIDS, MICH.). **2545**

0897-8913 See PC DISK QUARTERLY. **1198**

0897-8921 See MAGAZETTE (SHREVEPORT, LA.), THE. **2538**

0897-893X See PCGAMES. **1230**

0897-8956 See ... GIS GUIDE TO FOUR-YEAR COLLEGES, THE. **1825**

0897-8972 See NEW ENGLAND GAME & FISH. **4875**

0897-8980 See INDIANA GAME & FISH. **4873**

0897-8999 See NEBRASKA GAME & FISH. **4875**

0897-9022 See MID-ATLANTIC GAME & FISH. **4874**

0897-9065 See BUSINESS TO BUSINESS (PITTSFORD, N.Y.). **653**

0897-909X See CRS PUBLICATIONS' CAREER OPPORTUNITY INDEX (EAST-SOUTH-CENTRAL). **4203**

0897-9111 See SILVER SURFER. **4866**

0897-9138 See FUTURE ENERGY CONFERENCES AND SYMPOSIA. **1945**

0897-9154 See SOUTH CAROLINA GAME & FISH. **4878**

0897-9162 See WEST VIRGINIA GAME & FISH. **4880**

0897-9170 See OHIO GAME & FISH. **4876**

0897-9189 See NEW YORK GAME & FISH. **4875**

0897-9197 See IOWA GAME & FISH. **4873**

0897-9200 See GREAT PLAINS GAME & FISH. **4873**

0897-9219 See TRUCKERS/USA (TUSCALOOSA, ALA.). **5398**

0897-9227 See UTAH ADVANCE REPORTS. **3070**

0897-9243 See STUDIES IN THE ROMANTIC AGE. **3442**

0897-9251 See HEALTHWAYS. **4191**

0897-926X See WORCESTER POLYTECHNIC INSTITUTE STUDIES IN SCIENCE, TECHNOLOGY, AND CULTURE. **5170**

0897-9278 See AUGMENTATIVE COMMUNICATION NEWS. **1293**

0897-9286 See MARION ZIMMER BRADLEY'S FANTASY MAGAZINE. **3410**

0897-9308 See LOS ANGELES COMPUTER CURRENTS. **1193**

0897-9316 See WASHINGTON, D.C. COMPUTER CURRENTS. **1207**

0897-9324 See BOSTON COMPUTER CURRENTS. **1235**

0897-9383 See FLORIDA REAL ESTATE. **4837**

0897-9391 See WHITE WOLF MAGAZINE. **4867**

0897-9405 See COPY MAGAZINE. **4211**

0897-9413 See VAN BUREN ECHOES. **2476**

0897-9472 See WORLD MONITOR. **2495**

0897-9499 See DIRECTIONS : A NEWSLETTER FROM EBSCO PUBLISHING. **3206**

0897-9502 See ARCTIC SOUNDER, THE. **5628**

0897-9545 See PAX CHRISTI USA. **4985**

0897-9588 See BEREAVEMENT (CARMEL, IND.). **4577**

0897-9634 See MEDICARE ADVISOR. **5295**

0897-9669 See UNCAPTIVE MINDS. **2714**

0897-9677 See PROBLEMS IN RESPIRATORY CARE. **3951**

0897-9685 See JOURNAL OF CHILD AND ADOLESCENT PSYCHIATRIC AND MENTAL HEALTH NURSING. **3928**

0897-9715 See LYCEUM TIMES, THE. **3409**

0897-9723 See GLEANER (KOKOMO, IND.). **4960**

0897-9774 See MEDIGUIDE TO PEDIATRICS. **3906**

0897-9790 See CHILDREN'S WRITER'S & ILLUSTRATOR'S MARKET. **3374**

0897-9804 See INSPIRATIONAL WRITER'S MARKET. **3396**

0897-9812 See NOVEL & SHORT STORY WRITER'S MARKET. **3419**

0897-9839 See LIVE OAK (OAKLAND, CALIF. 1982), THE. **2458**

0897-9847 See NETWORK (CHARLOTTE, N.C.), THE. **5297**

0897-9871 See ANTIVIRAL AGENTS BULLETIN. **3551**

0897-991X See CALS REPORT. **3476**

0897-9979 See BUSINESS TAX REPORT. **3097**

0898-0012 See LOCAL AREA NETWORK MAGAZINE : LAN, THE. **1193**

0898-0055 See TRAVEL PREVIEW. **5496**

0898-008X See MONOGRAPHIC SUPPLEMENT ... TO CATALOGING & CLASSIFICATION QUARTERLY. **420**

0898-0101 See JOURNAL OF HOLISTIC NURSING. **3858**

0898-0128 See LEATHER CONSERVATION NEWS. **3185**

0898-0179 See RESEARCH IN LAW AND POLICY STUDIES. **3039**

0898-0209 See REAL ESTATE FINANCE JOURNAL, THE. **4844**

0898-0233 See FIVE FINGERS REVIEW. **3388**

0898-0268 See TENDER LOVING CARE PRACTICE PROMOTIONS. **5522**

0898-0284 See CLEM LABINE'S TRADITIONAL BUILDING. **295**

0898-0306 See JOURNAL OF POLICY HISTORY. **4479**

0898-0330 See CIRCUIT RIDER (FRANKFORT, KY.), THE. **2728**

0898-0373 See NARTE NEWS. **1160**

0898-0403 See CELLULAR INVESTOR. **1151**

0898-0454 See EURASIAN LANGUAGE ARCHIVES. **3280**

0898-0489 See OSI PRODUCT & EQUIPMENT NEWS. **1198**

0898-0497 See BULLETIN (MISSISSIPPI AGRICULTURAL AND FORESTRY EXPERIMENT STATION). **69**

0898-0519 See PSYCHIATRIC LENGTH OF STAY BY DIAGNOSIS, UNITED STATES, SOUTHERN REGION. **3791**

0898-0527 See PSYCHIATRIC LENGTH OF STAY BY DIAGNOSIS, UNITED STATES, NORTHEASTERN REGION. **3791**

0898-0535 See PSYCHIATRIC LENGTH OF STAY BY DIAGNOSIS. UNITED STATES, WESTERN REGION. **3791**

0898-0543 See PSYCHIATRIC LENGTH OF STAY BY DIAGNOSIS, UNITED STATES. **3791**

0898-0721 See COLUMBIA BUSINESS LAW REVIEW. **3097**

0898-0756 See SCRAP PROCESSING AND RECYCLING. **4018**

0898-0829 See ECONOMIC FACT BOOK (DETROIT, MICH.). **1483**

0898-0845 See SEATTLE WEEKLY. **5762**

0898-090X See SLOAN'S GREEN GUIDE TO ANTIQUING IN NEW ENGLAND. **252**

0898-0926 See HOLISTIC EDUCATION REVIEW. **1751**

0898-1027 See FRANCE TELECOM NEWS. **1156**

0898-1086 See PENTHOUSE HOT TALK. **3996**

0898-1094 See INTERNATIONAL DIRECTORY OF RESOURCES FOR ARTISANS, THE. **373**

0898-1140 See NUEZ (NEW YORK, N.Y.), LA. **3419**

0898-1183 See APPLEWORKS JOURNAL. **1278**

0898-1191 See NORTHERN CALIFORNIA HOME & GARDEN. **2902**

0898-1221 See COMPUTERS & MATHEMATICS WITH APPLICATIONS (1987). **1179**

0898-1329 See ARMSTRONG CHRONICLES. **2438**

0898-1353 See CAREER PLANNING AND ADULT DEVELOPMENT NETWORK NEWSLETTER. **4202**

0898-1418 See KAUAI UPDATE, THE. **5482**

0898-1434 See TODAY'S IMAGE. **715**

0898-1485 See SOAP OPERA UPDATE. **2546**

0898-1493 See NATIONAL DIRECTORY OF CERTIFIED COUNSELORS. **1882**

0898-1507 See LASERS IN ENGINEERING. **1985**

0898-1515 See RTFI INDEX, THE. **810**

0898-154X See MERVEILLES & CONTES. **3411**

0898-1558 See DARIUS MILHAUD SOCIETY NEWSLETTER, THE. **4113**

0898-1574 See PERKINS PRESS. **2467**

0898-1582 See FILM & VIDEO FINDER. **4069**

0898-1604 See NUTRITION NEWSLINE. **4196**

0898-1655 See DECUBITUS (CHICAGO, ILL.). **3571**

0898-1663 See AILA MONTHLY MAILING. **3123**

0898-1671 See MONEY WATCH (WASHINGTON, D.C.). **1506**

0898-168X See NORTHWEST FLORIDA DAILY NEWS. **5650**

0898-1698 See REAL PROPERTY LAW REPORTER. **3035**

0898-1701 See DENVER HERALD DISPATCH. **5642**

0898-171X See INSIDE DPMA. **683**

0898-1744 See EASTERN REVIEW (NEW YORK, N.Y.). **415**

0898-1795 See INSIGHTS. **3217**

0898-1817 See CALIFORNIAN (EL CAJON, CALIF.), THE. **5633**

0898-1833 See SPECTACULAR SPIDER-MAN. **4866**

0898-1841 See BUSINESS & TAX PLANNING QUARTERLY. **645**

0898-1930 See KHOSANA : THE BULLETIN OF THE THAILAND/LAOS/CAMBODIA STUDIES GROUP OF THE SOUTHWEST ASIA COUNCIL, ASSOCIATION FOR ASIAN STUDIES. **2505**

0898-2007 See ADVANCES IN SOCIAL COGNITION. **5238**

0898-2015 See ONLINE ACCESS. **1248**

0898-2031 See NORTHWEST (NEW YORK, N.Y.). **2571**

0898-2066 See OSKALOOSA HERALD (OSKALOOSA, IOWA : 1977). **5672**

0898-2074 See SOUTH DAKOTA HALL OF FAME. **2546**

0898-2104 See JOURNAL OF LIPOSOME RESEARCH. **538**

0898-2112 See QUALITY ENGINEERING. **1992**

0898-2139 See EMPLOYERS NEGOTIATING SERVICE. **4646**

0898-2155 See AUTOMOTIVE INVESTOR. **5406**

0898-218X See CRS PUBLICATIONS' CAREER OPPORTUNITY INDEX (WESTERN). **4203**

0898-2228 See ADWEEK AGENCY DIRECTORY (EASTERN ED. 1986). **754**

0898-2279 See HEP ... COLLEGES AND UNIVERSITY COMPUTER DIRECTORY, THE. **1827**

0898-2317 See DIRECTORY OF POSTSECONDARY INSTITUTIONS. **1821**

0898-2333 See TRANSFER (SANTA BARBARA, CALIF.). **1205**

0898-2392 See MUSE (GRAHAM, N.C.). **3414**

0898-2414 See BIOSIS PREVIEWS SEARCH GUIDE. **448**

0898-2457 See COMMUNICATIONS LAW (1982). **2954**

ISSN Index

0898-2473 *See* DIAGNOSTIC IMAGING INTERNATIONAL. 3940

0898-249X *See* PSYCHIATRIC LENGTH OF STAY BY DIAGNOSIS, UNITED STATES, NORTH CENTRAL REGION. 3791

0898-2503 *See* PHILLYSPORT (PHILADELPHIA, PA.). 2543

0898-2511 *See* FAIRTEST EXAMINER, THE. 1746

0898-252X *See* AASA PROFESSOR, THE. 1859

0898-2538 *See* ACTIONLINE (SOUTHFIELD, MICH.). 5403

0898-2562 See BROWN UNIVERSITY CHILD AND ADOLESCENT BEHAVIOR LETTER, THE. 4578

0898-2627 *See* PRENTICE HALL'S FEDERAL TAXATION. INDIVIDUALS. 4741

0898-2635 *See* PRENTICE HALL'S FEDERAL TAXATION. CORPORATIONS, PARTNERSHIPS, ESTATES, AND TRUSTS. 4741

0898-2643 *See* JOURNAL OF AGING AND HEALTH. 3752

0898-2740 *See* JOURNAL OF HEALTHCARE EDUCATION AND TRAINING. 3595

0898-2759 *See* PHYSICIAN EXECUTIVE. 3916

0898-2767 See ORL-HEAD AND NECK NURSING. 3890

0898-2783 *See* ACUTE CARE THERAPEUTICS. 3546

0898-2813 *See* BIOTECH PATENT NEWS. 3688

0898-2821 *See* FEDERAL LABOR RELATIONS UPDATE. 1669

0898-2848 *See* BIOTECHNOLOGY THERAPEUTICS. 3690

0898-2929 *See* UNITED NATIONS RESOLUTIONS. SERIES 2, RESOLUTIONS AND DECISIONS OF THE SECURITY COUNCIL. 3137

0898-2937 *See* NBER WORKING PAPER SERIES. 1507

0898-2945 *See* EAST AURORA BEE. 5716

0898-2996 *See* BUZZWORM (BOULDER, COLO.). 2189

0898-3011 *See* SATORI. 2492

0898-3038 *See* HEMISPHERE (MIAMI, FLA.). 4475

0898-3070 *See* BUCKEYE OSTEOPATHIC PHYSICIAN. 4294

0898-3089 *See* CATALYST REVIEW NEWSLETTER, THE. 1050

0898-3097 *See* HISPANIC (WASHINGTON, D.C.). 2262

0898-3100 *See* ANNUAL REPORT / ADMINISTRATIVE CONFERENCE OF THE UNITED STATES. 4626

0898-3127 *See* MIND BODY HEALTH DIGEST. 3799

0898-3283 *See* AUSTRALIAN & NEW ZEALAND JOURNAL OF SERIALS LIBRARIANSHIP. 3193

0898-3313 *See* PRINTWEAR MAGAZINE. 5355

0898-3348 *See* T.H.E. JOURNAL. SOURCE GUIDE OF HIGH-TECHNOLOGY PRODUCTS FOR EDUCATION. 1225

0898-3380 *See* SUFISM (SAN RAFAEL, CALIF.). 5001

0898-3399 *See* WORLD GRAIN SITUATION AND OUTLOOK. 204

0898-3402 *See* DAILY REPORT. NEAR EAST & SOUTH ASIA. 1131

0898-3410 *See* TRIATHLETE (ALLENTOWN, PA.). 4927

0898-3437 *See* PHYTOCHEMICAL BULLETIN. 522

0898-347X *See* DAILY REPORT. EAST ASIA. 2503

0898-3496 *See* DAILY REPORT. WEST EUROPE. 2515

0898-3526 *See* BUSINESS LINE (SYLMAR, CALIF.). 650

0898-3550 *See* SOUTHERN CALIFORNIA WOODWORKER, THE. 635

0898-3569 *See* HEALTH & YOU (CINNAMINSON, N.J.). 2598

0898-3577 *See* COMPLIANCE ENGINEERING. 1152

0898-3690 *See* JPRS REPORT. SCIENCE & TECHNOLOGY. USSR, LIFE SCIENCES. 5122

0898-3712 *See* ATHENS DAILY NEWS, ATHENS BANNER-HERALD. 5652

0898-3720 *See* CAR AUDIO AND ELECTRONICS. 5316

0898-3747 *See* CONTEST BUSTER. 2531

0898-3860 *See* COLUMBUS LEDGER-ENQUIRER. 5653

0898-3879 *See* STATISTICAL ABSTRACT OF UTAH (SALT LAKE CITY, UTAH. 1987). 733

0898-3917 *See* ANNUAL REPORT / BONNEVILLE POWER ADMINISTRATION. 2035

0898-3925 *See* MISSOURI, NEW AND EXPANDING INDUSTRY. 1618

0898-3933 *See* RELIABILITY ASSESSMENT. 2079

0898-4018 *See* HANDBOOK : A PUBLICATION OF THE COLORADO COUNCIL ON HIGH SCHOOL-COLLEGE RELATIONS. 1749

0898-4042 See MEANS SITE WORK & LANDSCAPE COST DATA. 621

0898-4050 *See* EMERGING TRENDS IN REAL ESTATE. 4837

0898-4077 *See* SCIENCE FICTION, FANTASY, & HORROR. 3434

0898-4093 *See* ALUMNI MAGAZINE / COLUMBIA UNIVERSITY-PRESBYTERIAN HOSPITAL SCHOOL OF NURSING ALUMNI ASSOCIATION, INC. 3850

0898-4131 *See* JOURNAL OF THE ASSOCIATION OF FOOD AND DRUG OFFICIALS. 4787

0898-4204 *See* WORLD WAR II. 2633

0898-4212 *See* JOURNAL OF THE ABRAHAM LINCOLN ASSOCIATION. 2742

0898-4247 *See* U.S. AND WORLD WIDE TRAVEL ACCOMMODATIONS GUIDE. 5498

0898-4271 *See* POLITICAL RESOURCE DIRECTORY (NATIONAL ED.). 4489

0898-4298 *See* FEDERAL UPDATE. 4649

0898-4301 *See* SPORT PARACHUTIST'S SAFETY JOURNAL. 4854

0898-4328 *See* CEP RESEARCH REPORT. 1469

0898-4336 *See* INTERNATIONAL ECONOMY, THE. 1636

0898-4360 *See* PLAINDEALER (WICHITA, KAN. 1919), THE. 5678

0898-4387 *See* FLORIDA LEADER. 1824

0898-4468 *See* DATAPRO OFFICE PRODUCTS EVALUATION SERVICE. 4211

0898-4484 *See* CONTINENTAL BANK JOURNAL OF APPLIED CORPORATE FINANCE. 784

0898-4557 *See* GETTYSBURG REVIEW (1988). 3391

0898-4565 *See* POULTRY PROCESSING. 2353

0898-4581 *See* UPTOWN SAN DIEGO EXAMINER. 5641

0898-4603 *See* COLORADO SKI INDUSTRY CHARACTERISTICS AND FINANCIAL ANALYSIS. 4890

0898-4654 *See* AMERICAN STATISTICAL ASSOCIATION PROCEEDINGS OF THE BIOPHARMACEUTICAL SECTION. 4334

0898-4697 *See* ASGSB BULLETIN. 12

0898-4719 *See* GOLF FOR WOMEN : GFW. 4896

0898-4735 *See* DIRECTORY OF DANCE FACULTIES IN COLLEGES AND UNIVERSITIES, U.S. AND CANADA. 1313

0898-4786 *See* MARTIAL ARTS TRAINING. 4904

0898-4875 *See* SALUDOS HISPANOS. 2492

0898-4905 *See* DIRECTORY - NATIONAL RESEARCH COUNCIL (U.S.). FOOD AND NUTRITION BOARD (1982). 4190

0898-4921 *See* JOURNAL OF NEUROSURGICAL ANESTHESIOLOGY. 3967

0898-4964 *See* MINING JOURNAL (1954). 5693

0898-4980 *See* MODEL (NEW YORK, N.Y.). 762

0898-5006 *See* MEANS REPAIR & REMODELING COST DATA. 620

0898-5022 *See* CASE INDUSTRY DIRECTORY. 1173

0898-5049 *See* URBAN DESIGN & PRESERVATION QUARTERLY. 2837

0898-5065 *See* SOLAR EARTHBUILDER INTERNATIONAL'S EARTH & SUN. 627

0898-5073 *See* WEIRD TALES. 3452

0898-5081 *See* TAX TREATY NETWORKS. 3136

0898-5111 *See* CHINESE JOURNAL OF CONTEMPORARY MATHEMATICS. 3500

0898-512X *See* CHINESE JOURNAL OF BIOCHEMISTRY AND BIOPHYSICS. 485

0898-5138 *See* CHUAN HSUEH PAO. 543

0898-5146 *See* CHINESE JOURNAL OF ARID LAND RESEARCH. 1353

0898-5162 *See* RUNNING & FITNEWS. 2601

0898-5170 *See* INSURANCE ANTITRUST & TORT REFORM REPORT. 3100

0898-5197 *See* PLUM CREEK ALMANAC. 2468

0898-5227 *See* BIOBUSINESS SEARCH GUIDE. 643

0898-526X *See* ALDEN ADVANCE. 5694

0898-5308 *See* INDICATOR (SAINT PAUL, MINN. 1985). 2140

0898-5367 *See* NEWMAN REPORT, THE. 934

0898-5375 *See* OUTLOOK (SANTA MONICA, CALIF.), THE. 5638

0898-5405 *See* NEW JERSEY FACTS. 2540

0898-5421 *See* WADE WORLD. 2477

0898-543X *See* HASTINGS HERALD (SPOKANE, WASH.). 2452

0898-5448 *See* ROBERTSON REPORT. 2470

0898-5456 *See* PARKER PAPERS. 2466

0898-5472 *See* TENNESSEE QUERIES. 2474

0898-5480 *See* DEAF USA. 4386

0898-5499 See SERVICE & SUPPORT MANAGEMENT. 710

0898-5510 *See* JOURNAL OF FORENSIC ECONOMICS. 1499

0898-5561 *See* TODAY'S DISTRIBUTOR. 1629

0898-560X *See* COUNTRY INNS, BED & BREAKFAST. 2804

0898-5626 *See* ENTREPRENEURSHIP AND REGIONAL DEVELOPMENT. 672

0898-5634 *See* COMMERCIAL LEASING LAW & STRATEGY. 2953

0898-5642 *See* MANILA TIMES, USA, THE. 2490

0898-5650 *See* TOY SHOP. 2585

0898-5669 *See* PEDIATRIC PHYSICAL THERAPY. 3909

0898-5685 *See* HAZMAT WORLD. 2232

0898-5693 See JAPANESE TECHNOLOGY REVIEWS. SECTION B, COMPUTERS AND COMMUNICATION. 1114

0898-5693 See JAPANESE TECHNOLOGY REVIEWS. SECTION E, BIOTECHNOLOGY. 3693

0898-5693 See JAPANESE TECHNOLOGY REVIEWS. SECTION C, NEW MATERIALS. 5117

0898-5693 See JAPANESE TECHNOLOGY REVIEWS. SECTION A, ELECTRONICS. 2068

0898-5693 See JAPANESE TECHNOLOGY REVIEWS. SECTION D, MANUFACTURING ENGINEERING. 1981

0898-5723 *See* FSF HUMAN FACTORS BULLETIN & AVIATION MEDICINE. 22

0898-574X See AIRPORT OPERATIONS. 10

0898-5758 *See* FSF CABIN CREW SAFETY BULLETIN. 22

0898-5766 *See* OUTLOOK (WASHINGTON, D.C. : 1988). 623

0898-5774 See ACCIDENT PREVENTION (ARLINGTON, VA.). 3

0898-5812 *See* LAND DEGRADATION AND REHABILITATION. 177

0898-5820 *See* MUSCLE CARS OF THE 5421

0898-5847 *See* JOURNAL OF INTERNATIONAL AND COMPARATIVE SOCIAL WELFARE. 5292

0898-5871 *See* CURRENT TOPICS IN AIDS. 3669

0898-588X *See* STUDIES IN AMERICAN POLITICAL DEVELOPMENT. 4497

0898-5898 *See* LINGUISTICS AND EDUCATION. 3299

0898-5901 *See* LASER THERAPY. 4437

0898-5928 *See* GENERATIONAL JOURNAL, THE. 5246

0898-5952 *See* PERFORMANCE IMPROVEMENT QUARTERLY. 703

0898-5979 *See* FANTASY AND SCIENCE FICTION CONVENTIONEER'S GUIDE, THE. 3387

0898-5987 See JOURNAL OF THE AMERICAN VIOLA SOCIETY. 4126
0898-5995 See SEMINARS IN NUTRITION. 4199
0898-6029 See HOLISTIC MEDICINE (SEATTLE, WASH.). 3584
0898-6037 See CLINICAL PHARMACOLOGY AND TOXICOLOGY CONSULTANT. 4297
0898-6118 See LIBRARY AUTOMATION NEWS. 3224
0898-6126 See WOMAN'S ENTERPRI$E. 5569
0898-6185 See BEETHOVEN NEWSLETTER, THE. 4102
0898-6193 See VOICE OF WALDEN, THE. 2208
0898-6207 See PRIMATE CONSERVATION. 2202
0898-6215 See LET'S GO. THE BUDGET GUIDE TO PACIFIC NORTHWEST, WESTERN CANADA, AND ALASKA INCLUDING ALBERTA AND BRITISH COLUMBIA--VANCOUVER, BANFF AND LAKE LOUISE, CALGARY, GLACIER/WATERTON NATIONAL PARKS. 5483
0898-6231 See DISCERNING TRAVELER, THE. 5468
0898-6355 See COUNTRY JOURNAL (HARRISBURG, PA.). 2531
0898-6363 See COLORADO BUSINESS MAGAZINE : CBM. 658
0898-6371 See PFEIFFER'S OFFICIAL FREQUENT FLYER GUIDE. 5389
0898-6401 See NEW YORK DOCTOR, THE. 3620
0898-641X See VAN WERT AND SURROUNDING COUNTIES, OHIO. 2549
0898-6444 See LEGACY (LOS ANGELES, CALIF.). 5050
0898-6495 See HIGH/SCOPE EARLY CHILDHOOD POLICY PAPERS. 5246
0898-6525 See SKIN INC. 3722
0898-6541 See SPORTS MARKETING NEWS. 4923
0898-6568 See CELLULAR SIGNALLING. 534
0898-6606 See WATERWHEEL (SILVER SPRING, MD.). 5008
0898-6614 See ANNUAL CONFERENCE - COUNCIL OF LOGISTICS MANAGEMENT (U.S.). 860
0898-6622 See BULLETIN / AMERICAN ASSOCIATION FOR THE HISTORY OF NURSING. 3852
0898-6630 See GROWTH GENETICS & HORMONES. 3903
0898-6657 See AVMA DIRECTORY. 5505
0898-672X See AMERICAN SOCIETY OF HYPERTENSION SYMPOSIUM SERIES. 3794
0898-6770 See PERSPECTIVES IN HYPERTENSION SERIES. 3626
0898-6827 See AACAR BULLETIN OF THE ASSOCIATION FOR THE ADVANCEMENT OF CENTRAL ASIAN RESEARCH. 2644
0898-6886 See PULP & PAPER FORECASTER. 4238
0898-6894 See HPV NEWS (INDIANAPOLIS, IND.). 1977
0898-6908 See HUMAN POWER. 1977
0898-6916 See CAPITAL SOURCE, THE. 4636
0898-6924 See INTERNATIONAL JOURNAL OF CANCER. SUPPLEMENT. 3818
0898-6932 See GROLIER'S LEARNING TREE. 1748
0898-6967 See TENNESSEE COMMUNICABLE DISEASE BULLETIN. 4804
0898-6975 See KANSAS WILDLIFE & PARKS. 2197
0898-7033 See NEBRASKA DIRECTORY OF MANUFACTURERS AND THEIR PRODUCTS. 3485
0898-7076 See PUBLISHING & DISTRIBUTION FAX-SPEED NEWS FROM AMERICA : PDN. 4819
0898-7084 See LONG ISLAND HISTORICAL JOURNAL, THE. 2744
0898-7106 See RENTAL (FORT ATKINSON, WIS.). 707
0898-7149 See ELECTRONICS DISTRIBUTION TODAY. 2049
0898-719X See DEAF LIFE. 4386

0898-7270 See HOSPIMEDICA. 3584
0898-7297 See STATE LEGISLATIVE SOURCEBOOK. 4688
0898-7300 See ANNUAL BIBLIOGRAPHY OF MODERN ART / THE MUSEUM OF MODERN ART LIBRARY, NEW YORK. 333
0898-7351 See AMBULATORY HEALTH CARE STANDARDS MANUAL. 3775
0898-7386 See JOURNAL OF CLINICAL PRACTICE IN SEXUALITY, THE. 5187
0898-7491 See REPORT TO THE SENATE AND HOUSE COMMITTEES ON THE BUDGET, A. 1516
0898-753X See PRISCILLA PAPERS. 4988
0898-7564 See JOURNAL OF VETERINARY DENTISTRY. 5514
0898-7572 See PHOTOGRAPHIC INSIGHT. 4374
0898-7645 See LENDER LIABILITY NEWS. 3087
0898-7661 See URISA MEMBERSHIP DIRECTORY. 2838
0898-767X See TELEVISION BROADCAST. 1140
0898-7742 See MAINE ENVIRONMENT. 2197
0898-7750 See METHODS IN MOLECULAR AND CELLULAR BIOLOGY. 464
0898-7904 See PACIFIC ECONOMIC COOPERATION. 1511
0898-7912 See EXECUTIVE BRIEFING (NEW YORK, N.Y.). 867
0898-7955 See HANDEL'S NATIONAL DIRECTORY FOR THE PERFORMING ARTS. 385
0898-798X See CORPORATE TAXATION. 785
0898-7998 See BANKING LAW REVIEW. 3085
0898-8048 See RIVERS (FORT COLLINS, COLO.). 5539
0898-8056 See LOCUS (DENTON, TEX.). 2744
0898-8064 See MILITARY HISTORY OF THE SOUTHWEST. 4050
0898-8072 See PENGUIN GUIDE TO NEW YORK CITY, THE. 5488
0898-8102 See ACCOUNTING FOR LAW FIRMS. 736
0898-8161 See RADIOACTIVE WASTE MANAGEMENT HANDBOOK. 2240
0898-8242 See SSI UPDATE. 36
0898-8323 See BROWN UNIVERSITY STD UPDATE, THE. 4769
0898-8331 See GEMINI (ELMIRA, N.Y.). 2449
0898-8358 See YIVO NEWS. 5054
0898-8366 See LET'S GO. THE BUDGET GUIDE TO CALIFORNIA AND HAWAII INCLUDING RENO, LAS VEGAS, GRAND CANYON, AND BAJA CALIFORNIA. 5482
0898-8374 See STATE MUNICIPAL LEAGUE DIRECTORY. 4688
0898-8404 See SAINT LOUIS UNIVERSITY PUBLIC LAW REVIEW. 3045
0898-8420 See PERSPECTIVE (AUSTIN, TEX.). 1512
0898-8439 See RETAIL SYSTEMS ALERT. 957
0898-8463 See CANTIGUEIROS (LEXINGTON, KY.). 3372
0898-8498 See CBT DIRECTIONS. 1173
0898-8528 See DIRECTORY OF PROGRAMS IN LINGUISTICS IN THE UNITED STATES & CANADA. 3277
0898-8560 See HEALTHTALK (MERRICK, N.Y.). 2598
0898-8587 See HISTORICAL PERFORMANCE. 4121
0898-8609 See CONSTRUCTIONS. 3378
0898-8625 See LOCOMOTIVE ENGINEER NEWSLETTER, THE. 5432
0898-8633 See PROGRAM DIRECTORY / MASSACHUSETTS DEPARTMENT OF EDUCATION. 1775
0898-865X See MIAMI HERALD (MIAMI, FLA.). 5650
0898-8684 See TALISMAN (HOBOKEN, N.J.). 3472
0898-8749 See SAFE DRIVER. 5425
0898-8757 See MUSIC FOR THE LOVE OF IT. 4133

0898-8803 See WILDFLOWER (AUSTIN, TEX. 1984). 530
0898-8811 See SOURCE (WINTER PARK, FLA.). 712
0898-8838 See ADVANCES IN INORGANIC CHEMISTRY. 1035
0898-8900 See NICHI-BEI JOSEI JANARU. 5563
0898-8935 See PORTABLE OFFICE, THE. 1119
0898-8943 See KNIVES ILLUSTRATED. 2774
0898-8951 See SPLASH (ANAHEIM, CALIF.). 4920
0898-8986 See ALL CHEVY. 5403
0898-8994 See MUSTANG ILLUSTRATED. 5421
0898-9001 See ALL ABOUT BEER. 2363
0898-901X See DIGITAL TECHNICAL JOURNAL. 2113
0898-9052 See LUSOAMERICANO (NEWARK, N.J.). 5710
0898-9079 See RESTAURANT/HOTEL DESIGN INTERNATIONAL. 307
0898-9117 See NEW YORK TAX CASES (BUFFALO, N.Y.). 4738
0898-915X See AUDUBON ACTIVIST. 2211
0898-9222 See FINANCIAL AID FOR THE DISABLED AND THEIR FAMILIES. 1824
0898-9249 See JOURNAL OF MORPHOLOGY. SUPPLEMENT. 461
0898-9265 See FREEDOM MONITOR. 4522
0898-929X See JOURNAL OF COGNITIVE NEUROSCIENCE, THE. 3835
0898-9303 See AGRICULTURE, KENTUCKY'S PRIDE. 54
0898-9311 See SENTINEL-ECHO (LONDON, KY.), THE. 5682
0898-9346 See EASTERN CHALLENGE. 4954
0898-9427 See LEGAL VIDEO REVIEW. 3001
0898-9451 See CURRENT INDEX TO LEGAL PERIODICALS (SEATTLE, WASH.). 3080
0898-9494 See FLORIDA HOME & GARDEN. 2900
0898-9516 See WG & L TAX PLANNING ANNUAL. 4758
0898-9540 See AQUACULTURE MAGAZINE. BUYER'S GUIDE ... AND INDUSTRY DIRECTORY. 2296
0898-9559 See RETAILER NEWS. 957
0898-9567 See PROCEEDINGS OF THE ANNUAL MEETING OF THE DECISION SCIENCES INSTITUTE. 882
0898-9575 See AUTO/BIOGRAPHY STUDIES. 430
0898-9583 See SUGAKU EXPOSITIONS. 3537
0898-9591 See CHINESE JOURNAL OF GEOPHYSICS. 1404
0898-9621 See ACCOUNTABILITY IN RESEARCH. 5079
0898-9672 See FANTASY FOOTBALL. 4894
0898-9729 See ADULT FAITH RESOURCES NETWORKER. 4932
0898-9737 See INVENTORY AND CRUISING NEWSLETTER / JOHN BELL & ASSOCIATES. 2385
0898-9753 See EXECUTIVE REPORT ON MANAGED CARE, THE. 940
0898-9761 See JAPANESE INVESTMENT IN U.S. REAL ESTATE REVIEW. WESTERN REGION. 4839
0898-9788 See C USERS JOURNAL, THE. 1278
0898-9818 See FAIRFIELD COUNTY BUSINESS JOURNAL. 674
0898-9842 See ENCYCLOPEDIA OF PHYSICAL SCIENCE AND TECHNOLOGY. YEARBOOK. 5103
0898-9850 See WIRE TECHNOLOGY INTERNATIONAL. 4023
0898-9877 See IMS LIST, SANITATION COMPLIANCE AND ENFORCEMENT RATINGS OF INTERSTATE MILK SHIPPERS. 195
0898-9907 See CORPORATE COUNSEL'S INTERNATIONAL ADVISER. 3126
0898-9923 See CORPORATE COUNSEL'S MONITOR. 3098
0898-994X See PURCHASER'S LEGAL ADVISER. 951
0898-9966 See LAWYER'S BRIEF, THE. 2998
0898-9974 See GREENE GENES. 2452

ISSN Index

0899-0042 *See* CHIRALITY (NEW YORK, N.Y.). **972**

0899-0050 *See* BIRMINGHAM NEWS, THE. **5625**

0899-0085 *See* AMORY ADVERTISER (1957), THE. **5699**

0899-014X *See* REC NEWSLETTER, THE. **3530**

0899-0158 *See* NORTH AMERICAN NEW PRODUCT REPORT, THE. **3485**

0899-0174 *See* CORPORATE CONTROLLER. **661**

0899-0182 *See* CHIEF INFORMATION OFFICER JOURNAL. **1174**

0899-0190 *See* GREENPEACE (WASHINGTON, D.C.). **2173**

0899-0212 *See* NATIONAL DIRECTORY OF PERSONNEL CONSULTANTS BY SPECIALIZATION. **4206**

0899-0220 *See* SOMATOSENSORY & MOTOR RESEARCH. **5597**

0899-0239 *See* REPORT - EDUCATION DEVELOPMENT CENTER. **1778**

0899-0247 *See* EAST/WEST EDUCATION. **1737**

0899-0263 *See* AIDS CLINICAL DIGEST. **3663**

0899-031X *See* IMPACT PUMPS. **2115**

0899-0328 *See* INDIANAPOLIS MONTHLY. **2535**

0899-0387 *See* CHILE NEWSLETTER (BERKELEY, CALIF. 1984). **4637**

0899-0409 *See* ESSAYS AND MONOGRAPHS IN COLORADO HISTORY. **2732**

0899-0417 *See* NEWSMAKERS (DETROIT, MICH.). **434**

0899-0425 *See* NEWSLETTERS IN PRINT. **4817**

0899-045X *See* AQUARIUM FISH MAGAZINE. **4285**

0899-0468 *See* ASSETS PROTECTION SOURCEBOOK. **891**

0899-0506 *See* EAST COAST ANGLER. **2300**

0899-0530 *See* WALL STREET DIGEST, THE. **919**

0899-0662 *See* RECENT TITLES IN LAW FOR THE SUBJECT SPECIALIST. AGRICULTURE, ANIMAL, AND FOOD LAW. **3035**

0899-0670 *See* RECENT TITLES IN LAW FOR THE SUBJECT SPECIALIST. TAXATION AND ESTATE PLANNING. **4744**

0899-0689 *See* RECENT TITLES IN LAW FOR THE SUBJECT SPECIALIST. RESOURCE, ENVIRONMENTAL, AND ENERGY LAW. **3116**

0899-0697 *See* RECENT TITLES IN LAW FOR THE SUBJECT SPECIALIST. PROPERTY (REAL AND CHATTEL), AND CONSTRUCTION LAW. **3035**

0899-0727 *See* RECENT TITLES IN LAW FOR THE SUBJECT SPECIALIST. TRANSPORTATION AND MARITIME LAW. **3182**

0899-0735 *See* RECENT TITLES IN LAW FOR THE SUBJECT SPECIALIST. TRADE REGULATION AND ECONOMICS. **3035**

0899-0743 *See* RECENT TITLES IN LAW FOR THE SUBJECT SPECIALIST. TORTS, LIABILITY, AND INDEMNITY. **3035**

0899-0751 *See* RECENT TITLES IN LAW FOR THE SUBJECT SPECIALIST. TECHNOLOGY AND DESIGN PROTECTION. **3035**

0899-076X *See* RECENT TITLES IN LAW FOR THE SUBJECT SPECIALIST. MILITARY AND SECURITY LAW. **3183**

0899-0778 *See* RECENT TITLES IN LAW FOR THE SUBJECT SPECIALIST. MEDICINE AND HEALTH LAW. **3035**

0899-0794 *See* RECENT TITLES IN LAW FOR THE SUBJECT SPECIALIST. LABOR AND EMPLOYMENT. **3153**

0899-0808 *See* RECENT TITLES IN LAW FOR THE SUBJECT SPECIALIST. FAMILY LAW AND SOCIAL WELFARE. **3122**

0899-0816 *See* RECENT TITLES IN LAW FOR THE SUBJECT SPECIALIST. EVIDENCE, PRATICE, AND PROCEDURE. **3035**

0899-0824 *See* RECENT TITLES IN LAW FOR THE SUBJECT SPECIALIST. ENTERPRISE ORGANIZATION. **3035**

0899-0840 *See* RECENT TITLES IN LAW FOR THE SUBJECT SPECIALIST. CRIMINAL LAW, PROCEDURE AND CRIMINOLOGY. **3108**

0899-0859 *See* RECENT TITLES IN LAW FOR THE SUBJECT SPECIALIST. COPYRIGHT AND ENTERTAINMENT LAW. **3035**

0899-0867 *See* RECENT TITLES IN LAW FOR THE SUBJECT SPECIALIST. CONTRACT LEASE, AND SALES LAW. **3035**

0899-0875 *See* RECENT TITLES IN LAW FOR THE SUBJECT SPECIALIST. CONSTITUTIONAL LAW, HUMAN RIGHTS, AND CITIZENSHIP. **3093**

0899-0883 *See* RECENT TITLES IN LAW FOR THE SUBJECT SPECIALIST. COMMUNICATION LAW. **3035**

0899-0891 *See* RECENT TITLES IN LAW FOR THE SUBJET SPECIALIST. BANKING, FINANCE (INCLUDING SECURITIES), AND INVESTMENT. **3088**

0899-0913 *See* DAILY REPORT. LATIN AMERICA. **1131**

0899-093X *See* CHILD AND YOUTH CARE ADMINISTRATOR / NOVA UNIVERSITY, THE. **5277**

0899-0948 *See* CITY LIVING. **2531**

0899-0956 *See* JOURNAL OF APPLIED MANUFACTURING SYSTEMS, THE. **1613**

0899-1014 *See* ... BMUG NEWSLETTER, THE. **1172**

0899-1022 *See* SWIMMING POOL/SPA AGE. **4855**

0899-1057 *See* STOCKMAN GRASS FARMER, THE. **222**

0899-1138 *See* IMAGES OF EXCELLENCE. **2738**

0899-1146 *See* AGORA (PHILADELPHIA, PA.). **2672**

0899-1154 *See* EMERGE (NEW YORK, N.Y.). **2533**

0899-1227 *See* ADVANCES IN LIBRARY INFORMATION TECHNOLOGY. **3188**

0899-1235 *See* NEWSFACES IN HIGH TECHNOLOGY. **5133**

0899-126X *See* COMPUTER PROTOCOLS. **1177**

0899-1294 *See* AGRIBUSINESS NEWS FOR KENTUCKY. **48**

0899-1332 *See* QUAKER QUERIES. **2468**

0899-1340 *See* NEW JERSEY QUERIES. **2462**

0899-1359 *See* KENTUCKY QUERIES. **2456**

0899-1405 *See* WARY CANARY, THE. **2183**

0899-1413 *See* OUT WEST (SACRAMENTO, CALIF.). **5488**

0899-1421 *See* MUSCLECAR CLASSICS. **5421**

0899-1448 *See* AMERICAN LITERATURE REVIEW. **3360**

0899-1464 *See* AIDS LITIGATION REPORTER. **3739**

0899-1499 *See* ORSA JOURNAL ON COMPUTING. **1198**

0899-1502 *See* JOURNAL OF SUGAR BEET RESEARCH. **177**

0899-1510 *See* RE:VIEW (WASHINGTON, D.C.). **4393**

0899-1529 *See* FAMILY (BOSTON, MASS.), THE. **5029**

0899-1537 *See* ATO ALIVE. **1089**

0899-1545 *See* MICHIGAN VOTER, THE. **4482**

0899-1553 *See* READERS' GUIDE ABSTRACTS. CD-ROM. **2497**

0899-1561 *See* JOURNAL OF MATERIALS IN CIVIL ENGINEERING. **2025**

0899-1588 *See* RIGHT COLLEGE, THE. **1846**

0899-1642 *See* MAC SUBJECTS. **1194**

0899-1685 *See* K.A.R.D. FILES PRESENTS ABSHIRE ABSTRACTS, THE. **2456**

0899-1693 *See* KARD FILES ADAMSON ANCESTRY, THE. **2456**

0899-1707 *See* BILLINGSLEY YESTERDAY & TODAY. **2439**

0899-1715 *See* K.A.R.D. FILES PRESENTS BLAKELEY BANDWAGON, THE. **2456**

0899-1723 *See* K.A.R.D. FILES DYE DATA, THE. **2456**

0899-1731 *See* K.A.R.D. FILES PRESENTS LUTTRELL LINEAGES & DATA, THE. **2456**

0899-174X *See* K.A.R.D. FILES PRESENTS RAMBO REFERENCES, THE. **2456**

0899-1766 *See* WHO'S WHO IN INTELLECTUAL PROPERTY. **1309**

0899-1782 *See* U.S. ART. **367**

0899-1804 *See* P/PM TECHNOLOGY. **1620**

0899-1812 *See* PIONEER (BEMIDJI, MINN.), THE. **5698**

0899-1820 *See* LETCHER COUNTY COMMUNITY NEWS-PRESS. **5681**

0899-1839 *See* COMMONWEALTH-JOURNAL (SOMERSET, KY.), THE. **5680**

0899-1847 *See* PC/COMPUTING (NEW YORK, N.Y.). **1270**

0899-1855 *See* JOURNAL, PHYSICAL THERAPY EDUCATION. **4380**

0899-1871 *See* LINEAGE (COMMACK, N.Y.). **2458**

0899-1898 *See* SUPERMARKET ADVERTISING NEWSLETTER. **767**

0899-191X *See* ALLEN'S TRADEMARK DIGEST. **1301**

0899-1928 *See* AVIATION TRADESCAN. **41**

0899-1936 *See* SEAPORTS OF THE WESTERN HEMISPHERE. **5455**

0899-1960 *See* ORGAN MOUNTAIN TRAILBLAZER. **2752**

0899-1987 *See* MOLECULAR CARCINOGENESIS. **465**

0899-2002 *See* SCHOOLS ABROAD OF INTEREST TO AMERICANS. **1782**

0899-2010 *See* UPTIME (APPLE IIGS). **1206**

0899-2029 *See* AAR RAILROAD COST INDEXES. **5429**

0899-2061 *See* SACRAMENTAL LIFE. **4995**

0899-2169 *See* TRAVELING HEALTHY NEWSLETTER. **5497**

0899-2193 *See* STUDIES IN COMPARATIVE LITERATURE (LUBBOCK, TEX.). **3441**

0899-2207 *See* STATE YELLOW BOOK. **1929**

0899-2231 *See* ANNUAL REPORT / THE CONFERENCE BOARD. **1462**

0899-2320 *See* ANNAPOLITAN (ANNAPOLIS, MD.). **2528**

0899-2347 *See* SMART (NEW YORK, N.Y.). **2546**

0899-2355 *See* STUDENT SUCCESS TUTOR DIRECTORY. SARASOTA COUNTY. **1786**

0899-2363 *See* PUBLIC CULTURE. **328**

0899-2371 *See* RECENT AMERICAN HISTORY. **2756**

0899-2398 *See* DIABETIC TRAVELER, THE. **5468**

0899-2428 *See* HISTORY OF MATHEMATICS. **3507**

0899-2444 *See* WEST BEND DAILY NEWS. **5772**

0899-2452 See ARVADA JEFFERSON SENTINEL, THE. **5641**

0899-2460 *See* MICHIGAN TAX LAWYER. **3010**

0899-2517 *See* JOURNAL OF MUSCULOSKELETAL MEDICINE. **3805**

0899-2525 *See* FIELD ARTILLERY. **4044**

0899-2533 *See* DIRECTORY OF SERVICES FOR BLIND AND VISUALLY IMPAIRED PERSONS IN THE UNITED STATES. **4387**

0899-2576 *See* QUE PASA (TEANECK, N.J.). **2491**

0899-2584 *See* CHRISTIAN OBSERVER (MANASSAS, VA.). **4945**

0899-2622 *See* OCEAN SPORTS INTERNATIONAL. **4908**

0899-2673 *See* HLI REPORT. **2280**

0899-2681 *See* BOUNDARY WATERS JOURNAL, THE. **2188**

0899-2711 *See* HANDBOOK OF LASER SCIENCE AND TECHNOLOGY. **4434**

0899-2762 See FROMMER'S COMPREHENSIVE TRAVEL GUIDE. RIO. **5476**

0899-2770 *See* FROMMER'S SYDNEY. **5478**

0899-2789 See FROMMER'S COMPREHENSIVE TRAVEL GUIDE. SANTA FE, TAOS & ALBUQUERQUE. **5476**

0899-2800 *See* FROMMER'S TOURING GUIDE TO BRAZIL. **5478**

0899-2843 *See* ACTION COMICS WEEKLY. **4856**

0899-2843 *See* ACTION COMICS. **4856**

0899-2851 *See* MIDDLE EAST REPORT (NEW YORK, N.Y. : 1988). **2526**

0899-2908 *See* FROMMER'S NEW ORLEANS. **5477**

0899-2916 See FROMMER'S COMPREHENSIVE TRAVEL GUIDE. ATLANTIC CITY & CAPE MAY. **5475**

ISSN Index

0899-2924 See FROMMER'S COMPREHENSIVE TRAVEL GUIDE. ATHENS. 5475

0899-2932 See FROMMER'S COMPREHENSIVE TRAVEL GUIDE. LISBON, MADRID & THE COSTA DEL SOL. 5476

0899-3009 See BRIEF (HOUSTON, TEX.). 862

0899-3017 See LETTER (HOUSTON, TEX.). 875

0899-3025 See COMPUTER RAMBLINGS. 1266

0899-3041 See PACIFIC NORTHWEST WEED CONTROL HANDBOOK. 2427

0899-3068 See GIANNINI FOUNDATION RESEARCH REPORT (1987). 90

0899-3092 See MEDICAL TECHNOLOGY. 3612

0899-3106 See PROCEEDINGS OF THE CONFERENCE ON MEDIEVALISM. 2703

0899-3114 See JAMES JOYCE LITERARY SUPPLEMENT. 3345

0899-3165 See FROMMER'S COMPREHENSIVE TRAVEL GUIDE. MONTREAL & QUEBEC CITY. 5476

0899-3181 See FROMMER'S AMSTERDAM AND HOLLAND. 5474

0899-319X See FROMMER'S COMPREHENSIVE TRAVEL GUIDE. ROME. 5476

0899-3211 See FROMMER'S PHILADELPHIA. 5477

0899-322X See FROMMER'S BOSTON. 5474

0899-3262 See FROMMER'S COMPREHENSIVE TRAVEL GUIDE. LAS VEGAS. 5476

0899-3289 See JOURNAL OF SUBSTANCE ABUSE. 1346

0899-3297 See FROMMER'S COMPREHENSIVE TRAVEL GUIDE. AUSTRIA & HUNGARY. 5475

0899-3327 See FROMMER'S DOLLARWISE SKIING EUROPE PLUS SUMMER SKIING IN ARGENTINA. 5477

0899-3335 See FROMMER'S DOLLARWISE SOUTHWEST. 5477

0899-3351 See FROMMER'S COMPREHENSIVE TRAVEL GUIDE. FRANCE. 5475

0899-3408 See COMPUTER SCIENCE EDUCATION. 1177

0899-3440 See NEW RAIN. 3416

0899-3459 See TOPICS IN MAGNETIC RESONANCE IMAGING. 3947

0899-3467 See JOURNAL OF CHIROPRACTIC TECHNIQUE. 3805

0899-3475 See BARCLAYS UNITED STATES TENTH CIRCUIT SERVICE. 2940

0899-3483 See IDENTITY (CINCINNATI, OHIO). 380

0899-3505 See FISH AND WILDLIFE TECHNICAL REPORT. 2301

0899-3521 See GROUNDWATER POLLUTION NEWS. 2230

0899-353X See DIRECTORIES IN PRINT. 415

0899-3572 See REGISTER (KANSAS CITY, MO.), THE. 220

0899-3645 See OPERA ANNUAL U.S. 4143

0899-367X See NORTHEASTERN JOURNAL OF AGRICULTURAL AND RESOURCE ECONOMICS. 115

0899-3718 See JOURNAL OF MILITARY HISTORY, THE. 4048

0899-3726 See BUSINESS ACRONYMS. 645

0899-3750 See AVEC (PENNGROVE, CALIF.). 3365

0899-3785 See S.S.A. NEWSLETTER : A PUBLICATION OF THE SUDAN STUDIES ASSOCIATION. 2500

0899-3793 See GIVING USA UPDATE. 4336

0899-3815 See SPORTCARE & FITNESS. 4921

0899-3831 See EXEMPT ORGANIZATION TAX REVIEW, THE. 4723

0899-3858 See MECHANICAL ENGINEERING (MARCEL DEKKER, INC.). 2122

0899-3874 See MONOGRAPH - UNIVERSITY OF FLORIDA. AGRICULTURAL EXPERIMENT STATION. 109

0899-3882 See CURRENT THERAPY OF INFERTILITY. 3760

0899-3920 See ANIMAL SCIENCE RESEARCH REPORT (BLACKSBURG, VA.). 205

0899-3947 See CURRENT THERAPY IN INFECTIOUS DISEASE. 3713

0899-3963 See CURRENT THERAPY IN NEUROLOGICAL SURGERY. 3831

0899-3998 See AGBIOTECHNOLOGY NEWS. 3685

0899-4005 See EROTIC ART BY LIVING ARTISTS. 349

0899-4013 See WIND TURBINE WORLDWIDE CATALOG. 2001

0899-4056 See VACCINES (COLD SPRING HARBOR, N.Y.). 3649

0899-4099 See FROMMER'S BUDGET TRAVEL GUIDE. SPAIN ... ON $ ... A DAY. 5475

0899-4129 See DALLAS BUSINESS JOURNAL. 664

0899-4137 See HEALTH OF AMERICA'S CHILDREN, THE. 4780

0899-4161 See FINAL FRONTIER. 20

0899-417X See TURF NEWS. 2433

0899-4188 See FREDERICK FINDINGS. 2449

0899-4293 See KID CITY. 1065

0899-434X See PACIFIC TELECOMMUNICATIONS REVIEW. 1119

0899-4358 See CHINESE JOURNAL OF NUMERICAL MATHEMATICS AND APPLICATIONS. 3500

0899-4366 See HOME PLANS TO BUILD. 300

0899-4374 See HOME PLANS GUIDE. 300

0899-4382 See BLUE RIBBON HOME PLANS. 2899

0899-4390 See ORIGINAL HOME PLANS. 305

0899-4404 See GALLERY OF FINE HOME PLANS. 299

0899-451X See FISH AND WILDLIFE LEAFLET. 2193

0899-4560 See MORGAN DIRECTORY REVIEWS / MDR. 3232

0899-4579 See DATA ENTRY SERVICES DIRECTORY. 1257

0899-4587 See PHOTO OPPORTUNITY. 882

0899-4595 See CONTINGENCY PLANNING & RECOVERY JOURNAL : CPR-J. 1226

0899-4730 See ST. LOUIS ART MUSEUM ANNUAL REPORT, THE. 365

0899-479X See WAYNE INDEPENDENT, THE. 5740

0899-4803 See CULPEPER STAR-EXPONENT (1988). 5758

0899-4811 See ARCHIVES OF STD/HIV RESEARCH. 3666

0899-4838 See DISKWORLD FOR THE MACINTOSH. 1285

0899-4862 See OHIO NEWS (WOOSTER, OHIO). 197

0899-4927 See MERTON SEASONAL OF BELLARMINE COLLEGE, THE. 2490

0899-496X See U.S. BOAT & SHIP MODELER. 2779

0899-5028 See ST. CLOUD TIMES. 5698

0899-5052 See NCSL CONFERENCE REPORT. 3141

1042-5039 See WORLD ENVIRONMENT REPORT. 2248

0899-5141 See JOURNAL OF COST MANAGEMENT FOR THE MANUFACTURING INDUSTRY. 873

0899-515X See U.S. GENERAL IMPORTS. SCHEDULE A, COMMODITY GROUPINGS BY WORLD AREA AND COUNTRY. 855

0899-5168 See EARTH SCIENCES (DUBLIN, OHIO). 1355

0899-5273 See ANELLO CHE NON TIENE, L'. 3361

0899-5281 See CAL POLY SCHOLAR, THE. 1813

0899-529X See SKIPPING STONES. 1069

0899-5303 See FM STATION ADDRESS BOOK. 1132

0899-5362 See JOURNAL OF AFRICAN EARTH SCIENCES (AND THE MIDDLE EAST). 1384

0899-5370 See ANNUAL REVIEW OF NICARAGUAN SOCIOLOGY. 5239

0899-5400 See IMMIGRATION DIGEST. 2454

0899-5443 See DRUM. 3382

0899-5451 See ICUC. 2488

0899-5508 See WOMEN'S FASTPITCH WORLD. 4930

0899-5524 See USA FINANCIAL NEWS. 815

0899-5540 See AUTOMATED BUILDER. 2815

0899-5591 See ADOLESCENT PREGNANCY PREVENTION CLEARINGHOUSE. 5270

0899-5605 See MILITARY PSYCHOLOGY. 4051

0899-563X See LRC NEWSBRIEFS. 4736

0899-5648 See HERBALGRAM (AUSTIN, TEX.). 512

0899-5664 See STRATEGIC SYSTEMS. 1249

0899-5702 See BIOTECH BUSINESS. 3687

0899-5729 See MAINTENANCE TECHNOLOGY. 619

0899-5737 See PLATTE COUNTY GAZETTE (1988), THE. 5704

0899-5788 See AEG NEWS. 2018

0899-5826 See SAN ANTONIO. 2544

0899-5834 See MORE POWER. 1988

0899-5869 See CHILDREN'S HOSPITAL QUARTERLY. 3901

0899-5885 See CRITICAL CARE NURSING CLINICS OF NORTH AMERICA. 3854

0899-5893 See STITCHES MAGAZINE. 5356

0899-594X See SOUTHERN FOLKLORE. 2324

0899-5982 See CONSTRUCTION CLAIMS TRAINING GUIDE. 609

0899-6008 See PARTY & PAPER RETAILER. 956

0899-6059 See MONK (SAN FRANCISCO, CALIF.). 4604

0899-6075 See CITIES OF THE UNITED STATES. 4638

0899-6105 See SILVER (WHITTIER, CALIF.). 4019

0899-6113 See WEEKLY READER. SUMMER EDITION B. 1791

0899-6121 See WEEKLY READER. SUMMER EDITION C. 1071

0899-6164 See COPIER REVIEW. 4211

0899-6172 See NATIONAL DIRECTORY OF ART & ANTIQUE BUYERS & SPECIALISTS. 251

0899-6180 See MISSOURI JOURNAL OF MATHEMATICAL SCIENCES. 3523

0899-6199 See SEMINARY TIMES, THE. 4996

0899-6202 See LLAMA BANNER. 105

0899-6210 See HEALTH FACILITIES MANAGEMENT. 4779

0899-6237 See REHAB MANAGEMENT. 4382

0899-6253 See INDEX TO BLACK PERIODICALS. 2276

0899-627X See HERALD (RINCON, GA.), THE. 5654

0899-6318 See LIFE AT KEN-CARYL. 5643

0899-6342 See DAILY NEWS (GREENVILLE, MICH.), THE. 5691

0899-6350 See CRITTENDEN INSURANCE MARKETS, COMMERCIAL LINES. 2878

0899-6369 See PETROLEUM/C-STORE PRODUCTS. 4272

0899-6407 See KURT WEILL NEWSLETTER. 4128

0899-6458 See MISSOURI LIBRARIES. 3231

0899-6520 See ONAWA DEMOCRAT (ONAWA, IOWA : 1967). 5672

0899-6547 See ARMS CONTROL, DISARMAMENT AND INTERNATIONAL SECURITY. 4036

0899-658X See FORT HENRIETTA NEWSLETTER. 2734

0899-6601 See VIETNAM UPDATE. 2632

0899-6687 See TODAY NEWS. 5630

0899-6717 See DRIVE. 5440

0899-6725 See BROADCAST TECHNICAL DATA AND APPLICATION INFORMATION MANUAL. 4398

0899-6733 See AIDS NEWS REPORTER, THE. 3664

0899-6741 See CONFERENCE BOARD BRIEFING, THE. 864

0899-6806 See MOBIL ROAD ATLAS AND TRIP PLANNING GUIDE, UNITED STATES, CANADA, AND MEXICO. 2569

0899-6830 *See* BUSINESS BULLETIN (FRANKFORT, KY.). **646**

0899-6849 *See* TALKIN' TWINS BASEBALL. **4925**

0899-6865 *See* CURRENT THERAPY IN INTERNAL MEDICINE. **3796**

0899-6938 *See* CHIROPRACTIC RESEARCH JOURNAL. **3804**

0899-7039 *See* MAGAZINE ISSUES. **4816**

0899-7047 *See* CML ARMY CHEMICAL REVIEW. **4039**

0899-7071 *See* CLINICAL IMAGING. **3939**

0899-708X *See* NORTHLAND QUARTERLY, THE. **3418**

0899-7098 See FINANCE (BOSTON, MASS.). **4204**

0899-711X *See* ST. JOSEPH NEWS-PRESS/GAZETTE. **5704**

0899-7225 *See* FREE SPEECH YEARBOOK. **3093**

0899-7241 *See* WASHINGTON INSIGHT. **476**

0899-725X *See* MACINTOSH BUSINESS REVIEW. **691**

0899-7292 *See* CHRISTIAN NEW AGE QUARTERLY. **4945**

0899-7330 *See* EDUCATIONEWS (ALBANY, N.Y.). **1743**

0899-7373 *See* HOME OFFICE COMPUTING. **1267**

0899-7403 *See* AMERICAN JOURNAL OF KNEE SURGERY, THE. **3958**

0899-7411 *See* AMERICAN JOURNAL OF ASTHMA & ALLERGY FOR PEDIATRICIANS, THE. **3948**

0899-742X *See* AIDS/HIV RECORD. **3663**

0899-7438 *See* CAMPAIGNETWORKS (LIBERTY, MO.). **4467**

0899-7446 *See* UWLA LAW REVIEW. **3070**

0899-7462 *See* TRYON TIMES, THE. **2476**

0899-7470 *See* ASTHMA & ALLERGY ADVOCATE. **3667**

0899-7519 *See* PLASTIC RAP. **4457**

0899-7535 *See* AGFOCUS (MIDDLETOWN, N.Y.). **45**

0899-7543 *See* PETROLEUM INFORMATION'S NATIONAL EXPLORATION DAILY. **4273**

0899-7586 See INTERNATIONAL BRANDS AND THEIR COMPANIES. **683**

0899-7594 See INTERNATIONAL COMPANIES AND THEIR BRANDS. **683**

0899-7616 *See* DELAVAN ENTERPRISE AND THE DELAVAN REPUBLICAN, THE. **5767**

0899-7624 *See* CARSON PRESS, THE. **5725**

0899-7640 *See* NONPROFIT AND VOLUNTARY SECTOR QUARTERLY. **5299**

0899-7659 *See* JOURNAL OF AQUATIC ANIMAL HEALTH. **2306**

0899-7667 *See* NEURAL COMPUTATION. **1215**

0899-7675 *See* FROMMER'S NEW YORK. **5477**

0899-7691 *See* JOURNAL OF HUMANISM & ETHICAL RELIGION. **2251**

0899-7721 *See* ENTREPRENEURIAL ECONOMY REVIEW, THE. **1488**

0899-7764 *See* JOURNAL OF MEDIA ECONOMICS. **1115**

0899-7799 *See* INTERNATIONAL CONTRACT ADVISER. **3130**

0899-7829 *See* CHEMTRACTS. MACROMOLECULAR CHEMISTRY. **971**

0899-7837 *See* FOCUS ON PHYTOCHEMICAL PESTICIDES. **511**

0899-787X *See* INTV JOURNAL. **1133**

0899-7888 *See* PSI FORCE. **4865**

0899-7934 *See* ONLINE WITH ADULT AND CONTINUING EDUCATORS. **1801**

0899-7977 *See* ISI ATLAS OF SCIENCE. SOCIAL SCIENCES. **5204**

0899-7993 See FROHLINGER'S MARKETING REPORT. **924**

0899-8019 *See* KEY CARDIOLOGY. **3708**

0899-8035 *See* YEAR BOOK OF OCCUPATIONAL AND ENVIRONMENTAL HEALTH. **2871**

0899-806X *See* AMERICAN CERAMIC CIRCLE JOURNAL. **2586**

0899-8086 *See* TEMPLE LAW REVIEW. **3063**

0899-8108 *See* MORNING FAX, THE. **1160**

0899-8116 *See* MONKEYSHINES ON YOU!. **4863**

0899-8132 *See* EARLY KEYBOARD JOURNAL. **4116**

0899-8159 *See* CRYPTOSYSTEMS JOURNAL. **1181**

0899-8175 *See* SURGICAL PATHOLOGY. **3898**

0899-8205 *See* BIOMEDICAL INSTRUMENTATION & TECHNOLOGY. **3687**

0899-8213 *See* PHYSICS OF FLUIDS. A, FLUID DYNAMICS. **4416**

0899-8221 *See* PHYSICS OF FLUIDS. B, PLASMA PHYSICS. **4416**

0899-823X *See* INFECTION CONTROL AND HOSPITAL EPIDEMIOLOGY. **3735**

0899-8248 *See* IMPACT OF COMPUTING IN SCIENCE AND ENGINEERING. **3508**

0899-8256 *See* GAMES AND ECONOMIC BEHAVIOR. **3506**

0899-8272 *See* LIBIDO (CHICAGO, ILL.). **3405**

0899-8299 *See* JOURNAL OF IMA, THE. **3595**

0899-8302 *See* SERGER UPDATE, THE. **5185**

0899-8310 *See* SEWING UPDATE, THE. **5186**

0899-8329 *See* DISCOVERY FIVE HUNDRED : NEWSLETTER OF THE INTERNATIONAL COLUMBIAN QUINCENTENARY ALLIANCE LTD. **2731**

0899-8361 *See* LOVECRAFT STUDIES. **3409**

0899-837X *See* CONTEMPORARY DIALYSIS & NEPHROLOGY. **3989**

0899-8396 *See* WEALTH AND RICHES NEWSLETTER. **816**

0899-8418 *See* INTERNATIONAL JOURNAL OF CLIMATOLOGY : A JOURNAL OF THE ROYAL METEOROLOGICAL SOCIETY. **1426**

0899-8485 *See* EXTRA INCOME NEWS NEWSLETTER. **674**

0899-8493 *See* PEDIATRIC EXERCISE SCIENCE. **3908**

0899-8531 *See* HIGH RELIABILITY ELECTRONIC COMPONENTS. **2056**

0899-8612 *See* ANNUAL REPORT OF THE BOARD OF PHARMACY OF THE STATE OF ARIZONA. **4291**

0899-8620 *See* JOURNAL OF CONSUMER SATISFACTION, DISSATISFACTION, AND COMPLAINING BEHAVIOR. **1297**

0899-8698 *See* BREMER COUNTY INDEPENDENT (1959). **5668**

0899-8779 See APPRAISER NEWS. **4834**

0899-8809 *See* SUN-DIAMOND GROWER. **2432**

0899-8833 *See* EMPLOYEE OWNERSHIP REPORT, THE. **671**

0899-885X *See* JOURNAL OF INTENSIVE ENGLISH STUDIES. **3290**

0899-8922 *See* SAS BULLETIN. **282**

0899-8930 *See* KALIS SHOPPING CENTER LEASING DIRECTORY. **1501**

0899-8949 *See* MEDICAL GROUP MANAGEMENT JOURNAL. **3609**

0899-8965 *See* HEALTH LEGISLATION AND REGULATION. **2978**

0899-8973 *See* ENDODONTIC REPORT, THE. **1323**

0899-8981 *See* MEDICAL STAFF COUNSELOR, THE. **3915**

0899-9007 *See* NUTRITION (BURBANK, LOS ANGELES COUNTY, CALIF.). **4196**

0899-9023 See RADON DIRECTORY, THE. **1029**

0899-904X *See* MICHIGAN TRIAL REPORTER, THE. **3090**

0899-9066 *See* SCARLET & GRAY ILLUSTRATED. **4916**

0899-9090 *See* MICHIGAN WORKERS' COMPENSATION LAW REPORTER. **3152**

0899-9104 *See* PENNSYLVANIA WORKERS' COMPENSATION LAW REPORTER. **3153**

0899-9107 See MONEY INCOME TAX HANDBOOK, THE. **4737**

0899-9112 *See* ADDICTION NURSING NETWORK. **3850**

0899-9147 *See* FLEET'S GUIDE. **4837**

0899-9171 *See* AFAS QUARTERLY OF THE AUTOMOTIVE FINE ARTS SOCIETY. **5403**

0899-9228 *See* JOURNAL OF THE AMERICAN DEAFNESS AND REHABILITATION ASSOCIATION : JADARA. **4390**

0899-9244 *See* PSYCHOANALYTIC INQUIRY BOOK SERIES. **3934**

0899-9252 *See* PATHWAYS (CHESTNUT HILL, MASS.). **4673**

0899-9287 *See* HEALTHCARE FORUM JOURNAL, THE. **3583**

0899-9317 *See* WOLVES AND RELATED CANIDS. **5600**

0899-9333 *See* OURS (MINNEAPOLIS, MINN.). **5300**

0899-9341 *See* MICROPROCESSOR REPORT. **1270**

0899-9368 *See* PACIFIC BOATING ALMANAC. PACIFIC NORTHWEST & ALASKA. **595**

0899-9414 *See* ROCKFORD MAGAZINE. **1299**

0899-9422 *See* MAGNETIC RESONANCE QUARTERLY. **3943**

0899-9449 *See* AIDS (PHOENIX, ARIZ.). **3664**

0899-9457 *See* INTERNATIONAL JOURNAL OF IMAGING SYSTEMS AND TECHNOLOGY. **5115**

0899-9465 *See* WORLD NEUROLOGY. **3847**

0899-9473 *See* VIRGINIA LAWYER. **3072**

0899-9511 *See* ENVIRONMENTAL OUTLOOK (SEATTLE, WASH.). **2168**

0899-952X *See* EE PRODUCT NEWS. **2042**

0899-9538 *See* DAILY SPARKS TRIBUNE, THE. **5707**

0899-9546 *See* AIDS EDUCATION AND PREVENTION. **4764**

0899-9554 *See* ISDN NEWS. **1114**

0899-9562 *See* FAMILY PRACTICE ALERT. **3737**

0899-9570 *See* I LOVE CATS. **4286**

0899-9589 *See* FISHING FACTS (SOUTHERN ED.). **2303**

0899-9597 *See* FISHING FACTS (NORTHERN ED.). **2303**

0899-9635 *See* TORONTO HERALD, THE. **5744**

0899-9651 *See* MICHIGAN BUSINESS LAW JOURNAL, THE. **3102**

0899-966X *See* ELKTON RECORD, THE. **5743**

0899-9708 *See* PETA NEWS. **226**

0899-9775 *See* WATER SCOOTER. **596**

0899-9783 *See* COMPUTER WORKSTATIONS. **1241**

0899-9791 *See* HVAC PROFITMAKER. **2605**

0899-9805 *See* WHITE LEADER, THE. **5744**

0899-9821 *See* PREVIEW. **3241**

0899-983X *See* OJANCANO (CHAPEL HILL, N.C.). **3420**

0899-9848 *See* SANTA MONICA REVIEW : SMR. **3433**

0899-9856 *See* HERMENEUTICS OF ART. **352**

0899-9872 *See* STUDIES IN OLD GERMANIC LANGUAGES AND LITERATURES. **3442**

0899-9880 *See* AMERICAN UNIVERSITY STUDIES. SERIES XXVI, THEATER ARTS. **383**

0899-9899 *See* GERMAN LIFE AND CIVILIZATION. **2689**

0899-9902 *See* COMPARATIVE LITERATURE AND FILM STUDIES. **3377**

0899-9910 *See* CONFLICT AND CONSCIOUSNESS. **5242**

0899-9929 *See* STUDIA CLASSICA. **1080**

0899-9937 *See* REVISIONING PHILOSOPHY. **4359**

0899-9953 *See* SASSY (NEW YORK, N.Y. 1988). **1068**

0899-9988 *See* CHINESE JOURNAL OF SEMICONDUCTORS. **4399**

0899-9996 *See* HIGH ENERGY PHYSICS & NUCLEAR PHYSICS. **4447**

0900-0518 *See* SKALA. **309**

0900-1476 *See* KRAKS BLA BOG. **433**

0900-3177 *See* EKSPORT KOEBENHAVN. **833**

0900-338X *See* ARGOS. **1089**

0900-5579 *See* DANTEC INFORMATION. **2040**

0900-7962 See HEALTH STATISTICS IN THE NORDIC COUNTRIES / HELSESTATISTIKK I DE NORDISKE LAND / NOMESKO. **4810**

0900-8527 See PSYKOLOGISK SKRIFTSERIE AARHUS. **4614**

0900-8675 See NORTH-WESTERN EUROPEAN LANGUAGE EVOLUTION. SUPPLEMENT. **3306**

0901-0025 See MICRO PUBLICATIONS, SOCIAL SCIENCE SERIES. **5209**

0901-0319 See KOMMUNALE TAL FRA INDENRIGSMINISTERIET ... SKN. **4735**

0901-0815 See ARKOLOGISKE UDGRAVNINGER I DANMARK / RIGSANTIKVARENS ARKOLOGISKE SEKRETARIAT. **260**

0901-3393 See SCANDINAVIAN JOURNAL OF LABORATORY ANIMAL SCIENCE. **5521**

0901-4527 See ARBEJDSDIREKTORATETS OG ARBEJDSFORMIDLINGENS ARSSTATISTIK FOR **5322**

0901-5027 See INTERNATIONAL JOURNAL OF ORAL AND MAXILLOFACIAL SURGERY. **3966**

0901-6473 See NYT OM ARBEJDSMILJ SKANDINAVIEN I SKANDINAVIEN. **1696**

0901-7496 See MAGASIN FRA DET KONGELIGE BIBLIOTEK OG UNIVERSITETSBIBLIOTEKET I. **3229**

0901-8050 See NORDISK PEDAGOGIK. **1769**

0901-814X See BIMCO BULLETIN. **5447**

0901-8328 See SCANDINAVIAN JOURNAL OF THE OLD TESTAMENT : SJOT. **5019**

0901-9898 See TANDLGERNES NYE TIDSSKRIFT. **1336**

0901-9928 See PHARMACOLOGY & TOXICOLOGY. **4322**

0901-9936 See PHARMACOLOGY & TOXICOLOGY. SUPPLEMENT. **4322**

0902-0055 See ORAL MICROBIOLOGY AND IMMUNOLOGY. **1332**

0902-0063 See CLINICAL TRANSPLANTATION. **3566**

0902-0608 See ARSBERETNING. **4037**

0902-1116 See TEKNISK TRAFIKRAPPORT. **5445**

0902-2767 See KLINISK SYGEPLEJE. **3602**

0902-3752 See OIL & GAS FINANCE & ACCOUNTANCY. **749**

0902-4441 See EUROPEAN JOURNAL OF HAEMATOLOGY. **3771**

0902-4506 See EUROPEAN JOURNAL OF HAEMATOLOGY. SUPPLEMENTUM. **3771**

0902-5162 See EPSILON. **3279**

0902-6266 See YEARBOOK. (INTERNATIONAL WORK GROUP FOR INDIGENOUS AFFAIRS). **4514**

0902-7270 See KORT SAGT !. **3222**

0902-7351 See NORDIC JOURNAL OF INTERNATIONAL LAW. **3133**

0902-7521 See CULTURE & HISTORY (COPENHAGEN). **2614**

0902-7726 See INPUT-OUTPUT TABELLER OG ANALYSER. **1496**

0902-8099 See KUNST & KOMMUNIKATION DANSK UDG. **355**

0902-8234 See TEATERRAADETS INDSTILLINGER, FORSLAG OG KONKLUSIONER. **5369**

0902-9621 See WORKING PAPERS (KBENHAVNS DEIVERSITET. CENTER FOR AFRIKASTUDIER). **2501**

0903-0719 See GRN VIDEN. HAVEBRUG / STATENS PLANTEAVLSFORSG. **2417**

0903-0727 See GRN VIDEN. LANDBRUG / STATENS PLANTEAVLSFORSG. **173**

0903-1871 See DANSKE INFORMATIONSBASER. **1181**

0903-188X See MUSIK & FORSKNING. **4137**

0903-1936 See EUROPEAN RESPIRATORY JOURNAL, THE. **3949**

0903-2401 See HUMANIORA (COPENHAGEN, DENMARK : 1988). **2847**

0903-2703 See COPENHAGEN PAPERS IN EAST AND SOUTHEAST ASIAN STUDIES. **5243**

0903-2738 See ARBOG (HISTORISK-TOPOGRAFISK SELSKAB FOR GLADSAXE KOMMUNE). **2675**

0903-3483 See CURRENT TITLES IN DENTISTRY. **1338**

0903-4641 See APMIS : ACTA PATHOLOGICA, MICROBIOLOGICA ET IMMUNOLOGICA SCANDINAVICA. **3666**

0903-465X See APMIS. ACTA PATHOLOGICA, MICROBIOLOGICA ET IMMUNOLOGICA SCANDINAVICA. SUPPLEMENTUM. **3666**

0903-6296 See UNGDOMSSKOLEN (DENMARK. UNDERVISNINGSMINISTERIET. KONOMISK--STATISTISK KONTOR). **1788**

0903-6946 See FOLKETINGSTIDENDE. ARBOG OG REGISTRE. **4474**

0903-7837 See DANMARK I SPEJLET. **3380**

0903-7845 See UDENRIGS. **4498**

0903-8086 See VIRKSOMHEDEN VED SYGEHUSE ... / SUNDHEDSSTYRELSEN. **3793**

0903-8388 See ARBEJDSMARKEDETS HANDBOG KOEBENHAVN. 1974. **1651**

0903-8825 See DANSK MONSTERTIDENDE. **1303**

0903-9759 See NORTH EUROPEAN FOOD AND DAIRY JOURNAL. **2351**

0903-9783 See PUBLIKATION - SUNDHEDSMINISTERIET. LEVNEDSMIDDELSTYRELSEN. **2355**

0904-1850 See EUROPEAN RESPIRATORY JOURNAL. SUPPLEMENT, THE. **3949**

0904-1966 See MEDICINSK FDSELS- OG MISDANNELSESSTATISTIK / SUNDHEDSSTYRELSEN. **3765**

0904-213X See ACTA CHEMICA SCANDINAVICA (COPENHAGEN, DENMARK : 1989). **1049**

0904-2334 See KATALOG. **4371**

0904-2431 See STUDIES IN CENTRAL AND EAST ASIAN RELIGIONS : JOURNAL OF THE SEMINAR FOR BUDDHIST STUDIES, COPENHAGEN & AARHUS. **5022**

0904-2512 See JOURNAL OF ORAL PATHOLOGY & MEDICINE. **1327**

0904-3063 See JOURNAL OF WORLD EDUCATION (SNEDSTED, DENMARK). **1759**

0904-3101 See DANMARKS KLIMA. **1424**

0904-339X See KOMMUNALVALGENE I KOMMUNER OG AMTSKOMMUNER. **4480**

0904-3535 See SOCIAL KRITIK. **5259**

0904-4450 See ALKOHOL- OG NARKOTIKAMISBRUGET KBENHAVN. 1988. **1340**

0904-4698 See CDR PROJECT PAPER. **72**

0904-4701 See CDR WORKING PAPERS. **5093**

0904-6380 See NORDIC THEATRE STUDIES. **5367**

0904-6453 See AAU REPORTS / BOTANICAL INSTITUTE AARHUS UNIVERSITY. **496**

0904-8626 See COPENHAGEN DISCUSSION PAPERS. **2503**

0904-9681 See NEWS FROM DBDH. **2607**

0905-0167 See SCANDINAVIAN JOURNAL OF INFORMATION SYSTEMS. **1249**

0905-0965 See BERETNING FRA FINANSTILSYNET. **2875**

0905-2233 See EUROPEAN GENERATING SET DIRECTORY. **2054**

0905-3026 See TEATER-ET. **389**

0905-3883 See ATLETIK'EN. **4884**

0905-4527 See PHOTODERMATOLOGY, PHOTOIMMUNOLOGY & PHOTOMEDICINE. **3722**

0905-4650 See B70. **3193**

0905-5533 See MAGASIN FRA DET KONGELIGE BIBLIOTEK. **3229**

0905-5606 See SCAN-ENERGY ENGLISH ED. **1956**

0905-5908 See DANSK SOCIOLOGI. **5244**

0905-6157 See PEDIATRIC ALLERGY AND IMMUNOLOGY : OFFICIAL PUBLICATION OF THE EUROPEAN SOCIETY OF PEDIATRIC ALLERGY AND IMMUNOLOGY. **3675**

0905-6440 See DANSKE MALERMESTRE. **4223**

0905-6866 See INTERNATIONAL JOURNAL FOR THE JOINING OF MATERIALS, THE. **1979**

0905-6947 See INDOOR AIR. **2232**

0905-7161 See CLINICAL ORAL IMPLANTS RESEARCH. **1319**

0905-717X See IATROGENICS : THE OFFICIAL JOURNAL OF THE INTERNATIONAL SOCIETY FOR THE PREVENTION OF IATROGENIC COMPLICATIONS (ISPIC). **3585**

0905-7196 See ARABIAN ARCHAEOLOGY AND EPIGRAPHY. **256**

0905-7544 See UDGIFTSANALYSER. **4757**

0905-9180 See EUROPEAN RESPIRATORY REVIEW : AN OFFICIAL JOURNAL OF THE EUROPEAN RESPIRATORY SOCIETY. **3949**

0905-9199 See JOURNAL OF TRANSPLANT COORDINATION : OFFICIAL PUBLICATION OF THE NORTH AMERICAN TRANSPLANT COORDINATORS ORGANIZATION (NATCO). **3799**

0906-0308 See EUROPEAN STUDIES. **2687**

0906-060X See ICES MARINE SCIENCE SYMPOSIA. **1449**

0906-1746 See TIDSSKRIFT FOR DANSK FAAREAVL. **223**

0906-2181 See BERETNING - FRA STATENS PLANTEAVLSFORSOEG OG STATENS HUSDYRBRUGSFORSOEG. **65**

0906-219X See PSYKOLOGISK PDAGOGISK RADGIVNING. **4614**

0906-4702 See ACTA AGRICULTUR SCANDINAVICA. SECTION A, ANIMAL SCIENCE. **43**

0906-4710 See ACTA AGRICULTUR SCANDINAVICA. SECTION B, SOIL AND PLANT SCIENCE. **43**

0906-6691 See ECOLOGY OF FRESHWATER FISH. **2300**

0906-6705 See EXPERIMENTAL DERMATOLOGY. **3720**

0906-6713 See PERIODONTOLOGY 2000. **1333**

0906-6714 See BAILLIERE'S CLINICAL PAEDIATRICS. **3900**

0906-7043 See JORD OG VIDEN. **98**

0906-7272 See UPDATE & DIALOG. **5007**

0906-7590 See ECOGRAPHY. **2213**

0906-7639 See COPENHAGEN WORKING PAPERS IN LINGUISTICS. **3275**

0906-9666 See PROGRAM OF PLENARY SESSIONS AND ADVANCE ABSTRACTS OF SHORT COMMUNICATIONS. **3661**

0907-1717 See NYE BGER (BIBLIOTEKSCENTRALEN (DENMARK). **421**

0907-2055 See SCANDINAVIAN JOURNAL OF SOCIAL WELFARE. **5307**

0907-4449 See ACTA CRYSTALLOGRAPHICA. SECTION D, BIOLOGICAL CRYSTALLOGRAPHY. **1031**

0908-665X See XENOTRANSPLANTATION. **3652**

0908-8857 See JOURNAL OF AVIAN BIOLOGY. **5618**

0910-0040 See NIHON REITO KYOKAI RONBUNSHU. **2607**

0910-075X See QUARTERLY FORECAST OF JAPAN'S ECONOMY. **1594**

0910-0865 See KANKYO HENIGEN KENKYU. **2176**

0910-1349 See KYOTO-SHI REKISHI SHIRYOKAN KIYO. **2657**

0910-2000 See NOGYO KANKYO GIJUTSU KENKYUJO NENPO. **520**

0910-2027 See JAPANESE YEARBOOK ON BUSINESS HISTORY. **685**

0910-2043 See JAPAN JOURNAL OF INDUSTRIAL AND APPLIED MATHEMATICS. **3511**

0910-2205 See KIDORUI. **1357**

0910-3627 See SEITAI BOGYO. **473**

0910-3740 See MEDICAL IMMUNOLOGY. **3674**

0910-4186 See RINPAGAKU. **3676**

0910-4348 See CHUGOKU KENKYU GEPPO. **5195**

0910-4534 See JAPAN INSURANCE NEWS. **2885**

0910-4607 See INTERSECT. **4349**

0910-500X See EIBUNGAKU SHICHO. **3383**

0910-5042 See SOSHIRAN ENGLISH ED. **3677**

0910-5050 See JAPANESE JOURNAL OF CANCER RESEARCH : GANN. **3818**

0910-5115 See NETTAI RINGYO 1984. **2389**

0910-5158 See KAGOSHIMA-KEN KANKYO SENTA SHOHO. **2176**

ISSN Index

0910-5719 *See* INSURANCE. SEIMEI HOKEN TOKEI-GO. 2897

0910-5727 *See* INSURANCE. SONGAI HOKEN TOKUBETSU TOKEI-GO. 2897

0910-6073 *See* KOSANKINBYO KENKYUSHO ZASSHI. 3602

0910-6340 *See* ANALYTICAL SCIENCES : THE INTERNATIONAL JOURNAL OF THE JAPAN SOCIETY FOR ANALYTICAL CHEMISTRY. 1013

0910-6545 *See* BIO INDUSTRY. 5088

0910-6707 *See* JAPAN COMPUTER QUARTERLY. 1260

0910-7908 *See* JAPAN ENGLISH PUBLICATIONS IN PRINT. 4829

0910-8017 *See* NIHON KENCHIKU GAKKAI KEIKAKUKEI RONBUN HOKOKUSHU. 622

0910-8025 *See* NIHON KENCHIKU GAKKAI KOZOKEI RONBUN HOKOKUSHU. 2027

0910-8300 *See* JAPAN ECONOMIC ALMANAC. 1569

0910-8327 *See* HEART AND VESSELS. 3705

0910-8629 *See* CHUBU DAIGAKU KOGAKUBU KIYO. 1968

0910-8637 *See* SHOKUHIN TO BISEIBUTSU. 2357

0910-9102 *See* DATA REPORT OF HYDROGRAPHIC OBSERVATIONS. 1354

0910-9722 *See* HIGASHI NIHON SHIGAKU ZASSHI. 1324

0911-0119 *See* GRAPHS AND COMBINATORICS. 3507

0911-0305 *See* MEMOIRS OF THE FACULTY OF ENGINEERING AND DESIGN, KYOTO INSTITUTE OF TECHNOLOGY. SERIES OF SCIENCE AND TECHNOLOGY. 5128

0911-0402 *See* ONSEIGAKKAI KAIHO. 3308

0911-050X *See* FUKUOKA KOGYO DAIGAKU EREKUTORONIKUSU KENKYUJO SHOHO. 2055

0911-0682 *See* JUNSHIN GAKUHO. 2849

0911-0704 *See* CONTROL THEORY AND ADVANCED TECHNOLOGY. 1180

0911-0755 *See* JOICFP NEWS. 589

0911-0836 *See* SHINZO PESHINGU. 3710

0911-0844 *See* NIHON KANGO KYOKAI CHOSA KENKYU HOKOKU. 3862

0911-1166 *See* GOSEI SENZAI KENKYUKAISHI. 976

0911-1247 *See* JOURNAL OF INTERNATIONAL ECONOMIC STUDIES. 794

0911-1557 *See* SHIKYO KENKYU. 3436

0911-2316 *See* KONBATEKKU. 4235

0911-3053 *See* ELECTRONIC PACKAGING TECHNOLOGY. 4218

0911-3622 *See* BULLETIN OF CENTRE FOR INFORMATICS. 3198

0911-4319 *See* KACHIKU KOKINZAI KENKYUKAIHO. 5515

0911-4785 *See* KAGOSHIMA-KEN CHAGYO SHIKENJO KENKYU HOKOKU. 102

0911-484X *See* KAIGAI SHAKAI HOSHO JOHO. 5294

0911-5544 *See* TECHNO JAPAN. 5163

0911-5943 *See* O PLUS E. 1118

0911-6028 *See* ORAL RADIOLOGY. 1332

0911-6044 *See* JOURNAL OF NEUROLINGUISTICS. 3291

0911-615X *See* SAN'IN CHIIKI KENKYU. 2394

0911-6168 *See* SAN'IN CHIIKI KENKYU. SHIRO-HEN. 2394

0911-6575 *See* NOGYO SEIBUTSU SHIGEN KENKYUJO KENKYU HOKOKU. 179

0911-7008 *See* TOKYO BUSINESS TODAY. 715

0911-7067 *See* NIHON SAKUMOTSU GAKKAI TOHOKU SHIBU KAIHO. 179

0911-7482 *See* CROWNED WITH THORNS. 4506

0911-7806 *See* X-SEN BUNSEKI NO SHINPO. 4442

0911-9450 *See* NOGYO KANKYO GIJUTSU KENKYUJO HOKOKU. 113

0911-9485 *See* KYUSHU KYORITSU DAIGAKU KENKYU HOKOKU. KOGAKUBU. 1985

0911-9647 *See* METALWORKING, ENGINEERING AND MARKETING. 4011

0912-0009 *See* JOURNAL OF CLINICAL BIOCHEMISTRY AND NUTRITION. 489

0912-0025 *See* YAMANASHI IKA DAIGAKU ZASSHI. 3652

0912-0076 *See* NEW ERA OF TELECOMMUNICATIONS IN JAPAN. 1160

0912-0289 *See* SEIMITSU KOGAKKAI SHI. 1996

0912-1048 *See* PROCEEDINGS OF JAPANESE SOCIETY OF SUGAR BEET TECHNOLOGISTS. 183

0912-2036 *See* JAPANESE JOURNAL OF PSYCHIATRY AND NEUROLOGY, THE. 3928

0912-2184 *See* TSUCHI TO BISEIBUTSU. 190

0912-2311 *See* ABSTRACTS OF SCIENCE AND TECHNOLOGY IN JAPAN: ENERGY TECHNOLOGY. 5173

0912-3016 *See* SHIGA IKA DAIGAKU ZASSHI. 3641

0912-3474 *See* JAPAN UPDATE. 1569

0912-3814 *See* ECOLOGICAL RESEARCH. 2214

0912-5361 *See* NIHONGO JANARU. 3306

0912-5434 *See* OPTOELECTRONICS (TOKYO). 2074

0912-5566 *See* OKI TECHNICAL REVIEW. 5136

0912-6112 *See* TOKEI SURI. 3538

0912-7305 *See* KASOKUKI KAGAKU TOKYO. 5123

0912-8859 *See* SHIKOKU KOKENKAIHO. 1996

0912-9200 *See* JOURNAL OF THE CERAMIC SOCIETY OF JAPAN. 2591

0912-9243 *See* ANNUAL OF THE JAPANESE BIBLICAL INSTITUTE. 5014

0912-9715 *See* TAMIYA MODEL MAGAZINE INTERNATIONAL. 2778

0912-9731 *See* NOSON KEIKAKU GAKKAISHI. 2829

0913-0071 *See* SUIZO. 3801

0913-0322 *See* SEIRIGAKU KENKYUJO GIJUTSUKA HOKOKU. 5156

0913-0748 *See* UNIX MAGAZINE. 1206

0913-140X *See* RINSAN SHIKENJOHO. 2394

0913-1442 *See* RIRON TO HOHO. 5256

0913-1507 *See* STUDIES IN MEDIEVAL ENGLISH LANGUAGE AND LITERATURE. 3326

0913-2090 *See* GAS REVIEW NIPPON. 4258

0913-2384 *See* KAGAKU RYOHO NO RYOIKI (1987). 3601

0913-283X *See* GAS & CHEMICAL REPORTER. 4257

0913-3615 *See* LANGUAGE RESEARCH BULLETIN / ICU. 3296

0913-4182 *See* CHIKASUI GAKKAI SHI. 1413

0913-4239 *See* CHUGOKU NOGYO SHIKENJO KENKYU HOKOKU. 73

0913-4549 *See* BAIOMASU HENKAN KEIKAKU KENKYU HOKOKU. 443

0913-4700 *See* REVIEW OF JAPANESE CULTURE AND SOCIETY. 2663

0913-4794 *See* KOBELCO TECHNOLOGY REVIEW. 5123

0913-4867 *See* MAGUNESHUMU KYOTO. 985

0913-5006 *See* DRUG DELIVERY SYSTEM. 4300

0913-5227 *See* NIHON KASEI GAKKAISHI. 2792

0913-557X *See* PLANT SPECIES BIOLOGY. 524

0913-5707 *See* DENSHI JOHO TSUSHIN GAKKAI RONBUNSHI. A. 2041

0913-6339 *See* DENKI GAKKAI RONBUNSHI. D, SANGYO OYO BUMONSHI. 2040

0913-6800 *See* SUGADAIRA KOGEN JIKKEN SENTA KENKYU HOKOKU. 4172

0913-8005 *See* TOSHOKAN KYORYOKU TSUSHIN. 3253

0913-8188 *See* COMMUNICATIONS IN APPLIED CELL BIOLOGY. 452

0913-8668 *See* JOURNAL OF ANESTHESIA. 3683

0913-8773 *See* JAPAN REVIEW OF INTERNATIONAL AFFAIRS. 4526

0913-882X *See* NIHON YOTON GAKKAISHI. 5593

0913-9907 *See* AKITA DAIGAKU KOZAN GAKUBU SHIGEN CHIGAKU KENKYU SHISETSU HOKOKU. 2185

0914-0026 *See* BUSINESS TOKYO. 653

0914-1855 *See* JOURNAL OF THE MAMMALOGICAL SOCIETY OF JAPAN. 5589

0914-2029 *See* PROCEEDINGS OF THE NIPR SYMPOSIUM ON ANTARCTIC GEOSCIENCES. 1391

0914-2037 *See* PROCEEDINGS OF THE NIPR SYMPOSIUM ON POLAR METEOROLOGY AND GLACIOLOGY. 1433

0914-2177 *See* KYOTO PASTEUR KENKYUJO KENKYU HOKOKU. 5125

0914-2568 *See* HYBRIDS. 513

0914-3238 *See* NEW ORCHIDS. 2425

0914-3319 *See* NIPPON INSATSU GAKKAISHI. 4567

0914-3491 *See* JIBI INKOKA, TOKEIBU GEKA 1988. 3888

0914-3505 *See* CONGENITAL ANOMALIES. 543

0914-3793 *See* KYUSHU DAIGAKU KINO BUSSHITSU KAGAKU KENKYUJO HOKOKU. 2104

0914-4404 *See* PROCEEDINGS OF THE ICMR SEMINAR. 3630

0914-4935 *See* SENSORS AND MATERIALS. 1996

0914-5087 *See* JOURNAL OF CARDIOLOGY. 3706

0914-5230 *See* JATI COURIER. 5417

0914-5400 *See* NIHON SERAMIKKUSU KYOKAI GAKUJUTSU RONBUNSHI. 2592

0914-5621 *See* PROCEEDINGS OF THE NIPR SYMPOSIUM ON ANTARCTIC METEORITES. 398

0914-563X *See* PROCEEDINGS OF THE NIPR SYMPOSIUM ON POLAR BIOLOGY. 557

0914-6628 *See* ZAIRYO TO PUROSESU. 2002

0914-6644 See YASAI CHAGYO SHIKENJO KENKYU HOKOKU. A, YASAI, KAKI. 2434

0914-6652 See YASAI CHAGYO SHIKENJO KENKYU HOKOKU. B, CHAGYO. 2373

0914-675X *See* KUMAMOTO JOURNAL OF MATHEMATICS. 3516

0914-711X *See* YAMANASHI-KEN KOGYO GIJUTSU SENTA KENKYU HOKOKU. 5171

0914-7470 *See* HUMAN CELL : OFFICIAL JOURNAL OF HUMAN CELL RESEARCH SOCIETY. 537

0914-7594 *See* APN. APPAREL PRODUCTION NEWS. 1081

0914-7675 *See* NIHON SHOKUHIN TEION HOZO GAKKAISHI. 2351

0914-8035 *See* JOURNAL OF AMERICAN AND CANADIAN STUDIES, THE. 2740

0914-854X *See* SANGYO GIJUTSU SOGO KENKYUJO HOKOKU. 5149

0914-8809 *See* JSME INTERNATIONAL JOURNAL. SERIES I, SOLID MECHANICS, STRENGTH OF MATERIALS. 2119

0914-8817 *See* JSME INTERNATIONAL JOURNAL. SERIES 2, FLUIDS ENGINEERING, HEAT TRANSFER, POWER, COMBUSTION, THERMOPHYSICAL PROPERTIES. 2119

0914-8825 *See* JSME INTERNATIONAL JOURNAL. SERIES 3, VIBRATION, CONTROL ENGINEERING, ENGINEERING FOR INDUSTRY. 2119

0914-899X *See* HITACHI CABLE REVIEW. 2155

0914-9007 *See* MANAGEMENT & COORDINATION. 876

0914-9198 *See* JOURNAL OF TOXICOLOGIC PATHOLOGY. 3896

0914-9244 *See* JOURNAL OF PHOTOPOLYMER SCIENCE AND TECHNOLOGY. 5119

0914-9260 *See* JOURNAL OF THE COMMUNICATIONS RESEARCH LABORATORY. 1159

0914-9279 *See* TSUSHIN SOGO KENKYUJO KIHO. 1123

0914-9457 *See* NIHON JIKI KYOMEI IGAKKAI ZASSHI. 3695

0914-9465 *See* ARCHIVES OF HISTOLOGY AND CYTOLOGY. 532

0914-9635 *See* JAPANESE JOURNAL OF ENDOUROLOGY AND ESWL. 3990

0914-9783 *See* GANKO : GANSEKI KOBUTSU KOSHO GAKKAI SHI. 1355

0915-0021 *See* NATIONAL ASTRONOMICAL OBSERVATORY REPRINT. 397

0915-0471 See MIE DAIGAKU SEIBUTSU SHIGEN GAKUBU KIYO. 2308
0915-0544 See NKK TECHNICAL REVIEW. 5134
0915-1168 See TORAIBOROJISUTO. 2130
0915-1478 See FUJI FIRUMU KENKYU HOKOKU. 4369
0915-1559 See ISIJ INTERNATIONAL / IRON AND STEEL INSTITUTE OF JAPAN. 1613
0915-1699 See PROCEEDINGS OF JAPANESE SYMPOSIUM ON PLASMA CHEMISTRY. 989
0915-1702 See CG. CAR GRAPHIC. 5409
0915-1729 See LEISURE & RECREATION. 4851
0915-1869 See HYOMEN GIJUTSU. 1025
0915-194X See HIROSHIMA KENRITSU SEIBU KOGYO GIJUTSU SENTA KENKYU HOKOKU. 5110
0915-2326 See NTT R & D. 1161
0915-2334 See NTT REVIEW. 1161
0915-2350 See JOURNAL OF THE JAPANESE SOCIETY OF COMPUTATIONAL STATISTICS. 3515
0915-3160 See NEW BREEZE. 1118
0915-3179 See WAKAYAMA-KEN EISEI KOGAI KENKYU SENTA NENPO. 2183
0915-3594 See MATERIARU RAIFU. 2106
0915-3640 See PUBLICATIONS OF THE NATIONAL ASTRONOMICAL OBSERVATORY OF JAPAN. 399
0915-3780 See MIZUSAWA KANSOKU SENTA GIHO. 1358
0915-3942 See JOURNAL OF ROBOTICS AND MECHATRONICS. 1214
0915-437X See YAMANASHI-KEN EISEI KOGAI KENKYUJO NENPO. 4808
0915-4841 See ACCESS NIPPON. 890
0915-499X See BULLETIN OF THE INSTITUTE OF TROPICAL AGRICULTURE, KYUSHU UNIVERSITY. 69
0915-5457 See REPORT OF STUDY GROUP ON INTERNATIONAL ISSUES, FAPRC. 126
0915-5635 See DIGESTIVE ENDOSCOPY : OFFICIAL JOURNAL OF THE JAPAN GASTROENTEROLOGICAL ENDOSCOPY SOCIETY. 3744
0915-5651 See JOURNAL OF ADVANCED SCIENCE / SOCIETY OF ADVANCED SCIENCE. 5118
0915-5805 See JAPANESE JOURNAL OF ENTOMOLOGY TOKYO. 1989. 5610
0915-6194 See JOURNAL OF ENVIRONMENTAL SCIENCE LABORATORY. 2176
0915-6321 See REPORT OF THE NATIONAL OBSERVATORY OF JAPAN. 399
0915-6380 See SHOWA UNIVERSITY JOURNAL OF MEDICAL SCIENCES, THE. 3641
0915-7476 See NEWSLETTER FOR INTERNATIONAL COLLABORATION. 112
0915-8669 See IGAKU KENSA. 3585
0915-8847 See KASSEI SANSO, FURI RAJIKARU. 983
0915-907X See CELL SCIENCE. 451
0915-9444 See NATURAL HISTORY RESEARCH. 2219
0915-9452 See CHIBA KENRITSU CHUO HAKUBUTSUKAN SHIZENSHI KENKYU HOKOKU. 4164
0915-9517 See AIKI NEWS ENGLISH ED. 2595
0915-9606 See HOCHUDOKU. 3740
0915-9975 See HIRAGANA TAIMUZU. 2504
0916-0388 See GLASS TOKYO. 1986, THE. 2590
0916-085X See NIHON IYO MASU SUPEKUTORU GAKKAI KOENSHU. 3622
0916-0930 See HITACHI KINZOKU GIHO. 4003
0916-1139 See YAKUBUTSU DOTAI. 4200
0916-1198 See DIRECTORY OF JAPANESE SCIENTIFIC PERIODICALS. 5174
0916-1465 See TOSHIBA'S SELECTED PAPERS ON SCIENCE & TECHNOLOGY. 5166
0916-1554 See TANPAKUSHITSU KOGAKU KISO KENKYU SENTA DAYORI. 1048
0916-1562 See SUISAN KAIYO KENKYU. 2314
0916-1589 See YOYUEN OYOBI KOON KAGAKU. 996

0916-1740 See SHIGEN TO SOZAI. 2151
0916-1821 See MATERIALS TRANSACTIONS, JIM. 4008
0916-2313 See OHU DAIGAKU SHIGAKUSHI. 1331
0916-3182 See SEMENTO KONKURITO RONBUNSHU. 627
0916-3646 See KOKUSAI KANKEI KENKYU. KOKUSAI KANKEI-HEN. 4527
0916-3654 See KOKUSAI KANKEI KENKYU. KOKUSAI BUNKA-HEN. 4527
0916-3786 See HIKAKU SEIRI SEIKAGAKU. 488
0916-3808 See NIHON RODO KEBNKYU ZASSHI. 1695
0916-3905 See KAGOSHIMA-KEN KOGYO GIJUTSU SENTA KENKYU HOKOKU. 5122
0916-4405 See SHINRIN SOGO KENKYUJO KENKYU HOKOKU. 2395
0916-4456 See ZAIKEN HOKOKU. 5172
0916-4553 See JFCC REVIEW. 2591
0916-4650 See ECONOMIC JOURNAL OF HOKKAIDO UNIVERSITY. 1483
0916-4804 See NIHON ISHINKIN GAKKAI ZASSHI. 576
0916-4812 See NIHON SETCHAKU GAKKAI SHI. 1027
0916-572X See CONNECTIVE TISSUE TOKYO. 1989. 3568
0916-6009 See MATHEMATICS JOURNAL OF TOYAMA UNIVERSITY. 3521
0916-6076 See YOSHA. 1031
0916-6386 See LANCET NIHONGO-BAN, THE. 3603
0916-6521 See REPORT OF MATERIALS SCIENCE AND TECHNOLOGY. 2108
0916-6572 See SHIZUOKA-KEN SHIZUOKA KOGYO GIJUTSU SENTA KENKYU HOKOKU. 5157
0916-6823 See KOSHU EISEI KENKYU. 4788
0916-684X See YASAI CHAGYO SHIKENJO KENKYU HOKOKU. A, YASAI, KAKI. 2434
0916-6858 See YASAI CHAGYO SHIKENJO KENKYU HOKOKU. B, CHAGYO. 2373
0916-7005 See JAPAN JOURNAL OF INDUSTRIAL AND APPLIED MATHEMATICS. 3511
0916-7064 See ASAHI GARASU ZAIDAN KENKYU HOKOKU. 2586
0916-7250 See JOURNAL OF VETERINARY MEDICAL SCIENCE. 5514
0916-7315 See KYUSHU DAIGAKU RIGAKUBU KENKYU HOKOKU. CHIKYU WAKUSEI KAGAKU. 1386
0916-7390 See MEMOIRS OF THE FACULTY OF SCIENCE, KYUSHU UNIVERSITY. SERIES D, EARTH AND PLANETARY SCIENCES. 1387
0916-7781 See JPG LETTER. 2505
0916-7838 See ABD. ASIAN/PACIFIC BOOK DEVELOPMENT. 4822
0916-8311 See BULLETIN OF PRECISION AND INTELLIGENCE LABORATORY. 3476
0916-8370 See JOURNAL OF OCEANOGRAPHY. 1450
0916-8451 See BIOSCIENCE, BIOTECHNOLOGY, AND BIOCHEMISTRY. 3687
0916-8478 See JAPANESE JOURNAL OF HUMAN GENETICS, THE. 548
0916-8508 See IEICE TRANSACTIONS ON FUNDAMENTALS OF ELECTRONICS, COMMUNICATIONS AND COMPUTER SCIENCES. 1157
0916-8516 See IEICE TRANSACTIONS ON COMMUNICATIONS. 1112
0916-8524 See IEICE TRANSACTIONS ON ELECTRONICS. 2064
0916-8532 See IEICE TRANSACTIONS ON INFORMATION AND SYSTEMS. 5111
0916-8737 See JOURNAL OF SMOOTH MUSCLE RESEARCH. 3805
0916-877X See JAPAN 21ST. 685
0916-9636 See HYPERTENSION RESEARCH, CLINICAL AND EXPERIMENTAL. 3706
0916-9997 See SHIGEN TO TANKYO. 2205
0917-0332 See ASAHI SHIMBUN JAPAN ACCESS. 2501
0917-0480 See ZAIRYO TO KANKYO. 2002

0917-0537 See SCIENTIFIC REPORTS OF CETACEAN RESEARCH. 5597
0917-0553 See RURDS. REVIEW OF URBAN AND REGIONAL DEVELOPMENT STUDIES. 2835
0917-0855 See HAIKIBUTSU GAKKAISHI. 2230
0917-0863 See ROAD HOME, THE. 5443
0917-1673 See IEICE TRANSACTIONS ON COMMUNICATIONS. 1112
0917-1673 See IEICE TRANSACTIONS ON INFORMATION AND SYSTEMS. 5111
0917-1673 See IEICE TRANSACTIONS ON ELECTRONICS. 2064
0917-1673 See IEICE TRANSACTIONS ON FUNDAMENTALS OF ELECTRONICS, COMMUNICATIONS AND COMPUTER SCIENCES. 1157
0917-1746 See HOBUNSHU / KYOTO DAIGAKU GENSHIRO JIKKENJO GAKUJUTSU KOENKAI. 1053
0917-2300 See KYORITSU JOSHI TANKI DAIGAKU SEIKATSU KAGAKUKA KIYO. 462
0917-2394 See PEDIATRIC DENTAL JOURNAL : INTERNATIONAL JOURNAL OF JAPANESE SOCIETY OF PEDIATRIC DENTISTRY. 1332
0917-4427 See JOURNAL OF PROTOZOOLOGY RESEARCH. 462
0917-4540 See DIAMOND FILMS AND TECHNOLOGY. 4001
0917-5555 See PURINTO KAIRO GAKKAI DENJI TOKUSEI KENKYU BUKAI KOKAI KENKYUKAI RONBUNSHU. 2078
0917-7221 See USUI GIJUTSU SHIRYO. 5541
0917-7507 See SEXUAL SCIENCE. 5188
0917-8260 See OZONEWS IN JAPAN. 2179
0917-9720 See NOGYO KIKAI GAKKAI KYUSHU SHIBUSHI. 113
0918-4406 See JAPAN ... MARKETING AND ADVERTISING YEARBOOK. 761
0918-4422 See MID-TERM ECONOMIC FORECAST. 1505
0918-516X See JAPAN CHRISTIAN REVIEW, THE. 4967
0918-5739 See CLINICAL PEDIATRIC ENDOCRINOLOGY. 3727
0918-6158 See BIOLOGICAL & PHARMACEUTICAL BULLETIN. 4293
0918-7960 See ANTHROPOLOGICAL SCIENCE : JOURNAL OF THE ANTHROPOLOGICAL SOCIETY OF NIPPON. 229
0918-8959 See ENDOCRINE JOURNAL. 3729
0918-9440 See JOURNAL OF PLANT RESEARCH. 516
0919-0589 See APO PRODUCTIVITY JOURNAL. 62
0919-1380 See BANK OF JAPAN QUARTERLY BULLETIN. 775
0919-2050 See JOURNAL OF ATMOSPHERIC ELECTRICITY. 1426
0919-3758 See SEIBUTSU KOGAKKAI SHI / SEIBUTSU-KOGAKU KAISHI. 3696
0919-6080 See ENERGY IN JAPAN. 1940
0919-8172 See INTERNATIONAL JOURNAL OF UROLOGY. 3990
0919-8822 See NEWSLETTER FOR INTERNATIONAL COLLABORATION. 112
0920-0223 See NAMENS ZWOLLE. 1506
0920-0401 See MANUSCRIPTS OF THE MIDDLE EAST. 4830
0920-0517 See TIJDSCHRIFT VOOR SOCIALE GEZONDHEIDSZORG : TSG : 14-DAAGS BLAD VAN DE ALGEMENE NEDERLANDSE VERENIGING VOOR SOCIALE GEZONDHEIDSZORG. 4805
0920-0649 See TIJDSCHRIFT VOOR OUDE MUZIEK. 4156
0920-1009 See VORMEN UIT VUUR. 2595
0920-119X See ARBEIDSOMSTANDIGHEDEN. 2859
0920-1211 See EPILEPSY RESEARCH. 3832
0920-1327 See CULTUREN. 2684
0920-1580 See NETHERLANDS JOURNAL OF HOUSING AND ENVIRONMENTAL RESEARCH. 2829

ISSN Index

0920-1610 *See* MARITIME INFORMATION REVIEW. 3181

0920-1629 *See* WIEDERHALL. 310

0920-1637 *See* CLINICAL NEUROPSYCHOLOGIST, THE. 3830

0920-1742 *See* FISH PHYSIOLOGY AND BIOCHEMISTRY. 2301

0920-203X *See* CHINA INFORMATION. 4468

0920-2099 *See* EISMA 'S VAKPERS. 4223

0920-2110 *See* OPTIMA FARMA. 4318

0920-2153 *See* EUROPEAN NEWSLETTER ON QUALITY ASSURANCE. 3780

0920-2307 *See* MATERIALS SCIENCE REPORTS. 2106

0920-234X *See* ICCA JOURNAL. 1230

0920-2706 *See* TRENDS IN TELECOMMUNICATIONS. 1168

0920-2862 *See* BIBLIOGRAFISCHE ATTENDERINGSLIJST VOOR DOCENTEN NEERLANDISTIEK IN HET BUITENLAND / BUREAU VOOR DE BIBLIOGRAFIE VAN DE NEERLANDISTIEK, KONINKLIJKE BIBLIOTHEEK, ONDER AUSPICIEN VAN DE NEDERLANDSE TAALUNIE. 409

0920-2870 *See* SOCIAAL RECHT. 5308

0920-3036 *See* K-THEORY. 3516

0920-3060 *See* CRITICAL THEORY. 3275

0920-3079 *See* PRAGMATICS & BEYOND COMPANION SERIES. 3311

0920-315X *See* INTERNATIONAL TAX ADVISOR, THE. 2984

0920-3168 *See* ALERT / REDACTIONELE VERANTWOORDELIJKHEID VAN HET MINISTERIE VAN BINNENLANDSE ZAKEN. 1072

0920-3192 *See* ORGAN YEARBOOK, THE. 4144

0920-3206 *See* CARDIOVASCULAR DRUGS AND THERAPY. 3701

0920-3273 *See* VERPLEEGKUNDE. 3870

0920-3796 *See* FUSION ENGINEERING AND DESIGN. 2155

0920-4105 *See* JOURNAL OF PETROLEUM SCIENCE & ENGINEERING. 4262

0920-427X *See* ARGUMENTATION. 4341

0920-4520 See NEDERLANDS TIJDSCHRIFT VOOR DERMATOLOGIE & VENEREOLOGIE. 3722

0920-4741 *See* WATER RESOURCES MANAGEMENT (DORDRECHT, NETHERLANDS). 5547

0920-4792 *See* YEARBOOK OF EUROPEAN STUDIES. 2525

0920-4849 *See* SER-BULLETIN. 1710

0920-5047 *See* MORSKOI GIDROFIZICHESKII ZHURNAL. 1453

0920-5071 *See* JOURNAL OF ELECTROMAGNETIC WAVES AND APPLICATIONS. 2068

0920-5268 *See* APPLIED CARDIOPULMONARY PATHOPHYSIOLOGY : ACP. 3699

0920-5438 *See* PROGRESS IN BIOMEDICAL ENGINEERING. 3696

0920-5446 *See* DEVELOPMENTS IN PALEONTOLOGY AND STRATIGRAPHY. 4227

0920-5489 *See* COMPUTER STANDARDS & INTERFACES. 1178

0920-5578 *See* DIAMANT-, GOUD- EN ZILVERVERWERKENDE INDUSTRIE, SIERADENINDUSTRIE. 2914

0920-5632 *See* NUCLEAR PHYSICS. SECTION B, PROCEEDINGS SUPPLEMENT. 4449

0920-5691 *See* INTERNATIONAL JOURNAL OF COMPUTER VISION. 1190

0920-5861 *See* CATALYSIS TODAY. 966

0920-6221 *See* STUDIES IN HUMAN SOCIETY. 5263

0920-623X *See* SUPPLEMENTS TO VIGILIAE CHRISTIANAE. 5001

0920-6280 *See* JOURNAAL NV/BV. 2986

0920-6299 *See* INTERNATIONAL JOURNAL OF FLEXIBLE MANUFACTURING SYSTEMS. 3481

0920-654X *See* JOURNAL OF COMPUTER-AIDED MOLECULAR DESIGN. 1229

0920-7554 *See* SUIKERINDUSTRIE, ZETMEEL- EN ZETMEELDERIVATENINDUSTRIE. 1628

0920-7724 *See* JAARBOEK VOOR DE GESCHIEDENIS VAN BEDRIJF EN TECHNIEK. 5117

0920-7775 *See* ANUARIO INTERAMERICANO DE DERECHOS HUMANOS. 4504

0920-7783 *See* STICHTING & VERENIGING. 405

0920-7848 *See* CANCER PHARMACOLOGY ANNUAL, THE. 3812

0920-7996 *See* AT SOURCE : A QUARTERLY FOR DEVELOPMENT. 5086

0920-8380 *See* GRONDVERZET & BOUWTRANSPORT. 615

0920-8399 *See* SUPPLEMENTUM EPIGRAPHICUM GRAECUM. 1080

0920-8534 *See* FEMS MICROBIOLOGY IMMUNOLOGY. 562

0920-8542 *See* JOURNAL OF SUPERCOMPUTING, THE. 1192

0920-8550 *See* JOURNAL OF FINANCIAL SERVICES RESEARCH. 794

0920-8569 *See* VIRUS GENES. 571

0920-8607 *See* BRILL'S STUDIES IN INTELLECTUAL HISTORY. 2612

0920-8771 *See* ILEIA NEWSLETTER. 174

0920-9026 *See* CREOLE LANGUAGE LIBRARY. 3275

0920-9034 *See* JOURNAL OF PIDGIN AND CREOLE LANGUAGES. 3291

0920-9069 *See* CYTOTECHNOLOGY (DORDRECHT). 535

0920-9832 *See* PROGRESS IN HPLC. 990

0920-9964 *See* SCHIZOPHRENIA RESEARCH. 3936

0921-0083 *See* STATISTIEK VAN HET BEROEPSONDERWIJS. BEROEPSBEGELEIDEND ONDERWIJS EN VORMINGSEREK, CURSORISCH ONDERNEMERSONDERWIJS / CBS, CENTRAAL BUREAU VOOR DE STATISTIEK, HOOFDAFDELING STATISTIEKEN VAN ONDERWIJS EN WETENSCHAPPEN. 5342

0921-0091 *See* STATISTIEK VAN HET HOGER BEROEPSONDERWIJS. INSTELLINGEN EN STUDENTEN / CBS, CENTRAAL BUREAU VOOR DE STATISTIEK, HOOFDAFDELING STATISTIEKEN VAN ONDERWIJS EN WETENSCHAPPEN. 1916

0921-0296 *See* JOURNAL OF INTELLIGENT & ROBOTIC SYSTEMS. 1220

0921-030X *See* NATURAL HAZARDS (DORDRECHT). 2178

0921-0350 *See* STATISTIEK VAN HET BASISONDERWIJS, HET SPECIAAL ONDERWIJS EN HET VOORTGEZET SPECIAAL ONDERWIJS. SCHOLEN EN LEERLINGEN. 1785

0921-0423 *See* PROGRESS IN BIOTECHNOLOGY. 492

0921-0687 *See* BIOACTIVE MOLECULES. 480

0921-0709 *See* TECHNIQUES IN THE BEHAVIORAL AND NEURAL SCIENCES. 4620

0921-142X *See* ZEVENTIENDE EEUW, DE. 2634

0921-2442 *See* PRAKTIJKBLAD VOOR MEDEZEGGENSCHAP. 946

0921-2507 *See* DQR STUDIES IN LITERATURE. 3382

0921-2515 *See* AVANT GARDE (AMSTERDAM, NETHERLANDS). 315

0921-2523 *See* TEORIA LITERARIA, TEXTO Y TEORIA. 3445

0921-2531 *See* AUSTRALIAN PLAYWRIGHTS. 5361

0921-2558 *See* BLOCK (ALMELO). 4104

0921-2566 *See* IPO ANNUAL PROGRESS REPORT. 514

0921-2574 *See* VANGNET. 3947

0921-2582 *See* DRUG-INDUCED DISORDERS. 4300

0921-2590 *See* VIRUS RESEARCH. SUPPLEMENT. 571

0921-2604 *See* GENETIC ENGINEERING AND BIOTECHNOLOGY YEARBOOK. 3692

0921-2639 *See* WATER TREATMENT. 5548

0921-2647 *See* ADVANCES IN HUMAN FACTORS / ERGONOMICS. 2109

0921-2728 *See* JOURNAL OF PALEOLIMNOLOGY. 461

0921-2736 *See* COMPUTER SCIENCE IN ECONOMICS AND MANAGEMENT. 1177

0921-2973 *See* LANDSCAPE ECOLOGY. 2218

0921-299X *See* BIOTHERAPY (DORDRECHT). 448

0921-3163 *See* STUDIES IN MANAGEMENT SCIENCE AND SYSTEMS. 887

0921-3198 *See* DEVELOPMENTS IN GEOCHEMISTRY. 974

0921-3287 *See* PAIN RESEARCH AND CLINICAL MANAGEMENT. 3625

0921-3376 *See* THEORY AND DECISION LIBRARY. 3253

0921-3449 *See* RESOURCES, CONSERVATION AND RECYCLING. 2204

0921-3457 *See* CAHIERS VAN DE STICHTING BIO-WETENSCHAPPEN EN MAATSCHAPPIJ. 3561

0921-3732 *See* EUROPEAN CANCER NEWS. 3816

0921-3740 *See* CULTURAL DYNAMICS. 5243

0921-3767 *See* MATHEMATICAL PHYSICS STUDIES. 4412

0921-3775 *See* FRONTIERS OF MEDICAL AND BIOLOGICAL ENGINEERING. 3692

0921-383X *See* EFM. EURO FLEXO MAGAZINE. 4564

0921-4348 *See* TIJDSCHRIFT VOOR ERGONOMIE. 2130

0921-4410 *See* CANCER CHEMOTHERAPY AND BIOLOGICAL RESPONSE MODIFIERS. 3810

0921-4488 *See* SMALL RUMINANT RESEARCH. 5597

0921-4526 *See* PHYSICA B. CONDENSED MATTER. 4414

0921-4534 *See* PHYSICA C. SUPERCONDUCTIVITY. 4414

0921-4755 *See* KUNST EN BELEID IN NEDERLAND. 356

0921-4771 *See* PROBUS. 3312

0921-481X *See* TIJDSCHRIFT VOOR SOCIAAL WETENSCHAPPELIJK ONDERZOEK VAN DE LANDBOUW. 141

0921-4828 *See* STATISTIEK VAN HET BASISONDERWIJS, HET SPECIAAL ONDERWIJS EN HET VOORTGEZET SPECIAAL ONDERWIJS. PERSONEEL. 1805

0921-4933 *See* AMSTERDAMS SOCIOLOGISCH TIJDSCHRIFT 1988. 5239

0921-5018 *See* NETHERLANDS JOURNAL OF CARDIOLOGY : THREE-MONTHLY ISSUE OF THE NETHERLANDS HEART FOUNDATION AND THE NETHERLANDS SOCIETY OF CARDIOLOGY, THE. 3708

0921-5034 *See* LANGUAGE AND COMPUTERS. 3294

0921-5077 *See* GEDRAG EN ORGANISATIE. 4587

0921-5093 *See* MATERIALS SCIENCE & ENGINEERING. A, STRUCTURAL MATERIALS : PROPERTIES, MICROSTRUCTURE AND PROCESSING. 2105

0921-5107 *See* MATERIALS SCIENCE & ENGINEERING. B, SOLID-STATE MATERIALS FOR ADVANCED TECHNOLOGY. 2105

0921-5131 *See* E.R.M. JOURNAAL. 2042

0921-5360 *See* GEDRAG & GEZONDHEID. 4587

0921-562X *See* TGO. TIJDSCHRIFT VOOR THERAPIE, GENEESMIDDEL EN ONDERZOEK. 4330

0921-5832 *See* TIJDSCHRIFT VOOR VERZORGENDEN. 4805

0921-5891 *See* HOBBES STUDIES. 4348

0921-5956 *See* INDUSTRIAL METROLOGY. 4030

0921-6111 *See* DIEPZEE. 3462

0921-6154 *See* LITERATUURINFORMATIE PERSONEELSBELEID EN ORGANISATIE. 690

0921-6200 See POLITIE MAGAZINE. 3172

0921-7126 *See* AI COMMUNICATIONS. 1210

0921-7134 *See* ASYMPTOTIC ANALYSIS. 3496

0921-7169 *See* PERIODIEKE RAPPORTAGE - LANDBOUW-ECONOMISCH INSTITUUT. 1512

ISSN Index

0921-7606 See SELECTIEF DEN HAAG. 1991. 5156

0921-8009 See ECOLOGICAL ECONOMICS. 2213

0921-8041 See ARCHIS. 288

0921-8106 See INDUSTRIAL CRISIS QUARTERLY. 682

0921-8181 See GLOBAL AND PLANETARY CHANGE. 1356

0921-8211 See NORMALISATIE MAGAZINE. 4032

0921-8254 See FEMS MICROBIOLOGY. 562

0921-8319 See JOURNAL OF LIPID MEDIATORS. 1042

0921-8343 See GGD-NIEWS (GRAVENHAGE). 4776

0921-8637 See BEAM MODIFICATION OF MATERIALS. 4433

0921-8696 See NEUROSCIENCE RESEARCH. SUPPLEMENT. 3843

0921-8734 See MUTATION RESEARCH. DNAGING : GENETIC INSTABILITY AND AGING. 550

0921-8769 See NEDERLANDS TIJDSCHRIFT VOOR ANESTHESIOLOGIE. 3683

0921-8777 See MUTATION RESEARCH. DNA REPAIR. 466

0921-8831 See ADVANCED POWDER TECHNOLOGY. 5080

0921-8890 See ROBOTICS AND AUTONOMOUS SYSTEMS. 1216

0921-8912 See ANALYTICAL CELLULAR PATHOLOGY. 532

0921-8971 See JOURNAL OF APPLIED PHYCOLOGY. 514

0921-898X See SMALL BUSINESS ECONOMICS. 1520

0921-9315 See REIDEL TEXTS IN THE MATHEMATICAL SCIENCES. 3530

0921-9331 See MECHANICS AND MATHEMATICAL METHODS. THIRD SERIES, ACOUSTIC, ELECTROMAGNETIC, AND ELASTIC WAVE SCATTERING. 4428

0921-9668 See PLANT FOODS FOR HUMAN NUTRITION (DORDRECHT). 4197

0921-9684 See GEZIN LISSE. 2280

0921-9749 See MECHANICS AND MATHEMATICAL METHODS SECOND SERIES, THERMAL STRESSERS. 4428

0921-9757 See ENERGY IN WORLD AGRICULTURE. 81

0921-9862 See INTERNATIONAL YEARBOOK OF NEPHROLOGY. 3990

0921-9986 See WALL STREET JOURNAL (EUROPE). 5778

0922-0895 See OPLEIDING & ONTWIKKELING. 1770

0922-1026 See FINANCIEEL OVERHEIDSMANAGEMENT. 4649

0922-1166 See TALEN GRONINGEN. 3327

0922-1425 See JAPAN AND THE WORLD ECONOMY. 1636

0922-1433 See BONES. 262

0922-1476 See MARITIME ANTHROPOLOGICAL STUDIES : MAST. 241

0922-1565 See LEIDEN JOURNAL OF INTERNATIONAL LAW. 3132

0922-1611 See TRIAKEL GRONINGEN. 3870

0922-2197 See PLATTELANDS POST ('S-GRAVENHAGE. 1988). 120

0922-2367 See AUDIO VIDEO TOTAAL. 1293

0922-2782 See VELDWERK AMSTERDAM. 2912

0922-2928 See AANSPRAAK AMSTERDAM. 938

0922-2936 See JOURNAL OF EMPIRICAL THEOLOGY : JET. 4969

0922-2995 See JOURNAL OF QUANTITATIVE ANTHROPOLOGY. 239

0922-3061 See ADVANCES IN SUICIDOLOGY. 3919

0922-3282 See RAPPORT - INSTITUUT VOOR VEEVOEDINGSONDERZOEK. 220

0922-338X See JOURNAL OF FERMENTATION AND BIOENGINEERING. 565

0922-3495 See YEARBOOK OF MORPHOLOGY. 3334

0922-2782 See INZET AMSTERDAM. 2910

0922-3576 See GROENTEN + FRUIT. VOLLEGRONDSGROENTEN. 2417

0922-3576 See GROENTEN + FRUIT. FRUIT. 2417

0922-3576 See GROENTEN + FRUIT. PADDESTOELEN. 2417

0922-3576 See GROENTEN + FRUIT. ALGEMEEN. 2417

0922-3576 See GROENTEN + FRUIT. GLASGROENTEN. 2417

0922-4106 See EUROPEAN JOURNAL OF PHARMACOLOGY. MOLECULAR PHARMACOLOGY SECTION. 4303

0922-4122 See INFORMATIEF NVR. 4455

0922-4238 See REFLECTION. 4990

0922-4777 See READING & WRITING. 3314

0922-4939 See LANDENDOCUMENTATIEMAPPEN. 2568

0922-5072 See SEMIOTIC CROSSROADS. 3320

0922-5307 See LASERS AND LIGHT IN OPHTHALMOLOGY. 3876

0922-5579 See STUDIES IN POLYMER SCIENCE. 993

0922-5773 See JOURNAL OF VLSI SIGNAL PROCESSING. 2070

0922-6028 See RESTORATIVE NEUROLOGY AND NEUROSCIENCE. 3845

0922-6168 See RESEARCH ON CHEMICAL INTERMEDIATES. 1057

0922-6184 See QUARTERLY BULLETIN / DE NEDERLANDSCHE BANK N.V. 805

0922-6419 See LANDINRICHTING UTRECHT. 4660

0922-6435 See EXPERIMENTAL ASTRONOMY. 395

0922-6443 See REAL-TIME SYSTEMS. 1201

0922-6540 See VERBINDING ROTTERDAM. 1168

0922-6567 See MACHINE TRANSLATION. 1194

0922-6702 See JAARBOEK VAN HET CENTRAAL BUREAU VOOR GENEALOGIE EN VAN HET ICONOGRAFISCH BUREAU. 2455

0922-680X See JOURNAL OF REGULATORY ECONOMICS. 843

0922-6842 See BIBLIOGRAFIE VAN NEDERLANDS NATIONAEL EN INTERNATIONAAL ONDERZOEK OP SOCIAAL-WETENSCHAPPELIJK TERREIN. 5226

0922-7210 See NIDI RAPPORT. 4555

0922-7415 See VERZEKERINGS MAGAZINE. 2856

0922-744X See NG. NIEUWSBLAD GEZONDHEIDSZORG. 3621

0922-775X See JAARBOEK / ORANJE-NASSAU MUSEUM. 4089

0922-7857 See INFORMATION BULLETIN / INTERNATIONAL ASSOCIATION ON THE POLITICAL USE OF PSYCHIATRY (IAPUP). 3926

0922-7911 See BULLETIN - ROYAL TROPICAL INSTITUTE. 450

0922-842X See PRAGMATICS & BEYOND NEW SERIES. 3311

0922-954X See COMPUTERWORLD NEDERLAND. 1180

0922-9558 See VELDSTUDIES / FACULTEIT DER RUIMTELIJKE WETENSCHAPPEN. GEOGRAFISCH INSTITUUT. RIJKSUNIVERSITEIT GRONINGEN. 2578

0922-9833 See EPILEPSY RESEARCH. SUPPLEMENT. 3575

0923-0033 See OCULI. 360

0923-019X See ADVANCES IN TEST ANXIETY RESEARCH. 4572

0923-0203 See DETAILHANDEL IN BLOEMEN, PLANTEN EN TUINBENODIGDHEDEN, DIEREN EN DIERBENODIGDHEDEN / CENTRAAL BUREAU VOOR DE STATISTIEK, HOOFDAFDELING STATISTIEKEN VAN BIENNENLANDSE HANDEL EN DIENSTVERLENING. 2435

0923-0211 See JOURNAL OF REHABILITATION SCIENCES. 4390

0923-0408 See INFORMATION AND DECISION TECHNOLOGIES (AMSTERDAM). 2116

0923-0416 See RODOPI PERSPECTIVES ON MODERN LITERATURE. 3431

0923-0459 See MACHINE INTELLIGENCE AND PATTERN RECOGNITION. 1215

0923-0467 See CHEMICAL ENGINEERING JOURNAL AND THE BIOCHEMICAL ENGINEERING JOURNAL, THE. 2010

0923-0475 See ELECTRON MICROSCOPY IN BIOLOGY AND MEDICINE. 454

0923-0483 See POSTMODERN STUDIES. 3424

0923-0645 See MARKETING LETTERS. 931

0923-0750 See JOURNAL OF INCLUSION PHENOMENA AND MOLECULAR RECOGNITION IN CHEMISTRY. 1054

0923-0769 See OOGST. 180

0923-084X See CLINICAL NEUROPHYSIOLOGY UPDATES. 3830

0923-1137 See REACTIVE POLYMERS. 1047

0923-1668 See MAANDSTATISTIEK VAN DE BUITENLANDSE HANDEL. 844

0923-1730 See OILFIELD REVIEW / SCHLUMBERGER. 4270

0923-179X See BIOSEPARATION. 3687

0923-1811 See JOURNAL OF DERMATOLOGICAL SCIENCE. 3721

0923-182X See LANGUAGE INTERNATIONAL. 3295

0923-2370 See NEDERLANDS TIJDSCHRIFT VOOR ZWAKZINNIGENZORG. 3931

0923-2486 See VOETBAL INTERNATIONAL SPECIAL. 4928

0923-2494 See RESEARCH IN IMMUNOLOGY (PARIS). 3676

0923-2508 See RESEARCH IN MICROBIOLOGY. 569

0923-2516 See RESEARCH IN VIROLOGY (PARIS). 569

0923-2524 See URGENCES MEDICALES (PARIS). 3649

0923-2532 See IMMUNO ANALYSE & BIOLOGIE SPECIALISEE. 458

0923-2958 See CELESTIAL MECHANICS AND DYNAMICAL ASTRONOMY. 394

0923-3482 See ERFGOED VAN INDUSTRIE EN TECHNIEK. 2686

0923-4128 See HUSSERLIANA DEN HAAG. 4349

0923-4195 See OFCOR, COMPARATIVE STUDY. 116

0923-4284 See BEYOND APARTHEID. 1464

0923-4365 See WAGENINGSE SOCIOLOGISCHE STUDIES : WSS. 5265

0923-4748 See JOURNAL OF ENGINEERING AND TECHNOLOGY MANAGEMENT. 1982

0923-4764 See WAPITI MAASTRICHT. 3452

0923-4861 See WETLANDS ECOLOGY AND MANAGEMENT. 2222

0923-5108 See B & B. BOUW EN BEHEER. 861

0923-5582 See LIST OF JOURNALS ABSTRACTED. 3660

0923-5957 See MARKETING AND RESEARCH TODAY : THE JOURNAL OF THE EUROPEAN SOCIETY FOR OPINION AND MARKETING RESEARCH. 731

0923-5965 See SIGNAL PROCESSING. IMAGE COMMUNICATION. 2081

0923-6082 See MULTIDIMENSIONAL SYSTEMS AND SIGNAL PROCESSING. 1196

0923-6198 See 2E WERELD. 4503

0923-6287 See ROTTERDAMS JAARBOEKJE. 2707

0923-666X See HSB INTERNATIONAL. 5450

0923-6805 See CHINA EARTH SCIENCES. 1353

0923-7054 See AVPROF AMSTERDAM. 5315

0923-7135 See INCOGNITA (LEIDEN, NETHERLANDS). 2848

0923-7488 See BOS NIEUWSLETTER. 2376

0923-7534 See ANNALS OF ONCOLOGY : OFFICIAL JOURNAL OF THE EUROPEAN SOCIETY FOR MEDICAL ONCOLOGY. 3808

0923-7577 See LANCET ED. FRANCAISE. 3603

0923-7992 See OPEN ECONOMIES REVIEW. 1511

0923-8174 See JOURNAL OF ELECTRONIC TESTING. 2069

0923-8182 See MULTI-MEDIA COMPUTING. 1196

0923-9073 See SYMBOLA ET EMBLEMATA. 2712

0923-9669 See KAPITAALGOEDERENVOORRAAD / CENTRAAL BUREAU VOOR DE STATISTIEK, HOOFDAFDELING STATISTIEKEN VAN KAPITAALGOEDERENVOORRAAD EN BALANSEN. 905

0923-9790 See DELINEAVIT ET SCULPSIT. 378

0923-9820 See BIODEGRADATION (DORDRECHT). 2225

0924-0136 See JOURNAL OF MATERIALS PROCESSING TECHNOLOGY. 2103

0924-0314 See BRILL'S STUDIES IN EPISTEMOLOGY, PSYCHOLOGY AND PSYCHIATRY. 4578

0924-0608 See REVISTA EUROPEA DE ESTUDIOS LATINOAMERICANOS Y DEL CARIBE. EUROPEAN REVIEW OF LATIN AMERICAN AND CARIBBEAN STUDIES. 5216

0924-073X See ECONOMISCH BEELD. 1559

0924-0829 See TRACTRIX. 5166

0924-0837 See STATISTIEK VAN HET LAGER BEROEPSONDERWIJS. PERSONEEL / CBS, CENTRAAL BUREAU VOOR DE STATISTIEK, HOOFDAFDELING STATISTIEKEN VAN ONDERWIJS EN WETENSCHAPPEN. 1785

0924-090X See NONLINEAR DYNAMICS. 1989

0924-1868 See USER MODELING AND USER-ADAPTED INTERACTION. 1206

0924-1884 See TARGET. 3327

0924-1914 See PROSTAGLANDINS, LEUKOTRIENES, AND CANCER. 3823

0924-1949 See CURRENT PLANT SCIENCE AND BIOTECHNOLOGY IN AGRICULTURE. 507

0924-2023 See GEODETICAL INFO MAGAZINE. 1405

0924-2139 See MECHANICS OF STRUCTURAL SYSTEMS. 4429

0924-2147 See MECHANICS ANALYSIS. 2106

0924-2244 See TRENDS IN FOOD SCIENCE & TECHNOLOGY. 2360

0924-2287 See INTERNATIONAL JOURNAL OF HEALTH SCIENCES. 4785

0924-2554 See MEDISCHE INSTRUMENTEN- EN ORTHOPEDISCHE ARTIKELENINDUSTRIE, TANDTECHNISCHE WERKPLAATSEN / CENTRAAL BUREAU VOOR DE STATISTIEK, HOOFDAFDELING STATISTIEDEN VAN INDUSTRIE EN BOUWNIJVERHEID. 3614

0924-2708 See ACTA NEUROPSYCHIATRICA. 3826

0924-2716 See ISPRS JOURNAL OF PHOTOGRAMMETRY AND REMOTE SENSING. 2067

0924-2937 See PODIUMKUNSTEN. 387

0924-3046 See ADVANCED COMPOSITE MATERIALS : THE OFFICIAL JOURNAL OF THE JAPAN SOCIETY OF COMPOSITE MATERIALS. 2100

0924-3054 See ARTIFICIAL ORGANS TODAY : THE OFFICIAL INTERNATIONAL JOURNAL OF THE JAPANESE SOCIETY FOR ARTIFICIAL ORGANS. 3553

0924-3089 See PROCESS CONTROL & QUALITY. 2016

0924-3453 See SCHOOL EFFECTIVENESS AND SCHOOL IMPROVEMENT. 1871

0924-3461 See INFORMATION, COMPUTER, COMMUNICATIONS POLICY. 1188

0924-3542 See STUDIES IN COMPUTER SCIENCE AND ARTIFICIAL INTELLIGENCE. 1217

0924-3585 See GROENTEN + FRUIT. VOLLEGRONDSGROENTEN. 2417

0924-3585 See GROENTEN + FRUIT. FRUIT. 2417

0924-3585 See GROENTEN + FRUIT. PADDESTOELEN. 2417

0924-3585 See GROENTEN + FRUIT. ALGEMEEN. 2417

0924-3585 See GROENTEN + FRUIT. GLASGROENTEN. 2417

0924-3860 See EUROPEAN JOURNAL OF MORPHOLOGY. 3679

0924-3984 See STEREOCHEMISTRY OF ORGANOMETALLIC AND INORGANIC COMPOUNDS. 993

0924-3992 See MECHATRONIC SYSTEMS ENGINEERING. 1220

0924-4107 See APOTHEEK IN PRAKTIJK. 4292

0924-4115 See PROFIEL VAN BEROEPSONDERWIJS EN VOLWASSENENEDUCATIE. 1775

0924-4204 See ANNALES DE L'INSTITUT PASTEUR ACTUALITES. 5083

0924-4247 See SENSORS AND ACTUATORS. A, PHYSICAL. 2080

0924-4301 See NIEUWSBRIEF MILIEUTECHNOLOGIE. 2178

0924-4611 See SERIES ENTOMOLOGICA. 5613

0924-4646 See STUDIES IN INDUSTRIAL ORGANIZATION. 887

0924-4662 See STUDIES IN LINGUISTICS AND PHILOSOPHY. 3326

0924-4824 See JURISPRUDENTIE VOOR GEMEENTEN. 4659

0924-5251 See KUNST & MUSEUMJOURNAAL (DUTCH EDITION). 355

0924-526X See KUNST & MUSEUMJOURNAAL (ENGLISH EDITION). 356

0924-5308 See DEVELOPMENTS IN CIVIL AND FOUNDATION ENGINEERING. 2022

0924-5359 See DEVELOPMENTS IN VETERINARY VIROLOGY. 5509

0924-5480 See FORESTRY SCIENCES. 2382

0924-5812 See IFIP CONGRESS SERIES. 1187

0924-5863 See INTERNATIONAL FOOD INGREDIENT. 2345

0924-6282 See MILIEU MAGAZINE ALPHEN AAN DEN RIJN. 2177

0924-6304 See MAB 'S-GRAVENHAGE. 747

0924-6460 See ENVIRONMENTAL AND RESOURCE ECONOMICS. 2166

0924-6479 See INTERNATIONAL JOURNAL OF RISK & SAFETY IN MEDICINE, THE. 3589

0924-6495 See MINDS AND MACHINES (DORDRECHT). 1215

0924-6509 See NORTH-HOLLAND MATHEMATICAL LIBRARY. 3237

0924-6533 See CANCER THERAPY UPDATE. 3812

0924-655X See GRONINGER ARBEITEN ZUR GERMANISTISCHEN LINGUISTIK. 3284

0924-669X See APPLIED INTELLIGENCE. 1211

0924-6703 See DISCRETE EVENT DYNAMIC SYSTEMS. 1282

0924-6711 See DATA SECURITY DIGEST EMMELOORD. 1226

0924-7025 See STEM-, SPRAAK- EN TAALPATHOLOGIE. 4619

0924-7165 See VAKBLAD VOOR DE HANDEL IN AARDAPPELEN, GROENTEN EN FRUIT. 190

0924-7696 See STUDIES IN TEXTILE AND COSTUME HISTORY. 5356

0924-7815 See DISCUSSION PAPER - CENTER FOR ECONOMIC RESEARCH. 1591

0924-7947 See ARCHIVES OF GERONTOLOGY AND GERIATRICS. SUPPLEMENT. 3749

0924-7963 See JOURNAL OF THE EUROPEAN ASSOCIATION OF MARINE SCIENCES AND TECHNIQUES. 1450

0924-7963 See JOURNAL OF MARINE SYSTEMS. 1450

0924-8323 See PROCEEDINGS OF THE KONINKLIJKE NEDERLANDSE AKADEMIE VAN WETENSCHAPPEN (1990). 5140

0924-8328 See PROCEEDINGS OF THE ROYAL NETHERLANDS ACADEMY OF ARTS AND SCIENCES: BIOLOGICAL, CHEMICAL, GEOLOGICAL, PHYSICAL AND MEDICAL SCIENCES. 5141

0924-8447 See SUPPLEMENT TO INTERNATIONAL JOURNAL OF GYNECOLOGY AND OBSTETRICS. 3768

0924-8455 See GERIATRIC NEPHROLOGY AND UROLOGY. 3990

0924-8463 See ARTIFICIAL INTELLIGENCE AND LAW. 1211

0924-8579 See INTERNATIONAL JOURNAL OF ANTIMICROBIAL AGENTS. 3588

0924-8625 See SPACE COMMUNICATIONS. 1164

0924-865X See REVIEW OF QUANTITATIVE FINANCE AND ACCOUNTING. 751

0924-8986 See INDIAN THOUGHT LEIDEN. 2653

0924-9265 See DISCRETE MATHEMATICS AND APPLICATIONS. 3504

0924-9303 See ECMA FOLDING CARTON BULLETIN ENGLISH ED. 4233

0924-9338 See EUROPEAN PSYCHIATRY. 3925

0924-9389 See STUDIES IN CHRISTIAN MISSION. 5000

0924-9419 See HOOGSTEDER MERCURY, THE. 352

0924-9605 See CA TECHNIEK. 1173

0924-977X See EUROPEAN NEUROPSYCHOPHARMACOLOGY : THE JOURNAL OF THE EUROPEAN COLLEGE OF NEUROPSYCHOPHARMACOLOGY. 3832

0924-980X See ELECTROENCEPHALOGRAPHY AND CLINICAL NEUROPHYSIOLOGY/ ELECTROMYOGRAPHY AND MOTOR CONTROL. 3832

0924-9907 See JOURNAL OF MATHEMATICAL IMAGING AND VISION. 3513

0925-0042 See SOLID MECHANICS AND ITS APPLICATIONS. 2129

0925-0182 See OPTISCHE IN FOTOTECHNISCHE INDUSTRIE, KLOKKEN- EN UURWERKINDUSTRIE / CENTRAAL BUREAU VOOR DE STATISTIEK, HOOFDAFDELING STATISTIEKEN VAN INDUSTRIE EN BOUWNIJVERHEID. 2916

0925-0832 See INTERNATIONAL VAT MONITOR. 4733

0925-0885 See CARIBBEAN ABSTRACTS / EDITED AND PUBLISHED BY THE DEPARTMENT OF CARIBBEAN STUDIES OF THE ROYAL INSTITUTE OF LINGUISTICS AND ANTHROPOLOGY. 5227

0925-0980 See POLITIE MAGAZINE. 3172

0925-0999 1263

0925-1014 See JOURNAL OF AQUATIC ECOSYSTEM HEALTH. 555

0925-1022 See DESIGNS, CODES AND CRYPTOGRAPHY. 2041

0925-1030 See ANALOG INTEGRATED CIRCUITS AND SIGNAL PROCESSING. 2035

0925-1049 See NEDERLANDSE MILIEULITERATUUR. 2178

0925-1057 See DOSSIER HERTOGENBOSCH. 1480

0925-1332 See ART VIEW VIANEN. 340

0925-1413 See SCAN (WAGENINGEN). 2204

0925-1421 See STUDIES IN ANCIENT MEDICINE. 3643

0925-1618 See INTERNATIONAL JOURNAL OF PHARMACOGNOSY. 4308

0925-1650 See BODEM ALPHEN AAN DEN RIJN. 2162

0925-1669 See ECONOMIC AND SOCIAL HISTORY IN THE NETHERLANDS. 1556

0925-2096 See INTERNATIONAL JOURNAL OF APPLIED ELECTROMAGNETICS IN MATERIALS. 4444

0925-2312 See NEUROCOMPUTING (AMSTERDAM). 1215

0925-2738 See JOURNAL OF BIOMOLECULAR NMR. 461

0925-2762 See AGRILOPER WAGENINGEN. 54

0925-2819 See TIJDSCHRIFT VOOR GENEESKUNDE & ETHIEK. 3646

0925-2916 See BRILL'S INDOLOGICAL LIBRARY. 2647

0925-2932 See ADFOMEDIA HANDBOEK. 1103

0925-3440 See VERZEKERINGS MAGAZINE. 2856

0925-3467 See OPTICAL MATERIALS. 4439

0925-4005 See SENSORS AND ACTUATORS. B, CHEMICAL. 2081

0925-4218 See HAAGSE MONITOR. 678

0925-4439 See BIOCHIMICA ET BIOPHYSICA ACTA. MOLECULAR BASIS OF DISEASE. 482

0925-4560 See JOURNAL FOR GENERAL PHILOSOPHY OF SCIENCE. 4350

0925-4641 See EEC NEWSLETTER. 3127

0925-4668 See DYNAMICS AND CONTROL. 2113

0925-4676 See JOURNAL OF SYSTEMS INTEGRATION. 1192

0925-4692 See INFLAMMOPHARMACOLOGY. 3587

0925-4757 See REINARDUS : YEARBOOK OF THE INTERNATIONAL REYNARD SOCIETY. 3428

0925-4773 See MECHANISMS OF DEVELOPMENT. 464

0925-482X See VROUWENBELANGEN LEIDEN. 5568

0925-4927 See PSYCHIATRY RESEARCH : NEUROIMAGING SECTION. 3934

0925-4986 See TRANSPUTER AND OCCAM ENGINEERING SERIES. 1249

0925-4994 See CRIME, LAW, AND SOCIAL CHANGE. 3161

0925-5001 See JOURNAL OF GLOBAL OPTIMIZATION : AN INTERNATIONAL JOURNAL DEALING WITH THEORETICAL AND COMPUTATIONAL ASPECTS OF SEEKING GLOBAL OPTIMA AND THEIR APPLICATIONS IN SCIENCE, MANAGEMENT AND ENGINEERING. 3513

0925-5052 See INFORMATIZATION AND THE PUBLIC SECTOR. 1189

0925-5060 See EUROPEAN WATER POLLUTION CONTROL : OFFICIAL PUBLICATION OF THE EUROPEAN WATER POLLUTION CONTROL ASSOCIATION (EWPCA). 5533

0925-5125 See MOLECULAR ENGINEERING. 1988

0925-5206 See ADVANCES IN ECHO-CONTRAST. 3938

0925-5214 See POSTHARVEST BIOLOGY AND TECHNOLOGY. 182

0925-5273 See INTERNATIONAL JOURNAL OF PRODUCTION ECONOMICS. 1612

0925-5281 See CHEMOMETRICS AND INTELLIGENT LABORATORY SYSTEMS : LABORATORY INFORMATION MANAGEMENT. 1014

0925-5338 See NEDERLANDS TIJDSCHRIFT VOOR FOTONICA. 4413

0925-5397 See ELEKTRO MAGAZINE EDITIE DETAIL. 2051

0925-5672 See POLYTECHNISCH TIJDSCHRIFT. ELEKTRONICA ELEKTROTECHNIEK (1990). 2075

0925-5710 See INTERNATIONAL JOURNAL OF HEMATOLOGY. 3772

0925-5745 See PC ACTIVE. 1270

0925-5842 See SCIENCE AND INDUSTRY. 5150

0925-6032 See KANTOORMANAGEMENT (AMSTERDAM). 874

0925-6164 See SCREENING: JOURNAL OF THE INTERNATIONAL SOCIETY OF NEONATAL SCREENING. 3768

0925-6318 See KOUDE MAGAZINE. 2606

0925-6512 See BRILL'S JAPANESE STUDIES LIBRARY. 2647

0925-6563 See FARMING SYSTEMS ANALYSIS PAPER. 86

0925-6660 See NONLINEAR TOPICS IN THE MATHEMATICAL SCIENCES. 3524

0925-6830 See ARCHITECT. THEMA. 288

0925-7535 See SAFETY SCIENCE. 2869

0925-7721 See COMPUTATIONAL GEOMETRY. 3501

0925-7845 See JAARBOEK MONUMENTENZORG. 301

0925-7977 See CA TECHNIEK. 1173

0925-8051 See FOOD PERSONALITY. 2339

0925-8275 See VISUM NIEUWS. 1853

0925-8388 See JOURNAL OF ALLOYS AND COMPOUNDS. 4006

0925-8434 See LASERS IN MEDICINE. 3604

0925-8531 See JOURNAL OF LOGIC, LANGUAGE, AND INFORMATION. 4350

0925-854X See NATURAL LANGUAGE SEMANTICS. 3305

0925-8558 See JOURNAL OF EAST ASIAN LINGUISTICS. 3290

0925-8574 See ECOLOGICAL ENGINEERING. 1971

0925-8604 See NEDERLANDS TIJDSCHRIFT VOOR DERMATOLOGIE & VENEREOLOGIE. 3722

0925-9392 See STUDIES IN EAST EUROPEAN THOUGHT. 4362

0925-9406 See GELUID ALPHEN AAN DEN RIJN. 5316

0925-9635 See DIAMOND AND RELATED MATERIALS. 4001

0925-9678 See GROENTEN + FRUIT. VOLLEGRONDSGROENTEN. 2417

0925-9686 See GROENTEN + FRUIT. GLASGROENTEN. 2417

0925-9694 See GROENTEN + FRUIT. FRUIT. 2417

0925-9708 See GROENTEN + FRUIT. ALGEMEEN. 2417

0925-9716 See GROENTEN + FRUIT. PADDESTOELEN. 2417

0925-9724 See COMPUTER SUPPORTED COOPERATIVE WORK : CSCW : AN INTERNATIONAL JOURNAL. 1232

0925-9759 See EUROPEAN TAX HANDBOOK. 4722

0925-9848 See ADVANCES IN MRI CONTRAST. 3938

0925-9856 See FORMAL METHODS IN SYSTEM DESIGN. 1247

0925-9864 See GENETIC RESOURCES AND CROP EVOLUTION. 511

0925-9872 See INFORMATION TECHNOLOGY AND THE LAW: AN INTERNATIONAL BIBLIOGRAPHY. 3129

0925-9880 See REVIEW OF CENTRAL AND EAST EUROPEAN LAW. 3135

0925-9899 See JOURNAL OF ALGEBRAIC COMBINATORICS. 3511

0925-9902 See JOURNAL OF INTELLIGENT INFORMATION SYSTEMS: INTEGRATING ARTIFICIAL INTELLIGENCE AND DATABASE TECHNOLOGIES. 1214

0926-0447 See VOEDING & MILIEU. 1300

0926-1524 See POVERTY AND DEVELOPMENT. 2911

0926-2040 See SOLID STATE NUCLEAR MAGNETIC RESONANCE. 4421

0926-2067 See IMMUNOASSAY KIT DIRECTORY. SERIES A, CLINICAL CHEMISTRY, THE. 3586

0926-2245 See DIFFERENTIAL GEOMETRY AND ITS APPLICATIONS. 3503

0926-2261 See BRILL'S SERIES IN JEWISH STUDIES. 5046

0926-227X See JOURNAL OF COMPUTER SECURITY. 1227

0926-2326 See STUDIES IN INTERRELIGIOUS DIALOGUE. 5000

0926-2601 See POTENTIAL ANALYSIS : AN INTERNATIONAL JOURNAL DEVOTED TO THE INTERACTIONS BETWEEN POTENTIAL THEORY, PROBABILITY THEORY, GEOMETRY AND FUNCTIONAL ANALYSIS. 3527

0926-261X See BIOETHICS YEARBOOK. 444

0926-2644 See GROUP DECISION AND NEGOTIATION. 5201

0926-3225 See ISNAR SMALL-COUNTRIES STUDY PAPER. 98

0926-3241 See VIP. VAKBLAD VOOR IMAGE PROCESSING. 1221

0926-3314 See RENDEMENT. AMSTERDAM. 884

0926-3373 See APPLIED CATALYSIS. B : ENVIRONMENTAL. 2161

0926-3411 See NFM-THEMAREEKS AMSTERDAM. 4075

0926-3543 See AMOEBA AMSTERDAM. 1976. 4161

0926-3837 See GEOGRAFIE. 2562

0926-4183 See SELECTIEF DEN HAAG. 1991. 5156

0926-4213 See SCHIP EN WERF DE ZEE. 4183

0926-4264 See NEDERLANDS TIJDSCHRIFT VOOR NATUURKUNDE (AMSTERDAM. 1991). 5132

0926-4345 See ANALYTICAL SPECTROSCOPY LIBRARY. 4433

0926-4957 See GENEVA PAPERS ON RISK AND INSURANCE THEORY. 2881

0926-5112 See FLUID MECHANICS AND ITS APPLICATIONS. 2089

0926-5473 See IFIP TRANSACTIONS. COMPUTER SCIENCE AND TECHNOLOGY. 1247

0926-5481 See IFIP TRANSACTIONS B: COMPUTER APPLICATIONS IN TECHNOLOGY. 1229

0926-5589 See DEVELOPMENTS IN AGRICULTURAL ECONOMICS. 79

0926-5805 See AUTOMATION IN CONSTRUCTION. 599

0926-6003 See COMPUTATIONAL OPTIMIZATION AND APPLICATIONS. 3502

0926-6070 See EDUCATION AND SOCIETY IN THE MIDDLE AGES AND RENAISSANCE. 2615

0926-6364 See RANDOM OPERATORS AND STOCHASTIC EQUATIONS. 1244

0926-6410 See COGNITIVE BRAIN RESEARCH. 3830

0926-6690 See INDUSTRIAL CROPS AND PRODUCTS. 174

0926-6801 See JOURNAL OF HIGH SPEED NETWORKS. 1242

0926-6917 See EUROPEAN JOURNAL OF PHARMACOLOGY : ENVIRONMENTAL TOXICOLOGY AND PHARMACOLOGY SECTION. 4303

0926-6976 See GROOTCONSUMENT AMSTERDAM. 2790

0926-7220 See SCIENCE & EDUCATION. 1904

0926-7638 See RSG. RICHTING SPORT-GERICHT. 1904

0926-860X See APPLIED CATALYSIS A : GENERAL. 2008

0926-874X See TILBURG FOREIGN LAW REVIEW. 3064

0926-8782 See DISTRIBUTED AND PARALLEL DATABASES. 1254

0926-910X See AVANTGARDE (NEDERLANDSE ED.). 5551

0926-9282 See MECHANICS AND PHYSICS OF DISCRETE SYSTEMS. 4429

0926-9495 See TROPICAL RESOURCE MANAGEMENT PAPERS. 142

0926-9703 See INDIAN THOUGHT LEIDEN. 2653

0926-9851 See JOURNAL OF APPLIED GEOPHYSICS. 1407

0926-9959 See JOURNAL OF THE EUROPEAN ACADEMY OF DERMATOLOGY AND VENEREOLOGY : JEADV. 3721

0927-0248 See SOLAR ENERGY MATERIALS AND SOLAR CELLS : AN INTERNATIONAL JOURNAL DEVOTED TO PHOTOVOLTAIC, PHOTOTHERMAL, AND PHOTOCHEMICAL SOLAR ENERGY CONVERSION. 1957

0927-0256 See COMPUTATIONAL MATERIALS SCIENCE. 2101

0927-0523 See ITALIAN STUDIES IN LAW : A REVIEW OF LEGAL PROBLEMS / EDITED BY THE ITALIAN ASSOCIATION OF COMPARATIVE LAW. 2985

0927-0574 See NIEUWE DROGIST. 4318

0927-0655 See RSP-BULLETIN LELYSTAD. 131

0927-1368 See BABY & PEUTER. 5183

0927-2704 See REFLECTOR DEN BOSCH. 5255

0927-2720 See BLIKOPENER DEN BOSCH. 5240

0927-2852 See APPLIED CATEGORICAL STRUCTURES. 3494

0927-3026 See ERFGOED VAN INDUSTRIE EN TECHNIEK. 2686

0927-3034 See LANGUAGES OF DESIGN. 3296

0927-3042 See CANCER TREATMENT AND RESEARCH. 3812

0927-3522 See INTERNATIONAL JOURNAL OF MARINE AND COASTAL LAW, THE. 3130

0927-4898 See PROFIEL VAN BEROEPSONDERWIJS EN VOLWASSENENEDUCATIE. 1775

0927-5371 See LABOUR ECONOMICS. 1685

0927-538X See PACIFIC-BASIN FINANCE JOURNAL. 802

0927-5398 See JOURNAL OF EMPIRICAL FINANCE. 794

0927-5401 See CLINICAL TRIALS AND META-ANALYSIS. 4297

0927-5568 See INTERNATIONAL JOURNAL OF CHILDREN'S RIGHTS, THE. 3121

0922-355X See INZET AMSTERDAM. 2910

0927-5770 See INZET AMSTERDAM. 2910

0927-5657 See INZET AMSTERDAM. 2910

0927-5908 See INTERNATIONAL JOURNAL ON GROUP RIGHTS. 3130

0927-5940 See INTERNATIONAL TAX AND PUBLIC FINANCE. 4733

0927-6440 See COMPOSITE INTERFACES. 973

0927-6467 See RUSSIAN JOURNAL OF NUMERICAL ANALYSIS AND MATHEMATICAL ANALYSIS. 3532

0927-6505 See ASTROPARTICLE PHYSICS. 4398

0927-6513 See MICROPOROUS MATERIALS. 986

0927-6947 See SET-VALUED ANALYSIS. 3534

0927-7056 See INTERFACE SCIENCE. 4428

0927-7099 See COMPUTATIONAL ECONOMICS. 1470

0927-748X See VORMEN UIT VUUR. 2595

0927-7544 See JOURNAL OF REAL ESTATE LITERATURE. 3400

0927-7641 See STADSWERK. 2031

0927-7757 See COLLOIDS AND SURFACES. A, PHYSICOCHEMICAL AND ENGINEERING ASPECTS. 1051

0927-7765 See COLLOIDS AND SURFACES B: BIOINTERFACES. 1051

0927-7951 See COMPUTATIONAL MECHANICS ADVANCES. 2112

0927-796X See MATERIALS SCIENCE AND ENGINEERING : R-REPORTS. 1986

0927-8311 See NIEUWSBRIEF / NEDERLANDS FOTOARCHIEF. 4372

0927-9806 See RAADSADVIEZEN / RAAD VOOR DE KUNST. 328

0928-0197 See CLINICAL AND DIAGNOSTIC VIROLOGY. 561

0928-0200 See EAST-WEST JOURNAL OF NUMERICAL MATHEMATICS. 3504

0928-0219 See JOURNAL OF INVERSE AND ILL-POSED PROBLEMS. 3513

0928-0529 See EUROPEAN VIDEO JOURNAL OF CARDIOLOGY, THE. 3704

0928-0707 See JOURNAL OF SOL-GEL SCIENCE AND TECHNOLOGY. 5120

0928-0758 See EUROPA REGIONAAL CUIJK. 673

0928-0987 See EUROPEAN JOURNAL OF PHARMACEUTICAL SCIENCES. 4303

0928-1045 See JOURNAL OF COMPUTER AIDED MATERIALS DESIGN. 1191

0928-1231 See PHARMACY WORLD & SCIENCE : PWS. 4324

0928-1371 See EUROPEAN JOURNAL ON CRIMINAL POLICY AND RESEARCH. 3164

0928-1436 See GIM. GEODETICAL INFO MAGAZINE. 1406

0928-1509 See ADVANCES IN X-RAY CONTRAST. 3938

0928-1541 See IAWA JOURNAL / INTERNATIONAL ASSOCIATION OF WOOD ANATOMISTS. 2401

0928-2998 See TIJDSCHRIFT VOOR HYGIENE EN INFEKTIEPREVENTIE. 3793

0928-4109 See EXKIES 'S-GRAVENHAGE. 350

0928-4249 See VETERINARY RESEARCH. 5526

0928-4257 See JOURNAL OF PHYSIOLOGY, PARIS. 583

0928-432X See ASIAN YEARBOOK OF INTERNATIONAL LAW. 3124

0928-4346 See INTERNATIONAL HEPATOLOGY COMMUNICATIONS. 3797

0928-4680 See PATHOPHYSIOLOGY. 584

0928-4869 See SIMULATION PRACTICE AND THEORY. 1244

0928-4931 See MATERIALS SCIENCE & ENGINEERING. C, BIOMIMETIC MATERIALS, SENSORS AND SYSTEMS. 1986

0928-6500 See PREPRESS COMPUTING MAGAZINE. 1263

0928-7329 See TECHNOLOGY AND HEALTH CARE : OFFICIAL JOURNAL OF THE EUROPEAN SOCIETY FOR ENGINEERING AND MEDICINE. 3644

0928-7655 See RESOURCE AND ENERGY ECONOMICS. 1955

0928-8244 See FEMS IMMUNOLOGY AND MEDICAL MICROBIOLOGY. 3669

0928-8503 See OVERHEIDSMANAGEMENT : VAKBLAD VOOR FINANCIEN AUTOMATISERING EN PERSONEEL 7 ORGANISATIE. 4672

0928-8759 See CRIMINOLOGY, PENOLOGY AND POLICE SCIENCE ABSTRACTS. 3080

0928-8910 See AUTOMATED SOFTWARE ENGINEERING. 1284

0928-9313 See GLOBAL JOURNAL ON CRIME AND CRIMINAL LAW. 3165

0928-9380 See ISLAMIC LAW AND SOCIETY. 5043

0928-9801 See EUROPEAN REVIEW OF PRIVATE LAW. 2967

0928-9917 See AGING AND COGNITION. 4572

0929-0141 See MODERN MEDICINE (NEDERLANDSE ED.). 3617

0929-0273 See EUROPEAN JOURNAL OF HEALTH LAW. 2967

0929-0761 See DEAD SEA DISCOVERIES. 4952

0929-077X See ANCIENT CIVILIZATIONS FROM SCYTHIA TO SIBERIA. 2673

0929-0907 See PRAGMATICS & COGNITION. 3311

0929-1016 See BIOLOGICAL RHYTHM RESEARCH. 445

0929-1199 See JOURNAL OF CORPORATE FINANCE. 793

0929-1261 See EUROPEAN JOURNAL OF LAW AND ECONOMICS. 2967

0929-1393 See APPLIED SOIL ECOLOGY : A SECTION OF AGRICULTURE, ECOSYSTEMS & ENVIRONMENT. 163

0929-1873 See EUROPEAN JOURNAL OF PLANT PATHOLOGY. 509

0929-1881 See ADVANCED PERFORMANCE MATERIALS. 2100

0929-189X See APPLIED COMPOSITE MATERIALS. 2100

0929-1903 See CANCER GENE THERAPY. 3811

0929-2233 See EDI LAW REVIEW, THE. 2965

0929-2985 See NORMALISATIE-NIEUWS (DELFT). 4032

0929-4929 1183

0929-5011 See DOS-WIN SPECIAL. 1183

0929-5305 See JOURNAL OF THROMBOSIS AND THROMBOLYSIS. 3600

0929-5313 See JOURNAL OF COMPUTATIONAL NEUROSCIENCE. 3835

0929-5585 See DESIGN AUTOMATION FOR EMBEDDED SYSTEMS. 1219

0929-5593 See AUTONOMOUS ROBOTS. 1212

0929-5607 See ADSORPTION. 959

0929-6174 See JOURNAL OF QUANTITATIVE LINGUISTICS. 3291

0929-6212 See WIRELESS PERSONAL COMMUNICATIONS. 1124

0929-6646 See JOURNAL OF THE FORMOSAN MEDICAL ASSOCIATION / TAI-WAN I CHIH. 3598

0929-693X See ARCHIVES DE PEDIATRIE : ORGANE OFFICIEL DE LA SOCIETE FRANCAISE DE PEDIATRIE. 3900

0929-7049 See CHILD NEUROPSYCHOLOGY. 3923

0929-7316 See BENJAMINS TRANSLATION LIBRARY. 3268

0929-7855 See JOURNAL OF LIPID MEDIATORS AND CELL SIGNALLING. 1042

0929-791X See MILIEUSTRATEGIE ALPHEN AAN DEN RIJN. 1994. 2177

0929-8215 See JOURNAL OF NEW MUSIC RESEARCH. 4126

0929-8266 See EUROPEAN JOURNAL OF ULTRASOUND. 3941

0929-9629 See MONTE CARLO METHODS AND APPLICATIONS. 5129

0929-9637 See PRIMARY SENSORY NEURON. 5139

0929-9645 See TRANSPORT LOGISTICS. 5395

0929-9971 See TERMINOLOGY. 1123

0929-9998 See FUNCTIONS OF LANGUAGE. 3283

0930-0252 See BAUEN IN BETON. 600

0930-0317 See LECTURE NOTES IN EARTH SCIENCES. 1357

0930-035X See ROUX'S ARCHIVES OF DEVELOPMENTAL BIOLOGY. 541

0930-0430 See BASF AGRICULTURAL NEWS. 65

0930-0597 See BILANZ & BUCHHALTUNG. 739

0930-0708 See MINERALOGY AND PETROLOGY. 1442

0930-1038 See SURGICAL AND RADIOLOGIC ANATOMY (ENGLISH ED.). 3680

0930-1127 See MUNCHENER BEITRAEGE ZUR MEDIAVISTIK UND RENAISSANCE-FORSCHUNG. 3304

0930-1151 See ZEITSCHRIFT FUER PHYSIK. A, HADRONS AND NUCLEI. 4451

0930-1178 See ARZTLICHE MONATSHEFTE. 3553

0930-1208 See HEIDELBERGER ALTHISTORISCHE BEITRAEGE UND EPIGRAPHISCHE STUDIEN. 1077

0930-1461 See FORENSIC SCIENCE PROGRESS. 3740

0930-2794 See SURGICAL ENDOSCOPY. 3976

0930-3286 See GESCHICHTE IM WESTEN. 2689

0930-343X See EUROPEAN JOURNAL OF PLASTIC SURGERY. 3964

0930-3472 See SYMPTOME. 4363

0930-3677 See VERBANDTECHNIK. 3649

0930-3847 See EUROPEAN COATINGS JOURNAL. 4223

0930-3855 See WIRTSCHAFTSRECHTLICHE BLAETTER : WBL. 3104

0930-4061 See SUPPLEMENT (DARMSTADT). 3643

0930-4282 See SPEKTRUM DER AUGENHEILKUNDE : ZEITSCHRIFT DER OSTERREICHISCHEN OPHTHALMOLOGISCHEN GESELLSCHAFT, OOG. 3879

0930-4304 See ABHANDLUNGEN DER AKADEMIE DER WISSENSCHAFTEN IN GOTTINGEN. PHILOLOGISCH-HISTORISCHE KLASSE. 1073

0930-4320 See GBF MONOGRAPHS / GESELLSCHAFT FUER BIOTECHNOLOGISCHE FORSCHUNG. 3692

0930-4460 See LERNFELD BETRIEB. 690

0930-4622 See MTA. 3915

0930-4827 See VITAMINE, MINERALSTOFFE, SPURENELEMENTE IN MEDIZIN, ERNAHRUNG UND UMWELT. 4200

0930-4878 See HIERZULAND NICHT NUR BADISCHES VON RHEIN, NECKAR UND MAIN : ORGAN DES ARBEITSKREISES HEIMATPFLEGE NORDBADEN / REGIERUNGSBEZIRK KARLSRUHE. 2517

0930-4967 See REGENSBURGER TRICHTER, DER. 3530

0930-5157 See PIK. PRAXIS DER INFORMATIONSVERARBEITUNG UND KOMMUNIKATION. 1199

0930-5181 See INFORMATION MANAGEMENT (MUNCHEN). 682

0930-522X See OBERRHEINISCHE STUDIEN KARLSRUHE. 2701

0930-5440 See BERICHTE - INSTITUT FUER PHONETIK DER UNIVERSITAT ZU KOLN. 3268

0930-5874 See FORUM MODERNES THEATER. 5364

0930-6447 See TIERARZTLICHE PRAXIS. SUPPLEMENT. 5523

0930-6544 See FISCH-MAGAZIN (WALDSOLMS). 1746

0930-6552 See FISH INTERNATIONAL. 2301

0930-6897 See HERMENEIA. 352
0930-7044 See BERICHTE DES FORSCHUNGSZENTRUMS WALDOKOSYSTEME/WALDSTERBEN REIHE A. 2376
0930-7516 See CHEMICAL ENGINEERING & TECHNOLOGY. 2009
0930-7575 See CLIMATE DYNAMICS. 1421
0930-7591 See MUSIK MAGAZIN. 4137
0930-777X See INTERNATIONAL POLYMER PROCESSING. 4455
0930-7818 See MUECKE. 1765
0930-8040 See ULTRASCHALL IN KLINIK UND PRAXIS. 3648
0930-8148 See BERICHTE DER BIOLOGISCHEN ANSTALT HELGOLAND. 443
0930-8318 See GIATROS HNO. 3888
0930-8326 See GIATROSERTHOPAEDIE. 3881
0930-8490 See PPS-REPORT. 1621
0930-8555 See COLONIA ROMANICA. 295
0930-861X See ZEITSCHRIFT FUER AUSLANDISCHES UND INTERNATIONALES ARBEITS UND SOZIALRECHT. 3155
0930-8938 See BIOTECHNOLOGY MONOGRAPHS. 3689
0930-8954 See MUSIK-ALMANACH (KASSEL, GERMANY). 4137
0930-8989 See SPRINGER PROCEEDINGS IN PHYSICS. 4422
0930-8997 See ZIBALDONE (MUNCHEN). 3456
0930-9152 See JAHRBUCH BIOTECHNOLOGIE. 3693
0930-9160 See IMMUNOASSAY TECHNOLOGY. 3670
0930-9225 See ZEITSCHRIFT FUER HERZ THORAX UND GEFAESSCHIRURGIE. 3978
0930-9276 See TECHNISCHE MITTEILUNGEN KRUPP (DEUTSCH AUSG.). 1629
0930-9284 See TECHNISCHE MITTEILUNGEN KRUPP (ENGLISH ED.). 4021
0930-9292 See QUELLEN UND FORSCHUNGEN ZUR GESCHICHTE DER STADT MUNSTER. 2704
0930-9381 See ZEITSCHRIFT FUER INTERNATIONALE ERZIEHUNGS- UND SOZIALWISSENSCHAFTLICHE FORSCHUNG. 1792
0930-9535 See ADVANCES IN FORENSIC HAEMOGENETICS. 3770
0930-9977 See 1999. 4539
0931-0037 See DEUTSCHE ZEITSCHRIFT FUER ONKOLOGIE. 3816
0931-0185 See HAMBURGISCHE GESCHICHTS- UND HEIMATBLATTER. 2690
0931-0347 See ORTHODOXIE HEUTE. 5040
0931-041X See PEDIATRIC NEPHROLOGY (BERLIN, WEST). 3909
0931-0428 See FUNDAMENTA PSYCHIATRICA. 3925
0931-0509 See NEPHROLOGY, DIALYSIS, TRANSPLANTATION. 3992
0931-0827 See ISDN-REPORT. 1191
0931-0983 See ZEITSCHRIFT FUER UMWELTPOLITIK & UMWELTRECHT. 3117
0931-1084 See PETRI NET NEWSLETTER. 1199
0931-1181 See DARMSTADT CONCRETE : ANNUAL JOURNAL ON CONCRETE AND CONCRETE STRUCTURES. 612
0931-1408 See BIOTEC (STUTTGART). 3687
0931-1513 See NATURA & MED. 3775
0931-1785 See JOURNAL OF PHYTOPATHOLOGY 1986. 100
0931-1793 See JOURNAL OF VETERINARY MEDICINE. SERIES B. 5514
0931-184X See JOURNAL OF VETERINARY MEDICINE. SERIES A. 5514
0931-1890 See TREES (BERLIN, WEST). 2397
0931-1955 See STOCHASTIC HYDROLOGY AND HYDRAULICS. 1418
0931-2048 See JOURNAL OF APPLIED ENTOMOLOGY 1986. 5610
0931-2234 See HANDBUCH DER WIRTSCHAFTSDATENBANKEN. 679

0931-2250 See ZEITSCHRIFT FUER ACKER- UND PFLANZENBAU. 148
0931-2277 See FORSCHUNGSREPORT, ERNAHRUNG, LANDWIRTSCHAFT, FORSTEN. 88
0931-2439 See JOURNAL OF ANIMAL PHYSIOLOGY AND ANIMAL NUTRITION (1986). 5513
0931-2447 See SONDERBAENDE ZUR STRAHLENTHERAPIE UND ONKOLOGIE. 3642
0931-2471 See DEUTSCHE AUSGLEICHSBANK. 787
0931-2668 See JOURNAL OF ANIMAL BREEDING AND GENETICS (1986). 548
0931-2838 See JOURNAL OF TRACE ELEMENTS AND ELECTROLYTES IN HEALTH AND DISEASE. 3600
0931-3079 See EDITIO. 3341
0931-3125 See CIM-PRAXIS. 1218
0931-3230 See JAPANINFO. 685
0931-3311 See MUSIK-KONZEPTE. 4137
0931-380X See KALENDER FUER DEN BIOGARTEN. 462
0931-3850 See TRIATHLON UND SPORTWISSENSCHAFT. 4927
0931-4091 See FORUM HOMOSEXUALITAT UND LITERATURE. 3388
0931-4113 See CRYPTOGAMIC STUDIES. 507
0931-4202 See ADVANCES IN ETHOLOGY (1987). 4571
0931-4393 See DBZ. DEUTSCHE BRIEFMARKEN-ZEITUNG. 2773
0931-4857 See MITTEILUNGSBLATT - MUSEUMSVERBAND FUER NIEDERSACHSEN UND BREMEN E.V. 4091
0931-5020 See EMPIRISCHE PADAGOGIK. 1744
0931-5195 See SPRINGER SERIES IN SURFACE SCIENCES. 4422
0931-5918 See BUNDESFIRMENREGISTER. BAND 1, NORD- UND WESTDEUTSCHLAND 1986. 644
0931-5985 See FETT WISSENSCHAFT TECHNOLOGIE : ORGAN DER DEUTSCHEN GESELLSCHAFT FUER FETTWISSENSCHAFT E.V. / FAT SCIENCE TECHNOLOGY. 1024
0931-6183 See RECHTSPRECHUNG FRANKFURT. 3036
0931-6221 See ENGINEERING & AUTOMATION. 1972
0931-6280 See VEROFFENTLICHUNGEN DER URGESCHICHTLICHEN SAMMLUNGEN DES LANDESMUSEUMS ZU HANNOVER. 4097
0931-6795 See PSYCHOPHARMACOLOGY SERIES. 4326
0931-704X See JOURNAL OF MATERIALS ENGINEERING AND PERFORMANCE. 2118
0931-7058 See JOURNAL OF MATERIALS ENGINEERING. 2103
0931-7112 See KUNST + UNTERRICHT 1985. 356
0931-7198 See ZEITSCHRIFT FUER KUNSTTECHNOLOGIE UND KONSERVIERUNG. 369
0931-7260 See SPRINGER SERIES IN ELECTRONICS AND PHOTONICS. 2082
0931-7597 See CHEM INFORM. 1011
0931-8283 See STOFFWECHSELKRANKHEITEN. 3733
0931-8313 See JAHRBUCH ... / MANNER VOM MORGENSTERN, HEIMATBUND AN ELB- UND WESERMUNDUNG. 322
0931-8658 See JOURNAL OF ECONOMICS (VIENNA, AUSTRIA). 1593
0931-8739 See MUNCHNER GEOWISSENSCHAFTLICHE ABHANDLUNGEN. REIHE B, ALLGEMEINE UND ANGEWANDTE GEOLOGIE. 1389
0931-8771 See QUANTITATIVE STRUCTURE-ACTIVITY RELATIONSHIPS. 4327
0931-8801 See RWI-KONJUNKTURBERICHTE. 1625
0931-9077 See KRP. KOSTENRECHNUNGSPRAXIS 1977. 689
0931-9190 See REINRAUMTECHNIK. 5145
0931-9506 See PROTEIN SEQUENCES & DATA ANALYSIS. 470

0931-9700 See PHARMA TECHNOLOGIE JOURNAL. 4319
0931-9808 See MEDIEN KONKRET. 1117
0931-9913 See ANNALES UNIVERSITATIS SARAVIENSIS. MEDICINAE. SUPPLEMENT. 3550
0932-0067 See ARCHIVES OF GYNECOLOGY AND OBSTETRICS. 3757
0932-0113 See PARASITOLOGY RESEARCH (1987). 468
0932-0229 See JAHRBUCH / BAYERISCHE AKADEMIE DER SCHONEN KUNSTE. 322
0932-0377 See JAHRBUCH DES RHEIN-SIEG-KREISES. 2518
0932-0393 See PROFESSIONAL PRODUCTION. 4076
0932-0458 See MILITARGESCHICHTLICHES BEIHEFT ZUR EUROPAISCHEN WEHRKUNDE WIHRWISSENSCHAFTLICHE RUNDSCHAU. 4050
0932-0482 See ZWF CIM. 2132
0932-0555 See SPORTVERLETZUNG, SPORTSCHADEN. 3956
0932-0776 See ZEITSCHRIFT FUR NATURFORSCHUNG. 996
0932-0784 See ZEITSCHRIFT FUER NATURFORSCHUNG. 4425
0932-0814 See VETERINARY AND COMPARATIVE ORTHOPAEDICS AND TRAUMATOLOGY. 5524
0932-142X See PROTOZOENFAUNA. 470
0932-1543 See REDEN-BERATER, DER. 1120
0932-2205 See EXCELLENCE IN ECOLOGY. 2216
0932-2221 See ZEITSCHRIFT FUER KATALANISTIK. 3335
0932-2353 See SPRINGER SERIES IN BIOPHYSICS. 496
0932-2361 See BGA SCHRIFTEN. 4768
0932-2558 See TECHNOLOGIE & MANAGEMENT. 887
0932-2655 See ALTE UHREN UND MODERNE ZEITMESSUNG. 335
0932-2744 See FOOD MARKETING & TECHNOLOGY. 2338
0932-2760 See ONKOLOGISCHES JOURNAL / INFORMATIONSDIENST, BEHRINGWERKE AG. 3822
0932-2876 See IDIS-LITERATURLISTE. ARBEITSMEDIZIN / IDIS. 3797
0932-2973 See DEUTSCH-AMERIKANISCHE GESCHAFTSBEZIEHUNGEN. 665
0932-3031 See ADVANCES IN ELECTROPHORESIS. 2034
0932-3147 See MUNCHENER GEOGRAPHISCHE ABHANDLUNGEN REIHE B. 2569
0932-3279 See ERGEBNISSE DER INTERNISTISCHEN ONKOLOGIE. 3816
0932-3333 See ART BUYER'S HANDBOOK. 338
0932-3635 See JAHRBUCH DER BUEROKOMMUNIKATION. 872
0932-3708 See ABWASSERTECHNIK 1983. 2222
0932-3791 See CONSILIUM CEDIP PRACTICUM. 4298
0932-383X See ELEKTROTECHNIK UND INFORMATIONSTECHNIK : E&I. 2052
0932-3848 See FORTSCHRITTE DER OPERATIVEN DERMATOLOGIE. 3720
0932-3856 See SCHRIFTENREIHE DER BUNDESANSTALT FUER ARBEITSSCHUTZ. FORSCHUNG. 4801
0932-3902 See KERNTECHNIK (1987). 2156
0932-3910 See GRUNDSCHULZEITSCHRIFT, DIE. 1895
0932-3961 See GABLERS MAGAZIN. 868
0932-4011 See EXPERIMENTAL BRAIN RESEARCH SERIES. 3833
0932-4194 See MATHEMATICS OF CONTROL, SIGNALS, AND SYSTEMS : MCSS. 1986
0932-4240 See IDIS-LITERATURLISTE. SUCHTINFORMATION / IDIS. 1345
0932-4313 See INFORMATIONEN FRESENIUS FUR KRANKENSCHWESTERN UND KRANKENPFLEGER. 3857
0932-433X See SCHMERZ, DER. 3639

0932-4461 See ZEITSCHRIFT FUER ALTHEBRAISTIK. 3335

0932-4569 See JOURNAL OF INSTITUTIONAL AND THEORETICAL ECONOMICS : JITE. 5206

0932-4658 See WISSENSCHAFTLICHE REIHE / ZENTRALINSTITUT FUER DIE KASSENARZTLICHE VERSORGUNG IN DER BUNDESREPUBLIK DEUTSCHLAND. 2896

0932-4682 See INSTAND SCHRIFTENREIHE / INSTITUT FUR STANDARDISIERUNG UND DOKUMENTATION IM MEDIZINISCHEN LABORATORIUM E.V. (INSTAND). 3588

0932-4712 See SCHRIFTENREIHE DER BUNDESANSTALT FUER ARBEITSSCHUTZ. GEFAHRLICHE ARBEITSSTOFFE. 2870

0932-4712 See GEFAHRLICHE ARBEITSSTOFFE. 4776

0932-4739 See EUROPEAN JOURNAL OF PROTISTOLOGY. 562

0932-478X See SCHRIFTENREIHE DER BUNDESANSTALT FEUR ARBEITSSCHUTZ. REGELWERKE. 4801

0932-481X See SCHRIFTENREIHE DER BUNDESANSTALT FEUR ARBEITSSCHUTZ. SONDERSCHRIFT. 4801

0932-4828 See SCHRIFTENREIHE DER BUNDESANSTALT F...UR ARBEITSSCHUTZ. TAGUNGSBERICHT. 4801

0932-4836 See SCHRIFTENREIHE DER BUNDESANSTALT FUER ARBEITSSCHUTZ. FORSCHUNGSANWENDUNG. 4801

0932-5026 See STATISTICAL PAPERS (BERLIN, GERMANY). 5340

0932-5034 See IDIS-LITERATURLISTE. SOZIALMEDIZIN / IDIS. 4783

0932-5468 See ELEKTOR AACHEN. 2051

0932-5476 See SOZIALANTHROPOLOGISCHE ARBEITSPAPIERE / FU BERLIN, INSTITUT FUER ETHNOLOGIE, SCHWERPUNKT SOZIALANTHROPOLOGIE. 245

0932-5611 See FORTSCHRITTE DER MEDIZIN. SUPPLEMENT : DIE KONGRESSINFORMATION FUER DIE PRAXIS. 3577

0932-593X See ADVANCES IN SYSTEM ANALYSIS. 1964

0932-6111 See ORPHEUS BERLIN. 4145

0932-6138 See KUNSTSTOFFE FEUR DIE ELEKTRONIK UND OPTIK. 5076

0932-6154 See FARMING SYSTEMS AND RESOURCE ECONOMICS IN THE TROPICS. 2414

0932-6200 See GI. GESUNDHEITS-INGENIEUR (1985). 2230

0932-6251 See JAHRBUCH DER WERBUNG IN DEUTSCHLAND, OSTERREICH UND DER SCHWEIZ. 761

0932-6510 See METHODIKA. 5209

0932-6588 See BILDGEBENDE VERFAHREN IN DER NEURORADIOLOGIE. 3828

0932-6596 See KINDERHEILKUNDE UND JUGENDMEDIZIN. 3906

0932-6936 See FREMDSPRACHEN LEHREN UND LERNEN. 3282

0932-7754 See LITERATUR-SCHNELLDIENST KUNSTSTOFFE, KAUTSCHUK, FASERN. 5126

0932-7770 See JAHRBUCH PHARMALABOR. 4309

0932-7991 See GLOTTOMETRIKA. 3284

0932-8092 See MACHINE VISION AND APPLICATIONS. 1252

0932-8114 See ZEITSCHRIFT FUER SEXUALFORSCHUNG. 5188

0932-8122 See HEBAMME, DIE. 3762

0932-8408 See TEL AVIVER JAHRBUCH FUR DEUTSCHE GESCHICHTE / HERAUSGEGEBEN VOM INSTITUT FUR DEUTSCHE GESCHICHTE. 5053

0932-8610 See ADOLESCENT AND PEDIATRIC GYNECOLOGY. 3756

0932-8629 See BOTANICA ACTA. 503

0932-8661 See GIATROS DERMATOLOGIE. 3720

0932-8823 See BRENNPUNKTE DER SPORTWISSENSCHAFT / HERAUSGEGEBEN VON DER DEUTSCHEN SPORTHOCHSCHULE KOLN. 4888

0932-9196 See PRAXIS DER ANASTHESIOLOGIE UND INTENSIVMEDIZIN. 3972

0932-9315 See FORST UND HOLZ (HANNOVER, GERMANY : 1988). 2383

0932-9706 See HANDBUCH ZUM NEUEN TESTAMENT. 5016

0932-9714 See MATATU. 3410

0932-9951 See KIRCHLICHE ZEITGESCHICHTE. 4972

0933-0089 See RWI-MITTEILUNGEN. 3637

0933-0321 See DOKUMENTATIONEN DES STADTARCHIVS NEUSS. 4087

0933-0445 See INTERNATIONAL JOURNAL OF FETO-MATERNAL MEDICINE. 3762

0933-0453 See INTERNATIONAL JOURNAL OF EXPERIMENTAL AND CLINICAL CHEMOTHERAPY. 3818

0933-050X See FAT-SCHRIFTENREIHE. 5414

0933-0704 See GEOWISSENSCHAFTEN (WEINHEIM AN DER BERGSTRASSE, GERMANY). 1356

0933-081X See MEINE FAMILIE & ICH. 2519

0933-1093 See EXPERIMENTELLE UND KLINISCHE HYPNOSE : ZEITSCHRIFT DER DEUTSCHEN GESELLSCHAFT FUER HYPNOSE. 2858

0933-1271 See PERSPEKTIVEN DER FORSCHUNG UND IHRER FORDERUNG / DFG, DEUTSCHE FORSCHUNGSGEMEINSCHAFT. 5138

0933-1433 See JOURNAL OF POPULATION ECONOMICS. 4554

0933-1557 See DOS INTERNATIONAL. 1183

0933-1719 See HUMOR (BERLIN, GERMANY). 4589

0933-1743 See NORD-SUD AKTUELL. 4530

0933-1883 See SOCIOLINGUISTICA. 3322

0933-1891 See NUCLEIC ACIDS AND MOLECULAR BIOLOGY. 491

0933-1905 See INTERNATIONALE JAHRESBIBLIOGRAPHIE DER KONGRESSBERICHTE. 417

0933-2022 See MITTEILUNG (DEUTCHE FORSCHUNGSGEMEINSCHAFT. KOMMISSION FUR WASSERFORSCHUNG). 5536

0933-2367 See NEUE KERAMIK. 3466

0933-2421 See CANADIANA ROMANICA. 3372

0933-2480 See CHANCE (NEW YORK). 3499

0933-257X See KOLNER MUSEUMS-BULLETIN. 4090

0933-2715 See NEUROLINGUISTIK : ZEITSCHRIFT FUER APHASIEFORSCHUNG UND -THERAPIE. 4381

0933-2766 See WOHNRECHTLICHE BLAETTER. 3076

0933-2790 See JOURNAL OF CRYPTOLOGY. 3512

0933-2855 See BTH. BODENBELAGE, TAPETEN, HEIMTEXTILIEN. FUSSBODEN-ZEITUNG. 633

0933-3053 See SYSTEM FAMILIE. 2286

0933-3347 See LUZIFER-AMOR. 4603

0933-3525 See SCHRIFTENREIHE DES DEUTSCHEN KINDERHILFSWERKES E.V. 3911

0933-3630 See SOIL TECHNOLOGY. 187

0933-3657 See ARTIFICIAL INTELLIGENCE IN MEDICINE. 1211

0933-3770 See BM. BANK UND MARKT + TECHNIK. 921

0933-4017 See RESTAURO MUNCHEN. 363

0933-4173 See JPC. JOURNAL OF PLANAR CHROMATOGRAPHY, MODERN TLC. 983

0933-4548 See VERSICHERUNGSMEDIZIN. 3649

0933-4556 See OBOE, FAGOTT. 4142

0933-4807 See PTERIDINES. 5143

0933-5137 See MATERIALWISSENSCHAFT UND WERKSTOFFTECHNIK. 2106

0933-5315 See BIOS : ZEITSCHRIFT FUER BIOGRAPHIEFORSCHUNG UND ORAL HISTORY. 3269

0933-5846 See ARCHIVE FOR MATHEMATICAL LOGIC. 3496

0933-5854 See BIOMETALS. 483

0933-5927 See F & S. FILTRIEREN UND SEPARIEREN. 2012

0933-6540 See DISTRICT HEATING INTERNATIONAL. 2604

0933-6788 See UPDATE IN INTENSIVE CARE AND EMERGENCY MEDICINE. 3649

0933-6885 See MUSIK-, TANZ- UND KUNSTTHERAPIE. 4138

0933-7105 See MARKTFORSCHUNG & MANAGEMENT. 879

0933-7407 See MYCOSES. 576

0933-7415 See GOLF-MAGAZIN HAMBURG. 1987. 4896

0933-7598 See DAMPF & REISE, UBERSEEISCHE BAHNEN. 5431

0933-7741 See FORUM MATHEMATICUM. 3506

0933-7814 See DEUTSCHER FORSCHUNGSDIENST. GERMAN RESEARCH SERVICE. SPECIAL SCIENCE REPORTS. 5099

0933-7946 See ARTHROSKOPIE. 3960

0933-7954 See SOCIAL PSYCHIATRY AND PSYCHIATRIC EPIDEMIOLOGY. 3936

0933-808X See SCHUHTECHNIK 1987. 1087

0933-811X See ENDOSKOPIE HEUTE. 3574

0933-8217 See EMPLOYEE COUNSELLING TODAY. 4586

0933-8241 See MENSCH UND BUERO. 4212

0933-8241 See MENSCH & BUERO. 4212

0933-8357 See AUSSENDIENST-INFORMATIONEN. TRAININGSKURS FUR SYSTEMATISCHES VERKAUFEN. 2874

0933-842X See PRAXIS DER KLINISCHEN VERHALTENSMEDIZIN UND REHABILITATION. 3932

0933-8667 See DESIGN & ELEKTRONIK. 2041

0933-8853 See AMERICAS (BONN, GERMANY). 2527

0933-9027 See ZEITSCHRIFT FUER ANGEWANDTE UMWELTFORSCHUNG. 2183

0933-9094 See RUCKERT ZU EHREN : EINE SCHRIFTENREIHE DER RUCKERT-GESELLSCHAFT. 3470

0933-9418 See BAYREUTHER GEOWISSENSCHAFTLICHE ARBEITEN. 2556

0933-9434 See MICROSOFT-SYSTEM-JOURNAL. 1195

0933-9914 See MAYO CLINIC HEALTH LETTER (GERMAN ED.). 4790

0934-0351 See ZEITSCHRIFT FUER PHOTOGRAMMETRIE UND FERNERKUNDUNG. 2580

0934-0378 See FILM & FAKTEN : EIN MAGAZIN DER FSK. 4069

0934-0378 See FILM UND FARBE. 4070

0934-0394 See AUTOMOBIL-PRODUKTION. 5405

0934-0505 See WISSENSCHAFTLICHE BEITRAEGE AUS EUROPAISCHEN HOCHSCHULEN REIHE 11 MATHEMATIK. 3541

0934-0696 See ZEITSCHRIFT FUER TURKEISTUDIEN : ZFTS. 2668

0934-0734 See BIOMEDICAL PROGRESS. 3557

0934-0769 See EVANGELIUM UND WISSENSCHAFT. 4957

0934-0785 See GLAUBE UND DENKEN : JAHRBUCH DER KARL-HEIM-GESELLSCHAFT. 4960

0934-0866 See PARTICLE & PARTICLE SYSTEMS CHARACTERIZATION. 988

0934-0874 See TRANSPLANT INTERNATIONAL. 3976

0934-0882 See SEXUAL PLANT REPRODUCTION. 527

0934-1129 See AIDS WIESBADEN. 3665

0934-1730 See KUENSTLER (MUENCHEN). 323

0934-215X See COLLECTION CONTACTOLOGIA. 3873

0934-2400 See EUROPEAN ARCHIVES OF OTO-RHINO-LARYNGOLOGY. SUPPLEMENT. 3888

0934-2842 See DOS EXTRA. 1183

0934-3148 See MED-REPORT. 3607

0934-3237 See ST-MAGAZIN 68000ER. 1230

0934-3482 See MULLMAGAZIN. 2236

0934-3504 See UMWELTWISSENSCHAFTEN UND SCHADSTOFF-FORSCHUNG : ORGAN DER ARBEITSGEMEINSCHAFT UMWELTCHEMIE UND OKOTOXIKOLOGIE DER GESELLSCHAFT DEUTSCHER CHEMIKER. 2245

0934-361X See DACHAUER HEFTER. 2685

0934-3792 See DECHEMA BIOTECHNOLOGY CONFERENCES. 3691

0934-3962 See INSTRUMENTENBAU ZEITSCHRIFT, MUSIK INTERNATIONAL : IZ. 4122

0934-4217 See MEDIA SELECTION. 692

0934-4365 See SCIENTIFIC DRILLING. 1410

0934-4373 See STRUCTURAL OPTIMIZATION. 2129

0934-4640 See MITTEILUNGEN - DEUTSCHE GESELLSCHAFT FUR PHARMAKOLOGIE UND TOXIKOLOGIE. 4316

0934-4853 See SPIELRAUM. 2601

0934-5043 See FORMAL ASPECTS OF COMPUTING. 1247

0934-5116 See MITTEILUNGEN DER GESELLSCHAFT FUER PFLANZENBAUWISSENSCHAFTEN. 518

0934-5337 See FORSCHUNGEN ZU PAUL VALERY. 3388

0934-5693 See IMMOBILIEN-BERATER. 4839

0934-5841 See SOFTWARE-KURIER FUER MEDIZINER UND PSYCHOLOGEN. 1203

0934-5906 See WIREWORLD. 2001

0934-6112 See ADVANCES IN DISEASE VECTOR RESEARCH. 5604

0934-6449 See FOLK MICHEL. 4118

0934-6503 See LITERATURMAGAZIN. 3407

0934-666X See ZEITSCHRIFT FUER KULTURTECHNIK UND LANDENWICKLUNG. 148

0934-6694 See OPERATIVE ORTHOPADIE UND TRAUMATOLOGIE. 3883

0934-6724 See KTS ZEITSCHRIFT FUER INSOLVENZRECHT : KONKURS, TREUHAND, SANIERUNG. 2993

0934-6767 See STATISTISCHE RUNDSCHAU NORDRHEIN-WESTFALEN. 1522

0934-683X See BR. BAUSTOFF-RECYCLING + DEPONIETECHNIK. 5089

0934-7054 See FBM FERTIGUNGS-TECHNOLOGIE. 4001

0934-7062 See GESCHMACKSMUSTERBLATT. 2974

0934-7321 See WERKSTOFF UND INNOVATION. 631

0934-7348 See POWDER HANDLING & PROCESSING. 2148

0934-7453 See MEDIAEVISTIK. 2623

0934-7887 See EINBECKER JAHRBUCH. 2686

0934-7909 See NATUR-UND GANZHEITSMEDIZIN : NGM. 3619

0934-8387 See PNEUMOLOGIE. 3950

0934-8506 See MITTEILUNGEN - GESELLSCHAFT DEUTSCHER CHEMIKER, FACHGRUPPE GESCHICHTE DER CHEMIE. 986

0934-8727 See PROTOPLASMA. SUPPLEMENTUM. 5595

0934-8778 See NJW-COR COMPUTERREPORT : DER NEUEN JURISTISCHEN WOCHENSCHRIFT : INFORMATIONSMANAGEMENT AND BUROORGANISATION IN DER JUSTISCHEN PRAXIS. 3017

0934-8832 See MATRIX (STUTTGART). 3606

0934-8840 See ZENTRALBLATT FUER BAKTERIOLOGIE. 571

0934-8859 See ZENTRALBLATT FUER HYGIENE UND UMWELTMEDIZIN. 4809

0934-8913 See NIKEPHOROS : ZEITSCHRIFT FUER SPORT & KULTUR IM ALTERTUM. 4908

0934-9200 See NEUE KRIMINALPOLITIK. 3108

0934-9219 See AN-ALFABETEN, DIE. 1060

0934-9235 See BIOMETRIE UND INFORMATIK IN MEDIZIN UND BIOLOGIE. 447

0934-9340 See BRAUWELT INTERNATIONAL. 2365

0934-943X See BIOTECHNOLOGY IN AGRICULTURE AND FORESTRY. 3689

0934-9545 See PROGRESS IN PHARMACOLOGY AND CLINICAL PHARMACOLOGY. 4326

0934-9669 See THROMBOTIC AND HAEMORRHAGIC DISORDERS. 3774

0934-9669 See THROMBOTIC AND HEMORRHAGIC DISORDERS. 3645

0934-9723 See EUROPEAN JOURNAL OF CLINICAL MICROBIOLOGY & INFECTIOUS DISEASES. 562

0934-9758 See VAKUUM IN DER PRAXIS. 4424

0934-9820 See EICOSANOIDS. 3729

0934-9839 See RESEARCH IN ENGINEERING DESIGN. 1994

0934-9847 See RESEARCH IN NONDESTRUCTIVE EVALUATION. 1994

0935-0020 See PERFUSION : DURCHBLUTUNGSSTORUNGEN UND ARTERIOSKLEROSE IN KLINIK UND PRAXIS. 3626

0935-0195 See ADVANCES IN APPLIED NEUROLOGICAL SCIENCES. 3826

0935-0209 See ENVIRONMENTAL TOXIN SERIES. 2229

0935-0241 See KONZERNE IN SCHAUBILDERN. 689

0935-0276 See BTS : BUERO, TECHNIK, SYSTEME. 4210

0935-0373 See C-MAGAZIN. 4941

0935-0381 See CONTROLLING. 1181

0935-0411 See REGIONAL CANCER TREATMENT. 3823

0935-0454 See AZUR-CAMPING-MAGAZIN. 4848

0935-0519 See GARTENKUNST, DIE. 2416

0935-1043 See BIOTECHNOLOGY FOCUS. 3689

0935-1108 See LEONARDO (KISSING). 302

0935-1175 See CONTINUUM MECHANICS AND THERMODYNAMICS. 2112

0935-1183 See STRUCTURED PROGRAMMING. 1204

0935-1221 See EUROPEAN JOURNAL OF MINERALOGY (STUTTGART). 1439

0935-123X See BERICHTE DER DEUTSCHEN MINERALOGISCHEN GESELLSCHAFT. 1438

0935-1523 See GIS. GEO-INFORMATIONS-SYSTEME. 1356

0935-1531 See IRAN FOCUS. 1497

0935-1574 See GV SWISS. 2343

0935-1701 See INTENSIVE CARE MEDICINE SUPPLEMENT. 3588

0935-1906 See NEW DEVELOPMENT IN BIOSCIENCES. 467

0935-2023 See INDUSTRIEBAU HANNOVER. 617

0935-2147 See CRYPTOGAMIC BOTANY. 507

0935-2325 See BILDUNG UND KULTURPFLEGE IN BAYERN. 1728

0935-2422 See MITTEILUNGEN - MUSEUM FOLKWANG ESSEN. 4091

0935-2562 See MUSIKFORUM : REFERATE UND INFORMATIONEN DES DEUTSCHEN MUSIKRATES. 4138

0935-2694 See NEW TECH NEWS MUNICH. 5133

0935-2937 See PSYCHOMED. 4613

0935-3216 See TW-PADIATRIE. 3648

0935-3224 See TW NEUROLOGIE, PSYCHIATRIE. 3847

0935-3518 See HISTORISCHE SPRACHFORSCHUNG. 3285

0935-462X See ELLE (MUNICH, GERMANY). 5555

0935-4956 See ASTRONOMY AND ASTROPHYSICS REVIEW, THE. 392

0935-4964 See THEORETICAL AND COMPUTATIONAL FLUID DYNAMICS. 4423

0935-5596 See TRENDLETTER. 716

0935-560X See HISTORY AND MEMORY. 2619

0935-5626 See TROPICAL BRYOLOGY. 529

0935-5758 See WIK. ZEITSCHRIFT FUER WIRTSCHAFT, KRIMINALITAT UND SICHERHEIT. 5177

0935-5901 See PZ WISSENSCHAFT : PHARMAZEUTISCHE ZEITUNG, WISSENSCHAFTSAUSGABE. 4327

0935-6304 See JOURNAL OF HIGH RESOLUTION CHROMATOGRAPHY : HRC. 1017

0935-6339 See JOURNAL OF MANUAL MEDICINE. 3596

0935-6347 See VLIESSTOFF NONWOVEN INTERNATIONAL. 5359

0935-7092 See BIOORGANIC MARINE CHEMISTRY. 2212

0935-7114 See DISSERTATIONEN ZUR KUNSTGESCHICHTE. 319

0935-7157 See AUS HESSISCHEN MUSEEN. 343

0935-7254 See METALLURGICAL PLANT AND TECHNOLOGY INTERNATIONAL : MPT. 4010

0935-7335 See ETHIK IN DER MEDIZIN. 2250

0935-736X See HEART AND VESSLES. SUPPLEMENT. 3705

0935-7556 See SEMITICA VIVA-SERIES DIDACTICA. 3320

0935-8064 See PRESSE UND SPRACHE. 2923

0935-8072 See RUSSISTIK. 3318

0935-8927 See JUMA. DAS JUGENDMAGAZIN. 1759

0935-8943 See LARYNGO- RHINO- OTOLOGIE. 3889

0935-9060 See KRIEG UND LITERATUR. 2696

0935-9621 See PADERBORNER GEOGRAPHISCHE STUDIEN. 2572

0935-9648 See ADVANCED MATERIALS (WEINHEIM). 2100

0935-9680 See IX-MULTIUSER-MULTITASKING-MAGAZIN. 1191

0936-0018 See HAMBURGER BEITRAEGE ZUR FRIEDENSFORSCHUNG UND SICHERHEITSPOLITIK. 4523

0936-0085 See WORLD GUIDE TO LIBRARIES. 3260

0936-014X See INSTRUMENTENBAUREPORT. 4123

0936-0530 See ENGLISH TRANSLATIONS OF GERMAN STANDARDS CATALOGUE / ISSUED BY DIN DEUTSCHES INSTITUT FUER NORMUNG E.V. 4030

0936-0948 See DOKUMENTATION NATUR UND LANDSCHAFT. 2191

0936-1235 See CONTACTOLOGIA. 3873

0936-1375 See HANDBUCH DER DATENBANKEN FUER NATURWISSENSCHAFT, TECHNIK, PATENTE. 1185

0936-1502 See ONKOLOGISCHE KLINIK. 3822

0936-174X See JOURNAL OF PERINATAL MEDICINE SUPPLEMENT. 3764

0936-1928 See EURO-FOCUS RATINGEN. 4215

0936-2002 See TW-UROLOGIE, NEPHROLOGIE. 3993

0936-2479 See BLUEGRASS-BUEHNE. 4104

0936-2835 See EXCEPTIONALITY : THE OFFICIAL JOURNAL OF THE DIVISION FOR RESEARCH OF THE COUNCIL FOR EXCEPTIONAL CHILDREN. 1879

0936-2975 See ADVANCES IN FEED TECHNOLOGY. 199

0936-3076 See JOURNAL OF NEURAL TRANSMISSION. PARKINSON'S DISEASE AND DEMENTIA SECTION. 3835

0936-3734 See GARTNERBORSE, GARTENWELT. 2416

0936-3777 See KINEMATOGRAPH FRANKFURT. 4073

0936-384X See VERZEICHNIS DER NEUERWERBUNGEN - JOHN F. KENNEDY-INSTITUT FUER NORDAMERIKASTUDIEN, FREIE UNIVERSITAT BERLIN BIBLIOTHEK. 427

0936-4242 See LICHTENBERG-JAHRBUCH. 3405

0936-4315 See PC-NETZE. 1199

0936-451X See VIERTELJAHRESBERICHTE PROBLEMS OF INTERNATIONAL COOPERATION. 4537

0936-4595 See GESELLSCHAFT FUER KANADA-STUDIEN : MITTEILUNGEN. 2734

0936-5214 See SYNLETT. 1048

0936-577X See CLIMATE RESEARCH. 1422

0936-5796 *See* HISTORISCHE MITTEILUNGEN. 2619
0936-5893 *See* RDE. RECHT DER ELEKTRIZITATSWIRTSCHAFT. 1954
0936-5907 *See* COGNITIVE LINGUISTICS. 3274
0936-6318 *See* EUROPEAN DAIRY MAGAZINE. 194
0936-6555 *See* CLINICAL ONCOLOGY : A JOURNAL OF THE ROYAL COLLEGE OF RADIOLOGISTS. 3815
0936-6652 *See* ROFO. FORTSCHRITTE AUF DEM GEBIETE DER RONTGENSTRAHLEN UND DER NEUEN BILDGEBENDEN VERFAHREN. 3946
0936-6768 *See* REPRODUCTION IN DOMESTIC ANIMALS 1990. 5520
0936-6903 *See* BIOLOGIE HEUTE. 446
0936-6911 *See* ELEKTRONENMIKROSKOPIE : MITTEILUNGEN DER DEUTSCHEN GESELLSCHAFT FUER ELEKTRONENMIKROSKOPIE E.V. 572
0936-7160 *See* PERINATALMEDIZIN : OFFIZIELLES MITTEILUNGSBLATT DER DEUTSCHEN GESELLSCHAFT FUER PERINATALE MEDIZIN. 3767
0936-7195 *See* WISSENSCHAFTLICHE MITTEILUNGEN. 2579
0936-8051 *See* ARCHIVES OF ORTHOPAEDIC AND TRAUMA SURGERY. 3959
0936-8671 *See* ARBEITEN AUS DEM PAUL-EHRLICH-INSTITUT (BUNDESAMT FUER SERA UND IMPFSTOFFE) ZU FRANKFUERT A.M. 3666
0936-8787 *See* ZEITSCHRIFT FUER PLANUNG : ZP. 890
0936-9104 *See* MIKROWELLEN- & HF-MAGAZIN. 2072
0936-9198 *See* SOZIALVERSICHERUNGS-BERATER. 5310
0936-9244 *See* SKEPTIKER. 4243
0936-9589 *See* PHARMACOPSYCHIATRY SUPPLEMENT. 4323
0936-9902 *See* ICHTHYOLOGICAL EXPLORATION OF FRESHWATERS. 2305
0936-9937 *See* JOURNAL OF EVOLUTIONARY ECONOMICS. 1593
0937-0277 *See* PFLEGEN AMBULANT. 3627
0937-0420 *See* DLR-NACHRICHTEN : MITTEILUNGSBLATT DER DEUTSCHEN FORSCHUNGSANSTALT FUER LUFT- UND RAUMFAHRT. 18
0937-0633 *See* FRESENIUS' JOURNAL OF ANALYTICAL CHEMISTRY. 1015
0937-082X *See* LANDERBERICHT. HAITI. 2512
0937-0978 *See* CLINICAL PHARMACOLOGY. 4296
0937-1478 *See* LEBENSMITTELCHEMIE : ZEITSCHRIFT DER LEBENSMITTELCHEMISCHEN GESELLSCHAFT, FACHGRUPPE IN DER GESELLSCHAFT DEUTSCHER CHEMIKER. 2348
0937-1532 *See* PARODONTOLOGIE : DIE ZEITSCHRIFT FUER DIE PRAXIS. 1332
0937-1583 *See* PROFI MUNSTER. 122
0937-1591 *See* INTERNATIONAL JOURNAL OF MEDICAL MICROBIOLOGY AND HYGIENE ABSTRACTS OF MICROBIOLOGY, VIROLOGY, PARASITOLOGY, PREVENTIVE MEDICINE AND ENVIRONMENTAL HYGIENE. 564
0937-1958 *See* BIER & GETRANKE. 2364
0937-2032 *See* PPMP. PSYCHOTHERAPIE, PSYCHOSOMATIK, MEDIZINISCHE PSYCHOLOGIE. 4608
0937-2148 *See* CHEMISTRY OF PLANT PROTECTION. 506
0937-2156 *See* CURRENT TOPICS IN INFECTIOUS DISEASES AND CLINICAL MICROBIOLOGY. 3713
0937-2180 *See* FAMILIE UND RECHT : FUR. 3120
0937-261X *See* JAHRBUCH / BORSENVEREIN DES DEUTSCHEN BUCHHANDELS E.V. 4829
0937-289X *See* KRANKENHAUSPSYCHIATRIE. 3930
0937-3004 See MEDWELT COMPACT. 3615
0937-3195 *See* APPLIED PROBABILITY. 3495
0937-3446 *See* MESSEN & PRUFEN (1990). 1987

0937-3462 *See* INTERNATIONAL UROGYNECOLOGY JOURNAL. 3763
0937-3543 *See* MISS B ENGLISH ED. 1086
0937-3756 *See* BBR : WASSER UND ROHRBAU. 5531
0937-3764 *See* IT. IBEROAMERICANA DE TECHNOLOGIAS. 5117
0937-3977 *See* LEICA FOTOGRAFIE INTERNATIONAL. 4371
0937-4051 *See* APPROXIMATION & OPTIMIZATION. 3495
0937-4167 *See* KONSTRUKTIONSPRAXIS. 2120
0937-4450 *See* EUROPEAN JOURNAL FOR HIGH ABILITY. 1878
0937-4477 *See* EUROPEAN ARCHIVES OF OTO-RHINO-LARYNGOLOGY. 3888
0937-552X *See* PRAEVENTION UND REHABILITATION. 3629
0937-597X *See* KARTEN. 795
0937-6186 *See* KW HEUTE. 4007
0937-6348 *See* MS & T : MILITARY SIMULATION & TRAINING. 4052
0937-6429 *See* WIRTSCHAFTSINFORMATIK. 1263
0937-7069 *See* LASER-PRAXIS. 4437
0937-714X *See* REVUE UNIVERSELLE DES DROITS DE L'HOMME. 4512
0937-7204 *See* EUROPAISCHE ZEITSCHRIFT FUER WIRTSCHAFTSRECHT : EUZW. 2967
0937-7247 *See* SCHLESWIG-HOLSTEIN. 2708
0937-7271 2152
0937-7409 *See* CHEMOECOLOGY. 971
0937-7441 See RFE/RL RESEARCH REPORT. 1138
0937-7654 *See* EDS MAGAZINE : OFFICIAL JOURNAL OF THE E.E.C. DENTAL STUDENTS COMMITTEE. 1323
0937-7735 *See* FRANCIA 1 MITTELALTER. 2616
0937-7743 *See* FRANCIA 2 FRUHE NEUZEIT. 2616
0937-7751 *See* FRANCIA 3 19./20. JAHRHUNDERT. 2616
0937-7794 *See* LANDERBERICHT. GUATEMALA / [STATISTISCHES BUNDESAMT]. 2551
0937-7816 *See* LANDERBERICHT. JAMAIKA. 2512
0937-7824 *See* LANDERBERICHT. BIRMA. 2506
0937-7859 *See* LANDERBERICHT. LIBYEN. 2499
0937-7891 *See* LANDERBERICHT. TURKEI. 2506
0937-7913 *See* LANDERGBERICHT. VEREINIGTE STAATEN. 2537
0937-7921 *See* LANDERBERICHT. PHILIPPINEN. 2506
0937-7948 *See* LANDERBERICHT. PARAGUAY / [STATISTISCHES BUNDESAMT]. 2551
0937-7972 *See* LANDERBERICHT. MALAYSIA / STATISTISCHES BUNDESAMT. 5331
0937-8243 *See* EUROPEAN JOURNAL FOR FLUID POWER, OIL-HYDRAULICS AND PNEUMATICS. 2089
0937-8340 *See* MODERN METHODS OF PLANT ANALYSIS (1985). 518
0937-8898 *See* FACHMEDIEN GESUNDHEIT 1989. 3576
0937-907X *See* ACTA DEMOGRAPHICA / DEUTSCHE GESELLSCHAFT FUER BEVOLKERUNGSWISSENSCHAFT. 1589
0937-9134 *See* FEED MAGAZINE. 201
0937-9258 *See* COKEMAKING INTERNATIONAL. 2137
0937-9347 *See* APPLIED MAGNETIC RESONANCE. 4397
0937-938X *See* ETHIK UND SOZIALWISSENSCHAFTEN. 2250
0937-941X *See* OSTEOPOROSIS INTERNATIONAL : A JOURNAL ESTABLISHED AS RESULT OF COOPERATION BETWEEN THE EUROPEAN FOUNDATION FOR OSTEOPOROSIS AND THE NATIONAL OSTEOPOROSIS FOUNDATION OF THE USA. 3806
0937-9614 *See* DISKURS : STUDIEN ZU KINDHEIT, JUGEND, FAMILIE UND GESELLSCHAFT. 2278
0937-9649 *See* REVISTA SIEMENS (PORTUGUESE EDITION). 2079

0937-9819 *See* RECHTSMEDIZIN BERLIN. 3742
0937-9827 *See* INTERNATIONAL JOURNAL OF LEGAL MEDICINE. 3741
0937-9924 *See* EXPORT-POLYGRAPH INTERNATIONAL 1990. 4565
0937-9975 *See* LANDERBERICHT. KOREA, DEMOKRATISCHE VOLKSREPUBLIK. 5331
0938-0108 *See* MICROGRAVITY SCIENCE AND TECHNOLOGY. 4412
0938-0337 *See* AGRIBIOLOGICAL RESEARCH. 48
0938-0914 *See* STEPPKE. 1069
0938-0922 *See* IN-VITRO-DIAGNOSTICA-NACHRICHTEN. 3797
0938-0949 *See* COASTAL AND ESTUARINE STUDIES. 1968
0938-1236 *See* EURO PRINTER. 4564
0938-1279 *See* APPLICABLE ALGEBRA IN ENGINEERING, COMMUNICATION AND COMPUTING. 3494
0938-1287 *See* SHOCK WAVES. 4429
0938-1643 *See* SCHIFF & HAFEN/SEEWIRTSCHAFT. 5455
0938-1953 *See* SURVEYS ON MATHEMATICS FOR INDUSTRY. 1997
0938-202X *See* JULIT. 3401
0938-2259 *See* ECONOMIC THEORY. 1591
0938-2763 *See* ADVANCES IN COMPARATIVE AND ENVIRONMENTAL PHYSIOLOGY. 577
0938-3611 *See* JAHRESBERICHT / BAYERISCHE STAATSGEMALDESAMMLUNGEN. 238
0938-4472 *See* LANDERBERICHT. INDONESIEN. 5331
0938-4707 *See* LANDERBERICHT. VEREINIGTE ARABISCHE EMIRATE. 2506
0938-474X *See* LANDERBERICHT. NIEDERLANDE / STATISTISCHES BUNDESAMT. 5331
0938-5193 *See* ADVANCES IN ELECTROCHEMICAL SCIENCE AND ENGINEERING. 1033
0938-5207 *See* EQUIPMENT, CORROSION, AND CORROSION PROTECTION. 2012
0938-5215 *See* SAFETY, ENVIRONMENTAL PROTECTION, AND ANALYSIS. 2181
0938-5398 *See* LANDERBERICHT. AFGHANISTAN / [STATISTISCHES BUNDESAMT]. 5331
0938-5428 *See* EUROPEAN JOURNAL OF INTERNATIONAL LAW. 3128
0938-555X *See* POST-POLITISCHE INFORMATION. 4491
0938-5584 *See* BIOTECHNOLOGY (FRANKFURT 1991). 3689
0938-5807 *See* EQUIPMENT, CORROSION, AND CORROSION PROTECTION. 2012
0938-6033 *See* SOZIALWISSENSCHAFTLICHER FACHINFORMATIONSDIENST. MIGRATION UND ETHNISCHE MINDERHEITEN : SOFID / INFORMATIONSZENTRUM SOZIALWISSENSCHAFTEN. 1921
0938-6076 *See* SOZIALWISSENSCHAFTLICHER FACHINFORMATIONSDIENST. SOZIALPOLITIK / INFORMATIONSZENTRUM SOZIALWISSENSCHAFTEN. 5263
0938-6513 *See* BIBLIOGRAPHIEN DES FORSCHUNGSZENTRUMS JULICH. 410
0938-7390 *See* NOTFALLVORSORGE UND ZIVILE VERTEIDIGUNG. 1073
0938-7412 *See* HERZSCHRITTMACHERTHERAPIE & ELEKTROPHYSIOLOGIE. 2056
0938-7501 *See* BIOTECH FORUM EUROPE. 3688
0938-765X *See* LASERMEDIZIN : ORGAN DER DEUTSCHEN GESELLSCHAFT FUER LASERMEDIZIN. 3969
0938-7706 *See* JOURNAL OF SYSTEMS ENGINEERING. 1983
0938-7714 *See* COMPARATIVE HAEMATOLOGY INTERNATIONAL. 3771
0938-7927 *See* ACQUISA. 952
0938-7986 *See* KOGNITIONSWISSENSCHAFT. 4602
0938-7994 *See* EUROPEAN RADIOLOGY. 3941
0938-8249 *See* MIR. MANAGEMENT INTERNATIONAL REVIEW 1990. 695

0938-863X See JAHRBUCH DER VILLA VIGONI. **3398**

0938-880X See MID FRANKFURT. **5129**

0938-8974 See JOURNAL OF NONLINEAR SCIENCE. **5119**

0938-8982 See LEARNING DISABILITIES RESEARCH AND PRACTICE. **1881**

0938-8990 See MAMMALIAN GENOME. **463**

0938-9008 See NONLINEAR SCIENCE TODAY. **5134**

0938-9016 See PAIN DIGEST. **3625**

0938-9067 See WRP. WASCHEREI- & REINIGUNGSPRAXIS 1990. **1632**

0938-9245 See NEW VISTAS IN DRUG RESEARCH. **4318**

0938-9334 See BONNER JAHRBUCHER DES RHEINISCHEN LANDESMUSEUMS IN BONN UND DES RHEINISCHEN AMTES FUER BODENDENKMALPFLEGE IM LANDSCHAFTSVERBAND RHEINLAND UND DES VEREINS VON ALTERTUMSFREUNDEN IM RHEINLANDE. **2679**

0938-9369 See DMZ, LEBENSMITTELINDUSTRIE UND MILCHWIRTSCHAFT. **2334**

0938-9407 See FORTSCHRITTE DER DIAGNOSTIK. **3577**

0938-9563 See MODELING OF GEO-BIOSPHERE PROCESSES. **1358**

0938-9806 See TILE & BRICK INTERNATIONAL. **630**

0938-9849 See PE. PLAST EUROPE. **4457**

0938-9865 See MITTEILUNGEN DES VEREINS DEUTSCHER EMAILFACHLEUTE E.V. (1990). **4224**

0939-0146 See CRITICAL REVIEWS IN NEUROSURGERY : CR. **3963**

0939-0154 See BIBLIOGRAPHIE ZUR SYMBOLIK, IKONOGRAPHIE UND MYTHOLOGIE. ERGANZUNGSBAND. **4939**

0939-0359 See CM. CONTROLLER-MAGAZIN 1988. **1590**

0939-0421 See DEUTSCHE NATIONALBIBLIOGRAPHIE UND BIBLIOGRAPHIE DES IM AUSLAND ERSCHIENEN DEUTSCHSPRACHIGEN VEROFFENTLICHUNGEN. REIGE A. ESCHIENENE. **414**

0939-043X See DEUTSCHE NATIONALBIBLIOGRAPHIE UND BIBLIOGRAPHIE DER IM AUSLAND ERSCHIENEN DEUTSCHSPRACHIGEN VEROFFENTLICHUNGEN. REIHE B, MONOGRAPHIEN UND PERIODIKA AUSSERHALB DES VERLAGSBUCHHANDELS. WOCHENTLICHES VERZEICHNIS / BEARBEITER UND HERAUSGEBER, DIE DEUTSCHE BIBLIOTHEK. **414**

0939-0448 See TW DERMATOLOGIE : ARZTLICHE KOSMETOLOGIE. **406**

0939-0480 See DEUTSCHE NATIONALBIBLIOGRAPHIE UND BIBLIOGRAPHIE DER IM AUSLAND ERSCHIENEN DEUTSCHSPRACHIGEN VEROFFENTLICHUNGEN. MONOGRAPHIEN UND PERIODIKA DES VERLAGSBUCHHANDELS UND AUSSERHALB DES VERLAGSBUCHHANDELS. WOCHENTLICHES VERZEICHNIS. WOCHENREGISTER ZU REIHE A UND REIHE B / BEARBEITER UND HERAUSGEBER, DIE DEUTSCHE BIBLIOTHEK. **414**

0939-0553 See DEUTSCHE NATIONALBIBLIOGRAPHIE UND BIBLIOGRAPHIE DER IM AUSLAND ERSCHIENEN DEUTSCHSPRACHIGEN VEROFFENTLICHUNGEN. REIHE C, KARTEN, VIERTELJAHRLICHES VERZEICHNIS / BEARBEITER UND HERAUSGEBER, DIE DEUTSCHE BIBLIOTHEK. **4813**

0939-0588 See DEUTSCHE NATIONALBIBLIOGRAPHIE UND BIBLIOGRAPHIE DER IM AUSLAND ERSCHIENEN DEUTSCHSPRACHIGEN VEROFFENTLICHUNGEN. **414**

0939-0634 See DEUTSCHE NATIONALBIBLIOGRAPHIE UND BIBLIOGRAPHIE DER IM AUSLAND ERSCHIENEN DEUTSCHSPRACHIGEN VEROFFENTLICHUNGEN. REIHE N, VORANKUNDIGUNGEN MONOGRAPHIEN UND PERIODIKA (CIP). WOCHENTLICHES VERZEICHNIS / BEARBEITER UND HERAUSGEBER, DIE DEUTSCHE BIBLIOTHEK. **414**

0939-0642 See DEUTSCHE NATIONALBIBLIOGRAPHIE UND BIBLIOGRAPHIE DER IM AUSLAND ERSCHIENEN DEUTSCHSPRACHIGEN VEROFFENTLICHUNGEN. REIHE T, MUSIKTONTRAGER MONATLICHES VERZEICHNIS. **4114**

0939-141X See APR EUROPE. **4232**

0939-1517 See JOURNAL OF NEUROLOGY SUPPLEMENT. **3836**

0939-1533 See ARCHIVE OF APPLIED MECHANICS (1991). **2109**

0939-1916 See BINNENSCHIFFAHRT : ZEITSCHRIFT FEUR BINNENSCHIFFAHRT UND WASSERSTRASSEN. **5378**

0939-2327 See SIMMEL NEWSLETTER / [PRESENTED BY THE GEORG SIMMEL-GESELLSCHAFT E V., BIELEFELD]. **5258**

0939-2378 See NACHRICHTENBLATT DER VERMESSUNGS- UND KATASTERVERWALTUNG RHEINLAND-PFALZ. **2027**

0939-2475 See TEXTS IN APPLIED MATHEMATICS. **4429**

0939-2602 See HMD. THEORIE UND PRAXIS DER WIRTSCHAFTSINFORMATIK. **1186**

0939-2661 See ANASTHESIOLOGIE, INTENSIVMEDIZIN, NOTFALLMEDIZIN, SCHMERZTHERAPIE : AINS. **3682**

0939-267X See AKTUELLE RADIOLOGIE. **3938**

0939-2963 See FORSCHUNGSBERICHT / DEUTSCHE FORSCHUNGSANSTALT FUER LUFT- UND RAUMFAHRT. **21**

0939-3072 See EUROPEAN TRANSACTIONS ON ELECTRICAL POWER ENGINEERING. **2054**

0939-3331 See APOTHEKENHELFERIN HEUTE. **4292**

0939-334X See GESCHICHTE DER PHARMAZIE. **4306**

0939-351X See MEDIZIN, GESELLSCHAFT, UND GESCHICHTE : JAHRBUCH DES INSTITUTS FUER GESCHICHTE DER MEDIZIN DER ROBERT BOSCH STIFTUNG. **3615**

0939-3625 See ECONOMIC SYSTEMS. **1558**

0939-3773 See LANDERBERICHT. JAPAN. **2506**

0939-3781 See HALBASIEN. **3392**

0939-3854 See LANDERBERICHT. ZAIRE. **2499**

0939-4451 See AMINO ACIDS. **960**

0939-4753 See NUTRITION, METABOLISM, AND CARDIOVASCULAR DISEASES : NMCD. **3708**

0939-4818 See RESEARCH NOTES IN NEURAL COMPUTING. **3845**

0939-4893 See TATIGKEITSBERICHT - GEOLOGISCHES LANDESAMT NORDRHEIN-WESTFALIA. **1399**

0939-4974 See EUROPEAN JOURNAL OF CLINICAL CHEMISTRY AND CLINICAL BIOCHEMISTRY. **487**

0939-5075 See ZEITSCHRIFT FUR NATURFORSCHUNG. **476**

0939-5121 See THEOLOGIE FUER DIE PARXIS. **5003**

0939-5369 See EVREISKII ZHURNAL. **5047**

0939-5512 See DIALEKTIK. **4345**

0939-5555 See ANNALS OF HEMATOLOGY. **3770**

0939-5687 See THUERINGER ZAHNAERZTEBLATT. **1336**

0939-5911 See SUCHT. **3643**

0939-6071 See POLITICS AND THE INDIVIDUAL. **4490**

0939-6292 See MEDIZIN OHNE NEBENWIRKUNGEN. **4315**

0939-6314 See VEGETATION HISTORY AND ARCHAEOBOTANY. **529**

0939-6322 See JOURNAL OF MATERNAL-FETAL INVESTIGATION : THE OFFICIAL JOURNAL OF FRENCH SOCIETY OF ULTRASOUND IN MEDICINE AND BIOLOGY ... [ET AL.]. **3763**

0939-6365 See EUROPEAN JOURNAL OF PAIN, THE. **3575**

0939-6411 See EUROPEAN JOURNAL OF PHARMACEUTICS AND BIOPHARMACEUTICS : OFFICIAL JOURNAL OF ARBEITSGEMEINSCHAFT FUER PHARMAZEUTISCHE VERFAHRENSTECHNIK E.V. **4303**

0939-6780 See EUROPEAN JOURNAL OF CARDIAC PACING AND ELECTROPHYSIOLOGY. **3704**

0939-6896 See LANDERBERICHT. THAILAND. **2506**

0939-690X See LAENDERBERICHT. TSCHAD / STATISTISCHES BUNDESAMT. **5330**

0939-7116 See KLINISCHE NEURORADIOLOGIE. **3943**

0939-7248 See EUROPEAN JOURNAL OF PEDIATRIC SURGERY : OFFICIAL JOURNAL OF AUSTRIAN ASSOCIATION OF PEDIATRIC SURGERY ... ZEITSCHRIFT FUER KINDERCHIRURGIE. **3964**

0939-7418 See MACHINE VIBRATION. **2120**

0939-7698 See BEILSTEIN CURRENT FACTS IN CHEMISTRY [COMPUTER FILE] / BEILSTEIN INSTITUT. **1039**

0939-7701 See FORSCHUNGSVORHABEN / ZENTRALSTELLE FUER AGRARDOKUMENTATION UND -INFORMATION. **88**

0939-7922 See ZEITSCHRIFT FUER PHYSIK. A, HADRONS AND NUCLEI. **4451**

0939-8414 See FIRST CLASS ALFELD. **2805**

0939-8600 See JOURNAL OF EXPERIMENTAL ANIMAL SCIENCE (1991). **5513**

0939-8767 See THEMA UMWELT (OSNABRUCK). **426**

0939-9488 See PHARMACEUTICAL AND PHARMACOLOGICAL LETTERS. **4320**

0939-9534 See INFORMATIK IN DER LAND-, FORST- UND ERNAHRUNGSWIRTSCHAFT. **95**

0939-978X See PHLEBOLOGIE STUTTGART. **3709**

0939-9909 See IK. ZEITSCHRIFT FUER INDUSTRIEKAUFLEUTE. **1609**

0940-0117 See INTERFERENZEN. **1979**

0940-032X See GIT SPEZIAL. CHROMATOGRAPHIE. **1015**

0940-0788 See LANGUAGES OF THE WORLD. **3296**

0940-0842 See EUROPEAN SPACE REPORT. **18**

0940-0907 See LANDERBERICHT. BRASILIEN / STATISTISCHES BUNDESAMT. **5331**

0940-1334 See EUROPEAN ARCHIVES OF PSYCHIATRY AND CLINICAL NEUROSCIENCE. **3925**

0940-1555 See DEUTSCHE ZEITSCHRIFT FUER WIRTSCHAFTSRECHT. **2960**

0940-225X See ACADEMIE SPECTRUM. **5079**

0940-2268 See SEMINAR SOPHUS LIE : DARMSTADT, ERLANGEN, GREIFSWALD, LEIPZIG. **3533**

0940-2454 See DEUTSCHE GARTNERPOST. **2413**

0940-2470 See EUROPEAN PRODUCTION ENGINEERING : EPE. **1975**

0940-2721 See DEUTSCHE NATIONALBIBLIOGRAPHIE UND BIBLIOGRAPHIE DER IM AUSLAND ERSCHIENEN DEUTSCHSPRACHIGEN VEROFFENTLICHUNGEN. REIHE D, MONOGRAPHIEN UND PERIODIKA -- HALBJAHRESVERZEICHNIS. **4813**

0940-2993 See EXPERIMENTAL AND TOXICOLOGIC PATHOLOGY : OFFICIAL JOURNAL OF THE GESELLSCHAFT FUR TOXIKOLOGISCHE PATHOLOGIE. **3980**

0940-3256 See ORNITHOLOGISCHER ANZEIGER / HERAUSGEGEBEN VON DER ORNITHOLOGISCHEN GESELLSCHAFT IN BAYERN E.V. **5619**

ISSN Index

0940-3264 See ORTHOPEDIE TRAUMATOLOGIE : EUROPEAN JOURNAL OF ORTHOPAEDIC SURGERY & TRAUMATOLOGY : ORGANE OFFICIEL DE LA SOCIETE D'ORTHOPEDIE ET DE TRAUMATOLOGIE DE L'EST DE LA FRANCE (SOTEST) ET DU GROUPE D'ETUDE POUR LA CHIRURGIE OSSEUSE (GECO). 3884

0940-3507 See KUHN-ARCHIV. 177

0940-3825 See BERLIN-BRANDENBURGISCHE BAUWIRTSCHAFT. 600

0940-4117 3214

0940-4171 See EUROPAISCHE SICHERHEIT. 4043

0940-4961 See JUMA. DAS JUGENDMAGAZIN. 1759

0940-5151 See ECONOMIC QUALITY CONTROL. 1484

0940-5429 See ACTA DIABETOLOGICA. 3726

0940-5437 See INTERNATIONAL JOURNAL OF CLINICAL AND LABORATORY RESEARCH. 458

0940-5542 See BIOPRACTICE : INTERNATIONAL JOURNAL OF APPLIED BIOLOGY, BIOTECHNOLOGY, AND BIONICS. 447

0940-6360 See MYCORRHIZA. 518

0940-6581 See GEOBOTANISCHE KOLLOQUIEN. 2216

0940-6581 See GEOBOTANISCHE KOLLOQUIEN. 2216

0940-6689 See PHYSIKALISCHE MEDIZIN, REHABILITATIONSMEDIZIN, KURORTMEDIZIN. 3627

0940-6689 See PHYSIKALISCHE MEDIZIN. 4381

0940-6719 See EUROPEAN SPINE JOURNAL : OFFICIAL PUBLICATION OF THE EUROPEAN SPINE SOCIETY, THE EUROPEAN SPINAL DEFORMITY SOCIETY, AND THE EUROPEAN SECTION OF THE CERVICAL SPINE RESEARCH SOCIETY. 3964

0940-6735 See CHEMOTHERAPIE-JOURNAL. 3814

0940-6743 See PC-PRAXIS 1989. 1199

0940-7278 See INTERNATIONAL FASHION TRENDS. 1085

0940-7391 See INTERNATIONAL JOURNAL OF CULTURAL PROPERTY. 1305

0940-7936 See KIDNEY: A CURRENT SURVEY OF WORLD LITERATURE. 3991

0940-7944 See BIBLIOTHEKS-INFO. 3195

0940-8029 See WINDOS. 1207

0940-8541 See F. O. LICHT'S INTERNATIONAL SUGAR AND SWEETENER REPORT. 83

0940-855X See DEUTSCHE ZAHN-, MUND-, UND KIEFERHEILKUNDE MIT ZENTRALBLATT. 1322

0940-8606 See ADVANCES IN CHILD NEUROPSYCHOLOGY. 4571

0940-9092 See KONTINENZ. 3747

0940-9467 See TECHNOLOGY STUDIES. 5164

0940-9505 See ENDODONTIE. 1323

0940-9602 See ANNALS OF ANATOMY. 3678

0940-9653 See MICROBIAL RELEASES : VIRUSES, BACTERIA, FUNGI. 566

0940-9912 See EPITHELIAL CELL BIOLOGY. 536

0940-9998 See FOCUS MUL : ZEITSCHRIFT FUER WISSENSCHAFT, FORSCHUNG UND LEHRE AN DER MEDIZINISCHEN UNIVERSITAT ZU LUBECK. 3576

0941-0007 See AUSZUGE AUS DEN EUROPAISCHEN PATENTSCHRIFTEN. TEIL I, GRUND- UND ROHSTOFFINDUSTRIE, CHEMIE UND HUTTENWESEN, BAUWESEN, BERGBAU. 1301

0941-0015 See AUSZUGE AUS DEN EUROPAISCHEN PATENTSCHRIFTEN. TEIL II, ELEKTROTECHNIK, PHYSIK, FEINMECHANIK UND OPTIK, AKUSTIK. 1301

0941-0023 See AUSZUGE AUS DEN EUROPAISCHEN PATENTSCHRIFTEN. TEIL III, UBRIGE VERARBEITUNGSINDUSTRIE UND ARBEITSVERFAHREN, MASCHINEN- UND FAHRZEUGBAU, ERNAHRUNG, LANDWIRTSCHAFT. 1301

0941-018X See ZENTRALBLATT FUER BAKTERIOLOGIE. SUPPLEMENT. 571

0941-0198 See CLINICAL INVESTIGATOR, THE. 3565

0941-0295 See AEROSOL SPRAY REPORT : INTERNATIONAL PERIODICAL FOR THE AEROSOL AND SPRAY INDUSTRY. 1020

0941-0589 See ZEV, DET, GLASERS ANNALEN, DIE EISENBAHNTECHNIK. 5438

0941-0635 See APPLIED SIGNAL PROCESSING. 1255

0941-0643 See NEURAL COMPUTING & APPLICATIONS. 3839

0941-1046 See PRAXISMAGAZIN. 3629

0941-1216 See JOURNAL FUER PRAKTISCHE CHEMIE, CHEMIKER-ZEITUNG. 979

0941-1291 See SURGERY TODAY. 3975

0941-1348 See MILCHRIND. 215

0941-1461 See JAHRBUCH FUER PADAGOGIK. 1755

0941-1968 See OFFENE SYSTEME. 1197

0941-2131 See KLINISCHES LABOR. 5123

0941-2360 See WT PRODUKTION UND MANAGEMENT. 1632

0941-2778 See HEER MELSUNGEN. 4045

0941-2786 See HEER MELSUNGEN. 4045

0941-2794 See HEER MELSUNGEN. 4045

0941-2808 See HEER MELSUNGEN. 4045

0941-2921 See GERMAN JOURNAL OF OPHTHALMOLOGY. 3875

0941-293X See OPHTHALMOLOGE : ZEITSCHRIFT DER DEUTSCHEN OPHTHALMOLOGISCHEN GESELLSCHAFT, DER. 3877

0941-2948 See METEOROLOGISCHE ZEITSCHRIFT / HERAUSGEGEBEN VON DER DEUTSCHEN METEOROLOGISCHEN GESELLSCHAFT, OSTERREICHISCHEN GESELLSCHAFT FEUR METEOROLOGIE, SCHWEIZERISCHEN GESELLSCHAFT FUER GEOPHYSIK. 1431

0941-3596 See PLAST EUROPE : PE : KUNSTSTOFFE. 4457

0941-3596 See PE. PLAST EUROPE. 4457

0941-3790 See GESUNDHEITSWESEN, DAS. 4776

0941-3804 See CAHIERS D'ONCOLOGIE. 3810

0941-388X See STEEL & MATERIALS TECHNOLOGY. 4020

0941-4185 See INDUSTRIAL LASER HANDBOOK, THE. 4435

0941-4193 See MITTEILUNGEN DES BAYERISCHEN NOTARVEREINS, DER NOTARKASSE UND DER LANDESNOTARKAMMER BAYERN. 2519

0941-4355 See SUPPORTIVE CARE IN CANCER : OFFICIAL JOURNAL OF THE MULTINATIONAL ASSOCIATION OF SUPPORTIVE CARE IN CANCER. 3824

0941-4428 See PSYCHOANALYSE: KLINIK UND KULTURKRITIK. 4610

0941-505X See RFE/RL RESEARCH REPORT. 1138

0941-5092 See EUROPEAN ASPHALT MAGAZINE. 614

0941-6501 See NEUE BILDENDE KUNST. 359

0941-682X See MEDWELT COMPACT. 3615

0941-7494 See MOBILFUNK HEIDELBERG. 1117

0941-7567 See ZEISS INFORMATION WITH JENA REVIEW. 4442

0941-7583 See STUCK, PUTZ, TROCKENBAU. 3488

0941-7680 See PA. PRODUKTIONSAUTOMATISIERUNG. 1621

0941-7842 See MITTEILUNGEN DER KARL-MAY-GESELLSCHAFT. 3412

0941-8393 See DATZ : AQUARIEN TERRARIEN. 2773

0941-9500 See NEUROLOGY, PSYCHIATRY AND BRAIN RESEARCH. 3841

0941-9683 See LOGOS, NEUE FOLGE. 4352

0941-9772 See BASIC AND CLINICAL ASPECTS OF NEUROSCIENCE. 3828

0941-9780 See REIHE INFORMATIK. 1201

0941-9950 See WISSENSCHAFTLICHE ZEITSCHRIFT DER TECHNISCHEN UNIVERSITAT CHEMNITZ. 995

0942-010X See AUSTRIAN JOURNAL OF PUBLIC AND INTERNATIONAL LAW 1991. 3124

0942-0118 See GARTENBAU MAGAZIN. 2407

0942-1173 See BMT : BAUMASCHINENTECHNIK. 601

0942-136X See KONTRASTE FREIBURG. 1992. 5031

0942-2056 See KNEE SURGERY, SPORTS TRAUMATOLOGY, ARTHROSCOPY. 3969

0942-2366 See UHREN 1992. 367

0942-251X See APPLIED DATA AND KNOWLEDGE ENGINEERING. 1965

0942-2919 See SPRACHTYPOLOGIE UND UNIVERSALIENFORSCHUNG. 3323

0942-3028 See INTERNATIONALE ZEITSCHRIFT FUER PHILOSOPHIE. 4349

0942-332X See BERICHTE AUS TECHNIK UND WISSENSCHAFT / LINDE. 5087

0942-3478 See MOMBERGER AIRPORT INFORMATION. 29

0942-3915 See INGENIEUR FUER POST UND TELEKOMMUNIKATION, DER. 1978

0942-4318 See DEUTSCHE NATIONALBIBLIOGRAPHIE UND BIBLIOGRAPHIE DER IM AUSLAND ERSCHIENENEN DEUTSCHSPRACHIGEN VEROFFENTLICHUNGEN. REIHE E, MONOGRAPHIEN UND PERIODIKA -- FUNFJAHRESVERZEICHNIS / BEARBEITER UND HERAUSGEBER: DIE DEUTSCHE BIBLIOTHEK. 414

0942-4962 See MULTIMEDIA SYSTEMS. 1118

0942-5276 See AKTUELLE AUGENHEILKUNDE. 3871

0942-5276 See AKTUELLE AUGENHEILKUNDE. 498

0942-5594 See NONLINEAR DIGEST. 3524

0942-5608 See NON-LINEAR WORLD. 3524

0942-5616 See MATHEMATICAL LOGIC QUARTERLY. 3519

0942-6027 See ENDOSCOPIC SURGERY AND ALLIED TECHNOLOGIES. 3964

0942-721X See INTERNATIONAL VOLLEY TECH. 4901

0942-8151 See FASHION GUIDE DUSSELDORF. 1084

0942-8194 See TIZ PULVER + SCHUETTGUT MAGAZIN. 2152

0942-8704 See HISTORISCHE ANTHROPOLOGIE. 237

0942-8917 See COMPARAISON. 3377

0942-8925 See ABDOMINAL IMAGING. 3938

0943-0938 See APPLIED PARASITOLOGY. 3552

0943-1454 See KLEBEN UND DICHTEN. 1055

0943-1837 See AKTUELLE ENDOKRINOLOGIE. 3726

0943-2337 See ARCHIV FUER POST UND TELEKOMMUNIKATION. 1149

0943-2914 See DEUTSCHES BIENEN JOURNAL. 78

0943-4011 See JOURNAL FUER RECHTSPOLITIK. 4478

0943-4569 See ALLIANZ REPORT. 2109

0943-691X See HISTORISCH POLITISCHE MILLEILUNGEN. 4523

0943-7444 See KNOWLEDGE ORGANIZATION : KO. 3221

0943-7533 See CHINA MONTHLY DATA / INSTITUTE OF ASIAN AFFAIRS. 4468

0943-8149 See ZEITSCHRIFT FUER GESUNDHEITSPSYCHOLOGIE. 4622

0943-8750 See BANKENSTATISTIK / DEUTSCHE BUNDESBANK. 726

0943-8769 See KAPITALMARKTSTATISTIK / DEUTSCHE BUNDESBANK. 730

0943-8785 See SAISONBEREINIGTE WIRTSCHAFTSZAHLEN / DEUTSCHE BUNDESBANK. 1538

0943-898X See OPHTHALMOLOGISCHE NACHRICHTEN. 3877

0944-0291 See ROHRBLATT : MAGAZIN FUER OBOE, KLARINETTE, FAGOTT UND SAXOPHON. 4151

0944-1166 See JOURNAL OF HEPATO-BILIARY-PANCREATIC SURGERY. 3967
0944-1174 See JOURNAL OF GASTROENTEROLOGY. 3747
0944-1921 See ARCHIVE OF FISHERY AND MARINE RESEARCH. 2296
0944-2006 See ZOOLOGY : ANALYSIS OF COMPLEX SYSTEMS, ZACS. 5603
0944-2774 See INFORMATIONSTECHNIK UND TECHNISCHE INFORMATIK : IT + TI / ORGAN DER FACHBEREICHE 3 "TECHNISCHE INFORMATIK UND ARCHITEKTUR VON RECHENSYSTEMEN" UND 4 "INFORMATIONSTECHNIK UND TECHNISCHE NUTZUNG DER INFORMATIK" DER GI E.V. 1188
0944-5013 See MICROBIAL RESEARCH. 566
0944-5196 See MEDICAL & SURGICAL DERMATOLOGY : A CRITICAL GUIDE TO THE WORLD LITERATURE. 3721
0944-5277 See E.T.A. HOFFMANN-JAHRBUCH : MITTEILUNGEN DER E.T.A. HOFFMANN-GESELLSCHAFT. 3462
0944-5706 See JEWISH STUDIES QUARTERLY. 5049
0944-5943 See AMBULANT OPERIEREN. 3548
0944-6877 See PSYCHO PHARMAKO THERAPIE. 4326
0944-6885 See MEDIZINPRODUKTE JOURNAL. 3615
0944-7032 See PKA AKTUELL. 4325
0944-7105 See SEXUOLOGIE. 5188
0944-7113 See PHYTOMEDICINE. 3627
0944-8918 See PFLEGE AKTUELL / DBFK, DEUTSCHER BERUFSVERBAND FUER PFLEGEBERUFE. 3867
0945-0459 See KI LUFT UND KAELTETECHNIK. 618
0945-053X See MATRIX BIOLOGY : JOURNAL OF THE INTERNATIONAL SOCIETY FOR MATRIX BIOLOGY. 464
0945-1439 See MAJESTAS. 2622
0945-2737 See STANDORT CHEMIE. 993
0945-7917 See KIEFERORTHOPAEDIE : DIE ZEITSCHRIFT FUER DIE PRAXIS. 1329
0945-8182 See MICROBIOLOGY EUROPE. 567
0945-9111 See GARTNERBORSE. 2416
0945-9618 See CHEMICAL TECHNOLOGY EUROPE. 1022
0946-0470 See EUROMATERIALS. 2102
0946-1965 See INTERNATIONAL JOURNAL OF CLINICAL PHARMACOLOGY AND THERAPEUTICS. 4308
0946-2716 See JOURNAL OF MOLECULAR MEDICINE. 3596
0946-3151 See STOMATOLOGIE. 1336
0946-4441 See IBI DIENST. 2920
0947-0077 See Q-PRAXIS. 1623
0947-031X See DENKMALPFLEGE, DIE. 296
0949-138X See FABIAN NEWSLETTER. 4474
0950-0170 See WORK, EMPLOYMENT AND SOCIETY. 1718
0950-0189 See SCOTTISH LIBRARIES (1987). 3248
0950-0197 See BATHROOMS. 600
0950-0235 See DIALOGUE ON DIARRHOEA. 3796
0950-0294 See MEDICAL LABORATORY SCIENCES. SUPPLEMENT. 3610
0950-0510 See HEAT SHOCK PROTEINS. 488
0950-0561 See ONCOGENES. 550
0950-057X See OXYGEN RADICALS. 491
0950-0588 See PROTEASES & INHIBITORS. 470
0950-0618 See CONSTRUCTION & BUILDING MATERIALS. 608
0950-0642 See WINDIRECTIONS. 1960
0950-0669 See BICYCLE MAGAZINE. 428
0950-0693 See INTERNATIONAL JOURNAL OF SCIENCE EDUCATION. 5115
0950-0707 See SCIENCE, TECHNOLOGY & DEVELOPMENT. 5153
0950-0715 See SHEPPARD'S BOOK DEALERS IN THE BRITISH ISLES. 4832

0950-0731 See ARAB AFFAIRS. 2610
0950-0782 See LANGUAGE AND EDUCATION. 3294
0950-0790 See EVALUATION & RESEARCH IN EDUCATION. 1745
0950-0804 See JOURNAL OF ECONOMIC SURVEYS. 1570
0950-0839 See PHILOSOPHICAL MAGAZINE LETTERS. 4414
0950-091X See BASIN RESEARCH. 1366
0950-1029 See WORLD OIL TRADE. 4282
0950-1037 See FINANCIAL TIMES NORTH SEA LETTER AND EUROPEAN OFFSHORE NEWS. 1944
0950-1045 See OIL & ENERGY TRENDS. 4268
0950-107X See IEE PROCEEDINGS. PART H, MICROWAVES, ANTENNAS, AND PROPAGATION. 2058
0950-1401 See HANDBOOK OF GEOPHYSICAL EXPLORATION SECTION 1 SEISMIC EXPLORATION. 1406
0950-1487 See POWER INTERNATIONAL. 2124
0950-1584 See LEADSCAN. 4025
0950-1592 See ZINCSCAN. 4025
0950-1630 See STAFFORDSHIRE STUDIES. 2710
0950-1649 See MULTICULTURAL REVIEW. 2268
0950-1657 See HORTUS (FARNHAM). 2419
0950-1711 See NATURAL PRODUCT UPDATES. 1012
0950-1746 See FORKTAIL. 5617
0950-1800 See WHARTON REPORT. 1207
0950-1878 See FOOT AND MOUTH DISEASE BULLETIN. 5510
0950-1940 See INSULATION JOURNAL (RICKMARSWORTH). 617
0950-1991 See DEVELOPMENT (CAMBRIDGE). 541
0950-2009 See PHOTOGRAPHY (LONDON, ENGLAND : 1986). 4374
0950-2025 See SESAME BULLETIN. 3321
0950-2114 See IMAGE TECHNOLOGY (LONDON). 4072
0950-2181 See TRADITIONAL HOMES. 2903
0950-219X See TRADITIONAL INTERIOR DECORATION. 2903
0950-222X See EYE (LONDON, ENGLAND). 3874
0950-2238 See ASSIA. APPLIED SOCIAL SCIENCES INDEX & ABSTRACTS. 5226
0950-2262 See WORLD COPPER DATABOOK. 4024
0950-2289 See MASONRY INTERNATIONAL. 620
0950-2378 See NEW FORMATIONS. 3348
0950-2386 See CULTURAL STUDIES (LONDON, ENGLAND). 5197
0950-2424 See NEWSLETTER - CENTRE FOR HEALTH ECONOMICS. 4793
0950-2505 See COPYRIGHT WORLD. 1303
0950-2513 See PATENT WORLD. 1307
0950-2564 See TRADEMARK WORLD. 1309
0950-2645 See INSOLVENCY INTELLIGENCE. 2983
0950-2688 See EPIDEMIOLOGY AND INFECTION. 3713
0950-2742 See SOUROZH. 4998
0950-2815 See AUSTRALIAN MATHEMATICAL SOCIETY LECTURE SERIES. 3496
0950-3005 See BRITISH REVIEW OF BULIMIA + ANOREXIA NERVOSA. 3559
0950-303X See IBM SYSTEM USER. 1186
0950-3110 See AL-MASAQ. 5189
0950-3153 See PRACTICE BIRMINGHAM. 5301
0950-3234 See TURKEY MONITOR. 4757
0950-3293 See FOOD QUALITY AND PREFERENCE. 2339
0950-3366 See POWER ENGINEERING JOURNAL. 2075
0950-3374 See REGULATORY AFFAIRS BULLETIN. 4327
0950-3420 See PAPER FOCUS. 4236
0950-3439 See ROYALTY MONTHLY. 2707

0950-3471 See HISTORICAL RESEARCH : THE BULLETIN OF THE INSTITUTE OF HISTORICAL RESEARCH. 2618
0950-3501 See BAILLIERE'S CLINICAL ANAESTHESIOLOGY. 3682
0950-351X See BAILLIERE'S CLINICAL ENDOCRINOLOGY AND METABOLISM. 3726
0950-3528 See BAILLIERE'S CLINICAL GASTROENTEROLOGY. 3743
0950-3536 See BAILLIERE'S CLINICAL HAEMATOLOGY. 3770
0950-3552 See BAILLIERE'S CLINICAL OBSTETRICS AND GYNAECOLOGY. 3757
0950-3579 See BAILLIERE'S CLINICAL RHEUMATOLOGY. 3803
0950-3676 See DESIGN WEEK. 2899
0950-3730 See AGRA EUROPE. MILK PRODUCTS. 191
0950-382X See MOLECULAR MICROBIOLOGY. 568
0950-3846 See INTERNATIONAL JOURNAL OF LEXICOGRAPHY. 3287
0950-3889 See CONSTRUCTION LAW REPORTS (LONDON, ENGLAND). 2956
0950-4109 See INTERNATIONAL JOURNAL OF LAW AND THE FAMILY. 3121
0950-4125 See REFERENCE REVIEWS. 1928
0950-4206 See LEGAL JOURNALS INDEX. 3000
0950-4214 See GAS SEPARATION & PURIFICATION. 4258
0950-4222 See INDUSTRY & HIGHER EDUCATION. 1611
0950-4230 See JOURNAL OF LOSS PREVENTION IN THE PROCESS INDUSTRIES. 2099
0950-429X See CLASSICAL GUITAR. 1075
0950-4478 See PAPER EUROPEAN DATA BOOK. 4236
0950-4540 See WORLD ADVERTISING REVIEW. 382
0950-4591 See CURRENT PROBLEMS IN EPILEPSY. 3831
0950-4699 See TRANSACTIONS OF THE LANCASHIRE AND CHESHIRE ANTIQUARIAN SOCIETY. 2713
0950-4753 See KEY ABSTRACTS. ADVANCED MATERIALS. 2005
0950-4761 See KEY ABSTRACTS. ANTENNAS & PROPAGATION. 2005
0950-477X See KEY ABSTRACTS. ARTIFICIAL INTELLIGENCE. 2005
0950-4788 See KEY ABSTRACTS. COMPUTER COMMUNICATIONS & STORAGE. 2005
0950-4796 See KEY ABSTRACTS. COMPUTING IN ELECTRONICS AND POWER. 2005
0950-480X See KEY ABSTRACTS. ELECTRONIC INSTRUMENTATION. 2005
0950-4818 See KEY ABSTRACTS. MEASUREMENTS IN PHYSICS. 4426
0950-4826 See KEY ABSTRACTS. OPTOELECTRONICS. 2006
0950-4834 See KEY ABSTRACTS. POWER SYSTEMS AND APPLICATIONS. 1209
0950-4842 See KEY ABSTRACTS. ROBOTICS & CONTROL. 1209
0950-4850 See KEY ABSTRACTS. SEMICONDUCTOR DEVICES. 2006
0950-4869 See KEY ABSTRACTS. SOFTWARE ENGINEERING. 1209
0950-4877 See KEY ABSTRACTS. TELECOMMUNICATIONS. 1125
0950-494X See AGRAFILE. GRAIN & OILSEEDS. 161
0950-4958 See AGRAFILE. LIVESTOCK & MEAT. 46
0950-5075 See ARABIAN COMPUTER NEWS. 1235
0950-5245 See HERITAGE (BURNHAM-ON-CROUCH, ENG.). 2690
0950-5377 See INSURANCE & REINSURANCE SOLVENCY REPORT. 2883
0950-5423 See INTERNATIONAL JOURNAL OF FOOD SCIENCE AND TECHNOLOGY. 2345
0950-5431 See SCIENCE AS CULTURE. 5151

0950-5458 *See* ADVISER (WOLVERHAMPTON). 1293

0950-5474 *See* PC DEALER. 1238

0950-5482 *See* DEC COMPUTING. 1182

0950-5490 *See* DRIVERS AND CONTROLS. 1971

0950-5563 *See* INTERNATIONAL SERIES OF MONOGRAPHS ON PHYSICS (UK). 4406

0950-5571 *See* MEDICAL HISTORY. SUPPLEMENT. 3609

0950-558X *See* MARITIME DEFENCE. 4179

0950-5628 *See* BULLETIN - INSTITUTE OF MATHEMATICS AND ITS APPLICATIONS. 3498

0950-5644 *See* BULLETIN OF THE SCOTTISH GEORGIAN SOCIETY. 294

0950-5830 *See* RESCUE NEWS. 280

0950-5849 *See* INFORMATION AND SOFTWARE TECHNOLOGY. 1260

0950-5857 *See* LIPID REVIEW. 3708

0950-5903 *See* APPLIED MATHEMATICS AND ENGINEERING SCIENCE TEXTS. 3495

0950-5911 *See* GASTROENTEROLOGY INTERNATIONAL. 3745

0950-6101 *See* GAY TIMES LONDON. 1984. 2794

0950-6128 *See* KEESING'S RECORD OF WORLD EVENTS. 4480

0950-6144 *See* CHEMICAL BUSINESS UPDATE. 1011

0950-6209 *See* CORPORATE BRIEFING. 2956

0950-6284 *See* CAMBRIDGE TRACTS IN MATHEMATICS. 3499

0950-6292 *See* CAMBRIDGE STUDIES IN RUSSIAN LITERATURE. 3372

0950-6322 *See* CAMBRIDGE STUDIES IN FRENCH. 4343

0950-6330 *See* CAMBRIDGE STUDIES IN ADVANCED MATHEMATICS. 3499

0950-6349 *See* BROWNING SOCIETY NOTES. 3369

0950-6438 *See* DEVELOPMENTS IN SWEETENERS. 2333

0950-6551 *See* WATER & WASTE TREATMENT (1985). 2247

0950-656X *See* EUROPEAN DIRECTORY OF MARKETING INFORMATION SOURCES. 924

0950-6608 *See* INTERNATIONAL MATERIALS REVIEWS. 4004

0950-6659 *See* PHYSIOTHERAPY INDEX : CURRENT AWARENESS TOPICS SERVICES. 4382

0950-6667 *See* COMPLEMENTARY MEDICINE INDEX : CURRENT AWARENESS TOPICS SERVICES. 3567

0950-6675 *See* OCCUPATIONAL THERAPY INDEX : CURRENT AWARENESS TOPICS SERVICE. 1883

0950-6756 *See* COMPENDIA. 3274

0950-6764 *See* DEVELOPMENT POLICY REVIEW. 2909

0950-7051 *See* KNOWLEDGE-BASED SYSTEMS (GUILDFORD, SURREY). 1193

0950-7086 *See* NATIONAL LIBRARY OF SCOTLAND NEWS. 3233

0950-7116 *See* WELDING INTERNATIONAL. 4028

0950-7361 *See* EUROPEAN COMMUNITIES LEGISLATION : CURRENT STATUS. 3128

0950-737X *See* EYEPIECE. 4369

0950-7388 *See* ISM. INFORMATION SECURITY MONITOR. 1227

0950-7450 *See* EASTERN EUROPE NEWSLETTER. 2515

0950-7515 *See* SOCIAL SECURITY STATISTICS. 5267

0950-7582 *See* POPULATION PROJECTIONS AREA. 4557

0950-771X *See* FEED COMPOUNDER. 200

0950-7841 *See* PALMER'S IN COMPANY. 3024

0950-8163 *See* NOISE & VIBRATION IN INDUSTRY : NVI. 1620

0950-821X *See* EUROPEAN JOURNAL OF VASCULAR SURGERY. 3964

0950-8465 *See* RIGHTS AND HUMANITY. 4512

0950-8473 *See* DIA LONDON. 1479

0950-849X *See* RESEARCH MONOGRAPHS IN BANKING AND FINANCE. 808

0950-8686 *See* WATER CHEMISTRY OF NUCLEAR REACTOR SYSTEMS. 5542

0950-8708 *See* PROCEEDINGS OF THE INSTITUTE OF PETROLEUM. 4275

0950-8724 *See* CURRENT MEDICAL LITERATURE / REVERSIBLE OBSTRUCTIVE AIRWAYS DISEASE. 3949

0950-8864 *See* COGITO (BRISTOL, ENGLAND). 4344

0950-8945 *See* SHEFFIELD AND SOUTH YORKSHIRE CHAMBERS OF COMMERCE DIRECTORY. 851

0950-902X *See* AFRICA ANALYSIS. 1460

0950-916X *See* COI. COUNTERTRADE AND OFFSET INTELLIGENCE. 827

0950-9224 *See* CONTEMPORARY RECORD : THE JOURNAL OF THE INSTITUTE OF CONTEMPORARY BRITISH HISTORY. 2684

0950-9232 *See* ONCOGENE. 3821

0950-9240 *See* JOURNAL OF HUMAN HYPERTENSION. 3707

0950-9305 *See* ANNUAL REPORT OF THE POLICE COMPLAINTS AUTHORITY. 3157

0950-9526 *See* QUARRY MANAGEMENT. 2149

0950-9550 *See* HOCKEY DIGEST (HARROW). 4899

0950-9585 *See* JOURNAL OF THE SIMPLIFIED SPELLING SOCIETY. 1759

0950-9615 *See* PROCEEDINGS OF THE BRITISH MASONRY SOCIETY. 624

0950-9623 *See* FOOD SCIENCE & TECHNOLOGY TODAY. 2340

0950-9658 *See* SUPERSTORE MANAGEMENT INTERNATIONAL. 958

0950-9720 *See* FOCUS ON CHRISTIAN-MUSLIM RELATIONS. 4959

0950-9879 *See* INFORMATION WORLD REVIEW. 1277

0951-001X *See* TRANSACTIONS OF THE ANCIENT MONUMENTS SOCIETY. 366

0951-0079 *See* ABSTRACTS OF WORKING PAPERS IN ECONOMICS : THE OFFICIAL JOURNAL OF THE AWPE DATABASE. 1459

0951-0192 *See* BRITISH JOURNAL OF CLINICAL AND SOCIAL PSYCHIATRY. 3922

0951-0257 *See* ANNUAL REPORT / ANIMAL AND GRASSLAND RESEARCH INSTITUTE. 205

0951-0427 *See* INKSHED. 3464

0951-0443 *See* SCOTTISH CIVIL LAW REPORTS. 3091

0951-0524 *See* INFORMATION SERVICE NEWS AND ABSTRACTS / ADVISORY, CONCILIATION AND ARBITRATION SERVICE, WORK RESEARCH UNIT. 942

0951-0605 *See* CHILDREN & SOCIETY. 1061

0951-0621 *See* BIODETERIORATION ABSTRACTS. 2183

0951-0680 *See* MINOR ORES AND MINERALS. 2146

0951-0699 *See* LAW REPORTS OF THE COMMONWEALTH. CONSTITUTIONAL AND ADMINISTRATIVE LAW REPORTS. 3093

0951-0818 *See* DEVELOPMENTAL AND CELL BIOLOGY. 536

0951-0826 *See* COMBROAD. 1130

0951-0850 *See* ARUP JOURNAL. 292

0951-0869 *See* METALLURGICAL JOURNAL. 4010

0951-0893 *See* ELT JOURNAL. 3278

0951-0966 *See* AFRICAN CONCORD. 2636

0951-1105 *See* EFAC BULLETIN. 4955

0951-113X *See* REFUGEE ISSUES. 1921

0951-1288 *See* FINGERPRINT WHORLD. 3164

0951-130X *See* FOODNEWS. 2341

0951-1326 *See* FOLK ROOTS. 4118

0951-1512 *See* BUSINESS EDUCATION TODAY. 647

0951-1547 *See* EDIBLE NUT MARKET REPORT. 170

0951-1555 *See* INTERNATIONAL POPULAR BRIDGE MONTHLY. 4851

0951-158X *See* AUTOMOTIVE INDUSTRY DATA LTD. 5406

0951-1830 *See* JOURNAL OF AMBULATORY MONITORING. 3593

0951-1857 *See* NETWORK PAPER / ODI, RURAL DEVELOPMENT FORESTRY NETWORK. 2389

0951-1873 *See* NETWORK PAPER / ODI, AGRICULTURAL ADMINISTRATION (RESEARCH AND EXTENSION) NETWORK. 111

0951-1873 *See* DISCUSSION PAPER - AGRICULTURAL ADMINISTRATION, RESEARCH AND EXTENSION, NETWORK. 79

0951-192X *See* INTERNATIONAL JOURNAL OF COMPUTER INTEGRATED MANUFACTURING. 3481

0951-208X *See* BIOTECHNOLOGY TECHNIQUES. 3689

0951-2187 *See* ILP MAGAZINE. 1677

0951-2195 *See* WORLD MAGAZINE (LONDON, ENGLAND). 2579

0951-2233 *See* WORLD ALUMINIUM DATABOOK. 4023

0951-2292 *See* UEA PAPERS IN LINGUISTICS. 3330

0951-2500 *See* AMMONITE GILLINGHAM, DORSET. 2318

0951-2500 *See* AMMONITE. 3360

0951-256X *See* CYCLODEXTRIN NEWS. 1041

0951-2578 *See* JOURNAL / INSTITUTE OF STERILE SERVICES MANAGEMENT. 3592

0951-2640 *See* HEAVY HORSE WORLD. 2799

0951-2667 *See* ALCUIN/GROW LITURGICAL STUDY. 4933

0951-2721 *See* ENIGMA VARIATIONS NEWS. 4043

0951-2748 *See* PACIFIC REVIEW (OXFORD, ENGLAND). 4486

0951-3019 *See* COUNTRY HOMES AND INTERIORS. 2899

0951-3175 *See* MARKET LETTER. 4314

0951-3248 *See* INSTITUTE OF PHYSICS CONFERENCE SERIES. 4405

0951-3558 *See* INTERNATIONAL JOURNAL OF PUBLIC SECTOR MANAGEMENT, THE. 4657

0951-3574 *See* ACCOUNTING, AUDITING & ACCOUNTABILITY JOURNAL. 736

0951-3590 *See* GYNECOLOGICAL ENDOCRINOLOGY. 3730

0951-3604 *See* GLOBAL INVESTOR. 899

0951-3639 *See* CORPORATE MONEY. 785

0951-3752 *See* ANNUAL REVIEW / FRESHWATER FISHERIES LABORATORY, PITLOCHRY. 2295

0951-3760 *See* ANNUAL REVIEW / MARINE LABORATORY ABERDEEN. 1446

0951-3914 *See* HOLOGRAPHICS INTERNATIONAL. 4434

0951-418X *See* PTR. PHYTOTHERAPY RESEARCH. 525

0951-4198 *See* RAPID COMMUNICATIONS IN MASS SPECTROMETRY. 1018

0951-4309 *See* TESTS OF AGROCHEMICALS AND CULTIVARS. 4248

0951-4554 *See* FOOD, COSMETICS AND DRUG PACKAGING 1986. 4219

0951-4600 *See* OCCUPATIONAL HEALTH REVIEW (LONDON). 2866

0951-4635 *See* NEWSLETTER - BRITISH LIBRARY. SCIENCE REFERENCE AND INFORMATION SERVICE. 5133

0951-4686 *See* TELECOMMS REGULATION REVIEW. 1165

0951-4708 *See* CUBA BUSINESS. 663

0951-4767 *See* MONEY WEEK. 696

0951-4848 *See* HEALTH SERVICES MANAGEMENT RESEARCH : AN OFFICIAL JOURNAL OF THE ASSOCIATION OF UNIVERSITY PROGRAMS IN HEALTH ADMINISTRATION. 3781

0951-4937 *See* CONTEMPORARY WALES : AN ANNUAL REVIEW OF ECONOMIC AND SOCIAL RESEARCH. 1471

0951-497X *See* THEOSOPHICAL HISTORY. 5004

0951-5038 *See* JOURNAL OF BRITISH MUSIC THERAPY. 4125

0951-5070 See COUNSELLING PSYCHOLOGY QUARTERLY. 4583
0951-5089 See PHILOSOPHICAL PSYCHOLOGY. 4608
0951-5100 See ENVIRONMENT DIGEST. 2165
0951-5208 See BRITISH PERFORMING ARTS YEARBOOK. 384
0951-5216 See GERIATRIC CARDIOVASCULAR MEDICINE. 3751
0951-5224 See HIGHER EDUCATION QUARTERLY / SOCIETY FOR RESEARCH INTO HIGHER EDUCATION. 1828
0951-5240 See COMPUTER-INTEGRATED MANUFACTURING SYSTEMS. 1228
0951-5291 See BIOENGINEERING NOW. 3686
0951-5305 See NERC NEWS / NATURAL ENVIRONMENT RESEARCH COUNCIL. 2219
0951-5380 See AJ FOCUS. 287
0951-5429 See INTERNATIONAL JOURNAL OF THEOLOGY AND PHILOSOPHY IN AFRICA : TPA, THE. 4966
0951-547X See NEW MEXICO REAL ESTATE LAW REPORTER. 3016
0951-5666 See AI & SOCIETY. 1210
0951-5704 See DRAUGHTING & DESIGN. 1183
0951-5720 See BUTTERWORTHS LAW DIGEST MALAYSIA, SINGAPORE AND BRUNEI. 2945
0951-5747 See WORLD ELECTRONICS COMPANIES FILE. 2086
0951-578X See STEAM COAL. 852
0951-5798 See GRAIN (LONDON, ENGLAND). 838
0951-581X See FOREST PRODUCTS. 2380
0951-5836 See LIQUID CHEMICALS. 984
0951-5852 See CYCLING WEEKLY. 428
0951-5879 See CONTAINERISATION INTERNATIONAL WORLD DIRECTORY OF LINER SHIPPING AGENTS. 829
0951-6050 See CAB INTERNATIONAL DATABASE NEWS. 1253
0951-6158 See WORKS ISSUED BY THE HAKLUYT SOCIETY. 2579
0951-6204 See BRITISH REVIEW OF NEW ZEALAND STUDIES : BRONZS. 5193
0951-6298 See JOURNAL OF THEORETICAL POLITICS. 4479
0951-631X See SOCIAL HISTORY OF MEDICINE : THE JOURNAL OF THE SOCIETY FOR THE SOCIAL HISTORY OF MEDICINE. 3641
0951-6328 See JOURNAL OF REFUGEE STUDIES. 1919
0951-6433 See BIOFACTORS (OXFORD). 483
0951-6824 See OFFICE SECRETARY. 4207
0951-6832 See SEATRADE REVIEW. 5455
0951-6859 See BENCHMARK OBAN. 2111
0951-6875 See SPECIAL CHILDREN (BIRMINGHAM). 1885
0951-6913 See ANTIQUE (LONDON). 249
0951-7162 See AUTOMATED MANUFACTURING STRATEGY. 1217
0951-7197 See ADVANCES IN CEMENT RESEARCH. 598
0951-7200 See GASKELL SOCIETY JOURNAL, THE. 3389
0951-7359 See WATER AND ENVIRONMENTAL MANAGEMENT : JOURNAL OF THE INSTITUTION OF WATER AND ENVIRONMENTAL MANAGEMENT. 2247
0951-7367 See CURRENT OPINION IN PSYCHIATRY. 3924
0951-7375 See CURRENT OPINION IN INFECTIOUS DISEASES. 3713
0951-7383 See CURRENT OPINION IN NEUROLOGY AND NEUROSURGERY. 3831
0951-7472 See FERTILIZER WEEK. 1606
0951-7537 See GOVERNMENT COMPUTING. 1238
0951-7626 See TEACHER TRAINER. 1906
0951-7677 See FRONTIER. 4542
0951-7693 See PR WORLD. 764
0951-7715 See NONLINEARITY (BRISTOL). 3524
0951-7758 See EUROPEAN ADVERTISING & MEDIA FORECAST, THE. 759
0951-7766 See QUARTERLY SURVEY OF ADVERTISING EXPENDITURE. 765
0951-7782 See AIRCARGO NEWS INTERNATIONAL. 5375
0951-7812 See DIY SUPERSTORE. 2333
0951-7820 See STATIONERY TRADE NEWS. 713
0951-7855 See NUT EDUCATION REVIEW. 1769
0951-7871 See ENGINEERING SERVICES MANAGEMENT. 1974
0951-807X See RECENT ADVANCES IN CARDIAC ARRHYTHMIAS. 3709
0951-8088 See ATRIUM (LONDON). 292
0951-8207 See JOURNAL FOR THE STUDY OF THE PSEUDEPIGRAPHA. 4968
0951-8223 See MOORES & ROWLAND'S ORANGE TAX GUIDE. 4737
0951-8231 See MOORES & ROWLAND'S YELLOW TAX GUIDE. 4737
0951-824X See GROUPWORK LONDON. 5286
0951-8312 See OCEAN & COASTAL MANAGEMENT. 1453
0951-8320 See RELIABILITY ENGINEERING & SYSTEM SAFETY. 1993
0951-8339 See MARINE STRUCTURES. 4179
0951-838X See BOOKS AND PERIODICALS ONLINE. 3257
0951-8398 See INTERNATIONAL JOURNAL OF QUALITATIVE STUDIES IN EDUCATION : QSE. 1754
0951-8584 See HMSO ANNUAL CATALOGUE. 417
0951-8673 See WORLD AIRLINE FLEETS NEWS. 5400
0951-8711 See WHITAKER'S BOOKBANK CD-ROM SERVICE. 3256
0951-872X See GABBITAS, TRUMAN & THRING GUIDE TO BOARDING SCHOOLS AND COLLEGES, THE. 1747
0951-8819 See PANOSCOPE. 1511
0951-8827 See AT PRESS. 4631
0951-8835 See CATALOGUE AMENDMENT SERVICE. 4637
0951-919X See BUSINESS & ECONOMICS REVIEW. 645
0951-9327 See INFORMATION UPDATE/ DATABASE TECHNOLOGY. 1188
0951-9424 See ENVIRONMENT BUSINESS. 2165
0951-9580 See JOURNAL OF ORTHOPAEDIC RHEUMATOLOGY. 3882
0951-9599 See LIPID FILE. 3708
0951-9602 See CURRENT MEDICAL LITERATURE-INFECTIOUS DISEASES. 3980
0951-9610 See CURRENT MEDICAL LITERATURE / PAEDIATRICS. 3902
0951-9610 See CURRENT MEDICAL LITERATURE. PAEDIATRICS / THE ROYAL SOCIETY OF MEDICINE. 3902
0951-9629 See CURRENT MEDICAL LITERATURE / NEPHROLOGY AND UROLOGY. 3989
0951-9734 See RETAIL BUSINESS. MARKET SURVEYS / ECONOMIST INTELLIGENCE UNIT. 956
0951-9815 See COMMUNITY LIVING. 5280
0951-9882 See SALMON FARMING. 2312
0951-9904 See ONLINE HELIDATA. 31
0951-9998 See ENGINEERED MATERIALS ABSTRACTS. 2004
0952-0287 See WELDING ABSTRACTS / WELDING INSTITUTE. 4028
0952-0317 See DRUG TARGETING. 4301
0952-0384 See BIO-ELECTRONICS & BIOSENSORS. 443
0952-0406 See PROTEINS, POST-TRANSLATIONAL PROCESSING. 470
0952-0414 See RIBOSOMES & TRANSLATION. 551
0952-0422 See MEMBRANE LIPIDS. 490
0952-0481 See BRITISH JOURNAL OF ADDICTION. 1341
0952-0562 See ANNUAL OF CARDIAC SURGERY. 3959
0952-0600 See PULMONARY PHARMACOLOGY (EDINBURGH). 3951
0952-0627 See CURRENT PRACTICE IN SURGERY. 3963
0952-0643 See GULLET. 3579
0952-0686 See WIRE (LONDON, ENGLAND). 4159
0952-0708 See ICA. INTERNATIONAL COLOUR AUTHORITY. 5351
0952-1097 See ICSU SHORT REPORTS. 488
0952-1127 See INNOVATION IN MICROBIOLOGY SERIES. 563
0952-116X See ISLAMIC DEFENCE REVIEW. 4046
0952-1178 See JOURNAL OF HYPERTENSION. SUPPLEMENT. 3707
0952-1380 See SHEEP DAIRY NEWS. 221
0952-1402 See NEW FARMER AND GROWER. 111
0952-1453 See AGROFORESTRY ABSTRACTS. 2398
0952-147X See BIOTECHNOLOGY INFORMATION NEWS. 3689
0952-1488 See SCOTTISH BUSINESS INSIDER. 709
0952-1542 See CONTAMINATION CONTROL ABSTRACTS. 2183
0952-1895 See GOVERNANCE (OXFORD). 4651
0952-1909 See JOURNAL OF HISTORICAL SOCIOLOGY. 5249
0952-1917 See RATIO JURIS. 3034
0952-1941 See EUROPEAN JOURNAL OF ANAESTHESIOLOGY. SUPPLEMENT. 3682
0952-195X See KEESING'S UK RECORD. 4527
0952-1976 See ENGINEERING APPLICATIONS OF ARTIFICIAL INTELLIGENCE. 1212
0952-2131 See AIRLINER PRODUCTION LIST. 10
0952-2271 See HEALTH SERVICE JOURNAL, THE. 4781
0952-231X See OCCUPATIONAL PENSIONS. 2889
0952-2360 See PLAYBACK LONDON. 3241
0952-2433 See H.M. QUEEN ELIZABETH THE QUEEN MOTHER FELLOWSHIP. 3580
0952-2506 See LABOUR MARKET QUARTERLY REPORT. GREAT BRITAIN. 1686
0952-2638 See TOPICS IN NEUROCHEMISTRY AND NEUROPHARMACOLOGY. 3846
0952-2654 See HTFS DIGEST (1987). 2004
0952-2700 See GEOTITLES. 1363
0952-2832 See RESEARCH BULLETIN / BRITISH LIBRARY RESEARCH AND DEVELOPMENT DEPARTMENT. 3245
0952-2875 See CAT WORLD BRIGHTON. 5507
0952-2948 See BULLETIN OF TANZANIAN AFFAIRS. 2638
0952-3278 See PROSTAGLANDINS, LEUKOTRIENES, AND ESSENTIAL FATTY ACIDS. 3631
0952-3332 See ARCHAEOLOGICAL COMPUTING NEWSLETTER. 256
0952-3359 See UNIGRAM. X. 1249
0952-3367 See INTERNATIONAL JOURNAL OF THE HISTORY OF SPORT, THE. 4901
0952-3383 See BRITISH JOURNAL OF SPECIAL EDUCATION. 1876
0952-3391 See ESAO PROCEEDINGS / EUROPEAN SOCIETY FOR ARTIFICIAL ORGANS. 3575
0952-3480 See NMR IN BIOMEDICINE. 3622
0952-3499 See JMR. JOURNAL OF MOLECULAR RECOGNITION. 460
0952-357X See FOOD BIOTECHNOLOGY (LONDON). 3692
0952-3626 See DIRECTORY OF EUROPEAN INDUSTRIAL & TRADE ASSOCIATIONS. 1604
0952-3758 See AMBULANCE MANAGEMENT INTERNATIONAL. 3723
0952-3820 See EUROMARKETING : THE WEEKLY EUROPEAN NEWS BULLETIN FROM ADVERTISING AGE. 759
0952-3847 See PROGRESS IN RURAL POLICY AND PLANNING. 2832
0952-3863 See PLANT VARIETIES & SEEDS. 2427
0952-3871 See JOURNAL OF HUMAN NUTRITION AND DIETETICS. 4193

ISSN Index

0952-391X *See* EUROPEAN JOURNAL OF INTERCULTURAL STUDIES. **2261**

0952-3960 *See* EXPLOSIVES ENGINEERING. **2012**

0952-3987 *See* EMI. EDUCATIONAL MEDIA INTERNATIONAL. **1894**

0952-4096 *See* BILINGUAL FAMILY NEWSLETTER, THE. **2277**

0952-4290 *See* AFRICA NEWSFILE. **1544**

0952-4622 *See* BIOACOUSTICS (BERKHAMSTED). **5578**

0952-4630 *See* SPORTS MEDICINE BULLETIN (LONDON, ENGLAND). **3956**

0952-4649 *See* JOURNAL OF DESIGN HISTORY. **2099**

0952-4738 *See* RESEARCH & SURVEY IN NATURE CONSERVATION. **2203**

0952-4746 *See* JOURNAL OF RADIOLOGICAL PROTECTION. **4436**

0952-4975 *See* STUDIES IN ANCIENT CHRONOLOGY. **2631**

0952-5041 *See* JOURNAL OF MOLECULAR ENDOCRINOLOGY. **3731**

0952-5211 *See* MATERIALS EDGE. **4008**

0952-5238 *See* VISUAL NEUROSCIENCE. **3847**

0952-5300 *See* TOPICS IN ENGINEERING. **1999**

0952-5424 *See* PROGRESS IN TOURISM, RECREATION, AND HOSPITALITY MANAGEMENT. **5489**

0952-5432 *See* INTERNATIONAL JOURNAL OF OPTOELECTRONICS. **4435**

0952-5475 *See* MONTHLY NEWSLETTER FOR THE DATACOMM'S INDUSTRY. **1238**

0952-5505 *See* IRON AND STEEL INDUSTRY ANNUAL STATISTICS FOR THE UNITED KINGDOM. **4025**

0952-5513 *See* JOURNAL OF THE HISTORIC FARM BUILDINGS GROUP. **618**

0952-5556 *See* YEARBOOK OF CO-OPERATIVE ENTERPRISE. **1544**

0952-5734 *See* WORLD TRADE STEEL. **1540**

0952-5734 *See* WORLD TRADE STEEL. **1632**

0952-5742 *See* WORLD TRADE STAINLESS, HIGH SPEED AND OTHER ALLOY STEEL. **4026**

0952-5793 *See* SURVEYING TECHNICIAN. **2032**

0952-5807 *See* STRUCTURAL ENGINEERING REVIEW. **2031**

0952-617X *See* INTERNATIONAL JOURNAL OF COMPARATIVE LABOUR LAW AND INDUSTRIAL RELATIONS, THE. **3149**

0952-6196 *See* NEW MATERIALS KOREA. **2107**

0952-620X *See* THOMAS COOK EUROPEAN TIMETABLE. **5437**

0952-6293 *See* ANNUAL OF GASTROINTESTINAL ENDOSCOPY. **3743**

0952-6315 *See* INTERNATIONAL JOURNAL OF COMPUTERS IN ADULT EDUCATION AND TRAINING. **1190**

0952-6390 *See* PRIESTS & PEOPLE. **5034**

0952-6439 *See* SCOTTISH LITERARY JOURNAL. SUPPLEMENT. **3434**

0952-648X *See* STAND MAGAZINE. **3439**

0952-6498 *See* SCOTTISH ECONOMIC BULLETIN. **1583**

0952-6757 *See* PHONOLOGY. **3310**

0952-6803 *See* INTERNATIONAL STEEL STATISTICS : SUMMARY TABLES. **4025**

0952-6862 *See* INTERNATIONAL JOURNAL OF HEALTH CARE QUALITY ASSURANCE. **4785**

0952-6900 *See* ENGINEERING PLASTICS. **4455**

0952-6919 *See* COMPOSITE POLYMERS. **4454**

0952-6951 *See* HISTORY OF THE HUMAN SCIENCES. **5201**

0952-7001 *See* WHAT'S NEW IN BUSINESS INFORMATION. **719**

0952-701X *See* FASHION FORECAST INTERNATIONAL. **1084**

0952-7052 *See* KEY ABSTRACTS. MACHINE VISION. **1209**

0952-7060 *See* KEY ABSTRACTS. MICROELECTRONICS AND PRINTED CIRCUITS. **2005**

0952-7079 *See* KEY ABSTRACTS. MICROWAVE TECHNOLOGY. **2005**

0952-7125 *See* OFFSHORE CENTRES REPORT. **4267**

0952-7168 *See* REVIEWS ON IMMUNOASSAY TECHNOLOGY. **3676**

0952-7222 *See* ANNUAL REPORT / THE ROWETT RESEARCH INSTITUTE. **5503**

0952-7427 *See* AIDS LETTER, THE. **3664**

0952-7494 *See* CURRENT MEDICAL LITERATURE ORTHOPAEDICS. **3881**

0952-7516 *See* ASIAN COMMUNICATIONS. **1149**

0952-7524 *See* SOUTHSCAN. **4496**

0952-7583 *See* BRITISH JOURNAL OF ENTOMOLOGY AND NATURAL HISTORY. **4163**

0952-7613 *See* WORLD INTELLECTUAL PROPERTY REPORT. **1309**

0952-7648 *See* JOURNAL OF MEDITERRANEAN ARCHAEOLOGY. **271**

0952-7788 *See* UK PESTICIDE GUIDE, THE. **4248**

0952-7907 *See* CURRENT OPINION IN ANAESTHESIOLOGY. **3682**

0952-7915 *See* CURRENT OPINION IN IMMUNOLOGY. **3668**

0952-7923 *See* INFORMATION TECHNOLOGY & LEARNING. **1286**

0952-8040 *See* SOUTHERN AFRICAN REVIEW OF BOOKS. **3438**

0952-8059 *See* INTERNATIONAL JOURNAL FOR THE SEMIOTICS OF LAW. **2984**

0952-8067 *See* ASIA PACIFIC INTERNATIONAL JOURNAL OF BUSINESS LOGISTICS. **640**

0952-8075 *See* CURRENT AIDS LITERATURE. **3668**

0952-8083 *See* COMMONWEALTH YEARBOOK, THE. **4639**

0952-8091 *See* INTERNATIONAL JOURNAL OF COMPUTER APPLICATIONS IN TECHNOLOGY. **1190**

0952-813X *See* JOURNAL OF EXPERIMENTAL & THEORETICAL ARTIFICIAL INTELLIGENCE. **1214**

0952-8156 *See* HABS. HOUSING ABSTRACTS. **2823**

0952-8172 *See* MOLECULAR BIOTHERAPY. **465**

0952-8180 *See* JOURNAL OF CLINICAL ANESTHESIA. **3683**

0952-8199 *See* FAMILY COURT REPORTER. **3120**

0952-8210 *See* LEISURE OPPORTUNITIES. **4852**

0952-8229 *See* PSYCHOLOGIST, THE. **4612**

0952-8245 *See* BULLETIN - OVERSEAS DEVELOPMENT NATURAL RESOURCES INSTITUTE. **70**

0952-8369 *See* JOURNAL OF ZOOLOGY (1987). **5589**

0952-8377 *See* ECN CHEMSCOPE. **974**

0952-8407 *See* CHELYS (VIOLA DA GAMBA SOCIETY). **4109**

0952-8571 *See* FRANCO-BRITISH STUDIES : JOURNAL OF THE BRITISH INSTITUTE IN PARIS. **3282**

0952-8733 *See* HIGHER EDUCATION POLICY. **1828**

0952-8768 *See* SOFTWARE FOR ENGINEERING AND WORKSTATIONS. **1203**

0952-8776 *See* RISK (LONDON. 1987). **810**

0952-8784 *See* LONDON DIRECTORY FOR TRADE AND INDUSTRY, THE. **844**

0952-8822 *See* THIRD TEXT. **366**

0952-8865 *See* PROGRAM LONDON. 1987. **1248**

0952-8873 *See* JOURNAL OF ENVIRONMENTAL LAW. **3113**

0952-8911 *See* ENGINEERING OPTICS : AN INSTITUTE OF PHYSICS JOURNAL. **1973**

0952-892X *See* DOCUMENT SUPPLY NEWS. **3208**

0952-8962 *See* ORGANIC FARMING INDEX. **117**

0952-8997 *See* NEWSLETTER OF THE JEWISH LAW ASSOCIATION. **5051**

0952-9136 *See* CHILD ABUSE REVIEW. **5277**

0952-9500 *See* JOURNAL OF DRUG DEVELOPMENT. **4311**

0952-9543 *See* CONSUMER USA. **1296**

0952-956X *See* EUROPEAN ELECTRICAL APPLIANCES MARKETING DIRECTORY. **2054**

0952-9594 *See* RETAIL MONITOR INTERNATIONAL. **957**

0952-9608 *See* MENTAL HANDICAP RESEARCH. **3930**

0952-9616 *See* SCIENCE AND TECHNOLOGY POLICY. **5151**

0952-9748 *See* EDUCATION BULLETIN COUNCIL FOR BRITISH ARCHAEOLOGY. **267**

0952-9756 *See* CHINA-BRITAIN TRADE REVIEW. **827**

0952-9764 *See* DIRECT RESPONSE. **923**

0952-987X *See* BOOKS MAGAZINE. **4826**

0952-987X *See* BOOKS (LONDON,1987). **4826**

0952-9950 *See* CLOVER NEWSPAPER INDEX. **5811**

0953-0061 *See* IMA JOURNAL OF MATHEMATICS APPLIED IN BUSINESS AND INDUSTRY. **3508**

0953-0096 *See* AIDS ACTION. **3663**

0953-0223 *See* INTERNATIONAL FINANCING REVIEW. **792**

0953-024X *See* NATIONAL GALLERIES OF SCOTLAND EDINBURGH. 1987. **4093**

0953-0258 *See* EUROPEAN DIRECTORY OF NON-OFFICIAL STATISTICAL SOURCES. **5327**

0953-0282 *See* SIPRI YEARBOOK 1987. **4535**

0953-0355 *See* GOLDSMITHS REVIEW. **2914**

0953-0398 *See* WHITAKER'S BOOKS IN PRINT. **427**

0953-0401 *See* WHITAKER'S BOOKS IN PRINT [MICROFORM]. **427**

0953-041X *See* WHITAKER'S BOOK LIST. **427**

0953-0428 *See* AREE. ANNUAL REVIEW OF ENVIRONMENTAL EDUCATION. **2161**

0953-0460 *See* SERIALS (OXFORD, ENGLAND). **3249**

0953-0495 *See* HEART LONDON. 1987. **3705**

0953-0576 *See* RADIO CONTROL MODEL CARS. **2777**

0953-0584 *See* MODEL RAILWAYS (1987). **2775**

0953-0592 *See* PRACTICAL WARGAMER. **2777**

0953-0673 *See* ALIMENTARY PHARMACOLOGY & THERAPEUTICS SUPPLEMENT. **4290**

0953-0681 *See* DESIGN & APPLIED ARTS INDEX. **334**

0953-0711 *See* EUROBUSINESS (LONDON). **672**

0953-0754 *See* GEORGE ELIOT, GEORGE HENRY LEWES NEWSLETTER, THE. **3390**

0953-0800 *See* REGIONAL FURNITURE. **252**

0953-0975 *See* WASTE & ENVIRONMENT TODAY. NEWS JOURNAL. **2246**

0953-1033 *See* OIL & ENERGY TRENDS ANNUAL STATISTICAL REVIEW. **4284**

0953-1084 *See* COMMISSION OF THE EUROPEAN COMMUNITIES HEALTH SERVICES RESEARCH SERIES. **4771**

0953-1130 *See* RUSKIN NEWSLETTER, THE. **4096**

0953-1262 *See* KEY ABSTRACTS. HIGH-TEMPERATURE SUPERCONDUCTORS. **2005**

0953-1424 *See* MAGNESIUM RESEARCH : OFFICIAL ORGAN OF THE INTERNATIONAL SOCIETY FOR THE DEVELOPMENT OF RESEARCH ON MAGNESIUM. **3605**

0953-1513 *See* LEARNED PUBLISHING. **4816**

0953-1580 *See* AIDS INFORMATION. **3664**

0953-203X *See* OFF ROAD AND 4 WHEEL DRIVE. **5422**

0953-2048 *See* SUPERCONDUCTOR SCIENCE & TECHNOLOGY. **4445**

0953-2110 *See* MAINTENANCE FARNHAM. **1985**

0953-2161 *See* YOGA AND HEALTH. **4365**

0953-2188 *See* FRUIT GROWER MAIDSTONE. **172**

0953-220X *See* JOURNAL OF ARCHITECTURAL THEORY AND CRITICISM / UIA. **302**

0953-2226 *See* BIOTECH KNOWLEDGE SOURCES. **3688**

0953-2331 *See* 3D LONDON. **1169**

0953-2366 *See* TUBE & PIPE TECHNOLOGY. **4023**

0953-2404 See TEXTILE TECHNOLOGY INTERNATIONAL. 5358
0953-2412 See STEEL TECHNOLOGY INTERNATIONAL. 4020
0953-2455 See ANNUAL REPORT / HORTICULTURE RESEARCH INTERNATIONAL. 2409
0953-2463 See CROP PROTECTION DIRECTORY UNITED KINGDOM ED. 169
0953-2501 See CURRENT MEDICAL LITERATURE-GERIATRICS. 3750
0953-2579 See ACCOUNTING WORLD. 738
0953-2617 1761
0953-2625 See INSIDE IT. 1189
0953-2714 See INTERNATIONAL INSIDER. 1496
0953-2773 See ORIGINS BIBLICAL CREATION SOCIETY. 4984
0953-2781 See AQUACULTURE INFORMATION SERIES. 2295
0953-2919 See EDINBURGH ANTHROPOLOGY. 235
0953-3028 See GREEN TEACHER (BRITISH EDITION). 2173
0953-3133 See QUALITY OF MARKETS QUARTERLY. 912
0953-3222 See OXFORD ENGINEERING SCIENCE SERIES. 1990
0953-3257 See COMPUTERS IN AFRICA. 1179
0953-3362 See OPCS MONITOR. LEGAL ABORTIONS / OFFICE OF POPULATION CENSUS & SURVEYS. 4555
0953-4016 See SOVIET TECHNOLOGY ALERT. 5159
0953-4075 See JOURNAL OF PHYSICS. B : ATOMIC, MOLECULAR, AND OPTICAL PHYSICS. 4409
0953-4091 See HP WORLD : THE INDEPENDENT EUROPEAN MAGAZINE FOR HEWLETT PACKARD COMPUTER USERS. 1186
0953-4148 See SAC ECONOMIC REPORT. 131
0953-4180 See BEHAVIOURAL NEUROLOGY. 3828
0953-4377 See PRISON REPORT. 3108
0953-4385 See CHRISTIAN HERALD WORTHING. 5058
0953-4431 See CLINICAL EYE AND VISION CARE. 3873
0953-4466 See AQUATIC ENVIRONMENT PROTECTION : ANALYTICAL METHODS. 2211
0953-4474 See APPLE BUSINESS. 1171
0953-4776 See SOFT DRINKS MANAGEMENT INTERNATIONAL. 2371
0953-4806 See ENCYCLOPEDIA OF MATHEMATICS AND ITS APPLICATIONS. 3505
0953-4814 *See* JOURNAL OF ORGANIZATIONAL CHANGE MANAGEMENT. 874
0953-4822 See GERMAN TEACHING. 3283
0953-4857 See WORLD WAR II INVESTIGATOR. 2633
0953-4962 See CAST METALS. 3999
0953-4970 See DEFENCE SYSTEMS MODERNISATION. 4040
0953-4997 See ECONOMIC AWARENESS. 1482
0953-5004 See LLOYDS BANK ANNUAL REVIEW. 1572
0953-5047 See FOOD MAGAZINE LONDON. 1988. 2338
0953-5055 See ONLINE BUSINESS SOURCEBOOK. 1275
0953-5217 See COMPUTER AUDIT UPDATE. 1256
0953-5225 See SOCIAL WORK AND SOCIAL SCIENCES REVIEW. 5309
0953-5233 See GENDER & HISTORY. 5557
0953-5284 See NETWORK WEEK. 1160
0953-5314 See ECONOMIC SYSTEMS RESEARCH. 1485
0953-5349 See OOPS REPORT, THE. 1280
0953-5365 See BIOLOGICAL SCIENCES REVIEW. 445
0953-5411 See GULF STATES NEWSLETTER. 1493
0953-542X See BRITANNIA MONOGRAPH SERIES. 411

0953-5438 See INTERACTING WITH COMPUTERS. 1189
0953-5543 See OR INSIGHT. 1770
0953-5551 See EXPERT SYSTEMS FOR INFORMATION MANAGEMENT. 1212
0953-556X See INTERNATIONAL JOURNAL OF INFORMATION AND LIBRARY RESEARCH. 3218
0953-5586 See CAP LEGISLATION. 72
0953-5594 See CAP WEEKLY. 72
0953-5632 See ICB. 790
0953-5640 See REACTIONS (LONDON). 2891
0953-5683 See IEE REVIEW. 2058
0953-5705 See BRITISH EQUAL OPPORTUNITIES CASES. 2943
0953-5985 See IEE MATERIALS & DEVICES SERIES. 2057
0953-6000 See AIRING EDINBURGH. 1211
0953-6132 See OWEN'S AFRICA BUSINESS DIRECTORY. 702
0953-6191 See BULLETIN OF THE SUTTON HOO RESEARCH COMMITTEE. 264
0953-6205 See EUROPEAN JOURNAL OF INTERNAL MEDICINE. 3796
0953-6612 See PRACTICE NURSE. 3867
0953-6620 See FUTURES AND OPTIONS WORLD. 924
0953-6639 See PROFESSIONAL ENGINEERING. 2127
0953-6698 See MODERN PAINTERS (LONDON, ENGLAND). 358
0953-6779 See PALLIATIVE CARE INDEX. 3625
0953-6787 See CURRENT MEDICAL LITERATURE. BREAST AND PROSTRATE CANCER/THE ROYAL SOCIETY OF MEDICINE. 3759
0953-6833 See COMMUNITY EYE HEALTH. 3873
0953-6841 See TELEVISION BUSINESS INTERNATIONAL : TBI. 1140
0953-685X See BUSINESS STUDIES. 653
0953-6884 See ANNUAL REVIEW / THE EDINBURGH SCHOOL OF AGRICULTURE. 62
0953-6906 See WESTERN EUROPE. 2525
0953-6973 See JOURNAL (ROYAL INSTITUTE OF BRITISH ARCHITECTS : OVERSEAS ED.). 302
0953-7007 See NATIONAL MUSEUMS OF SCOTLAND ... REPORT. 4093
0953-7031 See PRIVATE BANKER INTERNATIONAL. 804
0953-7104 See PLATELETS. 3773
0953-7112 See CURRENT ANAESTHESIA AND CRITICAL CARE. 3963
0953-7139 See URBAN TRANSPORT INTERNATIONAL. 5399
0953-7147 See DISTRIBUTION BUSINESS. 954
0953-7155 See OCCASIONAL PAPER / SOCIETY OF ANTIQUARIES OF LONDON. 2701
0953-7252 See PARALLELOGRAM INTERNATIONAL. 1198
0953-7279 See PROFESSIONAL CALENDAR. 3242
0953-7287 See PRODUCTION PLANNING & CONTROL. 1622
0953-7325 See TECHNOLOGY ANALYSIS & STRATEGIC MANAGEMENT. 5163
0953-7414 See TOXIC SUBSTANCES BULLETIN. 3983
0953-7511 See BULLETIN / BRITISH SOCIETY FOR MUSIC THERAPY. 4105
0953-7554 See TROTSKYIST INTERNATIONAL. 4548
0953-7562 See MYCOLOGICAL RESEARCH. 575
0953-7589 See HYDROTITLES DIDCOT. 1363
0953-7708 See PC MAGAZINE. 1271
0953-7767 See RESEARCH MONOGRAPHS IN PARALLEL AND DISTRIBUTED COMPUTING. 1201
0953-7856 See IMI. INTERACTIVE MEDIA INTERNATIONAL. 1113
0953-7899 See PUBLISHERS REPORTS. 4819
0953-7929 See MULTINATIONAL EMPLOYER. 944

0953-8089 See CRAWFORD'S DIRECTORY OF CITY CONNECTIONS. 4641
0953-816X See EUROPEAN JOURNAL OF NEUROSCIENCE, THE. 3832
0953-8178 See INTERNATIONAL IMMUNOLOGY. 3672
0953-8186 See INTERNATIONAL JOURNAL OF REFUGEE LAW. 3130
0953-8194 See JOURNAL OF NEUROENDOCRINOLOGY. 3836
0953-8208 See UTILITAS. 2253
0953-8240 See COACH AND BUS WEEK. 5411
0953-8259 See REVIEW OF POLITICAL ECONOMY. 4494
0953-8348 See KEY INDICATORS. 2307
0953-8402 See NETWORK MONITOR. 1196
0953-8429 See TELECOM WORLD. 1165
0953-8534 See HEALTH SERVICES MANAGEMENT. 3781
0953-8542 See WILTON PARK PAPERS. 4538
0953-8550 See GARDENS OF ENGLAND AND WALES 1988. 2416
0953-8577 See PARAGRAPH POOLE. 2851
0953-8585 See PHYSICS WORLD. 4416
0953-8674 See CONSERVATION BULLETIN. 4087
0953-8690 See CANMAKER AND CANNER, THE. 4218
0953-8771 See INTERACTIVE UPDATE. 1189
0953-8860 See FISH TRADER YEARBOOK. 2301
0953-895X See TOPIC WINDSOR. 1788
0953-8984 See JOURNAL OF PHYSICS. CONDENSED MATTER : AN INSTITUTE OF PHYSICS JOURNAL. 4409
0953-9026 See SHELL AGRICULTURE 1988. 134
0953-9182 See CONTEMPORARY REVIEWS IN OBSTETRICS AND GYNAECOLOGY. 3759
0953-9212 See SERVICE MANAGEMENT. 5157
0953-9263 See BUSINESS INFORMATION BASICS. 649
0953-931X See CRAFT HISTORY. 371
0953-9344 See PROGRAM NOW. 1281
0953-9611 See GEOGRAPHICAL ABSTRACTS. HUMAN GEOGRAPHY. 2580
0953-9638 See LIBRARY WORK. 3228
0953-9743 See HOSPITAL MANAGEMENT INTERNATIONAL / INTERNATIONAL HOSPITAL FEDERATION. 3784
0953-9794 See BASE METAL CONCENTRATES. 3998
0953-9816 See AFRICAN WOMAN. 5550
0953-9859 *See* JOURNAL OF WILDERNESS MEDICINE. 3600
0953-9875 See CLINICAL SPORTS MEDICINE. 3953
0953-9891 See PAINT & INK INTERNATIONAL. 4224
0953-9905 See BSA ANNUAL REPORT. 602
0953-9964 See EDUCATION AND THE LAW. 1738
0954-0075 See LUBRICATION SCIENCE. 1985
0954-0083 See HIGH PERFORMANCE POLYMERS. 977
0954-0091 See CONNECTION SCIENCE. 1212
0954-0105 See FOOD AND AGRICULTURAL IMMUNOLOGY. 563
0954-0121 See AIDS CARE. 3663
0954-0172 See YEARBOOK OF WORLD ELECTRONICS DATA ... VOL. 2, AMERICA, JAPAN & ASIA PACIFIC. 2086
0954-0180 See YEARBOOK OF WORLD ELECTRONICS DATA ... VOL. 1, WEST EUROPE. 2086
0954-0253 See GENDER AND EDUCATION. 5187
0954-0261 See INTERNATIONAL REVIEW OF PSYCHIATRY (ABINGDON, ENGLAND). 3927
0954-027X See JOURNAL OF HARD MATERIALS. 5118
0954-0369 See GETTING ABOUT BRITAIN. 5478
0954-0393 See ELECTRONIC PAYMENTS INTERNATIONAL. 671
0954-0423 See MUSEUM REPORTER. 4092

0954-0504 *See* GEOGRAPHICAL ABSTRACTS : PHYSICAL GEOGRAPHY. 2580

0954-0512 *See* GEOLOGICAL ABSTRACTS. 1362

0954-0547 *See* CAMBRIDGE STUDIES IN POPULATION, ECONOMY AND SOCIETY IN PAST TIME. 4550

0954-0628 *See* OFFSHORE INVESTMENT. 910

0954-0695 *See* ELECTRONICS & COMMUNICATIONS ENGINEERING JOURNAL. 2049

0954-0725 *See* JOURNAL OF REPRODUCTION & FERTILITY. ABSTRACT SERIES / SOCIETY FOR THE STUDY OF FERTILITY. 583

0954-0741 *See* PHYSIOTHERAPY IN SPORT. 3955

0954-0822 *See* SPECIAL EDUCATIONAL NEEDS ABSTRACTS. 1797

0954-0881 *See* VIGIL. 3451

0954-0911 *See* SOLDERING & SURFACE MOUNT TECHNOLOGY : JOURNAL OF THE SMART (SURFACE MOUNT & RELATED TECHNOLOGIES) GROUP. 4019

0954-092X *See* ROYAL AIR FORCE YEARBOOK. 34

0954-0954 *See* AUSTRALIAN STUDIES. 2669

0954-0962 *See* PUBLIC MONEY & MANAGEMENT. 4743

0954-0970 *See* BUNYAN STUDIES. 3370

0954-1020 *See* ANTARCTIC SCIENCE. 5084

0954-1063 *See* AKTUELL AUF DEUTSCH. 2513

0954-1071 *See* HOME FURNISHINGS TONBRIDGE. 2906

0954-1098 *See* LIVING EARTH (BRISTOL). 105

0954-1179 *See* BULLETIN OF JUDAEO-GREEK STUDIES. 5046

0954-1306 *See* OXFORD TODAY. 2521

0954-1314 *See* JOURNAL OF INTERNATIONAL FINANCIAL MANAGEMENT & ACCOUNTING. 747

0954-1381 *See* LITHIUM (EDINBURGH). 4314

0954-139X *See* REVIEWS IN MEDICAL MICROBIOLOGY : A JOURNAL OF THE PATHOLOGICAL SOCIETY OF GREAT BRITAIN AND IRELAND. 3634

0954-1438 *See* INTERIOR LONDON. 5352

0954-1446 *See* EUROPEAN JOURNAL OF COGNITIVE PSYCHOLOGY, THE. 4586

0954-1608 *See* CV : JOURNAL OF ART AND CRAFTS. 372

0954-1675 *See* EUROPEAN VENTURE CAPITAL JOURNAL : EUROPEAN VCJ. 1490

0954-1748 *See* JOURNAL OF INTERNATIONAL DEVELOPMENT. 1500

0954-1810 *See* ARTIFICIAL INTELLIGENCE IN ENGINEERING. 1211

0954-1837 *See* DIAGNOSTICS BUSINESS. 665

0954-190X *See* ODI INDEX TO DEVELOPMENT LITERATURE. 3419

0954-1985 *See* ECONOMICS & POLITICS (OXFORD, ENGLAND). 1486

0954-206X *See* SOCIAL INVENTIONS. 5259

0954-2116 *See* NEW WELSH REVIEW, THE. 3416

0954-2191 *See* THEOLOGICAL BOOK REVIEW. 5003

0954-2264 *See* OPTICAL COMPUTING & PROCESSING. 1277

0954-2299 *See* CHEMICAL SPECIATION AND BIOAVAILABILITY. 2162

0954-2361 *See* NEW STATESMAN & SOCIETY. 5210

0954-237X *See* RADAR BULLETIN. 4393

0954-2396 *See* REFLECTIONS ON HIGHER EDUCATION. 1843

0954-254X *See* JOURNAL OF SOVIET MILITARY STUDIES, THE. 4048

0954-2582 *See* VASCULAR MEDICINE REVIEW. 3802

0954-2612 *See* IT LINK. 3219

0954-2655 1906

0954-2809 *See* LAW FOR BUSINESS. 3101

0954-2833 *See* PC BUSINESS SOFTWARE. 1270

0954-2892 *See* INTERNATIONAL JOURNAL OF PUBLIC OPINION RESEARCH. 5248

0954-2957 *See* ASIA PACIFIC INTERNATIONAL MANAGEMENT REVIEW. 860

0954-2965 *See* KEROUAC CONNECTION. 3401

0954-2981 *See* EASTERN BLOC ENERGY. 1937

0954-3007 *See* EUROPEAN JOURNAL OF CLINICAL NUTRITION. 4190

0954-3082 *See* EXPLORATIONS IN SOCIOLOGY. 5245

0954-3201 *See* DISPENSING OPTICS. 4215

0954-3244 *See* EPJOURNAL. 4814

0954-3333 *See* PULMONARY PHARMACOLOGY SHEFFIELD. 4327

0954-3384 *See* SEARCHLIGHT SOUTH AFRICA. 4546

0954-3465 See INTERNATIONAL JOURNAL OF FOOD SCIENCES AND NUTRITION. 4192

0954-349X *See* STRUCTURAL CHANGE AND ECONOMIC DYNAMICS. 1522

0954-3538 *See* NEW MATERIALS INTERNATIONAL. 1619

0954-3589 *See* CURRENT MILITARY & POLITICAL LITERATURE. 4061

0954-3600 *See* CD-ROM NEWSLETTER ALTON. 1276

0954-3635 *See* SOCIALIST LAWYER. 4547

0954-3732 *See* JOURNAL - NATIONAL ASSOCIATION OF CAREERS AND GUIDANCE TEACHERS. 1756

0954-3732 *See* CAREER EDUCATION AND GUIDANCE. 1730

0954-3848 *See* JANE'S AIR LAUNCHED WEAPONS. 4046

0954-3880 *See* PARKS, GOLF COURSES & SPORTS GROUNDS (1975). 4707

0954-3899 *See* JOURNAL OF PHYSICS. G: NUCLEAR AND PARTICLE PHYSICS. 4448

0954-3945 *See* LANGUAGE VARIATION AND CHANGE. 3296

0954-3988 *See* FAST FERRY INTERNATIONAL. 593

0954-4054 *See* PROCEEDINGS OF THE INSTITUTION OF MECHANICAL ENGINEERS. PART B, JOURNAL OF ENGINEERING MANUFACTURE. 2126

0954-4062 *See* PROCEEDINGS OF THE INSTITUTION OF MECHANICAL ENGINEERS. PART C, JOURNAL OF MECHANICAL ENGINEERING SCIENCE. 2126

0954-4070 *See* PROCEEDINGS OF THE INSTITUTION OF MECHANICAL ENGINEERS. PART D, JOURNAL OF AUTOMOBILE ENGINEERING. 2126

0954-4089 *See* PROCEEDINGS OF THE INSTITUTION OF MECHANICAL ENGINEERS. PART E, JOURNAL OF PROCESS MECHANICAL ENGINEERING. 2126

0954-4097 *See* PROCEEDINGS OF THE INSTITUTION OF MECHANICAL ENGINEERS. PART F, JOURNAL OF RAIL AND RAPID TRANSIT. 2126

0954-4100 *See* PROCEEDINGS OF THE INSTITUTION OF MECHANICAL ENGINEERS. PART G, JOURNAL OF AEROSPACE ENGINEERING. 32

0954-4119 *See* PROCEEDINGS OF THE INSTITUTION OF MECHANICAL ENGINEERS. PART H, JOURNAL OF ENGINEERING IN MEDICINE. 3696

0954-4127 *See* TOTAL QUALITY MANAGEMENT. 888

0954-416X *See* AFRICAN LANGUAGES AND CULTURES. 3262

0954-4178 *See* ARTSCRIBE. 342

0954-4194 *See* SCIENCE & CHRISTIAN BELIEF. 4995

0954-4224 *See* NUTRITION RESEARCH REVIEWS. 4197

0954-4240 *See* DECANTER (LONDON. 1985). 2366

0954-4755 *See* ORTHOPAEDIC PRODUCT NEWS. 3883

0954-478X *See* TQM MAGAZINE (INTERNATIONAL ED.). 888

0954-4828 *See* JOURNAL OF ENGINEERING DESIGN. 2099

0954-4836 *See* MBA REVIEW. 1835

0954-4879 *See* TERRA NOVA. 1411

0954-495X See WASTE & ENVIRONMENT TODAY. BIBLIOGRAPHIC JOURNAL. 2246

0954-5395 *See* HUMAN RESOURCE MANAGEMENT JOURNAL. 942

0954-5514 *See* INSURANCE SYSTEMS INTERNATIONAL. 2884

0954-5581 *See* DIAMOND INSIGHT. 2914

0954-562X *See* GOOD NEWS EXETER. 4960

0954-5697 *See* VOICE OF THE ARAB WORLD. INTELLIGENCE REPORT. 2509

0954-576X *See* JOURNAL OF HEALTH AND SAFETY, THE. 4786

0954-5794 *See* DEVELOPMENT AND PSYCHOPATHOLOGY. 4584

0954-5824 *See* ENVIRONMENTAL ENGINEERING (BURY SAINT EDMUNDS, ENG. : 1988). 1975

0954-5832 *See* AEROSPACE COMPOSITES & MATERIALS. 5

0954-5867 *See* CAMBRIDGE OPERA JOURNAL. 4107

0954-5875 *See* UNITED KINGDOM MEAT MARKET REVIEW. 223

0954-593X *See* ANTIQUE CLOCKS. 2916

0954-6030 *See* POLITICS AND SOCIETY IN GERMANY, AUSTRIA, AND SWITZERLAND. 5254

0954-6111 *See* RESPIRATORY MEDICINE. 3951

0954-6154 *See* EDI UPDATE LONDON. 4721

0954-6219 *See* HOLSTEIN FRIESIAN JOURNAL (RICKMANSWORTH). 195

0954-6235 *See* VENDING INTERNATIONAL. 2360

0954-6235 *See* VENDING INTERNATIONAL. 937

0954-6286 *See* PC YEAR BOOK. 1245

0954-6316 *See* TRANSACTIONS OF THE YORKSHIRE DIALECT SOCIETY. 3329

0954-6324 *See* WILDFOWL (SLIMBRIDGE). 5621

0954-6510 *See* WORLDAIDS. 3677

0954-6529 *See* MECHANICAL INCORPORATED ENGINEER. 2122

0954-6545 *See* REVOLUTIONARY RUSSIA. 2706

0954-6553 *See* TERRORISM AND POLITICAL VIOLENCE. 4536

0954-6561 *See* MULTI-USER COMPUTING. 1242

0954-6634 *See* JOURNAL OF DERMATOLOGICAL TREATMENT, THE. 3721

0954-6642 *See* APPLIED AND THEORETICAL ELECTROPHORESIS. 1013

0954-6650 *See* JOURNAL OF THE HISTORY OF COLLECTIONS. 4090

0954-6782 *See* AFRICAN REVIEW OF BUSINESS AND TECHNOLOGY. 5081

0954-6820 *See* JOURNAL OF INTERNAL MEDICINE. 3798

0954-6839 *See* SLOVO (LONDON, ENGLAND). 4496

0954-691X *See* EUROPEAN JOURNAL OF GASTROENTEROLOGY & HEPATOLOGY. 3744

0954-6928 *See* CORONARY ARTERY DISEASE. 3703

0954-7010 *See* ANNUAL REPORT / MACAULAY LAND USE RESEARCH INSTITUTE. 163

0954-7029 *See* BULLETIN - SOMERSET INDUSTRIAL ARCHAEOLOGICAL SOCIETY. 265

0954-7037 *See* TROUT NEWS. 2315

0954-7053 *See* TAXATION INTERNATIONAL. 4755

0954-7096 *See* THREADS LONDON. 1205

0954-7118 *See* INTERNATIONAL JOURNAL OF GLOBAL ENERGY ISSUES. 1948

0954-7126 *See* MAPPING AWARENESS. 1194

0954-712636 *See* MAPPING AWARENESS & GIS EUROPE. 1242

0954-7169 *See* JOURNAL OF MUSEUM ETHNOGRAPHY / MUSEUM ETHNOGRAPHERS' GROUP. 239

0954-7185 *See* POULTRY JOURNAL 1987. 218

0954-7274 *See* TAX JOURNAL, THE. 4753

0954-7304 *See* EDUCATIONAL & TRAINING TECHNOLOGY INTERNATIONAL : ETTI. 1741

0954-7479 See COMPUTING, COMMUNICATIONS & MEDIA TREND MONITOR. **1180**

0954-7487 See CRITIQUE (LONDON). **3205**

0954-7517 See ASIA PACIFIC INTERNATIONAL JOURNAL OF MARKETING. **921**

0954-7541 See INTERNATIONAL JOURNAL OF WINE MARKETING. **2368**

0954-7649 See JANE'S AIRPORT REVIEW. **25**

0954-7762 See NURSING TIMES (1987). **3865**

0954-7800 See SOCIETY FOR THE STUDY OF HUMAN BIOLOGY SYMPOSIUM SERIES. **473**

0954-7843 See COUNTRY TIMES AND LANDSCAPE. **296**

0954-7894 See CLINICAL AND EXPERIMENTAL ALLERGY. **3667**

0954-7940 See IT TRAINING. **1223**

0954-8106 See COMPANY ACCOUNTANT. **741**

0954-8211 See RADIOGRAPHY TODAY. **4441**

0954-8521 See PHILLIPS INTERNATIONAL PAPER DIRECTORY. **4237**

0954-853X See GAS INDUSTRY DIRECTORY. **4257**

0954-8548 See BENN'S GUIDE. **600**

0954-8602 See REVIEWS IN CONTEMPORARY PHARMACOTHERAPY. **4328**

0954-867X See ZZAP! 64. **1245**

0954-8750 See GQ (UK EDITION). **3995**

0954-8769 See SCOTTISH BOOK COLLECTOR. **4819**

0954-8874 See DEAN ARCHAEOLOGY. **266**

0954-8890 See AFRICAN JOURNAL OF INTERNATIONAL AND COMPARATIVE LAW. **3122**

0954-8912 See ARABIAN BUSINESS COMPUTING. **1171**

0954-8947 See SURGICAL NURSE. **3870**

0954-8963 See CULTURAL TRENDS. **318**

0954-898X See NETWORK (BRISTOL). **1196**

0954-9153 See KEY ABSTRACTS. BUSINESS AUTOMATION. **2005**

0954-917X See I T L G. **5161**

0954-920X See QUESTIONS (BIRMINGHAM). **1903**

0954-9226 See BASELINE LONDON. **4564**

0954-9773 See TOBACCO TRADE MARKETING DIRECTORY. **5374**

0954-9803 See BIG PAPER. **824**

0954-982X See BIOCHEMIST LONDON. **481**

0954-9889 See INTERNATIONAL JOURNAL OF NEURAL NETWORKS. **1213**

0954-9897 See AGBIOTECH NEWS AND INFORMATION. **149**

0954-9900 See PALAEONTOLOGY NEWSLETTER. **4229**

0954-9927 See ANGLO-NORMAN STUDIES ... : PROCEEDINGS OF THE BATTLE CONFERENCE. **2673**

0955-0569 See DEVELOPMENT BIBLIOGRAPHIES. **415**

0955-0666 See DURHAM MEDIEVAL TEXTS. **3382**

0955-0674 See CURRENT OPINION IN CELL BIOLOGY. **535**

0955-095X See NEW HORIZON (LONDON, ENGLAND). **5044**

0955-0984 See REHABILITATION INDEX / THE BRITISH LIBRARY, MEDICAL INFORMATION SERVICE. **4382**

0955-1034 See ARCHIVE SERVICES STATISTICS ... ESTIMATES. **2479**

0955-1077 See AMIGA USER INTERNATIONAL. **1264**

0955-1182 See RAW VISION. **363**

0955-1204 See PSA CONTRACTS BULLETIN. **1513**

0955-1247 See JANE'S INTELLIGENCE REVIEW. **4047**

0955-1298 See CONTINENTAL MODELLER. **2773**

0955-1328 See AUTOMOBILE (COBHAM). **5405**

0955-1433 See VECTOR LONDON. **1206**

0955-1476 See CURRENT MEDICAL LITERATURE. RADIOLOGY. **3940**

0955-1514 See PROC. - BRIGHTON CROP PROT. CONF., PESTS DIS. **182**

0955-1514 See BRIGHTON CROP PROTECTION CONFERENCE--WEEDS. **165**

0955-1603 See REPORT - PROUDMAN OCEANOGRAPHIC LABORATORY. **1456**

0955-1662 See SECURITY JOURNAL. **3176**

0955-1697 See INITIATIVE EUROPE MONITOR. **682**

0955-2057 See MUSEUM NEWS LONDON. **4092**

0955-2065 See HEALTH MANPOWER MANAGEMENT. **3582**

0955-2111 See COMPUTER INDUSTRY GUIDE. **1176**

0955-2170 See NCVO NEWS. **5297**

0955-2197 See INTELLECTUAL PROPERTY IN BUSINESS BRIEFING. **1304**

0955-2219 See JOURNAL OF THE EUROPEAN CERAMIC SOCIETY. **2591**

0955-2235 See PROGRESS IN GROWTH FACTOR RESEARCH. **990**

0955-2308 See ADULTS LEARNING. **1799**

0955-2340 See JOURNAL OF ISLAMIC STUDIES (OXFORD, ENGLAND). **5043**

0955-2359 See 20 CENTURY BRITISH HISTORY. **2671**

0955-2367 See ASIAN PHILOSOPY. **4341**

0955-2448 See LIVING MARXISM. **4543**

0955-2758 See CTN LONDON. **663**

0955-2804 See EMULSION POLYMERISATION AND POLYMER EMULSIONS. **4223**

0955-2839 See JOURNAL OF THE ASSOCIATION OF OBSTETRIC AND GYNAECOLOGICAL PHYSIOTHERAPISTS. **3764**

0955-2847 See MINERALS INDUSTRY INTERNATIONAL : BULLETIN OF THE INSTITUTION OF MINING AND METALLURGY. **1442**

0955-2863 See JOURNAL OF NUTRITIONAL BIOCHEMISTRY, THE. **4193**

0955-3002 See INTERNATIONAL JOURNAL OF RADIATION BIOLOGY. **3942**

0955-3010 See BITS. BSI INFORMATION TECHNOLOGY SERVICES. **5465**

0955-3045 See CLIMBER AND HILL WALKER. **4849**

0955-3541 See ONCOLOGY RESEARCH. **3822**

0955-355X See COMPUTER OPTICS. **1177**

0955-3681 See EUROPEAN JOURNAL OF IMPLANT AND REFRACTIVE SURGERY, THE. **3874**

0955-3835 See TECHNICAL DIAGNOSTICS AND NONDESTRUCTIVE TESTING. **1998**

0955-3843 See CONTEMPORARY EUROPEAN AFFAIRS. **1552**

0955-3886 See TRANSFUSION SCIENCE. **3647**

0955-3894 See PHARMACEUTICAL MANUFACTURING REVIEW. **3486**

0955-3959 See INTERNATIONAL JOURNAL ON DRUG POLICY, THE. **1345**

0955-4041 See EUROPEAN COMMUNICATIONS. **1111**

0955-4238 See BIRD KEEPER. **5615**

0955-4262 See CARE OF THE ELDERLY. **3750**

0955-4270 See ACIS : JOURNAL OF THE ASSOCIATION FOR CONTEMPORARY IBERIAN STUDIES. **3260**

0955-4319 See COMPUTER-AIDED PROCESS CONTROL ABSTRACTS. **1232**

0955-4386 See COIN NEWS (HINDHEAD, ENGLAND). **2780**

0955-4408 See INTERNATIONAL SHIPPING REVIEW. **5450**

0955-4416 See EUROPEAN FOOD AND DRINK REVIEW. **2334**

0955-4424 See GAMES INTERNATIONAL. **4861**

0955-4475 See JOURNAL OF CHILD LAW, THE. **2987**

0955-470X See TRANSPLANTATION REVIEWS (ORLANDO, FLA.). **3977**

0955-4777 See NEW MATERIALS WORLD. **5132**

0955-4785 See MARKETING BREAKTHROUGHS. **930**

0955-4823 See WORLD INSURANCE REPORT CORPORATE. **2896**

0955-4882 See EUROPEAN ACCOUNTING FOCUS. **743**

0955-4955 See Q (LONDON). **4148**

0955-5102 See TUMOUR MARKER UPDATE. **3825**

0955-5129 See ANGLO JAPANESE JOURNAL. **1632**

0955-534X See EUROPEAN BUSINESS REVIEW. **673**

0955-5358 See HEALTHY CITIES. **4782**

0955-5404 See EUROFOOD. **2334**

0955-5439 See ELECTRICITY INTERNATIONAL. **2045**

0955-5803 See JAPAN FORUM (OXFORD, ENGLAND). **2654**

0955-5889 See AUTOCAR & MOTOR. **5405**

0955-5986 See FLOW MEASUREMENT AND INSTRUMENTATION. **2089**

0955-6036 See PSYCHIATRIC BULLETIN OF THE ROYAL COLLEGE OF PSYCHIATRISTS. **3933**

0955-6214 See INTERNATIONAL JOURNAL OF CAREER MANAGEMENT, THE. **4205**

0955-6222 See INTERNATIONAL JOURNAL OF CLOTHING SCIENCE AND TECHNOLOGY. **1085**

0955-6230 See EXECUTIVE SECRETARY. **674**

0955-6230 See EXECUTIVE SECRETARY BRADFORD. **4204**

0955-632X See PANAMAX BULK CARRIERS. **848**

0955-6354 See LAND MANAGEMENT AND ENVIRONMENTAL LAW REPORT : LME LAW REPORT. **3113**

0955-6419 See BUSINESS STRATEGY REVIEW. **653**

0955-6427 See DURHAM MODERN LANGUAGE SERIES. **3278**

0955-6621 See BIOTECHNOLOGY EDUCATION. **3689**

0955-663X See ANNUAL REVIEW OF ADDICTIONS RESEARCH AND TREATMENT. **1341**

0955-6648 See CURRENT ADVANCES IN ECOLOGICAL & ENVIRONMENTAL SCIENCES. **2183**

0955-6664 See JOURNAL OF NUTRITIONAL MEDICINE. **4193**

0955-6915 See SKY INTERNATIONAL. **2493**

0955-7024 See SCOTTISH WORLD. **5813**

0955-7040 See INDUSTRIAL CORROSION ABSTRACTS. **2013**

0955-7059 See MIXING AND SEPARATION TECHNOLOGY ABSTRACTS. **2015**

0955-7105 See BUYERS' GUIDE FOR COSMETICS & TOILETRIES MANUFACTURERS SUPPLIERS. **402**

0955-7288 See BUSINESS TRAVELER INTERNATIONAL. **5465**

0955-7369 See DRILLING NEWS. **4255**

0955-7458 See PESTICIDES REGISTER, THE. **4247**

0955-7490 See ALEXANDRIA (ALDERSHOT). **3189**

0955-7571 See CAMBRIDGE REVIEW OF INTERNATIONAL AFFAIRS. **4467**

0955-7644 See ENGINEERING IN MINIATURE. **2773**

0955-7717 See BIOMEDICAL MATERIALS. **3556**

0955-7806 See PAPER EUROPE. **4236**

0955-7873 See JOURNAL OF INTERNAL MEDICINE. SUPPLEMENT. **3799**

0955-792X See JOURNAL OF LOGIC AND COMPUTATION. **1214**

0955-7970 See RESEARCH HIGHLIGHTS IN SOCIAL WORK. **5255**

0955-7989 See CASE STUDIES FOR PRACTICE. **5276**

0955-7997 See ENGINEERING ANALYSIS WITH BOUNDARY ELEMENTS. **1972**

0955-8047 See VOLLEYBALL WORLD. **4928**

0955-8055 See AVIONICS INTERNATIONAL. **14**

0955-8063 See AIRCRAFT MAINTENANCE INTERNATIONAL. **9**

0955-808X See EUROPEAN BUSINESS JOURNAL. **673**

0955-8160 See BRITISH JOURNAL OF PODIATRIC MEDICINE & SURGERY. 3917
0955-8209 See ALUMINIUM TODAY. 2100
0955-8241 See LOGISTICS (STAMFORD). 950
0955-8357 See WOMEN IN MANAGEMENT REVIEW. 735
0955-8500 See REVMEDIA LONDON. 1183
0955-8543 See HYPERMEDIA. 1223
0955-8586 See ORGANOMETALLIC CHEMISTRY IN THE USSR. 1045
0955-8658 See PROPERTY FINANCE. 804
0955-8683 See MIDIRS MIDWIFERY DIGEST. 3765
0955-8780 See TALKING POLITICS. 4497
0955-8810 See BEHAVIOURAL PHARMACOLOGY. 4293
0955-8829 See PSYCHIATRIC GENETICS. 551
0955-8950 See ENGLISH REVIEW OXFORD. 3279
0955-9000 See WINGSPAN HIGH WYCOMBE. 40
0955-9051 See REPORT FOR ... - INSTITUTE OF ARABLE CROPS RESEARCH. 184
0955-9078 See CASE SEARCH MONTHLY. 2949
0955-9469 See OUR DOGS MANCHESTER. 4287
0955-9841 See COMBAT AND SURVIVAL MAGAZINE. 4039
0955-9930 See INTERNATIONAL JOURNAL OF IMPOTENCE RESEARCH. 3589
0956-0122 See EX LONDON. 18
0956-0157 See WATER & SEWAGE INTERNATIONAL. 5542
0956-0157 See WATER & ENVIRONMENT INTERNATIONAL. 5541
0956-0521 See COMPUTING SYSTEMS IN ENGINEERING. 1969
0956-053X See WASTE MANAGEMENT (ELMSFORD). 2246
0956-0580 See DOD'S REPORT. 1605
0956-0629 See GEOACTIVE. 2561
0956-0661 See PHARMACEUTICAL BUSINESS NEWS. 4320
0956-0726 See MODERN HISTORY REVIEW. 2623
0956-0904 See USA AND CANADA. 2578
0956-0939 See PIG VETERINARY JOURNAL. 5518
0956-098X See BOXING MONTHLY. 4888
0956-1110 See DISCUSSION PAPER SERIES - UNIVERSITY OF LEEDS. SCHOOL OF BUSINESS AND ECONOMIC STUDIES. 79
0956-1242 See ANNUAL REPORT - NATIONAL COUNCIL FOR EDUCATIONAL TECHNOLOGY. 1725
0956-1250 See PESTICIDE OUTLOOK. 4246
0956-1498 See BUSINESS BANKER INTERNATIONAL. 781
0956-2257 See CRITICAL ISCHAEMIA. 3569
0956-2273 See EUROPA WORLD YEAR BOOK, THE. 4473
0956-2281 See PIC : PEOPLE IN CAMERA. 4375
0956-2311 See HYPERTENSION ANNUAL. 3705
0956-2362 See WHAT SATELLITE. 1124
0956-2478 See ENVIRONMENT AND URBANIZATION. 2165
0956-2559 See OTC NEWS & MARKET REPORT. 4318
0956-2737 See HEC FORUM. 3783
0956-2753 See UNIX NEWS LONDON. 1249
0956-277X See PRIMARY GEOGRAPHER. 2573
0956-2828 See UNITED STATES AIR FORCE YEARBOOK. 4059
0956-2834 See JOURNAL OF PHILOSOPHY AND THE VISUAL ARTS. 4350
0956-2893 See ARTHUR ANDERSEN CORPORATE REGISTER, THE. 639
0956-2931 See AUDIO VISUAL DIRECTORY. 1126
0956-2982 See MATERIALS RECLAMATION HANDBOOK. 2105
0956-3016 See WHO'S WHO IN THE CITY / STOCK EXCHANGE PRESS. 920
0956-3075 See CLINICAL INTENSIVE CARE : INTERNATIONAL JOURNAL OF CRITICAL & CORONARY CARE MEDICINE. 3703
0956-3113 See CHILDREN AND WAR. 5195

0956-3202 See ANTIVIRAL CHEMISTRY & CHEMOTHERAPY. 961
0956-3253 See MANAGEMENT CONSULTANT INTERNATIONAL. 876
0956-3261 See EC FINANCIAL INDUSTRY MONITOR. 788
0956-327X See LIFE INSURANCE INTERNATIONAL. 2887
0956-3288 See BANK FINANCIAL MANAGEMENT INTERNATIONAL. 774
0956-3385 See COMPUTING & CONTROL ENGINEERING JOURNAL. 1228
0956-375X See IEE PROCEEDINGS. F, RADAR AND SIGNAL PROCESSING. 1156
0956-3768 See IEE PROCEEDINGS. G, CIRCUITS, DEVICES, AND SYSTEMS. 2058
0956-3776 See IEE PROCEEDINGS. I, COMMUNICATIONS, SPEECH, AND VISION. 1156
0956-3784 See ASIAN REVIEW OF BUSINESS AND TECHNOLOGY. 640
0956-3806 See DIESEL CAR. 5412
0956-4187 See PROGRESS IN RURAL POLICY AND PLANNING. 2832
0956-4223 See INTERNATIONAL JOURNAL OF SERVICE INDUSTRY MANAGEMENT. 872
0956-4241 See ASI JOURNAL LONDON. 292
0956-4314 See CHINA STUDY JOURNAL. 4943
0956-4624 See INTERNATIONAL JOURNAL OF STD & AIDS. 3672
0956-4683 See WASTE PAPER NEWS. 4239
0956-5000 See JOURNAL OF THE CHEMICAL SOCIETY. FARADAY TRANSACTIONS. 1055
0956-5221 See SCANDINAVIAN JOURNAL OF MANAGEMENT. 885
0956-523X See GROWTH REGULATION. 547
0956-5280 See PAPERS IN AGRICULTURAL AND FOOD ECONOMICS NORTHERN IRELAND. 118
0956-5353 See WIDEWORLD OXFORD. 2495
0956-5361 See ANCIENT MESOAMERICA. 254
0956-540X See GEOPHYSICAL JOURNAL INTERNATIONAL. 1405
0956-5507 See CYTOPATHOLOGY (OXFORD). 535
0956-5515 See JOURNAL OF INTELLIGENT MANUFACTURING. 1214
0956-5558 See CARDS INTERNATIONAL. 655
0956-5574 See BARCLAYS ECONOMIC REVIEW. 778
0956-5590 See FAILSAFE LONDON. 1296
0956-5620 See CRICKET LIFE INTERNATIONAL. 4891
0956-5663 See BIOSENSORS & BIOELECTRONICS. 484
0956-6120 See WORKING BRIEF - UNEMPLOYMENT UNIT. 1719
0956-6163 See ENVIRONMENTAL MANAGEMENT AND HEALTH. 2168
0956-618X See ECCLESIASTICAL LAW JOURNAL : THE JOURNAL OF THE ECCLESIASTICAL LAW SOCIETY. 2965
0956-6333 See ABERDEEN PETROLEUM QUARTERLY. 4248
0956-6511 See CURRENT MEDICAL LITERATURE-BREAST CANCER. 3759
0956-666X See LIPID TECHNOLOGY. 984
0956-6732 See OFFSHORE BUSINESS. 2094
0956-6740 See REPORT - UNIVERSITY OF NEWCASTLE UPON TYNE. DEPARTMENT OF AGRICULTURAL ECONOMICS AND FOOD MARKETING. 126
0956-6783 See FOOD EUROPE ENGLISH ED. 2337
0956-7143 See COMPOSITES MANUFACTURING. 2101
0956-7151 See ACTA METALLURGICA ET MATERIALIA. 3996
0956-716X See SCRIPTA METALLURGICA ET MATERIALIA. 4018
0956-7429 See CRIMINAL LAWYER, THE. 3106
0956-7895 See DISCUSSION PAPER - ECONOMICS RESEARCH CENTRE. 1591

0956-7925 See EUROPEAN JOURNAL OF APPLIED MATHEMATICS. 3505
0956-7933 See RURAL HISTORY. 5256
0956-7968 See JOURNAL OF FUNCTIONAL PROGRAMMING. 1279
0956-7976 See PSYCHOLOGICAL SCIENCE. 4611
0956-8115 See NURSING THE ELDERLY : IN HOSPITAL, HOMES AND THE COMMUNITY. 3865
0956-8131 See DAIRY INDUSTRY NEWSLETTER. 193
0956-8409 See FILM AND TELEVISION HANDBOOK / BRITISH FILM INSTITUTE. 4069
0956-8719 See PHOTO ANSWERS. 4372
0956-9014 See RESEARCH ON LATIN AMERICA IN THE HUMANITIES AND SOCIAL SCIENCES IN THE UNIVERSITIES AND POLYTECHNICS OF THE UNITED KINGDOM. 2853
0956-9081 See NB. NEW BUILDER. 622
0956-9227 See PAINTING & DECORATING (LONDON, ENGLAND). 4224
0956-9359 See DEVELOPMENTS IN SOCIOLOGY. 5244
0956-960X See HUMAN ANTIBODIES AND HYBRIDOMAS. 457
0956-9618 See SEPARATIONS TECHNOLOGY. 1996
0956-9758 See WORLD ARCHITECTURE (LONDON. 1989). 311
0956-9979 See VIRUS BULLETIN. 1227
0957-0004 See TRAINING TOMORROW. 4691
0957-0020 See ARGUMENTS & FACTS INTERNATIONAL. 639
0957-0039 See EUROPEAN BUSINESS INTELLIGENCE BRIEFING. 673
0957-0063 See SPACE INSURANCE REPORT. 2894
0957-0144 See HISTORY & COMPUTING. 1186
0957-0233 See MEASUREMENT SCIENCE & TECHNOLOGY. 4412
0957-0241 See NEWSLETTER / ROYAL COMMISSION ON THE HISTORICAL MONUMENTS OF ENGLAND. 2700
0957-0276 See DEER FARMING INVERNESS. 5581
0957-0306 See CAMBRIDGE STUDIES IN BIOLOGICAL ANTHROPOLOGY. 233
0957-0322 See TEXTS AND DISSERTATIONS. 2855
0957-0349 See INTERNATIONAL MONOGRAPHS ON OBESITY SERIES. 2598
0957-0381 See REPORTS ON RHEUMATIC DISEASES (1985). 3806
0957-0381 See REPORTS ON RHEUMATIC DISEASES (1985). 3806
0957-0411 See ARBITRATION INTERNATIONAL. 3124
0957-0446 See DIAMOND INTERNATIONAL. 2914
0957-0462 See CURRENT CARDIOVASCULAR PATENTS. CARDIOVASCULAR FAST-ALERT. 3704
0957-0578 See UKIC GRAPEVINE. 4097
0957-0837 See IRISH HERITAGE LINKS. 2454
0957-0853 See RUSSIA EXPRESS. 1625
0957-0942 See NEW ERA IN EDUCATION. 1767
0957-0950 See CONSENSUS FORECASTS. 1471
0957-0950 See LATIN AMERICA CONSENSUS FORECASTS. 1502
0957-0985 See OCCASIONAL PAPER / WYE COLLEGE, UNIVERSITY OF LONDON, DEPARTMENT OF AGRICULTURE, HORTICULTURE AND THE ENVIRONMENT. 116
0957-1035 See BLACK COUNTRY BUSINESS DIRECTORY (SOUTH EDITION). 643
0957-1043 See HEMEL HEMPSTEAD & DISTRICT BUSINESS DIRECTORY. 679
0957-1094 See COMMERCE BUSINESS DIRECTORIES REDDITCH ED. 658
0957-1124 See WATFORD BUSINESS DIRECTORY. 719
0957-1248 See ABBEY CHRONICLE. 3457
0957-1264 See JOURNAL OF WINE RESEARCH / THE INSTITUTE OF MASTERS OF WINE. 2368

0957-1272 See ATMOSPHERIC ENVIRONMENT. PART B, URBAN ATMOSPHERE. 2161

0957-1280 See MATHEMATICS REVIEW. 3521

0957-1299 See INTERNATIONAL MINDS : THE QUARTERLY JOURNAL OF PSYCHOLOGICAL INSIGHT INTO INTERNATIONAL AFFAIRS. 4525

0957-1329 See SMALL ENTERPRISE DEVELOPMENT. 711

0957-1388 See MORTGAGE FINANCE MONTHLY. 800

0957-154X See HISTORY OF PSYCHIATRY. 3926

0957-1558 See FRENCH CULTURAL STUDIES. 2846

0957-1671 1153

0957-1728 See WHICH? WAY TO HEALTH. 2602

0957-1736 See LANGUAGE LEARNING JOURNAL : THE JOURNAL OF THE ASSOCIATION OF LANGUAGE LEARNING. 3295

0957-1744 See FRANCOPHONIE RUGBY. 3282

0957-1760 See RUSISTIKA : THE RUSSIAN JOURNAL OF THE ASSOCIATION FOR LANGUAGE LEARNING. 3318

0957-1787 See UTILITIES POLICY. 4693

0957-1817 See ASIA PACIFIC DUTY-FREE. 823

0957-1853 See PROJECT MANAGER TODAY. 883

0957-2279 See PERSONAL COMPUTER MAGAZINE (LONDON). 1272

0957-2341 See MACWORLD (LONDON). 1194

0957-2422 See SCICAT SCIENCE REFERENCE AND INFORMATION SERVICE. 992

0957-2481 See AUTOMOTIVE SPECIAL REPORT. 5407

0957-2791 See LIBRARY MONITOR. 3226

0957-2902 See BOUNDARY ELEMENTS ABSTRACTS AND NEWSLETTER. 1966

0957-2945 See COMPUTER SYSTEMS EUROPE. 1246

0957-2953 See ELECTRONICS EDUCATION (LONDON). 2049

0957-297X See WELSH JOURNAL OF EDUCATION, THE. 1791

0957-3038 See OBSTETRICS & GYNECOLOGY REVIEW. 3766

0957-3100 See DRUGLINK LONDON. 1344

0957-3178 See DESKTOP PUBLISHING COMMENTARY. 4813

0957-3224 See AUTOMATED OFFICE ABSTRACTS. 1217

0957-3518 See ENDOTHELIUM. 454

0957-3526 See GENE EXPRESSION. 545

0957-3666 See EC ENERGY MONTHLY. 1937

0957-3704 See RIGHT START. 1068

0957-3828 See INVERT MAGAZINE. 429

0957-3844 See TV ZONE. 1142

0957-3933 See BRIDES OF BERKSHIRE. 5552

0957-3941 See BRIDES OF DEVON & CORNWALL. 5552

0957-395X See BRIDES OF HERTS, BUCKS & BEDS. 5552

0957-3968 See BRIDES OF SOMERSET. 5552

0957-3976 See BRIDES OF SURREY. 5552

0957-3984 See BRIDES OF YORKSHIRE & HUMBERSIDE. 5552

0957-4042 See WOMEN. 5569

0957-4085 See C & L APPLICATIONS. 3199

0957-4107 See CHILD SAFETY REVIEW. 4771

0957-4115 See DEVELOPMENT JOURNAL (LONDON). 4642

0957-4158 See MECHATRONICS (OXFORD). 1195

0957-4166 See TETRAHEDRON, ASYMMETRY. 994

0957-4174 See EXPERT SYSTEMS WITH APPLICATIONS. 1212

0957-4190 See PAPILLOMAVIRUS REPORT. 3626

0957-4212 See MANAGER UPDATE. 1689

0957-4239 See ARABIC SCIENCES AND PHILOSOPHY : A HISTORICAL JOURNAL. 5085

0957-4271 See JOURNAL OF VESTIBULAR RESEARCH. 3889

0957-4344 See INTERNATIONAL JOURNAL OF CONTINUING ENGINEERING EDUCATION. 1979

0957-4352 See INTERNATIONAL JOURNAL OF ENVIRONMENT AND POLLUTION. 2174

0957-4360 See MICRONUTRIENT NEWS AND INFORMATION. 4194

0957-4425 See INTERNATIONAL BROADCASTING. 1133

0957-4484 See NANOTECHNOLOGY (BRISTOL). 1988

0957-4522 See JOURNAL OF MATERIALS SCIENCE. MATERIALS IN ELECTRONICS. 2069

0957-4530 See JOURNAL OF MATERIALS SCIENCE. MATERIALS IN MEDICINE. 3694

0957-4565 See NOISE & VIBRATION WORLDWIDE. 2178

0957-4581 See SNACK FOOD INTERNATIONAL. 936

0957-4611 See TELECOMMS ABSTRACTS. 1165

0957-4751 See CURRENT RESEARCH IN FRENCH STUDIES AT UNIVERSITIES & POLYTECHNICS IN THE UNITED KINGDOM & IRELAND. 3276

0957-476X See INTERNATIONAL JOURNAL OF RADIOACTIVE MATERIALS TRANSPORT. 4435

0957-4778 See ADVANCED MATERIALS TECHNOLOGY. 5080

0957-4824 See HEALTH PROMOTION INTERNATIONAL. 4781

0957-4832 See JOURNAL OF PUBLIC HEALTH MEDICINE. 3597

0957-4964 See INTERNATIONAL JOURNAL OF COGNITIVE EDUCATION & MEDIATED LEARNING. 1753

0957-4980 See MOBILE BUSINESS. 695

0957-5022 See SUGAR INDUSTRY ABSTRACTS / [CAB INTERNATIONAL, BUREAU OF HORTICULTURE AND PLANTATION CROPS IN ASSOCIATION WITH TATE & LYLE PLC]. 157

0957-5073 See POLAR AND GLACIOLOGICAL ABSTRACTS. 2572

0957-5138 See DENTAL LABORATORY NOTTINGHAM. 1321

0957-5189 See FOOD PACKER INTERNATIONAL. 4219

0957-5235 See BLOOD COAGULATION & FIBRINOLYSIS : AN INTERNATIONAL JOURNAL IN HAEMOSTASIS AND THROMBOSIS. 3795

0957-5243 See CANCER CAUSES & CONTROL : CCC. 3810

0957-5499 See SCOTLIT ABERDEEN. 3434

0957-5545 See RECENT ADVANCES IN CLINICAL PHARMACOLOGY AND TOXICOLOGY. 4327

0957-5685 See EUROPEAN SEMICONDUCTOR. 2054

0957-5790 See BUILDING REFURBISHMENT. 604

0957-5812 See DUNS EUROPA. 669

0957-5820 See PROCESS SAFETY AND ENVIRONMENTAL PROTECTION. 2180

0957-5839 See CURRENT PAEDIATRICS. 3902

0957-5847 See CURRENT OBSTETRICS AND GYNAECOLOGY. 3759

0957-588X See BBC GOOD FOOD. 2328

0957-5960 See CONTEMPORARY BRITAIN : AN ANNUAL REVIEW. 2684

0957-6053 See LOGISTICS INFORMATION MANAGEMENT. 3229

0957-6061 See INTEGRATED MANUFACTURING SYSTEMS. 2116

0957-6215 See ALLONS. 1723

0957-6436 See VITAMIN CONNECTION. 4200

0957-6509 See PROCEEDINGS OF THE INSTITUTION OF MECHANICAL ENGINEERS. PART A, JOURNAL OF POWER AND ENERGY. 2126

0957-6517 See STREETWISE : THE MAGAZINE OF URBAN STUDIES. 2836

0957-6525 See YOUR CLASSIC. 5429

0957-655X See OIL PACKER INTERNATIONAL. 4220

0957-6606 See MUSIC TECHNOLOGY (ELY). 4135

0957-6762 See REVIEW OF AGRICULTURAL ENTOMOLOGY. 5604

0957-6770 See REVIEW OF MEDICAL AND VETERINARY ENTOMOLOGY. 5604

0957-6789 See HELMINTHOLOGICAL ABSTRACTS. 5604

0957-6797 See NEMATOLOGICAL ABSTRACTS. 478

0957-6851 See JOURNAL OF ASIAN PACIFIC COMMUNICATION. 1114

0957-7041 See FERMENT (LONDON). 2367

0957-7238 See ITE RESEARCH PUBLICATION. 2217

0957-7270 See BRIDES OF EAST ANGLIA. 5552

0957-7289 See BRIDES OF SCOTLAND. 5552

0957-7432 See BRIDES OF BRISTOL BATH & AVON. 5552

0957-7440 See BRIDES OF NORTH EAST ENGLAND. 5552

0957-7505 See POSTHARVEST NEWS AND INFORMATION. 155

0957-7572 See INTERNATIONAL JOURNAL OF TECHNOLOGY AND DESIGN EDUCATION. 5115

0957-7580 See SPECIAL VEHICLE ENGINEER. 1997

0957-767X See EUROPEAN JOURNAL OF NON-DESTRUCTIVE TESTING, THE. 5104

0957-7718 See MINERVA (LONDON. 1989). 275

0957-7734 See EQUINE VETERINARY EDUCATION. 2798

0957-7742 See HEALTH ESTATE JOURNAL : JOURNAL OF THE INSTITUTE OF HOSPITAL ENGINEERING. 3781

0957-7858 See REFUGEE COMMUNITY NEWS. 1921

0957-798X See PATON WELDING JOURNAL, THE. 4027

0957-8005 See TEACHING EARTH SCIENCES. 1360

0957-8536 See LAW AND CRITIQUE. 2994

0957-8544 See NEWSLETTER - UK ONLINE USER GROUP. 1275

0957-8625 See DAIRY MARKETS WEEKLY. 193

0957-8714 See HEADLINES. 1864

0957-8765 See VOLUNTAS : INTERNATIONAL JOURNAL OF VOLUNTARY AND NON-PROFIT ORGANISATIONS. 4339

0957-8773 See CHARTERED BUILDER (ASCOT, 1989). 607

0957-8811 See EUROPEAN JOURNAL OF DEVELOPMENT RESEARCH, THE. 2909

0957-882X See EQUAL OPPORTUNITIES REVIEW. DISCRIMINATION CASE LAW DIGEST. 3148

0957-8870 See AMENITY MANAGEMENT. 4848

0957-8897 See WORLD CERAMICS ABSTRACTS. 2595

0957-8943 See ELLE DECORATION BRITISH ED. 2900

0957-8978 See JOURNAL : PAPER OF THE NATIONAL UNION OF CIVIL AND PUBLIC SERVANTS. 4704

0957-9044 See NEWS - NATIONAL CAMPAIGN FOR THE ARTS. 326

0957-9052 See ENVIRONMENTAL PROTECTION BULLETIN. 2229

0957-9125 See NEWSPAPER FOCUS. 5812

0957-9133 See INTELLIGENT TUTORING MEDIA. 1213

0957-9249 See BATTERIES INTERNATIONAL. 2036

0957-9265 See DISCOURSE & SOCIETY. 5198

0957-9346 See MEDICAL LAW REPORTS. 3008

0957-9575 See EDUCATION LIBRARIES JOURNAL. 3209

0957-9656 See LOGOS. 4830

0957-9664 See CMBH CRIMINAL BEHAVIOUR AND MENTAL HEALTH. 3160

0957-9672 See CURRENT OPINION IN LIPIDOLOGY. 3704

0957-9710 See ADMINISTRATIVE LAW REPORTS. 2927

0957-9729 See ADVANCED METALS TECHNOLOGY. 3997

0957-9737 See ELECTRONIC MATERIALS AND PROCESSING. 2047
0957-9869 See BUSINESS RESEARCH GUIDE HEADLAND. 652
0958-0328 See VACHER'S PARLIAMENTARY COMPANION. 4693
0958-0336 See VACHER'S EUROPEAN COMPANION & CONSULTANTS' REGISTER. 4693
0958-0344 See PHYTOCHEMICAL ANALYSIS. 522
0958-0441 See TIMES LAW REPORTS. 3065
0958-0549 See EXTRUSION COMMUNIQUE. 2334
0958-0581 See JOURNAL OF PHARMACEUTICAL MEDICINE : THE OFFICIAL JOURNAL OF THE SOCIETY OF PHARMACEUTICAL MEDICINE. 4312
0958-0670 See EXPERIMENTAL PHYSIOLOGY. 580
0958-0824 See PAPER ASIA NEWS : THE ASIAN PULP & PAPER NEWSLETTER. 4235
0958-126X See JANE'S NATO HANDBOOK. 4047
0958-1278 See REPORT / HYDRAULICS RESEARCH STATION. 2095
0958-1596 See CRITICAL PUBLIC HEALTH. 4772
0958-1669 See CURRENT OPINION IN BIOTECHNOLOGY. 3691
0958-1758 See MUSEUM DEVELOPMENT. 4092
0958-1790 See INSIDE INFORMATION WHITCHURCH. 1189
0958-1820 See CARRIAGE DRIVING. 2798
0958-1847 See CONSERVATION UPDATE : NEWSLETTER OF THE CONSERVATION UNIT, MUSEUMS & GALLERIES COMMISSION. 348
0958-188X See ROUGE. 2796
0958-1952 See EUROPEAN MICROSCOPY AND ANALYSIS. 572
0958-1987 See PERIOD LIVING. 2902
0958-2002 See SCOTTISH ARCHAEOLOGICAL NEWS. 282
0958-2029 See RESEARCH EVALUATION. 5146
0958-2053 See CORPORATE FINANCE (LONDON). 785
0958-2118 See MEMBRANE TECHNOLOGY. 3695
0958-2126 See ENVIRONMENT & INDUSTRY DIGEST. 2192
0958-2541 See PROFESSIONAL INVESTOR. 912
0958-2584 See RHEUMATOLOGY REVIEW (EDINBURGH). 3807
0958-2592 See FOOT, THE. 3881
0958-2606 See PHOTORESEARCHER / EUROPEAN SOCIETY FOR THE HISTORY OF PHOTOGRAPHY. 4375
0958-2770 See NEWSBRIEF - UNITED SOCIETY FOR THE PROPAGATION OF THE GOSPEL. 4981
0958-2789 See UNITED SOCIETY FOR THE PROPAGATION OF THE GOSPEL ISSUES. 5006
0958-3017 See DESIGN & TECHNOLOGY TEACHING. 5099
0958-305X See ENERGY & ENVIRONMENT. 1939
0958-3076 See FOREIGN INVESTMENT IN THE US. 899
0958-3157 See BIOCONTROL SCIENCE & TECHNOLOGY. 164
0958-3165 See NANOBIOLOGY : JOURNAL OF RESEARCH ON NANOSCALE LIVING SYSTEMS. 539
0958-319X See SPECTROCHIMICA ACTA REVIEWS. 4441
0958-319X See SPECTROCHIMICA ACTA REVIEWS [MICROFORM]. 4441
0958-3246 See SEAFOOD NEWS FOR UK AND IRELAND. 2357
0958-3467 See SEARCH YORK. 5307
0958-353X See THOMSON'S INTERNATIONAL BANKING REGULATOR. 814
0958-3629 See CATALYST OXFORD. 5092
0958-3637 See HINDSIGHT CAMBRIDGE. 2617
0958-367X See AUDIT BRIEFING. 4712
0958-3785 See INTERNATIONAL MONEY MARKETING. 902
0958-3858 5056

0958-3866 See EUROPEAN BOOKSELLER. 4828
0958-3939 See PERESTROIKA ANNUAL. 4487
0958-3971 See EXILE LONDON. 1918
0958-4021 See INLOGOV INFORMS. 4657
0958-4579 See IBM FUTURES. 1186
0958-4609 See LEGAL BUSINESS. 2999
0958-465X See SOFTWARE SYSTEMS AND TECHNIQUES ABSTRACTS. 1291
0958-4668 See MICRO ABSTRACTS. 1269
0958-479X See SAFETY & HEALTH PRACTITIONER. 4800
0958-4846 See UFO TIMES. 38
0958-4935 See CONTEMPORARY SOUTH ASIA. 2503
0958-4986 See MEDAL NEWS HINDHEAD. 1989. 2781
0958-501X See OPERA NOW. 4144
0958-5036 See MICROGRAVITY QUARTERLY. 4412
0958-5052 See EDI ANALYSIS. 866
0958-5176 See CURRICULUM JOURNAL. 1892
0958-5184 See JOURNAL OF FORENSIC PSYCHIATRY, THE. 3928
0958-5192 See INTERNATIONAL JOURNAL OF HUMAN RESOURCE MANAGEMENT, THE. 943
0958-5206 See ACCOUNTING BUSINESS AND FINANCIAL HISTORY. 736
0958-5214 See INTERNATIONAL COMPANY AND COMMERCIAL LAW REVIEW. 3100
0958-5222 See IPMS BULLETIN. 5116
0958-5443 See REPORT FOR THE YEAR ... / JANE AUSTEN SOCIETY. 3429
0958-5451 See TRANSACTIONS OF THE GAELIC SOCIETY OF INVERNESS. 3329
0958-5664 See BRITISH MUSIC. 4105
0958-5702 See POPSI. 422
0958-5737 See POSITIVE HEALTH. 4795
0958-6024 See PAPER TECHNOLOGY (1989). 4236
0958-6253 See UNIX/BUSINESS. 1239
0958-6407 See ARCHITECTURE TODAY. 290
0958-6415 See ISSUES IN REPRODUCTIVE AND GENETIC ENGINEERING : JOURNAL OF INTERNATIONAL FEMINIST ANALYSIS. 3693
0958-6601 See OXFORD MONOGRAPHS ON BIOGEOGRAPHY. 468
0958-6644 See PHILOSOPHICAL MAGAZINE. B, PHYSICS OF CONDENSED MATTER, STRUCTURAL, ELECTRONIC, OPTICAL, AND MAGNETIC PROPERTIES. 4414
0958-6679 See IR. INVESTOR RELATIONS. 903
0958-6687 See DENTAL HISTORIAN. 1320
0958-6709 See SUMMIT OXFORD. 3537
0958-6857 See OVERSEAS BROADCASTERS CIRCUIT. 1136
0958-6946 See INTERNATIONAL DAIRY JOURNAL. 195
0958-7039 See BRIDES OF THE NORTH WEST. 5552
0958-7349 See NEW CONSUMER. 1298
0958-7373 See STEAM CLASSIC. 5437
0958-7462 See FERRARI WORLD. 5415
0958-7489 4202
0958-7578 See TRANSFUSION MEDICINE. 3802
0958-7594 See INTERNATIONAL TAX REVIEW. 4733
0958-7608 See JOURNAL OF BIOLOGICAL CURATION. 4090
0958-7683 See SHIPPING BOURNEMOUTH. 5456
0958-8140 See LANGUAGE AND LITERACY NEWS. 1899
0958-8221 See COMPUTER ASSISTED LANGUAGE LEARNING. 3274
0958-8515 See TELECOMEUROPA'S ISDN NEWSLETTER. 1165
0958-8523 See TELECOMEUROPA'S PERSONAL COMMUNICATIONS NEWSLETTER. 1165
0958-8574 See DTI QA REGISTER. 1605
0958-868X See JOURNAL OF PROPERTY FINANCE. 4839

0958-8787 See TANKER CHARTER RECORD. 5457
0958-8825 See ANNUAL VOLUME / THE OLD WATER-COLOUR SOCIETY'S CLUB. 337
0958-9236 See JOURNAL OF GENDER STUDIES. 5559
0958-9287 See JOURNAL OF EUROPEAN SOCIAL POLICY. 2518
0958-9309 See ASIAMONEY. 891
0958-9341 See DAM ENGINEERING. 2088
0958-9376 See CURRENT MEDICAL LITERATURE. GENERAL PRACTICE / THE ROYAL SOCIETY OF MEDICINE. 3737
0958-9384 See CURRENT MEDICAL LITERATURE / HOSPITAL PHARMACY. 4298
0958-9414 See INTERNATIONAL MONOGRAPHS IN NUTRITION, METABOLISM, AND OBESITY. 4192
0958-9422 See NEW DRUGS AND NOVEL COMPOUNDS IN MEDICINE AND PHARMACOLOGY. 4317
0958-9465 See CEMENT & CONCRETE COMPOSITES. 606
0958-9732 See SPECIAL STUDIES IN AGRICULTURAL ECONOMICS - UNIVERSITY OF READING, DEPARTMENT OF AGRICULTURAL ECONOMICS & MANAGEMENT. 137
0958-9767 See INTERNATIONAL LITIGATION PROCEDURE. 3130
0958-9775 See RESIDENTIAL ACCOMMODATION FOR ELDERLY PEOPLE WITH PHYSICAL OR VISUAL DISABILITIES / WELSH OFFICE. 4393
0958-9961 See INTERNATIONAL JOURNAL OF MICROGRAPHICS & OPTICAL TECHNOLOGY. 1277
0959-0188 See FOCUS, FIBRE OPTIC COMMUNICATION & USER SYSTEMS. 1155
0959-0196 See ENERGY UTILITIES. 1488
0959-020X See GENETIC ENGINEER & BIOTECHNOLOGIST, THE. 3692
0959-0218 See MINIBUS LONDON. 1078
0959-0552 See INTERNATIONAL JOURNAL OF RETAIL & DISTRIBUTION MANAGEMENT. 955
0959-0587 See MOUSE GENOME. 466
0959-0838 See GLASS PRODUCTION TECHNOLOGY INTERNATIONAL. 2590
0959-0889 See LAWYERS IN EUROPE. 3132
0959-1117 See NETBALL MAGAZINE. 4907
0959-1346 See AGING AND AGING DISORDERS. 3749
0959-1389 See ABC EXECUTIVE FLIGHT PLANNER EUROPE, MIDDLE EAST, AFRICA. 5459
0959-146X See RECRUITMENT AND DEVELOPMENT REPORT. 946
0959-1524 See JOURNAL OF PROCESS CONTROL. 3482
0959-1591 See ACCESS BY DESIGN. 287
0959-2113 See BEST OF BUSINESS INTERNATIONAL. 642
0959-2164 See TECHNICAL REPORT - LONG ASHTON RESEARCH STATION, WEED RESEARCH DEPARTMENT. 2432
0959-2199 See IDS EUROPEAN REPORT. 1677
0959-2253 See EDINBURGH WORKING PAPERS IN APPLIED LINGUISTICS. 3278
0959-2296 See DIPLOMACY AND STATECRAFT. 4520
0959-2318 See SMALL WARS AND INSURGENCIES. 4057
0959-2350 See INFORMATION MANAGEMENT & TECHNOLOGY / ANBAR ABSTRACTS. 5175
0959-2369 See SSCR JOURNAL. 283
0959-2431 See JOURNAL OF SMOKING-RELATED DISORDERS, THE. 3981
0959-2512 See HOSPITAL BED USE STATISTICS / WELSH OFFICE [AND] WELSH HEALTH COMMON SERVICES AUTHORITY. 3783
0959-2598 See REVIEWS IN CLINICAL GERONTOLOGY. 3754
0959-2601 See SOUTH EAST ASIA MONITOR. 1584
0959-2687 See PROFESSIONAL HOTEL & RESTAURANT INTERIORS. 2902

0959-2695 See JOURNAL OF FRENCH LANGUAGE STUDIES. 3290

0959-2709 See BIRD CONSERVATION INTERNATIONAL. 5615

0959-289X See INTERNATIONAL JOURNAL OF OBSTETRIC ANESTHESIA. 3763

0959-2903 See MEDICAL AUDIT NEWS. 748

0959-2911 See ABC EXECUTIVE FLIGHT PLANNER. ASIA, PACIFIC. 5459

0959-2954 See JOURNAL OF INFORMATION SYSTEMS. 1248

0959-2989 See BIO-MEDICAL MATERIALS AND ENGINEERING. 3686

0959-3004 See CTISS FILE. 1222

0959-3101 See FAIRPLAY WORLD SHIPPING DIRECTORY. 5449

0959-3160 See MOUNTAIN EAR. 4875

0959-3268 See QUALITY FORUM (LONDON). 4032

0959-3314 See GASTROENTEROLOGY & RHEUMATOLOGY IN PRACTICE. 3745

0959-3330 See ENVIRONMENTAL TECHNOLOGY. 2170

0959-3438 See BUTTERWORTH LECTURES. 2945

0959-3535 See FEMINISM & PSYCHOLOGY. 5555

0959-3543 See THEORY & PSYCHOLOGY. 4620

0959-3608 See MANCHESTER GUARDIAN WEEKLY (1985). 5812

0959-3632 See TRAFODION ANRHYDEDDUS GYMDEITHAS Y CYMMRODORION. 3447

0959-3640 See ANNUAL REPORT - YORK GEORGIAN SOCIETY. 5228

0959-3683 See PUBLICATIONS OF THE ENGLISH GOETHE SOCIETY. 3426

0959-3780 See GLOBAL ENVIRONMENTAL CHANGE. 2172

0959-3799 See ENTERTAINMENT LAW REVIEW. 2966

0959-3845 See INFORMATION TECHNOLOGY & PEOPLE (WEST LINN, OR.). 870

0959-3853 See PHARMAKRITIK INTERNATIONAL. 4324

0959-3950 See MATHS & STATS. 3522

0959-3969 See INTERNATIONAL REVIEW OF RETAIL DISTRIBUTION CONSUMER RESEARCH. 955

0959-3985 See PHYSIOTHERAPY THEORY AND PRACTICE. 4382

0959-3993 See WORLD JOURNAL OF MICROBIOLOGY & BIOTECHNOLOGY. 571

0959-4213 See ARAM PERIODICAL. 2767

0959-4213 See ARAM PERIODICAL. 3266

0959-4272 See MAN. MUSEUM ARCHAEOLOGISTS NEWS. 273

0959-4299 See POSTGRADUATE EDUCATION FOR GENERAL PRACTICE. 3738

0959-437X See CURRENT OPINION IN GENETICS AND DEVELOPMENT. 544

0959-4388 See CURRENT OPINION IN NEUROBIOLOGY. 453

0959-440X See CURRENT OPINION IN STRUCTURAL BIOLOGY. 453

0959-4493 See VETERINARY DERMATOLOGY. 5525

0959-4752 See LEARNING AND INSTRUCTION : THE JOURNAL OF THE EUROPEAN ASSOCIATION FOR RESEARCH ON LEARNING AND INSTRUCTION. 1899

0959-4779 See ESSAYS IN COGNITIVE PSYCHOLOGY. 5245

0959-4906 See INDEX OF CONFERENCE PROCEEDINGS. ANNUAL CUMULATION. 3214

0959-4914 See CURRENT SERIALS RECEIVED. 3205

0959-4922 See BRITISH REPORTS, TRANSLATIONS AND THESES RECEIVED BY THE BRITISH LIBRARY DOCUMENT SUPPLY CENTRE. 3197

0959-4957 See IMMUNOLOGY AND INFECTIOUS DISEASES. 3671

0959-4965 See NEUROREPORT. 3842

0959-4973 See ANTI-CANCER DRUGS. 3979

0959-5090 See INTERNATIONAL JOURNAL OF CONSTRUCTION MAINTENANCE & REPAIR, THE. 618

0959-5236 See DRUG AND ALCOHOL REVIEW. 1343

0959-5244 See MOLECULAR NEUROPHARMACOLOGY. 3838

0959-5619 See ONLINE FILES. 1275

0959-5740 See AKTUELL. 3262

0959-5805 See PLANNING HISTORY. 2702

0959-5813 See BROADCAST SYSTEMS INTERNATIONAL. 1128

0959-5864 See MECHANICS OF CREEP BRITTLE MATERIALS. 2106

0959-6038 See INTERNATIONAL CEMENT REVIEW. 617

0959-6062 See NEW COATINGS & SURFACES. 1027

0959-6089 See TANK CONTAINER WORLD. 5457

0959-6119 See INTERNATIONAL JOURNAL OF CONTEMPORARY HOSPITALITY MANAGEMENT. 2807

0959-6127 See WORLD CERAMICS & REFRACTORIES. 2595

0959-6186 See TRAVEL INDUSTRY MONITOR. 5496

0959-6259 See CAD USER. 1222

0959-6321 See BIOLOGICAL RESEARCH IN NORWICH. 445

0959-6402 See INTERNATIONAL JOURNAL OF SIGN LINGUISTICS. 3287

0959-6410 See ISLAM & CHRISTIAN MUSLIM RELATIONS. 5042

0959-6429 See DATACOMMS BOOK, THE. 1257

0959-6518 See PROCEEDINGS OF THE INSTITUTION OF MECHANICAL ENGINEERS. PART I, JOURNAL OF SYSTEMS & CONTROL ENGINEERING. 2126

0959-6526 See JOURNAL OF CLEANER PRODUCTION. 1613

0959-6569 See WORK IN PROGRESS - UNIVERSITY OF EDINBURGH. DEPARTMDENT OF LINGUISTICS. 3333

0959-6631 See INTELLIGENT HIGHWAY, THE. 5441

0959-6658 See GLYCOBIOLOGY (OXFORD). 487

0959-6682 See PRESCRIBER. 3629

0959-6836 See HOLOCENE (SEVENOAKS). 1382

0959-6879 See BRITISH JOURNAL OF PHYTOTHERAPY, THE. 504

0959-6909 See MODEL ENGINEERS' WORKSHOP. 2775

0959-6933 See HOT SHOE INTERNATIONAL. 4370

0959-6941 See EUROPEAN BUSINESS LAW REVIEW. 3099

0959-7042 See ENVIRONMENT BUSINESS. 2165

0959-7050 See WORLD AIR POWER JOURNAL. 40

0959-7174 See WAVES IN RANDOM MEDIA. 4424

0959-7271 See WHICH LONDON SCHOOL?. 1791

0959-7441 See MERGERS & ACQUISITIONS ABSTRACTS / ANBAR. 693

0959-7727 See OXFORD ENERGY FORUM. 1952

0959-7735 See EUROTECHNOLOGY. 5104

0959-7743 See CAMBRIDGE ARCHAEOLOGICAL JOURNAL. 265

0959-793X See DUMFRIES AND GALLOWAY COURIER. 2919

0959-8022 See ACCOUNTING, MANAGEMENT, AND INFORMATION TECHNOLOGIES. 737

0959-8030 See ANNUAL REVIEW OF FISH DISEASES. 2295

0959-8049 See EUROPEAN JOURNAL OF CANCER (1990). 3816

0959-8103 See POLYMER INTERNATIONAL. 4459

0959-8111 See PLASTICS, RUBBER AND COMPOSITES PROCESSING AND APPLICATIONS. 4458

0959-8138 See BMJ. BRITISH MEDICAL JOURNAL (CLINICAL RESEARCH ED.). 3557

0959-8146 See BMJ. BRITISH MEDICAL JOURNAL (INTERNATIONAL ED.). 3557

0959-8278 See EUROPEAN JOURNAL OF CANCER PREVENTION. 3817

0959-8286 See INSTRUMENTATION & CONTROL ENGINEERING. 2065

0959-8332 See ELECTRONICS WORLD + WIRELESS WORLD. 2050

0959-8421 See LICENSING REVIEW. 3003

0959-8464 See CHEMISTRY REVIEW. 971

0959-8472 See PHYSICS REVIEW DEDDINGTON. 4416

0959-8480 See POLITICS REVIEW. 4491

0959-8499 See SOCIOLOGY REVIEW. 5262

0959-888X See FIBA BASKETBALL MONTHLY. 4894

0959-8928 See INFORMATION RESEARCH NEWS. 3216

0959-8936 See STRATEGIES (BIRMINGHAM). 1905

0959-8944 See BOXING WEEKLY. 4888

0959-9010 See EAST EUROPE BUSINESS FOCUS. 670

0959-9134 See O.S.B.E.R. OIL SPILL BULLETIN AND ENVIRONMENTAL REVIEW. 2238

0959-9266 See PAPER & PACKAGING ANALYST. 4221

0959-9320 See PORT ENGINEERING MANAGEMENT. 624

0959-9428 See JOURNAL OF MATERIALS CHEMISTRY. 981

0959-9436 See MENDELEEV COMMUNICATIONS / ROYAL SOCIETY OF CHEMISTRY, [AKADEMIIA NAUK SSSR]. 985

0959-9576 See FOCUS ON AFRICA : BBC MAGAZINE. 2499

0959-9584 See EUROPE 2000 YEOVIL. 2687

0959-9673 See INTERNATIONAL JOURNAL OF EXPERIMENTAL PATHOLOGY. 3895

0959-972X See BULLETIN OF THE ROYAL COLLEGE OF PATHOLOGISTS. 3893

0959-9754 See WATER LAW. 5543

0959-9851 See CLINICAL AUTONOMIC RESEARCH : OFFICIAL JOURNAL OF THE CLINICAL AUTONOMIC RESEARCH SOCIETY. 3565

0959-9886 See JOURNAL OF ALTERNATIVE AND COMPLEMENTARY MEDICINE. 3593

0959-9916 See JOURNAL OF PROPERTY RESEARCH. 4839

0959-9959 See GROUND ENGINEERING YEARBOOK. 2024

0959-9983 See PAPERS PRESENTED AT THE ... INDUSTRIAL MINERALS INTERNATIONAL CONGRESS. 4014

0960-0035 See INTERNATIONAL JOURNAL OF PHYSICAL DISTRIBUTION & LOGISTICS MANAGEMENT. 871

0960-0124 See PC TODAY MACCLESFIELD. 1199

0960-0159 See CONFLICT INTERNATIONAL. 4518

0960-0175 See JOURNAL OF THE MOSCOW PHYSICAL SOCIETY : JMPS. 4410

0960-0183 See MUSEUM ABSTRACTS INTERNATIONAL. 4092

0960-0248 See WORLD COUNTERTRADE & BARTER NEWS. 858

0960-0604 See ANTHROPOLOGICAL JOURNAL ON EUROPEAN CULTURES. 229

0960-0752 See MEDIEVAL HISTORY. 2698

0960-0760 See JOURNAL OF STEROID BIOCHEMISTRY AND MOLECULAR BIOLOGY, THE. 462

0960-0779 See CHAOS, SOLITONS AND FRACTALS. 3499

0960-0833 See SOFTWARE TESTING, VERIFICATION & RELIABILITY. 1291

0960-085X See EUROPEAN JOURNAL OF INFORMATION SYSTEMS. 1184

0960-0884 See SOVIET LIGHTWAVE COMMUNICATIONS. 4441

0960-0892 See ISSUE DESIGN MUSEUM. 4089

0960-0906 See SOFTWARE MANAGEMENT. 1291

0960-0949 See WORLD ARBITRATION & MEDIATION REPORT. 3138

0960-0981 See EUROPEAN INSURANCE MARKET. 2879

0960-1295 See MSCS (CAMBRIDGE). 1195

0960-1317 See JOURNAL OF MICROMECHANICS AND MICROENGINEERING : STRUCTURES, DEVICES, AND SYSTEMS. 2069

0960-135X See EUROPEAN JOURNAL OF CLINICAL INVESTIGATION SUPPLEMENT. 3575

0960-1449 See MEDIUM COMPANIES OF EUROPE. 692

0960-1481 See RENEWABLE ENERGY. 1954

0960-1511 See ANTHROPOLOGY AND RELATED DISCIPLINES / INTERNATIONAL CURRENT AWARENESS SERVICES. 230

0960-152X See ECONOMICS AND RELATED DISCIPLINES / INTERNATIONAL CURRENT AWARENESS SERVICES. 1486

0960-1538 See POLITICAL SCIENCE AND RELATED DISCIPLINES / INTERNATIONAL CURRENT AWARENESS SERVICES. 4490

0960-1546 See SOCIOLOGY AND RELATED DISCIPLINES / INTERNATIONAL CURRENT AWARENESS SERVICES. 5262

0960-1570 See SELECT : NATIONAL BIBLIOGRAPHIC SERVICE NEWSLETTER. 3248

0960-1619 See PERSONNEL TRAINING AND EDUCATION. 3241

0960-1627 See MATHEMATICAL FINANCE : AN INTERNATIONAL JOURNAL OF MATHEMATICS, STATISTICS AND FINANCIAL THEORY. 3518

0960-1635 See GAS WORLD INTERNATIONAL. 4258

0960-1643 See BRITISH JOURNAL OF GENERAL PRACTICE, THE. 3737

0960-1686 See ATMOSPHERIC ENVIRONMENT. PART A, GENERAL TOPICS. 2225

0960-2003 See EUROPEAN WORK AND ORGANISATIONAL PSYCHOLOGIST, THE. 4587

0960-2011 See NEUROPSYCHOLOGICAL REHABILITATION. 4605

0960-233X See PARKS NEWBURY. 2202

0960-2356 See UTILITIES LAW REVIEW. 3070

0960-250X See PRIMARY HEALTH CARE MANAGEMENT. 3739

0960-2585 See SEED SCIENCE RESEARCH. 133

0960-2593 See COMPUTER AUDIT UPDATE. 1256

0960-2615 See WRU NEWS & ABSTRACTS. 1207

0960-2712 See JOURNAL OF PROPERTY VALUATION & INVESTMENT. 4839

0960-2720 See EUROPEAN JOURNAL OF THEOLOGY. 4957

0960-2941 See INTERNATIONAL JOURNAL OF ORTHOPAEDIC TRAUMA. 3882

0960-2992 See CHEMICAL INDUSTRY EUROPE. 968

0960-3085 See FOOD AND BIOPRODUCTS PROCESSING : TRANSACTIONS OF THE INSTITUTION OF CHEMICAL ENGINEERS, PART C. 2336

0960-3107 See APPLIED FINANCIAL ECONOMICS. 1633

0960-3115 See BIODIVERSITY AND CONSERVATION. 2188

0960-3123 See INTERNATIONAL JOURNAL OF ENVIRONMENTAL HEALTH RESEARCH. 2174

0960-3131 See JOURNAL OF ELECTRONICS MANUFACTURING. 2069

0960-314X See PHARMACOGENETICS. 4321

0960-3158 See PROCESSING OF ADVANCED MATERIALS. 5142

0960-3168 See REVIEWS IN FISH BIOLOGY AND FISHERIES. 2311

0960-3174 See STATISTICS AND COMPUTING. 1210

0960-3182 See GEOTECHNICAL AND GEOLOGICAL ENGINEERING. 2139

0960-3204 See ITALIAN CARS. 5417

0960-3247 See ADVANCED SEARCHER. 3187

0960-3271 See HUMAN & EXPERIMENTAL TOXICOLOGY. 3981

0960-3352 See DOWNLINK : SATELLITE & CABLE INDUSTRY NEWS. 1153

0960-3360 See NIR NEWS. 4413

0960-3409 See MATERIALS AT HIGH TEMPERATURES. 2105

0960-3751 See BEAUTY COUNTER LONDON. 402

0960-376X See COMMUNITY PHARMACY LONDON. 4297

0960-3913 See PORTFOLIO MAGAZINE EDINBURGH. 4375

0960-3964 See CLINICAL AND LABORATORY HAEMATOLOGY. SUPPLEMENT. 3771

0960-3999 See PUBLIC OPINION AND BROADCASTING STANDARDS / BROADCASTING STANDARDS COUNCIL. 1136

0960-4286 See EDINBURGH JOURNAL OF BOTANY. 508

0960-4405 See NO-DIG INTERNATIONAL. 2027

0960-4634 See EDI IN FINANCE. 5102

0960-5002 See MANAGING INTELLECTUAL PROPERTY. 1306

0960-5037 See CURRENT BIOTECHNOLOGY. 3656

0960-5045 See PROCESS AND CHEMICAL ENGINEERING. 2006

0960-5053 See THEORETICAL CHEMICAL ENGINEERING. 2007

0960-5061 See WHICH EUROPEAN DATABASE?. 1255

0960-5185 See BUILDING AND CIVIL ENGINEERING RESEARCH FOCUS. 2019

0960-5290 See CONTEMPORARY HYPNOSIS : THE JOURNAL OF THE BRITISH SOCIETY OF EXPERIMENTAL AND CLINICAL HYPNOSIS. 2857

0960-5371 See BRITISH JOURNAL OF PSYCHIATRY. SUPPLEMENT, THE. 3922

0960-5428 See ADVANCES IN NEUROIMMUNOLOGY. 3826

0960-5592 See TRANSFUSION MEDICINE. SUPPLEMENT. 3774

0960-6009 See I.O.S. CRUISE REPORT. 1449

0960-6033 See MUSIC. 4132

0960-6130 See EUROPEAN RESEARCH IN REGIONAL SCIENCE. 5104

0960-6319 See CENTRAL BANKING. 782

0960-6491 See INDUSTRIAL AND CORPORATE CHANGE. 1610

0960-6513 See PERSPECTIVES IN INFORMATION MANAGEMENT. 3241

0960-653X See WORLD PUBLISHING MONITOR. 4822

0960-6548 See PHARMACEUTICAL PHYSICIAN. 4320

0960-6556 See ART NEWSPAPER. 339

0960-6661 See TECHNICAL CERAMICS INTERNATIONAL. 2594

0960-667X See MICROWAVE ENGINEERING EUROPE. 2072

0960-6696 See MONOGRAPHS ON STATISTICS AND APPLIED PROBABILITY. 5333

0960-670X See GEMINI (HERSTMONCEUX, EAST SUSSEX). 390

0960-7315 See RIG MARKET FORECAST. 4277

0960-7404 See SURGICAL ONCOLOGY. 3824

0960-7412 See PLANT JOURNAL : FOR CELL AND MOLECULAR BIOLOGY, THE. 523

0960-7420 See EUROPEAN JOURNAL OF IMMUNOGENETICS : OFFICIAL JOURNAL OF THE BRITISH SOCIETY FOR HISTOCOMPATABILITY AND IMMUNOGENETICS. 3669

0960-7439 See INTERNATIONAL JOURNAL OF PAEDIATRIC DENTISTRY / THE BRITISH PAEDONDONTIC SOCIETY [AND] THE INTERNATIONAL ASSOCIATION OF DENTISTRY FOR CHILDREN. 1325

0960-7447 See GLOBAL ECOLOGY AND BIOGEOGRAPHY LETTERS. 2216

0960-748X See NEW TIMES : THE JOURNAL OF DEMOCRATIC LEFT. 5210

0960-7560 See HOMEOSTASIS IN HEALTH AND DISEASE : INTERNATIONAL JOURNAL DEVOTED TO INTEGRATIVE BRAIN FUNCTIONS AND HOMEOSTATIC SYSTEMS. 3833

0960-7609 See GENERAL STUDIES REVIEW. 2487

0960-7641 See IEE PROCEEDINGS. A, SCIENCE, MEASUREMENT AND TECHNOLOGY. 2057

0960-764X See IEE PROCEEDINGS. SCIENCE, MEASUREMENT AND TECHNOLOGY. 2058

0960-7692 See ULTRASOUND IN OBSTETRICS AND GYNAECOLOGY. 3769

0960-7722 See CELL PROLIFERATION. 534

0960-7773 See CONTEMPORARY EUROPEAN HISTORY. 2684

0960-779X See EYE : THE INTERNATIONAL REVIEW OF GRAPHIC DESIGN. 378

0960-7889 See REGULATORY AFFAIRS JOURNAL. 3633

0960-7919 See ENGINEERING MANAGEMENT JOURNAL. 1973

0960-7943 See EUROFOOD MONITOR. 2334

0960-796X See BRITISH JOURNAL OF CURRICULUM AND ASSESSMENT. 1889

0960-7986 See AWARDS FOR POSTGRADUATE STUDY AT COMMONWEALTH UNIVERSITIES. 1811

0960-7994 See JANE'S HIGH-SPEED MARINE CRAFT. 4047

0960-832X See MILLION BRIGHTON. 3412

0960-8524 See BIORESOURCE TECHOLOGY. 2225

0960-8532 See TREASURY BULLETIN. 4757

0960-8648 See ISSUES IN ARCHITECTURE ART AND DESIGN. 301

0960-8702 See LATIN AMERICAN ECONOMY & BUSINESS. 1637

0960-8710 See NEGOCIOS AL DIA. 698

0960-877X See WATCHWORDS GCSE ENGLISH REVIEW. 3332

0960-8788 See BRITISH JOURNAL FOR THE HISTORY OF PHILOSOPHY. 4342

0960-8796 See GREEN ENGINEERING. 2173

0960-8869 See INTERNATIONAL ECONOMIC OUTLOOK / CENTRE FOR ECONOMIC FORECASTING, LONDON BUSINESS SCHOOL. 1636

0960-8923 See OBESITY SURGERY. 3970

0960-8931 See MELANOMA RESEARCH. 3821

0960-894X See BIOORGANIC & MEDICINAL CHEMISTRY LETTERS. 1039

0960-8966 See NEUROMUSCULAR DISORDERS : NMD. 3806

0960-8974 See PROGRESS IN CRYSTAL GROWTH AND CHARACTERIZATION OF MATERIALS. 1033

0960-9024 See CIVIL AVIATION TRAINING : CAT. 16

0960-9199 See NEWSHEET - COUNCIL FOR ENVIRONMENTAL EDUCATION. 2178

0960-9555 See LINCOLNSHIRE PAST & PRESENT. 2697

0960-9768 See JOURNAL OF CANCER CARE. 3819

0960-9776 See BREAST : OFFICIAL JOURNAL OF THE EUROPEAN SOCIETY OF MASTOLOGY, THE. 3758

0960-9784 See INTERNATIONAL FOOD SAFETY NEWS. 2345

0960-9822 See CURRENT BIOLOGY. 452

0960-9857 See JOURNAL OF ADVANCES IN HEALTH AND NURSING CARE. 3858

0960-9911 See OPEN SYSTEMS (SUTTON, SURREY, ENGLAND). 1243

0960-9989 See EXPLORATION INTERNATIONAL NEWS. 4256

0961-0006 See JOURNAL OF LIBRARIANSHIP AND INFORMATION SCIENCE. 3220

0961-0286 See CPN. CRIME PREVENTION NEWS. 3161

0961-0421 See BAILLIERE'S CLINICAL NEUROLOGY. 3828

0961-0464 See FRUIT & VEGETABLE MARKETS. 89

0961-0480 See CAMBRIDGE FUTURES CHARTS. 1467

0961-0804 See PRACTITIONERS' CHILD LAW BULLETIN. 3030

0961-088X See BIOMEDICAL LETTERS. 3556

0961-0898 See DENDRON : AN INTERNATIONAL BIOMEDICAL JOURNAL FOR RESEARCH IN NEUROSCIENCE. 3831
0961-0901 See CHROMATIN. 543
0961-1096 See RACECAR ENGINEERING. 5423
0961-1118 See WORLD PHARMACEUTICAL STANDARDS REVIEW. 4333
0961-1142 See AFRICA FORUM. 2501
0961-1215 See LEONARDO MUSIC JOURNAL : LMJ : JOURNAL OF THE INTERNATIONAL SOCIETY FOR THE ARTS, SCIENCES AND TECHNOLOGY. 4128
0961-124X See AUDIT TUNBRIDGE WELLS. 641
0961-1290 See III-VS REVIEW. 2064
0961-1347 See PERSPECTIVES IN ENERGY. 1953
0961-1371 See PLAINSONG AND MEDIEVAL MUSIC. 4146
0961-1428 See DISASTER MANAGEMENT. 1073
0961-1444 See NONRENEWABLE RESOURCES. 2201
0961-1452 See QUANTUM LONDON. 3033
0961-2025 See WOMEN'S HISTORY REVIEW. 5571
0961-2033 See LUPUS. 3721
0961-205X See SOCIAL DEVELOPMENT. 1805
0961-2076 See MEAT FOCUS INTERNATIONAL. 215
0961-2114 See BROKER (LONDON). 2876
0961-2149 See OXFORD STUDIES IN COMPARATIVE EDUCATION. 1771
0961-2246 See CURRENT MEDICAL LITERATURE. THROMBOSIS. 3771
0961-2513 See AVMARK AVIATION ECONOMIST. 14
0961-2564 See CIVIL PROTECTION. 1072
0961-2580 See RECREATION MELTON MOWBRAY. 4854
0961-2653 See BJR SUPPLEMENT. 3939
0961-2742 See ANBAR ACCOUNTING & FINANCE ABSTRACTS. 726
0961-2793 See EAST ASIA EXPRESS. 670
0961-3218 See BUILDING RESEARCH AND INFORMATION : THE INTERNATIONAL JOURNAL OF RESEARCH, DEVELOPMENT AND DEMONSTRATION. 604
0961-3226 See MAJOR COMPANIES OF THE FAR EAST AND AUSTRALASIA. 691
0961-3501 See SMALL ANIMALS. 5522
0961-3552 See ADVANCES IN ENGINEERING SOFTWARE (1992). 1964
0961-3730 See INTERNATIONAL FIRE AND SECURITY PRODUCT NEWS. 2291
0961-4141 See KEW RICHMOND. 516
0961-4206 See PRIVATISATION INTERNATIONAL. 1639
0961-4249 See ARCHBOLD NEWS. 3105
0961-4524 See DEVELOPMENT IN PRACTICE. 2909
0961-4532 See CARRYING STREAM, THE. 2683
0961-4559 See JEWELLERY INTERNATIONAL. 2914
0961-4575 See LIBRARIES DIRECTORY. 3223
0961-4591 See PALLIATIVE CARE INDEX. 3625
0961-463X See TIME & SOCIETY. 4364
0961-4664 See FRESHWATER FORUM. 456
0961-4710 See INDUSTRIAL WASTE MANAGEMENT. 2232
0961-4729 See CLEANING INDUSTRY YEARBOOK. 5349
0961-4745 See IMPACT AGBIOBUSINESS. 681
0961-5032 See CLOCKMAKER (HINCKLEY). 2772
0961-5237 See CLASSICAL CATALOGUE. 5316
0961-5261 See TREASURY TODAY. 752
0961-5326 See INTERNATIONAL CORPORATE LAW. 3100
0961-5423 See EUROPEAN JOURNAL OF CANCER CARE / THE OFFICIAL JOURNAL OF THE EUROPEAN ONCOLOGY NURSING SOCIETY. 3855
0961-5539 See INTERNATIONAL JOURNAL OF NUMERICAL METHODS FOR HEAT & FLUID FLOW. 1980

0961-5555 See MIDIRS MIDWIFERY DIGEST. 3765
0961-5628 See GEOSCIENTIST. 1380
0961-5962 See PERIOD HOUSE & ITS GARDEN. 2902
0961-6055 See JOURNAL OF BRITISH PODIATRIC MEDICINE LONDON 1991. 3918
0961-6071 See REPORT / IGER. 126
0961-625X See MINIMALLY INVASIVE THERAPY. 3970
0961-6284 See WORLD TELEMEDIA. 1169
0961-7256 See BANKING LAW REPORTS. 2939
0961-7264 See REINSURANCE LAW REPORTS. 3037
0961-7272 See CALVINISM TODAY. 4942
0961-7388 See AIRCRAFT VALUE NEWSLETTER. 9
0961-754X See COMMON KNOWLEDGE. 2844
0961-7590 See COMMUNICATIONS MIDDLE EAST AFRICA. 1108
0961-7612 See INFORMATION MANAGEMENT REPORT. 1157
0961-7655 See POTATO REVIEW. 182
0961-7671 See INTERNATIONAL JOURNAL OF PHARMACY PRACTICE. 4309
0961-7752 See MARKETING SUCCESS. 932
0961-7787 See CLINICIAN'S MANUAL ON HYPERLIPIDEMIA. 3703
0961-8082 See TOTAL QUALITY REVIEW, THE. 888
0961-8163 See OFFSHORE ENGINEERING INFORMATION BULLETIN. 3238
0961-8171 See BONDHOLDER / IFR, THE. 779
0961-818X See PROJECT FINANCE INTERNATIONAL. 804
0961-8295 See PALMER'S IN COMPANY. 3024
0961-8333 See PRACTICE MARKETING. 935
0961-8368 See PROTEIN SCIENCE : A PUBLICATION OF THE PROTEIN SOCIETY. 493
0961-8414 See ARCHIMEDES WORLD. 1171
0961-8422 See LONDON DEFENCE STUDIES. 4049
0961-8481 See AHORA. 3262
0961-933X See NEW STUDIES IN ATHLETICS. 4907
0961-9356 See ENVIRONMENTAL POLICY AND PRACTICE. 2168
0961-9526 See COMPOSITES ENGINEERING. 2101
0961-9534 See BIOMASS & BIOENERGY. 1933
0961-9712 See EUROPROPERTY LONDON. 897
0961-9755 See BDA NEWS. 1317
0961-978X See FEEDS & FEEDING. 201
0961-9836 See MAGHREB QUARTERLY. 1573
0961-9836 See MAGHREB QUARTERLY REPORT. 1573
0962-0036 See DIRECTORY OF RESEARCH WORKERS IN AGRICULTURE AND ALLIED SCIENCES. 153
0962-0184 See PEAK PERFORMANCE. 4853
0962-0214 See INTERNATIONAL STUDIES IN SOCIOLOGY OF EDUCATION. 1754
0962-029X See JOURNAL OF INFORMATION TECHNOLOGY FOR TEACHER EDUCATION. 1757
0962-0311 See INSTITUTION OF WATER OFFICERS JOURNAL. 5534
0962-0605 See MAMMOGRAPH ABSTRACTS : BREAST CANCER SCREENING REFERENCES. 3820
0962-0648 See EARLY MODERN HISTORY. 2686
0962-1016 See OUTDOORS ILLUSTRATED. 4877
0962-1040 See EASTERN EUROPE AND THE COMMONWEALTH OF INDEPENDENT STATES. 1925
0962-1067 See JOURNAL OF CLINICAL NURSING. 3858
0962-1083 See MOLECULAR ECOLOGY. 2218
0962-1091 See GYNAECOLOGICAL ENDOSCOPY. 3761
0962-1105 See JOURNAL OF SLEEP RESEARCH. 3597

0962-1113 See INTEGRATED ENVIRONMENTAL MANAGEMENT. 2174
0962-1369 See JOURNAL OF BUSINESS ECONOMICS. 1498
0962-1377 See JOURNAL OF CELTIC LINGUISTICS. 3289
0962-1423 See BRITISH JOURNAL OF MEDICAL ECONOMICS, THE. 1465
0962-1474 See FINANCIAL MARKETING UPDATE. 1491
0962-1539 See BOLTON EVENING NEWS. 5811
0962-1792 See THEATRE RECORD. 5371
0962-1830 See SPECTRUM : THE QUARTERLY MAGAZINE OF THE INDEPENDENT TELEVISION COMMISSION. 1139
0962-1849 See APPLIED & PREVENTIVE PSYCHOLOGY : JOURNAL OF THE AMERICAN ASSOCIATION OF APPLIED AND PREVENTIVE PSYCHOLOGY. 4574
0962-2152 See WOMAN ALIVE. 5009
0962-2225 See SUPERSTORE MANAGEMENT INTERNATIONAL. 958
0962-2519 See TARGET MANAGEMENT DEVELOPMENT REVIEW. 887
0962-2543 See CENTRAL EUROPEAN. 1633
0962-2624 See TRUST LAW INTERNATIONAL : PENSION FUNDS, COMMERCIAL TRUSTS, AND CHARITIES. 918
0962-2640 See GUITAR MAGAZINE. 4120
0962-2780 See ECONOMIC AND FINANCIAL COMPUTING. 1482
0962-2799 See REPRODUCTIVE MEDICINE REVIEW. 3767
0962-2802 See STATISTICAL METHODS IN MEDICAL RESEARCH. 3642
0962-3566 See PARKING REVIEW. 5442
0962-3582 See DRUG TARIFF. 4721
0962-3590 See HOLLIS EUROPE. 760
0962-3647 See ADVANCES IN GEOPHYSICAL RESEARCH. 1402
0962-3752 See OIL & GAS FINANCE AND ACCOUNTING. 749
0962-3825 See TELECOMEUROPA'S EASTERN EUROPE NEWSLETTER. 1165
0962-3876 See CEPS PAPER. 4468
0962-3922 See FLOPPY ANBAR (MCB UNIVERSITY PRESS). 1185
0962-4694 See JOURNAL OF DESIGN AND MANUFACTURING. 3482
0962-4740 See ENVIRONEWS SHREWSBURY. 2165
0962-4929 See ACTA NUMERICA. 3490
0962-6220 See LOCAL TRANSPORT TODAY. 5386
0962-6298 See POLITICAL GEOGRAPHY. 2572
0962-6484 See SALMON NET. 2312
0962-7146 See TRANSPORTATION PLANNING SYSTEMS. 5396
0962-7162 See FLUID ABSTRACTS. PROCESS ENGINEERING. 2004
0962-7170 See FLUID ABSTRACTS. CIVIL ENGINEERING. 2004
0962-7189 See TRIBOLOGY AND CORROSION ABSTRACTS. 2017
0962-7286 See ANIMAL WELFARE. 225
0962-7308 See GRAPHICS INTERNATIONAL. 379
0962-7448 See BOTANIC GARDENS MICROPROPAGATION NEWS. 503
0962-7472 See CRESCENDO & JAZZ MUSIC. 4113
0962-7480 See OCCUPATIONAL MEDICINE. 3623
0962-7871 See JOURNAL - SOCIAL HISTORY CURATORS GROUP. 4090
0962-7944 See GREENPEACE BUSINESS. 2173
0962-8266 See GROUP TRAVEL ORGANISER. 5478
0962-8312 See EUROPEAN MEDIA BULLETIN. 1132
0962-8428 See PHILOSOPHICAL TRANSACTIONS - ROYAL SOCIETY OF LONDON. PHYSICAL SCIENCES AND ENGINEERING. 4414
0962-8436 See PHILOSOPHICAL TRANSACTIONS OF THE ROYAL SOCIETY OF LONDON. SERIES B; BIOLOGICAL SCIENCES. 468

ISSN Index

0962-8444 See PROCEEDINGS. MATHEMATICAL AND PHYSICAL SCIENCES / THE ROYAL SOCIETY. 4417

0962-8444 See PROCEEDINGS. MATHEMATICAL AND PHYSICAL SCIENCES / THE ROYAL SOCIETY. 3527

0962-8452 See PROCEEDINGS. BIOLOGICAL SCIENCES / THE ROYAL SOCIETY. 469

0962-8479 See TUBERCLE AND LUNG DISEASE : THE OFFICIAL JOURNAL OF THE INTERNATIONAL UNION AGAINST TUBERCULOSIS AND LUNG DISEASE. 3952

0962-8770 See BUSINESS ETHICS: A EUROPEAN REVIEW. 2249

0962-8789 See PRIMARY LIFE. 1902

0962-8797 See REVIEW OF EUROPEAN COMMUNITY AND INTERNATIONAL ENVIRONMENTAL LAW. 3116

0962-8819 See TRANSGENIC RESEARCH. 552

0962-8827 See CLINICAL DYSMORPHOLOGY. 451

0962-9262 See SCANDINAVIAN INTERNATIONAL BUSINESS REVIEW. 709

0962-9327 See GC/MS UPDATE. PART A ENVIRONMENTAL. 2172

0962-9335 See GC/MS UPDATE PART B BIOMEDICAL, CLINICAL, DRUGS. 4305

0962-9343 See QUALITY OF LIFE RESEARCH. 4392

0962-9351 See MEDIATORS OF INFLAMMATION. 3607

0962-9467 See GREENPEACE BUSINESS. 2173

0962-9475 See BBC ACORN USER. 1171

0962-9505 See IFAC SYMPOSIA SERIES. 1219

0963-0112 See CURRENT MEDICAL LITERATURE / OPHTHALMOLOGY. 3874

0963-0171 See SHEPPARD'S BOOK DEALERS IN EUROPE. 4832

0963-0252 See PLASMA SOURCES SCIENCE AND TECHNOLOGY. 4417

0963-0538 See EUROPEAN ACCOUNTANCY YEARBOOK. 743

0963-0597 See TELECOM WORLD. 1165

0963-0643 See CURRENT OPINION IN UROLOGY. 3989

0963-0651 See JOURNAL OF SEISMIC EXPLORATION. 1408

0963-0678 See RADIO TECHNOLOGY INTERNATIONAL. 1137

0963-0880 See JOURNAL OF TROPICAL & GEOGRAPHICAL NEUROLOGY : THE OFFICIAL JOURNAL OF THE RESEARCH GROUP ON TROPICAL NEUROLOGY OF THE WORLD FEDERATION OF NEUROLOGY. 3837

0963-1046 See REVENUE LONDON. 3039

0963-1054 See LOCAL AUTHORITY LAW. 3169

0963-1070 See GEORGIAN GROUP JOURNAL, THE. 299

0963-116X See DEFENCE HELICOPTER. 17

0963-1674 See CONFLICT INTERNATIONAL. 4518

0963-1690 See CREATIVITY AND INNOVATION MANAGEMENT. 864

0963-1798 See JOURNAL OF OCCUPATIONAL AND ORGANIZATIONAL PSYCHOLOGY. 4598

0963-1801 See CAMBRIDGE QUARTERLY OF HEALTHCARE ETHICS : CQ : THE INTERNATIONAL JOURNAL FOR HEALTHCARE ETHICS COMMITTEES. 3561

0963-2654 See JOURNAL OF NATURAL GEOMETRY. 3514

0963-2719 See ENVIRONMENTAL VALUES. 2170

0963-3235 See ANNUAL REPORT / HORTICULTURE RESEARCH INTERNATIONAL. 2409

0963-3464 See BMD (LONDON). 921

0963-4029 See CAMBRIDGE EVENING NEWS. 5811

0963-4770 See CHARLESTON MAGAZINE, THE. 3374

0963-4894 See WORLD FOOD REGULATION REVIEW. 2361

0963-5084 See PUBLIC NETWORK EUROPE. 1514

0963-5386 See JOURNAL OF ONE-DAY SURGERY. 3968

0963-5483 See COMBINATORICS, PROBABILITY & COMPUTING : CPC. 3500

0963-5572 See INDEX TO MEED. MIDDLE EAST ECONOMIC DIGEST. 1566

0963-5580 See ADVANCES IN SPEECH, HEARING, AND LANGUAGE PROCESSING. 3261

0963-5637 See ELECTROCHEMICAL SCIENCE AND TECHNOLOGY OF POLYMERS. 975

0963-5696 See ANNUAL BULLETIN - BRITISH SOCIETY FOR PLANT GROWTH REGULATION. 499

0963-5696 See NEWSLETTER - BRITISH SOCIETY FOR PLANT GROWTH REGULATION. 519

0963-5750 See CADCAM LONDON. 1231

0963-5866 See INTERNATIONAL PIG TOPICS. 213

0963-5920 See EPE. 2053

0963-6412 See SECURITY STUDIES. 4535

0963-6420 See AFRO-ASIAN JOURNAL OF NEMATOLOGY. 5574

0963-6536 See REPORT - UNIVERSITY OF NEWCASTLE UPON TYNE. DEPARTMENT OF AGRICULTURAL ECONOMICS AND FOOD MARKETING. 126

0963-6625 See PUBLIC UNDERSTANDING OF SCIENCE. 5143

0963-6706 See CONSTRUCTIONAL LAW. 2956

0963-6749 See ANNUAL BULLETIN - BRITISH SOCIETY FOR PLANT GROWTH REGULATION. 499

0963-6757 See JOURNAL OF SEXUAL HEALTH. 5187

0963-6897 See CELL TRANSPLANTATION. 3795

0963-6927 See TWI JOURNAL. 4028

0963-6935 See ADVANCED COMPOSITES LETTERS. 2100

0963-6986 See MACROMOLECULAR STRUCTURES. 985

0963-7001 See NEWSLETTER - BRITISH SOCIETY FOR PLANT GROWTH REGULATION. 519

0963-7036 See SOVIET & EASTERN EUROPEAN REPORT. 3136

0963-7133 See JOURNAL OF AUDIOLOGICAL MEDICINE. 3889

0963-7141 See CAMBRIDGE NONLINEAR SCIENCE SERIES. 5092

0963-7214 See CURRENT DIRECTIONS IN PSYCHOLOGICAL SCIENCE : A JOURNAL OF THE AMERICAN PSYCHOLOGICAL SOCIETY. 4583

0963-7257 See MARKET RESEARCH REPORTER. 906

0963-7273 See EUROPEAN JOURNAL OF DISORDERS OF COMMUNICATION. 1111

0963-7346 See ENGINEERING SCIENCE AND EDUCATION JOURNAL. 1974

0963-7362 See INTERNATIONAL ENVIRONMENTAL TECHNOLOGY. 2174

0963-7486 See INTERNATIONAL JOURNAL OF FOOD SCIENCES AND NUTRITION. 4192

0963-7494 See RELIGION, STATE & SOCIETY : THE KESTON JOURNAL. 4991

0963-8016 See JOURNAL OF POLITICAL PHILOSOPHY. 4350

0963-8024 See JOURNAL OF AFRICAN ECONOMIES. 1637

0963-8156 See UNITED KINGDOM OIL AND GAS. 4281

0963-8172 See QUALITY IN HEALTH CARE : QHC. 3632

0963-8180 See EUROPEAN ACCOUNTING REVIEW. 743

0963-8199 See JOURNAL OF INTERNATIONAL TRADE AND ECONOMIC DEVELOPMENT. 1637

0963-8237 See JOURNAL OF MENTAL HEALTH. 3929

0963-8245 See PUBLIC PROCUREMENT LAW REVIEW. 3033

0963-8253 See FORUM FOR PROMOTING 3-19 COMPREHENSIVE EDUCATION. 1747

0963-8288 See DISABILITY AND REHABILITATION. 4387

0963-8334 See CONTEMPORARY LEGEND : THE JOURNAL OF THE INTERNATIONAL SOCIETY FOR CONTEMPORARY LEGEND RESEARCH. 2319

0963-8474 See EUROPEAN POLYMERS PAINT COLOUR JOURNAL. 4223

0963-8601 See PREP SCHOOL. 1774

0963-8687 See JOURNAL OF STRATEGIC INFORMATION SYSTEMS, THE. 1248

0963-8695 See NDT & E INTERNATIONAL : INDEPENDENT NONDESTRUCTIVE TESTING AND EVALUATION. 1988

0963-9268 See URBAN HISTORY. 2838

0963-9284 See ACCOUNTING EDUCATION. 736

0963-9292 See ECOTOXICOLOGY LONDON. 2215

0963-9306 See JOURNAL OF PROGRAMMING LANGUAGES. 1280

0963-9314 See SOFTWARE QUALITY JOURNAL. 1203

0963-9446 See UK TRADE BULLETIN IMPORTS & EXPORTS OF FISH & FISH PRODUCTS. 2315

0963-9462 See EARLY MEDIEVAL EUROPE. 2686

0963-9470 See LANGUAGE AND LITERATURE. 3294

0963-9489 See MODERN & CONTEMPORARY FRANCE. 5209

0963-9535 See PROJECT FINANCE INTERNATIONAL. 804

0963-9640 See INTELLIGENT SYSTEMS ENGINEERING. 1979

0963-9659 See PURE AND APPLIED OPTICS: JOURNAL OF THE EUROPEAN OPTICAL SOCIETY PART A. 4440

0963-9675 See BULLETIN / INSTITUTE OF ADVANCED LEGAL STUDIES (UNIVERSITY OF LONDON). 2944

0963-9969 See FOOD RESEARCH INTERNATIONAL. 2339

0964-0029 See MICROSOFT MAGAZINE. 1270

0964-0037 See EUROPEAN CURRENT LAW : MONTHLY DIGEST. 2967

0964-010X See DISABILITY NEWS. 4387

0964-0142 See MARKETING SURVEYS INDEX. 932

0964-0282 See SOCIAL ANTHROPOLOGY : THE JOURNAL OF THE EUROPEAN ASSOCIATION OF SOCIAL ANTHROPOLOGISTS. 245

0964-0401 See CZECHOSLOVAKIA, MAJOR BUSINESSES / DUN & BRADSTREET INTERNATIONAL. 664

0964-0428 See JOURNAL OF ECONOMIC REFORM AND TRANSFORMATION. 1637

0964-0568 See JOURNAL OF ENVIRONMENTAL PLANNING AND MANAGEMENT. 2826

0964-0606 See JOURNAL OF TEACHER DEVELOPMENT. 1899

0964-0681 See WORLD HOCKEY. 4930

0964-069X See IMPACT AGBIOINDUSTRY. 3693

0964-1645 See LC-MS UPDATE. 5125

0964-1807 See APPLIED SUPERCONDUCTIVITY. 2035

0964-1816 See COMPLEXITY: AN INTERNATIONAL JOURNAL OF COMPLEX AND ADAPTIVE SYSTEMS. 5096

0964-1823 See EXPLORATION AND MINING GEOLOGY : JOURNAL OF THE GEOLOGICAL SOCIETY OF CIM. 2138

0964-1866 See THERAPEUTIC COMMUNITIES. 3645

0964-1955 See EUROPEAN JOURNAL OF CANCER. PART B : ORAL ONCOLOGY. 3817

0964-198X See ADVERSE DRUG REACTIONS AND TOXICOLOGICAL REVIEWS. 3978

0964-2366 See MANUFACTURING BREAKTHROUGH. 3483

0964-2633 See JOURNAL OF INTELLECTUAL DISABILITY RESEARCH. 4598

0964-2706 See AWARDS FOR UNIVERSITY TEACHERS AND RESEARCH WORKERS. 1727

0964-3397 See INTENSIVE & CRITICAL CARE NURSING : THE OFFICIAL JOURNAL OF THE BRITISH ASSOCIATION OF CRITICAL CARE NURSES. 3857

0964-3400 *See* ALPHANUMERIC REPORTS PUBLICATIONS INDEX. 3189
0964-4008 *See* GERMAN POLITICS. 4474
0964-4016 *See* ENVIRONMENTAL POLITICS. 2168
0964-413X *See* PROJECT FINANCE INTERNATIONAL. 804
0964-4156 *See* PROFESSIONAL CARE OF MOTHER AND CHILD. 3767
0964-4164 *See* FOOD SAFETY & SECURITY. 2340
0964-4199 *See* CABINET MAKER LONDON. 1990. 633
0964-4326 *See* UKRAINIAN REPORTER. 4537
0964-4563 *See* TOBACCO CONTROL. 4805
0964-4571 *See* MONTHLY BULLETIN OF INDICES PRICE ADJUSTMENT FORMULAE FOR CONSTRUCTION CONTRACTS. 633
0964-4636 *See* NOROIL CONTACTS. 4266
0964-4946 *See* EVENING NEWS (NORWICH. 1991). 5812
0964-5292 *See* EDUCATION ECONOMICS. 1739
0964-5322 *See* ENVIRONMENT INFORMATION BULLETIN. 2165
0964-5586 *See* ANIMATOR ST. ALBANS. 4063
0964-5691 *See* OCEAN & COASTAL MANAGEMENT. 1453
0964-5985 *See* VAT PLANNING. 4757
0964-5993 *See* TECHNICAL TEXTILES INTERNATIONAL. 5356
0964-6221 *See* CHESS (OXFORD). 4858
0964-6337 *See* INTERPRETATION NEWSLETTER. 2692
0964-6604 *See* POULTRY SCIENCE REVIEWS. 218
0964-6639 *See* SOCIAL & LEGAL STUDIES. 3056
0964-671X *See* CLEARING & SETTLEMENT. 783
0964-6841 *See* SOFTWARE DEVELOPMENT MONITOR. 1290
0964-6906 *See* HUMAN MOLECULAR GENETICS. 547
0964-704X *See* JOURNAL OF THE HISTORY OF THE NEUROSCIENCES. 490
0964-7058 *See* ASIA PACIFIC JOURNAL OF CLINICAL NUTRITION. 4187
0964-7082 *See* WALTHAM INTERNATIONAL FOCUS. 5527
0964-7104 *See* BRITISH ARCHAEOLOGICAL BIBLIOGRAPHY. 286
0964-7554 *See* GROWTH FACTORS & CYTOKINES. 581
0964-7570 *See* PARASITOLOGY. 3626
0964-7589 *See* SIGNAL TRANSDUCTION & CYCLIC NUCLEOTIDES. 493
0964-7597 *See* CHOLESTEROL AND LIPOPROTEINS. 485
0964-7600 *See* MAMMARY GLAND. 464
0964-7627 *See* LIBRARY TECHNOLOGY NEWS LTN. 3227
0964-7686 *See* BASE METALS MONTHLY. 3998
0964-7694 *See* STEEL MARKETS MONTHLY. 4020
0964-7775 *See* MUSEUM MANAGEMENT AND CURATORSHIP (1990). 4092
0964-816X *See* CHURCH OF ENGLAND NEWSPAPER : CEN. 2514
0964-8305 *See* INTERNATIONAL BIODETERIORATION & BIODEGREDATION. 1356
0964-8313 *See* DRUGS PREVENTION INITIATIVE PROGRESS REPORT / HOME OFFICE ; [PREPARED BY THE HOME OFFICE CENTRAL DRUGS PREVENTION UNIT]. 4302
0964-8410 *See* CORPORATE GOVERNANCE. 864
0964-8461 *See* CURRENT SENTENCING PRACTICE NEWS. 2958
0964-8496 *See* GAS MATTERS. 4257
0964-8550 *See* EUROPEAN BUSINESS INFORMATION SOURCEBOOK. 673
0964-8585 *See* COMMERCE BUSINESS DIRECTORIES REDDITCH ED. 658
0964-8712 *See* CURRENT ADVANCES IN APPLIED MICROBIOLOGY & BIOTECHNOLOGY. 477

0964-8720 *See* CURRENT ADVANCES IN ENDOCRINOLOGY AND METABOLISM. 3656
0964-8747 *See* CURRENT ADVANCES IN IMMUNOLOGY & INFECTIOUS DISEASES. 3656
0964-8755 *See* GREEN ENERGY MATTERS. 4259
0964-8844 *See* CLIENT SERVER. 1174
0964-8895 *See* SEATRADE REVIEW. 5455
0964-8992 *See* HORTICULTURIST/ INSTITUTE OF HORTICULTURE, THE. 2419
0964-9107 *See* GREENHOUSE GASES BULLETIN. 2140
0964-9204 *See* CAPITAL TAXES NEWS AND REPORTS. 4717
0964-9271 *See* PRACTICE NURSING. 3867
0964-928X *See* SURFACE COATINGS INTERNATIONAL : JOCCA, JOURNAL OF THE OIL AND COLOUR CHEMISTS' ASSOCIATION. 4225
0964-9301 *See* INTERNATIONAL SECURITIES LENDING. 792
0964-9425 *See* WOMEN IN MANAGEMENT REVIEW. 735
0964-962X *See* HAZARDOUS SUBSTANCES (SUDBURY). 2231
0964-9700 *See* MILITARY FIREFIGHTER. 2291
0964-9719 *See* INDUSTRIAL FIRE JOURNAL. 2291
0965-030X *See* ELECTRONIC AND ELECTRICAL ENGINEERING. 2046
0965-0326 *See* TECHNOLOGY COMMERCIALISATION (EUROPE ED.). 5163
0965-0350 *See* EASTERN EUROPE ANALYST. 1481
0965-0407 *See* ONCOLOGY RESEARCH. 3822
0965-0482 *See* ENVIRONMENT, TECHNOLOGY AND INDUSTRY. 2166
0965-0504 *See* CURRENT ADVANCES IN PROTEIN BIOCHEMISTRY. 478
0965-0504 *See* CURRENT ADVANCES IN PROTEIN CHEMISTRY. 478
0965-0512 *See* CURRENT ADVANCES IN TOXICOLOGY. 3656
0965-0644 *See* INTERNATIONAL MARINE BUSINESS. 684
0965-0717 *See* EC FOOD LAW. 2965
0965-075X *See* INTERNATIONAL JOURNAL OF SELECTION AND ASSESSMENT. 943
0965-0792 *See* EDUCATIONAL ACTION RESEARCH. 1741
0965-0822 *See* WORLD TIN STATISTICS. 4024
0965-0830 *See* WORLD NICKEL STATISTICS. 4024
0965-089X *See* PROCEEDINGS OF THE INSTITUTION OF CIVIL ENGINEERS. CIVIL ENGINEERING. 2029
0965-0903 *See* PROCEEDINGS OF THE INSTITUTION OF CIVIL ENGINEERS. MUNICIPAL ENGINEER. 2029
0965-0911 *See* PROCEEDINGS OF THE INSTITUTION OF CIVIL ENGINEERS. STRUCTURES AND BUILDINGS. 2029
0965-092X *See* PROCEEDINGS OF THE INSTITUTION OF CIVIL ENGINEERS, TRANSPORT. 2029
0965-0946 *See* PROCEEDINGS OF THE INSTITUTION OF CIVIL ENGINEERS. WATER, MARITIME AND ENERGY. 2094
0965-1004 *See* WHICH SCHOOL? FOR SPECIAL NEEDS. 1886
0965-125X *See* CONFERENCE & INCENTIVE TRAVEL. 5467
0965-1403 *See* FAMILY SPENDING / CENTRAL STATISTICAL OFFICE. 1490
0965-156X *See* DEBATTE OXFORD. 2845
0965-1748 *See* INSECT BIOCHEMISTRY AND MOLECULAR BIOLOGY. 5609
0965-1802 *See* ADVANCES IN ALS/MND. 3826
0965-1896 *See* AIR PICTORIAL INTERNATIONAL. 8
0965-190X *See* RCD. ROCK COMPACT DISC MAGAZINE. 4148
0965-2035 *See* ELECTRONIC DOCUMENTS. 5102
0965-2051 *See* FOREST. 5373

0965-206X *See* JOURNAL OF TISSUE VIABILITY. 538
0965-2140 *See* ADDICTION. 1338
0965-2299 *See* COMPLEMENTARY THERAPIES IN MEDICINE. 3567
0965-2302 *See* ACCIDENT AND EMERGENCY NURSING. 3850
0965-2396 *See* EDUCATION AFTER SIXTEEN. 1738
0965-240X *See* LANGUAGES IN EUROPE. 1761
0965-2507 *See* OLDIE (LONDON). 2520
0965-254X *See* JOURNAL OF STRATEGIC MARKETING. 929
0965-3031 *See* NETWORK WEEK. 1160
0965-3147 *See* WASTE PLANNING. 2246
0965-3570 *See* ASIA PACIFIC JOURNAL OF QUALITY MANAGEMENT. 860
0965-3597 *See* IN COMPETITION. 2980
0965-366X *See* HOME COOKING. 2790
0965-3775 *See* INTERNATIONAL WHO'S WHO OF WOMEN, THE. 5559
0965-3783 *See* WORLD DIRECTORY OF DIPLOMATIC REPRESENTATION. 4705
0965-3813 *See* ENVIRONMENT RISK. 2166
0965-3821 *See* INFORMATION WORLD EN ESPANOL. 3217
0965-3848 *See* XYZ DIRECTION. 369
0965-4283 *See* HEALTH EDUCATION. 1855
0965-4313 *See* EUROPEAN PLANNING STUDIES. 2822
0965-4380 *See* JOURNAL OF AGSI. 3219
0965-4488 *See* WASTE & ENVIRONMENT TODAY. NEWS JOURNAL. 2246
0965-4496 *See* WASTE & ENVIRONMENT TODAY. BIBLIOGRAPHIC JOURNAL. 2246
0965-450X *See* BOOTH'S NIC BRIEF. 2876
0965-4682 *See* FOOD INDUSTRY BULLETIN. 2337
0965-4690 *See* FOOD LAUNCH AWARENESS BULLETIN. 2338
0965-4704 *See* FREIGHT MANAGEMENT INTERNATIONAL. 5383
0965-4712 *See* PANEL BUILDING. 305
0965-4739 *See* PREMISES & FACILITIES MANAGEMENT. 4214
0965-528X *See* INTERNATIONAL YEARBOOK OF LAW, COMPUTERS, AND TECHNOLOGY. 2984
0965-528X *See* INTERNATIONAL YEARBOOK OF LAW, COMPUTERS AND TECHNOLOGY. 5116
0965-531X *See* BIBLE PUZZLER. 5056
0965-5395 *See* FETAL AND MATERNAL MEDICINE REVIEW. 3760
0965-5425 *See* COMPUTATIONAL MATHEMATICS AND MATHEMATICAL PHYSICS. 3501
0965-5433 *See* ELECTRICAL TECHNOLOGY. 2045
0965-5441 *See* PETROLEUM CHEMISTRY. 4272
0965-545X *See* POLYMER SCIENCE. 989
0965-5751 *See* CLINICIAN IN MANAGEMENT. 3913
0965-5948 *See* POLLUTION PREVENTION LONDON. 2239
0965-6219 *See* PRACTICAL PC. 1200
0965-6545 *See* SOFTWARE FUTURES. 1290
0965-6812 *See* IMAGING : AN INTERNATIONAL JOURNAL OF CLINICO-RADIOLOGICAL PRACTICE. 3942
0965-7053 *See* ARBITRATION AND DISPUTE RESOLUTION LAW JOURNAL, THE. 3124
0965-7231 *See* BUILDINGS & FACILITIES MANAGEMENT FOR THE PUBLIC SECTOR. 605
0965-7576 *See* REVIEW OF INTERNATIONAL ECONOMICS. 1639
0965-7991 *See* PERSONAL INJURIES AND QUANTUM REPORTS. 1701
0965-8106 *See* SILSOE LINK. 134
0965-8203 *See* PORT ENGINEERING MANAGEMENT. 624
0965-8211 *See* MEMORY. 4603
0965-8297 *See* BRITISH MUSEUM MAGAZINE. 4085

0965-8335 *See* INTERNATIONAL JOURNAL OF HEALTH INFORMATICS. **3857**

0965-8416 *See* LANGUAGE AWARENESS. **3295**

0965-8564 *See* TRANSPORTATION RESEARCH. PART A, POLICY AND PRACTICE. **5397**

0965-8629 *See* MOTOR INSURANCE MARKET. **2888**

0965-867X *See* MEMBERS' HANDBOOK & BUYERS' GUIDE : THE GREEN BOOK / THE INSTITUTION OF AGRICULTURAL ENGINEERS. **160**

0965-9269 *See* EXCHANGE & MART NORTH/MIDLAND ED. **5812**

0965-9587 *See* SCREEN FINANCE. **4077**

0965-9595 *See* BIOTECHNOLOGY BUSINESS NEWS. **3688**

0965-9676 *See* EAST EUROPEAN INSURANCE REPORT. **2879**

0965-9749 *See* MARXIST REVIEW. LONDON. **4543**

0965-9757 *See* CURRICULUM STUDIES. **1892**

0965-9773 *See* NANOSTRUCTURED MATERIALS. **2107**

0965-9978 *See* ADVANCES IN ENGINEERING SOFTWARE (1992). **1964**

0965-9986 *See* DENTAL WORLD / FDI. **1322**

0966-002X *See* EUROPEAN MACHINING. **2114**

0966-0100 *See* PLANT GENETIC RESOURCES ABSTRACTS. **479**

0966-0259 *See* EUROSLOT OLDHAM. **4860**

0966-0399 *See* SELL'S BUILDING & CONSTRUCTION INDEX. **627**

0966-0410 *See* HEALTH & SOCIAL CARE IN THE COMMUNITY. **5287**

0966-0429 *See* JOURNAL OF NURSING MANAGEMENT. **3859**

0966-0453 *See* ASIA PACIFIC HANDBOOK. **640**

0966-0461 *See* BRITISH JOURNAL OF NURSING : BJN. **3852**

0966-0844 *See* BIOMETALS. **483**

0966-0879 *See* JOURNAL OF CONTINGENCIES AND CRISIS MANAGEMENT. **873**

0966-0941 *See* SPECTROSCOPY EUROPE. **4442**

0966-095X *See* BRITISH JOURNAL OF HOLOCAUST EDUCATION. **2679**

0966-1050 *See* CARF. CAMPAIGN AGAINST RACISM & FASCISM 1991. **4467**

0966-114X *See* SCICAT SCIENCE REFERENCE AND INFORMATION SERVICE. **992**

0966-1530 *See* PERIOD HOUSE & ITS GARDEN. **2902**

0966-1646 *See* EUROPEAN ENVIRONMENTAL LAW REVIEW. **3112**

0966-1743 *See* URBAN STREET ENVIRONMENT, THE. **5446**

0966-1913 *See* RISC USER. **1202**

0966-212X *See* MARKET INFORMATION. **906**

0966-2138 *See* BUSINESS INFORMATION FROM GOVERNMENT. **649**

0966-2839 *See* EUROPEAN SECURITY. **4521**

0966-2847 *See* LOW INTENSITY CONFLICT AND LAW ENFORCEMENT. **3169**

0966-2995 *See* HARPIES & QUINES. **5558**

0966-3266 See BASIC REPORTS. **4037**

0966-3274 *See* TRANSPLANT IMMUNOLOGY. **3677**

0966-3371 *See* KNOWLEDGE, THE. **1134**

0966-3452 *See* CENTRAL ASIA BRIEF. **5042**

0966-3541 *See* BUSINESS EUROPA. **648**

0966-369X *See* GENDER, PLACE AND CULTURE: A JOURNAL OF FEMINIST GEOGRAPHY. **5268**

0966-4033 *See* PLAYING-CARD WORLD. **4865**

0966-4661 *See* DRINKS FILE. **2366**

0966-4734 *See* EUROPEAN PACKAGING. **4219**

0966-4793 *See* TRENDS IN POLYMER SCIENCE REGULAR ED. **994**

0966-4858 *See* EUROPEAN HANDBOOK. **673**

0966-4890 *See* BRUSHES INTERNATIONAL DIRECTORY. **2810**

0966-4904 *See* ENVIRONMENTAL PROTECTION TECHNOLOGY. **2169**

0966-4955 *See* INTERNATIONAL CAR PARK DESIGN & CONSTRUCTION TRENDS. **5441**

0966-6346 *See* DANCE NOW. **1312**

0966-6362 *See* GAIT & POSTURE. **3578**

0966-6532 *See* AMBULATORY SURGERY. **3958**

0966-6745 *See* TAKING STOCK LONDON. 1992. **3252**

0966-6796 *See* MICROBIAL CLEANUP. **566**

0966-6907 *See* COLLEGE MANAGEMENT TODAY. **864**

0966-6923 *See* JOURNAL OF TRANSPORT GEOGRAPHY. **2567**

0966-7318 *See* POULTRY SCIENCE SYMPOSIUM SERIES. **218**

0966-7369 *See* JOURNAL OF PENTECOSTAL THEOLOGY. **5062**

0966-761X *See* LLOYD'S CASUALTY WEEK. **5451**

0966-7660 *See* OVERSEAS JOBS EXPRESS. **4208**

0966-7687 *See* WORLD PHARMACEUTICALS REPORT. **4333**

0966-7717 *See* EUROPEAN MARKETING POCKET BOOK. **924**

0966-7733 *See* INTERNATIONAL BROKER, THE. **2884**

0966-7822 *See* POLYMER GELS AND NETWORKS. **2015**

0966-7849 *See* COMPUTER FINANCE. **1236**

0966-7873 *See* NETWORK COMPUTING. **1243**

0966-789X *See* VOICE LONDON. 1992. **3891**

0966-7903 *See* OCCUPATIONAL THERAPY INTERNATIONAL. **4381**

0966-7970 *See* EAST EUROPEAN BUSINESS INFORMATION. **670**

0966-8136 *See* EUROPE-ASIA STUDIES. **2687**

0966-8225 *See* PROPERTY REVIEW OXFORD. **4843**

0966-8330 *See* SHIPBUILDING & SHIPREPAIR. **5456**

0966-8349 *See* LOCATION SCIENCE. **5208**

0966-8373 *See* EUROPEAN JOURNAL OF PHILOSOPHY. **4346**

0966-842X *See* TRENDS IN MICROBIOLOGY (REGULAR ED.). **570**

0966-8519 *See* JOURNAL OF HEART VALVE DISEASE, THE. **3707**

0966-8608 *See* EUROPEAN MARKET & MEDIA FACT. **1490**

0966-8772 *See* BHI PLUS [COMPUTER FILE]. **2857**

0966-8799 *See* LISA PLUS [COMPUTER FILE]. **3259**

0966-9035 *See* BAOBAB ARID LANDS INFORMATION NETWORK. **2555**

0966-9051 *See* BIOIMAGING. **4433**

0966-906X *See* HAZARDS IN THE OFFICE. **2862**

0966-9086 *See* WINDOW ON CHEMOMETRICS. **1031**

0966-9094 *See* WINDOW ON DRUG MONITORING. **5169**

0966-9175 *See* BASIC REPORTS. **4037**

0966-9248 *See* JOURNAL OF INFORMATION NETWORKING. **1242**

0966-9272 *See* ENVIRONMENT MATTERS (INTERNATIONAL). **2166**

0966-9582 *See* JOURNAL OF SUSTAINABLE TOURISM. **5481**

0966-9647 *See* ABC AND D. ARCHITECT BUILDER CONTRACTOR AND DEVELOPER. **287**

0966-9698 *See* RADNEWS TEDDINGTON. **4225**

0966-9795 *See* INTERMETALLICS. **4004**

0966-9809 *See* OLE. OPTO & LASER EUROPE. **4438**

0966-9884 *See* WORLD BOWLS. **4930**

0967-0106 *See* SECURITY DIALOGUE. **4495**

0967-0149 *See* THERAPEUTIC IMMUNOLOGY. **3677**

0967-0262 *See* EUROPEAN JOURNAL OF PHYCOLOGY. **509**

0967-0386 *See* AUTOMOTIVE INTERIORS INTERNATIONAL. **5406**

0967-0424 *See* RELOCATION HANDBOOK. **4846**

0967-0513 *See* LAND CONTAMINATION & RECLAMATION. **2176**

0967-0637 *See* DEEP-SEA RESEARCH. PART I, OCEANOGRAPHIC RESEARCH PAPERS. **1448**

0967-0645 *See* DEEP-SEA RESEARCH. PART II, TOPICAL STUDIES IN OCEANOGRAPHY. **1448**

0967-0653 *See* OCEANOGRAPHIC LITERATURE REVIEW. **1363**

0967-0661 *See* CONTROL ENGINEERING PRACTICE. **2163**

0967-067X *See* COMMUNIST AND POST-COMMUNIST STUDIES. **4540**

0967-070X *See* TRANSPORT POLICY. **5395**

0967-0726 *See* CONSTRUCTION REPAIR. **610**

0967-0742 *See* MEDICAL LAW REVIEW. **3008**

0967-0750 *See* ECONOMICS OF TRANSITION, THE. **1486**

0967-0769 *See* INTERNATIONAL JOURNAL OF LAW AND INFORMATION TECHNOLOGY. **2984**

0967-0793 *See* RUSSIAN ECONOMIC TRENDS. **1583**

0967-0874 *See* INTERNATIONAL JOURNAL OF PEST MANAGEMENT. **96**

0967-0912 *See* STEEL IN TRANSLATION. **4020**

0967-1056 *See* INTERNATIONAL SHIPPING REVIEW. **5450**

0967-1773 *See* POLICING POLICY. **3172**

0967-1994 *See* ZYGOTE. **476**

0967-2052 *See* VOICE INTERNATIONAL. **1168**

0967-2109 *See* CARDIOVASCULAR SURGERY : OFFICIAL JOURNAL OF THE INTERNATIONAL SOCIETY FOR CARDIOVASCULAR SURGERY. **3702**

0967-2265 *See* RUSSIA AND THE SUCCESSOR STATES BRIEFING SERVICE. **4495**

0967-2273 *See* V & A CONSERVATION JOURNAL. **4097**

0967-2486 *See* PRINTWEAR & PROMOTION. **4569**

0967-2494 See PRINTWEAR & PROMOTION. **4569**

0967-2508 *See* CORE. COATINGS, REGULATIONS AND THE ENVIRONMENT. **4226**

0967-2559 *See* INTERNATIONAL JOURNAL OF PHILOSOPHICAL STUDIES, THE. **4349**

0967-2567 *See* EUROPEAN JOURNAL OF THE HISTORY OF ECONOMIC THOUGHT, THE. **1560**

0967-2648 *See* HIGH INTEGRITY SYSTEMS. **1247**

0967-2680 *See* JOURNAL OF PRODUCTS AND TOXICS LIABILITY. **2989**

0967-3334 *See* PHYSIOLOGICAL MEASUREMENT. **3695**

0967-3393 *See* ANARCHIST STUDIES. **4539**

0967-3466 *See* INTELPROP NEWS. **1305**

0967-3849 *See* CHROMOSOME RESEARCH. **3563**

0967-3865 *See* PRIMARY SCHOOL MANAGER. **1868**

0967-3873 *See* GOVERNMENT AND MUNICIPAL BUYERS GUIDE. **4651**

0967-3881 *See* HEALTH CARE BUYERS GUIDE. **950**

0967-389X *See* LABORATORY EQUIPMENT BUYERS GUIDE. **5125**

0967-3911 *See* POLYMERS & POLYMER COMPOSITES. **4459**

0967-3962 *See* TRAINING MATTERS. **332**

0967-411X *See* BOUNDARY AND SECURITY BULLETIN. **861**

0967-4128 *See* BOUNDARY AND TERRITORY BRIEFINGS. **861**

0967-4136 *See* SOUTH PACIFIC LAW REPORTS. **3057**

0967-439X *See* AIRCRAFT TECHNOLOGY ENGINEERING & MAINTENANCE. **1964**

0967-4422 *See* METAL CD. **4131**

0967-4608 *See* ECUMENE. **2560**

0967-4764 *See* URBAN FOCUS LONDON. **2714**

0967-4845 *See* BRITISH JOURNAL OF BIOMEDICAL SCIENCE. **3690**

0967-523X *See* TREASURY MANAGEMENT INTERNATIONAL. **814**

0967-5302 *See* FOOD FILE. **2337**

0967-537X ISSN Index

0967-537X *See* OIL & GAS RUSSIA & POST SOVIET REPUBLICS. HYDROCARBONS BRIEF. **4269**

0967-5698 *See* HORIZONS LONDON. 1991. **5480**

0967-5744 *See* ROYALTY DIGEST. **2522**

0967-5868 *See* JOURNAL OF CLINICAL NEUROSCIENCE. **3594**

0967-5892 *See* GROCER FOOD & DRINK DIRECTORY, THE. **2342**

0967-5914 *See* PROJECT FINANCE INTERNATIONAL. **804**

0967-6090 *See* ONLINE FILES. **1275**

0967-6120 *See* AQUACULTURE INTERNATIONAL. **2295**

0967-621X *See* CRONER'S PREMISES MANAGEMENT. **865**

0967-635X *See* COMPANY INFORMATION. **658**

0967-6368 *See* TOP 100 BUSINESS LIBRARIES. **3253**

0967-6376 *See* BUSINESS NEWSLETTERS DIRECTORY. **651**

0967-6384 *See* MARKET PROFILES. **906**

0967-6392 *See* BUSINESS STATISTICS LONDON. **5324**

0967-6406 *See* WHERE TO BUY BUSINESS INFORMATION. **720**

0967-652X *See* INTERNATIONAL INSTITUTE OF MANAGEMENT DATABASES PLUS. **871**

0967-6562 *See* LAWYERS' EUROPE. **2998**

0967-6597 *See* PESTICIDES NEWS. **2179**

0967-6813 *See* HEADS OF SCIENCE. **5109**

0967-7003 *See* ENGINEERING MATERIALS. **1973**

0967-7119 *See* FAMILY MATTERS LONDON. **2968**

0967-7720 *See* JOURNAL OF MEDICAL BIOGRAPHY. **3967**

0967-7755 *See* SPORTS PHYSIOLOGY & MEDICINE. **3956**

0967-7836 *See* POLICY IMPACT ANALYSIS. **120**

0967-7844 *See* EUROCHEM MONITOR. **82**

0967-7852 *See* EC PACKAGING REPORT. **80**

0967-8115 *See* OCCUPATIONAL PENSIONS LAW REPORTS. **3152**

0967-8123 *See* CD-ROM INFORMATION PRODUCTS. **1264**

0967-828X *See* SOUTH EAST ASIA RESEARCH. **2508**

0967-8298 *See* CURRENT OPINION IN INVESTIGATIONAL DRUGS. **4298**

0967-8344 *See* CRONER'S HEALTH & SAFETY AT WORK. **2861**

0967-8638 *See* MATERIALS WORLD : THE JOURNAL OF THE INSTITUTE OF MATERIALS. **2106**

0967-9618 *See* FOCUS ON TIN. **4002**

0967-9650 *See* EUROPEAN SURFACE TREATMENT. **2114**

0967-9782 *See* BRITISH CERAMIC TRANSACTIONS. **2586**

0968-0136 *See* PRACTICAL FARM IDEAS QUARTERLY. **160**

0968-0160 *See* KNEE, THE. **3806**

0968-0349 *See* TAGLINE (OLNEY). **4820**

0968-042X *See* PHARMACY TODAY LONDON. **4323**

0968-0446 *See* BULLETIN OF THE NATURAL HISTORY MUSEUM. BOTANY SERIES. **505**

0968-0454 *See* BULLETIN OF THE NATURAL HISTORY MUSEUM. ENTOMOLOGY SERIES. **5606**

0968-0462 *See* BULLETIN OF THE NATURAL HISTORY MUSEUM. GEOLOGY SERIES. **1370**

0968-0470 *See* BULLETIN OF THE NATURAL HISTORY MUSEUM. ZOOLOGY SERIES. **5579**

0968-0519 *See* JOURNAL OF ENDOTOXIN RESEARCH. **3595**

0968-0829 *See* STRATEGIC INSIGHTS INTO QUALITY. **713**

0968-0896 *See* BIOORGANIC & MEDICINAL CHEMISTRY. **962**

0968-090X *See* TRANSPORTATION RESEARCH. PART C, EMERGING TECHNOLOGIES. **5397**

0968-1043 *See* SOURCE JOURNALS IN METALS & MATERIALS. **4019**

0968-1302 *See* PAIN REVIEWS. **3625**

0968-1361 *See* TRANSLATION AND LITERATURE. **3447**

0968-1418 *See* BUTTERWORTHS EC CASE CITATOR AND SERVICE. **2945**

0968-1647 *See* FOOD SAFETY CONCERNS BULLETIN, THE. **2340**

0968-1655 *See* PEOPLE & THE PLANET / IPPF, UNFPA, IUCN. **4556**

0968-2082 *See* COLLABORATIVE COMPUTING. **1175**

0968-2090 *See* INTERNATIONAL INSURANCE LAW REVIEW. **2984**

0968-2147 *See* ANIMAL WORLD HORSHAM. **225**

0968-2414 *See* TEACHING & LEARNING BULLETIN. **1906**

0968-2422 *See* COUNTRY PROFILE. THE GAMBIA, GUINEA-BISSAU, CAPE VERDE. **1554**

0968-2481 *See* BRITISH ELECTIONS AND PARTIES YEARBOOK. **4634**

0968-2627 *See* NETWORK PAPER / ODI, RURAL DEVELOPMENT FORESTRY NETWORK. **2389**

0968-2732 *See* CARIBBEAN AND CENTRAL AMERICA REPORT. **1468**

0968-2783 *See* JOURNAL OF ELECTRONIC MATERIAL APPLICATIONS. **2068**

0968-2864 *See* FOCUS ON GENDER. **5557**

0968-3097 *See* BNB ON CD-ROM [COMPUTER FILE]. **3196**

0968-3224 *See* WORLD COAL DORKING. **2153**

0968-3321 *See* WATER & ENVIRONMENT MANAGEMENT. **5542**

0968-3445 *See* WAR IN HISTORY. **2633**

0968-3623 *See* EVENING CHRONICLE (OLDHAM). **5812**

0968-4026 *See* INTERNATIONAL TRADE FINANCE. **684**

0968-4050 *See* CHILDREN LOOKED AFTER BY LOCAL AUTHORITIES IN WALES / WELSH OFFICE / PLANT Y GOFELIR AM DANYNT GAN AWDURDODAU LLEOL CYMRU / Y SWYDDFA GYMREIG. **5278**

0968-4328 *See* MICRON : THE INTERNATIONAL RESEARCH AND REVIEW JOURNAL FOR MICROSCOPY. **573**

0968-4425 *See* EARTHLINES. **2164**

0968-4875 *See* TRAINING FOR QUALITY. **948**

0968-4883 *See* QUALITY ASSURANCE IN EDUCATION. **1869**

0968-4891 *See* EMPOWERMENT IN ORGANIZATIONS. **866**

0968-5227 *See* INFORMATION MANAGEMENT & COMPUTER SECURITY. **1188**

0968-5480 *See* AIDS ABSTRACTS : INTERNATIONAL LITERATURE ON ACQUIRED IMMUNODEFICIENCY SYNDROME AND RELATED RETROVIRUSES. **3663**

0968-5588 *See* STATISTICS OF EDUCATION AND TRAINING IN WALES. SCHOOLS / WELSH OFFICE / YSTADEGAU ADDYSG A HYFFORDDIANT YNG NGHYMRU. YSGOLION / Y SWYDDFA GYMREIG. **1785**

0968-5685 *See* BIOLOGICAL PRODUCTS. **445**

0968-574X *See* FOOD INGREDIENTS & PROCESSING INTERNATIONAL. **2337**

0968-574X *See* FOOD INGREDIENTS AND ANALYSIS INTERNATIONAL. **2337**

0968-6053 *See* CURRENT DIAGNOSTIC PATHOLOGY. **3570**

0968-6118 *See* ICB MAGAZINE. **900**

0968-6185 *See* PREMONITIONS ARRETON. **3425**

0968-6266 *See* NEWSLETTER - WOMEN HERITAGE AND MUSEUMS. **4094**

0968-6347 *See* UTILITY FINANCE. **1630**

0968-6673 *See* GENDER, WORK AND ORGANISATION. **5246**

0968-7122 *See* JAPAN FINANCE AND ECONOMIC REVIEW. **793**

0968-7130 *See* JAPAN MANAGEMENT REVIEW. **872**

0968-7262 *See* CHOIR & ORGAN. **4109**

0968-7513 *See* ANNUAL REGISTER OF BOOK VALUES. EARLY PRINTED BOOKS. **4821**

0968-7521 *See* ANNUAL REGISTER OF BOOK VALUES. MODERN FIRST EDITIONS. **4823**

0968-7548 *See* ANNUAL REGISTER OF BOOK VALUES. VOYAGES, TRAVEL & EXPLORATION. **407**

0968-7610 *See* ADDICTION ABSTRACTS. **1338**

0968-7637 *See* DRUGS : EDUCATION, PREVENTION AND POLICY. **1344**

0968-7645 *See* EUROPEAN UROLOGY UPDATE SERIES. **3990**

0968-7661 *See* POTATO BUSINESS WORLD. **2353**

0968-7688 *See* MOLECULAR MEMBRANE BIOLOGY. **491**

0968-8137 *See* TRUST MONITOR & GRANT NEWS. **815**

0968-8234 *See* RETAIL MONITOR INTERNATIONAL. **957**

0968-8689 *See* CENTRAL ASIA AND THE CAUCASUS IN WORLD AFFAIRS. **656**

0968-8773 *See* CELLULAR & MOLECULAR BIOLOGY RESEARCH. **534**

0968-8803 *See* EXECUTIVE SYSTEMS INTERNATIONAL NEWSLETTER. **674**

0968-8838 *See* CARERS WORLD. **4385**

0968-9249 *See* COMMUNITY CARE MANAGEMENT & PLANNING. **4639**

0969-0239 *See* CELLULOSE. **3562**

0969-059X *See* EUROPEAN QUALITY. : THE OFFICIAL JOURNAL OF THE EUROPEAN ORGANIZATION FOR QUALITY. **1606**

0969-0700 *See* JOURNAL OF WOUND CARE. **3600**

0969-1049 *See* OUTLOOK NEW CHURCH. GENERAL CONFERENCE. **4984**

0969-1189 *See* CV GUIDE TO THE ARTS. **372**

0969-1200 *See* NEWSLETTER - SCOTTISH CIVIC TRUST. **2700**

0969-1375 *See* OCCULT OBSERVER, THE. **4242**

0969-1405 *See* YEARBOOK - SALMON AND TROUT ASSOCIATION. **2316**

0969-1650 *See* DIRT BIKE RIDER. GRAND PRIX SPECIAL. **4081**

0969-2053 *See* COMPUTERGRAM WEEKLY. **1178**

0969-2126 *See* STRUCTURE. **540**

0969-2290 *See* REVIEW OF INTERNATIONAL POLITICAL ECONOMY. **4534**

0969-2509 *See* ECONOMICS AND BUSINESS EDUCATION. **1486**

0969-2681 *See* HENSTON VETERINARY EQUINE VADE MECUM. **5511**

0969-3483 *See* UKRAINE BUSINESS REVIEW. **717**

0969-3637 *See* INDUSTRIAL RELATIONS LAW BULLETIN. **3149**

0969-3653 *See* GLYCOSYLATION AND DISEASE. **3579**

0969-3769 *See* GEODRILLING INTERNATIONAL. **1405**

0969-3823 *See* QUEKETT JOURNAL OF MICROSCOPY, THE. **573**

0969-3912 *See* BUTTERWORTH'S EC LEGISLATION IMPLEMENTATOR. **2945**

0969-4110 *See* GOVERNMENT PROPERTY CONTRACTS BULLETIN. **4652**

0969-4218 *See* MINING ENVIRONMENTAL MANAGEMENT. **1408**

0969-434X *See* PROFESSIONAL UPDATE. **3630**

0969-4978 *See* PRIMARY CARE MANAGEMENT. **3739**

0969-5893 *See* CLINICAL PSYCHOLOGY : SCIENCE AND PRACTICE. **4581**

0969-5931 *See* INTERNATIONAL BUSINESS REVIEW. **683**

0969-594X *See* ASSESSMENT IN EDUCATION: PRINCIPLES, POLICY AND PRACTICE. **1726**

0969-5958 *See* INTERNATIONAL JOURNAL OF THE LEGAL PROFESSION. **2984**

0969-5990 *See* POLYMER RECYCLING. **1028**

0969-6016 *See* INTERNATIONAL TRANSACTIONS IN OPERATIONAL RESEARCH : A JOURNAL OF THE INTERNATIONAL FEDERATION OF OPERATIONAL RESEARCH SOCIETIES. **1191**

0969-6202 *See* FOCUS ON ELECTRONICS CHEMICALS. **975**

0969-6210 *See* FOCUS ON PIGMENTS. 975
0969-6229 *See* FOCUS ON DIAGNOSTICS. 975
0969-6431 *See* CAREERS GUIDANCE TODAY. 4202
0969-6725 *See* AIR TRAFFIC MANAGEMENT. 8
0969-692X *See* CURRENT CLINICAL CANCER. 3815
0969-6989 *See* JOURNAL OF RETAILING AND CONSUMER SERVICES. 955
0969-6997 *See* JOURNAL OF AIR TRANSPORT MANAGEMENT. 26
0969-7012 *See* EUROPEAN JOURNAL OF PURCHASING AND SUPPLY MANAGEMENT. 949
0969-7128 *See* GENE THERAPY. 545
0969-7330 *See* NURSING ETHICS. 3864
0969-7764 *See* EUROPEAN URBAN AND REGIONAL STUDIES. 2822
0969-8043 *See* APPLIED RADIATION AND ISOTOPES : INCLUDING DATA, INSTRUMENTATION AND METHODS FOR USE IN AGRICULTURE, INDUSTRY AND MEDICINE. 4433
0969-806X *See* RADIATION PHYSICS AND CHEMISTRY. 4419
0969-8868 *See* CURRENT OPINION IN SURGICAL INFECTIONS. 3963
0969-9015 *See* LEARN FOR YOURSELF. 1801
0969-9260 *See* PROGRESS IN PALLIATIVE CARE. 3867
0969-9767 *See* OBJECT-ORIENTED SYSTEMS. 1248
0969-9961 *See* NEUROBIOLOGY OF DISEASE. 3620
0969-997X *See* FISHERIES MANAGEMENT AND ECOLOGY. 2302
0969-9988 *See* ENGINEERING CONSTRUCTION & ARCHITECTURAL MANAGEMENT. 2023
0970-0048 *See* INTERNATIONAL LIBRARY MOVEMENT. 3218
0970-0080 *See* FUSION ASIA. 2504
0970-0102 *See* IAPQR TRANSACTIONS. 5328
0970-0129 *See* COMPUTERS TODAY. 1179
0970-0137 *See* JOURNAL OF STRUCTURAL ENGINEERING. 2026
0970-0153 *See* ANNALS OF BIOLOGY (LUDHIANA). 442
0970-0161 *See* STRATEGIC ANALYSIS. 4058
0970-017X *See* STRATEGIC DIGEST. 4058
0970-0188 *See* NISSAT NEWSLETTER. 5134
0970-020X *See* ORIENTAL JOURNAL OF CHEMISTRY. 988
0970-0242 *See* GURU NANAK JOURNAL OF SOCIOLOGY. 5246
0970-0277 *See* OSMANIA PAPERS IN LINGUISTICS. 3308
0970-0285 *See* SHIPPING & MARINE INDUSTRIES JOURNAL. 5456
0970-0293 *See* SOCIAL SCIENTIST (NEW DELHI). 5221
0970-0307 *See* GANITA BHARATI. 3506
0970-0315 *See* ADVANCES IN BIOSCIENCES. 440
0970-0358 *See* INDIAN JOURNAL OF PLASTIC SURGERY. 3966
0970-0382 *See* COMMUNICATIO SOCIALIS YEARBOOK. 4949
0970-0404 *See* INDIAN JOURNAL OF PLANT SCIENCES. 513
0970-0420 *See* ENVIRONMENT & ECOLOGY. 454
0970-0447 *See* JOURNAL OF THE MANAGEMENT PROFESSIONALS ASSOCIATION. 874
0970-0455 *See* ACTA CIENCIA INDICA. MATHEMATICS. 3490
0970-048X *See* ELT FORUM JOURNAL OF ENGLISH STUDIES. 3278
0970-0501 *See* SPACE : JOURNAL OF SCHOOL OF PLANNING AND ARCHITECTURE, NEW DELHI. 309
0970-051X *See* INDIAN JOURNAL OF VETERINARY MEDICINE. 5512
0970-0609 *See* JOURNAL OF THE K.R. CAMA ORIENTAL INSTITUTE. 4971

0970-0617 *See* ANNUAL REPORT ON INDIAN EPIGRAPHY FOR... / DEPARTMENT OF ARCHAEOLOGY. 255
0970-0692 *See* JADAVPUR JOURNAL OF COMPARATIVE LITERATURE. 3398
0970-0714 *See* RECORDS OF THE ZOOLOGICAL SURVEY OF INDIA. MISCELLANEOUS PUBLICATION. OCCASIONAL PAPER. 5596
0970-0765 *See* BULLETIN OF PURE & APPLIED SCIENCES. SECTION A, ANIMAL SCIENCE. 5579
0970-0811 *See* INDIAN JOURNAL OF PHYSICAL & NATURAL SCIENCES. SECTION A. 5112
0970-0838 *See* JOURNAL OF POLYMER MATERIALS. 982
0970-0846 *See* JOURNAL OF AQUACULTURE IN THE TROPICS. 2306
0970-0889 *See* BIO-SCIENCE RESEARCH BULLETIN. 444
0970-0897 *See* INDIAN JOURNAL OF BEHAVIOUR. 4589
0970-0943 *See* CLIS OBSERVER. 3202
0970-1036 *See* MIMS INDIA. 4316
0970-1052 *See* LIBRARY PROGRESS (INTERNATIONAL). 3226
0970-1087 *See* SOCIAL SCIENCE INTERNATIONAL. 5220
0970-1095 *See* INDIAN JOURNAL OF MARKETING GEOGRAPHY, THE. 2566
0970-1125 *See* JEEVADHARA (ENGLISH ED.). 4967
0970-1168 *See* HINDUSTAN YEAR-BOOK AND WHO'S WHO. 5012
0970-1184 *See* INDIAN COCOA, ARECANUT & SPICES JOURNAL. 174
0970-1222 *See* VIDYAJYOTI (DELHI). 5038
0970-1249 *See* JOURNAL OF THE RAMANUJAN MATHEMATICAL SOCIETY. 3515
0970-1257 *See* TIBETAN MEDICINE. 3645
0970-1273 *See* AVIAN RESEARCH : OFFICIAL JOURNAL OF THE INDIAN POULTRY CLUB. 206
0970-1281 *See* HIMALAYAN CHEMICAL AND PHARMACEUTICAL BULLETIN : HCPB. 1025
0970-129X *See* INDIAN JOURNAL OF NATURAL PRODUCTS. 4307
0970-1311 *See* STEEL INDIA. 4020
0970-1346 *See* JOURNAL OF COMMUNITY GUIDANCE AND RESEARCH. 4595
0970-1346 *See* INDIAN JOURNAL OF COMMUNITY GUIDANCE SERVICE. 4784
0970-1354 *See* INDIAN JOURNAL OF GEOLOGY. 1382
0970-1389 *See* INDIAN BOTANICAL CONTRACTOR. 513
0970-1435 *See* MLBD NEWSLETTER. 3232
0970-1478 See JOURNAL OF PHASE EQUILIBRIA. 4006
0970-1494 *See* JOURNAL OF TROPICAL FORESTRY. 2386
0970-1532 *See* INDIAN JOURNAL OF QUANTITATIVE ECONOMICS. 1494
0970-1575 *See* PERSPECTIVES IN EDUCATION (BARODA). 1773
0970-1583 *See* ENERGY OPPORTUNITIES. 1941
0970-1591 *See* INDIAN JOURNAL OF UROLOGY. 3990
0970-1672 *See* MAAS JOURNAL OF ISLAMIC SCIENCE. 5043
0970-1753 *See* ENCOLOGY. 2215
0970-1761 *See* INSIDE OUTSIDE. 2901
0970-1850 *See* INTERNATIONAL INFORMATION, COMMUNICATION & EDUCATION. 3218
0970-1893 *See* JOURNAL OF SURFACE SCIENCE AND TECHNOLOGY. 5120
0970-1915 *See* INDIAN JOURNAL OF CLINICAL BIOCHEMISTRY. 488
0970-1958 *See* POULTRY ADVISER. 218
0970-1982 *See* INDIAN JOURNAL OF FORENSIC SCIENCES : THE OFFICIAL PUBLICATION OF THE FORENSIC SCIENCE SOCIETY OF INDIA. 3741
0970-1990 *See* JOURNAL OF RECENT ADVANCES IN APPLIED SCIENCES. 462

0970-2016 *See* INDIAN JOURNAL OF RADIOLOGY & IMAGING, THE. 3942
0970-2083 *See* JOURNAL OF INDUSTRIAL POLLUTION CONTROL. 2234
0970-2091 *See* INDIAN JOURNAL OF APPLIED AND PURE BIOLOGY. 458
0970-2105 *See* PURATATTVA NEW DELHI. 279
0970-2113 *See* LUNG INDIA. 3950
0970-2121 *See* ANNALS OF PAEDIATRIC SURGERY. 3900
0970-2199 *See* JOURNAL OF PIERRE FAUCHARD ACADEMY. INDIA SECTION. 1327
0970-2202 See IGCAR. 2156
0970-2210 *See* IGCAR. 2156
0970-2288 *See* BIBLE BHASHYAM (ENGLISH ED.). 5014
0970-230X *See* NARENDRA DEVA JOURNAL OF AGRICULTURAL RESEARCH. 110
0970-2318 *See* ELECTRICITY CONSERVATION QUARTERLY. 1937
0970-2334 *See* BULLETIN OF THE INDIAN VACUUM SOCIETY. 4399
0970-2423 *See* CASHEW COCHIN. 72
0970-2431 *See* INDIAN JOURNAL OF NATURAL RUBBER RESEARCH. 5076
0970-2504 *See* TRENDS IN LIFE SCIENCES. 493
0970-2520 *See* INDIAN PSYCHOLOGIST. 4589
0970-2539 *See* JOURNAL OF PLANT SCIENCE RESEARCH, THE. 516
0970-2563 *See* INDIAN JOURNAL OF CANCER CHEMOTHERAPHY. 3818
0970-2571 *See* LIGHT OF LIFE. 4974
0970-258X *See* NATIONAL MEDICAL JOURNAL OF INDIA, THE. 3619
0970-2628 *See* STANDARDS INDIA. 4032
0970-2741 *See* INDIAN FERN JOURNAL. 513
0970-275X *See* JOURNAL OF INDIAN WATER WORKS ASSOCIATION. 5535
0970-2776 *See* JOURNAL OF OILSEEDS RESEARCH. 176
0970-2814 *See* JOURNAL OF THE INSTITUTE OF ASIAN STUDIES. 2656
0970-2822 *See* INDIAN JOURNAL OF VIROLOGY. 458
0970-2830 *See* POETCRIT MARANDA. 3468
0970-2857 *See* INTERNATIONAL JOURNAL OF ANIMAL SCIENCES. 213
0970-289X *See* ENERGY MANAGEMENT : QUARTERLY JOURNAL OF NATIONAL PRODUCTIVITY COUNCIL. 1940
0970-2903 *See* HIMALAYAN JOURNAL OF ENVIRONMENT AND ZOOLOGY. 2216
0970-2946 *See* IEEMA JOURNAL. 3480
0970-3004 *See* LIVESTOCK ADVISER. 5515
0970-3012 *See* PESTOLOGY (BOMBAY). 4247
0970-3020 *See* PROGRESSIVE HORTICULTURE. 2429
0970-308X *See* JOURNAL OF THE INDIAN SOCIETY FOR COTTON IMPROVEMENT. 177
0970-3098 *See* PETROLEUM ASIA JOURNAL. 4272
0970-3136 *See* CHEMICAL BUSINESS. 2009
0970-3179 *See* ANNALS OF AGRICULTURAL RESEARCH. 59
0970-3209 *See* INDIAN JOURNAL OF ANIMAL NUTRITION. 212
0970-3292 *See* COLEMANIA (BANGALORE). 5607
0970-3349 *See* INDIAN JOURNAL OF SOIL CONSERVATION. 174
0970-3357 *See* JOURNAL OF RURAL DEVELOPMENT (HYDERABAD, INDIA). 5206
0970-3411 *See* JOURNAL OF THE ANTHROPOLOGICAL SURVEY OF INDIA, THE. 239
0970-342X *See* INDIAN JOURNAL OF PLANT PATHOLOGY. 513
0970-3438 *See* DAIRY GUIDE. NEW DELHI. 193
0970-3446 *See* ENERGY ENVIRONMENT MONITOR. 1940
0970-3500 *See* JOURNAL OF EDUCATION AND SOCIAL CHANGE. 1756

0970-356X ISSN Index

0970-356X *See* DISABILITIES AND IMPAIRMENTS. 4387

0970-3586 *See* ADVANCES IN PLANT SCIENCES (MUZAFFARNAGAR, INDIA). 498

0970-3594 *See* JOURNAL OF HYDROBIOLOGY. 461

0970-3640 *See* COMPANY LAW JOURNAL. ANNUAL REVIEW, THE. 3098

0970-373X *See* BIODIGEST DEHRA DUN. 444

0970-3810 *See* JOURNAL OF APHIDOLOGY. 5610

0970-3845 *See* RESEARCH JOURNAL OF PLANT AND ENVIRONMENT. 526

0970-3888 *See* PACIFIC AND ASIAN JOURNAL OF ENERGY. 1952

0970-3918 *See* TRANSACTIONS OF INDIAN SOCIETY OF DESERT TECHNOLOGY. 142

0970-3926 *See* PHARMACOPSYCHOECOLOGIA VARANASI. 4608

0970-3934 *See* TELEMATICS INDIA. 1167

0970-3950 *See* MAPAN. JOURNAL OF METROLOGY SOCIETY OF INDIA. 1430

0970-4027 *See* JOURNAL OF THE DIABETIC ASSOCIATION OF INDIA. SCIENTIFIC SECTION. 3731

0970-4116 *See* JOURNAL : SCIENCE, TECHNOLOGY & MEDICINE. 5122

0970-4124 *See* RUBBER BOARD BULLETIN. 5077

0970-4140 *See* JOURNAL OF THE INDIAN INSTITUTE OF SCIENCE 1960. 5120

0970-4183 *See* JOURNAL OF THE ANDAMAN SCIENCE ASSOCIATION. 5120

0970-4205 *See* JOURNAL OF FINANCIAL MANAGEMENT AND ANALYSIS. 794

0970-423X *See* METALS MATERIALS AND PROCESSES. 2107

0970-4299 *See* INDIAN SHIPPING. 5450

0970-4302 *See* INDIAN JOURNAL OF LIBRARY SCIENCE. 3215

0970-4345 *See* INDIAN JOURNAL OF CRIMINOLOGY & CRIMINALISTICS, THE. 3166

0970-4396 *See* JOURNAL OF THE VIVEKANANDA INSTITUTE OF MEDICAL SCIENCES. 3600

0970-454X *See* DEMOGRAPHY INDIA. 4552

0970-4639 *See* BULLETIN OF PURE & APLIED SIENCES. SEC. F, GEOLOGY. 1370

0970-4728 *See* ILA BULLETIN. 3214

0970-4809 *See* AKASHVANI (NEW DELHI). 1126

0970-4825 *See* BANASTHALI PATRIKA, THE. 1089

0970-4841 *See* INTERNATIONAL REVIEW OF MODERN SOCIOLOGY. 5248

0970-4884 *See* CROP RESEARCH (HISAR). 169

0970-4914 *See* PLANT DISEASE RESEARCH. 523

0970-5112 *See* CECIDOLOGIA INTERNATIONALE. 5580

0970-5120 *See* JOURNAL OF THE INDIAN ACADEMY OF MATHEMATICS, THE. 3515

0970-5139 *See* SCIENCE AND ENVIRONMENT. 5150

0970-5147 *See* CHANDRABHAGA. 3373

0970-5155 *See* INDUSTRIAL INDIA : OFFICIAL ORGAN OF THE ALL-INDIA MANUFACTURERS' ORGANIZATION. 1610

0970-5295 *See* MEMOIRS OF THE ASTRONOMICAL SOCIETY OF INDIA. 397

0970-5309 *See* JOURNAL OF ARTS & IDEAS. 323

0970-5317 *See* JOURNAL OF ENGINEERING GEOLOGY. 1982

0970-5686 *See* TEXINCON AHMEDABAD. 5357

0970-5732 *See* JOURNAL OF BIOLOGICAL CONTROL. 460

0970-5767 *See* JOURNAL OF PHYTOLOGICAL RESEARCH. 515

0970-5880 *See* SAMYA SHAKTI : A JOURNAL OF WOMEN'S STUDIES. 5566

0970-5945 *See* JOURNAL OF NATURE CONSERVATION. 2218

0970-5953 *See* PHYSICS EDUCATION (MADRAS). 1841

0970-6070 *See* JOURNAL OF THE INDIAN SOCIETY OF ORIENTAL ART. 354

0970-6186 *See* EXPORT GAZETTE. 834

0970-6232 *See* JOURNAL OF ENGLISH STUDIES (WARANGAL), THE. 3290

0970-6240 *See* BHARATIYA SUGAR. 164

0970-6305 *See* ASIAN ECONOMIC AND SOCIAL REVIEW, THE. 1547

0970-6313 *See* LECTURES ON MATHEMATICS AND PHYSICS. 3516

0970-6380 *See* INDIAN JOURNAL OF PULSES RESEARCH. 513

0970-6399 *See* INDIAN JOURNAL OF AGRICULTURAL BIOCHEMISTRY. 94

0970-6429 *See* INDIAN JOURNAL OF HILL FARMING. 2420

0970-6437 *See* CONCEPT NEWS. 5196

0970-6577 *See* BULLETIN OF PURE & APPLIED SCIENCES. SEC. E, MATHEMATICS. 3498

0970-6623 *See* MDI MANAGEMENT JOURNAL. 692

0970-6704 *See* MOVING TECHNOLOGY. 5130

0970-6720 *See* CEMENT ABSTRACTS. 606

0970-6852 *See* ARCHITECTS INDIA. 288

0970-714X *See* JOURNAL OF LIBRARY AND INFORMATION SCIENCE (DELHI). 3220

0970-7328 *See* INTERNATIONAL JOURNAL OF MANAGEMENT AND SYSTEMS. 871

0970-7557 *See* NIS SCIENTIFIC JOURNAL. 4908

0970-7573 *See* VET MHOW. 5523

0970-7972 *See* INDIAN SOCIO-LEGAL JOURNAL. 2981

0970-8103 *See* KFRI RESEARCH REPORT. 2386

0970-8154 *See* DESIDOC BULLETIN. 1110

0970-8324 *See* SEVARTHAM. 4996

0970-8332 *See* JOURNAL OF ENGLISH AND FOREIGN LANGUAGES. 3290

0970-8340 *See* CIEFL BULLETIN NEW SERIES. 3273

0970-8480 *See* JOURNAL OF INDIAN ASSOCIATION FOR ENVIRONMENTAL MANAGEMENT. 2234

0970-860X *See* THIRD WORLD SCIENCE & ENVIRONMENT PERSPECTIVES. 5165

0970-8685 *See* HEALTH FOR THE MILLIONS. 4779

0970-9037 *See* JOURNAL OF ECOBIOLOGY. 2217

0970-9045 *See* URBAN INDIA. 2838

0970-9061 *See* IASSI QUARTERLY. 5202

0970-9169 *See* GANITA SANDESH. 3506

0970-9274 *See* JOURNAL OF HUMAN ECOLOGY (DELHI). 2218

0970-938X *See* BIOMEDICAL RESEARCH. 3687

0970-9517 *See* JOURNAL OF FRESHWATER BIOLOGY. 555

0970-9525 *See* CHEMICAL DIGEST DELHI. 968

0970-955X *See* INDIAN JOURNAL OF MEDICAL RESEARCH. SECTION A, INFECTIOUS DISEASES. 3586

0970-9568 *See* INDIAN JOURNAL OF MEDICAL RESEARCH. SECTION B, BIOMEDICAL RESEARCH OTHER THAN INFECTIOUS DISEASES. 3586

0970-9584 *See* UNIVERSITY ADMINISTRATION. OSMANIA UNIVERSITY. HYDERABAD. 1852

0970-9703 *See* TISGLOW NEW DELHI. 2182

0970-972X *See* ANNALS OF THE NATIONAL ASSOCIATION OF GEOGRAPHERS, INDIA. 2554

0970-9843 *See* JOURNAL OF THE INSTITUTION OF ENGINEERS (INDIA). INTERDISCIPLINARY PANELS. 1983

0970-9878 *See* BULLETIN OF THE DEPARTMENT OF MARINE SCIENCES. 553

0970-9916 *See* VAGARTHA (NEW DELHI). 3450

0970-9924 *See* ANNALS OF PLANT PHYSIOLOGY AKOLA. 2408

0970-9940 *See* PRACI BHASA-VIJNAN (CALCUTTA). 3311

0970-9991 *See* JOURNAL OF ENERGY, HEAT AND MASS TRANSFER. 4431

0971-0116 *See* CURRENT NEMATOLOGY. 507

0971-0426 *See* INDIAN JOURNAL OF FIBRE & TEXTILE RESEARCH. 5351

0971-0507 *See* ADVANCES IN HORTICULTURE AND FORESTRY. 2407

0971-0523 *See* ASIAN JOURNAL OF CHEMISTRY REVIEWS. 961

0971-0566 *See* INDIAN JOURNAL OF FINANCE AND RESEARCH. 870

0971-0701 *See* JOURNAL OF VETERINARY AND ANIMAL SCIENCES. 5514

0971-071X *See* JOURNAL INTERNATIONAL MEDICAL SCIENCES ACADEMY. 3592

0971-0728 *See* POWDER METALLURGY SCIENCE AND TECHNOLOGY. 4015

0971-0752 *See* POULTRY TODAY & TOMORROW. 218

0971-085X *See* TIDE : TERI INFORMATION DIGEST ON ENERGY. 1959

0971-1031 *See* JOURNAL OF VETERINARY PARASITOLOGY. 5514

0971-104X *See* INDIAN JOURNAL OF ZOOLOGICAL SPECTRUM. 5586

0971-118X *See* SAFE ENERGY & ENVIRONMENT. 1956

0971-1422 *See* JOURNAL OF THE INDIAN FISHERIES ASSOCIATION. 2307

0971-1562 *See* PERSPECTIVES IN PSYCHOLOGICAL RESEARCHES. 4607

0971-1627 *See* INDIAN JOURNAL OF HETEROCYCLIC CHEMISTRY / PUBLISHED IN ASSOCIATION WITH NATIONAL ACADEMY OF CHEMISTRY AND BIOLOGY (INDIA). 978

0971-1716 *See* INTERNATIONAL BIOSCIENCE SERIES. 458

0971-1724 *See* JOURNAL OF RESEARCH RANCHI. 100

0971-1937 *See* INDIAN JOURNAL OF VETERINARY ANATOMY. 5512

0971-1988 *See* JOURNAL OF INFORMATION SCIENCE AND TECHNOLOGY. 3220

0971-1996 *See* POPULATION RESEARCH ABSTRACT. 4558

0971-2038 *See* URJA OIL AND GAS INTERNATIONAL. 4281

0971-2097 *See* POLITICAL ECONOMY JOURNAL OF INDIA : A QUARTERLY JOURNAL OF THE CENTRE FOR INDIAN DEVELOPMENT STUDIES. 1512

0971-2119 *See* JOURNAL OF APPLIED ANIMAL RESEARCH. 5513

0971-2313 *See* RHEEDEA (CALICUT). 526

0971-2356 *See* INDIAN JOURNAL OF AGRICULTURAL ENGINEERING, THE. 95

0971-2402 *See* ASIAN JOURNAL OF PLANT SCIENCE. 500

0971-2542 *See* INDIAN JOURNAL OF PETROLEUM GEOLOGY. 4260

0971-2852 *See* BYWORD NEW DELHI. 2486

0971-2976 *See* JOURNAL OF THE NATIONAL BOTANICAL SOCIETY. 516

0971-3336 *See* PSYCHOLOGY AND DEVELOPING SOCIETIES. 4612

0971-3425 *See* ASIAN TEXTILE JOURNAL. 5348

0971-3557 *See* JOURNAL OF ENTREPRENEURSHIP, THE. 687

0971-3719 *See* JOURNAL OF MYCOPATHOLOGICAL RESEARCH. 575

0971-457X *See* INDIAN JOURNAL OF CHEMICAL TECHNOLOGY. 1025

0971-457X *See* INDIAN JOURNAL OF ENGINEERING & MATERIALS SCIENCES. 1978

0971-52155 *See* INDIAN JOURNAL OF GENDER STUDIES. 5203

0971-5223 *See* INTERNATIONAL JOURNAL OF PUNJAB STUDIES. 2768

0971-524X *See* INDIAN PSYCHOLOGICAL ABSTRACTS AND REVIEWS. 4589

0980-0611 *See* ADALIA. 44

0980-0875 *See* COSMETIQUE NEWS PARIS. 403

0980-1367 *See* INDUSTRIE DU CUIR (PARIS, FRANCE : 1987). 3184

0980-1472 *See* REVUE INTERNATIONALE DE SYSTEMIQUE. 1252

0980-1529 *See* IX-MAGAZINE PARIS. 1229

0980-157X *See* ANNALES DE LA FOUNDATION FYSSEN. 228

0980-2282 *See* REVUE DE PRESSE CHAMPAGNE-ARDENNE ACTUALITES. 708

0980-2797 *See* REVUE DES REVUES, LA. 424

0980-322X See FIT : FORMATION INFORMATIQUE TECHNOLOGIE. 3211
0980-3904 See CONTRACEPTION, FERTILITE, SEXUALITE. 588
0980-5338 See ST MAGAZINE. 4866
0980-7527 See ARDECHE ARCHEOLOGIE. 259
0980-8396 See CHEF PARIS, LE. 2789
0980-8493 See TRADITION MAGAZINE. 4157
0980-9465 See ATELIER PARIS, L'. 2898
0980-949X See BULLETIN DE DOCUMENTATION / MINISTERE DE L'ENVIRONNEMENT. 2162
0981-0560 See INFIRMIERE MAGAZINE, L'. 3857
0981-1095 See LILLE MEDICAL (1987). 3604
0981-1842 See DESSOUS MODE INTERNATIONAL. 1083
0981-4183 See LINEAIRES. 5126
0981-6402 See INFO PC (NEUILLY-SUR-SEINE). 1268
0981-6445 See VAISSEAU DE PIERRES. 310
0981-8715 See ECONOMIE AND GESTION AGRO-ALIMENTAIRE. 81
0981-8936 See BATTEUR MAGAZINE. 4102
0981-9428 See PLANT PHYSIOLOGY AND BIOCHEMISTRY. 524
0982-0582 See RIO DE LA PLATA. 3431
0982-1783 See HISTOIRE & MESURE. 2617
0982-2232 See BULLETIN DU BUREAU NATIONAL DE METROLOGIE. 4029
0982-3417 See BIBLIOGRAPHIE - INSTITUT NATIONAL DE LA RECHERCHE AGRONOMIQUE, DEPARTEMENT D'ECONOMIE ET DE LA SOCIOLOGIE RURALES. 151
0982-3425 See SPEAK UP PARIS. 3322
0982-3573 See CAHIERS DU BARREAU DE PARIS, LES. 2946
0982-460X See LETTRE D'INFORMATION DU C.E.E, LA. 1687
0982-6246 See PARCS PARIS. 1987. 2202
0982-6548 See REVUE DE BIBLIOLOGIE. 3430
0982-6904 See JOYCE. 3400
0982-801X See BULLETIN OFFICIEL DES IMPOTS. 825
0982-8044 See BULLETIN DE GESTION FISCALE DES ENTREPRISES. 825
0982-8354 See STUDIO MAGAZINE. 2903
0982-8567 See DERMATOLOGIE PRATIQUE. 3719
0982-8648 See BLAIREAU PARIS. 3338
0982-9156 See AUTOMOBILE MAGAZINE, L'. 5406
0983-0537 See JOURNAL DE LA MARINE MARCHANDE ET DU TRANSPORT MULTIMODAL. 5450
0983-1509 See ARABIES. 2637
0983-1592 See AEROSPACE WORLD : BUSINESS & TECHNOLOGY. 5
0983-1851 See CAHIERS DE LA FONDATION, LES. 654
0983-1924 See REFERENCES DE LA POSTE PARIS. 1147
0983-2424 See ENQUETES ET DOCUMENTS / CENTRE DE RECHERCHES SUR L'HISTOIRE DU MONDE ATLANTIQUE, UNIVERSITE DE NANTES. 2686
0983-3943 See BULLETIN - AMIS DE GUSTAVE COURBET. 345
0983-5075 See PRECEPTA MEDICA. 3629
0983-6802 See LAMY DROIT DE L'INFORMATIQUE. 2993
0983-737X See AGENCE CAMBODGE - LAOS. 4462
0983-8201 See OPA PRATIQUE. 3890
0984-1466 See TUTTI INSIEME PARIS. 2494
0984-2810 See REVUE DU BOIS STRASBOURG. 2404
0984-421X See FRANCE TENNIS DE TABLE MAGAZINE. 4895
0984-4708 See 30 MILLIONS D'AMIS PARIS. 1987. 5572
0984-4759 See AUTRE MONDE (PARIS. 1987), L'. 4241
0984-4783 See AGORA PARIS. 1986. 2249

0984-5259 See STATISTIQUES ENERGETIQUES PARIS. 1963
0984-5453 See RAPPORT ANNUEL / OFFICE NATIONAL DES FORETS. 2391
0984-7677 See HISTOIRE & GENEALOGIE PARIS. 2453
0984-7685 See ISLAM ET SOCIETES AU SUD DU SAHARA. 5043
0984-7847 See CUNI SCIENCES LEMPDES. 209
0984-7979 See VERRE (PARIS, FRANCE). 2595
0984-8274 See ZNAKI CZASU. 5011
0984-8541 See DOCUMENTATION REFUGIES PARIS. 1918
0984-8541 See DOCUMENTATION-REFUGIES. 4472
0984-8916 See FRANCE TELECOM ED. NATIONALE. 1156
0984-9521 See MARCHES AFRICAINS PARIS. 1988. 845
0985-0120 See ATHAREP. 5274
0985-0503 See FRANCE COMPOSITES. 2102
0985-0562 See NUTRITION CLINIQUE ET METABOLISME. 4196
0985-0732 See SEMINAIRE D'ANALYSE (CLERMONT-FERRAND, FRANCE). 1847
0985-0791 See COLLECTION CXP CATALOGUES DE PROGICIELS. 1284
0985-1402 See VERTIGO (PARIS, FRANCE). 4079
0985-2174 See SYNTHESE FINANCIERE, LA. 813
0985-2220 See FTS FRENCH TECHNOLOGY SURVEY. 5106
0985-2395 See ARCHIVES PERPIGNAN. 4063
0985-2549 See REVUE JURIDIQUE DU CENTRE QUEST. 3043
0985-2654 See FLASH JAPON. 455
0985-2662 See FLASH ETAT-UNIS. 455
0985-3111 See GEODINAMICA ACTA. 2561
0985-3286 See MARSYAS PARIS. 358
0985-3766 See DEVELOPPEMENT PERSONNEL. 1110
0985-5556 See TECHNIQUE CHAUSSURE MAROQUINERIE MODE. 3186
0985-5637 See TOLERIE PONTAULT-COMBAULT. 4022
0985-5939 See SOCIOCRITICISM MONTPELLIER. 3437
0985-9861 See MES CONFIDENCES EROTIQUES. 5188
0986-1351 See AS. ACTUALITE DE LA SCENOGRAPHIE. 4063
0986-1653 See ENSEIGNEMENT PHILOSOPHIQUE, L'. 4365
0986-1793 See PCM LE PONT. 5442
0986-2684 See ANNUAIRE DE LA SOCIETE DES AMIS DU VIEUX STRASBOURG. 2674
0986-2900 See RADIOCOMMUNICATIONS MAGAZINE. 1162
0986-2943 See ENVIRONNEMENT & TECHNIQUE. 2171
0986-5748 See FRANCE-ECO-PECHE. 2304
0986-7236 See CAHIER DE CONJONCTURE DE L'ANDESE, LE. 1633
0986-7481 See VOICI PARIS. 5568
0986-9042 See ANNUAIRE - ASSOCIATION D'ALSACE POUR LA CONSERVATION DES MONUMENTS NAPOLEONIENS. 2674
0986-9050 See JOURNAL DES ENFANTS ED. NATIONALE, LE. 1755
0987-0113 See COUP D'OEIL GRANDVILLIERS. 3874
0987-0210 See MUSEES STRASBOURG. 4091
0987-0717 See SCIENCES ET NATURE. 5154
0987-1209 See DIABOLO TOULOUSE. 3341
0987-2213 See CAHIERS POUR CROIRE AUJOURD'HUI. 4942
0987-237X See GULLIVORE PARIS. 1749
0987-2507 See EBA NEWSLETTER. 788
0987-2825 See JOURNAL DE MEDECINE PRATIQUE. 3592
0987-3090 See MEMOIRE DE TRAME. 3231
0987-3260 See PLEIN DROIT : LA REVUE DE GISTI. 1702

0987-3368 See REVUE D'ECONOMIE FINANCIERE. 1518
0987-3872 See LETTRE D'ORION MAGAZINE, LA. 2915
0987-4119 See TELECOMS RESEAUX INTERNATIONAL. 1166
0987-6014 See NETCOM ISSY-LES-MOULINEAUX. 1118
0987-6030 See REPERTOIRE (MONTPELLIER, FRANCE). 1929
0987-6960 See INHARMONIQUES. 4122
0987-7053 See NEUROPHYSIOLOGIE CLINIQUE. 3841
0987-7541 See STRATEGIES GOURMANDES PARIS. 2358
0987-7738 See LANGUES ORIENTALES ANCIENNES PHILOLOGIE ET LINGUISTIQUE. 3296
0987-7940 See BULLETIN / SOCIETE INTERNATIONALE D'ETUDES YOURCENARIENNES. 3370
0988-0321 See MIROIR DE L'HISTOIRE. 2623
0988-1476 See ELLE DECORATION NEUILLY-SUR-SEINE. 2900
0988-1557 See BULLETIN DE LA SOCIETE ARIEGEOISE DES SCIENCES LETTRES ET ARTS. 316
0988-1808 See VIEUX MARLY, LE. 2715
0988-1824 See RECHERCHE ET FORMATION PARIS. 1987. 1843
0988-1875 See BULLETIN DE LA SOCIETE DES AMIS DU VIEUX CHINON. 2680
0988-1999 See BIBLIOTHEQUE JEAN GENET. 3195
0988-2022 See ESPACES ET RESSOURCES MARITIMES. 5449
0988-3266 See INRA SCIENCES SOCIALES. 5203
0988-3452 See COMPUTER DATA STORAGE NEWSLETTER. 1276
0988-3754 See RAIRO. INFORMATIQUE THEORIQUE ET APPLICATIONS. 1261
0988-4068 See NERVURE PARIS. 3931
0988-4319 See JOURNAL D'ACOUSTIQUE. 4452
0988-4343 See LETTRE DES CUISINISTES, DES BAINISTES ET DES ELECTROMENAGISTES, LA. 2791
0988-5730 See SYSTEMES EXPERTS PARIS. 5161
0988-6249 See INNOVATIVE PACKAGING PARIS. 4219
0988-629X See RFM REVUE FRANCAISE DES METALLURGISTES. 4018
0988-6990 See GYNECOLOGIE OBSTETRIQUE PRATIQUE. 3761
0988-7199 See BULLETIN - CEDRI. 1918
0988-7679 See PHOTOGRAPHIES MAGAZINE. 4374
0988-8233 See TOUT EN CARTES. 1524
0988-9183 See ADMINISTRATEUR DU CREDIT AGRICOLE, L'. 44
0988-9477 See BULLETIN DU GROUPE D'HISTOIRE ET D'ARCHEOLOGIE DE BUZANCAIS. 2681
0989-0165 See AFFICHE PARIS. 335
0989-1013 See MUSCLE & FITNESS. 2600
0989-1323 See TRIBUNE DE L'EXPANSION, LA. 855
0989-1773 See REPERAGES NANTES. 1988. 3429
0989-1900 See OPTION FINANCE ED. FRANCAISE. 802
0989-1994 See BULLETIN SIGNALETIQUE - DOC MNE. 208
0989-2192 See STIMULOGRAPHY. 3710
0989-2648 See AGRO PERFORMANCES. 55
0989-2672 See TENSIOLOGIE. 3710
0989-2869 See FORTUNE FRANCE. 677
0989-3059 See BULLETIN DE LA SOCIETE DES AMIS DE LA BIBLIOTHEQUE DE L'ECOLE POLYTECHNIQUE. 5090
0989-3091 See CUISINE ACTUELLE. 2789
0989-3105 See OPHTALMOLOGIE (PARIS). 3877
0989-4985 See HEBDO-TEX, L'. 5351

0989-5086 See BULLETIN D'INFORMATION ET DE DOCUMENTATION - CENTRE NATIONAL DE FORMATION, DOCUMENTATION ET COOPERATION INTERNATIONALE DE LA DIRECTION GENERALE DE LA CONCURRENCE, DE LA CONSOMMATION ET DE LA REPRESSION DES FRAUDES. **1466**

0989-5876 See RAPPORT ANNUEL DU SERVICE HYDROGRAPHIQUE ET OCEANOGRAPHIQUE DE LA MARINE. **1455**

0989-6023 See LIGEIA. **324**

0989-6139 See VALENTIANA VALENCIENNES. **285**

0989-6171 See THERAPEUTIQUE ACTUELLE : TA. **3645**

0989-6228 See PUBLICATION DE L'OBSERVATOIRE ASTRONOMIQUE DE STRASBOURG. SERIE ASTRONOMIE ET SCIENCES HUMAINES. **398**

0989-6333 See THURIES MAGAZINE. **2793**

0989-6961 See REGATE INTERNATIONAL PARIS. (1987). **595**

0989-6988 See COMPTES RENDUS DE L'ACADEMIE D'AGRICULTURE DE FRANCE. **76**

0989-7100 See ROBOTS EXPERT PARIS. **1230**

0989-7445 See ACTUALITES EXPATRIATION PARIS. **1918**

0989-7925 See REVUE D'HISTOIRE DES FACULTES DE DROIT ET DE LA SCIENCE JURIDIQUE. **3043**

0989-8107 See DOMOTIQUE NEWS PARIS. **5101**

0989-8220 See RAIL PARIS, LE. **5435**

0989-8972 See BIOLOGICAL STRUCTURES AND MORPHOGENESIS. **3679**

0990-0632 See PRODUCTIONS ANIMALES (PARIS, 1988). **5519**

0990-0845 See SUBAQUA MARSEILLE. **4924**

0990-1310 See OXYMAG : JOURNAL D'INFORMATION PROFESSIONNELLE DES INFIRMIERS ANESTHESISTES. **3683**

0990-2473 See ANNUAIRE DE LA SOCIETE D'HISTOIRE ET D'ARCHEOLOGIE DE DAMBACH-LA-VILLE, BARR, OBERNAI. **2674**

0990-5413 See EDUCATION ECONOMIE (PARIS). **1591**

0990-6029 See SEMAINE AMEUBLEMENT INFORMATION, LA. **2903**

0990-6479 See GLAMOUR PARIS. **5557**

0990-7440 See AQUATIC LIVING RESOURCES (MONTROUGE). **2296**

0990-7939 See MEMOIRES OPTIQUES & SYSTEMES. **1277**

0990-915X See HISTOIRES DE DEVELOPPEMENT LYON. **2910**

0991-1367 See BULLETIN DE LA SOCIETE D'HISTOIRE MODERNE. **2612**

0991-1960 See COMPUTER AIDED DESIGN. FRENCH EDITION. **1231**

0991-2428 See TERRITOIRES PARIS. 1988. **4690**

0991-2738 See DROIT DE L'INFORMATIQUE ET DES TELECOMS. **1153**

0991-8248 See INFO PRESSE PARIS. **1495**

0991-8787 See BELLES HISTOIRES DE POMME D'API PARIS. 1972, LES. **1060**

0991-9325 See INDUSTRIES GRAPHIQUES PARIS. **4566**

0991-9708 See NOUVEL EDUCATEUR CANNES, LE. **1769**

0992-065X See AIR ACTION. **6**

0992-0757 See LEVANT (MONTPELLIER, FRANCE). **2658**

0992-1788 See TECHNOLOGIES PARIS. 1988. **5163**

0992-2016 See ATARI MAGAZINE. **1264**

0992-2059 See HISTOIRE DE L'ART (PARIS, 1988). **321**

0992-2164 See MEILLEURES ADRESSES DES TRAITEMENTS THERMIQUES, LES. **693**

0992-3012 See APPLE MAGAZINE LES ULIS. **1171**

0992-3020 See NTI. NOUVELLES TECHNOLOGIES DE L'INFORMATION. **5135**

0992-3039 See JOURNAL OF MEDECINE NUCLEAIRE ET BIOPHYSIQUE. **495**

0992-3233 See BANQUE & DROIT PARIS. **778**

0992-390X See PARTENAIRES PARIS. 1985. **702**

0992-4361 See EUROPEAN JOURNAL OF SOLID STATE AND INORGANIC CHEMISTRY. **1036**

0992-4426 See POLISH AGRICULTURE. **120**

0992-4663 See EJHP, EUROPEAN JOURNAL OF HOSPITAL PHARMACY. **4302**

0992-4922 See EPHEMERA NANCY. **2686**

0992-5120 See SVM MAC PARIS. **1204**

0992-5163 See PROFESSION POLITIQUE PARIS. **4492**

0992-5279 See LITTERATURES CLASSIQUES. **3408**

0992-5597 See MODES & TECHNIQUES INTERNATIONAL. **1086**

0992-5899 See SCIENCE & VIE JUNIOR. **5151**

0992-5945 See OPTION/BIO PARIS. **467**

0992-6054 See PARTICULIER IMMOBILIER PARIS. 1986, LE. **2285**

0992-6151 See BULLETIN - HCEIA. **1342**

0992-647X See PUBLICATIONS DE L'INSTITUT DE MATHEMATIQUE DE L'UNIVERSITE DE STRASBOURG. **3529**

0992-7158 See REVUE DES SCIENCES DE L'EAU (PARIS). **5539**

0992-7662 See GRAND ANGLE SUR L'EMPLOI ISSY-LES-MOULINEAUX. **1676**

0992-7689 See ANNALES GEOPHYSICAE (1988). **1402**

0992-8154 See AUTO PLUS PARIS. **5405**

0992-8421 See DOSSIERS BREVETS... CENTRE DU DROIT DE L'ENTREPRISE. **1304**

0992-9215 See RENCONTRE - MOUVEMENT CHRETIEN DE PROFESSIONS SOCIALES. **5304**

0992-986X See REVUE INTERNATIONALE DE PSYCHOLOGIE SOCIALE. **4617**

0993-0701 See PUCK (CHARLEVILLE-MEZIERES). **2777**

0993-0787 See GRAIN DE SOLEIL PARIS. **5030**

0993-2097 See SCRIPT (PARIS, 1988). **4077**

0993-2801 See LETTRE DE CLEO, LA. **1224**

0993-3522 See RESEAUX ET CHALEUR (ORLEANS). **1955**

0993-4871 See ANTHROPOLOGIE VISUELLE. **229**

0993-538X See ATELIER ASEMI. **231**

0993-6165 See DOSSIERS DU CEPED, LES. **4552**

0993-9067 See LETTRE DES MUSEES ET DES EXPOSITIONS. **4090**

0993-9199 See MONITEUR HOSPITALIER, LE. **3789**

0993-9717 See PEDIATRIE PRATIQUE PARIS. **3910**

0994-0235 See AFRICA ENERGY & MINING. **1931**

0994-1541 See REVUE SCIENTIFIQUE ET TECHNIQUE DE LA DEFENSE. **4056**

0994-1894 See ELECTRONIQUE EUROPE 2000 PARIS. **2050**

0994-2556 See MINES & CARRIERES. **2145**

0994-2653 See ABRICOT PARIS. **2325**

0994-3749 See BULLETIN DE L'IREPP. **1144**

0994-3919 See REPRODUCTION HUMAINE ET HORMONES. **3733**

0994-4370 See PHARMACIE RURALE PARIS. **4321**

0994-4478 See MONITEUR INTERNAT PARIS, LE. **4316**

0994-5490 See ETUDES LAWRENCIENNES NANTERRE. **3386**

0994-6993 See PHILIPPINES INFORMATION PARIS. **4511**

0994-7590 See TECHNICAL REVIEW / GEC ALSTHOM. **2083**

0994-7736 See CAHIERS DU LACITO PARIS. **3272**

0994-7744 See LINGUISTIQUE AFRICAINE (PARIS, FRANCE). **3299**

0994-8899 See GALLIA INFORMATIONS : PREHISTORIE ET HISTORIE. **2689**

0994-9895 See IMMUNOCLONES. **458**

0995-0583 See VENDREDI. **4548**

0995-1121 See IMAGES DOC PARIS. **4370**

0995-2187 See ARGOS LE PERREUX. **3363**

0995-2721 See EUROPEAN SPONSORSHIP NEWSLETTER PARIS, THE. **1635**

0995-3310 See METIS (PARIS, FRANCE). **3302**

0995-3671 See BULLETIN DE LIAISON DU CNDT. **1342**

0995-4228 See VOYAGES D'AFFAIRES PARIS. **718**

0995-4325 See PUBLICATIONS MATHEMATIQUES DE LA FACULTE DES SCIENCES DE BESANCON ANALYSE NON LINEAIRE. **3529**

0995-4945 See ENTREPRISE & CARRIERES PARIS. **1489**

0995-5178 See AGRICULTURES ACTUALITE. **161**

0995-616X See PROFESSIONAL TRANSLATOR & INTERPRETER. **3312**

0995-6492 See REUSSIR- LAIT ELEVAGE. **198**

0995-6794 See TRAVAUX DE LITTERATURE : T.L. **3447**

0995-6840 See PARTICULIER PRATIQUE PARIS, LE. **2285**

0995-709X See HISTORAMA SPECIAL. **2617**

0995-9181 See ANNALES DE LA SOCIETE SCIENTIFIQUE ET LITTERAIRE DE CANNES ET DE L'ARRONDISSEMENT DE GRASSE. **4161**

0996-3634 See RECHERCHES REGIONALES: COTE D'AZUR ET CONTREES LIMITROPHES. **2704**

0996-4703 See AU SERVICE DE L'ENSEIGNEMENT. FRANCAIS. **1888**

0996-553X See OFFICIEL DES DERMATOLOGISTES ET VENEREOLOGISTES, L'. **3722**

0996-5750 See ANNUAIRE HISTORIQUE DE LA VILLE DE MULHOUSE. **2674**

0996-5882 See PERFORMANCES MARSEILLE. **1773**

0996-5904 See TRANSEUPHRATENE PARIS. **2632**

0996-5912 See REFERENCES DESIGN MALAKOFF. **375**

0996-7826 See LETTRE. FRENCH TV MARKET NEWSLETTER, LA. **1159**

0996-8067 See TOP VENTES BOULOGNE-BILLANCOURT. **716**

0996-8296 See ANESTHESIE REANIMATION PRATIQUE PARIS. **3681**

0996-8393 See REVUE BIBLIOGRAPHIQUE - TOXIBASE LYON. **1350**

0996-8407 See TRESORERIE PARIS. **4691**

0996-9888 See LETTRE AFRIQUE EXPANSION, LA. **4480**

0996-9942 See HUMORESQUES. **3344**

0997-0274 See ENSEMBLE. **1744**

0997-0509 See ANNUAIRE DE L'INDUSTRIE PHARMACEUTIQUE EN FRANCE. **4291**

0997-055X See ANNALES DU GROUPE NUMISMATIQUE DU COMTAT ET DE PROVENCE. **2779**

0997-0568 See ANNUAIRE DE LA SOCIETE DES AMIS DU PALAIS DES PAPES ET DES MONUMENTS D'AVIGNON. **2610**

0997-1122 See BULLETIN MENSUEL DE STATISTIQUE AGRICOLE (PARIS). **152**

0997-1327 See REVUE DU MONDE MUSULMAN ET DE LA MEDITERRANEE. **5044**

0997-1734 See BULLETIN - SOCIETE D'HISTOIRE DE HUNINGUE ET DE SA REGION. **2681**

0997-2676 See GUIDE DU CADEAU ET DES ARTS DE LA TABLE. **351**

0997-3192 See INSEE PREMIERE. **1496**

0997-3753 See AVIATION DESIGN THIAIS. **13**

0997-3907 See BULLETIN D'ETUDES PARNASSIENNES ET SYMBOLISTES. **3461**

0997-5047 See BULLETIN JOLY PARIS. **825**

0997-5306 See BULLETIN ARCHEOLOGIQUE DU COMITE DES TRAVAUX HISTORIQUES ET SCIENTIFIQUES. FASCICULE B, AFRIQUE DU NORD. **262**

0997-5322 See BULLETIN ARCHEOLOGIQUE DU COMITE DES TRAVAUX HISTORIQUES ET SCIENTIFIQUES. FASCICULE A, ANITQUITES NATIONALES / MINISTERE DE L'EDUCATION NATIONALE. **262**

0997-5373 See SAVOIRS LASALLE. **245**

0997-5489 See PUBLICATIONS DE L'INSTITUT DE RECHERCHE MATHEMATIQUES DE RENNES. **3529**

0997-654X See 01 REFERENCES (PARIS). **2484**

0997-7139 See MONDE DU RENSEIGNEMENT 1988, LE. **4051**

0997-721X See EDUCATION & MANAGEMENT LE PERREUX-SUR-MARNE. **1738**

0997-7287 See ACTUALITIES MEDICALES INTERNATIONALES. HYPERTENSION. **3697**

0997-7538 See EUROPEAN JOURNAL OF MECHANICS. A. SOLIDS. **4427**

0997-7546 See EUROPEAN JOURNAL OF MECHANICS. B. FLUIDS. **4402**

0997-7554 See ATIP. ASSOCIATION TECHNIQUE DE L'INDUSTRIE PAPETIERE 1989. **4232**

0997-9565 See TECHNOLOGIES MECANIQUES SENLIS. **2130**

0997-9638 See QUALITE SANTE PARIS. **3632**

0998-0113 See SOCIOLOGIE SANTE. **4803**

0998-2221 See WAKOU TOULOUSE. **1790**

0998-416X See AGRESTE. CONJONCTURE, CONJONCTURE GENERALE. **46**

0998-4178 See AGRESTE. ANALYSES & ETUDES, CAHIERS. **46**

0998-4186 See AGRESTE. ANALYSES & ETUDES. **46**

0998-4194 See MONITEUR ARCHITECTURE AMC, LE. **303**

0998-4313 See DICTIONNAIRE PERMANENT DROIT EUROPEEN DES AFFAIRES. **2960**

0998-4321 See REVUE D'IMAGERIE MEDICALE. **3946**

0998-4364 See ACTA PALYNOLOGICA : AP. **5080**

0998-4399 See HERBA GALLICA CHEMILLE. **512**

0998-4747 See INSEE RESULTATS. EMPLOI-REVENUS. **1680**

0998-4771 See HORIZON. SCIENCES DE LA TERRE. **1363**

0998-4828 See INSEE CADRAGE. ECONOMIE GENERALE. **1496**

0998-4836 See INSEE. CADRAGE ET INSEE RESULTATS SYSTEME PRODUCTIF. **5329**

0998-4844 See INSEE. CADRAGE ET INSEE RESULTATS EMPLOIS REVENUS. **5329**

0998-4852 See INSEE. CADRAGE ET INSEE RESULTATS CONSOMMATIONS ET MODES DE VIE. **1534**

0998-4860 See INSEE CADRAGE. DEMOGRAPHIE-SOCIETE. **4553**

0998-4895 See INSEE RESULTATS. SYSTEME PRODUCTIF. **1496**

0998-4909 See TECHNIQUES & EQUIPEMENTS DE PRODUCTION PARIS. **1629**

0998-4933 See PATISSERIE BOULANGERIE NEUILLY-SUR-SEINE. **2353**

0998-495X See MOTOCULTURE MAGAZINE NEUILLY-SUR-SEINE. **2424**

0998-5956 See DEMEURE HISTORIQUE PARIS, LA. **296**

0998-6553 **1109**

0998-6650 See PROCESS CESSON-SEVIGNE. **197**

0998-678X See BULLETIN BIBLIOGRAPHIQUE O.R.S.T.O.M. SANTE. **3655**

0998-8041 See ESTAMPILLE, L'OBJET D'ART, L'. **320**

0999-2413 See CAHIERS DE L'ACADEMIE ANQUETIN NEUILLY-SUR-SEINE, LES. **1090**

0999-4084 See ARTS ET METIERS MAGAZINE PARIS. **315**

0999-582X See ETUDES TELECOM PARIS. **1154**

0999-5919 See APPLE UTILISATEUR LES ULIS. **1171**

0999-6338 See MEDECIN BIOPATHOLOGISTE PARIS, LE. **3607**

0999-7148 See MER & BATEAUX PARIS. **594**

0999-7342 See SCIENCE ILLUSTREE BAGNOLET. **5152**

0999-7385 See SANG, THROMBOSE, VAISSEAUX : STV. **3710**

0999-7822 See ESPACE SOCIAL EUROPEEN PARIS. **5244**

1000-0119 See HANG KUNG CHIH SHIH. **22**

1000-0224 See ZIRAN KEXUESHI YANJIU. **1361**

1000-0240 See PING CHUAN TUNG TU. **1391**

1000-0267 See AGRO-ENVIRONMENTAL PROTECTION. **55**

1000-0267 See NUNG YEH HUAN CHING PAO HU. **2237**

1000-0496 See SHANDONG YIKE DAXUE XUEBAO. **3640**

1000-0550 See CHENJI XUEBAO. **1371**

1000-0577 See HSI TUNG KO HSUEH YU SHU HSUEH. **3508**

1000-0607 See ZHENCI YANJIU. **3653**

1000-0615 See SHUICHAN XUEBAO. **557**

1000-0739 See DONGWU FENLEI XUEBAO. **5581**

1000-0747 See SHIYOU KANTAN KAIFA. **4278**

1000-081X See GAODENG XUEXIAO JISUAN SHUXUE XUEBAO. **3506**

1000-0879 See LIXUE YU SHIJIAN. **4428**

1000-0887 See YING YUNG SHU HSUEH HO LI HSUEH. **3541**

1000-0895 See QIGONG YU KEXUE. **2601**

1000-0925 See NEIRANJI GONGCHENG. **2123**

1000-0933 See SHENG TAI HSUEH PAO. **2221**

1000-1034 See SHENGWU FANGZHI TONGBAO. **473**

1000-1093 See BINGGONG XUEBAO. **4038**

1000-1298 See NONGYE JIXIE XUEBAO. **160**

1000-1328 See YU HANG HSUEH PAO. **40**

1000-1476 See ZHONGGUO FANGZHI DAXUE XUEBAO. **5360**

1000-1514 See BEIJING NONGYE GONGCHENG DAXUE XUEBAO. **65**

1000-1522 See PEI-CHING LIN YEH TA HSUEH HSUEH PAO. **2390**

1000-1530 See BEIJING YIKE DAXUE XUEBAO. **3555**

1000-1565 See HEBEI DAXUE XUEBAO ZIRAN KEXUE BAN. **5201**

1000-1581 See HEBEI YIXUEYUAN XUEBAO. **3583**

1000-1611 See TAIYUAN GONGYE DAXUE XUEBAO. **5161**

1000-1638 See NEIMENGGU DAXUE XUEBAO (ZIRAN KEXUE BAN). **5132**

1000-1727 See SHENYANG YAOXUEYUAN XUEBAO. **4329**

1000-1743 See ZHEJIANG YIKE DAXUE XUEBAO. **3653**

1000-1786 See DONGWUXUE JIKAN. **5581**

1000-193X See SHANGHAI NONGXUEYUAN XUEBAO. **134**

1000-1956 See NANJING HANGKONG XUEYUAN XUEBAO. **29**

1000-2006 See NANJING LINYE DAXUE XUEBAO. **2388**

1000-2022 See NANJING QIXIANG XUEYUAN XUEBAO. **1432**

1000-2030 See NANJING NONGYE DAXUE XUEBAO. **110**

1000-209X See ZHEJIANG GONGXUEYUAN XUEBAO. **2002**

1000-2383 See TI CHIU KO HSUEH : WU-HAN TI CHIH HSUEH YUAN HSUEH PAO. **1361**

1000-2405 See WUHAN GONGYE DAXUE XUEBAO. **5171**

1000-243X See HUBEI YIXUEYUAN XUEBAO. **3585**

1000-2464 See SHENJING JINGSHEN JIBING ZAZHI. **3846**

1000-2537 See HUNAN SHIFAN DAXUE XUEBAO (ZIRAN KEXUE BAN). **5111**

1000-2553 See GUANGXI NONGXUEYUAN XUEBAO. **91**

1000-2650 See SICHUAN NONGYE DAXUE XUEBAO. **134**

1000-274X See XIBEI DAXUE XUEBAO ZIRAN KEXUE BAN. **1096**

1000-2758 See XIBEI GONGYE DAXUE XUEBAO. **5171**

1000-2804 See LAN-CHOU TA HSUEH HSUEH PAO. SHE HUI KO HSUEH PAN. **5208**

1000-2871 See BOLI YU TANGCI. **2586**

1000-3002 See ZHONGGUO YAOLIXUE YU DULIXUE ZAZHI. **3984**

1000-3029 **5119**

1000-3053 See REDAI HAIYANG. **1455**

1000-3061 See SHENGWU GONGCHENG XUEBAO. **3696**

1000-3118 See GUJIZHUI DONGWU XUEBAO. **4227**

1000-3193 See RENLEIXUE XUEBAO. **244**

1000-3223 See BINGDUXUE ZAZHI. **560**

1000-3231 See GANGUANG KEXUE YU GUANGHUAXUE. **4370**

1000-3258 See DIWEN WULI XUEBAO. **4402**

1000-3290 See WULI XUEBAO. **4425**

1000-3525 See ZHONGHUA WUSHU. **2602**

1000-3541 See BEIFANG LUNCONG. **5192**

1000-3851 See FUHE CAILIAO XUEBAO. **2102**

1000-3924 See SHANGHAI NONYE XUEBAO. **134**

1000-3932 See HUAGONG ZIDONGHUA JI YIBIAO. **2013**

1000-3975 See SHANGHAI HUANJING KEXUE. **2181**

1000-4076 See XIBEI SHI-DI. **2668**

1000-4084 See GUTI RUNHUA. **2115**

1000-4106 See TUN-HUANG YEN CHIU / TUN-HUANG WEN WU YEN CHIU SO PIEN. **2667**

1000-4149 See RENKOU YU JINGJI. **4559**

1000-4181 See CHUNG-KUO CHING CHI WEN TI. **1551**

1000-4254 See TU SHU KUAN TSA CHIH. **3254**

1000-4343 See ZHONGGUO XITU XUEBAO. **4024**

1000-4432 See YANKE XUEBAO. **3880**

1000-4440 See JIANGSU NONGYE XUEBAO. **98**

1000-4556 See BOPUXUE ZAZHI. **4434**

1000-4610 See CHUNG-HUA CHI KUNG / CHUAN KUO CHUNG I HSUEH HUI CHI KUNG KO YEN HUI CHU PAN. **4380**

1000-4734 See KUANGWU XUEBAO. **1441**

1000-4742 See DIANDU YU HUANBAO. **2041**

1000-484X See ZHONGGUO MIANYIXUE ZAZHI. **3677**

1000-4874 See SHUI DONGLIXUE YANJIU YU JINZHAN. **1418**

1000-4890 See SHENGTAIXUE ZAZHI. **2221**

1000-4912 See BINGQI ZHISHI. **4038**

1000-5048 See ZHONGGUO YAOKE DAXUE XUEBAO. **4333**

1000-5072 See CHI NAN HSUEH PAO. CHE HSUEH SHE HUI KO HSUEH. **1815**

1000-5277 See FUJIAN SHIFAN DAXUE XUEBAO (ZIRAN KEXUE BAN). **5106**

1000-5331 See NANJING YIXUEYUAN XUEBAO. **3618**

1000-5358 See HEBEI GONGXUEYUAN XUEBAO. **5109**

1000-5382 See TUNG-PEI LIN YEH TA HSUEH HSUEH PAO. **2397**

1000-5625 See HUNAN YIKE DAXUE XUEBAO. **3585**

1000-565X See HUANAN LIGONG DAXUE XUEBAO ZIRAN KEXUE BAN. **5111**

1000-5668 See BEIJING HUAGONG XUEYUAN XUEBAO ZIRAN KEXUE BAN. **1021**

1000-5684 See JILIN NONGYE DAXUE XUEBAO. **98**

1000-579X See CHIANG-HSI SHIH FAN TA HSUEH HSUEH PAO. CHE HSUEH SHE HUI KO HSUEH PAN. **5195**

1000-5811 See XIBEI QINGGONGYE XUEYUAN XUEBAO. **5171**

1000-5854 See HEBEI SHIFAN DAXUE XUEBAO ZIRAN KEXUE BAN. **5109**

1000-5897 See HA'ERBIN KEXUE JISHU DAXUE XUEBAO. **5108**

1000-5900 See XIANGTAN DAXUE ZIRAN KEXUE XUEBAO. **5171**

1000-5919 See BEIJING DAXUE XUEBAO ZHEXUE SHEHUI KEXUE BAN. **4342**

1000-6087 See RENKOU YANJIU. **4559**

1000-632X See ZHONGGUO MIANHUA. 5360
1000-6419 See ZHONGGUO SHOUYI KE-JI. 5528
1000-6435 See TSO WU PIN CHUNG TZU YUAN. 189
1000-6524 See YANSHI KUANGWUXUE ZAZHI. 1445
1000-6532 See KUANGCHAN ZONGHE LIYONG. 1441
1000-6567 See ZHUZI YANJIU HUIKAN. 191
1000-6613 See HUAGONG JINZHAN. 2012
1000-6648 See HSIN LI KO HSUEH. 4588
1000-6656 See WUSUN JIANCE. 2001
1000-6699 See ZHONGHUA NEIFENMI DAIXIE ZAZHI. 3733
1000-6710 See ZHONGGUO YUNDONG YIXUE ZAZHI. 3957
1000-6818 See WULI HUAXUE XUEBAO. 995
1000-6893 See HANGKONG XUEBAO. 22
1000-6923 See ZHONGGUO HUANJING KEXUE. 2183
1000-6931 See YUANZINENG KEXUE JISHU. 2159
1000-7091 See HUA PEI NUNG HSUEH PAO. 93
1000-7164 See GONGYE WEISHENG YU ZHIYEBING. 2862
1000-7377 See SHAANXI YIXUE ZAZHI. 3640
1000-7423 See ZHONGGUO JISHENGCHONGXUE YU JISHENGCHONGPING ZAZHI. 3653
1000-7555 See GAOFENZI CAILIAO KEXUE YU GONGCHENG. 976
1000-7571 See YEJIN FENXI. 4024
1000-758X See ZHONGGUO KONGJIAN KEXUE JISHU. 41
1000-7806 See ZHONGHUA ZHENGXING SHAOSHANG WAIKE ZAZHI. 3978
1000-7830 See KAOGU YU WENWU. 272
1000-8047 See ZHONGGUO GUOSHU. 191
1000-8055 See HANGKONG DONGLI XUEBAO. 22
1000-8144 See SHIYOU HUAGONG. 4278
1000-8152 See KONGZHI LILUN YU YINGYONG. 1985
1000-8160 See TAIWAN HAIXIA. 1457
1000-8179 See ZHONGGUO ZHONGLIU LINCHUANG. 3825
1000-8306 See TSAI CHING KO HSUEH. 1525
1000-8365 See ZHUZAO JISHU. 4024
1000-8438 See DAXUE HUAXUE. 974
1000-8489 See QINGBAO KEXUE. 3243
1000-8543 See SHENGWU HUAXUE ZAZHI. 3696
1000-8551 See HO NUNG HSUEH PAO. 92
1000-8667 See CHUNG YANG MIN TSU TA HSUEH HSUEH PAO / ZHONGYANG MINZU DAXUE XUEBAO. 2258
1000-8713 See SEPU. 1019
1000-8721 See BINGDU XUEBAO. 560
1000-8845 See XINJIANG DIZHI. 1401
1000-9000 See JOURNAL OF COMPUTER SCIENCE AND TECHNOLOGY. 1191
1000-9027 See JOURNAL OF CHEMICAL INDUSTRY AND ENGINEERING (CHINA). 2014
1000-9094 See CHINA ECONOMIC NEWS. 1469
1000-9094 See JOURNAL OF MEDICAL COLLEGES OF PLA. 3596
1000-9116 See ACTA SEISMOLOGICA SINICA. 1402
1000-9140 See BEIJING REVIEW. 4465
1000-9191 See JOURNAL OF MATHEMATICAL RESEARCH AND EXPOSITION. 3513
1000-9221 See APPROXIMATION THEORY AND ITS APPLICATIONS. 3495
1000-9310 See CINA, LA. 827
1000-9345 See CHI HSIEH KUNG CHENG HSUEH PAO. 2111
1000-9361 See CHINESE JOURNAL OF AERONAUTICS. 16
1000-940X See JOURNAL OF PARTIAL DIFFERENTIAL EQUATIONS. 3514
1000-9450 See ACTA METALLURGICA SINICA. SERIES B, PROCESS METALLURGY & MISCELLANEOUS. 3997

1000-9507 See BUILDING IN CHINA. 603
1000-9515 See ACTA GEOLOGICA SINICA : JOURNAL OF THE GEOLOGICAL SOCIETY OF CHINA. 1364
1000-9574 See ACTA MATHEMATICA SINICA. NEW SERIES. 3490
1000-9590 See SYSTEMS SCIENCE AND MATHEMATICAL SCIENCES / EDITED BY INSTITUTE OF SYSTEMS SCIENCE, CHINESE ACADEMY OF SCIENCES. 3538
1000-985X See RENGONG JINGTI XUEBAO. 1033
1000-9965 See JINAN DAXUE XUEBAO ZIRAN KEXUE YU YIXUE BAN. 3592
1000-9973 See ZHONGGUO TIAOWEIPIN. 2361
1001-0017 See HUAXUE YU ZHANHE. 2013
1001-0327 See JIANGHAN KAOGU. 271
1001-0408 See ZHONGGUO YAOFANG. 4333
1001-0505 See DONGNAN DAXUE XUEBAO. 5101
1001-053X See PEI-CHING KO CHI TA HSUEH HSUEH PAO. 4014
1001-0610 See HSIEN TAI WU LI CHIH SHIH / MODERN PHYSICS. 4404
1001-0645 See BEIJING LIGONG DAXUE XUEBAO. 5087
1001-0718 See CHINESE JOURNAL OF BOTANY. 506
1001-0742 See JOURNAL OF ENVIRONMENTAL SCIENCES (CHINA). 2234
1001-0939 See ZHONGHUA JIEHE HE HUXI ZAZHI. 3952
1001-1455 See BAOZHA YU CHONGJI. 4452
1001-1498 See LINYE KEXUE YANGJIU. 2387
1001-1560 See CAILIAO BAOHU. 966
1001-1579 See DIANCHI. 5099
1001-1625 See GUISUANYAN TONGBAO. 1036
1001-1803 See RIYONG HUAXUE GONGYE. 1029
1001-1935 See NAIHUO CAILIAO. 4013
1001-2052 See HUAGONG YEJIN. 2013
1001-2389 See SHOUDU YIXUEYUAN XUEBAO. 3641
1001-2478 See SHANGHAI MIANYIXUE ZAZHI. 3676
1001-2486 See GUOFANG KE-JI DAXUE XUEBAO. 4045
1001-2494 See ZHONGGUO YAOXUE ZAZHI (1989). 4334
1001-3555 See FENZI CUIHUA. 455
1001-3725 See YIBIAO CAILIAO. 5171
1001-3776 See ZHEJIANG LINYE KE JI. 2398
1001-3865 See HUANJING WURAN YU FANGZHI. 2232
1001-3911 See GUOWAI ZAOZHI. 4234
1001-4020 See LI HUA JIANYAN. HUAXUE FENCE. 4007
1001-4055 See TUIJIN JISHU. 2000
1001-4101 See SHIYOU LIANZHI. 4278
1001-4144 See ZHONGGUO HANGTIAN. 41
1001-4160 See JISUANJI YU YINGYONG HUAXUE. 1191
1001-4241 See SHIJIE LINYE YANJIU. 2395
1001-4276 See WUYI KEXUE. 4174
1001-4454 See ZHONGYAOCAI. 3654
1001-4861 See WUJI HUAXUE XUEBAO. 1038
1001-4977 See ZHUZAO. 4024
1001-5078 See CHI KUANG YU HUNG WAI. 4434
1001-5116 See ANHUI CHIAO YU HSUEH YUAN HSUEH PAO / JOURNAL OF ANHUI INSTITUTE OF EDUCATION. 1724
1001-5302 See ZHONGGUO ZHONGYAO ZAZHI. 3653
1001-5493 See LIZI JIAOHUAN YU XIFU. 984
1001-604X See CHINESE JOURNAL OF CHEMISTRY. 972
1001-6058 See JOURNAL OF HYDRODYNAMICS. 2092
1001-6511 See SCIENCE IN CHINA. SERIES A, MATHEMATICS, PHYSICS, ASTRONOMY & TECHNOLOGICAL SCIENCES. 5152
1001-652X See SCIENCE IN CHINA. SERIES B, CHEMISTRY, LIFE SCIENCES & EARTH SCIENCES. 5152

1001-6538 See CHINESE SCIENCE BULLETIN. 5094
1001-6627 See ZHONGGUO JISHENGCHONGBING FANGZHI ZAZHI. 3653
1001-6678 See GONGYE WEISHENGWU. 563
1001-6813 See ZHONGGUO PIGE. 3186
1001-7216 See ZHONGGUO SHUIDAO KEXUE. 2361
1001-7313 See YINGYONG QIXIANG XUEBAO. 1437
1001-7364 See JOURNAL OF FRUIT SCIENCE. 100
1001-7488 See LINYE KEXUE (1979). 2387
1001-7631 See HUAXUE FANYING GONGCHENG YU GONGYI. 2013
1001-8042 See NUCLEAR SCIENCE AND TECHNIQUES. 4449
1001-8158 See ZHONGGUO TUDI KEXUE. 1361
1001-8255 See ZHONGGUO YIYAO GONGYE ZAZHI. 4334
1001-8417 See CHINESE CHEMICAL LETTERS. 1023
1001-8654 See MUCAI GONGYE. 2403
1001-8689 See ZHONGGUO KANGSHENGSU ZAZHI. 4333
1001-8719 See SHIYOU XUEBAO. SHIYOU JIAGONG. 4278
1001-8859 See ZHONGGUO CHUBAN NIANJIAN / CHINA PUBLISHING YEARBOOK. 4820
1001-8867 See CHUNG-KUO TU SHU KUAN HSUEH PAO. 3202
1001-909X See DONGHAI HAIYANG. 554
1001-9294 See CHINESE MEDICAL SCIENCES JOURNAL. 3563
1001-9383 See HEBEI SHENG KEXUEYUAN XUEBAO. 5109
1001-9391 See ZHONGHUA LAODONG WEISHENG ZHIYEBING ZAZHI. 2871
1001-943X See HUNAN DAXUE XUEBAO. 1092
1001-9448 See GUANGDONG YIXUE. 3579
1001-9456 See SULIAO (BEIJING). 4460
1001-9499 See LINYE KE-JI. 2387
1001-9626 See SHENGWU SHUXUE XUEBAO. 3534
1001-9707 See HEBEI DIZHI XUEYUAN XUEBAO. 1382
1002-0071 See PROGRESS IN NATURAL SCIENCE : COMMUNICATION OF STATE KEY LABORATORIES OF CHINA. 5142
1002-011X See SHIJIE LISHI. 2629
1002-056X See WEISHENGWUXUE ZAZHI. 571
1002-0837 See HANGTIAN YIXUE YU YIXUE GONGCHENG. 3580
1002-0926 See KUNCHONGXUE YANJIU JIKAN. 5611
1002-0942 See ANNALS OF DIFFERENTIAL EQUATIONS. WEI FEN FANG CHENG NIEN KAN. 3494
1002-1302 See JIANGSU NONGYE KEXUE. 98
1002-204X See NINGXIA NONG-LIN KE-JI. 113
1002-4611 See CHUNG-HUA JEN MIN KUNG HO KUO TSUI KAO JEN MIN FA YUAN KUNG PAO. 2950
1002-4980 See CHIU SHIH. 4517
1002-5030 See KUO CHI HUO I. 843
1002-6800 See CHUNG-KUO PIEN CHIANG SHIH TI YEN CHIU. 2683
1002-7742 See ZHONGGUO HANGTIAN. 41
1002-8889 See RURAL ECONOMY AND SOCIETY. 1519
1003-5370 See CHUNG-KUO CHUNG HSI I CHIEH HO TSA CHIH. 3564
1004-2490 See HAIYANG YUYE. 2305
1005-0302 See JOURNAL OF MATERIALS SCIENCE & TECHNOLOGY. 5119
1005-3026 See TUNG-PEI TA HSUEH HSUEH PAO. TZU JAN KO HSUEH PAN. 5167
1010-0091 See ABSTRACTS OF CHINESE MEDICINES : ACME. 3543
1010-0423 See INTERNATIONAL PHARMACY JOURNAL. 4309

1010-0466 See HISTORIA LATINOAMERICANA EN EUROPA. 2617

1010-061X See JOURNAL OF EVOLUTIONARY BIOLOGY. 548

1010-0652 See ZEITSCHRIFT FUER PAEDAGOGISCHE PSYCHOLOGIE. 4622

1010-0695 See TAEHAN HANUI HAKHOE CHI. 3644

1010-0725 See TUNG WU CHE HSUEH CHUAN HSI LU / TUNG WU TA HSUEH. 4364

1010-0849 See ACTA PHARMACEUTICA TURCICA. 4289

1010-0962 See RE METALLICA, DE. 4017

1010-0970 See NESTLE RESEARCH NEWS. 4195

1010-1098 See ALEXANDRIA SCIENCE EXCHANGE. 5082

1010-1179 See INTERNATIONAL CRUDE OIL AND PRODUCT PRICES. 4261

1010-1349 See LUCRARI STIINTIFICE - INSTITUTUL DE CERCETARI SI PROIECTARI PENTRU VALORIFICAREA SI INDUSTRIALIZAREA LEGUMELOR SI FRUCTELOR. 105

1010-1365 See FAO AGRICULTURAL SERVICES BULLETIN. 83

1010-1578 See CIENCIAS Y TECNICA EN LA AGRICULTURA. PROTECCION DE PLANTAS. 74

1010-1608 See JOURNAL OF EAST ASIAN AFFAIRS, THE. 2655

1010-1640 See PLANTBESKERMINGSNUUS. 525

1010-1845 See CIIR JUSTICE PAPERS. 4518

1010-1853 See CIIR NEWS. 4518

1010-2000 See CIENCIA Y TECNICA EN LA AGRICULTURA. MECANIZACION DE LA AGRICULTURA. 74

1010-206X See JOURNAL DE GENEVE ET GAZETTE DE LAUSANNE. 5811

1010-2108 See JOURNAL DE GENEVE ET GAZETTE DE LAUSANNE. 5811

1010-2566 See PROCEEDINGS OF THE ... ENTOMOLOGICAL CONGRESS - ENTOMOLOGICAL SOCIETY OF SOUTHERN AFRICA. 5613

1010-2744 See MRL BULLETIN OF RESEARCH AND DEVELOPMENT. 1988

1010-2752 See REVISTA DE PROTECCION VEGETAL. 185

1010-3376 See ANALYSE NUMERIQUE ET LA THEORIE DE L'APPROXIMATION, L'. 3493

1010-3422 See CHEVAL (WIEN). 2798

1010-3465 See KLASGIDS. 3293

1010-3481 See KENYA COFFEE. 177

1010-3503 See CAFE PERU - CENTRAL DE COOPERATIVAS AGRARIAS CAFE PERU. 165

1010-3538 See VETERINARY DRUG REGISTRATION NEWSLETTER. 5525

1010-3562 See PAKISTAN SEAFOOD DIGEST. 2352

1010-3589 See BULETINUL INFORMATIV AL ACADEMIEI DE STIINTE AGRICOLE SI SILVICE. 2376

1010-3597 See BLATTER DER RILKE-GESELLSCHAFT. 3367

1010-3600 See ARCHITHESE (1914). 291

1010-3619 See APE, L'. 62

1010-3627 See CINEMA (ZURICH, SWITZERLAND). 4066

1010-3635 See INVESTIGATIONS ON CETACEA. 5587

1010-3643 See CAHIERS INTERNATIONAUX D'HISTOIRE ECONOMIQUE ET SOCIALE. 1550

1010-3716 See KENYA REVIEW. 1571

1010-3740 See LIBYAN JOURNAL OF AGRICULTURE, THE. 105

1010-3783 See RURAL DEMOGRAPHY. 4560

1010-3791 See JUTE AND JUTE FABRICS, BANGLADESH. 5353

1010-3821 See ARQUITECTURA CUBA. 292

1010-3856 See KUNSTHISTORISCHES JAHRBUCH GRAZ. 356

1010-3872 See ECCLESIA ORANS. 4954

1010-3902 See SABRAO JOURNAL. 527

1010-3910 See JOURNAL OF BIOLOGICAL SCIENCES RESEARCH. 460

1010-397X See NATURAL RESOURCES/WATER SERIES. 2199

1010-3996 See BELARUSKAIA MOVA. 3268

1010-4011 See BELARUSKAJA LITARATURA. 3366

1010-4038 See SAVINGS BANKS INTERNATIONAL. 810

1010-4054 See IPH YEARBOOK. 4234

1010-4089 See ARCHITHESE (1980). 291

1010-4127 See AFRICAN JOURNAL OF SOCIOLOGY. 5238

1010-4135 See ACCOUNTANT (NAIROBI), THE. 735

1010-4151 See BOLETIM MENSAL DE ESTATISTICA. 5323

1010-416X See ASIAN MONETARY MONITOR. 640

1010-4208 See SRI LANKA JOURNAL OF TEA SCIENCE. 2371

1010-4283 See TUMOR BIOLOGY. 3824

1010-4569 See AIOLIKA GRAMMATA. 3358

1010-5182 See JOURNAL OF CRANIO-MAXILLO-FACIAL SURGERY. 3967

1010-5204 See LIN YEH SHIH YEN SO YEN CHIU PAO KAO CHI KAN. 2387

1010-5220 See OPUSCULA ZOOLOGICA FLUMINENSIA. 5612

1010-5239 See STI REVUE. 5160

1010-5395 See ASIA-PACIFIC JOURNAL OF PUBLIC HEALTH : ASIA-PACIFIC ACADEMIC CONSORTIUM FOR PUBLIC HEALTH. 4767

1010-5433 See ANALELE UNIVERSITATII BUCURESTI. MATEMATICA. 3492

1010-5441 See SEAMIC INFORMATION RETRIEVAL ON CURRENT LITERATURE. SERIES M, MALARIA. 4802

1010-5492 See MANUSCRIPTUM. 3410

1010-5506 See ANALE DE ISTORIE. 4625

1010-5522 See AFRICAN ENVIRONMENT. 2159

1010-5549 See MALAWIAN GEOGRAPHER, THE. 2568

1010-5557 See AMERIKANSKII EZHEGODNIK. 2527

1010-5565 See NEW CLASSIC. 3415

1010-559X See BERNER KUNSTMITTEILUNGEN. 343

1010-562X See NONGSA SIHOM YON'GU NONMUNJIP. WONYE P'YON. 2426

1010-5824 See INTERNATIONAL ARACHIS NEWSLETTER. 174

1010-5980 See REVISTA DE CIENCIAS MATEMATICAS. 3531

1010-6030 See JOURNAL OF PHOTOCHEMISTRY AND PHOTOBIOLOGY. A, CHEMISTRY. 1054

1010-6049 See GEOCARTO INTERNATIONAL. 2561

1010-6103 See SARHAD JOURNAL OF AGRICULTURE. 132

1010-6146 See VEROFFENTLICHUNGEN DER BUNDESANSTALT FUER ALPENLANDISCHE LANDWIRTSCHAFT GUMPENSTEIN / BUNDESMINISTERIUM FUER LAND- UND FORSTWIRTSCHAFT. 144

1010-6367 See JAMAICAN HISTORICAL REVIEW, THE. 2740

1010-6960 See TURKIYE ENTOMOLOJI DERGISI. 5614

1010-7053 See SAFETY AND HEALTH AT WORK : ILO-CIS BULLETIN. 2872

1010-7215 See LATERANUM. 4972

1010-7266 See LAOGRAPHIA. 2321

1010-7274 See LINGUISTIQUE ET SCIENCES HUMAINES. 3299

1010-7363 See DIOTIMA. 4345

1010-7576 See DOGA. TURK BIYOLOJI DERGISI. 454

1010-7584 See DOGA. TURK TIP VE ECZACILIK DERGISI. 3573

1010-7592 See DOGA. TURK VETERINERLIK VE HAYVANCILIK. 5509

1010-7614 See DOGA. TURK KIMYA DERGISI. 974

1010-7630 See DOGA. TURKISH JOURNAL OF PHYSICS. 4402

1010-7649 See DOGA. TURKISH JOURNAL OF VETERINARY AND ANIMAL SCIENCES. 5509

1010-7649 See DOGA. TURK TARIM VE ORMANCLK DERGISI. 80

1010-7940 See EUROPEAN JOURNAL OF CARDIO-THORACIC SURGERY : OFFICIAL JOURNAL OF THE EUROPEAN ASSOCIATION FOR CARDIO-THORACIC SURGERY. 3964

1010-8017 See PRAKTIESE TEOLOGIE IN S.A. 4987

1010-8092 See HUMAN RESOURCE MANAGEMENT. 941

1010-8149 See ESRA NEWSLETTER. 1668

1010-8262 See JOURNAL OF COMPARATIVE PHYSICAL EDUCATION AND SPORT / ISCPES, INTERNATIONAL SOCIETY ON COMPARATIVE PHYSICAL EDUCATION AND SPORT. 1856

1010-8408 See ISSUES IN BIOMEDICINE. 459

1010-8424 See JOURNAL OF THE HONG KONG MEDICAL ASSOCIATION. 3598

1010-8734 See IFES REVIEW. 4964

1010-8793 See NATO ASI SERIES. SERIES H, CELL BIOLOGY. 539

1010-9099 See WORLD FOOD PROGRAMME JOURNAL. 2913

1010-9501 See UDT NEWSLETTER. 3254

1010-9609 See WHO DRUG INFORMATION. 4332

1010-9919 See OLD TESTAMENT ESSAYS. 5018

1010-9935 See ODTU GELISME DERGISI. 2911

1010-9943 See GAZETA MATEMATICA (BUCHAREST, ROMANIA : 1974). 3506

1010-9994 See GREEK ECONOMIC REVIEW. 1493

1011-002X See PAKISTAN ECONOMIC AND SOCIAL REVIEW. 1577

1011-0054 See SPORE (ENGLISH ED.). 137

1011-0070 See OZS, OSTERREICHISCHE ZEITSCHRIFT FUER SOZIOLOGIE. 5253

1011-016X See GODO GODO. 2639

1011-0186 See PAPIER AUS OESTERREICH. 4236

1011-0240 See RIGHTS (GENEVA, SWITZERLAND). 1308

1011-0267 See PROGRESS IN BASIC AND CLINICAL PHARMACOLOGY. 4326

1011-0283 See SKIN PHARMACOLOGY. 3723

1011-0410 See REVISTA PERUANA DE CIENCIAS SOCIALES : RPCS. 5216

1011-0887 See DOGA. TURK BOTANIK DERGISI. 508

1011-0917 See DOGA BILIM DERGISI. SERI D2, TARIM V ORMANCILIK. 80

1011-0925 See DOGA BILIM DERGISI. SERI D1, VETERINERLIK VE HAYVANCILIK. 5509

1011-1344 See JOURNAL OF PHOTOCHEMISTRY AND PHOTOBIOLOGY. B, BIOLOGY. 1054

1011-1557 See ATHENA (ATHENI). 1089

1011-1603 See SEA WIND. 2205

1011-1778 See DEMOCRACY INTERNATIONAL. 4471

1011-1891 See ROUTES PARIS. 1986. 1995

1011-2014 See HANGUK KOMI YONGUSO YONGU POGOSO. 5585

1011-2057 See VETERINER FAKULTESI DERGISI. SELCUK UNIVERSITESI. 5527

1011-226X See QUEST (LUSAKA, ZAMBIA). 4358

1011-2359 See CHINA CURRENT LAWS. 2950

1011-2367 See ASIAN-AUSTRALASIAN JOURNAL OF ANIMAL SCIENCES. 5504

1011-2588 See FOOD IRRADIATION NEWSLETTER. 2337

1011-2693 See URANIUM NEWSLETTER. 995

1011-288X See DOULEUR ET ANALGESIE. 3573

1011-2901 See GERATRIE FUER DIE TAEGLICHE PRAXIS. 3751

1011-291X See PHARMACOLOGY AND THE SKIN. 3722

1011-2928 See LITHIUM THERAPY MONOGRAPHS. 3605

1011-2952 See DIRECTORY OF UNITED NATIONS SERIAL PUBLICATIONS. 3208

1011-2979 See CHINESE AROUND THE WORLD. 4943

1011-3010 See GREGORIOS O PALAMAS. 4961

1011-3029 See JOURNAL OF PACIFIC STUDIES. 2669

1011-3258 See EVOLUTIONARY TRENDS IN PLANTS. 509

1011-3398 See MARMARA UNIVERSITESI ECZACILIK DERGISI. 4314

1011-3436 See SOUTH AFRICAN JOURNAL OF ECONOMIC HISTORY : [JOURNAL OF THE ECONOMIC HISTORY SOCIETY OF SOUTHERN AFRICA], THE. 1584

1011-3487 See SOUTH AFRICAN JOURNAL OF HIGHER EDUCATION. 1847

1011-3509 See NASHRIYYAH-I SHIMI VA-MUHANDISI-I SHIMI-I IRAN. 987

1011-3649 See IP ASIA: INTELLECTUAL PROPERTY, MARKETING AND COMMUNICATIONS LAW. 1305

1011-372X See CATALYSIS LETTERS. 1050

1011-3738 See TEACHING AND TRAINING IN GERIATRIC MEDICINE. 3755

1011-3797 See BULLETIN DES TRANSPORTS INTERNATIONAUX FERROVIAIRES / ZEITSCHRIFT FUER DEN INTERNATIONALEN EISENBAHNVERKEHR. 5430

1011-3924 See BULLETIN OF THE CHEMICAL SOCIETY OF ETHIOPIA. 1021

1011-3983 See BULLETIN (ARTICLE 19 ORGANIZATION). 4504

1011-4025 See ANALELE UNIVERSITATII DIN GALATI. FASCICULA VI, TEHNOLOGIA SI CHIMIA PRODUSELOR ALIMENTARE. 5082

1011-405X See MESSAGE OLYMPIQUE. 4904

1011-4149 See PEOPLE DYNAMICS. 944

1011-4173 See ENVIRONMENTAL HEALTH (COPENHAGEN). 2167

1011-4181 See HELLENIKA STOMATOLOGIKA CHRONIKA. 1324

1011-4203 See SCHWEIZER MONATSSCHRIFT FUER ZAHNMEDIZIN. 1335

1011-4386 See PHARMAKLINIK (MADRID). 4324

1011-4548 See WORLD COMPETITION. 3104

1011-4726 See JAHRBUCH DES VEREINS FUER GESCHICHTE DER STADT WIEN. 2694

1011-4750 See EASTERN AFRICA ECONOMIC REVIEW. 1480

1011-4831 See GERIATRICA. 3751

1011-4858 See FOREIGN TRADE STATISTICS OF ASIA AND THE PACIFIC. 836

1011-4866 See CARINDEX, SCIENCE & TECHNOLOGY. 5174

1011-5110 See SOUTH PACIFIC PERIODICALS INDEX. 425

1011-5145 See SOUTH PACIFIC RESEARCH REGISTER. 5159

1011-5153 See HEALTH SERVICES INTERNATIONAL. 4781

1011-5498 See MADOQUA (WINDHOEK. 1975). 4167

1011-5544 See UPDATE. 5225

1011-5714 See JIAOYU XINLIXUEBAO. 4592

1011-5765 See CARIBBEAN AFFAIRS. 2511

1011-5773 See WHO AIDS SERIES. 3677

1011-582X See SHAKESPEARE IN SOUTHERN AFRICA : JOURNAL OF THE SHAKESPEARE SOCIETY OF SOUTHERN AFRICA. 5368

1011-5846 See DIRECTIONS SUVA. 3206

1011-596X See ASIAN HOSPITAL. 3777

1011-601X See PAKISTAN JOURNAL OF PHARMACEUTICAL SCIENCES. 4319

1011-6125 See STEREOTACTIC AND FUNCTIONAL NEUROSURGERY. 3975

1011-6311 See ANNUAL ECONOMIC SURVEY (PORT OF SPAIN, TRINIDAD AND TOBAGO). 1545

1011-6370 See DEVELOPMENT (ROME). 2909

1011-6435 See RAPA BULLETIN. 2508

1011-6524 See RENAL PHYSIOLOGY AND BIOCHEMISTRY. 3993

1011-6559 See OPTOELEKTRONIKA I POLUPROVODNIKOVAA TEHNIKA. 2074

1011-6583 See EPITHEORESE KLINIKES FARMAKOLOGIAS KAI FARMAKOKINETIKES INTERNATIONAL ED. 4303

1011-663X See AFRICAN JOURNAL OF INTERNATIONAL LAW, THE. 3122

1011-6656 See ERATOSTHENES THESSALONIKE. 2560

1011-6672 See NEW TRENDS IN LIPID MEDIATORS RESEARCH. 467

1011-6702 See JOURNAL OF WORLD TRADE. 843

1011-6710 See SWISS CONTAMINATION CONTROL. 2244

1011-6788 See ZHONGHUA MINGUO WAIKE YIXUE HUI ZAZHI. 3978

1011-6842 See ZHONGHUA MINGUO XINZANGXUE HUI ZAZHI. 3711

1011-6877 See ZEITSCHRIFT FUER GERONTOPSYCHOLOGIE & -PSYCHIATRIE. 3755

1011-6966 See INFUSIONSTHERAPIE UND TRANSFUSIONSMEDIZIN. 3772

1011-6974 See BEITRAEGE ZUR INFUSIONSTHERAPIE. 3555

1011-6982 See ANIMAL MODELS OF PSYCHIATRIC DISORDERS. 3920

1011-730X See ADALET DERGISI. 2927

1011-7547 See SUID-AFRIKAAN, DIE. 1523

1011-7571 See MEDICAL PRINCIPLES AND PRACTICE. 3611

1011-7601 See JOURNAL FOR THE STUDY OF RELIGION. 4967

1011-7768 See TRAVEL BUSINESS ANALYST ASIA ED. 5495

1011-7903 See BULLETIN DE L'UNION INTERNATIONALE CONTRE LA TUBERCULOSE ET LES MALADIES RESPIRATOIRES. 3949

1011-792X See MAIN SCIENCE AND TECHNOLOGY INDICATORS. 5126

1011-7989 See ESCRITURA (CARACAS). 3342

1011-7997 See ESPMENA BULLETIN. 3280

1011-839X See CIRES, CAHIERS IVOIRIENS DE RECHERCHE ECONOMIQUE ET SOCIALE. 1551

1011-8527 See SOUTH AFRICAN JOURNAL OF CRIMINAL JUSTICE. 3109

1011-8780 See FAO QUARTERLY BULLETIN OF STATISTICS. 153

1011-8829 See INTERNATIONAL CATALOGUING AND BIBLIOGRAPHIC CONTROL : QUARTERLY BULLETIN OF THE IFLA UBCIM PROGRAMME. 417

1011-8845 See STUDII TEOLOGICE. 5040

1011-8918 See CONTRIBUTIONS TO GENERAL ALGEBRA. 3502

1011-8934 See JOURNAL OF KOREAN MEDICAL SCIENCE. 3595

1011-9019 See CREACTION. 1819

1011-9086 See NEWSLETTER & GALLERY GUIDE / NATIONAL PALACE MUSEUM. 4094

1011-9094 See GUGONG XUESHU JIKAN. 351

1011-923X See ACTUALITES COMMUNAUTAIRES. 3122

1011-9485 See STUDII - INSTITUTUL DE CERCETARI SI PROIECTARI PENTRU GOSPODARIREA APELOR. EPURAREA APELOR. 2244

1011-9493 See HANGUK KONCHUNG HAKHOE CHI. 5609

1011-9981 See BANGLADESH JOURNAL OF MICROBIOLOGY. 443

1011-999X See BULLETIN SIGNALETIQUE - INSTITUT NATIONAL AGRONOMIQUE EL HARRACH. 70

1012-0211 See PARATERETES : PERIODIKE EKDOSE LOGOU KAI TECHNES, O. 3422

1012-0238 See CAHIERS LIGURES DE PREHISTOIRE ET DE PROTOHISTOIRE. 2613

1012-0319 See SPECIALISED NATIONAL COUNCILS' MAGAZINE, THE. 5223

1012-0335 See SPECIAL PUBLICATION / BERMUDA BIOLOGICAL STATION FOR RESEARCH, INC. 2221

1012-0343 See PROCEEDINGS - INTERNATIONAL SYMPOSIUM ON SUBSCRIBER LOOPS AND SERVICES. 2076

1012-0386 See DIFFUSION AND DEFECT DATA. [PT. A], DEFECT AND DIFFUSION FORUM. 1051

1012-0394 See DIFFUSION AND DEFECT DATA. [PT. B], SOLID STATE PHENOMENA : SSP. 1051

1012-0408 See JOURNAL OF KOREAN APPLIED ECOLOGY. 2218

1012-0424 See ELLENIKE GASTROENTEROLOGIA. 3744

1012-0491 See BULLETIN D'INFORMATION SPORTIVE BRUXELLES. 4888

1012-0602 See SCIENTIFIC JOURNAL OF ORIENTEERING. 4917

1012-0750 See SOUTH AFRICAN JOURNAL OF GEOLOGY. 1397

1012-1617 See REVISTA GEOGRAFICA VENEZOLANA. 2575

1012-1692 See ECOTROPICOS : REVISTA DE LA SOCIEDAD VENEZOLANA DE ECOLOGIA. 2215

1012-1730 See VOLLEYBALL ROME. 4928

1012-1773 See ANNALES DE LA FACULTE DES SCIENCES. SERIE III, BIOLOGIE -BIOCHIMIE : AFS / UNIVERSITE DE YAOUNDE. 480

1012-229X See DELTION TES HISTORIKES KAI ETHNOLOGIKES HETAIREIAS TES HELLADOS. 2319

1012-2311 See DELTION BIBLIKON MELETON. 5016

1012-2338 See STUDI D'ITALIANISTICA NELL'AFRICA AUSTRALE. 2273

1012-2435 See IMACS ANNALS ON COMPUTING AND APPLIED MATHEMATICS. 1187

1012-2443 See ANNALS OF MATHEMATICS AND OF ARTIFICIAL INTELLIGENCE. 1211

1012-2516 See BIONEWS ATHENS. 2161

1012-2532 See BIOPOLITICS ATHENS. 2161

1012-2591 See JOURNAL OF BUSINESS AND SOCIETY. 1569

1012-2710 See ICC COMMERCIAL CRIME INTERNATIONAL. 1609

1012-2796 See S.A. ARGIEFBLAD. 2483

1012-3172 See REVISTA CUBANA DE HEMATOLOGIA INMUNOLOGIA Y HEMOTERAPIA. 3635

1012-3202 See BULETINUL INSTITUTULUI POLITEHNIC BUCURESTI. SERIA ENERGETICA. 2111

1012-3288 See POWER BOAT AND SKI. 595

1012-3326 See MAGAZINE / BANQUE DE LA REPUBLIQUE D'HAITI. 797

1012-3334 See ASIAN VENTURE CAPITAL JOURNAL, THE. 891

1012-3466 See MAGALLAT AL-BUHUT AL-ZIRA'IYYAT WA-AL-MAWARID AL-MA'IYYAT. AL-INTAG AL-HAYAWANI. 106

1012-3474 See MAGALLAT AL-BUHUT AL-ZIRA'IYYAT WA-AL-MAWARID AL-MA'IYYAT. AL-INTAG AL-NABATI. 106

1012-3482 See MAGALLAT AL-BUHUT AL-ZIRA'IYYAT WA-AL-MAWARID AL-MA'IYYAT. AL-TURBAT WA-MASADIR AL-MIYAH. 106

1012-3520 See CHINA SOURCES. HARDWARE. 2810

1012-3962 See TEA BULLETIN. 2371

1012-4195 See ZHONGYANG YANJIUYUAN LISHI YUYAN YANJIUSUO JIKAN. 2510

1012-4411 See ACOPS YEARBOOK / ADVISORY COMMITTEE ON POLLUTION OF THE SEA, LONDON. 2223

1012-4543 See PRO MUNDI VITA STUDIES. 5034

1012-490X See EDI POLICY SEMINAR REPORT, AN. 1487

1012-4926 See CIMBEBASIA : JOURNAL OF THE STATE MUSEUM, WINDHOEK. 5095

1012-4934 See UNIDIR NEWSLETTER / UNITED NATIONS INSTITUTE FOR DISARMAMENT RESEARCH. 4059

1012-5299 See MINTEK BULLETIN. 2146

1012-5329 See DISEASE INFORMATION. 5509

1012-5655 See BILDGEBUNG (BASEL). 3939

1012-5833 See ROMISCHES OSTERREICH. 2707

1012-5949 See BANGLADESH VETERINARIAN, THE. 5505

1012-5965 See MAGALLAT AL-DILTA LI-L-ULUM. 5126

1012-5973 See ASSIUT VETERINARY MEDICAL JOURNAL. 5504

1012-6465 See JAHRBUCH FUER ZEITGESCHICHTE. 2694

1012-6511 See DISCUSSION PAPER / UNITED NATIONS RESEARCH INSTITUTE FOR SOCIAL DEVELOPMENT. 1480

1012-6570 See INFORMATION BULLETIN / INTERNATIONAL ASSOCIATION FOR THE STUDY OF THE CULTURES OF CENTRAL ASIA. 2654

1012-6694 See CHILD NEPHROLOGY AND UROLOGY. 3989

1012-6880 See INTECOL NEWSLETTER. 2217

1012-6910 See BUVISINDI (REYKJAVIK). 70

1012-7100 See TECHNICAL COMMUNICATION (SOUTH AFRICA. DEPT. OF AGRICULTURE AND WATER SUPPLY). 140

1012-7410 See PASTURAS TROPICALES. 118

1012-7720 See IFPRA BULLETIN. 4706

1012-7895 See PRO JUVENTUTE. 1068

1012-8026 See SOCIAL INDICATORS OF DEVELOPMENT. 1521

1012-8042 See NEWSLETTER OF THE INTERNATIONAL ACADEMY FOR THE STUDY OF TOURISM. 5486

1012-8050 See INNOVATION IN SOCIAL SCIENCE RESEARCH. 5203

1012-8069 See DISCUSSION PAPER - IFC. 2909

1012-8115 See EMERGING STOCK MARKETS FACTBOOK. 897

1012-8263 See TRANSITION. 5225

1012-8328 See IT ASIA. 2566

1012-8360 See ICAA NEWS. 1345

1012-8417 See INTERNATIONAL TEXTILE BULLETIN. DYEING/PRINTING/FINISHING. 5352

1012-8425 See INTERNATIONAL TEXTILE BULLETIN. FABRIC FORMING. 5352

1012-8603 See JOURNAL OF PETROLEUM RESEARCH. 4262

1012-8611 See JOURNAL OF NEPAL CHEMICAL SOCIETY, NEPAL CHEMICAL SOCIETY. 982

1012-8638 See SEAMIC INFORMATION RETRIEVAL ON CURRENT LITERATURE. SERIES I, CAMPYLOBACTER. 4802

1012-8646 See SEAMIC INFORMATION RETRIEVAL ON CURRENT LITERATURE. SERIES J, VIRAL DIARRHEA. 4802

1012-8654 See SEAMIC INFORMATION RETRIEVAL ON CURRENT LITERATURE. SERIES K, DYSENTERY, BACILLARY. 4802

1012-8689 See ADVANCES IN CONTRACEPTIVE DELIVERY SYSTEMS. 587

1012-8697 See JOPSOM. JOURNAL OF PREVENTIVE AND SOCIAL MEDICINE. 3592

1012-8719 See IPTC NEWS. 1158

1012-8727 See TECHNICAL BULLETINS / WORLD FERTILITY SURVEY. 4560

1012-8778 See NAGRA INFORMIERT. 2237

1012-8786 See PROFESSIONAL PAPERS (SAUDI ARABIA. DEPUTY MINISTRY FOR MINERAL RESOURCES). 1392

1012-8832 See BULLETIN OF THE FACULTY OF EARTH SCIENCES. 1352

1012-8875 See JOURNAL OF PAEDIATRICS, OBSTETRICS, AND GYNAECOLOGY. 3905

1012-8956 See LABOR + SPRECHSTUNDE / SCHWEIZERISCHER VERBAND DER ARZTGEHILFINNEN. 1685

1012-8964 See PEDIATRIA (LIMA, PERU). 3907

1012-8999 See CHEMISTRY IN SRI LANKA. 971

1012-909X See IIASA COLLABORATIVE PROCEEDINGS SERIES. 1187

1012-9103 See ZIMBABWE NURSE, THE. 3871

1012-912X See SCHRIFTENREIHE INFANS CEREBROPATHICUS. 3936

1012-9197 See PROBIN HITAISHI. 3754

1012-9243 See EARTHQUAKE ENGINEERING - EUROPEAN SYMPOSIUM ON EARTHQUAKE ENGINEERING. 2022

1012-9391 See AFRICA PERSPECTIVE. 2636

1012-9405 See AFRIKA MATHEMATICA. 3491

1012-9421 See AK JOURNAL. 3547

1012-9464 See BOLETIN DE LA BIBLIOTECA NACIONAL (CARACAS). 2724

1012-9472 See BOLETIN DEL ARCHIVO GENERAL DE LA NACION (SANTO DOMINGO). 2480

1012-9480 See BOLETIN DEL SECRETARIADO TECNICO. 861

1012-9529 See BOLETIN ESTADISTICO TRIMESTRAL (INSTITUTO NACIONAL DE ESTADISTICA). (BOLIVIA). 1530

1012-9545 See INTERNATIONAL TEXTILE MANUFACTURING. 5352

1012-9588 See MELITA THEOLOGICA. 4976

1012-960X See BOLETIN / ACADEMIA VENEZOLANA DE LA LENGUA CORRESPONDIENTE DE LA ESPANOLA. 3368

1012-9685 See PROPOSED PROGRAM AND BUDGET ESTIMATES - PAN AMERICAN HEALTH ORGANIZATION. 4797

1012-9707 See CLIPPER (BASEL), THE. 2331

1012-9790 See REVISTA DE HISTORIA (HEREDIA). 2758

1012-9871 See NINS. NEW ISSUES IN NEUROSCIENCES. 3843

1012-9987 See ENCEPHALARTOS. 2413

1013-0047 See RHINOLOGY. SUPPLEMENT. 3897

1013-0306 See BANGLADESH JOURNAL OF TRAINING AND DEVELOPMENT. 64

1013-0314 See PGRC/E-ILCA GERMPLASM NEWSLETTER. 521

1013-0764 See JOURNAL OF RURAL DEVELOPMENT. 100

1013-090X See JIAOYU ZILIAO YU TUSHUGUAN XUE. 3219

1013-0942 See REPUBLIC OF CHINA YEARBOOK. 2663

1013-1116 See TYDSKRIF VIR CHRISTELIKE WETENSKAP. 5006

1013-1191 See PEAKE STUDIES. 3422

1013-1396 See BULLETIN DE LIAISON DE DEMOGRAPHIE AFRICAINE. 4550

1013-1493 See BOTSWANA JOURNAL OF EARTH SCIENCES. 1352

1013-1644 See EDUCATIONAL AND PSYCHOLOGICAL MEASUREMENT. 4585

1013-171X See AFRICAN CHRISTIAN STUDIES. 4933

1013-1809 See JOURNAL OF ECONOMICS AND INTERNATIONAL RELATIONS. 1570

1013-1930 See AL-NASRAT AL-TIBIYYA AL-ARABIYYAT. 3547

1013-2007 See TEXTE ZUR GESCHICHTE DER PRAVENTIVMEDIZIN : TGP / HERAUSGEGEBEN VON ERWIN BRAUN GESELLSCHAFT FUR PRAVENTIVMEDIZIN. 3645

1013-2015 See EDI SEMINAR PAPER, AN. 1487

1013-204X See NEUE ASPEKTE RADIOLOGISCHER DIAGNOSTIK UND THERAPIE : JAHRBUCH ... DER SCHWEIZERISCHEN GESELLSCHAFT FUR RADIOLOGIE UND NUKLEARMEDIZIN. 3944

1013-2058 See SCHWEIZERISCHE RUNDSCHAU FUER MEDIZIN PRAXIS. 3801

1013-2104 See BIBLIOGRAFIA GEOLOGICA SI GEOFIZICA A REPUBLICII SOCIALISTE ROMANIA. 1367

1013-2120 See BUSINESS VENEZUELA. 653

1013-2163 See REVISTA DE LA ACADEMIA HONDURENA DE GEOGRAFIA E HISTORIA. 2483

1013-2171 See LINGUISTIQUE ET SCIENCES HUMAINES. 3299

1013-2287 See CONTROL CIBERNETICA Y AUTOMATIZACION. 1250

1013-2309 See DOSTOEVSKY STUDIES : JOURNAL OF THE INTERNATIONAL DOSTOEVSKY SOCIETY. 3382

1013-2392 See AL-'ILM WA-AL-TIKNULUGIYA. 5082

1013-2511 See ISSUES & STUDIES. 4526

1013-2732 See ZHONGHUA ZHENJUNXUEHUI HUIKAN. 577

1013-3097 See CANCER PAIN RELEASE. 3812

1013-3119 See ABB REVIEW. 2109

1013-3224 See CYPRUS JOURNAL OF ECONOMICS, THE. 1479

1013-333X See EDI DEVELOPMENT POLICY CASE SERIES. ANALYTICAL CASE STUDIES. 1487

1013-3348 See EDI DEVELOPMENT POLICY CASE SERIES. TEACHING CASES. 1487

1013-3429 See POLICY & RESEARCH SERIES. 803

1013-3445 See ZIMBABWE JOURNAL OF EDUCATIONAL RESEARCH : ZJER. 1792

1013-3453 See NARCOTIC DRUGS : ESTIMATED WORLD REQUIREMENTS FOR ..., STATISTICS FOR 4316

1013-3488 See ANNALES VALAISANNES. 2674

1013-3534 See ANNALES FRIBOURGEOISES. 2674

1013-364X See REAL TIME MAGAZINE. 1221

1013-3666 See SA JOURNAL OF FOOD SCIENCE AND NUTRITION, THE. 4199

1013-3968 See CHONNAM JOURNAL OF MEDICAL SCIENCES. 3563

1013-4050 See AIRLINE CODING DIRECTORY. 9

1013-4069 See ESTUDIOS DEL DESARROLLO. 5199

1013-4204 See MITROPOLIA ARDEALULUI. 5032

1013-4255 See SARGETIA. 4096

1013-431X See BERMUDA JOURNAL OF ARCHAEOLOGY AND MARITIME HISTORY. 261

1013-4476 See SWISS MATERIALS. 1997

1013-4492 See SOCIAL SECURITY DOCUMENTATION. PACIFIC SERIES. 1711

1013-4514 See WORLD TRADE MATERIALS. 858

1013-4689 See CPE NEWSLETTER. 1877

1013-5065 See HALLE SUD. 5479

1013-5235 See CHRONIQUE DES NATIONS UNIES. 3126

1013-5294 See PHARMEUROPA ED. FRANCAISE. 4324

1013-5316 See SCIENCE INTERNATIONAL LAHORE. 5152

1013-5332 See BULLETIN MENSUEL - BANQUE DE LA REPUBLIQUE DU BURUNDI. 780

1013-5375 See CHUNGGUK KYONGJE SOKPO. 1470

1013-543X See DACCA UNIVERSITY STUDIES. PART A, THE. 318

1013-5464 See ARAB OIL (ARAB OIL PUB. CO. : 1980.). 4250

1013-5480 See AIR QUALITY IN SELECTED URBAN AREAS. 2223

1013-5499 See INDEX MEDICUS FOR WHO SOUTH-EAST ASIA REGION. 3586

1013-6444 See NATURALIST PORT ELIZABETH, THE. 4168

1013-655X See SIDWAYA. 5779

1013-6835 See TRIBUNE DE L'ORGUE, LA. 4157

1013-6916 See JAHRESBERICHT - ZURCHER KUNSTGESELLSCHAFT. 354

1013-6924 See REVUE HISTORIQUE VAUDOISE. 2706

1013-6959 See JAHRESBERICHTE / HISTORISCHES MUSEUM BASEL. 4089

1013-6991 See JAHRBUCH FUER DIE GESCHICHTE DES PROTESTANTISMUS IN OSTERREICH. 5061

1013-7009 See UNGYONG MULLI. 4424

1013-7335 See COURIER. AFRICA-CARIBBEAN-PACIFIC-EUROPEAN COMMUNITIES, THE. 1554

1013-7424 See DEMENTIA (BASEL, SWITZERLAND). 3831

1013-7432 See ARBITRATION MATERIALS. 2936

1013-7459 See BASLER BEITRAEGE ZUR CHIRURGIE. 3960

1013-7696 See ZHONGHUA MINGUO XIAOHUA XIYI XUEHUI ZAZHI. 3748

1013-7769 See TELEMA (KINSHASA). 5002

1013-7777 See BUTLLETI OFICIAL DEL PRINCIPAT D'ANDORRA. 2945

1013-7785 See AIDS HEALTH PROMOTION, EXCHANGE. 3663

1013-784X See BULLETIN - CAVE EXPLORATION GROUP OF EAST AFRICA. 1403

1013-7866 See INTERNATIONAL JOURNAL OF SEDIMENT RESEARCH. 1383

1013-8129 See DIAGNOSTIC ONCOLOGY. 3816

1013-834X See SEAMIC INFORMATION RETRIEVAL ON CURRENT LITERATURE. SERIES A: TYPHOID AND PARA-TYPHOID FEVERS, AND SALMONELLA FOOD POISONING. 4802

1013-8471 See JOURNAL FOR SEMITICS. 3289

1013-8501 See GESTION DE L'ENSEIGNEMENT SUPERIEUR. 1825

1013-851X See HIGHER EDUCATION MANAGEMENT (PARIS, FRANCE). 1828

1013-8609 See CEREAL RUSTS AND POWDERY MILDEWS BULLETIN. 166

1013-8919 See TIROLER HEIMAT. 2712

1013-9087 See ANNALS OF DERMATOLOGY. 3717

1013-9222 See INTERNATIONAL SYMPOSIUM ON THE PHARMACOLOGY OF THERMOREGULATION. 4309

1013-9230 See CARIBBEAN LAW AND BUSINESS. 3097

1013-9281 See OCEAN MODELLING. 1453

1013-9338 See ECMI NEWSLETTER. 3504

1013-9370 See NONGSA SIHOM YON'GU NONMUNJIP. T'OYANG PIRYO P'YON. 2425

1013-9389 See NONGSA SIHOM YON'GU NONMUNJIP. CHANGMUL POHO P'YON. 114

1013-9397 See NONGSA SIHOM YON'GU NONMUNJIP. CHON-T'UKCHAK P'YON. 114

1013-9400 See NONGSA SIHOM YON'GU NONMUNJIP. CH'UKSAN P'YON. 5517

1013-9419 See NONGSA SIHOM YON'GU NONMUNJIP. KACH'UK UISAENG P'YON. 5517

1013-9427 See NONGSA SIHOM YON'GU NONMUNJIP. NONG KIGYE-NONGGYONG-CHAMOP-NONGRI-KYUNI P'YON. 114

1013-9435 See NONGSA SIHOM YON'GU NONMUNJIP. SAENGMYONG KONGHAK P'YON. 3695

1013-9443 See NONGSA SIHOM YON'GU NONMUNJIP. SUDO P'YON. 114

1013-9567 See BARRICADA INTERNACIONAL (ENGLISH ED.). 2511

1013-9796 See ILLIMANI. 2738

1013-980X See INAZUCAR. 2344

1013-9818 See JOURNAL OF THE SRI LANKA BRANCH OF THE ROYAL ASIATIC SOCIETY. 2656

1013-9826 See KEY ENGINEERING MATERIALS. 2104

1013-9850 See CIENCIA Y TECNICA EN LA AGRICULTURA. RIEGO Y DRENAJE. 2088

1013-9869 See CIENCIA Y TECNICA EN LA AGRICULTURA. TABACO. 5372

1013-9877 See SOUTH PACIFIC JOURNAL OF NATURAL SCIENCE, THE. 4172

1013-9877 See COMMONWEALTH QUARTERLY. 3377

1013-9885 See IRAN AGRICULTURAL RESEARCH. 97

1013-9893 See MONTHLY ECONOMIC SURVEY - INTERNATIONAL COMMERCIAL BANK OF CHINA. 1506

1013-9915 See INFORMATION CIRCULAR / SOUTH PACIFIC COMMISSION. 96

1013-9958 See ASIAN BUSINESS & INDUSTRY. 1598

1013-9966 See OESTERREICH IN GESCHICHTE UND LITERATUR MIT GEOGRAPHIE. 2701

1013-9974 See BULLETIN OF THE INTERNATIONAL TEST COMMISSION AND OF THE DIVISION OF PSYCHOLOGICAL ASSESSMENT OF THE IAAP. 4579

1013-9982 See CYTOKINES. 535

1014-0107 See AIRCRAFT TYPE DESIGNATORS. 9

1014-0255 See AFRICA RECOVERY. 1596

1014-1561 See INIS. AUTHORITY LIST FOR CORPORATE ENTRIES AND REPORT NUMBER PREFIXES. 4426

1014-191X See RAPA PUBLICATION. 2662

1014-2339 See ANIMAL GENETIC RESOURCES INFORMATION. 542

1014-2347 See AL-NASHRAH AL-WABAIYAH LI-IQLIM SHARQ AL-BAHR AL-MUTAWASSIT. 3712

1014-3351 See TECHNICAL DOCUMENT / FAO REGIONAL OFFICE FOR ASIA AND THE PACIFIC. ASIA AND PACIFIC PLANT PROTECTION COMMISSION. 140

1014-370X See UNCTAD REVIEW. 1640

1014-4498 See ACCIDENT/INCIDENT REPORTING ADREP. 3

1014-4994 See ECONOMIC STUDIES / UNITED NATIONS ECONOMIC COMMISSION FOR EUROPE. 1485

1014-6334 See ARAB AND NEAR EAST PLANT PROTECTION NEWSLETTER. 500

1014-6539 See U.N. OBSERVER & INTERNATIONAL REPORT. 3137

1014-6911 See EAST-WEST JOINT VENTURES NEWS. 670

1014-6954 See WORLD ANIMAL REVIEW / REVUE MONDIALE DE ZOOTECHNIE / REVISTA MUNDIAL DE ZOOTECNIA. 224

1014-703X See DOCUMENTOS DE DERECHO SOCIAL. 1664

1014-7063 See DOCUMENTS DE DROIT SOCIAL - BUREAU INTERNATIONAL DU TRAVAIL. 2963

1014-7071 See LABOUR LAW DOCUMENTS. 3151

1014-711X See IARC MONOGRAPHS ON THE EVALUATION OF CARCINOGENIC RISKS TO HUMANS. SUPPLEMENT. 3818

1014-7268 See PROCEEDINGS OF THE WORLD BANK ANNUAL CONFERENCE ON DEVELOPMENT ECONOMICS. 1513

1014-7276 See WTO NEWS. 5500

1014-7306 See TRAVEL AND TOURISM BAROMETER : TTB. 5495

1014-739X See SDA WORKING PAPER SERIES. 2912

1014-7411 See TRADE POLICY REVIEW. THE EUROPEAN COMMUNITIES. 854

1014-8159 See MERCADOS AGRARIOS. PRECIOS / COMISION DE LAS COMUNIDADES EUROPEAS / LANDSBRUGSMARKEDER. PRISER / KOMMISSIONEN FOR DE EUROPAEISKE FAELLESSKABER / AGRICULTURAL MARKETS. PRICES / COMMISSION OF THE EUROPEAN COMMUNITIES. 155

1014-8221 See OTO-RHINO-LARYNGOLOGIA NOVA. 3890

1014-8590 See WORLD BANK POLICY RESEARCH BULLETIN. 816

1014-8647 See UNEP REGIONAL SEAS REPORTS AND STUDIES. 1458

1014-8906 See GLOBAL ECONOMIC PROSPECTS AND THE DEVELOPING COUNTRIES. 1492

1014-9015 See ILCA ... ANNUAL REPORT AND PROGRAMME HIGHLIGHTS. 212

1014-9066 See DISCUSSION PAPERS / ECONOMIC COMMISSION FOR EUROPE. 1480

1014-9201 See GLOBEFISH HIGHLIGHTS. 2304

1014-949X See UNEP ENVIRONMENTAL MANAGEMENT GUIDELINES. 2208

1014-9538 See REPORTS OF MEETINGS OF EXPERTS AND EQUIVALENT BODIES. 1456

1014-9562 See TRANSNATIONAL CORPORATIONS. 716

1014-9600 See DAILY SUBSISTANCE ALLOWANCE RATES. 1634

1014-9759 See MONTH AT UNESCO, THE. 4979

1014-9783 See POVERTY AND SOCIAL POLICY PAPER. 5301

1014-997X See STUDIES OF ECONOMIES IN TRANSFORMATION. 1523

1015-0005 See JOURNAL OF THE INSTITUTE OF CHARTERED ACCOUNTANTS OF SRI LANKA. 747

1015-0021 See FU JEN STUDIES : LITERATURE & LINGUISTICS. 3283

1015-0048 See LOCAL GOVERNMENT IN SOUTHERN AFRICA. 4662

1015-0064 See QUARTERLY REVIEW - CIPEC. 1623

1015-0072 See ANNUAL REPORT / KENYA TUBERCULOSIS AND RESPIRATORY DISEASES RESEARCH CENTRE. 3948

1015-0099 See SA MERCANTILE LAW JOURNAL / SA TYDSKRIF VIR HANDELSREG. 3045

1015-0129 See KUNSTHISTORIKER. 356

1015-0145 See CHEMICAL IMMUNOLOGY. 3667

1015-0498 See GRAZER LINGUISTISCHE STUDIEN. 3284

1015-0714 See HEAVY OILER. 4259

1015-079X See DISCOVERY AND INNOVATION. 5101

1015-0811 See OSTERREICHISCHE ZEITSCHRIFT FUER STATISTIK UND INFORMATIK. 2352

1015-0862 See IN SITU (LUSAKA). 300

1015-0870 See JOURNAL OF BANGLADESH COLLEGE OF PHYSICIANS & SURGEONS. 3593

1015-0889 See BANGLADESH RENAL JOURNAL. 3988

1015-0935 See NATAL MUSEUM JOURNAL OF HUMANITIES. 2851

1015-1540 See AGRICULTURAL POLICIES, MARKETS, AND TRADE. 51

1015-1621 See AQUATIC SCIENCES. 1412

1015-1680 See SELECTED BIBLIOGRAPHY ON IRRIGATION MANAGEMENT, A. 186

1015-1702 See COMPARATIVE PHYSIOLOGY : CELLULAR AND MOLECULAR APPROACH TO COMPARATIVE PHYSIOLOGY. 579

1015-180X See TARIH ENSTITUSU DERGISI. 2631

1015-1915 See CAMERA AUSTRIA. 4367

1015-2008 See PATHOBIOLOGY (BASEL). 3896

1015-2059 See HONGKONG PAPERS IN LINGUISTICS AND LANGUAGE TEACHING. 3286

1015-213X See ACP BASIC STATISTICS. 1528

1015-2172 See LUCUARI STIINTIFICE - INSTITUTUL AGRONOMIC "NICOLAE BALESCU", BUCURESTI. SERIA E. IMBUNATATIRI FUNCIARE. 2568

1015-2199 See UNITED NATIONS SYSTEM OF ORGANIZATIONS ... AND DIRECTORY OF SENIOR OFFICIALS. 3137

1015-227X See LLOYD'S LIST MARITIME ASIA. 5451

1015-2296 See JOURNAL OF BLACK THEOLOGY IN SOUTH AFRICA. 4968

1015-2512 See DIRE PARIS. 1988. 4472

1015-2830 See MAJOLLAH-'I BASTANSHINASI VA-TARIKH. 273

1015-2857 See NASHR-I RIYAZI. 3523

1015-2881 See CYPRUS REVIEW, THE. 4471

1015-3055 See PAKISTAN JOURNAL OF AGRICULTURE, AGRICULTURAL ENGINEERING & VETERINARY SCIENCES. 118

1015-3470 See JAHRESBERICHT - SCHWEIZERISCHES LANDESMUSEUM ZURICH. 4089

1015-356X See JOURNAL OF ECONOMIC INTEGRATION. 1637

1015-3640 See METEOROLOGY AND HYDROLOGY BUCURESTI. 1431

1015-3837 See FETAL DIAGNOSIS AND THERAPY. 3760

1015-3845 See MAGNESIUM AND TRACE ELEMENTS. 985

1015-3918 See ANKARA UNIVERSITESI ECZACILIK FAKULTESI DERGISI. 4290

1015-4159 See EXTERNAL DEBT STATISTICS. 1532

1015-4442 See ARAB GULF JOURNAL OF SCIENTIFIC RESEARCH. 5085

1015-4760 *See* PHARMACEUTICAL & COSMETIC REVIEW. 4320

1015-4965 *See* ORIENTEERING WORLD. 4911

1015-4965 *See* ORIENTEERING WORLD : ORIENTIERUNGSLAUF AUS ALLER WELT. 4911

1015-5007 *See* CARDIOSCIENCE. 3701

1015-5023 *See* ASIAMAC JOURNAL. 2110

1015-5295 *See* ASTRONOMI VE FIZIK DERGISI / ISTANBUL UNIVERSITESI, FEN FAKULTESI. 391

1015-5449 *See* WORLD COMPETITIVENESS REPORT. 1641

1015-5473 *See* ASCOM TECHNISCHE MITTEILUNGEN. 1149

1015-5481 *See* ASCOM TECHNICAL REVIEW. 5086

1015-549X *See* PRETEXTS. 3350

1015-5759 *See* EUROPEAN JOURNAL OF PSYCHOLOGICAL ASSESSMENT. 4587

1015-616X *See* OSTERREICHISCHES JAHRBUCH FUER INTERNATIONALE POLITIK. 4530

1015-6186 *See* FISHERIES BULLETIN (PRETORIA). 2302

1015-6283 *See* PECUNIA. BRUXELLES, DE. 881

1015-6305 *See* BRAIN PATHOLOGY. 3829

1015-6321 *See* JOURNAL OF THE BAHRAIN MEDICAL SOCIETY. 3598

1015-6356 *See* SECURITE, ENVIRONEMENT. 2870

1015-6798 *See* MUSIK UND GOTTESDIENST. 4138

1015-6828 *See* ZIMBABWE LIBRARIAN, THE. 3257

1015-6844 *See* P. T. T. I. STUDIES. 1146

1015-6879 *See* CARIBBEAN JOURNAL OF AFRICAN STUDIES. 2638

1015-6941 *See* MEDEDELING. 1387

1015-7891 *See* JOURNAL OF PARAMETRICS. 747

1015-7999 *See* SOUTH AFRICAN COMPUTER JOURNAL SUID-AFRIKAANSE REKENAARTYDSKRIF. 1203

1015-8014 *See* COMPLEAT GOLFER. 4891

1015-8049 *See* BULLETIN - GEOLOGICAL SURVEY (PRETORIA). 1369

1015-8057 *See* PROCEEDINGS / INTERNATIONAL ZURICH SEMINAR ON DIGITAL COMMUNICATIONS. 1200

1015-8138 *See* A.T.A. JOURNAL. 5347

1015-8146 *See* GENETIC COUNSELING (GENEVA, SWITZERLAND). 545

1015-8219 *See* BULLETIN DU SERVICE DE LA PROTECTION DES VEGETAUX. 69

1015-8480 *See* CARTOGRAPHICA HELVETICA. 2581

1015-8499 *See* ALAFUA AGRICULTURAL BULLETIN. 57

1015-8502 *See* IRETA'S SOUTH PACIFIC AGRICULTURAL NEWS. 97

1015-8553 *See* REVISTA CENIC. 991

1015-8634 *See* BULLETIN OF THE KOREAN MATHEMATICAL SOCIETY. 3498

1015-8987 *See* CELLULAR PHYSIOLOGY AND BIOCHEMISTRY. 534

1015-9274 *See* ANTIKE WELT SONDERNUMMER. 2610

1015-9584 *See* ASIAN JOURNAL OF SURGERY. 3960

1015-9592 *See* GAZI UNIVERSITESI, ECZACILIK FAKULTESI DERGISI. 4305

1015-9606 *See* ANALELE UNIVERSITATII DIN GALATI. FASCICULA I, STIINTE SOCIALE SI UMANISTE. 5190

1015-9762 *See* IAR NEWSLETTER OF AGRICULTURAL RESEARCH. 93

1015-9770 *See* CEREBROVASCULAR DISEASES. 3829

1015-9924 *See* EUROSTAT. AGRICULTURAL PRICES. PRICE INDICES AND ABSOLUTE PRICES. QUARTERLY STATISTICS. 153

1016-0019 *See* BEIHEFTE ZUR SYDOWIA. 574

1016-0469 *See* MANEJO INTEGRADO DE PLAGAS. 107

1016-0566 *See* JINDAI ZHONGGUO SHI YANJIU TONGXUN. 2694

1016-0582 *See* BANKO JANAKARI : A JOURNAL OF FORESTRY INFORMATION FOR NEPAL. 2375

1016-0809 *See* TEMPORALE. 332

1016-0884 *See* SAENGHWAHAK NYUSU. 3696

1016-0922 *See* BIOLOGICAL SIGNALS. 532

1016-1104 *See* JOURNAL OF SCIENCES, ISLAMIC REPUBLIC OF IRAN. 5119

1016-121X *See* OPTIONS MEDITERRANEENNES. SERIE A : SEMINAIRES MEDITERRANEENS. 117

1016-1228 *See* OPTIONS MEDITERRANEENNES. SERIE B : ETUDES ET RECHERCHES. 117

1016-1317 *See* IWRB NEWS. 2196

1016-1503 *See* ZIMBABWE SCIENCE NEWS, THE. 5172

1016-1511 *See* ZIMBABWE VETERINARY JOURNAL. 5528

1016-152X *See* ZED. ZIMBABWE ENVIRONMENT & DESIGN. 311

1016-1538 *See* FU JEN STUDIES : NATURAL SCIENCES. 5106

1016-1546 *See* WORLD MONEY OUTLOOK. 817

1016-1562 *See* JAHRESBERICHT - SCHWEIZERISCHE AKADEMIE DER MEDIZINISCHEN WISSENSCHAFTEN (1988). 3591

1016-1570 *See* BULLETIN - CREDIT SUISSE (ENGLISH ED.). 780

1016-1597 *See* PUNJAB UNIVERSITY JOURNAL OF ZOOLOGY. 5596

1016-2240 *See* REVIEW OF RURAL AND URBAN PLANNING IN SOUTHERN AND EASTERN AFRICA : JOURNAL OF THE ASSOCIATION OF RURAL & URBAN PLANNERS IN SOUTHERN & EASTERN AFRICA. 2834

1016-2291 *See* PEDIATRIC NEUROSURGERY. 3909

1016-2410 *See* REVUE GABONAISE D'POLITIQUES, ECONOMIQUES, ET JURIDIQUES. 4684

1016-2437 *See* PROCEEDINGS - INTERNATIONAL CONFERENCE ON LARGE HIGH VOLTAGE ELECTRIC SYSTEMS (CIGRE). 2076

1016-2461 *See* REVUE AFRICAINE DE THEOLOGIE. 4993

1016-264X *See* ZEITSCHRIFT FUER NEUROPSYCHOLOGIE. 4622

1016-2690 *See* INFORMATION - VMS. 4089

1016-2712 *See* JAHRBUCH FUER LANDESKUNDE VON NIEDEROSTERREICH. 2518

1016-2879 *See* SCHWEIZER KUNST. 364

1016-3158 *See* MITTEILUNGEN DER EIDGENOSSISCHEN FORSCHUNGSANSTALT FUER WALD, SCHNEE UND LANDSCHAFT. 2388

1016-3263 *See* IUFRO WORLD SERIES. 2385

1016-3328 *See* COMPUTATIONAL COMPLEXITY. 3501

1016-3476 *See* JOURNAL OF MEDITERRANEAN STUDIES. 2848

1016-3573 *See* ETLIK VETERINER MIKROBIYOLOJI DERGISI. 5510

1016-4162 *See* ZHONGWAI ZAZHI. 3356

1016-443X *See* GEOMETRIC AND FUNCTIONAL ANALYSIS : GAFA. 3507

1016-460X *See* SUCEAVA. 2712

1016-4731 *See* AIDS ANALYSIS AFRICA. 3663

1016-4855 *See* ARCHIVA ZOOTECHNICA. 5576

1016-4901 *See* INDOOR ENVIRONMENT : THE JOURNAL OF INDOOR AIR INTERNATIONAL. 2174

1016-4928 *See* IOP NEWSLETTER. 514

1016-5142 *See* PEDIATRIK CERRAHI DERGISI. 3910

1016-5150 *See* TURK ANESTEZIYOLOJI VE REANIMASYON CEMIYETI MECMUASI. 3684

1016-5169 *See* TURK KARDIYOLOJI DERNEGI ARSIVI. 3711

1016-5584 *See* JOURNAL OF COPTIC STUDIES. 2640

1016-5711 *See* SUDAN JOURNAL OF ANIMAL PRODUCTION, THE. 5522

1016-572X *See* EUROPA FORUM LUXEMBOURG. 4521

1016-5975 *See* NUCLEAR EUROPE WORLDSCAN. 2157

1016-6254 *See* OSTERREICHISCHE BEITRAGE ZU METEOROLOGIE UND GEOPHYSIK. 1433

1016-6262 *See* VERHALTENSTHERAPIE BASEL. 3937

1016-6359 *See* EVERTON'S GENEALOGICAL HELPER. 2446

1016-6505 *See* BIOTECH PRODUCTS INTERNATIONAL. 5088

1016-7048 *See* NOUVELLES DE LA FIPESO, LES. 1769

1016-7293 *See* ARKITEKTUR OG SKIPULAG. 292

1016-7560 *See* IFA CONGRESS SEMINAR SERIES. 1494

1016-796X *See* PUBLIC TRANSPORT INTERNATIONAL. 5390

1016-8478 *See* MOLECULES AND CELLS. 539

1016-8664 *See* STRUCTURAL ENGINEERING INTERNATIONAL : JOURNAL OF THE INTERNATIONAL ASSOCIATION FOR BRIDGE AND STRUCTURAL ENGINEERING (IABSE). 5393

1016-8699 *See* INTERNATIONAL CHILD HEALTH. 4785

1016-9075 *See* NEW GROUND. 2178

1016-9113 *See* EGE TIP DERGISI. 3574

1016-927X *See* SPECIES (BROOKFIELD). 2205

1016-961X *See* BULLETIN DES ANTIQUITES LUXEMBOURGEOISES. 2681

1016-9660 *See* CINE & MEDIA. 1106

1016-9857 *See* PASOS SAN JOSE. 4985

1017-0243 *See* DEMOCRACY IN ACTION. 4471

1017-0405 *See* STATISTICA SINICA. 3536

1017-0510 *See* WIRTSCHAFTS-GEOGRAPHISCHE STUDIEN. 2579

1017-0529 *See* TAI-DIAN HENENG YUEKAN. 2159

1017-0588 *See* BAURECHT. 2940

1017-0596 *See* ESTUDIOS SOCIALES (SANTO DOMINGO). 5199

1017-0626 *See* PAKISTAN JOURNAL OF HYDROCARBON RESEARCH. 1045

1017-1142 *See* HARPA. 4120

1017-1371 *See* GLOOM, BOOM AND DOOM REPORT, THE. 1492

1017-1398 *See* NUMERICAL ALGORITHMS. 3525

1017-1584 *See* ZEITSCHRIFT FUER UNFALLCHIRURGIE UND VERSICHERUNGSMEDIZIN. 3653

1017-1592 *See* TAATIGKEITSBERICHT DER OESTERREICHISCHEN AKADEMIE DER WISSENSCHAFTEN. 5161

1017-1606 *See* IARC MONOGRAPHS ON THE EVALUATION OF CARCINOGENIC RISKS TO HUMANS. 3818

1017-1711 *See* PEDMED. 3626

1017-2106 *See* IN-NAZZJON TAGHNA HAMRUN. 5806

1017-2270 *See* INDUSTRIA USOARA (1974). 3184

1017-2300 *See* ZHONGGUO YUWEN (TAIPEI). 3336

1017-2572 *See* JARD. JOURNAL OF AGE RELATED DISORDERS. 3752

1017-2696 *See* UNSERE HEIMAT. 2671

1017-2734 *See* DIRECTION OF TRADE STATISTICS (ELECTRONIC ED.). 831

1017-284X *See* ICC INTERNATIONAL COURT OF ARBITRATION BULLETIN, THE. 3129

1017-2947 *See* VOILA LUXEMBOURG. 2524

1017-3285 *See* FACHSPRACHE 1990. 3281

1017-4397 *See* HSING TA KUNG CHENG HSUEH PAO. 1977

1017-4559 *See* CURRENT LEGAL SOCIOLOGY. 5243

1017-4648 *See* ENVIRONMENTAL STRATEGY & PLANNING : BULLETIN OF THE COMMISSION ON ENVIRONMENTAL STRATEGY AND PLANNING OF THE WORLD CONSERVATION UNION. **2193**

1017-4699 *See* SPECIALIST KARACHI. **3642**

1017-5156 *See* ZIMBABWE AGRICULTURAL JOURNAL. **149**

1017-5199 *See* CHINA TELECOMMUNICATIONS CONSTRUCTION. **1130**

1017-5199 *See* CHINA TELECOMMUNICATIONS CONSTRUCTION. **1151**

1017-5415 *See* NEW CONTRAST. **3415**

1017-5547 *See* INTERNATIONALES WAFFEN-MAGAZIN. **4046**

1017-5563 *See* BEITRAGE ZUR PALAONTOLOGIE VON OSTERREICH. **4226**

1017-5598 *See* SYSTEMATIC AND ECOGEOGRAPHIC STUDIES ON CROP GENEPOOLS / INTERNATIONAL BOARD FOR PLANT GENETIC RESOURCES. **528**

1017-5644 *See* REVUE ROUMAINE DE NEUROLOGIE ET PSYCHIATRIE (1990). **3845**

1017-5652 *See* IRANIAN JOURNAL OF AGRICULTURAL SCIENCE. **97**

1017-5679 *See* NEWSLETTER. ASSOCIATION OF PACIFIC SYSTEMATISTS. **519**

1017-5695 *See* FINANZ JOURNAL. **4726**

1017-5725 *See* ERH SHIH I SHIH CHI. **2651**

1017-5776 *See* RAPID REPORTS. AGRICULTURE, FORESTRY, AND FISHERIES / EUROSTAT. **124**

1017-5989 *See* PEDIATRIC AND ADOLESCENT MEDICINE. **3908**

1017-6241 *See* LIBRARY NEWS. **3226**

1017-6276 *See* PEST ADVISORY LEAFLET. **4246**

1017-6462 *See* CHUNG-KUO WEN CHE YEN CHIU CHI KAN. **3375**

1017-6713 *See* P+ : EUROPEAN PARTICIPATION MONITOR. **881**

1017-6721 *See* EUROPEAN JOURNAL OF PHYSICAL MEDICINE & REHABILITATION. **4380**

1017-6748 *See* ASIAN LIBRARIES. **3192**

1017-6764 *See* CARIBBEAN JOURNAL OF MATHEMATICAL AND COMPUTING SCIENCES. **3499**

1017-6772 *See* AFRICAN DEVELOPMENT REVIEW. **768**

1017-6950 *See* XIII MAGAZINE (BRUXELLES). **1169**

1017-7515 *See* ISO NEWS : THE QUARTERLY MAGAZINE OF THE INTERNATIONAL SOCIETY OF ORGANBUILDERS. **4124**

1017-7566 *See* CHAILLOT PAPERS. **4039**

1017-7620 *See* ZEITSCHRIFT FUER KULTUR, POLITIK, KIRCHE. **5011**

1017-7698 *See* MEDICAL JOURNAL OF EGE UNIVERSITY. **3610**

1017-7825 *See* JOURNAL OF MICROBIOLOGY AND BIOTECHNOLOGY. **566**

1017-785X *See* RETAIL NEWS LETTER ED. FRANCAISE. **957**

1017-849X *See* BULLETIN DE LA SOCIETE D'HISTOIRE ET D'ARCHEOLOGIE DE GENEVE. **2680**

1017-8678 *See* MAGALLAT MATHAF AL-TARIH AL-TABII (BAGDAD). **4167**

1017-8686 *See* PROGRESS IN APPLIED MICROCIRCULATION (ENGLISH ED.). **3630**

1017-8716 *See* CHINA'S MILITARY : THE PLA IN **4039**

1017-8937 *See* ANALES DEL CARIBE. **2841**

1017-9410 *See* TEHRAN TIMES TEHRAN. **1123**

1017-9909 *See* JOURNAL OF ELECTRONIC IMAGING. **2068**

1018-0303 *See* REAL TIME MAGAZINE. **1221**

1018-0532 *See* REVUE ROUMAINE DE VIROLOGIE (1990). **569**

1018-0753 *See* SOUTH AFRICAN JOURNAL OF ART AND ARCHITECTURAL HISTORY. **365**

1018-0818 *See* BANGLADESH JOURNAL OF CROP SCIENCE. **2410**

1018-0826 *See* EUROPEAN RESEARCH LIBRARIES COOPERATION : THE LIBER QUARTERLY. **3209**

1018-1008 *See* REVISTA OLIMPICA. **4915**

1018-1172 *See* JOURNAL OF VASCULAR RESEARCH. **3707**

1018-1210 *See* CARAPHIN NEWS. **506**

1018-1342 *See* DOSSIER - WOMEN LIVING UNDER MUSLIM LAWS. **5554**

1018-1385 *See* POWER BOAT AND SKI. **595**

1018-1520 *See* SUB-SAHARAN MONITOR. **1523**

1018-1555 *See* QUARTERLY INDEX TO PERIODICAL LITERATURE, EASTERN AND SOUTHERN AFRICA. **3427**

1018-1806 *See* HELIA (NOVI SAD). **2418**

1018-208X *See* TRENDS IN PRIVATE INVESTMENT IN DEVELOPING COUNTRIES. **918**

1018-2101 *See* PRAGMATICS : QUARTERLY PUBLICATION OF THE INTERNATIONAL PRAGMATICS ASSOCIATION. **3311**

1018-2438 *See* INTERNATIONAL ARCHIVES OF ALLERGY AND IMMUNOLOGY. **3672**

1018-2500 *See* PROCEEDINGS OF PARASITOLOGY. **568**

1018-2926 *See* CARIBBEAN REVIEW OF BOOKS. **3373**

1018-3442 *See* LANGUAGE PROJECTS' REVIEW. **3295**

1018-3590 *See* MAGALLAT GAMIAT AL-MALIK SAUD. AL-ULUM AL-ZIRAIYYAT. **106**

1018-3760 See REVUE OLYMPIQUE. **4915**

1018-4317 *See* BOLLETTINO - MONUMENTI, MUSEI E GALLERIE PONTIFICIE. **344**

1018-4325 *See* MEMOIR - GEOLOGICAL SURVEY OF NAMIBIA. **1387**

1018-4619 *See* FRESENIUS ENVIRONMENTAL BULLETIN. **2172**

1018-4627 *See* MEDICAL MICROBIOLOGY LETTERS : AN INTERNATIONAL JOURNAL FOR RAPID COMMUNICATIONS ON ALL ASPECTS OF MEDICAL AND CLINICAL MICROBIOLOGY. **566**

1018-4635 *See* ICLAS NEWS. **5111**

1018-4635 *See* ICLAS NEWS. **5511**

1018-4783 *See* ISSN COMPACT. **3219**

1018-4813 *See* EUROPEAN JOURNAL OF HUMAN GENETICS : EJHG. **544**

1018-4864 *See* TELECOMMUNICATION SYSTEMS. **1165**

1018-4899 *See* GENERAL PUBLICATIONS CATALOG - INTERNATIONAL IRRIGATION MANAGEMENT INSTITUTE. **172**

1018-4902 *See* FOREIGN INVESTMENT ADVISORY SERVICE OCCASIONAL PAPER. **899**

1018-502X *See* FAT-BERICHTE. **86**

1018-5054 *See* MAKROMOLEKULARE CHEMIE: THEORY AND SIMULATIONS, DIE. **985**

1018-5089 *See* PAS RESEARCH PAPER SERIES. **802**

1018-5097 *See* TECHNICAL PAPERS - INTERNATIONAL FINANCE CORPORATION. **813**

1018-5275 *See* ADLI TP DERGISI. **3739**

1018-5291 *See* ASIA-PACIFIC JOURNAL OF RURAL DEVELOPMENT. **1463**

1018-533X *See* VETERINARY BIOTECHNOLOGY NEWSLETTER / OFFICE INTERNATIONAL DES EPIZOOTIES. **5525**

1018-5666 *See* JOURNAL OF LAUGHTER IN TEACHING/TRAINING : JOLT, THE. **1898**

1018-5739 *See* SIGMA : THE BULLETIN OF EUROPEAN STATISTICS. **5338**

1018-5763 *See* REVISTA DE INTERPRETACION BIBLICA LATINOAMERICANA : RIBLA. **5019**

1018-5925 *See* EOQ QUALITY. **1606**

1018-6107 *See* BURGENLANDISCHE HEIMATBLATTER. **5580**

1018-6212 *See* REVISTA DE LA SANIDAD DE LA POLICIA NACIONAL DEL PERU. **4799**

1018-6247 *See* APPLIED FLUORESCENCE TECHNOLOGY. **4433**

1018-6255 *See* BIOMETHODS (BASEL). **447**

1018-6301 *See* BULLETIN OF IRANIAN MATHEMATICAL SOCIETY. **3498**

1018-6441 *See* IN DIE SKRIFLIG. **4964**

1018-7057 *See* JOURNAL OF THE GEOLOGICAL SOCIETY OF CHINA. **1385**

1018-7235 *See* GATEKEEPER SERIES. **89**

1018-7286 *See* BALTIC INDEPENDENT, THE. **5800**

1018-7391 See EBU TECHNICAL REVIEW. **1110**

1018-7782 *See* EXPERIMENTAL NEPHROLOGY. **3990**

1018-7928 *See* ULTRAHIGH- AND HIGH-SPEED PHOTOGRAPHY, VIDEOGRAPHY, AND PHOTONICS. **4377**

1018-8029 *See* PLANT TISSUE CULTURE. **524**

1018-8568 *See* AGRIPROMO ABIDJAN. **2813**

1018-8592 *See* JOURNAL OF AFRICAN RELIGION AND PHILOSOPHY. **4350**

1018-8657 *See* PREPARING FOR THE FUTURE : ESA'S TECHNOLOGY PROGRAMME QUARTERLY. **31**

1018-8665 *See* DERMATOLOGY (BASEL). **3719**

1018-872X *See* UNIVERS DU FRANCAIS SEVRES, L'. **1788**

1018-8843 *See* GYNAKOLOGISCH-GEBURTSHILFLICHE RUNDSCHAU. **3761**

1018-8851 *See* EGE UNIVERSITESI ZIRAAT FAKULTESI DERGISI. **81**

1018-8916 *See* NATURAL IMMUNITY. **3675**

1018-8975 *See* EAST AFRICA JOURNAL OF EVANGELICAL THEOLOGY. **4954**

1018-8983 *See* BRIDGE (HONG KONG). **4940**

1018-9041 *See* CLAN. CARIBBEAN LABORATORY ACTION NEWS. **3564**

1018-9068 *See* JOURNAL OF INVESTIGATIONAL ALLERGOLOGY & CLINICAL IMMUNOLOGY. **3674**

1018-9181 *See* PROCEEDINGS OF THE INTERNATIONAL CONGRESS ON HIGH SPEED PHOTOGRAPHY AND PHOTONICS. **4375**

1018-9327 *See* PEB EXCHANGE. **1772**

1018-9688 *See* SOUTHERN AFRICAN JOURNAL OF AQUATIC SCIENCES. **2313**

1019-0449 *See* TUNG WU SHE HUI HSUEH PAO. **5264**

1019-0600 *See* BULLETIN DE L'INSTITUT INTERNATIONAL DE DROIT D'EXPRESSION FRANCAISE. **2944**

1019-0716 *See* APPLICATIONS OF ARTIFICIAL INTELLIGENCE: KNOWLEDGE-BASED SYSTEMS. **1211**

1019-0732 *See* BEIRUT REVIEW, THE. **4516**

1019-1127 *See* SWISS ECONOMIC NEWS. **1523**

1019-1135 *See* ROMANTIC REASSESSMENT. **3432**

1019-1224 *See* TAP CHI SINH HOC. **474**

1019-1291 *See* OSTEOLOGIE. **3800**

1019-1801 *See* OIBF INFO. **1620**

1019-1984 *See* AGROFORESTERIA (TURRIALBA). **55**

1019-2530 *See* CURRENT COMMERCIAL CASES. **2499**

1019-3316 *See* HERALD OF THE RUSSIAN ACADEMY OF SCIENCES. **5109**

1019-4126 *See* TRENDS IN SOCIAL SECURITY. **1715**

1019-4363 *See* EVALUATION RESULTS FOR ... WORLD BANK. **1561**

1019-438X *See* PAKISTAN JOURNAL OF CLINICAL PSYCHOLOGY. **4606**

1019-4681 *See* TARIH VE TOPLUM : AYLK ANSIKLOPEDIK DERGI. **2712**

1019-4754 *See* UGRA MITTEILUNGEN. **4570**

1019-4835 *See* JUGGLERS' WORLD. **4902**

1019-5076 *See* CARIBBEAN WEEK. **5778**

1019-5149 *See* TURKISH NEUROSURGERY. **3847**

1019-5297 *See* LIKARSKA SPRAVA. **3604**

1019-5815 *See* DEVELOPMENTAL BRAIN DYSFUNCTION. **3831**

1019-6196 *See* PEOPLE DYNAMICS. **944**

1019-6242 *See* BASLER LEHRBUCHER. **3497**

1019-6404 *See* ZIMBABWE ENGINEER (1992). **2002**

1019-6439 *See* INTERNATIONAL JOURNAL OF ONCOLOGY. **3818**

1019-6544 See OFCOR DISCUSSION PAPER. 116
1019-6587 See EBU TECHNICAL REVIEW. 1110
1019-6773 See ENZYME & PROTEIN. 580
1019-7079 See MALAWI JOURNAL OF SCIENCE & TECHNOLOGY. 5127
1019-7168 See ADVANCES IN COMPUTATIONAL MATHEMATICS. 3491
1019-8113 See REVISTA ECUATORIANA DE NEUROLOGIA. 3845
1019-8334 See AIDS BULLETIN TYGERBERG. 3711
1019-8350 See BMJ. BRITISH MEDICAL JOURNAL (SOUTH AFRICAN ED.). 3557
1019-8466 See INFUSIONSTHERAPIE UND TRANSFUSIONSMEDIZIN. 3772
1019-9829 See SHORT-TERM ECONOMIC INDICATORS, TRANSITION ECONOMIES / CENTRE FOR CO-OPERATION WITH THE ECONOMIES IN TRANSITION / INDICATEURS ECONOMIQUES A COURT TERME, ECONOMIES EN TRANSITION / CENTRE POUR LA COOPERATION AVEC LES ECONOMIES EN TRANSITION. 1520
1020-0029 See WORLD OF WORK : THE MAGAZINE OF THE ILO. 1720
1020-007X See GLOBAL AIDSNEWS: THE NEWSLETTER OF THE WORLD HEALTH ORGANIZATION GLOBAL PROGRAMME ON AIDS. 3713
1020-0339 See DEVELOPMENT EDUCATION EXCHANGE PAPERS : DEEP. 1735
1021-0296 See REVISTA NICARAGUENSE DE ENTOMOLOGIA. 5613
1021-0601 See KUNSTSTOFFE SYNTHETICS. 4456
1021-1667 See EUR-OP NEWS DEUTSCHE AUSG. 1489
1021-1721 See JOURNAL DE GENEVE ET GAZETTE DE LAUSANNE. 5811
1021-2000 See CIVIL ENGINEERING YEOVILLE. 2021
1021-2000 See CIVIL ENGINEERING : MAGAZINE OF THE SOUTH AFRICAN INSTITUTION OF CIVIL ENGINEERS / SIVIELE INGENIEURSWESE. 2021
1021-2019 See JOURNAL OF THE SOUTH AFRICAN INSTITUTION OF CIVIL ENGINEERS / JOERNAAL VAN DIE SUID-AFRIKAANSE INSTITUUT VAN SIVIELE INGENIEURS. 2026
1021-2353 See FRONTIER-FREE EUROPE / COMMISSION OF THE EUROPEAN COMMUNITIES, DIRECTORATE-GENERAL FOR AUDIOVISUAL MEDIA, INFORMATION, COMMUNICATION AND CULTURE. 1562
1021-3287 See TRENDS AND POLICIES IN PRIVATISATION / CENTRE FOR CO-OPERATION WITH EUROPEAN ECONOMIES IN TRANSITION / TENDANCES ET POLITIQUES DES PRIVATISATIONS / CENTRE POUR LA COOPERATION AVEC LES ECONOMIES EUROPEENNES EN TRANSITION. 1524
1021-335X See ONCOLOGY REPORTS. 3822
1021-3589 See AFRICAN ENTOMOLOGY. 5605
1021-3600 See PETROLEUM INFORMATION SERVICE. 4273
1021-3740 See ASIAN AIR TRANSPORT. 5377
1021-4186 See MULTINATIONAL SERVICE. 846
1021-4224 See MONTHLY REPORT ON EUROPE. 2519
1021-4240 See AGRI-SERVICE INTERNATIONAL. 47
1021-4437 See RUSSIAN JOURNAL OF PLANT PHYSIOLOGY : A COMPREHENSIVE RUSSIAN JOURNAL ON MODERN PHYTOPHYSIOLOGY. 527
1021-495X See MEMBERSHIP DIRECTORY / INTERNATIONAL ASSOCIATION OF AQUATIC AND MARINE SCIENCE LIBRARIES AND INFORMATION CENTERS. 1452
1021-500X See ISSN REGISTER. TAPE EDITION. 3219
1021-5506 See ZOOLOGICAL STUDIES. 5602
1021-562X See IASA JOURNAL / INTERNATIONAL ASSOCIATION OF SOUND ARCHIVES. 5317
1021-6278 See GENOME PRIORITY REPORTS. 546

1021-643X See NOISE/NEWS INTERNATIONAL. 2028
1021-7401 See NEUROIMMUNOMODULATION. 3840
1021-7762 See FOLIA PHONIATRICA ET LOGOPAEDICA : OFFICIAL ORGAN OF THE INTERNATIONAL ASSOCIATION OF LOGOPEDICS AND PHONIATRICS (IALP). 3888
1021-7770 See JOURNAL OF BIOMEDICAL SCIENCE. 3594
1021-7789 See EUROCAT [COMPUTER FILE]. 416
1021-8459 See TIMINN REYKJAVIK. 5802
1021-9722 See NONLINEAR DIFFERENTIAL EQUATIONS AND APPLICATIONS. 3524
1022-0038 See WIRELESS NETWORKS. 2086
1022-0267 See ASIA LAW. 2937
1022-0461 See SOUTH AFRICAN JOURNAL OF INTERNATIONAL AFFAIRS, THE. 4535
1022-1336 See MACROMOLECULAR RAPID COMMUNICATIONS. 985
1022-1344 See MACROMOLECULAR THEORY AND SIMULATIONS. 985
1022-1352 See MACROMOLECULAR CHEMISTRY AND PHYSICS. 985
1022-1360 See MACROMOLECULAR SYMPOSIA. 985
1022-1492 See CBN NEWSLETTER. 166
1022-2502 See DHAKA UNIVERSITY JOURNAL OF SCIENCE, THE. 5099
1022-5536 See JOURNAL OF ORTHOPAEDIC SURGERY. 3882
1022-6117 See SCIENCE EDUCATION INTERNATIONAL. 1782
1022-663X See AGRARFORSCHUNG BERN. 46
1022-6699 See SCHWEIZERISCHE ZEITSCHRIFT FUER MEDIZIN UND TRAUMATOLOGIE. 3955
1022-6877 See EUROPEAN ADDICTION RESEARCH. 1344
1022-7059 See EUREKA NEWS. 5103
1023-3830 See INFLAMMATION RESEARCH. 3587
1030-0090 See AIRBORNE MAGAZINE. 8
1030-0112 See AUSTRALASIAN JOURNAL OF SPECIAL EDUCATION. 1875
1030-0120 See BULLETIN - ENVIRONMENTAL PROTECTION AUTHORITY, WESTERN AUSTRALIA. 2162
1030-0155 See ACCESS (VICTORIA, AUSTRALIA). 1802
1030-0236 See AUSTRALIAN EARLY CHILDHOOD NEWSLETTER. 1802
1030-0457 See NEWSLETTER - GEOLOGICAL SOCIETY OF AUSTRALIA INC. SPECIALIST GROUP ON SOLID - EARTH GEOPHYSICS. 1409
1030-0481 See SOUTH AUSTRALIAN GEOGRAPHICAL JOURNAL. 2576
1030-1046 See CRIME AND JUSTICE BULLETIN. 3161
1030-1429 See ENVIRONMENT INSTITUTE OF AUSTRALIA NEWSLETTER. 2165
1030-1887 See AUSTRALIAN SYSTEMATIC BOTANY. 501
1030-1933 See AUSTRALIAN THERAPEUTIC DEVICE BULLETIN / DEPARTMENT COMMUNITY SERVICES AND HEALTH. 3554
1030-1968 See PARENTS SHOPPING GUIDE. 2285
1030-1976 See INDIAN OCEAN POLICY PAPERS. 1566
1030-2077 See EXHAUST AND UNDERCAR. 5414
1030-2379 See INSURANCE LAW JOURNAL (SYDNEY, N.S.W.). 2883
1030-2476 See PERIODICALS IN PRINT, AUSTRALIA, NEW ZEALAND & PAPUA NEW GUINEA. 422
1030-2581 See CONSTRUCT IN STEEL. 608
1030-2646 See FAMILY MATTERS (MELBOURNE, VIC.). 2279
1030-2662 See SILICON CHIP. 2081
1030-2883 See DULWICH CENTRE NEWSLETTER. 4585
1030-3316 See ANNUAL REPORT / INDUSTRY RESEARCH AND DEVELOPMENT BOARD. 1597

1030-360X See CHINA PAPER. 2648
1030-3812 See ASSIG NEWSLETTER. 3192
1030-3839 See ANTITHESIS. 2842
1030-3847 See IMPACT SYDNEY, 1986. 3113
1030-391X See DIRECTIONS IN GOVERNMENT. 4472
1030-407X See JOURNAL OF TEACHING PRACTICE. 1899
1030-4177 See IPA REVIEW (1986). 4733
1030-4312 See CONTINUUM (MT. LAWLEY, W.A.). 4067
1030-4428 See LUCAS. 4975
1030-4614 See AGRICULTURAL SCIENCE. MELBOURNE. 52
1030-4649 See SCITECH TECHNOLOGY DIRECTORY. 5156
1030-469X See WILD PRAHRAN. 4880
1030-4711 See IVF AND GIFT PREGNANCIES AUSTRALIA AND NEW ZEALAND / NATIONAL PERINATAL STATISTICS UNIT; FERTILITY SOCIETY OF AUSTRALIA. 3763
1030-4851 See NEW SOUTH WALES COAL INDUSTRY PROFILE. 2147
1030-4932 See REDOUBT. 3428
1030-5033 See AUSTRALASIAN PUBLIC LIBRARIES AND INFORMATION SERVICES. 3193
1030-5289 See NATIONAL AIDS BULLETIN / AUSTRALIAN FEDERATION OF AIDS ORGANISATIONS INC. 3715
1030-5467 See THIRD OPINION. 2511
1030-6072 See HEALTH FORUM. 4779
1030-6110 See NEWSLETTER. 4511
1030-6137 See PC WEEK (AUSTRALIAN EDITION). 1199
1030-617X See AUSTRALIAN JOURNAL OF LITURGY. 4937
1030-6390 See JOURNAL OF VIETNAMESE STUDIES. 2656
1030-6412 See OCEANIA MONOGRAPHS, THE. 242
1030-6641 See NATIONAL GUIDE TO GOVERNMENT. 4668
1030-7036 See THOMSON'S CONSTRUCTION AUSTRALIA. 630
1030-7222 See AUSTRALIAN JOURNAL OF LABOUR LAW. 3144
1030-7230 See JOURNAL OF CONTRACT LAW. 2987
1030-7664 See AUSTRALIAN INDUSTRY TRENDS. 1598
1030-7745 See ANSTO/E. 5084
1030-7907 See TEACHER UNIONIST. 1786
1030-7915 See AUSTRALIAN NUGGET JOURNAL. 3998
1030-8474 See FEEDBACK (SYDNEY, N.S.W.). 211
1030-8512 See BACTERIAL WILT NEWSLETTER. 560
1030-858X See ACT PAPERS IN ADULT EDUCATION AND TRAINING. 1799
1030-8768 See TELL. 5002
1030-8784 See NATIONAL MARKET PLACE NEWS. 2350
1030-8954 See AUSTRALIAN BIRDKEEPER. 5615
1030-8989 See ESTIMATED RESIDENT POPULATION BY MARITAL STATUS, AGE AND SEX, AUSTRALIA. 4552
1030-9047 See AUSTRALIAN NATIONAL ACCOUNTS. GROSS PRODUCT, EMPLOYMENT AND HOURS WORKED. 1654
1030-9179 See ESTIMATED RESIDENT POPULATION BY COUNTRY OF BIRTH, AGE AND SEX, AUSTRALIA / AUSTRALIAN BUREAU OF STATISTICS. 4552
1030-9527 See ABARE RESEARCH REPORT. 42
1030-9667 See AUSTRALIAN DEFENCE 2000. 4037
1030-9713 See CRAFT & DECORATING. 371
1030-9748 See PLANT VARIETIES JOURNAL. 2428
1030-9837 See ON THE RECORDS. 3022

1030-9853 ISSN Index

1030-9853 See SIL - AAIB OCCASIONAL PAPERS. 3321

1030-9861 See SIL - AAIB OCCASIONAL PAPERS. 3321

1030-9985 *See* VIETNAM TODAY. 4537

1031-0134 See BULLETIN OF THE AUSTRALIAN METEOROLOGICAL AND OCEANOGRAPHIC SOCIETY. 1421

1031-0193 *See* COMMERCIAL FINANCE AUSTRALIA. 727

1031-0320 *See* HOUSING FINANCE FOR OWNER OCCUPATION, AUSTRALIA. 2840

1031-0533 *See* APPARENT CONSUMPTION OF FOODSTUFFS AND NUTRIENTS, AUSTRALIA. 2362

1031-0541 *See* AUSTRALIA AT A GLANCE. 1923

1031-0673 *See* PUBLICATIONS ISSUED - AUSTRALIAN BUREAU OF STATISTICS. 423

1031-0894 *See* JOB PROSPECTS AUSTRALIA. 4205

1031-1009 *See* PARTNERS IN RESEARCH FOR DEVELOPMENT. 118

1031-1017 *See* ACORN JOURNAL. 3850

1031-1211 *See* GERARD HENDERSON'S MEDIA WATCH. 1112

1031-1343 *See* BUSINESS WHO'S WHO PRODUCTS AND TRADENAMES GUIDE. 727

1031-1378 *See* ANNUAL REPORT / CURTIN UNIVERSITY OF TECHNOLOGY. 5084

1031-1580 *See* REPORT / CSIRO, DIVISION OF ANIMAL HEALTH. 5520

1031-170X *See* AUSTRALIAN COLLEGE OF MIDWIVES INCORPORATED JOURNAL. 3554

1031-2315 *See* BUSINESS DIRECTIONS. 647

1031-2331 *See* INDIAN OCEAN REVIEW, THE. 2510

1031-2765 *See* NATIONAL INCOME AND EXPENDITURE CANBERRA. 4738

1031-282X *See* ACTIVE (BELCONNEN). 4881

1031-2943 *See* AUSTRALIAN RELIGION STUDIES REVIEW. 4937

1031-3001 *See* TERROR AUSTRALIS: THE AUSTRALIAN HORROR & FANTASY MAGAZINE. 3445

1031-3079 *See* RURAL BUSINESS MAGAZINE. 131

1031-3249 *See* AUSTRALIAN CONCRETE CONSTRUCTION. 599

1031-332X *See* QUARTERLY SUMMARY / NATIONAL AUSTRALIA BANK. 806

1031-3575 *See* INTER ALIA ADELAIDE. 1864

1031-3613 *See* REPRODUCTION, FERTILITY, AND DEVELOPMENT. 586

1031-3745 *See* BUILDING CONSTRUCTION MATERIALS AND EQUIPMENT. 603

1031-3796 *See* RESOURCE RICHMOND. 5777

1031-3966 *See* PC SUPPORT ADVISOR (SYDNEY). 1271

1031-4067 *See* NATIONAL SOCIAL SCIENCE SURVEY REPORT / RESEARCH SCHOOL OF SOCIAL SCIENCES, AUSTRALIAN NATIONAL UNIVERSITY. 5210

1031-444X *See* EDUCATION AUSTRALIA ANNANDALE. 1738

1031-4555 *See* OLDE MACHINERY MART. 2123

1031-461X *See* AUSTRALIAN HISTORICAL STUDIES. 2668

1031-4695 *See* WEEKLY TIMES TECHNICAL ANNUAL. 161

1031-4709 *See* ANNUAL REPORT AND ACCOUNTS - HOWARD FLOREY INSTITUTE OF EXPERIMENTAL PHYSIOLOGY AND MEDICINE. 3726

1031-4717 *See* RESEARCH REPORT - ROYAL PRINCE ALFRED HOSPITAL. 3634

1031-4822 *See* AUSTRALIAN INVESTMENT. 891

1031-4830 *See* AUSTRALIAN MOTHER AND BABY. 2277

1031-4997 *See* V.C.O.S.S. NOTICEBOARD. 5313

1031-5187 *See* AUSTRALIAN LIBRARIES : ALED. 3193

1031-5225 *See* ANNUAL REPORT / WATER AUTHORITY OF WESTERN AUSTRALIA. 5530

1031-5411 *See* NAATI NEWS. 3304

1031-5462 *See* AUSTRALIAN FILM DATA. 4064

1031-5543 *See* INFORMATION CIRCULAR - OCCUPATIONAL SUPERANNUATION GROUP. 1679

1031-556X *See* MINERALS AND ENERGY RESEARCH NEWS. 2144

1031-5810 *See* AUSTRALIAN FRANCHISING. 641

1031-5969 *See* PACIFECON SURVEY OF DEVELOPMENT ACTIVITY IN NEW ZEALAND. 2911

1031-6280 *See* DONKEY DIGEST. 5582

1031-6434 *See* NONVIOLENCE TODAY. 4484

1031-6574 *See* LINC BELCONNEN. 1386

1031-6590 *See* INFORMATION BULLETIN - CHILDREN'S COURT OF NEW SOUTH WALES. 2982

1031-6620 *See* YOUR RETIREMENT CHIPPENDALE. 5182

1031-6892 *See* HANDBOOK - AUSTRALIAN ACADEMY OF TECHNOLOGICAL SCIENCES AND ENGINEERING. 5109

1031-6914 *See* AUSTRALIAN, ASIAN AND PACIFIC ELECTRICAL WORLD. 2036

1031-6981 *See* PACIFIC REPORT (RED HILL). 702

1031-7104 *See* GOVERNMENT FINANCE STATISTICS, AUSTRALIA. 4698

1031-7112 *See* PUBLIC SECTOR DEBT, AUSTRALIA. 4699

1031-7511 *See* PSYCHOLOGICAL TEST BULLETIN. 4611

1031-7740 *See* ANNUAL REPORT / FORESTRY COMMISSION OF TASMANIA. 2375

1031-7805 *See* JAC COURSES DIRECTORY. 1755

1031-8216 *See* ANSTO TECHNOLOGY. 4446

1031-8313 *See* JOURNAL OF STUDIES IN JUSTICE. 5250

1031-8364 *See* CCH JOURNAL OF ASIAN PACIFIC TAXATION, THE. 4717

1031-8380 *See* MINE LIFE. 2144

1031-8453 *See* AD 2000. 4932

1031-9379 *See* PACIFIC RESEARCH : A PERIODICAL OF THE PEACE RESEARCH CENTRE, AUSTRALIAN NATIONAL UNIVERSITY. 4530

1031-953X *See* INFONET. 5113

1031-9573 *See* TASMANIAN POCKET YEAR BOOK. 1929

1031-9964 *See* RESEARCH REPORT / CSIRO DIVISION OF OCEANOGRAPHY. 1456

1032-0024 *See* SAFETY AND TRAINING NEWS. 2869

1032-0407 *See* REPORT - WOOD UTILISATION RESEARCH CENTRE, DEPARTMENT OF CONSERVATION AND LAND MANAGEMENT. 2404

1032-0431 *See* ACLIS NEWS. 3187

1032-0458 *See* VOX CANBERRA. 1790

1032-0512 *See* AUSTRALIAN BUREAU OF STATISTICS PUBLICATIONS TO BE RELEASED IN 408

1032-0539 *See* OCCASIONAL PAPER - BUREAU OF TRANSPORT AND COMMUNICATIONS ECONOMICS. 1509

1032-0865 *See* DIRECTORY OF HOUSING RELATED STATISTICS. 2840

1032-0954 *See* HOTEL EXECUTIVE, THE. 2806

1032-0989 *See* OCCUPATIONAL HEALTH MAGAZINE. 2866

1032-1071 *See* SOFTWARE PRODUCTIVITY REVIEW. 1291

1032-111X *See* ANNUAL REPORT / MINERALS AND ENERGY RESEARCH INSTITUTE OF WESTERN AUSTRALIA. 1932

1032-1195 *See* ENGINEERS AUSTRALIA. 1974

1032-125X *See* FRESHWATER FISHING AUSTRALIA. 2304

1032-1314 *See* ICHTHYOLITH ISSUES. 5586

1032-1322 *See* AUSTRALIAN JOURNAL OF NUTRITION AND DIETETICS. 4187

1032-1403 *See* CSIRO WATER RESOURCES SERIES. 5532

1032-1438 *See* LIBRARIES ALONE. 3223

1032-1640 *See* IDIOM 23. 3395

1032-1810 *See* CCH JOURNAL OF AUSTRALIAN TAXATION, THE. 4717

1032-1829 *See* NATIONAL LIBRARY OF AUSTRALIA NEWS. 3233

1032-1896 *See* ANNUAL REPORT / DEPARTMENT OF TRANSPORT AND COMMUNICATIONS. 5376

1032-1942 *See* AUSTRALIAN ART EDUCATION. 343

1032-2019 *See* ANNUAL REPORT / DEPARTMENT OF FOREIGN AFFAIRS AND TRADE. 822

1032-2205 *See* ACSJC OCCASIONAL PAPERS. 4503

1032-2302 *See* GEMS WODEN. 3506

1032-2396 *See* DISABLED AND AGED PERSONS AUSTRALIA ... PRELIMINARY RESULTS. 4395

1032-240X *See* AUSTRALIAN BUILDING, CONSTRUCTION AND HOUSING. 599

1032-2426 *See* AUSTRALIAN JOURNAL OF SOIL AND WATER CONSERVATION. 5530

1032-2892 *See* SYDNEY REVIEW 1988. 331

1032-3007 *See* CIT TASK FORCE REPORT. 5095

1032-3449 *See* AUSTRALASIAN SHIPS & PORTS. 5447

1032-3627 See ASIA PACIFIC JOURNAL OF HUMAN RESOURCES. 938

1032-3759 *See* PORK JOURNAL. 218

1032-3767 *See* MILNE'S POULTRY DIGEST. 215

1032-3899 *See* SOUND AND IMAGE. DEE WHY. 1139

1032-3945 *See* ACCART NEWS. 5501

1032-4410 *See* GERIACTION. 3751

1032-5298 *See* FOOD AUSTRALIA : OFFICIAL JOURNAL OF CAFTA AND AIFST. 2336

1032-5441 *See* ANNUAL REPORT - CSIRO DIVISION OF SOILS (1987). 162

1032-5506 *See* SPORTS TRAINERS DIGEST : A CONTINUING EDUCATION SERVICE OF THE AUSTRALIAN SPORTS MEDICINE FEDERATION / NATIONAL SPORTS TRAINERS SCHEME. 3956

1032-5565 *See* ELECTRICITY WEEK. 2046

1032-5999 *See* EARTH SCIENCES AT ANU. 1354

1032-6111 *See* TREESPEAK ADELAIDE. 2207

1032-6138 *See* AUSTRALIA'S HEALTH / AUSTRALIAN INSTITUTE OF HEALTH. 4768

1032-6189 *See* AQUALINK. 4883

1032-6499 *See* AMERICAR AUSTRALIA. 5403

1032-6626 *See* AUSTRALIAN EQUINE VETERINARIAN. 2797

1032-6634 *See* POLICY (CENTRE FOR INDEPENDENT STUDIES (N.S.W.)). 4487

1032-6898 *See* STANDARD FOR THE UNIFORM SCHEDULING OF DRUGS AND POISONS. 4330

1032-805X *See* CATALOGUE OF PUBLICATIONS. 5325

1032-8068 *See* AUSTRALIAN AND NEW ZEALAND BIOTECHNOLOGY DIRECTORY. 3686

1032-8106 *See* RESEARCH BULLETIN - DEPARTMENT OF CONSERVATION AND LAND MANAGEMENT WESTERN AUSTRALIA. 2203

1032-870X *See* RETAIL BANKING PRODUCTS SURVEY. AT CALL DEPOSITS. 809

1032-8718 *See* RETAIL BANKING PRODUCTS SURVEY. TERM DEPOSITS. 809

1032-8726 *See* RETAIL BANKING PRODUCTS SURVEY. CONTINUING CREDIT. 809

1032-8734 *See* RETAIL BANKING PRODUCTS SURVEY. TERM LOANS. 809

1032-8742 *See* RETAIL BANKING PRODUCTS SURVEY. CREDIT CARDS. 809

1032-8793 *See* STATE AND REGIONAL PROJECTIONS. BULLETIN. 4563

1032-9005 *See* ACTION NETWORK. 5178

1032-9366 *See* AIRCRAFT & AEROSPACE. 9

1032-9552 *See* DAIRY ECONOMICS RESEARCH REPORT. 193

1032-9617 *See* NEWSLETTER - NATIONAL ASSOCIATION FOR THE VISUAL ARTS. 326

1032-9625 *See* BIRTH ST. LEONARDS. 2277

1032-9722 *See* AGRICULTURE & RESOURCES QUARTERLY. 53

1033-0216 *See* ARTWORK MAGAZINE. 342

ISSN Index

1033-0682 *See* BROKER REPORT INDEX. 893
1033-0801 *See* TEA NEWS SYDNEY. 3327
1033-1069 *See* TODAY'S MOTOR. 2130
1033-1115 *See* AGENDA PARKVILLE. 312
1033-1247 *See* FISHING BOAT WORLD. 2303
1033-1352 *See* AUSTRALIAN RECORD AND MUSIC REVIEW. 4101
1033-1360 *See* LAND AND WATER RESEARCH NEWS. 1357
1033-1425 *See* HEALTH AT WORK NEWSLETTER. 2863
1033-1867 *See* FABRICATIONS : THE JOURNAL OF THE SOCIETY OF ARCHITECTURAL HISTORIANS, AUSTRALIA & NEW ZEALAND. 298
1033-1875 *See* ERGONOMICS AUSTRALIA. 2114
1033-1891 *See* UNESCO AUSTRALIA / AUSTRALIAN NATIONAL COMMISSION FOR UNESCO. 3137
1033-2014 *See* EXCHANGE LILYFIELD. 673
1033-2170 *See* MATHEMATICS EDUCATION RESEARCH JOURNAL. 3520
1033-2391 *See* UNION ISSUES. 1716
1033-2464 *See* INDEPENDENT TEACHER FORTITUDE VALLEY. 1896
1033-2626 *See* AUSTRALASIAN RELIGION INDEX. 4937
1033-2731 *See* BIENNIAL REPORT / DIVISION OF WILDLIFE AND ECOLOGY. 5578
1033-2774 *See* AMREP RESOURCE POLITICS. 2133
1033-2839 *See* LEGAL EDUCATION REVIEW. 2999
1033-2863 *See* IVS ANNUAL CROWS NEST. 5512
1033-2898 *See* DEFENCE INDUSTRY AND AEROSPACE REPORT. 4040
1033-3010 *See* AUSTRALIAN NATIONAL ACCOUNTS. CAPITAL STOCK. 4696
1033-3061 *See* WEED CONTROL IN SUMMER CROPS. 145
1033-3665 *See* SUMMARY OF STATISTICS - AUSTRALIAN BUREAU OF STATISTICS. VICTORIAN OFFICE. 4701
1033-3673 *See* AUSTRALIAN GARDEN HISTORY. 2409
1033-3711 See ANZLIC NEWS. 4630
1033-3738 *See* WHAT RESEARCH SAYS TO THE SCIENCE AND MATHEMATICS TEACHER. 1908
1033-3908 *See* RESEARCH REPORT - CSIRO DIVISION OF MINERAL AND PROCESS ENGINEERING. 2150
1033-3967 *See* CROP PROTECTION BULLETIN. 169
1033-3975 *See* STAGES MELBOURNE. 388
1033-40253 *See* ART MONTHLY AUSTRALIA. 339
1033-4149 *See* WESTERN FISHERIES MAGAZINE. 2316
1033-4505 *See* BOND LAW REVIEW. 2943
1033-4513 *See* DOWN UNDER QUILTS. 5183
1033-4777 *See* CRIMINOLOGY AUSTRALIA : QUARTERLY JOURNAL OF THE AUSTRALIAN INSTITUTE OF CRIMINOLOGY. 3163
1033-4890 *See* EDUCATION MONITOR MELBOURNE. 1740
1033-5196 *See* PROSPECT PERTH. 2148
1033-5609 *See* REPS BODYBUILDING AUSTRALIA. 2601
1033-5722 *See* AUSTRALIAN FOREIGN AFFAIRS AND TRADE. 824
1033-596X *See* EEO ANNUAL REPORT - AUSTRALIAN INDUSTRY DEVELOPMENT CORPORATION. 1605
1033-6001 *See* AUSTRALIA'S SURFING LIFE ANNUAL. 4885
1033-6044 *See* AUSTRALIAN LIQUOR TRADER. 2364
1033-6060 *See* AUSTRALIAN COUNTRY STYLE. 2510
1033-6133 *See* EMPLOYMENT INJURIES, TASMANIA. 2872
1033-6192 *See* AUSTRALIA AND WORLD AFFAIRS. 4516
1033-6257 *See* SOVIET REVIEW. 1522

1033-6273 *See* NURSING AND HEALTH SCIENCE EDUCATION REVIEW. 3863
1033-6273 *See* INFORMATION AND SOCIETY. 5247
1033-6281 *See* MULTICULTURAL EDUCATION REVIEW. 1765
1033-6656 *See* AUSTRALIAN SUGAR CRAFT. 2328
1033-6885 *See* PRINT PRODUCTION DIRECTORY. 4568
1033-6893 *See* TODAY'S LIFE SCIENCE. 5166
1033-7369 *See* FAST FOURS & ROTARIES. 5414
1033-7423 *See* HOT METAL. 4027
1033-7466 *See* AUSTRALIAN CORPORATIONS AND SECURITIES REPORTS. 3096
1033-758X *See* STATIONERY NEWS. 713
1033-7660 *See* CHILD SAFETY LIBRARY NEWS. 4771
1033-7741 See AUSTRALIAN AND NEW ZEALAND CATALOGUE OF NEW FILMS AND VIDEOS, THE. 4064
1033-792X *See* SHHH NEWS. 4393
1033-7954 *See* AUSTRALIAN AND NEW ZEALAND WINE INDUSTRY DIRECTORY. 2363
1033-8160 *See* STAR AUSTRALIS. 1360
1033-8292 *See* JOE WEIDER'S MUSCLE AND FITNESS AUSTRALIAN ED. 2599
1033-8306 *See* TASFORESTS. 2396
1033-839X *See* AUSTRALIA AND TOMORROWS PACIFIC / FOR AUSTRALIA. 4631
1033-8624 *See* AGSA NEWSLETTER. 542
1033-8640 *See* STATISTICS WEEKLY. 5342
1033-8713 *See* CULTURE AND POLICY / ICPS. 2845
1033-8772 *See* SUMMARY OF CROPS AUSTRALIA. 157
1033-8934 *See* AUGUSTA MELBOURNE. 293
1033-8977 *See* SPORTSNETWORK. 4923
1033-9280 *See* AQIS BULLETIN. 2327
1033-9345 *See* AUSTRALIAN INSOLVENCY BULLETIN. 2938
1033-9434 *See* AUSTRALIAN WOMEN'S BOOK REVIEW. 5551
1033-9612 *See* BUSINESS TO BUSINESS SOUTH AUSTRALIA. 653
1033-9752 *See* TRANSPORT AND COMMUNICATIONS INDICATORS. 5395
1033-9957 *See* INDEPENDENT MONTHLY, THE. 4476
1034-0408 See JOURNAL OF CORPORATE MANAGEMENT, THE. 3101
1034-0475 4696
1034-0505 *See* INTERNATIONAL TRADE IN SERVICES, AUSTRALIA. 730
1034-0580 *See* PERIPHERY LISMORE. 374
1034-0785 *See* AUSTRALIAN BOOK COLLECTOR. 4823
1034-1218 *See* AUSTRALIAN SYSTEMATIC BOTANY SOCIETY NEWSLETTER. 501
1034-1412 *See* OCCASIONAL PAPER - CENTRE FOR ENVIRONMENTAL STUDIES, UNIVERSITY OF TASMANIA. 2179
1034-148X *See* INTERDATA LEISURE & TOURISM HANDBOOK, THE. 5480
1034-1854 *See* ANNUAL REPORT - AUSTRALIAN COUNCIL OF LIBRARIES AND INFORMATION SERVICES. 3190
1034-2338 *See* AFR INVESTOR. 636
1034-3024 *See* PUBLIC LAW REVIEW. 3033
1034-3040 *See* JOURNAL OF BANKING AND FINANCE LAW AND PRACTICE. 793
1034-3059 *See* AUSTRALIAN DISPUTE RESOLUTION JOURNAL. 2938
1034-3075 *See* PLUMBING AND MECHANICAL CONNECTION. 2607
1034-3326 *See* NETWORKING : THE TAFE LEARN NETWORK NEWSLETTER. 1767
1034-3350 *See* JOURNAL OF HIGHER EDUCATION. 1832
1034-361X *See* ANTARCTIC AND SOUTHERN OCEANS LAW AND POLICY OCCASIONAL PAPERS. 3123

1034-3938 *See* AUSTRALIAN GOLF DIGEST ... HANDBOOK. 4885
1034-4101 *See* ARCHITECT DESIGNED HOUSES. 288
1034-4128 *See* ETHOS PAPERS. 1894
1034-4608 *See* AUSTRALIAN PRODUCT LIABILITY REPORTER. 4768
1034-4810 *See* JOURNAL OF PAEDIATRICS AND CHILD HEALTH. 3905
1034-4837 *See* TCF INDUSTRY ADVISOR. 1087
1034-4888 *See* DAWSON'S LOCAL PINK PAGES. BRISBANE WATERS. 1924
1034-4896 *See* DAWSON'S LOCAL PINK PAGES. MACARTHUR. 1924
1034-490X *See* DAWSON'S LOCAL PINK PAGES. ST. GEORGE. 1925
1034-4918 *See* DAWSON'S LOCAL PINK PAGES. NEWCASTLE. 1924
1034-4926 *See* DAWSON'S LOCAL PINK PAGES. WOLLONGONG. 1925
1034-4942 *See* AUSTRALASIAN JOURNAL OF COMBINATORICS, THE. 3496
1034-5051 *See* IMMIGRATION UPDATE. 1919
1034-5329 *See* CURRENT ISSUES IN CRIMINAL JUSTICE. 3163
1034-5337 *See* TODAY MONA VALE. 2182
1034-5671 *See* SCHOOLS, AUSTRALIA ... PRELIMINARY. 1797
1034-5809 See AUSTRALIAN FARM JOURNAL. 64
1034-5876 *See* GREENWEEK. 2194
1034-6066 *See* AUSTRALIAN "BEGG ORTHODONTICS" NEWSLETTER. 1317
1034-6074 *See* RURAL RESEARCH. 131
1034-6147 *See* TODAY'S FEED LOTTING. 223
1034-6171 *See* AUSTRALIAN DEER FARMING. 64
1034-6244 *See* LITERATURE BASE. 3407
1034-6384 *See* SYDNEY'S CHILD. 2286
1034-652X *See* AUSTRALIAN JOURNAL OF MARRIAGE & FAMILY. 2276
1034-6627 *See* AUSTRALIAN CRIMINOLOGY INFORMATION BULLETIN. 3158
1034-6686 *See* OFFICE PRODUCTS NEWS (DARLINGHURST). 4213
1034-6740 *See* EDUCATION ACTION WAGGA WAGGA. 1738
1034-6775 *See* AUSIMM BULLETIN / THE AUSTRALASIAN INSTITUTE OF MINING AND METALLURGY, THE. 2134
1034-6783 *See* AUSIMM PROCEEDINGS. 2134
1034-7313 *See* IMPORT BANKSTOWN. 839
1034-7356 *See* ANNUAL REPORT - NORTHERN TERRITORY. DEPARTMENT OF PRIMARY INDUSTRY AND FISHERIES. 2294
1034-7380 *See* ANNUAL REPORT - QUEENSLAND. DEPARTMENT OF RESOURCE INDUSTRIES. 2133
1034-747X *See* ECONOMIC UPDATE ULTIMO. 1486
1034-7496 *See* TELECOMMUNICATIONS MANAGEMENT AND MARKETING NEWSLETTER. 1165
1034-7577 *See* HISTORY FORUM BRIDGEWATER. 1896
1034-7747 *See* REVENUE LAW JOURNAL. 4746
1034-8042 *See* AUSTRALIAN LIBRARY REVIEW. 3193
1034-8085 *See* BICYCLING AUSTRALIA. 428
1034-8360 *See* EDI RESEARCH AUSTRALIA. 1183
1034-8506 *See* INTERNATIONAL TAX HANDBOOK / HORWATH INTERNATIONAL. 4733
1034-8794 *See* MINES AND ENERGY REVIEW. 2145
1034-9006 *See* AUSTRALIAN GOURMET TRAVELLER 1989. 2328
1034-9154 *See* ASL. 3192
1034-9219 *See* BIENNIAL REPORT / CSIRO AUSTRALIAN ANIMAL HEALTH LABORATORY. 5505
1034-9243 *See* PAPERS VICTORIA PARK. 1067
1034-9294 *See* STREETBIKE. 4083
1034-9553 *See* AUSTRALIAN ILLAWARRA DAIRYMAN. 192

ISSN Index

1034-9685 *See* AUSTRALIAN BANKING STATISTICS - RESERVE BANK OF AUSTRALIA. 773

1035-0233 *See* EPA REVIEW. 2171

1035-0357 *See* AUSTRALIAN PURCHASING AND SUPPLY (WATERLOO). 949

1035-0462 *See* AUSTRALIAN JOURNAL OF ADULT AND COMMUNITY EDUCATION. 1799

1035-0500 *See* DESIGNINK. 297

1035-0764 *See* AUSTRALIAN TOXIC NETWORK NEWS. 2225

1035-0772 *See* CHILDREN AUSTRALIA. 5278

1035-0977 *See* FACET TALK. 2773

1035-1051 *See* AUTO MARKET REPORT. 5405

1035-1094 *See* ETHNIC COMMUNITIES' REFERENCE YEARBOOK. 2260

1035-1108 See HOUSE & HOME WOODWORKER. 634

1035-1205 *See* AUREALIS MT. WAVERLEY. 3364

1035-1272 *See* SEWTRADE C F I YEARBOOK AND DIRECTORY. 1087

1035-1515 *See* AUSTRALIAN GEOMAGNETISM REPORT. 1351

1035-1841 *See* CERAMICS PADDINGTON. 2588

1035-1914 *See* AUSTRALIAN FARM MANAGER, THE. 64

1035-2015 *See* WHO AUDITS AUSTRALIA? (1987). 753

1035-2287 *See* FIREPOINT ROSEVILLE. 2290

1035-2295 *See* AUSTRALIAN CAPITAL TERRITORY LEGISLATION CATALOGUE. 2938

1035-2600 See AUSTRALIAN PAEDIATRIC NURSE. 3852

1035-3046 *See* ECONOMIC AND LABOUR RELATIONS REVIEW : ELRR, THE. 2861

1035-3062 *See* DIRECTORY OF MINISTERIAL ADVISERS AND ASSISTANTS. 4697

1035-3127 *See* ISLAND. SANDY BAY. 3397

1035-3127 *See* ISLAND. 3397

1035-3380 *See* INDEX TO CHINA DAILY. 417

1035-3437 *See* AUSCON CLAYTON. 315

1035-3593 *See* NEWSLETTER OF THE SPECIALIST GROUP IN TECTONICS & STRUCTURAL GEOLOGY. 1389

1035-3615 *See* PENSIONERS VOICE (SYDNEY). 2889

1035-364X *See* AUSTRALIAN PROPERTY MARKET INVESTMENT STRATEGY REPORT. 891

1035-3682 *See* ETHNIC SCHOOLS IN FOCUS. 1745

1035-3712 *See* WILDLIFE RESEARCH. 5600

1035-4107 *See* INDUSTRY REVIEW DEAKIN. 1612

1035-4247 *See* MEMOIRS OF THE MUSEUM OF VICTORIA. ANTHROPOLOGY AND HISTORY. 4091

1035-4298 *See* TIMBERTRADER NEWS (1990). 2405

1035-4425 *See* JOURNAL FOR SOCIAL JUSTICE STUDIES. 5249

1035-4549 *See* FISHERIES RESEARCH REPORT (PERTH). 2193

1035-4573 *See* AUSSIE SPORTS ACTION. 4884

1035-4611 *See* AUSTRALIAN CLAY JOURNAL AND CERAMIC NEWS. 2586

1035-4662 *See* JOURNAL OF TOURISM STUDIES, THE. 5481

1035-4727 *See* OPEN LETTER GEELONG. 1883

1035-4816 *See* LISWA NEWSLETTER. 3228

1035-4832 *See* ANNUAL SURVEY OF VICTORIAN PUBLIC LIBRARIES / VICTORIAN MINISTRY FOR THE ARTS. 3191

1035-4859 *See* VIVA MT. LAWLEY. 2275

1035-493X *See* WESTERN ANGLER. 2316

1035-5391 *See* GUIDE TO NEW AUSTRALIAN BOOKS. 3392

1035-5693 *See* MIMS DISEASE INDEX. 3715

1035-5723 *See* MIMS CROWS NEST. 4315

1035-6150 *See* ENVIRONMENTAL LAW REPORTER SYDNEY. 3111

1035-624X *See* HINTERALIA. 3213

1035-641X *See* AUSTRALIAN CAMERA CRAFT AND SHOOTING VIDEO. 4367

1035-6576 *See* BULLETIN OF THE AUSTRALIAN METEOROLOGICAL AND OCEANOGRAPHIC SOCIETY. 1421

1035-6754 *See* 21.C. 2609

1035-6878 *See* ANNUAL AUSTRALIAN NOTICES TO MARINERS IN FORCE ON 1ST JANUARY. 4174

1035-6959 *See* COMMUNICATIONS REPORT. SYDNEY. 1152

1035-7068 *See* SYDNEY PAPERS, THE. 1640

1035-7319 *See* AUSTRALIAN JOURNAL OF PUBLIC HEALTH. 4768

1035-7602 *See* STATISTICAL REPORT - AUSTRALIA. ARMY OFFICE. 1 PSYCHOLOGICAL RESEARCH UNIT. 4619

1035-767X See ABARE RESEARCH REPORT. 42

1035-7718 *See* AUSTRALIAN JOURNAL OF INTERNATIONAL AFFAIRS. 4516

1035-7823 *See* ASIAN STUDIES REVIEW. 2646

1035-8005 *See* AUSTRALIAN AND NEW ZEALAND CATALOGUE OF NEW FILMS AND VIDEOS, THE. 4064

1035-803X See ABARE RESEARCH REPORT. 42

1035-8544 *See* INTERNATIONAL ENVIRONMENTAL UPDATE. 2174

1035-865X *See* AUSTRALIAN ECONOMIC INDICATORS. 1464

1035-8714 *See* NEW ZEALAND MEDIA GUIDE. 1118

1035-8803 *See* AUSTRALIAN WRITER'S JOURNAL, THE. 3460

1035-8811 *See* AUSTRALIAN JOURNAL OF ANTHROPOLOGY, THE. 231

1035-9079 *See* AVIATION REPORT. SYDNEY. 13

1035-915X *See* SPORTS & LEISURE RETAILER. 958

1035-9176 *See* TOY & HOBBY RETAILER. 2585

1035-9338 *See* AUS.GEO NEWS. 1366

1035-9508 *See* VIDEOCAMERA AND ELECTRONIC IMAGING. 1142

1035-9621 *See* AUSTRALIAN PARAPSYCHOLOGICAL REVIEW. 4240

1035-9656 See AUSTRALIAN WRITER'S JOURNAL, THE. 3460

1035-9796 *See* RESEARCH PAPER. 2393

1036-0212 *See* ELECTRONICS AUSTRALIA WITH ETI. 2049

1036-0220 *See* BIENNIAL RESEARCH REPORT. 66

1036-0352 *See* INFORMATION TECHNOLOGY INDEX. 1188

1036-0417 *See* AUSTRALIAN CURRENT LAW. REPORTER. 2938

1036-0425 *See* AUSTRALIAN CURRENT LAW. LEGISLATION. 2938

1036-0573 *See* LEISURE OPTIONS. 4852

1036-0867 *See* ADVISORY BULLETIN. 44

1036-0875 *See* AUSTRALASIAN SCIENCE MAG. 5087

1036-0913 *See* CHIROPRACTIC JOURNAL OF AUSTRALIA. 4379

1036-1073 *See* HEALTH PROMOTION JOURNAL OF AUSTRALIA. 3582

1036-1146 *See* AUSTRALIAN JOURNAL OF POLITICAL SCIENCE. 4464

1036-1162 *See* CONSUMER ACTION CANBERRA. 1294

1036-1243 *See* SIL - AAIB OCCASIONAL PAPERS. 3321

1036-126X *See* GREEN LEFT WEEKLY. 4542

1036-1367 *See* ANNUAL REPORT - CSIRO. COAL AND ENERGY TECHNOLOGY. 1932

1036-1421 *See* IN OTHER WORDS NUNAWADING. 3286

1036-1456 *See* BOND MANAGEMENT REVIEW. 861

1036-1499 *See* REPORT - AUSTRALIAN-AMERICAN EDUCATIONAL FOUNDATION. 1778

1036-1510 See ACCOUNTING & ASC COMPLIANCE. 736

1036-1561 *See* VOICES : THE QUARTERLY JOURNAL OF THE NATIONAL LIBRARY OF AUSTRALIA. 3255

1036-1669 *See* AUSTRALIAN LITERARY AWARDS AND FELLOWSHIPS. 3337

1036-1693 *See* SUCCESSFUL SELLING & MANAGING. 937

1036-1723 *See* BACKGROUND PAPER - ECONOMIC PLANNING ADVISORY COUNCIL. 1464

1036-1820 *See* AUSTRALIAN LIBRARY TECHNICIANS ASSOCIATION NEWS. 3193

1036-1871 See AM NEWS BOX HILL. 859

1036-1901 *See* HEALTHCOVER SYDNEY. 2598

1036-2045 *See* ART READING MATERIAL. 340

1036-2185 *See* MUNICIPAL MANAGER, QUEENSLAND. 4667

1036-2207 See DESKTOP MAGAZINE. 1233

1036-2606 *See* DIRECTORY OF TOURISM STATISTICS. 5500

1036-2649 *See* DEMOGRAPHY, QUEENSLAND. 4561

1036-2657 *See* DEMOGRAPHY, SOUTH AUSTRALIA. 4561

1036-2916 *See* CREATION EX NIHILO TECHNICAL JOURNAL. 4951

1036-3181 *See* PERIOD HOME RENOVATOR BUYER'S GUIDE. 2907

1036-3254 *See* AUSTRALIAN ROAD AND TRACK. 5404

1036-3491 *See* AUSTRALIA'S SURFING LIFE. 4885

1036-3831 *See* AUSTRALIAN & NEW ZEALAND PHYSICIST : A PUBLICATION OF THE AUSTRALIAN INSTITUTE OF PHYSICS & THE NEW ZEALAND INSTITUTE OF PHYSICS, THE. 4398

1036-384X *See* PHOTO & VIDEO RETAILER. 4372

1036-3858 *See* WAATL CIRCULAR. 3256

1036-3912 *See* WEB ABBOTSFORD. 1908

1036-4005 *See* HEALTH TRANSITION REVIEW : THE CULTURAL, SOCIAL, AND BEHAVIOURAL DETERMINANTS OF HEALTH. 4781

1036-4099 *See* WORKING PAPERS ON LANGUAGE, GENDER & SEXISM. 3333

1036-4242 *See* AUSTRALIAN FARMERS' AND DEALERS' JOURNAL. 158

1036-5060 *See* AUSTRALIAN PAEDIATRIC NURSE. 3852

1036-5117 *See* WORKPLACE MELBOURNE. 1719

1036-5141 *See* SCHOOL EDUCATION NEWS. 1782

1036-5915 *See* GREETINGS AND GIFTS. 2584

1036-5931 *See* NETWORK ARMIDALE. 1767

1036-6008 *See* EAST ASIAN HISTORY. 2650

1036-6474 *See* AUSTRALIAN FARM JOURNAL. 64

1036-6709 *See* LANGUAGE AND LANGUAGE EDUCATION. 3294

1036-7128 *See* AUSTRALASIAN BIOTECHNOLOGY. 3685

1036-7314 *See* AUSTRALIAN CRITICAL CARE : OFFICIAL JOURNAL OF THE CONFEDERATION OF AUSTRALIAN CRITICAL CARE NURSES. 3851

1036-7810 *See* WING SPAN (MOONEE PONDS). 5621

1036-7918 *See* JOURNAL OF JUDICIAL ADMINISTRATION. 2987

1036-8124 *See* ON THE LEVEL ASHFIELD. 2600

1036-8701 *See* FILMNEWS. 4071

1036-904X *See* FOREIGN TRADE, AUSTRALIA. MERCHANDISE IMPORTS / AUSTRALIAN BUREAU OF STATISTICS. 729

1036-918X *See* SOUTH AUSTRALIAN NEWSLETTER. 4496

1036-9449 *See* FOREIGN TRADE, AUSTRALIA. MERCHANDISE EXPORTS / AUSTRALIAN BUREAU OF STATISTICS. 729

1036-9457 *See* AUSTRALIAN JOURNAL OF MUSIC THERAPY, THE. 3554

1036-9589 *See* COMMONWEALTH BILLS TABLE AND ASSOCIATED MATERIAL. 2953

1036-9686 *See* COMPASS KENSINGTON. 4949

1036-9872 See RANGELAND JOURNAL, THE. 2391

1036-9988 See PRIVATISATION REPORT. 4675

1037-0242 See INDEPENDENT REPORTER JOLIMONT. 1751

1037-051X See APRG REPORT. 5439

1037-0544 See INTERNATIONAL JOURNAL OF SALT LAKE RESEARCH. 5115

1037-0641 See MILNE'S PRIME BEEF. 215

1037-0838 See AUSTRALIAN JOURNAL OF JEWISH STUDIES. 2256

1037-1176 See NORTHERN TERRITORY IN FOCUS. 2670

1037-1311 See OZ ARTS MAGAZINE. 327

1037-1354 See HOUSE & HOME WOODWORKER. 634

1037-1435 See ASIA-PACIFIC DEFENCE REPORTER ANNUAL REFERENCE EDITION. 4037

1037-1648 See INSIDE SPORT CAMMERAY. 4900

1037-1842 See MOOREANA : JOURNAL OF THE PALMETUM. 518

1037-1869 See ACCOUNTING & ASC COMPLIANCE. 736

1037-2105 See AUSTRALIAN JOURNAL OF OTO-LARYNGOLOGY : THE OFFICIAL JOURNAL OF THE AUSTRALIAN SOCIETY OF OTO-LARYNGOLOGY HEAD AND NECK SURGERY. 3887

1037-3292 See AUSTRALIAN TRAINING REVIEW. 1911

1037-3314 See ANNUAL REPORT - AUSTRALIAN INSTITUTE OF MARINE SCIENCE 1987. 1351

1037-339X See CROSS STITCH. 5183

1037-3500 See BIENNIAL REPORT / DIVISION OF ENTOMOLOGY, CSIRO. 5606

1037-3535 See AUSTRALIAN DRILLING. 1966

1037-3748 See WORK BOAT WORLD. 597

1037-4124 See AUSTRALIAN JOURNAL OF CORPORATE LAW. 3096

1037-4299 See CHINA PAPER. 2648

1037-4973 See ANNUAL REPORT - AUSTRALIAN LAND INFORMATION COUNCIL. 2554

1037-5104 See EDUCATION ALTERNATIVES. 1738

1037-5171 See ANNUAL REPORT / DEPARTMENT OF PLANNING AND HOUSING. 2814

1037-5457 See PRACTICAL HYDROPONICS. 2428

1037-566X See HANDBOOK AND COURSES DIRECTORY - DIVISION OF TECHNICAL AND FURTHER EDUCATION, EDUCATION DEPARTMENT HOBART. 1749

1037-5678 See SUMMARY OF CROPS, WESTERN AUSTRALIA. 157

1037-5759 See CSIRO SPACE INDUSTRY NEWS. 17

1037-5783 See ROAD & TRANSPORT RESEARCH : [A JOURNAL OF AUSTRALIAN AND NEW ZEALAND RESEARCH AND PRACTICE]. 5443

1037-5945 See ANNUAL REPORT - OFFICE OF ENERGY PLANNING ADELAIDE. 1932

1037-6178 See CONTEMPORARY NURSE : A JOURNAL FOR THE AUSTRALIAN NURSING PROFESSION. 3854

1037-6267 See CHARTAC ACCOUNTANCY NEWS. 740

1037-6275 See CHARTAC TAX PLANNING NEWS. 740

1037-6445 See AM NEWS BOX HILL. 859

1037-6615 See NATIONAL HIV/AIDS LEGAL LINK NEWSLETTER. 3013

1037-6720 See ARCHERY ACTION WITH OUTDOOR CONNECTIONS. 4884

1037-6917 See NATIONAL DIRECTORY OF ABORIGINAL AND TORRES STRAIT ISLANDER ORGANISATIONS. 2268

1037-6992 See COMMERCIAL PHOTOGRAPHY IN AUSTRALIA. 4368

1037-700X See NADIE AUSTRALIA JOURNAL, THE. 1765

1037-7107 See MATERIALS AUSTRALIA. 4008

1037-7603 See DESKTOP MAGAZINE. 1233

1037-812X See WHO WEEKLY. 2511

1037-8286 See ABARE RESEARCH REPORT. 42

1037-8480 See PERMACULTURE INTERNATIONAL JOURNAL. 119

1037-8529 See CAD USER AUSTRALIA NEW ZEALAND. 1173

1037-8782 See INTERNATIONAL INVESTMENT POSITION, AUSTRALIA. 730

1037-888X See FOREIGN TRADE, AUSTRALIA, MERCHANDISE EXPORTS, DETAILED COMMODITY TABLES. 729

1037-9177 See SUMMARY OF CRIMINAL COURT PROCEEDINGS, WESTERN AUSTRALIA. 3109

1037-9606 See TAFE NSW HANDBOOK. 1916

1037-9630 See ANZLIC NEWS. 4630

1037-9687 See T & D. 887

1037-969X See ALTERNATIVE LAW JOURNAL. 3179

1037-9886 See ELECTRICITY AND GAS, AUSTRALIA. 1962

1038-0124 See PROSPECTUS AND HANDBOOK - UNIVERSITY OF MELBOURNE. 1843

1038-1317 See OIL AND GAS GAZETTE. 4268

1038-1430 See BUSINESS QUEENSLAND. 652

1038-1562 See AUSTRALIAN JOURNAL OF LANGUAGE AND LITERACY / ARA, THE. 3267

1038-1643 See AUSTRALIAN JOURNAL OF MEDICAL SCIENCE. 3554

1038-1775 See EDUCATIONAL HISTORIAN, THE. 1741

1038-1872 See GAZETTE - LAW SOCIETY OF THE AUSTRALIAN CAPITAL TERRITORY. 2973

1038-2062 See CTC NEWSLETTER. 663

1038-2097 See PACIFIC CONSERVATION BIOLOGY. 2201

1038-2410 See JOURNAL OF CORPORATE MANAGEMENT, THE. 3101

1038-4111 See ASIA PACIFIC JOURNAL OF HUMAN RESOURCES. 938

1038-4286 See AUSTRALIAN NATIONAL ACCOUNTS FINANCIAL ACCOUNTS. 4696

1038-4871 See ISLAND ARC, THE. 1383

1038-5231 See TECHNICAL COMPUTING (ALEXANDRIA). 1204

1038-5282 See AUSTRALIAN JOURNAL OF RURAL HEALTH, THE. 3554

1038-6300 See INDEX TO THE HISTORICAL MICROFICHE SERIES. 1926

1038-6424 See HISTORICAL MICROFICHE SERIES. 1926

1038-6491 See COMMERCIAL BANKING PRODUCTS SURVEY. COMMERCIAL LOANS. 783

1038-6505 See COMMERCIAL BANKING PRODUCTS SURVEY. BUSINESS CHEQUE ACCOUNTS. 783

1038-6726 See INSIGHT : AUSTRALIAN FOREIGN AFFAIRS AND TRADE ISSUES. 4524

1038-6793 See WAVELENGTHS NORTH RYDE. 1361

1038-6920 See ACIAR PROCEEDINGS. 43

1038-6963 See WORLD ACROBATICS. 389

1038-7609 See FINANCIAL ESTIMATES OF COMMONWEALTH PUBLIC TRADING ENTERPRISES, AUSTRALIA. 729

1038-8400 See TIRRA LIRRA. 3446

1038-8451 See GLOBAL AGENDA. 2172

1039-0081 See YOUR MORTGAGE MAGAZINE. 817

1039-1010 See ARENA MAGAZINE. 4540

1039-2017 See NEWSLETTER - REMOTE SENSING ASSOCIATION OF AUSTRALASIA. 1358

1039-3013 See LIST. LIBRARY AND INFORMATION SCIENCE TRENDS. 3228

1039-4001 See AUSTRALIAN & NEW ZEALAND JOURNAL OF VOCATIONAL EDUCATION RESEARCH. 1911

1039-6594 See AUSTRALIAN CAPITAL TERRITORY IN FOCUS. 4696

1039-6616 See AUSTRALIAN LAW LIBRARIAN. 2939

1039-7213 See LOCAL GOVERNMENT AND ENVIRONMENTAL REPORTS OF AUSTRALIA, THE. 4662

1039-7469 See GP GENERAL PRACTITIONER. 3738

1039-7841 See AUSTRALIAN JOURNAL OF INFOMATION SYSTEMS, THE. 1727

1039-8112 See GAS DISTRIBUTION INDUSTRY AND PERFORMANCE INDICATORS. 4257

1040-0001 See TRAVEL COLLECTOR. 2778

1040-0036 See WG&L PENSION AND BENEFITS FACT BOOK. 919

1040-0079 See QUALITY RESOURCE MONITOR. 3632

1040-0109 See FISHERMAN (LONG ISLAND, METROPOLITAN NEW YORK ED.), THE. 2302

1040-0117 See FISHERMAN (NEW JERSEY, DELAWARE BAY ED.), THE. 4894

1040-0125 See FISHERMAN (NEW ENGLAND ED.), THE. 2302

1040-0176 See HEALTHCARE ISSUES & TRENDS. 4782

1040-0192 See MEALEY'S LITIGATION REPORT. ASBESTOS PROPERTY ACTIONS. 3007

1040-0214 See DISCRETE SEMICONDUCTORS. POWER SEMICONDUCTORS. 4401

1040-0222 See DISCRETE SEMICONDUCTORS. THYRISTORS. 4402

1040-0230 See DISCRETE SEMICONDUCTORS. TRANSISTORS. 4402

1040-0230 See DISCRETE SEMICONDUCTORS. SURFACE-MOUNTED DISCRETE SEMICONDUCTORS. 1971

1040-0249 See DISCRETE SEMICONDUCTORS. DIODES. 2042

1040-0257 See JOURNAL OF CRITICAL ILLNESS, THE. 3595

1040-0265 See REFLEXIONES (SANTA FE, N.M.). 5490

1040-0303 See SCIENTIFIC REPORT - FOX CHASE CANCER CENTER. 3823

1040-0311 See CORPORATE CASHFLOW. 784

1040-032X See AREA CODE HANDBOOK. 1149

1040-0346 See PHOTOGRAPHY IN NEW YORK. 4374

1040-0354 See NPGA REPORTS. 4267

1040-0362 See BOOKS BY BLACK WOMEN. 4825

1040-0370 See JOURNAL OF INTERACTIVE INSTRUCTION DEVELOPMENT. 1192

1040-0397 See ELECTROANALYSIS (NEW YORK, N.Y.). 1014

1040-0400 See STRUCTURAL CHEMISTRY. 993

1040-0419 See CREATIVITY RESEARCH JOURNAL. 5196

1040-0435 See ASSISTIVE TECHNOLOGY. 4384

1040-0443 See HUMAN RESOURCE EXECUTIVE. 941

1040-0451 See FIDIA RESEARCH FOUNDATION SYMPOSIUM SERIES. 3833

1040-0486 See CURRENT PROBLEMS IN DERMATOLOGY (CHICAGO, ILL.). 3719

1040-0494 See POSITIVE INK. 1774

1040-0516 See NORTHWEST SALES GUIDE TO HIGH-TECH COMPANIES. 5134

1040-0524 See SOUTHWEST SALES GUIDE TO HIGH-TECH COMPANIES. 5159

1040-0532 See SOUTH CENTRAL SALES GUIDE TO HIGH-TECH COMPANIES. 5159

1040-0540 See NORTH CENTRAL SALES GUIDE TO HIGH-TECH COMPANIES. 5134

1040-0559 See EASTERN GREAT LAKES SALES GUIDE TO HIGH-TECH COMPANIES. 5102

1040-0567 See SOUTHEAST SALES GUIDE TO HIGH-TECH COMPANIES. 5159

1040-0575 See MID-ATLANTIC SALES GUIDE TO HIGH-TECH COMPANIES. 5128

1040-0583 See NEW YORK METRO SALES GUIDE TO HIGH-TECH COMPANIES. 5133

1040-0591 See NEW ENGLAND SALES GUIDE TO HIGH-TECH COMPANIES. 5132

1040-0605 See AMERICAN JOURNAL OF PHYSIOLOGY. LUNG CELLULAR AND MOLECULAR PHYSIOLOGY. 3948

1040-0656 See NWSA JOURNAL. 5563

1040-0664 See QUALITY ASSURANCE BULLETIN. 883

1040-0672 See STATISTICS, TEXTBOOKS AND MONOGRAPHS. 5342

1040-0680 See MINNESOTA WILDLIFE REPORT. 2198

1040-0729 See EDUCATING AT-RISK YOUTH. 5284

1040-0753 See FORESIGHT (WESTLAKE VILLAGE, CALIF.). 868

1040-077X See BEST OF INDIA, THE. 5463

1040-0788 See BEST OF MOROCCO, THE. 5463

1040-0850 See SUMMER INSTITUTE OF LINGUISTICS AND THE UNIVERSITY OF TEXAS AT ARLINGTON PUBLICATIONS IN LINGUISTICS. 3327

1040-0885 See TOP SHELF. 5073

1040-0893 See FLORIDA ARCHITECTURE (1966). 298

1040-0907 See DISCRETE SEMICONDUCTORS. OPTOELECTRONICS. 2042

1040-0915 See DISCRETE SEMICONDUCTORS. SUGGESTED REPLACEMENTS. 2042

1040-0931 See PHARMACEUTICAL NEWS CAPSULE (SPECIAL ED.). 4320

1040-094X See BARBIE BAZAAR. 2583

1040-0958 See WORK & FAMILY LIFE. 2287

1040-0974 See NEW RELIGIOUS MOVEMENTS. 4981

1040-0990 See BUYOUTS (WELLESLEY HILLS, MASS.). 654

1040-1008 See JOHN BURTON'S WORKERS' COMPENSATION MONITOR. 2885

1040-1024 See CITIZEN AGENDA. 3110

1040-1067 See MOBIL TRAVEL GUIDE. SOUTHEAST. 5485

1040-1075 See MOBIL TRAVEL GUIDE. NORTHEAST. 5485

1040-1091 See PETERSON'S GRANTS FOR GRADUATE STUDY. 1840

1040-1105 See HANSEN REPORT ON AUTOMOTIVE ELECTRONICS, THE. 2056

1040-1121 See VOICE, THE. 2293

1040-113X See SAN FRANCISCO/BAY AREA POWER BOOK, THE. 2759

1040-1156 See DIRECTORY OF WOMEN'S MEDIA. 5554

1040-1237 See ANNALS OF CLINICAL PSYCHIATRY. 3920

1040-127X See ALMANAC OF FAMOUS PEOPLE. 429

1040-1296 See MAIL ORDER PRODUCT GUIDE. 691

1040-1334 See TEACHING AND LEARNING IN MEDICINE. 3644

1040-1342 See PRESS REPORT, THE. 3629

1040-1350 See UNDERSTANDING OUR GIFTED. 1886

1040-1369 See CQ AMATEUR RADIO ... BUYER'S GUIDE. 1130

1040-1377 See REGIONALE WEST. 307

1040-1423 See MID AMERICA FARMER GROWER, THE. 108

1040-1431 See SUPER SCIENCE (RED ED.). 4866

1040-144X See SUPER SCIENCE (BLUE ED.). 4866

1040-1466 See JOURNAL OF ESTHETIC DENTISTRY. 1327

1040-1482 See PRODUCTIVITY SOFTWARE. 1289

1040-1504 See LYONS DAILY NEWS (1929). 5677

1040-1512 See EPA COMPENDIUM OF REGISTERED PESTICIDES. VOLUME 1. HERBICIDES AND PLANT REGULATORS. 4244

1040-1520 See EPA COMPENDIUM OF REGISTERED PESTICIDES. VOLUME 2. FUNGICIDES AND NEMATICIDES. 4244

1040-1547 See MINORITY MBA. 695

1040-1555 See DIRECTORY OF NATIONAL ENVIRONMENTAL ORGANIZATIONS. 2164

1040-1571 See BIRMINGHAM POST-HERALD. 5625

1040-1598 See NIGERIAN FRONTLINE NEWS. 1118

1040-1628 See INFORMATION RESOURCES MANAGEMENT JOURNAL. 3216

1040-1636 See GOVERNMENT MICRO USER'S GUIDE, THE. 1267

1040-1644 See ELLIPSIS (LOS GATOS, CALIF.). 3384

1040-1679 See ENGINEERING HORIZONS (VAN NUYS, CALIF.). 1973

1040-1687 See WORLD MAP DIRECTORY, THE. 2583

1040-1725 See ENVIRONMENTAL HOTLINE. 2171

1040-1733 See DEBATES IN CLINICAL SURGERY. 3963

1040-1741 See YEAR BOOK OF ONCOLOGY. 3825

1040-175X See YEAR BOOK OF PLASTIC, RECONSTRUCTIVE, AND AESTHETIC SURGERY. 3977

1040-1784 See NORTHWEST PORTFOLIO. 2571

1040-1822 See PATHWAYS FOR YOUNG ADULTS. STUDENT. 4985

1040-1830 See PATHWAYS FOR YOUNG ADULTS. TEACHER. 4985

1040-1903 See COOKING EDGE, THE. 2332

1040-192X See SCIENCE FICTION & FANTASY BOOK REVIEW ANNUAL. 3434

1040-1938 See CHARIHO TIMES (1993), THE. 5741

1040-2004 See TRIBOLOGY TRANSACTIONS. 2000

1040-2012 See RLE CURRENTS. 1216

1040-2020 See BELLCORE EXCHANGE. 1150

1040-2047 See NEW DAY HERALD, THE. 4186

1040-2098 See TODAY'S AQUARIST (DEVON, CONN.). 4879

1040-211X See PUBLIC ART REVIEW. 362

1040-2136 See STRATEGIES (LOS ANGELES, CALIF.). 4497

1040-2152 See JOURNAL OF STONE DISEASE, THE. 3968

1040-2160 See LONG ISLAND MENTAL HEALTH CLINICIAN : JOURNAL OF CENTRAL NASSAU GUIDANCE & COUNSELING SERVICES, INC. 3930

1040-2179 See INFOCUS (PORTLAND, OR.). 870

1040-2217 See CONTEMPORARY PERSPECTIVES IN REHABILITATION. 3568

1040-2225 See ADVOCATE (DENVER, COLO.). 4285

1040-2241 See RUXTON REPORT, THE. 751

1040-2276 See FERGUSON FILES. 2448

1040-2284 See NATSO TRUCKERS NEWS. 5388

1040-2292 See LOS ANGELES THEATRE & ENTERTAINMENT REVIEW. 5365

1040-2306 See MEDICAL GROUP MANAGEMENT WASHINGTON REPORT. 3788

1040-2349 See ALABAMA MAGAZINE. 2527

1040-2365 See P / PURDUE UNIVERSITY, COOPERATIVE EXTENSION SERVICE. 217

1040-2373 See NURSING ... I.V. DRUG HANDBOOK. 3864

1040-2381 See LAKE AND RESERVOIR MANAGEMENT. 2235

1040-2411 See FISH AND WILDLIFE RESEARCH. 2193

1040-2446 See ACADEMIC MEDICINE. 1806

1040-2454 See JOURNAL OF COMPUTING IN TEACHER EDUCATION. 1897

1040-2489 See CLARKSVILLE TIMES, THE. 5748

1040-2497 See PRIMARY CARE REPORTS. 3629

1040-2519 See ANNUAL REVIEW OF PLANT PHYSIOLOGY AND PLANT MOLECULAR BIOLOGY. 500

1040-2527 See PLASTICS ENGINEERING (NEW YORK, N.Y.). 1990

1040-2608 See CURRENT PERSPECTIVES ON AGING AND THE LIFE CYCLE. 2278

1040-2616 See GUIDE TO COOKING SCHOOLS, THE. 2343

1040-2640 See CALIFORNIA PARALEGAL MAGAZINE. 2946

1040-2659 See PEACE REVIEW (PALO ALTO, CALIF.). 4531

1040-2748 See LOUISIANA SOCIAL STUDIES JOURNAL. 5208

1040-2756 See COMBUSTION (NEW YORK, N.Y. : 1989). 2112

1040-2772 See VIDEO TECHNOLOGY NEWSLETTER. 4378

1040-2802 See EMERGING TECHNOLOGIES (ALEXANDRIA, VA.). 4043

1040-2861 See JOURNAL OF MENTAL HEALTH COUNSELING. 5292

1040-2926 See NATIONAL ESTIMATOR. 2889

1040-2934 See INVESTAMERICA (SAN FRANCISCO, CALIF.). 902

1040-3019 See CHRISTO, EN. 4946

1040-3078 See RADIATION EMBRITTLEMENT. 4440

1040-3108 See CONCURRENCY (CHICHESTER, ENGLAND). 1180

1040-3124 See EARTH IN SPACE. 1404

1040-3140 See GOOD FOOD + FITNESS A WINNING LIFESTYLE. 2342

1040-3167 See STORYBOARD (ANAHEIM HILLS, CALIF.). 388

1040-3175 See LAGNIAPPE LETTER. 1637

1040-3183 See LAGNIAPPE QUARTERLY MONITOR. 1615

1040-3205 See FOCUSES (BOONE, N.C.). 2919

1040-3213 See SCIENTIFIC AMERICAN LIBRARY SERIES. 5155

1040-323X See MATURE INVESTOR, THE. 906

1040-3272 See EMBEDDED SYSTEMS PROGRAMMING. 1228

1040-3337 See STANDARD-TIMES (WAKEFIELD, R.I), THE. 5741

1040-3361 See SOVIET SCIENTIFIC REVIEWS SUPPLEMENT SERIES. PHYSIOLOGY AND GENERAL BIOLOGY. 587

1040-3396 See UNDERGRADUATE CHEMISTRY. 995

1040-340X See CGS NEWSLETTER. 2442

1040-3434 See RESTAURANT MANAGEMENT INSIDER. 5072

1040-3469 See LINK (ASHLAND, MASS.). 5295

1040-3485 See INVENT! (WOODLAND HILLS, CALIF.). 1305

1040-3507 See MOBIL TRAVEL GUIDE. WASHINGTON, D.C. 5485

1040-3558 See READING EDGE (CROWNSVILLE, MD.), THE. 3244

1040-3582 See OLD-TIME HERALD. 4143

1040-3590 See PSYCHOLOGICAL ASSESSMENT. 4610

1040-3612 See SYLLECTA CLASSICA. 1080

1040-3620 See SISKIYOU COUNTY (CA) SERIES. 2545

1040-3647 See CAHIERS DU DIX-SEPTIEME. 3371

1040-3663 See POWERBOAT REPORTS. 595

1040-3736 See LEISURE BEVERAGE INSIDER NEWSLETTER. 2369

1040-3760 See LIBERATOR (1988), THE. 5251

1040-3779 See WRITING LAB NEWSLETTER. 3334

1040-3957 See RESPONSE (LEBANON, PA.). 3634

1040-3965 See FOR THE LOVE OF CROSS STITCH. 5184

1040-3981 See JOURNAL OF FINANCIAL PLANNING (DENVER, COLO.). 794

1040-399X See CALHOUN CHRONICLE AND THE GRANTSVILLE NEWS, THE. 5763

1040-4023 See LICENSING JOURNAL, THE. 1616

1040-4066 See CORE MEDLINE/EBSCO CD-ROM. 3569

1040-4074 See COMPREHENSIVE MEDLINE/EBSCO CD-ROM. 3567

1040-4090 See ARIZONA ATTORNEY. 2936

1040-4163 See SUBSTANCE ABUSE REPORT (NEW YORK, N.Y.). 1349

1040-418X See TELECOMMUNICATIONS WEEK (NEW YORK, N.Y.). 1166

1040-4198 See JOB SAFETY CONSULTANT. 2864

1040-4201 See CORPORATE SECURITY (NEW YORK, N.Y.). 5176

1040-421X *See* CREATIVE MANAGEMENT (NEW YORK, N.Y.). **864**

1040-4228 *See* DRUGS IN THE WORKPLACE. **1344**

1040-4236 *See* SAFETY AND SECURITY FOR SUPERVISORS. **885**

1040-4252 *See* PERSONNEL POLICY BRIEFS. **945**

1040-4279 *See* ALBUQUERQUE MONTHLY. **2527**

1040-4287 *See* MAGICAL BLEND MAGAZINE. **4242**

1040-4309 *See* ADVANCES IN ENVIRONMENT, BEHAVIOR, AND DESIGN. **2159**

1040-4317 *See* CALIFORNIA ARCHITECTURE AND ARCHITECTS. **294**

1040-4333 *See* LIBRARY HI TECH BIBLIOGRAPHY. **3258**

1040-4384 *See* ADVANCES IN SERIALS MANAGEMENT. **3188**

1040-4430 *See* PROFESSIONAL GENEALOGISTS OF ARKANSAS NEWSLETTER. **2468**

1040-4449 *See* ADAMS CHRONICLE, THE. **1300**

1040-4457 *See* QUILTING TODAY. **5185**

1040-449X *See* AGGS NEWS VIEWS. **4811**

1040-4503 *See* NETWARE TECHNICAL JOURNAL. **1288**

1040-452X *See* MOLECULAR REPRODUCTION AND DEVELOPMENT. **541**

1040-4546 *See* FOODSERVICE OPERATORS GUIDE. **2341**

1040-4554 See CARIBBEAN DIGEST. **2258**

1040-4589 See PRIMARY CARE MEDICINE DRUG ALERTS. **4325**

1040-4651 *See* PLANT CELL, THE. **539**

1040-4694 *See* UPDATE - INTERNATIONAL COUNCIL FOR COMPUTERS IN EDUCATION (U.S.). **1225**

1040-4708 *See* SECRETARY'S LETTER (ENGLEWOOD, N.J.). **4209**

1040-4724 *See* SIGNAL (EMMETT, IDAHO), THE. **3437**

1040-4805 *See* GEORGIA REAL ESTATE LAW LETTER. **2974**

1040-4813 *See* GEORGIA EMPLOYMENT LAW LETTER. **3148**

1040-4821 *See* FAMILY FINDER (HEIDELBERG, GERMANY). **2447**

1040-483X *See* GESTOS (IRVINE, CALIF.). **5364**

1040-4848 *See* TRANSCRIPT. **1123**

1040-4872 *See* OHIO FACTS (DALLAS, TEX.). **2541**

1040-4880 *See* URBAN TRANSPORTATION MONITOR, THE. **5399**

1040-4937 *See* SHERLOCKIAN TIDBITS. **3436**

1040-4961 *See* MILITARY IMAGES. **4050**

1040-5003 *See* COMPUTER REVIEW INDEX. **1208**

1040-502X *See* JOURNAL OF TAXATION OF S CORPORATIONS, THE. **795**

1040-5038 *See* UNIX TODAY!. **1206**

1040-5054 *See* COMPOSITES IN MANUFACTURING. **3477**

1040-5119 *See* STUDIES IN SPECULATIVE FICTION. **3442**

1040-5208 *See* JOURNAL OF THE INTERNATIONAL ASSOCIATION OF ZOO EDUCATORS. **5589**

1040-5216 *See* WORLD BASEBALL MAGAZINE. **4930**

1040-5232 *See* HUMAN RESOURCES PROFESSIONAL (NEW YORK, N.Y.), THE. **942**

1040-5267 *See* IMPORTCAR & TRUCK. **5416**

1040-5313 *See* INDOOR AIR QUALITY UPDATE. **2606**

1040-5321 *See* CONCRETE TRADER, THE. **608**

1040-533X *See* QUEST (WHEATON, ILL.), THE. **4358**

1040-5372 *See* PUNISHER (NEW YORK, N.Y. 1987), THE. **4865**

1040-5380 *See* SOUTHEASTERN MASSACHUSETTS BUSINESS DIGEST. **712**

1040-5399 *See* LEADERSHIP FOR STUDENT ACTIVITIES. **1761**

1040-5402 *See* COMMUTER / REGIONAL AIRLINE NEWS. **5380**

1040-5410 *See* AIRLINE FINANCIAL NEWS. **10**

1040-5437 *See* NEWS FROM NATIVE CALIFORNIA. **2749**

1040-547X *See* HOME PLANNER. **616**

1040-5488 *See* OPTOMETRY AND VISION SCIENCE. **4217**

1040-550X *See* JOURNAL OF SOFTWARE MAINTENANCE. **1288**

1040-5518 *See* NEEDLEPOINT PLUS. **5185**

1040-5534 *See* PREMIUM CHANNELS TV BLUEPRINT. **1136**

1040-5542 *See* LOADSTAR 128 QUARTERLY. **1288**

1040-5631 *See* AMS STUDIES IN LIBRARY AND INFORMATION SCIENCE. **3189**

1040-5682 *See* AUTHORS & ARTISTS FOR YOUNG ADULTS. **3365**

1040-5704 *See* PEPTIDE RESEARCH. **1046**

1040-5712 *See* MENSAJERO (SAN FRANCISCO, CALIF.), EL. **2746**

1040-5763 *See* BEST AMERICAN POETRY, THE. **3460**

1040-5798 *See* SPORT PILOT HOT KITS & HOMEBUILTS. **36**

1040-5801 *See* SHIH TZU REPORTER, THE. **4288**

1040-581X *See* HERB COMPANION, THE. **2343**

1040-5828 *See* FACILITY ISSUES. **867**

1040-5852 *See* ADVANCES IN VLSI SERIES. **4396**

1040-5879 See AUGUSTA (AUGUSTA, GA.). **2722**

1040-5917 *See* LAN TIMES. **1242**

1040-5992 *See* MHQ (NEW YORK, N.Y.). **4049**

1040-600X *See* SUCCESSFUL HOTEL MARKETER, THE. **2809**

1040-6018 *See* AIBC BULLETIN. **1419**

1040-6026 *See* ENVIRONMENTAL CLAIMS JOURNAL. **3111**

1040-6042 *See* C++ REPORT, THE. **1278**

1040-6050 *See* RT (LOS ANGELES, CALIF.). **3952**

1040-6077 *See* OSAGE COUNTY CHRONICLE (BURLINGAME, KAN. : 1983). **5678**

1040-6093 *See* NEWS 3X/400. **1238**

1040-6123 *See* TV PROGRAM STATS. **1141**

1040-6166 *See* QUALITY ASSURANCE IN HEALTH CARE. **4797**

1040-6182 *See* QUATERNARY INTERNATIONAL. **1393**

1040-6190 *See* ELECTRICITY JOURNAL, THE. **4761**

1040-6212 *See* HOBBY GREENHOUSE. **2418**

1040-6247 *See* AIDS UPDATES. **3665**

1040-6255 *See* HOMILETICS (NORTH CANTON, OHIO). **4963**

1040-6263 *See* HOSPITAL STRATEGY REPORT. **3785**

1040-628X *See* INDIA TIMES (LOS GATOS, CALIF.). **5203**

1040-6328 *See* BROWN UNIVERSITY DIGEST OF ADDICTION THEORY AND APPLICATION. **1341**

1040-6344 *See* BOOK/LOS ANGELES, THE. **4824**

1040-6352 *See* IDEAS & INFORMATION ABOUT DEVELOPMENT EDUCATION. **1751**

1040-6360 *See* BUSINESS JOURNAL OF UPPER EAST TENNESSEE AND SOUTHWEST VIRGINIA. **650**

1040-6387 *See* JOURNAL OF VETERINARY DIAGNOSTIC INVESTIGATION. **5514**

1040-6395 *See* DUN'S DIRECTORY OF SERVICE COMPANIES. **1605**

1040-6433 *See* HEURISTICS (ROCKVILLE, MD.). **1229**

1040-6441 *See* STUDIES IN THE DEVELOPMENT OF MODERN MATHEMATICS. **3537**

1040-6484 *See* PC TODAY. **1271**

1040-6506 *See* ARKANSAS BAPTIST (1987). **5055**

1040-6514 *See* HARPER HERALD (HARPER, TEX. 1917), THE. **5750**

1040-6522 *See* ATHENS DAILY REVIEW. **5746**

1040-6557 *See* SINGLE DAD'S MAGAZINE. **2286**

1040-6565 *See* TML TEXAS TOWN & CITY. **4691**

1040-659X *See* CATECHUMENATE (CHICAGO, ILL.). **4942**

1040-6611 *See* ENVIRONMENT & ART LETTER. **349**

1040-6638 *See* POLYCYCLIC AROMATIC COMPOUNDS. **988**

1040-6646 *See* ONLINE HOTLINE NEWS SERVICE. **1197**

1040-676X *See* CHRONICLE OF PHILANTHROPY, THE. **4335**

1040-6778 *See* AIDS SCAN. **3664**

1040-6794 *See* ALLIANCE LIFE. **4933**

1040-6867 *See* INSURANCE MARKETING INSIDER. **2884**

1040-6883 *See* VICTORIA (NEW YORK, N.Y.). **5567**

1040-6921 *See* INTERNATIONAL INVESTOR'S DIRECTORY. **902**

1040-6948 *See* NIELSEN MARKETING TRENDS (ENGLISH ED.). **934**

1040-6964 *See* ALBANY PRESERVATION REPORT. **2718**

1040-6972 *See* VICTORIA'S ERA. **2632**

1040-6999 *See* MUSEUM STORE. **4092**

1040-7022 *See* MOBILE DATA REPORT. **1242**

1040-7030 *See* RESTAURANT WINE. **5073**

1040-7057 *See* YOUR PERSONAL BEST. **4622**

1040-7065 *See* BUYER'S GUIDE TO MEDICAL TOYS & BOOKS FOR TODDLERS THROUGH TEENS. **2583**

1040-7073 *See* SOVIET TECHNOLOGY REVIEWS. SECTION C, WELDING AND SURFACING REVIEWS. **4027**

1040-7081 *See* CAS BIOTECH UPDATES. ENZYMES IN BIOTECHNOLOGY. **3690**

1040-709X *See* CAS BIOTECH UPDATES. CELL & TISSUE CULTURE. **3690**

1040-7103 *See* CAS BIOTECH UPDATES. PRODUCT PURIFICATION & SEPARATION. **1021**

1040-7111 *See* CA SELECTS: AIDS & RELATED IMMUNODEFICIENCIES. **997**

1040-712X *See* CA SELECTS: CHEMICAL ENGINEERING OPERATIONS. **999**

1040-7138 *See* CA SELECTS: CHEMILUMINESCENCE. **999**

1040-7146 *See* CA SELECTS: CHEMISTRY OF IR, OS, RH, & RU. **999**

1040-7154 *See* CA SELECTS: COMPOSITE MATERIALS (POLYMERIC). **1000**

1040-7162 *See* CA SELECTS: DRUG DELIVERY SYSTEMS & DOSAGE FORMS. **1001**

1040-7170 *See* CA SELECTS: OXIDATION CATALYSTS. **1006**

1040-7189 *See* CA SELECTS: ORGANOSULFUR CHEMISTRY (JOURNALS). **1006**

1040-7197 *See* CA SELECTS: MEMBRANE SEPARATION. **1005**

1040-7200 *See* CA SELECTS: PAPER CHEMISTRY. **1007**

1040-7219 *See* CA SELECTS: OXIDE SUPERCONDUCTORS. **1006**

1040-726X *See* EDUCATIONAL PSYCHOLOGY REVIEW. **4586**

1040-7278 *See* JOURNAL OF CLUSTER SCIENCE. **981**

1040-7286 *See* JOURNAL OF COMPUTER-ASSISTED MICROSCOPY. **1223**

1040-7294 *See* JOURNAL OF DYNAMICS AND DIFFERENTIAL EQUATIONS. **3512**

1040-7308 *See* NEUROPSYCHOLOGY REVIEW. **3842**

1040-7316 *See* 9-1-1 MAGAZINE. **1103**

1040-7340 *See* PAS MEMO. **2830**

1040-7359 *See* HAWORTH SERIES ON WOMEN. **5558**

1040-7383 *See* SEMINARS IN SPINE SURGERY. **3974**

1040-7391 *See* DIFFERENCES (BLOOMINGTON, IND.). **5554**

1040-7405 *See* BOOTBLACK (BOYNTON BEACH, FLA.). **3368**

1040-7413 *See* ECOLOGICAL PSYCHOLOGY. **4585**

1040-7421 *See* MERIDIAN - MAP & GEOGRAPHY ROUND TABLE (AMERICAN LIBRARY ASSOCIATION). **2582**

1040-7448 *See* LIGHT OF CONSCIOUSNESS. **4973**

1040-7464 *See* WHO'S WHO OF AMERICAN HIGH SCHOOL BASKETBALL COACHES. **4929**

1040-7472 *See* WORKSTATION REPORT, THE. **4214**

1040-7480 *See* PROFILES IN HEALTHCARE MARKETING. **935**

1040-7537 *See* F & B MARKETPLACE. **924**

1040-757X *See* FANTASY FRONTIERS. **373**

1040-7588 *See* INTERNATIONAL MEDICAL TRIBUNE SYNDICATE. **3589**

1040-760X See HIGH SCHOOL WRITER, THE. **2920**

1040-7618 See BRICKER'S INTERNATIONAL DIRECTORY. VOL. 2, SHORT-TERM UNIVERSITY-BASED EXECUTIVE PROGRAMS. **862**

1040-7650 *See* ASSISTANTSHIPS AND GRADUATE FELLOWSHIPS IN THE MATHEMATICAL SCIENCES. **1810**

1040-7669 *See* SPECTROSCOPY INTERNATIONAL. **993**

1040-7685 *See* JOURNAL OF MICROCOLUMN SEPARATIONS, THE. **981**

1040-7707 *See* SCHOOL MATES. **4866**

1040-7758 *See* BLACK ALUMNI NETWORK NEWSLETTER. **1101**

1040-7782 *See* NUMERICAL HEAT TRANSFER. PART A, APPLICATIONS. **4432**

1040-7790 *See* NUMERICAL HEAT TRANSFER. PART B, FUNDAMENTALS. **4432**

1040-7804 *See* WHO'S WHO IN THE FISH INDUSTRY, CANADA. **2316**

1040-7812 *See* ART & ACADEME. **337**

1040-7820 *See* COAL (CHICAGO, ILL. : 1988). **2137**

1040-7847 *See* JOURNAL OF THEORETICAL GRAPHICS AND COMPUTING. **1234**

1040-788X *See* TRACES OF INDIANA AND MIDWESTERN HISTORY. **2763**

1040-7898 *See* GENERAL SURGERY REPORT. **3965**

1040-7901 *See* EMERGENCY PHYSICIAN REPORT. **3574**

1040-791X *See* INFECTIOUS DISEASE REPORT. **4784**

1040-7928 *See* LITERATURE AND THE SCIENCES OF MAN. **3407**

1040-7936 *See* MARYLAND MAGAZINE (1988). **2745**

1040-7952 *See* ADVANCES IN SECOND MESSENGER AND PHOSPHOPROTEIN RESEARCH. **577**

1040-8061 *See* PUNTOS. **5214**

1040-807X *See* FACEPLATE. **4176**

1040-8088 See CHRISTIAN PARENTING TODAY. **2278**

1040-8126 *See* IDEA TODAY. **1313**

1040-8134 *See* JOY OF HERBS, THE. **2422**

1040-8142 *See* TRAVEL AND TOURISM INDEX, THE. **5495**

1040-8150 *See* VERANDA (ATLANTA, GA.). **2903**

1040-8169 *See* P-O-P TIMES. **763**

1040-8207 *See* AMERICAN JOURNAL OF GERMANIC LINGUISTICS AND LITERATURES. **3263**

1040-8223 *See* MINE REGULATION REPORTER. **3010**

1040-8231 *See* ASIA TIMES (LOS GATOS, CALIF.). **2501**

1040-824X *See* ANNUAL REVIEW OF OCEAN AFFAIRS--LAW & POLICY, MAIN DOCUMENTS. **3123**

1040-8258 *See* FULLTEXT SOURCES ONLINE. **3211**

1040-8290 *See* SUPER BMX & FREESTYLE. **429**

1040-8304 *See* BIOPHARM (EUGENE, OR.). **4293**

1040-8347 *See* CRITICAL REVIEWS IN ANALYTICAL CHEMISTRY. **1014**

1040-8363 *See* CRITICAL REVIEWS IN CLINICAL LABORATORY SCIENCES. **3894**

1040-8371 *See* CRITICAL REVIEWS IN DIAGNOSTIC IMAGING. **3940**

1040-838X *See* CRITICAL REVIEWS IN ENVIRONMENTAL CONTROL. **2163**

1040-8398 *See* CRITICAL REVIEWS IN FOOD SCIENCE AND NUTRITION. **2332**

1040-8401 *See* CRITICAL REVIEWS IN IMMUNOLOGY. **3668**

1040-841X *See* CRITICAL REVIEWS IN MICROBIOLOGY. **561**

1040-8428 *See* CRITICAL REVIEWS IN ONCOLOGY/HEMATOLOGY. **3815**

1040-8436 *See* CRITICAL REVIEWS IN SOLID STATE AND MATERIALS SCIENCES. **4401**

1040-8444 *See* CRITICAL REVIEWS IN TOXICOLOGY. **3980**

1040-8460 *See* MARKETING RESEARCH (CHICAGO, ILL.). **932**

1040-8479 *See* KEY INTERVENTIONAL RADIOLOGY. **3943**

1040-8495 *See* FOREFRONT (COLUMBUS, OHIO). **4215**

1040-8509 *See* AIRBRUSH ACTION. **369**

1040-8517 *See* NEWSLETTER / ASIAN/PACIFIC AMERICAN LIBRARIANS ASSOCIATION. **3235**

1040-8541 *See* VOYAGER INTERNATIONAL. **2579**

1040-8576 *See* M/E/A/N/I/N/G (NEW YORK, N.Y.). **324**

1040-8584 *See* HOLINESS DIGEST. **4963**

1040-8622 *See* CHRISTIAN IRELAND TODAY. **4945**

1040-869X *See* CURRENT OPINION IN RADIOLOGY. **3940**

1040-8703 *See* CURRENT OPINION IN PEDIATRICS. **3902**

1040-8711 *See* CURRENT OPINION IN RHEUMATOLOGY. **3804**

1040-8720 *See* EUROFISH REPORT. **2300**

1040-872X *See* CURRENT OPINION IN OBSTETRICS & GYNECOLOGY. **3759**

1040-8738 *See* CURRENT OPINION IN OPHTHALMOLOGY. **3874**

1040-8746 *See* CURRENT OPINION IN ONCOLOGY. **3815**

1040-8754 *See* PM NET WORK, THE. **882**

1040-8800 *See* JOURNAL OF PROSTHETICS AND ORTHOTICS. **3597**

1040-8827 *See* CEREBROVASCULAR AND BRAIN METABOLISM REVIEWS. **3562**

1040-886X *See* STRATEGY & TACTICS (CAMBRIA, CALIF.). **4058**

1040-8878 *See* DIESEL PROGRESS ENGINES & DRIVES. **2112**

1040-8886 *See* CHALLENGER (BUFFALO, N.Y.), THE. **5714**

1040-8908 *See* NEW DANCE REVIEW, THE. **1314**

1040-8924 *See* DATA DISPENSER. **1819**

1040-8932 *See* DESKTOP PUBLISHING DIGEST. **4813**

1040-8959 *See* RAM RESEARCH BANKCARD UPDATE. **806**

1040-8991 *See* UNIVERSITY PRESS BOOK NEWS. **427**

1040-9009 *See* WATER RESOURCES ABSTRACTS (COLLEGE PARK, MD.). **5544**

1040-9017 *See* BOURBON TIMES (PARIS, KY.). **5679**

1040-9033 *See* OSBORNE COUNTY FARMER (OSBORNE, KAN. : 1958). **5678**

1040-9068 *See* MODERN SHORT STORIES. **3412**

1040-9076 *See* FOOD INDUSTRY REPORT. **2337**

1040-9122 See CITIZEN PARTICIPATION (CLEVELAND, OHIO). **4717**

1040-9165 *See* DIABETES SPECTRUM. **3728**

1040-9203 *See* CONNECTICUT ENVIRONMENT. **2163**

1040-9238 *See* CRITICAL REVIEWS IN BIOCHEMISTRY AND MOLECULAR BIOLOGY. **486**

1040-9246 *See* CREDIT UNION DIRECTOR. **785**

1040-9254 *See* BAKING & SNACK SYSTEMS. **2328**

1040-9270 *See* NBC BRIEF. **4052**

1040-9289 *See* EARLY EDUCATION AND DEVELOPMENT. **1737**

1040-9335 *See* REAL PEOPLE. **2544**

1040-936X *See* FROMMER'S CHICAGO. **5475**

1040-9378 *See* FROMMER'S COMPREHENSIVE TRAVEL GUIDE. BELGIUM, HOLLAND & LUXEMBOURG. **5475**

1040-9386 *See* FROMMER'S CALIFORNIA WITH KIDS. **5475**

1040-9394 *See* FROMMER'S DOLLARWISE SOUTHEAST ASIA. **5477**

1040-9408 See FROMMER'S COMPREHENSIVE TRAVEL GUIDE. AUSTRALIA. **5475**

1040-9416 *See* BT CATALYST. **3690**

1040-9467 *See* FIRST FOR WOMEN. **5557**

1040-9483 *See* EUGENE O'NEILL REVIEW, THE. **3386**

1040-9513 *See* FELL'S GUIDE TO COLLEGE MONEY FOR THE ASKING IN FLORIDA. **1824**

1040-9556 *See* RESEARCH ON NEGOTIATION IN ORGANIZATIONS. **884**

1040-9564 *See* JOURNAL OF JASTRO : THE OFFICIAL JOURNAL OF THE JAPANESE SOCIETY FOR THERAPEUTIC RADIOLOGY AND ONCOLOGY, THE. **3819**

1040-9599 *See* MONOGRAPHS IN INTERNATIONAL STUDIES. SOUTHEAST ASIA SERIES. **2659**

1040-9602 *See* JOURNAL FOR QUALITY AND PARTICIPATION, THE. **1681**

1040-9645 *See* COMPETITIVE INTELLIGENCER. **659**

1040-967X *See* METAL STAMPING. **4027**

1040-9718 *See* PLC INSIDER'S NEWSLETTER, THE. **1265**

1040-9912 *See* INTERNATIONAL LOW VISION DIRECTORY. **3875**

1040-9920 *See* CASINOS : THE INTERNATIONAL CASINO GUIDE. **4858**

1040-9955 See SCRAPE (PHOENIX, ARIZ.). **2545**

1041-0023 *See* ENCYCLOPEDIA OF ASSOCIATIONS. INTERNATIONAL ORGANIZATIONS. **1925**

1041-0031 *See* INFORMATION STANDARDS QUARTERLY. **3217**

1041-004X *See* ADVANCES IN PARENTERAL SCIENCES. **4289**

1041-0058 *See* IN SERVICE REVIEWS IN RESPIRATORY THERAPY. **3949**

1041-0082 *See* IN SERVICE REVIEWS IN RADIOLOGIC TECHNOLOGY. **3942**

1041-0090 *See* IN SERVICE REVIEWS IN NUCLEAR MEDICINE. **3848**

1041-0104 *See* IN SERVICE REVIEWS IN DIAGNOSTIC MEDICAL SONOGRAPHY. **3586**

1041-0120 *See* SOYA WORLD. **136**

1041-0139 *See* ... AMERICAN-JEWISH MEDIA DIRECTORY, THE. **755**

1041-0228 *See* PROBLEMS IN VETERINARY MEDICINE. **5518**

1041-0236 *See* HEALTH COMMUNICATION. **4779**

1041-0244 See BRIEFING (SHAWNEE MISSION, KAN.). **5193**

1041-0260 *See* CALIFORNIA SALES GUIDE TO HIGH-TECH COMPANIES. **5092**

1041-0376 *See* GAME PLAYER'S NINTENDO BUYER'S GUIDE. **4861**

1041-0384 *See* JOURNAL OF VISION REHABILITATION (LINCOLN, NEB.). **3876**

1041-0392 *See* ACCOUNTING EDUCATORS' JOURNAL, THE. **736**

1041-0406 *See* EARTH ISLAND JOURNAL. **2164**

1041-0422 *See* DESIGN TIMES. **2899**

1041-052X *See* ELECTRO MANUFACTURING. **3478**

1041-0651 *See* RESCUE MAGAZINE. **4799**

1041-0708 *See* STORYQUARTERLY (NORTHBROOK, ILL.). **3440**

1041-0716 *See* MICROSCOPE TECHNOLOGY & NEWS. **573**

ISSN Index

1041-0740 See VERDICTS, SETTLEMENTS & TACTICS. 3070

1041-0759 See CROCHET WORLD SPECIAL. 5183

1041-0791 See PLASTICSBRIEF. INJECTION MOLDING NEWSLETTER. 4459

1041-0805 See PLASTICS BRIEF/ REINFORCED PLASTICS NEWSLETTER. 4457

1041-0813 See PLASTICS BRIEF/ EXTRUSION AND BLOW MOLDING NEWSLETTER. 4457

1041-0821 See PLASTICS BRIEF/ DESIGN AND MATERIALS NEWSLETTER. 4457

1041-083X See PLASTICS BRIEF/ THERMOPLASTIC MARKETING NEWSLETTER. 4457

1041-0857 See PRACTICAL WIRELESS. 1136

1041-0864 See MINORITY BUSINESS REVIEW (HEMPSTEAD, N.Y.). 695

1041-0872 See BALTIMORE MESSENGER (1985), THE. 5685

1041-0880 See OWINGS MILLS TIMES. 5686

1041-0945 See FREE LUNCH. 3463

1041-0961 See MORAVIAN (1989), THE. 4979

1041-102X See AD ASTRA (WASHINGTON, D.C.) 3

1041-1135 See IEEE PHOTONICS TECHNOLOGY LETTERS. 4435

1041-1151 See MAGAZINE ARTICLE SUMMARIES (CD-ROM ED.). 2497

1041-116X See COMPARATIVE PATHOLOGY BULLETIN. 3894

1041-1232 See GROWTH, DEVELOPMENT, AND AGING. 456

1041-1240 See CANADIAN ANCESTRAL TIES. 2441

1041-1275 See AURORA ADVERTISER (AURORA, MO. : 1914), THE. 5702

1041-1291 See WISCONSIN WOODS & WATER. 4881

1041-1305 See CERAMICS MAGAZINE. 2588

1041-1321 See INDEX AND ABSTRACT DIRECTORY, THE. 3258

1041-1380 See RHODE ISLAND MONTHLY. 5490

1041-1410 See SCIENCE WORLD (1987). 5154

1041-1453 See TAA REPORT. 4832

1041-1488 See JOB TRAINING AND PLACEMENT REPORT. 872

1041-1534 See WASHINGTON POST INDEX (ANN ARBOR, MICH.). 5694

1041-1569 See TENNESSEE REGISTER, THE. 5746

1041-1585 See APPRAISAL REVIEW & MORTGAGE UNDERWRITING JOURNAL. 4834

1041-1615 See WALT DISNEY'S MICKEY & DONALD. 4867

1041-1658 See COLUMBIA BASIN HERALD. 5760

1041-1666 See UTAH FARMER-STOCKMAN. 143

1041-1674 See MONTANA FARMER-STOCKMAN. 216

1041-1682 See IDAHO FARMER-STOCKMAN. 212

1041-1712 See CORPORATE TRENDTRAC. 662

1041-1747 See NORTH CAROLINA LAWYERS WEEKLY. 3018

1041-1763 See ACCESSIONS LIST, BRAZIL AND URUGUAY. 406

1041-178X See PARENT & CHILD. 2284

1041-1798 See KIDSCIENCE (MANKATO, MINN.). 1804

1041-1801 See FEMINISMS (COLUMBUS, OHIO). 5556

1041-1860 See HENINGER/NOELL WEEKLY M&A "GREEN SHEET", THE. 790

1041-1887 See MIZZOU INTERNATIONAL DIRECTORY. 1836

1041-1933 See FILM & VIDEO (LOS ANGELES, CALIF.). 4069

1041-1968 See DAKOTA OUTDOORS. 4871

1041-2018 See SCHAU INS LAND. SOUND RECORDING. 2522

1041-2050 See PLASTICS MATERIALS. ADHESIVES. 1056

1041-2115 See J.K. LASSER'S PERSONAL INVESTMENT ANNUAL. 904

1041-2166 See CABINET MANUFACTURING & FABRICATIONS. 3476

1041-2174 See HERE'S HELP (RENO, NEV.). 5287

1041-2182 See RT IMAGE. 3946

1041-2212 See BESTIA (KIRKSVILLE, MO.). 3366

1041-2255 See CABELL RECORD. 5763

1041-2271 See FAMILY PRACTICE NEWSLETTER, THE. 3576

1041-2344 See ASHRAE HANDBOOK. HEATING, VENTILATING, AND AIR-CONDITIONING SYSTEMS AND EQUIPMENT. 2603

1041-2344 See ASHRAE HANDBOOK. 2603

1041-2352 See GREAT IDEAS FOR LONG TERM CARE. 3579

1041-2360 See CHIROPRACTIC PRODUCTS. 3563

1041-2379 See SOUTHWEST TECHNOLOGY REPORT. 2082

1041-2433 See JOURNAL OF THE MUSEUM OF FINE ARTS, BOSTON. 4090

1041-245X See APPLIED VIROLOGY RESEARCH. 559

1041-2492 See PIANO STYLIST & JAZZ WORKSHOP, THE. 4146

1041-2506 See FLOOR COVERING BUSINESS. 2905

1041-2514 See SOUTH AMBOY CITIZEN (SOUTH AMBOY, N.J. 1884), THE. 5711

1041-2530 See AT&T DATALINE. 1149

1041-2549 See FOCUS (AUSTIN, TEX. 1989). 1185

1041-2573 See EXEMPLARIA (BINGHAMTON, N.Y.). 3386

1041-2581 See ASSEMBLY (WEST POINT, N.Y.). 1101

1041-2638 See MACRAE'S STATE INDUSTRIAL DIRECTORY. CONNECTICUT, RHODE ISLAND. 1616

1041-2654 See CALIFORNIA REGULATORY NOTICE REGISTER. 2946

1041-2662 See ISLANDER (GULF SHORES, ALA.), THE. 5627

1041-2697 See GIS FORUM, THE. 3212

1041-2700 See WETA (WASHINGTON, D.C.). 1143

1041-2719 See PACIFIC FARMER-STOCKMAN. 118

1041-2727 See PACIFIC FARMER-STOCKMAN. 118

1041-2735 See ROTORCRAFT (CLINTON, LA.). 34

1041-2743 See INTERNATIONAL JOURNAL OF FINANCE, THE. 4732

1041-2778 See ILLINOIS FACTS. 1926

1041-2786 See JUST HORSIN' AROUND. 2800

1041-2808 See JOURNAL OF MANAGEMENT SYSTEMS, THE. 943

1041-2824 See SPACE NUCLEAR POWER SYSTEMS. 36

1041-2832 See SICKNESS & WELLNESS PUBLICATIONS. 3641

1041-2840 See RESTAURANT INDEX. 5072

1041-2859 See INDEX TO THE SPORTING NEWS. 4899

1041-2875 See GARDENER'S EYE, THE. 2415

1041-2891 See TIME TABLE OF HISTORY. SCIENCE AND INNOVATION. 715

1041-2905 See JOURNAL OF ESSENTIAL OIL RESEARCH, THE. 1026

1041-2913 See ENGINEERING INDEX BIOENGINEERING AND BIOTECHNOLOGY ABSTRACTS. 2004

1041-2921 See HOXIE SENTINEL (HOXIE, KAN. : 1931). 5676

1041-293X See TELEGRAPH HERALD (1935). 5673

1041-2956 See CDMARC SUBJECTS. 3201

1041-2956 See CDMARC SUBJECTS. 3201

1041-2964 See CDMARC NAMES. 1174

1041-2972 See JOURNAL OF THE AMERICAN ACADEMY OF NURSE PRACTITIONERS. 3860

1041-3030 See CONTEMPORARY SSOCIAL PSYCHOLOGY. 4582

1041-3073 See SITE SELECTION & INDUSTRIAL DEVELOPMENT. 4847

1041-3081 See CROWLEY REVIEW. 2332

1041-3111 See 13TH STREET JOURNAL, THE. 311

1041-3138 See AMERICAN RODDER. 5403

1041-3146 See TATTOO (AGOURA HILLS, CALIF.). 2493

1041-3170 See WALT DISNEY'S DONALD DUCK ADVENTURES. 4867

1041-3200 See JOURNAL OF APPLIED SPORT PSYCHOLOGY. 4594

1041-3235 See AMERICAN CLINICAL LABORATORY. 3548

1041-3243 See PBI EXCHANGE. 5300

1041-3324 See BRANCH FOUR. 4517

1041-3405 See INTERNATIONAL LAW PRACTICUM. 3130

1041-3456 See BLUE RIDGE COUNTRY. 2529

1041-3480 See PATHOLOGY (PHILADELPHIA, PA.). 3897

1041-3499 See ADOLESCENT MEDICINE (PHILADELPHIA, PA.). 3546

1041-3510 See HOMEOWNER'S GUIDE TO GLASS, THE. 2591

1041-3529 See WORLD OF WINNERS. 1124

1041-3537 See FLORIDA EMPLOYMENT LAW LETTER. 3148

1041-3545 See JOURNAL OF MEDICAL HUMANITIES, THE. 3596

1041-3553 See COUNTRY FORECASTS. 1472

1041-3642 See TRAVEL SOUTH (1989). 2548

1041-3669 See BULL'S EYE (LYNBROOK, N.Y.). 2917

1041-3707 See NEW BUSINESS OPPORTUNITIES (IRVINE, CALIF.). 698

1041-3782 See POPULAR STATISTICS. 3527

1041-3839 See ISSUES & VIEWS. 2264

1041-3855 See INTERNATIONAL QUARTERLY (CHESTERLAND, OHIO). 3100

1041-3863 See ENVIRONMENTAL COUNSELOR, THE. 3111

1041-3871 See CORPORATE ANALYST, THE. 3098

1041-388X See AQUA (DULUTH, MINN.). 2810

1041-3928 See CHINESE COMPARATIST. 3374

1041-3936 See BLUE SWAN REVIEW : GUIDE TO WOMEN'S FASHION CATALOGS, THE. 1082

1041-3944 See INTERNATIONAL THIRD WORLD STUDIES JOURNAL & REVIEW. 4526

1041-3952 See JOURNAL OF PROPRIETARY RIGHTS, THE. 2989

1041-4010 See BRITISH TRAVEL LETTER. 5465

1041-4029 See PATRIOT (HARRISBURG, PA. : DAILY). 5738

1041-4037 See WEST COAST STUDIES. 4560

1041-4231 See AIRPORT MANAGEMENT. 10

1041-4231 See AIRPORT BUSINESS. 637

1041-4258 See TUFF STUFF. 2779

1041-4282 See SERVICE MANUAL. CAMARO. 5425

1041-4290 See DOMESTIC CARS SERVICE & REPAIR. 5413

1041-4320 See IMAGING TECHNOLOGY REPORT. 1277

1041-4347 See IEEE TRANSACTIONS ON KNOWLEDGE AND DATA ENGINEERING. 2063

1041-4460 See LEADER (ANDERSON, IND.). 4973

1041-4487 See ACQUIRED IMMUNE DEFICIENCY SYNDROME NEWSLETTER. 3662

1041-4541 See INTERNATIONAL SATELLITE DIRECTORY. 1113

1041-4657 See ZOOLOGICAL RECORD SERIAL SOURCES. 5602

1041-4665 See INTERNATIONAL ENVIRONMENTAL AFFAIRS. 2195

1041-4673 See JOURNAL OF MANUFACTURING, THE. 3482

1041-469X See D.C. TRACTS. 3804

1041-4703 See PETERSEN'S FISHING. 4912

1041-4746 See RAILROAD TEN-YEAR TRENDS. 5435

1041-4754 See PRESS-REPUBLICAN. 5720

1041-4762 See FISH & GAME HIGHLIGHTS. 4872
1041-4770 See BCS UPDATE. 1171
1041-4789 See UPDATE (ANNAPOLIS, MD.). 3069
1041-4797 See JOURNAL OF PROPERTY TAXATION. 4734
1041-4800 See NEW ENGLAND RUNNER. 4907
1041-4827 See COMMUNITY EDUCATION RESEARCH DIGEST. 1733
1041-4851 See THEMA (METAIRIE, LA.). 3446
1041-4886 See FEDERAL POET, THE. 3463
1041-4959 See CARING PEOPLE (WASHINGTON, D.C.). 2844
1041-5017 See RADIO FINANCIAL REPORT / NAB. 1137
1041-5041 See DRUG INTERACTION PROGRAM FOR IBM-PC AND COMPATIBLES. 4300
1041-5114 See LOYOLA CONSUMER LAW REPORTER. 3004
1041-5130 See ASBESTOS PROPERTY LITIGATION REPORTER. 599
1041-5173 See DBMS (REDWOOD CITY, CALIF.). 1254
1041-5203 See TRAVEL LEISURE & ENTERTAINMENT NEWS MEDIA. 5496
1041-5211 See DIRECTORY OF THEATRE TRAINING PROGRAMS. 5363
1041-5289 See ROUNDUP QUARTERLY, THE. 3432
1041-5335 See AFGE GOVERNMENT STANDARD. 4701
1041-536X See ACLS OCCASIONAL PAPER. 2841
1041-5378 See AUDIO/VIDEO INTERIORS. 5315
1041-5394 See ALGEBRA, LOGIC AND APPLICATIONS. 3491
1041-5416 See HIGH SPEED DIESELS & DRIVES. 5416
1041-5424 See GAME PLAYER'S MS-DOS STRATEGY GUIDE. 1185
1041-5440 See DIO (BALTIMORE, MD.). 395
1041-5459 See GUIDE TO GRANTS & FELLOWSHIPS IN LINGUISTICS. 3284
1041-5483 See EARTHQUEST (BOULDER, COLO.). 1355
1041-5505 See RESEARCH REPORT - HEALTH EFFECTS INSTITUTE. 2242
1041-553X See HOSTA JOURNAL : A PUBLICATION OF THE AMERICAN HOSTA SOCIETY, THE. 513
1041-5548 See GEORGETOWN JOURNAL OF LEGAL ETHICS, THE. 2974
1041-5564 See DANCEBAG (NORMAN, OKLA.). 1312
1041-5572 See DIRECTORY OF LEADING PRIVATE COMPANIES, INCLUDING CORPORATE AFFILIATIONS. 666
1041-5602 See WORLD AQUACULTURE. 2316
1041-5610 See PRO (FORT ATKINSON, WIS.). 2428
1041-5653 See NATIONAL INFORMATION STANDARDS SERIES. 3233
1041-5718 See DISABILITY STUDIES QUARTERLY : DSQ. 4387
1041-5726 See COMMUNITY COLLEGE WEEK. 1817
1041-5734 See MOTORCYCLE TOURING. 5485
1041-5742 See CAPITAL SPORTS FOCUS. 4889
1041-5769 See WALNUT COUNCIL BULLETIN. 2398
1041-5793 See I.D. CHECKING GUIDE. 4655
1041-5858 See RESEARCH IN MICROPOLITICS. 4493
1041-5866 See HUMAN RIGHTS BULLETIN (BERKELEY, CALIF.). 4508
1041-5882 See REVIEW OF PSYCHIATRY. 3935
1041-5904 See LABOR'S HERITAGE. 1685
1041-5963 See NEWSLETTER - AMERICAN COUNCIL OF LEARNED SOCIETIES. 5234
1041-5971 See NEWS. 1694
1041-6048 See STAGES (NORWOOD, N.J.). 5369
1041-6072 See HEALTH TECHNOLOGY TRENDS. 3583

1041-6080 See LEARNING AND INDIVIDUAL DIFFERENCES. 1761
1041-6099 See ASSESSMENT UPDATE. 1810
1041-6102 See INTERNATIONAL PSYCHOGERIATRICS / IPA. 3752
1041-6129 See MILITARY TOWN AND INSTALLATION. 4051
1041-6137 See BUSINESS TELECOMMUNICATIONS DIRECTORY. 1150
1041-6145 See EUROPE 1992. 1489
1041-617X See ANIMATION MAGAZINE. 4063
1041-6196 See CUED SPEECH CENTER LINES. 4386
1041-6226 See CUED SPEECH ANNUAL. 3276
1041-6234 See ON CUE. 1770
1041-6250 See WATKINS REVIEW & EXPRESS, THE. 5722
1041-6277 See NEW CHOICES FOR THE BEST YEARS. 5180
1041-6323 See PA TIMES. 4672
1041-6331 See DIRECTORY OF PUBLIC ELEMENTARY AND SECONDARY EDUCATION AGENCIES. 1736
1041-6366 See MUSKY HUNTER MAGAZINE. 4875
1041-6374 See YALE JOURNAL OF LAW & THE HUMANITIES. 3076
1041-6390 See INSTALLMENT CREDIT REPORT. 791
1041-6447 See EDUCATION REPORTS (WASHINGTON, D.C.). 1740
1041-6501 See MEDICAL STAFF LEADER. 3611
1041-6544 See PENNY STOCK INSIGHT. 910
1041-6552 See MISSOURI QUERIES. 2461
1041-6560 See NEW YORK STATE QUERIES. 2462
1041-6587 See TIES (PHILADELPHIA, PA.). 5165
1041-6633 See REPORT ON THE ... SALARY BUDGET SURVEY. 1707
1041-6714 See TRANSDEX INDEX. 426
1041-6722 See FEDERAL-STATE-LOCAL GOVERNMENT DIRECTORY, THE. 4648
1041-6730 See WEST'S OKLAHOMA DECISIONS. 3074
1041-6749 See ADVANCES IN WORKING CAPITAL MANAGEMENT. 636
1041-679X See APPLIED LANGUAGE LEARNING. 3266
1041-682X See CONNECT (BRATTLEBORO, VT.). 1733
1041-6862 See ROCKEFELLER ARCHIVE CENTER NEWSLETTER. 2483
1041-6900 See NOVA QUARTERLY. 1093
1041-6943 See PUBLIC COMMUNICATIONS MAGAZINE. 1120
1041-6951 See FELL'S UNITED STATES COIN BOOK. 2781
1041-696X See SPORTS MEDICINE STANDARDS AND MALPRACTICE REPORTER, THE. 3956
1041-6994 See AVISTA FORUM. 316
1041-701X See NEWSLETTER - PENNSYLVANIA STATE UNIVERSITY. ENVIRONMENTAL RESOURCES RESEARCH INSTITUTE. 2237
1041-7060 See ADVANCES IN PUBLIC INTEREST ACCOUNTING. 738
1041-7095 See DAILY NEWS (MIDDLESBORO, KY. 1981). 5680
1041-7109 See HARLAN DAILY ENTERPRISE, THE. 5680
1041-7117 See COMMUNICATOR (WASHINGTON, D.C. 1988). 2918
1041-7133 See COMPUTER SOFTWARE. 1226
1041-7176 See AMERICAN LUTHERIE. 4099
1041-7222 See CERTIFIED MANAGEMENT ACCOUNTANT EXAMINATION. QUESTIONS AND UNOFFICIAL ANSWERS (MONTVALE, N.J.). 863
1041-7249 See CONFERENCE RECORD OF ... ANNUAL PULP AND PAPER INDUSTRY TECHNICAL CONFERENCE. 4233
1041-7273 See DIRECTORY OF THEATRE FACULTIES IN COLLEGES AND UNIVERSITIES, U.S. AND CANADA. 5363

1041-7281 See MIJU HAN'GUK ILBO. 5647
1041-729X See ELECTRICAL CONSTRUCTION ESTIMATOR. 2044
1041-7311 See FRANCHISING WORLD. 677
1041-7370 See EASTERN EUROPEAN AND SOVIET ADVANCED MATERIALS REPORT, THE. 1971
1041-7419 See AEROSPACE INTELLIGENCE. 5
1041-7427 See CONTRACTING INTELLIGENCE. 4640
1041-746X See INTERNATIONAL DEFENSE INTELLIGENCE. 4046
1041-7494 See TRAVERSO (CLAVERACK, N.Y.). 4157
1041-7508 See AFFLUENT MARKETS ALERT. 859
1041-7516 See YOUTH MARKETS ALERT. 938
1041-7524 See MINORITY MARKETS ALERT. 906
1041-7559 See GREAT LAKES MONITOR. 1132
1041-7567 See JOURNAL OF CHINESE LAW. 2987
1041-7648 See BIOSTATISTICA (DAVENPORT, IOWA). 477
1041-7699 See STUDIO SOUND (SHAWNEE MISSION, KAN.). 5319
1041-7729 See GLBAMES NEWSLETTER. 2794
1041-777X See MONTGOMERY COUNTY GENEALOGICAL SOCIETY QUARTERLY. 2461
1041-7826 See ADVANCES IN SMALL ANIMAL MEDICINE AND SURGERY. 5501
1041-7834 See BOOKLURE (PASADENA, CALIF.). 3368
1041-7893 See COMMUNICATION SERIALS. 1107
1041-7915 See COMPUTERS IN LIBRARIES. 3203
1041-7923 See ACADEMIC AND LIBRARY COMPUTING. 1265
1041-794X See SOUTHERN COMMUNICATION JOURNAL, THE. 1122
1041-7958 See AMERICAN MACHINIST (1988). 2109
1041-7974 See ACLS ALERT. 3697
1041-8024 See HOW TO FIND COMPANY INTELLIGENCE IN STATE DOCUMENTS. 680
1041-8105 See ENVIRONMENT WEEK. 2166
1041-8113 See TODAY'S WOODWORKER. 635
1041-8156 See MACINTOSH BUYER'S GUIDE, THE. 1194
1041-8164 See F.O.C. REVIEW. 3387
1041-8172 See ENVIRONMENTAL MANAGEMENT REVIEW (ROCKVILLE, MD.). 3112
1041-8199 See REALITY (HOUSTON, TEX.). 1334
1041-8237 See MIDRANGE SYSTEMS. 1274
1041-8253 See REALITY NOW (HOUSTON, TEX.). 1334
1041-830X See LOG HOME LIVING. 302
1041-8318 See AIRPORT NOISE REPORT. 10
1041-8385 See QUI PARLE. 2852
1041-8466 See APPALACHIAN FAMILIES. 2437
1041-8474 See TVI REPORT. 4537
1041-8482 See BUSINESS & THE CONTEMPORARY WORLD (WALTHAM, MASS. 1991). 645
1041-8490 See VOICE OF THE DIABETIC. 3733
1041-8520 See NETWORK FOR PUBLIC SCHOOLS. 1767
1041-8563 See MICROCOMPUTER SOLUTIONS (U.S. ED.). 1269
1041-8644 See FOLKLORE HISTORIAN (MIDDLETOWN, DAUPHIN COUNTY, PA.), THE. 2320
1041-8660 See FAMILY RESOURCE COALITION REPORT. 2280
1041-875X See SINO-WESTERN CULTURAL RELATIONS JOURNAL. 4535
1041-892X See YEAR BOOK OF OTOLARYNGOLOGY. HEAD AND NECK SURGERY, THE. 3977
1041-9039 See PHILADELPHIA PAPERS, THE. 4531
1041-9063 See BULLETIN / THE J. PAUL GETTY TRUST. 346

1041-908X *See* INDUSTRY REPORT ON SUPERVISORY MANAGEMENT COMPENSATION. **942**

1041-9136 *See* TRANSPORTATION (CLEVELAND, OHIO). **5396**

1041-9144 *See* COATINGS, DYES & PIGMENTS. **4223**

1041-9152 *See* BUILDING PRODUCTS (CLEVELAND, OHIO). **604**

1041-9268 *See* IOWA CROPS AND WEATHER / IOWA CROP AND LIVESTOCK REPORTING SERVICE. **175**

1041-9276 See COMMON GROUND (DES MOINES, IOWA). **5028**

1041-9306 *See* MISSISSIPPI OUTDOORS (1987). **4874**

1041-9314 *See* ADVENTURE TRAVEL (EMMAUS, PA.). **5460**

1041-9373 *See* FODOR'S ... POCKET GUIDE TO THE BAHAMAS. **5473**

1041-9381 *See* ALLEN COUNTY-FORT WAYNE HISTORICAL SOCIETY BULLETIN. **2718**

1041-9411 *See* REGIONAL THEATRE DIRECTORY. **5367**

1041-9454 *See* CABOT'S MUTUAL FUND NAVIGATOR. **4716**

1041-9462 *See* EDUCATION MONITOR. **1740**

1041-9470 *See* FOX (NEW YORK, N.Y. 1984). **3995**

1041-9489 *See* SAFETY BRIEF. **4801**

1041-9551 *See* NINTENDO POWER. **4864**

1041-9756 *See* OLDER TRUCK BLUE BOOK, THE. **5422**

1041-9764 *See* STATE UNIVERSITY OF NEW YORK RESEARCH. **1848**

1041-9772 *See* RV WEST MAGAZINE. **4854**

1041-9780 *See* PRESENTATION PRODUCTS MAGAZINE. **704**

1041-9799 *See* RHONDA WHITE-WARNER'S TIDBITS. **2492**

1041-9861 *See* SOCIOCRITICISM. **5260**

1041-9918 *See* CURRENT OPINION IN ORTHOPAEDICS. **3881**

1041-9926 *See* POTATO EYES. **3424**

1041-9969 *See* ECONOMIC DEVELOPER. **1482**

1041-9977 *See* DAILY TRIBUNE (MOUNT CLEMENS, MICH.). **5691**

1042-0053 *See* FUND RAISER'S GUIDE TO RELIGIOUS PHILANTHROPY. **4336**

1042-0088 *See* CHALLENGES (WASHINGTON, D.C. 1987). **656**

1042-0134 *See* LEFT BUSINESS OBSERVER. **1503**

1042-0150 *See* RADIATION EFFECTS AND DEFECTS IN SOLIDS. **1057**

1042-0169 *See* SYNTHESIS (ASHEVILLE, N.C.). **3062**

1042-0193 *See* ABSTRACTS IN HUMAN-COMPUTER INTERACTION. **1208**

1042-0304 *See* PRE- (PRAIRIE VILLAGE, KAN.). **4818**

1042-0355 *See* KANSAS DIRECTORY OF COMMERCE, THE. **820**

1042-0371 *See* CENTRO DE ESTUDIOS PUERTORRIQUENOS BULLETIN. **2613**

1042-0398 *See* CORRELATIVE NEUROANATOMY (EAST NORWALK, CONN.). **3830**

1042-041X *See* PSYCHIATRIC ABSTRACTS AND COMMENT. **3933**

1042-0460 *See* VOICE PROCESSING MAGAZINE. **1206**

1042-0487 *See* PRO PRINCIPAL. **1868**

1042-0517 *See* RESIDENTIAL FLORIDA REAL ESTATE. **4846**

1042-0533 *See* AMERICAN JOURNAL OF HUMAN BIOLOGY. **441**

1042-0541 *See* JOURNAL OF AGRICULTURAL EDUCATION. **99**

1042-0614 *See* WASTE AGE'S RECYCLING TIMES. **2246**

1042-0622 See FUN ZONE, THE. **4861**

1042-0630 *See* SOLAR TODAY. **1957**

1042-0649 *See* SOUNDTRACK (RINGWOOD, N.J.). **5319**

1042-0657 *See* EXECUTIVE STRATEGIES (NEW YORK, N.Y.). **867**

1042-0665 *See* DIRECTORY OF U.S. TRADEMARKS, THE. **1303**

1042-0681 *See* PC-SIG MAGAZINE. **1289**

1042-0681 *See* SHAREWARE MAGAZINE. **1202**

1042-0711 *See* ADVANCED IMAGING (WOODBURY, N.Y.). **1276**

1042-072X *See* QUALITY AND PRODUCTIVITY PLUS. **706**

1042-0746 *See* BUSINESS INFORMATION ALERT. **3199**

1042-0827 *See* POMONA COLLEGE TODAY. **1841**

1042-0843 *See* YOUR FAVORITE COUNTRY STARS. **4160**

1042-0851 *See* ANNOUNCER (COLLEGE PARK, MD.). **4397**

1042-0878 *See* FAMILY INFORMATION SERVICES. **2279**

1042-0908 *See* MICROSOFT CD-ROM YEARBOOK, THE. **1195**

1042-0940 *See* ICHNOS (CHUR, SWITZERLAND). **269**

1042-0959 *See* APPLIED THERMAL SCIENCES. **2097**

1042-0967 *See* ELECTRONICS AND COMMUNICATIONS IN JAPAN. PART 3, FUNDAMENTAL ELECTRONIC SCIENCE. **2049**

1042-0991 *See* PHARMACY TODAY (WASHINGTON, D.C.). **4323**

1042-1009 *See* HEARTLAND BOATING. **593**

1042-1092 See GP (ATLANTA, GA.). **1324**

1042-1122 *See* CERAMIC TRANSACTIONS. **2587**

1042-1130 *See* COMPUTER IMAGES. **377**

1042-1149 *See* ORBIT VIDEO. **4075**

1042-119X *See* DEMOCRAT (EMMETSBURG, IOWA). **5669**

1042-1203 *See* REPORTER (EMMETSBURG, IOWA). **5672**

1042-1238 *See* CHANNEL GUIDE (MILWAUKEE, WIS.). **1106**

1042-1254 *See* NORTHWESTERN FINANCIAL REVIEW. **801**

1042-1262 *See* MUSIC RESEARCH FORUM. **4134**

1042-1300 *See* JOURNAL OF MANAGEMENT IN PRACTICE. **874**

1042-1319 *See* JOURNAL OF INFORMATION TECHNOLOGY MANAGEMENT. **873**

1042-1343 *See* DIVING WORLD (VAN NUYS, CALIF.). **4893**

1042-1386 *See* BROWN UNIVERSITY LONG-TERM CARE LETTER, THE. **4769**

1042-1394 *See* ALCOHOLISM & DRUG ABUSE WEEK. **1340**

1042-1408 See JOURNAL OF PUBLIC RELATIONS RESEARCH. **761**

1042-1459 *See* ARCHIVES AND MUSEUM INFORMATICS TECHNICAL REPORT. **2479**

1042-1467 *See* ARCHIVES & MUSEUM INFORMATICS. **1217**

1042-1629 *See* EDUCATIONAL TECHNOLOGY RESEARCH AND DEVELOPMENT. **1743**

1042-1696 *See* VETERINARY MANAGEMENT UPDATE. **5525**

1042-170X *See* POPULAR ELECTRONICS (1989). **2075**

1042-1726 *See* JOURNAL OF COMPUTING IN HIGHER EDUCATION. **1832**

1042-1742 See AMERICAN MANUFACTURERS DIRECTORY. **3475**

1042-1769 *See* FLEET MANAGEMENT NEWS (PORT READING, N.J.). **5382**

1042-1785 *See* EAGLES (NEW MARKET, FREDERICK COUNTY, MD.). **373**

1042-1858 *See* GEORGETOWN INTERNATIONAL ENVIRONMENTAL LAW REVIEW. **3112**

1042-1866 *See* SEMINARS DIRECTORY. **710**

1042-1882 *See* JOHNS HOPKINS MEDICAL LETTER HEALTH AFTER 50, THE. **3592**

1042-1890 *See* AMERICAN INVENTOR (BLOOMINGTON, IND.). **5082**

1042-1912 *See* PUBLIC GAMING INTERNATIONAL. **4743**

1042-1920 *See* NAVAL HISTORY. **4180**

1042-1939 *See* ENERGY AND ENGINEERING SCIENCE SERIES. **4402**

1042-198X *See* AMATEUR TELEVISION QUARTERLY. **1148**

1042-2021 *See* ADVANCED DEVELOPMENT. **1874**

1042-203X *See* UNIVERSITY OF TEXAS LIFETIME HEALTH LETTER, THE. **4806**

1042-2048 *See* HELICOPTER SAFETY (ARLINGTON, VA.). **23**

1042-2102 *See* WALKING MAGAZINE, THE. **2602**

1042-2129 *See* MEDIAGUIDE (MORRISTOWN, N.J.). **2922**

1042-2145 *See* FLORAL & NURSERY TIMES. **511**

1042-2161 *See* VISIONS OF NEW MEXICO. **2765**

1042-217X *See* CROCKER COMMUNICATION RESOURCES NEWSLETTER. **663**

1042-2250 *See* CONTEMPORARY UROLOGY. **3989**

1042-2277 *See* MANY VOICES. **4603**

1042-2285 *See* CAPITAL CONSORTIUM'S NORTH CAROLINIA GIVING. **5276**

1042-2307 *See* FIRESIDE SENTINEL : THE ALEXANDRIA LIBRARY, LLOYD HOUSE NEWSLETTER, THE. **2733**

1042-2315 See VOLUNTEERISM (NEW YORK, N.Y.). **5267**

1042-2323 *See* TIMES-NEWS (HENDERSONVILLE, N.C.). **5724**

1042-2420 *See* DIRECTORY OF WOMEN ENTREPRENEURS, THE. **667**

1042-2455 *See* TODAY IN MEDICINE. CARDIOVASCULAR DISEASE. **3711**

1042-2471 *See* ANCIENT CONTROVERSY. **4515**

1042-251X *See* EI DIGEST. **2227**

1042-2528 *See* FOCUS ON OHIO DENTISTRY. **1323**

1042-2544 *See* BILLBOARD'S NASHVILLE 615 / COUNTRY MUSIC SOURCEBOOK. **4103**

1042-2579 *See* PHYSICAL THERAPY TODAY. **4381**

1042-2587 *See* ENTREPRENEURSHIP THEORY AND PRACTICE. **672**

1042-2595 *See* DATABASE REVIEW. **1253**

1042-2617 *See* ACCESS CONTROL. **2034**

1042-2625 *See* PHYSICIAN'S MARKETING & MANAGEMENT. **3627**

1042-2633 *See* WHO'S WHO IN LIVE ANIMAL TRADE & TRANSPORT. **224**

1042-2706 *See* ON CARL. **3239**

1042-2722 *See* PRACTICAL PERIODONTICS AND AESTHETIC DENTISTRY. **1333**

1042-2757 *See* SENSORS BUYER'S GUIDE. **3488**

1042-2781 *See* FDC REPORTS. HEALTH NEWS DAILY. **4775**

1042-2838 *See* TODAY IN MEDICINE DIABETOLOGY AND ENDOCRINOLOGY. **3733**

1042-2846 *See* TODAY IN MEDICINE. RESPIRATORY DISEASE. **3952**

1042-2935 *See* GREATER CAROLINAS REGIONAL INDUSTRIAL BUYING GUIDE. **1607**

1042-2943 *See* PC GAMES (PETERBOROUGH, N.H.). **4864**

1042-296X *See* IEEE TRANSACTIONS ON ROBOTICS AND AUTOMATION. **1212**

1042-296X *See* IEEE TRANSACTIONS ON ROBOTICS AND AUTOMATION. **1213**

1042-2978 *See* EMERGENCY DEPARTMENT LAW. **2965**

1042-3028 *See* FORMSMFG. **676**

1042-3036 *See* TAN MAGAZINE. **405**

1042-3087 *See* PERSONAL INVESTING NEWS. **911**

1042-3141 *See* ASSOCIATION MEETINGS. **756**

1042-3168 *See* TENNESSEE ENVIRONMENTAL LAW LETTER. **3063**

1042-3184 *See* SECURITIES ARBITRATION. **3047**

1042-3192 *See* STUDIES IN QUALITATIVE METHODOLOGY. **5223**

1042-3265 *See* JOURNAL OF NAVAJO EDUCATION. **1758**

1042-3281 See CANALES (NEW YORK, N.Y.). 2486

1042-329X See BLACK HEALTH. 4768

1042-3354 See NEWS-GAZETTE (CHAMPAIGN, ILL.). 5661

1042-3370 See INTERNATIONAL BANKING FOCUS. 792

1042-3419 See MUSCOGIANA (COLUMBUS, GA.). 2461

1042-3427 See AMERICAN ROSE REGISTRY. 2408

1042-3443 See MUSICAL AMERICA (1987). 4136

1042-346X See JOURNAL OF LASER APPLICATIONS. 4435

1042-3494 See CATHOLIC WORLD (1989), THE. 5027

1042-3508 See ELECTRONICS WORLD (LAKE ZURICH, ILL.). 2050

1042-3516 See MID SPORTS. 4904

1042-3524 See QUARTERLY - PLANT GROWTH REGULATOR SOCIETY OF AMERICA. 2429

1042-3559 See SPEAK OUT FOR CHILDREN. 2286

1042-3575 See PC DIGEST RATINGS REPORT. 1270

1042-3621 See MORNING NEWS TRIBUNE. 5761

1042-363X See PROGRESS IN AIDS PATHOLOGY. 4796

1042-3664 See INSIDE TEXAS RUNNING. 4900

1042-3672 See CV (NEW YORK, N.Y.). 4203

1042-3680 See NEUROSURGERY CLINICS OF NORTH AMERICA. 3970

1042-3699 See ORAL AND MAXILLOFACIAL SURGERY CLINICS OF NORTH AMERICA. 3971

1042-3729 See SPECTRA (SYRACUSE, N.Y.). 4096

1042-3737 See EPSIG NEWS. 2053

1042-3761 See TAMPA TRIBUNE, THE. 5651

1042-3834 See JOURNAL OF THE SOCIETY OF BASQUE STUDIES IN AMERICA. 2695

1042-3850 See MEANS PLUMBING COST DATA. 2607

1042-3869 See NCCA ILLUSTRATED MEN'S AND WOMEN'S BASKETBALL RULES. 4907

1042-3877 See NCAA MEN'S AND WOMEN'S BASKETBALL RULES AND INTERPRETATIONS. 4907

1042-3885 See POLITICAL CHRONICLE, THE. 4489

1042-3915 See JOURNAL OF FIRE PROTECTION ENGINEERING. 2291

1042-3931 See JOURNAL OF INVASIVE CARDIOLOGY, THE. 3707

1042-394X See SPORTS ILLUSTRATED FOR KIDS. 1069

1042-3966 See COMMON CAUSE/COLORADO. 2531

1042-4032 See INTERNATIONAL JOURNAL OF HUMANITIES AND PEACE, THE. 2848

1042-4067 See JOURNAL OF GYNECOLOGIC SURGERY. 3763

1042-4075 See MA REPORT (FAIRFAX, VA.), THE. 3674

1042-4083 See EXCHANGE (TUSCALOOSA, ALA.). 1746

1042-4091 See MANAGED CARE LAW OUTLOOK. 3006

1042-4105 See SUPERCONDUCTOR INDUSTRY. 5161

1042-4121 See NEWS JOURNAL (WILMINGTON, DEL.), THE. 5647

1042-413X See INITIATIVES MICROFORM : [JOURNAL OF NAWDAC]. 1830

1042-413X See INITIATIVES (WASHINGTON, D.C.). 1864

1042-4148 See REVIEWS OF WEED SCIENCE. 2430

1042-4156 See ADVANCES IN MEMBRANE FLUIDITY. 440

1042-4172 See DIRECTORY OF STATE COURT CLERKS AND COUNTY COURTHOUSES. 4644

1042-4199 See BLACK HERITAGE UNVEILED NEWSLETTER. 2611

1042-4229 See WASHINGTON VIEW. 2549

1042-4245 See SCHOOL LIBRARY MEDIA FOLDERS OF IDEAS FOR LIBRARY EXCELLENCE. 3248

1042-4261 See HULBERT FINANCIAL DIGEST, THE. 900

1042-4296 See INTELLIGENCE (NEW YORK, N.Y. 1984). 1189

1042-4326 See NEWSPAPER INVESTOR. 909

1042-4334 See IHN NEWS. 1113

1042-4350 See PEABODY ESSAYS IN MUSIC HISTORY. 4145

1042-4423 See ABSTRACTS OF CLINICAL CARE GUIDELINES. 3654

1042-4431 See JOURNAL OF INTERNATIONAL FINANCIAL MARKETS, INSTITUTIONS & MONEY. 1637

1042-444X See JOURNAL OF MULTINATIONAL FINANCIAL MANAGEMENT. 1637

1042-4458 See JOURNAL OF INTERLIBRARY LOAN & INFORMATION SUPPLY. 3220

1042-4601 See PRACTICAL HOMEOWNER. 624

1042-461X See VIRGINIA EMPLOYMENT LAW LETTER. 3155

1042-4644 See FOLIO'S MEDICAL DIRECTORY OF CONNECTICUT AND RHODE ISLAND. 3914

1042-4695 See LAN TECHNOLOGY. 1242

1042-4717 See PSYCHWARE SOURCEBOOK. 1775

1042-4725 See GREEN COUNTY REVIEW. 2452

1042-4741 See PUBLIC BUDGETING AND FINANCIAL MANAGEMENT. 4743

1042-4784 See AIDS UPDATE (RESTON, VA.). 3665

1042-4849 See WOMAN. 5568

1042-4911 See CHILTON'S AIR CONDITIONING AND HEATING MANUAL. 5410

1042-5039 See GREENHOUSE EFFECT REPORT. 2230

1042-5055 See JOURNAL OF CHIROPRACTIC EDUCATION, THE. 3805

1042-5063 See NERA ENERGY OUTLOOK. 1507

1042-508X See COMPOUNDINGS. 4253

1042-511X See WINGING IT. 5600

1042-5152 See WORDPERFECT (OREM, UTAH). 1292

1042-5160 See NEWS & VIEWS (PITTSBURGH, PA.). 5298

1042-5179 See DNA SEQUENCE. 453

1042-5195 See INCENTIVE (NEW YORK, N.Y. 1988). 760

1042-5209 See ENVIRONMENTAL LAB. 5103

1042-5217 See BUSINESS & MANAGEMENT EDUCATION FUNDING ALERT. 1813

1042-5225 See BOURBON NEWS-MIRROR (1971). 5663

1042-5268 See JOURNAL OF VASCULAR MEDICINE AND BIOLOGY. 462

1042-5276 See SOPHISTICATE'S BLACK HAIR STYLES AND CARE GUIDE. 405

1042-5284 See WRESTLING SUPERSTARS. 4931

1042-5330 See IDEAS PLUS. 1896

1042-5349 See RANKING THE BANKS / AMERICAN BANKER. 806

1042-5381 See HEAVEN BONE. 3393

1042-539X See ANIMATO! (CAMBRIDGE, MASS.). 4063

1042-5489 See REGIONAL INDUSTRIAL BUYING GUIDE. CAPITAL CITIES. 1624

1042-5497 See REGIONAL INDUSTRIAL BUYING GUIDE. GREATER ALLEGHENY. 1624

1042-5500 See REGIONAL INDUSTRIAL BUYING GUIDE. GREATER DELAWARE VALLEY. 1624

1042-5519 See REGIONAL INDUSTRIAL BUYING GUIDE. GREATER NEW YORK. 1624

1042-5527 See REGIONAL INDUSTRIAL BUYING GUIDE. NORTH CENTRAL TRI-STATE. 1624

1042-5551 See REGIONAL INDUSTRIAL BUYING GUIDE. NORTHERN OHIO. 1624

1042-556X See REGIONAL INDUSTRIAL BUYING GUIDE. OHIO VALLEY. 1624

1042-5586 See REGIONAL INDUSTRIAL BUYING GUIDE. WESTERN NEW ENGLAND. 1624

1042-5675 See PROFESSIONAL LAWYER : PL / SPECIAL COORDINATING COMMITTEE ON PROFESSIONALISM, AMERICAN BAR ASSOCIATION CENTER FOR PROFESSIONAL RESPONSIBILITY, THE. 3032

1042-5683 See CLASSIC AUTO RESTORER. 5411

1042-5713 See GASTROENTEROLOGIST'S CLINICAL UPDATE. 3745

1042-5721 See JOURNAL OF C LANGUAGE TRANSLATION, THE. 1279

1042-5756 See DELAWARE CORPORATE LITIGATION REPORTER. 3099

1042-5764 See LENDER LIABILITY LITIGATION REPORTER. 3087

1042-5772 See STOCKHOLDERS & CREDITORS NEWS SERVICE CONCERNING LTV CORPORATION, ET AL. 3103

1042-5780 See STOCKHOLDERS & CREDITORS NEWS SERVICE CONCERNING ASBESTOS BANKRUPTCIES. 3103

1042-5810 See NATIONAL BULLETIN ON POLICE MISCONDUCT. 3170

1042-587X See BERKSHIRE MAGAZINE. 2723

1042-590X See FLORIDA BUSINESS (CLEVELAND, OHIO). 675

1042-5918 See CHRIE COMMUNIQUE. 2804

1042-5985 See AMERICAN UNIVERSITY STUDIES. SERIES XXVII, FEMINIST STUDIES. 5550

1042-6019 See STANDARDS AND RECOMMENDED PRACTICES FOR INSTRUMENTATION AND CONTROL. 1997

1042-6086 See COMMUNICATIONSWEEK INTERNATIONAL. 1108

1042-6094 See WEEKEND WOODWORKING PROJECTS. 2779

1042-6108 See HANDGUNNING. 4898

1042-6116 See INBOUND/OUTBOUND. 926

1042-6167 See CATALOG HANDBOOK. 656

1042-6175 See BUSINESS OPPORTUNITIES HANDBOOK. 651

1042-6205 See AUTO PRICES ALMANAC. 5405

1042-6213 See AMERICAS REVIEW (HOUSTON, TEX.). 3360

1042-6221 See AQUACULTURE SITUATION AND OUTLOOK REPORT. 5530

1042-6248 See COUNTRY INNS AND BACK ROADS. NORTH AMERICA. 2804

1042-6256 See NSAA NEWS. 4908

1042-6280 See CA CRAFT CONNECTION, THE. 370

1042-6299 See FISHERIES REVIEW (FORT COLLINS, COLO.). 2317

1042-6302 See FOXTALK (FEDERAL WAY, WASH.). 1279

1042-6329 See AUDIOTEX DIRECTORY & BUYER'S GUIDE. 1149

1042-6337 See JOURNAL OF BUSINESS & ENTREPRENEURSHIP. 686

1042-6353 See BIRNBAUM'S PORTUGAL. 5464

1042-6353 See BIRNBAUM'S SPAIN. 5464

1042-637X See PALM BEACH BOOKS OF FACTS & FIRSTS, THE. 1928

1042-6388 See STUDENT ASSISTANCE JOURNAL. 1349

1042-6426 See WOLF! (CLIFTON HEIGHTS, PA.). 4881

1042-6434 See HOW TO AVOID RIPPING YOUR HAIR OUT WHEN PURCHASING NEW OR USED FOREIGN OR DOMESTIC TAX FREE CARS DIRECT STATESIDE, OVERSEAS OR CANADA. 5416

1042-6442 See CLEANFAX (COLUMBUS, OHIO). 5349

1042-6450 See GUN TESTS. 4045

1042-6469 See AT YOUR SERVICE (BIRMINGHAM, ALA.). 3192

1042-6507 See PHOSPHORUS, SULFUR, AND SILICON AND THE RELATED ELEMENTS. 1037

1042-654X See HARVARD BUSINESS SCHOOL CATALOG OF TEACHING MATERIALS. 679

1042-6566 See NEW AGE RETAILER. 4186

1042-6574 See HAZ PACKS. 2230

1042-6590 See PARTNERSHIPS IN EDUCATION JOURNAL. 1772

1042-6604 See SOUTHERN READER. 3438

1042-6620 See WISCONSIN GOLF. 4930

1042-6647 See EX LIBRIS (PORTSMOUTH, N.H.). 3386

1042-671X See BARTON COUNTY GENEALOGICAL SOCIETY QUARTERLY. 2438

1042-6736 See MUSICWORLD (NEW YORK, N.Y.). 4137

1042-6787 See ARIZONA BLUE CHIP ECONOMIC FORECAST. 1463

1042-6795 See WESTERN BLUE CHIP ECONOMIC FORECAST. 1526

1042-6817 See FORUM. 4838

1042-6833 See BULLETIN DE LA SOCIETE AMERICAINE DE PHILOSOPHIE DE LANGUE FRANCAISE. 4343

1042-6841 See NATIONAL UNDERWRITER (PROPERTY & CASUALTY / RISK & BENEFITS MANAGEMENT EDITION). 2889

1042-6906 See CITIZEN (HAMTRAMCK, MICH.), THE. 5691

1042-6922 See LENS AND EYE TOXICITY RESEARCH. 3604

1042-6930 See INTELLIGENT NETWORK NEWS. 1113

1042-6965 See AMERICA OGGI. 5709

1042-699X See HEALTH SENTRY. 2598

1042-704X See ORTHOPEDIC PRODUCT NEWS. 3884

1042-7074 See SWIMMING POOL & SPA INDUSTRY MARKET REPORT. 1628

1042-7082 See JACARANDA REVIEW, THE. 3398

1042-7090 See COMPUTER DAILY. 1176

1042-7104 See BLACK ARTS ANNUAL. 344

1042-7112 See NEW AGE LINK'S LETTER LINK : THE SPIRITUAL AWARENESS NETWORK. 4186

1042-7139 See BREAD PUDDING UPDATE. 2789

1042-7147 See POLYMERS FOR ADVANCED TECHNOLOGIES. 1028

1042-7163 See HETEROATOM CHEMISTRY. 976

1042-718X See SEMINARS IN DENTAL HYGIENE. 1335

1042-7198 See GUIDE OF CHINESE TRADING. 838

1042-7201 See FORENSIC SCIENCE REVIEW. 3740

1042-721X See FEDERAL COMPUTER MARKET REPORT. 1237

1042-7228 See CABLE WORLD. 1150

1042-7252 See SOFTWARE INDUSTRY REPORT. 1290

1042-7260 See JOURNAL OF ZOO AND WILDLIFE MEDICINE : OFFICIAL PUBLICATION OF THE AMERICAN ASSOCIATION OF ZOO VETERINARIANS. 5514

1042-7279 See DISSERTATION ABSTRACTS INTERNATIONAL. C, WORLDWIDE. 1821

1042-7309 See JOURNAL OF MANAGEMENT SCIENCE & POLICY ANALYSIS. 4658

1042-7325 See RESELLER MANAGEMENT. 1239

1042-7333 See INSURANCE TIMES (NEWTON, MASS.). 2884

1042-7368 See FISKE GUIDE TO COLLEGES, THE. 1824

1042-7392 See ANTIQUE POWER MAGAZINE. 249

1042-7406 See CAR COLLECTING & INVESTING. 5409

1042-7414 See AUTO SERVICE TODAY. 5377

1042-7430 See IN-SERVICE REVIEWS IN CLINICAL LABORATORY SCIENCE. 3586

1042-749X See CHINESE JOURNAL OF BIOTECHNOLOGY. 3690

1042-7503 See RFE/RL RESEARCH REPORT. 1138

1042-752X See NORTH AMERICAN JOURNAL OF ECONOMICS AND FINANCE. 1508

1042-7562 See IN-SITE (VERNON HILLS, ILL.). 2420

1042-7589 See ADOLESCENT COUNSELOR. 4571

1042-7597 See VIETNAM GENERATION. 2765

1042-7643 See WEAVER'S (SIOUX FALLS, S.D.). 5359

1042-7678 See MET GOLFER, THE. 4904

1042-7694 See VIDEO INVESTOR. 4377

1042-7708 See BULLETIN - ASSOCIATION FOR THE ADVANCEMENT OF AUTOMOTIVE MEDICINE. 5439

1042-7732 See BACKWOODS. 64

1042-7872 See DIAGNOSTIC RADIOLOGY (1982). 3940

1042-7937 See PASSENGER TRAIN ANNUAL. 5433

1042-7961 See JOURNAL OF WOMEN'S HISTORY. 5559

1042-7988 See INTERNATIONAL JOURNAL OF COMPUTER AIDED VLSI DESIGN. 2066

1042-7996 See LEARNING CENTER DIGEST, THE. 1761

1042-8011 See WORLD RESOURCE REVIEW. 2210

1042-802X See PLASTICS NEWS (AKRON, OHIO). 4458

1042-8038 See OAHU UPDATE, THE. 5487

1042-8046 See HAWAII, THE BIG ISLAND UPDATE. 5479

1042-8054 See OAHU. 5487

1042-8062 See HAWAII, THE BIG ISLAND. 5479

1042-8089 See JAWETZ, MELNICK & ADELBERG'S MEDICAL MICROBIOLOGY. 564

1042-8127 See TODAY'S INVESTOR. 917

1042-8143 See KNOWLEDGE ACQUISITION. 1214

1042-8194 See LEUKEMIA & LYMPHOMA. 3820

1042-8208 See GREAT STREAM REVIEW. 3392

1042-8216 See PRIMARY SOURCES AND ORIGINAL WORKS. 3241

1042-8224 See JOURNAL OF MULTICULTURAL SOCIAL WORK. 5292

1042-8232 See JOURNAL OF PROGRESSIVE HUMAN SERVICES. 5292

1042-8275 See OCEANOGRAPHY (WASHINGTON, D.C.). 1454

1042-8291 See FROMMER'S BELGIUM, HOLLAND & LUXEMBOURG. 5474

1042-8364 See ANNUAL BENZENE & DERIVATIVES. 4249

1042-8380 See SOCIAL PLANNING, POLICY & DEVELOPMENT ABSTRACTS. 5266

1042-8437 See FROMMER'S BUDGET TRAVEL GUIDE. WASHINGTON, D.C. ... ON $ ... A DAY. 5475

1042-8461 See HORIZON (CHICAGO, ILL.). 4963

1042-8496 See DAILY PRESS (1988). 5634

1042-8534 See DESIGN MANAGEMENT. 865

1042-8569 See SMALLMOUTH (EDGEFIELD, S.C.). 2313

1042-8623 See CD-ROM ENDUSER. 1174

1042-8631 See CAIN AND SCOTT APARTMENT INVESTMENT STUDY, THE. 4835

1042-864X See CAMOES CENTER QUARTERLY. 2613

1042-8658 See GAMEPRO (BELMONT, CALIF.). 4861

1042-8704 See BUSINESS FOR CENTRAL NEW JERSEY. 862

1042-878X See TRACK AND FIELD AND CROSS COUNTRY RULE BOOK. 4926

1042-8798 See OFFICIAL PGA TOUR BOOK. 4910

1042-8836 See CBMR MONOGRAPHS. 4108

1042-8860 See ADVANCES IN POWDER METALLURGY & PARTICULATE MATERIALS. 3997

1042-895X See GASTROENTEROLOGY NURSING. 3856

1042-9018 See YEARBOOK / ASSOCIATION FOR SUPERVISION AND CURRICULUM DEVELOPMENT OF THE NATIONAL EDUCATION ASSOCIATION. 1909

1042-9042 See DIRECTORY OF MEMBER AGENCIES - CHILD WELFARE LEAGUE OF AMERICA (1986). 5283

1042-9069 See BLACK & WHITE & READ ALL OVER. 410

1042-9085 See RENTAL MANAGEMENT. 707

1042-9107 See BREEDER FORUM. 4286

1042-9115 See CORPORATE REAL ESTATE EXECUTIVE. 4836

1042-9123 See FOOD ARTS. 2336

1042-9158 See MCGRAW-HILL'S TECH TRANSFER REPORT. 1618

1042-9166 See EMERALD CITY COMIX AND STORIES. 3384

1042-9174 See RACING GREYHOUNDS. 4865

1042-9212 See KENTUCKY LAW SUMMARY. 2992

1042-9220 See CWRU - CASE WESTERN RESERVE UNIVERSITY. 1091

1042-9255 See SOFTWARE QUALITY WORLD. 1291

1042-9263 See BIG CITY MUSIC. 4103

1042-9271 See ATLANTA KIDS MAGAZINE. 1060

1042-928X See ACCOUNTING DEPARTMENT MANAGEMENT & ADMINISTRATION REPORT. 736

1042-931X See WORLD OPERA SCHEDULE. 4159

1042-9336 See PUBLIC FAX DIRECTORY, THE. 1162

1042-9379 See PEANUT GROWER, THE. 180

1042-9433 See PENSION HANDBOOK. 3026

1042-9549 See COLORADO WOMAN. 5553

1042-9557 See $TARTING $MART. 715

1042-9573 See JOURNAL OF FINANCIAL INTERMEDIATION. 904

1042-9581 See POWER REPORT ON AUTOMOTIVE MARKETING, THE. 5423

1042-9603 See CALIFORNIA REPORT ON AUTOMOTIVE MARKETING, THE. 5408

1042-9611 See ANNALS OF PHARMACOTHERAPY, THE. 4291

1042-962X See REFRACTIVE & CORNEAL SURGERY. 3878

1042-9638 See BALDWIN'S OHIO SCHOOL LAW JOURNAL. 1727

1042-9646 See CONTEMPORARY INTERNAL MEDICINE. 3796

1042-9662 See SPORTS CAR INTERNATIONAL. 5425

1042-9670 See ACADEMIC PSYCHIATRY. 3918

1042-9689 See NEW ENGLAND REAL ESTATE NEWS. 4842

1042-9697 See AQUATICS INTERNATIONAL. 4883

1042-9719 See WASHINGTON HISTORY. 2765

1042-9808 See LATIN AMERICAN ART. 356

1042-9832 See RANDOM STRUCTURES AND ALGORITHMS. 3530

1042-9859 See EDUCATION AND TRAINING IN MENTAL RETARDATION. 1878

1042-9980 See LOUISIANA LIFE (1989). 2537

1043-0075 See BLK (LOS ANGELES, CALIF.). 2793

1043-0083 See PJG (MIAMI, FLA.). 2427

1043-0210 See PENTHOUSE FORUM (1988). 3996

1043-0261 See V.I.P. ADDRESS BOOK. 435

1043-0342 See HUMAN GENE THERAPY. 547

1043-0369 See STALSBY/WILSON'S PETROLEUM SUPPLY AMERICAS. 4279

1043-0377 See STALSBY/WILSON'S PETROLEUM SUPPLY EUROPE. 4279

1043-0458 See PIONEER RECORD. 2467

1043-0474 See COALDAT MARKETING REPORT. SUPPLIER FORMAT (1988). 1935

1043-0490 See WISCONSIN LAWYER. 4695

1043-0539 See JOURNAL OF TAXATION OF EXEMPT ORGANIZATIONS, THE. 4735

1043-0547 See FAULKNER & GRAY'S BANKRUPTCY LAW REVIEW. 2968

1043-0628 See NEW YORK CIVIL MOTION CITATOR. 3016

1043-0644 See NETWORK NEWS & VIEWS. 1767

1043-0652 See AMERICAN GAS. 4249

1043-0660 See CLINICAL CONSULTATIONS IN OBSTETRICS AND GYNECOLOGY. 3758

1043-0679 See SEMINARS IN THORACIC AND CARDIOVASCULAR SURGERY. 3974

1043-0687 See EQUATOR (SAN FRANCISCO, CALIF. 1991), THE. 4346

1043-0695 See COMMUNIQUE (COLUMBUS, OHIO). 4949
1043-0717 See DEFENCE ECONOMICS. 4040
1043-0725 See MISSIONARY TIDINGS (WINONA LAKE, IND.). 4978
1043-0733 See CANCER BIOTHERAPY. 3810
1043-0768 See ACKNOWLEDGE : THE WINDOW LETTER. 1283
1043-0806 See BURIED TREASURE (WESTLAKE, OHIO). 1060
1043-0814 See POETICS. 3468
1043-0849 See BARKER, THE. 5505
1043-0857 See ADJUNCT MENTOR, THE. 1807
1043-0865 See SATELLITE BUSINESS NEWS. 1121
1043-0873 See TAX EXEMPT FINANCING. 3062
1043-089X See LAWN, GARDEN, AND FARM TRACTOR TRADE-IN GUIDE. 159
1043-092X See NATIONAL DIRECTORY OF ARTS INTERNSHIPS. 325
1043-0946 See SEARCH (DEVON, PA.). 2903
1043-0989 See PROCEEDINGS / CONFERENCE ON ARTIFICIAL INTELLIGENCE APPLICATIONS. 1216
1043-0997 See SCIENCE WEEKLY. LEVEL F. 1904
1043-1020 See JOURNAL OF ARTIFICIAL INTELLIGENCE IN EDUCATION. 1213
1043-1039 See LIVE ANIMAL TRADE & TRANSPORT MAGAZINE. 226
1043-1047 See TAEKWONDO WORLD. 2601
1043-1055 See JOURNAL OF COMPUTING IN CHILDHOOD EDUCATION. 1224
1043-1187 See FAXON PLANNING REPORT, THE. 3210
1043-1195 See OFFICIAL GUIDE TO AMERICAN HISTORIC INNS, THE. 2808
1043-1209 See REPORT ON DISABILITY PROGRAMS. 4393
1043-1217 See NETWORK MANAGEMENT SYSTEMS & STRATEGIES. 1243
1043-1225 See CHRISTIAN COMMUNICATOR, THE. 4944
1043-1241 See CBMR DIGEST. 4108
1043-1306 See STRATEGIES FOR HEALTHCARE EXCELLENCE. 3793
1043-1314 See PC LAPTOP COMPUTERS MAGAZINE. 1270
1043-1322 See CULTURAL DIVERSITY AT WORK. 1662
1043-1365 See INTERNATIONAL SOCIAL MOVEMENT RESEARCH. 5248
1043-1489 See SEMINARS IN COLON & RECTAL SURGERY. 3974
1043-1497 See SYCAMORE REVIEW. 3443
1043-1500 See CARDOZO STUDIES IN LAW AND LITERATURE. 2948
1043-1535 See WORLD ALMANAC OF U.S. POLITICS, THE. 4500
1043-1543 See AIDS CLINICAL CARE. 3711
1043-1578 See SOCIAL JUSTICE (SAN FRANCISCO, CALIF.). 3177
1043-1659 See ARIZONA FACTS. 2721
1043-1667 See ESTIMATE, THE. 4520
1043-1675 See COMMERCIAL PROPERTY NEWS. 4835
1043-1691 See ARCHAEOLOGICAL METHOD AND THEORY. 257
1043-1721 See JOURNAL OF THE SOCIETY FOR HEALTH SYSTEMS. 4788
1043-1756 See GEMUTLICHKEIT (HAYWARD, CALIF.). 2561
1043-1772 See BREEDER FORUM. 4286
1043-1780 See OPHTHALMIC DRUG FACTS. 3877
1043-1802 See BIOCONJUGATE CHEMISTRY. 483
1043-1810 See OPERATIVE TECHNIQUES IN OTOLARYNGOLOGY--HEAD AND NECK SURGERY. 3890
1043-1845 See COALDAT MARKETING REPORT. PRODUCING DISTRICT FORMAT (1988). 1935
1043-1888 See CREDIT UNION FINANCIAL PROFILES. 786

1043-190X See BARRON'S GUIDE TO GRADUATE BUSINESS SCHOOLS. 642
1043-1942 See IN-PLANT REPRODUCTIONS (1988). 4566
1043-1950 See SHELBY STAR, THE. 5724
1043-2035 See PROFESSIONAL BOATBUILDER MAGAZINE. 595
1043-2043 See DIRECTORY OF WORLD LEADERS & FACTBOOK. 4472
1043-2051 See PROFESSIONAL LICENSING REPORT. 4208
1043-2086 See CAMPUS-FREE COLLEGE DEGREES. 1813
1043-2094 See AGAINST THE GRAIN (CHARLESTON, S.C.). 3188
1043-2140 See EAST ASIA AND THE WESTERN PACIFIC. 2650
1043-2167 See NATIONAL FORUM OF SPECIAL EDUCATION JOURNAL. 1882
1043-2191 See SUPERVISOR (ENGLEWOOD, N.J.), EL. 2871
1043-2221 See NEW WOMEN/NEW CHURCH. 4981
1043-223X See RED THE NET. HOTLINE, LA. 1777
1043-2248 See JOURNAL OF STATE GOVERNMENT, THE. 4479
1043-2256 See JOURNAL OF THE CALIFORNIA DENTAL ASSOCIATION. 1328
1043-2264 See NEW FEDERALIST. 4484
1043-2280 See MATURE TRAVELER. 5484
1043-2302 See TEXAS PRINTER. 4570
1043-2310 See LECTIONARY HOMILETICS. 4973
1043-2345 See ROW (PETALUMA, CALIF.). 4915
1043-2361 See NEW YORK OPERA NEWSLETTER, THE. 386
1043-237X See LIBRARY TALK. 3227
1043-240X See HUMOR AND CARTOON MARKETS. 380
1043-2418 See SUPER GROUP MAGAZINE. 1204
1043-2450 See NORTH AMERICAN FISHERMAN. 2309
1043-2485 See FIRE PROTECTION CONTRACTOR, THE. 2289
1043-2493 See EXPLORATIONS. SPECIAL SERIES. 2846
1043-254X See JOURNAL OF DENTAL HYGIENE. 1326
1043-2558 See FLUID / PARTICLE SEPARATION JOURNAL. 1024
1043-2590 See MUSTANG!. 2801
1043-2604 See CLINICAL DIGEST SERIES. DERMATOLOGY. 3718
1043-2620 See NEWS MEDIA YELLOW BOOK OF WASHINGTON AND NEW YORK, THE. 1118
1043-2639 See MAYBERRY GAZETTE, THE. 1134
1043-2671 See TODAY'S ECONOMY (DENVER, COLO.). 1524
1043-268X See REPORT ON DEFENSE PLANT WASTES. 4055
1043-2698 See ENVIRONMENTAL LIABILITY REPORT, THE. 2168
1043-2752 See REGULATORY AFFAIRS. 3792
1043-2760 See TRENDS IN ENDOCRINOLOGY AND METABOLISM. 3733
1043-2795 See NATIONAL JEWISH NEWS, THE. 5051
1043-2809 See APPALACHIAN READER, THE. 5273
1043-285X See IBC'S MONEY MARKET INSIGHT. 900
1043-2884 See ENVIRONMENTAL SOFTWARE REPORT. 2170
1043-2906 See GROWING EDGE (CORVALLIS, OR.), THE. 2418
1043-2949 See GREEN SHEET (MURRAY, UTAH), THE. 1826
1043-2957 See O'DWYER'S PR SERVICES REPORT. 763
1043-2981 See INFECTIOUS DISEASE AND THERAPY. 3714
1043-299X See FISH AND FISH EGG DISTRIBUTION REPORT OF THE NATIONAL FISH HATCHERY SYSTEM. 2301

1043-3023 See ILVS REVIEW. 4089
1043-3031 See CLINICAL ABSTRACTS/CURRENT THERAPEUTIC FINDINGS. 4296
1043-3074 See HEAD & NECK. 3965
1043-3082 See EXECUTIVE ACTION REPORT. 3100
1043-3104 See DEALER PROGRESS. 78
1043-3163 See RECOVERY NOW. 3633
1043-3198 See CLINICAL PRACTICE OF GYNECOLOGY. 3759
1043-3201 See CQ AMATEUR RADIO ... BEGINNER'S GUIDE TO AMATEUR RADIO. 1130
1043-321X See BREAST DISEASES. 3758
1043-3236 See PRESS (ELMHURST, ILL. : OAK BROOK ED.). 5661
1043-3252 See ADVANCES IN BIOMATERIALS (LANCASTER, PA.). 3546
1043-3309 See JOURNAL OF AGRICULTURAL ECONOMICS RESEARCH, THE. 99
1043-3317 See ARS CERAMICA. 2586
1043-3325 See PARTING GIFTS. 3467
1043-3333 See EVERGREEN CHRONICLES, THE. 2794
1043-3341 See ECHOES (BLAINE, ME.). 2732
1043-3473 See MYSTERY READERS JOURNAL. 3414
1043-3511 See NCA QUARTERLY. 1766
1043-352X See BOOK NEWSLETTER (MINNEAPOLIS, MINN.). 3338
1043-3538 See NEW WORLD (1989), THE. 5033
1043-3546 See DAIRY, FOOD AND ENVIRONMENTAL SANITATION. 2333
1043-3635 See 2000 AD PRESENTS. 1059
1043-3678 See CAIN AND SCOTT MARKET SUMMARY, THE. 4835
1043-3694 See INFOTEXT (IRVINE, CALIF.). 1113
1043-3767 See AIRCRAFT BLUEBOOK-PRICE DIGEST. 9
1043-3805 See KANSAS WORKING PAPERS IN LINGUISTICS. 3293
1043-383X See CABIRION AND GAY BOOKS BULLETIN, THE. 2793
1043-3848 See ARS LYRICA. 3460
1043-3856 See REPORT ON GUATEMALA. 5215
1043-3880 See OPEN MINDS. 4606
1043-3937 See CITY GUIDE (NEW YORK, N.Y.). 5466
1043-3961 See WEST-TAX PREPARER TO ACCOMPANY WEST'S FEDERAL TAXATION. 4758
1043-3996 See CONTEMPORARY TOPICS IN PURE AND APPLIED CONDENSED MATTER SCIENCE. 5097
1043-4046 See ADVANCES IN PHYSIOLOGY EDUCATION. 577
1043-4054 See TRANSPORTATION BUILDER. 5396
1043-4062 See CONSTITUTIONAL POLITICAL ECONOMY. 3092
1043-4070 See JOURNAL OF THE HISTORY OF SEXUALITY. 5187
1043-4119 See PLASTIC SURGERY NEWS (ARLINGTON HEIGHTS, ILL.). 3972
1043-4135 See JUDGE DREDD. 2489
1043-4143 See NATIONAL DIRECTORY OF ADDRESSES AND TELEPHONE NUMBERS (MARINA DEL REY, CALIF.), THE. 1118
1043-4151 See COLUMBIAN (VANCOUVER, WASH.). 5760
1043-4194 See VISIONS. 2601
1043-4208 See DX MAGAZINE, THE. 1154
1043-4224 See SCIENTIFIC SLEUTHING REVIEW. 5155
1043-4232 See PROFESSIONAL CLEANING JOURNAL. 1703
1043-4259 See OKC ACTION. 2542
1043-4275 See FLORIDA STATE UNIVERSITY RESEARCH IN REVIEW. 1824
1043-4291 See POST (MIDDLEBURG, PA. 1976), THE. 5738

1043-4313 See YORK DAILY RECORD (YORK, PA. : 1973). 5741

1043-433X See NEWSLETTER / IEEE PROFESSIONAL COMMUNICATION SOCIETY. 2073

1043-4356 See JOURNAL OF CARDIOVASCULAR TECHNOLOGY (NEW YORK, N.Y.). 3694

1043-4364 See PEAK PERFORMANCE SELLING. 881

1043-4372 See MAILING LIST COMPANIES AND CATAGORIES ... DIRECTORY. 1145

1043-4380 See 1992, THE EXTERNAL IMPACT OF EUROPEAN UNIFICATION. 1632

1043-4488 See COUNTRY AMERICA. 4112

1043-4518 See JOURNAL OF GASTROINTESTINAL MOTILITY. 3747

1043-4526 See ADVANCES IN FOOD AND NUTRITION RESEARCH. 4186

1043-4534 See HARVARD PAPERS IN BOTANY. 512

1043-4542 See JOURNAL OF PEDIATRIC ONCOLOGY NURSING. 3859

1043-4577 See BERLITZ TRAVELER'S GUIDE TO MEXICO, THE. 5462

1043-4585 See PENGUIN GUIDE TO PORTUGAL, THE. 5488

1043-4593 See PENGUIN GUIDE TO SPAIN, THE. 5488

1043-4607 See PENGUIN GUIDE TO GREECE, THE. 5488

1043-4631 See RATIONALITY AND SOCIETY. 5214

1043-464X See FIRE RESISTANT MATERIALS AND PRODUCTS, PATENTS AND ABSTRACTS. 2290

1043-4666 See CYTOKINE (PHILADELPHIA, PA.). 453

1043-4674 See NEW BIOLOGIST, THE. 467

1043-4682 See SEMINARS IN CELL BIOLOGY. 473

1043-4690 See LET'S GO. THE BUDGET GUIDE TO ITALY (INCLUDING TUNISIA). 5483

1043-4712 See PROCEEDINGS OF THE INTERNATIONAL AIR CARGO FORUM. 5390

1043-4739 See TALES OF THE NINJA WARRIORS. 1070

1043-4771 See PAINTBALL (BURBANK, LOS ANGELES COUNTY, CALIF.). 4864

1043-4852 See CATALOG OF NEW FOREIGN AND INTERNATIONAL LAW TITLES. 3126

1043-4895 See CENTRAL VIRGINIA HERITAGE. 2442

1043-495X See LITE FLYER SAFETY ALERT ACTIONGRAM. 27

1043-4968 See LITE FLYER. 27

1043-4976 See SIM INDUSTRIAL MICROBIOLOGY NEWS. 2017

1043-4992 See HARRISON NEWS-HERALD. 5728

1043-500X See JOURNAL OF OFFENDER MONITORING. 3167

1043-5026 See FOLK ART MESSENGER. 350

1043-5050 See PACIFIC REVIEW (SAN BERNARDINO, CALIF.). 2542

1043-5085 See ASPEN MAGAZINE. 2528

1043-5093 See STAMPING QUARTERLY. 4020

1043-5158 See SOUTHEASTERN COLLEGE ART CONFERENCE REVIEW. 331

1043-5174 See BARLEY GENETICS NEWSLETTER. 200

1043-5212 See PACIFIC NORTHWEST EXECUTIVE. 702

1043-5255 See COMPARATIVE LABOR LAW JOURNAL. 3145

1043-5379 See AMICA NEWS BULLETIN, THE. 4100

1043-5417 See MARKETING TO DOCTORS. 932

1043-545X See COLUMBINE FAX DIRECTORY. 1151

1043-5468 See BEAUTIFUL GLASS FOR HOME & OFFICE. 2586

1043-5492 See BOWHUNTING WORLD. 4869

1043-5506 See LABOR RELATIONS REFERENCE MANUAL. 3151

1043-5522 See BIBLICAL PREACHING JOURNAL. 4939

1043-5557 See CORTLAND COUNTY CONNECTION. 77

1043-5565 See NOISE REGULATION REPORT. 2179

1043-5573 See WORLD TABLES (BALTIMORE, MD.). 1641

1043-5662 See INTERNATIONAL TRADE REPORTER. IMPORT REFERENCE MANUAL. 842

1043-5670 See INTERNATIONAL TRADE REPORTER. EXPORT REFERENCE MANUAL. 842

1043-5727 See SOCIOCRITICISM (NEW YORK, N.Y.). 5260

1043-5743 See IRISH STUDIES (NEW YORK, N.Y.). 2693

1043-5751 See STUDIES IN GERARD MANLEY HOPKINS. 3472

1043-5786 See STUDIES IN EUROPEAN THOUGHT. 5223

1043-5794 See STUDIES IN ITALIAN CULTURE. LITERATURE IN HISTORY. 246

1043-5808 See NEW GERMAN-AMERICAN STUDIES. 2269

1043-5816 See EMORY STUDIES IN EARLY CHRISTIANITY. 4956

1043-5824 See ALLSTATE MOTOR CLUB RV SALES, RENTAL & SERVICE DIRECTORY. 5375

1043-5832 See ALLSTATE MOTOR CLUB AMERICA'S FAVORITE NATIONAL PARKS. 5460

1043-5905 See PHARM-AID (CHATHAM, N.J.). 4319

1043-593X See GRAND LEDGE INDEPENDENT. 5692

1043-5964 See LABOR ARBITRATION INDEX (ANNUAL SUMMARY). 3150

1043-5972 See ATMOSPHERE CRISIS, THE. 5192

1043-5999 See TULSA KIDS. 1071

1043-6057 See INSECT WORLD (LANSING, MICH.). 1064

1043-6065 See BOVE & RHODES INSIDE REPORT ON DESKTOP PUBLISHING AND MULTIMEDIA. 1263

1043-6081 See HEALTH LAW JOURNAL OF OHIO. 2977

1043-609X See JOURNAL OF NIH RESEARCH, THE. 461

1043-6103 See AAPG TREATISE OF PETROLEUM GEOLOGY. ATLAS OF OIL AND GAS FIELDS. 4248

1043-6138 See TRAVEL PUBLISHING NEWS. 5496

1043-6146 See HARLOW REPORT, GEOGRAPHIC INFORMATION SYSTEMS, THE. 869

1043-6227 See BUSINESS & ECONOMIC REPORT. 1550

1043-6251 See ACP HEALTH LIBRARY. 3543

1043-626X See PROGRESS IN ELECTROMAGNETICS RESEARCH. 4445

1043-6278 See PROBLEMS IN OPTOMETRY. 4217

1043-6359 See SELECTED BIBLIOGRAPHY OF MATERIALS AND RESOURCES ON WOMEN, A. 5566

1043-6367 See DISCRETE SEMICONDUCTORS. DIRECT ALTERNATE SOURCES. 2042

1043-6375 See SOUTHERN LINKS (HILTON HEAD ISLAND, S.C.). 4919

1043-6383 See BRIDGE TODAY!. 4858

1043-6405 See NEW JERSEY LAKE SURVEY MAP GUIDE. 2570

1043-643X See CHINESE HISTORIANS. 2649

1043-6448 See CAD/CAM, CAE, SURVEY, REVIEW, AND BUYERS' GUIDE. 1173

1043-6464 See JOURNAL OF MICROCOMPUTER SYSTEMS MANAGEMENT. 1192

1043-6537 See BEST OF MACAU, THE. 5463

1043-6545 See BEST OF HONG KONG, THE. 5463

1043-6553 See BEST OF CHINA WITH HONG KONG AND MACAU, THE. 5463

1043-6596 See JOURNAL OF TRANSCULTURAL NURSING. 3860

1043-6618 See PHARMACOLOGICAL RESEARCH. 4322

1043-6669 See DIRECTORY OF THE NATIONAL ASSOCIATION OF ADVISORS FOR THE HEALTH PROFESSIONS. 3913

1043-6677 See BLACK ETHNIC COLLECTIBLES. 2256

1043-6685 See HAWAII ANNUAL ECONOMIC REPORT. 1565

1043-6774 See WESTCHESTER FAMILY. 1071

1043-6790 See PARTICLE WORLD. 4450

1043-6839 See IMPRESSIONS (DALLAS, TEX.). 1085

1043-6863 See SPECIAL ISSUES. 425

1043-6871 See PROCEEDINGS / SYMPOSIUM ON LOGIC IN COMPUTER SCIENCE. 1200

1043-6898 See BALLOT ACCESS NEWS. 4465

1043-6928 See LITERATURE, INTERPRETATION, THEORY. 3407

1043-6995 See CANCER DETECTION AND PREVENTION. SUPPLEMENT. 3811

1043-7002 See CATALOG OF AMERICAN NATIONAL STANDARDS. 4030

1043-7010 See ICE RIVER. 3395

1043-7029 See AMERRIKUA! (SCHUYLER FALLS, N.Y.). 2255

1043-707X See ADVANCES IN MAGNETIC RESONANCE. SUPPLEMENT. 4443

1043-7118 See DISTRIBUTOR'S & WHOLESALER'S ADVISOR, THE. 866

1043-7134 See INTERNATIONAL JOURNAL OF RESEARCH AND ENGINEERING (POSTAL APPLICATION). 1145

1043-724X See AMERICAN BANKER CORPORATE SURVEY. 769

1043-7274 See FEDERAL EQUAL OPPORTUNITY REPORTER. 1669

1043-7312 See LAND RIG NEWSLETTER, THE. 4263

1043-7320 See INDEPENDENT ENERGY. 1946

1043-7347 See CONCEPTS IN MAGNETIC RESONANCE. 4443

1043-7355 See LEGAL MANAGEMENT. 3000

1043-7371 See FEDERAL INCOME TAX REGULATIONS (1986). 4724

1043-7398 See JOURNAL OF ELECTRONIC PACKAGING. 2069

1043-7428 See PARTNER'S REPORT (NEW YORK, N.Y. 1989). 881

1043-7460 See NATURAL RESOURCES (COLLEGE PARK, MD.). 2199

1043-7479 See ARCTIC & ANTARCTIC REGIONS. 1351

1043-7495 See CANADIAN NEWSPAPER CIRCULATION FACTBOOK. 5781

1043-7533 See LARGE ANIMAL VETERINARIAN COVERING HEALTH & NUTRITION. 5515

1043-755X See ADVANCED MUNICIPAL BONDS WORKSHOP. 2928

1043-7576 See PRO WRESTLING ILLUSTRATED. 4913

1043-7584 See COMBAT HANDGUNS. 4039

1043-7592 See STUDIES IN DANCE HISTORY. 1314

1043-7606 See INDOOR AIR REVIEW. 1609

1043-7665 See TRADING POST (COLUMBIA, MD.). 4059

1043-7797 See JOURNAL OF SOCIAL WORK EDUCATION. 5293

1043-7800 See COOPERATIVE FORECASTING. TECHNICAL REPORT. 1471

1043-786X See ENVIRONMENTAL MANAGER. 2228

1043-7878 See TRUE VINE. 5040

1043-7908 See BUSINESS RANKINGS ANNUAL. 652

1043-7916 See JOURNAL OF SOVIET NATIONALITIES. 2266

1043-7967 See CHRONICLE OF HIGHER EDUCATION ALMANAC, THE. 1815

1043-8009 See RADIO CONTROL BOAT MODELER. 375

1043-8017 See CLEANROOMS (FLEMINGTON, N.J.). 2860

1043-8033 See CHINESE JOURNAL OF ENGINEERING THERMOPHYSICS. 2101

1043-8092 See LASER FOCUS WORLD. 4437

1043-8157 See MONDAY DEVELOPMENTS. 5296

1043-8165 See DR. FOX'S NEW HEALTH JOURNAL. 4774

1043-8173 See WHO'S WHO IN COLLECTIBLES AND ANTIQUES. 252

1043-8181 See GAMEROOM (NEW ALBANY, IND.). 4861

1043-8270 See VAN, PICKUP, SPORT UTILITY BUYER'S GUIDE. 5427

1043-8319 See ID SYSTEM BUYER'S GUIDE. 1494

1043-8343 See WORLD REPORT (WHITESTONE, N.Y.). 3454

1043-8378 See STUDENT GUIDE TO THE SAT. 1848

1043-8416 See MEALEY'S LITIGATION REPORTS. INSURANCE INSOLVENCY. 3008

1043-8467 See INSIGHT INTO COURTS. 2982

1043-8491 See CANCER PREVENTION (BALTIMORE, MD.). 3812

1043-853X See KENTUCKY LIVING. 2536

1043-8572 See WASHINGTON CRIME NEWS SERVICES' NARCOTICS DEMAND REDUCTION DIGEST. 1350

1043-8580 See STUDIES OF WORLD LITERATURE IN ENGLISH. 3442

1043-8599 See ECONOMICS OF INNOVATION AND NEW TECHNOLOGY. 5102

1043-8629 See MSA PROFILE. 1506

1043-8637 See COPING (FRANKLIN, TENN.). 3815

1043-8688 See FOLIO'S PUBLISHING NEWS. 4815

1043-8734 See MELPOMENE (MINNEAPOLIS, MINN.). 5561

1043-8807 See NEBRASKA LIBRARIES. 3233

1043-8823 See ISSUES IN CHILD ABUSE ACCUSATIONS. 5291

1043-8831 See HOME-TECH REMODELING AND RENOVATION COST ESTIMATOR. 2900

1043-884X See ONTHEBUS (LOS ANGELES, CALIF.). 3420

1043-8858 See FARM CHEMICALS INTERNATIONAL. 84

1043-8939 See CITY & STATE DIRECTORIES IN PRINT. 1924

1043-8963 See ONCOGENES AND GROWTH FACTORS ABSTRACTS. 3661

1043-898X See CONTEMPORARY PACIFIC, THE. 2510

1043-8998 See HUMAN CAPITAL. 869

1043-9021 See ALLSTATE MOTOR CLUB GREAT NATIONAL PARK VACATIONS. 5460

1043-9056 See ENVIRONMENTAL SOFTWARE DIRECTORY. 2170

1043-9064 See ATARIAN VIDEO GAME MAGAZINE. 4857

1043-9129 See SELMA TIMES-JOURNAL, THE. 5628

1043-9137 See FLORICULTURE DIRECTIONS. 2414

1043-9145 See DESIGN WITH FLOWERS. 372

1043-9161 See PACE BUYER'S GUIDES. USED CAR PRICES. 5422

1043-9226 See TRADEWEEK (LOS ANGELES, CALIF.). 854

1043-9250 See UNITED SENIORS HEALTH REPORT. 5182

1043-934X See SPACE COMMERCE. 35

1043-9366 See YALE JOURNAL OF LAW AND FEMINISM. 3076

1043-9374 See BIOGRAPHY REVIEW. 430

1043-9382 See AIRCRAFT BLUEBOOK MARKETLINE. 9

1043-9455 See BLACK SACRED MUSIC. 4103

1043-9463 See POLICING AND SOCIETY. 3172

1043-9471 See METHODS IN NEUROSCIENCES. 3838

1043-951X See CHINA ECONOMIC REVIEW. 1469

1043-9579 See VIDEOS FOR BUSINESS AND TRAINING. 1143

1043-9587 See MERRILLVILLE HERALD, THE. 5665

1043-9595 See LITTLE PEOPLE'S PRESS, THE. 2922

1043-9617 See ASIC & EDA. 4398

1043-9641 See NOUVELLES ESTHETIQUES (AMERICAN ED.), LES. 405

1043-9714 See STOCKHOLDERS & CREDITORS NEWS SERVICE CONCERNING EASTERN AIRLINES, INC. / CONTINENTAL AIRLINES, INC. 37

1043-9722 See DIRECTORY OF SEASONAL/HOLIDAY CRAFT BOUTIQUES. 5268

1043-979X See WOMEN WITH WHEELS. 5428

1043-9811 See HARPER'S BIOCHEMISTRY. 488

1043-982X See ESD TECHNOLOGY. 1975

1043-9838 See NATIONAL HOME-WORK NEWS. 879

1043-9854 See NINA LYTTON'S OPEN SYSTEMS ADVISOR. 1238

1043-9862 See JOURNAL OF CONTEMPORARY CRIMINAL JUSTICE. 3167

1043-9900 See NATIONAL ARTIST SURVEY. 359

1043-9935 See COSMIC SOFTWARE CATALOG. 1228

1043-9986 See ENDOCRINE PATHOLOGY UPDATE. 3729

1044-0003 See INTERNATIONAL JOURNAL OF ORIENTAL MEDICINE. 4308

1044-0011 See S'VARA (NEW YORK, N.Y.). 4363

1044-002X See JOURNAL OF EUROPEAN BUSINESS, THE. 1613

1044-0046 See JOURNAL OF SUSTAINABLE AGRICULTURE. 100

1044-0054 See JOURNAL OF PHARMACY TEACHING. 4312

1044-0062 See MISSISSIPPI WILDLIFE. 4874

1044-0070 See MESSENGER (TROY, ALA.), THE. 5627

1044-0089 See MID-CITIES NEWS, THE. 5752

1044-0097 See GRAND PRAIRIE NEWS (GRAND PRAIRIE, TEX.). 5750

1044-0100 See ALTERNATIVES REPORT, THE. 5502

1044-0151 See VICA JOURNAL. 4209

1044-016X See AIR POWER HISTORY. 8

1044-0178 See DYNAMIC PREACHING. 4954

1044-0186 See ARIZONA BAPTIST BEACON (ARIZONA SOUTHERN BAPTIST CONVENTION). 4936

1044-0194 See BARCLAYS LAW LIBRARY. 2940

1044-0224 See EQUINE IMAGES. 373

1044-0267 See NELSON'S GUIDE TO INSTITUTIONAL RESEARCH. 909

1044-0283 See GLOBAL FINANCE JOURNAL. 789

1044-0305 See JOURNAL OF THE AMERICAN SOCIETY FOR MASS SPECTROMETRY. 1017

1044-033X See ENVIRONMENTAL AND URBAN ISSUES. 2821

1044-0348 See MCGREGOR MIRROR AND THE CRAWFORD SUN, THE. 5752

1044-0380 See PRATTVILLE PROGRESS (PRATTVILLE, ALA.), THE. 5628

1044-0399 See CHARLOTTE SUN HERALD. 5649

1044-0410 See NOTES ON ANTHROPOLOGY AND INTERCULTURAL COMMUNITY WORK. 242

1044-0445 See AV MARKET PLACE. 726

1044-0453 See DIRECTORY OF ORGANIZATIONS IN EDUCATIONAL MANAGEMENT. 1736

1044-0488 See HOPSCOTCH (SARATOGA SPRINGS, N.Y.). 1064

1044-0534 See AFTERLOSS (RANCHO MIRAGE, CALIF.). 4572

1044-0623 See ANUARIO BIBLIOGRAFICO DE HISTORIA DEL PENSAMIENTO IBERO E IBEROAMERICANO. 3362

1044-0631 See HAZARDOUS AND INDUSTRIAL WASTE. 2230

1044-064X See CHINESE JOURNAL OF AUTOMATION. 1968

1044-0666 See RECRUITMENT, RETENTION, & RESTRUCTURING REPORT. 3868

1044-0666 See RECRUITMENT & RETENTION REPORT. 3868

1044-0690 See CHOICES IN RESPIRATORY MANAGEMENT. 3949

1044-0704 See MODELL'S DRUGS IN CURRENT USE AND NEW DRUGS. 4316

1044-0720 See DISNEY'S DUCKTALES. 1063

1044-0720 See DISNEY'S DUCKTALES. 1063

1044-0755 See JOURNAL OF COMPUTING & SOCIETY. 5205

1044-0771 See ALLSTATE MOTOR CLUB GREAT CAMPING VACATIONS, NORTHWEST. 5460

1044-078X See FROMMER'S TOURING GUIDE TO LENINGRAD/MOSCOW. 5478

1044-0801 See U.S. ROLLER SKATING. 4927

1044-0844 See CHICAGO ENTERPRISE. 1601

1044-0887 See WHO'S WHO IN ENTERTAINMENT. 335

1044-0933 See HISPANIC MEDIA & MARKET SOURCE. 925

1044-0941 See QUALITY EXECUTIVE, THE. 884

1044-0976 See GEORGIA COUNTY GUIDE, THE. 5327

1044-1026 See LIVING BLUES BLUES DIRECTORY. 4129

1044-1034 See REJOICE! (UNIVERSITY, MISS.). 4149

1044-1042 See OLD TIME COUNTRY. 4143

1044-1093 See DOING BUSINESS WITH THE USSR. 669

1044-1107 See NRTA BULLETIN. 5180

1044-1115 See CALIFORNIA RULES OF COURT. FEDERAL. 3139

1044-1123 See AARP BULLETIN. 5177

1044-1174 See ARLINGTON NEWS (1989). 5746

1044-1190 See MOBILE PRODUCT NEWS. 1160

1044-1204 See PGA MAGAZINE (1989). 4912

1044-1239 See SYSTEMS 3X/400. 1204

1044-1247 See SPOTLIGHT (BROOKLYN, N.Y.). 2512

1044-131X See MACINTOSH MARKET REPORT. 1194

1044-1336 See MOVIES USA. 4075

1044-1344 See U.S. TOY COLLECTOR MAGAZINE. 2585

1044-1360 See SF UNIQUE VACATION SELECTIONS. 5491

1044-1387 See ANARCHY (COLUMBIA, MO.). 4539

1044-1395 See PHYSICIANS' DESK REFERENCE FOR NONPRESCRIPTION DRUGS. 4324

1044-1417 See PATTERSON'S ELEMENTARY EDUCATION. 1772

1044-1425 See PHOTONICS DIRECTORY, THE. 4440

1044-1522 See OBESITY & HEALTH. 4197

1044-1549 See AMERICAN JOURNAL OF RESPIRATORY CELL AND MOLECULAR BIOLOGY. 3948

1044-1557 See OPHTHALMOLOGY REPORT. 3878

1044-1573 See TOLSTOY STUDIES JOURNAL. 3447

1044-1581 See CATHOLIC ANSWER, THE. 5025

1044-1603 See RADIO INK. 1137

1044-1638 See PERFORMANCE PRACTICE REVIEW. 4145

1044-1654 See JOURNAL OF THE STUDENT NATIONAL MEDICAL ASSOCIATION. 3599

1044-1662 See INSTITUTIONAL REAL ESTATE LETTER, THE. 4839

1044-1700 See CD REVIEW (HANCOCK, N.H.). 4108

1044-1743 See BULLETIN - HUDSON FAMILY ASSOCIATION, SOUTH. 2440

1044-1794 See COMPUTER COUNSEL. 864

1044-1816 See INTERNATIONAL PETROLEUM STATISTICS REPORT. 4261

1044-1840 *See* TRAINING DIRECTORY FOR BUSINESS AND INDUSTRY. **716**

1044-1891 *See* ARAMCO WORLD (1987). **2768**

1044-1905 *See* OLD LAWRENCE REMINISCENCES. **2465**

1044-193X *See* HUMAN RIGHTS IN SWEDEN. **4509**

1044-1948 *See* MICHIGAN BANKER (LANSING, MICH.). **798**

1044-1964 *See* ST. CLAIR NEWS-AEGIS. **5628**

1044-1980 *See* AOHA TODAY!. **3777**

1044-2022 *See* CLEARING UP. CALIFORNIA ENERGY MARKETS. **1601**

1044-2030 See MOLECULAR BIOLOGY OF THE CELL. **539**

1044-2049 *See* ACUTE TOXICITY DATA. **3978**

1044-2057 *See* DIASPORA (NEW YORK, N.Y.). **5198**

1044-2073 *See* JOURNAL OF DISABILITY POLICY STUDIES, THE. **4389**

1044-209X *See* SENIOR HEALTH DIGEST. **4802**

1044-2103 *See* PSYCHOANALYTIC BOOKS. **4610**

1044-2111 *See* HARVARD BUSINESS SCHOOL CORE COLLECTION. **416**

1044-2138 *See* AIDS INFORMATION SOURCEBOOK. **3664**

1044-2189 *See* PERSONNEL ALERT (MAYWOOD, N.J.), THE. **945**

1044-2197 *See* CONTEMPORARY MUSICIANS. **4111**

1044-2200 *See* PRACTICAL FORESTRY. **2390**

1044-2243 *See* EXECUTIVES ON THE MOVE. **867**

1044-2251 See FROMMER'S COMPREHENSIVE TRAVEL GUIDE. CANADA. **5475**

1044-226X *See* FROMMER'S EGYPT. **5477**

1044-2278 See FROMMER'S COMPREHENSIVE TRAVEL GUIDE. PORTUGAL. **5476**

1044-2286 See FROMMER'S COMPREHENSIVE TRAVEL GUIDE. NEW ENGLAND. **5476**

1044-2308 See FROMMER'S COMPREHENSIVE TRAVEL GUIDE. NEW YORK STATE. **5476**

1044-2316 See FROMMER'S COMPREHENSIVE TRAVEL GUIDE. THE CAROLINAS & GEORGIA. **5477**

1044-2316 See FROMMER'S COMPREHENSIVE TRAVEL GUIDE. VIRGINIA. **5477**

1044-2324 *See* GEORGIA ENVIRONMENTAL LAW LETTER. **3112**

1044-2375 See FROMMER'S COMPREHENSIVE TRAVEL GUIDE. CARIBBEAN. **5475**

1044-2383 *See* FROMMER'S COMPREHENSIVE TRAVEL GUIDE. BERMUDA & THE BAHAMAS. **5475**

1044-2391 See FROMMER'S COMPREHENSIVE TRAVEL GUIDE. FLORIDA. **5475**

1044-2413 *See* FROMMER'S BELGIUM, HOLLAND & LUXEMBOURG. **5474**

1044-2529 *See* BONSAI TODAY. **2410**

1044-2618 *See* WILDLIFE REHABILITATION TODAY. **227**

1044-2634 *See* MICHIGAN JOURNAL OF COUNSELING AND DEVELOPMENT. **4604**

1044-2782 *See* NEW TIMES (SEATTLE, WASH.). **4186**

1044-2790 *See* JOURNAL OF HEALTH & HEALING (WILDWOOD, GA.). **2599**

1044-2812 *See* MEANS ELECTRICAL CHANGE ORDER COST DATA. **2071**

1044-2839 *See* LAKE STATION HERALD. **5665**

1044-2847 See CAD INDUSTRY DIRECTORY (HARDWARE ED.). **1231**

1044-2871 *See* CED (DENVER, COLO.). **1130**

1044-2944 *See* BRITISH-AMERICAN DEAL REVIEW, THE. **1633**

1044-2979 *See* JOURNAL OF ASIAN AND AFRICAN AFFAIRS. **4527**

1044-2987 *See* CATALOG OF CURRENT LAW TITLES. **2949**

1044-3061 *See* GARBAGE (BROOKLYN, NEW YORK, N.Y.). **2194**

1044-307X *See* OBG MANAGEMENT. **3766**

1044-3096 *See* ALMANAC OF HIGHER EDUCATION, THE. **1808**

1044-3118 *See* SPORT PSYCHOLOGY TRAINING BULLETIN. **4921**

1044-3134 *See* NYPIRG AGENDA. **1298**

1044-3142 *See* NEWSLETTER FOR DENTISTS. **1331**

1044-3150 *See* ELECTRONIC MUSIC EDUCATOR. **1240**

1044-3193 *See* CONSUMER REPORTS HEALTH LETTER. **4772**

1044-3207 *See* OCCUPATIONAL THERAPY PRACTICE. **1883**

1044-3223 *See* CANADA-U.S. OUTLOOK. **4716**

1044-3231 *See* FINANCIAL MARKETING LETTER, THE. **924**

1044-324X *See* STATE AND REGIONAL ASSOCIATIONS OF THE UNITED STATES. **713**

1044-3266 *See* KEYBOARD CLASSICS. **4127**

1044-3274 See PREPARING A TOXIC TORT CASE FOR TRIAL. **3030**

1044-3312 *See* ULTIMATE NETWORKING DIRECTORY, THE. **1205**

1044-3479 *See* SOUTH FLORIDA ENVIRONMENTAL READER (ELECTRONIC ED.). **2243**

1044-3479 *See* SOUTH FLORIDA ENVIRONMENTAL READER (PRINT ED.). **2243**

1044-3487 *See* CHICANO INDEX, THE. **2635**

1044-3509 *See* INTERNATIONAL EDUCATOR (WEST BRIDGEWATER, MASS.), THE. **1897**

1044-3525 *See* CORPORATE DIRECTORY, THE. **661**

1044-3576 *See* GARDEN STATE HOME & GARDEN. **2900**

1044-3584 See TODAY'S FACILITY MANAGER. **2903**

1044-3622 *See* GEM & LAPIDARY QUARTERLY. **2914**

1044-3630 *See* BATON ROUGE DAILY NEWS. **5683**

1044-3657 *See* STARKVILLE DAILY NEWS. **5702**

1044-3665 *See* INDONESIA NEWS SERVICE. **2505**

1044-3746 *See* INSTANT AND SMALL COMMERCIAL PRINTER. **4566**

1044-3797 *See* EMERGENCY PEDIATRICS. **3903**

1044-3800 *See* OCLC ANNUAL REPORT. **3238**

1044-3851 *See* HEIDELBERG BULLETIN, THE. **1092**

1044-3886 *See* PRO-ACTION. **3242**

1044-3894 *See* FAMILIES IN SOCIETY. **5285**

1044-3967 *See* INDEX TO AV PRODUCERS & DISTRIBUTORS. **1896**

1044-3975 *See* DEFENSE MARKETING INTERNATIONAL. **4041**

1044-3983 *See* EPIDEMIOLOGY (CAMBRIDGE, MASS.). **3734**

1044-4009 *See* CRAFT INTERNATIONAL. **371**

1044-4017 *See* JOINT COMMISSION PERSPECTIVES. **3786**

1044-4025 *See* PRO NE NATA : PRN. **3867**

1044-405X *See* HORN BOOK GUIDE TO CHILDREN'S AND YOUNG ADULT BOOKS, THE. **1064**

1044-4068 *See* INTERNATIONAL JOURNAL OF CONFLICT MANAGEMENT, THE. **871**

1044-4076 *See* HEALTH CARE STANDARDS. **4778**

1044-4106 *See* NEWS-TIMES (DANBURY, CONN.), THE. **5646**

1044-4122 *See* JOURNAL OF VASCULAR TECHNOLOGY, THE. **3708**

1044-4130 *See* AKRON TAX JOURNAL. **4708**

1044-4149 *See* DIONYSOS (SUPERIOR, WISC.). **1342**

1044-4211 *See* ACPM NEWS. **3544**

1044-422X *See* BIOLOGICAL THERAPIES IN PSYCHIATRY NEWSLETTER. **3922**

1044-4238 *See* SOUTH CAROLINA LAWYER. **3057**

1044-4246 *See* HERALD-TIMES (BLOOMINGTON, IND.), THE. **5664**

1044-4262 *See* SYSTEMS INTEGRATION. **1274**

1044-4289 *See* BEACON (1989), THE. **5709**

1044-4297 *See* SERIAL SOURCES OF THE BIOSIS PREVIEWS DATABASE. **473**

1044-4300 *See* JOURNAL OF APPLIED FIRE SCIENCE. **2291**

1044-4319 *See* HOTLINE ON OBJECT-ORIENTED TECHNOLOGY. **1186**

1044-4327 *See* ON THE ROAD (BROOKLYN, NEW YORK, N.Y.). **3239**

1044-4343 *See* PERSONAL FINANCIAL PLANNING (BOSTON, MASS.). **803**

1044-4351 *See* UNITED STATES-GERMAN ECONOMIC YEARBOOK. **717**

1044-4386 *See* STANFORD LAW & POLICY REVIEW. **3058**

1044-4416 *See* MANILA TIMES INTERNATIONAL. **5637**

1044-4440 *See* DIRECTORY OF AMERICAN YOUTH ORGANIZATIONS. **1062**

1044-4467 *See* FEDERAL MARKETING HANDBOOK AND YEARBOOK, THE. **924**

1044-4521 *See* IFDC REPORT (FRENCH ED.). **174**

1044-453X *See* WOLVERINE. **4867**

1044-4556 *See* CONFERENCE RECORD - IEEE INTERNATIONAL CONFERENCE ON COMMUNICATIONS. **1152**

1044-4610 *See* PUNISHER WAR JOURNAL, THE. **4865**

1044-4637 *See* ORIGINAL RECIPES. **2792**

1044-4688 *See* POCKET LIST OF RAILROAD OFFICIALS (INTERNATIONAL ED.), THE. **5434**

1044-4696 *See* ADVANCES IN OXYGENATED PROCESSES. **440**

1044-470X *See* TAIWAN REGISTER. **4847**

1044-4718 *See* ASIAN FINANCE DIRECTORY. **1463**

1044-4734 *See* DIRECTORY OF ASIAN HIGH TECH COMPANIES IN THE UNITED STATES. **5100**

1044-4742 *See* INVENTING AND PATENTING SOURCEBOOK. **1305**

1044-4750 *See* CLARION TECH JOURNAL, THE. **5095**

1044-4769 *See* CAPITAL (ALBANY, N.Y.). **2486**

1044-4785 *See* LAX (GLENDALE, CALIF.). **1193**

1044-4793 *See* PROFESSIONAL SOUND (DURANGO, COLO. : 1989). **4453**

1044-4807 *See* ORIENTAL RUG REVIEW. **2902**

1044-4823 *See* BULLETIN - UNIVERSITY OF CALIFORNIA (SYSTEM). DIVISION OF AGRICULTURE AND NATURAL RESOURCES. **70**

1044-4858 *See* OCLC/AMIGOS COLLECTION ANALYSIS CD. **3238**

1044-4882 *See* MONOGRAPHS IN CLINICAL PEDIATRICS. **3906**

1044-4890 *See* YEAR BOOK OF NEONATAL AND PERINATAL MEDICINE, THE. **3769**

1044-4904 *See* AMERICAN COUNTRY CHRISTMAS. **369**

1044-4947 *See* STATE PROFILE (WASHINGTON, D.C. 1984). **1522**

1044-4971 *See* NATIONAL WILDLIFE FEDERATION SCIENTIFIC AND TECHNICAL SERIES. **4875**

1044-4998 *See* PRINCIPAL'S REPORT (NEW YORK, N.Y.). **882**

1044-5005 *See* MANAGEMENT ACCOUNTING RESEARCH. **747**

1044-503X *See* PERSONAL ADVANTAGE/FINANCIAL. **703**

1044-5080 *See* HAZARDOUS WASTE DRIVER SAFETY MANUAL, THE. **2231**

1044-5110 *See* ATOMIZATION AND SPRAYS. **2008**

1044-5153 *See* MIRABELLA (NEW YORK, N.Y.). **5561**

1044-5323 *See* SEMINARS IN IMMUNOLOGY. **3676**

1044-5331 *See* HELLAS. **3393**

1044-5463 *See* JOURNAL OF CHILD AND ADOLESCENT PSYCHOPHARMACOLOGY. **3928**

1044-5471 *See* JOURNAL OF CLINICAL LASER MEDICINE & SURGERY. **3967**

1044-548X *See* SENIOR HEALTH CARE. **4802**

1044-5498 *See* DNA AND CELL BIOLOGY. **544**

1044-5528 See WHO'S WHO IN THE EGG AND POULTRY INDUSTRIES IN THE UNITED STATES AND CANADA. 224
1044-5544 See CROSSROADS (SPRINGDALE, ARK.). 5281
1044-5633 See SERIES IN PSYCHOSOCIAL EPIDEMIOLOGY. 3936
1044-5706 See OUTLOOK (WASHINGTON, D.C. 1989). 5564
1044-5714 See ACCOUNTING TODAY. 738
1044-5757 See JOHN MACMURRAY STUDIES. 4350
1044-5765 See SEMINARS IN NEUROSCIENCES. 3846
1044-5773 See SEMINARS IN VIROLOGY. 570
1044-5781 See SEMINARS IN DEVELOPMENTAL BIOLOGY. 473
1044-579X See SEMINARS IN CANCER BIOLOGY. 3824
1044-5803 See MATERIALS CHARACTERIZATION. 4008
1044-5854 See PXE AWARENESS. 3631
1044-5897 See NEWSLETTER / VIRGINIA BEACH GENEALOGICAL SOCIETY. 2464
1044-5943 See EDUCATORS GUIDE TO FREE FILMSTRIPS AND SLIDES. 1893
1044-6036 See WESCON CONFERENCE RECORD (1979). 2085
1044-6044 See SOCIAL SCIENCES CITATION INDEX (COMPACT DISC ED.). 5221
1044-6052 See SCIENCE CITATION INDEX (COMPACT DISC ED.). 5176
1044-6079 See MAGAZINE TREND REPORT. 762
1044-6133 See FODOR'S ... TORONTO. 5473
1044-6168 See SOUTHERN CALIFORNIA TDD COMMUNITY DIRECTORY. 5310
1044-6257 See GUNS MAGAZINE. 4897
1044-6265 See EMPLOYEE BENEFIT NEWS. 1665
1044-629X See TRENDS IN HEALTH CARE, LAW & ETHICS. 2253
1044-6303 See MEXICO SERVICE. 2512
1044-6354 See VIDEONEWS INTERNATIONAL (HOLLYWOOD, CALIF.). 1143
1044-6370 See TRUSTEE'S LETTER, THE. 1788
1044-6389 See HEAD'S LETTER, THE. 1750
1044-6400 See ILLINOIS MEDICINE. 3585
1044-6419 See JOURNAL OF LAW AND HEALTH. 3741
1044-646X See GRAPHIC ARTS BLUE BOOK (NORTHEASTERN ED.). 378
1044-6486 See OWL CREEK JOURNAL, THE. 3421
1044-6494 See ASHLAND THEOLOGICAL JOURNAL. 4936
1044-6508 See CANCER CHRONICLES, THE. 3811
1044-6516 See CONSUMER MAGAZINES DIGEST : NUTRITION AND FOOD-RELATED HEALTH TOPICS. 4189
1044-6524 See DAKOTA COUNTY GENEALOGIST, THE. 2444
1044-6583 See NATURAL PHYSIQUE. 4906
1044-6605 See NATIONAL DIRECTORY OF HOME MORTGAGE LENDERS, THE. 801
1044-6648 See FELA REPORTER AND RAILROAD LIABILITY MONITOR. 2970
1044-6672 See DEVELOPMENTAL IMMUNOLOGY. 3669
1044-6699 See OUR WORLD (DAYTONA BEACH, FLA.). 5487
1044-6745 See ALF. 4856
1044-6753 See JOURNAL OF THE PENNSYLVANIA ACADEMY OF SCIENCE. 5121
1044-677X See JOURNAL OF RESEARCH OF THE NATIONAL INSTITUTE OF STANDARDS AND TECHNOLOGY. 4031
1044-6796 See RETAIL INFO SYSTEMS NEWS. 956
1044-6834 See VICKERS BOND TRADERS GUIDE. 919
1044-6850 See VICKERS STOCK TRADERS GUIDE. 919
1044-6893 See PROVOKING THOUGHTS. 4609

1044-6915 See PENNSYLVANIA QUERIES. 2467
1044-6923 See IRISH QUERIES. 2454
1044-6931 See IOWA QUERIES. 2454
1044-694X See INDIANA QUERIES. 2454
1044-7024 See MANUFACTURING USA. 3484
1044-7032 See SELECTED READINGS IN ORAL AND MAXILLOFACIAL SURGERY. 1335
1044-7059 See NATIONAL AMATEUR ASTRONOMY NEWS. 397
1044-7083 See DRUG INTERACTIONS AND SIDE EFFECTS INDEX. 4300
1044-7172 See DOCTOR STRANGE, SORCERER SUPREME. 372
1044-7180 See MARVEL COMICS PRESENTS. 4863
1044-7199 See AFRO TIMES (BROOKLYN, N.Y.). 5713
1044-7202 See COMMUNICO. 5230
1044-727X See AIR SAFETY WEEK. 8
1044-7288 See VIDEO MAGAZINE. 1142
1044-7318 See INTERNATIONAL JOURNAL OF HUMAN-COMPUTER INTERACTION. 1220
1044-7350 See 3-D DATA. 2436
1044-7377 See WOMEN'S SPORTS EXPERIENCE, THE. 4930
1044-7385 See ADVANCING THE CONSUMER INTEREST. 1293
1044-7393 See MOLECULAR AND CHEMICAL NEUROPATHOLOGY. 3838
1044-7423 See PROBATE PRACTICE REPORTER. 3118
1044-7431 See MOLECULAR AND CELLULAR NEUROSCIENCES. 3838
1044-7474 See BNA'S BANKRUPTCY LAW REPORTER. 3085
1044-7482 See WORLD MINE PRODUCTION OF SILVER. 4024
1044-7512 See DOOR (EL CAJON, CALIF.). 4954
1044-7539 See OPELIKA AUBURN NEWS. 5627
1044-7555 See SEDONA RED ROCK NEWS. 5630
1044-758X See BUSINESS FORMS, LABELS & SYSTEMS. 4211
1044-7598 See NATIONAL NEWSLETTER - ASSOCIATED GENERAL CONTRACTORS OF AMERICA. 1619
1044-7601 See AUDIO WEEK. 5315
1044-7644 See TRACKING THE UPCOMING BESTSELLERS. 4833
1044-7652 See CONNECTIONS. 5467
1044-7660 See LAWYER'S MONTHLY CATALOG. 2998
1044-7695 See ENVIRONMENTAL & LAND USE AADMINISTRATIVE LAW REPORTER ER FALR. 3111
1044-7733 See EVANSTON REVIEW, THE. 5660
1044-7741 See FROMMER'S NORTHWEST. 5477
1044-775X See BASICALLY BUCKLES. 2771
1044-7768 See WESTERN RETAILER. 889
1044-7784 See HOW TO FIND BUSINESS INTELLIGENCE IN WASHINGTON. 680
1044-7822 See PARKE COUNTY SENTINEL. 5666
1044-7857 See CHORUS! (DULUTH, GA.). 4109
1044-789X See DR. DOBB'S JOURNAL (1989). 1267
1044-7903 See SPORT TRUCK. 5425
1044-7911 See ESTATE & FINANCIAL PLANNERS ALERT. 3118
1044-792X See LOUISIANA QUERIES. 2458
1044-7938 See MARYLAND QUERIES. 2459
1044-7946 See WOUNDS (KING OF PRUSSIA, PA.). 3652
1044-7970 See GRAPHIC ARTS BLUE BOOK. 4565
1044-7989 See GRAPHIC ARTS BLUE BOOK (SOUTHEASTERN ED.). 378
1044-7997 See ADVANCES IN SOFTWARE SCIENCE AND TECHNOLOGY. 1284
1044-8004 See HUMAN RESOURCE DEVELOPMENT QUARTERLY. 941
1044-8012 See AIRCRAFT TECHNICIAN. 9

1044-8039 See PUBLIC PRODUCTIVITY & MANAGEMENT REVIEW. 4705
1044-8071 See HYPERTENSION INDEX & REVIEWS. 3705
1044-811X See INTERNATIONAL JOURNAL OF BIOSOCIAL AND MEDICAL RESEARCH. 5248
1044-8136 See JOURNAL OF CORPORATE ACCOUNTING AND FINANCE. 746
1044-8144 See MOLECULAR CRYSTALS AND LIQUID CRYSTALS. LETTERS SECTION (1991). 1032
1044-8179 See CE COMPUTING REVIEW. 2020
1044-8195 See AVENGERS WEST COAST. 4857
1044-8209 See TROPOS (EAST LANSING, MICH.). 3330
1044-8217 See FAMILIES AND DISABILITY NEWSLETTER. 4388
1044-825X See ANNUAL DIRECTORY OF WORLD LEADERS. 4626
1044-8268 See AMUSEMENT INDUSTRY BUYERS GUIDE. 4856
1044-8306 See ANTIC'S AMIGA PLUS. 1170
1044-8314 See JOURNAL OF THE ASSOCIATION OF AVIAN VETERINARIANS. 5513
1044-8322 See NEW CATHOLIC EXPLORER. 5033
1044-8330 See ROCKY MOUNTAIN FOOD DEALER BULLETIN : NEWSLETTER FOR MEMBERS OF THE ROCKY MOUNTAIN FOOD DEALERS ASSOCIATION, THE. 2356
1044-8357 See ACTA PHYSICA SINICA. 4395
1044-8403 See CHINESE JOURNAL OF POPULATION SCIENCE. 4551
1044-8500 See OZARKSWATCH (SPRINGFIELD, MO.). 2542
1044-8527 See GRAPHIC ARTS BLUE BOOK (METROPOLITAN NEW YORK-NEW JERSEY ED.). 4565
1044-8535 See GRAPHIC ARTS BLUE BOOK (MIDWESTERN ED.). 378
1044-8578 See NEW WORDS DIGEST. 1882
1044-8608 See STYLES MAGAZINE. 405
1044-8616 See SALON NEWS MAGAZINE. 405
1044-8632 See NEUTRON NEWS. 987
1044-8683 See WALTERS (BALTIMORE, MD.), THE. 368
1044-8705 See AMERICAN SALON'S GREEN BOOK. 402
1044-8756 See LAMPLIGHTER (CHICAGO, ILL.). 3182
1044-8764 See INFOPERSPECTIVES INTERNATIONAL. 1238
1044-8799 See NACORE'S ... COMPENSATION & BENEFITS SURVEY. 2888
1044-8829 See DIRECTORY OF ENGINEERING DOCUMENT SOURCES. 3207
1044-8853 See NOTICIERO ALFONSI. 2701
1044-8888 See CHESS IN INDIANA. 4858
1044-890X See CHINA AND PACIFIC RIM LETTER. 2502
1044-8934 See SINGLE HOUND. 3471
1044-8942 See ST. THOMAS LAW REVIEW. 3058
1044-8985 See JOURNAL OF INTERDISCIPLINARY LITERARY STUDIES. 3400
1044-9000 See FLORIDA COACHING DIRECTORY. 4895
1044-9086 See GEORGIA FACTS. 2734
1044-9108 See GUIDE TO PHOTOGRAPHY WORKSHOPS & SCHOOLS. 4370
1044-9167 See ED MANAGEMENT. 3724
1044-9221 See TECHNICAL, TRADE, & BUSINESS SCHOOL DATA HANDBOOK. MIDWEST/WEST REGIONS. 1916
1044-923X See FODOR'S WAIKIKI. 5474
1044-9264 See GREATER CINCINNATI BUSINESS RECORD, THE. 678
1044-9345 See CALIFORNIA ARBITRATIONS. 2946
1044-9353 See SHOSHONE NEWS-PRESS. 5657
1044-937X See JOURNAL OF AMERICAN DRAMA AND THEATRE, THE. 5365
1044-940X See VERMONT MAGAZINE. 2549

1044-9418 *See* JOURNAL OF TAXATION OF ESTATES & TRUSTS, THE. 3118

1044-9450 *See* REGIONAL AVIATION WEEKLY. 33

1044-9469 *See* AIRPORTS (WASHINGTON, D.C.). 11

1044-9493 *See* WATER ENVIRONMENT & TECHNOLOGY. 2247

1044-9523 *See* CELL GROWTH & DIFFERENTIATION. 533

1044-9574 *See* EMPLOYMENT OPPORTUNITIES (ATHLETICS). 4894

1044-9612 *See* U.S. GEOLOGICAL SURVEY PROFESSIONAL PAPER. 1400

1044-9647 *See* RADIO-CHICAGO. 1137

1044-9663 *See* PLASTICS WEEK (NEW YORK, N.Y.). 4458

1044-9779 *See* INFECTIOUS DISEASES IN CHILDREN. 3714

1044-9809 *See* FOX FAMILY FACTS. 2449

1044-985X *See* RADIO PROMOTION BULLETIN. 1120

1044-9876 *See* AGENDA OF REGULATIONS. 2153

1044-9884 *See* CSR ADVISOR, THE. 2878

1044-9892 *See* ELECTRONIC MESSAGING NEWS. 1110

1044-9906 *See* WHO'S WHO IN ATHLETICS IN AMERICAN COLLEGES AND UNIVERSITIES. 4929

1044-9922 *See* COLUMBIAN-PROGRESS, THE. 5700

1045-0017 *See* HAWAII, WASHINGTON, ALASKA, OREGON COACHING DIRECTORY : AN OFFICIAL PUBLICATION OF THE NATIONAL INTERSCHOLASTIC ATHLETIC ADMINISTRATORS ASSOCIATION, THE ALASKA INTERSCHOLASTIC ATHLETIC ADMINISTRATORS ASSOCIATION, AND THE WASHINGTON SECONDARY SCHOOL ATHLETIC ADMINISTRATORS ASSOCIATION. 4898

1045-0041 *See* DIRECTORY OF COMPANIES OFFERING DIVIDEND REINVESTMENT PLANS. 896

1045-0076 *See* SPHENISCID PENGUIN NEWSLETTER : SPN. 5598

1045-0084 *See* REQUEST (MINNEAPOLIS, MINN.). 4149

1045-0114 *See* CD REVIEW DIGEST. CLASSICAL. 4108

1045-0122 *See* CD REVIEW DIGEST. JAZZ, POPULAR, ETC. 4108

1045-0130 *See* RESOLUTION TRUST REPORTER. 809

1045-0149 *See* FLY ROD & REEL. 2304

1045-0203 *See* INDUSTRIAL COMPUTING PLUS PROGRAMMABLE CONTROLS. 1238

1045-0246 *See* RESCUE (SOLANA BEACH, CALIF.). 3634

1045-0300 *See* GERMAN POLITICS AND SOCIETY. 5200

1045-0319 *See* GUIDE TO OBTAINING MINORITY BUSINESS DIRECTORIES. 678

1045-0343 *See* WORLD DREDGING, MINING & CONSTRUCTION. 2153

1045-0394 *See* NAVSO NEWS. 5297

1045-0416 *See* REGISTER OF AMERICAN YACHTS. 595

1045-0459 *See* SOUTHEASTERN REGULATORY ALERT. 3057

1045-0483 *See* FABRICS & ARCHITECTURE. 298

1045-0491 *See* WE'RE LIVING IN FUNNY TIMES. 3452

1045-053X *See* GUAM BUSINESS NEWS. 678

1045-0548 *See* ... GUIDE TO THE NATION'S HOSPICES, THE. 3579

1045-0564 *See* WORLD CULTURES. 5269

1045-0580 *See* NATURAL RESOURCES, ENERGY, AND ENVIRONMENTAL LAW. 3114

1045-0602 *See* HOBBYISTS' SOURCEBOOK. 2774

1045-0629 *See* PICTURE PERFECT. 4375

1045-0637 *See* JOURNAL OF CHEMICAL TRANSPORT & INDUSTRIAL HISTORY. 1026

1045-067X *See* JOURNAL OF RAILWAY TANK CARS. 5432

1045-0688 *See* ADVANCES IN METAL-ORGANIC CHEMISTRY. 1039

1045-0734 *See* EDUCATION LITERATURE REVIEW. 1740

1045-0750 *See* SPECIAL EFFECTS & STUNTS GUIDE. 4078

1045-0769 *See* PLASTICS MATERIALS. PLASTICS. 4458

1045-0815 *See* CREATOR (WICHITA, KAN.). 4113

1045-0823 *See* IJCAI (UNITED STATES). 1213

1045-0831 *See* STORY (VIENNA, AUSTRIA). 3440

1045-084X *See* JOURNAL : THE LITERARY MAGAZINE OF THE OHIO STATE UNIVERSITY, THE. 3400

1045-0904 *See* PHOEBE (ONEONTA, N.Y.). 5564

1045-0920 *See* INTERNATIONAL REVIEW OF AFRICAN AMERICAN ART, THE. 353

1045-0955 *See* ELECTRONIC MATERIALS TECHNOLOGY NEWS. 2047

1045-1005 *See* BREAD FOR THE WORLD NEWSLETTER. 5275

1045-1013 *See* LAS AMERICAS. 2743

1045-1021 *See* MISSISSIPPI COAST. 2539

1045-103X *See* KOOKS MAGAZINE. 4242

1045-1056 *See* BIOLOGICALS. 445

1045-1064 *See* JOURNAL OF TECHNOLOGY EDUCATION. 5120

1045-1129 *See* STOCHASTICS AND STOCHASTICS REPORT. 3536

1045-1153 *See* ALA NEWS (VERNON HILLS, ILL.). 2929

1045-1188 *See* PEN WORLD. 2776

1045-120X *See* PETERSEN'S ROD & CUSTOM. 5423

1045-1234 *See* PREVUE (READING, PA.). 1119

1045-1307 See LANE GUIDE (WESTERN ED.). 796

1045-1366 *See* EXCALIBUR. 4860

1045-1439 *See* SEC ACCOUNTING & REPORTING UPDATE SERVICE. 751

1045-1447 *See* ACCOUNTING & AUDITING UPDATE SERVICE. 736

1045-1463 *See* LENDER LIABILITY LAW REPORT. 3087

1045-1471 *See* JOURNAL OF S CORPORATION TAXATION. 4735

1045-1498 *See* VOICE TECHNOLOGY NEWS. 2131

1045-151X See GUIDE TO U.S. FOUNDATIONS, THEIR TRUSTEES, OFFICERS, AND DONORS. 4338

1045-1579 *See* REPORT TO THE PRESIDENT AND CONGRESS / NATIONAL AGRICULTURAL RESEARCH AND EXTENSION USERS ADVISORY BOARD. 126

1045-1595 *See* ADULT LEARNING. 1799

1045-1625 *See* GOULD'S CRIMINAL LAW HANDBOOK OF NEW YORK. 3107

1045-1668 *See* NATIONAL CONTRACT MANAGEMENT JOURNAL (1979). 879

1045-1684 *See* DIRECTORY OF MEMBER AGENCIES IN THE UNITED STATES AND CANADA. 5283

1045-1706 *See* OFF-HOLLYWOOD REPORT, THE. 4075

1045-1757 *See* DOBERMAN QUARTERLY. 4286

1045-1765 *See* HOSPITAL COST MANAGEMENT AND ACCOUNTING. 3783

1045-1773 *See* PHOENIX (1989). 2543

1045-1854 *See* PLASTIC CANVAS! MAGAZINE. 374

1045-1870 *See* SEMINARS IN PEDIATRIC INFECTIOUS DISEASES. 3716

1045-1889 *See* INNOVATIONS IN POLYMER/ENGINEERING PLASTICS. 2102

1045-1943 *See* CITY LIGHTS REVIEW. 3376

1045-1951 *See* FUND RAISER'S GUIDE TO HUMAN SERVICE FUNDING. 4336

1045-1978 *See* AUTOPARTS REPORT, THE. 5407

1045-2001 *See* PROGRESS IN NEUROENDOCRINIMMUNOLOGY. 3732

1045-201X *See* HEPCATS. 5074

1045-2044 *See* PROJECT BREED DIRECTORY. 2252

1045-2087 *See* NSGA RETAIL FOCUS. 4908

1045-2133 See GUIDE TO PRIVATE FORTUNES. 678

1045-2192 *See* DAILY REPORT. EAST ASIA. INDEX. 1130

1045-2206 *See* COMPLETE CAR COST GUIDE, THE. 5412

1045-2230 *See* ASIA TODAY (WASHINGTON, D.C.). 2646

1045-2249 *See* BEHAVIORAL ECOLOGY. 2211

1045-2257 *See* GENES, CHROMOSOMES & CANCER. 545

1045-2273 *See* SUBMISSION SOURCEBOOK FOR CREATIVE CLASSROOM PUBLISHING, THE. 1786

1045-2303 *See* AFRICAN COMMENTARY. 2497

1045-232X *See* BUSINESS PROFITABILITY DATA. 651

1045-2338 *See* PERMUTED MEDICAL SUBJECT HEADINGS. 3240

1045-2354 *See* CRITICAL PERSPECTIVES ON ACCOUNTING. 742

1045-2397 *See* HIGH TECH CERAMICS NEWS. 2590

1045-2427 *See* NUESTRAS RAICES (QUARTERLY). 2465

1045-2508 *See* LEASING SOURCEBOOK. 1615

1045-2559 *See* EAST TENNESSEE TODAY. 866

1045-2591 *See* HOBO JUNGLE : A QUARTERLY JOURNAL OF NEW WRITING. 2488

1045-2613 *See* INTERNATIONAL DIRECTORY OF NUCLEAR CONTRACT SERVICE FIRMS. 4657

1045-263X *See* SUPERVISORY MANAGEMENT (1989). 947

1045-2648 *See* HARNESS HANDBOOK, THE. 2799

1045-2664 *See* ALABAMA MANUFACTURERS REGISTER. 3475

1045-2680 *See* CHEMTRACTS. BIOCHEMISTRY AND MOLECULAR BIOLOGY. 485

1045-2699 *See* INTERNATIONAL JOURNAL OF HUMAN FACTORS IN MANUFACTURING, THE. 1220

1045-2710 *See* CEE NEWS. 2038

1045-2729 *See* HUMAN ECOLOGY & ENERGY BALANCING SCIENTIST, THE. 4783

1045-2737 *See* FODOR'S WILLIAMSBURG, JAMESTOWN & YORKTOWN. 5474

1045-2745 *See* FODOR'S I-75 MICHIGAN TO FLORIDA. 5471

1045-2761 *See* GRANT$ FOR HIGHER EDUCATION. 4336

1045-277X *See* FODOR'S MEXICO CITY AND ACAPULCO. 5472

1045-2796 *See* RANDOM LENGTHS YEARBOOK (1985). 2404

1045-2877 *See* AIDS CLINICAL REVIEW. 3663

1045-2885 *See* VIDEO EVENT. 4079

1045-2907 *See* GARVIN'S LARGE PRINT READER. 3389

1045-2923 *See* DEADLY IMPULSE. 3380

1045-2966 *See* BOOK AUTHOR'S NEWSLETTER. 3368

1045-2974 *See* WELLSPRING (LONG LAKE, MINN.). 3452

1045-2990 *See* CHANNELMARKER LETTER. 1601

1045-3040 *See* WOODWORK (ROSS, CALIF.). 635

1045-3059 *See* OGLE COUNTY LIFE, ROCK VALLEY SHOPPER, THE. 5661

1045-3067 *See* BEST OF SPAIN, THE. 5463

1045-3075 *See* BEST OF MADRID, THE. 5463

1045-3083 *See* BEST OF CATALUNYA, THE. 5463

1045-3091 *See* BEST OF ANDALUCIA, THE. 5463

1045-3105 *See* BEST OF PORTUGAL, THE. 5463

1045-3148 *See* STEAM ELECTRIC MARKET ANALYSIS. 1958

1045-3172 *See* BRITISH JOURNAL OF MANAGEMENT. 862

1045-3199 *See* MERIWETHER CONNECTIONS. 2460

1045-3253 *See* NORTH CAROLINA ARCHITECTURE. 305

1045-3296 *See* MARITIME ABSTRACTS. 5452

1045-3334 See FEDGAZETTE (MINNEAPOLIS, MINN.). 675

1045-3342 See DIRECTORY OF LAWYER REFERRAL SERVICES (1976). 2962

1045-3350 See NEWSLINE (SPRINGFIELD, VA.). 5133

1045-3385 See EMERGENCY SERVICES SOURCEBOOK. 4774

1045-3393 See VIDEO RATING GUIDE FOR LIBRARIES. 3255

1045-3407 See MARRIAGE CONNECTION. 2283

1045-3415 See KENTUCKY ADVANCED TECHNOLOGY DIRECTORY, THE. 5123

1045-3423 See LEGACY. 2744

1045-3555 See MARINE FISH MONTHLY. 2308

1045-3563 See LISP POINTERS. 1280

1045-3598 See AMERICAN KITE. 4882

1045-361X See HOLLYWOOD MAGAZINE. 2488

1045-3652 See INFORMATION CATALOG, THE. 682

1045-3679 See AMERICAN LOBBYISTS DIRECTORY. 4463

1045-3695 See JOURNAL OF MANAGERIAL ISSUES. 874

1045-3717 See EMIGRE (BERKELEY, CALIF.). 378

1045-3733 See PERSPECTIVES IN NEUROLOGICAL SURGERY. 3971

1045-3741 See PERSPECTIVES IN GENERAL SURGERY. 3971

1045-375X See PERSPECTIVES IN ORTHOPAEDIC SURGERY. 3972

1045-3806 See PLASTICS CANVAS CORNER. 4458

1045-3814 See CELEBRATIONS TO CROSS STITCH AND CRAFT. 5183

1045-3822 See BUSINESS GUIDE TO ATLANTA. 648

1045-3830 See SCHOOL PSYCHOLOGY QUARTERLY. 4618

1045-3857 See EUROPEAN COMMUNITY (SYRACUSE, N.Y.), THE. 1489

1045-3865 See AMERICAN GOVERNANCE. 4625

1045-3873 See JOURNAL OF CARDIOVASCULAR ELECTROPHYSIOLOGY. 3707

1045-3881 See ASIA PACIFIC TRAVEL. 5461

1045-389X See JOURNAL OF INTELLIGENT MATERIAL SYSTEMS AND STRUCTURES. 5118

1045-3911 See SHEET MUSIC MAGAZINE. EASY PLAY. 4153

1045-3962 See PT DISTRIBUTOR, THE. 2127

1045-3970 See SCHOOL AND COLLEGE (CLEVELAND, OHIO). 1846

1045-3989 See TESTIMONY OF TRUTH, THE. 5003

1045-3997 See GARLAND NEWS (1989), THE. 5750

1045-4004 See RICHARDSON NEWS. 5754

1045-4020 See QUARTERLY COMPLETION REPORT. 4276

1045-4055 See GRAND RAPIDS BUSINESS JOURNAL. 678

1045-4160 See PRECISION MACHINERY. INCORPORATING LIFE SUPPORT TECHNOLOGY. 3696

1045-4195 See ARIZONA STATISTICAL ABSTRACT : A ... DATA HANDBOOK. 5322

1045-4209 See FIVE HUNDRED. 2733

1045-4241 See FLORIDA LAW REVIEW. 2971

1045-4268 See MASSAGE (DAVIS, CALIF.). 2599

1045-4292 See MARTHA'S KIDLIT NEWSLETTER. 1066

1045-4314 See CAREER FUTURES. 4202

1045-4322 See COMMUNITY ECONOMICS (GREENFIELD, MASS.). 2818

1045-4349 See WALPOLE SOCIETY NOTE BOOK, THE. 332

1045-4365 See BILINGUALISM TODAY. 3269

1045-4373 See RUG HOOKING. 375

1045-4403 See CRITICAL REVIEWS IN EUKARYOTIC GENE EXPRESSION. 486

1045-4411 See CRITICAL REVIEWS IN ORAL BIOLOGY AND MEDICINE. 1319

1045-4438 See JOURNAL OF APPLIED AQUACULTURE. 2306

1045-4446 See JOURNAL OF FOOD PRODUCTS MARKETING. 2346

1045-4470 See HUMAN GENOME ABSTRACTS. 478

1045-4489 See BSI HISTORY PROJECT, THE. 3197

1045-4497 See AGE OF REVOLUTION AND ROMANTICISM, THE. 5073

1045-4527 See SEMINARS IN ARTHROPLASTY. 3974

1045-4543 See CAPTN. JACK'S TIDE AND ... CURRENT ALMANAC. 4175

1045-456X See DIRECTORY OF HISTORICAL ORGANIZATIONS IN THE UNITED STATES AND CANADA. 4087

1045-4578 See DOLLAR LINES. 1605

1045-4594 See HISTORIC BRASS SOCIETY NEWSLETTER. 4121

1045-4616 See HISTORIC BRASS SOCIETY JOURNAL. 4121

1045-4624 See HYPERLINK MAGAZINE. 1186

1045-4756 See OHIO GEOLOGY NEWSLETTER. 1390

1045-4764 See ARCTIC RESEARCH OF THE UNITED STATES. 2555

1045-4802 See ARIZONA GEOLOGY. 1366

1045-4837 See ANNUAL REPORT / NATIONAL COMMISSION ON LIBRARIES AND INFORMATION SCIENCE. 3190

1045-4853 See TEACHING ELEMENTARY PHYSICAL EDUCATION. 1805

1045-4861 See JOURNAL OF APPLIED BIOMATERIALS. 3798

1045-487X See DAILY GLOBE (WORTHINGTON, MINN.). 5695

1045-4918 See GREATER LOS ANGELES 3-D MAP. 2582

1045-4969 See AGENDA NEW YORK. 5271

1045-4977 See CHRISTIAN EARLY CHILDHOOD CONNECTION : METHODS AND MATERIALS FOR THE PRE-SCHOOL YEARS. 1732

1045-5027 See GLASS AUDIO. 4404

1045-5051 See BROWN UNIVERSITY FAMILY THERAPY LETTER, THE. 2277

1045-5108 See METROPOLITAN ALMANAC (1989). 2538

1045-5116 See FLOOR COVERING NEWS / U.S.A. 2905

1045-5140 See N-SCALE (EDMONDS, WASH.). 5433

1045-5175 See CONKLIN'S GUIDE. 317

1045-5183 See VIRGINIA ENVIRONMENTAL LAW JOURNAL. 3117

1045-5191 See TRADE CASES. 3104

1045-5205 See JOYFUL CHILD JOURNAL. 2282

1045-5256 See DIRECTORY OF CHEMICAL PRODUCERS, CANADA. 1023

1045-5299 See REVISIONIST LETTERS. 2627

1045-5418 See PEDIATRIC AIDS AND HIV INFECTION. 3675

1045-5485 See NURSE PRACTITIONER FORUM. 3863

1045-5493 See JUNIOR HIGH MAGAZINE ABSTRACTS. 1795

1045-5515 See STORY TIME STORIES THAT RHYME NEWSLETTER. 1069

1045-5523 See BASIC AND CLINICAL BIOSTATISTICS. 476

1045-5698 See EDI (DALLAS, TEX.). 1258

1045-5701 See PC COMPUTER MAINTENANCE ANNUAL. 1270

1045-5728 See ENERGY ANALYST (SILVER SPRING, MD.). 1938

1045-5736 See JOURNAL OF DEMOCRACY. 4478

1045-5744 See KAET MAGAZINE. 1134

1045-5752 See CAPITALISM, NATURE, SOCIALISM. 2212

1045-5779 See INCAST (DALLAS, TEX.). 4003

1045-5795 See AUDIOTEX UPDATE. 1282

1045-5825 See MAC/CHICAGO (CHICAGO, ILL.). 1193

1045-5841 See TRAVELLERS AGENDA. 5497

1045-5868 See CALIFORNIAN (TEMECULA, CALIF.), THE. 5633

1045-5876 See JOURNAL OF RELIGION IN PSYCHOTHERAPY. 3929

1045-5930 See ASPEN INSTITUTE QUARTERLY (QUEENSTOWN, MD.), THE. 5192

1045-5965 See QUICK & EASY QUILTING. 5185

1045-599X See ENVIRONMENTAL LAW JOURNAL OF OHIO. 3111

1045-6007 See JOURNAL OF WORLD HISTORY. 2621

1045-6015 See JEWISH LAW IN CONTEXT. 5049

1045-6023 See AMS STUDIES IN GERMAN LITERATURE AND CULTURE. 3361

1045-6031 See AQUATIC SCIENCES AND FISHERIES ABSTRACTS. PART 3 : AQUATIC POLLUTION AND ENVIRONMENTAL QUALITY. 2317

1045-6058 See HIDA MANUFACTURERS DIRECTORY. 4782

1045-6066 See HORSEMAN'S CONNECTION OF OREGON. 2800

1045-6171 See TECHNICAL, TRADE, & BUSINESS SCHOOL DATA HANDBOOK. NORTHEAST/SOUTHEAST REGIONS. 1916

1045-6198 See OPERATING PERFORMANCE REPORT FOR THE PHCP WHOLESALE/DISTRIBUTION INDUSTRY. PVF DISTRIBUTING INDUSTRY. 2607

1045-6201 See DIRECTORY OF MAJOR MAILERS & WHAT THEY MAIL. 923

1045-6295 See GUITAR WORLD. 4120

1045-6317 See MAINE MANUFACTURING DIRECTORY. 3483

1045-6325 See INTERNATIONAL SOLAR ENERGY INTELLIGENCE REPORT. 1948

1045-6368 See LIE GROUPS. HISTORY, FRONTIERS, AND APPLICATIONS. 5208

1045-6376 See ROCK-OUT! (RIVER EDGE, N.J.). 4150

1045-6392 See METAL MUSCLE. 4131

1045-6422 See FIBER OPTICS MAGAZINE. 1155

1045-6430 See COAL MINE DIRECTORY, UNITED STATES AND CANADA. 2137

1045-6481 See JOURNAL MICHIGAN PHARMACIST. 4310

1045-6503 See TURF WEST. 2433

1045-6562 See TELECOM OUTLOOK : THE TELECOMMUNICATIONS & DATA COMMUNICATIONS NEWSLETTER. 1164

1045-6619 See NOTES ON MODERN IRISH LITERATURE. 3418

1045-6627 See ELECTRONIC WORLD NEWS. 2048

1045-6635 See LATIN AMERICAN ANTIQUITY. 273

1045-6643 See JUST-IN-TIME & QUICK RESPONSE NEWS. 843

1045-6651 See FAX & BUSINESS DIRECTORY. 1111

1045-666X See NIF REPORT. 2660

1045-6678 See HENRY HERALD, THE. 5653

1045-6694 See NEUROSURGICAL CONSULTATIONS. 3843

1045-6716 See POLYLINGUA (HOUGHTON, MICH.). 3311

1045-6724 See BAYVIEWS (OAKLAND, CALIF.). 3193

1045-6740 See PERMAFROST AND PERIGLACIAL PROCESSES. 1391

1045-6767 See HUMAN NATURE (HAWTHORNE, N.Y.). 2847

1045-6775 See INSIDE TURBO PASCAL. 1268

1045-6791 See INSIDE TURBO C. 1287

1045-6805 See DIRECTORY OF CONSTRUCTION LAW FIRMS, THE. 2962

1045-6821 See ADVANCES IN STATISTICAL ANALYSIS AND STATISTICAL COMPUTING. 5320

1045-6899 See FROMMER'S COMPREHENSIVE TRAVEL GUIDE. JAPAN. 5476

1045-7011 See CREATING EXCELLENCE. 663

1045-7046 See IN CONTROL (HOUSTON, TEX.). 1609

ISSN Index

1045-7070 See ALASKA OIL SPILL REPORTER. 4249

1045-7089 See FACILITIES PLANNING NEWS. 298

1045-7097 See PERSPECTIVES ON POLITICAL SCIENCE. 4487

1045-7127 See PROCEEDINGS ... ANNUAL CONFERENCE OF THE TROPICAL AND SUBTROPICAL FISHERIES TECHNOLOGICAL SOCIETY OF THE AMERICAS. 2310

1045-716X See MEDIA BUSINESS. 1116

1045-7186 See AMERICAN VOLLEYBALL. 4883

1045-7194 See DESIGN MANAGEMENT JOURNAL. 1970

1045-7216 See CAR CORRAL. 5409

1045-7240 See PC FAST FACTS. 1270

1045-7313 See LAB REPORT. 3603

1045-7348 See WOOD DIGEST. 635

1045-7410 See CANCER (CD-ROM ED.). 3810

1045-7429 See FARIBAULT COUNTY REGISTER (1989). 5695

1045-7445 See CONNECTION, THE. 1279

1045-7496 See CATHOLIC WEEK, THE. 5625

1045-7577 See LATIN AMERICAN ANTHROPOLOGY REVIEW, THE. 240

1045-7585 See PROUT PRESS (WASHINGTON, D.C.). 5647

1045-764X See TEXAS INDEX. 2763

1045-7682 See SWAMP ROOT. 3443

1045-7704 See WOMEN & GUNS. 5569

1045-7798 See BUSINESS LIBRARY REVIEW. 650

1045-7828 See JAPANESE JOURNAL OF TRIBOLOGY. 2117

1045-7836 See PEGASUS (NORWALK, CONN.). 3423

1045-7879 See AUERBACH INFORMATION MANAGEMENT. 1256

1045-7909 See MANOA. 3347

1045-795X See MECHANICAL MUSIC. 4130

1045-7968 See HIGHER EDUCATION TUITION. 1828

1045-7984 See JOURNAL OF MYOCARDIAL ISCHEMIA, THE. 3707

1045-7992 See WRIGHT STUDIES. 311

1045-8042 See INTERNATIONAL JOURNAL OF AFRICAN DANCE. 1313

1045-8050 See BLACK AMERICANS INFORMATION DIRECTORY. 2256

1045-8077 See JOURNAL OF THE URBAN AND REGIONAL INFORMATION SYSTEMS ASSOCIATION. 2826

1045-8093 See NEW AMERICAN PRESS, THE. 5650

1045-8115 See SCHOOL BOARD NEWS (ALEXANDRIA, VA.). 1871

1045-8158 See PHOTO DISTRICT NEWS (EASTERN ED.). 4373

1045-8166 See GENEALOGICAL JOURNAL OF JEFFERSON COUNTY, NEW YORK. 2450

1045-8182 See OLD NEWS IS GOOD NEWS ANTIQUES GAZETTE, THE. 252

1045-8190 See NASE RODINA (SAINT PAUL, MINN.). 2461

1045-8298 See USP DI. APPROVED DRUG PRODUCTS AND LEGAL REQUIREMENTS. 4332

1045-831X See SECURITY SALES. 5177

1045-8336 See AMADOR LEDGER DISPATCH. 5633

1045-8352 See DIRECTORY OF PORTABLE DATABASES. 1183

1045-8395 See JOURNAL OF BEHAVIORAL OPTOMETRY. 4216

1045-845X See RADIOACTIVITY & RADIOCHEMISTRY. 1029

1045-8484 See TAX GUIDE (NEW YORK, N.Y.). 4752

1045-8522 See CA SELECTS: ANTIBACTERIAL AGENTS. 997

1045-8565 See CAS BIOTECH UPDATES. COMMERCIAL FERMENTATION. 1021

1045-8581 See CAS BIOTECH UPDATES. DNA & RNA PROBES. 450

1045-859X See CAS BIOTECH UPDATES. NUCLEIC ACID & PROTEIN SEQUENCES. 450

1045-8611 See ENVIRONMENTAL BUSINESS JOURNAL. 2166

1045-8638 See HOUSTON REAL ESTATE TRENDS. 4838

1045-8697 See BUSINESS PRESS (FORT WORTH, TEX.), THE. 651

1045-8727 See ARCHIVES REPORT / CALIFORNIA WATER RESOURCES CENTER, UNIVERSITY OF CALIFORNIA. 5530

1045-8751 See SPECIAL EFFECTS. 4078

1045-8816 See DECORATIVE RUG, THE. 2904

1045-8875 See TQS NEWS. 2274

1045-8883 See THOMSON SAVINGS DIRECTORY. 814

1045-8891 See TULANE CIVIL LAW FORUM. 3091

1045-8905 See TRANSNATIONAL LAWYER, THE. 3136

1045-8913 See ART OF CALIFORNIA. 313

1045-893X See WOMEN AND INTERNATIONAL DEVELOPMENT ANNUAL, THE. 5569

1045-8948 See GROWING CHURCHES. 5060

1045-8956 See CONSUMER ADVANTAGE INSIDERS VEHICLE MARKET DIGEST. 5412

1045-8999 See SOUTH DAKOTA CROP & LIVESTOCK REPORTER. 136

1045-9006 See BARCLAYS UNITED STATES SEVENTH CIRCUIT SERVICE. 2940

1045-9030 See MILLING DIRECTORY BUYER'S GUIDE. 202

1045-9073 See NCOA NETWORKS. 5180

1045-9081 See LAW PRACTICE MANAGEMENT (CHICAGO, ILL.). 2996

1045-9146 See EDUCOM REVIEW. 1822

1045-9170 See CRS REVIEW. 4470

1045-9219 See IEEE TRANSACTIONS ON PARALLEL AND DISTRIBUTED SYSTEMS. 1259

1045-9227 See IEEE TRANSACTIONS ON NEURAL NETWORKS. 1229

1045-9235 See IEEE LTS : THE MAGAZINE OF LIGHTWAVE TELECOMMUNICATIONS SYSTEMS. 4434

1045-9243 See IEEE ANTENNAS & PROPAGATION MAGAZINE. 2058

1045-926X See JOURNAL OF VISUAL LANGUAGES AND COMPUTING. 1192

1045-9308 See FROMMER'S COMPREHENSIVE TRAVEL GUIDE. SEATTLE & PORTLAND. 5476

1045-9324 See FROMMER'S COMPREHENSIVE TRAVEL GUIDE. BARCELONA. 5475

1045-9367 See HOME IMPROVEMENT CENTER. 616

1045-9456 See SHAKESPEARE YEARBOOK. 3435

1045-9464 See HELICOPTER EQUIPMENT LISTS & PRICES. TURBINE ENGINE HELICOPTERS : H.E.L.P. 22

1045-9472 See BANK SYSTEMS + TECHNOLOGY. 776

1045-9499 See NATIONAL FAX DIRECTORY. 1160

1045-9545 See POWER MEDIA SELECTS. 1119

1045-9553 See TALK SHOW "SELECTS". 1140

1045-9677 See PERSONAL INJURY DEFENSE REPORTER. 3090

1045-9693 See DJ TIMES. 1131

1045-9723 See LINK (TROY, MICH.). 761

1045-9731 See GLOBAL PRAYER DIGEST. 237

1045-9758 See FLORIDA JOURNAL OF PUBLIC HEALTH. 4776

1045-9812 See ESTHETIC DENTISTRY UPDATE (PHILADELPHIA, PA.). 1323

1045-9820 See UNIVERSAL ALMANAC, THE. 1929

1045-9863 See PROFESSIONAL CAREERS SOURCEBOOK. 4208

1045-9871 See CATHER STUDIES. 3373

1045-988X See PREVENTING SCHOOL FAILURE. 1884

1045-991X See UTOPIAN STUDIES. 4548

1045-9936 See POLICIES IN REVIEW. 2890

1045-9960 See AMERICAN SCHLESWIG-HOLSTEIN HERITAGE SOCIETY NEWSLETTER. 2437

1045-9987 See SIMS SEEKER, THE. 2472

1046-008X See GREAT AMERICAN STORIES. 2488

1046-0144 See TREATISE OF PETROLEUM GEOLOGY REPRINT SERIES. 4280

1046-0292 See PENN SOUNDS. 4145

1046-0330 See FREQUENT FLYER. 5474

1046-0349 See DIRECTORY / AMERICAN BAR ASSOCIATION. 2961

1046-039X See HIGH TECH SEPARATIONS NEWS. 1015

1046-0403 See SNOW BOARDER. 4919

1046-0411 See BIOLOGUE AND THE REGIONAL BIOMASS ENERGY PROGRAM REPORTS. 1933

1046-0438 See ASBESTOS MANAGEMENT SOURCEBOOK. 599

1046-0446 See PARENTS MAKE THE DIFFERENCE!. 2285

1046-0454 See VALLEY MAGAZINE (SELINSGROVE, PA.). 5498

1046-0462 See BELGIAN LACES. 2438

1046-0470 See AMERICAN AMATEUR JOURNALIST, THE. 2770

1046-0551 See PUBLICATIONS OF THE LOUISIANA GEOLOGICAL SURVEY. 1392

1046-056X See MISSISSIPPI BUSINESS DIRECTORY. 695

1046-0616 See ALDUS MAGAZINE. 1284

1046-0691 See DAILY REPORT. NEAR EAST & SOUTH ASIA. INDEX. 1131

1046-0713 See DAILY REPORT. SUB-SAHARAN AFRICA. INDEX (1989). 1131

1046-0748 See CASE MANAGEMENT RESOURCE GUIDE: A DIRECTORY OF HOMECARE, REHABILITATION, MENTAL HEALTH AND LONG TERM CARE SERVICES. 4771

1046-0756 See JOURNAL OF MUSCLE FOODS. 2347

1046-0764 See CURRENT OPINION IN DENTISTRY. 1319

1046-0837 See VIDEO INSIDER. 1142

1046-0845 See THINKING FAMILIES. 1787

1046-0934 See SOUTH CAROLINA BUSINESS DIRECTORY. 712

1046-0950 See WORLD SATELLITE DIRECTORY (POTOMAC, MD.), THE. 1169

1046-0993 See AERO SUN-TIMES. 1931

1046-1000 See WHOM NEWSLETTER / WOMEN HISTORIANS OF THE MIDWEST. 2633

1046-1019 See MESSAGE (1993). 5043

1046-1027 See SCOTT COUNTY IOWAN. 2760

1046-1051 See A.U.A. TODAY. 3987

1046-1310 See CURRENT PSYCHOLOGY (NEW BRUNSWICK, N.J.). 4584

1046-1337 See BARCLAYS UNITED STATES SECOND CIRCUIT SERVICE. 2940

1046-1353 See JOB READY. 1681

1046-137X See MOVING AHEAD (CHICAGO, ILL.). 3618

1046-1388 See CRUISES & TOURS. 5467

1046-1396 See COLLECTIONS OF THE MASSACHUSETTS HISTORICAL SOCIETY. 2728

1046-1434 See WORLD NEWSMAP OF THE WEEK. 1792

1046-1442 See BULLETIN OF THE CALIFORNIA NATIVE PLANT SOCIETY. 505

1046-1469 See JOURNAL OF THE TRANSPORTATION RESEARCH FORUM. 5385

1046-1485 See EXCHANGE (ALEXANDRIA, VA.). 2193

1046-1493 See EPIGRAM (1988). 1241

1046-154X See LAWN & LANDSCAPE MAINTENANCE. 2423

1046-1566 See 20/20. 821

1046-1582 See BEDROOM MAGAZINE. 2485

1046-1590 See DAILY NEWS (HAVRE, MONT.), THE. 5705

1046-1604 See BIKER (AGOURA HILLS, CALIF.). 4080

1046-1612 See DAILY SUN-NEWS. 5760

1046-1620 See BANKERS MIDDLE MARKET LENDING LETTER. 776
1046-1639 See EATING WELL. 4190
1046-1647 See HOSPITAL EDITORS' IDEA EXCHANGE. 1112
1046-1655 See HONG KONG REGISTER. 4838
1046-1663 See NEWS - LIBRARY OF CONGRESS. NATIONAL LIBRARY SERVICE FOR THE BLIND AND PHYSICALLY HANDICAPPED. 4391
1046-1671 See 1992 LECTURE SERIES WORKING PAPERS. 2717
1046-168X See BUSINESS DIGEST. 647
1046-1701 See FITNESS CYCLING. 2597
1046-171X See TACD JOURNAL. 4620
1046-1736 See INCOME PLU$. 681
1046-1744 See COMPUTERS IN MUSIC RESEARCH. 4111
1046-1752 See MARLIN DEMOCRAT (1989). 5752
1046-1795 See CARDIOTHORACIC AND VASCULAR ANESTHESIA UPDATE. 3682
1046-1833 See DAILY NONPAREIL (1976), THE. 5669
1046-1868 See FLETCHER FORUM OF WORLD AFFAIRS, THE. 4521
1046-1876 See CONSUMER CONFIDENCE SURVEY. 1294
1046-1906 See TARGETED DIAGNOSIS AND THERAPY. 3644
1046-1914 See SOLAR INDICES BULLETIN. 1411
1046-1922 See SCIENCE FICTION AND FANTASY BOOK REVIEW INDEX. 3459
1046-1957 See ELLE DECOR. 2900
1046-1965 See SERVICE NEWS (YARMOUTH, ME.). 2081
1046-1973 See JOBSON'S BEVERAGE DYNAMICS. 2368
1046-1981 See MICROSOFT WORKS IN EDUCATION. 1900
1046-199X See AMERICAN JOURNAL OF CONTACT DERMATITIS. 3717
1046-2023 See METHODS (SAN DIEGO, CALIF.). 490
1046-2058 See CECIL WHIG, THE. 5686
1046-2082 See PED FORUM. 4704
1046-2104 See VACATION STUDY ABROAD (NEW YORK, N.Y.). 5498
1046-2112 See PET FOCUS. 4287
1046-2147 See 3/16 SCALE RAILROADING. 5429
1046-2155 See TRENDS IN HIGH SCHOOL MEDIA. 2925
1046-2163 See TRENDS IN COLLEGE MEDIA. 2925
1046-2171 See MARKET GUIDE, THE. 906
1046-218X See AGNI (BOSTON, MASS.). 3358
1046-2201 See PLASTICS RECYCLING AS A FUTURE BUSINESS OPPORTUNITY : PROCEEDINGS, TECHNOLOGY EXCHANGE PROGRAM. 4458
1046-2252 See COLLECTIONS (COLUMBIA, S.C.). 4087
1046-2279 See JAMES BURNSIDE BULLETIN OF RESEARCH, THE. 2740
1046-2333 See INTERSTATE OIL & GAS COMPACT & COMMITTEE BULLETIN, THE. 4261
1046-2341 See DISPATCH - COLUMBIA UNIVERSITY. CENTER FOR AMERICAN CULTURE STUDIES, THE. 2731
1046-2368 See BULLETIN (NEW YORK STATE ARCHEOLOGICAL ASSOCIATION : 1987). 264
1046-2392 See LOS ANGELES READER. 2537
1046-2406 See PETERSON'S REGISTER OF HIGHER EDUCATION. 1841
1046-2414 See FOOD PROFESSIONAL'S GUIDE, THE. 2339
1046-249X See COURT MANAGER, THE. 3140
1046-2511 See MILITARY (SACRAMENTO, CALIF.). 4051
1046-252X See CUSTOMER SERVICE REPORT. 865
1046-2627 See NEWSLETTER - CATALOG OF LANDSCAPE RECORDS IN THE UNITED STATES (PROJECT). 2425

1046-266X See INTERNATIONAL BANK DIRECTORY. 792
1046-2686 See DIRECTORY OF CITY POLICY OFFICIALS. 4643
1046-2694 See PHYSICIANS' DESK REFERENCE (COMPACT DISK ED.). 4324
1046-2708 See SANTA FEAN MAGAZINE (SANTA FE, N.M.). 2545
1046-2724 See LEDGE, THE. 3465
1046-2767 See COMPLETE MEMBERSHIP DIRECTORY OF THE INTERACTIVE MULTIMEDIA ASSOCIATION, THE. 1222
1046-2775 See WORKERS' COMP ADVISOR (CALIFORNIA ED.). 2896
1046-2791 See PEDIATRIC DENTISTRY TODAY. 1332
1046-2821 See AMERICAN ENTOMOLOGIST (LANHAM, MD.). 5605
1046-283X See COMPUTATIONAL MATHEMATICS AND MODELING. 3501
1046-2872 See EXHIBIT REVIEW, THE. 759
1046-2880 See FANCY FOOD. 2335
1046-2899 See AMERICA'S CIVIL WAR. 2720
1046-2902 See VIETNAM (LEESBURG, VA.). 2632
1046-2929 See NACAC BULLETIN. 1866
1046-2937 See TEXT AND PERFORMANCE QUARTERLY. 389
1046-2996 See YEARBOOK - ILLINOIS CREDIT UNION LEAGUE (1988). 817
1046-302X See TRIBUNE-COURIER (1989). 5683
1046-3046 See PLASTIC WASTE STRATEGIES. 4221
1046-3070 See MONEY LAUNDERING ALERT. 3087
1046-3089 See WASHINGTON FLYER MAGAZINE. 5499
1046-3127 See WICHITA EAGLE (1989), THE. 5679
1046-3143 See ANNUAL REPORT - HARVARD UNIVERSITY. MUSEUM OF COMPARATIVE ZOOLOGY. 5576
1046-316X See RECREATION RESOURCES. 4854
1046-3186 See ELECTRICITY SUPPLY & DEMAND FOR ... THE REGIONAL RELIABILITY COUNCILS OF THE NORTH AMERICAN ELECTRIC RELIABILITY COUNCIL. 4761
1046-3216 See MASSACHUSETTS PRIMER / MASSACHUSETTS TAXPAYERS FOUNDATION, INC, A. 4737
1046-3232 See SYMPHONY (WASHINGTON, D.C.). 4155
1046-3267 See SANDLAPPER (1990). 2628
1046-3283 See EUROPEAN REVIEW OF SOCIAL PSYCHOLOGY. 5245
1046-3291 See INDEPENDENT INVESTOR (MIAMI BEACH, FLA.). 901
1046-3305 See CLINICAL BIOTECHNOLOGY. 3691
1046-333X See ... ANNUAL, DEVELOPING HUMAN RESOURCES, THE. 938
1046-3348 See COLORADO REVIEW (1985). 3340
1046-3356 See ONCOLOGY ISSUES. 3822
1046-3364 See RESEARCH & TEACHING IN DEVELOPMENTAL EDUCATION. 1884
1046-3380 See JOURNAL OF THE INTERNATIONAL COUNCIL FOR HEALTH, PHYSICAL, EDUCATION, AND RECREATION. 1856
1046-3410 See NEWSLETTER ON SERIALS PRICING ISSUES. 3236
1046-3429 See VETERANS ADVOCATE (WASHINGTON, D.C.), THE. 3071
1046-3445 See TOURO JOURNAL OF TRANSNATIONAL LAW. 3136
1046-350X See HARVARD UNIVERSITY ART MUSEUMS REVIEW. 4088
1046-3534 See HANDBOOK OF SEC ACCOUNTING AND DISCLOSURE. 744
1046-3550 See MULTIMEDIA REVIEW. 1196
1046-3569 See ADOPTION. 2276
1046-3607 See JOURNAL OF THE AMERICAN MOSQUITO CONTROL ASSOCIATION. SUPPLEMENT. 3741
1046-3631 See FEDERAL INDEX (1985). 2969

1046-3674 See WORK IN PROGRESS (STONE CENTER FOR DEVELOPMENTAL SERVICES AND STUDIES). 4622
1046-3755 See ADVERTISING RESEARCH DIRECTORY. 754
1046-3771 See SUPPLIER SELECTION & MANAGEMENT REPORT. 887
1046-3798 See EXALTATION. 4958
1046-3801 See CONTEMPORARY PRAISE. 5058
1046-381X See WORSHIP (NASHVILLE, TENN.). 5069
1046-3852 See CAR STEREO (DURANGO, COLO.). 5409
1046-3860 See VIDEO & TELEVISION. 1142
1046-3879 See GUITARS & MUSICAL INSTRUMENTS. 4120
1046-3887 See PROCEEDINGS / NATIONAL SYMPOSIUM ON MINING, HYDROLOGY, SEDIMENTOLOGY AND RECLAMATION. 1417
1046-3925 See EXPO (WAUCONDA, ILL.). 867
1046-3933 See HISPANIC AMERICANS INFORMATION DIRECTORY. 2262
1046-3976 See ENDOCRINE PATHOLOGY. 3729
1046-400X See JOURNAL OF CALIFORNIA TAXATION, THE. 2987
1046-4174 See DIRECT (STAMFORD, CONN.). 923
1046-4204 See PHILLIPS COUNTY HISTORICAL REVIEW. 2754
1046-4239 See DECLASSIFIED DOCUMENTS CATALOG, THE. 414
1046-4247 See BALLEW FAMILY JOURNAL, THE. 2438
1046-4255 See COLLEGE MEDIA DIRECTORY, THE. 1816
1046-4263 See DIRECTORY OF INTERNATIONAL CORPORATE GIVING IN AMERICA. 4335
1046-4328 See NEW YORK LAW SCHOOL JOURNAL OF HUMAN RIGHTS. 4511
1046-4336 See OHIO LIBRARIES (COLUMBUS, OHIO. 1988). 3239
1046-4344 See OHIO STATE JOURNAL ON DISPUTE RESOLUTION. 3022
1046-4352 See PIMA MAGAZINE. 4237
1046-4360 See JOURNAL OF HEALTH AND HOSPITAL LAW : A PUBLICATION OF THE AMERICAN ACADEMY OF HOSPITAL ATTORNEYS OF THE AMERICAN HOSPITAL ASSOCIATION. 2987
1046-4395 See TRADE SHOWS WORLDWIDE. 767
1046-4468 See NETWORK COMPUTING. 1243
1046-4522 See APA MAGAZINE. 4366
1046-4549 See REDIRECTIONS (KIRKLAND, WASH.). 884
1046-4603 See HEALTHCARE RECRUITMENT RESOURCE GUIDE. 3583
1046-4603 See HEALTHCARE RECRUITMENT RESOURCE GUIDE. 3583
1046-4611 See TRANSWORLD SNOWBOARDING. 4927
1046-4638 See WILD WEST (LEESBURG, VA.). 2766
1046-476X See ARIZONA TREND AZ. 2528
1046-4778 See WORLD M&A NETWORK. 816
1046-4875 See MOUNTAIN & CITY BIKING. 429
1046-4883 See JOURNAL OF ARCHITECTURAL EDUCATION (WASHINGTON, D.C. : 1984). 301
1046-4948 See TRIAD (FARMINGTON, MICH.). 3647
1046-4956 See CHECKS & CHECKING. 741
1046-4964 See SMALL GROUP RESEARCH. 5258
1046-4972 See JOURNAL OF NURSING RESEARCH. 3859
1046-4980 See ... INFORMATION PLEASE SPORTS ALMANAC, THE. 4900
1046-4999 See ART AT AUCTION IN AMERICA. 338
1046-5022 See DRAMA/THEATRE TEACHER, THE. 5364
1046-5049 See OWNERS AT WORK. 1543
1046-5057 See BUSINESS TRAVEL MANAGEMENT. 653

1046-5081 See ACTUARIAL REVIEW, THE. 2872
1046-5111 See CURRENT PROBLEMS IN UROLOGY. 3989
1046-5146 See ADWEEK AGENCY DIRECTORY (SOUTHWESTERN ED.). 755
1046-5189 See BIOMEDICAL NEWS SOURCE MIDWEST. 3557
1046-5197 See AMERICAN BAR, THE. 2932
1046-5219 See MOLECULAR DYNAMICS NEWS. 986
1046-5235 See REUNIONS (MILWAUKEE, WIS.). 2470
1046-5243 See SHADOW PLAY. 3435
1046-5286 See MOBILE SATELLITE NEWS (POTOMAC, MD.). 1160
1046-5294 See ENVIRONMENTAL TOPICS. 2170
1046-5316 See INSIDE MEDIA (STAMFORD, CONN.). 760
1046-5332 See PROGRESSIVE GROCER'S DIRECTORY OF CONVENIENCE STORES. 956
1046-5340 See VICKERS DIRECTORY OF INSTITUTIONAL INVESTORS. 919
1046-5359 See LOCKWOOD-POST'S DIRECTORY OF THE PULP, PAPER AND ALLIED TRADES. 4235
1046-5367 See STREET ROD ACTION. 5426
1046-5421 See N.A. WAY MAGAZINE, THE. 1347
1046-543X See JOURNAL OF VITAL CHRISTIANITY, A. 4971
1046-543X See BOTTLED WATER REPORTER. 2365
1046-5448 See INTERNATIONAL BRAIN DOMINANCE REVIEW. 4590
1046-5456 See SUNWORLD. (PETERBOROUGH, N.H.). 1272
1046-5480 See ALL ABOUT BUSINESS IN HAWAII. 637
1046-5502 See MARSHALL NEWS MESSENGER. 5752
1046-5545 See SENECA SEARCHERS. 2472
1046-5553 See SOUTH CAROLINA PROGRAM FOR LIBRARY DEVELOPMENT, THE. 3250
1046-560X See JOURNAL OF SCIENCE TEACHER EDUCATION. 1898
1046-5626 See CORPORATE RISK MANAGEMENT. 662
1046-5634 See MAS (NEW YORK, N.Y.). 2267
1046-5693 See TRILOGY. 5648
1046-5723 See ADVANCES IN SOLID-STATE CHEMISTRY. 1049
1046-5766 See ADVANCES IN THEORETICALLY INTERESTING MOLECULES. 1039
1046-5774 See GUIDE TO ACCREDITED CAMPS. 1064
1046-5790 See SAZZ (NEW YORK, N.Y.). 5566
1046-5871 See ALASKA'S INSIDE PASSAGE TRAVELER : SEE MORE, SPEND LESS!. 5460
1046-5901 See CHARBONNEAU CONNECTION. 2442
1046-5928 See PROTEIN EXPRESSION AND PURIFICATION. 551
1046-5944 See CASE TRENDS. 1227
1046-5952 See SEMINAIRE DE THEORIE DES NOMBRES / SEMINAIRE DELANGE-PISOT-POITOU. 3533
1046-6029 See FIREHEART (MAYNARD, MASS.). 4185
1046-6045 See RSA NEWSLETTER, THE. 1121
1046-6045 See VIDEO INVESTOR, THE. 1168
1046-6053 See MAINE (AUBURN, ME.). 2745
1046-6061 See MOBILE SATELLITE REPORTS. 1160
1046-607X See VIDEO SOFTWARE MAGAZINE. 4377
1046-6088 See MONTANA GRAIN NEWS. 203
1046-6096 See AMERICAN OFFICE DEALER. 4210
1046-6142 See CHICAGO USED CAR SELLER'S GUIDE, THE. 5410
1046-6150 See REPORT ON LITERACY PROGRAMS. 5305
1046-6185 See CHICAGO GALLERY NEWS. 4086

1046-6193 See TEACHER MAGAZINE. 1906
1046-6223 See DESIGNSOURCE (1989). 612
1046-6231 See CONVERGENCE (WASHINGTON, D.C.). 4506
1046-6266 See YEAR BOOK OF NEPHROLOGY, THE. 3994
1046-6339 See TREES FROM THE GROVE. 2476
1046-6355 See MAINSTREAM NEWS. 4391
1046-641X See COUNCIL OF GENEALOGY COLUMNISTS NEWSLETTER. 2444
1046-6444 See DISCUSSION PAPER PROGRAM / CASUALTY ACTUARIAL SOCIETY. 2879
1046-6460 See PRIMA BALLERINA. 1314
1046-6479 See WILDLIFE & FISH WORLDWIDE. VOLUME 1. 2209
1046-6487 See CASUALTY ACTUARIAL SOCIETY FORUM. 2877
1046-6568 See PENNSYLVANIA ENVIRONMENTAL LAW LETTER. 3115
1046-6606 See IACM BULLETIN OF THE INTERNATIONAL ASSOCIATION FOR COMPUTATIONAL MECHANICS. 2115
1046-6614 See IMAGE FILE. 4089
1046-6673 See JOURNAL OF THE AMERICAN SOCIETY OF NEPHROLOGY. 3991
1046-669X See JOURNAL OF MARKETING CHANNELS. 928
1046-6703 See STATE REPRODUCTIVE HEALTH MONITOR. 591
1046-672X See PROCEEDINGS OF THE INTERNATIONAL CONGRESS ON EXPERIMENTAL MECHANICS. 1992
1046-6770 See PROCEEDINGS OF THE ... INTERNATIONAL MODAL ANALYSIS CONFERENCE & EXHIBIT. 1992
1046-6789 See PROCEEDINGS OF THE SOCIETY FOR EXPERIMENTAL MECHANICS. 4429
1046-6819 See LEARNING DISABILITIES (PITTSBURGH, PA.). 1881
1046-6835 See POLICE LIABILITY REVIEW. 3172
1046-6851 See WINE EDUCATOR, THE. 2372
1046-6940 See SPACE NEWS (SPRINGFIELD, VA.). 36
1046-6959 See DEVELOPMENTS IN CARDIOLOGY. 3704
1046-6967 See WAR, LITERATURE, AND THE ARTS. 3452
1046-6975 See CAMPUS OUTREACH. 1813
1046-6983 See MEETINGS INMED. 3615
1046-7009 See FOREST & CONSERVATION HISTORY. 2379
1046-7017 See SPORTING NEWS ROTISSERIE & FANTASY BASEBALL LEAGUE GUIDE, THE. 4922
1046-7041 See ABNF JOURNAL, THE. 3850
1046-705X See FOOD STRUCTURE. 2340
1046-7076 See PRACTICAL REVIEWS IN DERMATOLOGY. 3722
1046-7092 See SHEPARD'S NEW YORK MISCELLANEOUS CASE NAMES CITATOR. 3052
1046-7106 See PRACTICAL REVIEWS IN ORTHODONTICS. 1333
1046-7114 See AMERICAN PAPERMAKER (1991). 4232
1046-7122 See AMERICAN PAPERMAKER (1991). 4232
1046-7130 See AMERICAN PAPERMAKER (1991). 4232
1046-7157 See TIRE RETREADING/REPAIR JOURNAL, THE. 5078
1046-7165 See CLINICAL ADVANCES IN GASTROENTEROLOGY. 3743
1046-7203 See WHO'S WHO IN AMERICAN EDUCATION (OWINGS MILLS, MD.). 1791
1046-7211 See INTERNATIONAL NEW PRODUCT NEWSLETTER. 5115
1046-7254 See JOURNAL - MICHIGAN ASSOCIATION OF TEACHER EDUCATORS, THE. 1897
1046-7262 See DIAL-A-FAX DIRECTORY. 1153
1046-7289 See OFFICIAL IDENTIFICATION AND PRICE GUIDE TO ANTIQUE & MODERN DOLLS, THE. 252

1046-7335 See KTB (FOX LAKE, FLA.). 2622
1046-7386 See CYTOMETRY. SUPPLEMENT. 535
1046-7394 See SOUTH CAROLINA NURSE, THE. 3869
1046-7408 See AMERICAN JOURNAL OF REPRODUCTIVE IMMUNOLOGY : AJRI. 3666
1046-7416 See JOURNAL OF SURGICAL ONCOLOGY. SUPPLEMENT. 3820
1046-7459 See NURSING DIAGNOSIS. 3864
1046-7467 See AACN CLINICAL ISSUES IN CRITICAL CARE NURSING. 3849
1046-7475 See NAACOG'S CLINICAL ISSUES IN PERINATAL AND WOMEN'S HEALTH NURSING. 3765
1046-7491 See JOURNAL OF EMPLOYEE OWNERSHIP LAW AND FINANCE, THE. 1682
1046-7513 See UNITED STATES INSTITUTE OF PEACE JOURNAL. 4537
1046-7548 See WHY - WORLD HUNGER YEAR. 2912
1046-7599 See HUMAN COMMUNICATION AND ITS DISORDERS (NORWOOD, N.J.). 1112
1046-7718 See WESTAF'S NATIONAL ARTS JOBBANK. 333
1046-7785 See PROFESSIONALS AND THEIR ADDICTIONS. 4796
1046-7823 See VIKING UPDATE. 4928
1046-7858 See MOVIE STATS. 1125
1046-7890 See JOURNAL OF CLINICAL ETHICS, THE. 2251
1046-7912 See LIES OF OUR TIMES. 4481
1046-7947 See AGRICULTURAL BUILDING COST GUIDE (1987). 598
1046-7963 See PATTON'S ... FANTASY BASEBALL PRICE GUIDE. 2776
1046-8005 See GRAPHIC ARTS BLUE BOOK (WEST COAST ED.). 378
1046-8013 See OPEN SEASON GUIDE. 2889
1046-8021 See E (NORWALK, CONN.). 2164
1046-8064 See RESEARCH IN THE SOCIAL SCIENTIFIC STUDY OF RELIGION. 4992
1046-8110 See HUDSON'S SUBSCRIPTION NEWSLETTER DIRECTORY. 2488
1046-8188 See ACM TRANSACTIONS ON INFORMATION SYSTEMS : PUBLICATION OF THE ASSOCIATION FOR COMPUTING MACHINERY. 1255
1046-8196 See CHF NEWSBRIEFS. 2817
1046-820X See STATISTICAL YEARBOOK / CHICAGO MERCANTILE EXCHANGE. 5356
1046-8226 See CRB COMMODITY YEAR BOOK. 830
1046-8242 See BEST IN ADVERTISING, THE. 756
1046-8250 See JOBSON'S LIQUOR HANDBOOK. 2368
1046-8293 See LIVINGSTON COUNTY NEWS (GENESEO, N.Y.). 5718
1046-8315 See DON KORN'S BREAKTHROUGH INVESTING. 897
1046-8358 See BRIDGES (SEATTLE, WASH.). 5552
1046-8366 See INTERNATIONAL PERMACULTURE SOLUTIONS JOURNAL, THE. 97
1046-8374 See CRIMINAL LAW FORUM. 3106
1046-8390 See UNIVERSITY OF KANSAS PALEONTOLOGICAL CONTRIBUTIONS (1992), THE. 4231
1046-8404 See YOUNG VOICES (OLYMPIA, WASH.). 1072
1046-8412 See INTERNATIONAL GIS SOURCEBOOK. 2566
1046-8447 See PROMO NEWS. 935
1046-8471 See ART ISSUES. 339
1046-8501 See COLLEGE FINANCIAL FACTS. 1816
1046-8544 See INTERSTATE SECURITIES TELEPHONE AND ELECTRIC UTILITIES ATLAS, THE. 4761
1046-8595 See PRINTINGNEWS. EAST. 4568
1046-8633 See CEDAR CREEK PILOT. 5748
1046-865X See HERALD (HAYWARD, CALIF.), THE. 5635

1046-8684 See NEW MEDIA NEWS (BOSTON, MASS.). 1197
1046-8692 See CRISP THESAURUS. 3204
1046-8749 See WASHINGTON PARK ARBORETUM BULLETIN. 2433
1046-8757 See JOURNAL OF PRACTICAL APPLICATIONS OF SPACE. 26
1046-8765 See BIBLIOGRAPHIC GUIDE TO EAST ASIAN STUDIES. 2634
1046-8773 See MUTUAL FUND PERFORMANCE REPORT. 908
1046-8781 See SIMULATION & GAMING. 1283
1046-8803 See INVESTMENT & TAX SHELTER BLUE BOOK. 4733
1046-8838 See ANNUAL FAA AVIATION FORECAST CONFERENCE PROCEEDINGS. 11
1046-8900 See HEALTH & MEDICAL CARE DIRECTORY. 3780
1046-8919 See MINNESOTA MEDIA DIRECTORY (MIDWEST ED.). 1117
1046-8927 See TBC NEWS. 4394
1046-8943 See MANHATTAN OFFICE BUILDINGS. MIDTOWN SOUTH. 4840
1046-8978 See FODOR'S ... POCKET GUIDE TO SAN FRANCISCO. 5473
1046-8986 See AMERICAN PHOTO. 4366
1046-9001 See VISUAL RESOURCES ASSOCIATION BULLETIN. 368
1046-9036 See SELLING ADVANTAGE, THE. 886
1046-9079 See MILITARY & AEROSPACE ELECTRONICS. 4050
1046-9095 See AIR MEDICAL JOURNAL. 3547
1046-9109 See MICHIGAN EMPLOYMENT LAW LETTER. 3152
1046-9125 See FANTASY BASEBALL. 4894
1046-9176 See UCLA LATIN AMERICAN STUDIES. 2764
1046-9184 See WRITER'S GUIDELINES (PITTSBURG, MO.). 2925
1046-9192 See MICHIGAN ENVIRONMENTAL LAW LETTER. 3114
1046-9206 See OHIO EMPLOYMENT LAW LETTER. 3153
1046-9214 See TEXAS EMPLOYMENT LAW LETTER. 3154
1046-9257 See KENTUCKY COMMERCE. 820
1046-9265 See PORT OF NEW ORLEANS RECORD. 849
1046-9303 See INFORMATION MANAGEMENT BULLETIN. 1188
1046-932X See INTEGRATED IMAGE. 1189
1046-9338 See WDA JOURNAL. 1337
1046-9354 See ALLERGY PROCEEDINGS. 3666
1046-9389 See NORTH STONE REVIEW, THE. 3418
1046-9400 See PACE BUYER'S GUIDES. NEW CAR PRICES. 5422
1046-9427 See TWIN PLANT NEWS. 855
1046-9443 See ANNUAL REPORT - SCRIPPS INSTITUTION OF OCEANOGRAPHY (1984). 1446
1046-9486 See COAL TRANSPORTATION STATISTICS. 1439
1046-9508 See CUPA JOURNAL (WASHINGTON, D.C.: 1987). 939
1046-9516 See NIDA RESEARCH MONOGRAPH. 1347
1046-9540 See PARK CITY MAIN STREET MAP. 2583
1046-9575 See BUSINESS NEW HAMPSHIRE MAGAZINE. 650
1046-9613 See TRIBE (BALTIMORE, MD.). 2796
1046-9621 See MOSCOW INTERNATIONAL BUSINESS. 696
1046-9648 See INSIDE MICROSOFT WORKS. 1268
1046-9656 See INSIDE WORDPERFECT. 1287
1046-9672 See CONNECTICUT TECHNOLOGY DIRECTORY. 5096
1046-9680 See TERRITORIAL SEA JOURNAL. 3182
1046-980X See DESIGN PROCESSES NEWSLETTER. 2097

1046-9834 See AFGHANISTAN STUDIES JOURNAL. 2501
1046-9869 See THEATRICAL INDEX. 5371
1046-9958 See INGRAM'S (KANSAS CITY, MO.). 870
1046-9966 See REAL ESTATE/ENVIRONMENTAL LIABILITY NEWS. 4844
1046-9990 See LITURGY 90. 5031
1047-000X See FOSTER'S BOTANICAL & HERB REVIEWS. 2415
1047-0018 See SLAVIC AND EAST EUROPEAN PERFORMANCE. 5368
1047-0042 See RESEARCH IN URBAN SOCIOLOGY. 5255
1047-0123 See SPECIAL REPORT ON LIVING. 5263
1047-014X See STROKE CONNECTION. 5312
1047-0166 See TENNESSEE PHARMACIST. 4330
1047-0212 See FAVONIUS SUPPLEMENTARY VOLUME. 1076
1047-0239 See PROPAGANDA REVIEW. 764
1047-031X See ALABAMA LIVING (MONTGOMERY, ALA.). 2527
1047-0328 See CHRISTMAS (BIRMINGHAM, ALA.). 371
1047-0336 See JOURNAL OF CLINICAL RESEARCH AND PHARMACOEPIDEMIOLOGY. 4311
1047-0387 See ATTENTION AND PERFORMANCE. 4575
1047-0433 See SRDS REPORT, THE. 766
1047-045X See TGA-PC (ARLINGTON, VA.). 1850
1047-0476 See JOE FRANKLIN'S NOSTALGIA. 2489
1047-0484 See RISK, ISSUES IN HEALTH & SAFETY. 4800
1047-0492 See JOURNAL OF COMMUNICATIONS TECHNOLOGY. 1159
1047-0549 See IN HEALTH. 3586
1047-059X See EMPLOYMENT, HOURS, AND EARNINGS, UNITED STATES. 1666
1047-062X See TRANSPORTATION NEWS DIGEST, THE. 5396
1047-0638 See FAMILY PRACTICE PEDIATRICS. 3737
1047-0670 See BRIDGEVILLE AREA NEWS. 5735
1047-0697 See SEWICKLEY HERALD (1968), THE. 5739
1047-0719 See FOCUS (SAN FRANCISCO, CALIF.). 3669
1047-0735 See DEVELOP (CUPERTINO, CALIF.). 1182
1047-0743 See CALIFORNIA BANKRUPTCY JOURNAL. 782
1047-0751 See EDMUND'S NEW CAR PRICES. 5413
1047-076X See EDMUND'S CAR SAVVY. 5413
1047-0808 See OPHTHALMOLOGY ALERT. 3877
1047-0905 See PERSPECTIVES ON SOCIAL PROBLEMS. 5253
1047-0913 See VAN HOC (GARDEN GROVE, CALIF.). 3450
1047-0956 See FAMILY TREE (DAYTON, OHIO). 2447
1047-1006 See COMPARATIVE STATE POLITICS. 4469
1047-1014 See HEARTBEAT. 4962
1047-1057 See KOINONIA (PRINCETON, N.J.). 4972
1047-1065 See CURRENT DEFERRALS. 1662
1047-1073 See CANADIAN-AMERICAN PUBLIC POLICY. 826
1047-112X See PRIME RATE UPDATE SERVICE. 803
1047-1170 See VALLEY COURIER (ALAMOSA, COLO.). 5644
1047-1200 See JOURNAL OF NONLINEAR BIOLOGY. 495
1047-1227 See SEMINARS IN CHIROPRACTIC. 3640
1047-126X See RESEARCH IN ASIAN ECONOMIC STUDIES. 1639

1047-1324 See CONGRESS AND THE NATION. 4469
1047-1359 See MIN FAX. 2828
1047-1367 See TECHNOTES DBASE IV. 1273
1047-1413 See FLORIDA LAND OWNER MAGAZINE. 4837
1047-1448 See JOURNAL OF DISABILITY. 4389
1047-1499 See OUTLAW BIKER TATTOO REVUE. 5269
1047-1618 See SPECIAL EDUCATOR, THE. 1885
1047-1634 See QUILTMAKER (WHEATRIDGE, COLO.). 5185
1047-1642 See YOUTH MINISTRY QUARTERLY. 1072
1047-1669 See COMPETITION ANGLER. 4871
1047-1677 See MARKETING TO WOMEN (1989). 5561
1047-1693 See DIGITAL DIRECTIONS REPORT. 1258
1047-1707 See PROMO (DANBURY, CONN.). 935
1047-174X See BLOOD REVIEW, THE. 3367
1047-1782 See FLORIDA RULES OF COURT. STATE. 3140
1047-1804 See FLORIDA BUSINESS DIRECTORY. 676
1047-1812 See SCOUT MID-RANGE SOFTWARE DIRECTORY. 1202
1047-1847 See CHRISTIAN COMPUTING MAGAZINE. 1174
1047-1855 See PRUFROCK JOURNAL, THE. 1884
1047-1863 See MEDICARE COMPLIANCE ALERT. 2888
1047-1871 See TOPPS MAGAZINE. 4926
1047-1901 See STAGE DIRECTIONS (WEST SACRAMENTO, CALIF.). 5368
1047-191X See FUTURE CHOICES. 5286
1047-1936 See ARIZONA EPISCOPALIAN, THE. 5055
1047-1952 See MOBILE OFFICE. 695
1047-1960 See MUSCLE POWER. 2600
1047-1979 See INTERNATIONAL JOURNAL OF CLINICAL ACUPUNCTURE. 3589
1047-1987 See POLITICAL ANALYSIS. 4488
1047-2002 See ADVANCES IN SOCIAL SCIENCE METHODOLOGY. 5238
1047-2010 See ADVANCES IN SOCIAL SCIENCE AND COMPUTERS. 5189
1047-2061 See AUTOGLASS (MCLEAN, VA.). 2586
1047-2088 See ABSTRACT BULLETIN OF THE INSTITUTE OF PAPER SCIENCE AND TECHNOLOGY. 4240
1047-210X See SPORTBOSTON (PHILADELPHIA, PA.). 4921
1047-2169 See CIVIC ARTS REVIEW, THE. 5242
1047-2223 See BODY BOARDING. 4887
1047-2258 See BIRMINGHAM POETRY REVIEW. 3460
1047-2320 See GOOD NEWS (NEW BERLIN, WIS.). 4961
1047-2339 See WORD & WITNESS. 5069
1047-2347 See INDEPENDENT BUSINESS : IB. 681
1047-2355 See SCHWANN OPUS. 5318
1047-2371 See SPECTRUM (CHATSWORTH, CALIF.). 4154
1047-2398 See NOVA (BROOKFIELD, WIS.). 5033
1047-2436 See STOCKS, BONDS, BILLS, AND INFLATION YEARBOOK. 916
1047-2452 See COMPUTER-ASSISTED COMPOSITION JOURNAL, THE. 1292
1047-2495 See MIAMI MEDICAL LETTER EN ESPANOL. 3616
1047-2509 See MIAMI MEDICAL LETTER. 3616
1047-2517 See NEWSLETTER OF THE AMERICAN INSTITUTE OF STRESS, THE. 3621
1047-2525 See FISHERIES PRODUCT NEWS. 2302
1047-255X See FAMILY BUSINESS. 674
1047-2568 See PROFILES. 1775
1047-2576 See ACADEMIC YEAR ABROAD. 1721
1047-2592 See UPSCALE (ATLANTA, GA.). 2274

1047-2665 See VIVARIUM (LAKESIDE, CALIF.), THE. 5599

1047-2703 See FLORIDA BUSINESS DIRECTORY. 676

1047-272X See SPECIAL REPORT ON HEALTH. 4803

1047-2746 See NEW AGE ENCYCLOPEDIA. 4186

1047-2770 See NEWSLETTER - BUCKS COUNTY GENEALOGICAL SOCIETY. 2463

1047-2797 See ANNALS OF EPIDEMIOLOGY. 3734

1047-2800 See WOMEN'S HEALTH ADVISER POSTER. 5570

1047-2819 See BUSINESS LAW JOURNAL (CORAL GABLES, FLA.), THE. 3096

1047-2827 See LEADER'S EUROPE 1992 LAW & STRATEGY. 2998

1047-2843 See TENNESSEE ILLUSTRATED. 2493

1047-2886 See SPECIAL REPORT - WHITTLE COMMUNICATIONS. 2546

1047-286X See SPECIAL REPORT ON PERSONALITIES. 4619

1047-2878 See SPECIAL REPORT ON FAMILY. 2286

1047-2886 See SPECIAL REPORT, FICTION. 3439

1047-2908 See INSIDE MARKET DATA. 926

1047-2967 See MANUFACTURED HOME MERCHANDISER. 2827

1047-2975 See HOTELS (NEWTON, MASS.). 2807

1047-3068 See OLD NEWS (MARIETTA, PA.). 2625

1047-3114 See MOODY'S INDUSTRY REVIEW. 907

1047-3130 See WHO'S WHO IN HR. 437

1047-3149 See HRMAGAZINE (ALEXANDRIA, VA.). 941

1047-3157 See HRNEWS (ALEXANDRIA, VA.). 941

1047-3165 See WHEELS (DETROIT, MICH.). 5428

1047-3173 See PAMTECO TRACINGS. 2466

1047-3203 See JOURNAL OF VISUAL COMMUNICATION AND IMAGE REPRESENTATION. 1234

1047-3211 See CEREBRAL CORTEX (NEW YORK, N.Y. 1991). 3829

1047-322X See APPLIED OCCUPATIONAL AND ENVIRONMENTAL HYGIENE. 2859

1047-3289 See JOURNAL OF THE AIR & WASTE MANAGEMENT ASSOCIATION. 2196

1047-3297 See ARTS & CULTURE FUNDING REPORT. 314

1047-3300 See MINORITY FUNDING REPORT. 5296

1047-3351 See BOUND BROOK CHRONICLE (1971). 5709

1047-336X See ENVIRONMENTAL CONTRACTOR MAGAZINE. 614

1047-3378 See CRUISE INDUSTRY NEWS (ANNUAL). 5467

1047-3394 See STATE AND LOCAL STATISTICS SOURCES. 4563

1047-3424 See DIAL IN. 3206

1047-3467 See ORAL HISTORY INDEX. 2625

1047-3475 See VIETNAM STUDIES BULLETIN. 2667

1047-3513 See ADVENTURE GAMES FOR MICROCOMPUTERS. 1230

1047-3572 See AMERICAN ENTERPRISE (WASHINGTON, D.C.), THE. 638

1047-3645 See ADVANCES IN CARBOCATION CHEMISTRY. 1038

1047-3777 See IN VIEW. 1829

1047-3793 See PHYSICIAN'S WEEKLY. 3627

1047-3815 See PET CARE REPORT. 4287

1047-3831 See BIG PICTURE (KNOXVILLE, TENN.). 2485

1047-384X See PRE-PARENT ADVISER. 2285

1047-3858 See GO!. 5478

1047-3874 See CAMPUS VOICE (KNOXVILLE, TENN.). 1813

1047-3882 See BEST OF BUSINESS QUARTERLY. 642

1047-3890 See SOURCE BOOK MAGAZINE. 886

1047-3912 See PURSUITS. 434

1047-3947 See VICTORIAN SAMPLER. 2903

1047-3955 See COUNTRY SAMPLER. 2899

1047-3963 See FOX VALLEY LIVING. 2487

1047-3971 See SECOND STONE, THE. 2796

1047-4048 See CONSUMERS REPORTS NEWS DIGEST. 1296

1047-4064 See LITOVSKII FIZICHESKII SBORNIK. 4411

1047-4110 See SAN FRANCISCO PERFORMING ARTS LIBRARY AND MUSEUM SERIES. 388

1047-4137 See ENTERTAINMENT LITIGATION REPORTER. 2966

1047-4153 See HARTFORD COURANT, THE. 5645

1047-417X See NEWS LIBRARY NEWS. 3234

1047-4242 See SOUTHWEST SAMPLER. 2903

1047-4269 See KING'S COAL EXPORT REPORT. 2142

1047-4285 See KING'S PETROLEUM COKE REPORT. 2142

1047-4293 See CAREER WAVES. 4202

1047-4315 See DIRTY LINEN. 4115

1047-434X See PERSONAL REPORT. PRACTICE DEVELOPMENT AND WEALTH ACCUMULATION FOR THE PERIODONTIST, THE. 1333

1047-4358 See CLACKAMAS LEGACY. 2443

1047-4382 See HOT LINE CONSTRUCTION EQUIPMENT MONTHLY UPDATE. 616

1047-4412 See JOURNAL OF EDUCATIONAL AND PSYCHOLOGICAL CONSULTATION. 1757

1047-4420 See VINTAGE FASHIONS. 1088

1047-4447 See WORKPLACE TRENDS. 948

1047-4463 See GAUNTLET. 5246

1047-4501 See EXOTIC CARS QUARTERLY. 5414

1047-451X See 24HOURS (SANTA MONICA, CALIF.). 2526

1047-4528 See PUNCTURE (SAN FRANCISCO, CALIF.). 4148

1047-4544 See SIG FORTH. 1281

1047-4552 See MEDITERRANEAN QUARTERLY. 4528

1047-4595 See REVIEW OF BUSINESS STUDIES, THE. 708

1047-4609 See SEASONS (OAKLAND, CALIF.). 4802

1047-4625 See COUNTRY FOLK ART MAGAZINE. 318

1047-4633 See WOMBLE, CARLYLE, SANDRIDGE & RICE'S NORTH CAROLINA ENVIRONMENTAL LAW LETTER. 3076

1047-4641 See HOLLAND & KNIGHT'S FLORIDA ENVIRONMENTAL & LAND USE LETTER. 3113

1047-4668 See RECOMMENDED COUNTY INNS. 2809

1047-4676 See FURNITURE RETAILER (GREENSBORO, N.C.). 2905

1047-4730 See WORLD BIO LICENSING & PATENT REPORT. 3697

1047-4749 See HAWAII NURSE, THE. 3856

1047-4773 See QA REVIEW. 4797

1047-4781 See AGEXPORTER (WASHINGTON, D.C.). 45

1047-4803 See INTERNATIONAL BULLETIN FOR THE RECONSTRUCTION & DEVELOPMENT OF ARMENIA. 2910

1047-482X See INTERNATIONAL JOURNAL OF OSTEOARCHAEOLOGY. 270

1047-4838 See JOM (1989). 4006

1047-4854 See CORPORATE INTELLIGENCE. 661

1047-4862 See ABSTRACTS IN SOCIAL GERONTOLOGY. 3654

1047-4951 See VINEYARD & WINERY MANAGEMENT. 2371

1047-496X See BOCOEX INDEX, THE. 1172

1047-4978 See GRAIN & FEED MARKETING. 201

1047-4994 See ART OF THE WEST. 340

1047-5028 See INFLAMMATORY DISEASE AND THERAPY. 3587

1047-5052 See FODOR'S HEALTHY ESCAPES. 5471

1047-5060 See FODOR'S THE UPPER GREAT LAKES REGION. 5473

1047-5079 See AICPA'S UNIFORM CPA EXAM, THE. 738

1047-5087 See PENNSYLVANIA RULES OF COURT. FEDERAL. 3142

1047-5125 See AUTONOMIC NERVOUS SYSTEM, THE. 3827

1047-5133 See BANK BAILOUT LITIGATION NEWS. 774

1047-5141 See FIRST THINGS (NEW YORK, N.Y.). 4959

1047-5192 See BERKELEY PLANNING JOURNAL. 2816

1047-5230 See HELLER REPORT ON EDUCATIONAL TECHNOLOGY AND TELECOMMUNICATIONS MARKETS, THE. 5109

1047-5257 See ESSAYS IN PUBLIC WORKS HISTORY. 5245

1047-529X See NEVADA CASINO JOURNAL. 4864

1047-5303 See PLAYER (ATLANTIC CITY, N.J.), THE. 4865

1047-5311 See QUALITY LETTER FOR HEALTHCARE LEADERS, THE. 3791

1047-5354 See EUROPEAN CLINICAL LABORATORY. 3575

1047-5370 See INTERRACE (SCHENECTADY, N.Y.). 2264

1047-5400 See OHIO ARCHIVIST (1987), THE. 3239

1047-5427 See AS PICTURE PROFESSIONAL. 4366

1047-5443 See BLUE BOOK BUILDING AND CONSTRUCTION (FLORIDA ED.). 601

1047-546X See ALL-AROUND, THE. 4882

1047-5486 See ABINGDON PREACHER'S ANNUAL. 4931

1047-5524 See NORTH CAROLINA STATE BAR NEWSLETTER, THE. 3018

1047-5532 See WHRO MAGAZINE. 1143

1047-5559 See AUTOINC. 5405

1047-5583 See ELECTRONICS MANUFACTURERS DIRECTORY. 3478

1047-5613 See HERITAGE (AUSTIN, TEX.). 2736

1047-5672 See WORLD SHRIMP FARMING (BIMONTHLY REPORT). 2316

1047-5680 See FODOR'S SHOPPING IN EUROPE. 5473

1047-5699 See FAMILY AND CONCILIATION COURTS REVIEW. 3120

1047-5834 See CPA PROFIT REPORT. 742

1047-5893 See SAN LUIS OBISPO COUNTY GENEALOGICAL SOCIETY, INC. 2471

1047-5974 See MATHEMATICA JOURNAL, THE. 3518

1047-5982 See MODERN LOGIC. 3523

1047-5990 See CONSERVATIVE REVIEW (WASHINGTON, D.C.). 1471

1047-6016 See NEWS-DISPATCH (MICHIGAN CITY, IND.). 5666

1047-6059 See CE/Q MEDICAL NEWSLETTER. 3795

1047-6067 See INSIDE MICROSOFT BASIC. 1268

1047-6075 See INSIDE MICROSOFT C. 1287

1047-6083 See CLAYTON-FILLMORE REPORT, THE. 4835

1047-6105 See FLORIDA BUSINESS SOUTHWEST. 676

1047-6121 See BULLETIN / GERMAN GENEALOGICAL SOCIETY OF AMERICA. 2440

1047-6202 See FASTIE REPORT, THE. 1184

1047-6210 See TEACHING EDUCATION (COLUMBIA, S.C.). 1906

1047-6245 See BULLETIN - ALBERT HOFMANN FOUNDATION. 4578

1047-6261 See PRACTICAL LITIGATOR, THE. 3030

1047-627X See HUMANISTIC MATHEMATICS NETWORK JOURNAL. 3508

1047-630X See PETROLEUM MARKET INTELLIGENCE. 4273

1047-6318 See DIRECCION (KANSAS CITY, MO.). 4953

1047-6326 See VETERINARY FORUM. 5525

1047-6385 See MEALEY'S LITIGATION REPORTS. BANKING INSOLVENCY. **797**

1047-6393 *See* COMPANIES AND THEIR BRANDS. **1303**

1047-6407 *See* BRANDS AND THEIR COMPANIES. **1302**

1047-6415 *See* FLIGHT TRAINING. **21**

1047-6423 *See* MARYLAND HIGH-TECH DIRECTORY. **5127**

1047-6458 *See* COMPUTERS IN HR MANAGEMENT. **1179**

1047-6466 *See* CALIFORNIA INSURANCE LAW & REGULATION REPORTER. **2946**

1047-6482 *See* LAW OFFICE TECHNOLOGY REVIEW. **1193**

1047-6555 *See* GMP TRENDS. **3480**

1047-6571 *See* PAYROLL PRACTITIONER'S MONTHLY. **1701**

1047-6598 *See* PEOPLE SEARCHING NEWS. **5301**

1047-6636 *See* COASTAL COURIER (HINESVILLE, GA.), THE. **5653**

1047-6768 *See* FODOR'S CAPE COD, MARTHA'S VINEYARD, NANTUCKET. **5471**

1047-6822 *See* BONNER COUNTY DAILY BEE. **5656**

1047-6830 *See* MISSOURI MAGAZINE (SAINT LOUIS, MO.). **2539**

1047-6857 *See* TULANE ENVIRONMENTAL LAW JOURNAL. **3117**

1047-6865 *See* UNDERGROUND WINE JOURNAL, THE. **2371**

1047-6903 *See* HOSPITAL BLUE BOOK (OFFICIAL NATIONAL ED.). **3783**

1047-692X *See* ATI DIRECTORY. **5348**

1047-6938 *See* OPTICS AND PHOTONICS NEWS. **4439**

1047-6946 *See* BIBLICAL REFLECTIONS ON MODERN MEDICINE. **4939**

1047-6954 *See* GENERAL SURGERY (GLENDALE, CALIF.). **3965**

1047-6989 *See* LIT PAGE, THE. **3228**

1047-6997 *See* GREENLINE GUIDE TO RESIDENTIAL ARCHITECTS. **299**

1047-7004 *See* GRAPHICS DESIGN JOURNAL, THE. **379**

1047-7039 *See* ORGANIZATION SCIENCE. **881**

1047-7047 *See* INFORMATION SYSTEMS RESEARCH. **1188**

1047-7055 *See* ELDERLAW REPORT, THE. **2965**

1047-7071 *See* REQUIREMENTS FOR CERTIFICATION OF TEACHERS, COUNSELORS, LIBRARIANS, ADMINISTRATORS FOR ELEMENTARY AND SECONDARY SCHOOLS. **1870**

1047-708X *See* NEWS / INDIANA HISTORICAL SOCIETY. **2749**

1047-7128 *See* SOAP OPERA WEEKLY. **2546**

1047-7136 *See* AMERICAN WORKER, THE. **1643**

1047-7160 *See* DAILY DUNKLIN DEMOCRAT, THE. **5703**

1047-7187 *See* SERVICE INSIDER (NORWALK, CONN.). **886**

1047-7217 *See* SOCIAL STUDIES REVIEW (NEW YORK, N.Y.). **5222**

1047-7225 *See* GOOD COUNTRY PEOPLE. **2320**

1047-7233 *See* JAPANESE INVESTMENT IN U.S. AND CANADIAN REAL ESTATE DIRECTORY. **4839**

1047-7268 See CABLE IN THE CLASSROOM. **1129**

1047-7276 *See* HEALTHCARE TRENDS & TRANSITION. **3583**

1047-7314 *See* COUNSELOR (ARLINGTON, VA.), THE. **1342**

1047-7454 See INTERNATIONAL DIRECTORY OF CONTEMPORARY MUSIC. INSTRUMENTATION. **4123**

1047-7462 *See* NTH MAN. **4864**

1047-7497 *See* DIRECTORY OF CERTIFIED UNITARY AIR-CONDITIONERS, UNITARY AIR-SOURCE HEAT PUMPS, SOUND-RATED OUTDOOR UNITARY EQUIPMENT. **2604**

1047-7527 *See* AMERICAN GINSENG TRENDS. **1596**

1047-7535 *See* TRUCK SAFETY NEWS. **5398**

1047-7551 *See* MINING WORLD NEWS. **2146**

1047-7594 *See* JOURNAL OF ROMAN ARCHAEOLOGY. **271**

1047-7667 *See* TEXAS TREES. **2396**

1047-7705 *See* EXPERTEASE (FEDERAL WAY, WASH.). **1184**

1047-7713 *See* VIDEO MANAGEMENT. **889**

1047-773X *See* ORGANIC SYNTHESIS. **1045**

1047-7764 See INTERNATIONAL DRUG PREVENTION QUARTERLY OF THE NAE PROJECT, THE. **2910**

1047-7799 *See* REGIONAL DIRECTORY OF MINORITY & WOMEN-OWNED BUSINESS FIRMS (CENTRAL ED.). **706**

1047-7802 *See* REGIONAL DIRECTORY OF MINORITY AND WOMEN-OWNED BUSINESS FIRMS (EASTERN ED.). **706**

1047-7837 *See* JOURNAL OF NATUROPATHIC MEDICINE, THE. **3596**

1047-7845 *See* JOURNAL OF RELIGIOUS & THEOLOGICAL INFORMATION. **3220**

1047-7853 *See* FROMMER'S COMPREHENSIVE TRAVEL GUIDE. TORONTO. **5477**

1047-7861 *See* FROMMER'S SALT LAKE CITY. **5477**

1047-787X *See* FROMMER'S COMPREHENSIVE TRAVEL GUIDE, SAN DIEGO. **5476**

1047-7888 *See* FROMMER'S COMPREHENSIVE TRAVEL GUIDE. ATLANTA. **5475**

1047-7896 *See* FROMMER'S COMPREHENSIVE TRAVEL GUIDE. TAMPA & ST. PETERSBURG. **5477**

1047-790X *See* FROMMER'S COMPREHENSIVE TRAVEL GUIDE. MIAMI. **5476**

1047-7918 *See* INTERNATIONAL REVIEW OF STRATEGIC MANAGEMENT. **872**

1047-7926 *See* MANAGE IT. **5127**

1047-7942 *See* SOUTHERN SOCIAL STUDIES JOURNAL. **5222**

1047-7977 *See* TRANSPACIFIC (VENICE, CALIF.). **2274**

1047-8000 *See* ... COIN WORLD GUIDE TO U.S. COINS, PRICES, AND VALUE TRENDS, THE. **2780**

1047-8035 *See* UNIVERSITY OF FLORIDA JOURNAL OF LAW AND PUBLIC POLICY. **3068**

1047-8043 *See* SCIENCE WATCH. **5154**

1047-8051 *See* NEW PITTSBURGH COURIER (CITY ED.). **5738**

1047-806X *See* NEW PITTSBURGH COURIER (NATIONAL ED.). **5738**

1047-8108 *See* CA SELECTS: NITROGEN FIXATION. **1005**

1047-8183 *See* CA SELECTS: ALZHEIMER'S DISEASE & RELATED MEMORY DYSFUNCTIONS. **997**

1047-8221 *See* MACBARGAIN CONNECTION NEWSLETTER : MONEY-SAVING NEWS AND INFO ABOUT APPLE MACINTOSH PRODUCTS AND SERVICES. **1194**

1047-823X *See* DANCE INK. **1312**

1047-8248 *See* EDUCATIONAL FOUNDATIONS (ANN ARBOR, MICH.). **1741**

1047-8272 *See* PURTI RESEARCH SUMMARIES. **4762**

1047-8280 *See* PERRYMAN REPORT, THE. **1512**

1047-8310 *See* JOURNAL OF HIGH TECHNOLOGY MANAGEMENT RESEARCH. **1614**

1047-8329 *See* PROFILES, PATHWAYS, AND DREAMS. **434**

1047-8345 *See* CONFECTIONER (1989), THE. **2332**

1047-8353 *See* INFORM (RICHMOND, VA.). **301**

1047-8388 *See* TECHNICAL & SKILLS TRAINING. **4209**

1047-840X *See* PSYCHOLOGICAL INQUIRY. **4611**

1047-8477 *See* JOURNAL OF STRUCTURAL BIOLOGY. **462**

1047-8485 *See* METROPOLITAN UNIVERSITIES. **1835**

1047-8507 *See* INTERNATIONAL JOURNAL OF OPTICAL COMPUTING. **1190**

1047-8515 *See* DEFAMATION & DISPARAGEMENT. **2959**

1047-854X *See* WIN MAGAZINE (VAN NUYS, CALIF.). **4867**

1047-8566 *See* PERSONAL INJURY NEWSLETTER. **3026**

1047-8620 *See* EQUINE ATHLETE, THE. **2798**

1047-8639 *See* VETERINARY PRACTICE STAFF. **5526**

1047-8663 *See* BEHAVIOROLOGY (MORGANTOWN, W. VA.). **4577**

1047-8698 *See* INTERNATIONAL BUSINESS CLIMATE, THE. **683**

1047-871X *See* MONOCLONAL ANTIBODIES (NEW YORK, N.Y.). **539**

1047-8736 *See* GLOBAL CUSTODIAN. **899**

1047-8760 *See* DMS WORLD MISSILES FORECAST. **4043**

1047-8833 *See* NORTHEAST REAL ESTATE NEWS. **4842**

1047-8841 *See* RETAIL STORE IMAGE. **2903**

1047-885X *See* STEWART'S GUIDE TO ANTIQUE & COLLECTIBLE SHOPS COVERING LOS ANGELES COUNTY. **252**

1047-8892 *See* FAULKNER & GRAY'S MEDICINE & HEALTH. **3576**

1047-8949 *See* CONSOLIDATED RETURNS TAX REPORT. **2955**

1047-8957 *See* WEAPONS COMPLEX MONITOR. **4061**

1047-8981 *See* ANNUAL WORLD'S BEST SF, THE. **3362**

1047-9066 *See* SINGLE TODAY (LAPORTE, IND.). **2493**

1047-9120 *See* OCULAR SURGERY NEWS INTERNATIONAL EDITION. **3971**

1047-9163 *See* SHEPARD'S CITATIONS FOR ANNOTATIONS. **3049**

1047-918X *See* JOBSON'S HANDBOOK ADVANCE. **2368**

1047-921X *See* VIDEODISC COMPENDIUM FOR EDUCATION AND TRAINING, THE. **1790**

1047-9228 *See* GEORGIA JOURNAL OF SOUTHERN LEGAL HISTORY, THE. **2974**

1047-9317 *See* ALTAMONT NEWS, THE. **5658**

1047-9325 *See* GRAPHIC ARTS MONTHLY (1987). **379**

1047-9341 *See* STANDARD & POOR'S CREDITSTATS. **812**

1047-935X *See* RELEASE 1.0. **1239**

1047-9422 *See* INFERTILITY AND REPRODUCTIVE MEDICINE CLINICS OF NORTH AMERICA. **3762**

1047-9430 *See* JOURNAL OF DATABASE ADMINISTRATION. **1192**

1047-9449 *See* DISCIPLESHIP TRAINING. **4954**

1047-9473 *See* PRIVATE VARNISH. **5434**

1047-9481 *See* CALIFORNIA FOOD. **2330**

1047-949X *See* ALCTS NEWSLETTER. **3189**

1047-9511 *See* CARDIOLOGY IN THE YOUNG. **3701**

1047-9546 *See* FIRST BOSTON WORKING PAPER SERIES. **1491**

1047-9562 *See* INSIDE WRESTLING. **4900**

1047-9619 *See* SAN DIEGO COUNTY BUSINESS DIRECTORY. **709**

1047-9627 *See* INTERNATIONAL JOURNAL OF DIGITAL AND ANALOG COMMUNICATION SYSTEMS. **1158**

1047-9635 *See* SOUTHEASTERN JOURNAL OF MUSIC EDUCATION. **4154**

1047-9651 *See* PHYSICAL MEDICINE AND REHABILITATION CLINICS OF NORTH AMERICA. **4392**

1047-966X *See* CD-ROM MARKET PLACE. **1174**

1047-9716 *See* JOURNAL OF AFRICAN RESEARCH. **2640**

1047-9759 *See* AMERICAN FINANCIAL DIRECTORY. **769**

1047-9791 *See* HOLT ADVISORY, THE. **900**

1047-9821 See SAFE MONEY REPORT. **708**

1047-9848 *See* PSYCHOTHERAPY TODAY. **4614**

1047-9856 See METRO (WINTER PARK, FLA.). 2902

1047-9902 See WARREN PUBLISHING'S CABLE & STATION COVERAGE ATLAS. 1168

1047-9953 See DOING BUSINESS IN KENYA. 668

1047-9961 See MONTHLY SURVEY OF LIFE INSURANCE SALES IN THE UNITED STATES (1986). 2888

1048-0021 See INTERNATIONAL REVIEW OF PSYCHIATRY. 3927

1048-0056 See TAMPA BAY LIFE (TAMPA, FLA.). 2547

1048-0080 See SHEPARD'S FEDERAL CASE NAMES CITATOR, THIRD CIRCUIT CASES. 3050

1048-0099 See SHEPARD'S FEDERAL CASE NAMES CITATOR, FOURTH CIRCUIT CASES. 3049

1048-0102 See SHEPARD'S FEDERAL CASE NAMES CITATOR, FIFTH CIRCUIT CASES. 3049

1048-0145 See PHOTO DISTRICT NEWS. (WESTERN ED.). 4373

1048-0153 See PHOTO DISTRICT NEWS (SOUTHERN ED.). 4373

1048-0161 See PHOTO DISTRICT NEWS (MIDWESTERN ED.). 4373

1048-0196 See CABINETMAKER (CHICAGO, ILL.). 633

1048-020X See GORMAN'S NEW PRODUCT NEWS. 678

1048-0234 See SHEPARD'S FEDERAL CASE NAMES CITATOR, SIXTH CIRCUIT CASES. 3049

1048-0242 See SHEPARD'S FEDERAL CASE NAMES CITATOR, SEVENTH CIRCUIT CASES. 3049

1048-0250 See SHEPARD'S FEDERAL CASE NAMES CITATOR, EIGHTH CIRCUIT CASES. 3049

1048-0293 See GATFWORLD (PITTSBURGH, PA.). 378

1048-0307 See STEELS ALERT. 4021

1048-0331 See SHEPARD'S FEDERAL CASE NAMES CITATOR, DISTRICT OF COLUMBIA CIRCUIT CASES. 3049

1048-034X See SHEPARD'S FEDERAL CIRCUIT CASE NAMES CITATOR. 3050

1048-0374 See TAFT GUIDE TO CORPORATE GIVING CONTACTS. 5312

1048-0455 See WINE COUNTRY INTERNATIONAL. 2372

1048-0501 See INTERACTIVE HEALTHCARE NEWSLETTER. 4784

1048-0528 See MEGABUCKING (STERLING HEIGHTS, MICH.). 692

1048-0579 See SHEPARD'S FEDERAL LABOR LAW CASE NAMES CITATOR. 3154

1048-0587 See SHEPARD'S BANKRUPTCY CASE NAMES CITATOR. 3048

1048-0633 See CATALOG PRODUCT NEWS. 949

1048-0641 See HOMEWORLD BUSINESS. 1608

1048-0684 See SHEPARD'S MICHIGAN CASE NAMES CITATOR. 3051

1048-0706 See LABORATORY REGULATION NEWS. 5125

1048-0714 See NEVADA GOLF AND TENNIS. 4907

1048-0722 See OVERSEAS BUSINESS. 702

1048-0757 See SHEPARD'S CALIFORNIA CASE NAMES CITATOR. 3049

1048-0773 See SHEPARD'S LOUISIANA CASE NAMES CITATOR. 3051

1048-079X See SHEPARD'S NEW YORK SUPREME COURT APPELLATE DIVISION CASE NAMES CITATOR. 3053

1048-082X See SHEPARD'S INSURANCE LAW CITATIONS. 3051

1048-0846 See SHEPARD'S MEDICAL MALPRACTICE CITATIONS. 3051

1048-0862 See WORLD CLASS ENTERTAINMENT. 2495

1048-0870 See GENERALIST PAPERS, THE. 3390

1048-0919 See MINORITY BUSINESS ENTREPRENEUR. 695

1048-0935 See TODAY'S REFINERY. 4280

1048-0943 See SCIENTIFIC AMERICAN. SPECIAL ISSUE. 5155

1048-0951 See COLLECTORS BULLETIN (CANTON, ILL.). 2780

1048-096X See SHEPARD'S FLORIDA CASE NAME CITATOR. 3050

1048-1036 See REPLACEMENT ASSEMBLIES ESTIMATING GUIDE. 5424

1048-1060 See FODOR'S ... VIRGIN ISLANDS. 5474

1048-1079 See TRAVEL & HOSPITALITY CAREER DIRECTORY. 4209

1048-115X See ECONOMIC PERSPECTIVES (1989). 789

1048-1222 See RESEARCH IN INEQUALITY AND SOCIAL CONFLICT. 1581

1048-1273 See SHEPARD'S UNIFORM COMMERCIAL CODE CASE CITATIONS. 3054

1048-129X See RIVER CITY (MEMPHIS, TENN.). 3431

1048-1303 See SEAFOOD YELLOW PAGES. 2313

1048-1311 See RESULTS ... ANNUAL SURVEY OF CORPORATE RELOCATION POLICIES. 707

1048-1354 See STORYTELLING MAGAZINE. 2324

1048-1370 See DIRECTORY OF NORTH AMERICAN GUIDE AND CHARTERBOAT SERVICES. 593

1048-1389 See GOVERNMENT ACCOUNTING AND AUDITING UPDATE. 744

1048-1494 See MUSIC INTERNATIONAL (RUSSIAN ED.). 4134

1048-1532 See NATURAL BODY & FITNESS. 2600

1048-1540 See ADVANCES IN MARKETING AND PUBLIC POLICY. 920

1048-1559 See ADVANCES IN FUTURES AND OPTIONS RESEARCH. 636

1048-1591 See RESEARCH IN SOCIAL POLICY. 5255

1048-1605 See LIVESTOCK AND POULTRY UPDATE. 214

1048-1648 See JOURNAL FOR CORPORATE GROWTH. 685

1048-1656 See PROCEEDINGS OF THE ... EASTERN STATES CONFERENCE ON LINGUISTICS. 3312

1048-1680 See AMYGDALA (SAN CRISTOBAL, N.M.). 3492

1048-1699 See ARRL ANTENNA BOOK, THE. 1126

1048-1788 See BIORESEARCH TODAY. FOOD & DRUG LEGISLATION. 2941

1048-1818 See BIORESEARCH TODAY. ANTIVIRAL AGENTS. 483

1048-1826 See BIORESEARCH TODAY. ALZHEIMER'S DISEASE & SENILE DEMENTIAS. 3828

1048-1842 See IMPLANT DENTISTRY. 1324

1048-1877 See PRODUCCION Y DISTRIBUCION. 705

1048-1885 See PSYCHOANALYTIC DIALOGUES. 4610

1048-1990 See JOURNAL OF GENERAL ORTHODONTICS. 1327

1048-2059 See LANDIS' LANDINGS. 2457

1048-2091 See AIRPORT MAGAZINE. 10

1048-2121 See TAXLINE (CINCINNATI, OHIO). 4755

1048-2172 See LOST CREEK LETTERS. 3408

1048-2180 See SCHERZO. 4152

1048-2199 See ORALL NEWSLETTER. 3239

1048-2202 See NEW YORK STATE STUDENT LEADER. 1837

1048-2237 See YUMA DAILY SUN, THE. 5712

1048-2245 See SARASOTA MAGAZINE. 2545

1048-227X See RT RECRUITER. 3946

1048-2288 See WORLD DIRECTORY OF ENERGY CONSERVATION AND RENEWABLE ENERGY SOFTWARE FOR MICROCOMPUTERS. 1960

1048-2296 See IMAGING RETAIL NEWS. 1113

1048-2318 See SOUTHERN LIVING ... GARDEN ANNUAL. 2431

1048-2342 See TAIWAN STUDIES NEWSLETTER. 2666

1048-2350 See DIRECTORY OF TAIWAN SCHOLARS. 5198

1048-2431 See JOURNAL OF TEXAS CATHOLIC HISTORY AND CULTURE / TEXAS CATHOLIC HISTORICAL SOCIETY, THE. 5031

1048-2482 See JOURNAL OF AMERICAN ORGANBUILDING. 4125

1048-2539 See KOREA REPORT. 4480

1048-2563 See WHO,S WHO IN PROFESSIONAL PHOTOGRAPHY. 4378

1048-2644 See BEST IN EXHIBITION DESIGN, THE. 756

1048-2652 See SPACE FAX DAILY. 36

1048-2660 See FROMMER'S COMPREHENSIVE TRAVEL GUIDE. BERLIN. 5475

1048-2687 See CRNA. 3682

1048-2709 See MICHIGAN THEOLOGICAL JOURNAL. 4977

1048-2717 See CHASE INVESTMENT PERFORMANCE DIGEST. 656

1048-2733 See LEGISLATIVE BULLETIN - NEW YORK STATE SCHOOL BOARDS ASSOCIATION. 1865

1048-2741 See MUSIC LIBRARY. MUSICAL SOUND RECORDINGS. 5317

1048-275X See CREDIT & COLLECTION MANAGEMENT BULLETIN. 663

1048-2768 See FOURTH CIRCUIT AND DISTRICT OF COLUMBIA BANKRUPTCY COURT REPORTER, THE. 2972

1048-2784 See COMPARATIVE STATISTICS OF INDUSTRIAL AND OFFICE REAL ESTATE MARKETS. 4836

1048-2814 See EMPLOYEE BENEFIT ISSUES. 1665

1048-2822 See LAFAYETTE BUSINESS DIGEST. 689

1048-2830 See COST OF LIVING INDEX (LOUISVILLE, KY.). 1471

1048-2849 See WORLD CHAMBER OF COMMERCE DIRECTORY. 821

1048-2873 See BRIO (POMONA, CALIF.). 2277

1048-2881 See BREAKAWAY (POMONA, CALIF.). 2277

1048-2911 See NEW SOLUTIONS. 4793

1048-292X See VOICES IN ITALIAN AMERICANA. 3451

1048-2954 See EXECUTIVE EDGE. 2597

1048-2962 See INTERNATIONAL AG-SIEVE. 96

1048-2997 See WINKLER COUNTY NEWS, THE. 5756

1048-3004 See EDUCATION INTERFACE GUIDE TO VOLUNTARY SUPPORT. 1739

1048-3039 See OEM OFF-HIGHWAY. 3485

1048-3047 See EDI FORUM. 671

1048-3055 See PUBLISHING & PRODUCTION EXECUTIVE. 4819

1048-3063 See FEDERATION HIGHLIGHTS. 5533

1048-3152 See HUNTSVILLE HISTORICAL REVIEW, THE. 2738

1048-3160 See HERB, SPICE, AND MEDICINAL PLANT DIGEST, THE. 2418

1048-3217 See MEDIMARK RESEARCH MAGAZINE TOTAL AUDIENCES REPORT. 933

1048-3225 See MEDIMARK RESEARCH MAGAZINE QUALITATIVE AUDIENCES REPORT. 933

1048-3276 See TERRORISM, AN INTERNATIONAL RESOURCE FILE. INDEX. 4536

1048-3306 See TAX NOTES INTERNATIONAL. 4753

1048-3314 See MCKNIGHT'S LONG-TERM CARE NEWS. 5295

1048-3330 See CONSUMERS DIRECTORY OF CERTIFIED EFFICIENCY RATINGS FOR RESIDENTIAL HEATING AND WATER HEATING EQUIPMENT. 2604

1048-3365 See WICHITA JOURNAL. 5679

1048-3373 See HIGH SCHOOL WRITER, THE. 2920

1048-3403 See FAXON REPORT, THE. 3210

1048-3411 See PETERSON'S JOB OPPORTUNITIES FOR BUSINESS AND LIBERAL ARTS GRADUATES. 703

1048-342X See PETERSON'S JOB OPPORTUNITIES FOR ENGINEERING, SCIENCE, AND COMPUTER GRADUATES. 4208

1048-3438 See DIRECTORY OF GALLERIES FOR THE FINE ARTIST. 4087

1048-3462 See SERVICE INDUSTRY NEWSLETTER. 710

1048-3535 See MACINTOSH DISCOUNT REPORTER NEWSLETTER, THE. 1194

1048-3624 See WEST'S NEW YORK SUPPLEMENT. 3074

1048-3659 See QUICK & EASY CRAFTS. 5185

1048-3675 See PRATT TRIBUNE (PRATT, KAN. : 1964). 5678

1048-3683 See COLORADO BANKRUPTCY COURT REPORTER, THE. 2952

1048-3713 See GENERAL MUSIC TODAY. 4119

1048-3721 See STANFORD HUMANITIES REVIEW. 2855

1048-373X See DIRECTORY OF WIRE COMPANIES OF NORTH AMERICA. 2113

1048-3748 See TULANE MARITIME LAW JOURNAL. 3182

1048-3756 See AETHLON (SAN DIEGO, CALIF.). 4882

1048-3764 See CABLE CONTACTS YEARBOOK. 1150

1048-3772 See INDEPENDENT LIVING (1989). 4389

1048-3780 See WEST'S SOUTH WESTERN REPORTER. 3075

1048-3799 See WEST'S SOUTHERN REPORT. 3075

1048-3845 See NEW ELECTRIC RAILWAY JOURNAL, THE. 5433

1048-3896 See SCHOOL HEALTH ALERT. 1782

1048-3926 See TENNESSEE MANAGED CARE. 3645

1048-3950 See WORD OF MOUTH (SAN ANTONIO, TEX.). 1886

1048-3969 See CROSS-STITCH QUICK & EASY. 372

1048-4051 See FEDERAL DATA REPORT. 4647

1048-406X See CD-ROM SHOPPERS GUIDE. 1174

1048-4078 See FEDERAL FACILITIES ENVIRONMENTAL JOURNAL. 3112

1048-4116 See STAR-HERALD (KOSCIUSKO, MISS.), THE. 5702

1048-4124 See 21ST CENTURY CHRISTIAN MAGAZINE. 4931

1048-4159 See TASK FORCE REPORT. 3937

1048-4167 See HEALTHTEXAS (AUSTIN, TEX.). 3782

1048-4205 See GEORGETOWN JOURNAL OF LANGUAGES & LINGUISTICS, THE. 3283

1048-4418 See DIRECTORY OF WOMEN HISTORIANS. 2615

1048-4442 See COMPUTER COMPENDIUM. 1176

1048-4477 See HOSPITAL PATIENT RELATIONS REPORT. 3784

1048-4485 See AIR TOXICS REPORT. 2223

1048-4493 See MEDICAL WASTE NEWS. 3612

1048-4507 See CLASSIC CD (U.S. ED.). 4110

1048-4523 See PACE (HUNTINGTON, IND.). 4984

1048-4612 See DEFENSE TECHNOLOGY BUSINESS. 4042

1048-4620 See CLARKE BURTON REPORT. 1106

1048-4639 See DIGITAL DESKTOP REVIEW. 1182

1048-4647 See PERRY'S ENVIRONMENT AND THE LAW DIGEST. 3115

1048-4663 See DIRECTORY OF COLLEGE & UNIVERSITY FOODSERVICE. 1820

1048-4671 See DIRECTORY OF RECREATIONAL MARINE PRODUCT DEALERS. 593

1048-471X See DALHOUSIE UNIVERSITY, SCHOOL OF LIBRARY AND INFORMATION STUDIES SERIES. 3205

1048-4736 See ADVANCES IN THE STUDY OF ENTREPRENEURSHIP, INNOVATION, AND ECONOMIC GROWTH. 1460

1048-4744 See ANNUAL REPORT / NORTH AMERICAN ELECTRIC RELIABILITY COUNCIL. 2035

1048-4760 See ADVANCES IN MATHEMATICAL PROGRAMMING AND FINANCIAL PLANNING. 859

1048-4779 See YEARBOOK (COUNCIL ON TECHNOLOGY TEACHER EDUCATION (U.S.). 1917

1048-4825 See TWENTIETH CENTURY PETROLEUM STATISTICS. 4285

1048-4833 See STANFORD SLAVIC STUDIES. 3324

1048-4876 See CULTURE & AGRICULTURE. 78

1048-4892 See IN-FISHERMAN ANGLING ADVENTURES TRAVEL GUIDE. 4873

1048-4906 See WEST'S FEDERAL RULES DECISIONS. 3074

1048-4949 See WILDLIFE CONSERVATION. 2209

1048-4965 See AMERICA'S NEW FOUNDATIONS. 5271

1048-4981 See WASHINGTON CEO. 719

1048-499X See MIDWEST ALLIANCE IN NURSING JOURNAL / MAIN. 3861

1048-5015 See ARMY MAN. 2485

1048-5074 See CALIFORNIA FIRE SERVICE, THE. 2288

1048-5090 See EXTENDED ABSTRACTS / MATERIALS RESEARCH SOCIETY. 2102

1048-5104 See GPS WORLD. 2565

1048-5112 See ENTERTAINMENT MARKETING LETTER. 924

1048-5120 See ITEM PROCESSING REPORT. 793

1048-5139 See TRAVEL MEXICO EVENTS. 5496

1048-5155 See TRAVEL MEXICO UPDATE. 5496

1048-5163 See TRAVEL MEXICO MAGAZINE. 5496

1048-5171 See CARIBBEAN EVENTS MAGAZINE. 2530

1048-5198 See TAPPING THE NETWORK JOURNAL. 887

1048-5201 See HOSPITAL LITIGATION REPORTER. 2979

1048-521X See SOFTWARE TAXATION LETTER. 3056

1048-5236 See STRATEGIC PLANNING FOR ENERGY AND THE ENVIRONMENT. 1958

1048-5244 See BOATS & GEAR. 592

1048-5252 See JOURNAL OF NONPARAMETRIC STATISTICS. 5329

1048-5260 See PRESCHOOLERS AT CHURCH AND HOME. 4890

1048-5287 See EUROPEAN JOURNAL OF SERIALS LIBRARIANSHIP. 3209

1048-5309 See ASOTIN COUNTY AMERICAN. 5760

1048-5317 See TODAY'S FDA. 1336

1048-5325 See MASCA RESEARCH PAPERS IN SCIENCE AND ARCHAEOLOGY. 274

1048-5341 See QUICK & EASY PLASTIC CANVAS. 375

1048-535X See LATINFINANCE (CORAL GABLES, FLA.). 796

1048-5384 See REFERENCE POINTS. 3244

1048-5392 See CALLAGHAN'S LAW REVIEW DIGEST. 2947

1048-5406 See SOUTH DADE NEWS LEADER. 5651

1048-5562 See HEALTHLINES (WACO, TEX.). 4782

1048-5597 See DIABETES NEWS DIGEST. 3728

1048-5600 See AMERICAN PROGRAMMER. 1284

1048-5635 See PROCEEDINGS OF THE SECTION ON STATISTICAL GRAPHICS. 5336

1048-5678 See SCIENTIFIC INFORMATION BULLETIN. 5155

1048-5759 See INSIDE FLYER. 5384

1048-5945 See ARRIS (ATLANTA, GA.). 292

1048-597X See JOURNAL OF ERITREAN STUDIES. 2848

1048-5996 See APPROVED DRUG PRODUCTS WITH THERAPEUTIC EQUIVALENCE EVALUATIONS. 4292

1048-6119 See WINSTON CUP ILLUSTRATED. 4930

1048-6135 See AMS ... MANAGEMENT SALARIES REPORT. 860

1048-6194 See CAR MODELER. 2772

1048-6216 See GLOBAL AFRICA. 2499

1048-6259 See QUARTERLY REPORT OF THE INTER-AMERICAN TROPICAL TUNA COMMISSION, THE. 2311

1048-6313 See SCIENCE & ENGINEERING INDICATORS. 1996

1048-6380 See NUEVO TEXTO CRITICO. 3419

1048-6526 See CHICAGO BEAR REPORT. 4890

1048-6534 See AREA DEVELOPMENT SITES & FACILITY PLANNING. 4834

1048-6542 See PUBLIC-ACCESS COMPUTER SYSTEMS REVIEW (ELECTRONIC ED.), THE. 1201

1048-6550 See NATIONAL SURVEY OF CORPORATE LAW DEPARTMENTS COMPENSATION AND ORGANIZATION PRACTICES. 3102

1048-6593 See MODERN MICROBIOLOGICAL METHODS. 568

1048-6615 See OHIO SLAVIC & EAST EUROPEAN NEWSLETTER. 2701

1048-6666 See OPERATIVE TECHNIQUES IN ORTHOPAEDICS. 3883

1048-6682 See NONPROFIT MANAGEMENT & LEADERSHIP. 880

1048-6690 See MEDICAL DEVICE TECHNOLOGY. 3608

1048-6747 See CLIMATE DIAGNOSTICS BULLETIN. 1421

1048-6798 See COMPUTERS AND THE HISTORY OF ART. 348

1048-6801 See CONTEMPORARY THEATRE REVIEW. 5363

1048-6836 See SUPERCOMPUTING REVIEW. 1204

1048-6852 See WORD WIZE. 4868

1048-6860 See PRINTINGNEWS. MIDWEST. 4568

1048-6879 See OE REPORTS. 4438

1048-6933 See MANAGING END-USER COMPUTING. 1268

1048-6976 See MICROCELL REPORT. 1160

1048-6984 See EATING DISORDERS REVIEW (VAN NUYS, CALIF.). 4190

1048-7042 See SCIENCE GLOBAL SECURITY MONOGRAPH SERIES. 5151

1048-7069 See ALASKA BUSINESS DIRECTORY. 637

1048-7077 See WASHINGTON D.C. AREA BUSINESS DIRECTORY. 719

1048-7085 See DELAWARE BUSINESS DIRECTORY. 665

1048-7093 See FLORIDA BUSINESS DIRECTORY. 676

1048-7115 See MAINE BUSINESS DIRECTORY. 691

1048-7123 See MARYLAND BUSINESS DIRECTORY. 692

1048-7131 See MASSACHUSETTS BUSINESS DIRECTORY (OMAHA, NEB.). 692

1048-714X See NEW HAMPSHIRE BUSINESS DIRECTORY. 698

1048-7158 See NEW JERSEY BUSINESS DIRECTORY. 698

1048-7166 See RHODE ISLAND BUSINESS DIRECTORY. 708

1048-7174 See VERMONT BUSINESS DIRECTORY. 718

1048-7190 See ARKANSAS BUSINESS DIRECTORY. 639

1048-7220 See GEORGIA BUSINESS DIRECTORY. 677

1048-7255 See INDIANA BUSINESS DIRECTORY. 682

1048-7263 See IOWA BUSINESS DIRECTORY. 684

1048-728X See KENTUCKY BUSINESS DIRECTORY. 688

1048-7387 See CURRENT POLITICS AND ECONOMICS OF RUSSIA. 4470

1048-7468 *See* STEVENSON CLASSICAL COMPACT DISC GUIDE. 4154

1048-7492 *See* REAL ESTATE SYNDICATIONS. 4845

1048-7514 *See* GERIATRIC CARE NEWS. 3751

1048-7565 *See* CURRENT HOUSING REPORTS. H-150, AMERICAN HOUSING SURVEY FOR THE UNITED STATES IN 2820

1048-7573 *See* ECONOMIC PERSPECTIVES. AGRICULTURAL CREDIT OUTLOOK. 1484

1048-759X *See* HIV/AIDS SURVEILLANCE. 3670

1048-776X *See* NIST SPECIAL PUBLICATION. 4413

1048-7840 See CHEMTRACTS. INORGANIC CHEMISTRY. 1036

1048-7883 See EARTH WORK. 2192

1048-7891 *See* FLORIDA RUNNING. 2597

1048-793X *See* SHOTS (DANVILLE, KY.). 4376

1048-7948 *See* CORRIDOR REAL ESTATE JOURNAL, THE. 4836

1048-7972 *See* GALE DIRECTORY OF PUBLICATIONS AND BROADCAST MEDIA. 1132

1048-8030 *See* RAPTOR REPORT. 5620

1048-8057 *See* SOUTHERN QUERIES : THE CONTACT MAGAZINE FOR PEOPLE SEARCHING FOR THEIR SOUTHERN ANCESTORS. 2473

1048-8065 *See* FORTUNE DIGEST. 677

1048-809X *See* WHO'S WEALTHY IN AMERICA. 720

1048-8111 *See* AQUA TERRA (EUREKA SPRINGS, ARK.). 5530

1048-812X *See* ETHIOPIAN ART AND CULTURE CODEX / THE ETHIOPIAN ART AND CULTURE CHRONICLES SOCIETY, THE. 2639

1048-8138 *See* TROPICAL LEPIDOPTERA. 5614

1048-8154 *See* NATIONAL DIRECTORY OF NONPROFIT ORGANIZATIONS. 4338

1048-8170 *See* CLARENDON NEWS (1990), THE. 5748

1048-8197 *See* FOOD DISTRIBUTION MAGAZINE : FDM. 2337

1048-8219 *See* ARTES GRAFICAS (PORT SAINT LUCIE, FLA.). 341

1048-8227 *See* ROCKWALL COUNTY JOURNAL-SUCCESS. 5754

1048-8235 *See* TEXAS EMS MESSENGER. 4805

1048-8243 *See* PLAY METER MAGAZINE. 4864

1048-8251 *See* PAPER INDUSTRY (MONTGOMERY, ALA.). 4236

1048-826X *See* PANEL WORLD. 2403

1048-8324 *See* NEW MYSTERY. 3416

1048-8340 *See* SIGTC CONNECTIONS. 1225

1048-8359 *See* T.I.E. NEWS. 1164

1048-8383 *See* MAGAZINE OF AMERICA'S BEST RECIPES, THE. 4194

1048-8391 *See* DIET AND HEALTH MAGAZINE. 4189

1048-8405 *See* HEALTH & FITNESS MAGAZINE FOR HEALTHY, SOUND LIVING : HF. 4777

1048-8413 *See* SPECIALTY COOKING. 4199

1048-8472 *See* HOLISTIC RESOURCE MANAGEMENT NEWSLETTER. 93

1048-8537 *See* HOME LANDSCAPE PLANS. 2418

1048-8545 *See* NEW ATHENAEUM (LEWISTON, N.Y.). 4980

1048-857X *See* MEDIEVAL FOLKLORE. 2322

1048-8596 *See* EDWARDIAN (LEWISTON, N.Y.). 1091

1048-8618 *See* WILLA CATHER YEARBOOK, THE. 3453

1048-8626 *See* YEARBOOK OF WOMEN STUDIES, A. 5572

1048-8642 *See* SCIENCE & RELIGION NEWS. 4995

1048-8650 *See* CULTURAL VISTAS. 2845

1048-8685 *See* GREAT MODEL RAILROADS. 5431

1048-8693 *See* LYCEUM TECHNICAL JOURNAL. 1985

1048-8707 *See* WARD'S BUSINESS DIRECTORY OF U.S. PRIVATE AND PUBLIC COMPANIES. 718

1048-8731 *See* FORENSIC DRUG ABUSE ADVISOR, THE. 1344

1048-8758 *See* GO (TORRANCE, CALIF.). 429

1048-8766 *See* CORDOVA TIMES, THE. 5629

1048-8774 *See* DISTRIBUTOR SALES. 5695

1048-8782 *See* WICHITA COMMERCE. 857

1048-8790 *See* CONCEPTIONS SOUTHWEST. 317

1048-8804 *See* CAMCORDER (VENTURA, CALIF.). 4367

1048-8812 *See* BUSINESS JOURNAL (1988), THE. 649

1048-8820 *See* QUANTUM (WASHINGTON, D.C.). 3530

1048-8839 *See* KIDS CLUB MAGAZINE. 1065

1048-8863 *See* QUARKXPRESS IN-DEPTH. 1289

1048-8871 *See* OUTDOOR WOMAN. 4877

1048-8898 *See* CAREER PILOT. 16

1048-891X *See* INTERNATIONAL JOURNAL OF GYNECOLOGICAL CANCER. 3818

1048-8928 *See* OEM INTEGRATOR, THE. 3485

1048-8936 *See* BIMONTHLY REVIEW OF LAW BOOKS. 2941

1048-8952 *See* ALASKA PUBLIC AFFAIRS JOURNAL, THE. 1461

1048-8987 *See* PROCEEDINGS OF THE ANNUAL HEALTH CARE INFORMATION AND MANAGEMENT SYSTEMS CONFERENCE. 3791

1048-8995 *See* MACINTOSH-AIDED DESIGN. 1194

1048-9002 *See* JOURNAL OF VIBRATION AND ACOUSTICS. 4453

1048-9053 *See* CARTOGRAPHIC PERSPECTIVES. 2581

1048-907X *See* ASH SMOKING AND HEALTH REVIEW. 4767

1048-910X *See* MIRKIN REPORT. 2600

1048-9118 *See* AT-THE-PARK (CHICAGO, ILL.). 4857

1048-9150 *See* WAGS RAG. 2477

1048-9207 *See* AVIONICS REVIEW. 14

1048-9215 *See* TACKLE TEST. 2314

1048-9223 *See* LANGUAGE ACQUISITION. 3294

1048-9398 *See* HAZARDOUS WASTE LITIGATION. 2977

1048-9401 *See* EARLY DRAMA, ART, AND MUSIC REVIEW, THE. 319

1048-9428 *See* HAWAIIAN SUGAR MANUAL. 91

1048-9487 *See* LAMBDA BOOK REPORT. 2795

1048-9533 *See* JOURNAL OF APPLIED MATHEMATICS AND STOCHASTIC ANALYSIS. 1282

1048-9568 *See* CONCHO RIVER REVIEW. 3377

1048-9576 *See* UNIVERSITY OF HARTFORD STUDIES IN LITERATURE. 3449

1048-9584 *See* TRUCK ENGINEERING. 5426

1048-9711 *See* LIBRARY OF CONGRESS SUBJECT HEADINGS. 3226

1048-9738 *See* EDMUND'S ... IMPORT CAR PRICES. 5413

1048-9819 *See* BADGER TRUCKER. 5377

1048-9843 *See* LEADERSHIP QUARTERLY, THE. 875

1048-9851 *See* CONTINGENCIES (WASHINGTON, D.C.). 2878

1048-9886 *See* JOURNAL OF THE ASSOCIATION FOR ACADEMIC MINORITY PHYSICIANS. 3914

1048-9924 See ST. PETERSBURG MATHEMATICAL JOURNAL. 3536

1048-9940 *See* WOLVERINE (ANN ARBOR, MICH.), THE. 4930

1049-0000 *See* GOLF & SPORTSTURF. 2417

1049-0035 *See* BEFORE AND AFTER. 4824

1049-0043 *See* BATS (AUSTIN, TEX.). 2188

1049-0078 *See* JOURNAL OF ASIAN ECONOMICS. 1498

1049-0116 *See* WHOLESALE-BY-MAIL CATALOG, THE. 767

1049-0140 *See* WORLD MUSIC CONNECTIONS. 4159

1049-0159 *See* SOAP OPERA WORD-FIND. 4866

1049-0175 *See* MICHIGAN 4-H TODAY. 5233

1049-0183 *See* TEENAGE MUTANT NINJA TURTLES MAGAZINE. 4866

1049-0191 *See* GARFIELD MAGAZINE. 2533

1049-0221 *See* PROCEEDINGS OF THE ILLINOIS MOSQUITO AND VECTOR CONTROL ASSOCIATION. 5613

1049-023X *See* PREHOSPITAL AND DISASTER MEDICINE. 3629

1049-0248 *See* NOVA LAW REVIEW. 3019

1049-0256 *See* NATIONAL BUSINESS EDUCATION YEARBOOK (1987). 697

1049-0264 *See* YEARBOOK OF EDUCATION LAW, THE. 1874

1049-0272 *See* NAVAL LAW REVIEW. 3183

1049-0280 *See* JOURNAL OF ENVIRONMENTAL LAW AND LITIGATION. 3113

1049-0299 *See* ST. JOHN'S JOURNAL OF LEGAL COMMENTARY. 3058

1049-0302 *See* CELLULAR CLOCKS. 534

1049-0337 See SOFTWARE DIRECTORY. SYSTEMS & UTILITIES. 1290

1049-0345 See SOFTWARE DIRECTORY. SYSTEMS & UTILITIES. 1290

1049-0396 *See* CURLEY. 3379

1049-0434 *See* ENTERTAINMENT WEEKLY. 385

1049-0450 *See* SPOT (HOUSTON, TEX.). 4377

1049-0574 *See* COAL VOICE. 1439

1049-0655 *See* STOUGHTON COURIER HUB (STOUGHTON, WIS. : 1981). 5771

1049-071X *See* WINDOWS SHOPPER'S GUIDE, THE. 1207

1049-0736 *See* NORTHEAST POWER REPORT. 2074

1049-0744 *See* INDEPENDENT POWER REPORT. 2064

1049-0779 *See* PEACE REPORTER. 1772

1049-0787 *See* ANNUAL REVIEW OF HEAT TRANSFER. 4427

1049-0795 *See* INSIDE WORD FOR WINDOWS. 1287

1049-0809 *See* JOYCE STUDIES ANNUAL. 3400

1049-0833 *See* CD-ROM PROFESSIONAL. 1276

1049-085X *See* BEHAVIOR, HEALTH AND AGING. 3749

1049-0892 *See* DEAD OF NIGHT. 2319

1049-0914 See EMPLOYEE TERMINATIONS LAW BULLETIN (1991). 1665

1049-0965 *See* PS, POLITICAL SCIENCE & POLITICS. 4492

1049-1015 *See* CHEMICAL MONITOR, THE. 1022

1049-1023 *See* CALIFORNIA TRUCKER. 5378

1049-1058 *See* MIT WORKING PAPERS IN LINGUISTICS. 3302

1049-1139 *See* ACCOUNTANT'S WEEKLY TAX REPORT. 736

1049-1163 *See* TV ENTERTAINMENT. 1141

1049-118X See SPANG ROBINSON REPORT ON INTELLIGENT SYSTEMS, THE. 1217

1049-121X *See* C2C CURRENTS JAPAN. MATERIALS. 654

1049-1228 *See* C2C CURRENTS JAPAN. CHEMISTRY. 964

1049-1236 *See* C2C CURRENTS JAPAN. ELECTRONICS. 2037

1049-1244 *See* C2C CURRENTS JAPAN. COMPUTERS. 1172

1049-1252 *See* C2C ABSTRACTS JAPAN. CERAMICS. 2595

1049-1260 *See* C2C ABSTRACTS JAPAN. ANALYTICAL CHEMISTRY. 996

1049-1279 *See* C2C ABSTRACTS JAPAN. CHEMICAL ENGINEERING. 996

1049-1287 *See* C2C ABSTRACTS JAPAN. CRYSTALLOGRAPHY. 996

1049-1295 *See* C2C ABSTRACTS JAPAN. HYDROCARBONS. 996

1049-1309 *See* C2C ABSTRACTS JAPAN. INORGANIC CHEMISTRY. 996

1049-1317 *See* C2C ABSTRACTS JAPAN. MATERIALS SCIENCES. 5174

1049-1325 *See* C2C ABSTRACTS JAPAN. ORGANIC CHEMISTRY. 1040

1049-1333 *See* C2C ABSTRACTS JAPAN. PHYSICAL CHEMISTRY. **996**

1049-1341 *See* C2C ABSTRACTS JAPAN. PLASTICS. **4461**

1049-135X *See* C2C ABSTRACTS JAPAN. POLYMER CHEMISTRY. **996**

1049-1368 *See* C2C ABSTRACTS JAPAN. SURFACE CHEMISTRY. **997**

1049-1376 *See* C2C ABSTRACTS JAPAN. TEXTILES. **5360**

1049-1384 *See* C2C ABSTRACTS JAPAN. METALS. **4025**

1049-1392 *See* RECONSTRUCTION (CAMBRIDGE, MASS.). **2271**

1049-1422 *See* TRANSPORT HISTORY MONOGRAPH. **5437**

1049-1449 See BERLITZ TRAVELLER'S GUIDE TO SAN FRANCISCO & NORTHERN CALIFORNIA, THE. **5463**

1049-1457 See BERLITZ TRAVELLER'S GUIDE TO LONDON, THE. **5463**

1049-1465 *See* PENGUIN GUIDE TO TURKEY. **5488**

1049-1473 *See* CAPTAIN N, THE GAME MASTER. **4858**

1049-1562 *See* INTEGRATED WASTE MANAGEMENT. **2233**

1049-1716 See MEMBER DIRECTORY - AMERICAN HISTORICAL PRINT COLLECTORS SOCIETY. **358**

1049-1767 *See* CAPITOL WEEKLY. **2918**

1049-1775 *See* BANK MANAGEMENT (ROLLING MEADOWS, ILL.). **775**

1049-1783 *See* SEPTS (SAINT PAUL, MINN.), THE. **2472**

1049-1791 *See* CALORIE CONTROL COMMENTARY. **4188**

1049-1813 See DRINKING, DRUGS & DRIVING. **1343**

1049-1821 *See* NORTON NOTES. **2284**

1049-1872 *See* NIE INFORMATION SERVICE. **4817**

1049-1880 *See* NEBRASKA FARMER, THE. **111**

1049-2062 *See* SKOLER, ABBOTT, HAYES & PRESSER'S MASSACHUSETTS EMPLOYMENT LAW LETTER. **3154**

1049-2089 *See* JOURNAL OF HEALTH CARE FOR THE POOR AND UNDERSERVED. **4786**

1049-2119 *See* U.S. MAYOR. **4692**

1049-2127 *See* JOURNAL OF MANAGEMENT ACCOUNTING RESEARCH. **747**

1049-2135 *See* AFSM INTERNATIONAL. **1235**

1049-2194 *See* CAPACITY MANAGEMENT REVIEW. **1173**

1049-2216 *See* BLANCO COUNTY NEWS. **5747**

1049-2275 *See* JOURNAL OF CRANIOFACIAL SURGERY, THE. **3967**

1049-233X *See* JOURNAL OF THE HELMINTHOLOGICAL SOCIETY OF WASHINGTON. **5589**

1049-2364 *See* NEWSLETTER - MACRO SYSTEMS. INSTITUTE FOR RESOURCE DEVELOPMENT. DEMOGRAPHIC AND HEALTH SURVEYS. **4793**

1049-2372 See PROPERTY MANAGEMENT MONTHLY. **4843**

1049-2399 *See* OSSIPEE VALLEY TIMES. **5708**

1049-2402 *See* HAVING A BABY. **2280**

1049-2445 *See* INTEGRATED CIRCUITS. MICROPROCESSORS. **2065**

1049-250X *See* ADVANCES IN ATOMIC, MOLECULAR, AND OPTICAL PHYSICS. **959**

1049-2526 *See* VIDYA (SANTA BARBARA, CALIF.). **5045**

1049-2542 *See* AVIION NEWS. **1171**

1049-2585 *See* RESEARCH ON ECONOMIC INEQUALITY. **1517**

1049-2631 *See* VILLANOVA ENVIRONMENTAL LAW JOURNAL, THE. **3117**

1049-2666 *See* TIBET PRESS WATCH. **2666**

1049-2704 *See* TITLES MAGAZINE. **2925**

1049-2712 See OFFICIAL PROPERTY MANAGEMENT DIRECTORY (METROPOLITAN WASHINGTON), THE. **4842**

1049-2747 *See* GREEN CONSUMER LETTER, THE. **2172**

1049-2771 *See* GLOBAL PERSPECTIVES ON HEPATITIS : NEWSLETTER OF THE INTERNATIONAL TASK FORCE ON HEPATITIS B IMMUNIZATION. **3797**

1049-2801 *See* MATHEMATICAL CHEMISTRY. **985**

1049-2828 *See* SPECIAL EDUCATION, TEACHER. **1885**

1049-2852 *See* POOL & BILLIARD MAGAZINE. **4912**

1049-2879 *See* NEW JERSEY BUSINESS SOURCE BOOK, THE. **698**

1049-2917 *See* MONTAIGNE STUDIES. **3413**

1049-2968 *See* IDEAL HOME PLANS. **300**

1049-3018 *See* GRAND ISLAND INDEPENDENT. **5706**

1049-3050 *See* MANUFACTURERS AND PROCESSORS DIRECTORY, SOUTH DAKOTA. **3483**

1049-3085 *See* ANNUAL REPORT (COLONIAL WILLIAMSBURG FOUNDATION). **2528**

1049-3158 *See* GOOD PACKAGING MAGAZINE. **4219**

1049-3166 See CALIFORNIA FRUIT GROWER ANNUAL. **2330**

1049-3174 *See* BAKERY NEWSLETTER. **2328**

1049-3190 *See* COPY EDITOR. **4813**

1049-3239 *See* FORT CONCHO AND THE SOUTH PLAINS JOURNAL. **2734**

1049-3247 *See* PERSPECTIVES IN CLINICAL MEDICINE. **3626**

1049-3255 *See* DEPARTMENT CHAIR, THE. **1862**

1049-3263 *See* S&P'S HIGH YIELD QUARTERLY. **913**

1049-3271 *See* BLACKFIRE. **2257**

1049-328X *See* KUUMBA (LOS ANGELES, CALIF.). **3403**

1049-3298 *See* BLACK LACE. **2793**

1049-3301 *See* ACM TRANSACTIONS ON MODELING AND COMPUTER SIMULATION : A PUBLICATION OF THE ASSOCIATION FOR COMPUTING MACHINERY. **1282**

1049-331X *See* ACM TRANSACTIONS ON SOFTWARE ENGINEERING AND METHODOLOGY. **1227**

1049-3344 *See* NELSON'S EARNINGS OUTLOOK. **801**

1049-3352 *See* SITUATION AND OUTLOOK REPORT. VEGETABLES AND SPECIALTIES. **2431**

1049-3379 *See* CONTEMPORARY CHRISTIAN MUSIC (1986). **4111**

1049-3387 *See* WHITE ROCKER (1990), THE. **5756**

1049-3433 See TODAY CEDAR HILL. **5755**

1049-3441 See TODAY LANCASTER. **5755**

1049-3700 *See* MACHINE KNITTERS SOURCE, THE. **374**

1049-3719 See FIAT LUX / UNIVERSITY OF CALIFORNIA, RIVERSIDE. **1091**

1049-3743 *See* NOPA DEALER OPERATING RESULTS. **4212**

1049-376X *See* LEGAL BULLETIN - UNITED STATES LEAGUE OF SAVINGS INSTITUTIONS. **3087**

1049-3859 *See* MOVIE MAKER. **4075**

1049-3867 *See* WOMEN'S HEALTH ISSUES. **5571**

1049-3875 *See* TRAINING AND DEVELOPMENT YEARBOOK. **734**

1049-3921 *See* BMWE JOURNAL. **1655**

1049-3948 *See* GAMEROOM (NEW ALBANY, IND.). **4861**

1049-3964 *See* PERFECT LAWYER, THE. **1292**

1049-3972 *See* BACK FORTY (ALEXANDRIA, VA.), THE. **2188**

1049-4057 *See* DOING BUSINESS IN GERMANY. **667**

1049-4073 *See* GRAIN GUIDE. **201**

1049-4081 *See* DOING BUSINESS IN THE NETHERLANDS ANTILLES. **668**

1049-4103 *See* GAS STATS. **4258**

1049-4197 *See* ANNUAL INDEX TO THE CURRENT DIGEST OF THE SOVIET PRESS. **407**

1049-4200 *See* NEW YORK BEIJING DIRECTORY, THE. **4669**

1049-4316 *See* BBI NEWSLETTER, THE. **642**

1049-4324 *See* TECHTRANSFER NEWS. **3644**

1049-4340 *See* LOOK BACK AT BOB DYLAN. **4129**

1049-4383 See ASIAN M&A AND INVESTMENT DATABASE. **891**

1049-4383 *See* JAPAN M&A REPORTER. **793**

1049-4421 *See* BETWEEN THE LINES (WASHINGTON, D.C.). **4465**

1049-4499 *See* HEALTHCARE TECHNOLOGY BUSINESS OPPORTUNITIES. **3583**

1049-4545 *See* FRUIT GARDENER, THE. **2415**

1049-4553 *See* NAILPRO (VAN NUYS, CALIF.). **405**

1049-4561 *See* THIS ROCK. **5004**

1049-457X *See* MANAGED CARE INSIGHTS. **3606**

1049-4596 *See* INDIVIDUAL INVESTOR (NEW YORK, N.Y.). **790**

1049-460X *See* CAPE COD HOME & GARDEN. **2412**

1049-4618 *See* HARROWSMITH COUNTRY LIFE. **2534**

1049-4685 *See* APPLIED MATHEMATICS SERIES. **3495**

1049-4715 *See* ENVIRONMENTAL WASTE MANAGEMENT. **2229**

1049-474X *See* TEXAS TEEN!. **1070**

1049-4766 *See* GEORGE MASON UNIVERSITY CIVIL RIGHTS LAW JOURNAL. **3090**

1049-4820 *See* INTERACTIVE LEARNING ENVIRONMENTS. **1753**

1049-4839 *See* CUTTING EDGE, THE. **2487**

1049-4855 *See* WORKING SMART (NEW YORK, N.Y.). **889**

1049-4871 *See* DENTAL OFFICE. **1321**

1049-488X *See* SITUATION AND OUTLOOK REPORT. OIL CROPS. **4278**

1049-4901 *See* CARNATION NUTRITION EDUCATION SERIES. **4188**

1049-491X *See* WORKSTATION NEWS. **1207**

1049-4928 *See* LINK, THE. **1193**

1049-4936 *See* COVINGTON NEWS (COVINGTON, GA.), THE. **5653**

1049-5045 *See* ADVENTURES (SILVER SPRING, MD). **754**

1049-507X *See* CELLULAR TECHNOLOGY. **1151**

1049-5096 *See* SHEPARD'S LABOR ARBITRATION CITATIONS. **3154**

1049-510X *See* ETHNICITY & DISEASE. **3735**

1049-5118 *See* SEMINARS IN GASTROINTESTINAL DISEASE. **3748**

1049-5142 *See* JOURNAL OF NONPROFIT & PUBLIC SECTOR MARKETING. **928**

1049-5150 *See* JOURNAL OF NUTRITIONAL IMMUNOLOGY. **4193**

1049-5177 *See* SCRIBES JOURNAL OF LEGAL WRITING, THE. **3047**

1049-524X *See* RESOURCE NOTES / UNIVERSITY OF NEBRASKA--LINCOLN, CONSERVATION AND SURVEY DIVISION. **1395**

1049-5258 *See* ADVANCES IN NEURAL INFORMATION PROCESSINGS SYSTEMS. **1210**

1049-5282 *See* AMA FREIDA. **3548**

1049-5304 *See* JOURNAL OF THE NEW YORK INSTITUTE OF LEGAL RESEARCH, THE. **2989**

1049-5312 *See* BRADYLINE. **5089**

1049-5320 *See* INSIDE DOS. **1268**

1049-5347 *See* MEALEY'S LITIGATION REPORT. REINSURANCE. **3007**

1049-5398 *See* ANIMAL BIOTECHNOLOGY. **5502**

1049-5452 *See* QUAYLE QUARTERLY, THE. **4677**

1049-5517 *See* DEPARTMENT OF STATE PUBLICATION. BACKGROUND NOTES SERIES. **2559**

1049-5541 *See* CONTROL (CHICAGO, ILL.). **3477**

1049-5568 *See* FOOD BUSINESS (CHICAGO, ILL.). **2336**

1049-5630 See NELSON'S GUIDE TO INVESTMENT CONSULTANTS. 909

1049-5665 See ENCOUNTERS (ALBUQUERQUE, N.M.). 2732

1049-5851 See INSTRUCTOR (1990). 1896

1049-5886 See GEOLOGICAL SOCIETY OF AMERICA DATA REPOSITORY. MICROFORM. 1378

1049-5908 See MEAT BUSINESS MAGAZINE. 2349

1049-5940 See SOVIET AEROSPACE & TECHNOLOGY. 5159

1049-5967 See SERVICE SAVVY. 886

1049-5983 See LEADING EDGE (PROVO, UTAH), THE. 3404

1049-6033 See JOURNAL OF LIGHT CONSTRUCTION (NATIONAL ED.), THE. 618

1049-6076 See DIRECTORY OF TEXAS WHOLESALERS. 831

1049-6092 See STATISTICAL FACT BOOK - DIRECT MARKETING ASSOCIATION (U.S.). 1300

1049-6122 See DEPAUL BUSINESS LAW JOURNAL. 3099

1049-6149 See INSIDE EPA'S SUPERFUND REPORT. 3113

1049-6211 See TRAVEL 50 & BEYOND. 5494

1049-622X See CRACKING THE GRE. 1819

1049-6300 See INTERNATIONAL SECURITIES IDENTIFICATION DIRECTORY. 902

1049-6319 See NEW YORK FAMILY LAW UPDATE. 3122

1049-6343 See JOURNAL OF PREVENTIVE PSYCHIATRY AND ALLIED DISCIPLINES. 3929

1049-6351 See VACATION HOME REPORT. 4855

1049-636X See PERSPECTIVES. 4208

1049-6378 See JOURNAL OF INTERNATIONAL TAXATION. 4734

1049-6386 See GALACTIC CENTRAL BIBLIOGRAPHIES FOR THE AVID READER. 416

1049-6394 See GALACTIC CENTRAL PUBLISHER CHECKLISTS. 4815

1049-6432 See GEORGIA LIVING. 2488

1049-6459 See EC BRIEF. 2965

1049-6467 See JOURNAL OF VEGETABLE CROP PRODUCTION. 177

1049-6475 See JOURNAL OF HERBS, SPICES & MEDICINAL PLANTS. 2421

1049-6483 See JOURNAL OF EURO MARKETING. 927

1049-6491 See JOURNAL OF PROMOTION MANAGEMENT. 874

1049-6505 See JOURNAL OF AGRICULTURAL & FOOD INFORMATION. 99

1049-6513 See CONTEMPORARY THEATER STUDIES. 5363

1049-6572 See PAPER PILE QUARTERLY. 4236

1049-6602 See NATURE PHOTOGRAPHER. 4372

1049-6645 See 1992 AND BEYOND. 1632

1049-6696 See AMERICAN GENEALOGY MAGAZINE. 2437

1049-670X See GRAPE GROWER (FRESNO, CALIF.). 173

1049-6718 See DICKINSON PRESS (DICKINSON, N.D. 1942), THE. 5725

1049-6726 See MR (NORWALK, CONN.). 955

1049-6734 See ADVANCES IN ENDOCRINOLOGY AND METABOLISM. 3726

1049-6750 See DAILY TRIBUNE NEWS (CARTERSVILLE, GA.), THE. 5653

1049-6785 See REPORT OF CRIMINAL OFFENSES AND ARRESTS. 3174

1049-684X See NATIONAL TRIAL LAWYER (NATIONAL ED.). 3014

1049-6963 See RADON DIRECTORY, THE. 1029

1049-7013 See RTC PROPERTY DISPOSITION REPORT. 4847

1049-7021 See CORNELL COOPERATIVE EXTENSION AGRICULTURAL NEWS. 76

1049-7064 See ADWEEK CLIENT/BRAND DIRECTORY (NATIONAL ED.). 755

1049-7145 See WNC BUSINESS JOURNAL. 723

1049-7153 See AMERICAN LETTERS & COMMENTARY. 3360

1049-717X See GOURMAN REPORT. A RATING OF GRADUATE AND PROFESSIONAL PROGRAMS IN AMERICAN AND INTERNATIONAL UNIVERSITIES, THE. 1825

1049-7188 See GOURMAN REPORT. A RATING OF UNDERGRADUATE PROGRAMS IN AMERICAN AND INTERNATIONAL UNIVERSITIES, THE. 1825

1049-7218 See DIRECTORY OF TELEFACSIMILE SITES IN NORTH AMERICAN LIBRARIES. 1153

1049-7242 See CHARLES CITY PRESS (1951). 5669

1049-7250 See EDUCATION IN FOCUS. 1739

1049-7315 See RESEARCH ON SOCIAL WORK PRACTICE. 5305

1049-7323 See QUALITATIVE HEALTH RESEARCH. 4797

1049-7374 See OBSERVER (RIO RANCHO, N.M.), THE. 5712

1049-7382 See X-MEN CLASSIC. 4868

1049-7404 See ENVIRONMENT LIBRARY. 2165

1049-7412 See COMPUTER SELECT. 1284

1049-7420 See ENERGY LIBRARY. 1940

1049-7455 See SCAPE (LOS ANGELES, CALIF.). 2492

1049-7463 See STROKE. CLINICAL UPDATES. 3643

1049-7579 See NIST BUILDING SCIENCE SERIES. 622

1049-7714 See POLITICAL ARCHIVES OF RUSSIA. 4545

1049-7722 See JOURNAL OF MULTINATIONAL STRATEGIES, THE. 1637

1049-7730 See SCIENCE PROBE!. 5152

1049-7757 See FOUR HUNDRED (NEW YORK, N.Y.), THE. 1267

1049-7765 See POLAR LIBRARIES BULLETIN. 3241

1049-7803 See NEWSLETTER / AMERICAN SOCIETY OF INTERNATIONAL LAW. 3133

1049-782X See AERODINE'S FLY-IN RESTAURANT GUIDE. 5070

1049-7838 See COUNTY COMMENT. 4641

1049-7927 See NASDAQ YELLOW BOOK. 696

1049-7935 See FINANCIAL YELLOW BOOK. 1926

1049-7943 See CORPORATE YELLOW BOOK. 1924

1049-7951 See INTERNATIONAL CORPORATE YELLOW BOOK. 871

1049-796X See CATALOG OF CURRENT LAW TITLES, ANNUAL. 2949

1049-7978 See LAWYERS MONTHLY CATALOG, ANNUAL. 2998

1049-7986 See BNA'S MEDICARE REPORT. 5275

1049-8001 See INTERNATIONAL JOURNAL OF WILDLAND FIRE, THE. 2291

1049-801X See INTERNATIONAL FIBER JOURNAL. 5352

1049-8044 See PRENTICE HALL'S FEDERAL TAXATION. INDIVIDUALS (ANNOTATED INSTRUCTOR'S ED.). 4741

1049-8052 See PIXEL (WATSONVILLE, CALIF.). 1234

1049-815X See AMERICAN WRITING (PHILADELPHIA, PA.). 312

1049-8168 See WHO'S INVENTING WHAT?. 1309

1049-8176 See SESSION WEEKLY. 4686

1049-8257 See ALL-IN-ONE BUSINESS CONTACTBOOK. 637

1049-8265 See DEALMAKERS (BELLE MEAD, N.J.), THE. 4836

1049-8338 See FREMONT TRIBUNE. 5706

1049-8435 See PRENTICE HALL'S FEDERAL TAXATION. CORPORATIONS, PARTNERSHIPS, ESTATES, AND TRUSTS (ANNOTATED INSTRUCTOR'S ED.). 4741

1049-8443 See WEST VIRGINIA SOUTHERN BAPTIST, THE. 5069

1049-8478 See CHILTON'S GUIDE TO CHASSIS ELECTRONICS AND POWER ACCESSORIES. GENERAL MOTORS. 5410

1049-8478 See CHILTON'S GUIDE TO CHASSIS ELECTRONICS & POWER ACCESSORIES. FORD/CHRYSLER/JEEP/EAGLE. 5410

1049-8478 See CHILTON'S GUIDE TO CHASSIS ELECTRONIC CONTROLS AND POWER ACCESSORIES. IMPORT CARS AND TRUCKS. 5410

1049-8494 See GREAT LAKES VEGETABLE GROWERS NEWS, THE. 173

1049-8508 See EUROPEAN INVESTMENT IN U.S. AND CANADIAN REAL ESTATE DIRECTORY. 4837

1049-8540 See WHO'S WHO IN AMERICA (JUNIOR & SENIOR HIGH SCHOOL VERSION). 427

1049-8583 See PACE BUYER'S GUIDES. NEW CAR PRICES. 5422

1049-8591 See YEARBOOK / EVANGELICAL FREE CHURCH OF AMERICA. 5069

1049-8621 See WHO'S WHO IN WRITERS, EDITORS & POETS, UNITED STATES & CANADA. 427

1049-863X See KYOWVA GENEALOGICAL SOCIETY NEWS LETTER. 2457

1049-8672 See DEPARTMENT OF DEFENSE FACT BOOK. 4042

1049-8699 See QUALITY DIGEST. 1705

1049-880X See MEDICAL GROUP MANAGEMENT MARKETERS GUIDEPOST. 933

1049-8834 See ARTERIOSCLEROSIS AND THROMBOSIS. 3699

1049-8850 See JOURNAL OF AQUATIC FOOD PRODUCTS TECHNOLOGY. 2306

1049-8869 See MUSICAL PERFORMANCE. 4136

1049-8877 See ENVIRONMENTAL WATCH (CHICAGO, ILL.). 4837

1049-8893 See BNA'S NATIONAL ENVIRONMENT WATCH. 2162

1049-8907 See JOURNAL OF VISUALIZATION AND COMPUTER ANIMATION, THE. 1234

1049-8915 See INTERNETWORKING (CHICHESTER, ENGLAND). 1242

1049-8923 See INTERNATIONAL JOURNAL OF ROBUST AND NONLINEAR CONTROL. 1980

1049-8931 See INTERNATIONAL JOURNAL OF METHODS IN PSYCHIATRIC RESEARCH. 3927

1049-8966 See RN-AIDSLINE. 3868

1049-8974 See PHOTOPRO (TITUSVILLE, FLA.). 4375

1049-8990 See CYCLING SCIENCE. 428

1049-9032 See FLORIDA THOROUGHBRED TIMES. 2799

1049-9040 See EUROPA 1992. 833

1049-9059 See CLL JOURNAL : COMPUTER-ASSISTED ENGLISH LANGUAGE LEARNING JOURNAL. 3274

1049-9067 See JOURNAL - AMERICAN PSYCHOLOGICAL ASSOCIATION. DIVISION OF CONSULTING PSYCHOLOGY. 4592

1049-9083 See GLOBAL ENVIRONMENTAL CHANGE REPORT. 2216

1049-9091 See AMERICAN JOURNAL OF HOSPICE AND PALLIATIVE CARE, THE. 5271

1049-913X See WINDOWS/DOS DEVELOPER'S JOURNAL. 1273

1049-9156 See PHARMACEUTICAL PROCESSING. 4321

1049-9164 See BRIDGEPORT POST, THE. 5645

1049-9172 See DISPLAY & DESIGN IDEAS. 759

1049-9199 See VIEWPOINT. 2632

1049-9210 See NONPROFIT COMPUTER SOURCEBOOK. 1238

1049-9229 See WHO'S WHO IN ATHLETICS IN AMERICAN HIGH SCHOOLS. 436

1049-9237 See WHO'S WHO IN ATHLETICS IN AMERICAN JUNIOR COLLEGES. 436

1049-9261 See ACOUSTIC GUITAR. 4098

1049-9296 See ENERGYLETTERS (CORAL GABLES, FLA.). 1943

1049-9334 See CALIFORNIA EMPLOYMENT LAW LETTER. 3145

1049-9342 See ARIZONA ENVIRONMENTAL LAW LETTER. 2936

1049-9350 See MISSOURI ENVIRONMENTAL LAW LETTER. **3114**

1049-9350 See KANSAS-IOWA ENVIRONMENTAL LAW LETTER. **3113**

1049-9369 *See* ALABAMA EMPLOYMENT LAW LETTER. **3143**

1049-9377 *See* MARYLAND EMPLOYMENT LAW LETTER. **3151**

1049-9385 *See* ILLINOIS EMPLOYMENT LAW LETTER. **3149**

1049-9407 *See* CRITICAL REVIEWS IN SURFACE CHEMISTRY. **1051**

1049-9431 *See* GARDENS & COUNTRYSIDES. **5478**

1049-9458 *See* TIMES-GEORGIAN (CARROLLTON, GA.). **5655**

1049-9466 *See* TEXAS CHILD CARE. **1070**

1049-9482 *See* KIND TEACHER. **1760**

1049-958X See INCITE INFORMATION. **5247**

1049-9601 *See* AUTO TRIM & RESTYLING NEWS. **5405**

1049-9636 *See* SMALL BUSINESS START-UP INDEX. **711**

1049-9644 *See* BIOLOGICAL CONTROL. **4244**

1049-9652 *See* CVGIP. GRAPHICAL MODELS AND IMAGE PROCESSING. **1233**

1049-9660 *See* CVGIP. IMAGE UNDERSTANDING. **1233**

1049-9679 *See* INTERNATIONAL JOURNAL OF SPORT MEDICINE. **3954**

1049-9709 *See* INNER WOMAN. **5559**

1049-9717 *See* FAMILIA DE HOY, LA. **2278**

1049-9725 *See* INSIDE HOUSING. **617**

1049-9741 *See* BULLETIN / AMERICAN ACADEMY OF ORTHOPAEDIC SURGEONS. **3880**

1049-9768 *See* PETERSEN'S BOWHUNTING. **4877**

1049-9776 *See* MACHIAVELLI STUDIES. **3409**

1049-978X See INCITE INFORMATION. **4815**

1049-9822 *See* BUSINESSWEST (SPRINGFIELD, MASS.). **654**

1049-9830 *See* TAXATION AND MERGERS & ACQUISITIONS. **4755**

1049-9849 *See* INVENTORY REDUCTION REPORT. **872**

1049-9865 *See* NOTES ON COMPUTING (1987). **1261**

1049-9946 *See* CAREER FOCUS FOR TODAY'S RISING HISPANIC PROFESSIONAL. **4202**

1049-9954 *See* CAREER FOCUS FOR TODAY'S RISING BLACK PROFESSIONAL. **4202**

1049-9962 *See* COMMON LOT. **5058**

1049-9970 *See* BALLOONS TODAY. **2528**

1050-0014 *See* AFRICAN TECHNOLOGY FORUM. **5081**

1050-0022 *See* RETURN (WASHINGTON, D.C.), THE. **2272**

1050-0030 *See* PADUCAH SUN (1978), THE. **5682**

1050-0049 *See* IALL JOURNAL OF LANGUAGE LEARNING TECHNOLOGIES, THE. **3286**

1050-0057 *See* EPISCOPAL LIFE. **5059**

1050-009X *See* CRANIO CLINICS INTERNATIONAL. **3569**

1050-0111 *See* HOPE BOLETIN DE SALUD. **4783**

1050-0162 *See* PRENTICE HALL'S FEDERAL TAXATION. COMPREHENSIVE VOLUME (COMPLIMENTARY INSTRUCTOR'S COPY). **4741**

1050-0170 *See* PRENTICE HALL'S FEDERAL TAXATION. COMPREHENSIVE VOLUME. **4741**

1050-0197 *See* PROBLEMS IN PLASTIC AND RECONSTRUCTIVE SURGERY. **3972**

1050-0200 *See* ECONOMIC TIMES (NEW YORK, N.Y.). **1485**

1050-0219 *See* SOLUTIONS FOR BETTER HEALTH. **5222**

1050-0251 *See* CHILTON'S MOTORCYCLE AND ATV REPAIR MANUAL. **4081**

1050-0316 *See* GIFT BASKET REVIEW. **2584**

1050-0324 *See* MIDNIGHT ENGINEERING. **1987**

1050-0340 *See* DAILY GAZETTE (1990), THE. **5715**

1050-0367 *See* ALLIANCE ALERT. ELECTRONICS/COMPUTER HARDWARE/INDUSTRIAL AUTOMATION. **1235**

1050-0391 *See* COLORADO JOURNAL OF INTERNATIONAL ENVIRONMENTAL LAW AND POLICY. **3110**

1050-0405 *See* SAINT PAUL PIONEER PRESS (SAINT PAUL, MINN. : 1990 : A.M. ED.). **5698**

1050-043X *See* TECHNOLOGY ACCESS REPORT. **5163**

1050-0448 *See* AFRAID (ANAHEIM, CALIF.). **1596**

1050-0472 *See* JOURNAL OF MECHNICAL DESIGN (1990). **2118**

1050-0545 *See* JOURNAL OF THE AMERICAN ACADEMY OF AUDIOLOGY. **3889**

1050-0553 *See* CABLE-TELCO REPORT, THE. **1150**

1050-0561 *See* EUROPEAN RADIO. **1111**

1050-0650 *See* OCULAR THERAPEUTICS AND MANAGEMENT. **3623**

1050-0758 *See* ACCESS (CHICAGO, ILL.). **1315**

1050-0782 *See* FX WEEK. **677**

1050-0790 *See* POCKET PAGES. **2776**

1050-0804 *See* HIGHWAY RESEARCH ABSTRACTS (1990). **2004**

1050-0812 See EAE (RENTON, WASH.), THE. **2259**

1050-0820 *See* MOODY'S ... ANNUAL BOND RECORD. **907**

1050-0839 *See* AMERICAN SEAFOOD INSTITUTE REPORT. **2294**

1050-091X *See* BUSINESS ALABAMA MONTHLY. **645**

1050-1045 *See* STUDIES IN WEIRD FICTION. **3442**

1050-1096 *See* HUDSON VALLEY BUSINESS JOURNAL (ORANGE COUNTY ED.). **680**

1050-1134 *See* CHILTON'S ELECTRONIC ENGINE CONTROLS MANUAL. EUROPEAN CARS AND LIGHT TRUCKS. **5410**

1050-1142 *See* CHILTON FUEL INJECTION & ELECTRONIC ENGINE CONTROLS. ASIA. **2038**

1050-1150 *See* FUEL INJECTION & ELECTRONIC ENGINE CONTROLS. AUDI, BMW, JAGUAR, MERCEDES-BENZ, PEUGEOT, SAAB, STERLING, VOLKSWAGEN, VOLVO. **2055**

1050-1169 *See* CHILTON'S EMISSION, DIAGNOSIS, TUNE-UP AND SERVICE MANUAL. DOMESTIC CARS AND LIGHT TRUCKS. **5410**

1050-1185 *See* GREENFIELD OBSERVER (1984). **5767**

1050-1193 *See* EMPLOYMENT HEALTH LAW & BENEFITS. **3147**

1050-1207 **5410**

1050-1282 *See* IRAC JOURNAL. **4658**

1050-1339 *See* CENTRAL NORTH CAROLINA JOURNAL. **2530**

1050-1347 *See* ADVANCED RECOVERY WEEK. **4249**

1050-1363 *See* IRV'S BODYBUILDING DIGEST. **2599**

1050-1398 *See* TOPICS CATALOG. **1141**

1050-1401 *See* ROCKDALE CITIZEN, THE. **5654**

1050-141X *See* DIVORCE LITIGATION. **3120**

1050-1460 *See* PORT TOWNSEND JEFFERSON COUNTY LEADER, THE. **5762**

1050-1495 *See* KING'S COALSTATS. MONTHLY COAL GUIDE. ELECTRIC UTILITIES REPORT. **2142**

1050-1509 *See* KING'S COALSTATS. MONTHLY COAL GUIDE. MINE PRICE REPORT. **2142**

1050-1517 *See* KING'S COALSTATS. MONTHLY COAL GUIDE. MINE PRODUCTION REPORT. **2142**

1050-1525 *See* KING'S COALSTATS. ELECTRIC UTILITIES REPORT. **2142**

1050-1533 *See* KING'S COALSTATS. MONTHLY COAL GUIDE. **2142**

1050-1576 *See* INFORMATION ADVISOR, THE. **682**

1050-1606 *See* INTERNATIONAL JOURNAL OF SPORT NUTRITION. **4192**

1050-1630 *See* MAIMONIDEAN STUDIES. **4352**

1050-1649 *See* KING'S COALSTATS. FOB MINE PRICES. **2142**

1050-1665 *See* KING'S COALSTATS. COAL PRODUCTION REPORT. **2142**

1050-1681 *See* MUSIC INC. **4134**

1050-169X *See* KING'S COALSTATS. GRAIN EXPORT REPORT. **843**

1050-1703 *See* KING'S COALSTATS. INTERNATIONAL COAL TRADE. **2142**

1050-1711 *See* KING'S COALSTATS. PETROLEUM COKE EXPORT REPORT. **2142**

1050-172X *See* KING'S COALSTATS. COAL EXPORT REPORT. **2142**

1050-1738 *See* TRENDS IN CARDIOVASCULAR MEDICINE. **3711**

1050-1754 See JOURNAL OF PETROLEUM MARKETING : JPM / PMAA, THE. **4262**

1050-1789 *See* SULLIVAN'S RETAIL PERFORMANCE MONITOR. **958**

1050-1797 *See* INSTITUTE (NEW YORK, N.Y.), THE. **2065**

1050-1800 *See* DESKTOP COMMUNICATIONS. **1182**

1050-1827 *See* INTERNATIONAL JOURNAL OF MICROWAVE AND MILLIMETER-WAVE COMPUTER-AIDED ENGINEERING. **2066**

1050-1835 *See* PTSD RESEARCH QUARTERLY. **3631**

1050-1843 *See* FOOD SAFETY NOTEBOOK. **2340**

1050-186X *See* MARKETER, THE. **930**

1050-1932 *See* NATURAL RESOURCES TAX REVIEW, THE. **2199**

1050-1975 *See* BITS & PIECES (FAIRFIELD, N.J.). **861**

1050-1983 *See* LEADER (CORNING, N.Y.), THE. **5717**

1050-2041 *See* LANDERS FILM & VIDEO REVIEWS. **4073**

1050-2076 *See* HOFSTRA PROPERTY LAW JOURNAL. **2978**

1050-2084 *See* CLANTON ADVERTISER, THE. **5625**

1050-2092 *See* TRADITIONAL DWELLINGS AND SETTLEMENTS REVIEW. **5225**

1050-2114 *See* MANAGEMENT PORTFOLIO. **877**

1050-2130 *See* REVIEW / OHIO COUNCIL FOR THE SOCIAL STUDIES, THE. **4494**

1050-2149 *See* AVIATION EMPLOYMENT MONTHLY : AVIATION & AEROSPACE EMPLOYMENT OPPORTUNITIES. **13**

1050-2173 *See* QIGONG (SAN FRANCISCO, CALIF.). **4913**

1050-2254 *See* LOCKSMITH LEDGER INTERNATIONAL. **2812**

1050-2262 *See* DOUBLE-GUN JOURNAL, THE. **4893**

1050-2270 *See* IOWA INTERLINK. **4657**

1050-2289 *See* JOURNAL OF RELIGIOUS GERONTOLOGY. **5180**

1050-2297 *See* PRO ADMINISTRATOR. **882**

1050-2300 *See* DAILY CALIFORNIAN. **5634**

1050-2343 *See* RECORDS MANAGEMENT QUARTERLY (1986). **884**

1050-2351 *See* LATIN AMERICAN POPULATION HISTORY BULLETIN. **2743**

1050-2378 *See* STATE DATA AND DATABASE FINDER. **1204**

1050-2416 *See* HOME POWER. **1946**

1050-2467 *See* NORTHVILLE RECORD (NORTHVILLE, MICH. : 1871). **5693**

1050-2483 See DEFENSE & AEROSPACE ELECTRONICS. **2040**

1050-2491 *See* DISNEY ADVENTURES. **1062**

1050-253X *See* HAWORTH SERIES IN INTERNATIONAL LIBRARY ACQUISITIONS. **3213**

1050-2548 *See* ART REFERENCE SERVICES QUARTERLY. **340**

1050-2556 *See* JOURNAL OF DIVORCE & REMARRIAGE. **2281**

1050-2580 *See* WALT DISNEY'S GOOFY ADVENTURES. **1071**

1050-2599 *See* DISNEY'S CHIP'N'DALE RESCUE RANGERS. **1063**

1050-2602 *See* ROGER RABBIT. **1068**

1050-2610 See JOURNAL OF LIGHT CONSTRUCTION (NEW ENGLAND ED), THE. 618

1050-2629 See JOURNAL OF LIGHT CONSTRUCTION (NATIONAL ED.), THE. 618

1050-2637 See JOURNAL OF LIGHT CONSTRUCTION (NATIONAL ED.), THE. 618

1050-267X See YORK DISPATCH, THE. 5741

1050-2688 See EMERGING FOOD R & D REPORT. 2334

1050-270X See MCMAHON HEAVY CONSTRUCTION COST GUIDE. 2027

1050-2718 See HARRIS MARYLAND INDUSTRIAL DIRECTORY. 1608

1050-2726 See SYSTEMS THINKER, THE. 887

1050-2777 See SOUND & IMAGE. 4154

1050-2866 See SOVIET INTELLIGENCE & ACTIVE MEASURES. 4535

1050-2939 See FROMMER'S COMPREHENSIVE TRAVEL GUIDE. DELAWARE, MARYLAND, PENNSYLVANIA & THE NEW JERSEY SHORE. 5475

1050-2947 See PHYSICAL REVIEW. A. 4415

1050-2955 See CORNELL EAST ASIA SERIES. 2503

1050-298X See EUROPEAN TV SPORTS. 1111

1050-3005 See CNY BUSINESS JOURNAL, THE. 657

1050-3013 See WELDING-BRAZING-SOLDERING DIGEST. 4028

1050-3056 See LEGAL RESEARCHER'S DESK REFERENCE, THE. 3000

1050-3080 See NEW PACIFIC (SEATTLE, WASH.), THE. 2540

1050-3099 See CARLYLE ANNUAL. 3373

1050-3145 See ALTERNATIVE ENERGY DIGESTS. 1931

1050-3153 See WASTE INFORMATION DIGESTS. 2246

1050-3188 See AGING ACTION ALERT. 5271

1050-3196 See LANDLORD-TENANT RELATIONS REPORT. 2827

1050-320X See CORPORATE GROWTH REPORT, THE. 661

1050-3234 See HOUSING THE ELDERLY REPORT. 5179

1050-3242 See FEDERAL ASSISTANCE MONITOR. 1490

1050-3250 See SENIOR LAW REPORT. 3048

1050-3285 See ENVIRONMENT HAWAII. 2165

1050-3293 See COMMUNICATION THEORY. 1107

1050-3307 See PSYCHOTHERAPY RESEARCH. 4614

1050-3331 See NATIONAL MORTGAGE NEWS. 801

1050-3366 See FLORIDA COMMUNICATION JOURNAL, THE. 1111

1050-3404 See JOURNAL OF BIBLICAL ETHICS IN MEDICINE. 2251

1050-3447 See PUBLIC ASSISTANCE REPORT (SILVER SPRING, MD.). 5303

1050-3463 See MINORITIES IN BUSINESS INSIDER. 1690

1050-3471 See AIM (GLENDALE, CALIF.). 2609

1050-3536 See PLANET THREE. 5213

1050-3560 See FRONTIER CHRONICLES. 2616

1050-3579 See EUROPEAN CABLE/PAY TV. 1110

1050-3641 See RADIOSCAN MAGAZINE (SPANISH ED.). 1120

1050-365X See SPORTS CARD TRADER. 2778

1050-3668 See FREE QUERIES. 2449

1050-3692 See SUN (BREMERTON, WASH.), THE. 5762

1050-3706 See ASIAN LEASING JOURNAL, THE. 2501

1050-3730 See RUSSIAN COMMONWEALTH BUSINESS LAW REPORT. 3103

1050-3749 See SCHOOL SHOP/TECH DIRECTIONS. 1915

1050-3757 See FINDING A JOB IN THE NONPROFIT SECTOR. 4204

1050-3773 See PASADENA CITIZEN (1990). 5753

1050-379X See LOUISIANA BANKER (1989), THE. 797

1050-3803 See SENIOR MEDIA GUIDE. 936

1050-3811 See CD-HOUSING REGISTER, THE. 2817

1050-3846 See LEE COUNTY EAGLE, THE. 5627

1050-3862 See GENETIC ANALYSIS, TECHNIQUES AND APPLICATIONS. 545

1050-3919 See CONTEMPORARY DRAMATISTS. 431

1050-3943 See STUDIES OF HIGH TEMPERATURE SUPERCONDUCTORS. 2082

1050-396X See COMPUTER NEWS INTERNATIONAL. 1177

1050-3978 See RESOLUTION. 1201

1050-3986 See JOURNAL OF ECONOMIC ARCHAEOLOGY, THE. 2781

1050-3994 See INTERNATIONAL DOLL WORLD. 2774

1050-4036 See AMERICAN TRAPPER. 2186

1050-4044 See HOLLAND SENTINEL (1977), THE. 5692

1050-4060 See CONSTRUCTION INJURY LIABILITY MONTHLY. 609

1050-4095 See DAILY PRESS (ASHLAND, WIS.), THE. 5766

1050-4109 See AMERICAN REVIEW OF INTERNATIONAL ARBITRATION, THE. 2933

1050-4125 See CHRISTIAN STUDIES (AUSTIN, TEX.). 4946

1050-415X See NEW DELTA REVIEW. 3415

1050-4184 See TELEGRAM & GAZETTE. 5690

1050-4214 See NEW ENGLAND CHRISTIAN. 4980

1050-4273 See ISSUES IN APPLIED LINGUISTICS. 3288

1050-4281 See JOURNAL OF CHEMICAL EDUCATION. SOFTWARE, A. 980

1050-429X See JOURNAL OF CHEMICAL EDUCATION. SOFTWARE, B. 980

1050-4303 See JOURNAL OF CHEMICAL EDUCATION. SOFTWARE, C. 980

1050-432X See COURIER-POST (CHERRY HILL, N.J.). 5709

1050-4354 See INTERNATIONAL OOP DIRECTORY. 1287

1050-4435 See TRADITIONAL QUILTWORKS. 5186

1050-4443 See YEAR BOOK OF ULTRASOUND, THE. 4453

1050-4451 See OPTOMETRY (CHICAGO, ILL.). 4217

1050-4524 See SOUTHERN COLLEGIATE ACCOUNTANT, THE. 751

1050-4591 See NEW YORKER STAATS-ZEITUNG (1991). 5719

1050-4648 See FISH AND SHELLFISH IMMUNOLOGY. 5584

1050-4672 See APS OBSERVER. 4575

1050-4710 See PROPERTY/CASUALTY INSURANCE FACTS. 2891

1050-4729 See PROCEEDINGS / IEEE INTERNATIONAL CONFERENCE ON ROBOTICS AND AUTOMATION. 1221

1050-4745 See TORAH U-MADDA JOURNAL, THE. 5005

1050-4753 See BEHAVIORAL RESEARCH IN ACCOUNTING. 739

1050-4788 See WRITING CONCEPTS. 2926

1050-4796 See DOLL DESIGNS. 372

1050-480X See GOOD OLD DAYS. SPECIAL ISSUES (1991). 3391

1050-4818 See BULLETIN OF THE GLOBAL VOLCANISM NETWORK. 1352

1050-4826 See MONEY LAUNDERING LAW REPORT. 3011

1050-4842 See OCCASIONAL PAPERS OF THE MUSEUM OF NATURAL SCIENCE. 5593

1050-4850 See CURRENT WORLD AFFAIRS. 4040

1050-4877 See REVIEW OF ARCHAEOLOGY, THE. 280

1050-4885 See RENEW AMERICA REPORT, THE. 2241

1050-4915 See DIRECTORY OF BUYOUT FINANCING SOURCES. 788

1050-4931 See MALIBU TIMES. 5637

1050-494X See HOME MAGAZINE'S BEST IDEAS KITCHEN AND BATH. 2900

1050-4974 See PENSIONS & INVESTMENTS (1990). 911

1050-5008 See CLINICAL NUTRITION (PHILADELPHIA, PA.). 4189

1050-5059 See FORMER U.S.S.R. MONITOR. 2688

1050-5067 See PUBLIC PERSPECTIVE, THE. 5336

1050-5083 See ISRAEL STUDIES BULLETIN. 2768

1050-5105 See SUN-TIMES (HEBER SPRINGS, ARK.). 5632

1050-5121 See BOWLING MAGAZINE (1988). 4888

1050-513X See NINE (SEATTLE, WASH.). 1135

1050-5164 See ANNALS OF APPLIED PROBABILITY, THE. 3494

1050-5172 See DUN'S ASIA / PACIFIC KEY BUSINESS ENTERPRISES. 669

1050-5180 See FODOR'S SKIING IN NORTH AMERICA. 5473

1050-5199 See SKIPPER'S ALMANAC (SOUTHERN U.S. ED.). 4183

1050-5229 See DIRECTORY OF MEMBERS - APPRAISAL INSTITUTE (U.S.). 4836

1050-5245 See AEROSPACE PROPULSION (WASHINGTON, D.C. 1990). 5

1050-5253 See ASTHMA MANAGEMENT. 3948

1050-5261 See ANTISENSE RESEARCH & DEVELOPMENT. 578

1050-5296 See IDISHER KEMFER. 2504

1050-530X See NATIONAL DENTAL ASSOCIATION JOURNAL. 1330

1050-5326 See ENERGY & CONSCIOUSNESS. 1939

1050-5334 See XENOPHILIA. 3473

1050-5350 See JOURNAL OF GAMBLING STUDIES. 5292

1050-5369 See TARIK (CHICAGO, ILL.). 1523

1050-5385 See LECCIONES CRISTIANAS PARA JOVENES. LIBRO DEL MAESTRO. 4973

1050-5393 See LECCIONES CHRISTIANAS PARA JOVENES. ALUMNO. 4973

1050-5415 See PACE BUYER'S GUIDES. USED CAR PRICES. 5422

1050-5423 See PACE BUYER'S GUIDES. FOREIGN CAR PRICES NEW & USED. 5422

1050-5466 See INTERNATIONAL DIRECTORY OF IMPORTERS. NORTH AMERICA, THE. 841

1050-5474 See BUSINESS LEADS INTERNATIONAL. 650

1050-5490 See NEW YORK LATINO. 2269

1050-5512 See NEW HAMPSHIRE PREMIER. 2540

1050-5520 See INTERNATIONAL DIRECTORY OF IMPORTERS. AFRICA, THE. 841

1050-5547 See INTERNATIONAL DIRECTORY OF IMPORTERS. SOUTH/CENTRAL AMERICA, THE. 841

1050-5555 See INTERNATIONAL DIRECTORY OF IMPORTERS. EUROPE, THE. 841

1050-5563 See INTERNATIONAL DIRECTORY OF IMPORTERS. MIDDLE EAST, THE. 841

1050-5601 See GAME PLAYERS STRATEGY GUIDE TO GAME BOY GAMES. 1230

1050-561X See ANIMAL WELFARE INFORMATION CENTER NEWSLETTER. 225

1050-5628 See METRIC TODAY. 4031

1050-5644 See CAMPUS WATCH. 1814

1050-5660 See SOLAR INDUSTRY JOURNAL. 1957

1050-5717 See SHOOTING SPORTSMAN (WILLIAMSPORT, PA.). 4878

1050-575X See HEALTHCARE HAZARDOUS MATERIALS MANAGEMENT. 4782

1050-5806 See LEADER (LANSING, KAN.), THE. 5677

1050-5830 See NATIONAL DIRECTORY OF CATALOGS, THE. 847

1050-5857 See NATIONAL UNDERWRITER PROFILES. LIFE INSURERS. 2889

1050-5873 See COLBY QUARTERLY. 3376

1050-5881 See PROSTATE. SUPPLEMENT, THE. 3992

1050-6004 See PUBLIC-ACCESS COMPUTER SYSTEMS NEWS. 1201

1050-6012 See THIS WEEK IN PEACHTREE CITY. 5655

1050-6063 See NORTHERN VIRGINIA MAGAZINE. 2541

1050-6071 See AFRICAN-AMERICAN JOURNAL OF CHIROPRACTIC. 2254

1050-6098 See ARL. 3191

1050-6101 See HUMAN GENOME NEWS. 547

1050-6144 See OFFICIAL ... IDENTIFICATION AND PRICE GUIDE TO ANTIQUES AND COLLECTIBLES, THE. 252

1050-6152 See TOURISM'S TOP TWENTY. 5494

1050-6160 See TRAINING DIRECTORS' FORUM NEWSLETTER. 947

1050-6217 See NURSERY BUSINESS GROWER. 2426

1050-625X See TREATMENT ISSUES. 3677

1050-6284 See JOURNAL OF GLOBAL BUSINESS : JGB. 687

1050-6306 See SOCIOLOGICAL PRACTICE REVIEW. 5261

1050-6357 See NATIONAL UNDERWRITER PROFILES. HEALTH INSURERS. 2889

1050-6365 See NATIONAL UNDERWRITER PROFILES. PROPERTY / CASUALTY INSURERS. 2889

1050-639X See JUST GO!. 5482

1050-6403 See TEXAS ENVIRONMENT. 2182

1050-6411 See JOURNAL OF ELECTROMYOGRAPHY AND KINESIOLOGY. 3805

1050-642X See CLINICAL JOURNAL OF SPORT MEDICINE. 3953

1050-6438 See NEUROSURGERY QUARTERLY. 3970

1050-6454 See LINTON TRAINER'S RESOURCE DIRECTORY, THE. 943

1050-6470 See ANESTHESIOLOGIST'S CLINICAL UPDATE. 3681

1050-6489 See PSYCHIATRIST'S CLINICAL UPDATE. 3934

1050-6497 See MAQUILA (EL PASO, TEX.). 1617

1050-6519 See JOURNAL OF BUSINESS AND TECHNICAL COMMUNICATION. 1114

1050-656X See MUTUAL FUND ADVISOR. 908

1050-6586 See AMERICAN JOURNAL OF RHINOLOGY. 3886

1050-6675 See EAST TEXAS MEDICINE. 3573

1050-6802 See HIPPO MAGAZINE. 3393

1050-6810 See AGRICOLA. 150

1050-6861 See VERMONT MONITOR. 2183

1050-6896 See NUCLEAR PHYSICS NEWS. 4449

1050-6918 See OPTOMETRY CLINICS : THE OFFICIAL PUBLICATION OF THE PRENTICE SOCIETY. 4217

1050-6926 See JOURNAL OF GEOMETRIC ANALYSIS, THE. 3513

1050-6934 See JOURNAL OF LONG-TERM EFFECTS OF MEDICAL IMPLANTS. 3595

1050-6977 See PROGRESS IN PROBABILITY. 3542

1050-6993 See DATEK IMAGING SUPPLIES MONTHLY, THE. 4564

1050-7000 See PENINSULA DAILY NEWS. 5761

1050-7019 See IMAGING BUSINESS REPORT, THE. 2064

1050-7043 See PRODUCT DATA INTERNATIONAL. 5142

1050-7051 See JOURNAL OF HOSPITALITY & LEISURE MARKETING. 4851

1050-7078 See SKYBOX (CINCINNATI, OHIO). 4918

1050-7086 See CALLIOPE (PETERBOROUGH, N.H.). 2613

1050-7108 See PARENTS AND CHILDREN TOGETHER. 2284

1050-7116 See TEXAS ENERGY (1989). 1959

1050-7124 See ENVIRONMENTAL PROTECTION WEEK. 2169

1050-7132 See HOUSTON TIMES-JOURNAL. 5654

1050-7256 See THYROID (NEW YORK, N.Y.). 3733

1050-7272 See PACE BUYER'S GUIDES. DOMESTIC & FOREIGN TRUCK & VAN PRICES NEW & USED. 5389

1050-7280 See INFINITY LIMITED. 3396

1050-7310 See LANGUAGE OF DEFENSE : HANDBOOK OF ACRONYMS AND TERMINOLOGY. 4048

1050-7361 See YELLOWED PAGES. 2478

1050-737X See FODOR'S BAJA & THE PACIFIC COAST RESORTS. 5470

1050-740X See MINNESOTA HOCKEY. 4905

1050-7418 See PET VETERINARIAN. 5518

1050-7485 See OUTDOOR NETWORK NEWSLETTER, THE. 1771

1050-7493 See AMERICAN HARMONICA ASSOCIATES NEWSLETTER. 4099

1050-7507 See FIRST DAYS RECORD : A JOURNAL OF LIBERAL RELIGIOUS RESPONSES, THE. 4959

1050-7620 See ALEXANDRIA GAZETTE PACKET. 5758

1050-7647 See MY WEEKLY READER. SUMMER EDITION A. 1066

1050-7655 See FAUQUIER TIMES-DEMOCRAT. 5758

1050-7698 See SOUTH CAROLINA BUSINESS. 712

1050-771X See MISSION HANDBOOK. USA/CANADA PROTESTANT MINISTRIES OVERSEAS. 4978

1050-7760 See TINY TOON ADVENTURES MAGAZINE. 4867

1050-785X See BASS PLAYER. 4102

1050-7868 See EQ (CUPERTINO, CALIF.). 4116

1050-7906 See UNION (1987), THE. 5641

1050-7930 See REVIEW OF BOOKS ON THE BOOK OF MORMON. 4993

1050-7949 See IN BETWEEN YEARS, THE. 2281

1050-7965 See AI DIRECTORY. 1210

1050-8031 See TRILOGY (LEXINGTON, KY.). 5313

1050-8112 See COMPUTERIZATION AND NETWORKING OF MATERIALS DATABASES. 1178

1050-8163 See ZILLIONS (MOUNT VERNON, N.Y.). 1300

1050-8171 See ASSEMBLY (CAROL STREAM, ILL.). 2110

1050-818X See INSIDE DOT & TRANSPORTATION WEEK. 5384

1050-821X See KIND NEWS JR. 2197

1050-835X See MAIRENA (RIO PIEDRAS, SAN JUAN, P.R.). 3465

1050-8376 See INTERNATIONAL BRANDS AND THEIR COMPANIES. 683

1050-8384 See INTERNATIONAL COMPANIES AND THEIR BRANDS. 683

1050-8392 See JOURNAL OF RESEARCH ON ADOLESCENCE. 4601

1050-8406 See JOURNAL OF THE LEARNING SCIENCES, THE. 1759

1050-8414 See INTERNATIONAL JOURNAL OF AVIATION PSYCHOLOGY, THE. 4591

1050-8422 See ETHICS & BEHAVIOR. 2250

1050-8430 See GENOME ANALYSIS. 546

1050-8457 See NATIONAL DOG REVIEW. 4287

1050-8481 See INTERNATIONAL ECONOMIC INSIGHTS. 1636

1050-849X See CANCER SURVEY (COLD SPRINGS HARBOR, N.Y.). 3812

1050-852X See MASSACHUSETTS, CONNECTICUT, RHODE ISLAND VERDICT REPORTER, THE. 3090

1050-8597 See PEOPLE OF DESTINY. 4986

1050-8627 See ECONOMIC AND DEMOGRAPHIC ALMANAC OF WASHINGTON COUNTIES AND CITIES. 4552

1050-866X See PETROLEUM POLITICS. 4273

1050-8686 See TRANSMISSION & DISTRIBUTION INTERNATIONAL. 2085

1050-8694 See DIRECTORY OF FOREIGN INVESTMENT IN THE U.S. 896

1050-8708 See BATON ROUGE KIDS. 1060

1050-8767 See GP (ATLANTA, GA.). 1324

1050-8775 See ANESTHESIA MALPRACTICE PROTECTOR. 3681

1050-8783 See PERIODONTICS FOR GPS. 1333

1050-8864 See YIVO ANNUAL. 5054

1050-8910 See DMS WORLD HELICOPTER INVENTORY & FORECAST. 18

1050-8945 See BOATING WORLD. 592

1050-897X See MEALEY'S EUROPEAN ENVIRONMENTAL LAW REPORT. 3114

1050-8996 See HBO'S GUIDE TO MOVIES ON VIDEOCASSETTE AND CABLE TV. 4370

1050-9011 See BOB NUROCK'S ADVISORY. 643

1050-902X See HMO MANAGERS LETTER. 3783

1050-9038 See HMO MAGAZINE. 2882

1050-9070 See INTERNATIONAL SPECTRUM. 1190

1050-9089 See ROGERIAN NURSING SCIENCE NEWS. 3869

1050-9100 See SHEPARD'S FLORIDA EXPRESS CITATIONS. 3050

1050-9119 See SHEPARD'S OHIO EXPRESS CITATIONS. 3053

1050-9127 See DG REVIEW. 1182

1050-9135 See HEALTHCARE INFORMATICS. 3782

1050-9143 See SITUATION AND OUTLOOK REPORT. FEED. 203

1050-9151 See SITUATION AND OUTLOOK REPORT. DAIRY. 198

1050-916X See SIGMICRO NEWSLETTER (1988). 1281

1050-9186 See REMITTANCE AND DOCUMENT PROCESSING TODAY. 5145

1050-9194 See PATHOLOGY PATTERNS. 3897

1050-9208 See QUARTERLY REVIEW OF FILM AND VIDEO. 4076

1050-9224 See DESIGN (WASHINGTON, D.C., 1980). 2918

1050-9232 See RISK & INSURANCE. 2892

1050-9259 See TRUCK, VAN, AND 4X4 BOOK, THE. 5427

1050-9291 See ADVANCES IN TELECOMMUNICATIONS MANAGEMENT. 1148

1050-933X See GUIDE TO HOSPITALITY AND TOURISM EDUCATION, THE. 1826

1050-9348 See MISHPACHA (VIENNA, VA.). 5051

1050-9372 See GREAT LIBRARY PROMOTION IDEAS. 924

1050-9402 See RACONTEUR. 2627

1050-9410 See MARKET--EUROPE. 845

1050-9453 See NEW YORK INTERNATIONAL LAW REVIEW. 3133

1050-9496 See ADVANCES IN TELEMATICS. 1148

1050-9518 See OLD-TIME CROCHET. 374

1050-9526 See SOUTHWEST STOCKMAN. 222

1050-9585 See EUROPEAN ROMANTIC REVIEW. 3386

1050-9607 See CONTEMPORARY MANAGEMENT IN INTERNAL MEDICINE. 3796

1050-9615 See CONTEMPORARY MANAGEMENT IN OBSTETRICS AND GYNECOLOGY. 3759

1050-9631 See HIPPOCAMPUS (NEW YORK, N.Y.). 3797

1050-964X See REPORT ON PEDIATRIC INFECTIOUS DISEASES, THE. 3715

1050-9658 See LABORATORY MEDICINE ABSTRACT AND COMMENT. 3603

1050-9674 See JOURNAL OF OFFENDER REHABILITATION. 3167

1050-9682 See CAR AND DRIVER YEARBOOK (DANBURY, CONN.). 5409

1050-9690 See ANNUAL SYMPOSIUM PROCEEDINGS / SOCIETY OF FLIGHT TEST ENGINEERS. 12

1050-9712 See BACKWOODS HOME MAGAZINE. 2485

1050-9720 See NEW ENGLAND THEATRE JOURNAL. 5366

ISSN Index

1050-9739 See STUDIES IN MEDIEVAL AND RENAISSANCE TEACHING. 2711

1050-9763 See SEPM SHORT COURSE NOTES. 4230

1050-9771 See FODOR'S ... BARBADOS. 5470

1050-978X See COPIER SPECIFICATION GUIDE. 4211

1050-9801 See ... NATIONAL OSTRICH/EXOTICS DIRECTORY, THE. 216

1050-981X See ... NATIONAL OSTRICH/RATITE DIRECTORY, THE. 216

1050-9836 See WORKERS' COMPENSATION LAW REVIEW. 3076

1050-9844 See CARTOGRAPHY AND GEOGRAPHIC INFORMATION SYSTEMS. 2581

1050-9852 See NATIONAL DIRECTORY OF CORPORATE GIVING. 4338

1050-9887 See CMA MATTERS. 4110

1050-9941 See HERB AND SPICE SAMPLER. 2343

1050-995X See YEAR BOOK OF HEALTH CARE MANAGEMENT. 4808

1050-9976 See HEALTH CARE 500, THE. 4778

1050-9984 See MEDICAL UTILIZATION REVIEW DIRECTORY. 3612

1050-9992 See CANCER THERAPY REPORTS. 3812

1051-0087 See INTERGOVERNMENTAL AIDS REPORTS. 4784

1051-0109 See RECYCLING TODAY (MUNICIPAL (POST-CONSUMER) MARKET ED.). 2241

1051-0117 See PROCEEDINGS / IEEE ... ULTRASONICS SYMPOSIUM. 2076

1051-0230 See SPECTATOR (LOS ANGELES, CALIF.). 4078

1051-0249 See NORTHSTAR NEWS & ANALYSIS. 2270

1051-0265 See PRACTICAL REVIEWS IN PEDIATRIC DENTISTRY. 1333

1051-0273 See BUSINESS OPPORTUNITIES IN EASTERN EUROPE. 651

1051-0281 See FLAVOR AND FRAGRANCE MATERIALS. 1024

1051-0303 See APERIODICITY AND ORDER. 3998

1051-0443 See JOURNAL OF VASCULAR AND INTERVENTIONAL RADIOLOGY. 3943

1051-046X See FLY FISHING DIRECTORY, THE. 4872

1051-0508 See TRANSACTIONS OF THE IRON & STEEL SOCIETY. 4022

1051-0559 See TRANSFORMING ANTHROPOLOGY : A PUBLICATION OF THE ASSOCIATION OF BLACK ANTHROPOLOGISTS. 246

1051-0567 See PLASTICS & ENVIRONMENT. 4457

1051-0575 See CROSSROADS (OAKLAND, CALIF.). 4470

1051-0583 See WATER FARMING JOURNAL. 2315

1051-0591 See KENNER/METAIRIE LIVING. 5684

1051-0605 See JOURNAL OF THE NEW ENGLAND LUTHERAN HISTORICAL SOCIETY. 4971

1051-0680 See COMPUTER & OFFICE PRODUCT EVALUATIONS. 1176

1051-0737 See REDI REALTY REPORT. 4846

1051-0745 See GREENWICH MAGAZINE. 2488

1051-0761 See ECOLOGICAL APPLICATIONS. 2213

1051-077X See CURRENT OBSTETRIC MEDICINE. 3759

1051-0788 See NEWSLETTER - WILLEM MENGELBERG SOCIETY. 4141

1051-0818 See ACCESS (LANSING, MICH.). 3186

1051-0850 See ANNUAL REPORT - COLORADO. DEPT. OF HIGHWAYS. 5438

1051-0915 See CLARKE BURTON NEWS ANALYSIS. 1240

1051-0923 See SURVEILLANT (WASHINGTON, D.C.). 4058

1051-0931 See PUBLIC LIBRARY WATCH. 3243

1051-0974 See COMMUNICATION STUDIES. 1107

1051-1016 See BRAILLE SCORES CATALOG. VOCAL. 4105

1051-1032 See SCREEN PLAY (DALLAS, TEX.). 388

1051-1067 See INTERNATIONAL SAMPE ELECTRONICS CONFERENCE. 2117

1051-1075 See CAREER WOMAN. 5553

1051-1091 See RECYCLING TODAY (SCRAP PROCESSING MARKET ED.). 2241

1051-1113 See APS MONOGRAPH SERIES. 500

1051-1229 See ENVIRONMENTAL OUTLOOK. 2229

1051-1237 See CASTING DESIGN & APPLICATION. 3999

1051-1253 See JOURNAL OF CRIMINAL JUSTICE EDUCATION. 3167

1051-1377 See JOURNAL OF HOUSING ECONOMICS. 2826

1051-1393 See RISC MANAGEMENT. 1202

1051-1407 See METALWORKING DISTRIBUTOR, THE. 4011

1051-1431 See ARGUMENTATION AND ADVOCACY. 1104

1051-144X See JOURNAL OF VISUAL LITERACY. 3292

1051-1466 See ITAA PROCEEDINGS. NATIONAL MEETING. 5353

1051-1482 See HOUSING POLICY DEBATE. 2825

1051-1490 See NEUROSURGICAL OPERATIVE ATLAS. 3970

1051-1504 See BEST OF ANDORRA, THE. 2678

1051-1539 See ANNUAL INSTITUTE, SECURITIES ACTIVITIES OF BANKS. 3084

1051-1555 See MULTISTATE CORPORATE TAX GUIDE. 4738

1051-1636 See TARGET (WHEELING, ILL.). 4222

1051-1679 See DEMOCRATS (WASHINGTON, D.C.). 4471

1051-1725 See MIDNIGHT ZOO. 3411

1051-1733 See NORTHWESTERN NATURALIST : A JOURNAL OF VERTEBRATE BIOLOGY. 4169

1051-1741 See REVIEW OF BANKING & FINANCIAL SERVICES, THE. 3040

1051-1776 See JAPAN POLITICAL RESEARCH. 4478

1051-1792 See BROADCASTING & CABLE MARKET PLACE. 1128

1051-1806 See PERSPECTIVES ON MARKETING MANAGEMENT. 934

1051-1822 See MUSIC RETAILING. 4134

1051-1830 See MEMBERSHIP DIRECTORY OF THE AMERICAN PSYCHOLOGICAL SOCIETY. 4603

1051-1849 See DAVE HEEREN'S BASKETBALL ABSTRACT. 4892

1051-1865 See JOURNAL OF AFRO-LATIN AMERICAN STUDIES AND LITERATURES, THE. 3399

1051-189X See FIBER OPTICS WEEKLY UPDATE. 1155

1051-1903 See FDDI NEWS. 1111

1051-1911 See FIBER OPTICS BUSINESS NEWSLETTER. 1155

1051-192X See FIBER TO THE HOME. 1155

1051-1938 See CABLEOPTICS NEWSLETTER. 1150

1051-1946 See FIBER OPTIC SENSORS AND SYSTEMS. 4403

1051-1962 See LOCAL AREA NETWORKS. 1193

1051-1970 See PRIMUS (TERRE HAUTE, IND.). 3527

1051-1997 See FOOTBALL, BASKETBALL & HOCKEY COLLECTOR. 2773

1051-2004 See DIGITAL SIGNAL PROCESSING. 1182

1051-2020 See BIOMEDICAL SCIENCE AND TECHNOLOGY. 3687

1051-208X See BNAC COMMUNICATOR. 1105

1051-2136 See STAFDA ... DIRECTORY. 1627

1051-2144 See ENDOCRINOLOGIST, THE. 3729

1051-2144 See ENDOCRINOLOGIST (BALTIMORE, MD.), THE. 3729

1051-2179 See WBF BODYBUILDING LIFESTYLES : THE OFFICIAL PUBLICATION OF THE WORLD BODYBUILDING FEDERATION. 2602

1051-2187 See TOY TRUCKER & CONTRACTOR. 2778

1051-2217 See DOCUMENT MANAGEMENT TECHNOLOGY. 1258

1051-2225 See UNIVERSITY OF MIAMI ENTERTAINMENT & SPORTS LAW REVIEW. 3069

1051-225X See NASA TOTAL QUALITY MANAGEMENT ... ACCOMPLISHMENT REPORT. 30

1051-2276 See JOURNAL OF RENAL NUTRITION. 3991

1051-2284 See JOURNAL OF NEUROIMAGING. 3836

1051-2292 See JOURNAL OF THE INTERNATIONAL FEDERATION OF CLINICAL CHEMISTRY. 983

1051-2306 See AMERICAN ENVIRONMENTAL LABORATORY. 2160

1051-2373 See OH! IDAHO. 2541

1051-242X See FLORIDA MUNICIPAL PROFILES. 1926

1051-2438 See PSR QUARTERLY (BALTIMORE, MD.), THE. 3631

1051-2446 See ASSISTED REPRODUCTIVE REVIEWS. 3757

1051-2454 See EDMS JOURNAL. 1183

1051-2470 See MILITARY & COMMERCIAL FIBER BUSINESS. 4438

1051-2500 See ISPNEWS (FRAMINGHAM, MASS.). 1191

1051-2616 See GALLUP POLL MONTHLY, THE. 5327

1051-2624 See ENTREPRENEURIAL WOMAN. 5555

1051-2632 See PHYSICIAN MARKETPLACE UPDATE. 3627

1051-2705 See JOURNAL OF HYDRAULIC ENGINEERING (WASHINGTON, D.C.). 2092

1051-2721 See COMPLETE MEMBERSHIP DIRECTORY OF THE INTERACTIVE MULTIMEDIA ASSOCIATION, THE. 1222

1051-2780 See AGRICULTURAL LAW DIGEST. 50

1051-2799 See MARKETING BRIEFING. 930

1051-2837 See ENVIRONMENTAL MANAGEMENT (DENVER, COLO.). 2228

1051-2853 See CONTRIBUTIONS TO AFRICAN AMERICAN LITERATURE AND AFRICAN STUDIES. 3378

1051-2896 See WORLD SCREEN NEWS. 389

1051-290X See BOWKER'S COMPLETE VIDEO DIRECTORY. 4378

1051-2977 See INFLATION MEASURES FOR SCHOOLS & COLLEGES. 1830

1051-2993 See THESAURUS OF ERIC DESCRIPTORS. 1798

1051-3000 See NORTHWESTERN LINDQUIST-ENDICOTT REPORT, THE. 4207

1051-3116 See CLEAN FUELS REPORT, THE. 4253

1051-3124 See TELEPHONE WEEK. 1167

1051-3140 See RESEARCH SERIES / UNIVERSITY OF ARKANSAS, FAYETTVILLE. AGRICULTURAL EXPERIMENT STATION. 128

1051-3183 See CITY (SAN FRANCISCO, CALIF. 1989), THE. 2531

1051-3221 See HAZTECH NEWS. 2232

1051-323X See BACKHOME (MOUNTAIN HOME, N.C.). 2528

1051-3248 See JOURNAL OF ENERGETICS AND FLUIDS ENGINEERING. 2091

1051-3272 See PEDIATRIC MANAGEMENT. 3908

1051-3299 See ASSISTANT EDITOR. 3192

1051-3310 See LINGUA FRANCA : THE REVIEW OF ACADEMIC LIFE. 1834

1051-3337 See ANNIE'S QUICK & EASY PATTERN CLUB. 5347

1051-3345 See MISSIONS TODAY (MEMPHIS, TENN.). 4978

1051-3396 See AUTOMATED AGENCY REPORT, THE. 2036

1051-340X See FORWARD (NEW YORK, N.Y.). 5716

1051-3442 See MILLION DOLLAR DIRECTORY, TOP 50,000 COMPANIES. 695

1051-3450 See PENNSYLVANIA MINUTEMAN, THE. 5235

1051-3469 See RESOURCES FOR CHILD CARE. 2285

1051-3507 See USSR DOCUMENTS ANNUAL. 2509

1051-3558 See AMERICAN CATHOLIC PHILOSOPHICAL QUARTERLY. 4340

1051-3590 See TV NEWS CONTACTS. 1141

1051-3663 See LEGAL ASSISTANT TODAY (1990). 2999

1051-371X See TOPICS ON THE CULTURE OF THE AMERICAN SOUTH. 2548

1051-3744 See PROFESSIONAL NEGLIGENCE LAW REPORTER. 3032

1051-3760 See HUMAN RESOURCES BRIEFING. 942

1051-3787 See HAWAIIAN ISLAND HOME. 299

1051-3825 See ASIATIC HERPETOLOGICAL RESEARCH. 5577

1051-3833 See PCN NEWS. 1119

1051-3868 See STUDENT TRAVELER (KNOXVILLE, TENN.). 5491

1051-3914 See CA SELECTS. FOOD, DRUGS, & COSMETICS. 1002

1051-3922 See CA SELECTS: HYPERTENSION & ANTIHYPERTENSIVES. 1003

1051-3957 See CAS BIOTECH UPDATES. SLOW-RELEASE PHARMACEUTICALS. 4295

1051-3973 See WORLDWIDE NATURAL GAS INDUSTRY DIRECTORY. 4282

1051-3981 See EL&P ELECTRIC UTILITY INDUSTRY SOFTWARE DIRECTORY. 2043

1051-399X See UNITED NATIONS RESOLUTIONS.SERIES 3, RESOLUTIONS AND DECISIONS OF THE ECONOMIC AND SOCIAL COUNCIL. 4537

1051-4015 See PAIS INTERNATIONAL IN PRINT. 5227

1051-4023 See NEW HAMPSHIRE BAR NEWS. 3015

1051-4031 See NEW YORK CARIB NEWS, THE. 5718

1051-4058 See YEARBOOK OF EXPERTS, AUTHORITIES & SPOKESPERSONS. AN ENCYCLOPEDIA OF SOURCES. 1930

1051-4066 See LAN REPORTER. 1242

1051-4090 See TEXTILE & TEXT. 5357

1051-4120 See TUBE & PIPE QUARTERLY, THE. 4023

1051-4147 See MUNDO HISPANICO (ATLANTA, GA.). 5654

1051-4155 See X MAGAZINE. 2495

1051-4163 See ASR NEWS : AUTOMATIC SPEECH RECOGNITON NEWS. 1104

1051-4171 See PRESCRIBING REFERENCE FOR OBSTETRICIANS & GYNECOLOGISTS. 3767

1051-4201 See INTERNATIONAL BIBLIOGRAPHY OF WILDLAND FIRE. 2291

1051-4236 See HAWORTH SERIES IN DRUG THERAPY FOR ADDICTION PROBLEMS. 1344

1051-4295 See RAISING ARIZONA KIDS. 2285

1051-4341 See NURSING RECRUITMENT & RETENTION. 3865

1051-4546 See IN THE FIELD (CHICAGO, ILL.). 4089

1051-4597 See FOOTPRINTS (MARIETTA, GA.). 2487

1051-4600 See NATIONAL KNIFE MAGAZINE, THE. 2775

1051-4694 See INTERNATIONAL REVIEW OF COMPARATIVE PUBLIC POLICY. 4657

1051-4716 See SURVEY OF EXECUTIVE ENGINEERING COMPENSATION. 1997

1051-4732 See BETE (MIAMI, FLA.), LA. 3366

1051-4775 See BNA'S WORKERS' COMPENSATION REPORT. 1656

1051-4791 See RESEARCH & EDUCATION NETWORKING. 1221

1051-4805 See ELECTRONIC NETWORKING. 1241

1051-4813 See AMERICAN SHORT FICTION. 3360

1051-483X See ABERDEEN'S CONSTRUCTION MARKETING TODAY. 597

1051-4848 See ABERDEEN'S PAVEMENT MAINTENANCE. 5438

1051-4856 See ABERDEEN'S PARKING AREA MAINTENANCE & INTERNATIONAL SWEEPER. 2222

1051-4872 See NATIONAL JOB BANK, THE. 4206

1051-4880 See INSIGHT ON THE NEWS (WASHINGTON, D.C.). 4477

1051-4961 See LADYBUG (PERU, ILL.). 1066

1051-4988 See DIRECTORY OF LEGISLATIVE LEADERS. 4643

1051-5011 See FANTASY COMMENTATOR. 3387

1051-5054 See MIDSOUTH POLITICAL SCIENCE JOURNAL. 4482

1051-5062 See AMERICAN LITERARY REVIEW. 3360

1051-5097 See NARAS JOURNAL. 5318

1051-5143 See IEVANHELSKYI RANOK. 5061

1051-5240 See ALABAMA INDUSTRIAL DIRECTORY. 2133

1051-5313 See HARVARD HEART LETTER. 3705

1051-533X See LEGAL QUARTERLY DIGEST OF MINE SAFETY AND HEALTH DECISIONS. 3000

1051-5364 See IRANSHINASI (BETHESDA, MD.). 3397

1051-5410 See NEURAL NETWORK NEWS. 1215

1051-5488 See MOVIE MARKETPLACE. 4372

1051-5518 See MARTINDALE-HUBBELL BAR REGISTER, THE. 3006

1051-5526 See ABERDEEN'S CONCRETE CONSTRUCTION. 597

1051-5615 See BLUE CHIP JOB GROWTH UPDATE. 1465

1051-5623 See FACTS ABOUT ALASKA (1990). 2533

1051-564X See JOBSON'S CHEERS. 2368

1051-5658 See REMEDIATION (NEW YORK, N.Y.). 2180

1051-5666 See FORUM INSIDER, THE. 2449

1051-5682 See TECHNOLOGY FOR HOME CARE. 3644

1051-5690 See ELEKTOR ELECTRONICS USA. 4402

1051-5704 See MINNESOTA MEDIA DIRECTORY (TWIN CITIES ED. 1991). 1117

1051-5720 See CLEANING MANAGEMENT MAGAZINE. 863

1051-5739 See TRI-VALLEY HERALD (1990). 5641

1051-578X See FLEX AND SPEX INFORMATION BULLETIN. 3576

1051-5836 See BIBLIOGRAPHY OF LATIN AMERICAN AND CARIBBEAN BIBLIOGRAPHIES. 410

1051-5844 See HUMAN SERVICE YELLOW PAGES OF MASSACHUSETTS. 5288

1051-5852 See HISTORIC NEIGHBORHOODS NEWSLETTER. 2824

1051-5925 See AFVA EVALUATIONS. 4062

1051-5941 See REVIEW - INSTITUTE OF NUCLEAR POWER OPERATIONS (U.S.). 4451

1051-5968 See LULLWATER REVIEW. 3409

1051-6018 See SPORTING NEWS HOCKEY, THE. 4922

1051-6069 See MILITARY COST HANDBOOK. 4050

1051-6093 See NATIONAL ORGANIZATIONS OF STATE GOVERNMENT OFFICIALS DIRECTORY. 4668

1051-6174 See ASTRONOMICAL CALENDAR. 391

1051-6204 See PERSPECTIVES IN EDUCATION AND DEAFNESS. 4392

1051-6239 See INFORMATION INDUSTRY DIRECTORY. 3216

1051-6247 See WORLDWIDE TRAVEL INFORMATION CONTACT BOOK. 5500

1051-6255 See GOLOB'S OIL POLLUTION BULLETIN. 2230

1051-628X See BEVERLY HILLS BAR ASSOCIATION JOURNAL. 2941

1051-6336 See FODOR'S ... CANCUN, COZUMEL, YUCATAN PENINSULA. 5471

1051-6360 See INTERNATIONAL ENERGY OUTLOOK. 1947

1051-6433 See LIBERAL OPINION WEEK. 5671

1051-6441 See SISMODINAMICA (DURHAM, N.H.). 2031

1051-6492 See POST-POLIO DIRECTORY. 3628

1051-6514 See CORPORATE PHILANTHROPY IN RHODE ISLAND. 4335

1051-6557 See OIL INDUSTRY OUTLOOK. 4269

1051-6565 See OIL INDUSTRY OUTLOOK. 4269

1051-6573 See EQUIPMENT LEASING & ASSET BASED BORROWING REPORT INCLUDING CURRENT RATES AND SOURCES. 866

1051-6581 See PSYCHIC ALMANAC, THE. 4242

1051-662X See GENOTYPE-BY-ENVIRONMENT, INTERACTION, AND PLANT BREEDING SYMPOSIUM. 511

1051-6646 See RODALE'S FOOD AND NUTRITION LETTER. 4199

1051-6670 See THEORETICAL STUDIES IN SECOND LANGUAGE ACQUISITION. 3328

1051-6689 See GAIAN SCIENCE FOR GEOPHYSIOLOGY RESEARCHERS & TEACHERS. 1405

1051-6700 See CONNECTIONS (PROVIDENCE, R.I.). 1276

1051-6719 See SLOAN'S GREEN GUIDE TO ANTIQUING IN NEW ENGLAND. 252

1051-6778 See CARD INDUSTRY DIRECTORY. 740

1051-6786 See JOURNAL OF FARMING SYSTEMS RESEARCH-EXTENSION. 100

1051-6794 See CELLS AND MATERIALS. 534

1051-6808 See FROMMER'S NORTHWEST. 5477

1051-6816 See FROMMER'S INDIA ON $ ... A DAY. 5477

1051-6824 See FROMMER'S COMPREHENSIVE TRAVEL GUIDE. BED & BREAKFAST, NORTH AMERICA. 2805

1051-6840 See FROMMER'S COMPREHENSIVE TRAVEL GUIDE. ST. LOUIS & KANSAS CITY. 5476

1051-6859 See FROMMER'S COSTA RICA, GUATEMALA & BELIZE ON $ ... A DAY. 5477

1051-6867 See ZORA NEALE HURSTON FORUM, THE. 3456

1051-6905 See HI-TECH COACHING & TRAINING. 1855

1051-6913 See SENIOR CARE PROFESSIONAL. 5181

1051-6921 See FASHION & CRAFTS (PALM COAST, FLA.). 373

1051-6956 See SKYWAYS (POUGHKEEPSIE, N.Y.). 35

1051-6964 See GFOA NEWSLETTER. 4727

1051-6972 See REPORT FROM THE INSTITUTE FOR PHILOSOPHY & PUBLIC POLICY. 5215

1051-6980 See FROMMER'S COMPREHENSIVE TRAVEL GUIDE. MINNEAPOLIS & ST. PAUL. 5476

1051-7022 See YALE JOURNAL OF LAW AND LIBERATION, THE. 4514

1051-7073 See INVESTMENT BENCHMARKS. 902

1051-7103 See JOURNAL / PHILADELPHIA SOCIAL STUDIES COUNCIL, THE. 5207

1051-712X See JOURNAL OF BUSINESS-TO-BUSINESS MARKETING. 927

1051-7170 See HARVARD SCIENCE REVIEW (1992). 5109

1051-7197 See TRACKING EASTERN EUROPE. 917

1051-7200 See SURGICAL LAPAROSCOPY AND ENDOSCOPY. 3976

1051-7227 See CHEMTRACTS. INORGANIC CHEMISTRY. 1036

1051-7235 See TOXICOLOGY METHODS. 3984

1051-7316 See GREEN MARKETING REPORT. 925

1051-7324 *See* FLEXO (RONKONKOMA, N.Y.). 4565

1051-7332 *See* AGENCY EXAMINER, THE. 1460

1051-7359 *See* PAYMENT SYSTEMS WORLDWIDE. 802

1051-7367 *See* TRIBUNE BUSINESS WEEKLY. 716

0550-8401 4739

1051-7405 *See* USA TODAY (INTERNATIONAL ED.). 5722

1051-7421 *See* ... ALBERT LEA TRIBUNE, THE. 5694

1051-7480 *See* ORANGE COUNTY BUSINESS JOURNAL (NEWPORT BEACH, CALIF.). 701

1051-7510 *See* BUSINESS PHILADELPHIA. 651

1051-7545 *See* C2C CURRENTS JAPAN. MANUFACTURING. 3476

1051-7642 *See* CHINESE AMERICA, HISTORY AND PERSPECTIVES. 2258

1051-7685 *See* DAITA. 3669

1051-7693 *See* US DEPARTMENT OF STATE DISPATCH. 4692

1051-7707 *See* INTEGRATED CIRCUITS. SURFACE-MOUNTED ICS. 2066

1051-7715 See DISCRETE SEMICONDUCTORS. SURFACE-MOUNTED DISCRETE SEMICONDUCTORS. 1971

1051-7731 *See* MEDIAQUEST (BOSTON, MASS.). 5252

1051-7758 *See* GOLF TIPS. 4897

1051-7782 *See* COMPREHENSIVE MENTAL HEALTH CARE. 4582

1051-7804 *See* ZOOMER & CO. 2287

1051-7839 *See* HANDBOOK OF COMMUNICATIONS SYSTEMS MANAGEMENT. YEARBOOK. 1156

1051-7871 *See* LIBERATION AND MARXISM. 4543

1051-7901 *See* SITUATION AND OUTLOOK REPORT. FRUIT AND TREE NUTS. 135

1051-791X *See* SITUATION AND OUTLOOK SERIES. WESTERN EUROPE AGRICULTURE AND TRADE REPORT. 135

1051-7928 *See* SITUATION AND OUTLOOK REPORT. COTTON AND WOOL. 5356

1051-7936 *See* DELTA COUNCIL NEWS, THE. 78

1051-8010 *See* QUARTERLY BANK AND SAVINGS & LOAN RATING SERVICE. 804

1051-8037 *See* ADVANCES IN SOVIET MATHEMATICS. 3491

1051-8045 *See* USSR JOURNAL OF THEORETICAL AND APPLIED MECHANICS. 2131

1051-8053 *See* RUSSIAN JOURNAL OF ENGINEERING THERMOPHYSICS. 1995

1051-8061 *See* INTERNATIONAL MARKET ALERT. 841

1051-807X *See* WEEKLY INTERNATIONAL MARKET ALERT. 857

1051-8118 *See* REVUSER (PHILADELPHIA, PA.). 1289

1051-8126 *See* PULSO DEL PERIODISMO. 2923

1051-8134 *See* ANGOLA UPDATE. 1104

1051-8177 *See* MANGAJIN (ATLANTA, GA.). 380

1051-8193 *See* DESIGN FOR LEADERSHIP. 1862

1051-8207 *See* IEEE MICROWAVE AND GUIDED WAVE LETTERS. 2060

1051-8215 *See* IEEE TRANSACTIONS ON CIRCUITS AND SYSTEMS FOR VIDEO TECHNOLOGY. 1133

1051-8223 *See* IEEE TRANSACTIONS ON APPLIED SUPERCONDUCTIVITY. 2061

1051-824X *See* MAST (MADISON, WIS.). 1145

1051-8258 *See* DERMATOLOGY (BIENNIAL). 3719

1051-8266 *See* AI APPLICATIONS. 1210

1051-8304 *See* FLORIDA TODAY. 5649

1051-8592 *See* MS-DOS COLLECTION. 1288

1051-869X *See* SITUATION AND OUTLOOK SERIES. PACIFIC RIM AGRICULTURE AND TRADE REPORT. 135

1051-8703 *See* SITUATION AND OUTLOOK SERIES. CHINA AGRICULTURE AND TRADE REPORT. 135

1051-8738 *See* FUSION FACTS (SALT LAKE CITY, UTAH). 1945

1051-8746 *See* NEW JERSEY TRIAL LAWYER, THE. 3015

1051-8762 *See* FAITH & RENEWAL. 4958

1051-8886 *See* TESOL MATTERS. 1907

1051-8967 *See* AMERICAN JOURNAL OF CASE MANAGEMENT, THE. 5190

1051-8975 *See* MUSIC ALIVE. 4132

1051-8983 *See* CIRCULATION IDEA SERVICE. 4813

1051-9017 *See* JOB JARGON. 4205

1051-9033 *See* WORLD BOXING. 4930

1051-9076 *See* FLORACULTURE INTERNATIONAL. 2414

1051-9084 *See* DIAMOND DEPOSITIONS, SCIENCE AND TECHNOLOGY. 1023

1051-9130 *See* FERTILIZER MARKETS. 87

1051-9149 *See* SITUATION AND OUTLOOK REPORT. RICE. 135

1051-919X *See* OKLAHOMA DIRECTORY OF MANUFACTURERS AND PROCESSORS. 1620

1051-9246 *See* INTRODUCING COMPUTERS. 1260

1051-9335 *See* TRAVELIN' (EUGENE, OR.). 5497

1051-9351 See SUN HERALD (ENGLEWOOD ED.). 5651

1051-9432 See SENSOR BUSINESS DIGEST. 3487

1051-9440 See MANUFACTURING AUTOMATION. 3483

1051-9467 *See* LIFELINE (TORRANCE, CALIF.). 4194

1051-9483 *See* BUDAYA (SHOREVIEW, MINN.). 2647

1051-9505 See FAIRS AND FESTIVALS, NORTHEAST AND SOUTHEAST. 4850

1051-9513 See FAIRS AND FESTIVALS, NORTHEAST AND SOUTHEAST. 4850

1051-9521 *See* STRAIGHTTALK -- FROM THE DESK OF THE CHIEF ECONOMIST 1522

1051-953X *See* MULTIMEDIA COMPUTING & PRESENTATIONS. 908

1051-9602 *See* NONPROFIT MANAGEMENT STRATEGIES. 5299

1051-9629 *See* CIVIL ENGINEERING NEWS (MARIETTA, GA.). 2021

1051-9637 *See* 3TECH (SANTA CLARA, CALIF.). 1240

1051-9653 *See* WORSHIP WORKS. 5010

1051-9661 *See* MRO ALERT. 3012

1051-967X *See* WINTER PARK SUN OUTLOOK. 5651

1051-9688 *See* TRANSGENICA (LEVITTOWN, PA). 3697

1051-9696 *See* PARADOX DEVELOPER'S JOURNAL. 1289

1051-9726 *See* HEALTH WATCH (LOUISVILLE, KY.). 4782

1051-9734 *See* INSIDE MICROSOFT WINDOWS. 1287

1051-9777 See MARYLAND BEVERAGE JOURNAL. 2369

1051-9785 See WASHINGTON BEVERAGE JOURNAL. 2372

1051-9793 *See* AEROSPACE & DEFENSE SCIENCE. 5

1051-9815 *See* WORK : A JOURNAL OF PREVENTION, ASSESSMENT, AND REHABILITATION. 4808

1051-9823 *See* NEBRASKA ENGLISH AND LANGUAGE ARTS JOURNAL. 3414

1051-9831 *See* RECYCLED PAPER NEWS. 2241

1051-9858 *See* GEO INFO SYSTEMS. 2561

1051-9866 See CHRISTIAN COUNSELING TODAY. 4944

1051-9912 *See* SLVGS QUERY QUARTERLY, THE. 2472

1051-9939 *See* S & L- SAVINGS BANK FINANCIAL QUARTERLY. 810

1051-9963 *See* AIC SERIES. 2293

1051-9971 *See* FUTURE HOME TECHNOLOGY NEWS. 1111

1051-9998 *See* PLASMA DEVICES AND OPERATIONS. 5138

1052-0015 *See* JOURNAL OF SMALL FRUITS & VITICULTURE. 100

1052-0031 *See* DIRECTORY OF FOREIGN MANUFACTURERS IN THE UNITED STATES. 3477

1052-0066 *See* NEWSLETTER - WESTERN ASSOCIATION FOR ART CONSERVATION. 326

1052-0082 *See* BEHAVIOR ANALYSIS DIGEST. 4576

1052-0120 *See* INSIDER'S GUIDE TO BOOK EDITORS AND PUBLISHERS, THE. 4815

1052-0139 *See* CRYOGAS INTERNATIONAL. 2112

1052-018X *See* MAINE SCHOLAR, THE. 2850

1052-0201 *See* A'S & B'S OF ACADEMIC SCHOLARSHIPS (1987), THE. 1810

1052-0279 *See* WORLD AGRICULTURAL PRODUCTION. 147

1052-0287 *See* AIDS BIBLIOGRAPHY. 3654

1052-0295 *See* BIOTECHNIC & HISTOCHEMISTRY. 532

1052-0309 *See* DIPLOMATIC RECORD, THE. 4471

1052-0325 *See* MEDICAL DIRECTIONS (MERCER ISLAND, WASH.). 3608

1052-0341 *See* UPSIDE (U.S. ED.). 1239

1052-0406 *See* NINETEENTH CENTURY PROSE. 3417

1052-0414 *See* NEWS / BECKMAN CENTER FOR THE HISTORY OF CHEMISTRY. 987

1052-0457 *See* RESEARCH IN ACCOUNTING REGULATION. 750

1052-0465 *See* ADVANCES IN EATING DISORDERS. 3919

1052-0481 *See* MONOGRAPHS IN INTERNATIONAL STUDIES. AFRICA SERIES. 2642

1052-049X *See* NETWORKING MANAGEMENT. 1243

1052-0511 *See* THEATER THREE. 5370

1052-0597 *See* EDUCATED TRAVELER, THE. 5469

1052-0600 *See* JOURNAL OF MATHEMATICAL SYSTEMS, ESTIMATION, AND CONTROL. 3514

1052-0627 *See* CLINICIAN REVIEWS. 3566

1052-0635 *See* DEFENSE CLEANUP. 2227

1052-0643 *See* COMPUTATIONAL POLYMER SCIENCE. 4454

1052-0716 *See* NORTH AMERICAN DIRECTORY OF CONTRACT MANUFACTURERS IN ELECTRONICS. 2074

1052-0724 See INTERNATIONAL JOURNAL OF COMMUNICATIVE PSYCHOANALYSIS AND PSYCHOTHERAPY, THE. 3927

1052-0805 *See* DOLL ARTISTRY. 2773

1052-0856 *See* CAD/CAM WATCH. 1173

1052-0899 *See* WRESTLER (ROCKVILLE CENTRE, N.Y.), THE. 4930

1052-0910 See BEST OF METAL, THE. 4103

1052-0929 *See* BRITISH CAR. 5408

1052-0953 *See* MEMBRANE QUARTERLY. 1027

1052-0961 *See* MINITRUCKIN' (ANAHEIM, CALIF.). 4905

1052-0996 *See* BALTIMORE/ANNAPOLIS. 641

1052-1011 *See* CARIBBEAN TRAVEL AND LIFE. 5466

1052-102X *See* GUARDIANS OF THE GALAXY. 4862

1052-1062 *See* JOURNAL OF CLEAN TECHNOLOGY AND ENVIRONMENTAL SCIENCES. 2175

1052-1070 *See* JOURNAL OF GENETIC AND DEVELOPMENTAL TOXICOLOGY. 3981

1052-1151 *See* RELIGION AND AMERICAN CULTURE. 4990

1052-1186 *See* PC NOVICE. 1271

1052-1208 *See* CANADA REGISTER. 4835

1052-1356 *See* MOUNTAIN EAGLE (TANNERSVILLE, N.Y.), THE. 5718

1052-1372 *See* P&T (LAWRENCEVILLE, N.J.). 3625

1052-1380 *See* PRINCE GEORGE'S COUNTY GENEALOGICAL SOCIETY BULLETIN. 2468

1052-1453 See SKULL BASE SURGERY. 3974
1052-150X See BUSINESS ETHICS QUARTERLY. 647
1052-1542 See ENVIRONMENTAL SAFETY ALERT. 2229
1052-1550 See JOURNAL OF POLLUTION PREVENTION. 2234
1052-1569 See BRIDGE (OAK PARK, MICH.), THE. 3369
1052-1577 See HARVARD HEALTH LETTER. 3580
1052-1607 See INSIDE TRACK (HAMMONTON, N.J.). 4851
1052-1615 See TRAVELIN TALK NEWSLETTER, THE. 5497
1052-1658 See INFORMATION SERVICES UPDATE. 3216
1052-1666 See ANDRE GAYOT'S TASTES, WITH THE BEST OF GAULT MILLAU. 2326
1052-1674 See ACQUISITION ISSUES. 4708
1052-1682 See BOOMERANG! (SAN FRANCISCO, CALIF.). 1060
1052-1712 See MODERN ARTS CRITICISM. 358
1052-1747 See CASH MANAGEMENT PERFORMANCE REPORT. 782
1052-1755 See GREEN MARKETALERT. 2173
1052-1763 See WOMEN'S RECOVERY NETWORK. 5571
1052-181X See MARTIN LUTHER KING, JR. MEMORIAL STUDIES IN RELIGION, CULTURE, AND SOCIAL DEVELOPMENT. 5251
1052-1941 See DATAPRO SOFTWARE FINDER (MICROCOMPUTER ED.). 1285
1052-195X See DATAPRO SOFTWARE FINDER (COMPLETE ED.). 1285
1052-1968 See DATAPRO SOFTWARE FINDER (MID-RANGE/MAINFRAME ED.). 1285
1052-1984 See CA SELECTS: OMEGA THREE FATTY ACIDS & FISH OIL. 1006
1052-2026 See RETIREMENT OPPORTUNITIES. 885
1052-2077 See ADVANCES IN CYCLOADDITION. 1038
1052-2131 See EUROPEAN PACKAGING NEWSLETTER AND WORLD REPORT. 4219
1052-214X See JOURNAL OF RESTAURANT & FOODSERVICE MARKETING. 5071
1052-2158 See JOURNAL OF FAMILY SOCIAL WORK. 5291
1052-2166 See GENE EXPRESSION. 545
1052-2174 See VIDEO JOURNAL OF ECHOCARDIOGRAPHY. 3711
1052-2182 See VIDEO JOURNAL OF COLOR FLOW IMAGING. 3947
1052-2190 See FAX & BUSINESS DIRECTORY. 1111
1052-2212 See WHAT DO I READ NEXT?. 3256
1052-2220 See AWARDS ALMANAC. 1799
1052-2239 See NEWS OF THE EARTH. 2178
1052-2247 See SUNDEW GARDENS REPORTS. 2432
1052-2255 See AGRI-TOPICS (BELTSVILLE, MD.). 48
1052-2263 See JOURNAL OF VOCATIONAL REHABILITATION. 4380
1052-2271 See MOODY (CHICAGO, ILL.). 4979
1052-231X See ADULT BASIC EDUCATION (ATHENS, GA.). 1799
1052-2336 See EXECUTIVE'S MANUAL OF PERSONAL SECRETARIES, THE. 4211
1052-2379 See CALIFORNIA LAWYERS. 2946
1052-2433 See TODAY IN MISSISSIPPI. 2084
1052-2468 See ECOLOGICAL RESEARCH SERIES. 2214
1052-2484 See URBAN FORESTS. 2397
1052-2522 See 73 AMATEUR RADIO TODAY. 1125
1052-2573 See CREATIVE FORECASTING. 5281
1052-2581 See TECHNICAL SUPPORT. 1249
1052-262X See ADVANCES IN LIBRARY RESOURCE SHARING. 3188
1052-2638 See CD-ROMS IN PRINT (CD-ROM VERSION). 1276
1052-2662 See INSIDE 1-2-3 RELEASE 3. 1287

1052-2689 See VIOLENCE UPDATE. 4621
1052-2727 See ALASKA'S WILDLIFE. 4868
1052-2824 See MASB JOURNAL. 1866
1052-2840 See EMORY INTERNATIONAL LAW REVIEW. 3128
1052-2859 See JOURNAL OF DISPUTE RESOLUTION. 2987
1052-2867 See MICHIGAN JOURNAL OF INTERNATIONAL LAW. 3132
1052-2875 See JOURNAL OF THE AMERICAN SOCIETY OF CLU & CHFC. 2886
1052-2883 See JOURNAL OF THE IES. 2176
1052-2891 See NEW DIRECTIONS FOR ADULT AND CONTINUING EDUCATION. 1801
1052-2905 See SURVEYING AND LAND INFORMATION SYSTEMS. 2583
1052-2913 See ADMINISTRATIVE LAW JOURNAL (WASHINGTON, D.C.), THE. 3091
1052-2921 See CALIFORNIA REAL PROPERTY JOURNAL. 2946
1052-293X See ARKANSAS LAW NOTES. 2937
1052-2964 See EMPLOYMENT LAW COUNSELOR. 3147
1052-2972 See LAW DEPARTMENT MANAGEMENT ADVISER. 875
1052-3030 See MISSION INN MUSUEM JOURNAL. 4091
1052-3049 See THIRD WORLD LIBRARIES. 3253
1052-3057 See JOURNAL OF STROKE AND CEREBROVASCULAR DISEASES. 3837
1052-3065 See ANALYTICAL CONSUMER. 1293
1052-3073 See FINANCIAL COUNSELING AND PLANNING. 898
1052-309X See NATIONAL MEDICAL-LEGAL JOURNAL. 3013
1052-3103 See CACD JOURNAL. 5276
1052-3146 See HOSPITAL PHARMACIST REPORT. 4306
1052-3154 See BAKUNIN (DAVIS, CALIF.). 3338
1052-3170 See TUROK'S CHOICE. 4157
1052-3219 See WESTERN LINKS (HILTON HEAD ISLAND, S.C.). 4929
1052-3243 See NEIL SPERRY'S GARDENS. 2425
1052-3278 See PATTON (TOMS RIVER, N.J.). 2467
1052-3324 See DRUMS & DRUMMING. 4115
1052-3332 See HOFSTRA LABOR LAW JOURNAL. 3149
1052-3359 See CHEST SURGERY CLINICS OF NORTH AMERICA. 3961
1052-3367 See ORACLE NEWS. 1198
1052-3383 See SPACE EXPLORATION TECHNOLOGY. 35
1052-3405 See JOURNAL OF CORPORATE DISCLOSURE AND CONFIDENTIALITY. 3101
1052-3413 See NATURAL GAS LAWYER'S JOURNAL, THE. 3014
1052-3421 See WISCONSIN WOMEN'S LAW JOURNAL. 3075
1052-343X See SOUTH TEXAS LAW REVIEW. 3057
1052-3448 See PACE YEARBOOK OF INTERNATIONAL LAW. 3133
1052-3456 See CRSP DAILY EXCESS RETURNS FILE. 895
1052-3464 See MONTHLY MASTER/MONTHLY RETURNS. 907
1052-3502 See COMPUTER PRICE WATCH. 1244
1052-3545 See DOWLINE. 788
1052-3561 See MIDRANGE COMPUTING. 1195
1052-3634 See MONTEVALLO TODAY. 1102
1052-3642 See OERI BULLETIN. 1770
1052-3669 See BULLETIN OF THE FLORIDA MUSEUM OF NATURAL HISTORY. BIOLOGICAL SCIENCES. 4164
1052-3707 See RESEARCH & SOCIETY. 5215
1052-3723 See BEAM'S DIRECTORY OF INTERNATIONAL TOURIST EVENTS. 5462
1052-374X See TRIBUNE SYOSSET, JERICHO. 5721
1052-3758 See JUST BETWEEN US. 3465

1052-3774 See LEGACY (FORT COLLINS, COLO.). 4706
1052-3790 See COVENANT DISCIPLESHIP QUARTERLY. 4951
1052-3804 See DISCIPULOS RESPONSABLES. 4954
1052-3820 See QUICK ANSWER, THE. 1255
1052-3901 See JOURNAL OF LAPAROENDOSCOPIC SURGERY. 3967
1052-391X See CURRENT NEWS ON FILE. 2532
1052-3928 See JOURNAL OF PROFESSIONAL ISSUES IN ENGINEERING EDUCATION AND PRACTICE. 2026
1052-3944 See POSTAL WATCH. 1147
1052-3952 See FRENCH AMERICAN REVIEW. 2688
1052-3979 See CHARITABLE ORGANIZATIONS OF THE U.S. 4335
1052-3987 See REPORT ON UROLOGIC TECHNIQUES, THE. 3993
1052-3995 See TREATING ABUSE TODAY. 5313
1052-4010 See CURRENT PROBLEMS IN UROLOGY. 3989
1052-4029 See COLLECTION AGENCY REPORT. 658
1052-4037 See WHO'S WHO IN PHOTOGRAPHY (PLYMOUTH, VT.). 4378
1052-4053 See DISC. 1183
1052-407X See CAR DEALER INSIDER (1990). 5409
1052-4088 See RESTAURANT MANAGEMENT INSIDER. 5072
1052-4096 See NATIONAL GARDENING. 2425
1052-410X See TEACHER'S GUIDE TO CLASSROOM MANAGEMENT. 1906
1052-4118 See CAR RENTAL & LEASING INSIDER. 5409
1052-4142 See MINILAB DEVELOPMENTS. 1618
1052-4169 See BEAUTY EDUCATION. 402
1052-4207 See AIDS TREATMENT NEWS. 3664
1052-4215 See NASHVILLE BUSINESS AND LIFESTYLES. 2490
1052-4231 See VIRGINIA MEDICAL QUARTERLY : VMQ. 3650
1052-424X See GAMC NEWS JOURNAL. 868
1052-4290 See SYNDICATION NEWS. 1140
1052-4355 See PORTER, WRIGHT, MORRIS & ARTHUR'S OHIO ENVIRONMENTAL LAW LETTER. 3115
1052-4363 See PENNSYLVANIA EMPLOYMENT LAW LETTER. 3153
1052-4371 See KENTUCKY EMPLOYMENT LAW LETTER. 3150
1052-438X See ON! (PETERBOROUGH, N.H.). 1197
1052-4452 See MILWAUKEE JOURNAL, THE. 5769
1052-4479 See MILWAUKEE SENTINEL (1883), THE. 5769
1052-4533 See STUDIA PHILONICA ANNUAL, THE. 4362
1052-4541 See BAR LETTER - STATE BAR OF NEVADA. 2940
1052-4614 See ADDICTION & RECOVERY. 1338
1052-4622 See REAL ESTATE SECURITIES & CAPITAL MARKETS. 4845
1052-4630 See GOURMET NEWS (YARMOUTH, ME.). 2342
1052-4649 See LAW REPORTER (WASHINGTON, D.C.). 2996
1052-4657 See IN CONTEXT (CROWNSVILLE, MD.). 2738
1052-4665 See IN CONTEXT (CROWNSVILLE, MD.). 2738
1052-4673 See IN CONTEXT (CROWNSVILLE, MD.). 2738
1052-4754 See C-L-A-S-S FORUM. 3199
1052-4770 See PLANNED GIVING TODAY. 4338
1052-4789 See DUSTY DOG CHAPBOOK SERIES. 3462
1052-4800 See JOURNAL ON EXCELLENCE IN COLLEGE TEACHING. 1833
1052-4819 See STERN'S SOURCEFINDER. 947

1052-4851 See POETRY CRITICISM. 3469

1052-486X See CONTEMPORARY DOLL MAGAZINE. 2773

1052-4878 See PHILOMEL (PHILADELPHIA, PA.). 3423

1052-4894 See MEDICAL OFFICE MANAGER. 3788

1052-4908 See RESOURCE RECYCLING'S PLASTICS RECYCLING UPDATE. 4460

1052-4916 See RESOURCE RECYCLING'S BOTTLE/CAN RECYCLING UPDATE. 2242

1052-4924 See MEDICAL RECORDS BRIEFING. 3788

1052-4975 See SEAWAYS' SHIPS IN SCALE. 4183

1052-5017 See TRANSFORMATIONS (WAYNE, N.J.). 5225

1052-5025 See SECONDS (NEW YORK, N.Y.). 4152

1052-5092 See DIVIDEND REINVESTMENT PLANS. 896

1052-5114 See STATE OF COLORADO TELEPHONE DIRECTORY. 766

1052-5122 See EDUCATIONAL RESEARCH NEWSLETTER. 1742

1052-5149 See NEUROIMAGING CLINICS OF NORTH AMERICA. 3840

1052-5157 See GASTROINTESTINAL ENDOSCOPY CLINICS OF NORTH AMERICA. 3746

1052-5165 See GREAT PLAINS RESEARCH. 4166

1052-5173 See GSA TODAY. 1381

1052-5203 See HUMANIST ALMANAC AND DATEBOOK, A. 4348

1052-522X See ALBERTSEN'S (INTERNATIONAL ED.). 407

1052-5238 See U.S. & FOREIGN DIPLOMATIC CONTACTS. 4691

1052-5300 See REVIEW-HERALD, THE. 5639

1052-5319 See APPALACHIA. BULLETIN ISSUE. 4869

1052-5327 See IOWA LAWYER. 2985

1052-5351 See PROCEEDINGS / BELTWIDE COTTON CONFERENCES. 182

1052-536X See SPECIAL REFERENCE BRIEFS. 137

1052-5378 See QUICK BIBLIOGRAPHY SERIES - NATIONAL AGRICULTURAL LIBRARY. 124

1052-5386 See ARS. 63

1052-5394 See JOURNAL FOR HAWAIIAN AND PACIFIC AGRICULTURE. 99

1052-5408 See INTERNATIONAL NEMATOLOGY NETWORK NEWSLETTER. 5586

1052-5432 See ADVANCES IN PLANT SCIENCES SERIES. 498

1052-5440 See BRIDGE (GLASSBORO, N.J.), THE. 1861

1052-5491 See CHEVY HIGH PERFORMANCE. 5410

1052-5505 See TRIBAL COLLEGE. 1851

1052-5521 See QUARTERLY BYTE, THE. 4843

1052-5548 See DAVID ANTHONY KRAFTS COMICS INTERVIEW. 4859

1052-5564 See SPECIALTY STORE SERVICE BULLETIN. 958

1052-5572 See NEWSPAPERS & TECHNOLOGY. 5644

1052-5629 See JOURNAL OF MANAGEMENT EDUCATION (NEWBURY PARK, CALIF.). 873

1052-5653 See SHEPARD'S COLORADO CASE NAMES CITATOR. 3049

1052-5696 See SHEPARD'S ALASKA CASE NAMES CITATOR. 3048

1052-5718 See SHEPARD'S WISCONSIN CASE NAMES CITATOR. 3055

1052-5726 See PROGRESSIVE LIBRARIAN. 3242

1052-5777 See GOVERNMENT CONTRACT, COSTS, PRICING & ACCOUNTING REPORT. 744

1052-5785 See MARTHA'S VINEYARD. 107

1052-5831 See NEWSLINE - (COLUMBIA UNIVERSITY. GRADUATE SCHOOL OF ARCHITECTURE PLANNING AND PRESERVATION). 304

1052-5882 See CELLULAR AND MOLECULAR MECHANISMS OF INFLAMMATION. 484

1052-5912 See STANGER'S INVESTMENT ADVISOR. 916

1052-5920 See SHEPARD'S HAWAII CASE NAMES CITATOR. 3050

1052-5939 See SHEPARD'S INDIANA CASE NAMES CITATOR. 3050

1052-5955 See SHEPARD'S KANSAS CASE NAMES CITATOR. 3051

1052-5971 See SHEPARD'S MAINE CASE NAMES CITATOR. 3051

1052-6099 See JOURNAL OF THE INTERNATIONAL ACADEMY OF HOSPITALITY RESEARCH, THE. 1501

1052-6102 See PROCEEDINGS / A & WMA ANNUAL MEETING. 2180

1052-6129 See MONOGRAPH SERIES OF THE WEED SCIENCE SOCIETY OF AMERICA. 178

1052-6153 See BIOTECHNOLOGY HANDBOOKS. 3689

1052-6161 See MARYLAND GRAPEVINE, THE. 178

1052-6188 See JOURNAL OF MACHINERY MANUFACTURE AND RELIABILITY. 2118

1052-6196 See SOVIET JOURNAL OF HEAVY MACHINERY. 2129

1052-6226 See DATAPRO COMPETITIVE EDGE IN COMMUNICATIONS, THE. 1109

1052-6234 See SIAM JOURNAL ON OPTIMIZATION. 3535

1052-6242 See VIRTUAL REALITY REPORT. 1283

1052-6307 See SHEPARD'S NEVADA CASE NAMES CITATOR. 3052

1052-6315 See SHEPARD'S NEBRASKA CASE NAMES CITATOR. 3052

1052-6331 See COMMON SENSE ON ENERGY AND OUR ENVIRONMENT. 1935

1052-6358 See WORKERS COMPENSATION OUTLOOK (BOSTON, MASS.). 1719

1052-6366 See ACCESS TO WANG. 1264

1052-648X See SHORT STORY (COLUMBIA, S.C.). 3436

1052-6552 See COMMUNITY HEALTH FUNDING REPORT. 5280

1052-6560 See PAGEMAKER IN-DEPTH. 1289

1052-6579 See PC SOURCES. 1199

1052-6587 See PRESS (LITTLETON, COLO.). 1086

1052-6609 See DALTON'S NEW YORK METROPOLITAN DIRECTORY. 664

1052-6641 See SHEPARD'S PUERTO RICO CASE NAMES CITATOR. 3053

1052-6668 See SHEPARD'S TENNESSEE CASE NAMES CITATOR. 3054

1052-6676 See SHEPARD'S VIRGINIA CASE NAMES CITATOR. 3055

1052-6684 See SHEPARD'S WEST VIRGINIA CASE NAMES CITATOR. 3055

1052-6714 See CONNECTICUT SUPERIOR COURT REPORTS. 2955

1052-6730 See OCEAN AND COASTAL LAW MEMO. 3182

1052-6765 See TD&T (NEW YORK, N.Y.). 5369

1052-6773 See MONOGRAPHS - NATIONAL CANCER INSTITUTE (U.S.). 3821

1052-6781 See SAAS BULLETIN, BIOCHEMISTRY AND BIOTECHNOLOGY. 3696

1052-682X See PACKAGE TRAVEL. 4220

1052-6838 See CONFERENCE PROCEEDINGS / ANNUAL ADVANCED RESEARCH TECHNIQUES FORUM. 829

1052-6846 See JOURNAL OF SCHOOL LEADERSHIP. 1865

1052-696X See WASHINGTON REPORTER (WASHINGTON, D.C.), THE. 5648

1052-6986 See MASSACHUSETTS PHARMACY JOURNAL. 4314

1052-6994 See STONE WORLD. 2151

1052-7001 See JOURNAL OF HOUSING RESEARCH. 2826

1052-701X See OPEN SYSTEMS REPORT. 1243

1052-7036 See FOREIGN POLICY BULLETIN (WASHINGTON, D.C.). 4522

1052-7060 See PROFESSIONS EDUCATION RESEARCHER QUARTERLY : PERQ. 1775

1052-7133 See COMPLETE HOCKEY BOOK. 4891

1052-7192 See TBI'S WORLD GUIDE. 1140

1052-7206 See BUSINESS AND THE ENVIRONMENT. 2162

1052-7214 See INTELLIGENT SOFTWARE STRATEGIES. 1287

1052-7311 See BOOKKEEPER'S JOURNAL FOR DENTAL PRACTICES, THE. 1317

1052-7338 See ... NEWCOMER'S GUIDE TO FLORIDA BUSINESS, THE. 699

1052-7346 See OPTOMETRIC ECONOMICS. 4216

1052-7354 See WHO'S WHO AMONG HISPANIC AMERICANS. 2275

1052-7443 See SELLER'S GUIDE TO GOVERNMENT PURCHASING. 4747

1052-7540 See ALLEGANY AGRICULTURE. 57

1052-7559 See SCAW NEWSLETTER. 227

1052-7575 See HOSTETLER MEMO FOR BROKERS ONLY, THE. 790

1052-7591 See SPORTING NEWS ... FANTASY BASEBALL OWNER'S MANUAL, THE. 4922

1052-7605 See INSIDE WORD (PC ED.). 1287

1052-7613 See AQUATIC CONSERVATION. 2211

1052-763X See GAME PLAYERS SEGA GUIDE. 4861

1052-7648 See SYMPHONIUM (PITTSBURGH, PA.). 4155

1052-7656 See COMMUNITY ALTERNATIVES. 5279

1052-7664 See LOOKING FOR EMPLOYMENT IN FOREIGN COUNTRIES. 690

1052-7737 See DIRECTORY OF SELECTED RESEARCH & POLICY CENTERS WORKING ON WOMEN'S ISSUES, A. 5554

1052-7788 See RESEARCH IN FINANCIAL SERVICES. 808

1052-7842 See WORLD SATELLITE ANNUAL, THE. 1169

1052-7869 See MISSISSIPPI WORKERS' COMPENSATION REPORTER. 2888

1052-7877 See THESAURUS OF METALLURGICAL TERMS. 4021

1052-7893 See ASCP WASHINGTON REPORT ON NATIONAL AND STATE LABORATORY ISSUES. 3893

1052-7958 See AMERICAN PSYCHOANALYST, THE. 4573

1052-7982 See NEWSLETTER / AMERICAN FEDERATION FOR CLINICAL RESEARCH. 3621

1052-8008 See MARKETING EDUCATION REVIEW. 930

1052-8032 See NEW AGE LINK'S LETTER LINK : THE SPIRITUAL AWARENESS NETWORK. 4186

1052-8040 See RECEPTOR (CLIFTON, N.J. JOURNAL). 493

1052-8091 See MINOR PLANET BULLETIN, THE. 397

1052-813X See BNA CALIFORNIA ENVIRONMENT REPORTER. 3110

1052-8156 See SOVIET INDEPENDENT BUSINESS DIRECTORY : SIBD. 713

1052-8164 See CONSTRUCTIVE CRITICISM. 4582

1052-8202 See BULLETIN OF THE GENERAL THEOLOGICAL CENTER OF MAINE. 4941

1052-8261 See EDUCATION INTERFACE SERIES. 1740

1052-8342 See CORPORATE GOVERNANCE SERVICE. VOTING RESULTS. 895

1052-8350 See ANNUAL COMPUTER LAW INSTITUTE. 2934

1052-8377 See WASHINGTON COURT RULES. STATE. 3072

1052-8385 See WASHINGTON COURT RULES. FEDERAL. 3072

1052-8415 See OTTERWISE (PORTLAND, ME.). 1067

1052-8431 See LONG ISLAND BUSINESS DIRECTORY & BUYERS GUIDE, THE. 690

1052-8512 See DOCUMENT - AFRIKA BARAZA. 2639

1052-8547 See KEYSTONE GAZETTE (BELLEFONTE, PA. : 1989). 5737

1052-8563 See M (NEW YORK, N.Y. 1991). 1085

1052-8571 See MICROSOFT NETWORKING JOURNAL. 1288

1052-858X See OHIO GENEALOGICAL SOCIETY NEWSLETTER, THE. 2465

1052-861X See INSIDE COLLECTOR, THE. 251

1052-8733 See HOSPITAL REVENUE REPORT. 3785

1052-8741 See GARY NORTH'S RARE COIN INVESTMENT REVIEW. 2781

1052-8806 See PARTNERSHIP FEDERAL AND STATE INCOME TAX REPORTING. 4740

1052-8814 See VOX MAGAZINE (NEW YORK, N.Y. 1990). 3451

1052-8822 See NORTHERN CALIFORNIA BUSINESS DIRECTORY (NEWPORT BEACH, CALIF.). 699

1052-8849 See COUNTRY EXTRA. 2531

1052-8938 See HORACE (PROVIDENCE, R.I.). 1829

1052-8946 See CALIFORNIA LAND USE AND PLANNING LAW. 2817

1052-9020 See KENNEDY SCHOOL CASE CATALOG, THE. 875

1052-9063 See CURRENT BIBLIOGRAPHIES IN MEDICINE. 3656

1052-9098 See MATCHING GIFT DETAILS. 4338

1052-9101 See NEWSLETTER - MISSISSIPPI ARCHAEOLOGICAL ASSOCIATION (1983). 276

1052-9136 See GENERAL AVIATION NEWS AND FLYER. 22

1052-9144 See CHILTON'S GUIDE TO FUEL INJECTION AND ELECTRONIC ENGINE CONTROLS. CHEVROLET CARS AND TRUCKS. 5411

1052-9144 See CHILTON'S GUIDE TO FUEL INJECTION AND ELECTRONIC ENGINE CONTROLS. BUICK, OLDS, PONTIAC CARS AND TRUCKS. 5410

1052-9152 See MEDICAL RESEARCH FUNDING NEWS. 3611

1052-9179 See CONSUMER GUIDE TO HOME ENERGY SAVINGS. 2810

1052-9187 See INTERNATIONAL CONTRIBUTIONS TO LABOUR STUDIES. 1680

1052-9225 See CHINA STATISTICAL YEARBOOK. 5325

1052-9233 See SURVEYS IN DIFFERENTIAL GEOMETRY. 3537

1052-9241 See JOURNAL OF CULINARY PRACTICE. 2346

1052-9268 See INTERNATIONAL VIDEO JOURNAL OF ENGINEERING RESEARCH. 1980

1052-9276 See REVIEWS IN MEDICAL VIROLOGY. 569

1052-9284 See JOURNAL OF COMMUNITY AND APPLIED SOCIAL PSYCHOLOGY. 5249

1052-9292 See INTERNATIONAL PETROLEUM ABSTRACTS INCORPORATING OFFSHORE ABSTRACTS. 4261

1052-9306 See BIOLOGICAL MASS SPECTROMETRY. 1013

1052-9314 See THEOLOGY & PUBLIC POLICY. 5004

1052-9381 See ALLIANCE LETTER. 2718

1052-9411 See QUALITY ASSURANCE (SAN DIEGO, CALIF.). 5143

1052-942X See RANDOM LENGTHS EXPORT. 2404

1052-9438 See NEW YORK REVIEW OF SCIENCE FICTION, THE. 3416

1052-9454 See BULLETIN - SPECIAL LIBRARIES ASSOCIATION. EDUCATION DIVISION. 3198

1052-9470 See INSIDE HYPERCARD. 1287

1052-9489 See INSIDE TURBO C++. 1287

1052-9551 See DIAGNOSTIC MOLECULAR PATHOLOGY. 3894

1052-9578 See MARKET SHARE REPORTER. 930

1052-9586 See GUIDE TO INTERNATIONAL EDUCATION IN THE UNITED STATES. 1748

1052-9624 See CIRCLE TRACK. 4890

1052-9632 See CONSUMER PRODUCT LITIGATION REPORTER. 2956

1052-9640 See PENSION FUND LITIGATION REPORTER. 3025

1052-9713 See MORGAN STANLEY CAPITAL INTERNATIONAL PERSPECTIVE (MONTHLY). 908

1052-9721 See MORGAN STANLEY CAPITAL INTERNATIONAL PERSPECTIVE (QUARTERLY). 908

1052-9764 See MEMBERSHIP DIRECTORY - SOCIETY FOR NEUROSCIENCE. 4603

1052-9829 See FAYETTEVILLE OBSERVER-TIMES, THE. 5723

1052-987X See ASIA TODAY INTERNATIONAL. 2646

1052-9896 See DIRECTORY OF POLITICAL PERIODICALS. 5675

1052-9942 See ... INTERNATIONAL MERGER YEARBOOK, THE. 684

1052-9950 See JOURNAL OF ANALYTIC SOCIAL WORK. 5291

1052-9977 See PICTURE FRAMING MAGAZINE. 2776

1052-9985 See PARKING SECURITY REPORT. 4795

1053-0002 See OAG BUSINESS TRAVEL PLANNER (NORTH AMERICAN ED.). 2808

1053-0010 See NORTH SOUTH TRADER'S CIVIL WAR. 2624

1053-0045 See HILO TIMES, THE. 5656

1053-0169 See COMMUNICATION EDGE, THE. 1106

1053-0185 See STURM DIETER'S RESTAURANT GUIDE, OKLAHOMA CITY. 5073

1053-0193 See OSHKAABEWIS NATIVE JOURNAL. 3421

1053-0215 See STOCKHOLDERS & CREDITORS NEWS SERVICE CONCERNING ASBESTOS BANKRUPTCIES. 3103

1053-0258 See UTILITIES INDUSTRY LITIGATION REPORTER. 3070

1053-0274 See WRONGFUL DISCHARGE REPORT. 3155

1053-0304 See SHOOTER'S GUIDE (CALIFORNIA ED.). 4878

1053-0312 See NELSON'S DIRECTORY OF PLAN SPONSORS AND TAX-EXEMPT FUNDS. 909

1053-0339 See EAST ASIAN INVESTMENT IN U.S. AND CANADIAN REAL ESTATE DIRECTORY. 4837

1053-0347 See CASH FLOW ENHANCEMENT REPORT. 863

1053-0363 See HR MANAGERS LEGAL REPORTER. 3149

1053-0398 See COMICS SCENE. 4859

1053-0428 See INFORMATION INDUSTRY SCAN. 1188

1053-0444 See HOME OFFICE WORKER. 680

1053-0452 See CLINICS IN APPLIED NUTRITION. 4189

1053-0460 See CLEARINGHOUSE DIRECTORY, THE. 1924

1053-0479 See JOURNAL OF PSYCHOTHERAPY INTEGRATION. 4600

1053-0487 See JOURNAL OF OCCUPATIONAL REHABILITATION. 2864

1053-0495 See JOURNAL OF INORGANIC AND ORGANOMETALLIC POLYMERS. 981

1053-0509 See JOURNAL OF FLUORESCENCE. 4435

1053-0517 See DIFFERENTIAL GEOMETRY AND APPLICATIONS. 3503

1053-0525 See RECYCLING RELATED NEWSLETTERS, PUBLICATIONS, PERIODICALS, ETC. : AN UPDATING REFERENCE. 2180

1053-0533 See REPORT OF INVESTIGATION - FLORIDA GEOLOGICAL SURVEY (1987). 1394

1053-0606 See ADVANCES IN LONG-TERM CARE. 5270

1053-0614 See ACROSS THE BORDER (BLOOMINGTON, MINN.). 2436

1053-0649 See ALLIANCE ALERT. MEDICAL/HEALTH. 3775

1053-0657 See ALLIANCE ALERT. COMMUNICATIONS. 1104

1053-0665 See ALLIANCE ALERT. SOFTWARE/INFORMATION SERVICES. 1235

1053-0673 See ALLIANCE ALERT. CHEMICALS/MATERIALS/AGRICULTURE. 1020

1053-0703 See MAIL (MILFORD, PA.). 1145

1053-072X See CLINICAL CHIROPRACTIC REPORT. 4380

1053-0746 See NUDE PACIFIC TRAVEL GUIDE. 5486

1053-0754 See RESPONSIVE COMMUNITY, THE. 5256

1053-0762 See HOME GROUND. 2824

1053-0770 See JOURNAL OF CARDIOTHORACIC AND VASCULAR ANESTHESIA. 3683

1053-0789 See JOURNAL OF SOCIAL DISTRESS AND THE HOMELESS. 5293

1053-0797 See DREAMING (NEW YORK, N.Y.). 580

1053-0800 See JOURNAL OF CHILD AND ADOLESCENT GROUP THERAPY. 4594

1053-0819 See JOURNAL OF BEHAVIORAL EDUCATION. 1880

1053-0827 See KMT (SAN FRANCISCO, CALIF.). 272

1053-0886 See NCAA MANUAL. 4907

1053-0894 See AIDS READER, THE. 3664

1053-0908 See BOWSER DIRECTORY OF SMALL STOCKS, THE. 893

1053-0924 See ELECTRONIC ATLAS NEWSLETTER, THE. 1183

1053-0932 See WEBB REPORT : A NEWSLETTER ON SEXUAL HARASSMENT BY SUSAN L. WEBB, THE. 3179

1053-0967 See MEMBERSHIP DIRECTORY / AMERICAN COLLEGE OF PHYSICIANS. 1927

1053-1017 See CONTRACT AND CAPTIVE ELECTRONIC MANUFACTURING AND PRINTED CIRCUIT PRODUCTION. 2039

1053-1068 See RADIO NEW YORK : LISTENER'S GUIDE TO RADIO PROGRAMMING IN THE GREATER NEW YORK AREA. 1137

1053-1084 See NATIONAL DISABILITY LAW REPORTER. 3013

1053-1092 See ALLERGIC DISEASE AND THERAPY. 3665

1053-1106 See CDIAC COMMUNICATIONS. 1421

1053-1114 See CHILTON'S AIR CONDITIONING AND HEATING MANUAL. 5410

1053-1130 See CHILTON'S GUIDE TO CHASSIS ELECTRONICS & POWER ACCESSORIES. FORD/CHRYSLER/JEEP/EAGLE. 5410

1053-1173 See IRS PRACTICE ALERT. 4734

1053-1181 See CIVIL WAR NEWS, THE. 2728

1053-122X See CURRENT TOPICS IN PHOTOVOLTAICS. 4401

1053-1238 See QUARTERLY BULLETIN OF THE COMPUTER SOCIETY OF THE IEEE TECHNICAL COMMITTEE ON DATA ENGINEERING. 1254

1053-1254 See RESEARCH IN INTERNATIONAL BUSINESS AND INTERNATIONAL RELATIONS. 1639

1053-1270 See EASTERN EUROPEAN AND SOVIET ADVANCED MATERIALS REPORT, THE. 1971

1053-1297 See NEW ENGLAND REVIEW (1990). 3415

1053-1319 See PAS (EVANSTON, ILL.). 2642

1053-1327 See AMERICAN FESTIVAL MAGAZINE. 312

1053-1351 See NEW MATURE WOMAN. 5562

1053-136X See FIELD GUIDES TO COLLECTING SHAKER ANTIQUES. 250

1053-1378 See EDUCATIONAL RANKINGS ANNUAL. 1822

1053-1386 See COUNTERPOINT (WASHINGTON, D.C.). 1877

1053-1394 See NATURAL RESOURCES METABASE. 2199

1053-1408 See CONSUMER REPORTS ON CD-ROM (BEGINNER'S ED.). 1471

1053-1416 See CONSUMER REPORTS ON CD-ROM (ADVANCED USER'S ED.). 1471

1053-1424 See CONSUMER REFERENCE DISC. 1295

1053-1432 See WOMEN, WATER AND SANITATION. 2248

1053-1440 See ENVIRONMENTAL PERIODICALS BIBLIOGRAPHY ON CD-ROM. 2184

1053-1459 See WEIGHT CONTROL DIGEST (CONSUMER ED.), THE. 4200

1053-1467 See INSIDE QUATTRO PRO. 1287

1053-1521 See BECKETT FOOTBALL CARD MONTHLY. 4887

1053-1556 See PROCESS (WASHINGTON, D.C.). 2354

1053-1564 See DRUG & MARKET DEVELOPMENT. 4299

1053-1572 See WORLDWISE (HANOVER, N.H.). 5709

1053-1580 See ON Q (MILWAUKEE, WIS.). 944

1053-1599 See EXECUTIVE BRIEFING, CASE. 1228

1053-1645 See DAVE HEEREN'S BASKETBALL ABSTRACT. 4892

1053-1653 See AFPC POLICY WORKING PAPER. 45

1053-1661 See SPANG ROBINSON REPORT ON HIGH PERFORMANCE COMPUTING. 1203

1053-170X See CREATIVE TRAINING TECHNIQUES. 939

1053-1718 See TOTAL QUALITY NEWSLETTER. 888

1053-1726 See FRONT-LINE SERVICE. 941

1053-1734 See SERVICE EDGE, THE. 886

1053-1742 See FORMAT (ANN ARBOR, MICH.). 1209

1053-1750 See INTERNATIONAL EDUCATION FORUM (PULLMAN, WASHINGTON). 1831

1053-1769 See SHEPARD'S ILLINOIS TORT REPORTER. 3050

1053-1793 See WRITER'S GUIDELINES (PITTSBURG, MO.). 2925

1053-1807 See JOURNAL OF MAGNETIC RESONANCE IMAGING. 3942

1053-1815 See YOUTH ILLUSTRATOR, THE. 5011

1053-1823 See CHILTON'S GUIDE TO CHASSIS ELECTRONIC CONTROLS AND POWER ACCESSORIES. IMPORT CARS AND TRUCKS. 5410

1053-1831 See COLOR WHEEL. 3377

1053-184X See ADVANCES IN INFORMATION STORAGE SYSTEMS. 1170

1053-1858 See JOURNAL OF PUBLIC ADMINISTRATION RESEARCH AND THEORY. 4659

1053-1866 See CONTRIBUTIONS IN ASIAN STUDIES. 2649

1053-1874 See JOB HUNTER'S SOURCEBOOK. 4205

1053-1459 See WEIGHT CONTROL DIGEST (DALLAS, TEX. 1992), THE. 4200

1053-1890 See CHILD AND YOUTH CARE FORUM. 5278

1053-1904 See COACHING CLINIC'S BASKETBALL COACH. 4890

1053-1912 See E.T. IDEAS. 1737

1053-1920 See POSTMODERN CULTURE. 2852

1053-1955 See NEW JERSEY LAWYERS DIARY AND MANUAL. 3015

1053-1998 See TRAVEL REVIEW, THE. 5496

1053-2013 See CRAFTS RELATED NEWSLETTERS, PERIODICALS, AND PUBLICATIONS ETC. 372

1053-2021 See BARGAIN HUNTERS AND BUDGETEERS OPPORTUNITY NEWSLETTER. 1293

1053-203X See JOURNAL OF THE FRESHMAN YEAR EXPERIENCE. 1833

1053-2048 See FRESHMAN YEAR EXPERIENCE NEWSLETTER, THE. 1825

1053-2064 See ROD & CUSTOM (1990). 5424

1053-2137 See JOURNAL OF HUMAN MUSCLE PERFORMANCE. 3805

1053-2161 See STRESS AND EMOTION. 4619

1053-2188 See CHILTON'S EMISSION CONTROLS APPLICATION GUIDE. 5410

1053-2196 See CHILTON'S EMISSION CONTROL MANUAL. 5410

1053-2277 See COUNTRY GALLERY. 371

1053-2285 See CAKALELE (HONOLULU, HAWAII). 2647

1053-2331 See FACT FINDER (JAMESTOWN, N.Y.), THE. 940

1053-2374 See ROSTER OF MEMBERSHIP AND RESOURCE GUIDE / EMPLOYEE RELOCATION COUNCIL. 1929

1053-2382 See APPAREL PERSONNEL POLICIES & BENEFITS SURVEY. 1650

1053-2404 See ATLANTIC TRADE REPORT & GLOBAL DEFENSE INDUSTRY. 4037

1053-2420 See KIDS' TIME OUT. 1065

1053-2439 See FROMMER'S BUDGET TRAVEL GUIDE. SPAIN ... ON $ ... A DAY. 5475

1053-2455 See FROMMER'S COMPREHENSIVE TRAVEL GUIDE. NEW MEXICO. 5476

1053-2463 See FROMMER'S COLORADO. 5475

1053-2471 See FROMMER'S ARIZONA. 5474

1053-2498 See JOURNAL OF HEART AND LUNG TRANSPLANTATION, THE. 3967

1053-2501 See INTERNATIONAL DIRECTORY OF CONSULTANTS AND CONTRACTORS ACTIVE IN EASTERN EUROPE, AN. 618

1053-2528 See ANNUAL REVIEW OF SEX RESEARCH. 5186

1053-2536 See NELSON'S GUIDE TO PENSION FUND CONSULTANTS. 909

1053-2544 See EQUITIES (NEW YORK, N.Y.). 897

1053-2552 See USED CARS INSIDER. 5427

1053-2560 See NEWPORT DAILY NEWS. 5741

1053-2587 See INNOVATING (RENSSELAERVILLE, N.Y.). 870

1053-2609 See WHAT'S WORKING IN PARENT INVOLVEMENT. 1791

1053-2617 See JOURNAL OF THE NEW ENGLAND GARDEN HISTORY SOCIETY. 2421

1053-2625 See LABYRINTH (BOSTON, MASS.). 2422

1053-2633 See COWBOY MAGAZINE. 2532

1053-2668 See ADEPT REPORT, THE. 1315

1053-2684 See THREE VILLAGE HERALD. 5721

1053-2749 See MINORITIES & WOMEN IN BUSINESS. 5561

1053-2765 See OZARK HAPPENINGS NEWSLETTER. 2466

1053-2781 See ANNUAL REPORT - PULP AND PAPER FOUNDATION (1988). 4232

1053-282X See GOVERNMENT DISC. 1, US FEDERAL GOVERNMENT [COMPUTER FILE], THE. 4651

1053-2838 See LIFE & HEALTH INSURANCE SALES. 2886

1053-2846 See HIGHLAND PARK NEWS (HIGHLAND PARK, ILL.). 5660

1053-2854 See DIRECTORY OF FINE ART REPRESENTATIVES & CORPORATIONS COLLECTING ART. 349

1053-2870 See ABERDEEN'S PAVEMENT MAINTENANCE TRADER. 5438

1053-2889 See REVIEW (WINSLOW, WASH.), THE. 5762

1053-2897 See AFRICA COMMUNICATIONS. 1103

1053-2943 See LIFE AFTER DEATH, AN ISLAMIC PERSPECTIVE. 5043

1053-2951 See EDUCATION IN ISLAM. 5042

1053-2986 See RESIDENTIAL BUILDING COST GUIDE (MILWAUKEE, WIS. : 1986). 626

1053-3001 See DODGE REMODELING & RETROFIT COST DATA. 613

1053-3060 See FLORIDA LAND OWNER. 4837

1053-3087 See BLITZ CHESS. 4857

1053-3338 See NAVA NEWS / NORTH AMERICAN VEXILLOLOGICAL ASSOCIATION. 2623

1053-3362 See ADVOCATE - MINNESOTA EDUCATION ASSOCIATION. 1860

1053-3494 See PROCEEDINGS - AMERICAN MERCHANT MARINE AND MARITIME INDUSTRY CONFERENCE. 5454

1053-3605 See BUZZ (LOS ANGELES, CALIF.). 2529

1053-363X See LAMBDA RISING NEWS. 4829

1053-3648 See SUPERMARKET STRATEGIC ALERT. 2359

1053-3656 See HR HORIZONS. 941

1053-3664 See JOURNAL / CALIFORNIA TRADITIONAL MUSIC SOCIETY. 2321

1053-3672 See ... DEVELOPMENT REPORT CARD FOR THE STATES, THE. 1555

1053-3699 See DISCOUNT AND WHOLESALE PRINTING NEWSLETTER. 4564

1053-3729 See MOLECULAR CRYSTALS AND LIQUID CRYSTALS SCIENCE AND TECHNOLOGY SECTION B, NONLINEAR OPTICS. 4438

1053-377X See JOURNAL OF ENERGY, NATURAL RESOURCES & ENVIRONMENTAL LAW. 3113

1053-380X See CHOREOGRAPHY AND DANCE STUDIES. 1311

1053-3826 See KELLER'S INDUSTRIAL SAFETY REPORT. 2865

1053-3834 See COMPUTER USER'S SURVIVAL MAGAZINE, THE. 1178

1053-3842 See PUNCH IN INTERNATIONAL TRAVEL & ENTERTAINMENT MAGAZINE. 5489

1053-3869 See PORTFOLIO (ZEPHYRHILLS, FLA.). 4375

1053-3877 See ARTHURIAN YEARBOOK, THE. 3364

1053-3923 See BEHAVIORAL HEALTH MANAGEMENT. 1341

1053-4083 See ACTION ALERT (WASHINGTON, D.C. 1980). 5550

1053-4156 See ARTISTS RESOURCE GUIDE TO NEW ENGLAND, THE. 341

1053-4164 See CALIFORNIA REAL ESTATE TRENDS. FORECAST FOR HOUSING AND THE ECONOMY. 4835

1053-4180 See ENVIRONMENTAL HISTORY REVIEW : EHR. 2228

1053-4199 See SOCCER INTERNATIONAL. 4919

1053-4202 See ANTHROPOLOGY OF CONSCIOUSNESS. 230

1053-4210 See DIRECTORY OF DIRECTORY PUBLISHERS. 4813

1053-4229 See JOBS IN HIGHER EDUCATION. 4205

1053-4237 See UKRAINIAN BUSINESS DIGEST. 717

1053-4245 See JOURNAL OF EXPOSURE ANALYSIS AND ENVIRONMENTAL EPIDEMIOLOGY. 2176

1053-4253 See POLLUTION PREVENTION REVIEW. 2239

1053-4261 See ADVANCED LABANOTATION. 1310

1053-427X See RECURSIVE REASONING REPORTS. 2271

1053-4288 See AP3SCEP2SWP (HOUSTON, TEX.). 1642

1053-4296 See SEMINARS IN RADIATION ONCOLOGY. 3824

1053-4318 See AUTO SERVICE INSIDER. 5405

1053-4326 See ONLY THE BEST. 1224

1053-4334 See ULTRAHIGH- AND HIGH-SPEED PHOTOGRAPHY, VIDEOGRAPHY, AND PHOTONICS. 4377

1053-4423 See MAWEWI (MAHWAH, N.J.). 2538

1053-4490 See ADVANCES IN APPLIED BIOTECHNOLOGY SERIES. 3685

1053-4504 See BREEZE (CAPE CORAL, FLA.), THE. 5649

1053-4512 See INTERVENTION IN SCHOOL AND CLINIC. 1880

1053-4547 See AMAZING COMPUTING FOR THE COMMODORE AMIGA. 1264

1053-4555 See OCEAN COUNTY REVIEW. 5711

1053-4563 See FOLIO'S PUBLISHING NEWS. 4815

1053-4571 See DIGEST FOR HOME FURNISHERS. 2905

1053-461X See WINSTON CUP SCENE. 4930

1053-4628 See JOURNAL OF CLINICAL PEDIATRIC DENTISTRY, THE. 1326

1053-4644 See MOTION CONTROL. 2123

1053-4652 *See* FEDERAL STAFFING DIGEST. **4703**

1053-4660 *See* INTERNATIONAL MERGER LAW. **684**

1053-4679 *See* EASTERN EUROPE ON FILE. **2686**

1053-4695 *See* SMALL BUSINESS FORUM. **711**

1053-4725 *See* ENVIRONMENTAL TOXICOLOGY AND WATER QUALITY. **3980**

1053-4733 *See* NESBITT MEMORIAL LIBRARY JOURNAL. **2624**

1053-475X *See* EI ENVIRONMENTAL SERVICES DIRECTORY. **2227**

1053-4768 *See* EXCEPTIONAL HUMAN EXPERIENCE. **4243**

1053-4776 *See* WINE ON LINE. **2372**

1053-4792 *See* SMARANDACHE FUNCTION JOURNAL. **3536**

1053-4806 *See* KOREA BRIEFING. **2506**

1053-4814 *See* LEISURE AND FAMILY FUN: LAFF. **4851**

1053-4822 *See* HUMAN RESOURCE MANAGEMENT REVIEW. **942**

1053-4830 *See* SIGART BULLETIN. **1217**

1053-489X *See* CITIZEN-STANDARD, THE. **5735**

1053-4911 *See* SOUTHWESTERN (DENTON, TEX.), THE. **5182**

1053-492X *See* WORKSITE WELLNESS WORKS. **4200**

1053-4938 *See* CALIFORNIA WATER LAW & POLICY REPORTER. **3110**

1053-4946 *See* GIBSON COUNTY LINES. **2451**

1053-4997 *See* JAPAN NOTEBOOK. **2654**

1053-5314 *See* MOVIES ON TV AND VIDEOCASSETTE. **1135**

1053-5322 *See* WEST'S MISSISSIPPI CASES REPORTED IN SOUTHERN REPORTER, SECOND SERIES. **3074**

1053-5349 *See* IOMA'S REPORT ON CONTROLLING BENEFITS COSTS FOR LAW, DESIGN, CPA, AND OTHER PROFESSIONAL SERVICE FIRMS. **872**

1053-5357 *See* JOURNAL OF SOCIO-ECONOMICS. **1570**

1053-5381 *See* INTERNATIONAL JOURNAL OF OFFSHORE AND POLAR ENGINEERING. **1980**

1053-539X *See* ST. CROIX COUNTY STAR. **5771**

1053-542X *See* NORTHFIELD NEWS, THE. **5697**

1053-5446 *See* PLANETARY CITIZEN : HONORING THE EARTH, HUMANITY, AND THE SACRED IN ALL LIFE. **4357**

1053-5454 *See* DANCING USA. **1313**

1053-5470 *See* NEWS FOR INVESTORS. **909**

1053-5497 *See* SOUTH AFRICA REPORTER. **851**

1053-5500 *See* CASE MANAGEMENT ADVISOR. **3778**

1053-5543 *See* BUENASALUD (ED. NACIONAL). **2596**

1053-556X *See* RISK & BENEFITS JOURNAL, THE. **2892**

1053-5578 *See* TAILS (PADUCAH, KY.). **1087**

1053-5586 *See* INFANT-TODDLER INTERVENTION. **3904**

1053-5594 *See* DATA RESOURCE MANAGEMENT. **865**

1053-5616 *See* ARIZONA JEWISH POST. **5629**

1053-5624 *See* WATER RESOURCES ABSTRACTS. VOLUME 1. **5544**

1053-5632 *See* CONTRACT DESIGN. **2904**

1053-5705 *See* NEWS MESSENGER (MARSHALL, TEX.). **5752**

1053-5748 *See* PALESTINE HERALD-PRESS. **5753**

1053-5780 *See* SHEPARD'S MASSACHUSETTS EXPRESS CITATIONS. **3051**

1053-5799 *See* SHEPARD'S FEDERAL MERIT SYSTEMS CITATIONS. **3050**

1053-5802 *See* WORLD COGENERATION. **2132**

1053-5829 *See* DONALD R. MORRIS NEWSLETTER. **4520**

1053-5837 *See* KITH 'N KIN (FREMONT, OHIO). **2457**

1053-587X *See* IEEE TRANSACTIONS ON SIGNAL PROCESSING. **2064**

1053-5888 *See* IEEE SIGNAL PROCESSING MAGAZINE. **2060**

1053-5918 *See* STEWART'S GUIDE TO ANTIQUE & COLLECTIBLES SHOPS. **252**

1053-5926 *See* TEAMREHAB REPORT. **4382**

1053-5942 *See* TRUCK SALES & LEASING. **5398**

1053-5950 *See* FODOR'S SAN DIEGO. **5473**

1053-6035 *See* ILLUSTRATED DIRECTORY OF HANDICAPPED PRODUCTS, THE. **4389**

1053-6124 *See* WHO'S WHO BUYERS GUIDE TO ELECTRONIC SOURCES (MIDWESTERN ED.). **2085**

1053-6132 *See* WHO'S WHO BUYERS GUIDE TO ELECTRONIC SOURCES (NORTHEASTERN ED.). **2086**

1053-6140 *See* WHO'S WHO BUYERS GUIDE TO ELECTRONIC SOURCES (SOUTHEASTERN ED.). **2086**

1053-6159 *See* WHO'S WHO BUYERS GUIDE TO ELECTRONIC SOURCES (SOUTHWESTERN ED.). **2086**

1053-6175 *See* MOODY'S UNIT INVESTMENT TRUSTS. **908**

1053-6183 *See* INDIANA ENVIRONMENTAL LAW LETTER. **2981**

1053-6191 *See* INDIANA EMPLOYMENT LAW LETTER. **3149**

1053-6205 *See* PC TECHNIQUES. **1289**

1053-6213 *See* INTERACTIVE WORLD. **1113**

1053-623X *See* ATHENS MAGAZINE (ATHENS, GA. 1989). **2528**

1053-6256 *See* VIZIONS (CAMDEN, ME.). **1124**

1053-6272 *See* DISNEY BABIES OUT & AROUND / DISNEY. **1062**

1053-6280 *See* MINNIE 'N ME, THE BEST FRIENDS COLLECTION. **1066**

1053-6302 *See* CHILTON'S GUIDE TO CHASSIS ELECTRONICS AND POWER ACCESSORIES. GENERAL MOTORS. **5410**

1053-6337 *See* LAKEWOOD SENTINEL (1990). **5643**

1053-6345 *See* NEVADA BEVERAGE ANALYST. **2369**

1053-6353 *See* PROFESSIONAL BUILDER & REMODELER. **624**

1053-6396 *See* FAXON GUIDE TO CD-ROM. **1185**

1053-640X *See* EUROPEAN FACULTY DIRECTORY. **1823**

1053-6418 *See* GREEN2000 (WEST CHESTER, PA.). **2173**

1053-6426 *See* MOLECULAR MARINE BIOLOGY AND BIOTECHNOLOGY. **556**

1053-6450 *See* PRODUCERS QUARTERLY. **1162**

1053-654X *See* JOBS IN RECESSIONARY TIMES POSSIBILITY NEWSLETTER. **1681**

1053-6566 *See* ENTERPRISE SYSTEMS JOURNAL. **1184**

1053-6582 *See* ARKANSAS BUSINESS. **639**

1053-6590 *See* TENNESSEAN (1972), THE. **5746**

1053-6620 *See* GRAND ROUNDS PRESS, THE. **3579**

1053-6671 *See* BEST OF THE SUPERSTARS, THE. **383**

1053-668X *See* ATCHISON MAGAZINE. **2528**

1053-6698 *See* TEXAS BUSINESS DIRECTORY. **715**

1053-6728 *See* TECHNOLOGY & LEARNING. **1225**

1053-6736 *See* DUKE JOURNAL OF COMPARATIVE & INTERNATIONAL LAW. **3127**

1053-6744 *See* CREDIT UNION EXECUTIVE (MADISON, WIS. 1989). **786**

1053-6760 *See* SOFTWARE ENGINEERING. **1996**

1053-6825 *See* NATIONAL DIRECTORY OF RETIREMENT FACILITIES. **5180**

1053-6825 *See* DIRECTORY OF RETIREMENT FACILITIES, THE. **5179**

1053-685X *See* DALTON'S PHILADELPHIA METROPOLITAN DIRECTORY. **664**

1053-6868 *See* SECOND SOURCE BIOMEDICAL. **3696**

1053-6876 *See* SECOND SOURCE IMAGING. **3640**

1053-6884 *See* JUKEBOX COLLECTOR. **4127**

1053-6892 *See* SHEPARD'S MISSOURI EXPRESS CITATIONS. **3052**

1053-6906 *See* ONALASKA COMMUNITY LIFE. **5769**

1053-6949 *See* LNG OBSERVER, THE. **4263**

1053-6981 *See* JOURNAL OF NARRATIVE AND LIFE HISTORY. **3400**

1053-699X *See* JOURNAL OF JEWISH THOUGHT & PHILOSOPHY, THE. **5050**

1053-7015 *See* 3X/400 INFORMATION MANAGEMENT. **858**

1053-7031 *See* PHOTOGRAPHIC ART MARKET. **4374**

1053-704X *See* BLACK EMPLOYMENT & EDUCATION. **643**

1053-7104 *See* GREENHOUSE PRODUCT NEWS. **2417**

1053-7147 *See* VISUAL ANTHROPOLOGY REVIEW. **247**

1053-7155 *See* EAST/WEST EXECUTIVE GUIDE. **832**

1053-7163 *See* INITIAL PUBLIC OFFERINGS ANNUAL. **1612**

1053-718X *See* THINK & GROW RICH NEWSLETTER. **888**

1053-7198 *See* I.B.I. GUIDE. **2115**

1053-721X *See* ... TRAVEL CONSULTANTS DIRECTORY, THE. **5495**

1053-7236 *See* POOL PLAYER'S NATIONAL POCKET BILLIARDS DIRECTORY, THE. **4865**

1053-7260 *See* HOME HOW-TO NEWS. **2811**

1053-7279 *See* PHONEFICHE, COMMUNITY CROSS-REFERENCE GUIDE. **1119**

1053-7287 *See* JOURNAL OF GLOBAL BUSINESS (HARRISONBURG, VA.). **687**

1053-7325 *See* NEW WARRIORS, THE. **4864**

1053-7333 *See* BROWN'S DIRECTORY OF INSTRUCTIONAL PROGRAMS (K-8). READING. **1802**

1053-7341 *See* BROWN'S DIRECTORY OF INSTRUCTIONAL PROGRAMS (K-8). WHOLE LANGUAGE/LITERATURE. **1890**

1053-735X *See* BROWN'S DIRECTORY OF INSTRUCTIONAL PROGRAMS (K-8). LANGUAGE ARTS/SPELLING/HANDWRITING. **1889**

1053-7368 *See* BROWN'S DIRECTORY OF INSTRUCTIONAL PROGRAMS (K-8). SOCIAL STUDIES. **1889**

1053-7376 *See* BROWN'S DIRECTORY OF INSTRUCTIONAL PROGRAMS (K-8). MATHEMATICS / PREPARED AND COMPILED BY BROWN PUBLISHING NETWORK. **1802**

1053-7384 *See* BROWN'S DIRECTORY OF INSTRUCTIONAL PROGRAMS (K-8). SCIENCE/HEALTH / PREPARED AND COMPILED BY BROWN PUBLISHING NETWORK. **1889**

1053-7392 *See* BROWN'S DIRECTORY OF INSTRUCTIONAL PROGRAMS (7-12). LANGUAGE ARTS / PREPARED AND COMPILED BY BROWN PUBLISHING NETWORK. **1889**

1053-7406 *See* BROWN'S DIRECTORY OF INSTRUCTIONAL PROGRAMS (7-12). FOREIGN LANGUAGE. **1889**

1053-7414 *See* BROWN'S DIRECTORY OF INSTRUCTIONAL PROGRAMS (7-12). SOCIAL STUDIES / PREPARED AND COMPILED BY BROWN PUBLISHING NETWORK. **1889**

1053-7422 *See* BROWN'S DIRECTORY OF INSTRUCTIONAL PROGRAMS (7-12). MATHEMATICS. **1889**

1053-7430 *See* BROWN'S DIRECTORY OF INSTRUCTIONAL PROGRAMS (7-12). SCIENCE/HEALTH. **5090**

1053-7449 *See* BROWN'S DIRECTORY OF INSTRUCTIONAL PROGRAMS (7-12). VOCATIONAL EDUCATION. **1911**

1053-7457 *See* EAE (RENTON, WASH.), THE. **2259**

1053-7465 *See* DEVELOPMENTS IN NANOTECHNOLOGY. **5099**

1053-749X *See* COMPLICATIONS IN SURGERY. **3963**

1053-7503 *See* RECHARGER (RIVERSIDE, CALIF.). **2241**

1053-7511 See COLUMBIA NEWS-TIMES, THE. 5653

1053-7538 See NORTHWEST PARKS & WILDLIFE. 4169

1053-7619 See EAST ROCHESTER POST-HERALD. 5716

1053-7627 See CLOAK AND DAGGER (1990). 377

1053-7635 See CHILTON'S GUIDE TO FUEL INJECTION AND ELECTRONIC ENGINE CONTROLS. CHRYSLER CARS AND TRUCKS. 5411

1053-7635 See CHILTON'S GUIDE TO FUEL INJECTION AND ELECTRONIC ENGINE CONTROLS. FORD CARS AND TRUCKS. 5411

1053-766X See SMALL BUSINESS CONTROLLER, THE. 711

1053-7694 See CAS JOURNAL. 4108

1053-7740 See STATES IN PROFILE. 5339

1053-7791 See SONG HITS' HEARTBREAKERS. 4153

1053-7805 See SUN CHRONICLE (ATTLEBORO, MASS.). 5690

1053-7813 See ASIAN MEDICINE. 3553

1053-783X See INTERNATIONAL PUBLIC WORKS REVIEW. 4657

1053-7848 See DALIBRARY. 1233

1053-7856 See COMPUTING ARCHIVE. 1180

1053-7864 See IN PERSPECTIVE OF THE BLACK AMERICAN VETERAN. 4045

1053-7880 See DIRECTORY OF ENVIRONMENTAL GROUPS IN THE NEWLY INDEPENDENT STATES AND BALTIC NATIONS, THE. 2163

1053-7899 See MSW MANAGEMENT. 2236

1053-7902 See NATIONAL DIRECTORY OF REAL ESTATE ATTORNEYS, THE. 3013

1053-7929 See AC'S TECH FOR THE COMMODORE AMIGA. 1170

1053-7937 See WRITING ABOUT WOMEN. 3454

1053-8011 See HOBBY INDEX. 2774

1053-802X See ZOOLOGICAL RECORD SEARCH GUIDE, THE. 5601

1053-8097 See CHROMATOGRAM (SAN RAMON, CALIF.). 972

1053-8100 See CONSCIOUSNESS AND COGNITION. 4582

1053-8119 See NEUROIMAGE (SAN DIEGO, CALIF.). 3840

1053-8127 See JOURNAL OF BACK AND MUSCULOSKELETAL REHABILITATION. 3805

1053-8135 See NEUROREHABILITATION (READING, MASS.). 3842

1053-8151 See JOURNAL OF EARLY INTERVENTION. 1880

1053-816X See UROLOGIC NURSING. 3870

1053-8216 See MISSISSIPPI COAST HISTORICAL & GENEALOGICAL SOCIETY. 2461

1053-8259 See JOURNAL OF EXPERIENTIAL EDUCATION, THE. 1880

1053-8283 See SHEPARD'S CALIFORNIA EXPRESS CITATIONS. 3049

1053-8291 See INTERNATIONAL IMAGING SOURCE BOOK. 1190

1053-8305 See MEMBERSHIP DIRECTORY - NATIONAL ROOFING CONTRACTORS' ASSOCIATION. 621

1053-8313 See EURO CABLE TV PROGRAMMING. 1110

1053-8321 See MEDIAWATCH (ALEXANDRIA, VA.). 1117

1053-833X See WRITER'S N.W. 4820

1053-8348 See BEHAVIOR AND PHILOSOPHY. 4576

1053-8356 See AMERICAN JOURNAL OF NUMISMATICS (1989). 2779

1053-8364 See JOURNAL OF PHILOSOPHICAL RESEARCH. 4350

1053-8372 See JOURNAL OF THE HISTORY OF ECONOMIC THOUGHT. 1500

1053-8402 See AMS OFFICE, PROFESSIONAL & DATA PROCESSING SALARIES REPORT. 1643

1053-8437 See ELECTROPHYSIOLOGICAL APPROACH TO THE DIAGNOSIS OF ARRHYTHMIAS, AN. 3704

1053-8445 See JOURNAL OF PROGRESSIVE LEGAL THOUGHT. 2989

1053-8453 See DIRECTORY OF FORESTRY AND NATURAL RESOURCES COMPUTER SOFTWARE. 1182

1053-8496 See QUANTA (PITTSBURGH, PA.). 3427

1053-8542 See INSIGHT (CHICAGO, ILL.). 745

1053-8550 See JOURNAL OF IMMUNOTHERAPY. 3674

1053-8569 See PHARMACOEPIDEMIOLOGY AND DRUG SAFETY. 4321

1053-8607 See STATS (ALEXANDRIA, VA.). 5344

1053-8623 See AFRICAN FARMER (ENGLISH ED.). 45

1053-8631 See BASTA! (CHICAGO, ILL.). 4938

1053-8658 See BOND BUYER'S MUNICIPAL MARKETPLACE, THE. 892

1053-8704 See COMICS BUYER'S GUIDE PRICE GUIDE. 4859

1053-8712 See JOURNAL OF CHILD SEXUAL ABUSE. 5291

1053-8720 See JOURNAL OF GAY & LESBIAN SOCIAL SERVICES. 2794

1053-8739 See JOURNAL OF COLLEGE & UNIVERSITY FOODSERVICE. 2345

1053-8747 See POPULAR CULTURE IN LIBRARIES. 3241

1053-8755 See JOURNAL OF MINISTRY IN ADDICTION & RECOVERY. 1346

1053-8763 See AFRICA INVESTMENT MONITOR. 890

1053-8771 See POLITICAL RISK YEARBOOK. VOL. 6, EUROPE. COUNTRIES OF THE EUROPEAN COMMUNITY. 4532

1053-878X See POLITICAL RISK YEARBOOK. VOL. 7, EUROPE. OUTSIDE THE EUROPEAN COMMUNITY. 4532

1053-8828 See INSIDE PR. 760

1053-8852 See ENVIRONTECH (OAKLAND GARDENS, N.Y.). 2171

1053-8860 See TECHNICAL BRIEF (YALE SCHOOL OF DRAMA. DEPT. OF TECHNICAL DESIGN AND PRODUCTION). 389

1053-8879 See NUTRI-TOPICS (HEALTH PROFESSIONAL/RESEARCHER). 4195

1053-8887 See NUTRI-TOPICS (CONSUMER). 4195

1053-8895 See NUTRI-TOPICS / FOOD AND NUTRITION INFORMATION CENTER, NATIONAL AGRICULTURAL LIBRARY. 4195

1053-8917 See REALSCAN. BROWARD COUNTY. 4845

1053-8925 See REALSCAN. DADE COUNTY. 4845

1053-8933 See AJCU HIGHER EDUCATION REPORT. 1807

1053-8941 See DIRECTORY / ASSOCIATION OF JESUIT COLLEGES AND UNIVERSITIES JESUIT SECONDARY EDUCATION ASSOCIATION. 1820

1053-8968 See PTN (MELVILLE, N.Y.). 4376

1053-8976 See RECORD (TROY, N.Y.). 5720

1053-8992 See LOUISIANA MANUFACTURERS REGISTER. 3482

1053-900X See TEXT TECHNOLOGY. 1205

1053-9026 See CABLE CONTACTS. 1129

1053-9034 See FOOD AND DRUG LAW REPORTS. 2971

1053-9069 See DIRECTORY OF VIDEO RETAILERS. 1131

1053-9093 See AIDS UPDATE (ALBANY, N.Y.). 3664

1053-9123 See CLAY TIMES-JOURNAL, THE. 5625

1053-9131 See BELTON JOURNAL (BELTON, TEX. : 1923). 5747

1053-9158 See WORLDWIDE BROCHURES (PRINT ED.). 5500

1053-9190 See ENVIRONMENT, HEALTH & SAFETY MANAGEMENT. 4774

1053-9212 See BIG BOPPER, THE. 383

1053-9239 See SUNEXPERT (BROOKLINE, MASS.). 1204

1053-9247 See PAINTED HILLS REVIEW. 3421

1053-9263 See CENTRAL BUSINESS REVIEW. 656

1053-9328 See TEST INDUSTRY REPORTER, THE. 2130

1053-9360 See TRAVEL AGENT. 5494

1053-9379 See MCGRAW-HILL'S UTILITY ENVIRONMENT REPORT. 4761

1053-9425 See DAIRY FIELD (1991). 193

1053-9433 See COMMUNICATIONS QUARTERLY. 1152

1053-9484 See BEST OF THE REPUBLIC OF KOREA, THE. 5463

1053-9514 See INTERNATIONAL PRODUCTIVITY JOURNAL. 1612

1053-9549 See AACD LEGAL SERIES, THE. 2926

1053-9557 See INTERNATIONAL JOURNAL OF OCCUPATIONAL HEALTH AND TOXICOLOGY. 2864

1053-959X See FLORIDA RAILROAD DIRECTORY. 5431

1053-9603 See AGRI-VIEW. 150

1053-9611 See CANCER ECONOMICS. 3811

1053-9638 See WORDPERFECT REPORT. 1292

1053-9689 See MORNING NEWS (SPRINGDALE, ARK.), THE. 5632

1053-9697 See CLINICAL DERMATOLOGY. 3718

1053-9700 See CARIBBEAN PERSPECTIVES. 2727

1053-9719 See RAM RESEARCH'S CARDTRAK. 1299

1053-9727 See PHYSICIANS' GUIDE TO RARE DISEASES. 3627

1053-9743 See EMPHASIS (LIMA, OHIO). 4956

1053-9751 See PUBLIC PULSE, THE. 5214

1053-9778 See CROSSCURRENTS (NEW BRUNSWICK, N.J.). 234

1053-9794 See CMS PROCEEDINGS. 4110

1053-9808 See COMPUTER SCIENCE. VERY LARGE SCALE INTEGRATION. 1177

1053-9832 See NONWOVENS MARKETS AND FIBER STRUCTURES REPORT. 5354

1053-9840 See PROFILE. 1869

1053-9859 See WORLD GEOPHYSICAL NEWS. 4282

1053-9867 See FEDERAL SENTENCING REPORTER : FSR. 3164

1053-9891 See CREATION SPIRITUALITY. 4951

1053-993X See SPECTRUM REPORT : NEWS AND ANALYSIS ON THE GLOBAL FREQUENCY ALLOCATION BATTLE, THE. 1122

1053-9948 See NEWSLETTER OF THE ERNST KRENEK ARCHIVE. 4141

1053-9972 See REPORTER. 5770

1053-9980 See COUNTRY VICTORIAN ACCENTS. 2899

1053-9999 See EL DORADO TIMES, THE. 5675

1054-0032 See ADVANCES IN INSTRUMENTATION AND CONTROL. 5081

1054-0032 See ADVANCES IN INSTRUMENTATION AND CONTROL. 5081

1054-0040 See MONTESSORI LIFE. 1882

1054-0067 See EARTH CARE ANNUAL. 2213

1054-0075 See CAMPAIGN (WASHINGTON, D.C. 1991). 4467

1054-013X See NIST TECHNICAL NOTE. 4031

1054-0156 See PRO FOOTBALL ILLUSTRATED. 4913

1054-027X See RANDOL MINING DIRECTORY. 2149

1054-0296 See COUPLES (BOSTON, MASS.). 2794

1054-0326 See BUSINESS LAW SECTION NEWSLETTER. 3096

1054-0407 See CIRCUITS ASSEMBLY. 2038

1054-0415 See COMPUTER PUBLISHING MAGAZINE. 1177

1054-044X See JOURNAL OF OCCUPATIONAL MEDICINE AND TOXICOLOGY. 3981

1054-0458 See REAL ESTATE NEWSLINE (KNOXVILLE, TENN.). 4844

1054-0466 See NGAN PHNG. 3417

1054-0474 See RURAL ELECTRIFICATION MAGAZINE (1987). 1543

1054-0555 See ADWEEK AGENCY DIRECTORY (MIDWESTERN EDITION). 754

1054-0563 See GIS APPLICATION NOTE. 2384

1054-0636 See EDWARD C. ARMSTRONG MONOGRAPHS ON MEDIEVAL LITERATURE, THE. 3383

1054-0652 See NEW YORK NEWSREEL. 4075

1054-0717 See ACOUSTIC PERFORMER. 4098

1054-0725 See EMERGENCY MEDICINE NEWS. 3724

1054-0733 See INSURANCE & TECHNOLOGY. 2883

1054-075X See ORGONOMIC FUNCTIONALISM (RANGELEY, ME.). 3932

1054-0784 See COMPUTHINK WINDOWS WATCHER, THE. 1180

1054-0806 See AMA WINTER EDUCATORS' CONFERENCE. 921

1054-0814 See DBS REPORT, THE. 1109

1054-0830 See JOURNAL OF REGRESSION THERAPY, THE. 4600

1054-0849 See SITUATION AND OUTLOOK REPORT. LIVESTOCK AND POULTRY. 222

1054-0873 See NEW HISTORICISM, THE. 3415

1054-089X See JOURNAL OF DATA & COMPUTER COMMUNICATIONS. 1260

1054-0903 See ECONOMIC DEVELOPMENT ABROAD. 2821

1054-0946 See GUIDE TO SOCIAL SCIENCE AND RELIGION. 5012

1054-0954 See ADVANCES IN MOLECULAR MODELING. 440

1054-0970 See LABMEDICA (WILTON, CONN.). 3603

1054-0997 See FLARE FIRST EDITION. 378

1054-1055 See EJOURNAL (ALBANY, N.Y.). 1183

1054-1063 See CREDIT INSURANCE NEWSLETTER, THE. 2878

1054-1071 See GREAT LAKES MONITOR. 1132

1054-1136 See TIMBER FRAME HOMES. 630

1054-1144 See CHILDREN'S MINISTRY. 4943

1054-1209 See CAL-OSHA REPORTER. 2860

1054-1225 See PROFIT MANAGEMENT. 883

1054-1233 See TOTAL PRODUCTIVE MAINTENANCE : TPM. 888

1054-1365 See CHICAGO JEWISH STAR. 5659

1054-1373 See ILLNESS CRISIS & LOSS. 2251

1054-1381 See ICARUS (NEW YORK, N.Y. : 1991). 3395

1054-139X See JOURNAL OF ADOLESCENT HEALTH. 3593

1054-1403 See STUDIES ON CERVANTES AND HIS TIMES. 3442

1054-1411 See ALATEEN TALK. 1339

1054-1462 See ADVANCED OFFICE TECHNOLOGIES REPORT. 1170

1054-1500 See CHAOS (WOODBURY, N.Y.). 4399

1054-1551 See CROSSSTITCH SAMPLER. 5183

1054-156X See FENESTRATION ... BUYERS' GUIDE. 1606

1054-1578 See ENGLISH LEADERSHIP QUARTERLY. 1863

1054-1608 See EASTERN EUROPEAN ENERGY REPORT. 1937

1054-1624 See ETHNOMUSICOLOGY RESEARCH DIGEST. 4117

1054-1632 See SNAIL'S PACE REVIEW : A BIANNUAL LITTLE MAGAZINE OF CONTEMPARY POETRY, THE. 3471

1054-1640 See INDIAN-AMERICAN (NEW YORK, N.Y.), THE. 2263

1054-1675 See RECORD (SOMERVILLE, MASS.). 4512

1054-1683 See WASHINGTON WEEKLY (WASHINGTON, D.C. 1989). 5073

1054-1713 See BOOKKEEPER'S JOURNAL FOR DENTAL PRACTICES, THE. 1317

1054-1721 See JOURNAL OF ORGANIZATIONAL COMPUTING. 874

1054-1756 See FORGING (CLEVELAND, OHIO). 4565

1054-1802 See JOURNAL OF URBAN AND CULTURAL STUDIES. 1759

1054-1810 See NEPHROLOGY EXCHANGE, THE. 3992

1054-1829 See FRIENDS OF THE EARTH. 2216

1054-1837 See GOD'S WORLD TODAY. 1063

1054-187X See PEDIATRIC PULMONOLOGY. SUPPLEMENT. 3909

1054-1888 See ADVANCES IN HEALTH ECONOMICS AND HEALTH SERVICES RESEARCH. SUPPLEMENT. 3546

1054-1918 See WEST'S FEDERAL TAXATION. CORPORATION, S CORPORATION, AND PARTNERSHIP PRACTICE SETS. 719

1054-1942 See TELECOMMUNICATIONS REPORTS INTERNATIONAL. 1166

1054-1950 See FROM THE GYM TO THE JURY. 2972

1054-1985 See PROGRESSIVE PERIODICALS DIRECTORY. 4822

1054-2000 See DIRECTORY OF INSTITUTE/COMPONENT OFFICERS. 297

1054-2027 See ASFA MARINE BIOTECHNOLOGY ABSTRACTS. 553

1054-2043 See TDR (1988). 5369

1054-206X See UNIVERSITY OF CHICAGO GEOGRAPHY RESEARCH PAPER. 2578

1054-2116 See SOYBEAN GENETICS NEWSLETTER. 188

1054-2167 See FAIRES & FESTIVALS. 4861

1054-2175 See HOOSIER GENEALOGIST, THE. 2454

1054-2213 See DICK VITALE'S BASKETBALL. 4892

1054-2256 See RADIO CONTROL ACTION SERIES. 2777

1054-2264 See MARKETPLACE MAGAZINE. 692

1054-2280 See REHABILITATION TODAY. 3792

1054-2299 See WRITER'S NETWORK, THE. 2926

1054-2310 See ANCESTRY TRAILS. 2437

1054-2329 See TV ETC. 1141

1054-2337 See HISPANIC OUTLOOK IN HIGHER EDUCATION, THE. 1829

1054-2353 See NURSE AUTHOR & EDITOR. 3862

1054-2361 See OHIO'S OFFICIAL SOURCEBOOK. 381

1054-237X See ... SOUTHEAST SOURCEBOOK, THE. 766

1054-2388 See MARKETING EXECUTIVE REPORT. 930

1054-2396 See PPO LETTER, THE. 2890

1054-2434 See INDUSTRIA GRAFICA & ARTES GRAFICAS. 1610

1054-2485 See MACON TELEGRAPH. 5654

1054-2523 See MEDICINAL CHEMISTRY RESEARCH. 4315

1054-2531 See PROCEEDINGS OF THE ... ANNUAL CONFERENCE / ASSOCIATION FOR POPULATION/FAMILY PLANNING LIBRARIES AND INFORMATION CENTERS INTERNATIONAL. 2285

1054-2604 See STATE ENVIRONMENT REPORT. 3116

1054-2620 See IT'S A FANZINE. 4862

1054-2639 See MUSE, MUSIC SEARCH. 4132

1054-2647 See INSIDE IVHS. 5384

1054-2655 See MAD RIVER. 3409

1054-2663 See MEXICO BUSINESS MONTHLY. 906

1054-2671 See HAYKAKAN ELLOPEYJ : KALIFORNIAHAY ENDARDZAK HERATSUTSAK. 2262

1054-268X See OCLC CJK350 NEWSLETTER. 3238

1054-2698 See SUPERCONDUCTIVITY REVIEW. 2082

1054-2701 See SUPREME COURT YEARBOOK, THE. 3061

1054-2728 See CATHOLIC COURIER (1989). 5025

1054-2736 See PORTABLE OFFICE (PETERBOROUGH, N.H.). 1272

1054-2744 See JAWETZ, MELNICK & ADELBERG'S MEDICAL MICROBIOLOGY. 564

1054-2760 See BOARDWATCH MAGAZINE. 1274

1054-2825 See INSIDE HOLLYWOOD. 385

1054-2841 See KENTUCKY CHECKLIST OF STATE PUBLICATIONS. 418

1054-2868 See KIDS DISCOVER. 1065

1054-2876 See BUGLE (COTTONWOOD, ARIZ.), THE. 5629

1054-2884 See PHILOSOPHICAL INQUIRIES. 4355

1054-2914 See TITLE LIST OF DOCUMENTS MADE PUBLICLY AVAILABLE. 4691

1054-2957 See HEALTH AND SEXUALITY. 4778

1054-3007 See JOURNAL OF CONSTRUCTION ACCOUNTING & TAXATION. 618

1054-3015 See KASUN RE'O BEDTIME STORIES. 3401

1054-3023 See JOURNAL OF LEGAL ECONOMICS. 1500

1054-3066 See MEDICAL NEWS REPORT. 3610

1054-3082 See DIRECTORY OF HIGH VOLUME INDEPENDENT DRUG STORES. 831

1054-3090 See FREEDOM REVIEW. 4508

1054-3104 See LISTEN (NEW YORK, N.Y. 1991). 4129

1054-3120 See STUDIES ON THE SHOAH. 2711

1054-3139 See ICES JOURNAL OF MARINE SCIENCE. 1449

1054-3147 See CLASSIC CYCLE REVIEW. 4948

1054-3163 See DESIGN COST AND DATA. 297

1054-318X See SUPER FORD. 5426

1054-3260 See ELECTRIC GENERATING AND DISTRIBUTING COMPANIES. 2043

1054-3287 See NATIONAL ENVIRONMENTAL SCORECARD, THE. 2178

1054-3309 See OFFICIAL MEETING FACILITIES GUIDE, EUROPE. 2808

1054-3317 See ... BANKING TECHNOLOGY DIRECTORY, THE. 777

1054-335X See AVIATION HERITAGE. 13

1054-3376 See ELF (TONAWANDA, N.Y.). 3341

1054-3384 See SOCIAL SERVICES EMPLOYMENT BULLETIN. 5309

1054-3406 See JOURNAL OF BIOPHARMACEUTICAL STATISTICS. 4310

1054-3414 See POLYMER REACTION ENGINEERING. 1990

1054-3422 See BEST OF TV GUIDE CROSSWORDS, THE. 4857

1054-3449 See WAKONDA TIMES. 5744

1054-3457 See DAILY RECORD (1989). 5642

1054-3465 See REFLEX (SEATTLE, WASH.). 329

1054-3473 See EXPERIENCE : THE MAGAZINE OF THE SENIOR LAWYERS DIVISION, AMERICAN BAR ASSOCIATION. 2968

1054-3511 See SUPERVISOR'S QUALITY CLINIC. 714

1054-3562 See JAPANESE GOLF COURSE INVESTMENT REPORT. 904

1054-3589 See ADVANCES IN PHARMACOLOGY. 4289

1054-3600 See HIGH SCHOOL WRESTLING RULES. 4898

1054-3619 See DIRECTORY - ACADEMY OF ACCOUNTING HISTORIANS. 742

1054-3627 See ZAGAT UNITED STATES TRAVEL SURVEY. WESTERN STATES. 2810

1054-3627 See ZAGAT UNITED STATES TRAVEL SURVEY. CENTRAL STATES. 2810

1054-3686 See PUSH! (NEW YORK, N.Y.). 382

1054-3716 See CALEDONIAN-RECORD (SAINT JOHNSBURY, VT.). 5757

1054-3724 See LASERJET JOURNAL. 4566

1054-3791 See NEWS BUREAU CONTACTS. 1135

1054-3821 See CAMPUS CRIME. 3159

1054-383X See MARITIMEWEEK (ARLINGTON, VA.). 3181

1054-3848 See PROPERTY MANAGEMENT MONTHLY. 4843

1054-3856 See HOW TO BUY A NEW OR USED POWER BOAT WITHOUT GETTING BURNED. 593

1054-3872 See JOURNAL OF THE AMERICAN ACADEMY FOR THE PRESERVATION OF OLD-TIME COUNTRY MUSIC, THE. 4126

1054-3880 See NETWORK (NEWARK, N.J.), THE. 5044

1054-3929 See PARADIGM SHIFT : PATRICIA SEYBOLD'S GUIDE TO THE INFORMATION REVOLUTION. 1198

1054-3953 See AD/SOLUTIONS REPORT. 1170

1054-3988 See UPLINE (CHARLOTTESVILLE, VA.). 717

1054-3996 See CDMARC BIBLIOGRAPHIC. 413

1054-4003 See EC INDUSTRIAL REPORT. 1481

1054-4011 See PEN-BASED COMPUTING. 1248

1054-402X See WILEY EMPLOYMENT LAW UPDATE. 3155

1054-4038 See OFFICIAL MAJOR LEAGUE BASEBALL STAT BOOK, THE. 4909

1054-4046 See ENTREPRENEURIAL COUPLES. 672

1054-4054 See LAW FIRMS YELLOW BOOK. 1927

1054-4062 See MUNICIPAL YELLOW BOOK. 1927

1054-4070 See ASSOCIATIONS YELLOW BOOK. 1923

1054-4089 See BEST BED & BREAKFAST IN ENGLAND, SCOTLAND & WALES, THE. 2804

1054-4100 See ASBESTOS WORKERS JOURNAL. 1654

1054-4119 See BIOETHICS FORUM. 2249

1054-4127 See GOUSHA TRUCKER'S ROAD ATLAS. 5440

1054-4135 See HANDGUNS FOR SPORT & DEFENSE. 4898

1054-4178 See GUINNESS BOOK OF SPORTS RECORDS, THE. 4897

1054-4208 See FOCUS (BURBANK, CALIF.). 4241

1054-4240 See FEATURE NEWS PUBLICITY OUTLETS. 5736

1054-4267 See TECHNOLOGY ALERT (PLANTATION, FLA.). 5163

1054-4275 See MANAGEMENT MATTERS (PLANTATION, FLA.). 943

1054-4283 See VOICES OF THE AFRICAN DIASPORA. 2275

1054-4305 See CRYONICS (RIVERSIDE, CALIF.). 3569

1054-4313 See WORLD BANK WATCH, THE. 816

1054-433X See COVER STORY INDEX, THE. 2531

1054-4437 See CRSP INDICES FILES. 895

1054-4542 See GUINNESS BOOK OF SPORTS RECORDS, THE. 4897

1054-4585 See ORIGINAL ... HIGHWAY 17 ALMANAC & GAZETTEER, THE. 1927

1054-4593 See SELLING TO THE OTHER EDUCATIONAL MARKETS. 936

1054-4607 See AMERIKAI MAGYAR LEVELESTAR. 2673

1054-4615 See DOCUMENT MANAGEMENT TECHNOLOGY SOURCEBOOK. 1971

1054-4623 See NEW JERSEY LAKE SURVEY FISHING MAPS GUIDE. 2309

1054-4631 See AMIGAWORLD TECH JOURNAL, THE. 1264

1054-464X See BLACK BOOK STOCK. 4367

1054-4666 See ARCHITECTUS (SAINT PAUL, MINN.). 290

1054-4674 See GAUER DISTINGUISHED LECTURE IN LAW AND PUBLIC POLICY, THE. 2973

1054-4682 See JOURNAL OF HOME & CONSUMER HORTICULTURE. 2421

1054-4690 See ENSEMBLE (SANTA ANA, CALIF.). 5364

1054-4704 See CHINESE MEDICINE AND HEALTH. 3563

1054-4747 See IDEAS UNLIMITED (WASHINGTON, D.C.). 2791

1054-4771 See SHEPARD'S ENVIRONMENTAL LIABILITY IN COMMERCIAL TRANSACTIONS REPORTER. 3116

1054-478X See MEANS PLUMBING CHANGE ORDER COST DATA. 2606

1054-4798 See MEANS MECHANICAL CHANGE ORDER COST DATA. 620

1054-4801 See RURAL LIVING (A&N ELECTRIC COOPERATIVE ED.). 131

1054-481X See VITRO TECHNICAL JOURNAL. 2000

1054-4828 See AUTOMOTIVE ELECTRONICS JOURNAL. 5406

1054-4836 See MEN'S HEALTH (MAGAZINE). 2599

1054-4887 See APPLIED COMPUTATIONAL ELECTROMAGNETICS SOCIETY JOURNAL. 4443

1054-4909 See CONSUMER INFORMATION APPLIANCE. 1295

1054-4933 See INTERNATIONAL DOCUMENTS REVIEW. 4524

1054-5026 See COMPUTER ECONOMIC$ REPORT (INTERNATIONAL ED.). 1176

1054-5034 See BELL'S ALASKA, YUKON & BRITISH COLUMBIA TRAVEL GUIDE. 5462

1054-5042 See TIME TABLE OF HISTORY. BUSINESS, POLITICS, AND MEDIA. 2631

1054-5050 See ROY ANDERSON'S ROAD WORK SAFETY REPORT. 5444

1054-5069 See CREDIT RISK MANAGEMENT REPORT. 785

1054-5131 See CHEMICAL PACKAGING REVIEW, THE. 2162

1054-514X See T.E. NOTES. 3354

1054-5166 See LEMPESIS REPORT ON PERSONAL COMPUTING. 1193

1054-5182 See ATLANTA BUSINESS MAKERS & SHAKERS SERIES. 640

1054-5190 See NEW JERSEY MEDIA GUIDE. 1118

1054-5204 See TODAY'S HEALTHCARE MANAGER. 3793

1054-5212 See RE ARTS & LETTERS : REAL. 329

1054-5409 See CABLE IN THE CLASSROOM. 1129

1054-5417 See SUBSCRIBER NEWS : PRACTICAL INFORMATION FOR USERS OF FATE, FET, FIT, AND FGT. 1204

1054-5425 See DENTAL ADVISOR PLUS, THE. 1320

1054-5441 See AURA (FORT WORTH, TEX.). 2528

1054-545X See HISTORY OF WOMEN RELIGIOUS NEWS AND NOTES. 4963

1054-5468 See DATA CAPTURE CASE STUDIES AND TECHNOLOGY. 5099

1054-5476 See IN VITRO CELLULAR & DEVELOPMENTAL BIOLOGY. PLANT. 513

1054-5816 See EMC TEST & DESIGN. 2053

1054-5840 See MICHIGAN PROFESSIONAL ENGINEER (1990). 1987

1054-5859 See GOVERNMENT & POLITICS ALERT. 4651

1054-5875 See COMMONS (HARRISONBURG, VA.), THE. 1090

1054-5891 See NEW KOREA (LOS ANGELES, CALIF.). 5637

1054-5905 See STUDENT SPORTS (CAL-HI SPORTS ED.). 4924

1054-5913 See AAPPO JOURNAL. 3775

1054-5921 See CONFERENCE RECORD / IEEE GLOBAL TELECOMMUNICATIONS CONFERENCE & EXHIBITION. 1152

1054-5948 See ADA COMPLIANCE GUIDE. 4383

1054-5956 See FUND ACTION. 899

1054-5972 See OFFICIAL IDENTIFICATION AND PRICE GUIDE TO POTTERY & PORCELAIN, THE. 374

1054-5980 See SUNWORLD. (PETERBOROUGH, N.H.) 1272

1054-5999 See APPRAISER NEWS. 4834

1054-6006 See FISHERIES OCEANOGRAPHY. 1449

1054-6243 See RUSSIA (SYRACUSE, N.Y.). 1595

1054-6308 See UKRAINE (SYRACUSE, N.Y.). 1587

1054-6340 See PITTSBURGH QUARTERLY : A MAGAZINE FOR CREATIVE FICTION, POETRY & NONFICTION, THE. 3423

1054-6359 See NORTH CAROLINA EMPLOYMENT LAW LETTER. 3152

1054-6367 See MINNESOTA EMPLOYMENT LAW LETTER. 3152

1054-6375 See MISSOURI EMPLOYMENT LAW LETTER. 3152

1054-6421 See HOUSEMENDING NOTEBOOK. 616

1054-6464 See E&P ENVIRONMENT. 1439

1054-6472 See DEFENSE & AEROSPACE ELECTRONICS. 2040

1054-6499 See EASTERN EUROPEAN & SOVIET TELECOM REPORT. 1154

1054-6510 See USSR NEWS & INFORMATION DIGEST [COMPUTER FILE] : USSR-D / COMPILED & EDITED BY JOHN B HARLAN. 2714

1054-6529 See CHELSEA RECORD (CHELSEA, MASS.), THE. 5688

1054-6561 See ATLANTIC CONTROL STATES/VIRGINIA BEVERAGE JOURNAL. 2363

1054-657X See ATLANTIC CONTROL STATES/NORTH CAROLINA BEVERAGE JOURNAL. 2363

1054-6588 See STUDIES ON SOVIET ECONOMIC DEVELOPMENT. 1640

1054-6596 See SOVIET ARCHIVES OF INTERNAL MEDICINE. 3801

1054-660X See LASER PHYSICS. 4411

1054-6618 See PATTERN RECOGNITION AND IMAGE ANALYSIS. 3526

1054-6634 See MATHEMATICAL MODELING. 3519

1054-6669 See INTERNATIONAL DIRECTORY OF CONTEMPORARY MUSIC. COMPOSERS. 4123

1054-6677 See INTERNATIONAL DIRECTORY OF CONTEMPORARY MUSIC. INSTRUMENTATION. 4123

1054-6723 See MAGIC MAGAZINE (ORLANDO, FLA.). 4904

1054-674X See FITNESS PLUS. 2597

1054-6774 See SAN DIEGO WRITERS MONTHLY. 2924

1054-6790 See CONTRIBUTIONS IN LATIN AMERICAN STUDIES. 2729

1054-6804 See PUTTING OUT : A PUBLISHING RESOURCE GUIDE FOR LESBIAN & GAY WRITERS. 3426

1054-6812 See SALES & USE TAX ALERT. 4747

1054-6839 See DOING BUSINESS IN SENEGAL. 668

1054-6847 See ELECTRONIC NEWS (1991). 2047

1054-6855 See INFORMATION SERIES - NATIONAL TRUST FOR HISTORIC PRESERVATION IN THE UNITED STATES. 2739

1054-6863 See KENNEDY INSTITUTE OF ETHICS JOURNAL. 2252

1054-6871 See RAMDIL SOCIAL SCIENCE RESOURCE GUIDES. 5214

1054-691X See DUKE JOURNAL OF COMPARATIVE & INTERNATIONAL LAW. 3127

1054-6936 See ECONOMIC DEVELOPMENT MONITOR. 1482

1054-6944 See ACADEMIC STUDIES SERIES / JOINT KOREA-U.S. ACADEMIC SYMPOSIUM. 1544

1054-6952 See MEDIA LETTER (CORAL GABLES, FLA.). 845

1054-6960 See WIRELESS INVESTOR. 1169

1054-6995 See BRIEFINGS ON JCAHO. 4769

1054-7002 See KIDSPORTS (ARLINGTON, VA.). 1065

1054-7045 See AEROSPACE PRODUCTS. 5

1054-707X See NEWS-REPORT (BICKNELL, IND.). 5666

1054-7126 See YOUTH MINISTRY QUARTERLY. 5038

1054-7134 See INFORMATION CENTER QUARTERLY REPORTS. 870

1054-7142 See HAZMAT NEWS. 2231

1054-7150 See SOUTHERN SHIPPER. 5457

1054-724X See TEXT AND PRESENTATION. 5369

1054-7258 See MULTIMEDIA & VIDEODISC MONITOR. 1619

1054-7304 See CREDIT UNION TECHNOLOGY. 786
1054-7312 See WORKPLACE INJURY REPORTER. 1719
1054-7355 See MEMBERSHIP DIRECTORY / ALOA, ASSOCIATED LOCKSMITHS OF AMERICA, INC. 4206
1054-7436 See COMMUTER AIR INTERNATIONAL. 5380
1054-7444 See FM RADIO LOG. 1111
1054-7452 See TRADE. 2548
1054-7460 See PRESENCE (CAMBRIDGE, MASS.). 1216
1054-7479 See AMERICAN PERIODICALS : A JOURNAL OF HISTORY, CRITICISM, AND BIBLIOGRAPHY. 4812
1054-7495 See HYMNOLOGY ANNUAL, THE. 4122
1054-7517 See ENVIRONMENT TODAY. 2166
1054-7541 See AIPE FACILITIES. 1964
1054-755X See BROCKWAY RECORD, THE. 5735
1054-7568 See DIRECTORY OF NON-FACULTY BARGAINING AGENTS IN INSTITUTIONS OF HIGHER EDUCATION. 1663
1054-7576 See PORTABLE OFFICE. BUYER'S GUIDE 4214
1054-7606 See VINYAR TENGWAR. 3332
1054-7665 See VISIONMONDAY (NEW YORK, N.Y.). 4217
1054-7673 See NCRTL SPECIAL REPORT. 1901
1054-7681 See HANDBOOK OF COMPARATIVE ECONOMIC POLICIES. 1493
1054-769X See GRANT/ACCESS. 4652
1054-7703 See CELLULAR & MOBILE INTERNATIONAL. 1151
1054-772X See YEAR BOOK OF CLINICAL MICROBIOLOGY. 571
1054-7738 See CLINICAL NURSING RESEARCH. 3853
1054-7746 See STATEMENTS (CHICAGO, ILL. 1985). 309
1054-7762 See CURRENT JOBS FOR GRADUATES. 4203
1054-7789 See SCANDAL SHEET. 4865
1054-7819 See WORKERS' COMP ADVISOR (CALIFORNIA ED.). 2896
1054-7835 See BRICKER'S INTERNATIONAL DIRECTORY. VOL. 1, LONG-TERM UNIVERSITY-BASED EXECUTIVE PROGRAMS. 862
1054-7843 See BRICKER'S INTERNATIONAL DIRECTORY. VOL. 2, SHORT-TERM UNIVERSITY-BASED EXECUTIVE PROGRAMS. 862
1054-7932 See NORRIDGE HARWOOD HEIGHTS NEWS. 5661
1054-7940 See COUNTRYSIDE (BARRINGTON, ILL.). 5659
1054-7959 See WORLDWIDE PETROLEUM PHONE/FAX/TELEX DIRECTORY. 4282
1054-7967 See INSIDE IMMIGRATION : THE PRACTICE ADVISORY. 1919
1054-7983 See LINCOLN JOURNAL (LINCOLN, NEB.). 5706
1054-8017 See ENVIRONMENTAL FINANCE (NEW YORK, N.Y.). 2167
1054-8025 See INSIDE JAPAN : HARVARD'S UNDERGRADUATE JAPAN JOURNAL. 2654
1054-8033 See HOME SCHOOL RESEARCHER. 1751
1054-8068 See PACIFIC RIM ENTREPRENEUR. ASIAN MARKET UPDATE. 848
1054-8076 See MOBILE HOME & RV TRAILER GUIDE, NEW & USED VALUES. 5387
1054-8084 See EXOTIC CARS QUARTERLY. 5414
1054-8106 See BOXING TODAY (NEW YORK, N.Y. 1991). 4888
1054-8122 See ELLERY QUEEN'S MYSTERY MAGAZINE. 5074
1054-8149 See HERALD TRIBUNE CROSSWORD PUZZLES ONLY. 4862
1054-8165 See HERALD TRIBUNE CROSSWORDS & OTHER WORD GAMES. 4862
1054-8173 See PAGEMAKER IN-DEPTH (WINDOWS ED.). 1198

1054-8238 See NATIONAL YELLOW BOOK OF FUNERAL DIRECTORS, THE. 2407
1054-8246 See TREASURE FACTS. 4855
1054-8254 See MACARONI (MINNEAPOLIS, MINN.). 2537
1054-8270 See CENTRAL CITIES SIGHT AND SOUND. 384
1054-8289 See FUTURE OF CHILDREN / CENTER FOR THE FUTURE OF CHILDREN, THE DAVID AND LUCILE PACKARD FOUNDATION, THE. 5286
1054-8297 See ENVIRONMENTAL LAW ANTHOLOGY. 3111
1054-8300 See ANNUAL RESEARCH REPORT / RICE RESEARCH STATION. 163
1054-8319 See FRUIT CROPS FACT SHEET. 172
1054-8327 See EXPORT SALES AND MARKETING MANUAL. 834
1054-8335 See EUROPE 1992 AND BEYOND (MINNEAPOLIS, MINN.). 833
1054-8351 See VIRGINIA FACTS (DALLAS, TEX.). 2765
1054-836X See ON TRACK (HARLINGEN, TEX.). 4911
1054-8378 See THEATRE TOPICS. 5371
1054-8386 See SEMIOTICS AND THE HUMAN SCIENCES. 5218
1054-8394 See JOURNAL OF MULTISTATE TAXATION, THE. 4734
1054-8408 See JOURNAL OF TRAVEL AND TOURISM MARKETING. 5482
1054-8424 See HAWAII BAR JOURNAL (1992). 2977
1054-8459 See DAILY LEDGER, POST DISPATCH. 5634
1054-8483 See MONTHLY DIGESTS OF SOVIET ELECTRONICS PAPERS. 2073
1054-8491 See SIMPSONS ILLUSTRATED. 388
1054-8505 See CLINICS IN COMMUNICATION DISORDERS. 3887
1054-8513 See PHYSICAL THERAPY PRACTICE. 4381
1054-8521 See TODAY IN MEDICINE. FAMILY PRACTICE. 3739
1054-853X See INTERNATIONAL JOURNAL OF ENERGY, ENVIRONMENT, ECONOMICS. 1947
1054-8556 See COGNIZER REPORT. 1175
1054-8580 See WOMAN DIVER. 4930
1054-8637 See WORLD TRADE (IRVINE, CALIF.). 858
1054-8645 See AI REVIEW OF PRODUCTS, SERVICES, AND RESEARCH. 1964
1054-867X See PC ADVISOR. 1198
1054-8688 See CURRENT THOUGHTS AND TRENDS. 5012
1054-8696 See INTELLIGENT SYSTEMS REPORT. 1213
1054-8718 See OH! ZONE. 2179
1054-8726 See FAMILY DYNAMICS OF ADDICTION QUARTERLY. 1344
1054-8734 See JOURNAL OF UROGENITAL PATHOLOGY. 3991
1054-8742 See GLOBAL TRADE WHITE PAGES. 838
1054-8769 See BLACK HISTORY MONTHLY (LITTLE ROCK, ARK.). 2256
1054-8777 See DICKENS' UNIVERSE. 3381
1054-8793 See NFPA JOURNAL. 2292
1054-8807 See CARDIOVASCULAR PATHOLOGY. 3701
1054-8815 See RADIOLOGICAL INSPECTION REPORTS. 2240
1054-8823 See WORLD LETTER (IOWA CITY, IOWA). 3454
1054-884X See GAME PLAYERS NINTENDO GUIDE. 4861
1054-8866 See IMMUNIZATION ALERT, THE. 4784
1054-8874 See CHRONICLE OF LATIN AMERICAN ECONOMIC AFFAIRS. 1469
1054-8882 See CENTRAL AMERICA UPDATE (ALBUQUERQUE, N.M.). 4467
1054-8890 See SOURCEMEX [COMPUTER FILE]. 1521

1054-8890 See SOURCEMEX (ALBUQUERQUE, N.M.). 1521
1054-8904 See GUIDE TO PHOTOGRAPHY WORKSHOPS & SCHOOLS. 4370
1054-8912 See MUSCLE MUSTANGS & FAST FORDS. 5421
1054-8939 See JOURNAL OF REGULATION AND SOCIAL COSTS. 1500
1054-8955 See CALIFORNIA TRADESHOW & EXHIBIT CALENDAR. 757
1054-8963 See ARIZONA EVENTS CALENDAR. 313
1054-898X See FOOTWEAR PLUS. 1084
1054-8998 See CLEARING (ELIZABETHTOWN, N. Y.), THE. 2818
1054-903X See SHEPARD'S OKLAHOMA EXPRESS CITATIONS. 3053
1054-9048 See RADIOWEEK. 1138
1054-9056 See COMPASS (SYRACUSE, N.Y.). 5412
1054-9099 See PRODUCTION RESOURCE, THE. 1622
1054-9102 See BIBLIOGRAPHIES AND INDEXES IN LATIN AMERICAN AND CARIBBEAN STUDIES. 2723
1054-9110 See REFERENCE GUIDES TO ARCHIVAL AND MANUSCRIPT SOURCES IN WORLD HISTORY. 2627
1054-9153 See MAGNOLIA (WINSTON-SALEM, N.C.). 2424
1054-9161 See DIRECTORY OF MASTER GARDENING PROGRAMS IN THE UNITED STATES AND CANADA. 2413
1054-917X See CURRENTS IN EMERGENCY CARDIAC CARE. 3704
1054-9188 See NCPHS NEWSLETTER. 1146
1054-9196 See FACILITY STRATEGIES. 1155
1054-9218 See ABSTRACTS IN INFECTIOUS DISEASE. 3711
1054-9226 See GENEVA CHRONICLE (BERKELEY, CALIF.). 2262
1054-9277 See OFFICIAL GUIDE FOR THE TRANSPORTATION OF HAZARDOUS MATERIALS, THE. 2238
1054-9315 See GRID NEWS (LANSING, MICH.). 1277
1054-9323 See EQUINE BUSINESS JOURNAL. 1084
1054-9331 See WILEY CONSTRUCTION LAW UPDATE. 631
1054-9358 See SEARCH (NEW YORK, N.Y. 1991). 3640
1054-9366 See NEW VOICES IN POETRY AND PROSE. 3416
1054-9390 See ISLA (MANGILAO, GUAM). 238
1054-9404 See LITERATI INTERNAZIONALE. 3406
1054-9412 See NOVO DIABETES CARE PROFILE. 3732
1054-9447 See NUCLEAR PLANT MAINTENANCE NEWSLETTER. 2157
1054-9463 See BANKRUPTCY YEARBOOK AND ALMANAC, THE. 777
1054-9471 See NATIONAL DIRECTORY OF COURTS OF LAW, THE. 3013
1054-948X See HUMAN RIGHTS WATCH WORLD REPORT. 4509
1054-951X See REFINING & GAS PROCESSING INDUSTRY : WORLDWIDE. 4276
1054-9536 See ARIZONA DAILY SUN (FLAGSTAFF, ARIZ.). 5629
1054-9552 See ROCKY MOUNTAIN GARDENER. 2430
1054-9587 See TODAY'S WOMAN. 5567
1054-9595 See AMERICAN WOMAN (NEW YORK, N.Y. 1991). 5550
1054-9609 See DIAGNOSTICS INTELLIGENCE. 3571
1054-9641 See NATURE SOUTH. 4169
1054-9668 See MICROELECTRONICS MANUFACTURING TECHNOLOGY. 2072
1054-9676 See LIBRARY MOSAICS. 3226
1054-9684 See MINNEAPOLIS AREA REALTOR. 4841

1054-9692 See DOCUMENT IMAGE AUTOMATION. 1277

1054-9706 See DOCUMENT IMAGE AUTOMATION UPDATE. 1277

1054-9714 See JOURNAL OF PHASE EQUILIBRIA. 4006

1054-9757 See BEST VACATION RENTALS. CARIBBEAN. 5463

1054-9765 See BEST VACATION RENTALS, EUROPE :A TRAVELER'S GUIDE TO COTTAGES, CONDOS, AND CASTLES. 5463

1054-9781 See AFRICAN CHRONICLE, THE. 2636

1054-979X See TECHSCAN (NEW YORK, N.Y.). 5165

1054-9803 See PCR METHODS AND APPLICATIONS. 1045

1054-9811 See JOURNAL OF SUSTAINABLE FORESTRY. 2386

1054-982X See TEXTILE FINANCIAL OUTLOOK. ENGINEERING. 5357

1054-9838 See MIDDLE EAST CIVIL AVIATION. 28

1054-9846 See H & R BLOCK ... INCOME TAX GUIDE. 4730

1054-9919 See OERI BULLETIN. 1770

1054-9935 See SATELLITE LEARNING. 1846

1054-9986 See FULD & COMPANY LETTER, THE. 1635

1054-9994 See CASH RICH COS. 782

1055-0038 See IN THE COMPANY OF POETS. 3464

1055-0054 See HEALING HEALTHCARE NETWORK NEWSLETTER. 3581

1055-0097 See ARIZONA HIGH TECH DIRECTORY. 2036

1055-0100 See BALDWIN'S OHIO SCHOOL LAW JOURNAL. 1727

1055-0119 See SOUTHWEST BUSINESS REVIEW (SAN MARCOS, TEX.). 713

1055-0127 See AFRICAN ANVIL AND BUSINESS NEWS, THE. 637

1055-0135 See SLIDE GUITARIST. 4153

1055-0178 See POCKET PDR [COMPUTER FILE]. 3628

1055-0186 See DRUG INTERACTIONS AND SIDE EFFECTS SYSTEM. 4300

1055-0224 See WRITERS' WORKSHOP. 2926

1055-0232 See THUNDERMUG REPORT. 3446

1055-0259 See POWDER COATING. 1991

1055-0267 See VIDEO ANNUAL, THE. 3255

1055-0283 See INSIDE MCI. 1157

1055-0305 See WOUND BALLISTICS REVIEW. 3179

1055-0321 See PRATT CITY COMMUNITY NEWSPAPER. 5628

1055-033X See HACK'D (WOODBRIDGE, VA.). 4081

1055-0348 See WAVES (SPRING VALLEY, CALIF.). 2096

1055-0356 See ABERDEEN'S CONCRETE TRADER. 597

1055-0364 See DECOY MAGAZINE. 2773

1055-0380 See AIDS & SOCIETY. 3663

1055-0399 See EDI WORLD. 2042

1055-0461 See COLLEGE BROADCASTER. 1130

1055-0488 See TRAVEL SMARTER. 5496

1055-0496 See AMERICAN JOURNAL ON ADDICTIONS, THE. 1340

1055-050X See JOURNAL OF PSYCHOTHERAPY PRACTICE AND RESEARCH, THE. 3929

1055-0518 See CHILD ASSESSMENT NEWS. 4580

1055-0526 See ENGINEERING DEPARTMENT MANAGEMENT & ADMINISTRATION REPORT. 866

1055-0534 See MBA NEWSLETTER, THE. 692

1055-0542 See INTELLIGENT SYSTEMS : THE NEWSLETTER OF THE FOUNDATION FOR INTELLIGENT SYSTEMS IN THE SOCIAL SCIENCES, ARTS & HUMANITIES. 5204

1055-0550 See BLACK HISTORY IS NO MYSTERY. 2256

1055-0577 See INSIDE QUICKBASIC. 1189

1055-0607 See SOVIET AGRICULTURAL SCIENCES. 136

1055-0607 See DAIRY FIELD (1991). 193

1055-0615 See AMERICAN SKIER. 4883

1055-0623 See CORPORATE GIVING DIRECTORY. 4335

1055-0658 See DAILY GRAPHS. NASDAQ (OTC)/AMERICAN STOCK EXCHANGE. 895

1055-0666 See CONSUMER MEDIA TECH. 1109

1055-0674 See AMERICAN BUNGALOW. 598

1055-0682 See BEST OF KERVIN FONDREN, THE. 3460

1055-0690 See MINORITY LITERARY EXPO. 3347

1055-0704 See COLORBAT LAB PRO. 347

1055-0712 See PERIO REPORTS. 1332

1055-0720 See SECURITIES OPERATIONS MAGAZINE. 913

1055-0763 See NEW HAMPSHIRE GENEALOGICAL RECORD, THE. 2462

1055-0771 See DEALMAKERS (BELLE MEAD, N.J.), THE. 4836

1055-0801 See U.S. CONSTITUTION REVIEW, THE. 3067

1055-081X See FILM COMPOSERS GUIDE. 4069

1055-0828 See TELEVISION DIRECTORS GUIDE. 1140

1055-0836 See FILM ACTORS GUIDE. 4069

1055-0844 See TODAY'S MANAGER. 888

1055-0852 See WHO IS WHO (WAYNESVILLE, N.C.). 2183

1055-0860 See EDUCATION IN THE PUBLIC EYE : THE NATIONAL PRESS REVIEW OF COMMUNITY ISSUES IN EDUCATION. 1739

1055-0879 See BEST PLACES TO STAY IN MEXICO. 5463

1055-0887 See JOURNAL OF ADDICTIVE DISEASES. 1345

1055-0895 See RANDOM LENGTHS YARDSTICK. 2391

1055-0909 See WORKS (ALTADENA, CALIF.). 5010

1055-0917 See MOVIELINE (LOS ANGELES, CALIF.). 4075

1055-0925 See JOURNAL OF ECONOMICS AND FINANCE. 1499

1055-0933 See SENIOR YELLOW PAGES. 424

1055-0976 See BLACK AND GAY. 2256

1055-0984 See METAPHOR (SAN JOSE, CALIF.). 1093

1055-0992 See METROPOLITAN (SAN JOSE, CALIF.). 1801

1055-1026 See STARCH TESTED COPY. 766

1055-1042 See SOVIET PERSPECTIVES. 2710

1055-1050 See INDOOR AIR REVIEW. 1609

1055-1069 See NATIONAL LEGAL EXCHANGE. 3013

1055-1077 See AMERICAN BANKER. CONSUMER SURVEY. 769

1055-1123 See SUBSEA-DATA-BASE (HOUSTON, TEX.). 1523

1055-1131 See ENTERTAINMENT EMPLOYMENT NETWORK. 1667

1055-114X See ENTERTAINMENT EMPLOYMENT WEEKLY. 1667

1055-1158 See RESEARCH IN RELIGION AND FAMILY--BLACK PERSPECTIVES. 2272

1055-1166 See WILD EARTH. 2183

1055-1174 See GUIDE TO ORANGE COUNTY FREELANCE MARKETS. 678

1055-1182 See HRD DIGEST AND ABSTRACTS. 2847

1055-1190 See OYE! (NEW YORK, N.Y.). 1902

1055-1204 See LISTO (NEW YORK, N.Y.). 2537

1055-1212 See SCHOLASTIC MATH POWER. 3533

1055-1220 See COPAINS (NEW YORK, N.Y.). 2531

1055-1239 See ENCORE! (NEW YORK, N.Y. 1991). 2533

1055-1247 See AGENDA (NEW YORK, N.Y. 1991). 1723

1055-128X See LAW OFFICE COMPUTING. 2996

1055-1298 See SOLID WASTE MANAGEMENT ECONOMICS REPORT : SWMER. 2243

1055-1336 See OUR GIFTED CHILDREN. 1883

1055-1344 See SIBERIAN ADVANCES IN MATHEMATICS. 3535

1055-1352 See CURRENT ISSUES IN EXERCISE SCIENCE. 2596

1055-1360 See JOURNAL OF LINGUISTIC ANTHROPOLOGY. 239

1055-1379 See JOURNAL OF NUTRITION IN RECIPE & MENU DEVELOPMENT. 4193

1055-1387 See JOURNAL OF TREE FRUIT PRODUCTION. 177

1055-1395 See NY SCHOOL BOARDS. 1868

1055-1409 See JR. HIGH MINISTRY. 4971

1055-1468 See FOREIGN TRADE (MCLEAN, VA.). 836

1055-1476 See IMAGES (RESTON, VA.). 3941

1055-1522 See OUR MEN. 3996

1055-1573 See WORLD FINANCE (WASHINGTON, D.C.). 1641

1055-1581 See REFLECTIONS ON REALITY. 4990

1055-159X See DIXON ARNETT'S CALIFORNIA COMMENT FROM WASHINGTON, DC. 4472

1055-1603 See PHYSICIAN MANAGER. 3791

1055-162X See EYEBEAM (AUSTIN, TEX.). 350

1055-1700 See CYCLE PROJECTIONS. 787

1055-1719 See WINDOW ON THE ARTS, LITERATURE, AND SOCIETY, THE. 333

1055-1727 See ROGER! ROGER!. 2544

1055-176X See MEDIAWEEK (NEW YORK, N.Y.). 933

1055-1778 See OFFICIAL CITY GUIDE. 5487

1055-1808 See LAN COMPUTING. 1193

1055-1913 See TEXAS CRIMINAL LAW AND MOTOR VEHICLE HANDBOOK. 3109

1055-1921 See GEORGIA BYWAYS. 2734

1055-1948 See JOURNAL OF THE WRITERS GUILD OF AMERICA. WEST. 3400

1055-1964 See N.A.D.A. SMALL BOAT APPRAISAL GUIDE. 594

1055-1972 See N.A.D.A. LARGE BOAT APPRAISAL GUIDE. 594

1055-2022 See ADWEEK'S GUIDE TO NEW ENGLAND MARKETS & MEDIA. 920

1055-2049 See HORIZONTN FUN KULTUR UN LEBN / WORKMEN'S CIRCLE. 5247

1055-2057 See DRUG THERAPY (WALTHAM, MASS.). 4301

1055-2073 See JOURNAL OF SOUTHEAST ASIA BUSINESS. 687

1055-2081 See R & R MILITARY RETIREE: RETIREMENT & RELOCATION MILITARY RETIREE. 4054

1055-209X See SINE (HESPERIA, CALIF.). 2081

1055-2103 See WORLDWIDE ACCOUNTING, BUSINESS, AND EDUCATION JOURNAL, THE. 753

1055-2146 See ISAAC ASIMOV'S SCIENCE FICTION MAGAZINE (1990). 3397

1055-2154 See INVESTOR'S ENVIRONMENTAL REPORT / IRRC, ENVIRONMENTAL INFORMATION SERVICE. 903

1055-2162 See BIOTECHNOLOGY, CURRENT PROGRESS. 3689

1055-2170 See EDMUND'S PRESENTS ... ECONOMY CAR BUYING GUIDE. 5414

1055-2189 See EDMUND'S PRESENTS ... NEW CAR PRICE ANNUAL. 5414

1055-2197 See EDMUND'S PRESENTS ... CAR, VAN & TRUCK PREVIEW. 5414

1055-2200 See EDMUND'S PRESENTS ... CAR SAVVY. 5414

1055-2219 See EDMUND'S PRESENTS ... MUSCLE CAR BUYER'S GUIDE. 5414

1055-2227 See ALASKAMEN USA. 5550

1055-2243 See THRUST FOR EDUCATIONAL LEADERSHIP. 1873

1055-2278 See VESTNIK (OWINGS MILLS, MD.). 2275

1055-2286 See ART & DESIGN NEWS. 376

1055-2294 See BECKETT FOOTBALL CARD MONTHLY. 4887

1055-2316 See MONOGRAPHS IN WORLD ARCHAEOLOGY. 275

1055-2324 See SHOPPER'S GUIDE (COLORADO SPRINGS, COLO.), THE. 1299

1055-2340 See SPRAY TECHNOLOGY & MARKETING. 4222

1055-2359 See PEDIATRIC OPTOMETRY & VISION THERAPY. 4217

1055-2367 See FULL-TIME DADS. 2280

1055-2375 See INVESTMENT VISION. 903

1055-2383 See GEOPHYSICAL ABSTRACTS IN PRESS. 1405

1055-2405 See PRESENTFUTURES REPORT, THE. 1621

1055-2421 See FAULKNER & GRAY'S ... EUROPEAN BUSINESS DIRECTORY. 675

1055-2448 See CHILD CARE DIRECTORY & FAMILY RESOURCE GUIDE (DENVER METRO ED.), THE. 2277

1055-2456 See TAX PENALTIES : THE COMPLETE GUIDE TO PENALTIES UNDER THE INTERNAL REVENUE SERVICE. 4753

1055-2464 See STUDIES IN ANTHROPOLOGY AND HISTORY. 246

1055-2472 See ALI-ABA REAL ESTATE COURSE MATERIALS JOURNAL. 4834

1055-2480 See ALI-ABA TAX COURSE MATERIALS JOURNAL. 4709

1055-2510 See SHEPARD'S ARIZONA EXPRESS CITATIONS. 3048

1055-2545 See ASSOCIATION PUBLISHING. 4812

1055-2561 See TEXAS INDUSTRY ENVIRONMENTAL ALERT. 3116

1055-257X See LOUISIANA INDUSTRY ENVIRONMENTAL ALERT. 2177

1055-2588 See NEW JERSEY INDUSTRY ENVIRONMENTAL ALERT. 2178

1055-2596 See PENVISION NEWS. 1621

1055-2626 See LEADER (ANDERSON, IND.). 4973

1055-2634 See NFO REPORTER, THE. 112

1055-2685 See GOLDMINE (1985). 2774

1055-2693 See GENEALOGICAL SOCIETY OF CHICKASAW COUNTY, THE. 2450

1055-2715 See DETROIT NEWS (DETROIT, MICH.), THE. 5691

1055-2723 See SYNDICATED COLUMNIST CONTACTS. 2924

1055-2758 See DETROIT FREE PRESS (DETROIT, MICH., 1858). 5691

1055-2766 See NMFS FISHERIES MARKET NEWS REPORT. 2309

1055-2774 See STEP-BY-STEP ELECTRONIC DESIGN. 1235

1055-2782 See DRINKING WATER & BACKFLOW PREVENTION. 5533

1055-2804 See INTERCULTURAL STUDIES. 5204

1055-2812 See BBS CALLERS DIGEST. 1274

1055-2820 See SEN TEX. 5181

1055-2839 See EUROPEAN HOME VIDEO. 1111

1055-2863 See RECORDS OF WILLS, SURROGATES COURT, STATEN ISLAND, NEW YORK (RICHMOND COUNTY). 3036

1055-2863 See RECORD OF WILLS : SURROGATES COURT. STATEN ISLAND, NEW YORK. 2469

1055-2871 See CROSS STITCHER, THE. 5183

1055-291X See BFLO JOURNAL. 2723

1055-2952 See DRUG STORE NEWS FOR THE PHARMACIST. 4301

1055-2960 See WXXI (ROCHESTER, N.Y.). 1143

1055-2979 See STALLION DIRECTORY. 2802

1055-3010 See MEMBERSHIP DIRECTORY. 4130

1055-3037 See PUBLIC POLICY AND AGING REPORT, THE. 5181

1055-3045 See JOURNAL OF ET NURSING. 3858

1055-3053 See TIMES-PICAYUNE (NEW ORLEANS, LA. 1986), THE. 5684

1055-3061 See ABERDEEN EXAMINER (ABERDEEN, MISS.: 1866). 5704

1055-307X See MEALEY'S LITIGATION REPORTS. PUNITIVE DAMAGES & TORT REFORM. 2887

1055-3088 See JOURNAL OF NURSING JOCULARITY. 3859

1055-3096 See JOURNAL OF INFORMATION SYSTEMS EDUCATION. 1192

1055-310X See JOURNAL OF INFORMATION SYSTEMS EDUCATION. 1192

1055-3134 See TENNESSEE NURSE. 3870

1055-3142 See FLASH. (LOS ANGELES/WEST ED.). 378

1055-3150 See BIOGERON (BLOOMINGTON, IND.). 3556

1055-3169 See TODAY'S FAMILY (ST. PAUL, MINN.). 2286

1055-3177 See NOVON (SAINT LOUIS, MO.). 520

1055-3185 See INTERNATIONAL JOURNAL OF ORGANIZATIONAL ANALYSIS. 684

1055-3193 See BANK INVESTMENT REPRESENTATIVE. 775

1055-3207 See SURGICAL ONCOLOGY CLINICS OF NORTH AMERICA. 3824

1055-3215 See ISLAND TIMES (HILTON HEAD ISLAND, S.C.). 5742

1055-3223 See FEED & GRAIN. 200

1055-3231 See PLUMBING, HEATING, PIPING. 2607

1055-324X See JOURNAL OF AMERICAN HEALTH POLICY, THE. 5291

1055-3258 See MICROCOMPUTER TRAINER, THE. 1269

1055-3266 See CIVIL WAR REGIMENTS. 2728

1055-3274 See INTEGRATED MANUFACTURING (ROCKFORD, ILL.). 3481

1055-3290 See JOURNAL OF THE ASSOCIATION OF NURSES IN AIDS CARE, THE. 3860

1055-3304 See O'DWYER'S FARA REPORT. 700

1055-3339 See COLOR BUSINESS REPORT. 1231

1055-3355 See INDIANAPOLIS 500 YEARBOOK, THE. 5417

1055-3371 See GLOBAL CONNECTOR, THE. 869

1055-3401 See SINGLE STYLE FOR WRITERS DIALOGUE GROUP. 3437

1055-3428 See QUICK REFERENCE GUIDE TO SCHOOL DROPOUTS. 1776

1055-3436 See US2U AMERICAN TECHNOLOGY REPORTER. 5168

1055-3460 See BUILDER'S BEST HOME DESIGNS. 602

1055-3479 See CUSTOM HOME. 296

1055-3487 See DIRECTORY OF DIPLOMATES / AMERICAN BOARD OF FAMILY PRACTICE. 3737

1055-3495 See HAZARDOUS WASTE MANAGEMENT & BUSINESS OPPORTUNITIES NEWSLETTER / CAE CONSULTANTS INC. 2231

1055-3517 See HEALTH BENEFITS LETTER. 4778

1055-3525 See BRUCE REPORT, THE. 862

1055-3533 See NAACOG'S WOMEN'S HEALTH NURSING SCAN. 3862

1055-3541 See MEDIA BOND INVESTOR. 906

1055-355X See JOURNAL OF THE FLORIDA MOSQUITO CONTROL ASSOCIATION. 4787

1055-3568 See BUSINESS SPEAKER'S DIGEST. 652

1055-3584 See SITE WORLD. 914

1055-3614 See OBJECT MAGAZINE. 1288

1055-3622 See STEP-BY-STEP GUIDE TO LOWERING YOUR INCOME TAX 50-90%, THE. 4750

1055-3630 See 21ST CENTURY POLICY REVIEW. 2253

1055-3649 See INTERNATIONAL PARALLELS. 841

1055-3657 See INTERNATIONAL FRIENDSHIP MAGAZINE. 2791

1055-3665 See LIBRARIES AND INFORMATION SERVICES TODAY : THE YEARLY CHRONICLE. 3223

1055-3703 See RESPONSE (LOS ANGELES, CALIF.). 2272

1055-3746 See EITF ABSTRACTS. 743

1055-3789 See PAUL KAGAN'S RECORD OF TV STATION DEALS. 1136

1055-3835 See JOURNAL OF ADDICTIONS & OFFENDER COUNSELING. 4593

1055-3851 See MRI BANKERS' GUIDE TO FOREIGN CURRENCY. 800

1055-3878 See DRYDEN THEATRE, CURTIS THEATRE AT THE INTERNATIONAL MUSEUM OF PHOTOGRAPHY AT GEORGE EASTMAN HOUSE : [SCHEDULE OF EVENTS]. 4369

1055-3916 See INFORMATION SEARCHER. 1752

1055-3924 See OPPORTUNITY EVALUATION NEWSLETTER. 881

1055-3940 See GLOBAL COMMUNIQUE/ THE EDP AUDITORS ASSOCIATION, INC. 744

1055-4084 See LITIGATION APPLICATIONS. 3003

1055-4122 See REGULATORY COMPLIANCE UPDATE. 2180

1055-4130 See OUR WRITE MIND. 3421

1055-4149 See CONCH REPUBLIC MAGAZINE. 2531

1055-4157 See EARLY CHILDHOOD LAW AND POLICY REPORTER. 2965

1055-4165 See METROPOLITAN NEW YORK BUSINESS AND MARKET GUIDE, THE. 693

1055-4173 See UNIVERSITY PRESS BOOKS FOR PUBLIC AND SECONDARY SCHOOL LIBRARIES. 3255

1055-4181 See TECHNOLOGY AND DISABILITY. 4394

1055-419X See KALMIOPSIS (ASHLAND, OR.). 516

1055-4203 See DISNEY'S TALE SPIN. 1063

1055-4211 See JOURNAL OF RTC REAL ESTATE. 4839

1055-422X See SAN JOAQUIN AGRICULTURAL LAW REVIEW. 3046

1055-4238 See RESEARCH REVIEW - COLORADO. DIVISION OF WILDLIFE. 4878

1055-4246 See UNDERGROUND STORAGE TANK GUIDE. 1929

1055-4319 See CAMPUS SECURITY REPORT. 4770

1055-4394 See WALLCOVERINGS, WINDOWS & INTERIOR FASHION. 2903

1055-4408 See ABERDEEN'S MAGAZINE OF MASONRY CONSTRUCTION. 597

1055-4440 See MODERN WOODWORKING. 634

1055-4467 See HERALD-SUN (DURHAM, N.C.), THE. 5723

1055-4491 See QUARTERLY / ALLIANCE AGAINST FRAUD IN TELEMARKETING, COORDINATED BY THE NATIONAL CONSUMERS' LEAGUE. 3174

1055-4505 See DWELLING CONSTRUCTION UNDER THE UNIFORM MECHANICAL CODE. 613

1055-4513 See JOURNAL OF TRANSLATION AND TEXTLINGUISTICS. 3292

1055-4548 See BTN (BIRMINGHAM, ALA.). 1150

1055-4556 See INSURANCE & LIABILITY REPORTER. 2883

1055-4564 See FRATERNA (CENTRAL POINT, OR.). 2415

1055-4580 See SOVIET LAW & BUSINESS NEWS. 3103

1055-4610 See VIET NAM HAI NGOAI. 1929

1055-4629 See SHEPARD'S WISCONSIN EXPRESS CITATIONS. 3055

1055-4645 See ALABAMA BUSINESS & ECONOMIC INDICATORS. 637

1055-4661 See LANDSMEN (WASHINGTON, D.C.). 2457

1055-4688 See GUIDE TO GRADUATE PROGRAMS IN CRIMINAL JUSTICE AND CRIMINOLOGY. 3165

1055-470X See AMERICAN BREWER (HAYWARD, CALIF.). 2363

1055-4726 See BATTALION (COLLEGE STATION, TEX. 1893), THE. 1089

1055-4734 See POWER EQUIPMENT TRADE. 634

1055-4742 See BOOK LINKS. 4824

1055-4750 See SECOND LANGUAGE INSTRUCTION/ACQUISITION ABSTRACTS. 3320

1055-4769 See ACADEMIC AND LIBRARY COMPUTING. 1265

1055-4777 See REFERENCE DESK : QUARTERLY JOURNAL OF THE ENCYCLOPEDISTS: INTERNATIONAL ENCYCLOPEDIA SOCIETY. 1928

1055-4785 See DISC GOLF JOURNAL. 4893

1055-4815 See JASON AND THE ARGONAUTS. 380

1055-4831 See SUPPRESSED! (PLYMOUTH, MICH.). 2762

1055-484X See TRICYCLE (NEW YORK, N.Y.). 5022

1055-4858 See EXECUTIVE FLIGHT PLANNER. AMERICAS. 5469

1055-4874 See SPRING FEVER. 4866

1055-4882 See WALT DISNEY'S HOLIDAY PARADE. 4867

1055-4904 See INTERNATIONAL CREATIVITY NETWORK NEWSLETTER : ICN. 1753

1055-4912 See WASHINGTON WOMAN NEWS. 5568

1055-4920 See GOVERNMENT AFFAIRS UPDATE. 2590

1055-4947 See COMMUNITY BANK MARKETING / BANK MARKETING ASSOCIATION. 783

1055-4998 See FOUNDATION REPORTER (1990). 5286

1055-4998 See FOUNDATION REPORTER (1990). 4727

1055-5005 See HERALD (ROCKPORT, TEX. 1990), THE. 5750

1055-5013 See IHD, THE HANDBOOK. 2901

1055-5056 See JOURNAL OF PETROLEUM MARKETING : JPM / PMAA, THE. 4262

1055-5072 See COMPUTERCRAFT (HICKSVILLE, N.Y.). 1266

1055-5099 See HAZARDOUS WASTE CASE LAW UPDATE. 2231

1055-5129 See BIOGERON ... LIFE EXTENSION MANUAL. 3556

1055-5137 See MILESTONES IN ANESTHESIA. 3683

1055-5161 See JOURNAL OF THE AMERICAN SOCIETY OF OCULARISTS, THE. 3876

1055-5188 See MEMORY CARD SYSTEMS & DESIGN. 1195

1055-5196 See AMES HIGH ALUMNI NEWSLETTER. 1101

1055-520X See INDIVIDUAL WITH DISABILITIES EDUCATION LAW REPORT. 2982

1055-5218 See MOLECULAR CRYSTALS AND LIQUID CRYSTALS. LETTERS SECTION (1991). 1032

1055-5234 See INSIDE BT. 1157

1055-5242 See INDOOR AIR BULLETIN. 2174

1055-5250 See HEALTHCARE ENVIRONMENTAL MANAGEMENT SYSTEM. 4782

1055-5269 See SURFACE SCIENCE SPECTRA. 4442

1055-5277 See FJC DIRECTIONS. 3140

1055-5285 See MOBILE PRODUCTS INTERNATIONAL. 1117

1055-5293 See UFPSS FRIENDSHIP. 3449

1055-5307 See ERISA LITIGATION REPORTER. 3148

1055-5315 See FROMMER'S PARIS ON ... $ A DAY. 5477

1055-5323 See FROMMER'S BUDGET TRAVEL GUIDE. MADRID ... ON $ ... A DAY. 5475

1055-5331 See FROMMER'S BUDGET TRAVEL GUIDE. LONDON ... ON $ ... A DAY. 5475

1055-534X See FROMMER'S STOCKHOLM ON ... $ A DAY. 5478

1055-5358 See FROMMER'S COPENHAGEN ON ... $ A DAY. 5477

1055-5366 See FROMMER'S BERLIN ON ... $ A DAY. 5474

1055-5374 See FROMMER'S COMPREHENSIVE TRAVEL GUIDE. BANGKOK. 5475

1055-5382 See FROMMER'S COMPREHENSIVE TRAVEL GUIDE. DELAWARE, MARYLAND, PENNSYLVANIA & THE NEW JERSEY SHORE. 5475

1055-5390 See FROMMER'S SCOTLAND. 5477

1055-5404 See FROMMER'S ENGLAND. 5477

1055-5412 See FROMMER'S THAILAND. 5478

1055-5439 See FROMMER'S COMPREHENSIVE TRAVEL GUIDE. NEPAL. 5476

1055-5447 See FROMMER'S COMPREHENSIVE TRAVEL GUIDE. THE VIRGIN ISLANDS. 5477

1055-5498 See MAJOR TAX PLANNING. 4736

1055-5536 See MUSIC CATALOG (WASHINGTON, D.C.), THE. 4133

1055-5544 See KERN REPORT, THE. 688

1055-5552 See SLIM FAST MAGAZINE. 2601

1055-5560 See CHILTON'S AIR CONDITIONING AND HEATING LABOR GUIDE. 5410

1055-5579 See MARKETSOURCE (CHICAGO, ILL.). 1504

1055-5587 See INTERNATIONAL TRADE ALERT (BALTIMORE, MD.). 841

1055-5595 See OB/GYN ROUNDS. 3766

1055-5609 See ONE MEADWAY. 3349

1055-5617 See HARRIS MARYLAND INDUSTRIAL DIRECTORY. 1608

1055-5625 See BIRNBAUM'S BAHAMAS, TURKS & CAICOS. 5463

1055-5641 See BIRNBAUM'S CANCUN, COZUMEL, AND ISLA MUJERES. 5464

1055-565X See BIRNBAUM'S SPAIN. 5464

1055-5668 See BIRNBAUM'S PORTUGAL. 5464

1055-5676 See BIRNBAUM'S IXTAPA & ZIHUATENEJO. 5464

1055-5684 See BIRNBAUM'S BERMUDA. 5463

1055-5692 See USSR BUSINESS GUIDE & DIRECTORY. 856

1055-5749 See INSURANCE PHONE BOOK & DIRECTORY. 2884

1055-5781 See ERNST & YOUNG'S OIL AND GAS FEDERAL INCOME TAXATION. 4255

1055-579X See DIRECTORY OF NORTH AMERICAN MILITARY AVIATION COMMUNICATIONS, VHF/UHF. CENTRAL. 18

1055-5803 See DIRECTORY OF NORTH AMERICAN MILITARY AVIATION COMMUNICATIONS, VHF/UHF. SOUTHEASTERN. 18

1055-5811 See DIRECTORY OF NORTH AMERICAN MILITARY AVIATION COMMUNICATIONS, VHF/UHF. WESTERN. 18

1055-582X See DIRECTORY OF NORTH AMERICAN MILITARY AVIATION COMMUNICATIONS, VHF/UHF. NORTHEASTERN. 18

1055-5854 See STREET SONGS. 3440

1055-5935 See ABORTION AND FAMILY PLANNING BIBLIOGRAPHY. 587

1055-5951 See MEDICAL MONITOR. 3610

1055-596X See GUIDE TO FEDERAL FUNDING FOR GOVERNMENTS AND NONPROFITS. 4653

1055-596X See GRANT UPDATE! FOR GUIDE TO FEDERAL FUNDING FOR GOVERNMENTS & NONPROFITS. 4729

1055-5978 See CORPORATE CLEVELAND. 661

1055-6001 See INTERNATIONAL JOURNAL OF PURCHASING AND MATERIALS MANAGEMENT. 950

1055-601X See BARBIE (NEW YORK, N.Y. 1990). 4857

1055-6028 See LOWERING YOUR CHOLESTEROL. 2599

1055-6036 See YOUR CHILD'S HEALTH AND DEVELOPMENT. 2287

1055-6044 See NATIONAL DIGEST OF HEALTH AND MEDICINE. 3618

1055-6052 See HOW YOU CAN STOP SMOKING. 2598

1055-6060 See VIDEO PROPHILES. 1142

1055-6087 See GUIDE TO LITERARY AGENTS & ART/PHOTO REPS. 321

1055-6095 See ASIAPACIFIC BRIEFING PAPER. 2646

1055-6109 See ADOPTION THERAPIST. 5270

1055-6117 See NATURALIST (DANVILLE, VT.), THE. 2199

1055-6141 See GUIA DE TELEVISION Y ENTRETENIMEINTO. 1132

1055-615X See INTERNATIONAL JOURNAL OF INTELLIGENT SYSTEMS IN ACCOUNTING, FINANCE & MANAGEMENT. 745

1055-6192 See BOCA NATIONAL PROPERTY MAINTENANCE CODE. 2816

1055-6230 See EMC TECHNOLOGY. 2053

1055-6249 See EMPLOYMENT LITIGATION REPORTER. 3147

1055-6265 See BN HISTORIAN, THE. 2723

1055-6273 See MR (SAN FRANCISCO, CALIF.). 3944

1055-6281 See DRUG DETECTION REPORT. 3163

1055-629X See PHYSICIAN'S PAYMENT UPDATE. 3627

1055-6311 See 1:87 SCALE. 5375

1055-632X See LIBRO DEL ANO (CHICAGO, ILL.). 1927

1055-6354 See VALUE LINE INVESTMENT SURVEY (CANADIAN ED.), THE. 918

1055-6370 See WORCESTER MEDICINE. 3651

1055-6400 See OOPS MESSENGER. 1280

1055-6427 See HIGHLIGHTS OF THE YEAR 1356

1055-6532 See GREAT PLAINS GAME & FISH. 4873

1055-6540 See MID-ATLANTIC GAME & FISH. 4874

1055-6559 See CAMDEN COUNTY TRIBUNE. 5652

1055-6567 See SLIDE ATLAS OF CURRENT RADIOLOGY. 3947

1055-6575 See SLIDE ATLAS OF CURRENT OPHTHALMOLOGY. 3879

1055-6621 See EXPLORER (MERCED, CALIF.), THE. 2560

1055-6656 See CLEFT PALATE-CRANIOFACIAL JOURNAL. 3564

1055-6680 See BOCA NATIONAL PLUMBING CODE, THE. 2603

1055-6699 See JOURNAL OF HEALTH EDUCATION. ASSOCIATION FOR THE ADVANCEMENT OF HEALTH EDUCATION. 4786

1055-6710 See DIRECTORY OF PROFESSIONAL GENEALOGISTS. 2445

1055-6737 See AMERICAN ANGLER (INTERVALE, N.H.). 2294

1055-6745 See EMPLOYMENT LITIGATION REPORTER. 3147

1055-6761 See NORTHWEST PUBLIC POWER BULLETIN. 1951

1055-677X See COMPUTATIONAL FLUID DYNAMICS (NEW YORK, N.Y.). 1175

1055-6788 See OPTIMIZATION METHODS AND SOFTWARE. 1198

1055-6796 See ASTRONOMICAL AND ASTROPHYSICAL TRANSACTIONS. 391

1055-6818 See NURSING QUALITY CONNECTION. 3865

1055-6826 See BIO-BIBLIOGRAPHIES IN ART AND ARCHITECTURE. 334

1055-6834 See CHILTON'S GEARBOX FLUID SERVICE LOCATOR. 5410

1055-6842 See CHILTON'S QUICK LUBRICATION GUIDE. 5411

1055-6850 See TOURING AMERICA. 5493

1055-6869 See BROWNSTONE MYSTERY GUIDES. 3369

1055-6877 See IEEE LTS : THE MAGAZINE OF LIGHTWAVE TELECOMMUNICATIONS SYSTEMS. 4434

1055-6893 See GREEN BOOK (WOBURN, MASS.), THE. 2172

1055-6907 See WEB (SANTA CRUZ, CALIF.), THE. 3452

1055-6915 See MAGNETIC AND ELECTRICAL SEPARATION. 4444

1055-6923 See NETWARE PROGRAMMER'S JOURNAL. 1196

1055-7008 See AMANECER (ENGLISH ED.). 4933

1055-713X See PROGRESS IN NEURAL NETWORKS. 1244

1055-7148 See INTERNATIONAL JOURNAL OF NETWORK MANAGEMENT. 1113
1055-7156 See CAPABILITIES (CHICAGO, ILL.). 1967
1055-7164 See COMICS MANIFESTO, THE. 4859
1055-7172 See BIOMATERIALS, ARTIFICIAL CELLS, AND IMMOBILIZATION BIOTECHNOLOGY. 3686
1055-7180 See INTERNATIONAL STUDIES IN SOCIAL CHANGE. 5249
1055-7199 See HOOVER'S HANDBOOK OF WORLD BUSINESS. 680
1055-7202 See HOOVER'S HANDBOOK OF AMERICAN BUSINESS. 1608
1055-7229 See CONTRIBUTIONS TO CELLULAR AND MOLECULAR ENDOCRINOLOGY. 535
1055-7245 See GEORGIA COURT RULES AND PROCEDURE. FEDERAL. 3140
1055-7288 See INTERNATIONAL INDUSTRIAL ENGINEERING CONFERENCE PROCEEDINGS. 2099
1055-730X See PREMISES LIABILITY REPORT. 3030
1055-7318 See STRATEGIC DEVELOPMENTS IN BIOTECHNOLOGY / NORTH CAROLINA BIOTECHNOLOGY CENTER. 3696
1055-7326 See THOREAU RESEARCH NEWSLETTER. 4363
1055-7334 See CONFLUENCE (BELPRE, OHIO). 3340
1055-7342 See CONNECTICUT TECHNOLOGY RESOURCE GUIDE. 5096
1055-7350 See MACINTOSH CONSTRUCTION FORUM. 1194
1055-7385 See AFRO-AMERICAN HISTORY KIT (7TH GRADE AND ABOVE ED.). 2717
1055-7393 See AFRO-AMERICAN HISTORY KIT (K-6 ED.). 2637
1055-7407 See PROSPECTUS. 4217
1055-7415 See DRUMMER (SAN FRANCISCO, CALIF.). 2794
1055-7431 See DIABLO BUSINESS. 665
1055-7466 See HEALTH SYSTEMS REVIEW. 3782
1055-7490 See INTERNATIONAL JOURNAL OF MATHEMATICAL AND STATISTICAL SCIENCES. 5115
1055-7504 See LOTUS ON WINDOWS. 1288
1055-7512 See JOURNAL OF INDIVIDUAL EMPLOYMENT RIGHTS. 1682
1055-7520 See GLIMMER TRAIN STORIES. 3391
1055-7547 See JOURNAL OF ENVIRONMENTAL QUALITY MANAGEMENT. 2175
1055-7555 See JOURNAL OF QUALITY ENVIRONMENTAL MANAGEMENT. 2176
1055-7563 See JOURNAL OF ENVIRONMENTAL QUALITY (NEW YORK, N.Y.). 2175
1055-7571 See TOTAL QUALITY ENVIRONMENTAL MANAGEMENT. 2182
1055-758X See JOURNAL OF ENVIRONMENTAL REGULATION. 2175
1055-7598 See ENVIRONMENTAL REGULATION. 2169
1055-7601 See ANESTHESIA & PAIN CONTROL IN DENTISTRY. 1316
1055-761X See PARADOXIST MOVEMENT, THE. 4354
1055-7628 See AMERICAN SALARIES AND WAGES SURVEY. 1643
1055-7636 See GLOBAL AFRICA (WASHINGTON, D.C.). 2639
1055-7644 See TEMPORARY CULTURE. 3444
1055-7652 See COMPARISON REPORT ON ENGINEERING DOCUMENT MANAGEMENT (EDMS) SYSTEMS. 1969
1055-7660 See BRYN MAWR CLASSICAL REVIEW. 1075
1055-7725 See ROAD & REC. 5391
1055-7741 See READY, SET, GO! IN-DEPTH (1992). 4569
1055-775X See JACKSON COUNTY BANNER (BROWNSTOWN, IND.). 5665
1055-7768 See SYSTEMS 3X/400. 1204
1055-7776 See COPPER JOURNAL, THE. 1602

1055-7784 See REVIEW OF BOOKS IN EDUCATION. 1779
1055-7792 See BORNEO RESEARCH COUNCIL MONOGRAPH SERIES. 232
1055-7806 See SUN HERALD (CHARLOTTE ED.). 5651
1055-7814 See CITIZEN PARTICIPATION (CLEVELAND, OHIO). 4717
1055-7822 See BUSINESS MACHINE DEALER. 4211
1055-7830 See WINNING (ALLENTOWN, PA.). 429
1055-7857 See WAKE TREASURES. 2477
1055-7865 See CORPORATE ENVIRONMENTAL OFFICER MAGAZINE. 2163
1055-7873 See CORPORATE PSYCHOLOGY. 4583
1055-789X See JOURNAL OF TECHNOLOGY IN MATHEMATICS. 3515
1055-7903 See MOLECULAR PHYLOGENETICS AND EVOLUTION. 549
1055-7911 See YOGA INTERNATIONAL. 4186
1055-792X See AWARD-WINNING BOOKS FOR CHILDREN AND YOUNG ADULTS. 3365
1055-7938 See FAMILY VIOLENCE & SEXUAL ASSAULT BULLETIN. 5285
1055-7954 See UKRAINIAN BIOCHEMISTRY. 494
1055-7997 See ULTRASOUND SOURCEBOOK & REFERENCE GUIDE. 3648
1055-8004 See JAPAN TECHNOLOGY MONITOR. 5117
1055-8020 See SPORTS MARKET PLACE. 4923
1055-8047 See CHINA INFORMATION BULLETIN (PORTLAND, OR.). 2648
1055-8071 See COOKBOOK COLLECTOR, THE. 2332
1055-808X See ADVANCES IN GASTROINTESTINAL RADIOLOGY. 3794
1055-8098 See IMAGING SERVICE BUREAU NEWS. 1609
1055-8179 See BECKETT BASKETBALL MAGAZINE. 2771
1055-8195 See FEDERAL CIRCUIT BAR JOURNAL, THE. 2969
1055-8209 See INTERNATIONAL POLICY CASE SERIES. 684
1055-8217 See BUSINESS CONCEPTS. 646
1055-8225 See CREDIT & FINANCE. 785
1055-8233 See MOTOR WORLD (LOS ANGELES, CALIF.). 5420
1055-8241 See HEALTH DIET & NUTRITION. 4191
1055-825X See GOVERNMENT PROGRAMS. 4652
1055-8268 See NATIONAL AUCTIONS & SALES. 1298
1055-8276 See U.S. IMMIGRATION. 1921
1055-8284 See ECONOMIC HOME OWNER, THE. 2821
1055-8292 See CURRENT EMPLOYMENT. 4203
1055-8306 See AMERICAN SENIOR, THE. 5178
1055-8314 See IDEAL TRAVELER. 5480
1055-8322 See DIABETES CONSULTANT. 3727
1055-8330 See NEURODEGENERATION (PHILADELPHIA, PA.). 3839
1055-8349 See AACN NURSING SCAN IN CRITICAL CARE. 3849
1055-8365 See EXPORT YELLOW PAGES, THE. 835
1055-8373 See COAST GUARD LETTER. 4175
1055-8381 See NACM BANKRUPTCY REORGANIZATION GUIDE. 800
1055-839X See PYM NEWS: A PUBLICATION OF THE RELIGIOUS SOCIETY OF FRIENDS. 4988
1055-8403 See EVENING HERALD (SHEHANDOAH, PA. : 1969). 5736
1055-8411 See EARTH FIRST! (1991). 2164
1055-842X See NIHILISTIC REVIEW, THE. 3417
1055-8438 See CAT LOVERS : THE OFFICIAL CLA CLUB MAGAZINE. 4286
1055-8446 See SANTA FE LITERARY REVIEW. 3352
1055-8454 See TELECOMMUNICATIONS DIRECTORY (DETROIT, MICH.). 1165

1055-8462 See INTERNATIONAL JOURNAL OF SYSTEMS AUTOMATION, RESEARCH & APPLICATIONS. 1247
1055-8470 See INTERNATIONAL JOURNAL IN COMPUTER SIMULATION. 1282
1055-8489 See MAXINE'S PAGES. 2538
1055-8519 See DIRECTORY OF AMERICAN INDIAN LAW ATTORNEYS. 2961
1055-8535 See WEEKLY SALE & DISCOUNT MAGAZINE (LOS ANGELES ED.). 719
1055-856X See MICHIGAN FEMINIST STUDIES. 5561
1055-8578 See HERBAL ROSE REPORT, THE. 2418
1055-8586 See SEMINARS IN PEDIATRIC SURGERY. 3974
1055-8608 See SCOREBOARD (OWINGS MILLS, MD. NORTHWEST ED.). 4917
1055-8624 See MUSEUMEDIA (MILWAUKEE, WISC.). 4093
1055-8667 See SHEPARD'S NEW JERSEY INSURANCE LAW & REGULATION REPORTER. 3052
1055-8683 See EDUCATIONAL IRM QUARTERLY. 1223
1055-8705 See ISBA NEWS. 2985
1055-873X See AMERICAN ASSOCIATION OF CHRISTIAN COUNSELORS MEMBERSHIP REGISTRY. 4933
1055-8756 See ANDEAN PAST. 254
1055-8799 See SOUTHWESTERN ENTOMOLOGIST. SUPPLEMENT (WESLACO, TEX.). 5613
1055-8845 See EARTH FIRST! (1991). 2164
1055-8853 See FOUR DRAGONS GUIDEBOOK : A COMPREHENSIVE GUIDE TO HONG KONG, THAILAND, SINGAPORE, TAIWAN, THE. 5474
1055-8861 See THAILAND GUIDEBOOK, THE. 5492
1055-887X See RADIO FUN. 1137
1055-8888 See JOURNAL OF INDEPENDENT RESEARCH. 1757
1055-8896 See JOURNAL OF EDUCATIONAL MULTIMEDIA AND HYPERMEDIA. 1224
1055-890X See PARKING TECHNOLOGY. 5389
1055-8926 See CAD INDUSTRY DIRECTORY (HARDWARE ED.). 1231
1055-8934 See NEW HEALTH STANDARD JOURNAL, THE. 2600
1055-8942 See KANSAS JOURNAL OF LAW & PUBLIC POLICY, THE. 2992
1055-8950 See ADWEEK AGENCY DIRECTORY (NATIONAL ED.). 755
1055-8969 See SCHIFF REPORT, THE. 4801
1055-8977 See KENNEDY LIBRARY QUARTERLY, EASTERN WASHINGTON UNIVERSITY. 3221
1055-8985 See GUILT & GARDENIAS / THE ARTS COUNCIL. 3392
1055-8993 See F. PAUL PACULT'S SPIRIT JOURNAL. 2367
1055-9051 See PIPELINE (ST. PAUL, MINN.). 1119
1055-9051 See PIPELINE (ST. PAUL, MINN.). 1119
1055-9086 See PLACES TO PRACTICE (INTERNAL MEDICINE/CARDIOLOGY ED.). 3800
1055-9094 See APPLIED H.R.M. RESEARCH. 938
1055-9108 See LEADERSHIP (FORT WORTH, TEX.). 5294
1055-9140 See DRINKING WATER RESEARCH : AN UPDATE FROM THE AWWA RESEARCH FOUNDATION. 5533
1055-9159 See VISTAS (LUBBOCK, TEX.). 5313
1055-9175 See OIL SPILL U.S. LAW REPORT. 3022
1055-9183 See HEALTHCARE STAFFING MANAGEMENT. 3782
1055-9191 See AMERICAN HOLIDAY & LIFE. 5268
1055-9205 See ASPHALT CONTRACTOR, THE. 5439
1055-9213 See STATE OF AMERICA'S CHILDREN. 5311
1055-9213 See VISION FOR AMERICA'S FUTURE: AN AGENDA FOR THE 1990S, A. 5313

1055-9221 See CDF'S CHILD, YOUTH, AND FAMILY FUTURES CLEARINGHOUSE. 5276

1055-9256 See GAMEPLAN COLLEGE FOOTBALL ... ANNUAL PREVIEW. 4896

1055-9272 See THINK (SAN ANTONIO, TEX.). 1805

1055-9280 See HDTV REPORT. 1132

1055-9299 See INTERAMERICAN OPPORTUNITIES BRIEFING. 683

1055-9302 See BUYER'S GUIDE (NATIONAL GLASS ASSOCIATION (U.S.)). 2587

1055-9345 See NEW INFORMATION NEWS. 1118

1055-9361 See CLINIGUIDE TO RHEUMATOLOGY. 3804

1055-937X See SEMINARS IN AVIAN AND EXOTIC PET MEDICINE. 5522

1055-9396 See GREEN INDEX. 2173

1055-940X See BARBIE FASHION. 4857

1055-9418 See ADVANCED MATERIALS IN AEROSPACE APPLICATIONS. 3

1055-9426 See MATHEMATICAL WORLD. 3520

1055-9450 See ROBERTSON'S CURRENT COMPETITION. 2080

1055-9469 See SHEPARD'S CALIFORNIA CONSTRUCTION LAW REPORTER. 3049

1055-9477 See CHAPTER 11 UPDATE. 783

1055-9485 See FAILED LBO LITIGATION REPORTER. 3086

1055-9507 See SHEPARD'S CONNECTICUT EXPRESS CITATIONS. 3049

1055-9515 See HERITAGE COUNTRY. 2736

1055-9531 See PROGRESS (CAVE CITY, KY. 1988), THE. 5682

1055-9566 See AUDIO'S GUIDE TO SURROUND SOUND. 5315

1055-9590 See TRIBORO BANNER. 5740

1055-9604 See NEVADA GOLF AND TENNIS. 4907

1055-9612 See DRUG DESIGN AND DISCOVERY. 4300

1055-9620 See TECHNOLOGY FOR CRITICAL CARE NURSES. 3870

1055-9639 See COMIC RELIEF. 4859

1055-9663 See MAINTENANCE EXECUTIVE. 1617

1055-9698 See STATISTICS ON FUEL USED TO GENERATE ELECTRICITY BY THE ELECTRIC UTILITY INDUSTRY. 1958

1055-9701 See COLOR PUBLISHING. 4813

1055-9760 See TRAINING & DEVELOPMENT (ALEXANDRIA, VA.). 947

1055-9787 See MONEYPLU$ NEWS. 799

1055-9795 See EAST-WEST CENTER VIEWS. 1822

1055-9809 See IN DEPTH (WASHINGTON, D.C.). 4476

1055-9825 See BACK STAGE SHOOT. 756

1055-9833 See AMERICAN DREAM CARS, 1946-1972. 5403

1055-9868 See NEW MYTHS. 3416

1055-9884 See HEAVEN EARTH. 2652

1055-9892 See ENVISIONEERING. 1975

1055-9914 See RESEARCH IN CONTEMPORARY AND APPLIED GEOGRAPHY. 2574

1055-9922 See REMOTE SENSING OF EARTH RESOURCES (ALBUQUERQUE, N.M.), THE. 4419

1055-9957 See MINING BUSINESS DIGEST. 2145

1055-9965 See CANCER EPIDEMIOLOGY, BIOMARKERS & PREVENTION. 3811

1055-9973 See IMAGE BUILDER. 870

1055-9981 See CREDIT REPORT MAGAZINE : CR : A PUBLICATION OF THE NATIONAL CONSUMER ADVOCATE ASSOCIATION. 1296

1055-999X See MODERN DRAMATISTS RESEARCH AND PRODUCTION SOURCEBOOKS. 3412

1056-0009 See INTERNATIONAL INFORMATION SYSTEMS. 871

1056-0017 See APICS, THE PERFORMANCE ADVANTAGE. 860

1056-0025 See PAUL EDWARDS' TRAVEL CONFIDENTIAL. 5488

1056-0033 See MINNESOTA AACR 2 TRAINERS SERIES. 3231

1056-005X See CZECHOSLOVAK AND CENTRAL EUROPEAN JOURNAL. 2685

1056-0114 See ROCKY MOUNTAIN GAME & FISH. 4878

1056-0122 See CALIFORNIA GAME & FISH. 4870

1056-0130 See BREAKTHROUGH (HAMMOND, LA.). 2771

1056-0157 See SOILS (INDEPENDENCE, MO.). 187

1056-0173 See TURNAROUND LETTER, THE. 918

1056-022X See NORTH AMERICAN STEEL MARKET OUTLOOK. 4014

1056-0254 See COMMUTER / REGIONAL AIRLINE NEWS INTERNATIONAL. 16

1056-0289 See NEWSINDEX FOR SMALL BUSINESS ENTREPRENEURS, THE. 699

1056-0297 See ESPERANTOUSA. 3280

1056-0300 See SOCIAL STUDIES AND THE YOUNG LEARNER. 5221

1056-0319 See AMERICAN JAILS. 3156

1056-0327 See LAUGHING BEAR NEWSLETTER. 4816

1056-0343 See CRAFT SUPPLY MAGAZINE. 371

1056-0378 See O'LOCHLAINNS PERSONAL JOURNAL OF IRISH FAMILIES. 2465

1056-0386 See MICROLEADS VENDOR DIRECTORY. 1245

1056-0394 See MEMBERSHIP DIRECTORY / MARYLAND GENEALOGICAL SOCIETY. 2460

1056-0440 See TTS BLUE BOOK OF TRUCKING COMPANIES. 5398

1056-0467 See IMMINENCE! (ARLINGTON, VA.). 2263

1056-0483 See AFRICAN MIRROR (WASHINGTON, D.C.), THE. 2637

1056-0505 See TEEN BEAT ALL STARS. 1070

1056-0513 See TEEN BEAT. 1070

1056-053X See DIABETES, PREVENTION AND THERAPY. 3728

1056-0548 See INSIGHTS : A JOURNAL OF THE FACULTY OF AUSTIN SEMINARY. 4965

1056-0556 See WINDOWS (AUSTIN, TEX.). 5009

1056-0777 See BANK MIDYEAR REVIEW. TEXAS. 775

1056-0793 See RADTECH REPORT. 4419

1056-0866 See LIFE SCIENCE LAB PRODUCTS. 463

1056-0874 See SOUTHERN GLENN GLEANINGS NEWSLETTER. 2473

1056-0904 See CLASS UPDATE. 3202

1056-0939 See BANTAM'S HAWAII. 5462

1056-0963 See TELEVISION DATATRAK. 1140

1056-0998 See HANDBOOK OF SYSTEMS MANAGEMENT, DEVELOPMENT AND SUPPORT. YEARBOOK. 1286

1056-1005 See EDUCATION INTERFACE NATIONAL GUIDE TO EDUCATOR EMPOWERMENT. 1739

1056-1013 See PENNSYLVANIA EDUCATION & EMPLOYMENT WEEKLY. 1772

1056-1021 See SOUTHWESTERN ARCHIVIST. 3250

1056-103X See OUT IN VIDEO. 387

1056-1064 See INIQUITY (SAN DIEGO, CALIF.). 2535

1056-1072 See CONTENTION (BLOOMINGTON, IND.). 5196

1056-1080 See AIDS RESEARCH REVIEWS. 3664

1056-1099 See INTERNATIONAL DIRECTORY OF CONSULTANTS AND CONTRACTORS ACTIVE IN WESTERN EUROPE, AN. 618

1056-1102 See PRACTICAL ENVIRONMENTAL REGULATION. 2180

1056-1129 See MCGRAW-HILL HEALTH LETTER. 2599

1056-1137 See LEGAL OPINION LETTER / WASHINGTON LEGAL FOUNDATION. 3000

1056-120X See NWFN NEWSJOURNAL : A WOMEN'S FITNESS RESOURCE. 2600

1056-1218 See SHEPARD'S ELDER CARE/LAW NEWSLETTER. 3119

1056-1226 See LAWYER'S WORD : A NEWSLETTER FOR LAWYERS USING MICROSOFT WORD AND OTHER MICROSOFT PRODUCTS, THE. 1288

1056-1285 See CHILTON'S CHASIS ELECTRONICS SERVICE MANUAL. ASIAN CARS AND TRUCKS. 5410

1056-1293 See ADMINISTRATIVE FOCUS. 1859

1056-1307 See CHILTON'S CHASSIS ELECTRONICS SERVICE MANUAL. EUROPEAN. 2038

1056-1323 See WINNEBAGO INDIAN NEWS. 5707

1056-1404 See ENERGY NEWSBRIEF, THE. 1941

1056-1412 See INTEGRATED MESSAGING NEWS. 1157

1056-1420 See INNER SOUND OF LIFE, THE. 3464

1056-1447 See WINE BUSINESS INSIDER. 2372

1056-1455 See MOTORCYCLE ROAD RACER ILLUSTRATED. 4082

1056-1471 See CONTEMPORARY TOPICS IN LABORATORY ANIMAL SCIENCE. 5508

1056-148X See EARTH (WAUKESHA, WIS.). 1355

1056-1498 See GOLIARD (WOOSTER, OHIO). 3391

1056-1528 See CALIFORNIA LIBRARIES. 3199

1056-1536 See IMPACT PUMP NEWS & PATENTS. 2115

1056-1544 See IMPACT VALVE NEWS & PATENTS. 2115

1056-1579 See EXHIBITION DIRECTORY. 350

1056-1587 See MISSISSIPPI MEMORIES. 2461

1056-1595 See OKAY AMERICA. 2542

1056-1684 See NEWSPAPER ABSTRACTS. 2464

1056-1781 See READINGS IN INTRODUCTORY MACROECONOMICS. 1515

1056-179X See EUROPE DRUG & DEVICE REPORT. 4303

1056-182X See COMPARISON REPORT ON ENGINEERING DOCUMENT MANAGEMENT (EDMS) SYSTEMS. 1969

1056-1838 See CPU REVIEW. 1091

1056-1862 See OFFICIAL HOTEL GUIDE. 2808

1056-1870 See PACE BUYER'S GUIDES. TRUCK FACTS. 5422

1056-1889 See PACE BUYER'S GUIDES. CAR FACTS. 5422

1056-1900 See HEALTH NEWS & REVIEW. 4191

1056-1935 See MOLECULAR MATERIAL. 986

1056-1943 See COMPASS PATHFINDER. 3962

1056-1951 See DIGEST OF GERIATRICS. 3750

1056-196X See LEGAL PUBLISHER, THE. 4816

1056-1978 See INSIGHTS FOR LIFE. 4965

1056-1986 See HELP FOR LIVING. 5061

1056-1994 See ANSWERS FOR LIFE'S QUESTIONS. 4935

1056-2001 See SUNDAY SCHOOL LEADER. SMALLER CHURCH ED, THE. 5068

1056-201X See SUNDAY SCHOOL LEADER (LARGER CHURCH ED.), THE. 5068

1056-2028 See LAW FIRM PARTNERSHIP REPORT. 2995

1056-2036 See CQ RESEARCHER, THE. 4470

1056-2044 See INFECTIOUS AGENTS AND DISEASE. 3714

1056-2052 See UPHOLSTERY DESIGN & MANUFACTURING. 3489

1056-2095 See CGS NEWSLETTER. 2442

1056-2125 See MORNING ADVOCATE (BATON ROUGE, LA.). 5684

1056-2133 See NEW AMERICAN FARMER. 111

1056-2141 See JOURNAL OF CLINICAL PSYCHIATRY ADVANCES IN PSYCHIATRIC TREATMENT MONOGRAPH SERIES, THE. 3928

1056-215X See GREEK-AMERICAN REVIEW. 2262

1056-2168 See ALABAMA FACTS. 2717

1056-2176 See DYNAMIC SYSTEMS AND APPLICATIONS. 3504

1056-2184 See SOUTHERN LAW JOURNAL (ABILENE, TEX.). 3057

1056-2206 See TAFT'S WEALTHWATCHER. 714

1056-2214 See RESPONSE! (ROCKVILLE, MD.). 4339
1056-2222 See 501 (C)OMPUTING NEWS : AN INFORMATION NEWSLETTER SERVING THE 501(C) NON-PROFIT COMMUNITY. 1169
1056-2230 See DOJ ALERT, THE. 3140
1056-2265 See NANTUCKET JOURNAL (NANTUCKET, MASS. 1987). 2747
1056-2273 See FOLDING KAYAKER. 4895
1056-2281 See EUROPEAN CELLULAR. 1154
1056-229X See TREK, LIFE-CENTERED BIBLE STUDY FOR SENIOR HIGHS. STUDENTS LEAFLETS. 5020
1056-2303 See TREK, LIFE-CENTERED BIBLE STUDY FOR SENIOR HIGHS. TEACHER IDEA BOOK. 5020
1056-2311 See TREK, LIFE-CENTERED BIBLE STUDY FOR JUNIOR HIGHS. STUDENTS LEAFLETS. 5020
1056-232X See TREK, LIFE-CENTERED BIBLE STUDY FOR JUNIOR HIGHS. TEACHER IDEA BOOK. 5005
1056-2338 See VANGUARD ADVISER, THE. 815
1056-2346 See BRASS MODELER & COLLECTOR. 2771
1056-2354 See ETHIOPIAN REVIEW. 2639
1056-2370 See ADIRONDACK MOUNTAIN CLUB : [NEWSLETTER], THE. 4868
1056-2389 See HEALTH POLICY ANNUAL. 4780
1056-2419 See FORT LUPTON PRESS (1981). 5643
1056-2443 See JOURNAL / NATIONAL SOCIETY OF FUND RAISING EXECUTIVES, THE. 761
1056-2451 See ADVENTURE GAMES FOR MICROCOMPUTERS. 1230
1056-246X See CDC BULLETIN : A PUBLICATION OF THE CURRICULUM DEVELOPMENT COUNCIL FOR SOUTHERN NEW JERSEY. 1890
1056-2478 See JOURNAL OF MEDICAL EDUCATION TECHNOLOGIES. 3596
1056-2486 See CALIFORNIA APARTMENT INVESTMENT SURVEY (SACRAMENTO COUNTY ED.), THE. 2816
1056-2494 See SOUTHERN CALIFORNIA LEGAL RESOURCE MANUAL. 3057
1056-2508 See NORTHERN CALIFORNIA LEGAL RESOURCE MANUAL. 3018
1056-2516 See CHICANO DATABASE ON CD-ROM. 2258
1056-2516 See CHICANO DATABASE. 2258
1056-2532 See MOTORIST (ALLENTOWN, PA.). 5420
1056-2540 See FACS OF THE WEEK. 898
1056-2559 See FASHION JEWELRY PLUS. 2914
1056-2575 See JOURNAL OF SOLID WASTE. 2234
1056-2583 See INTERNATIONAL ACCOUNTING SUMMARIES. 745
1056-2591 See SAGARIN REVIEW, THE. 3432
1056-2605 See AMERICAN CURRENTS (WASHINGTON, D.C.). 2718
1056-2613 See OXYGEN (SAN FRANCISCO, CALIF.). 3349
1056-263X See JOURNAL OF DEVELOPMENTAL AND PHYSICAL DISABILITIES. 4389
1056-2648 See TURF & ORNAMENTAL CHEMICALS REFERENCE: T&OCR. 143
1056-2656 See EDUCATION GRANTS ALERT. 1739
1056-2664 See NASHVILLE INDEX. 2539
1056-2672 See LIFE SCIENCE BOOK REVIEW. 5126
1056-2680 See HANDS-ON ENGLISH. 3285
1056-2699 See TECH MARKET SOUTH. 853
1056-2702 See JOURNAL OF ENVIRONMENTAL ENGINEERING. 1982
1056-2761 See FAA AVIATION SAFETY JOURNAL. 19
1056-277X See CAREERS & THE DISABLED. 4202
1056-280X See BUYERS GUIDE - NATIONAL SOFT DRINK ASSOCIATION. 2365
1056-2877 See MONTHLY MUSIC REPORT. 4132
1056-2915 See MIRA (SAN FRANCISCO, CALIF.). 3675

1056-294X See PAIN MANAGEMENT UPDATE. 3625
1056-2974 See CHEVY ACTION. 5410
1056-3008 See PULSE (SALT LAKE CITY, UTAH). 5565
1056-3032 See HOSPITAL NEWS FOR HEALTHCARE PROVIDERS (NORTHERN NEW ENGLAND ED.). 3784
1056-3040 See HOSPITAL NEWS FOR HEALTHCARE PROVIDERS. (EASTERN MASS/BOSTON ED.). 3784
1056-3083 See WILLIAMSPORT SUN-GAZETTE. 5740
1056-3091 See NURSING SCAN IN ADMINISTRATION. 3865
1056-3113 See LICTON SPRINGS REVIEW / A NORTH SEATTLE COMMUNITY COLLEGE LITERARY GUILD PUBLICATION. 3346
1056-3121 See J.K. LASSER'S MONTHLY TAX LETTER. 4734
1056-3164 See ENVIRONMENTAL REGULATORY ADVISOR. 3112
1056-3172 See OVATION REPORT ON COST EFFECTIVE PRODUCTS, THE. 3625
1056-3199 See FOCUS (WASHINGTON, D.C. 1990). 1824
1056-3202 See SAN DIEGO COMMERCE. 850
1056-3210 See FARMLIFE. 194
1056-3245 See MID-ATLANTIC THOROUGHBRED. 2800
1056-327X See FOODREVIEW (WASHINGTON, D.C.). 2341
1056-3288 See BLOUNT COUNTIAN, THE. 5625
1056-330X See MEDIGUIDE TO SPECIAL PROBLEMS IN OPHTHALMOLOGY. 3876
1056-3318 See WILDERNESS SERIES. 4880
1056-3326 See OWNERS & OFFICERS OF PRIVATE COMPANIES. 702
1056-3334 See POLITICAL WARFARE. 4532
1056-3342 See JEWISH TELEVIMAGE REPORT. 5049
1056-3369 See OFFICIAL USSR MINISTRY OF HEALTH DIRECTORY OF HEALTH RESOURCES, THE. 4794
1056-3377 See CROES LETTER, THE. 372
1056-3385 See KAMAAINA'S GUIDE TO HAWAII'S DIVE SHOPS & TOUR OPERATIONS. 5482
1056-3393 See MOTHER ROAD JOURNAL, THE. 4905
1056-3423 See FOURTH SEASON. 5179
1056-3431 See PEST MANAGEMENT & CROP DEVELOPMENT BULLETIN. 181
1056-3466 See ANNUAL REVIEW OF ENERGY AND THE ENVIRONMENT. 1932
1056-3482 See NATIONAL ENQUIRER (NEW YORK, N.Y. 1957). 2539
1056-3490 See CERAMIC ABSTRACTS CD-ROM. 2587
1056-3504 See INCITE INFORMATION. 5247
1056-3504 See INCITE INFORMATION. 4815
1056-3512 See BUSINESS SERIALS. 652
1056-3547 See CHICAGO BOWLER, INC, THE. 4890
1056-358X See CHINESE OUR MISSIONS WORLD. 4943
1056-3644 See CHRISTIAN JOURNAL (FORT WORTH, TEX.). 4945
1056-3660 See NIGHTMARES ON ELM STREET. 4864
1056-3679 See QUANTUM LEAP. 4865
1056-3709 See CHILD'S PLAY (WHEELING, W. VA.). 377
1056-3806 See YOUR PRESENCE. 5269
1056-3814 See IMAGE SCH. RELEASE. 1829
1056-3830 See DARKHAWK (NEW YORK, N.Y.). 4859
1056-3857 See GLOBAL TRADE TALK. 838
1056-3873 See HUA WEN ZA ZHI. 2263
1056-389X See CRITICAL LEGAL ISSUES. 2957
1056-3903 See BIOLOGIC THERAPY OF CANCER UPDATES. 3809
1056-3911 See JOURNAL OF ALGEBRAIC GEOMETRY. 3511

1056-392X See ISLAND ESCAPES. 5481
1056-3938 See SOLAR, MAN OF THE ATOM. 4866
1056-3946 See WORLD WRESTLING FEDERATION BATTLEMANIA. 4930
1056-3954 See LOTUS (MUSKOGEE, ILL.). 4603
1056-3962 See REGENT UNIVERSITY LAW REVIEW. 3037
1056-3970 See STUDIES ON THEMES AND MOTIFS IN LITERATURE. 3442
1056-3997 See MID-WESTERN EDUCATIONAL RESEARCHER (1991). 1764
1056-4004 See QI (FAIRFAX, VA.). 2601
1056-4020 See VITAL TIMES. 5182
1056-4055 See MARYLAND TECHNOLOGY RESOURCE GUIDE. 5127
1056-4063 See ENGINE POWER PERSPECTIVE. 2113
1056-4063 See POWER PRODUCTS BUSINESS. 2124
1056-408X See JOURNAL REVIEWS FOR SCHOOL ADMINISTRATORS. 1865
1056-4098 See MEDICAL MALPRACTICE - OB/GYN LITIGATION REPORTER. 3741
1056-4128 See FORDHAM ENTERTAINMENT, MEDIA & INTELLECTUAL PROPERTY LAW FORUM. 2971
1056-4209 See SNOW GOER (WAYZATA, MINN.). 4919
1056-4217 See SHEPARD'S COLORADO EXPRESS CITATIONS. 3049
1056-4225 See LEATHER CRAFTERS JOURNAL, THE. 374
1056-4241 See CHALLENGING THE LITERARY CANON. 3373
1056-425X See NINETEENTH-CENTURY STUDIES (ANN ARBOR, MICH.). 3417
1056-4276 See FIAT LUX / UNIVERSITY OF CALIFORNIA, RIVERSIDE. 1091
1056-4284 See CHICAGO BEAR REPORT. 4890
1056-4292 See STOCKHOLDERS & CREDITORS NEWS SERVICE CONCERNING EASTERN AIRLINES, INC. / CONTINENTAL AIRLINES, INC. 37
1056-4314 See PATRIOT REVIEW, THE. 1094
1056-4322 See AMERICA AT LARGE. 2527
1056-4330 See GALE'S AUTO SOURCEBOOK. 5415
1056-4349 See DRAMA CRITICISM (DETROIT, MICH. : 1991). 5363
1056-4357 See BIRNBAUM'S BOSTON. 5464
1056-4365 See BIRNBAUM'S CHICAGO. 5464
1056-4373 See BIRNBAUM'S WESTERN EUROPE. 5465
1056-4381 See BIRNBAUM'S BARCELONA. 5463
1056-439X See BIRNBAUM'S EASTERN EUROPE. 5464
1056-4403 See BIRNBAUM'S SAN FRANCISCO. 5464
1056-4411 See BIRNBAUM'S VENICE. 5464
1056-442X See BIRNBAUM'S ROME. 5464
1056-4438 See BIRNBAUM'S PARIS. 5464
1056-4446 See BIRNBAUM'S NEW YORK. 5464
1056-4454 See BIRNBAUM'S MIAMI & FT. LAUDERDALE. 5464
1056-4462 See BIRNBAUM'S LOS ANGELES. 5464
1056-4470 See BIRNBAUM'S LONDON. 5464
1056-4489 See BIRNBAUM'S FLORENCE. 5464
1056-4497 See MODERN GENETICS. 549
1056-4500 See CHINA BUSINESS MONITOR. 656
1056-4527 See COLLECT, I. 2772
1056-4535 See WOMEN WRITERS OF ITALY. 3454
1056-4543 See ORTHOPEDIC RESIDENT, THE. 3884
1056-4551 See GROOM'S GUIDE, THE. 3995
1056-456X See WORLDWIDE FRANCHISE DIRECTORY. 958
1056-4578 See ANNUAL REVIEW OF WOMEN IN WORLD RELIGIONS, THE. 4935
1056-4586 See POLLUTION PREVENTION ADVISOR. 2239

1056-4594 See NONPROFIT INSIGHTS. 4739
1056-4616 See JUNTA TRIBUNE-DEMOCRAT, LA. 5636
1056-4624 See HOOSIER UNITED METHODIST NEWS. 5061
1056-4659 See HORN REVIEW, THE. 2640
1056-4667 See MINNESOTA POLITICAL ACTION REPORT. 4482
1056-4675 See SOCIAL STUDIES TEXAN, THE. 5222
1056-4683 See WORKPLACE AND THE LAW, THE. 1719
1056-4705 See RAP MASTERS. 4148
1056-4713 See HOTEL & TRAVEL INDEX (ABC INTERNATIONAL ED.). 23
1056-4721 See GERMANY (SYRACUSE, N.Y.). 1564
1056-473X See INJURIES, WOUNDS, AND MULTIPLE BODY DAMAGES. 3587
1056-4748 See MALPRACTICE BI-WEEKLY NEWSLETTER INDEX OF FRAUD, MEDICAL MISTAKES, DIAGNOSTIC ERRORS, AND ADVERSE REACTIONS, INCLUDING ILLNESSES AND DISEASES CAUSED BY DOCTORS. 3741
1056-4764 See ARKANSAS DENTISTRY. 1316
1056-4772 See AMERICAN PAPERMAKER (1991). 4232
1056-4780 See ULTIMATE FITNESS FOR A LIFETIME. 2601
1056-4829 See NEW YORK TAX UPDATE. 749
1056-4837 See LEGO DACTA DEALER NEWS. 1615
1056-4853 See VALLEY GAZETTE, THE. 5740
1056-487X See NUNC PRO TUNC. 3020
1056-4888 See PHASE AND CYCLE. 3468
1056-4896 See IMMUNOLOGICAL DISORDERS UPDATE. 3671
1056-490X See GREEN BUSINESS LETTER, THE. 2172
1056-4926 See JOURNAL OF MANAGEMENT INQUIRY. 874
1056-4934 See EUROPEAN EDUCATION. 1745
1056-4942 See PUBLIC AND ACCESS SERVICES QUARTERLY. 3243
1056-4950 See JOURNAL OF PHARMACEUTICAL CARE IN PAIN & SYMPTOM CONTROL. 4311
1056-4969 See STUDIES IN PHENOMENOLOGICAL THEOLOGY. 5001
1056-4977 See WIRELESS COMPUTING. 1207
1056-4985 See RX REPORT. 4329
1056-4993 See CHILD AND ADOLESCENT PSYCHIATRIC CLINICS OF NORTH AMERICA. 3923
1056-5000 See IBERICA. 3395
1056-5019 See MONOGRAPHS IN LINGUISTICS. 3304
1056-5027 See ORACLE STORY. 3420
1056-5035 See ORACLE POETRY. 3467
1056-5043 See JAPAN HOTEL AND RESORT INVESTMENT REPORT. 2807
1056-5051 See AIR JOBS DIGEST. 7
1056-506X See REDEMPTION DIGEST AND CORPORATE ACTIONS. 807
1056-5078 See FOOD PRODUCTS & EQUIPMENT. 2339
1056-5094 See NONPROFIT REPORT (BOSTON, MASS.), THE. 749
1056-5108 See MANN-MALLIN FANTASY BASEBALL GUIDE, THE. 4904
1056-5116 See GREAT AMERICAN BASEBALL STAT BOOK. 4897
1056-5124 See NGOUI VIET DAILY NEWS. ENGLISH SECTION. 5637
1056-5132 See HOUSING MARKET STATISTICS. 2824
1056-5140 See HOUSING ECONOMICS. 2824
1056-5159 See FORECAST OF HOUSING ACTIVITY. 2823
1056-5167 See PFLUGERVILLE PRESS, THE. 5753
1056-5175 See MAN! (AUSTIN, TEX.). 3995
1056-5191 See APPLIED CYTOGENETICS. 542

1056-5272 See SWEET'S INDUSTRIAL CONSTRUCTION & RENOVATION CATALOG FILE. 1997
1056-5280 See POLITICAL AND ECONOMIC CONDITIONS IN SOUTHERN AFRICA. 1578
1056-5299 See SOTO STATES ANTHROPOLOGIST, THE. 245
1056-5329 See LEAD BELLY LETTER. 4128
1056-5353 See BOXING REGISTRY'S RATINGS GUIDE. 4888
1056-540X See PC PUBLISHING AND PRESENTATIONS. 1263
1056-5426 See SWEET'S ELECTRICAL ENGINEERING & REPORT CATALOG FILE. 2083
1056-5442 See PIB'S BUSINESS & INCENTIVES. 703
1056-5469 See CFO'S REPORT FOR TREASURERS, FINANCIAL OFFICERS & BUSINESS MANAGERS, THE. 656
1056-5477 See LYMPHOKINE AND CYTOKINE RESEARCH. 538
1056-5485 See GOLF MAGAZINE (1991). 4896
1056-5493 See GOLF MAGAZINE (1991). 4896
1056-5507 See Z MAGAZINE (BOSTON, MASS.). 4501
1056-5531 See WESTWORDS (SAN MARINO, CALIF.). 2484
1056-554X See MESSAGE IN THE MUSIC. 4131
1056-5558 See WISCONSIN CAREER DIRECTIONS. 4210
1056-5604 See GSI REPORT ON REAL ESTATE AND FACILITY MANAGEMENT AUTOMATION. 4838
1056-5647 See SWEET'S CATALOG FILE. PRODUCTS FOR ENGINEERING AND RETROFIT, ELECTRICAL AND RELATED PRODUCTS. 2083
1056-5663 See ATOMS & WASTE. 2225
1056-5671 See PHASE III PROFILES. 4324
1056-568X See BULLETIN / POLISH GENEALOGICAL SOCIETY, CALIFORNIA. 2441
1056-5696 See LAW OFFICE AUTOMATOR, THE. 2996
1056-5701 See INTERNATIONAL AIR REVIEW. 24
1056-5728 See INTERNATIONAL MILITARY REVIEW. 4657
1056-5744 See NEO-TECH REPORT, THE. 5132
1056-5760 See FAMA (TEANECK, N.J.). 2533
1056-5787 See FROMMER'S COMPREHENSIVE TRAVEL GUIDE. NEW ENGLAND. 5476
1056-5795 See FROMMER'S COMPREHENSIVE TRAVEL GUIDE. ROME. 5476
1056-5841 See ROYCROFT REVIEW, THE. 363
1056-5868 See STRESS MANAGEMENT ADVISOR. 4619
1056-5876 See NEWSLETTER - SOUTH AND MESO-AMERICAN INDIAN INFORMATION CENTER (1990). 2269
1056-5914 See CORE ANALYTE. 973
1056-599X See CLINICAL CHEMISTRY (CHICAGO, ILL.). 972
1056-6007 See BAKING BUYER. 2328
1056-6015 See KANSAS CITY COMMERCE. 820
1056-6023 See PAGE (CHICAGO, ILL.), THE. 1263
1056-6031 See JOURNAL - ILLINOIS. OFFICE OF THE COMMISSIONER OF SAVINGS AND RESIDENTIAL FINANCE, THE. 793
1056-6074 See MEMBERSHIP DIRECTORY - ASSOCIATION FOR INVESTMENT MANAGEMENT AND RESEARCH. 906
1056-6090 See DIE CASTING INDUSTRY BLUE BOOK. 1604
1056-6104 See BIB TELEVISION PROGRAMMING SOURCE BOOKS. 1127
1056-6112 See DIRECTORY OF EMPLOYEE LEASING FIRMS, A. 1663
1056-6120 See OCCASIONAL PAPERS / SWENSON SWEDISH IMMIGRATION RESEARCH CENTER. 1920
1056-6139 See INTERDISCIPLINARY HUMANITIES. 2848
1056-6147 See WHO'S WHO OF AMERICAN BUSINESS LEADERS. 720

1056-6155 See I.H.I. GUIDE HOSES. 3480
1056-6163 See IMPLANT DENTISTRY. 1324
1056-6171 See JOURNAL OF APPLIED POULTRY RESEARCH. 213
1056-618X See ADVANCES IN HYPERTENSION. 3698
1056-6198 See YSB (WASHINGTON, D.C.). 2275
1056-621X See ALLIANCE PLUS. 3189
1056-6228 See BB'S HEALTH WATCH. 2596
1056-6244 See BUSINESS INSIGHT. 649
1056-6252 See BLOUNT JOURNAL, THE. 2439
1056-6279 See HOOVER'S HANDBOOK OF WORLD BUSINESS. 680
1056-6279 See HOOVER'S HANDBOOK OF AMERICAN BUSINESS. 1608
1056-6287 See AMERICAS COMMON MARKET NEWS, THE. 822
1056-6309 See HISTORIC PRESERVATION FORUM. 2618
1056-6325 See SOCIAL STUDIES REVIEW (MILLBRAE, CALIF.). 5222
1056-6333 See FAMILYFUN (NEW YORK, N.Y.). 2280
1056-6341 See INSIDE LOBBYING. 4657
1056-635X See BOOK RIGHTS REPORT. 4825
1056-6368 See VITAL ISSUES (WASHINGTON, D.C.). 2275
1056-6376 See WHO'S PRINTING WHAT? (NEWSLETTER). 4570
1056-6392 See JOURNAL OF VETERINARY EMERGENCY AND CRITICAL CARE (SANTA BARBARA, CALIF.). 5514
1056-6406 See GLOBAL MEETING LINE, INC. [COMPUTER FILE] : MEETINGS DATA BASE MANAGEMENT. 869
1056-6414 See GAME PLAYERS PC ENTERTAINMENT. 4861
1056-6465 See MINNESOTA MEDIA DIRECTORY (TWIN CITIES ED. 1991). 1117
1056-6473 See SHOP 'TIL YA DROP. 1299
1056-649X See GRANTS FOR FOREIGN AND INTERNATIONAL PROGRAMS. 4337
1056-6554 See WG&L TAX PLANNING CHECKLISTS. 4758
1056-6708 See WHO'S WHO WORLDWIDE REGISTRY. 439
1056-6716 See JOURNAL OF SPORT REHABILITATION. 3954
1056-6724 See SPORT SCIENCE REVIEW (CHAMPAIGN, ILL.). 4921
1056-6732 See QUARTERLY - ASSOCIATION OF PROFESSIONAL GENEALOGISTS (U.S.). 2468
1056-6740 See POLITICAL CORRECTION. 4489
1056-6759 See WACKY WORLD OF PEAFOWL REPORT, THE. 5620
1056-6767 See OREGON HEALTH FORUM. 4795
1056-6783 See PASSAGES (EVANSTON, ILL.). 2851
1056-6791 See OPERA SCENE (DURHAM, N.C.). 386
1056-6805 See FESTIVAL OF AMERICAN FOLKLIFE / SMITHSONIAN INSTITUTION AND NATIONAL PARK SERVICE. 2319
1056-6813 See CAPACITOR INDUSTRY NEWSLETTER : BIMONTHLY NEWS FOR THE FILM CAPACITOR TRADE AND ALLIED DIELECTRIC MARKETS. 1600
1056-683X See NOBO (HARLEM HEIGHTS, N.Y.). 2270
1056-6872 See OFFICIAL IOWA MANUFACTURERS DIRECTORY. 3485
1056-6945 See ... FILM FINANCIAL RECORD, THE. 4069
1056-6953 See NEWSLETTER / BLAIR COUNTY GENEALOGICAL SOCIETY. 2463
1056-6961 See BARNES BULLETIN 2.0. 2438
1056-697X See KIPLINGER'S PERSONAL FINANCE MAGAZINE. 795
1056-697X See KIPLINGER'S PERSONAL FINANCE MAGAZINE [MICROFORM]. 795
1056-6996 See VERMONT GOVERNMENT DIRECTORY. 4693

1056-7011 *See* STATE EXECUTIVE DIRECTORY ANNUAL. **4687**

1056-702X *See* WILDLAND/URBAN INTERFACE. **2293**

1056-7038 *See* DIGITAL MEDIA. **2113**

1056-7046 *See* CONDENSED MATTER NEWS. **4401**

1056-7054 *See* ENVIRONMENTAL ENGINEERING (NEW YORK, N.Y.). **2167**

1056-7062 *See* ENA'S NURSING SCAN IN EMERGENCY CARE. **3855**

1056-7070 *See* LOWER COLUMBIA BUSINESS. **691**

1056-7089 *See* LIVE POETS. **3465**

1056-7097 *See* OPERATIVE ORTHOPAEDICS UPDATES. **3883**

1056-7100 *See* PUBLIC ASSISTANCE REPORT (SILVER SPRING, MD.). **5303**

1056-7119 *See* ADVANCED INTELLIGENT NETWORKS REPORT. **1240**

1056-7127 *See* GPS REPORT. **1156**

1056-7135 *See* USER'S GUIDE TO ARTICLE 80, A. **2293**

1056-7151 *See* PROGRESS IN EXPERIMENTAL PERSONALITY AND PSYCHOPATHOLOGY RESEARCH. **3932**

1056-716X *See* BETTER HOMES AND GARDENS DECORATIVE WOODCRAFTS. **633**

1056-7186 *See* NEUROSCIENCE FACTS. **3842**

1056-7194 *See* INDUSTRIAL BIOPROCESSING. **1946**

1056-7208 *See* TECHNIQUES IN DIAGNOSTIC PATHOLOGY (BALTIMORE, MD.). **3898**

1056-7216 *See* URBAN MISSION. **5007**

1056-7224 *See* RELIGION & PUBLIC EDUCATION. **1777**

1056-7232 *See* BANK RESOLUTION REPORTER. **776**

1056-7240 *See* MOVING FORWARD : THE NATIONAL NEWSPAPER FOR PEOPLE WITH DISABILITIES. **4391**

1056-7275 *See* FEDERAL EXECUTIVE DIRECTORY ANNUAL. **4648**

1056-733X *See* WEST VIRGINIA SCHOOL JOURNAL (1990). **1791**

1056-7348 *See* NEWS FROM THE OCEANOGRAPHER OF THE NAVY. **4181**

1056-7364 *See* DOS RESOURCE GUIDE. **1202**

1056-7372 *See* CONSUMER ELECTRONICS BUYER'S GUIDE. **2039**

1056-7380 *See* AMERICAN GOSPEL MAGAZINE. **4099**

1056-7399 *See* PHLI ENVIRONMENTAL LIFE LETTER, THE. **2179**

1056-7402 *See* WIDE SMILES. **5314**

1056-7410 *See* BIBLIOGRAPHIES OF BATTLES AND LEADERS. **4061**

1056-7429 *See* LEFT BANK. **3404**

1056-7437 *See* JOURNAL OF ORTHOPAEDIC TECHNIQUES. **3882**

1056-7461 *See* MANAGED CARE WEEK. **3788**

1056-747X *See* DEFENSE & AEROSPACE ELECTRONICS. **2040**

1056-7488 *See* SLENDER SENSE. **2601**

1056-7496 *See* ACADEMIC ABSTRACTS. **2496**

1056-750X *See* PURCHASING PERFORMANCE BENCHMARKS FOR THE U.S. COMPUTER AND TELECOMMUNICATIONS EQUIPMENT INDUSTRY. **951**

1056-7518 *See* GEOCHEMISTRY AND COSMOCHEMISTRY. **976**

1056-7542 *See* CROSS STITCH! MAGAZINE. **372**

1056-7550 *See* SHAWNEE SUN (SHAWNEE, OKLA.), THE. **5732**

1056-7569 *See* LEGISLATIVE UPDATE - ALABAMA COUNCIL FOR SCHOOL ADMINISTRATION AND SUPERVISION. **1866**

1056-7585 *See* EIKENBURG & STILES' TEXAS ENVIRONMENTAL LAW LETTER. **2965**

1056-7593 *See* CURRENT POLITICS AND ECONOMICS OF JAPAN. **4370**

1056-7623 *See* RACING FOR KIDS. **1068**

1056-7682 *See* WASHINGTON APPLE PI. **1207**

1056-7690 *See* PRICE WATERHOUSE INVESTOR'S TAX ADVISER (POCKET BOOKS), THE. **4741**

1056-7712 *See* FODOR'S ... POCKET GUIDE TO NEW YORK CITY. **5472**

1056-7739 *See* D.C. ZONING NEWS, THE. **2820**

1056-7747 *See* HELICOPTER EQUIPMENT LISTS & PRICES. RECIPROCATING ENGINE HELICOPTERS. **22**

1056-7755 *See* OFFICIAL HELICOPTER BLUE BOOK. RECIPROCATING ENGINE HELICOPTERS. **31**

1056-7763 *See* OFFICIAL HELICOPTER BLUE BOOK. TURBINE ENGINE HELICOPTERS. **31**

1056-778X *See* BRIGHT (MIDDLETOWN, CALIF.), THE. **4940**

1056-7798 *See* BOTTOM LINE, THE. **644**

1056-7801 *See* CONSTRUCTION MANAGEMENT JOURNAL. **610**

1056-781X *See* KINESIS (WHITEFISH, MONT.). **3402**

1056-7828 *See* MINORITY BUILDER GAZETTE, THE. **621**

1056-7836 *See* WOMAN'S DAY HELPFUL HINTS LETTER. **2793**

1056-7844 *See* CLIENT SERVER REPORT, THE. **1174**

1056-7852 *See* BUSINESS VISUALIZATION. **1172**

1056-7860 *See* JOURNAL OF CHEMICAL VAPOR DEPOSITION. **980**

1056-7879 *See* INTERNATIONAL JOURNAL OF EDUCATIONAL REFORM. **1754**

1056-7887 *See* SPORTS ILLUSTRATED ... SPORTS ALMANAC, THE. **4923**

1056-7895 *See* INTERNATIONAL JOURNAL OF DAMAGE MECHANICS. **1979**

1056-7909 *See* VACCINE RESEARCH. **3677**

1056-7917 *See* MEDIEVAL AND EARLY MODERN MYSTICISM. **4242**

1056-7925 *See* WSN EXPRESS. **40**

1056-7933 *See* PRACTICAL ENDODONTICS. **1333**

1056-7941 *See* TESOL JOURNAL. **1907**

1056-795X *See* U.S.A. GULF COAST OIL & GAS INDUSTRY DIRECTORY. **4281**

1056-7976 *See* SMALLTALK REPORT, THE. **1281**

1056-7984 *See* IOMA'S REPORT ON REDUCING BENEFITS COSTS. **872**

1056-7992 *See* HISPANIC AMERICANS (BOULDER, COLO.). **2262**

1056-800X *See* RESEARCH & EXPLORATION. **4171**

1056-8018 *See* TERRA NOVA (WASHINGTON, D.C.). **4536**

1056-8034 *See* BEST AMERICAN SPORTS WRITING, THE. **4887**

1056-8042 *See* UP FROM DEPRESSION. **2601**

1056-8050 *See* BPRC TECHNICAL REPORT. **2556**

1056-8077 *See* ASEE PRISM. **1965**

1056-8093 *See* CPJ UPDATE. **4506**

1056-8115 *See* BANKRISK (STAMFORD, CONN.). **777**

1056-8123 *See* GOVERNMENTAL RISK MANAGEMENT REPORTS. **2881**

1056-8131 *See* OUTLAW BIKER TATTOO REVUE SPECIALS. **5269**

1056-814X *See* CAPTIVE INSURANCE COMPANY DIRECTORY. **2877**

1056-8158 *See* CAPTIVE INSURANCE COMPANY REPORTS. **2877**

1056-8174 *See* FRANKFORT AREA NEWS. **2533**

1056-8182 *See* HUNTER & SPORT HORSE. **2800**

1056-8190 *See* PAPERS IN REGIONAL SCIENCE : THE JOURNAL OF THE REGIONAL SCIENCE ASSOCIATION INTERNATIONAL. **2830**

1056-8204 *See* SHEPARD'S TEXAS EXPRESS CITATIONS. **3054**

1056-8263 *See* OFFSHORE WORLDWIDE. **4853**

1056-8271 *See* CEDARTOWN STANDARD (1950). **5652**

1056-828X *See* JOURNAL OF LIGHT CONSTRUCTION (NATIONAL ED.), THE. **618**

1056-8298 *See* TREKWEST (SACRAMENTO, CALIF.). **5497**

1056-8301 *See* TRADEWEEK (LOS ANGELES, CALIF.). **854**

1056-8328 *See* OUTLOOK (OTHELLO, WASH.), THE. **5761**

1056-8336 *See* TORRE DE PAPEL (IOWA CITY, IOWA). **3447**

1056-8344 *See* REALSCAN. PALM BEACH COUNTY [COMPUTER FILE] : REAL ESTATE MARKET INFORMATION SYSTEMS. **4845**

1056-845X *See* BIG BLUE REVIEW. **4887**

1056-8468 *See* BRITISH MARQUE CAR CLUB NEWS. **5408**

1056-8476 *See* EUROPEAN CAR. **5414**

1056-8484 *See* CAMERA & DARKROOM. **4367**

1056-8492 *See* TODAY'S JEWISH FAMILY. **5053**

1056-8506 *See* YANKEE DOODLER MAGAZINE, THE. **2550**

1056-8514 *See* STATE PARK AND RECREATION UPDATE. **4708**

1056-8522 *See* PLANETARY CITIZEN : HONORING THE EARTH, HUMANITY, AND THE SACRED IN ALL LIFE. **4357**

1056-8530 *See* CHIROHEALTH (FULLERTON, CALIF.). **2596**

1056-8557 *See* FOCUS, ISRAEL. **2651**

1056-8573 *See* ORION COMPUTER PRICE WATCH. **1245**

1056-8581 *See* VINTAGE GUITAR. **4158**

1056-859X *See* OFFICE EQUIPMENT. **700**

1056-8603 *See* PHANTASTIC PHINDS FOR PHYS. ED. **1857**

1056-8611 *See* SIMPLY SEAFOOD. **2357**

1056-862X *See* GUIDE TO MARTIN COUNTY. **5479**

1056-8638 *See* SOUTHEASTERN STATES MINING DIRECTORY. **2151**

1056-8662 *See* JOURNAL OF PROFESSIONAL BOOKKEEPING AND MANAGEMENT, THE. **747**

1056-8670 *See* SEMINARS IN PERIOPERATIVE NURSING. **3869**

1056-8689 *See* AFROCENTRIC SCHOLAR, THE. **2254**

1056-8697 *See* TOMART'S ACTION FIGURE DIGEST. **2778**

1056-8700 *See* ANNUAL REVIEW OF BIOPHYSICS AND BIOMOLECULAR STRUCTURE. **494**

1056-8719 *See* JOURNAL OF PHARMACOLOGICAL AND TOXICOLOGICAL METHODS. **4312**

1056-8727 *See* JOURNAL OF DIABETES AND ITS COMPLICATIONS. **3731**

1056-8735 *See* DIRECTORY OF CONSTRUCTION LAW FIRMS, THE. **2962**

1056-8751 *See* ACP JOURNAL CLUB. **3794**

1056-8816 See MOLECULAR CRYSTALS AND LIQUID CRYSTALS SCIENCE AND TECHNOLOGY SECTION C, MOLECULAR MATERIALS. **1033**

1056-8816 See MOLECULAR CRYSTALS AND LIQUID CRYSTALS SCIENCE AND TECHNOLOGY: SECTION A, MOLECULAR CRYSTALS AND LIQUID CRYSTALS. **1032**

1056-8816 See MOLECULAR CRYSTALS AND LIQUID CRYSTALS SCIENCE AND TECHNOLOGY SECTION D, DISPLAY AND IMAGING. **4438**

1056-8875 *See* QUARTERLY / DUTCH FAMILY HERITAGE SOCIETY. **2469**

1056-8905 *See* JUSTICE (WASHINGTON, D.C.). **2992**

1056-8921 *See* NUEVA INTERNACIONAL. **4485**

1056-893X *See* LGB TELEGRAM. **5385**

1056-8948 *See* CHICAGO ENVIRONMENT, THE. **2162**

1056-8956 *See* NEONATAL PHARMACOLOGY QUARTERLY. **4317**

1056-8972 See JOURNAL OF QUESTIONED DOCUMENT EXAMINATION. **3167**

1056-8980 *See* SHEPARD'S ALABAMA EXPRESS CITATIONS. **3048**

1056-9006 *See* OZAUKEE COUNTY NEWS GRAPHIC. **5770**

1056-9014 *See* NATURAL TOXINS. **3983**

ISSN Index

1056-9030 *See* ENFORCEMENT ACTIONS. **2155**

1056-9049 *See* LICENSEE CONTRACTOR AND VENDOR INSPECTION STATUS REPORT. **4662**

1056-9057 *See* LICENSEE EVENT REPORT (LER) COMPILATION. **3003**

1056-9065 *See* WEEKLY INFORMATION REPORT - U.S. NUCLEAR REGULATORY COMMISSION. **2159**

1056-9073 *See* MARINES (WASHINGTON, D.C.). **4049**

1056-9081 *See* NRC TELEPHONE DIRECTORY. **4670**

1056-9111 *See* APPELBAUM/GRISSO REPORT ON LAW AND MENTAL HEALTH, THE. **2936**

1056-912X *See* CARDEALS (WASHINGTON, D.C.). **4889**

1056-9138 *See* BIOLOGICAL EFFECTS OF NONIONIZING ELECTROMAGNETIC RADIATION DIGEST UPDATE (PHILADELPHIA, PA.). **3686**

1056-9162 *See* STANDARD & POOR'S STRUCTURED FINANCE. **915**

1056-9189 *See* STUDIES IN THIRD WORLD SOCIETIES. **5223**

1056-9219 *See* INTERNATIONAL JOURNAL OF COMMERCE AND MANAGEMENT. **841**

1056-9227 *See* CHAPTER ONE FOR THE UNPUBLISHED WRITER IN ALL OF US. **2918**

1056-9235 See WCOE (CARMICHAEL, CALIF.). **631**

1056-9243 *See* FAMILY TIMES (EAU CLAIRE, WIS.). **2280**

1056-9251 *See* INFECTIOUS DISEASE NEWS. **3714**

1056-9278 *See* REPUBLICAN UPDATE. **4493**

1056-9286 *See* INTERNAL MEDICINE (PLAINSBORO, N.J.). **3797**

1056-9324 *See* PHOTONICS EUROPEAN DIRECTORY. **3486**

1056-9340 *See* GUIDE TO FEDERAL FUNDING FOR ANTI-DRUG PROGRAMS. **1344**

1056-9413 *See* FOIA UPDATE. **2919**

1056-9537 *See* JOURNAL / AGRI-MARK INC. **195**

1056-9545 *See* WEEKLY READER OF HOUSING AND COMMUNITY NEWS, THE. **2839**

1056-9561 *See* REGIONAL REPORT ON TOP MANAGEMENT COMPENSATION. **884**

1056-9588 *See* PREVENTING INJURY. **2868**

1056-9596 *See* MISSOURI FACTS. **2747**

1056-960X *See* SOUTH CAROLINA FACTS. **2761**

1056-9618 *See* INTERSTUDY QUALITY EDGE, THE. **3590**

1056-9626 *See* DIRECTORY OF GRANTS FOR FOREIGN STUDY AND RESEARCH IN LAW. **1821**

1056-9634 *See* ASTRO-WEATHER (CENTRAL TIME ED.). **1420**

1056-9642 *See* ASTRO-WEATHER (EASTERN TIME ED.). **1420**

1056-9669 *See* ASTRO-WEATHER (MOUNTAIN TIME ED.). **1420**

1056-9677 *See* CERTIFIED NEWS : A NEWSLETTER FOR CERTIFIED CLINICAL AND HEALTH & FITNESS PROFESSIONALS. **3953**

1056-9693 *See* FREE STUFF FOR KIDS (DEEPHAVEN, MINN.). **1063**

1056-9707 *See* CONSERVATION IMPACT. **168**

1056-974X *See* 370/390 DATA BASE MANAGEMENT. **1252**

1056-9782 *See* TRACKKER (FORT WORTH, TEX.). **752**

1056-991X See INTERACTIONS BIBLIOGRAPHY, THE. **417**

1056-9928 *See* PRACTITIONERS GUIDE TO SUCCESSFUL TAX PRACTICE. **4741**

1057-0012 *See* HAZARDOUS WASTE & HAZARDOUS MATERIALS TRANSPORT DIRECTORY, THE. **2231**

1057-0020 *See* AMERICAN/OVERSEAS INVESTOR, THE. **890**

1057-0055 *See* LAST WORD (FRIENDSWOOD, TEX.), THE. **2922**

1057-0071 *See* COMMUNICATION & COMPUTER NEWS. **1106**

1057-008X *See* HENLEIN-HEINLEIN CHANTICLEER : NEWSLETTER OF THE HENLEIN-HEINLEIN FAMILY ASSOCIATION, THE. **2453**

1057-0098 *See* DIRECT CONTRACTING & HOSPITAL MANAGED CARE. **3779**

1057-0136 *See* GOLD BOOK. OLDER VEHICLES, THE. **5415**

1057-0160 *See* MATERIAL INFORMATION. **5354**

1057-0179 *See* HOT STOVE BASEBALL. **4899**

1057-0187 *See* ELECTRIC TROLLING MOTOR REPAIR FOR MR. & MS. FIX-IT. **593**

1057-0195 *See* YOUTH IN DISCOVERY. BIBLE STUDY CARDS. **5020**

1057-0209 *See* YOUTH IN ACTION. BIBLE STUDY CARDS. **5020**

1057-0217 *See* BIBLE BOOK STUDY FOR YOUTH. BIBLE STUDY CARDS. **5014**

1057-0225 *See* REBOOTING (PITTSBURGH, PA.). **1993**

1057-0241 *See* ELECTRICAL CODE WATCH. **2044**

1057-0268 *See* OUTDOOR RAILROADER. **5433**

1057-0276 *See* MOVIE GUIDE (CHICAGO, ILL.). **4075**

1057-0292 *See* JOURNAL OF SOCIAL THEORY IN ART EDUCATION, THE. **354**

1057-0306 *See* TRACTOR MAGAZINE, THE. **161**

1057-0314 *See* WESTERN JOURNAL OF COMMUNICATION. **1124**

0194-780X See R/C MODEL BOATS & RACING. **4914**

1057-0330 *See* FAT FENDERED STREET RODS. **5414**

1057-0349 *See* INSURANCE SOUTH MAGAZINE. **2884**

1057-0365 *See* DOCUMENT MANAGEMENT (SCOTTSDALE, ARIZ.). **1258**

1057-0381 *See* MAIN STREET MESSAGE. **5483**

1057-039X *See* PAUL MCCARTNEY MAGAZINE. **4145**

1057-0411 *See* CONVENIENCE STORE PEOPLE. **864**

1057-042X *See* CATERING IMPACT. **2330**

1057-0454 *See* OAG DESKTOP FLIGHT GUIDE (WORLDWIDE ED.). **5486**

1057-0535 *See* GOLD BOOK. CONTEMPORARY VEHICLES, THE. **5415**

1057-0551 *See* STUDIES IN TRANSNATIONAL LEGAL POLICY. **3136**

1057-0578 *See* DIRECTORY OF POLITICAL PERIODICALS. **5675**

1057-0586 *See* STATE REFERENCE PUBLICATIONS. **4688**

1057-0594 *See* LOBBYING RESOURCE DIRECTORY. **4662**

1057-0608 *See* MEDIEVAL PHILOSOPHY AND THEOLOGY. **4352**

1057-0624 *See* PERSECUTION OF HUMAN RIGHTS MONITORS. **4511**

1057-0675 *See* GOVERNING FLORIDA. **4728**

1057-0705 *See* NEW SENSE BULLETIN. **4605**

1057-0713 *See* HYDROGEN LETTER, THE. **977**

1057-0748 See CHINA RIGHTS FORUM. **4505**

1057-0756 *See* WRITER'S FORUM (CINCINNATI, OHIO). **3454**

1057-0772 *See* WRITER'S WORLD (BIG STONE GAP, VA.). **2926**

1057-0799 *See* WIND SURFING. **4929**

1057-0802 *See* JOURNAL OF MATERNAL-FETAL MEDICINE, THE. **3763**

1057-0829 *See* JOURNAL OF GLAUCOMA. **3876**

1057-0837 *See* JOURNAL OF MUSIC TEACHER EDUCATION. **4126**

1057-0845 *See* INSIGHT INTO AMERICAN LIFE & OPINIONS REVEALED BY POLLS & SURVEYS. **2739**

1057-0853 *See* LOBBY MONITOR, THE. **4481**

1057-0861 *See* HOW TO GET RICHES FROM GOD SCRIPTURALLY. **5017**

1057-087X *See* PROTECTION OFFICER NEWS. **3173**

1057-0888 *See* FINDER BINDER. THE SACRAMENTO, STOCKTON AND NORTHERN CALIFORNIA UPDATED NEWS MEDIA DIRECTORY. **1111**

1057-0896 *See* SWITZERLAND, JEWEL OF EUROPE. **2712**

1057-090X *See* REA REPORT, THE. **1515**

1057-0918 *See* OAG DESKTOP FLIGHT GUIDE (NORTH AMERICAN ED.). **5486**

1057-0926 See CQ RESEARCHER, THE. **4470**

1057-0934 *See* MUSIC OF THE BABA ALLAUDDIN GHARANA AS TAUGHT BY ALI AKBAR KHAN AT THE ALI AKBAR COLLEGE OF MUSIC, THE. **4134**

1057-0942 *See* ELECTRONIC IMAGING REPORT. **1183**

1057-0950 *See* AEROSPACE FINANCIAL NEWS. **5**

1057-1000 *See* MEALEY'S LITIGATION REPORTS. BANKING INSOLVENCY. **797**

1057-1019 *See* NOTISES (EVANSTON, ILL.). **3237**

1057-1159 *See* APPLE LIBRARY USERS GROUP NEWSLETTER. **1171**

1057-1191 *See* AEROSPACE DAILY'S AEROGRAM. **5**

1057-1213 *See* GLOBAL AGENDA, A. **4522**

1057-123X *See* YOUR MONEY (CHICAGO, ILL.). **920**

1057-1256 *See* ADVANCES IN PATHOLOGY AND LABORATORY MEDICINE. **3892**

1057-1272 *See* WEST HARTFORD NEWS. **5646**

1057-1337 *See* DIRECTORY OF ELECTRONIC JOURNALS, NEWSLETTERS, AND ACADEMIC DISCUSSION LISTS. **4813**

1057-137X *See* FETUS (NASHVILLE, TENN.), THE. **3761**

1057-1396 *See* WORLD CHAMPIONSHIP WRESTLING MAGAZINE : WCW. **4930**

1057-140X *See* VIDEO CONFERENCING : ANALYSIS OF AN EMERGING TECHNOLOGY. **1123**

1057-1418 *See* DENTISTRY (HAMILTON, ONT.). **1322**

1057-1485 *See* OSHA WEEK. **2868**

1057-1515 *See* PORTUGUESE STUDIES REVIEW. **2703**

1057-1523 *See* JOURNAL OF MINISTRY MARKETING & MANAGEMENT. **928**

1057-1531 *See* SOVIET UPDATE. **2710**

1057-1558 *See* MY FIRST MAGAZINE. **1066**

1057-1590 *See* APS BULLETIN / AMERICAN PAIN SOCIETY. **578**

1057-1604 *See* INSTANT HITS. **4072**

1057-1620 *See* GLOBAL NETWORKS. **1185**

1057-1639 *See* PERSPECTIVES ON ADDICTIONS NURSING. **3867**

1057-1655 *See* NATIONAL MINORITY POLITICS. **2268**

1057-1663 *See* SPECIAL BULLETIN / MISSISSIPPI AGRICULTURAL AND FORESTRY EXPERIMENT STATION. **136**

1057-1698 *See* AGRONOMY NOTES / UNIVERSITY OF KENTUCKY, COLLEGE OF AGRICULTURE, DEPARTMENT OF AGRONOMY. **162**

1057-171X *See* ENVIRONMENTAL PROTECTION NEWS. **2169**

1057-1736 *See* CAMCORE BULLETIN ON TROPICAL FORESTRY. **2377**

1057-1796 *See* LOCAL GOVERNMENT BULLETIN. **4662**

1057-1809 *See* SHEEP RESEARCH JOURNAL. **221**

1057-1825 See LAWYERS MONTHLY CATALOG, ANNUAL. **2998**

1057-185X *See* RCGS NEWSLETTER. **2469**

1057-1922 *See* RESEARCH IN RURAL SOCIOLOGY AND DEVELOPMENT. **5255**

1057-1930 *See* RURAL ENTERPRISE (MENOMONEE FALLS, WIS.). **131**

1057-1949 *See* EC - UNIVERSITY OF ARKANSAS, FAYETTEVILLE. COOPERATIVE EXTENSION SERVICE. **80**

1057-1981 *See* CCPS/AICHE DIRECTORY OF CHEMICAL PROCESS SAFETY SERVICES. **967**

1057-199X See HEALTHY OFFICE REPORT, THE. 2863

1057-2015 See SINGLES SOLUTIONS. 3996

1057-2023 See INTERNATIONAL FINE ART COLLECTOR. 353

1057-204X See PARK & GROUNDS MANAGEMENT. 4707

1057-2058 See FROMMER'S COMPREHENSIVE TRAVEL GUIDE. HONOLULU & OAHU. 5476

1057-2082 See ABUI NETWORK NEWS. 636

1057-2104 See NEW YORK REAL ESTATE JOURNAL. 4842

1057-2120 See ANIMAL AGRICULTURE UPDATE NEWSLETTER / COOPERATIVE EXTENSION SERVICE, UNIVERSITY OF MARYLAND SYSTEM, DEPARTMENT OF ANIMAL SCIENCES. 58

1057-2139 See FORESTRY REPORT R8-FR. 2382

1057-2163 See WATER PROTECTION, CONSERVATION, MANAGEMENT. 5543

1057-218X See PRACTICAL AQUACULTURE & LAKE MANAGEMENT. 2310

1057-2252 See TECHNICAL COMMUNICATION QUARTERLY. 1122

1057-2260 See ANALGESIAFILE (SAN ANTONIO, TEXAS). 3549

1057-2279 See GAS DAILY'S GAS STORAGE REPORT. 4257

1057-2287 See JOURNAL OF SMALL BUSINESS FINANCE, THE. 687

1057-2295 See CURRENT POLITICS AND ECONOMICS OF RUSSIA. 4470

1057-2309 See CURRENT POLITICS AND ECONOMICS OF EUROPE. 4470

1057-2317 See INTERNATIONAL INFORMATION & LIBRARY REVIEW, THE. 3218

1057-2333 See 1-2-3 FOR WINDOWS REPORT, THE. 1169

1057-235X See BASEBALL MAGAZINE (BELLEVILLE, ILL.). 4886

1057-2368 See REMINISCE (GREENDALE, WIS.). 2544

1057-2414 See INTERNATIONAL JOURNAL OF NAUTICAL ARCHAEOLOGY, THE. 270

1057-2430 See GRAZIER (CORVALLIS, OR.), THE. 90

1057-2457 See ANIMAL DAMAGE CONTROL. 58

1057-2465 See WREP. 147

1057-2473 See STAGE FIVE ADOLESCENCE. 1069

1057-2554 See DATA ENTRY/DATA CONVERSION SERVICES DIRECTORY. 1181

1057-2570 See ROOTS & BRANCHES. 5338

1057-2600 See PROBE (BELTSVILLE, MD.). 525

1057-2619 See DAIRY FOODS NEWSLETTER. 193

1057-266X See JOURNAL FOR PREACHERS. 4967

1057-2694 See PRACTICAL WINERY/VINEYARD. 2370

1057-2708 See SEAFOOD TREND NEWSLETTER. 2357

1057-2724 See FOREST WATCH. 2381

1057-2732 See ADVANCES IN MAGNETIC AND OPTICAL RESONANCE. 4443

1057-2759 See FOOD, DRUG, COSMETIC, AND MEDICAL DEVICE LAW DIGEST. 2971

1057-2791 See FROMMER'S COMPREHENSIVE TRAVEL GUIDE. FLORIDA. 5475

1057-2805 See MOLECULAR GENETIC MEDICINE. 549

1057-2821 See WONDER (SOUND BEACH, N.Y.). 2550

1057-283X See JOURNAL - ILLINOIS. OFFICE OF THE COMMISSIONER OF SAVINGS AND RESIDENTIAL FINANCE, THE. 793

1057-2848 See BIG BOND BOOK, THE. 892

1057-2856 See MICHIGAN HUNTING & FISHING. 4874

1057-2864 See DESIGN FIRM MANAGEMENT & ADMINISTRATION REPORT. 865

1057-2872 See CARIBBEAN ETHNOLOGY. 2258

1057-2880 See NATIONAL TEACHING & LEARNING FORUM, THE. 1901

1057-2899 See MLA DIRECTORY OF SCHOLARLY PRESSES IN LITERATURE AND LANGUAGE. 3412

1057-2902 See OBSERVATIONS (CARY, N.C.). 1288

1057-2910 See FLARE ADVENTURES. 378

1057-2929 See LADY ARCANE. 380

1057-2953 See GREEN COUNTRY SCIENCE & ENGINEERING JOURNAL. 1976

1057-2961 See RELIGIOUS LEADERS OF AMERICA (DETROIT, MICH.). 4992

1057-2996 See KIDS (STORRS, CONN.). 5294

1057-3003 See VIRGINIA GARDENER, THE. 2433

1057-3011 See KIDDIE BAZAAR. 1065

1057-302X See MICHIGAN UPPER PENINSULA BUSINESS REGISTER. 694

1057-3038 See MICHIGAN NORTHWESTERN REGION BUSINESS REGISTER. 694

1057-3046 See MICHIGAN NORTHEASTERN REGION COUNTIES BUSINESS REGISTER. 694

1057-3054 See MICHIGAN BAY-MIDLAND-SAGINAW COUNTIES BUSINESS REGISTER. 694

1057-3062 See MICHIGAN CENTRAL REGION BUSINESS REGISTER. 694

1057-3070 See MICHIGAN THUMB REGION BUSINESS REGISTER. 694

1057-3089 See MICHIGAN ALLEGAN-MUSKEGON-OTTAWA COUNTIES BUSINESS REGISTER. 694

1057-3097 See MICHIGAN BERRIEN-CASS-ST. JOSEPH BUSINESS REGISTER. 694

1057-3100 See MICHIGAN CALHOUN-KALAMAZOO COUNTIES BUSINESS REGISTER. 694

1057-3119 See MICHIGAN INGHAM-JACKSON COUNTIES BUSINESS REGISTER. 694

1057-3127 See MICHIGAN LIVINGSTON-WASHTENAW COUNTIES BUSINESS REGISTER. 1618

1057-3135 See MICHIGAN BRANCH-HILLSDALE-LENAWEE-MONROE COUNTIES BUSINESS REGISTER. 694

1057-3143 See MICHIGAN KENT COUNTY BUSINESS REGISTER. 694

1057-3151 See MICHIGAN GENESEE COUNTY BUSINESS REGISTER. 694

1057-3178 See MICHIGAN NORTH OAKLAND COUNTY BUSINESS REGISTER. 694

1057-3186 See MICHIGAN SOUTH OAKLAND COUNTY BUSINESS REGISTER. 694

1057-3194 See MICHIGAN CITY OF DETROIT BUSINESS REGISTER. 694

1057-3208 See MICHIGAN WESTERN WAYNE COUNTY BUSINESS REGISTER. 694

1057-3216 See ANNUAL PROGRESS REPORT / SOUTHEAST RESEARCH STATION, LOUISIANA AGRICULTURAL EXPERIMENT STATION. 205

1057-3224 See LONGWOOD GRADUATE PROGRAM SEMINARS, THE. 2424

1057-3240 See MINNESOTA MEDIA DIRECTORY (MIDWEST ED.). 1117

1057-3259 See SUNDAY BY SUNDAY. 5001

1057-3275 See SAVVY SHOPPER, THE. 5490

1057-3291 See HABILITATIVE MENTAL HEALTHCARE NEWSLETTER, THE. 3926

1057-3305 See STANDARD & POOR'S COMMERCIAL PAPER GUIDE. 812

1057-3321 See JOURNAL OF THE CHRONIC FATIGUE SYNDROMES. 3598

1057-333X See AEROSPACE DAILY'S WEEKLY BRIEFING. 5

1057-3348 See INTERNATIONAL GIS SOURCEBOOK. 2566

1057-3380 See SHEPARD'S ILLINOIS EXPRESS CITATIONS. 3050

1057-3453 See CULINARY TRENDS. 2332

1057-3461 See ADVANCES IN PARALLEL COMPUTING (GREENWICH, CONN.). 1170

1057-347X See IDAHO MANUFACTURING DIRECTORY. 3480

1057-3526 See NAHAM MANAGEMENT JOURNAL, THE. 3789

1057-3542 See FARM STORE. 85

1057-3569 See READING & WRITING QUARTERLY. 1884

1057-3577 See CYANOSIS (SANTA ROSA, CALIF.). 318

1057-3593 See EARLY DEVELOPMENT AND PARENTING. 1803

1057-3607 See CITY JOURNAL (NEW YORK, N.Y.), THE. 4468

1057-3623 See STATE RANKINGS (LAWRENCE, KAN.). 5339

1057-3631 See JOURNAL OF NURSING CARE QUALITY. 3859

1057-3682 See FREEDOM SPEECH. 5635

1057-3704 See OTOLARYNGOLOGY, AUDIOLOGY : AN ILLUSTRATED DESK DIARY. 3890

1057-3720 See ENTERTAINMENT ATLANTA : YOUR HOUR-BY-HOUR GUIDE TO ENTERTAINMENT ATLANTA. 319

1057-3771 See NORTHSHORE CITIZEN (1990). 5761

1057-378X See MASSAGE (DAVIS, CALIF.). 2599

1057-3801 See DOING BUSINESS IN SOUTH AFRICA. 668

1057-381X See DOING BUSINESS IN ZIMBABWE. 669

1057-3828 See DOING BUSINESS IN BELGIUM (NEW YORK, N.Y. 1978). 667

1057-3844 See DOING BUSINESS IN INDIA. 668

1057-3887 See DOING BUSINESS IN SPAIN (NEW YORK, N.Y. 1980). 668

1057-3909 See DOING BUSINESS IN SINGAPORE. 668

1057-3925 See DOING BUSINESS IN JAPAN (1975). 668

1057-3968 See BULLETIN - NATIONAL TROPICAL BOTANICAL GARDEN. 505

1057-4018 See FROMMER'S COMPREHENSIVE TRAVEL GUIDE. AUSTRIA & HUNGARY. 5475

1057-4131 See ANALGESIA COMPUTERFILE. 3958

1057-414X See HONOLULU WEEKLY. 5656

1057-4166 See MISSOURI ENVIRONMENTAL LAW LETTER. 3114

1057-4174 See KANSAS-IOWA ENVIRONMENTAL LAW LETTER. 3113

1057-4182 See DIRECT (BUFFALO, N.Y.). 2532

1057-4190 See COUNCIL CHRONICLE (URBANA, ILL.), THE. 1803

1057-4247 See INDUSTRIAL ENERGY TECHNOLOGY. 1946

1057-4263 See INTERNATIONAL JOURNAL OF ARTS MEDICINE. 3588

1057-428X See CONTINUING CARE. 5280

1057-4298 See ENVIRONMENTAL PROTECTION (WACO, TEX.). 2169

1057-4441 See CAR COLLECTOR & CAR CLASSICS MAGAZINE. 5409

1057-445X See PERIODONTICS FOR GPS. 1333

1057-4506 See DIMENSIONS (WINONA, MINN.). 1182

1057-4514 See ACM LETTERS ON PROGRAMMING LANGUAGES AND SYSTEMS. 1277

1057-4522 See INTEGRATED CIRCUITS. INTERFACE. 2065

1057-4530 See INTEGRATED CIRCUITS. DIGITAL. 2065

1057-4557 See GUINNESS BOOK OF RECORDS (NEW YORK, N.Y.). 1926

1057-4565 See DIRECTORY OF NEW MEXICO MANUFACTURERS (1991). 1604

1057-462X See BERLITZ TRAVELLER'S GUIDE TO GERMANY, THE. 5463

1057-4689 See BERLITZ TRAVELLER'S GUIDE TO AUSTRALIA, THE. 5462

1057-4697 See BERLITZ TRAVELLER'S GUIDE TO THE CARIBBEAN, THE. 5463

1057-4700 See BERLITZ TRAVELLER'S GUIDE TO HAWAII, THE. 5463

1057-4719 See BERLITZ TRAVELLER'S GUIDE TO IRELAND, THE. 5463

1057-4727 See BERLITZ TRAVELLER'S GUIDE TO SAN FRANCISCO & NORTHERN CALIFORNIA, THE. 5463

1057-4735 See BERLITZ TRAVELLER'S GUIDE TO ENGLAND & WALES, THE. 5462

1057-4743 See BERLITZ TRAVELLER'S GUIDE TO NEW YORK CITY, THE. 5463

1057-4751 See BERLITZ TRAVELLER'S GUIDE TO LONDON, THE. 5463

1057-476X See BERLITZ TRAVELLER'S GUIDE TO FRANCE, THE. 5462

1057-4786 See BERLITZ TRAVELER'S GUIDE TO MEXICO, THE. 5462

1057-4816 See LEADERSHIP WITH A HUMAN TOUCH. 875

1057-4883 See CRB FUTURES MARKET SERVICE. 895

1057-4921 See RANDOL BUYER'S GUIDE. 2149

1057-4956 See EUROPEAN ELECTRO-OPTICS. 4434

1057-5006 See HOUSEHOLD VEHICLES ENERGY CONSUMPTION. 1946

1057-5014 See ... BUSINESS ONE IRWIN BUSINESS AND INVESTMENT ALMANAC, THE. 651

1057-5022 See HARVARD MENTAL HEALTH LETTER, THE. 3926

1057-5049 See MOUNTAIN, PLAIN AND GARDEN. 518

1057-5057 See HARVARD HUMAN RIGHTS JOURNAL. 4508

1057-5065 See AIDS/HIV TREATMENT DIRECTORY. 3663

1057-5073 See JOURNAL OF HEALTH CARE BENEFITS. 2885

1057-509X See HERALD OF THE RUSSIAN ACADEMY OF SCIENCES. 5109

1057-5111 See DIRECTORY OF UNITED STATES IMPORTERS (1991). 831

1057-512X See DIRECTORY OF UNITED STATES IMPORTERS (1991). 831

1057-512X See DIRECTORY OF UNITED STATES EXPORTERS. 831

1057-5219 See INTERNATIONAL REVIEW OF FINANCIAL ANALYSIS. 792

1057-5227 See SPARK (CINCINNATI, OHIO). 1069

1057-526X See PRIVATE EQUITY ANALYST, THE. 911

1057-5278 See DIRECTORY OF ENGINEERING GRADUATE STUDIES & RESEARCH. 1970

1057-5286 See DIRECTORY OF ENGINEERING AND ENGINEERING TECHNOLOGY UNDERGRADUATE PROGRAMS. 1970

1057-5316 See FROHLINGER'S MARKETING REPORT. 924

1057-5375 See FIBER OPTICS BUSINESS NEWSLETTER. 1155

1057-5383 See MAN (BOSTON, MASS.). 1194

1057-5391 See WIRELESS TELECOMMUNICATIONS. 1169

1057-5413 See ARTWORLD HOTLINE. 315

1057-5472 See BEST BED & BREAKFAST IN ENGLAND, SCOTLAND & WALES, THE. 2804

1057-5480 See CLINICAL DENTAL BRIEFING. 1319

1057-5537 See AIRPORT OPERATIONS. 10

1057-5561 See ACCIDENT PREVENTION (ARLINGTON, VA.). 3

1057-557X See FLIGHT SAFETY FOUNDATION NEWS. 21

1057-5588 See FLIGHT SAFETY DIGEST (1988). 21

1057-5596 See ATTORNEY'S GUIDE TO STATE BAR ADMISSION REQUIREMENTS. 2938

1057-5618 See EN ROUTE TECHNOLOGY. 1184

1057-5626 See INVESTMENT MANAGEMENT TECHNOLOGY. 903

1057-5634 See NATURAL PRODUCT LETTERS. 491

1057-5642 See AMERICA'S FINEST COMPANIES. 638

1057-5677 See INTERNATIONAL CRIMINAL JUSTICE REVIEW. 2983

1057-5715 See JOURNAL OF RADIATION CURING AND RADIATION CURING. 4436

1057-5723 See PSYCHOANALYSIS AND PSYCHOTHERAPY. 3934

1057-5731 See PATHFINDER (DALLAS, TEX.). 2906

1057-5766 See FCC RECORD. 1155

1057-5774 See LISTS OF PARTIES EXCLUDED FROM FEDERAL PROCUREMENT OR NONPROCUREMENT PROGRAMS. 4662

1057-5782 See DOE THIS MONTH. 1936

1057-5790 See WEEKLY PETROLEUM STATUS REPORT / U.S. DEPARTMENT OF ENERGY, ENERGY INFORMATION ADMINISTRATION. 4282

1057-5804 See FEDERAL ADP AND TELECOMMUNICATIONS STANDARDS INDEX. 1185

1057-5812 See DECISIONS OF THE OFFICE OF ADMINISTRATIVE LAW JUDGES AND OFFICE OF ADMINISTRATIVE APPEALS. 3092

1057-5820 See JOB SAFETY & HEALTH QUARTERLY. 2864

1057-5839 See AWIS MAGAZINE. 5087

1057-5871 See NIH RECORD, THE. 4794

1057-588X See CANCERGRAM. SERIES CB19, ANTITUMOR AND ANTIVIRAL AGENTS MECHANISM OF ACTION. 3813

1057-5898 See CANCERGRAM. SERIES CB20 ANTITUMOR AND ANTIVIRAL AGENTS EXPERIMENTAL THERAPEUTICS TOXICOLOGY PHARMACOLOGY. 3813

1057-5901 See CANCERGRAM. SERIES CT01 CANCER DETECTION AND MANAGEMENT BIOLOGICAL MARKERS. 3813

1057-591X See CANCERGRAM. SERIES CT02 CANCER DETECTION AND MANAGEMENT NUCLEAR MEDICINE. 3813

1057-5928 See CANCERGRAM. SERIES CT14 CANCER DETECTION AND MANAGEMENT DIAGNOSTIC RADIOLOGY. 3813

1057-5936 See CANCERGRAM. SERIES CT05 LYMPHOMAS DIAGNOSIS TREATMENT. 3813

1057-5944 See CANCERGRAM. SERIES CT06, CLINICAL CANCER IMMUNOLOGY AND BIOLOGICAL THERAPY. 3813

1057-5960 See CANCERGRAM. SERIES CT08 LUNG CANCER. DIAGNOSIS TREATMENT. 3813

1057-5979 See CANCERGRAM. SERIES CT09 BREAST CANCER DIAGNOSIS TREATMENT PRE-CLINICAL BIOLOGY. 3813

1057-6002 See TELECOM TEN YEAR CALENDAR. 1165

1057-6010 See REYNOLDS RECORDS. 2470

1057-6029 See MARQUETTE SPORTS LAW JOURNAL. 3006

1057-6037 See LANGUAGE AND LITERATURE (SAN ANTONIO, TEX.). 3294

1057-607X See BIOTECHNOLOGY CITATION INDEX. 3689

1057-6088 See CHEMISTRY CITATION INDEX. 1011

1057-6096 See NEUROSCIENCE CITATION INDEX. 3842

1057-610X See STUDIES IN CONFLICT AND TERRORISM. 5263

1057-6185 See ... SOUTHEAST SOURCEBOOK, THE. 766

1057-6193 See GUIDE LINES (ROUND ROCK, TEX.). 865

1057-6215 See ADAMHA NEWS (1990). 1338

1057-6223 See FDA VETERINARIAN. 5510

1057-6266 See FROMMER'S COMPREHENSIVE TRAVEL GUIDE. CRUISES. 5475

1057-6274 See LET'S GO. THE BUDGET GUIDE TO LONDON. 5483

1057-6290 See ADVANCES IN MEDICAL SOCIOLOGY. 5238

1057-6304 See WHO'S WHO BUYERS GUIDE TO ELECTRONIC SOURCES (MIDWESTERN ED.). 2085

1057-6320 See WHO'S WHO BUYERS GUIDE TO ELECTRONIC SOURCES (SOUTHWESTERN ED.). 2086

1057-6339 See WHO'S WHO BUYERS GUIDE TO ELECTRONIC SOURCES (SOUTHEASTERN ED.). 2086

1057-6347 See WHO'S WHO BUYERS GUIDE TO ELECTRONIC SOURCES (NORTHEASTERN ED.). 2086

1057-6355 See BOOKWAYS (AUSTIN, TEX.). 4827

1057-6371 See NEWSLINE / AMERICAN MEDICAL ASSOCIATION AUXILIARY, INC. 3621

1057-6436 See AMERICA'S WONDERFUL LITTLE HOTELS & INNS. THE ROCKY MOUNTAINS AND THE SOUTHWEST. 2804

1057-6436 See AMERICA'S WONDERFUL LITTLE HOTELS & INNS. THE MIDWEST. 2803

1057-6460 See RAJANI PUBLICATIONS U.S.A., INC. 329

1057-6533 See WILSON BUSINESS ABSTRACTS. 735

1057-655X See MUSTANG & FORDS. 5421

1057-6614 See FELINE PRACTICE (1990). 5510

1057-6622 See CANINE PRACTICE (1990). 5507

1057-6681 See MONTANA MANUFACTURERS DIRECTORY. 3485

1057-6703 See FUND WATCH. 899

1057-6711 See INVESTOR'S DIGEST (FORT LAUDERDALE, FLA.). 903

1057-6800 See X-FORCE (NEW YORK, N.Y.). 4868

1057-6819 See X-MEN (NEW YORK, N.Y.). 4868

1057-6835 See RAJANI PUBLICATIONS U.S.A., INC. 329

1057-6851 See TENNIS ILLUSTRATED. 4925

1057-686X See WESTCHESTER COUNTY BUSINESS JOURNAL. 719

1057-6878 See DIRECTORY OF UNITED STATES EXPORTERS. 831

1057-6908 See CONDITIONING FOR CYCLING. 4891

1057-6940 See FOOD BUSINESS OPPORTUNITIES. 676

1057-6959 See FOOD BUSINESS ANNUAL. 2336

1057-7017 See TASK FORCE REPORT / COUNCIL FOR AGRICULTURAL SCIENCE AND TECHNOLOGY. 139

1057-7025 See HALL OF THE STATES MANDATE MONITOR. 4653

1057-7033 See RETAIL PROFIT FORUM. 957

1057-7041 See SILICON GRAPHICS WORLD. 1235

1057-7076 See CROCHET WORLD SPECIAL. 5183

1057-7114 See MEMORIAL'S SENIOR HEALTH UPDATE. 4790

1057-7122 See IEEE TRANSACTIONS ON CIRCUITS & SYSTEMS. PART 1, FUNDAMENTAL THEORY AND APPLICATIONS. 2061

1057-7130 See IEEE TRANSACTIONS ON CIRCUITS AND SYSTEMS. PART 2, ANALOG AND DIGITAL SIGNAL PROCESSING. 2061

1057-7149 See IEEE TRANSACTIONS ON IMAGE PROCESSING. 2062

1057-7157 See JOURNAL OF MICROELECTROMECHANICAL SYSTEMS. 2069

1057-7262 See EQUIPMENT WORLD. 5103

1057-7351 See PURCHASING PERFORMANCE BENCHMARKS FOR THE U.S. FOOD MANUFACTURING INDUSTRY. 951

1057-7378 See CABLE AVAILS. 756

1057-7394 See INFLATION MEASURES FOR SCHOOLS & COLLEGES. 1830

1057-7408 See JOURNAL OF CONSUMER PSYCHOLOGY: OFFICIAL JOURNAL OF THE SOCIETY FOR CONSUMER PSYCHOLOGY. 761

1057-7416 See MEDIA STUDIES JOURNAL. 1117

1057-7424 See BIOMEDICAL NEWS SOURCE MIDWEST. 3557

1057-7432 See JOURNAL OF EXPRESSIVE THERAPY. 4597

1057-7459 See FAIRFAX (COLUMBIA, MD.). 3387

1057-7467 See SOVIET BUSINESS REPORT, THE. 713

1057-7521 See DEFAULTED BONDS NEWSLETTER. 896

1057-753X See AMBULATORY RECORD MONITOR. 3776
1057-7556 See WEARABLE CRAFTS. 5186
1057-7610 See DIRECTORY OF FOOTWEAR & RELATED ACCESSORIES BUYERS. 1083
1057-7629 See VITAL AND HEALTH STATISTICS. SERIES 21. DATA ON NATALITY, MARRIAGE, AND DIVORCE. 4563
1057-7645 See FROMMER'S COMPREHENSIVE TRAVEL GUIDE. NEW ORLEANS. 5476
1057-770X See BANTAM'S SCOTLAND. 5462
1057-7718 See BANTAM'S AUSTRALIA. 5462
1057-7726 See BANTAM'S AUSTRALIA. 5462
1057-7734 See BANTAM'S SOVIET UNION. 5462
1057-7769 See INTERCULTURAL COMMUNICATION STUDIES. 5247
1057-7785 See FOOD NEWS FOR CONSUMERS / UNITED STATES DEPT. OF AGRICULTURE, FOOD SAFETY AND QUALITY SERVICE. 2338
1057-7793 See ACCEPTED MEAT AND POULTRY EQUIPMENT. 158
1057-7858 See TURKEYS (1985). 223
1057-7866 See LAYERS AND EGG PRODUCTION. 214
1057-7874 See LIVESTOCK SLAUGHTER. SUMMARY. 214
1057-7890 See ECONOMIC INDICATORS OF THE FARM SECTOR. COSTS OF PRODUCTION. MAJOR FIELD CROPS. 170
1057-7912 See NONCITRUS FRUITS & NUTS. MID-YEAR SUPPLEMENT. 114
1057-7920 See RICE STOCKS. 185
1057-7939 See INFORMATION TECHNOLOGY NEWSLETTER (HARRISBURG, PA.). 3217
1057-7971 See LADY'S CIRCLE PATCHWORK QUILTS PRESENTS QUILT CRAFT. 5184
1057-798X See SOFTWARE DIRECTORY. MASTER INDEX. 1290
1057-803X See WHO'S PRINTING WHAT (DIRECTORY). 4570
1057-8048 See FODOR'S HEALTHY ESCAPES. 5471
1057-8056 See CORPORATE FINANCE (NEW YORK, N.Y. 1991). 785
1057-8080 See LIFESTYLE ZIP CODE ANALYST, THE. 1298
1057-8102 See CIRCUIT RIDER (COLORADO SPRINGS, COLO.), THE. 4948
1057-8153 See ACCIDENT RECONSTRUCTION JOURNAL. 5403
1057-8161 See SHEPARD'S PENNSYLVANIA EXPRESS CITATIONS. 3053
1057-817X See WALT DISNEY'S SUMMER FUN. 4867
1057-8188 See RSAP NEWSLETTER. 3260
1057-8196 See METRO MAGAZINE. 5386
1057-8234 See SPOTLIGHT CASTING MAGAZINE. 4078
1057-8242 See WORLD AGRICULTURE (WASHINGTON, D.C. 1991). 147
1057-8250 See VIDEO SHOPPER. 1142
1057-8269 See FINE ART INDEX (NORTH AMERICAN ED.), THE. 350
1057-8277 See DESIGNERS WORLD. 2900
1057-8285 See ASIAN IC CONNECTION, THE. 1598
1057-8293 See INFORMATION PLEASE ENVIRONMENTAL ALMANAC, THE. 2174
1057-8307 See JOURNAL OF MILITARY AVIATION. 26
1057-8315 See SPORTS MEDICINE, TRAINING, AND REHABILITATION. 3956
1057-8323 See NURSING STAFF DEVELOPMENT INSIDER. 3865
1057-8331 See PENNSYLVANIA FISHERMAN. 4877
1057-834X See ELECTRONIC PUBLIC INFORMATION NEWSLETTER. 4645
1057-8358 See JOURNAL OF ASIAN MARTIAL ARTS. 2599
1057-8366 See DREAM (SAN DIEGO, CALIF.). 2532
1057-8374 See COGNIZER REPORT. 1175

1057-8390 See ESTIMATION AND TRACKING : PRINCIPLES AND TECHNIQUES. 3505
1057-8404 See STATE TAX NOTES (PRINT). 4750
1057-8447 See SITUATION AND OUTLOOK REPORT. AGRICULTURAL RESOURCES. 135
1057-8498 See GEOGRAPHIC REFERENCE REPORT. 1492
1057-8501 See HUNTER & SPORT HORSE. 2800
1057-8544 See WINE BUSINESS INSIDER. 2372
1057-8641 See BROOKINGS PAPERS ON ECONOMIC ACTIVITY. MICROECONOMICS. 1465
1057-8684 See DOING BUSINESS IN THE UNITED STATES (NEW YORK, N.Y. 1980). 669
1057-8714 See GLOBAL GUARANTY'S CREDIT ENHANCEMENT AND FINANCIAL GUARANTY DIRECTORY. 2881
1057-8722 See STUDENT LEADER (MADISON, WIS.). 1786
1057-8765 See U.S. IMPORTS OF MERCHANDISE. 855
1057-8773 See U.S. EXPORTS OF MERCHANDISE. 855
1057-8781 See COUNTY & CITY DATA BOOK (CD-ROM ED.). 5326
1057-8854 See RANKING THE BANKS / AMERICAN BANKER. 806
1057-8889 See OFFICE COMPUTING REPORT. 1197
1057-8919 See ANTITRUST REPORT (WASHINGTON, D.C. 1991). 3096
1057-8927 See REPORT OF ASSOCIATION FOR INVESTMENT MANAGEMENT AND RESEARCH CORPORATE INFORMATION COMMITTEE. 912
1057-8943 See ADVANCES IN BIOPHYSICAL CHEMISTRY. 479
1057-8951 See ADVANCES IN MOLECULAR ELECTRONIC STRUCTURE THEORY. 1039
1057-896X See JCT, AN INTERDISCIPLINARY JOURNAL OF CURRICULUM STUDIES. 1897
1057-8986 See THOMSON BANK DIRECTORY. 814
1057-8994 See PERSPECTIVES IN PERSONALITY. 4607
1057-9001 See AFRICAN AMERICAN JOURNAL. 2254
1057-9044 See FLORIDA COLLEGE COMMUNIQUE. 1091
1057-9052 See CANCERGRAM. SERIES CT15, CLINICAL TREATMENT OF CANCER. RADIATION THERAPY. 3813
1057-9060 See CANCERGRAM. SERIES CT12 SARCOMAS AND RELATED TUMORS. DIAGNOSIS TREATMENT. 3813
1057-9079 See CANCERGRAM. SERIES CT11 NEOPLASIA OF THE HEAD AND NECK DIAGNOSIS TREATMENT. 3813
1057-9087 See CANCERGRAM. SERIES CT10 PEDIATRIC ONCOLOGY. 3813
1057-9095 See SGNA NEWS. 3748
1057-9109 See CANCERGRAM. SERIES CT16, GENITO-URINARY CANCERS. DIAGNOSIS, TREATMENT. 3813
1057-9117 See CANCERGRAM. SERIES CT17 GYNECOLOGIC TUMORS. DIAGNOSIS TREATMENT. 3813
1057-9125 See CANCERGRAM. SERIES CT18, NERVOUS SYSTEM MALIGNANCIES. DIAGNOSIS, TREATMENT. 3814
1057-9133 See CANCERGRAM. SERIES CT21 ENDOCRINE TUMORS. DIAGNOSIS TREATMENT PATHOPHYSIOLOGY. 3814
1057-9141 See CANCERGRAM. SERIES CT22 MELANOMA AND OTHER SKIN CANCER DIAGNOSIS TREATMENT. 3814
1057-915X See CANCERGRAM. SERIES CT23, LEUKEMIAS AND MULTIPLE MYELOMA. DIAGNOSIS, TREATMENT. 3814
1057-9184 See INSIDER TRAVEL SECRETS. 5480
1057-9192 See SOAP OPERA MAGAZINE (LANTANA, FLA.). 2546
1057-9206 See DEVELOPING NATIONS. 1634
1057-9214 See JOURNAL OF MULTICRITERIA ANALYSIS. 4598

1057-9222 See COMPANIES PARTICIPATING IN THE DEPARTMENT OF DEFENSE SUBCONTRACTING PROGRAM. 4039
1057-9230 See HEALTH ECONOMICS. 4779
1057-9249 See PSYCHO-ONCOLOGY (CHICHESTER, ENGLAND). 3823
1057-9257 See ADVANCED MATERIALS FOR OPTICS AND ELECTRONICS. 5080
1057-9265 See JOURNAL OF STRATEGIC CHANGE. 687
1057-9273 See DR. JULIAN WHITAKER'S HEALTH & HEALING. 2596
1057-929X See OUR SUNDAY VISITOR'S CATHOLIC HERITAGE. 5034
1057-932X See POBEREZE (PHILADELPHIA, PA.). 2271
1057-9338 See AUGUSTINIAN JOURNEY. 4937
1057-9346 See SORKINS' MAGAZINE. 712
1057-9354 See MEDICINE, EXERCISE, NUTRITION, AND HEALTH. 3613
1057-9362 See FIBEROPTIC APPLICATIONS 4434
1057-9397 See FDA ENFORCEMENT REPORT. 1344
1057-9400 See REPORTER - NATIONAL CENTER FOR RESEARCH RESOURCES (U.S.). 3634
1057-9419 See ASA NEWSLETTER - APPLIED SCIENCE AND ANALYSIS, INC, THE. 4037
1057-9451 See FAMILY PEDIGREES. 2447
1057-946X See FAMILY HISTORIAN QUARTERLY, THE. 2447
1057-9478 See COMPUTING IN MUSICOLOGY. 1240
1057-9486 See OFFICIAL PROPERTY MANAGEMENT DIRECTORY (METROPOLITAN WASHINGTON), THE. 4842
1057-9508 See ERNST & YOUNG TAX GUIDE, THE. 4721
1057-9532 See USA TODAY BASEBALL WEEKLY. 4928
1057-9540 See REDS REPORT. 4914
1057-9559 See WESTMINSTER REVIEW (NEW WILMINGTON, PA.), THE. 3453
1057-9567 See MICROSTATION MANAGER. 1195
1057-9575 See A & W BASICS IN MEDICINE SERIES. 3543
1057-9583 See QUALITY OBSERVER, THE. 884
1057-9591 See DOCTOR VETERINARIAN QUICK REVIEW. 5509
1057-9605 See DOCTOR VETERINARIAN BOARD REVIEW. 5509
1057-9621 See NOTICES TO AIRMEN. 30
1057-963X See AIRMAN'S INFORMATION MANUAL. BASIC FLIGHT INFORMATION AND ATC PROCEDURES. 10
1057-9648 See FAA AVIATION NEWS (1987). 19
1057-9656 See CENSUS AND YOU. 4561
1057-9664 See MONTHLY & SEASONAL WEATHER OUTLOOK. 1431
1057-9672 See COMMERCE PUBLICATIONS UPDATE. 828
1057-9680 See U.S. MERCHANDISE TRADE. 1630
1057-9699 See QUARTERLY SUMMARY OF FEDERAL, STATE, AND LOCAL TAX REVENUE. 4743
1057-9702 See TRADE AND EMPLOYMENT. 853
1057-9710 See CHILTON'S DISTRIBUTION (1986). 5379
1057-9745 See MINERALS TODAY. 1442
1057-9753 See RODALE'S STRAIGHT TALK. 1068
1057-9761 See VINCENT VOICES. 2476
1057-9834 See RAND MCNALLY WORLD FACTS & MAPS. 1928
1057-9893 See ON THE AIR MAGAZINE. 1135
1057-9907 See BUYER'S GUIDE / THOROUGHBRED TIMES, BLOODSTOCK RESEARCH, THE. 2797
1057-9915 See INFLATION MEASURES FOR SCHOOLS & COLLEGES. 1830
1057-9958 See QUARTERLY BULLETIN - UNITED STATES. BUREAU OF ALCOHOL, TOBACCO AND FIREARMS. 4677

1057-9982 *See* COMPUTER BUYING WORLD. 1244

1057-9990 *See* STANDARDIZED REGULATIONS. 4687

1058-000X *See* MAXIMUM TRAVEL PER DIEM ALLOWANCES FOR FOREIGN AREAS. 5484

1058-0018 *See* U.S. DEPARTMENT OF STATE INDEXES OF LIVING COSTS ABROAD, QUARTERS ALLOWANCES, AND HARDSHIP DIFFERENTIALS. 4560

1058-0042 *See* MASTER INDEX TO DIRECTORY OF CORPORATE AFFILIATIONS, INTERNATIONAL DIRECTORY OF CORPORATE AFFILIATIONS, LEADING PRIVATE COMPANIES. 692

1058-0123 *See* SPECIAL WARFARE : THE PROFESSIONAL BULLETIN OF THE JOHN F. KENNEDY SPECIAL WARFARE CENTER AND SCHOOL. 4057

1058-014X *See* PRIME CONTRACT AWARDS IN LABOR SURPLUS AREAS. 4054

1058-0158 *See* DIRECTORY OF DCAA OFFICES. 4643

1058-0166 *See* INNOVATIONS IN UROLOGY NURSING. 3857

1058-0212 *See* MOBILE BEAT INTERNATIONAL. 4131

1058-0220 *See* GUITAR SCHOOL. 4120

1058-0239 *See* BIOTREATMENT NEWS. 5088

1058-0247 *See* COMPETITIVE INTELLIGENCE REVIEW. 659

1058-0255 *See* MAGAZINE ARTICLE SUMMARIES FULL TEXT SELECT. 2497

1058-0263 *See* RICKEY ROOTS & REVELS. 2470

1058-028X *See* HEALTHCARE ISSUES & TRENDS. 4782

1058-0298 *See* DELHI PRESS. 5728

1058-0301 *See* PRIME CONTRACT AWARDS BY STATE. 4674

1058-0328 *See* WORLDWIDE MANPOWER DISTRIBUTION BY GEOGRAPHICAL AREA. 4062

1058-0344 *See* STEVEN DWORMAN'S INFORMERCIAL MARKETING REPORT. 937

1058-0352 *See* PUBLICATIONS IN FOOD MICROBIOLOGY. 569

1058-0360 *See* AMERICAN JOURNAL OF SPEECH-LANGUAGE PATHOLOGY. 4383

1058-0379 *See* EDMS JOURNAL. 1183

1058-0387 *See* CONSUMER HEALTH SAFETY DIGEST. 4772

1058-0395 *See* SCRAPE (PHOENIX, ARIZ.). 2545

1058-0409 *See* WORKS OF ART (CHICAGO, ILL.). 333

1058-0417 *See* QUALITY QUIPS. 884

1058-0425 *See* EARTH SCIENCE OPPORTUNITIES. 1354

1058-0433 *See* BASEBALL CARD UPDATE. 2771

1058-045X *See* SPIE HOLOGRAPHICS INTERNATIONAL DIRECTORY & RESOURCE GUIDE. 4442

1058-0468 *See* JOURNAL OF ASSISTED REPRODUCTION AND GENETICS. 3763

1058-0476 *See* JOURNAL OF FAMILY AND ECONOMIC ISSUES. 2281

1058-0492 See NEWMEDIA (SAN MATEO, CALIF.). 1118

1058-0506 *See* INTERNATIONAL EMPLOYMENT GAZETTE. 4205

1058-0514 *See* IDAHI VELFAIYAR JARNAL. 5289

1058-0530 *See* INFORMATION SYSTEMS MANAGEMENT. 870

1058-0557 *See* LRA TRADE UNION ADVISOR. 1688

1058-0565 *See* MISSION AND MINISTRY. 5064

1058-0573 *See* INSTITUTE FOR MATH MANIA PRESENTS WONDERFUL IDEAS, THE. 3509

1058-0603 *See* POLK'S BANK DIRECTORY (INTERNATIONAL ED.). 803

1058-0611 *See* POLK'S BANK DIRECTORY (NORTH AMERICAN ED.). 803

1058-062X *See* NORTHROP FRYE NEWSLETTER. 4353

1058-0638 *See* SINGLES CHOICE. 3996

1058-0646 *See* WELL SERVICE MARKET REPORT. 2248

1058-0654 *See* BLUE RYDER. 2529

1058-0662 *See* ACADEMIC ABSTRACTS FULL TEXT SELECT. 2484

1058-0670 *See* SHOCK AND VIBRATION TECHNOLOGY REVIEW. 1996

1058-0751 *See* AMAZING STORIES (1986). 3360

1058-076X *See* DCAA CONTRACT AUDIT MANUAL. 4040

1058-0808 *See* GAMA NEWS JOURNAL. 2881

1058-0824 *See* GPO SALES PUBLICATIONS REFERENCE FILE. 4652

1058-0832 *See* CONSUMER REPORTS ON HEALTH. 1295

1058-0859 *See* EMPLOYMENT AND TRENDS AS OF 4702

1058-0867 *See* DOMESTIC MAIL MANUAL. 1144

1058-0875 *See* INTERNATIONAL MAIL MANUAL. 1145

1058-0891 *See* GPO NEW SALES PUBLICATIONS (1991). 4652

1058-093X *See* SURFACE MODIFICATION TECHNOLOGY NEWS. 1030

1058-0948 *See* FLAME RETARDANCY NEWS. 2290

1058-0980 *See* HAIRDO IDEAS. 404

1058-0999 *See* BLACK HAIR CARE. 402

1058-1006 *See* TRANSNATIONAL LAW & CONTEMPORARY PROBLEMS : A JOURNAL OF THE UNIVERSITY OF IOWA COLLEGE OF LAW. 3136

1058-1014 *See* AVIATION NEWS FROM SOUTH FLORIDA. 13

1058-1022 *See* WORLD PERSPECTIVES (MADISON, WIS.). 4501

1058-1030 *See* TELEVISION LISTING CO. 1141

1058-1057 *See* BALTIC BUSINESS REPORT. 892

1058-1065 *See* COASTAL NEWS (DESTIN, FLA.). 5466

1058-1073 *See* BROWN UNIVERSITY CHILD AND ADOLESCENT BEHAVIOR LETTER, THE. 4578

1058-1081 *See* PROFESSIONAL MODEL NEWSLETTER. 2777

1058-109X *See* EPI-LOG (DUNLAP, TENN.). 1131

1058-1103 *See* MENTAL HEALTH WEEKLY. 4604

1058-112X *See* JOHNS HOPKINS CENTER FOR ALTERNATIVES TO ANIMAL TESTING : NEWSLETTER, THE. 3592

1058-1138 *See* PR - TEXAS AGRICULTURAL EXPERIMENT STATION. 121

1058-1189 *See* PLANTS FOR TOXICITY ASSESSMENT. 4325

1058-1200 *See* DRIPPS' INTRODUCTION TO ANESTHESIA. 3682

1058-1219 *See* READERS' GUIDE ABSTRACTS (SCHOOL AND PUBLIC LIBRARY ED.). 3259

1058-1227 *See* CHEMICAL SCIENCES GRADUATE SCHOOL FINDER. 969

1058-1235 *See* FUNDING DECISION MAKERS. 5286

1058-1243 *See* JOURNAL OF PERINATAL EDUCATION, THE. 3764

1058-1251 *See* PURCHASING PERFORMANCE BENCHMARKS FOR THE U.S. TRANSPORTATION INDUSTRY / CAPS, CENTER FOR ADVANCED PURCHASING STUDIES. 5390

1058-126X *See* ALL IN COMMUNICATIONS. 1103

1058-1278 *See* REVUE - NEW YORK UNIVERSITY. INSTITUTE OF FRENCH STUDIES. 2706

1058-1294 *See* INTERSTUDY COMPETITIVE EDGE, THE. 4785

1058-1308 *See* EMPLOYMENT LAW REPORT (ROSEMOUNT, MINN.). 3147

1058-1316 *See* CONTEMPORARY BLACK BIOGRAPHY. 2259

1058-1324 *See* AID FOR EDUCATION REPORT. 1723

1058-1332 *See* MUNICIPAL ENVIRONMENTAL JOURNAL. 2178

1058-1359 *See* RETIREMENT OPPORTUNITIES. 885

1058-1367 *See* JOURNAL OF ENVIRONMENTAL PERMITTING. 2987

1058-1383 *See* ARROYO (TUCSON, ARIZ.). 5530

1058-1421 *See* SPINE REHABILITATION. 3642

1058-1537 *See* SCHOLASTIC NEWSTIME (1989). 1781

1058-1561 *See* CREDIT UNION DIRECTORS NEWSLETTER. 785

1058-157X *See* DOLLS IN MINIATURE : THE MAGAZINE. 2773

1058-1588 *See* JOURNAL OF SPINE RESEARCH. 3597

1058-1596 *See* BEVERLY HILLS 90210, THE OFFICIAL MAGAZINE. 383

1058-1618 *See* WORLD TRADE RESOURCES GUIDE. 858

1058-1626 *See* SERVICE INDUSTRIES USA. 1626

1058-1634 *See* ISSUES IN THE POSTMODERN THEORY OF EDUCATION. 1755

1058-1650 *See* MVP VIDEO JOURNAL OF GENERAL SURGERY. 3970

1058-1669 *See* AMUSE USA. 4856

1058-1677 *See* OB/GYN RESIDENT, THE. 3766

1058-1685 *See* INTERNAL MEDICINE RESIDENT. 3797

1058-1693 *See* PSYCHIATRIC RESIDENT. 3933

1058-1707 *See* REGULATED CHEMICALS DIRECTORY. 991

1058-1715 *See* METROPOLITAIN (ARLINGTON, VA.). 3411

1058-1731 *See* SIRS GLOBAL PERSPECTIVES. 4535

1058-174X *See* HISTORY (BOCA RATON, FLA.). 2619

1058-1758 *See* ECONOMICS (BOCA RATON, FLA.). 1486

1058-1766 *See* WORLD AFFAIRS (BOCA RATON, FLA.). 4538

1058-1774 *See* GOVERNMENT (BOCA RATON, FLA.). 4651

1058-1782 *See* NASHVILLE CABLEGUIDE. 1135

1058-1820 *See* SPRINGWELLS UPDATE. 1784

1058-1847 *See* LEGEND (WASHINGTON, D.C.). 3404

1058-1871 *See* GOOD OLD DAYS. SPECIAL ISSUES (1991). 3391

1058-1936 *See* CORE ANALYTE. 973

1058-1944 *See* WORLD GUIDE TO TELEVISION & PROGRAMMING. 1143

1058-1995 *See* RESEARCH IN THIRD WORLD ACCOUNTING. 750

1058-2029 *See* COSMOS (WASHINGTON, D.C.). 5230

1058-2045 *See* YOUNKIN FAMILY NEWS BULLETIN. 2478

1058-2088 *See* REGIONAL INDUSTRIAL BUYING GUIDE. UPSTATE NEW YORK. 2128

1058-2096 *See* CALIFORNIA AND HAWAII PUBLISHING MARKET PLACE. 4813

1058-2118 *See* RECRUITMENT SOLUTION, THE. 765

1058-2126 *See* JOURNAL OF EAST TENNESSEE HISTORY, THE. 2741

1058-2134 *See* WASHINGTON GEOLOGY. 1401

1058-2215 *See* SPECIAL MAP / GEOLOGICAL SURVEY OF ALABAMA, ENERGY RESOURCES DIVISION. 1397

1058-2274 *See* PRACTICAL SURVIVAL. 4877

1058-2282 *See* TECHNOLOGY NY REPORT. 5164

1058-2304 *See* FROMMER'S COMPREHENSIVE TRAVEL GUIDE. CARIBBEAN. 5475

1058-2320 *See* PLAYING FOR K.E.E.P.S. (TOTS ED.). 1774

1058-2339 *See* PRINT PRICE INDEX. 381

1058-2347 *See* BIOGRAPHY TODAY. 430

1058-2355 *See* GOODALE'S DIRECTORY OF CLASSIFIED ADVERTISING. 759

1058-2371 *See* AMS INTERNATIONAL STUDIES. 3360

1058-238X *See* AMS ANCIENT AND CLASSICAL STUDIES. 1074

1058-2398 *See* AMS STUDIES IN CULTURAL HISTORY. 2609

1058-2401 See COMPARATIVE MEDICINE. 5508
1058-241X See DRUG TARGETING AND DELIVERY. 3573
1058-2428 See US BLACK ENGINEER. 2274
1058-2436 See JOURNAL OF BONE AND JOINT SURGERY (COMPUTER FILE), THE. 3966
1058-2444 See HARD COPY OBSERVER, THE. 1608
1058-2452 See JOURNAL OF MUSCULOSKELETAL PAIN. 3805
1058-2460 See EL&P ELECTRIC UTILITY INDUSTRY SOFTWARE DIRECTORY. 2043
1058-2479 See EL & P U.S. ELECTRIC UTILITY INDUSTRY DIRECTORY. 4759
1058-2487 See INTERNATIONAL ENERGY STATISTICS SOURCEBOOK. 1963
1058-2495 See PLAYING FOR K.E.E.P.S. (TEEN ED.). 1774
1058-2509 See ABERATIONS (WALNUT CREEK, CALIF.). 3357
1058-2517 See MIDNIGHT ZOO. 3411
1058-2533 See EXPORT COMMUNICATIONS : EC. 834
1058-2541 See FROMMER'S BUDGET TRAVEL GUIDE. MEXICO ... ON $ ... A DAY. 5475
1058-255X See NORTH CAROLINA RULES OF COURT. FEDERAL. 3018
1058-2568 See NORTH CAROLINA RULES OF COURT. STATE. 3018
1058-2576 See SPACE YEAR. 36
1058-2592 See ADVERTISING OPTIONS PLUS : SRDS DIRECTORY OF OUT-OF-HOME MEDIA. 754
1058-2606 See COMPUTER COMPENDIUM. 1176
1058-2630 See FILM PRODUCERS, STUDIOS, AGENTS, AND CASTING DIRECTORS GUIDE. 4070
1058-2657 See DIRECTORY OF ILLINOIS POLITICAL LEADERS. 4643
1058-2673 See ARCHAEOLOGY IN THE BIBLICAL WORLD. 257
1058-2703 See COUNTY SEAT SCRAPS. 2444
1058-2711 See MEDICAL WASTE MONITOR. 3612
1058-2738 See JOURNAL OF SHOULDER AND ELBOW SURGERY. 3968
1058-2754 See ELEMENTARY MODULE SERIES. 3504
1058-2762 See LOBBYING & INFLUENCE ALERT. 4481
1058-2789 See SHOOTER'S RAG. 4376
1058-2797 See DETWILER DIRECTORY OF MEDICAL MARKET SOURCES, THE. 3571
1058-2800 See NETWARE SOLUTIONS. 1196
1058-2819 See HEART DISEASE AND STROKE. 3705
1058-2878 See FINANCIAL YELLOW BOOK. 1926
1058-2886 See NASDAQ YELLOW BOOK. 696
1058-2894 See INTERNATIONAL CORPORATE YELLOW BOOK. 871
1058-2908 See CORPORATE YELLOW BOOK. 1924
1058-2916 See ASAIO JOURNAL (1992). 3960
1058-2975 See GUNS & WEAPONS FOR LAW ENFORCEMENT. 3165
1058-2983 See HAIR CUT AND STYLE. 404
1058-3041 See MEN'S WORKOUT. 3996
1058-3068 See PROFILES INTERNATIONAL. 2543
1058-3076 See COMMERCIAL TRAILER BLUE BOOK. 949
1058-3084 See JOURNAL FROM THE RADICAL REFORMATION, A. 4968
1058-3130 See ORION (NEW YORK, N.Y.). 4170
1058-3165 See FROMMER'S BUDGET TRAVEL GUIDE. MEXICO ... ON $ ... A DAY. 5475
1058-3173 See WASHINGTON, D.C. MARKETING DIRECTORY. 938
1058-319X See SOUTHERN BAPTIST HANDBOOK (1991). 4998
1058-3211 See KENTUCKY RULES OF COURT. FEDERAL : INCLUDING AMENDMENTS RECEIVED THROUGH OCTOBER 1 2992
1058-322X See KENTUCKY RULES OF COURT. STATE. 2992

1058-3238 See LOCATION UPDATE. 4074
1058-3246 See SKI TECH. 4918
1058-3297 See HYPHEN MAGAZINE. 3395
1058-3300 See REVIEW OF FINANCIAL ECONOMICS. 1518
1058-3343 See DELL LOGIC PUZZLES. 4860
1058-3378 See THIS IS LAGUNA. 5492
1058-3416 See NORTH SOUTH. 4484
1058-3467 See CORNELL ALUMNI NEWS. 1101
1058-3475 See SLEEPWALKER (NEW YORK, N.Y.). 4866
1058-3483 See SPINAL NETWORK'S NEW MOBILITY. 3975
1058-3491 See LOCAL GOVERNMENT MONITOR. 4663
1058-3548 See TRAINING & CONDITIONING. 2601
1058-3556 See EGREGIOUS STEAMBOAT JOURNAL, THE. 4176
1058-3572 See AMERICAN MUSIC RESEARCH CENTER JOURNAL, THE. 4099
1058-3580 See COLOR DESKTOP PUBLISHING PRODUCTS MONTHLY. 1263
1058-3599 See CENTRAL PENN BUSINESS JOURNAL. 656
1058-3637 See POMERANIAN REGISTRY, THE. 4287
1058-3645 See INDUSTRIAL WATER TREATMENT. 5534
1058-3653 See MINNESOTA VENTURES. 695
1058-3661 See CARDIOLOGY IN THE ELDERLY. 3701
1058-3734 See COUNTRY ALMANAC (NEW YORK, N.Y.). 1924
1058-3750 See WEEKEND WOOD PROJECTS. 635
1058-3769 See COUNTRY WOOD PROJECTS. 371
1058-3807 See EASY-TO-BUILD WOOD PROJECTS. 634
1058-3815 See WOOD PROJECTS (NEW YORK, N.Y. 1991). 635
1058-3823 See COMPLETE BOOK OF AUTOPISTOLS : BUYER'S GUIDE. 4891
1058-3831 See VIETNAM (SYRACUSE, N.Y.). 4499
1058-384X See PUBLIC INTEREST LAW REVIEW, THE. 3033
1058-3904 See CRAIGHEAD'S INTERNATIONAL BUSINESS, TRAVEL, AND RELOCATION GUIDE TO 71 COUNTRIES. 5467
1058-3912 See JOURNAL OF ENVIRONMENTAL HYDROLOGY. 1416
1058-3920 See GLOBAL INVESTMENT TECHNOLOGY. 899
1058-3947 See JOURNAL OF AMERICAN-EAST ASIAN RELATIONS, THE. 4527
1058-3955 See ENVIRONMENT DAILY (ARLINGTON, VA.). 2165
1058-3963 See CONSUMER BANKRUPTCY NEWS. 2956
1058-3971 See TAX NOTES INTERNATIONAL WEEKLY NEWS. 3062
1058-398X See NEW "DIVERS SPEAK OUT" ... DIVE TRAVEL DIRECTORY, THE. 5485
1058-403X See CUSTOM WOODWORKING BUSINESS. 634
1058-4056 See PERIODIC JOURNAL OF BIBLIOGRAPHY, THE. 422
1058-4072 See WEEKEND WOODWORKER ANNUAL, THE. 635
1058-4080 See CTFA ... INTERNATIONAL BUYERS' GUIDE. 403
1058-4110 See BEST PAPERS PROCEEDINGS / ATLANTIC ECONOMIC SOCIETY. 1464
1058-4129 See BIOLOGICAL ABSTRACTS ON COMPACT DISC. 477
1058-4137 See BIOLOGICAL ABSTRACTS / RRM ON COMPACT DISC. 444
1058-4153 See DISTRIBUTED COMPUTING MONITOR. 1241
1058-4161 See OPEN INFORMATION SYSTEMS. 1248
1058-4188 See DIRECTIONS FOR PENNSYLVANIA SINGLES!. 5554

1058-420X See XIB (SAN DIEGO, CALIF.). 3473
1058-4218 See ELECTRICAL DESIGN AND INSTALLATION. 4761
1058-4226 See POLITICAL PULSE'S EDUCATION BEAT. 1774
1058-4234 See BOWERS BUSINESS BAROMETER. 644
1058-4285 See GLOBAL STANDARDS & SPECIFICATIONS BULLETIN. 1976
1058-4293 See CALIFORNIA EMPLOYER ADVISOR. 1658
1058-4307 See MICHIGAN MUNICIPAL LIABILITY AND PROPERTY POOL BULLETIN. 4665
1058-4315 See CARIBBEAN INTERNATIONAL (ALBANY, N.Y.). 2511
1058-4323 See UNIVERSITY OF DETROIT MERCY LAW REVIEW. 3068
1058-434X See PURCHASING PERFORMANCE BENCHMARKS FOR THE U.S. AEROSPACE/DEFENSE CONTRACTING INDUSTRY / CAPS, CENTER FOR ADVANCED PURCHASING STUDIES. 951
1058-4358 See YEARBOOK OF BLOW MOLDED PACKAGING, THE. 4461
1058-4382 See ADVANCES IN MULTIDIMENSIONAL LUMINESCENCE. 1012
1058-4455 See CFP TODAY. 783
1058-4471 See HAYS COUNTY FREE PRESS. 5750
1058-4587 See INTEGRATED FERROELECTRICS. 2066
1058-4595 See CPNEWS (SACRAMENTO, CALIF.). 2596
1058-4609 See POLITICAL COMMUNICATION. 4489
1058-4617 See JOURNAL OF BIG BEND STUDIES. 2740
1058-4706 See NEUROLAW LETTER, THE. 3015
1058-4722 See U.S./CANADA PROFILES. 5498
1058-4730 See INFORMATION PUBLISHING. 2920
1058-4749 See PRINT PUBLISHING FOR THE SCHOOL MARKET. 4818
1058-4757 See WASHINGTON RETAIL WEEKLY. 958
1058-4773 See CHALLENGES (MIDDLETOWN, CONN.). 1061
1058-4781 See CROSSWORDS TO RELAX WITH. 4859
1058-4803 See SUPERMARKET FLORAL. 2432
1058-4811 See RELAX (BANNOCKBURN, ILL.). 5490
1058-482X See NATIONAL PARALEGAL REPORTER. 3014
1058-482X See NATIONAL PARALEGAL REPORTER. 3014
1058-4838 See CLINICAL INFECTIOUS DISEASES. 3712
1058-4862 See GUIDES TO MAJOR SOCIAL SCIENCE DATA BASES. 5201
1058-4870 See WOMEN'S WORK (MONTESANO, WASH.). 1718
1058-4897 See GUIDE TO BUSINESS VALUATIONS. 678
1058-4919 See DESKBOOK ENCYCLOPEDIA OF AMERICAN SCHOOL LAW. 2960
1058-4927 See CHICAGO METRO MARKET MEDIA DIRECTORY. 1106
1058-4935 See CHICAGO MEDIA UPDATE. 1106
1058-4943 See FROMMER'S COMPREHENSIVE TRAVEL GUIDE. THE CAROLINAS & GEORGIA. 5477
1058-4943 See FROMMER'S COMPREHENSIVE TRAVEL GUIDE. VIRGINIA. 5477
1058-4951 See FROMMER'S FAMILY TRAVEL GUIDE. SAN FRANCISCO WITH KIDS. 5477
1058-496X See FROMMER'S FAMILY TRAVEL GUIDE. LOS ANGELES WITH KIDS. 5477
1058-4978 See FROMMER'S FAMILY TRAVEL GUIDE. WASHINGTON, D.C., WITH KIDS. 5477
1058-4986 See CHANGING VIEWS IN SURGICAL ONCOLOGY. 3814
1058-4994 See INTERNATIONAL REVIEW OF STUDIES ON EMOTION. 4592

1058-5001 *See* HUMAN RESOURCE LINE, THE. 1677

1058-5028 *See* RESEARCH IN COMMUNITY SOCIOLOGY. 5255

1058-5044 *See* SITUATION (ENCINITAS, CALIF.), THE. 811

1058-5052 *See* AAA WORLD (VIRGINIA ED.). 5459

1058-5095 *See* MIGRATION WORLD MAGAZINE. 1920

1058-5109 *See* REPORT ON EXEMPT OVERTIME PLANS AND PRACTICES. 1707

1058-5125 See COMPLETE CAR BUYER'S GUIDE, THE. 5412

1058-5133 *See* CGS NEWS - CALIFORNIA GENEALOGICAL SOCIETY. 2442

1058-5222 See KENTUCKY RULES OF COURT. FEDERAL : INCLUDING AMENDMENTS RECEIVED THROUGH OCTOBER 1 2992

1058-5222 See KENTUCKY RULES OF COURT. STATE. 2992

1058-5249 See COMPLETE CATALOG - LIBRARY OF CONGRESS. CATALOGING DISTRIBUTION SERVICE, THE. 3203

1058-5257 *See* COMPLETE CATALOG - LIBRARY OF CONGRESS. CATALOGING DISTRIBUTION SERVICE, THE. 3203

1058-529X *See* CRIME BEAT. 3161

1058-5303 *See* THE POINT (HANCOCK, MICH.), TO. 366

1058-532X *See* GAS (SAN CARLOS, CALIF.). 3463

1058-5397 *See* REPORT ON THE AMERICAS. 2757

1058-5400 *See* SUN OBSERVER (U.S. ED.), THE. 1204

1058-5419 *See* BOARD MEMBER: NATIONAL CENTER FOR NONPROFIT BOARDS. 861

1058-5427 *See* TEXAS JOURNAL OF WOMEN AND THE LAW. 5567

1058-5435 *See* ILLINOIS REGISTER OF EXPERT WITNESSES, THE. 2980

1058-546X *See* PRODUCT & PROCESS INNOVATION. 2099

1058-5494 *See* NORTHERN VIRGINIA MARKETING DIRECTORY. 934

1058-5516 *See* CHILD ABUSE, NEGLECT, AND THE FOSTER CARE SYSTEM. 2950

1058-5567 *See* OFFICIAL NEW YORK STATE EDUCATION DEPARTMENT REPORTS. 1770

1058-5575 *See* INTERNATIONAL VISITOR. 5481

1058-5583 *See* PARENT CARE (BETHANY, OKLA.). 2284

1058-5591 *See* X RESOURCE, THE. 1207

1058-5605 *See* PLANNING COMMISSIONERS JOURNAL. 2831

1058-5613 *See* JOURNAL OF AFRICAN POLICY STUDIES. 2640

1058-5621 *See* STUDIES IN SOUTHERN ITALIAN AND ITALIAN AMERICAN CULTURE. 2273

1058-563X *See* AMERICAN INDIAN STUDIES. 2255

1058-5656 *See* LIMITED INFINITY. 3405

1058-5664 *See* PEOPLE, PROPERTY, PROSPECTS. 1512

1058-5680 *See* BLACK COLLEGES AND UNIVERSITIES LISTING. 2256

1058-5702 *See* MEXICO TRADE AND LAW REPORTER. 846

1058-5710 *See* PADDLER (FALLBROOK, CALIF.). 4877

1058-5729 *See* WINE SPECTATOR ULTIMATE GUIDE TO BUYING WINE, THE. 2372

1058-5737 *See* CRESTLINE COURIER-NEWS. 5634

1058-5745 *See* FREE TRADE ADVISORY : THE BIWEEKLY ADVISORY ON HOW THE NORTH AMERICAN FREE TRADE TALKS WILL AFFECT YOUR BUSINESS AND INVESTMENTS IN MEXICO. 837

1058-5761 *See* DISCOVERING AND EXPLORING NEW JERSEY'S FISHING STREAMS. 4871

1058-577X *See* EXCLUSIVELY MALLS : CHICAGO'S METROPOLITAN MALL RESOURCE AND REFERENCE DIRECTORY. 954

1058-5796 *See* INTERNATIONAL DIRECTORY OF CONSULTANTS AND CONTRACTORS ACTIVE IN THE UNITED STATES AND CANADA, AN. 1979

1058-580X *See* INTERNATIONAL DIRECTORY OF CONSULTANTS AND CONTRACTORS ACTIVE IN THE MIDDLE EAST AND AFRICA, AN. 683

1058-5826 *See* ALBERTSEN'S SINGLES DIRECTORY. 3994

1058-5834 *See* JOURNAL OF CHEMICAL AND BIOCHEMICAL KINETICS. 1054

1058-5842 *See* OFFSHORE INTERNATIONAL NEWSLETTER, THE. 4267

1058-5850 *See* GULF OF MEXICO DRILLING REPORT. 1608

1058-5869 *See* OFFSHORE FIELD DEVELOPMENT INTERNATIONAL. 1620

1058-5885 *See* GULF OF MEXICO NEWSLETTER. 1608

1058-5893 *See* INTERNATIONAL JOURNAL OF PLANT SCIENCES. 514

1058-5893 *See* INTERNATIONAL JOURNAL OF PLANT SCIENCES. MICROFORM. 514

1058-5907 *See* NATIONAL BAPTIST PREACHERWOMAN SERMON SERIES, THE. 5065

1058-5915 *See* AMS HENRY JAMES STUDIES. 3360

1058-5931 *See* CRA BULLETIN. 4641

1058-594X *See* GREEN-KEEPING (ANNANDALE-ON-HUDSON, N.Y.). 2194

1058-5958 *See* BECKETT HOCKEY MONTHLY. 4887

1058-6008 *See* INTERNATIONAL OFFSHORE RIG OWNERS & PERSONNEL DIRECTORY. 4261

1058-6016 See 2 TO 22 DAYS IN GERMANY, AUSTRIA, AND SWITZERLAND. 5458

1058-6024 See 2 TO 22 DAYS IN SPAIN AND PORTUGAL. 5459

1058-6040 See 2 TO 22 DAYS IN THE ROCKIES. 5459

1058-6059 *See* 2 TO 22 DAYS IN GERMANY, AUSTRIA, AND SWITZERLAND. 5458

1058-6067 *See* 2 TO 22 DAYS IN SPAIN AND PORTUGAL. 5459

1058-6075 *See* 2 TO 22 DAYS IN THE AMERICAN SOUTHWEST. 5459

1058-6083 *See* 2 TO 22 DAYS IN THE ROCKIES. 5459

1058-6091 *See* 2 TO 22 DAYS IN NORWAY, SWEDEN, AND DENMARK. 5459

1058-6105 *See* 2 TO 22 DAYS IN GREAT BRITAIN. 5458

1058-6113 *See* 2 TO 22 DAYS AROUND THE GREAT LAKES. 5458

1058-613X *See* IEG DIRECTORY OF SPONSORSHIP MARKETING. 926

1058-6148 *See* R'S RELATIVES, THE. 2471

1058-6156 *See* AFRICENTRIC MONITOR, THE. 2637

1058-6164 *See* GOLD NEWS (WASHINGTON, D.C.). 1440

1058-6180 *See* IEEE ANNALS OF THE HISTORY OF COMPUTING. 1187

1058-6210 *See* FOUNDATION DIRECTORY. PART 2, A GUIDE TO GRANT PROGRAMS, $25,000-$100,000, THE. 4336

1058-6229 See AVC PRESENTATION DEVELOPMENT & DELIVERY. 641

1058-6288 *See* MISSOURI JOURNAL OF HEALTH, PHYSICAL EDUCATION, RECREATION AND DANCE. 1857

1058-6318 *See* MINORITIES & SUCCESS. 879

1058-6326 *See* CHIPS OFF THE WRITER'S BLOCK CATHARSIS. 2918

1058-6342 *See* ERNST & YOUNG'S TAX-SAVING STRATEGIES / ERNST & YOUNG. 4721

1058-6369 *See* WOMEN'S STUDIES INDEX. 5571

1058-6377 *See* PETERSON'S GRANTS FOR GRADUATE STUDY. 1840

1058-6385 *See* AOHA : A PUBLICATION OF THE AMERICAN OSTEOPATHIC HOSPITAL ASSOCIATION. 3551

1058-6393 *See* CONFERENCE RECORD / ASILOMAR CONFERENCE ON SIGNALS, SYSTEMS & COMPUTERS. 2039

1058-6407 *See* JOURNAL OF ECONOMICS & MANAGEMENT STRATEGY. 873

1058-6415 *See* QUALITY HEALTHCARE & OUTCOMES. 3632

1058-6431 *See* SCHOOL EXECUTIVE (PHILADELPHIA, PA.). 1871

1058-644X *See* BIBLIOGRAPHIC GUIDE TO MIDDLE EASTERN STUDIES. 2768

1058-6458 *See* EXPERIMENTAL MATHEMATICS. 3505

1058-6482 *See* EARLY CHILDHOOD REPORTER. 1878

1058-6490 See BUSINESS LEADER (RALEIGH, N.C.). 650

1058-6504 *See* ANNUAL WORKERS' COMPENSATION CONFERENCE, THE. 1650

1058-6539 *See* COMPETITIONS (LOUISVILLE, KY.). 295

1058-6571 *See* ETHICAL MANAGEMENT. 2249

1058-6598 *See* SCOTT KING'S DIABETES INTERVIEW. 3676

1058-6601 *See* MACPREPRESS. 2489

1058-661X *See* ECONOMIC REFORM TODAY. 1484

1058-6628 *See* AIR POLLUTION CONSULTANT, THE. 2223

1058-6636 *See* LIFE POSITIVE!. 875

1058-6644 *See* DELAWARE DIVISION OF LIBRARIES NEWSLETTER, THE. 3205

1058-6652 *See* KEEN ON NEW YORK SURVEY OF TOP-RATED SERVICES, THE. 3995

1058-6660 *See* PSYCSCAN. NEUROPSYCHOLOGY. 4623

1058-6679 *See* STANDARD & POOR'S CREDITWEEK. MUNICIPAL. 915

1058-6687 *See* IMMUNOMETHODS (SAN DIEGO, CALIF.). 3672

1058-6695 *See* WIRELESS SATELLITE & BROADCASTING. 1143

1058-6709 *See* WIRELESS SPECTRUM MANAGEMENT. 1124

1058-6717 *See* WIRELESS CELLULAR. 1124

1058-6725 *See* WIRELESS PCN TELECOMMUNICATIONS. 1169

1058-6733 *See* TECHNOLOGY TUTORIALS ENTERPRISE NETWORKING. 1244

1058-6741 *See* NEUROPROTOCOLS (ORLANDO, FLA.). 3841

1058-6768 *See* LIBRES (KENT, OHIO). 3228

1058-6776 *See* NATIONAL PSYCHOLOGIST, THE. 4605

1058-6806 *See* CONNEXIONS (MANASSAS, VA.). 1241

1058-6857 *See* MANVILLE NEWS, THE. 5710

1058-689X *See* CORPORATE GIVING YELLOW PAGES (1992). 5281

1058-6938 *See* INSIDE FREELANCE. 1287

1058-6954 *See* 1-2-3 FOR MACINTOSH REPORT, THE. 1283

1058-6962 *See* ILR JOURNAL, THE. 3464

1058-6970 *See* NEW ENGLAND BIENNIAL : [CATALOG] : A JURIED EXHIBITION OF NEW ENGLAND PHOTOGRAPHERS / ORGANIZED BY THE PHOTOGRAPHIC RESOURCE CENTER. 4372

1058-6989 *See* ADDICTION RESEARCH. 1338

1058-7004 *See* AVIATION EUROPE (WASHINGTON, D.C.). 13

1058-7012 *See* LAND USE FORUM. 2993

1058-7020 *See* NATIONAL QUERIES FORUM, THE. 2462

1058-7039 *See* AQUATICS INTERNATIONAL. 4883

1058-7071 *See* PARADOX INFORMANT. 1280

1058-708X *See* BETA (SAN FRANCISCO, CALIF.). 3667

1058-7098 *See* TRAVEL BOOKS WORLDWIDE. 5495

1058-711X *See* DIAMOND DUDS. 319

1058-7136 *See* TELLTALES (STERLING, VA.). 1070

1058-7179 See WORKERS' COMP ADVISOR (OHIO ED.). 1719
1058-7187 See VISUAL ANTHROPOLOGY REVIEW. 247
1058-7195 See REVIEW OF AGRICULTURAL ECONOMICS. 128
1058-7217 See WOMEN IN THE ARTS / THE NATIONAL MUSEUM OF WOMEN IN THE ARTS. 369
1058-7233 See METRO (WINTER PARK, FLA.). 2902
1058-7241 See NEWS BULLETIN / THE MUSICAL BOX SOCIETY INTERNATIONAL. 4140
1058-725X See MOLECULAR CRYSTALS AND LIQUID CRYSTALS SCIENCE AND TECHNOLOGY: SECTION A, MOLECULAR CRYSTALS AND LIQUID CRYSTALS. 1032
1058-7268 See MOLECULAR CRYSTALS AND LIQUID CRYSTALS SCIENCE AND TECHNOLOGY SECTION B, NONLINEAR OPTICS. 4438
1058-7276 See MOLECULAR CRYSTALS AND LIQUID CRYSTALS SCIENCE AND TECHNOLOGY SECTION C, MOLECULAR MATERIALS. 1033
1058-7284 See MOLECULAR CRYSTALS AND LIQUID CRYSTALS SCIENCE AND TECHNOLOGY SECTION D, DISPLAY AND IMAGING. 4438
1058-7292 See JAPANESE TECHNOLOGY REVIEWS. SECTION A, ELECTRONICS. 2068
1058-7306 See JAPANESE TECHNOLOGY REVIEWS. SECTION B, COMPUTERS AND COMMUNICATION. 1114
1058-7314 See JAPANESE TECHNOLOGY REVIEWS. SECTION C, NEW MATERIALS. 5117
1058-7322 See JAPANESE TECHNOLOGY REVIEWS. SECTION D, MANUFACTURING ENGINEERING. 1981
1058-7330 See JAPANESE TECHNOLOGY REVIEWS. SECTION E, BIOTECHNOLOGY. 3693
1058-7349 See JAPANESE JOURNAL OF FUZZY THEORY AND SYSTEMS. 3511
1058-7357 See VIDEOSCOPIC SURGERY. 3977
1058-7365 See BNA'S EASTERN EUROPE REPORTER. 892
1058-7373 See BNA CALIFORNIA EMPLOYEE RELATIONS REPORT. 1655
1058-7381 See TUEBOR TERRA. 2207
1058-7411 See MACINTOSH ADVERTISING REPORT. 762
1058-7438 See KINESIOLOGY AND MEDICINE FOR DANCE. 1313
1058-7470 See ISDN USER MAGAZINE. 1191
1058-7489 See ADVANCES IN POLYMER BLENDS AND ALLOYS TECHNOLOGY. 4453
1058-7497 See ADVANCES IN TAXATION. 4708
1058-7500 See ARS MUSICA DENVER. 4101
1058-7535 See NEUROLOGICAL DISEASE AND THERAPY. 3840
1058-7632 See REFORMA ECONOMICA HOY. 1516
1058-7667 See FAIRBANKS ARTS : A PUBLICATION OF THE FAIRBANKS ARTS ASSOCIATION. 320
1058-7683 See NORTE SUR. 2571
1058-7691 See POWYS NOTES. 3350
1058-7705 See IMAGING NEWS (ALEXANDRIA, VA.). 1113
1058-7713 See ADVANCED WIRELESS COMMUNICATIONS. 1103
1058-773X See WINNER (NAGS HEAD, N. C.). 4621
1058-7756 See OUTDOOR & TRAVEL PHOTOGRAPHY. 4372
1058-7764 See CREDIT UNION TIMES. 786
1058-7780 See CONTRACTORS JOURNAL, THE. 611
1058-7829 See STRATEGIES FOR HEALTHCARE EXCELLENCE. 3793
1058-7845 See LMT (NORWALK, CONN.). 1329
1058-7888 See CD SUMMARY. 3712
1058-7926 See BIKER (AGOURA HILLS, CALIF.). 4080

1058-7934 See HOME CARE SALARY & BENEFITS REPORT. 5287
1058-7950 See CEO, INTERNATIONAL STRATEGIES. 1601
1058-7977 See ... DIRECTORY. ASSOCIATIONS. NORTH EAST REGION, THE. 1604
1058-7985 See ... DIRECTORY. ASSOCIATIONS. EAST NORTH CENTRAL REGION, THE. 5230
1058-7993 See ... DIRECTORY. ASSOCIATIONS. WEST NORTH CENTRAL REGION, THE. 5230
1058-8000 See ... DIRECTORY. ASSOCIATIONS. SOUTH ATLANTIC REGION, THE. 5230
1058-8019 See ... DIRECTORY. ASSOCIATIONS. SOUTH CENTRAL REGION, THE. 5230
1058-8027 See ... DIRECTORY. ASSOCIATIONS. MOUNTAIN REGION, THE. 5230
1058-8027 See DIRECTORY. ASSOCIATIONS. WESTERN REGION. 1604
1058-8108 See JOURNAL OF NATURAL TOXINS. 4311
1058-8108 See JOURNAL OF NATURAL TOXINS. 3981
1058-8124 See CURRENT NEWS ON FILE. 2532
1058-8132 See APSNEWS. 4398
1058-8159 See CATHOLIC WORLD REPORT, THE. 5027
1058-8167 See MUSIC REFERENCE SERVICES QUARTERLY. 4134
1058-8183 See VETERINARY RADIOLOGY & ULTRASOUND. 5526
1058-8191 See FRESH TRACKS. 385
1058-8205 See CALIFORNIA LAND USE LAW & POLICY REPORTER. 2946
1058-8213 See NEFESH. 5051
1058-8221 See NATIONAL VOLUNTEERS IN PARKS DIRECTORY (U.S. ED.). 4875
1058-823X See WAR RESEARCH INFO SERVICE. 4060
1058-8248 See ROGER RABBIT'S TOONTOWN. 4865
1058-8256 See SLOT MACHINE-JUKE BOX COLLECTOR. 2778
1058-8272 See EVELYN WAUGH NEWSLETTER AND STUDIES. 432
1058-8299 See FREEMAN REPORTS. MASS STORAGE OUTLOOK. 1237
1058-8329 See CCRA NEWSLETTER : THE OFFICIAL MONTHLY NEWSLETTER OF THE CAMPUS COMPUTER RESELLERS ALLIANCE, THE. 1244
1058-8337 See JOURNAL OF SOIL CONTAMINATION. 176
1058-8353 See LITERARY SCANNER. 3346
1058-837X See AUSTIN TEXAS MAGAZINE. 818
1058-8388 See DEVELOPMENTAL DYNAMICS. 3679
1058-8396 See EARLY INTERVENTION. 5284
1058-8434 See BECKETT HOCKEY MONTHLY. 4887
1058-8442 See VERMONT GOLF JOURNAL & DIRECTORY. 4928
1058-8450 See NBER WORKING PAPER SERIES ON HISTORICAL FACTORS IN LONG-RUN GROWTH. 1575
1058-8485 See CLLI'S COMMERCIAL PROPERTY LAW DIGESTS. 2951
1058-8493 See WESTERN AMERICA VACATION TRAVELER. 5499
1058-854X See NELSON'S DIRECTORY OF REAL ESTATE INVESTMENTS. 4842
1058-8558 See CHRISTIAN BEGINNINGS. 4944
1058-8566 See DISCRETE SEMICONDUCTORS. SUGGESTED REPLACEMENTS. 2042
1058-8604 See FLORIDA JURY VERDICT REVIEW AND ANALYSIS. 3089
1058-8612 See SCARLET STREET. 3433
1058-8620 See MILITARY GROCER. 4050
1058-8647 See SOAP OPERA PANORAMA. 2546
1058-8655 See PROCEEDINGS OF THE INDUSTRIAL COMPUTING CONFERENCE. 1200
1058-8663 See JOURNAL OF PUBLIC SAFETY COMPUTING, THE. 4787

1058-8671 See INSIDE JAPANESE SUPPORT. 5290
1058-8736 See GEST-GUEST QUARTERLY. 2451
1058-8760 See CCAR JOURNAL (1991). 5046
1058-8787 See PIQUALITY. 1199
1058-8795 See NEWS FOR KIDS. 1067
1058-885X See RETAIL BANKING REPORT. 809
1058-8906 See AUTHORLINE - SAS INSTITUTE. 3365
1058-8930 See SOCIOLOGICAL STUDIES OF CHILD DEVELOPMENT. 5261
1058-8957 See ADVANCES IN STATISTICAL SIGNAL PROCESSING. 1170
1058-8965 See COMPUSERVE MAGAZINE. 1240
1058-8981 See EARTH CHANGES REPORT, THE. 4185
1058-904X See COMPOSITES INDUSTRY MONTHLY. 1969
1058-9058 See NCO JOURNAL, THE. 4052
1058-9074 See SOLID WASTE & POWER. 2243
1058-9082 See ALIGNMENT TECH/TALK. 5403
1058-9112 See GATHERING OF THE TRIBES, A. 3390
1058-9120 See CONTRIBUTIONS TO THE STUDY OF ART AND ARCHITECTURE. 348
1058-9139 See APS JOURNAL. 3552
1058-9155 See ADOPTIVE FAMILIES TOGETHER : AFT. 2276
1058-9163 See WASHINGTON TECHNOLOGY. 5169
1058-918X See ELECTRONIC GAMING MONTHLY. 4860
1058-9236 See MULTICULTURAL REVIEW. 2268
1058-9244 See SCIENTIFIC PROGRAMMING. 5155
1058-9252 See CENTRAL CITIES SIGHT AND SOUND. 384
1058-9260 See CONTRACTOR'S BUSINESS MANAGEMENT REPORT. 864
1058-9287 See PETERSON'S GRANTS FOR POST-DOCTORAL STUDY. 1840
1058-9309 See ILLINOIS STEWARD, THE. 2195
1058-9317 See CIRCUIT NEWS. 2038
1058-9325 See CIRCUIT NEWS ASSEMBLY. 2038
1058-9333 See CIRCUIT NEWS MAGAZINE. 2038
1058-9341 See WASHINGTON BEVERAGE JOURNAL. 2372
1058-935X See MARYLAND BEVERAGE JOURNAL. 2369
1058-9376 See AUTOMOTIVE RECYCLING. 5407
1058-9384 See WHRO MAGAZINE. 1143
1058-9503 See 3D ARTIST. 376
1058-9511 See ARAB WOMEN YEAR 2000. 5551
1058-9538 See ABSTRACT ME. 3357
1058-9546 See CIRCUIT NEWS. 2038
1058-9554 See CIRCUIT NEWS ASSEMBLY. 2038
1058-9570 See CIRCUIT NEWS MAGAZINE. 2038
1058-9600 See SHEPARD'S KENTUCKY EXPRESS CITATIONS. 3051
1058-9678 See R.E.P. (OVERLAND PARK, KAN.). 5318
1058-9686 See WORLDWIDE OFFSHORE CONTRACTORS & EQUIPMENT DIRECTORY. 4285
1058-9716 See BACON'S BUSINESS/FINANCIAL DIRECTORY. 756
1058-9732 See SHEPARD'S GEORGIA EXPRESS CITATIONS. 3050
1058-9740 See CHEMICAL OCEANOGRAPHY. 1447
1058-9759 See NONDESTRUCTIVE TESTING AND EVALUATION. 2123
1058-9767 See DOE NEW TECHNOLOGY. 1936
1058-9783 See WORDPERFECT FOR WINDOWS MAGAZINE. 1292
1058-9805 See AFRICAN WILDLIFE UPDATE. 4868
1058-9813 See PROGRESS IN PEDIATRIC CARDIOLOGY. 3709
1058-9821 See WEEKEND WOODCRAFTS. 2907

1058-983X *See* COLLECTION AGENCY DIRECTORY. **1602**

1058-9856 *See* TEEN SET. **1070**

1058-9864 *See* TOPICS IN FAMILY PSYCHOLOGY AND COUNSELING. **4620**

1058-9872 See INSIDE SPRINT CORP. **1157**

1058-9899 *See* ENGLEWOOD HERALD, THE. **5642**

1058-9902 *See* INTERGENERATIONAL ISSUES IN SPEECH, HEARING, AND LANGUAGE. **3287**

1058-9910 *See* BEST OF KERVIN FONDREN, THE. **3460**

1058-9929 *See* CIVIL ENGINEERING STUDIES. CONSTRUCTION MATERIALS RESEARCH SERIES. **2021**

1058-997X *See* STUDIES IN MODERN ART. **331**

1058-9988 *See* BULLETIN / AMERICAN ASSOCIATION OF UNIVERSITY WOMEN. **1812**

1059-0021 *See* WELCOME TO THE USA. **5499**

1059-0048 *See* PRO-FUND NOTES. **5301**

1059-0056 *See* OFFICIAL IDENTIFICATION AND PRICE GUIDE TO POSTCARDS, THE. **2775**

1059-0072 *See* DIRECTORY OF NATURAL GAS VEHICLE REFUELING STATIONS, PRODUCTS, AND SERVICES. **5413**

1059-0080 *See* DIGITAL INFORMATION GROUP'S INFORMATION INDUSTRY BULLETIN. **3206**

1059-0137 *See* ENTREPRENEURSHIP, INNOVATION AND CHANGE. **672**

1059-0145 *See* JOURNAL OF SCIENCE EDUCATION AND TECHNOLOGY. **5119**

1059-0153 *See* BIOMIMETICS (NEW YORK, N.Y.). **1966**

1059-0161 *See* JOURNAL OF ARCHAEOLOGICAL RESEARCH. **271**

1059-0196 *See* JOURNAL OF DURASSIAN STUDIES. **3399**

1059-0242 *See* TODAY'S TEAM. **3646**

1059-0269 See HANDLING CORPORATE EMPLOYMENT PROBLEMS. **1676**

1059-0277 *See* HANDLING CORPORATE EMPLOYMENT PROBLEMS. **1676**

1059-0307 *See* TODAY'S FACILITY MANAGER. **2903**

1059-034X *See* FLORIDA SUNLINK NEWS : SCHOOL LIBRARY MEDIA NETWORK / UNIVERSITY OF CENTRAL FLORIDA, COLLEGE OF EDUCATION. **3211**

1059-0366 *See* MTS=IP2S, INNOVATORS & INNOVATIONS. **1765**

1059-0374 *See* CRAWFORD COUNTY IOWA GENEALOGICAL SOCIETY. **2444**

1059-0390 *See* TAX RETURN PREPARER'S GUIDE. **4754**

1059-0412 *See* LET'S GO. THE BUDGET GUIDE TO NEW YORK CITY. **5483**

1059-0447 *See* S & P'S INSURER SOLVENCY REVIEW (LIFE-HEALTH ED.). **2893**

1059-0455 *See* S & P'S INSURER SOLVENCY REVIEW (PROPERTY-CASUALTY ED.). **2893**

1059-0471 *See* CLINICAL ENDOCRINOLOGY (NEW YORK, N.Y.,1992). **3727**

1059-048X *See* JOURNAL OF BANKRUPTCY, LAW, AND PRACTICE. **793**

1059-0501 *See* JOURNAL OF ENVIRONMENTAL SCIENCE AND HEALTH. PART C, ENVIRONMENTAL CARCINOGENESIS & ECOTOXICOLOGY REVIEWS. **2234**

1059-0536 *See* PERSPECTIVA (SOUTH HADLEY, MASS.). **3310**

1059-0544 *See* BROADBAND NETWORKING NEWS. **1127**

1059-0552 *See* TACTICAL TECHNOLOGY. **5161**

1059-0560 *See* INTERNATIONAL REVIEW OF ECONOMICS & FINANCE. **1497**

1059-0587 *See* YEAR BOOK OF DERMATOLOGIC SURGERY. **3723**

1059-0595 *See* EDUCATION SPECIAL INTEREST SECTION NEWSLETTER. **1878**

1059-0609 *See* TECHNOLOGY SPECIAL INTEREST SECTION NEWSLETTER. **5164**

1059-0625 *See* BREEDER FORUM. **4286**

1059-0633 *See* ESSENTIAL NEWS. **5630**

1059-0641 *See* MARINE RESPONSE BULLETIN : WEST COAST OIL SPILL PREVENTION AND RESPONSE. **4264**

1059-065X *See* GLBAMES NEWSLETTER. **2794**

1059-0668 *See* REPTILE & AMPHIBIAN MAGAZINE. **5596**

1059-0676 *See* CREATIVE READING. **3378**

1059-0684 *See* QUILT (NEW YORK, N.Y.). **375**

1059-0706 *See* WRESTLING EYE. **4931**

1059-0714 *See* WRESTLING FURY. **4931**

1059-0722 *See* COMPENSATION AND WORKING CONDITIONS. **1660**

1059-0730 *See* NORTH AMERICAN BED & BREAKFAST REGISTRY, THE. **2808**

1059-0749 *See* MATRIX NEWS. **1242**

1059-0773 *See* DEATHLOK. **378**

1059-0803 *See* FAMILY TREE QUARTERLY : A PUBLICATION OF THE COBB COUNTY, GEORGIA, GENEALOGICAL SOCIETY, INC. **2447**

1059-082X *See* FURKINDRED (SEATTLE, WASH.). **378**

1059-0838 *See* GREEN LIBRARY JOURNAL (BERKELEY, CALIF. 1992). **2173**

1059-0846 *See* FUTUREBUS+ DESIGN. **1241**

1059-0854 *See* EDUCATION (HORSHAM, PA.). **1739**

1059-0862 *See* SPORTS FAN'S CONNECTION. **4922**

1059-0870 *See* PEDIATRIC EMERGENCY & CRITICAL CARE. **3908**

1059-0889 *See* AMERICAN JOURNAL OF AUDIOLOGY. **4383**

1059-0897 *See* SOUND TIMES. **5319**

1059-0900 *See* CINEFOCUS. **4066**

1059-0919 *See* GALE ENVIRONMENTAL SOURCEBOOK. **2172**

1059-0927 *See* REVOLUTION (STATEN ISLAND, N.Y.). **3868**

1059-0935 *See* WISCONSIN NEWMONTH. **2550**

1059-0986 *See* FRESNO BUSINESS AND INDUSTRY NEWS : SERVING THE GREATER FRESNO/CLOVIS METROPOLITAN AREA. **677**

1059-0994 *See* VETERINARY MEDICAL REVIEW (COLUMBIA, MO.). **5525**

1059-1001 *See* AUTOCEPHALOUS ORTHODOX CHURCHES, THE. **4937**

1059-101X *See* CRACKING THE ACT. **1819**

1059-1028 *See* WIRED (SAN FRANCISCO, CALIF.). **1207**

1059-1036 *See* INTERNATIONAL TRAN SCRIPT. **5249**

1059-1044 *See* WORKPLACE SAFETY AWARENESS PROGRAM. **2871**

1059-1052 *See* JOURNAL OF THE SOUTHERN ORTHOPAEDIC ASSOCIATION. **3883**

1059-1079 *See* PAPERS OF ROBERT TREAT PAINE, THE. **3422**

1059-1125 *See* OAH NEWSLETTER. **2751**

1059-1133 *See* APPROACHES TO TEACHING WORLD LITERATURE. **3363**

1059-1168 *See* EARLY DRAMA, ART, AND MUSIC REFERENCE SERIES. **319**

1059-1230 *See* IN YOUR FACE. **2263**

1059-1257 *See* BANKING POLICY REPORT. **3085**

1059-1265 *See* DOING BUSINESS IN CYPRUS. **667**

1059-1281 *See* DOING BUSINESS IN SWEDEN. **668**

1059-1311 *See* SEIZURE (LONDON, ENGLAND). **3846**

1059-1338 *See* JOURNAL (NEW ULM, MINN.). **5696**

1059-1362 *See* COVER-TO-COVER WITH CASPR. **3204**

1059-1400 *See* INSIDE MORTGAGE FINANCE'S CRA/HMDA UPDATE. **791**

1059-1419 *See* MORNINGSTAR CLOSED-END FUNDS. **908**

1059-1427 *See* MORNINGSTAR MUTUAL FUNDS ONDISC. **908**

1059-1435 *See* VARIABLE ANNUITY PERFORMANCE REPORT. **919**

1059-1443 *See* MORNINGSTAR MUTUAL FUNDS. **908**

1059-1478 *See* PRODUCTION AND OPERATIONS MANAGEMENT. **883**

1059-1494 *See* AMERICAN JOURNAL OF PAIN MANAGEMENT. **3548**

1059-1508 *See* FTMS MULTICULTURAL EDUCATION REVIEW. **1895**

1059-1516 *See* ORTHOPAEDIC PHYSICAL THERAPY CLINICS OF NORTH AMERICA. **4381**

1059-1524 *See* MOLECULAR BIOLOGY OF THE CELL. **539**

1059-1540 *See* ADVANCES IN NEUROSCIENCE. **3826**

1059-1621 *See* HSUS NEWS. **226**

1059-163X *See* DIRECTORY OF EXECUTIVE RECRUITERS (CORPORATE ED.), THE. **939**

1059-164X *See* EQUAL MEANS. **5555**

1059-1672 *See* GUNS & AMMO ... HANDGUN ANNUAL. **2811**

1059-1680 *See* PETERSEN'S PREVIEW ... PRO FOOTBALL. **4912**

1059-1710 *See* BOSTON PARENTS' PAPER, THE. **2277**

1059-1729 *See* IR & R NEWS REPORT / SECTION OF INDIVIDUAL RIGHTS AND RESPONSIBILITIES. **2985**

1059-1753 *See* PETERSEN'S ... ANNUAL TURKEY HUNTING. **4877**

1059-1788 *See* INSIDE VISUAL BASIC. **1287**

1059-1818 *See* NEW YORK AMSTERDAM NEWS (1962). **5718**

1059-1923 *See* MARKET NICHES IN **692**

1059-1931 *See* WORLD & SCIENCE, THE. **5170**

1059-194X *See* SOLDIERS TODAY. **4057**

1059-1958 *See* SITUATIONS DIGEST. **2545**

1059-1966 *See* PBC TRAVEL NEWSLETTER. **702**

1059-1974 *See* PBC TAX BRIEFS. **4740**

1059-1982 *See* PBC SENIOR NEWSLETTER. **702**

1059-1990 *See* PBC SCIENCE BRIEFS. **5137**

1059-2008 *See* PBC IMMIGRATION BRIEFS. **1920**

1059-2016 *See* PBC HOUSING BRIEFS. **2830**

1059-2024 *See* PBC GOVERNMENT PROGRAMS NEWSLETTER. **4673**

1059-2032 *See* PBC FEDERAL TAX GUIDE. **4740**

1059-2040 *See* PBC EMPLOYMENT BRIEFS. **4208**

1059-2059 *See* PBC CREDIT BRIEFS. **802**

1059-2067 *See* PBC COMPREHENSIVE HEALTH BRIEFS. **4795**

1059-2075 *See* PBC BUSINESS GUIDE. **702**

1059-2083 *See* PBC AUTO GUIDE. **5423**

1059-2091 *See* INNOVATIONS & IDEAS. **5114**

1059-2105 *See* MICHIGAN MUNICIPAL LEAGUE AND MICHIGAN ASSOCIATION OF MUNICIPAL ATTORNEYS MONOGRAPH SERIES. **3010**

1059-2113 *See* ANALOG SCIENCE FICTION & FACT. **3361**

1059-2121 *See* HELLENIC TIMES. **5717**

1059-2148 *See* INSIDE FLORIDA POLITICS. **4477**

1059-2156 *See* LIPPINCOTT'S REVIEWS. RADIOLOGY. **3943**

1059-2164 *See* POPULAR COMMUNICATIONS COMMUNICATIONS GUIDE. **1119**

1059-2172 *See* GAME PLAYERS NINTENDO GUIDE. **4861**

1059-2180 *See* GAME PLAYERS PC ENTERTAINMENT. **4861**

1059-2202 *See* CLEAN FUEL VEHICLE WEEK. **4253**

1059-2210 *See* SIDEWALKS (ANOKA, MINN.). **3436**

1059-2245 *See* VIDEO INK. **332**

1059-2253 *See* EARTHLETTER. **5284**

1059-2369 *See* ORGANIZER (SAN FRANCISCO, CALIF.), THE. **5638**

1059-2393 *See* FBN (SPARTA, N.J.). **2335**

1059-2407 *See* WINDOWS/DOS DEVELOPER'S JOURNAL. **1273**

1059-2423 *See* CJ EUROPE. **3160**

1059-2431 *See* INSTITUTE ON AGING NEWSLETTER. **5179**

1059-2458 See ASIAN AMERICANS INFORMATION DIRECTORY. 2255
1059-2466 See TREASURES IN NEEDLEWORK. 376
1059-2474 See AMERICAN BANK LAWYER, THE. 2932
1059-2512 See SPECIAL PUBLICATION / FOREST RESEARCH LAB, SCHOOL OF FORESTRY, OREGON STATE UNIVERSITY. 2395
1059-2539 See LIVING BETTER. 2791
1059-2563 See GROWER (STORRS, CONN.). 173
1059-2571 See PETERSEN'S PREVIEW ... COLLEGE FOOTBALL. 4912
1059-2636 See SAN FRANCISCO DAILY JOURNAL (1990). 3046
1059-2644 See PROCEEDINGS / BELTWIDE COTTON CONFERENCES. 182
1059-2660 See ILLUSTRATED LIGHT. 4370
1059-2725 See ONLINE JOURNAL OF CURRENT CLINICAL TRIALS, THE. 3624
1059-2733 See LIVING PULPIT, THE. 4974
1059-2741 See IOMA'S REPORT ON MANAGING 401 (K) PLANS. 903
1059-275X See MARKET. ASIA PACIFIC. 930
1059-2768 See INTER-VIEWS (PHILADELPHIA, PA.). 5247
1059-2776 See IEE BRIEF. 1751
1059-2784 See CA SELECTS: MOLECULAR MODELING (BIOCHEMICAL ASPECTS). 1005
1059-2830 See FROMMER'S COMPREHENSIVE TRAVEL GUIDE. FRANCE. 5475
1059-2849 See DOING BUSINESS IN THE NETHERLANDS (NEW YORK, N.Y. 1980). 668
1059-2857 See DOING BUSINESS IN THE PEOPLE'S REPUBLIC OF CHINA. 669
1059-2881 See PLUMB LINE (ONEONTA, ALA.), THE. 4986
1059-289X See ENERGY NEWSBRIEF, THE. 1941
1059-2938 See VIDEO GAMES & COMPUTER ENTERTAINMENT. 1231
1059-2946 See 2 TO 22 DAYS IN EUROPE / RICK STEVES. 5458
1059-2954 See 2 TO 22 DAYS IN THE PACIFIC NORTHWEST. 5459
1059-2962 See 2 TO 22 DAYS IN NEW ENGLAND / ANNE E. WRIGHT. 5459
1059-2970 See MARINE DIGEST AND TRANSPORTATION NEWS. 845
1059-2997 See ANVIL MAGAZINE. 2797
1059-3039 See INDEPENDENT POWER MARKETS QUARTERLY. 4761
1059-3047 See RESOURCE BOOK, REAL ESTATE. LOS ANGELES COUNTY. 4846
1059-3055 See CLEVELAND ENTERPRISE (CLEVELAND, OHIO. 1991). 1601
1059-3063 See DEAF SPORTS REVIEW. 4892
1059-3071 See NATIONAL HOUSING REGISTER. 2829
1059-308X See SCHOOL COMMUNITY JOURNAL, THE. 1782
1059-3098 See ERNST & YOUNG RESOURCE GUIDE TO GLOBAL MARKETS, THE. 1634
1059-311X See ORTHOPAEDIC NETWORK NEWS. 3883
1059-3128 See INTEGRATED CIRCUITS. LINEAR. 2065
1059-3144 See ODAN NEWSLETTER. 5033
1059-3152 See JOURNAL OF SUNG-YUAN STUDIES. 2505
1059-3160 See GAS & LIQUID CHROMATOGRAPHY LITERATURE, ABSTRACTS & INDEX. 1011
1059-3179 See INDY REVIEW. 4900
1059-3187 See LAWRENCE'S DEALER PRINT PRICES. 356
1059-3195 See LETTER TO LIBRARIES ONLINE [COMPUTER FILE] : A NEWSLETTER OF THE OREGON STATE LIBRARY. 3223
1059-3209 See FUN E LAFFS. 4861
1059-3217 See SEXY LAFFS. 2545
1059-3225 See ADULT STUDENT GUIDE. 4932
1059-3233 See ADULT TEACHER GUIDE. 4932

1059-3241 See NURSERY TEACHER GUIDE (SPRINGFIELD, MO.). 4983
1059-325X See BEGINNER TEACHER GUIDE. 4938
1059-3268 See PRIMARY TEACHER GUIDE. 5066
1059-3276 See PRIMARY ONE STUDENT GUIDE. 5066
1059-3284 See PRIMARY TWO STUDENT GUIDE. 5066
1059-3292 See BABY & TODDLER TEACHER GUIDE. 4937
1059-3306 See MIDDLER TEACHER GUIDE. 4977
1059-3314 See MIDDLER STUDENT GUIDE. 4977
1059-3322 See JUNIOR TEACHER GUIDE. 4971
1059-3330 See TEEN TEACHER GUIDE (SPRINGFIELD, MO.). 5002
1059-3349 See TEEN STUDENT GUIDE (SPRINGFIELD, MO.). 1070
1059-3357 See HI-TEEN TEACHER GUIDE. 4962
1059-3365 See HI-TEEN STUDENT GUIDE. 4962
1059-3373 See JUNIOR STUDENT GUIDE. 4971
1059-3381 See SENIOR ADULT STUDENT GUIDE. 4996
1059-339X See PRESCHOOL CHILDREN'S CHURCH TEACHER GUIDE. 4987
1059-3403 See PRIMARY CHILDREN'S CHURCH TEACHER GUIDE. 4987
1059-3411 See MIDDLER & JUNIOR CHILDREN'S CHURCH TEACHER GUIDE. 4977
1059-342X See KEEP FLORIDA BEAUTIFUL. 2235
1059-3438 See UNIVERSAL MEDICAL DEVICE NOMENCLATURE SYSTEM. 3648
1059-3454 See GARLAND REFERENCE LIBRARY OF THE HUMANITIES. 2846
1059-3470 See CLIENT/SERVER COMPUTING. 1174
1059-3489 See IMPLANT SOCIETY, THE. 3586
1059-3497 See AMERICAN COUNSELOR. 4572
1059-3500 See NC HOME. 2902
1059-3519 See STARS FOR STUDENTS, CLASS ACTS. 1784
1059-3527 See TAMPA BAY REVIEW CHAPBOOK SERIES. 3444
1059-3535 See MAJOR CONCEPTS IN POLITICS AND POLITICAL THEORY. 4481
1059-3551 See ERNEST BECKER. 3925
1059-356X See PROCEEDINGS OF THE FIRST BIANNUAL INTERNATIONAL CONFERENCE ON ADVANCES IN MANAGEMENT. 883
1059-3640 See INTERNATIONAL JOURNAL OF INTELLIGENT SYSTEMS IN ACCOUNTING, FINANCE & MANAGEMENT. 745
1059-3667 See FACILITY MANAGEMENT JOURNAL : A PUBLICATION OF THE INTERNATIONAL FACILITY MANAGEMENT ASSOCIATION. 867
1059-3683 See INSIDE CONTACTS U.S.A. METRO TUCSON MARKETING DIRECTORY. 682
1059-3713 See MURPHY MATES. 2461
1059-3764 See TEENSCOPE MAGAZINE. 1070
1059-3772 See SPECIALTY REFERENCES. APPLICATION NOTES. 2082
1059-3799 See ALL-UNIVERSITY GERONTOLOGY CENTER PUBLIC POLICY SERIES. 5178
1059-3802 See CANCER WATCH. 3813
1059-3810 See INTERNATIONAL REFERENCE. 5329
1059-3829 See PENNSYLVANIA ART EDUCATOR, THE. 1772
1059-3837 See HUNTING HORIZONS. 4873
1059-3845 See VACATION RENTAL MAGAZINE. 5498
1059-3853 See GADGETS FOR DIVERS. 4895
1059-3861 See CAREERS INTERNATIONAL. 4202
1059-387X See INSIDE TRAC, THE. 926
1059-3888 See CELLULAR PEOPLE / PUBLISHED IN ASSOCIATION WITH THE INTERNATIONAL REGISTRY FOR CELLULAR PROFESSIONALS (IRCP). 1106
1059-3896 See CAREER PLANNING GUIDE FOR PHYSICAL AND OCCUPATIONAL THERAPISTS. 4379

1059-390X See ENVIROBUSINESS REPORT. 2165
1059-3918 See QUALITY BRIEFING. 1623
1059-3950 See FINANCIAL WOMAN TODAY. 5556
1059-3969 See ANDREWS' PROFESSIONAL LIABILITY LITIGATION REPORTER. 3084
1059-3985 See DELL EASY FAST 'N' FUN CROSSWORDS. 4860
1059-3993 See OFF THE SHELF (HUMBLE, TEX.). 3420
1059-4027 See DONOSY (WASHINGTON, D.C.). 2487
1059-4035 See FACILITY FAST FACTS. 759
1059-4043 See IMAGING TECHNOLOGY NEWS : THE NEWSLETTER FOR IMAGING END USERS. 4435
1059-4051 See FRANKLINTONIAN (COLUMBUS, OHIO), THE. 2449
1059-406X See CONSTRUCTION BUSINESS REVIEW. 609
1059-4078 See INVIRONMENT (BUFFALO GROVE, ILL.). 2175
1059-4094 See SCHOOL LAW REPORTER. 3046
1059-4108 See OBJECT-ORIENTED STRATEGIES. 880
1059-4116 See MEALEY'S LITIGATION REPORTS. LEAD. 3008
1059-4140 See NEW MIAMI. 698
1059-4159 See UNIX SYSTEM PRICE PERFORMANCE GUIDE. 1250
1059-4167 See JOURNAL OF WORKERS COMPENSATION, THE. 2886
1059-4175 See WHO'S DOING WHAT?. 2912
1059-4183 See WORLD AIRLINE NEWS. 40
1059-4205 See ALLERGY CONNECTIONS. 3665
1059-4221 See INTERNATIONAL EDUCATOR (WASHINGTON, D.C.). 1753
1059-423X See STABILIZATION AND SOLIDIFICATION OF HAZARDOUS, RADIOACTIVE, AND MIXED WASTES. 2243
1059-4256 See ADVANCES IN SILICON CHEMISTRY. 1035
1059-4280 See ALBANY LAW JOURNAL OF SCIENCE & TECHNOLOGY. 2929
1059-4302 See CIVIL WAR SERIALS & BIBLIOGRAPHY. 2728
1059-4310 See SETON HALL JOURNAL OF SPORT LAW. 3048
1059-4329 See JOURNAL OF SUPREME COURT HISTORY. 4659
1059-4337 See STUDIES IN LAW, POLITICS AND SOCIETY. 5263
1059-440X See ASIAN CINEMA. 4063
1059-4434 See ARCHITECTURE/GEORGIA. 290
1059-4469 See ANNUAL CONFERENCE PROCEEDINGS - NATIONAL COUNCIL ON FAMILY RELATIONS. 2276
1059-4477 See AMERICAN AIREDALE, THE. 4285
1059-4485 See GLOBAL TELECOM REPORT. 1156
1059-4493 See PACK & PADDLE. 4911
1059-4507 See SPE MEMBERSHIP DIRECTORY. 4279
1059-4515 See AMERICAN CHARACTER, THE. 2249
1059-4523 See OKLAHOMA MANUFACTURERS REGISTER. 1620
1059-4531 See MATERIALS MANAGEMENT IN HEALTH CARE. 3788
1059-454X See TECHNOLOGY FOR EMERGENCY CARE NURSES. 3870
1059-4558 See UCC INTERCHANGE. 889
1059-4566 See QUEST (WASHINGTON, D.C. 1991). 4171
1059-4590 See CPA'S PC NETWORK ADVISOR. 1241
1059-4604 See USCSAR REPORTS / THE UNITED STATES CENTER FOR SOVIET-AMERICAN RELATIONS. 4537
1059-4620 See MISSISSIPPI CONSTRUCTION. 621
1059-468X See HAZARDOUS WASTE STRATEGIES UPDATE. 3112

1059-4698 See LEBANON FILE / COUNCIL OF LEBANESE AMERICAN ORGANIZATIONS. 2658

1059-4701 See AMERICAN SINGLES MAGAZINE. 3994

1059-4744 See WEEKLY REVIEW (EMMONS, MINN.), THE. 5699

1059-4760 See OGGI 7. 5711

1059-4779 See RAIVAAJA (FITCHBURG, MASS.). 5690

1059-4795 See HOCKEY TODAY (NEW YORK, N.Y.). 4899

1059-4809 See LIVE WIRE (NEW YORK, N.Y. 1991). 4129

1059-4817 See SHOUT! (NEW YORK, N.Y.). 4153

1059-4825 See COLLEGE FOOTBALL TODAY. 4890

1059-4833 See PRO FOOTBALL TODAY. 4913

1059-4876 See ELK RIVER REVIEW. 3384

1059-4922 See NATIONAL SERVICE NEWSLETTER. 5297

1059-4930 See LEAD DETECTION & ABATEMENT REPORT. 4788

1059-4973 See INDIA JOURNAL, THE. 2653

1059-4981 See SOUTH ASIA CURRENTS [COMPUTER FILE]. 2665

1059-5007 See COLOR (ATLANTA, GA.). 2258

1059-5015 See COMMONS (HARRISONBURG, VA.), THE. 1090

1059-5023 See SOLUTIONS FOR LONG-TERM CARE ADMINISTRATION. 3792

1059-504X See COLORADO EMPLOYMENT LAW LETTER. 3145

1059-5058 See LOUISIANA EMPLOYMENT LAW LETTER. 3151

1059-5066 See WISCONSIN EMPLOYMENT LAW LETTER. 3155

1059-5074 See ILLINOIS ENVIRONMENTAL LAW LETTER. 2980

1059-5082 See TENNESSEE LAW ENFORCEMENT BULLETIN. 3177

1059-5090 See TENNESSEE REAL ESTATE LAW LETTER. 3063

1059-5104 See BAPTIST HERITAGE JOURNAL, THE. 4938

1059-5112 See A TO Z. 2185

1059-5120 See MANAGING TODAY'S FAMILY. 2283

1059-5155 See BOATING WORLD. 592

1059-518X See ANDERSON'S OHIO CASE LOCATOR. 2933

1059-5201 See SPECIAL REPORT - WHITTLE COMMUNICATIONS. 2546

1059-521X See LIVING BIRD (1991). 5618

1059-5252 See TODAY'S FAMILY HOME PLANS. 310

1059-5260 See CD-ROM HANDBOOK. 3201

1059-5279 See ROCK HEROES PRESENTS 4150

1059-5287 See INTERIORS & SOURCES. 2901

1059-5295 See FISHERMAN (FLORIDA ED.), THE. 2302

1059-5325 See SOLSTICE (ANN ARBOR, MICH.). 2576

1059-5341 See SOUTHWEST PUBLISHING MARKET PLACE : A COMPREHENSIVE DIRECTORY OF MARKETS, RESOURCES, AND OPPORTUNITIES FOR WRITERS. 4819

1059-5368 See MUSTANG & FORDS. 5421

1059-5384 See SELF-STORAGE RENTAL GUIDE (SOUTHERN CALIFORNIA ED.). 1299

1059-5392 See WHO'S WHO OF THE ASIAN PACIFIC RIM. 2509

1059-5406 See AMS STUDIES IN 19TH CENTURY LITERATURE AND CULTURE. 3360

1059-5414 See SHEPARD'S CALIFORNIA ENVIRONMENTAL LAW & REGULATION REPORTER. 3116

1059-5422 See COMPETITIVENESS REVIEW. 5242

1059-5457 See DIGITAL GAMES REVIEW. 4860

1059-5465 See COMMUNICATION & COMPUTER NEWS. 1106

1059-5511 See IN CONTEXT (CROWNSVILLE, MD.). 2738

1059-552X See REAL-TIME INTERFACE. 1201

1059-5643 See TEAM LICENSING BUSINESS. 1628

1059-5651 See COMMAND MAGAZINE (SAN LUIS OBISPO, CALIF.). 4039

1059-566X See NOTIONS, POTIONS. 3418

1059-5694 See NORTH COUNTY BLADE-CITIZEN, THE. 5637

1059-5708 See ASSAULT RIFLES. 4037

1059-5716 See COMPLETE GUIDE TO 45'S. 4891

1059-5724 See SMALL BLOCK CHEVY. 5425

1059-5732 See CUSTOM PAINT & BODY. 5412

1059-5740 See CAMAROS (LOS ANGELES, CALIF.). 5408

1059-5759 See RIFLE & SHOTGUN ANNUAL. 4915

1059-5767 See BIG GAME HUNTING. 4869

1059-5775 See USED 4 X 4 BUYER'S GUIDE. 5427

1059-5783 See COMPLETE GUIDE TO 9MM. 4871

1059-5805 See PETERSEN'S ... COLLEGE BASKETBALL. 4912

1059-5813 See ENERGY, ECONOMICS AND CLIMATE CHANGE. 1940

1059-583X See GUIDE TO RESTAURANTS AND BARS. 5071

1059-5856 See CAREERS & MAJORS. 1730

1059-5872 See SARMATIAN REVIEW, THE. 2708

1059-5880 See TOY COLLECTOR & PRICE GUIDE. 2585

1059-5902 See NEW DIRECTION (LOS ANGELES, CALIF.). 4980

1059-5910 See INFO-SOUTH ABSTRACTS. 1534

1059-5929 See FAIRS AND FESTIVALS, NORTHEAST AND SOUTHEAST. 4850

1059-5937 See FRONT PAGE NEWS PLUS BUSINESS. 2920

1059-5953 See TRADITIONAL MUSICLINE, THE. 4157

1059-5988 See GLOBAL STUDIES. JAPAN AND THE PACIFIC RIM. 2651

1059-5996 See VACATION AND TRAVEL TOUR GUIDEBOOK, THE. 5498

1059-6011 See GROUP & ORGANIZATION MANAGEMENT. 869

1059-6038 See HR FOCUS. 941

1059-6046 See GENERAL CONSTRUCTION COSTBOOK. 615

1059-6100 See UNIQUE OPPORTUNITIES. 3793

1059-6119 See FREELANCE GRAPHICS REPORT, THE. 378

1059-6127 See NATIONAL AIR AND SPACE MUSEUM OCCASIONAL PAPER SERIES. 30

1059-6135 See FUN ZONE, THE. 4861

1059-6143 See GREEN CAR JOURNAL. 5415

1059-6151 See TEACHING LEARNING PROCESS, THE. 1907

1059-6178 See SAFE BULLETIN : SCAM AND FRAUD EXCHANGE, THE. 3176

1059-6186 See MALECKI ON INSURANCE. 2887

1059-6208 See JASHNVARAH (LOS ANGELES, CALIF.). 2265

1059-6224 See GUARDIAN (LEXINGTON, KY.), THE. 2250

1059-6232 See ASBESTOS MDL 875 UPDATE. 2937

1059-6259 See SOBER TIMES. 1349

1059-6275 See FLORIDA JURY VERDICT REPORTER. 2971

1059-6313 See PAINT CHECK. 4853

1059-633X See PRENTICE HALL CREATIVE SECRETARY'S LETTER, THE. 4208

1059-6348 See TURF CENTRAL. 2433

1059-6356 See TAX RETURN PREPARER'S LETTER. 4754

1059-6364 See TAPER & SHAVE. 4925

1059-6372 See FREEDOM WRITER (GREAT BARRINGTON, MASS.). 4960

1059-6399 See RAPID PROTOTYPING REPORT. 1201

1059-6402 See ENLACE (WASHINGTON, D.C. 1991). 1488

1059-6461 See DAILY HOME. 5626

1059-647X See BEACHES LEADER, THE. 5649

1059-6488 See EARTH JOURNAL (BOULDER, COLO.). 2164

1059-6526 See PENNSYLVANIA COMMERCIAL REAL ESTATE. 4842

1059-6534 See PENNSYLVANIA REAL ESTATE. 4842

1059-6542 See CLARISWORKS JOURNAL. 1174

1059-6550 See SMALL BUSINESS LETTER, THE. 711

1059-6569 See COMPILER, THE. 3160

1059-6593 See LIFE-LINE (NATIONAL HYDROCEPHALUS FOUNDATION). 3604

1059-6607 See GOULD'S PRIVATE SECURITY REPORTER : SERVING THE HOSPITALITY AND REAL ESTATE INDUSTRIES. 4838

1059-6615 See ABOVEGROUND TANK UPDATE. 4033

1059-6631 See EMF KEEPTRACK. 2966

1059-6674 See KEN GERBINO'S SMART INVESTING. 905

1059-6712 See WCOE (CARMICHAEL, CALIF.). 631

1059-6720 See METRO PHOENIX MARKETING DIRECTORY. 933

1059-678X See HAWAII ARTS MONTHLY : A PUBLICATION OF HAWAII PUBLIC RADIO. 321

1059-6801 See PUBLICATIONS IN PRINT (WASHINGTON, D.C.). 5035

1059-681X See CABLE SYSTEM MANAGER. 1105

1059-6828 See FEDERAL COURT APPOINTMENTS REPORT. 2969

1059-6836 See FAXON HEALTH INFORMATION CATALOG. 4775

1059-6844 See FAXON BUSINESS INFORMATION CATALOG. 675

1059-6852 See FAXON GUIDE TO SERIALS. 3210

1059-6860 See SYZYGY (STANFORD, CALIF.). 5002

1059-6879 See EMILY DICKINSON JOURNAL, THE. 3384

1059-6887 See U.S. BEER MARKET. 2371

1059-6909 See AMERITECH INDUSTRIAL PURCHASING GUIDE. GEORGIA/ALABAMA/EASTERN & CENTRAL TENNESSEE. 948

1059-7018 See COMPUTER TAPE OUTLOOK. HALF-INCH PRODUCTS / BY ROBERT C. ABRAHAM AND RAYMOND C. FREEMAN, JR. 1236

1059-7050 See LOCAL CLIMATOLOGICAL DATA. MIDDLETOWN/HARRISBURG INTL. APT. MONTHLY SUMMARY. 1429

1059-7069 See JOURNAL OF TECHNOLOGY AND TEACHER EDUCATION. 1758

1059-7077 See ORANGE COUNTY BUSINESS DIRECTORY. 701

1059-7085 See CALIFORNIA TECHNOLOGY REGISTER. 5092

1059-7093 See CONTRA COSTA COUNTY COMMERCE AND INDUSTRY DIRECTORY. 829

1059-7107 See CURRENT ISSUES IN MIDDLE LEVEL EDUCATION. 1734

1059-7115 See JOURNAL OF WOMEN'S HEALTH. 3600

1059-7123 See ADAPTIVE BEHAVIOR. 4571

1059-7166 See MISSISSIPPI PRESS (PASCAGOULA, MISS.), THE. 5701

1059-7182 See UCGM (NORTH CHARLESTON, S.C.). 4157

1059-7204 See RAM UPDATE. 5072

1059-7220 See DIRECTORY, INVESTOR-OWNED HOSPITALS, RESIDENTIAL TREATMENT FACILITIES AND CENTERS, HOSPITAL MANAGEMENT COMPANIES, HEALTH SYSTEMS. 3779

1059-7239 See PRACTICES (CINCINNATI, OHIO). 306

1059-7255 See AMS STUDIES IN RELIGIOUS TRADITION. 4934

1059-7263 See ARTLANTA. 342

1059-7298 See FIRE AND ARSON INVESTIGATOR, THE. 2288

1059-731X See INFORMATION & INTERACTIVE SERVICES REPORT. 1157

1059-7328 See PROCEEDINGS - UNITED STATES. BUREAU OF THE CENSUS. 5336

1059-7344 See LOTUS WORKS REPORT, THE. 1193

1059-7352 See BIOTECHNOLOGY DIRECTORY (NEW YORK, N.Y.), THE. 3689

1059-7395 See NEW STUDIES ON THE LEFT. 5210

1059-7409 See ACCREDITATION MANUAL FOR HOSPITALS / THE JOINT COMMISSION. 3775

1059-7417 See EDUCATIONAL FACILITY PLANNER. 1863

1059-7433 See DIRECTORY OF REGISTERED INVESTMENT ADVISORS. 896

1059-7441 See INVESTMENT SPECIALTIES GUIDE. 903

1059-745X See NARA PYLON : OFFICIAL PUBLICATION OF THE NATIONAL AIR RACING ASSOCIATION. 4905

1059-7476 See BRIDE'S & YOUR NEW HOME. 2277

1059-7484 See NEW ALASKA OUTDOORS, THE. 4875

1059-7492 See STORYBOARD (MANGILAO, GUAM). 3440

1059-7514 See ION CHANNELS. 488

1059-7522 See METHODS IN PLANT BIOCHEMISTRY. 518

1059-7565 See HEADACHE QUARTERLY. 3833

1059-759X See IN THE WIND (ANGOURA HILLS, CALIF.). 4081

1059-7603 See FROMMER'S BUDGET TRAVEL GUIDE. HAWAII ... ON $ ... A DAY. 5475

1059-7638 See SCHOOL EXECUTIVE (PHILADELPHIA, PA.). 1871

1059-7654 See ACCOUNTANT'S TAX WEEKLY. 736

1059-7670 See NORDSTJERNAN (1991). 5719

1059-7689 See ART NOW GALLERY GUIDE. INTERNATIONAL. 340

1059-7700 See JOURNAL OF GENETIC COUNSELING. 548

1059-7719 See ALLTON-ALTON-AULTON ASSOCIATION FAMILY NEWSLETTER. 2436

1059-7727 See NEBRASKA MANUFACTURERS REGISTER. 3485

1059-7786 See LITURGICAL MINISTRY. 4974

1059-7794 See HUMAN MUTATION. 547

1059-7808 See INTERNATIONAL GUIDE TO AFROCENTRIC MERCHANDISE. 2264

1059-7816 See INTERNATIONAL OFFSHORE OIL COMPANY DIRECTORY. 4261

1059-7905 See ADVENTIST THEOLOGICAL SOCIETY MONOGRAPHS. 4932

1059-7913 See PAAC NOTES (CHICAGO, ILL.). 3715

1059-793X See STUDENT SPORTS (CAL-HI SPORTS ED.). 4924

1059-7964 See CORPORATE DIRECTORY OF U.S. PUBLIC COMPANIES, THE. 661

1059-8006 See METAL EDGE. 4131

1059-8022 See RESEARCH BULLETIN - WASHINGTON STATE UNIVERSITY. COLLEGE OF AGRICULTURE AND HOME ECONOMICS. RESEARCH CENTER. 127

1059-8057 See MOODY'S HANDBOOK OF NASDAQ STOCKS. 907

1059-8065 See MMAP LOG. 275

1059-8073 See PILLSBURY FAST AND HEALTHY MAGAZINE. 4197

1059-8081 See INTOUCH (KNOXVILLE, TENN.). 1325

1059-809X See ERNST & YOUNG TAX GUIDE, THE. 4721

1059-8154 See ALTERNATIVE INDEX. 5814

1059-8162 See CENTRALIA SENTINEL. 5658

1059-8197 See MOSAIC (BLOOMINGTON, IND.). 2747

1059-8200 See MARKETOOLS (HERNDON, VA.). 932

1059-8227 See INSIDE U.S.A. VOLLEYBALL. 4900

1059-8243 See CUED SPEECH JOURNAL. 4386

1059-826X See RESEARCH REPORT - ILLINOIS STATE WATER SURVEY. 5538

1059-8278 See 2 TO 22 DAYS IN FRANCE. 5458

1059-8308 See CAUDA PAVONIS. 2844

1059-8324 See JOURNAL OF EXPERIMENTAL ZOOLOGY. SUPPLEMENT. 5587

1059-8359 See SEEK-A-WORD. 4866

1059-8367 See AUTO RACEPAGES. 4885

1059-8375 See ST. WILLIBRORD STUDIES IN PHILOSOPHY AND RELIGION. 4999

1059-8405 See JOURNAL OF SCHOOL NURSING, THE. 3860

1059-8413 See SBN UPDATE. 1121

1059-8456 See VETERINARY UPDATE (LARGE ANIMALS). 5527

1059-8472 See CORCORAN (WASHINGTON, D.C.). 348

1059-8545 See NEW JERSEY TRAFFIC DIRECTORY (STATEWIDE ED.), THE. 5442

1059-8553 See ARISTOS (TACOMA, WASH.). 3363

1059-8561 See CONSOLIDATED TREATIES & INTERNATIONAL AGREEMENTS. CURRENT DOCUMENT SERVICE, EUROPEAN COMMUNITY. 4519

1059-8596 See JOURNAL OF FIXED INCOME, THE. 904

1059-8650 See JOURNAL OF MUSEUM EDUCATION, THE. 4090

1059-8707 See PROCEEDINGS OF THE SAN DIEGO SOCIETY OF NATURAL HISTORY. 4170

1059-8715 See HUNTERDON REVIEW (LEBANON, N.J.). 5710

1059-8723 See CONNECTICUT WEEKLY AGRICULTURAL REPORT. 76

1059-8766 See CRAFT SUPPLY MAGAZINE. 371

1059-8804 See AIDSMONTHLY (TREATMENT ED.). 3665

1059-8812 See AIDSMONTHLY (JOURNAL ED.). 3665

1059-8820 See AIDSMONTHLY (HEALTHCARE ED.). 3665

1059-8839 See AIDSMONTHLY (EDUCATION ED.). 1723

1059-8847 See AIDSMONTHLY (BUSINESS AND FINANCE ED.). 5271

1059-8855 See AIDSMONTHLY (GOVERNMENT ED.). 3665

1059-8863 See AIDSMONTHLY (PSYCHOSOCIAL ED.). 3665

1059-8871 See AIDSMONTHLY (LEGAL ED.). 3665

1059-888X See AIDSMONTHLY (WORKPLACE ED.). 3665

1059-8898 See AIDSMONTHLY (RESEARCH ED.). 3665

1059-8901 See AIDSMONTHLY (INTERNATIONAL ED.). 3665

1059-891X See AIDSMONTHLY (SERVICE ORGANIZATION ED.). 3665

1059-8928 See CANCERMONTHLY (BREAST CANCER ED.). 3814

1059-8936 See CANCERMONTHLY (SMOKING AND LUNG CANCER ED.). 3814

1059-8944 See CANCERMONTHLY (CARCINOGENESIS AND EPIDEMIOLOGY ED.). 3814

1059-8952 See CANCERMONTHLY (SOLID TUMOR ED.). 3814

1059-8960 See CANCERMONTHLY (AIDS RELATED CANCER ED.). 3814

1059-8979 See CANCERMONTHLY (CANCER TREATMENT/GENE THERAPY ED.). 3814

1059-8987 See CANCERMONTHLY (JOURNAL ED.). 3814

1059-8995 See CANCERMONTHLY (RESEARCH ED.). 3814

1059-9010 See CANCERMONTHLY (EDUCATION AND HEALTHCARE ED.). 4770

1059-9029 See CANCERMONTHLY (BUSINESS AND FINANCE ED.). 3814

1059-9037 See CANCERMONTHLY (INTERNATIONAL ACTIVITIES ED.). 3814

1059-9053 See JOURNAL OF NATURAL RESOURCES AND LIFE SCIENCES EDUCATION. 100

1059-907X See MEDICAL SOFTWARE REVIEWS. 3611

1059-9088 See CATHOLIC MUSIC EDUCATOR. 4108

1059-9096 See COUNTY AND CITY EXTRA. 5326

1059-910X See MICROSCOPY RESEARCH AND TECHNIQUE. 573

1059-9126 See FIDELIO (WASHINGTON, D.C.). 2533

1059-9134 See REFERENCE GUIDES TO NATIONAL LEGAL SYSTEMS. 3142

1059-9142 See CARD COLLECTOR'S PRICE GUIDE. 2772

1059-9169 See MEN'S EXERCISE. 2599

1059-9177 See KENTUCKY AFIELD. 4874

1059-9185 See SCHOLARS OF EARLY MODERN STUDIES. 2708

1059-9207 See PARENTS' GUIDE TO CHILDREN'S ENTERTAINMENT. 1136

1059-9231 See JOURNAL OF ASIA-PACIFIC BUSINESS. 685

1059-924X See JOURNAL OF AGROMEDICINE. 3593

1059-9258 See JOURNAL OF RELIGION IN DISABILITY & REHABILITATION. 4970

1059-9266 See WARD'S SALES PROSPECTOR. 718

1059-9274 See TODAY'S SCIENCE ON FILE. 5166

1059-9290 See NELSON'S GUIDE TO INSTITUTIONAL RESEARCH. 909

1059-938X See HEALTH (SAN FRANCISCO, CALIF.). 4781

1059-9401 See COMICS RETAILER. 2773

1059-941X See JOURNAL OF PROSTHODONTICS. 1327

1059-9436 See BUSINESS LAW TODAY / THE MAGAZINE OF THE ABA SECTION OF BUSINESS LAW. 3097

1059-9452 See INTERNATIONAL GUIDE TO AFROCENTRIC EVENTS. 2264

1059-9460 See INTERNATIONAL GUIDE TO AFROCENTRIC TALENT. 2264

1059-9487 See CALIFORNIA NOTARY BULLETIN. 4636

1059-9495 See JOURNAL OF MATERIALS ENGINEERING AND PERFORMANCE. 2118

1059-9509 See JOURNAL OF STONE DISEASE, THE. 3968

1059-9576 See SEWANEE THEOLOGICAL REVIEW. 4996

1059-9630 See JOURNAL OF THERMAL SPRAY TECHNOLOGY. 4006

1059-9657 See TV 2 (SAINT PAUL, MINN.). 1141

1059-9681 See NORTHWEST TRAVEL. 5486

1059-9711 See NUGGET (SAN FRANCISCO, CALIF.), THE. 2465

1059-9762 See KURIER (ORANGE, VA), DER. 2457

1059-9770 See U.S.-JAPAN WOMEN'S JOURNAL. ENGLISH SUPPLEMENT. 5567

1059-9924 See REGIONAL INDUSTRIAL BUYING GUIDE BY STANDARD INDUSTRIAL CLASSIFICATION CODE. UPSTATE NEW YORK. 1623

1059-9959 See WORKSTATION (AUSTIN, TEX.). 1207

1059-9967 See UNISYS WORLD OPEN SYSTEMS NEWS. 1206

1059-9975 See RISC WORLD. 1265

1059-9983 See NCR CONNECTION. 697

1059-9991 See DIGITAL'S RDB WORLD. 1182

1060-0027 See PARENT WORKSHOP, THE. 2284

1060-0051 See JOURNAL OF INFUSIONAL CHEMOTHERAPY, THE. 3819

1060-0086 See CRUISES & TOURS. 5467

1060-0094 See WHERE TO RETIRE. 5182

1060-0159 See CATHOLIC NEWS & HERALD, THE. 5026

1060-0167 See NEW YORK GUARDIAN, THE. 5711

1060-0191 See FODOR'S NOVA SCOTIA, PRINCE EDWARD ISLAND, AND NEW BRUNSWICK. 5472

1060-0221 See FORTRAN JOURNAL. 1185

1060-0280 See ANNALS OF PHARMACOTHERAPY, THE. 4291

1060-0353 See STUDENT LEADER NEWS SERVICE. 1849

1060-0388 See SPANG ROBINSON REPORT ON INTELLIGENT SYSTEMS, THE. 1217

1060-0396 See CYBERNETICS AND SYSTEMS ANALYSIS. 1251

1060-0418 See RECEIVABLES REPORT, THE. 807

1060-054X See PURCHASING PERFORMANCE BENCHMARKS FOR THE CARBON STEEL INDUSTRY / CAPS, CENTER FOR ADVANCED PURCHASING STUDIES. 4017

1060-0558 See CONTEMPORARY TOPICS IN LABORATORY ANIMAL SCIENCE. 5508

1060-0655 See DOMESTIC AFFAIRS. 4472

1060-0671 See AFRICAN-AMERICAN ARCHAEOLOGY. 253

1060-068X See HANDGUNNING. 4898

1060-071X See SPECIAL PUBLICATION / SOCIETY FOR SEDIMENTARY GEOLOGY. 4231

1060-0876 See SOCIOLOGICAL VIEWPOINTS. 5261

1060-0884 See GLOBAL JUSTICE. 4523

1060-0906 See GLOBAL TRADE. 838

1060-0922 See INITIATIVE (AUSTIN, TEX.), THE. 1189

1060-0949 See COLLIN CHRONICLES. 2443

1060-0973 See SOURCEBOOK FOR SCIENCE, MATHEMATICS, AND TECHNOLOGY EDUCATION. 5158

1060-1066 See WINDOWS MAGAZINE. 1282

1060-1074 See SCO MAGAZINE. 1249

1060-1147 See JACK ANDERSON CONFIDENTIAL (1992). 4478

1060-1171 See HALLS GRAPHIC, THE. 5745

1060-1309 See MEASURE OF EXCELLENCE / LAURANCE D. LINFORD, A. 2745

1060-1317 See AUTOCAD WORLD. 1171

1060-1325 See JOURNAL OF MACROMOLECULAR SCIENCE. PURE AND APPLIED CHEMISTRY. 1042

1060-1333 See CLINICAL RESEARCH AND REGULATORY AFFAIRS. 4297

1060-135X See INSIGHT (SAN FRANSISCO, CALIF.). 3857

1060-1368 See SPEEDNEWS DEFENSE BIWEEKLY. 36

1060-1376 See COMPUTER RESELLER SOURCES. 1177

1060-1384 See SYSTEMS & NETWORK INTEGRATION. 1291

1060-1392 See MANAGED HEALTHCARE. 4789

1060-1392 See MANAGED HEALTHCARE NEWS. 4789

1060-1406 See SYSTEMS & NETWORK INTEGRATION. 1291

1060-1414 See ENVIRONMENT WATCH. LATIN AMERICA. 672

1060-1465 See CHARTS, GRAPHS & STATS INDEX. 5325

1060-1473 See DIRECTORY OF PACKAGING SOURCES. 4218

1060-1481 See INVESTMENT INFORMATION DIRECTORY (SEATTLE, WASH.). 902

1060-149X See JOURNAL OF PRE-RAPHAELITE STUDIES (1992), THE. 2848

1060-1503 See VICTORIAN LITERATURE & CULTURE. 3450

1060-1511 See CONSUMER REPORTS TRAVEL BUYING GUIDE. 5467

1060-152X See JOURNAL OF PEDIATRIC ORTHOPEDICS. PART B. 3882

1060-1538 See EVOLUTIONARY ANTHROPOLOGY / ISSUES, NEWS AND REVIEWS. 236

1060-1554 See MASSACHUSETTS TECHNOLOGY RESOURCE GUIDE. 5127

1060-1600 See GREATER SILICON VALLEY TECHNOLOGY RESOURCE GUIDE. 5108

1060-1635 See BULLETIN / COUNCIL OF SOCIETIES FOR THE STUDY OF RELIGION. 4940

1060-1759 See DIRECTORY OF PUBLISHED PROCEEDINGS. SERIES MLS, MEDICAL/LIFE SCIENCES. 3572

1060-1848 See EARTH SPACE REVIEW. 1355

1060-1872 See OPERATIVE TECHNIQUES IN SPORTS MEDICINE. 3955

1060-1880 See EUROPEAN CONSULTANTS DIRECTORY. 673

1060-1902 See SENSOR BUSINESS DIGEST. 3487

1060-2011 See ABSTRACTS OF THE ... GENERAL MEETING OF THE AMERICAN SOCIETY FOR MICROBIOLOGY. 476

1060-2070 See Z PAPERS. 4548

1060-2100 See ELECTRONICS MANUFACTURERS DIRECTORY. 3478

1060-2135 See HERALDO DE SANTIDAD (1992), EL. 4962

1060-2178 See LOTUS ONE SOURCE. CD/CORPORATE. U.S. PUBLIC COS. 691

1060-2208 See BUSINESS PUBLISHING (CAROL STREAM, ILL.). 4812

1060-2240 See DAILY JAPAN DIGEST, THE. 4471

1060-2259 See WEEKLY JAPAN DIGEST, THE. 4500

1060-2275 See STUDENTS AID NEWSLETTER. 1849

1060-2399 See AMERITECH INDUSTRIAL PURCHASING GUIDE. FLORIDA. 948

1060-2410 See ADVANCES IN CONNECTIONIST AND NEURAL COMPUTATION THEORY. 1210

1060-250X See SINGAPORE REPORT ON THE GROWTH TRIANGLE. 851

1060-2518 See EASTERN EUROPE FINANCE. 832

1060-2526 See SF WEEKLY (SAN FRANCISCO, CALIF.). 5640

1060-2534 See TODAY'S PARTS MANAGER. 1999

1060-2542 See PLAGUE WATCH. 5213

1060-2550 See SPORTING GOODS INTELLIGENCE. 937

1060-2569 See ARTISTIC TRAVELER, THE. 5461

1060-2585 See ORANGE COUNTY REPORTER (SANTA ANA, CALIF.). 3023

1060-2607 See MARINE SOCIETY VIEWS. 4049

1060-2666 See NONCITRUS FRUITS AND NUTS. SUMMARY. 114

1060-2712 See MANUFACTURING AUTOMATION. 3483

1060-2739 See CREDIT & COLLECTION MANAGERS' LETTER. 785

1060-2747 See TIMES (PAWTUCKET, R.I.), THE. 5741

1060-278X See MACROMOLECULAR REPORTS. 985

1060-2801 See BECKETT FOCUS ON FUTURE STARS. 2485

1060-2860 See SALES & MARKETING SURVEY / SHESHUNOFF. 936

1060-2895 See ALASKA MARINE RESOURCE QUARTERLY. 1446

1060-2909 See HEALTH CARE FEDERAL REGISTER ALERT. 4778

1060-2917 See CHIEFS OF STATE & CABINET OFFICERS FOR NATIONS OF THE WORLD. 4637

1060-2933 See GUIDE TO AUDITS OF EMPLOYEE BENEFIT PLANS. 744

1060-2941 See BRIEFING (SHAWNEE MISSION, KAN.). 5193

1060-2941 See BRIEFING, THE COMPREHENSIVE SOURCE FOR INTERNATIONAL SECURITY INTELLIGENCE. 4517

1060-2968 See YEAR BOOK OF TRANSPLANTATION. 3978

1060-2976 See DAILY ENVIRONMENT REPORT. 3110

1060-3026 See WINNEBAGO INDIAN NEWS. 5707

1060-3042 See THEATRE CRAFTS INTERNATIONAL. 5370

1060-3085 See JOURNAL OF THE INTERAMERICAN MEDICAL AND HEALTH ASSOCIATION. 3598

1060-3093 See BRIDGEWATER-DAVIS PACIFIC INTELLIGENCE UPDATE. 4517

1060-3107 See MINNESOTA ARTS DIRECTORY. 358

1060-3131 See MEDICAL EXECUTIVE COMMITTEE REPORTER, THE. 4790

1060-314X See FAIRCHILDE INTERNATIONAL LIBRARY INSTITUTE : [NEWSLETTER] / FILI. 3210

1060-3166 See GIFTED EDUCATION REVIEW. 1879

1060-3174 See JOURNAL OF CLASSROOM MANAGEMENT. 1897

1060-3182 See ACKERMAN WAREHOUSING FORUM. 636

1060-3190 See CALIFORNIA HOMES AND LIFESTYLES. 2899

1060-3212 See PRAEGER SERIES IN CRIMINOLOGY AND CRIME CONTROL POLICY. 3173

1060-3220 See O&P BUSINESS NEWS. 700

1060-3239 See CHOICE$ (RESEARCH TRIANGLE PARK, N.C.). 783

1060-3247 See AIC NEWS : NEWSLETTER OF THE AMERICAN INSTITUTE FOR CONSERVATION OF HISTORIC AND ARTISTIC WORKS. 335

1060-3255 See ASHEVILLE CITIZEN-TIMES. 5722

1060-3263 See NEWSLETTER / AUSTIN FAMILIES ASSOCIATION OF AMERICA. 2463

1060-3271 See JOURNAL OF AOAC INTERNATIONAL. 1016

1060-3344 See INFORMATION TECHNOLOGY SERVICES MEMBER DIRECTORY. 5113

1060-3409 See MARJORIE KINNAN RAWLINGS JOURNAL OF FLORIDA LITERATURE, THE. 3410

1060-3417 See COAST BUSINESS. 657

1060-3441 See DERMATOLOGY NURSING. 3719

1060-3476 See JEFFERSON JIMPLECUTE. 5751

1060-3484 See HOUSTON POST (1932). 5751

1060-3506 See BANK TECHNOLOGY NEWS. 776

1060-3514 See NFL SUPERPRO. 4864

1060-3522 See NOPA OFFICE MARKET UPDATE. 4212

1060-3565 See MIS MANAGEMENT REVIEW. 1195

1060-3573 See EUROPEAN ENVIRONMENTAL BUSINESS NEWS, THE. 2171

1060-3581 See SAT-VIEW. 34

1060-3603 See FAMILY BUSINESS ADVISOR, THE. 674

1060-362X See ATLANTIC COAST COLLEGIATE SPORTS MAGAZINE. 4884

1060-3646 See PELHAM JOURNAL, THE. 5654

1060-3654 See NMFS FISHERIES MARKET NEWS REPORT. 2309

1060-3662 See ARTNEWS INTERNATIONAL DIRECTORY OF CORPORATE ART COLLECTIONS. 342

1060-3670 See CAWP NEWS & NOTES. 5553

1060-3689 See SIMULATION DIGEST. 1283

1060-3697 See SHEPARD'S NEW JERSEY EXPRESS CITATIONS. 3052

1060-3700 See VERB (ATLANTA, GA.). 3450

1060-3719 See FROMMER'S FAMILY TRAVEL GUIDE. NEW YORK CITY WITH KIDS. 5477

1060-3727 See FROMMER'S COMPREHENSIVE TRAVEL GUIDE. PUERTO VALLARTA, MANZANILLO & GUADALAJARA. 5476

1060-3735 See REMODEL NOW. 2903

1060-3743 See JOURNAL OF SECOND LANGUAGE WRITING. 3291

1060-3751 See STRATEGIC SYSTEMS. 1249

1060-376X See SIOUXLAND EVENTS. 4854

1060-3778 See COUNTRY INNS AND BACK ROADS. NEW ENGLAND. 5467

1060-3786 See COUNTRY INNS AND BACK ROADS. CALIFORNIA. 5467

1060-3808 See RETAIL INFO SYSTEMS NEWS. 956

1060-3816 See WORLD AT LARGE, THE. 2550

1060-3840 See UFCW LOCAL 1428 MESSENGER. 1715

1060-3859 See ZOOSCAPE (LOS ANGELES, CALIF.). 5603

1060-3875 See BIRNBAUM'S HONOLULU. 5464

1060-3883 See BIRNBAUM'S PUERTO VALLARTA. 5464

1060-3891 See GLOBAL VISIONS. 4523

1060-3905 See ABOUT ... TIME. 2526

1060-3921 See BLACK PAGES OF AMERICA (WASHINGTON, D.C., METROPOLITAN ED.). 2257

1060-393X See WASHINGTON MASONIC TRIBUNE : THE OFFICIAL MAGAZINE OF THE MASONIC GRAND LODGE OF WASHINGTON. 5237

1060-3948 See RESOURCE BOOK, REAL ESTATE. ORANGE, RIVERSIDE & SAN BERNARDINO COUNTIES. 4846

1060-3956 See SINGING NEWS MAGAZINE, THE. 4153

1060-3964 See SOFTWARE MARKETING JOURNAL. 1291

1060-3972 See ON POINTE. 1314

1060-3999 See JOURNAL OF RAPID METHODS AND AUTOMATION IN MICROBIOLOGY. 2347

1060-4006 See DINOSAUR REVIEW (BOULDER, COLO.), THE. 4227

1060-4014 See UNIFORM ZONING CODE. 631

1060-4030 See BA PAPYRUS. 370

1060-4065 See VIRGINIA LEGAL DESKBOOK : THE COMMON SENSE APPROACH. 3072

1060-4081 See PROCEEDINGS OF THE BUSINESS LAW SECTION ANNUAL MEETING. 3102

1060-4154 See INDIANA BUSINESS MAGAZINE. 682

1060-4189 See NOTISUR (ALBUQUERQUE, N.M.). 4530

1060-4197 See NEUROLOGY CHRONICLE. 3841

1060-4200 See DIRECTORY OF PLANT BIOTECHNOLOGY COMPANIES IN USA/ BY FORE. 508

1060-4235 See STAKE (SAN FRANCISCO, CALIF.), THE. 3439

1060-4243 See PERTINENT LEGISLATION AFFECTING NURSES : PLAN. 3867

1060-4251 See STURZA'S MEDICAL INVESTMENT LETTER. 916

1060-426X See SCHOOL SECURITY REPORT. 1871

1060-4316 See RIDER COLLEGE. 1102

1060-4332 See ARKANSAS DEMOCRAT GAZETTE. 5631

1060-4367 See DOMES (MILWAUKEE, WIS.). 2768

1060-4375 See ROBOT EXPLORER. 1202

1060-4383 See COLORADO REAL ESTATE JOURNAL. 4835

1060-4405 See CHILTON'S MEDIUM/HEAVY DUTY TRUCK SERVICE MANUAL. 5411

1060-4413 See CHILTON'S NISSAN REPAIR MANUAL. 5411

1060-443X See CHILTON'S LABOR GUIDE MANUAL. 1659

1060-4448 See WRITING IN OHIO. 3455

1060-4456 See PHARMACOLOGY COMMUNICATIONS. 4322

1060-4502 See TODAY'S COLLECTOR. 752

1060-4537 See PHARMACY BUSINESS. 4323

1060-4545 See ELDER UPDATE. 5179

1060-4553 See DAILY ITEM (WHITE PLAINS, N.Y.), THE. 5715

1060-4596 See LIGHT & ISLAMIC REVIEW, THE. 5043

1060-460X See HERALD STATESMAN. 5717

1060-4642 See ASSET INTERNATIONAL (GREENWICH, CONN.). 891

1060-4650 See WEDGE (WILLOW STREET, PA.), THE. 2477

1060-4677 See ELECTRONIC GAMING RETAIL NEWS. 4860

1060-4685 See SUPER GAMING. 4866

1060-4707 See ANTI-DRUG FUNDING ALERT. 4630

1060-4723 See DAILY ARGUS (WHITE PLAINS, N.Y.), THE. 5715

1060-4731 See NSI ADVISORY. 4670

1060-474X See B.B. DUCKWOOD'S WORD SEARCH IN RUSSIAN. 4857

1060-4774 See SHEPARD'S VIRGINIA EXPRESS CITATIONS. 3055

1060-4804 See DIRT WHEELS. 4893

1060-4812 See NORTHWEST PARKS & WILDLIFE. 4169

1060-488X See MORRISON ENVIRONMENTAL DIRECTORY. 1988

1060-4898 See MONTGOMERY COUNTY BUSINESS DIRECTORY. 696

1060-491X See STATE TAX NOTES (MICROFICHE). 4749

1060-4936 See PHOTO ELECTRONIC IMAGING. 4373

1060-4944 See TAX COURT PETITIONS. 4762

1060-4952 See PANEL STUDY OF INCOME DYNAMICS. 1511

1060-4960 See NATIONAL LONGITUDINAL SURVEY OF YOUTH, THE. 5252

1060-5037 See YEAR IN REVIEW - CRANBROOK INSTITUTE OF SCIENCE. 4097

1060-5045 See COGEL BLUE BOOK. 4639

1060-5053 See EARTH WORK. 2192

1060-507X See OBSTETRICS & GYNECOLOGY REVIEW. 3766

1060-5088 See PRESIDENTS & PRIME MINISTERS. 4492

1060-5118 See LABORATORY INDUSTRY REPORT. 1615

1060-5134 See CONNECTICUT COLLEGE MAGAZINE. 1091

1060-5193 See MEDICAL INDUSTRY EXECUTIVE. 3609

1060-5207 See ARVADA JEFFERSON SENTINEL, THE. 5641

1060-5215 See LAKEWOOD JEFFERSON SENTINEL (1991), THE. 5643

1060-5223 See WHEAT RIDGE JEFFERSON SENTINEL, THE. 5644

1060-5231 See MOROCCO COURIER, THE. 5665

1060-5258 See PETROGRAM (TALLAHASSEE, FLA.). 4271

1060-5266 See FRESH MEN. 2533

1060-5274 See CHILDREN'S WRITER. 3374

1060-5282 See HIGH COLOR. 1233

1060-5304 See TERM FREQUENCY LIST. 4280

1060-5312 See FRANKLIN PIERCE TIMES. 2304

1060-5320 See THEATREFORUM (LA JOLLA, CALIF.). 5371

1060-5339 See ECONOMIC DEVELOPMENT DIGEST (WASHINGTON, D.C.). 1482

1060-5355 See MEDICARE AND MEDICAID LAW REPORTER. 3009

1060-5398 See PENNSYLVANIA LAWN, AND GARDEN MAGAZINE. 2427

1060-5436 See PENNSYLVANIA BUSINESS MAGAZINE. 702

1060-5444 See FISHING TRIP MAGAZINE. 4872

1060-5452 See HUNTING TRIP MAGAZINE. 4873

1060-5460 See PENNSYLVANIA GOLFER MAGAZINE. 4912

1060-5487 See JOURNAL OF AHIMA. 3786

1060-5495 See FOUNTAIN COUNTY NEIGHBOR. 5664

1060-5517 See HEALTH PROMOTION PRACTITIONER. 4781

1060-5525 See SIN CENSURA (WASHINGTON, D.C.). 2760

1060-5568 See NORTHEAST MISSISSIPPI HISTORICAL & GENEALOGICAL SOCIETY QUARTERLY, THE. 2464

1060-5576 See AMERICAN PHARMACY TECHNICIAN JOURNAL, THE. 4290

1060-5606 See SCRIBE (WASHINGTON, D.C.), THE. 2273

1060-5622 See WELFARE TO WORK. 5314

1060-5630 See VOCATIONAL CAREERS SOURCEBOOK. 4209

1060-5649 See TECHNOS (BLOOMINGTON, IND.). 1787

1060-5657 See JOURNAL OF HEALTH INFORMATION MANAGEMENT RESEARCH, THE. 4787

1060-5665 See WASHINGTON GREEN. 1526

1060-5673 See READMORE REPORTER, THE. 3632

1060-5681 See TELINDE'S OPERATIVE GYNECOLOGY UPDATES. 3769

1060-569X See RUSSIAN BUSINESS REPORTS. 708

1060-5703 See SANKOFA JOURNAL : THE AUTHENTIC VOICE OF THE TRADITIONAL HEALERS OF AFRICA. 4329

1060-5711 See BIBLIOGRAPHIES OF THE STATES OF THE UNITED STATES. 410

1060-5770 See INTERNATIONAL DIRECTORY OF CONSULTANTS AND CONTRACTORS ACTIVE IN THE MIDDLE EAST AND AFRICA, AN. 683

1060-5789 See NELSON'S DIRECTORY OF INSTITUTIONAL REAL ESTATE. 4842

1060-5797 See REMODELING ... COSTBOOK / BNI, BUILDING NEWS. 626

1060-5851 See POST-SOVIET GEOGRAPHY. 2573

1060-586X See POST-SOVIET AFFAIRS. 1513

1060-5894 See RUSSIAN ECONOMY AND BUSINESS DIGEST. 1519

1060-5908 See NEW WAVE WRESTLING. 4907

1060-5916 See HR COMPUTING. 1186

1060-5924 See IOMA'S REPORT ON CONTROLLING LAW FIRM COSTS. 2984

1060-5932 See ROVER REGISTER, THE. 5392

1060-5967 See WORTH (BOSTON, MASS.). 920

1060-5991 See ADMINISTRATIVE OPHTHALMOLOGY. 3871

1060-6009 See PURCHASING PERFORMANCE BENCHMARKS FOR THE U.S. CONSTRUCTION/ENGINEERING INDUSTRY. 625

1060-6017 See ISSUES IN AGRICULTURAL DATABASE MARKETING. 927

1060-6025 See NATIONAL DIRECTORY OF CORPORATE DISTRESS SPECIALISTS, THE. 697

1060-6033 See OCLC SELECTED TITLES. 3238

1060-6041 See JOURNAL OF INVITATIONAL THEORY AND PRACTICE. 1898

1060-605X See HEALTH ONE MEDICAL JOURNAL. 3582

1060-6084 See INTERNATIONAL QUARTERLY (TALLAHASS., FLA.). 3396

1060-6092 See ZA ZAGOLOVKAMI. 3077

1060-6106 See DECA DIMENSIONS. 1912

1060-6114 See OHIO RESTAURANT HOTLINE. 5072

1060-6130 See DAILY REFLECTOR (GREENVILLE, N.C.). 5723

1060-6149 See ETHIOPIAN (CHANTILLY, VA.), THE. 2499

1060-6157 See EAST EUROPE & THE REPUBLICS. 1480

1060-6165 See NEWS-REPORT (BICKNELL, IND.). 5666

1060-6173 See KNOX COUNTY DAILY NEWS (BICKNELL, IND. : 1991). 5665

1060-6629 See NYSE WEEKLY STOCK BUYS. 910

1060-6645 See ADVANCE NOTICE (PRINCETON, N.J.). 3187

1060-6653 See LEAD ABATEMENT NEWS. 5294

1060-6661 See CHILD LABOR MONITOR. 1659

1060-6688 See HARPOON (BUFFALO, N.Y.). 4862

1060-670X See JAZZ REVIEW AND COLLECTOR'S DISCOGRAPHY, THE. 4125

1060-6718 See HEAVY EQUIPMENT & FARM MACHINERY MAGAZINE. 159

1060-6726 See PARTY SOURCE. 2585

1060-6734 See IN PROCESS (NEW YORK, N.Y.). 322

1060-6750 See ACADEMIC ABSTRACTS FULL TEXT ELITE. 2496

1060-6769 See MAGAZINE ARTICLE SUMMARIES FULL TEXT ELITE. 2497

1060-6815 See LEUKEMIA & LYMPHOMA REVIEWS. 3820

1060-6823 See RECEPTORS AND CHANNELS. 990

1060-6831 See ROD & CUSTOM ANNUAL. 5424

1060-684X See DARK SHADOWS (WHEELING, W. VA.). 348

1060-6858 See SAN FRANCISCO PERFORMING ARTS LIBRARY AND MUSEUM SERIES. 388

1060-7153 See GTRI TECHNICAL JOURNAL. 1976

1060-7161 See WHIDBEY NEWS-TIMES. 5763

1060-7188 See NEWMEDIA (SAN MATEO, CALIF.). 1118

1060-7196 See ZAGAT UNITED STATES TRAVEL SURVEY. WESTERN STATES. 2810

1060-720X See ZAGAT UNITED STATES TRAVEL SURVEY. CENTRAL STATES. 2810

1060-7250 See ANNUAL MEETING OF THE SOCIETY FOR ORGANIC PETROLOGY. ABSTRACTS AND PROGRAM. 1458

1060-7595 See WONDER MAN. 4867

1060-7609 See MT TODAY. 3618

1060-7625 See SHEPARD'S EVIDENCE CITATIONS. 3049

1060-7633 See SHEPARD'S NORTH CAROLINA EXPRESS CITATIONS. 3053

1060-7684 See MUMPS COMPUTING. 1196

1060-7692 See LIFTOFF (GRAND RAPIDS, MICH.). 27

1060-7706 See PUBLIC HEALTH UPDATE (WASHINGTON, D.C.). 4797

1060-7714 See PUBLIC HEALTH MACROVIEW. 4797

1060-7722 See BARGAIN HUNTERS GUIDE. ATLANTA/ATHENS AREA. 824

1060-7730 See BEST PLACES TO STAY IN THE ROCKY MOUNTAIN STATES. 2804

1060-7749 See BEST PLACES TO STAY IN THE MIDWEST. 5463

1060-7757 See BEST PLACES TO STAY IN THE SOUTH. 5463

1060-7765 See COOKBOOK REVIEW, THE. 2789

1060-7781 See OHIO EMPLOYMENT PRACTICES LAW MONTHLY. 3153

1060-779X See WEEKLY PUZZLER, THE. 4867

1060-7803 See NEWS- INTERNET SOCIETY (PRINT ED.). 1243

1060-7838 See HOSPITAL'S MEDICARE POLICY & PAYMENT REPORT, THE. 3786

1060-7889 See NONPROFIT ALMANAC. 5299

1060-7900 See WORLD WIDE SHIPPING. 5458

1060-7951 See SAN MATEO COUNTY COMMERCE & INDUSTRY DIRECTORY. 1625

1060-7978 See INTERPRET YOUR DREAMS. 4592

1060-8001 See LITTLE MERMAID MAGAZINE, THE. 1066

1060-8036 See NORTHEAST & MIDWEST MINING DIRECTORY. 2147

1060-8044 See SOUTHEASTERN STATES MINING DIRECTORY. 2151

1060-8052 See ANCIENT WISDOM FOR MODERN LIVING. 4340

1060-8095 See CHEMICAL WEAPONS CONVENTION BULLETIN. 4039

1060-815X See INTERNATIONAL DRUG PREVENTION QUARTERLY OF THE NAE PROJECT, THE. 2910

1060-8168 See EMERSON'S AUDITOR CHANGE REPORT. 743

1060-8184 See SMALL BUSINESS EMPLOYEE ASSISTANCE. 711

1060-8222 See CLEVELAND PARENT. 2278

1060-8230 See BUSINESS LEADER (RALEIGH, N.C.). 650

1060-8249 See TRADES (NEW ORLEANS, LA.). 854

1060-8265 See JOURNAL OF MEN'S STUDIES, THE. 3995

1060-8273 See MISSILE MONITOR. 4051

1060-8281 See MINNESOTA TECHNOLOGY. 5129

1060-829X See ST. JOHN'S OBELISK, THE. 1095

1060-8303 See WOMEN IN HIGHER EDUCATION. 1854

1060-832X See SCHOLASTIC ART. 364

1060-8338 See MEDICAL DEVICE APPROVAL LETTER. 3608

1060-8362 See BASICS OF SWAPS. 892

1060-8400 See COMPLETE CAR BUYER'S GUIDE, THE. 5412

1060-8419 See SPORTBIKE (NEW YORK, N.Y.). 4921

1060-8427 See SMART DRUG NEWS. 3641

1060-8435 See NATIONAL BOOK OF LISTS, THE. 1619

1060-8494 See JOURNAL FOR QUALITY AND PARTICIPATION. PROFILES OF SERVICES AND PRODUCTS FOR EXCELLENCE, THE. 1613

1060-8508 See AMERICANS TALK ISSUES. 5239

1060-8516 See IBC/DONOGHUE'S MONEY FUND DIRECTORY. 900

1060-8524 See IBC/DONOGHUE'S MUTUAL FUNDS ALMANAC. 900

1060-8532 See CANA, INC. 3852

1060-8540 See CITY JOURNAL (NEW YORK, N.Y.), THE. 4468

1060-8583 See UPSIDEDOWN (WOBURN, MASS.). 5007

1060-8621 See COOPERATIVE CATALOGING NEWS. 3204

1060-8648 See ENVIRONMENTAL SAFETY ALERT. 2229

1060-8672 See HAWG (MT. MORRIS, N.Y.). 4898

1060-8702 See GLOBAL STOCK GUIDE. 789

1060-8710 See CIFAR'S GLOBAL COMPANY HANDBOOK. 657

1060-8729 See EMERSON'S PROFESSIONAL SERVICES REVIEW : PSR. 743

1060-8745 See CAPTAIN PLANET AND THE PLANETEERS. 4858

1060-8753 See RUSSIA (SYRACUSE, N.Y.). 1595

1060-8826 See LANDWATCH (REDLANDS, CALIF.). 4840

1060-8893 See ROLLING VENTURES. 708

1060-8931 See QRM (WASHINGTON, D.C.). 4148

1060-894X See IMAGINGWORLD (CAMDEN, ME.). 4212

1060-8958 See TEACHING OPPORTUNITIES (NORTH BRUNSWICK, N.J.). 1907

1060-8966 See TOTAL FOOD SERVICE : TFS. 2360

1060-9040 See COMPUTER CASES. 1176

1060-9083 See PASS CHRISTIAN REVIEW, THE. 2543

1060-9105 See EUROSCOPE INC. 4647

1060-913X See PROGRESS IN LIVER DISEASES (PHILADELPHIA, PA.). 3800

1060-9172 See FAMILY PLANNING MANAGER, THE. 5285

1060-9180 See BEVERAGE AISLE. 2364

1060-9202 See ARTS & HUMANITIES CITATION INDEX (COMPACT DISC ED.). 314

1060-9210 See NATIONAL TRIAL LAWYER (NEW YORK ED.). 3014

1060-9253 See HEALTHCARE HUMAN RESOURCES. 3914

1060-930X See WORK-FAMILY ROUNDTABLE. 2287

1060-9350 See HOSPITALITY RESEARCH JOURNAL. 2806

1060-9369 See EPILEPSY USA. 3832

1060-9385 See PREVENTION'S LOSE WEIGHT GUIDEBOOK. 2600

1060-9393 See RUSSIAN EDUCATION AND SOCIETY. 1781

1060-9431 See HEROLD'S OIL SHARE MARKET PERFORMANCE. 679

1060-9458 See SLS REPORT, THE. 3975

1060-9474 See SOVIET OBSERVER (NEW YORK, N.Y.). 2710

1060-9490 See GREAT BATTLES. 2617

1060-9547 See VIRTUAL REALITY WORLD. 1217

1060-9563 See RODALE'S SCUBA DIVING. 4915

1060-9571 See ZUZU'S PETALS QUARTERLY. 3456

1060-9601 See SPEECH MAKERS NEWSLETTER. 1122

1060-961X See THRIFT SHOPPING IN YOUR NEIGHBORHOOD. 1300

1060-9636 See PROFESSIONAL REPORT : A PUBLICATION OF THE SOCIETY OF INDUSTRIAL AND OFFICE REALTORS. 4843

1060-9725 See FUELOIL & OIL HEAT WITH AIR CONDITIONING. 4257

1060-9741 See WORLD AGRICULTURE (WASHINGTON, D.C. 1991). 147

1060-9865 See TAX-RELATED DOCUMENTS. 4754

1060-9873 See GREENWICH REGISTER: THE DIRECTORY OF PERSONNEL MANAGERS, HUMAN RESOURCE EXECUTIVES AND CORPORATE RECRUITERS, THE. 941

1060-9881 See NOVA JOURNAL OF ALGEBRA AND GEOMETRY. 3525

1060-989X See WALL STREET & TECHNOLOGY. 919

1060-9903 See LOUIS RUKEYSER'S WALL STREET. 905

1060-9911 See SOCCER JR. 1069

1060-992X See OPTICAL MEMORY & NEURAL NETWORKS. 1215

1060-9938 See NATURALIST (DANVILLE, VT.), THE. 2199

1060-9954 See NEW JERSEY ENVIRONMENTAL LAW LETTER. 3115

1060-9962 See LANDSCAPE ARCHITECT & SPECIFIER NEWS. 2422

1060-9970 See TRADING CARDS. 2778

1060-9989 See CELLS AND MATERIALS. SUPPLEMENT. 534

1060-9997 See STAR GUIDE. 2493

1061-0014 See STATUTES & DECISIONS. 3059

1061-0022 See ST. PETERSBURG MATHEMATICAL JOURNAL. 3536

1061-0030 See RS/MAGAZINE (BROOKLINE, MASS.). 1202

1061-0057 See AMERICAN DRAMA. 5361

1061-0081 See BUSINESS ETHICS REVIEW. 2249

1061-0146 See SUMMARY REPORTER. 3061

1061-0154 See SOCIOLOGICAL RESEARCH. 5261

1061-0219 See PREPAID HEALTHCARE ASSEMBLY DIRECTORY : ... REPORT BASED ON ... DATA / MEDICAL GROUP MANAGEMENT ASSOCIATION. 3791

1061-0227 See HOME CARING. 5288

1061-0235 See PENTON'S CONTROLS & SYSTEMS. 3486

1061-0251 See OCCUPATIONAL HYGIENE. 2866

1061-026X See JOURNAL OF MARINE ENVIRONMENTAL ENGINEERING. 2176

1061-0278 See SUPRAMOLECULAR CHEMISTRY. 993

1061-0294 See COLORADO PRIVATE ELEMENTARY AND SECONDARY SCHOOLS. 1732

1061-0308 See ANIMATION JOURNAL. 4063

1061-0316 See MEDIA AND FILM. 325

1061-0324 See INTERNATIONAL OBSERVER (WASHINGTON, D.C.). 2620

1061-0340 See SECRECY & GOVERNMENT BULLETIN. 4685

1061-0359 See PRIMARY CARE MEDICINE DRUG ALERTS. 4325

1061-0383 See CONTEMPORARY ONCOLOGY. 3815

1061-0405 See JOURNAL OF RUSSIAN AND EAST EUROPEAN PSYCHOLOGY. 4601

1061-0413 See JOURNAL OF RUSSIAN AND EAST EUROPEAN PSYCHIATRY. 3929

1061-0421 See JOURNAL OF PRODUCT & BRAND MANAGEMENT, THE. 761

ISSN Index

1061-043X *See* GUIDELINE FOR THE PREPARATION OF A HAZARD COMMUNICATION RIGHT-TO-KNOW PROGRAM / PREPARED BY HAZARDOUS COMMUNICATION AND RIGHT-TO-KNOW TASK FORCE, AMERICAN BOILER MANUFACTURERS ASSOCIATION. **2230**

1061-0480 *See* NOCTILUCA (NORWOOD, MASS.). **3467**

1061-0499 *See* RECOMMENDED VIDEOS FOR SCHOOLS. **1138**

1061-0529 *See* GERMAN ANCESTRY. **2451**

1061-0537 *See* COOKBOOK (STEUBEN, ME.). **2332**

1061-0553 *See* JOURNAL OF ART & ENTERTAINMENT LAW. **2987**

1061-0731 *See* DUN'S REGIONAL BUSINESS DIRECTORY. TENNESSEE METROS AREA. **670**

1061-0758 *See* DUN'S REGIONAL BUSINESS DIRECTORY. COLUMBUS AREA. **670**

1061-0790 *See* DUN'S REGIONAL BUSINESS DIRECTORY. OKLAHOMA/ARKANSAS AREA. **670**

1061-0804 *See* DUN'S REGIONAL BUSINESS DIRECTORY. NORTHERN NEW YORK STATE AREA. **670**

1061-0812 *See* DUN'S REGIONAL BUSINESS DIRECTORY. SAN ANTONIO AREA. **670**

1061-0839 *See* OPEN SYSTEMS TODAY. **1248**

1061-0855 *See* STANDARD & POOR'S RATINGS HANDBOOK. **915**

1061-0871 *See* UNIFICATION NEWS. **5006**

1061-0901 *See* HASTINGS WOMEN'S LAW JOURNAL. **2977**

1061-0952 *See* ON COURSE (SPRINGFIELD, MO.). **4983**

1061-0987 *See* MINNESOTA GUIDEBOOK TO STATE AGENCY SERVICES. **4665**

1061-0995 *See* FLORIDA SDB DIRECTORY : A DIRECTORY OF MINORITY-OWNED MANUFACTURERS. **676**

1061-1010 *See* PICKING THE "RIGHT" BIBLE STUDY PROGRAM. **5018**

1061-1029 *See* RICHLAND COUNTY NEWS-MONITOR. **5726**

1061-1037 *See* STRAT FAN. **4866**

1061-1088 *See* CRABB NEWSLETTER, THE. **2444**

1061-1118 *See* DESIGNNET (AUSTIN, TEX.). **1233**

1061-1126 *See* DUN'S REGIONAL BUSINESS DIRECTORY. CENTRAL INDIANA. **669**

1061-1134 *See* DUN'S REGIONAL BUSINESS DIRECTORY. CHARLOTTE/GREENSBORO AREA. **669**

1061-1177 *See* DUN'S REGIONAL BUSINESS DIRECTORY. MICHIGAN METROS (EXCLUDING DETROIT) AREA. **670**

1061-1185 *See* DUN'S REGIONAL BUSINESS DIRECTORY. NORTHERN CALIFORNIA. **670**

1061-1193 *See* DUN'S REGIONAL BUSINESS DIRECTORY. ORLANDO/JACKSONVILLE AREA. **670**

1061-1207 *See* DUN'S REGIONAL BUSINESS DIRECTORY. GEORGIA (EXCLUDING ATLANTA) AREA. **1605**

1061-124X *See* ROMANCE OF LIFE. **5565**

1061-1258 *See* WHO OWNS CORPORATE AMERICA. **919**

1061-1266 *See* MAJOR DONORS. **4338**

1061-1274 *See* CORPORATE AND FOUNDATION GRANTS. **660**

1061-1282 *See* SOCIAL SCIENCES CITATION INDEX WITH ABSTRACTS. **5221**

1061-1290 *See* SCIENCE CITATION INDEX WITH ABSTRACTS. **5176**

1061-1304 *See* UKRAINE (SYRACUSE, N.Y.). **1587**

1061-1355 *See* DUN'S REGIONAL BUSINESS DIRECTORY. ST. LOUIS AREA. **670**

1061-1371 *See* AD BUSINESS REPORT. **753**

1061-141X *See* FUELOIL & OIL HEAT WITH AIR CONDITIONING. **4257**

1061-1428 *See* RUSSIAN SOCIAL SCIENCE REVIEW. **5217**

1061-1444 *See* WBF IN ACTION. **1717**

1061-1452 *See* PROGRESS IN PAPER RECYCLING. **4237**

1061-1479 *See* ECRITIQUE (IOWA CITY, IOWA). **3383**

1061-1495 *See* BETTER TEACHING. **1727**

1061-1509 *See* POLICE COMPUTER REVIEW. **1289**

1061-155X *See* ENVIRONMENTAL CONTRACT OPPORTUNITY REPORT, THE. **2167**

1061-1568 *See* WOMEN'S SPORTS EXPERIENCE, THE. **4930**

1061-1576 *See* COMPENSATION & BENEFITS ALERT. **658**

1061-1606 *See* MULTIVAC UPDATE. **4413**

1061-1622 *See* WARFIELD'S BUSINESS RECORD. **719**

1061-1673 *See* DIRECTORY OF MEMBERS - APPRAISAL INSTITUTE (U.S.). **4836**

1061-1681 *See* THOMSON CREDIT UNION DIRECTORY. **814**

1061-1711 *See* INTERNATIONAL JOURNAL OF ANGIOLOGY, THE. **3706**

1061-172X *See* CORPORATE HEALTH PROMOTION TODAY. **4772**

1061-1754 *See* CALIFORNIA/NEVADA HORSEMAN'S DIRECTORY. **2797**

1061-1789 *See* GUERNSEY GAZETTE, THE. **5772**

1061-1797 *See* AUTOMATIC MERCHANDISER. **2328**

1061-1843 *See* POLICY STUDIES PAPERS. **1702**

1061-186X *See* JOURNAL OF DRUG TARGETING. **4311**

1061-1878 *See* JEFFERSONIANA (MARTINSVILLE, VA.). **4166**

1061-1886 *See* MORNINGSTAR JAPAN. **696**

1061-1894 *See* R&D INNOVATOR. **5144**

1061-1908 *See* PRATT CITY COMMUNITY NEWSPAPER. **5628**

1061-1924 *See* MIDDLE EAST POLICY. **4528**

1061-1932 *See* CHINESE EDUCATION AND SOCIETY. **1731**

1061-1940 *See* RUSSIAN POLITICS AND LAW. **3045**

1061-1959 *See* ANTHROPOLOGY & ARCHEOLOGY OF EURASIA. **229**

1061-1967 *See* RUSSIAN STUDIES IN PHILOSOPHY. **4360**

1061-1975 *See* RUSSIAN STUDIES IN LITERATURE. **3432**

1061-1983 *See* RUSSIAN STUDIES IN HISTORY. **2628**

1061-1991 *See* PROBLEMS OF ECONOMIC TRANSITION. **1513**

1061-2009 *See* RUSSIAN & EAST EUROPEAN FINANCE AND TRADE. **850**

1061-2017 *See* ISSUES & INQUIRY IN COLLEGE LEARNING AND TEACHING. **1831**

1061-2033 *See* HARRIS MANUFACTURERS DIRECTORY (SOUTHEAST ED.). **3480**

1061-2041 *See* HARRIS MANUFACTURERS DIRECTORY (NORTHEAST ED.). **3480**

1061-205X *See* HARRIS MANUFACTURERS DIRECTORY (WEST & SOUTHWEST ED.). **3480**

1061-2068 *See* HARRIS MANUFACTURERS DIRECTORY (SOUTHWEST ED.), THE. **3480**

1061-2076 *See* HARRIS MANUFACTURERS DIRECTORY (NATIONAL ED.). **3480**

1061-2084 *See* PRACTITIONERS 1120S DESKBOOK. **1513**

1061-2106 *See* GUIDE TO RETAIL SHOPS. **954**

1061-2114 *See* AMERICAN WHOLESALERS AND DISTRIBUTORS DIRECTORY. **1597**

1061-2130 *See* JOURNAL OF OPTIMAL NUTRITION, THE. **4193**

1061-2157 *See* NEW CHOICES FOR RETIREMENT LIVING. **5298**

1061-2165 *See* SANCTUARY (DENVER, COLO.). **5036**

1061-2181 *See* SOUTHERN CALIFORNIA BUSINESS DIRECTORY. **712**

1061-219X *See* AMERICAN MANUFACTURERS DIRECTORY. **3475**

1061-2203 *See* INSTRUMENT BUSINESS OUTLOOK. **1612**

1061-222X *See* RHODE ISLAND MEDICINE. **3637**

1061-2246 *See* MINORITY LITERARY EXPO (BIRMINGHAM, ALA.). **3347**

1061-2254 *See* TEE SHORTS. **3444**

1061-2270 *See* GENESIS REPORT/RX, THE. **4306**

1061-2289 *See* GENESIS REPORT/DX, THE. **3578**

1061-2300 *See* PACKAGING PRODUCTIVITY. **4221**

1061-2335 *See* DRUG GMP REPORT. **4300**

1061-2343 *See* TRANSITIONS ABROAD. **1788**

1061-2351 *See* BILL & TED'S EXCELLENT COMIC BOOK. **4857**

1061-2424 *See* SPORTING CLAYS. **4879**

1061-2505 *See* PIQUE (NEW YORK, N.Y.). **4375**

1061-253X *See* MADERA HERITAGE QUARTERLY. **2459**

1061-2564 *See* WE THE PEOPLE (WASHINGTON, D.C.: 1992). **3073**

1061-2572 *See* CALS JOURNAL. **1173**

1061-2602 See MICHIGAN INSURANCE HANDBOOK. **2888**

1061-2610 *See* MICHIGAN INSURANCE HANDBOOK. **2888**

1061-2629 *See* INSIDE BT. **1157**

1061-2637 *See* INSIDE GTE. **1113**

1061-2688 *See* SYS ADMIN (LAWRENCE, KAN.). **1249**

1061-2696 *See* MARYLAND REGISTER CONTRACT WEEKLY. **4664**

1061-2718 *See* BREAD MACHINE NEWSLETTER, THE. **2329**

1061-2734 *See* TIMELINE (PALO ALTO, CALIF.). **4498**

1061-284X *See* THOMAS FOOD INDUSTRY REGISTER. **2359**

1061-2890 *See* INVESTOR'S BUSINESS DAILY. **903**

1061-2920 *See* ACAPA SERIAL. **1632**

1061-2971 *See* RESTORATIVE ECOLOGY. **2220**

1061-3056 *See* 1992 DIRECTORY OF AGING RESOURCES. **5269**

1061-3072 *See* GPLLA NEWSLETTER. **3212**

1061-3099 *See* CYBEREDGE JOURNAL. **1181**

1061-3102 *See* RETIRED OFFICER MAGAZINE (ALEXANDRIA, VA.), THE. **4055**

1061-3145 *See* AIRPORT MANAGEMENT. **10**

1061-3153 *See* FEDERAL REGIONAL YELLOW BOOK. **1925**

1061-3161 *See* ZALE CORPORATION BANKRUPTCY NEWS. **817**

1061-317X *See* R.H. MACY & CO. BANKRUPTCY NEWS. **806**

1061-3188 See ADVANCE FOR HEALTH INFORMATION PROFESSIONALS. **4210**

1061-3196 *See* WATER SCOOTER BUSINESS. **596**

1061-320X *See* SESSER-VALIER TIMES. **5662**

1061-3218 *See* COUNTRY COURIER (HINCKLEY, ILL.). **5659**

1061-3234 *See* SIMPLY CROSS STITCH. **5186**

1061-3242 *See* ADCOM (BOSTON, MASS.). **754**

1061-3269 *See* ADVANCE FOR HEALTH INFORMATION PROFESSIONALS. **4210**

1061-3285 *See* JOB SEEKER'S GUIDE TO PRIVATE AND PUBLIC COMPANIES. **4205**

1061-3293 *See* INSIDE DBASE. **1279**

1061-3315 *See* ATLAS OF THE ORAL AND MAXILLOFACIAL SURGERY CLINICS OF NORTH AMERICA. **3960**

1061-3323 *See* DIVE TRAINING. **4893**

1061-3331 *See* UNIVERSITY OF SAN FRANCISCO MARITIME LAW JOURNAL. **3182**

1061-334X *See* DIRECTORY OF CONNECTICUT AND RHODE ISLAND HIGH TECHNOLOGY COMPANIES, THE. **1604**

1061-3358 *See* DIRECTORY OF MASTERCARD AND VISA CREDIT CARD SOURCES, THE. **788**

1061-3366 *See* FIELDING'S HAWAII. **5470**

1061-3374 *See* MECHANICAL/ELECTRICAL ... COSTBOOK / BNI, BUILDING NEWS. **621**

1061-3390 *See* INSIDER REPORTING AND LIABILITY UNDER SECTION 16 OF THE SECURITIES EXCHANGE ACT OF 1934. **2982**

1061-3420 See MICROBEAM ANALYSIS (NEW YORK, N.Y.). 4438

1061-3439 See ISSX PROCEEDINGS. 4309

1061-3447 See STANFORD LAW ALUM. 3058

1061-3455 See JOURNAL OF QUESTIONED DOCUMENT EXAMINATION. 3167

1061-3471 See BIOTECHNOLOGY WEEK. 3690

1061-348X See MIDLIFE WOMAN. 5561

1061-3498 See VIKING (INKSTER, MICH.), THE. 1096

1061-3501 See WINDOWS TECH JOURNAL. 1282

1061-351X See KAKO (NEW YORK, N.Y.), LES. 2536

1061-3528 See APPLIED MICROWAVE MAGAZINE. 4433

1061-3536 See IN RE, EAGLE-PICHER INDUSTRIES, INC., ET AL. 790

1061-3552 See CAL SCIENCES. 5092

1061-3560 See COUNTRYPLACE (BIRMINGHAM, ALA.). 2531

1061-3579 See SANDHILLS REVIEW, THE. 3433

1061-3587 See TRUDY'S TIME-PERIODS. 3448

1061-3595 See TRANSPORTING HAZARDOUS MATERIALS. 2245

1061-3609 See INFORMED LIBRARIAN, THE. 3217

1061-3625 See LITIGATION SERVICES RESOURCE DIRECTORY. 3003

1061-365X See CALIFORNIA ENVIRONMENTAL LAW REPORTER. 3110

1061-3676 See CREDIT UNION $50 MILLION YEARBOOK. 785

1061-3692 See IMPROVED RECOVERY WEEK. 1609

1061-3706 See JOURNAL OF CASE MANAGEMENT. 3787

1061-3714 See GLOBAL COMPANY NEWS DIGEST. 678

1061-3722 See GARDEN LITERATURE. 2434

1061-3730 See AFRIKA MIX. 1125

1061-3749 See JOURNAL OF NURSING MEASUREMENT. 3859

1061-3757 See PURCHASING PERFORMANCE BENCHMARKS FOR THE PAPER INDUSTRY. 4238

1061-3765 See HOME STUDIO FORUM. 4370

1061-3773 See COMPUTER APPLICATIONS IN ENGINEERING EDUCATION. 1969

1061-3781 See BULLETIN OF AMERICAN ODONATOLOGY. 5579

1061-379X See WASHINGTON, D.C. INTERNSHIP DIRECTORY. 1790

1061-3811 See METAGAME (SOMERVILLE, MASS.). 3411

1061-3838 See POINT LINE POLY. PC. 1199

1061-3846 See MARKETING MANAGEMENT (CHICAGO, ILL.). 931

1061-3862 See INTERNATIONAL JOURNAL OF SELF-PROPAGATING HIGH-TEMPERATURE SYSTEM. 1980

1061-3870 See VANDERWICKEN'S FINANCIAL DIGEST. 815

1061-3900 See CALIFORNIA REPUBLIC. 2529

1061-3919 See SHANGRI-LA (WASHINGTON, D.C.). 3471

1061-3927 See MIRACLES MAGAZINE. 4977

1061-3935 See ENVIRONMENTAL ISSUES REPORT. 2168

1061-396X See BETTER WORLD. 4577

1061-3978 See ADVOCATE (BATON ROUGE, LA.), THE. 5683

1061-3986 See CUTTING HORSE. 2798

1061-3994 See NEIL SPERRY'S GARDENS. 2425

1061-401X See TAX FACTS. INSURANCE AND EMPLOYEE BENEFITS ED. 2894

1061-4028 See TAX FACTS. INVESTMENTS ED. 917

1061-4036 See NATURE GENETICS. 550

1061-4052 See 'LECTRIC AUTO NEWS. 5418

1061-4060 See OLSON'S BOOK OF LIBRARY CLIP ART. 361

1061-4079 See HOUSEPLANT MAGAZINE. 2420

1061-4087 See JOURNAL - AMERICAN PSYCHOLOGICAL ASSOCIATION. DIVISION OF CONSULTING PSYCHOLOGY. 4592

1061-4109 See HAWAII'S VOICES. 5558

1061-4117 See COPING NEWSLETTER. 5553

1061-4125 See PERSONAL HEALTH REPORTER. 4795

1061-4133 See COMMUNICATOR (NASHVILLE, TENN., 1992), THE. 4949

1061-4176 See TURNAROUNDS & WORKOUTS. EUROPE. 815

1061-4184 See TURNAROUNDS & WORKOUTS. SURVEY. 4848

1061-4192 See MEDICAL RECORD RISKS, CLAIMS & LITIGATION. 3008

1061-4214 See FILM ANNUAL. 4069

1061-4222 See HOME BASED HOMERUN. 680

1061-4230 See AMERICA'S CENSORED NEWSLETTER. 2917

1061-4249 See BOARD LEADERSHIP. 861

1061-4257 See CASE STUDIES IN GREAT LAKES ARCHAEOLOGY. 265

1061-4265 See ORIGINAL GREAT SMOKY MOUNTAIN SAMPLER, THE. 5487

1061-4273 See CORPORATE FUNDERS OPERATING IN MISSOURI. 661

1061-4311 See INTELLIMOTION (RICHMOND, CALIF.). 5384

1061-4338 See ASORN NEWS. 3851

1061-4346 See TEACHING AND LEARNING LITERATURE WITH CHILDREN AND YOUNG ADULTS. 1906

1061-4354 See ABA JOURNAL OF AFFORDABLE HOUSING & COMMUNITY DEVELOPMENT LAW. 2812

1061-4370 See MDA REPORTS. 3606

1061-4397 See MENOPAUSE NEWS. 3765

1061-4400 See GUITAR CLASSICS, THE. 4120

1061-4427 See SOUTH DAKOTA HALL OF FAME. 2546

1061-4435 See ENNAANIN ETTO. 2615

1061-4486 See NEBRASKA EPISCOPALIAN, THE. 5065

1061-4494 See INSIDE FLYER. 5384

1061-4508 See FAIRFIELD LEDGER (1966). 5670

1061-4516 See BEACON (SPIRIT LAKE, IOWA). 5668

1061-4524 See STN (NEW YORK, N.Y.). 4924

1061-4567 See HEARTHSIDE READER, THE. 3393

1061-4575 See BREAST DISEASES UPDATES. 3558

1061-4583 See WITZ (PENNGROVE, CALIF.). 3453

1061-4605 See DELAWARE BUSINESS REVIEW. 665

1061-4613 See EXTENSION NEWS & ADVISOR. 83

1061-4656 See OFFICE TECHNOLOGY MANAGEMENT (GARDEN CITY, N.Y.). 880

1061-4664 See EASTWEST NATURAL HEALTH. 2596

1061-4699 See YANKEE TRAVELER (DUBLIN, N.H.), THE. 5500

1061-4710 See COMMUNICATIONS OF THE WORKSHOP FOR SCIENTIFIC LINGUISTICS. 3274

1061-4729 See COOKING CONTEST NEWSLETTER, THE. 2332

1061-4737 See MODEL CALL / RICHARD POIRIER MODEL & TALENT AGENCY. 1086

1061-4745 See EXEMPLARY PRACTICES IN EDUCATION : EPIE. 1746

1061-4753 See NURSING HOMES (1991). 3790

1061-4761 See PRIVATE FLEET DIRECTORY, THE. 5390

1061-477X See TTS NATIONAL MOTOR CARRIER DIRECTORY. 5398

1061-4796 See ONE TO ONE (UPPER DARBY, PA.). 5018

1061-480X See INSIDE INDIANA. 4851

1061-4818 See FIREFIGHTER'S NEWS. 2290

1061-4834 See FIELDING'S SCANDINAVIA. 5470

1061-4842 See FIELDING'S AUSTRALIA. 5469

1061-4850 See COMPLETE GUIDE TO SPECIAL INTEREST VIDEOS, THE. 4368

1061-494X See HERMES (LANSING, MICH.). 839

1061-4958 See KEE PRODUCTIONS PRESENTS THE INTERCESSORY BIBLE JOURNAL. 5017

1061-4966 See YOUNG INDIANA JONES CHRONICLES, THE. 3456

1061-4982 See INDIANA INTERNATIONAL & COMPARATIVE LAW REVIEW. 3129

1061-5008 See EDUCATION TECHNOLOGY NEWS. 1223

1061-5024 See GAS DAILY NATURAL GAS MARKETING. INDUSTRY DIRECTORY. 4257

1061-5032 See JOR QUARTERLY. 4125

1061-5067 See EARTH SATELLITE CATALOG. 18

1061-5105 See POST AND COURIER, THE. 5743

1061-5202 See ADL ON THE FRONTLINE. 2254

1061-5210 See RELIGION AND THE SOCIAL ORDER. 4991

1061-5261 See PRAEGER SERIES IN TRANSFORMATIONAL POLITICS AND POLITICAL SCIENCE. 4492

1061-527X See CLERGY FOCUS. 4948

1061-5288 See CORPORATE LIBRARY UPDATE. 3204

1061-5296 See MISNOMER (PRESTONBURG, KY.). 3466

1061-530X See INTERNATIONAL JOURNAL OF PHILOSOPHY, PSYCHOLOGY, AND SPIRITUALITY. 4349

1061-5318 See HEMATOPOIETIC THERAPY. 3797

1061-5326 See GANG JOURNAL, THE. 3165

1061-5334 See IFCI FIRE CODE JOURNAL. 2291

1061-5342 See CA SELECTS: BISMUTH CHEMISTRY. 998

1061-5350 See SPACE STATION FREEDOM NEWS. 36

1061-5369 See NEURAL, PARALLEL AND SCIENTIFIC COMPUTATIONS. 1197

1061-5377 See CARDIOLOGY IN REVIEW. 3701

1061-5385 See CELL ADHESION AND COMMUNITATION. 532

1061-5393 See BIRNBAUM'S TORONTO. 5464

1061-5407 See BIRNBAUM'S VANCOUVER. 5464

1061-5415 See BIRNBAUM'S MONTREAL. 5464

1061-5423 See BIRNBAUM'S LAS VEGAS. 5464

1061-5431 See BIRNBAUM'S NEW ORLEANS. 5464

1061-544X See BIRNBAUM'S WASHINGTON DC. 5464

1061-5458 See MAXWELL COMPACT LIBRARIES. AIDS. 3674

1061-5466 See BIRDS OF NORTH AMERICA, THE. 5616

1061-5474 See DOWN MEMORY LANE (LAKELAND, FLA.). 2532

1061-5512 See SPORTS CARD PRICE GUIDE MONTHLY. 4922

1061-5539 See FARM FORESTRY NEWS. 2379

1061-5547 See ABUI NETWORK NEWS. 636

1061-5555 See BANK TECHNOLOGY REPORT. 5087

1061-5563 See CRANBURY PRESS, THE. 5709

1061-561X See TEXAS ALCALDE. 1103

1061-5636 See QIRAAT SIYASIYAH. 4492

1061-5652 See CABLE TV FINANCE (1992). 1129

1061-5679 See RUSSIAN FAR EAST UPDATE. 1519

1061-5733 See MAPLE TECHNICAL NEWSLETTER, THE. 1280

1061-5741 See TELEVISION & CABLE UPDATE. 1140

1061-575X See PROGRESS IN VETERINARY NEUROLOGY. 5519

1061-5768 See PROGRESS IN VETERINARY & COMPARATIVE OPHTHALMOLOGY. 5519

1061-5776 See UNDERCURRENTS: MYSTIC MARINELIFE AQUARIUM QUARTERLY. 5599

1061-5792 See INTIMATE FASHION NEWS. 1085

1061-5806 See ANXIETY, STRESS AND COPING. 4574

1061-5865 See INSIDE PC TOOLS. 1287

1061-5873 See INSIDE WORKS FOR WINDOWS. 1287

1061-5881 See NATIONAL CHRONICLE (WASHINGTON, D.C.), THE. 5647

1061-5938 See EPIGRAPHIC SOCIETY OCCASIONAL PAPERS, THE. 267

1061-5997 See CEO'S REPORT ON COST CUTTING. 939

1061-6004 See GASTROINTESTINAL DISEASES TODAY. 3745

1061-6012 See PLATTSBURGH STUDIES IN THE HUMANITIES. 2852

1061-6020 See CLS MARKET PLACE. 657

1061-6039 See DEVELOPING YOUR CREATIVE WRITING STYLE AND LEARNING THE CRAFT OF WRITING. 3381

1061-6047 See PERSPECTIVES GLOBALES DES LA HEPATITIS. 3715

1061-6055 See BERKELEY MODELS OF GRAMMAR. 3268

1061-6071 See MONOGRAPHS IN P/M SERIES. 4013

1061-608X See CLINICAL TRIALS. 3740

1061-6098 See EMERGING PHARMACEUTICALS. 4303

1061-6101 See PAKISTAN (BOULDER, COLO.). 2507

1061-611X See GAMER'S CONNECTION, THE. 4861

1061-6128 See JOURNAL OF HEMATOTHERAPHY. 3798

1061-6136 See STEPHEN CRANE STUDIES. 3440

1061-6152 See REFRIGERATED & FROZEN FOODS. 2355

1061-6160 See SPECTRUM (WHEATON, ILL.). 4999

1061-6179 See BLACK HILLS PIONEER (1989), THE. 5743

1061-6225 See NATIONAL BAPTIST WOMEN CLERGY DIRECTORY, THE. 5065

1061-6292 See JOURNAL OF THE OUGHTRED SOCIETY, THE. 3515

1061-6306 See AGING & NEUROSCIENCE. 577

1061-6314 See TRENDS, BIOTECHNOLOGY : INFORMATION AND ISSUES FOR PHARMACISTS. 4331

1061-6322 See PARTNERS IN PHARMACEUTICAL CARE. 4319

1061-6330 See SEED & CROPS INDUSTRY. 186

1061-6349 See COUNTRYSIDE (NEW YORK, N.Y. 1990). 2486

1061-6357 See COLLEGE HOCKEY. 4890

1061-6365 See TEXTURE (NORMAN, OKLA.). 3445

1061-6403 See COMPUTER INFO. 1176

1061-6411 See REVIEW - INSTITUTE OF NUCLEAR POWER OPERATIONS (U.S.). 4451

1061-6446 See HEALTH AND MEDICINE. 4777

1061-6489 See HANDBOOK ON LOUISIANA FAMILY LAW. 3121

1061-6519 See CROSSWORDS (WALNUT CREEK, CALIF.). 4081

1061-6535 See MINNESOTA WRITING PROJECT. 3412

1061-6543 See EUROPEAN BUSINESS LETTER. 833

1061-656X See RCDA (NEW YORK, N.Y.). 4989

1061-6578 See HASTINGS COMMUNICATIONS AND ENTERTAINMENT LAW JOURNAL (COMM/ENT). 2977

1061-6586 See MIDWEST PUREBRED DOGPOST!, THE. 226

1061-6616 See NEXTWORLD (SAN FRANCISCO, CALIF.). 1197

1061-6624 See ELECTRONIC NEWS (1991). 2047

1061-6632 See RESIDENTS' PRESCRIBING REFERENCE. 3634

1061-6659 See HERALD OF CHRISTIAN SCIENCE (AUDIO CASSETTE ED.), THE. 4962

1061-6667 See HOME MAGAZINE'S BUILDING/REMODELING PLANNER. 616

1061-6675 See BRAINSTORMER (BELLINGHAM, MASS.). 861

1061-6683 See TRANSCENDING LIMITS. 4243

1061-6691 See CD-DIS (ARLINGTON, VA.). 2908

1061-6705 See RADIO REGULARS. 1137

1061-6721 See EZHEKVARTALNIK KHRISTIANSKOI NAUKI. BIBLEISKIE UROKI. 5016

1061-673X See CTVRTLETNIK KRESTANSKE VEDY. BIBLICKE LEKCE. 5016

1061-6756 See SAMPLER & ANTIQUE NEEDLEWORK QUARTERLY. 375

1061-6764 See MAJOR CHANGES IN STATE MEDICAID PROGRAMS. 5295

1061-6772 See MARINE BLUE BOOK (OVERLAND PARK, KAN.). 594

1061-6780 See PUBLISHING TRENDS & TRENDSETTERS. 4819

1061-6845 See DEFENSE INTELLIGENCE JOURNAL. 4041

1061-6861 See RAPPORT (LOS ANGELES, CALIF.). 388

1061-687X See SPORTSTURF (1992). 2431

1061-6888 See JUST-IN-TIME & QUICK RESPONSE NEWS. 843

1061-690X See EILRICH FAMILY SNAPSHOTS. 2446

1061-6918 See GUN TRADER. 4897

1061-6934 See SPORT MARKETING QUARTERLY. 4920

1061-6969 See CLINICAL IMMUNOLOGY DIGEST. 3668

1061-6977 See X, THE FUTURE OF SEX. 5188

1061-6985 See OLD OTOHATCHER DISTRICT REPORTER. 2465

1061-6993 See NEBRASKA ENGLISH JOURNAL. 1093

1061-7019 See MISSISSIPPI SAXOPHONE. 4131

1061-7035 See ASHI TECHNICAL JOURNAL OF HOME INSPECTION AND IN-SERVICE BUILDING COMPONENT FAILURES. 2815

1061-7043 See STANDARD & POOR'S QIB. 915

1061-7051 See AMERICA'S BEST MONEY MANAGERS. 890

1061-706X See HAZARDOUS MATERIALS CONTROL BUYER'S GUIDE AND SOURCE BOOK (SILVER SPRING, MD. 1991). 2231

1061-7108 See GENERAL PRACTICE SECTION DIRECTORY AND OPERATING MANUAL. 2973

1061-7116 See DAILY AMERICAN REPUBLIC. 5703

1061-7132 See INSIDER'S GUIDE TO GRADUATE PROGRAMS IN CLINICAL PSYCHOLOGY. 4590

1061-7140 See MILES TO GO. 4905

1061-7159 See MARKETER'S GUIDE TO MEDIA. 1116

1061-7175 See NON-SPORT MARKETPLACE. 2775

1061-7183 See INTERACTION (COARSEGOLD, CALIF.). 4862

1061-7191 See RECOVERY TODAY. 5304

1061-7205 See RADIO CONTROL MODEL CARS AND TRUCKS. 2777

1061-7213 See RADIO CONTROL MODEL CARS (1992). 2777

1061-723X See SOUTHERN AFRICA (DENVER, COLO.). 2643

1061-7264 See FORTRAN FORUM. 1279

1061-7272 See LAWYER'S REGISTER INTERNATIONAL BY SPECIALTIES AND FIELDS OF LAW INCLUDING A DIRECTORY OF CORPORATE COUNSEL. 3101

1061-7310 See VIETNAM INSIGHT. 4514

1061-7329 See WEISS RESEARCH'S INSURANCE SAFETY DIRECTORY. 2896

1061-7337 See INTERNAMERICA (NEEDHAM, MASS.). 1680

1061-7345 See GULF WAR CLAIMS REPORTER. 3128

1061-7353 See BEST PLACES TO STAY IN THE MID-ATLANTIC STATES. 2804

1061-7361 See JOURNAL OF SOCIAL AND EVOLUTIONARY SYSTEMS. 5250

1061-737X See CLUTCH (FRANKFORT, KY.). 3340

1061-7388 See CHILTON'S GUIDE TO FUEL INJECTION AND ELECTRONIC ENGINE CONTROLS. CHRYSLER CARS AND TRUCKS. 5411

1061-7396 See CHILTON'S GUIDE TO FUEL INJECTION AND ELECTRONIC ENGINE CONTROLS. FORD CARS AND TRUCKS. 5411

1061-740X See CHILTON'S GUIDE TO FUEL INJECTION AND ELECTRONIC ENGINE CONTROLS. BUICK, OLDS, PONTIAC CARS AND TRUCKS. 5410

1061-7418 See CHILTON'S GUIDE TO FUEL INJECTION AND ELECTRONIC ENGINE CONTROLS. CHEVROLET CARS AND TRUCKS. 5411

1061-7434 See CITATIONS FOR SERIAL LITERATURE. 3202

1061-7469 See GEOGRAPHIC REFERENCE REPORT. 1492

1061-7485 See PROCEEDINGS OF FLICC FORUMS ON FEDERAL INFORMATION POLICIES. 4675

1061-7507 See LLEWELLYN'S DAILY PLANETARY GUIDE & ASTROLOGER'S DATEBOOK. 390

1061-7566 See RUSSIAN JOURNAL OF COMPUTATIONAL MECHANICS. 2128

1061-7574 See GEOCRYOLOGY (MOSCOW, R.S.F.S.R.). 1355

1061-7582 See PHYSICS OF HIGH ENERGY DENSITY. 4416

1061-7590 See MATHEMATICAL MODELING AND COMPUTATIONAL EXPERIMENT. 3519

1061-7604 See NEW YORKER STAATS-ZEITUNG (1991). 5719

1061-7620 See HOSPITAL MANAGED CARE & DIRECT CONTRACTING. 3784

1061-7639 See PUBLIC MANAGER (POTOMAC, MD.), THE. 4676

1061-7647 See INSIDE NETWARE. 1287

1061-7655 See JOURNAL - ASSOCIATION FOR HEALTHCARE PHILANTHROPY (U.S.). 3786

1061-7663 See A/E/C SYSTEMS COMPUTER SOLUTIONS. 1246

1061-768X See ABOUT WOMEN ON CAMPUS. 1720

1061-7701 See PALATE AND SPIRIT. 2352

1061-7728 See EMPLOYEE ASSISTANCE PROFESSIONAL REPORT. 1665

1061-7736 See SUPERVISORS REPORT. 2871

1061-7787 See ENVIRONMENTAL TOXICOLOGY NEWSLETTER. / COOPERATIVE EXTENSION, UNIVERSITY OF CALIFORNIA. 2170

1061-7825 See PROTECTION REPORT R8. 2391

1061-7884 See NATIVE MONTHLY READER. 2747

1061-7906 See SHEPARD'S NEW YORK STATUTE EXPRESS CITATIONS. 3053

1061-7914 See SHEPARD'S NEW YORK SUPPLEMENT EXPRESS CITATIONS. 3053

1061-7930 See SURVEY NOTES / UTAH GEOLOGICAL SURVEY. 1399

1061-7957 See INDIANA ENVIRONMENTAL STATUTES. 3113

1061-7981 See DIVERSITY & DIVISION. 5244

1061-799X See OAG CRUISE AND SHIPLINE GUIDE. 5453

1061-8090 See NORTHEAST JOURNAL OF TRANSPORTATION, THE. 5388

1061-8112 See PASSING SHOW (NEW YORK, N.Y.). 5367

1061-8198 See AMERICANS TALK ISSUES. 5239

1061-8228 See JOURNAL / ECONOMIC POLICY INSTITUTE. 1498

1061-8244 See ION NEWSLETTER / THE INSTITUTE OF NAVIGATION, THE. 4177

1061-8252 See GRO NEWSLETTER / NASA GODDARD SPACE FLIGHT CENTER. 395

1061-8295 See ALABAMA AUTOMOTIVE REPORT. 5403

1061-8309 See RUSSIAN JOURNAL OF NONDESTRUCTIVE TESTING. 2128

1061-8317 See TV STATION LOG. 1142

1061-8325 See FM RADIO LOG. 1111

1061-8333 See VARIEGATED GOSPEL. 5007

1061-8341 See MORNING (NEW YORK, N.Y.). 325

1061-835X See RANDOM & COMPUTATIONAL DYNAMICS. 2127

1061-8368 See OHIO SPORTS ALMANAC. 4910

1061-8376 See MUSIC MADNESS MAGAZINE. 4134

1061-8384 See VIRUS NEWS AND REVIEWS. 1206

1061-8457 See KURDISH LIFE. 2769

1061-8465 See SALESFYI (CHICAGO, ILL.). 885

1061-8473 See KOSHER BUSINESS. 1615

1061-8481 See DIRT (NEW YORK, N.Y.). 3995

1061-8538 See JOURNEYMEN (CANDIA, N.H.). 3995

1061-8562 See INTERNATIONAL JOURNAL OF COMPUTATIONAL FLUID DYNAMICS. 2116

1061-8570 See AMERICAN CAUCUS. 4463

1061-8597 See MOSCOW PULLMAN DAILY NEWS. 5657

1061-8600 See JOURNAL OF COMPUTATIONAL AND GRAPHICAL STATISTICS. 5329

1061-8619 See PACIFIC ASIAN BUSINESS REVIEW. 702

1061-8627 See HOW TO DEFEND AND UPHOLD YOUR RIGHTS VS. THE POLICE. 3165

1061-8635 See BUSINESS AND LEGAL START-UP DIRECTORY FOR ENTREPRENEURS, THE. 645

1061-8643 See WORKPLACE ISSUES & ANSWERS. 2253

1061-8651 See NEW YORK UNIVERSITY ENVIRONMENTAL LAW JOURNAL. 3115

1061-866X See CONTAMINATION ALERT. 4772

1061-8678 See TIDEWATER VIRGINIA FAMILIES. 2475

1061-8686 See SPACE SHUTTLE DATABASE REPORT. 36

1061-8694 See JOURNAL OF CREATIVE VISUAL LEARNING, THE. 1756

1061-8732 See LIGHTHOUSE (CAMBRIDGE, MASS.). 5560

1061-8759 See DATA USERS GUIDE - GEOLOGICAL SURVEY (U.S.). 1373

1061-8767 See COLLEGIATE JOURNAL, THE. 4771

1061-8775 See CORPORATE CONDUCT QUARTERLY. 2957

1061-8783 See CBP'S GUIDE TO BLACK CHARLOTTE. 2258

1061-8864 See CHICAGO ARTS & COMMUNICATION. 317

1061-8872 See AMERICAN INVESTOR (RESEARCH TRIANGLE PARK, N.C.). 890

1061-8880 See AFRICAN STOCK MARKETS. 890

1061-8899 See CHICANO-LATINO LAW REVIEW. 2950

1061-8902 See ADVANCES IN STRAIN IN ORGANIC CHEMISTRY. 1039

1061-8910 See ADVANCES IN QUANTITATIVE ANALYSIS OF FINANCE AND ACCOUNTING. 738

1061-8929 See ADVANCES IN THE IMPLEMENTATION AND IMPACT OF COMPUTER SYSTEMS. 1246

1061-8937 See ADVANCES IN ELECTRON TRANSFER CHEMISTRY. 1038

1061-8945 See ADVANCES IN BIOSENSORS. 440

1061-8953 See ROOFING MATERIALS GUIDE. 627

1061-8961 See ARCHAEOLOGICAL FIELDWORK OPPORTUNITIES BULLETIN. 256

1061-9011 See FLOWERING PLANT INDEX. 2415

1061-9038 See MEMBERSHIP DIRECTORY - AMERICAN ASTRONOMICAL SOCIETY (1984). 397

1061-9046 See OP-ED (BELLINGHAM, WASH.). 2542

1061-9054 See N.A.D.A. OFFICIAL USED CAR GUIDE (RETAIL CONSUMER ED.). 5421

1061-9070 See PLAYBOY'S CAREER GIRLS. 3996

1061-9089 See PLAYBOY'S GIRLS OF THE WORLD. 3996

1061-9119 See ... CUSTOMER SERVICE MANAGER'S GUIDE, THE. 865

1061-9127 See NUCLEAR PHYSICS NEWS. 4449

1061-9135 See AAZPA ANNUAL REPORT ON CONSERVATION AND SCIENCE. 2185

1061-9143 See U.S. CHEMICAL INDUSTRY STATISTICAL HANDBOOK. 1030

1061-916X See INDIANA ENVIRONMENTAL RULES. 3113

1061-9178 See OFFICIAL MAJOR LEAGUE BASEBALL ROOKIE LEAGUE MAGAZINE FOR KIDS. 4909

1061-9186 See CURRENT POLITICS AND ECONOMICS OF RUSSIA. 4470

1061-9194 See PROFIT (ARMONK, N.Y.). 705

1061-9208 See RUSSIAN JOURNAL OF MATHEMATICAL PHYSICS. 4420

1061-9224 See SHIPYARD CHRONICLE. 4183

1061-9232 See ILF CALENDAR NEWSLETTER. 3395

1061-9240 See WORLD SCANNER REPORT : A JOURNAL OF VHF-UHF SCANNER TECHNOLOGY & ENGINEERING, THE. 2001

1061-9259 See CASE MANAGER. 2877

1061-9267 See MEDIA MONITOR (DANVILLE, CALIF.). 1116

1061-9291 See ON TAP (MORGANTOWN, W.VA.). 5300

1061-9305 See INTERNATIONAL WINE MARKET: IMPACT DATABANK REPORT, THE. 2368

1061-9321 See JOURNAL OF INFORMATION ETHICS. 2251

1061-933X See COLLOID JOURNAL OF THE RUSSIAN ACADEMY OF SCIENCES. 5095

1061-9348 See JOURNAL OF ANALYTICAL CHEMISTRY (NEW YORK, N.Y.). 1016

1061-9364 See JOURNAL OF ONCOLOGY MANAGEMENT, THE. 3819

1061-9380 See STUDIES IN MUSLIM-JEWISH RELATIONS. 5000

1061-9399 See AMERICAN MODELER (RALEIGH, N.C.). 2771

1061-9410 See LAW FIRM BENEFITS. 2995

1061-9429 See FROMMER'S JAMAICA, BARBARDOS. 5477

1061-9461 See CHARITABLE GIVING TECHNIQUES. 4717

1061-9518 See JOURNAL OF INTERNATIONAL ACCOUNTING AUDITING & TAXATION. 747

1061-9526 See ELECTRO- AND MAGNETOBIOLOGY. 454

1061-9534 See CHINESE ENVIRONMENT & DEVELOPMENT. 2558

1061-9542 See HERALD-LEADER (SILOAM SPRINGS, ARK.). 5631

1061-9550 See EDMS COMPARISON REPORT. 1971

1061-9585 See ALABAMA INDUSTRIAL DIRECTORY. 2133

1061-9607 See MHFA UPDATE. 2828

1061-9615 See NETWORK CONNECTION. 4980

1061-964X See CAMPAIGN (WASHINGTON, D.C. 1991). 4467

1061-9658 See CALIFORNIA FRUIT GROWER ANNUAL. 2330

1061-9674 See FROM THE STATE CAPITALS. EMPLOYEE POLICY FOR THE PRIVATE & PUBLIC SECTORS. 4703

1061-9682 See FROM THE STATE CAPITALS. ENVIRONMENTAL REGULATION. 2230

1061-9690 See FROM THE STATE CAPITALS. THE OUTLOOK FROM THE STATE CAPITALS. 2972

1061-9704 See FROM THE STATE CAPITALS. PUBLIC SAFETY & JUSTICE POLICIES. 3165

1061-9712 See FROM THE STATE CAPITALS. ECONOMIC DEVELOPMENT. 1492

1061-9739 See CN LINES. 5430

1061-9755 See ENVIRONMENTAL INDEX, THE. 2168

1061-9763 See OLDTIMERS (AUGUSTA, GA.). 4143

1061-9771 See NUTHING SACRED. 3419

1061-978X See PASTOR'S TAX & MONEY. 4985

1061-9801 See ILLINOIS AUDUBON. 4166

1061-981X See METROPOLITAN RICHMOND APARTMENTS FOR RENT. 2828

1061-9836 See SOUTH ASIAN HANDBOOK (NEW YORK, N.Y.). 5491

1061-9844 See THAILAND, INDOCHINA & BURMA HANDBOOK. 5492

1061-9852 See INDONESIA, MALAYSIA & SINGAPORE HANDBOOK. 5480

1061-9887 See TEXTURE MINIATURE. 3472

1061-9909 See AMERICAS WATCH. 4503

1061-9917 See WORLD BUSINESS ACADEMY PERSPECTIVES. 723

1061-9925 See AT WORK (SAN FRANCISCO, CALIF.). 4201

1061-9933 See SMALL TOWN OBSERVER, THE. 2835

1061-9976 See KENNEL HEALTHLINE. 5515

1061-9992 See SUTTON SEARCHERS. 2474

1062-0028 See BUSINESS ONE IRWIN INVESTOR'S HANDBOOK, THE. 893

1062-0036 See AT RANDOM. 4812

1062-0044 See ADVANCES IN CARBOHYDRATE ANALYSIS. 959

1062-0060 See CHILTON'S COMMERCIAL CARRIER JOURNAL FOR PROFESSIONAL FLEET MANAGERS. 5379

1062-0079 See CHANGE NOTICE, THE. 607

1062-0087 See LIVE LETTERS. 3408

1062-0095 See STRAIGHT TALK (PLEASANTVILLE, N.Y.). 1069

1062-0109 See SIERRA LEONE REVIEW, THE. 2643

1062-0125 See JOURNAL OF ENGINEERING PHYSICS AND THERMOPHYSICS. 4408

1062-0133 See DIRECTORY OF STATE BAR PUBLIC SERVICE ACTIVITIES AND PROGRAMS. 4644

1062-0141 See MANHATTAN USER'S GUIDE. 2568

1062-015X See GASLIGHT (CLEVELAND, MINN.). 3389

1062-0168 See WRITING AND EDITING FOR SCIENCE AND TECHNOLOGY. 5171

1062-0176 See ADA WATCH. 4383

1062-0192 See FOOD PAPER (LOS ANGELES, CALIF.), THE. 2338

1062-0249 See ACADEMIC NURSE, THE. 4201

1062-0265 See JOURNAL OF THE GREATER HOUSTON DENTAL SOCIETY, THE. 1328

1062-0273 See JOURNAL FOR HEALTHCARE QUALITY. 3858

1062-0281 See ASEPSIS (ARLINGTON, TEX.). 3553

1062-029X See HARVARD DENTAL BULLETIN. 1324

1062-0303 See JOURNAL OF VASCULAR NURSING. 3860

1062-0311 See NORTHWESTERN DENTAL RESEARCH. 1331

1062-032X See HEALTHCARE BOTTOM LINE. 3782

1062-0346 See DENTAL IMPLANTOLOGY UPDATE. 1321

1062-0370 See USB MOLECULAR BIOLOGY REAGENTS/PROTOCOLS. 475

1062-0427 See WHODUZZIT? (NEW YORK, N.Y.). 4378

1062-0443 See NEW PARADIGM DIGEST. 5252

1062-0451 See MONASH SOFTWARE LETTER. 1288

1062-046X See STUDIES IN DEFENCE ECONOMICS. 1523

1062-0478 See SPARROW. 3471

1062-0486 See BANDELE'S ANNUAL VENDOR'S GUIDE TO AFRICAN-AMERICAN EVENTS. 2256

1062-0508 See ERIC IDENTIFIER AUTHORITY LIST. 1795

1062-0591 See STUDIES IN FRENCH THEATRE. 5369

1062-0605 See U.S.A. OIL INDUSTRY'S ENVIRONMENTAL DIRECTORY. 4281

1062-0613 See DEFENSE CONTRACT AWARDS. 4041

1062-063X See SOUTH DAKOTA WRITERS. 3438

1062-0648 See NATURAL FIBERS FACT BOOK. 5354

1062-0656 See JOURNAL OF MATERIALS MANUFACTURING AND PROCESSING SCIENCE. 3482

1062-0664 See APT FOR LIBRARIES. 3191

1062-0672 See CUBA REPORT, THE. 2614

1062-0680 See LAW & SEXUALITY. 2795

1062-0699 See DOG WATCH (STUDIO CITY, CALIF.). 4286

1062-0702 See NORTH AMERICAN STEEL MARKET OUTLOOK. 4014

1062-0710 See NETWORK DATA MANAGEMENT, MARKET STRATEGY REPORT. 1619

1062-0729 See THOMSON DESKTOP FINANCIAL DIRECTORY : ROUTING NUMBER INDEX. 814

1062-0737 See RADIO & TELEVISION CAREER DIRECTORY. 1137

1062-0745 See KERR'S COST DATA FOR LANDSCAPE CONSTRUCTION. 2422

1062-0788 See DIRECTIONS IN MENTAL HEALTH COUNSELING. 4585

1062-080X See UN-COMMON SENSE (LONG BEACH, CALIF.). 3648

1062-0834 See ENVIRONMENTAL RISK WATCH. 2169

1062-0842 See DESKTOP MARKETING ALERT. 923

1062-0907 See NIMA/NELSON DIRECTORY OF MINORITY AND WOMAN-OWNED INVESTMENT MANAGERS. 910

1062-0931 See PRAEGER SERIES IN PRESIDENTIAL STUDIES. 4492

1062-094X See TODAY'S CHEMIST AT WORK. 994

1062-0958 See SPECTRUM (NEW YORK, N.Y. : 1992). 2500

1062-0966 See AMERICAN CENTER FOR DESIGN JOURNAL. 287

1062-1008 See CREDIT CARD INSIDER REPORT, THE. 785

1062-1024 See JOURNAL OF CHILD AND FAMILY STUDIES. 2281

1062-1032 See MARK SPIVAK'S FLORIDA WINE BULLETIN. 2369

1062-1059 See INFORMATION FUTURES. 1113

1062-1083 See PERSPECTIVES - AMERICAN BAR ASSOCIATION. COMMISSION ON WOMEN IN THE PROFESSION. 3029

1062-1121 See DIETARY MANAGER. 4189

1062-1148 See BENEFITS (CLEARWATER, FLA.). 1655

1062-1156 See WELLNESS MANAGEMENT. 4807

1062-1164 See PUZZLER (MINNETONKA, MINN.), THE. 4865

1062-1172 See WORLD BUSINESS DIRECTORY (DETROIT, MICH.). 723

1062-1180 See CURRENT CONTENTS ON DISKETTE. PHYSICAL, CHEMICAL & EARTH SCIENCES. 1362

1062-1199 See PORT LAVACA WAVE, THE. 5753

1062-1202 See CUERO RECORD, THE. 5748

1062-1210 See DIVING & SNORKELING QUARTERLY. 4893

1062-1237 See JOURNAL OF VAISNAVA STUDIES, THE. 4971

1062-1245 See CITIZENS HEALTH ALERT. 4771

1062-1261 See GLOBAL BUSINESS WHITE PAPERS. 677

1062-1288 See MAYAN LINGUISTICS NEWSLETTER. 3301

1062-1342 See QED STATE-BY-STATE SCHOOL GUIDE [MASSACHUSETTS]. 1776

1062-1385 See DON THE BEAR SERIES. 1063

1062-1407 See SPECIAL ISSUES IN GEOSCIENCE. 1360

1062-1415 See NORTHWEST COLORADO OFFICIAL TRAVEL GUIDE. 5486

1062-1423 See NITE-WRITER'S LITERARY ARTS JOURNAL. 3417

1062-1431 See CLEVELAND NOW. 2531

1062-1458 See ACC CURRENT JOURNAL REVIEW. 3697

1062-1466 See GOVERNMENT DIRECTORY OF ADDRESSES AND TELEPHONE NUMBERS, THE. 4651

1062-1466 See LONG DISTANCE DIRECTORY OF GOVERNMENT ADDRESSES AND TELEPHONE NUMBERS. 4663

1062-1474 See LEADERSHIP EDUCATION. 875

1062-1482 See GAUGE RAIL-ROADING, O. 2773

1062-1601 See ARIZONA ANTHROPOLOGIST. 231

1062-161X See SOCIETY OF VERTEBRATE PALEONTOLOGY MEMOIR. 4231

1062-1628 See SECURITY MANAGEMENT BULLETIN. 886

1062-1679 See DUN'S HEALTHCARE REFERENCE BOOK. 3780

1062-1687 See PREPARING A TOXIC TORT CASE FOR TRIAL. 3030

1062-1717 See THOMSON SAVINGS DIRECTORY. 814

1062-1776 See SUPERCONDUCTIVITY BULLETIN. 1958

1062-1806 See MIND MATTERS. 4604

1062-1814 See BREAST IMPLANT LITIGATION REPORTER. 2943

1062-1822 See PENNSYLVANIA CIVIL APPELLATE REPORTER. 3090

1062-1830 See ASIAN AMERICAN POLICY REVIEW. 2255

1062-1849 See CHALLENGE (WASHINGTON, D.C. 1989). 4943

1062-1857 See DIRECTORY OF MUTUAL FUNDS / INVESTMENT COMPANY INSTITUTE. 896

1062-1865 See REGIONAL REVIEW (BOSTON, MASS.). 807

1062-189X See ARCHAEOASTRONOMY & ETHNOASTRONOMY NEWS. 391

1062-192X See CHEVY HIGH PERFORMANCE. 5410

1062-1946 See DIRECTORY OF U.S. HOSPITALS. 3780

1062-1962 See NATIONAL EDUCATION GOALS REPORT, THE. 1766

1062-1989 See MCGRAW-HILL DIRECTORY OF MANAGEMENT FACULTY, THE. 879

1062-2063 See PURCHASING PERFORMANCE BENCHMARKS FOR THE U.S. APPLIANCE INDUSTRY. 951

1062-2071 See SPORTING NEWS INSIDER REPORT, THE. 4922

1062-2098 See DRAGON MAGAZINE. 4860

1062-2098 See INTERACTIVE WORLD. 1113

1062-2152 See REPORTS ON RESEARCH - WOODS HOLE OCEANOGRAPHIC INSTITUTION. 1456

1062-2160 See REPORTS ON RESEARCH - WOODS HOLE OCEANOGRAPHIC INSTITUTION. 1456

1062-2195 See AAAS HANDBOOK. 5079

1062-2209 See WI CPA. 753

1062-2284 See PLAYBOY PRESENTS INTERNATIONAL PLAYMATES. 3996

1062-2292 See URBAN REPORT (WASHINGTON, D.C.), THE. 2838

1062-2306 See HISTORY AND LANGUAGE. 2619

1062-2322 See RESTAURANT SERVICE REPORT. 5073

1062-2330 See TROUBLED COMPANY PROSPECTOR, THE. 716

1062-239X See PERSPECTIVES ON BIOINORGANIC CHEMISTRY. 1037

1062-2403 See ZAGAT LOS ANGELES, SO. CALIFORNIA RESTAURANT SURVEY. 5073

1062-2446 See AMERICAN LAW REPORTS. ALR 5TH, ANNOTATIONS AND CASES. 2932

1062-2454 See NEONATAL INTENSIVE CARE. 3765

1062-2462 See 1ST PLACE MARKETING. 920

1062-2470 See LAW & BUSINESS DIRECTORY OF LITIGATION ATTORNEYS. 3090

1062-2489 See BARRON'S GUIDE TO LAW SCHOOLS. 1811

1062-2527 See TRINITY FORUM READING, THE. 3447

1062-2535 See CPS EXPRESS. 2957

1062-2543 See MAN (CHICAGO, ILL.). 2267

1062-2551 See JOURNAL FOR HEALTHCARE QUALITY. 3858

1062-256X See PACIFIC FARMER-STOCKMAN. 118

1062-2578 See TRUCK, VAN AND 4X4 BOOK. 5427

1062-2578 See MINIVAN, PICKUP, AND 4X4 BOOK, THE. 5419

1062-2594 See OMNIFORCE (BROOKLYN, NEW YORK, N.Y.). 4864

1062-2616 See LONG-TERM CARE EXECUTIVE NETWORK. 3605

1062-2624 See RISK MANAGER'S LAW ALERT. 3044

1062-2640 See S.H.A.R.E. (TUKWILA, WASHINGTON). 5306

1062-2683 See AVC PRESENTATION DEVELOPMENT & DELIVERY. 641

1062-2691 See MAINE AGRICULTURAL REPORT. 106

1062-2705 See FRESH TRENDS. 2341

1062-2713 See PEOPLE IN THE NEWS. 434

1062-2721 See ROCK CREEK CURRENT, THE. 5647

1062-273X See COLUMBIA HEIGHTS BUSINESS NEWS. 658

1062-2748 See TODAY'S BEAUTY TRENDS. 405

1062-2764 See ILLINOIS JOURNAL OF HEALTH, PHYSICAL EDUCATION, RECREATION, AND DANCE. 1751

1062-2772 See MATURE GROUP TRAVELER. 5484

1062-2799 See IIR REVIEW, THE. 2863

1062-2837 See BREAK POINT WITH CHARLES COLSON. 4940

1062-2845 See MAGIC (LAKEWOOD, CALIF.). 4863

1062-2918 See MOUNTAIN BIKING (1992). 429

1062-2926 See JUVENILE AND FAMILY JUSTICE TODAY. 2992

1062-2934 See ODESSA RECORD, THE. 5761

1062-2942 See ANIMALS' VOICE MAGAZINE, THE. 225

1062-2950 See ENGLAND'S FINEST LOGIC PROBLEMS. 4860

1062-2969 See JOURNAL OF COGNITIVE REHABILITATION, THE. 3835

1062-2985 See ANACOSTIA GRAPE VINE, THE. 5647

1062-3027 See CURRENT CONTENTS ON DISKETTE. LIFE SCIENCES. J1200. 5174

1062-3035 See BEAUTYFACTS (NEW YORK, N.Y.). 402

1062-3051 See INTERNATIONAL JOURNAL OF COMMUNICATIVE PSYCHOANALYSIS AND PSYCHOTHERAPY, THE. 3927

1062-306X See METAGAME (SOMERVILLE, MASS.). 3411

1062-3078 See CURRENT CONTENTS ON DISKETTE. LIFE SCIENCES. J600. 5174

1062-3086 See FOCUS ON GLOBAL CHANGE. 2172

1062-3094 See CURRENT CONTENTS ON DISKETTE WITH ABSTRACTS. PHYSICAL, CHEMICAL & EARTH SCIENCES. 1362

1062-3108 See CURRENT CONTENTS ON DISKETTE WITH ABSTRACTS. LIFE SCIENCES. 5174

1062-3116 See CURRENT CONTENTS ON DISKETTE WITH ABSTRACTS. CLINICAL MEDICINE. 3656

1062-3124 See CURRENT CONTENTS ON DISKETTE WITH ABSTRACTS. AGRICULTURE, BIOLOGY & ENVIRONMENTAL SCIENCES. 152

1062-3132 See CURRENT CONTENTS ON DISKETTE. ENGINEERING, TECHNOLOGY & APPLIED SCIENCES. 1970

1062-3140 See CURRENT CONTENTS ON DISKETTE. SOCIAL & BEHAVIORAL SCIENCES. 5197

1062-3159 *See* CURRENT CONTENTS ON DISKETTE. CLINICAL MEDICINE. **3656**

1062-3167 *See* CURRENT CONTENTS ON DISKETTE. AGRICULTURE, BIOLOGY & ENVIRONMENTAL SCIENCES. **152**

1062-3175 *See* EMERGING ISSUES IN BIOMEDICAL POLICY. **3574**

1062-3183 *See* NEW HORIZONS IN ADULT EDUCATION. **1882**

1062-3191 *See* EXPORTERS RESOURCES DIRECTORY. **835**

1062-3205 *See* PAYING LESS FOR COLLEGE. **1839**

1062-323X *See* EASY & FUN WORD SEEK PUZZLES. **4860**

1062-3248 *See* WARLOCK AND THE INFINITY WATCH. **382**

1062-3264 *See* AMERICAN JOURNAL OF CRITICAL CARE. **3850**

1062-3280 *See* FUTURECAST (LA CANADA, CALIF.). **1492**

1062-3302 *See* JAPAN WATCH, USA. **1498**

1062-3310 *See* MANAGING TECHNOLOGY TODAY. **878**

1062-3329 *See* ENDOTHELIUM (NEW YORK, N.Y.). **536**

1062-3337 *See* DRINKING, DRUGS & DRIVING. **1343**

1062-3345 *See* APPLIED IMMUNOHISTOCHEMISTRY. **480**

1062-3353 *See* NORTHWEST LITERARY FORUM. **3349**

1062-3361 *See* VARIABLE ANNUITY SOURCEBOOK. **2895**

1062-337X *See* YEAR BOOK OF NEURORADIOLOGY, THE. **3947**

1062-3388 *See* MANAGED CARE (LANGHORNE, PA.). **3788**

1062-3396 *See* ISLANDS OF ALOHA, THE. **5481**

1062-340X *See* HAVERSACK (TICONDEROGA, N.Y. 1991), THE. **2736**

1062-3418 *See* SAGAMORE PUBLISHING'S BOOK LOOK. **3247**

1062-3426 *See* DONKEY TALK. **4954**

1062-3434 *See* WRITING FOR OUR LIVES. **3454**

1062-3442 *See* COASTLINES (STONY BROOK, N.Y.). **2299**

1062-3450 *See* UNCLASSIFIED (WASHINGTON, D.C.). **5177**

1062-3485 *See* HEROLD'S OIL HEADLINER. **4260**

1062-3507 *See* STATISTICS USERS NETWORK. **5342**

1062-3515 *See* CABLE NETWORK INVESTOR. **781**

1062-3523 *See* PSYCHIATRY MALPRACTICE PROTECTOR. **3934**

1062-3558 *See* KARATE PROFILES MADE IN AMERICA. **4903**

1062-3574 *See* RUSSIA, EURASIAN STATES, AND EASTERN EUROPE. **2508**

1062-3582 *See* HERDER YEARBOOK: PUBLICATIONS OF THE INTERNATIONAL HERDER SOCIETY. **212**

1062-3590 *See* BIOLOGY BULLETIN OF THE RUSSIAN ACADEMY OF SCIENCES. **446**

1062-3604 *See* RUSSIAN JOURNAL OF DEVELOPMENTAL BIOLOGY. **472**

1062-3612 *See* DRY CRIK REVIEW. **3462**

1062-3620 *See* EXPRESS-TIMES, THE. **5736**

1062-3639 *See* ETHIOPIAN BUSINESS MAGAZINE. **672**

1062-3647 *See* COMPUTER FREEBIE$. **1176**

1062-3655 *See* BERLITZ TRAVELLER'S GUIDE TO NEW ENGLAND, THE. **5463**

1062-3663 *See* BERLITZ TRAVELLER'S GUIDE TO THE SOUTHWEST, THE. **5463**

1062-3671 See CORPORATE DETROIT. **661**

1062-368X *See* CORPORATE DETROIT. **661**

1062-3698 *See* ABC TODAY. **597**

1062-3701 *See* JOURNAL OF IMAGING SCIENCE AND TECHNOLOGY, THE. **5118**

1062-371X *See* YOUR PATIENT & FITNESS IN ENDOCRINOLOGY. **3733**

1062-3736 *See* ENVIRONMENTAL PHYSICIAN, THE. **3574**

1062-3744 *See* FUEL REFORMULATION. **4257**

1062-3752 *See* WCW COLLECTORS EDITIONS. **4929**

1062-3760 *See* APPLICATIONS AND SOLUTIONS. **5085**

1062-3787 *See* EWP UPDATE, THE. **1155**

1062-3817 *See* OHIO UST CLAIMS DIGEST. **3022**

1062-3825 *See* BLACK TALENT NEWS. **383**

1062-385X *See* REAL PEOPLE, REAL JOBS. **1705**

1062-3884 *See* LATIN AMERICAN TELECOM REPORT. **1115**

1062-3892 *See* SURFER'S JOURNAL, THE. **4924**

1062-3906 *See* FEMME FATALES OF THE FILMS. **320**

1062-3930 *See* SWARTZLANDER DESCENDANTS, THE. **2474**

1062-3949 *See* STUDIES ON MANUFACTURING ENGINEERING AND PRODUCTION MANAGEMENT. **1997**

1062-3957 *See* ENVIRONMENTAL BUILDING NEWS : A NEWSLETTER ON ENVIRONMENTALLY SUSTAINABLE DESIGN & CONSTRUCTION. **614**

1062-3965 *See* REVIEWS IN PESTICIDE TOXICOLOGY. **4248**

1062-3981 *See* TEMPTATION OF SAINT ANTHONY, THE. **4620**

1062-4031 *See* AMERICAN LISZT SOCIETY STUDIES SERIES. **4099**

1062-4147 *See* WESTERN ENERGY. **1960**

1062-4155 *See* PROBE. **5139**

1062-4163 *See* WOMEN'S HEALTH LETTER. **3651**

1062-4171 *See* NOBODY QUARTERLY, THE. **3418**

1062-418X *See* WINDOW MARKETPLACE. **1631**

1062-4201 See INTERNATIONAL SADDLERY AND APPAREL JOURNAL. **2800**

1062-421X *See* RESEARCH REPORT - NORTH CENTRAL WEED SCIENCE SOCIETY (U.S.). **128**

1062-4228 *See* JOURNAL OF RESEARCH IN RURAL EDUCATION. **1758**

1062-4236 *See* HEALTHY KIDS. 4-10 YEARS. **2598**

1062-4244 *See* NATIONAL NEWS - AMERICAN LEGION AUXILIARY. **5234**

1062-4260 *See* INGHAM COUNTY NEWS. **5692**

1062-4279 *See* TOWNE COURIER. **5694**

1062-4309 See NORTHEAST JOURNAL OF TRANSPORTATION, THE. **5388**

1062-4317 *See* 22 DAYS AROUND THE WORLD. **5459**

1062-4325 *See* 2 TO 22 DAYS IN ASIA. **5458**

1062-4333 *See* 2 TO 22 DAYS IN AUSTRALIA. **5458**

1062-4341 *See* 2 TO 22 DAYS IN FLORIDA. **5458**

1062-435X *See* 2 TO 22 DAYS IN HAWAII. **5459**

1062-4368 *See* WBF BODYBUILDING LIFESTYLES : THE OFFICIAL PUBLICATION OF THE WORLD BODYBUILDING FEDERATION. **2602**

1062-4465 See 2 TO 22 DAYS IN THAILAND. **5459**

1062-4473 *See* 2 TO 22 DAYS IN NEW ZEALAND. **5459**

1062-449X *See* INDUSTRIAL NATION. **2535**

1062-4503 *See* COMICS VALUES ANNUAL. **4849**

1062-4511 *See* EXEMPLARIA HISPANICA. **2733**

1062-452X *See* MACAUTHORITY (LOUISVILLE, KY.), THE. **1288**

1062-4546 *See* JOURNAL OF PHARMACY & LAW, THE. **4312**

1062-4562 *See* HEALTH FACILITIES REPORT. **3781**

1062-4570 *See* 2 TO 22 DAYS IN THAILAND. **5459**

1062-4589 *See* GREEN BOOK REPORT, THE. **2172**

1062-4597 *See* SERVICE EMPLOYEES UNION. **1710**

1062-4600 *See* BILL BOARD : LEGISLATIVE NEWS FOR OHIO JUDGES / OHIO JUDICIAL CONFERENCE. **2941**

1062-4643 *See* THESE CELESTIAL TIMES. **4243**

1062-4651 *See* LATIN AMERICAN ADVISOR, THE. **1503**

1062-466X *See* GLOBAL NOMAD, THE. **5231**

1062-4686 *See* FOUNDATION & CORPORATE GRANTS ALERT. **4336**

1062-4694 *See* RPCV WRITERS & READERS. **3432**

1062-4708 *See* CREATIVE TRANSFORMATION. **4951**

1062-4724 *See* TELEPHONE WEEK. **1167**

1062-4732 *See* SURGICAL PRODUCTS. **3976**

1062-4759 *See* MUSICIANS GUIDE TO TOURING & PROMOTION, THE. **4137**

1062-4767 *See* FRONTIER PERSPECTIVES. **5106**

1062-4775 *See* FROMMER'S COMPREHENSIVE TRAVEL GUIDE, PUERTO RICO. **5476**

1062-4783 *See* AFRICAN AMERICAN REVIEW. **3358**

1062-4791 *See* COLORADO COMPUTER RESOURCES. **1175**

1062-4805 *See* HUMANE INNOVATIONS AND ALTERNATIVES. **226**

1062-4821 *See* CURRENT OPINION IN NEPHROLOGY AND HYPERTENSION. **3989**

1062-483X *See* WEST ALLIS POST-ENTERPRISE, THE. **5772**

1062-4856 *See* NEW BERLIN ENTERPRISE. **5769**

1062-4902 *See* WEST ALLIS ENTERPRISE (WEST ALLIS, WIS. 1967). **5771**

1062-4929 *See* ANNUAL REPORT / DEPARTMENT OF AGRICULTURE. **60**

1062-4961 *See* ENVIRONMENTAL DISCOVERY. **2167**

1062-5003 *See* UNIX USER. **1206**

1062-5011 *See* COAL CITY REVIEW. **3376**

1062-502X *See* APHELION (SANTA ANA, CALIF.). **4857**

1062-5038 *See* JOURNAL OF NORTHEAST-AFRICAN STUDIES, THE. **2640**

1062-5062 *See* UPLINE (CHARLOTTESVILLE, VA.). **717**

1062-5070 *See* MANCHESTER JOURNAL (MANCHESTER, VT.), THE. **5708**

1062-5089 *See* PUBLIC ART ISSUES. **362**

1062-5100 *See* BOOKS IN PRINT PLUS. **411**

1062-5119 *See* AMERICAN BUSINESS DISK, THE. **638**

1062-5127 *See* ABI/INFORM ONDISC. **725**

1062-5135 *See* SECURITIZATION DIRECTORY & HANDBOOK. **811**

1062-5151 *See* CATALOGUE OF YEASTS. **506**

1062-5178 *See* PREDICTIONS & PRESCRIPTIONS. **882**

1062-5194 *See* HIGHWAY & HEAVY CONSTRUCTION PRODUCTS. **5440**

1062-5216 *See* POLICE OFFICERS JOURNAL, THE. **1702**

1062-5224 *See* JOE FELLEGY'S MILLE LACS FISHING DIGEST. **4874**

1062-5232 *See* ROGER TORY PETERSON INSTITUTE'S BIRDS, BATS & BUTTERFLIES. **5620**

1062-5259 *See* EMPOWERMENT! (WASHINGTON, D.C.). **4473**

1062-5283 *See* CHAC MOL NEWSLETTER. **2511**

1062-5321 *See* ABILITY MAGAZINE (IRVINE, CALIF.). **2484**

1062-5348 *See* DEVELOPERS AND BUILDERS NEWS. **2821**

1062-5356 *See* GREAT LAKES WETLANDS. **2216**

1062-5364 *See* TRENDS IN HEALTH CARE, LAW & ETHICS. **2253**

1062-5380 *See* FSMBNEWSLINE (FORT WORTH, TEX.). **3577**

1062-5399 *See* COOPERATIVE TECHNOLOGY RD&D REPORT. **5097**

1062-5445 *See* HISTORY OF SCIENCE AND TECHNOLOGY. **5110**

1062-5453 *See* TAFT AND UNIVERSITY OF CINCINNATI SERIES IN LATIN AMERICAN AND HISPANIC AMERICAN THEATRE. **5369**

1062-5488 *See* BIOMEDICAL ENGINEERING CITATION INDEX. **3686**

1062-5496 See MATERIALS SCIENCE CITATION INDEX. 5127
1062-5518 See HITCHCOCK ANNUAL. 4072
1062-5526 See EMF HEALTH & SAFETY DIGEST. 4774
1062-5534 See CRACKING THE GRE. 1819
1062-5569 See DA UPDATE. 1319
1062-5577 See ERIC (BOSTON, MASS.). 1745
1062-5607 See STANDARD & POOR'S DIRECTORY OF DIVIDEND REINVESTMENT PLANS. 915
1062-5615 See MEXICAN WAR QUARTERLY. 2746
1062-5631 See NATIONAL CONFERENCE OF BAR FOUNDATIONS' FOUNDATION FORUM. 3013
1062-5658 See REFINING & GAS PROCESSING INDUSTRY : WORLDWIDE. 4276
1062-5674 See POINT LINE POLY. HOST. 1990
1062-5690 See BRIEF (FORT LAUDERDALE, FLA.). 862
1062-5704 See HANDBOOK OF GYNECOLOGY & OBSTETRICS. 3762
1062-5712 See GRAY AREAS. 2534
1062-5720 See ONS NURSING SCAN IN ONCOLOGY. 3866
1062-5798 See SOUTHEAST POWER REPORT. 2082
1062-581X See SOUND SAFETY. 136
1062-5828 See SAFETY BRIEFS. WESTERN REGION. 5257
1062-5844 See TRIBUNE (SCRANTON, PA. 1990), THE. 5740
1062-5860 See PURCHASING PERFORMANCE BENCHMARKS FOR THE NONFERROUS METALS INDUSTRY. 951
1062-5879 See COMMERCIAL REAL ESTATE PROPERTY DIRECTORY. 4836
1062-5887 See TEMPLE POLITICAL & CIVIL RIGHTS LAW REVIEW. 4513
1062-5895 See ALPHA FORUM. 1252
1062-5909 See TEXAS FUNERAL SERVICES DIRECTORY. 2407
1062-5925 See BASICS OF SWAPS. 892
1062-5992 See PUBLIC EMPLOYEE MAGAZINE, THE. 4705
1062-6018 See FLUID POWER SERVICE CENTER. 2089
1062-6026 See HAZMAT TRANSPORTATION MANAGEMENT. 5383
1062-6034 See EMU TODAY & TOMORROW. 5582
1062-6050 See JOURNAL OF ATHLETIC TRAINING. 1856
1062-6069 See PSYCHOANALYST : A MONOGRAPH OF THE WESTCHESTER CENTER FOR THE STUDY OF PSYCHOANALYSIS AND PSYCHOTHERAPY AND THE PSYCHOANALYTIC ASSOCIATION OF THE WESTCHESTER CENTER, THE. 4610
1062-6093 See GARDEN TOURIST, THE. 2415
1062-6107 See HEALTH BUSINESS. 925
1062-6131 See STATE IRM ORGANIZATIONAL STRUCTURES. 4688
1062-614X See FORMER U.S.S.R. MONITOR. 2688
1062-6158 See BUSINESS & THE CONTEMPORARY WORLD (WALTHAM, MASS. 1991). 645
1062-6166 See OCCASIONAL PAPER - FREEDOM FORUM MEDIA STUDIES CENTER. 2923
1062-6182 See CRYPTIC SCHOLAR, THE. 611
1062-6190 See APT COMMUNIQUE. 288
1062-6212 See UNIVERSITY OF BALTIMORE JOURNAL OF ENVIRONMENTAL LAW. 3117
1062-6220 See COLUMBIA JOURNAL OF GENDER AND LAW. 2953
1062-6239 See HARVARD REVIEW OF PHILOSOPHY, THE. 4347
1062-6247 See DENEUVE (SAN FRANCISCO, CALIF.). 2794
1062-6255 See JUST PEACE (WASHINGTON, D.C.). 5559
1062-6271 See JOURNAL OF COMMERCIAL LENDING, THE. 793

1062-628X See VOICES FROM THE ATTIC. 5568
1062-6298 See SACRED RIVER. 5565
1062-6301 See NEWS / SOCIETY OF ARCHITECTURAL HISTORIANS, SOUTHERN CALIFORNIA CHAPTER. 304
1062-6344 See PEN COMPUTER REPORT. 1199
1062-6352 See NATIONAL REGISTER OF COMMERCIAL REAL ESTATE, THE. 4842
1062-6360 See HOLART REPORT. 352
1062-6379 See CAT'S EAR. 3461
1062-6387 See SUN DANCER REVIEW. 3443
1062-6395 See OPTOMETRIC BUSINESS STRATEGIST. 3878
1062-6409 See BLUFFS READER, THE. 3368
1062-6417 See DEPRESSION (NEW YORK, N.Y.). 4584
1062-6425 See TALKING BETTAS. 4288
1062-6441 See UNDERWRITER ALERT. 2895
1062-645X See EDI MONTHLY REPORT. 4645
1062-6468 See DELAWARE COUNTY GENEALOGIST. 2445
1062-6506 See CONGRESSIONAL INFORMATION BUREAU. 4175
1062-6549 See CISTERCIAN STUDIES QUARTERLY. 5027
1062-6565 See QUARTERLY NEWSLETTER - WOMEN'S THEOLOGICAL CENTER (BOSTON, MASS.). 4989
1062-6573 See MARGARET SANGER PAPERS PROJECT NEWSLETTER. 589
1062-6603 See L.A. 411. 4073
1062-6638 See MOBILE OFFICE MAGAZINE'S CELLULAR BUYERS' GUIDE. 1117
1062-6646 See TEXAS MUSIC INDUSTRY DIRECTORY, THE. 4156
1062-6719 See LEGAL ISSUES IN RECREATION ADMINISTRATION. 4706
1062-6727 See COLE PAPERS, THE. 2918
1062-6743 See CTDNEWS (PHILADELPHIA, PA.). 3569
1062-6751 See JOURNAL OF GENDER STUDIES (SOUTH PORTLAND, ME.). 3995
1062-6808 See ELECTRICAL CONTACTS. 2044
1062-6816 See FODOR'S ... RUSSIA, THE REPUBLICS AND THE BALTICS. 5473
1062-6824 See INFORMATION CENTER QUARTERLY REPORTS. 870
1062-6832 See INTERNATIONAL JOURNAL OF ENVIRONMENTALLY CONSCIOUS MANUFACTURING. 3481
1062-6859 See BARNES BULLETIN 2.0. 2438
1062-6867 See NED BACKGROUNDER: A FORUM FOR THE STUDY OF THE NATIONAL ENDOWMENT FOR DEMOCRACY AND OTHER U.S. GOVERNMENT DEMOCRATIZATION PROGRAMS, THE. 4483
1062-6891 See CD-ROM DIRECTORY ON DISC, THE. 1276
1062-6913 See BEST OF METAL, THE. 4103
1062-6921 See OVERSEAS BUILDER. 623
1062-6956 See PLAY (GAINESVILLE, FLA.). 4864
1062-6964 See COMIC ART STUDIES. 377
1062-6972 See DIASPORA (MAGNOLIA, ARK.). 3381
1062-6980 See OFFICIAL ... PRICE GUIDE TO BASKETBALL CARDS, THE. 2775
1062-6999 See ROBERT FROST REVIEW, THE. 3431
1062-7006 See HORIZONS OF VIETNAMESE THOUGHT AND EXPERIENCE. 5268
1062-7022 See HARVARD SCIENCE REVIEW (1992). 5109
1062-7030 See MATHUSER. 3522
1062-7049 See ON BALANCE (DENVER, COLO.). 4606
1062-7103 See MOUNTAIN BIKE ACTION TRAVEL GUIDE. 5485
1062-7111 See MOUNTAIN BIKE ACTION PARTS AND ACCESSORIES GUIDE. 429
1062-7146 See INTERNATIONAL SADDLERY AND APPAREL JOURNAL. 2800
1062-7162 See STANDARDS OF MEDICAL CARE. 3642

1062-7197 See EDUCATIONAL ASSESSMENT. 1741
1062-7200 See HIGHWAYMAN (WILLOW STREET, PA.), THE. 2453
1062-7219 See GOOSE (WILLOW STREET, PA.), THE. 2452
1062-7227 See OFFICIAL PRICE GUIDE TO HOCKEY AND BASKETBALL CARDS. 2776
1062-7243 See OPERA AMERICA NEWSLINE. 386
1062-726X See JOURNAL OF PUBLIC RELATIONS RESEARCH. 761
1062-7278 See INTERACTIONS BIBLIOGRAPHY, THE. 417
1062-7308 See TAX DIGEST (SANTA BARBARA, CALIF.). 3062
1062-7316 See RETIREMENT HOUSING BUSINESS REPORT. 2834
1062-7324 See FOODSERVICE YEARBOOK INTERNATIONAL. 2341
1062-7332 See MENOPAUSE MANAGEMENT. 5561
1062-7340 See REGISTER OF NORTH AMERICAN HOSPITALS. 3792
1062-7367 See FYI EVERYWOMAN'S RESOURCE GUIDE TO L.I. 5557
1062-7375 See JOURNAL OF GLOBAL INFORMATION MANAGEMENT. 3220
1062-7383 See CAGED BIRD HOBBYIST. 5616
1062-7391 See JOURNAL OF MINING SCIENCE. 2142
1062-7405 See INSIDE COMICS (GLASSBORO, N.J.). 4862
1062-7413 See BARNSTORMER (FORT WAYNE, IND.), THE. 14
1062-7421 See LAW AND POLITICS BOOK REVIEW. 2994
1062-7448 See GALENA GENEALOGY. 2449
1062-7456 See POINT OF VIEW. 4487
1062-7472 See FOCUS (WASHINGTON, D.C. 1991). 2172
1062-7480 See QUALIFIED PLAN UPDATE. 912
1062-7499 See IRA BULLETIN (BRAINERD, MINN.). 904
1062-7529 See WASTE MANAGEMENT NEWS (WACO, TEX.). 2246
1062-7537 See MED-SURG NURSING QUARTERLY. 3861
1062-7545 See ADVENTURE FLORIDA. 5460
1062-7553 See INNOVATIONS & RESEARCH IN CLINICAL SERVICES, COMMUNITY SUPPORT, AND REHABILITATION. 3926
1062-7561 See BEST AMERICAN SHORT PLAYS, THE. 5362
1062-757X See R/C MODEL BOATS & RACING. 4914
1062-7634 See VOYAGEUR (GREEN BAY, WIS.). 2633
1062-7650 See WORKSTATION REPORT'S ... BUYER' GUIDE TO OFFICE FURNITURE, THE. 4214
1062-7693 See UCC BULLETIN. 3067
1062-7715 See EXTRA!, EXTRA! (GREENSBURG, PA.). 4647
1062-7723 See HOW ON EARTH!. 4192
1062-7731 See WORLD MEDICAL REVIEWS IN PARKINSON'S DISEASE. 3651
1062-774X See WORLD MEDICAL REVIEWS IN GLAUCOMA. 3880
1062-7766 See TRADEMARK TRENDS. 1309
1062-7774 See BOARD REPORT FOR GRAPHIC ARTISTS. 377
1062-7782 See PINCKNEY DISTRICT CHAPTER QUARTERLY. 2467
1062-7790 See LONE STAR LITERARY QUARTERLY. 3408
1062-7812 See AMERICAN GIRL (MIDDLETON, WIS.). 1060
1062-7839 See NEW MEDIA IN EDUCATION & ENTERTAINMENT. 763
1062-7855 See POLLOCK POTPOURRI. 2468
1062-7901 See PHASE TRANSITIONS AND CRITICAL PHENOMENA. 4414
1062-791X See GIS NEWSLETTER. 1381

1062-7928 *See* OUT (NEW YORK, N.Y.). 2795

1062-7936 *See* IOMA'S REPORT ON CONTROLLING BENEFITS COSTS FOR LAW, DESIGN, CPA, AND OTHER PROFESSIONAL SERVICE FIRMS. 872

1062-7944 *See* JOURNAL OF QUANTUM NONLINEAR PHENOMENA. 4410

1062-7952 *See* NFAIS YEARBOOK OF THE INFORMATION INDUSTRY, THE. 3236

1062-7960 *See* MARYLAND ENVIRONMENTAL LAW LETTER. 3114

1062-7987 *See* EUROPEAN REVIEW (CHICHESTER, ENGLAND). 1745

1062-7995 *See* PROGRESS IN PHOTOVOLTAICS. 2077

1062-8002 *See* INTERNATIONAL JOURNAL OF THE STRUCTURAL DESIGN OF TALL BUILDINGS, THE. 2025

1062-8010 *See* DIRECTORY OF PUBLICATIONS RESOURCES. 4814

1062-8029 *See* DOING BUSINESS IN PARAGUAY. 668

1062-8053 *See* SIBERIAN JOURNAL OF COMPUTER MATHEMATICS. 3535

1062-8061 *See* NURSING HISTORY REVIEW. 3864

1062-807X *See* CREDIT UNION LEGAL LETTER. 2957

1062-8088 *See* JOURNAL OF THE COIN LAUNDRY AND DRYCLEANING INDUSTRY, THE. 1026

1062-8096 *See* HAZARDOUS EMERGENCY RESPONSE. 5287

1062-810X *See* COLORADO SPRINGS BUSINESS JOURNAL, THE. 658

1062-8118 *See* AMERICAS TRADE & FINANCE. 769

1062-8134 *See* FREE SPIRIT (MIAMI, FLA.). 4388

1062-8142 *See* SRA JOURNAL. 5159

1062-8150 *See* CLINICAL MICROBIOLOGY REPORTS. 3712

1062-8169 *See* COIN DEALER NEWSLETTER, THE. 2780

1062-8207 *See* CREATIVE OUTLETS. 1603

1062-8215 *See* SPORTS-N-REVIEW. 4923

1062-8223 *See* LONG ISLAND EXPRESS QUARTERLY. 4852

1062-824X *See* PONIECKI NEWSLETTER/INFORMATOR. 2923

1062-8266 *See* TRENDS MAGAZINE. 5523

1062-8274 *See* NEBRASKA CATTLEMAN. 216

1062-8312 *See* ARTWORLD EUROPE. 342

1062-8371 *See* COURIER (BROCKTON, MASS.), THE. 4859

1062-838X *See* MURKY AT BEST. 325

1062-8398 *See* SUPER PROJECTS. 1628

1062-8401 *See* CANCER BIOTHERAPY. 3810

1062-841X *See* CARROLL COUNTY HISTORICAL QUARTERLY (1992). 2727

1062-8428 *See* PARDIS (WEST ORANGE, N.J.). 2270

1062-8444 *See* FRONTERAS (ARLINGTON, TEX.). 2581

1062-8460 *See* LOUPE (SANTA MONICA, CALIF.). 2915

1062-8495 *See* WORLD (COOS BAY, OR.), THE. 5734

1062-8509 *See* COMPUTER SELECT. 1284

1062-8517 See COMPUTER SELECT. 1284

1062-8525 *See* COMPACT D/SEC. 658

1062-855X *See* FLORA-LINE, THE. 2435

1062-8576 *See* EXPERIMENTAL ROCKET FLYER. 18

1062-8584 *See* AFRICA TODAY (NEW YORK, N.Y.). 4462

1062-8592 *See* SPORTS MEDICINE AND ARTHROSCOPY REVIEW. 3956

1062-8606 *See* AMERICAN JOURNAL OF MEDICAL QUALITY. 3776

1062-8649 *See* PENNSYLVANIA ARCHITECT. 305

1062-8665 *See* FOOD CHANNEL, THE. 2336

1062-8681 *See* CA SELECTS: METALLIC GLASSES. 1005

1062-869X *See* CA SELECTS: SHAPE MEMORY ALLOYS. 1009

1062-8703 *See* CA SELECTS: TECHNICAL CERAMICS. 1010

1062-8738 *See* BULLETIN OF THE RUSSIAN ACADEMY OF SCIENCES. PHYSICS. 4399

1062-8746 *See* WIRELINE (DALLAS, TEX.). 1337

1062-8762 *See* SPACE TIMES (SEATTLE, WASH.). 36

1062-8770 *See* WRITING RIGHT NEWSLETTER. 3473

1062-8789 *See* PEDIATRIC ROUNDS. 3909

1062-8797 *See* CRYSTAL MOUNTAIN MINING QUARTERLY. 1439

1062-8800 *See* ENGINEERING DOCUMENTATION ADVISOR, THE. 1973

1062-8819 *See* ART IMAGE MAGAZINE. 313

1062-8827 *See* CHEMICAL VAPOR DEPOSITION PATENTS. 1302

1062-8843 *See* POPULAR COMMUNICATIONS SUMMER COMMUNICATIONS GUIDE. 1119

1062-8894 *See* VSDA MEMBERSHIP DIRECTORY. 1143

1062-8908 *See* SANSEVIERIA JOURNAL, THE. 2430

1062-8916 *See* STUDIES ON DEFENCE ECONOMICS. 1523

1062-8924 *See* JOURNAL OF FINANCIAL ENGINEERING, THE. 1982

1062-8932 *See* LANE GUIDE (WESTERN ED.). 796

1062-8940 *See* LEGAL ASSISTANT'S NOTEBOOK. VOL. 1, SOUTHERN CALIFORNIA ED, THE. 2999

1062-8959 *See* LEGAL ASSISTANT'S NOTEBOOK (NORTHERN CALIFORNIA ED.), THE. 2999

1062-8991 *See* WORKFORCE STRATEGIES. 948

1062-9009 *See* QUICKTIME FORUM, THE. 1120

1062-9033 *See* FINANCIAL PREDICTIONS. 675

1062-9041 *See* FREEMAN (WAUKESHA, WIS.), THE. 5767

1062-905X *See* CHAMBER PROGRESS / DODGE CITY AREA CHAMBER OF COMMERCE, THE. 819

1062-9076 *See* EARTH FORUM. 2213

1062-9084 *See* AFFORDABLE CARIBBEAN, THE. 5460

1062-9092 *See* NURSES' DRUG GUIDE. 3863

1062-9106 *See* TAX-RELATED DOCUMENTS. 4754

1062-9122 *See* ULTRA HAWK. 382

1062-9130 *See* SAL-NEWS (ROCKVILLE, MD.). 1519

1062-9173 *See* MALCONTENT, THE. 3409

1062-9181 *See* TRAVELER'S GUIDE TO WORLD RADIO. 1141

1062-9211 *See* GREEN BOOK. NEW YORK/NEW JERSEY, THE. 2172

1062-922X *See* CONFERENCE PROCEEDINGS / IEEE INTERNATIONAL CONFERENCE ON SYSTEMS, MAN, AND CYBERNETICS. 1250

1062-9238 *See* GETTING THE LOW-DOWN ON EMPLOYERS AND A LEG-UP ON THE JOB MARKET. 4204

1062-9254 *See* HOSPITALITY DESIGN. 2900

1062-9289 *See* DIET BUSINE$$ BULLETIN, THE. 4189

1062-9297 *See* PHYS ED JOURNAL OF SPORTS MEDICINE, THE. 3955

1062-9300 *See* RESEARCH NOTES. 4534

1062-9327 *See* BLUE CHIP JOB GROWTH UPDATE. 1465

1062-9343 *See* DIRECTORY OF WORLD MANUFACTURED FIBER PRODUCERS. 1605

1062-9351 *See* TECH DIRECTIONS. 1916

1062-936X *See* SAR AND QSAR IN ENVIRONMENTAL RESEARCH. 992

1062-9378 *See* NEW VIEWS (FORREST CITY, ARK.). 2540

1062-9386 *See* POETRY IN PENNSYLVANIA. 3469

1062-9394 *See* DRIVER (MIAMI, FLA.). 4893

1062-9408 *See* NORTH AMERICAN JOURNAL OF ECONOMICS AND FINANCE. 1508

1062-9416 *See* DEOSNEWS (UNIVERSITY PARK, PA.). 1735

1062-9424 *See* EFFECTOR ONLINE. 1110

1062-9440 *See* QUALITY & PRODUCTIVITY ONE HUNDRED NEWSLETTER. 705

1062-9459 *See* ART ON SCREEN. 340

1062-9467 *See* ART ON SCREEN CLOSE-UPS. 340

1062-9475 *See* PSYCHOTHERAPY LETTER, THE. 4614

1062-9483 *See* TRANSIT RESEARCH ABSTRACTS (1992). 5395

1062-9505 *See* LATVIAN DIMENSIONS. 2267

1062-9513 *See* MUSSELMAN'S ORIGINAL PRO BASKETBALL SCOUTING HANDBOOK. 4905

1062-9521 *See* MIDWEST JEWISH WEEK, THE. 5051

1062-953X *See* NEBRASKA LAW NEWSLETTER. 3014

1062-9548 *See* CHEAP RELIEF. 4580

1062-9556 *See* MEMORIES PLUS. 5180

1062-9564 *See* IN/FIRE ETHICS. 2251

1062-9572 *See* FACTS ON FILE NEWS DIGEST CD-ROM. 2487

1062-9580 *See* ELECTRONIC SWEET'S. 614

1062-9599 *See* SOCIETY AND NATURE. 2182

1062-9610 *See* KIT CAR ILLUSTRATED. 2774

1062-9629 *See* SPORT COMPACT CAR. 5425

1062-9653 *See* CONDO VACATIONING. 4849

1062-9661 *See* PORTRAITS (NEW YORK, N.Y.). 4375

1062-967X *See* SCIENCE AND TECHNOLOGY OF BUILDING SEALS, SEALANTS, GLAZING AND WATERPROOFING. 5150

1062-9696 *See* SHOPNOTES (DES MOINES, IOWA). 375

1062-970X *See* CHRISTIAN ADVOCATE (AUSTIN, TEX.). 4944

1062-9718 *See* FORUM OF THE AMERICAN TARANTULA SOCIETY. 5609

1062-9734 *See* COMPUTER ASSISTED REHABILITATION THERAPY. 1176

1062-9742 *See* WORKWATCH (BELLINGHAM, WASH.). 1719

1062-9769 *See* QUARTERLY REVIEW OF ECONOMICS AND FINANCE, THE. 1515

1062-9777 *See* OLYMPIA & YORK BANKRUPTCY NEWS. 802

1062-9785 *See* MICROSCOPY SOCIETY OF AMERICA BULLETIN. 573

1062-9920 *See* JOURNAL OF CHIROPRACTIC TECHNIQUE. 3805

1062-9939 *See* DAILY REPORT. CENTRAL EURASIA. INDEX. 1130

1062-9947 *See* HOSPITAL NEWS. WISCONSIN. 3784

1062-9971 *See* BLUEBOOK (CAMBRIDGE, MASS.), THE. 2942

1062-9998 *See* AMERICA'S WONDERFUL LITTLE HOTELS & INNS. THE ROCKY MOUNTAINS AND THE SOUTHWEST. 2804

1063-0007 *See* AMERICA'S WONDERFUL LITTLE HOTELS & INNS. THE MIDWEST. 2803

1063-0015 *See* MASORET (NEW YORK, N.Y.). 5051

1063-0023 *See* COMPLETE DIRECTORY FOR PEOPLE WITH DISABILITIES, THE. 4385

1063-0058 *See* INDUSTRY REPORT ON TECHNICIAN AND SKILLED TRADES PERSONNEL COMPENSATION. 1679

1063-0074 *See* KELLEY BLUE BOOK MANUFACTURED HOUSING USED VALUE GUIDE. 2826

1063-0155 *See* WASHINGTON COUNTS. 145

1063-0198 *See* HORTTECHNOLOGY (ALEXANDRIA, VA.). 2419

1063-0244 *See* AUDIOFILE (PORTLAND, ME.). 1104

1063-0252 *See* SMALL BUSINESS SPOTLIGHT NEWS. 711

1063-0260 *See* INFRASTRUCTURE FINANCE. 791

1063-0279 *See* CLINICAL PERFORMANCE AND QUALITY HEALTH CARE. 3566

1063-0287 See ACCOUNTING AND TAX INDEX. 725

1063-0295 See BONE & JOINT DISEASES. 3803

1063-0325 See VIEW POINTS (FULLERTON, CALIF.). 1123

1063-0333 See INTERNATIONAL TENNIS. 4901

1063-0341 See GEN GUIDE TO BIOTECHNOLOGY COMPANIES. 3692

1063-035X See MANAGING SENIORCARE. 5295

1063-0392 See SUBURBAN TRIBUNE, THE. 5755

1063-0414 See POWER EQUIPMENT TRADE. 634

1063-0422 See MOTORSPORTS WEEKLY. 4905

1063-0449 See BLACK PAGES OF AMERICA (BALTIMORE METROPLITAN ED.). 2256

1063-0457 See BLACK PAGES OF AMERICA (HAMPTON ROADS METROPOLITAN ED.). 2257

1063-0473 See BLACK PAGES OF AMERICA. 2256

1063-0481 See EXECUTIVE'S TAX REPORT. 4723

1063-0481 See EXECUTIVE'S TAX REPORT. 743

1063-049X See INTERNATIONAL BULLETIN OF WILDLAND FIRE. 2291

1063-0503 See 3W REGISTER OF CHINESE BUSINESS. 1596

1063-0511 See HOME SALES. 4838

1063-0538 See CHECK-UP (SAN DIEGO, CALIF.). 4771

1063-0546 See SERIALS & NEWSPAPERS IN MICROFORM. 424

1063-0554 See WOMEN'S INFORMATION DIRECTORY. 5571

1063-0570 See EXPRESS (CHICAGO, ILL.). 5660

1063-0589 See EQUAL TIME (MENTOR, OHIO). 5555

1063-0619 See ADVANCES IN DETAILED REACTION MECHANISMS. 1038

1063-0627 See HARVARD AIDS INSTITUTE SERIES ON GENE REGULATION OF HUMAN RETROVIRUSES. 3670

1063-0635 See DUN & BRADSTREET COMMENTS ON THE ECONOMY. 1480

1063-0686 See WILEY LIBRARIANS' NEWSLETTER. 4833

1063-0708 See PROCESS ANALYTICAL CHEMISTRY SOURCE BOOK. 1018

1063-0716 See SPECIALTY AUTO MARKETPLACE. 5425

1063-0724 See NORTH CAROLINA LITERARY REVIEW. 3418

1063-0732 See JOURNAL OF URBAN TECHNOLOGY, THE. 2826

1063-0740 See RUSSIAN JOURNAL OF MARINE BIOLOGY. 557

1063-0767 See DIVING (BLOOMSBURG, PA.). 4893

1063-0775 See CARIBBEAN DIGEST. 2258

1063-0813 See UNICAMERAL UPDATE. 4692

1063-0821 See COURT MANAGEMENT & ADMINISTRATION REPORT. 2957

1063-0856 See DIRECTORY OF NATIVE HAWAIIAN-OWNED BUSINESSES, THE. 667

1063-0902 See AFS WORLD. 1722

1063-0937 See AETHERIUS SOCIETY NEWSLETTER, THE. 4932

1063-0945 See HEALTHY KIDS. BIRTH-3. 2598

1063-0953 See ARKANSAS WILDLIFE. 2187

1063-0961 See FEDSTAT (ALEXANDRIA, VA.). 4553

1063-097X See EMPLOYEE TERMINATIONS LAW BULLETIN (1991). 1665

1063-0988 See PROCEEDINGS / THE ... ANNUAL IEEE INTERNATIONAL ASIC CONFERENCE AND EXHIBIT. 2077

1063-1011 See BRE (HOLLYWOOD, CALIF.). 1127

1063-102X See SAN DIEGO UNION-TRIBUNE (1992). 5639

1063-1054 See MARRIAGE (SAINT PAUL, MINN.). 2283

1063-1089 See OFFICIAL ... NCAA BASKETBALL. 4909

1063-1100 See ELECTRONIC SIMULATION. 2048

1063-1119 See SOCIETY & ANIMALS. 5222

1063-1127 See GET A CLUE: GUIDE TO CORNELL & ITHACA, NY. 1091

1063-1135 See INTERNATIONAL CONSTRUCTION DIRECTORY. INTERNATIONAL SECTION. 617

1063-1143 See HUNT-SCANLON'S EXECUTIVE RECRUITERS OF NORTH AMERICA. 4204

1063-1151 See AGRICULTURAL & ENVIRONMENTAL BIOTECHNOLOGY ABSTRACTS. 150

1063-116X See ENVIRONMENTAL VIEWPOINTS. 2170

1063-1178 See MEDICAL & PHARMACEUTICAL BIOTECHNOLOGY ABSTRACTS. 3660

1063-1208 See ECONOMY AT A GLANCE, THE. 1487

1063-1216 See QUARTERLY DEC JOURNAL. 706

1063-1232 See DIRECTORY OF CALIFORNIA LICENSED CONTRACTORS (NORTHERN ED.). 613

1063-1240 See DIRECTORY OF CALIFORNIA LICENSED CONTRACTORS (SOUTHERN ED.). 613

1063-1259 See WORLDWIDE GOVERNMENT DIRECTORY, REGIONAL EDITION. THE FORMER SOVIET BLOC. 2716

1063-1267 See FREE PRESS (COLUMBUS, OHIO), THE. 2920

1063-1283 See RAPPAGES (BEVERLY HILLS, CALIF.). 4148

1063-1291 See GASTROENTEROLOGY MEDICINE TODAY. 3745

1063-1305 See ARIS (PITTSBURGH, PA.). 291

1063-1313 See HEAT TRANSFER RECENT CONTENTS. 2115

1063-1321 See EXPOSE: THE VISUAL ARTS MAGAZINE. 350

1063-133X See SWORDS & PLOUGHSHARES. 4536

1063-1348 See AUDIOTEX NEWS. 1149

1063-1356 See REVIEW - PATIENT FOCUSED CARE ASSOCIATION. 5306

1063-1364 See GUIDE TO MARINES IN REUNION. 4176

1063-1372 See LOST TREASURE'S TREASURE CACHE. 4852

1063-1380 See STORIES THAT RHYME EVERY TIME KIDS PAGES. 1069

1063-1399 See NELSON'S DIRECTORY OF 'NEGLECTED STOCK' OPPORTUNITIES. 909

1063-1437 See BARNA REPORT, THE. 4938

1063-1445 See SALES IMPROVEMENT FOR PROFESSIONALS. 708

1063-1453 See INTERNATIONAL CONSTRUCTION DIRECTORY. USA SECTION. 618

1063-1461 See BELIZE DATA GUIDE. 5266

1063-147X See SOFTWARE HANDBOOK (PLYMOUTH MEETING, PA.). 1290

1063-1488 See MICROSYSTEMS HANDBOOK. 1270

1063-1496 See PERIPHERALS HANDBOOK. 1272

1063-1518 See PUCK STOPS HERE!, THE. 4913

1063-1534 See AUSTIN LAWYER'S MAGAZINE. 2938

1063-1577 See FISHING HOLES. 4872

1063-1585 See HAWAII BAR JOURNAL (1992). 2977

1063-1607 See INTERIOR LANDSCAPE. 2420

1063-1615 See CFC REPORT. 5093

1063-1623 See KANSAS OPTOMETRIC JOURNAL. 4216

1063-164X See PUBLIC-ACCESS COMPUTER SYSTEMS REVIEW, THE. 3243

1063-1666 See POEM FINDER ON DISC. 3468

1063-1674 See INTERNATIONAL JOURNAL OF MICROCIRCUITS AND ELECTRONIC PACKAGING, THE. 4219

1063-1690 See STATISTICAL ABSTRACT OF THE UNITED STATES (ENLARGED PRINT ED.). 5340

1063-1704 See HMO PERFORMANCE DIGEST. 5287

1063-1712 See DIRECTORY OF MEDICAL REHABILITATION PROGRAMS. 3572

1063-1739 See PUBLICITY AND MEDIA RESOURCES FOR BOOK PUBLISHERS. 4818

1063-1747 See HOW TO BE A PERFECT COOK. 2791

1063-1763 See MID-ATLANTIC ALMANACK, THE. 2538

1063-1771 See PUBLICATIONS (TOPOR & ASSOCIATES). 1843

1063-1798 See OUTREACH (WASHINGTON, D.C. 1992). 702

1063-1801 See CONFIGURATIONS (BALTIMORE, MD.). 5096

1063-1887 See JOURNAL WATCH (SOUND RECORDING). 5317

1063-1909 See NHAC VIET. 4141

1063-1968 See REPORT ON HUMAN RESOURCES COMPENSATION. 5305

1063-1984 See CENTRAL CITIES SOURCEBOOK, THE. 757

1063-2123 See BLOOMBERG (PRINCETON, N.J.). 892

1063-2166 See JOURNAL OF BIBLICAL COUNSELING, THE. 4968

1063-2220 See CLARK'S BANK DEPOSITS AND PAYMENTS MONTHLY. 783

1063-2239 See JOURNAL OF END USER COMPUTING. 1192

1063-2263 See ADVANCES IN PRESERVATION AND ACCESS. 3188

1063-2271 See DOS USER'S JOURNAL. 1292

1063-2301 See MONEY MANAGER REVIEW. 907

1063-2433 See DICKINSON'S FDA INSPECTION. 4642

1063-2441 See DICKINSON'S PHARMACY. 4299

1063-245X See MEETINGS REPORTS. CNS. 3838

1063-2468 See MEETING REPORTS, CARDIOVASCULAR. 3708

1063-2476 See PENSION BENEFITS. 911

1063-2492 See TEEN WORLD, THE MAGAZINE FOR TOMORROW'S LEADERS. 1070

1063-2522 See STATE-BY-STATE SUMMARY OF SOFTWARE SALES & USE TAX. 1204

1063-2565 See SSSA SPECIAL PUBLICATION. 188

1063-2573 See PAUL KAGAN'S BOX OFFICE CHAMPIONS. DIRECTORS. 4076

1063-2654 See QUALITY SERVICE UPDATE. 884

1063-2662 See TOOL WATCH. 1205

1063-2697 See VANGUARD (EDUCATION INFORMATION NETWORK (LOS ANGELES, CALIF.)). 2796

1063-2700 See MACAUTHORITY SOFTWARE CONNECTION. 1288

1063-2719 See WORDPERFECT SOFTWARE CONNECTION. 1292

1063-2727 See INSIDE WORDPERFECT WINDOWS. 1287

1063-2735 See COST CONTROLLER, THE. 864

1063-2913 See ARTS EDUCATION POLICY REVIEW. 314

1063-2921 See JOURNAL OF ARTS MANAGEMENT, LAW, AND SOCIETY. 323

1063-293X See CONCURRENT ENGINEERING : RESEARCH AND APPLICATIONS. 1969

1063-3014 See MERRILL'S ILLINOIS LEGAL TIMES. 3009

1063-3111 See BNA'S AMERICANS WITH DISABILITIES ACT MANUAL. NEWSLETTER. 4384

1063-312X See COMPUTER ARTIST. 1232

1063-3146 See INSIDE OS/2. 1287

1063-3286 See BIOGRAPHY INDEX (CD-ROM ED.). 439

1063-3294 See HUMANITIES INDEX (CD-ROM ED.). 2857

1063-3308 See SOCIAL SCIENCES INDEX (CD-ROM ED.). 5228

1063-3316 See MLA INTERNATIONAL BIBLIOGRAPHY. 3303

1063-3324 See GP (ATLANTA, GA.). 1324

1063-3332 *See* PREHOSPITAL CARE REPORTS. 3725

1063-3340 *See* THINK TANK DIRECTORY. 4690

1063-3375 *See* CURRICULUM PRODUCT NEWS : CPN. 1892

1063-3413 *See* DAYTON BUSINESS REPORTER. 664

1063-3588 *See* NDT UPDATE. 4052

1063-3596 *See* BIOETHICS BULLETIN (WASHINGTON, D.C.). 2941

1063-360X *See* NEW DEVELOPMENTS IN MEDICINE & DRUG THERAPY. 4317

1063-3618 See TOY COLLECTOR & PRICE GUIDE. 2585

1063-3626 *See* MAINE NATURALIST (STEUBEN, ME.). 4167

1063-3685 *See* NARRATIVE (COLUMBUS, OHIO). 3414

1063-3782 *See* EMPLOYMENT AND EARNINGS REPORT FOR ALASKA AND ... CENSUS AREAS. 1666

1063-3804 *See* LABOR MARKET INFORMATION DIRECTORY. 1683

1063-3839 *See* WALL STREET NETWORK NEWS. 1244

1063-3863 *See* AAA WORLD (ALASKA, HAWAII ED.). 5459

1063-3871 *See* AAA WORLD (LOUISIANA, MISSISSIPPI ED.). 5459

1063-388X *See* AAA WORLD (MASSACHUSETTS, NEW HAMPSHIRE ED.). 5459

1063-3898 *See* AAA WORLD (TEXAS, NEW MEXICO, OKLAHOMA ED.). 5459

1063-3987 *See* ARCHIVES OF FAMILY MEDICINE. 3736

1063-3995 *See* CLINICAL PSYCHOLOGY AND PSYCHOTHERAPY. 4581

1063-4002 *See* LED LAMPS & DISPLAYS. 2070

1063-4029 *See* EAST EUROPEAN INVESTMENT MAGAZINE. 897

1063-4053 *See* AUDITOR-TRAK (ATLANTA, GA.). 739

1063-4061 *See* HEALTH LAW WEEK. 2978

1063-407X *See* SYSTEMS INTEGRATION BUSINESS. 1274

1063-4088 *See* SCIENTIFIC & APPLIED PHOTOGRAPHY. 4376

1063-4134 *See* TOWARD FREEDOM (1990). 4536

1063-4169 *See* FOODS INTELLIGENCE ON COMPACT DISC. 2362

1063-4258 *See* ATOMIC ENERGY (NEW YORK, N.Y.). 2154

1063-4266 *See* JOURNAL OF EMOTIONAL AND BEHAVIORAL DISORDERS. 4596

1063-4282 *See* INTERVENTIONAL CARDIOLOGY NEWSLETTER. 3706

1063-4290 *See* REAL ESTATE WORKOUTS & ASSET MANAGEMENT. 4845

1063-4312 *See* ST. JOSEPH NEWS-PRESS (1992). 5704

1063-4320 *See* IMAGING (NEW YORK, N.Y.). 1187

1063-4339 *See* STEEL INDUSTRY UPDATE. 4020

1063-4363 *See* WORKFORCE (WASHINGTON, D.C.). 1719

1063-4460 *See* JOURNAL OF AFRICAN AMERICAN MALE STUDIES. 2265

1063-4541 *See* VESTNIK ST. PETERSBURG UNIVERSITY: MATHEMATICS. 3540

1063-455X *See* JOURNAL OF WATER CHEMISTRY AND TECHNOLOGY. 2234

1063-4568 *See* UKRAINIAN CHEMISTRY JOURNAL. 994

1063-4576 *See* JOURNAL OF SUPERHARD MATERIALS. 4006

1063-4584 *See* OSTEOARTHRITIS AND CARTILAGE. 3806

1063-4630 *See* FILIPINAS (SAN FRANCISCO, CALIF.). 2261

1063-4657 *See* MEN'S JOURNAL (NEW YORK, N.Y.). 3996

1063-4703 *See* FAMILYSEARCH. INTERNATIONAL GENEALOGICAL INDEX. U.S. AND CANADA. 2448

1063-4711 *See* FAMILYSEARCH. INTERNATIONAL GENEALOGICAL INDEX. BRITISH ISLES. 2447

1063-472X *See* FAMILYSEARCH. INTERNATIONAL GENEALOGICAL INDEX. WALES. 2448

1063-4738 *See* FAMILYSEARCH. INTERNATIONAL GENEALOGICAL INDEX. DENMARK. 2448

1063-4932 *See* IRS TAX PRACTICE INSIDER, THE. 4734

1063-5084 *See* COTTON QUARTERLY, THE. 3378

1063-5092 *See* TEACHING AND LEARNING LITERATURE WITH CHILDREN AND YOUNG ADULTS. 1906

1063-5106 *See* VIDEO MOVIES (BREMERTON, WASH.). 1142

1063-5122 *See* MAGMA (BLUE BELL, PA.). 3943

1063-5157 *See* SYSTEMATIC BIOLOGY. 474

1063-5173 *See* SRC ORANGE BOOK OF 5-TREND LONG-TERM O-T-C CHARTS, THE. 812

1063-5203 *See* APPLIED AND COMPUTATIONAL HARMONIC ANALYSIS. 3494

1063-5211 *See* BULLETIN OF THE RUSSIAN ACADEMY OF SCIENCES, DIVISION OF CHEMICAL SCIENCE. 963

1063-5246 *See* ANALYTICAL METHODS AND INSTRUMENTATION. 1020

1063-5262 See EAST EUROPEAN INVESTMENT MAGAZINE. 897

1063-5319 *See* BEAT (LOS ANGELES, CALIF. 1989). 4102

1063-5335 *See* HEALTH CARE BILLER, THE. 4778

1063-5386 *See* LIBRARIANS COLLECTION LETTER. 3223

1063-5408 *See* NEW ENGLAND LIBRARIES. 3233

1063-5432 *See* CONFERENCE PROCEEDINGS / AUTOFACT. 3477

1063-5467 *See* ADVANCES IN MOLECULAR VIBRATIONS AND COLLISION DYNAMICS. 1049

1063-5475 *See* DIRECTORY. ASSOCIATIONS. WESTERN REGION. 1604

1063-5513 *See* SAN DIEGO COMMERCE. 850

1063-5521 See V.P.I.'S IMPRINTABLES TODAY. 4570

1063-553X *See* ALEXANDRIA TIMES-TRIBUNE (1992), THE. 5662

1063-5599 *See* WHO'S WHO IN SCIENCE AND ENGINEERING. 5169

1063-5718 *See* EUROPEAN BUSINESS SERVICES DIRECTORY. 673

1063-5734 *See* PHILOSOPHY OF MUSIC EDUCATION REVIEW. 4146

1063-5742 *See* SUCCESSFUL RETIREMENT. 5182

1063-5769 *See* COLONIAL LATIN AMERICAN HISTORICAL REVIEW. 2728

1063-5777 *See* ATLAS OF THE UROLOGIC CLINICS OF NORTH AMERICA. 3988

1063-5823 *See* CURRENT TOPICS IN MEMBRANES. 535

1063-5866 *See* RURAL CONDITIONS AND TRENDS. 131

1063-5955 *See* ENVIRONMENT WATCH. EAST EUROPE, RUSSIA & EURASIA. 2166

1063-6145 *See* PERSPECTIVES ON SCIENCE. 5137

1063-620X *See* APPLAUSE/BEST PLAYS THEATER YEARBOOK, THE. 5361

1063-6269 *See* POINTS EAST. 5052

1063-634X *See* CULTUREFRONT (NEW YORK, N.Y.). 2845

1063-6382 *See* PROCEEDINGS / INTERNATIONAL CONFERENCE ON DATA ENGINEERING. 1254

1063-6471 *See* NEW MEDIA SHOWCASE. 1234

1063-6498 *See* COMPLETE DRUG REFERENCE, THE. 4297

1063-651X *See* PHYSICAL REVIEW E. STATISTICAL PHYSICS, PLASMAS, FLUIDS, AND RELATED INTERDISCIPLINARY TOPICS. 4415

1063-6528 *See* IEEE TRANSACTIONS ON REHABILITATION ENGINEERING. 3693

1063-6536 *See* IEEE TRANSACTIONS ON CONTROL SYSTEMS TECHNOLOGY. 1977

1063-6552 *See* IEEE PARALLEL & DISTRIBUTED TECHNOLOGY : SYSTEMS & APPLICATIONS. 1187

1063-6560 *See* EVOLUTIONARY COMPUTATION. 1247

1063-6579 *See* PROFESSIONAL ETHICS (GAINESVILLE, FLA.). 2252

1063-6587 *See* SALES PRODUCTIVITY REVIEW!, THE. 885

1063-6595 *See* WORCESTER BUSINESS JOURNAL. 723

1063-6676 *See* IEEE TRANSACTIONS ON SPEECH AND AUDIO PROCESSING. 5317

1063-6692 *See* IEEE/ACM TRANSACTIONS ON NETWORKING. 1241

1063-6706 *See* IEEE TRANSACTIONS ON FUZZY SYSTEMS. 1187

1063-679X *See* POLAND BUSINESS REPORT. 703

1063-6803 *See* ORGANIC FARMER (MONTPELIER, VT.). 117

1063-6889 *See* PROCEEDINGS / SYMPOSIUM ON COMPUTER ARITHMETIC. 3528

1063-6919 *See* PROCEEDINGS / CVPR, IEEE COMPUTER SOCIETY CONFERENCE ON COMPUTER VISION AND PATTERN RECOGNITION. 1200

1063-6927 *See* PROCEEDINGS OF THE INTERNATIONAL CONFERENCE ON DISTRIBUTED COMPUTING SYSTEMS. 1243

1063-6994 *See* BRANSON TRI-LAKES DAILY NEWS. 5702

1063-7060 *See* INSPEC ONDISC. 2065

1063-7095 *See* INTERNATIONAL APPLIED MECHANICS. 2116

1063-7109 *See* PROCEEDINGS - IEEE COMPUTER SOCIETY SYMPOSIUM ON RESEARCH IN SECURITY AND PRIVACY. 1227

1063-7176 *See* PALAEOCLIMATES. 4228

1063-7184 *See* ATMOSPHERE-OCEAN SYSTEM, THE. 1446

1063-7192 *See* PARALLEL ALGORITHMS AND APPLICATIONS. 1248

1063-7222 *See* PRIVACY TIMES. 3031

1063-7281 *See* FORD FOUNDATION REPORT, THE. 1824

1063-729X *See* JOURNEYS (BLOOMINGTON, ILL.). 4862

1063-7311 *See* MECHANICAL ENGINEERING ABSTRACTS. 2006

1063-732X *See* MATERIALS SCIENCE AND ENGINEERING ABSTRACTS. 2006

1063-7338 *See* CIVIL AND STRUCTURAL ENGINEERING ABSTRACTS. 2003

1063-7346 *See* ENVIRONMENTAL ENGINEERING ABSTRACTS. 2184

1063-7354 *See* MANUFACTURING AND PROCESS ENGINEERING ABSTRACTS. 1985

1063-7389 *See* NEW HORIZONS (BALTIMORE, MD.). 3620

1063-7397 *See* RUSSIAN MICROELECTRONICS. 1202

1063-7419 *See* DICKINSON JOURNAL OF ENVIRONMENTAL LAW & POLICY. 2960

1063-7427 See DICKINSON JOURNAL OF ENVIRONMENTAL LAW & POLICY. 2960

1063-7443 *See* CUSTOMS RECORD. 3126

1063-7451 *See* CAROLINA GARDENER. 2412

1063-746X *See* CORDAGE NEWS. 5349

1063-7478 *See* INTERNATIONAL ASSOCIATION OF PANORAMIC PHOTOGRAPHERS :. 4370

1063-7494 *See* ADULT CONTEMPORARY MUSIC RESEARCH LETTER, THE. 4098

1063-7508 *See* TEACHER CERTIFICATION REQUIREMENTS IN ALL FIFTY STATES. 1905

1063-7516 *See* SOCIAL LIST OF WASHINGTON, D.C. AND SOCIAL PRECEDENCE IN WASHINGTON, THE. 4686

1063-7532 *See* IRISH EDITION. 2264

1063-7540 *See* VALLEY VOICE (COLD SPRING, N.Y.). 2549

1063-7559 *See* BERKSHIRE REVIEW (PITTSFIELD, MASS.), THE. 2528

1063-7567 See SNOQUALMIE VALLEY REPORTER. 5762
1063-7575 See COMMENTS FROM THE FRIENDS. 4949
1063-7591 See COREL MAGAZINE. 1233
1063-7621 See COLUMBIA GORGE VISITOR & RECREATION GUIDE (1992). 4849
1063-763X See COLUMBIA GORGE VISITOR & RECREATION GUIDE (1992). 4849
1063-7648 See GORGE GUIDE. 4850
1063-7656 See GORGE GUIDE. 4850
1063-7664 See NDTA NETWORK. 3839
1063-7672 See CHRISTIAN COMPUTING MAGAZINE. 1174
1063-7702 See TRIBUNE (TABOR CITY), THE. 5724
1063-7710 See ACOUSTICAL PHYSICS. 4452
1063-7729 See ASTRONOMY REPORTS. 393
1063-7737 See ASTRONOMY LETTERS. 392
1063-7745 See CRYSTALLOGRAPHY REPORTS. 1031
1063-7753 See PHYSICS-DOKLADY. 4415
1063-7761 See JOURNAL OF EXPERIMENTAL AND THEORETICAL PHYSICS. 4409
1063-777X See LOW TEMPERATURE PHYSICS. 4411
1063-7788 See PHYSICS OF ATOMIC NUCLEI. 4450
1063-7796 See PHYSICS OF PARTICLES AND NUCLEI. 4450
1063-780X See PLASMA PHYSICS REPORTS. 4417
1063-7818 See QUANTUM ELECTRONICS (NEW YORK, N.Y. 1993). 2078
1063-7826 See SEMICONDUCTORS (NEW YORK, N.Y.). 4421
1063-7834 See PHYSICS OF THE SOLID STATE. 4416
1063-7842 See TECHNICAL PHYSICS. 4423
1063-7850 See TECHNICAL PHYSICS LETTERS. 4423
1063-7869 See PHYSICS, USPEKHI. 4416
1063-7877 See PEOPLE AND EDUCATION. 1772
1063-7885 See CIGAR AFICIONADO. 5372
1063-7893 See WOOD MAGAZINE'S SUPER SCROLLSAW PATTERNS. 635
1063-7915 See CHRONICLE FINANCIAL AID GUIDE. 1815
1063-7931 See WORLD PULSE. 5010
1063-794X See LIFELINES FOR YOUTH TEACHER. 4973
1063-7974 See PROVIDENCE (PROVIDENCE, R.I.). 2626
1063-7982 See COMIC BOOK COLLECTOR. 4859
1063-8016 See JOURNAL OF DATABASE MANAGEMENT. 1254
1063-8024 See ALAMO AREA SQUARE AND ROUND DANCE ASSOCIATION NEWSLETTER. 1310
1063-8067 See FDA MEDICAL BULLETIN. 4305
1063-8091 See GAS SHALES TECHNOLOGY REVIEW. 4258
1063-8156 See LEGACY (MONROEVILLE, ALA.). 2458
1063-8164 See NORTHWEST SAILBOARD. 4908
1063-8172 See WINDSURFING CALIFORNIA. 4929
1063-8180 See SAILBOARD RETAILER. 4916
1063-8202 See TEXAS EMS MAGAZINE. 4805
1063-8210 See IEEE TRANSACTIONS ON VERY LARGE SCALE INTEGRATION (VLSI) SYSTEMS. 1187
1063-8245 See HANDBOOK / ASSOCIATION OF AMERICAN LAW SCHOOLS. 2976
1063-8253 See HANDBOOK / ASSOCIATION OF AMERICAN LAW SCHOOLS. 2976
1063-8288 See EUROPEAN WHOLESALERS AND DISTRIBUTORS DIRECTORY. 1606
1063-8296 See AVID (CUPERTINO, CALIF.). 1171
1063-8326 See ELECTRONIC GAMES. 4860
1063-8334 See TURBOFORCE (LOMBARD, ILL.). 4867

1063-8369 See COMPUTER REPORT & THE PC STREET PRICE INDEX. 1246
1063-8377 See STANZA (MEDFORD, N.J.). 3472
1063-8407 See FORESIGHT (RESTON, VA.). 676
1063-8415 See PAGELAND PROGRESSIVE JOURNAL, THE. 5743
1063-8423 See GLOBAL ACCESS TO STD DIAGNOSTICS. 3713
1063-8431 See EDGE (HACKETTSTOWN, N.J.). 1241
1063-8466 See OBSERVER (HERNDON, VA.), THE. 5759
1063-8490 See BEHAVIORAL HEALTHCARE TOMORROW. 4768
1063-8512 See PRO ECCLESIA (NORTHFIELD, MINN.). 4988
1063-8520 See IMPULSE (CHAMPAIGN, ILL.). 1313
1063-8539 See JOURNAL OF COMBINATORIAL DESIGNS. 3512
1063-8547 See SURGICAL RESIDENT, THE. 3976
1063-8555 See FAMILY PRACTICE RESIDENT, THE. 3737
1063-8563 See RADIOLOGY RESIDENT, THE. 3946
1063-8571 See ANESTHESIOLOGY RESIDENT, THE. 3681
1063-8598 See COMMERCIAL AVIATION NEWS. 16
1063-8601 See DISTRICT OF COLUMBIA LAW REVIEW. 2963
1063-861X See ADJUNCT INFO. 1089
1063-8628 See QUALITY MANAGEMENT IN HEALTH CARE. 884
1063-8652 See JOURNAL OF AGING AND PHYSICAL ACTIVITY. 3752
1063-8679 See M (NEW YORK, N.Y. 1991). 1085
1063-8695 See APPLIED SCIENCE & TECHNOLOGY INDEX (CD-ROM ED.). 5173
1063-8709 See COMPENDEX PLUS. 2003
1063-8717 See SCITECH REFERENCE PLUS. 5176
1063-8784 See CDMARC SERIALS. 3201
1063-8792 See AHFS DRUG INFORMATION. 4290
1063-8806 See CURRENT COMMUNICATIONS IN CELL & MOLECULAR BIOLOGY. 535
1063-8822 See PENNINGTON CENTER NUTRITION SERIES. 4197
1063-8881 See LA POINTE, A. 2457
1063-889X See LA POINTE, A. 2457
1063-892X See CHILDREN & YOUTH FUNDING REPORT. 5278
1063-8938 See END PAPERS (ARLINGTON, VA.). 4828
1063-8946 See PHARMACOLOGY, TOXICOLOGY & THERAPEUTICS. 4322
1063-8954 See FILMMAKER (LOS ANGELES, CALIF.). 4071
1063-8970 See COMBAT EDGE, THE. 16
1063-9004 See SATISFACTION (EVANS, GA.). 3792
1063-9012 See CURRENT BOOKS MAGAZINE. 3341
1063-9047 See PAYTECH (NEW YORK, N.Y.). 749
1063-9055 See SOAP OPERA ILLUSTRATED. 2546
1063-9071 See HOW TO ADOPT YOUR BABY PRIVATELY. 5288
1063-908X See SPAULDING & SLYE REPORT. GREATER BOSTON, THE. 4847
1063-9098 See SPAULDING & SLYE REPORT. GREATER BOSTON, THE. 4847
1063-9101 See SPAULDING & SLYE REPORT. WASHINGTON, D.C, THE. 4847
1063-9128 See INTERNATIONAL POETRY REVIEW (GREENSBORO, N.C.). 3464
1063-9136 See P-A-M BULLETIN. 3526
1063-9160 See SEW BEAUTIFUL. 5185
1063-9187 See CHURCH WORSHIP. 4948
1063-9195 See TRIBOMATERIALS NEWS. 4424
1063-9209 See FTCA NEWS. 2972
1063-9233 See ORGANIZER MAILING, THE. 4671

1063-9241 See BEND OF THE RIVER. 4162
1063-925X See LANE REPORT, THE. 689
1063-9268 See CONTRACT EMPLOYMENT WEEKLY. 4203
1063-9276 See DICK VINOCUR'S FOOTPRINTS. 4564
1063-9314 See WEEKLY HARDWOOD REVIEW. 2405
1063-9322 See HARDWOOD REVIEW EXPORT. 2401
1063-9330 See SKEPTIC (ALTADENA, CALIF.). 5158
1063-9349 See ULTRA CYCLING. 4927
1063-9357 See KENTUCKY JOURNAL (LEXINGTON, KY.). 2536
1063-9373 See DISABILITY ISSUES. 4387
1063-942X See RESTAURANT MARKETING STRATEGIES. 5072
1063-9438 See TELL (CINCINNATI, OHIO). 5002
1063-9454 See CIVIL RIGHTS MONITOR. 2613
1063-9489 See SHELBY COUNTY REPORTER (1955). 5628
1063-9497 See TCI (NEW YORK, N.Y.). 5369
1063-9594 See OHIO ENVIRONMENTAL MONTHLY. 3115
1063-9608 See PLAYBOY'S BEAUTY QUEENS. 3996
1063-9616 See PLAYBOY'S CALENDER GIRLS. 3996
1063-9624 See SALMON MAGAZINE. 2312
1063-9632 See NATIVE AMERICANS INFORMATION DIRECTORY. 2268
1063-9640 See SOUTHERN RE-ENACTING VETERAN, THE. 4854
1063-9659 See KIDS COPY. 1065
1063-9667 See VLSI DESIGN. 2085
1063-9675 See EYEBALL (ST. LOUIS, MO.). 3387
1063-9721 See NELSON'S 401(K) MARKETPLACE DIRECTORY. 698
1063-973X See TOWARD AN ELECTRONIC PATIENT RECORD. 1205
1063-9748 See DIRECTORY OF U.S. GOVERNMENT SOFTWARE FOR MAINFRAMES AND MICROCOMPUTERS. 1285
1063-9772 See GLOBAL GEORGIA. 838
1063-9799 See HISTORY SOURCE. 2635
1063-9802 See SOCIAL SCIENCE SOURCE. 5227
1063-9810 See HEALTH SOURCE (PEABODY, MASS.). 2602
1063-9829 See NETWORK 2D. 3014
1063-9837 See GEOGRAFFITY (BLACKSBURG, VA.). 2517
1063-9845 See OUR SCHOOLS USA. 1771
1063-9888 See LEGAL EDGE, THE. 2999
1063-990X See OHIO REPORT (COLUMBUS, OHIO). 4671
1063-9926 See ADAIR COUNTY REVIEW. 2436
1063-9942 See FAMUAN (TALLAHASSEE, FLA.), THE. 5649
1063-9950 See CROSS COUNTRY STITCHING. 5183
1063-9977 See DEVELOPMENTS IN MENTAL HEALTH LAW. 2960
1063-9985 See DIRECTORY OF THE FOREST PRODUCTS INDUSTRY. 2400
1063-9993 See AMERITECH INDUSTRIAL PURCHASING GUIDE. NEW YORK, WESTERN PENNSYLVANIA. 948
1064-0029 See SANDY PARKER REPORTS. 3185
1064-0037 See FURMAN HUMANITIES REVIEW. 2846
1064-0053 See GIFTED EDUCATION PRESS QUARTERLY. 1879
1064-007X See ON GUARD (NEW YORK, N.Y.). 4053
1064-0096 See BOX N' CHEST. 3369
1064-010X See AUSTRALIAN EXPATRIATE, THE. 2668
1064-0118 See GREEN PRINTS. 2417
1064-0126 See THRUST (AUSTIN, TEX.). 3446

ISSN Index

1064-0134 See BLACK & WHITE (BIRMINGHAM, ALA.). 2485

1064-0142 See ATLANTIC TIDE & CURRENT ALMANAC (NORTHEAST ED.). 4175

1064-0185 See LEAF (FORT COLLINS, COLO.), THE. 2197

1064-0207 See OUR VOICE (NEW YORK, N.Y. 1990). 3890

1064-0223 See BUSINESS ETHICS RESOURCE. 648

1064-0266 See EATING DISORDERS. 4585

1064-0312 See LONDON THEATRE NEWS. 5365

1064-0320 See MISSISSIPPI RECORDS. 2461

1064-0339 See QUICK TRIPS TRAVEL LETTER. 5489

1064-0347 See NICHE (BALTIMORE, MD.). 955

1064-0355 See DIRECTORY OF INTELLECTUAL PROPERTY ATTORNEYS. 2962

1064-0363 See LAW & BUSINESS DIRECTORY OF ENVIRONMENTAL ATTORNEYS. 3114

1064-0371 See LAW & BUSINESS DIRECTORY OF BANKRUPTCY ATTORNEYS. 3087

1064-038X See AUGUSTA (AUGUSTA, GA.). 2722

1064-0398 See LOGIA (FORT WAYNE, INDIANA). 4974

1064-0401 See LAND USE LAW REPORT. 2993

1064-041X See HISTORICAL GENEALOGICAL MAGAZINE SPECIALIZING IN CLINTON AND BOONE COUNTIES. 2453

1064-0444 See NORTH JERSEY COMPUTERUSER. 1197

1064-0452 See LEONARD'S ANNUAL PRICE INDEX OF PRINTS, POSTERS & PHOTOGRAPHS. 4371

1064-0460 See AQUATIC SCIENCES & FISHERIES ABSTRACTS (CD-ROM ED.). 2316

1064-0479 See NTIS BIBLIOGRAPHIC DATABASE. 5175

1064-0495 See WORLD AVIATION DIRECTORY. BUYER'S GUIDE. 40

1064-0509 See WORLD AVIATION DIRECTORY. BUYER'S GUIDE. 40

1064-0517 See PERSPECTIVES ON DEVELOPMENTAL NEUROBIOLOGY. 468

1064-0525 See CANCER RESEARCH, THERAPY & CONTROL. 3812

1064-0541 See CHILDREN'S BOOK BAG, THE. 3374

1064-055X See COMPETITION PLUS. 5412

1064-0568 See WE THE PEOPLE (NORTH READING, MASS.). 4500

1064-0576 See INNOVATIVE IDEAS. 1612

1064-0584 See TANTRA (TORREON, N.M.). 4363

1064-0614 See PLANT AND EQUIPMENT EXPENDITURES AND PLANS. 1621

1064-0622 See SOUTH WHIDBEY RECORD. 5762

1064-0649 See IN THE MARKETPLACE. 4964

1064-0657 See KATAHDIN TIMES. 5685

1064-0665 See WINCHESTER STAR (WINCHESTER, VA.). 5760

1064-0703 See CALL BOARD (SAN FRANCISCO, CALIF.). 5362

1064-072X See NEW DIRECTIONS (NEW YORK, N.Y. 1979). 1767

1064-0738 See ANCESTOR UPDATE. 2437

1064-0746 See JOURNAL OF ABSTRACTS (AND ARTICLES) IN INTERNATIONAL EDUCATION. 1795

1064-0762 See NEW YORK STATE GFOA NEWSLETTER. 801

1064-0770 See QURANIC GUIDANCE. 5044

1064-0819 See LESBIAN HERSTORY ARCHIVES NEWSLETTER. 2795

1064-0827 See GETTING READY. 1063

1064-0843 See MUTUAL FUND MONTHLY. 800

1064-0851 See STAT NEWS. 5373

1064-086X See TOBACCO-FREE YOUTHREPORTER. 5373

1064-0886 See DA&DSM MONITOR. 4760

1064-0894 See NAVIGATOR (NORFOLK, VA.), THE. 2462

1064-0908 See OHIO HIGH SCHOOL ATHLETE, THE. 4910

1064-0916 See HISPANIC HOTLINE. 4204

1064-0924 See FIELDING'S BENELUX. 5470

1064-0932 See FIELDING'S ALPINE EUROPE. 5469

1064-0940 See FIELDING'S BRITAIN. 5470

1064-0959 See ANNUAL REPORT, SECTION OF PUBLIC UTILITY, COMMUNICATIONS AND TRANSPORTATION LAW. 4759

1064-0991 See FIELDING'S SPAIN AND PORTUGAL. 5470

1064-1009 See LET'S GO. THE BUDGET GUIDE TO GREECE & TURKEY. 5483

1064-1068 See POF NEWSLETTER. 4440

1064-1076 See TELECOM STANDARDS NEWSLETTER. 1165

1064-1084 See JOURNAL OF WOMEN'S MINISTRIES. 4971

1064-1092 See AREEA REPORT, THE. 4834

1064-1106 See FAMILY TREE (HOWARD COUNTY, MD), THE. 2447

1064-1114 See KIDSNET (WASHINGTON, D.C.). 1134

1064-119X See MARINE GEORESOURCES & GEOTECHNOLOGY. 1986

1064-1203 See PRACTICE MANAGEMENT AND MARKETING NEWS IN PEDIATRIC DENTISTRY. 1333

1064-1211 See KEY WORDS. 3221

1064-122X See FULLERENE SCIENCE AND TECHNOLOGY. 5106

1064-1238 See FROMMER'S COMPREHENSIVE TRAVEL GUIDE. HONOLULU & OAHU. 5476

1064-1246 See JOURNAL OF INTELLIGENT & FUZZY SYSTEMS. 5118

1064-1254 See ELECTRIC VEHICLE DIGEST. 5414

1064-1262 See REVIEWS IN FISHERIES SCIENCE. 2312

1064-1270 See BETTER BUSINESS BULLETIN (NORTH PALM BEACH, FLA.), THE. 643

1064-1289 See ABOVEGROUND TANK STATE REGULATORY GUIDE. 2926

1064-1297 See EXPERIMENTAL AND CLINICAL PSYCHOPHARMACOLOGY. 4587

1064-1300 See WANT'S THEATRE DIRECTORY. 5372

1064-1343 See MATRIX (WASHINGTON, D.C. 1992). 1220

1064-1351 See FOR YOUR INFORMATION (SAN DIEGO, CALIF.). 3211

1064-136X See FIVE STONES, THE. 5060

1064-1394 See PROGRAMMABLE LOGIC, NEWS & VIEWS. 1239

1064-1408 See INDIA BUSINESS & INDUSTRY NEWSLETTER. 681

1064-1416 See FROMMER'S COMPREHENSIVE TRAVEL GUIDE, YUCATAN. 5477

1064-1424 See BEING WELL. 3555

1064-1459 See U.S. MILITARY AIRCRAFT DATA BOOK. 38

1064-1467 See U.S. WEAPON SYSTEMS COSTS. 4059

1064-1475 See MEALEY'S LITIGATION REPORTS. TOXIC TORTS. 3008

1064-1491 See REAL ESTATE CAPITAL MARKETS REPORT. 1515

1064-1505 See ADA IC NEWSLETTER. 1278

1064-1513 See EXPORT LEADS. 834

1064-153X See VIZ (HATTIESBURG, MISS.). 3451

1064-1548 See REIMBURSEMENT UPDATE SALT LAKE CITY, UTAH. 706

1064-1556 See NEWS NOTES - MARYKNOLL JUSTICE AND PEACE OFFICE. 4530

1064-1580 See JUILLIARD JOURNAL, THE. 386

1064-1599 See AMBC NEWS. 205

1064-1602 See CHRISTIAN ANTHROPOLOGY. 233

1064-1610 See WHEELER'S INLAND EMPIRE. 1526

1064-1629 See STRATTON MAGAZINE. 4924

1064-1645 See SOUTHWEST NEWSWEEK, THE. 5682

1064-1653 See WHO'S WHO IN THE INTERNATIONAL PERSONNEL MANAGEMENT ASSOCIATION. 948

1064-1661 See BUSINESS NEWS (EUGENE, OR.), THE. 651

1064-1688 See MAINSHEET (SAN FRANCISCO, CALIF.). 594

1064-170X See FIDELITY INSIGHT. 898

1064-1718 See AMERICA'S BEST QUILTING PROJECTS. 5183

1064-1734 See JOURNAL OF CURRENT ISSUES AND RESEARCH IN ADVERTISING. 761

1064-1742 See HOMETOWN PRESS. 2534

1064-1750 See SUPPORT@FTP.COM (WAKEFIELD, MASS.). 1204

1064-1769 See HIDDEN JOB MARKET. 4204

1064-1785 See RICHMOND SURROUNDINGS. 4854

1064-1793 See O'KEEFE'S GUIDE. MID-ATLANTIC REGIONAL DIRECTORY. 5300

1064-1807 See PETROLEUM INDUSTRY PROFILES. 4273

1064-1831 See HOT SHEET (FAIRFIELD, WASH.). 2290

1064-184X See INTERNATIONAL BIBLIOGRAPHIC BULLETIN OF WILDLAND FIRE. 2291

1064-1858 See JOURNAL OF MAGNETIC RESONANCE. SERIES A. 4444

1064-1866 See JOURNAL OF MAGNETIC RESONANCE. SERIES B. 4444

1064-1874 See FLORIDA ENVIRONMENTAL COMPLIANCE UPDATE. 3112

1064-1912 See CORPORATE FINANCING WEEK - INSTITUTIONAL INVESTOR (FIRM). 785

1064-1955 See HYPERTENSION IN PREGNANCY. 3762

1064-1963 See CLINICAL AND EXPERIMENTAL HYPERTENSION (1993). 3703

1064-1971 See ON CAMPUS (WASHINGTON, D.C.). 1839

1064-1998 See EL SOL (SALINAS, CALIF.). 5635

1064-2013 See DELAWARE GAZETTE (DELAWARE, OHIO 1932), THE. 5728

1064-2021 See PERRYSBURG MESSENGER-JOURNAL. 5730

1064-2048 See GREETINGS MAGAZINE. 2584

1064-2056 See KIDSTAR 1250. 1065

1064-2064 See SPACE 2000. 1291

1064-2072 See TOBACCO-FREE YOUTHREPORTER. 5373

1064-2080 See HERE'S HELP (RENO, NEV.). 5287

1064-2129 See ENVIRONMENTAL LAW NEWS (SAN FRANCISCO, CALIF.). 3111

1064-2137 See BNA'S HEALTH LAW REPORTER. 2942

1064-2145 See KEY SOLUTIONS. 1984

1064-2153 See DEPOT MILITAIRE. 4042

1064-217X See LIFE DESIGNS. 2599

1064-2188 See PENNSTATE SPORTS MEDICINE NEWSLETTER. 3955

1064-2269 See JOURNAL OF COMMUNICATIONS TECHNOLOGY & ELECTRONICS. 2068

1064-2277 See FLUID MECHANICS RESEARCH. 2114

1064-2285 See HEAT TRANSFER RESEARCH. 2056

1064-2293 See EURASIAN SOIL SCIENCE. 1355

1064-2307 See JOURNAL OF COMPUTER AND SYSTEMS SCIENCES INTERNATIONAL. 1191

1064-2315 See JOURNAL OF AUTOMATION AND INFORMATION SCIENCES. 1220

1064-234X See LINTON TRAINER'S RESOURCE DIRECTORY, THE. 943

1064-2358 See REPORTS - NATIONAL CENTER FOR SCIENCE EDUCATION (U.S.). 1778

1064-2366 See DIESEL & GAS TURBINE WORLDWIDE CATALOG (1992). 2112

1064-2374 See MASSACHUSETTS ENVIRONMENTAL COMPLIANCE UPDATE. 3114

1064-2382 *See* CONNECTICUT ENVIRONMENTAL COMPLIANCE UPDATE. 2955

1064-2390 *See* NEW JERSEY EMPLOYMENT LAW LETTER. 3152

1064-2404 *See* GRAY'S SPECIALTY CAR VALUE GUIDE. 5415

1064-2412 *See* BUSINESSGRAM (TAMPA, FLA.). 654

1064-2439 *See* DISTANCE EDUCATION AND TECHNOLOGY NEWSLETTER. 1736

1064-2455 *See* BIOREMEDIATION REPORT, THE. 1966

1064-2463 *See* THACKERAY NEWSLETTER, THE. 3445

1064-2471 *See* BUSINESS PICTURE, THE. 651

1064-251X *See* BIOPROBES (EUGENE, OR.). 5088

1064-2560 *See* IMSA JOURNAL. 5441

1064-2579 *See* CUE MAGAZINE. 4850

1064-2595 *See* JOURNAL OF THE BRAXTON HISTORICAL SOCIETY. 2742

1064-2609 *See* C.A.R.E. PACKAGE, THE. 3370

1064-2617 *See* OMAK-OKANOGAN COUNTY CHRONICLE, THE. 5761

1064-2625 *See* UNIVERSAL ACADEMIA. 3472

1064-2641 See O'CONNOR REPORT (SEATTLE, WASH.). 4794

1064-265X *See* O'CONNOR REPORT (SEATTLE, WASH.). 4794

1064-2668 *See* PROFESSIONAL VCR REPAIR TRAINING MANUAL AND BUSINESS PLAN, THE. 2812

1064-2676 *See* TV VIDEO. 1142

1064-2684 *See* GLQ (NEW YORK, N.Y.). 2794

1064-2692 *See* PATENTIMAGES (NEW HAVEN, CONN.). 1307

1064-2722 *See* ADVANCES IN DEVELOPMENTAL BIOCHEMISTRY. 479

1064-2730 *See* NEWSLETTER / RENTON HISTORICAL SOCIETY AND MUSEUM. 4094

1064-2757 *See* FREE TIME. 2533

1064-2765 *See* PRO BIKE NEWS. 429

1064-2811 *See* CONSULTING SERVICES. 973

1064-2900 *See* LOIRE VALLEY INSIGHT GUIDES. 5483

1064-2986 *See* QUAD CITY REPORTER, THE. 705

1064-301X *See* BIBLION (NEW YORK, N.Y.). 2843

1064-3036 *See* FROMMER'S COMPREHENSIVE TRAVEL GUIDE. AUSTRALIA. 5475

1064-3044 *See* FROMMER'S COMPREHENSIVE TRAVEL GUIDE. CALIFORNIA. 5475

1064-3060 *See* FROMMER'S COMPREHENSIVE TRAVEL GUIDE. ATHENS. 5475

1064-3079 *See* INTERTEC RECREATIONAL VEHICLE TRADE-IN GUIDE. 5481

1064-3095 *See* DECORATING DIGEST CRAFT AND HOME PROJECTS. 372

1064-3125 *See* DIGEST - ANTENNAS AND PROPAGATION SOCIETY SYMPOSIUM. 5099

1064-3257 *See* SECRET OF THE PROS, THE. 2778

1064-3389 *See* CRITICAL REVIEWS IN ENVIRONMENTAL SCIENCE AND TECHNOLOGY. 2163

1064-3397 *See* HAPPENINGS IN SAN DIEGO COUNTY. 2534

1064-3427 *See* FROMMER'S COMPREHENSIVE TRAVEL GUIDE. BARCELONA. 4478

1064-3435 *See* FROMMER'S COMPREHENSIVE TRAVEL GUIDE. BED & BREAKFAST, NORTH AMERICA. 2805

1064-3443 *See* FROMMER'S COMPREHENSIVE TRAVEL GUIDE. CANADA. 5475

1064-3486 *See* EASTERN EXPRESS (OMAHA, NEB.). 3208

1064-3494 See EASTERN EXPRESS (OMAHA, NEB.). 3208

1064-3540 *See* FLESNEWS. 1804

1064-3567 *See* TRENTONIAN (TRENTON, N.J.), THE. 5711

1064-3575 *See* ZIGZAG'S MONDAY MORNING QUARTERBACK. 2907

1064-3583 *See* DEFENSE MERGERS & ACQUISITIONS. 665

1064-3591 *See* FRENCH ANCESTORS : HERITAGE OF THE FRENCH SETTLERS IN WESTERN OHIO. 2734

1064-3613 *See* WINTER PARK-MAITLAND OBSERVER. 5651

1064-3621 *See* OUTSTATE BUSINESS. 702

1064-363X *See* PSYCHOTRAIN (FAYETTEVILLE, ARK.). 3426

1064-3699 *See* NEWS DIMENSIONS. 5647

1064-3753 *See* LIFERAFT (COLORADO SPRINGS, COLO.). 875

1064-377X *See* DATATRENDS REPORT ON DEC, THE. 1237

1064-3818 *See* AIR TRAFFIC CONTROL QUARTERLY. 8

1064-3826 *See* INTERNATIONAL DIRECTORY OF PRIMATOLOGY. 5586

1064-3834 *See* AMERICAN FASTENER JOURNAL. 1596

1064-3842 *See* ORL-HEAD AND NECK NURSING. 3890

1064-3850 *See* TEXAS JOB FINDER. 4209

1064-3877 *See* ATLANTA TRIBUNE (ROSWELL, GA.). 640

1064-3893 *See* MARKETING REPORT, THE. 932

1064-3907 *See* COMMUNICATIONS STANDARDS REVIEW. 829

1064-394X *See* ADMINISTRATIVE JUDICIARY NEWS AND JOURNAL, THE. 3138

1064-3958 *See* DUKE ENVIRONMENTAL LAW & POLICY FORUM. 2964

1064-4059 *See* QUEST : FOR A POSITIVE LIFESTYLE. 2796

1064-4083 *See* VIRGINIA FRUIT AND VEGETABLE MARKET INFORMATION. 2360

1064-4091 *See* CHEMUNG VALLEY REPORTER. 5714

1064-4121 *See* EATING AWARENESS & SELF ENHANCEMENT NEWSLETTER. 2597

1064-4148 *See* REPORT ON MEDICAL GUIDELINES & OUTCOMES RESEARCH. ANNOTATED DIRECTORY OF MEDICAL PRACTICE GUIDELINES. 3633

1064-4156 *See* TRENCHLESS TECHNOLOGY. 5167

1064-4164 *See* OLD TOY SOLDIER. 2585

1064-4172 *See* DECLARATION (INDEPENDENCE, VA.), THE. 5758

1064-4199 *See* TARIFF NEWS. 5394

1064-4237 *See* HEALING (SACRAMENTO, CALIF.). 4777

1064-4261 *See* TOXIC CRUSADERS. 4867

1064-430X *See* BUSINESS AND INCENTIVE STRATEGIES. 756

1064-4318 *See* BRANDWEEK (NEW YORK, N.Y.). 756

1064-4326 *See* INTERPERSONAL COMPUTING AND TECHNOLOGY. 1191

1064-4342 *See* REGULATORY COMPLIANCE WATCH. 807

1064-4377 *See* GRANTS FOR WOMEN AND GIRLS. 4337

1064-4393 *See* ISSO NEWSLETTER, THE. 25

1064-4431 *See* INDEPENDENT NEWSPAPER FROM RUSSIA. 5759

1064-4458 *See* JACK ANDERSON CONFIDENTIAL (1992). 4478

1064-4466 *See* SALES & MARKETING ONE HUNDRED NEWSLETTER. 936

1064-4482 *See* COSMEP NEWSLETTER (1981). 4813

1064-4490 *See* CROSS POINT. 4951

1064-4512 *See* SEATTLE'S CHILD. 2286

1064-4520 *See* VIEWFINDER (LEWISTON, MAINE). 1143

1064-4539 *See* DELAVAN ENTERPRISE (1992), THE. 5767

1064-4555 *See* AUDACITY (NEW YORK, N.Y.). 1547

1064-4563 *See* PHYSICIAN COMPENSATION AND PRODUCTION SURVEY. 3627

1064-4571 *See* COST SURVEY (1992). 3778

1064-4598 *See* BUSINESS OWNER (NEWPORT BEACH, CALIF.). 651

1064-4601 *See* CHEMICAL INFORMATION ALERT. 968

1064-461X *See* SOUTH CAROLINA EMPLOYMENT LAW LETTER. 3154

1064-4628 *See* PACE BUYER'S GUIDES. DOMESTIC & FOREIGN TRUCK, VAN, 4X4 PRICES, NEW & USED. 5422

1064-4636 *See* SRDS MEDIA & MARKET PLANNER. HEALTHCARE MARKETS. 766

1064-4644 *See* CHATHAM COURIER, THE ROUGH NOTES, THE. 5714

1064-4660 *See* PAIS INTERNATIONAL. 1511

1064-4679 *See* CONGRESSIONAL MASTERFILE 2. 2955

1064-4709 *See* TRANSACTIONS OF THE ACADEMY OF INSURANCE MEDICINE: 1992, VOLUME LXXVI. 2894

1064-4725 *See* EUROPEAN MICROBIOLOGY. 562

1064-4733 *See* PUBLICITY DIRECTORY FOR THE DESIGN, ENGINEERING, AND BUILDING INDUSTRIES, THE. 625

1064-4741 *See* PLANT'S REVIEW OF BOOKS. 4831

1064-475X *See* BUSINESS THEATER. 5362

1064-4768 *See* VIRGINIA ACQUACULTURE MARKET NEWS REPORT. 2315

1064-4776 *See* LESBIAN CONTRADICTION. 2795

1064-4784 *See* DESOTO TIMES (1981). 5700

1064-4806 *See* GRAYS HARBOR BEACON. 5761

1064-4814 *See* NATIONAL FIRE & ARSON REPORT, THE. 3170

1064-4822 *See* HAMMER & DOLLY. 5416

1064-4830 *See* NORTH CAROLINA BEACON. 5724

1064-4849 *See* CHILD HEALTH ALERT. 4771

1064-4857 *See* RESEARCH IN GLOBAL STRATEGIC MANAGEMENT. 884

1064-489X *See* WORKING IT OUT. 1719

1064-4903 *See* CONNECTICUT EMPLOYMENT LAW LETTER. 3145

1064-4911 *See* NONPROFIT MARKETING REPORT. 934

1064-492X *See* BIKE (MIDDLETOWN, R.I.), THE. 4887

1064-4938 *See* RECYCLING SOURCEBOOK. 2241

1064-4954 *See* COHOCTON JOURNAL, THE. 2613

1064-4962 *See* ASSERTIVE UTILIZATION MANAGEMENT REPORT, THE. 3553

1064-4970 *See* EARTH BOUND. 3462

1064-5004 *See* REAL TIME GRAPHICS. 1235

1064-5012 *See* WIDENER JOURNAL OF PUBLIC LAW. 3075

1064-5020 *See* EMF, STUDIES IN EARLY MODERN FRANCE. 2686

1064-5055 *See* FAX-STAT ON DRUGS. 4305

1064-5063 *See* VIEWPOINTS (ATLANTA, GA.). 5069

1064-5071 *See* VIOLENT KIN!. 3178

1064-5101 *See* TOPICS IN VETERINARY MEDICINE. 5523

1064-5128 *See* MEANS SITE WORK & LANDSCAPE COST DATA. 621

1064-5136 *See* CRISIS INTERVENTION AND TIME-LIMITED TREATMENT. 5281

1064-5144 *See* BIBLIOGRAPHY OF NATIVE NORTH AMERICANS ON DISC. 410

1064-5152 *See* SOUTH FLORIDA CONTINUING EDUCATION NEWS. 1802

1064-5160 See PHASE EQUILIBRIA DIAGRAMS (ANNUAL). 2593

1064-5179 See PHASE EQUILIBRIA DIAGRAMS (FINAL COMPILATION). 2593

1064-5187 *See* FROMMER'S COMPREHENSIVE TRAVEL GUIDE. SEATTLE & PORTLAND. 5476

1064-5195 *See* FROMMER'S COMPREHENSIVE TRAVEL GUIDE. LAS VEGAS. 5476

1064-5209 *See* FROMMER'S COMPREHENSIVE TRAVEL GUIDE. SANTA FE, TAOS & ALBUQUERQUE. 5476

1064-5225 See FROMMER'S COMPREHENSIVE TRAVEL GUIDE. LISBON, MADRID & THE COSTA DEL SOL. 5476

1064-5233 See FROMMER'S COMPREHENSIVE TRAVEL GUIDE. JAPAN. 5476

1064-5241 See FROMMER'S COMPREHENSIVE TRAVEL GUIDE. RIO. 5476

1064-525X See FROMMER'S COMPREHENSIVE TRAVEL GUIDE. ATLANTIC CITY & CAPE MAY. 5475

1064-5268 See FROMMER'S COMPREHENSIVE TRAVEL GUIDE. PORTUGAL. 5476

1064-5276 See FROMMER'S COMPREHENSIVE TRAVEL GUIDE. NEW YORK STATE. 5476

1064-5284 See FROMMER'S COMPREHENSIVE TRAVEL GUIDE. MONTREAL & QUEBEC CITY. 5476

1064-5306 See GUIDE TO THE ATLANTA UNIVERSITY CENTER AND ATLANTA, THE. 1827

1064-5314 See ISO 9000 REGISTERED COMPANY DIRECTORY, UNITED STATES / COMPILED BY QUALITY SYSTEMS UPDATE. 684

1064-5349 See KEY TO ROUTING NUMBERS. 795

1064-5365 See BIG PICTURE (ALEXANDRIA, VA.), THE. 892

1064-5373 See UTILITY FORECASTER, THE. 4762

1064-5381 See UMI ABI/INFORM--BUSINESS PERIODICALS ONDISC. 734

1064-5403 See PROCEEDINGS OF THE ASSOCIATION FOR EDUCATION IN JOURNALISM AND MASS COMMUNICATION SOUTHEAST COLLOQUIUM. 2923

1064-5411 See MUSICIAN MAGAZINE SPECIAL EDITION SERIES. 4137

1064-542X See FAMILY ENTERTAINMENT CENTER. 4861

1064-5438 See ETHICS ROUNDTABLE. 2250

1064-5446 See SLIDE ATLAS OF OPHTHALMIC LASER SURGERY. 3879

1064-5454 See MANAGED CARE QUALITY. 1617

1064-5462 See ARTIFICIAL LIFE. 5086

1064-5470 See JOURNAL SUBSCRIPTION CATALOG / THE ASSOCIATION OF AMERICAN UNIVERSITY PRESSES. 4821

1064-5489 See BLOUNT COUNTY HISTORICAL SOCIETY. 2723

1064-5500 See SRDS MEDIA & MARKET PLANNER. ARCHITECTURAL & CONSTRUCTION MARKETS. 628

1064-5527 See LAFAYETTE COUNTY HERITAGE NEWS. 2457

1064-5543 See CALL CENTER MAGAZINE. 1151

1064-556X See LATIN MASS, THE. 5031

1064-5586 See MILLENNIUM FILM JOURNAL. 4074

1064-5594 See REPORT / CUCURBIT GENETICS COOPERATIVE. 184

1064-5608 See MAHD BULLETIN. 3229

1064-5616 See SBORNIK. MATHEMATICS. 3532

1064-5624 See DOKLADY. MATHEMATICS. 3504

1064-5632 See IZVESTIYA. MATHEMATICS. 3511

1064-5640 See UNOFFICIAL GUIDE TO LAS VEGAS, THE. 5498

1064-5675 See MEMBER NEWS / MINNESOTA HISTORICAL SOCIETY. 2746

1064-5683 See INDUSTRY ENGINEER. 1978

1064-5691 See VIRGINIA (BERRYVILLE, VA.). 2765

1064-573X See SPORTS ADVANTAGE. 4922

1064-5748 See SRDS ... TRADESHOW CATALOG, THE. 766

1064-5756 See BRANDADVANTAGE (WILMETTE, ILL.). 1293

1064-5764 See MEDIASCOPE. CHICAGO MARKET & MEDIA PLANNER. 762

1064-5772 See MEDIASCOPE. SOUTHERN CALIFORNIA MARKET & MEDIA PLANNER. 762

1064-587X See RADIO INK. 1137

1064-5896 See BUILDING SYSTEMS BUILDER. 605

1064-5896 See BUILDING SYSTEMS BUILDER. 605

1064-590X See FOOD AND DRUG LAW JOURNAL. 2971

1064-5918 See WEEKLY BULLETIN - CALIFORNIA. STATE BANKING DEPT. 816

1064-5934 See EMERGENCY MEDICAL UPDATE. 3724

1064-5942 See NEW JERSEY ECONOMIC INDICATORS (1976). 1536

1064-5950 See LESBIAN AND GAY STUDIES NEWSLETTER : LGSN. 2795

1064-5969 See SLIDE ATLAS OF CURRENT CARDIOLOGY. 3710

1064-5977 See SWEET B'S PAD. 1070

1064-5993 See WINDOWS & DOS USER'S GUIDE. 1207

1064-6000 See ADVANCES IN STRUCTURAL BIOLOGY. 479

1064-6027 See FLASHY BUT CHEAP. 1233

1064-6043 See HARRISONBURG-ROCKINGHAM HISTORICAL SOCIETY NEWSLETTER. 2736

1064-6051 See WRITING ON THE EDGE. 3455

1064-6078 See NAHE (WESTWOOD, MASS.). 4792

1064-6094 See TURKEY CALL. 4879

1064-6108 See ARC NEWS (REDLANDS, CALIF.). 1284

1064-6116 See SCENE ENTERTAINMENT WEEKLY. 330

1064-6124 See BROADCASTING ABROAD. 1128

1064-6132 See MULLENS ADVOCATE, THE. 5764

1064-6140 See WASTE MINIMIZATION UPDATE. 2246

1064-6159 See GEORGIA PTA TODAY. 1748

1064-6167 See FAMILY LIFE MATTERS. 2279

1064-6175 See HOWARD JOURNAL OF COMMUNICATIONS, THE. 1112

1064-6183 See DANCE PAGES MAGAZINE. 1312

1064-6280 See DEALERSCOPE MERCHANDISING GOLDBOOK. 2811

1064-6302 See FEMME FATALE. 4861

1064-6310 See VALUE LINE EARNINGS FORECASTS. 717

1064-6329 See FOOD LABELING NEWS. 2338

1064-6337 See PORTABLE MBA EXECUTIVE SERVICE, THE. 704

1064-6345 See INTERNATIONAL JOURNAL OF FLEXIBLE AUTOMATION AND INTEGRATED MANUFACTURING. 3481

1064-637X See RUSSIA AND COMMONWEALTH BUSINESS LAW REPORT. 3103

1064-6418 See TWINE LINE : OHIO SEA GRANT PROGRAM NEWSLETTER. 2315

1064-6434 See HORIZONS (GAMBRILLS, MD.). 4388

1064-6442 See MIAMI HURRICANE, THE. 5650

1064-6469 See WEED PRESS. 5641

1064-6477 See MOUNT SHASTA HERALD. 5637

1064-6493 See NEWS AND ISSUES (NEW YORK, N.Y.). 5298

1064-6507 See BOICE LYDELL'S SPORT KARATE INTERNATIONAL. 4887

1064-6531 See DELAY LETTER, THE. 923

1064-6558 See FLORIDA GROWER'S ORNAMENTAL OUTLOOK. 87

1064-6590 See PHYSICAL THERAPY FORUM (KING OF PRUSSIA, PA. 1994). 4381

8750-0968 See PHYSICAL THERAPY FORUM (KING OF PRUSSIA, PA. 1994). 4381

1064-6620 See ARTSOURCE (RENAISSANCE, CALIF.). 315

1064-6639 See MULTIMEDIA WEEK. 1118

1064-6647 See JOURNAL OF ACTUARIAL PRACTICE. 2885

1064-6655 See JOURNAL OF OROFACIAL PAIN. 3837

1064-6663 See ELEMENTA (YVERDON, SWITZERLAND). 3278

1064-6671 See SPE DRILLING AND COMPLETIONS. 4278

1064-668X See SPE PRODUCTION AND FACILITIES. 4279

1064-6698 See LIPPINCOTT'S ORAL AND MAXILLOFACIAL SURGERY. 1329

1064-6701 See SUMMER JOBS (PRINCETON, N.J.). 4209

1064-671X See BRAIN, MIND & COMMON SENSE. 4578

1064-6728 See HEALTH & FITNESS TRIAD. 2598

1064-6736 See PAGEMAKER IN-DEPTH (1992). 1198

1064-6795 See GOVERNMENT CONTRACTS & SUBCONTRACT LEADS DIRECTORY. 4651

1064-6809 See CONGRESSIONAL QUARTERLY'S POLITICS IN AMERICA. 4469

1064-6833 See INDEPENDENT TELEVISION. 1133

1064-6841 See INSIDER'S GUIDE TO PERSONAL WELLNESS. 2598

1064-685X See MENTAL HEALTH-HUMAN RESOURCES CONFERENCE GUIDE. 3616

1064-6868 See V.P.I.'S IMPRINTABLES TODAY. 4570

1064-6876 See LAKE OCONEE FREE PRESS, THE. 5654

1064-6892 See HOCKEY (BLOOMINGTON, MINN.). 4898

1064-6892 See HOCKEY, ART OF THE STATE. 4898

1064-6906 See ISLAND HOME. 301

1064-6914 See SOUTHWEST CONTRACTOR (PHOENIX, ARIZ.). 628

1064-6957 See CAPITOL CURRENTS. 4637

1064-6973 See NEWS FOR ENTREPRENEURIAL MOTHERS. 699

1064-6981 See ACCENT (MARLBORO, MASS.). 2254

1064-699X See BIOMEDICAL LIBRARY ACQUISITIONS BULLETIN [COMPUTER FILE]. 3196

1064-7007 See COMPUTER PARTNER LEADS. 1177

1064-7015 See SCIENCE IS ELEMENTARY. 5152

1064-7023 See JOURNAL OF EMOTIONAL AND BEHAVIORAL PROBLEMS. 4596

1064-7112 See AVC PRESENTATION FOR THE VISUAL COMMUNICATOR. 641

1064-7120 See READY, SET, GO! IN-DEPTH (1992). 4569

1064-7139 See AMERICAN HARPOON, THE. 2527

1064-7147 See DEFENSE ORGANIZATION SERVICE. 4042

1064-7155 See HBJ MILLER ACCOUNTANTS' LEGAL LIABILILTY. 744

1064-7163 See HBJ MILLER COMPREHENSIVE LOCAL AUDIT GUIDE. 744

1064-7228 See PAUL KAGAN'S BOX OFFICE CHAMPIONS. PRODUCERS. 387

1064-7236 See PAUL KAGAN'S BOX OFFICE CHAMPIONS. ACTORS/ACTRESSES. 387

1064-7244 See PAUL KAGAN'S BOX OFFICE CHAMPIONS. SCREENWRITERS. 387

1064-7260 See JACKSONVILLE PATRIOT. 5631

1064-7309 See GARFIELD COUNTY NEWS (TROPIC, UTAH). 5756

1064-7317 See SPOKESMAN-REVIEW (1894), THE. 5762

1064-7325 See QUILTESSENCE (THIEF RIVER FALLS, MINN.). 5185

1064-7333 See OCCUPATIONAL BRIEFS / CGP. 4207

1064-7368 See DORSANEO'S TEXAS CODES AND RULES. CIVIL LITIGATION. 2964

1064-7406 See FACIAL PLASTIC SURGERY CLINICS OF NORTH AMERICA. 3965

1064-7414 See RIGHT GUIDE (ANN ARBOR, MICH.), THE. 4495

1064-7422 See ENVIRONMENT CONNECTIONS. 2165

1064-7430 See DIVERSITY & DIVISION. 5244

1064-7449 See INFECTIOUS DISEASES IN OBSTETRICS AND GYNECOLOGY. 3762

1064-7473 See AMERICAN SMALL FARM MAGAZINE. 58

1064-7481 See AMERICAN JOURNAL OF GERIATRIC PSYCHIATRY, THE. 3749

1064-749X *See* DIRECTORY OF THE WOOD PRODUCTS INDUSTRY (1992). **2400**

1064-7503 *See* PREVENTION'S QUICK AND HEALTHY LOW-FAT COOKING. **2353**

1064-7511 *See* NEW BOOKTALKER, THE. **4830**

1064-752X *See* JOURNAL OF COMMUNICATION AND TRANSFORMATIONAL MYTH. **2321**

1064-7538 *See* DANCE/MOVEMENT THERAPY ABSTRACTS. **1312**

1064-7546 *See* JOURNAL OF ENVIRONMENTAL POLYMER DEGRADATION. **981**

1064-7554 *See* JOURNAL OF MAMMALIAN EVOLUTION. **239**

1064-7562 *See* JOURNAL OF MATERIALS SYNTHESIS AND PROCESSING. **2104**

1064-7570 *See* JOURNAL OF NETWORK AND SYSTEMS MANAGEMENT. **1242**

1064-7589 *See* PAINTBOX (LOS ANGELES, CALIF.). **1067**

1064-7597 *See* INSIDE EDGE FOR MEN. **3995**

1064-7627 *See* FLOOR FOCUS. **615**

1064-7643 *See* FODOR'S NOVA SCOTIA, PRINCE EDWARD ISLAND, AND NEW BRUNSWICK. **5472**

1064-7651 *See* BIOMASS ENERGY DIRECTORY. **1934**

1064-7678 *See* EARNINGS GUIDE (NEW YORK, N.Y.). **897**

1064-7686 *See* PORT OF HOUSTON. **5389**

1064-7724 *See* PRACTITIONERS 5500 DESKBOOK. **3030**

1064-7732 *See* GUIDE TO TEXAS FRANCHISE TAX. **2976**

1064-7740 *See* ROCKBRIDGE DAILY PRESS. **5759**

1064-7945 *See* JIM GILREATH'S EXECUTIVE JOB SEARCH GAZETTE. **4205**

1064-7953 *See* FACE (MALIBU, CALIF.). **2533**

1064-7961 *See* PROFESSIONAL SCHOLAR. **2852**

1064-797X *See* PHARMACY CADENCE. **4323**

1064-7988 *See* QUALITY OF LIFE. **3867**

1064-7996 *See* FOR THE BRIDE BY DEMETRIOS (UNITED KINGDOM ED.). **2280**

1064-8003 *See* FACULTY GRANTS DIRECTORY. **1746**

1064-8011 *See* JOURNAL OF STRENGTH AND CONDITIONING RESEARCH. **4902**

1064-802X *See* U.S.-MEXICO FREE TRADE REPORTER. **856**

1064-8038 *See* BEST'S AGENTS GUIDE. LIFE-HEALTH. **2875**

1064-8046 *See* ERGONOMICS IN DESIGN. **1975**

1064-8062 *See* LITERARY IMAGE. **3406**

1064-8070 *See* COLOR LIFE. **2794**

1064-8119 *See* ASPEN'S NURSE EXECUTIVE NETWORK. **3851**

1064-8127 *See* BUSINESS & FINANCE CAREER DIRECTORY. **781**

1064-816X *See* ENVIRONMENTAL UPDATE (NEW YORK, N.Y.). **2170**

1064-8186 *See* LIGHT (CHICAGO, ILL.). **3405**

1064-8208 *See* ELECTROCHEMICAL SOCIETY INTERFACE, THE. **975**

1064-8224 *See* PARTY TIMES. **2352**

1064-8232 *See* TRUE NEWS (NEW YORK, N.Y.). **2548**

1064-8259 *See* NEW PROFESSIONAL, THE. **4207**

1064-8267 *See* NEW PROFESSIONAL SURVEY, THE. **4207**

1064-8275 *See* SIAM JOURNAL ON SCIENTIFIC COMPUTING. **3535**

1064-8380 *See* GENERAL PERIODICALS ONDISC (RESEARCH 1 ED.). **2496**

1064-8429 *See* WORLD WASTES. **2248**

1064-8488 See INDEPENDENT NEWSPAPER FROM RUSSIA. **5759**

1064-8496 *See* DIRECTORY OF HEALTH CARE GROUP PURCHASING ORGANIZATIONS. **3779**

1064-850X *See* PRODUCT SOS. **3630**

1064-8526 *See* PRODUCT DEVELOPMENT DIRECTORY. **3630**

1064-8534 *See* PRODUCT TESTING WITH CONSUMERS FOR RESEARCH GUIDANCE. **1622**

1064-8542 *See* APPLIED CLINICAL TRIALS. **4292**

1064-8577 *See* TOBACCO & HEALTH. **5373**

1064-8585 *See* WORKING TOGETHER (SEATTLE, WASH.). **5314**

1064-8623 *See* EXECUTIVE REPORT ON CUSTOMER SATISFACTION. **867**

1064-8658 *See* VISIONS MAGAZINE (BOSTON, MASS.). **4378**

1064-8674 *See* ISLAND SCENE. **2599**

1064-8682 *See* YOU! (AGOURA HILLS, CALIF.). **5038**

1064-8712 *See* NEUROSCIENCE NEWSLETTER (COLLEGE STATION, TEX.). **3842**

1064-8755 *See* CONNECTIONS (ASSOCIATION OF AMERICAN COLLEGES). **1091**

1064-8771 *See* ETHICS & PSYCHOTHERAPY. **2250**

1064-878X *See* SOFTWARE MANUFACTURING NEWS. **1203**

1064-8801 *See* POWER USER. **1199**

1064-881X *See* TABLETALK (LAKE MARY, FLA.). **5002**

1064-8844 *See* BEST OF HAIRDO IDEAS, THE. **402**

1064-8852 *See* GREEN ALTERNATIVES FOR HEALTH AND THE ENVIRONMENT. **2172**

1064-8860 *See* SOFT WATCH. **1209**

1064-8887 *See* RUSSIAN PHYSICS JOURNAL. **4420**

1064-895X *See* BUTLER COUNTY BANNER AND THE GREEN RIVER REPUBLICAN, THE. **5679**

1064-8968 *See* OKLAHOMA LIVING. **2542**

1064-8976 *See* HOMBRE INTERNACIONAL. **3995**

1064-8984 *See* AMERICA'S AGENDA. **1724**

1064-9018 *See* DIRECTORY OF PANAMANIAN BUSINESSES, ASSOCIATIONS AND ORGANIZATIONS IN THE UNITED STATES. **2731**

1064-9026 *See* QUE PASA PANAMA! NEWSLETTER. **2756**

1064-9034 *See* FROM INFORMATION TO EDUCATION. **1747**

1064-9042 *See* INTERNATIONAL EXPLORATION NEWSLETTER. **4261**

1064-9050 *See* FREELANCE WRITER'S NEWSLETTER (KNOXVILLE, TENN.). **2920**

1064-9093 *See* COUNTERTERRORISM & SECURITY REPORT. **4519**

1064-9239 *See* CHRISTIAN READER, THE. **4945**

1064-928X *See* ACCESS MEXICO. **920**

1064-9298 *See* BONNERS FERRY HERALD. **5656**

1064-931X *See* WHO'S WHO IN THE FISH INDUSTRY, CENTRAL & SOUTH AMERICA. **2316**

1064-9328 *See* 2 TO 22 DAYS IN ITALY. **5459**

1064-9352 *See* TERRORISM, SECOND SERIES. **4059**

1064-9395 *See* BETTY (MAMARONECK, N.Y.). **4857**

1064-9433 *See* TV BLUEPRINT. **1141**

1064-9476 *See* BOND COUNSEL. **892**

1064-9506 *See* BEHAVIOR AND SOCIAL ISSUES. **4576**

1064-9549 *See* MERIDIAN STAR (1914), THE. **5701**

1064-9557 *See* VARIETY AND DAILY VARIETY TELEVISION REVIEWS. **1142**

1064-9638 *See* GRAPHIC ARTS BULLETIN OF THE INSTITUTE OF PAPER SCIENCE AND TECHNOLOGY. **334**

1064-9654 *See* TOWN AND COUNTRY MAGAZINE PERSONAL NAME INDEX. **426**

1064-9670 *See* CALIFORNIA AGRICULTURAL EXPORTS ANNUAL BULLETIN AND STATISTICAL APPENDIX. **71**

1064-9689 *See* MRI CLINICS OF NORTH AMERICA. **3944**

1064-9697 *See* RUSSIAN OIL & GAS GUIDE. **4277**

1064-9700 *See* GI CANCER. **3817**

1064-9719 *See* CHIP'S CLOSET CLEANER. **2530**

1064-9743 *See* LEGACY (MONROEVILLE, ALA.). **2458**

1064-9751 *See* CHRISTO, EN. **4946**

1064-9778 *See* SPE COMPUTER APPLICATIONS. **4278**

1064-9786 *See* N.D.A. (SKOKIE, ILL.), THE. **4316**

1064-9832 *See* PACIFIC BASIN/ASEAN BUSINESS. **702**

1064-9859 *See* I/E (CHANDLER, ARIZ.). **4122**

1064-9867 *See* JOURNAL OF PASTORAL THEOLOGY. **4969**

1064-9913 *See* NATIONAL TRADE DATA BANK, THE. **847**

1064-993X *See* NEWSPAPER ABSTRACTS ONDISC. **5814**

1064-9948 *See* 100 DESIGNERS' FAVORITE ROOMS. **2898**

1064-9999 *See* KIN HUNTERS. **2456**

1065-0008 *See* RESPONSIVE PHILANTHROPY. **4339**

1065-0016 *See* HISTORIC MAURY. **2737**

1065-0024 *See* HISTORY NOTES / LAKE CHELAN HISTORICAL SOCIETY. **2453**

1065-0032 *See* FEDERAL MANAGER'S EDGE, THE. **868**

1065-0067 *See* FOODTALK (SAN FRANCISCO, CALIF.). **4191**

1065-0075 *See* POSITIVE ALTERNATIVES. **1513**

1065-0083 *See* FAYETTE REVIEW, THE. **5728**

1065-0091 *See* MSPB ALERT. **3012**

1065-0113 *See* ETHICS & POLICY. **2250**

1065-0148 *See* MICROTIMES (PLEASANT HILL, CALIF.). **1270**

1065-0156 *See* SOUTHWEST (FLAGSTAFF, AZ.). **3438**

1065-0164 *See* FULTON-HICKMAN GENEALOGICAL JOURNAL. **2449**

1065-0180 *See* AFRICAN-AMERICAN BUSINESS. **637**

1065-0210 *See* FIRELINE. **2290**

1065-0229 *See* MUSIC VIDEO MAGAZINE. **4135**

1065-0237 *See* BULLETIN - SEARCH FOR COMMON GROUND (ORGANIZATION). INITIATIVE FOR PEACE AND COOPERATION IN THE MIDDLE EAST. **4517**

1065-0245 *See* MINIATURE QUILTS. **5185**

1065-0253 *See* PEOPLE TRENDS. **881**

1065-0261 *See* PENNSYLVANIA BUSINESS AND TECHNOLOGY. **5137**

1065-027X *See* ORIGINAL WNC BUSINESS JOURNAL, THE. **701**

1065-0288 *See* MCCALL'S CROCHET PATTERNS. **5185**

1065-0296 *See* COLLEGIATE TRENDS (RIDGEWOOD, N.J.). **1817**

1065-0342 *See* BORDERLANDS (AUSTIN, TEX.). **3460**

1065-0350 *See* INDIANA JOURNAL OF HISPANIC LITERATURES. **3396**

1065-0369 *See* COLLEGE MARKETING ANNUAL. **1816**

1065-0377 *See* LIMBAUGH LETTER, THE. **4481**

1065-0385 *See* $AVE OUR PLANET. **2161**

1065-0393 *See* INFORMATION MARKETPLACE DIRECTORY. **682**

1065-0415 *See* INTERCONNECTION TECHNOLOGY. **1189**

1065-0423 *See* PATENT INDEX. **4271**

1065-0431 *See* LITERATURE INDEX. **4263**

1065-044X *See* PATENT ABSTRACTS. PETROLEUM SUBSTITUTES. **1307**

1065-0458 *See* PATENT ABSTRACTS. PETROLEUM PROCESSES. **1307**

1065-0466 *See* PATENT ABSTRACTS. PETROLEUM & SPECIALTY PRODUCTS. **1307**

1065-0474 *See* PATENT ABSTRACTS. CHEMICAL PRODUCTS. **1307**

1065-0482 *See* PATENT ABSTRACTS. AGRICULTURALS. **1307**

1065-0490 *See* LITERATURE ABSTRACTS. HEALTH & ENVIRONMENT. **2184**

1065-0504 See LITERATURE ABSTRACTS. PETROLEUM SUBSTITUTES. 4284

1065-0512 See LITERATURE ABSTRACTS. PETROLEUM REFINING & PETROCHEMICALS. 4284

1065-0520 See LITERATURE ABSTRACTS. TRANSPORTATION & STORAGE. 4284

1065-0539 See LITERATURE ABSTRACTS. CATALYSTS & CATALYSIS. 4284

1065-0547 See LITERATURE & PATENT ABSTRACTS. OILFIELD CHEMICALS. 4284

1065-0555 See ADVANCED PACKAGING. 2034

1065-0571 See COMMON-SENSE GUIDE TO AMERICAN COLLEGES, THE. 1817

1065-061X See NEW YORK FAMILY PHYSICIAN. 3738

1065-0636 See DISPATCH CONGRESS NEWS. 2731

1065-0644 See TODAY LANCASTER. 5755

1065-0652 See NEWS FOR NETWORK USERS. 1243

1065-0660 See INFORMATION FOR NETWORK USERS. 1241

1065-0679 See HEALTH PLANNING AND ADMINISTRATION. 3659

1065-0687 See PERSONAL MEDICAL ADVISOR. 3626

1065-0695 See OKLAHOMA POLITICS. 4485

1065-0709 See PRISON LIFE. 3173

1065-0717 See CURRENT TECHNIQUES IN SURGERY. 3963

1065-0725 See MEDIGUIDE TO DEPRESSION IN PRIMARY CARE. 3614

1065-0733 See WOMAN'S LIFE (NEW YORK, N.Y. 1993). 5569

1065-0741 See CAMPUS-WIDE INFORMATION SYSTEMS. 1218

1065-075X See OCLC SYSTEMS AND SERVICES. 3238

1065-0768 See 1-2-3 SOFTWARE CONNECTION. 1283

1065-0776 See SOFTWARE CONNECTION, DOS. 1290

1065-0784 See WINDOWS SOFTWARE CONNECTION. 1292

1065-0792 See AUTO SOUND & SECURITY. 5405

1065-0806 See WESTERN RESOURCES WRAP-UP. 2208

1065-0865 See STEVE WILSON REPORT, THE. 3353

1065-0873 See YOUR ASSOCIATE IN SACRAMENTO FOR SPECIAL EDUCATION. 1887

1065-0881 See JENKS HEALTHCARE BUSINESS REPORT. 3786

1065-089X See HIGH YIELD SECURITIES JOURNAL. 900

1065-092X See ATRIUM GROUP ADVISORY, THE. 3192

1065-0962 See PENNSYLVANIA LAW JOURNAL (1992). 3025

1065-0970 See FEDERAL EMPLOYEES NEWS DIGEST. 4702

1065-0989 See TOPICS IN HEALTH INFORMATION MANAGEMENT. 4805

1065-1004 See BANKING LAW BRIEFS. 3085

1065-1012 See BISHOP REPORT, THE. 643

1065-1047 See BEHAVIOR AND SOCIAL ISSUES. 4576

1065-1055 See EUROPE 92 (PORT WASHINGTON, N.Y.). 2967

1065-1063 See REGULATORY ANALYST. MEDICAL WASTE. 3633

1065-108X See PUMPS AND SYSTEMS. 2127

1065-1098 See WORLDWIDE GOVERNMENT REPORT. 4695

1065-1101 See AT THE MUSEUM. 343

1065-111X See PCS, THE REGULATORY CHALLENGE. 1119

1065-1128 See PERRY HERALD (1912). 5720

1065-1136 See JOURNAL OF AVIATION/AEROSPACE EDUCATION & RESEARCH, THE. 26

1065-1144 See GREENWOOD LAKE AND WEST MILFORD NEWS. 5717

1065-1152 See MOJAVE DESERT NEWS, THE. 5637

1065-1179 See MUSIC LIBRARIAN. 4134

1065-1209 See WESTERLY SUN, THE. 5741

1065-1217 See SONOMA SEARCHER, THE. 2473

1065-1241 See CHRISTIAN SCIENCE SENTINEL (RADIO ED.). 2530

1065-125X See MONEY INCOME TAX HANDBOOK, THE. 4737

1065-1276 See 3-DIMENSIONAL ILLUSTRATORS AWARDS ANNUAL. 376

1065-1284 See PEDIATRIC REPORT'S CHILD HEALTH NEWSLETTER. 3909

1065-1292 See CAROLINA AGENT, THE. 2877

1065-1306 See NEW LEADERS, THE. 880

1065-1314 See PROFESSIONAL SKIER, THE. 4913

1065-1330 See GARMENT MANUFACTURERS INDEX. 1084

1065-1349 See INTERNATIONAL PERSPECTIVES IN SOFTWARE ENGINEERING. 1229

1065-1357 See TABER'S CYCLOPEDIC MEDICAL DICTIONARY. 3644

1065-1403 See HEALTH CARE STATE RANKINGS. 4778

1065-142X See FOOD IRRADIATION UPDATE. 2338

1065-1438 See JOURNAL OF MEDICAL SPEECH-LANGUAGE PATHOLOGY. 4390

1065-1462 See BROWARD TIMES, THE. 2257

1065-1470 See SUFFOLK COUNTY NEWS, THE. 5721

1065-1489 See PROCEDURAL SKILLS AND OFFICE TECHNOLOGY BULLETIN. 3791

1065-1497 See FOOD INSIGHT. 2337

1065-1500 See INTERNATIONAL EXAMINER (SEATTLE, WASH. 1973). 2654

1065-1519 See MOVEMENT THEATRE QUARTERLY. 5366

1065-1527 See IN GOOD TILTH. 94

1065-1535 See DESTINATION DISCOVERY. 2532

1065-1543 See ARTSPEAK (NEW YORK, N.Y.). 342

1065-1586 See INTERNATIONAL TRAVEL IMMUNIZATIONS. 3590

1065-1594 See PACIFIC COAST JOURNAL (CAMPBELL, CALIF.). 3421

1065-1632 See NORTHERN VIRGINIA SUN. 5759

1065-1640 See GMP HORIZONS. 1676

1065-1659 See PHILANTHROPIC TRENDS DIGEST, THE. 4338

1065-1667 See ALTERNATIVE PRESS (CLEVELAND, OHIO). 4099

1065-1675 See IFCO NEWS. 4964

1065-1713 See TEXTILE MANUFATURING. 5358

1065-1748 See GOLD COAST GAZETTE (SEA CLIFF, N.Y.). 5716

1065-1756 See COUNTRY FOLKS GROWER. 77

1065-1764 See TERROR, INC. 4866

1065-1799 See JOURNAL OF PHARMACEUTICAL CARE IN AIDS/HIV TREATMENT. 3674

1065-1802 See BICYCLE TRAVELER, THE. 4887

1065-1810 See HEALTH NEWS DIGEST (MARLBOROUGH, MASS.). 4780

1065-1829 See SCIENCE FICTION AGE (HERNDON, VA.). 3434

1065-1853 See JOURNAL OF FINANCIAL & STRATEGIC DECISIONS. 4734

1065-1861 See ALABAMA SCHOOL BOARDS. 1723

1065-187X See DIRECTORY OF SPARC-BASED HARDWARE PRODUCTS & COMPANINES. 1264

1065-1888 See NEW YORK BUSINESS ENVIRONMENT. 3115

1065-1896 See REGULATORY UPDATE (PHILADELPHIA, PA.). 3037

1065-1918 See HIP REPORT, THE. 4388

1065-1969 See POSITIVELY FOR KIDS. 2285

1065-1977 See TOTAL TRIATHLON ALMANAC, THE. 4926

1065-1993 See EH & S DIGEST. 2164

1065-2027 See GIS LAW. 2974

1065-2035 See NUTS & VOLTS MAGAZINE. 4413

1065-2043 See MEADOWLARK (EVANSTON, ILL.). 5618

1065-2078 See COMPUTER SCIENCE SYLLABUS. 1177

1065-2094 See TRENDS JOURNAL (RHINEBECK, N.Y.), THE. 1524

1065-2108 See NEWSLETTER OF THE GARDEN CONSERVANCY, THE. 2425

1065-2124 See SPINAL NETWORK'S NEW MOBILITY. 3975

1065-2140 See BUFFALO SPORTS NEWS, THE. 4888

1065-2167 See PATENT ABSTRACTS. POLYMERS. 1307

1065-2183 See ENR DIRECTORY OF CONTRACTORS. WEST REGION. 614

1065-2205 See ENR DIRECTORY OF CONTRACTORS. MIDWEST REGION. 614

1065-2213 See ENR DIRECTORY OF CONTRACTORS. SOUTH REGION. 614

1065-223X See BULLETIN FOR BIBLICAL RESEARCH. 5015

1065-2299 See CHART CONNECTION, THE. 370

1065-2302 See INTERNATIONAL SEARCH AND RESCUE TRADE ASSOCIATION (INSARTA). 5290

1065-2310 See INSIDER FORECLOSURE GUIDE. 4839

1065-2329 See NEWSLETTER / NORTH AMERICAN SOCIETY OF OCEANIC HISTORY. 4181

1065-2345 See STAR-DEMOCRAT (EASTON, MD.), THE. 5687

1065-2388 See CRITICAL REVIEWS IN MULTIPHASE SCIENCE AND TECHNOLOGY. 5097

1065-2396 See NELSON'S TECHRESOURCE. 909

1065-240X See TEX AND TUG NEWS. 1205

1065-2418 See PERIODONTAL CLINICAL INVESTIGATIONS : OFFICIAL PUBLICATION OF THE NORTHEASTERN SOCIETY OF PERIODONTISTS. 1333

1065-2426 See BEYOND BORDERS. 1655

1065-2442 See WRITTEN AND SPOKEN HINDI. 3334

1065-2450 See OFFICIAL CRUISE GUIDE. 5487

1065-2469 See INTEGRAL TRANSFORMS AND SPECIAL FUNCTIONS. 5114

1065-2477 See GASTROENTEROLOGIST (BOSTON, MASS.), THE. 3745

1065-2485 See PRIMARY SEARCH. 1796

1065-2493 See VIRGINIA MANUFACTURERS DIRECTORY. 3489

1065-2507 See MARYLAND MANUFACTURERS DIRECTORY (EVANSTON, ILL.). 3484

1065-2523 See BODY CONTOURING SURGERY. 3960

1065-2566 See ASPIRE INTERNATIONAL NEWSLETTER. 3553

1065-2590 See TECHJOURNAL (SANTA CLARA, CALIF.). 2493

1065-2655 See EASTSIDE PARENT. 2278

1065-268X See COUNTY NEIGHBORS (PUNXSUTAWNEY, PA.). 5735

1065-2698 See ASIMOV'S SCIENCE FICTION. 3364

1065-2701 See FESTIVAL MANAGEMENT & EVENT TOURISM. 5469

1065-271X See VIRTUAL REALITY MARKET PLACE. 1217

1065-2728 See VEGGIE LIFE. 2360

1065-2736 See INSIDE WORKERS' COMPENSATION. 1680

1065-2744 See JOURNAL OF THERMAL INSULATION AND BUILDING ENVELOPES. 618

1065-2760 See METHODS & TECHNIQUES FOR THE CLINICAL LABORATORY. 3616

1065-2787 See INDEX OF MAJORS AND GRADUATE DEGREES. 1830

1065-2817 See HOSPITAL LAW MANUAL BULLETIN. 3740

1065-2841 See FINANCIAL TIMES INDUSTRIAL COMPANIES. CHEMICALS. 1024

1065-285X See PONY EXPRESS (GAINESVILLE, FLA.). 4170

1065-2868 See RUSSIAN COMMONWEALTH BUSINESS LAW REPORT. 3103

1065-2876 See TODAY CEDAR HILL. 5755

1065-2884 See TIFTON GAZETTE (DAILY), THE. 5655

1065-2914 See VOICES (RENO, NEV.). 2796

1065-2922 See CROSSWORD CHALLENGE. 4859

1065-2930 See WORD SEARCH CHALLENGE. 4868

1065-2965 See MATHEMATICA IN EDUCATION. 1763

1065-2973 See NORTH CAROLINA GEOGRAPHER, THE. 2571

1065-2981 See SECRET GUIDE TO MUSIC AND OTHER GREAT STUFF YOU'RE UNLIKELY TO FIND ANYWHERE ELSE, THE. 4152

1065-299X See INTERACTIVE MEDIA BUSINESS. 1113

1065-3007 See TELECONFERENCING NEWS. 1166

1065-3023 See REGGAE REPORT. 4149

1065-3031 See PARAPSYCHOLOGY, NEW AGE, AND THE OCCULT. 4242

1065-304X See COLUMBIA DOCUMENTS OF ARCHITECTURE AND THEORY. 295

1065-3058 See HEALTH CARE ANALYSIS. 3581

1065-3066 See SELLING EDGE, THE. 710

1065-3074 See MOLECULAR AND CELLULAR DIFFERENTIATION. 465

1065-3090 See JOURNAL OF FLOW VISUALIZATION AND IMAGE PROCESSING. 2091

1065-3104 See BNA CALIFORNIA SAFETY & HEALTH REPORT. 4768

1065-3112 See 1650-1850 (NEW YORK, N.Y.). 4339

1065-3155 See HOSPICE SALARY & BENEFITS REPORT. 3783

1065-3171 See ORACLE MAGAZINE. 1198

1065-318X See ST. THOMAS LAW REVIEW. 3058

1065-3201 See COMPUTERS IN ENGINEERING. 1969

1065-3260 See SUPERMARKET SCOOP. 2359

1065-3287 See SACRAMENTO NEWS & REVIEW. 2544

1065-3341 See JOURNAL OF SAFE MANAGEMENT OF DISRUPTIVE AND ASSAULTIVE BEHAVIOR, THE. 3168

1065-3376 See GAME PLAYERS SEGA GUIDE. 4861

1065-3406 See CONTINUOUS JOURNEY. 864

1065-3414 See 5-STAR INVESTOR. 890

1065-3422 See NGV NEWS. 4266

1065-3457 See AMERICAN JOURNAL OF ADOPTION REFORM. 5271

1065-3473 See VANTAGE (WORCESTER, MASS.). 2895

1065-3481 See WINDOWS USER. 1207

1065-349X See STEM TO STERN (CLAYTON, CALIF.). 4183

1065-3562 See HISTORIC PRESERVATION NEWS. 2618

1065-3570 See ENVIRONMENTAL TRADE EVENT PREVIEW. 2170

1065-3600 See ZIMMERMAN CASH FLOW LETTER, THE. 817

1065-3619 See PYRAMID (BURKE, VA.). 804

1065-3627 See WINDOWS REPORT, THE. 1292

1065-3643 See PPC ACCOUNTING AND AUDITING UPDATE, THE. 749

1065-3651 See PALLET ENTERPRISE. 2403

1065-366X See TIGHTWAD GAZETTE. 2793

1065-3678 See LOW-INCOME HOUSING TAX CREDIT ADVISOR. 3004

1065-3694 See ANTIQUE & COLLECTORS REPRODUCTION NEWS. 248

1065-3740 See HARVEY COUNTY INDEPENDENT, THE. 5676

1065-3775 See AMERICAN FOOD AND AG EXPORTER. 2326

1065-3783 See SEMPER REFORMANDA. 4996

1065-3805 See WILLAPA HARBOR HERALD, THE. 5763

1065-383X See NEWSLETTER / AMERICAN ASSOCIATION OF PASTORAL COUNSELORS. 4981

1065-3848 See MINDFIELD (NEW YORK, N.Y.). 4604

1065-3872 See KIDSPRINT TIMES. 1804

1065-3880 See BUCKEYE INDEPENDENT, THE. 5629

1065-3929 See MACROMEDIA USER JOURNAL. 1115

1065-3937 See MANAGING EMPLOYEE HEALTH BENEFITS. 878

1065-397X See STROKE & DAGGER. 388

1065-4011 See WESTERN OBLATE STUDIES. 2766

1065-402X See SOAP OPERA BOOK, THE. 2546

1065-4038 See ALABAMA HEALTH CARE IN PERSPECTIVE. 4764

1065-4046 See ALASKA HEALTH CARE IN PERSPECTIVE. 4764

1065-4054 See ARIZONA HEALTH CARE IN PERSPECTIVE. 4767

1065-4062 See ARKANSAS HEALTH CARE IN PERSPECTIVE. 4767

1065-4070 See CALIFORNIA HEALTH CARE IN PERSPECTIVE. 4770

1065-4089 See COLORADO HEALTH CARE IN PERSPECTIVE. 4771

1065-4097 See CONNECTICUT HEALTH CARE IN PERSPECTIVE. 4772

1065-4100 See DELAWARE HEALTH CARE IN PERSPECTIVE. 4773

1065-4119 See FLORIDA HEALTH CARE IN PERSPECTIVE. 4775

1065-4127 See GEORGIA HEALTH CARE IN PERSPECTIVE. 4776

1065-4135 See HAWAII HEALTH CARE IN PERSPECTIVE. 4777

1065-4143 See IDAHO HEALTH CARE IN PERSPECTIVE. 4783

1065-4151 See ILLINOIS HEALTH CARE IN PERSPECTIVE. 4784

1065-416X See INDIANA HEALTH CARE IN PERSPECTIVE. 4784

1065-4178 See IOWA HEALTH CARE IN PERSPECTIVE. 4785

1065-4186 See KANSAS HEALTH CARE IN PERSPECTIVE. 4788

1065-4194 See KENTUCKY HEALTH CARE IN PERSPECTIVE. 4788

1065-4208 See LOUISIANA HEALTH CARE IN PERSPECTIVE. 4789

1065-4216 See MAINE HEALTH CARE IN PERSPECTIVE. 4789

1065-4224 See MARYLAND HEALTH CARE IN PERSPECTIVE. 4789

1065-4232 See MASSACHUSETTS HEALTH CARE IN PERSPECTIVE. 4789

1065-4240 See MICHIGAN HEALTH CARE IN PERSPECTIVE. 4791

1065-4259 See MINNESOTA HEALTH CARE IN PERSPECTIVE. 4791

1065-4267 See MISSISSIPPI HEALTH CARE IN PERSPECTIVE. 4791

1065-4275 See MISSOURI HEALTH CARE IN PERSPECTIVE. 4791

1065-4283 See MONTANA HEALTH CARE IN PERSPECTIVE. 4791

1065-4291 See NEBRASKA HEALTH CARE IN PERSPECTIVE. 4793

1065-4305 See NEVADA HEALTH CARE IN PERSPECTIVE. 4793

1065-4313 See NEW HAMPSHIRE HEAALTH CARE IN PERSPECTIVE. 4793

1065-4321 See NEW MEXICO HEALTH CARE IN PERSPECTIVE. 4793

1065-433X See NEW YORK HEALTH CARE IN PERSPECTIVE. 4793

1065-4348 See NORTH CAROLINA HEALTH CARE IN PERSPECTIVE. 4794

1065-4356 See NORTH DAKOTA HEALTH CARE IN PERSPECTIVE. 4794

1065-4364 See OHIO HEALTH CARE IN PERSPECTIVE. 4794

1065-4372 See OKLAHOMA HEALTH CARE IN PERSPECTIVE. 4794

1065-4380 See OREGON HEALTH CARE IN PERSPECTIVE. 4795

1065-4399 See PENNSYLVANIA HEALTH CARE IN PERSPECTIVE. 4795

1065-4402 See RHODE ISLAND HEALTH CARE IN PERSPECTIVE. 4800

1065-4410 See SOUTH CAROLINA HEALTH CARE IN PERSPECTIVE. 4803

1065-4429 See SOUTH DAKOTA HEALTH CARE IN PERSPECTIVE. 4803

1065-4437 See TENNESSEE HEALTH CARE IN PERSPECTIVE. 4804

1065-4445 See TEXAS HEALTH CARE IN PERSPECTIVE. 4805

1065-4453 See UTAH HEALTH CARE IN PERSPECTIVE. 4806

1065-4461 See VERMONT HEALTH CARE IN PERSPECTIVE. 4806

1065-447X See VIRGINIA HEALTH CARE IN PERSPECTIVE. 4806

1065-4488 See WASHINGTON HEALTH CARE IN PERSPECTIVE. 4807

1065-4496 See WEST VIRGINIA HEALTH CARE IN PERSPECTIVE. 4807

1065-450X See WISCONSIN HEALTH CARE IN PERSPECTIVE. 4807

1065-4518 See WYOMING HEALTH CARE IN PERSPECTIVE. 4808

1065-4526 See NEW JERSEY HEALTH CARE IN PERSPECTIVE. 4793

1065-4585 See FROMMER'S BUDGET TRAVEL GUIDE. WASHINGTON, D.C. ... ON $ ... A DAY. 5475

1065-4593 See FODOR'S ... BERLIN. 5470

1065-4607 See FODOR'S BUDAPEST. 5471

1065-4631 See FLY! (BALDWIN, N.Y.). 4118

1065-464X See ISSUES & OBSERVATIONS. 872

1065-4658 See JOB FINDER FOR HIGH TECH SILICON VALLEY. 4205

1065-4666 See DISCUSSIONS IN DIETETICS. 4190

1065-4682 See INSIDE TAE KWON DO. 4900

1065-4690 See JOURNAL OF CHICANA STUDIES. 2741

1065-4704 See CANCER PRACTICE. 3812

1065-4712 See CONTEMPORARY MUSIC FORUM. 4111

1065-4720 See HARRIS NORTH CAROLINA MANUFACTURERS DIRECTORY. 3480

1065-4747 See HARRIS SOUTH CAROLINA MANUFACTURERS DIRECTORY. 3480

1065-4755 See HARRIS GEORGIA MANUFACTURERS DIRECTORY. 3480

1065-4763 See SPALDING BOOK OF RULES AND ... SPORTS ALMANAC. 4920

1065-4844 See ESC! (DEKALB, ILL.). 3385

1065-4852 See EVANGELICAL MORMON OUTREACH QUARTERLY, THE. 4957

1065-4887 See DELAWARE GENEALOGIST, THE. 2445

1065-4895 See WINE NEWS (CORAL GABLES, FLA.), THE. 2372

1065-4917 See THEATRE SYMPOSIUM. 5371

1065-495X See YOUR CHICAGO EXPRESS. 2897

1065-4968 See BUILDING RESEARCH JOURNAL. 604

1065-500X See PHASE EQUILIBRIA DIAGRAMS (FINAL COMPILATION). 2593

1065-5034 See PHASE EQUILIBRIA DIAGRAMS (ANNUAL). 2593

1065-5050 See GALE GLOBAL ACCESS. ASSOCIATIONS. 5231

1065-5069 See FISHING VESSELS OF THE UNITED STATES. 2303

1065-5077 See PT (ALEXANDRIA, VA.). 4382

1065-5085 See ERS UPDATE (HONOLULU, HAWAII). 1668

1065-5093 See MORE FREE STUFF FOR KIDS. 1066

1065-5115 See EXECUTIVE SUMMARY OF CALIFORNIA EDUCATION. 1746

1065-5123 See IVHS JOURNAL. 5441

1065-5131 See JOURNAL OF ENHANCED HEAT TRANSFER: AN INTERNATIONAL JOURNAL OF THEORY AND APPLICATION IN HIGH-PERFORMANCE HEAT AND MASS TRANSFER. 4431

1065-514X See VLSI DESIGN (PHILADELPHIA, PA.). 1206

1065-5158 See IMPORTERS MANUAL USA. 839

1065-5166 See ALUMNI DIRECTORY / STOCKTON STATE COLLEGE. 1099

1065-5174 See INTERNATIONAL JOURNAL OF TRANSPORTATION POLICY. 5384

1065-5182 See TEACHERS IN FOCUS. 1787

1065-5190 See AT YOUR BEST. 2596

1065-5212 See BORSCHT (MINNEAPOLIS, MINN.). 316

1065-5247 See NEW NONWOVENS WORLD, THE. 5354

1065-5263 See FORT NORFOLK COURIER. 2734

1065-5301 See ALABAMA IN PERSPECTIVE. 5320

1065-531X See ALASKA IN PERSPECTIVE (LAWRENCE, KAN.). 5320

1065-5328 See ARIZONA IN PERSPECTIVE. 5322

1065-5336 See ARKANSAS IN PERSPECTIVE. 5322

1065-5344 See CALIFORNIA IN PERSPECTIVE. 5324

1065-5352 See COLORADO IN PERSPECTIVE. 5325

1065-5360 See CONNECTICUT IN PERSPECTIVE. 5325

1065-5379 See DELAWARE IN PERSPECTIVE. 5326

1065-5387 See FLORIDA IN PERSPECTIVE. 5327

1065-5395 See GEORGIA IN PERSPECTIVE. 5327

1065-5409 See HAWAII IN PERSPECTIVE. 5328

1065-5417 See IDAHO IN PERSPECTIVE. 5328

1065-5425 See ILLINOIS IN PERSPECTIVE. 5328

1065-5433 See INDIANA IN PERSPECTIVE. 5328

1065-5441 See IOWA IN PERSPECTIVE. 5329

1065-545X See KANSAS IN PERSPECTIVE. 5330

1065-5468 See KENTUCKY IN PERSPECTIVE. 5330

1065-5476 See LOUISIANA IN PERSPECTIVE. 5332

1065-5484 See MAINE IN PERSPECTIVE. 5332

1065-5492 See MARYLAND IN PERSPECTIVE. 5332

1065-5506 See MASSACHUSETTS IN PERSPECTIVE. 5332

1065-5514 See MICHIGAN IN PERSPECTIVE. 5333

1065-5522 See MINNESOTA IN PERSPECTIVE. 5333

1065-5530 See MISSISSIPPI IN PERSPECTIVE. 5333

1065-5549 See MISSOURI IN PERSPECTIVE (LAWRENCE, KAN.). 5333

1065-5557 See MONTANA IN PERSPECTIVE. 5333

1065-5565 See NEBRASKA IN PERSPECTIVE. 5334

1065-5573 See NEW JERSEY IN PERSPECTIVE. 5334

1065-5581 See NEW HAMPSHIRE IN PERSPECTIVE. 5334

1065-559X See NEVADA IN PERSPECTIVE. 5334

1065-5603 See NEW YORK IN PERSPECTIVE. 5334

1065-5611 See NORTH CAROLINA IN PERSPECTIVE. 5334

1065-562X See NORTH DAKOTA IN PERSPECTIVE (LAWRENCE, KAN.). 5334

1065-5638 See OHIO IN PERSPECTIVE. 5335

1065-5646 See OKLAHOMA IN PERSPECTIVE. 5335

1065-5654 See OREGON IN PERSPECTIVE. 5335

1065-5662 See PENNSYLVANIA IN PERSPECTIVE. 5336

1065-5670 See RHODE ISLAND IN PERSPECTIVE. 5337

1065-5689 See SOUTH CAROLINA IN PERSPECTIVE. 5338

1065-5697 See SOUTH DAKOTA IN PERSPECTIVE. 5338

1065-5700 See TENNESSEE IN PERSPECTIVE. 5345

1065-5719 See TEXAS IN PERSPECTIVE. 5345

1065-5727 See UTAH IN PERSPECTIVE. 5345

1065-5735 See VERMONT IN PERSPECTIVE. 5345

1065-5751 See WASHINGTON IN PERSPECTIVE. 5346

1065-576X See WEST VIRGINIA IN PERSPECTIVE. 5346

1065-5778 See WISCONSIN IN PERSPECTIVE. 5346

1065-5786 See WYOMING IN PERSPECTIVE. 5346

1065-5794 See NEW MEXICO IN PERSPECTIVE. 5334

1065-5824 See ADVANCES IN POWDER METALLURGY & PARTICULATE MATERIALS. 3997

1065-5832 See LINK (DURHAM, N.C.), THE. 5295

1065-5840 See JOURNAL OF NEOPLATONIC STUDIES, THE. 4350

1065-5859 See COLLECTIONS SERVICES NEWS. 3203

1065-5867 See PINK BOOK (MOUNTAIN VIEW, CALIF.), THE. 5185

1065-5875 See BUSINESS AND SOCIETY BRIEFING. 645

1065-5883 See WAZO WEUSI. 2275

1065-5905 See OZONE NEWS. 5212

1065-5913 See UNITED YOUTH DIGEST. 5006

1065-5921 See AGENT & MANAGER. 859

1065-5956 See F&S INDEX PLUS TEXT. INTERNATIONAL. 729

1065-5964 See F&S INDEX PLUS TEXT. UNITED STATES. 729

1065-5980 See SEED & CROPS INDUSTRY. 186

1065-6049 See GRADUATE FACULTY AND PROGRAMS IN POLITICAL SCIENCE. 4475

1065-6073 See BLOOD WEEKLY. 3770

1065-6081 See ISOLATION AND PURIFICATION. 978

1065-609X See RADIOACTIVE WASTE MANAGEMENT AND ENVIRONMENTAL RESTORATION. 2240

1065-6103 See WORKBOOK'S SINGLE IMAGE. 382

1065-6111 See MICROPRENEUR (NORTHWOOD, N.H.) 1269

1065-612X See BIOPEOPLE (SAN MATEO, CALIF.). 447

1065-6146 See SOFTWARE ECONOMICS LETTER. 1290

1065-6154 See WRITING IT RIGHT. 2926

1065-6162 See AIDS DIRECTORY, THE. 3663

1065-6189 See HP PALMTOP PAPER, THE. 1186

1065-6219 See JOURNAL OF RESEARCH ON CHRISTIAN EDUCATION. 4970

1065-6227 See EUROPEAN COMMUNITY BUSINESS LAW. SOURCEBOOK. 3100

1065-6235 See EUROPEAN COMMUNITY BUSINESS LAW. HANDBOOK. 3100

1065-6243 See CURRENT OPINION IN GENERAL SURGERY. 3963

1065-6251 See CURRENT OPINION IN HEMATOLOGY. 3771

1065-626X See CURRENT OPINION IN PERIODONTOLOGY. 1319

1065-6278 See CURRENT OPINION IN COSMETIC DENTISTRY. 1319

1065-6286 See SDB/PRIMES. 709

1065-6294 See BERLITZ TRAVELLER'S GUIDE BERLIN, THE. 5462

1065-6324 See MAP REPORT (KANKAKEE, ILL.), THE. 2582

1065-6340 See VEGETARIAN GOURMET. 2360

1065-6375 See FEDERAL LABORATORY CONSORTIUM HANDBOOK SERIES. 5104

1065-6383 See ARMS CONTROL DISCUSSION PAPERS. 4036

1065-6391 See CISSM PAPERS. 4518

1065-6405 See HELPING CHILDREN LEARN. 1750

1065-6413 See INSIGHTS & STRATEGIES. 791

1065-6421 See HUNGRY POET, THE. 3464

1065-643X See INTERNATIONAL TATTO ART. 5268

1065-6448 See HARVARD UNIVERSITY ART MUSEUMS BULLETIN. 351

1065-6456 See FINANCIAL OFFICER'S TAX & MANAGEMENT REPORT. 868

1065-6480 See UTILITY SPOTLIGHT. 1525

1065-6529 See PAYROLL CURRENTLY. 4740

1065-6537 See ERIC (PEABODY, MASS.). 1745

1065-6545 See PHYSICIAN'S MEDLINE PLUS. 3661

1065-6553 See MAGILL'S SURVEY OF CINEMA. 4074

1065-6561 See MAGLEV NEWS. 4444

1065-657X See COMPOST SCIENCE & UTILIZATION. 2226

1065-6588 See ENVIRONMENTAL SATELLITE DATA RESEARCH. 2169

1065-6596 See DRUGS OF CHOICE FROM THE MEDICAL LETTER. 4302

1065-660X See CHILTON'S CHASSIS ELECTRONIC SERVICE MANUAL. CHRYSLER. 5410

1065-6618 See CHILTON'S CHASSIS ELECTRONIC SERVICE MANUAL. FORD. 5410

1065-6626 See CHILTON'S HEAVY DUTY TRUCK SERVICE MANUAL. 5411

1065-6634 See CHILTON'S TRANSMISSION DIAGNOSTIC MANUAL. 5411

1065-6642 See PERFORMING ARTS HEALTH NEWS. 4795

1065-6650 See TIGER TRIBE. 5523

1065-6669 See INTERCHANGE (CARRBORO, N.C.). 5290

1065-6677 See EXPORT EN ESPANOL. 2811

1065-6685 See AUTO & TRUCK INTERNATIONAL. 5404

1065-6693 See AUTO & TRUCK INTERNATIONAL EN ESPANOL. 5404

1065-6707 See PACE BUYER'S GUIDES. FOREIGN AND JAPANESE CAR PRICES, NEW & USED. 5422

1065-6766 See CLINICAL NEUROSCIENCE (NEW YORK, N.Y.). 3830

1065-6774 See TQM IN HIGHER EDUCATION. 1850

1065-6782 See MAGNET NEWSLETTER, THE. 1804

1065-6790 See EAST/WEST BUSINESS & TRADE. 832

1065-6812 See ANABAPTIST TIMES, THE. 4934

1065-6839 See STATE CONSTITUTIONAL COMMENTARIES AND NOTES. 3058

1065-6855 See FUTURES INDUSTRY (WASHINGTON, D.C.). 1492

1065-6863 See CROSSROADS (SUNNYVALE, CALIF.). 4951

1065-6871 See TAP CHI NGI DAN. 2666

1065-688X See SERIES IN CHICANA CRITICAL ISSUES. 2760

1065-6898 See INSIDE MOTOROLA. 1157

1065-6901 See ED-TECH REVIEW. 1223

1065-691X See STAR TREK FEDERATION SCIENCE (TEACHER'S GUIDE). 5160

1065-6928 See STAR TREK FEDERATION SCIENCE (EXHIBIT GUIDE). 5160

1065-6944 See JOBS AVAILABLE (WESTERN ED.). 4205
1065-6952 See ENGINEERING AUTOMATION REPORT. 1972
1065-6960 See EXPLORING BOOKS. 3210
1065-6995 See CELL BIOLOGY INTERNATIONAL. 533
1065-7002 See CONTEMPORARY URBAN STUDIES. 2819
1065-7010 See TIMBER TIMES. 2405
1065-7029 See CRIME PREVENTION STUDIES. 3162
1065-7037 See ADAC REPORT. 4383
1065-707X See ENTREZ (BETHESDA, MD.). 3692
1065-7088 See GENERAL SURGERY & LAPAROSCOPY NEWS. 3965
1065-710X See BREATHE! (LA QUINTA, CALIF.). 4769
1065-7118 See EXECUTIVE PHARMACY REPORT. 4304
1065-7134 See BOTTOM TIME. 4887
1065-7142 See STEPHENS' OHIO PLASTICS DIRECTORY. 4460
1065-7150 See CHANTEH (ARLINGTON, VA.). 5242
1065-7177 See DATA PROCESSING MANAGER'S BULLETIN. 865
1065-7185 See OFFICE & BRANCH MANAGER'S BULLETIN. 880
1065-7207 See NCBA COOPERATIVE BUSINESS JOURNAL. 697
1065-7215 See CHRISTIAN PARENTING TODAY. 2278
1065-7223 See CONSUMER ELECTRONICS EDGE, THE. 2039
1065-7231 See HARRIS MARYLAND MANUFACTURERS DIRECTORY. 3480
1065-724X See RACZ' FINANCIAL DIRECTORY. 806
1065-7258 See JOURNAL OF FOOD LIPIDS. 2346
1065-7274 See BIOETHICS FORUM. 2249
1065-7282 See CALIFORNIA PHILANTHROPY REPORT. 4334
1065-7290 See SOFTAWARENESS (AUSTIN, TEX.). 1290
1065-7304 See JOURNAL OF RUSSIAN TECHNOLOGY. 5119
1065-7312 See ERNEST & YOUNG NEW YORK, NEW JERSEY, CONNECTICUT STATE TAX GUIDE, THE. 4721
1065-7320 See INSIDE VIEW (IRVING, TEX.). 3834
1065-7339 See GRADUATE STUDIES IN MATHEMATICS. 3507
1065-7355 See ADVANCED CEMENT-BASED MATERIALS. 598
1065-7371 See GEOMBINATORICS : [A MINI-JOURNAL OF OPEN PROBLEMS OF COMBINATORIAL AND DISCRETE GEOMETRY AND RELATED AREAS] / UNIVERSITY OF COLORADO AT COLORADO SPRINGS AND CENTER FOR EXCELLENCE IN MATHEMATICAL EDUCATION. 3506
1065-738X See TEAM LICENSING BUSINESS. 1628
1065-741X See MASTERING PEDIATRIC DENTISTRY. 1329
1065-7428 See LATIN AMERICAN LAW & BUSINESS REPORT. 3101
1065-7436 See ELECTRICAL DESIGN & MFG. 2044
1065-7444 See LMA BUSINESSLETTER, THE. 215
1065-7452 See DIGITAL NEWS & REVIEW. 1246
1065-7460 See AUSTIN DAILY RECORD. 2938
1065-7509 See BIOCHEMISTRY & BIOPHYSICS CITATION INDEX. 481
1065-7525 See MENTAL HEALTH RAP. 5296
1065-7533 See ASTRO CASTER. 390
1065-7541 See RADIATION ONCOLOGY INVESTIGATIONS. 3823
1065-755X See JOURNAL OF CREATIVE WRITING AND BIBLIOTHERAPY, THE. 2921
1065-7568 See JOURNAL OF ENVIRONMENTAL STATISTICS. 2176

1065-7576 See LAB LAW REPORTER. 2993
1065-7584 See ASTRO AGENTS. 389
1065-7622 See AMERICAN CITIZENS REVIEW. 2527
1065-7630 See CURRENT DRUG THERAPY. 4298
1065-7649 See SPORT RIDER. 4921
1065-7657 See MULTILINGUAL COMPUTING. 1196
1065-7665 See STUDIES OF VACUUM ULTRAVIOLET AND X-RAY PROCESSES. 4442
1065-7703 See SELECTED NEW ACQUISITIONS / CALIFORNIA ACADEMY OF SCIENCES, LIBRARY. 3248
1065-7711 See ISRAEL STUDIES BULLETIN. 2768
1065-772X See FOOD PRODUCT DESIGN. 2339
1065-7738 See QUEST (GRAND RAPIDS, MICH.). 32
1065-7746 See DIAGNOSTIC NUTRITION NETWORK. 4189
1065-7754 See HOME SCHOOL ADVANTAGE. 1751
1065-7762 See PREFERRED STOCK (DENVER, COLO.). 2543
1065-7770 See ILLINOIS TECHNOLOGY RESOURCE GUIDE. 5112
1065-7789 See DOROTHY KAMM'S PORCELAIN COLLECTOR'S COMPANION. 2773
1065-7797 See MONMOUTH'S EARLY REPORT. 1691
1065-786X See GAS SHALES TECHNOLOGY REVIEW. 4258
1065-7886 See BRAZOSPORT FACTS, THE. 5747
1065-7894 See DAILY ARDMOREITE, THE. 5731
1065-7908 See SAN ANTONIO EXPRESS-NEWS. 5754
1065-7967 See NY FOOD LETTER, THE. 2351
1065-7975 See SOUTH CAROLINA ENVIRONMENTAL COMPLIANCE UPDATE. 2243
1065-7983 See FURIOUS FICTIONS. 3389
1065-8009 See INFORMATION SYSTEMS IN GROUP PRACTICE SURVEY. 3587
1065-8025 See ADHD REPORT, THE. 1874
1065-8033 See ALCHEMIST JOURNAL, THE. 960
1065-8041 See NEW YORK TECHNOLOGY RESOURCE GUIDE. 5133
1065-805X See OLLANTAY THEATER MAGAZINE. 5367
1065-8068 See AMERICAN INDIAN RELIGIONS. 4933
1065-8076 See BNA'S STATE ENVIRONMENT & SAFETY REGULATORY MONITORING REPORT. 2162
1065-8092 See INSPIRATION (PITTSBURGH, PA.). 4965
1065-8114 See CAPITAL IDEAS / FROM THE NATIONAL TAXPAYERS UNION FOUNDATION. 4716
1065-8130 See ARTS REACH. 315
1065-8157 See CUSTOM HOME PLANS. 612
1065-8165 See BANK FRAUD. 774
1065-8173 See OR REPORTS. 3971
1065-8181 See DRAGONS' QUEST, THE. 4241
1065-819X See HARVARD UNIVERSITY ART MUSEUMS REVIEW. 4088
1065-8203 See INDEX LOS ANGELES TIMES-ORANGE COUNTY SECTIONS. 1286
1065-822X See URBAN ISSUES IN SOCIAL WORK. 5313
1065-8238 See FEDERAL LABOR RELATIONS ... DESK BOOK. 1669
1065-8246 See COMPUTER VIRUS DEVELOPMENTS QUARTERLY. 1178
1065-8254 See WILLIAM AND MARY BILL OF RIGHTS JOURNAL, THE. 3075
1065-8262 See LUSOAMERICANO CALIFORNIA. 5636
1065-8270 See COLLEGE SPORTS (RUTHERFORD, N.J.). 4890
1065-8289 See HEALING WOMAN, THE. 5287
1065-8297 See HUMANISTIC MATHEMATICS NETWORK JOURNAL. 3508

1065-8300 See MULTIMEDIA BUSINESS REPORT. 1117
1065-8327 See OFFICIAL STRIP JOINT GUIDE : THE O.S.J.G, THE. 3996
1065-8335 See HANOVER REPORT, THE. 1608
1065-8343 See RANDOM REALITIES. 3427
1065-836X See POET'S GUILD. 3470
1065-8386 See CHRISTIAN HOME JOURNAL, THE. 4945
1065-8408 See DREISSENA POLYMORPHA INFORMATION REVIEW. 5582
1065-8416 See MENDOCINO COUNTY OUTLOOK. 5637
1065-8424 See GLOBAL TELECOM. 1156
1065-8432 See HOTELBUSINESS (HAUPPAUGE, N.Y.). 2806
1065-8459 See WHO'S WHO IN THE PEACE CORPS. 438
1065-8467 See SHERMAN'S COMPLETE GUIDE TO BUSINESS LOAN SOURCES. 811
1065-8475 See INSIDE OBJECTVISION. 1189
1065-8483 See JOURNAL OF APPLIED BIOMECHANICS. 3694
1065-8491 See P.S.I. GUIDE, PREFIX/SUFFIX IDENTIFICATION FOR BEARINGS. 3309
1065-8505 See INSIDE SPRINT CORP. 1157
1065-8521 See BLUE BOOK OF PRINTING AND GRAPHIC ARTS BUYERS. 377
1065-853X See HOUSTON REAL ESTATE FINANCE SOURCEBOOK. 4838
1065-8548 See ENVIRONMENTAL CHANGE. 2167
1065-8564 See WJCT MAGAZINE. 1143
1065-8580 See CRM PROCEEDINGS & LECTURE NOTES. 3502
1065-8599 See CRM MONOGRAPH SERIES / CENTRE DE RECHERCHES MATHEMATIQUES. 3502
1065-8602 See KLIATT (WELLESLEY, MASS.). 3221
1065-8610 See CORPORATE COMPUTING. 1241
1065-8645 See PC VISION. 1271
1065-8653 See DEFENSE CONVERSION. 4041
1065-8661 See GAS TRANSPORTATION REPORT. 4258
1065-867X See GAS DAILY'S GAS MARKETS WEEK. 4257
1065-8688 See AIRCRAFT VALUE NEWSLETTER. 9
1065-8696 See ELECTRIC UTILITY WEEK'S DEMAND-SIDE REPORT. 4761
1065-870X See INDEPENDENT POWER MARKETS QUARTERLY. 4761
1065-8769 See ANCILLARY PROFITS. 1597
1065-8785 See GHOST RIDER & BLAZE : SPIRITS OF VENGEANCE. 4862
1065-8815 See SHEPARD'S MICHIGAN EXPRESS CITATIONS. 3051
1065-8904 See SEAWAYS' SHIPS IN SCALE. 4183
1065-8947 See NEWSPAPERS ONLINE. 1927
1065-898X See INFORMATION SYSTEMS SECURITY. 1226
1065-9056 See PERIODICAL SOURCE INDEX (FORT WAYNE, IND.). 2467
1065-9072 See LETTER OF CREDIT LAW AND ANNOTATIONS. 3002
1065-9080 See WILLA / WOMEN IN LITERATURE AND LIFE ASSEMBLY. 3453
1065-9099 See PC PRESENTATIONS, PRODUCTIONS. 1271
1065-9110 See CROSSROADS (UNIVERSITY, MISS.). 2730
1065-9129 See POLITICAL RESEARCH QUARTERLY. 4489
1065-9137 See AUTOINTELLIGENCE NEW CAR DECISION MAKER. VOL. 1, SMALL CARS, SPORTY CARS, MID-SIZE SEDANS. 5405
1065-9145 See AUTOINTELLIGENCE NEW CAR DECISION MAKER. VOL. 2, LARGE, LUXURY & HIGH PERFORMANCE CARS, SPORT UTILITY VEHICLES, STATION WAGONS & COMPACT VANS. 5405
1065-9161 See SCHWANN SPECTRUM. 5318

1065-917X *See* NEW SCIENCE CENTERS SUPPORT PROGRAM INFORMATION SERVICE BULLETIN. 5132

1065-920X *See* EPA WATCH. 2171

1065-9234 *See* SUPERCROSS. 4083

1065-9250 *See* CATHAY. 3461

1065-9277 *See* OSHA CD-ROM. 2867

1065-9285 *See* LAW-RELATED CD-ROM UPDATE. 2996

1065-9293 *See* CONSULTING PSYCHOLOGY JOURNAL. 4582

1065-9366 *See* JOURNAL OF BOOK OF MORMON STUDIES, THE. 4968

1065-9374 *See* RUSSIAN AND EAST EUROPEAN STUDIES IN AESTHETICS AND THE PHILOSOPHY OF CULTURE. 363

1065-9382 *See* PRINCETON PAPERS IN NEAR EASTERN STUDIES. 2662

1065-9390 *See* MEALEY'S LITIGATION REPORTS. INTELLECTUAL PROPERTY. 3008

1065-9412 *See* INTERPHARMACY FORUM. 4309

1065-9447 *See* EDUCATORS' TECH EXCHANGE : AN EDUTECH PUBLICATION FOR THE ACADEMIC COMPUTING COMMUNITY. 1223

1065-9447 *See* CAMPUS TECH. 1730

1065-9471 *See* HUMAN BRAIN MAPPING. 3833

1065-9498 *See* INTERNAL MEDICINE BULLETIN. 3797

1065-9501 *See* SAGA INTERNATIONAL AVIATOR. 34

1065-951X *See* SAGA DIRECTORY OF INTERNATIONAL AVIATION PRODUCTS AND SERVICES. 34

1065-9528 *See* MONOGRAPHS IN LINGUISTICS AND THE PHILOSOPHY OF LANGUAGE. 3304

1065-9536 *See* OFFICIAL COMPUTER USER'S TRAVEL COMPANION (NORTH AMERICAN ED.). 1197

1065-9560 *See* OFFICIAL COMPUTER USER'S TRAVEL COMPANION (ASIAN ED.). 1197

1065-9579 *See* OFFICIAL COMPUTER USER'S TRAVEL COMPANION (EUROPEAN ED.). 1197

1065-9587 *See* OKLAHOMA COURT RULES AND PROCEDURE. FEDERAL. 3022

1065-9641 *See* WINDOWS SOURCES. 1207

1065-965X *See* MEDIA AND THE LAW (GREENWICH, CONN.). 1134

1065-9668 *See* JOURNAL OF BIOCHEMICAL ORGANIZATION. 489

1065-9722 *See* FUTURES CHARTS. 837

1065-982X *See* TB WEEKLY. 3716

1065-9889 *See* PROCEEDINGS OF THE SOCIETY OF MAGNETIC RESONANCE IN MEDICINE. 4445

1065-9900 *See* MICROQUEST REPORT. 5128

1065-9935 *See* CAREERS & COLLEGES. 4202

1065-9943 *See* FEDERAL EEO UPDATE. 2969

1065-996X *See* MEDICAL TECHNOLOGY STOCK LETTER. 906

1065-9986 *See* DATA SECURITY LETTER. 1181

1065-9994 *See* MARKETING PULSE, THE. 931

1066-0011 *See* TONER TECHNOLOGY MONTHLY. 4214

1066-0062 *See* PITTSBURGH CITY PAPER. 2543

1066-0119 *See* GEORGIA COUNTY GOVERNMENT. 4650

1066-0127 *See* RUSSIA AND HER NEIGHBORS. 5217

1066-0151 *See* REPORT ON CORPORATE EDUCATIONAL SUPPORT. 1915

1066-016X *See* NUCLEAR SAFETY & CLEANUP REPORT. 2237

1066-0240 *See* MEANS BUILDING CONSTRUCTION COST DATA. 620

1066-0291 *See* GAZETTE (CEDAR RAPIDS, IOWA), THE. 5670

1066-033X *See* IEEE CONTROL SYSTEMS. 2059

1066-0348 *See* EMERGENCY SERVICES SOURCEBOOK. 4774

1066-0380 *See* BENCHMARKS (DENTON, TEX.). 1171

1066-0429 *See* QUARTERLY JOURNAL OF MUSIC TEACHING AND LEARNING, THE. 4148

1066-0437 *See* QUARTERLY JOURNAL OF MUSIC TEACHING AND LEARNING, THE. 4148

1066-0445 *See* FOUNDATION GIVING. 4336

1066-0453 *See* COUNTRY FEVER. 4112

1066-0569 *See* AGBIOTECH STOCK LETTER. 3685

1066-0585 *See* RABBINICS TODAY. 5052

1066-0607 *See* BEAN MARKET NEWS. 65

1066-0623 *See* ALUMINIUM INDUSTRY ABSTRACTS. 4025

1066-0658 *See* BIBLIOGRAPHIES AND INDEXES IN POPULAR CULTURE. 410

1066-0674 *See* PROFESSIONAL PUBLISHING UPDATE. 4818

1066-0704 *See* PHOTOGRAPHIC BUYERS GUIDE. 4374

1066-0739 *See* CAMPUS SAFETY JOURNAL. 3159

1066-0763 *See* MODAL ANALYSIS. 2122

1066-078X *See* FLIGHT TRAINING ACADEMIC ENHANCER. BOOK 2, INSTRUMENTS. 21

1066-0887 *See* NATIONAL DIRECTORY OF COMMUNITY NEWSPAPERS (1992). 5697

1066-0925 *See* HARMONIZED TARIFF SCHEDULE OF THE UNITED STATES. 4730

1066-0933 *See* COMPARATIVE STATISTICS OF INDUSTRIAL AND OFFICE REAL ESTATE MARKETS. 4836

1066-0941 *See* JOURNAL OF COLLEGE AND ADULT READING AND LEARNING. 1832

1066-1018 *See* NON-PROFIT LEGAL & TAX LETTER. 4739

1066-1085 *See* MSL LAW REVIEW. 3012

1066-1107 *See* AIDS ABSTRACTS (ATLANTA, GA.). 3654

1066-1115 *See* LOUISIANA ENVIRONMENTAL COMPLIANCE UPDATE. 3114

1066-1123 *See* OKLAHOMA EMPLOYMENT LAW LETTER. 3022

1066-1131 *See* ALABAMA ENVIRONMENTAL COMPLIANCE UPDATE. 3109

1066-114X *See* CA SELECTS: COMPOSITE MATERIALS (METALLIC). 1000

1066-1158 *See* CA SELECTS: COMPOSITE MATERIALS (CERAMIC). 1000

1066-1166 *See* CA SELECTS: ALUMINUM-LITHIUM & ALUMINUM-CERIUM ALLOYS. 997

1066-1174 *See* CA SELECTS: STRESS CORROSION - METALS. 1010

1066-1204 *See* VILLAGE CRIER (TOMS RIVER, N.J.), THE. 5712

1066-1263 *See* STS MISSION PROFILES : COMPLETE SPACE SHUTTLE MISSION COVERAGE. 37

1066-1271 *See* SMU LAW REVIEW. 3056

1066-1298 *See* SHEPARD'S WASHINGTON EXPRESS CITATIONS. 3055

1066-1344 *See* LATINO STUDIES JOURNAL. 2267

1066-1409 *See* PROCEEDINGS / EUROPEAN CONFERENCE ON DESIGN AUTOMATION AND THE EUROPEAN EVENT IN ASIC DESIGN. 1221

1066-1417 *See* SPECIAL EVENTS NEWS. 2358

1066-1425 *See* OPAC DIRECTORY. 1198

1066-145X *See* INTERNATIONAL GAMING & WAGERING BUSINESS. 4657

1066-1468 *See* JOURNAL OF CHILD-CARE ADMINISTRATION. 5291

1066-1506 *See* GEORGETOWN REVIEW (GEORGETOWN, KY.). 3390

1066-1514 *See* MUSIC INDEX ON CD-ROM, THE. 4134

1066-1530 *See* PIANO (PORT TOWNSEND, WASH.). 4146

1066-1778 *See* U.S. CORPORATIONS DOING BUSINESS ABROAD. 716

1066-1786 *See* HEALTH & MEDICAL YEAR BOOK. 3581

1066-1816 *See* SINO-U.S. TRADING ALMANAC. 851

1066-1972 *See* STANLEY & KILCULLEN'S FEDERAL INCOME TAX LAW. 3058

1066-2030 *See* SPOT RADIO. 1139

1066-2065 *See* PENINSULA GATEWAY, THE. 5761

1066-2103 *See* PATENT ABSTRACTS. ENVIRONMENT, TRANSPORT & STORAGE. 1307

1066-2138 *See* SCHWANN OPUS. 5318

1066-2154 *See* PICKWORLD IRVINE, CALIF. 1199

1066-2162 *See* NATIONAL DIRECTORY OF ORGANIC WHOLESALERS. 2350

1066-2197 *See* DEFINED PROVIDENCE. 3462

1066-2243 *See* INTERNET RESEARCH. 1242

1066-2251 *See* MARYLAND PROCUREMENT REPORT, THE. 4664

1066-2316 *See* AMERICAN JOURNAL OF CRIMINAL JUSTICE : AJCJ. 3156

1066-2367 *See* GETTING THE MOST FOR YOUR MEDICAL DOLLAR. 1297

1066-2375 *See* JMR ABSTRACTS. 2005

1066-2421 *See* BROWN'S BUSINESS REPORTER. 644

1066-2448 *See* BASEBALL QUARTERLY REVIEWS. 4886

1066-2553 *See* ENVIRONMENTAL COMPLIANCE (MADISON, CONN.). 3111

1066-2596 *See* BUSINESS LEGAL MATERIALS, RUSSIA. 2945

1066-260X *See* BREAKTHROUGH STRATEGIES. 2485

1066-2669 *See* WORKERS' COMP MANAGED CARE. 2896

1066-2707 *See* METEOROLOGICAL & GEOASTROPHYSICAL ABSTRACTS. 1363

1066-2731 *See* REFERENCE DATA FOR ENGINEERS : RADIO, ELECTRONICS, COMPUTER, AND COMMUNICATIONS. 2079

1066-274X *See* CD-ROM WORLD. 1276

1066-2758 *See* HUMAN RESOURCES FORECAST. 942

1066-2782 *See* BORN TO SHOP. NEW ENGLAND. 1293

1066-2790 *See* BORN TO SHOP. PARIS. 1293

1066-2847 *See* TEACHING TOLERANCE. 5264

1066-2863 *See* CINCINNATI JUDAICA REVIEW. 5047

1066-288X *See* CRITICAL MATRIX. 5554

1066-2898 *See* SUPER SNACK NEWS. 1070

1066-291X *See* HOOVER'S MASTERLIST OF MAJOR U.S. COMPANIES. 680

1066-2936 *See* UNDERSEA & HYPERBARIC MEDICINE. 3697

1066-2944 *See* VOICES (WASHINGTON, D.C.). 3870

1066-2952 *See* ONLY FOR KIDS MINI MAG. 1067

1066-2960 *See* ONE WOMAN'S OPINION. 5563

1066-2979 *See* FROM THE OLDE BOOKSHELF. 4828

1066-3002 *See* OIL DAILY'S LUBRICANTS WORLD, THE. 4269

1066-3053 *See* AFROTECH ENVIRONMENTALIST. 2159

1066-3312 *See* COUNTRY MUSIC CITY NEWS. 4112

1066-3355 *See* NORTHWEST ARKANSAS TIMES (FAYETTEVILLE, AR.). 5632

1066-3452 *See* ALTERNATIVE ORANGE, THE. 1089

1066-3479 *See* AL-FAJR : JERUSALEM PALESTINIAN WEEKLY. 2254

1066-3487 *See* FLORIDA TAX REVIEW. 4727

1066-3533 *See* PERSPECTIVES ON THE MEDICAL TRANSCRIPTION PROFESSION. 3626

1066-3584 *See* ANERA NEWSLETTER. 1918

1066-3614 *See* AWHONN'S CLINICAL ISSUES IN PERINATAL AND WOMEN'S HEALTH NURSING. 3757

1066-3622 *See* RADIOCHEMISTRY (NEW YORK, N.Y.). 990

1066-3630 *See* READERLY/WRITERLY TEXTS. 3351

1066-3649 *See* COLLECTOR'S SOURCE. 2772

1066-3657 *See* INTERNATIONAL REVIEW OF PSYCHIATRY (WASHINGTON, D.C.). 3927

1066-369X See RUSSIAN MATHEMATICS. 3532

1066-3703 See CODE OF FEDERAL REGULATIONS UPDATE. 21 CFR, DRUGS AND MEDICAL DEVICES. 4297

1066-3711 See PROCEEDINGS OF THE THEMATIC CONFERENCE ON REMOTE SENSING FOR MARINE AND COASTAL ENVIRONMENTS. 2180

1066-3746 See BIBLIOGRAPHIES AND INDEXES ON SPORTS HISTORY. 4856

1066-3754 See SOUTHERN BUSINESS REVIEW & FORECAST. 712

1066-3851 See SEMINARS FOR NURSE MANAGERS. 3869

1066-3894 See PACIFIC TELECOMMUNICATIONS REVIEW. 1119

1066-3959 See MASTER'S SEMINARY JOURNAL, THE. 4976

1066-3983 See STONE COUNTY LEADER (1956). 5632

1066-4033 See BRANSON'S COUNTRY REVIEW. 4105

1066-4068 See BLUES ACCESS. 4104

1066-4076 See AMERICAN ART THERAPY ASSOCIATION NEWSLETTER. 4572

1066-4106 See REMINERALIZE THE EARTH. 184

1066-4114 See CAPSULES AND COMMENTS IN ONCOLOGY NURSING. 3853

1066-4149 See MEDICINE (NEW YORK, N.Y. 1993). 3614

1066-4157 See JOURNAL OF CHEMICAL EDUCATION. SOFTWARE. D. 980

1066-4173 See ART MATERIALS TODAY. 339

1066-4181 See HOT ROD SWIMSUIT SPECIAL. 3995

1066-419X See INSIDE MOTOCROSS MAGAZINE. 4081

1066-4726 See DOLL WORLD (BERNE, IND.). 372

1066-4734 See CC PERFORMANCE CAR. 5409

1066-4807 See FAMILY JOURNAL (ALEXANDRIA, VA.), THE. 2279

1066-4815 See CAPSULES AND COMMENTS IN CRITICAL CARE NURSING. 3853

1066-4823 See VESTAL PRESS RESOURCE CATALOGUE, THE. 427

1066-4831 See BILYEU BLOOD LINES. 2439

1066-4858 See ZARUBEZNAA PERIODICESKAA PECAT NA RUSSKOM AZYKE. 2525

1066-4939 See FROMMER'S COMPREHENSIVE TRAVEL GUIDE. ACAPULCO, IXTAPA & TAXCO. 5475

1066-4947 See SIERRA LEONE REVIEW, THE. 2643

1066-4963 See SWINE HEALTH AND PRODUCTION. 222

1066-5005 See ADVANCES IN CLASSICAL TRAJECTORY METHODS. 1049

1066-5056 See DEMENTIA REVIEWS. 3924

1066-5099 See STEM CELLS (DAYTON, OHIO). 540

1066-5110 See PLAYBOY'S TWINS. 3996

1066-5234 See JOURNAL OF EUKARYOTIC MICROBIOLOGY, THE. 5587

1066-5277 See JOURNAL OF COMPUTATIONAL BIOLOGY. 461

1066-5285 See RUSSIAN CHEMICAL BULLETIN. 992

1066-5307 See MATHEMATICAL METHODS OF STATISTICS. 3519

1066-5315 See CHEMICAL HERITAGE. 968

1066-534X See I.V.U.N. NEWS. 3949

1066-5366 See PETERSON'S GUIDE TO PRIVATE SECONDARY SCHOOLS. 1773

1066-5404 See CLEARINGHOUSE BULLETIN / CARRYING CAPACITY NETWORK. 2163

1066-5455 See ABRASAX (CORPUS CHRISTI, TEX.). 4240

1066-5471 See FIRSTS (LOS ANGELES, CALIF.). 4821

1066-5498 See DATA BASE MANAGEMENT (WILWAUKEE, WIS.). 1253

1066-5501 See INDIAN COUNTRY TODAY. 5743

1066-5544 See BUREAU OF MINES INFORMATION CIRCULAR. 2135

1066-5544 See INFORMATION CIRCULAR - UNITED STATES. BUREAU OF MINES. 2140

1066-5552 See REPORT OF INVESTIGATIONS - UNITED STATES. BUREAU OF MINES. 2149

1066-5552 See REPORT OF INVESTIGATIONS - UNITED STATES. BUREAU OF MINES. 2149

1066-5595 See NATIONAL DIRECTORY OF LAW ENFORCEMENT ADMINISTRATORS, CORRECTIONAL INSTITUTIONS, AND RELATED GOVERNMENTAL AGENCIES. 3170

1066-5609 See NATIONAL DIRECTORY OF FIRE CHIEFS, RESCUE & EMERGENCY DEPARTMENTS. 2291

1066-5633 See INDEPENDENT SCHOLAR, THE. 1829

1066-5684 See EQUITY & EXCELLENCE IN EDUCATION. 1744

1066-5706 See MEN'S CONFIDENTIAL. 3995

1066-5730 See CA SELECTS: GEOCHEMISTRY. 1003

1066-5749 See LWML QUARTERLY ECHO. 4975

1066-5862 See FEDERAL REGISTER MONITOR, THE. 2970

1066-6001 See ENVIRONMENT WATCH. WESTERN EUROPE. 672

1066-6060 See RACER (TUSTIN, CALIF.). 4914

1066-6095 See DAILY WASHINGTON LAW REPORTER, THE. 2958

1066-6184 See NURSING DEPARTMENT COMPENSATION REPORT. 3864

1066-6257 See JUDO JOURNAL. 4902

1066-6273 See ALEXANDRIA PORT GAZETTE PACKET. 5758

1066-6281 See CLASSIC AMUSEMENTS. 2772

1066-6303 See IRS TECHNICAL ADVICE MEMORANDUMS AND IRS LETTER RULINGS. 4734

1066-6311 See HON VIET (GARDEN GROVE, CALIF.). 2263

1066-6346 See EVENTS USA. 4850

1066-6494 See ATD, N.A.D.A. OFFICIAL HEAVY DUTY TRUCK GUIDE. 5404

1066-677X See CLINICAL PRACTICE GUIDELINES. 3566

1066-6834 See .22 RIMFIRE. 4881

1066-6958 See VIEWCAMERA (SACRAMENTO, CALIF.). 4378

1066-7008 See DRUGS IN DEVELOPMENT. 4302

1066-7016 See INTERNATIONAL JOURNAL OF RADIATION HYGIENE. 4435

1066-7024 See MARKET LATIN AMERICA. 691

1066-7059 See ELIZABETHAN REVIEW, THE. 3384

1066-7083 See IMPRINTING BUSINESS. 1085

1066-7245 See COUNTRY SAMPLER'S WEST. 2899

1066-7253 See ACCESS ADVISOR. 1283

1066-7261 See FOXPRO ADVISOR. 1286

1066-7342 See COLORADO FIELD ORNITHOLOGISTS' JOURNAL. 5617

1066-7350 See FINANCE, INSURANCE & REAL ESTATE USA. 2880

1066-7385 See GREEN EGG. 4241

1066-7423 See TODAY'S COLLECTOR (IOLA, WIS.). 2778

1066-7458 See BETHEL JOURNAL-PRESS, THE. 5727

1066-7504 See DESIGN TECHNOLOGIES. 2097

1066-7512 See DAILY SENTINEL-STAR, THE. 5700

1066-7555 See INSIDE VISUAL BASIC FOR WINDOWS. 1287

1066-7598 See COMPUTER RETAIL WEEK. 1244

1066-7601 See WHO'S WHO ELECTRONICS BUYERS GUIDE (MIDWESTERN ED.). 2086

1066-761X See WHO'S WHO ELECTRONICS BUYERS GUIDE (NORTHEASTERN ED.). 2086

1066-7628 See WHO'S WHO ELECTRONICS BUYERS GUIDE (SOUTHEASTERN ED.). 2086

1066-7644 See WHO'S WHO ELECTRONICS BUYERS GUIDE (SOUTHWESTERN ED.). 2086

1066-7709 See GALE'S LITERARY INDEX. 3389

1066-7733 See NATIONAL TRIAL LAWYER (FLORIDA ED.). 3014

1066-7741 See RX CONSULTANT, THE. 4328

1066-7776 See OUT & ABOUT (NEW HAVEN, CONN.). 2795

1066-7792 See DISCOVERING AUTHORS. 3381

1066-7814 See CANADIAN JOURNAL OF APPLIED PHYSIOLOGY. 579

1066-7822 See INFO SECURITY NEWS. 1226

1066-7857 See MATERIALS TECHNOLOGY (NEW YORK, N.Y.). 2106

1066-7865 See JOURNAL OF CLINICAL RESEARCH AND DRUG DEVELOPMENT (1993). 4310

1066-789X See NEW FORTUNES. 801

1066-7903 See WEALTH RANKINGS. 719

1066-7911 See SMART ACCESS. 1255

1066-7970 See BEECHER CITY JOURNAL. 5658

1066-8071 See NEWS-DEMOCRAT & LEADER. 5682

1066-8098 See ROTOR & WING (1992). 34

1066-825X See MEDICAL CARE PRODUCTS. 3788

1066-8268 See VIBRATIONS (CLARENDON HILLS, ILL.). 4424

1066-8292 See AMERICAN CHESS JOURNAL (CAMBRIDGE, MASS.). 4856

1066-8322 See FRONTIERS IN HEADACHE RESEARCH. 3577

1066-8411 See BRIDGEPORT LAW REVIEW. 2943

1066-842X See STATE IRM ORGANIZATIONAL STRUCTURES. 4688

1066-8446 See MCCLAIN CO. OK HISTORICAL AND GENEALOGICAL SOCIETY QUARTERLY NEWSLETTER. 2459

1066-8489 See DISTRIBUTION (RADNOR, PA. 1992). 5381

1066-8527 See PROCESS SAFETY PROGRESS. 1028

1066-8586 See 'GBH (BOSTON, MASS.). 1132

1066-8608 See PROCEEDINGS OF THE ... ANNUAL CONFERENCE ON TAXATION HELD UNDER THE AUSPICES OF THE NATIONAL TAX ASSOCIATION-TAX INSTITUTE OF AMERICA. 4742

1066-8683 See COGENERATION AND COMPETITIVE POWER JOURNAL. 2039

1066-8691 See ASSOCIATION SOURCE. 640

1066-873X See MCGRAW-HILL'S FEDERAL TECHNOLOGY REPORT. 1618

1066-8764 See FEDERAL EQUAL OPPORTUNITY ... DESK BOOK. 4702

1066-8810 See VARIETY'S VIDEO DIRECTORY PLUS. 4377

1066-8845 See ANDREW SEYBOLD'S OUTLOOK ON MOBILE COMPUTING. 1170

1066-8888 See VLDB JOURNAL, THE. 1255

1066-8896 See FEDERAL SUPPORT FOR NONPROFITS. 4335

1066-8926 See COMMUNITY COLLEGE JOURNAL OF RESEARCH AND PRACTICE. 1817

1066-8934 See GALE DIRECTORY OF DATABASES. 1237

1066-8969 See INTERNATIONAL JOURNAL OF SURGICAL PATHOLOGY. 3895

1066-8977 See AMERICAN SOCIETY OF POST ANESTHESIA NURSES (ASPAN). 3851

1066-9078 See NEWS - HEALTHCARE INFORMATION AND MANAGEMENT SYSTEMS SOCIETY. 3790

1066-9175 See EARTH SUMMIT UPDATE. 2164

1066-9264 See CDA/WIESENBERGER MUTUAL FUNDS UPDATE. 894

1066-9353 See KAMAI FORUM. 5636

1066-937X See MENNINGER LETTER, THE. 3930

1066-940X See BLACK AUTHORS BOOKS IN PRINT. 4824

1066-9442 See DIABETES REVIEWS (ALEXANDRIA, VA.). 3728

1066-9477 See DEVELOPMENTAL POLICY STUDIES. 5326

1066-9493 See OPTIV (MCLEAN, VA.). 1198

1066-9507 See MINORITY & WOMEN DOCTORAL DIRECTORY. **1836**

1066-954X See ENVIRONMENT & DEVELOPMENT / APA, AMERICAN PLANNING ASSOCIATION. **2165**

1066-9574 See OFFICIAL POLICY RESOLUTIONS ADOPTED AT THE ANNUAL CONFERENCE OF MAYORS. **4671**

1066-9612 See RUSSIAN FIBER OPTICS AND TELECOMMUNICATIONS BUSINESS. **1163**

1066-9698 See DIRECTORY OF COMPUTER & SOFTWARE RETAILERS (TAMPA, FLA.). **1237**

1066-9701 See SHOPPING CENTER DIRECTORY. **1299**

1066-9736 See DIRECTORY OF BUYOUT FINANCING SOURCES. **788**

1066-9779 See DIRECTORY OF LEADING PRIVATE COMPANIES, INCLUDING CORPORATE AFFILIATIONS. **666**

1066-9795 See MASTER'S THESES DIRECTORIES. THE ARTS AND SOCIAL SCIENCES. **324**

1066-9817 See JOURNAL OF MANUAL & MANIPULATIVE THERAPY, THE. **3882**

1066-9868 See JOURNAL OF EAST-WEST BUSINESS. **686**

1066-9884 See PSYCHOANALYTIC ABSTRACTS. **4622**

1066-9973 See INTERNET WORLD'S ON INTERNET. **1242**

1066-999X See RUSSIAN LIFE. **2522**

1067-0068 See DECORATIVE ARTS PAINTING. **372**

1067-0165 See SUBSTANCE ABUSE FUNDING NEWS. **1349**

1067-0246 See MEALEY'S LITIGATION REPORTS. BREAST IMPLANTS. **3008**

1067-0432 See TREASURY AND RISK MANAGEMENT. **1524**

1067-0580 See COMMITTEE ON EAST ASIAN LIBRARIES DIRECTORY. **2613**

1067-0688 See MATHEMATICAL MODELLING AND SCIENTIFIC COMPUTING. **3519**

1067-0718 See AIDS TARGETED INFORMATION. **3664**

1067-0769 See WASHINGTON JOB SOURCE, THE. **4209**

1067-0777 See HILLARY CLINTON QUARTERLY, THE. **2534**

1067-0815 See DOCUMENT DELIVERY WORLD. **1183**

1067-084X See U.S. GEOLOGICAL SURVEY CIRCULAR. **1400**

1067-0904 See RENTAL PRODUCT NEWS (1992). **707**

1067-098X See DISABLED OUTDOORS MAGAZINE. **4387**

1067-1013 See E&P HEALTH, SAFETY AND ENVIRONMENT. **4255**

1067-1021 See GAS PROCESSING AND PIPELINING. **4257**

1067-103X See OFFSHORE TECHNOLOGY (TULSA, OKLA.). **4267**

1067-1048 See AIRPOWER (GRANADA HILLS, LOS ANGELES, CALIF.). **11**

1067-1064 See WOOD TECHNOLOGY. **2406**

1067-1072 See DIRECTORY OF COMPUTER & SOFTWARE RETAILERS (TAMPA, FLA.). **1237**

1067-1196 See BIOTECH DAILY. **3687**

1067-1269 See MEDICAL LITIGATION ALERT. **3008**

1067-1293 See SOFTWARE ENGINEERING STRATEGIES. **1290**

1067-1358 See MUTUAL FUND BUYER'S GUIDE. **908**

1067-1412 See TEXARKANA USA QUARTERLY (1987). **2474**

1067-1439 See TODAY'S ASTROLOGER. **390**

1067-1455 See FLORIDA SHIPPER MAGAZINE, THE. **5449**

1067-1463 See ARTS & CRAFTS RETAILER. **314**

1067-1498 See APARTMENT LETTER, THE. **772**

1067-1579 See CARD DECK ADVERTISING SOURCE. **757**

1067-1595 See INFO WORLD DIRECT. **1188**

1067-1633 See EATING DISORDERS REVIEW (CHICHESTER, ENGLAND). **4585**

1067-1684 See VISUAL SOCIOLOGY. **5265**

1067-1757 See SAVINGS & COMMUNITY BANKER. **810**

1067-1765 See CHATHAM RECORD, THE. **5723**

1067-1773 See CHATHAM NEWS (SILER CITY, N.C.), THE. **5723**

1067-1803 See COMMUNITY COLLEGE JOURNAL. **1817**

1067-182X See LIFESTYLE MARKET ANALYST, THE. **929**

1067-1862 See WEST ALLIS POST (1992), THE. **5772**

1067-1919 See JOURNAL OF UROLOGIC PATHOLOGY. **3991**

1067-1927 See WOUND REPAIR AND REGENERATION. **3651**

1067-1951 See FOOD HISTORY NEWS. **2337**

1067-1994 See TOPEKA CAPITAL-JOURNAL (TOPEKA, KAN. : MORNING ED.). **5678**

1067-2036 See LAPAROSCOPIC SURGERY UPDATE. **3604**

1067-2079 See LONG ISLAND UPDATE. **2537**

1067-2214 See HEALTH CARE REFORM WEEK. **3581**

1067-2222 See P FORM. **361**

1067-2249 See PIECEWORK (LOVELAND, COLO.). **374**

1067-2338 See ILLINOIS WORKERS' COMPENSATION LAW BULLETIN. **2980**

1067-2346 See OPHTHALMOLOGY RESIDENT, THE. **3878**

1067-2354 See NEW DENTIST (THOROFARE, N.J.), THE. **1330**

1067-2370 See HEM/ONC ANNALS. **3772**

1067-2400 See PENNSYLVANIA PERSONAL INJURY REPORTER. **3025**

1067-2427 See PERSONAL INJURY VERDICT REVIEWS. **3026**

1067-2516 See JOURNAL OF FOOT AND ANKLE SURGERY, THE. **3967**

1067-2583 See NATIONAL ENVIRONMENTAL JOURNAL, THE. **2178**

1067-2591 See SHEPARD'S TENNESSEE EXPRESS CITATIONS. **3054**

1067-2818 See BIOTECH BUYERS' GUIDE. **3687**

1067-2834 See BOSTONIA (BOSTON, MASS. 1986). **3368**

1067-2850 See ITAA PROCEEDINGS. NATIONAL MEETING. **5353**

1067-2982 See DOING BUSINESS IN THE RUSSIAN FEDERATION. **2964**

1067-3105 See ALCOHOL ISSUES INSIGHTS. **2363**

1067-3121 See CONTROLS DIGEST. **1181**

1067-3202 See EXPLORER KNIFE JOURNAL. **4894**

1067-3229 See HARVARD REVIEW OF PSYCHIATRY. **3926**

1067-3237 See THIRD FORCE (1993). **4513**

1067-3415 See GOLF PRO. **4897**

1067-3717 See DATA MANAGEMENT REVIEW. **1253**

1067-3768 See SUPPORT LINE (CHICAGO, ILL.). **4199**

1067-3806 See TED : THE ELECTRICAL DISTRIBUTORS MAGAZINE. **2084**

1067-3849 See VIDEO SERVICES NEWS / PHILLIPS BUSINESS INFORMATION, INC. **4377**

1067-3881 See PIANO & KEYBOARD. **4146**

1067-411X See PACKAGING TECHNOLOGY & ENGINEERING. **4221**

1067-4128 See ILLINOIS REVIEW, THE. **3344**

1067-4136 See RUSSIAN JOURNAL OF ECOLOGY. **2220**

1067-4144 See GREAT LAKES LOG. **5449**

1067-4195 See MEDICAL OUTCOMES & GUIDELINES ALERT. **3610**

1067-4209 See BAKER & DANIELS' INDIANA ENVIRONMENTAL COMPLIANCE UPDATE. **3110**

1067-4217 See DIRECTORY OF NATIONAL HELPLINES. **1296**

1067-4241 See DAILY NEWS-PRESS. (CASTLE ROCK, COLO. : 1987). **5642**

1067-4284 See HISTORIANS OF NETHERLANDISH ART NEWSLETTER. **352**

1067-4357 See CIVIC CENTER NEWSOURCE. **5634**

1067-4365 See ESCONDIDO NEWS-REPORTER. **5635**

1067-439X See PRODUCER (PORT WASHINGTON, N.Y.). **1162**

1067-4454 See NFI BLUE BOOK. **2309**

1067-4489 See PUBLIC SECTOR QUALITY REPORT. **732**

1067-4535 See ALSA SWIMMERS' GUIDE. **4882**

1067-4551 See IOMA'S REPORT ON SALARY SURVEYS. **684**

1067-4640 See JOURNAL OF ANTHROPOSOPHIC MEDICINE. **3593**

1067-4713 See ADA POLICY & LAW. **2927**

1067-4748 See LEGENDS SPORTS MEMORABILIA. **4903**

1067-4764 See PROFESSIONAL REPORT : A PUBLICATION OF THE SOCIETY OF INDUSTRIAL AND OFFICE REALTORS. **4843**

1067-4780 See NEWSLETTER - NAFSA: ASSOCIATION OF INTERNATIONAL EDUCATORS (WASHINGTON, D.C.). **1768**

1067-4799 See AVIATION (LEESBURG, VA.). **13**

1067-4861 See DIRECTORY - STATE BAR OF GEORGIA. **2962**

1067-4918 See FORBES MEDIAGUIDE 500. **2919**

1067-4926 See FORBES MEDIACRITIC. **2919**

1067-4934 See FEDERAL CLAIMS REPORTER. **2969**

1067-4942 See TURKEY & TURKEY HUNTING. **4879**

1067-4977 See SOUTH DAKOTA HIGH LINER MAGAZINE. **2493**

1067-4993 See ARCHIVAL ISSUES : JOURNAL OF THE MIDWEST ARCHIVES CONFERENCE. **2479**

1067-5027 See JOURNAL OF THE AMERICAN MEDICAL INFORMATICS ASSOCIATION. **3597**

1067-5051 See VASCULAR FORUM. **3649**

1067-5094 See RUNNING WILD. **4916**

1067-5132 See IN PRINT (TRENTON, N.J.). **4815**

1067-5213 See CALIFORNIA JAZZ NOW. **4106**

1067-5221 See ATM NEWSLETTER. **4398**

1067-523X See WEBSTER'S WAGON WHEEL. **2477**

1067-5256 See STREET ROD PICKUPS. **5426**

1067-5264 See FUNDAMENTAL AND CLINICAL CARDIOLOGY. **3704**

1067-5337 See INDUSTRIAL WASTEWATER. **5534**

1067-5345 See PHOTONICS AND OPTOELECTRONICS. **4440**

1067-5418 See AUDIT RISK ALERT. **739**

1067-5582 See JOURNAL OF IMMUNOTHERAPY WITH EMPHASIS ON TUMOR IMMUNOLOGY : OFFICIAL JOURNAL OF THE SOCIETY FOR BIOLOGICAL THERAPY. **3674**

1067-5604 See AMC OUTDOORS. **4868**

1067-5639 See CIRCLE (MINNEAPOLIS, MINN.), THE. **2258**

1067-5671 See ADVANCES IN SERVICES MARKETING AND MANAGEMENT. **920**

1067-568X See ADVANCES IN DNA SEQUENCE SPECIFIC AGENTS. **1012**

1067-5698 See ADVANCES IN MEDICINAL CHEMISTRY. **1039**

1067-5701 See ADVANCES IN GENOME BIOLOGY. **440**

1067-571X See ADVANCES IN HETEROCYCLIC NATURAL PRODUCT SYNTHESIS. **1038**

1067-5779 See 2 TO 22 DAYS IN GREAT BRITAIN. **5458**

1067-5817 See JOURNAL OF APPLIED STATISTICAL SCIENCE. **5329**

1067-585X See CORNELL FOCUS. **77**

1067-5914 See FRED TROST'S PRACTICAL SPORTSMAN. **4895**

1067-5922 See WALSH COUNTY RECORD (1992), THE. 5726
1067-5957 See OHIO'S OFFICIAL SOURCEBOOK. 381
1067-5973 See HISTORICAL GARDENER, THE. 2418
1067-6058 See ENVIRONMENTAL LAW AND MANAGEMENT. 3111
1067-6066 See 2 TO 22 DAYS IN NEW ZEALAND. 5459
1067-6090 See SCIENTIFIC INVESTMENT. 913
1067-6120 See ON PRODUCTION AND POST-PRODUCTION. 4075
1067-6147 See CONDENSED MATTER AND MATERIALS COMMUNICATIONS. 1031
1067-6163 See CORPORATE GOVERNANCE ADVISOR, THE. 3099
1067-6171 See INTERNATIONAL COMPUTER LAWYER, THE. 2983
1067-618X See BURAFF'S LITIGATION REPORTS. BANK LAWYER LIABILITY. 3085
1067-6228 See MORNINGSTAR MUTUAL FUND 500. 908
1067-6244 See FM TECHNOLOGY REPORT. 1185
1067-6252 See WARREN'S CABLE REGULATION MONITOR. 1168
1067-6317 See GLOBAL TELEPHONY. 1156
1067-6333 See LOCAL TELECOM COMPETITION NEWS. 1159
1067-6341 See JOURNAL OF EARLY CHRISTIAN STUDIES. 4968
1067-635X See EAST/WEST EXECUTIVE GUIDE. 832
1067-6384 See SAN DIEGO EXECUTIVE. 709
1067-6430 See MARKET DATA RETRIEVAL'S CIC SCHOOL DIRECTORY. ALABAMA. 1762
1067-6538 See MARKET DATA RETRIEVAL'S CIC SCHOOL DIRECTORY. IDAHO. 1762
1067-6554 See MARKET DATA RETRIEVAL'S CIC SCHOOL DIRECTORY. INDIANA. 1762
1067-6643 See MARKET DATA RETRIEVAL'S CIC SCHOOL DIRECTORY. MINNESOTA. 1762
1067-6651 See MARKET DATA RETRIEVAL'S CIC SCHOOL DIRECTORY. MISSISSIPPI. 1763
1067-6791 See MARKET DATA RETRIEVAL'S CIC SCHOOL DIRECTORY. PENNSYLVANIA. 1763
1067-6899 See MARKET DATA RETRIEVAL'S CIC SCHOOL DIRECTORY. WISCONSIN. 1763
1067-6945 See POLLSTAR (FRESNO, CALIF.). 4146
1067-697X See JAPAN'S EXPANDING U.S. MANUFACTURING PRESENCE. 904
1067-6996 See ANDREWS' TOXIC TORTS ANNUAL. 2933
1067-7003 See ELECTRONIC DOCUMENT MANAGEMENT SYSTEMS JOURNAL. 1183
1067-7062 See FAIRCHILD'S TEXTILE & APPAREL FINANCIAL DIRECTORY. 5350
1067-716X See LATEST WORD (PHILADELPHIA, PA.), THE. 3604
1067-7208 See ENVIRONMENTAL EXECUTIVE DIRECTORY. 2167
1067-7224 See DIGITAL SYSTEMS JOURNAL. 1182
1067-7232 See COVERTACTION QUARTERLY. 1073
1067-7267 See ANNUAL QUALITY CONGRESS TRANSACTIONS. 5083
1067-7283 See FAMILY VIOLENCE & SEXUAL ASSAULT BULLETIN. 5285
1067-7313 See WENDELL'S REPORT FOR CONTROLLERS. 753
1067-733X See MED AD NEWS. 4314
1067-7372 See BROWN UNIVERSITY GERIATRIC RESEARCH APPLICATION DIGEST, THE. 3750
1067-7380 See MINERVA HISTORICAL SOCIETY QUARTERLY. 2623
1067-7402 See MORE FROM THE SHORE. 2461
1067-7453 See NATIONAL INSTITUTE OF JUSTICE JOURNAL. 3170
1067-750X See BLUE BOOK OF COLLEGE ATHLETICS FOR SENIOR, JUNIOR & COMMUNITY COLLEGES, THE. 4887

1067-7542 See CURRENT DIGEST OF THE POST-SOVIET PRESS, THE. 4502
1067-7666 See BERKELEY JOURNAL OF EMPLOYMENT AND LABOR LAW. 3144
1067-7712 See OSTRICH NEWS. 217
1067-7739 See HOME-BASED & SMALL BUSINESS NETWORK. 680
1067-7755 See VALLEY NEWS (FULTON, N.Y.), THE. 5722
1067-7828 See FOUNDATION 1000, THE. 4336
1067-7887 See CONSUMER MULTIMEDIA REPORT. 1152
1067-7925 See FOUNDATION 1000, THE. 4336
1067-795X See IMMUNODEFICIENCY (CHUR, SWITZERLAND). 3670
1067-814X See DRUG, ALCOHOL, AND OTHER ADDICTIONS. 1343
1067-8158 See OAG POCKET FLIGHT GUIDE (WORLDWIDE ED.). 5487
1067-8182 See JOURNAL OF TRANSNATIONAL LAW & POLICY. 3131
1067-8204 See INSIDE MICROSOFT ACCESS. 1287
1067-8212 See RUSSIAN JOURNAL OF NON-FERROUS METALS. 4018
1067-8239 See JOURNAL OF THE NEUROMUSCULOSKELETAL SYSTEM. 3805
1067-828X See JOURNAL OF CHILD & ADOLESCENT SUBSTANCE ABUSE. 1345
1067-8328 See CRAFT CONNECTION. 371
1067-8360 See MACTECH MAGAZINE. 1280
1067-8433 See JOURNAL OF THE AMERICAN REAL ESTATE AND URBAN ECONOMICS ASSOCIATION. 4839
1067-8506 See DIRECTORY OF ARTISTS USING SCIENCE AND TECHNOLOGY. 349
1067-8530 See SPECTRUM (LEXINGTON, KY.). 4686
1067-8573 See NATIONAL INSTITUTE OF JUSTICE JOURNAL. 3170
1067-8646 See AESCLEPIUS (MARTINEZ, CALIF.). 287
1067-8654 See AMERICAN JOURNALISM REVIEW. 2917
1067-8697 See ROAD RIDER'S MOTORCYCLE CONSUMER NEWS. 5391
1067-8808 See BULLETIN - DAVID AND ALFRED SMART MUSEUM OF ART. 345
1067-8867 See STAINED GLASS (LEE'S SUMMIT, MO.). 2594
1067-8964 See FOCUS ON VETERINARY SCIENCE & MEDICINE. 5510
1067-8980 See MEMBER DIRECTORY - AMERICAN HISTORICAL PRINT COLLECTORS SOCIETY. 358
1067-9014 See INTERNATIONAL DIRECTORY OF ENGINEERING SOCIETIES AND RELATED ORGANIZATIONS. 1979
1067-9022 See DIRECTORY OF ENGINEERING GRADUATE STUDIES & RESEARCH. 1970
1067-9030 See UCLA WORKING PAPERS IN PHONETICS. 3330
1067-9073 See MATHEMATICAL NOTES (ROSSIISKAIA AKADEMIIA NAUK). 3519
1067-909X See INOCULUM (ITHACA, N.Y.). 5114
1067-9197 See TAG (STERLING, VA.). 1281
1067-9294 See ELECTRONICS NOW. 2050
1067-9359 See DESIGN METHODS. 297
1067-9375 See DAILY GRAPHS. NASDAQ (OTC)/AMERICAN STOCK EXCHANGE. 895
1067-9391 See MANAGEMENT IN PRACTICE (NEWPORT NEWS, VA.). 943
1067-9456 See APA NEWSLETTERS ON THE BLACK EXPERIENCE, COMPUTER USE, FEMINISM, LAW, MEDICINE, TEACHING. 4341
1067-9464 See APA NEWSLETTERS ON THE BLACK EXPERIENCE, COMPUTER USE, FEMINISM, LAW, MEDICINE, TEACHING. 4341
1067-9502 See CRITICAL CARE ALERT. 3569
1067-9537 See STRATEGIES & SOLUTIONS. 4804
1067-957X See MARKET DATA RETRIEVAL'S CIC SCHOOL DIRECTORY. DISTRICT OF COLUMBIA. 1762
1067-9588 See NATURAL HEALTH. 2600

1067-960X See MARKET DATA RETRIEVAL'S CIC SCHOOL DIRECTORY. ARKANSAS. 1866
1067-9774 See ELECTION CENTER REPORTS. 4473
1067-9804 See ASIC & EDA. 4398
1067-9812 See AUDIOVISUAL JOURNAL OF CATARACT & IMPLANT SURGERY. 3872
1067-9847 See POSITIONS (DURHAM, N.C.). 243
1067-9871 See FOOD INVESTMENT REPORT. 2337
1067-991X See AIR MEDICAL JOURNAL. 3547
1068-0055 See JOURNAL OF ASIAN BUSINESS. 685
1068-0063 See TENNESSEE & KENTUCKY QUERIES. 2474
1068-0187 See GUATEMALA BULLETIN. 4508
1068-0195 See OHIO BEEF CATTLE RESEARCH & INDUSTRY REPORT. 217
1068-0233 See SPACE AVAILABLE. 35
1068-025X See BANK INSURANCE SURVEY REPORT. 2875
1068-0292 See STORYWORKS (NEW YORK, N.Y.). 1805
1068-0365 See HIGH-PERFORMANCE COMPUTING REVIEW. 1186
1068-0373 See MODERN SCREEN'S COUNTRY MUSIC. 4131
1068-0403 See HEALTHCARE PR NEWS. 3782
1068-0500 See ULRICH'S PLUS. 3254
1068-0586 See GLOBAL CITY REVIEW. 3343
1068-0640 See CLINICAL PULMONARY MEDICINE. 3703
1068-0667 See JOURNAL OF ADULT DEVELOPMENT. 4593
1068-0675 See CLIPPER ADVISOR. 1284
1068-073X See PRIMARY VOICES K-6. 1805
1068-0802 See HEALTHCARE PACKAGING. 4219
1068-0810 See MEMBERSHIP DIRECTORY - AMERICAN ASSOCIATION OF EQUINE PRACTITIONERS. 5516
1068-0845 See NATIONAL BOYCOTT NEWS. 1298
1068-0853 See HEALTHCARE SYSTEM REFORM ALERT. 5201
1068-0861 See AMERICAN BANKRUPTCY INSTITUTE LAW REVIEW, THE. 2932
1068-0896 See JOURNAL OF INVESTING, THE. 904
1068-0918 See ACA JOURNAL / AMERICAN COMPENSATION ASSOCIATION. 938
1068-0950 See SQL FORUM. 1204
1068-0969 See NATURE OF ILLINOIS, THE. 2200
1068-0977 1162
1068-1019 See MEDICARE AND MEDICAID LAW BULLETIN. 2888
1068-1027 See TRUSTEESHIP (WASHINGTON, D.C.). 1851
1068-1159 See INVESTMENT COMPANY SERVICE DIRECTORY, THE. 902
1068-1191 See CLINICAL INVESTIGATOR NEWS. 3565
1068-1213 See BNA'S HEALTH CARE POLICY REPORT. 3557
1068-1256 See 1949-50-51 FORD/MERCURY OWNERS MAGAZINE. 5403
1068-1264 See INSIDER REAL ESTATE GUIDE, THE. 4839
1068-1299 See GAS DAILY'S NG. 4257
1068-1302 See POWDER METALLURGY AND METAL CERAMICS. 4015
1068-1310 See ZWEIG LETTER, THE. 890
1068-1345 See GRAND TIMES. 5179
1068-1396 See IBM INTERNET JOURNAL. 1186
1068-154X See CUSTOMER SERVICE MANAGER'S LETTER. 663
1068-1620 See RUSSIAN JOURNAL OF BIOORGANIC CHEMISTRY. 493
1068-1647 See BLIND SPOT PHOTOGRAPHY. 4367
1068-1744 See THIS OLD TRUCK. 5426
1068-1809 See GAME PLAYERS NINTENDO-SEGA. 4861

1068-1817 See TOMORROW'S NATION. 5699

1068-1876 See TODAY'S DAILY NEWS. (LAKE HAVASU CITY). 5630

1068-1884 See LAKE HAVASU CITY HERALD. 5630

1068-1892 See PETERSEN'S MUSCLECAR RESTORATION & PERFORMANCE. 5423

1068-1906 See CONSUMER BANKRUPTCY NEWS DESK BOOK. 2956

1068-1957 See SIGNATURE (PRAIRIE VILLAGE, KAN.). 4569

1068-1965 See REPTILES (IRVINE, CALIF.). 4287

1068-199X See RECAREERING NEWSLETTER. 4209

1068-2023 See DISPATCH CENTER MANAGEMENT. 1153

1068-2090 See JOURNAL OF SLAVIC LINGUISTICS. 3292

1068-2112 See WALLEYE IN-SIDER. 2315

1068-2120 See CREDIT UNION MANAGER NEWSLETTER. 786

1068-2147 See GLASS ART (BROOMFIELD, COLO.). 2589

1068-2198 See BUSINESS-EDUCATION REPORT. 1729

1068-2252 See CURRENT REVIEW OF CEREBROVASCULAR DISEASE. 3570

1068-2287 See BORN TO SHOP. GREAT BRITAIN. 1293

1068-235X See SHEPARD'S CLEAN AIR ACT REPORTER. 3116

1068-2406 See EDUCATION REFORM DIGEST. 1740

1068-2422 See KANSAS CITY SMALL BUSINESS MONTHLY. 688

1068-2449 See WOMEN AGAINST SEXUAL HARASSMENT RAG, THE. 5569

1068-2465 See MEDICARE MANAGER. 2888

1068-2473 See PAGAN MUSE & WORLD REPORT. 4186

1068-2511 See NEA-AKTIVIST (ANCHORAGE, ALASKA). 1766

1068-2554 See TRAVELAMERICA (EVANSTON, ILL.). 5497

1068-2619 See ACTION SPORTS (SOUTH LAGUNA, CALIF.). 4881

1068-2627 See SPECIALTY CAR. 5425

1068-2635 See HANDGUNS (LOS ANGELES, CALIF.). 4898

1068-2643 See ASBESTOS & LEAD ABATEMENT REPORT. 4767

1068-2716 See NCSL LEGISBRIEF. 4668

1068-2805 See AGRICULTURAL AND RESOURCE ECONOMICS REVIEW. 49

1068-2821 See COOK'S ILLUSTRATED. 2789

1068-2872 See METAL EDGE. 4131

1068-2899 See BUSINESS RECORD, THE. 652

1068-2902 See SERVICE & SUPPORT MANAGEMENT. 710

1068-2937 See COLORADO SCHOOL OF MINES QUARTERLY REVIEW OF ENGINEERING, SCIENCE, EDUCATION AND RESEARCH. 2137

1068-2953 See DR. WILLIAM CAMPBELL DOUGLASS' SECOND OPINION. 3573

1068-302X See NEWSLETTER FROM DICK B. ON THE SPIRITUAL ROOTS OF ALCOHOLICS ANONYMOUS, A. 4981

1068-3038 See BUSINESS REFERRAL DIRECTORY / GREATER SAN DIEGO CHAMBER OF COMMERCE. 652

1068-3097 See CURRENT OPINION IN ENDOCRINOLOGY & DIABETES. 3727

1068-3100 See FOOT AND ANKLE QUARTERLY. 3918

1068-3151 See MISSIO APOSTOLICA : JOURNAL OF THE LUTHERAN SOCIETY FOR MISSIOLOGY. 4977

1068-316X See PSYCHOLOGY, CRIME & LAW. 4612

1068-3178 See ANNUAL OF DRUG THERAPY. 4291

1068-3208 See BUBBA MAGAZINE. 2529

1068-3240 See OUTDOOR DELAWARE. 2201

1068-3267 See UNDISCOVERED COUNTRIES JOURNAL. 3449

1068-3356 See BULLETIN OF THE LEBEDEV PHYSICS INSTITUTE. 4399

1068-3372 See JOURNAL OF CONTEMPORARY PHYSICS. 4408

1068-347X See COLLECTING TOYS. 2584

1068-3526 See ETHICS & LOBBYING. 2250

1068-3542 See ERISA AND BENEFITS LAW JOURNAL. 1667

1068-3550 See ADVANCES IN INTERPENETRATING POLYMER NETWORKS. 959

1068-3593 See FODOR'S ... AFFORDABLE FRANCE. 5470

1068-3623 See JOURNAL OF CONTEMPORARY MATHEMATICAL ANALYSIS. 3512

1068-3631 See CABLE T.V. AND NEW MEDIA LAW & FINANCE. 1129

1068-3658 See HYDROLYSIS AND WOOD CHEMISTRY. 4234

1068-3666 See JOURNAL OF FRICTION AND WEAR. 1982

1068-3674 See RUSSIAN AGRICULTURAL SCIENCES. 131

1068-3682 See RUSSIAN BIOTECHNOLOGY. 3696

1068-3690 See RUSSIAN CASTINGS TECHNOLOGY. 4018

1068-3704 See RUSSIAN CHEMICAL INDUSTRY. 1029

1068-3712 See RUSSIAN ELECTRICAL ENGINEERING. 2080

1068-3720 See RUSSIAN JOURNAL OF HEAVY MACHINERY. 2128

1068-3739 See RUSSIAN METEOROLOGY AND HYDROLOGY. 1434

1068-3747 See RUSSIAN PROGRESS IN VIROLOGY. 570

1068-3755 See SURFACE ENGINEERING AND APPLIED ELECTROCHEMISTRY. 1997

1068-3763 See BANK SECURITIES REPORT. 776

1068-378X See TEACHING AND CHANGE. 1906

1068-3798 See BNA'S HEALTH CARE ELECTRONIC DATA REPORT. 3557

1068-3801 See GEORGE MASON INDEPENDENT LAW REVIEW. 2973

1068-3844 See MULTICULTURAL EDUCATION (SAN FRANCISCO, CALIF.). 1765

1068-3879 See CURRENT TECHNIQUES IN INTERVENTIONAL RADIOLOGY. 3940

1068-4034 See SAFE MONEY REPORT. 708

1068-4077 See SHEPARD'S MINNESOTA EXPRESS CITATIONS. 3052

1068-4107 See CURRENT TECHNIQUES IN ARTHROSCOPY. 3963

1068-414X See MEALEY'S LITIGATION REPORTS. D&O LIABILITY. 3008

1068-4158 See CONSUMER PRODUCT AND MANUFACTURER RATINGS. 3477

1068-4166 See CHINA RIGHTS FORUM. 4505

1068-4204 See EMPLOYEE BENEFITS COUNSELOR. 1665

1068-4239 See IOMA'S REPORT ON COMPENSATION & BENEFITS FOR LAW OFFICES. 1681

1068-4271 See GREENPACKAGING 2000. 4219

1068-4409 See BULLETIN - ALBERT HOFMANN FOUNDATION. 4578

1068-4425 See COMPUTERS & MINING. 2138

1068-4433 See FLORIDA INSIGHT. 4649

1068-4468 See NIGHT SONGS. 3459

1068-4514 See PRIVATE CABLE INVESTOR. 1136

1068-4581 See OCCUPATIONAL COMPENSATION SURVEY--PAY AND BENEFITS. GARY-HAMMOND, INDIANA, METROPOLITAN AREA. 1696

1068-4611 See OCCUPATIONAL COMPENSATION SURVEY--PAY AND BENEFITS. DALLAS, TEXAS, METROPOLITAN AREA / U.S. DEPARTMENT OF LABOR, BUREAU OF LABOR STATISTICS. 1696

1068-4751 See PERSONNEL EXECUTIVES CONTACTBOOK. 945

1068-476X See PRISM (NEW YORK, N.Y., 1993). 3867

1068-4778 See RISC WORLD. 1265

1068-4794 See COLLECTORS' INFORMATION BUREAU'S COLLECTIBLES MARKET GUIDE & PRICE INDEX. 2772

1068-4808 See COLLECTORS' INFORMATION BUREAU'S COLLECTIBLES MARKET GUIDE & PRICE INDEX. 2772

1068-4883 See ADVANCES IN STRAWBERRY RESEARCH. 44

1068-4980 See ENVIRONMENTAL BUYERS' GUIDE. 2228

1068-5200 See OPTICAL FIBER TECHNOLOGY. 4439

1068-5286 See IDEA LETTER FOR HEALTH CARE MANAGERS, THE. 3786

1068-5308 See PSYCHOPHARMACOLOGY UPDATE. 4326

1068-5316 See F-D-C REPORTS. NONPRESCRIPTION PHARMACEUTICALS AND NUTRITIONALS. 4304

1068-5324 See PRESCRIPTION PHARMACEUTICALS AND BIOTECHNOLOGY. 4325

1068-5340 See INPSIDER (ATLANTA, GA.), THE. 4241

1068-5391 See PRODUCER REPORT. 4147

1068-5405 See MEALEY'S LITIGATION REPORTS. AMERICANS WITH DISABILITIES ACT. 3007

1068-5502 See JOURNAL OF AGRICULTURAL AND RESOURCE ECONOMICS. 99

1068-5553 See OPEN INFORMATION SYSTEMS. 1248

1068-557X See SPEC NEWSLETTER. 2082

1068-5669 See MICROSOFT C/C++ DEVELOPER'S JOURNAL. 1288

1068-5685 See MINIMALLY INVASIVE SURGICAL NURSING. 3861

1068-5693 See BIOENGINEERING ABSTRACTS (1993). 3655

1068-5774 See OSTRICH NEWS RATITE DIRECTORY, THE. 5517

1068-5804 See SHEPARD'S ENVIRONMENTAL LIABILITY, ENFORCEMENT & PENALTIES REPORTER. 3116

1068-5812 See TACKLE TESTER. 2778

1068-5820 See MONROE EVENING TIMES (MONROE, WIS. 1898). 5769

1068-5839 See WATERWORLD REVIEW. 5548

1068-5871 See COMMLAW CONSPECTUS. 2953

1068-5936 See OAKLAND TRIBUNE (OAKLAND, CALIF. 1991). 5638

1068-5944 See CLOVIS INDEPENDENT (CLOVIS, CALIF. 1946), THE. 5634

1068-5952 See FITNESS AND SPORTS REVIEW INTERNATIONAL. 1855

1068-5987 See OFARI'S BI-MONTHLY. 4485

1068-6061 See JOURNAL OF TRANSNATIONAL MANAGEMENT DEVELOPMENT. 874

1068-607X See PRIMARY CARE UPDATE FOR OB/GYNS. 3767

1068-6088 See CAPSULES & COMMENTS IN NURSING LEADERSHIP & MANAGEMENT. 3853

1068-6193 See BONSAI MAGAZINE. 2410

1068-624X See PITTSBURGH POST-GAZETTE (PITTSBURGH, PA. 1978). 5738

1068-6266 See DISTRIBUTED COMPUTING MONITOR. 1241

1068-6282 See AIDS ARTICLE SUMMARIES. 3663

1068-6304 See ERISA TOP 25,000 COMPANIES : THE RED BOOK OF PENSION FUNDS. 672

1068-641X See FIELDING'S SHOPPING EUROPE. 954

1068-6452 See ACCOUNTING TECHNOLOGY. 738

1068-6533 See SECTION 504 COMPLIANCE HANDBOOK. SUPPLEMENT. 4393

1068-6673 See GREENWOOD AND SOUTHSIDE CHALLENGER, THE. 5664

1068-6681 See DES MOINES BUSINESS RECORD. 665

1068-669X See RUSSIAN FOREST SCIENCES. 2394

1068-6738 See SCIENTIFIC AMERICAN FRONTIERS (MAGAZINE). 3639
1068-6746 See SCIENTIFIC AMERICAN SCIENCE & MEDICINE. 3639
1068-6800 See BUCK NAKED CRIME FIGHTER. 4858
1068-6827 See BROADCASTING & CABLE. 1128
1068-6835 See OS/2 MONTHLY. 1198
1068-6924 See PDR LIBRARY ON CD ROM WITH THE MERCK MANUAL. 4319
1068-6967 See QUALITY MANAGEMENT JOURNAL, THE. 946
1068-6983 See HETEROGENEOUS CHEMISTRY REVIEWS. 977
1068-6991 See LOWER EXTREMITY, THE. 3883
1068-7149 See LITIGATION UNDER THE FEDERAL OPEN GOVERNMENT LAWS. 4481
1068-7181 See APPLIED ENERGY. 2109
1068-722X See BIRNBAUM'S SANTA FE, TAOS, ALBUQUERQUE. 5464
1068-7238 See BIRNBAUM'S GERMANY. 5464
1068-7319 See SAN DIEGO ECONOMIC BULLETIN. 1519
1068-7378 See EFFECTIVE SCHOOL PRACTICES. 1894
1068-7386 See FEDERAL INFORMATION RESOURCES MANAGEMENT REGULATION AND BULLETINS THROUGH TRANSMITTAL CIRCULAR. 4648
1068-7416 See TRAVEL ALERT BULLETIN. 5495
1068-7432 See ENVIRONMENTAL TESTING & ANALYSIS. 2170
1068-7459 See ADVANCES IN SUPRAMOLECULAR CHEMISTRY. 1039
1068-7491 See PROCEEDINGS OF THE ... IEEE FREQUENCY CONTROL SYMPOSIUM. 4418
1068-7629 See MUCOSAL IMMUNOLOGY UPDATE : OFFICIAL PUBLICATION OF THE SOCIETY FOR MUCOSAL IMMUNOLOGY. 3675
1068-7645 See KUNG FU MASTERS. 4903
1068-7653 See ROCK & RAP CONFIDENTIAL. 4150
1068-7696 See WHO'S WHO IN LATIN AMERICA (NEW YORK, N.Y.). 437
1068-770X See HEALTH NEWS & BREAKTHROUGHS. 2598
1068-7777 See JOURNAL OF INFECTIOUS DISEASE PHARMACOTHERAPY. 4311
1068-7912 See COLLEGE BOUND (EVANSTON, ILL.). 1816
1068-7939 See SUN HERALD (ENGLEWOOD ED.). 5651
1068-7971 See RUSSIAN GEOLOGY AND GEOPHYSICS. 1396
1068-798X See RUSSIAN ENGINEERING RESEARCH. 2128
1068-7998 See RUSSIAN AERONAUTICS. 34
1068-8005 See ST. PETERSBURG UNIVERSITY MECHANICS BULLETIN. 2129
1068-8021 See ACJ (PLATTE CITY, MO.). 204
1068-8153 See PERFORMING ARTS STUDIES. 387
1068-8161 See RUSSIAN THEATRE ARCHIVE. 5368
1068-820X See MATERIALS SCIENCE (NEW YORK, N.Y.). 2106
1068-8218 See SOUTHERN CULTURES. 5263
1068-8285 See CPA SOFTWARE NEWS, THE. 662
1068-8374 See SECURITY TECHNOLOGY NEWS. 1227
1068-8382 See ADVANCE ACS ABSTRACTS. 959
1068-8412 See TERRY SHANNON ON DEC. 1205
1068-848X See CQ AMATEUR RADIO ... BEGINNER'S GUIDE TO AMATEUR RADIO. 1130
1068-8501 See WOMEN OF THE EAST, INC. 5570
1068-8560 See ARCHITECTURAL SPECIFIER. 289
1068-8595 See APPLIED BEHAVIORAL SCIENCE REVIEW. 4574
1068-8617 See SANTA BARBARA REVIEW. 3433
1068-882X See NEVADA LAWYER. 3015
1068-8838 See HOSPITALS & HEALTH NETWORKS. 3785

1068-8897 See PPT EXPRESS. 5301
1068-8919 See AMERICAS WATCH. 4503
1068-8943 See WEST'S FEDERAL TAXATION. INDIVIDUAL PRACTICE SETS. 4758
1068-896X See TILLER (ALEXANDRIA, VA.), THE. 4184
1068-9206 See EDUCATORS GUIDE TO FREE VIDEOTAPES. 1743
1068-9265 See ANNALS OF SURGICAL ONCOLOGY. 3959
1068-9281 See PROCEEDINGS OF THE INTERNATIONAL SYMPOSIUM ON REMOTE SENSING AND GLOBAL ENVIRONMENTAL CHANGE. 1409
1068-9311 See MEDICAL DEVICE REGISTER : SUPPLEMENT. 3608
1068-9397 See SOURCE JOURNALS IN METALS & MATERIALS. 4019
1068-9494 See IRIS (ATLANTA, GA.). 3344
1068-9508 See CURRENT OPINION IN OTOLARYNGOLOGY & HEAD AND NECK SURGERY. 3887
1068-9516 See VIRGINIA ENVIRONMENTAL COMPLIANCE UPDATE. 3117
1068-9583 See JOURNAL OF CLINICAL PSYCHOLOGY IN MEDICAL SETTINGS. 4595
1068-9591 See JOURNAL OF REHABILITATION AND HEALTH. 3597
1068-9605 See INTERNATIONAL JOURNAL OF WIRELESS INFORMATION NETWORKS. 1242
1068-9699 See WORKGROUP COMPUTING REPORT. 4214
1068-9761 See LIGHT & ENGINEERING. 2070
1068-9818 See POSTSECONDARY EDUCATION OPPORTUNITY. 1842
1068-9826 See CABLE TV REGULATION (1993). 1129
1068-9931 See BROWN FAMILY NEWS AND GENEALOGICAL SOCIETY, THE. 2440
1068-9958 See INVESTMENT COMPANIES YEARBOOK. 902
1068-9982 See NORTHEAST ANTHROPOLOGY. 242
1069-0050 See LIGHTING ANSWERS. 619
1069-0085 See PETERSON'S GUIDE TO COLLEGES IN THE SOUTH. 1841
1069-0115 See INFORMATION SCIENCES, APPLICATIONS. 3216
1069-0190 See INQUIRY & ANALYSIS. 2982
1069-0212 See KEYSTONE WATER QUALITY MANAGER. 5535
1069-0298 See ARIZONA GREAT OUTDOORS. 4869
1069-031X See JOURNAL OF INTERNATIONAL MARKETING (EAST LANSING, MICH.). 928
1069-0344 See LOG HOMES MAGAZINE DESIGN, CONSTRUCTION & FINANCE ISSUE. 619
1069-0360 See NEWSLETTER - KANSAS ANTHROPOLOGICAL ASSOCIATION (1989). 242
1069-0379 See KANSAS ANTHROPOLOGIST, THE. 239
1069-0409 See OPEN SYSTEMS PRODUCTS DIRECTORY. 1198
1069-045X See CYTOPATHOLOGY ANNUAL. 535
1069-0506 See SHEPARD'S KANSAS EXPRESS CITATIONS. 3051
1069-0557 See EL&P U.S. ELECTRIC UTILITY INDUSTRY SOFTWARE DIRECTORY. 2043
1069-0573 See ADVANCES IN HUMAN ECOLOGY. 5238
1069-0727 See JOURNAL OF CAREER ASSESSMENT. 4205
1069-0832 See LIBRARIANS AT LIBERTY. 3223
1069-0840 See CONTEMPORARY GERONTOLOGY. 3750
1069-0913 See PC SOFTDIR. 1289
1069-093X See POLITICAL ARCHIVES OF RUSSIA. 4545
1069-0956 See INSIDE PARADOX FOR WINDOWS. 1287
1069-0964 See ADVANCES IN BUSINESS MARKETING AND PURCHASING. 920

1069-0999 See ARCHIE'S PAL JUGHEAD COMICS. 4857
1069-1081 See RUSSIAN GOVERNMENT TODAY. 4684
1069-1170 See ETHNIC AMERICAN EXPERIENCE. 2260
1069-126X See NETWORK ECONOMICS LETTER. 4413
1069-1286 See RADIOLOGIST (BALTIMORE, MD.), THE. 3945
1069-1316 See COLLEGE & UNDERGRADUATE LIBRARIES. 3203
1069-1324 See CRIME PREVENTION FUNDING NEWS. 3162
1069-1340 See PUBLIC ASSISTANCE FUNDING REPORT. 5303
1069-1359 See DISABILITY FUNDING NEWS. 5284
1069-1367 See PETERSON'S GUIDE TO VOCATIONAL AND TECHNICAL SCHOOLS. EAST. 1915
1069-1375 See PETERSON'S GUIDE TO VOCATIONAL AND TECHNICAL SCHOOLS. WEST. 1915
1069-1383 See PETERSON'S SPORTS SCHOLARSHIPS AND COLLEGE ATHLETIC PROGRAMS. 1841
1069-1448 See COSMETIC BENCH REFERENCE. 403
1069-1456 See AIDS WEEKLY. 3665
1069-1510 See REPROGRAPHICS & DESIGN IMAGING. 4569
1069-1685 See TOY COLLECTOR & PRICE GUIDE. 2585
1069-1693 See AMERICAN RACING CLASSICS. 4883
1069-1707 See BENEFITS & COMPENSATION SOLUTIONS. 938
1069-1715 See OFFICIAL RAILWAY GUIDE (FREIGHT SERVICE ED.), THE. 5433
1069-1731 See INVESTMENT ADVISOR (SHREWSBURY, N.J.). 902
1069-1766 See MINISTRY CURRENTS. 4977
1069-1774 See LARGE ANIMAL VETERINARY REPORT. 5515
1069-1847 See KANSAS INSURANCE AGENT & BROKER. 2886
1069-1944 See MEDICAL PRACTICE MANAGEMENT NEWS. 3788
1069-2029 See INSIDE ARTS. 385
1069-2037 See SAFETY (WATERFORD, CONN.). 2870
1069-207X See KIN KOLLECTING. 2457
1069-2088 See ANIMATRIX (LOS ANGELES, CALIF.). 4063
1069-2118 See SAFETY MANAGEMENT (WATERFORD, CONN.). 2869
1069-2134 See RELATIONAL DATABASE JOURNAL. 1255
1069-2150 See OAG TRAVEL PLANNER (PACIFIC ASIA ED.). 5487
1069-2177 See SIGNPOST FOR NORTHWEST TRAILS (1988). 4878
1069-2207 See MARYSVILLE JOURNAL-TRIBUNE. 5729
1069-2215 See OWEN WISTER REVIEW. 1094
1069-2282 See SPORTS CARDS. 2778
1069-2355 See CHICAGO ... MEDIA SOURCEBOOK. 757
1069-2460 See GELLIS & KAGAN'S CURRENT PEDIATRIC THERAPY. 3903
1069-2479 See PLENTY GOOD ROOM. 4986
1069-2509 See INTEGRATED COMPUTER AIDED ENGINEERING. 1229
1069-2533 See JOURNAL OF CUSTOMER SERVICE IN MARKETING & MANAGEMENT. 873
1069-2614 See KILLSHOT (PADUCAH, KY.). 4903
1069-2630 See PEPTIDE SCIENCES. 988
1069-2657 See CORPS REPORT, THE. 2088
1069-2665 See GEOGRAPHICAL SYSTEMS. 2563
1069-2673 See JOURNAL OF GYNECOLOGIC TECHNIQUES. 3763

1069-2681 See NEWS TRIBUNE (WOODBRIDGE, N.J.). **5711**

1069-269X See PERSONAL REPORT. PRACTICE DEVELOPMENT AND WEALTH ACCUMULATION FOR THE PERIODONTIST, THE. **1333**

1069-2789 See HOLISTIC RESOURCE MANAGEMENT QUARTERLY. **93**

1069-2800 See SLAVIC AND EAST EUROPEAN PERFORMANCE. **5368**

1069-2819 See WHITTIER DAILY NEWS. **5641**

1069-2827 See PASADENA STAR-NEWS. **5638**

1069-2843 See GLOBAL TRADE & TRANSPORTATION. **838**

1069-2851 See SMARTMONEY (NEW YORK, N.Y.). **712**

1069-286X See TRAVEL NEWS AMERICAS. **5496**

1069-2894 See MCCALL'S NEEDLEWORK. **5185**

1069-3017 See MIAMI HERALD ALMANAC OF FLORIDA POLITICS, THE. **4481**

1069-3041 See DUN & BRADSTREET'S KEY BUSINESS DIRECTORY OF LATIN AMERICA. **669**

1069-3130 See INTERNATIONAL JOURNAL OF FERTILITY AND MENOPAUSAL STUDIES. **3762**

1069-3181 See NEW EUROPE LAW REVIEW. **3015**

1069-3211 See GREEN MAN, THE. **4241**

1069-3238 See PACE BUYER'S GUIDES. NEW & USED IMPORT CAR PRICES. **5422**

1069-3254 See TOY & HOBBY WORLD INTERNATIONAL. **2585**

1069-3416 See WIRELESS DATA NEWS. **1124**

1069-3424 See SEMINARS IN RESPIRATORY AND CRITICAL CARE MEDICINE. **3952**

1069-3475 See SUNBELT FOODSERVICE. **2359**

1069-3629 See GROUND WATER MONITORING & REMEDIATION. **1413**

1069-3637 See PWA NEWSLINE. **3715**

1069-367X See PROCEEDINGS - IIE INTEGRATED SYSTEMS CONFERENCE. **2099**

1069-3769 See COMPUTERS IN EDUCATION JOURNAL. **1179**

1069-384X See COMPUTING RESEARCH NEWS. **1180**

1069-3971 See CROSS-CULTURAL RESEARCH. **5197**

1069-4021 See EMBEDDED COMPUTER TRENDS. **1184**

1069-4064 See JOURNAL OF PENSION BENEFITS. **2885**

1069-4099 See CD-ROM TODAY. **1276**

1069-4110 See CRITICAL REVIEWS IN PHARMACOLOGY. **4298**

1069-417X See ANTIMICROBICS AND INFECTIOUS DISEASES NEWSLETTER. **559**

1069-4188 See AMERICAN FURNITURE. **2904**

1069-420X See OUTSIDE KIDS. **1067**

1069-4218 See WARNING LETTER BULLETIN. **4332**

1069-4277 See INTERNATIONAL MEDIA GUIDE. BUSINESS/PROFESSIONAL THE AMERICAS. **760**

1069-4285 See KEYBOARD CLASSICS & PIANO STYLIST. **4127**

1069-4358 See PLASTICS DIGEST. **4458**

1069-4374 See ACCESSASIA (SEATTLE, WASH.). **4623**

1069-4404 See SOCIOLOGY OF RELIGION. **4998**

1069-4447 See WORLDWIDE BUSINESS PRACTICES REPORT. **724**

1069-451X See DISPATCH/NEWS (SPRINGFIELD, ILL.). **2731**

1069-4560 See HOMECARE DIRECTION. **3584**

1069-4579 See VACUUM PHYSICS AND TECHNOLOGY. **4424**

1069-4587 See CURRENT TOXICOLOGY. **3980**

1069-4595 See ELECTROMAGNETOEFFECT (COMMACK, N.Y.). **2046**

1069-4641 See EUROSERIALS (BINGHAMTON, N.Y.). **3209**

1069-4706 See PITTSBURGH HISTORY. **2754**

1069-4714 See IMPORTCAR (1993). **5416**

1069-4722 See COASTLAND TIMES, THE. **5723**

1069-4730 See JOURNAL OF ENGINEERING EDUCATION (WASHINGTON, D.C.). **1982**

1069-4749 See EDUCATION AND TECHNOLOGY. **1738**

1069-4757 See NATIONAL SCHOOL MARKET INDEX. **1901**

1069-4773 See BIOTECH REPORTER. **3688**

1069-4781 See RELIGION IN EASTERN EUROPE. **4991**

1069-4862 See CATHOLIC PARENT (HUNTINGTON, IND.). **5026**

1069-4951 See FUTURE AT WORK, THE. **868**

1069-4994 See POWER ENGINEERING INTERNATIONAL. **2075**

1069-5109 See FDA NEWS. **2335**

1069-5117 See BNA PENSION & BENEFITS REPORTER. **1655**

1069-5141 See ANTIQUE DOLL WORLD. **249**

1069-5168 See ORGANIZATIONS OF STATE GOVERNMENT OFFICIALS DIRECTORY. **4671**

1069-5176 See GEORGE D. HALL'S DIRECTORY OF NEW JERSEY MANUFACTURERS. **3479**

1069-5184 See INSIDE TUCSON BUSINESS. **683**

1069-5230 See BIO-CRITICAL SOURCE BOOKS ON MUSICAL PERFORMANCE. **4103**

1069-5281 See HOTHEAD PAISAN. **2794**

1069-529X See COMPUTER GRAPHICS PROCEEDINGS, ANNUAL CONFERENCE SERIES. **1232**

1069-5303 See ELECTRONICS AND COMMUNICATIONS ABSTRACTS. **2003**

1069-5346 See UKRAINIAN MATHEMATICS JOURNAL. **3540**

1069-5451 See JOURNAL OF COMPUTER AND SOFTWARE ENGINEERING. **1230**

1069-5478 See STREET BEAT (PITTSBURGH, PA.). **3440**

1069-5494 See INTERNATIONAL CABLE. **1133**

1069-5540 See CALCIUM AND CALCIFIED TISSUE ABSTRACTS. **3655**

1069-5591 See TOTAL QUALITY IN HOSPITALITY. **2809**

1069-5621 See LAN (SAN FRANCISCO, CALIF.). **1242**

1069-5648 See FAMILY PRACTICE MANAGEMENT. **3737**

1069-5656 See FRINGE WARE REVIEW. **1237**

1069-5834 See CHINA REVIEW INTERNATIONAL. **2648**

1069-5842 See CURRENT REVIEW OF SPORTS MEDICINE. **3953**

1069-5850 See CURRENT REVIEW OF PAIN. **3570**

1069-5869 See JOURNAL OF FOURIER ANALYSIS AND APPLICATIONS, THE. **3512**

1069-5893 See LACROSSE MAGAZINE. **4903**

1069-5907 See BANKERS NEWS. **776**

1069-5923 See RELOCATION COMPASS. **884**

1069-6113 See PRO/E, THE MAGAZINE. **1200**

1069-6164 See SERIALS IN MICROFORM (ANN ARBOR, MICH. 1993). **3249**

1069-6334 See KANSAS CITY METRO BUSINESS DIRECTORY. **688**

1069-6393 See HIGH SCHOOL GIRLS GYMNASTICS RULES AND MANUAL. **4898**

1069-6504 See PETERSON'S STUDY ABROAD. **1773**

1069-6520 See PATIENT OUTCOMES. **3790**

1069-6547 See UNDERWATER NEWS & TECHNOLOGY. **1458**

1069-6563 See ACADEMIC EMERGENCY MEDICINE. **3723**

1069-6571 See HEALTH CARE MANAGEMENT. **3781**

1069-6644 See CABLEFAX (DENVER, COLO.). **1105**

1069-6652 See POLITICAL WOMAN (WHITE PLAINS, N.Y.). **4490**

1069-6725 See UNIVERSAL HEALTHCARE ALMANAC, THE. **3648**

1069-6784 See ACCESS USA NEWS. **4383**

1069-6814 See OS2 PROFESSIONAL. **1289**

1069-6822 See SHOOTING SPORTS USA. **4917**

1069-6857 See DIALOGUE (LARGE PRINT ED.). **4386**

1069-6865 See DIALOGUE (BRAILLE ED.). **4386**

1069-6873 See DIALOGUE (CASSETTE ED.). **4386**

1069-6911 See SECURE RETIREMENT. **913**

1069-6970 See JOURNAL OF THE CLINICAL ORTHOPAEDIC SOCIETY. **3883**

1069-7004 See FOCUS ON. SPORTS, SCIENCE AND MEDICINE. **4895**

1069-708X See EW DESIGN ENGINEERS' HANDBOOK & MANUFACTURERS DIRECTORY. **4043**

1069-7098 See MARCH FOR LIFE. **589**

1069-711X See TAX FEATURES. **4752**

1069-7144 See VEERY (CHICAGO, ILL.). **3355**

1069-7225 See ECONOMIC QUARTERLY / FEDERAL RESERVE BANK OF RICHMOND. **1484**

1069-7268 See HETERODOXY (STUDIO CITY, LOS ANGELES, CALIF.). **4476**

1069-7276 See IRON GAME HISTORY. **2599**

1069-7292 See ADVANCES IN VASCULAR SURGERY. **3958**

1069-7438 See JOURNAL OF NEURO-AIDS. **3835**

1069-7446 See TEACHING MUSIC. **4156**

1069-7500 See WASHINGTON TELECOM NEWS. **1168**

1069-7829 See EMPLOYMENT LAW STRATEGIST. **3147**

1069-7837 See LAWYER'S WEEKLY USA. **2998**

1069-7853 See SHEPARD'S OREGON EXPRESS CITATIONS. **3053**

1069-7985 See CHILE PEPPER. **2331**

1069-8051 See UPSOUTH (BOWLING GREEN, KY.). **3449**

1069-806X See FFA NEW HORIZONS. **87**

1069-8124 See POLICY ANALYSIS (CATO INSTITUTE). **4487**

1069-8175 See BMD MONITOR. **4038**

1069-8205 See AFRICAN HERALD, THE. **5746**

1069-8264 See AUTOGRAPH COLLECTOR. **2438**

1069-8299 See COMMUNICATIONS IN NUMERICAL METHODS IN ENGINEERING. **3501**

1069-8302 See BIOCHEMISTRY AND MOLECULAR BIOLOGY INTERNATIONAL. **482**

1069-837X See JOURNAL OF HIV/AIDS PREVENTION & EDUCATION FOR ADOLESCENTS & CHILDREN. **4787**

1069-8426 See OFFICIAL PRICE GUIDE TO BEER CANS (1993), THE. **2775**

1069-8434 See TEXAS BUSINESS STATUTES AND SECURITIES RULES. **3104**

1069-8787 See OB/GYN ANNALS. **3766**

1069-8825 See STUDIES IN THE DECORATIVE ARTS. **375**

1069-8957 See REMINISCE EXTRA. **2544**

1072-5911 See MASTER'S THESES DIRECTORIES. **1835**

1069-8981 See FLORIDA JOB BANK, THE. **4204**

1069-921X See FAIR EMPLOYMENT PRACTICES GUIDELINES. **940**

1069-9228 See PC MANAGER'S LETTER. **881**

1069-9309 See FISH & FISHERIES WORLDWIDE. **2301**

1069-9317 See NEWSLETTER - SOUTH BEND AREA GENEALOGICAL SOCIETY. **4555**

1069-9333 See YVGS FAMILY FINDERS. **2478**

1069-9384 See PSYCHONOMIC BULLETIN & REVIEW. **4613**

1069-9473 See CHARIHO TIMES (1993), THE. **5741**

1069-9511 See SHEPARD'S NORTH CAROLINA STATUTES CITATIONS. **3053**

1069-9899 See GLOBAL FINANCIAL REPORT ON TELECOMMUNICATIONS AND COMPUTER COMPANIES. **789**

1069-9953 See PC MAGAZINE EN ESPANOL. **1199**

1069-9988 See EDUCATION INVESTOR, THE. **1740**

1070-0056 *See* JOURNAL OF MICROELECTRONIC SYSTEMS INTEGRATION. **1248**

1070-0099 *See* CLEAN AIR PERMITS. **2951**

1070-0102 *See* RISK MANAGEMENT LETTER, THE. **2892**

1070-0145 See SOFTWARE PROCESS, QUALITY & ISO 9000. **1291**

1070-0161 *See* (THE) BRAVE NEW TICK. **2796**

1070-0242 *See* JEWELERS' CIRCULAR-KEYSTONE (1990). **2914**

1070-0285 *See* PINK SHEET ON THE LEFT (1993), THE. **4487**

1070-0358 *See* PERCEPTIONS (TOLEDO, OH.). **3423**

1070-0536 *See* PRIVACY & AMERICAN BUSINESS. **704**

1070-0560 *See* SUNBONNET CRAFTS. **5186**

1070-0609 *See* FAMILY SYSTEMS. **2280**

1070-065X *See* REGIONAL AIR INTERNATIONAL. **33**

1070-0692 *See* JOINT FORCE QUARTERLY. **4047**

1070-079X *See* READ-EASY MEN'S AND WOMEN'S BASKETBALL RULES. **4914**

1070-0870 *See* KURDISH STUDIES. **2769**

1070-0900 *See* ONCOLOGIST'S POCKET GUIDE, THE. **3821**

1070-0927 **220**

1070-096X *See* SUBMARINE FIBER OPTIC COMMUNICATIONS SYSTEMS. **1164**

1070-0978 *See* HEALTHSERVICE LEADER, THE. **4782**

1070-0994 *See* CONNECT (ANN ARBOR, MICH.). **1180**

1070-101X *See* SOFWIN REPORTS. **1203**

1070-1192 *See* SOCIOLOGICAL THEORY ABSTRACTS. **5261**

1070-1214 *See* SCHOLASTIC EARLY CHILDHOOD TODAY. **1805**

1070-1362 *See* VIEW (BEDFORD, N.H.). **735**

1070-1370 *See* NURSING HOME MEDICINE. **3790**

1070-1400 *See* INDIGENOUS WOMAN. **2264**

1070-1702 *See* POWER TRANSMISSION DESIGN ... GUIDE TO PT PRODUCTS. **2124**

1070-1753 *See* POLITICAL ANIMAL (1993), THE. **4488**

1070-213X *See* SHEPARD'S ENVIRONMENTAL REGULATION SUMMARIES. **3116**

1070-2199 *See* SIN INTERNATIONAL. **4153**

1070-2210 *See* FINANCIAL MANAGER'S REPORT ON COST CUTTING, THE. **940**

1070-2318 *See* ENCYCLOPEDIA OF ASSOCIATIONS CD-ROM. **1925**

1070-2334 *See* INVESTMENT COMPANIES (CDA/WIESENBERGER (FIRM)). **902**

1070-2342 *See* CHAMBER EXECUTIVE NETWORK, THE. **818**

1070-2431 *See* HOME HEALTH PRODUCTS. **2598**

1070-2458 *See* JOURNAL OF GROUP THEORY IN PHYSICS. **4409**

1070-2466 *See* NUCLEIC ACIDS ABSTRACTS (1994). **478**

1070-2555 *See* PUBLIC DOMAIN REPORT. **328**

1070-2717 *See* ACCESSIONS LIST, EASTERN AND SOUTHERN AFRICA. **406**

1070-2733 *See* CORNELL MAGAZINE. **1101**

1070-2741 *See* CHAPEL HILL NEWS (CHAPEL HILL, N.C. 1992). **5723**

1070-2792 *See* MONITOR (ROCKVILLE, MD.). **1270**

1070-2830 *See* GENOME SCIENCE & TECHNOLOGY. **546**

1070-289X *See* IDENTITIES (YVERDON, SWITZERLAND). **2263**

1070-2911 *See* SPIDER (PERU, ILL.). **1069**

1070-2938 *See* LOS ANGELES LETTER, THE. **4663**

1070-2989 *See* INTERNATIONAL PRIVATE POWER QUARTERLY. **2067**

1070-3004 *See* EMERGENCY RADIOLOGY. **3941**

1070-3047 *See* ALTERNATIVES (WASHINGTON, D.C.). **4625**

1070-308X *See* WOMEN'S HEALTH NURSING SCAN (1993). **3871**

1070-3160 *See* CULTURAL DIVERSITY AT WORK. **1662**

1070-3217 *See* STATE RECYCLING LAWS UPDATE (QUARTERLY ED.). **2244**

1070-3241 *See* JOINT COMMISSION JOURNAL ON QUALITY IMPROVEMENT, THE. **3786**

1070-3276 *See* RUSSIAN ELECTROCHEMISTRY. **1035**

1070-3284 *See* RUSSIAN JOURNAL OF COORDINATION CHEMISTRY. **992**

1070-3292 *See* RUSSIAN PLANT PHYSIOLOGY. **527**

1070-3314 *See* NATIONAL DIRECTORY OF CHURCHES, SYNAGOGUES, AND OTHER HOUSES OF WORSHIP. **4980**

1070-3322 *See* PROFESSIONAL AND OCCUPATIONAL LICENSING DIRECTORY. **4208**

1070-3365 *See* AMERICANS TRAVELING ABROAD. **5461**

1070-3373 *See* MUTUAL FUND MARKET NEWS. **908**

1070-3411 *See* REMINGTON REPORT, THE. **706**

1070-3500 *See* OUTBOARD BOAT BLUE BOOK. **594**

1070-3535 *See* NEW ECONOMY (LONDON, ENGLAND). **1507**

1070-3586 *See* SCHOOL TRANSPORTATION NEWS. **5392**

1070-3608 *See* DIAGNOSTIC AND THERAPEUTIC ENDOSCOPY. **3571**

1070-3632 *See* RUSSIAN JOURNAL OF GENERAL CHEMISTRY. **992**

1070-3667 *See* PROTEIN PROFILE. **470**

1070-3756 *See* CIVIL WAR CHRONICLES. **2728**

1070-3853 *See* LANDSCAPE DESIGN (VAN NUYS, CALIF.). **2423**

1070-3896 *See* WORDPERFECT FOR THE LAW OFFICE. **3076**

1070-3950 *See* DIRECTORY OF COMPUTER AND HIGH TECHNOLOGY GRANTS. **1182**

1070-3969 *See* ASIAN AMERICAN NEWS (HOUSTON, TEX.). **2255**

1070-4027 *See* EMF HEALTH REPORT. **454**

1070-4035 *See* MEALEY'S LITIGATION REPORTS. PREMISES LIABILITY. **3008**

1070-4043 *See* MEALEY'S LITIGATION REPORTS. PATENTS. **3008**

1070-4051 *See* MANAGING OFFICE TECHNOLOGY. **878**

1070-4078 *See* DELL MATH PUZZLES AND LOGIC PROBLEMS. **4860**

1070-4205 *See* WORKERS WORLD WW. **4500**

1070-4272 *See* RUSSIAN JOURNAL OF APPLIED CHEMISTRY. **992**

1070-4280 *See* JOURNAL OF ORGANIC CHEMISTRY OF THE USSR. **1043**

1070-437X *See* JOURNAL OF TURFGRASS MANAGEMENT. **2422**

1070-4469 *See* NORTHEAST OIL AND GAS WORLD. **4267**

1070-4477 *See* FODOR'S CRUISES AND PORTS OF CALL. **5471**

1070-4485 *See* FODOR'S THE UPPER GREAT LAKES REGION. **5473**

1070-4515 *See* OFFICIAL MEETING FACILITIES GUIDE, NORTH AMERICA. **2808**

1070-4523 *See* CRITICAL CARE MANAGEMENT. **3569**

1070-4531 *See* CONSTRUCTION PRODUCTS. **610**

1070-454X *See* TRANSPUTER COMMUNICATIONS. **1205**

1070-4574 *See* CLASSIC CD (U.S. ED.). **4110**

1070-4590 *See* FODOR'S THE NETHERLANDS, BELGIUM, LUXEMBOURG. **5473**

1070-4604 *See* NEWSLETTER OF THE GYPSY LORE SOCIETY. **2323**

1070-468X *See* NORTH CAROLINA NATURALIST. **4169**

1070-4701 *See* VIBE (NEW YORK, N.Y.). **2494**

1070-4795 *See* SEARCHER (MEDFORD, N.J.). **1202**

1070-4833 *See* JOURNAL OF NATURAL RESOURCES & ENVIRONMENTAL LAW. **3113**

1070-485X *See* LEADING EDGE (TULSA, OKLA.). **1408**

1070-4884 *See* DIESEL & GAS TURBINE WORLDWIDE CATALOG (1992). **2112**

1070-4914 *See* GULF COAST OIL AND GAS WORLD. **4259**

1070-4922 *See* COUNTY LINES (PRINCETON, IND.). **2444**

1070-4965 *See* JOURNAL OF ENVIRONMENT & DEVELOPMENT, THE. **1499**

1070-499X *See* WILDLIFE REVIEW & FISHERIES REVIEW. **2209**

1070-5007 *See* WILDLIFE WORLDWIDE. **2210**

1070-5015 *See* REVISTA FARMACEUTICA (SAN JUAN, P.R.). **4328**

1070-5104 *See* MODERN SCREEN'S COUNTRY MUSIC. **4131**

1070-5112 *See* ALZHEIMER'S CARE GUIDE. **5271**

1070-5163 *See* JACKSONVILLE (JACKSONVILLE, FLA.). **2536**

1070-5198 *See* UNDERSTANDING JAPAN (DENVER, COLO.). **2667**

1070-5228 *See* MONEY MARKET DIRECTORY OF TAX-EXEMPT ORGANIZATIONS, THE. **4338**

1070-5287 *See* CURRENT OPINION IN PULMONARY MEDICINE. **3570**

1070-5295 *See* CURRENT OPINION IN CRITICAL CARE. **3570**

1070-5309 *See* SOCIAL WORK RESEARCH. **5309**

1070-5317 *See* SOCIAL WORK ABSTRACTS. **5267**

1070-5325 *See* NUMERICAL LINEAR ALGEBRA WITH APPLICATIONS. **3525**

1070-5341 *See* CREATING QUALITY K-12. **1862**

1070-535X *See* SEMINARS IN RADIOLOGIC TECHNOLOGY. **3946**

1070-5384 *See* ADVANCES IN CLINICAL OPHTHALMOLOGY. **3871**

1070-5392 *See* ADVANCES IN OBSTETRICS AND GYNECOLOGY (ST. LOUIS, MO.). **3756**

1070-5422 *See* JOURNAL OF COMMUNITY PRACTICE. **2826**

1070-5457 *See* SOFTWARE PROCESS, QUALITY & ISO 9000. **1291**

1070-549X *See* FEMINISM AND THE SOCIAL SCIENCES. **5200**

1070-5503 *See* INTERNATIONAL JOURNAL OF BEHAVIORAL MEDICINE. **4591**

1070-5511 *See* STRUCTURAL EQUATION MODELING. **3536**

1070-566X *See* EAA SPORT AVIATION FOR KIDS. **18**

1070-5740 *See* ATC MARKET REPORT. **12**

1070-5767 *See* REHABILITATION NURSING RESEARCH. **3868**

1070-5775 *See* SLAVIC SYNTAX NEWSLETTER, THE. **3321**

1070-5848 *See* JEWISH NEWS OF GREATER PHOENIX. **5630**

1070-5856 *See* SF UNIQUE VACATION SELECTIONS. **5491**

1070-597X *See* MCGRAW-HILL'S CANCER & GENETICS REPORT. **3820**

1070-5988 *See* BUILDING RENOVATION (CLEVELAND, OHIO). **604**

1070-6046 *See* GEOARCHIVE ON CD-ROM. **1376**

1070-6097 *See* 3X/400 SYSTEMS MANAGEMENT. **1169**

1070-6100 *See* WESTERN OIL AND GAS WORLD. **4282**

1070-6224 *See* PERSPECTIVES IN APPLIED NUTRITION. **4197**

1070-6232 *See* SWE (NEW YORK, N.Y.). **1997**

1070-6364 *See* NEW JERSEY RULES OF COURT. **3015**

1070-6380 *See* FODOR'S ... THE U.S. & BRITISH VIRGIN ISLANDS. **5473**

1070-6399 *See* FODOR'S ... MIAMI & THE KEYS. **5472**

1070-6402 *See* FODOR'S ... DISNEY WORLD & THE ORLANDO AREA. **5471**

1070-6437 See MIAMI DAILY BUSINESS REVIEW. 5718

1070-6488 See PROCEEDINGS ... ANNUAL GENERAL MEETING. 5077

1070-6569 See HARSH MISTRESS. 3393

1070-6585 See APPLIED SOCIAL PROBLEMS AND INTERVENTION STRATEGIES. 4575

1070-6593 See LAND MOBILE RADIO NEWS. 1134

1070-6607 See PCS NEWS. 1119

1070-6615 See PETERSON'S JOB OPPORTUNITIES IN BUSINESS. 4208

1070-6631 See PHYSICS OF FLUIDS (1994). 4416

1070-664X See PHYSICS OF PLASMAS. 4416

1070-6674 See PELIZZA'S POSITIVE PRINCIPLES FOR BETTER LIVING. 4607

1070-6690 See LIGHTHOUSE (UNIVERSITY PARK, PA.), THE. 4128

1070-6720 See MACINTOSH TIPS & TRICKS (PRINT). 1194

1070-6755 See AGRICULTURAL FINANCE DATABOOK (WASHINGTON, D.C. 1989). 50

1070-6771 See CHANGING MEDICAL MARKETS. 922

1070-678X See DOING RIGHT THINGS RIGHT. 669

1070-6828 See INVENTING TOMORROW'S SCHOOLS. 1754

1070-6836 See ALADDIN'S WINDOW. 3994

1070-6844 See EXPANSE (BALTIMORE, MD.). 3386

1070-6887 See FODOR'S ... HONG KONG. 5471

1070-6895 See FODOR'S CHINA. 5471

1070-6909 See FODOR'S ... LAS VEGAS, RENO, TAHOE. 5472

1070-700X See ABAA NEWSLETTER, THE. 4811

1070-7263 See THERAPISTS AND ALLIED HEALTH PROFESSIONALS CAREER DIRECTORY. 3917

1070-7271 See MEDICAL TECHNOLOGISTS AND TECHNICIANS CAREER DIRECTORY. 3915

1070-728X See COMPUTING AND SOFTWARE DESIGN CAREER DIRECTORY. 1236

1070-7298 See MENTAL HEALTH AND SOCIAL WORK CAREER DIRECTORY. 3915

1070-7328 See ELMONT HERALD. 5716

1070-7336 See NYCAP NEWS. 2179

1070-7352 See AMERICAN CURRENTS. 2294

1070-7395 See SAYING IT BETTER. 3319

1070-7409 See DELANEY REPORT, THE. 865

1070-745X See RECORD ENTERPRISE (PLYMOUTH, N.H.), THE. 5709

1070-7522 See TAFRIJA (TUCKER, GA.). 389

1070-7549 See FOUR DIRECTIONS (TELLICO PLAINS, TENN.), THE. 3388

1070-7557 See CLASSICS CHRONICLE. 3376

1070-7573 See SCREEN (CHICAGO, ILL.). 4077

1070-7611 See BANK DIRECTOR (BRENTWOOD, TENN.). 774

1070-762X See NETWORKER (ASHEVILLE, N.C.), THE. 4186

1070-7719 See STATE HOUSE WATCH. 4687

1070-7727 See NEW UNIONIST (MINNEAPOLIS, MINN.). 1694

1070-7735 See FULTON COUNTY IMAGES. 2616

1070-7751 See RAIL MART, THE. 5434

1070-7778 See HUGHSTON HEALTH ALERT. 3954

1070-7786 See SICANGU SUN TIMES. 2273

1070-7794 See GIA QUARTERLY. 4119

1070-7808 See GILCREASE JOURNAL. 351

1070-7816 See GEORGIA OFFICIAL AND STATISTICAL REGISTER. 4650

1070-7824 See YOUR GUIDE TO FLORIDA SCHOLARSHIPS AND OTHER FINANCIAL ASSISTANCE PROGRAMS. 1854

1070-7832 See GUIDE TO FLORIDA STATE PROGRAMS, A. 4338

1070-7840 See COMPLETE GUIDE TO FLORIDA FOUNDATIONS, THE. 4335

1070-7875 See DIAKONEO (NEW ORLEANS, LA.). 4953

1070-7964 See GUIDE TO PRIVATE FORTUNES. 678

1070-8014 See NATIVE NORTH AMERICAN ALMANAC. 2268

1070-8022 See JOURNAL OF NEURO-OPHTHALMOLOGY. 3876

1070-8030 See JOURNAL OF BRONCHOLOGY. 3950

1070-8049 See OTOLARYNGOLOGY JOURNAL CLUB JOURNAL, THE. 3890

1070-8057 See CONTAINER & PACKAGING RECYCLING UPDATE. 2226

1070-8073 See RESTORATION SERIALS INDEX. 4993

1070-8081 See RELOCATABLE BUSINESS. 706

1070-809X See SARAH STAMBLER'S MARKETING WITH TECHNOLOGY NEWS. 936

1070-8103 See LAKE MARTIN LIVING MAGAZINE. 4851

1070-8111 See POLICE AND SECURITY NEWS. 3171

1070-812X See NORTHBOUND (EAGLE RIVER, WIS.). 2201

1070-8138 See PROTESTANT REFORMED THEOLOGICAL JOURNAL. 4988

1070-8146 See CHAOS NETWORK, THE. 5242

1070-8154 See CONNECTIONS (MINNEAPOLIS, MINN. 1993). 4386

1070-8170 See SHERIFF (ALEXANDRIA, VA.). 3176

1070-8243 See BUSHWHACKER MUSINGS : VERNON COUNTY HISTORICAL SOCIETY NEWSLETTER. 2725

1070-8251 See COUNTRY DANCE & SONG SOCIETY NEWS. 1311

1070-826X See CREATIVE EXHIBITING TECHNIQUES. 758

1070-8294 See AUTO AGE DEALER BUSINESS. 5404

1070-8316 See NEBRASKA JUVENILE COURT REPORT. 5297

1070-8324 See SWEET'S CATALOG FILE. HOMEBUILDING & REMODELING. 629

1070-8340 See BIG RIVER. 2297

1070-8421 See ANTIQUE MAP PRICE RECORD & HANDBOOK. 2580

1070-8502 See INTRODUCTION TO FEDERAL INCOME TAXES, AN. 4733

1070-8588 See SOFTWARE DEVELOPMENT. 1290

1070-8596 See STACKS (SAN FRANCISCO, CALIF.). 1244

1070-860X See ORLANDO SPECTATOR, THE. 5650

1070-8642 See FODOR'S ACAPULCO, IXTAPA, ZIHUATANEJO. 5470

1070-8677 See BULLETIN - NORTHERN ARIZONA GENEALOGICAL SOCIETY. 2440

1070-874X See CONNECTICUT POST (BRIDGEPORT, CONN.). 5645

1070-8855 See TRAVEL & TOURISM EXECUTIVE REPORT. 5495

1070-8871 See NYQUIST REPORT ON FUNDING FOR COMMUNITY, JUNIOR, AND TECHNICAL COLLEGES. 1838

1070-8898 See FROM THE BROTHERS GRIMM. 2320

1070-8901 See ARTJOB/BANK (SANTA FE, N.M.). 314

1070-8928 See ELECTRICITY DAILY REPORT, THE. 1488

1070-8944 See PERSPECTIVES IN COVENANT EDUCATION. 1773

1070-8979 See PERIOPERATIVE OPTIONS AND OPPORTUNITIES. 3626

1070-9061 See SUCCESSFUL FUND RAISING. 4339

1070-907X See ACQUISITIONS, MERGERS, SPIN-OFFS, AND OTHER RESTRUCTURINGS. 636

1070-910X See HARVARD WOMEN'S HEALTH WATCH. 3762

1070-9142 See GREATER CHICAGO JOB BANK, THE. 4204

1070-9150 See HEALTH CARE 1000, THE. 4778

1070-9169 See ACCRA COST OF LIVING INDEX. 1460

1070-9193 See FINANCE (BOSTON, MASS.). 4204

1070-9207 See DARTNELL'S ... SALES FORCE COMPENSATION SURVEY. 1662

1070-9215 See FINANCE & TREASURY. 898

1070-9231 See ECONOMIC ANALYSIS OF UNITED STATES SKI AREAS. 4893

1070-9266 See NEW YORK WASTE REPORTER. 2237

1070-9274 See ACTS FACTS. 2858

1070-9282 See COUNTDOWN / JUVENILE DIABETES FOUNDATION INTERNATIONAL. 3727

1070-9320 See POSITIVELY PASTA!. 2353

1070-9363 See JAPAN SOCIETY NEWSLETTER. 2654

1070-9371 See INDIANA ENGLISH. 3286

1070-938X See OFFICIAL OFFICE MACHINES & BUSINESS EQUIPMENT USED PRICES GUIDE BLUE BOOK, THE. 4214

1070-9401 See A. MAGAZINE. 2253

1070-941X See JOURNAL OF BANK COST & MANAGEMENT ACCOUNTING, THE. 746

1070-9428 See JOURNAL OF HYMENOPTERA RESEARCH. 5610

1070-9479 See PORTHOLE (DEERFIELD BEACH, FLA.). 5489

1070-9495 See CONTRA MUNDUM. 4950

1070-9533 See HIGH SCHOOL MAGAZINE, THE. 1864

1070-9541 See RADWASTE MAGAZINE. 2241

1070-955X See COMPARATIVE CULTURES AND LITERATURE. 3377

1070-9568 See INTERNATIONAL FIGURE SKATING. 4900

1070-9592 See ADHESIVES & SEALANTS INDUSTRY. 1020

1070-9622 See SHOCK AND VIBRATION. 1996

1070-969X See QUAKE (NEW YORK, N.Y.). 1068

1070-9711 See CLASSICAL RUSSIA. 1076

1070-9746 See BIRNBAUM'S BERLIN. 5463

1070-9754 See SOCCER MAGAZINE (TITUSVILLE, FLA.). 4919

1070-9762 See JOURNAL OF OPTICAL TECHNOLOGY. 4436

1070-9789 See JOURNAL OF ADVANCED MATERIALS. 1981

1070-9797 See ANXIETY (NEW YORK, N.Y.). 4574

1070-9835 See NUDE & NATURAL. 2491

1070-9851 See INTERNET LETTER, THE. 1242

1070-986X See IEEE MULTIMEDIA. 1187

1070-9878 See IEEE TRANSACTIONS ON DIELECTRICS AND ELECTRICAL INSULATION. 2061

1070-9886 See IEEE TRANSACTIONS ON COMPONENTS, PACKAGING, AND MANUFACTURING TECHNOLOGY. PART A. 3480

1070-9894 See TRANSACTIONS ON COMPONENTS, PACKAGING & MANUFACTURING TECHNOLOGY PART B : TRANSACTIONS ON COMPONENTS, PACKAGING & ADVANCED PACKAGING. 4222

1070-9908 See IEEE SIGNAL PROCESSING LETTERS. 1977

1070-9924 See IEEE COMPUTATIONAL SCIENCE AND ENGINEERING. 1187

1070-9932 See IEEE ROBOTICS AND AUTOMATION MAGAZINE. 1219

1070-9940 See LI GUIDE TO DINING & WINING NEWSLETTER. 2348

1070-9967 See LAW ENFORCEMENT LEGAL REVIEW. 3107

1070-9975 See GLOBAL AUTOMOTIVE REVIEW AND OUTLOOK. 5415

1070-9983 See ANNALS OF EARTH. 1351

1070-9991 See VIDEO WATCHDOG. 4079

1071-0000 See STATE-OF-THE-ART RESEARCH SUMMARIES. 3755

1071-0019 See GLADWIN COUNTY RECORD AND BEAVERTON CLARION, THE. 5692

1071-0035 See ANIMAL PEOPLE. 225

1071-0043 See RAVEN (TRENTON, N.J.). 5214
1071-006X See REPORT ON HEALTHCARE INFORMATION MANAGEMNET. 3792
1071-0191 See NEWS BULLETIN / THE MUSICAL BOX SOCIETY INTERNATIONAL. 4140
1071-0248 See NEWS INDIA-TIMES. 2269
1071-0256 See COUNTRY VICTORIAN DECORATING & LIFESTYLE. 2899
1071-0302 See AMERITECH INDUSTRIAL PURCHASING GUIDE. UPSTATE NEW YORK, WESTERN PENNSYLVANIA. 949
1071-0337 See MOULTON ADVERTISER (1933), THE. 5627
1071-0353 See AUSTIN LAWYER'S MAGAZINE. 2938
1071-040X See FUND YOUR WAY THROUGH COLLEGE. 1825
1071-0418 See CAREERISM NEWSLETTER. 4385
1071-0450 See SAM NAGAGAMA'S ECONOMIC PERSPECTIVES. 1519
1071-0477 See PENSION, PROFIT-SHARING, WELFARE, AND OTHER COMPENSATION PLANS. 3153
1071-0507 See ARCHAEOLOGY AND BIBLICAL RESEARCH. 257
1071-0515 See REFLECTIONS (TAZEWELL, TENN.). 2756
1071-0523 See BUSH-MEETING DUTCH, THE. 4941
1071-054X See TAZEWELL GENEALOGICAL MONTHLY (1985). 2474
1071-0566 See TEXAS VETERINARIAN. 5522
1071-0574 See BLOWING ROCKET, THE. 5722
1071-0582 See HOSPITAL NEWS (PITTSBURGH, PA. 1986). 3784
1071-0590 See GRASSROOTS ECONOMIC ORGANIZING NEWSLETTER. 1592
1071-0604 See TRADE NEWS SERVICE, THE. 1630
1071-0612 See NEAL SPELCE AUSTIN LETTER, THE. 1507
1071-0620 See KIDS CUE. 5643
1071-0639 See NEWSLETTER - ASSOCIATION FOR CHINESE MUSIC RESEARCH. 4140
1071-0663 See ASIAN AVIATION NEWS. 12
1071-0671 See PETERSON'S JOB OPPORTUNITIES IN HEALTH CARE. 4208
1071-068X See PETERSON'S JOB OPPORTUNITIES IN ENGINEERING AND TECHNOLOGY. 4208
1071-0698 See MULTIMEDIA MONITOR. 1619
1071-0728 See INSIDE AUTOCAD. 1247
1071-0752 See INTERNATIONAL ANNALS OF ADOLESCENT PSYCHIATRY. 3926
1071-0825 See FEDERAL INCOME TAXATION. 4724
1071-0868 See OLD-HOUSE JOURNAL'S HISTORIC HOUSE PLANS, THE. 305
1071-0906 See ARCHIVES OF STD/HIV RESEARCH. 3666
1071-0949 See OPERATIVE TECHNIQUES IN PLASTIC AND RECONSTRUCTIVE SURGERY. 3971
1071-0973 See WORLD OF INVENTION. 5170
1071-0981 See WORLD OF SCIENTIFIC DISCOVERY. 5171
1071-099X See AMERICAN COST OF LIVING SURVEY. 638
1071-1007 See FOOT & ANKLE INTERNATIONAL. 3918
1071-1015 See FINE ART & ANTIQUES INTERNATIONAL. 320
1071-1023 See JOURNAL OF VACUUM SCIENCE & TECHNOLOGY. B, MICROELECTRONICS AND NANOMETER STRUCTURES PROCESSING, MEASUREMENT AND PHENOMENA. 4410
1071-1090 See WORLD BEER REVIEW. 2373
1071-1112 See HOOD COUNTY GENEALOGICAL SOCIETY. 2453
1071-1147 See CUSTOM TAILOR, THE. 1479
1071-1201 See NATIONAL GUIDE TO FUNDING IN HEALTH. 3619

1071-1260 See NATIONAL OIL & LUBE NEWS, THE. 4265
1071-1279 See AUBURN PLAINSMAN, THE. 5625
1071-1317 See C4I NEWS. 1212
1071-1325 See AIRLINE MARKETING NEWS. 10
1071-1333 See MARINE TECHNOLOGY NEWS. 4179
1071-135X See TELEMEDIA NEWS AND VIEWS. 1167
1071-1384 See AWI QUARTERLY. 226
1071-1392 See SAILING QUARTERLY. 596
1071-1406 See MACOMB DAILY, THE. 5692
1071-1414 See AAAD BULLETIN, THE. 4881
1071-1422 See SOS INTERNATIONAL NEWSLETTER. 1349
1071-1430 See AUTOMOTIVE & TRANSPORTATION INTERIORS. 5406
1071-1457 See PRIVATE SCHOOL MONITOR. 1774
1071-1570 See EUROPEAN MEDIA BUSINESS & FINANCE. 673
1071-1619 See AUTOHARP QUARTERLY. 4101
1071-1627 See MICHIGAN OPTOMETRIST, THE. 4216
1071-1635 See SALMONID (HARPERS FERRY, W.VA.). 2312
1071-1643 See OKLAHOMA WOMEN'S FRONT PAGE NEWS. 5563
1071-1651 See PHILADELPHIA ARCHITECT. 306
1071-1686 See NEW YORK CITY POETRY CALENDAR. 3466
1071-1716 See NEWS OF ORANGE COUNTY, THE. 5724
1071-1724 See POLICE COLLECTORS NEWS. 3172
1071-1740 See MARKET CHARTS INC. 1504
1071-1759 See INDY CAR RACING MAGAZINE. 4900
1071-1767 See WFS QUARTERLY. 2293
1071-1775 See WORLD TRADE NEWS (CLEVELAND, OHIO). 858
1071-1783 See CONSUMER ACTION NEWS / CONSUMER ACTION. 829
1071-1791 See CHAMBER MUSIC (NEW YORK, N.Y.). 4108
1071-1805 See REAL TRENDS. 4845
1071-1813 See PROCEEDINGS OF THE HUMAN FACTORS AND ERGONOMICS SOCIETY ... ANNUAL MEETING. 2125
1071-183X See PETERSON'S JOB OPPORTUNITIES IN THE ENVIRONMENT. 4208
1071-1864 See TRADITION (WALNUT, IOWA). 4157
1071-1880 See COLORADO WOMEN'S YELLOW PAGES. 5553
1071-1902 See GRIDIRON COACH. 4897
1071-1910 See SINGER REPORT ON MANAGED CARE SYSTEMS AND TECHNOLOGY, THE. 5158
1071-1937 See MADISON CO. MUSINGS. 2459
1071-1945 See QUALITY ABSTRACTS. 883
1071-1953 See PLANNING HISTORY PRESENT. 2831
1071-197X See SKAGIT VALLEY HERALD. 5762
1071-2011 See MILITARY HISTORY OF THE WEST. 4050
1071-202X See GUIDE TO U.S. FOUNDATIONS, THEIR TRUSTEES, OFFICERS, AND DONORS. 4338
1071-2038 See BANK SECURITIES REPORT. 776
1071-2186 See LAS VEGAS BUSINESS PRESS. 5708
1071-2194 See PROTOCOL DIGEST. 4054
1071-2216 See COMPUTER CONFERENCE ANALYSIS NEWSLETTER, THE. 1236
1071-2232 See JOURNAL OF WILDLIFE REHABILITATION. 2196
1071-2240 See CONTINUOUS IMPROVEMENT. 3477
1071-2259 See PC STREET PRICE INDEX, THE. 1248
1071-2267 See NRC CALENDAR, THE. 3020

1071-2275 See WISER NOW. 3755
1071-2313 See MICHIGAN GOLFER. 4904
1071-2321 See CITIZEN ADVOCACY FORUM. 5279
1071-233X See ORIGINAL NEWS PEPPER, THE. 3907
1071-2348 See JACKSON COUNTY CHRONICLES. 2739
1071-2364 See ANALYST WATCH. 890
1071-2372 See PHC PROFIT REPORT. 2607
1071-2445 See POWER DELIVERY PRODUCT NEWS. 1953
1071-247X See ELECTRONIC MARKETPLACE REPORT. 2047
1071-2488 See COMPUTER MARKETING & DISTRIBUTION REPORT. 864
1071-2496 See PRIMARY CARE NEWSLETTER. 5301
1071-250X See COMMODITIES (WASHINGTON, D.C.). 4000
1071-2526 See ONCE UPON A TIME (ST. PAUL, MINN.). 1067
1071-2569 See SPACE AND SECURITY NEWS. 35
1071-2577 See KAHPERD JOURNAL (BOWLING GREEN, KY.). 1856
1071-2585 See HOUSING NEW JERSEY. 2824
1071-2593 See LIBRARY CAT NEWSLETTER, THE. 4287
1071-2607 See NORWAY CURRENT, THE. 5693
1071-2615 See NYLON HIGHWAY. 1409
1071-2623 See Q-DEX (LISLE, ILL.). 3033
1071-2631 See PATENT INTELLIGENCE AND TECHNOLOGY REPORT. 1307
1071-264X See DIRECTORY OF LIBRARY AUTOMATION SOFTWARE, SYSTEMS, AND SERVICES. 3207
1071-2690 See IN VITRO CELLULAR & DEVELOPMENTAL BIOLOGY. ANIMAL. 537
1071-2720 See ACADEMIC SEARCH. 2496
1071-2739 See MAGAZINE SEARCH. 2497
1071-2747 See VOCATIONAL SEARCH. 1798
1071-2755 See MIDDLE SEARCH. 1795
1071-2801 See MUSIC FROM CHINA NEWSLETTER. 4133
1071-2828 See CHILD AND ADOLESCENT MENTAL HEALTH CARE. 4580
1071-2836 See JOURNAL OF RUSSIAN LASER RESEARCH. 4436
1071-2879 See BUILDING OKLAHOMA (OKLAHOMA CITY, OKLA. 1989). 603
1071-2895 See TWIN TERRITORIES (MUSKOGEE, OKLA. 1990). 2494
1071-2917 See CONTEMPORARY TIMES. 864
1071-2941 See HOUSTON SUN, THE. 5751
1071-295X See INTERFACE (SANTA MONICA, CALIF.). 1189
1071-2968 See INSIDE OPERATIONS. 1189
1071-2976 See CANDLE COMPUTER REPORT. 1173
1071-2984 See BEGINNINGS : THE OFFICIAL NEWSLETTER OF THE AMERICAN HOLISTIC NURSES' ASSOCIATION. 3852
1071-3018 See SCIENCE FICTION EYE. 3434
1071-3131 See BULLETIN - AMERICAN CONTRACT BRIDGE LEAGUE (1993), THE. 4858
1071-3158 See PASSAGES (WASHINGTON, D.C.). 590
1071-3182 See ABYA YALA NEWS. 2253
1071-3190 See BEE CULTURE. 65
1071-3212 See DAILY DIGEST (UNITED STATES. FEDERAL COMMUNICATIONS COMMISSION). 1153
1071-3220 See AUTOMOTIVE INTELLIGENCE REPORTS' METALWORKING. 3998
1071-3239 See FISH AND WILDLIFE INFORMATION EXCHANGE NEWSLETTER. 2193
1071-3255 See MANAGEMENT & DOCTORS. 3915
1071-328X See CLIMATE ALERT. 1421
1071-328X See MEANING OF LIFE, THE. 4352
1071-3425 See AUTOGRAPH COLLECTOR. 2438

1071-3441 See SOFTWARE DIRECTORY. SYSTEMS & UTILITIES. 1290

1071-3476 See GLENDALE NEWS-PRESS (1993). 5635

1071-3492 See VALENCIA COUNTY NEWS-BULLETIN. 5713

1071-3506 See CIBOLA COUNTY BEACON. 5712

1071-3514 See ARIZONA INDUSTRIAL DIRECTORY. 3475

1071-3530 See DIRECTORY, JUVENILE & ADULT CORRECTIONAL DEPARTMENTS, INSTITUTIONS, AGENCIES & PAROLING AUTHORITIES / AMERICAN CORRECTIONAL ASSOCIATION. 3163

1071-3581 See JOURNAL OF NUCLEAR CARDIOLOGY. 3707

1071-3646 See FINANCIAL TECHNOLOGY REVIEW. 898

1071-3670 See PLANTFINDER (PEMBROKE PINES, FLA.). 2428

1071-3697 See LANDSCAPE & NURSERY DIGEST. 2422

1071-3719 See TRAVERSE (TRAVERSE CITY, MICH.). 2494

1071-3751 See COLLEGE PLANNING QUARTERLY. 1732

1071-376X See ACADEMY ACCENTS. 4931

1071-3778 See ETHICS & MEDICS. 3575

1071-3786 See TODAY'S CHICAGO WOMAN. 5567

1071-3808 See PROFILE (SOUTH PORTLAND, ME.). 705

1071-3816 See CODE ONE. 16

1071-3905 See SOCIAL REGISTER. 425

1071-3956 See OM REVIEW. 880

1071-4065 See MERGERSTAT REVIEW. 693

1071-4073 See CLUBHOUSE (BERRIEN SPRINGS, MICH.). 4948

1071-4103 See SCIPHERS (COLLEGE STATION, TEX.). 2924

1071-4111 See SOBERING THOUGHTS. 1349

1071-412X See CLINICAL AND DIAGNOSTIC LABORATORY IMMUNOLOGY (PRINT). 3667

1071-4138 See CLINICAL AND DIAGNOSTIC LABORATORY IMMUNOLOGY (CD-ROM). 3667

1071-4154 See PERSPECTIVE (BOSTON, MASS. 1990). 4531

1071-4162 See COLLECTOR (HUNTER, N.Y.), THE. 2772

1071-4170 See RECORD ROUNDUP (NORTH CAMBRIDGE, MASS.). 4149

1071-4189 See QUARTERLY OF THE NATIONAL ASSOCIATION FOR OUTLAW AND LAWMAN HISTORY, INC. 2756

1071-4197 See REPORT ON TELECOM ADVERTISING & PUBLISHING, TA. 1120

1071-4200 See BRETHREN IN CHRIST HISTORY AND LIFE. 5057

1071-4243 See OHIO TAX REVIEW. 4739

1071-4251 See GOLD COAST. 2534

1071-4324 See PROJECT FINANCE MONTHLY, THE. 804

1071-4383 See ADULT LIFE AND WORK STUDY GUIDE. 5054

1071-4391 See LEONARDO ELECTRONIC ALMANAC. 324

1071-4413 See REVIEW OF EDUCATION/PEDAGOGY/CULTURAL STUDIES, THE. 1779

1071-4448 See SARATOGIAN (SARATOGA SPRINGS, N.Y., 1910), THE. 5720

1071-4480 See SHERMAN SENTINEL, THE. 2493

1071-4510 See ANNUITY & LIFE INSURANCE SHOPPER. 891

1071-4529 See NEWSPAPER ADVERTISING SOURCE. 763

1071-4537 See CONSUMER MAGAZINE & AGRI-MEDIA SOURCE. 1295

1071-4545 See PRINT MEDIA PRODUCTION SOURCE. 764

1071-4553 See HISPANIC MEDIA & MARKET SOURCE. 925

1071-4561 See DIRECT MARKETING LIST SOURCE. 923

1071-4596 See SPOT TV & CABLE SOURCE. 1139

1071-460X See HEALTH-CARE MEDIA SOURCE. 760

1071-4626 See CARD DECK ADVERTISING SOURCE. 757

1071-4634 See ARCHITECTURAL & CONSTRUCTION MEDIA SOURCE. 288

1071-4650 See COMMUNITY PUBLICATION SOURCE. 757

1071-4669 See RADIO LOCAL MARKETS SOURCE. 765

1071-4685 See SOUTHERN CALIFORNIA MEDIA SOURCEBOOK. 766

1071-4707 See RADIO ADVERTISING SOURCE. 765

1071-4782 See HOME COOKING. 2790

1071-4790 See MIDCONTINENT OIL AND GAS WORLD. 4264

1071-4804 See SOUTHWEST OIL AND GAS WORLD. 4278

1071-4839 See NACLA REPORT ON THE AMERICAS (1993). 1506

1071-4960 See PROBLEM ASSET REPORTER. 804

1071-4995 See TURF WEST. 2433

1071-5096 See PHARMACEUTICAL DAILY. 3695

1071-5126 See GYPSY BLOOD REVIEW. 3392

1071-5134 See DALLAS/FORT WORTH REAL ESTATE FINANCE SOURCEBOOK. 4836

1071-5142 See AUSTIN REAL ESTATE FINANCE SOURCEBOOK. 4834

1071-5185 See SHEPHERD EXPRESS. 5770

1071-5215 See MESSAGE (1993). 5043

1071-5320 See CONSENT MANUAL (SACRAMENTO, CALIF.). 3778

1071-538X See ENVIRONMENTAL REMEDIATION TECHNOLOGY. 2169

1071-5401 See HAWVER'S CAPITOL REPORT. 4654

1071-5452 See OLDER CAR / TRUCK RED BOOK. 5422

1071-5517 See SEMINARS IN LAPAROSCOPIC UURGERY. 3974

1071-555X See NATURAL BODYBUILDING AND FITNESS. 4906

1071-5568 See JOURNAL OF CULTURAL DIVERSITY. 5206

1071-5576 See JOURNAL OF THE SOCIETY FOR GYNECOLOGIC INVESTIGATION. 3764

1071-5584 See NORTH AMERICAN OUTLOOK. 4739

1071-5622 See OAH COUNCIL OF CHAIRS NEWSLETTER. 2751

1071-5657 See MOUTH. 4391

1071-569X See ANALGESIA (ELMSFORD, N.Y.). 3681

1071-5711 See PEDIATRIC PRIMARY CARE. 3909

1071-5754 See JOURNAL OF WOUND, OSTOMY, AND CONTINENCE NURSING. 3860

1071-5762 See FREE RADICAL RESEARCH. 1052

1071-5819 See INTERNATIONAL JOURNAL OF HUMAN-COMPUTER STUDIES. 1190

1071-5878 See TASTE OF HOME. 2547

1071-5975 See DCQFORUM (SILVER SPRING, MD.). 612

1071-605X See IMAGINE (BALTIMORE, MD.). 1751

1071-6068 See MODERNISM/MODERNITY (BALTIMORE, MD.). 3412

1071-6092 See SPECIAL TECHNOLOGIES. 5159

1071-6114 See CHEMISTRY REVIEWS. 971

1071-6262 See NATIONAL HEAD INJURY FOUNDATION'S TBI CHALLENGE!, THE. 3619

1071-6270 See PROCEEDINGS OF THE ELECTRICAL ELECTRONICS INSULATION CONFERENCE & ELECTRICAL MANUFACTURING & COIL WINDING. 2076

1071-6327 See COOK REPORT ON INTERNET, NREN, THE. 1181

1071-6521 See ARIZONA FARMER (1993). 62

1071-653X See UTAH FARMER (1993). 143

1071-6548 See PACIFIC FARMER. 118

1071-6564 See BAILLIERE'S CLINICAL INFECTIOUS DISEASES. 3712

1071-6580 See INFECTION CONTROL IN LONG-TERM CARE FACILITIES NEWSLETTER. 4784

1071-6661 See PHILANTHROPY MONTHLY, THE. 4338

1071-670X See GREAT BATTLES. 2617

1071-6734 See GUARDIAN (LEXINGTON, KY.), THE. 2250

1071-6777 See ALUMNI DIRECTORY / DICKINSON COLLEGE. 1098

1071-6947 See AES (SERIES). 1931

1071-6971 See BEST PLAYS OF ..., THE. 5362

1071-7013 See BURBANK BANNER. 2441

1071-7218 See CANCERWEEKLY (ATLANTA, GA.). 3814

1071-7226 See CANCER RESEARCHER WEEKLY. 3812

1071-7242 See LAW OFFICE ADMINISTRATOR. 875

1071-7250 See PEOPLE'S CULTURE (KANSAS CITY, KAN.). 4544

1071-7269 See FREETHOUGHT HISTORY. 4347

1071-7277 See REFORMATION & REVIVAL JOURNAL. 4990

1071-7323 See OBESITY RESEARCH. 3623

1071-7358 See LOUISIANA ARCHAEOLOGY. 273

1071-7366 See BEREAVEMENT & LOSS RESOURCES. 4577

1071-7471 See MARKET DATA RETRIEVAL'S SALES MANAGER'S GUIDE TO THE U.S. SCHOOL MARKET. 1763

1071-7544 See DRUG DELIVERY. 4299

1071-7560 See DOODY'S HEALTH SCIENCES BOOK REVIEW JOURNAL. 5101

1071-7579 See MAGHREB REPORT. 2499

1071-7625 See SUCCESSFUL RESTRUCTURINGS. 3091

1071-7641 See JOURNAL OF INTERIOR DESIGN. 2901

1071-779X See CELLULAR MARKET FORECASTS. 1151

1071-7900 See VIETNAM MARKET WATCH. 718

1071-796X See DIRECTORY OF POLITICAL NEWSLETTERS (1994). 4472

1071-8036 See COUNTRY COLLECTIBLES. 371

1071-8222 See KIRSCHNER'S INSURANCE DIRECTORIES. PACIFIC NORTHWEST. 2886

1071-8230 See KIRSCHNER'S INSURANCE DIRECTORIES. NORTHERN CALIFORNIA. 2886

1071-8249 See KIRSCHNER'S INSURANCE DIRECTORY. SOUTHERN CALIFORNIA. 2886

1071-8265 See INVESTMENT COMPANY REGULATION. 3101

1071-832X See IN-PLANT PRINTER (1993). 4565

1071-8419 See STATION & STORE PRODUCTS. 4279

1071-846X See JOURNAL OF MUTUAL FUND SERVICES, THE. 904

1071-8478 See ECOS (LEXINGTON, KY.). 2192

1071-8524 See ELECTRONIC CLAIMS PROCESSING REPORT. 671

1071-8532 See TREASURY MANAGER'S REPORT. 814

1071-8567 See DOCUMENT MANAGEMENT & WINDOWS IMAGING. 1258

1071-8680 See EXECUTIVE HEALTH'S GOOD HEALTH REPORT. 2597

1071-8710 See AFRICAN-AMERICAN ALMANAC, THE. 2254

1071-8729 See CEMETERIES OF THE U.S. 2442

1071-8842 See OPTICS INDEX (PRINT). 4439

1071-8869 See FOOD AND DRUG REPORT. 2971

1071-8923 See ENVIRONMENTAL SCIENCE REVIEW. 2170

1071-8931 See NEWS MEDIA YELLOW BOOK. 1927

1071-8958 See COMPLETE SUPER BOWL BOOK, THE. 4891

1071-8966 See DIRECTORY, PROCEEDINGS, AND HANDBOOK. 5100

1071-8990 See OEM MAGAZINE. 1248
1071-9059 See WORKSHOPS FOR LEGAL ASSISTANTS. EMPLOYEE BENEFITS. 3076
1071-9067 See WORKSHOPS FOR LEGAL ASSISTANTS. BANKRUPTCY. 3076
1071-9075 See WORKSHOPS FOR LEGAL ASSISTANTS. LITIGATION, LEGAL RESEARCH AND WRITING, ENVIRONMENTAL LAW AND TOXIC TORT LITIGATION. 3769
1071-9091 See SEMINARS IN PEDIATRIC NEUROLOGY. 3846
1071-9105 See AMERICA, BUSINESS TODAY. 638
1071-9121 See LAW TECHNOLOGY PRODUCT NEWS. 2997
1071-9156 See INKS (COLUMBUS, OHIO). 380
1071-9164 See JOURNAL OF CARDIAC FAILURE. 3706
1071-9466 See NTIS ALERT. REGIONAL & URBAN PLANNING & TECHNOLOGY. 2829
1071-9474 See NTIS ALERT. REGIONAL & URBAN PLANNING & TECHNOLOGY. 2829
1071-9482 See NTIS ALERT. REGIONAL & URBAN PLANNING & TECHNOLOGY. 2829
1071-9555 See WARD'S PRIVATE COMPANY PROFILES. 718
1071-9571 See DIRECTORY OF PACKAGING SOURCES. 4218
1071-961X See SHEPARD'S INDIANA EXPRESS CITATIONS. 3051
1071-9628 See PACIFIC OIL AND GAS WORLD. 4271
1071-9679 See ADVANCES IN DISTRIBUTION CHANNEL RESEARCH. 920
1071-9717 See BORN TO SHOP. GREAT BRITAIN. 1293
1071-9830 See BLACK SECRETS. 2257
1071-9903 See CHURCH MUSIC REPORT : TCMR, THE. 4109
1071-9946 See MINORITY NURSE NEWSLETTER. 3861
1071-9997 See FOCUS ON SECURITY. 3211
1072-0030 See ADVANCED INTELLIGENT NETWORK NEWS. 1240
1072-0065 See NEWS & RECORD (GREENSBORO, N.C.) 5724
1072-0103 See PAIS (PEABODY, MASS.). 5227
1072-0170 See SOCCER RULES. 4919
1072-0235 See CONFERENCE BOARD'S MEMBERSHIP UPDATE, THE. 864
1072-0316 See JOURNAL OF LEGAL ASPECTS OF SPORT. 2988
1072-0332 See FAMILY LIFE (NEW YORK, N.Y.). 2279
1072-0359 See NEWSLETTER / DUBUQUE COUNTY-KEY CITY GENEALOGICAL SOCIETY. 2463
1072-0367 See ASIAN AMERICAN AND PACIFIC ISLANDER JOURNAL OF HEALTH. 4768
1072-0391 See FODOR'S PACIFIC NORTH COAST. 5472
1072-0502 See LEARNING & MEMORY (COLD SPRING HARBOR, N.Y.). 4602
1072-0510 See EXTRA INNINGS. 1855
1072-0537 See JOURNAL OF CONSTRUCTIVIST PSYCHOLOGY. 4595
1072-0561 See PROFESSIONAL BUILDER (1993). 624
1072-057X See COLORADO ENVIRONMENTAL COMPLIANCE UPDATE. 3110
1072-0588 See WASHINGTON EMPLOYMENT LAW LETTER. 3155
1072-0596 See WASHINGTON ENVIRONMENTAL COMPLIANCE UPDATE. 3117
1072-0618 See ADVANCES IN VASCULAR BIOLOGY. 441
1072-0758 See FSIS FOOD SAFETY REVIEW. 2342
1072-0839 See MATHEMATICS TEACHING IN THE MIDDLE SCHOOL. 3521
1072-0847 See BEHAVIORAL INTERVENTIONS. 3921
1072-0863 See FOCUS & OPINION, INTERNAL MEDICINE. 3796

1072-1029 See ENVIRONMENTAL COMMUNICATOR. 2167
1072-1037 See MIRROR (1984). 3169
1072-1061 See BDS (CULVER CITY, CALIF.). 4887
1072-1150 See AGENDA, JEWISH EDUCATION. 1723
1072-1223 See PAPER RECYCLER. 2238
1072-1274 See GOLF PRO. 4897
1072-1290 See STANDARD AND POOR'S HIGH YIELD DIRECTIONS. 1522
1072-1436 See CHRISTIAN EDUCATION COUNSELOR. 5058
1072-1444 See KINDERGARTEN TEACHER GUIDE. 4972
1072-1460 See PRESCHOOL TEACHER GUIDE. 4987
1072-1517 See INSTRUCTIONAL STRATEGIES. 683
1072-1525 See DETROIT LABOR NEWS. 1662
1072-155X See RUSSIAN PETROLEUM INVESTOR. 4277
1072-1568 See LEADER (1993), THE. 5647
1072-1622 See SHEPARD'S MARYLAND EXPRESS CITATIONS. 3051
1072-1630 See CLINICAL AND EXPERIMENTAL METABOLISM. 3668
1072-1711 See COMPUTER TELEPHONY. 1178
1072-172X See NEW DIRECTIONS FOR PHILANTHROPIC FUNDRAISING. 5298
1072-1797 See AIRPORT BUSINESS. 637
1072-1800 See LINDSAY GAZETTE. 5636
1072-1819 See WOODLAKE ECHO AND THE THREE RIVERS CURRENT. 5641
1072-1827 See FARMERSVILLE HERALD (FARMERSVILLE, CALIF.). 5635
1072-1835 See ENVIRONMENTAL CAREER DIRECTORY. 2167
1072-1924 See BACH PERSPECTIVES. 4101
1072-1932 See BUSINESS OF MANAGED CARE. 3777
1072-1959 See ELECTRONIC MESSAGING UPDATE. 1110
1072-1983 See ZOOLOGICAL RECORD ON CD. 5604
1072-2041 See MICHIGAN CITIZEN. 5693
1072-2076 See NCBE FORUM. 1766
1072-2386 See DEFENSE ACQUISITION REPORT. 4040
1072-2416 See ENVIROLINE (FINDLAY, OHIO). 2165
1072-2432 See GREENWICH (GREENWICH, CONN.). 2488
1072-2440 See AMERICAN CONCHOLOGIST. 5574
1072-2521 See FITZPATRICK'S JOURNAL OF CLINICAL DERMATOLOGY. 3720
1072-2580 See OEM INDUSTRY. 3485
1072-2815 See MANAGED HEALTH CARE DIRECTORY. 3788
1072-298X See FOOD PLANT STRATEGIES. 2339
1072-303X See JOURNAL OF INTERLIBRARY LOAN, DOCUMENT DELIVERY & INFORMATION SUPPLY. 3220
1072-3072 See ENTREZ. REFERENCES. 486
1072-3080 See GLOBAL POSITIONING & NAVIGATION NEWS. 4176
1072-3129 See QUAD REPORT, THE. 2202
1072-3145 See AIRCRAFT MAINTENANCE TECHNOLOGY. 9
1072-3188 See TRAINING MEDIA REVIEW. 1123
1072-3374 See JOURNAL OF MATHEMATICAL SCIENCES. 3513
1072-3544 See COMPU-MART (RICHARDSON, TEX.). 1236
1072-3595 See MANN FANTASY BASEBALL GUIDE, THE. 4904
1072-3617 See HOME CARE REPORT. 3584
1072-3625 See RENAISSANCE (ARDMORE, PA.). 2271
1072-3714 See MENOPAUSE (NEW YORK, N.Y.). 3616
1072-3730 See SPINE LETTER. 3885

1072-3757 See COMMUNICATIONS IN RELIABILITY, MAINTAINABILITY, AND SUPPORTABILITY. 1968
1072-3773 See PUBLIC SECTOR JOB BULLETIN. 4209
1072-3846 See DAILY STOCK PRICE RECORD. NASDAQ. 896
1072-4044 See UNIXWORLD'S OPEN COMPUTING. 1265
1072-4052 See AFRICAN-AMERICAN SITES & INSIGHTS. 5460
1072-4109 See ADVANCES IN ANATOMIC PATHOLOGY. 3892
1072-4117 See MATH HORIZONS. 3518
1072-4133 See EUROPEAN EATING DISORDERS REVIEW. 4586
1072-4656 See DOWN THE ROAD. 4203
1072-4710 See ARCHIVES OF PEDIATRICS & ADOLESCENT MEDICINE. 3900
1072-4745 See SOCIAL POLITICS. 5259
1072-4761 See INTERNATIONAL JOURNAL OF INDUSTRIAL ENGINEERING. 2099
1072-477X See OLDER AMERICANS INFORMATION DIRECTORY. 5180
1072-4893 See AMERICAN RIDER. 5375
1072-5040 See JOURNAL OF THIRD WORLD SPECTRUM. 4527
1072-5067 See AONE'S LEADERSHIP PROSPECTIVES. 3851
1072-5083 See ENVIRONMENTAL ENCYCLOPEDIA. 2167
1072-5091 See HOW PRODUCTS ARE MADE. 680
1072-5113 See GAS TRANSACTIONS REPORT. 4258
1072-5121 See TAUNTON'S FINE COOKING. 2359
1072-5156 See BALLROOM REVIEW, THE. 1311
1072-5245 See INTERNATIONAL JOURNAL OF STRESS MANAGEMENT. 4591
1072-5369 See JOURNAL OF ARCHAEOLOGICAL METHOD AND THEORY. 271
1072-5490 See HEALTH CARE ETHICS USA. 3581
1072-5520 See INTERACTIONS (NEW YORK, N.Y.). 1189
1072-558X See WILD STEELHEAD AND ATLANTIC SALMON. 4855
1072-5598 See PARTS BUSINESS. 5423
1072-561X See ROGER EBERT'S VIDEO COMPANION. 4077
1072-5636 See ROCKY MOUNTAIN LIVESTOCK JOURNAL. 220
1072-5644 See FRIGHTEN THE HORSES. 5187
1072-575X See CHICAGO JOB BANK, THE. 4203
1072-5903 See MASTER'S THESES DIRECTORIES. 1835
1072-5911 See MASTER'S THESES DIRECTORIES. EDUCATION. 1835
1072-592X See ADAMS JOBS ALMANAC, THE. 4201
1072-6039 See MEDICAL WASTE ANALYST. 3612
1072-6063 See LOG HOMES ILLUSTRATED. 619
1072-611X See CONSERLINE (WASHINGTON, D.C.). 3204
1072-6136 See IRWIN BUSINESS AND INVESTMENT ALMANAC, THE. 684
1072-6144 See WORLD GUIDE TO TELEVISION & FILM. 1143
1072-6241 See CHILD THERAPY NEWS, THE. 4580
1072-625X See SLAM (NEW YORK, N.Y.). 4919
1072-6373 See PLASTIC CANVAS WORLD. 5185
1072-6381 See DOLL COLLECTOR'S PRICE GUIDE. 5183
1072-639X See DESSERTS! (BERNE, IND.). 2333
1072-6756 See WESTERN KENTUCKY JOURNAL. 2766
1072-7167 See KNITTING DIGEST. 5184
1072-7175 See OUTDOOR ILLINOIS (SPRINGFIELD, ILL.). 4877
1072-7191 See HONOLULU ADVERTISER, THE. 5656
1072-7361 See AG CHEM NEW COMPOUND REVIEW. 45

1072-7469 *See* CHILTON'S DRIVEABILITY MANUAL. ASIAN. **5410**

1072-7477 *See* CHILTON'S DRIVEABILITY MANUAL. CHRYSLER. **5410**

1072-7485 *See* CHILTON'S DRIVEABILITY MANUAL. EUROPEAN. **5410**

1072-7493 *See* CHILTON'S DRIVEABILITY MANUAL. FORD. **5410**

1072-7507 *See* CHILTON'S CASCADE EMISSION CONTROL APPLICATION GUIDE. **5410**

1072-7515 *See* JOURNAL OF THE AMERICAN COLLEGE OF SURGEONS. **3968**

1072-7655 *See* DIMENSIONP2S (KILGORE, TEX.). **3381**

1072-7787 *See* BAPTISTS TODAY. **4938**

1072-7795 *See* INTERNATIONAL LEGAL STRATEGY : ILS. **2984**

1072-7825 *See* ATLANTIC MONTHLY (1993), THE. **2485**

1072-7833 *See* CALIFORNIA REGULATORY LAW BULLETIN. **2946**

1072-7965 *See* JOURNAL OF PRACTICAL HYGIENE, THE. **1327**

1072-7973 *See* LAND USE & ENVIRONMENT FORUM. **3114**

1072-7981 *See* KIT CAR. **5418**

1072-8112 *See* MILITARY & POLICE UNIFORM ASSOCIATION NEWSLETTER, THE. **2795**

1072-8295 *See* MCCALL'S QUILTING. **5185**

1072-8368 *See* NATURE STRUCTURAL BIOLOGY. **466**

1072-8392 *See* CURRENT REVIEW OF MAGNETIC RESONANCE IMAGING. **3570**

1072-8422 *See* FASTEST STREET CARS IN AMERICA. **5414**

1072-8457 *See* COMPLETE GUIDE TO .38/.357. **4891**

1072-8538 *See* MASCULINITIES : OFFICIAL PUBLICATION OF THE MEN'S STUDIES ASSOCIATION, NATIONAL ORGANIZATION FOR MEN AGAINST SEXISM. **3995**

1072-8619 *See* SUN (1993). **5721**

1072-8651 *See* MANUFACTURING MARKET INSIDER. **3484**

1072-8740 *See* OCTANE WEEK. **4267**

1072-8759 *See* OXY-FUEL NEWS. **4271**

1072-8767 *See* ALCOHOL OUTLOOK. **4249**

1072-8953 *See* ANCIENT CITY GENEALOGIST, THE. **2437**

1072-902X *See* NATIONAL DIRECTORY OF CHILDREN, YOUTH & FAMILIES SERVICES. **5297**

1072-9143 *See* PENNSYLVANIA ENVIRONMENTAL COMPLIANCE UPDATE. **3115**

1072-9151 *See* WISCONSIN ENVIRONMENTAL COMPLIANCE UPDATE. **3117**

1072-916X *See* MINNESOTA ENVIRONMENTAL COMPLIANCE UPDATE. **3114**

1072-9178 *See* NEW YORK EMPLOYMENT LAW LETTER. **3152**

1072-9216 *See* CHOREOGRAPHY AND DANCE ARCHIVE. **1311**

1072-9224 *See* CONVERGE (SUNNYVALE, CALIF.). **1109**

1072-9232 *See* APEX OF THE M. **3460**

1072-9259 *See* QUILTER'S TREASURY. **5185**

1072-9267 *See* AG RETAILER. **45**

1072-9291 *See* ACTION SPORTS RETAILER (1993). **952**

1072-9321 *See* PUBLIC SAFETY ON-LINE. **1162**

1072-9356 *See* EASY MONEY (WESTPORT, CONN.). **670**

1072-9453 *See* REPORT ON MICROSOFT, THE. **1201**

1072-947X *See* GEORGIAN MATHEMATICAL JOURNAL. **3507**

1072-9933 *See* VXI JOURNAL. **1206**

1072-9984 *See* LITIGATION COMMITTEE NEWSLETTER. **3003**

1073-0028 *See* BASIC AND CLINICAL ONCOLOGY. **3809**

1073-0265 *See* OIL & GAS INTERESTS NEWSLETTER. **4268**

1073-0338 *See* OAG OFFICIAL TRAVELER. TRAVEL GUIDE. **2808**

1073-046X *See* ENTREPRENEUR NEWSLETTER. **672**

1073-0478 *See* ILLAHEE (SEATTLE, WASH.). **2173**

1073-0508 *See* INTERNATIONAL JOURNAL OF THE CLASSICAL TRADITION. **1077**

1073-0516 *See* TRANSACTIONS ON COMPUTER-HUMAN INTERACTION. **1221**

1073-0540 *See* ... NATIONAL ORGANIC DIRECTORY, THE. **2350**

1073-0680 *See* WEARABLE CRAFTS. **5186**

1073-0729 *See* OS/2 DEVELOPER. **1198**

1073-0885 *See* ANNUAL REVIEW OF COMMUNICATIONS. **1149**

1073-0893 *See* MIDWEST MUSEUMS CONFERENCE NEWS BRIEF. **4091**

1073-1059 *See* ELECTRONIC BUSINESS BUYER. **2046**

1073-1105 *See* JOURNAL OF LAW, MEDICINE & ETHICS, THE. **2988**

1073-1113 *See* CIJE ON DISC. **1793**

1073-1164 *See* NETWORK ADMINISTRATOR. **1243**

1073-1180 *See* CELL VISION. **534**

1073-1199 *See* ARTIFICIAL CELLS, BLOOD SUBSTITUTES, AND IMMOBILIZATION BIOTECHNOLOGY. **3553**

1073-1202 *See* MEDICAL IMAGING (PORTSMOUTH, R.I.). **3609**

1073-1210 *See* BIOMEDICAL TECHNOLOGY MANAGEMENT. **3687**

1073-1229 *See* CURRENT CONTENTS. LIFE SCIENCES (CD-ROM VERSION). **5174**

1073-1237 *See* CURRENT CONTENTS. CLINICAL MEDICINE (CD-ROM VERSION). **3656**

1073-1245 *See* CURRENT CONTENTS. AGRICULTURE, BIOLOGY & ENVIRONMENTAL SCIENCES (CD-ROM VERSION). **152**

1073-1253 *See* CURRENT CONTENTS. PHYSICAL, CHEMICAL & EARTH SCIENCES (CD-ROM VERSION). **1362**

1073-130X *See* JOURNAL OF SEDIMENTARY RESEARCH. SECTION A, SEDIMENTARY PETROLOGY AND PROCESSES. **1459**

1073-1318 *See* JOURNAL OF SEDIMENTARY RESEARCH. SECTION B, STRATIGRAPHY AND GLOBAL STUDIES. **1459**

1073-1326 *See* SPORTS REVIEW WRESTLING (AMBLER, PA.). **4923**

1073-1547 *See* OS/2 MAGAZINE. **1198**

1073-1555 *See* AFTER SCHOOL MAGAZINE. **1807**

1073-1644 *See* CLINICAL ADVANCES IN CARDIO-RESPIRATORY CARE. **3949**

1073-1768 *See* PROCEEDINGS OF THE ... NATIONAL AGRICULTURAL PLASTICS CONGRESS. **4459**

1073-1776 *See* AGRI-PLASTICS REPORT, THE. **47**

1073-1784 *See* HOME PC. **1267**

1073-1954 *See* GENERAL SCIENCE SOURCE. **5175**

1073-1962 *See* HUMANITIES SOURCE. **2857**

1073-2012 *See* ACCEPTABLE RISK. **636**

1073-2209 *See* CHRISTIAN'S EXPOSITOR. **4946**

1073-225X *See* FORUM - OHIO COALITION FOR THE EDUCATION OF HANDICAPPED CHILDREN. **1879**

1073-2268 *See* NJ VOTER. **4669**

1073-2357 *See* WORLD FOOD CHEMICAL NEWS. **2361**

1073-2721 *See* NSCA JOURNAL. **1857**

1073-273X *See* REDBOOK (CHAGRIN FALLS, OHIO), THE. **2407**

1073-2780 *See* MATHEMATICAL RESEARCH LETTERS. **3520**

1073-2837 *See* TOPICS IN CLINICAL CHIROPRACTIC. **3807**

1073-3027 *See* MFE COLLECTORS' BOOKLINE. **3411**

1073-3108 *See* CABLING INSTALLATION & MAINTENANCE. **1105**

1073-3124 *See* JOURNAL OF ITALIAN FOOD & WINE. **2347**

1073-3213 *See* WILEY BUSINESS INTELLIGENCE REPORTS. ALGERIA. **720**

1073-3221 *See* WILEY BUSINESS INTELLIGENCE REPORTS. ANGOLA. **720**

1073-323X *See* WILEY BUSINESS INTELLIGENCE REPORTS. ARGENTINA. **720**

1073-3248 *See* WILEY BUSINESS INTELLIGENCE REPORTS. AUSTRIA. **720**

1073-3256 *See* WILEY BUSINESS INTELLIGENCE REPORTS. AUSTRALIA. **720**

1073-3264 *See* WILEY BUSINESS INTELLIGENCE REPORTS. AZERBAIJAN. **720**

1073-3272 *See* WILEY BUSINESS INTELLIGENCE REPORTS. BAHAMAS. **720**

1073-3280 *See* WILEY BUSINESS INTELLIGENCE REPORTS. BELGIUM. **720**

1073-3299 *See* WILEY BUSINESS INTELLIGENCE REPORTS. BAHRAIN. **720**

1073-3302 *See* WILEY BUSINESS INTELLIGENCE REPORTS. BANGLADESH. **720**

1073-3310 *See* WILEY BUSINESS INTELLIGENCE REPORTS. BOLIVIA. **720**

1073-3329 *See* WILEY BUSINESS INTELLIGENCE REPORTS. BOTSWANA. **720**

1073-3337 *See* WILEY BUSINESS INTELLIGENCE REPORTS. BRUNEI. **720**

1073-3345 *See* WILEY BUSINESS INTELLIGENCE REPORTS. BRAZIL. **720**

1073-3361 *See* WILEY BUSINESS INTELLIGENCE REPORTS. CANADA. **721**

1073-337X *See* WILEY BUSINESS INTELLIGENCE REPORTS. CAMEROON. **720**

1073-3396 *See* WILEY BUSINESS INTELLIGENCE REPORTS. CHINA. **721**

1073-340X *See* WILEY BUSINESS INTELLIGENCE REPORTS. COLOMBIA. **721**

1073-3418 *See* WILEY BUSINESS INTELLIGENCE REPORTS. COSTA RICA. **721**

1073-3426 *See* WILEY BUSINESS INTELLIGENCE REPORTS. CUBA. **721**

1073-3434 *See* WILEY BUSINESS INTELLIGENCE REPORTS. CZECH REPUBLIC. **721**

1073-3450 *See* WILEY BUSINESS INTELLIGENCE REPORTS. ECUADOR. **721**

1073-3469 *See* WILEY BUSINESS INTELLIGENCE REPORTS. EGYPT. **721**

1073-3477 *See* WILEY BUSINESS INTELLIGENCE REPORTS. EL SALVADOR. **721**

1073-3485 *See* WILEY BUSINESS INTELLIGENCE REPORTS. ESTONIA. **721**

1073-3493 *See* WILEY BUSINESS INTELLIGENCE REPORTS. FINLAND. **721**

1073-3507 *See* WILEY BUSINESS INTELLIGENCE REPORTS. FRANCE. **721**

1073-3515 *See* WILEY BUSINESS INTELLIGENCE REPORTS. GABON. **721**

1073-3523 *See* WILEY BUSINESS INTELLIGENCE REPORTS. GERMANY. **721**

1073-3531 *See* WILEY BUSINESS INTELLIGENCE REPORTS. GHANA. **721**

1073-354X *See* WILEY BUSINESS INTELLIGENCE REPORTS. GREECE. **721**

1073-3558 *See* WILEY BUSINESS INTELLIGENCE REPORTS. GUATEMALA. **721**

1073-3566 *See* WILEY BUSINESS INTELLIGENCE REPORTS. GUYANA. **721**

1073-3574 *See* WILEY BUSINESS INTELLIGENCE REPORTS. HAITI. **721**

1073-3582 *See* WILEY BUSINESS INTELLIGENCE REPORTS. HUNGARY. **721**

1073-3590 *See* WILEY BUSINESS INTELLIGENCE REPORTS. HONG KONG. **721**

1073-3604 *See* WILEY BUSINESS INTELLIGENCE REPORTS. HONDURAS. **721**

1073-3612 *See* WILEY BUSINESS INTELLIGENCE REPORTS. INDONESIA. **721**

1073-3620 *See* WILEY BUSINESS INTELLIGENCE REPORTS. INDIA. **721**

1073-3639 *See* WILEY BUSINESS INTELLIGENCE REPORTS. IRELAND. **721**

1073-3647 *See* WILEY BUSINESS INTELLIGENCE REPORTS. IRAN. **721**

1073-3655 See WILEY BUSINESS INTELLIGENCE REPORTS. IRAQ. 721
1073-3663 See WILEY BUSINESS INTELLIGENCE REPORTS. ISRAEL. 721
1073-3671 See WILEY BUSINESS INTELLIGENCE REPORTS. ITALY. 721
1073-3698 See WILEY BUSINESS INTELLIGENCE REPORTS. JAMAICA. 721
1073-3701 See WILEY BUSINESS INTELLIGENCE REPORTS. JAPAN. 721
1073-371X See WILEY BUSINESS INTELLIGENCE REPORTS. JORDAN. 721
1073-3728 See WILEY BUSINESS INTELLIGENCE REPORTS. KAZAKHSTAN. 721
1073-3736 See WILEY BUSINESS INTELLIGENCE REPORTS. KENYA. 722
1073-3744 See WILEY BUSINESS INTELLIGENCE REPORTS. KOREA. 722
1073-3752 See WILEY BUSINESS INTELLIGENCE REPORTS. KUWAIT. 722
1073-3760 See WILEY BUSINESS INTELLIGENCE REPORTS. LEBANON. 722
1073-3779 See WILEY BUSINESS INTELLIGENCE REPORTS. LIBYA. 722
1073-3787 See WILEY BUSINESS INTELLIGENCE REPORTS. LUXEMBOURG. 722
1073-3795 See WILEY BUSINESS INTELLIGENCE REPORTS. MALAYSIA. 722
1073-3809 See WILEY BUSINESS INTELLIGENCE REPORTS. MOROCCO. 722
1073-3817 See WILEY BUSINESS INTELLIGENCE REPORTS. MOZAMBIQUE. 722
1073-3825 See WILEY BUSINESS INTELLIGENCE REPORTS. NIGERIA. 722
1073-3833 See WILEY BUSINESS INTELLIGENCE REPORTS. NICARAGUE. 722
1073-3841 See WILEY BUSINESS INTELLIGENCE REPORTS. NETHERLANDS. 722
1073-385X See WILEY BUSINESS INTELLIGENCE REPORTS. NORWAY. 722
1073-3868 See WILEY BUSINESS INTELLIGENCE REPORTS. NEW ZEALAND. 722
1073-3876 See WILEY BUSINESS INTELLIGENCE REPORTS. OMAN. 722
1073-3884 See WILEY BUSINESS INTELLIGENCE REPORTS. PAKISTAN. 722
1073-3914 See WILEY BUSINESS INTELLIGENCE REPORTS. PARAGUAY. 722
1073-3922 See WILEY BUSINESS INTELLIGENCE REPORTS. PHILIPPINES. 722
1073-3930 See WILEY BUSINESS INTELLIGENCE REPORTS. POLAND. 722
1073-3949 See WILEY BUSINESS INTELLIGENCE REPORTS. PORTUGAL. 722
1073-3957 See WILEY BUSINESS INTELLIGENCE REPORTS. PERU. 722
1073-3965 See WILEY BUSINESS INTELLIGENCE REPORTS. PUERTO RICO. 722
1073-3973 See WILEY BUSINESS INTELLIGENCE REPORTS. RUSSIA. 722
1073-3981 See WILEY BUSINESS INTELLIGENCE REPORTS. SOUTH AFRICA. 722
1073-399X See WILEY BUSINESS INTELLIGENCE REPORTS. SAUDI ARABIA. 722
1073-4007 See WILEY BUSINESS INTELLIGENCE REPORTS. SENEGAL. 722
1073-4015 See WILEY BUSINESS INTELLIGENCE REPORTS. SLOVAK REPUBLIC. 722
1073-4023 See WILEY BUSINESS INTELLIGENCE REPORTS. SINGAPORE. 722
1073-4031 See WILEY BUSINESS INTELLIGENCE REPORTS. SPAIN. 722
1073-404X See WILEY BUSINESS INTELLIGENCE REPORTS. SRI LANKA. 722
1073-4058 See WILEY BUSINESS INTELLIGENCE REPORTS. SUDAN. 722
1073-4066 See WILEY BUSINESS INTELLIGENCE REPORTS. SWITZERLAND. 723
1073-4074 See WILEY BUSINESS INTELLIGENCE REPORTS. SYRIA. 723
1073-4082 See WILEY BUSINESS INTELLIGENCE REPORTS. TAIWAN. 723
1073-4090 See WILEY BUSINESS INTELLIGENCE REPORTS. TAJIKISTAN. 723

1073-4104 See WILEY BUSINESS INTELLIGENCE REPORTS. THAILAND. 723
1073-4112 See WILEY BUSINESS INTELLIGENCE REPORTS. TANZANIA. 723
1073-4120 See WILEY BUSINESS INTELLIGENCE REPORTS. TUNISIA. 723
1073-4139 See WILEY BUSINESS INTELLIGENCE REPORTS. TURKEY. 723
1073-4236 See WILEY BUSINESS INTELLIGENCE REPORTS. MEXICO. 722
1073-4260 See WILEY BUSINESS INTELLIGENCE REPORTS. SWEDEN. 723
1073-4414 See DICKINSON'S FDA REVIEW. 4642
1073-4457 See TECHNOLOGY MANAGEMENT (NEW YORK, N.Y.). 888
1073-449X See AMERICAN JOURNAL OF RESPIRATORY AND CRITICAL CARE MEDICINE. 3948
1073-4600 See AFRICAN RURAL AND URBAN STUDIES. 2813
1073-4651 See INDUSTRIAL PAINT & POWDER. 4224
1073-4716 See PETERSEN'S GOLFING. 4912
1073-4724 See PETERSEN'S AUTOTRONICS. 5318
1073-4732 See CUSTOM & CLASSIC TRUCKS. 5412
1073-4740 See 5.0 MUSTANG. 5403
1073-4759 See MULTIMEDIA WORLD. 1196
1073-4805 See BORLAND C++ DEVELOPER'S JOURNAL. 1284
1073-4813 See WEBSTER AGRICULTURAL LETTER, THE. 145
1073-5186 See BIRD BREEDER. 4285
1073-5437 See YEAR BOOK OF ANESTHESIA AND PAIN MANAGEMENT, THE. 3684
1073-5518 See AVIATION / LATIN AMERICA AND THE CARIBBEAN. 13
1073-5585 See HOME FURNISHINGS EXECUTIVE (GREENSBORO, N.C.). 2906
1073-5615 See METALLURGICAL AND MATERIALS TRANSACTIONS. B, PROCESS METALLURGY AND MATERIALS PROCESSING SCIENCE. 4010
1073-5623 See METALLURGICAL AND MATERIALS TRANSACTIONS. PHYSICAL METALLURGY AND MATERIALS SCIENCE. 4010
1073-5720 See CANADIAN EMPLOYMENT LAW FOR U.S. COMPANIES. 3145
1073-5828 See JOURNAL OF ARTIFICIAL NEURAL NETWORKS. 1242
1073-5836 See TEACHING CHILDREN MATHEMATICS. 3538
1073-5852 See BUZZWORM'S EARTH JOURNAL. 2162
1073-5879 See MAGICAL BLEND (1989). 4242
1073-5976 See BULLETIN / INSTITUTE FOR THEOLOGICAL ENCOUNTER WITH SCIENCE AND TECHNOLOGY. 4941
1073-6077 See JOURNAL OF CHILD AND ADOLESCENT PSYCHIATRIC NURSING. 3858
1073-6085 See MOLECULAR BIOTECHNOLOGY. 3695
1073-6107 See DISCIPLINE NETWORK (MIDDLE/HIGH SCHOOL ED.). 1736
1073-6123 See DISCIPLINE NETWORK (ELEMENTARY SCHOOL ED.). 1736
1073-6255 See ANNUAL OF THE SOCIETY FOR THE STUDY OF CAUCASIA, THE. 3265
1073-6301 See ANALYST DIRECTORY. LISTED BY COMPANY. 890
1073-631X See EARNINGS FORECASTER. 897
1073-6379 See CLINICAL DATA MANAGEMENT. 863
1073-6417 See NATURAL GAS FOCUS. 4265
1073-6425 See PETROSYSTEMS WORLD. 1265
1073-6506 See INSIDE AMBULATORY CARE. 3724
1073-6514 See INSIDE CASE MANAGEMENT. 870
1073-6573 See FODOR'S THE HIMALAYAN COUNTRIES. 5473
1073-6646 See STATE DIRECTORY OF NEW ELECTRIC POWER PLANTS. 4762

1073-6662 See TAG'S CHANNEL COMPASS. 937
1073-6697 See INTERNATIONAL JOURNAL OF KURDISH STUDIES, THE. 2768
1073-676X See SAN DIEGO JUSTICE JOURNAL. 3046
1073-6840 See STRENGTH AND CONDITIONING. 1858
1073-6867 See BIG BEAR GRIZZLY. 5633
1073-6891 See SAN DIEGO HOME/GARDEN LIFESTYLES. 2792
1073-6948 See NATIONAL PACKING NEWS. 2351
1073-7111 See FLEXIBLE BENEFITS. 2881
1073-7774 See JOURNAL OF CARDIOVASCULAR DIAGNOSIS AND PROCEDURES. 3694
1073-7782 See EMERGENCY AND OFFICE PEDIATRICS. 3903
1073-7820 See PETERSON'S GUIDE TO NURSING PROGRAMS. 3867
1073-7995 See INTERNATIONAL MEDIA GUIDE. BUSINESS/PROFESSIONAL, ASIA/PACIFIC, MIDDLE EAST/AFICA. 760
1073-8002 See INTERNATIONAL MEDIA GUIDE. BUSINESS/PROFESSIONAL, ASIA/PACIFIC, MIDDLE EAST/AFICA. 760
1073-8010 See INTERNATIONAL MEDIA GUIDE. BUSINESS/PROFESSIONAL, ASIA/PACIFIC, MIDDLE EAST/AFICA. 760
1073-8126 See INFORMATION NETWORKS. 1113
1073-8142 See COLLECTIBLES, COUNTRY & AMERICANA. 2772
1073-8169 See DR. ATKINS' HEALTH REVELATIONS. 3573
1073-8339 See NEW YORK IRISH HISTORY. 2700
1073-8355 See EXPANSION MANAGEMENT. 674
1073-8363 See CHEROKEE TRACER, THE. 2443
1073-838X See BEYOND GERMANNA. 2439
1073-841X See DANGEROUS ASSIGNMENTS. 4507
1073-8444 See CREATIVE BUSINESS. 663
1073-8568 See ASSESSMENT JOURNAL. 4711
1073-8576 See NEW JERSEY REVIEW OF LITERATURE, THE. 3415
1073-8584 See NEUROLOGIST, THE. 3840
1073-8673 See RISK (CONCORD, N.H.). 5148
1073-8800 See JOURNAL / RHODE ISLAND BAR ASSOCIATION. 2990
1073-886X See ADDICTIONS NURSING. 3850
1073-8924 See MARKEE (SANFORD, FLA.). 4074
1073-8932 See TOY & HOBBY WORLD (1993). 2585
1073-8983 See LICENSING BUSINESS REVIEW. 1306
1073-8991 See LICENSING REPORTER EUROPE. 1306
1073-9149 See INSTRUMENTATION SCIENCE AND TECHNOLOGY. 3588
1073-922X See GAME DEVELOPER. 1185
1073-9335 See SAFETYLINE / NAVAL SAFETY CENTER. 4182
1073-9394 See MILKING SHORTHORN JOURNAL (1993). 215
1073-9408 See MOTORCYCLE CONSUMER NEWS. 4082
1073-9459 See MICHIGAN ENVIRONMENTAL COMPLIANCE UPDATE. 3114
1073-9483 See PHYSICAL THERAPY REIMBURSEMENT NEWS. 4381
1073-9718 See IMAGING DECISIONS. 3942
1073-9998 See RESCUE-EMS MAGAZINE. 4799
1074-0228 See HALF TONES TO JUBILEE. 3463
1074-0236 See HUSTLER, THE. 760
1074-0244 See MIDDLE EAST & SOUTH ASIA FOLKLORE BULLETIN, THE. 2322
1074-0252 See CAVALRY JOURNAL, THE. 2613
1074-0422 See KANSAS EMPLOYMENT LAW LETTER. 3150
1074-0430 See MISSISSIPPI EMPLOYMENT LAW LETTER. 3152
1074-0457 See PEABODY ESSEX MUSEUM COLLECTIONS. 2753
1074-0481 See CONTRACTOR'S PRICING GUIDE. RESIDENTIAL DETAILED COSTS. 611

1074-049X *See* CONTRACTOR'S PRICING GUIDE. RESIDENTIAL SQUARE FOOT COSTS. **611**

1074-0511 *See* INDUSTRIAL CONTROLS INTELLIGENCE & THE PLC INSIDER'S NEWSLETTER. **1188**

1074-0554 *See* JUNIOR TENNIS. **4902**

1074-0619 *See* ASIAN M&A AND INVESTMENT DATABASE. **891**

1074-0708 *See* JOURNAL OF AGRICULTURAL AND APPLIED ECONOMICS. **99**

1074-0740 *See* AUSTIN CHRONICLE, THE. **2528**

1074-0791 *See* NIP (CINCINNATI, OHIO. 1993). **2491**

1074-0805 *See* VOICE OF CHORUS AMERICA, THE. **4158**

1074-0953 *See* MEANS FACILITIES MAINTENANCE & REPAIR COST DATA. **620**

1074-1038 *See* VIRTUAL REALITY SPECIAL REPORT. **1206**

1074-1216 *See* FODOR'S ... EUROPE'S GREAT CITIES. **5471**

1074-1240 *See* JOURNAL OF DERIVATIVES, THE. **904**

1074-1291 *See* HAZARDOUS WASTE UPDATE SERVICE, THE. **2231**

1074-1542 *See* JOURNAL OF CHEMICAL CRYSTALLOGRAPHY. **1032**

1074-1593 *See* TIMELINES (EUGENE, OR). **2253**

1074-1674 *See* NTIS ALERT. BUSINESS & ECONOMICS. **700**

1074-1682 *See* MAJOR MASS MARKET MERCHANDISERS. **1085**

1074-1690 *See* NEW STEEL. **4013**

1074-1798 *See* CROCHET DIGEST. **5183**

1074-1917 *See* HARVARD JOURNAL OF HISPANIC POLICY. **2262**

1074-2158 *See* WEISS RESEARCH'S INSURANCE SAFETY DIRECTORY. **2896**

1074-2395 *See* JOURNAL OF THE PHYSICIANS ASSOCIATION FOR AIDS CARE. **3674**

1074-2425 *See* GAME PLAYERS SEGA NINTENDO. **4861**

1074-2654 *See* NONPROFIT MANAGEMENT DIGEST. **880**

1074-2670 *See* CARLYLE STUDIES ANNUAL. **3373**

1074-2727 *See* FEDERAL ADVISORY DIRECTORY. **4647**

1074-2816 *See* CURRENT CANCER THERAPEUTICS. **3815**

1074-2883 *See* AIDS & TB WEEKLY ARTICLE SUMMARIES. **3547**

1074-2905 *See* INFECTION CONTROL WEEKLY. **3714**

1074-2921 *See* VACCINE WEEKLY. **3677**

1074-2956 *See* BEYOND BEHAVIOR. **1876**

1074-2972 *See* WATER ENVIRONMENT LABORATORY SOLUTIONS. **2247**

1074-3022 *See* LIVER TRANSPLANTATION AND SURGERY. **3969**

1074-3057 *See* NEWSNET (STANFORD, CALIF.). **2700**

1074-3227 *See* THEORY AND PRACTICE OF OBJECT SYSTEMS. **1249**

1074-326X *See* PARENTLIFE (NASHVILLE, TENN.). **2284**

1074-3499 *See* BERLIN REPORTER, THE. **5708**

1074-3502 *See* KASHRUS MAGAZINE. **2347**

1074-3529 *See* CONTEMPORARY ECONOMIC POLICY. **1471**

1074-3596 *See* NEWBERRY NEWSLETTER, A. **3234**

1074-3642 *See* CARETAKER GAZETTE, THE. **4203**

1074-3650 *See* WILD FOREST REVIEW. **2398**

1074-3715 *See* IRP REPORT. **2067**

1074-3790 *See* MAPLE TECHNICAL NEWSLETTER, THE. **1280**

1074-3898 *See* IOMA'S REPORT ON MANAGING LITIGATION COSTS. **2984**

1074-3936 *See* COMMUNITY CABLE LETTER. **1152**

1074-3995 *See* MICROCOMPUTER ABSTRACTS. **1269**

1074-4037 *See* FOCUS SYSTEMS JOURNAL ENCYCLOPEDIA. **1279**

1074-407X *See* MICROLITHOGRAPHY WORLD. **2072**

1074-410X *See* DELANO RECORD. **5634**

1074-4274 *See* HOUSE (WESTHAMPTON BEACH, N.Y.). **2901**

1074-4452 *See* WORKPLACE VITALITY. **2871**

1074-4487 *See* DAILY REGISTER (OELWEIN, IOWA). **5669**

1074-4541 *See* HOME HEALTH CARE REIMBURSEMENT REPORT. **4783**

1074-455X *See* TILE DESIGN & INSTALLATION. **2594**

1074-4665 *See* HISTORIC TRAVELER, THE. **2618**

1074-469X *See* BEI-JING ZHI CHUN. **4465**

1074-4762 *See* VOICES FROM THE MIDDLE. **1908**

1074-4770 *See* HEALTH MANAGEMENT TECHNOLOGY. **3582**

1074-4851 *See* TECHNOLOGY CONNECTION. **1205**

1074-4983 *See* AMERICAN BICYCLIST MAGAZINE. **427**

1074-5017 *See* NAEDA EQUIPMENT DEALER. **160**

1074-5092 *See* CASWELL MESSENGER, THE. **5722**

1074-5238 *See* HERITAGE QUEST MAGAZINE. **2453**

1074-5289 *See* EMERALD OF SIGMA PI FRATERNITY, INTERNATIONAL, THE. **1822**

1074-5297 *See* SHOOT (NEW YORK, N.Y.). **765**

1074-5351 *See* INTERNATIONAL JOURNAL OF COMMUNICATION SYSTEMS. **1158**

1074-5475 *See* JOBS IN HIGHER EDUCATION. **4205**

1074-5521 *See* CHEMISTRY & BIOLOGY. **451**

1074-5599 *See* TAIWAN STUDIES. **2509**

1074-567X *See* HISTORIC HUNTSVILLE QUARTERLY OF LOCAL ARCHITECTURE AND PRESERVATION, THE. **300**

1074-5696 *See* COMPASS & TAPE. **2581**

1074-5742 *See* CASS COUNTY CONNECTIONS. **2442**

1074-5769 *See* SCORE (NASHVILLE, TENN.). **4152**

1074-5831 *See* VITALITY (DALLAS, TEX.). **2602**

1074-5858 *See* TAX PRACTICE & CONTROVERSIES. **752**

1074-6064 *See* HEALTHCARE CD-ROM DIRECTORY. **3583**

1074-6099 *See* FORTNIGHTLY : THE NORTH AMERICAN UTILITIES BUSINESS MAGAZINE. **4761**

1074-6218 *See* JOURNAL OF ENDOVASCULAR SURGERY. **3967**

1074-6242 *See* READ-EASY BASKETBALL RULES. **4914**

1074-6250 *See* UNITY IN A MULTICULTURAL U.S.A. **4513**

1074-6269 *See* IC CARD SYSTEMS & DESIGN. **1187**

1074-6293 *See* BENEFITS & COMPENSATION UPDATE. **1655**

1074-6331 *See* NONPROFIT FINANCIAL ADVISOR. **801**

1074-6404 *See* RELATIONAL DATABASE JOURNAL. **1255**

1074-6730 *See* NATURAL GAS STATISTICS SOURCEBOOK. **4284**

1074-679X *See* MAGAZINE OF ARTIFICIAL INTELLIGENCE IN FINANCE, THE. **1194**

1074-682X *See* SHERIDAN PRESS (SHERIDAN, WYO.), THE. **5772**

1074-6870 *See* LITERATURE ABSTRACTS. CATALYSTS / ZEOLITES. **4284**

1074-7109 *See* HOUSTON CHRONICLE (1912). **5751**

1074-7117 *See* ABERDEEN AMERICAN-NEWS. **5743**

1074-7427 *See* NEUROBIOLOGY OF LEARNING AND MEMORY. **466**

1074-7443 *See* CHINESE JOURNAL OF ADVANCED SOFTWARE RESEARCH. **1284**

1074-7532 *See* ADVANCES IN EXPERT SYSTEMS FOR MANAGEMENT. **1210**

1074-7567 *See* ADVANCES IN CELL AND MOLECULAR BIOLOGY OF MEMBRANES. **440**

1074-7575 *See* ADVANCES IN NEURAL SCIENCE. **3826**

1074-7613 *See* IMMUNITY (CAMBRIDGE, MASS.). **3670**

1074-7729 *See* CLEAN AIR ACT COMPLIANCE GUIDE UPDATE. **3110**

1074-777X *See* DOG INDUSTRY NEWSLETTER. **4286**

1074-7788 *See* CAT INDUSTRY NEWSLETTER. **4286**

1074-7869 *See* HISTORICAL ABSTRACTS ON DISC [COMPUTER FILE]. **2618**

1074-7931 *See* NEUROLOGIST (BALTIMORE, MD.), THE. **3840**

1074-8091 *See* WEST VIRGINIA NURSE. **3871**

1074-8105 *See* DISPUTE RESOLUTION JOURNAL. **2963**

1074-8334 *See* HOSPITAL PAYMENT & INFORMATION MANAGEMENT. **3784**

1074-8342 *See* NEWS-SUN (SEBRING, FLA.), THE. **5650**

1074-8350 *See* AMERICAN SHIPPER (1991). **822**

1074-8385 *See* SECURITIES MARKETING NEWS. **811**

1074-8407 *See* JOURNAL OF FAMILY NURSING. **3858**

1074-8628 *See* ACOG TECHNICAL BULLETIN. **3756**

1074-8636 *See* PHARMACEUTICAL & BIOTECH DAILY. **4320**

1074-8695 *See* NUEXCO REVIEW. **2157**

1074-875X *See* CCD ASTRONOMY. **394**

1074-8784 *See* GEORGETOWN MAGAZINE (1993). **1825**

1074-8806 *See* BAILLIERE'S CLINICAL PSYCHIATRY. **3921**

1074-8881 *See* SPACE FAX DAILY (GLOBAL ED.). **36**

1074-8903 *See* IOMA'S REPORT ON MANAGING CREDIT, RECEIVABLES & COLLECTIONS. **793**

1074-8911 *See* DIGITAL UNIX NEWS. **1182**

1074-8970 *See* PROCEEDINGS - INTERNATIONAL CONFERENCE ON COMPUTER LANGUAGES. **1200**

1074-9098 *See* CHEMICAL HEALTH & SAFETY. **2860**

1074-9144 *See* 21ST CENTURY AFRO REVIEW. **2253**

1074-9152 *See* RODALE'S AMERICAN WOODWORKER. **635**

1074-9306 *See* ADVANCED SYSTEMS. **1265**

1074-9357 *See* TOPICS IN STROKE REHABILITATION. **4382**

1074-939X *See* ENDOCRINOLOGY AND METABOLISM (LONDON, ENG.). **3729**

1074-9667 *See* DIRECTORY OF HISPANIC EXPERTS, THE. **2731**

1074-9845 *See* GOVERNMENTAL SERVICES NEWSLETTER (ASHLAND, MO.). **4652**

1075-0045 *See* NEW ENERGY NEWS. **1951**

1075-0096 *See* BANNER (CUBA, ILL.), THE. **207**

1075-0169 *See* HEALTHY WEIGHT JOURNAL. **4191**

1075-0207 *See* APPLIED MICROWAVE & WIRELESS. **4433**

1075-0223 *See* WGL TAX JOURNAL DIGEST, THE. **4758**

1075-0231 *See* NATIONAL LAMB & WOOL GROWER. **110**

1075-024X *See* HEALTH ALLIANCE ALERT. **2881**

1075-0274 *See* MEANS CONCRETE & MASONRY COST DATA. **620**

1075-0282 *See* WAREHOUSING / DISTRIBUTION DIRECTORY. **857**

1075-0347 *See* JOURNAL OF BIBLICAL STORYTELLING. **5017**

1075-0363 See BE-HOLD (BINGHAMTON, N.Y.). 4367
1075-0371 See BROWBEAT. 4105
1075-038X See 21ST CENTURY FUELS. 4248
1075-0479 See MULTIMEDIA SCHOOLS. 1196
1075-0487 See ALIMENTOS BALANCEADOS PARA ANIMALES. 205
1075-0495 See EMERGING TECHNOLOGY (AMERICAN SOCIETY OF CIVIL ENGINEERS). 2023
1075-0517 See MCD WAREHOUSING DISTRIBUTION DIRECTORY. 845
1075-0533 See MEANS CONCRETE COST DATA. 620
1075-055X See DERMASCOPE (DALLAS, TEX.). 403
1075-0592 See PRIVATE POWER EXECUTIVE. 1953
1075-0606 See HEALTH LAW LITIGATION REPORTER. 3740
1075-0665 See LEAD POISONING REPORT. 4788
1075-0711 See FODOR'S VIRGINIA & MARYLAND. 5474
1075-0754 See ISSUES IN PSYCHOANALYTIC PSYCHOLOGY. 4592
1075-0789 See MEANS FACILITIES CONSTRUCTION COST DATA. 620
1075-0886 See PROCEEDINGS OF THE ... MEETING / ASSOCIATION OF RESEARCH LIBRARIES. 3242
1075-0924 See METHODS OF LOGIC IN COMPUTER SCIENCE. 1195
1075-1084 See NATIONAL REFERRAL ROSTER. 4842
1075-1106 See CD-ROM NEWS EXTRA. 1276
1075-1130 See CLINTON MONTHLY, THE. 4468
1075-122X See BREAST JOURNAL. 3558
1075-1262 See SOVIET AND POST-SOVIET REVIEW, THE. 4496
1075-1416 See ACCOUNTING HISTORIANS NOTEBOOK, THE. 737
1075-1483 See WIRELESS CABLE INVESTOR. 1169
1075-1548 See OAG TRAVEL PLANNER (EUROPEAN ED.). 2808
1075-1629 See ADVANCES IN METAL AND SEMICONDUCTOR CLUSTERS. 1035
1075-1653 See DIFFERENT DRUMMER MAGAZINE. 2378
1075-1688 See RAND MCNALLY ROAD ATLAS & TRIP PLANNER. 5490
1075-1874 See HOUSTON TIMES-JOURNAL. 5654
1075-1920 See HIGH SCHOOL SOFTBALL UMPIRES MANUAL. 4898
1075-2013 See DIGEST OF POLYMER DEVELOPMENTS. SER. 3, STYRENICS AND ACRYLICS. 2012
1075-203X See CORRECTIONS ALERT. 3161
1075-2056 See TOTAL QUALITY REVIEW, THE. 888
1075-217X See BARNEY MAGAZINE. 1060
1075-2188 See HOME HEALTH FOCUS. 3856
1075-2196 See ARCHAEOLOGICAL PROSPECTION. 257
1075-2307 See BROWN'S DIRECTORY OF INSTRUCTIONAL PROGRAMS (7-12). TECHNICAL/VOCATIONAL EDUCATION, HOME ECONOMICS. 1911
1075-2412 See DERIVATIVES WEEK. 787
1075-248X See NEWSLETTER - MONROE COUNTY HISTORICAL SOCIETY (WIS.). 2750
1075-2528 See REPORT ON OBJECT ANALYSIS AND DESIGN. 1201
1075-2560 See EXPLORATIONS (LA JOLLA, CALIF.). 1449
1075-2595 See TEXAS ENVIRONMENTAL COMPLIANCE UPDATE. 3116
1075-2617 See JOURNAL OF PEPTIDE SCIENCE. 1043
1075-2749 See UCLA MAGAZINE (1989). 1103
1075-2765 See AMERICAN JOURNAL OF THERAPEUTICS. 3549
1075-2846 See GLOBAL GOVERNANCE. 4475

1075-2889 See WEIGHT CONTROL DIGEST (DALLAS, TEX. 1992), THE. 4200
1075-2951 See NEW ASIA REVIEW. 2507
1075-3028 See NEW FOOD & DRUG PACKAGING, THE. 4220
1075-3109 See 16 (NEW YORK, N.Y.). 1059
1075-3133 See PAGEANTRY (ALTAMONTE SPRINGS, FLA.). 2542
1075-3184 See FAMILIES IN CRISIS FUNDING REPORT. 5285
1075-3354 See AGRICULTURAL NEWS (HAMDEN, N.Y.). 50
1075-3605 See BULLETIN / CAPE COD GENEALOGICAL SOCIETY. 2440
1075-3664 See TRW REDI REALTY REPORT. 4848
1075-3753 See NATIONAL NETWORK (DALLAS, TEX.). 3619
1075-380X See MEALEY'S LITIGATION REPORTS. INSURANCE FRAUD. 2887
1075-3869 See LEADERSHIP DIRECTORIES ON CD-ROM. 689
1075-3885 See SCHOOL FOODSERVICE & NUTRITION. 2356
1075-413X See WIRELESS TELECOM INVESTOR. 1169
1075-4210 See INTERNATIONAL JOURNAL OF TRAUMA NURSING. 3857
1075-4261 See BIOSPECTROSCOPY (NEW YORK, N.Y.). 484
1075-4342 See PHYSICAL THERAPY FORUM (KING OF PRUSSIA, PA. 1994). 4381
1075-4512 See INVESTMENT LAWYER, THE. 2984
1075-4628 See HART COUNTY NEWS-HERALD. 5680
1075-4636 See APARTMENT ADVISOR, THE. 772
1075-475X See ANCESTRY (SALT LAKE CITY, UTAH). 2437
1075-5179 See VARIABLE ANNUITY/LIFE PERFORMANCE REPORT / MORNINGSTAR. 919
1075-5209 See STATE TRENDS FORECASTS. 4688
1075-525X See FIBER OPTICS YELLOW PAGES. 1155
1075-5268 See FIBER OPTICS YELLOW PAGES. 1155
1075-5276 See INTERNATIONAL ISDN YELLOW PAGES. 1190
1075-5470 See SCIENCE COMMUNICATION. 5151
1075-5535 See JOURNAL OF ALTERNATIVE AND COMPLEMENTARY MEDICINE (NEW YORK, N.Y.), THE. 3593
1075-5594 See METAL HEAT TREATING. 4009
1075-5926 See MOBIL TRAVEL GUIDE. FREQUENT TRAVELERS' GUIDE TO MAJOR CITIES. 5484
1075-6116 See DGA NEWS. 4067
1075-6302 See JOURNAL - AMERICAN SOCIETY OF SUGAR CANE TECHNOLOGISTS. FLORIDA DIVISIONS. 175
1075-6477 See AMIA NEWSLETTER. 4063
1075-6507 See ANNUAL MEMBERSHIP DIRECTORY - NATIONAL ASSOCIATION OF ADVISORS FOR THE HEALTH PROFESSIONS. 3913
1075-6531 See HOLLYWOOD AGENTS/MANAGERS DIRECTORY. 4072
1075-6671 See KIPLINGER'S RETIREMENT REPORT. 4480
1075-6701 See BEHAVIORAL HEALTH MANAGEMENT. 1341
1075-6752 See INSIDE THE LEGISLATURE. 4477
1075-6809 See AMERICAN NATIONAL STANDARDS CATALOG. 4029
1075-6833 See ANNUAL REPORT TO CONGRESS / UNITED STATES CONSUMER PRODUCT SAFETY COMMISSION. 1293
1075-7015 See GEOLOGY OF ORE DEPOSITS. 1440
1075-7384 See QUICK N EASY COUNTRY COOKIN. 2792
1075-7821 See PCIA JOURNAL. 1161

1075-7856 See ROCKY MOUNTAIN MAGAZINE (STAMFORD, CONN.). 2544
1075-7961 See PROCEEDINGS - ANNUAL PITTSBURGH COAL CONFERENCE. 1953
1075-7988 See PROCEEDINGS OF THE AESF ANNUAL TECHNICAL CONFERENCE, THE. 2076
1075-802X See BUILDING SUPPLY HOME CENTERS (NORTHEAST ED.). 605
1075-8038 See BUILDING SUPPLY HOME CENTERS (MIDWEST ED.). 605
1075-8046 See BUILDING SUPPLY HOME CENTERS (WEST ED.). 605
1075-8054 See BUILDING SUPPLY HOME CENTERS (SOUTH ED.). 605
1075-8143 See JEWELRY MARKETING REVIEW. 927
1075-8216 See PROBLEMS OF POST-COMMUNISM. 4545
1075-8313 See PROCEEDINGS ... ANNUAL PITTSBURGH COAL CONFERENCE. 1953
1075-8321 See HUAMAN RESOURCES AND PRACTICE AND IDEAS. 869
1075-8534 See FEDERAL BAR COUNCIL NEWS. 2969
1075-8550 See WILLIAMS REPORT. 1124
1075-8704 See VIDEO TOASTER USER. 1235
1075-8852 See LEBANON LIGHT. 1093
1075-8917 See WESTERN STYLES. 2550
1075-9018 See BUSINESS CLAIMS CASUALTY BULLETIN. 2877
1075-9034 See MEXICAN ENVIRONMENTAL BUSINESS. 693
1075-9050 See NAFTA DIGEST / NORTH AMERICAN FREE TRADE AGREEMENT INFORMATION CENTER, THE GRADUATE SCHOOL OF INTERNATIONAL TRADE & BUSINESS ADMINISTRATION, LAREDO STATE UNIVERSITY. 847
1075-9069 See MARINE OFFICER. 4049
1075-9417 See MECHANICS OF COMPOSITE MATERIALS AND STRUCTURE. 2106
1075-9611 See ARIZONA EMPLOYMENT LAW LETTER. 3144
1075-962X See IOWA EMPLOYMENT LAW LETTER. 3150
1075-9719 See N-COMPASS (LINCOLN, NEB.). 3232
1075-9964 See ANAEROBE (LONDON, ENGLAND). 441
1076-0008 See U.S. COLLEGE HOCKEY MAGAZINE. 4927
1076-0326 See TECHNIQUE (HYATTSVILLE, MD.). 1122
1076-0342 See JOURNAL OF INFRASTRUCTURE SYSTEMS. 2025
1076-0415 See CD-ROM POCKET GUIDE. 1276
1076-0423 See STANDARD & POOR'S GLOBAL SECTOR REVIEW. 812
1076-0431 See JOURNAL OF ARCHITECTURAL ENGINEERING. 2025
1076-0512 See DERMATOLOGIC SURGERY. 3719
1076-058X See ROUND BOBBIN. 5185
1076-0814 See EASY APPROACH. 1183
1076-0830 See INSTYLE (NEW YORK, N.Y.). 2535
1076-1020 See ADOPTIVE FAMILIES. 5270
1076-1047 See CAPITATION & MEDICAL PRACTICE. 3562
1076-1500 See GRANTSEEKER, THE. 4653
1076-1519 See DRUG & CRIME PREVENTION FUNDING NEWS. 4774
1076-1551 See MOLECULAR MEDICINE (CAMBRIDGE, MASS.). 3618
1076-1608 See JOURNAL OF CLINICAL RHEUMATOLOGY. 3594
1076-1799 See COLLEGE PLACEMENT COUNCIL DIRECTORY. 1817
1076-2167 See MORNINGSTAR VARIABLE ANNUITY/LIFE SOURCEBOOK. 2888
1076-2175 See GIFTED CHILD TODAY MAGAZINE. 1879
1076-2183 See LIVESTOCK, DAIRY AND POULTRY SITUATION AND OUTLOOK. 105

ISSN Index

1076-2191 See ADVANCES IN WOUND CARE. 3546

1076-2620 See IS BUDGET. 1260

1076-2701 See SPORT ROCKETRY. 2778

1076-2752 See JOURNAL OF OCCUPATIONAL AND ENVIRONMENTAL MEDICINE. 3596

1076-2787 See COMPLEXITY (NEW YORK, N.Y.). 3501

1076-2809 See ALTERNATIVE AND COMPLEMENTARY THERAPIES. 3548

1076-2825 See ECOSYSTEM HEALTH AND MEDICINE. 3573

1076-2833 See QUINTESSENCE (CHICAGO, ILL.). 3661

1076-3112 See IBSNAT VIEWS. 93

1076-3279 See TISSUE ENGINEERING. 3646

1076-3333 See RESOURCE (SAINT JOSEPH, MICH.). 1994

1076-3376 See HOW TO PREPARE AN INITIAL PUBLIC OFFERING. 3100

1076-3600 See MERGER YEARBOOK, THE. 693

1076-3619 See MERGER YEARBOOK, THE. 693

1076-3678 See CUSTOM RODDER. 5412

1076-3708 See ASIAN M&A AND INVESTMENT DATABASE. 891

1076-3740 See ROCKVILLE CENTRE'S LONG ISLAND NEWS AND THE OWL. 5720

1076-3872 See VETERINARY CLINICAL NUTRITION. 5525

1076-3902 See AMERICAN-CANADIAN GENEALOGIST. 2436

1076-3929 See GRAIN, WORLD MARKETS AND TRADE. 202

1076-3937 See PLATT'S METALS WEEK. 4015

1076-3961 See FOUNDATION NEWS & COMMENTARY. 4336

1076-397X See JOURNAL OF PHARMACEUTICAL SCIENCE AND TECHNOLOGY. 4312

1076-4100 See IS AUDIT & CONTROL JOURNAL. 1260

1076-4240 See WIRELESS DESIGN & DEVELOPMENT. 1169

1076-4356 See COLLECTIBLE NEWSPAPERS. 2772

1076-4488 See SMALL BUSINESS HEALTH REFORM WATCH. 4803

1076-4526 See PHILLIPS BUSINESS INFORMATION'S INTERACTIVE VIDEO NEWS. 4372

1076-4607 See VETERINARY & COMPARATIVE OPHTHALMOLOGY. 5524

1076-4631 See FORT COLLINS TRIANGLE REVIEW. 5643

1076-464X See AFCPE NEWSLETTER. 768

1076-4747 See STN'S JOURNAL OF TRAUMA NURSING. 3870

1076-4763 See CARDIOVASCULAR NETWORK NEWS. 3701

1076-4798 See EMPLOYMENT OPPORTUNITIES, USA. 4204

1076-4852 See GWINNETT POST-TRIBUNE. 5653

1076-4941 See F&S INDEX UNITED STATES ANNUAL. 675

1076-4976 See WORLD OILSEED SITUATION AND OUTLOOK. 1631

1076-5174 See JOURNAL OF MASS SPECTROMETRY. PART A. 1017

1076-5778 See ASPIRE (NASHVILLE, TENN.). 2596

1076-5786 See ATHLETIC TRAINING (ST. LOUIS, MO.). 3953

1076-6014 See BRIEFINGS ON LONG-TERM CARE REGULATIONS. 4769

1076-6030 See RESPIRATORY CARE MANAGER. 3951

1076-6286 See BIOMATERIALS SCIENCE AND ENGINEERING. 3686

1076-6294 See MICROBIAL DRUG RESISTANCE, MECHANISMS, EPIDEMIOLOGY, AND DISEASE. 3736

1076-6464 See ENVIRO/ENERGYLINE ABSTRACTS PLUS. 2184

1076-6502 See R & R (LOS ANGELES, CALIF.). 1137

1076-6588 See F&S INDEX INTERNATIONAL ANNUAL. 1606

1076-6596 See F&S INDEX EUROPE ANNUAL (1993). 674

1076-7266 See WHARTON JOURNAL-SPECTATOR, THE. 5756

1076-7363 See BUSINESS WOMEN'S NETWORK DIRECTORY, THE. 653

1076-7428 See MASTERING CLINICAL PEDIATRIC DENTISTRY. 1329

1076-7568 See SHRIMP NEWS INTERNATIONAL. 2313

1076-769X See NATIONAL PRISON PROJECT JOURNAL, THE. 3170

1076-7754 See FAMILY PC. 1184

1076-7762 See CURRENT ISSUES IN PUBLIC HEALTH. 4773

1076-7843 See DIRECTORY OF CONVENTIONS. SOUTHEAST CONVENTION GUIDE. 758

1076-7851 See DIRECTORY OF CONVENTIONS. WEST CONVENTION GUIDE. 758

1076-786X See DIRECTORY OF CONVENTIONS. CENTRAL CONVENTION GUIDE. 758

1076-7878 See DIRECTORY OF CONVENTIONS. NORTHEAST & MID-ATLANTIC CONVENTION GUIDE. 758

1076-7975 See ELECTRONIC GREEN JOURNAL. 2165

1076-819X See ESTATE PLANNER'S ALERT (1994). 3118

1076-8408 See HIGH SPEED TRANSPORT NEWS. 4443

1076-8424 See IDB PROJECTS. 1635

1076-8432 See ACCOUNTABILITY NEWS FOR HEALTH CARE MANAGERS. 859

1076-8858 See AVIATION HISTORY. 13

1076-8866 See AMERICAN HISTORY. 2719

1076-8920 See HAZARDOUS SUBSTANCES & PUBLIC HEALTH. 2173

1076-8939 See BULLETINS. 644

1076-8971 See PSYCHOLOGY, PUBLIC POLICY, AND LAW. 4613

1076-898X See JOURNAL OF EXPERIMENTAL PSYCHOLOGY. APPLIED. 4596

1076-9021 See APPROVED VARIETY PUZZLES PLUS CROSSROADS. 4857

1076-9102 See CRANK (PHILADELPHIA, PA.). 4113

1076-9110 See SLAP. 4854

1076-9188 See TOXIC SUBSTANCE MECHANISMS. 3983

1076-9242 See DYSLEXIA (CHICHESTER, ENGLAND). 1878

1076-9285 See WORLD INTELLIGENCE REVIEW. 3356

1076-9668 See CHRISTIAN COUNSELING TODAY. 4944

1076-9714 See PROGRAMMER'S PROVANTAGE COMPUTER PRODUCTS BUYER'S GUIDE. 1281

1076-979X See SUBSTANCE ABUSE LETTER. 1349

1076-9862 See COMPUTER LIFE. 1177

1076-9897 See TEEN LIFE (SPRINGFIELD, MO.). 5002

1076-9986 See JOURNAL OF EDUCATIONAL AND BEHAVIORAL STATISTICS. 1795

1077-0119 See GERBINO INVESTMENT LETTER, THE. 899

1077-0291 See FBC (MADISON, ALA.). 1233

1077-0739 See WHO GOT IN?. 1853

1077-0771 See DIRECTORY (COLLEGE PLACEMENT COUNCIL). 1820

1077-0887 See SINGLES & LEADERS NEWSLETTER. 4997

1077-095X See BULLETIN (CALIFORNIA CENTRAL COAST GENEALOGICAL SOCIETY : 1993). 2440

1077-1034 See BIOLOGICAL ANALYSIS AND IMAGING METHODS. 3556

1077-1042 See PEDIATRIC PATHOLOGY AND LABORATORY MEDICINE. 3897

1077-1123 See OTOLOGY-NEUROTOLOGY (NEW YORK, N.Y.). 3624

1077-1131 See BABYBUG (PERU, ILL.). 1060

1077-1719 See HOSPITAL AND HEALTH ADMINISTRATION INDEX. 3659

1077-2014 See REAL-TIME IMAGING. 1201

1077-2111 See EDMUND'S VAN, PICKUP, SPORT UTILITY. 5414

1077-2197 See VIOLENCE AND ABUSE ABSTRACTS. 5267

1077-2537 See ENVIRONMENTAL SOLUTIONS. 2229

1077-2839 See PHARMACY TODAY. 4323

1077-2847 See JOURNAL OF PELVIC SURGERY. 3968

1077-2936 See NEW SCHOOLS, NEW COMMUNITIES. 1768

1077-3215 See FAMILIA DE LA CIUDAD, LA. 2278

1077-3525 See INTERNATIONAL JOURNAL OF OCCUPATIONAL AND ENVIRONMENT HEALTH. 2175

1077-3703 See OVER THE EDGE. 4877

1077-4092 See SINGLE-PARENT FAMILY. 2286

1077-4173 See NET GUIDE. 1275

1077-4440 See MULTIMEDIA NETWORK TECHNOLOGY REPORT. 1196

1077-4610 See JOURNAL OF SECONDARY GIFTED EDUCATION : JSGE, THE. 1881

1077-4696 See PHILLIPS BUSINESS INFORMATION'S COMMUNICATIONS STANDARDS NEWS. 1243

1077-5048 See SOCIOLOGICAL IMAGINATION. 5260

1077-5285 See PETROLEUM FINANCE WEEK. 4272

1077-5544 See EVERYDAY TLC. 1894

1077-5625 See SCHOLASTIC COACH AND ATHLETIC DIRECTOR. 4917

1077-5684 See LESBIAN REVIEW OF BOOKS, THE. 2795

1077-5862 See PC GRAPHICS & VIDEO. 1234

1077-5870 See PROCESS HEATING. 4432

1077-6265 See JOURNAL OF COMPUTER ABSTRACTS AND RESEARCH. 1209

1077-6710 See HUMAN RIGHTS WATCH/AMERICAS. 4509

1077-694X See JOURNALISM & MASS COMMUNICATION ABSTRACTS. 2921

1077-6958 See JOURNALISM & MASS COMMUNICATION EDUCATOR. 2921

1077-6966 See JOURNALISM & MASS COMMUNICATION MONOGRAPHS. 2921

1077-6974 See TILE DESIGN & INSTALLATION. 2594

1077-6982 See VITAL CHRISTIANITY (1994). 5008

1077-6990 See JOURNALISM & MASS COMMUNICATION QUARTERLY. 2921

1077-8039 See BARRON'S (CHICOPEE, MASS.). 642

1077-8292 See OPHTHALMOLOGY WORLD NEWS. 3878

1077-8519 See CHITTY'S LAW JOURNAL AND FAMILY LAW REVIEW. 3120

1077-9043 See BIANNUAL NEWSLETTER OF THE CONFERENCE GROUP ON ITALIAN POLITICS & SOCIETY, THE. 4516

1077-9817 See ACCREDITATION MANUAL FOR HEALTH CARE NETWORKS. VOL. 2, SCORING GUIDELINES. 3775

1078-0068 See FERRARI'S PLACES OF INTEREST. 2794

1078-0076 See ACCREDITATION MANUAL FOR HEALTH CARE NETWORKS. VOL. 1, STANDARDS. 3775

1078-0203 See FAST AND HEALTHY MAGAZINE. 2597

1078-0262 See STANDARD & POOR'S NASDAQ AND REGIONAL EXCHANGE PROFILES. 915

1078-0289 See HOME FASHIONS. 2900

1078-0343 See YOUR DOG. 5527

1078-0475 See ENVIRONMENTAL HEALTH PERSPECTIVES. SUPPLEMENTS. 2597

1078-0726 See JOURNAL OF ACCOUNTING, TAXATION AND FINANCE FOR BUSINESS, THE. 746

1078-1005 See ISDN USER NEWSLETTER. 1191

1078-1161 See JOURNAL OF OFFSHORE FINANCE AND TAX. 795

1078-1528 See CONNECTOR SPECIFIER. 1180

1078-2028 See INTER-AMERICAN TRADE AND INVESTMENT LAW. 840

1078-2362 See FLORIDA COMP. 1675

1078-2370 See OPEN COMPUTING. 1264

1078-2613 See SOUTHERN SEMINARY. 4998

1078-2842 See GENE THERAPY WEEKLY. 545

1078-2850 See INFECTIOUS DISEASE WEEKLY. 3672

1078-2869 See INTERNAL MEDICINE WEEKLY. 3797

1078-2877 See LUNG DISEASE WEEKLY. 3950

1078-2885 See PHARMACEUTICAL INDUSTRY WEEKLY. 4320

1078-2893 See UNIVERSITY BIOMED WEEKLY. 3697

1078-2907 See HEALTH LETTER ON THE CDC. 4780

1078-2958 See WB (GREENDALE, WIS.). 4929

1078-313X See STOCKHOLDERS & CREDITORS NEWS SERVICE CONCERNING ASBESTOS BANKRUPTCIES. 3103

1078-3466 See INTERNATIONAL JOURNAL OF POWER & ENERGY SYSTEMS. 1948

1078-3482 See INTERNATIONAL JOURNAL OF SUPERCOMPUTER APPLICATIONS AND HIGH PERFORMANCE COMPUTING, THE. 1287

1078-389X See COMBO (EVANSTON, ILL.). 4859

1078-4454 See DERMATOPATHOLOGY: PRACTICAL & CONCEPTUAL. 3720

1078-4500 See AMERICAN JOURNAL OF ANESTHESIOLOGY, THE. 3680

1078-4519 See AMERICAN JOURNAL OF ORTHOPEDICS, THE. 3880

1078-4632 See NETGUIDE (MANHASSET, N.Y.). 1196

1078-5108 See DOING BUSINESS IN THE RUSSIAN FEDERATION. 2964

1078-523X See NORTHERN BUSINESS INFORMATION'S TELECOM PERSPECTIVES. 1161

1078-5558 See MUSIC CITY NEWS (1994). 4133

1078-5612 See COLORADO WHEAT GROWER. 167

1078-5809 See B.P.I.A. BUSINESS PRODUCTS INDUSTRY REPORT. 4210

1078-5949 See CHICAGO SOURCEBOOK. 757

1078-6503 See LODGING MAGAZINE. 2807

1078-6856 See JOURNAL OF THE AMERICAN HEALTH CARE, THE. 5293

1078-7178 See APPIC DIRECTORY. 4574

1079-4573 See INSIDE THE NEW COMPUTER INDUSTRY. 1189

1079-6673 See RUBY'S PEARLS ELECMAG. 3432

1100-049X See FAKTA EUROPA. 1561

1100-0678 See PLANERA BYGGA BO. 2830

1100-116X See ALTERNATIV ODLING. 57

1100-1186 See CROP PRODUCTION SCIENCE. 169

1100-1283 See STUDIES IN INTERNATIONAL ECONOMICS & GEOGRAPHY. 1640

1100-1801 See ACTA PHARMACEUTICA NORDICA. 4289

1100-2298 See SVENSK EXEGETISK ARSBOK. 5020

1100-3006 See BEST 'N' MOST IN DFS, THE. 824

1100-3227 See FOOD LABORATORY NEWS. 2338

1100-3456 See SKRIFTER - NORDISKA GENBANKEN. 551

1100-4096 See NORDIC JOURNAL OF FRESHWATER RESEARCH. 2309

1100-4231 See TEKNIK I TRANSPORT. 5394

1100-5203 See BILDTIDNINGEN. 4367

1100-6323 See TIDSKRIFT FOR MEDICINSK OCH TEKNISK FOTOGRAFI. 4377

1100-8091 See STUDIA SEMINARII LATINI UPSALIENSIS. 3325

1100-8679 See WORKING PAPER / SWEDISH UNIVERSITY OF AGRICULTURAL SCIENCES, INTERNATIONAL RURAL DEVELOPMENT CENTRE. 147

1100-9233 See JOURNAL OF VEGETATION SCIENCE. 516

1100-956X See NEW SCANDINAVIAN TECHNOLOGY. 5132

1101-1165 See SPRAK OCH STIL. 3323

1101-1262 See EUROPEAN JOURNAL OF PUBLIC HEALTH. 4775

1101-2706 See SCANDINAVIAN DAIRY INFORMATION - SDI. 198

1101-2706 See SCANDINAVIAN DAIRY INFORMATION. 198

1101-3192 See NATURMILJON I SIFFROR. 2200

1101-3354 See SKOGSINDUSTRIERNA. 4239

1101-4989 See SWEDEN INTERNATIONAL. 714

1101-5179 See NORDIC ROAD & TRANSPORT RESEARCH. 5442

1101-5462 See LUND ART PRESS. 303

1101-6345 See CURRENT SWEDEN / THE SWEDISH INSTITUTE. 2514

1101-6965 See ELEKTRONIKTIDNINGEN. 2052

1101-7341 See ENVIRO. 2228

1101-766X See SVENSK PAPPERSTIDNING. NORDISK CELLULOSA. 4239

1101-8429 See ACTA REGIAE SOCIETATIS SCIENTIARUM ET LITTERARUM GOTHOBURGENESIS. BIOMEDICA. 3871

1101-9506 See SKOG & FORSKNING. 2395

1101-9948 See LUND MONOGRAPHS IN SOCIAL ANTHROPOLOGY. 240

1102-0822 See POPULAR HISTORIA. 2703

1102-3937 See STUDIES ON CRIME AND CRIME PREVENTION. 3177

1102-4151 See EUROPEAN JOURNAL OF SURGERY, THE. 3964

1102-4712 See LUND DISSERTATIONS IN SOCIOLOGY. 5251

1102-5824 See NORDISK ARKITEKTURFORSKNING. 305

1102-6065 See KONKURRENS/ UITGAVEN AV STATENS PRIS- OCH KONKURRENSVERK I SAMARBETE MED NARINGSFRIHETSOMBUDSMANNEN OCH MARKNADSDOMSTOLEN. 1502

1102-6103 See IATUL NEWS. 3214

1102-6480 See SCANDINAVIAN JOURNAL OF NUTRITION NARINGSFORSKNING. 4199

1102-6650 See KEMIVARLDEN. 1055

1102-7355 See CURRENT SWEDISH ARCHAEOLOGY. 266

1102-7495 See ELEKTRONIKTIDNINGEN. 2052

1102-769X See LUND STUDIES IN ETHICS AND THEOLOGY. 2252

1103-5897 See GFF. 1381

1103-8128 See SCANDINAVIAN JOURNAL OF OCCUPATIONAL THERAPY. 3639

1105-0136 See VALKANIKA SYMMEIKTA. 2714

1105-0462 See HRONIKA AISTHETIKES. 322

1105-0519 See MENIAIO STATISTIKO DELTIO - TRAPEZA TES HELLADOS. 731

1105-073X See PLATON. 1079

1105-0772 See BUZANTINA (THESSALONIKE). 2682

1105-0950 See ARCHAIOLOGIKE EPHEMERIS : EKDIDOMENE TES ARCHAIOLOGIKES HETAIREIAS. 258

1105-0969 See PRAKTIKA TES EN ATHENAIS ARCHAIOLOGIKES HETAIREIAS. 278

1105-1000 See FILOLOGIKE PROTOHRONIA. 3281

1105-1019 See MNEMOSUNE (ATHENAI). 1078

1105-154X See THEOLOGIA ATHENAI. 5003

1105-1590 See REVUE EUROPEENNE DE DROIT PUBLIC. 3094

1105-1663 See ISTORIKA, TA. 2620

1105-2120 See FILOSOFIA (ATHENAI). 4346

1105-235X See PHILOSOPHICAL INQUIRY. 4355

1105-2473 See PLANODION. 3424

1105-2651 See EPITHEORESE ZOOTEHNIKES EPISTEMES. 5583

1105-5758 See DELTION HRISTIANIKES ARHAIOLOGIKES ETAIREIAS. 266

1110-1423 See VETERINARY MEDICAL JOURNAL GIZA. 227

1111-0171 See ALGERIE - ACTUALITE. 5777

1115-201X See NIGERIAN STAGE, THE. 5366

1115-232X See OGBOMOSO JOURNAL OF THEOLOGY. 4983

1115-3067 See IITA RESEARCH. 94

1115-4489 See MEDIA REVIEW. 1134

1120-009X See JOURNAL OF CHEMOTHERAPY (FLORENCE). 3594

1120-0391 See ARCHIVIO MONALDI PER LE MALATTIE DEL TORACE. 3948

1120-0413 See ALTREITALIE. 1918

1120-0499 See GIORNALE INTERNAZIONALE DI DERMATOLOGIA PEDIATRICA. 3720

1120-0634 2626

1120-0677 See STORIA DELLE RELAZIONI INTERNATIONALI. 4535

1120-0685 See ALTRA EUROPA / CENTRO RUSSIA CRISTIANA, L'. 4933

1120-1289 5381

1120-1657 See DIFESA OGGI. 4042

1120-1681 See PROTEC. 2220

1120-1762 See RAGIUSAN. RASSEGNA GIURIDICA DELLA SANITA. 3034

1120-1770 See ITALIAN JOURNAL OF FOOD SCIENCE. 2345

1120-1797 See PHYSICA MEDICA. 3627

1120-1819 See EDIZIONI PER LA CONSERVAZIONE. 4828

1120-1908 See ALTA FREQUENZA. RIVISTA DI ELETTRONICA. 2034

1120-1932 See MEDIAPLUSNEWS. 692

1120-1967 See MODA IN. 2490

1120-2068 See PANORAMA FLORICOLO. 521

1120-219X See GIORNALE DELL'INSTALLATORE TELEFONICO, IL. 1976

1120-2343 See K : INTERNATIONAL CERAMICS MAGAZINE. 2592

1120-2351 See CONTATTO ELETTRICO. 1936

1120-236X See HABITAT UFFICIO. 2900

1120-2386 See OFFICE FURNITURE. 4213

1120-2424 See YACHT PREMIERE ENGLISH ED. 4856

1120-2505 See DST (MILANO, ITALY ; 1988). 2022

1120-253X See SFOGLIALIBRO. 4819

1120-2556 See PERSPECTIVES IN E.N.T.-IMMUNOLOGY. 3675

1120-2637 See PORTE & CANCELLI. 1621

1120-2831 See RASSEGNA DI PENSIONISTICA. 5304

1120-2971 See PREVENZIONE OGGI. 3629

1120-2998 See BOLLETINO - CONSOB. 779

1120-3005 See VITA IN CAMPAGNA. 144

1120-3137 See JOURNAL OF SPORTS TRAUMATOLOGY AND RELATED RESEARCH. 4902

1120-3226 See VERONA ILLUSTRATA : RIVISTA DEL MUSEO DI CASTELVECCHIO. 367

1120-3277 See ALISEI. 11

1120-3420 See RIVISTA DI STUDI CANADESI. 3431

1120-3455 See OTORINOLARINGOLOGIA PEDIATRICA, L'. 3890

1120-3544 See PAESAGGIO URBANO. 2830

1120-3587 See LOGISTICA MANAGEMENT. 876

1120-3625 3990

1120-3633 See ATTIVITA FISICA & SPORT. 4884

1120-3714 See ADOLESCENZA. 1059

1120-3730 See CARDIOLOGIA PER IMMAGINI. 3700

1120-3749 See GIORNALE ITALIANO DI FARMACIA CLINICA. 4306

1120-3757 See GASTROENTEROLOGIA CLINICA. 3745

ISSN Index

1120-3765 See JOURNAL OF IMMUNOLOGICAL RESEARCH : JIR : THE JOURNAL OF THE ITALIAN FEDERATION OF IMMUNOLOGICAL SOCIETIES. **3673**

1120-3773 See MEDICINA E INFORMATICA. **3613**

1120-379X See RICERCA & PRATICA. **3637**

1120-3811 See MICROCIRCOLAZIONE OGGI. **3616**

1120-3862 See EUROPEAN TRANSACTIONS ON TELECOMMUNICATIONS AND RELATED TECHNOLOGIES. **1155**

1120-4052 See FLORA MEDITERRANEA. **510**

1120-4060 See BOCCONEA. **502**

1120-4133 See AUTOTRASPORTO DI MERCI, L'. **5377**

1120-4141 See CIRCOLAZIONE STRADALE. **5379**

1120-415X See MOTORIZZAZIONE, LA. **5387**

1120-4176 See PATENTE DI GUIDA, LA. **5389**

1120-4222 See STABILITY & APPLIED ANALYSIS OF CONTINUOUS MEDIA. **3536**

1120-432X See AMICA. **5550**

1120-4397 See ELLE ED. ITALIANA. **5555**

1120-4451 See PIU BELLA. **5564**

1120-4486 See VISTO. **2494**

1120-4583 See SPEAK UP MILANO. **3322**

1120-4621 See CARTELLINA, LA. **4108**

1120-4826 See MINERVA BIOTECHNOLOGICA. **465**

1120-4966 See CLASSICI URANIA. **5074**

1120-5032 See ECONOMIA & MANAGEMENT. **1481**

1120-5067 See GAZZETTA DELLO SPORT, LA. **5804**

1120-5164 See MINISISTEMI. **1195**

1120-527X See STARBENE MILANO. **3642**

1120-5318 See RIVISTA DELLA BORSA. **821**

1120-5377 See GT. Il GIORNALE DEL TERMOIDRAULICO. **2090**

1120-544X See BOLLETTINO UFFICIALE DEGLI IDROCARBURI E DELLA GEOTERMIA / MINISTERO DELL'INDUSTRIA, DEL COMMERCIO E DELL'ARTIGIANATO, DIREZIONE GENERALE DELLE MINIERE, UFFICIO NAZIONALE MINERARIO PER GLI IDROCARBURI E LA GEOTERMIA. **4252**

1120-5539 See TITOLO : RIVISTA SCIENTIFICO-CULTURALE D'ARTE CONTEMPORANEA. **366**

1120-5679 See SAHARA (SEGRATE). **2492**

1120-5695 See RIVISTA INTERNAZIONALE DIRITTO COMUNE. **3045**

1120-5768 See AMICIZIA PALERMO. **2484**

1120-5784 See MEDIA PRODUCTION. **1117**

1120-5997 See ITALIAN BUSINESS REVIEW. **685**

1120-6012 See AGRO-INDUSTRY HI-TECH. **55**

1120-6020 See AVVENIRE. **5804**

1120-6039 See RISTORAZIONE COLLETTIVA. **2356**

1120-608X See MESSAGGERO VENETO. **5804**

1120-6195 See GIORNALE DELLA MUSICA, IL. **4119**

1120-6330 See ATTI DELLA ACCADEMIA NAZIONALE DEI LINCEI. RENDICONTI LINCEI. MATEMATICA E APPLICAZIONI. **3496**

1120-6349 See ATTI DELLA ACCADEMIA NAZIONALE DEI LINCEI. RENDICONTI LINCEI. SCIENZE FISICHE E NATURALI. **5086**

1120-6373 See GIORNALE ITALIANO DI ALLERGOLOGIA E IMUNOLOGIA CLINICA. **3670**

1120-6381 See CASA SUI CAMPI, LA. **2904**

1120-639X See COLLETTIVITA CONVIVENZE. **4771**

1120-6403 See MEDIT. **107**

1120-6454 See GALVANOTECNICA & NUOVE FINITURE. **487**

1120-6535 See REGIME DELLE IMPORTAZIONI, ESPORTAZIONI E NORME VALUTARIE. **1639**

1120-6721 See EUROPEAN JOURNAL OF OPHTHALMOLOGY. **3874**

1120-673X See SIMG : MEDICINA GENERALE. **3641**

1120-6772 See ABITARE CON ARTE. **2898**

1120-687X See ARCHIVIO DELLA NUOVA PROCEDURA PENALE. **2936**

1120-6888 See ARGOMENTI DI GERONTOLOGIA. **3749**

1120-7000 See HIP INTERNATIONAL : THE JOURNAL OF CLINICAL AND EXPERIMENTAL RESEARCH ON HIP PATHOLOGY AND THERAPY. **3804**

1120-7108 See DIAGNOSIS MILANO. **3571**

1120-7183 See RENDICONTI DI MATEMATICA E DELLE SUE APPLICAZIONI (1981). **3531**

1120-7248 See FIRENZE IERI, OGGI, DOMANI. **2516**

1120-7302 See MATERIALS ENGINEERING MODENA. **2105**

1120-7353 See MONDO DELLA BIBBIA, IL. **5018**

1120-7388 See MOCT-MOST: ECONOMIC POLICY IN TRANSITIONAL ECONOMIES. **1505**

1120-7507 See PEDIATRICS EDIZIONE ITALIANA. **3910**

1120-754X See RE. REGIONE EUROPA. **1639**

1120-7558 See RIVISTA ITALIANA DI CHIRURGIA MAXILLO-FACCIALE. **3974**

1120-7736 See LEI MILANO. 1976. **5560**

1120-7787 See VOGUE ITALIA. BAMBINI (MILAN, ITALY : 1982). **1088**

1120-7795 See VOGUE PELLE. **1088**

1120-7884 See TILE ITALIA. **2594**

1120-7892 See GIAIDS. GIORNALE ITALIANO DELL' AIDS. **3669**

1120-7906 See QTGO. QUADERNI DI TECNICA E GESTIONE OSPEDALIERA. **3791**

1120-7965 See DIRITTO & PRATICA DEL LAVORO / IPSOA. **3146**

1120-8066 See PC WORLD ITALIA. **1271**

1120-8260 See FONTI MUSICALI IN ITALIA, LE. **4118**

1120-8368 See PROFESSIONAL PULIZIE. **2127**

1120-8376 See LABORATORIO 2000. **984**

1120-8392 See G & B : GIORNALE DI CLINIA MEDICA & BASI RAZIONALI DELLA TERAPIA. **3578**

1120-8422 See AION. SLAVISTICA : ANNALI DELL'ISTITUTO UNIVERSITARIO ORIENTALE DI NAPOLI / DIPARTIMENTO DI STUDI DELL'EUROPA ORIENTALE, SEZIONE SLAVISTICA. **3262**

1120-8465 See M. MACINTOSH MAGAZINE. **1264**

1120-849X See ACHAB ROMA. **3357**

1120-8627 See PEDAGOGIA MEDICA. **3626**

1120-8635 See ARGOMENTI DI CARDIOLOGIA. **3699**

1120-8651 See ARGOMENTI DI GASTROENTEROLOGIA CLINICA. **3743**

1120-866X See ARGOMENTI DI NEUROLOGIA. **3827**

1120-8678 See BOLLETTINO DI FARMACOSORVEGLIANZA. **3558**

1120-8694 See DISEASES OF THE ESOPHAGUS : OFFICIAL JOURNAL OF THE INTERNATIONAL SOCIETY FOR DISEASES OF THE ESOPHAGUS / I.S.D.E. **3887**

1120-8708 See JOURNAL OF EMERGENCY SURGERY AND INTENSIVE CARE, THE. **3967**

1120-8724 See OPTOLASER MILANO. **2074**

1120-8732 See T & T. TRASPORTI E TRAZIONE. **5393**

1120-8902 See POLITECNICO MILANO. 1988. **306**

1120-8945 See STATISTICHE DELL'AGRICOLTURA, ZOOTECNIA E MEZZI DI PRODUZIONE. **222**

1120-9151 See RIVISTA ITALIANA DI ACQUACOLTURA / ASSOCIAZIONE PISCICOLTORI ITALIANI (A.P.I.). **557**

1120-9232 See QUADERNI EMILIANI. **2832**

1120-9461 See FINANZA IMPRESE E MERCATI. **835**

1120-9879 See HIGH BLOOD PRESSURE AND CARDIOVASCULAR PREVENTION. **3705**

1120-9992 See BASIC AND APPLIED MYOLOGY : BAM. **3803**

1121-0311 See DELFINO ROMA, IL. **2487**

1121-0494 See MUSICALIA LUCCA. **4137**

1121-0524 See ARTE DOCUMENTO. **340**

1121-0753 See LETTERATURA ITALIANA. AGGIORNAMENTO BIBLIOGRAFICO. **3459**

1121-0788 See A.M. AMMINISTRAZIONE & MANAGEMENT. **4623**

1121-0958 See CAUSE DI MORTE (1989). **5325**

1121-1008 See STATISTICHE DALLA SANITA. **4804**

1121-1288 See STOP MILANO. **2523**

1121-1350 See NATOM. FARMACIA NATURALE. **3619**

1121-1431 See ANIMAL BIOLOGY. **5502**

1121-1490 See BOLLETTINO AIB. **3196**

1121-1555 See INSEGNARE RELIGIONE. **4965**

1121-1563 See ORA DI RELIGIONE, L'. **4983**

1121-158X See WORLD OF BEER, THE. **2373**

1121-1628 See EUTOPIA. **268**

1121-1644 See INFORMAZIONI SUI FARMACI. **4308**

1121-1709 See ITALIAN JOURNAL OF MINERAL & ELECTROLYTE METABOLISM. **489**

1121-175X See BENISSIMO MILANO. **1082**

1121-1792 See DOVE MILANO. **5468**

1121-1814 See TELEPIU MILANO. **2493**

1121-1881 See SEMINARS IN DERMATOLOGY ED. ITALIANA. **3722**

1121-189X See EPIDEMIOLOGIA E PSICHIATRIA SOCIALE. **3734**

1121-1938 See BIBLIOGRAPHISCHE INFORMATIONEN ZUR ITALIENISCHEN GESCHICHTE IM. 19 UND 20. JAHUNDERT. **410**

1121-2047 See MECCANICA OGGI. **2121**

1121-208X See WATT MILANO. **5169**

1121-2098 See ACTA TECHNOLOGIAE ET LEGIS MEDICAMENTI. **3545**

1121-2179 See ACTA PHILOSOPHICA ROMA. **4339**

1121-2233 See JOURNAL OF PREVENTIVE MEDICINE AND HYGIENE. **4787**

1121-2438 See AMMINISTRAZIONE & FINANZA ORO. **769**

1121-2462 See ARCHIVI & COMPUTER. **1171**

1121-2810 See MEDIFAX ROMA. **3614**

1121-2861 See BOLLETTINO QUINDICINALE - AUTORITA GARANTE DELLA CONCORRENZA E DEL MERCATO. **825**

1121-2993 See CAMMINANDO INSIEME. **3339**

1121-3108 See BOLINA ROMA. **592**

1121-323X See NICOLAUS. STUDI STORICI. **2624**

1121-3337 See PC PROFESSIONALE. **1199**

1121-3450 See AUTOTECNICA LOCATE TRIULZI. **2110**

1121-371X See PROMOTEC. AGGIORNAMENTO ELETTRICO. **2077**

1121-4074 See RIVISTA DI DIRITTO TRIBUTARIO. **3044**

1121-4112 See OPERA MILANO. 1987, L'. **4143**

1121-4228 See MICRO & MACRO MARKETING. **933**

1121-5305 See BOLLETTINO UFFICIALE DEL TOTOCALCIO. **2485**

1121-5496 See UOMO HARPER'S BAZAAR. **1088**

1121-550X **1088**

1121-5542 See PARALLELI ROZZANO. **3349**

1121-5550 See QUATTRORUOTINE ROZZANO. **2777**

1121-5585 See TUTTOTRASPORTI ROZZANO. **5427**

1121-5593 See TUTTO TRASPORTI PASSEGGERI. **5398**

1121-5607 See VOLARE ROZZANO. **39**

1121-6093 See CERAMICA ACTA. **2587**

1121-6336 See COSTRUIRE MILANO. **611**

1121-6379 See NO LIMITS WORLD. **4876**

1121-6425 See BOLLETTINO STORICO DELLA CITTA DI FOLIGNO / ACCADEMIA FULGINIA DI LETTERE, SCIENZE E ARTI. **2679**

1121-6433 See BOLLETTINO DI STUDI E RICERCHE. **1812**

1121-6840 See CODICE DELLA STRADA. **5379**
1121-6875 See CONCERTINO MILANO. **2845**
1121-6956 See CERAMICANTICA FERRARA. **2588**
1121-7081 See LABOUR ROMA. **1686**
1121-7375 See HARPER'S BAZAAR ITALIA. **1085**
1121-7499 See PRESENTE E LA STORIA, IL. **2626**
1121-7995 See ELEVATORI MODERNI : SOLLEVAMENTO E TRASPORTO A FUNE. **5381**
1121-8290 See MODELLINA MILANO. **1086**
1121-8320 See BIMBI DI ELEGANTISSIMA. **1082**
1121-8428 See JN. JOURNAL OF NEPHROLOGY. **3990**
1121-8940 See GEOGRAPHIA ANTIQUA. **2562**
1121-9696 See VETERA CHRISTIANORUM. **5007**
1122-0279 See CONFINIA CEPHALALGICA. **3568**
1122-1305 See PIMPA MILANO. **327**
1122-195X See AION. SLAVISTICA : ANNALI DELL'ISTITUTO UNIVERSITARIO ORIENTALE DI NAPOLI / DIPARTIMENTO DI STUDI DELL'EUROPA ORIENTALE, SEZIONE SLAVISTICA. **3262**
1122-2824 See AEI. AUTOMAZIONE ENEGIA INFORMAZIONE. **2034**
1122-8660 See EUROPEAN JOURNAL OF FOOT AND ANKLE SURGERY. **3964**
1122-8687 See INTERNATIONAL JOURNAL OF SURGICAL SCIENCES. **3966**
1122-8695 See ENDOSURGERY. **3964**
1130-0108 See REVISTA ESPANOLA DE ENFERMEDADES DIGESTIVAS. **3747**
1130-0124 See ESPACIO, TIEMPO Y FORMA. SERIE 7, HISTORIA DEL ARTE : REVISTA DE LA FACULTAD DE GEOGRAFIA E HISTORIA / UNIVERSIDAD NACIONAL DE EDUCACION A DISTANCIA. **349**
1130-0280 See SOLDADURA Y TECNOLOGIAS DE UNION. **4019**
1130-0426 See NEUVA REVISTA DE POLITICA, CULTURA Y ARTE. **5210**
1130-0523 See PROGRESOS EN DIAGNOSTICO PRENATAL. **3767**
1130-0965 See CORE JOURNALS EN ENFERMEDADES PULMONARES. **3949**
1130-1406 See REVISTA IBEROAMERICANA DE MICOLOGIA. **576**
1130-149X See SI..., ENTONCES... . **4618**
1130-2089 See ANTHROPOS. SUPLEMENTOS. **2842**
1130-2097 See ISEGORIA : REVISTA DE FILOSOFIA MORAL Y POLITICA / INSTITUTO DE FILOSOFIA. **4350**
1130-2283 See ANALES DE QUIMICA (MADRID. 1990). **960**
1130-2682 See COOPERATIVISMO E ECONOMIA SOCIAL. **1471**
1130-2747 See GALERIA ANTIQUARIA. **350**
1130-2917 See VINO Y GASTRONOMIA. **190**
1130-2976 See TRABAJO SOCIAL Y SALUD. **5312**
1130-3204 See ETOLOGIA. **5583**
1130-3794 See D'A PALMA DE MALLORCA. **296**
1130-4014 See CADRIOLOGIA & HIPERTENSION. **3700**
1130-4405 See REVISTA DE LA MEDICINA TRADICIONAL CHINA. **3635**
1130-4413 See ANDALUCIA ECONOMICA. **1462**
1130-4553 See INFORMACIO ESTADISTICA DEL DEPARTAMENT DE TREBALL. **1679**
1130-4723 See REVISTA DE LA ACADEMIA CANARIA DE CIENCIAS. **5148**
1130-4758 See BUTLLETI DE LES SOCIETATS CATALANES DE FISICA, QUIMICA, MATEMATIQUES I TECNOLOGIA. **4399**
1130-4855 See ALTA FIDELIDAD EN AUDIO Y EN VIDEO. **1126**
1130-4936 See DOCUMENTOS A. **2685**
1130-5134 See ARCHIVES OF OPTHALMOLOGY ED. ESPANOLA. BARCELONA. **3872**
1130-5762 See LABORATORIO DE ARTE : REVISTA DEL DEPARTAMENTO DE HISTORIA DEL ARTE. **356**
1130-6017 See ITEA. PRODUCCION VEGETAL. **175**
1130-6157 See MAYAB (MADRID). **5209**

1130-622X See REVISTA MICROSOFT PARA PROGRAMADORES. **1239**
1130-6343 See FARMACIA HOSPITALARIA. **4304**
1130-6971 See ELECTRONICA & COMUNICACIONES MAGAZINE. **1110**
1130-7390 See ACTUALIDAD CIVIL. LEGISLACION. **3088**
1130-765X See PROFESIONES Y EMPRESAS. **1703**
1130-7854 See PANORAMA ENGLISH ED. **4095**
1130-796X See SUELO Y PLANTA. **188**
1130-8109 See ARAL MADRID. **2327**
1130-8508 See REVISTA DE LENGUA Y LITERATURA CATALANA, GALLEGA Y VASCA. **3316**
1130-9121 See REVISTA DE LA ECONOMIA SOCIAL Y DE LA EMPRESA. **1518**
1130-9571 See EPI. EQUIPOS PRODUCTOS INDUSTRIALES. **1606**
1130-958X See RFE. REVISTA FORESTAL ESPANOLA. **2394**
1130-9865 See PANORAMA ENGLISH ED. **4095**
1130-9946 See ACTUALIDAD ADMINISTRATIVA MADRID. **2927**
1130-9954 See PC ACTUAL. **1198**
1131-4184 See CONSULTA MADRID. 1983. **3568**
1131-5253 See CIENCIA PHARMACEUTICA. **3740**
1131-558X See REVISTA DE ANTROPOLOGIA SOCIAL / DEPARTAMENTO DE ANTROPOLOGIA SOCIAL, FACULTAD DE CIENCIAS POLITICAS Y SOCIOLOGIA, UNIVERSIDAD COMPLUTENSE DE MADRID. **244**
1131-5814 See ANTROPOLOGIA. **230**
1131-5997 See VINO Y GASTRONOMIA. **190**
1131-799X See REVISTA ESPANOLA DE CIENCIA Y TECNOLOGIA DE ALIMENTOS / EDITADA POR EL CONSEJO SUPERIOR DE INVESTIGACIONES CIENTIFICAS. **2356**
1131-8694 See COMERCIO E INDUSTRIA DE LA MADERA. **633**
1131-8848 See FLORENTIA ILIBERRITANA. **3388**
1131-897X See MADERPRESS BARCELONA. **634**
1131-9151 See LAZARILLO SALAMANCA. **3296**
1131-9178 See REVISTA GALLEGA DE PATOLOGIA DIGESTIVA. **3897**
1132-0273 See CUADERNOS DE MEDICINA PSICOSOMATICA. **3759**
1132-029X See ACTUALIDAD OBSTETRICO GINECOLOGICA MADRID. **3756**
1132-1261 See NOTICIARIO DE HISTORIA AGRARIA. **115**
1133-0376 See ANALES DE FISICA. **4396**
1133-0686 See TEST (MADRID). **5345**
1133-9535 See NUEVO LUNES, EL. **1509**
1140-4264 See JAPON ECONOMIE ET SOCIETE PARIS. **1498**
1140-4639 See REVUE FRANCAISE DE TRANSFUSION ET D'HEMOBIOLOGIE : BULLETIN DE LA SOCIETE NATIONALE DE TRANSFUSION SANGUINE. **3773**
1140-5031 See JAMA H (ED. FRANCAISE). **3591**
1140-5228 See CONJONCTURE ET PREVISION / REPUBLIQUE FRANCAISE, MINISTERE DE L'ECONOMIE, DES FINANCES ET DU BUDGET. **1552**
1140-5252 See INSEE ETUDES. **1496**
1140-5325 See REVUE EUROPEENNE DE DERMATOLOGIE ET DE MST. **3722**
1140-6011 See ACTIVITE PHILOSOPHIQUE ET SOCIALE, SCIENTIFIQUE, MEDICALE ET LITTERAIRE, L'. **2841**
1140-7123 See ANNUAIRE DE L'ADMINISTRATION DES DIRECTIONS REGIONALES DE L'INDUSTRIE ET DE LA RECHERCHE. **2133**
1140-7387 See BULLETIN DE LA COMMISSION HISTORIQUE DU DEPARTEMENT DU NORD. **2680**
1140-7409 See BULLETIN ARCHEOLOGIQUE DU VEXIN FRANCAIS / CENTRE DE RECHERCHES ARCHEOLOGIQUES DU VEXIN FRANCAIS. **262**
1140-7425 See BULLETIN DES AMIS DE MONTLUCON. **2681**

1140-7530 See CAHIERS DE SAINT-MICHEL DE CUXA, LES. **346**
1140-7581 See COURRIER PROFESSIONNEL PARIS, LE. **1144**
1141-1325 See REVUE DE LA HAUTE-AUVERGNE. **2853**
1141-135X See BULLETIN DE LA SOCIETE HISTORIQUE ET ARCHEOLOGIQUE DU PERIGORD. **2681**
1141-1791 See NICE HISTORIQUE. **2700**
1141-5134 See ENGLISH AUDIO REVIEWS ENGLISH ED. **3692**
1141-5177 See MUSIQUE SACREE 1947, LA. **4139**
1141-5886 See REVUE DU GYNECOLOGUE OBSTETRICIEN. **3768**
1141-9946 See NOUVEL AFRIQUE ASIE, LE. **4484**
1142-1983 See ALCOOLOGIE (PARIS). **2363**
1142-2300 See BULLETIN - AIDE AUX CROYANTS DE L'URSS. **4940**
1142-2505 See HORIZON. OCEANOGRAPHIE HYDROBIOLOGIE. **1363**
1142-2513 See HORIZON. SCIENCES ECONOMIQUES ET SOCIALES. **1533**
1142-2521 See HORIZON. SCIENCES DU MONDE VEGETAL ET ANIMAL. **478**
1142-2599 See ESTHETICA (PARIS, 1989). **404**
1142-2815 See RESEAUX PARIS. 1989. **3245**
1142-2858 See BULLETIN DE LA COMMISSION BANCAIRE. **644**
1142-2866 See TPH. THERAPEUTIQUE ET PRATIQUE HOSPITALIERES PARIS. **3646**
1142-2904 See QUATERNAIRE : BULLETIN DE L'ASSOCIATION FRANCAISE POUR L'ETUDE DU QUATERNAIRE : INTERNATIONAL JOURNAL OF THE FRENCH QUATERNARY ASSOCIATION. **1393**
1142-2998 See ANNALES SCIENTIFIQUES DE L'UNIVERSITE DE FRANCHE-COMTE. BIOLOGIE-ECOLOGIE. **441**
1142-3080 See INSEE METHODES. **1496**
1142-3218 See AGRESTE, SER. BULL. **47**
1142-3250 See BIBLIOGRAPHIE NATIONALE FRANCAISE. LIVRES : NOTICES ETABLES PAR LA BIBLIOTHEQUE NATIONALE. **410**
1142-4877 See SCIENCES & AVENIR. HORS SERIE. **5154**
1142-4966 See HERALDIQUE ET GENEALOGIE VILLAINE-LA-JUHEL. **2453**
1142-5067 See CONNAISSANCE DE L'EURE. **2845**
1142-7086 See ACTION COMMERCIALE, MANUELS. **920**
1142-852X See HOMMES & MIGRATIONS. **1919**
1143-2462 See SPORTING GOODS INTELLIGENCE (BRY-SUR-MARNE). **4921**
1143-354X See RELATIONS ECOLES PROFESSIONS. **1843**
1143-3760 See TRANSFIL EUROPE PARIS. **1168**
1143-4325 See COURRIER EUROPEEN DE L'ENTREPRISE PARIS, LE. **830**
1143-4627 See ENTENTE EUROPEENNE POUR L'ENVIRONNEMENT PARIS. **2192**
1143-6360 See VIDEOTEX & RNIS MAGAZINE. **1123**
1143-676X See FESTIN, LE. **320**
1143-7375 See FILIERES VIANDE ET PECHE LEVALLOIS-PERRET. **2335**
1143-7405 See CULTIVAR 1989. **77**
1143-7723 See SINGULARITE LYON. **3535**
1144-0546 See NEW JOURNAL OF CHEMISTRY (1987). **987**
1144-2433 See SERVICE NEWS PARIS. **886**
1144-3464 See BULLETIN D'INFORMATIONS SCIENTIFIQUES - INSTITUT PASTEUR. **5091**
1144-4924 See CAHIERS DE PHILOSOPHIE POLITIQUE ET JURIDIQUE. **1060**
1144-5742 See ELECTRONIQUE RADIO PLANS PARIS. **2050**
1145-0320 See CAHIERS DE L'EXPRESS (PARIS), LES. **2514**
1145-0673 See INC HEBDO CONSOMMATEURS ACTUALITES. **1297**

1145-0762 See JOURNAL INTERNATIONAL DE BIOETHIQUE. 460

1145-0835 See D'ARCHITECTURES : D'A. 296

1145-1378 See REVUE DE L'IRES, LA. 1518

1145-1408 See CHRONIQUE INTERNATIONALE PARIS. 1470

1145-2099 See DEVELOPPEURS LEVALLOIS-PERRET. 4836

1145-4881 See LETTRE MENSUELLE DE FRANCE PHARMACIE LABORATOIRES, LA. 4314

1145-5187 See URBANISMES & ARCHITECTURE. 2838

1145-5268 See CAHIERS DE L'IPAG NANCY. 4466

1145-5799 See VIGNE PARIS, LA. 2371

1145-7295 See BULLETIN DE LA SOCIETE ARCHEOLOGIQUE CHAMPENOISE 1954. 263

1145-7325 See BULLETIN DE LA SOCIETE ARCHEOLOGIQUE, HISTORIQUE ET ARTISTIQUE, LE VIEUX PAPIER, POUR L'ETUDE DE LA VIE ET DES MRS D'AUTREFOIS. 263

1145-8488 See AFFICHES DE NORMANDIE, LES. 755

1145-8690 See ACTUALITES SOCIALES HEBDOMADAIRES. 5269

1145-9646 See LETTRE DE L'EDI PARIS, LA. 1115

1146-0024 See FRANCE ITALIE. 4474

1146-1497 See CFE INDUSTRIE. 2038

1146-190X See LETTRE TOURISTIQUE PARIS, LA. 5483

1146-1918 See LETTRE TOURISTIQUE PARIS, LA. 5483

1146-2132 See REVUE MARITIME 1990, LA. 4182

1146-2965 See CLEIRPPA INFOS PARIS. 3750

1146-5018 See PASCAL. VOL. 4, TERRE, OCEAN, ESPACE. 1363

1146-5034 See PASCAL. 215, BIOTECHNOLOGIES. 3695

1146-5077 See PASCAL. T 260, ZOOLOGIE FONDAMENTALE ET APPLIQUEE DES INVERTEBRES. 5594

1146-5093 See PASCAL. T 295, BATIMENT TRAVAUX PUBLICS. 2006

1146-5107 See PASCAL. F 10, MECANIQUE, ACOUSTIQUE ET TRANSFERT DE CHALEUR. 4453

1146-5123 See PASCAL. F 17, CHIMIE GENERALE MINERALE ET ORGANIQUE. 988

1146-5166 See PASCAL. F 25, TRANSPORTS TERRESTRES ET MARITIMES. 5389

1146-5174 See PASCAL. F 40, MINERALOGIE, GEOCHIMIE, GEOLOGIE EXTRATERRESTRE. 1359

1146-5182 See PASCAL. F 41, GISEMENTS METALLIQUES ET NON METALLIQUES. 4014

1146-5239 See PASCAL. F 46, HYDROLOGIE, GEOLOGIE DE L'INGENIEUR, FORMATIONS SUPERFICIELLES. 1417

1146-5247 See PASCAL. F 47, PALEONTOLOGIE. 4230

1146-5255 See PASCAL. F 52, BIOCHIMIE, BIOPHYSIQUE MOLECULAIRE, BIOLOGIE MOLECULAIRE ET CELLULAIRE. 492

1146-5271 See PASCAL. F 54, REPRODUCTION DES VERTEBRES, EMBRYOLOGIE DES VERTEBRES ET DES INVERTEBRES. 5594

1146-5301 See PASCAL. F 70, PHARMACOLOGIE, TRAITEMENTS MEDICAMENTEUX. 4319

1146-5344 See PASCAL. E 18, CHROMATOGRAPHIE. 988

1146-5360 See PASCAL. E 27, METHODES DE FORMATION ET TRAITEMENT DES IMAGES. 4426

1146-5387 See PASCAL. E29, SEMICONDUCTEURS, MATERIAUX ET COMPOSANTS. 2074

1146-5425 See PASCAL. E34, ROBOTICS, CONTROL THEORY AND INDUSTRIAL PROCESSES AUTOMATION. 1215

1146-545X See PASCAL. E 48, ENVIRONNEMENT COSMIQUE TERRESTRE, ASTRONOMIE ET GEOLOGIE EXTRATERRESTRE. 398

1146-5476 See PASCAL. E 57, BIOLOGIE MARINE. 468

1146-5484 See PASCAL. E 58, GENETIQUE. 550

1146-5492 See PASCAL. E 61, MICROBIOLOGIE. 468

1146-5506 See PASCAL. E 62, IMMUNOLOGIE. 3675

1146-5514 See PASCAL. E 63, TOXICOLOGIE. 3983

1146-5549 See PASCAL. 68, GENETIQUE HUMAINE. 550

1146-5581 See PASCAL. E 74, PNEUMOLOGIE. 3950

1146-559X See PASCAL. 75, CARDIOLOGIE ET APPAREIL CIRCULATOIRE. 3709

1146-5603 See PASCAL. E 76, GASTROENTEROLOGIE, FOIE, PANCREAS, ABDOMEN. 3747

1146-5611 See PASCAL. E 77, NEPHROLOGIE, VOIES URINAIRES. 3992

1146-562X See PASCAL. E 78, NEUROLOGIE. 3844

1146-5670 See PASCAL. E 83, ANESTHESIE ET REANIMATION. 3844

1146-5697 See PASCAL. E 89, CANCER. 3822

1146-5751 See AGRESTE. SERIES, BULLETIN BIMESTRIEL DE STATISTIQUE AGRICOLE DES PAYS DE LA LOIRE. 150

1146-5786 See COURANTS PARIS. 1990. 5532

1146-609X See ACTA OECOLOGICA (MONTROUGE). 2210

1146-7363 See ANNUAIRE DE LA SOCIETE D'HISTOIRE DU VAL ET DE LA VILLE DE MUNSTER. 2674

1146-7371 See ANNUAIRE DE LA SOCIETE D'HISTOIRE DES REGIONS DE THANN-GUEBWILLER. 2674

1147-1999 See BOTTIN ADMINISTRATIF. 4634

1147-7806 See SECHERESSE MONTROUGE. 1360

1147-7970 See PSYCHIATRIE MAGAZINE ROYAN. 3933

1147-9558 See REPERTOIRE DES GEOGRAPHES FRANCAIS PARIS. 2574

1148-1757 See ECHOS DE L'EXPORTATION PARIS, LES. 832

1148-2141 See TRAVAUX DU LABORATOIRE D'ANTHROPOLOGIE ET DE PREHISTOIRE DES PAYS DE LA MEDITERRANEE OCCIDENTALE. 246

1148-2893 See REVUE TECHNIQUE - GEC ALSTHOM. 2079

1148-3164 See LETTRE DE REPORTERS SANS FRONTIERES, LA. 2922

1148-3555 See INTERNATIONAL DOMOTIQUE NEWS PARIS. 5115

1148-4322 See SON, MUSIQUE, VIDEO MAG. 4377

1148-4675 See DECISION MICRO PARIS. 5099

1148-4683 See CAHIERS DE L'EUROPE PARIS. 5276

1148-5167 See AGRESTE. CONJONCTURE, PROVENCE ALPES COTE D'AZUR. 47

1148-5361 See AGRESTE. SERIES, LE BULLETIN DE FRANCHE-COMTE. 47

1148-5493 See EUROPEAN CYTOKINE NETWORK. 536

1148-5558 See AGRESTE. SERIES, BULLETIN MENSUEL LANGUEDOC-ROUSSILLON. 47

1148-5566 See ESPACE BUREAU PARIS. 4211

1148-5612 See AGRESTE. CONJONCTURE, PRODUCTIONS ANIMALES. 204

1148-5620 See AGRESTE. CONJONCTURE, GRANDES CULTURES. 46

1148-5639 See AGRESTE. CONJONCTURE, FRUITS. 161

1148-5647 See AGRESTE. CONJONCTURE, LAIT ET PRODUITS LAITIERS. 191

1148-5655 See AGRESTE. CONJONCTURE, LEGUMES. 161

1148-5663 See AGRESTE. CONJONCTURE, VITICULTURE. 161

1148-5671 See AGRESTE. CONJONCTURE, RHONE-ALPES. 47

1148-6023 See MONUMENTS ET MEMOIRES PARIS. 275

1148-7194 See TRANSFORMATIONS (PARIS). 310

1148-7305 See BUREAUX D'ETUDES 1990. 1172

1148-750X See STRATEGIES DU MANAGEMENT PARIS. 887

1148-7666 See TRIBUNE DES INDUSTRIES DE LA LANGUE, LA. 3330

1148-7771 See BUGEY, LE. 2612

1148-7852 See BULLETIN DE L'ACADEMIE DU VAR. 1075

1148-7860 See BULLETIN DE LA DIANA MONTBRISON. 2680

1148-795X See BULLETIN ANNUEL DE LA SOCIETE D'ARCHEOLOGIE ET D'HISTOIRE DU TONNEROIS. 262

1148-7968 See BULLETIN DE LA SOCIETE DE L'HISTOIRE DE PARIS ET DE L'ILE-DE-FRANCE. 2680

1148-8093 See MEMOIRES DE LA SOCIETE ROYALE D'HISTOIRE ET D'ARCHEOLOGIE DE TOURNAI. 274

1148-8298 See BULLETIN DE LA SOCIETE SCHONGAUER DE COLMAR. 2681

1148-8395 See BULLETIN DU MUSEE BASQUE. 4085

1148-8557 See BULLETIN DE LA SOCIETE DES LETTRES, SCIENCES ET ARTS DE LA CORREZE. 2843

1148-859X See BULLETIN DE LA SOCIETE HISTORIQUE ET ARCHEOLOGIQUE DE LANGRES. 2681

1148-8859 See BATI HIGH TECH MAGAZINE. 600

1148-9227 See KAIROS. 4351

1148-9480 See LETTRE - EUROSANTE, LA. 4789

1149-0039 See CAHIERS DE RHEOLOGIE, LES. 450

1149-0276 See SESSION D'ETUDES BIENNALE DE PHYSIQUE NUCLEAIRE. 4451

1149-0306 See BULLETIN TECHNIQUE - GATTEFOSSE REPORT. 5092

1149-0349 See MEMOIRES DE L'ACADEMIE DE METZ. 1078

1149-2031 See EVOCATIONS CREMIEU. 2688

1149-3305 See PAYS D'AUGE LISIEUX. 1951, LE. 2521

1149-6770 See BULLETIN DE LA SOCIETE ARCHEOLOGIQUE D'EURE-ET-LOIR. 263

1149-767X See RECUEIL DE L'ASSOCIATION DES AMIS DU VIEUX HAVRE. 2705

1149-8080 See MEMOIRES DE LA SOCIETE D'HISTOIRE ET D'ARCHEOLOGIE DE CHALON-SUR-SAONE. 274

1149-932X See BULLETIN - SOCIETE ARCHEOLOGIQUE DE SENS. 264

1150-1448 See AGRESTE. DONNEES, BULLETIN DE STATISTIQUE AGRICOLE REUNION. 150

1150-1529 See AGRESTE. SERIES, AVICULTURE. 204

1150-1537 See AGRESTE. SERIES, LE BULLETIN TRIMESTRIEL LIMOUSIN. 47

1150-1588 See BIBLIOGRAPHY OF THE HISTORY OF ART : BHA. 334

1150-1677 See COSMETICA DISTRIBUTION LEVALLOIS-PERRET. 403

1150-1693 See AGRESTE. CONJONCTURE, POITOU-CHARENTES. 47

1150-1707 See AGRESTE. CONJONCTURE, NOTE DE CONJONCTURE AGRICOLE MIDI-PYRENEES. 46

1150-1723 See AGRESTE. DONNEES, BULLETIN DE STATISTIQUE AGRICOLE HAUTE ET BASSE-NORMANDIE. 150

1150-1731 See AGRESTE. SERIES, BULLETIN DE STATISTIQUE AGRICOLE REGION MIDI-PYRENEES. 150

1150-1898 See AGRESTE. DONNEES, BULLETIN BOURGOGNE. 149

1150-1901 See AGRESTE. DONNEES, BULLETIN DE STATISTIQUE AGRICOLE D'AQUITAINE. 150

1150-1987 See AGRESTE. ANALYSES & ETUDES, COUP D'OEIL SUR RHONE-ALPES. 46

1150-2037 See AGRESTE. SERIES, BULLETIN ALSACE. 47

1150-224X See AGRESTE. CONJONCTURE, BULLETIN REGIONAL CHAMPAGNE-ARDENNE. 149

1150-3637 See ANNALES DE L'IRETIJ MONTPELLIER, LES. 2933

1150-4447 See MAGHREB CONFIDENTIEL PARIS. 4481

1150-5966 See MEDECINE FOETALE ET ECHOGRAPHIE EN GYNECOLOGIE. 3607

1150-6652 See REVUE INTERNATIONALE DE PSYCHOPATHOLOGIE PARIS. 3936

1150-8809 See CAHIERS SCIENTIFIQUES DU TRANSPORT CAEN, LES. 1467

1151-0285 See JOURNAL INTERNATIONAL DES SCIENCES DE LA VIGNE ET DU VIN. 2368

1151-0985 See JOURNAL INTERNATIONAL DES SCIENCES DE LA VIGNE ET DU VIN. 175

1151-2709 See BULLETIN DE LA SOCIETE DE MYTHOLOGIE FRANCAISE. 2318

1151-3195 See ACTUALITES SPORT ET MEDECINE ROYAN. 3953

1151-3551 See REVUE DE BIOTHERAPIE VETERINAIRE. 5520

1151-5422 See ETHIQUE. 2250

1152-0647 See METHODES ET TECHNIQUES DE L'INGENIEUR PARIS. 1987

1152-5096 See DOSSIERS ET DEBATS - INSTITUT INTERNATIONAL D'ADMINISTRATION PUBLIQUE. 4645

1152-6653 See VIVRE ENSEMBLE PARIS. 1790

1152-8400 See REVUE DU LITTORAL. 4616

1152-8427 See CAHIERS DU CRABB MONT-SAINT-AIGNAN, LES. 781

1152-9172 See REVUE DES AFFAIRES EUROPEENNES. 4534

1152-9563 See SPORT ET VIE DIJON. 4920

1153-0863 See JOURNAL DU SIDA PARIS, LE. 3592

1153-2254 See BULLETIN DE L'INSTITUT DES ACTUAIRES FRANCAIS. 644

1153-2424 See ANNALES DE CHIRURGIE DE LA MAIN ET DU MEMBRE SUPERIEUR. 3958

1153-2521 See BULLETIN DE LA SOCIETE ARCHEOLOGIQUE DE TOURAINE. 263

1153-2599 See BULLETIN HISTORIQUE ET SCIENTIFIQUE DE L'AUVERGNE 1933. 2843

1153-2661 See BULLETIN DE LA SOCIETE ARCHEOLOGIQUE DE TARN-ET-GARONNE. 316

1153-3072 See BOIS DE FEU & ENERGIE NOGENT-SUR-MARNE. 1934

1153-3277 See BULLETIN DE LA SOCIETE D'HISTOIRE ET D'ARCHEOLOGIE DE VICHY ET DE SES ENVIRONS. 2680

1153-4664 See OLEOSCOPE PARIS. 117

1154-1105 See CAOUTCHOUCS & PLASTIQUES PARIS. 5075

1154-1342 See REVUE ARCHEOLOGIQUE DE BORDEAUX. 281

1154-2675 See FLASH ESPACE TOULOUSE. 395

1154-2829 See SYSTEME D PRATIQUE PARIS. 1886

1154-368X See BULLETIN DE LA SOCIETE HISTORIQUE ET ARCHEOLOGIQUE DE CORBEIL, DE L'ESSONNE ET DU HUREPOIX. 2681

1154-4368 See BABAR PARIS. 1060

1154-516X See COURRIER INTERNATIONAL PARIS. 2486

1154-5399 See EURO POP BOOK PARIS. 2515

1154-5445 See LIVRE INTERNATIONAL DES VENTES PARIS, LE. 357

1154-5658 See OPTIONS MONTREUIL. 1511

1154-6433 See MAINTENANCE & ENTREPRISE PARIS. 1985

1154-7138 See JESUS PARIS. 1973. 4967

1154-7707 See PRECIS ANALYTIQUE DES TRAVAUX DE L'ACADEMIE DES SCIENCES, BELLES-LETTRES ET ARTS DE ROUEN. 2852

1154-9041 See AVIRON (FRANCE). 4885

1155-1087 See REVUE OFFICIELLE DE LA SOCIETE FRANCAISE D'ORL ET DE PATHOLOGIE CERVICO-FACIALE. 3891

1155-2492 See REALITES THERAPEUTIQUES EN DERMATO-VENEROLOGIE. 3722

1155-3219 See GENESES. 5200

1155-3480 See DEFENSE & TECHNOLOGIE INTERNATIONAL PARIS. 4041

1155-4029 See ANALYSES COMPARATIVES - COMMISSION BANCAIRE PARIS. 770

1155-4037 See AGRESTE. DONNEES, BULLETIN DE STATISTIQUE AGRICOLE GUADELOUPE. 150

1155-4088 See AGRESTE. SERIES, LE BULLETIN POITOU-CHARENTES. 47

1155-4274 See REVUE DU MARCHE UNIQUE EUROPEEN. 1639

1155-4304 See JOURNAL DE PHYSIQUE. I (LES ULIS). 4408

1155-4312 See JOURNAL DE PHYSIQUE. II (LES ULIS). 4408

1155-4320 See JOURNAL DE PHYSIQUE. III (LES ULIS). 4408

1155-4339 See JOURNAL DE PHYSIQUE. IV (LES ULIS). 4408

1155-4452 See REVUE DE NEUROPSYCHOLOGIE / SOCIETE DE NEUROPSYCHOLOGIE DE LANGUE FRANCAISE. 3845

1155-4479 See AGRESTE. DONNEES, BULLETIN DE STATISTIQUE AGRICOLE MARTINIQUE. 150

1155-4487 See AGRESTE. SERIES, ANIMAUX HEBDO. 204

1155-4495 See AGRESTE. SERIES, COMMERCE EXTERIEUR BOIS ET DERIVES. 2399

1155-5645 See PAEDIATRIC ANAESTHESIA. 3907

1156-1556 See MOTORISATION (PARIS). 160

1156-1602 See TOP CULTURES (FRANCE). 141

1156-1653 See INRA MENSUEL LES DOSSIERS. 2385

1156-2560 See NOTE D'INFORMATION ECONOMIQUE - COMITE PROFESSIONNEL DU PETROLE. 4267

1156-2897 See SMFA ACTUALITES PARIS. 627

1156-3133 See OFFICIEL DES TRANSPORTS PARIS, L'. 5388

1156-4148 See ANGLE DROIT PARIS. 2933

1156-4407 See MINUTE PARIS. 1993. 1764

1156-4903 See CONSEIL INFORMATIQUE A LA DIRECTION GENERALE, LE. 5096

1156-5233 See JOURNAL DE MYCOLOGIE MEDICALE PARIS. 575

1156-7198 See ARCHEOLOGIE ISLAMIQUE. 259

1156-833X See RECHERCHES, HANDICAPS ET VIE CHRETIENNE. 5304

1156-962X See RECYCLAGE RECUPERATION PARIS. 2220

1157-0466 See THANATOLOGIE (PARIS). 4363

1157-075X See MEMOIRES. 2850

1157-1055 See BULLETIN DES TRANSPORTS ET DE LA LOGISTIQUE PARIS. 5378

1157-1152 See ELECTRONIQUE PARIS. 1990. 2050

1157-1209 See BIOLOGISTE ET PRATICIEN PARIS. 446

1157-1497 See S.T.P. PHARMA PRATIQUES : TECHNIQUES REGLEMENTATIONS. 4329

1157-3546 See AGRESTE. SERIES, BULLETIN DE STATISTIQUE AGRICOLE ILE DE FRANCE. 150

1157-3554 See AGRESTE. CONJONCTURE, REGION ILE-DE-FRANCE. 47

1157-3694 See FRANCIS BULLETIN SIGNALETIQUE. 519, PHILOSOPHIE. 4347

1157-3708 See FRANCIS BULLETIN SIGNALETIQUE. 520, SCIENCES DE L'EDUCATION. 1747

1157-3716 See FRANCIS BULLETIN SIGNALETIQUE. 521, SOCIOLOGIE. 5245

1157-3724 See FRANCIS BULLETIN SIGNALETIQUE. 522, HISTOIRE DES SCIENCES ET DES TECHNIQUES. 5106

1157-3732 See FRANCIS BULLETIN SIGNALETIQUE. 523, HISTOIRE ET SCIENCES DE LA LITTERATURE. 3389

1157-3740 See FRANCIS BULLETIN SIGNALETIQUE. 524, SCIENCES DU LANGAGE. 3282

1157-3759 See FRANCIS BULLETIN SIGNALETIQUE. 525, PREHISTOIRE ET PROTOHISTOIRE. 236

1157-3767 See FRANCIS BULLETIN SIGNALETIQUE. 526, ART ET ARCHEOLOGIE. 268

1157-3775 See FRANCIS BULLETIN SIGNALETIQUE. 527, HISTOIRE ET SCIENCES DES RELIGIONS. 4959

1157-3783 See FRANCIS BULLETIN SIGNALETIQUE. 528, BIBLIOGRAPHIE INTERNATIONALE DE SCIENCE ADMINISTRATIVE. 868

1157-3791 See FRANCIS BULLETIN SIGNALETIQUE. 529, ETHNOLOGIE. 236

1157-3805 See FRANCIS BIBLIOGRAPHIE GEOGRAPHIQUE INTERNATIONALE. 531. 2561

1157-383X See FRANCIS. 617, ECODOC / RESEAU D'INFORMATION EN ECONOMIE GENERALE. 1491

1157-4127 See REVUE NOIRE. 330

1157-4445 See ELECTRONIQUE INTERNATIONAL HEBDO PARIS. 2050

1157-4569 See GDS INFO PARIS. 211

1157-5417 See RELATIONS INTERNATIONALES ET STRATEGIQUES. 4533

1157-5662 See MANAGEMENT ET CONJONCTURE SOCIALE PARIS. 877

1157-6049 See MAITRISE PARIS. 4206

1157-6197 See DECISION SANTE NEUILLY-SUR-SEINE. 2596

1157-6472 See EPARGNE & FINANCE PARIS. 1591

1157-688X See CONSERVATION RESTAURATION DES BIENS CULTURELS PARIS. 348

1157-741X See CHOCS (VILLENEUVE-SAINT-GEORGES). 2154

1157-7452 See LIBRESENS PARIS. 5062

1157-8181 See CONTRACEPTION, FERTILITE, SEXUALITE. 588

1157-8394 See FLASH INFORMATIONS - CHAMBRE DE COMMERCE FRANCO-SOVIETIQUE. 819

1157-8637 See COMMUNICATIONS & STRATEGIES MONTPELLIER. 1175

1157-996X See CULTURES ET CONFLITS. 4519

1158-2626 See RENAISSANCE DU VIEUX METZ, LA. 329

1158-4270 See DO RE MI PARIS. 1063

1158-5803 See NOUS DEUX COLLECTION. 2520

1160-5634 See BULLETIN - SOCIETE ACADEMIQUE DU BAS-RHIN POUR LE PROGRES DES SCIENCES, DES LETTRES, DES ARTS ET DE LA VIE ECONOMIQUE. 317

1160-9907 See SEMIOTIQUES / CENTRE NATIONAL DE LA RECHERCHE SCIENTIFIQUE, INSTITUT NATIONAL DE LA LANGUE FRANCAISE, URL7-ANALYSE DU DISCOURS. 3320

1161-0301 See EUROPEAN JOURNAL OF AGRONOMY. 171

1161-1804 See CLUB INFORMATIONS NANTERRE. 1968

1161-2258 See COSMOPOLITAN (PARIS). 5554

1161-3157 See UNIVERS MAC PARIS. 1206

1161-4951 See METROLOGIE PRATIQUE ET LEGALE. 4031

1161-7721 See REVUE DE LA MANCHE. 281

1161-7748 See ACHATS ET ENTREPRISE PARIS. 948

1161-8043 See COURRIER DE LA PLANETE PARIS. 5097

1161-8566 See TAMIYA MODEL MAGAZINE INTERNATIONAL FALQUEMONT. 2778

1161-8884 See EUROPE PLURILINGUE. 2487

1161-899X See COIFFURE ET STYLES PARIS. 403

1161-9147 See JOURNAL DE PATHOLOGIE DIGESTIVE. 3746

1161-9317 See TUT. TEXTILES A USAGES TECHNIQUES. 5359

1162-1982 See QUALITE EN MOUVEMENT PARIS LA DEFENSE. 4032

1162-325X See PHILOSOPHIE POLITIQUE PARIS. 1991. 4487

1162-387X See TRANSPORT MAGAZINE PARIS. 5395

1162-5724 See OFFICIEL DE LA FOURRURE 1960, L'. 3185

1162-8774 See BULLETIN ET MEMOIRES - SOCIETE D'EMULATION DE MONTBELIARD. 2681

1163-0736 See OFFICIEL DES TRANSPORTS PARIS, L'. 5388

1163-1651 See MISE A JOUR EN DROIT D'AUTEUR, LA. 3010

1163-1961 See SEIN PARIS, LE. 3640

1163-2283 See QUALITA PARIS. 2852

1163-2747 See SECRET PARIS. 710

1163-4723 See SOINS. FORMATION, PEDAGOGIE, ENCADREMENT : AVEC LA PARTICIPATION DU CEEIEC. 3869

1163-6262 See BABAR PARIS. 1060

1163-765X See CAHIERS DE L'ICP RAPPORT DE RECHERCHE, LES. 3271

1163-9180 See TELECOMS RESEAUX INTERNATIONAL. 1166

1164-0359 See MADAME JOURS DE FRANCE. 2519

1164-0642 See DIRECTORY OF FRENCH VIDEOTEX DATABASES FOR COMPANIES. 1254

1164-0863 See INDUSTRIES GRAPHIQUES PARIS. 4566

1164-1711 See MEILLEURES ADRESSES DE LA FONDERIE PARIS, LES. 845

1164-4079 See MACADAM NICE. 5441

1164-5431 See BULLETIN SIGNALETIQUE UCD DE JOUY-EN-JOSAS. 5580

1164-5563 See EUROPEAN JOURNAL OF SOIL BIOLOGY. 171

1164-5571 See FUNDAMENTAL AND APPLIED NEMATOLOGY. 456

1164-6993 See PHYTOMA, LA DEFENSE DES VEGETAUX. 120

1164-7027 See ENTREPRISE / A POUR AFFAIRES, L'. 672

1164-7701 See INDICATEUR OFFICIEL VILLE A VILLE. 2982

1164-8589 See ENFANCE MAJUSCULE PARIS. 3164

1165-0265 See MAISON FRANCE ISRAEL / CHAMBRE DE COMMERCE FRANCE-ISRAEL. 844

1165-0478 See EUROPEAN JOURNAL OF MEDICINE. 3575

1165-4651 See CT INFOS PARIS. 2332

1165-8606 See DECISIONS MEDIAS. 1109

1166-0600 See FICHES PRATIQUES DE LA FORMATION CONTINUE MISE A JOUR, LES. 1746

1166-2344 See PARIS CAPITALE... - PMR ED. FRANCAISE. 2521

1166-245X See BFCE MULTIDEVISES. 1464

1166-3081 See JOURNAL OF APPLIED NON-CLASSICAL LOGICS. 3511

1166-3286 See ACTION FRANCAISE HEBDO, L'. 4461

1166-4738 See GENIE LOGICIEL & SYSTEMES EXPERTS. 1286

1166-4770 See SVM MAC PARIS. 1204

1166-5300 See TRANSCRIPTASE : REVUE CRITIQUE DE L'ACTUALIT,E SCIENTIFIQUE INTERNATIONALE SUR LE SIDA. 3677

1166-7729 See AGRO MAGAZINE PARIS. 55

1166-8261 See REVUE ARCHEOLOGIQUE DE L'OUEST. SUPPLEMENT. 281

1166-9829 See ANAMNESES VILLEJUIF. 2610

1167-1122 See EUROPEAN JOURNAL OF DERMATOLOGY : EJD. 3720

1167-1416 See AGRESTE CONJONCTURE NORD-PAS-DE-CALAIS. 46

1167-2064 See BUSINESS DIGEST PARIS. 647

1167-2501 See SOLUTIONS TELEMATIQUES PARIS. 1121

1167-3648 See BULLETIN DE LA BIBLIOTHEQUE FORNEY ET DE SES AMIS. 5229

1167-4563 See AGRESTE. ANALYSES & ETUDES, TRAJECTOIRES BRETAGNE. 46

1167-492X See PREHISTOIRE ANTHROPOLOGIE MEDITERRANEENNES. 243

1167-5128 See ANALYSES COMPARATIVES - COMMISSION BANCAIRE PARIS. 770

1167-5217 See CAHIERS VERTS DE L'ECONOMIE PARIS, LES. 1467

1167-539X See PRODUITS FRAIS LEVALLOIS-PERRET. 2354

1167-7287 See INDUSTRIES PARIS. 1611

1167-9603 See CT INFOS PARIS. 2332

1167-9786 See BULLETIN DES NATURALISTES DES YVELINES / PUBLICATION DE L'ASSOCIATION DES NATURALISTES DES YVELINES. 4163

1168-1179 See ESPACES LATINO-AMERICAINS. 4473

1168-1209 See CHRONIQUES - GRET. 5094

1168-3392 See RATP SAVOIR FAIRE PARIS. 5390

1168-3961 See LETTRE DE LA FRANCOPHONIE. 1761

1168-6448 See CREEZ! LOISIRS CLICHY. 865

1168-6944 See TRIBUNE PARIS. 1992, LA. 855

1169-0356 See DIMANCHES BIOLOGIQUES DE LARIBOISIERE 453

1169-0402 See CAHIERS DE MARS, LES. 4038

1169-2421 See PAYS D'ALBE, LE. 2702

1169-7075 See BILAN ECONOMIQUE ET SOCIAL. 1548

1169-8152 See NATATION (PARIS). 4852

1170-1803 See HORTICULTURE IN NEW ZEALAND : JOURNAL OF THE ROYAL NEW ZEALAND INSTITUTE OF HORTICULTURE. 2419

1170-229X See DRUGS & AGING. 4302

1170-4268 See NATIONAL BUSINESS OUTLOOK. 800

1170-4616 See STOUT CENTRE REVIEW : JOURNAL OF THE STOUT RESEARCH CENTRE FOR THE STUDY OF NEW ZEALAND HISTORY AND CULTURE. 2671

1170-5469 See NZTD DOMESTIC RESEARCH SERIES. 5486

1170-5485 See NEWSLETTER - EUBIOS ETHICS INSTITUTE. 2252

1170-5698 See PROCEEDINGS OF THE NEW ZEALAND GEOGRAPHY CONFERENCE. 2573

1170-747X See CONSUMER EXPENDITURE STATISTICS. 1471

1170-7690 See PHARMACOECONOMICS. 4321

1170-814X See LMS ALERT. NEUROPSYCHOTHERAPEUTICS. 4314

1170-831X See NZTD REGIONAL RESEARCH SERIES. 5486

1170-8395 See BULLETIN - BRANZ. 605

1170-8875 See ANTIMICROBIAL NEWSLETTER. 559

1170-9103 See NEW ZEALAND BOOKS. 4831

1170-9456 See REPORT - DSIR CHEMISTRY. 991

1170-9758 See SHADOWS CHRIST CHURCH. 3947

1171-0195 See NEW ZEALAND JOURNAL OF MEDICAL LABORATORY SCIENCE. 3621

1171-0462 See NEW ZEALAND JOURNAL OF OCCUPATIONAL THERAPY. 2865

1171-0829 See NEW ZEALAND PRINTER MAGAZINE. 4567

1171-2031 See PROGRAMME PROFILES. 1513

1171-2961 See TRANS TASMAN. 854

1171-347X See GP WEEKLY. 3738

1171-3631 See ASMAL AUSTRALIA TRAVEL. 5462

1171-3690 See ASMAL NEW ZEALAND TRAVEL. 5462

1171-3771 See NEW ZEALAND SPORTSWOMAN. 4908

1171-445X See NEW ZEALAND MUSEUMS JOURNAL. 359

1171-5375 See NEW ZEALAND MANUFACTURER 1992. 3485

1171-7092 See NEW ZEALAND EXTERNAL RELATIONS AND TRADE RECORD. 847

1171-8536 See ARTS ADVOCATE WELLINGTON. 342

1171-8587 See COMMUNITY MOVES. 4385

1171-9672 See WOOL MARKET REVIEW. 5360

1172-0360 See DRUGS & THERAPY PERSPECTIVES : FOR RATIONAL DRUG SELECTION AND USE. 4302

1172-0719 See PROCEEDINGS OF THE NEW ZEALAND PLANT PROTECTION CONFERENCE. 525

1172-1979 See NURSING NEW ZEALAND. 3864

1172-2827 See PROCEEDINGS OF THE NEW ZEALAND INSTITUTE OF ARGRICULTURAL SCIENCE & THE NEW ZEALAND SOCIETY HORTICULTURAL SCIENCE ANNUAL CONVENTION. 122

1172-3300 See NATIONAL BUSINESS OUTLOOK. 800

1172-5958 See JOURNAL OF PHYSICAL EDUCATION NEW ZEALAND. 1856

1172-7039 See CLINICAL IMMUNOTHERAPEUTICS. 4296

1172-7047 See CNS DRUGS : THE CLINICAL REVIEW OF DRUGS AND THERAPEUICS IN PSYCHIATRY AND NEUROLOGY. 4297

1172-7195 See NEW ZEALAND FOREIGN AFFAIRS AND TRADE RECORD. 847

1172-8299 See PHARMACORESOURCES : WORLD PHARMACOECONOMIC NEWS, VIEWS, AND PRACTICAL APPLICATION. 4323

1180-0135 See RELIGIOLOGIQUES (MONTREAL). 4990

1180-0178 See RAPPORT SUR LES PROJETS / LA SOCIETE CANADIENNE DE LA CROIX-ROUGE. 5304

1180-0186 See TOURIST GUIDE, GREATER QUEBEC AREA. 5494

1180-0305 See GUIDE TOURISTIQUE, LANAUDIERE. 5479

1180-0313 See TOURIST GUIDE, LANAUDIERE. 5494

1180-0410 See IDRC ACQUIRES. 417

1180-0488 See KOMPASS NATIONAL. 689

1180-0488 See KOMPASS NATIONAL. KOMPASS CANADA : REGISTER OF CANADIAN INDUSTRY AND TRADE. 689

1180-050X See CANADIAN WATER WELL. 5532

1180-0666 See GATHERINGS (PENTICTON). 3390

1180-0682 See CONFRATERNITAS (TORONTO). 4949

1180-081X See NEWSLETTER / KEMPTVILLE & DISTRICT HISTORICAL SOCIETY. 2749

1180-0852 See TOGETHER (OTTAWA). 5264

1180-0933 See A/R/C, ARCHITECTURE, RESEARCH, CRITICISM. 286

1180-1050 See ACTION-SANTE (TORONTO). 3545

1180-1204 See BILAN SAINT-LAURENT. 5378

1180-1220 See ST. LAWRENCE UPDATE. 5393

1180-1239 See REFLECTIONS ON CANADIAN LITERACY : RCL. 1884

1180-1271 See ENAP, CARREFOUR UNVERSITAIRE DE L'ADMINISTRATION PUBLIQUE, PLAN DE DEVELOPMENT. 4646

1180-1395 See VITAL NEXUS. 2253

1180-1417 See NEWSLETTER. 519

1180-1468 See COURTLINK (VANCOUVER). 2957

1180-1506 See SUSTAINABLE FARMING. 138

1180-1565 See PENSION COMMISSION OF ONTARIO BULLETIN, THE. 4740

1180-159X See FLEURS, PLANTES ET JARDINS. 2414

1180-1670 See HOLE. 3394

1180-176X See CANADIAN LAW LIBRARIES. 2948

1180-1816 See INFO OCEANS (HALIFAX). 554

1180-1883 See NIPISSING VOYAGEUR. 2464

1180-1913 See SPAA PROVINCIAL NEWSLETTER. 1885

1180-193X See CRITICAL MASS (HALIFAX). 3462

1180-2014 See CONNECTIONS - ONTARIO. MINISTRY OF CULTURE AND COMMUNICATIONS. 3204

1180-2065 See CANADIAN AUTOMOTIVE TECHNICIAN. 5408

1180-2189 See LONG TERM CARE MONITOR. 3605

1180-2251 See ORCHARD (KELOWNA). 117

1180-2332 See CANADIAN JOURNAL OF INFECTIOUS DISEASES, THE. 3712

1180-2391 See HEALTH REPORTS. SUPPLEMENT. LIST OF CANADIAN HOSPITALS. 3781

1180-2413 See TUBERCULOSIS STATISTICS / STATISTICS CANADA, CANADIAN CENTRE FOR HEALTH INFORMATION. 3662

1180-2421 See HEALTH REPORTS. SUPPLEMENT. CAUSES OF DEATH. 4553

1180-243X See HEALTH REPORTS. SUPPLEMENT. SURGICAL PROCEDURES AND TREATMENTS. 3965

1180-2448 See MORTALITY, SUMMARY LIST OF CAUSES / STATISTICS CANADA, CANADIAN CENTRE FOR HEALTH INFORMATION. 4555

1180-2456 See HEALTH REPORTS. SUPPLEMENT. HOSPITAL STATISTICS, PRELIMINARY ANNUAL REPORT. 3781

1180-2499 See LOBBY DIGEST & PUBLIC AFFAIRS MONTHLY, THE. 4662

1180-2588 See WCAT IN FOCUS. 3073

1180-260X See BUSINESS ROUNDS. 3913

1180-2677 See GAZETTE DU GRANIT, LA. 2734

1180-2863 See OBSERVATIONS (OTTAWA). 2571

1180-2901 See WANDERING VOLHYNIANS. 2715

1180-3037 See HEALTH REPORTS. SUPPLEMENT. MENTAL HEALTH STATISTICS. 4588

1180-3045 See HEALTH REPORTS. SUPPLEMENT. LIST OF RESIDENTIAL CARE FACILITIES IN CANADA. 5287

1180-3045 See LIST OF RESIDENTIAL CARE FACILITIES / STATISTICS CANADA, CANADIAN CENTRE FOR HEALTH INFORMATION. 5295

1180-3053 See HEALTH REPORTS. SUPPLEMENT. CANCER IN CANADA. 3817

1180-3061 See THERAPEUTIC ABORTIONS - CANADIAN CENTRE FOR HEALTH INFORMATION. 3769

1180-307X See HEALTH REPORTS. SUPPLEMENT. LIFE TABLES, CANADA AND PROVINCES. 4562

1180-3088 See HEALTH REPORTS. SUPPLEMENT. BIRTHS. 3762

1180-3096 See HEALTH REPORTS. SUPPLEMENT. DEATHS. 4810

1180-3118 See MARRIAGES / STATISTICS CANADA, CANADIAN CENTRE FOR HEALTH INFORMATION. 2287

1180-3126 See HEALTH REPORTS. SUPPLEMENT. DIVORCES. 2287

1180-3169 See QUARTERLY FINANCIAL STATISTICS FOR ENTERPRISES. 732

1180-3223 See CCI NEWSLETTER OTTAWA. 2189

1180-3258 See VIE SANS FRONTIERES. 4621

1180-338X See DISKUSSIONS (GUELPH). 1183

1180-3401 See UPDATE - INTERNATIONAL ASSOCIATION FOR PUBLISHING EDUCATION. 4820

1180-341X See JURISELECTION (QUEBEC). 2990

1180-3444 See FIL DE LIAISON. 5231

1180-3479 See FRONTIERES (MONTREAL). 5200

1180-3533 See RECUEIL DES DECISIONS / COMITES D'APPEL DE LA FONCTION PUBLIQUE. 4679

1180-3568 See EXPOSURE (SASKATOON). 2334

1180-3584 See CANADIAN GOVERNMENT BOND REGISTER. 893

1180-3592 See ACQUISITIONS LIST - CANADIAN MUSEUM OF NATURE. LIBRARY SERVICES. 3187

1180-3630 See BRITISH COLUMBIA TRANSFER GUIDE. 1812

1180-3673 See HANDBOOK TO GRADUATE PROGRAMMES IN HISTORY IN CANADA. 2617

1180-3681 See BULLETIN / CANADIAN INSTITUTE OF ACTUARIES. 2876

1180-3703 See TECHNOLOGY WATCH (WILLOWDALE). 1205

1180-3711 See EVANS REPORT. 1184

1180-3762 See CANADIAN COMPOSER. 4107

1180-3819 See WORKING TITLE. 333

1180-3908 See STOCKLISTS AND NEWS SERVICE FOR CARPET AND FLOORCOVERING BUYERS, THE. 5356

1180-3916 See SALUT MONTREAL! (ED. FRANCAISE). 2759

1180-3983 See SANTE QUEBEC : REVUE DE LA CORPORATION PROFESSIONNELLE DES INFIRMIERES ET INFIRMIERS AUXILIAIRES DU QUEBEC. 3869

1180-3991 See INTERNATIONAL JOURNAL OF CANADIAN STUDIES. 2739

1180-4009 See ENVIRONMETRICS (LONDON, ONT.). 2170

1180-4270 See FORET DE CHEZ-NOUS (1990). 2382

1180-4289 See INTERNATIONAL VOICEPOWER DIRECTORY & BUYERS GUIDE, THE. 1612

1180-4491 See ANNUAL GUIDE TO SYNCHRONIZED SWIMMING. 4883

1180-4602 See INSIDE ROUTES. 5384

1180-4629 See ARCTIC CIRCLE. 2611

1180-467X See HIGHER EDUCATION GROUP ANNUAL. 1828

1180-4696 See MARKETPLACE (TORONTO). 845

1180-4734 See SYNTHESIS (OTTAWA). 1786

1180-4823 See CANADA-U.S. BUSINESS LAW REVIEW. 3097

1180-4831 See REVUE DE DROIT MEDIA & COMMUNICATIONS. 1163

1180-4882 See JOURNAL OF PSYCHIATRY & NEUROSCIENCE. 3929

1180-4890 See PAY EQUITY NEWSLETTER / NOVA SCOTIA PAY EQUITY COMMISSION, THE. 1701

1180-4912 See BLOOD DONOR DIGEST. 5275

1180-4963 See NEW PERSPECTIVES (ARMDALE). 1901

1180-4998 See KEY STATISTICS, ELEMENTARY AND SECONDARY EDUCATION IN ONTARIO. 1760

1180-503X See RAPPORT / CITIZEN ADVOCACY, OTTAWA-CARLETON. 5303

1180-5080 See SPORTING TIMES (VERNON). 4922

1180-5099 See PARTICLEBOARD, WAFERBOARD, AND FIBREBOARD. 2403

1180-5137 See P.O.V. : A NEWSLETTER FOR MANITOBA ACTORS. 5367

1180-5145 See WORD (ST. JOHN'S). 2925

1180-5196 See NS TRAILS. 2751

1180-5242 See BULLETIN DE LA FONDATION DE L'UQAM (ENGLISH ED.). 1812

1180-5323 See NORTHWEST EVANGELICAL BAPTIST JOURNAL. 5065

1180-5358 See DECISIONS - MEDICAL RESEARCH COUNCIL (CANADA). 3571

1180-5455 See HORIZONS (WINNIPEG. 1990). 321

1180-5463 See ANNUAL REPORT / FORENSIC PSYCHIATRIC SERVICES COMMISSION OF BRITISH COLUMBIA. 3920

1180-548X See STATISTICS CANADA PUBLICATIONS LIST. 4822

1180-5501 See PSYCHIATRIE, RECHERCHE ET INTERVENTION EN SANTE MENTALE DE L'ENFANT : P.R.I.S.M.E. 3934

1180-5579 See IMAGES D'OUTREMONT. 2738

1180-5633 See FISH FARM NEWS, THE. 2301

1180-5668 See FRONTIERS (POINTE-CLAIRE). 3692

1180-5714 See ROAMING ROOTS. 2470

1180-5730 See STATISTIQUES PRINCIPALES, LEDUCATION A LELEMENTAIRE ET AU SECONDAIRE EN ONTARIO. 1805

1180-5765 See ON OUR WAY (PRINCE ALBERT). 3420

1180-5781 See (M)OTHER TNGUES. 3413

1180-5838 See NHIC NEWSLETTER. 3621

1180-5862 See WOODWORKING SOURCER. 635

1180-5897 See QUARTERLY SHIPMENTS OF HOUSEHOLD FURNITURE PRODUCTS. 2907

1180-5900 See PACK OF PROCESSED ASPARAGUS. 2352

1180-5919 See PACK OF SELECTED PROCESSED FRUITS (EXCL. APPLES). 2352

1180-5919 See PACK OF SELECTED PROCESSED FRUITS (EXCL. APPLES). 2352

1180-5927 See PACK OF PROCESSED PEAS. 2352

1180-5935 See PACK OF PROCESSED CORN. 2352

1180-5943 See PACK OF CANNED TOMATOES AND TOMATO PRODUCTS. 2352

1180-5951 See PACK OF PROCESSED BEANS, GREEN AND WAX. 2352

1180-596X See PACK OF PROCESSED CARROTS. 2352

1180-5978 See PACK OF SELECTED PROCESSED VEGETABLES. 2352

1180-5986 See PACK OF APPLES AND APPLE PRODUCTS. 2352

1180-6761 See BOITE A NOUVELLES. 5780

1180-7563 See ON THE MOVE (SASKATOON). 1857

1180-7644 See PLEIN-JOUR SUR LA MANICOUAGAN, LE. 5793

1180-8047 See COUNTRY (TORONTO). 4112

1180-9132 See CAPITAL REGION DEVELOPMENTS. 1600

1180-9175 See PAPERTREE LETTER. 4236

1180-9183 See ONESTEP FORWARD. 4207

1180-9205 See IN TOUCH. 1804

1180-9353 See ISTC NEW BRUNSWICK/PRINCE EDWARD ISLAND. 1613

1180-9353 See ISTC NEW BRUNSWICK/PRINCE EDWARD ISLAND. 5117

1180-9434 See ANNUAIRE DE JURISPRUDENCE ET DE DOCTRINE DU QUEBEC. 2934

1180-9531 See BUSINESS DIRECTORY : A COMPREHENSIVE GUIDE FOR BUYING BUSINESS-TO-BUSINESS GOODS AND SERVICES IN THE HAMILTON/BURLINGTON AREA. 647

1180-9558 See ILLUMINATIONS (VANCOUVER). 373

1180-9647 See DUNHILL PERSONAL INJURY AND DEATH REPORTS. 2964

1180-9663 See AVIATION TODAY (PORT CREDIT). 14

1180-9671 See WHERE VANCOUVER. 5499

1180-968X See CANADIAN QUAKER HISTORY JOURNAL. 2258

1180-999X See PRAIRIE-HOTELIER. 2809

1181-1358 See NORTHERN ONTARIO CATALOG. 3237

1181-3369 See CANADIAN PATENT. 1302

1181-3385 See CANCORP DOCUMENTS SERVICE. 655

1181-3474 See ORO-VESPRA INDEPENDENT [MICROFORM]. 5792

1181-3598 5780

1181-4292 See SOLEIL DE COLOMBIE-BRITANNIQUE. 5794

1181-6023 See NEWS FROM THE CANADIAN MUSICAL HERITAGE SOCIETY. 4140

1181-604X See AU COURANT - CANADIAN COUNCIL FOR INTERNATIONAL CO-OPERATION. 2907

1181-6058 See PRACTICAL OPTOMETRY. 4217

1181-6074 See MOTHER OF THYME. 5561

1181-6090 See TALENT CATALOGUE / ACTRA ATLANTIC CANADA. 389

1181-6139 See HEALTHIER YOUTH. 2598

1181-6341 See TODAYS SKATER. 4926

1181-6414 See PROSPECTOR : EXPLORATION AND INVESTMENT BULLETIN, THE. 2149

1181-6430 See ISSUES (VANCOUVER. 1990). 1497

1181-652X See EUROPE'92, LES QUATRE VENTS. 867

1181-6554 See GEIST (VANCOUVER). 3390

1181-6562 See PULP & PAPER CANADA GRADE DIRECTORY. 4238

1181-6627 See LABOUR FORCE ANNUAL AVERAGES. 1535

ISSN Index

1181-6635 See BOOK PUBLISHING (OTTAWA). 4812

1181-6643 See TELEVISION VIEWING. 4560

1181-6708 See FILM AND VIDEO (OTTAWA). 4080

1181-6724 See EXPORTS BY COUNTRIES (OTTAWA). 835

1181-6805 See STEPPIN' OUT (SUDBURY). 4154

1181-6910 See PHONE LINK : THE OFFICIAL NEWSLETTER OF KIDS HELP PHONE. 5301

1181-6945 See CINEMAS (MONTREAL). 4067

1181-6988 See FITNESS WORKS!. 2597

1181-7003 See AUTOMATION SYSTEMS. 1218

1181-7070 See REPORT / WELLAND CANALS SOCIETY. 1625

1181-7372 See REFLETS DU NORD. 2756

1181-7488 See PROBLEMATIQUE (DOWNSVIEW). 4492

1181-7496 See NORTHERNHER (YELLOWKNIFE). 5563

1181-7534 See JOURNAL OF ENVIRONMENTAL LAW AND PRACTICE. 3113

1181-7550 See CAHIERS DE LA NCT. 5362

1181-7720 See DIARY / CANADIANS FOR HEALTH RESEARCH. 4773

1181-7739 See INTERVENTIONS SONORES. 4124

1181-7747 See DEPARTMENT STORE MONTHLY SALES, BY PROVINCE AND METROPOLITAN AREA (FRENCH EDITION 1991). 953

1181-7747 See DEPARTMENT STORE MONTHLY SALES, BY PROVINCE AND METROPOLITAN AREA (ENGLISH EDITION 1991). 953

1181-781X See STATISTICS INFOGRAM. 2870

1181-7828 See EARTHKEEPER MAGAZINE. 2164

1181-7917 See DIGITAL EVOLUTION MAGAZINE. 1131

1181-7941 See BULLETIN D'INFORMATION DE L'APCRIQ. 5378

1181-795X See CANADIAN ENVIRONMENTAL REGULATION & COMPLIANCE NEWS. 2162

1181-8034 See IMPACT - UNIVERSITE DU QUEBEC. 1829

1181-8077 See CANADIAN OIL INDUSTRY MERGER AND ACQUISITION REPORT. 4253

1181-8107 See NATIONAL NETWORK NEWS. 4052

1181-8131 See BUSINESS SOURCE, THE. 652

1181-8204 See VOICEPOWER REVIEW, THE. 1168

1181-8212 See LUMINA (MONTREAL). 3837

1181-8328 See VIE CONTINUE, LA. 5182

1181-8336 See ANNUAL REPORT - BRITISH COLUMBIA. MINISTRY OF ENVIRONMENT (1989). 2160

1181-8360 See BUDDHISM AT THE CROSSROADS. 5020

1181-8409 See UNIVERSITE EN OUTAOUAIS, L'. 1852

1181-8441 See ARTEFACT (MONTREAL). 341

1181-845X See ADOPTION HELPER. 5270

1181-8514 See SUCCES (LAVAL). 331

1181-8522 See SFP (MONTREAL). 4152

1181-8565 See REFLET (HULL). 1777

1181-8646 See PRODUCT CATALOGUE - ONTARIO. ADDICTION RESEARCH FOUNDATION. 422

1181-8654 See FORUM - CANADIAN TELEMATICS FORUM. 1111

1181-8689 See CAMP DITES-VOUS?. 4849

1181-8697 See BYWORDS (OTTAWA). 3461

1181-8700 See ENVIRONMENTAL REVIEWS. 2215

1181-8778 See NCBHR COMMUNIQUE. 2252

1181-8794 See RESIDENTIAL CARE FACILITIES, AGED / STATISTICS CANADA, CANADIAN CENTRE FOR HEALTH INFORMATION. 3754

1181-8824 See RELIEF (MONTREAL). 3792

1181-8832 See HEALTH REPORTS. SUPPLEMENT. RESIDENTIAL CARE FACILITIES. 5287

1181-9006 See DIGEST OF MUNICIPAL & PLANNING LAW, THE. 2961

1181-9014 See FROM SEA TO SEA. 2449

1181-9030 See CARDIOLOGY CONSULTANT. 3700

1181-9049 See CONSULTATIONS EN CARDIOLOGIE. 3703

1181-912X See CANADIAN ONCOLOGY NURSING JOURNAL. 3853

1181-912X See CANADIAN ONCOLOGY NURSING JOURNAL. 3853

1181-9189 See BULLETIN DE LAUDEM. 4106

1181-9219 See ORATOR (OTTAWA). 5033

1181-9243 See JUSTICE RESEARCH NOTES. 2991

1181-9286 See OUVROIR (SAINTE-MARIE-DE-BEAUCE). 4984

1181-9294 See ANNUAL REPORT / BRITISH COLUMBIA ACID MINE DRAINAGE TASK FORCE. 2133

1181-9340 See NATIONAL JOURNAL OF CONSTITUTIONAL LAW. 3093

1181-9340 See NATIONAL JOURNAL OF CONSTITUTIONAL LAW. 3093

1181-9359 See NATIONAL REAL PROPERTY LAW REVIEW. 4842

1181-9367 See DIRECTIONS - B.C. HYDRO. 4643

1181-9391 See PEACE AND ENVIRONMENT NEWS. 2179

1181-9405 See OEIL NU. 327

1181-9413 See NEWSLETTER - CANADIAN WAR MUSEUM. FRIENDS OF THE CANADIAN WAR MUSEUM. 4052

1181-943X See HARBOUR MAGAZINE ON ART AND EVERYDAY LIFE. 351

1181-9464 See STATISTIQUES SUR L'INDUSTRIE DU MEUBLE. 635

1181-9480 See EDUCATORS' NOTEBOOK. 1743

1181-9510 See POLYMER NETWORKS & BLENDS. 1046

1181-955X See AGRICULTURE ET COOPERATION. 53

1181-957X See HISTORICAL LABOUR FORCE STATISTICS. 1533

1181-9626 See PEOPLE (VANCOUVER). 1512

1181-9677 See SEQUELS (TORONTO). 3435

1181-9707 See ECOSOURCE. 2164

1181-974X See EQUITY NEWSLETTER (TORONTO). 4388

1181-9782 See VEGETABLE GARDEN RESEARCH. 2433

1181-9790 See OPTIMA (MONTREAL). 374

1181-9820 See NURSERY CROP PRODUCTION GUIDE FOR COMMERCIAL GROWERS. 180

1181-9839 See TSIG NEWSLETTER. 3254

1181-9847 See SOFTWARE DEVELOPMENT AND COMPUTER SERVICE INDUSTRY / STATISTICS CANADA, SERVICES, SCIENCE AND TECHNOLOGY DIVISION. 1203

1181-9960 See MULTI-FACT. 3708

1181-9979 See SCHOOL LIBRARY ADVOCATE. 3248

1182-0055 See OFF THE RECORD (TORONTO. 1990). 2482

1182-0063 See SASKATCHEWAN MEDICAL JOURNAL. 3638

1182-008X See FREE SPEECH MONITOR. 4508

1182-0187 See INFORMATION UPDATE - CANADIAN STANDARDS ASSOCIATION. 1978

1182-0195 See INNFOCUS (NORTH VANCOUVER). 2807

1182-0209 See NEWSLETTER / NOVA SCOTIA LIBRARY ASSOCIATION. 3235

1182-0470 See PROFESSIONAL RENOVATION. 2903

1182-0691 See MAGAZINES AND NEWSPAPERS - CALGARY PUBLIC LIBRARY. 5789

1182-0802 See INSTRUCTIONS RESPECTING VOCATIONAL TRAINING IN THE YOUTH AND ADULT SECTORS OF SCHOOL BOARDS. 1913

1182-0993 See WORLD BUSINESS (OTTAWA). 723

1182-1000 See PORC QUEBEC. 217

1182-1248 See FARMERS' CHOICE. 85

1182-1353 See FOCUS / SOCIETY FOR MANITOBANS WITH DISABILITIES. 4388

1182-1507 See MEDECINE MODERNE, RAPPORT SPECIAL. 3607

1182-1574 See MONTFORT A LA UNE. 5297

1182-1590 See CANADIAN RESOURCES & PENNYMINES ANALYST. 894

1182-1701 See DIRECTORY / MENNONITE CONFERENCE OF EASTERN CANADA. 5059

1182-1981 See WHERE CALGARY. 4867

1182-2015 See AGROPUR NOUVELLES. 56

1182-2155 See NEWSTIME - PUBLIC SERVICE ALLIANCE OF CANADA. NATIONAL COMPONENT. 4669

1182-2163 See ACTUALITE - ALLIANCE DE LA FONCTION PUBLIQUE DU CANADA. ELEMENT NATIONAL. 1642

1182-2376 See ALBERTA WASTE MATERIALS EXCHANGE. 2223

1182-2589 See JOURNAL PLUS, LE. 5232

1182-2600 See ALBERTA GUIDE TO SPORTFISHING. 4868

1182-3062 See INTERNATIONAL GUIDE, EDMONTON. 5481

1182-3089 See OTTAWA VALLEY OFFICIAL TRAVEL GUIDE. 5487

1182-3097 See CANADIAN INFORMATION PROCESSING. 1173

1182-3100 See ECHO. 5783

1182-3178 See ANISHINABEK NEWS. 2720

1182-3348 See ANNUAL REPORT - BRITISH COLUMBIA TRADE DEVELOPMENT CORPORATION. 822

1182-3429 See KIDS PARADE. 1085

1182-3852 See GUIDE DE LA DECLARATION D'EFFECTIF SCOLAIRE (DCS). 1748

1182-3976 See RELEASE (VANCOUVER). 4149

1182-4042 See DIRECTORY/BUYERS' GUIDE AND DAILY PLANNER. 819

1182-4166 See MARKET INSIDER BULLETIN. 1504

1182-4271 See WEST COAST LINE. 3452

1182-4301 See JUST NEWS. 4659

1182-4441 See DIRECTIONS - BRITISH COLUMBIA PREMIER'S ADVISORY COUNCIL FOR PERSONS WITH DISABILITIES. 4386

1182-4506 See WORKPLAN (TORONTO). 2210

1182-4573 See BULLETIN DE RCI. 1128

1182-4581 See RCI NEWSLETTER. 1138

1182-476X See FORMATION PROFESSIONNELLE DES JEUNES ET DES ADULTES DANS LES COMMISSIONS SCOLAIRES, INSTRUCTION, LA. 1747

1182-4867 See ALBERTA COORDINATED HOME CARE PROGRAM DIRECTORY. 4764

1182-4948 See THEATRE, DANSE, MUSIQUE, ARTS MULTIDISCIPLINAIRES ET MULTIMEDIAS. 332

1182-4980 See YOUNG VOICES, YOUR VOICES. 3456

1182-5049 See ICIDH INTERNATIONAL NETWORK. 5289

1182-5316 See DECISION - TRIBUNAL CANADIEN DU COMMERCE EXTERIEUR. 2959

1182-543X See PARAGRAPH (STRATFORD). 3422

1182-5480 See DAIRY RESEARCH REPORT (GUELPH). 194

1182-5510 See ESQUISSES (MONTREAL). 298

1182-5529 See BYLAWS & DIRECTORY / ONTARIO SCHOOL COUNSELLORS' ASSOCIATION. 1861

1182-5561 See BULLETIN - ONTARIO HANDWEAVERS AND SPINNERS. 370

1182-557X See B.C. GOAT NEWS. 207

1182-5758 See DIRECTORY OF CANADIAN EDUCATION & TRAINING PROGRAMS IN AQUACULTURE RELATED FIELDS. 554

1182-5790 See PACIFIC FOOD & DRINK NEWS. 2352

1182-5804 See GEORGIAN SUN. 5785

1182-5804 See GEORGIAN SUN. 5785

1182-5812 See MIRROR MONTREAL. 1990. 2539

1182-5847 See TAXES FEDERALES ET PROVINCIALES SUR LES PRODUITS PETROLIERS. 4280

1182-5944 See NEWSLETTER - OPERA LYRA OTTAWA. 386

1182-6002 *See* CALENDAR OF THE UNIVERSITY OF VICTORIA COLLEGE, COBOURG, FOR THE ACADEMIC YEAR 1730

1182-6096 *See* YELLOWHEAD STAR. 5798

1182-610X *See* CORPUS WORKERS' COMPENSATION HANDBOOK. 2878

1182-6126 *See* NORTH INTERLAKE ECHO. 5791

1182-6169 *See* MATRIART (TORONTO). 358

1182-6304 *See* HOROSCOPE (ANDRE MAURICE). 4241

1182-6312 *See* HOROSCOPE (VERONIQUE CHARPENTIER). 390

1182-6371 *See* ENERMARK NEWS. 954

1182-6436 *See* COMPLEXE NBR. 2088

1182-6606 *See* REGISTER AND FIRM INDEX / THE ALBERTA ASSOCIATION OF ARCHITECTS. 307

1182-6630 *See* SUMMERFOLK MUSIC & CRAFTS FESTIVAL. 4155

1182-6649 *See* NIAGARA'S HISTORICAL MUSEUMS ... DIRECTORY. 2750

1182-6665 *See* CLIPPING SERVICE. 5279

1182-722X *See* CANADIAN LINK. 2258

1182-7556 *See* REPERTOIRE DES USINES QUEBECOISES DE PLACAGES, DE CONTRE-PLAQUES ET DE PANNEAUX AGGLOMERES A BASE DE BOIS / MINISTERE DE L'ENERGIE ET DES RESSOURCES, DIRECTION DU DEVELOPPEMENT INDUSTRIEL. 4679

1182-7696 *See* OUTAOUAIS FORESTIER. 2390

1182-7718 *See* ALBERTA ADVISORY COUNCIL ON WOMEN'S ISSUES. 5550

1182-7823 *See* LEGISLATIVE ASSEMBLY OF ALBERTA. 4661

1182-7858 *See* SOILUTIONS (EDMONTON). 187

1182-7890 *See* MANAGEMENT PLAN / PRIVATE COLLEGES ACCREDITATION BOARD. 1866

1182-803X *See* GERMAN AMERICAN TRADE. 837

1182-8323 *See* LAURENTIAN SUN. 5788

1182-851X *See* PORC EXPRESS. 217

1182-8757 *See* ISSUES (PENTICTON). 4241

1182-8765 *See* CATTLE FEEDER, THE. 208

1182-8781 *See* FOCUS - ONTARIO VETERINARY MEDICAL ASSOCIATION. 5510

1182-8897 *See* ACCESS / ARNN, ASSOCIATION OF REGISTERED NURSES OF NEWFOUNDLAND. 3850

1182-8900 *See* DAIRY FARMER (LONDON, ONT.). 193

1182-8919 *See* MONTHLY COMMENTARY AND OUTLOOK. 110

1182-8935 *See* ENVIRONMENT LIBRARY ACQUISITIONS LIST - NEW BRUNSWICK. DEPT. OF THE ENVIRONMENT. LIBRARY. 3209

1182-8986 *See* NOVA SCOTIA FARM COMPUTING NEWS, THE. 1197

1182-8994 *See* BOWER'S DIRECTORY FOR GREATER METROPOLITAN TORONTO. 2556

1182-901X *See* WRITE ANGLES. 2925

1182-9028 *See* CONTACT / PLENTY CANADA. 5097

1182-9044 *See* PORCUPINE PRESS. 5793

1182-9052 *See* COMPUTER & TELECOM INDUSTRY UPDATE. 4211

1182-9095 *See* COLLINGWOOD CONNECTION, THE. 5782

1182-9125 *See* SASKATCHEWAN HORIZONTAL WELL SUMMARY. 2150

1182-9133 *See* AGRI-FOOD BUSINESS IN P.E.I. 47

1182-9192 *See* CAREER INFO CUS. 1911

1182-9265 *See* FLASH (BANFF). 4895

1182-946X *See* DISENPLUS (MONTREAL). 3924

1182-9478 *See* RENAISSANCE (CHICOUTIMI). 2601

1182-963X *See* ANTIBIOTHERAPIE AUJOURD'HUI. 3551

1182-9648 *See* ANTIBACTERIAL REVIEW. 3551

1182-9699 *See* TRAVEL COURIER (TORONTO). 5495

1182-9745 *See* ENVIRONMENT & PUBLIC SAFETY TODAY. 4774

1182-977X See WCB UPDATE. 1717

1182-9796 *See* 4-H NORTHERN NEWS. 42

1182-9818 *See* CONSTRUCTION NORTHWEST. 610

1182-9869 *See* CONTACT - NEW BRUNSWICK. DEPT. OF EDUCATION. 1733

1182-9877 *See* ALUMNI DIRECTORY / UNIVERSITY OF GUELPH. 1100

1182-9923 *See* CANADIAN HOTEL AND RESTAURANT (1990). 2804

1182-9931 *See* PRESS INDEPENDENT. 2543

1182-994X See WESTCOAST REFLECTIONS. 5182

1182-9958 *See* ENGLISH RIDER. 2798

1182-9966 *See* SOOKE STANDARD, THE. 5794

1182-9974 *See* COUNTRY CONNECTION (NORTH BATTLEFORD). 5782

1182-9982 *See* ASBESTOS WATCH. 599

1183-0042 *See* TPS ET LES TAXES A LA CONSOMMATION, LA. 4756

1183-0050 *See* LETTRE FISCALE QUEBECOISE. 4661

1183-0069 *See* ATLANTIC JOURNAL OF OPPORTUNITY. 1598

1183-0077 *See* HARMONY (OTTAWA). 2173

1183-0115 *See* SEATTLE & AREA AIRPORT BUSINESS DIRECTORY. 710

1183-0190 *See* BULLETEN - CANADA-USSR BUSINESS COUNCIL. 644

1183-0204 *See* AVIATION CANADA MAGAZINE. 13

1183-0212 *See* BRITISH COLUMBIA MEDIA GUIDE. 1105

1183-0247 *See* NEW DEMOCRATIC ALTERNATIVE. 4483

1183-0247 *See* NEW DEMOCRATIC ALTERNATIVE. 4483

1183-0271 *See* RECUEIL EN MATIERE DE PROTECTION DU TERRITOIRE AGRICOLE. 3037

1183-028X *See* PROGRAM AND ABSTRACTS OF THE CANADIAN PALEONTOLOGY CONFERENCE ... AND PANDER SOCIETY MEETING. 4230

1183-0298 *See* FIELD GUIDE TO THE PALEONTOLOGY OF ... / CANADIAN PALEONTOLOGY CONFERENCE, A. 4227

1183-0409 *See* CIDEM EXPRESS. 1470

1183-045X *See* PROVIDER (VANCOUVER). 2285

1183-0484 *See* FAST (COMMUNITY LEADERS' ED.). 5179

1183-0611 See CASE LAW DIGESTS. 2949

1183-062X *See* LEGISLATION (SCARBOROUGH). 3001

1183-0654 *See* BOUNTY INFANT CARE GUIDE, THE. 2277

1183-0662 *See* GUIDE BOUNTY DES SOINS AU NOURRISSON. 2280

1183-0689 *See* GUIDE BOUNTY DE LA GROSSESSE, LE. 3579

1183-0786 *See* EBAUCHES (SAINT-FELIX-DE-KINGSEY). 3383

1183-0832 *See* BONNET DE NUIT, LE. 3368

1183-0840 *See* INFO-GENEALOGIE (SAINTE-FOY). 2454

1183-0875 *See* NORTHERN RESEARCH AND EDUCATION AT YUKON COLLEGE. 2751

1183-0891 *See* ATTENTE (LONGUEUIL). 2528

1183-1049 *See* ON SCENE (CALGARY). 3725

1183-1073 *See* MATERIAL HISTORY REVIEW. 2745

1183-1081 *See* PUBLIC SECTOR MANAGEMENT (TORONTO). 4705

1183-112X *See* NORTHERN MARINER : JOURNAL OF THE CANADIAN NAUTICAL RESEARCH SOCIETY LE MARIN DU NORD : REVUE DE SOCIETE CANADIENNE POUR LA RECHERCHE NAUTIQUE, THE. 4181

1183-1138 *See* NOIR D'ENCRE. 360

1183-1170 *See* NEWSOURCES (HALIFAX). 1805

1183-1219 *See* BIBLIO-CLIP : BULLETIN D'INFORMATION DU SERVICE DES BBLIOTHEQUES DE L'UQAM. 3194

1183-1243 *See* CANADIAN JOURNAL OF DRAMA AND THEATRE, THE. 5362

1183-1278 *See* BULLETIN OF THE INSTITUTE OF COMBINATORICS AND ITS APPLICATIONS. 3498

1183-1316 *See* LANGUAGE ABUSE FORUM. 3294

1183-1324 *See* PROFIT (TORONTO). 705

1183-1340 *See* HEARTHEALTH. 2598

1183-1359 *See* FORUM INTERNATIONAL (MONTREAL. 1991). 4522

1183-1359 *See* INTERNATIONAL FORUM : BULLETIN OF THE JEANNE SAUVE YOUTH FOUNDATION. 5290

1183-1448 *See* THOMPSON-OKANAGAN DEVELOPMENT REGION MANUFACTURERS DIRECTORY. 3489

1183-1499 *See* BLOOD & APHORISMS. 3367

1183-1553 *See* BENEVOLONS! (ST-TITE). 5274

1183-160X *See* SEMA (TORONTO). 5257

1183-1634 *See* PENSION TAX REPORTS. 4740

1183-1650 *See* REPERTOIRE DE PROGRAMMES DE BOURSES INTERNATIONALES POUR LES CANADIENS ET LES RESSORTISSANTS ETRANGERS. 1844

1183-1693 *See* CIRCUIT (MONTREAL. 1991). 4110

1183-1766 *See* HOGTOWN HERALDRY. 2453

1183-1804 *See* EMPLOYMENT EQUITY REVIEW, THE. 1666

1183-1812 *See* REPERTOIRE DE L'ENSEIGNEMENT A DISTANCE EN FRANCAIS. 1844

1183-1820 *See* LISTEN (ENGLISH EDITION, OTTAWA). 4390

1183-1820 *See* LISTEN (FRENCH EDITION, OTTAWA). 4390

1183-1839 *See* UMBRELLA (BELLEVILLE). 332

1183-1847 *See* VALLEY (BURNSTOWN). 2764

1183-1855 *See* TRENDS (SCARBOROUGH). 716

1183-1863 *See* NAZARETH (COMBERMERE). 5033

1183-188X *See* POUR MIEUX ENTREPRENDRE. 704

1183-1898 *See* POUR MIEUX ENTREPRENDRE : A PUBLICATION OF THE COMMITTEE ON SMALL BUSINESS. 704

1183-1936 *See* TOUR DES PONTS, LE. 5796

1183-1944 *See* CORE (NORTH YORK). 1818

1183-1987 *See* CANADA WEST TRAVEL NEWS. 5465

1183-1995 *See* C.A.P. JOURNAL / THE CANADIAN ASSOCIAION OF PRINCIPALS. 1861

1183-2029 *See* ODYSSEY (TORONTO. 1991). 3467

1183-2045 *See* CARTOUCHE ENGLISH EDITION (CALGARY). 2581

1183-2045 *See* CARTOUCHE FRENCH EDITION (CALGARY). 2581

1183-2053 *See* GAUCHE, LA. 4542

1183-2096 *See* A PROPOS (MONTREAL). 3630

1183-2118 *See* AHA!!!--THE PREACHER'S RESEARCH ASSISTANT. 4933

1183-2142 *See* MONTREAL PASSIONS. 2747

1183-2142 *See* MONTREAL PASSIONS. 5485

1183-2185 *See* COLLECTORS' CHRONICLE, THE. 2772

1183-2215 *See* TRADITION D'AVENIR. 1095

1183-2274 *See* SAWT KANADA. 2545

1183-2282 *See* FORUM - CANADIAN URBAN TRANSIT ASSOCIATION. 5382

1183-2282 *See* FORUM - CANADIAN URBAN TRANSIT ASSOCIATION. 5382

1183-2290 *See* HEBDO, PUBLI-MAISON. 2534

1183-2312 *See* KINXIONS (RICHMOND). 2457

1183-2339 *See* CHURCH BUSINESS. 4947

1183-2355 *See* ECODECISION (MONTREAL). 2192

1183-2355 *See* ECODECISION (MONTREAL). 2192

1183-2363 See ACCES A L'INFORMATION EXPRESS. 406
1183-2428 See NORTHERN AQUACULTURE. 2309
1183-2487 See FRANCOPHONIES D'AMERIQUE. 2261
1183-2509 See CANADIAN JOURNAL OF ONCOLOGY, THE. 3810
1183-2517 See CANADIAN JOURNAL OF OB/GYN & WOMEN'S HEALTH CARE, THE. 3758
1183-2614 See ANNUAL REPORT - NEW BRUNSWICK. DEPT. OF INTERGOVERNMENTAL AFFAIRS. 4628
1183-2681 See WEST FORTY-NINTH. 3452
1183-269X See BULLETIN DBSF. 5275
1183-2703 See OPUNTIA (CALGARY). 3420
1183-2738 See ENTRE-NOUS - ASSOCIATION CANADIENNE DE LA DYSTROPHIE MUSCULAIRE. 4388
1183-2754 See SECURITE & STRATEGIES, ASIE. 4535
1183-2770 See PROCEEDINGS ... ANNUAL MEETING OF THE CANADIAN TRANSPORTATION RESEARCH FORUM. 5390
1183-2894 See LAKEHEAD FOREST : A NEWSLETTER FROM THE SCHOOL OF FORESTRY, LAKEHEAD UNIVERSITY, THE. 2386
1183-2916 See CHANGEMENTS (MONTREAL). 827
1183-3025 See VOTRE SANTE (TORONTO), A. 2602
1183-3033 See CHARLTON HOCKEY CARD PRICE GUIDE, THE. 2772
1183-3076 See EMPLOYMENT BULLETIN - CANADA LAW BOOK INC. 3147
1183-3084 See JOURNAL SUPER-MERITAS, LE. 2536
1183-3092 See OPTIONS - CENTRALE DE L'ENSEIGNEMENT DU QUEBEC. 2752
1183-3149 See ACCESS (GLOUCESTER). 4383
1183-3173 See HORSE ACTION (WINFIELD). 2799
1183-3181 See CALYX (TORONTO). 3901
1183-3203 See OVERSEAS EMPLOYMENT NEWSLETTER. 4208
1183-3211 See CHIMERE (SHERBROOKE). 3374
1183-322X See EXCEPTIONALITY EDUCATION CANADA. 1879
1183-3246 See MCGOLDRICK'S CANADIAN CUSTOMS TARIFF HARMONIZED SYSTEM. 845
1183-3254 See CANADIAN BIODIVERSITY. 450
1183-3297 See UNIVERSITY GUIDE ACCOUNTANCY. 753
1183-3343 See COMMENTAIRE SUR LA TPS. 4718
1183-3416 See FISHERIES NEWS. 2302
1183-3440 See CABARET VERT. 3370
1183-3521 See BRITISH COLUMBIA BIRDS. 5616
1183-3548 See ETAT DES FORETS AU CANADA, RAPPORT AU PARLEMENT, L'. 2379
1183-3564 See HOME OFFICE : THE OFFICIAL PUBLICATIN OF THE NATIONAL HOME BUSINESS INSTITUTE, INC. 869
1183-3580 See OFFICIAL REPORT OF DEBATES (HANSARD) - ONTARIO. LEGISLATIVE ASSEMBLY. SELECT COMMITTEE ON ONTARIO IN CONFEDERATION. 4485
1183-3637 See NOUVELLE ACROPOLE (MONTREAL). 4354
1183-3661 See MARTELLO PAPERS. 4528
1183-3726 See MURRAY MATTERS. 2461
1183-3734 See MEMBERSHIP DIRECTORY - CANADIAN ASSOCIATION OF COLLEGE AND UNIVERSITY STUDENT SERVICES. 1835
1183-3734 See MEMBERSHIP DIRECTORY - CANADIAN ASSOCIATION OF COLLEGE AND UNIVERSITY STUDENT SERVICES. 1835
1183-3742 See PAPERPLATES (TORONTO). 2542
1183-3785 See APPLESEED QUARTERLY. 3363
1183-3793 See LITERACY WORKS. 1762
1183-3815 See LIAISON-CEICI (ENGLISH ED.). 1761

1183-3955 See NATIONAL DIRECTORY FOR SOFTWARE ADAPTATION. 1288
1183-4048 See DANCEHALL (TORONTO). 4113
1183-4056 See CCTA NEWSLETTER. 1814
1183-4072 See ONTARIO CRICKET "PITCH". 4911
1183-4110 See CAHIERS - CEGEP DE LIMOILOU. DEPARTEMENT DE FRANCAIS. 3370
1183-4110 See CAHIERS - CEGEP DE LIMOILOU. DEPARTEMENT DE FRANCAIS. 3370
1183-4153 See ACTS IN ACTION. 4932
1183-417X See GREEN ENERGY UPDATE. 1945
1183-4196 See ENVIROSOURCE (HULL. ENGLISH ED.). 4646
1183-420X See ENVIROSOURCE (HULL. ED. FRANCAISE). 2171
1183-4269 See CANADIAN OFFICIAL, THE. 4889
1183-4307 See EXPLORATEUR (MONTREAL). 1323
1183-4323 See EXPRESS PLUS. 5784
1183-4331 See HEALTHY EXCHANGE (OTTAWA). 2598
1183-4331 See HEALTHY EXCHANGE (OTTAWA). 4782
1183-4374 See OTTAWA-CARLETON HEADLINER. 118
1183-4404 See CBIE RESEARCH. 1731
1183-4412 See BCEI RECHERCHES. 1811
1183-4420 See DEPECHE-TPS : BULLETIN MENSUEL DE TPS CANADA-QUEBEC. 4720
1183-4455 See BULLETIN LA PARENTELE : BULLETIN DE L'ASSOCIATION DES FAMILLES MARCHAND. 2440
1183-4501 See KIDS PARADE. 1085
1183-4528 See BULLETIN / CANADIAN ENVIRONMENTAL NETWORK. 2162
1183-4528 See BULLETIN / CANADIAN ENVIRONMENTAL NETWORK. 2162
1183-4544 See PETA JOURNAL. 1773
1183-4609 See NEWS / CANADIAN CENTRE FOR STUDIES IN PUBLISHING. 4817
1183-4676 See DAVIS ON EXECUTIVE COMPENSATION. 1662
1183-4692 See MORIARTY ON EXECUTIVE PENSIONS. 879
1183-4749 See INSERVICE QUARTERLY. 5290
1183-4757 See FOCUS ON EDUCATION (TORONTO). 4369
1183-479X See CRCS NEWSLETTER / CENTRE FOR RESEARCH ON CULTURE AND SOCIETY, CARLETON UNIVERSITY. 5243
1183-4803 See GUIDE DE L'ENVIRONNEMENT. 2173
1183-482X See POUVOIRS PUBLICS AU QUEBEC. 4674
1183-4846 See MONDE DU LOISIR ET DES SPORTS AU QUEBEC. 4905
1183-4854 See FAIT FRANCAIS EN AMERIQUE DU NORD. 2733
1183-4889 See OPTION GRAND AIR. 4876
1183-4943 See INJURY PREVENTION NEWS. 2598
1183-4951 See INDEPENDENT STUDY LINK. 1830
1183-4978 See REPERTOIRE DES JOURNALISTES DU QUEBEC ET ANNUAIRE DES ENTREPRISES DE PRESSE. 2924
1183-4986 See SOCIAL ISSUES NEWS. 4997
1183-5044 See HARLEQUIN WORLD'S BEST ROMANCES. 5074
1183-5052 See IGLU. INSTITUTO DE GESTION Y LIDERAZGO UNIVERSITARIO. 1829
1183-5052 See IGLU. INSTITUTO DE GESTION Y LIDERAZGO UNIVERSITARIO. 1829
1183-515X See MONDE ALPHABETIQUE / LE REGROUPEMENT DES GROUPES POPULAIRES EN ALPHABETISATION DU QUEBEC, LE. 1764
1183-5206 See UNITY DEBATE, THE. 4692
1183-5214 See PORTAL (NANAIMO). 3424
1183-5249 See LIBERTAS (ENGLISH EDITION MONTREAL). 4510
1183-5389 See MONITOR (RICHMOND HILL). 1619

1183-5400 See SHIP'S LOG (AMHERSTBURG). 4183
1183-5435 See ATLANTIC REGION ... AVIATION BUSINESS DIRECTORY. 12
1183-5443 See MECHA-PRESS. 1313
1183-5451 See MAGAZINE DES UTILISATEURS FORTUNE 1000. 876
1183-5486 See REPERTOIRE DES INSTITUTIONS - ONTARIO. DIRECTION DE L'ACCES A L'INFORMATION ET DE LA PROTECTION DE LA VIE PRIVEE. 4679
1183-5494 See VERNON'S BUSINESS SOURCES, HAMILTON & NIAGARA AREA EDITION FOR SELECTED COMMUNITIES. 718
1183-5532 See T.A.C. NEWS. 5393
1183-5540 See INFO DOCUMENTATION (DRUMMONDVILLE). 3215
1183-5559 See SIGNATURE (TORONTO). 4819
1183-5591 See EASY LIVING (SURREY-DELTA ED. 1991). 2532
1183-5672 See CAMPANILOIS (SAINTE-FOY). 2726
1183-5699 See JONQUIEROIS (JONQUIERE). 4658
1183-5702 See CANADIAN JOURNAL OF INFECTION CONTROL : THE OFFICIAL JOURNAL OF THE COMMUNITY & HOSPITAL INFECTION CONTROL ASSOCIATION-CANADA, THE. 4770
1183-5796 See HIGHLIGHTS OF AGRICULTURAL AND FOOD RESEARCH IN ONTARIO. 92
1183-580X See SENS DES AFFAIRES (OTTAWA. PRINTEMPS 1990). 3917
1183-5834 See HERITAGE NOTES (LOUISBOURG). 2736
1183-5869 See NORTHERN VOICE. 2201
1183-5877 See KANADA EXPLORER. 5482
1183-5990 See CANADIAN OUTBOARD MOTOR DEALERS BLUE BOOK. 592
1183-6024 See 2ND TIER, THE. 3543
1183-6040 See PLANET TODAY. 2179
1183-6091 See LINK'AGE (TORONTO). 5295
1183-627X See SURVOL CHAUDIERE-APPALACHES. 1628
1183-6288 See HIKE CANADA. 4873
1183-6296 See ECONOMIC OUTLOOK FOR INDUSTRIAL COUNTRIES. 1557
1183-630X See EARTHKEEPING ONTARIO. 80
1183-6326 See FNV : LE MAGAZINE DE LA FONDATION NOR-VAL. 5285
1183-6342 See EXPANDING HORIZONS, PSYCHIATRIC RESEARCH BULLETIN. 3925
1183-6369 See VIE ETUDIANTE. 1853
1183-6377 See WATERLINE (WINDSOR). 4929
1183-6393 See PARENTALK (RICHMOND HILL). 2284
1183-6415 See RESEAU PRESSE. 1625
1183-6423 See EXPERIENCE TRILLIUM : THE OFFICIAL PUBLICATION OF TRILLIUM TERMINAL 3 - TORONTO, CANADA. 5382
1183-644X See NEWS - ONTARIO. MINISTRY OF COMMUNITY AND SOCIAL SERVICES. 5298
1183-6458 See NOUVELLES - ONTARIO. MINISTERE DES SERVICES SOCIAUX ET COMMUNAUTAIRES. 5299
1183-6466 See ENVIRONMENTAL DIGEST. 2167
1183-6474 See BULLETIN DE RENSEIGNEMENTS, LA TAXE DE VENTE AU DETAIL / DIRECTION DE LA TAXE DE VENTE AU DETAIL. 4715
1183-6482 See PERSPECTIVES ROSEMONT / COLLEGE DE ROSEMONT. 1840
1183-6490 See BULLETIN DE LIAISON - SOCIETE CANADIENNE D'HISTOIRE DE L'EGLISE CATHOLIQUE. 5024
1183-6547 See JUNIOR MODE. 2282
1183-6598 See REPERTOIRE DES RESSOURCES CULTURELLES DES ILES-DE-LA-MADELEINE. 329
1183-6709 See HEAD OFFICE AT HOME. 679
1183-6792 See EXPRESSION : BULLETIN DE L'ASSOCIATION DES JURISTES D'EXPRESSION FRANCAISE DE L'ONTARIO (AJEFO), L'. 2968

1183-6814 See DIRECTORY OF PUBLIC COMPANIES IN CANADA. 667
1183-6822 See VECTOR PUBLIC OPINION REPORT. 5265
1183-6830 See WARBLER (TORONTO). 4708
1183-6938 See INVITATION A L'OPERA. 385
1183-6938 See INVITATION A L'OPERA. 385
1183-6962 See ICON (TORONTO). 322
1183-7004 See ALBERTA FIELD/POOL PRODUCTION AND INJECTION MONTHLY SUPPLEMENT. 4249
1183-708X See REID'S ADMINISTRATIVE LAW LETTER. 3037
1183-7098 See CHARLTON STANDARD CATALOGUE OF CANADIAN TIRE CASH BONUS COUPONS, THE. 5379
1183-7101 See CHARLTON STANDARD CATALOGUE OF THE CANADIAN NUMISMATIC ASSOCIATION'S MEDALS AND AWARDS, THE. 2780
1183-7128 See VISTA (EDMONTON). 1790
1183-7144 See CITE LIBRE (1991). 5466
1183-7160 See ENERGY MARKET UPDATE. 1941
1183-7179 See ENERGY MARKET UPDATE. 1941
1183-725X See UNIWORLD (OTTAWA). 1789
1183-7306 See CANADIAN JOURNAL OF APPLIED SPECTROSCOPY. 4434
1183-7314 See DRIVER/EDUCATION (TORONTO). 5413
1183-7349 See GENIE EN FORMATION. 1976
1183-7373 See GUIDE TO THE TORONTO REGION'S TOP EMPLOYERS. 1608
1183-7381 See LETTRES ET RENCONTRES DU CASIER POSTAL. 2537
1183-7446 See CLAYTON CONSUMER REPORT. 1294
1183-7454 See REHABILITATION TECHNOLOGY. 3696
1183-7454 See REHABILITATION TECHNOLOGY. 3696
1183-7489 See REPERTOIRE TOURISTIQUE (MONTREAL). 5490
1183-7500 See PROVOQUE (LONGUEUIL). 219
1183-7659 See SOUNDNOTES (TORONTO). 4154
1183-7667 See JOURNAL OF ENGINEERING FOR INTERNATIONAL DEVELOPMENT. 1982
1183-7675 See CELIBATAIRES MAGAZINE. 3994
1183-7705 See GUIDE, AGENCIES, BOARDS & COMMISSIONS, GOVERNMENT OF ONTARIO, A. 4653
1183-7713 See GUIDE DES ORGANISMES, CONSEILS ET COMMISSIONS DU GOUVERNEMENT DE L'ONTARIO. 4653
1183-773X See CONSERVATION AUTHORITY DIRECTORY. 2190
1183-7772 See POWER SMART ANNUAL REPORT. 1953
1183-7853 See CALGARY & AREA AVIATION BUSINESS DIRECTORY. 5378
1183-7861 See EDMONTON & AREA AVIATION BUSINESS DIRECTORY. 5381
1183-7888 See DEPARTMENT STORE MONTHLY SALES, BY PROVINCE AND METROPOLITAN AREA (FRENCH EDITION 1991). 953
1183-7888 See DEPARTMENT STORE MONTHLY SALES, BY PROVINCE AND METROPOLITAN AREA (ENGLISH EDITION 1991). 953
1183-7985 See CONTINUING EDUCATION IN NURSING, A DIRECTORY. 3854
1183-7985 See CONTINUING EDUCATION IN NURSING, A DIRECTORY. 3854
1183-7993 See POLITIQUE ET ENVIRONNEMENT / GROUPE D'ETUDES ET DE RECHERCHES SUR LES POLITIQUES ENVIRONNEMENTALES. 4491
1183-8159 See CROC CLASSIQUE. 318
1183-8329 See MCDONALD QUARTERLY. 5295
1183-8337 See PAN DEL MUERTO. 3421
1183-8434 See CLAYTON HOUSING REPORT. 2818
1183-8442 See CLAYTON HOUSING FORECAST. 2818
1183-8450 See CLAYTON COMPLETIONS REPORT. 2818

1183-8485 See EMPLOYERS' HUMAN RIGHTS & EQUITY REPORT. 1665
1183-8566 See CANQUA NEWSLETTER. 1353
1183-8620 See MESURES GLOBALES DE PRODUCTIVITE (1989). 1690
1183-868X See RAPPORT ANNUEL - QUEBEC (PROVINCE). COMITE DE DEONTOLOGIE POLICIERE. 4678
1183-8701 See LIBRARY DIRECTIONS : A NEWSLETTER OF UNIVERSITY OF MANITOBA LIBRARIES. 3225
1183-8728 See TALK B.A.C. 331
1183-8779 See PARENTS REPORT / THE INTERNATIONAL SCHOLARSHIP FOUNDATION. 1839
1183-8795 See ENVIRONMENTAL DIGEST (OWEN SOUND). 2228
1183-8809 See RECYCLING CANADA. 2241
1183-885X See JAPAN FOUNDATION PROGRAMS AVAILABLE IN CANADA, THE. 2654
1183-8868 See INFO-PARENTS. 2281
1183-8892 See PRESS FOR CONVERSION. 4054
1183-8949 See QUATRE VENTS (OTTAWA). 884
1183-8965 See STUDIO NORTH. 574
1183-899X See ECONOMICS OF CONFEDERATION. 1486
1183-9007 See MECHANICAL BUYER & SPECIFIER. PLUMBING, PIPING & HEATING. 2607
1183-9015 See MECHANICAL BUYER & SPECIFIER. HVAC/REFRIGERATION. 2607
1183-904X See ACCOUNTING ENQUIRIES. 736
1183-9139 See CANADIAN WOOD PRODUCTS (1992). 1600
1183-9155 See CULTURE SERVICE BULLETIN. 318
1183-9163 See EXTENSION (TORONTO). 378
1183-9201 See ACTION PREVENTION (SAINTE-FOY). 3156
1183-9236 See CLIENT (MONTREAL). 863
1183-9260 See DIRECTORY OF MEMBERS / THE CANADIAN HISTORICAL ASSOCIATION. 2731
1183-9260 See DIRECTORY OF MEMBERS / THE CANADIAN HISTORICAL ASSOCIATION. 2731
1183-9309 See ANNUAL REPORT - ONTARIO INSURANCE COMMISSION. 2873
1183-9309 See ANNUAL REPORT - ONTARIO INSURANCE COMMISSION. 2873
1183-935X See LUMINANCE (MONTREAL). 4975
1183-9414 See CAD SYSTEMS. 1231
1183-9473 See MONITOR (TORONTO). 5790
1183-966X See STEPTEXT (TORONTO). 5369
1183-9678 See DISABILITY DIGEST. 5284
1183-9686 See TIMBERLINE (PEMBROKE). 2475
1183-9708 See INTERNATIONAL CONTRACT (DOWNSVIEW). 2901
1183-9791 See BULLETIN - COUNTY OF CARLETON LAW ASSOCIATION. 2944
1183-9856 See FLEET SAFETY & HEALTH. 2862
1183-9929 See PRODUCTEUR PLUS, LE. 122
1183-9937 See IOUDAIOS REVIEW. 5048
1183-997X See ANNUAL REPORT / MENTAL HEALTH COMMISSION OF NEW BRUNSWICK. 4766
1183-997X See ANNUAL REPORT / MENTAL HEALTH COMMISSION OF NEW BRUNSWICK. 4766
1183-9996 See DENTAL STUDY CLUB. 1321
1184-0021 See ATLANTIC BEEF. 206
1184-0161 See RAPPORT ... INSUFFISANCE RENALE AU CANADA. 3992
1184-017X See WESTMOUNT BULLETIN (1990). 4695
1184-017X See WESTMOUNT BULLETIN (1990). 4695
1184-0188 See SANG-LIENS. 5306
1184-020X See REPERTOIRE DES RESSOURCES EN SEXUALITE, LE. 5188
1184-0218 See MEMBERSHIP DIRECTORY / CANADIAN SOCIETY FOR CHEMICAL ENGINEERING. 2015

1184-0269 See SURREY-DELTA MAGAZINE (JUNE 1990). 2547
1184-0293 See ANNOTATED TREMEEAR'S CRIMINAL CODE. 3105
1184-0307 See ANNUAL CRAFT FAIRS IN ONTARIO. 370
1184-0315 See DAVID INGRAM'S THE ULTIMATE YEAR ROUND TAX GUIDE. 4719
1184-0323 See DAVID INGRAM'S THE ULTIMATE YEAR ROUND TAX GUIDE. 4719
1184-0331 See CANADIAN RULE BOOK FOR TACKLE FOOTBALL. 4889
1184-0374 See WEEKLY HERALD (MONTREAL). 5797
1184-0390 See NOVA SCOTIA PICTORIAL COUNTRY INNS, BED & BREAKFAST AND MUCH MORE. 2808
1184-0412 See DEVELOPMENTAL DISABILITIES BULLETIN. 4386
1184-0420 See CMC YEARBOOK. 5058
1184-0439 See DIRECTORY/BUYERS' GUIDE AND DAILY PLANNER. 819
1184-0455 See TIMES FEMNIST. 5567
1184-0471 See LOBBYISTS REGISTRATION ACT ANNUAL REPORT. 4481
1184-0498 See MAJOR EVENTS. 5483
1184-051X See ATLANTIC LIFESTYLE BUSINESS. 641
1184-0528 See OFFICE SUPPLIES BUSINESS MAGAZINE, THE. 4213
1184-0536 See OFFICE PRODUCTS GOLD BOOK. 4213
1184-0552 See INTERFAX (OTTAWA). 4657
1184-0587 See NOTICE OF DECISION ON PUBLIC INTEREST REPRESENTATIONS. 848
1184-0641 See BULLETIN - CANADIAN ASSOCIATION OF JOURNALISTS. 2917
1184-065X See NEWSLETTER - CANADIAN MUSEUM OF FLIGHT AND TRANSPORTATION (1990). 30
1184-0676 See P.A.G.E. NEWS. 1771
1184-0692 See USC COUNTRY PROFILE. INDONESIA. 2912
1184-0714 See USC COUNTRY PROFILE. SWAZILAND. 2912
1184-0722 See USC COUNTRY PROFILE. NEPAL. 2912
1184-0730 See USC COUNTRY PROFILE. MALI. 2912
1184-0757 See USC COUNTRY PROFILE. LESOTHO. 2912
1184-0765 See RETIREMENT GUIDE. 5181
1184-0846 See BULLETIN DE L'AMIE. 5275
1184-0854 See BULLETIN - CANADIAN ASSOCIATION FOR COMPOSITE STRUCTURES AND MATERIALS. 2101
1184-0870 See STUDENT VENTURE CAPITAL PROGRAM. 1522
1184-0900 See SALARY ADMINISTRATION POLICIES AND PRACTICES IN CANADA. 1709
1184-1052 See CANADIAN TRANSPORTATION LOGISTICS. 5448
1184-1060 See ELORA SENTINEL, THE. 5784
1184-1087 See ITALIAN LINK. 2264
1184-1117 See PARLONS AFFAIRES DANS LES LAURENTIDES. 702
1184-1125 See PREFACE (SASKATOON. 1990). 3241
1184-1133 See MANITOBA CEC NEWS. 1882
1184-115X See ATLANTIC SILENT NEWS. 4384
1184-1451 See MINUTES OF PROCEEDINGS AND EVIDENCE OF THE SUB-COMMITTEE ON THE STATUS OF WOMEN OF THE STANDING COMMITTEE ON HEALTH AND WELFARE, SOCIAL AFFAIRS, SENIORS AND ON THE STATUS OF WOMEN. 5561
1184-146X See LEISURE WORLD. 5482
1184-1478 See NEWSLETTER / B.C. ALLIANCE CONCERNED WITH EARLY PREGNANCY AND PARENTHOOD. 5298
1184-1494 See WARD'S TAX TREATIES. 4758
1184-1508 See SADDLE & STRIKER (1990). 382
1184-1516 See MAGAZINE MARKETS & FEES. 4816

ISSN Index

1184-1524 See HUMANE TRAPPING PROGRAM ANNUAL REPORT. 226

1184-1575 See CHAROLAIS ROUNDUP. 209

1184-1605 See MANITOBA RESTAURANT NEWS. 5071

1184-163X See ALBERTA STABLE DIRECTORY. 2796

1184-1664 See OIL MARKET UPDATE. 4269

1184-1737 See DIALOGUE FOR ENGINEERS & GEOSCIENTISTS. 1970

1184-1753 See DIRECTORY OF SERVICES. 5283

1184-1761 See NICKLE'S OIL AND GAS STATISTICS QUARTERLY. 4284

1184-177X See CANADIAN RESIDENTIAL HEATING SURVEY (1990). 2604

1184-1796 See DIRECTORY & SERVICES GUIDE - CANADIAN ASSOCIATION OF WAREHOUSING AND DISTRIBUTION SERVICES. 1604

1184-1796 See DIRECTORY & SERVICES GUIDE - CANADIAN ASSOCIATION OF WAREHOUSING AND DISTRIBUTION SERVICES. 1604

1184-1818 See GUIDE RESSOURCES (1991). 4588

1184-1834 See MEMBERSHIP DIRECTORY / ACCIS. 1835

1184-1842 See VOTRE GUIDE QUOTIDIEN. 3541

1184-1869 See CONSOMMATION (MONTREAL). 4719

1184-1877 See ECOZOO. 5582

1184-1885 See REVUE DE CARTO-QUEBEC. 2583

1184-1907 See AVIATION SAFETY, ULTRALIGHT AND BALLOON. 14

1184-1990 See EGLISE DE SAINT-JEROME. 5029

1184-2059 See REVUE DU CHEVAL ARABE DU QUEBEC, LA. 2802

1184-2075 See ANNUAL REPORT - CANADA-ALBERTA SOIL CONSERVATION INITIATIVE. 162

1184-2083 See SPEC CHECK. QUEBEC & ATLANTIC REPORT. 628

1184-2091 See SPEC CHECK. ONTARIO REPORT. 628

1184-2105 See SPEC CHECK. PRAIRIE & TERRITORIES REPORT. 628

1184-2113 See SPEC CHECK. BRITISH COLUMBIA & YUKON REPORT. 628

1184-227X See SCIENCE BULLETIN (OTTAWA). 4495

1184-2288 See OUTLOOK - EDMONTON ART GALLERY. 361

1184-2326 See REPERTOIRE TELEPHONIQUE - QUEBEC (PROVINCE). MINISTERE DES AFFAIRES CULTURELLES. 4680

1184-2369 See COMPUTER DEALER NEWS (1990). 1236

1184-2512 See INTERNATIONAL CONTRACT (DOWNSVIEW). 2901

1184-2628 See ANNUAL CRAFT SHOWS IN ONTARIO / CRAFT RESOURCE CENTRE. 370

1184-2644 See P.A.G.E. JOURNAL. 4530

1184-2652 See HOMILY HINTS. 4963

1184-2679 See WESTERN SKIER. 4929

1184-2687 See ALBERTA GAME WARDEN, THE. 4868

1184-2695 See CANADIAN STAGE PRESS. 5362

1184-2709 See BROWSE (WEST HILL. 1991). 5579

1184-2717 See DIRECTIONS - ONTARIO COUNCIL OF TEACHERS OF ENGLISH. 3381

1184-2814 See HEBDO PENINSULE. 5786

1184-2849 See PROCEEDINGS AT THE OPENING OF THE LEGISLATIVE ASSEMBLY OF THE PROVINCE OF ONTARIO. 4675

1184-2970 See STATISTIQUES DE L'ADMISSION - UNIVERSITE DE MONTREAL. BUREAU DES ADMISSIONS. 1848

1184-2989 See BOOK OF SPECIAL DAYS. 1923

1184-5139 See JOURNAL (PENETANGUISHENE). 5787

1184-602X See SOURCES FOR SUCCESSFUL SMALL BUSINESS FINANCING IN CANADA. 712

1184-6038 See LISTE DES NOUVELLES ACQUISITIONS - HOPITAL SAINT-VINCENT, OTTAWA, ONT. BIBLIOTHEQUE. 3605

1184-6070 See DIRECTORY OF MUNICIPAL AND PROVINCIAL HERITAGE PROPERTY IN SASKATCHEWAN (1990). 2615

1184-6097 See RENDEZ-VOUS (QUEBEC). 4149

1184-616X See STRATEGIC PLAN - CANADA MORTGAGE AND HOUSING CORPORATION. 4689

1184-6178 See IMPRESSIONS/EXPRESSIONS (WINNIPEG). 3286

1184-6186 See ECOLES SECONDAIRES DE LA CECM, LES. 1737

1184-6194 See DIRECTORY OF CANADIAN DENTAL ASSOCIATION. 1322

1184-6194 See DIRECTORY OF CANADIAN DENTAL ASSOCIATION. 1322

1184-6208 See FACT BOOK - SASKATCHEWAN ROUGHRIDERS, FOOTBALL TEAM. 4894

1184-6216 See THUNDER BAY MUSEUM NEWSLETTER. 4097

1184-6224 See KOOTENAY WEEKLY EXPRESS, THE. 4851

1184-6259 See BILAN SOCIO-ECONOMIQUE, REGION DE LA COTE-NORD. 1464

1184-6283 See DIALOGUE - ANGLICAN CHURCH OF CANADA. DIOCESE OF ONTARIO. 4953

1184-6291 See GOLF GUIDE, ANNUAL GOLF COURSE DIRECTORY, BRITISH COLUMBIA, ALBERTA, SASKATCHEWAN. 4896

1184-6305 See REFLECTIONS (ORILLIA). 3428

1184-6313 See NATIONAL INVENTORY OF ACADEMIC & TRAINING COURSES IN PROGRAM & PROJECT EVALUATION. 420

1184-633X See INDUSTRIAL PROJECT SEARCH. ALBERTA & N.W.T. 617

1184-6356 See INDUSTRIAL PROJECT SEARCH. MANITOBA, SASKATCHEWAN, NORTHWEST ONTARIO. 617

1184-6364 See REVUE COMMERCE & INDUSTRIE. 850

1184-6399 See MICMAC MALISEET NATION NEWS. 5789

1184-6402 See MICMAC MALISEET NATION NEWS. 5789

1184-6518 See MINES AND MINERALS INFORMATION CIRCULAR. 2145

1184-6542 See BRIDGING THE GAP (CALGARY). 4940

1184-6569 See CATTW BULLETIN. 1890

1184-6577 See MANUEL D'INTERPRETATION ET D'APPLICATION DES CONVENTIONS COLLECTIVES F.T.Q. (U.E.S. LOCAL 298 ET S.C.F.P.) ... EN VIGUEUR DANS LES CENTRES D'ACCUEIL MEMBRES DE L'ASSOCIATION DES CENTRES D'ACCUEIL DU QUEBEC. 1690

1184-678X See WESTWORD (EDMONTON). 2925

1184-6801 See FAMILY TIMES (TORONTO). 5285

1184-6828 See LINK TO THE ONTARIO SOCIETY OF OCCUPATIONAL THERAPISTS, THE. 3605

1184-6941 See INFORMATION CIRCULAR - GEOLOGICAL SURVEY OF CANADA (1990). 1382

1184-695X See DRUG FACT SHEET. 4300

1184-6968 See RENSEIGNEMENTS SUR LES MEDICAMENTS. 4327

1184-7190 See CANADIAN LEGAL SERVICES DIRECTORY. 2948

1184-7204 See ACTUALITES BIBLIQUES. 5013

1184-7239 See ECHANGES - ECOLE DES HAUTES ETUDES COMMERCIALES, MONTREAL, QUEBEC. 671

1184-7247 See MINERVE DE SAINT-LAURENT, LA. 1836

1184-7255 See TOURISM TODAY OTTAWA. 5493

1184-7379 See NEWSLETTER (CANADIAN MAGAZINE PUBLISHERS ASSOCIATION). 4817

1184-7387 See BRUCE BULLETIN. 2440

1184-7409 See PREFERRED SHARE QUARTERLY. 911

1184-7417 See TRAPPER (NORTH BATTLEFORD. 1990). 4879

1184-7425 See GITES DU PASSANT AU QUEBEC. 2805

1184-745X See WARD'S TAX LAW AND PLANNING. INTERPRETATION BULLETINS. 4758

1184-7468 See WARD'S TAX LAW AND PLANNING. INFORMATION CIRCULARS AND RULINGS. 4758

1184-7476 See CODE CRIMINEL, L.R.C. (1985), CH. C-46, ET LOIS CONNEXES. 2951

1184-7484 See LOIS DU TRAVAIL. 3004

1184-7506 See CODE DE PROCEDURE CIVILE (EDITIONS THEMIS). 2951

1184-7514 See CODE DE PROCEDURE CIVILE DU QUEBEC, L.R.Q. C-25, ET LOIS ET REGLEMENTS CONNEXES. 2951

1184-7530 See FREDERICTON, NEW BRUNSWICK, ATLANTIC CANADA TOUR PLANNING MANUAL. 5474

1184-7549 See FAX BY TWIGG. 835

1184-7557 See COMPUTING & COMMUNICATIONS NEWSLETTER. 1180

1184-7565 See TALENT CATALOGUE / ACTRA ATLANTIC CANADA. 389

1184-7573 See VICTORIA BOULEVARD. 332

1184-7581 See COASTLINES (SURREY). 3376

1184-7603 See KINDRED SPIRITS OF P.E.I. 3401

1184-7786 See INTERLAKE LEADER. 5786

1184-7794 See BLAINE LAKE JOURNAL. 5780

1184-7832 See WESTCOAST REFLECTIONS. 5182

1184-7840 See CITL MEMBERSHIP DIRECTORY. 5379

1184-7956 See EDUCATION STATISTICS (FREDERICTON). 1740

1184-7956 See EDUCATION STATISTICS (FREDERICTON). 1740

1184-7980 See DEPARTMENTAL EXPENDITURE ESTIMATES SUPPLEMENT GUIDELINES. 4720

1184-7999 See DEPARTMENTAL EXPENDITURE ESTIMATES SUPPLEMENT GUIDELINES. 4720

1184-8006 See REPORT OF ACTIVITIES - MINERALS DIVISION (WINNIPEG). 1394

1184-8103 See INFO SOURCE (ENGLISH ED.). 4656

1184-8111 See INFO SOURCE (ED. FRANCAISE). 4656

1184-8170 See VARIETES DE POMMES DE TERRE AU CANADA. 144

1184-8367 See OFF THE SHELF (TORONTO). 3238

1184-8448 See CONFERENCE PROCEEDINGS - SOCIETY FOR THE ADVANCEMENT OF GIFTED EDUCATION. CONFERENCE. 1877

1184-8472 See SPINAL CORD SOCIETY CANADA. 3642

1184-8626 See LUMIERE D'ENCRE. 3409

1184-8677 See COURRIER FRANCAIS (1991). 3275

1184-8758 See DIALOGUE - FONDATION ASIE PACIFIQUE DU CANADA. 4519

1184-8774 See BULLETIN DE LA SDIE. 3125

1184-8782 See PUBLICS (MONTREAL). 765

1184-8839 See CONTACT / CANADIAN COUNCIL FOR NATIVE BUSINESS. 864

1184-8901 See THEOLOGICAL DIGEST & OUTLOOK. 5003

1184-891X See GALLUP REPORT (TORONTO. 1990). 5246

1184-8928 See MEMBERSHIP ROSTER / ALBERTA REGISTERED DIETITIANS ASSOCIATION. 4194

1184-8936 See MEMBERSHIP ROSTER / ALBERTA REGISTERED DIETITIANS ASSOCIATION. 4194

1184-8944 See OVTA NEWS. 5488

1184-8952 See MATH JOURNAL, THE. 3518

1184-9045 See PROPOSITION TARIFAIRE. 1513

1184-9207 See BRITISH COLUMBIA BUSINESS INDICATORS. 644

1184-9223 See BUSINESS FORMATIONS AND FAILURES. 648

1184-9231 See ECONOMIC STATISTICS REPORT. 1485

1184-9312 See SCCUQ-INFO. 1710

1184-9339 See CHANTIERS JEUNESSE. 5277

1184-9347 See DEPARTMENT OF INDUSTRY, TRADE AND TOURISM AND LOTTERIES FUNDED PROGRAMS, FITNESS AND SPORT DIRECTORATES, SUPPLEMENTARY INFORMATION FOR LEGISLATIVE REVIEW, ... EXPENDITURE ESTIMATES. **4720**

1184-9444 See COMPARAISONS INTERPROVINCIALES DU FINANCEMENT DES UNIVERSITES : ... RAPPORT DU COMITE TRIPARTITE SUR LES COMPARAISONS INTERPROVINCIALES. **1818**

1184-9509 See ANNUAL SALARY SURVEYS. INFORMATION SYSTEMS REPORT. **1650**

1184-9509 See ANNUAL SALARY SURVEYS. ADMINISTRATIVE & FINANCE REPORT / KPMG, PEAT MARWICK STEVENSON & KELLOGG, MANAGEMENT CONSULTANTS. **1650**

1184-9517 See ANNUAL SALARY SURVEYS. INFORMATION SYSTEMS REPORT. **1650**

1184-9525 See ANNUAL SALARY SURVEYS. ADMINISTRATIVE & FINANCE REPORT / KPMG, PEAT MARWICK STEVENSON & KELLOGG, MANAGEMENT CONSULTANTS. **1650**

1184-969X See ONTARIO BLUEWATER VISITOR GUIDE. **5487**

1184-9703 See REPORTER - BRITISH COLUMBIA LIBRARY ASSOCIATION. **3245**

1184-972X See PLEIN-JOUR SUR LA MANICOUAGAN, LE. **5793**

1184-9738 See CANADIAN MINING LIFE & EXPLORATION NEWS. **2136**

1184-9754 See NS TRAILS. **2751**

1184-9762 See INFOOD (EDMONTON). **2344**

1184-9770 See OUTPUT (RICHMOND HILL). **1224**

1184-9789 See AVIRON CANADIEN. **591**

1184-9797 See NEWSTIME - PUBLIC SERVICE ALLIANCE OF CANADA. NATIONAL COMPONENT. **4669**

1184-9800 See ACTUALITE - ALLIANCE DE LA FONCTION PUBLIQUE DU CANADA. ELEMENT NATIONAL. **1642**

1184-9819 See BUSINESS DIRECTORY : A COMPREHENSIVE GUIDE FOR BUYING BUSINESS-TO-BUSINESS GOODS AND SERVICES IN THE HAMILTON/BURLINGTON AREA. **647**

1184-9827 See CFCM REPORT. **4943**

1184-9851 See ALBERTA GOVERNMENT PUBLICATIONS QUARTERLY LIST. **407**

1184-986X See B.C. EXPORTER. **824**

1185-0175 See PEEL LABOUR. **1701**

1185-0183 See CARIBOO MINER. **2136**

1185-0213 See DIRECT LINE (SASKATOON). **1153**

1185-0264 See NEWS FROM WORKERS' COMPENSATION. **1694**

1185-0310 See VANCOUVER STEP (1991). **332**

1185-0353 See BRUCE BULLETIN. **2440**

1185-0361 See POLICE GOVERNOR. **3172**

1185-0388 See ALERT (CALGARY). **2159**

1185-040X See LAND CLAIMS NEWSLETTER. **2993**

1185-0418 See ANNUAL REPORT / NEWFOUNDLAND FARM PRODUCTS CORPORATION. **61**

1185-0744 See INTER COOP. **1542**

1185-0957 See GREEN LIVING. **2194**

1185-135X See OFSAA BULLETIN. **4910**

1185-1627 See CITT NEWSLETTER. **5363**

1185-1635 See ECHANGER POUR MIEUX FAIRE. **4850**

1185-1708 See CHICKEN FORUM. **209**

1185-1708 See CHICKEN FORUM. **209**

1185-1716 See ARBITRAGE, POINTS SAILLANTS. **1652**

1185-1724 See ADJUDICATION/ARBITRATION HIGHLIGHTS. **1642**

1185-1759 See SIGNAL (LONDON, ONT.). **3249**

1185-1783 See DOLPHIN UPDATE. **5449**

1185-1821 See NEWSLETTER / ATWATER INSTITUTE. **1118**

1185-1856 See CANADIAN SPORTSCARD COLLECTOR. **2772**

1185-1864 See ALTERNATIVE VOICE, THE. **5780**

1185-1872 See REGENT PARK T.O.!. **5793**

1185-1880 See TIMES OF SRI LANKA, THE. **5796**

1185-1899 See CASTLEGAR SUN, THE. **5781**

1185-1902 See RESEARCH BIWEEKLY. **1517**

1185-1953 See PARTNERS (KANATA). **5137**

1185-197X See ASTRO (MONTREAL). **4240**

1185-1988 See VITALITE. **2253**

1185-1996 See APERCU, L'. **5273**

1185-202X See NOUVELLES DU BUREAU NATIONAL. **5486**

1185-2119 See FARM FAMILY WEST. **84**

1185-2143 See MID-CANADA OUTDOORS. **4874**

1185-2151 See PATRONS PICK TORONTO'S FAVOURITE RESTAURANTS. **5072**

1185-216X See MLD CANADIAN TRAVELLER. **5484**

1185-2178 See FARMER-RANCHER. **85**

1185-2186 See MISSISSAUGA BUSINESS TIMES. **695**

1185-2194 See WILD OATS (WINNIPEG). **204**

1185-2208 See FORUM - CANADIAN URBAN TRANSIT ASSOCIATION. **5382**

1185-2208 See FORUM - CANADIAN URBAN TRANSIT ASSOCIATION. **5382**

1185-2275 See NATIVE SPORTS & CULTURE NEWS. **2268**

1185-2437 See PROGRAMME DE PERFECTIONNEMENT, PERFECTIONNEMENT COLLECTIF POUR LE PERSONNEL DES SERVICES DE L'EDUCATION DES ADULTES. **1802**

1185-2453 See PROGRAMME DE PERFECTIONNEMENT, PERFECTIONNEMENT COLLECTIF. **1775**

1185-247X See CHASSE AU QUEBEC, PRINCIPALES REGLES, LA. **4871**

1185-2488 See USA FACTS. **5345**

1185-2526 See CONTEMPORARY UROLOGY (MISSISSAUGA). **3989**

1185-2534 See LAW INFORMANT, THE. **2995**

1185-2542 See OWITT NEWS. **5564**

1185-2607 See FIRE PROTECTION VIDEO, FILM AND SLIDE CATALOGUE. **2289**

1185-2658 See HANDBOOK FOR CLASSROOM STUDENTS/ ALBERTA DISTANCE LEARNING CENTRE. **1749**

1185-2682 See HANDBOOK FOR NON-CLASSROOM STUDENTS / ALBERTA DISTANCE LEARNING CENTRE. **1749**

1185-2836 See ALBERTA GUIDE TO SPORTFISHING. **4868**

1185-2984 See ANNUAL REPORT / ALBERTA HEALTH. **4765**

1185-3077 See STRIVE (OTTAWA). **813**

1185-3093 See VANCOUVER SUBURBAN DIRECTORY. **5498**

1185-3107 See COMMUNITY INITIATIVES. **1817**

1185-3131 See GUIDA MENSILE. **2735**

1185-3158 See SHAIR INTERNATIONAL FORUM. **2545**

1185-3360 See SALMON ARM AND DISTRICT CHAMBER OF COMMERCE BUSINESS DIRECTORY. **821**

1185-3387 See COUNTRY ROADS (VANCOUVER). **77**

1185-3417 See DIRECTORY OF CANADIANISTS IN ALBERTA. **2731**

1185-3425 See SES CANADA FOCUS. **2760**

1185-3433 See PERFORMING ARTS & ENTERTAINMENT IN CANADA. **387**

1185-345X See WHAT'S HAPPENING MAGAZINE (BELLEVILLE. 1991). **389**

1185-3476 See STUDIO FILE. **366**

1185-3549 See GERMAN PRESS (TORONTO. 1991). **5785**

1185-3565 See ANNUAL SALARY SURVEYS. EXECUTIVE COMPENSATION REPORT. **1650**

1185-3573 See ANNUAL SALARY SURVEYS. PRODUCTION & DISTRIBUTION REPORT. **1650**

1185-3638 See NURSING BC. **3863**

1185-3794 See OILWEEK PULSE. **4270**

1185-3816 See INSIDE OLA SUPPLEMENT, OPINION SURVEY, AN. **1680**

1185-3948 See MANITOBA CONSTITUTIONAL TASK FORCE. **4664**

1185-3972 See LABOUR MARKET DEVELOPMENTS. **1686**

1185-3999 See UPDATE / SASKATCHEWAN ROUND TABLE ON ENVIRONMENT AND ECONOMY. **2183**

1185-4073 See DUN'S REGIONAL DIRECTORY OF SERVICE COMPANIES. TORONTO. **670**

1185-4219 See OFFICE LEASING DIRECTORY. **4842**

1185-4235 See REGISTER OF CANADIAN HONOURS, THE. **2469**

1185-4235 See REGISTER OF CANADIAN HONOURS, THE. **2469**

1185-4731 See WASTE BUSINESS WEST. **2246**

1185-474X See WASTE BUSINESS WEST. **2246**

1185-4839 See SASKATCHEWAN GAME MANAGEMENT. **4878**

1185-4863 See WOMEN IN MANAGEMENT. **889**

1185-4901 See WASAGA STAR TIMES. **5797**

1185-5088 See NEWSLETTER TRENDS. **4817**

1185-524X See CHIEF EXECUTIVES COMPENSATION IN CANADA. **1659**

1185-5304 See NATURAL GAS MARKET UPDATE. **847**

1185-5347 See COMMUNITY SCENE. **5280**

1185-5460 See RAPPORT D'ACTIVITES / LE BUREAU DE LA STATISTIQUE DU QUEBEC. **5337**

1185-5479 See INTERNATIONAL ABSTRACTS, PEDIATRIC UROLOGY. **3990**

1185-5614 See CHATHAM THIS WEEK. **5781**

1185-5614 See CHATHAM THIS WEEK. **5781**

1185-572X See CANADIAN LODGING OUTLOOK. **2804**

1185-5738 See CANADIAN LODGING OUTLOOK. **2804**

1185-5762 See STATE OF THE ENVIRONMENT, REPORT FOR MANITOBA. **2221**

1185-5800 See COMMUNITY PROFILE, STETTLER. **1470**

1185-5940 See VISIONS / CANADIAN MENTAL HEALTH ASOCIATION, B.C. DIVISION. **4806**

1185-5959 See TENDANCES CHEZ LES OISEAUX. **5620**

1185-5967 See BIRD TRENDS. **5615**

1185-6084 See TUSAGATSAIT (YELLOWKNIFE). **3330**

1185-622X See WHITBY COMMUNITY SERVICES DIRECTORY. **5314**

1185-6238 See WHITBY COMMUNITY SERVICES DIRECTORY. **5314**

1185-6351 See OBSERVATEUR (TORONTO). **5791**

1185-653X See CANADA'S CAPITAL, OURS IN COMMON. ANNUAL REPORT. **2817**

1185-6629 See CAHIERS PEDAGOGIQUES DE LA MONTEREGIE, LES. **1730**

1185-7099 See PERSPECTIVES - ONTARIO WORKERS' COMPENSATION INSTITUTE. **1701**

1185-7145 See ISLAND FISH FINDER MAGAZINE. **4874**

1185-720X See REVUE CANADIENNE DE LIPIDOLOGIE. **3636**

1185-7250 See BULLETIN - COPYRIGHT BOARD CANADA. **1302**

1185-7331 See INF-O-RAL (VERDUN). **1324**

1185-8591 See ALLIANCE (WHITE ROCK). **2294**

1185-877X See SUMMARIES OF DECISIONS / SOCIAL ASSISTANCE REVIEW BOARD. **5312**

1185-8788 See DYNAMO (VANCOUVER). **4893**

1185-880X See NARC (KITCHENER). **325**

1185-8834 See SPANZINE (VANCOUVER). **4569**

1185-8877 See NATURE ALERT. **2199**

1185-8923 See GUIDE TO A WORLD OF LEARNING. **1748**

1185-9075 See MANUEL D'EXPLOITATION FORESTIERE DES TERRES DE LA COURONNE. **2387**

ISSN Index

1185-9164 See SASKATCHEWAN CRIMES COMPENSATION BOARD ANNUAL REPORT. 3176

1185-9318 See CATALOGUE-REPERTOIRE DES CREATEURS-CONCEPTEURS. 317

1185-9326 See COMCAR REVIEW. 5380

1185-9334 See MEMBERSHIP DIRECTORY / THE CANADIAN SOCIETY OF ANIMAL SCIENCE. 5516

1185-9369 See WELLAND TOURISM NEWS / TOURISM OF WELLAND NIAGARA. 5499

1185-9504 See PINK & BLUE DIRECTORY, THE. 5564

1185-9598 See FORESTRY ON THE HILL. 2382

1185-9628 See PUBLICATIONS CATALOGUE / INSTITUTE FOR RESEARCH IN CONSTRUCTION. 625

1185-9628 See PUBLICATIONS CATALOGUE - INSTITUTE FOR RESEARCH IN CONSTRUCTION (OTTAWA). 633

1185-9652 See STATUTORY PUBLICATIONS, PRICE LIST - MANITOBA. OFFICE OF THE QUEEN'S PRINTER (ENGLISH EDITION). 3059

1185-9652 See STATUTORY PUBLICATIONS, PRICE LIST - MANITOBA. OFFICE OF THE QUEEN'S PRINTER (FRENCH EDITION). 3059

1185-9660 See ANNUAL REPORT - CANADIAN COUNCIL OF MINISTERS OF THE ENVIRONMENT. 5272

1185-9660 See ANNUAL REPORT - CANADIAN COUNCIL OF MINISTERS OF THE ENVIRONMENT. 2160

1185-9679 See CANADA-U.S. TRADE DISPUTES. 826

1185-9687 See DIFFERENDS COMMERCIAUX ENTRE LE CANADA ET LES ETATS-UNIS. 831

1185-9717 See CLASSICAL MUSIC MAGAZINE (MISSISSAUGA). 4110

1185-975X See COUNTRY ROADS MAGAZINE (CARP). 2729

1185-9792 See CANADIAN RULE BOOK FOR TACKLE FOOTBALL. 4889

1185-9806 See PROGRAMS AT WORK / BRITISH COLUMBIA FORESTRY ASSOCIATION. 2391

1185-9814 See CANADIAN JOURNAL OF QUALITY IN HEALTH CARE, THE. 4770

1185-9938 See CULTURES INTERNATIONAL. 5243

1185-9938 See CULTURES INTERNATIONAL. 5243

1185-9946 See NATIVE AGENDA, NEWS. 4668

1185-9954 See PROGRAMME POUR LES AUTOCHTONES, NOUVELLES, LE. 4675

1186-0006 See BULLETIN - CANADIAN MEDICAL ASSOCIATION. 3559

1186-0014 See QUARTERLY OUTLOOK FOR MAJOR FINANCIAL MARKETS. 805

1186-0022 See QUARTERLY OUTLOOK FOR MAJOR FINANCIAL MARKETS. 805

1186-0049 See GERMINATOR (LETHBRIDGE). 173

1186-0057 See ALLPOINTS (WILLOWDALE). 859

1186-0103 See THE POINT (VICTORIA), TO. 1787

1186-0170 See TURF & RECREATION. 2433

1186-0189 See ECHANGE DU YWCA QUEBEC, L'. 5554

1186-0294 See COMMUNICATION STOCKS AND THE TSE 300. 895

1186-0308 See ROUND TABLE NEWS. 1519

1186-0340 See BUSINESS TO BUSINESS QUINTE. 653

1186-0367 See LEXIQUE - ONTARIO. MINISTERE DES SERVICES SOCIAUX ET COMMUNAUTAIRES. 5294

1186-0375 See MINUTES OF PROCEEDINGS AND EVIDENCE OF THE SPECIAL JOINT COMMITTEE OF THE SENATE AND THE HOUSE OF COMMONS ON PROCESS FOR AMENDING THE CONSTITUTION OF CANADA. 4482

1186-0391 See CREATE: JOURNAL OF THE CREATIVE AND EXPRESSIVE ARTS THERAPIES EXCHANGE. 4583

1186-0405 See REPORT - BRITISH COLUMBIA. LEGISLATIVE ASSEMBLY. SELECT STANDING COMMITTEE ON FINANCE, CROWN CORPORATIONS AND GOVERNMENT SERVICES. 807

1186-0413 See NEWMARKET BUSINESS REPORT. 699

1186-043X See REPERTOIRE DES PROJETS DE RECHERCHE DU PAREA. 1844

1186-0480 See YOUTH EXCHANGE PROGRAMS. 1792

1186-0545 See SASKATCHEWAN CRIMES COMPENSATION BOARD ANNUAL REPORT. 3176

1186-091X See MW-Q. 800

1186-0928 See MARKET MONITOR (TORONTO). 906

1186-1029 See CANADIAN STEEL STOCKS. 894

1186-1037 See CANADIAN TECHNOLOGY MONTHLY. 894

1186-1053 See ECONOMIC ADVISOR (TORONTO). 1556

1186-1126 See SAWT KANADA. 2545

1186-1193 See COLLINGWOOD LIFE & PICTORIAL. 2728

1186-1215 See CATALOGUE DES PRODUITS EN FRANCAIS. 412

1186-1231 See REPERTOIRE DES ARTISTES ET DES ARTISANS DE SAINT-EUSTACHE. 329

1186-124X See ADIQ (MONTREAL). 1596

1186-1258 See VESTIBULLES (MONTREAL). 382

1186-1274 See PARLONS AFFAIRES, BEAUCE-ETCHEMINS. 702

1186-1282 See INFO DOCUMENTATION (DRUMMONDVILLE). 3215

1186-1304 See INFO-GENEALOGIE (SAINTE-FOY). 2454

1186-1355 See PRECIS DE CONCORDANCE DE LA CONVENTION COLLECTIVE F.P.S.S.S.(C.E.Q.) ... EN VIGUEUR DANS LES CENTRES D'ACCUEIL MEMBRES DE L'ASSOCIATION DES CENTRES D'ACCUEIL DU QUEBEC. 1702

1186-1363 See PRECIS DE CONCORDANCE DE LA CONVENTION COLLECTIVE U.Q.I.I. ... EN VIGUEUR DANS LES CENTRES D'ACCUEIL MEMBRES DE L'ASSOCIATION DES CENTRES D'ACCUEIL DU QUEBEC. 803

1186-1371 See PRECIS DE CONCORDANCE DE LA CONVENTION COLLECTIVE C.S.D.-F.A.S. ... EN VIGUEUR DANS LES CENTRES D'ACCUEIL MEMBRES DE L'ASSOCIATION DES CENTRES D'ACCEUIL DU QUEBEC. 1702

1186-1398 See BUILDING AND CONSTRUCTION TRADES TODAY. 602

1186-1460 See GRADUATE COMPUTERWORLD. 1238

1186-1487 See TAX REFORM AND RETIREMENT SAVINGS (TORONTO). 917

1186-1509 See CONNECTIONS (GRIMSBY). 784

1186-1525 See VILLAGE OF YORKVILLE VOICE, THE. 5797

1186-1568 See CANADIAN COMMENT. 2037

1186-1797 See PROFESSIONAL SOUND (TORONTO). 4453

1186-1886 See GUIDE PRATIQUE DE L'ORGANISATEUR DE CONGRES, RIMOUSKI LA PREFERENCE. 5479

1186-1975 See CANADIAN BASE METAL EQUITIES. 893

1186-1983 See CANADIAN BASE METAL EQUITIES. 893

1186-2017 See NOVI SKRIZALI. 4982

1186-2025 See REFLET TEMISCAMIEN, LE. 5793

1186-2033 See CANADIAN MILL PRODUCT NEWS. 4233

1186-2165 See MONTREAL TRIBUNE (1990). 5790

1186-2246 See RESPITE CARE SERVICES FOR SENIORS IN METROPOLITAN TORONTO. 5181

1186-2262 See PUBLICATIONS DU BUREAU DE LA STATISTIQUE DU QUEBEC, LES. 423

1186-2289 See PLAISIR DES JEUX (MONTREAL). 4864

1186-2300 See COMPONENT ACCEPTANCE DIRECTORY, PLASTICS PROGRAM. 4454

1186-2335 See TRENDS IN HAMILTON-WENTWORTH. 5264

1186-2378 See MUSIC '91 (VANCOUVER). 4132

1186-2394 See YOUTH FISHERIES EDUCATION PROGRAM : [NEWSLETTER]. 2316

1186-2432 See PROPOS (QUEBEC), A. 5254

1186-2785 See BULLETIN DU PROGRAMME D'EDUCATION SCOLAIRE SUR LES PECHES. 4870

1186-2858 See MEDICAL REVIEW OF MEETINGS & LISTINGS, THE. 3611

1186-2947 See GRAND ROUNDS IN INFECTIOUS DISEASES. 3713

1186-3064 See ASSINIBOIA TODAY. 5780

1186-4265 See ORO-VESPRA INDEPENDENT [MICROFORM]. 5792

1186-429X See YORKTON THIS WEEK & ENTERPRISE. 5798

1186-4303 See GREENBORO HUNT CLUB PARK NEWS [MICROFORM]. 5785

1186-4893 See ORILLIA TODAY [MICROFORM]. 5792

1186-4907 See SCUGOG CITIZEN [MICROFORM]. 5794

1186-5393 See MORNING CHRONICLE (HALIFAX. TRI-WEEKLY ED.). 5812

1186-5601 See NORTHUMBERLAND PUBLISHERS' WEEKENDER. 5791

1186-6012 See ANNUAIRE DES MEMBRES ... ET MANUEL DE REFERENCE / ABQ, ASSOCIATION BETON QUEBEC. 598

1186-6020 See JOURNAL JEUNESSE TIMOTHEE. 4968

1186-6047 See DIRECTORY OF MERGERS & ACQUISITIONS IN CANADA. 666

1186-6055 See IN TUNE (EDMONTON). 4122

1186-608X See M.A.S.B.O. NEWS. 1762

1186-6098 See PEACE RIVER, ALASKA HIGHWAY TOUR AND VACATION GUIDE. 5488

1186-6101 See PEACE RIVER, ALASKA HIGHWAY TOUR AND VACATION GUIDE. 5488

1186-611X See TEEN ARTS CONNECTION/TORONTO. 366

1186-6152 See LIST OF CSA CERTIFIED ELEVATOR EQUIPMENT. 2120

1186-6217 See CARREFOUR BIO-ALIMENTAIRE. 2330

1186-690X See EASTMAIN 1 HYDROELECTRIC DEVELOPMENT. 1481

1186-6918 See AMENAGEMENT HYDROELECTRIQUE D'EASTMAN 1, L'. 1931

1186-7035 See LEMOYNE-TILLY LIGNE A 735 KV. 2197

1186-7043 See LEMOYNE-TILLY 735-KV LINE. 1985

1186-7175 See FORAGE SEED UPDATE. 88

1186-723X See SOURCE (EDMONTON). 4686

1186-7477 See INSIDE ENTERTAINMENT. 385

1186-7515 See FOLK MUSIC CATALOGUE. 4118

1186-7523 See FOLK MUSIC CATALOGUE. 4118

1186-7558 See ALASKA TRANSPORTER : THE OFFICIAL PUBLICATION OF THE ALASKA TRUCKING ASSOCIATION, INC. 5375

1186-7604 See EFFECTIF SCOLAIRE ..., MANUEL D'OPERATIONS DES SYSTEMES INFORMATIQUES (DCS). 1743

1186-7620 See PERSPECTIVE REGIONALE DE DEVELOPPEMENT DE LA MAIN-D'OEUVRE POUR L'ANNEE. 4673

1186-7639 See MAGAZINE DES VEHICULES UTILITAIRES ANCIENS, LE. 5386

1186-7671 See VANCOUVER EAST NEWS. 5797

1186-768X See VANCOUVER SOUTH NEWS (1991). 5797

1186-7698 See VANCOUVER EAST NEWS. 5797

1186-7779 See PROVOQUE (LONGUEUIL). 219

1186-7787 See DISCOVERING ALBERTA. 5468

1186-7914 See SUNSHINE CIRCLE TOUR MAGAZINE : SUNSHINE COAST AND VANCOUVER ISLAND, THE. 5491

1186-7949 See OFFICIAL TRAVELLER'S GUIDE TO CANADA, THE. 5487

1186-7965 *See* BRITISH COLUMBIA MIGRATION HIGHLIGHTS. 4550

1186-7973 *See* VANCOUVER ISLAND GAS PIPELINE UPDATE. 4281

1186-799X *See* NORTHERN YUKON NATIONAL PARK. 4707

1186-799X *See* NORTHERN YUKON NATIONAL PARK. 4707

1186-8023 *See* OUTDOOR EDGE. 4876

1186-8058 *See* MEMBERSHIP DIRECTORY / CANADIAN SOCIETY FOR INDUSTRIAL SECURITY. 2865

1186-8058 *See* MEMBERSHIP DIRECTORY / CANADIAN SOCIETY FOR INDUSTRIAL SECURITY. 2865

1186-8090 *See* SASKATCHEWAN STATE OF THE ENVIRONMENT REPORT. 2204

1186-818X *See* BILAN SOCIO-ECONOMIQUE, REGION DE LA GASPESIE--ILES-DE-LA-MADELEINE. 5275

1186-8201 *See* HEALTH CARE PRODUCTS AND CAPABILITIES IN ALBERTA. 3581

1186-8295 *See* PROGRAM OF STUDIES - NEWFOUNDLAND. DIVISION OF PROGRAM DEVELOPMENT. 1903

1186-8325 *See* COALITION OF UNIONS NEWSLETTER. 1659

1186-835X *See* ASSUREUR DES COMMERCES, L'. 2874

1186-8368 *See* RIVE CULTURELLE. 388

1186-8392 *See* STRATEGY REPORT - MANITOBA. WASTE REDUCTION AND PREVENTION BRANCH. 2244

1186-8449 *See* ECHANGE DE DOCUMENTS INFORMATISES AU CANADA. 866

1186-8473 *See* GAZETTE DU GRANIT, LA. 2734

1186-849X *See* TLRC DIRECTORY. 2585

1186-8503 *See* TLRC DIRECTORY. 2585

1186-8511 *See* REPERTOIRE TLRC. 3245

1186-8619 *See* STELCO INC. 4750

1186-8635 *See* DOFASCO (TORONTO). 788

1186-8643 *See* IPSCO INC. / MIDLAND WALWYN RESEARCH. 4734

1186-8694 *See* CLIA LOSS PREVENTION BULLETIN / CANADIAN LAWYERS INSURANCE ASSOCIATION. 2951

1186-8759 *See* BULLETIN DE L'IRDAP : UN SERVICE D'INFORMATION DE L'INSTITUT DE RECHERCHES EN DONS ET EN AFFAIRES PUBLIQUES. 5275

1186-8783 *See* CURRENTS (CALGARY). 1181

1186-8872 *See* WINGS : WOMEN IN NEWS GATHERING. 2925

1186-8937 *See* BULLETIN MARIE DE L'INCARNATION. 4941

1186-8945 *See* NEPENTHES (MONTREAL). 3415

1186-8953 *See* DESTINATION INTEGRATION. 5281

1186-8953 *See* DESTINATION INTEGRATION. 5281

1186-9100 *See* PREVIEW - CANADIAN CONSTRUCTION ASSOCIATION. 624

1186-9119 *See* APERCU - ASSOCIATION CANADIENNE DE LA CONSTRUCTION. 599

1186-9208 *See* B.C. RETAILER. 952

1186-9216 *See* NATIONAL BULLETIN / MECHANICAL CONTRACTORS ASSOCIATION OF CANADA. 2027

1186-9240 *See* ZOOM IN : NEW FILMS AND VIDEOS FROM THE NATIONAL FILM BOARD OF CANADA. 4080

1186-9275 *See* QUARTERLY STEEL COMMENT. 4017

1186-9291 *See* ABORIGINAL BUSINESS COURIER. 2526

1186-9321 *See* GUIDE DES AUTOS USAGEES, LE. 5415

1186-9348 *See* CULTURAL EVENTS - NATIONAL LIBRARY OF CANADA. 318

1186-9461 *See* CAMBRIDGE, ONTARIO, CANADA ... TOURIST GUIDEBOOK. 5465

1186-947X *See* CAMBRIDGE, ONTARIO, CANADA ... TOURIST GUIDEBOOK. 5465

1186-950X *See* NEXUS NEWSLETTER. 1768

1186-950X *See* NEXUS NEWSLETTER / MOVEMENT FOR CANADIAN LITERACY. 1768

1186-9666 *See* DISABILITY TODAY (ST. CATHARINES). 4387

1186-9798 *See* ASSOCIATIONS CANADA. 5228

1186-9798 *See* ASSOCIATIONS CANADA. 5228

1186-9925 *See* COUNTRY ROADS MAGAZINE (CARP). 2729

1187-001X *See* LIBERTAS (ENGLISH EDITION MONTREAL). 4510

1187-0125 *See* ENVIRONMENTAL COMPLIANCE REPORT, THE. 3111

1187-0176 *See* MAGAZINE AFFAIRES PLUS. 797

1187-0265 *See* CUSTOMER INFORMATION - BRITISH COLUMBIA. PURCHASING COMMISSION. 949

1187-0273 *See* RECHERCHE-DEVELOPPEMENT POUR LES FORMATEURS DES SECTEURS TECHNIQUE ET PROFESSIONNEL. 1777

1187-0281 *See* RECHERCHE-DEVELOPPEMENT POUR LES FORMATEURS DES SECTEURS TECHNIQUE ET PROFESSIONNEL. 1777

1187-029X *See* INFO RENOVATION. SECTEUR RIVE-SUD. 617

1187-0303 *See* INFO RENOVATION. SECTEUR EST DE MTL. 617

1187-0362 *See* NEWSLETTER - OPERA LYRA OTTAWA. 386

1187-0370 *See* ONTARIO SOCIAL ACTION NEWSLETTER, THE. 5300

1187-0389 *See* ONTARIO SOCIAL ACTION NEWSLETTER, THE. 5300

1187-0400 *See* RPNABC PROFILE. 3869

1187-0419 *See* REPERTOIRE DES BIBLIOTHEQUES UNIVERSITAIRES QUEBECOISES. 3245

1187-0524 *See* CAD SYSTEMS. 1231

1187-0559 *See* CHILD CARE (KITCHENER). 2277

1187-0621 *See* PROGRAMME D'AIDE ... DU MINISTERE DES AFFAIRES CULTURELLES AIDE AUX ARTISTES PROFESSIONNELS. 328

1187-063X *See* SUPPORT FOR PROFESSIONAL ARTISTS. 331

1187-0664 *See* EXTRA! EXTRA! NEWSPAPERS ACROSS CANADA. 5784

1187-0672 *See* TOM TAC, LE REGIONAL. 5796

1187-0680 *See* TOM TAC, LE REGIONAL. 5796

1187-0699 *See* GABRIOLA SOUNDER, THE. 5785

1187-0702 *See* GABRIOLA SOUNDER, THE. 5785

1187-0761 *See* ALBERTA BEEF (1991). 205

1187-077X *See* EXTENSION (TORONTO). 378

1187-0788 *See* RENOVER (OUTREMONT). 626

1187-0796 *See* THUNDER BAY METRO TRADE INDEX. 853

1187-080X *See* ECONOMIC REFORM (TORONTO). 1484

1187-0818 *See* BULLETIN - CANADIAN INTRAMURAL RECREATION ASSOCIATION. 4849

1187-0826 *See* BULLETIN / CASCA, CANADIAN ANTHROPOLOGY SOCIETY. 232

1187-0850 *See* IMMERSION REGISTRY. 3286

1187-0877 *See* TRENDS IN HAMILTON-WENTWORTH. 5264

1187-0893 *See* RAPPORT ANNUEL / REGIE DES LOTERIES DU QUEBEC. 4678

1187-0990 *See* WHO'S WHO (ONTARIO ED.). 1263

1187-1121 *See* WESTERN GEOGRAPHY. 2579

1187-1164 *See* WOUND & SKIN CARE. 3723

1187-1202 *See* CANADIAN ENVIRONMENTAL DIRECTORY. 2162

1187-1261 *See* COMPOSITES REPORT / FIBERGLAS CANADA INC. 4454

1187-127X *See* BULLETIN SUR LES COMPOSITES. 4454

1187-1334 *See* CAMPING, CARAVANING (MONTREAL). 4870

1187-1490 *See* VOCATIONAL EDUCATION FOR YOUNG PERSONS AND ADULTS IN SCHOOL BOARDS. 1917

1187-1571 *See* BULLETIN / ROYAL ASTRONOMICAL SOCIETY OF CANADA. 394

1187-1725 *See* PHOTO SELECTION (1991). 4373

1187-1733 *See* WEEKLY SUMMARY - BRITISH COLUMBIA SECURITIES COMMISSION (1989). 919

1187-1768 *See* RECHERCHE DEVELOPPEMENT AU QUEBEC, LA. 5145

1187-1776 *See* CATALOGUE DES FOURNITURES ET DU MOBILIER. 4211

1187-1857 *See* REGLES DU JEU CANADIENNES POUR LE FOOTBALL AVEC PLAQUE. 4914

1187-1865 *See* REGLES DU JEU CANADIENNES POUR LE FOOTBALL AVEC PLAQUE. 4914

1187-2136 *See* ANNUAIRE DES COMMISSIONS SCOLAIRES. 1724

1187-2144 *See* REPERTOIRE DES INSTITUTIONS - ONTARIO. DIRECTION DE L'ACCES A L'INFORMATION ET DE LA PROTECTION DE LA VIE PRIVEE. 4679

1187-2144 *See* DIRECTORY OF INSTITUTIONS - ONTARIO. FREEDOM OF INFORMATION AND PRIVACY BRANCH. 4643

1187-2160 *See* ANNUAL REPORT / CANADIAN CENTRE FOR MANAGEMENT DEVELOPMENT. 4627

1187-2160 *See* ANNUAL REPORT-CANADIAN CENTRE FOR MANAGEMENT DEVELOPMENT. 860

1187-2195 *See* GUIDE TO THE HANDLING AND DISPOSAL OF HAZARDOUS SUBSTANCES IN THE SCHOOLS, A. 2230

1187-2233 *See* BULLETIN AMI. 3559

1187-225X *See* PERIODICALS / OTTAWA PUBLIC LIBRARY. 3240

1187-225X *See* PERIODICALS - OTTAWA PUBLIC LIBRARY (1991). 3240

1187-2268 *See* GUIDE DE L'ACHETEUR ANNUEL - EXPOSITION COMMERCIALE DE L'HORTICULTURE ORNEMENTALE. 2418

1187-2292 *See* GUIDE DE L'ACHETEUR ANNUEL - EXPOSITION COMMERCIALE DE L'HORTICULTURE ORNEMENTALE. 2418

1187-2306 *See* DIRECTORY OF THE ASSOCIATION OF PROFESSIONAL ENGINEERS AND GEOSCIENTISTS OF THE PROVINCE OF BRITISH COLUMBIA. 1971

1187-2454 *See* ANNUAL REPORT - NEW BRUNSWICK ARTS BOARD. 313

1187-2454 *See* ANNUAL REPORT / NEW BRUNSWICK ARTS BOARD. 313

1187-2462 *See* MINUTES OF PROCEEDINGS AND EVIDENCE OF THE STANDING COMMITTEE ON HOUSE MANAGEMENT. 4665

1187-2470 *See* MINUTES OF PROCEEDINGS AND EVIDENCE OF THE SUB-COMMITTEE ON PRIVATE MEMBERS BUSINESS OF THE STANDING COMMITTEE ON HOUSE MANAGEMENT. 4666

1187-2470 *See* MINUTES OF PROCEEDINGS AND EVIDENCE OF THE SUB-COMMITTEE ON PRIVATE MEMBERS BUSINESS OF THE STANDING COMMITTEE ON HOUSE MANAGEMENT. 4666

1187-2489 *See* PROCEEDINGS OF THE STANDING SENATE COMMITTEE ON PRIVILEGES, STANDING RULES AND ORDERS. 4675

1187-2608 *See* "CRISS-CROSS" MONTREAL METROPOLITAIN. 5467

1187-2608 *See* "CRISS-CROSS" MONTREAL METROPOLITAIN. 5467

1187-2691 *See* TABLES CHAMPETRES ET PROMENADES A LA FERME AU QUEBEC. 5073

1187-2691 *See* TABLES CHAMPETRES ET PROMENADES A LA FERME AU QUEBEC. 5073

1187-2705 *See* ARIA NEWS. 5315

1187-2713 *See* PATRIMOINE TRIFLUVIEN. 2830

1187-2721 *See* PATRIMOINE TRIFLUVIEN. 2830

1187-2861 *See* COMPAGNIES, SOCIETES PAR ACTIONS ET FAILLITE. 3089

1187-2896 *See* MINUTES OF PROCEEDINGS AND EVIDENCE OF THE STANDING COMMITTEE ON OFFICIAL LANGUAGES. 3302

1187-2942 *See* MANITOBA PRODUCTION STATISTICS REPORT. 1536

1187-2950 *See* ISTC NEW BRUNSWICK/PRINCE EDWARD ISLAND. 1613

1187-2950 See ISTC NEW BRUNSWICK/PRINCE EDWARD ISLAND. 5117

1187-2977 See GUIDE DE LA DECLARATION D'EFFECTIF SCOLAIRE (DCS). 1748

1187-2985 See NETWORK WORLD CANADA. 1197

1187-3000 See PRINCE EDWARD ISLAND MUNICIPAL DIRECTORY. 4674

1187-3043 See UPDATE - SOCIAL SCIENCE FEDERATION OF CANADA. 5225

1187-3043 See UPDATE / SOCIAL SCIENCE FEDERATION OF CANADA. 5225

1187-3183 See EXCLUSIVE (OTTAWA). 5469

1187-3264 See PLAN - BRITISH COLUMBIA. RESOURCE MANAGEMENT BRANCH. 1359

1187-3272 See RIGHTS AND LIBERTIES. 4512

1187-3280 See ROCKY MOUNTAIN HOUSE LIEU HISTORIQUE NATIONAL. 2759

1187-3299 See ROCKY MOUNTAIN HOUSE NATIONAL HISTORIC SITE. 2759

1187-3388 See GERMAN PRESS (TORONTO. 1991). 5785

1187-3396 See ALBERTA DEMOCRAT, THE. 4462

1187-3469 See MEMBERSHIP ROSTER - AUTOMOTIVE RETAILERS ASSOCIATION (WINNIPEG). 955

1187-3485 See PEACEKEEPING & INTERNATIONAL RELATIONS. 4531

1187-3493 See NEWS CORPORATION. 1118

1187-3507 See NEWS CORPORATION. 1118

1187-3523 See NATIVE SPORTS & CULTURE NEWS. 2268

1187-3531 See EASTWORD (HALIFAX). 3383

1187-3566 See PROGRAMS AT WORK / BRITISH COLUMBIA FORESTRY ASSOCIATION. 2391

1187-3612 See CLEAN CURRENTS / HALIFAX HARBOUR CLEANUP INC. 2226

1187-3663 See NEWS / FEDERAL-PROVINCIAL ENVIRONMENTAL ASSESSMENT REVIEW PANEL, HALIFAX-DARTMOUTH METROLITAN WASTEWATER MANAGEMENT SYSTEM. 2237

1187-3728 See ANNUAL REPORT - NATIONAL MUSEUM OF SCIENCE AND TECHNOLOGY (OTTAWA). 4083

1187-3736 See RAPPORT ANNUEL - MUSEE NATIONAL DES SCIENCES ET DE LA TECHNOLOGIE (OTTAWA). 5144

1187-3779 See CANADIAN HOSPITAL FORUM. 3778

1187-3787 See STRAIGHT FACTS ON PHARMACEUTICAL PRICES, MANUFACTURING AND RESEARCH, THE. 4330

1187-3949 See KAIKU (TORONTO). 2266

1187-3957 See EDMONTON FACTS. 2732

1187-4090 See REPERTOIRE DES ETABLISSEMENTS D'ENSEIGNEMENT SUPERIEUR MEMBRES DE L'AUPELF-UREF. 1844

1187-4104 See REPERTOIRE INTERNATIONAL DES DEPARTMENTS ET DES CENTRES DETUDES FRANCAISES. 3315

1187-4112 See REPERTOIRE DES ENSEIGNANTS ET CHERCHEURS DES INSTITUTIONS D'ENSEIGNEMENT SUPERIEUR MEMBRES DE L'AUPELF-UREF (AFRIQUE, CARAIBE, OCEAN INDIEN). 1844

1187-4147 See MANAGER NEWSLETTER. 1145

1187-4147 See MANAGER NEWSLETTER. 878

1187-4198 See OMCA RESOURCE GUIDE. 1620

1187-421X See GITES DU PASSANT AU QUEBEC. 2805

1187-421X See GITES DU PASSANT AU QUEBEC. 2805

1187-4295 See CANADIAN TRANSPORTATION LOGISTICS. 5448

1187-4309 See STRATEGY (TORONTO. 1991). 937

1187-4317 See ACCESS GUIDE TO GOVERNMENT RECORDS AND INFORMATION. 4623

1187-4333 See ACCESS GUIDE TO GOVERNMENT RECORDS AND INFORMATION. 4623

1187-435X See MAGAZINE ENFANTS, LE. 1066

1187-4376 See CANADIAN BLACK BOOK, USED TRUCK AND VAN GUIDE. 5408

1187-4392 See BULLETIN DE LA F.A.A.F., N.-B, LE. 69

1187-4406 See MINUTES OF PROCEEDINGS AND EVIDENCE OF THE SUB-COMMITTEE ON HEALTH ISSUES OF THE STANDING COMMITTEE ON HEALTH AND WELFARE, SOCIAL AFFAIRS, SENIORS AND THE STATUS OF WOMEN. 4791

1187-4406 See MINUTES OF PROCEEDINGS AND EVIDENCE OF THE SUB-COMMITTEE ON HEALTH ISSUES OF THE STANDING COMMITTEE ON HEALTH AND WELFARE, SOCIAL AFFAIRS, SENIORS AND THE STATUS OF WOMEN. 4791

1187-4414 See MINUTES OF PROCEEDINGS AND EVIDENCE OF THE SUB-COMMITTEE ON DEVELOPMENT AND HUMAN RIGHTS OF THE STANDING COMMITTEE ON EXTERNAL AFFAIRS AND INTERNATIONAL TRADE. 4510

1187-4414 See MINUTES OF PROCEEDINGS AND EVIDENCE OF THE SUB-COMMITTEE ON DEVELOPMENT AND HUMAN RIGHTS OF THE STANDING COMMITTEE ON EXTERNAL AFFAIRS AND INTERNATIONAL TRADE. 4510

1187-4430 See MINUTES OF PROCEEDINGS AND EVIDENCE OF THE SPECIAL COMMITTEE ON THE ACT RESPECTING CUSTOMS. 4737

1187-4430 See MINUTES OF PROCEEDINGS AND EVIDENCE OF THE SPECIAL COMMITTEE ON THE ACT RESPECTING CUSTOMS. 4665

1187-4457 See LABOUR MARKET DEVELOPMENTS. 1686

1187-452X See MINUTES OF PROCEEDINGS AND EVIDENCE OF THE SUB-COMMITTEE ON FINANCIAL INSTITUTIONS LEGISLATION OF THE STANDING COMMITTEE ON FINANCE. 798

1187-452X See MINUTES OF PROCEEDINGS AND EVIDENCE OF THE SUB-COMMITTEE ON FINANCIAL INSTITUTIONS LEGISLATION OF THE STANDING COMMITTEE ON FINANCE. 3087

1187-4546 See CORPORATE PLAN SUMMARY, CAPITAL BUDGET SUMMARY, OPERATING BUDGET SUMMARY. 5097

1187-4562 See SANFORD EVANS GOLD BOOK, OFFICIAL SNOWMOBILE DATA AND USED PRICES. 5392

1187-4570 See CANADIAN GLOBAL ALMANAC, THE. 1924

1187-4589 See TAX TIPS - DOANE, RAYMOND, PANNELL. 4754

1187-4619 See MANDAT (WILLOWDALE. 1991). 691

1187-4627 See REVUE CURLING QUEBEC, LA. 4915

1187-4635 See BUSINESS TODAY, CONSTRUCTION NEWS. 606

1187-4651 See COMMERCE (RED DEER). 828

1187-466X See MS TORONTO (1991). 4391

1187-4678 See CHILD CARE (KITCHENER). 2277

1187-4775 See MARCHE (MONTREAL). 4904

1187-4813 See FORMATION GENERALE DES JEUNES, L'EDUCATION PRESCOLAIRE, L'ENSEIGNEMENT PRIMAIRE ET L'ENSEIGNEMENT SECONDAIRE, INSTRUCTION, LA. 1747

1187-4821 See MATHEMATIQUE 3031, DEFINITION DU DOMAINE, EXAMENS DE FIN D'ETUDES SECONDAIRES, DE JANVIER ... ET JUIN . 3521

1187-483X See MATHEMATIQUE 3032, DEFINITION DU DOMAINE, EXAMENS DE FIN D'ETUDES SECONDAIRES, DE JANVIER ... ET JUIN . 3521

1187-4848 See TETE-A-TETE (OTTAWA. 1991). 1141

1187-4848 See TETE-A-TETE (OTTAWA. 1991). 1141

1187-4945 See LIAISON - CANADIAN ASSOCIATION OF LEGAL ASSISTANTS. 3003

1187-4945 See LIAISON - CANADIAN ASSOCIATION OF LEGAL ASSISTANTS. 3003

1187-4953 See NORD-EST PLUS. 5790

1187-497X See TESL MANITOBA. 1907

1187-4988 See VIVRE A PIERREFONDS. 2765

1187-4988 See VIVRE A PIERREFONDS. 2549

1187-4996 See BULLETIN - ONTARIO. SOCIAL ASSISTANCE REVIEW BOARD. 5275

1187-4996 See BULLETIN - ONTARIO. SOCIAL ASSISTANCE REVIEW BOARD. 4635

1187-5011 See PERSPECTIVES - ST. BONIFACE GENERAL HOSPITAL. 3790

1187-5011 See PERSPECTIVES - ST. BONIFACE GENERAL HOSPITAL. 3791

1187-502X See GUIDE RESSOURCES (1991). 4588

1187-5038 See BULLETIN DE L'AMIE. 5275

1187-5062 See PHYSICIAN'S NEWSLETTER - SASKATCHEWAN. SASKATCHEWAN HEALTH. 3627

1187-5216 See KEY (VICTORIA). 4660

1187-5313 See INFO-DETAIL / LE CONSEIL QUEBECOIS DU COMMERCE DE DETAIL. 840

1187-5321 See INFO-DETAIL (1991 ENGLISH ED.). 840

1187-5356 See CANADIAN AUTOMOTIVE FLEET. FACT BOOK. 5378

1187-5399 See MARIE-CLEMENT STAUB, A.A., SKETCHES OF HIS LIFE AND WORK. 4975

1187-5402 See MARIE-CLEMENT STAUB, A.A., SKETCHES OF HIS LIFE AND WORK. 4975

1187-5410 See PERE MARIE-CLEMENT STAUB, A., SON EXEMPLE, SA PAROLE, SON OEUVRE. 5034

1187-5429 See PERE MARIE-CLEMENT STAUB, A., SON EXEMPLE, SA PAROLE, SON OEUVRE. 5034

1187-5437 See NEWS - ONTARIO FEDERATION OF INDEPENDENT SCHOOLS. 1768

1187-5453 See AUDIO VISUAL CATALOGUE / LIBRARY, JUSTICE INSTITUTE OF BRITISH COLUMBIA. 408

1187-5658 See QUOI DE NEUF? / OMPAC, ORGANISATION MONTREALAISE DES PERSONNES ATTEINTES DE CANCER. 5303

1187-5666 See MODIFICATION DE LA LIGNE RIVIERE-DU-LOUP-SAINT-CLEMENT. 2198

1187-5674 See INTER-VIH. 3672

1187-5704 See FAMILY TO FAMILY. 2280

1187-5712 See FAMILY TO FAMILY. 2280

1187-5879 See CONFECTIONNEURS A FORFAIT DU QUEBEC, LES. 1602

1187-5887 See TODAY'S SENIORS HOUSING CHOICES GUIDE. 2837

1187-5917 See SUPPLEMENTARY INFORMATION FOR LEGISLATIVE REVIEW, REVENUE ESTIMATES. 813

1187-600X See REPERTOIRE DE L'ENSEIGNEMENT A DISTANCE EN FRANCAIS. 1844

1187-6026 See CANADIAN ELECTRONICS (WILLOWDALE). 2038

1187-6212 See URBAN CENTRE, THE. 4692

1187-6255 See PLAN D'ENTREPRISE DE CANMET. 1443

1187-6301 See FORTHCOMING BOOKS - NATIONAL LIBRARY OF CANADA. 3211

1187-6360 See HALTON-PEEL BRANCH NEWSLETTER. 2452

1187-645X See PROPERTY AND CASUALTY INSURANCE. 2891

1187-645X See PROPERTY AND CASUALTY INSURANCE. 2891

1187-6468 See REAL ESTATE DEVELOPMENT (OTTAWA). 4844

1187-6492 See MINUTES OF PROCEEDINGS AND EVIDENCE OF THE SUB-COMMITTEE ON INTERNATIONAL TRADE OF THE STANDING COMMITTEE ON EXTERNAL AFFAIRS AND INTERNATIONAL TRADE. 846

1187-6506 See MINUTES OF PROCEEDINGS AND EVIDENCE OF THE SUB-COMMITTEE ON THE BANK OF CANADA OF THE STANDING COMMITTEE ON FINANCE. 799

1187-6506 See MINUTES OF PROCEEDINGS AND EVIDENCE OF THE SUB-COMMITTEE ON THE BANK OF CANADA OF THE STANDING COMMITTEE ON FINANCE. 799

1187-6514 See MINUTES OF PROCEEDINGS AND EVIDENCE OF THE SUB-COMMITTEE ON NATIONAL SECURITY OF THE STANDING COMMITTEE ON JUSTICE AND THE SOLICITOR GENERAL. 4666

1187-6611 See AVENIR MONTREAL. 1991. 1464

1187-662X See PRODUCTEUR LAITIER (BEDFORD. 1990). 198

1187-6859 See BULLETIN - CANADIAN ASSOCIATION FOR COMPOSITE STRUCTURES AND MATERIALS. 2101

1187-7081 See INFO CANADA (DOWNSVIEW). 1188

1187-7111 See DIRECT MARKETING NEWS (MARKHAM). 923

1187-7154 See LISTE DES RAPPORTS ANNUELS, BIBLIOTHEQUE PRINCIPALE JE, LIST OF ANNUAL REPORTS, MAIN LIBRARY (JE). 4662

1187-7154 See LISTE DES RAPPORTS ANNUELS, BIBLIOTHEQUE PRINCIPALE JE. 4662

1187-7162 See IMAGES (MONTREAL. 1991). 2535

1187-7162 See IMAGES (MONTREAL. 1991). 2535

1187-7200 See REAL PROPERTY ASSESSMENT. YEAR ONE. 4845

1187-7219 See DIRECTORY OF DISABILITY MEDIA IN CANADA. 4386

1187-7227 See DIRECTORY OF SPIRITUALIST ORGANIZATIONS IN CANADA. 4953

1187-7243 See ANNUAL REPORT - MENTAL HEALTH COMMISSION OF NEW BRUNSWICK. REGION II. 3920

1187-7286 See DIRECTORY / CANADIAN SOCIETY OF ZOOLOGISTS. 5581

1187-7316 See SPECIAL NOTICE - ONTARIO MUNICIPAL EMPLOYEES RETIREMENT BOARD. 4705

1187-7367 See CYCLES THEN AND NOW. 787

1187-7375 See CANADIAN MAPLE LEAF REPORT, THE. 1468

1187-7405 See HEALTHCARE ADVOCATE (EDMONTON). 3782

1187-7472 See WELLSPRING (EDMONTON). 2602

1187-7480 See WELLSPRING (EDMONTON). 2602

1187-7502 See INCOME TAX ACT AND REGULATIONS, DEPARTMENT OF FINANCE TECHNICAL NOTES. 4731

1187-760X See SOMMAIRE - SYNDICAT DE L'ASSOCIATION DES JURISTES DE L'ETAT. 3056

1187-7669 See EDUNEUF (OTTAWA). 3855

1187-7693 See QUEBEC MARINE FISHERIES, MONTHLY LANDING STATISTICS BY SPECIES. 2311

1187-7715 See UNION LIST OF PERIODICALS - TORONTO HEALTH LIBRARIES ASSOCIATION. 426

1187-7723 See UNION LIST OF PERIODICALS - TORONTO HEALTH LIBRARIES ASSOCIATION. 426

1187-7758 See BULLETIN - ASSOCIATION DES PATHOLOGISTES DU QUEBEC. 3893

1187-7863 See JOURNAL OF AGRICULTURAL & ENVIRONMENTAL ETHICS. 2251

1187-7979 See CAMPING, CARAVANING (MONTREAL). 4870

1187-7987 See CAMPING, CARAVANING (MONTREAL). 4870

1187-8193 See INTERNATIONAL VOICEPOWER DIRECTORY & BUYERS GUIDE, THE. 1612

1187-8266 See SUPPLEMENTARY INFORMATION ..., PAYMENTS TO INDIVIDUALS. 813

1187-8304 See NOTES FROM MOTHER EARTH'S CENTRE. 326

1187-8320 See PARTNERS (CALGARY). 4271

1187-8401 See INFORMATION AND APPLICATION GUIDE / CANADIAN STUDIES AND SPECIAL PROJECTS DIRECTORATE. 2739

1187-841X See EDUCATION STATISTICS (FREDERICTON). 1740

1187-841X See EDUCATION STATISTICS (FREDERICTON). 1740

1187-8606 See IVANOUVELLES (MONTREAL). 872

1187-8606 See IVANOUVELLES (MONTREAL). 872

1187-8681 See DEBROUILLARDS (MONTREAL). 1062

1187-8711 See REPERTOIRE / CORPORATION DES TRADUCTEURS, TRADUCTRICES, TERMINOLOGUES ET INTERPRETES DU NOUVEAU-BRUNSWICK. 3315

1187-872X See ICI BOUCHERVILLE. 4655

1187-8746 See CAMFORD CHEMICAL REPORT. 966

1187-8754 See MANITOBA LEGAL SERVICES DIRECTORY. 3180

1187-8924 See AFFIRMATIVE ACTION FORUM (SASKATOON). 1642

1187-9130 See EFFECTIF SCOLAIRE ..., MANUEL D'OPERATIONS DES SYSTEMES INFORMATIQUES (DCS). 1743

1187-919X See CANADIAN MAPLE LEAF REPORT, THE. 1468

1187-922X See GUIDE DES MEMBRES DE LA STQ. 3284

1187-922X See GUIDE DES MEMBRES DE LA STQ (FRENCH EDITION). 3284

1187-9319 See CONTACT - ONTARIO EQUESTRIAN FEDERATION. 2798

1187-9327 See CONTACT - ONTARIO EQUESTRIAN FEDERATION. 2798

1187-936X See RECRUITING & SUPERVISION TODAY. 946

1187-9378 See RECRUITING & SUPERVISION TODAY. 946

1187-9475 See MAGAZINE CARGUIDE. 5418

1187-9580 See BOTTIN DE L'INDUSTRIE DE LA MUSIQUE AU QUEBEC. 4104

1187-967X See TIRE TALK. 5312

1187-9947 See PROPOSITION TARIFAIRE. 1513

1188-0007 See SILENCE -- ON TOURNE (MONTREAL). 388

1188-0066 See IMPERIAL QUARTERLY MAGAZINE. 2517

1188-0163 See COTTAGER (VICTORIA BEACH. MANITOBA ED.). 384

1188-021X See ANNUAL REPORT / ENVIRONMENTAL APPEAL BOARD. 3109

1188-0236 See PATIENT OF THE MONTH PROGRAM. 3626

1188-0244 See SEMINARS IN PEDIATRIC GASTROENTEROLOGY AND NUTRITION. 3911

1188-0252 See LAPAROSCOPIC SURGERY. 3969

1188-0260 See DRUGS IN SPORTS. 1344

1188-0368 See PROVING GROUND : ENVIRONMENTAL RESEARCH & TECHNOLOGY DEVELOPMENT, THE. 5142

1188-0376 See TIN TYPE : AMHERSTBURG HISTORIC SITES ASSOCIATION NEWSLETTER. 2763

1188-0384 See YRL NEWS & VIEWS. 3257

1188-0392 See ACAP NEWS. 2185

1188-0481 See EDUCATION FUNDING MODEL, THE. 1739

1188-0511 See VERTIGO. 376

1188-052X See KIT AB' AL -ILM'. 3221

1188-0589 See TENDANCES (MONTREAL. 1991). 888

1188-0619 See PUBLIC SECTOR EMPLOYMENT AND REMUNERATION / STATISTICS CANADA, PUBLIC INSTITUTIONS DIVISION, EMPLOYMENT SECTION. 4705

1188-0635 See INTERIOR MOTIVES. 2901

1188-0686 See CONTACT - CEGEP DE CHICOUTIMI. 1818

1188-0759 See INVITATION A L'OPERA. 385

1188-0759 See INVITATION A L'OPERA. 385

1188-0783 See CCMC NEWS. 606

1188-0856 See CHRONIQUES DU PROTECTEUR DU CITOYEN. 4637

1188-0945 See NATIONAL ROUND TABLE REVIEW, THE. 1507

1188-0945 See NATIONAL ROUND TABLE REVIEW. 2178

1188-102X See DIRECTORY OF MEMBERS OF THE ASSOCIATION OF TRANSLATORS AND INTERPRETERS OF ONTARIO. 3277

1188-102X See DIRECTORY OF MEMBERS OF THE ASSOCIATION OF TRANSLATORS AND INTERPRETERS OF ONTARIO. 3277

1188-1089 See KINGSTON RELATIONS. 2457

1188-1305 See INFORMATION PROCESSING COMPENSATION SURVEY. 1679

1188-1321 See NORD OUEST (SAINT-BASILE). 326

1188-1356 See INFO-FAC. 5289

1188-1380 See GUIDE UNIVERSITAIRE DE LA MEDECINE. 3579

1188-1429 See NEWSLETTER - LONDON (ONT.). PLANNING DIVISION. 2829

1188-1461 See CAHIERS DE LA NCT. 5362

1188-1496 See MUSIQUE VIVANTE. 4139

1188-1518 See CMJ CANADA. 4110

1188-1542 See ACTUALITE GOUVERNEMENTALE / COMMUNICATION-QUEBEC, BAS-SAINT-LAURENT, L'. 4624

1188-1577 See MEDIA MANAGER : A PUBLICATION OF THE ASSOCIATION OF MEDIA MANAGERS, THE. 1116

1188-1631 See CUMULUS (WOOD MOUNTAIN). 3462

1188-164X See JOURNAL OF THE MILITARY HISTORY SOCIETY OF MANITOBA. 4048

1188-1771 See PHYSICIAN'S GUIDE FOR TRAVEL & MEDICAL CONVENTION PLANNING. 3791

1188-1852 See ARTWALK MAGAZINE. 315

1188-1879 See CHARACTERISTICS OF DUAL-EARNER FAMILIES. 2277

1188-1887 See CNA TODAY. 3854

1188-1887 See CNA TODAY. 3854

1188-1917 See GLOBAL FOCUS. 869

1188-1941 See METRO IN VIEW. 1574

1188-195X See POSTECRAN. 387

1188-1968 See RAPPORT ANNUEL / INSTITUT DE POLICE DU QUEBEC. 3174

1188-2026 See CANADIAN CORPORATE COUNSEL. 655

1188-2034 See REPORT - CANADIAN RED CROSS SOCIETY. NEW BRUNSWICK DIVISION. 5305

1188-2131 See APPOINT (JONQUIERE). 1810

1188-2247 See CORONER (SAINTE-FOY). 4772

1188-2255 See PRAIRIE PROGRESS NEWSLETTER. 1513

1188-2344 See FORRUM (MONTREAL). 4305

1188-2387 See PARLIAMENTARY WEEKLY QUARTERLY REPORT, THE. 4487

1188-245X See EVALUATION EN ACTION, L'. 1746

1188-2492 See SURFACES (MONTREAL). 331

1188-2492 See SURFACES (MONTREAL). 331

1188-2506 See 2 MONDES. 5361

1188-2522 See RESOURCES 2000. 1121

1188-2549 See BIRDERS JOURNAL. 5616

1188-2565 See NEWS BRIEF - ENVIRONMENTAL LAW CENTRE (EDMONTON). 3115

1188-2603 See CHAPELHOW CHRONICLE AND COMMUNITY NEWS. 4039

1188-2670 See REDACTEUR (MONTREAL). 626

1188-2697 See CENTRAL ALBERTA BITS & BYTES. 1266

1188-2778 See VANCOUVER & AREA ... AVIATION BUSINESS DIRECTORY. 39

1188-2794 See STREET ADDRESS DIRECTORY, OTTAWA-HULL (FRENCH EDITION 1992). 425

1188-2794 See STREET ADDRESS DIRECTORY, OTTAWA-HULL (ENGLISH EDITION 1992). 425

1188-2867 See ONTARIO FISCAL OUTLOOK. 4739

1188-2875 See PERSPECTIVES BUDGETAIRES DE L'ONTARIO. 4741

1188-2891 See ARNEWS ANNUAL REPORT. 2375

1188-2948 See CASE LAW DIGESTS. 2949

1188-2972 See GARDENING IN ALBERTA. 2416

1188-2980 See SELF-STARTER (MARKHAM). 765

1188-2999 See IRC PERSPECTIVES. 4658

1188-3006 See PERSPECTIVES / COMMISSAIRE A L'INFORMATION ET A LA PROTECTION DE LA VIE PRIVEE/ONTARIO. 4673

1188-3022 See LET'S TALK GREEN. 2177

1188-3022 See LET'S TALK GREEN. 2177

1188-3030 See PRINTING SOURCE. 4568

1188-3081 See CANADIAN CASE AND STATUTE CITATIONS / REFERENCES JURISPRUDENTIELLES ET LEGISLATIVES CANADIENNES. 2947

1188-3081 See CANADIAN CASE AND STATUTE CITATIONS. 2947

1188-3146 See INTERACTIONS (TILLSONBURG). 2174

1188-3162 See CINEMATOGRAPHE, LE. 4067

1188-3359 See DECLENCHEUR (MALARTIC). 1603

1188-3375 See FOCUS SOUTH. 1635

1188-3383 See COMPUTING & COMMUNICATIONS NEWSLETTER. 1180

1188-360X See WATERSHED SENTINEL, THE. 2208

1188-3669 See LEADERSHIP IN HEALTH SERVICES. 3787

1188-3758 See MAGAZINE ARCHIMED. 2482

1188-3766 See MOTS ET DE CRAIE, DE. 1765

1188-3774 See CANADIAN JOURNAL OF URBAN RESEARCH. 2817

1188-3960 See STUDENT ADVOCATE (OTTAWA. 1992). 1848

1188-3960 See STUDENT ADVOCATE (OTTAWA. 1992). 1848

1188-4045 See CAHIERS PROFESSIONNELS, LES. 5276

1188-4053 See FIRE RESEARCH NEWS. 2289

1188-4126 See WORKSIGHT (EDMONTON). 1719

1188-4169 See CANADA COMMUNICABLE DISEASE REPORT. 4770

1188-4169 See CANADA COMMUNICABLE DISEASE REPORT. 4770

1188-4258 See DALHOUSIE JOURNAL OF LEGAL STUDIES. 2959

1188-4274 See ASSOCIATIONS QUEBEC. 5229

1188-4282 See ART ET CULTURE AU QUEBEC. 313

1188-4290 See SCIENCE ET TECHNOLOGIE AU QUEBEC. 5151

1188-4304 See ECONOMIE ET AFFAIRES AU QUEBEC. 671

1188-4347 See REVIEW - NORTH-SOUTH INSTITUTE (OTTAWA). 1625

1188-4347 See REVUE : UN BULLETIN DE L'INSTITUT NORD-SUD. 1625

1188-4428 See SOURCE (MONTREAL. 1992). 5310

1188-4444 See NOEUD (CHARLESBOURG). 2389

1188-4517 See CANADIAN JOURNAL OF HUMAN SEXUALITY, THE. 5187

1188-4525 See INTERNATIONAL SEMINARS IN PAEDIATRIC GASTROENTEROLOGY AND NUTRITION. 3746

1188-455X See CANADIAN BIOTECH NEWS. 3690

1188-4584 See ZEBRA MUSSEL WATCH. 5600

1188-4584 See MOULES ZEBREES, ALERTE. 5592

1188-4827 See HAMILTON LAWYER. 2976

1188-4886 See DIRECTORY OF SUBSTANCE ABUSE ORGANIZATIONS IN CANADA. 1343

1188-4886 See DIRECTORY OF SUBSTANCE ABUSE ORGANIZATIONS IN CANADA. 1343

1188-5017 See VOIR (QUEBEC). 332

1188-5033 See CAHIERS AFIDES. 1730

1188-5300 See PORTEURS DE LUMIERE. 4608

1188-5416 See LET'S GO RACIN'. 4903

1188-5424 See MANITOBA ARCHAEOLOGICAL JOURNAL. 273

1188-553X See AQUATIC SURVIVAL. 2296

1188-5556 See CANADIAN MULTI MEDIA MAGAZINE, THE. 1105

1188-5580 See PRESENCE (MONTREAL. 1992). 4987

1188-5831 See ESPACE MONTREAL (ENGLISH EDITION 1992). 1489

1188-5831 See ESPACE MONTREAL (FRENCH EDITION 1992). 1489

1188-6137 See SEARCH AND SEIZURE LAW REPORTER, THE. 3047

1188-6145 See EDITIONS AVIS DE RECHERCHE, LES. 5284

1188-6153 See NATIONAL DIRECTORY OF PUBLIC PRACTITIONERS / CGA CANADA. 748

1188-6153 See NATIONAL DIRECTORY OF PUBLIC PRACTITIONERS / CGA CANADA. 748

1188-6161 See REVUE ELECTORALE, SYNTHESES ET DOCUMENTS, LA. 4495

1188-620X See ACTIVE LIVING (TORONTO). 2595

1188-6226 See HUMAN RIGHTS TRIBUNE (OTTAWA). 4509

1188-6250 See HEALTH QUEST. 4781

1188-6331 See COMPUTERS IN SCHOOL LIBRARIES. 3203

1188-6641 See RESEARCH FILE, THE. 2601

1188-665X See ENERGY STATISTICS HANDBOOK. 1942

1188-665X See ENERGY STATISTICS HANDBOOK. 1942

1188-6676 See MONTREAL & AREA AVIATION BUSINESS DIRECTORY (FRENCH EDITION). 29

1188-6676 See MONTREAL & AREA AVIATION BUSINESS DIRECTORY. 29

1188-6749 See CAHIER DE L'ENVOLEE LUMIERE. 4941

1188-6773 See BOURSES D'EXCELLENCE POUR DES ETUDES DE CYCLES SUPERIEURS, DE PERFECTIONNEMENT ET DE REINTEGRATION A LA RECHERCHE ..., GUIDE DU BOURSIER, LES. 1812

1188-679X See TEACHING LIBRARIAN. 3252

1188-6870 See QUARTERLY / WORLD AFFAIRS CANADA, THE. 4533

1188-6870 See QUARTERLY / WORLD AFFAIRS CANADA, THE. 4533

1188-7494 See LITERARY REVIEW OF CANADA, THE. 3406

1188-7605 See CANADIAN CHILD PSYCHIATRIC BULLETIN, THE. 3922

1188-7702 See TRUDEL, NADEAU INFO. 3066

1188-7710 See CYBERSUIT ARKADYNE. 377

1188-7834 See CORPORATE TAX PLANNING. 4719

1188-7907 See INFO SOURCE. GUIDE TO SOURCES OF FEDERAL GOVERNMENT INFORMATION. 4656

1188-8172 See CHOICES (LONDON, ONT.). 5279

1188-8296 See MEMOIRES VIVES MONTREAL. 303

1188-8296 See MEMOIRES VIVES (MONTREAL). 274

1188-8377 See WIRAZU, NA. 4930

1188-8482 See ENSEMBLE - CONFERENCE BOARD OF CANADA. NATIONAL BUSINESS AND EDUCATION CENTRE. 1744

1188-8539 See LIAISON / CONSEIL REGIONAL DE L'ENVIRONNEMENT CHAUDIERE-APPALACHES. 2197

1188-8555 See BIERE MAG. 2329

1188-8652 See PARLIAMENTARY DIRECTORY (OTTAWA. 1992). 4672

1188-8709 See TAC TECHNICAL BULLETIN. 5394

1188-8717 See LAPIN MAGAZINE. 5515

1188-875X See ALERTA (TORONTO). 4503

1188-8911 See BARLEY COUNTRY. 65

1188-9004 See MINERAL INDUSTRY QUARTERLY REPORT. 1441

1188-9551 See REGISTRE CANADIEN DES PROPRIETES PATRIMONIALES, ... RAPPORT ANNUEL, LE. 4679

1188-9578 See ONTARIO MUSEUM ANNUAL. 4095

1188-9640 See MARTIN'S ONTARIO CRIMINAL PRACTICE. 3108

1188-9705 See SKILLSLINK LISTER NEWS. 1802

1188-9918 See TREASURE TRAILS. 5497

1188-9926 See ROULANT MA BOSSE, EN. 1519

1188-9950 See RUNGH (VANCOUVER). 330

1189-010X See NOWOCZESNY BIZNESMEN. 700

1189-0347 See PEOPLE OF ACTION. 2179

1189-0355 See POINT SUR LES PROJETS DU SAINT-MAURICE, LE. 2220

1189-038X See STATISTICAL UPDATE. 5341

1189-041X See MANUEL D'INTERPRETATION ET D'APPLICATION DE LA CONVENTION COLLECTIVE F.I.I.Q. ... EN VIGUEUR DANS LES CENTRES D'ACCUEIL MEMBRES DE L'ASSOCIATION DES CENTRES D'ACCUEIL DU QUEBEC. 1689

1189-0657 See CLIPBOARD. 4771

1189-069X See WELLAND & PELHAM BUSINESS BOOK, THE. 719

1189-072X See JOURNAL DES DEBATS - QUEBEC (PROVINCE). ASSEMBLEE NATIONALE. COMMISSION D'ETUDE SUR TOUTE OFFRE D'UN NOUVEAU PARTENARIAT DE NATURE CONSTITUTIONELLE. 4658

1189-0762 See JOURNAL DES DEBATS - QUEBEC (PROVINCE). ASSEMBLEE NATIONALE. COMMISSION D'ETUDE DES QUESTIONS AFFERENTES A L'ACCESSION DU QUEBEC A LA SOUVERAINETE. 4658

1189-0770 See SUPPLEMENTARY INFORMATION FOR LEGISLATIVE REVIEW, EXPENDITURE ESTIMATES - MANITOBA., CIVIL SERVICE COMMISSION. EMPLOYEE BENEFITS AND OTHER PAYMENTS. 4689

1189-2005 See PROCEEDINGS OF THE STANDING SENATE COMMITTEE ON TRANSPORT AND COMMUNICATIONS. 1119

1189-3001 See HURONIA YEARLY VACATION PLANNER. 5480

1189-3087 See RAPPORT D'ACTIVITES / CENTRE QUEBECOIS DE COORDINATION SUR LE SIDA. 4798

1189-3109 See BOARDWALK (SURREY). 316

1189-3125 See ANNUAL REPORT - CANADA. GOVERNMENT TELECOMMUNICATIONS AGENCY. 1149

1189-3125 See ANNUAL REPORT - CANADA. GOVERNMENT TELECOMMUNICATIONS AGENCY. 1149

1189-3257 See LEGAL FOR LIFE. 796

1189-3273 See DIRECTORY OF CANADIAN MARINE OILSPILL SPECIALISTS. 2227

1189-3281 See EDMONTON JEWISH LIFE. 5783

1189-329X See FITNESS, PHYSICAL HEALTH AND RECREATION EDUCATION (EASTERN U.S. ED.). 2597

1189-3303 See FITNESS, PHYSICAL HEALTH AND RECREATION EDUCATION (WESTERN U.S. ED.). 2597

1189-3311 See GREATER KINGSTON, ONTARIO CANADA, VISITOR'S GUIDE. 5478

1189-3397 See SPOTLIGHTING PLAYS ON ALCOHOL AND OTHER DRUGS. 5368

1189-3419 See ONTARIO'S ACCESS AND PRIVACY LEGISLATION, AN ANNOTATION. 3023

1189-3478 See ASSESSMENT HIGHLIGHTS. GRADE 3 SCIENCE ACHIEVEMENT TESTING PROGRAM. 1726

1189-3516 See PERSPECTIVE, EN. 1578

1189-3524 See BULLETIN DE LIAISON ACCESSSIBLE. 5275

1189-3532 See ASSESSMENT HIGHLIGHTS. GRADE 9 SOCIAL STUDIES ACHIEVEMENT TESTING PROGRAM. 1726

1189-3540 See LOOKING AHEAD (VANCOUVER). 4129

1189-3575 See WESTCOAST LOGGER. 2405

1189-363X See CP RAIL SYSTEM NEWS. 5430

1189-3672 See MINUTES OF PROCEEDINGS AND EVIDENCE OF THE ABORIGINAL LIAISON COMMITTEE OF THE SPECIAL JOINT COMMITTEE ON A RENEWED CANADA (FRENCH EDITION). 2747

1189-3672 See MINUTES OF PROCEEDINGS AND EVIDENCE OF THE ABORIGINAL LIAISON COMMITTEE OF THE SPECIAL JOINT COMMITTEE ON A RENEWED CANADA (ENGLISH EDITION). 2746

1189-3958 See APPRENTISSAGE ET SOCIALISATION (1991). 1875

1189-4067 *See* CAHIER D'INFORMATION ..., INDUSTRIE, MICT, QUEBEC. **1600**

1189-4172 *See* BERRY & VEGETABLE INFORMER. **65**

1189-4199 *See* BC HEALTH AND DISEASE SURVEILLANCE. **4768**

1189-4210 *See* TRANSCRIPT OF STANDING COMMITTEE ON PUBLIC ACCOUNTS. **4756**

1189-4245 *See* FAMILY JUSTICE BULLETIN. **3120**

1189-4296 *See* FUNDING OF EDUCATION IN ALBERTA, A SCHOOL FINANCE BROCHURE, THE. **1747**

1189-4407 *See* MANITOBA PARKS AND WILDERNESS. **4707**

1189-4512 *See* NEW PARKS NORTH. **4707**

1189-4555 *See* ANNUAL CRAFT SHOWS IN ONTARIO / CRAFT RESOURCE CENTRE. **370**

1189-4563 *See* TANGENCE. **3444**

1189-4571 See BUSINEST. **1600**

1189-458X *See* BUSINEST. **1600**

1189-461X *See* CIMI NEWS. **4086**

1189-4695 *See* YOU TORONTO. 1990. **1088**

1189-4709 *See* CANADIAN FEDERAL GOVERNMENT HANDBOOK. **4636**

1189-4717 *See* BRITISH COLUMBIA SCHOOL BUS. **5378**

1189-475X *See* HEALTH VISION. **4782**

1189-4830 *See* GOLF INTERNATIONAL. **4896**

1189-4849 *See* GOLF VACATIONS (BURLINGTON). **4897**

1189-4873 *See* LEISURE WATCH CANADA. **4707**

1189-4881 *See* NEWSLETTER : A PUBLICATION OF THE ALBERTA TEACHERS' ASSOCIATION, ENGLISH AS A SECOND LANGUAGE COUNCIL. **1901**

1189-4911 *See* ENTDECKEN SIE BRITISCH KOLUMBIEN, KANADA. **5469**

1189-4954 See CONTACTS AND COURSES, WHO'S WHO IN CANADIAN PLACEMENT. **1818**

1189-5012 *See* FOCAL POINT. **4071**

1189-5055 *See* AFRICAN ORACLE, THE. **5779**

1189-5071 *See* JOURNAL DU VILLAGE D'EMILIE, LE. **5365**

1189-5136 *See* AGENDA DES JURISTES, L'. **2928**

1189-5152 *See* KANAWA MAGAZINE FOR RECREATIONAL PADDLING IN CANADA. **4874**

1189-5993 *See* OFFICE LEASING DIRECTORY. **4842**

1189-6051 *See* BOULEVARD MAGAZINE (VICTORIA). **316**

1189-6078 *See* ICO. INTELLIGENCE ARTIFICIELLE ET SCIENCES COGNITIVES AU QUEBEC. **5111**

1189-623X *See* FAMILY GUIDE (TORONTO). **1063**

1189-6264 See BUILDING MANAGEMENT & DESIGN. **862**

1189-6892 *See* COMMON GROUND. (OTTAWA). **1732**

1189-7090 *See* CHINA ANALYST. **783**

1189-7163 *See* MSLA JOURNAL. **3232**

1189-7627 *See* OPERATIONAL REVIEW ... FARM DEBT REVIEW BOARDS. **117**

1189-9565 *See* REVUE QUEBECOISE DE SCIENCE POLITIQUE. **4495**

1189-9808 *See* VANDANCE INTERNATIONAL. **1314**

1189-9816 *See* DANCE INTERNATIONAL (VANCOUVER). **1312**

1189-9956 *See* CANADIAN ORCHESTRAS AND YOUTH ORCHESTRAS DIRECTORY. **4107**

1189-9999 *See* NEWSLETTER - HALIFAX DISTRICT SCHOOL BOARD, LIBRARY DEPT. (1989). **3235**

1191-0054 *See* HEALTHY INTERCHANGE. **4782**

1191-0100 *See* BODYCHECK (NEPEAN). **4887**

1191-0135 *See* KAMLOOPS LIVING. **5482**

1191-0305 *See* REPORT ON ENVIRONMENTAL RESEARCH, TECHNOLOGY DEVELOPMENT AND AWARENESS ACTIVITIES. **2181**

1191-0313 *See* ANNUAL REPORT / SASKATOON HEALTH SERVICES AUTHORITY. **4766**

1191-0321 *See* ANNUAL REPORT - SASKATCHEWAN. TRIPARTITE BEEF ADMINISTRATION BOARD. **206**

1191-033X *See* ANNUAL REPORT - SASKATCHEWAN. LABOUR RELATIONS BOARD. **1650**

1191-0348 *See* YOUR GUIDE TO FINANCIAL ASSISTANCE FOR BUSINESS IN ONTARIO. **817**

1191-0356 *See* YOUR GUIDE TO FINANCIAL ASSISTANCE FOR BUSINESS IN ATLANTIC CANADA. **724**

1191-047X *See* YOUR GUIDE TO CANADIAN EXPORT FINANCING. **858**

1191-0488 *See* YOUR GUIDE TO FINANCING BUSINESS GROWTH BY SELLING A PIECE OF THE PIE. **817**

1191-0496 *See* YOUR GUIDE TO PREPARING A PLAN TO RAISE MONEY FOR YOUR OWN BUSINESS. **725**

1191-050X *See* YOUR GUIDE TO FINANCIAL ASSISTANCE FOR BUSINESS IN WESTERN CANADA. **817**

1191-0518 *See* YOUR GUIDE TO STARTING & SELF-FINANCING YOUR OWN BUSINESS IN CANADA. **725**

1191-0526 *See* YOUR GUIDE TO FINANCIAL ASSISTANCE FOR BUSINESS IN QUEBEC. **817**

1191-0534 *See* YOUR GUIDE TO RAISING VENTURE CAPITAL FOR YOUR OWN BUSINESS IN CANADA. **725**

1191-0542 *See* YOUR GUIDE TO ARRANGING BANK & DEBT FINANCING FOR YOUR OWN BUSINESS IN CANADA. **817**

1191-0577 *See* CANADA IN TRANSIT. **5378**

1191-0690 *See* ACTION REGIONALE, L'. **5779**

1191-0755 *See* DEPECHE MAC. **1182**

1191-0763 *See* BENEFITS AND PENSIONS MONITOR. **861**

1191-0771 *See* TIMMINS TIMES, THE. **5796**

1191-0860 *See* CANADIAN SPEECHES, ISSUES OF THE DAY. **1105**

1191-0879 *See* GREATER TORONTO PROFESSIONAL AND SERVICE DIRECTORY. **615**

1191-0887 *See* CHECK IT OUT!. **3201**

1191-0909 *See* TINY WAILS. **366**

1191-0925 *See* MUSEUMNEWS (HALIFAX). **4093**

1191-0933 *See* SASK RIGHTS. **4512**

1191-1042 *See* INTER-ACTIF, L'. **1830**

1191-1069 *See* PIONNIER (SILLERY). **2467**

1191-1077 *See* VIESAGE (MONTREAL). **2895**

1191-1085 *See* CHAINON (MONTREAL. 1992). **1601**

1191-1115 *See* ARGUS ETHNIQUE. **5191**

1191-1123 *See* GUIDE SANTE (SILLERY). **2597**

1191-1131 *See* SEXUALITE NOUVELLE. **5188**

1191-1239 *See* EFFECTIF ETUDIANT - UNIVERSITE DE MONCTON. **1822**

1191-1255 *See* CIRCUMPOLAR NOTES. **5095**

1191-1255 *See* CIRCUMPOLAR NOTES / CIRCUMPOLAR AND SCIENTIFIC AFFAIRS DIRECTORATE, NORTHERN AFFAIRS PROGRAM, DEPARTMENT OF INDIAN AFFAIRS AND NORTHERN DEVELOPMENT. **5095**

1191-1441 See DIRECTION DES RESSOURCES EDUCATIVES FRANCAISES EN ACTION, LA. **1735**

1191-145X *See* DIRECTION DES RESSOURCES EDUCATIVES FRANCAISES EN ACTION, LA. **1735**

1191-1468 *See* CAAT TRACKS : INTERLIBRARY LOANS MANUAL. **3199**

1191-1514 *See* DIRECTORY OF CANADIAN REHABILITATION SERVICES. **4386**

1191-1522 *See* GUIDE EXPRESS DES VINS. **2367**

1191-1581 See ONTARIO SMALL CLAIMS COURT PRACTICE. **3023**

1191-159X *See* ONTARIO SMALL CLAIMS COURT PRACTICE. **3023**

1191-162X *See* CANADIAN SOCIAL STUDIES : THE HISTORY AND SOCIAL SCIENCE TEACHER. **1890**

1191-1670 *See* GULF ISLANDS GUARDIAN, THE. **5479**

1191-1700 *See* TRENDS AND ALTERNATIVES IN TESTING. **2253**

1191-1719 *See* CERR NEWS & VIEWS. **1353**

1191-1727 *See* PARENTS DE COEUR. **5300**

1191-1727 *See* PARENTS DE COEUR. **2284**

1191-2642 *See* SABIAN NEWS BEAT CATALOG. **4151**

1191-2650 *See* OTTAWA VALLEY OFFICIAL TRAVEL GUIDE. **5487**

1191-2693 *See* MMC : MEDIAS MAGNETIQUES CANADA. **4444**

1191-2707 *See* CMM : CANADIAN MEDIA MAG. **4443**

1191-3231 See IMPERIAL QUARTERLY MAGAZINE. **2517**

1191-3274 See FOREIGN GOVERNMENT AWARDS PROGRAM. **4649**

1191-3274 See PROGRAMME DE BOURSES DES GOUVERNEMENTS ETRANGERS / ADMINISTRE PAR LE CONSEIL INTERNATIONAL D'ETUDES CANADIENNES. **4675**

1191-3282 *See* FOREIGN GOVERNMENT AWARDS PROGRAM. **4649**

1191-3282 *See* PROGRAMME DE BOURSES DES GOUVERNEMENTS ETRANGERS / ADMINISTRE PAR LE CONSEIL INTERNATIONAL D'ETUDES CANADIENNES. **4675**

1191-3339 *See* CHRYSALIS CONNECTION. **5279**

1191-3363 *See* MEMBERSHIP DIRECTORY, PLANT SOURCE LIST. **2424**

1191-3371 *See* WESTBRIDGE ART MARKET REPORT. **368**

1191-3398 *See* REPORT ON THE BUDGET FOR THE DEVELOPMENT USES OF UNEMPLOYMENT INSURANCE. **5305**

1191-3398 *See* REPORT ON THE ... BUDGET FOR THE DEVELOPMENTAL USES OF UNEMPLOYMENT INSURANCE. **1707**

1191-3401 *See* AUTO SPORT (MONTREAL. 1992). **4885**

1191-3576 *See* ECONOMIC PLANNING JOURNAL IN FREE SOCIETIES FOR AGRICULTURE AND RELATED INDUSTRIES. **81**

1191-3576 *See* ECONOMIC PLANNING IN FREE SOCIETIES. **81**

1191-3851 *See* CIEL BLEU (SAINT-EDOUARD). **4890**

1191-386X *See* CRIME BUSTER (VANCOUVER). **3161**

1191-3959 *See* CORONER (SAINTE-FOY). **4772**

1191-3975 *See* RECORD BOOK / CANADIAN HOCKEY LEAGUE. **4914**

1191-3983 See MEDIA INFORMATION FOR THE ... IIHF WORLD JUNIOR HOCKEY CHAMPIONSHIPS / PREPARED BY THE CANADIAN HOCKEY LEAGUE. **4904**

1191-3991 *See* MEDIA INFORMATION FOR THE ... IIHF WORLD JUNIOR HOCKEY CHAMPIONSHIPS / PREPARED BY THE CANADIAN HOCKEY LEAGUE. **4904**

1191-4009 *See* CHRYSLER CUP CANADIAN HOCKEY LEAGUE EAST-WEST ALL-STAR CHALLENGE OFFICIAL GUIDE. **4890**

1191-4025 *See* ANCIENNE USINE A GAZ DE LA RUE VERDUN A QUEBEC, L'. **960**

1191-4238 *See* EUROPE BUSINESS TRAVEL ORGANIZER, THE. **673**

1191-4254 *See* TRANSCRIPT OF SELECT COMMITTEE ON THE CONSTITUTION (FRENCH EDITION). **4691**

1191-4297 *See* DISCOVERY NEWS. **3478**

1191-4335 *See* PARLONS PLEIN AIR, CHASSE, PECHE. **4877**

1191-4653 *See* STATEMENT ON NATIONAL SECURITY / BY THE SOLICITOR GENERAL OF CANADA. **4058**

1191-470X *See* PARC NATIONAL DES ILES-DU-SAINT-LAURENT, PLAN DE GESTION. **4707**

1191-4718 *See* ST. LAWRENCE ISLANDS NATIONAL PARK, MANAGEMENT PLAN REVIEW. **4708**

1191-4726 *See* PARC NATIONAL DES ILES-DE-LA-BAIE-GEORGIENNE, PLAN DE GESTION. **4707**

1191-4734 *See* GEORGIAN BAY ISLANDS NATIONAL PARK, MANAGEMENT PLANNING. **4706**

1191-4742 *See* VOIE NAVIGABLE TRENT-SEVERN, PLANIFICATION DE GESTION. **4694**

1191-4750 *See* TRENT-SEVERN WATERWAY, MANAGEMENT PLANNING. **4691**

1191-4785 *See* ARTWALK MAGAZINE. **315**

1191-5056 *See* CATALOGUE FRANCOPHONE CANADIEN DE DOCUMENTS EN ALPHABETISATION / GROUPE DE RESSOURCES DOCUMENTAIRES EN FRANCAIS. **412**

1191-5080 See ORTHOGRAPHE PLUS. **1770**

1191-5099 *See* ORTHOGRAPHE PLUS. **1770**

1183-708X See REID'S ADMINISTRATIVE LAW. **3037**

1191-677X *See* BULLETIN DU PROGRAMME DES EXAMENS EN VUE DU DIPLOME. FRANCAIS 30. **1729**

1191-6885 *See* WCB UPDATE. **1717**

1191-7423 *See* LISTE DES FILMS VISES PAR CATEGORIES DE SPECTATEURS, DIFFUSION PRIVEE. **4074**

1191-7431 *See* PROGRAMMES DE SUBVENTIONS ET DE BOURSES DE CARRIERE DU CONSEIL QUEBECOIS DE LA RECHERCHE SOCIALE. **5214**

1191-7733 *See* CANADA WATCH. **4636**

1191-7881 *See* ADMINISTRATIVE ASSISTANT'S UPDATE. **859**

1191-789X *See* TOURISM TODAY OTTAWA. **5493**

1191-7962 *See* METRO WEEKLY TELECASTER. **1134**

1191-7997 See AVIATION, AEROSPACE & DEFENCE UPDATE. **12**

1191-8004 *See* AVIATION, AEROSPACE & DEFENCE UPDATE. **12**

1191-8632 *See* PHOENIX (WATERLOO). **3468**

1191-8640 *See* BRITISH COLUMBIA & ALBERTA HOME BUSINESS REPORT. **644**

1191-887X *See* CANADIAN PAPERMAKER. **4233**

1191-9191 *See* REVUE ALERTE. **4800**

1191-923X *See* PRINCE GEORGE CITY DIRECTORY (BUSINESS ED.). **2573**

1191-9302 *See* RED DEER CITY DIRECTORY (1992). **2574**

1191-9310 *See* MONCTON CITY DIRECTORY (1992). **2569**

1191-9396 *See* VANCOUVER CITY DIRECTORY (1992). **2578**

1191-940X *See* SAINT JOHN CITY DIRECTORY (1992). **2575**

1191-9833 *See* WHAT'S NEW IN WELDING. **4023**

1191-9841 *See* BUILDING MANAGEMENT & DESIGN. **862**

1191-9868 *See* JOURNAL - ART GALLERY OF ONTARIO. **4090**

1192-0203 *See* ATLANTIC BUSINESS REPORT. **641**

1192-0238 *See* REVUE QUEBECOISE D'ERGOTHERAPIE. **4382**

1192-0254 *See* ANNUAL REPORT / FINANCIAL INSTITUTIONS COMMISSION. **771**

1192-0785 *See* HALTON-PEEL FARM NEWS. **91**

1192-1137 *See* B & D HEIR LINES. **2438**

1192-1145 *See* BILL PALMER'S WORD WATCHING. **3269**

1192-1188 *See* ABILITY NETWORK. **4503**

1192-1285 *See* GREEN TEACHER (TORONTO). **2173**

1192-1412 *See* FILIGRANE (MONTREAL). **3925**

1192-1854 *See* DIANOIA (CAMROSE). **1820**

1192-1900 *See* CHANTER (MONTREAL). **4109**

1192-1927 *See* LEFT HISTORY. **4480**

1192-2354 *See* POWER SMART ANNUAL REPORT. **1953**

1192-2427 *See* MAKING WAVES (PORT ALBERNI). **1504**

1192-2508 *See* REHAB & COMMUNITY CARE MANAGEMENT. **3633**

1192-2621 *See* JOURNAL OF ACCOUNTING CASE RESEARCH, THE. **746**

1192-2745 *See* CANADIAN AUTOWORLD. **5408**

1192-2796 *See* RESEAU - ASSOCIATION DES ENSEIGNANTES ET DES ENSEIGNANTS FRANCO-ONTARIENS. **1779**

1192-2958 *See* WOODSIDE REPORT, THE. **1960**

1192-3318 *See* EDUCATION ET FORMATION AU QUEBEC. **1739**

1192-3415 *See* CHRISTIAN COURIER. **5058**

1192-3636 *See* REVUE DE L'AMIE. **5306**

1192-3652 *See* ATLANTIC BOOKS TODAY. **4823**

1192-3857 *See* CAMIONNEURS/TRUCKERS MAGAZINE. **5408**

1192-4160 *See* CANADIAN INDEX (TORONTO). **5781**

1192-4241 *See* BAPTIST REVIEW OF THEOLOGY, THE. **4938**

1192-4578 *See* ENVIRONNEMENT (QUEBEC). **2171**

1192-5019 *See* EPICENTRE (CHICOUTIMI). **4646**

1192-5035 *See* COMMUNIQUE - ASSOCIATION CANADIENNE DE TELEVISION PAR CABLE (1992). **1130**

1192-523X *See* SUKCES W AMERYCE. **4924**

1192-5515 *See* ONTARIO MENNONITE HISTORY. **4983**

1192-5612 *See* IMMUNOLOGIST (TORONTO). **3671**

1192-5973 *See* MANUFACTURING & PROCESS AUTOMATION. **1220**

1192-6201 *See* BOARDROOM (WILLOWDALE). **861**

1192-6708 *See* HOUR (MONTREAL). **2535**

1192-6929 *See* MAGAZINE PROVIGO (ED. FRANCAISE). **2538**

1192-6937 *See* MAGAZINE PROVIGO (ENGLISH EDITION). **2538**

1192-7283 *See* INDUSTRIAL RELATIONS LEGISLATION IN CANADA. **3149**

1192-7445 *See* OFFICIAL STAR TREK FAN CLUB OF CANADA. **5234**

1192-7704 *See* AGRI-FOOD RESEARCH IN ONTARIO. **47**

1192-7755 *See* I.D.E.E (BRIGHAM). **5289**

1192-8190 *See* CHINOOK (CALGARY. 1993). **2443**

1192-8646 *See* INTERNET BUSINESS JOURNAL, THE. **1242**

1192-8700 *See* MYSTERY REVIEW, THE. **3414**

1193-011X *See* NOVA SCOTIA CRAFT NEWS / NSDCC. **374**

1193-0667 *See* RESUME D'ENQUETE. **4248**

1193-0721 *See* QUEEN'S PARK DIRECTORY. **4699**

1193-073X *See* WHO'S WHO (ONTARIO ED.). **1263**

1193-0748 *See* ECHOES (MEDICINE HAT). **4955**

1193-1043 *See* MINUTES OF PROCEEDINGS AND EVIDENCE OF THE SPECIAL COMMITTEE ON ELECTORAL REFORM. **4482**

1193-1043 *See* MINUTES OF PROCEEDINGS AND EVIDENCE OF THE SPECIAL COMMITTEE ON ELECTORAL REFORM (FRENCH EDITION). **4482**

1193-1051 *See* MODIFICATION AU TARIF. **846**

1193-1132 See CREATEURS QUEBECOIS. **372**

1193-1132 See CREATEURS QUEBECOIS. **372**

1193-1140 *See* CREATEURS QUEBECOIS. **372**

1193-1140 *See* CREATEURS QUEBECOIS. **372**

1193-1175 *See* SUBURBAN TORONTO CRISS-CROSS DIRECTORY. **5491**

1193-1248 *See* PERSPECTIVES / ALBERTA ASSOCIATION OF REGISTERED OCCUPATIONAL THERAPISTS. **3932**

1193-1272 *See* COMPUTER DEALER NEWS SOURCE GUIDE. **1236**

1193-1345 *See* DIRECTORY OF NATURAL GAS COMPANY OPERATIONS. **4760**

1193-1426 *See* ALGONQUIN PERIODICALS, UNION LISTING / ALGONQUIN RESOURCE CENTRE, STUDENT SERVICES DIVISION. **3189**

1193-1442 *See* REGULATORY TIMES, THE. **1954**

1193-1469 See TRENDS IN THE CANADIAN PC MARKET. **1273**

1193-1477 *See* TRENDS IN THE CANADIAN PC MARKET. **1273**

1193-1485 *See* OTTAWA BUSINESS QUARTERLY. **702**

1193-1493 *See* REVUE DE L'ACLA. **3316**

1193-1612 *See* PROCEEDINGS OF THE SUBCOMMITTEE ON SECURITY AND NATIONAL DEFENCE (FRENCH EDITION). **4054**

1193-1612 *See* PROCEEDINGS OF THE SUBCOMMITTEE ON SECURITY AND NATIONAL DEFENCE. **4054**

1193-1701 *See* PRACTITIONER'S INCOME TAX ACT, THE. **4741**

1193-171X *See* TODAY'S TIMES. **5182**

1193-1833 *See* INFO-PARENTS. **2281**

1193-1884 *See* MULTI-FACT. **3708**

1193-1922 *See* INNFOCUS (NORTH VANCOUVER). **2807**

1193-1981 *See* HISTORICAL STUDIES OTTAWA. 1990. **2618**

1193-199X *See* ETUDES D'HISTOIRE RELIGIEUSE. **2616**

1193-2074 *See* HAZARDOUS MATERIALS MANAGEMENT. **2231**

1193-2228 *See* REPERTOIRE QUEBECOIS DES RECUPERATEURS ET DES RECYCLEURS, LE. **2241**

1193-2325 *See* BULLETIN LS. **3198**

1193-2333 *See* LS NEWSLETTER. **3229**

1193-2430 *See* REPORT TO THE LEGISLATIVE ASSEMBLY OF BRITISH COLUMBIA ON THE PUBLIC ACCOUNTS. **4746**

1193-2449 *See* HR MANAGER'S SOURCEBOOK & BUYER'S GUIDE. **941**

1193-2481 See GENERAL INFORMATION AND GUIDELINES FOR THE SUMMER INDIVIDUAL EXCHANGE PROGRAM. **1748**

1193-249X *See* GENERAL INFORMATION AND GUIDELINES FOR THE SUMMER INDIVIDUAL EXCHANGE PROGRAM. **1748**

1193-2554 See JOURNAL LE MACAREUX. **4706**

1193-2554 See JOURNAL LE MACAREUX (FRENCH EDITION). **4706**

1193-2562 *See* JOURNAL LE MACAREUX. **4706**

1193-2562 *See* JOURNAL LE MACAREUX (FRENCH EDITION). **4706**

1193-2643 *See* MINUTES OF PROCEEDINGS AND EVIDENCE OF THE SUB-COMMITTEE ON INTERNATIONAL FINANCIAL INSTITUTIONS OF THE STANDING COMMITTEE ON FINANCE. **799**

1193-2643 *See* MINUTES OF PROCEEDINGS AND EVIDENCE OF THE SUB-COMMITTEE ON INTERNATIONAL FINANCIAL INSTITUTIONS OF THE STANDING COMMITTEE ON FINANCE (ENGLISH EDITION). **799**

1193-2651 *See* MINUTES OF PROCEEDINGS AND EVIDENCE OF THE SUB-COMMITTEE ON THE ST. LAWRENCE SEAWAY OF THE STANDING COMMITTEE ON TRANSPORT (FRENCH EDITON). **5387**

1193-2651 *See* MINUTES OF PROCEEDINGS AND EVIDENCE OF THE SUB-COMMITTEE ON THE ST. LAWRENCE SEAWAY OF THE STANDING COMMITTEE ON TRANSPORT. **5387**

1193-2724 *See* SERVICE QUALITY B.C. UPDATE. **4685**

1193-2732 *See* 1991 CENSUS OF CANADA, INFORMATION RELEASE. **4549**

1193-2759 *See* CONNECTION - ALBERTA. STUDENT PROGRAMS AND EVALUATION DIVISION. **1891**

1193-2805 *See* AMITIE SP : BULLETIN DE L'ASSOCIATION QUEBECOISE DES AMIS DE LA SCLEROSE EN PLAQUES. **3920**

1193-2813 *See* UKRAINIAN CANADIAN HERALD. **5796**

1193-2821 *See* FEDERAL LOBBYISTS, THE. **4474**

1193-2988 *See* CANADIAN MARKET PULP. **4232**

1193-3003 *See* ANNUAL REPORT FOR THE FISCAL YEAR ENDING ... / NOVA SCOTIA PROVINCIAL HEALTH COUNCIL. **4765**

1193-3046 *See* MAIS-GRAIN, RESULTATS D'ESSAIS ..., HYBRIDES RECOMMANDES EN ... / CONSEIL DES PRODUCTIONS VEGETALES DU QUEBEC. **106**

1193-3097 *See* ALBERTA PETROLEUM EQUIPMENT & SERVICES DIRECTORY. **4249**

1193-3100 *See* ABORIGINAL JUSTICE BULLETIN. **2926**

1193-3208 *See* CRAFT CONNECTION, THE. **371**

1193-3437 *See* COLLECTIVE BARGAINING IN NEW BRUNSWICK. **1660**

1193-3593 *See* WHO'S WHO (PQ/ATLANTIC ED.). **1263**

1193-3607 *See* WHO'S WHO (WESTERN CANADA ED.). **1263**

1193-3658 See GROCER TODAY. **838**

1193-3836 *See* REGLES BUDGETAIRES DU MINISTRE DES TRANSPORTS CONCERNANT LE TRANSPORT DES ELEVES. **4744**

1193-3879 *See* INCOME TAX BULLETINS, CIRCULARS, RULINGS. **4731**

1193-3968 *See* PERFORMER (TORONTO). **1314**

1193-400X See PLAN REGIONAL DE DEVELOPPEMENT DE LA MAIN-D'OEUVRE, REGION DE LANAUDIERE. **1702**

1193-4018 *See* PLAN REGIONAL DE DEVELOPPEMENT DE LA MAIN-D'OEUVRE, REGION DE LANAUDIERE. **1702**

1193-4034 *See* LOBBY DIGEST & PUBLIC AFFAIRS MONTHLY, THE. **4662**

1193-4069 *See* NATIONAL CHART. **4139**

1193-4077 *See* GRANDE PRAIRIE CITY DIRECTORY. **4652**

1193-414X *See* SOMMAIRE - SYNDICAT DE L'ASSOCIATION DES JURISTES DE L'ETAT. **3056**

1193-4263 *See* NEWSLETTER - CANADIAN ASSOCIATION OF SPORT SCIENCES. NATIONAL PHYSICAL FITNESS APPRAISAL CERTIFICATION AND ACCREDITATION PROGRAM. **1857**

1193-4816 See CCI NEWSLETTER OTTAWA. **2189**

1193-5073 *See* CONTACTS AND COURSES, WHO'S WHO IN CANADIAN PLACEMENT. **1818**

1193-509X *See* AUTO SPORTS MOTEUR, L'. **4885**

1193-5251 *See* PROCEEDINGS OF THE STANDING SENATE COMMITTEE ON PRIVILEGES, STANDING RULES AND ORDERS. **4675**

1193-5855 *See* LOGGER (VANCOUVER). **2402**

1193-5898 *See* COMMUNIQUE - CANADIAN CABLE TELEVISION ASSOCIATION 1992. **1130**

1193-6517 *See* CLAYTON COMPLETIONS REPORT. **2818**

1193-6541 *See* NEWSLETTER - ALBERTA HOME AND SCHOOL COUNCILS' ASSOCIATION. **1768**

1193-6665 *See* WHO PAYS WHAT. **4820**

1193-6886 *See* ESPOIR (LASALLE). **4473**

1193-6924 *See* MAGAZINE LUMIERE. **4603**

1193-7114 *See* ACCELERATOR (SASKATOON. 1988). **1887**

1193-7319 *See* EDULAW FOR CANADIAN SCHOOLS. **1743**

1193-7343 *See* CSRO. CANADIAN SPINAL RESEARCH ORGANIZATION. **3569**

1193-7351 *See* FOCUS AFRICA. **2639**

1193-7505 *See* CANADIAN FACILITY MANAGEMENT & DESIGN. **863**

1193-7513 *See* CONTACT - CANADIAN PROFESSIONAL SALES ASSOCIATION. **659**

1193-7521 *See* CONTACT - ASSOCIATION CANADIENNE DES PROFESSIONNELS DE LA VENTE. **659**

1193-7564 *See* NEWSLETTER / ASSOCIATION FOR CANADIAN THEATRE RESEARCH. **5366**

1193-7580 *See* DIRECTORY OF STATISTICS IN CANADA. **5326**

1193-767X *See* LIAISON - AMIS DU JARDIN BOTANIQUE DE MONTREAL. **2423**

1193-7912 *See* DIRECTORY / ECONOMIC DEVELOPERS ASSOCIATION OF CANADA. **1479**

1193-7998 *See* DIRECTORY / COLLEGE OF VETERINARIANS OF ONTARIO. [DISKETTE]. **5509**

1193-8021 *See* CANADIAN REALTOR NEWS. **4835**

1193-817X *See* CAUTG BULLETIN. **1890**

1193-8250 *See* TRANSPORTATION OF DANGEROUS GOODS REGULATIONS. **2245**

1193-8277 *See* AGRI-FOOD PERSPECTIVES. **47**

1193-8315 *See* SHARED VOICES. **3471**

1193-8536 *See* BULLETIN OF PROCEEDINGS - CANADA. SUPREME COURT. **2944**

1193-8544 *See* CARP. CANADIAN ASSOCIATION OF RETIRED PERSONS. **5178**

1193-8625 *See* C MAGAZINE (1992). **317**

1193-8722 *See* NEWSLETTER - ALBERTA TEACHERS' ASSOCIATION. RELIGIOUS AND MORAL EDUCATION COUNCIL. **4981**

1193-8757 See NATIONAL INTERNAL AUDITING LETTER, THE. **748**

1193-8765 *See* NATIONAL INTERNAL AUDITING LETTER, THE. **748**

1193-8781 *See* FLOOR COVERING PLUS. **615**

1193-8811 *See* UNITRADE SPECIALIZED CATALOGUE OF CANADIAN STAMPS. **2788**

1193-882X See UNITRADE CATALOGUE SPECIALISE DES TIMBRES CANADIENS. **2788**

1193-8838 *See* UNITRADE CATALOGUE SPECIALISE DES TIMBRES CANADIENS. **2788**

1193-9249 *See* CHANSONS (MONTREAL. 1992). **4108**

1193-9273 *See* CMS NOTES. **3500**

1193-9397 *See* NEW MOTHER (1992). **2284**

1193-9451 *See* COLLECTIONS OF THE ROYAL NOVA SCOTIA HISTORICAL SOCIETY. **2728**

1193-9524 *See* OSCA REPORTS (1990). **1868**

1193-9532 *See* V.I.T.A. NEWSLETTER (WINNIPEG. 1992). **1917**

1193-9540 *See* KINGSTON PUBLIC LIBRARY INQUIRER, THE. **3221**

1193-9575 *See* MATTHEWS MEDIA DIRECTORY. **1116**

1193-9737 *See* ANGLICAN CHURCH DIRECTORY / THE ANGLICAN CHURCH OF CANADA. **4934**

1193-9974 *See* CANADIAN AUTHOR (1992). **3372**

1194-0387 *See* LONDON NEWS (LONDON. EAST ED.). **5788**

1194-076X *See* ST. THOMAS COURIER. **5795**

1194-1030 *See* ELMIRA INDEPENDENT. **5784**

1194-1103 *See* ADVOCATE NEWSPAPER. **5779**

1194-2266 *See* ESPRIT DE CORPS, CANADIAN MILITARY THEN & NOW. **4043**

1194-2355 *See* DIRECTORY OF HAZARDOUS WASTE SERVICES. **2227**

1194-2967 *See* CANADIAN GAS RATES. **4760**

1194-305X *See* COMPUTER POST. **1177**

1194-3750 *See* ELECTRONIC DISSEMINATION PARTNERSHIPS. **4645**

1194-3963 *See* STUDENT LIBRARY HANDBOOK. **3251**

1194-398X *See* LANCASTER'S WRONGFUL DISMISSAL EMPLOYMENT LAW NEWS. **3151**

1194-4552 *See* LANCASTER'S CONSTRUCTION INDUSTRY EMPLOYMENT LAW NEWS. **3151**

1194-5303 *See* GEO PLEIN-AIR. **4896**

1194-6164 *See* SUSPOP NEWS. **4560**

1194-6180 *See* NEWSLETTER - INFANT FEEDING ACTION COALITION. **5298**

1194-6229 See LANCASTER'S EMPLOYMENT EQUITY REPORTER. **1687**

1194-6237 *See* LANCASTER'S EMPLOYMENT EQUITY REPORTER. **1687**

1194-6377 *See* CONTACT - ALBERTA POTTERS' ASSOCIATION (1992). **2588**

1194-689X *See* STATISTICAL REPORT - CANADIAN ASSOCIATION FOR GRADUATE STUDIES. **1848**

1194-7098 *See* SOLEIL DE COLOMBIE-BRITANNIQUE. **5794**

1194-823X *See* NEWS FROM THE OC CORRAL. **112**

1194-9589 *See* ALBERTA DAIRYMAN. **191**

1195-017X *See* ONTARIO PLANNING ACT. **3023**

1195-0188 *See* ONTARIO MUNICIPAL ACT. **3023**

1195-0196 *See* ONTARIO LABOUR AND EMPLOYMENT LEGISLATION. **3153**

1195-0242 *See* OMNIPRATICIEN (SCARBOROUGH). **3624**

1195-0390 *See* HOSPITAL MANAGEMENT SMARTS. **5786**

1195-0560 *See* FOREST PEOPLE (WILLOWDALE). **2380**

1195-0889 *See* ACCESS MAGAZINE (VANCOUVER). **1460**

1195-096X *See* CANADIAN JOURNAL OF INFORMATION AND LIBRARY SCIENCE, THE. **3199**

1195-1036 *See* GEOMATICA. **2582**

1195-163X *See* ONTARIO ENVIRONMENTAL LEGISLATION. **3115**

1195-1877 *See* TODAY'S EGG PRODUCER. **223**

1195-1893 *See* PARENT CARE / YOUR CHILD CARE NEWS-LINE. **2284**

1195-1982 *See* JOURNAL OF TRAVEL MEDICINE. **3600**

1195-1990 *See* MIND / BODY MEDICINE. **3617**

1195-2008 *See* PERIODONTAL INSIGHTS. **1333**

1195-227X *See* ARCHITECTURE AND DESIGN INSITE. **2898**

1195-2695 *See* INFIRMIERE DU QUEBEC. **3857**

1195-3101 *See* GLOBAL BIODIVERSITY. **456**

1195-3136 *See* ONTARIO LANDLORD AND TENANT LEGISLATION. **3022**

1195-3144 *See* FEDERAL AND ONTARIO INSOLVENCY LEGISLATION. **3100**

1195-3152 *See* ONTARIO REAL ESTATE LEGISLATION. **3023**

1195-3349 *See* SOURDS DU CANADA. **4393**

1195-3349 *See* DEAF CANADA. **4386**

1195-3365 *See* PACIFIC GILLNETTER. **2310**

1195-3616 *See* INFORMATION HIGHWAYS. **1188**

1195-4000 *See* HOSPITAL MORBIDITY - CANADIAN CENTRE FOR HEALTH INFORMATION. **3659**

1195-406X *See* CANCER IN CANADA (1989). **3811**

1195-4078 *See* THERAPEUTIC ABORTIONS - CANADIAN CENTRE FOR HEALTH INFORMATION. **3769**

1195-4086 *See* TUBERCULOSIS STATISTICS / STATISTICS CANADA, CANADIAN CENTRE FOR HEALTH INFORMATION. **3662**

1195-4108 *See* MORTALITY, SUMMARY LIST OF CAUSES / STATISTICS CANADA, CANADIAN CENTRE FOR HEALTH INFORMATION. **4555**

1195-4140 *See* MARRIAGES / STATISTICS CANADA, CANADIAN CENTRE FOR HEALTH INFORMATION. **2287**

1195-4167 *See* RESIDENTIAL CARE FACILITIES, AGED / STATISTICS CANADA, CANADIAN CENTRE FOR HEALTH INFORMATION. **3754**

1195-4175 *See* RESIDENTIAL CARE FACILITIES, MENTAL / STATISTICS CANADA, CANADIAN CENTRE FOR HEALTH INFORMATION. **5306**

1195-423X *See* TENANTS BULLETIN. **2836**

1195-4906 *See* TRAILS (WINDSOR). **2475**

1195-4981 *See* PARTNERS IN PRINT. **881**

1195-5015 *See* EUSKARIEN (QUEBEC). **2193**

1195-5023 *See* QUESNEL CARIBOO OBSERVER. **5793**

1195-5287 *See* NATURAL GAS EXPORTER. **4265**

1195-5325 *See* JOBS FOR YOUR FUTURE. **4205**

1195-5759 *See* TELECOM ADVISOR, THE. **1164**

1195-5767 *See* SPINAL COLUMNS. **4394**

1195-6038 *See* COMPENDIUM OF VETERINARY PRODUCTS. **5508**

1195-6747 *See* HEALTH PROMOTION IN CANADA. **4781**

1195-6755 *See* PROMOTION DE LA SANTE AU CANADA. **2240**

1195-6925 *See* CONTACT - ASSOCIATION DE SPINA-BIFIDA ET D'HYDROCEPHALIE DU QUEBEC. **4335**

1195-7956 *See* SPORT MAGAZINE. **4920**

1195-8472 *See* CANADIAN MILITARY HISTORY. **4038**

1195-9231 *See* C-JEUNES. **5276**

1195-9428 *See* FAMILY CONNECTIONS. **2279**

1196-0140 See OPERATIONAL REVIEW ... FARM DEBT REVIEW BOARDS. **117**

1196-054X *See* TELEPHONE DIRECTORY, OTTAWA-HULL. **4690**

1196-0612 *See* GRAND BABILLARD, LE. **4652**

1196-071X *See* MIRROR-EXAMINER. **5790**

1196-0809 *See* RADIOCOMM MAGAZINE. **1138**

1196-0817 *See* GROCER TODAY. **838**

1196-0833 *See* CANADIAN ENERGY TRENDS MONTHLY (1991). **1934**

1196-0906 *See* CANADIAN NATURAL GAS MARKET REPORT. **4253**

1196-1198 *See* THEATRE RESEARCH IN CANADA. **5371**

1196-1376 *See* CANADIAN RESOUCRES REVIEW. **2377**

1196-1880 LIST OF CSA CERTIFIED COMFORT CONDITIONING EQUIPMENT. **2606**

1196-1929 *See* OTTAWA JEWISH BULLETIN (1993). **2270**

1196-1961 *See* CANADIAN JOURNAL OF EXPERIMENTAL PSYCHOLOGY. **4579**

1196-2283 *See* APPAREL (SAINTE-ANNE-DE-BELLEVUE). **1081**

1196-278X *See* FORESTRY, OIL & GAS REVIEW. **2382**

1196-4081 *See* JOURNAL - CANADIAN SOCIETY FOR EDUCATION THROUGH ART. **323**

1196-4650 *See* MARKETING MAGAZINE (TORONTO). **931**

1196-4715 *See* I.T. MAGAZINE (TORONTO). **1259**

1196-4790 *See* FESTIVALS & ATTRACTIONS. **4850**

1196-5266 *See* REID'S ADMINISTRATIVE LAW. **3037**

1196-5290 *See* ANNUAL SURVEY OF PRESCRIPTION AND OVER-THE-COUNTER DRUGS. **4291**

1197-1193 *See* AVANT-POSTE (AMQUI). **5780**

1197-1495 *See* SALON MAGAZINE. **405**

1197-4303 *See* GALLUP POLL (TORONTO. 1993). **5246**

1197-4362 *See* INJURY PREVENTION NEWS. **2598**

1197-4532 *See* INITIATIVE (ST. JOHN). **5114**

1197-4699 *See* FUTURE CONSUMER NEWSLETTER. **1592**

1197-4710 *See* HEALTHCARE ADVOCATE (EDMONTON). **3782**

1197-4729 *See* CHCG PULSE. **3853**

1197-4982 *See* JOURNAL / CROHN'S AND COLITIS FOUNDATION OF CANADA, THE. **3746**

1197-5148 *See* DIRECTORY OF SOURCES FOR EDITORS, REPORTERS & RESEARCHERS, THE. **2919**

1197-5334 *See* FEDERATION NEWS / FEDERATION OF NOVA SCOTIAN HERITAGE. **2733**

1197-5865 *See* CCTANS NEWSLETTER. **1814**

1197-6578 *See* BULLETIN OF THE CANADIAN SOCIETY OF BIOCHEMISTRY AND MOLECULAR BIOLOGY. **484**

1197-7485 *See* ACQUISITIONS LIST - CANADIAN HOUSING INFORMATION CENTRE. **2813**

1197-8538 *See* ANNOTATED ONTARIO RULES OF CRIMINAL PRACTICE. **3105**

1197-8554 *See* ADVANCES IN PERITONEAL DIALYSIS. **3546**

1197-9704 *See* M5V MAGAZINE. **324**

1198-0281 *See* REPERE (MONTREAL. IMPRIME. 1994). **423**

1198-0400 *See* MISSION: JOURNAL OF MISSION STUDIES. **4978**

1198-046X *See* YOUR GUIDE TO GOVERNMENT FINANCIAL ASSISTANCE FOR BUSINESS IN ALBERTA. **724**

1198-0575 *See* YOUR GUIDE TO GOVERNMENT FINANCIAL ASSISTANCE FOR BUSINESS IN THE YUKON. **725**

1198-1180 *See* ANNUAL DIVIDEND RECORD. **639**

1198-3795 *See* ICIDH AND ENVIRONMENTAL FACTORS INTERNATIONAL NETWORK. **5289**

1198-3922 *See* LAST RIGHTS. **2252**

1198-4848 *See* ELECTRIC POWER STATISTICS. ANNUAL STATISTICS. **1962**

1198-7340 *See* SEMINARS IN HEADACHE MANAGEMENT. **3640**

1198-7421 *See* SEMINARS IN OTOLARYNGIC ALLERGY. **3676**

1198-743X *See* CLINICAL MICROBIOLOGY AND INFECTIOUS DISEASES. **561**

1198-8614 *See* JOURNAL OF CONFLICT STUDIES. **4527**

1199-0597 *See* EMERGING MARKETS ANALYST. **671**

1199-1429 *See* INTERNATIONAL TRADE BUSINESS PLAN. **97**

1199-1801 *See* AREAS SERVED BY NATURAL GAS. **4759**

1199-1836 *See* KEEPING TRACK. **159**

1199-1844 *See* BAOBAB INTERNATIONAL. **2908**

1199-2786 *See* HARDWARE MERCHANDISING (1993). **2811**

1199-6579 *See* TORONTO REGION TOP EMPLOYERS GUIDE. **1629**

1199-7699 *See* NUTRITION & MENTAL HEALTH. **4195**

1200-006X *See* LIST OF CSA CERTIFIED COMFORT CONDITIONING EQUIPMENT. **2606**

1200-1627 *See* AGRICULTURE CANADA ANNUAL REPORT. **53**

1200-1678 *See* LIST OF CSA CERTIFIED HEALTH CARE PRODUCTS AND SERVICES. **3605**

1200-2062 *See* HOUSE PRICE TRENDS. **4838**

1200-2275 *See* LIVING SAFETY. **4789**

1210-0455 *See* PRAGUE ECONOMIC PAPERS. **1513**

1210-0552 *See* NEURAL NETWORK WORLD. **1243**

1210-0668 *See* ENDOCRINE REGULATIONS (BRATISLAVA). **3729**

1210-0900 *See* PRAVNI PRAXE. **3030**

1210-115X *See* SBORNIK CESKE GEOGRAFICKE SPOLECNOSTI. **2576**

1210-1699 **1400**

1210-2059 *See* NOVY SLOVAK. **5810**

1210-2741 *See* NEW GLASS REVIEW (PRAHA). **2592**

1210-5546 *See* CZECH FOREIGN TRADE. **663**

1210-5759 *See* EUROPEAN JOURNAL OF ENTOMOLOGY. **5608**

1210-7697 *See* UHLI- RUDY- GEOLOGICKY PRUZKUM. **1400**

1210-7816 *See* CESKA A SLOVENSKA FARMACIE : CASOPIS CESKE FARMACEUTICKE SPOLECNOSTI A SLOVENSKE FARMACEUTICKE SPOLECNOSTI. **4295**

1215-007X *See* INDUSTRIE-ALMANACH UNGARN. **1611**

1215-0389 *See* ERDESZETI LAPOK : AZ ORSZAGOS ERDESZETI EGYESULET LAPJA. **2379**

1215-2439 *See* HUNGARIAN ECONOMIC REVIEW : HER. **839**

1215-282X *See* TAVLATOK. **5037**

1215-735X *See* BUDAPEST REVIEW OF BOOKS. **4827**

1216-1829 *See* ECONOMIC TRENDS IN EASTERN EUROPE. **1558**

1216-1993 *See* MAGYAR KOEZTARSASAG HELYNEVKOENYVE / KOEZPONTI STATISZTIKAI HIVATAL, A. **4663**

1216-4526 *See* HUNGARIAN AGRICULTURAL RESEARCH / MINISTRY OF AGRICULTURE, HUNGARY. **93**

1216-6626 *See* BIOLOGIA TANITASA SZEGED, A. **444**

1216-8076 *See* ACTA LINGUISTICA HUNGARICA. **3261**

1216-9803 *See* ACTA ETHNOGRAPHICA HUNGARICA. **227**

1217-8950 *See* ACTA MICROBIOLOGICA ET IMMUNOLOGICA HUNGARICA. **558**

1217-8969 *See* ACH, MODELS IN CHEMISTRY. **959**

1220-0522 *See* ROMANIAN JOURNAL OF MORPHOLOGY AND EMBRYOLOGY. **540**

1220-4749 *See* REVUE ROUMAINE DE MEDECINE INTERNE (1990). **3801**

1220-5168 *See* ROMANIAN ASTRONOMICAL JOURNAL. **399**

1220-5265 *See* STUDII SI CERCETARI DE GEOFIZICA / ACADEMIA ROMANA. **1411**

1220-5419 *See* REVUE ROUMAINE DE PSYCHOLOGIE / ACADEMIE ROUMAINE. **4617**

1220-5648 *See* ROMANIAN JOURNAL OF MINERAL DEPOSITS. **1396**

1220-5656 *See* ROMANIAN JOURNAL OF PALEONTOLOGY. **4230**

1220-580X *See* PEDIATRIA / ASOCIATIA MEDICALA ROMANA, SOCIETATEA ROMANA DE PEDIATRIE. **3907**

1220-580X *See* PEDIATRIE / UNIUNEA SOCIETATILOR DE STIINTE MEDICALE DIN ROMANIA. **3910**

1220-8485 *See* ROUMANIAN ARCHIVES OF MICROBIOLOGY AND IMMUNOLOGY. **3676**

1221-1451 *See* ROMANIAN REPORTS IN PHYSICS. **4420**

1225-0090 *See* MUNHON CHONGBO / THE LITERARY INFORMATION. **3459**

1225-4568 *See* STRUCTURAL ENGINEERING AND MECHANICS. **1997**

1230-0322 *See* POLISH JOURNAL OF FOOD AND NUTRITION SCIENCES / POLISH ACADEMY OF SCIENCES. **2353**

1230-0659 *See* WIES I PANSTWO. **146**

1230-2309 *See* SZACHISTA WARSZAWA. **4866**

1230-2856 *See* PRAWO PRZEDSIEBIORCY. **3030**

1230-3429 *See* TOPOLOGICAL METHODS IN NONLINEAR ANALYSIS. **3539**

1230-3534 *See* HUTNIK, WIADOMOSCI HUTNICZE. **4003**

1230-395X *See* SAT AUDIO VIDEO. **5318**

1230-4018 *See* MOWIA WIEKI 1992. **2699**

1235-0605 *See* VTT TIEDOTTEITA. **5169**

1235-0613 *See* VTT JULKAISUJA. **5169**

1235-1199 *See* PELIT 1992. **1272**

1235-1938 *See* STUDIA FENNICA. LINGUISTICA. **3324**

1235-1946 *See* STUDIA FENNICA. FOLKLORISTICA. **2324**

1235-2209 *See* DISCUSSION PAPERS / HELSINKI SCHOOL OF ECONOMICS, DEPARTMENT OF ECONOMICS. **1480**

1236-4746 *See* KOULUTUS. **1760**

1240-0866 *See* PHARMACEUTIQUES PARIS. **4321**

1240-0874 *See* URBANISME. **2838**

1240-1307 *See* NATURES-SCIENCES-SOCIETES. **5131**

1240-2095 *See* CAHIERS DE L'IREPP, LES. **1144**

1240-2419 *See* REVUE D'HISTOIRE DE BAYONNE, DU PAYS BASQUE ET DU BAS-ADOUR. **330**

1240-2494 *See* REVUE DOCUMENTAIRE - TOXIBASE LYON. **3983**

1240-3946 *See* PRODUCTIQUE AFFAIRES PARIS. **1216**

1240-4454 *See* INFOS JUNIOR PARIS. **4851**

1240-8751 *See* OFFICIEL DU CYCLE ET DE LA MOTO PARIS, L'. **4082**

1240-9863 *See* MEILLEURES ADRESSES DES TRAITEMENTS DE SURFACE, LES. **692**

1241-3682 *See* FEL ACTUALITES HEBDO : MARCHES EUROPEENS DES FRUITS ET LEGUMES. **171**

1241-5251 *See* CHAMBRE DE COMMERCE FRANCO-RUSSE. **819**

1241-5294 *See* MONDE ARABE PARIS. **4482**

1241-9257 *See* BULLETIN / CENTRE PIERRE LEON D'HISTOIRE ECONOMIQUE ET SOCIALE. **1549**

1242-0492 *See* MENSUEL DU CINEMA, LE. **4074**

1242-0565 *See* ELECTRICAL COMMUNICATION. **1154**

1242-2126 *See* COLLECTIVITES HOTELLERIE ET RESTAURATION PARIS. **5279**

1243-275X *See* ACTUALITE ET DOSSIER EN SANTE PUBLIQUE. **4763**

1243-3853 *See* KARATE, BUSHIDO. **4902**

1243-4442 *See* MEMOIRES DU MUSEUM NATIONAL D'HISTOIRE NATURELLE. **4167**

1243-4671 See INDICATEUR HORAIRES VILLE A VILLE. 2982

1243-6852 See CAHIERS DE L'ANIMATION, LES. 1730

1243-7492 See REVUE DES TELECOMMUNICATIONS PARIS. 1992. 1163

1243-7751 See MINUTE PARIS. 1993. 1764

1244-5460 See FAITS DE LANGUES EVRY. 3387

1246-6875 See BIGRE. 1172

1246-7391 See MEDECINE ET DROIT. 3607

1247-5793 See NOUVELLE REVUE D'AERONAUTIQUE ET D'ASTRONAUTIQUE. 30

1248-2722 See ENSEIGNEMENT SUPERIEUR & RECHERCHE PARIS. 1605

1248-9948 See TELE K7, TELE 7 VIDEO. 1140

1251-9103 See SOCIETE D'EMULATION DES COTES-D'AMOUR. 2630

1251-9812 See INTERFOLIO LEVALLOIS-PERRET. 301

1252-5367 See RECUEIL DES ACTES ADMINISTRATIFS DE LA PREFECTURE DES ARDENNES ET DES SERVICES DECONCENTRES DE L'ETAT. 4678

1252-607X See PARASITE : JOURNAL DE LA SOCIETE FRANCAISE DE PARASITOLOGIE. 468

1258-780X See METIERS DE LA PETITE ENFANCE. 3616

1315-0855 See VISION TECNOLOGICA / PUBLICACION DE INTEVEP, S.A. 4281

1320-1271 See AGSO JOURNAL OF AUSTRALIAN GEOLOGY & GEOPHYSICS. 1365

1320-1670 5490

1320-2340 See AUSTRALIAN DENTAL PRACTICE. 1317

1320-2677 See MUSEUM MATTERS. 4092

1320-3770 See MINING QUARTERLY. 2146

1320-4122 See WEEKLY WOOL INTERNATIONAL. 5359

1320-5331 See LAKES AND RESERVOIRS. 5535

1320-5358 See NEPHROLOGY. 3992

1320-5463 See PATHOLOGY INTERNATIONAL. 3897

1320-6133 See AUSTRALIAN ENTOMOLOGIST, THE. 5605

1320-7881 See NURSING INQUIRY. 3864

1320-9663 See SEAFOOD AUSTRALIA. 2357

1320-9787 See ASIA PACIFIC PAPERMAKER. 4232

1321-1609 See ACTIVE AND HEALTHY QUARTERLY. 4763

1321-2923 See RUSSIA, SIBERIA, MONGOLIA, AND NORTH KOREA TRAVEL NEWS. 5490

1321-408X See FRANCHISING. 677

1321-9820 See HQ MAGAZINE. 2510

1321-9855 2510

1322-0829 See PHYCOLOGICAL RESEARCH. 469

1322-350X See DIRECTORY OF ELECTRONIC SERVICES AND COMMUNICATION NETWORKS. 2042

1322-3518 See TELECOMMUNICATIONS STRATEGIES REPORT. 1166

1322-3526 See INFORMATION TECHNOLOGY MANAGEMENT. 5113

1322-3534 See CABLE AND PAY TV NEWSLETTER. 1128

1322-3992 See WOOL INTERNATIONAL INSIGHT. 5359

1322-4409 See FIA JOURNAL. 2597

1322-7114 See INTERNATIONAL JOURNAL OF NURSING PRACTICE. 3857

1330-0016 See FIZIKA B : A JOURNAL OF EXPERIMENTAL AND THEORETICAL PHYSICS. 4403

1330-0164 See ACTA MEDICA CROATICA : CASOPIS HRVATSKE AKADEMIJE MEDICINSKIH ZNANOSTI. 3544

1335-048X See FOREST GENETICS. 2380

1340-3540 See MYCOSCIENCE. 518

1350-0775 See MUSEUM INTERNATIONAL. 4092

1350-0872 See MICROBIOLOGY. 567

1350-0937 See GRAPHICS INTERNATIONAL. 379

1350-1402 See ADS INTERNATIONAL. 754

1350-1763 See JOURNAL OF EUROPEAN PUBLIC POLICY. 4658

1350-1771 See FORENSIC LINGUISTICS: THE INTERNATIONAL JOURNAL OF LANGUAGE AND THE LAW. 3282

1350-1933 See ASPECTS OF EDUCATIONAL AND TRAINING TECHNOLOGY. 1888

1350-2344 See IEE PROCEEDINGS. SCIENCE, MEASUREMENT AND TECHNOLOGY. 2058

1350-2352 See IEE PROCEEDINGS. ELECTRIC POWER APPLICATIONS. 2058

1350-2360 See IEE PROCEEDINGS. GENERATION, TRANSMISSION, AND DISTRIBUTION. 2058

1350-2379 See IEE PROCEEDINGS. CONTROL THEORY AND APPLICATIONS. 2057

1350-2387 See IEE PROCEEDINGS. COMPUTERS AND DIGITAL TECHNIQUES. 1229

1350-2395 See IEE PROCEEDINGS. RADAR, SONAR, AND NAVIGATION. 1156

1350-2409 See IEE PROCEEDINGS. CIRCUITS, DEVICES AND SYSTEMS. 2057

1350-2417 See IEE PROCEEDINGS. MICROWAVES, ANTENNAS AND PROPAGATION. 2058

1350-2425 See IEE PROCEEDINGS. COMMUNICATIONS. 1156

1350-2433 See IEE PROCEEDINGS. OPTOELECTRONICS. 2058

1350-245X See IEE PROCEEDINGS: VISION, IMAGE AND SIGNAL PROCESSING. 1156

1350-4010 See REPORTAGE; THE INTERNATIONAL MAGAZINE OF PHOTOJOURNALISM. 2924

1350-4126 See PERSONAL RELATIONSHIPS. 2285

1350-4150 See KELLY'S. 843

1350-4177 See ULTRASONICS SONOCHEMISTRY. 4424

1350-4339 See FICTION ON FICHE. 3387

1350-4347 See CHILDREN'S FICTION ON FICHE. 1061

1350-4460 See EUROPEAN AGRIBUSINESS. 82

1350-4487 See RADIATION MEASUREMENTS. 4440

1350-4495 See INFRARED PHYSICS & TECHNOLOGY. 4405

1350-4509 See INTERNATIONAL JOURNAL OF SUSTAINABLE DEVELOPMENT AND WORLD ECOLOGY, THE. 2217

1350-4533 See MEDICAL ENGINEERING & PHYSICS. 3695

1350-4541 See APOPTOSIS. 3551

1350-4592 See TOXICOLOGY AND ECOTOXICOLOGY NEWS. 3984

1350-4622 See ENVIRONMENTAL EDUCATION RESEARCH. 2167

1350-4630 See SOCIAL IDENTITIES. 5259

1350-4741 See EUROPEAN FINANCIAL SERVICES LAW. 2967

1350-4789 See SEALING TECHNOLOGY. 1029

1350-486X See APPLIED MATHEMATICAL FINANCE. 3494

1350-4894 See CONTEMPORARY ORGANIC SYNTHESIS. 1041

1350-4916 See MICROCIRCULATION. 3616

1350-5033 See CONSERVATION AND MANAGEMENT OF ARCHAEOLOGICAL SITES. 266

1350-5068 See EUROPEAN JOURNAL OF WOMEN'S STUDIES, THE. 5555

1350-5076 See MANAGEMENT LEARNING. 1617

1350-5851 See APPLIED ECONOMICS LETTERS. 1463

1350-6129 See AMYLOID: THE INTERNATIONAL JOURNAL OF EXPERIMENTAL AND CLINICAL INVESTIGATION. 3549

1350-6226 See JANE'S INTELLIGENCE REVIEW. 4047

1350-6269 See ORGANISATIONS AND PEOPLE - SUCCESSFUL DEVELOPMENT. 881

1350-6285 See VISUAL COGNITION. 4621

1350-6501 See PROCEEDINGS OF THE INSTITUTION OF MECHANICAL ENGINEERS. PART J, JOURNAL OF ENGINEERING TRIBOLOGY. 2126

1350-6773 See WORLD CLOTHING MANUFACTURER. 1088

1350-7265 See BERNOULLI. 5323

1350-7362 See MOBILE EUROPE. 1160

1350-7486 See EUROPEAN REVIEW OF HISTORY. 2687

1350-7508 See SCOTLANDS. 2854

1350-7516 See HUTHE PAPERS ON PUBLIC POLICY. 4655

1350-7532 See AUSTRIAN STUDIES. 3364

1350-7540 See CURRENT OPINION IN NEUROLOGY. 3831

1350-7583 See ISSUES IN ENVIRONMENTAL SCIENCE AND TECHNOLOGY. 5116

1350-9047 See CELL DEATH AND DIFFERENTIATION. 451

1350-9209 See CURRENT RESEARCH IN FRENCH STUDIES AT UNIVERSITIES IN THE UNITED KINGDOM & IRELAND. 3276

1350-9462 See PROGRESS IN RETINAL AND EYE RESEARCH. 3878

1350-9667 See AUDIO JOURNAL OF ONCOLOGY. 3553

1350-9837 See GRASSLANDS AND FORAGE ABSTRACTS. 153

1351 See JOURNAL OF ACCIDENT & EMERGENCY MEDICINE. 3725

1351-0002 See REDOX REPORT. 3633

1351-0029 See SPORTS, EXERCISE AND INJURY. 3956

1351-010X See BUILDING ACOUSTICS. 602

1351-0126 See JOURNAL OF PSYCHIATRIC AND MENTAL HEALTH NURSING. 3929

1351-0177 See PUBLISHING TECHNOLOGY REVIEW. 4819

1351-024X See LANGUAGE FORUM. 3295

1351-0266 See TEXTILE HORIZONS. 5358

1351-0266 See TEXTILE HORIZONS INTERNATIONAL. 5358

1351-0363 See JOURNAL OF FAR EASTERN BUSINESS. 687

1351-0487 See CONSTELLATIONS : AN INTERNATIONAL JOURNAL OF CRITICAL AND DEMOCRATIC THEORY. 4469

1351-0614 See PERSONNEL ASSISTANT'S HANDBOOK. 945

1351-0711 See OCCUPATIONAL AND ENVIRONMENTAL MEDICINE. 2866

1351-0754 See EUROPEAN JOURNAL OF SOIL SCIENCE. 171

1351-3214 See CELLULAR PHARMACOLOGY. 4295

1351-3249 See NATURAL LANGUAGE ENGINEERING. 1196

1351-3540 See PC GAMER. 4864

1351-3737 See TATE. 366

1351-3850 See PERSONAL INJURY LAW AND MEDICAL REVIEW. 3026

1351-3958 See ASIAN ECONOMIC JOURNAL : JOURNAL OF THE EAST ASIAN ECONOMIC ASSOCIATION. 1633

1351-4180 See FOCUS ON CATALYSTS. 975

1351-4199 See FOCUS ON PAPER CHEMICALS. 1024

1351-4202 See FOCUS ON SOLVENTS. 975

1351-4210 See FOCUS ON SURFACTANTS. 1024

1351-4288 See SOCIAL HOUSING. 5308

1351-4725 See WORLD BUSINESS & ECONOMIC REVIEW / COMPILED BY WALDEN PUBLISHING. 1527

1351-4954 See MANAGEMENT PAY REVIEW. 1689

1351-5055 See BENCHMARKING BRIEFING. 642

1351-5101 See EUROPEAN JOURNAL OF NEUROLOGY. 3832

1351-525X See NITRIC OXIDE. 3622

1351-5268 See ACTIVIN & INHIBIN. 3545

1351-5276 See EATING DISORDERS. 3573

1351-5284 See HELICOBACTER. 3583

1351-5292 See MYCOBACTERIA. 3618
1351-5314 See CELL CONTACT AND COMMUNICATION. 533
1351-5322 See LYSOSOMES & ENDOCYTOSIS. 3605
1351-5330 See OXYTOCIN AND VASOPRESSIN. 3732
1351-5543 See BANKING AUTOMATION BULLETIN FOR EUROPE. 777
1351-5756 See JUSTICE OF THE PEACE & LOCAL GOVERNMENT LAW. 4659
1351-5764 See LOCAL GOVERNMENT REVIEW REPORTS. 3004
1351-5802 See COMPETENCY. 2860
1351-6051 See JOURNAL OF PAY & REWARD MANAGEMENT. 874
1351-6337 See PHARMACEUTICAL SCIENCE COMMUNICATIONS. 4321
1351-7848 See INTERNATIONAL JOURNAL OF VEHICLE DESIGN SERIES B : HEAVY VEHICLE SYSTEMS. 5417
1351-8216 See HAEMOPHILIA. 3580
1351-8402 See RCOG DIPLOMATE, THE. 3767
1351-8488 See TUMOR TARGETING. 3647
1352-0229 See MANAGING INFORMATION. 878
1352-0237 See JOURNAL OF GOVERNMENT INFORMATION. 4658
1352-0431 See INTERNATIONAL BOND INVESTOR. 901
1352-0504 See JOURNAL OF VIRAL HEPATITIS. 3600
1352-061X See TRADING LAW AND TRADING LAW REPORTS. 3104
1352-0717 See ROAD LAW AND ROAD LAW REPORTS. 5443
1352-0849 See COUNTRY PROFILE. CONGO, SAO TOME AND PRINCIPE, GUINEA-BISSAU, CAPE VERDE / THE ECONOMIST INTELLIGENCE UNIT. 1552
1352-0938 See COUNTRY PROFILE. THE GAMBIA, MAURITANIA / EIU, THE ECONOMIST INTELLIGENCE UNIT. 1554
1352-2175 See AFRICAN STUDIES ABSTRACTS : THE ABSTRACTS JOURNAL OF THE AFRICAN STUDIES CENTRE, LEIDEN. 5226
1352-2310 See ATMOSPHERIC ENVIRONMENT. 1351
1352-2744 See ASIAN ART & CULTURE. 343
1352-2809 See INTERNATIONAL JOURNAL OF LEISURE. 4851
1352-3074 See WORLD CLASS DESIGN TO MANUFACTURE : WCDM. 3489
1352-3252 See LEGAL THEORY. 3001
1352-3538 See FOCUS ON INTERMEDIATES AND CONTRACT CHEMICALS. 975
1352-4127 See SOCIAL SCIENCES IN HEALTH. 5221
1352-4186 See NEW PLANTSMAN, THE. 2425
1352-4518 See EUROPEAN BUSINESS & ECONOMIC DIGEST. 673
1352-4739 See JAPANESE ECONOMIC REVIEW. 1498
1352-5581 See BUSINESS BASICS STAFF BULLETIN. 646
1352-5611 See HEALTH AND SAFETY MANAGER. 4778
1352-7266 See JOURNAL OF MARKETING COMMUNICATIONS. 928
1352-7592 See TEAM PERFORMANCE MANAGEMENT: AN INTERNATIONAL JOURNAL. 947
1352-7967 See HOSPITAL PHARMACIST, THE. 4306
1352-8505 See ENVIRONMENTAL AND ECOLOGICAL STATISTICS. 2215
1352-8513 See ILLUSTRATED CASE REPORTS IN GASTROENTEROLOGY. 3746
1352-8882 See ENVIRONMENT BUSINESS MAGAZINE. 2228
1352-8971 See AXIS: ACADEMIC COMPUTING & INFORMATION SYSTEMS. 1246
1352-9374 See VETERINARY TIMES. 5527
1352-9749 See PIG JOURNAL, THE. 5518

1353-1131 See JOURNAL OF CLINICAL FORENSIC MEDICINE. 3741
1353-1190 See REACTION!. 990
1353-1573 See IDS PENSIONS SERVICE BULLETIN. 3149
1353-2561 See SPILL SCIENCE AND TECHNOLOGY BULLETIN. 2243
1353-2677 See WORLD PAPER (TONBRIDGE). 4240
1353-3142 See COUNTRY REPORT. ISRAEL, THE OCCUPIED TERRITORIES / EIU, THE ECONOMIST INTELLIGENCE UNIT. 1474
1353-3258 See JOURNAL OF ORTHOPAEDICS. 3882
1353-329 See CHECKLIST OF UNIVERSITY INSTITUTIONS IN THE COMMONWEALTH. 1815
1353-3312 See INTERNATIONAL PEACEKEEPING. 4525
1353-3339 See PSYCHODYNAMIC COUNSELLING. 4610
1353-3347 See THERAPEUTIC WORK WITH CHILDREN. 1886
1353-3525 See EUROPEAN ENVIRONMENT LAW. 3112
1353-4505 See INTERNATIONAL JOURNAL FOR QUALITY IN HEALTH CARE : JOURNAL OF THE INTERNATIONAL SOCIETY FOR QUALITY IN HEALTH CARE. 3588
1353-4858 See NETWORK SECURITY NEWSLETTER. 1196
1353-5226 See INTEGRATED PEST MANAGEMENT REVIEWS. 4245
1353-5773 See AQUACULTURE NUTRITION. 552
1353-6117 See COMPLEMENTARY THERAPIES IN NURSING AND MIDWIFERY. 3567
1353-7784 See SPECTRUM : NEWSLETTER OF THE ROYAL OBSERVATORIES. 390
1353-8012 See JOURNAL OF VASCULAR INVESTIGATION. 3600
1353-8020 See PARKINSONISM AND RELATED DISORDERS. 3626
1353-8292 See JOURNAL OF HEALTH AND PLACE. 4786
1353-8853 See INFORMATION MANAGEMENT IN HEALTH CARE / FULL SERVICE. 870
1353-8861 See INFORMATION MANAGEMENT IN HEALTH CARE / IM & T SERVICE. 3587
1353-887X See INFORMATION MANAGEMENT IN HEALTH CARE / PRIMARY CARE SERVICE. 3587
1353-8888 See INFORMATION MANAGEMENT IN HEALTH CARE / HOSPITAL SYSTEMS SERVICE. 3786
1354-0793 See PETROLEUM GEOSCIENCE. 4272
1354-1013 See GLOBAL CHANGE BIOLOGY. 456
1354-1110 See BUSINESS REVIEW. 652
1354-1129 See PSYCHOLOY REVIEW. 4613
1354-2001 See AI WATCH. 1211
1354-2575 See INSIGHT (NORTHAMPTON). 2102
1354-3725 See EUROPEAN PUBLIC LAW. 2967
1354-4128 See AGRAFOOD ASIA. 46
1354-4195 See EARLY PREGNANCY: BIOLOGY AND MEDICINE. 3760
1354-5078 See NATIONS AND NATIONALISM. 4483
1354-5299 See FAR EAST FOCUS. 4775
1354-5701 See FEMINIST ECONOMICS. 1490
1354-571X See JOURNAL OF MODERN ITALIAN STUDIES. 3291
1354-5787 See AMERICAN JOURNAL OF MANAGEMENT DEVELOPMENT. 859
1354-6791 See MATHEMATICAL COGNITION. 3518
1354-7739 See BRADFORD STUDIES ON SOUTH EASTERN EUROPE. 2679
1354-7860 See JOURNAL OF ASIA PACIFIC ECONOMIES. 1498
1354-8166 See TOURISM ECONOMICS. 1524
1354-991X See EDINBURGH REVIEW OF THEOLOGY AND RELIGION. 4955
1354-9952 See INGENUITY. 1189

1355-2198 See STUDIES IN HISTORY AND PHILOSOPHY OF SCIENCE. PART B : MODERN PHYSICS. 4423
1355-2511 See JOURNAL OF QUALITY IN MAINTENANCE ENGINEERING. 874
1355-2538 See JOURNAL OF MARKETING PRACTICE : APPLIED MARKETING SCIENCE. 928
1355-2546 See JOURNAL OF MANAGEMENT HISTORY. 874
1355-2546 See RAPID PROTOTYPING JOURNAL. 1201
1355-2546 See BUSINESS PROCESS RE-ENGINEERING & MANAGEMENT JOURNAL. 862
1355-2554 See INTERNATIONAL JOURNAL OF ENTREPRENEURIAL BEHAVIOUR & RESEARCH. 683
1355-2554 See WORLD TRANSPORT POLICY & PRACTICE. 5400
1355-2570 See PRIMARY CARE PSYCHIATRY. 3932
1355-3224 See MUSCULOSKELETAL MANAGEMENT. 3806
1355-3259 See LEGAL AND CRIMINOLOGICAL PSYCHOLOGY. 3169
1355-4786 See HUMAN REPRODUCTION UPDATE. 581
1355-4794 See NEUROCASE. 3839
1355-557X See AQUACULTURE RESEARCH. 553
1355-5634 See STAINLESS STEELS MONTHLY. 4020
1355-6118 See JAPAN AUTO DIGEST. 5417
1355-6177 See JOURNAL OF THE INTERNATIONAL NEUROPSYCHOLOGICAL SOCIETY. 4602
1355-7939 See MAJOR UK COMPANIES HANDBOOK. 844
1355-8382 See RNA. THE OFFICIAL PUBLICATION OF THE RNA SOCIETY. 3637
1356-1308 See GENE THERAPY. 3578
1356-1316 See GLYCOBIOLOGY RESEARCH. 3579
1356-1324 See MOLECULAR BIOLOGY TECHNIQUES. 3618
1370-0081 See PEUPLES & LIBERATIONS BRUXELLES. 4487
1370-009X See ANTIPODES BRUXELLES. 4464
1370-0464 See ACTUALITES JURIDIQUES PHARMACEUTIQUES. 4289
1380-2224 See JOURNAL OF POROUS MATERIALS. 5119
1380-2933 See IMMUNOTECHNOLOGY. 3672
1380-3603 See CHRISTIAN BIOETHICS. 4944
1380-3611 See EDUCATIONAL RESEARCH AND EVALUATION. 1742
1380-3743 See MOLECULAR BREEDING. 986
1380-6084 See PINT NIEUWS. 2370
1380-6165 See AQUATIC GEOCHEMISTRY. 961
1380-6645 See REVIEW OF DERIVATIVES RESEARCH. 991
1380-6653 See REVIEW OF ACCOUNTING STUDIES. 751
1380-748X See INTERNATIONAL PEACEKEEPING. 4525
1380-7501 See MULTI MEDIA TOOLS AND APPLICATIONS. 1288
1380-7854 See MEDIEVAL ENCOUNTERS. 2623
1380-7870 See LIFETIME DATA ANALYSIS. 1193
1381-1177 See JOURNAL OF MOLECULAR CATALYSIS B : ENZYMATIC. 1054
1381-2386 See MITIGATION AND ADAPTATION STRATEGIES FOR GLOBAL CHANGE. 4482
1381-2416 See INTERNATIONAL JOURNAL OF SPEECH TECHNOLOGY. 5115
1381-2424 See MATHEMATICAL MODELLING OF SYSTEMS. 3519
1805-1157 See AONTAS NEWSLETTER. 1799
1830-2011 See FINANCIAL ENGINEERING AND THE JAPANESE MARKETS. 1975
1969-9546 See EUROPEAN JOURNAL OF EMERGENCY MEDICINE. 3575
5792-7290 See KIBBUTZ TRENDS. 4542

8750-0124 See SUPPLY LINE. 4058
8750-0183 See EARTHWATCH (BELMONT, MASS.). 2560
8750-0213 See SHERIDAN NEWS, THE. 5667
8750-0221 See ANGIER INDEPENDENT, THE. 5722
8750-023X See HARNETT COUNTY NEWS. 5723
8750-0256 See UTNE READER, THE. 2549
8750-0310 See OAG POCKET FLIGHT GUIDE (EUROPE & MIDDLE EAST ED.). 5486
8750-0418 See OUTER BANKS CURRENT. 5724
8750-0477 See ART & STYLE INTERNATIONAL. 402
8750-0507 See CONTEMPORARY PEDIATRICS (MONTVALE, N.J.). 3902
8750-0515 See GEORGIA ADVANCE SHEETS. 2974
8750-0558 See ALPHA FLIGHT. 4856
8750-0582 See ALLEGHANY HIGHLANDER, THE. 5758
8750-0590 See CONNEAUTVILLE COURIER (CONNEAUTVILLE, PA. : 1871). 5735
8750-0612 See LAUGH COMICS DIGEST MAGAZINE. 4862
8750-0620 See ARCHIE COMICS DIGEST MAGAZINE. 4857
8750-0639 See JUGHEAD WITH ARCHIE. 4862
8750-0655 See MOBILE HOME LIVING. 2828
8750-0698 See PRINSBURG NEWS. 5698
8750-0701 See WAURIKA NEWS-DEMOCRAT. 5733
8750-0728 See NEWSLETTER (SPINAL CORD SOCIETY (U.S.)). 3843
8750-0760 See KENTUCKY STANDARD, THE. 5681
8750-0779 See ANNA JOURNAL. 3851
8750-0795 See VALLEY TIMES (TIGARD, OR.). 5734
8750-0809 See SUNDAY WYOMING TRIBUNE-EAGLE. 5773
8750-0817 See WYOMING STATE TRIBUNE (CHEYENNE, WYO. : 1937). 5773
8750-0825 See WYOMING EAGLE, THE. 5773
8750-0841 See TIGARD TIMES. 5734
8750-0868 See WATERLOO COURIER CEDAR FALLS. 5673
8750-0876 See NEWS-SUN (KENDALLVILLE, IND.). 5666
8750-0884 See GILMER MIRROR, THE. 5750
8750-0922 See SUFFOLK SOURCE, THE. 5721
8750-0930 See RANDOM HARVEST WEEKLY. 5720
8750-0957 See HIGHLAND NEWS LEADER. 5660
8750-2119 See PHYSICAL THERAPY FORUM (KING OF PRUSSIA, PA. 1994). 4381
8750-0973 See CONNECTICUT LAW JOURNAL. 2955
8750-0981 See OAKLAND BUSINESS MONTHLY. 700
8750-1023 See HAUPPAGE NEWS. 5717
8750-104X See CENTRAL ISLIP NEWS (1984). 5714
8750-1058 See BELLEVILLE NEWS-DEMOCRAT. 5658
8750-1074 See SHEPARD'S GEORGIA CASE NAME CITATOR. 3050
8750-1082 See U.K. MAGAZINE. 2524
8750-1104 See SHEPARD'S CORPORATION LAW CITATIONS. 3103
8750-1112 See SHEPARD'S PARTNERSHIP LAW CITATIONS. 3103
8750-1120 See SHEPARD'S TEXAS CASE NAMES CITATOR. 3054
8750-1171 See CLINCH VALLEY NEWS, THE. 5758
8750-1236 See CONDO SALES REPORT. 4836
8750-1252 See RESORT DEVELOPMENT & OPERATION. 2809
8750-1260 See ORO VALLEY VOICE. 5630
8750-1287 See FISHING TACKLE RETAILER (1984). 675

8750-1317 See OREGONIAN (PORTLAND, OR. 1937), THE. 5734
8750-1333 See ACTION (REDONDO BEACH, CALIF.). 4932
8750-1376 See DALLAS NEW ERA, THE. 5653
8750-1392 See CENTRAL POST, THE. 5709
8750-1430 See VALLEY MAGAZINE (GRANADA HILLS, CALIF.). 1300
8750-1449 See MARTHA'S VINEYARD TIMES, THE. 5689
8750-1481 See ANTIQUE BOTTLE & GLASS COLLECTOR. 248
8750-1503 See TIMES-BULLETIN, THE. 5730
8750-1562 See UNION ADVOCATE. 5699
8750-1570 See BEDFORD BULLETIN (1984). 5758
8750-1651 See RUSSELL COUNTY NEWS (JAMESTOWN, KY.), THE. 5682
8750-1708 See SCANNER AND KING COUNTY LABOR NEWS, THE. 1710
8750-1732 See DUSTY TIMES. 4893
8750-1759 See LAMPASAS DISPATCH RECORD. 5751
8750-1767 See SUPER TEEN. 1070
8750-1791 See BELOIT DAILY CALL, THE. 5674
8750-1813 See CALIFORNIA PHYSICIAN. 3561
8750-1872 See WEST TOLEDOHERALD. 5731
8750-1880 See PUREBRED PICTURE, THE. 219
8750-1902 See ALVIN SUN, THE. 5746
8750-1929 See CHILDREN'S SERMONS SERVICE PLUS. 1062
8750-1937 See CURRENT NOTES. 1181
8750-1953 See SIGHTHOUND REVIEW. 4288
8750-1961 See BOSTON JEWISH TIMES, THE. 5688
8750-2003 See SUN (LAGRANGE, ILL.), THE. 5662
8750-2011 See LEAVEN (FRANKLIN PARK, ILL.). 2282
8750-202X See CAMERON CHRONICLE. 5747
8750-2038 See HERALD-DISPATCH (LOS ANGELES, CALIF. : 1981). 5635
8750-2046 See AIPE NEWSLINE. 1964
8750-2070 See SEMINOLE OUTLOOK. 5651
8750-2097 See ROSEBUD COUNTY PRESS. 5706
8750-2100 See MASS HIGH TECH. 5127
8750-2119 See PHYSICAL THERAPY FORUM (MIDDLE ATLANTIC ED.). 4381
8750-2127 See LIMOUSIN WORLD. 214
8750-2143 See PORTUGUESE AMERICAN, THE. 2271
8750-2151 See BAPTIST HOSPITAL FUND BULLETIN. 5274
8750-2186 See DENTISTRY TODAY. 1322
8750-2208 See SIGNAL (MONONA, WIS.). 1783
8750-2216 See NEWS (CLAREMONT GRADUATE SCHOOL). 1093
8750-2224 See PREPRESS BULLETIN, THE. 5034
8750-2240 See HERALD TRIBUNE CROSSWORDS & OTHER WORD GAMES. 4862
8750-2259 See CCC NEWS. 2277
8750-2267 See ISANTI COUNTY NEWS. 5696
8750-2275 See JOURNAL (KING GEORGE, VA.), THE. 5759
8750-2283 See UPDATE - GEORGIA ASSOCIATION OF EDUCATORS. 1789
8750-2321 See MDA NEWSMAGAZINE / MUSCULAR DYSTROPHY ASSOCIATION. 3806
8750-233X See TRAPPER AND PREDATOR CALLER, THE. 3186
8750-2348 See SANDARA. 5662
8750-2356 See SRC BLUE BOOK OF 5-TREND CYCLI-GRAPHS, THE. 914
8750-2364 See INDEPENDENT REPUBLICAN. 4476
8750-2380 See REPORTER (CASEY, ILL.). 5661
8750-2453 See ACCESSORIES. 1081
8750-2461 See SRC RED BOOK OF 5-TREND SECURITY CHARTS, THE. 914
8750-247X See DAILY AMERICAN (SOMERSET, PA.), THE. 5735
8750-2488 See ARMOUR CHRONICLE, THE. 5743

8750-250X See LEADER-TRIBUNE (FORT VALLEY, GA.), THE. 5654
8750-2518 See CORSICANA DAILY SUN. 5748
8750-2534 See VICTORIA (SAN DIEGO, CALIF). 5007
8750-2542 See TRIUMPH (LOS ANGELES, CALIF.). 5641
8750-2550 See INTERCORP. 683
8750-2585 See APMA NEWS. 3917
8750-2607 See WEST'S CRIMINAL LAW NEWS. 3109
8750-2615 See WEST'S ILLINOIS DECISIONS. 3074
8750-2623 See WEST'S CALIFORNIA REPORTER. 3074
8750-2658 See NEW JERSEY REPORTS AND NEW JERSEY SUPERIOR COURT REPORTS. 3142
8750-2674 See LYNCHBURG NEWS. 5729
8750-2720 See CITY SUN, THE. 5715
8750-2763 See ATTORNEYS PERSONNEL REPORT. 2938
8750-2836 See HOSPITAL PRACTICE (OFFICE EDITION). 3584
8750-2852 See CENTRAL FLORIDA MAGAZINE. 2530
8750-2895 See DAKOTA COUNTY TRIBUNE. 5695
8750-2925 See TOBACCO VALLEY NEWS. 5706
8750-295X See WESTERN WORLD AVON COLLECTORS NEWSLETTER. 2779
8750-3026 See FOOTHILLS SENTINEL. 5630
8750-3042 See HOROSCOPE GUIDE. 390
8750-3077 See BILDOR NEWS. 601
8750-3085 See OCULAR SURGERY NEWS. 3971
8750-3093 See MILLARD COUNTY CHRONICLE PROGRESS. 5757
8750-3115 See SAN ANTONIO EXPRESS-NEWS. 5754
8750-3123 See ENFIELD PRESS (1984), THE. 5645
8750-3158 See SBANE ENTERPRISE. 709
8750-3204 See STRATEGIC PLANNING AND ENERGY MANAGEMENT. 1958
8750-3212 See HOT BIKE. 4081
8750-3220 2491
8750-3247 See VIRGINIA LAW REPORTS. 3071
8750-3255 See AMERICAN THEATRE. 5361
8750-3271 See DREADSTAR. 4860
8750-328X See UFCW LEADERSHIP UPDATE. 1715
8750-3298 See STREET RODDING ILLUSTRATED. 5426
8750-3301 See VW TRENDS. 5428
8750-3328 See JOURNAL FOR THE OFFICE OF MENTAL RETARDATION & DEVELOPMENTAL DISABILITIES, THE. 5291
8750-3336 See CHILKAT VALLEY NEWS. 5629
8750-3352 See LAWRENCE COUNTY CENTENNIAL. 5744
8750-3379 See BERKS COUNTY LAW JOURNAL. 2941
8750-3417 See ROPERS SPORTS NEWS. 5639
8750-3425 See COASTAL OBSERVER (PAWLEYS ISLAND, S.C.). 5742
8750-3441 See OFFICE SYSTEMS (GEORGETOWN, CONN.). 4213
8750-345X See KITCHEN & BATH DESIGN NEWS. 2902
8750-3476 See JERICHO TRIBUNE, THE. 5717
8750-3484 See WALTHILL CITIZEN, THE. 5707
8750-3492 See POST-TRIBUNE (GARY, IND.). 5666
8750-3530 See FESTIVAL QUARTERLY. 4959
8750-3549 See RHODESIAN RIDGEBACK QUARTERLY, THE. 4287
8750-3557 See LABRADOR QUARTERLY : LQ, THE. 4287
8750-3603 See BOWLING DIGEST. 4888
8750-3670 See BUSINESS TRAVEL NEWS. 653
8750-3689 See LAKE NEWS, THE. 5681
8750-3697 See CULPEPPER LETTER, THE. 1285

8750-3719 See NORTH CADDO COUNTY NEWS, THE. 5732

8750-3735 See HOSPITAL & HEALTH SERVICES ADMINISTRATION. 3783

8750-3743 See SANTA GERTRUDIS TRIBUNE. 221

8750-376X See TIG BRIEF : THE INSPECTOR GENERAL. 4059

8750-3808 See SCLEOA UPDATE. 3176

8750-3832 See SCOTT COUNTY VIRGINIA STAR. 5759

8750-3867 See GOSHEN NEWS, THE. 5664

8750-3883 See THIEF RIVER FALLS TIMES. 5699

8750-3891 See SIERRA VISTA HERALD. 5630

8750-3913 See NEWS BEACON (FAIR LAWN, N.J.). 5814

8750-3921 See TIMES OF NORTHEAST BENTON COUNTY, THE. 5632

8750-393X See OKARCHE CHIEFTAIN, THE. 5732

8750-3948 See TAHOE DAILY TRIBUNE AND THE LAKE TAHOE NEWS. 5640

8750-3956 See PARKERSBURGH NEWS (1916). 5764

8750-3964 See PLUS (LONGVIEW, TEX.). 5753

8750-3972 See HARTSVILLE MESSENGER, THE. 5742

8750-3980 See NEWS-HERALD (MORGANTON, N.C.), THE. 5724

8750-4022 See IDAHO BUSINESS REVIEW, THE. 681

8750-4049 See COURIER-EXPRESS (DUBOIS, PA. : 1964). 5735

8750-4057 See WHOOT. 2550

8750-4081 See INDOOR GARDEN, THE. 2420

8750-409X See YALE ALUMNI MAGAZINE (1984). 1103

8750-4103 See AUTOMOTIVE PRODUCTS REPORT. 5407

8750-4219 See PULLER, THE. 160

8750-4286 See RETAIL NEWS WEST. 957

8750-4294 See SOUTHWEST JOURNAL OF BUSINESS AND ECONOMICS. 713

8750-4308 See CENTINELA (NAMPA, IDAHO), EL. 5057

8750-4316 See WEEKEND DESERT POST. 5641

8750-4367 See MARVEL AGE. 4863

8750-4375 See COMPUTER LIVING, NEW YORK. 1177

8750-4383 See AHOY! (NEW YORK, N.Y.). 1170

8750-4391 See RETAILER NEWS. 957

8750-4421 See GALVESTON (GALVESTON CHAMBER OF COMMERCE). 819

8750-4448 See LECCIONES DE LA ESCUELA SABATICA. 4973

8750-4499 See BRONX TIMES REPORTER. 5714

8750-4529 See MENSALOHA. 4603

8750-4537 See NORTH CASTLE NEWS. 5719

8750-4545 See RICHLAND COUNTY NEWS-MONITOR. 5726

8750-4561 See COUNTY PRESS (LAPEER, MICH.). 5691

8750-457X See MAUI NEWS, THE. 5656

8750-4588 See LOS ALTOS TOWN CRIER. 5636

8750-460X See RICE MARKET REPORT. 185

8750-4618 See MARIETTA DAILY JOURNAL (MARIETTA, GA.), THE. 5654

8750-4642 See NEW MEXICO EPIDEMIOLOGY REPORT. 3736

8750-4650 See XENIA DAILY GAZETTE, THE. 5731

8750-4669 See LEHI FREE PRESS. 5756

8750-4677 See CITIZEN (AMERICAN FORK, UTAH). 5756

8750-4685 See SAVANNAH EVENING PRESS. 5655

8750-4693 See NEWS HERALD (EAGLE BEND, MINN.), THE. 5697

8750-4723 See ARAUTO DA SANTIDADE, O. 5055

8750-4766 See GATOS TIMES-OBSERVER (GENERAL NEWS ED.), LOS. 5635

8750-4774 See HEATING, AIR CONDITIONING & PLUMBING PRODUCTS. 2605

8750-4782 See HERMISTON HERALD AND BUYER'S BONUS, THE. 5733

8750-4790 See PHARMACY NEWS AND REVIEW. 4323

8750-4804 See OIL & GAS TECHNOLOGY. 4269

8750-4863 See MONTECITO LIFE. 5637

8750-4871 See SCALE WOODCRAFT. 375

8750-4901 See DR. C.S. LOVETT'S MARANATHA FAMILY MINI-MAGAZINE. 4954

8750-4928 See HOME COMPUTER & SOFTWARE MERCHANDISING. 1267

8750-4960 See STANISLAUS FARM NEWS. 137

8750-4979 See HOME FURNISHINGS REPRESENTATIVES CONTACT. 2906

8750-4987 See ALEXANDRIA GAZETTE, THE. 5757

8750-4995 See FORDYCE NEWS-ADVOCATE. 5631

8750-5029 See NEWS-GAZETTE (SAINT CLOUD, FLA.). 5650

8750-5088 See TRI-STATE REAL ESTATE JOURNAL (CHERRY HILL, N.J.). 4848

8750-510X See REAL ESTATE SYNDICATION ALERT. 4845

8750-5126 See HOTEL/MOTEL SECURITY AND SAFETY MANAGEMENT. 2806

8750-5177 See WHITE COUNTY RECORD (JUDSONIA, ARK.). 5632

8750-5207 See LUTHERAN WOMEN'S MISSIONARY LEAGUE QUARTERLY ECHO / NEBRASKA DISTRICT SOUTH. 5063

8750-524X See MONITOR (MCALLEN, TEX.), THE. 5752

8750-5266 See BRIDGE (LAFAYETTE, IND.). 1089

8750-5274 See DAILY WORLD (HELENA, ARK.), THE. 5631

8750-5312 See SYLVESTER LOCAL NEWS, THE. 5655

8750-5339 See EVENING TIMES (WEST PALM BEACH, FLA.), THE. 5649

8750-5347 See SINFONIAN (1980), THE. 4153

8750-5355 See IMPERIAL COUNTY FARM BUREAU MONTHLY. 94

8750-5363 See HOLBROOK TRIBUNE-NEWS AND SNOWFLAKE HERALD. 5630

8750-5401 See MOVIE COLLECTOR'S WORLD. 2775

8750-5428 See INTERAMERICANA (RIO PIEDRAS, P.R.). 5808

8750-5436 See MCVILLE MESSENGER. 5725

8750-5444 See EDMORE HERALD. 5725

8750-5452 See PROVIDENCE VISITOR (1984), THE. 5741

8750-5460 See CORPUS CHRISTI MAGAZINE (1984). 662

8750-5479 See HILLSBORO ARGUS (HILLSBORO, OR.). 5733

8750-5495 See FAIRBANKS DAILY NEWS-MINER. 5629

8750-5525 See INDUSTRY NEWS (RICHMOND, VA.). 5071

8750-5533 See PIONEER (BIG RAPIDS, MICH.), THE. 5693

8750-5541 See HERALD-CITIZEN (COOKEVILLE, TENN.). 5745

8750-5568 See CPC EAST COAST REPORT, THE. 4254

8750-5584 See CPC PETRONEWS. 4254

8750-5606 See METROCREST NEWS, THE. 5752

8750-5649 See HOME & AWAY. 5479

8750-5665 See CEDAR FALLS CITIZEN, THE. 5669

8750-5673 See PREMIER HOG PRODUCER. 219

8750-5681 See SIERRA CLUB YODELER. 2205

8750-569X See MUSIC VIDEO RETAILER. 4135

8750-5703 See RITE IDEAS. 4994

8750-5711 See WINSLOW MAIL, THE. 5630

8750-5738 See GAZETTE (HURT, VA.), THE. 5758

8750-5746 See KALAMAZOO COLLEGE QUARTERLY. 1833

8750-5754 See OUTLOOK (GRAND RAPIDS, MICH.), THE. 5065

8750-5762 See AMERICAN RAILS. 5429

8750-5797 See PECAN SOUTH INCLUDING PECAN QUARTERLY. 181

8750-5800 See BANNER-PRESS, THE. 5747

8750-5827 See AMERICAN BMXER. MEMBERSHIP ED. 427

8750-5851 See BASEBALL CARDS. 2771

8750-5878 See AMERICAN SURVIVAL GUIDE. 2527

8750-5908 See MIDTOWN NEWS. 5732

8750-5916 See NORTH HILLS NEWS RECORD. 5738

8750-5932 See STAR (CHICAGO HEIGHTS, ILL.), THE. 5662

8750-5959 See TULSA WORLD (TULSA, OKLA.). 5733

8750-6009 See EAU CLAIRE COUNTY BUYER'S GUIDE. 1296

8750-6033 See EL PASO ECONOMIC REVIEW (1983), THE. 1488

8750-6041 See PLUMBING & MECHANICAL. 2607

8750-6106 See PROGRESSIVE RENTALS. 705

8750-6114 See CU IN CHICAGO. 2532

8750-6122 See SAN JUAN STAR, THE. 5808

8750-6149 See FINANCE AND COMMERCE (REGULAR DAILY ED.). 2970

8750-6181 See GPA BULLETIN, THE. 2920

8750-619X See TOMBALL SUN, THE. 5755

8750-622X See EPSONCONNECTION. 1184

8750-6238 See VALLEY CATHOLIC, THE. 5038

8750-6289 See EL DORADO GAZETTE, GEORGETOWN GAZETTE & TOWN CRIER. 5634

8750-6378 See LOUISBURG HERALD, THE. 5677

8750-6386 See EVENING CITIZEN (LACONIA, N.H.), THE. 5708

8750-6416 See DATAPRO MANAGEMENT OF OFFICE AUTOMATION. 4211

8750-6432 See ARIZONA FARMER-STOCKMAN. 62

8750-6505 See BRISTOL HERALD COURIER, BRISTOL VIRGINIA-TENNESSEAN. 5758

8750-6513 See ALBION NEW ERA, THE. 5662

8750-653X See WOMEN'S SPORTS AND FITNESS. 4930

8750-6548 See STAR TRIBUNE (ATTICA, IND.). 5667

8750-6580 See NATION'S BUILDING NEWS. 622

8750-6599 See SURAJ (1984). 2273

8750-6629 See HUNTING RETRIEVER. 4873

8750-6637 See STATE POLICY REPORTS. 4688

8750-6645 See IOWA COMMERCE. 842

8750-6653 See POWDER/BULK SOLIDS. 4221

8750-6696 See FULTON SUN, THE. 5703

8750-6726 See TOLEDO SPORTSMAN, THE. 4926

8750-6750 See MUNDAY COURIER, THE. 5752

8750-6769 See DAILY ILLINI (CHAMPAIGN-URBANA, ILL.), THE. 5659

8750-6785 See VILLE PLATTE GAZETTE, THE. 5684

8750-6807 See FLORIDA HOTEL & MOTEL JOURNAL. 2805

8750-6823 See OWYHEE AVALANCHE (HOMEDALE, IDAHO : 1985). 5657

8750-684X See GIFTED CHILDREN MONTHLY. 1879

8750-6858 See DATAPRO MANAGEMENT OF MICROCOMPUTER SYSTEMS. 1274

8750-6874 See INFORMATIONWEEK (MANHASSET, N.Y.). 1260

8750-6890 See SAN DIEGO BUSINESS JOURNAL. 709

8750-6963 See PORTSMOUTH DAILY TIMES (1984), THE. 5730

8750-6998 See LEMONT METROPOLITAN. 5661

8750-7005 See NOW-NYS ACTION REPORT. 5563

8750-7064 See EP NEWS SERVICE. 4956

8750-7145 See MILLAT-I BIDAR. 2770

8750-7188 See BAY VOICE, THE. 5691

8750-7196 See NEW LIFE (HOLLYWOOD, CALIF.). 2540

8750-7218 See MEETING MANAGER, THE. 692

8750-7242 See BOP. 2529

8750-7285 See UNDERWOOD NEWS, THE. 5726

8750-7307 See SUFFOLK COUNTY LIFE. 5721

8750-7315 See JOURNAL OF THE AMERICAN PODIATRIC MEDICAL ASSOCIATION. 3918

8750-7323 See FINCASTLE HERALD, THE. 5758

8750-7331 See BETTER TIMES (POMPANO BEACH, FLA. 1985). 2528

8750-734X See DAILY COMMERCIAL RECORDER, THE. 5748

8750-7374 See LIMOUSINE & CHAUFFEUR. 5385

8750-7390 See FRANKLIN CHALLENGER. 5664

8750-7412 See GRAPEVINE GAZETTE. 2534

8750-7455 See FOREST PARK NEWS. 5660

8750-751X See NEWS BULLETIN / FLORIDA COLLEGE. 1093

8750-7528 See DISPATCH (COOKEVILLE, TENN.). 5745

8750-7544 See PHYSICIAN ASSISTANT (1983). 3627

8750-7552 See DAILY DISPATCH (MOLINE, ILL.). 5659

8750-7587 See JOURNAL OF APPLIED PHYSIOLOGY (1985). 581

8750-7595 See COUNTRYSIDE AND SMALL STOCK JOURNAL (1985). 209

8750-7609 See INTERIOR JOURNAL (1984). 5681

8750-7625 See RALLS COUNTY HERALD-ENTERPRISE, THE. 5704

8750-765X See BMW OWNERS NEWS. 4080

8750-7668 See UNITED METHODIST CHRISTIAN ADVOCATE, THE. 5068

8750-7684 See GRANTSVILLE GAZETTE. 5756

8750-7706 See MILLIKIN QUARTERLY. 1836

8750-7714 See HARTFORD "AREA" NEWS, THE. 5743

8750-7730 See ACADEMIC LEADER. 1806

8750-7749 See DEACON DIGEST. 4952

8750-7757 See PUGET SOUND BUSINESS JOURNAL. 705

8750-7765 See CHRISTIAN MISSION. 4945

8750-7803 See BUSINESS UPDATE (SANTA ANA, CALIF.). 818

8750-782X See TIMBRE (WOODINVILLE, WASH.). 4156

8750-7862 See NEWS-VIRGINIAN, THE. 5759

8750-7897 See SHEPHERD (NEW WASHINGTON, OHIO), THE. 221

8750-7919 See VINTON MESSENGER, THE. 5760

8750-7927 See USC TROJAN FAMILY. 1096

8750-7943 See VETERINARY MEDICINE (1985). 5526

8750-7951 See TEXAS FISHERMAN. 2314

8750-7986 See RIVERSIDE COUNTY RECORD-NEWS. 5639

8750-8044 See NEW YORK STATE JURY VERDICT REVIEW AND ANALYSIS. 3090

8750-8052 See PENNSYLVANIA JURY VERDICT REVIEW AND ANALYSIS. 3090

8750-8060 See NEW JERSEY JURY VERDICT REVIEW AND ANALYSIS. 3090

8750-8079 See GET FIT. 2597

8750-8095 See LEADER (GARFIELD HEIGHTS, OHIO), THE. 5729

8750-8109 See WALKING HORSE WORLD. 2803

8750-8117 See SPORT FLYER. 4920

8750-8141 See KETTERING-OAKWOOD TIMES, THE. 5729

8750-8176 See INDIANA APOSTOLIC TRUMPET. 5061

8750-8184 See WALLCOVERINGS, WINDOWS & INTERIOR FASHION. 2903

8750-8214 See AMERICAN LAW REVIEW (DALLAS, TEX.), THE. 2932

8750-8230 See INDEPENDENT (FENTON, MICH.). 5692

8750-8249 See DAILY EVENING ITEM. 5688

8750-8257 See ALPINE SUN. 5633

8750-8273 See SAVANNAH MORNING NEWS, SAVANNAH EVENING PRESS (COASTAL EMPIRE ED.). 5655

8750-8281 See ARIZONA CATTLELOG (1985). 206

8750-829X See MISHAWAKA ENTERPRISE (MISHAWAKA, IND. : 1985). 5665

8750-8311 See LOCAL 1-FLM TEMPO. 3185

8750-8370 See NUTRITION & DIETARY CONSULTANT, THE. 4195

8750-8397 See TRANSPORTATION WORLDWIDE. 854

8750-846X See COLORADO NURSE (1985). 3854

8750-8478 See VEKER, DER. 5265

8750-8486 See PACIFIC RAIL NEWS. 5433

8750-8508 See REVIEW (SHIDLER, OKLA.), THE. 5732

8750-8516 See MASSCITIZEN. 3007

8750-8524 See GOODS & SERVICES BULLETIN, THE. 1297

8750-8591 See PLATEAU ELECTRIC NEWS. 2075

8750-863X See NALC RETIREE. 1692

8750-8656 See ORLANDO BUSINESS JOURNAL. 702

8750-8664 See KENILWORTH LEADER. 5710

8750-8680 See JACKPOT & RODEO NEWS. 4901

8750-8699 See CURRENTS IN AFFECTIVE ILLNESS. 4584

8750-8710 See WAREHOUSING REVIEW. 719

8750-8745 See LOVE LETTER, THE. 1762

8750-8788 See AUTHORITY (WASHINGTON, D.C.), THE. 2815

8750-8842 See YOUR HEALTH & SAFETY. 4808

8750-8869 See FASHION KNITTING. 5184

8750-8877 See CROCHET FANTASY. 5183

8750-8907 See CALIFORNIA ANGLER. 2298

8750-8915 See JOE WEIDER'S FLEX. 2599

8750-8974 See STING (CENTER SQUARE, PA.). 3440

8750-8990 See VETERINARY TECHNICIAN. 5527

8750-9016 See LOUISIANA SPORTSMAN. 4903

8750-9024 See ANTIQUE MARKET REPORT. 249

8750-9083 See TIMES (TRENTON, N.J. PRINCETON METRO ED.), THE. 5711

8750-9091 See INTER-COUNTY LEADER (FREDERIC, WIS.). 5768

8750-913X See HAWAII HERALD (1969). 2262

8750-9156 See EAST HARTFORD GAZETTE, THE. 5645

8750-9180 See BELLE FRANCE, LA. 5462

8750-9199 See FARMERS BRANCH TIMES. 5749

8750-9210 See STONE REVIEW. 2151

8750-9229 See ROADS & BRIDGES (DES PLAINS, ILL.). 2030

8750-9237 See JOURNAL OF IMAGING SCIENCE AND TECHNOLOGY, THE. 5118

8750-9245 See NORTH CREEK NEWS ENTERPRISE, THE. 5719

8750-927X See BUSINESS/NEW YORK. 651

8750-9296 5661

8750-9318 See AMERICAN WOODWORKER, THE. 633

8750-9326 See PREGONERO (WASHINGTON, D.C.), EL. 5647

8750-9369 See PROFESSIONAL SKATER, THE. 4913

8750-9377 See FIRM FOUNDATION. 5060

8750-9385 See WINSTON COUNTY JOURNAL, THE. 5702

8750-9393 See PASTA JOURNAL. 2352

8750-9407 See PHYSICIANS FINANCIAL NEWS. 803

8750-9415 See SYMPHONY USER'S JOURNAL, THE. 1291

8750-944X See CYLA QUARTERLY. 2958

8750-9474 See TEXAS PREVENTABLE DISEASE NEWS. 4805

8750-9504 See KITCHEN & BATH CONCEPTS. 2902

8750-9520 See BUSINESS DIGEST (DANBURY, CONN.). 647

8750-9539 See LMT (NORWALK, CONN.). 1329

8750-9555 See CREATIVE SALES MANAGER. 864

8750-9563 See WELCOME HOME. 2286

8750-9571 See MADERA TRIBUNE. 5636

8750-9598 See SUFFOLK NEWS-HERALD. 5759

8750-961X See EASTERN GAZETTE (1985), THE. 5685

8750-9628 See VAX PROFESSIONAL, THE. 1206

8750-9652 See CONTEMPORARY LONGTERM CARE. 5280

8750-9741 See MEDIGRAM (EAST LANSING, MICH. : 1985). 3614

8750-9768 See KNITTING ELEGANCE. 5184

8750-9776 See AFGHAN HOUND REVIEW, THE. 4285

8750-9792 See KENTUCKY AGRI-NEWS. 102

8750-9873 See TEXAS FARMER. 141

8750-9881 See MAPLE SYRUP JOURNAL, THE. 2348

8750-989X See BOSTON UNIVERSITY TODAY (1984). 1089

8755-0024 See APPLIED STOCHASTIC MODELS AND DATA ANALYSIS. 3495

8755-0032 See ADVANCES IN NEURAL AND BEHAVIORAL DEVELOPMENT. 3826

8755-0040 See CURRENT TOPICS IN HUMAN INTELLIGENCE. 4584

8755-0059 See KANSAS MEDICINE. 3601

8755-0067 See AFRICA INTERNATIONAL. 2636

8755-0075 See BRIEFS / AMERICAN INSTITUTE OF FISHERY RESEARCH BIOLOGISTS. 2297

8755-0083 See WESTERN TAX REVIEW. 4758

8755-0113 See DIEMEX-WHARTON MEXICAN PROJECT, THE. 1555

8755-013X See EXPORTERS' ENCYCLOPAEDIA, (1982). 835

8755-0199 See FREE RADICAL RESEARCH COMMUNICATIONS. 1052

8755-0229 See JOURNAL OF MEDICAL PRACTICE MANAGEMENT, THE. 3914

8755-0253 See PROFESSIONAL DOCUMENT RETRIEVAL. 3242

8755-0261 See RAUCH GUIDE TO THE U.S. PAINT INDUSTRY, THE. 4225

8755-0334 See IFMA ENCYCLOPEDIA OF THE FOODSERVICE INDUSTRY, THE. 2344

8755-0342 See PENNSYLVANIA BAR ASSOCIATION LAWYERS DIRECTORY. 3025

8755-0369 See TAX LITERATURE REPORT. 3062

8755-0393 See FORUM - UNITED STATES INFORMATION AGENCY (1982). 1895

8755-0415 See CITE (HOUSTON, TEX.). 295

8755-0423 See HOME MECHANIX. 634

8755-0431 See OFFICIAL GUIDE TO FOOD SERVICE AND HOSPITALITY MANAGEMENT CAREERS, THE. 4207

8755-044X See OFFICIAL GUIDE TO FLIGHT ATTENDANT CAREERS. 4207

8755-0458 See OFFICIAL GUIDE TO TRAVEL AGENT & TRAVEL CAREERS, THE. 4207

8755-0474 See OCEANS POLICY STUDY SERIES. 3182

8755-0490 See BULLETIN / AMERICAN CONIFER SOCIETY. 504

8755-0504 See JOURNAL OF LANGUAGE FOR INTERNATIONAL BUSINESS, THE. 3290

8755-0520 See WASHBURN COUNTY REGISTER (SHELL LAKE, WIS. : 1928). 5771

8755-0539 See PALMYRA ENTERPRISE. 5770

8755-0571 See PROGRESSIVE GROCER EXECUTIVE REPORT. 2354

8755-058X See LOCAL CLIMATOLOGICAL DATA. PADUCAH. KY., MONTHLY SUMMARY. 1429

8755-0598 See NEW FREEDOM QUARTERLY. 5366

8755-0628 See TAX MANAGEMENT REAL ESTATE JOURNAL. 3062

8755-0679 See FOREIGN COMMERCE HANDBOOK. 836

8755-0687 *See* WORLD AFFAIRS QUARTERLY. 4538

8755-0695 *See* EMPLOYER'S GUIDE TO LAW SCHOOLS. 2966

8755-0717 *See* BEVERAGE INDUSTRY ANNUAL MANUAL. 2364

8755-0776 *See* GAZETTE (MIAMI, FLA.), THE. 321

8755-0849 *See* BILATERAL TRADE OUTLOOK. 825

8755-0881 *See* DIEMEX-WHARTON. PROYECTO AUTOMOTRIZ. PROYECCIONES PREVIAS A LA JUNTA. 5412

8755-089X *See* BRAZILIAN ECONOMIC INDICATORS. 1549

8755-0911 *See* PACIFIC BASIN ECONOMIC OUTLOOK. 1577

8755-092X *See* LIVING MUSIC. 4129

8755-0962 *See* REFERENCE BOOKS BULLETIN. 3244

8755-0989 *See* GAME NEWS. 4861

8755-1020 *See* JOURNAL OF THE NATIONAL ASSOCIATION OF DOCUMENT EXAMINERS. 3168

8755-1039 *See* DIAGNOSTIC CYTOPATHOLOGY. 536

8755-1047 *See* EPSON WORLD. 1184

8755-1063 *See* TODO NATURAL DE NUEVA YORK. 4330

8755-1187 *See* ASAE STANDARDS. 1965

8755-1195 *See* OPTICAL MEMORY REPORT, THE. 1277

8755-1209 *See* REVIEWS OF GEOPHYSICS (1985). 1410

8755-1217 *See* HISTORY OF GEOPHYSICS. 1406

8755-1225 *See* JOURNAL OF PHARMACY TECHNOLOGY, THE. 4313

8755-1233 *See* UPDATE - UNIVERSITY OF SOUTH CAROLINA. DEPT. OF MUSIC. 4157

8755-1241 *See* HSA/NENY NEWS. 5288

8755-1284 *See* LABOR PAGE, THE. 1685

8755-1322 *See* SINTE GLESDA COLLEGE NEWS. 1095

8755-1411 *See* ANNUAL REPORT - NEWARK MUSEUM. 4083

8755-1470 *See* GAMEDAY. 4896

8755-1489 *See* BURMASS' TEX-OK-KAN OIL DIRECTORY. 4252

8755-1497 *See* LONG-TERM FORECAST. 1573

8755-1500 *See* LONG-TERM FORECAST. 1573

8755-1519 *See* WISCONSIN MEDICAL ALUMNI QUARTERLY. 1103

8755-1527 *See* ELECTRONIC SOURCE BOOK FOR SOUTHERN CALIFORNIA, THE. 2048

8755-1551 *See* INTERNATIONAL TAX SUMMARIES. 4733

8755-1586 *See* MARSHALL LOEB'S MONEY GUIDE. 797

8755-1608 *See* U.S. REAL ESTATE REGISTER. 4848

8755-1675 *See* AMERICAN COMPUTER LAW DIGEST. 2932

8755-1683 *See* SOYFOODS INDUSTRY AND MARKET, DIRECTORY AND DATABOOK, THE. 2358

8755-1713 *See* NAHC WILD GAME COOKBOOK. 2792

8755-1721 *See* JOHNSON JOURNAL. 2455

8755-173X *See* NEWSLETTER / NEW HAMPSHIRE SOCIETY OF GENEALOGISTS. 2463

8755-1748 *See* SOUTHERN GENEALOGICAL INDEX. 2473

8755-1756 *See* GERMAN CONNECTION, THE. 2451

8755-1780 *See* ABRAXAS (HOLLYWOOD, LOS ANGELES, CALIF.). 5041

8755-1799 *See* DIRECTOR'S REPORT FOR THE ARNOLD ARBORETUM, THE. 508

8755-1810 *See* MEETINGS (NEW YORK, N.Y. 1980). 3230

8755-1845 *See* UFF REACH. 1715

8755-1918 *See* RESOURCE REVIEW (ANCHORAGE, ALASKA). 2204

8755-1942 *See* ABSTRACTS OF PAPERS PRESENTED AT THE ... TOBACCO ROOT GEOLOGICAL SOCIETY CONFERENCE. 1364

8755-1977 *See* REGIONAL BUSINESS REVIEW. 849

8755-1985 *See* JOURNAL OF PROTECTIVE COATINGS & LININGS. 5119

8755-2000 *See* ERIGENIA. 509

8755-2019 *See* CENTER (AUSTIN, TEX.). 294

8755-2027 *See* SWIM (ARLINGTON, VA.). 4924

8755-2035 *See* PORTICUS. 362

8755-2094 *See* EDUCATIONAL MEDIA AND TECHNOLOGY YEARBOOK. 1893

8755-2124 *See* NETWORK RESOURCE REPORT, THE. 1160

8755-2132 *See* MICRO AND PERSONAL COMPUTERS USED IN THE CONVENIENCE STORE INDUSTRY. 1269

8755-2167 *See* WACONDA ROOTS AND BRANCHES. 2477

8755-2175 *See* EARLITEEN (TEACHER'S ED.). 5016

8755-2353 *See* DORCHESTER COUNTY GENEALOGICAL MAGAZINE, THE. 2445

8755-2361 *See* DATALINE (DALLAS, TEX.). 2959

8755-2396 *See* INDUSTRY NORMS AND KEY BUSINESS RATIOS. 745

8755-240X *See* HEALTH DATA SUMMARIES FOR CALIFORNIA COUNTIES. 4779

8755-2469 *See* IDAHO WILDLIFE. 4873

8755-2523 *See* CHILTON'S IMPO. 3476

8755-254X *See* CHILTON'S HARDWARE AGE (1984). 2810

8755-2566 *See* CHILTON'S INDUSTRIAL SAFETY & HYGIENE NEWS. 2860

8755-2582 *See* CORPORATE ARTNEWS. 348

8755-2590 *See* RESEARCH ROUNDUP. 1870

8755-2612 *See* INDIANA ROOTS. 2454

8755-2620 *See* LEADER IN ACTION. 1834

8755-2655 *See* CLOTH DOLL, THE. 371

8755-2663 *See* U.S. PRESS. 5687

8755-2671 *See* WHO'S MAILING WHAT!. 767

8755-268X *See* FALLEN LEAF MUSIC REFERENCE BOOKS. 4117

8755-2698 *See* FALLEN LEAF PUBLICATIONS IN CONTEMPORARY MUSIC. 4117

8755-2701 *See* DIALOGUES IN PEDIATRIC MANAGEMENT. 3903

8755-2744 *See* DETAILED MORTALITY STATISTICS, SOUTH CAROLINA. 5326

8755-2779 *See* REGIONAL SERVICES OUTLOOK. 1580

8755-2787 *See* OFFICIAL PRICE GUIDE TO SCIENCE FICTION & FANTASY COLLECTIBLES, THE. 2776

8755-2809 *See* PERSONAL INJURY VERDICT SURVEY MASSACHUSETTS EDITION. 3027

8755-2817 *See* PERSONAL INJURY VERDICT SURVEY RHODE ISLAND. 3028

8755-2825 *See* PERSONAL INJURY VERDICT SURVEY NEW JERSEY EDITION. 3027

8755-2841 *See* UTAH DIRECTORY OF BUSINESS AND INDUSTRY. 1630

8755-2884 *See* ANNUAL REPORT / OUTER CONTINENTAL SHELF OIL AND GAS LEASING AND PRODUCTION PROGRAM. 4250

8755-2892 *See* MEMBERSHIP DIRECTORY / NATIONAL ASSOCIATION FOR MUSIC THERAPY. 4130

8755-2914 *See* COLUMBIA (RHINEBECK, N.Y.), THE. 2443

8755-2930 *See* EARTHQUAKE SPECTRA. 2022

8755-2973 *See* HATCHERY PRODUCTION. SUMMARY. 212

8755-299X *See* JEWISH BOOK NEWS. 5048

8755-3023 *See* GOLDEN ROOTS OF THE MOTHER LODE, THE. 2451

8755-3058 *See* HYDROGEN ENERGY COORDINATING COMMITTEE ANNUAL REPORT-SUMMARY OF DOE HYDROGEN PROGRAMS. 1946

8755-3082 *See* MOST-PRESCRIBED DRUGS. 4316

8755-3139 *See* STAMP DEALER FORUM. 2787

8755-3147 *See* TEXAS EDUCATION NEWS. 1787

8755-3155 *See* TEACHING FOR EXCELLENCE. 1907

8755-3163 *See* AMERICAN FIREWORKS NEWS. 2007

8755-3171 *See* FORT SCOTT TRIBUNE, THE. 5675

8755-321X *See* SUCCESSFUL MARKETING TO SENIOR CITIZENS. 937

8755-3244 *See* PIERCE COUNTY HERALD (ELLSWORTH, WIS.). 5770

8755-3252 *See* ANNALS OF THE INSTITUTE FOR ORGONOMIC SCIENCE. 4291

8755-3260 *See* LINCOLN COUNTY RECORD (PIOCHE, NEV. : 1968). 5707

8755-3317 *See* FUTURES RESEARCH QUARTERLY. 5107

8755-3325 *See* CRITICA (LA JOLLA, CALIF.). 5243

8755-3384 *See* REVISTA DEL INSTITUTO GENEALOGICO E HISTORICO LATINOAMERICANO. 2470

8755-3392 *See* HOSPITAL MARKETING MONITOR. 869

8755-3406 *See* MARK LEIBOVIT'S THE VOLUME REVERSAL SURVEY. 797

8755-3422 *See* ALASKA MARINE RADIO DIRECTORY. 1148

8755-3449 *See* JOURNAL OF THIRD WORLD STUDIES. 1637

8755-3473 *See* COLLECTIONS (NEWARK, DEL.). 3203

8755-3511 *See* REPORT ON TELCO MARKETING, THE. 1163

8755-3546 *See* STANDARD METHODS FOR THE EXAMINATION OF WATER AND WASTEWATER. 2243

8755-3554 *See* STANDARD METHODS FOR THE EXAMINATION OF DAIRY PRODUCTS (1967). 4803

8755-3562 *See* OPINIONS (PHILATELIC FOUNDATION (NEW YORK, N.Y.)). 2786

8755-3589 *See* ROBINSON/ROBISON RESEARCHER, THE. 2470

8755-3600 *See* TORCH (INDIANAPOLIS, IND.). 5237

8755-3619 *See* REAL-TIME SIGNAL PROCESSING. 2078

8755-3627 *See* QUONDAM ET FUTURUS (BIRMINGHAM, ALA.). 3351

8755-3635 *See* CLAN DIGGER. 2443

8755-3651 *See* GATO TUERTO, EL. 3390

8755-366X *See* L.C. SUBJECT HEADINGS WEEKLY LISTS (DETROIT, MICH.). 3222

8755-3686 *See* SOUNDER (RANDOM LAKE, WIS.). 5770

8755-3694 *See* FENNIMORE TIMES. 5767

8755-3716 *See* HARVARD EDUCATION LETTER, THE. 1749

8755-3732 *See* CAAS NEWS. 4835

8755-3767 *See* WRESTLING MASTERS. 4931

8755-3805 *See* JOURNAL OF THE JOHANNES SCHWALM HISTORICAL ASSOCIATION, INC. 2742

8755-3813 *See* WALLACE-HOMESTEAD PRICE GUIDE TO DOLLS. 2585

8755-3821 *See* DIRECTORY OF DISTRIBUTORS. 831

8755-383X *See* ORGANIC CHEMISTRY OF DRUG SYNTHESIS, THE. 1044

8755-3848 *See* NEWS / PAN AMERICAN DEVELOPMENT FOUNDATION. 1619

8755-3856 *See* ZONING NEWS. 2839

8755-3864 *See* RESEARCH CENTER FOR THE ARTS AND HUMANITIES REVIEW. 329

8755-3899 *See* DUKE POLICY NEWS. 4645

8755-3902 *See* PRC NEWSLETTER. 4375

8755-3910 *See* ANAIS (LOS ANGELES, CALIF.). 3361

8755-3929 *See* SHOW HORSE (BANGOR, ME.). 2802

8755-3961 *See* OMRO HERALD, THE. 5769

8755-397X *See* PRINCETON TIMES-REPUBLIC. **5770**

8755-3988 *See* GREEN LAKE COUNTY REPORTER (GREEN LAKE, WIS. : 1983). **5767**

8755-3996 *See* IEEE CIRCUITS AND DEVICES MAGAZINE. **2059**

8755-4003 *See* BERLIN JOURNAL, THE. **5765**

8755-4011 *See* REPRESENTATIVE, FOX LAKE, WISCONSIN, THE. **5770**

8755-402X *See* ISRAEL MY GLORY. **4966**

8755-4038 *See* SECRETARIAL SERVICES TODAY. **4214**

8755-4046 *See* CONTROL OF COMMUNICABLE DISEASES IN MAN. **3713**

8755-4143 *See* COMLINE. **3203**

8755-4151 *See* MUTUAL FUND SOURCEBOOK. **908**

8755-416X *See* LEGAL NEWSLETTERS IN PRINT. **3082**

8755-4178 *See* JOURNAL OF FEMINIST STUDIES IN RELIGION. **4969**

8755-4208 *See* JOURNAL OF KENTUCKY STUDIES, THE. **3400**

8755-4216 *See* FISHERMAN (GRAND HAVEN, MICH.), THE. **2302**

8755-4259 *See* ACTIVITIES / CHEMICAL INDUSTRY INSTITUTE OF TOXICOLOGY. **3978**

8755-4267 *See* LIBRARY STATISTICS OF COLLEGES AND UNIVERSITIES IN THE PACIFIC NORTHWEST. **3259**

8755-4283 *See* EUROPEAN BULLETIN (LEXINGTON, MASS.). **1560**

8755-4291 *See* MUTUAL FUND MONITOR, THE. **800**

8755-4313 *See* LC & YOU. **404**

8755-4348 *See* APPRAISERS' INFORMATION EXCHANGE, THE. **4834**

8755-4356 *See* MEMBERSHIP DIRECTORY / INTERNATIONAL SOCIETY OF APPRAISERS. **693**

8755-4372 *See* FIREWORKS BUSINESS. **675**

8755-4380 *See* TSR HOTLINE. **888**

8755-4410 *See* LEGISLATIVE STATUS REPORT - UNITED STATES. VETERANS ADMINISTRATION. **3002**

8755-4453 *See* MITCHELL TECH SERVICE BULLETIN. **5419**

8755-4461 *See* AMERICAN LAWYER GUIDE TO LEADING LAW FIRMS, THE. **2932**

8755-450X *See* BULLETIN FROM THE HILL. **4941**

8755-4526 *See* TECHNICAL OFFICE, THE. **1239**

8755-4534 *See* WESTCHESTER HUMAN SERVICES DIRECTORY. **5314**

8755-4542 *See* HOSPITAL PRACTICE (HOSPITAL ED.). **3785**

8755-4550 *See* WOMEN AND LANGUAGE. **3333**

8755-4585 *See* SOVIET JOURNAL OF CONTEMPORARY PHYSICS. **4421**

8755-4593 *See* NEWSLETTER, EAST ASIAN ART & ARCHAEOLOGY. **360**

8755-4615 *See* COMPUTERS AND COMPOSITION. **1222**

8755-4631 *See* RECORD-COURIER (GARDNERVILLE, NEV.). **5708**

8755-464X *See* PROFILES (SOLANA BEACH, CALIF.). **1272**

8755-4658 *See* WHAT COLOR IS YOUR PARACHUTE?. **4210**

8755-4674 *See* NIH DATA BOOK. **3622**

8755-4682 *See* SEICHE, THE. **2205**

8755-4690 *See* ANNUAL PROGRESS REPORT, CHILKAT RIVER COOPERATIVE BALD EAGLE STUDY. **5576**

8755-4712 *See* SUPPLEMENT TO EMPLOYMENT, HOURS, AND EARNINGS, STATES AND AREAS. **1713**

8755-4720 *See* MOTORCYCLE DEALERNEWS MERCHANDISER. **4082**

8755-4747 *See* PATHWAYS (MAYNARDVILLE, TENN.). **2753**

8755-4763 *See* HEALTH ALERT (PASADENA, CALIF.). **4777**

8755-4771 *See* I. **2504**

8755-4836 *See* SEMIANNUAL REPORT TO THE CONGRESS - UNITED STATES. DEPT. OF TRANSPORTATION. OFFICE OF INSPECTOR GENERAL (1981). **5392**

8755-4909 *See* CALL-A.P.P.L.E. **1265**

8755-4917 *See* WASHINGTON REPORT ON MIDDLE EAST AFFAIRS, THE. **2526**

8755-4925 *See* MUNDUS ARABICUS. **3413**

8755-4933 *See* INTERNATIONAL MICROFORM JOURNAL OF LEGAL MEDICINE AND FORENSIC SCIENCES. **3741**

8755-4941 *See* ALTERNATIVE AGRICULTURE NEWS. **58**

8755-4968 *See* NICARAGUA (WASHINGTON, D.C. 1982). **2750**

8755-500X *See* AHA. **312**

8755-5093 *See* JOURNAL OF ENZYME INHIBITION. **461**

8755-5107 *See* EDUCATIONAL SOFTWARE SELECTOR, THE. **1285**

8755-5123 *See* NORTHEAST JOURNAL OF BUSINESS & ECONOMICS, THE. **1508**

8755-514X *See* NEBRASKA REVIEW (OMAHA, NEB.), THE. **2851**

0749-6567 *See* PERSONAL INJURY VERDICT REVIEWS. **3026**

0749-6559 *See* PERSONAL INJURY VERDICT REVIEWS. **3026**

8755-5182 *See* PERSONAL INJURY VERDICT REVIEWS. **3026**

8755-5190 *See* PERSONAL INJURY VERDICT REVIEWS. **3026**

8755-5220 *See* PERSONAL INJURY VERDICT REVIEWS. PHYSICIAN & HOSPITAL NEGLIGENCE. **3026**

8755-5204 *See* PERSONAL INJURY VERDICT REVIEWS. **3026**

8755-5220 *See* PERSONAL INJURY VERDICT REVIEWS. **3026**

8755-5212 *See* PERSONAL INJURY VERDICT REVIEWS. **3026**

0749-6583 *See* PERSONAL INJURY VERDICT REVIEWS. **3026**

8755-5271 *See* CORONARY CLUB BULLETIN, THE. **3703**

8755-531X *See* U.S. GEOLOGICAL SURVEY BULLETIN. **1400**

8755-5328 *See* INTERNATIONAL PERSPECTIVES IN PUBLIC HEALTH. **4785**

8755-5344 *See* WORTHINGTON DESCENDANTS. **2478**

8755-5352 *See* LESBIAN ETHICS. **2252**

8755-5360 *See* STUDIES IN SOCIAL WELFARE POLICIES AND PROGRAMS. **5312**

8755-5379 *See* ERISA NEWSLETTER, THE. **1667**

8755-5433 *See* FROMMER'S NEW YORK ON $ ... A DAY. **5477**

8755-5476 *See* POCKETBOOK OF PEDIATRIC ANTIMICROBIAL THERAPY. **4325**

8755-5492 *See* NATIONAL ENDOWMENT FOR THE HUMANITIES ... ANNUAL REPORT. **2851**

8755-5506 *See* ISTF NOUVELLES. **2385**

8755-5522 *See* OFFICIAL IDENTIFICATION GUIDE TO VICTORIAN FURNITURE, THE. **2906**

8755-5530 *See* OFFICIAL IDENTIFICATION GUIDE TO GLASSWARE, THE. **2592**

8755-5565 *See* AFRICAN INTELLIGENCE DIGEST. **2636**

8755-5573 *See* DIVER'S ALMANAC. **4893**

8755-559X *See* INDUSTRY WAGE SURVEY. BITUMINOUS COAL. **1679**

8755-562X *See* AMERICAN POLITICAL REPORT, THE. **4463**

8755-5654 *See* SALES & MARKETING ANALYSIS. **936**

8755-5670 *See* BULLETIN OF TAU BETA PI, THE. **5229**

8755-5697 *See* GOLDEN ROOTS OF THE MOTHER LODE. NEWSLETTER. **2451**

8755-5727 *See* CD DATA REPORT. **1276**

8755-5743 *See* PUBLICATIONS IN ARCHAEOLOGY (COLUMBIA, MO.). **279**

8755-5786 *See* MICRO SOFTWARE REPORT. **3231**

8755-5808 *See* VABA EESTI SONA. **5722**

8755-5816 *See* COMPUTER INSTRUCTOR, THE. **1222**

8755-5832 *See* BOOMBAH HERALD. **4104**

8755-5891 *See* LAWYER'S MEDICAL DIGEST. **2998**

8755-5905 *See* GENERAL MUSIC JOURNAL. **4119**

8755-593X *See* DIRECTORY OF FACILITIES OBLIGATED TO PROVIDE UNCOMPENSATED SERVICES BY STATE AND CITY. **3779**

8755-5956 *See* DIRECTORY - INTERSTATE OIL COMPACT COMMISSION. **4254**

8755-5964 *See* MEMBERSHIP DIRECTORY / INTERNATIONAL TRUMPET GUILD. **4130**

8755-5972 *See* DIRECTORY - AGRICULTURAL COMMUNICATORS IN EDUCATION (U.S.). **79**

8755-5980 *See* UNITED STATES CLAIMS COURT DIGEST. **3067**

8755-6006 *See* PACIFIC BASIN ECONOMIC UPDATE. **1577**

8755-6014 *See* PALATINE PATTER. **2466**

8755-6049 *See* JOURNAL OF TAXATION DIGEST, THE. **4735**

8755-6065 *See* SOFTWHERE. REAL ESTATE. **4847**

8755-6073 *See* HARDIN COUNTY HISTORICAL QUARTERLY. **2735**

8755-609X *See* OFFICIAL IDENTIFICATION GUIDE TO EARLY AMERICAN FURNITURE, THE. **2906**

8755-6103 *See* CASINO DIGEST. **4858**

8755-612X *See* INTERBEHAVIORIST, THE. **4590**

8755-6138 *See* INTERNATIONAL REAL ESTATE JOURNAL. **4839**

8755-6154 *See* RECORD COLLECTOR'S MONTHLY. **2777**

8755-6162 *See* INSURANCE COMPUTING NEWSLETTER. **2883**

8755-6189 *See* PACKAGING STRATEGIES. **4221**

8755-6235 *See* LICENSING LETTER, THE. **929**

8755-6243 *See* AIR QUALITY CONTROL FOR ARIZONA. **2223**

8755-626X *See* CAR AND DRIVER ROAD TEST ANNUAL. **5409**

8755-6286 *See* INFORMATION TODAY. **3217**

8755-6294 *See* REPORTS OF THE UNITED STATES TAX COURT. **3039**

8755-6316 *See* BIBLE REVIEW (WASHINGTON, D.C.). **5014**

8755-6324 *See* ROLLING STONE REVIEW, THE. **4151**

8755-6332 *See* INTERNATIONAL ASSOCIATION OF MARINE SCIENCE LIBRARIES AND INFORMATION CENTERS CONFERENCE SERIES. **3218**

8755-6359 *See* PERSONAL INJURY VERDICT SURVEY. NORTH CAROLINA EDITION. **3028**

8755-6367 *See* PERSONAL INJURY VERDICT SURVEY. OHIO EDITION. **3028**

8755-6375 *See* PERSONAL INJURY VERDICT SURVEY. NEW MEXICO EDITION. **3027**

8755-6383 *See* PERSONAL INJURY VERDICT SURVEY. NEW YORK EDITION. **3027**

8755-6391 *See* PERSONAL INJURY VERDICT SURVEY. NEW HAMPSHIRE EDITION. **3027**

8755-6405 *See* PERSONAL INJURY VERDICT SURVEY. OKLAHOMA EDITION. **3028**

8755-6413 *See* PERSONAL INJURY VERDICT SURVEY. ALABAMA EDITION. **3026**

8755-6421 *See* PERSONAL INJURY VERDICT SURVEY. TEXAS EDITION. **3028**

8755-643X *See* PERSONAL INJURY VERDICT SURVEY. TENNESSEE EDITION. **3028**

8755-6448 *See* PERSONAL INJURY VERDICT SURVEY. SOUTH CAROLINA EDITION. **3028**

8755-6456 *See* PERSONAL INJURY VERDICT SURVEY. SOUTH DAKOTA EDITION. **3028**

8755-6464 *See* PERSONAL INJURY VERDICT SURVEY. MONTANA EDITION. **3027**

8755-6472 *See* PERSONAL INJURY VERDICT SURVEY. MISSOURI EDITION. **3027**

8755-6480 *See* PERSONAL INJURY VERDICT SURVEY. MISSISSIPPI EDITION. **3027**

8755-6499 See PERSONAL INJURY VERDICT SURVEY. MICHIGAN EDITION. 3027

8755-6502 See PERSONAL INJURY VERDICT SURVEY MINNESOTA EDITION. 3027

8755-6510 See PERSONAL INJURY VERDICT SURVEY. WASHINGTON, D.C. EDITION. 3028

8755-6529 See PERSONAL INJURY VERDICT SURVEY. DELAWARE EDITION. 3026

8755-6537 See PERSONAL INJURY VERDICT SURVEY. MARYLAND EDITION. 3027

8755-6545 See PERSONAL INJURY VERDICT SURVEY. MAINE EDITION. 3027

8755-6553 See PERSONAL INJURY VERDICT SURVEY. WASHINGTON EDITION. 3028

8755-6561 See PERSONAL INJURY VERDICT SURVEY. WEST VIRGINIA EDITION. 3028

8755-657X See PERSONAL INJURY VERDICT SURVEY. VIRGINIA EDITION. 3028

8755-6588 See PERSONAL INJURY VERDICT SURVEY NEVADA EDITION. 3027

8755-6596 See PERSONAL INJURY VERDICT SURVEY. CONNECTICUT EDITION. 3026

8755-660X See PERSONAL INJURY VERDICT SURVEY. WISCONSIN EDITION. 3028

8755-6618 See PERSONAL INJURY VERDICT SURVEY. ALASKA EDITION. 3026

8755-6626 See PERSONAL INJURY VERDICT SURVEY. VERMONT EDITION. 3028

8755-6634 See PERSONAL INJURY VERDICT SURVEY. WYOMING EDITION. 3028

8755-6642 See PERSONAL INJURY VERDICT SURVEY. NEBRASKA EDITION. 3027

8755-6650 See PERSONAL INJURY VERDICT SURVEY. UTAH EDITION. 3028

8755-6669 See PERSONAL INJURY VERDICT SURVEY. IOWA EDITION. 3027

8755-6677 See PERSONAL INJURY VERDICT SURVEY. KANSAS EDITION. 3027

8755-6685 See PERSONAL INJURY VERDICT SURVEY. ILLINOIS EDITION. 3027

8755-6693 See PERSONAL INJURY VERDICT SURVEY. IDAHO EDITION. 3027

8755-6707 See PERSONAL INJURY VERDICT SURVEY. KENTUCKY EDITION. 3027

8755-6715 See PERSONAL INJURY VERDICT SURVEY. INDIANA EDITION. 3027

8755-6723 See PERSONAL INJURY VERDICT SURVEY. FLORIDA EDITION. 3026

8755-6731 See PERSONAL INJURY VERDICT SURVEY. COLORADO EDITION. 3026

8755-674X See PERSONAL INJURY VERDICT SURVEY. HAWAII EDITION. 3027

8755-6758 See PERSONAL INJURY VERDICT SURVEY. GEORGIA EDITION. 3026

8755-6766 See PERSONAL INJURY VERDICT SURVEY. OREGON EDITION. 3028

8755-6774 See PERSONAL INJURY VERDICT SURVEY. ARIZONA EDITION. 3026

8755-6782 See PERSONAL INJURY VERDICT SURVEY. ARKANSAS EDITION. 3026

8755-6790 See PERSONAL INJURY VERDICT SURVEY. CALIFORNIA EDITION. 3026

8755-6804 See PERSONAL INJURY VERDICT SURVEY. PENNSYLVANIA EDITION. 3028

8755-6812 See PERSONAL INJURY VERDICT SURVEY. NORTH DAKOTA EDITION. 3028

8755-6820 See PERSONAL INJURY VERDICT SURVEY. LOUISIANA EDITION. 3027

8755-6839 See SCIENCE OF TSUNAMI HAZARDS. 1456

8755-6847 See GEORGIA STATE UNIVERSITY LAW REVIEW. 2974

8755-6855 See GRASS ROOTS INTERNATIONAL FOLK RESOURCE DIRECTORY. 5268

8755-6863 See PEDIATRIC PULMONOLOGY. 3909

8755-6871 See IDEA INK. 5030

8755-6898 See MAMMOTH TRUMPET. 273

8755-6901 See CHRISTOPHER NEWS NOTES. 4946

8755-691X See ILLINOIS CONSTRUCTION LAW. 2980

8755-6928 See FOOTPRINTS IN MARION COUNTY. 2448

8755-6936 See DETROIT AUTOMOTIVE SERVICES. NEW CAR INVOICE GUIDE. 5412

8755-6952 See ALUMNI DIRECTORY / NEW YORK MILITARY ACADEMY. 1099

8755-6987 See SICILIA PARRA. 2273

8755-6995 See SPOONER ADVOCATE, THE. 5770

8755-7029 See PIATT COUNTY HISTORICAL AND GENEALOGICAL SOCIETY, THE. 2467

8755-7053 See ECONOMIC IMPACT ANALYSIS PROGRAM, THE ANNUAL REPORT. 2192

8755-707X See ANNUAL REPORT - MARYLAND HIGH BLOOD PRESSURE COMMISSION. 3699

8755-7088 See LAW & SOCIETY NEWSLETTER (DENVER, COLO.). 2994

8755-7118 See DIRECTORY OF COOPERATING AGENCIES. 5283

8755-7134 See CALL NEWS AND REVIEWS. 3272

8755-7142 See UNLISTED DRUGS. INDEX-GUIDE. 4331

8755-7169 See SOFTWARE REVIEWS ON FILE. 1291

8755-7193 See MACHEN FAMILY COURIER. 2459

8755-7207 See CARPENTER FAMILY COURIER. 2442

8755-7223 See JOURNAL OF PROFESSIONAL NURSING. 3860

8755-724X See RESEARCH & EXPLORATION. 4171

8755-7258 See ADVANCED TECHNOLOGY IN THE PACIFIC NORTHWEST. 5081

8755-7266 See MATRIX (URBANA, ILL.). 3466

8755-7282 See SGPB ALERT. 1520

8755-7290 See VIDEO NOW. 1168

8755-7347 See NEW YORK CITY ARTS FUNDING GUIDE. 326

8755-7371 See STRUCTURAL FOAM PLASTICS. 4460

8755-738X See DIGITAL & AUDIO/VIDEO DISCONTINUED DEVICES. 5316

8755-7398 See U.S. REGIONAL. 5345

8755-741X See SPITBALL. 3439

8755-7428 See NONVIOLENT ACTIVIST, THE. 3133

8755-7436 See PAN-AFRICAN SOCIAL SCIENCE REVIEW. 5212

8755-7444 See COVERAGE (CHAMPAIGN, ILL.), THE. 2878

8755-7452 See WEIRDBOOK. 5075

8755-7509 See REPORTER ON THE LEGAL PROFESSION. 3038

8755-7517 See SIMANTIKA. 3437

8755-7525 See MICROCOMPUTER REVIEW. 1269

8755-755X See TIKHOOKEANSKAIA GEOLOGIIA. ENGLISH. 1399

8755-7568 See CONSTRUCTION AND DESIGN LAW DIGEST. 2956

8755-7592 See NATIONAL PARLIAMENTARIAN. 4668

8755-7673 See HEART FAILURE. 3705

8755-7703 See CART NEWS MEDIA GUIDE. 4889

8755-7711 See CALIFORNIA LIBRARY TRUSTEES DIRECTORY. 3199

8755-7738 See TRAVEL AGENTS' ANNUAL PRODUCTION, UNITED STATES ONLY. 5495

8755-7754 See ANNUAL REPORT - NATIONAL COMMERCIAL FINANCE ASSOCIATION (U.S.). 771

8755-7770 See ILLINOIS TAX CLIMATE, THE. 4731

8755-7827 See UTAH ENERGY STATISTICAL ABSTRACT. 1963

8755-786X See REEL DIRECTORY, THE. 4077

8755-7878 See HUMAN ECOLOGIST, THE. 5202

8755-7886 See LABOR CONTRACT LAW BULLETIN. 3150

8755-7894 See ALTERNATIVE AQUACULTURE NETWORK. 552

8755-8181 See EMPLOYER-EMPLOYEE ALCOHOLISM ADVISOR. 1344

8755-8262 See REAL ESTATE SALES/CLOSINGS LAW BULLETIN. 4845

8755-8289 See NARCOTICS LAW BULLETIN. 3013

8755-8297 See SCHOOL LAW BULLETIN (BOSTON, MASS.). 1871

8755-8300 See ARREST LAW BULLETIN. 3158

8755-8319 See MUTUAL FUND REPORTER (MONTHLY ED.). 800

8755-8327 See MUTUAL FUND REPORTER QUARTERLY ED.). 800

8755-8335 See INTERNATIONAL POLITICAL ECONOMY YEARBOOK. 1636

8755-8343 See ROOTS DIGEST. 2471

8755-8378 See CPC NATIONAL DIRECTORY. 1818

8755-8416 See PENNSYLVANIA ETHNIC STUDIES NEWSLETTER. 2270

8755-8440 See FROMMER'S ISRAEL ON $ ... & $ ... A DAY. 5477

8755-8459 See DEKALB COUNTY HERITAGE. 2614

8755-8467 See EMERGENCY CARE QUARTERLY. 3724

8755-8564 See JOURNAL OF FLUID CONTROL, THE. 2091

8755-8572 See FIELD & STREAM (FAR WEST ED.). 4872

8755-8580 See FIELD & STREAM (NORTHEAST ED.). 4872

8755-8599 See FIELD & STREAM (MIDWEST ED.). 4872

8755-8602 See FIELD & STREAM (SOUTH ED.). 4872

8755-8610 See FIELD & STREAM (WEST ED.). 4872

8755-8629 See ECONOMIC DEVELOPMENT COMMENTARY. 1557

8755-8637 See CAD EDUCATOR, THE. 1231

8755-8645 See TURTLE NEWS. 1851

8755-8653 See COLORADO SPORTS MONTHLY. 4891

8755-8661 See ROCK POSTER MAGAZINE. 4151

8755-867X See NETWORK NEWS - NATIONAL WOMEN'S HEALTH NETWORK (U.S.). 4793

8755-8688 See HIGHWAY SAFETY PERFORMANCE. FATAL AND INJURY ACCIDENT RATES ON PUBLIC ROADS IN THE UNITED STATES. 5440

8755-8696 See ANNUAL SURVEY OF COLLEGES. 1793

8755-8718 See CUED ECONOMIC DEVELOPMENTS. 1603

8755-8742 See NEWSLETTER / AMERICAN AEROBICS ASSOCIATION. 2600

8755-8750 See JOURNAL OF APPLIED SEED PRODUCTION. 175

8755-8769 See TEACH (FORT WORTH, TEX.). 5002

8755-8785 See MAGAZINE OF SPECULATIVE POETRY, THE. 3465

8755-8815 See RAZA LAW JOURNAL, LA. 3034

8755-8823 See CONN'S CURRENT THERAPY. 3796

8755-8831 See THIRD WORLD RESOURCES. 2912

8755-884X See CREATIVE LIVING TODAY. 4583

8755-8858 See DIABETIC DIARY. 5282

8755-8866 See NORTHERN CALIFORNIA SUN. 1951

8755-8874 See MADISON INSTITUTE NEWSLETTER, THE. 240

8755-8912 See ISLAM INTERNATIONAL (DOVER, DEL.). 4478

8755-8955 See COMMUNICATION OPTIONS. 864

8755-8963 See MODERN CHINESE LITERATURE. 3412

8755-8971 See DEFOREST TIMES-TRIBUNE. 5767

8755-898X See CURRENT RESEARCH IN THE PLEISTOCENE. 235

8755-9005 See MEALEY'S LITIGATION REPORTS. INSURANCE. 3008

8755-9013 See ECOLOGICAL ILLNESS LAW REPORT. 3110

8755-9021 See LESBIAN-GAY LAW NOTES. 3002

8755-9048 See FOOTNOTES (RESTON, VA.). 4895

8755-9056 See ENNIS DAILY NEWS, THE. 5749

8755-9064 See HERITAGE (COOPERSTOWN, N.Y.). 2736

8755-9072 See PLEASANT GROVE REVIEW. 5757

8755-9080 See IDAHONIAN. 5657

8755-9099 See COUNTY LINES (ALBERT LEA, MINN.). 1542

8755-9110 See SALAMANCA PRESS. 5720

8755-9129 See FOOD REVIEWS INTERNATIONAL. 2339

8755-9137 See FAST FOLK MUSICAL MAGAZINE. 4117

8755-9145 See NUCLEAR ENGINEERING ENROLLMENTS AND DEGREES. 2156

8755-9153 See HEALTHCARE MARKET RESEARCH, REPORTS, STUDIES, & SURVEYS. 4782

8755-9161 See CONTACTS INFLUENTIAL. SOUTH ORANGE COUNTY. 660

8755-9188 See SOYFOODS. 4199

8755-9196 See HIGHWAY ACCIDENT REPORTS. SUMMARY FORMAT. 5440

8755-920X See LIFELINES (PLATTSBURGH, N.Y.). 2458

8755-9242 See ALA WHERE TO STAY BOOK, WEST. 2803

8755-9250 See FROMMER'S HAWAII ON $ ... A DAY. 5477

8755-9269 See INFO-LINE (WASHINGTON, D.C.). 1679

8755-9285 See FEDERAL ACQUISITION REPORT. 4647

8755-9315 See TODAY'S SPIRIT. 5740

8755-9323 See GREEN BAY CATHOLIC COMPASS, THE. 5030

8755-9331 See FREDERICKSBURG STANDARD RADIO POST. 5750

8755-934X See TERRE HAUTE GAZETTE (TERRE HAUTE, IND. : WEEKLY). 5667

8755-9358 See LIAOWANG (INTERNATIONAL ED.). 2506

8755-9390 See ATLA MASTERS AT WORK. 2937

8755-9404 See INTERFAITH ACTION FOR ECONOMIC JUSTICE. 4477

8755-9412 See POLICY NOTES. 4488

8755-9463 See CREWE, BURKEVILLE JOURNAL, THE. 5758

8755-948X See WINNSBORO NEWS (WINNSBORO, TEX. : 1908). 5756

8755-9498 See SONOMA INDEX-TRIBUNE, THE. 5640

8755-9501 See JEFFERSON REPORTER, THE. 5654

8755-9536 See OLD OREGON. 1094

8755-9544 See FARMLIFE. 194

8755-9552 See AMERICAN WEATHER OBSERVER. 1419

8755-9560 See SHOW MUSIC. 4153

8755-9579 See COMMUNICATIONS FOR BETTER LIVING. 3203

8755-9587 See WINSTON-SALEM MAGAZINE. 2550

8755-9595 See SAN GABRIEL VALLEY DAILY TRIBUNE. 5639

8755-9609 See INTERNATIONAL INVENTION REGISTER. 1305

8755-9706 See NARODNO ZEMEDELSKO ZNAME. 4482

8755-9714 See LIVING TREE NEWS, THE. 2458

8755-9730 See BEST'S EXECUTIVE DATA SERVICE. LIFE-HEALTH INDUSTRY MARKETING RESULTS. EXPERIENCE OF PUERTO RICO. 2875

8755-9749 See BRANCHING OUT FROM ST. CLAIR COUNTY, ILLINOIS. 2440

8755-9773 See CAMPING HOTLINE. 4870

8755-979X See HANDBOOK OF WAGES AND BENEFITS FOR CONSTRUCTION UNIONS. 1676

8755-9846 See ADLIB UPDATE. 3187

8755-9854 See NEWS AND JOURNAL (RIPLEY, MISS.). 2462

8755-9889 See MUTUAL FUND FORECASTER. 908

8756-0003 See INSIDE MORTGAGE FINANCE. 791

8756-0011 See CHICAGO ANTHROPOLOGY EXCHANGE. 233

8756-002X See SUBJECT GUIDE TO BOOK REVIEWS. 3251

8756-0038 See WATERFRONT NEWS. 596

8756-0046 See BAY AREA COMPUTER CURRENTS. 1171

8756-0054 See LEGISLATIVE NETWORK FOR NURSES. 3002

8756-0089 See RECORDS & RETRIEVAL REPORT, THE. 884

8756-0119 See CONTACTS INFLUENTIAL. LOS ANGELES COUNTY, SOUTHEAST L.A. : Cl. 660

8756-0127 See POWDER DIFFRACTION FILE ALPHABETICAL INDEX. INORGANIC PHASES. 1037

8756-0143 See SWAMPFOX. 2762

8756-0178 See DIRECTORY OF NEW JERSEY CERTIFIED NURSERIES AND PLANT DEALERS. 2413

8756-0216 See GUIDE TO THE AMERICAN RIGHT (KANSAS CITY, MO. 1984). 4502

8756-0259 See YANKEE HOMES. 4848

8756-0267 See ABBWA JOURNAL. 3357

8756-0291 See CREEPING BENT. 3462

8756-0313 See FLAT EARTH NEWS. 1405

8756-0321 See PACIFIC JOURNAL OF ORIENTAL MEDICINE, THE. 3625

8756-033X See ROCKY MOUNTAIN CAVING. 1410

8756-0348 See WYOMING GEO-NOTES. 1401

8756-0356 See NEHW HEALTH WATCH. 3862

8756-0364 See STROKING TIMES, THE. 4382

8756-0372 See PRACTICAL REAL ESTATE LAWYER, THE. 3030

8756-0380 See SINGLELIFE (MILWAUKEE, WIS.). 2493

8756-0399 See WANTED MISSING PERSONS. 5314

8756-0410 See CURRENT PROBLEMS IN OBSTETRICS, GYNECOLOGY AND FERTILITY. 3760

8756-0429 See CALVARY BAPTIST THEOLOGICAL JOURNAL. 5057

8756-0437 See SEMINARS IN SURGICAL ONCOLOGY. 3824

8756-0445 See BRENGLE BRANCHES. 2440

8756-047X See OCCASIONAL PAPERS ON ANTIQUITIES. 251

8756-0488 See DEVELOPMENT ANTHROPOLOGY NETWORK. 2908

8756-0518 See ANNUAL PROGRESS REPORT, TRACT C-A. 5083

8756-0534 See JOURNAL OF RESEARCH IN RURAL EDUCATION. 1758

8756-0542 See COWLITZ HISTORICAL QUARTERLY. 2730

8756-0550 See CEPA NEWSLETTER. 1231

8756-0577 See ADADATA. 1283

8756-0585 See ARCHIVES OF RESEARCH ON INDUSTRIAL CARCINOGENESIS. 3552

8756-0623 See INTERNATIONAL BUSINESSMAN. 792

8756-0631 See WORLD'S WORD. 3454

8756-064X See CONTACTS INFLUENTIAL. NORTH ORANGE COUNTY. 660

8756-0666 See BLACK BEAR. 3367

8756-0682 See CONTACTS INFLUENTIAL. TACOMA AND OLYMPIA. 660

8756-0690 See MARQUIS WHO'S WHO DIRECTORY OF COMPUTER GRAPHICS. 1234

8756-0747 See CONTACTS INFLUENTIAL. CENTRAL ORANGE COUNTY. 659

8756-0763 See REVIEW OF THE COMMODITY CREDIT CORPORATION'S FINANCIAL STATEMENTS. 809

8756-0798 See RIVER COUNTIES, THE. 2470

8756-0801 See WASHINGTON UNIVERSITY JOURNAL OF URBAN AND CONTEMPORARY LAW. 3073

8756-0828 See MASTERS AND MONUMENTS OF THE RENAISSANCE. 4130

8756-0836 See MOULTRIE COUNTY HERITAGE. 2461

8756-0860 See AMERICAN NATIONAL STANDARDS FOR INFORMATION SCIENCES. 3189

8756-0879 See JOURNAL OF PLASTIC FILM & SHEETING. 4456

8756-0917 See PRECIOUS METALS (TORONTO, ONT.). 4015

8756-0925 See NASSA NEWS. 325

8756-0941 See INFORMATION TIMES (1983). 3258

8756-0976 See CONTACTS INFLUENTIAL. SOUTH ORANGE COUNTY. 660

8756-1050 See SOFTWHERE. AGRI-BUSINESS. 1291

8756-1069 See SOFTWHERE. BANKING/FINANCE. 812

8756-1077 See SOFTWHERE. HEALTH CARE. 1291

8756-1085 See SOFTWHERE. ENGINEERING. 1291

8756-1093 See SOFTWHERE. INSURANCE. 1291

8756-1107 See SOFTWHERE. LEGAL. 1291

8756-1212 See CLASS/BRAND QTR$. 757

8756-1247 See CRUCIBLE (MERCEDES, TEX.), THE. 4951

8756-1263 See BENEFITS QUARTERLY. 1655

8756-1298 See CONTACTS INFLUENTIAL. ATLANTA, GEORGIA. 659

8756-1301 See LATIN AMERICAN ECONOMIC OUTLOOK. 1572

8756-131X See SHELBY COUNTY ANCESTORS. 2472

8756-1360 See TAX MANAGEMENT FINANCIAL PLANNING JOURNAL. 4753

8756-1379 See JOCK. 5187

8756-1387 See APARTMENT & CONDOMINIUM NEWS. 4834

8756-1395 See MEXICO TRAV'LER, THE. 5484

8756-1417 See JOURNAL OF SHIP PRODUCTION, THE. 4177

8756-1425 See SELF-HELP SOURCEBOOK, THE. 4618

8756-1476 See SATERN. 5307

8756-1484 See IRISH GENEALOGY DIGEST. 2454

8756-1492 See TRADE SECRET LAW REPORTER. 3065

8756-1514 See FOODLETTER. 2341

8756-1549 See MIND IN MOTION. 3466

8756-1565 See DIRECTORY OF BAR ASSOCIATIONS. 2961

8756-1611 See DIRECTORY OF THE NEW MEXICO BENCH AND BAR. 2962

8756-1638 See VIRGIN ISLANDS LABOR MARKET REVIEW. 1716

8756-1654 See OFFICIAL PRICE GUIDE TO COLLECTOR CARS, THE. 2776

8756-1670 See JOB INFORMATION LETTER. 4205

8756-1689 See ENDOCURIETHERAPY / HYPERTHERMIA ONCOLOGY. 3816

8756-1700 See NAVY NEWS & UNDERSEA TECHNOLOGY. 4180

8756-1727 See OCAW REPORTER. 1696

8756-1751 See CHRISTIAN EDUCATION DIGEST. 4944

8756-176X See SCIENCE WEEKLY. LEVEL B. 1904

8756-1778 See SCIENCE WEEKLY. LEVEL C. 1904

8756-1786 See SCIENCE WEEKLY. LEVEL D. 1904

8756-1794 See SCIENCE WEEKLY. LEVEL E. 1904

8756-1816 See INDEPENDENT BAPTIST VOICE, THE. 5061

8756-1840 See IDAHO ECONOMIC FORECAST, THE. 1566

ISSN Index

8756-1964 See HEAVY-ION REACTIONS. 4404

8756-1972 See BULLETIN OF THE ASSOCIATION FOR BUSINESS COMMUNICATION, THE. 862

8756-2006 See LEGAL REGISTER, METROPOLITAN WASHINGTON, THE. 3000

8756-2014 See METAL CONSTRUCTION NEWS. 621

8756-2049 See FIBER OPTICS NEWS. 4434

8756-2057 See REPORTER ON HUMAN REPRODUCTION AND THE LAW. 3038

8756-2081 See PARIS NEWS, THE. 5753

8756-209X See SECURITIES REGULATION LAW ALERT. 3047

8756-2111 See EXECUTIVE COMPENSATION REPORT (PARAMUS, N.J.). 1668

8756-212X See TAIWAN REVIEW. 3644

8756-2146 See FACULTY DIALOGUE. 4958

8756-2154 See CALIFORNIA TECHNOLOGY STOCK LETTER. 893

8756-2162 See IN THE WORKS (LITTLE ROCK, ARK.). 1913

8756-2170 See DIRECTORY OF RESIDENTIAL FACILITIES FOR EMOTIONALLY HANDICAPPED CHILDREN AND YOUTH. 3924

8756-2189 See IACD QUARTERLY. 4589

8756-2200 See JORNAL PORTUGUES (SAN PABLO, CALIF.). 5636

8756-2219 See LITERARY AGENTS OF NORTH AMERICA MARKETPLACE. 2922

8756-2235 See JOURNAL OF MODERN KOREAN STUDIES, THE. 2655

8756-2243 See ANNUAL REPORT - NATIONAL PSORIASIS FOUNDATION (U.S.). 3717

8756-2251 See ROSTER OF QUALIFIED ENGINEERING AND LAND SURVEYING FIRMS / LOUISIANA STATE BOARD OF REGISTRATION FOR PROFESSIONAL ENGINEERS AND LAND SURVEYORS. 2030

8756-226X See ANNUAL REVIEW - NATIONAL FUTURES ASSOCIATION (U.S.). 891

8756-2278 See SOUTHWESTERN JOURNAL OF ECONOMIC ABSTRACTS. 1522

8756-2286 See CHRONICLE / SOCIETY OF WINE EDUCATORS. 2366

8756-2294 See DYNIX DATALINE. 3208

8756-2308 See EXECUTIVE EXCELLENCE. 867

8756-2316 See FLORIDA PARISHES GENEALOGICAL NEWSLETTER. 2448

8756-2324 See AT&T TECHNICAL JOURNAL. 1149

8756-2340 See FIGHT BEAT. 4894

8756-2367 See ISLAMIC HORIZONS. 5043

8756-2375 See INDUSTRIAL & MARINE GAS TURBINE ENGINES. 2115

8756-2383 See INDEX TO NEW JERSEY LEGAL DECISIONS. 2981

8756-2405 See INJURIES IN OIL AND GAS DRILLING AND SERVICES. 2863

8756-2413 See HARD MONEY DIGEST. 790

8756-243X See AGCHEMPRICE. 45

8756-2464 See PANHANDLE HERALD, THE. 5753

8756-2537 See ELECTRONIC MAIL & MICRO SYSTEMS. 1154

8756-2553 See GREAT FOODS MAGAZINE. 2342

8756-260X See NEW RESEARCH IN MENTAL HEALTH. 4793

8756-2618 See NEW JERSEY POLITICAL ALMANAC. 4669

8756-2626 See NATIONAL POTATO GERMPLASM EVALUATION AND ENHANCEMENT REPORT. 179

8756-2634 See PC BUYERS GUIDE. 1270

8756-2642 See COMPUTER USER'S LEGAL REPORTER, THE. 2955

8756-2650 See PAFAMS UPDATE. 3625

8756-2766 See SOUTH FLORIDA PIONEERS. 2473

8756-2782 See REPORT OF THE DIRECTOR OF UNIVERSITY LIBRARIES TO THE VICE PRESIDENT OF UNIVERSITY SERVICES. 3245

8756-2812 See MASTERGUIDE. CENTRAL. 303

8756-2855 See MARKETING TECHNOLOGY. 932

8756-2871 See GARTENMOBEL INTERNATIONAL. 837

8756-2960 See CHIPPEWA HERALD-TELEGRAM. 5766

8756-2979 See JUSTIFICATIONS OF APPROPRIATION ESTIMATES FOR COMMITTEES ON APPROPRIATIONS - UNITED STATES DEPT. OF EDUCATION. 1865

8756-2987 See SERIAL NUMBER GUIDE. 627

8756-2995 See LABOR LAWYER, THE. 3150

8756-3002 See REGENERATION. 125

8756-3010 See AFTERWORDS. 5270

8756-3029 See HORUS (SILVER SPRINGS, MD.). 4963

8756-3037 See NATURAL GAS WEEK. 4266

8756-3053 See AMERICAN BUSINESS TREND SYNOPSIS, THE. 638

8756-3088 See CREATION SPIRITUALITY. 4951

8756-310X See HELPING OUT IN THE OUTDOORS. 4706

8756-3142 See IRON MOUNTAIN. 4966

8756-3150 See FUNCTIONAL ORTHODONTIST, THE. 1324

8756-3185 See MONEY OAK, THE. 799

8756-3207 See CLINICIAN'S RESEARCH DIGEST. 4581

8756-3231 See EMPLOYEE RELATIONS BULLETIN (NEW YORK, N.Y.). 1665

8756-324X See CARIBBEAN UPDATE. 655

8756-3282 See BONE (NEW YORK, N.Y.). 3803

8756-3320 See JOURNAL OF OCULAR PHARMACOLOGY. 3876

8756-3347 See INSIGHTS INTO CHRISTIAN EDUCATION. 4965

8756-3401 See VASCULAR VIEWS. 3649

8756-3428 See AMICUS CURIAE (CORAL GABLES, FLA.). 2933

8756-3436 See SMITH'S TABLES. 627

8756-3452 See YEAR BOOK OF PULMONARY DISEASE, THE. 3952

8756-3460 See YEAR BOOK OF REHABILITATION, THE. 3652

8756-3479 See BROOKFIELD ZOO BISON. 5578

8756-3487 See ROCK & SOUL. 4150

8756-3517 See SMOKE SIGNALS (MARYVILLE, MO.). 2472

8756-355X See POLICE CAREER DIGEST. 3171

8756-3630 See ADELPHIA LAW JOURNAL. 2927

8756-3711 See INSIDE F.E.R.C.'S GAS MARKET REPORT. 4260

8756-3746 See SPECIAL EDUCATION AND THE HANDICAPPED. 3057

8756-3789 See AMERICAN HOCKEY MAGAZINE. 4882

8756-3800 See ROSTER - ASSOCIATED GENERAL CONTRACTORS OF AMERICA. CAROLINAS BRANCH. 627

8756-3819 See RINGGOLD ROOTS. 2470

8756-3827 See MAGAZINE PEOPLE. 4816

8756-3835 See REAL ESTATE TAX DIGEST (ALBANY, N.Y.), THE. 4845

8756-3886 See SINGLE AUDIT INFORMATION SERVICE. 751

8756-3894 See TECHTRENDS. 1225

8756-3908 See GOREN BRIDGE LETTER. 4862

8756-3940 See NEWSCURRENTS (MADISON, WIS.). 5211

8756-3959 See MAYFLOWER DESCENDANT : A MAGAZINE OF PILGRIM GENEALOGY AND HISTORY, THE. 2459

8756-4017 See SENSOR TECHNOLOGY. 2080

8756-4041 See TRUCK BLUE BOOK LEASE GUIDE, RESIDUAL PROJECTIONS, THE. 5397

8756-405X See ADDICTION LETTER, THE. 1338

8756-4068 See CATHOLIC HEALTH WORLD. 3778

8756-4076 See CONNECTION TECHNOLOGY. 5096

8756-4084 See PUBFAX. 4818

8756-4092 See ALASKA BUSINESS MONTHLY. 637

8756-4114 See CAPITAL GAIN$. 782

8756-4149 See LOG/ON (LOUISVILLE, KY.). 1275

8756-4173 See ALKI. 3189

8756-4181 See PEA RIVER TRAILS. 2467

8756-4211 See PRIMARY CARDIOLOGY. 3709

8756-4254 See DIRECTORY OF ADMINISTRATORS OF COMMUNITY, TECHNICAL, AND JUNIOR COLLEGES. 1820

8756-4262 See ACCOUNTANTS' LIABILITY. 736

8756-4327 See MUDDY ROOTS. 2461

8756-4335 See THEATRE (WASHINGTON, D.C.). 5371

8756-4351 See ROSTER / THE BIRMINGHAM GENEALOGICAL SOCIETY, INC. 2471

8756-4459 See EUROPEAN TELECOMMUNICATIONS. 1155

8756-4467 See NEWSLETTER - CENTER FOR MIGRATION STUDIES (U.S.). 1920

8756-4475 See SUBNUCLEAR SERIES, THE. 4451

8756-4483 See NABP NEWSLETTER. 4316

8756-4491 See LITIGATION COURSE HANDBOOK SERIES. 3003

8756-4505 See WINGTIPS (LANSING, N.Y.). 5600

8756-4513 See HEALTHCARE ADVERTISING REVIEW. 760

8756-4521 See CENTRAL STATE BUSINESS REVIEW. 656

8756-453X See HEALTHLINES (ANN ARBOR, MICH.). 4782

8756-4548 See LITIGATION AND ADMINISTRATIVE PRACTICE SERIES. 3003

8756-4564 See MAGAZINE FOR CHRISTIAN YOUTH, THE. 4975

8756-4572 See DREXEL POLYMER NOTES. 4454

8756-4599 See QUARTERLY BENCHMARKS. 4614

8756-4602 See ECONOMETRIC INVESTING. 897

8756-4610 See LOSS, GRIEF & CARE. 4603

8756-4629 See JOURNAL OF GERIATRIC DRUG THERAPY. 3753

8756-4637 See NURADEEN. 5044

8756-4653 See AFRICAN ECHO. 2636

8756-4661 See BALLOON (IRVINE, CALIF.). 4384

8756-467X See SERIES IN HEALTH PSYCHOLOGY AND BEHAVIORAL MEDICINE, THE. 4618

8756-4696 See OTHER VOICES (HIGHLAND PARK, ILL.). 3421

8756-4726 See NASH NOTATIONS. 2461

8756-4734 See ASTHMA UPDATE. 3948

8756-4750 See TOBACCO GROWER, THE. 5374

8756-4785 See JOURNAL OF THETA ALPHA KAPPA. 4971

8756-4793 See JOURNAL OF DIAGNOSTIC MEDICAL SONOGRAPHY. 3595

8756-4866 See PROGRESS AND CHALLENGE, WASTE-TO-ENERGY PROJECTS. 2240

8756-4920 See THIS IS ALASKA. 5492

8756-4955 See OFFICIAL PRICE GUIDE TO COLLECTIBLE RECORDS, THE. 4143

8756-4963 See TYPE REPORTER, THE. 4621

8756-4971 See EMPLOYEE BENEFITS FOR NONPROFITS. 1665

8756-498X See NEW ORLEANS MENU, THE. 2351

8756-5048 See WELLNESS NEW MEXICO. 2602

8756-5064 See US AIR FORCE PLAN FOR DEFENSE RESEARCH SCIENCES. 4060

8756-5099 See LONG POND REVIEW. 3408

8756-5102 See L.O.H. CENTRAL CALIFORNIA INDUSTRIAL DIRECTORY, THE. 1615

8756-5129 See TRUCK & TRAILER BUYER'S GUIDE. 5397

8756-5137 See TAX PLANNING FOR THE TROUBLED BUSINESS. 715

8756-5153 See BAY PHIL, THE. 2784

8756-5161 See JAY SCHABACKER'S MUTUAL FUND INVESTING. 904

8756-517X See SPACEBUSINESS CONFERENCE DIGEST, THE. 1627

8756-5188 See PROEDUCATION. 1774

8756-5196 See OCLC MICRO. 3238

8756-5234 See OPEN DOORS (SANTA ANA, CALIF.). 4983

8756-5250 See VIDEO COMPUTING. 1142

8756-5277 See WORCESTER REVIEW, THE. 3473

8756-5293 *See* CORNELL EAST ASIA SERIES. 2503

8756-5307 *See* YEARBOOK ON INDIA'S FOREIGN POLICY. 4539

8756-5331 *See* L5 NEWS (TUCSON, ARIZ. : 1986). 27

8756-534X *See* GREENBOOK (NEW YORK, N.Y.). 925

8756-5358 *See* AMERICAN BMXER (NEWSSTAND EDITION). 428

8756-5374 *See* BAD FAITH LAW REPORT, THE. 2939

8756-5390 *See* PRIMARY CARE EMERGENCY DECISIONS. 3738

8756-5404 *See* KREATIVE KIDS KOPY FUNLETTERS. 4862

8756-5412 *See* TAX, SEC, AND ACCOUNTING ASPECTS OF CORPORATE ACQUISITIONS. 3104

8756-5439 *See* DATA BANKS. 4254

8756-5447 *See* DM & S ADP PLAN. 3573

8756-5455 *See* ARBITRATION TIMES. 2936

8756-5471 *See* GAS ENERGY REVIEW. 4257

8756-5501 *See* REVIEWS OF RENEWABLE ENERGY RESOURCES. 1956

8756-5528 *See* ASSEMBLY TECHNOLOGY BUYERS GUIDE. 1965

8756-5536 *See* FOREIGN MILITARY SALES, FOREIGN MILITARY CONSTRUCTION SALES AND MILITARY ASSISTANCE FACTS AS OF 4044

8756-5544 *See* SOUTHEAST CREATIVE DIRECTORY, THE. 331

8756-5579 *See* SERB WORLD U.S.A. 2760

8756-5587 *See* LEGISLETTER. 3002

8756-5595 *See* LEON HUNTERS DISPATCH, THE. 2458

8756-5609 *See* LININGTON LINEUP. 3405

8756-5633 *See* ZYZZYVA. 3457

8756-5641 *See* DEVELOPMENTAL NEUROPSYCHOLOGY. 3571

8756-565X *See* RING SYSTEMS HANDBOOK. SUPPLEMENT. 1047

8756-5668 *See* PENNSYLVANIA REVIEW (PITTSBURGH, PA.), THE. 3423

8756-5676 *See* CONTROLLERS' UPDATE, THE. 784

8756-5684 *See* CONTROLLERS QUARTERLY, THE. 1471

8756-5781 *See* FALCON (EASTERN AIR LINES, INC.). 19

8756-579X *See* FALCON DIGEST. 19

8756-5803 *See* CONTACTS INFLUENTIAL. SOUTH BAY. 660

8756-5811 *See* PALAESTRA (MACOMB, ILL.). 4392

8756-5838 *See* CONTACTS INFLUENTIAL. SOUTH CENTRAL KANSAS. 660

8756-5889 *See* CONTACTS INFLUENTIAL. LOS ANGELES COUNTY, LONG BEACH METRO. 660

8756-5897 *See* BUSINESS JOURNAL (SACRAMENTO, CALIF.). 650

8756-5919 *See* NUTRITION NEWS (RIVERSIDE, CALIF.). 4196

8756-5935 *See* DRUG AND DEVICE RECALL BULLETIN. 4299

8756-5943 *See* ETA SIGMA GAMMAN, THE. 4775

8756-596X *See* COMPUTING AND THE CLASSICS. 1222

8756-5986 *See* LIST OF PUBLICATIONS / ARKANSAS GEOLOGICAL COMMISSION. 1363

8756-6001 *See* MANAGEMENT COMPENSATION SURVEY OF THE INSURANCE INDUSTRY. 1689

8756-601X *See* NIH ALMANAC. 4794

8756-6044 *See* COLUMBUS DAILY ADVOCATE. 5675

8756-6060 *See* NUTRITION LEGISLATION NEWS. 3020

8756-6079 *See* BANKS IN INSURANCE REPORT. 3085

8756-6095 *See* AABB NEWS BRIEFS. 3769

8756-6168 *See* AIR PROFESSIONAL FILE, THE. 1807

8756-6206 *See* JOURNAL OF PEDIATRIC & PERINATAL NUTRITION. 3905

8756-6222 *See* JOURNAL OF LAW, ECONOMICS & ORGANIZATION. 2988

8756-6249 *See* CITYBUSINESS (NEW YORK, N.Y.). 657

8756-6257 *See* POPULAR MINING. 2148

8756-6265 *See* PROCEEDINGS / COINAGE OF THE AMERICAS CONFERENCE. 2783

8756-6273 *See* LOUISIANA RURAL ECONOMIST. 105

8756-6281 *See* INTERACTION (WASHINGTON, D.C. : 1981). 2195

8756-629X *See* ADMINISTRATION & MANAGEMENT SPECIAL INTEREST SECTION NEWSLETTER. 859

8756-632X *See* NRRI QUARTERLY BULLETIN. 4699

8756-6354 *See* CALYPSO LOG (LOS ANGELES, CALIF.). 1447

8756-6362 *See* DOLPHIN LOG. 1448

8756-6389 *See* ADWEEK (SOUTHEAST EDITION). 755

8756-6397 *See* SOMERSET HERALD (PRINCESS ANNE, MD. : 1985). 5687

8756-6400 *See* ATLANTIC NEWS-TELEGRAPH. 5668

8756-6419 *See* DEMOCRAT HERALD (BAKER, OR.). 5733

8756-6427 *See* FLORIDA KEYS KEYNOTER. 5649

8756-6435 *See* INSIDERS REPORT (SCOTTSDALE, ARIZ.). 901

8756-6443 *See* RUSHVILLE REPUBLICAN (RUSHVILLE, IND. : 1930 : DAILY). 5667

8756-6451 *See* HOKUBEI HOCHI. 5761

8756-646X *See* PORTLAND PHYSICIAN SCRIBE, THE. 3628

8756-6494 *See* FASTBACK. 1746

8756-6516 *See* DATAPRO MANAGEMENT OF APPLICATIONS SOFTWARE. 1254

8756-6567 *See* BIG SKY BUSINESS JOURNAL. 643

8756-6575 *See* PHILOSOPHY OF EDUCATION (EDWARDSVILLE, ILL.). 1902

8756-6583 *See* HOLOCAUST AND GENOCIDE STUDIES. 2691

8756-6591 *See* AMERICAN QUILTER. 5182

8756-6605 *See* GARDEN STATE REPORT. 4650

8756-6621 *See* ELECTRONICS & COMMUNICATIONS IN JAPAN. PART 1, COMMUNICATIONS. 2049

8756-663X *See* ELECTRONICS & COMMUNICATIONS IN JAPAN. PART 2, ELECTRONICS. 2049

8756-6648 *See* SOVIET JOURNAL OF COMMUNICATIONS TECHNOLOGY & ELECTRONICS. 2082

8756-6664 *See* IMAGE WORLD. 1092

8756-677X *See* ALUMNAE DIRECTORY / ZETA PHI BETA SORORITY, INC. 1808

8756-6788 *See* FACT BOOK - NEW YORK STOCK EXCHANGE. 898

8756-6796 *See* ENGINEERING APPLICATIONS OF COMPUTATIONAL HYDRAULICS. 2089

8756-6842 *See* ARMCHAIR RESEARCHERS. QUERIES & BOOK REVIEWS, THE. 2438

8756-6885 *See* ANNUAL REPORT - NATIONAL INSTITUTE OF DENTAL RESEARCH (U.S.). 1316

8756-6907 *See* SACOGE NEWS. 2471

8756-6923 *See* NEWS QUARTERLY OF THE MCDONOUGH COUNTY GENEALOGICAL SOCIETY. 2462

8756-6931 *See* WILL-GRUNDY COUNTIES GENEALOGICAL SOCIETY QUARTERLY. 2477

8756-694X *See* NEWSLETTER / CALIFORNIA GENEALOGICAL ASSOCIATION. 2463

8756-6990 *See* OPTOELECTRONICS, INSTRUMENTATION, AND DATA PROCESSING. 4440

8756-7008 *See* SOVIET SURFACE ENGINEERING & APPLIED ELECTROCHEMISTRY. 1035

8756-7040 *See* MICROCOMPUTER INDEX. 1209

8756-7059 *See* SPEER'S DIGEST OF TOXIC SUBSTANCES STATE LAW. 3116

8756-7083 *See* CATALOGUE - LAURENCE WITTEN RARE BOOKS. 4827

8756-7091 *See* LIQUEFIED GAS DIRECTORY OF AMERICA INC. WESTERN REGION. 4263

8756-7121 *See* FIBERWORKS QUARTERLY. 5351

8756-7156 *See* BIENNIAL REPORT OF EMPLOYMENT BY GEOGRAPHIC AREA. 4701

8756-7172 *See* IFAR REPORTS. 352

8756-7202 *See* SMALL PRESS BOOK REVIEW, THE. 4832

8756-7229 *See* WRIGHT FAMILY WORKBOOK. 2478

8756-7237 *See* BALL BEGINNINGS. 2438

8756-7245 *See* PUBLICATIONS / GYPSY LORE SOCIETY, NORTH AMERICAN CHAPTER. 2323

8756-7296 *See* AMERICAN HERITAGE OF INVENTION & TECHNOLOGY. 5082

8756-730X *See* CONSUMER SOFTWARE NEWS. 1284

8756-7326 *See* TOURO LAW REVIEW. 3065

8756-7334 *See* LOTUS (CAMBRIDGE, MASS.). 1288

8756-7342 *See* JOURNAL FOR COMPUTER USERS IN SPEECH AND HEARING. 4389

8756-7369 *See* LONE STAR HUMOR DIGEST, THE. 4863

8756-7385 *See* TORONTO STUDIES IN RELIGION. 5005

8756-7407 *See* HANDBELLS FOR DIRECTORS AND RINGERS. 4120

8756-7431 *See* TELECOMMUTING REVIEW. 1166

8756-7466 *See* DEVELOPMENT AND FOREIGN POLICY REPORT. 4519

8756-7482 *See* CATHOLIC CHALLENGE, THE. 5025

8756-7504 *See* CAMBRIDGE SCIENTIFIC BIOCHEMISTRY ABSTRACTS: PART 1 BIOLOGICAL MEMBRANES. 484

8756-7512 *See* CAMBRIDGE SCIENTIFIC BIOCHEMISTRY ABSTRACTS: PART 2 NUCLEIC ACIDS. 477

8756-7520 *See* CAMBRIDGE SCIENTIFIC BIOCHEMISTRY ABSTRACTS: PART 3 AMINO-ACIDS, PEPTIDES & PROTEINS. 484

8756-7547 *See* GENETIC, SOCIAL, AND GENERAL PSYCHOLOGY MONOGRAPHS. 4587

8756-7555 *See* COLLEGE TEACHING. 1817

8756-7571 *See* ANDERSON FAMILY COURIER. 2437

8756-758X *See* FATIGUE & FRACTURE OF ENGINEERING MATERIALS & STRUCTURES. 2102

8756-7598 *See* NURSING EXECUTIVE (HOSPITAL ED.). 3864

8756-7636 *See* AAG-AAG. 3459

8756-7679 *See* PERSPECTIVES (MANHATTAN, KAN.). 1840

8756-7687 *See* AI TRENDS (MONTHLY). 1211

8756-7695 *See* ART & OXYGEN. 338

8756-7717 *See* 1/1 (SAN FRANCISCO, CALIF.). 4098

8756-7733 *See* AGACCESS. 45

8756-7741 *See* ROBERTS REGISTOR. 2470

8756-775X *See* EVALUATOR (RIVER FOREST, ILL.). 320

8756-7784 *See* ROBERT G. ALLEN'S REAL ESTATE ADVISOR. 4847

8756-7792 *See* WWF MAGAZINE. 4931

8756-7822 *See* STEWART ALSOP'S P.C. LETTER. 1239

8756-7849 *See* WOMEN'S HEALTH UPDATE. 5571

8756-7857 *See* ICU FORUM. 3585

8756-7881 *See* COMMON SENSE PEST CONTROL QUARTERLY. 4244

8756-789X *See* CRAIN'S NEW YORK BUSINESS. 1478

8756-7911 See COMPUTERITER. 1266
8756-792X See LABOR AND EMPLOYMENT LAW NEWSLETTER. 3150
8756-7938 See BIOTECHNOLOGY PROGRESS. 3689
8756-7962 See FRANCHISE LAW JOURNAL. 3100
8756-7970 See JORDANS' JOURNEYS. 2455
8756-7989 See GENEAGRAM. 2449
8756-8012 See LUCRURI NOI SI VECHI. 4975
8756-8047 See OR MANAGER. 3866
8756-8055 See U.S. TAPE IMPORTS (MANIFEST EDITION). 856
8756-8063 See U.S. TAPE IMPORTS (STATISTICAL ED.). 856
8756-8071 See JOURNAL / HOUSTON ARCHEOLOGICAL SOCIETY. 271
8756-811X See PENN PALS. 2467
8756-8144 See ANNUAL REPORT - NATIONAL INSTITUTES OF HEALTH (U.S.). BIOMEDICAL ENGINEERING AND INSTRUMENTATION BRANCH. 3685
8756-8152 See TRANSACTIONS OF THE SOCIETY OF PETROLEUM ENGINEERS. 4280
8756-8160 See ISSUES IN LAW & MEDICINE. 2985
8756-8179 See CERAMICS AND CIVILIZATION. 2588
8756-8187 See CERAMIC SOURCE. 2587
8756-8225 See JOURNAL OF COLLEGE STUDENT PSYCHOTHERAPY. 4595
8756-8233 See DRUGS & SOCIETY (NEW YORK, N.Y.). 1344
8756-8292 See ANNUAL REPORT / ARKANSAS FORESTRY COMMISSION. 2374
8756-8314 See LOUISIANA FOREST PRODUCTS. 2402
8756-8322 See OKLAHOMA'S WATER QUALITY STANDARDS. 2238
8756-8357 See NEWSLETTER / THE AMERICAN BRAHMS SOCIETY. 4141
8756-8403 See HIGH PROFIT INVESTING. 900
8756-8411 See REAL ESTATE SYNDICATOR, THE. 4845
8756-842X See CAD/CIM ALERT. 1231
8756-8446 See FREMONT COUNTY NOSTALGIA NEWS. 2449
8756-8462 See TRACER - OHIO GENEALOGICAL SOCIETY. HAMILTON COUNTY CHAPTER, THE. 2475
8756-8470 See PROCEEDINGS - SOCIETY OF AUTOMOTIVE ENGINEERS. 1992
8756-8497 See TIME OUT (KANNAPOLIS, N.C.). 4926
8756-8500 See BOGUS REVIEW. 3368
8756-8519 See HOSPITAL ETHICS. 2251
8756-8535 See ESPIONAGE MAGAZINE. 5074
8756-8551 See BODY-MIND NETWORKS. 4768
8756-856X See OPERA-MUSICAL THEATER. 4143
8756-8578 See TECHNOLOGY FOR ANESTHESIA. 3684
8756-8586 See TECHNOLOGY FOR CARDIOLOGY. 3710
8756-8608 See TECHNOLOGY FOR MATERIALS MANAGEMENT. 3644
8756-8616 See TECHNOLOGY FOR RESPIRATORY THERAPY. 3952
8756-8624 See TECHNOLOGY FOR SURGERY. 3976
8756-8640 See G. W. REVIEW, THE. 3389
8756-8667 See FLUTIST QUARTERLY, THE. 4118
8756-8691 See JOURNAL OF WORLD PEACE, THE. 4527
8756-8705 See RURAL SPECIAL EDUCATION QUARTERLY. 1885
8756-8713 See HEALTH DEVICES INSPECTION AND PREVENTIVE MAINTENANCE SYSTEM. 4779
8756-873X See ADVANCED IMMIGRATION WORKSHOP. 2928
8756-8756 See SOUND WORDS (MIFFLINBURG, PA.). 4998
8756-8772 See FOOD BUSINESS MERGERS & ACQUISITIONS. 2336

8756-8780 See COMPUTER AIDED SELLING. 659
8756-8799 See TRAVEL INDUSTRY INDICATORS. 5495
8756-8810 See MACTUTOR. 1280
8756-8829 See COMPUTERS IN CHEMICAL EDUCATION NEWSLETTER. 973
8756-8845 See HARVEST STATES JOURNAL. 202
8756-8853 See SOUTHERN PACIFIC LOCOMOTIVE DIRECTORY. 5436
8756-8861 See SOCIETY NEWS (BROOMALL, PA.). 4153
8756-8888 See FORENSIC ACCOUNTING REVIEW. 3100
8756-8896 See VENTURE CAPITAL JOURNAL ... YEARBOOK. 815
8756-8942 See NEWSLETTER FOR RSEEA. 112
8756-8950 See PRESCRIPTION DRUGS. 4325
8756-8969 See ILLINOIS CODE OF CIVIL PROCEDURE AND COURT RULES. 3090
8756-9000 See LOW INCOME HOME ENERGY ASSISTANCE PROGRAM. 1949
8756-9019 See MAJOR AIRLINES ANALYSIS OF FULL YEAR ... FINANCIAL AND OPERATING RESULTS. 28
8756-9078 See OCCASIONAL PAPERS IN INTERCULTURAL LEARNING. 1769
8756-9086 See CONNECTIVE ISSUES. 3568
8756-9124 See MONEY & REAL ESTATE. 4841
8756-9132 See RAILSBACK LINES. 2469
8756-9175 See ABMS DIRECTORY OF CERTIFIED OPHTHALMOLOGISTS. 3871
8756-9205 See MARYLAND STANDARDS AND SPECIFICATIONS FOR SOIL EROSION AND SEDIMENT CONTROL. 178
8756-9213 See GEISHA GIRL PORCELAIN. 2589
8756-923X See MACHINERY OUTLOOK. 1616
8756-9248 See POLITICAL PULSE. 4489
8756-9256 See NORTH GEORGIA JOURNAL. 2750
8756-9280 See ENVIRONMENTAL LAW SECTION JOURNAL. 3111
8756-9299 See RESEARCH IN PHILOSOPHY & TECHNOLOGY. SUPPLEMENT. 5147
8756-9302 See TRANSPORTATION PRACTITIONERS JOURNAL. 5396
8756-9337 See ICSC MEMBERSHIP DIRECTORY. 681
8756-9353 See AUTO RACING/USA (DALLAS, TEX.). 4885
8756-9396 See INTRODUCTION TO QUALIFIED PENSION AND PROFIT-SHARING PLANS. 1680
8756-940X See VEHICLE IDENTIFICATION. 5427
8756-9418 See HERBERTIA (1984). 2418
8756-9523 See COMPENDIUM OF DRUG THERAPY. 3796
8756-9582 See COMPENDIUM OF DRUG & PATIENT INFORMATION. 3759
8756-9612 See BAPTIST CHALLENGE, THE. 5056
8756-9620 See MAINE BIRDLIFE. 4167
8756-9639 See BUSINESS MEDIA WEEK. 650
8756-9647 See LITALERT (VIENNA, VA.). 1306
8756-9655 See QUARTERLY REVIEW OF METHANE FROM COAL SEAMS TECHNOLOGY. 1392
8756-9663 See ARCHIVAL INFORMER, THE. 2479
8756-968X See ENDOSCOPY REVIEW. 3744
8756-9698 See CATHOLIC RESOURCE NEWSLETTER. 5026
8756-971X See JOURNAL OF THE AMERICAN MOSQUITO CONTROL ASSOCIATION. 4245
8756-9728 See PROJECT MANAGEMENT JOURNAL. 883
8756-9809 See WATER RESOURCES DATA. PUERTO RICO AND THE U.S. VIRGIN ISLANDS. 5545
8756-9817 See RESEARCHIN' OUACHITA-CALHOUN COUNTIES, AR. 2470
8756-9825 See INDUSTRY STANDARDS SERVICE. 1978
8756-9833 See SOFTWARE WRITERS MARKET (POMONA, N.Y.). 1291
8756-9841 See MAINE, NEW HAMPSHIRE, VERMONT ZIP+4 STATE DIRECTORY. 1145

8756-9892 See UNEMPLOYMENT INSURANCE QUALITY APPRAISAL RESULTS. 2895
8756-9930 See CHRISTIAN ACTIVIST, THE. 4944
8756-9965 See MOTC'S NOTEBOOK. 2283
8756-9981 See NEW BEGINNINGS (FRANKLIN PARK, ILL.). 5562
9036-1234 See NONWOVENS ABSTRACTS. 5360
0227-8669 See CANADIAN INDEX (TORONTO). 5781

Peer Reviewed Index

The following index lists all active serials in the Directory that contain peer reviewed / refereed articles or articles reviewed by colleagues. The country of publication and ISSN are provided when available. The page number in bold refers you to the complete serial listing in the Directory.

1:250,000 GEOLOGICAL SERIES. EXPLANATORY NOTES. (AT). **1364**

19TH CENTURY MUSIC. (US/0148-2076). **4098**

A & V, MONOGRAFIAS DE ARQUITECTURA Y VIVIENDA. (SP/0213-487X). **286**

A I M L S SELF ASSESSMENT PROGRAMMES SERIES. (AT). **3891**

A.M. AMMINISTRAZIONE & MANAGEMENT. (IT/1121-0788). **4623**

A.M.E. CHURCH REVIEW, THE. (US/0360-3725). **4931**

A. MAGAZINE. (US/1070-9401). **2253**

A.N.A. AUDIOLOGIA PROTESICA. (SP). **3885**

A.R. PRESS BOLETIN. (AG). **2484**

A.T.A. JOURNAL. (HK/1015-8138). **5347**

A.U.M.L.A. (AT/0001-2793). **3260**

AACN CLINICAL ISSUES IN CRITICAL CARE NURSING. (US/1046-7467). **3849**

AACN NURSING SCAN IN CRITICAL CARE. (US/1055-8349). **3849**

AACSB NEWSLINE. (US/0360-697X). **1806**

AANA JOURNAL. (US/0094-6354). **3849**

AAOHN JOURNAL. (US/0891-0162). **3849**

AAOHN NEWS / AMERICAN ASSOCIATION OF OCCUPATIONAL HEALTH NURSES, INC. (US/0746-620X). **3850**

AAPG BULLETIN. (US/0149-1423). **4248**

AAS HISTORY SERIES. (US/0730-3564). **3**

ABC TODAY. (US/1062-3698). **597**

ABEGWEIT REVIEW. (CN/0382-4632). **2253**

ABERDEEN'S PAVEMENT MAINTENANCE TRADER. (US/1053-2870). **5438**

ABHANDLUNGEN AUS DEM MATHEMATISCHEN SEMINAR DER HAMBURGISCHEN UNIVERSITAT. (GW/0025-5858). **3490**

ABHANDLUNGEN DER SENCKENBERGISCHEN NATURFORSCHENDEN GESELLSCHAFT. (GW/0365-7000). **4161**

ABNF JOURNAL, THE. (US/1046-7041). **3850**

ABORIGINAL LAW BULLETIN. (AT). **2926**

ABSTRACT REVIEW IN SCIENCE EXTENSION. (HU/0238-6178). **5079**

ABSTRACTS OF RESEARCH IN PASTORAL CARE AND COUNSELING. (US/0733-2599). **5012**

ABSTRACTS WITH PROGRAMS - GEOLOGICAL SOCIETY OF AMERICA. (US/0016-7592). **1364**

ACA JOURNAL / AMERICAN COMPENSATION ASSOCIATION. (US/1068-0918). **938**

ACADEMIC MEDICINE. (US/1040-2446). **1806**

ACADEMIC PSYCHIATRY. (US/1042-9670). **3918**

ACADEMY OF MANAGEMENT REVIEW, THE. (US/0363-7425). **859**

ACADIA QUARTERLY / ASSOCIATION FOR COMPUTER-AIDED DESIGN IN ARCHITECTURE. (US). **1231**

ACAFO. (AG). **4366**

ACAROLOGIA. (FR/0044-586X). **5573**

ACCA DOCKET. (US/0895-9544). **3094**

ACCIDENT ANALYSIS AND PREVENTION. (UK/0001-4575). **4763**

ACCIDENT PREVENTION. (CN/0044-5878). **2858**

ACCOUNTING AND BUSINESS RESEARCH. (UK/0001-4788). **736**

ACCOUNTING AND FINANCE. (AT/0110-5159). **736**

ACCOUNTING EDUCATORS' JOURNAL, THE. (US/1041-0392). **736**

ACCOUNTING FORUM (ADELAIDE, S. AUST.). (AT/0155-9982). **737**

ACCOUNTING HISTORIANS JOURNAL, THE. (US/0148-4184). **737**

ACCOUNTING, ORGANIZATIONS AND SOCIETY. (UK/0361-3682). **737**

ACCOUNTING REVIEW, THE. (US/0001-4826). **737**

ACCOUNTS OF CHEMICAL RESEARCH. (US/0001-4842). **958**

ACI MATERIALS JOURNAL. (US/0889-325X). **2018**

ACI STRUCTURAL JOURNAL. (US/0889-3241). **2018**

ACIS : JOURNAL OF THE ASSOCIATION FOR CONTEMPORARY IBERIAN STUDIES. (UK/0955-4270). **3260**

ACM COMPUTING SURVEYS. (US/0360-0300). **1170**

ACM TRANSACTIONS ON COMPUTER SYSTEMS. (US/0734-2071). **1246**

ACM TRANSACTIONS ON DATABASE SYSTEMS. (US/0362-5915). **1252**

ACM TRANSACTIONS ON GRAPHICS. (US/0730-0301). **1231**

ACM TRANSACTIONS ON MATHEMATICAL SOFTWARE. (US/0098-3500). **1283**

ACM TRANSACTIONS ON PROGRAMMING LANGUAGES AND SYSTEMS. (US/0164-0925). **1278**

ACORN JOURNAL. (AT/1031-1017). **3850**

ACORN JOURNAL : OFFICIAL JOURNAL OF THE AUSTRALIAN CONFEDERATION OF OPERATING ROOM NURSES. (AT/0156-3491). **3850**

ACOUSTICS LETTERS. (UK/0140-1599). **4452**

ACQUERELLO ITALIANO (AUDIOCASSETTE). (US). **2513**

ACQUIRED IMMUNE DEFICIENCY SYNDROME NEWSLETTER. (US/1041-4487). **3662**

ACQUISITIONS LIBRARIAN, THE. (US/0896-3576). **3187**

ACQUISIZIONI FUSIONI CONCORRENZA. (IT). **1596**

ACRONYMS. (US/0163-6774). **1170**

ACS SYMPOSIUM SERIES. (US/0097-6156). **959**

ACTA ACADEMIAE ABOENSIS. SERIES: B, MATHEMATICA ET PHYSICA. (FI/0001-5105). **3490**

ACTA ALIMENTARIA (BUDAPEST). (HU/0139-3006). **2325**

ACTA ANAESTHESIOLOGICA ITALICA. (IT/0374-4965). **3680**

ACTA ANAESTHESIOLOGICA SCANDINAVICA. (DK/0001-5172). **3680**

ACTA ANATOMICA. (SZ/0001-5180). **3678**

ACTA APPLICANDAE MATHEMATICAE. (NE/0167-8019). **3490**

ACTA ARITHMETICA. (PL/0065-1036). **3490**

ACTA ASTRONAUTICA. (UK/0094-5765). **3**

ACTA BELGICA HISTORIAE MEDICINAE : OFFICIAL JOURNAL OF THE BELGIAN ASSOCIATION FOR THE HISTORY OF MEDICINE. (BE). **3544**

ACTA BIOCHIMICA ET BIOPHYSICA HUNGARICA. (HU/0237-6261). **479**

ACTA BIOCHIMICA POLONICA. (PL/0001-527X). **479**

ACTA BIOQUIMICA CLINICA LATINOAMERICANA. (AG/0325-2957). **479**

ACTA BIOTECHNOLOGICA. (GW/0138-4988). **3685**

ACTA BIOTHEORETICA. (NE/0001-5342). **440**

ACTA BOTANICA MALACITANA. (SP/0210-9506). **497**

ACTA BOTANICA MEXICANA. (MX/0187-7151). **497**

ACTA BOTANICA NEERLANDICA. (NE/0044-5983). **497**

ACTA BOTANICA SINICA. (US/0095-4195). **497**

ACTA CARDIOLOGICA. (BE/0001-5385). **3697**

ACTA CHEMICA SCANDINAVICA (COPENHAGEN, DENMARK : 1989). (DK/0904-213X). **1049**

ACTA CHIMICA HUNGARICA. (HU/0231-3146). **959**

ACTA CHIRURGICA BELGICA. (BE/0001-5458). **3957**

ACTA CHIRURGICA ITALICA. (IT/0001-5466). **3957**

ACTA — Peer Reviewed Index

ACTA CLINICA BELGICA. (BE/0001-5512). **3544**

ACTA CRYSTALLOGRAPHICA. SECTION B, STRUCTURAL SCIENCE. (DK/0108-7681). **1031**

ACTA CRYSTALLOGRAPHICA. SECTION C, CRYSTAL STRUCTURE COMMUNICATIONS. (DK/0108-2701). **1031**

ACTA CYBERNETICA. (HU/0324-721X). **1250**

ACTA CYTOLOGICA. (US/0001-5547). **531**

ACTA DERMATO-VENEREOLOGICA. (SW/0001-5555). **3717**

ACTA ENDOCRINOLOGICA (COPENHAGEN). (DK/0001-5598). **3726**

ACTA ENTOMOLOGICA BOHEMOSLOVACA. (CS/0001-5601). **5604**

ACTA ENTOMOLOGICA CHILENA. (CL/0716-5072). **5604**

ACTA FARMACEUTICA BONAERENSE. (AG/0326-2383). **4288**

ACTA GASTRO-ENTEROLOGICA BELGICA. (BE/0001-5644). **3743**

ACTA GASTROENTEROLOGICA LATINOAMERICANA. (AG/0300-9033). **3794**

ACTA GENETICAE MEDICAE ET GEMELLOLOGIAE. (IT/0001-5660). **541**

ACTA GEOGRAPHICA SINICA. (CC/0375-5444). **2553**

ACTA GEOLOGICA SINICA : JOURNAL OF THE GEOLOGICAL SOCIETY OF CHINA. (CC/1000-9515). **1364**

ACTA HAEMATOLOGICA. (SZ/0001-5792). **3769**

ACTA HISTOCHEMICA. (GW/0065-1281). **531**

ACTA HISTOCHEMICA ET CYTOCHEMICA. (JA/0044-5991). **531**

ACTA HYDROBIOLOGICA SINICA. (CC/0559-9385). **552**

ACTA INFORMATICA. (GW/0001-5903). **1255**

ACTA IRANICA. DEUXIEME SERIE. HOMMAGES ET OPERA MINORA. (IR/0378-4215). **2767**

ACTA MATHEMATICA. (SW/0001-5962). **3490**

ACTA MATHEMATICA HUNGARICA. (HU/0236-5294). **3490**

ACTA MECHANICA. (AU/0001-5970). **2109**

ACTA MECHANICA SINICA. (CC/0567-7718). **4427**

ACTA MEDICA AUSTRIACA. (AU/0303-8173). **3794**

ACTA MEDICA OKAYAMA. (JA/0386-300X). **3544**

ACTA MICROBIOLOGICA HUNGARICA. (HU/0231-4622). **558**

ACTA NEUROCHIRURGICA. (AU/0001-6268). **3957**

ACTA NEUROLOGICA BELGICA. (BE/0300-9009). **3825**

ACTA NEUROLOGICA SCANDINAVICA. (DK/0001-6314). **3825**

ACTA NEUROPATHOLOGICA. (GW/0001-6322). **3892**

ACTA OBSTETRICIA ET GYNECOLOGICA SCANDINAVICA. (SW/0001-6349). **3756**

ACTA ODONTOLOGICA SCANDINAVICA. (NO/0001-6357). **1315**

ACTA OECONOMICA. (HU/0001-6373). **1460**

ACTA OPHTHALMOLOGICA. (DK/0001-639X). **3545**

ACTA ORTHOPAEDICA SCANDINAVICA. (DK/0001-6470). **3880**

ACTA PAEDIATRICA LATINA. (IT/0365-5504). **3899**

ACTA PATHOLOGICA JAPONICA. (JA/0001-6632). **3892**

ACTA PHARMACEUTICA NORDICA. (SW/1100-1801). **4289**

ACTA PHONIATRICA LATINA. (IT/0392-3088). **3885**

ACTA PHYSICA POLONICA, A. (PL/0587-4246). **4395**

ACTA PHYSICA POLONICA, B. (PL/0587-4254). **4445**

ACTA PHYSIOLOGICA HUNGARICA. (HU/0231-424X). **577**

ACTA PHYSIOLOGICA SCANDINAVICA. SUPPLEMENTUM. (UK/0302-2994). **577**

ACTA POLYMERICA. (GW/0323-7648). **5347**

ACTA PROTOZOOLOGICA. (PL/0065-1583). **5573**

ACTA PSIQUIATRICA Y PSICOLOGICA DE AMERICA LATINA. (AG/0001-6896). **3918**

ACTA PSYCHIATRICA SCANDINAVICA. (DK/0001-690X). **3919**

ACTA PSYCHOLOGICA. (NE/0001-6918). **4570**

ACTA SOCIETATIS BOTANICORUM POLONIAE. (PL/0001-6977). **497**

ACTA SOCIOLOGICA. (DK/0001-6993). **5237**

ACTA THERAPEUTICA. (BE/0378-0619). **4289**

ACTA THERIOLOGICA. (PL/0001-7051). **204**

ACTA TROPICA. (SZ/0001-706X). **3985**

ACTA VETERINARIA (BEOGRAD). (YU/0567-8315). **5501**

ACTA VETERINARIA HUNGARICA (BUDAPEST. 1983). (HU/0236-6290). **5501**

ACTA VETERINARIA SCANDINAVICA. (DK/0044-605X). **5501**

ACTA VIROLOGICA (ANGLICKA VERZE). (XR/0001-723X). **3545**

ACTA ZOOLOGICA MEXICANA. (MX/0065-1737). **5573**

ACTA ZOOLOGICA (STOCKHOLM). (SW/0001-7272). **5574**

ACTES DE LA RECHERCHE EN SCIENCES SOCIALES. (FR/0335-5322). **5189**

ACTES DE LECTURE, LES. (FR/0758-1475). **1722**

ACTION COMMERCIALE, MANUELS. (FR/1142-7086). **920**

ACTION IN TEACHER EDUCATION. (US/0162-6620). **1887**

ACTIVE SOLAR INSTALLATIONS SURVEY. (US/0738-4882). **1930**

ACTIVITIES, ADAPTATION & AGING. (US/0192-4788). **3748**

ACTUALIDAD BIBLIOGRAFICA DE FILOSOFIA Y TEOLOGIA. (SP/0211-4143). **4339**

ACUPUNCTURE & ELECTRO-THERAPEUTICS RESEARCH. (UK/0360-1293). **3545**

ACUSTICA. (GW/0001-7884). **4452**

AD CYCLE NEWSLETTER. (AT). **1170**

AD : REVISTA INTERNACIONAL DE DECORACION, DISENO Y ARQUITECTURA. (SP). **2898**

ADAPTIVE BEHAVIOR. (US/1059-7123). **4571**

ADDICTIVE BEHAVIORS. (UK/0306-4603). **1338**

ADFL BULLETIN. (US/0148-7639). **3261**

ADICCIONES PALMA DE MALLORCA. (SP/0214-4840). **1338**

ADLER (WIEN). (AU/0001-8260). **2436**

ADMINISTRATION & SOCIETY. (US/0095-3997). **4624**

ADMINISTRATION IN SOCIAL WORK. (US/0364-3107). **5270**

ADMINISTRATIVE LAW REVIEW. (US/0001-8368). **3092**

ADMINISTRATIVE SCIENCE QUARTERLY. (US/0001-8392). **4624**

ADMISSION REQUIREMENTS OF U.S. AND CANADIAN DENTAL SCHOOLS. (US/0091-729X). **1315**

ADNEWS (OCT. 13, 1981). (CN/0712-9041). **754**

ADOLESCENCE. (US/0001-8449). **1059**

ADOLESCENT AND PEDIATRIC GYNECOLOGY. (US/0932-8610). **3756**

ADOPTIVE FAMILIES. (US/1076-1020). **5270**

ADULT BASIC EDUCATION (ATHENS, GA.). (US/1052-231X). **1799**

ADULT EDUCATION QUARTERLY (AMERICAN ASSOCIATION FOR ADULT AND CONTINUING EDUCATION). (US/0741-7136). **1799**

ADVANCED COMPOSITE MATERIALS : THE OFFICIAL JOURNAL OF THE JAPAN SOCIETY OF COMPOSITE MATERIALS. (JA/0924-3046). **2100**

ADVANCES IN APPLIED MATHEMATICS. (US/0196-8858). **3491**

ADVANCES IN APPLIED MICROBIOLOGY. (US/0065-2164). **558**

ADVANCES IN APPLIED PROBABILITY. (UK/0001-8678). **3491**

ADVANCES IN BEHAVIOUR RESEARCH AND THERAPY. (UK/0146-6402). **4571**

ADVANCES IN BOTANICAL RESEARCH. (UK/0065-2296). **497**

ADVANCES IN CANCER RESEARCH. (US/0065-230X). **3808**

ADVANCES IN CATALYSIS. (US/0360-0564). **1049**

ADVANCES IN CHEMICAL PHYSICS. (US/0065-2385). **1049**

ADVANCES IN CHEMISTRY SERIES. (US/0065-2393). **959**

ADVANCES IN CHILD DEVELOPMENT AND BEHAVIOR. (US/0065-2407). **4571**

ADVANCES IN CHROMATOGRAPHY (NEW YORK, N.Y.). (US/0065-2415). **1038**

ADVANCES IN CLINICAL CHEMISTRY. (US/0065-2423). **3892**

ADVANCES IN COLLOID AND INTERFACE SCIENCE. (NE/0001-8686). **1049**

ADVANCES IN COMPUTERS. (US/0065-2458). **1255**

ADVANCES IN CONSUMER RESEARCH. (US/0098-9258). **1293**

ADVANCES IN CONTRACEPTION. (UK/0267-4874). **587**

ADVANCES IN DENTAL RESEARCH. (US/0895-9374). **1315**

ADVANCES IN DESCRIPTIVE PSYCHOLOGY. (US/0276-9913). **4571**

ADVANCES IN EATING DISORDERS. (US/1052-0465). **3919**

ADVANCES IN ECOLOGICAL RESEARCH. (UK/0065-2504). **2210**

ADVANCES IN ECONOMIC BOTANY. (US/0741-8280). **498**

ADVANCES IN ELECTRONICS AND ELECTRON PHYSICS. (US/0065-2539). **2034**

ADVANCES IN ENZYME REGULATION. (UK/0065-2571). **531**

ADVANCES IN ENZYMOLOGY AND RELATED SUBJECTS. (US/0065-258X). **479**

ADVANCES IN EXPLORATION IN GEOPHYSICS. (NE). **1365**

ADVANCES IN GENETICS. (US/0065-2660). **542**

ADVANCES IN HUMAN FACTORS / ERGONOMICS. (NE/0921-2647). **2109**

ADVANCES IN HUMAN GENETICS. (US/0065-275X). **542**

ADVANCES IN IMMUNOLOGY. (US/0065-2776). **3662**

ADVANCES IN LIPID RESEARCH. (US/0065-2849). **479**

ADVANCES IN MARINE BIOLOGY. (UK/0065-2881). **552**

ADVANCES IN MATHEMATICS (NEW YORK. 1965). (US/0001-8708). **3491**

ADVANCES IN MICROBIAL ECOLOGY. (US/0147-4863). **2211**

ADVANCES IN MRI CONTRAST. (US/0925-9848). **3938**

ADVANCES IN NEUROIMMUNOLOGY. (UK/0960-5428). **3826**

ADVANCES IN NURSING SCIENCE. (US/0161-9268). **3850**

ADVANCES IN ORGANOMETALLIC CHEMISTRY. (US/0065-3055). **1039**

ADVANCES IN PARASITOLOGY. (UK/0065-308X). **440**

ADVANCES IN PERSONALITY ASSESSMENT. (US/0278-2367). **4572**

ADVANCES IN PHYSICAL ORGANIC CHEMISTRY. (UK/0065-3160). **1049**

ADVANCES IN PHYSICS. (UK/0001-8732). **4396**

ADVANCES IN PHYSIOLOGY EDUCATION. (US/1043-4046). **577**

ADVANCES IN POLYMER SCIENCE. (GW/0065-3195). **1039**

ADVANCES IN PRIMATOLOGY. (US). **5574**

ADVANCES IN SOVIET MATHEMATICS. (US/1051-8037). **3491**

ADVANCES IN THE PSYCHOLOGY OF HUMAN INTELLIGENCE. (US/0278-2359). **4572**

ADVANCES IN VETERINARY SCIENCE AND COMPARATIVE MEDICINE. (US/0065-3519). **5501**

ADVANCES IN VIRUS RESEARCH. (US/0065-3527). **558**

ADVANCES IN WATER RESOURCES. (UK/0309-1708). **5528**

ADVANCES IN WORKING CAPITAL MANAGEMENT. (US/1041-6749). **636**

ADVANCES. THE JOURNAL OF MIND BODY HEALTH. (US). **3546**

ADVOCATE (BOISE, IDAHO), THE. (US/0515-4987). **2928**

AEB, ANALYTICAL & ENUMERATIVE BIBLIOGRAPHY. (US/0161-0376). **3457**

AEROESPACIO (BUENOS AIRES, ARGENTINA). (AG). **4**

AERONAUTICA & DIFESA. (IT/0394-820X). **4**

AERONAUTICAL JOURNAL, THE. (UK/0001-9240). **4**

AEROSOL SCIENCE AND TECHNOLOGY. (US/0278-6826). **1020**

AEROSPACE AMERICA. (US/0740-722X). **5**

AESTHETIC PLASTIC SURGERY. (US/0364-216X). **3958**

AEU. ARCHIV. FUER ELEKTRONIK UND UBERTRAGUNGSTECHNIK. (GW/0001-1096). **1148**

AFAS QUARTERLY OF THE AUTOMOTIVE FINE ARTS SOCIETY. (US/0899-9171). **5403**

AFERS INTERNACIONALS. (SP/0212-1786). **4461**

AFGHANISTAN STUDIES JOURNAL. (US/1046-9834). **2501**

AFINIDAD. (SP/0001-9704). **960**

AFRICA FORUM. (UK/0961-1142). **2501**

AFRICA QUARTERLY. (II/0001-9828). **2636**

AFRICA TODAY. (US/0001-9887). **4462**

AFRICAN AFFAIRS (LONDON). (UK/0001-9909). **4462**

AFRICAN ARTS. (US/0001-9933). **312**

AFRICAN ENTOMOLOGY. (SA/1021-3589). **5605**

AFRICAN JOURNAL OF ECOLOGY. (UK/0141-6707). **2211**

AFRICAN LANGUAGES AND CULTURES. (UK/0954-416X). **3262**

AFRICAN STUDIES (JOHANNESBURG). (SA/0002-0184). **227**

AFRICAN URBAN QUARTERLY. (US/0747-6108). **2813**

AFRICAN WOMAN. (UK/0953-9816). **5550**

AFRIKA JAHRBUCH. (GW). **4462**

AFRO-AMERICANS IN NEW YORK LIFE AND HISTORY. (US/0364-2437). **2254**

AFRO-ASIAN JOURNAL OF NEMATOLOGY. (UK/0963-6420). **5574**

AFRO-HISPANIC REVIEW. (US/0278-8969). **3262**

AGE AND AGEING. (UK/0002-0729). **3748**

AGE (OMAHA). (US/0161-9152). **3748**

AGENDA PARKVILLE. (AT/1033-1115). **312**

AGENTS AND ACTIONS. (SZ/0065-4299). **4289**

AGGRESSIVE BEHAVIOR. (US/0096-140X). **4572**

AGING, IMMUNOLOGY AND INFECTIOUS DISEASE. (US/0892-8762). **3662**

AGIS : ATTORNEY-GENERAL'S INFORMATION SERVICE. (AT/0312-4592). **2928**

AGORA, PAPELES DE FILOSOFIA. (SP). **4339**

AGORA PARIS. 1986. (FR/0984-4783). **2249**

AGRIBUSINESS NEWS FOR KENTUCKY. (US/0899-1294). **48**

AGRICULTURA (MADRID, SPAIN). (SP/0002-1334). **49**

AGRICULTURA TECNICA. (CL/0365-2807). **49**

AGRICULTURAL AND FOREST METEOROLOGY. (NE/0168-1923). **1419**

AGRICULTURAL ECONOMICS RESEARCH REPORT (MISSISSIPPI AGRICULTURAL AND FORESTRY EXPERIMENT STATION). (US). **50**

AGRICULTURAL ECONOMICS TECHNICAL PUBLICATION. (US/0883-0088). **50**

AGRICULTURAL ENGINEERING. (US/0002-1458). **1964**

AGRICULTURAL ENGINEERING AUSTRALIA. (AT/0044-6807). **50**

AGRICULTURAL FINANCE REVIEW. (US/0002-1466). **769**

AGRICULTURAL HISTORY. (US/0002-1482). **50**

AGRICULTURAL RESEARCH (WASHINGTON). (US/0002-161X). **51**

AGRICULTURAL SYSTEMS. (UK/0308-521X). **52**

AGRICULTURAL WATER MANAGEMENT. (NE/0378-3774). **52**

AGRICULTURE AND HUMAN VALUES. (US/0889-048X). **53**

AGRICULTURE, ECOSYSTEMS & ENVIRONMENT. (NE/0167-8809). **53**

AGRISCIENCE (OTTAWA). (CN/0840-8289). **54**

AGRISCIENTIA. (AG). **54**

AGROBOREALIS. (US/0002-1822). **55**

AGROCIENCIA. SERIE CIENCIA ANIMAL. (MX/0188-3038). **55**

AGROCIENCIA. SERIE FITOCIENCIA. (MX/0188-302X). **55**

AGROCIENCIA. SERIE MATEMATICAS APLICADAS, ESTADISTICA Y COMPUTACION. (MX/0188-3054). **3491**

AGROCIENCIA. SERIE PROTECCION VEGETAL. (MX/0188-3046). **55**

AGROCIENCIA. SERIE RECURSOS NATURALES RENOVABLES. (MX/0188-3062). **55**

AGROCIENCIA. SERIE SOCIOECONOMIA. (MX/0188-3070). **1461**

AGROFORESTRY SYSTEMS. (NE/0167-4366). **2211**

AGRONOMIE. (FR/0249-5627). **56**

AGRONOMIE TROPICALE, L'. (FR/0002-1946). **162**

AHFAD JOURNAL, THE. (SJ/0255-4070). **5550**

AI MAGAZINE. (US/0738-4602). **1211**

AIAA JOURNAL. (US/0001-1452). **6**

AIBC BULLETIN. (US/1040-6018). **1419**

AICHE JOURNAL. (US/0001-1541). **2007**

AIDS & PUBLIC POLICY JOURNAL. (US/0887-3852). **3663**

AIDS CARE. (UK/0954-0121). **3663**

AIDS EDUCATION AND PREVENTION. (US/0899-9546). **4764**

AIDS/HIV TREATMENT DIRECTORY. (US/1057-5065). **3663**

AIDS (LONDON). (UK/0269-9370). **3664**

AIDS RESEARCH AND HUMAN RETROVIRUSES. (US/0889-2229). **3664**

AIPE FACILITIES. (US/1054-7541). **1964**

AIR FAN. (FR/0223-0038). **4033**

AIR FORCE TIMES. (US/0002-2403). **4034**

AITIM : BOLETIN DE INFORMACION TECNICA / ASOCIACION DE INVESTIGACION TECHNICA DE LAS INDUSTRIAS DE LA MADERNA Y CORCHO. (PO). **2374**

AKTUELLE NEUROLOGIE. (GW/0302-4350). **3826**

AKTUELLE RHEUMATOLOGIE. (GW/0341-051X). **3802**

AL-GEZIRA. (SP/0213-2966). **2609**

ALABAMA BIRDLIFE. (US/0516-3870). **5614**

ALABAMA LITERARY REVIEW. (US/0890-1554). **3359**

ALABAMA MUNICIPAL JOURNAL, THE. (US/0002-4309). **4625**

ALABAMA PURCHASOR. (US/0002-4325). **948**

ALABAMA REVIEW, THE. (US/0002-4341). **2718**

ALASKA FISHERY RESEARCH BULLETIN. (US). **2293**

ALASKA MEDICINE. (US/0002-4538). **3547**

ALASKA'S WILDLIFE. (US/1052-2727). **4868**

ALBERTA (EDMONTON). (CN/0843-9931). **312**

ALBERTA JOURNAL OF EDUCATIONAL RESEARCH. (CN/0002-4805). **1723**

ALBUM. (SP). **2841**

ALCHERINGA (SYDNEY). (AT/0311-5518). **4226**

ALCOHOL AND ALCOHOLISM (OXFORD). (UK/0735-0414). **1339**

ALCOHOL (FAYETTEVILLE, N.Y.). (US/0741-8329). **1339**

ALCOHOL HEALTH AND RESEARCH WORLD. (US/0090-838X). **1339**

ALCOHOLISM : CLINICAL AND EXPERIMENTAL RESEARCH. (US/0145-6008). **1340**

ALCOHOLISM TREATMENT QUARTERLY. (US/0734-7324). **1340**

ALCOLOGIA. (IT/0394-9826). **1340**

ALEPH (MANIZALES, COLOMBIA). (CK/0120-0216). **3359**

ALERGIA (MEXICO). (MX/0002-5151). **3665**

ALGEBRA UNIVERSALIS. (CN/0002-5240). **3491**

ALGORITHMICA. (US/0178-4617). **1170**

ALI ANTICHE. (IT/0394-6185). **11**

ALIMENTA. (SZ/0002-5402). **2326**

ALIMENTARY PHARMACOLOGY & THERAPEUTICS. (UK/0269-2813). **4290**

ALISO. (US/0065-6275). **498**

ALLERGOLOGIA ET IMMUNOPATHOLOGIA. (SP/0301-0546). **3665**

ALLERGOLOGIE. (GW/0344-5062). **3665**

ALLERGY PROCEEDINGS. (US/1046-9354). **3666**

ALLGEMEINE FORST UND JAGDZEITUNG. (GW/0002-5852). **2374**

ALPHA BEAT SOUP. (CN/0838-391X). **3359**

ALTERNATIVES ECONOMIQUES DIJON. (FR/0247-3739). **1589**

ALTERNATIVES (PETERBOROUGH). (CN/0002-6638). **2159**

ALYTES. (FR/0753-4973). **5574**

AMBIENTE MEDICO : REVISTA DEL HOSPITAL J.A. FERNANDEZ. (AG/0326-0674). **3775**

AMBIENTE RISORSE SALUTE. (IT/0393-0521). **2160**

AMBIO. (SW/0044-7447). **2160**

AMBULATORY SURGERY. (UK/0966-6532). **3958**

AMEGHINIANA. (AG/0002-7014). **4226**

AMERASIA JOURNAL. (US/0044-7471). **2254**

AMERICAN ANNALS OF THE DEAF (WASHINGTON, D.C. 1886). (US/0002-726X). **4383**

AMERICAN ANTHROPOLOGIST. (US/0002-7294). **227**

AMERICAN ANTIQUITY; A QUARTERLY REVIEW OF AMERICAN ARCHAEOLOGY. (US/0002-7316). **253**

AMERICAN ARCHIVIST, THE. (US/0360-9081). **2478**

AMERICAN ART / NATIONAL MUSEUM OF AMERICAN ART, SMITHSONIAN INSTITUTION. (US). **336**

AMERICAN ASIAN REVIEW, THE. (US/0737-6650). **2645**

AMERICAN BANKRUPTCY LAW JOURNAL, THE. (US/0027-9048). **3084**

AMERICAN BEE JOURNAL. (US/0002-7626). **58**

AMERICAN BEHAVIORAL SCIENTIST (BEVERLY HILLS). (US/0002-7642). **5190**

AMERICAN BIOLOGY TEACHER, THE. (US/0002-7685). **441**

AMERICAN BIOTECHNOLOGY LABORATORY. (US/0749-3223). **3685**

AMERICAN BREWER (HAYWARD, CALIF.). (US/1055-470X). **2363**

AMERICAN BUSINESS LAW JOURNAL. (US/0002-7766). **3095**

AMERICAN CENTER FOR DESIGN JOURNAL. (US/1062-0966). **287**

AMERICAN CERAMIC SOCIETY BULLETIN. (US/0002-7812). **2586**

AMERICAN CRIMINAL LAW REVIEW, THE. (US/0164-0364). **3105**

AMERICAN ECONOMIC REVIEW, THE. (US/0002-8282). **1461**

AMERICAN EDUCATIONAL RESEARCH JOURNAL. (US/0002-8312). **1723**

AMERICAN ETHNOLOGIST. (US/0094-0496). **228**

AMERICAN FAMILY PHYSICIAN (1970). (US/0002-838X). **3736**

AMERICAN FERN JOURNAL. (US/0002-8444). **498**

AMERICAN GENEALOGIST (DES MOINES). (US/0002-8592). **2437**

AMERICAN HEART JOURNAL, THE. (US/0002-8703). **3698**

AMERICAN INDIAN AND ALASKA NATIVE MENTAL HEALTH RESEARCH. (US/0893-5394). **5271**

AMERICAN INDIAN CULTURE AND RESEARCH JOURNAL. (US/0161-6463). **2254**

AMERICAN INDIAN QUARTERLY. (US/0095-182X). **2255**

AMERICAN INDUSTRIAL HYGIENE ASSOCIATION JOURNAL. (US/0002-8894). **2858**

AMERICAN INVENTOR (BLOOMINGTON, IND.). (US/1042-1890). **5082**

AMERICAN JEWISH ARCHIVES. (US/0002-905X). **2255**

AMERICAN

AMERICAN JOURNAL OF ACUPUNCTURE. (US/0091-3960). **3548**

AMERICAN JOURNAL OF AGRICULTURAL ECONOMICS. (US/0002-9092). **58**

AMERICAN JOURNAL OF ALZHEIMER'S CARE AND RELATED DISORDERS & RESEARCH. (US/0895-5336). **3827**

AMERICAN JOURNAL OF CARDIAC IMAGING. (US/0887-7971). **3698**

AMERICAN JOURNAL OF CARDIOLOGY, THE. (US/0002-9149). **3698**

AMERICAN JOURNAL OF CASE MANAGEMENT, THE. (US/1051-8967). **5190**

AMERICAN JOURNAL OF CHINESE MEDICINE, THE. (US/0192-415X). **3548**

AMERICAN JOURNAL OF CLINICAL HYPNOSIS, THE. (US/0002-9157). **2857**

AMERICAN JOURNAL OF CLINICAL NUTRITION, THE. (US/0002-9165). **4187**

AMERICAN JOURNAL OF CLINICAL ONCOLOGY. (US/0277-3732). **3808**

AMERICAN JOURNAL OF CLINICAL PATHOLOGY. (US/0002-9173). **3892**

AMERICAN JOURNAL OF COMMUNITY PSYCHOLOGY. (US/0091-0562). **4573**

AMERICAN JOURNAL OF COMPARATIVE LAW, THE. (US/0002-919X). **3123**

AMERICAN JOURNAL OF CRIMINAL JUSTICE : AJCJ. (US/1066-2316). **3156**

AMERICAN JOURNAL OF CRITICAL CARE. (US/1062-3264). **3850**

AMERICAN JOURNAL OF DENTISTRY. (US/0894-8275). **1315**

AMERICAN JOURNAL OF DERMATOPATHOLOGY, THE. (US/0193-1091). **3717**

AMERICAN JOURNAL OF DISEASES OF CHILDREN (1960). (US/0002-922X). **3899**

AMERICAN JOURNAL OF DRUG AND ALCOHOL ABUSE, THE. (US/0095-2990). **1340**

AMERICAN JOURNAL OF ECONOMICS AND SOCIOLOGY, THE. (US/0002-9246). **5190**

AMERICAN JOURNAL OF EDUCATION (CHICAGO). (US/0195-6744). **1724**

AMERICAN JOURNAL OF EMERGENCY MEDICINE, THE. (US/0735-6757). **3723**

AMERICAN JOURNAL OF ENOLOGY AND VITICULTURE. (US/0002-9254). **2363**

AMERICAN JOURNAL OF EPIDEMIOLOGY. (US/0002-9262). **3734**

AMERICAN JOURNAL OF FAMILY THERAPY, THE. (US/0192-6187). **4573**

AMERICAN JOURNAL OF FORENSIC MEDICINE AND PATHOLOGY, THE. (US/0195-7910). **3739**

AMERICAN JOURNAL OF GASTROENTEROLOGY, THE. (US/0002-9270). **3743**

AMERICAN JOURNAL OF GERIATRIC CARDIOLOGY, THE. (US). **3698**

AMERICAN JOURNAL OF GERIATRIC PSYCHIATRY, THE. (US/1064-7481). **3749**

AMERICAN JOURNAL OF HEALTH PROMOTION. (US/0890-1171). **4764**

AMERICAN JOURNAL OF HEMATOLOGY. (US/0361-8609). **3770**

AMERICAN JOURNAL OF HOSPICE AND PALLIATIVE CARE, THE. (US/1049-9091). **5271**

AMERICAN JOURNAL OF HOSPITAL PHARMACY. (US/0002-9289). **4290**

AMERICAN JOURNAL OF HUMAN GENETICS. (US/0002-9297). **542**

AMERICAN JOURNAL OF HYPERTENSION. (US/0895-7061). **3698**

AMERICAN JOURNAL OF INDUSTRIAL MEDICINE. (US/0271-3586). **3548**

AMERICAN JOURNAL OF INFECTION CONTROL. (US/0196-6553). **3734**

AMERICAN JOURNAL OF JURISPRUDENCE (NOTRE DAME), THE. (US/0065-8995). **2932**

AMERICAN JOURNAL OF KIDNEY DISEASES. (US/0272-6386). **3988**

AMERICAN JOURNAL OF LAW & MEDICINE. (US/0098-8588). **2932**

AMERICAN JOURNAL OF LEGAL HISTORY, THE. (US/0002-9319). **2932**

AMERICAN JOURNAL OF MATHEMATICAL AND MANAGEMENT SCIENCES. (US/0196-6324). **3492**

AMERICAN JOURNAL OF MATHEMATICS. (US/0002-9327). **3492**

AMERICAN JOURNAL OF MEDICAL GENETICS. (US/0148-7299). **542**

AMERICAN JOURNAL OF MEDICAL QUALITY. (US/1062-8606). **3776**

AMERICAN JOURNAL OF MEDICINE, THE. (US/0002-9343). **3548**

AMERICAN JOURNAL OF NEPHROLOGY. (SZ/0250-8095). **3988**

AMERICAN JOURNAL OF NEURORADIOLOGY. (US/0195-6108). **3827**

AMERICAN JOURNAL OF OBSTETRICS AND GYNECOLOGY. (US/0002-9378). **3756**

AMERICAN JOURNAL OF OCCUPATIONAL THERAPY, THE. (US/0272-9490). **1874**

AMERICAN JOURNAL OF OPHTHALMOLOGY. (US/0002-9394). **3871**

AMERICAN JOURNAL OF ORTHODONTICS AND DENTOFACIAL ORTHOPEDICS. (US/0889-5406). **1315**

AMERICAN JOURNAL OF ORTHOPSYCHIATRY. (US/0002-9432). **3919**

AMERICAN JOURNAL OF OTOLARYNGOLOGY. (US/0196-0709). **3885**

AMERICAN JOURNAL OF OTOLOGY (NEW YORK, N.Y.), THE. (US/0192-9763). **3886**

AMERICAN JOURNAL OF PAIN MANAGEMENT. (US/1059-1494). **3548**

AMERICAN JOURNAL OF PATHOLOGY, THE. (US/0002-9440). **3892**

AMERICAN JOURNAL OF PEDIATRIC HEMATOLOGY/ONCOLOGY, THE. (US/0192-8562). **3900**

AMERICAN JOURNAL OF PERINATOLOGY. (US/0735-1631). **3756**

AMERICAN JOURNAL OF PHARMACEUTICAL EDUCATION. (US/0002-9459). **4290**

AMERICAN JOURNAL OF PHYSICAL ANTHROPOLOGY. (US/0002-9483). **228**

AMERICAN JOURNAL OF PHYSICAL MEDICINE & REHABILITATION. (US/0894-9115). **4379**

AMERICAN JOURNAL OF PHYSICS. (US/0002-9505). **4396**

AMERICAN JOURNAL OF PHYSIOLOGIC IMAGING. (US/0885-8276). **577**

AMERICAN JOURNAL OF PHYSIOLOGY. (US/0002-9513). **577**

AMERICAN JOURNAL OF PHYSIOLOGY : CELL PHYSIOLOGY. (US/0363-6143). **577**

AMERICAN JOURNAL OF PHYSIOLOGY : HEART AND CIRCULATORY PHYSIOLOGY. (US/0363-6135). **578**

AMERICAN JOURNAL OF POLITICAL SCIENCE. (US/0092-5853). **4463**

AMERICAN JOURNAL OF PREVENTIVE MEDICINE. (US/0749-3797). **3549**

AMERICAN JOURNAL OF PRIMATOLOGY. (US/0275-2565). **5574**

AMERICAN JOURNAL OF PSYCHIATRY, THE. (US/0002-953X). **3920**

AMERICAN JOURNAL OF PSYCHOLOGY, THE. (US/0002-9556). **4573**

AMERICAN JOURNAL OF PSYCHOTHERAPY. (US/0002-9564). **3920**

AMERICAN JOURNAL OF PUBLIC HEALTH (1971). (US/0090-0036). **4764**

AMERICAN JOURNAL OF RESPIRATORY CELL AND MOLECULAR BIOLOGY. (US/1044-1549). **3948**

AMERICAN JOURNAL OF RHINOLOGY. (US/1050-6586). **3886**

AMERICAN JOURNAL OF ROENTGENOLOGY (1976). (US/0361-803X). **3938**

AMERICAN JOURNAL OF SCIENCE (1880). (US/0002-9599). **5082**

AMERICAN JOURNAL OF SOCIOLOGY. (US/0002-9602). **5238**

AMERICAN JOURNAL OF SPORTS MEDICINE, THE. (US/0363-5465). **3953**

AMERICAN JOURNAL OF SURGERY, THE. (US/0002-9610). **3958**

AMERICAN JOURNAL OF SURGICAL PATHOLOGY, THE. (US/0147-5185). **3892**

AMERICAN JOURNAL OF THE MEDICAL SCIENCES, THE. (US/0002-9629). **3549**

AMERICAN JOURNAL OF THEOLOGY & PHILOSOPHY. (US/0194-3448). **4340**

AMERICAN JOURNAL OF TROPICAL MEDICINE AND HYGIENE, THE. (US/0002-9637). **3985**

AMERICAN JOURNAL OF VETERINARY RESEARCH. (US/0002-9645). **5502**

AMERICAN JOURNAL ON ADDICTIONS, THE. (US/1055-0496). **1340**

AMERICAN JOURNALISM. (US/0882-1127). **2917**

AMERICAN LABORATORY (FAIRFIELD). (US/0044-7749). **960**

AMERICAN LITERARY HISTORY. (US/0896-7148). **3360**

AMERICAN LITERARY REVIEW. (US/1051-5062). **3360**

AMERICAN MALACOLOGICAL BULLETIN. (US/0740-2783). **5574**

AMERICAN MATHEMATICAL MONTHLY, THE. (US/0002-9890). **3492**

AMERICAN MIDDLE SCHOOL EDUCATION. (US/0889-552X). **1860**

AMERICAN MIDLAND NATURALIST, THE. (US/0003-0031). **4161**

AMERICAN MINERALOGIST, THE. (US/0003-004X). **1437**

AMERICAN MUSIC RESEARCH CENTER JOURNAL, THE. (US/1058-3572). **4099**

AMERICAN NATURALIST, THE. (US/0003-0147). **4161**

AMERICAN PHARMACY. (US/0160-3450). **4290**

AMERICAN POLITICAL SCIENCE REVIEW, THE. (US/0003-0554). **4463**

AMERICAN POLITICS QUARTERLY. (US/0044-7803). **4463**

AMERICAN POTATO JOURNAL. (US/0003-0589). **162**

AMERICAN PROFESSIONAL CONSTRUCTOR, THE. (US/0146-7557). **2018**

AMERICAN REVIEW OF PUBLIC ADMINISTRATION. (US/0275-0740). **4625**

AMERICAN REVIEW OF RESPIRATORY DISEASE, THE. (US/0003-0805). **3948**

AMERICAN SCIENTIST. (US/0003-0996). **5082**

AMERICAN SECONDARY EDUCATION. (US/0003-1003). **1724**

AMERICAN SERIES IN MATHEMATICAL AND MANAGEMENT SCIENCES. (US/0883-6221). **3492**

AMERICAN SOCIOLOGICAL REVIEW. (US/0003-1224). **5238**

AMERICAN SPEECH. (US/0003-1283). **3263**

AMERICAN STATISTICIAN, THE. (US/0003-1305). **5320**

AMERICAN STUDIES INTERNATIONAL. (US/0883-105X). **2719**

AMERICAN STUDIES (LAWRENCE). (US/0026-3079). **2719**

AMERICAN SURGEON, THE. (US/0003-1348). **3958**

AMERICAN UNIVERSITY JOURNAL OF INTERNATIONAL LAW AND POLICY, THE. (US/0888-630X). **3123**

AMERICAN UNIVERSITY LAW REVIEW, THE. (US/0003-1453). **2933**

AMERICAN ZOOLOGIST. (US/0003-1569). **5574**

AMERICAS REVIEW (HOUSTON, TEX.). (US/1042-6213). **3360**

AMERIKASTUDIEN. (GW/0340-2827). **2720**

AMMONITE GILLINGHAM, DORSET. (UK/0951-2500). **2318**

ANAESTHESIA. (UK/0003-2409). **3680**

ANAESTHESIA AND INTENSIVE CARE. (AT/0310-057X). **3680**

ANAESTHESIST, DER. (GW/0003-2417). **3681**

ANALELE UNIVERSITATI DIN GALATI. FASCICULA II - MATEMATICA, FIZICA, MECANICA TEORETICA. (RM). **3492**

ANALELE UNIVERSITATII DIN GALATI. FASCICULA I, STIINTE SOCIALE SI UMANISTE. (RM/1015-9606). **5190**

ANALES. (SP/0034-0618). **4290**

ANALES DE LA ESTACION EXPERIMENTAL DE AULA DEI. (SP/0365-1800). **58**

ANALES DE LA LITERATURA ESPANOLA CONTEMPORANEA. (US/0272-1635). **3361**

ANALES DE LITERATURA HISPANOAMERICANA. (SP). **3361**

ANALES DEL INSTITUTO DE BIOLOGIA, UNIVERSIDAD NACIONAL AUTONOMA DE MEXICO. SERIE BOTANICA. (MX/0374-5511). **498**

ANALES DEL INSTITUTO DE BIOLOGIA, UNIVERSIDAD NACIONAL AUTONOMA DE MEXICO. SERIE ZOOLOGIA. (MX/0368-8720). **5575**

ANALES DEL INSTITUTO DE INVESTIGACIONES MARINAS DE PUNTA DE BETIN. (CK/0120-3959). **552**

ANALES DEL INSTITUTO DE MATEMATICAS. (MX/0185-0644). **3492**

ANALES ESPANOLES DE PEDIATRIA. (SP/0302-4342). **3900**

ANALES OTORRINOLARINGOLOGICOS IBERO-AMERICANOS. (SP/0303-8874). **3886**

ANALISIS FILOSOFICO. (AG/0326-1301). **4340**

ANALISIS FINANCIERO. (SP). **770**

ANALOG INTEGRATED CIRCUITS AND SIGNAL PROCESSING. (US/0925-1030). **2035**

ANALUSIS. (FR/0365-4877). **1012**

ANALYSE. (NE/0166-7688). **3549**

ANALYSIS OF VERBAL BEHAVIOR, THE. (US/0889-9401). **4573**

ANALYST (LONDON). (UK/0003-2654). **1012**

ANALYTIC TEACHING. (US/0890-5118). **4340**

ANALYTICA CHIMICA ACTA. (NE/0003-2670). **1012**

ANALYTICAL AND QUANTITATIVE CYTOLOGY AND HISTOLOGY. (US/0884-6812). **531**

ANALYTICAL BIOCHEMISTRY. (US/0003-2697). **479**

ANALYTICAL CHEMISTRY (WASHINGTON). (US/0003-2700). **1013**

ANALYTICAL INSTRUMENTATION. (US/0743-5797). **3549**

ANALYTICAL LETTERS. (US/0003-2719). **1013**

ANALYTICAL SCIENCES : THE INTERNATIONAL JOURNAL OF THE JAPAN SOCIETY FOR ANALYTICAL CHEMISTRY. (JA/0910-6340). **1013**

ANALYTISCHE PSYCHOLOGIE. (SZ/0301-3006). **4573**

ANATOMICAL RECORD, THE. (US/0003-276X). **3678**

ANATOMISCHER ANZEIGER. (GW/0003-2786). **3678**

ANATOMY AND EMBRYOLOGY. (GW/0340-2061). **3678**

ANCESTORING. (US/0272-0426). **2437**

ANCESTRY (SALT LAKE CITY, UTAH). (US/1075-475X). **2437**

ANCIENT PHILOSOPHY (PITTSBURGH, PA.). (US/0740-2007). **4340**

ANCIENT TL. (UK/0735-1348). **254**

ANCIENT WORLD, THE. (US/0160-9645). **254**

ANDROLOGIA (BERLIN, WEST). (GW/0303-4569). **3549**

ANESTHESIA AND ANALGESIA. (US/0003-2999). **3681**

ANESTHESIOLOGY (PHILADELPHIA). (US/0003-3022). **3681**

ANESTHESIOLOGY REVIEW. (US/0093-4437). **3681**

ANGEWANDTE BOTANIK. (GW/0066-1759). **499**

ANGEWANDTE CHEMIE. INTERNATIONAL EDITION IN ENGLISH. (GW/0570-0833). **960**

ANGEWANDTE MAKROMOLEKULARE CHEMIE. (SZ/0003-3146). **4454**

ANGIOLOGY. (US/0003-3197). **3794**

ANGLE ORTHODONTIST, THE. (US/0003-3219). **1316**

ANGLICAN AND EPISCOPAL HISTORY. (US/0896-8039). **5055**

ANGLICAN THEOLOGICAL REVIEW. (US/0003-3286). **4934**

ANGLICAN THEOLOGICAL REVIEW. SUPPLEMENTARY SERIES. (US/0097-4951). **4934**

ANIMAL BEHAVIOUR. (UK/0003-3472). **5575**

ANIMAL FEED SCIENCE AND TECHNOLOGY. (NE/0377-8401). **199**

ANIMAL GENETICS. (UK/0268-9146). **542**

ANIMAL KEEPERS' FORUM. (US/0164-9531). **5575**

ANIMAL LEARNING & BEHAVIOR. (US/0090-4996). **5575**

ANIMAL MODELS OF HUMAN DISEASE. (US). **3892**

ANIMAL REPRODUCTION SCIENCE. (NE/0378-4320). **5503**

ANIMATION JOURNAL. (US/1061-0308). **4063**

ANNALEN DER PHYSIK. (GW/0003-3804). **4396**

ANNALES ACADEMIAE SCIENTIARUM FENNICAE. SERIES A. I, MATHEMATICA (HELSINKI, FINLAND : 1975). (FI/0066-1953). **3493**

ANNALES BOTANICI FENNICI. (FI/0003-3847). **499**

ANNALES CHIRURGIAE ET GYNAECOLOGIAE. (FI/0355-9521). **3756**

ANNALES DE BIOLOGIE CLINIQUE (PARIS). (FR/0003-3898). **3892**

ANNALES DE BRETAGNE ET DES PAYS DE L'OUEST. (FR/0399-0826). **2674**

ANNALES DE CARDIOLOGIE ET D'ANGEIOLOGIE. (FR/0003-3928). **3698**

ANNALES DE CHIRURGIE. (FR/0003-3944). **3958**

ANNALES DE DERMATOLOGIE ET DE VENEREOLOGIE. (FR/0151-9638). **3717**

ANNALES DE GASTROENTEROLOGIE ET D'HEPATOLOGIE. (FR/0066-2070). **3743**

ANNALES DE GENETIQUE. (FR/0003-3995). **542**

ANNALES DE LA SOCIETE BELGE DE MEDECINE TROPICALE. (BE/0365-6527). **3985**

ANNALES DE LA SOCIETE ENTOMOLOGIQUE DE FRANCE. (FR/0037-9271). **5575**

ANNALES DE L'I.H.P. PHYSIQUE THEORIQUE. (FR/0246-0211). **4396**

ANNALES DE L'I.H.P. PROBABILITES ET STATISTIQUES. (FR/0246-0203). **3493**

ANNALES DE L'INSTITUT FOURIER. (FR/0373-0956). **3493**

ANNALES DE L'INSTITUT HENRI POINCARE. ANALYSE NON LINEAIRE. (FR/0294-1449). **3493**

ANNALES DE L'INSTITUT PHYTOPATHOLOGIQUE BENAKI. (GR/0365-5814). **499**

ANNALES DE MEDECINE INTERNE. (FR/0003-410X). **3794**

ANNALES DE MEDECINE VETERINAIRE. (BE/0003-4118). **5503**

ANNALES DE PARASITOLOGIE HUMAINE ET COMPAREE. (FR/0003-4150). **441**

ANNALES DE PATHOLOGIE. (FR/0242-6498). **3893**

ANNALES DE PEDIATRIE (PARIS). (FR/0066-2097). **3900**

ANNALES DE PHYSIQUE (PARIS). (FR/0003-4169). **4397**

ANNALES DE RADIOLOGIE. (FR/0003-4185). **3938**

ANNALES DE RECHERCHES VETERINAIRES. (FR/0003-4193). **5503**

ANNALES DE ZOOTECHNIE. (FR/0003-424X). **5575**

ANNALES D'ENDOCRINOLOGIE. (FR/0003-4266). **3726**

ANNALES DES SCIENCES FORESTIERES. (FR/0003-4312). **2374**

ANNALES DES SCIENCES MATHEMATIQUES DU QUEBEC. (CN/0707-9109). **3493**

ANNALES DES SCIENCES NATURELLES. (FR/0003-4320). **499**

ANNALES DES SCIENCES NATURELLES. ZOOLOGIE ET BIOLOGIE ANIMALE. (FR/0003-4339). **5575**

ANNALES DES TELECOMMUNICATIONS. (FR/0003-4347). **1148**

ANNALES D'UROLOGIE. (FR/0003-4401). **3988**

ANNALES MEDICO PSYCHOLOGIQUES. (FR/0003-4487). **4573**

ANNALES SCIENTIFIQUES DE L'ECOLE NORMALE SUPERIEURE. (FR/0012-9593). **3493**

ANNALI DEL DIPARTIMENTO DI FILOSOFIA / UNIVERSITA DE FIRENZE. (IT). **4341**

ANNALI DI CHIMICA. (IT/0003-4592). **961**

ANNALI DI MICROBIOLOGIA ED ENZIMOLOGIA. (IT/0003-4649). **558**

ANNALI ITALIANI DI MEDICINA INTERNA : ORGANO UFFICIALE DELLA SOCIETA ITALIANA DI MEDICINA INTERNA. (IT/0393-9340). **3794**

ANNALS OF AGRICULTURAL SCIENCE, MOSHTOHOR. (UA/0570-1791). **59**

ANNALS OF ALLERGY. (US/0003-4738). **3666**

ANNALS OF APPLIED BIOLOGY. (UK/0003-4746). **442**

ANNALS OF ARID ZONE. (II/0570-1791). **162**

ANNALS OF BEHAVIORAL MEDICINE. (US/0883-6612). **3654**

ANNALS OF BIOMEDICAL ENGINEERING. (US/0090-6964). **3685**

ANNALS OF BOTANY. (UK/0305-7364). **499**

ANNALS OF CLINICAL AND LABORATORY SCIENCE. (US/0091-7370). **3893**

ANNALS OF CLINICAL BIOCHEMISTRY. (UK/0004-5632). **480**

ANNALS OF CLINICAL PSYCHIATRY. (US/1040-1237). **3920**

ANNALS OF DISCRETE MATHEMATICS. (NE/0167-5060). **3494**

ANNALS OF DYSLEXIA. (US/0736-9387). **1874**

ANNALS OF EMERGENCY MEDICINE. (US/0196-0644). **3723**

ANNALS OF EPIDEMIOLOGY. (US/1047-2797). **3734**

ANNALS OF GLACIOLOGY. (UK/0260-3055). **1412**

ANNALS OF GLOBAL ANALYSIS AND GEOMETRY. (GW/0232-704X). **3494**

ANNALS OF HUMAN BIOLOGY. (UK/0301-4460). **442**

ANNALS OF HUMAN GENETICS. (UK/0003-4800). **542**

ANNALS OF INTERNAL MEDICINE. (US/0003-4819). **3794**

ANNALS OF IOWA. (US/0003-4827). **2720**

ANNALS OF MATHEMATICS. (US/0003-486X). **3494**

ANNALS OF MATHEMATICS AND OF ARTIFICIAL INTELLIGENCE. (NE/1012-2443). **1211**

ANNALS OF MATHEMATICS STUDIES. (US/0066-2313). **3494**

ANNALS OF MEDICINE (HELSINKI). (FI/0785-3890). **3550**

ANNALS OF NEUROLOGY. (US/0364-5134). **3827**

ANNALS OF NUCLEAR ENERGY. (UK/0306-4549). **2153**

ANNALS OF NUTRITION & METABOLISM. (SZ/0250-6807). **4187**

ANNALS OF OCCUPATIONAL HYGIENE, THE. (UK/0003-4878). **2858**

ANNALS OF OPHTHALMOLOGY (BIRMINGHAM). (US/0003-4886). **3872**

ANNALS OF OTOLOGY, RHINOLOGY & LARYNGOLOGY, THE. (US/0003-4894). **3886**

ANNALS OF PAEDIATRIC SURGERY. (II/0970-2121). **3900**

ANNALS OF PHYSICS. (US/0003-4916). **4397**

ANNALS OF PLASTIC SURGERY. (US/0148-7043). **3959**

ANNALS OF PROBABILITY, THE. (US/0091-1798). **3494**

ANNALS OF PUBLIC AND COOPERATIVE ECONOMY. (BE). **1462**

ANNALS OF PURE AND APPLIED LOGIC. (NE/0168-0072). **3494**

ANNALS OF REGIONAL SCIENCE, THE. (GW/0570-1864). **2814**

ANNALS OF SAUDI MEDICINE. (SU/0256-4947). **3550**

ANNALS OF SCIENCE. (UK/0003-3790). **5083**

ANNALS OF STATISTICS, THE. (US/0090-5364). **5321**

ANNALS OF SURGERY. (US/0003-4932). **3959**

ANNALS OF THE AMERICAN ACADEMY OF POLITICAL AND SOCIAL SCIENCE. (US/0002-7162). **5190**

ANNALS OF THE ASSOCIATION OF AMERICAN GEOGRAPHERS. (US/0004-5608). **2554**

ANNALS OF THE CARNEGIE MUSEUM. (US/0097-4463). **4162**

ANNALS OF THE ENTOMOLOGICAL SOCIETY OF AMERICA. (US/0013-8746). **5605**

ANNALS — Peer Reviewed Index

ANNALS OF THE INSTITUTE OF STATISTICAL MATHEMATICS. (JA/0020-3157). **3542**

ANNALS OF THE MISSOURI BOTANICAL GARDEN. (US/0026-6493). **499**

ANNALS OF THE NATAL MUSEUM, PIETERMARITZBURG. (SA/0304-0798). **4162**

ANNALS OF THE NEW YORK ACADEMY OF SCIENCES. (US/0077-8923). **5083**

ANNALS OF THE ROYAL COLLEGE OF SURGEONS OF ENGLAND. (UK/0035-8843). **3959**

ANNALS OF THE SOUTH AFRICAN MUSEUM. (SA/0303-2515). **4083**

ANNALS OF THE TRANSVAAL MUSEUM. (SA/0041-1752). **4162**

ANNALS OF THE UKRAINIAN ACADEMY OF ARTS AND SCIENCES IN THE UNITED STATES. (US/0503-1001). **2842**

ANNALS OF THORACIC SURGERY, THE. (US/0003-4975). **3959**

ANNALS OF TOURISM RESEARCH. (US/0160-7383). **5191**

ANNALS OF TROPICAL MEDICINE AND PARASITOLOGY. (UK/0003-4983). **3985**

ANNALS OF TROPICAL PAEDIATRICS. (UK/0272-4936). **3985**

ANNEE BIOLOGIQUE, L'. (SZ/0003-5017). **442**

ANNEE PSYCHOLOGIQUE, L'. (FR/0003-5033). **4574**

ANNUAL OF THE SOCIETY OF CHRISTIAN ETHICS, THE. (US/0732-4928). **4935**

ANNUAL REPORT ... / ARIZONA COUNCIL FOR THE DEAF. (US). **4383**

ANNUAL REPORT FOR ... / NEW YORK POWER AUTHORITY. (US). **4759**

ANNUAL REPORT / JUSTICE SOCIETY. (UK). **2934**

ANNUAL REPORT - LAND RESOURCE SCIENCE. UNIVERSITY OF GUELPH. (CN/0820-3997). **163**

ANNUAL REPORT OF THE INTER-AMERICAN TROPICAL TUNA COMMISSION. (US/0074-1000). **2295**

ANNUAL REPORT / THE OPEC FUND. (AU). **2907**

ANNUAL REPORTS IN MEDICINAL CHEMISTRY. (US/0065-7743). **4291**

ANNUAL REVIEW OF ANTHROPOLOGY. (US/0084-6570). **228**

ANNUAL REVIEW OF ASTRONOMY AND ASTROPHYSICS. (US/0066-4146). **391**

ANNUAL REVIEW OF BIOCHEMISTRY. (US/0066-4154). **480**

ANNUAL REVIEW OF CELL BIOLOGY. (US/0743-4634). **532**

ANNUAL REVIEW OF EARTH AND PLANETARY SCIENCES. (US/0084-6597). **1351**

ANNUAL REVIEW OF ECOLOGY AND SYSTEMATICS. (US/0066-4162). **2211**

ANNUAL REVIEW OF ENTOMOLOGY. (US/0066-4170). **5605**

ANNUAL REVIEW OF FLUID MECHANICS. (US/0066-4189). **2087**

ANNUAL REVIEW OF GENETICS. (US/0066-4197). **542**

ANNUAL REVIEW OF IMMUNOLOGY. (US/0732-0582). **3666**

ANNUAL REVIEW OF INFORMATION SCIENCE AND TECHNOLOGY. (US/0066-4200). **3191**

ANNUAL REVIEW OF MATERIALS SCIENCE. (US/0084-6600). **2100**

ANNUAL REVIEW OF MEDICINE. (US/0066-4219). **3551**

ANNUAL REVIEW OF NEUROSCIENCE. (US/0147-006X). **3827**

ANNUAL REVIEW OF NUCLEAR AND PARTICLE SCIENCE. (US/0163-8998). **4446**

ANNUAL REVIEW OF NUTRITION. (US/0199-9885). **4187**

ANNUAL REVIEW OF PHARMACOLOGY AND TOXICOLOGY. (US/0362-1642). **4291**

ANNUAL REVIEW OF PHYSICAL CHEMISTRY. (US/0066-426X). **1050**

ANNUAL REVIEW OF PHYSIOLOGY. (US/0066-4278). **578**

ANNUAL REVIEW OF PHYTOPATHOLOGY. (US/0066-4286). **500**

ANNUAL REVIEW OF PLANT PHYSIOLOGY AND PLANT MOLECULAR BIOLOGY. (US/1040-2519). **500**

ANNUAL REVIEW OF PSYCHOLOGY. (US/0066-4308). **4574**

ANNUAL REVIEW OF PUBLIC HEALTH. (US/0163-7525). **4767**

ANNUAL REVIEW OF SOCIOLOGY. (US/0360-0572). **5239**

ANNUAL STATUS REPORT ON FEMALE AND MALE STUDENTS AND EMPLOYEES IN VOCATIONAL EDUCATION (OKLAHOMA). (US). **1910**

ANO PEDAGOGICO. (SP/0577-8484). **1725**

ANPI MAGAZINE. (BE/0778-7383). **2288**

ANQ (LEXINGTON, KY.). (US/0895-769X). **3362**

ANSEARCHIN' NEWS. (US/0003-5246). **2437**

ANTARCTIC SCIENCE. (UK/0954-1020). **5084**

ANTHROPOLOGICA (OTTAWA). (CN/0003-5459). **228**

ANTHROPOLOGICAL FORUM. (AT/0066-4677). **229**

ANTHROPOLOGICAL PAPERS OF THE UNIVERSITY OF ALASKA. (US/0041-9354). **229**

ANTHROPOLOGICAL QUARTERLY. (US/0003-5491). **229**

ANTHROPOLOGIE (PARIS). (FR/0003-5521). **229**

ANTHROPOLOGY & EDUCATION QUARTERLY. (US/0161-7761). **230**

ANTHROPOLOGY TODAY. (UK/0268-540X). **230**

ANTHROPOS FRIBOURG. (SZ/0257-9774). **230**

ANTHROPOS. SUPLEMENTOS. (SP/1130-2089). **2842**

ANTHROPOZOOLOGICA PARIS. (FR/0761-3032). **5576**

ANTHROZOOS. (US/0892-7936). **5576**

ANTI-CANCER DRUG DESIGN. (UK/0266-9536). **3809**

ANTI-CANCER DRUGS. (UK/0959-4973). **3979**

ANTIBODY, IMMUNOCONJUGATES, AND RADIOPHARMACEUTICALS. (US/0892-7049). **3809**

ANTICANCER RESEARCH. (GR/0250-7005). **3809**

ANTICHITA VIVA. (IT/0003-5645). **337**

ANTICHTHON. (AT/0066-4774). **1074**

ANTIMICROBIAL AGENTS AND CHEMOTHERAPY. (US/0066-4804). **559**

ANTIPODAS : JOURNAL OF HISPANIC STUDIES OF THE UNIVERSITY OF AUCKLAND. (NZ/0113-2415). **3362**

ANTIQUITY. (UK/0003-598X). **255**

ANTITRUST BULLETIN. (US/0003-603X). **3095**

ANTIVIRAL RESEARCH. (US/0166-3542). **3551**

ANTONIE VAN LEEUWENHOEK. (NE/0003-6072). **559**

ANUARIO DE LINGUISTICA HISPANICA. (SP/0213-053X). **3266**

ANUARIO DE PSICOLOGIA. (SP). **4574**

ANUARIO IEHS. (AG/0326-9671). **2721**

ANUARIO JURIDICO. (MX/0185-3295). **2935**

ANXIETY (NEW YORK, N.Y.). (US/1070-9797). **4574**

AOPA PILOT, THE. (US/0001-2084). **12**

AORN JOURNAL. (US/0001-2092). **3851**

APCO BULLETIN, THE. (US/0001-2165). **4767**

APEC JOURNAL. (US/0893-0457). **1965**

APEX OF THE M. (US/1072-9232). **3460**

APHASIOLOGY. (UK/0268-7038). **3551**

APICOLTORE MODERNO, L'. (IT/0518-1259). **5605**

APIDOLOGIE. (FR/0044-8435). **5576**

APIS, THE. (US/0887-7386). **226**

APMIS : ACTA PATHOLOGICA, MICROBIOLOGICA ET IMMUNOLOGICA SCANDINAVICA. (DK/0903-4641). **3666**

APPALACHIAN JOURNAL. (US/0090-3779). **2721**

APPETITE. (UK/0195-6663). **4187**

APPLIED ACOUSTICS. (UK/0003-682X). **2097**

APPLIED AND ENVIRONMENTAL MICROBIOLOGY. (US/0099-2240). **559**

APPLIED AND THEORETICAL ELECTROPHORESIS. (UK/0954-6642). **1013**

APPLIED BIOCHEMISTRY AND BIOTECHNOLOGY. (US). **3685**

APPLIED CARDIOPULMONARY PATHOPHYSIOLOGY : ACP. (US/0920-5268). **3699**

APPLIED CATEGORICAL STRUCTURES. (NE/0927-2852). **3494**

APPLIED COGNITIVE PSYCHOLOGY. (UK/0888-4080). **4574**

APPLIED CYTOGENETICS. (US/1056-5191). **542**

APPLIED ECONOMICS. (UK/0003-6846). **1463**

APPLIED ENERGY. (UK/0306-2619). **1932**

APPLIED ENGINEERING IN AGRICULTURE. (US/0883-8542). **1965**

APPLIED ENTOMOLOGY AND ZOOLOGY. (JA/0003-6862). **5605**

APPLIED ERGONOMICS. (UK/0003-6870). **1965**

APPLIED GEOGRAPHY (SEVENOAKS). (UK/0143-6228). **2554**

APPLIED INTELLIGENCE. (NE/0924-669X). **1211**

APPLIED LINGUISTICS. (UK/0142-6001). **3266**

APPLIED MAGNETIC RESONANCE. (RU/0937-9347). **4397**

APPLIED MATHEMATICAL MODELLING. (UK/0307-904X). **3495**

APPLIED MATHEMATICS AND COMPUTATION. (US/0096-3003). **3495**

APPLIED MATHEMATICS AND OPTIMIZATION. (US/0095-4616). **3495**

APPLIED MECHANICS REVIEWS. (US/0003-6900). **2002**

APPLIED MICROBIOLOGY AND BIOTECHNOLOGY. (GW/0175-7598). **559**

APPLIED NUMERICAL MATHEMATICS : TRANSACTIONS OF IMACS. (NE/0168-9274). **3495**

APPLIED NURSING RESEARCH : ANR. (US/0897-1897). **3851**

APPLIED OCCUPATIONAL AND ENVIRONMENTAL HYGIENE. (US/1047-322X). **2859**

APPLIED OCEAN RESEARCH. (UK/0141-1187). **1446**

APPLIED OPTICS. (US/0003-6935). **4433**

APPLIED PHYSICS. A, SOLIDS AND SURFACES. (GW/0721-7250). **4397**

APPLIED PHYSICS. B, PHOTOPHYSICS AND LASER CHEMISTRY. (GW/0721-7269). **4433**

APPLIED PHYSICS LETTERS. (US/0003-6951). **4397**

APPLIED PLANT SCIENCE. (SA/0259-5605). **163**

APPLIED PSYCHOLINGUISTICS. (UK/0142-7164). **3266**

APPLIED PSYCHOLOGICAL MEASUREMENT. (US/0146-6216). **4574**

APPLIED PSYCHOLOGY. (UK/0269-994X). **4574**

APPLIED SCIENTIFIC RESEARCH. (NE/0003-6994). **2109**

APPLIED SPECTROSCOPY. (US/0003-7028). **4433**

APPLIED SPECTROSCOPY REVIEWS (SOFTCOVER ED.). (US/0570-4928). **1013**

APPLIED STATISTICS. (UK/0035-9254). **5322**

APPLIED SURFACE SCIENCE. (NE/0169-4332). **4397**

APPRENTICE (OTTAWA). (CN/0706-7399). **4857**

APPROPRIATE TECHNOLOGY. (UK/0305-0920). **5085**

APUA NEWSLETTER. (UK). **62**

AQUA FENNICA. (FI/0356-7133). **1412**

AQUACULTURAL ENGINEERING. (UK/0144-8609). **2295**

AQUACULTURE. (NE/0044-8486). **2295**

AQUARAMA. (FR/0151-6981). **4285**

AQUATIC BOTANY. (NE/0304-3770). **500**

AQUATIC INSECTS. (NE/0165-0424). **5605**

AQUATIC MAMMALS. (UK/0167-5427). **5576**

AQUATIC TOXICOLOGY (AMSTERDAM, NETHERLANDS). (NE/0166-445X). **3979**

AQUINAS JOURNAL. (CE). **5191**

ARAB GULF JOURNAL OF SCIENTIFIC RESEARCH. (SU/1015-4442). **5085**

ARAB LAW QUARTERLY. (UK/0268-0556). **2936**

ARABIAN JOURNAL FOR SCIENCE AND ENGINEERING. (UK/0377-9211). **5085**

ARAM PERIODICAL. (UK/0959-4213). **2767**

ARAM PERIODICAL. (UK/0959-4213). **3266**

ARBEITEN AUS DER KOMMISSION FUER GEOMORPHOLOGIE DER BAYERISCHEN AKADEMIE DER WISSENSCHAFTEN. (GW). **2555**

ARBEITSMEDIZIN, SOZIALMEDIZIN, PRAVENTIVMEDIZIN. (GW/0300-581X). **2859**

ARBITRATION INTERNATIONAL. (UK/0957-0411). **3124**

ARBITRATION JOURNAL, THE. (US/0003-7893). **2936**

ARC (OTTAWA). (CN/0705-6397). **3460**

ARCHAEOASTRONOMY. (UK/0142-7253). **256**

ARCHAEOLOGY. (US/0003-8113). **257**

ARCHAEOLOGY IN OCEANIA. (AT/0728-4896). **257**

ARCHAEOLOGY OF EASTERN NORTH AMERICA. (US/0360-1021). **257**

ARCHAEOMETRY. (UK/0003-813X). **257**

ARCHEOMATERIALS. (US/0891-2920). **259**

ARCHITECTURAL LIGHTING. (US/0894-0436). **289**

ARCHITECTURE MINNESOTA. (US/0149-9106). **290**

ARCHITECTURE TODAY. (UK/0958-6407). **290**

ARCHITECTUUR, BONWEN. (NE/0169-4421). **290**

ARCHIV DER MATHEMATIK. (SW/0003-889X). **3495**

ARCHIV DER PHARMAZIE (WEINHEIM). (GW/0365-6233). **4292**

ARCHIV FUER ACKER- UND PFLANZENBAU UND BODENKUNDE. (SW/0365-0340). **163**

ARCHIV FUER ELEKTROTECHNIK (BERLIN). (GW/0003-9039). **2036**

ARCHIV FUER EXPERIMENTELLE VETERINAERMEDIZIN. (GW/0003-9055). **5504**

ARCHIV FUER FISCHEREIWISSENSCHAFT. (GW/0003-9063). **2296**

ARCHIV FUER GEFLUGELKUNDE. (GW/0003-9098). **206**

ARCHIV FUER HYDROBIOLOGIE. (GW/0003-9136). **5530**

ARCHIV FUER PROTISTENKUNDE. (GW/0003-9365). **5576**

ARCHIV FUER TIERERNAHRUNG. (GW/0003-942X). **5504**

ARCHIV FUER TIERZUCHT. (GW/0003-9438). **206**

ARCHIVARIA. (CN/0318-6954). **2479**

ARCHIVE FOR HISTORY OF EXACT SCIENCES. (GW/0003-9519). **5085**

ARCHIVE FOR RATIONAL MECHANICS AND ANALYSIS. (GW/0003-9527). **4427**

ARCHIVES DES MALADIES DU COEUR ET DES VAISSEAUX. (FR/0003-9683). **3699**

ARCHIVES EUROPEENNES DE SOCIOLOGIE. (FR/0003-9756). **5240**

ARCHIVES FRANCAISES DE PEDIATRIE. (FR/0003-9764). **3900**

ARCHIVES INTERNATIONALES DE PHARMACODYNAMIE ET DE THERAPIE. (BE/0003-9780). **4292**

ARCHIVES ITALIENNES DE BIOLOGIE. (IT/0003-9829). **442**

ARCHIVES OF ANDROLOGY. (UK/0148-5016). **3678**

ARCHIVES OF COMPLEX ENVIRONMENTAL STUDIES : ACES. (FI/0787-0396). **2161**

ARCHIVES OF DERMATOLOGY. (US/0003-987X). **3718**

ARCHIVES OF DISEASE IN CHILDHOOD. (UK/0003-9888). **3900**

ARCHIVES OF EMERGENCY MEDICINE. (UK/0264-4924). **3723**

ARCHIVES OF ENVIRONMENTAL CONTAMINATION AND TOXICOLOGY. (US/0090-4341). **2161**

ARCHIVES OF ENVIRONMENTAL HEALTH. (US/0003-9896). **4767**

ARCHIVES OF FAMILY MEDICINE. (US/1063-3987). **3736**

ARCHIVES OF GENERAL PSYCHIATRY. (US/0003-990X). **3921**

ARCHIVES OF GERONTOLOGY AND GERIATRICS. (NE/0167-4943). **3749**

ARCHIVES OF INSECT BIOCHEMISTRY AND PHYSIOLOGY. (US/0739-4462). **5605**

ARCHIVES OF INTERNAL MEDICINE (1960). (US/0003-9926). **3795**

ARCHIVES OF NATURAL HISTORY. (UK/0260-9541). **4162**

ARCHIVES OF NEUROLOGY (CHICAGO). (US/0003-9942). **3827**

ARCHIVES OF OPHTHALMOLOGY. (US/0003-9950). **3872**

ARCHIVES OF ORAL BIOLOGY. (UK/0003-9969). **1316**

ARCHIVES OF PATHOLOGY & LABORATORY MEDICINE. (US/0003-9985). **3893**

ARCHIVES OF PEDIATRICS & ADOLESCENT MEDICINE. (US/1072-4710). **3900**

ARCHIVES OF PHYSICAL MEDICINE AND REHABILITATION. (US/0003-9993). **4379**

ARCHIVES OF PSYCHIATRIC NURSING. (US/0883-9417). **3851**

ARCHIVES OF SEXUAL BEHAVIOR. (US/0004-0002). **5186**

ARCHIVES OF SURGERY (CHICAGO. 1960). (US/0004-0010). **3959**

ARCHIVES OF VIROLOGY. (AU/0304-8608). **560**

ARCHIVOS DE BIOLOGIA Y MEDICINA EXPERIMENTALES. (CL/0004-0533). **442**

ARCHIVOS DE BRONCONEUMOLOGIA. (SP/0300-2896). **3948**

ARCHIVOS DE CRIMINOLOGIA, NEUROPSIQUIATRIA Y DISCIPLINAS CONEXAS. (EC). **3158**

ARCHIVOS DE MEDICINA DEL DEPORTE : PUBLICACION DE LA FEDERACION ESPANOLA DE MEDICINA DEL DEPORTE / FEMEDE. (SP/0212-8799). **3953**

ARCHIVOS DE NEUROBIOLOGIA. (SP/0004-0576). **3827**

ARCHIVOS DEL INSTITUTO DE CARDIOLOGIA DE MEXICO. (MX/0020-3785). **3699**

ARCHIVOS ESPANOLES DE UROLOGIA. (SP/0004-0614). **3988**

ARCHOLOGIAI ERTESITO. (HU/0003-8032). **259**

ARCTIC. (CN/0004-0843). **2555**

ARCTIC AND ALPINE RESEARCH. (US/0004-0851). **2555**

ARCTIC ANTHROPOLOGY. (US/0066-6939). **231**

ARCTIC MEDICAL RESEARCH. (FI/0782-226X). **3552**

ARDEA. (NE/0373-2266). **5614**

AREE. ANNUAL REVIEW OF ENVIRONMENTAL EDUCATION. (UK/0953-0428). **2161**

AREEA REPORT, THE. (US/1064-1092). **4834**

ARETE. (US/0885-9787). **5273**

ARGUMENT, DAS. (GW/0004-1157). **4341**

ARGUMENTATION. (NE/0920-427X). **4341**

ARGUMENTATION AND ADVOCACY. (US/1051-1431). **1104**

ARHIV PATOLOGIJ. (RU/0004-1955). **3893**

ARHIV ZA HIGIJENU RADA I TOKSIKOLOGIJU. (CR/0004-1254). **2859**

ARIZONA ANTHROPOLOGIST. (US/1062-1601). **231**

ARIZONA QUARTERLY, THE. (US/0004-1610). **3363**

ARIZONA REVIEW. (US/0004-1629). **639**

ARKANSAS BUSINESS. (US/1053-6582). **639**

ARKANSAS BUSINESS AND ECONOMIC REVIEW. (US/0004-1742). **639**

ARKANSAS FARM RESEARCH. (US/0004-1785). **62**

ARKANSAS HISTORICAL QUARTERLY, THE. (US/0004-1823). **2721**

ARKANSAS LIBRARIES. (US/0004-184X). **3191**

ARKIV FUER MATEMATIK. (SW/0004-2080). **3496**

ARMED FORCES AND SOCIETY. (US/0095-327X). **4035**

ARMENIAN REVIEW, THE. (US/0004-2366). **2501**

ARMY TIMES. (US/0004-2595). **4037**

ARQUITECTURA VIVA. (SP/0214-1256). **292**

ARQUIVOS DE BIOLOGIA E TECNOLOGIA. (BL/0365-0979). **443**

ARRIS (ATLANTA, GA.). (US/1048-5945). **292**

ARROZ EN LAS AMERICAS. (CK/0120-2634). **63**

ARS COMBINATORIA. (CN/0381-7032). **3496**

ARSC JOURNAL. (US). **5315**

ART CALENDAR (GREAT FALLS, VA.). (US/0893-3901). **338**

ART DOCUMENTATION. (US/0730-7187). **3192**

ART INDEX. (US/0004-3222). **334**

ART LAW AND ACCOUNTING REPORTER. (US/0886-1013). **2937**

ART PAPERS. (US/0278-1441). **340**

ART REFERENCE SERVICES QUARTERLY. (US/1050-2548). **340**

ART THERAPY : JOURNAL OF THE AMERICAN ART THERAPY ASSOCIATION. (US/0742-1656). **4575**

ART WORLD. (IT). **340**

ARTE CRISTIANA. (IT/0004-3400). **340**

ARTE LOMBARDA. (IT/0004-3443). **313**

ARTE NAIVE. (IT/0390-1319). **341**

ARTEFACT, THE. (AT/0044-9075). **260**

ARTERY. (US/0098-6127). **3795**

ARTHRITIS AND RHEUMATISM. (US/0004-3591). **3803**

ARTHRITIS CARE AND RESEARCH. (US/0893-7524). **3803**

ARTIFICIAL INTELLIGENCE. (NE/0004-3702). **1211**

ARTIFICIAL INTELLIGENCE AND LAW. (NE/0924-8463). **1211**

ARTIFICIAL INTELLIGENCE IN MEDICINE. (NE/0933-3657). **1211**

ARTIFICIAL INTELLIGENCE REVIEW, THE. (UK/0269-2821). **1211**

ARTIFICIAL ORGANS. (US/0160-564X). **3960**

ARTIFICIAL ORGANS TODAY : THE OFFICIAL INTERNATIONAL JOURNAL OF THE JAPANESE SOCIETY FOR ARTIFICIAL ORGANS. (NE/0924-3054). **3553**

ARTINF. (AG). **341**

ARTS REACH. (US/1065-8130). **315**

ARTWORLD EUROPE. (US/1062-8312). **342**

ARZNEIMITTEL FORSCHUNG. (GW/0004-4172). **4292**

ASA NEWSLETTER - APPLIED SCIENCE AND ANALYSIS, INC, THE. (US/1057-9419). **4037**

ASAIO JOURNAL (1992). (US/1058-2916). **3960**

ASB BULLETIN, THE. (US/0001-2386). **443**

ASEAN ECONOMIC BULLETIN. (SI/0217-4472). **1463**

ASEAN FOOD JOURNAL. (MY/0127-7324). **2327**

ASHLAND THEOLOGICAL JOURNAL. (US/1044-6494). **4936**

ASHRAE JOURNAL. (US/0001-2491). **2603**

ASIA PACIFIC PAPERMAKER. (AT/1320-9787). **4232**

ASIAN AMERICAN AND PACIFIC ISLANDER JOURNAL OF HEALTH. (US/1072-0367). **4768**

ASIAN AND AFRICAN STUDIES (JERUSALEM). (IS/0066-8281). **2638**

ASIAN AND PACIFIC MIGRATION JOURNAL : APMJ. (PH). **1918**

ASIAN ART. (US/0894-234X). **343**

ASIAN JOURNAL OF PHILOSOPHY, THE. (CC). **4341**

ASIAN MUSIC. (US/0044-9202). **4101**

ASIAN-PACIFIC ECONOMIC LITERATURE. (UK/0818-9935). **1530**

ASIAN PACIFIC JOURNAL OF ALLERGY AND IMMUNOLOGY. (TH/0125-877X). **3666**

ASIAN SURVEY. (US/0004-4687). **5192**

ASIAN THEATRE JOURNAL. (US/0742-5457). **383**

ASIAN YEARBOOK OF INTERNATIONAL LAW. (NE/0928-432X). **3124**

ASIATIC HERPETOLOGICAL RESEARCH. (US/1051-3825). **5577**

ASPECTS & DOCUMENTS. (BE). **773**

ASPECTS

Peer Reviewed Index

ASPECTS OF EDUCATION : JOURNAL OF THE INSTITUTE OF EDUCATION, THE UNIVERSITY OF HULL. (UK/0066-8672). **1726**

ASSISTIVE TECHNOLOGY. (US/1040-0435). **4384**

ASSOCIATION MANAGEMENT. (US/0004-5578). **640**

ASTERISQUE. (FR/0303-1179). **3496**

ASTRONOMISCHE NACHRICHTEN. (GW/0004-6337). **392**

ASTRONOMY AND ASTROPHYSICS (BERLIN). (GW/0004-6361). **392**

ASTRONOMY & ASTROPHYSICS. SUPPLEMENT SERIES. (FR/0365-0138). **392**

ASTROPHYSICAL JOURNAL. SUPPLEMENT SERIES, THE. (US/0067-0049). **393**

ASTROPHYSICAL JOURNAL, THE. (US/0004-637X). **393**

ASTROPHYSICAL LETTERS AND COMMUNICATIONS. (US/0888-6512). **393**

ASTROPHYSICS AND SPACE SCIENCE. (NE/0004-640X). **393**

ASTRUIM. (NE). **393**

ASYMPTOTIC ANALYSIS. (NE/0921-7134). **3496**

ATARI USER. (UK/0266-545X). **1264**

ATCP. (MX). **4232**

ATE NEWS LETTER. (US/0001-2718). **1888**

ATHANOR. (IT). **3267**

ATHEROSCLEROSIS. (NE/0021-9150). **3699**

ATLA : ALTERNATIVES TO LABORATORY ANIMALS. (UK/0261-1929). **3979**

ATLANTA HISTORY. (US/0896-3975). **2722**

ATLANTIC ECONOMIC JOURNAL. (US/0197-4254). **1464**

ATLANTIS (WOLFVILLE). (CN/0702-7818). **5551**

ATMOSPHERE-OCEAN. (CN/0705-5900). **1420**

ATOMIC DATA AND NUCLEAR DATA TABLES. (US/0092-640X). **4446**

ATOMIC SPECTROSCOPY. (US/0195-5373). **1013**

ATOMWIRTSCHAFT, ATOMTECHNIK. (GW/0365-8414). **2154**

ATR; AUSTRALIAN TELECOMMUNICATION RESEARCH. (AT/0001-2777). **1149**

ATTI DELLA FONDAZIONE GIORGIO RONCHI (1976). (IT/0391-2051). **4433**

AU FIL DU BOIS. (CN/0383-0047). **2399**

AUDIOLOGY. (SZ/0020-6091). **3886**

AUDIOTEX UPDATE. (US/1045-5795). **1282**

AUDITING. (US/0278-0380). **739**

AUERBACH INFORMATION MANAGEMENT. (US/1045-7879). **1256**

AUGUSTINIAN STUDIES. (US/0094-5323). **5024**

AUGUSTINUS. (SP/0004-802X). **4937**

AUK, THE. (US/0004-8038). **5615**

AURA (BIRMINGHAM, ALA.). (US/0889-7433). **3364**

AUSSENPOLITIK (ENGLISH EDITION). (GW/0587-3835). **4516**

AUSTRALASIAN BIOTECHNOLOGY. (AT/1036-7128). **3685**

AUSTRALASIAN BUS AND COACH. (AT). **5377**

AUSTRALASIAN DRAMA STUDIES. (AT/0810-4123). **5361**

AUSTRALASIAN JOURNAL OF AMERICAN STUDIES : AJAS. (AT/0705-7113). **2722**

AUSTRALASIAN JOURNAL OF SPECIAL EDUCATION. (AT/1030-0112). **1875**

AUSTRALASIAN PHYSICAL & ENGINEERING SCIENCES IN MEDICINE. (AT/0158-9938). **3685**

AUSTRALASIAN PUBLIC LIBRARIES AND INFORMATION SERVICES. (AT/1030-5033). **3193**

AUSTRALASIAN SHIPS & PORTS. (AT/1032-3449). **5447**

AUSTRALIA AND NEW ZEALAND JOURNAL OF DEVELOPMENTAL DISABILITIES. (AT/0726-3864). **4384**

AUSTRALIAN ABORIGINAL STUDIES (CANBERRA, A.C.T. : 1983). (AT/0729-4352). **2668**

AUSTRALIAN ACCOUNTANT, THE. (AT/0004-8631). **739**

AUSTRALIAN & NEW ZEALAND JOURNAL OF CRIMINOLOGY, THE. (AT/0004-8658). **3158**

AUSTRALIAN AND NEW ZEALAND JOURNAL OF MEDICINE. (AT/0004-8291). **3795**

AUSTRALIAN AND NEW ZEALAND JOURNAL OF OBSTETRICS AND GYNAECOLOGY. (AT/0004-8666). **3757**

AUSTRALIAN AND NEW ZEALAND JOURNAL OF OPHTHALMOLOGY. (AT/0814-9763). **3872**

AUSTRALIAN AND NEW ZEALAND JOURNAL OF PSYCHIATRY. (AT/0004-8674). **3921**

AUSTRALIAN & NEW ZEALAND JOURNAL OF SERIALS LIBRARIANSHIP. (US/0898-3283). **3193**

AUSTRALIAN AND NEW ZEALAND JOURNAL OF SOCIOLOGY, THE. (AT/0004-8690). **5240**

AUSTRALIAN AND NEW ZEALAND JOURNAL OF SURGERY. (AT/0004-8682). **3960**

AUSTRALIAN & NEW ZEALAND PHYSICIST : A PUBLICATION OF THE AUSTRALIAN INSTITUTE OF PHYSICS & THE NEW ZEALAND INSTITUTE OF PHYSICS, THE. (AT/1036-3831). **4398**

AUSTRALIAN & NEW ZEALAND STUDIES IN CANADA. (CN/0843-5049). **3364**

AUSTRALIAN AND NEW ZEALAND WINE INDUSTRY JOURNAL. (AT). **2363**

AUSTRALIAN ARCHAEOLOGY. (AT/0312-2417). **260**

AUSTRALIAN BOOKSELLER & PUBLISHER. (AT). **4823**

AUSTRALIAN-CANADIAN STUDIES. (AT/0810-1906). **2722**

AUSTRALIAN COLLEGE OF MIDWIVES INCORPORATED JOURNAL. (AT/1031-170X). **3554**

AUSTRALIAN COMPUTER JOURNAL, THE. (AT/0004-8917). **1256**

AUSTRALIAN CORPORATIONS AND SECURITIES REPORTS. (AT/1033-7466). **3096**

AUSTRALIAN CRITICAL CARE : OFFICIAL JOURNAL OF THE CONFEDERATION OF AUSTRALIAN CRITICAL CARE NURSES. (AT/1036-7314). **3851**

AUSTRALIAN CULTURAL HISTORY. (AT/0728-8433). **2668**

AUSTRALIAN DENTAL JOURNAL. (AT/0045-0421). **1317**

AUSTRALIAN ECONOMIC HISTORY REVIEW. (AT/0004-8992). **1547**

AUSTRALIAN ECONOMIC REVIEW. (AT/0004-9018). **1464**

AUSTRALIAN ENTOMOLOGICAL MAGAZINE. (AT/0311-1881). **5605**

AUSTRALIAN ENTOMOLOGIST, THE. (AT/1320-6133). **5605**

AUSTRALIAN EQUINE VETERINARIAN. (AT/1032-6626). **2797**

AUSTRALIAN EVANGEL. (AT/0812-4353). **4937**

AUSTRALIAN FARMERS' AND DEALERS' JOURNAL. (AT/1036-4242). **158**

AUSTRALIAN FOLKLORE. (AT/0819-0852). **2318**

AUSTRALIAN GEOGRAPHER. (AT/0004-9182). **2555**

AUSTRALIAN HAND WEAVER AND SPINNER / HAND WEAVERS AND SPINNERS GUILD OF NEW SOUTH WALES, THE. (AT). **5183**

AUSTRALIAN HISTORICAL STUDIES. (AT/1031-461X). **2668**

AUSTRALIAN HISTORY TEACHER. (AT/0312-2530). **1888**

AUSTRALIAN JOURNAL OF AGRICULTURAL ECONOMICS, THE. (AT/0004-9395). **64**

AUSTRALIAN JOURNAL OF AGRICULTURAL RESEARCH. (AT/0004-9409). **64**

AUSTRALIAN JOURNAL OF AUDIOLOGY, THE. (AT/0157-1532). **3886**

AUSTRALIAN JOURNAL OF BOTANY. (AT/0067-1924). **501**

AUSTRALIAN JOURNAL OF CHEMISTRY. (AT/0004-9425). **961**

AUSTRALIAN JOURNAL OF CLINICAL AND EXPERIMENTAL HYPNOSIS. (AT/0156-0417). **2857**

AUSTRALIAN JOURNAL OF COMMUNICATION. (AT/0811-6202). **1104**

AUSTRALIAN JOURNAL OF DAIRY TECHNOLOGY, THE. (AT/0004-9433). **192**

AUSTRALIAN JOURNAL OF EARLY CHILDHOOD. (AT/0312-5033). **1802**

AUSTRALIAN JOURNAL OF EARTH SCIENCES. (AT/0812-0099). **1351**

AUSTRALIAN JOURNAL OF ECOLOGY. (AT/0307-692X). **2211**

AUSTRALIAN JOURNAL OF EDUCATION, THE. (AT/0004-9441). **1726**

AUSTRALIAN JOURNAL OF EDUCATIONAL TECHNOLOGY. (AT/0814-673X). **1810**

AUSTRALIAN JOURNAL OF EXPERIMENTAL AGRICULTURE. (AT/0816-1089). **64**

AUSTRALIAN JOURNAL OF FORENSIC SCIENCES, THE. (AT/0045-0618). **3740**

AUSTRALIAN JOURNAL OF FRENCH STUDIES. (AT/0004-9468). **3364**

AUSTRALIAN JOURNAL OF GEODESY, PHOTOGRAMMETRY, AND SURVEYING. (AT/0159-8910). **2018**

AUSTRALIAN JOURNAL OF HOSPITAL PHARMACY. (AT/0310-6810). **4293**

AUSTRALIAN JOURNAL OF INFOMATION SYSTEMS, THE. (AT/1039-7841). **1727**

AUSTRALIAN JOURNAL OF LAW AND SOCIETY. (AT/0729-3356). **2938**

AUSTRALIAN JOURNAL OF LINGUISTICS. (AT/0726-8602). **3267**

AUSTRALIAN JOURNAL OF MANAGEMENT. (AT/0312-8962). **860**

AUSTRALIAN JOURNAL OF MARINE AND FRESHWATER RESEARCH. (AT/0067-1940). **1446**

AUSTRALIAN JOURNAL OF MEDICAL SCIENCE. (AT/1038-1643). **3554**

AUSTRALIAN JOURNAL OF PHYSICS. (AT/0004-9506). **4398**

AUSTRALIAN JOURNAL OF PLANT PHYSIOLOGY. (AT/0310-7841). **501**

AUSTRALIAN JOURNAL OF POLITICAL SCIENCE. (AT/1036-1146). **4464**

AUSTRALIAN JOURNAL OF POLITICS AND HISTORY, THE. (AT/0004-9522). **4464**

AUSTRALIAN JOURNAL OF PSYCHOLOGY. (AT/0004-9530). **4575**

AUSTRALIAN JOURNAL OF PUBLIC ADMINISTRATION. (AT/0313-6647). **4631**

AUSTRALIAN JOURNAL OF PUBLIC HEALTH. (AT/1035-7319). **4768**

AUSTRALIAN JOURNAL OF SCIENCE AND MEDICINE IN SPORT. (AT). **3953**

AUSTRALIAN JOURNAL OF SOCIAL ISSUES, THE. (AT/0157-6321). **5274**

AUSTRALIAN JOURNAL OF SOIL AND WATER CONSERVATION. (AT/1032-2426). **5530**

AUSTRALIAN JOURNAL OF SOIL RESEARCH. (AT/0004-9573). **164**

AUSTRALIAN JOURNAL OF TEACHER EDUCATION, THE. (AT/0313-5373). **1888**

AUSTRALIAN JOURNAL OF ZOOLOGY. (AT/0004-959X). **5577**

AUSTRALIAN JOURNALISM REVIEW : AJR. (AT/0810-2686). **2917**

AUSTRALIAN LIBRARY REVIEW. (AT/1034-8042). **3193**

AUSTRALIAN MAMMALOGY. (AT/0310-0049). **5577**

AUSTRALIAN MEDICAL RECORD JOURNAL / MEDICAL RECORD ASSOCIATION OF AUSTRALIA. (AT/0817-3907). **3777**

AUSTRALIAN NUGGET JOURNAL. (AT/1030-7915). **3998**

AUSTRALIAN OCCUPATIONAL THERAPY JOURNAL. (AT/0045-0766). **1875**

AUSTRALIAN OLYMPIAN. (AT). **4885**

AUSTRALIAN PODIATRIST. (AT/0311-3612). **3917**

AUSTRALIAN PRESCRIBER. (AT/0312-8008). **3554**

AUSTRALIAN PRODUCT LIABILITY REPORTER. (AT/1034-4608). **4768**

AUSTRALIAN PSYCHOLOGIST. (AT/0005-0067). **4575**

AUSTRALIAN REVIEW OF APPLIED LINGUISTICS. (AT/0155-0640). **3267**

AUSTRALIAN SHELL NEWS. (AT/0310-1304). **5577**

AUSTRALIAN SOCIAL WORK. (AT/0312-407X). **5274**

AUSTRALIAN STRING TEACHER. (AT/0312-9950). **4101**

AUSTRALIAN SURVEYOR. (AT/0005-0326). **2019**

AUSTRALIAN SYSTEMATIC BOTANY. (AT/1030-1887). **501**

AUSTRALIAN UNIVERSITIES' REVIEW, THE. (AT). **1810**

AUSTRALIAN VETERINARY JOURNAL. (AT/0005-0423). **5505**

AUSTRALIAN VETERINARY PRACTITIONER. (AT/0310-138X). **5505**

AUSTRALIA'S HEALTH / AUSTRALIAN INSTITUTE OF HEALTH. (AT/1032-6138). **4768**

AUTHORWARE MAGAZINE. (US). **1171**

AUTOGLASS (MCLEAN, VA.). (US/1047-2061). **2586**

AUTOMATICA E INSTRUMENTACION. (SP/0213-3113). **1217**

AUTOMATICA (OXFORD). (UK/0005-1098). **1217**

AUTOMATION AND REMOTE CONTROL. (US/0005-1179). **1218**

AUTOMAZIONE NAVALE, L'. (IT/0392-2294). **591**

AVALOKA. (US/0890-5541). **4937**

AVANCES EN ALIMENTACION Y MEJORA ANIMAL. (SP). **206**

AVANCES EN INVESTIGACION AGROPECUARIA. (MX/0188-7890). **64**

AVIAN DISEASES. (US/0005-2086). **5505**

AVIAN PATHOLOGY. (UK/0307-9457). **5505**

AVIATION SPACE AND ENVIRONMENTAL MEDICINE. (US/0095-6562). **3554**

AVTOMATIKA (KIEV). (UN/0572-2691). **1218**

AXONE (DARTMOUTH). (CN/0834-7824). **3852**

BABEL. (AT/0005-3503). **3267**

BACKGROUNDER / AUSTRALIA, DEPARTMENT OF FOREIGN AFFAIRS AND TRADE. (AT). **4632**

BAILLIERE'S CLINICAL ANAESTHESIOLOGY. (UK/0950-3501). **3682**

BAILLIERE'S CLINICAL ENDOCRINOLOGY AND METABOLISM. (UK/0950-351X). **3726**

BAILLIERE'S CLINICAL GASTROENTEROLOGY. (UK/0950-3528). **3743**

BAILLIERE'S CLINICAL OBSTETRICS AND GYNAECOLOGY. (UK/0950-3552). **3757**

BAILLIERE'S CLINICAL RHEUMATOLOGY. (UK/0950-3579). **3803**

BALANCE LONDON. (UK/0005-4216). **3555**

BALTIMORE BUSINESS JOURNAL. (US/0747-1823). **641**

BANCA Y FINANZAS. (CK/0120-7040). **773**

BANCHE E BANCHIERI. (IT/0390-1378). **774**

BANDAOTI XUEBAO. (CC/0253-4177). **2036**

BANKING ABSTRACTS. (IT). **777**

BANKING LAW ANTHOLOGY. (US/0737-2159). **3085**

BANKRISK (STAMFORD, CONN.). (US/1056-8115). **777**

BAPTIST REVIEW OF THEOLOGY, THE. (CN/1192-4241). **4938**

BARKER, THE. (US/1043-0849). **5505**

BARRISTER (PHILADELPHIA, PA.), THE. (US/0739-2494). **2940**

BASES PARIS. (FR/0765-1325). **1274**

BASIC RESEARCH IN CARDIOLOGY. (GW/0300-8428). **3699**

BASILISCO (OVIEDO, SPAIN). (SP/0210-0088). **4342**

BAT RESEARCH NEWS. (US/0005-6227). **5577**

BAYVIEWS (OAKLAND, CALIF.). (US/1045-6724). **3193**

BCIRA ABSTRACTS OF INTERNATIONAL LITERATURE ON METAL CASTINGS PRODUCTION. (UK/0268-3393). **3998**

BEAGLE : OCCASIONAL PAPERS OF THE TERRITORY MUSEUM OF ARTS AND SCIENCES, THE. (AT/0811-3653). **2843**

BEBIDAS. (US/0005-7533). **2364**

BEE CULTURE. (US/1071-3190). **65**

BEE WORLD. (UK/0005-772X). **5577**

BE'EMET?!. (IS/0334-973X). **1060**

BEETHOVEN NEWSLETTER, THE. (US/0898-6185). **4102**

BEHAVIOR ANALYST, THE. (US/0738-6729). **4576**

BEHAVIOR GENETICS. (US/0001-8244). **543**

BEHAVIOR MODIFICATION. (US/0145-4455). **4576**

BEHAVIOR THERAPY. (US/0005-7894). **4576**

BEHAVIORAL AND BRAIN SCIENCES, THE. (US/0140-525X). **4576**

BEHAVIORAL AND NEURAL BIOLOGY. (US/0163-1047). **5577**

BEHAVIORAL & SOCIAL SCIENCES LIBRARIAN. (US/0163-9269). **3193**

BEHAVIORAL ASSESSMENT. (US/0191-5401). **4576**

BEHAVIORAL ECOLOGY AND SOCIOBIOLOGY. (GW/0340-5443). **2212**

BEHAVIORAL MEDICINE (WASHINGTON, D.C.). (US/0896-4289). **3555**

BEHAVIORAL NEUROSCIENCE. (US/0735-7044). **4576**

BEHAVIORAL SCIENCE. (US/0005-7940). **4576**

BEHAVIOUR. (NE/0005-7959). **443**

BEHAVIOUR & INFORMATION TECHNOLOGY. (UK/0144-929X). **5087**

BEHAVIOUR CHANGE. (AT/0813-4839). **4577**

BEHAVIOUR RESEARCH AND THERAPY. (UK/0005-7967). **3921**

BEHAVIOURAL BRAIN RESEARCH. (NE/0166-4328). **3828**

BEHAVIOURAL PSYCHOTHERAPY. (UK/0141-3473). **4577**

BEIJING YIKE DAXUE XUEBAO. (CC/1000-1530). **3555**

BEIRUT REVIEW, THE. (LE/1019-0732). **4516**

BEITRAEGE ZUR TABAKFORSCHUNG INTERNATIONAL. (GW/0173-783X). **5372**

BELGISCHE FRUITREVUE. (BE/0005-8467). **2328**

BELOIT POETRY JOURNAL, THE. (US/0005-8661). **3460**

BENEFITS & COMPENSATION INTERNATIONAL. (UK/0268-764X). **2875**

BENEFITS QUARTERLY. (US/8756-1263). **1655**

BEREAVEMENT CARE. (UK/0268-2621). **5274**

BERICHTE DER BUNSENGESELLSCHAFT FUER PHYSIKALISCHE CHEMIE. (GW/0005-9021). **1050**

BERICHTE UBER LANDWIRTSCHAFT. (GW/0005-9080). **65**

BERKELEY INSIGHTS IN LINGUISTICS AND SEMIOTICS. (US/0893-6935). **3268**

BERKELEY JOURNAL OF SOCIOLOGY. (US/0067-5830). **5240**

BERKELEY PLANNING JOURNAL. (US/1047-5192). **2816**

BERKSHIRE GENEALOGIST, THE. (US/0887-0713). **2439**

BERYTUS ; ARCHAEOLOGICAL STUDIES. (LE/0067-6195). **261**

BEYOND BEHAVIOR. (US/1074-2956). **1876**

BIBLICAL BULLETIN. (US/0749-9280). **5015**

BIBLICAL THEOLOGY BULLETIN. (US/0146-1079). **5015**

BIBLIO 17. (FR). **3366**

BIBLIOGRAPHY OF THE HISTORY OF ART : BHA. (FR/1150-1588). **334**

BIJDRAGEN TIJDSCHRIFT VOOR FILOSOFIE EN THEOLOGIE. (NE). **4342**

BIJDRAGEN TOT DE DIERKUNDE. (NE/0067-8546). **578**

BIJDRAGEN TOT DE TAAL-, LAND- EN VOLKENKUNDE. (NE/0006-2294). **232**

BILTEN ZA HEMATOLOGIJU I TRANSFUZIJU. (YU/0350-2023). **3770**

BIO SYSTEMS. (IE/0303-2647). **444**

BIO/TECHNOLOGY (NEW YORK, N.Y. 1983). (US/0733-222X). **5088**

BIOACOUSTICS (BERKHAMSTED). (UK/0952-4622). **5578**

BIOCHEMICAL AND BIOPHYSICAL RESEARCH COMMUNICATIONS. (US/0006-291X). **481**

BIOCHEMICAL ARCHIVES. (US/0749-5331). **481**

BIOCHEMICAL GENETICS. (US/0006-2928). **543**

BIOCHEMICAL JOURNAL (LONDON. 1984). (UK/0264-6021). **481**

BIOCHEMICAL PHARMACOLOGY. (UK/0006-2952). **4293**

BIOCHEMICAL SOCIETY SYMPOSIA. (UK/0067-8694). **481**

BIOCHEMICAL SOCIETY TRANSACTIONS. (UK/0300-5127). **481**

BIOCHEMICAL SYSTEMATICS AND ECOLOGY. (UK/0305-1978). **481**

BIOCHEMIE UND PHYSIOLOGIE DER PFLANZEN. (GW/0015-3796). **502**

BIOCHEMISTRY AND CELL BIOLOGY. (CN/0829-8211). **481**

BIOCHEMISTRY (EASTON). (US/0006-2960). **482**

BIOCHEMISTRY INTERNATIONAL. (AT/0158-5231). **482**

BIOCHIMICA CLINICA. (IT/0393-0564). **482**

BIOCHIMICA ET BIOPHYSICA ACTA. (NE/0006-3002). **482**

BIOCHIMICA ET BIOPHYSICA ACTA. MOLECULAR BASIS OF DISEASE. (NE/0925-4439). **482**

BIOCHIMIE. (FR/0300-9084). **483**

BIOCYCLE. (US/0276-5055). **2225**

BIODEGRADATION (DORDRECHT). (NE/0923-9820). **2225**

BIOELECTROMAGNETICS. (US/0197-8462). **3556**

BIOESSAYS. (UK/0265-9247). **532**

BIOETHICS FORUM. (US/1065-7274). **2249**

BIOFACTORS (OXFORD). (UK/0951-6433). **483**

BIOFIZIKA. (RU/0006-3029). **494**

BIOFUTUR. (FR/0294-3506). **3686**

BIOGENIC AMINES. (UK/0168-8561). **483**

BIOGEOCHEMISTRY. (NE/0168-2563). **2188**

BIOGRAPHY INDEX. (US/0006-3053). **439**

BIOGRAPHY TODAY. (US/1058-2347). **430**

BIOLOGIA. (XO/0006-3088). **444**

BIOLOGIA MORA (VLADIVOSTOK). (RU/0134-3475). **553**

BIOLOGIA PLANTARUM. (XR/0006-3134). **502**

BIOLOGICAL AGRICULTURE & HORTICULTURE. (UK/0144-8765). **66**

BIOLOGICAL & AGRICULTURAL INDEX. (US/0006-3177). **477**

BIOLOGICAL BULLETIN (LANCASTER), THE. (US/0006-3185). **444**

BIOLOGICAL CHEMISTRY HOPPE-SEYLER. (GW/0177-3593). **483**

BIOLOGICAL CONSERVATION. (UK/0006-3207). **2188**

BIOLOGICAL CYBERNETICS. (GW/0340-1200). **1250**

BIOLOGICAL MASS SPECTROMETRY. (UK/1052-9306). **1013**

BIOLOGICAL NOTES (COLUMBUS). (US/0078-3986). **445**

BIOLOGICAL PAPERS OF THE UNIVERSITY OF ALASKA. (US/0568-8604). **445**

BIOLOGICAL PSYCHIATRY (1969). (US/0006-3223). **3921**

BIOLOGICAL PSYCHOLOGY. (NE/0301-0511). **4577**

BIOLOGICAL REVIEWS OF THE CAMBRIDGE PHILOSOPHICAL SOCIETY. (UK/0006-3231). **445**

BIOLOGICAL TRACE ELEMENT RESEARCH. (US/0163-4984). **483**

BIOLOGISCHES ZENTRALBLATT. (GW/0006-3304). **446**

BIOLOGY AND FERTILITY OF SOILS. (GW/0178-2762). **164**

BIOLOGY & PHILOSOPHY. (NE/0169-3867). **446**

BIOLOGY OF REPRODUCTION. (US/0006-3363). **578**

BIOLOGY OF THE CELL. (FR/0248-4900). **532**

BIOLOGY OF THE NEONATE. (SZ/0006-3126). **3900**

BIOMATERIALS. (UK/0142-9612). **3556**

BIOMEDICA BIOCHIMICA ACTA. (GW/0232-766X). **447**

BIOMEDICAL RESEARCH (TOKYO). (JA/0388-6107). **3557**

BIOMEDICAL SCIENCE AND TECHNOLOGY. (US/1051-2020). **3687**

BIOMEDICINE & PHARMACOTHERAPY. (FR/0753-3322). **3557**

BIOMEDIZINISCHE TECHNIK. (GW/0013-5585). **3687**

BIOMETRICS. (US/0006-341X). **5323**

BIOMETRIKA. (UK/0006-3444). **447**

BIOORGANIC

BIOORGANIC CHEMISTRY. (US/0045-2068). **1039**

BIOORGANICHESKAIA KHIMIIA. (RU/0132-3423). **1039**

BIOPHARM (EUGENE, OR.). (US/1040-8304). **4293**

BIOPHARMACEUTICS & DRUG DISPOSITION. (UK/0142-2782). **4293**

BIOPHYSICAL CHEMISTRY. (NE/0301-4622). **483**

BIOPOLYMERS. (US/0006-3525). **483**

BIOPROCESS ENGINEERING (BERLIN, WEST). (GW/0178-515X). **2008**

BIORHEOLOGY (OXFORD). (UK/0006-355X). **447**

BIOSCIENCE. (US/0006-3568). **448**

BIOSCIENCE REPORTS. (US/0144-8463). **532**

BIOSENSORS & BIOELECTRONICS. (UK/0956-5663). **484**

BIOSEPARATION. (NE/0923-179X). **3687**

BIOTEC (STUTTGART). (GW/0931-1408). **3687**

BIOTECHNIQUES. (US/0736-6205). **3557**

BIOTECHNOLOGIE. (NE). **448**

BIOTECHNOLOGY ADVANCES. (UK/0734-9750). **3688**

BIOTECHNOLOGY AND APPLIED BIOCHEMISTRY. (US/0885-4513). **3688**

BIOTECHNOLOGY AND BIOENGINEERING. (US/0006-3592). **3688**

BIOTECHNOLOGY LETTERS. (UK/0141-5492). **3689**

BIOTECHNOLOGY PROGRESS. (US/8756-7938). **3689**

BIOTECHNOLOGY TECHNIQUES. (UK/0951-208X). **3689**

BIOTECHNOLOGY THERAPEUTICS. (US/0898-2848). **3690**

BIOTROPICA. (US/0006-3606). **448**

BIRD STUDY. (UK/0006-3657). **5615**

BIRDS OF NORTH AMERICA, THE. (US/1061-5466). **5616**

BIRMINGHAM SLAVONIC MONOGRAPHS. (UK/0141-3805). **3269**

BIRTH (BERKELEY, CALIF.). (US/0730-7659). **3757**

BIT (NORDISK TIDSKRIFT FOR INFORMATIONSBEHANDLING). (DK/0006-3835). **1172**

BITACORA. (SP/0212-632X). **591**

BLACK HEALTH. (US/1042-329X). **4768**

BLIKI : TIMARIT UN FUGLA. (IC). **4163**

BLOCH-ALMANACH. (GW/0721-3743). **4342**

BLOOD. (US/0006-4971). **3770**

BLOOD COAGULATION & FIBRINOLYSIS : AN INTERNATIONAL JOURNAL IN HAEMOSTASIS AND THROMBOSIS. (UK/0957-5235). **3795**

BLOOD PRESSURE. (NO/0803-7051). **3699**

BLOOD PURIFICATION. (SZ/0253-5068). **3770**

BLOOD REVIEWS. (UK/0268-960X). **3770**

BLOUNT JOURNAL, THE. (US/1056-6252). **2439**

BLUMEA. (NE/0006-5196). **502**

BMJ. BRITISH MEDICAL JOURNAL (CLINICAL RESEARCH ED.). (UK/0959-8138). **3557**

BODENKULTUR (1964). (AU/0006-5471). **67**

BODLEIAN LIBRARY RECORD, THE. (UK/0067-9488). **3196**

BODY LEEDS. (UK/0006-5501). **5407**

BOGG (ARLINGTON, VA.). (US/0882-648X). **3368**

BOISE STATE UNIVERSITY WESTERN WRITERS SERIES. (US/0886-7348). **431**

BOLETIN / CENTRO DE ESTUDIOS MONETARIOS LATINOAMERICANOS. (MX). **779**

BOLETIN CHILENO DE PARASITOLOGIA. (CL/0365-9402). **449**

BOLETIN DE ANTROPOLOGIA AMERICANA. (MX/0252-841X). **232**

BOLETIN DE ESTUDIOS MEDICOS Y BIOLOGICOS. (MX/0067-9666). **449**

BOLETIN DE LA OFICINA SANITARIA PANAMERICANA. (US/0030-0632). **4769**

BOLETIN DE LA SOCIEDAD QUIMICA DEL PERU. (PE/0037-8623). **962**

BOLETIN DE LA SOCIEDAD VASCO-NAVARRA DE PEDIATRIA. (SP/0037-8658). **3901**

BOLETIN DE LITERATURA MEDIEVAL. (SP). **3368**

BOLETIN DEL INSTITUTO GEMOLOGICO ESPANOL. (SP/0210-7228). **2913**

BOLETIN ECONOMICO DE LA CONSTRUCCION 1956. (SP/0210-1947). **601**

BOLETIN INFORMATIVO TECHINT. (AG/0497-0292). **1599**

BOLLETTINO DEL LAVORO E DEI TRIBUTI. (IT/0394-6592). **3144**

BOLLETTINO DELLA SOCIETA GEOGRAFICA ITALIANA. (IT/0037-8755). **2556**

BOLLETTINO DI OCEANOLOGIA TEORICA ED APPLICATA. (IT/0393-196X). **1447**

BOLLETTINO DI ZOOLOGIA. (IT/0373-4137). **5578**

BOLLETTINO MALACOLOGICO. (IT/0394-7149). **5578**

BOLLETTINO UFFICIALE MINISTERO LAVORI PUBLICI. (IT). **2943**

BONE AND MINERAL. (NE/0169-6009). **3726**

BONE MARROW TRANSPLANTATION (BASINGSTOKE). (UK/0268-3369). **3558**

BONE (NEW YORK, N.Y.). (US/8756-3282). **3803**

BOOK REVIEW DIGEST. (US/0006-7326). **3356**

BOREAS. (NO/0300-9483). **1368**

BOSTON BAR JOURNAL. (US/0524-1111). **2943**

BOSTON REVIEW (CAMBRIDGE, MASS. : 1982). (US/0734-2306). **3368**

BOSTON UNIVERSITY LAW REVIEW. (US/0006-8047). **2943**

BOTANICA ACTA. (GW/0932-8629). **503**

BOTANICA HELVETICA. (SZ/0253-1453). **503**

BOTANICA MARINA. (GW/0006-8055). **503**

BOTANICAL BULLETIN OF ACADEMIA SINICA. (CH/0006-8063). **503**

BOTANICAL REVIEW, THE. (US/0006-8101). **503**

BOTHALIA. (SA/0006-8241). **504**

BOTTOM LINE (CHARLESTON, S.C.), THE. (US/0279-1889). **739**

BOUNDARY-LAYER METEOROLOGY. (NE/0006-8314). **1421**

BOUWKRONIEK : WEEKBLAD VOOR DE BOUW EN INDUSTRIE. (BE). **601**

BOUWWERELD. (NE/0026-5942). **602**

BRAIN. (UK/0006-8950). **3828**

BRAIN AND COGNITION. (US/0278-2626). **4577**

BRAIN & DEVELOPMENT (TOKYO. 1979). (JA/0387-7604). **3828**

BRAIN AND LANGUAGE. (US/0093-934X). **3828**

BRAIN, BEHAVIOR AND EVOLUTION. (SZ/0006-8977). **3828**

BRAIN RESEARCH BULLETIN. (US/0361-9230). **3829**

BRASIL PORTO ALEGRE. (BL/0103-751X). **3369**

BRAZILIAN JOURNAL OF MEDICAL AND BIOLOGICAL RESEARCH. (BL/0100-879X). **3558**

BREAST CANCER RESEARCH AND TREATMENT. (NE/0167-6806). **3809**

BRENNSTOFF-WAERME-KRAFT. (GW/0006-9612). **1934**

BRETHREN IN CHRIST HISTORY AND LIFE. (US/1071-4200). **5057**

BRIDGING THE GAP (LANCASTER). (CN/0840-7738). **2440**

BRIMLEYANA. (US/0193-4406). **5578**

BRITANNIA MONOGRAPH SERIES. (UK/0953-542X). **411**

BRITISH COLUMBIA MEDICAL JOURNAL. (CN/0007-0556). **3558**

BRITISH CORROSION JOURNAL. (UK/0007-0599). **2008**

BRITISH DENTAL JOURNAL. (UK/0007-0610). **1317**

BRITISH HEART JOURNAL. (UK/0007-0769). **3699**

BRITISH HOTELIER & RESTAURATEUR : OFFICIAL MAGAZINE OF THE BRITISH HOTELS, RESTAURANTS & CATERERS ASSOCIATION. (UK). **2804**

BRITISH JOURNAL FOR THE HISTORY OF SCIENCE, THE. (UK/0007-0874). **5089**

BRITISH JOURNAL FOR THE PHILOSOPHY OF SCIENCE, THE. (UK/0007-0882). **5089**

BRITISH JOURNAL OF ACADEMIC LIBRARIANSHIP. (UK/0269-0497). **3197**

BRITISH JOURNAL OF ANAESTHESIA. (UK/0007-0912). **3682**

BRITISH JOURNAL OF CANCER. (UK/0007-0920). **3809**

BRITISH JOURNAL OF CLINICAL PHARMACOLOGY. (UK/0306-5251). **4294**

BRITISH JOURNAL OF CLINICAL PRACTICE, THE. (UK/0007-0947). **3558**

BRITISH JOURNAL OF CLINICAL PSYCHOLOGY, THE. (UK/0144-6657). **4578**

BRITISH JOURNAL OF CRIMINOLOGY, DELINQUENCY AND DEVIANT SOCIAL BEHAVIOR, THE. (UK/0007-0955). **3158**

BRITISH JOURNAL OF DERMATOLOGY (1951). (UK/0007-0963). **3718**

BRITISH JOURNAL OF DEVELOPMENTAL PSYCHOLOGY, THE. (UK/0261-510X). **4578**

BRITISH JOURNAL OF EDUCATION AND WORK. (UK). **1728**

BRITISH JOURNAL OF EDUCATIONAL PSYCHOLOGY, THE. (UK/0007-0998). **4578**

BRITISH JOURNAL OF EDUCATIONAL STUDIES. (UK/0007-1005). **1728**

BRITISH JOURNAL OF EDUCATIONAL TECHNOLOGY. (UK/0007-1013). **1889**

BRITISH JOURNAL OF HAEMATOLOGY. (UK/0007-1048). **3771**

BRITISH JOURNAL OF HEALTHCARE COMPUTING, THE. (UK/0265-5217). **1172**

BRITISH JOURNAL OF HOSPITAL MEDICINE. (UK/0007-1064). **3559**

BRITISH JOURNAL OF INDUSTRIAL MEDICINE. (UK/0007-1072). **2859**

BRITISH JOURNAL OF INDUSTRIAL RELATIONS. (UK/0007-1080). **1656**

BRITISH JOURNAL OF MATHEMATICAL & STATISTICAL PSYCHOLOGY, THE. (UK/0007-1102). **4622**

BRITISH JOURNAL OF MEDICAL ECONOMICS, THE. (UK/0962-1423). **1465**

BRITISH JOURNAL OF MEDICAL PSYCHOLOGY. (UK/0007-1129). **4578**

BRITISH JOURNAL OF MENTAL SUBNORMALITY. (UK/0374-633X). **1876**

BRITISH JOURNAL OF MIDDLE EASTERN STUDIES. (UK). **2768**

BRITISH JOURNAL OF NEUROSURGERY. (UK/0268-8697). **3829**

BRITISH JOURNAL OF NON-DESTRUCTIVE TESTING. (UK/0007-1137). **2101**

BRITISH JOURNAL OF NUTRITION, THE. (UK/0007-1145). **4188**

BRITISH JOURNAL OF OBSTETRICS AND GYNAECOLOGY. (UK/0306-5456). **3758**

BRITISH JOURNAL OF OPHTHALMOLOGY. (UK/0007-1161). **3872**

BRITISH JOURNAL OF ORAL & MAXILLOFACIAL SURGERY, THE. (UK/0266-4356). **3961**

BRITISH JOURNAL OF PHARMACOLOGY. (UK/0007-1188). **4294**

BRITISH JOURNAL OF PHYSICAL EDUCATION. (UK/0144-3569). **1855**

BRITISH JOURNAL OF PLASTIC SURGERY. (UK/0007-1226). **3961**

BRITISH JOURNAL OF PODIATRIC MEDICINE & SURGERY. (UK/0955-8160). **3917**

BRITISH JOURNAL OF POLITICAL SCIENCE. (UK/0007-1234). **4466**

BRITISH JOURNAL OF PSYCHIATRY, THE. (UK/0007-1250). **3922**

BRITISH JOURNAL OF PSYCHOLOGY (1955). (UK/0007-1269). **4578**

BRITISH JOURNAL OF RADIOLOGY, THE. (UK/0007-1285). **3939**

BRITISH JOURNAL OF RHEUMATOLOGY. (UK/0263-7103). **3803**

BRITISH JOURNAL OF SOCIAL PSYCHOLOGY, THE. (UK/0144-6665). **4578**

BRITISH JOURNAL OF SOCIAL WORK, THE. (UK/0045-3102). **5275**

BRITISH JOURNAL OF SOCIOLOGY OF EDUCATION. (UK/0142-5692). **5241**

BRITISH JOURNAL OF SOCIOLOGY, THE. (UK/0007-1315). **5240**

BRITISH JOURNAL OF SURGERY. (UK/0007-1323). **3961**

BRITISH JOURNAL OF UROLOGY. (UK/0007-1331). **3988**

BRITISH LIBRARIANSHIP AND INFORMATION WORK. (UK). **3197**

BRITISH MEDICAL BULLETIN. (UK/0007-1420). **3559**

BRITISH PHYCOLOGICAL JOURNAL. (UK/0007-1617). **504**

BRITISH POULTRY SCIENCE. (UK/0007-1668). **207**

BRITISH REVIEW OF ECONOMIC ISSUES. (UK/0141-4739). **1465**

BRITISH TELECOMMUNICATIONS ENGINEERING. (UK/0262-401X). **1150**

BRITISH VETERINARY JOURNAL, THE. (UK/0007-1935). **5506**

BRITTONIA. (US/0007-196X). **504**

BRONTE SOCIETY PUBLICATIONS. TRANSACTIONS. (UK/0309-7765). **3369**

BROWN'S NAUTICAL ALMANAC; DAILY TIDE TABLES. (UK/0068-290X). **4175**

BRUEL & KJAER TECHNICAL REVIEW. (DK/0007-2621). **1967**

BRYOLOGIST, THE. (US/0007-2745). **504**

BUFFALO LAW REVIEW. (US/0023-9356). **2944**

BUILDING AND ENVIRONMENT. (UK/0360-1323). **602**

BUILDING RESEARCH AND INFORMATION : THE INTERNATIONAL JOURNAL OF RESEARCH, DEVELOPMENT AND DEMONSTRATION. (UK/0961-3218). **604**

BUILDING SERVICES ENGINEERING RESEARCH & TECHNOLOGY. (UK/0143-6244). **604**

BULLETIN. (FR). **5229**

BULLETIN - ASSOCIATION CANADIENNE POUR L'AVANCEMENT DES ETUDES NEERLANDAISES. (CN/0823-9487). **2680**

BULLETIN / BIBLIOGRAPHICAL SOCIETY OF AUSTRALIA AND NEW ZEALAND. (AT/0084-7852). **3198**

BULLETIN / BRITISH ARACHNOLOGICAL SOCIETY. (UK/0524-4994). **5579**

BULLETIN / CANADIAN SOCIETY FOR MESOPOTAMIAN STUDIES. (CN/0844-3416). **262**

BULLETIN / COLLEGE OF FORESTRY, WILDLIFE AND RANGE SCIENCES. (US). **2189**

BULLETIN / COLONIAL WATERBIRD SOCIETY. (US). **5616**

BULLETIN - COUNCIL FOR RESEARCH IN MUSIC EDUCATION. (US/0010-9894). **4105**

BULLETIN DE LA SOCIETE ARCHEOLOGIQUE ET HISTORIQUE DU LIMOUSIN. (FR). **263**

BULLETIN DE LA SOCIETE BELGE DE GEOLOGIE. (BE/0379-1807). **1368**

BULLETIN DE LA SOCIETE CHIMIQUE DE FRANCE (PARIS, FRANCE : 1985). (FR/0037-8968). **963**

BULLETIN DE LA SOCIETE DE L'HISTOIRE DU PROTESTANTISME FRANCAIS (1981). (FR/0037-9050). **5057**

BULLETIN DE LA SOCIETE GEOLOGIQUE DE FRANCE. (FR/0037-9409). **1368**

BULLETIN DE LA SOCIETE MATHEMATIQUE DE FRANCE. (FR/0037-9484). **3497**

BULLETIN DE LA SOCIETE ZOOLOGIQUE DE FRANCE. (FR/0037-962X). **5579**

BULLETIN DE L'ACADEMIE NATIONALE DE MEDICINE. (FR/0001-4079). **3559**

BULLETIN DE LIAISON DU CNDT. (FR/0995-3671). **1342**

BULLETIN DE L'INSTITUT PASTEUR. (FR/0020-2452). **3667**

BULLETIN DE L'UNION INTERNATIONALE CONTRE LA TUBERCULOSE ET LES MALADIES RESPIRATOIRES. (FR/1011-7903). **3949**

BULLETIN DES RECHERCHES AGRONOMIQUES DE GEMBLOUX. (BE/0435-2033). **69**

BULLETIN DES SCIENCES MATHEMATIQUES. (FR/0007-4497). **3498**

BULLETIN DES SOCIETES CHIMIQUES BELGES. (BE/0037-9646). **963**

BULLETIN D'INFORMATION ET DE LIAISON - ASSOCIATION DES SERVICES GEOLOGIQUES AFRICAINS. (FR/0396-8863). **1369**

BULLETIN D'INFORMATION SPORTIVE BRUXELLES. (BE/1012-0491). **4888**

BULLETIN FRANCAIS DE LA PECHE ET DE LA PISCICULTURE. (FR/0767-2861). **2298**

BULLETIN - GEOLOGICAL SURVEY OF WESTERN AUSTRALIA. (AT/0085-8137). **1369**

BULLETIN - ILLINOIS GEOGRAPHICAL SOCIETY. (US/0019-2031). **2557**

BULLETIN - KANSAS ORNITHOLOGICAL SOCIETY. (US/0022-8729). **5616**

BULLETIN (MISSISSIPPI AGRICULTURAL AND FORESTRY EXPERIMENT STATION). (US/0898-0497). **69**

BULLETIN - NEW JERSEY ACADEMY OF SCIENCE, THE. (US/0028-5455). **5091**

BULLETIN / NEW MEXICO STATE UNIVERSITY, AGRICULTURAL EXPERIMENT STATION. (US/0149-9866). **69**

BULLETIN (NEW SERIES) OF THE AMERICAN MATHEMATICAL SOCIETY. (US/0273-0979). **3498**

BULLETIN (NEW YORK STATE SCHOOL OF INDUSTRIAL AND LABOR RELATIONS). (US/0070-0134). **1657**

BULLETIN OF CANADIAN PETROLEUM GEOLOGY. (CN/0007-4802). **4252**

BULLETIN OF CARNEGIE MUSEUM OF NATURAL HISTORY. (US/0145-9058). **4164**

BULLETIN OF CONCERNED ASIAN SCHOLARS. (US/0007-4810). **2647**

BULLETIN OF DENTAL EDUCATION. (US/0007-4837). **1318**

BULLETIN OF EASTERN CARIBBEAN AFFAIRS. (BB). **2511**

BULLETIN OF ENTOMOLOGICAL RESEARCH. (UK/0007-4853). **5606**

BULLETIN OF ENVIRONMENTAL CONTAMINATION AND TOXICOLOGY. (US/0007-4861). **3979**

BULLETIN OF HISTORICAL RESEARCH IN MUSIC EDUCATION, THE. (US/0739-5639). **4106**

BULLETIN OF INDONESIAN ECONOMIC STUDIES. (AT/0007-4918). **1466**

BULLETIN OF MAGNETIC RESONANCE. (US/0163-559X). **4443**

BULLETIN OF MARINE SCIENCE. (US/0007-4977). **1447**

BULLETIN OF MATERIALS SCIENCE. (II/0250-4707). **5091**

BULLETIN OF MATHEMATICAL BIOLOGY. (US/0092-8240). **450**

BULLETIN OF PEACE PROPOSALS. (NO/0007-5035). **4466**

BULLETIN OF PURE & APPLIED SCIENCES. SEC. D, PHYSICS. (II). **4399**

BULLETIN OF PURE & APPLIED SCIENCES. SEC. E, MATHEMATICS. (II/0970-6577). **3498**

BULLETIN OF THE ALLYN MUSEUM. (US/0097-3211). **4086**

BULLETIN OF THE AMERICAN METEOROLOGICAL SOCIETY. (US/0003-0007). **1421**

BULLETIN OF THE AMERICAN MUSEUM OF NATURAL HISTORY. (US/0003-0090). **4164**

BULLETIN OF THE ASIA INSTITUTE. (US/0890-4464). **2647**

BULLETIN OF THE ASTRONOMICAL SOCIETY OF INDIA. (II/0304-9523). **394**

BULLETIN OF THE ATOMIC SCIENTISTS. (US/0096-3402). **5091**

BULLETIN OF THE AUSTRALIAN MATHEMATICAL SOCIETY. (AT/0004-9727). **3498**

BULLETIN OF THE AUSTRALIAN SOCIETY OF LEGAL PHILOSOPHY. (AT/0726-5239). **2945**

BULLETIN OF THE CALIFORNIA INSECT SURVEY. (US/0068-5631). **5606**

BULLETIN OF THE CHEMICAL SOCIETY OF JAPAN. (JA/0009-2673). **963**

BULLETIN OF THE EGYPTOLOGICAL SEMINAR. (US/0270-210X). **264**

BULLETIN OF THE EUROPEAN ASSOCIATION OF FISH PATHOLOGISTS. (NE/0108-0288). **2298**

BULLETIN OF THE EVANGELICAL PHILOSOPHICAL SOCIETY. (US). **4343**

BULLETIN OF THE HISTORY OF MEDICINE. (US/0007-5140). **3560**

BULLETIN OF THE INSTITUTE OF MARITIME AND TROPICAL MEDICINE IN GDYNIA. (PL/0324-8542). **3985**

BULLETIN OF THE INTERNATIONAL GROUP FOR THE STUDY OF MIMOSOIDEAE. (FR). **2411**

BULLETIN OF THE INTERNATIONAL ORGANIZATION FOR SEPTUAGINT AND COGNITE STUDIES. (US/0145-3890). **5046**

BULLETIN OF THE LONDON MATHEMATICAL SOCIETY, THE. (UK/0024-6093). **3498**

BULLETIN OF THE MALAYSIAN MATHEMATICAL SOCIETY. (MY/0126-6705). **3498**

BULLETIN OF THE MEDICAL LIBRARY ASSOCIATION. (US/0025-7338). **3198**

BULLETIN OF THE MENNINGER CLINIC. (US/0025-9284). **3922**

BULLETIN OF THE NEW YORK ACADEMY OF MEDICINE (1925). (US/0028-7091). **3560**

BULLETIN OF THE OHIO BIOLOGICAL SURVEY. (US/0078-3994). **450**

BULLETIN OF THE PSYCHONOMIC SOCIETY. (US/0090-5054). **4579**

BULLETIN OF THE SEISMOLOGICAL SOCIETY OF AMERICA. (US/0037-1106). **1403**

BULLETIN OF THE SOCIETY OF VECTOR ECOLOGISTS. (US/0146-6429). **2212**

BULLETIN OF THE TEXAS ORNITHOLOGICAL SOCIETY. (US/0040-4543). **5616**

BULLETIN OF THE TORREY BOTANICAL CLUB, THE. (US/0040-9618). **505**

BULLETIN OF THE WORLD HEALTH ORGANIZATION. (SZ/0042-9686). **3560**

BULLETIN OF VOLCANOLOGY. (GW/0258-8900). **1403**

BULLETIN - OHIO FLORISTS' ASSOCIATION. (US/0030-090X). **2434**

BULLETIN ON THE RHEUMATIC DISEASES. (US/0007-5248). **3804**

BULLETIN - OVERSEAS DEVELOPMENT NATURAL RESOURCES INSTITUTE. (UK/0952-8245). **70**

BULLETIN / POLISH GENEALOGICAL SOCIETY, CALIFORNIA. (US/1056-568X). **2441**

BULLETIN / SOUTHERN CALIFORNIA ACADEMY OF SCIENCES. (US/0038-3872). **5092**

BULLETIN - STATE OF ALASKA, ALASKA OIL AND GAS CONSERVATION COMMISSION. (US). **2189**

BULLETIN - UK CENTRE FOR ECONOMIC AND ENVIRONMENTAL DEVELOPMENT. (UK/0268-7402). **1466**

BULLETIN / VIRGINIA AGRICULTURAL EXPERIMENT STATION. (US/0096-6088). **70**

BULLETIN - YAKIMA VALLEY GENEALOGICAL SOCIETY. (US/0513-6776). **2441**

BUNGEI KENKYU. (JA). **3370**

BUNSEKI KAGAKU. (JA/0525-1931). **1014**

BURNS : JOURNAL OF THE INTERNATIONAL SOCIETY FOR BURN INJURIES. (UK/0305-4179). **3561**

BUSINESS & ECONOMIC REPORT. (US/1043-6227). **1550**

BUSINESS & PROFESSIONAL ETHICS JOURNAL. (US/0277-2027). **645**

BUSINESS AND SOCIETY. (US/0007-6503). **645**

BUSINESS ARCHIVES. (UK/0007-6538). **3199**

BUSINESS FORUM (LOS ANGELES, CALIF.). (US/0733-2408). **648**

BUSINESS HISTORY. (UK/0007-6791). **648**

BUSINESS HISTORY REVIEW. (US/0007-6805). **648**

BUSINESS HISTORY REVIEW. (US/0007-6805). **648**

BUSINESS LAW REVIEW LONDON. (UK/0143-6295). **3096**

BUSINESS LAWYER, THE. (US/0007-6899). **3097**

BUSINESS OPPORTUNITIES HANDBOOK. (US/1042-6175). **651**

BUSINESS PERIODICALS INDEX. (US/0007-6961). **727**

BUSINESS PROCESS RE-ENGINEERING & MANAGEMENT JOURNAL. (UK/1355-2546). **862**

BUTTERWORTHS CURRENT LAW. (NZ/0110-070X). **3125**

BUY BOOKS WHERE, SELL BOOKS WHERE. (US/0732-6599). **4812**

BVDA JOURNAL : BRITISH VETERINARY DENTAL ASSOCIATION. (UK). 5507
BYTE. (US/0360-5280). 1273
BYZANTINE AND MODERN GREEK STUDIES. (UK/0307-0131). 2682
BYZANTINE STUDIES. (US/0095-4608). 2682
C C C N (CALIFORNIA COMMUNITY CARE NEWS). (US). 2529
C-MAGAZIN. (GW/0935-0373). 4941
CA. (US/0007-9235). 3810
CAC NEWS - CHICAGO ARTISTS' COALITION. (US/0890-5908). 346
CACTUS AND SUCCULENT JOURNAL WOOLLAHRA. (AT/0526-7196). 2411
CAD CAM REPORT. (GW). 1227
CAD USER. (UK/0959-6259). 1222
CAFE, CACAO, THE. (FR/0007-9510). 165
CAHIER - DEPARTEMENT D'ECONNOMIQUE, FACULTE DES SCIENCES SOCIALES, UNIVERSITE LAVAL. (CN/0714-5659). 1467
CAHIERS DE BIOLOGIE MARINE. (FR/0007-9723). 553
CAHIERS DE FONTENAY, LES. (FR/0395-8418). 2844
CAHIERS DE PSYCHOLOGIE COGNITIVE. (FR/0249-9185). 4579
CAHIERS DE SOCIOLOGIE ECONOMIQUE ET CULTURELLE, ETHNOPSYCHOLOGIE. (FR/0761-9871). 5241
CAHIERS DE TOPOLOGIE ET GEOMETRIE DIFFERENTIELLE CATEGORIQUES. (FR). 3499
CAHIERS D'OUTRE-MER. (FR/0373-5834). 2557
CAHIERS DU CENTRE D'ETUDES DE L'ASIE DE L'EST. (CN/0839-4555). 2844
CAHIERS DU LABRAPS. (CN/0824-0736). 1813
CAHIERS ECONOMIQUES DE BRUXELLES. (BE/0008-0195). 1467
CAHIERS ETHNOLOGIQUES. (FR/0249-5635). 233
CAHIERS FRANCO-CANADIENS DE LOUEST. (CN/0843-9559). 3272
CAHIERS HENRI BOSCO. (FR). 431
CAHIERS INTERNATIONAUX DE SOCIOLOGIE. (FR/0008-0276). 5241
CAKALELE (HONOLULU, HAWAII). (US/1053-2285). 2647
CALAO. (FR/0335-6469). 1060
CALCIFIED TISSUE INTERNATIONAL. (US/0171-967X). 578
CALCUTTA LAW JOURNAL. (II). 2946
CALIFORNIA AGRICULTURE (BERKELEY, CALIF.). (US/0008-0845). 71
CALIFORNIA BUSINESS LAW REPORTER. (US/0199-669X). 3097
CALIFORNIA FISH AND GAME. (US/0008-1078). 2189
CALIFORNIA HEALTH LAW REPORT. (US). 2946
CALIFORNIA LABOR LETTER. (US). 1658
CALIFORNIA LAW REVIEW. (US/0008-1221). 2946
CALIFORNIA MANAGEMENT REVIEW. (US/0008-1256). 862
CALIFORNIA OPTOMETRY. (US/0273-804X). 4215
CALIFORNIA PEACE OFFICER, THE. (US/0199-7025). 3159

CALIFORNIA PLANT PATHOLOGY. (US/0094-3800). 505
CALIFORNIA PRISONER, THE. (US/0884-0075). 3159
CALIFORNIA SOCIOLOGIST. (US/0162-8712). 5241
CALPHAD. (US/0364-5916). 1050
CAMBRIA. (UK/0306-9796). 2557
CAMBRIDGE JOURNAL OF ECONOMICS. (UK/0309-166X). 1467
CAMBRIDGE MEDIEVAL CELTIC STUDIES. (UK/0260-5600). 3272
CANADA: THE STATE OF THE FEDERATION. (CN/0827-0708). 4636
CANADIAN ACOUSTICS. (CN/0711-6659). 2162
CANADIAN ADMINISTRATOR, THE. (CN/0008-2813). 1861
CANADIAN AERONAUTICS AND SPACE JOURNAL. (CN/0008-2821). 15
CANADIAN AGRICULTURAL ENGINEERING. (CN/0045-432X). 158
CANADIAN AND INTERNATIONAL EDUCATION. (CN/0315-1409). 1730
CANADIAN BAPTIST, THE. (CN/0008-2988). 4942
CANADIAN CAVER, THE. (CN/0833-0948). 4870
CANADIAN CERAMICS QUARTERLY. (CN/0831-2974). 2587
CANADIAN DENTAL ASSISTANTS' ASSOCIATION : JOURNAL. (CN/0833-8264). 1318
CANADIAN EMERGENCY NEWS. (CN/0847-947X). 4770
CANADIAN ENTOMOLOGIST, THE. (CN/0008-347X). 5606
CANADIAN ETHNIC STUDIES. (CN/0008-3496). 2257
CANADIAN FAMILY PHYSICIAN. (CN/0008-350X). 3737
CANADIAN GEMMOLOGIST. (CN/0226-7446). 2913
CANADIAN GEOGRAPHER. (CN/0008-3658). 2558
CANADIAN GEOTECHNICAL JOURNAL. (CN/0008-3674). 1352
CANADIAN ISSUES (ASSOCIATION FOR CANADIAN STUDIES). (CN/0318-8442). 2726
CANADIAN JOURNAL FOR THE STUDY OF ADULT EDUCATION. (CN/0835-4944). 1800
CANADIAN JOURNAL OF AFRICAN STUDIES. (CN/0008-3968). 2638
CANADIAN JOURNAL OF AGRICULTURAL ECONOMICS. (CN/0008-3976). 72
CANADIAN JOURNAL OF ANIMAL SCIENCE. (CN/0008-3984). 208
CANADIAN JOURNAL OF APPLIED SPECTROSCOPY. (CN/1183-7306). 4434
CANADIAN JOURNAL OF ARCHAEOLOGY. (CN/0705-2006). 265
CANADIAN JOURNAL OF BEHAVIOURAL SCIENCE. (CN/0008-400X). 4579
CANADIAN JOURNAL OF BOTANY. (CN/0008-4026). 505
CANADIAN JOURNAL OF CARDIOLOGY. (CN/0828-282X). 3700
CANADIAN JOURNAL OF CARDIOVASCULAR NURSING. (CN/0843-6096). 3700
CANADIAN JOURNAL OF CHEMICAL ENGINEERING, THE. (CN/0008-4034). 2008

CANADIAN JOURNAL OF CHEMISTRY. (CN/0008-4042). 966
CANADIAN JOURNAL OF CIVIL ENGINEERING. (CN/0315-1468). 2020
CANADIAN JOURNAL OF CRIMINOLOGY. (CN/0704-9722). 3159
CANADIAN JOURNAL OF EARTH SCIENCES. (CN/0008-4077). 1353
CANADIAN JOURNAL OF ECONOMICS, THE. (CN/0008-4085). 1468
CANADIAN JOURNAL OF EDUCATION. (CN/0380-2361). 1730
CANADIAN JOURNAL OF EDUCATIONAL COMMUNICATION. (CN/0710-4340). 1105
CANADIAN JOURNAL OF ELECTRICAL AND COMPUTER ENGINEERING. (CN/0840-8688). 1227
CANADIAN JOURNAL OF EXPERIMENTAL PSYCHOLOGY. (CN/1196-1961). 4579
CANADIAN JOURNAL OF FISHERIES AND AQUATIC SCIENCES. (CN/0706-652X). 2298
CANADIAN JOURNAL OF FOREST RESEARCH. (CN/0045-5067). 2377
CANADIAN JOURNAL OF GASTROENTEROLOGY, THE. (CN/0835-7900). 3743
CANADIAN JOURNAL OF HERBALISM. (CN/0848-9629). 2412
CANADIAN JOURNAL OF HISTORY. (CN/0008-4107). 2613
CANADIAN JOURNAL OF HISTORY OF SPORT. (CN/0712-9815). 4889
CANADIAN JOURNAL OF HUMAN SEXUALITY, THE. (CN/1188-4517). 5187
CANADIAN JOURNAL OF INFORMATION SCIENCE. (CN/0380-9218). 3199
CANADIAN JOURNAL OF IRISH STUDIES, THE. (CN/0703-1459). 3372
CANADIAN JOURNAL OF LAW AND SOCIETY. (CN/0829-3201). 2948
CANADIAN JOURNAL OF LINGUISTICS. (CN/0008-4131). 3272
CANADIAN JOURNAL OF MARKETING RESEARCH. (CN/0829-4836). 922
CANADIAN JOURNAL OF MATHEMATICS. (CN/0008-414X). 3499
CANADIAN JOURNAL OF MICROBIOLOGY. (CN/0008-4166). 560
CANADIAN JOURNAL OF NEUROLOGICAL SCIENCES. (CN/0317-1671). 3829
CANADIAN JOURNAL OF NURSING ADMINISTRATION. (CN/0838-2948). 3852
CANADIAN JOURNAL OF NURSING RESEARCH, THE. (CN/0844-5621). 3852
CANADIAN JOURNAL OF OPHTHALMOLOGY. (CN/0008-4182). 3873
CANADIAN JOURNAL OF PHYSICS. (CN/0008-4204). 4399
CANADIAN JOURNAL OF PHYSIOLOGY AND PHARMACOLOGY. (CN/0008-4212). 579
CANADIAN JOURNAL OF PLANT PATHOLOGY. (CN/0706-0661). 505
CANADIAN JOURNAL OF PLANT SCIENCE. (CN/0008-4220). 505
CANADIAN JOURNAL OF POLITICAL SCIENCE. (CN/0008-4239). 4467

CANADIAN JOURNAL OF PROGRAM EVALUATION, THE. (CN/0834-1516). 4636
CANADIAN JOURNAL OF PSYCHIATRY. (CN/0706-7437). 3923
CANADIAN JOURNAL OF PSYCHOLOGY. (CN/0008-4255). 4579
CANADIAN JOURNAL OF PUBLIC HEALTH. (CN/0008-4263). 4770
CANADIAN JOURNAL OF REHABILITATION. (CN/0828-0827). 4379
CANADIAN JOURNAL OF RESEARCH IN EARLY CHILDHOOD EDUCATION, THE. (CN/0827-0899). 1803
CANADIAN JOURNAL OF SCHOOL PSYCHOLOGY. (CN/0829-5735). 1730
CANADIAN JOURNAL OF SOCIOLOGY. (CN/0318-6431). 5241
CANADIAN JOURNAL OF SOIL SCIENCE. (US/0008-4271). 1371
CANADIAN JOURNAL OF SOIL SCIENCE. (CN/0008-4271). 166
CANADIAN JOURNAL OF SPORT SCIENCES. (US/0833-1235). 3953
CANADIAN JOURNAL OF STATISTICS, THE. (CN/0319-5724). 5325
CANADIAN JOURNAL OF SURGERY. (CN/0008-428X). 3961
CANADIAN JOURNAL OF URBAN RESEARCH. (CN/1188-3774). 2817
CANADIAN JOURNAL OF VETERINARY RESEARCH. (CN/0830-9000). 5507
CANADIAN JOURNAL OF WOMEN AND THE LAW. (CN/0832-8781). 2948
CANADIAN JOURNAL OF ZOOLOGY. (CN/0008-4301). 5580
CANADIAN JOURNAL ON AGING. (CN/0714-9808). 3750
CANADIAN LAW LIBRARIES. (CN/1180-176X). 2948
CANADIAN LIBRARY JOURNAL. (CN/0008-4352). 3200
CANADIAN MATHEMATICAL BULLETIN. (CN/0008-4395). 3499
CANADIAN METALLURGICAL QUARTERLY. (CN/0008-4433). 3999
CANADIAN MINERALOGIST, THE. (CN/0008-4476). 1438
CANADIAN MODERN LANGUAGE REVIEW, THE. (CN/0008-4506). 3272
CANADIAN NURSE (1924). (CN/0008-4581). 3852
CANADIAN ONCOLOGY NURSING JOURNAL. (CN/1181-912X). 3853
CANADIAN ONCOLOGY NURSING JOURNAL. (CN/1181-912X). 3853
CANADIAN PLANT DISEASE SURVEY. (CN/0008-476X). 72
CANADIAN PUBLIC ADMINISTRATION. (CN/0008-4840). 4636
CANADIAN PUBLIC POLICY. (CN/0317-0861). 1468
CANADIAN RAILWAY MODELLER. (CN/0849-2964). 5430
CANADIAN REFERENCE DIRECTORY ON BUSINESS PLANNING AND FUNDING. (CN). 655
CANADIAN REVIEW OF SOCIAL POLICY (1987). (CN/0836-303X). 5276
CANADIAN REVIEW OF SOCIOLOGY AND ANTHROPOLOGY, THE. (CN/0008-4948). 233
CANADIAN REVIEW OF STUDIES IN NATIONALISM. (CN/0317-7904). 2635
CANADIAN SCHOOL EXECUTIVE (1982). (CN/0228-0914). 1861

CANAL PARIS. (FR/0151-4989). **317**

CANCER. (US/0008-543X). **3810**

CANCER AND METASTASIS REVIEWS. (NE/0167-7659). **3810**

CANCER BIOCHEMISTRY BIOPHYSICS. (US/0305-7232). **3810**

CANCER CAUSES & CONTROL : CCC. (UK/0957-5243). **3810**

CANCER CHEMOTHERAPY AND PHARMACOLOGY. (GW/0344-5704). **3810**

CANCER DETECTION AND PREVENTION. (US/0361-090X). **3811**

CANCER FORUM. (AT/0311-306X). **3811**

CANCER GENETICS AND CYTOGENETICS. (US/0165-4608). **3811**

CANCER IMMUNOLOGY AND IMMUNOTHERAPY. (GW/0340-7004). **3811**

CANCER INVESTIGATION. (US/0735-7907). **3811**

CANCER LETTERS. (NE/0304-3835). **3811**

CANCER NURSING. (US/0162-220X). **3853**

CANCER PREVENTION (BALTIMORE, MD.). (US/1043-8491). **3812**

CANCER RESEARCH (BALTIMORE). (US/0008-5472). **3812**

CANCER SURVEYS. (US/0261-2429). **3812**

CANCER THERAPY UPDATE. (US/0924-6533). **3812**

CANCER TREATMENT REVIEWS. (UK/0305-7372). **3812**

CANDLE COMPUTER REPORT. (US/1071-2976). **1173**

CANPARA (1976). (CN/0227-5880). **4889**

CANTIGUEIROS (LEXINGTON, KY.). (US/0898-8463). **3372**

CAPITALISM, NATURE, SOCIALISM. (US/1045-5752). **2212**

CARBOHYDRATE POLYMERS. (UK/0144-8617). **1040**

CARBOHYDRATE RESEARCH. (NE/0008-6215). **1040**

CARBON (NEW YORK). (US/0008-6223). **1035**

CARBONATES AND EVAPORITES. (US/0891-2556). **1371**

CARCINOGENESIS (NEW YORK). (US/0143-3334). **3814**

CARDIOLOGY. (SZ/0008-6312). **3700**

CARDIOLOGY BOARD REVIEW. (US/0888-8418). **3700**

CARDIOLOGY IN THE YOUNG. (US/1047-9511). **3701**

CARDIOLOGY UPDATE. (US/0163-1675). **3701**

CARDIOPULMONARY PHYSICAL THERAPY JOURNAL. (US). **4379**

CARDIOSCIENCE. (IT/1015-5007). **3701**

CARDIOVASCULAR AND INTERVENTIONAL RADIOLOGY. (US/0174-1551). **3939**

CARDIOVASCULAR DRUGS AND THERAPY. (US/0920-3206). **3701**

CARDIOVASCULAR RESEARCH. (UK/0008-6363). **3702**

CARDIOVASCULAR REVIEWS & REPORTS. (US/0197-3118). **3702**

CARDIOVASCULAR RISK FACTORS. (CN/0842-537X). **3702**

CARDOZO STUDIES IN LAW AND LITERATURE. (US/1043-1500). **2948**

CARE CONNECTION, THE. (CN/0843-9966). **3853**

CARIBBEAN PORTS HANDBOOK. (JM). **5448**

CARIES RESEARCH. (SZ/0008-6568). **1318**

CARLYLE STUDIES ANNUAL. (US/1074-2670). **3373**

CAROUSEL NEWS & TRADER, THE. (US/0892-9769). **250**

CARREFOUR. (CN/0706-1250). **4343**

CARRIEROLOGIE. (CN/0820-5000). **1658**

CARRYING STREAM, THE. (UK/0961-4532). **2683**

CARTA INFORMATIVA PARA LOS SOCIOS. (ES). **818**

CARTOGRAPHIC JOURNAL, THE. (UK/0008-7041). **2581**

CARTOGRAPHY. (AT/0069-0805). **2581**

CARTOGRAPHY AND GEOGRAPHIC INFORMATION SYSTEMS. (US/1050-9844). **2581**

CARYOLOGIA. (IT/0008-7114). **450**

CAS JOURNAL. (US/1053-7694). **4108**

CASA DEL TIEMPO. (MX/0185-4275). **2511**

CASE MANAGER. (US/1061-9259). **2877**

CASSAVA BIBLIOGRAPHIC BULLETIN. (CK). **72**

CASSAVA NEWSLETTER. (CK/0120-1824). **166**

CASTANEA. (US/0008-7475). **506**

CATALAN REVIEW. (SP/0213-5949). **2258**

CATALOGING & CLASSIFICATION QUARTERLY. (US/0163-9374). **3200**

CATALYSIS. (UK/0140-0568). **1050**

CATALYSIS REVIEWS : SCIENCE AND ENGINEERING. (US/0161-4940). **2009**

CATALYSIS TODAY. (NE/0920-5861). **966**

CATALYST REVIEW NEWSLETTER, THE. (US/0898-3089). **1050**

CATENA (GIESSEN). (GW/0341-8162). **166**

CATERING & HEALTH. (UK/0267-3851). **2330**

CATHETERIZATION AND CARDIOVASCULAR DIAGNOSIS. (US/0098-6569). **3702**

CATHOLIC SCHOOL STUDIES: A JOURNAL OF EDUCATION FOR AUSTRALIAN & NEW ZEALAND CATHOLIC SCHOOLS. (AT). **1890**

CATO JOURNAL, THE. (US/0273-3072). **5195**

CAUDA PAVONIS. (US/1059-8308). **2844**

CAUSE/EFFECT. (US/0164-534X). **1814**

CD-ROM INFORMATION PRODUCTS. (UK/0967-8123). **1264**

CELESTIAL MECHANICS AND DYNAMICAL ASTRONOMY. (NE/0923-2958). **394**

CELL AND TISSUE RESEARCH. (GW/0302-766X). **533**

CELL BIOCHEMISTRY AND FUNCTION. (UK/0263-6484). **484**

CELL BIOLOGY AND TOXICOLOGY (PRINCETON SCIENTIFIC PUBLISHERS). (NE/0742-2091). **533**

CELL BIOLOGY INTERNATIONAL REPORTS. (UK/0309-1651). **533**

CELL BIOPHYSICS. (US/0163-4992). **495**

CELL CALCIUM (EDINBURGH). (UK/0143-4160). **533**

CELL (CAMBRIDGE). (US/0092-8674). **533**

CELL MOTILITY AND THE CYTOSKELETON. (US/0886-1544). **533**

CELL STRUCTURE AND FUNCTION. (JA/0386-7196). **534**

CELL VISION. (US/1073-1180). **534**

CELLULAR AND MOLECULAR BIOLOGY. (UK/0145-5680). **534**

CELLULAR AND MOLECULAR NEUROBIOLOGY. (US/0272-4340). **534**

CELLULAR IMMUNOLOGY. (US/0008-8749). **3667**

CELLULAR PHYSIOLOGY AND BIOCHEMISTRY. (SZ/1015-8987). **534**

CELLULAR SIGNALLING. (UK/0898-6568). **534**

CELLULOSE CHEMISTRY AND TECHNOLOGY. (RM/0576-9787). **1021**

CEMENT AND CONCRETE RESEARCH. (US/0008-8846). **2020**

CENIMM; CENTRO NACIONAL DE INVESTIGACIONES METALURGICAS. (SP). **4000**

CENTAURUS. (DK/0008-8994). **5093**

CENTER FOR STRATEGIC AND INTERNATIONAL STUDIES, GEORGETOWN UNIVERSITY, THE. (US/0272-2429). **4517**

CENTRAL AFRICAN JOURNAL OF MEDICINE. (RH/0008-9176). **3562**

CENTRAL & INNER ASIAN STUDIES. (US/0893-2301). **2648**

CENTRAL EUROPEAN HISTORY. (US/0008-9389). **2683**

CENTRAL TEXAS ARCHEOLOGIST. (US/0882-3693). **265**

CENTRE SCIENTIFIQUE ET TECHNIQUE DE LA CONSTRUCTION. (BE/0770-7274). **607**

CEPHALALGIA. (NO/0333-1024). **3829**

CERAMICS INTERNATIONAL. (IT/0272-8842). **2588**

CERAMURGIA. (IT/0045-6152). **2588**

CEREAL CHEMISTRY. (US/0009-0352). **1021**

CEREAL FOODS WORLD. (US/0146-6283). **2331**

CEREAL RESEARCH COMMUNICATIONS. (HU/0133-3720). **200**

CEREBROVASCULAR DISEASES. (SZ/1015-9770). **3829**

CEREBUS. (CN/0712-7774). **4858**

CERVANTES (GAINESVILLE, FLA.). (US/0277-6995). **431**

CEW, CHEMICAL ENGINEERING WORLD. (II/0009-2517). **2009**

CGST JOURNAL. (HK). **4943**

CHARLESTON MAGAZINE, THE. (UK/0963-4770). **3374**

CHARME MODA. (IT). **5553**

CHARTER (SYDNEY, AUSTRALIA). (AT). **740**

CHARTERED BUILDER (ASCOT, 1989). (UK/0957-8773). **607**

CHASQUI (WILLIAMSBURG, VA.). (US/0145-8973). **3374**

CHAT (TRYON), THE. (US/0009-1987). **5580**

CHAUTAUQUAN DAILY, THE. (US/0746-0414). **5714**

CHEMIA ANALITYCZNA. (PL/0009-2223). **1014**

CHEMICAL AND BIOCHEMICAL ENGINEERING QUARTERLY. (CI). **2009**

CHEMICAL & ENGINEERING NEWS. (US/0009-2347). **1022**

CHEMICAL ENGINEER (LONDON). (UK/0302-0797). **2009**

CHEMICAL ENGINEERING AND PROCESSING. (SZ/0255-2701). **2009**

CHEMICAL ENGINEERING COMMUNICATIONS. (US/0098-6445). **2009**

CHEMICAL ENGINEERING EDUCATION. (US/0009-2479). **2009**

CHEMICAL ENGINEERING JOURNAL AND THE BIOCHEMICAL ENGINEERING JOURNAL, THE. (SZ/0923-0467). **2010**

CHEMICAL ENGINEERING (NEW YORK). (US/0009-2460). **1034**

CHEMICAL ENGINEERING PROGRESS. (US/0360-7275). **2010**

CHEMICAL ENGINEERING RESEARCH & DESIGN. (UK/0263-8762). **2010**

CHEMICAL ENGINEERING SCIENCE. (UK/0009-2509). **2010**

CHEMICAL GEOLOGY. (NE/0009-2541). **1040**

CHEMICAL IMMUNOLOGY. (SZ/1015-0145). **3667**

CHEMICAL PHYSICS. (NE/0301-0104). **1050**

CHEMICAL PHYSICS LETTERS. (NE/0009-2614). **1050**

CHEMICAL RESEARCH IN TOXICOLOGY. (US/0893-228X). **3979**

CHEMICAL REVIEWS. (US/0009-2665). **969**

CHEMICAL SOCIETY REVIEWS. (UK/0306-0012). **969**

CHEMICKE LISTY. (XR/0009-2770). **969**

CHEMICO-BIOLOGICAL INTERACTIONS. (IE/0009-2797). **485**

CHEMIE IN UNSERER ZEIT. (GW/0009-2851). **969**

CHEMIEINGENIEURTECHNIK. (GW/0009-286X). **2010**

CHEMISCHE BERICHTE. (GW/0009-2940). **970**

CHEMISTRY AND INDUSTRY (LONDON). (UK/0009-3068). **970**

CHEMISTRY AND PHYSICS OF LIPIDS. (IE/0009-3084). **485**

CHEMISTRY AND TECHNOLOGY OF FUELS AND OILS. (US/0009-3092). **970**

CHEMISTRY IN BRITAIN. (UK/0009-3106). **970**

CHEMISTRY LETTERS. (JA/0366-7022). **1040**

CHEMISTRY OF FUNCTIONAL GROUPS, THE. (US). **971**

CHEMOMETRICS AND INTELLIGENT LABORATORY SYSTEMS : LABORATORY INFORMATION MANAGEMENT. (NE/0925-5281). **1014**

CHEMOSPHERE (OXFORD). (UK/0045-6535). **2226**

CHEMOTHERAPY (BASEL). (SZ/0009-3157). **3814**

CHEMTECH. (US/0009-2703). **1022**

CHESOPIEAN, THE. (US/0009-3300). 265

CHEST. (US/0012-3692). 3702

CHI HSIANG HSUEH PAO. (CC/0577-6619). 1421

CHICAGO. (US/0362-4595). 2530

CHIH WU SHENG LI HSUEH TUNG HSUN. (CC/0412-0914). 506

CHIHUA XUEBAO. (CC/0253-9837). 1050

CHILD ABUSE & NEGLECT. (US/0145-2134). 5277

CHILD & FAMILY BEHAVIOR THERAPY. (US/0731-7107). 4580

CHILD & YOUTH SERVICES. (US/0145-935X). 5278

CHILD CARE, HEALTH AND DEVELOPMENT. (UK/0305-1862). 3901

CHILD DEVELOPMENT. (US/0009-3920). 4580

CHILD NEPHROLOGY AND UROLOGY. (SZ/1012-6694). 3989

CHILD PSYCHIATRY AND HUMAN DEVELOPMENT. (US/0009-398X). 3923

CHILD SAFETY REVIEW. (UK/0957-4107). 4771

CHILD WELFARE. (US/0009-4021). 5278

CHILDHOOD EDUCATION. (US/0009-4056). 1803

CHILDREN AND YOUTH SERVICES REVIEW. (US/0190-7409). 5278

CHILDREN'S HEALTH CARE. (US/0273-9615). 3901

CHILD'S NERVOUS SYSTEM. (GW/0256-7040). 3902

CHILTON'S I&CS. (US/0746-2395). 1968

CHIMIA. (SZ/0009-4293). 1023

CHINA AND OURSELVES. (CN/0828-1602). 4943

CHINA EARTH SCIENCES. (NE/0923-6805). 1353

CHINA ECONOMIC REVIEW. (US/1043-951X). 1469

CHINA PLASTIC & RUBBER JOURNAL. (HK). 4454

CHINA QUARTERLY (LONDON). (UK/0305-7410). 2648

CHINAMAC JOURNAL. (HK). 3476

CHINESE ANNALS OF MATHEMATICS. SER. B. (CC/0252-9599). 3500

CHINESE JOURNAL OF CHEMISTRY. (CC/1001-604X). 972

CHINESE LAW AND GOVERNMENT. (US/0009-4609). 2950

CHINESE MUSIC. (US/0192-3749). 4109

CHINESE PHYSICS. (US/0273-429X). 4399

CHINESE PHYSICS LETTERS. (US/0256-307X). 4400

CHINESE SCIENCE BULLETIN. (CC/1001-6538). 5094

CHINESE SOCIOLOGY AND ANTHROPOLOGY. (US/0009-4625). 5242

CHINOPERL PAPERS. (US/0193-7774). 3375

CHIRALITY (NEW YORK, N.Y.). (US/0899-0042). 972

CHIRIBOTAN. (JA/0577-9316). 5094

CHIROPRACTIC JOURNAL OF AUSTRALIA. (AT/1036-0913). 4379

CHIROPRACTIC RESEARCH JOURNAL. (US/0899-6938). 3804

CHIRURG. (GW/0009-4722). 3961

CHIRURGIA DELLA TESTA E DEL COLLO : QUADERNI A.I.C.M.F., A.S.C.M.F.O.I. (IT). 3961

CHOSON ILBO (MIJU PAN). (US/0743-7056). 5715

CHRISTIAN EDUCATION JOURNAL. (US/0739-8913). 4944

CHRISTIAN HOME AND SCHOOL. (US). 2278

CHRISTIAN MEDICAL & DENTAL SOCIETY JOURNAL. (US). 3563

CHRISTIAN NEW AGE QUARTERLY. (US/0899-7292). 4945

CHRISTIAN NEWS (NEW HAVEN, MO.). (US/0009-5516). 4945

CHRISTIANITY & LITERATURE. (US/0148-3331). 3375

CHROMATOGRAPHIA. (GW/0009-5893). 1014

CHROMOSOMA. (GW/0009-5915). 534

CHRONICLE OF PARLIAMENTARY ELECTIONS. (SZ/0302-2498). 4637

CHRONICLE (OMAHA, NEB.), THE. (US/0030-2201). 4188

CHRONOBIOLOGIA. (IT/0390-0037). 3795

CHRONOBIOLOGY INTERNATIONAL. (UK/0742-0528). 451

CHRYSALIS (NEW YORK, N.Y.). (US/0888-9384). 4343

CHUNG WAI WEN HSUEH. (CH). 3375

CHUNG YANG YEN CHIU YUAN TUNG WU YEN CHUI SO CHI KAN. (CH/0001-3943). 5580

CHURCH & SYNAGOGUE LIBRARIES. (US/0009-6342). 3202

CHURCH GROWTH TODAY. (US). 4947

CHURCH OF ENGLAND NEWSPAPER : CEN. (UK/0964-816X). 2514

CICS UPDATE. (UK). 1278

CIENCIA PHARMACEUTICA. (SP). 4296

CIENCIAS MARINAS. (MX/0185-3880). 553

CIFRAS. (CK/0120-5331). 5799

CIM BULLETIN. (CN/0317-0926). 2136

CIMBEBASIA : JOURNAL OF THE STATE MUSEUM, WINDHOEK. (SX/1012-4926). 5095

CIMENTS, BETONS, PLATRES, CHAUX. (FR/0397-006X). 607

CINEMATOGRAPH. (US/0886-6570). 317

CIRCAEA : BULLETIN OF THE ASSOCIATION FOR ENVIRONMENTAL ARCHAEOLOGY. (UK/0268-425X). 266

CIRCUIT CELLAR INK. (US/0896-8985). 1227

CIRCUIT RIDER (SPRINGFIELD, ILL.), THE. (US/0741-8264). 2443

CIRCUITREE MAGAZINE. (US). 2038

CIRCUITS, SYSTEMS, AND SIGNAL PROCESSING. (US/0278-081X). 2039

CIRCULAIRE AUX PRETRES ET AUTRES AGENTS DE PASTORALE. (CN/0227-552X). 5027

CIRCULATION (NEW YORK, N.Y.). (US/0009-7322). 3702

CIRCULATION RESEARCH. (US/0009-7330). 3702

CIRCULATORY SHOCK. (US/0092-6213). 3702

CIRUGIA DEL URUGUAY. (UY/0009-7381). 3962

CIRUGIA PLASTICA IBERO-LATINOAMERICANA. (SP/0376-7892). 3962

CIRUGIA Y CIRUJANOS. (MX/0009-7411). 3962

CITEAUX, COMMENTARII CISTERCIENSES. (BE/0774-4919). 5027

CITY & SOCIETY. (US/0893-0465). 2818

CIUDAD DE DIOS, LA. (SP/0009-7756). 4948

CIVIL ENGINEER IN SOUTH AFRICA, THE. (SA/0009-7845). 2020

CIVIL ENGINEERING EDUCATION. (US/0884-1926). 2020

CIVIL ENGINEERING (NEW YORK, N.Y. 1983). (US/0885-7024). 2021

CIVIL ENGINEERING PRACTICE. (US/0886-9685). 2021

CIVIL ENGINEERING SYSTEMS. (UK/0263-0257). 2021

CIVIL PROTECTION. (UK/0961-2564). 1072

CIVIL WAR HISTORY. (US/0009-8078). 2728

CIVIL WAR REGIMENTS. (US/1055-3266). 2728

CIVILTA CLASSICA E CRISTIANA. (IT/0392-8632). 3273

CLADISTICS. (US/0748-3007). 451

CLARINET (POCATELLO, IDAHO), THE. (US/0361-5553). 4110

CLASSIC BIKE. (UK/0142-890X). 1294

CLASSICAL AND MODERN LITERATURE. (US/0197-2227). 1075

CLASSICAL ANTIQUITY. (US/0278-6656). 1075

CLASSICAL WORLD, THE. (US/0009-8418). 1076

CLAY MINERALS. (UK/0009-8558). 1438

CLAYS AND CLAY MINERALS. (US/0009-8604). 1438

CLE JOURNAL AND REGISTER, THE. (US). 2951

CLEVELAND CLINIC JOURNAL OF MEDICINE. (US/0891-1150). 3564

CLEVELAND MAGAZINE. (US/0160-8533). 2486

CLIMATIC CHANGE. (NE/0165-0009). 1422

CLINICA CHIMICA ACTA. (NE/0009-8981). 972

CLINICA E INVESTIGACION EN GINECOLOGIA Y OBSTETRICIA. (SP/0210-573X). 3758

CLINICA Y ANALISIS GRUPAL. (SP/0210-0657). 4581

CLINICAL AND EXPERIMENTAL ALLERGY. (UK/0954-7894). 3667

CLINICAL AND EXPERIMENTAL DERMATOLOGY. (UK/0307-6938). 3718

CLINICAL AND EXPERIMENTAL HYPERTENSION. PART A, THEORY AND PRACTICE. (US/0730-0077). 3703

CLINICAL AND EXPERIMENTAL HYPERTENSION. PART B, HYPERTENSION IN PREGNANCY. (US/0730-0085). 3758

CLINICAL AND EXPERIMENTAL IMMUNOLOGY. (UK/0009-9104). 3667

CLINICAL & EXPERIMENTAL METASTASIS. (UK/0262-0898). 3815

CLINICAL AND EXPERIMENTAL OPTOMETRY. (AT/0816-4622). 4215

CLINICAL AND EXPERIMENTAL PHARMACOLOGY & PHYSIOLOGY. (AT/0305-1870). 4296

CLINICAL AND EXPERIMENTAL RHEUMATOLOGY. (IT/0392-856X). 3565

CLINICAL AND INVESTIGATIVE MEDICINE. (UK/0147-958X). 3565

CLINICAL AND LABORATORY HAEMATOLOGY. (UK/0141-9854). 3771

CLINICAL AUTONOMIC RESEARCH : OFFICIAL JOURNAL OF THE CLINICAL AUTONOMIC RESEARCH SOCIETY. (UK/0959-9851). 3565

CLINICAL BIOCHEMISTRY (NEW YORK, N.Y.). (US/0009-9120). 485

CLINICAL BIOMECHANICS (BRISTOL). (UK/0268-0033). 3565

CLINICAL BIOTECHNOLOGY. (US/1046-3305). 3691

CLINICAL CARDIOLOGY (MAHWAH, N.J.). (US/0160-9289). 3703

CLINICAL CHEMISTRY (REFERENCE EDITION). (US/0009-9147). 972

CLINICAL EEG ELECTROENCEPHALOGRAPHY. (US/0009-9155). 3830

CLINICAL ENDOCRINOLOGY (OXFORD). (UK/0300-0664). 3727

CLINICAL GENETICS. (DK/0009-9163). 543

CLINICAL GERONTOLOGIST. (US/0731-7115). 3750

CLINICAL HEMORHEOLOGY. (US/0271-5198). 3771

CLINICAL IMAGING. (US/0899-7071). 3939

CLINICAL IMMUNOLOGY AND IMMUNOPATHOLOGY. (US/0090-1229). 3668

CLINICAL INSTRUMENT SYSTEMS : CIS. (US/0730-7578). 3691

CLINICAL INTENSIVE CARE : INTERNATIONAL JOURNAL OF CRITICAL & CORONARY CARE MEDICINE. (UK/0956-3075). 3703

CLINICAL JOURNAL OF PAIN, THE. (US/0749-8047). 3565

CLINICAL JOURNAL OF SPORT MEDICINE. (US/1050-642X). 3953

CLINICAL KINESIOLOGY. (US/0896-9620). 4380

CLINICAL LABORATORY SCIENCE. (US/0894-959X). 3566

CLINICAL LINGUISTICS & PHONETICS. (UK/0269-9206). 3274

CLINICAL MICROBIOLOGY REVIEWS. (US/0893-8512). 561

CLINICAL NEPHROLOGY. (GW/0301-0430). 3989

CLINICAL NEUROLOGY AND NEUROSURGERY. (NE/0303-8467). 3830

CLINICAL NEUROPATHOLOGY. (GW/0722-5091). 3894

CLINICAL NEUROPHARMACOLOGY. (US/0362-5664). 4296

CLINICAL NUCLEAR MEDICINE. (US/0363-9762). 3847

CLINICAL NURSE SPECIALIST. (US/0887-6274). 3853

CLINICAL NURSING RESEARCH. (US/1054-7738). 3853

CLINICAL NUTRITION. (UK/0261-5614). 4188

CLINICAL OBSTETRICS AND GYNECOLOGY. (US/0009-9201). 3759

CLINICAL ORTHOPAEDICS AND RELATED RESEARCH. (US/0009-921X). 3881

CLINICAL OTOLARYNGOLOGY AND ALLIED SCIENCES. (UK/0307-7772). **3887**

CLINICAL PEDIATRICS. (US/0009-9228). **3902**

CLINICAL PHARMACOKINETICS. (US/0312-5963). **4296**

CLINICAL PHARMACOLOGY AND THERAPEUTICS. (US/0009-9236). **4297**

CLINICAL PHARMACY. (US/0278-2677). **4297**

CLINICAL PHYSICS AND PHYSIOLOGICAL MEASUREMENT. (UK/0143-0815). **4400**

CLINICAL PHYSIOLOGY (OXFORD). (UK/0144-5979). **579**

CLINICAL PSYCHOLOGY REVIEW. (US/0272-7358). **4581**

CLINICAL RADIOLOGY. (UK/0009-9260). **3940**

CLINICAL REVIEWS IN ALLERGY. (US/0731-8235). **3668**

CLINICAL RHEUMATOLOGY. (BE/0770-3198). **3804**

CLINICAL SOCIAL WORK JOURNAL. (US/0091-1674). **5279**

CLINICAL SUPERVISOR, THE. (US/0732-5223). **4581**

CLINICAL THERAPEUTICS. (US/0149-2918). **4297**

CLINICAL TRANSPLANTATION. (DK/0902-0063). **3566**

CLINICAL VISION SCIENCES. (US/0887-6169). **3566**

CLINICIAN'S RESEARCH DIGEST. (US/8756-3207). **4581**

CLINICS IN CHEST MEDICINE. (US/0272-5231). **3566**

CLINICS IN DERMATOLOGY. (US/0738-081X). **3718**

CLINICS IN LABORATORY MEDICINE. (US/0272-2712). **3566**

CLINICS IN PERINATOLOGY. (US/0095-5108). **3759**

CLINICS IN PODIATRIC MEDICINE AND SURGERY. (US/0891-8422). **3917**

CLINICS IN SPORTS MEDICINE. (US/0278-5919). **3953**

CLINIQUE OPHTALMOLOGIQUE PARIS, LA. (FR/0009-9368). **3873**

CLIO (FORT WAYNE, IND.). (US/0884-2043). **3376**

CLOCKMAKER (HINCKLEY). (UK/0961-5032). **2772**

CLOTHING AND TEXTILES RESEARCH JOURNAL. (US/0887-302X). **5349**

CMAJ. CANADIAN MEDICAL ASSOCIATION JOURNAL. (CN/0820-3946). **3567**

CMI NEWSLETTER AND YEARBOOK. (NO). **3180**

CMIP PUBLICATIONS. (US). **2649**

CO-EXISTENCE (DORDRECHT). (NE/0587-5994). **4518**

COACHING DIRECTOR. (AT/0814-7752). **4890**

COALTRANS INTERNATIONAL. (UK). **2137**

COALTRANS WORCESTER PARK. (UK/0269-381X). **1935**

COASTAL ENGINEERING (AMSTERDAM). (NE/0378-3839). **1968**

COASTAL MANAGEMENT. (US/0892-0753). **2190**

COASTAL RESEARCH. (US/0271-5376). **1353**

CODE OF FEDERAL REGULATIONS INDEX. (US/0000-1058). **3079**

COGNITION. (SZ/0010-0277). **4581**

COGNITION AND INSTRUCTION. (US/0737-0008). **1891**

COGNITIVE DEVELOPMENT. (US/0885-2014). **4581**

COGNITIVE NEUROPSYCHOLOGY. (UK/0264-3294). **4581**

COGNITIVE PSYCHOLOGY. (US/0010-0285). **4581**

COGNITIVE SCIENCE. (US/0364-0213). **1212**

COGNITIVE THERAPY AND RESEARCH. (US/0147-5916). **4581**

COI. COUNTERTRADE AND OFFSET INTELLIGENCE. (UK/0950-916X). **827**

COLD REGIONS SCIENCE AND TECHNOLOGY. (NE/0165-232X). **1968**

COLECCIO HISTORICA. (SP). **2684**

COLEOPTERISTS' BULLETIN, THE. (US/0010-065X). **5580**

COLLECTED REPRINTS - UNIVERSITY OF GEORGIA MARINE INSTITUTE. (US/0072-1328). **553**

COLLECTION MANAGEMENT. (US/0146-2679). **3202**

COLLECTION OF CZECHOSLOVAK CHEMICAL COMMUNICATIONS. (UK/0010-0765). **973**

COLLECTIONS (COLUMBIA, S.C.). (US/1046-2252). **4087**

COLLEGE & RESEARCH LIBRARIES. (US/0010-0870). **3203**

COLLEGE AND UNIVERSITY. (US/0010-0889). **1816**

COLLEGE BAND DIRECTORS NATIONAL ASSOCIATION JOURNAL. (US/0742-8480). **4110**

COLLEGE LITERATURE. (US/0093-3139). **3376**

COLLEGE STUDENT AFFAIRS JOURNAL, THE. (US/0888-210X). **1817**

COLLEGE STUDENT JOURNAL. (US/0146-3934). **1817**

COLLEGIATE TRENDS (RIDGEWOOD, N.J.). (US/1065-0296). **1817**

COLLOID AND POLYMER SCIENCE. (GW/0303-402X). **1050**

COLLOIDS AND SURFACES. (NE/0166-6622). **1051**

COLLOQUE SCIENTIFIQUE INTERNATIONAL SUR LE CAFE : [PROCEEDINGS]. (SZ). **75**

COLLOQUIUM. (AT/0588-3237). **4948**

COLOMBIA MEDICA : CM. (CK/0120-8322). **3567**

COLONIAL LATIN AMERICAN HISTORICAL REVIEW. (US/1063-5769). **2728**

COLONIAL WATERBIRDS. (US/0738-6028). **5617**

COLOR PUBLISHING. (US/1055-9701). **4813**

COLOR RESEARCH AND APPLICATION. (US/0361-2317). **5095**

COLORADO GENEALOGIST, THE. (US/0010-1613). **2443**

COLORADO SCHOOL OF MINES QUARTERLY. (US/0163-9153). **2137**

COLUMBIA JOURNAL OF LAW AND SOCIAL PROBLEMS. (US/0010-1923). **2953**

COLUMBIA JOURNAL OF TRANSNATIONAL LAW. (US/0010-1931). **3126**

COLUMBIA JOURNAL OF WORLD BUSINESS, THE. (US/0022-5428). **658**

COLUMBIA LAW REVIEW. (US/0010-1958). **2953**

COLUMBIANA. (US/0893-276X). **2531**

COMBINATORICA (BUDAPEST. 1981). (NE/0209-9683). **3500**

COMBUSTION AND FLAME. (US/0010-2180). **1051**

COMBUSTION, EXPLOSION, AND SHOCK WAVES. (US/0010-5082). **1051**

COMBUSTION SCIENCE AND TECHNOLOGY. (US/0010-2202). **1051**

COMERCIO E INDUSTRIA (SAN SALVADOR, EL SALVADOR). (ES). **828**

COMMENTARII MATHEMATICI HELVETICI. (SZ/0010-2571). **3500**

COMMENTARY (NEW YORK). (US/0010-2601). **5047**

COMMERCE (HACKENSACK, N.Y.). (US/0745-077X). **658**

COMMERCIAL LAWS OF THE WORLD. CLASS C. (US). **3126**

COMMON MARKET LAW REVIEW. (NE/0165-0750). **2953**

COMMONWEALTH ESSAYS & STUDIES. (FR). **3377**

COMMUNICATIE. (BE/0771-7342). **1106**

COMMUNICATION EDUCATION. (US/0363-4523). **1106**

COMMUNICATION ET INFORMATION. (CN/0382-7798). **1106**

COMMUNICATION MONOGRAPHS. (US/0363-7751). **1107**

COMMUNICATION RESEARCH. (US/0093-6502). **1107**

COMMUNICATION SERIALS. (US/1041-7893). **1107**

COMMUNICATION STUDIES. (US/1051-0974). **1107**

COMMUNICATION THEORY. (US/1050-3293). **1107**

COMMUNICATIONES ARCHEOLOGICAE HUNGARIAE. (HU). **266**

COMMUNICATIONS & COGNITION. (BE/0378-0880). **1108**

COMMUNICATIONS IN ALGEBRA. (US/0092-7872). **3500**

COMMUNICATIONS IN APPLIED NUMERICAL METHODS. (UK/0748-8025). **3500**

COMMUNICATIONS IN LABORATORY MEDICINE. (UK/0267-3320). **3567**

COMMUNICATIONS IN MATHEMATICAL PHYSICS. (GW/0010-3616). **4400**

COMMUNICATIONS IN PARTIAL DIFFERENTIAL EQUATIONS. (US/0360-5302). **3501**

COMMUNICATIONS IN SOIL SCIENCE AND PLANT ANALYSIS. (US/0010-3624). **167**

COMMUNICATIONS IN THEORETICAL PHYSICS. (CC/0253-6102). **4400**

COMMUNICATIONS OF THE ACM. (US/0001-0782). **1175**

COMMUNICATIONS ON PURE AND APPLIED MATHEMATICS. (US/0010-3640). **3501**

COMMUNITY ALTERNATIVES. (US/1052-7656). **5279**

COMMUNITY & JUNIOR COLLEGE LIBRARIES. (US/0276-3915). **3203**

COMMUNITY BASED REHABILITATION NEWS : CBR. (UK). **4385**

COMMUNITY COLLEGE REVIEW. (US/0091-5521). **1817**

COMMUNITY DENTISTRY AND ORAL EPIDEMIOLOGY. (DK/0301-5661). **1319**

COMMUNITY DEVELOPMENT JOURNAL. (UK/0010-3802). **5242**

COMMUNITY EDUCATION JOURNAL. (US/0045-4736). **1733**

COMMUNITY EDUCATION RESEARCH DIGEST. (US/1041-4827). **1733**

COMMUNITY/JUNIOR COLLEGE. (US/0277-6774). **1817**

COMMUNITY MENTAL HEALTH JOURNAL. (US/0010-3853). **5280**

COMMUNITY RELATIONS REPORT (BARTLESVILLE, OKLA.), THE. (US/0736-7147). **757**

COMMUNITY SERVICES CATALYST. (US/0739-9227). **1800**

COMPARATIST, THE. (US/0195-7678). **3377**

COMPARATIVE BIOCHEMISTRY AND PHYSIOLOGY. A, COMPARATIVE PHYSIOLOGY. (UK/0300-9629). **579**

COMPARATIVE BIOCHEMISTRY AND PHYSIOLOGY. B, COMPARATIVE BIOCHEMISTRY. (UK/0305-0491). **486**

COMPARATIVE CIVILIZATIONS REVIEW. (US/0733-4540). **5196**

COMPARATIVE ECONOMIC STUDIES. (US/0888-7233). **1470**

COMPARATIVE EDUCATION. (UK/0305-0068). **1733**

COMPARATIVE EDUCATION REVIEW. (US/0010-4086). **1733**

COMPARATIVE IMMUNOLOGY, MICROBIOLOGY AND INFECTIOUS DISEASES. (UK/0147-9571). **561**

COMPARATIVE LABOR LAW JOURNAL. (US/1043-5255). **3145**

COMPARATIVE PHYSIOLOGY AND ECOLOGY. (II/0379-0436). **579**

COMPARATIVE POLITICAL STUDIES. (US/0010-4140). **4469**

COMPARATIVE POLITICS. (US/0010-4159). **4469**

COMPARATIVE STRATEGY. (US/0149-5933). **4518**

COMPARATIVE STUDIES IN SOCIETY AND HISTORY. (UK/0010-4175). **5196**

COMPARE. (UK/0305-7925). **1891**

COMPASS. (UK). **4469**

COMPEL. (IE/0332-1649). **2039**

COMPENDIUM (NEWTOWN, PA.). (US/0894-1009). **1319**

COMPENDIUM ON CONTINUING EDUCATION FOR THE PRACTICING VETERINARIAN, THE. (US/0193-1903). **5508**

COMPETITIVE ADVANCES. MATERIALS AND PROCESSES. (US). **5095**

COMPILATION OF STATE AND FEDERAL PRIVACY LAWS. (US/0882-9136). **2954**

COMPLEMENT PROFILES. (SZ). **3668**

COMPLEMENTARY MEDICINE INDEX : CURRENT AWARENESS TOPICS SERVICES. (UK/0950-6667). **3567**

COMPLICATIONS IN ORTHOPEDICS. (US/0887-1736). **3881**

COMPOSITE INTERFACES. (NE/0927-6440). **973**

COMPOSITE STRUCTURES. (UK/0263-8223). **2101**

COMPOSITES. (UK/0010-4361). **2101**

COMPOSITES SCIENCE AND TECHNOLOGY. (UK/0266-3538). **2101**

COMPOSITIO — Peer Reviewed Index

COMPOSITIO MATHEMATICA. (NE/0010-437X). **3501**

COMPOSITION STUDIES : FRESHMAN ENGLISH NEWS. (US). **3274**

COMPREHENSIVE PSYCHIATRY. (US/0010-440X). **3923**

COMPTES RENDUS DE L'ACADEMIE DES SCIENCES. SERIE II, MECANIQUE, PHYSIQUE, CHIMIE, SCIENCES DE L'UNIVERS, SCIENCES DE LA TERRE. (FR/0764-4450). **5096**

COMPTES RENDUS DE L'ACADEMIE DES SCIENCES. SERIE III, SCIENCES DE LA VIE. (FR/0764-4469). **5096**

COMPTES RENDUS DE THERAPEUTIQUE ET DE PHARMACOLOGIE CLINIQUE. (FR/0293-9908). **4297**

COMPTES RENDUS MATHEMATIQUES DE L'ACADEMIE DES SCIENCES. (CN/0706-1994). **3501**

COMPUTATIONAL ECONOMICS. (NE/0927-7099). **1470**

COMPUTATIONAL INTELLIGENCE. (CN/0824-7935). **1212**

COMPUTATIONAL OPTIMIZATION AND APPLICATIONS. (NE/0926-6003). **3502**

COMPUTATIONAL POLYMER SCIENCE. (US/1052-0643). **4454**

COMPUTATIONAL STATISTICS & DATA ANALYSIS. (NE/0167-9473). **3502**

COMPUTER AIDED DESIGN. (UK/0010-4485). **1231**

COMPUTER APPLICATIONS IN THE BIOSCIENCES. (UK/0266-7061). **1176**

COMPUTER COMMUNICATIONS. (UK/0140-3664). **1240**

COMPUTER DESIGN (WINCHESTER). (US/0010-4566). **1176**

COMPUTER ECONOMIC$ REPORT (INTERNATIONAL ED.). (US/1054-5026). **1176**

COMPUTER GRAPHICS FORUM : A JOURNAL OF THE EUROPEAN ASSOCIATION FOR COMPUTER GRAPHICS. (NE/0167-7055). **1232**

COMPUTER-INTEGRATED MANUFACTURING SYSTEMS. (UK/0951-5240). **1228**

COMPUTER JOURNAL. (UK/0010-4620). **1176**

COMPUTER LANGUAGES. (US/0096-0551). **1278**

COMPUTER (LONG BEACH, CALIF.). (US/0018-9162). **1266**

COMPUTER METHODS IN APPLIED MECHANICS AND ENGINEERING. (NE/0045-7825). **1256**

COMPUTER MUSIC JOURNAL. (US/0148-9267). **1240**

COMPUTER NETWORKS AND ISDN SYSTEMS. (NE/0169-7552). **1240**

COMPUTER PAPER (BRITISH COLUMBIA ED.). (CN/0840-3929). **1177**

COMPUTER PHYSICS COMMUNICATIONS. (NE/0010-4655). **4400**

COMPUTER PROTOCOLS. (US/0899-126X). **1177**

COMPUTER STANDARDS & INTERFACES. (SZ/0920-5489). **1178**

COMPUTER SUPPORTED COOPERATIVE WORK : CSCW : AN INTERNATIONAL JOURNAL. (NE/0925-9724). **1232**

COMPUTER SYSTEMS SCIENCE AND ENGINEERING. (UK/0267-6192). **1228**

COMPUTERIZED MEDICAL IMAGING AND GRAPHICS. (US/0895-6111). **3940**

COMPUTERS AND BIOMEDICAL RESEARCH. (US/0010-4809). **3691**

COMPUTERS & CHEMICAL ENGINEERING. (UK/0098-1354). **2011**

COMPUTERS & CHEMISTRY. (UK/0097-8485). **973**

COMPUTERS AND COMPOSITION. (US/8755-4615). **1222**

COMPUTERS & EDUCATION. (US/0360-1315). **1222**

COMPUTERS & FLUIDS. (UK/0045-7930). **2088**

COMPUTERS & GEOSCIENCES. (UK/0098-3004). **1178**

COMPUTERS & GRAPHICS. (US/0097-8493). **1232**

COMPUTERS & INDUSTRIAL ENGINEERING. (US/0360-8352). **2097**

COMPUTERS & OPERATIONS RESEARCH. (US/0305-0548). **1179**

COMPUTERS & STRUCTURES. (UK/0045-7949). **1228**

COMPUTERS AND THE HUMANITIES. (NE/0010-4817). **2844**

COMPUTERS, ENVIRONMENT AND URBAN SYSTEMS. (US/0198-9715). **2819**

COMPUTERS IN BIOLOGY AND MEDICINE. (US/0010-4825). **3691**

COMPUTERS IN EDUCATION JOURNAL. (US/1069-3769). **1179**

COMPUTERS IN HUMAN SERVICES. (US/0740-445X). **1179**

COMPUTERS IN INDUSTRY. (NE/0166-3615). **1228**

COMPUTERS IN NURSING. (US/0736-8593). **3854**

COMPUTERS IN THE SCHOOLS. (US/0738-0569). **1222**

COMPUTING. (AU/0010-485X). **1257**

COMPUTING IN MUSICOLOGY. (US/1057-9478). **1240**

COMPUTING SYSTEMS. (US/0895-6340). **1279**

COMUNI D'ITALIA. (IT/0394-8277). **4640**

COMUNICACION PSIQUIATRICA. (SP/0210-1424). **3923**

COMUNICACION Y SOCIEDAD. (SP/0214-0039). **1109**

COMUNICACIONES BIOLOGICAS. (AG/0326-1956). **452**

CONCEPTS IN MAGNETIC RESONANCE. (US/1043-7347). **4443**

CONCOURS MEDICAL. (FR/0010-5309). **3568**

CONDITION MONITORING AND DIAGNOSTIC TECHNOLOGY. (UK). **1969**

CONDO SALES REPORT. (US/8750-1236). **4836**

CONDOR (LOS ANGELES, CALIF.), THE. (US/0010-5422). **5617**

CONFLICT MANAGEMENT AND PEACE SCIENCE. (US/0738-8942). **4518**

CONFLICT QUARTERLY. (CN/0227-1311). **4518**

CONGENITAL ANOMALIES. (JA/0914-3505). **543**

CONGRESS & THE PRESIDENCY. (US/0734-3469). **4469**

CONGRESS PUBLICATIONS. (SZ). **2021**

CONGRESSUS NUMERANTIUM. (CN/0384-9864). **3502**

CONNECTICUT MEDICINE. (US/0010-6178). **3568**

CONNECTIVE TISSUE RESEARCH. (US/0300-8207). **580**

CONRAD GREBEL REVIEW, THE. (CN/0829-044X). **4950**

CONSENSUS (WINNIPEG). (CN/0317-1493). **4950**

CONSERVATION BIOLOGY. (US/0888-8892). **2190**

CONSTITUTIONAL FORUM. (CN/0847-3889). **3092**

CONSTITUTIONAL POLITICAL ECONOMY. (US/1043-4062). **3092**

CONSTRUCTION LAWYER, THE. (US/0272-0116). **2956**

CONSTRUCTION (LONDON, 1977). (UK/0142-0410). **609**

CONSTRUCTION MANAGEMENT AND ECONOMICS. (UK/0144-6193). **610**

CONSTRUCTIS. (UK). **611**

CONSTRUCTIVE APPROXIMATION. (US/0176-4276). **3502**

CONSULTANT (HACKENSACK). (US/0010-7069). **3568**

CONSULTANT PHARMACIST, THE. (US/0888-5109). **4298**

CONSUMER HEALTH. (US/0736-010X). **4772**

CONTACT DERMATITIS. (DK/0105-1873). **3718**

CONTACT (DON MILLS). (CN/0703-119X). **4836**

CONTACT LENS JOURNAL. (US/0096-2716). **3873**

CONTACT LENS JOURNAL (THORNTON HEATH, SURREY), THE. (UK/0306-9575). **4215**

CONTEMPORARY EDUCATIONAL PSYCHOLOGY. (US/0361-476X). **4582**

CONTEMPORARY FRENCH CIVILIZATION. (US/0147-9156). **2684**

CONTEMPORARY HYPNOSIS : THE JOURNAL OF THE BRITISH SOCIETY OF EXPERIMENTAL AND CLINICAL HYPNOSIS. (UK/0960-5290). **2857**

CONTEMPORARY INTERNAL MEDICINE. (US/1042-9646). **3796**

CONTEMPORARY JEWRY. (US/0147-1694). **2259**

CONTEMPORARY PACIFIC, THE. (US/1043-898X). **2510**

CONTEMPORARY PHYSICS. (UK/0010-7514). **4401**

CONTEMPORARY POLICY ISSUES. (US/0735-0007). **1471**

CONTEMPORARY PSYCHOANALYSIS. (US/0010-7530). **3923**

CONTEMPORARY PSYCHOLOGY. (US/0010-7549). **4582**

CONTEMPORARY SOUTHEAST ASIA. (SI/0129-797X). **2649**

CONTEMPORARY SSOCIAL PSYCHOLOGY. (US/1041-3030). **4582**

CONTEMPORARY TOPICS IN LABORATORY ANIMAL SCIENCE. (US/1060-0558). **5508**

CONTINENTAL SHELF RESEARCH. (UK/0278-4343). **1354**

CONTINGENCIES (WASHINGTON, D.C.). (US/1048-9851). **2878**

CONTINGENCY PLANNING & RECOVERY JOURNAL : CPR-J. (US/0899-4595). **1226**

CONTRACEPTION (STONEHAM). (US/0010-7824). **588**

CONTRIBUTIONS IN BIOLOGY AND GEOLOGY. (US/0160-5313). **452**

CONTRIBUTIONS IN MARINE SCIENCE. (US/0082-3449). **1448**

CONTRIBUTIONS TO GEOLOGY (LARAMIE). (US/0010-7980). **1372**

CONTRIBUTIONS TO INDIAN SOCIOLOGY. NEW SERIES. (US/0069-9667). **5243**

CONTRIBUTIONS TO MUSIC EDUCATION. (US/0190-4922). **4112**

CONTROL ENGINEERING. (US/0010-8049). **1219**

CONTROL THEORY AND ADVANCED TECHNOLOGY. (JA/0911-0704). **1180**

CONTROLLED CLINICAL TRIALS. (US/0197-2456). **3568**

CONTROLLERS MAGAZINE. (NE). **660**

CONVENIENCE STORE NEWS. (US/0194-8733). **660**

CONVULSIVE THERAPY. (US/0749-8055). **3568**

COOPERATION AND CONFLICT. (NO/0010-8367). **4470**

COORDINATION CHEMISTRY REVIEWS. (SZ/0010-8545). **1051**

COPEIA. (US/0045-8511). **5581**

COPPER STUDIES. (US/0091-2204). **4000**

CORAL REEFS. (GW/0722-4028). **1448**

CORELLA. (AT/0155-0438). **5617**

CORNEA. (US/0277-3740). **3873**

CORNELL EAST ASIA SERIES. (US/1050-2955). **2503**

CORNELL INTERNATIONAL LAW JOURNAL. (US/0010-8812). **3126**

CORNELL LAW REVIEW. (US/0010-8847). **2956**

CORNELL VETERINARIAN, THE. (US/0010-8901). **5508**

CORNERSTONE (CHICAGO, ILL.). (US/0275-2743). **4950**

CORNSTALK GAZETTE. (AT/0818-7339). **384**

CORONARY ARTERY DISEASE. (US/0954-6928). **3703**

CORONICA, LA. (US/0193-3892). **3275**

CORRIERE EUROPEO. (IT). **1634**

CORROSION (HOUSTON, TEX.). (US/0010-9312). **2011**

CORROSION SCIENCE. (UK/0010-938X). **2011**

CORTEX. (IT/0010-9452). **3830**

COSMETICA DISTRIBUTION LEVALLOIS-PERRET. (FR/1150-1677). **403**

COSMETICS & TOILETRIES. (IT). **403**

COUNCIL OF GENEALOGY COLUMNISTS NEWSLETTER. (US/1046-641X). **2444**

COUNSELING INTERVIEWER, THE. (US/0160-6794). **4583**

COUNSELING PSYCHOLOGIST, THE. (US/0011-0000). **4583**

COUNTDOWN (ATHENS, OHIO). (US/0746-8830). **17**

COUNTRY MUSIC NEWS (OTTAWA). (CN/0714-8356). **4112**

COUNTRY-SIDE. (UK/0011-023X). **2213**

COUNTRY TODAY, THE. (US/0192-9658). **5766**

COURRIER DE LA SCLEROSE EN PLAQUES, LE. (FR/0290-5736). **3569**

COURRIER DU CENTRE INTERNATIONAL D'ETUDES POETIQUES. (BE/0577-1757). **3461**

COYUNTURA ANDINA. (CK). **1554**

COYUNTURA ECONOMICA. (CK/0120-3576). **1554**

CPA JOURNAL (1975), THE. (US/0732-8435). **742**

CPA'S PC NETWORK ADVISOR. (US/1059-4590). **1241**

CPL BIBLIOGRAPHY. (US/0743-1635). **2840**

CPOA TRAINING BULLETIN. (US). **3161**

CRANIO. (US/0886-9634). **3569**

CRAZYHORSE (LITTLE ROCK, ARK.). (US/0011-0841). **3462**

CREATION RESEARCH QUARTERLY. (US/0092-9166). **5097**

CREATIVE CHILD AND ADULT QUARTERLY, THE. (US/0884-4291). **1877**

CREATIVE TRANSFORMATION. (US/1062-4708). **4951**

CRIME AND DELINQUENCY. (US/0011-1287). **3161**

CRIME LABORATORY DIGEST. (US/0743-1872). **3080**

CRIME, LAW, AND SOCIAL CHANGE. (NE/0925-4994). **3161**

CRIMINAL JUSTICE AND BEHAVIOR. (US/0093-8548). **4583**

CRIMINAL JUSTICE ETHICS. (US/0731-129X). **2249**

CRIMINAL JUSTICE REVIEW (ATLANTA, GA.). (US/0734-0168). **3162**

CRIMINAL LAW FORUM. (US/1046-8374). **3106**

CRIMINAL LAW REVIEW (LONDON, ENGLAND). (UK/0011-135X). **3106**

CRIMINOLOGY (BEVERLY HILLS). (US/0011-1384). **3163**

CRITICA (LA JOLLA, CALIF.). (US/8755-3325). **5243**

CRITICAL CARE CLINICS. (US/0749-0704). **3779**

CRITICAL CARE MEDICINE. (US/0090-3493). **3723**

CRITICAL CARE NURSE. (US/0279-5442). **3854**

CRITICAL CARE NURSING QUARTERLY. (US/0887-9303). **3854**

CRITICAL PUBLIC HEALTH. (UK/0958-1596). **4772**

CRITICAL REVIEW (NEW YORK, N.Y.). (US/0891-3811). **4470**

CRITICAL REVIEWS IN ANALYTICAL CHEMISTRY. (US/1040-8347). **1014**

CRITICAL REVIEWS IN BIOTECHNOLOGY. (US/0738-8551). **3691**

CRITICAL REVIEWS IN CLINICAL LABORATORY SCIENCES. (US/1040-8363). **3894**

CRITICAL REVIEWS IN DIAGNOSTIC IMAGING. (US/1040-8371). **3940**

CRITICAL REVIEWS IN MICROBIOLOGY. (US/1040-841X). **561**

CRITICAL REVIEWS IN ONCOGENESIS. (US/0893-9675). **3815**

CRITICAL REVIEWS IN SOLID STATE AND MATERIALS SCIENCES. (US/1040-8436). **4401**

CRITICAL REVIEWS IN THERAPEUTIC DRUG CARRIER SYSTEMS. (US/0743-4863). **4298**

CRITICAL SOCIOLOGY. (US/0896-9205). **5243**

CRITICAL STUDIES IN MASS COMMUNICATION. (US/0739-3180). **1109**

CRITICAL THEORY. (NE/0920-3060). **3275**

CROATICA CHEMICA ACTA. (CI/0011-1643). **973**

CROP PROTECTION (GUILDFORD, SURREY). (UK/0261-2194). **169**

CROP SCIENCE. (US/0011-183X). **169**

CROSS-CULTURAL RESEARCH. (US/1069-3971). **5197**

CROSSCURRENTS (NEW BRUNSWICK, N.J.). (US/1053-9778). **234**

CROSSOSOMA. (US/0891-9100). **507**

CROSSROADS (DE KALB, ILL.). (US/0741-2037). **2503**

CRUSADER (MEMPHIS). (US/0011-2151). **5058**

CRUSTACEANA. (NE/0011-216X). **5581**

CRUSTACEANA. SUPPLEMENT. (NE/0167-6563). **5581**

CRUX OF THE NEWS. (US/0591-2296). **4952**

CRYO LETTERS. (UK/0143-2044). **452**

CRYOBIOLOGY. (US/0011-2240). **452**

CRYOGENICS (GUILFORD). (UK/0011-2275). **4401**

CRYPTOGAMIE. ALGOLOGIE. (FR/0181-1568). **452**

CRYPTOGAMIE. BRYOLOGIE, LICHENOLOGIE. (FR/0181-1576). **507**

CRYPTOGAMIE. MYCOLOGIE (1979). (FR/0181-1584). **507**

CRYPTOZOOLOGY. (US/0736-7023). **5581**

CRYSTAL RESEARCH AND TECHNOLOGY (1979). (GW/0232-1300). **1031**

CSR HOTLINE. (US/0894-6418). **1153**

CTNS BULLETIN. (US/0889-8243). **5098**

CUADERNOS DE ACTUALIDAD INTERNACIONAL. (VE/0798-0841). **5197**

CUADERNOS DE ESTUDIOS BORJANOS. (SP). **2684**

CUADERNOS DE ETNOLOGIA Y ETNOGRAFIA DE NAVARRA. (SP/0590-1871). **234**

CUADERNOS DE INVESTIGACION FILOLOGICA. (SP/0211-0547). **3276**

CULTURA E NATURA. (IT). **5243**

CULTURAL FUTURES RESEARCH. (US/0748-772X). **234**

CULTURE & TRADITION. (CN/0701-0184). **2319**

CULTURE, MEDICINE AND PSYCHIATRY. (NE/0165-005X). **3924**

CUMULATIVE BOOK INDEX, THE. (US/0011-300X). **3458**

CURA REPORTER. (US). **2819**

CURATIONIS (PRETORIA). (SA/0379-8577). **3854**

CURATOR (NEW YORK, N.Y.). (US/0011-3069). **4087**

CURRENT ANTHROPOLOGY. (US/0011-3204). **234**

CURRENT EYE RESEARCH. (UK/0271-3683). **3874**

CURRENT GENETICS. (GW/0172-8083). **544**

CURRENT HISTORY (1941). (US/0011-3530). **2614**

CURRENT MEDICAL LITERATURE-INFECTIOUS DISEASES. (UK/0951-9602). **3980**

CURRENT MEDICAL LITERATURE / NEPHROLOGY AND UROLOGY. (UK/0951-9629). **3989**

CURRENT MEDICAL RESEARCH AND OPINION. (UK/0300-7995). **3570**

CURRENT MICROBIOLOGY. (US/0343-8651). **561**

CURRENT OPINION IN CARDIOLOGY. (UK/0268-4705). **3704**

CURRENT OPINION IN GASTROENTEROLOGY. (UK/0267-1379). **3744**

CURRENT OPINION IN IMMUNOLOGY. (UK/0952-7915). **3668**

CURRENT OPINION IN INFECTIOUS DISEASES. (UK/0951-7375). **3713**

CURRENT OPINION IN NEUROLOGY AND NEUROSURGERY. (UK/0951-7383). **3831**

CURRENT OPINION IN THERAPEUTIC PATENTS. (UK). **1303**

CURRENT PROBLEMS IN CANCER. (US/0147-0272). **3815**

CURRENT PROBLEMS IN CARDIOLOGY. (US/0146-2806). **3704**

CURRENT PROTOCOLS IN MOLECULAR BIOLOGY. (US). **453**

CURRENT PSYCHOLOGY (NEW BRUNSWICK, N.J.). (US/1046-1310). **4584**

CURRENT REFERENCES IN FISH RESEARCH. (US/0739-540X). **2317**

CURRENT SCIENCE. (II/0011-3891). **5098**

CURRENT THERAPEUTIC RESEARCH. (US/0011-393X). **4298**

CURRENT TOPICS IN CELLULAR REGULATION. (US/0070-2137). **535**

CURRENT TOPICS IN INFECTION. (UK). **3713**

CURRICULUM AND TEACHING. (AT/0726-416X). **1734**

CURRICULUM INQUIRY. (US/0362-6784). **1892**

CUTIS (NEW YORK, N.Y.). (US/0011-4162). **3719**

CYBERNETICA. (BE/0011-4227). **1250**

CYBERNETICS AND SYSTEMS. (US/0196-9722). **1250**

CYPRUS JOURNAL OF ECONOMICS, THE. (CY/1013-3224). **1479**

CYTOBIOS. (UK/0011-4529). **535**

CYTOGENETICS AND CELL GENETICS. (SZ/0301-0171). **544**

CYTOMETRY (NEW YORK, N.Y.). (US/0196-4763). **535**

CYTOPATHOLOGY (OXFORD). (UK/0956-5507). **535**

CZECHOSLOVAK AND CENTRAL EUROPEAN JOURNAL. (US/1056-005X). **2685**

CZECHOSLOVAK JOURNAL OF PHYSICS. (XR/0011-4626). **4401**

CZECHOSLOVAK MATHEMATICAL JOURNAL. (XR/0011-4642). **3503**

D (DALLAS. 1978). (US/0164-8292). **2532**

D.H. LAWRENCE REVIEW, THE. (US/0011-4936). **3341**

DAEDALUS (CAMBRIDGE). (US/0011-5266). **5098**

DAEHAN HWAHAK HWOEJEE. (KO/0418-2472). **974**

DAIRY COUNCIL DIGEST. (US/0011-5568). **193**

DAIRY INDUSTRIES INTERNATIONAL. (UK/0308-8197). **193**

DALHOUSIE FRENCH STUDIES. (CN/0711-8813). **3379**

DALHOUSIE REVIEW, THE. (CN/0011-5827). **3380**

DALLAS MEDICAL JOURNAL. (US/0011-586X). **3570**

DALLAS POST TRIBUNE, THE. (US/0746-7303). **5749**

DALMO'MA. (US/0191-7722). **3462**

DALTON TRANSACTIONS. (UK/0300-9246). **1036**

DANA (DANMARKS FISKERI- OG HAVUNDERSGELSER). (DK/0106-553X). **554**

DANCE RESEARCH JOURNAL. (US/0149-7677). **1312**

DANISH MEDICAL BULLETIN. (DK/0011-6092). **3570**

DANSK ELFORSYNING. (DK). **2003**

DATA BASE. (US/0095-0033). **1257**

DATA NETWORKING / DATAPRO. (US). **1241**

DATA SECURITY LETTER. (US/1065-9986). **1181**

DATABASE PROGRAMMING & DESIGN. (US/0895-4518). **1253**

DATAMATION. (US/0011-6963). **1258**

DATAPRO REPORTS ON RETAIL AUTOMATION. (US/0730-8817). **1258**

DAVID Y GOLIATH : BOLETIN CLACSO. (AG/0325-0431). **2551**

DAXUE HUAXUE. (CC/1000-8438). **974**

DAY CARE AND EARLY EDUCATION. (US/0092-4199). **1803**

DEATH STUDIES. (US/0748-1187). **4584**

DEBATE (LIMA, PERU). (PE). **4471**

DEBATES EN SOCIOLOGIA. (PE). **5244**

DECISION SCIENCES. (US/0011-7315). **664**

DECUBITUS (CHICAGO, ILL.). (US/0898-1655). **3571**

DEEP-SEA RESEARCH. PART A. OCEANOGRAPHIC RESEARCH PAPERS. (UK/0198-0149). **1362**

DEFENSE MANUAL. (US/0191-877X). **3089**

DEFENSE NEWS (SPRINGFIELD, VA.). (US/0884-139X). **4041**

DEFENSE SCIENCE JOURNAL. (II/0011-748X). **4042**

DEGRE SECOND. (US/0148-561X). **3341**

DEGREES AND OTHER FORMAL AWARDS CONFERRED, KENTUCKY COLLEGES AND UNIVERSITIES / KENTUCKY CENTER FOR EDUCATION STATISTICS. (US). **1819**

DELAWARE GENEALOGICAL SOCIETY JOURNAL. (US/0731-3896). **2445**

DELAWARE HISTORY. (GW/0011-7765). **2730**

DELAWARE MEDICAL JOURNAL. (US/0011-7781). **3571**

DELAWARE TODAY (WILMINGTON, DEL. : 1983). (US). **2532**

DELOS. (US/0011-7951). **3462**

DELTION AUTOKINETISTIKES NOMOTHESIAS KAI NOMOLOGIAS. (GR). **2959**

DEMENTIA (BASEL, SWITZERLAND). (SZ/1013-7424). **3831**

DENKI KAGAKU OYOBI KOGYO BUTSURI KAGAKU. (JA/0366-9297). **1034**

DENTAL COMPUTER NEWSLETTER. (US/0738-9744). **1320**

DENTAL MATERIALS. (DK/0109-5641). **1321**

DEPARTMENT CHAIR, THE. (US/1049-3255). **1862**

DEPRESSION (NEW YORK, N.Y.). (US/1062-6417). **4584**

DERMATOLOGIC CLINICS. (US/0733-8635). **3719**

DERMATOLOGY NURSING. (US/1060-3441). **3719**

DESALINATION. (NE/0011-9164). **5532**

DESARROLLO ECONOMICO (BUENOS AIRES). (AG/0046-001X). **5198**

DESIGN METHODS. (US/1067-9359). **297**

DESIGNS, CODES AND CRYPTOGRAPHY. (NE/0925-1022). **2041**

DEUTSCHE ENTOMOLOGISCHE ZEITSCHRIFT. (GW/0012-0073). **5607**

DEUTSCHE LEBENSMITTEL-RUNDSCHAU. (GW/0012-0413). **2333**

DEUTSCHE MEDIZINISCHE WOCHENSCHRIFT. (GW/0012-0472). **3571**

DEUTSCHE ZEITSCHRIFT FUER PHILOSOPHIE. (GW/0012-1045). **4344**

DEVELOPING ECONOMIES, THE. (JA/0012-1533). **5198**

DEVELOPMENT AND CHANGE. (UK/0012-155X). **5198**

DEVELOPMENT (CAMBRIDGE). (UK/0950-1991). **541**

DEVELOPMENT, GROWTH & DIFFERENTIATION. (JA/0012-1592). **541**

DEVELOPMENT. SUPPLEMENT. (UK). **541**

DEVELOPMENTAL AND COMPARATIVE IMMUNOLOGY. (US/0145-305X). **3669**

DEVELOPMENTAL BIOLOGY. (US/0012-1606). **453**

DEVELOPMENTAL BRAIN DYSFUNCTION. (SZ/1019-5815). **3831**

DEVELOPMENTAL BRAIN RESEARCH. (NE/0165-3806). **3831**

DEVELOPMENTAL GENETICS. (US/0192-253X). **544**

DEVELOPMENTAL MEDICINE & CHILD NEUROLOGY. (UK/0012-1622). **3657**

DEVELOPMENTAL NEUROPSYCHOLOGY. (US/8756-5641). **3571**

DEVELOPMENTAL NEUROSCIENCE. (SZ/0378-5866). **3831**

DEVELOPMENTAL PHARMACOLOGY AND THERAPEUTICS. (SZ/0379-8305). **4299**

DEVELOPMENTAL PHYSIOPATHOLOGY & CLINICS. (IT). **3894**

DEVELOPMENTAL PSYCHOBIOLOGY. (US/0012-1630). **453**

DEVELOPMENTAL PSYCHOLOGY. (US/0012-1649). **4584**

DEVELOPMENTAL REVIEW. (US/0273-2297). **4584**

DEVELOPMENTS IN ATMOSPHERIC SCIENCE. (US/0167-5117). **1425**

DEVELOPMENTS IN CANCER RESEARCH. (US/0163-6146). **3816**

DEVELOPMENTS IN CELL BIOLOGY. (US/0165-2265). **536**

DEVELOPMENTS IN FOOD MICROBIOLOGY. (UK/0264-2670). **562**

DEVELOPMENTS IN FRACTURE MECHANICS. (UK). **1970**

DEVELOPMENTS IN GEOCHEMISTRY. (NE/0921-3198). **974**

DEVELOPMENTS IN GEOMATHEMATICS. (US). **1373**

DEVELOPMENTS IN INTERNATIONAL LAW. (NE). **3127**

DEVELOPMENTS IN MINERAL PROCESSING. (NE/0167-4528). **1439**

DEVELOPMENTS IN PETROLEUM SCIENCE. (NE/0376-7361). **4254**

DEVELOPMENTS IN PETROLOGY. (NE/0167-2894). **1458**

DEVELOPMENTS IN PLASTICS TECHNOLOGY. (UK). **4454**

DEVELOPMENTS IN SOLID EARTH GEOPHYSICS. (NE/0419-0297). **1404**

DEVELOPMENTS IN STRUCTURAL GEOLOGY. (NE). **1373**

DEVELOPMENTS IN VOLCANOLOGY. (NE). **1404**

DEVIANT BEHAVIOR. (US/0163-9625). **4584**

DEWITT POLYMER SERVICE. (US). **4454**

DIABETE & METABOLISME. (FR/0338-1684). **3727**

DIABETES CARE. (US/0149-5992). **3727**

DIABETES/METABOLISM REVIEWS. (US/0742-4221). **3728**

DIABETES (NEW YORK, N.Y.). (US/0012-1797). **3728**

DIABETES RESEARCH AND CLINICAL PRACTICE. (NE/0168-8227). **3728**

DIABETES RESEARCH AND CLINICAL PRACTICE. (NE/0168-8227). **3728**

DIABETES RESEARCH (EDINBURGH, LOTHIAN). (UK/0256-5985). **3728**

DIABETIC MEDICINE. (UK/0742-3071). **3728**

DIABETIC TRAVELER, THE. (US/0899-2398). **5468**

DIABETOLOGIA. (GW/0012-186X). **3728**

DIAGNOSTIC CYTOPATHOLOGY. (US/8755-1039). **536**

DIAGNOSTIC MICROBIOLOGY AND INFECTIOUS DISEASE. (US/0732-8893). **562**

DIAGNOSTIC MOLECULAR PATHOLOGY. (US/1052-9551). **3894**

DIAGNOSTIC ONCOLOGY. (SZ/1013-8129). **3816**

DIALECTICAL ANTHROPOLOGY. (NE/0304-4092). **235**

DIALOGO SOCIAL. (PN/0046-0206). **2614**

DIALYSIS & TRANSPLANTATION. (US/0090-2934). **3571**

DIANOIA (CAMROSE). (CN/1192-1854). **1820**

DIARIST'S JOURNAL. (US). **3381**

DICKINSON STUDIES. (US/0164-1492). **3462**

DIET AND HEALTH MAGAZINE. (US/1048-8391). **4189**

DIFFERENTIAL EQUATIONS. (US/0012-2661). **3503**

DIFFERENTIATION (LONDON). (GW/0301-4681). **536**

DIGESTION. (SZ/0012-2823). **3744**

DIGESTIVE DISEASES AND SCIENCES. (US/0163-2116). **3744**

DIGESTIVE DISEASES (BASEL). (SZ/0257-2753). **3744**

DIGITAL SIGNAL PROCESSING. (US/1051-2004). **1182**

DIMENSIONAL STONE. (US/0883-0258). **613**

DIMENSIONS OF CRITICAL CARE NURSING. (US/0730-4625). **3855**

DIONYSOS (SUPERIOR, WISC.). (US/1044-4149). **1342**

DIPLOMATIC HISTORY. (US/0145-2096). **2731**

DIRECTIONS SUVA. (FJ/1011-5846). **3206**

DIRECTORIO COMERCIAL E INDUSTRIAL DE EL SALVADOR. EL SALVADOR'S COMMERCIAL AND INDUSTRIAL DIRECTORY. (ES). **1604**

DIRECTORY - AGRICULTURAL COMMUNICATORS IN EDUCATION (U.S.). (US/8755-5972). **79**

DIRECTORY - CANADIAN PAYMENTS ASSOCIATION. (CN/0822-7152). **787**

DIRECTORY OF MAILING LIST COMPANIES. (US). **666**

DIRECTORY - SOUTH DAKOTA REAL ESTATE BOARD. (US/0731-9525). **4837**

DIRITTO ED ECONOMIA. (IT/0394-8366). **1479**

DIRITTO FALLIMENTARE E DELLE SOCIETA COMMERCIALI. (IT/0391-5239). **2963**

DISABLED OUTDOORS. (US). **4387**

DISASTERS. (UK/0361-3666). **5284**

DISCERNMENT. (US). **2249**

DISCLOSURES. (US). **743**

DISCOURSE. (UK/0159-6306). **1736**

DISCOURSE PROCESSES. (US/0163-853X). **3277**

DISCRETE & COMPUTATIONAL GEOMETRY. (US/0179-5376). **3503**

DISCRETE EVENT DYNAMIC SYSTEMS. (US/0924-6703). **1282**

DISCRETE MATHEMATICS. (NE/0012-365X). **3504**

DISCRETE MATHEMATICS AND APPLICATIONS. (NE/0924-9265). **3504**

DISCURSO. (PY/0737-8742). **3381**

DISEASE-A-MONTH. (US/0011-5029). **3572**

DISEASE MARKERS. (UK/0278-0240). **3713**

DISEASES OF THE COLON & RECTUM. (US/0012-3706). **3744**

DISPLAYS. (UK/0141-9382). **1228**

DISSENT (NEW YORK). (US/0012-3846). **4541**

DISTANCE EDUCATION. (AT/0158-7919). **1736**

DISTRIBUTED AND PARALLEL DATABASES. (US/0926-8782). **1254**

DISTRIBUTED COMPUTING. (GW/0178-2770). **1258**

DIWEN WULI XUEBAO. (CC/1000-3258). **4402**

DNA REPORTER. (US). **3855**

DOCTRINA PENAL. (AG). **3107**

DOCUMENTA OPHTHALMOLOGICA. (NE/0012-4486). **3874**

DOCUMENTALISTE (PARIS). (FR/0012-4508). **3208**

DOCUMENTS D'ANALISI GEOGRAFICA / [PUBLICACIONS DEL DEPARTAMENT DE GEOGRAFIA, UNIVERSITAT AUTONOMA DE BARCELONA]. (SP/0212-1573). **2560**

DOCUMENTS D'ARCHEOLOGIE MERIDIONALE. (FR/0184-1068). **266**

DOCUMENTS EXPERIENCES. (FR). **4954**

DOE THIS MONTH. (US/1057-5782). **1936**

DOG WATCH, THE. (AT). **4176**

DOKLADY AKADEMII NAUK SSSR. (RU/0002-3264). **1354**

DOLOR. (SP/0214-0659). **3573**

DOMES (MILWAUKEE, WIS.). (US/1060-4367). **2768**

DOMESTIC ANIMAL ENDOCRINOLOGY. (US/0739-7240). **3728**

DOORS AND HARDWARE. (US/0361-5294). **613**

DORIS LESSING NEWSLETTER. (US/0882-486X). **3382**

DOSSIER. L'UFFICIO TECNICO. (IT/0394-8315). **298**

DOSSIERS DU CEPED, LES. (FR/0993-6165). **4552**

DR. DOBB'S JOURNAL (1989). (US/1044-789X). **1267**

DREISER STUDIES. (US/0896-6362). **3382**

DRESS. (US/0361-2112). **1083**

DREVARSKY VYSKUM. (XO/0012-6136). **2400**

DRIVER (MIAMI, FLA.). (US/1062-9394). **4893**

DROIT ET CULTURES / REVUE SEMESTRIELLE ANTHROPOLOGIE ET D'HISTOIRE. (FR). **235**

DRUG AND ALCOHOL DEPENDENCE. (SZ/0376-8716). **1343**

DRUG AND CHEMICAL TOXICOLOGY (NEW YORK, N.Y. 1978). (US/0148-0545). **3980**

DRUG DEVELOPMENT AND INDUSTRIAL PHARMACY. (US/0363-9045). **4300**

DRUG DEVELOPMENT RESEARCH. (US/0272-4391). **4300**

DRUG INVESTIGATION. (NZ/0114-2402). **4300**

DRUG METABOLISM AND DISPOSITION. (US/0090-9556). **4300**

DRUG METABOLISM REVIEWS (SOFTCOVER ED.). (US/0360-2532). **4301**

DRUG THERAPY (NEW YORK, N.Y.). (US/0001-7094). **3573**

DRUG THERAPY TOPICS. (US/0882-6684). **4301**

DRUGS & SOCIETY (NEW YORK, N.Y.). (US/8756-8233). **1344**

DRUGS (NEW YORK, N.Y.). (US/0012-6667). **4302**

DRUGS UNDER EXPERIMENTAL AND CLINICAL RESEARCH. (SP/0378-6501). **4302**

DRYING TECHNOLOGY. (US/0737-3937). **1024**

DTW. DEUTSCHE TIERAERZTLICHE WOCHENSCHRIFT. (GW/0341-6593). **5509**

DUKE LAW JOURNAL. (US/0012-7086). **2964**

DUKE MATHEMATICAL JOURNAL. (US/0012-7094). **3504**

DURHAM ARCHAEOLOGICAL JOURNAL. (UK/0265-8038). **267**

DYES AND PIGMENTS. (UK/0143-7208). **4223**

DYNAMIC NUTRITION RESEARCH. (SZ) **4190**

DYNAMICS AND CONTROL. (US/0925-4668). **2113**

EAF JOURNAL. (CN/0831-3318). **1862**

EANHS BULLETIN. (KE/0374-7387). **4165**

EAR AND HEARING. (US/0196-0202). **3887**

EAR, NOSE & THROAT JOURNAL. (US/0145-5613). **3887**

EARLY CHINA. (US/0362-5028). **2650**

EARLY KEYBOARD JOURNAL. (US/0899-8132). **4116**

EARTH AND PLANETARY SCIENCE LETTERS. (NE/0012-821X). **1374**

EARTH, MOON, AND PLANETS. (NE/0167-9295). **395**

EARTH-SCIENCE REVIEWS. (NE/0012-8252). **1374**

EARTH SCIENCES HISTORY. (US/0736-623X). **1355**

EARTH SURFACE PROCESSES AND LANDFORMS. (UK/0197-9337). **1374**

EARTHCARE NORTHWEST. (US/0732-684X). **2192**

EARTHQUAKE ENGINEERING & STRUCTURAL DYNAMICS. (UK/0098-8847). **2022**

EARTH'S DAUGHTERS. (US/0163-0989). **3383**

EAST AFRICAN MEDICAL JOURNAL, THE. (KE/0012-835X). **3573**

EAST ASIAN HISTORY. (AT/1036-6008). **2650**

EAST EUROPEAN QUARTERLY. (US/0012-8449). **2686**

EAST TEXAS HISTORICAL JOURNAL. (US/0424-1444). **2732**

EAST/WEST EDUCATION. (US/0899-0247). **1737**

EAST-WEST JOURNAL OF NUMERICAL MATHEMATICS. (NE/0928-0200). **3504**

EASTERN EUROPEAN ECONOMICS. (US/0012-8775). **1481**

EATON COUNTY QUEST. (US). **2446**

EBA NEWSLETTER. (FR/0987-2507). **788**

ECCLESIA ORANS. (IT/1010-3872). **4954**

ECHOS DU CENTRE INTERNATIONAL D'ETUDES PEDAGOGIQUES DE SEVRES. (FR/0154-5280). **2686**

ECLOGAE GEOLOGICAE HELVETIAE. (SZ/0012-9402). **1374**

ECOLOGICAL ENTOMOLOGY. (UK/0307-6946). **5607**

ECOLOGICAL MODELLING. (NE/0304-3800). **2214**

ECOLOGICAL MONOGRAPHS. (US/0012-9615). **2214**

ECOLOGY LAW QUARTERLY. (US/0046-1121). **3110**

ECOLOGY OF FOOD AND NUTRITION. (US/0367-0244). **4190**

ECOLOGY (TEMPE). (US/0012-9658). **2214**

ECONOMETRIC THEORY. (US/0266-4666). **1591**

ECONOMETRICA. (US/0012-9682). **1481**

ECONOMIA E BANCA. (IT/0393-9243). **1481**

ECONOMIA INTERNAZIONALE. (IT/0012-981X). **1634**

ECONOMIA (LISBOA). (PO/0870-3531). **1481**

ECONOMIC AND INDUSTRIAL DEMOCRACY. (UK/0143-831X). **1664**

ECONOMIC AND LABOUR RELATIONS REVIEW : ELRR, THE. (AT/1035-3046). **2861**

ECONOMIC AND POLITICAL WEEKLY. (II/0012-9976). **1556**

ECONOMIC AND SOCIAL REVIEW, THE. (IE/0012-9984). **5199**

ECONOMIC AWARENESS. (UK/0953-4997). **1482**

ECONOMIC BOTANY. (US/0013-0001). **508**

ECONOMIC DEVELOPMENT AND CULTURAL CHANGE. (US/0013-0079). **1482**

ECONOMIC DEVELOPMENT REVIEW (SCHILLER PARK, ILL.). (US/0742-3713). **1483**

ECONOMIC GEOGRAPHY. (US/0013-0095). **1483**

ECONOMIC GEOLOGY AND THE BULLETIN OF THE SOCIETY OF ECONOMIC GEOLOGISTS. (US/0361-0128). **1374**

ECONOMIC HISTORY REVIEW, THE. (UK/0013-0117). **1557**

ECONOMIC INQUIRY. (US/0095-2583). **1483**

ECONOMIC JOURNAL (LONDON). (UK/0013-0133). **1483**

ECONOMIC MODELLING. (UK/0264-9993). **1591**

ECONOMIC RECORD, THE. (AT/0013-0249). **1484**

ECONOMIC REVIEW (CLEVELAND). (US/0013-0281). **1484**

ECONOMIC SYSTEMS RESEARCH. (UK/0953-5314). **1485**

ECONOMIC THEORY. (GW/0938-2259). **1591**

ECONOMICA (LONDON). (UK/0013-0427). **1486**

ECONOMICS AND PHILOSOPHY. (UK/0266-2671). **1486**

ECONOMICS LETTERS. (NE/0165-1765). **1486**

ECONOMIST, DE. (NE/0013-063X). **1559**

ECONOMY AND SOCIETY. (UK/0308-5147). **5199**

ECOTOXICOLOGY AND ENVIRONMENTAL SAFETY. (US/0147-6513). **2214**

ECUMENE. (UK/0967-4608). **2560**

ECUMENISM. (CN/0383-431X). **4955**

EDAV. EDUCAZIONE AUDIOVISIVA. (IT/0393-098X). **1737**

EDDA. (NO/0013-0818). **3341**

EDI FORUM. (US/1048-3047). **671**

EDI LAW REVIEW, THE. (UK/0929-2233). **2965**

EDI WORLD. (US/1055-0399). **2042**

EDIFICACION CRISTIANA. (SP). **4955**

EDUCATING ABLE LEARNERS, DISCOVERING & NURTURING TALENT. (US/0896-9574). **1878**

EDUCATION ALTERNATIVES. (AT/1037-5104). **1738**

EDUCATION AND SOCIETY (MELBOURNE). (AT/0726-2655). **1738**

EDUCATION & TREATMENT OF CHILDREN. (US/0748-8491). **1893**

EDUCATION AND URBAN SOCIETY. (US/0013-1245). **1738**

EDUCATION (CHULA VISTA). (US/0013-1172). **1738**

EDUCATION FOR INFORMATION. (NE/0167-8329). **1739**

EDUCATION FOR LIBRARY AND INFORMATION SERVICES, AUSTRALIA. (AT). **3209**

EDUCATION INDEX. (US/0013-1385). **1794**

EDUCATIONAL ADMINISTRATION AND HISTORY. MONOGRAPH. (UK/0140-0428). **1863**

EDUCATIONAL ADMINISTRATION QUARTERLY. (US/0013-161X). **1863**

EDUCATIONAL AND PSYCHOLOGICAL MEASUREMENT. (US/1013-1644). **4585**

EDUCATIONAL CONSIDERATIONS. (US/0146-9282). **1913**

EDUCATIONAL GERONTOLOGY. (US/0360-1277). **1800**

EDUCATIONAL LEADERSHIP : JOURNAL OF THE ASSOCIATION FOR SUPERVISION AND CURRICULUM DEVELOPMENT. (US/0013-1784). **1742**

EDUCATIONAL PHILOSOPHY AND THEORY. (AT/0013-1857). **1893**

EDUCATIONAL POLICY (LOS ALTOS, CALIF.). (US/0895-9048). **1742**

EDUCATIONAL PSYCHOLOGIST. (US/0046-1520). **4586**

EDUCATIONAL RESEARCH (WINDSOR). (UK/0013-1881). **1742**

EDUCATIONAL REVIEW (BIRMINGHAM). (UK/0013-1911). **1742**

EDUCATIONAL SERIES - NORTH DAKOTA GEOLOGICAL SURVEY. (US/0091-9004). **1374**

EDUCATIONAL STUDIES. (UK/0305-5698). **1743**

EDUCATIONAL STUDIES IN MATHEMATICS. (NE/0013-1954). **1743**

EDUCATIONAL TECHNOLOGY RESEARCH AND DEVELOPMENT. (US/1042-1629). **1743**

EDUCATORE. (IT). **1743**

EDULAW FOR CANADIAN SCHOOLS. (CN/1193-7319). **1743**

EDWARD SAPIR MONOGRAPH SERIES IN LANGUAGE, CULTURE, AND COGNITION. (US/0163-3848). **3278**

EEG-EMG. (GW). **3574**

EEO TRENDS AND ISSUES. (US/0740-204X). **1664**

EFM. EURO FLEXO MAGAZINE. (NE/0921-383X). **4564**

EGYPTIAN JOURNAL OF DAIRY SCIENCE. (UA/0378-2700). **2334**

EGYPTIAN JOURNAL OF PHYSICS. (UA/0376-8724). **4402**

EIGHT PEAK INDEX OF MASS SPECTRA. (UK). **675**

EIGHTEENTH CENTURY (LUBBOCK), THE. (US/0193-5380). **2686**

EISEI KAGAKU. (JA/0013-273X). **975**

EISMA 'S VAKPERS. (NE/0920-2099). **4223**

EKONOMICKO-MATEMATICKY OBZOR. (CS/0013-3027). **1591**

EKONOMICKY CASOPIS. (XO/0013-3035). **1488**

EKSPERIMENTALNAJA ONKOLOGIJA. (UN/0204-3564). **3816**

ELAEIS. (MY/0128-1828). **5102**

ELECTORAL STUDIES. (UK/0261-3794). **4645**

ELECTRIC MACHINES AND POWER SYSTEMS. (US/0731-356X). **2043**

ELECTRIC RATE BOOK. (US). **4760**

ELECTRICAL COMMUNICATION. (US/0013-4252). **1154**

ELECTRICAL EQUIPMENT LONDON. (UK/0013-4317). **2045**

ELECTROANALYSIS (NEW YORK, N.Y.). (US/1040-0397). **1014**

ELECTROCHIMICA ACTA. (UK/0013-4686). **1034**

ELECTROENCEPHALOGRAPHY AND CLINICAL NEUROPHYSIOLOGY. (IE/0013-4694). **3831**

ELECTROMAGNETICS. (US/0272-6343). **2046**

ELECTRON SPIN RESONANCE. (UK/0305-9758). **1015**

ELECTRONIC GREEN JOURNAL. (US/1076-7975). **2165**

ELECTRONIC LIBRARY. (UK/0264-0473). **3209**

ELECTRONIC PRODUCTS (1981). (US/0013-4953). **2048**

ELECTRONIC PUBLISHING. (UK/0894-3982). **4814**

ELECTRONICS INFORMATION & PLANNING. (II/0304-9876). **2049**

ELECTRONICS LETTERS. (UK/0013-5194). **2049**

ELECTROPHORESIS. (GW/0173-0835). **1015**

ELEKTRISCHE ENERGIE-TECHNIK. (GW/0170-2033). **1937**

ELEMENTARY SCHOOL JOURNAL. MICROFORM, THE. (US/0013-5984). **1743**

ELEMENTARY SCHOOL LIBRARY COLLECTION, THE. (US). **3209**

ELEPHANT (DETROIT, MICH.). (US/0737-108X). **5582**

ELIZABETHAN REVIEW, THE. (US/1066-7059). **3384**

ELSEVIER OCEANOGRAPHY SERIES. (NE/0422-9894). **1449**

ELVIS COSTELLO INFORMATION SERVICE. (NE). **4116**

EMBO JOURNAL. (UK/0261-4189). **454**

EMF HEALTH REPORT. (US/1070-4027). **454**

EMORY VICO STUDIES. (US/0883-6000). **4345**

EMPHASIS, NURSING. (US/0886-7143). **3855**

EMPIRISCHE PADAGOGIK. (GW/0931-5020). **1744**

EMPLOYEE ASSISTANCE QUARTERLY. (US/0749-0003). **2861**

EMPLOYEE COUNSELLING TODAY. (UK/0933-8217). **4586**

EMPLOYEE RELATIONS LAW JOURNAL. (US/0098-8898). **3146**

EMU. (AT/0158-4197). **5617**

ENABLE EXCHANGE NEWSLETTER. (US/0892-5496). **1184**

ENA'S NURSING SCAN IN EMERGENCY CARE. (US/1056-7062). **3855**

ENCLITIC. (US/0193-5798). **3342**

ENDEAVOUR (NEW SERIES). (UK/0160-9327). **5103**

ENDOCRINE RESEARCH. (US/0743-5800). **3729**

ENDOCRINE

ENDOCRINE REVIEWS. (US/0163-769X). **3729**

ENDOCRINOLOGIA JAPONICA. (JA/0013-7219). **3729**

ENDOCRINOLOGY AND METABOLISM CLINICS OF NORTH AMERICA. (US/0889-8529). **3729**

ENDOCRINOLOGY (PHILADELPHIA). (US/0013-7227). **3730**

ENDOCURIETHERAPY / HYPERTHERMIA ONCOLOGY. (US/8756-1689). **3816**

ENDODONTICS & DENTAL TRAUMATOLOGY. (DK/0109-2502). **1323**

ENDOSCOPY. (GW/0013-726X). **3744**

ENERGY AND BUILDINGS. (SZ/0378-7788). **614**

ENERGY & FUELS. (US/0887-0624). **1939**

ENERGY CONVERSION AND MANAGEMENT. (UK/0196-8904). **1939**

ENERGY ECONOMICS. (UK/0140-9883). **1940**

ENERGY (OXFORD). (UK/0360-5442). **1941**

ENERGY POLICY. (UK/0301-4215). **1941**

ENERGY SOURCES. (US/0090-8312). **1942**

ENERGY STUDIES REVIEW. (CN/0843-4379). **1942**

ENGEI GAKKAI ZASSHI. (JA/0013-7626). **2413**

ENGINEERING ANALYSIS WITH BOUNDARY ELEMENTS. (UK/0955-7997). **1972**

ENGINEERING AND MINING JOURNAL (1926). (US/0095-8948). **2138**

ENGINEERING DESIGN GRAPHICS JOURNAL. (US/0046-2012). **1972**

ENGINEERING FRACTURE MECHANICS. (US/0013-7944). **2102**

ENGINEERING GEOLOGY. (NE/0013-7952). **1973**

ENGINEERING IN MINIATURE. (UK/0955-7644). **2773**

ENGINEERING STRUCTURES. (UK/0141-0296). **2023**

ENGINEERING WITH COMPUTERS. (US/0177-0667). **1974**

ENGLISH LANGUAGE NOTES. (US/0013-8282). **3342**

ENGLISH LITERATURE IN TRANSITION, 1880-1920. (US/0013-8339). **3342**

ENLIGHTENMENT AND DISSENT. (UK/0262-7612). **4473**

ENTERPRISE SYSTEMS JOURNAL. (US/1053-6566). **1184**

ENTOMOLOGIA EXPERIMENTALIS ET APPLICATA. (NE/0013-8703). **5607**

ENTOMOLOGIA GENERALIS. (GW/0171-8177). **5607**

ENTOMOLOGICA SCANDINAVICA. (DK/0013-8711). **5607**

ENTOMOLOGICAL NEWS. (US/0013-872X). **5607**

ENTOMOLOGICAL RESEARCH BULLETIN. (KO). **5607**

ENTOMON. (II/0377-9335). **5608**

ENTREFILET (POINTE CLAIRE). (CN/0826-4546). **2334**

ENTREPRENEURSHIP AND REGIONAL DEVELOPMENT. (UK/0898-5626). **672**

ENVIRONMENT AND BEHAVIOR. (US/0013-9165). **2215**

ENVIRONMENT & PLANNING A. (UK/0308-518X). **2821**

ENVIRONMENT AND PLANNING. B, PLANNING & DESIGN. (UK/0265-8135). **2821**

ENVIRONMENT AND PLANNING. C, GOVERNMENT & POLICY. (UK/0263-774X). **4646**

ENVIRONMENT AND PLANNING. D, SOCIETY & SPACE. (UK/0263-7758). **5199**

ENVIRONMENT INTERNATIONAL. (UK/0160-4120). **2165**

ENVIRONMENTAL AND EXPERIMENTAL BOTANY. (UK/0098-8472). **509**

ENVIRONMENTAL AND RESOURCE ECONOMICS. (NE/0924-6460). **2166**

ENVIRONMENTAL APPROVALS IN CANADA : PRACTICE AND PROCEDURE. (CN). **3111**

ENVIRONMENTAL BIOLOGY OF FISHES. (NE/0378-1909). **2300**

ENVIRONMENTAL CARCINOGENESIS REVIEWS. (US/0882-8164). **3816**

ENVIRONMENTAL CONSERVATION. (SZ/0376-8929). **2193**

ENVIRONMENTAL EDUCATION AND INFORMATION. (UK/0144-9281). **2167**

ENVIRONMENTAL ENTOMOLOGY. (US/0046-225X). **5608**

ENVIRONMENTAL ETHICS. (US/0163-4275). **2167**

ENVIRONMENTAL GEOLOGY AND WATER SCIENCES. (US/0177-5146). **1375**

ENVIRONMENTAL GEOLOGY SERIES (NASHVILLE). (US/0362-8175). **1375**

ENVIRONMENTAL HEALTH PERSPECTIVES. (US/0091-6765). **4774**

ENVIRONMENTAL HISTORY REVIEW : EHR. (US/1053-4180). **2228**

ENVIRONMENTAL LAW ANTHOLOGY. (US/1054-8297). **3111**

ENVIRONMENTAL LAW (PORTLAND, ORE.). (US/0046-2276). **3111**

ENVIRONMENTAL LAW (WASHINGTON D.C.). (US/0748-8769). **3112**

ENVIRONMENTAL MANAGEMENT (NEW YORK). (US/0364-152X). **2168**

ENVIRONMENTAL MONITORING AND ASSESSMENT. (NE/0167-6369). **2168**

ENVIRONMENTAL POLLUTION (1987). (UK/0269-7491). **2229**

ENVIRONMENTAL PROFESSIONAL, THE. (US/0191-5398). **2169**

ENVIRONMENTAL PROGRESS. (US/0278-4491). **2229**

ENVIRONMENTAL PROTECTION BULLETIN. (UK/0957-9052). **2229**

ENVIRONMENTAL RESEARCH (NEW YORK, N.Y.). (US/0013-9351). **2169**

ENVIRONMENTAL SCIENCE & TECHNOLOGY. (US/0013-936X). **2169**

ENVIRONMENTAL TECHNOLOGY. (UK/0959-3330). **2170**

ENVIRONMENTAL TOXICOLOGY AND CHEMISTRY. (US/0730-7268). **2229**

ENVIRONMENTALIST, THE. (UK/0251-1088). **2193**

ENZYME. (SZ/0013-9432). **486**

EOHSI INFOLETTER. (US). **2171**

EPHEMERIDES MARIOLOGICAE. (SP/0425-1466). **4956**

EPIDEMIOLOGIC REVIEWS. (US/0193-936X). **3734**

EPIDEMIOLOGY AND INFECTION. (UK/0950-2688). **3713**

EPILEPSIA (COPENHAGEN). (NE/0013-9580). **3832**

EPILEPSY RESEARCH. (NE/0920-1211). **3832**

EPILOGUE (HALIFAX, N.S.). (CN/0836-088X). **3209**

EPISODES. (CN/0705-3797). **1375**

EPTA BULLETIN. (BE). **5059**

EQUINE VETERINARY JOURNAL. (UK/0425-1644). **5509**

ERASMUS OF ROTTERDAM SOCIETY YEARBOOK. (US/0276-2854). **1076**

ERDOL & KOHLE, ERDGAS, PETROCHEMIE. (GW/0014-0058). **4255**

ERGODIC THEORY AND DYNAMICAL SYSTEMS. (UK/0143-3857). **3505**

ERGONOMICS. (UK/0014-0139). **1251**

ERGONOMICS IN DESIGN. (US/1064-8046). **1975**

ERIC (PEABODY, MASS.). (US/1065-6537). **1745**

ERKENNTNIS. (NE/0165-0106). **4346**

ERNEST BECKER. (US/1059-3551). **3925**

ERROR TRENDS. (US). **2781**

ESA BULLETIN. (FR/0376-4265). **18**

ESA JOURNAL. (FR/0379-2285). **18**

ESPERIENZE LETTERARIE. (IT/0392-3495). **3385**

ESPIAL CANADIAN DATA BASE DIRECTORY, THE. (CN/0834-3888). **1259**

ESPRIT DE CORPS, CANADIAN MILITARY THEN & NOW. (CN/1194-2266). **4043**

ESSAYS AND REPORTS - LUTHERAN HISTORICAL CONFERENCE. (US/0090-3817). **5059**

ESSAYS IN ARTS AND SCIENCES. (US/0361-5634). **2846**

ESSAYS IN LITERATURE. (US/0094-5404). **3342**

ESSAYS IN THEATRE. (CN/0821-4425). **5364**

ESSEX ARCHAEOLOGY AND HISTORY : THE TRANSACTIONS OF THE ESSEX ARCHAEOLOGICAL SOCIETY. (UK/0308-3462). **2686**

ESSEX INSTITUTE HISTORICAL COLLECTIONS. (US). **2732**

EST MEDECINE. (FR/0248-9643). **3575**

ESTADISTICA ESPANOLA. (SP/0014-1151). **5327**

ESTIMATES OF LABOUR INCOME (OTTAWA). (CN/0318-9007). **1532**

ESTRENO. (US/0097-8663). **5364**

ESTUARIES. (US/0160-8347). **554**

ESTUDIOS DEL DESARROLLO. (INT/1013-4069). **5199**

ESTUDIOS - INSTITUTO DE ESTUDIO ECONOMICOS SOBRE LA REALIDAD ARGENTINA Y LATINOAMERICANA. (AG/0325-6928). **1489**

ESTUDIOS MADRID. (SP/0210-0525). **3385**

ESTUDIOS SOCIALES CENTROAMERICANOS. (CR/0303-9676). **5245**

ESTUDIOS SOCIALES (SANTO DOMINGO). (DR/1017-0596). **5199**

ESTUDIOS TERRITORIALES. (SP/0211-6871). **2822**

ETHICS. (US/0014-1704). **2250**

ETHICS & INTERNATIONAL AFFAIRS. (US/0892-6794). **4520**

ETHIOPIAN MEDICAL JOURNAL. (ET/0014-1755). **3575**

ETHNIC AND RACIAL STUDIES. (UK/0141-9870). **2260**

ETHNOHISTORY. (US/0014-1801). **2261**

ETHNOLOGY. (US/0014-1828). **235**

ETHOLOGY. (GW/0179-1613). **5583**

ETHOLOGY AND SOCIOBIOLOGY. (US/0162-3095). **4586**

ETHOLOGY, ECOLOGY & EVOLUTION. (IT/0394-9370). **5583**

ETHOS. (US/0091-2131). **4586**

ETUDES CANADIENNES. (FR/0153-1700). **2732**

EUGENE O'NEILL REVIEW, THE. (US/1040-9483). **3386**

EUPHORBIA JOURNAL, THE. (US/0737-8823). **2414**

EUPHORIA ET CACOPHORIA. (JA). **3720**

EUPHYTICA. (NE/0014-2336). **509**

EUROPA-ARCHIV. (GW/0014-2476). **4521**

EUROPEAN ACCOUNTING REVIEW. (UK/0963-8180). **743**

EUROPEAN APPLIED RESEARCH REPORTS. ENVIRONMENT AND NATURAL RESOURCES SECTION. (UK/0272-4626). **2171**

EUROPEAN APPLIED RESEARCH REPORTS. NUCLEAR SCIENCE AND TECHNOLOGY SECTION. (SZ/0379-4229). **2155**

EUROPEAN BIOPHYSICS JOURNAL. (GW/0175-7571). **495**

EUROPEAN BUSINESS JOURNAL. (UK/0955-808X). **673**

EUROPEAN BUSINESS LAW REVIEW. (UK/0959-6941). **3099**

EUROPEAN CANCER NEWS. (NE/0921-3732). **3816**

EUROPEAN COMPANION, THE. (UK). **4521**

EUROPEAN CONSORTIUM FOR POLITICAL RESEARCH NEWS. (UK). **4473**

EUROPEAN ECONOMIC REVIEW. (NE/0014-2921). **1489**

EUROPEAN ENVIRONMENTAL LAW REVIEW. (UK/0966-1646). **3112**

EUROPEAN HEART JOURNAL. (UK/0195-668X). **3704**

EUROPEAN INFORMATION SERVICE. (UK/0261-2747). **2516**

EUROPEAN JOURNAL OF ANAESTHESIOLOGY. (UK/0265-0215). **3682**

EUROPEAN JOURNAL OF APPLIED PHYSIOLOGY AND OCCUPATIONAL PHYSIOLOGY. (GW/0301-5548). **580**

EUROPEAN JOURNAL OF BIOCHEMISTRY. (GW/0014-2956). **487**

EUROPEAN JOURNAL OF CELL BIOLOGY. (GW/0171-9335). **536**

EUROPEAN JOURNAL OF CLINICAL INVESTIGATION. (GW/0014-2972). **3575**

EUROPEAN JOURNAL OF CLINICAL MICROBIOLOGY & INFECTIOUS DISEASES. (GW/0934-9723). **562**

EUROPEAN JOURNAL OF CLINICAL NUTRITION. (UK/0954-3007). **4190**

EUROPEAN JOURNAL OF CLINICAL PHARMACOLOGY. (GW/0031-6970). **4303**

EUROPEAN JOURNAL OF COMBINATORICS. (UK/0195-6698). **3505**

EUROPEAN JOURNAL OF COMMUNICATION (LONDON). (UK/0267-3231). **1111**

EUROPEAN JOURNAL OF DEVELOPMENT RESEARCH, THE. (UK/0957-8811). **2909**

EUROPEAN JOURNAL OF DISORDERS OF COMMUNICATION. (UK/0963-7273). **1111**

EUROPEAN JOURNAL OF DRUG METABOLISM AND PHARMACOKINETICS. (FR/0398-7639). **4303**

EUROPEAN JOURNAL OF EPIDEMIOLOGY. (NE/0392-2990). **3735**

EUROPEAN JOURNAL OF EPIDEMIOLOGY. (IT/0393-2990). **3735**

EUROPEAN JOURNAL OF FOREST PATHOLOGY. (GW/0300-1237). **2379**

EUROPEAN JOURNAL OF GASTROENTEROLOGY & HEPATOLOGY. (UK/0954-691X). **3744**

EUROPEAN JOURNAL OF HAEMATOLOGY. (DK/0902-4441). **3771**

EUROPEAN JOURNAL OF HUMAN GENETICS : EJHG. (SZ/1018-4813). **544**

EUROPEAN JOURNAL OF IMMUNOLOGY. (GW/0014-2980). **3669**

EUROPEAN JOURNAL OF IMPLANT AND REFRACTIVE SURGERY, THE. (FR/0955-3681). **3874**

EUROPEAN JOURNAL OF INFORMATION SYSTEMS. (UK/0960-085X). **1184**

EUROPEAN JOURNAL OF INTERCULTURAL STUDIES. (UK/0952-391X). **2261**

EUROPEAN JOURNAL OF MEDICINAL CHEMISTRY. (FR/0223-5234). **3575**

EUROPEAN JOURNAL OF MINERALOGY (STUTTGART). (GW/0935-1221). **1439**

EUROPEAN JOURNAL OF NEUROSCIENCE, THE. (UK/0953-816X). **3832**

EUROPEAN JOURNAL OF NUCLEAR MEDICINE. (GW/0340-6997). **3848**

EUROPEAN JOURNAL OF OPERATIONAL RESEARCH. (NE/0377-2217). **5104**

EUROPEAN JOURNAL OF ORIENTAL MEDICINE. (UK). **3575**

EUROPEAN JOURNAL OF PEDIATRICS. (GW/0340-6199). **3903**

EUROPEAN JOURNAL OF PERSONALITY. (UK/0890-2070). **4587**

EUROPEAN JOURNAL OF PHARMACOLOGY. (NE/0014-2999). **4303**

EUROPEAN JOURNAL OF PHARMACOLOGY. MOLECULAR PHARMACOLOGY SECTION. (NE/0922-4106). **4303**

EUROPEAN JOURNAL OF POLITICAL RESEARCH. (NE/0304-4130). **4473**

EUROPEAN JOURNAL OF POPULATION. (NE/0168-6577). **4553**

EUROPEAN JOURNAL OF PROTISTOLOGY. (GW/0932-4739). **562**

EUROPEAN JOURNAL OF PSYCHIATRY, THE. (SP/0213-6163). **3925**

EUROPEAN JOURNAL OF RADIOLOGY. (GW/0720-048X). **3941**

EUROPEAN JOURNAL OF SERIALS LIBRARIANSHIP. (US/1048-5287). **3209**

EUROPEAN JOURNAL OF SOCIAL PSYCHOLOGY. (UK/0046-2772). **5245**

EUROPEAN JOURNAL OF SOLID STATE AND INORGANIC CHEMISTRY. (FR/0992-4361). **1036**

EUROPEAN JOURNAL OF SURGICAL ONCOLOGY. (UK/0748-7983). **3817**

EUROPEAN MAC PROFESSIONAL. (SP). **1237**

EUROPEAN MICROSCOPY & ANALYSIS. (UK). **572**

EUROPEAN NEUROLOGY. (SZ/0014-3022). **3832**

EUROPEAN POLYMER JOURNAL. (UK/0014-3057). **1041**

EUROPEAN RESPIRATORY JOURNAL, THE. (DK/0903-1936). **3949**

EUROPEAN RESPIRATORY REVIEW : AN OFFICIAL JOURNAL OF THE EUROPEAN RESPIRATORY SOCIETY. (DK/0905-9180). **3949**

EUROPEAN REVIEW OF NATIVE AMERICAN STUDIES. (GW/0238-1486). **2261**

EUROPEAN SCIENCE EDITING : BULLETIN OF THE EUROPEAN ASSOCIATION OF SCIENCE EDITORS. (UK/0309-4715). **4815**

EUROPEAN SECURITY STUDIES. (UK). **4043**

EUROPEAN SURGICAL RESEARCH. (SZ/0014-312X). **3964**

EUROPEAN UROLOGY. (SZ/0302-2838). **3989**

EUROPEAN WATER POLLUTION CONTROL : OFFICIAL PUBLICATION OF THE EUROPEAN WATER POLLUTION CONTROL ASSOCIATION (EWPCA). (NE/0925-5060). **5533**

EUROPHYSICS LETTERS. (FR/0295-5075). **4402**

EUROPROPERTY LONDON. (UK/0961-9712). **897**

EVALUATION AND PROGRAM PLANNING. (US/0149-7189). **5285**

EVALUATION & THE HEALTH PROFESSIONS. (US/0163-2787). **3576**

EVALUATION REVIEW. (US/0193-841X). **5245**

EVELYN WAUGH NEWSLETTER AND STUDIES. (US/1058-8272). **432**

EVOLUTION. (US/0014-3820). **544**

EVOLUTIONARY ECOLOGY. (UK/0269-7653). **2216**

EVOLUTIONARY THEORY & REVIEW. (US). **236**

EX AUDITU : AN INTERNATIONAL JOURNAL OF THEOLOGICAL INTERPRETATION OF SCRIPTURE. (US). **4958**

EXCEPTIONAL CHILDREN. (US/0014-4029). **1878**

EXCHANGE. (NE/0166-2740). **4958**

EXE. (UK/0268-6872). **1184**

EXETER LINGUISTIC STUDIES. (UK/0309-4375). **3281**

EXETER STUDIES IN AMERICAN AND COMMONWEALTH ARTS. (UK). **320**

EXPEDITION. (US/0014-4738). **268**

EXPERIENTIA. (SZ/0014-4754). **5104**

EXPERIMENTAL AGING RESEARCH. (US/0361-073X). **3750**

EXPERIMENTAL AGRICULTURE. (UK/0014-4797). **82**

EXPERIMENTAL AND CLINICAL IMMUNOGENETICS. (SZ/0254-9670). **3669**

EXPERIMENTAL AND MOLECULAR PATHOLOGY. (US/0014-4800). **3894**

EXPERIMENTAL ASTRONOMY. (NE/0922-6435). **395**

EXPERIMENTAL BRAIN RESEARCH. (GW/0014-4819). **3832**

EXPERIMENTAL CELL RESEARCH. (US/0014-4827). **536**

EXPERIMENTAL EYE RESEARCH. (UK/0014-4835). **3874**

EXPERIMENTAL GERONTOLOGY. (UK/0531-5565). **3751**

EXPERIMENTAL HEMATOLOGY. (US/0301-472X). **3771**

EXPERIMENTAL LUNG RESEARCH. (US/0190-2148). **3949**

EXPERIMENTAL MECHANICS. (US/0014-4851). **4427**

EXPERIMENTAL MYCOLOGY. (US/0147-5975). **574**

EXPERIMENTAL NEPHROLOGY. (SZ/1018-7782). **3990**

EXPERIMENTAL NEUROLOGY. (US/0014-4886). **3833**

EXPERIMENTAL PARASITOLOGY. (US/0014-4894). **562**

EXPERIMENTAL TECHNIQUES (WESTPORT, CONN.). (US/0732-8818). **2114**

EXPERIMENTAL THERMAL AND FLUID SCIENCE. (US/0894-1777). **4427**

EXPERIMENTS IN FLUIDS. (GW/0723-4864). **2089**

EXPLORATION AND MINING GEOLOGY : JOURNAL OF THE GEOLOGICAL SOCIETY OF CIM. (UK/0964-1823). **2138**

EXPLORATION GEOPHYSICS (MELBOURNE). (AT/0812-3985). **4402**

EXPLORATIONS IN ECONOMIC HISTORY. (US/0014-4983). **1561**

EXPLORATIONS IN ETHNIC STUDIES. (US/0730-904X). **2261**

EXPLORATIONS IN KNOWLEDGE. (UK/0261-1376). **4346**

EXPLORATIONS IN RENAISSANCE CULTURE. (US/0098-2474). **2846**

EXPLORATIONS. SPECIAL SERIES. (US/1043-2493). **2846**

EXPONENT II. (US). **4958**

EXPORT SALES AND MARKETING MANUAL. (US/1054-8327). **834**

EXPOSITORY TIMES, THE. (UK/0014-5246). **5016**

EXTRAPOLATION. (US/0014-5483). **3342**

EYEPIECE. (UK/0950-737X). **4369**

F.O.C. REVIEW. (US/1041-8164). **3387**

FABRICATIONS : THE JOURNAL OF THE SOCIETY OF ARCHITECTURAL HISTORIANS, AUSTRALIA & NEW ZEALAND. (AT/1033-1867). **298**

FABRICS-FASHIONS. (US/0097-2495). **5350**

FACHSPRACHE. (AU/0251-1207). **3281**

FALMOUTH OUTLOOK, THE. (US/0891-8694). **5680**

FAMILIES AND DISABILITY NEWSLETTER. (US/1044-8217). **4388**

FAMILIES IN SOCIETY. (US/1044-3894). **5285**

FAMILLE QUEBEC. (CN/0318-0581). **2279**

FAMILY & COMMUNITY HEALTH. (US/0160-6379). **4775**

FAMILY AND CONCILIATION COURTS REVIEW. (US/1047-5699). **3120**

FAMILY LAW QUARTERLY. (US/0014-729X). **3120**

FAMILY MEDICINE. (US/0742-3225). **3737**

FAMILY PERSPECTIVE. (US/0014-7311). **2279**

FAMILY PLANNING PERSPECTIVES. (US/0014-7354). **588**

FAMILY PRACTICE. (UK/0263-2136). **3737**

FAMILY PRACTICE RESEARCH JOURNAL, THE. (US/0270-2304). **3737**

FAMILY PROCESS. (US/0014-7370). **2279**

FAMILY RELATIONS. (US/0197-6664). **2279**

FANTASY COMMENTATOR. (US/1051-5011). **3387**

FARE ELETTRONICA. (IT). **2054**

FARM & POWER EQUIPMENT DEALER. (US/0892-6085). **158**

FARMACEUTISCH TIJDSCHRIFT VOOR BELGIE. (BE/0369-9714). **4304**

FARMACI E TERAPIA. (IT/0393-9693). **4304**

FARMACOTERAPIA MADRID. (SP/0214-8935). **4305**

FASEB JOURNAL, THE. (US/0892-6638). **455**

FAT-SCHRIFTENREIHE. (GW/0933-050X). **5414**

FATIGUE & FRACTURE OF ENGINEERING MATERIALS & STRUCTURES. (UK/8756-758X). **2102**

FEBS LETTERS. (NE/0014-5793). **487**

FEDERAL PROBATION. (US/0014-9128). **3164**

FEDERAL SENTENCING REPORTER : FSR. (US/1053-9867). **3164**

FEDERAL TIMES. (US/0014-9233). **4703**

FELIX. (US). **320**

FEMINIST STUDIES. (US/0046-3663). **5556**

FEMS MICROBIOLOGY. (NE/0921-8254). **562**

FEMS MICROBIOLOGY LETTERS. (NE/0378-1097). **562**

FERNANDINA BEACH NEWS-LEADER. (US). **5649**

FERROELECTRICS. (US/0015-0193). **4402**

FERROELECTRICS. LETTERS SECTION. (US/0731-5171). **2054**

FERTILITY AND STERILITY. (US/0015-0282). **3576**

FERTILIZER RESEARCH. (NE/0167-1731). **171**

FETAL AND MATERNAL MEDICINE REVIEW. (UK/0965-5395). **3760**

FETUS (NASHVILLE, TENN.), THE. (US/1057-137X). **3761**

FEW-BODY SYSTEMS. (AU/0177-7963). **4447**

FIBER AND INTEGRATED OPTICS. (US/0146-8030). **4434**

FIBONACCI QUARTERLY, THE. (US/0015-0517). **3505**

FIELD CROPS RESEARCH. (NE/0378-4290). **172**

FIELD GUIDE - NEBRASKA GEOLOGICAL SURVEY. (US). **1375**

FILM & HISTORY (NEWARK, N.J.). (US/0360-3695). **4069**

FILM CRITICISM. (US/0163-5069). **4069**

FILM EN TELEVISIE EN VIDEO. (BE). **4069**

FILM QUARTERLY. (US/0015-1386). **4070**

FILM REVIEW ANNUAL. (US/0737-9080). **4070**

FILOZOFICKY CASOPIS (USTAV PRO FILOZOFII A SOCIOLOGII CSAV). (XR/0015-1831). **4347**

FILSON CLUB HISTORY QUARTERLY, THE. (US/0015-1874). **2733**

FINANCE QUARTERLY BULLETIN. (US). **4725**

FINANCIAL ANALYSTS JOURNAL, THE. (US/0015-198X). **898**

FINNISH GAME RESEARCH. (FI/0783-4365). **2216**

FIRE PROTECTION HANDBOOK. (US/0734-5984). **2289**

FIRE SAFETY JOURNAL. (SZ/0379-7112). **2290**

FIRE TECHNOLOGY. (US/0015-2684). **2290**

FISCH UND FANG. (GW/0015-2838). **4894**

FISH AND SHELLFISH IMMUNOLOGY. (UK/1050-4648). **5584**

FISH PHYSIOLOGY AND BIOCHEMISTRY. (NE/0920-1742). **2301**

FISHERIES (BETHESDA). (US/0363-2415). **2302**

FISHERIES RESEARCH. (NE/0165-7836). **2302**

FISHERY BULLETIN. (US/0090-0656). **2303**

FITOPATOLOGIA BRASILEIRA. (BL/0100-4158). **172**

FIZIOLOGICESKIJ ZURNAL. (UN/0201-8489). **580**

FLAMBOROUGH NEWS. (CN/0710-5339). **5784**

FLAMING CRESCENT, THE. (US). **4474**

FLANNERY O'CONNOR BULLETIN. (US/0091-4924). **432**

FLEISCHEREI. (GW/0015-3613). **2335**

FLEISCHWIRTSCHAFT, DIE. (GW/0015-363X). **211**

FLEXPACK MATERIALS & MARKETS BULLETIN. (UK). **4219**

FLORA (LONDON). (UK/0306-882X). **2435**

FLORA OF THE GUIANAS. SERIES A : PHANEROGAMAE. (GW). **511**

FLORIDA ALMANAC. (US/0361-9796). **2533**

FLORIDA COMMUNICATION JOURNAL, THE. (US/1050-3366). **1111**

FLORIDA ENTOMOLOGIST, THE. (US/0015-4040). **5608**

FLORIDA FIELD NATURALIST. (US/0738-999X). **5584**

FLORIDA REVIEW (ORLANDO, FLA.), THE. (US/0742-2466). **3463**

FLORIDA SCIENTIST. (US/0098-4590). **5105**

FLORIDA TAX REVIEW. (US). **2971**

FLORIDA WATER RESOURCES JOURNAL. (US/0896-1794). **5533**

FLOWERS&. (US/0199-4751). **2435**

FLUID DYNAMICS RESEARCH. (NE/0169-5983). **5105**

FLUID PHASE EQUILIBRIA. (NE/0378-3812). **1052**

FLUORIDE. (US/0015-4725). **487**

FLYING REVIEW. (US/0274-5798). **21**

FOCUS ON AFRICA : BBC MAGAZINE. (UK/0959-9576). **2499**

FOCUS ON CRITICAL CARE. (US/0736-3605). **3856**

FOCUS ON EXCEPTIONAL CHILDREN. (US/0015-511X). **1879**

FOCUS ON LEARNING PROBLEMS IN MATHEMATICS. (US/0272-8893). **1879**

FOCUS (ROCKVILLE). (US/0533-1242). **455**

FOLIA ARCHAEOLOGICA BUDAPEST. (HU/0133-2023). **268**

FOLIA BIOLOGICA. (XR/0015-5500). **455**

FOLIA BIOLOGICA (WARSZAWA). (PL/0015-5497). **5584**

FOLIA ENTOMOLOGICA MEXICANA. (MX/0430-8603). **5609**

FOLIA GEOBOTANICA & PHYTOTAXONOMICA. (XR/0015-5551). **511**

FOLIA HISTOCHEMICA ET CYTOBIOLOGICA. (PL/0239-8508). **536**

FOLIA MICROBIOLOGICA. (XR/0015-5632). **563**

FOLIA PARASITOLOGICA / CZECHOSLOVAK ACADEMY OF SCIENCE. (XR/0015-5683). **5584**

FOLIA PHONIATRICA. (SZ/0015-5705). **3888**

FOLIA PRIMATOLOGICA. (SZ/0015-5713). **5584**

FOLIA ZOOLOGICA (BRNO). (XR/0139-7893). **5584**

FOLK HARP JOURNAL. (US/0094-8934). **4118**

FOLKLORE AMERICANO. (PE/0071-6774). **2319**

FOLKLORE AND MYTHOLOGY STUDIES (LOS ANGELES, CALIF. : 1977). (US/0162-6280). **2320**

FOLKLORE BRABANCON. (BE/0015-590X). **2320**

FOLKLORE DE FRANCE. (FR/0015-5918). **2320**

FOLKLORE FORUM. (US/0015-5926). **2320**

FOOD ADDITIVES AND CONTAMINANTS. (UK/0265-203X). **2335**

FOOD AND BIOPRODUCTS PROCESSING : TRANSACTIONS OF THE INSTITUTION OF CHEMICAL ENGINEERS, PART C. (UK/0960-3085). **2336**

FOOD AND NUTRITION BULLETIN. (JA/0379-5721). **4191**

FOOD BIOTECHNOLOGY. (US/0890-5436). **3692**

FOOD CHEMISTRY. (UK/0308-8146). **1024**

FOOD MAGAZINE LONDON. 1988. (UK/0953-5047). **2338**

FOOD MANAGEMENT AMERSFOORT. (NE/0168-325X). **2338**

FOOD POLICY. (UK/0306-9192). **2339**

FOOD SCIENCE & TECHNOLOGY TODAY. (UK/0950-9623). **2340**

FOOD TECHNOLOGY (CHICAGO). (US/0015-6639). **2340**

FOOT & ANKLE. (US/0198-0211). **3881**

FOOT & ANKLE INTERNATIONAL. (US/1071-1007). **3918**

FOR FORMULATION CHEMISTS ONLY. (US/0887-736X). **975**

FOR THE LEARNING OF MATHEMATICS : AN INTERNATIONAL JOURNAL OF MATHEMATICS EDUCATION. (CN/0228-0671). **3505**

FORDHAM LAW REVIEW. (US/0015-704X). **2971**

FOREIGN AFFAIRS (NEW YORK, N.Y.). (US/0015-7120). **4521**

FOREIGN INVESTMENT IN THE US. (UK/0958-3076). **899**

FOREIGN LANGUAGE ANNALS. (US/0015-718X). **3282**

FOREIGN POLICY. (US/0015-7228). **4522**

FORENSIC OF PI KAPPA DELTA, THE. (US/0015-735X). **1111**

FORENSIC REPORTS. (US/0888-692X). **3740**

FORENSIC SCIENCE INTERNATIONAL. (SZ/0379-0738). **3740**

FOREST ECOLOGY AND MANAGEMENT. (NE/0378-1127). **2379**

FOREST RESEARCH (TORONTO). (CN/0704-2809). **2381**

FOREST SCIENCE. (US/0015-749X). **2381**

FORESTRY CHRONICLE, THE. (CN/0015-7546). **2381**

FORESTRY (LONDON). (UK/0015-752X). **2382**

FORET PRIVEE (1977), LA. (FR/0153-0216). **2382**

FORET WALLONE. (BE). **2382**

FORMAL METHODS IN SYSTEM DESIGN. (US/0925-9856). **1247**

FORME E LA STORIA, LE. (IT). **3388**

FORO INTERNACIONAL. (MX/0185-013X). **4474**

FORSCHUNG IM INGENIEURWESEN. (GW/0015-7899). **1975**

FORSTWISSENSCHAFTLICHES CENTRALBLATT. (GW/0015-8003). **2383**

FORSYTH COUNTY GENEALOGICAL SOCIETY JOURNAL, THE. (US/0741-8159). **2448**

FORTNIGHT (BELFAST). (IE/0046-4694). **3343**

FORTRAN JOURNAL. (US/1060-0221). **1185**

FORTSCHRITTE DER KIEFERORTHOPAEDIE. (GW/0015-816X). **1323**

FORTSCHRITTE DER NEUROLOGIE, PSYCHIATRIE. (GW/0720-4299). **3833**

FORTSCHRITTE DER PHYSIK (BERLIN : 1953). (GW/0015-8208). **4403**

FORTUNE. (US/0015-8259). **676**

FORUM FOR PROMOTING 3-19 COMPREHENSIVE EDUCATION. (UK/0963-8253). **1747**

FORUM FOR SOCIAL ECONOMICS, THE. (US/0736-0932). **1491**

FORUM LINGUISTICUM. (US/0163-0768). **3282**

FOSSILS AND STRATA. (NO/0300-9491). **1376**

FOUNDATIONS OF PHYSICS. (US/0015-9018). **4403**

FOUNDRYMAN, THE. (UK/0007-0718). **4002**

FOURRAGES. (FR). **201**

FRANCE COMPOSITES. (FR/0985-0503). **2102**

FRANCOPHONIE RUGBY. (UK/0957-1744). **3323**

FRANK. (FR/0738-9299). **3343**

FRANK NORRIS STUDIES. (US). **3389**

FRANKLIN LECTURES IN THE SCIENCES AND HUMANITIES, THE. (US/0533-0130). **5200**

FREE INQUIRY IN CREATIVE SOCIOLOGY. (US/0736-9182). **5246**

FREE MATERIALS FOR SCHOOLS AND LIBRARIES. (US/0836-0073). **1895**

FREE RADICAL BIOLOGY & MEDICINE. (US/0891-5849). **487**

FREE RADICAL RESEARCH COMMUNICATIONS. (SZ/8755-0199). **1052**

FREE SPIRIT (MIAMI, FLA.). (US/1062-8134). **4388**

FREE SPIRIT (MINNEAPOLIS, MINN.). (US/0895-2256). **1063**

FREMONTIA (SACRAMENTO, CALIF.). (US/0092-1793). **511**

FRENCH FORUM. (US/0098-9355). **3343**

FREQUENZ ZEITSCHRIFT FUER SCHWINGUNGS-UND SCHWACHSTROMTECHNIK. (GW/0016-1136). **2055**

FRESENIUS' JOURNAL OF ANALYTICAL CHEMISTRY. (GW/0937-0633). **1015**

FRESHMAN YEAR EXPERIENCE NEWSLETTER, THE. (US/1053-2048). **1825**

FRESHWATER BIOLOGY. (UK/0046-5070). **456**

FRIENDLY WORD, THE. (IE/0790-3642). **5060**

FRONTIERS (BOULDER). (US/0160-9009). **5557**

FRONTIERS IN AGING SERIES. (US/0271-955X). **3751**

FRONTIERS OF ENTREPRENEURSHIP RESEARCH : PROCEEDINGS OF THE ... ANNUAL BABSON COLLEGE ENTREPRENEURSHIP RESEARCH CONFERENCE. (US). **677**

FRONTIERS OF HORMONE RESEARCH. (SZ/0301-3073). **487**

FRUIT VARIETIES JOURNAL. (US/0091-3642). **2415**

FU JEN STUDIES : LITERATURE & LINGUISTICS. (CH/1015-0021). **3283**

FUEL (GUILFORD). (UK/0016-2361). **4256**

FUEL PROCESSING TECHNOLOGY. (NE/0378-3820). **1025**

FUJITSU SCIENTIFIC & TECHNICAL JOURNAL. (JA/0016-2523). **2055**

FULLERENE SCIENCE AND TECHNOLOGY. (US/1064-122X). **5106**

FUNCTION. (AT/0313-6825). **3506**

FUNCTIONAL ANALYSIS AND ITS APPLICATIONS. (US/0016-2663). **3506**

FUNDAMENTA MATHEMATICAE. (PL/0016-2736). **3506**

FUNDAMENTAL AND APPLIED TOXICOLOGY. (US/0272-0590). **3980**

FUNDAMENTAL & CLINICAL PHARMACOLOGY. (FR/0767-3981). **4305**

FUNGAL GENETICS NEWSLETTER. (US/0895-1942). **563**

FURMAN HUMANITIES REVIEW. (US/1064-0037). **2846**

FUSION ENGINEERING AND DESIGN. (NE/0920-3796). **2155**

FUSION TECHNOLOGY. (US/0748-1896). **2155**

FUTURES (LONDON). (UK/0016-3287). **1492**

FUTURICS. (US/0164-1220). **5107**

FUTURIST, THE. (US/0016-3317). **5107**

FUZZY SETS AND SYSTEMS. (NE/0165-0114). **3506**

GAIRM. (UK/0016-3929). **3343**

GAMA NEWS JOURNAL. (US/1058-0808). **2881**

GANG JOURNAL, THE. (US/1061-5326). **3165**

GARTENBAUWISSENSCHAFT. (GW/0016-478X). **2416**

GAS (BARCELONA, SPAIN). (SP). **4257**

GAS MATTERS. (UK/0964-8496). **4257**

GASLIGHT (CLEVELAND, MINN.). (US/1062-015X). **3389**

GASTROENTEROLOGIE CLINIQUE ET BIOLOGIQUE. (FR/0399-8320). **3745**

GASTROENTEROLOGY & ENDOSCOPY NEWS. (US/0883-8348). **3745**

GASTROENTEROLOGY CLINICS OF NORTH AMERICA. (US/0889-8553). **3745**

GASTROENTEROLOGY (NEW YORK, N.Y. 1943). (US/0016-5085). **3745**

GASTROINTESTINAL ENDOSCOPY. (US/0016-5107). **3746**

GASTROINTESTINAL RADIOLOGY. (US/0364-2356). **3941**

GAZETTE. (NE/0016-5492). **1111**

GAZETTE LEADER. (US). **5710**

GAZZETTA CHIMICA ITALIANA. (IT/0016-5603). **976**

GEAR TECHNOLOGY. (US/0743-6858). **2114**

GEBURTSHILFE UND FRAUENHEILKUNDE. (GW/0016-5751). **3761**

GEGENWARTSKUNDE. (GW/0016-5875). **5200**

GEMS & GEMOLOGY (GEMOLOGICAL INSTITUTE OF AMERICA : 1967). (US/0016-626X). **1439**

GENDAI KORIA. (JA). **2651**

GENE. (NE/0378-1119). **545**

GENE AMPLIFICATION AND ANALYSIS. (US/0275-2778). **545**

GENE EXPRESSION. (US/1052-2166). **545**

GENEALOGICAL COMPUTING. (US/0277-5913). **2450**

GENEALOGICAL JOURNAL (SALT LAKE CITY, UTAH). (US/0146-2229). **2450**

GENEALOGIST (NEW YORK), THE. (US/0197-1468). **2450**

GENEESMIDDELENBULLETIN. (NE/0304-4629). **4305**

GENERAL AND COMPARATIVE ENDOCRINOLOGY. (US/0016-6480). **3730**

GENERAL DENTISTRY. (US/0363-6771). **1324**

GENERAL HOSPITAL PSYCHIATRY. (US/0163-8343). **3925**

GENERAL PHARMACOLOGY. (UK/0306-3623). **4306**

GENERAL PHYSIOLOGY AND BIOPHYSICS. (XO/0231-5882). **580**

GENERAL RELATIVITY AND GRAVITATION. (US/0001-7701). **4403**

GENERAL RULES AND RULES OF PRACTICE. (US). **4259**

GENERATIONS (BALTIMORE). (US/0191-6939). **5047**

GENERATIONS (SAN FRANCISCO, CALIF.). (US/0738-7806). **5179**

GENES & DEVELOPMENT. (US/0890-9369). **545**

GENES, CHROMOSOMES & CANCER. (US/1045-2257). **545**

GENETIC EPIDEMIOLOGY. (US/0741-0395). **3735**

GENETIC EPISTEMOLOGIST, THE. (GW/0740-9583). **546**

GENETIC RESOURCES AND CROP EVOLUTION. (NE/0925-9864). **511**

GENETICA. (NE/0016-6707). **546**

GENETICAL RESEARCH. (UK/0016-6723). **546**

GENETICS (AUSTIN). (US/0016-6731). **546**

GENETIKA. (RU/0016-6758). **546**

GENEVA PAPERS ON RISK AND INSURANCE THEORY. (US/0926-4957). **2881**

GENIE LOGICIEL & SYSTEMES EXPERTS. (FR/1166-4738). **1286**

GENITOURINARY MEDICINE. (UK/0266-4348). **4776**

GENOME. (CN/0831-2796). **546**

GENOMICS (SAN DIEGO, CALIF.). (US/0888-7543). **546**

GEO-MARINE LETTERS. (US/0276-0460). **554**

GEOBIOS (LYON, FRANCE). (FR/0016-6995). **4227**

GEOBOTANISCHE KOLLOQUIEN. (GW/0940-6581). **2216**

GEOBOTANISCHE KOLLOQUIEN. (GW/0940-6581). **2216**

GEOCARTO INTERNATIONAL. (HK/1010-6049). **2561**

GEOCHEMICAL JOURNAL. (JA/0016-7002). **1376**

GEOCHIMICA ET COSMOCHIMICA ACTA. (US/0016-7037). **1376**

GEODERMA. (NE/0016-7061). **173**

GEOFIZIKA ZAGREB. (CI/0352-3659). **1405**

GEOFORUM. (UK/0016-7185). **1355**

GEOGRAFFITY (BLACKSBURG, VA.). (US/1063-9837). **2517**

GEOGRAFISKA ANNALER. SERIES A, PHYSICAL GEOGRAPHY. (SW/0435-3676). **2562**

GEOGRAFISKA ANNALER. SERIES B, HUMAN GEOGRAPHY. (NO/0435-3684). **2823**

GEOGRAPHICAL ANALYSIS. (US/0016-7363). **2562**

GEOGRAPHICAL BULLETIN (YPSILANTI, MICH.), THE. (US/0731-3292). **2563**

GEOGRAPHICAL JOURNAL, THE. (UK/0016-7398). **2563**

GEOGRAPHICAL MONOGRAPHS. (CN/0829-7622). **2563**

GEOGRAPHICAL REVIEW. (US/0016-7428). **2563**

GEOGRAPHISCHE ZEITSCHRIFT. (GW/0016-7479). **2564**

GEOGRAPHY. (UK/0016-7487). **2564**

GEOGRAPHY RESEARCH FORUM. (US/0333-5275). **2564**

GEOHIMIJA. (RU/0016-7525). **1377**

GEOJOURNAL. (GE/0343-2521). **2564**

GEOLOGICAL JOURNAL (CHICHESTER, ENGLAND). (UK/0072-1050). **1378**

GEOLOGICAL MAGAZINE. (UK/0016-7568). **1378**

GEOLOGICAL SOCIETY OF AMERICA BULLETIN. (US/0016-7606). **1378**

GEOLOGICAL SURVEY OF WYOMING, EDUCATIONAL SERIES. (US). **1355**

GEOLOGIE EN MIJNBOUW. (NE/0016-7746). **1379**

GEOLOGISCHE RUNDSCHAU. (GW/0016-7835). **1379**

GEOLOGY (BOULDER). (US/0091-7613). **1380**

GEOMAGNETIZM I AERONOMIJA. (RU/0016-7940). **4443**

GEOMETRIAE DEDICATA. (NE/0046-5755). **3507**

GEOMICROBIOLOGY JOURNAL. (US/0149-0451). **563**

GEOPHYSICAL AND ASTROPHYSICAL FLUID DYNAMICS. (US/0309-1929). **1405**

GEOPHYSICAL PROSPECTING. (NE/0016-8025). **1406**

GEOPHYSICAL RESEARCH LETTERS. (US/0094-8276). **1406**

GEOPHYSICS. (US/0016-8033). **1406**

GEORGE HERBERT JOURNAL. (US/0161-7435). **3390**

GEORGE WASHINGTON LAW REVIEW, THE. (US/0016-8076). **2973**

GEORGETOWN LAW JOURNAL, THE. (US/0016-8092). **2974**

GEORGIA BUSINESS AND ECONOMIC CONDITIONS. (US/0279-3857). **677**

GEORGIA JOURNAL OF SCIENCE. (US/0147-9369). **5107**

GEORGIA STATE BAR JOURNAL. (US/0016-8416). **2974**

GEORGIAN ANNUAL. (US). **4241**

GEOSCIENCE AND MAN. (US/0072-1395). **2564**

GEOSCIENCE CANADA. (CN/0315-0941). **1380**

GEOSCIENTIST. (UK/0961-5628). **1380**

GEOSTANDARDS NEWSLETTER. (FR/0150-5505). **1380**

GEOSUR / [ASOCIACION SUDAMERICANA DE ESTUDIOS GEOPOLITICOS E INTERNACIONALES]. (UY). **4522**

GEOTECHNIQUE. (UK/0016-8505). **2023**

GEOTEXTILES AND GEOMEMBRANES. (UK/0266-1144). **495**

GEOTIMES. (US/0016-8556). **1381**

GERIATRIC NEPHROLOGY AND UROLOGY. (NE/0924-8455). **3990**

GERIATRIC NURSING (NEW YORK). (US/0197-4572). **3856**

GERIATRICS. (US/0016-867X). **3751**

GERMAN QUARTERLY, THE. (US/0016-8831). **3390**

GERMAN STUDIES REVIEW. (US/0149-7952). **2689**

GERMAN TEACHING. (UK/0953-4822). **3283**

GERMANIC NOTES AND REVIEWS. (US). **2846**

GERONTOLOGIST, THE. (US/0016-9013). **3751**

GERONTOLOGY & GERIATRICS EDUCATION. (US/0270-1960). **3752**

GESCHAFTSBERICHT DER BUNDESBAHN-VERSICHERUNGSANSTALT. (GW). **1676**

GESCHICHTE UND GESELLSCHAFT (GOTTINGEN). (GW/0340-613X). **5201**

GIATROS HNO. (GW/0930-8318). **3888**

GIATROSERTHOPAEDIE. (GW/0930-8326). **3881**

GIATROSGYNAKOLOGIE. (GW/0177-9109). **3761**

GIATROSPAEDIATRIE. (GW/0177-9095). **3903**

GIATROSUROLOGIE. (GW/0178-7527). **3990**

GIFTED CHILD QUARTERLY, THE. (US/0016-9862). **1879**

GIFTED EDUCATION INTERNATIONAL. (UK/0261-4294). **1879**

GIORNALE BOTANICO ITALIANO (FLORENCE, ITALY : 1962). (IT/0017-0070). **512**

GIORNALE DELL' INSTALLATORE ELETTRICO, IL. (IT/0392-3630). **2056**

GIORNALE DELL' OFFICINA. (IT/0017-0240). **2115**

GIORNALE DELLA SUBFORNITURA, IL. (IT/0392-3622). **1607**

GIORNALE DELL'INSTALLATORE TELEFONICO, IL. (IT/1120-219X). **1976**

GIORNALE DI MEDICINA MILITARE. (IT/0017-0364). **3578**

GIORNALE ITALIANO DI ENTOMOLOGIA. (IT/0392-7296). **5609**

GLASGOW MATHEMATICAL JOURNAL. (UK/0017-0895). **3507**

GLASTECHNISCHE BERICHTE. (GW/0017-1085). **2590**

GLAUCOMA (MIAMI). (US/0164-4645). **3875**

GLENBOW (EXHIBITIONS AND EVENTS). (CN/0710-3697). **4088**

GLIA (NEW YORK, N.Y.). (US/0894-1491). **3833**

GLIMMER TRAIN STORIES. (US/1055-7520). **3391**

GLOBAL AND PLANETARY CHANGE. (NE/0921-8181). **1356**

GLOBAL JUSTICE. (US/1060-0884). **4523**

GLOBAL TAPESTRY. (UK). **3463**

GLYCOBIOLOGY (OXFORD). (UK/0959-6658). **487**

GLYCOCONJUGATE JOURNAL. (UK/0282-0080). **1025**

GOING DOWN SWINGING. (AT/0157-3950). **3391**

GOLDBELT GAZETTE. (CN/0849-8288). **5785**

GOLDSMITHS REVIEW. (UK/0953-0355). **2914**

GOTUJS' (TORONTO). (CN/0046-8061). **1064**

GOURD, THE. (US/0888-5672). **90**

GOVERNMENT AND OPPOSITION (LONDON). (UK/0017-257X). **4475**

GOVERNMENT INFORMATION QUARTERLY. (US/0740-624X). **3212**

GOVERNMENT PUBLICATIONS REVIEW (1982). (US/0277-9390). **3212**

GOVERNMENTAL RISK MANAGEMENT REPORTS. (US/1056-8123). **2881**

GOYA. (SP/0017-2715). **351**
GR. GROCERS REPORT. (US/0160-8894). **2342**
GRAEFE'S ARCHIVE FOR CLINICAL AND EXPERIMENTAL OPHTHALMOLOGY. (GW/0721-832X). **3875**
GRANA. (SW/0017-3134). **512**
GRANMA INTERNATIONAL. (CU/0864-4624). **5799**
GRAPHS AND COMBINATORICS. (JA/0911-0119). **3507**
GRASAS Y ACEITES (SEVILLA). (SP/0017-3495). **488**
GRASS AND FORAGE SCIENCE. (UK/0142-5242). **90**
GREAT BASIN NATURALIST, THE. (US/0017-3614). **4165**
GREAT CIRCLE. (AT/0156-8698). **4176**
GREAT LAKES ENTOMOLOGIST, THE. (US/0090-0222). **5609**
GREAT PLAINS SOCIOLOGIST, THE. (US/0896-0054). **5246**
GREEK, ROMAN AND BYZANTINE STUDIES. (US/0017-3916). **1077**
GREEN LIBRARY JOURNAL (BERKELEY, CALIF. 1992). (US/1059-0838). **2173**
GREENPEACE BUSINESS. (UK/0962-9467). **2173**
GROLIER POETRY PRIZE. (US/0743-7242). **3463**
GROSS DOMESTIC PRODUCT BY INDUSTRY (MONTHLY EDITION). (CN/0711-852X). **1533**
GROUND WATER AGE. (US/0046-645X). **5533**
GROUND WATER MONITORING REVIEW. (US/0277-1926). **1413**
GROUP DECISION AND NEGOTIATION. (US/0926-2644). **5201**
GROUP (NEW YORK. 1977). (US/0362-4021). **4588**
GROWTH AND CHANGE. (US/0017-4815). **2823**
GROWTH GENETICS & HORMONES. (US/0898-6630). **3903**
GUIA DEL ESTUDIANTE. (AG). **1826**
GUIA, EL. (SP). **321**
GUIDE TO CONSTRUCTION ACTIVITY IN MANHATTAN. (US). **4838**
GUIDEBOOK FOR THE ... ANNUAL FIELD CONFERENCE OF PENNSYLVANIA GEOLOGISTS. (US/0375-5630). **1381**
GULF COAST HISTORICAL REVIEW. (US/0892-9025). **2735**
GULF RESEARCH REPORTS. (US/0072-9027). **554**
GULLET. (UK/0952-0643). **3579**
GULLIVER (BARI, ITALY). (IT). **1112**
GUT. (UK/0017-5749). **3746**
GYNAKOLOGE (BERLIN). (GW/0017-5994). **3761**
GYNECOLOGIC ONCOLOGY. (US/0090-8258). **3817**
GYNECOLOGICAL ENDOCRINOLOGY. (UK/0951-3590). **3730**
GYOBYO KENKYU. (JA/0388-788X). **2304**
GYORUIGAKU ZASSHI. (JA/0021-5090). **2304**
HABITAT INTERNATIONAL. (UK/0197-3975). **2823**
HAEMATOLOGIA. (HU/0017-6559). **3797**

HAEMATOLOGICA (ROMA). (IT/0390-6078). **3772**
HAEMOSTASIS. (SZ/0301-0147). **3580**
HAKKOKOGAKU KAISHI. (JA/0385-6151). **3693**
HAND CLINICS. (US/0749-0712). **3881**
HANDBOEK ARBEIDS - EN MILIEUVEILIGHEID. (NE). **2862**
HANDBOOK OF SECURITY. (UK). **5177**
HAN'GUK CHUKSAN HAKHOE CHI. (KO/0367-5807). **5510**
HARDWICK GAZETTE, THE. (US/0744-5512). **5757**
HARVARD BUSINESS REVIEW. (US/0017-8012). **679**
HARVARD EDUCATIONAL REVIEW. (US/0017-8055). **1749**
HARVARD INTERNATIONAL LAW JOURNAL. (US/0017-8063). **3128**
HARVARD JOURNAL OF LAW & PUBLIC POLICY. (US/0193-4872). **2976**
HARVARD JOURNAL ON LEGISLATION. (US/0017-808X). **2977**
HARVARD LAW REVIEW. (US/0017-811X). **2977**
HARVARD LIBRARY BULLETIN. (US/0017-8136). **3213**
HARVARD THEOLOGICAL REVIEW, THE. (US/0017-8160). **4962**
HARVEY LECTURES, THE. (US/0073-0874). **3580**
HASTINGS COMMUNICATIONS AND ENTERTAINMENT LAW JOURNAL (COMM/ENT). (US/1061-6578). **2977**
HASTINGS CONSTITUTIONAL LAW QUARTERLY. (US/0094-5617). **3093**
HASTINGS INTERNATIONAL AND COMPARATIVE LAW REVIEW. (US/0149-9246). **3129**
HASTINGS LAW JOURNAL. (US/0017-8322). **2977**
HASTINGS WOMEN'S LAW JOURNAL. (US/1061-0901). **2977**
HAUTARZT. (GW/0017-8470). **3720**
HAWAII MEDICAL JOURNAL (1962). (US/0017-8594). **3581**
HAWAIIAN ARCHAEOLOGY. (US/0890-1678). **269**
HAZARDS. (UK/0267-7296). **2862**
HAZARDS AUSTRALIA. (AT). **2862**
HEADACHE. (US/0017-8748). **3833**
HEADACHE QUARTERLY. (US/1059-7565). **3833**
HEALTH AFFAIRS (MILLWOOD, VA.). (US/0278-2715). **4777**
HEALTH & ENVIRONMENT DIGEST. (US/0893-6242). **4777**
HEALTH AND HYGIENE (LONDON). (UK/0140-2986). **4777**
HEALTH & SAFETY. MICROFILE. (UK). **4778**
HEALTH CARE ETHICS USA. (US/1072-5490). **3581**
HEALTH CARE FINANCING REVIEW. (US/0195-8631). **2897**
HEALTH CARE FOR WOMEN INTERNATIONAL. (US/0739-9332). **3762**
HEALTH CARE MANAGEMENT REVIEW. (US/0361-6274). **3781**
HEALTH CARE SUPERVISOR, THE. (US/0731-3381). **3781**
HEALTH EDUCATION QUARTERLY. (US/0195-8402). **4779**

HEALTH INFORMATION AND LIBRARIES. (HU/0864-991X). **3213**
HEALTH MARKETING QUARTERLY. (US/0735-9683). **3582**
HEALTH PHYSICS (1958). (US/0017-9078). **4404**
HEALTH PLANNING AND ADMINISTRATION. (US/1065-0679). **3659**
HEALTH POLICY AND PLANNING. (UK/0268-1080). **4780**
HEALTH PROGRESS (SAINT LOUIS, MO.). (US/0882-1577). **3781**
HEALTH PROMOTION INTERNATIONAL. (UK/0957-4824). **4781**
HEALTH PROMOTION PRACTITIONER. (US/1060-5517). **4781**
HEALTH PSYCHOLOGY. (US/0278-6133). **4588**
HEALTH SERVICES RESEARCH. (US/0017-9124). **3582**
HEALTHCARE HAZARDOUS MATERIALS MANAGEMENT. (US/1050-575X). **4782**
HEALTHCARE INFORMATION MANAGEMENT. (US). **3782**
HEALTHLINE (SAN MATEO, CALIF.). (US/0736-7929). **2598**
HEALTHY PEOPLE. (US/0884-2094). **4782**
HEARING HEALTH. (US/0888-2517). **1297**
HEARING RESEARCH. (NE/0378-5955). **3888**
HEARSAY. (US). **4388**
HEART & LUNG. (US/0147-9563). **3856**
HEART FAILURE. (US/8755-7673). **3705**
HEAT RECOVERY SYSTEMS & CHP. (UK/0890-4332). **4430**
HEAT TRANSFER ENGINEERING. (US/0145-7632). **2012**
HEAT TREATMENT OF METALS. (UK/0305-4829). **4003**
HEBREW STUDIES. (US/0146-4094). **5048**
HEC FORUM. (NE/0956-2737). **3783**
HECATE. (AT/0311-4198). **5558**
HELICOPTER ANNUAL. (US/0739-5728). **22**
HELICTITE. (AT/0017-9973). **5109**
HELVETICA CHIMICA ACTA. (SZ/0018-019X). **976**
HELVETICA CHIRURGICA ACTA. (SZ/0018-0181). **3903**
HELVETICA PHYSICA ACTA. (SZ/0018-0238). **4404**
HEMATOLOGICAL ONCOLOGY. (UK/0278-0232). **3772**
HEMATOLOGY/ONCOLOGY CLINICS OF NORTH AMERICA. (US/0889-8588). **3772**
HEMET NEWS, THE. (US). **5635**
HEMISPHERE (MIAMI, FLA.). (US/0898-3038). **4475**
HEMOGLOBIN. (US/0363-0269). **3797**
HEPATO-GASTROENTEROLOGY. (GW/0172-6390). **3746**
HEPATOLOGY (BALTIMORE, MD.). (US/0270-9139). **3797**
HERALD OF LIBRARY SCIENCE. (II/0018-0521). **3213**
HERALDRY IN CANADA. (CN/0441-6619). **2453**

HERBALGRAM (AUSTIN, TEX.). (US/0899-5648). **512**
HERBERTIA (1984). (US/8756-9418). **2418**
HEREDITAS. (SW/0018-0661). **547**
HEREDITY. (UK/0018-067X). **547**
HERITAGE OF THE GREAT PLAINS. (US/0739-4772). **2736**
HERMATHENA. (IE/0018-0750). **4348**
HERMES AMERICANUS. (US/0741-1286). **3285**
HERPETOFAUNA. (AT). **5585**
HERPETOLOGICA. (US/0018-0831). **5585**
HERPETOLOGICAL JOURNAL, THE. (UK/0268-0130). **5585**
HERZ. (GW/0340-9937). **3705**
HERZ-KREISLAUF. (GW/0046-7324). **3705**
HESPERIA. (US/0018-098X). **1077**
HETEROCYCLES. (JA/0385-5414). **1041**
HEURISTICS (ROCKVILLE, MD.). (US/1040-6433). **1229**
HIGH ENERGY CHEMISTRY. (US/0018-1439). **1052**
HIGH PLAINS APPLIED ANTHROPOLOGIST. (US/0882-4894). **237**
HIGH TEMPERATURE. (US/0018-151X). **4431**
HIGH TEMPERATURE SCIENCE. (US/0018-1536). **1052**
HIGHER EDUCATION. (NE/0018-1560). **1828**
HIGHER EDUCATION QUARTERLY / SOCIETY FOR RESEARCH INTO HIGHER EDUCATION. (UK/0951-5224). **1828**
HIGHER EDUCATION RESEARCH AND DEVELOPMENT. (AT/0729-4360). **1828**
HIGHLIGHTS OF AGRICULTURAL RESEARCH. (US/0018-1668). **92**
HIGHWAYMAN (WILLOW STREET, PA.), THE. (US/1062-7200). **2453**
HILGARDIA. (US/0073-2230). **92**
HIMIKO-FARMACEVTICESKIJ ZURNAL. (RU/0023-1134). **4306**
HINDU-CHRISTIAN STUDIES BULLETIN. (CN/0844-4587). **5041**
HIPPO MAGAZINE. (US/1050-6802). **3393**
HIRAM POETRY REVIEW, THE. (US/0018-2036). **3464**
HISPAMERICA (COLLEGE PARK). (US/0363-0471). **3394**
HISPANIC JOURNAL. (US/0271-0986). **3394**
HISPANIC JOURNAL OF BEHAVIORAL SCIENCES. (US/0739-9863). **2262**
HISPANIC LINGUISTICS. (US/0742-5287). **3285**
HISTOCHEMICAL JOURNAL. (UK/0018-2214). **536**
HISTOIRE SOCIALE. (CN/0018-2257). **5201**
HISTOLOGY AND HISTOPATHOLOGY. (SP/0213-3911). **537**
HISTOPATHOLOGY. (UK/0309-0167). **3894**
HISTORIA CRITICA (BOGOTA, COLOMBIA). (CK). **2736**
HISTORIA DE LA REVOLUCION MEXICANA. (MX). **2736**
HISTORIA MATHEMATICA. (US/0315-0860). **3507**

HISTORIA MEXICANA. (MX/0185-0172). **2736**

HISTORIC BRASS SOCIETY JOURNAL. (US/1045-4616). **4121**

HISTORIC BRASS SOCIETY NEWSLETTER. (US/1045-4594). **4121**

HISTORIC ENVIRONMENT. (AT/0726-6715). **2669**

HISTORICA (LIMA). (PE/0252-8894). **2737**

HISTORICAL ARCHAEOLOGY. (US/0440-9213). **269**

HISTORICAL BULLETIN (MADISON, WIS.). (US/0275-1968). **2618**

HISTORICAL PRICING--PETROCHEMICALS. (US). **1025**

HISTORICAL REFLECTIONS. (CN/0315-7997). **2618**

HISTORICAL STUDIES IN EDUCATION. (CN/0843-5057). **1750**

HISTORICAL STUDIES IN THE PHYSICAL AND BIOLOGICAL SCIENCES. (US/0890-9997). **4404**

HISTORISCHE ZEITSCHRIFT. (GW/0018-2613). **2619**

HISTORY AND PHILOSOPHY OF THE LIFE SCIENCES. (UK/0391-9714). **457**

HISTORY (LONDON). (UK/0018-2648). **2619**

HISTORY OF EDUCATION QUARTERLY. (US/0018-2680). **1750**

HISTORY OF HIGHER EDUCATION ANNUAL. (US/0737-2698). **1829**

HISTORY OF POLITICAL ECONOMY. (US/0018-2702). **1565**

HISTORY OF SCIENCE. (UK/0073-2753). **5110**

HISTORY OF THE GENEVA BIBLE. (UK). **5017**

HISTORY SOURCE. (US/1063-9799). **2635**

HISTORY TEACHER (LONG BEACH, CALIF.), THE. (US/0018-2745). **1896**

HISTORY WORKSHOP. (UK/0309-2984). **2619**

HITOTSUBASHI JOURNAL OF ECONOMICS. (JA/0018-280X). **1493**

HNO. (GW/0017-6192). **3888**

HOLISTIC NURSING PRACTICE. (US/0887-9311). **3856**

HOLOCENE (SEVENOAKS). (UK/0959-6836). **1382**

HOLZ ALS ROH- UND WERKSTOFF. (GW/0018-3768). **2401**

HOLZFORSCHUNG. (GW/0018-3830). **2401**

HOME ENERGY (BERKELEY, CALIF.). (US/0896-9442). **1946**

HOME HEALTH CARE SERVICES QUARTERLY. (US/0162-1424). **5288**

HOME POWER. (US/1050-2416). **1946**

HOME SCHOOL RESEARCHER. (US/1054-8033). **1751**

HOMETOWN PRESS. (US/1064-1742). **2534**

HOMME. (FR/0439-4216). **237**

HOMO. (GW/0018-442X). **237**

HONG KONG LIBRARY ASSOCIATION JOURNAL. (HK). **3213**

HORECO. (SP). **5071**

HORIZONS (VILLANOVA). (US/0360-9669). **4963**

HORMONE AND METABOLIC RESEARCH. (GW/0018-5043). **3730**

HORMONE RESEARCH. (SZ/0301-0163). **3730**

HORMONES AND BEHAVIOR. (US/0018-506X). **3730**

HORN CALL, THE. (US/0046-7928). **4121**

HORNERO, EL. (AG/0073-3407). **5586**

HORTSCIENCE. (US/0018-5345). **2419**

HOSPICE JOURNAL, THE. (US/0742-969X). **5288**

HOSPITAL & COMMUNITY PSYCHIATRY. (US/0022-1597). **3926**

HOSPITAL & HEALTH SERVICES ADMINISTRATION. (US/8750-3735). **3783**

HOSPITAL COST MANAGEMENT AND ACCOUNTING. (US/1045-1765). **3783**

HOSPITAL FORMULARY. (US/0098-6909). **4306**

HOSPITAL LAW NEWSLETTER. (US/0738-0984). **3741**

HOSPITAL MORBIDITY - CANADIAN CENTRE FOR HEALTH INFORMATION. (CN/1195-4000). **3659**

HOSPITAL PHYSICIAN (SURGERY/EMERGENCY/SPECIALTIES ED.). (US/0888-2428). **3584**

HOSPITAL PRACTICE (OFFICE EDITION). (US/8750-2836). **3584**

HOSPITALITY & TOURISM EDUCATOR. (US). **2806**

HOSPITALS (CHICAGO, ILL. 1936). (US/0018-5973). **3786**

HOTELDOMANI. (IT). **2806**

HOUSTON JOURNAL OF MATHEMATICS. (US/0362-1588). **3507**

HOW TO DOUBLE YOUR INCOME. (US/0277-0334). **404**

HOWARD JOURNAL OF COMMUNICATIONS, THE. (US/1064-6175). **1112**

HRPLANNING NEWSLETTER, THE. (US/0733-0332). **941**

HUA HSUEH HSUEH PAO. (CC/0567-7351). **977**

HUANJING HUAXUE. (CC/0254-6108). **2173**

HUANJING KEXUE. (CC/0250-3301). **2173**

HUMAN ANTIBODIES AND HYBRIDOMAS. (US/0956-960X). **457**

HUMAN BIOLOGY. (US/0018-7143). **457**

HUMAN COMMUNICATION RESEARCH. (US/0360-3989). **1112**

HUMAN DEVELOPMENT. (SZ/0018-716X). **4588**

HUMAN EVOLUTION. (IT/0393-9375). **237**

HUMAN FACTORS. (US/0018-7208). **1251**

HUMAN HEREDITY. (SZ/0001-5652). **547**

HUMAN IMMUNOLOGY. (US/0198-8859). **3670**

HUMAN MOVEMENT SCIENCE. (NE/0167-9457). **5202**

HUMAN ORGANIZATION. (US/0018-7259). **237**

HUMAN PATHOLOGY. (US/0046-8177). **3895**

HUMAN RELATIONS (NEW YORK). (US/0018-7267). **5202**

HUMAN REPRODUCTION (OXFORD). (UK/0268-1161). **541**

HUMAN RESOURCE DEVELOPMENT QUARTERLY. (US/1044-8004). **941**

HUMAN RESOURCE MANAGEMENT. (US/0090-4848). **941**

HUMAN RIGHTS (CHICAGO, ILL.). (US/0046-8185). **2979**

HUMAN RIGHTS QUARTERLY. (US/0275-0392). **4509**

HUMAN SERVICE EDUCATION. (US/0890-5428). **1751**

HUMAN STUDIES. (NE/0163-8548). **4348**

HUMANE INNOVATIONS AND ALTERNATIVES. (US/1062-4805). **226**

HUMANE MEDICINE. (CN/0828-7090). **3585**

HUMANIST IN CANADA. (CN). **4348**

HUMANISTIC PSYCHOLOGIST, THE. (US/0887-3267). **4589**

HUMANITY & SOCIETY. (US/0160-5976). **5247**

HUME STUDIES. (US/0319-7336). **4348**

HUMOR (BERLIN, GERMANY). (GW/0933-1719). **4589**

HUNGARIAN JOURNAL OF INDUSTRIAL CHEMISTRY. (HU/0133-0276). **977**

HUNGARIAN STUDIES NEWSLETTER. (US/0194-164X). **2692**

HUNGRY MIND REVIEW. (US/0887-5499). **4829**

HUNTIA. (US/0073-4071). **513**

HUNTINGTON LIBRARY QUARTERLY, THE. (US/0018-7895). **352**

HUSSERL STUDIES. (NE/0167-9848). **4348**

HUSSERLIANA DEN HAAG. (NE/0923-4128). **4349**

HYBRIDOMA. (US/0272-457X). **3670**

HYDROBIOLOGIA. (NE/0018-8158). **457**

HYDROLOGICAL PROCESSES. (UK/0885-6087). **1414**

HYDROLOGICAL SCIENCE AND TECHNOLOGY. (US/0887-686X). **1415**

HYDROLOGICAL SCIENCES JOURNAL. (UK/0262-6667). **1415**

HYDROMETALLURGY. (NE/0304-386X). **4003**

HYGIE. (FR/0751-7149). **4783**

HYGIENE + MEDIZIN. (GW/0172-3790). **3585**

HYPATIA (EDWARDSVILLE, ILL.). (US/0887-5367). **5558**

HYPERFINE INTERACTIONS. (NE/0304-3843). **4443**

HYPERTENSION (DALLAS, TEX. 1979). (US/0194-911X). **3705**

I.D.E.E (BRIGHAM). (CN/1192-7755). **5289**

I. S. E. R. SECTOR REPORTS. (US). **1494**

IA. INGEGNERIA AMBIENTALE. (IT/0394-5871). **2232**

IA, THE JOURNAL OF THE SOCIETY FOR INDUSTRIAL ARCHEOLOGY. (US/0160-1040). **269**

IALL JOURNAL OF LANGUAGE LEARNING TECHNOLOGIES, THE. (US/1050-0049). **3286**

IATREIA MEDELLIN. (CK/0121-0793). **3585**

IAWA BULLETIN. (NE/0254-3915). **2401**

IBERIAN STUDIES. (UK/0307-3262). **2517**

IBIS (LONDON, ENGLAND). (UK/0019-1019). **5617**

IBM JOURNAL OF RESEARCH AND DEVELOPMENT. (US/0018-8646). **2056**

IBM SYSTEMS JOURNAL. (US/0018-8670). **1259**

ICARUS (NEW YORK, N.Y. 1962). (US/0019-1035). **395**

ICC INTERNATIONAL COURT OF ARBITRATION BULLETIN, THE. (FR/1017-284X). **3129**

ICCA JOURNAL. (CN/0920-234X). **1230**

ICE RIVER. (US/1043-7010). **3395**

ICELANDIC CANADIAN. (CN/0046-8452). **2263**

ICHTHYOLOGICAL EXPLORATION OF FRESHWATERS. (GW/0936-9902). **2305**

ICP INFORMATION NEWSLETTER. (US/0161-6951). **1015**

IDAHO ARCHAEOLOGIST. (US/0893-2271). **270**

IDAHO CITIES. (US). **4655**

IDAHO YESTERDAYS. (US/0019-1264). **2738**

IDESIA. (CL/0073-4675). **2195**

IDIOM 23. (AT/1032-1640). **3395**

IDS BULLETIN (UNIVERSITY OF SUSSEX. INSTITUTE OF DEVELOPMENT STUDIES : 1985). (UK). **1494**

IEE PROCEEDINGS. C, GENERATION, TRANSMISSION, AND DISTRIBUTION. (UK/0143-7046). **2057**

IEE PROCEEDINGS. CIRCUITS, DEVICES AND SYSTEMS. (UK/1350-2409). **2057**

IEE PROCEEDINGS. COMPUTERS AND DIGITAL TECHNIQUES. (UK/1350-2387). **1229**

IEE PROCEEDINGS. CONTROL THEORY AND APPLICATIONS. (UK/1350-2379). **2057**

IEE PROCEEDINGS. D, CONTROL THEORY AND APPLICATIONS. (UK/0143-7054). **2057**

IEE PROCEEDINGS. ELECTRIC POWER APPLICATIONS. (UK/1350-2352). **2058**

IEE PROCEEDINGS. F, RADAR AND SIGNAL PROCESSING. (UK/0956-375X). **1156**

IEE PROCEEDINGS. G, CIRCUITS, DEVICES, AND SYSTEMS. (UK/0956-3768). **2058**

IEE PROCEEDINGS. GENERATION, TRANSMISSION, AND DISTRIBUTION. (UK/1350-2360). **2058**

IEE PROCEEDINGS. MICROWAVES, ANTENNAS AND PROPAGATION. (UK/1350-2417). **2058**

IEE PROCEEDINGS. OPTOELECTRONICS. (UK/1350-2433). **2058**

IEE PROCEEDINGS. PART B. ELECTRIC POWER APPLICATIONS. (UK/0143-7038). **2058**

IEE PROCEEDINGS. PART E. COMPUTERS AND DIGITAL TECHNIQUES. (UK/0143-7062). **1229**

IEE PROCEEDINGS. PART H, MICROWAVES, ANTENNAS, AND PROPAGATION. (UK/0950-107X). **2058**

IEE PROCEEDINGS. PART J, OPTOELECTRONICS. (UK/0267-3932). **2058**

IEEE CIRCUITS AND DEVICES MAGAZINE. (US/8755-3996). **2059**

IEEE COMMUNICATIONS MAGAZINE. (US/0163-6804). **1157**

IEEE — Peer Reviewed Index

IEEE COMPUTER GRAPHICS AND APPLICATIONS. (US/0272-1716). **1233**

IEEE DESIGN & TEST OF COMPUTERS. (US/0740-7475). **1229**

IEEE ENGINEERING IN MEDICINE AND BIOLOGY MAGAZINE. (US/0739-5175). **3693**

IEEE EXPERT. (US/0885-9000). **1229**

IEEE JOURNAL OF OCEANIC ENGINEERING. (US/0364-9059). **2090**

IEEE JOURNAL OF QUANTUM ELECTRONICS. (US/0018-9197). **2060**

IEEE JOURNAL OF SOLID-STATE CIRCUITS. (US/0018-9200). **2060**

IEEE JOURNAL ON SELECTED AREAS IN COMMUNICATIONS. (US/0733-8716). **1157**

IEEE MICRO. (US/0272-1732). **1267**

IEEE PHOTONICS TECHNOLOGY LETTERS. (US/1041-1135). **4435**

IEEE SOFTWARE. (US/0740-7459). **1286**

IEEE SPECTRUM. (US/0018-9235). **2060**

IEEE TRANSACTIONS ON AEROSPACE AND ELECTRONIC SYSTEMS. (US/0018-9251). **2061**

IEEE TRANSACTIONS ON ANTENNAS AND PROPAGATION. (US/0018-926X). **2061**

IEEE TRANSACTIONS ON AUTOMATIC CONTROL. (US/0018-9286). **1219**

IEEE TRANSACTIONS ON BROADCASTING. (US/0018-9316). **1133**

IEEE TRANSACTIONS ON COMPONENTS, HYBRIDS AND MANUFACTURING TECHNOLOGY. (US/0148-6411). **2061**

IEEE TRANSACTIONS ON COMPUTER-AIDED DESIGN OF INTEGRATED CIRCUITS AND SYSTEMS. (US/0278-0070). **2061**

IEEE TRANSACTIONS ON COMPUTERS. (US/0018-9340). **1247**

IEEE TRANSACTIONS ON CONSUMER ELECTRONICS. (US/0098-3063). **2061**

IEEE TRANSACTIONS ON EDUCATION. (US/0018-9359). **2062**

IEEE TRANSACTIONS ON ELECTRICAL INSULATION. (US/0018-9367). **2062**

IEEE TRANSACTIONS ON ELECTROMAGNETIC COMPATIBILITY. (US/0018-9375). **2062**

IEEE TRANSACTIONS ON ELECTRON DEVICES. (US/0018-9383). **2062**

IEEE TRANSACTIONS ON ENERGY CONVERSION. (US/0885-8969). **2062**

IEEE TRANSACTIONS ON ENGINEERING MANAGEMENT. (US/0018-9391). **2062**

IEEE TRANSACTIONS ON GEOSCIENCE AND REMOTE SENSING. (US/0196-2892). **1406**

IEEE TRANSACTIONS ON INDUSTRY APPLICATIONS. (US/0093-9994). **2062**

IEEE TRANSACTIONS ON INSTRUMENTATION AND MEASUREMENT. (US/0018-9456). **2063**

IEEE TRANSACTIONS ON MAGNETICS. (US/0018-9464). **4443**

IEEE TRANSACTIONS ON MEDICAL IMAGING. (US/0278-0062). **3941**

IEEE TRANSACTIONS ON MICROWAVE THEORY AND TECHNIQUES. (US/0018-9480). **2063**

IEEE TRANSACTIONS ON NUCLEAR SCIENCE. (US/0018-9499). **2155**

IEEE TRANSACTIONS ON PATTERN ANALYSIS AND MACHINE INTELLIGENCE. (US/0162-8828). **1229**

IEEE TRANSACTIONS ON PLASMA SCIENCE. (US/0093-3813). **3693**

IEEE TRANSACTIONS ON POWER DELIVERY. (US/0885-8977). **2063**

IEEE TRANSACTIONS ON POWER SYSTEMS. (US/0885-8950). **2063**

IEEE TRANSACTIONS ON RELIABILITY. (US/0018-9529). **2063**

IEEE TRANSACTIONS ON ROBOTICS AND AUTOMATION. (US/1042-296X). **1212**

IEEE TRANSACTIONS ON SEMICONDUCTOR MANUFACTURING. (US/0894-6507). **2063**

IEEE TRANSACTIONS ON SOFTWARE ENGINEERING. (US/0098-5589). **1286**

IEEE TRANSACTIONS ON SYSTEMS, MAN, AND CYBERNETICS. (US/0018-9472). **1251**

IEEE TRANSACTIONS ON ULTRASONICS, FERROELECTRICS, AND FREQUENCY CONTROL. (US/0885-3010). **4452**

IEEE TRANSACTIONS ON VEHICULAR TECHNOLOGY. (US/0018-9545). **2064**

IFIP TRANSACTIONS. COMPUTER SCIENCE AND TECHNOLOGY. (NE/0926-5473). **1247**

IFLA JOURNAL. (GW/0340-0352). **3214**

IIE TRANSACTIONS. (US/0740-817X). **2098**

IKUSHUGAKU ZASSHI. (JA/0536-3683). **94**

ILLINOIS HISTORICAL JOURNAL. (US/0748-8149). **2738**

ILLINOIS JOURNAL OF MATHEMATICS. (US/0019-2082). **3508**

ILLINOIS SCHOOL RESEARCH AND DEVELOPMENT. (US/0163-822X). **1751**

ILLINOIS SCHOOLS JOURNAL. (US/0019-2236). **1896**

ILLNESS CRISIS & LOSS. (US/1054-1373). **2251**

ILVS REVIEW. (US/1043-3023). **4089**

IMA JOURNAL OF APPLIED MATHEMATICS. (UK/0272-4960). **3508**

IMA JOURNAL OF MATHEMATICAL CONTROL AND INFORMATION. (UK/0265-0754). **3508**

IMA JOURNAL OF MATHEMATICS APPLIED IN MEDICINE AND BIOLOGY. (UK/0265-0746). **3508**

IMA JOURNAL OF NUMERICAL ANALYSIS. (UK/0272-4979). **3508**

IMAGE AND VISION COMPUTING. (UK/0262-8856). **1233**

IMAGE--THE JOURNAL OF NURSING SCHOLARSHIP. (US/0743-5150). **3857**

IMAGES (RESTON, VA.). (US/1055-1476). **3941**

IMMIGRATION NEWSLETTER. (US/0145-3416). **1919**

IMMUNITAT UND INFEKTION. (GW/0340-1162). **3670**

IMMUNOASSAY KIT DIRECTORY. SERIES A, CLINICAL CHEMISTRY, THE. (NE/0926-2067). **3586**

IMMUNOBIOLOGY (1979). (GW/0171-2985). **3670**

IMMUNOGENETICS (NEW YORK). (US/0093-7711). **3670**

IMMUNOHEMATOLOGY. (US/0894-203X). **3772**

IMMUNOLOGIC RESEARCH. (SZ/0257-277X). **3670**

IMMUNOLOGICAL INVESTIGATIONS. (US/0882-0139). **3671**

IMMUNOLOGICAL REVIEWS. (DK/0105-2896). **3671**

IMMUNOLOGY. (UK/0019-2805). **3671**

IMMUNOLOGY AND ALLERGY CLINICS OF NORTH AMERICA. (US/0889-8561). **3671**

IMMUNOLOGY AND CELL BIOLOGY. (AT/0818-9641). **3671**

IMMUNOLOGY AND INFECTIOUS DISEASES. (UK/0959-4957). **3671**

IMMUNOLOGY LETTERS. (NE/0165-2478). **3671**

IMMUNOPHARMACOLOGY. (US/0162-3109). **3672**

IMMUNOPHARMACOLOGY AND IMMUNOTOXICOLOGY. (US/0892-3973). **3672**

IMPACT OF SCIENCE ON SOCIETY. (UK/0019-2872). **5112**

IMPOSTE LAVORO PREVIDENZA. (IT). **1677**

IN DIE SKRIFLIG. (SA/1018-6441). **4964**

IN SITU. (US/0146-2520). **1440**

IN THESE TIMES. (US/0160-5992). **5203**

IN VITRO CELLULAR & DEVELOPMENTAL BIOLOGY. ANIMAL. (US/1071-2690). **537**

IN VITRO CELLULAR & DEVELOPMENTAL BIOLOGY. PLANT. (US/1054-5476). **513**

IN VIVO (ATHENS). (GR/0258-851X). **458**

INA NEWSLETTER. (UK/0255-013X). **4227**

INC HEBDO CONSOMMATEURS ACTUALITES. (FR/1145-0673). **1297**

INCAST (DALLAS, TEX.). (US/1045-5779). **4003**

INCOME TAX AND FAMILY LAW HANDBOOK. (CN). **3121**

INDEPENDENCE. (AT). **1751**

INDIAN HIGHWAYS. (II/0376-7256). **5441**

INDIAN JOURNAL OF AGRICULTURAL SCIENCES, THE. (II/0019-5022). **95**

INDIAN JOURNAL OF AMERICAN STUDIES. (II/0019-5030). **2738**

INDIAN JOURNAL OF ANIMAL SCIENCES, THE. (II/0367-8318). **5511**

INDIAN JOURNAL OF APPLIED PSYCHOLOGY. (II/0019-5073). **4589**

INDIAN JOURNAL OF BIOCHEMISTRY & BIOPHYSICS. (II/0301-1208). **488**

INDIAN JOURNAL OF HEREDITY. (II/0374-826X). **548**

INDIAN JOURNAL OF MARINE SCIENCES. (II/0379-5136). **1450**

INDIAN JOURNAL OF MEDICAL RESEARCH. SECTION A, INFECTIOUS DISEASES. (II/0970-955X). **3586**

INDIAN JOURNAL OF MEDICAL RESEARCH. SECTION B, BIOMEDICAL RESEARCH OTHER THAN INFECTIOUS DISEASES. (II/0970-9568). **3586**

INDIAN JOURNAL OF PHARMACOLOGY. (II/0253-7613). **4307**

INDIAN JOURNAL OF PHYSIOLOGY AND PHARMACOLOGY. (II/0019-5499). **581**

INDIAN JOURNAL OF PURE AND APPLIED MATHEMATICS. (II/0019-5588). **3508**

INDIAN JOURNAL OF PURE & APPLIED PHYSICS. (II/0019-5596). **4405**

INDIAN JOURNAL OF RADIO & SPACE PHYSICS. (II/0367-8393). **4405**

INDIAN JOURNAL OF TECHNOLOGY. (II/0019-5669). **5112**

INDIAN PEDIATRICS. (II/0019-6061). **3904**

INDIAN VETERINARY JOURNAL, THE. (II/0019-6479). **5512**

INDIANA LAW JOURNAL (BLOOMINGTON). (US/0019-6665). **2982**

INDIANA MAGAZINE OF HISTORY. (US/0019-6673). **2739**

INDIANA MEDICINE. (US/0746-8288). **3587**

INDIANA MUSICATOR. (US/0273-9933). **4122**

INDIANA READING QUARTERLY. (US/0019-672X). **1896**

INDIANA UNIVERSITY MATHEMATICS JOURNAL. (US/0022-2518). **3509**

INDICE ESPANOL DE CIENCIA Y TECNOLOGIA. (SP/0210-9409). **5112**

INDIVIDUAL PSYCHOLOGY REPORTER. (US/0888-4595). **4590**

INDO-IRANIAN JOURNAL. (NE/0019-7246). **4349**

INDONESIA (ITHACA). (US/0019-7289). **2654**

INDOOR AIR. (DK/0905-6947). **2232**

INDOOR AIR BULLETIN. (US/1055-5242). **2174**

INDUSTRIA CARNICA LATINOAMERICANA, LA. (AG/0325-3414). **213**

INDUSTRIA PORCINA. (US/0279-7771). **213**

INDUSTRIA Y QUIMICA. (AG). **978**

INDUSTRIAL & ENGINEERING CHEMISTRY RESEARCH. (US/0888-5885). **2013**

INDUSTRIAL CERAMICS. (IT). **2591**

INDUSTRIAL CRISIS QUARTERLY. (NE/0921-8106). **682**

INDUSTRIAL ENGINEERING (NORCROSS, GA.). (US/0019-8234). **2098**

INDUSTRIAL HEALTH. (JA/0019-8366). **2863**

INDUSTRIAL MARKETING MANAGEMENT. (US/0019-8501). **926**

INDUSTRIAL RELATIONS & MANAGEMENT LETTER. (AT). **1678**

INDUSTRIAL RELATIONS (BERKELEY). (US/0019-8676). **1678**

INDUSTRIAL ROBOT, THE. (UK/0143-991X). **1219**

INDUSTRIE ALIMENTARI (PINEROLO). (IT/0019-901X). **2344**

INDUSTRIE CERAMIQUE, L'. (FR/0019-9044). **2591**

INDUSTRIE LACKIER BETRIEB. (GW/0019-9109). **4224**

INDUSTRY AND ENVIRONMENT (ENGLISH EDITION). (FR/0378-9993). **2863**

INDUSTRY DIGEST. (PH/0115-4419). **1612**

INFANCIA Y APRENDIZAJE. (SP/0210-3702). **4590**

INFANT BEHAVIOR & DEVELOPMENT. (US/0163-6383). **4590**

INFANT MENTAL HEALTH JOURNAL. (US/0163-9641). **4590**

INFANT-TODDLER INTERVENTION. (US/1053-5586). **3904**

INFANTRY. (US/0019-9532). **4046**

INFANTS AND YOUNG CHILDREN. (US/0896-3746). **3904**

INFECTION. (GW/0300-8126). **3714**

INFECTION AND IMMUNITY. (US/0019-9567). **563**

INFECTION CONTROL AND HOSPITAL EPIDEMIOLOGY. (US/0899-823X). **3735**

INFECTIOUS DISEASES IN OBSTETRICS AND GYNECOLOGY. (US/1064-7449). **3762**

INFLAMMATION. (US/0360-3997). **3587**

INFLAMMOPHARMACOLOGY. (NE/0925-4692). **3587**

INFO JOURNAL / INTERNATIONAL FORTEAN ORGANIZATION. (US/0019-0144). **4241**

INFOBRAZIL / CENTER OF BRAZILIAN STUDIES. (US/0736-8666). **1567**

INFOFISH INTERNATIONAL. (MY/0127-2012). **2305**

INFOR. INFORMATION SYSTEMS AND OPERATIONAL RESEARCH. (CN/0315-5986). **1259**

INFORMAL LOGIC (WINDSOR, ONT.). (CN/0824-2577). **4349**

INFORMATIK - FORSCHUNG UND ENTWICKLUNG. (GW/0178-3564). **1188**

INFORMATION AND COMPUTATION. (US/0890-5401). **1219**

INFORMATION AND REFERRAL. (US/0278-2383). **5289**

INFORMATION AND SOCIETY. (AT/1033-6273). **5247**

INFORMATION AND SOFTWARE TECHNOLOGY. (UK/0950-5849). **1260**

INFORMATION GRAMMATICALE (PARIS), L'. (FR/0222-9838). **3287**

INFORMATION RESOURCES MANAGEMENT JOURNAL. (US/1040-1628). **3216**

INFORMATION SCIENCES. (US/0020-0255). **3216**

INFORMATION SERIES - VIRGINIA POLYTECHNIC INSTITUTE AND STATE UNIVERSITY. COLLEGE OF AGRICULTURE AND LIFE SCIENCES. (US/0742-7425). **96**

INFORMATION SYSTEMS MANAGEMENT. (US/1058-0530). **870**

INFORMATION SYSTEMS (OXFORD). (UK/0306-4379). **1254**

INFORMATION SYSTEMS RESEARCH. (US/1047-7047). **1188**

INFORMATION TECHNOLOGY AND LIBRARIES. (US/0730-9295). **3217**

INFORMATION TECHNOLOGY AND THE LAW: AN INTERNATIONAL BIBLIOGRAPHY. (NE/0925-9872). **3129**

INFORMATION TECHNOLOGY MANAGEMENT. (AT/1322-3526). **5113**

INFRARED PHYSICS. (UK/0020-0891). **4405**

INGEGNERIA ALIMENTARE. LE CONSERVE ANIMALI. (IT/0394-588X). **2344**

INGENIERIA CIVIL MADRID. (SP/0213-8468). **2024**

INITIALES (HALIFAX). (CN/0710-4278). **3396**

INJURY. (UK/0020-1383). **3587**

INNERE MEDIZIN. (GW/0303-4305). **3797**

INORGANIC CHEMISTRY. (US/0020-1669). **1036**

INORGANIC MATERIALS. (US/0020-1685). **1036**

INORGANICA CHIMICA ACTA : BIOINORGANIC CHEMISTRY ARTICLES AND LETTERS. (SZ/0020-1693). **1036**

INQUIRY (CHICAGO). (US/0046-9580). **3587**

INQUIRY (OSLO). (NO/0020-174X). **4349**

INSECT SCIENCE AND ITS APPLICATION. (KE/0191-9040). **5609**

INSECTA MUNDI. (US/0749-6737). **5609**

INSECTES SOCIAUX. (FR/0020-1812). **5609**

INSIEME. (IT/0020-1871). **683**

INSIGHT (SAN FRANSISCO, CALIF.). (US/1060-135X). **3857**

INSIGHTS (SPRINGFIELD, OHIO). (US/0164-7709). **4965**

INSOLVENCY INTELLIGENCE. (UK/0950-2645). **2983**

INSTALADOR, EL. (SP). **2065**

INSTRUCTIONAL SCIENCE. (NE/0020-4277). **1896**

INSTRUMENTS AND EXPERIMENTAL TECHNIQUES (NEW YORK). (US/0020-4412). **4405**

INSURANCE MATHEMATICS & ECONOMICS. (NE/0167-6687). **2884**

INTECH. (US/0192-303X). **2065**

INTEGRAL EQUATIONS AND OPERATOR THEORY. (SZ/0378-620X). **3509**

INTEGRATION (AMSTERDAM). (NE/0167-9260). **2066**

INTELLIGENCE (NORWOOD). (US/0160-2896). **4590**

INTELLIGENT INSTRUMENTS & COMPUTERS. (US/0889-8308). **1220**

INTENSIVE CARE MEDICINE. (GW/0342-4642). **3588**

INTER-AMERICAN TRADE AND INVESTMENT LAW. (US/1078-2028). **840**

INTER CDI ETAMPES. (FR/0242-2999). **683**

INTERACTION - CANADIAN CHILD DAY CARE FEDERATION. (CN/0835-5819). **5290**

INTERBEHAVIORIST, THE. (US/8755-612X). **4590**

INTERCHANGE (SYDNEY, AUSTRALIA). (AT). **5017**

INTERCHANGE (TORONTO. 1984). (CN/0826-4805). **1753**

INTERCHANGE (TORONTO. 1984). (US/0826-4805). **1753**

INTERCIENCIA. (VE/0378-1844). **5114**

INTERDISCIPLINARY SCIENCE REVIEWS : ISR. (UK/0308-0188). **5114**

INTERFACE SCIENCE. (US/0927-7056). **4428**

INTERFACES (PROVIDENCE). (US/0092-2102). **871**

INTERLENDING & DOCUMENT SUPPLY. (UK/0264-1615). **3217**

INTERNASJONAL POLITIKK (OSLO, NORWAY). (NO/0020-577X). **4524**

INTERNATIONAL AFFAIRS (LONDON). (UK/0020-5850). **4524**

INTERNATIONAL AFFAIRS STUDIES. (PL/0867-4493). **4524**

INTERNATIONAL AND COMPARATIVE LAW QUARTERLY, THE. (UK/0020-5893). **3129**

INTERNATIONAL ANESTHESIOLOGY CLINICS. (US/0020-5907). **3683**

INTERNATIONAL ANGIOLOGY. (IT/0392-9590). **3966**

INTERNATIONAL ANNALS OF ADOLESCENT PSYCHIATRY. (US/1071-0752). **3926**

INTERNATIONAL CHORAL BULLETIN. (US/0896-0968). **4123**

INTERNATIONAL CLASSIFICATION. (GW/0340-0050). **3218**

INTERNATIONAL CLINICAL PSYCHOPHARMACOLOGY. (UK/0268-1315). **4308**

INTERNATIONAL COMMUNICATIONS IN HEAT AND MASS TRANSFER. (US/0735-1933). **4431**

INTERNATIONAL ECONOMIC REVIEW (PHILADELPHIA). (US/0020-6598). **1496**

INTERNATIONAL EDUCATION. (US/0160-5429). **1753**

INTERNATIONAL EDUCATION FORUM (PULLMAN, WASHINGTON). (US/1053-1750). **1831**

INTERNATIONAL ENCYCLOPEDIA OF COMPOSITES. (GW). **1979**

INTERNATIONAL ENDODONTIC JOURNAL. (UK/0143-2885). **1325**

INTERNATIONAL ENERGY STATISTICS SOURCEBOOK. (US/1058-2487). **1963**

INTERNATIONAL FAMILY PLANNING PERSPECTIVES. (US/0190-3187). **2281**

INTERNATIONAL FINANCE SECTION PUBLICATIONS. (US). **1496**

INTERNATIONAL FORUM ON INFORMATION AND DOCUMENTATION. (NE/0304-9701). **3218**

INTERNATIONAL HEPATOLOGY COMMUNICATIONS. (NE/0928-4346). **3797**

INTERNATIONAL HISTORY REVIEW, THE. (CN/0707-5332). **2620**

INTERNATIONAL HYDROGRAPHIC REVIEW, THE. (MC/0020-6946). **1415**

INTERNATIONAL INFORMATION, COMMUNICATION & EDUCATION. (II/0970-1850). **3218**

INTERNATIONAL JOURNAL. (CN/0020-7020). **2692**

INTERNATIONAL JOURNAL FOR NUMERICAL AND ANALYTICAL METHODS IN GEOMECHANICS. (UK/0363-9061). **2025**

INTERNATIONAL JOURNAL FOR NUMERICAL METHODS IN ENGINEERING. (UK/0029-5981). **1979**

INTERNATIONAL JOURNAL FOR NUMERICAL METHODS IN FLUIDS. (UK/0271-2091). **2091**

INTERNATIONAL JOURNAL FOR PHILOSOPHY OF RELIGION. (NE/0020-7047). **4965**

INTERNATIONAL JOURNAL FOR THE ADVANCEMENT OF COUNSELLING. (NE/0165-0653). **4591**

INTERNATIONAL JOURNAL FOR THE SEMIOTICS OF LAW. (UK/0952-8059). **2984**

INTERNATIONAL JOURNAL FOR VITAMIN AND NUTRITION RESEARCH. (SZ/0300-9831). **4192**

INTERNATIONAL JOURNAL FOR VITAMIN AND NUTRITION RESEARCH (SUPPLEMENT). (SZ/0300-9831). **4192**

INTERNATIONAL JOURNAL OF ACAROLOGY. (US/0164-7954). **5586**

INTERNATIONAL JOURNAL OF ADHESION AND ADHESIVES. (UK/0143-7496). **1053**

INTERNATIONAL JOURNAL OF AGING & HUMAN DEVELOPMENT, THE. (US/0091-4150). **5247**

INTERNATIONAL JOURNAL OF AMERICAN LINGUISTICS. (US/0020-7071). **3287**

INTERNATIONAL JOURNAL OF ANALYTICAL AND EXPERIMENTAL MODAL ANALYSIS, THE. (US/0886-9367). **2116**

INTERNATIONAL JOURNAL OF ANDROLOGY. (UK/0105-6263). **3588**

INTERNATIONAL JOURNAL OF ANGIOLOGY, THE. (US/1061-1711). **3706**

INTERNATIONAL JOURNAL OF APPLIED ELECTROMAGNETICS IN MATERIALS. (NE/0925-2096). **4444**

INTERNATIONAL JOURNAL OF APPLIED LINGUISTICS. (NO/0802-6106). **3287**

INTERNATIONAL JOURNAL OF ARTIFICIAL ORGANS, THE. (IT/0391-3988). **3798**

INTERNATIONAL JOURNAL OF ARTS MEDICINE. (US/1057-4263). **3588**

INTERNATIONAL JOURNAL OF BEHAVIORAL DEVELOPMENT. (NE/0165-0254). **4591**

INTERNATIONAL JOURNAL OF BIOCHEMISTRY, THE. (UK/0020-711X). **488**

INTERNATIONAL JOURNAL OF BIOLOGICAL MACROMOLECULES. (UK/0141-8130). **581**

INTERNATIONAL JOURNAL OF BIOLOGICAL MARKERS, THE. (IT/0393-6155). **3818**

INTERNATIONAL JOURNAL OF BIOMEDICAL COMPUTING. (UK/0020-7101). **3589**

INTERNATIONAL JOURNAL OF BIOMETEOROLOGY. (NE/0020-7128). **1426**

INTERNATIONAL JOURNAL OF BIOSOCIAL AND MEDICAL RESEARCH. (US/1044-811X). **5248**

INTERNATIONAL JOURNAL OF CANADIAN STUDIES. (CN/1180-3991). **2739**

INTERNATIONAL JOURNAL OF CANCER. (US/0020-7136). **3818**

INTERNATIONAL JOURNAL OF CARDIAC IMAGING. (US/0167-9899). **3706**

INTERNATIONAL JOURNAL OF CARDIOLOGY. (NE/0167-5273). **3706**

INTERNATIONAL JOURNAL OF CELL CLONING. (US/0737-1454). **537**

INTERNATIONAL JOURNAL OF CHEMICAL KINETICS. (US/0538-8066). **1053**

INTERNATIONAL JOURNAL OF CHILDREN'S RIGHTS, THE. (NE/0927-5568). **3121**

INTERNATIONAL JOURNAL OF CIRCUIT THEORY AND APPLICATIONS. (UK/0098-9886). **2066**

INTERNATIONAL JOURNAL OF CLIMATOLOGY : A JOURNAL OF THE ROYAL METEOROLOGICAL SOCIETY. (UK/0899-8418). **1426**

INTERNATIONAL JOURNAL OF CLINICAL AND EXPERIMENTAL HYPNOSIS, THE. (US/0020-7144). **2858**

INTERNATIONAL JOURNAL OF CLINICAL MONITORING AND COMPUTING. (NE/0167-9945). **1190**

INTERNATIONAL — Peer Reviewed Index

INTERNATIONAL JOURNAL OF CLINICAL NEUROPSYCHOLOGY, THE. (US/0749-8470). **4591**

INTERNATIONAL JOURNAL OF CLINICAL PHARMACOLOGY RESEARCH. (SZ/0251-1649). **4308**

INTERNATIONAL JOURNAL OF COAL GEOLOGY. (NE/0166-5162). **1383**

INTERNATIONAL JOURNAL OF COGNITIVE EDUCATION & MEDIATED LEARNING. (UK/0957-4964). **1753**

INTERNATIONAL JOURNAL OF COLORECTAL DISEASE. (GW/0179-1958). **3589**

INTERNATIONAL JOURNAL OF COMPUTER MATHEMATICS. (UK/0020-7160). **3509**

INTERNATIONAL JOURNAL OF COMPUTER SYSTEMS SCIENCE & ENGINEERING. (UK). **1190**

INTERNATIONAL JOURNAL OF COMPUTER VISION. (US/0920-5691). **1190**

INTERNATIONAL JOURNAL OF CONTINUING ENGINEERING EDUCATION. (SZ/0957-4344). **1979**

INTERNATIONAL JOURNAL OF CONTROL. (UK/0020-7179). **5115**

INTERNATIONAL JOURNAL OF COSMETIC SCIENCE. (UK/0142-5463). **404**

INTERNATIONAL JOURNAL OF DERMATOLOGY. (US/0011-9059). **3721**

INTERNATIONAL JOURNAL OF DEVELOPMENTAL BIOLOGY, THE. (SP/0214-6282). **541**

INTERNATIONAL JOURNAL OF DEVELOPMENTAL NEUROSCIENCE. (UK/0736-5748). **3834**

INTERNATIONAL JOURNAL OF EATING DISORDERS, THE. (US/0276-3478). **3798**

INTERNATIONAL JOURNAL OF EDUCOLOGY. (AT/0818-0563). **1754**

INTERNATIONAL JOURNAL OF ELECTRICAL ENGINEERING EDUCATION. (UK/0020-7209). **2066**

INTERNATIONAL JOURNAL OF ELECTRICAL POWER & ENERGY SYSTEMS. (UK/0142-0615). **2066**

INTERNATIONAL JOURNAL OF ENERGY RESEARCH. (UK/0363-907X). **1947**

INTERNATIONAL JOURNAL OF ENGINEERING FLUID MECHANICS. (US/0893-3960). **2091**

INTERNATIONAL JOURNAL OF ENGINEERING SCIENCE. (UK/0020-7225). **1980**

INTERNATIONAL JOURNAL OF ENVIRONMENTAL ANALYTICAL CHEMISTRY. (US/0306-7319). **1015**

INTERNATIONAL JOURNAL OF EPIDEMIOLOGY. (UK/0300-5771). **3735**

INTERNATIONAL JOURNAL OF FATIGUE. (UK/0142-1123). **2102**

INTERNATIONAL JOURNAL OF FERTILITY. (US/0020-725X). **581**

INTERNATIONAL JOURNAL OF FLEXIBLE MANUFACTURING SYSTEMS. (US/0920-6299). **3481**

INTERNATIONAL JOURNAL OF FOOD MICROBIOLOGY. (NE/0168-1605). **2345**

INTERNATIONAL JOURNAL OF FOOD SCIENCE AND TECHNOLOGY. (UK/0950-5423). **2345**

INTERNATIONAL JOURNAL OF FORECASTING. (NE/0169-2070). **684**

INTERNATIONAL JOURNAL OF FOUNDATIONS OF COMPUTER SCIENCE. (SI/0129-0541). **1190**

INTERNATIONAL JOURNAL OF FRACTURE. (NE/0376-9429). **2102**

INTERNATIONAL JOURNAL OF GAME THEORY. (GW/0020-7276). **3509**

INTERNATIONAL JOURNAL OF GENERAL SYSTEMS. (US/0308-1079). **1247**

INTERNATIONAL JOURNAL OF GERIATRIC PSYCHIATRY. (UK/0885-6230). **3752**

INTERNATIONAL JOURNAL OF GROUP PSYCHOTHERAPY, THE. (US/0020-7284). **3927**

INTERNATIONAL JOURNAL OF GYNAECOLOGY AND OBSTETRICS. (IE/0020-7292). **3762**

INTERNATIONAL JOURNAL OF GYNECOLOGICAL PATHOLOGY. (US/0277-1691). **3895**

INTERNATIONAL JOURNAL OF HEALTH SERVICES. (US/0020-7314). **4785**

INTERNATIONAL JOURNAL OF HEAT AND FLUID FLOW, THE. (US/0142-727X). **2116**

INTERNATIONAL JOURNAL OF HEAT AND MASS TRANSFER. (UK/0017-9310). **4431**

INTERNATIONAL JOURNAL OF HUMAN-COMPUTER INTERACTION. (US/1044-7318). **1220**

INTERNATIONAL JOURNAL OF HYDROGEN ENERGY. (UK/0360-3199). **1948**

INTERNATIONAL JOURNAL OF HYPERTHERMIA. (UK/0265-6736). **3589**

INTERNATIONAL JOURNAL OF IMMUNOPHARMACOLOGY. (UK/0192-0561). **4308**

INTERNATIONAL JOURNAL OF IMMUNOTHERAPY. (SZ/0255-9625). **3672**

INTERNATIONAL JOURNAL OF IMPACT ENGINEERING. (UK/0734-743X). **2103**

INTERNATIONAL JOURNAL OF INDUSTRIAL ORGANIZATION. (NE/0167-7187). **871**

INTERNATIONAL JOURNAL OF INFORMATION MANAGEMENT. (UK/0268-4012). **3218**

INTERNATIONAL JOURNAL OF INFRARED AND MILLIMETER WAVES. (US/0195-9271). **4435**

INTERNATIONAL JOURNAL OF INSECT MORPHOLOGY & EMBRYOLOGY. (UK/0020-7322). **5610**

INTERNATIONAL JOURNAL OF INTELLIGENT SYSTEMS. (US/0884-8173). **1213**

INTERNATIONAL JOURNAL OF INTERCULTURAL RELATIONS. (US/0147-1767). **5248**

INTERNATIONAL JOURNAL OF ISLAMIC AND ARABIC STUDIES. (US/0740-5375). **2768**

INTERNATIONAL JOURNAL OF LAW AND PSYCHIATRY. (US/0160-2527). **2984**

INTERNATIONAL JOURNAL OF LEPROSY AND OTHER MYCOBACTERIAL DISEASES. (US/0148-916X). **4785**

INTERNATIONAL JOURNAL OF LIFELONG EDUCATION. (UK/0260-1370). **1801**

INTERNATIONAL JOURNAL OF LOGISTICS MANAGEMENT, THE. (US). **684**

INTERNATIONAL JOURNAL OF MACHINE TOOLS & MANUFACTURE. (US/0890-6955). **2116**

INTERNATIONAL JOURNAL OF MAN-MACHINE STUDIES. (UK/0020-7373). **1251**

INTERNATIONAL JOURNAL OF MARINE AND COASTAL LAW, THE. (NE/0927-3522). **3130**

INTERNATIONAL JOURNAL OF MARITIME HISTORY. (CN/0843-8714). **4177**

INTERNATIONAL JOURNAL OF MASS SPECTROMETRY AND ION PROCESSES. (NE/0168-1176). **4405**

INTERNATIONAL JOURNAL OF MATERIALS & PRODUCT TECHNOLOGY. (SZ/0268-1900). **1980**

INTERNATIONAL JOURNAL OF MATHEMATICS. (SI/0129-167X). **3509**

INTERNATIONAL JOURNAL OF MATHEMATICS AND MATHEMATICAL SCIENCES. (US/0161-1712). **3509**

INTERNATIONAL JOURNAL OF MECHANICAL SCIENCES. (UK/0020-7403). **2116**

INTERNATIONAL JOURNAL OF MENTAL HEALTH. (US/0020-7411). **3927**

INTERNATIONAL JOURNAL OF MICROCIRCULATION: CLINICAL AND EXPERIMENTAL. (NE/0167-6865). **3798**

INTERNATIONAL JOURNAL OF MIDDLE EAST STUDIES. (UK/0020-7438). **2768**

INTERNATIONAL JOURNAL OF MINERAL PROCESSING. (NE/0301-7516). **2140**

INTERNATIONAL JOURNAL OF MINING AND GEOLOGICAL ENGINEERING. (UK/0269-0136). **2141**

INTERNATIONAL JOURNAL OF MODERN PHYSICS A. (SI/0217-751X). **4405**

INTERNATIONAL JOURNAL OF MODERN PHYSICS B. (SI/0217-9792). **4406**

INTERNATIONAL JOURNAL OF MORAL AND SOCIAL STUDIES. (UK/0267-9655). **2251**

INTERNATIONAL JOURNAL OF MULTIPHASE FLOW. (UK/0301-9322). **2067**

INTERNATIONAL JOURNAL OF MUSIC EDUCATION / INTERNATIONAL SOCIETY FOR MUSIC EDUCATION. (UK). **4123**

INTERNATIONAL JOURNAL OF NEURAL NETWORKS. (UK/0954-9889). **1213**

INTERNATIONAL JOURNAL OF NEURAL SYSTEMS. (SI/0129-0657). **1190**

INTERNATIONAL JOURNAL OF NEUROSCIENCE. (US/0020-7454). **3834**

INTERNATIONAL JOURNAL OF NON-LINEAR MECHANICS. (US/0020-7462). **4428**

INTERNATIONAL JOURNAL OF NURSING STUDIES. (UK/0020-7489). **3857**

INTERNATIONAL JOURNAL OF OBSTETRIC ANESTHESIA. (UK/0959-289X). **3763**

INTERNATIONAL JOURNAL OF OFFENDER THERAPY AND COMPARATIVE CRIMINOLOGY. (US/0306-624X). **3166**

INTERNATIONAL JOURNAL OF OFFSHORE AND POLAR ENGINEERING. (US/1053-5381). **1980**

INTERNATIONAL JOURNAL OF ONCOLOGY. (GR/1019-6439). **3818**

INTERNATIONAL JOURNAL OF OPTOELECTRONICS. (UK/0952-5432). **4435**

INTERNATIONAL JOURNAL OF ORTHOPAEDIC TRAUMA. (UK/0960-2941). **3882**

INTERNATIONAL JOURNAL OF PANCREATOLOGY. (NE/0169-4197). **3798**

INTERNATIONAL JOURNAL OF PARALLEL PROGRAMMING. (US/0885-7458). **1279**

INTERNATIONAL JOURNAL OF PATTERN RECOGNITION AND ARTIFICIAL INTELLIGENCE. (SI/0218-0014). **1213**

INTERNATIONAL JOURNAL OF PEDIATRIC OTORHINOLARYNGOLOGY. (NE/0165-5876). **3904**

INTERNATIONAL JOURNAL OF PHARMACEUTICS. (NE/0378-5173). **4308**

INTERNATIONAL JOURNAL OF PHARMACY PRACTICE. (UK/0961-7671). **4309**

INTERNATIONAL JOURNAL OF PLASTICITY. (US/0749-6419). **2103**

INTERNATIONAL JOURNAL OF POLYMERIC MATERIALS. (US/0091-4037). **978**

INTERNATIONAL JOURNAL OF POWDER METALLURGY (PRINCETON, N.J.). (US/0888-7462). **4004**

INTERNATIONAL JOURNAL OF PRESSURE VESSELS AND PIPING, THE. (UK/0308-0161). **2116**

INTERNATIONAL JOURNAL OF PRIMATOLOGY. (US/0164-0291). **5586**

INTERNATIONAL JOURNAL OF PRODUCTION RESEARCH. (UK/0020-7543). **871**

INTERNATIONAL JOURNAL OF PSYCHIATRY IN MEDICINE, THE. (US/0091-2174). **3927**

INTERNATIONAL JOURNAL OF PSYCHO-ANALYSIS, THE. (UK/0020-7578). **4591**

INTERNATIONAL JOURNAL OF PSYCHOLOGY. (NE/0020-7594). **4591**

INTERNATIONAL JOURNAL OF PSYCHOPHYSIOLOGY. (NE/0167-8760). **581**

INTERNATIONAL JOURNAL OF PSYCHOSOMATICS. (US/0884-8297). **3589**

INTERNATIONAL JOURNAL OF PUBLIC ADMINISTRATION. (US/0190-0692). **4657**

INTERNATIONAL JOURNAL OF QUANTUM CHEMISTRY. (US/0020-7608). **978**

INTERNATIONAL JOURNAL OF RADIATION APPLICATIONS AND INSTRUMENTATION. PART A, APPLIED RADIATION AND ISOTOPES. (UK/0883-2889). **4406**

INTERNATIONAL JOURNAL OF RADIATION APPLICATIONS AND INSTRUMENTATION. PART B, NUCLEAR MEDICINE AND BIOLOGY. (UK/0883-2897). **3848**

INTERNATIONAL JOURNAL OF RADIATION APPLICATIONS AND INSTRUMENTATION. PART E, NUCLEAR GEOPHYSICS, THE. (UK/0886-0130). **1407**

INTERNATIONAL JOURNAL OF RADIATION BIOLOGY. (UK/0955-3002). **3942**

INTERNATIONAL JOURNAL OF RADIATION- ONCOLOGY, BIOLOGY, PHYSICS. (US/0360-3016). **3818**

INTERNATIONAL JOURNAL OF RAPID SOLIDIFICATION. (UK/0265-0916). **4004**

INTERNATIONAL JOURNAL OF REFRIGERATION. (UK/0140-7007). **2606**

INTERNATIONAL JOURNAL OF REHABILITATION RESEARCH. (GW/0342-5282). **4389**

INTERNATIONAL JOURNAL OF REMOTE SENSING. (UK/0143-1161). **1980**

INTERNATIONAL JOURNAL OF RESEARCH AND ENGINEERING (POSTAL APPLICATION). (US/1043-7134). **1145**

INTERNATIONAL JOURNAL OF ROBOTICS RESEARCH, THE. (US/0278-3649). **1220**

INTERNATIONAL JOURNAL OF ROCK MECHANICS AND MINING SCIENCES & GEOMECHANICS ABSTRACTS. (UK/0148-9062). **2141**

INTERNATIONAL JOURNAL OF SATELLITE COMMUNICATIONS. (UK/0737-2884). **1158**

INTERNATIONAL JOURNAL OF SCIENCE AND TECHNOLOGY. (US/0891-5083). **5115**

INTERNATIONAL JOURNAL OF SCIENCE EDUCATION. (UK/0950-0693). **5115**

INTERNATIONAL JOURNAL OF SLAVIC LINGUISTICS AND POETICS. (US/0538-8228). **3287**

INTERNATIONAL JOURNAL OF SOCIAL ECONOMICS. (UK/0306-8293). **1496**

INTERNATIONAL JOURNAL OF SOCIAL EDUCATION, THE. (US/0889-0293). **5204**

INTERNATIONAL JOURNAL OF SOLIDS AND STRUCTURES. (US/0020-7683). **2025**

INTERNATIONAL JOURNAL OF SPELEOLOGY. (IT/0020-7691). **1407**

INTERNATIONAL JOURNAL OF SPORT BIOMECHANICS. (US/0740-2082). **495**

INTERNATIONAL JOURNAL OF SPORT PSYCHOLOGY. (IT/0047-0767). **4900**

INTERNATIONAL JOURNAL OF SPORTS MEDICINE. (GW/0172-4622). **3954**

INTERNATIONAL JOURNAL OF STD & AIDS. (UK/0956-4624). **3672**

INTERNATIONAL JOURNAL OF SUPERCOMPUTER APPLICATIONS, THE. (US/0890-2720). **1287**

INTERNATIONAL JOURNAL OF SYSTEMATIC BACTERIOLOGY. (US/0020-7713). **564**

INTERNATIONAL JOURNAL OF SYSTEMS SCIENCE. (UK/0020-7721). **2116**

INTERNATIONAL JOURNAL OF TECHNOLOGY AND DESIGN EDUCATION. (NE/0957-7572). **5115**

INTERNATIONAL JOURNAL OF TECHNOLOGY MANAGEMENT. (SZ/0267-5730). **5115**

INTERNATIONAL JOURNAL OF THE ADDICTIONS. (US/0020-773X). **1345**

INTERNATIONAL JOURNAL OF THE SOCIOLOGY OF LANGUAGE. (NE/0165-2516). **3287**

INTERNATIONAL JOURNAL OF THEORETICAL PHYSICS. (US/0020-7748). **4406**

INTERNATIONAL JOURNAL OF THERMOPHYSICS. (US/0195-928X). **4406**

INTERNATIONAL JOURNAL OF TISSUE REACTIONS. (SZ/0250-0868). **537**

INTERNATIONAL JOURNAL OF TROPICAL AGRICULTURE. (II/0254-8755). **97**

INTERNATIONAL JOURNAL OF URBAN AND REGIONAL RESEARCH. (UK/0309-1317). **2825**

INTERNATIONAL JOURNAL OF VEHICLE DESIGN. (SZ/0143-3369). **5417**

INTERNATIONAL JOURNAL OF WILDLAND FIRE, THE. (US/1049-8001). **2291**

INTERNATIONAL JOURNAL ON DRUG POLICY, THE. (UK/0955-3959). **1345**

INTERNATIONAL JOURNAL ON GROUP RIGHTS. (NE/0927-5908). **3130**

INTERNATIONAL JOURNAL ON WORLD PEACE. (US/0742-3640). **4524**

INTERNATIONAL LABMATE. (UK/0143-5140). **1015**

INTERNATIONAL LAW PRACTICUM. (US/1041-3405). **3130**

INTERNATIONAL MARINE BUSINESS. (UK/0965-0644). **684**

INTERNATIONAL MIGRATION (GENEVA, SWITZERLAND). (SZ/0020-7985). **1919**

INTERNATIONAL MIGRATION REVIEW : IMR. (US/0197-9183). **1919**

INTERNATIONAL MONEY MARKETING. (UK/0958-3785). **902**

INTERNATIONAL OIL AND GAS DEVELOPMENT YEARBOOK. PART 1: EXPLORATION. (US/0535-1634). **4261**

INTERNATIONAL OPHTHALMOLOGY. (NE/0165-5701). **3875**

INTERNATIONAL OPHTHALMOLOGY CLINICS. (US/0020-8167). **3875**

INTERNATIONAL ORGANIZATION. (US/0020-8183). **4525**

INTERNATIONAL ORTHOPAEDICS. (GW/0341-2695). **3882**

INTERNATIONAL PACKAGING ABSTRACTS. (UK/0260-7409). **4222**

INTERNATIONAL PERSPECTIVES ON EDUCATION AND SOCIETY. (US). **1754**

INTERNATIONAL PEST CONTROL. (UK/0020-8256). **4245**

INTERNATIONAL PHILOSOPHICAL QUARTERLY. (US/0019-0365). **4349**

INTERNATIONAL POLYMER PROCESSING. (GW/0930-777X). **4455**

INTERNATIONAL PSYCHOGERIATRICS / IPA. (US/1041-6102). **3752**

INTERNATIONAL PULP & PAPER DIRECTORY. (US/0097-2509). **4234**

INTERNATIONAL REGIONAL SCIENCE REVIEW. (US/0160-0176). **1497**

INTERNATIONAL REVIEW OF CHILDREN'S LITERATURE AND LIBRARIANSHIP. (UK/0269-0500). **3218**

INTERNATIONAL REVIEW OF EDUCATION. (NE/0020-8566). **1754**

INTERNATIONAL REVIEW OF PSYCHO-ANALYSIS, THE. (UK/0306-2643). **4592**

INTERNATIONAL REVIEW OF SOCIAL HISTORY. (NE/0020-8590). **5248**

INTERNATIONAL REVIEWS IN PHYSICAL CHEMISTRY. (UK/0144-235X). **1053**

INTERNATIONAL SECURITY. (US/0162-2889). **4525**

INTERNATIONAL SMALL BUSINESS JOURNAL. (UK/0266-2426). **684**

INTERNATIONAL SOCIAL SCIENCE JOURNAL. (FR/0020-8701). **5204**

INTERNATIONAL SOCIOLOGY. (UK/0268-5809). **5248**

INTERNATIONAL STUDIES NOTES. (US/0094-7768). **4525**

INTERNATIONAL STUDIES QUARTERLY. (US/0020-8833). **4525**

INTERNATIONAL SURGERY. (IT/0020-8868). **3966**

INTERNATIONAL TAX AND PUBLIC FINANCE. (NE/0927-5940). **4733**

INTERNATIONAL THIRD WORLD STUDIES JOURNAL & REVIEW. (US/1041-3944). **4526**

INTERNATIONAL TRADE JOURNAL, THE. (US/0885-3908). **841**

INTERNATIONAL YEARBOOK OF NEPHROLOGY. (US/0921-9862). **3990**

INTERNATIONALE REVUE DER GESAMTEN HYDROBIOLOGIE. (GW/0020-9309). **555**

INTERNIST (BERLIN), DER. (GW/0020-9554). **3798**

INTERPRETATION (THE HAGUE). (US/0020-9635). **4478**

INTERSCHOLASTIC ATHLETIC ADMINISTRATION. (US/0097-871X). **4901**

INTERVENTION IN SCHOOL AND CLINIC. (US/1053-4512). **1880**

INTERVIROLOGY. (SZ/0300-5526). **564**

INTI (PROVIDENCE, R.I.). (US/0732-6750). **3397**

INTIMATE FASHION NEWS. (US/1061-5792). **1085**

INVASION & METASTASIS. (SW/0251-1789). **537**

INVENTIONES MATHEMATICAE. (GW/0020-9910). **3510**

INVENTORY OF THE COLLECTIONS. (US/0095-2893). **4089**

INVERSE PROBLEMS. (UK/0266-5611). **3510**

INVERT MAGAZINE. (UK/0957-3828). **429**

INVESTIGATIONAL NEW DRUGS. (US/0167-6997). **3818**

INVESTIGATIVE RADIOLOGY. (US/0020-9996). **3942**

INVESTMENT COMPANIES (NEW YORK, N.Y. 1983). (US/0747-9484). **3100**

INVIRONMENT (BUFFALO GROVE, ILL.). (US/1059-4078). **2175**

INZYNIERIA CHEMICZNA I PROCESOWA. (PL/0208-6425). **2013**

IOWA JOURNAL OF COMMUNICATION. (US). **1114**

IOWA LAW REVIEW. (US/0021-0552). **2984**

IOWA SCIENCE TEACHERS' JOURNAL. (US/0021-0676). **5116**

IPN-BLATTER. (GW/0179-5775). **1755**

IPW BERICHTE. (GW/0046-970X). **1636**

IRAL, INTERNATIONAL REVIEW OF APPLIED LINGUISTICS IN LANGUAGE TEACHING. (GW/0019-042X). **3288**

IRANIAN STUDIES. (US/0021-0862). **2768**

IRISH BIRDS. (IE/0332-0111). **5617**

IRISH EDITION. (US/1063-7532). **2264**

IRISH EDUCATIONAL STUDIES. (IE/0332-3315). **1755**

IRISH GEOGRAPHY. (IE/0075-0778). **2566**

IRISH HERITAGE LINKS. (UK/0957-0837). **2454**

IRISH JOURNAL OF AGRICULTURAL RESEARCH. (IE/0578-7483). **97**

IRISH JOURNAL OF MEDICAL SCIENCE. (IE/0021-1265). **3590**

IRISH JOURNAL OF PSYCHOLOGICAL MEDICINE. (IE/0790-9667). **3927**

IRISH JOURNAL OF PSYCHOLOGY, THE. (IE/0303-3910). **4592**

IRISH NATURALISTS' JOURNAL, THE. (UK/0021-1311). **4166**

IRISH SLAVONIC STUDIES. (UK/0260-2067). **2692**

IRISH VETERINARY JOURNAL. (IE/0368-0762). **5512**

IRONMAKING & STEELMAKING. (UK/0301-9233). **4005**

IRRIGATION AND DRAINAGE SYSTEMS. (NE/0168-6291). **2091**

IRRIGATION SCIENCE. (GW/0342-7188). **175**

ISA TRANSACTIONS. (US/0019-0578). **5116**

ISIJ INTERNATIONAL / IRON AND STEEL INSTITUTE OF JAPAN. (JA/0915-1559). **1613**

ISIS. (US/0021-1753). **5116**

ISLA (MANGILAO, GUAM). (GU/1054-9390). **238**

ISOKINETICS AND EXERCISE SCIENCE. (US). **2599**

ISOTECH JOURNAL OF THERMOMETRY. (US). **5116**

ISOTOPENPRAXIS. (SW/0021-1915). **4406**

ISRAEL EXPLORATION JOURNAL. (IS/0021-2059). **270**

ISRAEL JOURNAL OF BOTANY. (IS/0021-213X). **514**

ISRAEL JOURNAL OF CHEMISTRY. (IS/0021-2148). **978**

ISRAEL JOURNAL OF ENTOMOLOGY. (IS/0075-1243). **5610**

ISRAEL JOURNAL OF MATHEMATICS. (IS/0021-2172). **3510**

ISRAEL JOURNAL OF MEDICAL SCIENCES. (IS/0021-2180). **3590**

ISRAEL JOURNAL OF ZOOLOGY. (IS/0021-2210). **5587**

ISRAEL SOCIAL SCIENCE RESEARCH. (IS). **5205**

ISSUES & STUDIES. (CH/1013-2511). **4526**

ISSUES IN CHILD ABUSE ACCUSATIONS. (US/1043-8823). **5291**

ISSUES IN COMPREHENSIVE PEDIATRIC NURSING. (US/0146-0862). **3857**

ISSUES IN INTEGRATIVE STUDIES. (US). **1755**

ISSUES IN LAW & MEDICINE. (US/8756-8160). **2985**

ISSUES IN MENTAL HEALTH NURSING. (US/0161-2840). **3858**

ISSUES IN SCIENCE AND TECHNOLOGY. (US/0748-5492). **5116**

ISSUES IN SOCIAL WORK EDUCATION / ASSOCIATION OF TEACHERS IN SOCIAL WORK EDUCATION. (UK/0261-4154). **5291**

ISSX PROCEEDINGS. (US/1061-3439). **4309**

ISTINA. (FR/0021-2423). **4966**

ITAA PROCEEDINGS. NATIONAL MEETING. (US/1067-2850). **5353**

ITALIA CONTEMPORANEA. (IT/0392-3568). **2693**

ITALIAN AMERICANA. (US/0096-8846). **2264**

ITALIAN JOURNAL OF BIOCHEMISTRY. (IT/0021-2938). **488**

ITALIAN — Peer Reviewed Index

ITALIAN JOURNAL OF FOOD SCIENCE. (IT/1120-1770). **2345**

ITALIAN JOURNAL OF GASTROENTEROLOGY, THE. (IT/0392-0623). **3746**

ITALIAN JOURNAL OF NEUROLOGICAL SCIENCES. (IT/0392-0461). **3834**

ITALIANIST. (UK/0261-4340). **3397**

ITAWAMBA SETTLERS. (US/0737-7932). **2455**

ITE JOURNAL. (US/0162-8178). **5384**

ITI. INTERNATIONAL TELECOMMUNICATIONS INTELLIGENCE. (UK/0268-9960). **1158**

IT'S HAPPENING. (US/0098-7549). **1880**

IZVESTIIA AKADEMII NAUK SSSR. FIZIKA ZEMLI. (RU/0002-3337). **4407**

IZVESTIIA AKADEMII NAUK SSSR. SERIIA BIOLOGICHESKAIA. (RU/0002-3329). **459**

IZVESTIIA VYSSHIKH UCHEBNYKH ZAVEDENII. FIZIKA / MINISTERSTVO VYSSHEGO OBRAZOVANIIA SSSR. (RU/0021-3411). **4407**

IZVESTIJA VYSSIH UCEBNYH ZAVEDENIJ. HIMIJA I HIMICESKAJA TEHNOLOGIJA. (RU/0579-2991). **979**

IZVESTIJA VYSSIH UCEBNYH ZAVEDENIJ. MATEMATIKA. (RU/0021-3446). **3510**

IZVESTIJA VYSSIH UCEBNYH ZAVEDENIJ. RADIOELEKTRONIKA. (UN/0021-3470). **2067**

IZVESTIJA VYSSIH UCEBNYH ZAVEDENIJ. RADIOFIZIKA. (RU/0021-3462). **1114**

IZVESTIJA VYSSIH UCEBNYH ZAVEDENIJ. AVIACIONNAJA TEHNIKA. (RU/0579-2975). **25**

J. IIC-CG : JOURNAL OF THE INTERNATIONAL INSTITUTE FOR CONSERVATION, CANADIAN GROUP. (CN/0381-0402). **353**

JAHRBUCH FUER SOZIALWISSENSCHAFT. (GW/0075-2770). **5205**

JAHRBUCHER FUER NATIONALOKONOMIE UND STATISTIK. (GW/0021-4027). **1497**

JAHRESBERICHT DES LANDESARBEITSAMTES TIROL. (AU). **1681**

JAMA : THE JOURNAL OF THE AMERICAN MEDICAL ASSOCIATION. (US/0098-7484). **3591**

JAMES BURNSIDE BULLETIN OF RESEARCH, THE. (US/1046-2279). **2740**

JAMES JOYCE LITERARY SUPPLEMENT. (US/0899-3114). **3345**

JANASAMKHYA. (II). **4554**

JANE'S ARMOURED FIGHTING VEHICLE RETROFIT SYSTEMS. (UK). **4046**

JAPAN COMPUTER QUARTERLY. (JA/0910-6707). **1260**

JAPAN QUARTERLY. (JA/0021-4590). **2654**

JAPANESE CIRCULATION JOURNAL. (JA/0047-1828). **3706**

JAPANESE JOURNAL OF CANCER RESEARCH : GANN. (JA/0910-5050). **3818**

JAPANESE JOURNAL OF CLINICAL ONCOLOGY. (JA/0368-2811). **3819**

JAPANESE JOURNAL OF MEDICAL SCIENCE & BIOLOGY. (JA/0021-5112). **3591**

JAPANESE JOURNAL OF OPHTHALMOLOGY. (JA/0021-5155). **3875**

JAPANESE JOURNAL OF PHARMACOLOGY. (JA/0021-5198). **4309**

JAPANESE JOURNAL OF PHYSIOLOGY, THE. (JA/0021-521X). **581**

JAPANESE JOURNAL OF PSYCHIATRY AND NEUROLOGY, THE. (JA/0912-2036). **3928**

JAPANESE JOURNAL OF RELIGIOUS STUDIES. (JA/0304-1042). **4967**

JAPANESE JOURNAL OF VETERINARY RESEARCH, THE. (JA/0047-1917). **5512**

JAPANESE PSYCHOLOGICAL RESEARCH. (JA/0021-5368). **4592**

JARQ. JAPAN AGRICULTURAL RESEARCH QUARTERLY. (JA/0021-3551). **98**

JAZZ REPORT (TORONTO). (CN/0843-3151). **4125**

JCT, JOURNAL OF COATINGS TECHNOLOGY. (US/0361-8773). **4224**

JCU : JOURNAL OF CLINICAL ULTRASOUND. (US/0091-2751). **3591**

JE TAI TI LI. (CC). **2567**

JEAN RHYS REVIEW. (US/0889-759X). **3399**

JEEVADHARA (ENGLISH ED.). (II/0970-1125). **4967**

JEI. JOURNAL OF ECONOMIC ISSUES. (US/0021-3624). **1592**

JEN KOU HSUEH KAN / KUO LI TAI-WAN TA HSUEH. (CH). **4554**

JET. JOURNAL OF EDUCATION FOR TEACHING. (UK/0260-7476). **1897**

JETP LETTERS. (US/0021-3640). **4408**

JEWISH EDUCATION NEWS. (US). **1755**

JEWISH QUARTERLY REVIEW (PHILADELPHIA, PA.). (US/0021-6682). **5049**

JIKKEN DOBUTSU. (JA/0007-5124). **3592**

JISUANJI YU YINGYONG HUAXUE. (CC/1001-4160). **1191**

JMA MANAGEMENT NEWS. (JA). **872**

JMR ABSTRACTS. (US/1066-2375). **2005**

JMR, JOURNAL OF MARKETING RESEARCH. (US/0022-2437). **927**

JOERNAAL VIR EIETYDSE : GESKIEDENIS EN INTERNASIONALE VERHOUDINGE. (SA). **2620**

JOHNS HOPKINS APL TECHNICAL DIGEST. (US/0270-5214). **1981**

JORNADAS. (MX). **5205**

JORNAL DA LIGA BRASILEIRA DE EPILEPSIA. (BL). **3834**

JOURNAL (AMERICAN ACADEMY OF GNATHOLOGIC ORTHOPEDICS). (US/0886-1064). **1325**

JOURNAL / AMERICAN WATER WORKS ASSOCIATION. (US/0003-150X). **5535**

JOURNAL - AMERICAN WINE SOCIETY. (US/0364-698X). **2368**

JOURNAL - CANADIAN DENTAL ASSOCIATION. (CN/0709-8936). **1325**

JOURNAL - CONNECTICUT STATE DENTAL ASSOCIATION, THE. (US/0010-6232). **1326**

JOURNAL D' ANALYSE MATHEMATIQUE (JERUSALEM). (IS/0021-7670). **3511**

JOURNAL DE CHIMIE PHYSIQUE ET DE PHYSICO-CHIMIE BIOLOGIQUE. (FR/0021-7689). **1053**

JOURNAL DE CHIRURGIE. (FR/0021-7697). **3966**

JOURNAL DE MATHEMATIQUES PURES ET APPLIQUEES. (FR/0021-7824). **3511**

JOURNAL DE TOXICOLOGIE CLINIQUE ET EXPERIMENTALE. (FR/0753-2830). **3981**

JOURNAL DES MALADIES VASCULAIRES. (FR/0398-0499). **3706**

JOURNAL D'UROLOGIE. (FR/0248-0018). **3990**

JOURNAL FOR GENERAL PHILOSOPHY OF SCIENCE. (NE/0925-4560). **4350**

JOURNAL FOR PEACE & JUSTICE STUDIES. (US). **4526**

JOURNAL FOR QUALITY AND PARTICIPATION, THE. (US/1040-9602). **1681**

JOURNAL FOR RESEARCH IN MATHEMATICS EDUCATION. (US/0021-8251). **3511**

JOURNAL FOR THE ANTHROPOLOGICAL STUDY OF HUMAN MOVEMENT AT NEW YORK UNIVERSITY. (US/0891-7124). **238**

JOURNAL FOR THE HISTORY OF ASTRONOMY. (UK/0021-8286). **396**

JOURNAL FOR THE SCIENTIFIC STUDY OF RELIGION. (US/0021-8294). **4967**

JOURNAL FOR THE STUDY OF RELIGION. (SA/1011-7601). **4967**

JOURNAL FOR THE THEORY OF SOCIAL BEHAVIOUR. (UK/0021-8308). **4593**

JOURNAL - FORENSIC SCIENCE SOCIETY. (UK/0015-7368). **3741**

JOURNAL FRANCAIS D'OPHTALMOLOGIE. (FR/0181-5512). **3875**

JOURNAL FROM THE RADICAL REFORMATION, A. (US/1058-3084). **4968**

JOURNAL FUER BETRIEBSWIRTSCHAFT. (AU/0344-9327). **685**

JOURNAL FUER DIE REINE UND ANGEWANDTE MATHEMATIK. (GW/0075-4102). **3511**

JOURNAL FUER HIRNFORSCHUNG. (GW/0021-8359). **3834**

JOURNAL FUER ORNITHOLOGIE. (GW/0021-8375). **5618**

JOURNAL / GERMAN-TEXAN HERITAGE SOCIETY, THE. (US). **2455**

JOURNAL MICHIGAN PHARMACIST. (US/1045-6481). **4310**

JOURNAL OF ABNORMAL CHILD PSYCHOLOGY. (US/0091-0627). **4593**

JOURNAL OF ABNORMAL PSYCHOLOGY (1965). (US/0021-843X). **4593**

JOURNAL OF ACADEMIC LIBRARIANSHIP. (US/0099-1333). **3219**

JOURNAL OF ACCOUNTANCY. (US/0021-8448). **746**

JOURNAL OF ACCOUNTING & ECONOMICS. (NE/0165-4101). **746**

JOURNAL OF ACCOUNTING AND PUBLIC POLICY. (US/0278-4254). **746**

JOURNAL OF ACCOUNTING CASE RESEARCH, THE. (CN/1192-2621). **746**

JOURNAL OF ACCOUNTING EDUCATION. (US/0748-5751). **746**

JOURNAL OF ACCOUNTING LITERATURE. (US/0737-4607). **746**

JOURNAL OF ACCOUNTING RESEARCH. (US/0021-8456). **746**

JOURNAL OF ACOUSTIC EMISSION. (US/0730-0050). **1981**

JOURNAL OF ACQUIRED IMMUNE DEFICIENCY SYNDROMES. (US/0894-9255). **3673**

JOURNAL OF ACTUARIAL PRACTICE. (US/1064-6647). **2885**

JOURNAL OF ADDICTIVE DISEASES. (US/1055-0887). **1345**

JOURNAL OF ADHESION SCIENCE AND TECHNOLOGY. (NE/0169-4243). **1053**

JOURNAL OF ADHESION, THE. (UK/0021-8464). **1053**

JOURNAL OF ADOLESCENCE (LONDON, ENGLAND). (UK/0140-1971). **3904**

JOURNAL OF ADOLESCENT CHEMICAL DEPENDENCY. (US/0896-7768). **1345**

JOURNAL OF ADOLESCENT HEALTH. (US/1054-139X). **3593**

JOURNAL OF ADVANCED COMPOSITION. (US/0731-6755). **3289**

JOURNAL OF ADVANCED NURSING. (UK/0309-2402). **3858**

JOURNAL OF ADVANCED TRANSPORTATION. (US/0197-6729). **5385**

JOURNAL OF ADVANCES IN HEALTH AND NURSING CARE. (UK/0960-9857). **3858**

JOURNAL OF ADVERTISING. (US/0091-3367). **761**

JOURNAL OF ADVERTISING RESEARCH. (US/0021-8499). **761**

JOURNAL OF AEROSOL SCIENCE. (UK/0021-8502). **1053**

JOURNAL OF AFFECTIVE DISORDERS. (NE/0165-0327). **3593**

JOURNAL OF AFRICAN EARTH SCIENCES (AND THE MIDDLE EAST). (UK/0899-5362). **1384**

JOURNAL OF AFRICAN HISTORY. (UK/0021-8537). **2640**

JOURNAL OF AFRICAN ZOOLOGY. (BE/0776-7943). **5587**

JOURNAL OF AGING & SOCIAL POLICY. (US/0895-9420). **5179**

JOURNAL OF AGING STUDIES. (US/0890-4065). **5249**

JOURNAL OF AGRICULTURAL & ENVIRONMENTAL ETHICS. (CN/1187-7863). **2251**

JOURNAL OF AGRICULTURAL AND FOOD CHEMISTRY. (US/0021-8561). **99**

JOURNAL OF AGRICULTURAL & FOOD INFORMATION. (US/1049-6505). **99**

JOURNAL OF AGRICULTURAL ECONOMICS. (UK/0021-857X). **99**

JOURNAL OF AGRICULTURAL EDUCATION. (US/1042-0541). **99**

JOURNAL OF AGRICULTURAL ENGINEERING RESEARCH. (UK/0021-8634). **1981**

JOURNAL OF AGRICULTURAL ENTOMOLOGY. (US/0735-939X). **5610**

JOURNAL OF AGRICULTURAL SCIENCE, THE. (UK/0021-8596). **99**

JOURNAL OF AGRICULTURE OF THE UNIVERSITY OF PUERTO RICO, THE. (PR/0041-994X). **99**

JOURNAL OF AGRICULTURE (SOUTH PERTH). (AT/0021-8618). **100**

JOURNAL OF AIR TRAFFIC CONTROL, THE. (US/0021-8650). **25**

JOURNAL OF AIRCRAFT. (US/0021-8669). **26**

JOURNAL OF ALCOHOL AND DRUG EDUCATION. (US/0090-1482). **1345**

JOURNAL OF ALGEBRA. (US/0021-8693). **3511**

JOURNAL OF ALGEBRAIC COMBINATORICS. (US/0925-9899). **3511**

JOURNAL OF ALGORITHMS. (US/0196-6774). **3511**

JOURNAL OF ALTERNATIVE AND COMPLEMENTARY MEDICINE (NEW YORK, N.Y.), THE. (US/1075-5535). **3593**

JOURNAL OF AMBULATORY CARE MANAGEMENT, THE. (US/0148-9917). **3786**

JOURNAL OF AMBULATORY CARE MARKETING. (US/0886-9723). **3725**

JOURNAL OF AMERICAN CULTURE. (US/0191-1813). **2740**

JOURNAL OF AMERICAN ETHNIC HISTORY. (US/0278-5927). **2265**

JOURNAL OF AMERICAN HISTORY, THE. (US/0021-8723). **2740**

JOURNAL OF ANALYTICAL AND APPLIED PYROLYSIS. (NE/0165-2370). **1016**

JOURNAL OF ANALYTICAL ATOMIC SPECTROMETRY. (UK/0267-9477). **1016**

JOURNAL OF ANALYTICAL PSYCHOLOGY. (UK/0021-8774). **4593**

JOURNAL OF ANALYTICAL TOXICOLOGY. (US/0146-4760). **3981**

JOURNAL OF ANATOMY. (UK/0021-8782). **3679**

JOURNAL OF ANDROLOGY. (US/0196-3635). **581**

JOURNAL OF ANIMAL ECOLOGY, THE. (UK/0021-8790). **5587**

JOURNAL OF ANIMAL SCIENCE. (US/0021-8812). **5513**

JOURNAL OF ANTHROPOLOGICAL ARCHAEOLOGY. (US/0278-4165). **271**

JOURNAL OF ANTHROPOLOGICAL RESEARCH. (US/0091-7710). **238**

JOURNAL OF ANTIBIOTICS (NIHON KOSEIBUSSHITSU GAKUJUTSU KYOGIKAI : 1968). (JA/0021-8820). **4310**

JOURNAL OF ANTIMICROBIAL CHEMOTHERAPY, THE. (UK/0305-7453). **564**

JOURNAL OF ANXIETY DISORDERS. (US/0887-6185). **4593**

JOURNAL OF APICULTURAL RESEARCH. (UK/0021-8839). **5587**

JOURNAL OF APPLIED AQUACULTURE. (US/1045-4438). **2306**

JOURNAL OF APPLIED BEHAVIOR ANALYSIS. (US/0021-8855). **4593**

JOURNAL OF APPLIED BEHAVIORAL SCIENCE, THE. (US/0021-8863). **5205**

JOURNAL OF APPLIED BUSINESS RESEARCH. (US/0892-7626). **685**

JOURNAL OF APPLIED CRYSTALLOGRAPHY. (DK/0021-8898). **1032**

JOURNAL OF APPLIED ECOLOGY, THE. (UK/0021-8901). **2217**

JOURNAL OF APPLIED ECONOMETRICS (CHICHESTER, ENGLAND). (UK/0883-7252). **1592**

JOURNAL OF APPLIED ELECTROCHEMISTRY. (UK/0021-891X). **1034**

JOURNAL OF APPLIED FIRE SCIENCE. (US/1044-4300). **2291**

JOURNAL OF APPLIED ICHTHYOLOGY. (GW/0175-8659). **2306**

JOURNAL OF APPLIED METEOROLOGY (1988). (US/0894-8763). **1426**

JOURNAL OF APPLIED NUTRITION, THE. (US/0021-8960). **4192**

JOURNAL OF APPLIED PHYCOLOGY. (NE/0921-8971). **514**

JOURNAL OF APPLIED PHYSIOLOGY (1985). (US/8750-7587). **581**

JOURNAL OF APPLIED POLYMER SCIENCE. (US/0021-8995). **2013**

JOURNAL OF APPLIED PROBABILITY. (UK/0021-9002). **3511**

JOURNAL OF APPLIED PSYCHOLOGY. (US/0021-9010). **4593**

JOURNAL OF APPLIED SEED PRODUCTION. (US/8755-8750). **175**

JOURNAL OF APPLIED SOCIAL PSYCHOLOGY. (US/0021-9029). **4594**

JOURNAL OF APPLIED SOCIAL SCIENCES, THE. (US/0146-4310). **5291**

JOURNAL OF APPLIED SOCIOLOGY - SOCIETY FOR APPLIED SOCIOLOGY (U.S.). (US/0749-0232). **5249**

JOURNAL OF APPLIED TOXICOLOGY. (UK/0260-437X). **3981**

JOURNAL OF APPROXIMATION THEORY. (US/0021-9045). **3512**

JOURNAL OF AQUACULTURE & AQUATIC SCIENCES. (US/0733-2076). **460**

JOURNAL OF AQUATIC ECOSYSTEM HEALTH. (NE/0925-1014). **555**

JOURNAL OF AQUATIC FOOD PRODUCTS TECHNOLOGY. (US/1049-8850). **2306**

JOURNAL OF AQUATIC PLANT MANAGEMENT. (US/0146-6623). **515**

JOURNAL OF ARAB AFFAIRS. (US/0275-3588). **4527**

JOURNAL OF ARACHNOLOGY, THE. (US/0161-8202). **5587**

JOURNAL OF ARCHAEOLOGICAL SCIENCE. (UK/0305-4403). **271**

JOURNAL OF ARCHITECTURAL AND PLANNING RESEARCH. (US/0738-0895). **301**

JOURNAL OF ARID ENVIRONMENTS. (UK/0140-1963). **1357**

JOURNAL OF ARIZONA HISTORY, THE. (US/0021-9053). **2740**

JOURNAL OF ASIAN AND AFRICAN AFFAIRS. (US/1044-2979). **4527**

JOURNAL OF ASIAN AND AFRICAN STUDIES (LEIDEN). (NE/0021-9096). **2769**

JOURNAL OF ASIAN BUSINESS. (US/1068-0055). **685**

JOURNAL OF ASIAN MARTIAL ARTS. (US/1057-8358). **2599**

JOURNAL OF ASIAN PACIFIC COMMUNICATION. (UK/0957-6851). **1114**

JOURNAL OF ASIAN STUDIES, THE. (US/0021-9118). **2655**

JOURNAL OF ASTROPHYSICS AND ASTRONOMY. (II/0250-6335). **396**

JOURNAL OF ATMOSPHERIC AND TERRESTRIAL PHYSICS. (UK/0021-9169). **1407**

JOURNAL OF ATMOSPHERIC CHEMISTRY. (NE/0167-7764). **1426**

JOURNAL OF AUSTRALIAN POLITICAL ECONOMY, THE. (AT/0156-5826). **1498**

JOURNAL OF AUTISM AND DEVELOPMENTAL DISORDERS. (US/0162-3257). **3928**

JOURNAL OF AUTOIMMUNITY. (UK/0896-8411). **3673**

JOURNAL OF AUTOMATED REASONING. (NE/0168-7433). **1220**

JOURNAL OF AUTOMATIC CHEMISTRY, THE. (UK/0142-0453). **1016**

JOURNAL OF AUTONOMIC PHARMACOLOGY. (UK/0144-1795). **4310**

JOURNAL OF AVIAN BIOLOGY. (DK/0908-8857). **5618**

JOURNAL OF BACTERIOLOGY. (US/0021-9193). **564**

JOURNAL OF BAHA'I STUDIES. (CN/0838-0430). **4968**

JOURNAL OF BANK COST & MANAGEMENT ACCOUNTING, THE. (US/1070-941X). **746**

JOURNAL OF BANKING & FINANCE. (NE/0378-4266). **793**

JOURNAL OF BANKING & FINANCE MICROFORM. (SZ/0378-4266). **793**

JOURNAL OF BASIC MICROBIOLOGY. (GW/0233-111X). **564**

JOURNAL OF BECKETT STUDIES. (US). **3399**

JOURNAL OF BEHAVIOR THERAPY AND EXPERIMENTAL PSYCHIATRY. (UK/0005-7916). **3928**

JOURNAL OF BEHAVIORAL MEDICINE. (US/0160-7715). **4594**

JOURNAL OF BEHAVIORAL OPTOMETRY. (US/1045-8395). **4216**

JOURNAL OF BIBLICAL ETHICS IN MEDICINE. (US/1050-3404). **2251**

JOURNAL OF BIOCHEMICAL AND BIOPHYSICAL METHODS. (NE/0165-022X). **489**

JOURNAL OF BIOCHEMICAL TOXICOLOGY. (US/0887-2082). **3981**

JOURNAL OF BIOCHEMISTRY (TOKYO). (JA/0021-924X). **489**

JOURNAL OF BIOENERGETICS AND BIOMEMBRANES. (US/0145-479X). **565**

JOURNAL OF BIOGEOGRAPHY. (UK/0305-0270). **2567**

JOURNAL OF BIOLOGICAL CHEMISTRY, THE. (US/0021-9258). **489**

JOURNAL OF BIOLOGICAL CURATION. (UK/0958-7608). **4090**

JOURNAL OF BIOLOGICAL EDUCATION. (UK/0021-9266). **460**

JOURNAL OF BIOLOGICAL PHYSICS. (NE/0092-0606). **495**

JOURNAL OF BIOLOGICAL REGULATORS AND HOMEOSTATIC AGENTS. (IT/0393-974X). **460**

JOURNAL OF BIOLUMINESCENCE AND CHEMILUMINESCENCE. (UK/0884-3996). **495**

JOURNAL OF BIOMECHANICAL ENGINEERING. (US/0148-0731). **3694**

JOURNAL OF BIOMECHANICS. (US/0021-9290). **582**

JOURNAL OF BIOMEDICAL ENGINEERING. (UK/0141-5425). **3694**

JOURNAL OF BIOMOLECULAR NMR. (NE/0925-2738). **461**

JOURNAL OF BIOMOLECULAR STRUCTURE & DYNAMICS. (US/0739-1102). **461**

JOURNAL OF BIOSCIENCES. (II/0250-5991). **461**

JOURNAL OF BIOSOCIAL SCIENCE. (UK/0021-9320). **5205**

JOURNAL OF BLACK STUDIES. (US/0021-9347). **2266**

JOURNAL OF BONE AND JOINT SURGERY. AMERICAN VOLUME (PRINT ED.). (US/0021-9355). **3882**

JOURNAL OF BONE AND JOINT SURGERY. BRITISH VOLUME. (UK/0301-620X). **3966**

JOURNAL OF BONE AND MINERAL RESEARCH. (US/0884-0431). **3805**

JOURNAL OF BRYOLOGY. (UK/0373-6687). **515**

JOURNAL OF BURN CARE & REHABILITATION, THE. (US/0273-8481). **3594**

JOURNAL OF BUSINESS & ECONOMIC STATISTICS. (US/0735-0015). **1534**

JOURNAL OF BUSINESS & ENTREPRENEURSHIP. (US/1042-6337). **686**

JOURNAL OF BUSINESS & FINANCE LIBRARIANSHIP. (US/0896-3568). **3219**

JOURNAL OF BUSINESS & INDUSTRIAL MARKETING, THE. (US/0885-8624). **927**

JOURNAL OF BUSINESS AND SOCIETY. (CY/1012-2591). **1569**

JOURNAL OF BUSINESS (CHICAGO, ILL.), THE. (US/0021-9398). **686**

JOURNAL OF BUSINESS ETHICS. (NE/0167-4544). **2251**

JOURNAL OF BUSINESS LOGISTICS. (US/0735-3766). **5385**

JOURNAL OF BUSINESS RESEARCH. (US/0148-2963). **686**

JOURNAL OF BUSINESS STRATEGIES. (US/0887-2058). **686**

JOURNAL OF BUSINESS VENTURING. (US/0883-9026). **686**

JOURNAL OF CALIFORNIA AND GREAT BASIN ANTHROPOLOGY. (US/0191-3557). **238**

JOURNAL OF CALIFORNIA LAW ENFORCEMENT. (US/0449-5063). **3167**

JOURNAL OF CANADIAN PETROLEUM TECHNOLOGY, THE. (CN/0021-9487). **4262**

JOURNAL OF CANADIAN POETRY. (CN/0705-1328). **3464**

JOURNAL OF CANADIAN STUDIES. (CN/0021-9495). **2740**

JOURNAL OF CANCER EDUCATION, THE. (US/0885-8195). **3819**

JOURNAL OF CANCER RESEARCH AND CLINICAL ONCOLOGY. (GW/0171-5216). **3819**

JOURNAL OF CARBOHYDRATE CHEMISTRY. (US/0732-8303). **1042**

JOURNAL OF CARDIOPULMONARY REHABILITATION. (US/0883-9212). **3706**

JOURNAL OF CARDIOVASCULAR ELECTROPHYSIOLOGY. (US/1045-3873). **3707**

JOURNAL OF CARDIOVASCULAR NURSING, THE. (US/0889-4655). **3858**

JOURNAL OF CARDIOVASCULAR PHARMACOLOGY. (US/0160-2446). **4310**

JOURNAL OF CARDIOVASCULAR SURGERY. (IT/0021-9509). **3966**

JOURNAL OF CASE MANAGEMENT. (US/1061-3706). **3787**

JOURNAL OF CATALYSIS. (US/0021-9517). **1053**

JOURNAL OF CELL BIOLOGY, THE. (US/0021-9525). **537**

JOURNAL OF CELL SCIENCE. (UK/0021-9533). **537**

JOURNAL OF CELLULAR BIOCHEMISTRY. (US/0730-2312). **489**

JOURNAL OF CELLULAR PHYSIOLOGY. (US/0021-9541). **582**

JOURNAL — Peer Reviewed Index

JOURNAL OF CEREAL SCIENCE. (UK/0733-5210). **176**

JOURNAL OF CEREBRAL BLOOD FLOW AND METABOLISM. (US/0271-678X). **582**

JOURNAL OF CHEMICAL AND ENGINEERING DATA. (US/0021-9568). **2014**

JOURNAL OF CHEMICAL DEPENDENCY TREATMENT. (US/0885-4734). **1345**

JOURNAL OF CHEMICAL ECOLOGY. (US/0098-0331). **2217**

JOURNAL OF CHEMICAL EDUCATION. (US/0021-9584). **980**

JOURNAL OF CHEMICAL ENGINEERING OF JAPAN. (JA/0021-9592). **2014**

JOURNAL OF CHEMICAL PHYSICS, THE. (US/0021-9606). **4408**

JOURNAL OF CHEMICAL RESEARCH. MINIPRINT. (UK/0308-2350). **980**

JOURNAL OF CHEMICAL RESEARCH. SYNOPSES. (UK/0308-2342). **980**

JOURNAL OF CHEMICAL THERMODYNAMICS, THE. (UK/0021-9614). **1054**

JOURNAL OF CHEMOTHERAPY (FLORENCE). (IT/1120-009X). **3594**

JOURNAL OF CHILD LANGUAGE. (UK/0305-0009). **3289**

JOURNAL OF CHILD NEUROLOGY. (US/0883-0738). **3904**

JOURNAL OF CHILD PSYCHOLOGY AND PSYCHIATRY AND ALLIED DISCIPLINES. (UK/0021-9630). **4594**

JOURNAL OF CHILD SEXUAL ABUSE. (US/1053-8712). **5291**

JOURNAL OF CHIROPRACTIC EDUCATION, THE. (US/1042-5055). **3805**

JOURNAL OF CHRISTIAN NURSING. (US/0743-2550). **3858**

JOURNAL OF CHROMATOGRAPHIC SCIENCE. (US/0021-9665). **1016**

JOURNAL OF CHROMATOGRAPHY. (NE/0021-9673). **1016**

JOURNAL OF CHROMATOGRAPHY. BIOMEDICAL APPLICATIONS. (NE/0378-4347). **980**

JOURNAL OF CITRICULTURE. (US). **176**

JOURNAL OF CLASSIFICATION. (US/0176-4268). **3512**

JOURNAL OF CLASSROOM INTERACTION, THE. (US/0749-4025). **1756**

JOURNAL OF CLEAN TECHNOLOGY AND ENVIRONMENTAL SCIENCES. (US/1052-1062). **2175**

JOURNAL OF CLIMATE. (US/0894-8755). **1426**

JOURNAL OF CLINICAL AND EXPERIMENTAL GERONTOLOGY. (US/0192-1193). **3753**

JOURNAL OF CLINICAL AND EXPERIMENTAL NEUROPSYCHOLOGY. (NE/0168-8634). **3834**

JOURNAL OF CLINICAL & LABORATORY IMMUNOLOGY. (UK/0141-2760). **3673**

JOURNAL OF CLINICAL BIOCHEMISTRY AND NUTRITION. (JA/0912-0009). **489**

JOURNAL OF CLINICAL CHILD PSYCHOLOGY. (US/0047-228X). **4594**

JOURNAL OF CLINICAL DENTISTRY, THE. (US/0895-8831). **1326**

JOURNAL OF CLINICAL ENDOCRINOLOGY AND METABOLISM, THE. (US/0021-972X). **3731**

JOURNAL OF CLINICAL EPIDEMIOLOGY. (UK/0895-4356). **3735**

JOURNAL OF CLINICAL ETHICS, THE. (US/1046-7890). **2251**

JOURNAL OF CLINICAL GASTROENTEROLOGY. (US/0192-0790). **3746**

JOURNAL OF CLINICAL IMMUNOASSAY. (US/0736-4393). **3673**

JOURNAL OF CLINICAL IMMUNOLOGY. (US/0271-9142). **3673**

JOURNAL OF CLINICAL LABORATORY ANALYSIS, THE. (US/0887-8013). **3594**

JOURNAL OF CLINICAL LASER MEDICINE & SURGERY. (US/1044-5471). **3967**

JOURNAL OF CLINICAL MICROBIOLOGY. (US/0095-1137). **565**

JOURNAL OF CLINICAL MONITORING. (US/0748-1977). **3594**

JOURNAL OF CLINICAL NEURO-OPHTHALMOLOGY. (US/0272-846X). **3875**

JOURNAL OF CLINICAL NEUROPHYSIOLOGY. (US/0736-0258). **3834**

JOURNAL OF CLINICAL ONCOLOGY. (US/0732-183X). **3819**

JOURNAL OF CLINICAL PATHOLOGY. (UK/0021-9746). **3895**

JOURNAL OF CLINICAL PERIODONTOLOGY. (DK/0303-6979). **1326**

JOURNAL OF CLINICAL PHARMACY AND THERAPEUTICS. (UK/0269-4727). **4310**

JOURNAL OF CLINICAL PSYCHIATRY, THE. (US/0160-6689). **3928**

JOURNAL OF CLINICAL PSYCHOANALYSIS. (US). **3928**

JOURNAL OF CLINICAL PSYCHOPHARMACOLOGY. (US/0271-0749). **4310**

JOURNAL OF COAL QUALITY, THE. (US/0732-8087). **1948**

JOURNAL OF COASTAL RESEARCH. (US/0749-0208). **1357**

JOURNAL OF COGNITIVE NEUROSCIENCE, THE. (US/0898-929X). **3835**

JOURNAL OF COGNITIVE PSYCHOTHERAPY, THE. (US/0889-8391). **4595**

JOURNAL OF COLLECTIVE NEGOTIATIONS IN THE PUBLIC SECTOR. (US/0047-2301). **1682**

JOURNAL OF COLLEGE ADMISSIONS, THE. (US/0734-6670). **1832**

JOURNAL OF COLLEGE & UNIVERSITY FOODSERVICE. (US/1053-8739). **2345**

JOURNAL OF COLLEGE MANAGEMENT. (UK). **1832**

JOURNAL OF COLLEGE SCIENCE TEACHING. (US/0047-231X). **5118**

JOURNAL OF COLLEGE STUDENT PSYCHOTHERAPY. (US/8756-8225). **4595**

JOURNAL OF COLLOID AND INTERFACE SCIENCE. (US/0021-9797). **1054**

JOURNAL OF COMBINATORIAL THEORY. SERIES A. (US/0097-3165). **3512**

JOURNAL OF COMBINATORIAL THEORY. SERIES B. (US/0095-8956). **3512**

JOURNAL OF COMMON MARKET STUDIES. (UK/0021-9886). **1569**

JOURNAL OF COMMONWEALTH & COMPARATIVE POLITICS, THE. (UK/0306-3631). **4478**

JOURNAL OF COMMUNICATION. (US/0021-9916). **1114**

JOURNAL OF COMMUNICATION DISORDERS. (US/0021-9924). **3835**

JOURNAL OF COMMUNICATION INQUIRY, THE. (US/0196-8599). **1114**

JOURNAL OF COMMUNITY HEALTH NURSING. (US/0737-0016). **3858**

JOURNAL OF COMMUNITY PSYCHOLOGY. (US/0090-4392). **4595**

JOURNAL OF COMPARATIVE ECONOMICS. (US/0147-5967). **1592**

JOURNAL OF COMPARATIVE FAMILY STUDIES. (CN/0047-2328). **2281**

JOURNAL OF COMPARATIVE NEUROLOGY (1911). (US/0021-9967). **3835**

JOURNAL OF COMPARATIVE PATHOLOGY. (UK/0021-9975). **3895**

JOURNAL OF COMPARATIVE PHYSIOLOGY. A, SENSORY, NEURAL, AND BEHAVIORAL PHYSIOLOGY. (GW/0340-7594). **582**

JOURNAL OF COMPARATIVE PHYSIOLOGY. B, BIOCHEMICAL, SYSTEMIC, AND ENVIRONMENTAL PHYSIOLOGY. (GW/0174-1578). **582**

JOURNAL OF COMPARATIVE PSYCHOLOGY (1983). (US/0735-7036). **4595**

JOURNAL OF COMPOSITE MATERIALS. (US/0021-9983). **2103**

JOURNAL OF COMPOSITES TECHNOLOGY & RESEARCH. (US/0884-6804). **2103**

JOURNAL OF COMPUTATIONAL AND APPLIED MATHEMATICS. (NE/0377-0427). **3512**

JOURNAL OF COMPUTATIONAL CHEMISTRY. (US/0192-8651). **981**

JOURNAL OF COMPUTATIONAL MATHEMATICS. (CC/0254-9409). **3512**

JOURNAL OF COMPUTATIONAL PHYSICS. (US/0021-9991). **4408**

JOURNAL OF COMPUTER-AIDED MOLECULAR DESIGN. (NE/0920-654X). **1229**

JOURNAL OF COMPUTER AND SYSTEM SCIENCES. (US/0022-0000). **1247**

JOURNAL OF COMPUTER-ASSISTED MICROSCOPY. (US/1040-7286). **1223**

JOURNAL OF COMPUTER ASSISTED TOMOGRAPHY. (US/0363-8715). **3942**

JOURNAL OF COMPUTER-BASED INSTRUCTION. (US/0098-597X). **1223**

JOURNAL OF COMPUTERS IN MATHEMATICS AND SCIENCE TEACHING, THE. (US/0731-9258). **1224**

JOURNAL OF COMPUTING IN CHILDHOOD EDUCATION. (US/1043-1055). **1224**

JOURNAL OF COMPUTING IN HIGHER EDUCATION. (US/1042-1726). **1832**

JOURNAL OF CONCHOLOGY. (UK/0022-0019). **5587**

JOURNAL OF CONFLICT RESOLUTION, THE. (US/0022-0027). **4527**

JOURNAL OF CONSTRUCTION ACCOUNTING & TAXATION. (US/1054-3007). **618**

JOURNAL OF CONSTRUCTIONAL STEEL RESEARCH. (UK/0143-974X). **618**

JOURNAL OF CONSULTING AND CLINICAL PSYCHOLOGY. (US/0022-006X). **4595**

JOURNAL OF CONSUMER AFFAIRS, THE. (US/0022-0078). **1297**

JOURNAL OF CONSUMER POLICY. (NE/0168-7034). **1297**

JOURNAL OF CONSUMER RESEARCH, THE. (US/0093-5301). **927**

JOURNAL OF CONTEMPORARY ASIA. (UK/0047-2336). **2655**

JOURNAL OF CONTEMPORARY CRIMINAL JUSTICE. (US/1043-9862). **3167**

JOURNAL OF CONTEMPORARY ETHNOGRAPHY. (US/0891-2416). **5249**

JOURNAL OF CONTEMPORARY HEALTH LAW AND POLICY, THE. (US/0882-1046). **2987**

JOURNAL OF CONTINUING EDUCATION IN THE HEALTH PROFESSIONS, THE. (CN/0894-1912). **3594**

JOURNAL OF CONTROLLED RELEASE. (NE/0168-3659). **981**

JOURNAL OF COOPERATIVE EDUCATION. (US/0022-0132). **1756**

JOURNAL OF COORDINATION CHEMISTRY. (US/0095-8972). **981**

JOURNAL OF CORPORATE MANAGEMENT, THE. (AT/1038-2410). **3101**

JOURNAL OF CORPORATE TAXATION, THE. (US/0094-0593). **4734**

JOURNAL OF COST ANALYSIS, THE. (US/0882-3871). **747**

JOURNAL OF COUNSELING AND DEVELOPMENT. (US/0748-9633). **1913**

JOURNAL OF COUNSELING PSYCHOLOGY. (US/0022-0167). **4595**

JOURNAL OF COUPLES THERAPY. (US/0897-4446). **2281**

JOURNAL OF CRANIOFACIAL GENETICS AND DEVELOPMENTAL BIOLOGY. (DK/0270-4145). **3805**

JOURNAL OF CREATIVE BEHAVIOR, THE. (US/0022-0175). **4596**

JOURNAL OF CRIMINAL JUSTICE. (US/0047-2352). **3167**

JOURNAL OF CRIMINAL LAW & CRIMINOLOGY. (US/0091-4169). **3107**

JOURNAL OF CRIMINAL LAW (HERTFORD). (UK/0022-0183). **3107**

JOURNAL OF CRITICAL CARE. (US/0883-9441). **3594**

JOURNAL OF CROSS-CULTURAL GERONTOLOGY. (NE/0169-3816). **3753**

JOURNAL OF CROSS-CULTURAL PSYCHOLOGY. (US/0022-0221). **4596**

JOURNAL OF CRUSTACEAN BIOLOGY. (US/0278-0372). **555**

JOURNAL OF CRYSTAL GROWTH. (NE/0022-0248). **1032**

JOURNAL OF CRYSTALLOGRAPHIC AND SPECTROSCOPIC RESEARCH. (US/0277-8068). **1032**

JOURNAL OF CULINARY PRACTICE. (US/1052-9241). **2346**

JOURNAL OF CULTURAL DIVERSITY. (US/1071-5568). **5206**

JOURNAL OF CURRICULUM AND SUPERVISION. (US/0882-1232). **1897**

JOURNAL OF CURRICULUM STUDIES. (UK/0022-0272). **1898**

JOURNAL OF CUTANEOUS PATHOLOGY. (DK/0303-6987). **3721**

JOURNAL OF DAIRY RESEARCH, THE. (UK/0022-0299). **195**

JOURNAL OF DAIRY SCIENCE. (US/0022-0302). **195**

JOURNAL OF DATABASE MANAGEMENT. (US/1063-8016). **1254**

JOURNAL OF DENTAL EDUCATION. (US/0022-0337). **1326**

JOURNAL OF DENTAL HYGIENE. (US/1043-254X). **1326**

JOURNAL OF DENTAL RESEARCH. (US/0022-0345). **1326**

JOURNAL OF DENTISTRY. (UK/0300-5712). **1326**

JOURNAL OF DENTISTRY FOR CHILDREN. (US/0022-0353). **1326**

JOURNAL OF DEPRESSION & STRESS. (US). **3928**

JOURNAL OF DERIVATIVES, THE. (US/1074-1240). **904**

JOURNAL OF DERMATOLOGIC SURGERY AND ONCOLOGY, THE. (US/0148-0812). **3967**

JOURNAL OF DERMATOLOGICAL SCIENCE. (NE/0923-1811). **3721**

JOURNAL OF DERMATOLOGICAL TREATMENT, THE. (UK/0954-6634). **3721**

JOURNAL OF DESIGN AND MANUFACTURING. (UK/0962-4694). **3482**

JOURNAL OF DEVELOPMENT ECONOMICS. (NE/0304-3878). **1569**

JOURNAL OF DEVELOPMENT STUDIES, THE. (UK/0022-0388). **1569**

JOURNAL OF DEVELOPMENTAL AND BEHAVIORAL PEDIATRICS. (US/0196-206X). **3904**

JOURNAL OF DEVELOPMENTAL PHYSIOLOGY. (UK/0141-9846). **3763**

JOURNAL OF DHARMA. (II/0253-7222). **4968**

JOURNAL OF DIAGNOSTIC MEDICAL SONOGRAPHY. (US/8756-4793). **3595**

JOURNAL OF DIFFERENTIAL EQUATIONS. (US/0022-0396). **3512**

JOURNAL OF DIFFERENTIAL GEOMETRY. (US/0022-040X). **3512**

JOURNAL OF DISABILITY POLICY STUDIES, THE. (US/1044-2073). **4389**

JOURNAL OF DISPERSION SCIENCE AND TECHNOLOGY. (US/0193-2691). **4428**

JOURNAL OF DISTANCE EDUCATION / REVUE DE L'ENSEIGNEMENT A DISTANCE. (CN/0830-0445). **1756**

JOURNAL OF DIVORCE & REMARRIAGE. (US/1050-2556). **2281**

JOURNAL OF DOCUMENT AND TEXT MANAGEMENT. (UK). **1192**

JOURNAL OF DOCUMENTATION. (UK/0022-0418). **3219**

JOURNAL OF DRUG DEVELOPMENT. (UK/0952-9500). **4311**

JOURNAL OF DRUG EDUCATION. (US/0047-2379). **1345**

JOURNAL OF DRUG ISSUES. (US/0022-0426). **1346**

JOURNAL OF DYNAMIC SYSTEMS, MEASUREMENT, AND CONTROL. (US/0022-0434). **1982**

JOURNAL OF EAST ASIAN LINGUISTICS. (NE/0925-8558). **3290**

JOURNAL OF EAST-WEST BUSINESS. (US/1066-9868). **686**

JOURNAL OF ECOLOGY, THE. (UK/0022-0477). **515**

JOURNAL OF ECONOMETRICS. (NE/0304-4076). **1592**

JOURNAL OF ECONOMIC AND SOCIAL INTELLIGENCE. (UK). **5206**

JOURNAL OF ECONOMIC BEHAVIOR & ORGANIZATION. (NE/0167-2681). **1498**

JOURNAL OF ECONOMIC DYNAMICS & CONTROL. (NE/0165-1889). **1499**

JOURNAL OF ECONOMIC EDUCATION, THE. (US/0022-0485). **1499**

JOURNAL OF ECONOMIC ENTOMOLOGY. (US/0022-0493). **5610**

JOURNAL OF ECONOMIC HISTORY, THE. (US/0022-0507). **1569**

JOURNAL OF ECONOMIC LITERATURE. (US/0022-0515). **1535**

JOURNAL OF ECONOMIC PERSPECTIVES, THE. (US/0895-3309). **1499**

JOURNAL OF ECONOMIC PSYCHOLOGY. (NE/0167-4870). **1593**

JOURNAL OF ECONOMIC STUDIES (BRADFORD). (UK/0144-3585). **1499**

JOURNAL OF ECONOMIC THEORY. (US/0022-0531). **1593**

JOURNAL OF ECONOMICS AND BUSINESS. (US/0148-6195). **1499**

JOURNAL OF ECONOMICS AND FINANCE. (US/1055-0925). **1499**

JOURNAL OF ECONOMICS (VIENNA, AUSTRIA). (AU/0931-8658). **1593**

JOURNAL OF ECUMENICAL STUDIES. (US/0022-0558). **4968**

JOURNAL OF EDUCATION FOR BUSINESS. (US/0883-2323). **687**

JOURNAL OF EDUCATION FOR LIBRARY AND INFORMATION SCIENCE. (US/0748-5786). **3220**

JOURNAL OF EDUCATIONAL COMPUTING RESEARCH. (US/0735-6331). **1224**

JOURNAL OF EDUCATIONAL GERONTOLOGY. (UK/0268-9987). **3753**

JOURNAL OF EDUCATIONAL ISSUES OF LANGUAGE MINORITY STUDENTS. (US). **1757**

JOURNAL OF EDUCATIONAL MEASUREMENT. (US/0022-0655). **1757**

JOURNAL OF EDUCATIONAL PSYCHOLOGY. (US/0022-0663). **4596**

JOURNAL OF EDUCATIONAL RESEARCH (WASHINGTON, D.C.), THE. (US/0022-0671). **1757**

JOURNAL OF EDUCATIONAL STATISTICS. (US/0362-9791). **1795**

JOURNAL OF EDUCATIONAL TECHNOLOGY SYSTEMS. (US/0047-2395). **1224**

JOURNAL OF EDUCATIONAL TELEVISION. (UK/0260-7417). **1757**

JOURNAL OF EDUCATIONAL THOUGHT. (CN/0022-0701). **1757**

JOURNAL OF ELASTICITY. (NE/0374-3535). **4428**

JOURNAL OF ELASTOMERS AND PLASTICS, THE. (US/0095-2443). **4456**

JOURNAL OF ELDER ABUSE & NEGLECT. (US/0894-6566). **5291**

JOURNAL OF ELECTROANALYTICAL CHEMISTRY AND INTERFACIAL ELECTROCHEMISTRY. (NE/0022-0728). **1034**

JOURNAL OF ELECTROCARDIOLOGY. (US/0022-0736). **3707**

JOURNAL OF ELECTROMAGNETIC WAVES AND APPLICATIONS. (NE/0920-5071). **2068**

JOURNAL OF ELECTRON SPECTROSCOPY AND RELATED PHENOMENA. (NE/0368-2048). **4435**

JOURNAL OF ELECTRONIC MATERIALS. (US/0361-5235). **2068**

JOURNAL OF ELECTRONIC TESTING. (US/0923-8174). **2069**

JOURNAL OF ELECTRONICS MANUFACTURING. (UK/0960-3131). **2069**

JOURNAL OF ELECTROSTATICS. (NE/0304-3886). **2069**

JOURNAL OF EMERGENCY NURSING. (US/0099-1767). **3858**

JOURNAL OF EMOTIONAL AND BEHAVIORAL PROBLEMS. (US/1064-7023). **4596**

JOURNAL OF EMPLOYEE OWNERSHIP LAW AND FINANCE, THE. (US/1046-7491). **1682**

JOURNAL OF EMPLOYMENT COUNSELING. (US/0022-0787). **4206**

JOURNAL OF END USER COMPUTING. (US/1063-2239). **1192**

JOURNAL OF ENDOCRINOLOGICAL INVESTIGATION. (IT/0391-4097). **3731**

JOURNAL OF ENDOCRINOLOGY, THE. (UK/0022-0795). **3731**

JOURNAL OF ENDODONTICS. (US/0099-2399). **1327**

JOURNAL OF ENDOUROLOGY. (US/0892-7790). **3990**

JOURNAL OF ENERGY AND DEVELOPMENT, THE. (US/0361-4476). **1948**

JOURNAL OF ENERGY & NATURAL RESOURCES LAW. (UK/0264-6811). **2987**

JOURNAL OF ENGINEERING FOR INDUSTRY. (US/0022-0817). **1982**

JOURNAL OF ENGINEERING MATERIALS AND TECHNOLOGY. (US/0094-4289). **2118**

JOURNAL OF ENGINEERING MATHEMATICS. (NE/0022-0833). **1982**

JOURNAL OF ENGINEERING MECHANICS. (US/0733-9399). **2118**

JOURNAL OF ENTOMOLOGICAL RESEARCH. (II/0378-9519). **5587**

JOURNAL OF ENTOMOLOGICAL SCIENCE. (US/0749-8004). **5610**

JOURNAL OF ENVIRONMENTAL BIOLOGY. (II/0254-8704). **2233**

JOURNAL OF ENVIRONMENTAL ECONOMICS AND MANAGEMENT. (US/0095-0696). **1499**

JOURNAL OF ENVIRONMENTAL ENGINEERING (NEW YORK N.Y.). (US/0733-9372). **2233**

JOURNAL OF ENVIRONMENTAL HEALTH. (US/0022-0892). **2175**

JOURNAL OF ENVIRONMENTAL HORTICULTURE. (US/0738-2898). **2421**

JOURNAL OF ENVIRONMENTAL LAW. (UK/0952-8873). **3113**

JOURNAL OF ENVIRONMENTAL MANAGEMENT. (UK/0301-4797). **2175**

JOURNAL OF ENVIRONMENTAL PSYCHOLOGY. (UK/0272-4944). **4596**

JOURNAL OF ENVIRONMENTAL QUALITY. (US/0047-2425). **2217**

JOURNAL OF ENVIRONMENTAL RADIOACTIVITY. (UK/0265-931X). **2233**

JOURNAL OF ENVIRONMENTAL SCIENCE AND HEALTH. PART A, ENVIRONMENTAL SCIENCE AND ENGINEERING. (US/0360-1226). **1982**

JOURNAL OF ENVIRONMENTAL SCIENCE AND HEALTH. PART B, PESTICIDES, FOOD CONTAMINANTS, AND AGRICULTURAL WASTES. (US/0360-1234). **2176**

JOURNAL OF ENVIRONMENTAL SYSTEMS. (US/0047-2433). **2176**

JOURNAL OF EPIDEMIOLOGY AND COMMUNITY HEALTH (1979). (UK/0143-005X). **3735**

JOURNAL OF EPILEPSY. (US/0896-6974). **3835**

JOURNAL OF EQUINE VETERINARY SCIENCE. (US/0737-0806). **2800**

JOURNAL OF ET NURSING. (US/1055-3045). **3858**

JOURNAL OF ETHIOPIAN STUDIES. (ET/0304-2243). **2640**

JOURNAL OF ETHNIC STUDIES, THE. (US/0091-3219). **2266**

JOURNAL OF ETHNOPHARMACOLOGY. (SZ/0378-8741). **4311**

JOURNAL OF ETHOLOGY. (JA/0289-0771). **239**

JOURNAL OF EURO MARKETING. (US/1049-6483). **927**

JOURNAL OF EVOLUTIONARY BIOCHEMISTRY AND PHYSIOLOGY. (US/0022-0930). **582**

JOURNAL OF EVOLUTIONARY BIOLOGY. (SZ/1010-061X). **548**

JOURNAL OF EVOLUTIONARY ECONOMICS. (GW/0936-9937). **1593**

JOURNAL OF EXPERIENTIAL EDUCATION, THE. (US/1053-8259). **1880**

JOURNAL OF EXPERIMENTAL & CLINICAL CANCER RESEARCH : CR. (IT/0392-9078). **3819**

JOURNAL OF EXPERIMENTAL BIOLOGY. (UK/0022-0949). **582**

JOURNAL OF EXPERIMENTAL BOTANY. (UK/0022-0957). **515**

JOURNAL OF EXPERIMENTAL CHILD PSYCHOLOGY. (US/0022-0965). **4596**

JOURNAL OF EXPERIMENTAL EDUCATION, THE. (US/0022-0973). **1898**

JOURNAL OF EXPERIMENTAL MARINE BIOLOGY AND ECOLOGY. (NE/0022-0981). **555**

JOURNAL OF EXPERIMENTAL MEDICINE, THE. (US/0022-1007). **3673**

JOURNAL OF EXPERIMENTAL PSYCHOLOGY : ANIMAL BEHAVIOR PROCESSES. (US/0097-7403). **4596**

JOURNAL OF EXPERIMENTAL PSYCHOLOGY : GENERAL. (US/0096-3445). **4596**

JOURNAL OF EXPERIMENTAL PSYCHOLOGY : HUMAN PERCEPTION AND PERFORMANCE. (US/0096-1523). **4597**

JOURNAL OF EXPERIMENTAL PSYCHOLOGY. LEARNING, MEMORY, AND COGNITION. (US/0278-7393). **4597**

JOURNAL OF EXPERIMENTAL SOCIAL PSYCHOLOGY. (US/0022-1031). **4597**

JOURNAL OF EXPERIMENTAL ZOOLOGY, THE. (US/0022-104X). **5587**

JOURNAL OF EXPOSURE ANALYSIS AND ENVIRONMENTAL EPIDEMIOLOGY. (US/1053-4245). **2176**

JOURNAL OF EXTENSION. (US/0022-0140). **1914**

JOURNAL OF EXTRA-CORPOREAL TECHNOLOGY, THE. (US/0022-1058). **3772**

JOURNAL OF FAMILY ISSUES. (US/0192-513X). **2282**

JOURNAL OF FAMILY LAW. (US/0022-1066). **3121**

JOURNAL OF FAMILY NURSING. (US/1074-8407). **3858**

JOURNAL OF FAMILY PRACTICE, THE. (US/0094-3509). **3738**

JOURNAL OF FAMILY PSYCHOLOGY. (US/0893-3200). **4597**

JOURNAL OF FAMILY PSYCHOTHERAPY. (US/0897-5353). **2282**

JOURNAL OF FAMILY SOCIAL WORK. (US/1052-2158). **5291**

JOURNAL OF FAMILY THERAPY. (UK/0163-4445). **3928**

JOURNAL OF FAMILY WELFARE, THE. (II/0022-1074). **589**

JOURNAL OF FEMINIST FAMILY THERAPY. (US/0895-2833). **2282**

JOURNAL OF FERROCEMENT. (TH/0125-1759). **632**

JOURNAL OF FERTILIZER ISSUES. (US/0748-4690). **176**

JOURNAL OF FIELD ARCHAEOLOGY. (US/0093-4690). **271**

JOURNAL OF FIELD ORNITHOLOGY. (US/0273-8570). **5618**

JOURNAL OF FINANCE (NEW YORK), THE. (US/0022-1082). **794**

JOURNAL OF FINANCIAL AND QUANTITATIVE ANALYSIS. (US/0022-1090). **794**

JOURNAL OF FINANCIAL & STRATEGIC DECISIONS. (US/1065-1853). **4734**

JOURNAL OF FINANCIAL ECONOMICS. (NE/0304-405X). **794**

JOURNAL OF FINANCIAL INTERMEDIATION. (US/1042-9573). **904**

JOURNAL OF FINANCIAL MANAGEMENT AND ANALYSIS. (II/0970-4205). **794**

JOURNAL OF FINANCIAL PLANNING (DENVER, COLO.). (US/1040-3981). **794**

JOURNAL OF FINANCIAL RESEARCH, THE. (US/0270-2592). **794**

JOURNAL OF FIRE SCIENCES. (US/0734-9041). **2291**

JOURNAL OF FISH BIOLOGY. (UK/0022-1112). **2306**

JOURNAL OF FISH DISEASES. (UK/0140-7775). **2306**

JOURNAL OF FISHERIES & AQUACULTURE. (PH/0115-690X). **2306**

JOURNAL OF FLUENCY DISORDERS. (US/0094-730X). **3595**

JOURNAL OF FLUID CONTROL, THE. (US/8755-8564). **2091**

JOURNAL OF FLUID MECHANICS. (UK/0022-1120). **2091**

JOURNAL OF FLUIDS ENGINEERING. (US/0098-2202). **2092**

JOURNAL OF FLUORESCENCE. (US/1053-0509). **4435**

JOURNAL OF FLUORINE CHEMISTRY. (SZ/0022-1139). **981**

JOURNAL OF FOLKLORE RESEARCH. (US/0737-7037). **2321**

JOURNAL OF FOOD BIOCHEMISTRY. (US/0145-8884). **2346**

JOURNAL OF FOOD DISTRIBUTION RESEARCH. (US/0047-245X). **2346**

JOURNAL OF FOOD PROCESSING AND PRESERVATION. (US/0145-8892). **2346**

JOURNAL OF FOOD PRODUCTS MARKETING. (US/1045-4446). **2346**

JOURNAL OF FOOD PROTECTION. (US/0362-028X). **2346**

JOURNAL OF FOOD QUALITY. (US/0146-9428). **2346**

JOURNAL OF FOOD SAFETY. (US/0149-6085). **2346**

JOURNAL OF FOOD SCIENCE. (US/0022-1147). **2346**

JOURNAL OF FOOD SCIENCE AND TECHNOLOGY. (II/0022-1155). **4193**

JOURNAL OF FORAMINIFERAL RESEARCH. (US/0096-1191). **5588**

JOURNAL OF FORECASTING. (UK/0277-6693). **5249**

JOURNAL OF FORENSIC ECONOMICS. (US/0898-5510). **1499**

JOURNAL OF FORENSIC IDENTIFICATION. (US/0895-173X). **3741**

JOURNAL OF FORENSIC SCIENCES. (US/0022-1198). **3741**

JOURNAL OF FORTH APPLICATION AND RESEARCH, THE. (US/0738-2022). **1279**

JOURNAL OF FRESHWATER ECOLOGY. (US/0270-5060). **2218**

JOURNAL OF FUNCTIONAL ANALYSIS. (US/0022-1236). **3513**

JOURNAL OF FUSION ENERGY. (US/0164-0313). **1949**

JOURNAL OF FUTURES MARKETS, THE. (US/0270-7314). **904**

JOURNAL OF GASTROENTEROLOGY AND HEPATOLOGY. (AT/0815-9319). **3747**

JOURNAL OF GAY & LESBIAN PSYCHOTHERAPY. (US/0891-7140). **2794**

JOURNAL OF GAY & LESBIAN SOCIAL SERVICES. (US/1053-8720). **2794**

JOURNAL OF GENERAL AND APPLIED MICROBIOLOGY, THE. (JA/0022-1260). **565**

JOURNAL OF GENERAL INTERNAL MEDICINE. (US/0884-8734). **3798**

JOURNAL OF GENERAL MICROBIOLOGY, THE. (UK/0022-1287). **565**

JOURNAL OF GENERAL PHYSIOLOGY, THE. (US/0022-1295). **582**

JOURNAL OF GENERAL PSYCHOLOGY, THE. (US/0022-1309). **4597**

JOURNAL OF GENERAL VIROLOGY, THE. (UK/0022-1317). **565**

JOURNAL OF GENETIC COUNSELING. (US/1059-7700). **548**

JOURNAL OF GENETIC PSYCHOLOGY, THE. (US/0022-1325). **4597**

JOURNAL OF GENETICS. (II/0022-1333). **548**

JOURNAL OF GENETICS & BREEDING. (IT/0394-9257). **548**

JOURNAL OF GEOCHEMICAL EXPLORATION. (NE/0375-6742). **2141**

JOURNAL OF GEODYNAMICS. (UK/0264-3707). **1384**

JOURNAL OF GEOGRAPHY (HOUSTON). (US/0022-1341). **2567**

JOURNAL OF GEOGRAPHY IN HIGHER EDUCATION. (UK/0309-8265). **2567**

JOURNAL OF GEOLOGY, THE. (US/0022-1376). **1385**

JOURNAL OF GEOMAGNETISM AND GEOELECTRICITY. (JA/0022-1392). **1407**

JOURNAL OF GEOPHYSICAL RESEARCH. (US/0148-0227). **1407**

JOURNAL OF GEOTECHNICAL ENGINEERING. (US/0733-9410). **1385**

JOURNAL OF GERIATRIC DRUG THERAPY. (US/8756-4629). **3753**

JOURNAL OF GERIATRIC PSYCHIATRY AND NEUROLOGY. (US/0891-9887). **3753**

JOURNAL OF GERONTOLOGICAL NURSING. (US/0098-9134). **3858**

JOURNAL OF GERONTOLOGICAL NURSING. (US/0098-9134). **3858**

JOURNAL OF GERONTOLOGICAL SOCIAL WORK. (US/0163-4372). **5292**

JOURNAL OF GERONTOLOGY (KIRKWOOD). (US/0022-1422). **3753**

JOURNAL OF GLACIOLOGY, THE. (UK/0022-1430). **1416**

JOURNAL OF GLOBAL INFORMATION MANAGEMENT. (US/1062-7375). **3220**

JOURNAL OF GLOBAL MARKETING. (US/0891-1762). **927**

JOURNAL OF GLOBAL OPTIMIZATION : AN INTERNATIONAL JOURNAL DEALING WITH THEORETICAL AND COMPUTATIONAL ASPECTS OF SEEKING GLOBAL OPTIMA AND THEIR APPLICATIONS IN SCIENCE, MANAGEMENT AND ENGINEERING. (NE/0925-5001). **3513**

JOURNAL OF GRAPH THEORY. (US/0364-9024). **3513**

JOURNAL OF GREAT LAKES RESEARCH. (US/0380-1330). **1416**

JOURNAL OF GYNECOLOGIC SURGERY. (US/1042-4067). **3763**

JOURNAL OF HALACHA AND CONTEMPORARY SOCIETY. (US/0730-2614). **5050**

JOURNAL OF HAND SURGERY (ST. LOUIS, MO.), THE. (US/0363-5023). **3967**

JOURNAL OF HAND THERAPY. (US/0894-1130). **4380**

JOURNAL OF HAZARDOUS MATERIALS. (NE/0304-3894). **2234**

JOURNAL OF HEAD TRAUMA REHABILITATION, THE. (US/0885-9701). **4380**

JOURNAL OF HEALTH ADMINISTRATION EDUCATION, THE. (US/0735-6722). **4786**

JOURNAL OF HEALTH AND SOCIAL BEHAVIOR. (US/0022-1465). **4786**

JOURNAL OF HEALTH & SOCIAL POLICY. (US/0897-7186). **5292**

JOURNAL OF HEALTH CARE CHAPLAINCY. (US/0885-4726). **4969**

JOURNAL OF HEALTH CARE FOR THE POOR AND UNDERSERVED. (US/1049-2089). **4786**

JOURNAL OF HEALTH ECONOMICS. (NE/0167-6296). **1499**

JOURNAL OF HEALTH EDUCATION. ASSOCIATION FOR THE ADVANCEMENT OF HEALTH EDUCATION. (US/1055-6699). **4786**

JOURNAL OF HEALTH OCCUPATIONS EDUCATION. (US/0890-6874). **3595**

JOURNAL OF HEALTH POLITICS, POLICY AND LAW. (US/0361-6878). **2987**

JOURNAL OF HEALTHCARE MATERIAL MANAGEMENT. (US/0889-2482). **3787**

JOURNAL OF HEAT TRANSFER. (US/0022-1481). **1983**

JOURNAL OF HELMINTHOLOGY. (UK/0022-149X). **5588**

JOURNAL OF HEMATOTHERAPHY. (US/1061-6128). **3798**

JOURNAL OF HEPATOLOGY. (NE/0168-8278). **3798**

JOURNAL OF HERBS, SPICES & MEDICINAL PLANTS. (US/1049-6475). **2421**

JOURNAL OF HEREDITY, THE. (US/0022-1503). **548**

JOURNAL OF HERPETOLOGY. (US/0022-1511). **5588**

JOURNAL OF HETEROCYCLIC CHEMISTRY. (US/0022-152X). **1042**

JOURNAL OF HIGH RESOLUTION CHROMATOGRAPHY : HRC. (GW/0935-6304). **1017**

JOURNAL OF HIGHER EDUCATION (COLUMBUS), THE. (US/0022-1546). **1833**

JOURNAL OF HISPANIC PHILOLOGY. (US/0147-5460). **3290**

JOURNAL OF HISTOCHEMISTRY AND CYTOCHEMISTRY, THE. (US/0022-1554). **537**

JOURNAL OF HISTORICAL GEOGRAPHY. (UK/0305-7488). **2567**

JOURNAL OF HISTORY AND POLITICS. (US/0228-6939). **2621**

JOURNAL OF HISTOTECHNOLOGY. (US/0147-8885). **538**

JOURNAL OF HOME ECONOMICS (WASHINGTON). (US/0022-1570). **2791**

JOURNAL OF HOMOSEXUALITY. (US/0091-8369). **2795**

JOURNAL OF HORTICULTURAL SCIENCE, THE. (UK/0022-1589). **2421**

JOURNAL OF HOSPITAL INFECTION, THE. (US/0195-6701). **3714**

JOURNAL OF HOSPITAL MARKETING. (US/0883-7570). **3787**

JOURNAL OF HOSPITALITY & LEISURE MARKETING. (US/1050-7051). **4851**

JOURNAL OF HOUSING FOR THE ELDERLY. (US/0276-3893). **2826**

JOURNAL OF HUMAN EVOLUTION. (UK/0047-2484). **239**

JOURNAL OF HUMAN HYPERTENSION. (UK/0950-9240). **3707**

JOURNAL OF HUMAN LACTATION. (US/0890-3344). **3763**

JOURNAL OF HUMAN MOVEMENT STUDIES. (UK/0306-7297). **583**

JOURNAL OF HUMAN NUTRITION AND DIETETICS. (UK/0952-3871). **4193**

JOURNAL OF HUMAN RESOURCES, THE. (US/0022-166X). **1914**

JOURNAL OF HUMANISTIC PSYCHOLOGY, THE. (US/0022-1678). **4597**

JOURNAL OF HYDRAULIC RESEARCH. (NE/0022-1686). **2092**

JOURNAL OF HYDROLOGY (AMSTERDAM). (NE/0022-1694). **1416**

JOURNAL OF HYDROLOGY, NEW ZEALAND. (NZ/0022-1708). **1416**

JOURNAL OF HYMENOPTERA RESEARCH. (US/1070-9428). **5610**

JOURNAL OF HYPERBARIC MEDICINE. (US/0884-1225). **3595**

JOURNAL OF HYPERTENSION. (US/0263-6352). **3707**

JOURNAL OF IMMUNOASSAY. (US/0197-1522). **3673**

JOURNAL OF IMMUNOLOGICAL METHODS. (NE/0022-1759). **3673**

JOURNAL OF IMMUNOLOGY (1950), THE. (US/0022-1767). **3673**

JOURNAL OF INCLUSION PHENOMENA AND MOLECULAR RECOGNITION IN CHEMISTRY. (NE/0923-0750). **1054**

JOURNAL OF INDIAN PHILOSOPHY. (NE/0022-1791). **4350**

JOURNAL OF INDIGENOUS STUDIES, THE. (CN/0838-4711). **2741**

JOURNAL OF INDO-EUROPEAN STUDIES : MONOGRAPH SERIES. (US/0895-7258). **5206**

JOURNAL OF INDUSTRIAL ECONOMICS, THE. (UK/0022-1821). **1614**

JOURNAL OF INDUSTRIAL MICROBIOLOGY. (NE/0169-4146). **565**

JOURNAL OF INDUSTRIAL TEACHER EDUCATION. (US/0022-1864). **1914**

JOURNAL OF INDUSTRIAL TECHNOLOGY / THE NATIONAL ASSOCIATION OF INDUSTRIAL TECHNOLOGY. (US/0882-6404). **5118**

JOURNAL OF INFECTION, THE. (UK/0163-4453). **3714**

JOURNAL OF INFECTIOUS DISEASE PHARMACOTHERAPY. (US/1068-7777). **4311**

JOURNAL OF INFECTIOUS DISEASES, THE. (US/0022-1899). **3714**

JOURNAL OF INFORMATION NETWORKING. (UK/0966-9248). **1242**

JOURNAL OF INFORMATION RECORDING MATERIALS (1985). (GW/0863-0453). **4371**

JOURNAL OF INFORMATION SCIENCE. (NE/0165-5515). **3220**

JOURNAL OF INFORMATION TECHNOLOGY MANAGEMENT. (US/1042-1319). **873**

JOURNAL OF INHERITED METABOLIC DISEASE. (UK/0141-8955). **3798**

JOURNAL OF INORGANIC AND ORGANOMETALLIC POLYMERS. (US/1053-0495). **981**

JOURNAL OF INORGANIC BIOCHEMISTRY. (US/0162-0134). **489**

JOURNAL OF INSECT PHYSIOLOGY. (UK/0022-1910). **5610**

JOURNAL OF INSURANCE MEDICINE (NEW YORK, N.Y.). (US/0743-6661). **2885**

JOURNAL OF INTELLIGENT & ROBOTIC SYSTEMS. (NE/0921-0296). **1220**

JOURNAL OF INTELLIGENT INFORMATION SYSTEMS: INTEGRATING ARTIFICIAL INTELLIGENCE AND DATABASE TECHNOLOGIES. (US/0925-9902). **1214**

JOURNAL OF INTELLIGENT MANUFACTURING. (UK/0956-5515). **1214**

JOURNAL OF INTELLIGENT SYSTEMS. (UK/0334-1860). **1214**

JOURNAL OF INTERAMERICAN STUDIES AND WORLD AFFAIRS. (US/0022-1937). **4527**

JOURNAL OF INTERDISCIPLINARY CYCLE RESEARCH. (NE/0022-1945). **461**

JOURNAL OF INTERDISCIPLINARY HISTORY, THE. (US/0022-1953). **2621**

JOURNAL OF INTERDISCIPLINARY STUDIES. (US/0890-0132). **4969**

JOURNAL OF INTERFERON RESEARCH. (US/0197-8357). **565**

JOURNAL OF INTERIOR DESIGN EDUCATION AND RESEARCH. (US/0147-0418). **2901**

JOURNAL OF INTERLIBRARY LOAN & INFORMATION SUPPLY. (US/1042-4458). **3220**

JOURNAL OF INTERNAL MEDICINE. (UK/0954-6820). **3798**

JOURNAL OF INTERNATIONAL AND COMPARATIVE SOCIAL WELFARE. (US/0898-5847). **5292**

JOURNAL OF INTERNATIONAL BUSINESS STUDIES. (CN/0047-2506). **687**

JOURNAL OF INTERNATIONAL CONSUMER MARKETING. (US/0896-1530). **928**

JOURNAL OF INTERNATIONAL DEVELOPMENT. (UK/0954-1748). **1500**

JOURNAL OF INTERNATIONAL ECONOMICS. (NE/0022-1996). **1637**

JOURNAL OF INTERNATIONAL FINANCIAL MARKETS, INSTITUTIONS & MONEY. (US/1042-4431). **1637**

JOURNAL OF INTERNATIONAL FOOD & AGRIBUSINESS MARKETING. (US/0897-4438). **2347**

JOURNAL OF INTERNATIONAL MARKETING (EAST LANSING, MICH.). (US/1069-031X). **928**

JOURNAL OF INTERNATIONAL MEDICAL RESEARCH, THE. (UK/0300-0605). **3595**

JOURNAL OF INTERNATIONAL MONEY AND FINANCE. (UK/0261-5606). **795**

JOURNAL OF INTERNATIONAL TRADE AND ECONOMIC DEVELOPMENT. (UK/0963-8199). **1637**

JOURNAL OF INTRAVENOUS NURSING. (US/0896-5846). **3858**

JOURNAL OF INVERTEBRATE PATHOLOGY. (US/0022-2011). **5611**

JOURNAL OF INVESTIGATIVE DERMATOLOGY, THE. (US/0022-202X). **3721**

JOURNAL OF INVESTIGATIVE SURGERY. (US/0894-1939). **3967**

JOURNAL OF INVESTING, THE. (US/1068-0896). **904**

JOURNAL OF INVITATIONAL THEORY AND PRACTICE. (US/1060-6041). **1898**

JOURNAL OF IRRIGATION AND DRAINAGE ENGINEERING. (US/0733-9437). **2092**

JOURNAL OF JAPANESE STUDIES, THE. (US/0095-6848). **2655**

JOURNAL OF KOREAN STUDIES (SEATTLE, WASH. : 1979), THE. (US/0731-1613). **2655**

JOURNAL OF LABELLED COMPOUNDS & RADIOPHARMACEUTICALS. (UK/0362-4803). **1054**

JOURNAL OF LABOR ECONOMICS. (US/0734-306X). **1500**

JOURNAL OF LABOR RESEARCH. (US/0195-3613). **1682**

JOURNAL OF LABORATORY AND CLINICAL MEDICINE, THE. (US/0022-2143). **3595**

JOURNAL OF LAPAROENDOSCOPIC SURGERY. (US/1052-3901). **3967**

JOURNAL OF LARYNGOLOGY AND OTOLOGY. (UK/0022-2151). **3889**

JOURNAL OF LATIN AMERICAN STUDIES. (UK/0022-216X). **2741**

JOURNAL OF LAW & ECONOMICS, THE. (US/0022-2186). **2988**

JOURNAL OF LAW & EDUCATION. (US/0275-6072). **1865**

JOURNAL OF LAW AND ETHICS IN DENTISTRY. (US/0894-8879). **1327**

JOURNAL OF LAW AND SOCIETY. (UK/0263-323X). **2988**

JOURNAL OF LEARNING DISABILITIES. (US/0022-2194). **1880**

JOURNAL OF LEGAL ASPECTS OF SPORT. (US/1072-0316). **2988**

JOURNAL OF LEGAL ECONOMICS. (US/1054-3023). **1500**

JOURNAL OF LEGAL EDUCATION. (US/0022-2208). **2988**

JOURNAL OF LEGAL MEDICINE (CHICAGO. 1979), THE. (US/0194-7648). **3741**

JOURNAL OF LEGAL STUDIES, THE. (US/0047-2530). **2988**

JOURNAL OF LEISURABILITY (1980). (CN/0711-222X). **4389**

JOURNAL OF LEISURE RESEARCH. (US/0022-2216). **4851**

JOURNAL OF LEUKOCYTE BIOLOGY. (US/0741-5400). **3799**

JOURNAL OF LIBRARY ADMINISTRATION. (US/0193-0826). **3220**

JOURNAL OF LIGHTWAVE TECHNOLOGY. (US/0733-8724). **4436**

JOURNAL OF LINGUISTICS. (UK/0022-2267). **3290**

JOURNAL OF LIPID MEDIATORS. (NE/0921-8319). **1042**

JOURNAL OF LIPID RESEARCH. (US/0022-2275). **583**

JOURNAL OF LIQUID CHROMATOGRAPHY. (US/0148-3919). **1017**

JOURNAL OF LOGIC, LANGUAGE, AND INFORMATION. (NE/0925-8531). **4350**

JOURNAL OF LOGIC PROGRAMMING, THE. (US/0743-1066). **1280**

JOURNAL OF LONG TERM CARE ADMINISTRATION, THE. (US/0093-4445). **3787**

JOURNAL OF LONG-TERM EFFECTS OF MEDICAL IMPLANTS. (US/1050-6934). **3595**

JOURNAL OF LOSS PREVENTION IN THE PROCESS INDUSTRIES. (UK/0950-4230). **2099**

JOURNAL OF LOW TEMPERATURE PHYSICS. (US/0022-2291). **4409**

JOURNAL OF LUMINESCENCE. (NE/0022-2313). **4436**

JOURNAL OF MACROECONOMICS. (US/0164-0704). **1500**

JOURNAL OF MACROMOLECULAR SCIENCE. PHYSICS. (US/0022-2348). **4409**

JOURNAL OF MAGNETIC RESONANCE. (US/0022-2364). **4444**

JOURNAL OF MAGNETIC RESONANCE IMAGING. (US/1053-1807). **3942**

JOURNAL OF MAGNETISM AND MAGNETIC MATERIALS. (NE/0304-8853). **4444**

JOURNAL OF MANAGEMENT. (US/0149-2063). **873**

JOURNAL OF MANAGEMENT INQUIRY. (US/1056-4926). **874**

JOURNAL OF MANAGEMENT SYSTEMS, THE. (US/1041-2808). **943**

JOURNAL OF MANIPULATIVE AND PHYSIOLOGICAL THERAPEUTICS. (US/0161-4754). **4380**

JOURNAL OF MANUAL & MANIPULATIVE THERAPY, THE. (US/1066-9817). **3882**

JOURNAL OF MANUFACTURING SYSTEMS. (US/0278-6125). **3482**

JOURNAL OF MARITAL AND FAMILY THERAPY. (US/0194-472X). **2282**

JOURNAL OF MARKETING. (US/0022-2429). **928**

JOURNAL OF MARKETING CHANNELS. (US/1046-669X). **928**

JOURNAL OF MARKETING FOR HIGHER EDUCATION. (US/0884-1241). **1833**

JOURNAL OF MARRIAGE AND THE FAMILY. (US/0022-2445). **2282**

JOURNAL OF MATERIALS CHEMISTRY. (UK/0959-9428). **981**

JOURNAL OF MATERIALS EDUCATION, THE. (US/0738-7989). **2103**

JOURNAL OF MATERIALS ENGINEERING AND PERFORMANCE. (US/1059-9495). **2118**

JOURNAL OF MATERIALS RESEARCH. (US/0884-2914). **2103**

JOURNAL OF MATERIALS SCIENCE LETTERS. (UK/0261-8028). **2103**

JOURNAL OF MATERIALS SCIENCE. MATERIALS IN ELECTRONICS. (UK/0957-4522). **2069**

JOURNAL OF MATERIALS SCIENCE. MATERIALS IN MEDICINE. (UK/0957-4530). **3694**

JOURNAL OF MATHEMATICAL ANALYSIS AND APPLICATIONS. (US/0022-247X). **3513**

JOURNAL OF MATHEMATICAL BIOLOGY. (AU/0303-6812). **461**

JOURNAL OF MATHEMATICAL ECONOMICS. (NE/0304-4068). **1500**

JOURNAL OF MATHEMATICAL IMAGING AND VISION. (US/0924-9907). **3513**

JOURNAL OF MATHEMATICAL PHYSICS. (US/0022-2488). **4409**

JOURNAL OF MATHEMATICAL PSYCHOLOGY. (US/0022-2496). **4598**

JOURNAL OF MATHEMATICAL SOCIOLOGY, THE. (US/0022-250X). **5250**

JOURNAL OF MATHEMATICS OF KYOTO UNIVERSITY. (JA/0023-608X). **3514**

JOURNAL OF MAYAN LINGUISTICS. (US/0195-475X). **3291**

JOURNAL OF MEDECINE NUCLEAIRE ET BIOPHYSIQUE. (FR/0992-3039). **495**

JOURNAL OF MEDIA ECONOMICS. (US/0899-7764). **1115**

JOURNAL OF MEDICAL AND VETERINARY MYCOLOGY. (UK/0268-1218). **575**

JOURNAL OF MEDICAL ENGINEERING & TECHNOLOGY. (UK/0309-1902). **3694**

JOURNAL OF MEDICAL ENTOMOLOGY. (US/0022-2585). **5611**

JOURNAL OF MEDICAL ETHICS. (UK/0306-6800). **3596**

JOURNAL OF MEDICAL GENETICS. (UK/0022-2593). **549**

JOURNAL OF MEDICAL MICROBIOLOGY. (UK/0022-2615). **565**

JOURNAL OF MEDICAL PRIMATOLOGY. (SZ/0047-2565). **5513**

JOURNAL OF MEDICAL SPEECH-LANGUAGE PATHOLOGY. (US/1065-1438). **4390**

JOURNAL OF MEDICAL VIROLOGY. (US/0146-6615). **565**

JOURNAL — Peer Reviewed Index

JOURNAL OF MEDICINE AND PHILOSOPHY, THE. (NE/0360-5310). **3596**

JOURNAL OF MEDICINE (WESTBURY). (US/0025-7850). **3596**

JOURNAL OF MEMBRANE BIOLOGY, THE. (US/0022-2631). **538**

JOURNAL OF MEMBRANE SCIENCE. (NE/0376-7388). **5119**

JOURNAL OF MEMORY AND LANGUAGE. (US/0749-596X). **4598**

JOURNAL OF MENNONITE STUDIES. (CN/0824-5053). **4969**

JOURNAL OF MEN'S STUDIES, THE. (US/1060-8265). **3995**

JOURNAL OF MENTAL HEALTH ADMINISTRATION. (US/0092-8623). **5292**

JOURNAL OF METAMORPHIC GEOLOGY. (UK/0263-4929). **1458**

JOURNAL OF METEOROLOGY. (UK/0307-5966). **1426**

JOURNAL OF MICROBIOLOGICAL METHODS. (NE/0167-7012). **566**

JOURNAL OF MICROCOMPUTER APPLICATIONS. (UK/0745-7138). **1268**

JOURNAL OF MICROENCAPSULATION. (UK/0265-2048). **4311**

JOURNAL OF MICROPALEONTOLOGY. (UK/0262-821X). **4227**

JOURNAL OF MICROSCOPY (OXFORD). (UK/0022-2720). **572**

JOURNAL OF MICROWAVE POWER AND ELECTROMAGNETIC ENERGY, THE. (US/0832-7823). **2069**

JOURNAL OF MIDDLE ATLANTIC ARCHAEOLOGY. (US/0883-9697). **271**

JOURNAL OF MILITARY HISTORY, THE. (US/0899-3718). **4048**

JOURNAL OF MIND AND BEHAVIOR, THE. (US/0271-0137). **4598**

JOURNAL OF MINISTRY IN ADDICTION & RECOVERY. (US/1053-8755). **1346**

JOURNAL OF MISSISSIPPI HISTORY, THE. (US/0022-2771). **2741**

JOURNAL OF MODERN AFRICAN STUDIES, THE. (UK/0022-278X). **2640**

JOURNAL OF MODERN HISTORY, THE. (US/0022-2801). **2621**

JOURNAL OF MODERN LITERATURE. (US/0022-281X). **3345**

JOURNAL OF MOLECULAR AND CELLULAR CARDIOLOGY. (UK/0022-2828). **3707**

JOURNAL OF MOLECULAR BIOLOGY. (UK/0022-2836). **461**

JOURNAL OF MOLECULAR CATALYSIS. (SZ/0304-5102). **1054**

JOURNAL OF MOLECULAR ENDOCRINOLOGY. (UK/0952-5041). **3731**

JOURNAL OF MOLECULAR EVOLUTION. (GW/0022-2844). **549**

JOURNAL OF MOLECULAR GRAPHICS. (UK/0263-7855). **1234**

JOURNAL OF MOLECULAR LIQUIDS. (NE/0167-7322). **982**

JOURNAL OF MOLECULAR NEUROSCIENCE. (US/0895-8696). **3835**

JOURNAL OF MOLECULAR SPECTROSCOPY. (US/0022-2852). **4436**

JOURNAL OF MOLECULAR STRUCTURE. (NE/0022-2860). **1054**

JOURNAL OF MOLECULAR STRUCTURE. THEOCHEM. (NE/0166-1280). **1054**

JOURNAL OF MOLLUSCAN STUDIES. (UK/0260-1230). **5588**

JOURNAL OF MONETARY ECONOMICS. (NE/0304-3932). **1500**

JOURNAL OF MONEY, CREDIT, AND BANKING. (US/0022-2879). **795**

JOURNAL OF MORAL EDUCATION. (UK/0305-7240). **1758**

JOURNAL OF MORPHOLOGY (1931). (US/0362-2525). **583**

JOURNAL OF MOTOR BEHAVIOR. (US/0022-2895). **583**

JOURNAL OF MULTI-CULTURAL AND CROSS-CULTURAL RESEARCH IN ART EDUCATION. (US/0740-1833). **354**

JOURNAL OF MULTILINGUAL AND MULTICULTURAL DEVELOPMENT. (UK/0143-4632). **3291**

JOURNAL OF MULTINATIONAL FINANCIAL MANAGEMENT. (US/1042-444X). **1637**

JOURNAL OF MULTIVARIATE ANALYSIS. (US/0047-259X). **3514**

JOURNAL OF MUSCLE RESEARCH AND CELL MOTILITY. (UK/0142-4319). **538**

JOURNAL OF MUSIC THEORY PEDAGOGY, THE. (US/0891-7639). **4126**

JOURNAL OF MUSIC THERAPY. (US/0022-2917). **4126**

JOURNAL OF NATURAL HISTORY. (UK/0022-2933). **4166**

JOURNAL OF NATURAL PRODUCTS. (US/0163-3864). **1043**

JOURNAL OF NATURAL TOXINS. (US/1058-8108). **4311**

JOURNAL OF NATUROPATHIC MEDICINE, THE. (US/1047-7837). **3596**

JOURNAL OF NAVAJO EDUCATION. (US/1042-3265). **1758**

JOURNAL OF NEAR EASTERN STUDIES. (US/0022-2968). **3291**

JOURNAL OF NEAR INFRARED SPECTROSCOPY. (UK). **4436**

JOURNAL OF NEGRO EDUCATION, THE. (US/0022-2984). **1758**

JOURNAL OF NEMATOLOGY. (US/0022-300X). **5588**

JOURNAL OF NERVOUS AND MENTAL DISEASE, THE. (US/0022-3018). **3835**

JOURNAL OF NEURAL TRANSMISSION. GENERAL SECTION : JNT. (AU/0300-9564). **3835**

JOURNAL OF NEURAL TRANSMISSION. PARKINSON'S DISEASE AND DEMENTIA SECTION. (AU/0936-3076). **3835**

JOURNAL OF NEURO-ONCOLOGY. (US/0167-594X). **3819**

JOURNAL OF NEUROBIOLOGY. (US/0022-3034). **3835**

JOURNAL OF NEUROCHEMISTRY. (US/0022-3042). **3836**

JOURNAL OF NEUROCYTOLOGY. (UK/0300-4864). **538**

JOURNAL OF NEUROENDOCRINOLOGY. (UK/0953-8194). **3836**

JOURNAL OF NEUROGENETICS. (SZ/0167-7063). **549**

JOURNAL OF NEUROIMMUNOLOGY. (NE/0165-5728). **3836**

JOURNAL OF NEUROLOGICAL & ORTHOPAEDIC MEDICINE & SURGERY, THE. (US/0890-6599). **3967**

JOURNAL OF NEUROLOGY. (GW/0340-5354). **3836**

JOURNAL OF NEUROLOGY, NEUROSURGERY AND PSYCHIATRY. (UK/0022-3050). **3836**

JOURNAL OF NEUROPATHOLOGY AND EXPERIMENTAL NEUROLOGY. (US/0022-3069). **3836**

JOURNAL OF NEUROPHYSIOLOGY. (US/0022-3077). **3836**

JOURNAL OF NEUROPSYCHIATRY AND CLINICAL NEUROSCIENCES, THE. (US/0895-0172). **3929**

JOURNAL OF NEUROSCIENCE METHODS. (NE/0165-0270). **3837**

JOURNAL OF NEUROSCIENCE NURSING, THE. (US/0888-0395). **3859**

JOURNAL OF NEUROSCIENCE RESEARCH. (US/0360-4012). **3837**

JOURNAL OF NEUROSCIENCE, THE. (US/0270-6474). **3836**

JOURNAL OF NEUROSURGERY. (US/0022-3085). **3837**

JOURNAL OF NEUROSURGICAL ANESTHESIOLOGY. (US/0898-4921). **3967**

JOURNAL OF NEW JERSEY POETS. (US/0363-4205). **3464**

JOURNAL OF NON-CRYSTALLINE SOLIDS. (NE/0022-3093). **2591**

JOURNAL OF NON-EQUILIBRIUM THERMODYNAMICS. (GW/0340-0204). **4431**

JOURNAL OF NON-NEWTONIAN FLUID MECHANICS. (NE/0377-0257). **2092**

JOURNAL OF NONLINEAR BIOLOGY. (US/1047-1200). **495**

JOURNAL OF NONPROFIT & PUBLIC SECTOR MARKETING. (US/1049-5142). **928**

JOURNAL OF NONVERBAL BEHAVIOR. (US/0191-5886). **4598**

JOURNAL OF NUCLEAR MATERIALS. (NE/0022-3115). **2156**

JOURNAL OF NUCLEAR MEDICINE (1978), THE. (US/0161-5505). **3848**

JOURNAL OF NUCLEAR MEDICINE TECHNOLOGY. (US/0091-4916). **3848**

JOURNAL OF NUCLEAR SCIENCE AND TECHNOLOGY. (JA/0022-3131). **2156**

JOURNAL OF NUMBER THEORY. (US/0022-314X). **3514**

JOURNAL OF NURSE-MIDWIFERY. (US/0091-2182). **3859**

JOURNAL OF NURSING ADMINISTRATION, THE. (US/0002-0443). **3859**

JOURNAL OF NURSING EDUCATION, THE. (US/0148-4834). **3859**

JOURNAL OF NURSING STAFF DEVELOPMENT : JNSD. (US/0882-0627). **3859**

JOURNAL OF NUTRITION EDUCATION. (US/0022-3182). **4193**

JOURNAL OF NUTRITION FOR THE ELDERLY. (US/0163-9366). **4193**

JOURNAL OF NUTRITION IN RECIPE & MENU DEVELOPMENT. (US/1055-1379). **4193**

JOURNAL OF NUTRITION, THE. (US/0022-3166). **4193**

JOURNAL OF NUTRITIONAL IMMUNOLOGY. (US/1049-5150). **4193**

JOURNAL OF NUTRITIONAL SCIENCE AND VITAMINOLOGY. (JA/0301-4800). **4193**

JOURNAL OF OBJECT-ORIENTED PROGRAMMING. (US/0896-8438). **1280**

JOURNAL OF OBSTETRIC, GYNECOLOGIC, AND NEONATAL NURSING : JOGNN. (US/0884-2175). **3859**

JOURNAL OF OCCUPATIONAL AND ORGANIZATIONAL PSYCHOLOGY. (UK/0963-1798). **4598**

JOURNAL OF OCCUPATIONAL MEDICINE. (US/0096-1736). **2864**

JOURNAL OF OCCUPATIONAL MEDICINE AND TOXICOLOGY. (US/1054-044X). **3981**

JOURNAL OF OCEANOGRAPHY. (JA/0916-8370). **1450**

JOURNAL OF OCULAR PHARMACOLOGY. (US/8756-3320). **3876**

JOURNAL OF OFFENDER MONITORING. (US/1043-500X). **3167**

JOURNAL OF OFFENDER REHABILITATION. (US/1050-9674). **3167**

JOURNAL OF ONE-DAY SURGERY. (UK/0963-5386). **3968**

JOURNAL OF OPERATIONS MANAGEMENT. (US/0272-6963). **1614**

JOURNAL OF OPERATOR THEORY. (RM/0379-4024). **3514**

JOURNAL OF OPHTHALMIC PHOTOGRAPHY, THE. (US/0198-6155). **3876**

JOURNAL OF OPTICS. (US/0150-536X). **4436**

JOURNAL OF OPTIMAL NUTRITION, THE. (US/1061-2130). **4193**

JOURNAL OF OPTIMIZATION THEORY AND APPLICATIONS. (US/0022-3239). **3514**

JOURNAL OF OPTOMETRIC VISION DEVELOPMENT (1976). (US/0149-886X). **4216**

JOURNAL OF ORAL AND MAXILLOFACIAL SURGERY. (US/0278-2391). **3968**

JOURNAL OF ORAL PATHOLOGY & MEDICINE. (DK/0904-2512). **1327**

JOURNAL OF ORAL REHABILITATION. (UK/0305-182X). **1327**

JOURNAL OF ORGANIC CHEMISTRY. (US/0022-3263). **1043**

JOURNAL OF ORGANIZATIONAL BEHAVIOR. (UK/0894-3796). **4598**

JOURNAL OF ORGANIZATIONAL BEHAVIOR MANAGEMENT. (US/0160-8061). **4599**

JOURNAL OF ORGANOMETALLIC CHEMISTRY. (SZ/0022-328X). **1043**

JOURNAL OF ORTHOPAEDIC RESEARCH. (US/0736-0266). **3882**

JOURNAL OF ORTHOPAEDIC RHEUMATOLOGY. (UK/0951-9580). **3882**

JOURNAL OF OTOLARYNGOLOGY, THE. (CN/0381-6605). **3889**

JOURNAL OF PACKAGING TECHNOLOGY. (US/0892-029X). **4219**

JOURNAL OF PAIN AND SYMPTOM MANAGEMENT. (US/0885-3924). **3596**

JOURNAL OF PALEOLIMNOLOGY. (NE/0921-2728). **461**

JOURNAL OF PALEONTOLOGY. (US/0022-3360). **4227**

JOURNAL OF PALESTINE STUDIES. (US/0377-919X). **2655**

JOURNAL OF PALLIATIVE CARE. (CN/0825-8597). **5292**

JOURNAL OF PAN AFRICAN STUDIES, THE. (US/0888-6601). **5206**

JOURNAL OF PARALLEL AND DISTRIBUTED COMPUTING. (US/0743-7315). **1260**

JOURNAL OF PARAMETRICS. (US/1015-7891). **747**

JOURNAL OF PARAPSYCHOLOGY, THE. (US/0022-3387). **4241**

JOURNAL OF PARASITOLOGY, THE. (US/0022-3395). **5588**

JOURNAL OF PARENTERAL SCIENCE AND TECHNOLOGY. (US/0279-7976). **4311**

JOURNAL OF PASTORAL CARE, THE. (US/0022-3409). **4969**

JOURNAL OF PASTORAL THEOLOGY. (US/1064-9867). **4969**

JOURNAL OF PEACE RESEARCH. (NO/0022-3433). **4527**

JOURNAL OF PEASANT STUDIES, THE. (UK/0306-6150). **5250**

JOURNAL OF PEDIATRIC & PERINATAL NUTRITION. (US/8756-6206). **3905**

JOURNAL OF PEDIATRIC ENDOCRINOLOGY, THE. (UK/0334-018X). **3905**

JOURNAL OF PEDIATRIC GASTROENTEROLOGY AND NUTRITION. (US/0277-2116). **3905**

JOURNAL OF PEDIATRIC HEALTH CARE. (US/0891-5245). **3905**

JOURNAL OF PEDIATRIC NURSING. (US/0882-5963). **3859**

JOURNAL OF PEDIATRIC ONCOLOGY NURSING. (US/1043-4542). **3859**

JOURNAL OF PEDIATRIC OPHTHALMOLOGY AND STRABISMUS. (US/0191-3913). **3905**

JOURNAL OF PEDIATRIC ORTHOPEDICS. PART B. (US/1060-152X). **3882**

JOURNAL OF PEDIATRIC PSYCHOLOGY. (US/0146-8693). **4599**

JOURNAL OF PEDIATRIC SURGERY. (US/0022-3468). **3968**

JOURNAL OF PEDIATRICS, THE. (US/0022-3476). **3905**

JOURNAL OF PERINATAL & NEONATAL NURSING, THE. (US/0893-2190). **3859**

JOURNAL OF PERINATAL EDUCATION, THE. (US/1058-1243). **3764**

JOURNAL OF PERINATAL MEDICINE. (GW/0300-5577). **3764**

JOURNAL OF PERIODONTAL RESEARCH. (DK/0022-3484). **1327**

JOURNAL OF PERIODONTOLOGY (1970). (US/0022-3492). **1327**

JOURNAL OF PERSONALITY. (US/0022-3506). **4599**

JOURNAL OF PERSONALITY AND SOCIAL PSYCHOLOGY. (US/0022-3514). **4599**

JOURNAL OF PESTICIDE SCIENCE (TOKYO, 1975). (JA/0385-1559). **4245**

JOURNAL OF PETROLEUM GEOLOGY. (UK/0141-6421). **4262**

JOURNAL OF PETROLEUM SCIENCE & ENGINEERING. (NE/0920-4105). **4262**

JOURNAL OF PETROLEUM TECHNOLOGY. (US/0149-2136). **4262**

JOURNAL OF PETROLOGY. (UK/0022-3530). **1458**

JOURNAL OF PHARMACEUTICAL AND BIOMEDICAL ANALYSIS. (UK/0731-7085). **4311**

JOURNAL OF PHARMACEUTICAL MARKETING & MANAGEMENT. (US/0883-7597). **4311**

JOURNAL OF PHARMACEUTICAL SCIENCES. (US/0022-3549). **4312**

JOURNAL OF PHARMACOBIO-DYNAMICS. (JA/0386-846X). **4312**

JOURNAL OF PHARMACOEPIDEMIOLOGY. (US/0896-6966). **3596**

JOURNAL OF PHARMACOKINETICS AND BIOPHARMACEUTICS. (US/0090-466X). **4312**

JOURNAL OF PHARMACY AND PHARMACOLOGY. (UK/0022-3573). **4312**

JOURNAL OF PHARMACY TEACHING. (US/1044-0054). **4312**

JOURNAL OF PHARMACY TECHNOLOGY, THE. (US/8755-1225). **4313**

JOURNAL OF PHASE EQUILIBRIA. (US/1054-9714). **4006**

JOURNAL OF PHILOSOPHICAL LOGIC. (NE/0022-3611). **3291**

JOURNAL OF PHONETICS. (UK/0095-4470). **3291**

JOURNAL OF PHOTOCHEMISTRY AND PHOTOBIOLOGY. A, CHEMISTRY. (SZ/1010-6030). **1054**

JOURNAL OF PHOTOCHEMISTRY AND PHOTOBIOLOGY. B, BIOLOGY. (SZ/1011-1344). **1054**

JOURNAL OF PHOTOGRAPHIC SCIENCE, THE. (UK/0022-3638). **4371**

JOURNAL OF PHYCOLOGY. (US/0022-3646). **515**

JOURNAL OF PHYSICAL AND CHEMICAL REFERENCE DATA. (US/0047-2689). **4409**

JOURNAL OF PHYSICAL CHEMISTRY (1952). (US/0022-3654). **1054**

JOURNAL OF PHYSICAL EDUCATION, RECREATION & DANCE. (US/0730-3084). **1856**

JOURNAL OF PHYSICAL OCEANOGRAPHY. (US/0022-3670). **1450**

JOURNAL OF PHYSICAL ORGANIC CHEMISTRY. (UK/0894-3230). **1043**

JOURNAL OF PHYSICS. B : ATOMIC, MOLECULAR, AND OPTICAL PHYSICS. (UK/0953-4075). **4409**

JOURNAL OF PHYSICS. CONDENSED MATTER : AN INSTITUTE OF PHYSICS JOURNAL. (UK/0953-8984). **4409**

JOURNAL OF PHYSICS. D : APPLIED PHYSICS. (UK/0022-3727). **4410**

JOURNAL OF PHYSICS. G: NUCLEAR AND PARTICLE PHYSICS. (UK/0954-3899). **4448**

JOURNAL OF PHYSIOLOGY (LONDON). (UK/0022-3751). **583**

JOURNAL OF PINEAL RESEARCH. (DK/0742-3098). **583**

JOURNAL OF PLANKTON RESEARCH. (US/0142-7873). **5588**

JOURNAL OF PLANNING EDUCATION AND RESEARCH. (US/0739-456X). **2826**

JOURNAL OF PLANT GROWTH REGULATION. (US/0721-7595). **515**

JOURNAL OF PLANT NUTRITION. (US/0190-4167). **515**

JOURNAL OF PLANT PHYSIOLOGY. (GW/0176-1617). **516**

JOURNAL OF PLANT PROTECTION IN THE TROPICS. (MY/0127-6883). **100**

JOURNAL OF PLASMA PHYSICS. (UK/0022-3778). **4410**

JOURNAL OF POLICE AND CRIMINAL PSYCHOLOGY. (US/0882-0783). **3167**

JOURNAL OF POLICY ANALYSIS AND MANAGEMENT. (US/0276-8739). **4479**

JOURNAL OF POLICY MODELING. (US/0161-8938). **5206**

JOURNAL OF POLITICAL ECONOMY, THE. (US/0022-3808). **1500**

JOURNAL OF POLITICAL SCIENCE (CLEMSON). (US/0098-4612). **4479**

JOURNAL OF POLITICS, THE. (US/0022-3816). **4479**

JOURNAL OF POLYMER ENGINEERING. (IS/0334-6447). **2104**

JOURNAL OF POLYMER SCIENCE. PART A, POLYMER CHEMISTRY. (US/0887-624X). **1043**

JOURNAL OF POLYMER SCIENCE. PART B, POLYMER PHYSICS. (US/0887-6266). **1043**

JOURNAL OF POPULATION ECONOMICS. (GW/0933-1433). **4554**

JOURNAL OF PORTFOLIO MANAGEMENT. (US/0095-4918). **904**

JOURNAL OF POST ANESTHESIA NURSING. (US/0883-9433). **3859**

JOURNAL OF POST KEYNESIAN ECONOMICS. (US/0160-3477). **1593**

JOURNAL OF POTATO PRODUCTION & POSTHARVEST HANDLING. (US). **176**

JOURNAL OF POWER SOURCES. (SZ/0378-7753). **2118**

JOURNAL OF PRACTICAL APPLICATIONS OF SPACE. (US/1046-8757). **26**

JOURNAL OF PRACTICAL APPROACHES TO DEVELOPMENTAL HANDICAP. (CN/0707-7807). **4390**

JOURNAL OF PRAGMATICS. (NE/0378-2166). **3291**

JOURNAL OF PRE-RAPHAELITE STUDIES (1992), THE. (US/1060-149X). **2848**

JOURNAL OF PRESSURE VESSEL TECHNOLOGY. (US/0094-9930). **2118**

JOURNAL OF PRISONERS ON PRISONS. (CN/0838-164X). **3167**

JOURNAL OF PROBATION AND PAROLE : THE JOURNAL OF THE NEW YORK STATE PROBATION OFFICERS ASSOCIATION. (US/0278-1042). **3167**

JOURNAL OF PRODUCT INNOVATION MANAGEMENT, THE. (US/0737-6782). **687**

JOURNAL OF PROFESSIONAL NURSING. (US/8755-7223). **3860**

JOURNAL OF PROFESSIONAL SERVICES MARKETING. (US/0748-4623). **929**

JOURNAL OF PROGRESSIVE HUMAN SERVICES. (US/1042-8232). **5292**

JOURNAL OF PROMOTION MANAGEMENT. (US/1049-6491). **874**

JOURNAL OF PROPERTY RESEARCH. (UK/0959-9916). **4839**

JOURNAL OF PROPULSION AND POWER. (US/0748-4658). **26**

JOURNAL OF PROSTHETIC DENTISTRY, THE. (US/0022-3913). **1327**

JOURNAL OF PROSTHETICS AND ORTHOTICS. (US/1040-8800). **3597**

JOURNAL OF PROTEIN CHEMISTRY. (US/0277-8033). **490**

JOURNAL OF PROTOZOOLOGY, THE. (US/0022-3921). **5588**

JOURNAL OF PSYCHIATRIC RESEARCH. (UK/0022-3956). **3929**

JOURNAL OF PSYCHOACTIVE DRUGS. (US/0279-1072). **1346**

JOURNAL OF PSYCHOHISTORY, THE. (US/0145-3378). **4599**

JOURNAL OF PSYCHOLINGUISTIC RESEARCH. (US/0090-6905). **3291**

JOURNAL OF PSYCHOLOGY AND CHRISTIANITY. (US/0733-4273). **4969**

JOURNAL OF PSYCHOLOGY & HUMAN SEXUALITY. (US/0890-7064). **4600**

JOURNAL OF PSYCHOLOGY AND THEOLOGY. (US/0091-6471). **4600**

JOURNAL OF PSYCHOLOGY, THE. (US/0022-3980). **4600**

JOURNAL OF PSYCHOPATHOLOGY AND BEHAVIORAL ASSESSMENT. (US/0882-2689). **4600**

JOURNAL OF PSYCHOSOCIAL ONCOLOGY. (US/0734-7332). **3819**

JOURNAL OF PSYCHOSOMATIC OBSTETRICS AND GYNAECOLOGY. (NE/0167-482X). **3764**

JOURNAL OF PSYCHOSOMATIC RESEARCH. (UK/0022-3999). **3597**

JOURNAL OF PSYCHOTHERAPY PRACTICE AND RESEARCH, THE. (US/1055-050X). **3929**

JOURNAL OF PUBLIC ADMINISTRATION RESEARCH AND THEORY. (US/1053-1858). **4659**

JOURNAL OF PUBLIC ECONOMICS. (NE/0047-2727). **4734**

JOURNAL OF PUBLIC HEALTH DENTISTRY. (US/0022-4006). **1328**

JOURNAL OF PUBLIC POLICY & MARKETING. (US/0743-9156). **929**

JOURNAL OF PULP AND PAPER SCIENCE. (CN/0826-6220). **4234**

JOURNAL OF PURE AND APPLIED ALGEBRA. (NE/0022-4049). **3514**

JOURNAL OF QUALITY IN MAINTENANCE ENGINEERING. (UK/1355-2511). **874**

JOURNAL OF QUALITY TECHNOLOGY. (US/0022-4065). **5119**

JOURNAL OF QUANTITATIVE ANTHROPOLOGY. (NE/0922-2995). **239**

JOURNAL OF QUANTITATIVE SPECTROSCOPY & RADIATIVE TRANSFER. (UK/0022-4073). **4436**

JOURNAL OF QUESTIONED DOCUMENT EXAMINATION. (US/1061-3455). **3167**

JOURNAL OF RADIATION RESEARCH. (JA/0449-3060). **4436**

JOURNAL OF RADIOANALYTICAL AND NUCLEAR CHEMISTRY. (SZ/0236-5731). **1017**

JOURNAL OF RADIOLOGICAL PROTECTION. (UK/0952-4746). **4436**

JOURNAL OF RAMAN SPECTROSCOPY. (UK/0377-0486). **4436**

JOURNAL OF RANGE MANAGEMENT. (US/0022-409X). **100**

JOURNAL OF RAPTOR RESEARCH, THE. (US/0892-1016). **5588**

JOURNAL OF READING. (US/0022-4103). **1898**

JOURNAL OF READING BEHAVIOR. (US/0022-4111). **1758**

JOURNAL OF READING EDUCATION. (US/0886-5701). **1758**

JOURNAL OF REAL ESTATE TAXATION. (US/0093-5107). **4734**

JOURNAL OF REALITY THERAPY. (US/0743-0493). **4600**

JOURNAL OF RECONSTRUCTIVE MICROSURGERY. (US/0743-684X). **3968**

JOURNAL — Peer Reviewed Index

JOURNAL OF REGIONAL SCIENCE. (US/0022-4146). **1500**

JOURNAL OF REGULATION AND SOCIAL COSTS. (US/1054-8939). **1500**

JOURNAL OF REGULATORY ECONOMICS. (US/0922-680X). **843**

JOURNAL OF REHABILITATION. (US/0022-4154). **5292**

JOURNAL OF REINFORCED PLASTICS AND COMPOSITES. (US/0731-6844). **2104**

JOURNAL OF RELIGION AND HEALTH. (US/0022-4197). **4969**

JOURNAL OF RELIGION IN PSYCHOTHERAPY. (US/1045-5876). **3929**

JOURNAL OF RELIGIOUS & THEOLOGICAL INFORMATION. (US/1047-7845). **3220**

JOURNAL OF RELIGIOUS GERONTOLOGY. (US/1050-2289). **5180**

JOURNAL OF REPRODUCTION & FERTILITY. (UK/0022-4251). **3597**

JOURNAL OF REPRODUCTIVE AND INFANT PSYCHOLOGY. (UK/0264-6838). **3764**

JOURNAL OF REPRODUCTIVE IMMUNOLOGY. (NE/0165-0378). **3674**

JOURNAL OF REPRODUCTIVE MEDICINE. (US/0024-7758). **3764**

JOURNAL OF RESEARCH IN CHILDHOOD EDUCATION. (US/0256-8543). **1758**

JOURNAL OF RESEARCH IN CRIME AND DELINQUENCY, THE. (US/0022-4278). **3167**

JOURNAL OF RESEARCH IN PERSONALITY. (US/0092-6566). **4601**

JOURNAL OF RESEARCH IN PHARMACEUTICAL ECONOMICS. (US/0896-6621). **4313**

JOURNAL OF RESEARCH IN RURAL EDUCATION. (US/1062-4228). **1758**

JOURNAL OF RESEARCH IN SCIENCE TEACHING. (US/0022-4308). **5119**

JOURNAL OF RESEARCH ON CHRISTIAN EDUCATION. (US/1065-6219). **4970**

JOURNAL OF RESEARCH ON THE LEPIDOPTERA, THE. (US/0022-4324). **5611**

JOURNAL OF RESOURCE MANAGEMENT AND TECHNOLOGY, THE. (US/0745-6999). **2234**

JOURNAL OF RETAILING. (US/0022-4359). **955**

JOURNAL OF RHEOLOGY (NEW YORK, N.Y.). (US/0148-6055). **4428**

JOURNAL OF RHEUMATOLOGY, THE. (CN/0315-162X). **3805**

JOURNAL OF RISK AND INSURANCE, THE. (US/0022-4367). **2885**

JOURNAL OF RISK AND UNCERTAINTY. (US/0895-5646). **1500**

JOURNAL OF ROBOTIC SYSTEMS. (US/0741-2223). **1214**

JOURNAL OF ROMAN ARCHAEOLOGY. (US/1047-7594). **271**

JOURNAL OF RURAL HEALTH, THE. (US/0890-765X). **4787**

JOURNAL OF RURAL STUDIES. (UK/0743-0167). **5250**

JOURNAL OF SAFETY RESEARCH. (US/0022-4375). **2864**

JOURNAL OF SCHOOL HEALTH, THE. (US/0022-4391). **4787**

JOURNAL OF SCHOOL LEADERSHIP. (US/1052-6846). **1865**

JOURNAL OF SCHOOL PSYCHOLOGY. (US/0022-4405). **4601**

JOURNAL OF SCIENCE AND MATHEMATICS EDUCATION IN SOUTHEAST ASIA. (MY/0126-7663). **1758**

JOURNAL OF SCIENTIFIC EXPLORATION. (US/0892-3310). **5120**

JOURNAL OF SECONDARY GIFTED EDUCATION : JSGE, THE. (US/1077-4610). **1881**

JOURNAL OF SECURITY ADMINISTRATION. (US/0195-9425). **3168**

JOURNAL OF SEDIMENTARY PETROLOGY. (US/0022-4472). **1458**

JOURNAL OF SEED TECHNOLOGY. (US/0146-3071). **176**

JOURNAL OF SEMI-CUSTOM ICS. (UK/0264-3375). **2069**

JOURNAL OF SERVICES MARKETING, THE. (US/0887-6045). **929**

JOURNAL OF SEX & MARITAL THERAPY. (US/0092-623X). **5187**

JOURNAL OF SEX RESEARCH, THE. (US/0022-4499). **5187**

JOURNAL OF SHIP RESEARCH. (US/0022-4502). **4177**

JOURNAL OF SHOULDER AND ELBOW SURGERY. (US/1058-2746). **3968**

JOURNAL OF SLAVIC LINGUISTICS. (US/1068-2090). **3292**

JOURNAL OF SMALL ANIMAL PRACTICE, THE. (UK/0022-4510). **5513**

JOURNAL OF SMALL BUSINESS MANAGEMENT. (US/0047-2778). **874**

JOURNAL OF SOCIAL AND CLINICAL PSYCHOLOGY. (US/0736-7236). **4601**

JOURNAL OF SOCIAL AND PERSONAL RELATIONSHIPS. (UK/0265-4075). **4601**

JOURNAL OF SOCIAL BEHAVIOR AND PERSONALITY. (US/0886-1641). **4601**

JOURNAL OF SOCIAL DEVELOPMENT IN AFRICA. (RH). **5206**

JOURNAL OF SOCIAL HISTORY. (US/0022-4529). **5206**

JOURNAL OF SOCIAL ISSUES, THE. (US/0022-4537). **5206**

JOURNAL OF SOCIAL POLICY. (UK/0047-2794). **5293**

JOURNAL OF SOCIAL PSYCHOLOGY, THE. (US/0022-4545). **4601**

JOURNAL OF SOCIAL RESEARCH (RANCHI). (II/0449-315X). **239**

JOURNAL OF SOCIAL SERVICE RESEARCH. (US/0148-8376). **5293**

JOURNAL OF SOCIAL WORK & HUMAN SEXUALITY. (US/0276-3850). **5293**

JOURNAL OF SOCIOLOGY AND SOCIAL WELFARE. (US/0191-5096). **5293**

JOURNAL OF SOIL AND WATER CONSERVATION. (US/0022-4561). **2196**

JOURNAL OF SOIL SCIENCE, THE. (UK/0022-4588). **176**

JOURNAL OF SOLAR ENERGY ENGINEERING. (US/0199-6231). **1949**

JOURNAL OF SOLID STATE CHEMISTRY. (US/0022-4596). **982**

JOURNAL OF SOLUTION CHEMISTRY. (US/0095-9782). **1055**

JOURNAL OF SOUND AND VIBRATION. (UK/0022-460X). **4452**

JOURNAL OF SOUTH ASIAN AND MIDDLE EASTERN STUDIES. (US/0149-1784). **2769**

JOURNAL OF SOUTH ASIAN LITERATURE. (US/0091-5637). **3400**

JOURNAL OF SOUTHERN AFRICAN STUDIES. (UK/0305-7070). **2641**

JOURNAL OF SOUTHWEST GEORGIA HISTORY, THE. (US/0739-1943). **2742**

JOURNAL OF SPACECRAFT AND ROCKETS. (US/0022-4650). **26**

JOURNAL OF SPECIAL EDUCATION, THE. (US/0022-4669). **1881**

JOURNAL OF SPEECH AND HEARING RESEARCH. (US/0022-4685). **4390**

JOURNAL OF SPEECH-LANGUAGE-HEARING ASSOCIATION OF VIRGINIA. (US). **3889**

JOURNAL OF SPEECH-LANGUAGE PATHOLOGY AND AUDIOLOGY. (CN/0848-1970). **4390**

JOURNAL OF SPORT & EXERCISE PSYCHOLOGY. (US/0895-2779). **4901**

JOURNAL OF SPORT AND SOCIAL ISSUES. (US/0193-7235). **5250**

JOURNAL OF SPORT HISTORY. (US/0094-1700). **4902**

JOURNAL OF SPORTS MEDICINE AND PHYSICAL FITNESS. (IT/0022-4707). **3954**

JOURNAL OF SPORTS SCIENCES. (UK/0264-0414). **4902**

JOURNAL OF STAFF, PROGRAM & ORGANIZATION DEVELOPMENT, THE. (US/0736-7627). **1898**

JOURNAL OF STATISTICAL PHYSICS. (US/0022-4715). **4410**

JOURNAL OF STATISTICAL PLANNING AND INFERENCE. (NE/0378-3758). **3514**

JOURNAL OF STEROID BIOCHEMISTRY AND MOLECULAR BIOLOGY, THE. (UK/0960-0760). **462**

JOURNAL OF STORED PRODUCTS RESEARCH. (UK/0022-474X). **2347**

JOURNAL OF STRAIN ANALYSIS FOR ENGINEERING DESIGN, THE. (UK/0309-3247). **2118**

JOURNAL OF STROKE AND CEREBROVASCULAR DISEASES. (US/1052-3057). **3837**

JOURNAL OF STRUCTURAL ENGINEERING. (II/0970-0137). **2026**

JOURNAL OF STRUCTURAL GEOLOGY. (UK/0191-8141). **1385**

JOURNAL OF STUDIES IN TECHNICAL CAREERS. (US/0163-3252). **1914**

JOURNAL OF STUDIES ON ALCOHOL. (US/0096-882X). **1346**

JOURNAL OF SUBSTANCE ABUSE TREATMENT. (US/0740-5472). **1346**

JOURNAL OF SUNG-YUAN STUDIES. (US/1059-3152). **2505**

JOURNAL OF SUPERCOMPUTING, THE. (US/0920-8542). **1192**

JOURNAL OF SUPERVISION AND TRAINING IN MINISTRY. (US/0160-7774). **4970**

JOURNAL OF SURGICAL ONCOLOGY. (US/0022-4790). **3820**

JOURNAL OF SURGICAL RESEARCH, THE. (US/0022-4804). **3968**

JOURNAL OF SURVEYING ENGINEERING. (US/0733-9453). **2026**

JOURNAL OF SUSTAINABLE AGRICULTURE. (US/1044-0046). **100**

JOURNAL OF SYMBOLIC COMPUTATION. (UK/0747-7171). **3514**

JOURNAL OF SYMBOLIC LOGIC, THE. (US/0022-4812). **3515**

JOURNAL OF SYSTEMS AND SOFTWARE, THE. (US/0164-1212). **1280**

JOURNAL OF SYSTEMS INTEGRATION. (US/0925-4676). **1192**

JOURNAL OF SYSTEMS MANAGEMENT. (US/0022-4839). **687**

JOURNAL OF TAXATION, THE. (US/0022-4863). **4735**

JOURNAL OF TEACHER EDUCATION. (US/0022-4871). **1865**

JOURNAL OF TEACHING IN INTERNATIONAL BUSINESS. (US/0897-5930). **688**

JOURNAL OF TEACHING IN SOCIAL WORK. (US/0884-1233). **5293**

JOURNAL OF TEACHING PRACTICE. (AT/1030-407X). **1899**

JOURNAL OF TEACHING WRITING. (US/0735-1259). **3292**

JOURNAL OF TECHNICAL WRITING AND COMMUNICATION. (US/0047-2816). **1115**

JOURNAL OF TECHNOLOGY EDUCATION. (US/1045-1064). **5120**

JOURNAL OF TERRAMECHANICS. (UK/0022-4898). **2026**

JOURNAL OF TESTING AND EVALUATION. (US/0090-3973). **1983**

JOURNAL OF TEXAS CATHOLIC HISTORY AND CULTURE / TEXAS CATHOLIC HISTORICAL SOCIETY, THE. (US/1048-2431). **5031**

JOURNAL OF TEXTURE STUDIES. (US/0022-4901). **2347**

JOURNAL OF THE ACADEMY OF MARKETING SCIENCE. (US/0092-0703). **929**

JOURNAL OF THE ACOUSTICAL SOCIETY OF AMERICA, THE. (US/0001-4966). **4452**

JOURNAL OF THE AIR & WASTE MANAGEMENT ASSOCIATION. (US/1047-3289). **2196**

JOURNAL OF THE ALABAMA ACADEMY OF SCIENCE, THE. (US/0002-4112). **5120**

JOURNAL OF THE AMERICAN ACADEMY OF CHILD AND ADOLESCENT PSYCHIATRY. (US/0890-8567). **3929**

JOURNAL OF THE AMERICAN ACADEMY OF DERMATOLOGY. (US/0190-9622). **3721**

JOURNAL OF THE AMERICAN ACADEMY OF NURSE PRACTITIONERS. (US/1041-2972). **3860**

JOURNAL OF THE AMERICAN ACADEMY OF PHYSICIAN ASSISTANTS. (US/0893-7400). **3597**

JOURNAL OF THE AMERICAN ACADEMY OF PSYCHOANALYSIS, THE. (US/0090-3604). **3930**

JOURNAL OF THE AMERICAN ANIMAL HOSPITAL ASSOCIATION, THE. (US/0587-2871). **5513**

JOURNAL OF THE AMERICAN CERAMIC SOCIETY. (US/0002-7820). **2591**

JOURNAL OF THE AMERICAN CHEMICAL SOCIETY. (US/0002-7863). **982**

JOURNAL OF THE AMERICAN COLLEGE OF CARDIOLOGY. (US/0735-1097). **3707**

JOURNAL OF THE AMERICAN COLLEGE OF DENTISTS, THE. (US/0002-7979). **1328**

JOURNAL OF THE AMERICAN COLLEGE OF NUTRITION. (US/0731-5724). **4194**

JOURNAL OF THE AMERICAN COLLEGE OF TOXICOLOGY. (US/0730-0913). **3982**

JOURNAL OF THE AMERICAN CREATIVITY ASSOCIATION. (US). **1758**

JOURNAL OF THE AMERICAN DENTAL ASSOCIATION (USA ED.), THE. (US/0002-8177). **1328**

JOURNAL OF THE AMERICAN DIETETIC ASSOCIATION. (US/0002-8223). **4194**

JOURNAL OF THE AMERICAN GERIATRICS SOCIETY. (US/0002-8614). **3753**

JOURNAL OF THE AMERICAN LEATHER CHEMISTS ASSOCIATION, THE. (US/0002-9726). **3184**

JOURNAL OF THE AMERICAN MEDICAL WOMEN'S ASSOCIATION (1972). (US/0098-8421). **3597**

JOURNAL OF THE AMERICAN MOSQUITO CONTROL ASSOCIATION. (US/8756-971X). **4245**

JOURNAL OF THE AMERICAN MUSICAL INSTRUMENT SOCIETY. (US/0362-3300). **4126**

JOURNAL OF THE AMERICAN OIL CHEMISTS' SOCIETY. (US/0003-021X). **1043**

JOURNAL OF THE AMERICAN OPTOMETRIC ASSOCIATION. (US/0003-0244). **4216**

JOURNAL OF THE AMERICAN PLANNING ASSOCIATION. (US/0194-4363). **2826**

JOURNAL OF THE AMERICAN PODIATRIC MEDICAL ASSOCIATION. (US/8750-7315). **3918**

JOURNAL OF THE AMERICAN PSYCHOANALYTIC ASSOCIATION. (US/0003-0651). **4601**

JOURNAL OF THE AMERICAN SOCIETY FOR HORTICULTURAL SCIENCE. (US/0003-1062). **2421**

JOURNAL OF THE AMERICAN SOCIETY FOR INFORMATION SCIENCE. (US/0002-8231). **3220**

JOURNAL OF THE AMERICAN SOCIETY FOR MASS SPECTROMETRY. (US/1044-0305). **1017**

JOURNAL OF THE AMERICAN SOCIETY FOR PSYCHICAL RESEARCH (1932). (US/0003-1070). **4242**

JOURNAL OF THE AMERICAN SOCIETY OF BREWING CHEMISTS. (US/0361-0470). **982**

JOURNAL OF THE AMERICAN SOCIETY OF ECHOCARDIOGRAPHY. (US/0894-7317). **3707**

JOURNAL OF THE AMERICAN SOCIETY OF NEPHROLOGY. (US/1046-6673). **3991**

JOURNAL OF THE AMERICAN STATISTICAL ASSOCIATION. (US/0162-1459). **5329**

JOURNAL OF THE AMERICAN STUDIES ASSOCIATION OF TEXAS. (US/0587-5064). **2742**

JOURNAL OF THE ARIZONA-NEVADA ACADEMY OF SCIENCE. (US/0193-8509). **1357**

JOURNAL OF THE ARKANSAS MEDICAL SOCIETY, THE. (US/0004-1858). **3598**

JOURNAL OF THE ASSOCIATION FOR COMPUTING MACHINERY. (US/0004-5411). **1192**

JOURNAL OF THE ASSOCIATION OF AVIAN VETERINARIANS. (US/1044-8314). **5513**

JOURNAL OF THE ASSOCIATION OF NURSES IN AIDS CARE, THE. (US/1055-3290). **3860**

JOURNAL OF THE ASSOCIATION OF PHYSICIANS OF INDIA. (II). **3799**

JOURNAL OF THE ASSOCIATION OF TEACHERS OF JAPANESE, THE. (US/0885-9884). **3292**

JOURNAL OF THE ASTRONAUTICAL SCIENCES, THE. (US/0021-9142). **26**

JOURNAL OF THE ATMOSPHERIC SCIENCES. (US/0022-4928). **1427**

JOURNAL OF THE AUSTRALIAN MATHEMATICAL SOCIETY. SERIES A : PURE MATHEMATICS AND STATISTICS. (AT/0263-6115). **3515**

JOURNAL OF THE AUSTRALIAN MATHEMATICAL SOCIETY. SERIES B : APPLIED MATHEMATICS, THE. (AT/0334-2700). **3515**

JOURNAL OF THE AUSTRALIAN NAVAL INSTITUTE. (AT/0312-5807). **4178**

JOURNAL OF THE AUSTRALIAN WAR MEMORIAL. (AT/0729-6274). **4048**

JOURNAL OF THE AUTONOMIC NERVOUS SYSTEM. (NE/0165-1838). **3837**

JOURNAL OF THE BRITISH CONTACT LENS ASSOCIATION. (UK/0141-7037). **3876**

JOURNAL OF THE CHEMICAL SOCIETY, CHEMICAL COMMUNICATIONS. (UK/0022-4936). **982**

JOURNAL OF THE CHEMICAL SOCIETY OF PAKISTAN. (PK/0253-5106). **982**

JOURNAL OF THE CHRISTIAN MEDICAL FELLOWSHIP. (UK). **4970**

JOURNAL OF THE COMMUNITY DEVELOPMENT SOCIETY. (US/0010-3829). **5250**

JOURNAL OF THE COPYRIGHT SOCIETY OF THE U.S.A. (US/0886-3520). **1305**

JOURNAL OF THE DAGUERREIAN SOCIETY. (US). **4371**

JOURNAL OF THE EARLY REPUBLIC. (US/0275-1275). **2742**

JOURNAL OF THE ELECTROCHEMICAL SOCIETY. (US/0013-4651). **1034**

JOURNAL OF THE ELECTROCHEMICAL SOCIETY OF INDIA. (II/0013-466X). **1026**

JOURNAL OF THE ELISHA MITCHELL SCIENTIFIC SOCIETY. (US/0013-6220). **5120**

JOURNAL OF THE ENTOMOLOGICAL SOCIETY OF SOUTHERN AFRICA. (SA/0013-8789). **5589**

JOURNAL OF THE EUROPEAN ASSOCIATION OF MARINE SCIENCES AND TECHNIQUES. (NE/0924-7963). **1450**

JOURNAL OF THE EXPERIMENTAL ANALYSIS OF BEHAVIOR. (US/0022-5002). **4601**

JOURNAL OF THE FLORIDA MEDICAL ASSOCIATION (1974). (US/0015-4148). **3598**

JOURNAL OF THE FRANKLIN INSTITUTE. (US/0016-0032). **5120**

JOURNAL OF THE FRESHMAN YEAR EXPERIENCE. (US/1053-203X). **1833**

JOURNAL OF THE GEOLOGICAL SOCIETY. (UK/0016-7649). **1385**

JOURNAL OF THE GEOLOGICAL SOCIETY OF INDIA. (II/0016-7622). **1385**

JOURNAL OF THE GRASSLAND SOCIETY OF SOUTHERN AFRICA, THE. (SA/0256-6702). **101**

JOURNAL OF THE HERPETOLOGICAL ASSOCIATION OF AFRICA. (SA/0441-6651). **5589**

JOURNAL OF THE HISTORY OF BIOLOGY. (NE/0022-5010). **462**

JOURNAL OF THE HISTORY OF ECONOMIC THOUGHT. (US/1053-8372). **1500**

JOURNAL OF THE HISTORY OF IDEAS. (US/0022-5037). **4351**

JOURNAL OF THE HISTORY OF MEDICINE AND ALLIED SCIENCES. (US/0022-5045). **3598**

JOURNAL OF THE HISTORY OF THE BEHAVIORAL SCIENCES. (US/0022-5061). **4601**

JOURNAL OF THE IDAHO ACADEMY OF SCIENCE. (US/0536-3012). **5120**

JOURNAL OF THE IES. (US/1052-2883). **2176**

JOURNAL OF THE ILLINOIS SPEECH & THEATRE ASSOCIATION. (US/0145-5516). **5365**

JOURNAL OF THE ILLUMINATING ENGINEERING SOCIETY. (US/0099-4480). **2069**

JOURNAL OF THE INDIAN ACADEMY OF MATHEMATICS, THE. (II/0970-5120). **3515**

JOURNAL OF THE INDIAN CHEMICAL SOCIETY. (II/0019-4522). **982**

JOURNAL OF THE INDIAN INSTITUTE OF SCIENCE. (II/0019-4964). **5120**

JOURNAL OF THE INDIAN SOCIETY OF SOIL SCIENCE. (II/0019-638X). **177**

JOURNAL OF THE INTERNATIONAL LISTENING ASSOCIATION : JILA. (US). **1115**

JOURNAL OF THE INTERNATIONAL PHONETIC ASSOCIATION. (UK/0025-1003). **3292**

JOURNAL OF THE IOWA ACADEMY OF SCIENCE, THE. (US/0896-8381). **5121**

JOURNAL OF THE IRISH COLLEGES OF PHYSICIANS AND SURGEONS. (IE/0374-8405). **3598**

JOURNAL OF THE IRISH FAMILY HISTORY SOCIETY. (IE/0790-7060). **2455**

JOURNAL OF THE IRISH SOCIETY FOR LABOUR LAW. (IE/0790-0473). **3150**

JOURNAL OF THE KAFKA SOCIETY OF AMERICA. (US/0894-6388). **3345**

JOURNAL OF THE KANSAS ENTOMOLOGICAL SOCIETY. (US/0022-8567). **5611**

JOURNAL OF THE KUWAIT MEDICAL ASSOCIATION, THE. (KU/0023-5776). **3598**

JOURNAL OF THE LONDON MATHEMATICAL SOCIETY. (UK/0024-6107). **3515**

JOURNAL OF THE LOUISIANA STATE MEDICAL SOCIETY, THE. (US/0024-6921). **3599**

JOURNAL OF THE MALACOLOGICAL SOCIETY OF AUSTRALIA. (AT/0085-2988). **5589**

JOURNAL OF THE MARINE BIOLOGICAL ASSOCIATION OF THE UNITED KINGDOM. (UK/0025-3154). **555**

JOURNAL OF THE MARKET RESEARCH SOCIETY. (UK/0025-3618). **929**

JOURNAL OF THE MATHEMATICAL SOCIETY OF JAPAN. (JA/0025-5645). **3515**

JOURNAL OF THE MECHANICS AND PHYSICS OF SOLIDS. (UK/0022-5096). **2104**

JOURNAL OF THE MEDICAL ASSOCIATION OF GEORGIA. (US/0025-7028). **3599**

JOURNAL OF THE MIDWEST FINANCE ASSOCIATION. (US/0272-6637). **905**

JOURNAL OF THE MISSISSIPPI ACADEMY OF SCIENCES. (US/0076-9436). **5121**

JOURNAL OF THE NATIONAL ASSOCIATION OF ADMINISTRATIVE LAW JUDGES. (US/0735-0821). **3093**

JOURNAL OF THE NATIONAL CANCER INSTITUTE. (US/0027-8874). **3820**

JOURNAL OF THE NATIONAL MEDICAL ASSOCIATION. (US/0027-9684). **3599**

JOURNAL OF THE NATIONAL SCIENCE COUNCIL OF SRI LANKA. (CE/0300-9254). **5121**

JOURNAL OF THE NEUROLOGICAL SCIENCES. (NE/0022-510X). **3837**

JOURNAL OF THE NEUROMUSCULOSKELETAL SYSTEM. (US/1067-8239). **3805**

JOURNAL OF THE NEW YORK ENTOMOLOGICAL SOCIETY. (US/0028-7199). **5589**

JOURNAL OF THE NEW YORK STATE NURSES ASSOCIATION, THE. (US/0028-7644). **3860**

JOURNAL OF THE NEW ZEALAND SOCIETY OF PERIODONTOLOGY. (NZ/0111-1485). **1328**

JOURNAL OF THE NORTH AMERICAN BENTHOLOGICAL SOCIETY. (US/0887-3593). **2218**

JOURNAL OF THE OPERATIONAL RESEARCH SOCIETY, THE. (UK/0160-5682). **3515**

JOURNAL OF THE OPERATIONS RESEARCH SOCIETY OF JAPAN. (JA/0453-4514). **5121**

JOURNAL OF THE OPTICAL SOCIETY OF AMERICA. A, OPTICS AND IMAGE SCIENCE. (US/0740-3232). **4437**

JOURNAL OF THE OPTICAL SOCIETY OF AMERICA. B, OPTICAL PHYSICS. (US/0740-3224). **4437**

JOURNAL OF THE PENNSYLVANIA ACADEMY OF SCIENCE. (US/1044-6753). **5121**

JOURNAL OF THE PHILOSOPHY OF SPORT. (US/0094-8705). **4902**

JOURNAL OF THE PHYSICAL SOCIETY OF JAPAN. (JA/0031-9015). **4410**

JOURNAL OF THE POLYNESIAN SOCIETY. (NZ/0032-4000). **3292**

JOURNAL OF THE RIO GRANDE VALLEY HORTICULTURAL SOCIETY. (US/0485-2044). **2421**

JOURNAL OF THE ROYAL ASTRONOMICAL SOCIETY OF CANADA, THE. (CN/0035-872X). **396**

JOURNAL OF THE ROYAL COLLEGE OF PHYSICIANS AND SURGEONS OF THE UNITED STATES OF AMERICA : JRCP&S. (US). **3968**

JOURNAL OF THE ROYAL COLLEGE OF PHYSICIANS OF LONDON. (UK/0035-8819). **3599**

JOURNAL OF THE ROYAL SOCIETY OF MEDICINE. (UK/0141-0768). **3599**

JOURNAL OF THE ROYAL SOCIETY OF MEDICINE. SUPPLEMENT. (UK). **3599**

JOURNAL OF THE ROYAL SOCIETY OF NEW ZEALAND. (NZ/0303-6758). **5121**

JOURNAL OF THE ROYAL SOCIETY OF WESTERN AUSTRALIA. (AT/0035-922X). **4166**

JOURNAL OF THE ROYAL STATISTICAL SOCIETY. SERIES A (GENERAL). (UK/0035-9238). **5330**

JOURNAL OF THE ROYAL STATISTICAL SOCIETY. SERIES A: (STATISTICS IN SOCIETY). (UK). **5330**

JOURNAL OF THE ROYAL STATISTICAL SOCIETY. SERIES B (METHODOLOGICAL). (UK/0035-9246). **5330**

JOURNAL OF THE SCIENCE OF FOOD AND AGRICULTURE. (UK/0022-5142). **2347**

JOURNAL OF THE SCIENCE SOCIETY OF THAILAND. (TH/0303-8122). **5121**

JOURNAL OF THE SOCIETY FOR ARMENIAN STUDIES. (US/0747-9301). **2656**

JOURNAL OF THE SOCIETY OF COSMETIC CHEMISTS. (US/0037-9832). **1026**

JOURNAL OF THE SOCIETY OF DYERS AND COLOURISTS. (UK/0037-9859). **1026**

JOURNAL OF THE SOCIETY OF LEATHER TECHNOLOGISTS AND CHEMISTS. (UK/0144-0322). **3184**

JOURNAL OF THE SOUTH AFRICAN INSTITUTE OF MINING & METALLURGY. (SA/0038-223X). **2142**

JOURNAL OF THE SOUTH AFRICAN VETERINARY ASSOCIATION. (SA/0301-0732). **5513**

JOURNAL OF THE SOUTH CAROLINA MEDICAL ASSOCIATION (1975). (US/0038-3139). **3599**

JOURNAL OF THE SOUTHERN ORTHOPAEDIC ASSOCIATION. (US/1059-1052). **3883**

JOURNAL OF THE SOUTHWEST. (US/0894-8410). **2742**

JOURNAL OF THE STEWARD ANTHROPOLOGICAL SOCIETY. (US/0039-1344). **239**

JOURNAL OF THE TENNESSEE ACADEMY OF SCIENCE. (US/0040-313X). **5121**

JOURNAL OF THE TILES & ARCHITECTURAL CERAMICS SOCIETY. (UK/0264-5157). **302**

JOURNAL OF THE UNIVERSITY OF KUWAIT, SCIENCE, THE. (KU/0376-4818). **5121**

JOURNAL OF THE VIOLIN SOCIETY OF AMERICA. (US/0148-6845). **4127**

JOURNAL OF THE WEST. (US/0022-5169). **2742**

JOURNAL OF THEOLOGY. (US/0361-1906). **4971**

JOURNAL OF THEORETICAL BIOLOGY. (UK/0022-5193). **462**

JOURNAL OF THERMAL ANALYSIS. (UK/0368-4466). **1055**

JOURNAL OF THERMAL BIOLOGY. (UK/0306-4565). **462**

JOURNAL OF THERMAL SPRAY TECHNOLOGY. (US/1059-9630). **4006**

JOURNAL OF THERMAL STRESSES. (UK/0149-5739). **2119**

JOURNAL OF THERMOPHYSICS AND HEAT TRANSFER. (US/0887-8722). **4431**

JOURNAL OF THETA ALPHA KAPPA. (US/8756-4785). **4971**

JOURNAL OF THIRD WORLD STUDIES. (US/8755-3449). **1637**

JOURNAL OF THORACIC AND CARDIOVASCULAR SURGERY. (US/0022-5223). **3968**

JOURNAL OF THORACIC IMAGING. (US/0883-5993). **3600**

JOURNAL OF TISSUE VIABILITY. (UK/0965-206X). **538**

JOURNAL OF TOXICOLOGY AND ENVIRONMENTAL HEALTH. (US/0098-4108). **3982**

JOURNAL OF TOXICOLOGY. CLINICAL TOXICOLOGY. (US/0731-3810). **3982**

JOURNAL OF TOXICOLOGY. CUTANEOUS AND OCULAR TOXICOLOGY. (US). **3982**

JOURNAL OF TOXICOLOGY. TOXIN REVIEWS. (US/0731-3837). **3982**

JOURNAL OF TRACE ELEMENTS AND ELECTROLYTES IN HEALTH AND DISEASE. (GW/0931-2838). **3600**

JOURNAL OF TRANSCULTURAL NURSING. (US/1043-6596). **3860**

JOURNAL OF TRANSPERSONAL PSYCHOLOGY, THE. (US/0022-524X). **4602**

JOURNAL OF TRANSPLANT COORDINATION : OFFICIAL PUBLICATION OF THE NORTH AMERICAN TRANSPLANT COORDINATORS ORGANIZATION (NATCO). (DK/0905-9199). **3799**

JOURNAL OF TRANSPORT ECONOMICS AND POLICY. (UK/0022-5258). **5385**

JOURNAL OF TRANSPORTATION ENGINEERING. (US/0733-947X). **2026**

JOURNAL OF TRAUMA, THE. (US/0022-5282). **3969**

JOURNAL OF TRAVEL AND TOURISM MARKETING. (US/1054-8408). **5482**

JOURNAL OF TREE FRUIT PRODUCTION. (US/1055-1387). **177**

JOURNAL OF TROPICAL & GEOGRAPHICAL NEUROLOGY : THE OFFICIAL JOURNAL OF THE RESEARCH GROUP ON TROPICAL NEUROLOGY OF THE WORLD FEDERATION OF NEUROLOGY. (UK/0963-0880). **3837**

JOURNAL OF TROPICAL ECOLOGY. (UK/0266-4674). **2218**

JOURNAL OF TROPICAL MEDICINE AND HYGIENE. (UK/0022-5304). **3986**

JOURNAL OF TURBOMACHINERY. (US/0889-504X). **2119**

JOURNAL OF TURFGRASS MANAGEMENT. (US/1070-437X). **2422**

JOURNAL OF UFO STUDIES, THE. (US/0730-5478). **26**

JOURNAL OF UKRAINIAN GRADUATE STUDIES. (CN/0701-1792). **2695**

JOURNAL OF ULTRASOUND IN MEDICINE. (US/0278-4297). **3943**

JOURNAL OF URBAN ECONOMICS. (US/0094-1190). **1501**

JOURNAL OF URBAN HISTORY. (US/0096-1442). **2621**

JOURNAL OF UROLOGICAL NURSING. (US/0738-7350). **3991**

JOURNAL OF UROLOGY, THE. (US/0022-5347). **3991**

JOURNAL OF VACUUM SCIENCE & TECHNOLOGY. A: VACUUM, SURFACES, AND FILMS. (US/0734-2101). **4410**

JOURNAL OF VAISNAVA STUDIES, THE. (US/1062-1237). **4971**

JOURNAL OF VALUE INQUIRY, THE. (NE/0022-5363). **4351**

JOURNAL OF VASCULAR AND INTERVENTIONAL RADIOLOGY. (US/1051-0443). **3943**

JOURNAL OF VASCULAR NURSING. (US/1062-0303). **3860**

JOURNAL OF VASCULAR SURGERY. (US/0741-5214). **3969**

JOURNAL OF VASCULAR TECHNOLOGY, THE. (US/1044-4122). **3708**

JOURNAL OF VEGETABLE CROP PRODUCTION. (US/1049-6467). **177**

JOURNAL OF VETERINARY EMERGENCY AND CRITICAL CARE (SANTA BARBARA, CALIF.). (US/1056-6392). **5514**

JOURNAL OF VETERINARY INTERNAL MEDICINE. (US/0891-6640). **5514**

JOURNAL OF VETERINARY PHARMACOLOGY AND THERAPEUTICS. (UK/0140-7783). **5514**

JOURNAL OF VIROLOGICAL METHODS. (NE/0166-0934). **566**

JOURNAL OF VIROLOGY. (US/0022-538X). **566**

JOURNAL OF VISION REHABILITATION (LINCOLN, NEB.). (US/1041-0384). **3876**

JOURNAL OF VISUAL IMPAIRMENT & BLINDNESS. (US/0145-482X). **4390**

JOURNAL OF VLSI SIGNAL PROCESSING. (US/0922-5773). **2070**

JOURNAL OF VOCATIONAL AND TECHNICAL EDUCATION. (US/0888-8639). **1914**

JOURNAL OF VOCATIONAL BEHAVIOR. (US/0001-8791). **4602**

JOURNAL OF VOCATIONAL HOME ECONOMICS EDUCATION. (US). **2791**

JOURNAL OF VOLCANOLOGY AND GEOTHERMAL RESEARCH. (NE/0377-0273). **1408**

JOURNAL OF WATER RESOURCES PLANNING AND MANAGEMENT. (US/0733-9496). **5535**

JOURNAL OF WEATHER MODIFICATION, THE. (US/0739-1781). **1427**

JOURNAL OF WILDLIFE DISEASES. (US/0090-3558). **5514**

JOURNAL OF WILDLIFE MANAGEMENT, THE. (US/0022-541X). **2196**

JOURNAL OF WIND ENGINEERING AND INDUSTRIAL AERODYNAMICS. (NE/0167-6105). **1983**

JOURNAL OF WOMEN & AGING. (US/0895-2841). **5559**

JOURNAL OF WOMEN'S HEALTH. (US/1059-7115). **3600**

JOURNAL OF WOMEN'S HISTORY. (US/1042-7961). **5559**

JOURNAL OF WOOD CHEMISTRY AND TECHNOLOGY. (US/0277-3813). **1055**

JOURNAL OF WORLD HISTORY. (US/1045-6007). **2621**

JOURNAL OF WORLD TRADE. (SZ/1011-6702). **843**

JOURNAL OF XIAN MEDICAL UNIVERSITY. (CC/0258-0659). **3600**

JOURNAL OF YOUTH AND ADOLESCENCE. (US/0047-2891). **5207**

JOURNAL OF ZOO AND WILDLIFE MEDICINE : OFFICIAL PUBLICATION OF THE AMERICAN ASSOCIATION OF ZOO VETERINARIANS. (US/1042-7260). **5514**

JOURNAL OF ZOOLOGY (1987). (UK/0952-8369). **5589**

JOURNAL ON EXCELLENCE IN COLLEGE TEACHING. (US/1052-4800). **1833**

JOURNAL - TIMBER DEVELOPMENT ASSOCIATION OF INDIA. (II/0377-936X). **2402**

JOURNALISM HISTORY. (US/0094-7679). **2921**

JPEN, JOURNAL OF PARENTERAL AND ENTERAL NUTRITION. (US/0148-6071). **4194**

JPMS; JOURNAL OF POLITICAL & MILITARY SOCIOLOGY. (US/0047-2697). **5250**

JSME INTERNATIONAL JOURNAL. SERIES 2, FLUIDS ENGINEERING, HEAT TRANSFER, POWER, COMBUSTION, THERMOPHYSICAL PROPERTIES. (JA/0914-8817). **2119**

JSME INTERNATIONAL JOURNAL. SERIES 3, VIBRATION, CONTROL ENGINEERING, ENGINEERING FOR INDUSTRY. (JA/0914-8825). **2119**

JSME INTERNATIONAL JOURNAL. SERIES I, SOLID MECHANICS, STRENGTH OF MATERIALS. (JA/0914-8809). **2119**

JUDICATURE. (US/0022-5800). **2990**

JURIDICA. (MX). **2990**

JURIST (WASHINGTON), THE. (US/0022-6858). **5031**

JURNAL FIZIK MALAYSIA. (MY). **4410**

JURY: A HANDBOOK OF LAW AND PROCEDURE, THE. (CN). **2991**

JUSTICE SYSTEM JOURNAL, THE. (US/0098-261X). **3141**

JUSTICE TRENDS. (AT/0157-6011). **4510**

JUVENILE & FAMILY COURT JOURNAL. (US/0161-7109). **3121**

K-THEORY. (NE/0920-3036). **3516**

KAGAKU KOGAKU RONBUNSHU. (JA/0386-216X). **2014**

KAGENNA. (SA). **2499**

KAHPER JOURNAL (RICHMOND, KY.). (US/0022-7269). **1856**

KAHPERD JOURNAL (PITTSBURG, KAN.). (US/0893-3316). **1857**

KALEIDOSCOPE (AKRON, OHIO), THE. (US/0748-8742). **3401**

KALKI (ORADELL). (US/0022-7994). **3345**

KALLIOPE. (US/0735-7885). **323**

KANAWA MAGAZINE FOR RECREATIONAL PADDLING IN CANADA. (CN/1189-5152). **4874**

KANSAS BUSINESS REVIEW (LAWRENCE. 1977). (US/0164-8632). **688**

KANSAS HISTORY. (US/0149-9114). **2743**

KANSAS MEDICINE. (US/8755-0059). **3601**

KANSAS WORKING PAPERS IN LINGUISTICS. (US/1043-3805). **3293**

KANTOOR EN EFFICIENCY. (NE). **4212**

KARDIOLOGIJA. (RU/0022-9040). **3708**

KAUTSCHUK + GUMMI KUNSTSTOFFE. (GW/0022-9520). **5076**

KEATS-SHELLEY REVIEW. (UK). **3401**

KEMIJA U INDUSTRIJI. (CI/0022-9830). **983**

KEMISK TIDSKRIFT. (SW/0039-6605). **983**

KENTUCKY COLLEGE AND UNIVERSITY ENROLLMENTS. (US). **1795**

KENTUCKY POETRY REVIEW. (US/0889-647X). **3345**

KERNTECHNIK (1987). (GW/0932-3902). **2156**

KEY OPTHALMOLOGY. (US/0886-8026). **3876**

KHIMIIA PRIRODNYKH SOEDINENII. (UZ/0023-1150). **1043**

KIDNEY INTERNATIONAL. (US/0085-2538). **3991**

KIKAI GIJUTSU KENKYUJO SHOHO. (JA/0388-4252). **5123**

KINESIOLOGY AND MEDICINE FOR DANCE. (US/1058-7438). **1313**

KINESIS (CARBONDALE, ILL.). (US/0023-1568). **4351**

KINETICS AND CATALYSIS. (US/0023-1584). **1044**

KIPLING JOURNAL. (UK/0023-1738). **3402**

KIRTLANDIA. (US/0075-6245). **4167**

KITABAT. (BA). **3402**

KITH 'N KIN (FREMONT, OHIO). (US/1053-5837). **2457**

KIVA (TUSCON, ARIZ.), THE. (US/0023-1940). **272**

KLEINTIER-PRAXIS. (GW/0023-2076). **5515**

KLINICESKAJA MEDICINA. (RU/0023-2149). **3602**

KLINISCHE MONATSBLATTER FUER AUGENHEILKUNDE. (GW/0023-2165). **3876**

KLINISCHE PADIATRIE. (GW/0300-8630). **3906**

KLINISCHES LABOR. (GW/0941-2131). **5123**

KNOWLEDGE-BASED SYSTEMS (GUILDFORD, SURREY). (UK/0950-7051). **1193**

KNOWLEDGE (BEVERLY HILLS, CALIF.). (US/0164-0259). **5207**

KOBUNSHI RONBUNSHU (TOKYO). (JA/0386-2186). **984**

KOEDOE. (SA/0075-6458). **5589**

KOERS. (SA/0023-270X). **4351**

KOGNITIONSWISSENSCHAFT. (GW/0938-7986). **4602**

KOLNER ZEITSCHRIFT FUER SOZIOLOGIE UND SOZIALPSYCHOLOGIE. (GW/0023-2653). **5251**

KOREAN JOURNAL OF PARASITOLOGY. (KO/0023-4001). **3715**

KOVOVE MATERIALY. (XO/0023-432X). **4007**

KRANKENHAUSTECHNIK. (GW/0720-3977). **3787**

KREFELD IMMIGRANTS AND THEIR DESCENDANTS. (US/0883-7961). **2457**

KRIGSHISTORISK TIDSSKRIFT. (DK). **2622**

KRIMINALISTIK. (GW/0023-4699). **3168**

KRISTALLOGRAFIJA. (RU/0023-4761). **1032**

KRITERION. (BL/0100-512X). **4351**

KUEI SUAN YEN HSUEH PAO. (CC/0454-5648). **1037**

KUNG CHI TUNG LI HSUEH HSUEH PAO. (CC/0258-1825). **4411**

KYBERNETES. (UK/0368-492X). **1252**

KYBERNETIKA. (XR/0023-5954). **1252**

KYKLOS. (SZ/0023-5962). **5208**

LAB REPORT. (US/1045-7313). **3603**

LABOR AND EMPLOYMENT LAW ANTHOLOGY. (US). **3150**

LABOR HISTORY. (US/0023-656X). **1683**

LABOR HOSPITALARIA. (SP/0211-8262). **3787**

LABOR LAW JOURNAL (CHICAGO). (US/0023-6586). **3150**

LABORATORIUM PRAKTIJK. (NE). **463**

LABORATORY ANIMAL SCIENCE (CHICAGO). (US/0023-6764). **5515**

LABORATORY ANIMALS (LONDON). (UK/0023-6772). **5515**

LABORATORY INVESTIGATION. (US/0023-6837). **3896**

LABORATORY MEDICINE. (US/0007-5027). **3603**

LABOUR (HALIFAX). (CN/0700-3862). **1686**

LABOUR HISTORY REVIEW. (UK). **1686**

LAIT, LE. (FR/0023-7302). **196**

LAKARTIDNINGEN. (SW/0023-7205). **3603**

LAMAR JOURNAL OF THE HUMANITIES. (US/0275-410X). **2849**

LAMBDA ALPHA JOURNAL OF MAN. (US/0047-3928). **240**

LAN MAGAZINE. (NE). **1242**

LANCET (BRITISH EDITION). (UK/0140-6736). **3603**

LANCET (NORTH AMERICAN EDITION), THE. (US/0099-5355). **3603**

LAND + WATER / MILIEUTECHNIEK. (NE). **2027**

LANDSCAPE AND URBAN PLANNING. (NE/0169-2046). **2827**

LANDSCAPE ARCHITECTURAL REVIEW. (CN/0228-6963). **2422**

LANDSCAPE ECOLOGY. (NE/0921-2973). **2218**

LANDSCAPE RESEARCH. (UK/0142-6397). **2423**

LANDTECHNIK, DIE. (GW/0023-8082). **159**

LANGENBECKS ARCHIV FUER CHIRURGIE. (GW/0023-8236). **3969**

LANGMUIR. (US/0743-7463). **1055**

LANGUAGE & COMMUNICATION. (UK/0271-5309). **3294**

LANGUAGE AND LITERATURE (SAN ANTONIO, TEX.). (US/1057-6037). **3294**

LANGUAGE AND SPEECH. (UK/0023-8309). **3295**

LANGUAGE (BALTIMORE). (US/0097-8507). **3295**

LANGUAGE FORUM. (UK/1351-024X). **3295**

LANGUAGE IN SOCIETY. (UK/0047-4045). **3295**

LANGUAGE LEARNING. (US/0023-8333). **3295**

LANGUAGE LEARNING JOURNAL : THE JOURNAL OF THE ASSOCIATION OF LANGUAGE LEARNING. (UK/0957-1736). **3295**

LANGUAGE TEACHER / JAPAN ASSOCIATION OF LANGUAGE TEACHERS, THE. (JA/0289-7938). **3296**

LANGUAGES OF DESIGN. (NE/0927-3034). **3296**

LANGUES ET LINGUISTIQUE. (CN/0226-7144). **3296**

LARGE ANIMAL VETERINARIAN COVERING HEALTH & NUTRITION. (US/1043-7533). **5515**

LARYNGOSCOPE, THE. (US/0023-852X). **3889**

LASER AND PARTICLE BEAMS. (UK/0263-0346). **4437**

LASER CHEMISTRY. (SZ/0278-6273). **984**

LASER NURSING. (US/0888-6075). **3861**

LASERS AND LIGHT IN OPHTHALMOLOGY. (NE/0922-5307). **3876**

LASERS IN SURGERY AND MEDICINE. (US/0196-8092). **3969**

LATIN AMERICAN ANTIQUITY. (US/1045-6635). **273**

LATIN AMERICAN INDIAN LITERATURES JOURNAL. (US/0888-5613). **3403**

LATIN AMERICAN LITERARY REVIEW. (US/0047-4134). **3345**

LATIN AMERICAN PERSPECTIVES. (US/0094-582X). **4542**

LATIN AMERICAN RESEARCH REVIEW. (US/0023-8791). **2743**

LAUREL REVIEW / WEST VIRGINIA WESLEYAN COLLEGE, THE. (US/0023-9003). **3404**

LAURISTON S. TAYLOR LECTURES IN RADIATION PROTECTION AND MEASUREMENTS. (US/0277-9196). **4788**

LAW AND CONTEMPORARY PROBLEMS. (US/0023-9186). **2994**

LAW AND HUMAN BEHAVIOR. (US/0147-7307). **2994**

LAW AND PHILOSOPHY. (NE/0167-5249). **2994**

LAW & SOCIAL INQUIRY. (US/0897-6546). **2994**

LAW & SOCIETY REVIEW. (US/0023-9216). **2994**

LAW COMPUTERS AND ARTIFICIAL INTELLIGENCE. (UK). **1214**

LAW ENFORCEMENT INTELLIGENCE ANALYSIS DIGEST. (US/0895-3945). **3168**

LAW ENFORCEMENT LEGAL REVIEW. (US/1070-9967). **3107**

LAW FOR BUSINESS. (UK/0954-2809). **3101**

LAW LIBRARY JOURNAL. (US/0023-9283). **3222**

LAWYERS IN EUROPE. (UK/0959-0889). **3132**

LAWYER'S REGISTER INTERNATIONAL BY SPECIALTIES AND FIELDS OF LAW INCLUDING A DIRECTORY OF CORPORATE COUNSEL. (US/1061-7272). **3101**

LC GC. (US/0888-9090). **984**

LEAD BELLY LETTER. (US/1056-5329). **4128**

LEADER-TELEGRAM. (US/0891-0227). **5768**

LEAF (FORT COLLINS, COLO.), THE. (US/1064-0185). **2197**

LEARNING AND INSTRUCTION : THE JOURNAL OF THE EUROPEAN ASSOCIATION FOR RESEARCH ON LEARNING AND INSTRUCTION. (UK/0959-4752). **1899**

LEARNING AND MOTIVATION. (US/0023-9690). **4602**

LEARNING DISABILITY QUARTERLY. (US/0731-9487). **1881**

LEARNING RESOURCES JOURNAL. (UK/0268-2125). **1834**

LEBANON LIGHT. (US/1075-8852). **1093**

LEBENSMITTEL-INDUSTRIE, DIE. (SZ/0024-0028). **2791**

LEBER, MAGEN, DARM. (GW/0300-8622). **3747**

LEDGER, THE. (US). **5677**

LEGACY (FORT COLLINS, COLO.). (US/1052-3774). **4706**

LEGAL REFERENCE SERVICES QUARTERLY. (US/0270-319X). **3000**

LEGAL THEORY. (UK/1352-3252). **3001**

LEGAL WRITING : THE JOURNAL OF THE LEGAL WRITING INSTITUTE. (US). **3001**

LEGISLATIVE STUDIES QUARTERLY. (US/0362-9805). **4480**

LEISURE STUDIES. (UK/0261-4367). **4852**

LENDER LIABILITY LAW REPORT. (US/1045-1463). **3087**

LENGAS. (FR/0153-0313). **3297**

LENGUAS MODERNAS (SANTIAGO). (CL/0716-0542). **3297**

LEPROSY REVIEW. (UK/0305-7518). **3604**

LETHAIA. (NO/0024-1164). **4227**

LETRAS FEMENINAS. (US/0277-4356). **3404**

LETRAS PENINSULARES. (US/0897-7542). **3404**

LETTERS IN APPLIED MICROBIOLOGY. (UK/0266-8254). **566**

LETTERS IN MATHEMATICAL PHYSICS. (NE/0377-9017). **4411**

LETTRE ADA, LA. (FR). **1280**

LETTRE DE LA SURETE DE FONCTIONNEMENT, LA. (FR). **1616**

LETTRE DE REPORTERS SANS FRONTIERES, LA. (FR/1148-3164). **2922**

LETTRES BOTANIQUES (PARIS). (FR/0181-1797). **517**

LEUKEMIA. (UK/0887-6924). **3820**

LEUKEMIA RESEARCH. (UK/0145-2126). **3820**

LEWISTON - PORTER SENTINEL. (US). **5718**

LEXIS. (PE/0254-9239). **3297**

LIBERAL EDUCATION (WASHINGTON, D.C.). (US/0024-1822). **1834**

LIBERATOR (1988), THE. (US/1040-3760). **5251**

LIBERTAS MATHEMATICA. (US/0278-5307). **3517**

LIBRARIES & CULTURE. (US/0894-8631). **4829**

LIBRARY ACQUISITIONS : PRACTICE AND THEORY. (US/0364-6408). **3223**

LIBRARY & ARCHIVAL SECURITY. (US/0196-0075). **3224**

LIBRARY AND INFORMATION SCIENCE. (JA/0373-4447). **3224**

LIBRARY & INFORMATION SCIENCE ABSTRACTS. (UK/0024-2179). **3258**

LIBRARY & INFORMATION SCIENCE RESEARCH. (US/0740-8188). **3224**

LIBRARY JOURNAL (1976). (US/0363-0277). **3225**

LIBRARY QUARTERLY (CHICAGO), THE. (US/0024-2519). **3226**

LIBRARY RESOURCES & TECHNICAL SERVICES. (US/0024-2527). **3227**

LIBRARY SCIENCE WITH A SLANT TO DOCUMENTATION. (II/0024-2543). **3227**

LIBRARY SOFTWARE REVIEW. (US/0742-5759). **1288**

LIBRARY TRENDS. (US/0024-2594). **3227**

LIBRI (KBENHAVN). (DK/0024-2667). **3228**

LICHENOLOGIST (LONDON). (UK/0024-2829). **517**

LIEBIGS ANNALEN DER CHEMIE. (GW/0170-2041). **984**

LIGAND

Peer Reviewed Index

LIGAND QUARTERLY NOTIZIE TECHNICHE. (IT) **3604**

LIGHTING RESEARCH & TECHNOLOGY. (UK/0024-3426). **2071**

LIJECNICKI VJESNIK. (CI/0024-3477). **3604**

LIMNOLOGY AND OCEANOGRAPHY. (US/0024-3590). **1451**

LINDBERGIA. (SW/0105-0761). **517**

LINEAR ALGEBRA AND ITS APPLICATIONS. (US/0024-3795). **3517**

LINGUA (AMSTERDAM, NETHERLANDS). (NE/0024-3841). **3298**

LINGUISTIC ANALYSIS. (US/0098-9053). **3298**

LINGUISTIC INQUIRY. (US/0024-3892). **3298**

LINGUISTICA ATLANTICA : JOURNAL OF THE ATLANTIC PROVINCES LINGUISTIC ASSOCATION. (CN). **3299**

LINGUISTICS. (NE/0024-3949). **3299**

LINGUISTICS AND PHILOSOPHY. (NE/0165-0157). **3299**

LINK (WOODLAND HILLS). (US). **3837**

LINKS : SOZIALISTISCHE ZEITUNG. (GW/0024-404X). **4543**

LINQ. (AT). **3405**

LIPID FILE. (UK/0951-9599). **3708**

LIPIDS. (US/0024-4201). **583**

LIPPINCOTT'S REVIEWS. RADIOLOGY. (US/1059-2156). **3943**

LIQUID CRYSTALS. (UK/0267-8292). **1032**

LISP AND SYMBOLIC COMPUTATION. (US/0892-4635). **1280**

LITE FLYER. (US/1043-4968). **27**

LITE FLYER SAFETY ALERT ACTIONGRAM. (US/1043-495X). **27**

LITERATURE AND BELIEF. (US/0732-1929). **3407**

LITERATURE AND PSYCHOLOGY. (US/0024-4759). **3407**

LITHIC TECHNOLOGY. (US/0197-7261). **273**

LITHOS. (NO/0024-4937). **1441**

LITTERATURES (MONTREAL). (CN/0838-1453). **3408**

LITTEREALITE. (CN/0843-4182). **3408**

LITUANUS. (US/0024-5089). **2697**

LIVER (COPENHAGEN). (DK/0106-9543). **3799**

LIVERPOOL LAW REVIEW, THE. (UK/0144-932X). **3003**

LIVESTOCK PRODUCTION SCIENCE. (NE/0301-6226). **214**

LIVING MUSIC. (US/8755-092X). **4129**

LOCAL GOVERNMENT STUDIES. (UK/0300-3930). **876**

LOCKE NEWSLETTER, THE. (UK/0307-2606). **4352**

LOCUS (DENTON, TEX.). (US/0898-8056). **2744**

LOGISTICS AND TRANSPORTATION REVIEW, THE. (CN/0047-4991). **5386**

LOGOS (SANTA CLARA, CALIF.). (US/0276-5667). **4352**

LONDON DEFENCE STUDIES. (UK/0961-8422). **4049**

LONDON LOG. (UK). **5483**

LONG ISLAND HISTORICAL JOURNAL, THE. (US/0898-7084). **2744**

LONG ISLAND POSTAL HISTORIAN. (US). **1145**

LONG RANGE PLANNING. (UK/0024-6301). **876**

LOSS, GRIEF & CARE. (US/8756-4610). **4603**

LOT OF BUNKUM. YEARBOOK, A. (US/0882-2425). **2458**

LOTTA CONTRO LA TUBERCOLOSI E LE MALATTIE POLMONARI SOCIALI. (IT/0368-7546). **3950**

LOUISIANA ARCHAEOLOGY. (US/1071-7358). **273**

LOUISIANA HISTORY. (US/0024-6816). **2745**

LOUISIANA LAW REVIEW. (US/0024-6859). **3004**

LOUVAIN BREWING LETTERS. (BE/0777-8805). **2369**

LUA NOVA. (BL). **4352**

LUBRICATION ENGINEERING. (US/0024-7154). **2120**

LUCAS. (AT/1030-4428). **4975**

LUFTWAFFEN-FORUM. (GW). **28**

LUNG. (GW/0341-2040). **3950**

LUTHERAN EDUCATOR. (US/0458-4988). **1762**

LUTRA. (NE/0024-7634). **5590**

LYMAN ENTOMOLOGICAL MUSEUM AND RESEARCH LABORATORY MEMOIR. (CN/0318-6784). **4090**

LYMPHOLOGY. (US/0024-7766). **3773**

LYON CHIRURGICAL. (SZ/0024-7782). **3969**

LYSOSOMES IN BIOLOGY AND PATHOLOGY. (NE). **463**

M.D. COMPUTING. (US/0724-6811). **1268**

M-SERIES MONOGRAPHS. (AT). **5483**

MAARAV. (US/0149-5712). **3300**

MAAS JOURNAL OF ISLAMIC SCIENCE. (II/0970-1672). **5043**

MAC/CHICAGO (CHICAGO, ILL.). (US/1045-5825). **1193**

MACCHINE. (IT/0024-8959). **2120**

MACHINE LEARNING. (US/0885-6125). **1215**

MACHINE TRANSLATION. (NE/0922-6567). **1194**

MACPLAS. (IT/0394-3453). **4456**

MACROMOLECULES. (US/0024-9297). **1044**

MADOQUA. (SA). **2197**

MADOQUA (WINDHOEK. 1975). (SX/1011-5498). **4167**

MADRONO. (US/0024-9637). **517**

MAGAZINE OF CONCRETE RESEARCH. (UK/0024-9831). **2027**

MAGILL'S SURVEY OF CINEMA. (US/1065-6553). **4074**

MAGNESIUM AND TRACE ELEMENTS. (SZ/1015-3845). **985**

MAGNETIC RESONANCE IMAGING. (US/0730-725X). **3943**

MAGNETIC RESONANCE IN CHEMISTRY : MRC. (UK/0749-1581). **1044**

MAGNETIC RESONANCE IN MEDICINE. (US/0740-3194). **3943**

MAGNETS IN YOUR FUTURE. (US/0887-5707). **3943**

MAGYAR PEDAGOGIA. (HU/0025-0260). **1762**

MAINE NATURALIST (STEUBEN, ME.). (US/1063-3626). **4167**

MAINE SCHOLAR, THE. (US/1052-018X). **2850**

MAINLINES (INDIANAPOLIS, IND.). (US/0278-9450). **3861**

MAKROMOLEKULARE CHEMIE (BASEL, SWITZERLAND : 1981). (SZ/0025-116X). **1044**

MAKROMOLEKULARE CHEMIE. MACROMOLECULAR SYMPOSIA, DIE. (SZ/0258-0322). **1044**

MAKROMOLEKULARE CHEMIE. RAPID COMMUNICATIONS, DIE. (SZ/0173-2803). **1044**

MALACOLOGICAL REVIEW. (US/0076-3004). **5590**

MALADIES CHRONIQUES AU CANADA. (CN/0228-8702). **3606**

MALAYSIAN JOURNAL OF PATHOLOGY, THE. (MY/0126-8635). **3896**

MALAYSIAN JOURNAL OF TROPICAL GEOGRAPHY. (MY/0127-1474). **2568**

MALCOLM LOWRY REVIEW, THE. (CN/0828-5020). **3347**

MALPRACTICE PREVENTION REPORTER. (US/0739-6031). **3005**

MALPRACTICE REPORTER. PODIATRY, THE. (US/0749-3495). **3005**

MAMMAL REVIEW. (UK/0305-1838). **5590**

MAMMALIA (PARIS). (FR/0025-1461). **5590**

MAN AND WORLD. (NE/0025-1534). **4352**

MAN (CHICAGO, ILL.). (US/1062-2543). **2267**

MAN IN INDIA. (II/0025-1569). **240**

MAN IN THE NORTHEAST. (US/0191-4138). **240**

MAN (LONDON). (UK/0025-1496). **240**

MANAGEMENT AND MARKETING ABSTRACTS. (UK/0308-2172). **731**

MANAGEMENT INFORMATION SYSTEMS QUARTERLY. (US/0276-7783). **1194**

MANAGEMENT INTERNATIONAL REVIEW. (GW/0025-181X). **877**

MANAGEMENT SCIENCE. (US/0025-1909). **878**

MANCHESTER SCHOOL OF ECONOMIC AND SOCIAL STUDIES, THE. (UK/0025-2034). **1504**

MANCUNION : THE OFFICIAL NEWSPAPER OF MANCHESTER UNIVERSITY STUDENTS UNION. (UK). **1093**

MANHATTAN OFFICE BUILDINGS. MIDTOWN. (US/0886-3725). **4840**

MANITOBA LAW JOURNAL (1966). (CN/0076-3861). **3006**

MANITOBA PSYCHOLOGIST. (CN/0711-1533). **4603**

MANKIND QUARTERLY. (US/0025-2344). **240**

MANOA. (US/1045-7909). **3347**

MANUSCRIPTA MATHEMATICA. (GW/0025-2611). **3517**

MAPLINE. SPECIAL NUMBER. (US). **2582**

MAPPING AWARENESS & GIS EUROPE. (UK/0954-712636). **1242**

MAPS NEWS. (US). **4975**

MARINE AND PETROLEUM GEOLOGY. (UK/0264-8172). **1386**

MARINE BEHAVIOUR AND PHYSIOLOGY. (US/0091-181X). **583**

MARINE BIOLOGY. (GW/0025-3162). **556**

MARINE CHEMISTRY. (NE/0304-4203). **1451**

MARINE ECOLOGY (BERLIN, WEST). (GW/0173-9565). **2218**

MARINE ECOLOGY. PROGRESS SERIES (HALSTENBEK). (GW/0171-8630). **2218**

MARINE ENVIRONMENTAL RESEARCH. (UK/0141-1136). **2177**

MARINE FISHERIES REVIEW. (US/0090-1830). **2308**

MARINE GEOLOGY. (NE/0025-3227). **1386**

MARINE GEOPHYSICAL RESEARCHES. (NE/0025-3235). **1451**

MARINE GEOTECHNOLOGY. (US/0360-8867). **1451**

MARINE MAMMAL SCIENCE. (US/0824-0469). **1452**

MARINE MICROPALEONTOLOGY. (NE/0377-8398). **4228**

MARINE ORNITHOLOGY. (SA). **5618**

MARINE POLICY. (UK/0308-597X). **1452**

MARINE POLLUTION BULLETIN. (UK/0025-326X). **2236**

MARINE TECHNOLOGY SOCIETY JOURNAL. (US/0025-3324). **1452**

MARITIME ANTHROPOLOGICAL STUDIES : MAST. (NE/0922-1476). **241**

MARJORIE KINNAN RAWLINGS JOURNAL OF FLORIDA LITERATURE, THE. (US/1060-3409). **3410**

MARKETING PULSE, THE. (US/1065-9994). **931**

MARKETING RESEARCH (CHICAGO, ILL.). (US/1040-8460). **932**

MARKETING SCIENCE (PROVIDENCE, R.I.). (US/0732-2399). **932**

MARKETING SUCCESS. (UK/0961-7752). **932**

MARKETING TREASURES. (US/0895-1799). **932**

MARKETING TRIBUNE. (IT). **692**

MARRIAGE & FAMILY REVIEW. (US/0149-4929). **2283**

MARYLAND MEDICAL JOURNAL (1985). (US/0886-0572). **3606**

MASONRY SOCIETY JOURNAL, THE. (US/0741-1294). **620**

MASS COMM REVIEW. (US/0193-7707). **1116**

MASS SPECTROMETRY. (UK/0305-9987). **1017**

MASS SPECTROMETRY REVIEWS. (US/0277-7037). **1017**

MASSACHUSETTS NURSE, THE. (US/0163-0784). **3861**

MASTERPLOTS II. (US). **3410**

MATATU. (NE/0932-9714). **3410**

MATEMATICA APLICADA E COMPUTACIONAL. (US/0101-8205). **3517**

MATERIAL CULTURE. (US/0883-3680). **241**

MATERIALS CHEMISTRY AND PHYSICS. (SZ/0254-0584). **1055**

MATERIALS EVALUATION. (US/0025-5327). **2105**

MATERIALS LETTERS. (NE/0167-577X). **2105**

MATERIALS PERFORMANCE. (US/0094-1492). **2105**

MATERIALS RESEARCH BULLETIN. (US/0025-5408). **2105**

MATERIALS SCIENCE & ENGINEERING. A, STRUCTURAL MATERIALS : PROPERTIES, MICROSTRUCTURE AND PROCESSING. (SZ/0921-5093). **2105**

MATERIALS SCIENCE & ENGINEERING. B, SOLID-STATE MATERIALS FOR ADVANCED TECHNOLOGY. (SZ/0921-5107). **2105**

MATERIALS SCIENCE AND TECHNOLOGY. (UK/0267-0836). **2105**

MATERIALWISSENSCHAFT UND WERKSTOFFTECHNIK. (GW/0933-5137). **2106**

MATHEMATICA SCANDINAVICA. (DK/0025-5521). **3518**

MATHEMATICAL AND COMPUTER MODELLING. (UK/0895-7177). **3518**

MATHEMATICAL BIOSCIENCES. (US/0025-5564). **464**

MATHEMATICAL GEOLOGY. (US/0882-8121). **1386**

MATHEMATICAL METHODS IN THE APPLIED SCIENCES. (GW/0170-4214). **3519**

MATHEMATICAL PROCEEDINGS OF THE CAMBRIDGE PHILOSOPHICAL SOCIETY. (UK/0305-0041). **3519**

MATHEMATICAL SOCIAL SCIENCES. (NE/0165-4896). **5208**

MATHEMATICAL SYSTEMS THEORY. (US/0025-5661). **3520**

MATHEMATICS AND COMPUTER EDUCATION. (US/0730-8639). **3520**

MATHEMATICS AND COMPUTERS IN SIMULATION. (NE/0378-4754). **1282**

MATHEMATICS OF COMPUTATION. (US/0025-5718). **3521**

MATHEMATICS OF OPERATIONS RESEARCH. (US/0364-765X). **3521**

MATHEMATICS OF THE USSR : IZVESTIJA. (US/0025-5726). **3521**

MATHEMATICS OF THE USSR : SBORNIK. (US/0025-5734). **3521**

MATHEMATICS TEACHER, THE. (US/0025-5769). **3521**

MATHEMATIKA. (UK/0025-5793). **3521**

MATHEMATISCHE ANNALEN. (GW/0025-5831). **3522**

MATHEMATISCHE NACHRICHTEN. (GW/0025-584X). **3522**

MATHEMATISCHE ZEITSCHRIFT. (GW/0025-5874). **3522**

MATRIX (STUTTGART). (GW/0934-8832). **3606**

MATURE MARKET REPORT. (US/0894-2609). **933**

MATURITAS. (IE/0378-5122). **3754**

MAYDICA. (IT/0025-6153). **107**

MAYO CLINIC PROCEEDINGS. (US/0025-6196). **3799**

MCGILL JOURNAL OF EDUCATION. (CN/0024-9033). **1763**

MCNEESE REVIEW, THE. (US/0885-467X). **3347**

MDI MANAGEMENT JOURNAL. (II/0970-6623). **692**

MEASUREMENT TECHNIQUES. (US/0543-1972). **2121**

MEAT PROBE. (CN/0826-4554). **2349**

MEAT SCIENCE. (UK/0309-1740). **215**

MECCANICA (MILAN). (NE/0025-6455). **4428**

MECHANICAL SYSTEMS AND SIGNAL PROCESSING. (UK/0888-3270). **2122**

MECHANICS OF COMPOSITE MATERIALS. (US/0191-5665). **2106**

MECHANICS OF MATERIALS. (NE/0167-6636). **2106**

MECHANICS OF STRUCTURES AND MACHINES. (US/0890-5452). **2106**

MECHANICS RESEARCH COMMUNICATIONS. (US/0093-6413). **4429**

MECHANISM AND MACHINE THEORY. (UK/0094-114X). **2122**

MECHANISMS OF AGEING AND DEVELOPMENT. (SZ/0047-6374). **584**

MECHATRONICS (OXFORD). (UK/0957-4158). **1195**

MEDECIN DU QUEBEC. (CN/0025-6692). **3607**

MEDECINE ET ARMEES. (FR/0300-4937). **4049**

MEDECINE ET MALADIES INFECTIEUSES. (FR/0399-077X). **3607**

MEDECINE SCIENCES : M/S. (FR/0767-0974). **464**

MEDECINE TROPICALE. (FR/0025-682X). **3986**

MEDIA, CULTURE & SOCIETY. (UK/0163-4437). **5251**

MEDIA MARKETING NEWS. (BE). **933**

MEDIA REPORT TO WOMEN. (US/0145-9651). **1117**

MEDIAEVAL STUDIES. (CN/0076-5872). **2697**

MEDICAL AND HEALTH ANNUAL. (US/0363-0366). **1927**

MEDICAL AND PEDIATRIC ONCOLOGY. (US/0098-1532). **3906**

MEDICAL AND VETERINARY ENTOMOLOGY. (UK/0269-283X). **5611**

MEDICAL AUDIT NEWS. (UK/0959-2903). **748**

MEDICAL CARE. (US/0025-7079). **3608**

MEDICAL CARE REVIEW. (US/0025-7087). **3608**

MEDICAL CLINICS OF NORTH AMERICA, THE. (US/0025-7125). **3608**

MEDICAL DECISION MAKING. (US/0272-989X). **1215**

MEDICAL EDUCATION. (UK/0308-0110). **3609**

MEDICAL FOCUS (WURZBURG, GERMANY). (GW/0724-8172). **3609**

MEDICAL HISTORY. (UK/0025-7273). **3609**

MEDICAL HISTORY. SUPPLEMENT. (UK/0950-5571). **3609**

MEDICAL HYPOTHESES. (UK/0306-9877). **3609**

MEDICAL INFORMATICS. (UK/0307-7640). **1261**

MEDICAL INTERFACE. (US/0896-4831). **3609**

MEDICAL JOURNAL OF AUSTRALIA. (AT/0025-729X). **3610**

MEDICAL LABORATORY SCIENCES. (UK/0308-3616). **3610**

MEDICAL LETTER ON DRUGS AND THERAPEUTICS EDITION FRANCAISE, THE. (SZ/0253-8512). **4314**

MEDICAL MALPRACTICE DEFENSE REPORTER, THE. (US/0893-8229). **3008**

MEDICAL MICROBIOLOGY AND IMMUNOLOGY. (GW/0300-8584). **566**

MEDICAL PHYSICS (LANCASTER). (US/0094-2405). **4412**

MEDICAL PROBLEMS OF PERFORMING ARTISTS. (US/0885-1158). **3611**

MEDICAL PROGRESS THROUGH TECHNOLOGY. (NE/0047-6552). **3695**

MEDICAL REFERENCE SERVICES QUARTERLY. (US/0276-3869). **3230**

MEDICAL TEACHER. (UK/0142-159X). **3611**

MEDICINA (BUENOS AIRES). (AG/0025-7680). **3613**

MEDICINA CLINICA. (SP/0025-7753). **3613**

MEDICINA DE REHABILITACION. (SP/0214-8714). **4381**

MEDICINAL RESEARCH REVIEWS. (US/0198-6325). **4315**

MEDICINE AND SCIENCE IN SPORTS AND EXERCISE. (US/0195-9131). **3955**

MEDICINE (BALTIMORE). (US/0025-7974). **3613**

MEDICINE, SCIENCE, AND THE LAW. (UK/0025-8024). **3742**

MEDIEN KONKRET. (GW/0931-9808). **1117**

MEDIEVAL CERAMICS. (UK). **2592**

MEDIEVAL PROSOPOGRAPHY. (US/0198-9405). **2698**

MEDISCH CONTACT. (NE). **3614**

MEDISTAT / WORLD MEDICAL MARKET ANALYSIS. (UK). **3614**

MEDIUM AEVUM. (UK/0025-8385). **3301**

MEDIZINISCHE KLINIK (MUNCHEN. 1983). (GW/0723-5003). **3615**

MEDIZINISCHE WELT. (GW/0025-8512). **3615**

MEGAMOT / MOSAD SOLD LEMAAN HA-YELED VEHA-NOAR. (IS/0025-8679). **5209**

MELBOURNE JOURNAL OF POLITICS. (AT/0085-3224). **4481**

MELUS. (US/0163-755X). **3410**

MELVILLE SOCIETY EXTRACTS. (US/0193-8991). **3411**

MEMBERSHIP DIRECTORY - AMERICAN CHAMBER OF COMMERCE IN EGYPT. (UA). **820**

MEMBERSHIP DIRECTORY / EL PASO COUNTY HISTORICAL SOCIETY. (US). **2746**

MEMBERSHIP DIRECTORY / NORTH AMERICAN LAKE MANAGEMENT SOCIETY. (US). **1505**

MEMBERSHIP LIST - AMERICAN MENSA LIMITED. (US/0363-3616). **5233**

MEMBRANE BIOCHEMISTRY. (US/0149-046X). **490**

MEMOIRES ET ETUDES SCIENTIFIQUES DE LA REVUE DE METALLURGIE. (FR/0245-8292). **4008**

MEMOIRS OF THE AMERICAN MATHEMATICAL SOCIETY. (US/0065-9266). **3522**

MEMOIRS OF THE ENTOMOLOGICAL SOCIETY OF CANADA. (CN/0071-075X). **5591**

MEMOIRS OF THE HOURGLASS CRUISES. (US/0085-0683). **556**

MEMOIRS OF THE MUSEUM OF VICTORIA. ANTHROPOLOGY AND HISTORY. (AT/1035-4247). **4091**

MEMOIRS OF THE QUEENSLAND MUSEUM. (AT/0079-8835). **4167**

MEMOIRS OF THE SOUTHERN CALIFORNIA ACADEMY OF SCIENCES. (US/0097-2622). **5128**

MEMORIAS DEL MUSEO DE HISTORIA NATURAL JAVIER PRADO. (PE/0457-9151). **4167**

MEMORY & COGNITION. (US/0090-502X). **4603**

MENNINGER LETTER, THE. (US/1066-937X). **3930**

MENSALOHA. (US/8750-4529). **4603**

MENTALITIES. (NZ/0111-8854). **4604**

MERCADO DE VALORES, EL. (MX/0025-9756). **798**

MERCER BULLETIN, THE. (CN/0714-6914). **1690**

MERCIAN GEOLOGIST. (UK/0025-990X). **1387**

MERIDIAN - MAP & GEOGRAPHY ROUND TABLE (AMERICAN LIBRARY ASSOCIATION). (US/1040-7421). **2582**

MERRILL-PALMER QUARTERLY (1960). (US/0272-930X). **4604**

MERTON ANNUAL, THE. (US/0894-4857). **4976**

MESSIANIC OUTREACH, THE. (US/0278-2782). **5051**

MESTER (LOS ANGELES). (US/0160-2764). **3411**

METABOLIC BRAIN DISEASE. (US/0885-7490). **3838**

METABOLISM, CLINICAL AND EXPERIMENTAL. (US/0026-0495). **3674**

METALL (BERLIN). (GW/0026-0746). **4009**

METALLOVEDENIE I TERMICHESKAYA OBRABOTKA METALLOV. (US/0026-0673). **4010**

METALLURGICAL AND MATERIALS TRANSACTIONS. PHYSICAL METALLURGY AND MATERIALS SCIENCE. (US/1073-5623). **4010**

METALLURGICAL TRANSACTIONS. A. PHYSICAL METALLURGY AND MATERIALS SCIENCE. (US/0360-2133). **4010**

METALLURGICAL TRANSACTIONS. B, PROCESS METALLURGY. (US/0360-2141). **4010**

METALLURGIST (NEW YORK). (US/0026-0894). **4010**

METALURGIA Y ELECTRICIDAD. (SP/0026-0991). **4011**

METAPHOR AND SYMBOLIC ACTIVITY. (US/0885-7253). **3411**

METEORITICS. (US/0026-1114). **1387**

METEOROLOGICAL MAGAZINE. (UK/0026-1149). **1430**

METEOROLOGY AND ATMOSPHERIC PHYSICS. (AU/0177-7971). **1431**

METHOD (LOS ANGELES, CALIF.). (US/0736-7392). **4353**

METHODOLOGY AND SCIENCE. (NE/0543-6095). **5209**

METHODS IN ENZYMOLOGY. (US/0076-6879). **490**

METHODS IN GENE TECHNOLOGY. (UK). **3695**

METHODS OF INFORMATION IN MEDICINE. (GW/0026-1270). **3616**

METROLOGIA. (GW/0026-1394). **4031**

MEXICAN ECONOMY : ECONOMIC AND FINANCIAL DEVELOPMENTS IN ... POLICIES FOR ... / BANCO DE MEXICO, THE. (MX). **798**

MEXICAN STUDIES. (US/0742-9797). **1505**

MIC / TECH-COMPUTERS. (US). **1248**

MIC-TECH-UNIX. (US). **1195**

MICHIGAN

MICHIGAN ACADEMICIAN. (US/0026-2005). **2850**

MICHIGAN ARCHAEOLOGIST. (US/0543-9728). **274**

MICHIGAN ASSOCIATION OF SPEECH COMMUNICATION JOURNAL, THE. (US). **1117**

MICHIGAN BOTANIST. (US/0026-203X). **518**

MICHIGAN CPA, THE. (US/0026-2064). **748**

MICHIGAN GERMANIC STUDIES. (US/0098-8030). **3302**

MICHIGAN HISTORICAL REVIEW, THE. (US/0890-1686). **2746**

MICHIGAN LAW REVIEW. (US/0026-2234). **3009**

MICHIGAN MATHEMATICAL JOURNAL, THE. (US/0026-2285). **3523**

MICHIGAN ROMANCE STUDIES. (US/0270-3629). **3302**

MICHIGAN VOTER, THE. (US/0899-1545). **4482**

MICKY MAUS. (GW). **1066**

MICROBEAM ANALYSIS. (US/0278-1727). **1012**

MICROBIAL ECOLOGY. (US/0095-3628). **2218**

MICROBIAL PATHOGENESIS. (UK/0882-4010). **3715**

MICROBIOLOGICA. (IT/0391-5352). **567**

MICROBIOLOGICAL REVIEWS. (US/0146-0749). **567**

MICROBIOLOGY AND IMMUNOLOGY. (JA/0385-5600). **3674**

MICROBIOS. (UK/0026-2633). **567**

MICROCHEMICAL JOURNAL. (US/0026-265X). **986**

MICROCIRCULATION, ENDOTHELIUM, AND LYMPHATICS. (US/0740-9451). **3616**

MICROELECTRONICS AND RELIABILITY. (UK/0026-2714). **2072**

MICRON AND MICROSCOPICA ACTA. (UK/0739-6260). **573**

MICROPALEONTOLOGY. (US/0026-2803). **4228**

MICROPOROUS MATERIALS. (NE/0927-6513). **986**

MICROPROCESSING AND MICROPROGRAMMING. (NE/0165-6074). **1269**

MICROPROCESSORS AND MICROSYSTEMS. (UK/0141-9331). **1230**

MICROSCOPIA ELECTRONICA Y BIOLOGIA CELULAR : ORGANO OFICIAL DE LAS SOCIEDADES LATINOAMERICANA DE MICROSCOPIA ELECTRONICA E IBEROAMERICANA DE BIOLOGIA CELULAR. (AG/0326-3142). **573**

MICROVASCULAR RESEARCH. (US/0026-2862). **3773**

MICROWAVE AND OPTICAL TECHNOLOGY LETTERS. (US/0895-2477). **2072**

MICROWAVE JOURNAL (EURO-GLOBAL ED.). (US/0192-6217). **2072**

MICROWAVES & RF. (US/0745-2993). **4438**

MID-AMERICAN JOURNAL OF BUSINESS. (US/0895-1772). **694**

MID-AMERICAN REVIEW OF SOCIOLOGY. (US/0732-913X). **5252**

MID-NORTH MONITOR, THE. (CN/0227-3853). **5789**

MIDDLE EAST JOURNAL, THE. (US/0026-3141). **2635**

MIDDLE EAST REPORT (NEW YORK, N.Y. : 1988). (US/0899-2851). **2526**

MIDDLE EASTERN STUDIES. (UK/0026-3206). **2769**

MIDDLE SCHOOL JOURNAL. (US/0094-0771). **1764**

MIDWEST ALLIANCE IN NURSING JOURNAL / MAIN. (US/1048-499X). **3861**

MIDWEST QUARTERLY (PITTSBURG), THE. (US/0026-3451). **2538**

MIDWESTERN FOLKLORE. (US/0894-4059). **2322**

MIGRATIONS SANTE. (FR/0335-7198). **4791**

MIKOLOGIJA I FITOPATOLOGIJA. (RU/0026-3648). **575**

MIKROCHIMICA ACTA. (AU/0026-3672). **1018**

MILCH-MARKETING. (GW). **196**

MILCHWISSENSCHAFT. (GW/0026-3788). **196**

MILITARY HISTORY OF THE WEST. (US/1071-2011). **4050**

MILITARY LAW REVIEW. (US/0026-4040). **3183**

MILITARY MEDICINE. (US/0026-4075). **3617**

MILLENNIUM. (UK/0305-8298). **4529**

MINDS AND MACHINES (DORDRECHT). (NE/0924-6495). **1215**

MINERAL AND ELECTROLYTE METABOLISM. (SZ/0378-0392). **3799**

MINERAL LAW NEWSLETTER. (US/0897-6694). **3010**

MINERALIUM DEPOSITA. (GW/0026-4598). **1441**

MINERALOGICAL MAGAZINE. (UK/0026-461X). **1441**

MINERALS ENGINEERING. (UK/0892-6875). **2144**

MINERVA (LONDON). (UK/0026-4695). **5129**

MINNESOTA HISTORY. (US/0026-5497). **2746**

MINNESOTA LAW REVIEW. (US/0026-5535). **3010**

MINNESOTA MEDICINE. (US/0026-556X). **3617**

MINORITY BUSINESS ENTREPRENEUR. (US/1048-0919). **695**

MINTEL LEISURE INTELLIGENCE. (UK). **4852**

MIRRORS : INTERNATIONAL HAIKU FORUM. (US). **3466**

MISCELLANEOUS PUBLICATIONS - MUSEUM OF ZOOLOGY, UNIVERSITY OF MICHIGAN. (US/0076-8405). **5591**

MISCELLANEOUS SERIES - NEW ZEALAND GEOGRAPHICAL SOCIETY. (NZ/0078-0022). **2569**

MISCELLANIA ZOOLOGICA. (SP/0211-6529). **5591**

MISSION AND MINISTRY. (US/1058-0565). **5064**

MISSISSIPPI BUSINESS EDUCATION ASSOCIATION JOURNAL. (US). **695**

MISSISSIPPI QUARTERLY, THE. (US/0026-637X). **2850**

MISSISSIPPI RN, THE. (US/0026-6388). **3861**

MISSOURI FOLKLORE SOCIETY JOURNAL. (US/0731-2946). **2322**

MISSOURI JOURNAL OF MATHEMATICAL SCIENCES. (US/0899-6180). **3523**

MISSOURI MEDICINE. (US/0026-6620). **3617**

MITTEILUNGEN - PTB. (GW/0030-834X). **5129**

MMW. MUNCHENER MEDIZINISCHE WOCHENSCHRIFT. (GW/0341-3098). **3617**

MOBILIA (AMSTERDAM). (NE/0165-5302). **2906**

MODELING, IDENTIFICATION AND CONTROL. (NO/0332-7353). **3523**

MODERN ASIAN STUDIES. (UK/0026-749X). **2659**

MODERN CHINA. (US/0097-7004). **2659**

MODERN DRAMA. (CN/0026-7694). **5366**

MODERN GREEK STUDIES YEARBOOK. (US/0884-8432). **2699**

MODERN LANGUAGE JOURNAL (BOULDER, COLO.), THE. (US/0026-7902). **3303**

MODERN MEDICINE (NEDERLANDSE ED.). (NE/0929-0141). **3617**

MODERN PATHOLOGY. (US/0893-3952). **3896**

MODERN PHYSICS LETTERS A. (SI/0217-7323). **4448**

MODERN SCHOOLMAN, THE. (US/0026-8402). **4353**

MOKUZAI GAKKAISHI. (JA/0021-4795). **2403**

MOLECULAR AND BIOCHEMICAL PARASITOLOGY. (NE/0166-6851). **465**

MOLECULAR AND CELLULAR BIOCHEMISTRY. (NE/0300-8177). **491**

MOLECULAR AND CELLULAR BIOLOGY. (US/0270-7306). **568**

MOLECULAR AND CELLULAR ENDOCRINOLOGY. (IE/0303-7207). **3732**

MOLECULAR AND CELLULAR NEUROSCIENCES. (US/1044-7431). **3838**

MOLECULAR AND CELLULAR PROBES. (UK/0890-8508). **465**

MOLECULAR AND CHEMICAL NEUROPATHOLOGY. (US/1044-7393). **3838**

MOLECULAR & GENERAL GENETICS : MGG. (GW/0026-8925). **549**

MOLECULAR BIOLOGY AND EVOLUTION. (US/0737-4038). **465**

MOLECULAR BIOLOGY OF THE CELL. (US/1059-1524). **539**

MOLECULAR BIOLOGY REPORTS. (NE/0301-4851). **465**

MOLECULAR BRAIN RESEARCH. (NE/0169-328X). **3838**

MOLECULAR CARCINOGENESIS. (US/0899-1987). **465**

MOLECULAR ENDOCRINOLOGY (BALTIMORE, MD.). (US/0888-8809). **3732**

MOLECULAR IMMUNOLOGY. (UK/0161-5890). **3675**

MOLECULAR MICROBIOLOGY. (UK/0950-382X). **568**

MOLECULAR NEUROBIOLOGY. (US/0893-7648). **3838**

MOLECULAR PHARMACOLOGY. (US/0026-895X). **4316**

MOLECULAR PHYSICS. (UK/0026-8976). **1056**

MONASH PUBLICATIONS IN GEOGRAPHY. (AT). **2569**

MONASH PUBLICATIONS IN HISTORY. (AT/0818-0032). **2623**

MONASH SOFTWARE LETTER. (US/1062-0451). **1288**

MONASH UNIVERSITY LAW REVIEW. (AT/0311-3140). **3011**

MONATSBERICHTE - OESTERREICHISCHES INSTITUT FUER WIRTSCHAFTSFORSCHUNG. (AU/0029-9898). **1505**

MONATSHEFTE FUER CHEMIE. (US/0026-9247). **986**

MONATSHEFTE FUER MATHEMATIK. (AU/0026-9255). **3523**

MONATSHEFTE FUER VETERINAERMEDIZIN. (GW/0026-9263). **5516**

MONATSSCHRIFT FUER KINDERHEILKUNDE. (GW/0026-9298). **3906**

MONDE DU RENSEIGNEMENT 1988, LE. (FR/0997-7139). **4051**

MONETARIA. (MX/0185-1136). **799**

MONEY AFFAIRS / CEMLA, CENTRE FOR LATIN AMERICAN MONETARY STUDIES. (MX). **1506**

MONOGRAPH / INSTITUTE OF APPLIED SOCIAL AND ECONOMIC RESEARCH. (PP). **5209**

MONOGRAPHIC REVIEW. (US/0885-7512). **3413**

MONOGRAPHIC SUPPLEMENT ... TO CATALOGING & CLASSIFICATION QUARTERLY. (US/0898-008X). **420**

MONOGRAPHS - ACADEMY OF NATURAL SCIENCES OF PHILADELPHIA. (US/0096-7750). **4168**

MONOGRAPHS IN ALLERGY. (SW/0077-0760). **3675**

MONOGRAPHS IN FETAL PHYSIOLOGY. (NE/0165-196X). **584**

MONOGRAPHS IN P/M SERIES. (US/1061-6071). **4013**

MONOGRAPHS OF MARINE MOLLUSCA. (US/0162-8321). **5591**

MONOGRAPHS. SOCIAL SCIENCES - UNIVERSITY OF FLORIDA. (US). **5209**

MONTAIGNE STUDIES. (US/1049-2917). **3413**

MONTANA BUSINESS QUARTERLY. (US/0026-9921). **1506**

MONTANA GRAIN NEWS. (US/1046-6088). **203**

MONTANA LIBRARY DIRECTORY, WITH STATISTICS OF MONTANA PUBLIC LIBRARIES. (US/0094-873X). **3259**

MONTH (LONDON. 1882), THE. (UK/0027-0172). **4979**

MONTHLY LABOR REVIEW. (US/0098-1818). **1691**

MONTHLY NOTICES OF THE ROYAL ASTRONOMICAL SOCIETY. (UK/0035-8711). **397**

MONTHLY PRESCRIBING REFERENCE. (US/0883-0266). **3618**

MONTHLY REVIEW (NEW YORK. 1949). (US/0027-0520). **4543**

MONTHLY WEATHER REVIEW. (US/0027-0644). **1432**

MONTHLY WEATHER REVIEW. NORTHERN TERRITORY / COMMONWEALTH OF AUSTRALIA, BUREAU OF METEOROLOGY, DEPARTMENT OF THE INTERIOR. (AT). **1432**

MONUMENTA ARCHAEOLOGICA (LOS ANGELES). (US/0363-7565). **275**

MONUMENTA NIPPONICA. (JA/0027-0741). **2659**

MONUMENTA SERICA. (GW/0254-9948). **2623**

MOODY STREET IRREGULARS. (US/0196-2604). **3413**

MOOREANA : JOURNAL OF THE PALMETUM. (AT/1037-1842). **518**

MOSELLE FRUIT. (FR). **2350**

MOSQUITO SYSTEMATICS. (US/0091-3669). **2177**

MOTHERING. (US/0733-3013). **2283**

MOTIF (COLUMBUS, OHIO). (US/0278-2286). **2322**

MOTIVATION AND EMOTION. (US/0146-7239). **4604**

MOTOR. (NE). **4082**

MOUNT SINAI JOURNAL OF MEDICINE, NEW YORK, THE. (US/0027-2507). **3618**

MOUNTAIN HOME NEWS. (US). **5657**

MOUNTAIN RESEARCH AND DEVELOPMENT. (US/0276-4741). **241**

MOUNTAINEER (SEATTLE, WASH.). (US/0027-2620). **4875**

MOUVEMENT SOCIAL, LE. (FR/0027-2671). **2623**

MOVEMENT DISORDERS. (US/0885-3185). **3838**

MRAX INFORMATION. (BE/0024-8320). **5209**

MULGA RESEARCH CENTRE JOURNAL. (AT/0818-8238). **41**

MULTI-MEDIA COMPUTING. (NE/0923-8182). **1196**

MULTICULTURAL REVIEW. (US/1058-9236). **2268**

MULTIDIMENSIONAL SYSTEMS AND SIGNAL PROCESSING. (US/0923-6082). **1196**

MULTIMEDIA MARKETS. (US). **933**

MULTIMEDIA MARKETS : INTERNATIONAL FORECAST SUPPLEMENT. (US). **934**

MULTIMEDIA TECHNOLOGIES AND SYSTEMS. (US). **1118**

MULTIPLE LINEAR REGRESSION VIEWPOINTS. (US/0195-7171). **3523**

MULTIVARIATE BEHAVIORAL RESEARCH. (US/0027-3171). **4605**

MUNDO EJECUTIVO. (MX). **800**

MUNDO NUEVO. (VE/0379-6922). **4529**

MUSCLE & NERVE. (US/0148-639X). **3838**

MUSCOGIANA (COLUMBUS, GA.). (US/1042-3419). **2461**

MUSIC LIBRARIAN. (US/1065-1179). **4134**

MUSIC PERCEPTION. (US/0730-7829). **4134**

MUSIC REFERENCE SERVICES QUARTERLY. (US/1058-8167). **4134**

MUSIC THEORY SPECTRUM. (US/0195-6167). **4135**

MUSIC THERAPY (NEW YORK, N.Y.). (US/0734-7367). **4135**

MUSICOLOGY AUSTRALIA. (AT/0814-5857). **4137**

MUSLIM WORLD LEAGUE JOURNAL, THE. (SU). **5044**

MUTAGENESIS. (UK/0267-8357). **549**

MUTATION BREEDING NEWSLETTER. (AU). **110**

MUTATION RESEARCH. DNA REPAIR. (NE/0921-8777). **466**

MVS UPDATE. (UK). **1280**

MYCOLOGIA. (US/0027-5514). **575**

MYCOLOGICAL RESEARCH. (UK/0953-7562). **575**

MYCOPATHOLOGIA (1975). (NE/0301-486X). **576**

MYCOTAXON. (US/0093-4666). **518**

MYSTICS QUARTERLY (IOWA CITY, IOWA). (US/0742-5503). **3414**

N.A.C.W.P.I JOURNAL. (US/0027-576X). **4139**

NAACOG'S WOMEN'S HEALTH NURSING SCAN. (US/1055-3533). **3862**

NACA NEWS. (US). **226**

NACADA JOURNAL / NATIONAL ACADEMIC ADVISING ASSOCIATION. (US/0271-9517). **1836**

NACHRICHTEN AUS DEM OFFENTLICHEN VERMESSUNGSDIENST NORDRHEIN-WESTFALEN. (GW). **2027**

NACHRICHTEN FUER DOKUMENTATION. (GW/0027-7436). **3232**

NACHRICHTENDIENST. (GW/0012-1185). **5297**

NAGOYA MATHEMATICAL JOURNAL. (JA/0027-7630). **3523**

NAHRUNG, DIE. (GW/0027-769X). **4194**

NAMES. (US/0027-7738). **2461**

NASHR-I DANISH. (IR/0259-9090). **5044**

NASHVILLE BUSINESS JOURNAL. (US/0889-2873). **696**

NATAL MUSEUM JOURNAL OF HUMANITIES. (SA/1015-0935). **2851**

NATION (NEW YORK, N.Y.), THE. (US/0027-8378). **3348**

NATIONAL ACADEMY SCIENCE LETTERS. (II/0250-541X). **5130**

NATIONAL ASSOCIATION OF SECRETARIES OF STATE HANDBOOK. (US/0547-4221). **4668**

NATIONAL DIRECTORY OF AIDS CARE. (US). **4792**

NATIONAL ENVIRONMENTAL JOURNAL, THE. (US/1067-2583). **2178**

NATIONAL ESTIMATOR. (US/1040-2926). **2889**

NATIONAL FORUM OF APPLIED EDUCATIONAL RESEARCH JOURNAL. (US/0895-3880). **1867**

NATIONAL FORUM OF EDUCATIONAL ADMINISTRATION AND SUPERVISION JOURNAL. (US/0888-8132). **1766**

NATIONAL FORUM OF SPECIAL EDUCATION JOURNAL. (US/1043-2167). **1882**

NATIONAL GEOGRAPHIC WORLD. (US/0361-5499). **2570**

NATIONAL GEOGRAPHICAL JOURNAL OF INDIA, THE. (II/0027-9374). **2570**

NATIONAL HOOKUP. (US/0194-4754). **4391**

NATIONAL MILK RECORDS. ANNUAL REPORT, ENGLAND & WALES. (UK). **197**

NATIONAL POLITICAL SCIENCE REVIEW. (US/0896-629X). **4483**

NATIONAL TAX JOURNAL. (US/0028-0283). **4738**

NATIONAL WEATHER DIGEST. (US/0271-1052). **1432**

NATIONALKONOMISK TIDSSKRIFT. (DK/0028-0453). **1507**

NATION'S BUSINESS. (US/0028-047X). **697**

NATIVE STUDIES REVIEW. (CN/0831-585X). **2268**

NATURAL AREAS JOURNAL. (US/0885-8608). **2199**

NATURAL HAZARDS (DORDRECHT). (NE/0921-030X). **2178**

NATURAL HISTORY. (US/0028-0712). **4168**

NATURAL LANGUAGE AND LINGUISTIC THEORY. (NE/0167-806X). **3305**

NATURAL LANGUAGE SEMANTICS. (US/0925-854X). **3305**

NATURAL PRODUCT REPORTS. (UK/0265-0568). **491**

NATURAL RESOURCES FORUM. (NE/0165-0203). **2199**

NATURAL RESOURCES JOURNAL. (US/0028-0739). **3115**

NATURE (LONDON). (UK/0028-0836). **5131**

NATURE, SOCIETY, AND THOUGHT. (US/0890-6130). **5210**

NATURE SOUTH. (US/1054-9641). **4169**

NATURWISSENSCHAFTEN, DIE. (GW/0028-1042). **5131**

NAUNYN-SCHMIEDEBERG'S ARCHIVES OF PHARMACOLOGY. (GW/0028-1298). **4317**

NAUTILUS (PHILADELPHIA), THE. (US/0028-1344). **5592**

NAVAL RESEARCH LOGISTICS. (US/0894-069X). **4180**

NAVY TIMES. (US/0028-1697). **4180**

NBER MACROECONOMICS ANNUAL. (US/0889-3365). **1593**

NCA/TCS NEWSLETTER. (US/0163-772X). **539**

NCEOA JOURNAL. (US/0889-8405). **1766**

NCRP REPORT. (US/0083-209X). **4793**

NEBRASKA BIRD REVIEW, THE. (US/0028-1816). **5592**

NEBRASKA LIBRARY ASSOCIATION QUARTERLY. (US/0028-1883). **3233**

NEBRASKA MEDICAL JOURNAL, THE. (US/0091-6730). **3619**

NEBRASKA SYMPOSIUM ON MOTIVATION. (US/0146-7875). **4605**

NEDERLANDS MELK- EN ZUIVELTIJSCHRIFT. (NE/0028-209X). **5132**

NEDERLANDSCHE LEEUW; MAANDBLAD VAN HET KONINKLIJK NEDERLANDSCH GENOOTSCHAP VOOR GESLACHT- EN WAPENKUNDE, DE. (NE). **2462**

NEFROLOGIA. (SP/0211-6995). **3991**

NEGOTIATION JOURNAL. (US/0748-4526). **4483**

NEMATOLOGICA. (NE/0028-2596). **466**

NEMOURIA. (US/0085-3887). **4169**

NEONATAL NETWORK. (US/0730-0832). **3906**

NEOPLASMA. (XO/0028-2685). **3821**

NEOTROPICA. (AG/0548-1686). **5592**

NEPHROLOGIE. (SZ/0250-4960). **3991**

NEPHROLOGY, DIALYSIS, TRANSPLANTATION. (UK/0931-0509). **3992**

NEPHROLOGY NEWS & ISSUES. (US/0896-1263). **3992**

NEPHRON. (SZ/0028-2766). **3992**

NERVENARZT. (GW/0028-2804). **3839**

NERVENHEILKUNDE. (GW/0722-1541). **3839**

NERVLINE. A MICROCOMPUTER INFORMATION RETRIEVAL SYSTEM IN THE CLINICAL NEUROSCIENCES. (US). **3839**

NERVURE PARIS. (FR/0988-4068). **3931**

NETHERLANDS INTERNATIONAL LAW REVIEW. (NE/0165-070X). **3133**

NETHERLANDS JOURNAL OF AGRICULTURAL SCIENCE. (NE/0028-2928). **111**

NETHERLANDS JOURNAL OF MEDICINE. (NE/0300-2977). **3800**

NETHERLANDS JOURNAL OF PLANT PATHOLOGY. (NE/0028-2944). **519**

NETHERLANDS JOURNAL OF SEA RESEARCH. (NE/0077-7579). **556**

NETHERLANDS JOURNAL OF ZOOLOGY. (NE/0028-2960). **5592**

NETWORKS (NEW YORK). (US/0028-3045). **5132**

NEUE HUTTE. (GW/0028-3207). **4013**

NEUES JAHRBUCH FUER MINERALOGIE. ABHANDLUNGEN. (GW/0077-7757). **1443**

NEUES JAHRBUCH FUER MINERALOGIE. MONATSHEFTE. (GW/0028-3649). **1443**

NEURAL COMPUTATION. (US/0899-7667). **1215**

NEURAL NETWORK WORLD. (XR/1210-0552). **1243**

NEURAL NETWORKS. (US/0893-6080). **1215**

NEURAL, PARALLEL AND SCIENTIFIC COMPUTATIONS. (US/1061-5369). **1197**

NEURO-CHIRURGIE. (FR/0028-3770). **3839**

NEURO ENDOCRINOLOGY LETTERS. (GW/0172-780X). **3732**

NEURO-OPHTHALMOLOGY (AMSTERDAM : AEOLUS PRESS. 1980). (NE/0165-8107). **3876**

NEUROBIOLOGY OF AGING. (US/0197-4580). **3839**

NEUROCHEMICAL RESEARCH. (US/0364-3190). **3839**

NEUROCHEMISTRY INTERNATIONAL. (US/0197-0186). **3839**

NEUROCHIRURGIA. (GW/0028-3819). **3970**

NEUROENDOCRINOLOGY. (SZ/0028-3835). **3840**

NEUROEPIDEMIOLOGY. (SZ/0251-5350). **3840**

NEUROIMMUNOMODULATION. (SZ/1021-7401). **3840**

NEUROLOGIA CROATICA : GLASILO UDRUZENJA NEUROLOGA JUGOSLAVIJE, OFFICIAL JOURNAL OF YUGOSLAV NEUROLOGICAL ASSOCIATION. (CI/0353-8842). **3840**

NEUROLOGIA PSICHIATRIA SCIENZE UMANE. (IT). **3931**

NEUROLOGIC CLINICS. (US/0733-8619). **3840**

NEUROLOGY. (US/0028-3878). **3840**

NEUROLOGY, INDIA. (II/0028-3886). **3841**

NEUROPATHOLOGY AND APPLIED NEUROBIOLOGY. (UK/0305-1846). **3896**

NEUROPEDIATRICS. (GW/0174-304X). **3841**

NEUROPEPTIDES

NEUROPEPTIDES (EDINBURGH). (UK/0143-4179). **3841**

NEUROPHARMACOLOGY. (UK/0028-3908). **4317**

NEUROPSYCHOBIOLOGY. (SZ/0302-282X). **3842**

NEUROPSYCHOLOGIA. (UK/0028-3932). **3842**

NEUROPSYCHOLOGY. (US/0894-4105). **4605**

NEUROPSYCHOPHARMACOLOGY (NEW YORK, N.Y.). (US/0893-133X). **3842**

NEURORADIOLOGY. (GW/0028-3940). **3842**

NEUROREHABILITATION (READING, MASS.). (US/1053-8135). **3842**

NEUROREPORT. (UK/0959-4965). **3842**

NEUROSCIENCE. (UK/0306-4522). **3842**

NEUROSCIENCE AND BIOBEHAVIORAL REVIEWS. (US/0149-7634). **3842**

NEUROSCIENCE LETTERS. (NE/0304-3940). **3842**

NEUROSCIENCE RESEARCH. (IE/0168-0102). **3842**

NEUROSCIENCE RESEARCH COMMUNICATIONS. (UK/0893-6609). **3843**

NEUROSURGERY. (US/0148-396X). **3970**

NEUROSURGICAL REVIEW. (GW/0344-5607). **3970**

NEUROTOXICOLOGY (PARK FOREST SOUTH). (US/0161-813X). **3843**

NEUROUROL. URODYN. (US/0733-2467). **3843**

NEVADA LAWYER. (US/1068-882X). **3015**

NEVADA REVIEW OF BUSINESS & ECONOMICS. (US/0148-5881). **698**

NEW BOOKBINDER, THE. (UK/0261-5363). **4830**

NEW CONVERSATIONS. (US/0360-0181). **4980**

NEW DIMENSIONS IN GIVING. (US). **4338**

NEW EDUCATION (MELBOURNE, VIC.). (AT). **1767**

NEW ELECTRONIC ENCYCLOPEDIA. [COMPUTER FILE], THE. (US). **1927**

NEW ENGLAND JOURNAL OF MEDICINE (OVERSEAS ED.). (US/0028-4793). **3620**

NEW ENGLAND JOURNAL OF MEDICINE, THE. (US/0028-4793). **3620**

NEW ENGLAND PROGRESS MAGAZINE. (US). **2607**

NEW ENGLAND READING ASSOCIATION JOURNAL. (US/0028-4882). **1901**

NEW ENGLAND RUNNER. (US/1041-4800). **4907**

NEW FORESTS. (NE/0169-4286). **2389**

NEW GENERATION COMPUTING. (JA/0288-3635). **1270**

NEW HAMPSHIRE GENEALOGICAL RECORD, THE. (US/1055-0763). **2462**

NEW IDEAS IN PSYCHOLOGY. (UK/0732-118X). **4605**

NEW JERSEY BUSINESS SOURCE BOOK, THE. (US/1049-2879). **698**

NEW JERSEY LAKE SURVEY FISHING MAPS GUIDE. (US/1054-4623). **2309**

NEW JERSEY MEDICINE. (US/0885-842X). **3620**

NEW LEFT REVIEW. (UK/0028-6060). **4544**

NEW LITERATURE REVIEW. (AT/0314-7495). **3348**

NEW PERSPECTIVES ON TURKEY. (TU/0896-6346). **5210**

NEW PHYTOLOGIST, THE. (UK/0028-646X). **519**

NEW PRODUCT REPORT, THE. (UK). **934**

NEW QUARTERLY. (CN/0227-0455). **3416**

NEW REPUBLIC (NEW YORK, N.Y.). (US/0028-6583). **2851**

NEW SCHOLAR, THE. (US/0028-6613). **5210**

NEW SCIENTIST (1971). (UK/0262-4079). **5132**

NEW STUDIES IN AESTHETICS. (US/0893-6005). **359**

NEW TECHNOLOGY IN THE HUMAN SERVICES. (UK). **5252**

NEW YORK FOLKLORE. (US/0361-204X). **2323**

NEW YORK INTERNATIONAL LAW REVIEW. (US/1050-9453). **3133**

NEW YORK STATE JOURNAL OF MEDICINE. (US/0028-7628). **3621**

NEW YORK TAX CASES (BUFFALO, N.Y.). (US/0898-9117). **4738**

NEW YORK TAX UPDATE. (US/1056-4829). **749**

NEW YORK UNIVERSITY JOURNAL OF INTERNATIONAL LAW & POLITICS. (US/0028-7873). **3133**

NEW YORK UNIVERSITY LAW REVIEW (1950). (US/0028-7881). **3016**

NEW ZEALAND DENTAL JOURNAL. (NZ/0028-8047). **1330**

NEW ZEALAND ENTOMOLOGIST, THE. (NZ/0077-9962). **5592**

NEW ZEALAND FISHERMAN. (NZ/0113-9606). **4908**

NEW ZEALAND GEOLOGICAL SURVEY BULLETIN. (NZ). **1389**

NEW ZEALAND GEOLOGICAL SURVEY PALEONTOLOGICAL BULLETIN. (NZ). **1389**

NEW ZEALAND JOURNAL OF AGRICULTURAL RESEARCH. (NZ/0028-8233). **112**

NEW ZEALAND JOURNAL OF BOTANY. (NZ/0028-825X). **519**

NEW ZEALAND JOURNAL OF CROP AND HORTICULTURAL SCIENCE. (NZ/0114-0671). **2425**

NEW ZEALAND JOURNAL OF ECOLOGY. (NZ/0110-6465). **2219**

NEW ZEALAND JOURNAL OF EDUCATIONAL STUDIES. (NZ/0028-8276). **1768**

NEW ZEALAND JOURNAL OF FORESTRY SCIENCE. (NZ/0048-0134). **2389**

NEW ZEALAND JOURNAL OF GEOLOGY AND GEOPHYSICS. (NZ/0028-8306). **1389**

NEW ZEALAND JOURNAL OF MARINE AND FRESHWATER RESEARCH. (NZ/0028-8330). **556**

NEW ZEALAND JOURNAL OF MEDICAL LABORATORY SCIENCE. (NZ/1171-0195). **3621**

NEW ZEALAND JOURNAL OF PSYCHOLOGY (CHRISTCHURCH. 1983). (NZ/0112-109X). **4605**

NEW ZEALAND JOURNAL OF SPORTS MEDICINE, THE. (NZ/0110-6384). **3955**

NEW ZEALAND JOURNAL OF ZOOLOGY. (NZ/0301-4223). **5592**

NEW ZEALAND MEDICAL JOURNAL. (NZ/0028-8446). **3621**

NEW ZEALAND NATURAL SCIENCES. (NZ/0113-7492). **1358**

NEW ZEALAND NURSING FORUM. (NZ/0110-7968). **3862**

NEW ZEALAND VETERINARY JOURNAL. (NZ/0048-0169). **5517**

NEWS CIRCLE, THE. (US/0193-1814). **2269**

NEWS IN PHYSIOLOGICAL SCIENCES. (US/0886-1714). **584**

NEWS / MONTANA STATE LIBRARY. (US). **3234**

NEWS PHOTOGRAPHER. (US/0199-2422). **4372**

NEWS, THE. (US). **5627**

NEWSLETTER / ASSOCIATION FOR CANADIAN THEATRE RESEARCH. (CN/1193-7564). **5366**

NEWSLETTER - AUSTRALIAN AND NEW ZEALAND SOCIETY OF NUCLEAR MEDICINE. (AT/0159-8376). **3848**

NEWSLETTER - DANISH CENTRE FOR TECHNICAL AIDS FOR REHABILITATION AND EDUCATION. (DK). **1882**

NEWSLETTER - EUBIOS ETHICS INSTITUTE. (NZ/1170-5485). **2252**

NEWSLETTER - LITTLE BIG HORN ASSOCIATES. (US/0459-5866). **2749**

NEWSLETTER OF THE AMERICAN COMMITTEE TO ADVANCE THE STUDY OF PETROGLYPHS AND PICTOGRAPHS. (US/0278-2871). **242**

NEWSLETTER OF THE NEW YORK STATE COUNCIL FOR THE SOCIAL STUDIES, THE. (US). **5211**

NEWSLINK. (US). **4606**

NEWSPAPER RESEARCH JOURNAL. (US/0739-5329). **4817**

NEXUS (HAMILTON, ONT.). (CN/0711-5342). **242**

NIAGARA - WHEATFIELD TRIBUNE. (US). **5719**

NIEREN- UND HOCKDRUCKKRANKHEITEN. (GW/0300-5224). **3622**

NIEUWE WISKRANT. (NE). **3524**

NIGERIAN LIBRARY AND INFORMATION SCIENCE REVIEW. (NR/0189-4412). **3236**

NIGRIZIA. (IT/0029-0173). **4982**

NIHON GENSHIRYOKU GAKKAISHI. (JA/0004-7120). **1951**

NIHON OYO DOBUTSU KONCHU GAKKAISHI. (JA/0021-4914). **5612**

NIHON SAKUMOTSU GAKKAI KIJI. (JA/0011-1848). **179**

NIHON SHOKUHIN KOGYO GAKKAI SHI. (JA/0029-0394). **2351**

NIHON SUISAN GAKKAI SHI. (JA/0021-5392). **2309**

NIMHANS JOURNAL. (II). **3931**

NIMROD (TULSA). (US/0029-053X). **3417**

NINETEENTH CENTURY CONTEXTS. (US/0890-5495). **3417**

NINETEENTH-CENTURY FRENCH STUDIES. (US/0146-7891). **3349**

NINETEENTH-CENTURY LITERATURE. (US/0891-9356). **3417**

NINETEENTH CENTURY PROSE. (US/1052-0406). **3417**

NINETEENTH-CENTURY STUDIES (CHARLESTON, S.C.). (US/0893-7931). **3417**

NIPH ANNALS. (NO/0332-5652). **4794**

NIPPON KAGAKUKAI (1972). (JA/0369-4577). **987**

NIPPON NOGEI KAGAKU KAISHI. (JA/0002-1407). **113**

NIR NEWS. (UK/0960-3360). **4413**

NOISE CONTROL ENGINEERING JOURNAL. (US/0736-2501). **2178**

NOMOS (FORTALEZA, BRAZIL). (BL). **3018**

NONLINEAR ANALYSIS. (UK/0362-546X). **3524**

NONLINEAR DYNAMICS. (NE/0924-090X). **1989**

NONPROFIT WORLD. (US). **5299**

NONWOVENS ABSTRACTS. (UK/9036-1234). **5360**

NORD REVY : TIDSSKRIFT FOR REGIONAL UDVIKLING, NAERINGSLIV, MILJOE. (NO/0802-8818). **2829**

NORDIC HYDROLOGY. (DK/0029-1277). **1416**

NORDIC JOURNAL OF BOTANY. (DK/0107-055X). **520**

NORDIC JOURNAL OF LINGUISTICS. (NO/0332-5865). **3306**

NORDISK PSYKOLOGI. (DK/0029-1463). **4606**

NORDISK TIDSSKRIFT FOR SPECIALPAEDAGOGIK. (NO/0048-0509). **1883**

NORMAS LEGALES. (PE). **3018**

NORSK ANTHROPOLOGISK TIDSSKRIFT. (NO/0802-7285). **242**

NORSK GEOLOGISK TIDSSKRIFT. (NO/0029-196X). **1390**

NORTH AMERICAN CULTURE. (US/0882-1968). **5253**

NORTH CAROLINA HISTORICAL REVIEW, THE. (US/0029-2494). **2750**

NORTH CAROLINA INSIGHT. (US). **4669**

NORTH CAROLINA LIBRARIES. (US/0029-2540). **3237**

NORTH CAROLINA LITERARY REVIEW. (US/1063-0724). **3418**

NORTH DAKOTA QUARTERLY, THE. (US/0029-277X). **2541**

NORTH WEST EUROPE COMPANY REPORT. (UK). **4266**

NORTHEAST GULF SCIENCE. (US/0148-9836). **1453**

NORTHEASTERN GEOLOGY. (US/0194-1453). **1390**

NORTHERN LIGHTS. (US). **2541**

NORTHERN PERSPECTIVE. (AT/0314-989X). **3418**

NORTHERN REVIEW (WHITEHORSE). (CN). **326**

NORTHWEST ANTHROPOLOGICAL RESEARCH NOTES. (US/0029-3296). **242**

NORTHWEST ENVIRONMENTAL JOURNAL, THE. (US/0749-7962). **2179**

NORTHWEST EUROPE UPSTREAM PETROLEUM DATABASE. (UK). **4267**

NORTHWEST FOLKLORE. (US/0029-3369). **2323**

NORTHWEST GEORGIA HISTORICAL & GENEALOGICAL QUARTERLY. (US/0887-588X). **2464**

NORTHWEST SCIENCE. (US/0029-344X). **5134**

NORTHWESTERN NATURALIST : A JOURNAL OF VERTEBRATE BIOLOGY. (US/1051-1733). **4169**

NORTHWESTERN UNIVERSITY LAW REVIEW. (US/0029-3571). **3019**

NOTE D'INFORMATION TECHNIQUE - CENTRE SCIENTIFIQUE ET TECHNIQUE DE LA CONSTRUCTION. (FR/0379-6264). **622**

NOTES AND RECORDS OF THE ROYAL SOCIETY OF LONDON. (UK/0035-9149). **5134**

NOTES ON AMERICA'S FOLK ART ENVIRONMENTS. (US). **360**

NOTICIARIO DE HISTORIA AGRARIA. (SP/1132-1261). **115**

NOTICIAS ALIADAS. (PE). **2512**

NOTIZIARIO DEL CENTRO DI DOCUMENTAZIONE. (IT/0392-4270). **421**

NOTULAE NATURAE OF THE ACADEMY NATURAL SCIENCES OF PHILADELPHIA. (US/0029-4608). **5134**

NOUS VOULONS LIRE PESSAC. (FR/0153-9027). **3349**

NOUVEAUX CAHIERS D'ALLEMAND. (FR/0758-170X). **3418**

NOVA HEDWIGIA. (GW/0029-5035). **520**

NOVA SCOTIA REAL PROPERTY PRACTICE MANUAL. (CN). **3019**

NOVENYTERMELES. (HU/0546-8191). **179**

NOVI DNI. (CN/0048-1017). **2270**

NOW DIG THIS. (UK). **4142**

NTT REVIEW. (JA/0915-2334). **1161**

NUC COMPACT : COMPACT NEWS IN NUCLEAR MEDICINE. (GW/0344-3752). **3848**

NUCLEAR ENERGY (1978). (UK/0140-4067). **1951**

NUCLEAR ENGINEERING INTERNATIONAL. (UK/0029-5507). **2157**

NUCLEAR FUSION. (AU/0029-5515). **4448**

NUCLEAR INSTRUMENTS & METHODS IN PHYSICS RESEARCH. SECTION A, ACCELERATORS, SPECTROMETERS, DETECTORS AND ASSOCIATED EQUIPMENT. (NE/0168-9002). **4449**

NUCLEAR INSTRUMENTS & METHODS IN PHYSICS RESEARCH. SECTION B, BEAM INTERACTIONS WITH MATERIALS AND ATOMS. (NE/0168-583X). **4449**

NUCLEAR MAGNETIC RESONANCE. (UK/0305-9804). **4444**

NUCLEAR MEDICINE COMMUNICATIONS. (UK/0143-3636). **3848**

NUCLEAR PHYSICS. A. (NE/0375-9474). **4449**

NUCLEAR SAFETY. (US/0029-5604). **2157**

NUCLEAR SCIENCE AND ENGINEERING. (US/0029-5639). **2157**

NUCLEAR TECHNOLOGY. (US/0029-5450). **2157**

NUCLEIC ACIDS RESEARCH. (UK/0305-1048). **491**

NUCLEOSIDES & NUCLEOTIDES. (US/0732-8311). **491**

NUESTRAS RAICES (QUARTERLY). (US/1045-2427). **2465**

NUEVA REVISTA DE FILOLOGIA HISPANICA. (MX/0185-0121). **3307**

NUMERICAL FUNCTIONAL ANALYSIS AND OPTIMIZATION. (US/0163-0563). **3525**

NUMERICAL HEAT TRANSFER. PART A, APPLICATIONS. (US/1040-7782). **4432**

NUMERICAL HEAT TRANSFER. PART B, FUNDAMENTALS. (US/1040-7790). **4432**

NUMERISCHE MATHEMATIK. (GW/0029-599X). **3525**

NUNG YEH HUAN CHING PAO HU. (CC/1000-0267). **2237**

NUOVA FINESTRA. (IT). **634**

NUOVO CIMENTO DELLA SOCIETA ITALIANA DI FISICA [SEZIONE] C, IL. (IT/0390-5551). **4413**

NUOVO CIMENTO DELLA SOCIETA ITALIANA DI FISICA, [SEZIONE] D. (IT/0392-6737). **4449**

NUOVO CIMENTO DELLA SOCIETA ITALIANA DI FIZICA. SEZIONE A. (IT/0369-4097). **4449**

NUOVO SAGGIATORE : BOLLETTINO DELLA SOCIETA ITALIANA DI FISICA, IL. (IT). **4413**

NURSE ANESTHESIA. (US/0897-7437). **3683**

NURSE PRACTITIONER FORUM. (US/1045-5485). **3863**

NURSE PRACTITIONER, THE. (US/0361-1817). **3863**

NURSE, THE PATIENT & THE LAW, THE. (US/0196-6790). **3020**

NURSING ADMINISTRATION QUARTERLY. (US/0363-9568). **3863**

NURSING & HEALTH CARE. (US/0276-5284). **3863**

NURSING AND HEALTH SCIENCE EDUCATION REVIEW. (AT/1033-6273). **3863**

NURSING CLINICS OF NORTH AMERICA, THE. (US/0029-6465). **3863**

NURSING DIAGNOSIS. (US/1046-7459). **3864**

NURSING ECONOMIC$. (US/0746-1739). **3864**

NURSING FORUM (HILLSDALE). (US/0029-6473). **3864**

NURSING HISTORY REVIEW. (US/1062-8061). **3864**

NURSING OUTLOOK. (US/0029-6554). **3865**

NURSING RESEARCH (NEW YORK). (US/0029-6562). **3865**

NURSING RSA. (SA/0258-1647). **3865**

NURSING SCAN IN ADMINISTRATION. (US/1056-3091). **3865**

NURSING SCAN IN RESEARCH. (US/0897-5647). **3865**

NURSING SCIENCE QUARTERLY. (US/0894-3184). **3865**

NURSINGCONNECTIONS (WASHINGTON, D.C.). (US/0895-2809). **3866**

NUTRITION AND CANCER. (US/0163-5581). **4195**

NUTRITION AND HEALTH (BERKHAMSTED). (UK/0260-1060). **4195**

NUTRITION (BURBANK, LOS ANGELES COUNTY, CALIF.). (US/0899-9007). **4196**

NUTRITION RESEARCH (NEW YORK, N.Y.). (US/0271-5317). **4196**

NUTRITION REVIEWS. (US/0029-6643). **4197**

NYAME AKUMA. (CN/0713-5815). **277**

NYENGO BOGO - RIMMOG NYUGJON NYENGUSO. (KO/0073-9294). **2390**

O.S.B.E.R. OIL SPILL BULLETIN AND ENVIRONMENTAL REVIEW. (UK/0959-9134). **2238**

OBESITY RESEARCH. (US/1071-7323). **3623**

OBSERVATORY, THE. (UK/0029-7704). **397**

OBSTETRICS AND GYNECOLOGY CLINICS OF NORTH AMERICA. (US/0889-8545). **3766**

OBSTETRICS AND GYNECOLOGY (NEW YORK. 1953). (US/0029-7844). **3766**

OCCASIONAL PAPER - MISSOURI ACADEMY OF SCIENCE. (US/0148-0944). **5135**

OCCASIONAL PAPER / SOCIETY OF ANTIQUARIES OF LONDON. (UK/0953-7155). **2701**

OCCASIONAL PAPERS. (SA/0065-387X). **2851**

OCCASIONAL PAPERS - APPLIED LINGUISTICS ASSOCIATION OF AUSTRALIA. (AT/0314-3937). **3307**

OCCASIONAL PAPERS - DEPT. OF ENGLISH LOCAL HISTORY, LEICESTER UNIVERSITY. (UK/0078-303X). **2701**

OCCASIONAL PAPERS OF THE MUSEUM OF ZOOLOGY, UNIVERSITY OF MICHIGAN. (US/0076-8413). **5593**

OCCASIONAL PAPERS (UNIVERSITY OF NEW MEXICO. MUSEUM OF SOUTHWESTERN BIOLOGY). (US/0749-2421). **2219**

OCCASIONAL PUBLICATIONS OF THE DEPARTMENT OF GEOGRAPHY (URBANA). (US/0271-0366). **2571**

OCCUPATIONAL MEDICINE (PHILADELPHIA, PA.). (US/0885-114X). **2867**

OCCUPATIONAL THERAPY IN HEALTH CARE. (US/0738-0577). **1883**

OCCUPATIONAL THERAPY IN MENTAL HEALTH. (US/0164-212X). **2867**

OCCUPATIONAL THERAPY INDEX : CURRENT AWARENESS TOPICS SERVICE. (UK/0950-6675). **1883**

OCCUPATIONAL THERAPY INTERNATIONAL. (UK/0966-7903). **4381**

OCCUPATIONAL THERAPY JOURNAL OF RESEARCH. (US/0276-1599). **1883**

OCEAN CHALLENGE. (UK). **1453**

OCEAN DEVELOPMENT AND INTERNATIONAL LAW. (US/0090-8320). **3182**

OCEAN ENGINEERING. (US/0029-8018). **2093**

OCEANIA. (AT/0029-8077). **2670**

OCEANOLOGICA ACTA. (FR/0399-1784). **1454**

OCEANUS (WOODS HOLE). (US/0029-8182). **1454**

ODONATOLOGICA. (NE/0375-0183). **467**

OECOLOGIA. (GW/0029-8549). **2219**

OFFICE SYSTEMS RESEARCH JOURNAL. (US/0737-8998). **700**

OHIO FISH AND WILDLIFE REPORT. (US/0085-4468). **2201**

OHIO JOURNAL OF SCIENCE, THE. (US/0030-0950). **5136**

OHIO NORTHERN UNIVERSITY LAW REVIEW. (US/0094-534X). **3021**

OHIO READING TEACHER. (US/0030-1035). **3308**

OHIO TAX REVIEW. (US/1071-4243). **4739**

OIKOS. (DK/0030-1299). **2220**

OIL & GAS JOURNAL. (US/0030-1388). **4268**

OKLAHOMA GEOLOGY NOTES. (US/0030-1736). **1443**

OLD COLONY MEMORIAL. (US). **5689**

OLD LYONS RECORDER, THE. (US). **5644**

OLD NORTHWEST, THE. (US/0360-5531). **2752**

OLEAGINEUX. (FR/0030-2082). **117**

OMEGA (FARMINGDALE). (US/0030-2228). **4606**

OMEGA (OXFORD). (UK/0305-0483). **880**

ON BALANCE (DENVER, COLO.). (US/1062-7049). **4606**

ON-LINE REVIEW. (UK/0309-314X). **1275**

ON-SHORE WEEKLY. (UK). **2147**

ONCODISC (PHILADELPHIA, PA.). (US/0897-5639). **3821**

ONCOGENE. (UK/0950-9232). **3821**

ONCOGENE RESEARCH. (US/0890-6467). **3821**

ONCOLOGY NURSING FORUM. (US/0190-535X). **3866**

ONDE ELECTRIQUE. (FR/0030-2430). **2074**

ONDERNEMEN. (BE/0772-3326). **5065**

ONDERSTEPOORT JOURNAL OF VETERINARY RESEARCH, THE. (SA/0030-2465). **5517**

ONE, TWO, THREE, FOUR. (US/0889-0536). **4143**

ONKOLOGIE. (SZ/0378-584X). **3822**

ONLINE & CDROM REVIEW : THE INTERNATIONAL JOURNAL OF ONLINE & OPTICAL INFORMATION SYSTEMS. (UK). **1275**

ONLINE HOTLINE NEWS SERVICE. (US/1040-6646). **1197**

ONLINE (WESTON, CONN.). (US/0146-5422). **1275**

ONOMASTICA CANADIANA. (CN/0078-4656). **3308**

ONS NURSING SCAN IN ONCOLOGY. (US/1062-5720). **3866**

ONTARIO CRAFT. (CN/0229-1320). **374**

ONTARIO GEOGRAPHY. (CN/0078-4850). **2571**

ONTARIO HISTORY. (CN/0030-2953). **2752**

OPEN LETTER GEELONG. (AT/1035-4727). **1883**

OPERA ANNUAL U.S. (US/0899-3645). **4143**

OPERA BOTANICA. (DK/0078-5237). **520**

OPERA JOURNAL, THE. (US/0030-3585). **4143**

OPERATIONS RESEARCH. (US/0030-364X). **3525**

OPERATIONS RESEARCH LETTERS. (NE/0167-6377). **5136**

OPERATIONS RESEARCH/MANAGEMENT SCIENCE. (US/0030-3658). **1209**

OPERATIONS RESEARCH/MANAGEMENT SCIENCE YEARBOOK. (US/0473-0496). **881**

OPERATIVE DENTISTRY. (US/0361-7734). **1332**

OPERATORE SANITARIO, L'. (IT/0392-5153). **3624**

OPHELIA. (DK/0078-5326). **556**

OPHTHALMIC & PHYSIOLOGICAL OPTICS. (UK/0275-5408). **4216**

OPHTHALMIC PAEDIATRICS AND GENETICS. (NE/0167-6784). **550**

OPHTHALMIC

OPHTHALMIC RESEARCH. (SZ/0030-3747). **3877**

OPHTHALMIC SURGERY. (US/0022-023X). **3971**

OPHTHALMOLOGICA (BASEL). (SZ/0030-3755). **3877**

OPHTHALMOLOGY (ROCHESTER, MINN.). (US/0161-6420). **3878**

OPTICA APPLICATA. (PL/0078-5466). **4438**

OPTICAL AND QUANTUM ELECTRONICS. (UK/0306-8919). **4439**

OPTICAL COMPUTING & PROCESSING. (UK/0954-2264). **1277**

OPTICAL ENGINEERING. (US/0091-3286). **4439**

OPTICS AND LASER TECHNOLOGY. (UK/0030-3992). **4439**

OPTICS AND LASERS IN ENGINEERING. (UK/0143-8166). **4439**

OPTICS COMMUNICATIONS. (NE/0030-4018). **4439**

OPTICS LETTERS. (US/0146-9592). **4439**

OPTIK (STUTTGART). (GW/0030-4026). **4440**

OPTIKA I SPEKTROSKOPIJA. (RU/0030-4034). **4440**

OPTIMAL CONTROL APPLICATIONS & METHODS. (UK/0143-2087). **1220**

OPTION/BIO PARIS. (FR/0992-5945). **467**

OPTOMETRY AND VISION SCIENCE. (US/1040-5488). **4217**

OR-SPEKTRUM. (GW/0171-6468). **5136**

ORAFO ITALIANO. (IT/0471-7376). **2915**

ORAL AND MAXILLOFACIAL SURGERY CLINICS OF NORTH AMERICA. (US/1042-3699). **3971**

ORAL MICROBIOLOGY AND IMMUNOLOGY. (DK/0902-0055). **1332**

ORAL SURGERY, ORAL MEDICINE, ORAL PATHOLOGY. (US/0030-4220). **1332**

ORAL TRADITION. (US/0883-5365). **2323**

ORBIS (PHILADELPHIA). (US/0030-4387). **4485**

ORDER (DORDRECHT). (NE/0167-8094). **3526**

OREGON PERSONAL INCOME TAX ANNUAL STATISTICS. (US). **4699**

ORGANIC GEOCHEMISTRY. (UK/0146-6380). **1390**

ORGANIC MASS SPECTROMETRY. (UK/0030-493X). **1018**

ORGANIC PREPARATIONS AND PROCEDURES INTERNATIONAL. (US/0030-4948). **1045**

ORGANIZATION DEVELOPMENT JOURNAL. (US/0889-6402). **881**

ORGANIZATION STUDIES. (GW/0170-8406). **5211**

ORGANIZATIONAL DYNAMICS. (US/0090-2616). **881**

ORGANOMETALLIC CHEMISTRY IN THE USSR. (UK/0955-8586). **1045**

ORGANOMETALLICS. (US/0276-7333). **1045**

ORGUE (PARIS), L'. (FR/0030-5170). **4145**

ORIENTAL INSECTS. (US/0030-5316). **5612**

ORIENTAL INSECTS MONOGRAPH. (US). **5612**

ORIGINAL NEWS PEPPER, THE. (US/1071-233X). **3907**

ORIGINS (LOMA LINDA). (US/0093-7495). **5136**

ORIGINS OF LIFE AND EVOLUTION OF THE BIOSPHERE. (NE/0169-6149). **467**

ORL; JOURNAL FOR OTO-RHINO-LARYNGOLOGY AND ITS BORDERLANDS. (SZ/0301-1569). **3890**

ORNIS FENNICA. (FI/0030-5685). **5619**

ORNIS SCANDINAVICA. (NO/0030-5693). **5619**

ORQUIDEA (MEXICO. 1971). (MX/0300-3701). **520**

ORSA JOURNAL ON COMPUTING. (US/0899-1499). **1198**

ORTHODOXIE HEUTE. (GW/0931-0347). **5040**

ORTHOPAEDIC REVIEW. (US/0094-6591). **3883**

ORTHOPEDIC CLINICS OF NORTH AMERICA, THE. (US/0030-5898). **3884**

ORTHOPEDIC NURSING / NATIONAL ASSOCIATION OF ORTHOPEDIC NURSES. (US/0744-6020). **3884**

ORTHOPEDICS (THOROFARE). (US/0147-7447). **3884**

ORYX. (UK/0030-6053). **2201**

OSAKA JOURNAL OF MATHEMATICS. (JA/0030-6126). **3526**

OSMOSE (MONTREAL). (CN/0829-5131). **3866**

OSTEUROPA (STUTTGART). (GW/0030-6428). **4486**

OSTRICH, THE. (SA/0030-6525). **5619**

OTHER SIDE OF THE BOAT. (US). **4984**

OTHER SIDE (SAVANNAH), THE. (US/0145-7675). **4984**

OTHER VOICES (HIGHLAND PARK, ILL.). (US/8756-4696). **3421**

OTOLARYNGOLOGIC CLINICS OF NORTH AMERICA, THE. (US/0030-6665). **3890**

OTOLARYNGOLOGY AND HEAD AND NECK SURGERY. (US/0194-5998). **3971**

OTTO NOVECENTO. (IT). **3421**

OUEST MEDICAL PARIS. (FR/0048-2366). **3625**

OUR VOICE (NEW YORK, N.Y. 1990). (US/1064-0207). **3890**

OUTDOOR OKLAHOMA. (US/0030-7106). **4877**

OUTLOOK ON AGRICULTURE. (UK/0030-7270). **118**

OVERLAND JOURNAL. (US/0738-1093). **2752**

OWL OF MINERVA, THE. (US/0030-7580). **4354**

OXFORD BULLETIN OF ECONOMICS AND STATISTICS. (UK/0305-9049). **1577**

OXFORD ECONOMIC PAPERS. (UK/0030-7653). **1594**

OXFORD REVIEW OF EDUCATION. (UK/0305-4985). **1771**

OXFORD REVIEWS OF REPRODUCTIVE BIOLOGY. (UK/0260-0854). **584**

OXFORD STUDIES IN COMPARATIVE EDUCATION. (UK/0961-2149). **1771**

OXIDATION COMMUNICATIONS. (BU/0209-4541). **1045**

OXIDATION OF METALS. (US/0030-770X). **4014**

OZONE : SCIENCE & ENGINEERING. (US/0191-9512). **1037**

OZS, OSTERREICHISCHE ZEITSCHRIFT FUER SOZIOLOGIE. (AU/1011-0070). **5253**

PAAC NOTES (CHICAGO, ILL.). (US/1059-7913). **3715**

PAC-FINDER SYSTEM 34/36 SOFTWARE DIRECTORY. (US/0741-4978). **1289**

PACE PETROLEUM COKE QUARTERLY. (US). **4271**

PACIFIC AFFAIRS. (CN/0030-851X). **4486**

PACIFIC ARTS. (US). **327**

PACIFIC HISTORICAL REVIEW. (US/0030-8684). **2753**

PACIFIC JOURNAL OF MATHEMATICS. (US/0030-8730). **3526**

PACIFIC NORTHWEST QUARTERLY. (US/0030-8803). **2753**

PACIFIC NORTHWESTERNER, THE. (US/0030-882X). **2753**

PACIFIC STUDIES. (US/0275-3596). **2670**

PACIFICA : AUSTRALIAN THEOLOGICAL STUDIES. (AT). **4984**

PACING AND CLINICAL ELECTROPHYSIOLOGY. (US/0147-8389). **3708**

PAEDIATRIC ANAESTHESIA. (FR/1155-5645). **3907**

PAGE (CHICAGO, ILL.), THE. (US/1056-6023). **1263**

PAIN (AMSTERDAM). (NE/0304-3959). **3896**

PAIN RESEARCH AND CLINICAL MANAGEMENT. (NE/0921-3287). **3625**

PAKISTAN DEVELOPMENT REVIEW. (PK/0030-9729). **1511**

PAKISTAN JOURNAL OF BOTANY. (PK/0556-3321). **520**

PAKISTAN JOURNAL OF SCIENTIFIC AND INDUSTRIAL RESEARCH. (PK/0030-9885). **5137**

PAKISTAN JOURNAL OF SCIENTIFIC RESEARCH. (PK/0552-9050). **5137**

PALAEOGEOGRAPHY, PALAEOCLIMATOLOGY, PALAEOECOLOGY. (NE/0031-0182). **4228**

PALAEONTOLOGY. (UK/0031-0239). **4229**

PALAEONTOLOGY NEWSLETTER. (UK/0954-9900). **4229**

PALAESTRA (MACOMB, ILL.). (US/8756-5811). **4392**

PALAIOS. (US/0883-1351). **4229**

PALEOBIOLOGY. (US/0094-8373). **4229**

PALEOBIOS. (US/0031-0298). **4229**

PALEOPATHOLOGY NEWSLETTER. (US/0148-4737). **278**

PALESTINE EXPLORATION QUARTERLY. (UK/0031-0328). **278**

PAN. (MX). **2352**

PAN-PACIFIC ENTOMOLOGIST, THE. (US/0031-0603). **5612**

PANCREAS. (US/0885-3177). **3800**

PANMINERVA MEDICA. (IT/0031-0808). **3625**

PANORAMA CONTITERO. (SP). **2352**

PAPER & BOARD ABSTRACTS. (UK/0307-0778). **4240**

PAPER MARKET DIGEST. (UK). **4236**

PAPERI JA PUU. (FI/0031-1243). **4236**

Peer Reviewed Index

PAPERS. (AT). **3422**

PAPERS AND DISCUSSIONS - ASSOCIATION OF MINE MANAGERS OF SOUTH AFRICA. (SA). **2147**

PAPERS AND RECORDS - THUNDER BAY HISTORICAL MUSEUM SOCIETY. (CN/0703-7058). **4095**

PAPERS IN AUSTRALIAN LINGUISTICS. (AT/0078-9062). **3309**

PAPERS OF THE LEEDS INTERNATIONAL LATIN SEMINAR. (UK). **1079**

PAPIER, DAS. (GW/0031-1340). **4236**

PAPUA NEW GUINEA MEDICAL JOURNAL. (PP/0031-1480). **3626**

PAR. PUBLIC ADMINISTRATION REVIEW POPULATION. (US/0033-3352). **4672**

PARADOX INFORMANT (US/1058-7071). **1280**

PARALLEL COMPUTING. (NE/0167-8191). **1248**

PARAPLEGIA. (UK/0031-1758). **4392**

PARASITOLOGY. (UK/0031-1820). **492**

PARASITOLOGY TODAY (REFERENCE ED.). (UK/0169-4707). **468**

PARAZITOLOGIJA. (RU/0031-1847). **468**

PARENTS AND CHILDREN TOGETHER. (US/1050-7108). **2284**

PARERGON. (AT/0313-6221). **1079**

PARLIAMENTARY AFFAIRS. (UK/0031-2290). **4672**

PARLIAMENTARY WEEKLY QUARTERLY REPORT, THE. (CN/1188-2387). **4487**

PARLIAMENTS, ESTATES & REPRESENTATION. (UK/0260-6755). **4487**

PARTICLE & PARTICLE SYSTEMS CHARACTERIZATION. (GW/0934-0866). **988**

PARTICULATE SCIENCE AND TECHNOLOGY. (US/0272-6351). **2015**

PARTISAN REVIEW (1936). (US/0031-2525). **4544**

PASADENA HERITAGE. (US/0889-5864). **2753**

PAST & PRESENT. (UK/0031-2746). **2625**

PASTORAL SCIENCES. (CN/0713-3383). **4985**

PASTURAS TROPICALES. (CK/1012-7410). **118**

PATHOLOGE, DER. (GW/0172-8113). **3896**

PATHOLOGIE ET BIOLOGIE (PARIS). (FR/0369-8114). **3896**

PATHOLOGY. (AT/0031-3025). **3897**

PATHOLOGY, RESEARCH AND PRACTICE. (GW/0344-0338). **3897**

PATIENT UPDATE. (CN/0847-8090). **3790**

PATTERN RECOGNITION. (UK/0031-3203). **1215**

PATTERN RECOGNITION AND IMAGE ANALYSIS. (US/1054-6618). **3526**

PATTERN RECOGNITION LETTERS. (NE/0167-8655). **1234**

PC GUIDE USA. CD-ROM. (US). **1198**

PC-SIG MAGAZINE. (US/1042-0681). **1289**

PEABODY JOURNAL OF EDUCATION. (US/0161-956X). **1772**

PEACE RESEARCH. (CN/0008-4697). **4531**

PEACEKEEPING & INTERNATIONAL RELATIONS. (CN/1187-3485). **4531**

PEAK RUNNING PERFORMANCE. (US). **4911**

PEANUT RESEARCH. (US/0479-7558). **180**

PEANUT SCIENCE. (US/0095-3679). **180**

PEASANT STUDIES. (US/0149-1547). **5212**

PEDIATRE, LE. (FR/0397-9180). **3907**

PEDIATRIC ALLERGY AND IMMUNOLOGY : OFFICIAL PUBLICATION OF THE EUROPEAN SOCIETY OF PEDIATRIC ALLERGY AND IMMUNOLOGY. (DK/0905-6157). **3675**

PEDIATRIC ANNALS. (US/0090-4481). **3908**

PEDIATRIC CARDIOLOGY. (US/0172-0643). **3908**

PEDIATRIC CLINICS OF NORTH AMERICA, THE. (US/0031-3955). **3908**

PEDIATRIC DERMATOLOGY. (US/0736-8046). **3908**

PEDIATRIC EMERGENCY & CRITICAL CARE. (US/1059-0870). **3908**

PEDIATRIC HEMATOLOGY AND ONCOLOGY. (US/0888-0018). **3773**

PEDIATRIC INFECTIOUS DISEASE JOURNAL, THE. (US/0891-3668). **3908**

PEDIATRIC NEPHROLOGY (BERLIN, WEST). (GW/0931-041X). **3909**

PEDIATRIC NEUROLOGY. (US/0887-8994). **3909**

PEDIATRIC NEUROSURGERY. (SZ/1016-2291). **3909**

PEDIATRIC NURSING. (US/0097-9805). **3866**

PEDIATRIC NURSING [MICROFORM]. (US/0097-9805). **3866**

PEDIATRIC PHYSICAL THERAPY. (US/0898-5669). **3909**

PEDIATRIC PRIMARY CARE. (US/1071-5711). **3909**

PEDIATRIC PULMONOLOGY. (US/8755-6863). **3909**

PEDIATRIC RADIOLOGY. (GW/0301-0449). **3944**

PEDIATRIC RESEARCH. (US/0031-3998). **3909**

PEDIATRIC SURGERY INTERNATIONAL. (GW/0179-0358). **3909**

PEDIATRIC THERAPEUTICS AND TOXICOLOGY. (US/0893-6218). **3909**

PEDIATRICS. EDICION ESPANOLA. (SP/0210-5721). **3910**

PEDIATRICS (EVANSTON). (US/0031-4005). **3910**

PEDOBIOLOGIA. (GW/0031-4056). **181**

PENNSYLVANIA FOLKLIFE. (US/0031-4498). **2754**

PENNSYLVANIA GEOGRAPHER, THE. (US/0553-5980). **2572**

PENNSYLVANIA GEOLOGY. (US/0048-3214). **1391**

PENNSYLVANIA HISTORY. (US/0031-4528). **2754**

PENNSYLVANIA MAGAZINE OF HISTORY AND BIOGRAPHY, THE. (US/0031-4587). **2754**

PENNSYLVANIA POLICE CRIMINAL LAW BULLETIN, THE. (US/0098-7174). **3171**

PEPTIDE RESEARCH. (US/1040-5704). **1046**

PEPTIDES (NEW YORK, N.Y, : 1980). (US/0196-9781). **492**

PERCEPTION & PSYCHOPHYSICS. (US/0031-5117). **4607**

PERCEPTION (OTTAWA). (CN/0704-5263). **5301**

PERCEPTUAL AND MOTOR SKILLS. (US/0031-5125). **4607**

PERFORMANCE EVALUATION. (NE/0166-5316). **1261**

PERFORMANCE (FORT WORTH, TEX.). (US/0882-9314). **387**

PERFORMANCES MARSEILLE. (FR/0996-5882). **1773**

PERFORMING ARTS & ENTERTAINMENT IN CANADA. (CN/1185-3433). **387**

PERIODICA MATHEMATICA HUNGARICA. (HU/0031-5303). **3526**

PERIODICUM BIOLOGORUM. (CI/0031-5362). **468**

PERIPHERY LISMORE. (AT/1034-0580). **374**

PERISTIL (ZAGREB). (CI/0553-6707). **362**

PERITONEAL DIALYSIS INTERNATIONAL. (US/0896-8608). **3800**

PERKIN TRANSACTIONS 1. (UK/0300-922X). **1046**

PERMAFROST AND PERIGLACIAL PROCESSES. (UK/1045-6740). **1391**

PERSONA Y DERECHO. (SP/0211-4526). **3090**

PERSONAL MEDICAL ADVISOR. (US/1065-0687). **3626**

PERSONALITY AND INDIVIDUAL DIFFERENCES. (UK/0191-8869). **4607**

PERSONALITY & SOCIAL PSYCHOLOGY BULLETIN. (US/0146-1672). **4607**

PERSONNEL JOURNAL. (US/0031-5745). **945**

PERSONNEL PSYCHOLOGY. (US/0031-5826). **4607**

PERSONNEL REVIEW. (UK/0048-3486). **945**

PERSOON EN GEMEENSCHAP. (BE/0031-5842). **1773**

PERSOONIA. (NE/0031-5850). **576**

PERSPECTIVA (SOUTH HADLEY, MASS.). (US/1059-0536). **3310**

PERSPECTIVES IN BIOLOGY AND MEDICINE. (US/0031-5982). **468**

PERSPECTIVES IN EDUCATION AND DEAFNESS. (US/1051-6204). **4392**

PERSPECTIVES IN MATHEMATICAL LOGIC. (GW/0344-4325). **3526**

PERSPECTIVES IN PSYCHIATRIC CARE. (US/0031-5990). **3866**

PERSPECTIVES MEDIEVALES. (FR/0338-2338). **3423**

PERSPECTIVES ON SCIENCE AND CHRISTIAN FAITH. (US/0892-2675). **4986**

PERSPECTIVES ON SOCIAL PROBLEMS. (US/1047-0905). **5253**

PERSPECTIVES ON THE HISTORY OF ECONOMIC THOUGHT. (UK). **1594**

PERSUASIONS (VICTORIA). (CN/0821-0314). **3423**

PERTANIKA. (MY/0126-6128). **119**

PERU ECONOMICO. (PE). **1578**

PESQUISA AGROPECUARIA BRASILEIRA. (BL/0100-204X). **119**

PESTICIDE BIOCHEMISTRY AND PHYSIOLOGY. (US/0048-3575). **4246**

PESTICIDE MANUAL. (UK). **4246**

PESTICIDE SCIENCE. (UK/0031-613X). **4246**

PET DEALER ANNUAL GUIDE. (US/0553-8572). **4287**

PETROLEUM ACCOUNTING AND FINANCIAL MANAGEMENT JOURNAL. (US). **4272**

PETROLEUM SERVICES WEEKLY SCOUTING SERVICE - OFF SHORE. (UK). **4273**

PHARMACEUTICA ACTA HELVETIAE. (SZ/0031-6865). **4319**

PHARMACEUTICAL ENGINEERING. (US/0273-8139). **4320**

PHARMACEUTICAL MARKETING. (UK). **4320**

PHARMACEUTICAL RESEARCH. (US/0724-8741). **4321**

PHARMACEUTICAL TIMES. (UK). **4321**

PHARMACEUTISCH WEEKBLAD. SCIENTIFIC EDITION. (NE/0167-6555). **4321**

PHARMACOLOGICAL REVIEWS. (US/0031-6997). **4322**

PHARMACOLOGY. (SZ/0031-7012). **4322**

PHARMACOLOGY & THERAPEUTICS (OXFORD). (UK/0163-7258). **4322**

PHARMACOLOGY & TOXICOLOGY. (DK/0901-9928). **4322**

PHARMACOLOGY, BIOCHEMISTRY AND BEHAVIOR. (US/0091-3057). **4322**

PHARMACOPEIAL FORUM. (US/0363-4655). **4322**

PHARMACOTHERAPY. (US/0277-0008). **4323**

PHARMAZEUTISCHE INDUSTRIE, DIE. (GW/0031-711X). **4324**

PHARMAZIE, DIE. (GW/0031-7144). **4324**

PHASE TRANSITIONS. (US/0141-1594). **4414**

PHELON'S DISCOUNT & JOBBING TRADE. (US). **956**

PHELON'S WOMEN'S APPAREL SHOPS. (US/0737-3430). **1086**

PHI DELTA KAPPAN. (US/0031-7217). **1773**

PHILADELPHIA ARCHITECT. (US/1071-1651). **306**

PHILIPPINE AGRICULTURIST, THE. (PH/0031-7454). **119**

PHILIPPINE JOURNAL OF BIOTECHNOLOGY. (PH/0117-0503). **3695**

PHILIPPINE JOURNAL OF WEED SCIENCE. (PH). **181**

PHILOLOGICAL QUARTERLY. (US/0031-7977). **3310**

PHILOLOGOS. (GR). **1079**

PHILOSOPHER, THE. (UK). **4355**

PHILOSOPHIA (RAMAT GAN). (IS/0048-3893). **4355**

PHILOSOPHICAL MAGAZINE. A, PHYSICS OF CONDENSED MATTER, DEFECTS AND MECHANICAL PROPERTIES. (UK/0141-8610). **4414**

PHILOSOPHICAL MAGAZINE. B, PHYSICS OF CONDENSED MATTER, STRUCTURAL, ELECTRONIC, OPTICAL, AND MAGNETIC PROPERTIES. (UK/0958-6644). **4414**

PHILOSOPHICAL MAGAZINE LETTERS. (UK/0950-0839). **4414**

PHILOSOPHICAL STUDIES. (NE/0031-8116). **4356**

PHILOSOPHICAL STUDIES IN EDUCATION. (US/0160-7561). **4356**

PHILOSOPHICAL TRANSACTIONS - ROYAL SOCIETY OF LONDON. PHYSICAL SCIENCES AND ENGINEERING. (UK/0962-8428). **4414**

PHILOSOPHIQUES. (CN/0316-2923). **4356**

PHILOSOPHY AND PHENOMENOLOGICAL RESEARCH. (US/0031-8205). **4356**

PHILOSOPHY & PUBLIC AFFAIRS. (US/0048-3915). **5212**

PHILOSOPHY AND SOCIAL ACTION. (II/0377-2772). **5253**

PHILOSOPHY OF MUSIC EDUCATION REVIEW. (US/1063-5734). **4146**

PHILOSOPHY OF SCIENCE (EAST LANSING). (US/0031-8248). **5138**

PHILOSOPHY OF THE SOCIAL SCIENCES. (US/0048-3931). **5212**

PHILOSOPHY TODAY (CELINA). (US/0031-8256). **4357**

PHOENICS JOURNAL OF COMPUTATIONAL FLUID DYNAMICS & ITS APPLICATIONS, THE. (UK). **1289**

PHOENIX (MINNEAPOLIS, MINN.), THE. (US/0893-4509). **4608**

PHONETICA. (SZ/0031-8388). **3310**

PHOTOCHEMISTRY AND PHOTOBIOLOGY. (UK/0031-8655). **1056**

PHOTOGRAMMETRIC ENGINEERING AND REMOTE SENSING. (US/0099-1112). **1990**

PHOTOGRAMMETRIC RECORD, THE. (UK/0031-868X). **2572**

PHOTONICS DIRECTORY, THE. (US/1044-1425). **4440**

PHOTOSYNTHESIS RESEARCH. (NE/0166-8595). **521**

PHOTOSYNTHETICA. (NE/0300-3604). **492**

PHYCOLOGIA (OXFORD). (UK/0031-8884). **521**

PHYSICA A. (NE/0378-4371). **4414**

PHYSICA B. CONDENSED MATTER. (NE/0921-4526). **4414**

PHYSICA C. SUPERCONDUCTIVITY. (NE/0921-4534). **4414**

PHYSICA. D. (NE/0167-2789). **4414**

PHYSICA SCRIPTA. (SW/0031-8949). **4414**

PHYSICA STATUS SOLIDI. A: APPLIED RESEARCH. (GW/0031-8965). **4414**

PHYSICA STATUS SOLIDI. B : BASIC RESEARCH. (GW/0370-1972). **4415**

PHYSICAL & OCCUPATIONAL THERAPY IN GERIATRICS. (US/0270-3181). **4381**

PHYSICAL & OCCUPATIONAL THERAPY IN PEDIATRICS. (US/0194-2638). **4381**

PHYSICAL REVIEW. A. (US/1050-2947). **4415**

PHYSICAL REVIEW B : CONDENSED MATTER. (US/0163-1829). **4415**

PHYSICAL REVIEW C : NUCLEAR PHYSICS. (US/0556-2813). **4450**

PHYSICAL REVIEW D : PARTICLES AND FIELDS. (US/0556-2821). **4415**

PHYSICAL REVIEW LETTERS. (US/0031-9007). **4415**

PHYSICAL THERAPY. (US/0031-9023). **4381**

PHYSICIAN EXECUTIVE. (US/0898-2759). **3916**

PHYSICIAN'S MEDLINE PLUS. (US/1065-6545). **3661**

PHYSICS AND CHEMISTRY OF GLASSES. (UK/0031-9090). **2593**

PHYSICS AND CHEMISTRY OF LIQUIDS. (US/0031-9104). **1056**

PHYSICS AND CHEMISTRY OF MINERALS. (GW/0342-1791). **1443**

PHYSICS ESSAYS. (CN/0836-1398). **4415**

PHYSICS IN MEDICINE & BIOLOGY. (UK/0031-9155). **479**

PHYSICS LETTERS : PART A. (NE/0375-9601). **4416**

PHYSICS LETTERS : PART B. (NE/0370-2693). **4450**

PHYSICS OF FLUIDS. A, FLUID DYNAMICS. (US/0899-8213). **4416**

PHYSICS OF THE EARTH AND PLANETARY INTERIORS. (NE/0031-9201). **1391**

PHYSICS REPORTS. (NE/0370-1573). **4416**

PHYSICS TODAY. (US/0031-9228). **4416**

PHYSIOLOGIA PLANTARUM. (DK/0031-9317). **521**

PHYSIOLOGICAL AND MOLECULAR PLANT PATHOLOGY. (UK/0885-5765). **521**

PHYSIOLOGICAL CHEMISTRY AND PHYSICS AND MEDICAL NMR. (US/0748-6642). **469**

PHYSIOLOGICAL ENTOMOLOGY. (UK/0307-6962). **5612**

PHYSIOLOGICAL REVIEWS. (US/0031-9333). **585**

PHYSIOLOGICAL ZOOLOGY. (US/0031-935X). **5594**

PHYSIOLOGY & BEHAVIOR. (US/0031-9384). **585**

PHYSIOTHERAPY. (UK/0031-9406). **4382**

PHYSIOTHERAPY IN SPORT. (UK/0954-0741). **3955**

PHYSIOTHERAPY INDEX : CURRENT AWARENESS TOPICS SERVICES. (UK/0950-6659). **4382**

PHYSIOTHERAPY THEORY AND PRACTICE. (UK/0959-3985). **4382**

PHYTOCHEMISTRY (OXFORD). (UK/0031-9422). **522**

PHYTOLOGIA. (US/0031-9430). **522**

PHYTOLOGIA MEMOIRS. (US). **522**

PHYTON (BUENOS AIRES). (AG/0031-9457). **522**

PHYTON (HORN). (AU/0079-2047). **522**

PHYTOPARASITICA. (IS/0334-2123). **522**

PHYTOPATHOLOGY. (US/0031-949X). **522**

PHYTOPROTECTION. (CN/0031-9511). **181**

PIECES OF EIGHT. (US). **803**

PIG IRON. (US/0362-5214). **3423**

PIQUALITY. (US/1058-8787). **1199**

PISMA V ZURNAL TEHNICESKOJ FIZIKI. (RU/0320-0116). **4417**

PITCH PIPE, THE. (US/0882-214X). **4146**

PITTSBURGH HISTORY. (US/1069-4706). **2754**

PLACENTA (EASTBOURNE). (UK/0143-4004). **539**

PLAINS ANTHROPOLOGIST. (US/0032-0447). **2271**

PLAINSONGS. (US). **3423**

PLANETARY AND SPACE SCIENCE. (UK/0032-0633). **398**

PLANNING & CHANGING. (US/0032-0684). **1774**

PLANNING PERSPECTIVES : PP. (UK/0266-5433). **2831**

PLANNING PRACTICE + RESEARCH. (UK/0269-7459). **2831**

PLANODION. (GR/1105-2473). **3424**

PLANT AND CELL PHYSIOLOGY. (JA/0032-0781). **523**

PLANT AND SOIL. (NE/0032-079X). **181**

PLANT & WORKS ENGINEERING. (UK). **1990**

PLANT BREEDING. (GW/0179-9541). **523**

PLANT, CELL AND ENVIRONMENT. (UK/0140-7791). **523**

PLANT CELL REPORTS. (GW/0721-7714). **539**

PLANT CELL, THE. (US/1040-4651). **539**

PLANT CELL, TISSUE AND ORGAN CULTURE. (NE/0167-6857). **523**

PLANT DISEASE. (US/0191-2917). **181**

PLANT FOODS FOR HUMAN NUTRITION (DORDRECHT). (NE/0921-9668). **4197**

PLANT GROWTH REGULATION. (NE/0167-6903). **523**

PLANT JOURNAL : FOR CELL AND MOLECULAR BIOLOGY, THE. (UK/0960-7412). **523**

PLANT MOLECULAR BIOLOGY. (NE/0167-4412). **550**

PLANT PATHOLOGY. (UK/0032-0862). **524**

PLANT PHYSIOLOGY (BETHESDA). (US/0032-0889). **524**

PLANT PROTECTION QUARTERLY. (AT/0815-2195). **120**

PLANT SCIENCE (LIMERICK). (IE/0168-9452). **524**

PLANT SYSTEMATICS AND EVOLUTION. (AU/0378-2697). **524**

PLANT VARIETIES & SEEDS. (UK/0952-3863). **2427**

PLANTA. (GW/0032-0935). **524**

PLANTA MEDICA. (GW/0032-0943). **4325**

PLASMA CHEMISTRY AND PLASMA PROCESSING. (US/0272-4324). **2015**

PLASMA NEWS REPORT. (US/0892-6352). **1028**

PLASMA PHYSICS AND CONTROLLED FUSION. (UK/0741-3335). **4450**

PLASMID. (US/0147-619X). **550**

PLASTIC AND RECONSTRUCTIVE SURGERY (1963). (US/0032-1052). **3972**

PLATING AND SURFACE FINISHING. (US/0360-3164). **4225**

PLAY & CULTURE. (US/0894-4253). **5213**

PLUMBING. (UK/0032-1656). **2607**

PLURILINGUA. (BE). **3310**

PM PLUS. (UK). **946**

PMI. POWDER METALLURGY INTERNATIONAL. (GW/0048-5012). **4015**

POET LORE. (US/0032-1966). **3468**

POETRY IRELAND REVIEW, THE. (IE/0332-2998). **3469**

POETS ON. (US/0146-3136). **3470**

POLAR BIOLOGY. (GW/0722-4060). **5594**

POLAR RECORD, THE. (UK/0032-2474). **5138**

POLAR RESEARCH. (NO). **1359**

POLEMIC. (AT). **3029**

POLICE COMPUTER REVIEW. (US/1061-1509). **1289**

POLICE JOURNAL (CHICHESTER). (UK/0032-258X). **3172**

POLICE LIABILITY REVIEW. (US/1046-6835). **3172**

POLICY AND POLITICS. (UK/0305-5736). **4487**

POLICY (CENTRE FOR INDEPENDENT STUDIES (N.S.W.)). (AT/1032-6634). **4487**

POLICY REVIEW (WASHINGTON). (US/0146-5945). **5213**

POLICY SCIENCES. (NE/0032-2687). **4488**

POLICY STUDIES. (UK/0144-2872). **4488**

POLICY STUDIES JOURNAL. (US/0190-292X). **4488**

POLISH AMERICAN STUDIES (CHICAGO, ILL.). (US/0032-2806). **2754**

POLISH JOURNAL OF OCCUPATIONAL MEDICINE AND ENVIRONMENTAL HEALTH. (PL/0867-8383). **3628**

POLISH JOURNAL OF PHARMACOLOGY AND PHARMACY. (PL/0301-0244). **4325**

POLISH REVIEW (NEW YORK. 1956), THE. (US/0032-2970). **5213**

POLITICA. (DK/0105-0710). **4488**

POLITICAL PSYCHOLOGY. (US/0162-895X). **4608**

POLITICAL QUARTERLY (LONDON. 1930). (UK/0032-3179). **4489**

POLITICAL RESEARCH QUARTERLY. (US/1065-9129). **4489**

POLITICAL SCIENCE. (NZ/0032-3187). **4490**

POLITICAL SCIENCE QUARTERLY. (US/0032-3195). **4490**

POLITICAL STUDIES. (UK/0032-3217). **4490**

POLITICAL THEORY. (US/0090-5917). **4490**

POLITICAL WARFARE. (US/1056-3334). **4532**

POLITICS & SOCIETY. (US/0032-3292). **5213**

POLITICS AND THE LIFE SCIENCES. (US/0730-9384). **4490**

POLITICS (MANCHESTER (GREATER MANCHESTER)). (UK/0263-3957). **4491**

POLITIKA EKONOMIE. (XR/0032-3233). **1512**

POLITIKON. (SA/0258-9346). **4491**

POLITIQUES DE POPULATION. (BE). **4556**

POLITY. (US/0032-3497). **4491**

POLYHEDRON. (UK/0277-5387). **1037**

POLYMER BULLETIN (BERLIN, WEST). (GW/0170-0839). **1056**

POLYMER COMPOSITES. (US/0272-8397). **4459**

POLYMER DEGRADATION AND STABILITY. (UK/0141-3910). **988**

POLYMER (GUILFORD). (UK/0032-3861). **1046**

POLYMER JOURNAL. (JA/0032-3896). **1046**

POLYMER NETWORKS & BLENDS. (CN/1181-9510). **1046**

POLYMER TESTING. (UK/0142-9418). **4459**

POPULAR CULTURE IN LIBRARIES. (US/1053-8747). **3241**

POPULATION AND DEVELOPMENT REVIEW. (US/0098-7921). **4556**

POPULATION AND ENVIRONMENT. (US/0199-0039). **4556**

POPULATION BULLETIN. (US/0032-468X). **4556**

POPULATION ESTIMATES FOR OREGON. (US). **4557**

POPULATION INDEX. (US/0032-4701). **4562**

POPULATION REPORTS. SERIES M, SPECIAL TOPICS (ENGLISH ED.). (US/0733-9135). **4558**

POPULATION RESEARCH AND POLICY REVIEW. (NE/0167-5923). **4558**

POPULATION STUDIES. (UK/0032-4728). **4558**

POROSHKOVAIA METALLURGIIA. (US/0038-5735). **4015**

PORT OF DETROIT WORLD HANDBOOK. (US/0160-5526). **5454**

PORTLAND PRESS HERALD, THE. (US). **5685**

POSIDONIA NEWSLETTER. (FR/0758-8623). **1455**

POST SCRIPT (JACKSONVILLE, FLA.). (US/0277-9897). **4076**

POSTGRADUATE EDUCATION FOR GENERAL PRACTICE. (UK/0959-4299). **3738**

POSTGRADUATE MEDICAL JOURNAL. (UK/0032-5473). **3628**

POSTGRADUATE MEDICINE. (US/0032-5481). **3628**

POSTHARVEST NEWS AND INFORMATION. (UK/0957-7505). **155**

POTATO EYES. (US/1041-9926). **3424**

POTENTIAL ANALYSIS : AN INTERNATIONAL JOURNAL DEVOTED TO THE INTERACTIONS BETWEEN POTENTIAL THEORY, PROBABILITY THEORY, GEOMETRY AND FUNCTIONAL ANALYSIS. (US/0926-2601). **3527**

POTTER COUNTY HISTORICAL SOCIETY QUARTERLY BULLETIN. (US/0895-0865). **2625**

POULTRY SCIENCE. (US/0032-5791). **218**

POUR. (FR/0245-9442). **5254**

POWDER METALLURGY. (UK/0032-5899). **4015**

POWDER TECHNOLOGY. (SZ/0032-5910). **2016**

POWER ENGINEERING (BARRINGTON, ILL.). (US/0032-5961). **2124**

PRACTICAL LAWYER, THE. (US/0032-6429). **3030**

PRACTICAL LITIGATOR, THE. (US/1047-6261). **3030**

PRACTICAL PERIODONTICS AND AESTHETIC DENTISTRY. (US/1042-2722). **1333**

PRACTICAL REAL ESTATE LAWYER, THE. (US/8756-0372). **3030**

PRACTICAL TAX LAWYER, THE. (US/0890-4898). **3030**

PRACTICAL WINERY/VINEYARD. (US/1057-2694). **2370**

PRACTICE NURSE. (UK/0953-6612). **3867**

PRACTITIONER (RESTON), THE. (US/0192-6160). **1868**

PRAGMATICS & BEYOND NEW SERIES. (NE/0922-842X). **3311**

PRAGMATICS : QUARTERLY PUBLICATION OF THE INTERNATIONAL PRAGMATICS ASSOCIATION. (BE/1018-2101). **3311**

PRAIRIE NATURALIST, THE. (US/0091-0376). **4170**

PRAKTISCHE TIERARZT. (GW/0032-681X). **5518**

PRAMANA. (II/0304-4289). **4417**

PRAXIS DER KINDERPSYCHOLOGIE UND KINDERPSYCHIATRIE. (GW/0032-7034). **4608**

PRE/TEXT. (US/0731-0714). **3311**

PRECAMBRIAN RESEARCH. (NE/0301-9268). **1391**

PRECISION ENGINEERING. (US/0141-6359). **2125**

PRENATAL DIAGNOSIS. (UK/0197-3851). **3767**

PRENSA (ORLANDO, FLA.), LA. (US/0888-756X). **5650**

PREPARATIVE BIOCHEMISTRY. (US/0032-7484). **492**

PREPRINT EXTENDED ABSTRACT - AMERICAN CHEMICAL SOCIETY. DIVISION OF ENVIRONMENTAL CHEMISTRY. (US/0740-0667). **989**

PREPRINTS - AMERICAN CHEMICAL SOCIETY. DIVISION OF PETROLEUM CHEMISTRY. (US/0569-3799). **1028**

PRESCRIBER. (UK/0959-6682). **3629**

PRESERVATION LAW REPORTER. (US/0882-715X). **3030**

PRESSE MEDICALE (1983), LA. (FR/0755-4982). **3629**

PREVENTION IN HUMAN SERVICES. (US/0270-3114). **4810**

PREVENTIVE MEDICINE (1972). (US/0091-7435). **3629**

PREVENTIVE VETERINARY MEDICINE. (NE/0167-5877). **5518**

PRIMARY CARE. (US/0095-4543). **3738**

PRIMARY CARE UPDATE FOR OB/GYNS. (US/1068-607X). **3767**

PRIMARY GEOGRAPHER. (UK/0956-277X). **2573**

PRIMARY SEARCH. (US/1065-2485). **1796**

PRIMARY SOURCES AND ORIGINAL WORKS. (US/1042-8216). **3241**

PRIMARY TEACHING STUDIES. (UK/0268-2176). **1902**

PRIMATES. (JA/0032-8332). **5594**

PRINCETON UNIVERSITY LIBRARY CHRONICLE, THE. (US/0032-8456). **2852**

PRINTING ABSTRACTS. (UK/0031-109X). **4570**

PRIORITIES. (US). **2601**

PRISON JOURNAL (PHILADELPHIA, PA.), THE. (US/0032-8855). **3173**

PRIVACY EN REGISTRATIE. (NE). **4512**

PRIVATE COMPANY SECRETARY'S MANUAL. (UK). **4208**

PRIVATE POST, THE. (UK). **2787**

PROBABILITY THEORY AND RELATED FIELDS. (GW/0178-8051). **3527**

PROBLEMAS BARCELONA. (SP/0032-9223). **4865**

PROBLEMAS DEL DESARROLLO. (MX/0301-7036). **1639**

PROBLEMI DI GESTIONE. (IT). **704**

PROBLEMISTA. (PL). **4865**

PROBLEMS OF COMMUNISM (WASHINGTON, D.C.). (US/0032-941X). **4545**

PROBLEMS OF ECONOMICS. (US/0032-9436). **1513**

PROBLEMY PRAWNE HANDLU ZAGRANICZNEGO. (PL). **3134**

PROCEEDINGS ... ANNUAL CONFERENCE / AGRONOMY SOCIETY OF NEW ZEALAND. (NZ/0110-6589). **121**

PROCEEDINGS ... ANNUAL CONFERENCE OF THE AMERICAN COUNCIL ON CONSUMER INTERESTS. (US/0275-1356). **1299**

PROCEEDINGS, ... ANNUAL MEETING, ELECTRON MICROSCOPY SOCIETY OF AMERICA. (US/0424-8201). **573**

PROCEEDINGS - ASTRONOMICAL SOCIETY OF AUSTRALIA. (AT/0066-9997). **398**

PROCEEDINGS - DEVON ARCHAEOLOGICAL SOCIETY. (UK/0305-5795). **279**

PROCEEDINGS - INSTITUTE OF REFRIGERATION. (UK/0073-9677). **2607**

PROCEEDINGS OF AMERICAN PEANUT RESEARCH AND EDUCATION SOCIETY, INC. (US/0197-8748). **183**

PROCEEDINGS OF THE ACADEMY OF NATURAL SCIENCES OF PHILADELPHIA. (US/0097-3157). **4170**

PROCEEDINGS OF THE AMERICAN CATHOLIC PHILOSOPHICAL ASSOCIATION. (US/0065-7638). **4357**

PROCEEDINGS OF THE AMERICAN MATHEMATICAL SOCIETY. (US/0002-9939). **3528**

PROCEEDINGS OF THE ANNUAL EASTERN SNOW CONFERENCE. (US/0424-1932). **1359**

PROCEEDINGS OF THE ANNUAL MEETING OF THE WESTERN SOCIETY FOR FRENCH HISTORY. (US/0099-0329). **2703**

PROCEEDINGS OF THE ARKANSAS ACADEMY OF SCIENCE. (US/0097-4374). **5140**

PROCEEDINGS OF THE ASIS ANNUAL MEETING. (US/0044-7870). **3242**

PROCEEDINGS OF THE BIOLOGICAL SOCIETY OF WASHINGTON. (US/0006-324X). **469**

PROCEEDINGS OF THE BRITISH SOCIETY FOR THE STUDY OF PROSTHETIC DENTISTRY. (UK). **1333**

PROCEEDINGS OF THE CONFERENCE OF THE AMERICAN ACADEMY OF ADVERTISING (1985). (US/0883-2404). **764**

PROCEEDINGS OF THE ... CONFERENCE OF THE INTERNATIONAL ORGANIZATION OF CITRUS VIROLOGISTS. (US/0074-7203). **183**

PROCEEDINGS OF THE EDINBURGH MATHEMATICAL SOCIETY. (UK/0013-0915). **3528**

PROCEEDINGS OF THE ENTOMOLOGICAL SOCIETY OF MANITOBA. (CN/0315-2146). **5613**

PROCEEDINGS OF THE ENTOMOLOGICAL SOCIETY OF ONTARIO. (CN/0071-0768). **5595**

PROCEEDINGS OF THE ENTOMOLOGICAL SOCIETY OF WASHINGTON. (US/0013-8797). **5595**

PROCEEDINGS OF THE IEEE. (US/0018-9219). **2076**

PROCEEDINGS OF THE INDIAN ACADEMY OF SCIENCE. EARTH AND PLANETARY SCIENCES. (II/0253-4126). **1359**

PROCEEDINGS OF THE INDIAN ACADEMY OF SCIENCES. CHEMICAL SCIENCES. (II/0253-4134). **989**

PROCEEDINGS OF THE INSTITUTION OF MECHANICAL ENGINEERS. PART I, JOURNAL OF SYSTEMS & CONTROL ENGINEERING. (UK/0959-6518). **2126**

PROCEEDINGS OF THE INTERAMERICAN SOCIETY FOR TROPICAL HORTICULTURE. (CR). **2429**

PROCEEDINGS OF THE LEEDS PHILOSOPHICAL AND LITERARY SOCIETY, LITERARY AND HISTORICAL SECTION. (UK/0024-0281). **5235**

PROCEEDINGS OF THE LEEDS PHILOSOPHICAL AND LITERARY SOCIETY. SCIENTIFIC SECTION. (UK/0369-9986). **2852**

PROCEEDINGS OF THE LINNEAN SOCIETY OF NEW SOUTH WALES. (AT/0370-047X). **4170**

PROCEEDINGS OF THE LONDON MATHEMATICAL SOCIETY. (UK/0024-6115). **3528**

PROCEEDINGS OF THE ... NATIONAL AGRICULTURAL PLASTICS CONGRESS. (US/1073-1768). **4459**

PROCEEDINGS OF THE NATIONAL CONFERENCE ON FLUID POWER. (US/0160-8428). **2095**

PROCEEDINGS OF THE NATIONAL SCIENCE COUNCIL, REPUBLIC OF CHINA. PART A, PHYSICAL SCIENCE AND ENGINEERING. (CH/0255-6588). **5141**

PROCEEDINGS OF THE NEW ZEALAND PLANT PROTECTION CONFERENCE. (NZ/1172-0719). **525**

PROCEEDINGS OF THE NEW ZEALAND SOCIETY OF ANIMAL PRODUCTION. (NZ/0370-2731). **219**

PROCEEDINGS OF THE NORTH DAKOTA ACADEMY OF SCIENCE. (US/0096-9214). **5141**

PROCEEDINGS OF THE NUTRITION SOCIETY. (UK/0029-6651). **4197**

PROCEEDINGS OF THE OKLAHOMA ACADEMY OF SCIENCE. (US/0078-4303). **5141**

PROCEEDINGS OF THE PMR CONFERENCE. (US/0272-8710). **1079**

PROCEEDINGS OF THE PREHISTORIC SOCIETY. (UK/0079-497X). **243**

PROCEEDINGS OF THE ROYAL SOCIETY OF EDINBURGH. SECTION A. MATHEMATICA. (UK/0308-2105). **3528**

PROCEEDINGS OF THE ROYAL SOCIETY OF EDINBURGH. SECTION B, BIOLOGICAL SCIENCES. (UK/0269-7270). **470**

PROCEEDINGS OF THE ROYAL SOCIETY OF QUEENSLAND. (AT/0080-469X). **5141**

PROCEEDINGS OF THE SAN DIEGO SOCIETY OF NATURAL HISTORY. (US/1059-8707). **4170**

PROCEEDINGS OF THE SOCIETY FOR EXPERIMENTAL BIOLOGY AND MEDICINE. (US/0037-9727). **3630**

PROCEEDINGS OF THE SOCIETY FOR EXPERIMENTAL MECHANICS. (US/1046-6789). **4429**

PROCEEDINGS OF THE SOUTH ATLANTIC PHILOSOPHY OF EDUCATION SOCIETY. (US). **1774**

PROCEEDINGS OF THE SOUTH CAROLINA HISTORICAL ASSOCIATION, THE. (US/0361-6207). **2755**

PROCEEDINGS OF THE TOPOLOGY CONFERENCE, THE. (US/0196-3880). **3528**

PROCEEDINGS OF THE WESTERN FOUNDATION OF VERTEBRATE ZOOLOGY. (US/0511-7550). **5595**

PROCEEDINGS - TAGA. (US/0082-2299). **381**

PROCEEDINGS / THE ANNUAL SYMPOSIUM ON COMPUTER APPLICATIONS IN MEDICAL CARE. (US). **3630**

PROCEEDINGS / THE SOIL AND CROP SCIENCE SOCIETY OF FLORIDA. (US/0096-4522). **183**

PROCESS CONTROL & QUALITY. (US/0924-3089). **2016**

PROCESSING OF ADVANCED MATERIALS. (UK/0960-3158). **5142**

PRODUCTION AND OPERATIONS MANAGEMENT. (US/1059-1478). **883**

PRODUCTION PLANNING & CONTROL. (UK/0953-7287). **1622**

PROFESSIONAL EDUCATOR, THE. (US/0196-786X). **1903**

PROFESSIONAL GEOGRAPHER, THE. (US/0033-0124). **2573**

PROFESSIONAL PSYCHOLOGY, RESEARCH AND PRACTICE. (US/0735-7028). **4609**

PROGRAM (ASLIB). (UK/0033-0337). **3242**

PROGRESS IN BIOPHYSICS AND MOLECULAR BIOLOGY. (US/0079-6107). **496**

PROGRESS IN BRAIN RESEARCH. (NE/0079-6123). **3844**

PROGRESS IN CARDIOVASCULAR DISEASES. (US/0033-0620). **3709**

PROGRESS IN CARDIOVASCULAR NURSING. (US/0889-7204). **3709**

PROGRESS IN ELECTROMAGNETICS RESEARCH. (US/1043-626X). **4445**

PROGRESS IN ENERGY AND COMBUSTION SCIENCE. (UK/0360-1285). **1954**

PROGRESS IN FOOD & NUTRITION SCIENCE. (UK/0306-0632). **4198**

PROGRESS IN HISTOCHEMISTRY AND CYTOCHEMISTRY. (GW/0079-6336). **540**

PROGRESS IN HUMAN GEOGRAPHY. (UK/0309-1325). **2573**

PROGRESS IN INORGANIC CHEMISTRY. (US/0079-6379). **1037**

PROGRESS IN LIPID RESEARCH. (UK/0163-7827). **1046**

PROGRESS IN MATERIALS SCIENCE. (UK/0079-6425). **2107**

PROGRESS IN MEDICAL VIROLOGY. (US/0079-645X). **569**

PROGRESS IN MUTATION RESEARCH. (US/0731-2849). **551**

PROGRESS IN NEURO-PSYCHOPHARMACOLOGY & BIOLOGICAL PSYCHIATRY. (UK/0278-5846). **4326**

PROGRESS IN NEUROBIOLOGY. (UK/0301-0082). **3844**

PROGRESS IN NUCLEAR MAGNETIC RESONANCE SPECTROSCOPY. (UK/0079-6565). **4450**

PROGRESS IN OCEANOGRAPHY. (UK/0079-6611). **1455**

PROGRESS IN ORGANIC COATINGS. (SZ/0300-9440). **4225**

PROGRESS IN PAPER RECYCLING. (US/1061-1452). **4237**

PROGRESS IN PARTICLE AND NUCLEAR PHYSICS. (UK/0146-6410). **4450**

PROGRESS

PROGRESS IN PHYSICAL GEOGRAPHY. (UK/0309-1333). **2573**

PROGRESS IN PLANNING. (UK/0305-9006). **2832**

PROGRESS IN POLYMER SCIENCE. (UK/0079-6700). **1047**

PROGRESS IN QUANTUM ELECTRONICS. (UK/0079-6727). **2077**

PROGRESS IN RUBBER AND PLASTICS TECHNOLOGY. (UK/0266-7320). **5077**

PROGRESS IN SOLID STATE CHEMISTRY. (UK/0079-6786). **1057**

PROGRESS IN SURFACE SCIENCE. (UK/0079-6816). **1057**

PROGRESS OF THEORETICAL PHYSICS. (JA/0033-068X). **4429**

PROGRESSIVE FISH-CULTURIST, THE. (US/0033-0779). **2311**

PROMETHEUS. (AT/0810-9028). **3242**

PROMOTION AND EDUCATION. (FR/0751-7149). **4797**

PROP. 65 NEWS. (US/0895-5042). **3115**

PROPERTY DISPOSITION HANDBOOK. (US). **2832**

PROPERTY MANAGEMENT. (LONDON). (UK/0263-7472). **4843**

PROSTAGLANDINS. (US/0090-6980). **585**

PROSTAGLANDINS, LEUKOTRIENES, AND ESSENTIAL FATTY ACIDS. (UK/0952-3278). **3631**

PROSTATE, THE. (US/0270-4137). **3800**

PROSTHETICS AND ORTHOTICS INTERNATIONAL. (DK/0309-3646). **4392**

PROTECTION OF METALS. (US/0033-1732). **4017**

PROTEE. (CN/0300-3523). **3312**

PROTEIN ENGINEERING. (UK/0269-2139). **492**

PROTEIN SCIENCE : A PUBLICATION OF THE PROTEIN SOCIETY. (US/0961-8368). **493**

PROTEINS. (US/0887-3585). **470**

PROTOPLASMA. (AU/0033-183X). **540**

PRUDENTIA. (NZ). **3426**

PRZEMYS CHEMICZNY. (PL/0033-2496). **2016**

PSICHIATRIA GENERALE E DELL'ETA EVOLUTIVA. (IT/0555-5299). **3932**

PSIHOLOGICESKIJ ZURNAL. (RU/0205-9592). **4609**

PSYCHE. (GW/0033-2623). **4609**

PSYCHE (CAMBRIDGE, MASS.). (US/0033-2615). **5595**

PSYCHIATRIC ANNALS. (US/0048-5713). **3933**

PSYCHIATRIC CLINICS OF NORTH AMERICA, THE. (US/0193-953X). **3933**

PSYCHIATRIC TIMES, THE. (US/0893-2905). **3933**

PSYCHIATRIE DE L'ENFANT, LA. (FR/0079-726X). **3933**

PSYCHIATRISCHE PRAXIS. (GW/0303-4259). **3934**

PSYCHIATRY RESEARCH. (IE/0165-1781). **3934**

PSYCHIATRY (WASHINGTON, D.C.). (US/0033-2747). **3934**

PSYCHOANALYTIC QUARTERLY, THE. (US/0033-2828). **4610**

PSYCHOLOGIA. (JA/0033-2852). **4610**

PSYCHOLOGICA BELGICA. (BE/0033-2879). **4610**

PSYCHOLOGICAL ASSESSMENT. (US/1040-3590). **4610**

PSYCHOLOGICAL BULLETIN. (US/0033-2909). **4610**

PSYCHOLOGICAL INQUIRY. (US/1047-840X). **4611**

PSYCHOLOGICAL MEDICINE. (UK/0033-2917). **4611**

PSYCHOLOGICAL PERSPECTIVES. (US/0033-2925). **4611**

PSYCHOLOGICAL RECORD, THE. (US/0033-2933). **4611**

PSYCHOLOGICAL REPORTS. (US/0033-2941). **4611**

PSYCHOLOGICAL REVIEW. (US/0033-295X). **4611**

PSYCHOLOGIE IN ERZIEHUNG UND UNTERRICHT. (GW/0342-183X). **1903**

PSYCHOLOGISCHE RUNDSCHAU. (GW/0033-3042). **4612**

PSYCHOLOGY AND AGING. (US/0882-7974). **4612**

PSYCHOLOGY AND SOCIOLOGY OF SPORT. (US/0885-7423). **4612**

PSYCHOLOGY IN THE SCHOOLS. (US/0033-3085). **4612**

PSYCHOLOGY OF WOMEN QUARTERLY. (UK/0361-6843). **5565**

PSYCHOLOGY, PUBLIC POLICY, AND LAW. (US/1076-8971). **4613**

PSYCHOMETRIKA. (US/0033-3123). **4613**

PSYCHONEUROENDOCRINOLOGY. (UK/0306-4530). **3732**

PSYCHOPATHOLOGY. (SZ/0254-4962). **3934**

PSYCHOPHARMACOLOGIA. (GW/0033-3158). **4326**

PSYCHOPHARMACOLOGY BULLETIN. (US/0048-5764). **4613**

PSYCHOPHYSIOLOGY. (US/0048-5772). **586**

PSYCHOSOCIAL REHABILITATION JOURNAL. (US/0147-5622). **3934**

PSYCHOSOMATIC MEDICINE. (US/0033-3174). **3631**

PSYCHOSOMATICS (WASHINGTON, D.C.). (US/0033-3182). **3631**

PSYCHOTHERAPY AND PSYCHOSOMATICS. (SZ/0033-3190). **3935**

PSYCHOTHERAPY IN PRIVATE PRACTICE. (US/0731-7158). **4614**

PSYCHOTHERAPY PATIENT, THE. (US/0738-6176). **3935**

PSYCHOTHERAPY RESEARCH. (US/1050-3307). **4614**

PSYCHOTROPICS (RENO, NEV.). (US/0895-5727). **3986**

PTA TODAY. (US/0195-2781). **1775**

PTERIDOLOGIA. (US/0749-7741). **525**

PUBLIC ADMINISTRATION AND DEVELOPMENT. (UK/0271-2075). **4675**

PUBLIC ADMINISTRATION (LONDON). (UK/0033-3298). **4704**

PUBLIC ART REVIEW. (US/1040-211X). **362**

PUBLIC CHOICE. (NE/0048-5829). **1514**

PUBLIC ENTERPRISE / INTERNATIONAL CENTER FOR PUBLIC ENTERPRISES IN DEVELOPING COUNTRIES. (YU/0351-3564). **2911**

PUBLIC FINANCE. (NE/0033-3476). **4743**

PUBLIC FINANCE QUARTERLY. (US/0048-5853). **4743**

PUBLIC HEALTH (LONDON). (UK/0033-3506). **4797**

PUBLIC HEALTH NURSING (BOSTON, MASS.). (US/0737-1209). **3867**

PUBLIC HISTORIAN, THE. (US/0272-3433). **2626**

PUBLIC INTEREST, THE. (US/0033-3557). **5214**

PUBLIC LAND AND RESOURCES LAW DIGEST, THE. (US/0148-6489). **3115**

PUBLIC LIBRARIES. (US/0163-5506). **3243**

PUBLIC LIBRARY QUARTERLY (NEW YORK, N.Y.). (US/0161-6846). **3243**

PUBLIC MANAGER (POTOMAC, MD.), THE. (US/1061-7639). **4676**

PUBLIC OPINION QUARTERLY. (US/0033-362X). **5254**

PUBLIC PERSONNEL MANAGEMENT. (US/0091-0260). **946**

PUBLIC POLICY AND ADMINISTRATION. (UK). **4676**

PUBLIC RELATIONS REVIEW (RIVERDALE, N.Y.). (US/0363-8111). **765**

PUBLIC SCHOOL FINANCE PROGRAMS OF THE UNITED STATES AND CANADA. (US). **1776**

PUBLIC WELFARE (WASHINGTON). (US/0033-3816). **5303**

PUBLICATION OF THE AMERICAN DIALECT SOCIETY. (US/0002-8207). **3312**

PUBLICATIONES MATHEMATICAL (DEBRECEN). (HU/0033-3883). **3529**

PUBLICATIONS - ASBL CENTRE D'HISTOIRE ET D'ART DE LA THUDINIE. (BE). **2626**

PUBLICATIONS MATHEMATIQUES. INSTITUT DES HAUTES ETUDES SCIENTIFIQUES. (FR/0073-8301). **3529**

PUBLICATIONS OF THE ARKANSAS PHILOLOGICAL ASSOCIATION. (US/0160-3124). **3312**

PUBLICATIONS OF THE ASTRONOMICAL SOCIETY OF JAPAN. (JA/0004-6264). **398**

PUBLICATIONS OF THE ASTRONOMICAL SOCIETY OF THE PACIFIC. (US/0004-6280). **398**

PUBLICATIONS OF THE INTERNATIONAL MARITIME ORGANIZATION. (UK). **4182**

PUBLICATIONS OF THE RESEARCH INSTITUTE FOR MATHEMATICAL SCIENCES. SERIES A. (JA/0034-5318). **3529**

PUBLICATIONS / TECHNICAL RESEARCH CENTRE OF FINLAND. (FI/0358-5069). **5143**

PUBLIUS. (US/0048-5950). **4492**

PUERTO RICO HEALTH SCIENCES JOURNAL. (PR/0738-0658). **3631**

PUPIL TRANSPORTATION NEWS. (US/0730-5443). **5390**

PURE AND APPLIED CHEMISTRY. (UK/0033-4545). **990**

PURE AND APPLIED GEOPHYSICS. (SZ/0033-4553). **1409**

PYNCHON NOTES. (US/0278-1891). **3426**

QEDEM MONOGRAPHS OF THE INSTITUTE OF ARCHAEOLOGY. (IS). **279**

QRB. QUALITY REVIEW BULLETIN. (US/0097-5990). **3791**

QUADERNI CALABRESI : QUADERNI DEL MEZZOGIORNO E DELLE ISOLE. (IT). **2521**

QUADERNI DI TERZO MONDO. (IT/0391-7312). **4492**

QUAESTIONES MATHEMATICAE : JOURNAL OF THE SOUTH AFRICAN MATHEMATICAL SOCIETY : TYDSKRIF VAN DIE SUID-AFRIKAANSE WISKUNDEVERENIGING. (SA/0379-9468). **3529**

QUAKER HISTORY. (US/0033-5053). **4989**

QUAKER LIFE. (US/0033-5061). **4989**

QUAKER YEOMEN, THE. (US/0737-8246). **2468**

QUALITY & QUANTITY. (NE/0033-5177). **3529**

QUALITY ASSURANCE AND UTILIZATION REVIEW : OFFICIAL JOURNAL OF THE AMERICAN COLLEGE OF UTILIZATION REVIEW PHYSICIANS. (US/0885-713X). **3632**

QUALITY BY DESIGN. (US/0893-360X). **625**

QUALITY CONTROL AND APPLIED STATISTICS. (US/0033-5207). **5176**

QUALITY IN HEALTH CARE : QHC. (UK/0963-8172). **3632**

QUALITY PROGRESS. (US/0033-524X). **1993**

QUANTITATIVE STRUCTURE-ACTIVITY RELATIONSHIPS. (GW/0931-8771). **4327**

QUARTER HORSE JOURNAL (1953), THE. (US/0164-6656). **2801**

QUARTERLY DEC JOURNAL. (US/1063-1216). **706**

QUARTERLY FORECAST OF JAPAN'S ECONOMY. (JA/0910-075X). **1594**

QUARTERLY JOURNAL OF ECONOMICS, THE. (US/0033-5533). **1514**

QUARTERLY JOURNAL OF ENGINEERING GEOLOGY, THE. (UK/0481-2085). **2029**

QUARTERLY JOURNAL OF EXPERIMENTAL PSYCHOLOGY. A, HUMAN EXPERIMENTAL PSYCHOLOGY, THE. (UK/0272-4987). **4614**

QUARTERLY JOURNAL OF EXPERIMENTAL PSYCHOLOGY. B, COMPARATIVE AND PHYSIOLOGICAL PSYCHOLOGY, THE. (UK/0272-4995). **4614**

QUARTERLY JOURNAL OF IDEOLOGY. (US/0738-9752). **5254**

QUARTERLY JOURNAL OF MATHEMATICS. (UK/0033-5606). **3530**

QUARTERLY JOURNAL OF MECHANICS AND APPLIED MATHEMATICS, THE. (UK/0033-5614). **2127**

QUARTERLY JOURNAL OF MEDICINE, THE. (UK/0033-5622). **3632**

QUARTERLY OF APPLIED MATHEMATICS. (US/0033-569X). **3530**

QUARTERLY REVIEW / NATIONAL WESTMINSTER BANK. (UK/0028-0399). **1514**

QUARTERLY REVIEW OF BIOLOGY, THE. (US/0033-5770). **471**

QUARTERLY REVIEWS OF BIOPHYSICS. (UK/0033-5835). **496**

QUATERNAIRE : BULLETIN DE L'ASSOCIATION FRANCAISE POUR L'ETUDE DU QUATERNAIRE : INTERNATIONAL JOURNAL OF THE FRENCH QUATERNARY ASSOCIATION. (FR/1142-2904). **1393**

QUATERNARY RESEARCH. (US/0033-5894). **1393**

QUATERNARY SCIENCE REVIEWS. (UK/0277-3791). **1393**

QUEEN OF PEACE WILDERNESS GAZETTE. (US). **4989**

QUEENSLAND ARCHAEOLOGICAL RESEARCH. (AT/0814-3021). **280**

QUEST (GRAND RAPIDS, MICH.). (US/1065-7738). **32**

QUEST (NATIONAL ASSOCIATION FOR PHYSICAL EDUCATION IN HIGHER EDUCATION). (US/0033-6297). **3955**

QUONDAM ET FUTURUS (BIRMINGHAM, ALA.). (US/8755-3627). **3351**

R & D MANAGEMENT. (UK/0033-6807). **5144**

RACING GREYHOUNDS. (US/1042-9174). **4865**

RADIATION AND ENVIRONMENTAL BIOPHYSICS. (GW/0301-634X). **496**

RADIATION EFFECTS AND DEFECTS IN SOLIDS. (US/1042-0150). **1057**

RADIATION PROTECTION DOSIMETRY. (UK/0144-8420). **4440**

RADIATION PROTECTION IN AUSTRALIA. (AT/0729-7963). **4798**

RADIATION PROTECTION MANAGEMENT. (US/0740-0640). **2868**

RADIATION RESEARCH. (US/0033-7587). **4441**

RADIATION THERAPIST: THE JOURNAL OF THE RADIATION ONCOLOGY SCIENCES. (US). **3944**

RADIO PROMOTION BULLETIN. (US/1044-985X). **1120**

RADIO SCIENCE. (US/0048-6604). **1409**

RADIOACTIVE WASTE MANAGEMENT AND THE NUCLEAR FUEL CYCLE. (SZ/0739-5876). **2240**

RADIOACTIVITY & RADIOCHEMISTRY. (US/1045-845X). **1029**

RADIOCARBON. (US/0033-8222). **1393**

RADIOCHIMICA ACTA. (US/0033-8230). **1057**

RADIOGRAPHER. (AT/0033-8273). **3632**

RADIOLOGE, DER. (GW/0033-832X). **3945**

RADIOLOGIC CLINICS OF NORTH AMERICA, THE. (US/0033-8389). **3945**

RADIOLOGIC TECHNOLOGY. (US/0033-8397). **3945**

RADIOLOGY. (US/0033-8419). **3945**

RADIOLOGY MANAGEMENT. (US/0198-7097). **3946**

RADIOPROTECTION. (FR/0033-8451). **4798**

RADIOSCAN MAGAZINE (SPANISH ED.). (US/1050-3641). **1120**

RADIOTEKHNIKA I ELEKTRONIKA. (RU/0033-8494). **2078**

RADIOTHERAPY AND ONCOLOGY. (NE/0167-8140). **3823**

RAGIUSAN. RASSEGNA GIURIDICA DELLA SANITA. (IT/1120-1762). **3034**

RAICES (MADRID, SPAIN). (SP/0212-6753). **2271**

RAIL PARIS, LE. (FR/0989-8220). **5435**

RAIRO. INFORMATIQUE THEORIQUE ET APPLICATIONS. (FR/0988-3754). **1261**

RAIRO : RECHERCHE OPERATIONNELLE. (FR/0399-0559). **5144**

RAM RESEARCH'S CARDTRAK. (US/1053-9719). **1299**

RAMUS. (AT/0048-671X). **1079**

RAND JOURNAL OF ECONOMICS, THE. (US/0741-6261). **1594**

RANDOM OPERATORS AND STOCHASTIC EQUATIONS. (NE/0926-6364). **1244**

RANGIFER. (NO/0333-256X). **5596**

RAPID COMMUNICATIONS (SUPPLEMENTS). (NE). **5596**

RAPPORT BIPM. (FR/0026-1394). **1434**

RAVEN (TRENTON, N.J.). (US/1071-0043). **5214**

RAW MATERIALS REPORT. (SW/0349-6287). **2203**

RBM, REVISTA BRASILEIRA DE MANDIOCA. (BL/0101-563X). **125**

RCDA. RELIGION IN COMMUNIST DOMINATED AREAS. (US/0034-3978). **4546**

REACTION KINETICS AND CATALYSIS LETTERS. (HU/0304-4122). **1057**

REACTIVE POLYMERS. (NE/0923-1137). **1047**

READING & WRITING. (NE/0922-4777). **3314**

READING RESEARCH AND INSTRUCTION. (US/0886-0246). **3314**

READING RESEARCH QUARTERLY. (US/0034-0553). **3314**

READING TEACHER, THE. (US/0034-0561). **3314**

REAL ANALYSIS EXCHANGE. (US/0147-1937). **3530**

REAL ESTATE ISSUES. (US/0146-0595). **4844**

REAL ESTATE REVIEW (BOSTON, MASS.). (US/0034-0790). **4845**

REAL ESTATE TODAY. (US/0034-0804). **4845**

REAL PROPERTY LAW REPORTER. (US/0898-1698). **3035**

REAL-TIME SYSTEMS. (US/0922-6443). **1201**

REALITES INDUSTRIELLES. (FR). **2149**

RECENT AMERICAN HISTORY. (US/0899-2371). **2756**

RECENT PROGRESS IN HORMONE RESEARCH. (US/0079-9963). **3733**

RECHERCHE AEROSPATIALE. (FR/0034-1223). **33**

RECHERCHE (PARIS. 1970). (FR/0029-5671). **5145**

RECORD - GEOLOGICAL SURVEY OF WESTERN AUSTRALIA. (AT/0728-2311). **1393**

RECORDS OF EARLY ENGLISH DRAMA. (CN/0700-9283). **5367**

RECORDS OF THE SOUTH AUSTRALIAN MUSEUM. (AT/0376-2750). **4095**

RECREATION CANADA (FRENCH EDITION). (CN/0031-2231). **4853**

RECUEIL DE MEDECINE VETERINAIRE. (FR/0034-1843). **5520**

RECUEIL DES TRAVAUX CHIMIQUES DES PAYS-BAS (1920). (NE/0165-0513). **991**

RECUPERARE. EDILIZIA DESIGN IMPIANTI. (IT/0392-4599). **307**

REFERENCE LIBRARIAN, THE. (US/0276-3877). **3244**

REFERENCE SERVICES REVIEW. (US/0090-7324). **1928**

REFLECTION. (NE/0922-4238). **4990**

REFLECTIONS (CHAMPAIGN, ILL.). (US/0739-9448). **307**

REFLECTIONS ON CANADIAN LITERACY : RCL. (CN/1180-1239). **1884**

REFUGEE UPDATE ENGLISH ED. (CN/0251-6500). **4512**

REGATTA. (UK). **4914**

REGIONAL ANESTHESIA. (US/0146-521X). **3684**

REGIONAL BUSINESS REVIEW. (US/8755-1977). **849**

REGIONAL JOURNAL OF SOCIAL ISSUES. (AT/0158-7102). **5255**

REGIONAL SCIENCE AND URBAN ECONOMICS. (NE/0166-0462). **2833**

REGIONAL STUDIES. (UK/0034-3404). **5215**

REGIONAL TOURISM MONITOR. (AT). **5490**

REGISTERED NURSE (TORONTO). (CN/0840-8831). **3868**

REGULATORY AFFAIRS. (US/1043-2752). **3792**

REGULATORY AFFAIRS JOURNAL. (UK/0960-7889). **3633**

REGULATORY PEPTIDES. (NE/0167-0115). **1047**

REGULATORY TOXICOLOGY AND PHARMACOLOGY. (US/0273-2300). **4327**

REHABILITACION (MADRID). (SP/0048-7120). **4382**

REHABILITATION COUNSELING BULLETIN. (US/0034-3552). **1884**

REHABILITATION INDEX / THE BRITISH LIBRARY, MEDICAL INFORMATION SERVICE. (UK/0955-0984). **4382**

REHABILITATION NURSING. (US/0278-4807). **3868**

REHABILITATION PSYCHOLOGY. (US/0090-5550). **4615**

RELACIONES MEXICO-ESTADOS UNIDOS, BIBLIOGRAFIA ANUAL. (MX). **4502**

RELATIONAL DATABASE JOURNAL. (US/1074-6404). **1255**

RELATIONS INDUSTRIELLES / INDUSTRIAL RELATIONS. (CN/0034-379X). **1706**

RELIABILITY ENGINEERING & SYSTEM SAFETY. (UK/0951-8320). **1993**

RELICS. (US/0034-3897). **2757**

RELIGION & PUBLIC EDUCATION. (US/1056-7224). **1777**

RELIGIOUS HUMANISM. (US/0034-4095). **4992**

REMEDIAL AND SPECIAL EDUCATION. (US/0741-9325). **1884**

REMOTE SENSING OF ENVIRONMENT. (US/0034-4257). **1410**

RENAISSANCE AND REFORMATION. (CN/0034-429X). **2705**

RENAISSANCE PAPERS. (US/0584-4207). **3428**

RENAL FAILURE. (US/0886-022X). **3992**

RENAL PHYSIOLOGY AND BIOCHEMISTRY. (SZ/1011-6524). **3993**

RENASCENCE. ESSAYS ON VALUES IN LITERATURE. (US/0034-4346). **3429**

RENDITIONS. (HK/0377-3515). **3429**

RENEGADE (BLOOMFIELD HILLS). (US). **3429**

REPERTOIRE DES GEOGRAPHES FRANCAIS PARIS. (FR/1147-9558). **2574**

REPORT FOR THE YEAR ... - MINERAL RESOURCES DEPARTMENT (FIJI). (FJ). **1360**

REPORT / IDAHO. PUBLIC UTILITIES COMMISSION. (US). **4680**

REPORT (INSTITUTE OF OCEANOGRAPHIC SCIENCES (GREAT BRITAIN)). (UK). **1456**

REPORT OF THE INTERNATIONAL WHALING COMMISSION. (UK/0143-8700). **5596**

REPORTS - CALIFORNIA COOPERATIVE OCEANIC FISHERIES INVESTIGATIONS. (US/0575-3317). **2311**

REPORTS FROM GENERAL PRACTICE. (UK/0557-3912). **3739**

REPORTS ON PROGRESS IN PHYSICS. (UK/0034-4885). **4419**

REPRESENTATIONS (BERKELEY, CALIF.). (US/0734-6018). **2853**

REPRODUCTION, FERTILITY, AND DEVELOPMENT. (AT/1031-3613). **586**

REPRODUCTION, NUTRITION, DEVELOPMENT. (FR). **4198**

RESEARCH AND INDUSTRY. (II/0034-513X). **5146**

RESEARCH & TEACHING IN DEVELOPMENTAL EDUCATION. (US/1046-3364). **1884**

RESEARCH COMMUNICATIONS IN CHEMICAL PATHOLOGY AND PHARMACOLOGY. (US/0034-5164). **4327**

RESEARCH COMMUNICATIONS IN SUBSTANCES OF ABUSE. (US/0193-0818). **1348**

RESEARCH EVALUATION. (UK/0958-2029). **5146**

RESEARCH FILE, THE. (CN/1188-6641). **2601**

RESEARCH IN DEVELOPMENTAL DISABILITIES. (US/0891-4222). **4615**

RESEARCH IN EXPERIMENTAL MEDICINE. (GW/0300-9130). **3634**

RESEARCH IN HIGHER EDUCATION. (US/0361-0365). **1845**

RESEARCH IN IMMUNOLOGY (PARIS). (FR/0923-2494). **3676**

RESEARCH IN MICROBIOLOGY. (FR/0923-2508). **569**

RESEARCH IN NONDESTRUCTIVE EVALUATION. (US/0934-9847). **1994**

RESEARCH IN NURSING & HEALTH. (US/0160-6891). **3868**

RESEARCH IN ORGANIZATIONAL BEHAVIOR. (US/0191-3085). **5255**

RESEARCH IN SCIENCE EDUCATION. (AT/0157-244X). **1779**

RESEARCH IN THE TEACHING OF ENGLISH. (US/0034-527X). **1903**

RESEARCH IN THIRD WORLD ACCOUNTING. (US/1058-1995). **750**

RESEARCH IN VETERINARY SCIENCE. (UK/0034-5288). **5520**

RESEARCH IN VIROLOGY (PARIS). (FR/0923-2516). **569**

RESEARCH MONOGRAPHS IN CELL AND TISSUE PHYSIOLOGY. (NE/0378-6129). **586**

RESEARCH ON AGING. (US/0164-0275). **3754**

RESEARCH ON CHEMICAL INTERMEDIATES. (NE/0922-6168). **1057**

RESEARCH POLICY. (NE/0048-7333). **5147**

RESEARCH

RESEARCH QUARTERLY FOR EXERCISE AND SPORT. (US/0270-1367). **1858**

RESEARCH REPORT / DEPARTMENT OF CIVIL ENGINEERING, UNIVERSITY OF QUEENSLAND. (AT). **2030**

RESEARCH REPORT - MISSISSIPPI AGRICULTURAL & FORESTRY EXPERIMENT STATION. (US/0147-2186). **128**

RESEARCH REPORT - WISCONSIN. DEPT. OF NATURAL RESOURCES. (US/0084-0556). **2204**

RESEARCH SERIES. (US/0882-2042). **280**

RESEARCH TECHNOLOGY MANAGEMENT. (US/0895-6308). **5147**

RESEARCHES ON POPULATION ECOLOGY. (JA/0034-5466). **2220**

RESIDENTIAL TREATMENT FOR CHILDREN & YOUTH. (US/0886-571X). **5306**

RESOLUTION. (US/1050-3978). **1201**

RESOURCE ATLAS - UNIVERSITY OF NEBRASKA, CONSERVATION AND SURVEY DIVISION. (US/0160-3094). **2574**

RESOURCE PUBLICATION - U.S. FISH AND WILDLIFE SERVICE. (US/0163-4801). **2204**

RESOURCE SHARING & INFORMATION NETWORKS. (US/0737-7797). **3245**

RESOURCES AND ENERGY. (NE/0165-0572). **1517**

RESOURCES, CONSERVATION AND RECYCLING. (NE/0921-3449). **2204**

RESOURCES IN AGING. (US/0892-0818). **5306**

RESOURCES IN EDUCATION. (US/0098-0897). **1779**

RESOURCES POLICY. (UK/0301-4207). **2204**

RESPIRATION. (SZ/0025-7931). **3951**

RESPIRATION PHYSIOLOGY. (NE/0034-5687). **586**

RESPIRATORY MEDICINE. (UK/0954-6111). **3951**

RESPONSA MERIDIANA. (SA/0486-5588). **3039**

RESPONSIVE COMMUNITY, THE. (US/1053-0754). **5256**

RESTORATION QUARTERLY. (US/0486-5642). **4993**

RESUSCITATION. (IE/0300-9572). **3951**

RETHINKING MARXISM. (US/0893-5696). **1594**

RETINA (PHILADELPHIA, PA.). (US/0275-004X). **3878**

RETIREMENT INDUSTRY JOURNAL, THE. (AT). **5181**

REVIEW OF AGRICULTURAL ECONOMICS. (US/1058-7195). **128**

REVIEW OF BLACK POLITICAL ECONOMY, THE. (US/0034-6446). **1517**

REVIEW OF BOOKS ON THE BOOK OF MORMON. (US/1050-7930). **4993**

REVIEW OF CENTRAL AND EAST EUROPEAN LAW. (NE/0925-9880). **3135**

REVIEW OF ECONOMIC STUDIES, THE. (UK/0034-6527). **1517**

REVIEW OF ECONOMICS AND STATISTICS, THE. (NE). **1538**

REVIEW OF EDUCATIONAL RESEARCH. (US/0034-6543). **1779**

REVIEW OF EXISTENTIAL PSYCHOLOGY AND PSYCHIATRY (1972). (US/0361-1531). **4615**

REVIEW OF FINANCIAL ECONOMICS. (US/1058-3300). **1518**

REVIEW OF INCOME AND WEALTH, THE. (US/0034-6586). **1518**

REVIEW OF NATIONAL LITERATURES. (US/0034-6640). **3351**

REVIEW OF PALAEOBOTANY AND PALYNOLOGY. (NE/0034-6667). **4230**

REVIEW OF POLITICS, THE. (US/0034-6705). **4494**

REVIEW OF PUBLIC PERSONNEL ADMINISTRATION. (US/0734-371X). **4705**

REVIEW OF RELIGIOUS RESEARCH. (US/0034-673X). **4993**

REVIEW OF SCIENTIFIC INSTRUMENTS. (US/0034-6748). **5147**

REVIEW OF SOCIAL ECONOMY. (UK/0034-6764). **1581**

REVIEW OF TEXAS BOOKS. (US/0892-6212). **4832**

REVIEWS IN BIOCHEMICAL TOXICOLOGY. (US/0163-7673). **3983**

REVIEWS IN CHEMICAL ENGINEERING. (UK/0264-8431). **2017**

REVIEWS IN CLINICAL GERONTOLOGY. (UK/0959-2598). **3754**

REVIEWS IN INORGANIC CHEMISTRY (LONDON, ENGLAND). (UK/0193-4929). **1037**

REVIEWS IN MINERALOGY. (US/0275-0279). **1444**

REVIEWS OF ENVIRONMENTAL CONTAMINATION AND TOXICOLOGY. (US/0179-5953). **2242**

REVIEWS OF GEOPHYSICS (1985). (US/8755-1209). **1410**

REVIEWS OF MODERN PHYSICS. (US/0034-6861). **4419**

REVISTA ANTIOGUENA DE ECONOMIA Y DESARROLLO. (CK/0121-0017). **1518**

REVISTA ARGENTINA DE MICOLOGIA : ORGANO DE DIFUSION DE LA SOCIEDAD ARGENTINA DE MICOLOGIA. (AG/0325-4755). **576**

REVISTA BIBLICA. (AG/0034-7078). **5019**

REVISTA BRASILEIRA DE GENETICA. (BL/0100-8455). **551**

REVISTA CHILENA DE DERECHO. (CL). **3040**

REVISTA CHILENA DE LITERATURA. (CL/0048-7651). **3430**

REVISTA CHILENA DE PEDIATRIA. (CL/0370-4106). **3911**

REVISTA COLOMBIANA DE MATEMATICAS. (CK/0034-7426). **3531**

REVISTA COLOMBIANA DE OBSTETRICIA Y GINECOLOGIA. (CK/0034-7434). **3768**

REVISTA DA ESCOLA DE BIBLIOTECONOMIA DA UFMG. (BL/0100-0829). **3246**

REVISTA DE BIOLOGIA MARINA. (CL/0080-2115). **557**

REVISTA DE BIOLOGIA TROPICAL. (CR/0034-7744). **3986**

REVISTA DE CHIMIE. (RM/0034-7752). **991**

REVISTA DE CIENCIA POLITICA (SANTIAGO). (CL/0716-1417). **4494**

REVISTA DE CIENCIAS SOCIALES (SAN JOSE). (CR/0482-5276). **5216**

REVISTA DE FARMACOLOGIA CLINICA Y EXPERIMENTAL. (SP). **4328**

REVISTA DE FILOSOFIA. (MX/0185-3481). **4359**

REVISTA DE FILOSOFIA DE LA UNIVERSIDAD DE COSTA RICA. (CR/0034-8252). **4359**

REVISTA DE FOMENTO SOCIAL. (SP/0015-6043). **5216**

REVISTA DE HISTORIA (HEREDIA). (CR/1012-9790). **2758**

REVISTA DE LA ASOCIACION ESPANOLA DE NEUROPSIQUIATRIA. (SP/0211-5735). **3935**

REVISTA DE LA ASOCIACION ODONTOLOGICA ARGENTINA. (AG/0004-4881). **1334**

REVISTA DE LA FACULTAD DE AGRONOMIA DE LA UNIVERSIDAD CENTRAL DE VENEZUELA. ALCANCE. (VE/0376-0030). **129**

REVISTA DE LA FACULTAD DE DERECHO DE LA UNIVERSIDAD COMPLUTENSE. (SP). **3041**

REVISTA DE LA SOCIEDAD DE OBSTETRICIA Y GINECOLOGIA DE BUENOS AIRES. (AG/0037-8542). **3768**

REVISTA DE LLENGUA I DRET. (SP/0212-5056). **1079**

REVISTA DE METALURGIA (MADRID). (SP/0034-8570). **4018**

REVISTA DE MICROBIOLOGIA. (BL/0001-3714). **569**

REVISTA DE NEURO-PSIQUIATRIA. (PE/0034-8597). **3845**

REVISTA DE PRE-HISTORIA. (BL). **2758**

REVISTA DE SAUDE PUBLICA. (BL/0034-8910). **4799**

REVISTA DE SOLDADURA. (SP/0048-7759). **4027**

REVISTA DEL ARCHIVO HISTORICO DEL GUAYAS. (EC). **2483**

REVISTA DEL DERECHO COMERCIAL Y DE LAS OBLIGACIONES. (AG/0556-6428). **3102**

REVISTA DEL DERECHO INDUSTRIAL. (AG/0326-0763). **3041**

REVISTA DO COLEGIO BRASILEIRO DE CIRURGIOES. (BL/0100-6991). **3973**

REVISTA DO INSTITUTO DE MEDICINA TROPICAL DE SAO PAULO. (BL/0036-4665). **3986**

REVISTA ESPANOLA DE ANESTESIOLOGIA Y REANIMACION. (SP/0034-9356). **3684**

REVISTA ESPANOLA DE CARDIOLOGIA. (SP/0300-8932). **3710**

REVISTA ESPANOLA DE DOCUMENTACION CIENTIFICA. (SP/0210-0614). **3246**

REVISTA ESPANOLA DE ENFERMEDADES DIGESTIVAS. (SP/1130-0108). **3747**

REVISTA ESPANOLA DE FISIOLOGIA. (SP/0034-9402). **586**

REVISTA ESPANOLA DE GERIATRIA Y GERONTOLOGIA. (SP/0211-139X). **3755**

REVISTA EUROPEA DE ESTUDIOS LATINOAMERICANOS Y DEL CARIBE. EUROPEAN REVIEW OF LATIN AMERICAN AND CARIBBEAN STUDIES. (NE/0924-0608). **5216**

REVISTA GEOFISICA. (MX/0252-9769). **1410**

REVISTA GEOGRAFICA DE CHILE TERRA AUSTRALIS. (CL/0378-8482). **2574**

REVISTA HISPANICA MODERNA. (US/0034-9593). **3430**

REVISTA INTERNACIONAL DE METODOS NUMERICOS PARA CALCULO Y DISEfNO EN INGENIERIA. (SP/0213-1315). **1994**

REVISTA JAVERIANA (BOGOTA). (CK/0120-3088). **2552**

REVISTA LATINOAMERICANA DE ESTUDIOS EDUCATIVOS. (MX/0185-1284). **1780**

REVISTA LATINOAMERICANA DE FILOSOFIA. (AG/0325-0725). **4359**

REVISTA LATINOAMERICANA DE MICROBIOLOGIA (1970). (MX/0187-4640). **569**

REVISTA LATINOAMERICANA DE PATOLOGIA. (VE/0300-9068). **3897**

REVISTA LATINOAMERICANA DE PSICOLOGIA. (CK/0120-0534). **4616**

REVISTA LATINOAMERICANA DE QUIMICA. (MX/0370-5943). **1047**

REVISTA LETRAS (CURITIBA). (BL/0100-0888). **3316**

REVISTA MATEMATICA IBEROAMERICANA. (SP/0213-2230). **3531**

REVISTA MEDICA DE CHILE. (CL/0034-9887). **3801**

REVISTA MEDICA DE PANAMA. (PN/0379-1629). **3636**

REVISTA MEXICANA DE ANESTESIOLOGIA Y REANIMACION. (MX/0185-1012). **3684**

REVISTA MEXICANA DE ASTRONOMIA Y ASTROFISICA. (MX/0185-1101). **399**

REVISTA MUSICAL CHILENA. (CL/0716-2790). **4150**

REVISTA PERUANA DE DERECHO DE LA EMPRESA. (PE). **3042**

REVISTA PORTUGUESA DE ESTOMATOLOGIA E CIRURGIA MAXILO-FACIAL. (PO/0035-0397). **1334**

REVISTA TELEGRAFICA ELECTRONICA. (AG/0035-0516). **2079**

REVISTA URUGUAYA DE DERECHO PROCESAL. (UY). **3042**

REVOLUTION (STATEN ISLAND, N.Y.). (US/1059-0927). **3868**

REVUE ANDRE MALRAUX. (CN/0839-458X). **3351**

REVUE ARBIDO. (SZ/0258-0772). **3246**

REVUE BIBLIOGRAPHIQUE - TOXIBASE LYON. (FR/0996-8393). **1350**

REVUE CANADIENNE DE PSYCHO-EDUCATION. (CN/0080-2492). **1780**

REVUE CANADIENNE D'ETUDES DU DEVELOPPEMENT. (CN/0225-5189). **1639**

REVUE DE CHIRURGIE ORTHOPEDIQUE ET REPARATRICE DE L'APPAREIL MOTEUR. (FR/0035-1040). **3973**

REVUE DE L'ACLA. (CN/1193-1493). **3316**

REVUE DE LARYNGOLOGIE, D'OTOLOGIE ET DE RHINOLOGIE. (FR/0035-1334). **3891**

REVUE DE MEDECINE INTERNE, LA. (FR/0248-8663). **3801**

REVUE DE MEDECINE VETERINAIRE. (FR/0035-1555). **5520**

REVUE DE METALLURGIE (PARIS). (FR/0035-1563). **4018**

REVUE D'EPIDEMIOLOGIE ET DE SANTE PUBLIQUE. (US/0398-7620). **3736**

REVUE DES INGENIEURS. (FR). **1360**

REVUE DES MALADIES RESPIRATOIRES. (FR/0761-8425). **3951**

REVUE DES SCIENCES DE L'EDUCATION. (CN/0318-479X). **1780**

REVUE D'ETUDES COMPARATIVES EST-OUEST. (FR/0338-0599). **4546**

REVUE D'INTEGRATION EUROPEENNE. (CN/0703-6337). **4494**

REVUE DU RHUMATISME ET DES MALADIES OSTEO-ARTICULAIRES. (FR/0035-2659). **3806**

REVUE ECONOMIQUE. (FR/0035-2764). **1595**

REVUE FRANCAISE D'ALLERGOLOGIE ET D'IMMUNOLOGIE CLINIQUE. (FR/0335-7457). **3676**

REVUE FRANCAISE DE PSYCHANALYSE : ORGANE OFFICIEL DE LA SOCIETE PSYCHANALYTIQUE DE PARIS. (FR/0035-2942). **4616**

REVUE FRANCAISE DE SOCIOLOGIE. (FR/0035-2969). **5256**

REVUE FRANCAISE DES CORPS GRAS. (FR/0035-3000). **1047**

REVUE FRANCOPHONE DE LA DEFICIENCE INTELLECTUELLE. (CN/0847-5733). **3845**

REVUE FRANCOPHONE DE LOUISIANE. (US/0890-9555). **3431**

REVUE FRONTENAC. (CN/0715-9994). **3431**

REVUE GENERALE DE THERMIQUE. (FR/0035-3159). **2128**

REVUE GEOGRAPHIQUE DES PYRENEES ET DU SUD-OUEST. (FR/0035-3221). **2575**

REVUE INTERNATIONALE DE LA CROIX-ROUGE. (SZ). **2911**

REVUE INTERNATIONALE DE PARODONTIE & DENTISTERIE RESTAURATRICE. (FR/0721-0078). **1335**

REVUE INTERNATIONALE DES HAUTES TEMPERATURES ET DES REFRACTAIRES. (US/0035-3434). **1057**

REVUE MARITIME 1990, LA. (FR/1146-2132). **4182**

REVUE NEUROLOGIQUE. (FR/0035-3787). **3845**

REVUE POLYTECHNIQUE. (SZ/0374-4256). **5148**

REVUE PRESCRIRE, LA. (FR/0247-7750). **3637**

REVUE QUEBECOISE DE LINGUISTIQUE THEORIQUE ET APPLIQUEE. (CN/0835-3581). **3317**

REVUE QUEBECOISE D'ERGOTHERAPIE. (CN/1192-0238). **4382**

REVUE ROUMAINE DE CHIMIE. (RM/0035-3930). **991**

REVUE SUISSE DE ZOOLOGIE. (SZ/0035-418X). **5596**

RHEOLOGICA ACTA. (GW/0035-4511). **4420**

RHETORIC REVIEW. (US/0735-0198). **3317**

RHETORIC SOCIETY QUARTERLY. (US/0277-3945). **3317**

RHETORICA. (US/0734-8584). **3317**

RHEUMATIC DISEASE CLINICS OF NORTH AMERICA. (US/0889-857X). **3807**

RHEUMATOLOGY INTERNATIONAL. (GW/0172-8172). **3807**

RHINOLOGY. SUPPLEMENT. (NE/1013-0047). **3897**

RHODORA. (US/0035-4902). **526**

RICERCHE ECONOMICHE. (IT/0035-5054). **1518**

RICERCHE PEDAGOGICHE. (IT). **1781**

RICHMOND COUNTY HISTORY. (US/0035-5119). **2759**

RILCE : REVISTA DE FILOLOGIA HISPANICA. (SP). **3431**

RINSHO SHINKEIGAKU. (JA/0009-918X). **3845**

RIRON TO HOHO. (JA/0913-1442). **5256**

RISK ANALYSIS. (US/0272-4332). **4800**

RISK (CONCORD, N.H.). (US/1073-8673). **5148**

RISK, ISSUES IN HEALTH & SAFETY. (US/1047-0484). **4800**

RISK MANAGEMENT LETTER, THE. (US/1070-0102). **2892**

RISORGIMENTO, IL. (IT/0035-5607). **2707**

RISQUE PAYS. (FR). **1639**

RIVER STYX. (US/0149-8851). **3431**

RIVERS (FORT COLLINS, COLO.). (US/0898-8048). **5539**

RIVERSEDGE. (US/0272-9598). **3431**

RIVISTA DEL DIRITTO COMMERCIALE E DEL DIRITTO GENERALE DELLE OBBLIGAZIONI. (IT/0035-5887). **3103**

RIVISTA DEL NUOVO CIMENTO. (IT/0035-5917). **4420**

RIVISTA DELLA SOCIETA ITALIANA DI SCIENZA DELL'ALIMENTAZIONE, LA. (IT/0391-4887). **2356**

RIVISTA DELLE TECNOLOGIE TESSILI. (IT/0394-5413). **5355**

RIVISTA DI BIOLOGIA. (IT/0035-6050). **472**

RIVISTA DI CARDIOLOGIA PREVENTIVA E RIABILITATIVA : ORGANO DELL'ASSOCIAZIONE NAZIONALE DEI CENTRI PER LE MALATTIE CARDIOVASCOLARI. (IT/0393-2028). **3710**

RIVISTA DI GRAMMATICA GENERATIVA. (IT). **3317**

RIVISTA DI MATEMATICA PURA ED APPLICATA. (IT). **3532**

RIVISTA DI NEURORADIOLOGIA. (IT). **3845**

RIVISTA DI PARASSITOLOGIA. (IT/0035-6387). **569**

RIVISTA GIURUDICA DELLA SCUOLA. (IT/0391-1845). **1870**

RIVISTA ITALIANA DELLE SOSTANZE GRASSE. (IT/0035-6808). **1029**

RIVISTA ITALIANA DI CHIRURGIA MAXILLO-FACCIALE. (IT/1120-7558). **3974**

RIVISTA ITALIANA DI PALEONTOLOGIA E STRATIGRAFIA. (IT/0035-6883). **4230**

RIVISTA SPERIMENTALE DI FRENIATRIA E MEDICINA LEGALE DELLE ALIENAZIONI MENTALI. (IT/0370-7261). **3936**

RLA, REVISTA DE LINGUISTICA TEORICA Y APLICADA. (CL/0033-698X). **3317**

RN-AIDSLINE. (US/1049-8966). **3868**

ROAD HOME, THE. (JA/0917-0863). **5443**

ROBERT FROST REVIEW, THE. (US/1062-6999). **3431**

ROBOTERSYSTEME. (GW/0178-0026). **1216**

ROBOTICA. (UK/0263-5747). **1216**

ROBOTICS AND COMPUTER-INTEGRATED MANUFACTURING. (US/0736-5845). **1216**

ROCAS Y MINERALES. (SP/0378-3316). **2150**

ROCK & ICE. (US/0885-5722). **4878**

ROCKY MOUNTAIN JOURNAL OF MATHEMATICS, THE. (US/0035-7596). **3532**

ROCKY MOUNTAIN REVIEW OF LANGUAGE AND LITERATURE. (US/0361-1299). **3431**

ROEPER REVIEW. (US/0278-3193). **1885**

ROLLERCOASTER! MAGAZINE. (US/0896-7261). **4865**

ROMANCE MONOGRAPHS, INC. (SERIES). (US). **3352**

ROMANCE PHILOLOGY. (US/0035-8002). **3318**

ROMANCE QUARTERLY. (US/0883-1157). **3318**

ROMANIC REVIEW. (US/0035-8118). **3431**

ROOFING, CLADDING & INSULATION. (UK). **626**

ROOFING MATERIALS GUIDE. (US/1061-8953). **627**

ROTUNDA (TORONTO). (CN/0035-8495). **4096**

ROUND UP (UNIVERSITY PARK, N.M.). (US/0744-5555). **5713**

ROYAL ASTRONOMICAL SOCIETY OF NEW ZEALAND VARIABLE STAR MONTHLY CIRCULARS M. (NZ). **399**

RQ. (US/0033-7072). **3247**

RRT. (CN/0831-2478). **3952**

RS. CUADERNOS DE REALIDADES SOCIALES. (SP/0302-7724). **5256**

RS. RIFIUTI SOLIDI. (IT/0394-5391). **2242**

RTW REVIEW. (US/0887-3003). **1087**

RUBBER CHEMISTRY AND TECHNOLOGY. (US/0035-9475). **5077**

RURAL EDUCATOR (FORT COLLINS), THE. (US/0273-446X). **1781**

RURAL ELECTRIC NEWS LETTER. (US/0747-4784). **4684**

RURAL HISTORY. (UK/0956-7933). **5256**

RURAL SOCIOLOGY. (US/0036-0112). **5257**

RURDS. REVIEW OF URBAN AND REGIONAL DEVELOPMENT STUDIES. (JA/0917-0553). **2835**

RUSSIAN ECONOMIC TRENDS. (UK/0967-0793). **1583**

RUSSIAN JOURNAL OF NUMERICAL ANALYSIS AND MATHEMATICAL ANALYSIS. (NE/0927-6467). **3532**

RUSSIAN LINGUISTICS. (NE/0304-3487). **3318**

RUSSIAN MATHEMATICAL SURVEYS. (UK/0036-0279). **3532**

RUSSKOE VOZROZHDENIE. (US/0222-1543). **5040**

RUTGERS ART REVIEW, THE. (US/0194-049X). **363**

RX CONSULTANT, THE. (US/1066-7741). **4328**

S.A.M. ADVANCED MANAGEMENT JOURNAL (1984). (US/0749-7075). **885**

S.A.M.P.E. QUARTERLY. (US/0036-0821). **1995**

S.T.A.L. (FR/0339-722X). **5521**

SA JOURNAL OF FOOD SCIENCE AND NUTRITION, THE. (SA/1013-3666). **4199**

SABER LEER. (SP/0213-6449). **3352**

SABORD, LE. (CN/0822-2908). **330**

SABRETACHE. (AT/0486-8013). **4056**

SACRAMENTO MEDICINE. (US/0886-2826). **3638**

SACRAMENTO NEWS & REVIEW. (US/1065-3287). **2544**

SAFARI (TUCSON, ARIZ.). (US/0199-5316). **4916**

SAFE JOURNAL. (US/0191-6319). **34**

SAGA-BOOK. (UK/0305-9219). **3432**

SAINTS HERALD. (US/0036-3251). **5067**

SALESIANUM. (IT/0036-3502). **5036**

SAM ADVANCED MANAGEMENT JOURNAL. (US). **885**

SAMPE JOURNAL. (US/0091-1062). **1995**

SAN DIEGO EXECUTIVE. (US/1067-6384). **709**

SANKHYA. SERIES A. (II/0581-572X). **5338**

SANKHYA. SERIES B. (II/0581-5738). **5338**

SARSIA. (NO/0036-4827). **557**

SAS BULLETIN. (US/0899-8922). **282**

SASKATCHEWAN ASSOCIATION OF SOCIAL WORKERS NEWSLETTER. (CN). **5306**

SASKATCHEWAN HISTORY. (CN/0036-4908). **2759**

SAUDI BULLETIN OF OPHTHALMOLOGY : OFFICIAL JOURNAL OF THE SAUDI OPHTHALMOLOGICAL SOCIETY. (SU). **3879**

SAUDI MEDICAL JOURNAL. (SU/0379-5284). **3638**

SAUL BELLOW JOURNAL. (US/0735-1550). **434**

SAUVEGARDE DES CHANTIERS. (FR/0036-505X). **627**

SCANDINAVIAN AUDIOLOGY. (SW/0105-0397). **3891**

SCANDINAVIAN-CANADIAN STUDIES. (CN/0823-1796). **2759**

SCANDINAVIAN JOURNAL OF CLINICAL & LABORATORY INVESTIGATION. (UK/0036-5513). **586**

SCANDINAVIAN JOURNAL OF DENTAL RESEARCH. (DK/0029-845X). **1335**

SCANDINAVIAN JOURNAL OF DEVELOPMENT ALTERNATIVES. (SW/0280-2791). **4535**

SCANDINAVIAN JOURNAL OF ECONOMICS, THE. (UK/0347-0520). **1520**

SCANDINAVIAN JOURNAL OF FOREST RESEARCH. (SW/0282-7581). **2394**

SCANDINAVIAN JOURNAL OF GASTROENTEROLOGY. (NO/0036-5521). **3747**

SCANDINAVIAN JOURNAL OF IMMUNOLOGY. (UK/0300-9475). **3676**

SCANDINAVIAN JOURNAL OF INFECTIOUS DISEASES. (NO/0036-5548). **3716**

SCANDINAVIAN JOURNAL OF METALLURGY. (SW/0371-0459). **4018**

SCANDINAVIAN JOURNAL OF NUTRITION NARINGSFORSKNING. (SW/1102-6480). **4199**

SCANDINAVIAN JOURNAL OF PSYCHOLOGY. (SW/0036-5564). **4617**

SCANDINAVIAN JOURNAL OF REHABILITATION MEDICINE. (SW/0036-5505). **3639**

SCANDINAVIAN JOURNAL OF RHEUMATOLOGY. (SW/0300-9742). **3807**

SCANDINAVIAN — Peer Reviewed Index

SCANDINAVIAN JOURNAL OF SOCIAL MEDICINE. (SW/0300-8037). **3639**

SCANDINAVIAN JOURNAL OF SOCIAL WELFARE. (DK/0907-2055). **5307**

SCANDINAVIAN JOURNAL OF STATISTICS. (SW/0303-6898). **5338**

SCANDINAVIAN JOURNAL OF THORACIC AND CARDIOVASCULAR SURGERY. (SW/0036-5580). **3974**

SCANDINAVIAN JOURNAL OF UROLOGY AND NEPHROLOGY. (SW/0036-5599). **3993**

SCANDINAVIAN JOURNAL OF WORK, ENVIRONMENT & HEALTH. (FI/0355-3140). **2870**

SCANDINAVIAN STUDIES: PUBLICATION OF THE SOCIETY FOR THE ADVANCEMENT OF SCANDINAVIAN STUDY. (US/0036-5637). **3433**

SCANNING. (US/0161-0457). **574**

SCHATZKAMMER DER DEUTSCHEN SPRACHE, DICHTUNG UND GESCHICHTE. (US/0740-1965). **3433**

SCHIZOPHRENIA BULLETIN. (US/0586-7614). **3936**

SCHIZOPHRENIA RESEARCH. (NE/0920-9964). **3936**

SCHNAUZER SHORTS. (US/0276-1521). **4288**

SCHOLARLY INQUIRY FOR NURSING PRACTICE. (US/0889-7182). **3869**

SCHOLARLY PUBLISHING. (CN/0036-634X). **4819**

SCHOOL ARTS. (US/0036-6463). **364**

SCHOOL EFFECTIVENESS AND SCHOOL IMPROVEMENT. (NE/0924-3453). **1871**

SCHOOL PSYCHOLOGY REVIEW. (US/0279-6015). **4618**

SCHOOL SOCIAL WORK JOURNAL. (US/0161-5653). **1871**

SCHUHTECHNIK 1987. (GW/0933-808X). **1087**

SCHWEIZER ARCHIV FUER TIERHEILKUNDE. (SZ/0036-7281). **5521**

SCHWEIZER WAFFEN-MAGAZIN. (SZ/0253-4878). **4056**

SCHWEIZERISCHE MEDIZINISCHE WOCHENSCHRIFT. (SZ/0036-7672). **3639**

SCIENCE AND CHILDREN. (US/0036-8148). **1904**

SCIENCE & EDUCATION. (NE/0926-7220). **1904**

SCIENCE & GLOBAL SECURITY. (US/0892-9882). **4535**

SCIENCE AND SOCIETY (NEW YORK. 1936). (US/0036-8237). **5218**

SCIENCE & TECHNOLOGY LIBRARIES (NEW YORK, N.Y.). (US/0194-262X). **3248**

SCIENCE EDUCATION (SALEM, MASS.). (US/0036-8326). **5151**

SCIENCE FICTION. (AT/0314-6677). **3434**

SCIENCE IN CHINA. SERIES A, MATHEMATICS, PHYSICS, ASTRONOMY & TECHNOLOGICAL SCIENCES. (CC/1001-6511). **5152**

SCIENCE IN NEW GUINEA. (PP/0310-4303). **5152**

SCIENCE OF COMPUTER PROGRAMMING. (NE/0167-6423). **1281**

SCIENCE OF THE TOTAL ENVIRONMENT, THE. (NE/0048-9697). **2181**

SCIENCE OF TSUNAMI HAZARDS. (US/8755-6839). **1456**

SCIENCE PROGRESS (1916). (UK/0036-8504). **5152**

SCIENCE SCOPE (WASHINGTON, D.C.). (US/0887-2376). **5153**

SCIENCE SERIES (LOS ANGELES). (US/0076-0943). **4171**

SCIENCE, TECHNOLOGY & HUMAN VALUES. (US/0162-2439). **5153**

SCIENCE (WASHINGTON, D.C.). (US/0036-8075). **5154**

SCIENCES DES ALIMENTS. (FR/0240-8813). **2356**

SCIENCES (NEW YORK), THE. (US/0036-861X). **5154**

SCIENTIA HORTICULTURAE. (NE/0304-4238). **2431**

SCIENTIFIC AMERICAN. (US/0036-8733). **5155**

SCIENTIFIC AMERICAN MEDICINE. (US/0194-9063). **3639**

SCIENTIFIC DRILLING. (GW/0934-4365). **1410**

SCIENTIST (PHILADELPHIA, PA.), THE. (US/0890-3670). **5156**

SCIENTOMETRICS. (NE/0138-9130). **5156**

SCIMA. (II). **1252**

SCOTIA. (US/0273-0693). **2709**

SCOTT KING'S DIABETES INTERVIEW. (US/1058-6598). **3676**

SCOTTISH GEOGRAPHICAL MAGAZINE. (UK/0036-9225). **2576**

SCOTTISH JOURNAL OF GEOLOGY. (UK/0036-9276). **1396**

SCOTTISH JOURNAL OF POLITICAL ECONOMY. (UK/0036-9292). **1595**

SCOTTISH JOURNAL OF RELIGIOUS STUDIES, THE. (UK/0143-8301). **4995**

SCOTTISH LANGUAGE. (UK/0264-0198). **3319**

SCOTTISH LITERARY JOURNAL. (UK/0305-0785). **3434**

SCOTTISH LITERARY JOURNAL. THE YEAR'S WORK IN SCOTTISH LITERARY AND LINGUISTIC STUDIES. (UK). **3319**

SCOTTISH MEDICAL JOURNAL. (UK/0036-9330). **3639**

SCOTTISH SLAVONIC REVIEW. (UK/0265-3273). **3319**

SCOTTISH TRADITION. (CN/0703-1580). **2545**

SCRIPTURA. (SA/0254-1807). **5019**

SEA SWALLOW, THE. (UK). **5620**

SEARCH (SYDNEY). (AT/0004-9549). **5156**

SEARCH YORK. (UK/0958-3467). **5307**

SECHERESSE MONTROUGE. (FR/1147-7806). **1360**

SECHZIG - NA UND ?. (GW). **5181**

SECOLAS ANNALS. (US/0081-2951). **2760**

SECOND LANGUAGE RESEARCH. (UK/0267-6583). **3320**

SECOND MESSENGER AND PHOSPHOPROTEINS. (US/0895-7479). **586**

SECOND OPINION (PARK RIDGE, ILL.). (US/0890-1570). **3640**

SECRETORY PROCESS, THE. (NE/0167-8523). **3640**

SECURITIES REGULATION LAW JOURNAL. (US/0097-9554). **3047**

SECURITY STUDIES. (UK/0963-6412). **4535**

SEDIMENTARY GEOLOGY. (NE/0037-0738). **1396**

SEDIMENTOLOGY. (UK/0037-0746). **1410**

SEED SCIENCE AND TECHNOLOGY. (NE/0251-0952). **186**

SEEDS (DECATUR, GA.). (US/0194-4495). **2912**

SEISMOLOGICAL RESEARCH LETTERS. (US/0895-0695). **1397**

SEIZURE (LONDON, ENGLAND). (UK/1059-1311). **3846**

SELECCIONES DE TEOLOGIA. (SP/0037-119X). **4996**

SELECTED PAPERS FROM THE WEST VIRGINIA SHAKESPEARE AND RENAISSANCE ASSOCIATION. (US/0885-9574). **3435**

SELECTED REPORTS IN ETHNOMUSICOLOGY. (US/0361-6622). **4152**

SEMAINE DES HOPITAUX. (FR/0037-1777). **3792**

SEMANA. (IS). **2508**

SEMANA ECONOMICA. (PE). **1520**

SEMICONDUCTOR SCIENCE AND TECHNOLOGY. (UK/0268-1242). **4420**

SEMIGROUP FORUM. (US/0037-1912). **3533**

SEMINARS IN ANESTHESIA. (US/0277-0326). **3684**

SEMINARS IN ARTHRITIS AND RHEUMATISM. (US/0049-0172). **3807**

SEMINARS IN DERMATOLOGY. (US/0278-145X). **3722**

SEMINARS IN DIAGNOSTIC PATHOLOGY. (US/0740-2570). **3898**

SEMINARS IN DIALYSIS. (US/0894-0959). **3640**

SEMINARS IN HEMATOLOGY. (US/0037-1963). **3774**

SEMINARS IN INTERVENTIONAL RADIOLOGY. (US/0739-9529). **3946**

SEMINARS IN LIVER DISEASE. (US/0272-8087). **3801**

SEMINARS IN NEPHROLOGY. (US/0270-9295). **3993**

SEMINARS IN NUCLEAR MEDICINE. (US/0001-2998). **3849**

SEMINARS IN ONCOLOGY. (US/0093-7754). **3824**

SEMINARS IN ONCOLOGY NURSING. (US/0749-2081). **3869**

SEMINARS IN PERINATOLOGY. (US/0146-0005). **3768**

SEMINARS IN REPRODUCTIVE ENDOCRINOLOGY. (US/0734-8630). **3733**

SEMINARS IN RESPIRATORY MEDICINE. (US/0192-9755). **3952**

SEMINARS IN SURGICAL ONCOLOGY. (US/8756-0437). **3824**

SEMINARS IN THROMBOSIS AND HEMOSTASIS. (US/0094-6176). **3774**

SEMINARS IN ULTRASOUND, CT, AND MR. (US/0887-2171). **3946**

SEMINARS IN VETERINARY MEDICINE AND SURGERY (SMALL ANIMALS). (US/0882-0511). **5522**

SEMPER REFORMANDA. (US/1065-3783). **4996**

SEPARATION AND PURIFICATION METHODS (SOFTCOVER ED.). (US/0360-2540). **1029**

SEPARATIONS TECHNOLOGY. (US/0956-9618). **1996**

SERIALS LIBRARIAN, THE. (US/0361-526X). **3249**

SERIE CIENTIFICA. INSTITUTO ANTARTICO CHILENO. (CL/0073-9871). **1360**

SERVANT, THE. (CN/0705-6338). **4996**

SERVICE NEWS PARIS. (FR/1144-2433). **886**

SERVICE STATION MANAGEMENT. (US/0488-3896). **5425**

SERVIZI SOCIALI. (IT). **4685**

SET-VALUED ANALYSIS. (NE/0927-6947). **3534**

SETON HALL JOURNAL OF SPORT LAW. (US/1059-4310). **3048**

SEVENTEENTH-CENTURY FRENCH STUDIES. (UK/0265-1068). **3435**

SEX ROLES. (US/0360-0025). **5257**

SEXUALITY AND LITERATURE. (US/0893-6889). **3435**

SEXUALLY TRANSMITTED DISEASES. (US/0148-5717). **4802**

SHAKESPEARE BULLETIN. (US/0748-2558). **5368**

SHAKESPEARE IN SOUTHERN AFRICA : JOURNAL OF THE SHAKESPEARE SOCIETY OF SOUTHERN AFRICA. (SA/1011-582X). **5368**

SHAREHOLDER REMEDIES IN CANADA. (CN). **3103**

SHELBY COUNTY REPORTER (1955). (US/1063-9489). **5628**

SHELDON'S MAJOR STORES AND CHAINS. (US). **957**

SHENG LI HSUEH PAO. (CC/0371-0874). **587**

SHENGWU GONGCHENG XUEBAO. (CC/1000-3061). **3696**

SHENGWU HUAXUE ZAZHI. (CC/1000-8543). **3696**

SHINING LIGHT. (US). **4997**

SHINRIGAKU KENKYU. (JA/0021-5236). **4618**

SHOCK WAVES. (GW/0938-1287). **4429**

SHOFAR (WEST LAFAYETTE, IND.). (US/0882-8539). **5052**

SHOKUBUTSUGAKU ZASSHI. (JA/0006-808X). **527**

SHOKUHIN EISEIGAKU ZASSHI. (JA/0015-6426). **4803**

SHORT LINE, THE. (US/0199-4050). **5436**

SHROUD SPECTRUM INTERNATIONAL. (US/0738-6524). **5157**

SHUI DONGLIXUE YANJIU YU JINZHAN. (CC/1000-4874). **1418**

SHUXUE WULI XUEBAO. (CC/0252-9602). **3534**

SI..., ENTONCES... . (SP/1130-149X). **4618**

SIAM JOURNAL ON APPLIED MATHEMATICS. (US/0036-1399). **3534**

SIAM JOURNAL ON COMPUTING. (US/0097-5397). **1262**

SIAM JOURNAL ON MATHEMATICAL ANALYSIS. (US/0036-1410). **3534**

SIAM JOURNAL ON MATRIX ANALYSIS AND APPLICATIONS. (US/0895-4798). **3534**

SIAM JOURNAL ON NUMERICAL ANALYSIS. (US/0036-1429). **3535**

SIAM JOURNAL ON SCIENTIFIC AND STATISTICAL COMPUTING. (US/0196-5204). **3535**

SIAM REVIEW. (US/0036-1445). **3535**

SIBERIAN MATHEMATICAL JOURNAL. (US/0037-4466). **3535**

SID CATO'S NEWSLETTER ON ANNUAL REPORTS. (US). **914**

SIDA, CONTRIBUTIONS TO BOTANY. (US/0036-1488). **527**

SIEMENS REVIEW. (GW/0302-2528). **2081**

SIGN LANGUAGE STUDIES. (US/0302-1475). **3321**

SIGNAL PROCESSING. (NE/0165-1684). **2081**

SIGNAL PROCESSING. IMAGE COMMUNICATION. (NE/0923-5965). **2081**

SIGNOS UNIVERSITARIOS : REVISTA DE LA UNIVERSIDAD DEL SALVADOR. (AG). **1847**

SIGNS (CHICAGO, ILL.). (US/0097-9740). **5566**

SILVAE GENETICA. (GW/0037-5349). **528**

SIMULATION & GAMING. (US/1046-8781). **1283**

SIMULATION PRACTICE AND THEORY. (NE/0928-4869). **1244**

SIMULATION (SAN DIEGO, CALIF.). (US/0037-5497). **1283**

SINFONIAN (1980), THE. (US/8750-5347). **4153**

SING OUT EAST DONCASTER. (AT/0818-0555). **4153**

SINGAPORE ECONOMIC REVIEW. (SI/0217-5908). **1584**

SINGAPORE JOURNAL OF TROPICAL GEOGRAPHY. (SI/0129-7619). **2576**

SINGLE HOUND. (US/1044-8934). **3471**

SINGLELIFE (MILWAUKEE, WIS.). (US/8756-0380). **2493**

SINGMUL HAKHOE CHI. (KO/0583-421X). **528**

SINO-JAPANESE STUDIES. (US). **2664**

SINO-WESTERN CULTURAL RELATIONS JOURNAL. (US/1041-875X). **4535**

SISMODINAMICA (DURHAM, N.H.). (US/1051-6441). **2031**

SIXTEENTH CENTURY JOURNAL, THE. (US/0361-0160). **2629**

SKELETAL RADIOLOGY. (US/0364-2348). **3947**

SKEPTIKER. (GW/0936-9244). **4243**

SKILLINGS' MINING REVIEW. (US/0037-6329). **2151**

SKULL BASE SURGERY. (US/1052-1453). **3974**

SLAVIC AND EAST EUROPEAN JOURNAL. (US/0037-6752). **3321**

SLEEP (NEW YORK, N.Y.). (US/0161-8105). **3641**

SLOAN MANAGEMENT REVIEW. (US/0019-848X). **886**

SMALL BUSINESS FORUM. (US/1053-4695). **711**

SMALL WARS AND INSURGENCIES. (UK/0959-2318). **4057**

SMARANDACHE FUNCTION JOURNAL. (US/1053-4792). **3536**

SMITH COLLEGE STUDIES IN SOCIAL WORK. (US/0037-7317). **5307**

SMRC-NEWSLETTER. (US/0584-5025). **2760**

SOAP, COSMETICS, CHEMICAL SPECIALTIES. (US/0091-1372). **1030**

SOCIAL ANALYSIS (ADELAIDE, S. AUST.). (AT/0155-977X). **5219**

SOCIAL ANARCHISM. (US/0196-4801). **4546**

SOCIAL BEHAVIOR AND PERSONALITY. (NZ/0301-2212). **5258**

SOCIAL BIOLOGY. (US/0037-766X). **551**

SOCIAL CHOICE AND WELFARE. (GW/0176-1714). **5308**

SOCIAL COGNITION. (US/0278-016X). **5258**

SOCIAL COMPASS. (UK/0037-7686). **5219**

SOCIAL CONCEPT. (US/0737-7762). **5219**

SOCIAL DYNAMICS. (SA/0253-3952). **5258**

SOCIAL EPISTEMOLOGY. (UK/0269-1728). **4361**

SOCIAL FORCES. (US/0037-7732). **5258**

SOCIAL HOUSING. (UK/1351-4288). **5308**

SOCIAL INDICATORS RESEARCH. (NE/0303-8300). **5219**

SOCIAL ISSUES RESOURCES SERIES. (US/0740-3127). **5308**

SOCIAL JUSTICE (SAN FRANCISCO, CALIF.). (US/1043-1578). **3177**

SOCIAL NETWORKS. (SZ/0378-8733). **5259**

SOCIAL PHILOSOPHY & POLICY. (UK/0265-0525). **5219**

SOCIAL POLICY. (US/0037-7783). **5259**

SOCIAL POLICY & ADMINISTRATION. (UK/0144-5596). **4686**

SOCIAL PROBLEMS. (US/0037-7791). **5220**

SOCIAL RESEARCH. (US/0037-783X). **5220**

SOCIAL SCIENCE & MEDICINE (1982). (US/0277-9536). **5220**

SOCIAL SCIENCE HISTORY. (US/0145-5532). **5220**

SOCIAL SCIENCE INFORMATION. (UK/0539-0184). **5220**

SOCIAL SCIENCE JOURNAL (FORT COLLINS), THE. (US/0362-3319). **5220**

SOCIAL SCIENCE QUARTERLY. (US/0038-4941). **5220**

SOCIAL SCIENCE RECORD. (US/0037-7872). **5221**

SOCIAL SCIENCE RESEARCH. (US/0049-089X). **5221**

SOCIAL SCIENCE SOURCE. (US/1063-9802). **5227**

SOCIAL SECURITY BULLETIN (WASHINGTON, D.C. : 1938). (US/0037-7910). **5308**

SOCIAL SERVICE REVIEW (CHICAGO), THE. (US/0037-7961). **5309**

SOCIAL STUDIES OF SCIENCE. (UK/0306-3127). **5221**

SOCIAL THEORY AND PRACTICE. (US/0037-802X). **5222**

SOCIAL WORK IN HEALTH CARE. (US/0098-1389). **5309**

SOCIAL WORK (NEW YORK). (US/0037-8046). **5309**

SOCIAL WORK RESEARCH & ABSTRACTS. (US/0148-0847). **5267**

SOCIAL WORK STELLENBOSCH. (SA/0037-8054). **5310**

SOCIAL WORK WITH GROUPS (NEW YORK. 1978). (US/0160-9513). **5310**

SOCIALISM AND DEMOCRACY. (US/0885-4300). **4546**

SOCIALIST REVIEW (SAN FRANCISCO). (US/0161-1801). **4547**

SOCIALIST STUDIES/ETUDES SOCIALIST: A CANADIAN ANNUAL. (CN). **5222**

SOCIETY & NATURAL RESOURCES. (US/0894-1920). **2205**

SOCIETY (NEW BRUNSWICK). (US/0147-2011). **5222**

SOCIO-ECONOMIC PLANNING SCIENCES. (US/0038-0121). **1521**

SOCIOBIOLOGY. (US/0361-6525). **5597**

SOCIOLOGIA RURALIS. (NE/0038-0199). **5260**

SOCIOLOGICAL ANALYSIS. (US/0038-0210). **4998**

SOCIOLOGICAL FOCUS (KENT, OHIO). (US/0038-0237). **5260**

SOCIOLOGICAL FORUM (RANDOLPH, N.J.). (US/0884-8971). **5260**

SOCIOLOGICAL INQUIRY. (US/0038-0245). **5260**

SOCIOLOGICAL METHODS & RESEARCH. (US/0049-1241). **5261**

SOCIOLOGICAL PERSPECTIVES. (US/0731-1214). **5261**

SOCIOLOGICAL QUARTERLY. (US/0038-0253). **5261**

SOCIOLOGICAL REVIEW, THE. (UK/0038-0261). **5261**

SOCIOLOGICAL SPECTRUM. (US/0273-2173). **5261**

SOCIOLOGICAL VIEWPOINTS. (US/1060-0876). **5261**

SOCIOLOGIE DU TRAVAIL (PARIS). (FR/0038-0296). **1711**

SOCIOLOGIJA SELA. (CI/0038-0326). **5262**

SOCIOLOGISK FORSKNING. (SW/0038-0342). **5262**

SOCIOLOGY OF EDUCATION ABSTRACTS. (UK/0038-0415). **1797**

SOCIOLOGY OF HEALTH & ILLNESS. (UK/0141-9889). **5262**

SOCIOLOGY (OXFORD). (UK/0038-0385). **5262**

SOCIONOMEN 1987. (SW/0283-1929). **5310**

SOFTWARE ABC. (GW). **1290**

SOFTWARE ENGINEERING JOURNAL. (UK/0268-6961). **1996**

SOFTWARE : PRACTICE & EXPERIENCE. (UK/0038-0644). **1291**

SOFTWARE TESTING, VERIFICATION & RELIABILITY. (UK/0960-0833). **1291**

SOIL & TILLAGE RESEARCH. (NE/0167-1987). **186**

SOIL BIOLOGY & BIOCHEMISTRY. (UK/0038-0717). **186**

SOIL SCIENCE. (US/0038-075X). **187**

SOIL SCIENCE AND PLANT NUTRITION (TOKYO). (JA/0038-0768). **187**

SOIL SCIENCE SOCIETY OF AMERICA JOURNAL. (US/0361-5995). **187**

SOIL USE AND MANAGEMENT. (UK/0266-0032). **187**

SOJOURN (SINGAPORE, SINGAPORE). (SI/0217-9520). **5222**

SOLAR ENERGY (PHOENIX, ARIZ.). (US/0038-092X). **1957**

SOLAR PHYSICS. (NE/0038-0938). **400**

SOLAR PROGRESS. (AT/0729-6436). **1957**

SOLID STATE COMMUNICATIONS. (US/0038-1098). **4421**

SOLID-STATE ELECTRONICS. (UK/0038-1101). **2081**

SOLID STATE IONICS. (NE/0167-2738). **4421**

SOLID STATE TECHNOLOGY. (US/0038-111X). **2081**

SOLVENT EXTRACTION AND ION EXCHANGE. (US/0736-6299). **1019**

SOMATIC CELL AND MOLECULAR GENETICS. (US/0740-7750). **551**

SOMATOTHERAPIES ET SOMATOLOGIE. (FR). **3642**

SORGHUM NEWSLETTER. (US/0584-1321). **136**

SOTSIOLOGICHESKIE ISSLEDOVANIIA. (RU/0132-1625). **5263**

SOUDAGE ET TECHNIQUES CONNEXES. (FR/0038-173X). **4027**

SOUTH AFRICAN BUILDER, THE. (SA). **627**

SOUTH AFRICAN GEOGRAPHICAL JOURNAL. (SA/0373-6245). **2576**

SOUTH AFRICAN JOURNAL OF ANIMAL SCIENCE. (SA/0375-1589). **222**

SOUTH AFRICAN JOURNAL OF CHEMISTRY. (SA/0379-4350). **992**

SOUTH AFRICAN JOURNAL OF ECONOMICS, THE. (SA/0038-2280). **1521**

SOUTH AFRICAN JOURNAL OF SCIENCE. (SA/0038-2353). **5158**

SOUTH AFRICAN JOURNAL OF SURGERY. (SA/0038-2361). **3975**

SOUTH AFRICAN JOURNAL OF WILDLIFE RESEARCH. (SA/0379-4369). **2205**

SOUTH AFRICAN LABOUR BULLETIN. (SA/0377-5429). **1711**

SOUTH AFRICAN MEDICAL JOURNAL. (SA/0038-2469). **3642**

SOUTH AFRICAN STATISTICAL JOURNAL. (SA/0038-271X). **3542**

SOUTH ASIA. (AT/0085-6401). **2664**

SOUTH ATLANTIC REVIEW. (US/0277-335X). **3322**

SOUTH AUSTRALIAN ORNITHOLOGIST. (AT/0038-2973). **5620**

SOUTH CAROLINA HISTORICAL MAGAZINE. (US/0038-3082). **2761**

SOUTH CAROLINA NURSE, THE. (US/1046-7394). **3869**

SOUTH CAROLINA REVIEW, THE. (US/0038-3163). **3353**

SOUTH CENTRAL REVIEW. (US/0743-6831). **3322**

SOUTH DAKOTA JOURNAL OF MEDICINE. (US/0038-3317). **3642**

SOUTH PACIFIC JOURNAL OF NATURAL SCIENCE, THE. (FJ/1013-9877). **4172**

SOUTH PIERCE COUNTY DISPATCH, THE. (US). **5762**

SOUTHAMPTON MEDICAL JOURNAL. (UK/0266-0342). **3642**

SOUTHEAST ASIA PROGRAM SERIES. (US). **2665**

SOUTHEAST ASIAN AFFAIRS. (SI/0377-5437). **4496**

SOUTHEASTERN ARCHAEOLOGY. (US/0734-578X). **282**

SOUTHEASTERN GEOGRAPHER. (US/0038-366X). **2576**

SOUTHEASTERN GEOLOGY. (US/0038-3678). **1397**

SOUTHEASTERN POLITICAL REVIEW. (US/0730-2177). **4496**

SOUTHERN — Peer Reviewed Index

SOUTHERN BAPTIST EDUCATOR, THE. (US/0038-3848). **5067**

SOUTHERN BUSINESS & ECONOMIC JOURNAL, THE. (US/0743-779X). **712**

SOUTHERN BUSINESS REVIEW. (US/0884-1373). **886**

SOUTHERN CALIFORNIA LAW REVIEW. (US/0038-3910). **3057**

SOUTHERN COMMUNICATION JOURNAL, THE. (US/1041-794X). **1122**

SOUTHERN ECONOMIC JOURNAL. (US/0038-4038). **1521**

SOUTHERN FOLKLORE. (US/0899-594X). **2324**

SOUTHERN HISTORIAN, THE. (US/0738-5102). **2761**

SOUTHERN HISTORY. (UK/0142-4688). **2710**

SOUTHERN HUMANITIES REVIEW. (US/0038-4186). **2854**

SOUTHERN JOURNAL OF AGRICULTURAL ECONOMICS. (US/0081-3052). **136**

SOUTHERN JOURNAL OF PHILOSOPHY, THE. (US/0038-4283). **4361**

SOUTHERN MEDICAL JOURNAL (BIRMINGHAM). (US/0038-4348). **3975**

SOUTHERN PARTISAN, THE. (US/0739-1714). **4496**

SOUTHERN REVIEW (ADELAIDE). (AT/0038-4526). **3353**

SOUTHERN RURAL SOCIOLOGY. (US/0885-3436). **5263**

SOUTHERN SOCIAL STUDIES JOURNAL. (US/1047-7942). **5222**

SOUTHERN STUDIES. (US/0735-8342). **2761**

SOUTHWEST JOURNAL OF LINGUISTICS. (US/0737-4143). **3322**

SOUTHWEST PHILOSOPHY REVIEW. (US/0897-2346). **4361**

SOUTHWESTERN ENTOMOLOGIST, THE. (US/0147-1724). **5613**

SOUTHWESTERN MASS COMMUNICATION JOURNAL. (US/0891-9186). **1122**

SOUTHWESTERN NATURALIST, THE. (US/0038-4909). **4172**

SOVIET AND EASTERN EUROPEAN FOREIGN TRADE. (US/0038-5263). **1640**

SOVIET & EASTERN EUROPEAN REPORT. (UK/0963-7036). **3136**

SOVIET ANTHROPOLOGY AND ARCHAEOLOGY. (US/0038-528X). **245**

SOVIET APPLIED MECHANICS. (US/0038-5298). **2129**

SOVIET ASTRONOMY LETTERS. (US/0360-0327). **400**

SOVIET ATOMIC ENERGY. (US/0038-531X). **2158**

SOVIET ECONOMY (SILVER SPRING, MD.). (US/0882-6994). **1640**

SOVIET ELECTROCHEMISTRY. (US/0038-5387). **1035**

SOVIET JOURNAL OF ECOLOGY, THE. (US/0096-7807). **2221**

SOVIET JOURNAL OF NONDESTRUCTIVE TESTING, THE. (US/0038-5492). **2031**

SOVIET JOURNAL OF NUCLEAR PHYSICS. (US/0038-5506). **4451**

SOVIET JOURNAL OF PSYCHOLOGY. (US/0891-2726). **4619**

SOVIET LAW AND GOVERNMENT. (US/0038-5530). **3057**

SOVIET MATERIALS SCIENCE. (US/0038-5565). **2108**

SOVIET PHYSICS-ACOUSTICS. (US/0038-562X). **4453**

SOVIET PHYSICS-SEMICONDUCTORS. (US/0038-5700). **4422**

SOVIET PLANT PHYSIOLOGY. (US/0038-5719). **528**

SOVIET SOIL SCIENCE. (US/0038-5832). **188**

SOVIET STUDIES. (UK/0038-5859). **4547**

SOVIET STUDIES IN PHILOSOPHY. (US/0038-5883). **4361**

SPACE NEWS (SPRINGFIELD, VA.). (US/1046-6940). **36**

SPACE POLICY. (UK/0265-9646). **36**

SPACE SCIENCE REVIEWS. (NE/0038-6308). **400**

SPEAKER AND GAVEL. (US/0584-8164). **3322**

SPECIAL CARE IN DENTISTRY. (US/0275-1879). **1335**

SPECIAL PUBLICATION - ACADEMY OF NATURAL SCIENCES OF PHILADELPHIA. (US/0097-3254). **1360**

SPECIAL PUBLICATION - CARNEGIE MUSEUM OF NATURAL HISTORY. (US/0145-9031). **4172**

SPECIAL PUBLICATION - COUNCIL FOR AGRICULTURAL SCIENCE AND TECHNOLOGY. (US/0194-407X). **137**

SPECIALITY PAPER & BOARD MATERIALS & MARKETS BULLETIN. (UK). **4222**

SPECIALTY COOKING. (US/1048-8413). **4199**

SPECTROCHIMICA ACTA. PART A : MOLECULAR SPECTROSCOPY. (UK/0584-8539). **4441**

SPECTROCHIMICA ACTA. PART B : ATOMIC SPECTROSCOPY. (UK/0584-8547). **4422**

SPECTROSCOPIC PROPERTIES OF INORGANIC AND ORGANOMETALLIC COMPOUNDS. (UK/0584-8555). **1019**

SPECTROSCOPY INTERNATIONAL. (US/1040-7669). **993**

SPECTROSCOPY LETTERS. (US/0038-7010). **4442**

SPECTRUM (SANTA BARBARA, CALIF.). (US/0038-7061). **1095**

SPEECH COMMUNICATION. (NE/0167-6393). **1122**

SPELD. (AT). **1885**

SPILL SCIENCE AND TECHNOLOGY BULLETIN. (UK/1353-2561). **2243**

SPINE (PHILADELPHIA, PA. 1976). (US/0362-2436). **3642**

SPIRIT & LIFE (CLYDE, MO.). (US/0038-7592). **4999**

SPOON RIVER POETRY REVIEW. (US). **3471**

SPORT & MEDICINA. (IT/0392-9647). **3956**

SPORT MARKETING QUARTERLY. (US/1061-6934). **4920**

SPORTS BUSINESS. (CN/0830-1921). **958**

SPORTS, PARKS & RECREATION LAW REPORTER, THE. (US/0893-8210). **3058**

SPRING. (US/0362-0522). **4619**

SPRINGER SEMINARS IN IMMUNOPATHOLOGY. (US/0344-4325). **3677**

SRI LANKA VETERINARY JOURNAL : THE OFFICIAL JOURNAL OF THE SRI LANKA VETERINARY ASSOCIATION, THE. (CE). **5522**

ST. MARK'S REVIEW. (AT/0036-3103). **4999**

STABILITY & APPLIED ANALYSIS OF CONTINUOUS MEDIA. (IT/1120-4222). **3536**

STAFF PAPERS - INTERNATIONAL MONETARY FUND. (US/0020-8027). **812**

STAHL UND EISEN. (GW/0340-4803). **4020**

STANFORD BUSINESS SCHOOL MAGAZINE. (US/0883-265X). **713**

STANFORD LAW REVIEW. (US/0038-9765). **3058**

STARKE, DIE. (GW/0038-9056). **993**

STATION NOTE - UNIVERSITY OF IDAHO FOREST, WILDLIFE AND RANGE EXPERIMENT STATION. (US/0073-4594). **2206**

STATISTICAL REPORT - STATE OF ALASKA, ALASKA OIL AND GAS CONSERVATION COMMISSION. (US/0273-1916). **2206**

STATISTICAL SCIENCE. (US/0883-4237). **5340**

STATISTICIAN, THE. (UK/0039-0526). **5341**

STATISTICS AND COMPUTING. (UK/0960-3174). **1210**

STATISTICS & PROBABILITY LETTERS. (NE/0167-7152). **3536**

STATISTICS IN MEDICINE. (UK/0277-6715). **3661**

STAUB, REINHALTUNG DER LUFT. (GW/0039-0771). **2244**

STEAM PASSENGER SERVICE DIRECTORY. (US/0081-542X). **5437**

STEEL RESEARCH. (GW/0177-4832). **4020**

STEREO-ATLAS OF OSTRACOD SHELLS; EDITED BY P.C. SYLVESTER-BRADLEY AND DAVID J. SIVETER. (UK). **557**

STEREOTACTIC AND FUNCTIONAL NEUROSURGERY. (SZ/1011-6125). **3975**

STEROIDS. (US/0039-128X). **473**

STOCHASTIC ANALYSIS AND APPLICATIONS. (US/0736-2994). **3536**

STOCHASTIC HYDROLOGY AND HYDRAULICS. (GW/0931-1955). **1418**

STOCHASTIC PROCESSES AND THEIR APPLICATIONS. (NE/0304-4149). **3536**

STOCK-TAKING ON THE EUROPEAN CONVENTION ON HUMAN RIGHTS. (FR/0252-0613). **4513**

STORIA DEL PENSIERO ECONOMICO. BOLLETTINO DI INFORMAZIONE. (IT). **1585**

STRASSENVERKEHRSSICHERHEIT IM JAHRE ... / HERAUSGEGEBEN VOM OSTERREICHISCHEN STATISTISCHEN ZENTRALAMT. (AU). **5444**

STRATEGIC MANAGEMENT JOURNAL. (UK/0143-2095). **887**

STRESS MEDICINE. (UK/0748-8386). **3643**

STROKE (1970). (US/0039-2499). **3710**

STRUCTURAL ENGINEERING AND MECHANICS. (KO/1225-4568). **1997**

STRUCTURAL ENGINEERING REVIEW. (UK/0952-5807). **2031**

STRUCTURAL SAFETY. (NE/0167-4730). **629**

STRUCTURES AND ENVIRONMENT HANDBOOK. (US/0149-1245). **629**

STRUGGLE : MATHEMATICS FOR LOW ATTAINERS. (UK). **1885**

STUDI CATTOLICI. (IT/0039-2901). **5036**

STUDI CLASSICI E ORIENTALI. (IT/0081-6124). **1080**

STUDI DI TEOLOGIA. (IT). **4999**

STUDIA BIOPHYSICA. (SZ/0081-6337). **496**

STUDIA GEOPHYSICA ET GEODAETICA. (XR/0039-3169). **1411**

STUDIA LOGICA. (PL/0039-3215). **4362**

STUDIA MATHEMATICA. (PL/0039-3223). **3536**

STUDIA PATAVINA. (IT/0039-3304). **5000**

STUDIA PHONETICA POSNANIENSIA. (PL/0861-2085). **3325**

STUDIES IN 20TH CENTURY LITERATURE. (US/0145-7888). **3354**

STUDIES IN AFRICAN LINGUISTICS. (US/0039-3533). **3325**

STUDIES IN AMERICAN DRAMA, 1945-PRESENT. (US/0886-7097). **5369**

STUDIES IN AMERICAN INDIAN LITERATURE. (US). **3441**

STUDIES IN AMERICAN JEWISH LITERATURE (ALBANY, N.Y.). (US/0271-9274). **3441**

STUDIES IN APPLIED MATHEMATICS (CAMBRIDGE). (US/0022-2526). **3537**

STUDIES IN BIBLIOGRAPHY AND BOOKLORE. (US/0039-3568). **5013**

STUDIES IN CANADIAN LITERATURE (FREDERICTON, N.B.). (CN/0380-6995). **3441**

STUDIES IN CENTRAL AND EAST ASIAN RELIGIONS : JOURNAL OF THE SEMINAR FOR BUDDHIST STUDIES, COPENHAGEN & AARHUS. (DK/0904-2431). **5022**

STUDIES IN CHRISTIAN ETHICS. (UK). **5000**

STUDIES IN COMPARATIVE COMMUNISM. (UK/0039-3592). **4548**

STUDIES IN COMPARATIVE INTERNATIONAL DEVELOPMENT. (US/0039-3606). **5223**

STUDIES IN CONTEMPORARY SATIRE. (US/0163-4143). **3441**

STUDIES IN EAST EUROPEAN THOUGHT. (NE/0925-9392). **4362**

STUDIES IN ECONOMIC ANALYSIS. (US/0198-8263). **1595**

STUDIES IN EIGHTEENTH-CENTURY CULTURE. (US/0360-2370). **2631**

STUDIES IN FAMILY PLANNING. (US/0039-3665). **591**

STUDIES IN HISTORY AND PHILOSOPHY OF SCIENCE. (UK/0039-3681). **5160**

STUDIES IN ICONOGRAPHY. (US/0148-1029). **5000**

STUDIES IN INTERRELIGIOUS DIALOGUE. (NE/0926-2326). **5000**

STUDIES IN LATIN AMERICAN POPULAR CULTURE. (US/0730-9139). **331**

STUDIES IN MATHEMATICAL AND MANAGERIAL ECONOMICS. (NE/0081-8194). **1523**

STUDIES IN MEDIEVAL AND RENAISSANCE TEACHING. (US/1050-9739). **2711**

STUDIES IN MODERN GERMAN LITERATURE. (US/0888-3904). **3442**

STUDIES IN MYCOLOGY. (NE/0166-0616). **576**

STUDIES IN ORGANIC CHEMISTRY (AMSTERDAM). (NE/0165-3253). **1047**

STUDIES IN PHILOSOPHY AND EDUCATION. (US/0039-3746). **4362**

STUDIES IN POLITICAL ECONOMY. (CN/0707-8552). **4497**

STUDIES IN RELIGION. (CN/0008-4298). **5001**

STUDIES IN ROMANCE LANGUAGES (LEXINGTON, KY.). (US/0085-6894). **3442**

STUDIES IN SOVIET THOUGHT. (NE/0039-3797). **4362**

STUDIES IN THE DECORATIVE ARTS. (US/1069-8825). **375**

STUDIES IN THE HUMANITIES. (US). **2855**

STUDIES IN THE ROMANTIC AGE. (US/0897-9243). **3442**

STUDIES OF HIGHER EDUCATION AND RESEARCH. (SW/0283-7692). **1849**

STUDIES OF ISRAELI SOCIETY. (US/0734-4937). **5263**

STUDIES ON MANUFACTURING ENGINEERING AND PRODUCTION MANAGEMENT. (UK/1062-3949). **1997**

STUDIES ON SOUTHEAST ASIA. (US). **2665**

SUCCESSFUL HOTEL MARKETER, THE. (US/1040-600X). **2809**

SUD; INFORMATION ECONOMIQUE : PROVENCE ALPES COTE D'AZUR. (FR). **1585**

SUID-AFRIKAANSE BOSBOUTYDSKRIF. (SA/0038-2167). **2396**

SUMMA. (AG/0325-4615). **309**

SUMMARIOS. (AG/0325-6448). **309**

SUMMER THEATRE DIRECTORY (DORSET, VT.). (US/0884-5840). **5369**

SUN AT WORK IN EUROPE. (UK/0269-1159). **1958**

SUNSTONE. (US/0363-1370). **5001**

SUPERCOMPUTER. (NE/0168-7875). **1204**

SUPERCONDUCTOR SCIENCE & TECHNOLOGY. (UK/0953-2048). **4445**

SUPERLATTICES AND MICROSTRUCTURES. (UK/0749-6036). **5161**

SUPERTRAX. (CN). **4855**

SURFACE & COATINGS TECHNOLOGY. (SZ/0257-8972). **2108**

SURFACE AND INTERFACE ANALYSIS : SIA. (UK/0142-2421). **1019**

SURFACE MOUNT TECHNOLOGY. (US/0893-3588). **2083**

SURFACE SCIENCE. (NE/0039-6028). **1058**

SURFACE SCIENCE REPORTS. (NE/0167-5729). **2083**

SURGERY. (US/0039-6060). **3975**

SURGERY, GYNECOLOGY & OBSTETRICS. (US/0039-6087). **3975**

SURGICAL AND RADIOLOGIC ANATOMY (ENGLISH ED.). (GW/0930-1038). **3680**

SURGICAL CLINICS OF NORTH AMERICA, THE. (US/0039-6109). **3975**

SURGICAL LAPAROSCOPY AND ENDOSCOPY. (US/1051-7200). **3976**

SURGICAL NEUROLOGY. (US/0090-3019). **3976**

SURGICAL TECHNOLOGIST, THE. (US/0164-4238). **3644**

SURREY ARCHAEOLOGICAL COLLECTIONS. (UK). **283**

SURVEY OF OPHTHALMOLOGY. (US/0039-6257). **3879**

SURVEYING AND LAND INFORMATION SYSTEMS. (US/1052-2905). **2583**

SURVEYING TECHNICIAN. (UK/0952-5793). **2032**

SURVEYS IN GEOPHYSICS. (NE/0169-3298). **1411**

SURVEYS ON MATHEMATICS FOR INDUSTRY. (AU/0938-1953). **1997**

SUSTAINABLE DEVELOPMENT. (CN/0840-4666). **2206**

SWEDISH DENTAL JOURNAL. (SW/0347-9994). **1336**

SWEDISH JOURNAL OF AGRICULTURAL RESEARCH. (SW/0049-2701). **139**

SYLLECTA CLASSICA. (US/1040-3612). **1080**

SYMBIOSIS (PHILADELPHIA, PA.). (US/0334-5114). **474**

SYMBOLIC INTERACTION. (US/0195-6086). **5264**

SYMPOSIUM / DEUTSCHKANADISCHE STUDIEN. (CN/0823-2458). **3443**

SYNTHESE (DORDRECHT). (NE/0039-7857). **4363**

SYNTHESIS AND REACTIVITY IN INORGANIC AND METAL-ORGANIC CHEMISTRY. (US/0094-5714). **994**

SYNTHESIS (STUTTGART). (GW/0039-7881). **1048**

SYNTHETIC COMMUNICATIONS. (US/0039-7911). **1048**

SYNTHETIC METALS. (SZ/0379-6779). **4021**

SYRACUSE NEW TIMES. (US/0893-844X). **2493**

SYSTEMATIC AND APPLIED MICROBIOLOGY. (GW/0723-2020). **570**

SYSTEMATIC BOTANY. (US/0363-6445). **528**

SYSTEMATIC ENTOMOLOGY. (UK/0307-6970). **5613**

SYSTEMATIC PARASITOLOGY. (NE/0165-5752). **5598**

SYSTEMS ANALYSIS, MODELLING, SIMULATION. (GW/0232-9298). **3537**

SYSTEMS & CONTROL LETTERS. (NE/0167-6911). **1998**

T.E.C. (PARIS). (FR/0397-6513). **2244**

TA NEA. (GR). **5802**

TACT : THE AIR CARGO TARIFF. (NE). **5394**

TAITO. (FI/0355-7421). **376**

TAKAHE CHRISTCHURCH. (NZ/0114-4138). **3444**

TALANTA (OXFORD). (UK/0039-9140). **1019**

TAMKANG JOURNAL OF MATHEMATICS. (CH/0376-4079). **3538**

TAMPA BAY BUSINESS JOURNAL. (US/0896-467X). **714**

TANG STUDIES. (US/0737-5034). **334**

TAPPI JOURNAL. (US/0734-1415). **4239**

TAR HEEL JUNIOR HISTORIAN. (US/0496-8913). **2762**

TAREAS. (PN/0494-7061). **5224**

TAX EXECUTIVE, THE. (US/0040-0025). **4752**

TAX EXEMPT FINANCING. (US/1043-0873). **3062**

TAX LAWS OF THE WORLD. CLASS B. (US). **4753**

TAXON. (GW/0040-0262). **529**

TBC NEWS. (US/1046-8927). **4394**

TE REO. (NZ/0494-8440). **3327**

TEACHER EDUCATION & PRACTICE. (US/0890-6459). **1905**

TEACHER EDUCATION AND SPECIAL EDUCATION. (US/0888-4064). **1886**

TEACHER EDUCATION QUARTERLY (CLAREMONT, CALIF.). (US/0737-5328). **1906**

TEACHERS COLLEGE RECORD (1970). (US/0161-4681). **1849**

TEACHING AND TEACHER EDUCATION. (UK/0742-051X). **1906**

TEACHING HISTORY (EMPORIA, KAN.). (US/0730-1383). **2631**

TEACHING OF PSYCHOLOGY. (US/0098-6283). **4620**

TEACHING SOCIOLOGY. (US/0092-055X). **5264**

TECHNICAL BULLETIN - WISCONSIN DEPARTMENT OF NATURAL RESOURCES. (US/0084-0564). **2206**

TECHNICAL COMMUNICATION QUARTERLY. (US/1057-2252). **1122**

TECHNICAL SERVICES QUARTERLY. (US/0731-7131). **3252**

TECHNISCHES MESSE : TM. (GW/0171-8096). **4033**

TECHNOLOGICAL FORECASTING AND SOCIAL CHANGE. (US/0040-1625). **5163**

TECHNOLOGY AND CULTURE. (US/0040-165X). **5163**

TECHNOLOGY IN SOCIETY. (US/0160-791X). **5164**

TECHNOLOGY REVIEW. (US/0040-1692). **5164**

TECHNOLOGY TEACHER, THE. (US/0746-3537). **5164**

TECHNOMETRICS. (US/0040-1706). **5176**

TECHNOSTYLE. (CN/0712-4627). **3444**

TECHNOVA. (HK). **1998**

TECHNOVATION. (NE/0166-4972). **1629**

TECHTRENDS. (US/8756-3894). **1225**

TECNICA ITALIANA. (IT/0040-1846). **2032**

TECNICA TEXTIL INTERNACIONAL. (SP/0040-1900). **5356**

TECNOLOGIA ELETTRICHE. INDUSTRIA ITALIANA ELETTROTECNICA ED ELETTRONICA. (IT/0390-6698). **2083**

TECNOLOGIE DEI SERVIZI PUBBLICI. (IT). **4690**

TECNOLOGIE MECCANICHE. (IT/0391-1683). **2130**

TECTONICS (WASHINGTON, D.C.). (US/0278-7407). **1411**

TECTONOPHYSICS. (NE/0040-1951). **1411**

TEELINE : THE SHORTHAND AND BUSINESS STUDIES MAGAZINE. (UK). **1850**

TEHO / TYOTEHOSEURA. (FI/0355-0567). **140**

TEJAS JOURNAL OF AUDIOLOGY AND SPEECH PATHOLOGY. (US/0738-8837). **3891**

TEKNOS. (IT). **5165**

TELECOMMUNICATION JOURNAL (ENGLISH EDITION). (SZ/0497-137X). **1165**

TELECOMMUNICATIONS AND RADIO ENGINEERING. (US/0040-2508). **1165**

TELECOMMUNICATIONS POLICY. (UK/0308-5961). **1166**

TELECOMMUNICATIONS STRATEGIES REPORT. (AT/1322-3518). **1166**

TELEX MEDITERRANNEE. (BE). **4536**

TEMA CELESTE. (IT). **366**

TEMPLE INTERNATIONAL AND COMPARATIVE LAW JOURNAL. (US/0889-1915). **3136**

TENNESSEE JOURNAL OF HEALTH, PHYSICAL EDUCATION, RECREATION, AND DANCE / TENNESSEE ASSOCIATION OF HEALTH, PHYSICAL EDUCATION, RECREATION, AND DANCE. (US/0890-1597). **1859**

TENNESSEE REGISTER, THE. (US/1041-1569). **5746**

TEOLOGIA Y VIDA. (CL/0049-3449). **5002**

TEORETICESKAJA I EKSPERIMENTALNAJA HIMIJA. (UN/0497-2627). **994**

TERAPEVTICESKIJ ARHIV. (RU/0040-3660). **3645**

TERATOGENESIS, CARCINOGENESIS, AND MUTAGENESIS. (US/0270-3211). **3824**

TERATOLOGY (PHILADELPHIA). (US/0040-3709). **474**

TERRITOIRES. (FR). **4498**

TERRITORIAL, THE. (US/0890-4235). **2547**

TERTIARY RESEARCH. (NE/0308-9649). **1399**

TERZO MONDO. (IT/0040-392X). **5264**

TESL REPORTER. (US/0886-0661). **1787**

TESOL QUARTERLY. (US/0039-8322). **3328**

TEST & MEASUREMENT WORLD. (US/0744-1657). **2084**

TESTO UNICO IMPOSTE DIRETTE. (IT). **3063**

TETRAHEDRON LETTERS. (UK/0040-4039). **1048**

TETSU TO HAGANE. (JA/0021-1575). **4021**

TEXAS AIRPORT DIRECTORY. (US). **37**

TEXAS DENTAL JOURNAL. (US/0040-4284). **1336**

TEXAS HEART INSTITUTE JOURNAL. (US/0730-2347). **3710**

TEXAS HEREFORD. (US/0744-4761). **222**

TEXAS JOURNAL OF POLITICAL STUDIES. (US/0191-0930). **4498**

TEXAS JOURNAL OF SCIENCE, THE. (US/0040-4403). **5165**

TEXAS LAW REVIEW. (US/0040-4411). **3064**

TEXAS MEDICINE. (US/0040-4470). **3645**

TEXAS PHARMACY. (US/0362-7926). **4330**

TEXINCON AHMEDABAD. (II/0970-5686). **5357**

TEXTILE ASIA. (HK/0049-3554). **5357**

TEXTILE ASIA INDEX. (HK). **5357**

TEXTILE CHEMIST AND COLORIST. (US/0040-490X). **5357**

TEXTILE RESEARCH JOURNAL. (US/0040-5175). **5358**

TEXTUAL STUDIES IN CANADA. (CN). **3355**

TEXTURES AND MICROSTRUCTURES. (US/0730-3300). **1033**

THEATRE & THERAPY. (UK). **5370**

THEATRE ANNUAL, THE. (US/0082-3821). **5370**

THEATRE HISTORY IN CANADA. (CN/0226-5761). **5370**

THEATRE/PUBLIC. (FR/0335-2927). **5371**

THEATRE RESEARCH IN CANADA. (CN/1196-1198). **5371**

THEATRE STUDIES. (US/0362-0964). **5371**

THEATRE TOPICS. (US/1054-8378). **5371**

THEMA (METAIRIE, LA.). (US/1041-4851). **3446**

THEOLOGOS, HO. (IT). **5004**

THEOLOGY & LIFE (HONG KONG). (HK/0253-3812). **5004**

THEORETICA CHIMICA ACTA. (GW/0040-5744). **1058**

THEORETICAL AND APPLIED CLIMATOLOGY. (AU/0177-798X). **1436**

THEORETICAL AND APPLIED FRACTURE MECHANICS. (NE/0167-8442). **4430**

THEORETICAL AND APPLIED GENETICS. (GW/0040-5752). **551**

THEORETICAL AND MATHEMATICAL PHYSICS. (US/0040-5779). **4423**

THEORETICAL COMPUTER SCIENCE. (NE/0304-3975). **1205**

THEORETICAL MEDICINE. (NE/0167-9902). **3645**

THEORETICAL POPULATION BIOLOGY. (US/0040-5809). **4560**

THEORIA/PRAXIS: A GRADUATE JOURNAL OF THEORY AND CRITICISM. (CN). **5224**

THEORY AND DECISION. (NE/0040-5833). **4363**

THEORY AND PRACTICE : JOURNAL OF THE MUSIC THEORY SOCIETY OF NEW YORK STATE. (US/0741-6156). **4156**

THEORY AND RESEARCH IN SOCIAL EDUCATION. (US/0093-3104). **5224**

THEORY AND SOCIETY. (NE/0304-2421). **5264**

THEORY OF PROBABILITY AND ITS APPLICATIONS. (UK/0040-585X). **3538**

THEOSOPHICAL HISTORY. (US/0951-497X). **5004**

THERAPEUTIC DRUG MONITORING. (US/0163-4356). **4330**

THERAPEUTISCHE UMSCHAU. (SZ/0040-5930). **3976**

THERAPIE. (FR/0040-5957). **4330**

THERIOGENOLOGY. (US/0093-691X). **5522**

THERIOS : REVISTA DE MEDICINA VETERINARIA Y PRODUCCION ANIMAL. (AG). **5523**

THERMAL ENGINEERING. (UK/0040-6015). **1998**

THERMOCHIMICA ACTA. (NE/0040-6031). **1058**

THERMOLOGY. (US/0882-3758). **3645**

THIN SOLID FILMS. (SZ/0040-6090). **2084**

THIRD WORLD PLANNING REVIEW. (UK/0142-7849). **2836**

THIS MAGAZINE. (CN/0381-3746). **2493**

THOMAS WOLFE REVIEW, THE. (US/0276-5683). **3446**

THORACIC AND CARDIOVASCULAR SURGEON, THE. (GW/0171-6425). **3976**

THORAX. (UK/0040-6376). **3952**

THOREAU SOCIETY BULLETIN, THE. (US/0040-6406). **3446**

THOUGHTS FOR ALL SEASONS. (US/0886-6481). **3446**

THROMBOSIS AND HAEMOSTASIS. (GW/0340-6245). **3801**

THROMBOSIS RESEARCH. (US/0049-3848). **3710**

THYMUS. (NE/0165-6090). **3677**

TIDE, DISTANCE AND SPEED TABLES. (UK). **4184**

TIDE : TERI INFORMATION DIGEST ON ENERGY. (II/0971-085X). **1959**

TIDEWATER VIRGINIA FAMILIES. (US/1061-8678). **2475**

TIDSSKRIFT FOR PLANTEAVL. (DK/0040-7135). **189**

TIDSSKRIFT FOR SAMFUNNSFORSKNING. (NO/0040-716X). **5224**

TIERARZTLICHE UMSCHAU. (GW/0049-3864). **5523**

TIJDSCHRIFT VOOR ECONOMISCHE EN SOCIALE GEOGRAFIE : TESG. (NE/0040-747X). **1524**

TIJDSCHRIFT VOOR GENEESKUNDE. (BE/0371-683X). **3802**

TIJDSCHRIFT VOOR MARKETING. (NE). **937**

TIJDSCHRIFT VOOR RECHTSGESCHIEDENIS. (NE/0040-7585). **3064**

TIJDSCHRIFT VOOR SEKSUOLOGIE. (NE/0167-5915). **5188**

TIJDSCHRIFT VOOR SOCIAAL WETENSCHAPPELIJK ONDERZOEK VAN DE LANDBOUW. (NE/0921-481X). **141**

TILE & DECORATIVE SURFACES. (US/0192-9550). **2907**

TISSUE & CELL. (UK/0040-8166). **540**

TISSUE ANTIGENS. (DK/0001-2815). **3802**

TJS SPEC. PUBL. (US/0145-0123). **5166**

TJUSTBYGDEN. (SW). **2712**

TO VIMA. (GR). **5802**

TOCQUEVILLE REVIEW, THE. (US/0730-479X). **5224**

TODAY IN MEDICINE. CARDIOVASCULAR DISEASE. (US/1042-2455). **3711**

TODAY IN MEDICINE. RESPIRATORY DISEASE. (US/1042-2846). **3952**

TODAY'S CHIROPRACTIC. (US/0091-2360). **3646**

TODAY'S CPA. (US/0889-4337). **752**

TOHOKU JOURNAL OF EXPERIMENTAL MEDICINE, THE. (JA/0040-8727). **3646**

TOHOKU MATHEMATICAL JOURNAL. (JA/0040-8735). **3538**

TOLUENE XYLENES ANNUAL. (US/0271-2660). **1030**

TOPEKA GENEALOGICAL SOCIETY QUARTERLY, THE. (US/0734-8495). **2475**

TOPICAL ISSUES IN PROCUREMENT SERIES. (US). **952**

TOPICS IN CLINICAL NUTRITION. (US/0883-5691). **4199**

TOPICS IN EARLY CHILDHOOD SPECIAL EDUCATION. (US/0271-1214). **1886**

TOPICS IN EMERGENCY MEDICINE. (US/0164-2340). **3725**

TOPICS IN ENVIRONMENTAL HEALTH. (NE/0166-2082). **4805**

TOPICS IN GERIATRIC REHABILITATION. (US/0882-7524). **3755**

TOPICS IN HEALTH INFORMATION MANAGEMENT. (US/0270-5230). **3793**

TOPICS IN INORGANIC AND GENERAL CHEMISTRY. (NE/0082-495X). **1038**

TOPICS IN LANGUAGE DISORDERS. (US/0271-8294). **3329**

TOPICS IN MOLECULAR PHARMACOLOGY. (NE/0167-7101). **4331**

TOPICS IN PHOTOSYNTHESIS. (NE/0378-6099). **529**

TOPOLOGIE STRUCTURALE STRUCTURAL TOPOLOGY. (CN/0226-9171). **3539**

TOPOLOGY AND ITS APPLICATIONS. (NE/0166-8641). **3539**

TOPOLOGY (OXFORD). (UK/0040-9383). **3539**

TOPOLOGY PROCEEDINGS. (US/0146-4124). **3539**

TORRE (RIO PIEDRAS (SAN JUAN, P.R.), LA. (PR/0040-9588). **3447**

TORRENS. (SP). **2713**

TOSCANA QUI. (IT). **332**

TOSHOKAN JOHO DAIGAKU KENKYU HOKOKU. (JA/0287-0010). **3253**

TOXICOLOGIC PATHOLOGY. (US/0192-6233). **3898**

TOXICOLOGICAL AND ENVIRONMENTAL CHEMISTRY. (UK/0277-2248). **3984**

TOXICOLOGIST, THE. (US/0731-9193). **3984**

TOXICOLOGY (AMSTERDAM). (IE/0300-483X). **3984**

TOXICOLOGY AND APPLIED PHARMACOLOGY. (US/0041-008X). **3984**

TOXICOLOGY AND INDUSTRIAL HEALTH. (US/0748-2337). **3984**

TOXICOLOGY IN VITRO. (UK/0887-2333). **3984**

TOXICOLOGY LETTERS. (NE/0378-4274). **3984**

TOXICON (OXFORD). (UK/0041-0101). **4331**

TOY & HOBBY WORLD. WEEKLY MARKET REPORT. (US). **958**

TRABAJOS DE INVESTIGACION OPERATIVA. (SP/0213-8204). **3539**

TRAC, TRENDS IN ANALYTICAL CHEMISTRY (PERSONAL EDITION). (NE/0165-9936). **1019**

TRACE ELEMENTS IN MEDICINE. (GW/0174-7371). **3647**

TRACES (MONTREAL). (CN/0841-6397). **1908**

TRADING POST (COLUMBIA, MD.). (US/1043-7665). **4059**

TRADITIONAL DWELLINGS AND SETTLEMENTS REVIEW. (US/1050-2092). **5225**

TRAFFIC BULLETIN - WILDLIFE TRADE MONITORING UNIT. (UK/0267-4297). **2207**

TRAINING AND DEVELOPMENT IN AUSTRALIA. (AT/0310-4664). **716**

TRANSACTIONAL ANALYSIS JOURNAL. (US/0362-1537). **4620**

TRANSACTIONS - INSTITUTE OF BRITISH GEOGRAPHERS (1965). (UK/0020-2754). **2577**

TRANSACTIONS OF THE AMERICAN ENTOMOLOGICAL SOCIETY (1890). (US/0002-8320). **5614**

TRANSACTIONS OF THE AMERICAN FISHERIES SOCIETY (1900). (US/0002-8487). **2315**

TRANSACTIONS OF THE AMERICAN MATHEMATICAL SOCIETY. (US/0002-9947). **3539**

TRANSACTIONS OF THE ANNUAL MEETING OF THE ORTHOPAEDIC RESEARCH SOCIETY. (US/0149-6433). **3885**

TRANSACTIONS OF THE ASAE. (US/0001-2351). **1999**

TRANSACTIONS OF THE CANADIAN SOCIETY FOR MECHANICAL ENGINEERING. (CN/0315-8977). **2130**

TRANSACTIONS OF THE CHARLES S. PIERCE SOCIETY. (US/0009-1774). **4364**

TRANSACTIONS OF THE INDIAN CERAMIC SOCIETY. (II/0371-750X). **2594**

TRANSACTIONS OF THE INSTITUTION OF ENGINEERS, AUSTRALIA. MULTI-DISCIPLINARY ENGINEERING. (AT/0812-3314). **1999**

TRANSACTIONS OF THE IRON & STEEL SOCIETY. (US/1051-0508). **4022**

TRANSACTIONS OF THE KANSAS ACADEMY OF SCIENCE (1903). (US/0022-8443). **5166**

TRANSACTIONS OF THE KENTUCKY ACADEMY OF SCIENCE. (US/0023-0081). **5166**

TRANSACTIONS OF THE MISSOURI ACADEMY OF SCIENCE. (US/0544-540X). **5166**

TRANSACTIONS OF THE ROYAL SOCIETY OF TROPICAL MEDICINE AND HYGIENE. (UK/0035-9203). **3987**

TRANSACTIONS OF THE SOCIETY FOR COMPUTER SIMULATION. (US/0740-6797). **1283**

TRANSACTIONS OF THE SOCIETY OF PETROLEUM ENGINEERS. (US/8756-8152). **4280**

TRANSACTIONS OF THE WESTERN SECTION OF THE WILDLIFE SOCIETY. (US/0893-214X). **2207**

TRANSACTIONS - SOCIETY OF ACTUARIES. (US/0037-9794). **2895**

TRANSCRIPT. (US/1040-4848). **1123**

TRANSCULTURAL PSYCHIATRIC RESEARCH REVIEW. (CN/0041-1108). **3937**

TRANSFUSION MEDICINE REVIEWS. (US/0887-7963). **3647**

TRANSFUSION (PHILADELPHIA). (US/0041-1132). **3774**

TRANSFUSION SCIENCE. (UK/0955-3886). **3647**

TRANSITION. (AT/0157-7344). **310**

TRANSITION METAL CHEMISTRY. (UK/0340-4285). **4022**

TRANSITION : THE NEWSLETTER ABOUT REFORMING ECONOMIES / TRANSITION AND MACRO-ADJUSTMENT, COUNTRY ECONOMICS DEPARTMENT, WORLD BANK. (US). **1640**

TRANSPLANT INTERNATIONAL. (GW/0934-0874). **3976**

TRANSPLANTATION. (US/0041-1337). **3647**

TRANSPLANTATION PROCEEDINGS. (US/0041-1345). **3977**

TRANSPORT IN POROUS MEDIA. (NE/0169-3913). **994**

TRANSPORT MANAGEMENT; THE BRITISH JOURNAL OF TRADE AND TRANSPORT. (UK/0041-1515). **5395**

TRANSPORT REVIEWS. (UK/0144-1647). **5396**

TRANSPORTATION (DORDRECHT). (NE/0049-4488). **5396**

TRANSPORTATION JOURNAL. (US/0041-1612). **5396**

TRANSPORTATION NEWS DIGEST, THE. (US/1047-062X). **5396**

TRANSPORTATION QUARTERLY. (US/0278-9434). **5397**

TRANSPORTATION RESEARCH. PART B : METHODOLOGICAL. (UK/0191-2615). **5397**

TRANSPORTATION SCIENCE. (US/0041-1655). **5397**

TRANSPUTER COMMUNICATIONS. (UK/1070-454X). **1205**

TRASGRESSIONI. (IT). **4498**

TRATTAMENTI E FINITURA. (IT/0041-1833). **4022**

TRAVAIL ET SOCIETE. (SZ/0378-5424). **1715**

TRAVAIL HUMAIN, LE. (FR/0041-1868). **4620**

TRAVAUX ET DOCUMENTS. (FR/0298-8879). **4536**

TRAVELIN TALK NEWSLETTER, THE. (US/1052-1615). **5497**

TREASURY MANAGEMENT INTERNATIONAL. (UK/0967-523X). **814**

TREE PHYSIOLOGY. (CN/0829-318X). **2397**

TRENDS & TECHNIQUES IN THE CONTEMPORARY DENTAL LABORATORY. (US/0746-8962). **1337**

TRENDS IN BIOTECHNOLOGY (REFERENCE ED.). (NE/0167-9430). **3697**

TRENDS IN ECOLOGY & EVOLUTION (AMSTERDAM). (UK/0169-5347). **2221**

TRENDS IN ENDOCRINOLOGY AND METABOLISM. (US/1043-2760). **3733**

TRENDS IN PHARMACOLOGICAL SCIENCES (REGULAR ED.). (UK/0165-6147). **4331**

TRI-CITY GENEALOGICAL SOCIETY BULLETIN, THE. (US/0496-1803). **2476**

TRIAD (FARMINGTON, MICH.). (US/1046-4948). **3647**

TRIAL ADVOCATE QUARTERLY. (US/0743-412X). **3066**

TRIBOLIUM INFORMATION BULLETIN. (US/0082-6391). **5604**

TRIBOLOGY INTERNATIONAL. (UK/0301-679X). **2108**

TRIMESTRE ECONOMICO, EL. (MX/0041-3011). **1640**

TROPICAL AGRICULTURE. (UK/0041-3216). **142**

TROPICAL AND GEOGRAPHICAL MEDICINE. (NE/0041-3232). **3987**

TROPICAL ANIMAL HEALTH AND PRODUCTION. (UK/0049-4747). **5523**

TROPICAL DOCTOR. (UK/0049-4755). **3987**

TROPICAL ECOLOGY. (II/0564-3295). **2222**

TROPICAL GRASSLANDS. (AT/0049-4763). **189**

TROPICAL LEPIDOPTERA. (US/1048-8138). **5614**

TROPICAL MEDICINE AND PARASITOLOGY. (GW/0177-2392). **3987**

TROPICAL PEST MANAGEMENT. (UK/0143-6147). **4248**

TROPICAL VETERINARIAN. (NR/0253-4851). **3987**

TRUTH SEEKER (SAN DIEGO, CALIF.), THE. (US/0041-3712). **5006**

TSITOLOGIIA. (RU/0041-3771). **540**

TSUDA-JUKU DAIGAKU KIYO. (JA/0287-7805). **2855**

TUG LINES. (US/0892-4961). **1281**

TULANE LAWYER. (US). **3066**

TULANE STUDIES IN GEOLOGY AND PALEONTOLOGY. (US/0041-4018). **1400**

TULANE STUDIES IN ZOOLOGY AND BOTANY. (US/0082-6782). **5599**

TUMORI. (IT/0300-8916). **3824**

TUMOUR BIOLOGY. (SZ/0289-5447). **475**

TURISMO D'ITALIA. (IT). **2809**

TURKISH JOURNAL OF PEDIATRICS, THE. (TU/0041-4301). **3912**

TURKISH STUDIES ASSOCIATION BULLETIN. (US/0275-6048). **3355**

TURNBULL LIBRARY RECORD, THE. (NZ/0110-1625). **3254**

TURRIALBA : REVISTA INTERAMERICANO DE CIENCIAS AGRICOLAS. (CR/0041-4360). **143**

TUTELA. (IT/0393-7798). **5313**

TUTTITALIA. (UK). **3330**

TYDSKRIF VIR VOLKSKUNDE EN VOLKSTAAL. (SA/0049-4933). **2325**

TZU TUNG HUA HSUEH PAO. (CC/0254-4156). **1221**

UBERSETZUNGEN, KERNTECHNISCHE REGELN. (GW). **2159**

UCLA HISTORICAL JOURNAL. (US/0276-864X). **2632**

UCLA LAW REVIEW. (US/0041-5650). **3067**

UCLA WORKING PAPERS IN PHONETICS. (US/1067-9030). **3330**

UKRAINIAN REPORTER. (UN/0964-4326). **4537**

UKRAINSKIJ FIZICESKIJ ZURNAL (KIEV, 1967). (UN/0503-1265). **4424**

UKRAINSKIJ HIMICESKIJ ZURNAL. (UN/0041-6045). **995**

ULSTER MEDICAL JOURNAL. (UK/0041-6193). **3648**

ULTRAMICROSCOPY. (NE/0304-3991). **574**

ULTRASCHALL IN DER MEDIZIN. (GW/0172-4614). **3648**

ULTRASONIC IMAGING. (US/0161-7346). **3802**

ULTRASONICS. (UK/0041-624X). **4424**

ULTRASOUND IN MEDICINE & BIOLOGY. (US/0301-5629). **3648**

ULTRASTRUCTURAL PATHOLOGY. (US/0191-3123). **3898**

UNAK (TORONTO). (CN/0044-1384). **1071**

UNCLASSIFIED (WASHINGTON, D.C.). (US/1062-3450). **5177**

UNDERSEA BIOMEDICAL RESEARCH. (US/0093-5387). **3697**

UNDERWATER MEDICINE AND RELATED SCIENCES. (US/0191-2534). **3648**

UNFALLCHIRURG, DER. (GW/0177-5537). **3725**

UNION MEDICALE DU CANADA. (CN/0041-6959). **3648**

UNIQUE (EAST HANOVER, N.J.). (US/0736-4083). **1244**

UNITED NATIONS RESOLUTIONS. SERIES 2, RESOLUTIONS AND DECISIONS OF THE SECURITY COUNCIL. (US/0898-2929). **3137**

UNIVERSALIST FRIENDS. (US). **5068**

UNIVERSALIST - QUAKER UNIVERSALIST GROUP. (UK/0267-6648). **5068**

UNIVERSITY COMPUTING : THE BULLETIN OF THE IUCC. (UK/0265-4385). **1852**

UNIVERSITY OF CALIFORNIA PUBLICATIONS IN MODERN PHILOLOGY. (US/0068-6492). **3331**

UNIVERSITY OF CHICAGO LAW REVIEW, THE. (US/0041-9494). **3068**

UNIVERSITY OF FLORIDA JOURNAL OF LAW AND PUBLIC POLICY. (US/1047-8035). **3068**

UNIVERSITY OF HAWAII LAW REVIEW. (US/0271-9835). **3068**

UNIVERSITY OF ILLINOIS LAW REVIEW. (US/0276-9948). **3068**

UNIVERSITY OF KANSAS SCIENCE BULLETIN, THE. (US/0022-8850). **5167**

UNIVERSITY OF MISSISSIPPI STUDIES IN ENGLISH, THE. (US/0278-310X). **3449**

UNIVERSITY OF NEW SOUTH WALES LAW JOURNAL, THE. (AT/0313-0096). **3069**

UNIVERSITY OF PENNSYLVANIA JOURNAL OF INTERNATIONAL BUSINESS LAW. (US/0891-9895). **3104**

UNIVERSITY OF PENNSYLVANIA LAW REVIEW. (US/0041-9907). **3069**

UNIVERSITY OF PITTSBURGH LAW REVIEW. (US/0041-9915). **3069**

UNIVERSITY OF TASMANIA LAW REVIEW. (AT/0082-2108). **3069**

UNIX NEWS LONDON. (UK/0956-2753). **1249**

UNSER WALD : ZEITSCRIFT DER SCHUTZGEMEINSCHAFT DEUTSCHER WALD. (GW). **2397**

UNTERRICHTSPRAXIS, DIE. (US/0042-062X). **3331**

UPSALA JOURNAL OF MEDICAL SCIENCES. (SW/0300-9734). **3649**

UPSTART CROW, THE. (US/0886-2168). **3449**

URBAN AFFAIRS QUARTERLY. (US/0042-0816). **2837**

URBAN ANTHROPOLOGY AND STUDIES OF CULTURAL SYSTEMS AND WORLD ECONOMIC DEVELOPMENT. (US/0894-6019). **247**

URBAN EDUCATION (BEVERLY HILLS, CALIF.). (US/0042-0859). **1789**

URBAN GEOGRAPHY. (US/0272-3638). **2578**

URBAN LAWYER, THE. (US/0042-0905). **3070**

URBAN LEAGUE REVIEW, THE. (US/0147-1740). **2274**

UROLOGE. AUSG. A, DER. (GW/0340-2592). **3993**

UROLOGIA. (IT/0391-5603). **3993**

UROLOGIA INTERNATIONALIS. (SZ/0042-1138). **3993**

UROLOGIC CLINICS OF NORTH AMERICA, THE. (US/0094-0143). **3993**

UROLOGIC NURSING. (US/1053-816X). **3870**

UROLOGIC RADIOLOGY. (US/0171-1091). **3994**

UROLOGICAL RESEARCH. (GW/0300-5623). **3994**

UROLOGY (RIDGEWOOD, N.J.). (US/0090-4295). **3994**

USAE. (US/0894-8194). **5687**

USER MODELING AND USER-ADAPTED INTERACTION. (NE/0924-1868). **1206**

USPEKHI KHIMII. (RU/0042-1308). **995**

USQR, UNION SEMINARY QUARTERLY REVIEW. (US/0362-1545). **5007**

UTAH BIRDS : JOURNAL OF THE UTAH ORNITHOLOGICAL SOCIETY. (US). **5620**

UTBLICK LANDSKAP. (SW). **310**

UTENSIL. (IT/0392-6567). **2131**

UTILITAS MATHEMATICA. (CN/0315-3681). **3540**

UTRECHT MICROPALEONTOLOGICAL BULLETINS. (NE/0083-4963). **4231**

VACCINE. (UK/0264-410X). **3649**

VACUUM. (UK/0042-207X). **4430**

VANDERBILT LAW REVIEW. (US/0042-2533). **3070**

VAROSI KOZLEKEDES. (HU/0133-0314). **5399**

VASA. (SZ/0301-1526). **3802**

VASCULAR SURGERY. (US/0042-2835). **3977**

VASCULUM, THE. (UK/0049-5891). **4173**

VAX PROFESSIONAL, THE. (US/8750-9628). **1206**

VEGETARIAN JOURNAL. (US/0885-7636 #y 0883-1165). **4200**

VEGETATIO. (NE/0042-3106). **529**

VEHICLE SYSTEM DYNAMICS. (NE/0042-3114). **2131**

VELDWERK AMSTERDAM. (NE/0922-2782). **2912**

VELIGER, THE. (US/0042-3211). **5599**

VENEREOLOGY : OFFICIAL PUBLICATION OF THE NATIONAL VENEREOLOGY COUNCIL OF AUSTRALIA. (AT). **3716**

VERA LEX. (US/0893-4851). **2253**

VERBA. (SP). **3331**

VERBINDING ROTTERDAM. (NE/0922-6540). **1168**

VERBONDSNIEUWS VOOR DE BELGISCHE SIERTEELT. (BE). **2436**

VERFAHRENSRICHTLINIEN FUER DIE MIKROBIOLOGISCHE DIAGNOSTIK. (GW/0720-9940). **570**

VESTNIK AKADEMII MEDITSINSKIKH NAUK SSSR. (RU/0002-3027). **3649**

VESTNIK AKADEMII NAUK SSSR. (RU/0002-3442). **5168**

VESTNIK DERMATOLOGII I VENEROLOGII. (RU/0042-4609). **3723**

VESTNIK HIRURGII IM. I.I. GREKOVA. (RU/0042-4625). **3994**

VESTNIK MOSKOVSKOGO UNIVERSITETA. SERIA IX : FILOLOGIIA. (RU/0130-0075). **3331**

VESTNIK OFTALMOLOGII. (RU/0042-465X). **3879**

VETERINARIA ARGENTINA. (AG/0326-4629). **5523**

VETERINARIA

VETERINARIA (MEXICO). (MX/0301-5092). **5523**

VETERINARY AND HUMAN TOXICOLOGY. (US/0145-6296). **5524**

VETERINARY CLINICS OF NORTH AMERICA. EQUINE PRACTICE, THE. (US/0749-0739). **5525**

VETERINARY CLINICS OF NORTH AMERICA. FOOD ANIMAL PRACTICE, THE. (US/0749-0720). **5525**

VETERINARY DERMATOLOGY. (UK/0959-4493). **5525**

VETERINARY IMMUNOLOGY AND IMMUNOPATHOLOGY. (NE/0165-2427). **5525**

VETERINARY MEDICINE (1985). (US/8750-7943). **5526**

VETERINARY MICROBIOLOGY. (NE/0378-1135). **5526**

VETERINARY PARASITOLOGY. (NE/0304-4017). **5526**

VETERINARY PATHOLOGY. (US/0300-9858). **5526**

VETERINARY QUARTERLY, THE. (NE/0165-2176). **5526**

VETERINARY RADIOLOGY & ULTRASOUND. (US/1058-8183). **5526**

VETERINARY RECORD. (UK/0042-4900). **5526**

VETERINARY RESEARCH COMMUNICATIONS. (NE/0165-7380). **5527**

VETERINARY SURGERY. (US/0161-3499). **5527**

VIATOR (BERKELEY). (US/0083-5897). **1080**

VIBRATIONAL SPECTRA AND STRUCTURE. (NE/0090-1911). **4442**

VICTORIA NATURALIST, THE. (CN/0049-612X). **4173**

VICTORIAN NATURALIST. (AT/0042-5184). **4173**

VICTORIAN PERIODICALS REVIEW. (US/0709-4698). **3355**

VICTORIAN POETRY. (US/0042-5206). **3450**

VICTORIAN REVIEW. (CN/0848-1512). **3450**

VIDA HISPANICA (1972). (UK/0308-4957). **3332**

VIDE, LES COUCHES MINCES, LE. (FR/0223-4335). **4424**

VIDEO JOURNAL OF COLOR FLOW IMAGING. (US/1052-2182). **3947**

VIDEO JOURNAL OF ECHOCARDIOGRAPHY. (US/1052-2174). **3711**

VIDEO : REVISTA DE CIRURGIA. (SP). **3977**

VIE ET MILIEU (1980). (FR/0240-8759). **2222**

VIES-A-VIES (MONTREAL. 1988). (CN/0842-1838). **4621**

VIETNAM GENERATION. (US/1042-7597). **2765**

VIRAL IMMUNOLOGY. (US/0882-8245). **3677**

VIRCHOWS ARCHIV. A, PATHOLOGICAL ANATOMY AND HISTOPATHOLOGY. (GW/0174-7398). **3898**

VIRGINIA CAVALCADE. (US/0042-6474). **2765**

VIRGINIA GEOGRAPHER, THE. (US/0042-6512). **2579**

VIRGINIA JOURNAL OF INTERNATIONAL LAW. (US/0042-6571). **3137**

VIRGINIA JOURNAL OF SCIENCE. (US/0042-658X). **5169**

VIRGINIA LAW REVIEW. (US/0042-6601). **3071**

VIRGINIA MEDICAL QUARTERLY : VMQ. (US/1052-4231). **3650**

VIRGINIA SOCIAL SCIENCE JOURNAL. (US/0507-1305). **5225**

VIRGINIA WOOLF MISCELLANY. (US/0736-251X). **3355**

VIROLOGY (NEW YORK, N.Y.). (US/0042-6822). **570**

VIRUS GENES. (US/0920-8569). **571**

VIRUS RESEARCH. (NE/0168-1702). **571**

VISIBLE LANGUAGE. (US/0022-2224). **4570**

VISION RESEARCH (OXFORD). (UK/0042-6989). **3879**

VISIONMONDAY (NEW YORK, N.Y.). (US/1054-7665). **4217**

VISUAL ARTS RESEARCH. (US/0736-0770). **368**

VISUAL NEUROSCIENCE. (US/0952-5238). **3847**

VISUM NIEUWS. (NE/0925-8275). **1853**

VITICULTURA ENOLOGIA PROFESIONAL. (SP). **145**

VLAAMS DIERGENEESKUNDIG TIJDSCHRIFT. (BE/0303-9021). **5527**

VOCATIONAL EVALUATION AND WORK ADJUSTMENT BULLETIN. (US/0160-8312). **4395**

VOICE LONDON. 1992. (UK/0966-789X). **3891**

VOICES (AMERICAN ACADEMY OF PSYCHOTHERAPISTS). (US/0042-8272). **3937**

VOLTA REVIEW, THE. (US/0042-8639). **4395**

VOLUNTAS : INTERNATIONAL JOURNAL OF VOLUNTARY AND NON-PROFIT ORGANISATIONS. (UK/0957-8765). **4339**

VOPROSY MEDICINSKOJ HIMII. (RU/0042-8809). **494**

VOPROSY ONKOLOGIJ. (RU/0507-3758). **3825**

VOPROSY PSIHOLOGII. (RU/0042-8841). **4621**

VOX BENEDICTINA. (CN/0715-8726). **5038**

VOX SANGUINIS. (SZ/0042-9007). **3774**

VOZ DE LA VALDERIA, LA. (SP). **2524**

VSE UPDATE. (UK). **1281**

VSTRECI (PHILADELPHIA, PA.). (US/0888-5257). **3473**

VTT JULKAISUJA. (FI/1235-0613). **5169**

WAGENINGEN AGRICULTURAL UNIVERSITY PAPERS. (NE). **145**

WAHKAW, THE. (US/0743-6483). **2477**

WALLACE STEVENS JOURNAL, THE. (US/0148-7132). **3473**

WALLRAF-RICHARTZ-JAHRBUCH. (GW/0083-7105). **368**

WAR, LITERATURE, AND THE ARTS. (US/1046-6967). **3452**

WARME- UND STOFFUBERTRAGUNG. (GW/0042-9929). **2131**

WASHINGTON APPLE PI. (US/1056-7682). **1207**

WASHINGTON GEOLOGY. (US/1058-2134). **1401**

WASHINGTON JOB SOURCE, THE. (US/1067-0769). **4209**

WASHINGTON LAW REVIEW (1967). (US/0043-0617). **3072**

WASHINGTON QUARTERLY, THE. (US/0163-660X). **4538**

WASTE MANAGEMENT & RESEARCH. (UK/0734-242X). **2246**

WASTE MINIMIZATION UPDATE. (US/1064-6140). **2246**

WATER, AIR, AND SOIL POLLUTION. (NE/0049-6979). **2247**

WATER AND ENVIRONMENTAL MANAGEMENT : JOURNAL OF THE INSTITUTION OF WATER AND ENVIRONMENTAL MANAGEMENT. (UK/0951-7359). **2247**

WATER ENGINEERING & MANAGEMENT. (US/0273-2238). **2096**

WATER INTERNATIONAL. (US/0250-8060). **5542**

WATER LAW. (UK/0959-9754). **5543**

WATER LAW NEWSLETTER (BOULDER, COLO. : 1976). (US/0737-044X). **3182**

WATER OPERATION AND MAINTENANCE BULLETIN. (US/0145-2800). **5543**

WATER POLLUTION RESEARCH JOURNAL OF CANADA. (CN/0197-9140). **2247**

WATER RESEARCH (OXFORD). (UK/0043-1354). **5543**

WATER RESOURCES BULLETIN (URBANA). (US/0043-1370). **5544**

WATER RESOURCES MANAGEMENT (DORDRECHT, NETHERLANDS). (NE/0920-4741). **5547**

WATER RESOURCES RESEARCH. (US/0043-1397). **5547**

WATER S. A. (SA/0378-4738). **5547**

WATER SCIENCE AND TECHNOLOGY. (UK/0273-1223). **5548**

WAVE MOTION. (NE/0165-2125). **3541**

WAVES IN RANDOM MEDIA. (UK/0959-7174). **4424**

WAY MAGAZINE, THE. (US/0277-0431). **5020**

WCCI FORUM. (US/0116-5461). **1908**

WEAR. (SZ/0043-1648). **2132**

WEATHER VANE (CHARLESTON, W. VA.), THE. (US/0043-1664). **3871**

WEBBIA. (IT/0083-7792). **530**

WEED RESEARCH. (UK/0043-1737). **530**

WEED SCIENCE. (US/0043-1745). **145**

WEEKLY LIST OF MONTANA STATE PUBLICATIONS RECEIVED BY MONTANA STATE LIBRARY. (US). **4694**

WEIGHTWATCHERS. (UK). **4200**

WELCOME HOME. (US/8750-9563). **2286**

WELDING JOURNAL. (US/0043-2296). **4028**

WELLNESS PERSPECTIVES. (US/0748-1764). **4807**

WELTWIRTSCHAFTLICHES ARCHIV. (GW/0043-2636). **5225**

WERKSTOFFE UND KORROSION. (GW/0043-2822). **4023**

WEST AFRICAN JOURNAL OF MEDICINE. (NR/0189-160X). **3650**

WEST INDIAN MEDICAL JOURNAL, THE. (JM/0043-3144). **3650**

WEST VIRGINIA MEDICAL JOURNAL. (US/0043-3284). **3650**

WESTERN AMERICAN LITERATURE. (US/0043-3462). **3453**

WESTERN BIRDS. (US/0160-1121). **5620**

WESTERN CANADIAN ANTHROPOLOGIST, THE. (CN/0829-0547). **247**

WESTERN GEOGRAPHICAL SERIES. (CN/0315-2022). **2579**

WESTERN JOURNAL OF BLACK STUDIES, THE. (US/0197-4327). **2275**

WESTERN JOURNAL OF MEDICINE, THE. (US/0093-0415). **3650**

WESTERN LEGAL HISTORY. (US/0896-2189). **3073**

WESTERN LIVING (VANCOUVER ED.). (CN/0824-0604). **2904**

WESTERN MARYLAND GENEALOGY. (US/0747-7805). **2477**

WESTERN METALWORKING DIRECTORY. (US). **4023**

WESTERN POLITICAL QUARTERLY, THE. (US/0043-4078). **4500**

WESTERN TAX REVIEW. (US/8755-0083). **4758**

WESTERN VIKING. (US). **2275**

WESTMINSTER THEOLOGICAL JOURNAL, THE. (US/0043-4388). **5009**

WETLANDS (WILMINGTON, N.C.). (US/0277-5212). **2208**

WG & L TAX PLANNING ANNUAL. (US/0898-9516). **4758**

WHALEWATCHER. (US/0273-4419). **5600**

WHO'S WHO IN ATHLETICS IN AMERICAN COLLEGES AND UNIVERSITIES. (US/1044-9906). **4929**

WHO'S WHO IN CANADIAN LITERATURE. (CN/0715-9366). **3453**

WIENER KLINISCHE WOCHENSCHRIFT. (AU/0043-5325). **3651**

WIENER MEDIZINISCHE WOCHENSCHRIFT. (AU/0043-5341). **3651**

WILD EARTH. (US/1055-1166). **2183**

WILDFLOWER (AUSTIN, TEX. 1984). (US/0898-8803). **530**

WILDFLOWER (AUSTIN, TEX. 1988). (US/0896-4858). **530**

WILDLIFE JOURNAL. (US/0893-6560). **2209**

WILDLIFE SOCIETY BULLETIN. (US/0091-7648). **2209**

WILLAMETTE LAW REVIEW. (US/0191-9822). **3075**

WILLIAM CARLOS WILLIAMS REVIEW. (US/0196-6286). **3356**

WILLIAMS REPORT. (US/1075-8550). **1124**

WILMINGTON JOURNAL (WILMINGTON, N.C.), THE. (US/0049-7649). **5724**

WILSON AND WILSON'S COMPREHENSIVE ANALYTICAL CHEMISTRY. (NE). **1020**

WILSON BULLETIN (WILSON ORNITHOLOGICAL SOCIETY), THE. (US/0043-5643). **5621**

WILSON LIBRARY BULLETIN. (US/0043-5651). **3256**

WIND ENGINEERING. (UK/0309-524X). **1437**

WINDLESS ORCHARD, THE. (US/0043-5716). **3473**

WINDOWS MAGAZINE. (FR). **2904**

WINDSOR YEARBOOK OF ACCESS TO JUSTICE, THE. (CN/0710-0841). **3075**

WINESBURG EAGLE, THE. (US/0147-3166). **439**

WINNIPEG SUN (1980). (CN/0711-3773). **5798**

WISCONSIN LAW REVIEW. (US/0043-650X). **3075**

WISCONSIN LAWYER. (US/1043-0490). **4695**

WISCONSIN MAGAZINE OF HISTORY. (US/0043-6534). **2766**

WISCONSIN SOCIOLOGIST, THE. (US/0043-6666). **5265**

WIZARD: THE GUIDE TO COMICS. (US). **2779**

WOMAN'S ART JOURNAL. (US/0270-7993). **368**

WOMEN & CRIMINAL JUSTICE. (US/0897-4454). **3179**

WOMEN & HEALTH. (US/0363-0242). **3769**

WOMEN AND LANGUAGE. (US/8755-4550). **3333**

WOMEN & PERFORMANCE. (US/0740-770X). **5372**

WOMEN & POLITICS. (US/0195-7732). **4500**

WOMEN & THERAPY. (US/0270-3149). **5569**

WOMEN POLICE MAGAZINE. (US). **3179**

WOMEN'S STUDIES JOURNAL. (NZ). **5571**

WONDER (SOUND BEACH, N.Y.). (US/1057-2821). **2550**

WOOD AND FIBER SCIENCE. (US/0735-6161). **2406**

WOOD SCIENCE AND TECHNOLOGY. (US/0043-7719). **2406**

WOOL TECHNOLOGY AND SHEEP BREEDING. (AT/0043-7875). **224**

WORCESTER POLYTECHNIC INSTITUTE STUDIES IN SCIENCE, TECHNOLOGY, AND CULTURE. (US/0897-926X). **5170**

WORDS BY SPECIALISTS. (US). **1791**

WORK AND OCCUPATIONS. (US/0730-8884). **4210**

WORK AND STRESS. (UK/0267-8373). **4621**

WORKING PAPERS ON LANGUAGE, GENDER & SEXISM. (AT/1036-4099). **3333**

WORKSITE WELLNESS WORKS. (US/1053-492X). **4200**

WORLD AFFAIRS (WASHINGTON). (US/0043-8200). **4538**

WORLD AQUACULTURE. (US/1041-5602). **2316**

WORLD ARCHAEOLOGY. (UK/0043-8243). **285**

WORLD BANK ECONOMIC REVIEW, THE. (US/0258-6770). **1631**

WORLD COGENERATION. (US/1053-5802). **2132**

WORLD DEVELOPMENT. (UK/0305-750X). **1641**

WORLD ECONOMY, THE. (UK/0378-5920). **1641**

WORLD EDUCATION NEWS & REVIEWS. (US/0897-6724). **1791**

WORLD HEALTH ORGANIZATION TECHNICAL REPORT SERIES. (SZ/0512-3054). **4808**

WORLD HISTORY BULLETIN. (US/0886-117X). **2633**

WORLD JOURNAL OF SURGERY. (US/0364-2313). **3977**

WORLD JOURNAL OF UROLOGY. (GW/0724-4983). **3994**

WORLD LITERATURE TODAY. (US/0196-3570). **3454**

WORLD OIL (HOUSTON, TEX.). (US/0043-8790). **4282**

WORLD POLICY JOURNAL. (US/0740-2775). **4538**

WORLD POLITICS. (US/0043-8871). **4538**

WORLD PUBLISHING MONITOR. (UK/0960-653X). **4822**

WORLD RESOURCE REVIEW. (US/1042-8011). **2210**

WORLD TELECOMMUNICATIONS MARKETFILE SERVICES. (UK). **1169**

WORLD TODAY, THE. (UK/0043-9134). **4539**

WORLD'S POULTRY SCIENCE JOURNAL. (UK/0043-9339). **224**

WOUND REPAIR AND REGENERATION. (US/1067-1927). **3651**

WPA, WRITING PROGRAM ADMINISTRATION. (US/0196-4682). **3454**

WRITING INSTRUCTOR, THE. (US/0277-7789). **3334**

WRITING ON THE EDGE. (US/1064-6051). **3455**

WRITTEN COMMUNICATION. (US/0741-0883). **1124**

WXXI (ROCHESTER, N.Y.). (US/1055-2960). **1143**

WYOMING CATHOLIC REGISTER, THE. (US/0746-5580). **5038**

X-RAY SPECTROMETRY. (UK/0049-8246). **1020**

XENOBIOTICA. (UK/0049-8254). **3984**

YACHT PREMIERE ENGLISH ED. (IT/1120-2424). **4856**

YAKUGAKU ZASSHI. (JA/0031-6903). **4333**

YALE JOURNAL OF BIOLOGY AND MEDICINE, THE. (US/0044-0086). **3652**

YALE LAW JOURNAL, THE. (US/0044-0094). **3077**

YEARBOOK - ASSOCIATION OF PACIFIC COAST GEOGRAPHERS. (US/0066-9628). **2579**

YEARBOOK FOR TRADITIONAL MUSIC. (US/0740-1558). **4159**

YEARBOOK OF EDUCATION LAW, THE. (US/1049-0264). **1874**

YEARBOOK OF LANGLAND STUDIES, THE. (US/0890-2917). **3473**

YEARBOOK OF PHYSICAL ANTHROPOLOGY (WASHINGTON). (US/0096-848X). **248**

YEAST CHICHESTER (WEST SUSSEX). (UK/0749-503X). **1048**

YICHUAN XUEBAO. (CC/0379-4172). **552**

YORK PAPERS IN LINGUISTICS. (UK/0307-3238). **3334**

YOUNG CHILDREN. (US/0044-0728). **1806**

YOUNG GENERATION. (SI). **1071**

YOUR CLASSIC. (UK/0957-6525). **5429**

YOUTH & SOCIETY. (US/0044-118X). **5265**

YOUTH THEATRE JOURNAL. (US/0892-9092). **5372**

YUKI GOSEI KAGAKU KYOKAISHI. (JA/0037-9980). **1049**

ZAPAD TODAY. (CN). **2275**

ZAPISKI RUSSKOI AKADEMICHESKOI GRUPPY V SSHA. (US). **1854**

ZBORNIK FILOZOFICKEJ FAKULTY UNIVERZITY KOMENSKEHO. ETHNOLOGIA SLAVICA. (XO/0083-4106). **248**

ZEITSCHRIFT FUER ACKER- UND PFLANZENBAU. (GW/0931-2250). **148**

ZEITSCHRIFT FUER ANGEWANDTE MATHEMATIK UND MECHANIK. (GW/0044-2267). **3541**

ZEITSCHRIFT FUER ANGEWANDTE MATHEMATIK UND PHYSIK : ZAMP. (SZ/0044-2275). **3541**

ZEITSCHRIFT FUER ANORGANISCHE UND ALLGEMEINE CHEMIE. (GW/0044-2313). **1038**

ZEITSCHRIFT FUER BERUFS- UND WIRTSCHAFTSPADAGOGIK 1980. (GW/0172-2875). **1918**

ZEITSCHRIFT FUER ENTWICKLUNGSPSYCHOLOGIE UND PADAGOGISCHE PSYCHOLOGIE. (GW/0049-8637). **1792**

ZEITSCHRIFT FUER ERNAHRUNGSWISSENSCHAFT. (GW/0044-264X). **4200**

ZEITSCHRIFT FUER EXPERIMENTELLE UND ANGEWANDTE PSYCHOLOGIE. (GW/0044-2712). **4622**

ZEITSCHRIFT FUER GASTROENTEROLOGIE. (GW/0044-2771). **3748**

ZEITSCHRIFT FUER GEBURTSHILFE UND PERINATOLOGIE. (GW/0300-967X). **3769**

ZEITSCHRIFT FUER GEOMORPHOLOGIE. (GW/0372-8854). **1401**

ZEITSCHRIFT FUER GERONTOLOGIE. (GW/0044-281X). **3755**

ZEITSCHRIFT FUER HERZ THORAX UND GEFAESSCHIRURGIE. (GW/0930-9225). **3978**

ZEITSCHRIFT FUER JAGDWISSENSCHAFT. (GW/0044-2887). **4931**

ZEITSCHRIFT FUER KARDIOLOGIE. (GW/0300-5860). **3711**

ZEITSCHRIFT FUER KINDER- UND JUGENDPSYCHIATRIE. (SZ/0301-6811). **3937**

ZEITSCHRIFT FUER KLINISCHE PSYCHOLOGIE, PSYCHOPATHOLOGIE UND PSYCHOTHERAPIE. (GW/0723-6557). **4622**

ZEITSCHRIFT FUER KRISTALLOGRAPHIE. (GW). **1033**

ZEITSCHRIFT FUER LEBENSMITTEL-UNTERSUCHUNG UND -FORSCHUNG. (GW/0044-3026). **2361**

ZEITSCHRIFT FUER METALLKUNDE (STUTTGART, GERMANY). (GW/0044-3093). **4024**

ZEITSCHRIFT FUER ORTHOPADIE UND IHRE GRENZGEBIETE. (GW/0044-3220). **3885**

ZEITSCHRIFT FUER PAEDAGOGIK. (GW/0044-3247). **1792**

ZEITSCHRIFT FUER PAEDAGOGISCHE PSYCHOLOGIE. (SZ/1010-0652). **4622**

ZEITSCHRIFT FUER PARAPSYCHOLOGIE UND GRENZGEBIETE DER PSYCHOLOGIE. (GW/0028-3479). **4243**

ZEITSCHRIFT FUER PFLANZENERHAHRUNG UND BODENKUNDE. (GW/0044-3263). **530**

ZEITSCHRIFT FUER PHYSIK. B, CONDENSED MATTER. (GW/0722-3277). **4425**

ZEITSCHRIFT FUER PHYSIK. C, PARTICLES AND FIELDS. (GW/0170-9739). **4425**

ZEITSCHRIFT FUER PHYSIK. D, ATOMS, MOLECULES AND CLUSTERS. (GW/0178-7683). **4425**

ZEITSCHRIFT FUER PLANUNG : ZP. (GW/0936-8787). **890**

ZEITSCHRIFT FUER PSYCHOLOGIE MIT ZEITSCHRIFT FUER ANGEWANDTE PSYCHOLOGIE. (GW/0044-3409). **4622**

ZEITSCHRIFT FUER PSYCHOSOMATISCHE MEDIZIN UND PSYCHOANALYSE. (GW/0340-5613). **3653**

ZEITSCHRIFT FUER RHEUMATOLOGIE. (GW/0340-1855). **3807**

ZEITSCHRIFT FUER SAUGETIERKUNDE. (GW/0044-3468). **476**

ZEITSCHRIFT FUER SOZIALPSYCHOLOGIE. (SZ/0044-3514). **4622**

ZEITSCHRIFT FUER WASSER- UND ABWASSER FORSCHUNG. (GW/0044-3727). **1419**

ZEITSCHRIFT FUER ZOOLOGISCHE SYSTEMATIK UND EVOLUTIONSFORSCHUNG. (GW/0044-3808). **5600**

ZEITSCHRIFT FUR GANZHEITSFORSCHUNG. (AU). **4365**

ZEITSCHRIFT FUR KULTUR, POLITIK, KIRCHE. (SW). **5070**

ZEITSCHRIFT FUR NATURFORSCHUNG. (GW/0939-5075). **476**

ZEITSCHRIFT FUR NATURFORSCHUNG. (GW/0932-0776). **996**

ZEITSCHRIFT FUR SCHWEIZERISCHE KIRCHENGESCHICHTE. REVUE D'HISTOIRE ECCLESIASTIQUE SUISSE. (SZ/0044-3484). **5011**

ZEITSCHRIFT FUR TIERZUCHTUNG UND ZUCHTUNGSBIOLOGIE (HAMBURG, GERMANY : 1939). (GW/0044-3581). **224**

ZENTRALBLATT FUER CHIRURGIE. (GW/0044-409X). **3978**

ZENTRALBLATT FUER GYNAKOLOGIE. (GW/0044-4197). **3769**

ZENTRALBLATT FUER MIKROBIOLOGIE. (GW/0232-4393). **571**

ZEOLITES. (US/0144-2449). **1038**

ZHONGGUO HANGTIAN. (CC/1002-7742). **41**

ZHONGGUO HUANJING KEXUE. (CC/1000-6923). **2183**

ZHONGGUO KANGSHENGSU ZAZHI. (CC/1001-8689). **4333**

ZHONGGUO YAOLI XUEBAO. (CC/0253-9756). **4333**

ZHONGHUA MINGUO XIAOERKE YIXUEHUI ZAZHI. (CH/0001-6578). **3912**

ZHURNAL FIZICHESKOI KHIMII. (RU/0044-4537). **1059**

ZHURNAL MIKROBIOLOGII, EPIDEMIOLOGII I IMMUNOBIOLOGII. (RU/0372-9311). **3678**

ZHURNAL NEORGANICHESKOI KHIMII. (RU/0044-457X). **1038**

ZHURNAL VYSSHEI NERVNOI DEIATELNOSTI IMENI I. P. PAVLOVA. (RU/0044-4677). **3847**

ZOO BIOLOGY. (US/0733-3188). **5601**

ZOOLOGICA SCRIPTA. (UK/0300-3256). **5601**

ZOOLOGICAL

ZOOLOGICAL JOURNAL OF THE LINNEAN SOCIETY. (UK/0024-4082). **5601**

ZOOLOGICAL RECORD. (CH). **5601**

ZOOLOGICAL SCIENCE. (JA/0289-0003). **5602**

ZOOLOGICESKIJ ZURNAL. (RU/0044-5134). **5602**

ZOOLOGISCHE JAHRBUCHER. ABTEILUNG FUER ALLGEMEINE ZOOLOGIE UND PHYSIOLOGIE DER TIERE. (GW/0044-5185). **5603**

ZOOLOGISCHE MEDEDELINGEN. (NE/0024-0672). **5603**

ZOOLOGISCHER ANZEIGER. (GW/0044-5231). **5603**

ZUCHTUNGSKUNDE. (GW/0044-5401). **476**

ZUCKERINDUSTRIE. (GW/0344-8657). **1031**

ZURNAL NEVROPATOLOGII I PSIHIATRII IM S.S. KORSAKOVA. (RU/0044-4588). **3847**

ZURNAL OBSCEJ BIOLOGI. (RU/0044-4596). **476**

ZURNAL ORGANICESKOJ HIMII. (RU/0514-7492). **1049**

ZURNAL TEHNICESKOJ FIZIKI. (RU/0044-4642). **4426**

ZVAIGZNOTA DEBESS. (LV/0135-129X). **401**

ZYGOTE. (UK/0967-1994). **476**

Serials available on CD-ROM

The following index lists all serials in the Directory that are available on CD-ROM. The country code and ISSN are provided when available as well as the Publisher name, address, and telephone/fax numbers. The page number in bold refers you to the complete serial listing in Volume I, II or III of the Directory.

A. MAGAZINE. (US/1070-9401). Metro East Publications Inc., 296 Elizabeth Street #2F, New York NY 10012. **Tel** (212)505-1416, 800 446-6235, FAX (212)505-2077. **2253**

A S T I S CURRENT AWARENESS BULLETIN. (CN/0705-8454). Arctic Institute of North America, University of Calgary, 2500 University Drive Northwest, Calgary Alberta T2N 1N4 Canada. **Tel** (403)220-7515, FAX (403)282-4609. **406**

A-V ONLINE [COMPUTER FILE]. (US). Silverplatter Information Inc., 100 River Ridge Drive, Norwood MA 02062. **Tel** (800)343-0064, (617)769-2599, FAX (617)235-1715. **1887**

AACN NURSING SCAN IN CRITICAL CARE. (US/1055-8349). NURSECOM Inc., 1211 Locust Street, Philadelphia PA 19107. **Tel** (215)545-7222, (800)242-6757, FAX (215)545-8107. **3849**

ABC DER DEUTSCHEN WIRTSCHAFT. CD-ROM. (GW). ABC Publishing Group, POB 100262, D-64202 Darmstadt Germany. **Tel** 011 49 6151 38920. **1596**

ABC POL SCI. ADVANCE BIBLIOGRAPHY OF CONTENTS: POLITICAL SCIENCE & GOVERNMENT. (US/0001-0456). ABC Clio Press, PO Box 1911, 130 Cremona, Santa Barbara CA 93117. **Tel** (805)968-1911, (800)422-2546, FAX (805)685-9685. **4501**

ABC WORLD AIRWAYS GUIDE, THE. (UK). Reed Travel Group / England, World Timetable Center, Church Street, Dunstable, Bedfordshire LU5 4HB England. **Tel** 011 44 582 600111, FAX 011 44 582 695348. **5460**

ABI/INFORM GLOBAL EDITION [COMPUTER FILE]. (US). University Microfilms International, 300 North Zeeb Road, Ann Arbor MI 48106-1346. **Tel** (313)761-4700, (800)521-0600 Exts. 2490, 2491, FAX (313)973-1540. **725**

ABI/INFORM ONDISC. (US/1062-5127). University Microfilms International, 300 North Zeeb Road, Ann Arbor MI 48106-1346. **Tel** (313)761-4700, (800)521-0600 Exts. 2490, 2491, FAX (313)973-1540. **725**

ABI/INFORM ONDISC: EXPRESS EDITION [COMPUTER FILE]. (US). University Microfilms International, 300 North Zeeb Road, Ann Arbor MI 48106-1346. **Tel** (313)761-4700, (800)521-0600 Exts. 2490, 2491, FAX (313)973-1540. **725**

ABRIDGED INDEX MEDICUS. (US/0001-3331). Superintendent of Documents, US Government Printing Office, Washington DC 20402. **Tel** (202)275-3328, FAX (202)786-2377. **3654**

ABRIDGED READERS' GUIDE TO PERIODICAL LITERATURE. (US/0001-334X). H W Wilson Company, 950 University Avenue, Bronx NY 10452. **Tel** (800)367-6770, (718)588-8400, FAX (718)590-1617, telex 4990003 HWILSON. **2496**

ABSTRACTS IN HUMAN-COMPUTER INTERACTION. (US/1042-0193). Ergosyst Associates Inc, 123 West Eighth Street, Suite 1012, Lawrence KS 66044-2605. **Tel** (913)842-7334, FAX (913)842-7348. **1208**

ABSTRACTS ON RURAL DEVELOPMENT IN THE TROPICS. (NE/0169-605X). Royal Tropical Institute, Information & Documentation, Mauritskade 63, 1092 AD Amsterdam Netherlands. **Tel** 11 31 20 5688330, FAX 11 31 20 6654423, telex 15080 KIT NL. **5189**

ABSTRACTS ON TROPICAL AGRICULTURE. (NE/0304-5951). Royal Tropical Institute, Information & Documentation, Mauritskade 63, 1092 AD Amsterdam Netherlands. **Tel** 11 31 20 5688330, FAX 11 31 20 6654423, telex 15080 KIT NL. **149**

ACADEMIC ABSTRACTS. (US/1056-7496). EBSCO Publishing / Boston, 83 Pine Street, Peabody MA 01960. **Tel** (800)653-2726 North America, (508)535-8500, FAX (508)535-8545. **2496**

ACADEMIC ABSTRACTS FULL TEXT ELITE. (US/1060-6750). EBSCO Publishing / Boston, 83 Pine Street, Peabody MA 01960. **Tel** (800)653-2726 North America, (508)535-8500, FAX100 (508)535-8545. **2496**

ACADEMIC ABSTRACTS FULL TEXT SELECT. (US/1058-0662). EBSCO Publishing / Boston, 83 Pine Street, Peabody MA 01960. **Tel** (800)653-2726 North America, (508)535-8500, FAX (508)535-8545. **2484**

ACADEMIC INDEX. [COMPUTER FILE]. (US). Information Access Company, 362 Lakeside Drive, Foster City CA 94404. **Tel** (800)227-8431. **2496**

ACADEMIC SEARCH. (US/1071-2720). EBSCO Publishing / Boston, 83 Pine Street, Peabody MA 01960. **Tel** (800)653-2726 North America, (508)535-8500, FAX (508)535-8545. **2496**

ACCOUNTING AND FINANCE. (AT/0110-5159). Accounting Association of Australia and New Zealand, c/o Department of Accounting and Finance, Faculty of Economics and Commerce, University of Melbourne, Parkville Vic 3052 Australia. **Tel** 011/61/3/344/5350, FAX 011/61/344/6681, telex AA40315. **736**

ACCOUNTING AND TAX DATABASE [ONLINE DATABASE]. (US). University Microfilms International, 300 North Zeeb Road, Ann Arbor MI 48106-1346. Tel (313)761-4700, (800)521-0600 Exts. 2490, 2491, FAX (313)973-1540. **725**

ACCOUNTING AND TAX INDEX. (US/1063-0287). University Microfilms International, 300 North Zeeb Road, Ann Arbor MI 48106-1346. Tel (313)761-4700, (800)521-0600 Exts. 2490, 2491, FAX (313)973-1540. **725**

ACTA PSIQUIATRICA Y PSICOLOGICA DE AMERICA LATINA. (AG/0001-6896). Acta Psiquiatrica Y Psicologica de America Latina, Malabia 2274 13 A, 1425 Buenos Aires Argentina. **Tel** 54 1 711998, FAX 54 1 8545602. **3918**

ACTA SOCIETATIS BOTANICORUM POLONIAE. (PL/0001-6977). Panstwowe Wydawn Naukowe, Miodowa 10, PO Box 391, 00251 Warsaw Poland. **497**

ADA BUFFET. CD-ROM. (US). Alde Publishing, PO Box 39326, Minneapolis MN 55396. **Tel** (612)474-3755. **1170**

ADA IC NEWSLETTER. (US/1064-1505). Ada Information Clearinghouse, c/o IIT Research Institute, PO Box 46593, Washington DC 20050-6593. Tel (703)635-1477, (800)232-4211, FAX (703)685-7019. 1278

ADA WHITESANDS. CD-ROM. (US). Alde Publishing, PO Box 39326, Minneapolis MN 55396. Tel (612)474-3755. 1170

ADONIS CD-ROM. (NE). ADONIS BV, PO Box 17005, 1001 JA Amsterdam Netherlands. **Tel** 011 31 20 6262629. **3685**

ADVANCES IN POLYMER TECHNOLOGY. (US/0730-6679). John Wiley & Sons, Inc., 605 Third Avenue, New York NY 10158-0012. **Tel** (212)850-6000, (212)850-6645, FAX (212)850-6088, telex 12-7063. **4453**

AGBIOTECH NEWS AND INFORMATION. (UK/0954-9897). CAB International Centre, Wallingford, Oxon OX10 8DE United Kingdom. **Tel** 44 491 832111, FAX 44 491 833508, telex 847964 (COMAGG G). **149**

AGRI/STATS I. CD-ROM. (US). Hopkins Technology, 421 Hazel Lane, Suite 120, Hopkins MN 55343. **Tel** (612)931-9376, FAX (612)931-9377. **150**

AGRICOLA. (US/1050-6810). Silverplatter Information Inc., 100 River Ridge Drive, Norwood MA 02062. **Tel** (800)343-0064, (617)769-2599, FAX (617)235-1715. **150**

AGRICOLA ; CRIS. (US/0897-3237). OCLC Asia Pacific Services, 6565 Frantz Road, Dublin OH 43017. **Tel** (800)848-5878, (614)764-6394 or 6000, FAX (614)764-6096. **48**

AGRICULTURAL & ENVIRONMENTAL BIOTECHNOLOGY ABSTRACTS. (US/1063-1151). Cambridge Scientific Abstracts, 7200 Wisconsin Avenue, #601, Bethesda MD 20814-4823. **Tel** (301)961-6750, (800)843-7751, FAX (301)961-6720. **150**

AGRICULTURAL ENGINEERING ABSTRACTS. (UK/0308-8863). CAB International Centre, Wallingford, Oxon OX10 8DE United Kingdom. **Tel** 44 491 832111, FAX 44 491 833508, telex 847964 (COMAGG G). **150**

AGRICULTURE & HUMAN RESOURCE SERIES AGRICULTURE. CD-ROM. (US). Alde Publishing, PO Box 39326, Minneapolis MN 55396. **Tel** (612)474-3755. **53**

AGRICULTURE MATERIALS IN LIBRARIES. (US/0895-5506). OCLC Asia Pacific Services, 6565 Frantz Road, Dublin OH 43017. **Tel** (800)848-5878, (614)764-6394 or 6000, FAX (614)764-6096. **3188**

AGRICULTURE

Serials available on CD-ROM

AGRICULTURE STATISTICS. CD-ROM. (US). Slater Hall Information Products, 1301 Pennsylvania Avenue Northwest, Washington DC 20004. **Tel** (202)393-2666. **54**

AGRIS [CD-ROM]. (US). Silverplatter Information Inc., 100 River Ridge Drive, Norwood MA 02062. **Tel** (800)343-0064, (617)769-2599, FAX (617)235-1715. **54**

AGRISEARCH [COMPUTER FILE] : CRIS, SIS-SPAAR, ICAR, ARRIP, AGREP. (US). Silverplatter Information Inc., 100 River Ridge Drive, Norwood MA 02062. **Tel** (800)343-0064, (617)769-2599, FAX (617)235-1715. **54**

AGROFORESTRY ABSTRACTS. (UK/0952-1453). CAB International Centre, Wallingford, Oxon OX10 8DE United Kingdom. **Tel** 44 491 832111, FAX 44 491 833508, telex 847964 (COMAGG G). **2398**

AHFS DRUG INFORMATION. (US/1063-8792). American Society of Hospital Pharmacists, 7272 Wisconsin Avenue, Bethesda MD 20814. **Tel** (301)657-3000, (301)657-4383, FAX (301)652-8278. **4290**

AIDS CLINICAL CARE. (US/1043-1543). New England Journal of Medicine, 1440 Main Street, Waltham MA 02154-1649. **Tel** (617)893-3800, (800)843-6356, FAX (617)647-5785, telex 5106015660 NEJM BOS UQ. **3711**

AIDS CRISIS, THE. (US/0893-7613). Social Issues Resources Crisis Inc, PO Box 2348, Boca Raton FL 33427-2348. **Tel** (407)994-0079, (800)327-0513. **3663**

AIR POWER HISTORY. (US/1044-016X). Air Power History, Virginia Military Institute, Lexington VA 24450. **Tel** (703)464-7468, FAX (703)464-5229. **8**

AIRBORNE ELECTRONICS FORECAST. (US). Forecast International / DMS Inc., 22 Commerce Road, Newtown CT 06470. **Tel** (203)426-0800, FAX (203)426-1964, telex 467615. **4034**

AIRBORNE RETROFIT & MODERNIZATION SYSTEMS FORECAST. (US). Forecast International / DMS Inc., 22 Commerce Road, Newtown CT 06470. **Tel** (203)426-0800, FAX (203)426-1964, telex 467615. **4034**

AL-SHARQ. (SU). Al-Sharikah Al-Sharqiyah Lil-Sihafah Wa-Al-Tibaah Wa-Al-Ilam Shari Al-Amir Muhammad Imarat Al-Zamil, PO Box 2662-2663, Al-Damman 31461 Saudi Arabia. **Tel** (03)8571011, FAX (03)8578055. **2767**

AL-TAMWIL WA-AL-TANMIYAH. (US/0250-7455). Finance and Development, International Monetary Fund Building, Washington DC 20431. **Tel** (202)623-8308. **4708**

ALA HANDBOOK OF ORGANIZATION AND MEMBERSHIP DIRECTORY. (US/0273-4605). American Library Association, 50 East Huron Street, Chicago IL 60611. **Tel** (312)944-6780, (800)545-2433, FAX (312)944-2641. **3188**

ALASKA BUSINESS DIRECTORY. (US/1048-7069). American Business Directory, 5711 South 86th Circle, Omaha NE 68127. **Tel** (402)593-4600, FAX (402)331-5481. **637**

ALISA. AUSTRALIAN LIBRARY AND INFORMATION SCIENCE ABSTRACTS. (AT/0810-9265). Library Publications / University of South Australia, Holbrook Road, Underdale SA 5032 Australia. **Tel** 011 61 8 3026258. **3257**

ALLIANCE PLUS. (US/1056-621X). Follett, 809 North Front Street, McHenry IL 60050. **Tel** (800)323-3397, FAX (815)344-8774. **3189**

ALLOYS INDEX. (US/0094-8233). American Society for Metals International, c/o Deborah Barthelmes, Materials Park OH 44073-0002. **Tel** (216)338-5151, FAX (216)338-4634, telex 980-619. **3997**

AMAZING MOBY. CD-ROM. (US). Alde Publishing, PO Box 39326, Minneapolis MN 55396. **Tel** (612)474-3755. **1284**

AMERICA, HISTORY AND LIFE ON DISC. COMPUTER FILE. (US/0002-7065). ABC Clio Press, PO Box 1911, 130 Cremona, Santa Barbara CA 93117. **Tel** (805)968-1911, (800)422-2546, FAX (805)685-9685. **2718**

AMERICA, HISTORY AND LIFE (SANTA BARBARA, CALIF. : 1989). (US/0002-7065). ABC Clio Press, PO Box 1911, 130 Cremona, Santa Barbara CA 93117. **Tel** (805)968-1911, (800)422-2546, FAX (805)685-9685. **2634**

AMERICAN ARCHIVIST, THE. (US/0360-9081). Society of American Archivists, 600 South Federal, Suite 504, Chicago IL 60605. **Tel** (312)922-0140, FAX (312)347-1452. **2478**

AMERICAN BANKER INDEX (ANN ARBOR, MICH.). (US/0893-2468). University Microfilms International, 300 North Zeeb Road, Ann Arbor MI 48106-1346. **Tel** (313)761-4700, (800)521-0600 Exts. 2490, 2491, FAX (313)973-1540. **769**

AMERICAN BOOK PRICES CURRENT. (US/0091-9357). Bancroft Parkman Inc, PO Box 1236, Old Litchfield Road, Washington CT 06793. **Tel** (203)868-7408, FAX (203)868-0080. **4823**

AMERICAN BOOK TRADE DIRECTORY. (US/0065-759X). R R Bowker, A Reed Reference Publishing Company, Part of Reed International PLC, PO Box 31, 121 Chanlon Drive, New Providence NJ 07974. **Tel** (908)464-6800, (800)521-8110, FAX (908)665-6688, telex 138-755. **4821**

AMERICAN BUSINESS DISK, THE. (US/1062-5119). American Business Information, 5711 South 86th Circle, PO Box 27347, Omaha NE 68127. **638**

AMERICAN CRAFT. (US/0194-8008). American Craft Council, 72 Spring Street, 6th Floor, New York NY 10012. **Tel** (212)274-0630, (800)562-1973. **369**

AMERICAN DOCTORAL DISSERTATIONS. (US/0065-809X). University Microfilms International, 300 North Zeeb Road, Ann Arbor MI 48106-1346. **Tel** (313)761-4700, (800)521-0600 Exts. 2490, 2491, FAX (313)973-1540. **1808**

AMERICAN FAMILY PHYSICIAN (1970). (US/0002-838X). American Academy of Family Physicians, 8880 Ward Parkway, Kansas City MO 64114. **Tel** (816)333-9700 ext. 1142, FAX (816)333-0303. **3736**

AMERICAN FAMILY PHYSICIAN. [CD-ROM]. (US). Creative Multimedia Corporation, 513 Northwest Avenue, Suite 400, Portland OR 97209. **Tel** (503)241-4351. **3736**

AMERICAN JOURNAL OF CRITICAL CARE. (US/1062-3264). American Association Critical Care Nurses, 101 Columbia, Alisa Veijo CA 92655. **Tel** (714)362-2000. **3850**

AMERICAN JOURNAL OF INTERNATIONAL LAW, THE. (US/0002-9300). American Society of International Law, 2223 Massachusetts Avenue Northwest, Washington DC 20008-2864. **Tel** (202)939-6000, FAX (202)797-7133. **3123**

AMERICAN LIBRARY DIRECTORY. (US/0065-910X). R R Bowker, A Reed Reference Publishing Company, Part of Reed International PLC, PO Box 31, 121 Chanlon Drive, New Providence NJ 07974. **Tel** (908)464-6800, (800)521-8110, FAX (908)665-6688, telex 138-755. **3257**

AMERICAN MANUFACTURERS DIRECTORY. (US/1061-219X). American Business Directory, 5711 South 86th Circle, Omaha NE 68127. **Tel** (402)593-4600, FAX (402)331-5481. **3475**

AMERICAN MEN & WOMEN OF SCIENCE. (US/0000-1287). R R Bowker, A Reed Reference Publishing Company, Part of Reed International PLC, PO Box 31, 121 Chanlon Drive, New Providence NJ 07974. **Tel** (908)464-6800, (800)521-8110, FAX (908)665-6688, telex 138-755. **5173**

AMERICAN MEN AND WOMEN OF SCIENCE: BIOLOGY. (US/0146-0048). R R Bowker, A Reed Reference Publishing Company, Part of Reed International PLC, PO Box 31, 121 Chanlon Drive, New Providence NJ 07974. **Tel** (908)464-6800, (800)521-8110, FAX (908)665-6688, telex 138-755. **5173**

AMERICAN MEN AND WOMEN OF SCIENCE: CHEMISTRY. (US/0146-0056). R R Bowker, A Reed Reference Publishing Company, Part of Reed International PLC, PO Box 31, 121 Chanlon Drive, New Providence NJ 07974. **Tel** (908)464-6800, (800)521-8110, FAX (908)665-6688, telex 138-755. **5173**

AMERICAN MEN AND WOMEN OF SCIENCE: CONSULTANTS. (US/0146-0064). R R Bowker, A Reed Reference Publishing Company, Part of Reed International PLC, PO Box 31, 121 Chanlon Drive, New Providence NJ 07974. **Tel** (908)464-6800, (800)521-8110, FAX (908)665-6688, telex 138-755. **5173**

AMERICAN MEN AND WOMEN OF SCIENCE: ECONOMICS. (US/0094-5315). R R Bowker, A Reed Reference Publishing Company, Part of Reed International PLC, PO Box 31, 121 Chanlon Drive, New Providence NJ 07974. **Tel** (908)464-6800, (800)521-8110, FAX (908)665-6688, telex 138-755. **5173**

AMERICAN MEN AND WOMEN OF SCIENCE: MEDICAL AND HEALTH SCIENCES. (US/0145-9996). R R Bowker, A Reed Reference Publishing Company, Part of Reed International PLC, PO Box 31, 121 Chanlon Drive, New Providence NJ 07974. **Tel** (908)464-6800, (800)521-8110, FAX (908)665-6688, telex 138-755. **5173**

AMERICAN MEN AND WOMEN OF SCIENCE: PHYSICS, ASTRONOMY, MATHEMATICS, STATISTICS, AND COMPUTER SCIENCE. (US/0146-003X). R R Bowker, A Reed Reference Publishing Company, Part of Reed International PLC, PO Box 31, 121 Chanlon Drive, New Providence NJ 07974. **Tel** (908)464-6800, (800)521-8110, FAX (908)665-6688, telex 138-755. **5173**

AMERICAN POTATO JOURNAL. (US/0003-0589). Potato Association of America, University of Maine, 5736 Holmes Hall, Orono ME 04469. **Tel** (207)581-3160. **162**

AMERICAN SPECTATOR (ARLINGTON, VA.), THE. (US/0148-8414). The American Spectator, 2020 North 14th Street, PO Box 549, Arlington VA 22216. **Tel** (703)243-3733, (800)341-1522. **3337**

AMERICAN STATISTICS INDEX. (US/0091-1658). Congressional Information Service Inc, 4520 East-West Highway, Suite 800, Bethesda MD 20814-3389. **Tel** (800)638-8380, (301)654-1550, FAX (301)654-4033, telex 292386 CIS UR. **4696**

ANALES DEL JARDIN BOTANICO DE MADRID (1979). (SP/0211-1322). Consejo Superior Investigacion Cientificas (CSIC), Vitruvio 8, 28006 Madrid Spain. **Tel** 011 34 1 5612833, FAX 011 34 1 4113077, telex 42182. **499**

ANALYTICAL ABSTRACTS. (UK/0003-2689). Royal Society of Chemistry, Thomas Graham House, Science Park, Cambridge CB4 4WF England. **Tel** 011 44 223 420066, FAX 011 44 223 423429, telex 818293 ROYAL. **996**

ANBAR ACCOUNTING & FINANCE ABSTRACTS. (UK/0961-2742). MCB University Press, 60 62 Toller Lane, Bradford West Yorkshire BD8 9BX England. **Tel** 011 44 274 499821, FAX 011 44 274 547143, telex 51317 MCBUNI G. **726**

ANBAR MARKETING & DISTRIBUTION ABSTRACTS. (UK/0305-0661). MCB University Press, 60 62 Toller Lane, Bradford West Yorkshire BD8 9BX England. **Tel** 011 44 274 499821, FAX 011 44 274 547143, telex 51317 MCBUNI G. **726**

ANBAR TOP MANAGEMENT ABSTRACTS. (UK). MCB University Press, 60 62 Toller Lane, Bradford West Yorkshire BD8 9BX England. **Tel** 011 44 274 499821, FAX 011 44 274 547143, telex 51317 MCBUNI G. **726**

ANIMAL BEHAVIOR ABSTRACTS. (US/0301-8695). Cambridge Scientific Abstracts, 7200 Wisconsin Avenue, #601, Bethesda MD 20814-4823. **Tel** (301)961-6750, (800)843-7751, FAX (301)961-6720. **5604**

ANIMAL BREEDING ABSTRACTS. (UK/0003-3499). CAB International Centre, Wallingford, Oxon OX10 8DE United Kingdom. **Tel** 44 491 832111, FAX 44 491 833508, telex 847964 (COMAGG G). **151**

ANIMALS AGENDA. (US/0892-8819). Animal Rights Network, 456 Monroe Turnpike, PO Box 1242, Darien CT 06820. **Tel** (203)452-0446, (800)825-0061, FAX (203)452-9543. **225**

ANNALS OF INTERNAL MEDICINE. (US/0003-4819). American College of Physicians, 6th Street and Race Street, Independence Mall West, Philadelphia PA 19106-1572. **Tel** (215)351-2600, (800)523-1546. **3794**

ANNUAIRE. (FR). Orsay, Institut de Physique Nucleaire, Orsay 91406 France. **Tel** 69417305, FAX 69416470, telex IPNORS 692 006 F. **4445**

ANNUAL REVIEW OF EUROPEAN EXPORT INDUSTRIES : FURNITURE. (GW). Industrieschau Verlagsgesellschaft MBH, PO Box 4034, Berliner Allee 8, W-6000 Darmstadt Germany. **Tel** (06151)33411, FAX (06151)33164, telex 419257. **2904**

ANNUAL STATE WATER-DATA REPORTS [COMPUTER FILE] : A DIGITAL REPRESENTATION OF THE HYDROLOGIC RECORDS OF THE UNITED STATES FOR ... . (US). US Department of the Interior / US Geological Survey, Books and Open-File Reports Section, Box 25425, Federal Center, Denver CO 80225-0425. **1412**

ANTARCTIC BIBLIOGRAPHY. (US/0066-4626). Superintendent of Documents, US Government Printing Office, Washington DC 20402. **Tel** (202)275-3328, FAX (202)786-2377. **3457**

ANTI-SUBMARINE WARFARE FORECAST. (US). Forecast International / DMS Inc., 22 Commerce Road, Newtown CT 06470. **Tel** (203)426-0800, FAX (203)426-1964, telex 467615. **4035**

ANTIMICROBIAL AGENTS AND CHEMOTHERAPY. (US/0066-4804). American Society for Microbiology, 1325 Massachusetts Avenue Northwest, Washington DC 20005-4171. **Tel** (202)737-3600, FAX (202)737-0367. **559**

Serials available on CD-ROM — BIBLIOGRAPHY

ANTIOCH REVIEW, THE. (US/0003-5769). Antioch Review, PO Box 148, Yellow Springs OH 45387. **Tel** (513)767-6389. **3337**

APCO BULLETIN, THE. (US/0001-2165). Association of Public Safety Communications Officers, 2040 S Ridgewood Ave, Suite 104, South Daytona FL 32119-2257. **Tel** (904)322-2500. **4767**

APPLIED AND ENVIRONMENTAL MICROBIOLOGY. (US/0099-2240). American Society for Microbiology, 1325 Massachusetts Avenue Northwest, Washington DC 20005-4171. **Tel** (202)737-3600, FAX (202)737-0367. **559**

APPLIED SCIENCE & TECHNOLOGY INDEX. (US/0003-6986). H W Wilson Company, 950 University Avenue, Bronx NY 10452. **Tel** (800)367-6770, (718)588-8400, FAX (718)590-1617, telex 4990003 HWILSON. **5173**

APPLIED SCIENCE & TECHNOLOGY INDEX (CD-ROM ED.). (US/1063-8695). H W Wilson Company, 950 University Avenue, Bronx NY 10452. **Tel** (800)367-6770, (718)588-8400, FAX (718)590-1617, telex 4990003 HWILSON. **5173**

AQUALINE ABSTRACTS. (UK/0263-5534). Water Research Centre, WRC PLC Frankland Road, Blagrove Swindon SN5 8YF England. **Tel** 011 44 793 511711, FAX 011 44 793 511712, telex 449541. **2002**

AQUAREF. (CN). WATDOC, Client Services, Interpretation and Access Division, Surveys and Information Systems Branch, Ecosystem Sciences and Evaluation Directorate, Environment Canada, Ottawa, Ontario K1A 0H3 Canada. **Tel** (819)953-1529, . **5549**

AQUATIC SCIENCES & FISHERIES ABSTRACTS (CD-ROM ED.). (US/1064-0460). Cambridge Scientific Abstracts, 7200 Wisconsin Avenue, #601, Bethesda MD 20814-4823. **Tel** (301)961-6750, (800)843-7751, FAX (301)961-6720. **2316**

AQUATIC SCIENCES AND FISHERIES ABSTRACTS. PART 1 : BIOLOGICAL SCIENCES AND LIVING RESOURCES. (US/0140-5373). Cambridge Scientific Abstracts, 7200 Wisconsin Avenue, #601, Bethesda MD 20814-4823. **Tel** (301)961-6750, (800)843-7751, FAX (301)961-6720. **2316**

AQUATIC SCIENCES AND FISHERIES ABSTRACTS. PART 2 : OCEAN TECHNOLOGY, POLICY AND NON-LIVING RESOURCES. (US/0140-5381). Cambridge Scientific Abstracts, 7200 Wisconsin Avenue, #601, Bethesda MD 20814-4823. **Tel** (301)961-6750, (800)843-7751, FAX (301)961-6720. **2316**

AQUATIC SCIENCES AND FISHERIES ABSTRACTS. PART 3 : AQUATIC POLLUTION AND ENVIRONMENTAL QUALITY. (US/1045-6031). Cambridge Scientific Abstracts, 7200 Wisconsin Avenue, #601, Bethesda MD 20814-4823. **Tel** (301)961-6750, (800)843-7751, FAX (301)961-6720. **2317**

ARCHIVOS DE MEDICINA DEL DEPORTE : PUBLICACION DE LA FEDERACION ESPANOLA DE MEDICINA DEL DEPORTE / FEMEDE. (SP/0212-8799). Federacion Espanola de Medicina del Deporte, Apartado 1027, 31080 Pamplona Spain. **Tel** 34 3 2007344, or 2011698. **3953**

ARCTIC & ANTARCTIC REGIONS. (US/1043-7479). National Information Services Corp, 3100 St Paul Street, Wyman Towers, Suite 6, Baltimore MD 21218. **Tel** (410)243-0797, FAX (410)243-0982. **1351**

ARERUGI. (JA/0021-4884). Nihon Arerugi Gakkai, (Japanese Society of Allergology), c/o Nihon Ika Daigaku Biseibutsu, Men Ekigaku Kyoshitsu, 1-5, Sendagi, 1 Chome, Bunkyoku, Tokyo 113 Japan. **3666**

ARITHMETIC TEACHER, THE. (US/0004-136X). National Council of Teachers of Mathematics, 1906 Association Drive, Reston VA 22091. **Tel** (703)620-9840, FAX (703)476-2970. **3496**

ARIZONA BUSINESS. (US/0093-0717). Arizona State University / Center for Business Research, College of Business-NBJ, Box 874406, Tempe AZ 85287-4406. **Tel** (602)965-3961, FAX (602)965-5458. **1463**

ARKANSAS BUSINESS DIRECTORY. (US/1048-7190). American Business Directory, 5711 South 86th Circle, Omaha NE 68127. **Tel** (402)593-4600, FAX (402)331-5481. **639**

ARQUIVOS DE NEURO-PSIQUIATRIA. (BL/0004-282X). Associacao Arquivos de Neuro-Psiquiatria, Caixa Postal 8877, 01065 970 Sao Paulo, SP Brazil. **Tel** 11 55 11 2898824, FAX 11 55 11 2898879. **3827**

ART INDEX. (US/0004-3222). H W Wilson Company, 950 University Avenue, Bronx NY 10452. **Tel** (800)367-6770, (718)588-8400, FAX (718)590-1617, telex 4990003 HWILSON. **334**

ART INDEX. CD-ROM. (US/0004-3222). H W Wilson Company, 950 University Avenue, Bronx NY 10452. **Tel** (800)367-6770, (718)588-8400, FAX (718)590-1617, telex 4990003 HWILSON. **334**

ARTBIBLIOGRAPHIES MODERN. (UK/0300-466X). ABC Clio Press, PO Box 1911, 130 Cremona, Santa Barbara CA 93117. **Tel** (805)968-1911, (800)422-2546, FAX (805)685-9685. **334**

ARTIFICIAL INTELLIGENCE ABSTRACTS. (US/0882-1410). R R Bowker, A Reed Reference Publishing Company, Part of Reed International PLC, PO Box 31, 121 Chanlon Drive, New Providence NJ 07974. **Tel** (908)464-6800, (800)521-8110, FAX (908)665-6688, telex 138-755. **1208**

ARTS & HUMANITIES CITATION INDEX (COMPACT DISC ED.). (US/1060-9202). Institute for Scientific Information, 3501 Market Street, Philadelphia PA 19104. **Tel** (215)386-0100, (800)523-1850, FAX (215)386-6362, telex 84-5305. **314**

ARTS & HUMANITIES CITATION INDEX (PRINT ED.). (US/0162-8445). Institute for Scientific Information, 3501 Market Street, Philadelphia PA 19104. **Tel** (215)386-0100, (800)523-1850, FAX (215)386-6362, telex 84-5305. **2857**

ASAIO JOURNAL (1992). (US/1058-2916). J.B. Lippincott Company, 227 East Washington Square, Philadelphia PA 19106-3780. **Tel** (215)238-4200 or 4454, FAX (215)238-4227. **3960**

ASFA AQUACULTURE ABSTRACTS. (US/0739-814X). Cambridge Scientific Abstracts, 7200 Wisconsin Avenue, #601, Bethesda MD 20814-4823. **Tel** (301)961-6750, (800)843-7751, FAX (301)961-6720. **2296**

ASFA MARINE BIOTECHNOLOGY ABSTRACTS. (US/1054-2027). Cambridge Scientific Abstracts, 7200 Wisconsin Avenue, #601, Bethesda MD 20814-4823. **Tel** (301)961-6750, (800)843-7751, FAX (301)961-6720. **553**

ASIA PACIFIC HANDBOOK. (UK/0966-0453). Extel Financial Ltd, Fitzroy House, 13-17 Epworth Street, London EC2A 4DL England. **Tel** 071 825 8000, FAX (0)71 251-2725, telex 884319 EXTELX G. **640**

ASIA-PACIFIC JOURNAL OF PUBLIC HEALTH : ASIA-PACIFIC ACADEMIC CONSORTIUM FOR PUBLIC HEALTH. (TH/1010-5395). APACPH Office Fac. Public Health, 420 1 Rasuithi Road Phyatmai, Bangkok 10400 Thailand. **Tel** 66-2-247-9669, FAX 246-5227, telex 84770 UNIMAHITH. **4767**

ASIANWEEK. (US/0195-2056). Asian Week, 811 Sacramento Street, San Francisco CA 94108. **Tel** (415)397-0220, FAX (415)397-7258. **5633**

ASSEMBLIES OF GOD HERITAGE. (US/0896-4394). Assemblies of God Archives, 1445 Boonville Avenue, Springfield MO 65802-1894. **Tel** (417)862-2781, (417)862-1447, FAX (417)862-8558. **4936**

ASSIA. APPLIED SOCIAL SCIENCES INDEX & ABSTRACTS. (UK/0950-2238). Bowker Saur Ltd., A Reed Reference Publishing Company, Part of Reed International PLC, 59-60 Grosvenor Street, London WIX 9DA England. **Tel** 011 44 71 4935841, FAX 011 44 71 4991590. **5226**

ASSIA PLUS [COMPUTER FILE]. (UK). Bowker Saur Ltd., A Reed Reference Publishing Company, Part of Reed International PLC, 59-60 Grosvenor Street, London WIX 9DA England. **Tel** 011 44 71 4935841, FAX 011 44 71 4991590. **5226**

ASTIS BIBLIOGRAPHY. (CN/0226-1685). Arctic Institute of North America, University of Calgary, 2500 University Drive Northwest, Calgary Alberta T2N 1N4 Canada. **Tel** (403)220-7515, FAX (403)282-4609. **5173**

ATLANTA CONSTITUTION : A GEORGIA INDEX, THE. (US/0093-1179). Georgia State University Publishing Services Division, University Plaza, Atlanta GA 30303. **Tel** (404)651-4253. **408**

AUSTRALIAN AND NEW ZEALAND CATALOGUE OF NEW FILMS AND VIDEOS, THE. (AT/1035-8005). Australian Catalogue, PO Box 204, Albert Park Victoria 3206 Australia. **Tel** 011 61 3 5255302, FAX 011 63 3 5372325. **4064**

AUSTRALIAN EDUCATION INDEX. (AT/0004-9026). Australian Council for Educational Research, 19 Prospect Hill Road, Camberwell VIC 3124 Australia. **Tel** 011 61 3 2775555. **1793**

AUSTRALIAN JOURNAL OF CHINESE AFFAIRS, THE. (AT/0156-7365). Contemporary China Centre, RSPAS, Anutech GPO Box 4, Canberra ACT 2601 Australia. **Tel** (06) 249 4150, FAX (06) 257 3642, telex AA62694 SOPAC. **2501**

AUSTRALIAN MASTER TAX GUIDE. (AT). CCH Australia Ltd, PO Box 230, North Ryde New South Wales, 2113 Australia. **Tel** 011 61 02 888 2555, FAX 011 61 02 888 7324. **4712**

AVERY INDEX TO ARCHITECTURAL PERIODICALS. (US). GK Hall & Co, 100 Front Street, Riverside NJ 08075. **Tel** (800)257-5755 ext. 2223. **293**

BANK LETTER. (US). Institutional Investor Inc., 488 Madison Avenue, New York NY 10022. **Tel** (212)303-3234, (212)303-3233, FAX (212)303-3353. **775**

BARRON'S PROFILES OF AMERICAN COLLEGES : DESCRIPTIONS OF THE COLLEGES / COMPILED AND EDITED BY THE COLLEGE DIVISION OF BARRON'S EDUCATIONAL SERIES. (US). Barron's Educational Series Inc., 250 Wireless Boulevard, Hauppauge NY 11788. **Tel** (800)645-3476, FAX (516)434-3723. **1811**

BEHAVIOR AND PHILOSOPHY. (US/1053-8348). Cambridge Center for Behavioral Studies, 11 Waterhouse Street, Cambridge MA 02138. **Tel** (617)491-9020, FAX (617)491-1072. **4576**

BEHAVIOR AND SOCIAL ISSUES. (US/1064-9506). Cambridge Center for Behavioral Studies, 11 Waterhouse Street, Cambridge MA 02138. **Tel** (617)491-9020, FAX (617)491-1072. **4576**

BEILSTEIN CURRENT FACTS IN CHEMISTRY [COMPUTER FILE] / BEILSTEIN INSTITUT. (GW/0939-7698). Springer-Verlag GmbH & Company KG, Heidelberger Platz 3, D 14197 Berlin Germany. **Tel** 011 49 30 8207223, FAX 011 49 30 8214091, telex 183 319 SPBLN D. **1039**

BEST BOOKS FOR CHILDREN : A CATALOG OF ... TITLES. (US). R R Bowker, A Reed Reference Publishing Company, Part of Reed International PLC, PO Box 31, 121 Chanlon Drive, New Providence NJ 07974. **Tel** (908)464-6800, (800)521-8110, FAX (908)665-6688, telex 138-755. **1060**

BHI PLUS [COMPUTER FILE]. (UK/0966-8772). Bowker Saur Ltd., A Reed Reference Publishing Company, Part of Reed International PLC, 59-60 Grosvenor Street, London WIX 9DA England. **Tel** 011 44 71 4935841, FAX 011 44 71 4991590. **2857**

BIB TELEVISION PROGRAMMING SOURCE BOOKS. (US/1056-6104). North American Publishing Company, 401 North Broad Street, Philadelphia PA 19108. **Tel** (215)238-5300, (800)777-8074, FAX (215)238-5283. **1127**

BIBLIOGRAFIA BRASILEIRA DE ODONTOLOGIA. (BL). Universidade de Sao Paulo / Faculdade de Odontologia 2227, 05508 Sao Paulo SP Brazil. **Tel** 011 813 6944, FAX 011 815 4272. **1337**

BIBLIOGRAFIA LATINOAMERICANA. 1, TRABAJOS PUBLICADOS POR LATINOAMERICANOS EN REVISTAS EXTRANJERAS. (MX). Centro de Informacion Cientifica y Humanistica, Apartado 70 392, Mexico 20 DF Mexico. **Tel** 011 52 5 5480208, 011 52 5 6223964. **408**

BIBLIOGRAFIA LATINOAMERICANA. 2, TRABAJOS SOBRE AMERICA LATINA PUBLICADOS EN REVISTAS EXTRANJERAS. (MX). Centro de Informacion Cientifica y Humanistica, Apartado 70 392, Mexico 20 DF Mexico. **Tel** 011 52 5 5480208, 011 52 5 6223964. **409**

BIBLIOGRAPHIE NATIONALE FRANCAISE DEPUIS 1970. CD-ROM. (UK). Chadwyck-Healey Limited, The Quorum Barnwell Road, Cambridge CB5 8SW England. **Tel** 011 44 223 215512, telex 9312102281 CH G. **410**

BIBLIOGRAPHIE NATIONALE FRANCAISE. LIVRES : NOTICES ETABLES PAR LA BIBLIOTHEQUE NATIONALE. (FR/1142-3250). Cercle de la Librairie, 35 rue Gregoire de Tours, F-75279 Paris Cedex 06 France. **Tel** 011 33 1 43291000, FAX 011 33 1 43296895, telex LIFRAN 270 838. **410**

BIBLIOGRAPHY AND INDEX OF GEOLOGY. (US/0098-2784). American Geological Institute, 4220 King Street, Alexandria VA 22302. **Tel** (703)379-2480, FAX (703)379-7563. **1361**

BIBLIOGRAPHY OF AGRICULTURE. (US/0006-1530). Oryx Press, 4041 North Central Avenue, #700, Phoenix AZ 85012-3397. **Tel** (800)279-ORYX, (602)265-2651, FAX (602)265-6250, (800)279-4663, (800)279-6799. **151**

BIBLIOGRAPHY OF ECONOMIC GEOLOGY. (UK/0016-7053). Geosystems Inc., PO Box 40, Didcot, Oxon OX11 9BX England. **Tel** 011 44 235 813913. **1361**

BIBLIOGRAPHY OF EDUCATION THESES IN AUSTRALIA. (AT/0811-0174). Australian Council for Educational Research, 19 Prospect Hill Road, Camberwell VIC 3124 Australia. **Tel** 011 61 3 2775555. **1793**

BIBLIOGRAPHY

Serials available on CD-ROM

BIBLIOGRAPHY OF NATIVE NORTH AMERICANS ON DISC. (US/1064-5144). ABC Clio Press, PO Box 1911, 130 Cremona, Santa Barbara CA 93117. **Tel** (805)968-1911, (800)422-2546, FAX (805)685-9685. **410**

BIBLIOGRAPHY ON COLD REGIONS SCIENCE AND TECHNOLOGY. (US/0149-3825). National Technical Information Service - NTIS, Room 2027S, 5285 Port Royal Road, Springfield VA 22161. **Tel** (703)487-4630, (703)487-4660, (703)487-4650, FAX (703)321-8547, telex 89-9405. **5088**

BINSTED'S DIRECTORY OF FOOD TRADE MARKS AND BRAND NAMES. (UK). Food Trade Press Ltd, Station House, Hortons Way, Westerham Kent TN16 1BZ England. **Tel** 011 44 689 50551, 011 44 689 53070, FAX 011 44 689 561285. **2329**

BIOCHEMISTRY & BIOPHYSICS CITATION INDEX. (US/1065-7509). Institute for Scientific Information, 3501 Market Street, Philadelphia PA 19104. **Tel** (215)386-0100, (800)523-1850, FAX (215)386-6362, telex 84-5305. **481**

BIOCONTROL NEWS AND INFORMATION. (UK/0143-1404). CAB International Centre, Wallingford, Oxon OX10 8DE United Kingdom. **Tel** 44 491 832111, FAX 44 491 833508, telex 847964 (COMAGG G). **151**

BIODETERIORATION ABSTRACTS. (UK/0951-0621). CAB International Centre, Wallingford, Oxon OX10 8DE United Kingdom. **Tel** 44 491 832111, FAX 44 491 833508, telex 847964 (COMAGG G). **2183**

BIOGRAPHY AND GENEALOGY MASTER INDEX. (US/0730-1316). Gale Research Inc., 835 Penobscot Building, 645 Griswold Street, Detroit MI 48226. **Tel** (800)877-GALE, (313)961-2242, FAX (313)961-6083, (800)414-5043, telex TWX 810-221-7086. **430**

BIOGRAPHY INDEX. (US/0006-3053). H W Wilson Company, 950 University Avenue, Bronx NY 10452. **Tel** (800)367-6770, (718)588-8400, FAX (718)590-1617, telex 4990003 HWILSON. **439**

BIOGRAPHY INDEX (CD-ROM ED.). (US/1063-3286). H W Wilson Company, 950 University Avenue, Bronx NY 10452. **Tel** (800)367-6770, (718)588-8400, FAX (718)590-1617, telex 4990003 HWILSON. **439**

BIOLOGICAL ABSTRACTS. (US/0006-3169). BioSciences Information Service, Biological Abstracts / BIOSIS, 2100 Arch Street, Philadelphia PA 19103-1399. **Tel** (800)523-4806 US, (215)587-4800 Pennsylvania and worldwide, FAX (215)587-2016, telex 831739. **477**

BIOLOGICAL ABSTRACTS ON COMPACT DISC. (US/1058-4129). BioSciences Information Service, Biological Abstracts / BIOSIS, 2100 Arch Street, Philadelphia PA 19103-1399. **Tel** (800)523-4806 US, (215)587-4800 Pennsylvania and worldwide, FAX (215)587-2016, telex 831739. **477**

BIOLOGICAL ABSTRACTS / RRM. (US/0192-6985). BioSciences Information Service, Biological Abstracts / BIOSIS, 2100 Arch Street, Philadelphia PA 19103-1399. **Tel** (800)523-4806 US, (215)587-4800 Pennsylvania and worldwide, FAX (215)587-2016, telex 831739. **477**

BIOLOGICAL ABSTRACTS / RRM ON COMPACT DISC. (US/1058-4137). BioSciences Information Service, Biological Abstracts / BIOSIS, 2100 Arch Street, Philadelphia PA 19103-1399. **Tel** (800)523-4806 US, (215)587-4800 Pennsylvania and worldwide, FAX (215)587-2016, telex 831739. **444**

BIOLOGICAL & AGRICULTURAL INDEX. (US/0006-3177). H W Wilson Company, 950 University Avenue, Bronx NY 10452. **Tel** (800)367-6770, (718)588-8400, FAX (718)590-1617, telex 4990003 HWILSON. **477**

BIOLOGICAL & AGRICULTURAL INDEX [COMPUTER FILE]. (US). H W Wilson Company, 950 University Avenue, Bronx NY 10452. **Tel** (800)367-6770, (718)588-8400, FAX (718)590-1617, telex 4990003 HWILSON. **477**

BIOLOGICAL EFFECTS OF NONIONIZING ELECTROMAGNETIC RADIATION DIGEST UPDATE (PHILADELPHIA, PA). (US/1056-9138). Information Ventures Inc., 1500 Locust Street, Suite 3216, Philadelphia PA 19102. **Tel** (215)732-9083, FAX (215)732-3754. **3686**

BIOMEDICAL ENGINEERING CITATION INDEX. (US/1062-5488). Institute for Scientific Information, 3501 Market Street, Philadelphia PA 19104. **Tel** (215)386-0100, (800)523-1850, FAX (215)386-6362, telex 84-5305. **3686**

BIOSIS PREVIEWS [ONLINE DATABASE]. (US). BioSciences Information Service, Biological Abstracts / BIOSIS, 2100 Arch Street, Philadelphia PA 19103-1399. **Tel** (800)523-4806 US, (215)587-4800 Pennsylvania and worldwide, FAX (215)587-2016, telex 831739. **477**

BIOTECHNOLOGY ABSTRACTS [COMPUTER FILE] / DERWENT PUBLICATIONS, LTD. (US). Silverplatter Information Inc., 100 River Ridge Drive, Norwood MA 02062. **Tel** (800)343-0064, (617)769-2599, FAX (617)235-1715. **3688**

BIOTECHNOLOGY CITATION INDEX. (US/1057-607X). Institute for Scientific Information, 3501 Market Street, Philadelphia PA 19104. **Tel** (215)386-0100, (800)523-1850, FAX (215)386-6362, telex 84-5305. **3689**

BIOTECHNOLOGY RESEARCH ABSTRACTS. (US/0733-5709). Cambridge Scientific Abstracts, 7200 Wisconsin Avenue, #601, Bethesda MD 20814-4823. **Tel** (301)961-6750, (800)843-7751, FAX (301)961-6720. **3655**

BIRKNER. (GW). Birkner & Co. Verlag, Postfach 540750, D 22507 Hamburg Germany. **Tel** 011 49 40 85308 401, FAX 011 49 40 85308 381. **4232**

BLACK COUNTRY BUSINESS DIRECTORY (SOUTH EDITION). (UK/0957-1035). Holcot Press Ltd, Station House, Station Road, Newport Pognell, Milton Keynes MK16 0AG England. **Tel** 0908-614477, FAX 0908-217425. **643**

BLACK ENTERPRISE. (US/0006-4165). Earl G. Graves Publishing Company, 130 Fifth Avenue, New York NY 10011. **Tel** (212)242-8000, FAX (212)989-8410. **643**

BLUE BOOK (NEW YORK, N.Y.). (US). Rubber World, PO Box 5451, 1867 West Narjet Street, Akron OH 44334-0451. **Tel** (216)864-2122, FAX (216)864-5298, telex 297690 RWMAG UR. **5075**

BMJ. BRITISH MEDICAL JOURNAL (INTERNATIONAL ED.). (UK/0959-8146). BMJ / British Medical Journal Publishing Group, British Medical Association House, Tavistock Square, London WC1H 9JR England. **Tel** 011 44 71 3874499, FAX 011 44 71 383 6402, telex 290034 HBJ MN. **3557**

BNB NBB COMPTES ANNUELS DES ENTREPRISES BELGES. CD-ROM. (BE). Banque National de Belgique, Boulevard de Berlaimont 14-B, 1000 Brussels Belgium. **Tel** 11 32 2 2212033, FAX 11 32 2 2213163. **739**

BNB ON CD-ROM [COMPUTER FILE]. (UK/0968-3097). Chadwyck-Healey Limited, The Quorum Barnwell Road, Cambridge CB5 8SW England. **Tel** 011 44 223 215512, telex 9312102281 CH G. **3196**

BOATING WORLD. (US/1059-5155). Billian Publishing Inc., 2100 Powers Ferry Road, Atlanta GA 30339. **Tel** (404)955-5656, FAX (404)952-0669. **592**

BOLLETTINO TRIBUTARIO D'INFORMAZIONI. (IT/0006-6893). Bollettino Tributario d'Informazione, Via L Manara 1, 20122 Milan Italy. **Tel** 011 39 2 540-1010. **2942**

BOLLETTINO UFFICIALE REGIONE : EMILIA ROMAGNA - PART III. (IT). Bollettino Ufficiale Emilia Romagna, Viale Silvani 6, 40122 Bologna Italy. **Tel** 011 39 51 284440, FAX 011 39 51 284841. **4633**

BOOK REVIEW DIGEST. (US/0006-7326). H W Wilson Company, 950 University Avenue, Bronx NY 10452. **Tel** (800)367-6770, (718)588-8400, FAX (718)590-1617, telex 4990003 HWILSON. **3356**

BOOK REVIEW DIGEST. CD-ROM. (US/0006-7326). H W Wilson Company, 950 University Avenue, Bronx NY 10452. **Tel** (800)367-6770, (718)588-8400, FAX (718)590-1617, telex 4990003 HWILSON. **4821**

BOOK REVIEW INDEX. (US/0524-0581). Gale Research Inc., 835 Penobscot Building, 645 Griswold Street, Detroit MI 48226. **Tel** (800)877-GALE, (313)961-2242, FAX (313)961-6083, (800)414-5043, telex TWX 810-221-7086. **4821**

BOOKS AND PERIODICALS ONLINE. (US/0951-838X). Library Alliance, Inc., 264 Lexington Avenue, Suite 4-C North, New York NY 10016. **Tel** (212)685-5297, FAX (212)213-6055. **3257**

BOOKS IN PRINT (NEW YORK). (US/0068-0214). R R Bowker, A Reed Reference Publishing Company, Part of Reed International PLC, PO Box 31, 121 Chanlon Drive, New Providence NJ 07974. **Tel** (908)464-6800, (800)521-8110, FAX (908)665-6688, telex 138-755. **411**

BOOKS IN PRINT PLUS. (US/1062-5100). R R Bowker, A Reed Reference Publishing Company, Part of Reed International PLC, PO Box 31, 121 Chanlon Drive, New Providence NJ 07974. **Tel** (908)464-6800, (800)521-8110, FAX (908)665-6688, telex 138-755. **411**

BOOKS IN PRINT SUPPLEMENT. (US/0000-0310). R R Bowker, A Reed Reference Publishing Company, Part of Reed International PLC, PO Box 31, 121 Chanlon Drive, New Providence NJ 07974. **Tel** (908)464-6800, (800)521-8110, FAX (908)665-6688, telex 138-755. **411**

BOOKS IN PRINT WITH BOOK REVIEWS PLUS [COMPUTER FILE]. (US). R R Bowker Electronic Publishing, A Reed Reference Publishing Company, Part of Reed International PLC, 121 Chanlon Drive, New Providence NJ 07974. **Tel** (908)323-3288. **3197**

BOOKS IN SERIES. (US/0000-0906). R R Bowker, A Reed Reference Publishing Company, Part of Reed International PLC, PO Box 31, 121 Chanlon Drive, New Providence NJ 07974. **Tel** (908)464-6800, (800)521-8110, FAX (908)665-6688, telex 138-755. **4826**

BOOKS OUT-OF-PRINT. (US/0000-0736). R R Bowker, A Reed Reference Publishing Company, Part of Reed International PLC, PO Box 31, 121 Chanlon Drive, New Providence NJ 07974. **Tel** (908)464-6800, (800)521-8110, FAX (908)665-6688, telex 138-755. **4826**

BOSTON SPA SERIALS ON CD-ROM. (UK). British Library Document Supply Centre, Boston Spa, Wetherby West Yorkshire LS23 7BQ England. **Tel** 0937 546060, FAX 0937 546333, telex 557381. **411**

BOTANICAL BULLETIN OF ACADEMIA SINICA. (CH/0006-8063). Institute of Botany, Academia Sinica, Nankang Taipei 11529 Taiwan. **Tel** 886-2-782-1605, FAX 886-2-7827954. **503**

BOWKER ANNUAL LIBRARY AND BOOK TRADE ALMANAC, THE. (US). R R Bowker, A Reed Reference Publishing Company, Part of Reed International PLC, PO Box 31, 121 Chanlon Drive, New Providence NJ 07974. **Tel** (908)464-6800, (800)521-8110, FAX (908)665-6688, telex 138-755. **3197**

BOWKER'S COMPLETE VIDEO DIRECTORY. (US/1051-290X). R R Bowker, A Reed Reference Publishing Company, Part of Reed International PLC, PO Box 31, 121 Chanlon Drive, New Providence NJ 07974. **Tel** (908)464-6800, (800)521-8110, FAX (908)665-6688, telex 138-755. **4378**

BRIGHAM YOUNG UNIVERSITY LAW REVIEW. (US/0360-151X). Brigham Young University / Law School Accounting, 358B JRCB, Provo UT 84602. **Tel** (801)378-6600, FAX (801)378-2188. **2943**

BRITISH EDUCATION INDEX. (UK/0007-0637). University of Leeds, Publications Office, Leeds LS2 9JT England. **Tel** 011 44 113 2335524, telex 556473. **1793**

BRITISH HUMANITIES INDEX. (UK/0007-0815). Bowker Saur Ltd., A Reed Reference Publishing Company, Part of Reed International PLC, 59-60 Grosvenor Street, London WIX 9DA England. **Tel** 011 44 71 4935841, FAX 011 44 71 4991590. **2857**

BRITISH NATIONAL BIBLIOGRAPHY. (UK/0007-1544). British Library / Bibliographic Service, Boston Spa, Wetherby West Yorkshire LS23 7BQ England. **Tel** 011 44 937 546160, FAX 011 44 937 546586, telex 557381. **3257**

BUILDINGS (CEDAR RAPIDS. 1947). (US/0007-3725). Stamats Communications Inc., 427 Sixth Avenue Southeast, Cedar Rapids IA 52406. **Tel** (319)364-6167, FAX (319)365-5421. **605**

BULLETIN OF THE ATOMIC SCIENTISTS. (US/0096-3402). Educational Foundation for Nuclear Science, 6042 South Kimbark Avenue, Chicago IL 60637. **Tel** (312)702-2555, FAX (312)702-0725. **5091**

BUSINESS ASAP [COMPUTER FILE]. (US). Information Access Company, 362 Lakeside Drive, Foster City CA 94404. **Tel** (800)227-8431. **726**

BUSINESS DATELINE. (US). University Microfilms International, 300 North Zeeb Road, Ann Arbor MI 48106-1346. **Tel** (313)761-4700, (800)521-0600 Exts. 2490, 2491, FAX (313)973-1540. **727**

BUSINESS ECONOMICS (CLEVELAND, OHIO). (US/0007-666X). NABE / National Association of Business Economists, 1233 20th Street NW Suite 505, Washington DC 20036. **Tel** (202)463-6223. **1466**

BUSINESS HISTORY. (UK/0007-6791). Frank Cass & Company Ltd, Newbury House, 890-900 Eastern Avenue, Newbury Park, Ilford, Essex IG2 7HH United Kingdom. **Tel** 011 44 81 599 8866, FAX 011 44 81 599 0984, telex 897719. **648**

BUSINESS INDEX. (US/0273-3684). Information Access Company, 362 Lakeside Drive, Foster City CA 94404. **Tel** (800)227-8431. **727**

BUSINESS INDICATORS. CD-ROM. (US). Slater Hall Information Products, 1301 Pennsylvania Avenue Northwest, Washington DC 20004. **Tel** (202)393-2666. **1550**

BUSINESS MEXICO. (MX/0187-1455). American Chamber of Commerce of Mexico, Lucerna 78/ Col Juarez, Mexico DF 06600 Mexico. **Tel** 011 52 5 7243826, or 7243800, FAX 011 52 5 7032911, telex 1771300. **650**

BUSINESS PERIODICALS INDEX. (US/0007-6961). H W Wilson Company, 950 University Avenue, Bronx NY 10452. **Tel** (800)367-6770, (718)588-8400, FAX (718)590-1617, telex 4990003 HWILSON. **727**

BUSINESS PERIODICALS INDEX. CD-ROM. (US/0007-6961). H W Wilson Company, 950 University Avenue, Bronx NY 10452. **Tel** (800)367-6770, (718)588-8400, FAX (718)590-1617, telex 4990003 HWILSON. **727**

BUSINESS SOURCE. [COMPUTER FILE]. (US). EBSCO Publishing / Boston, 83 Pine Street, Peabody MA 01960. **Tel** (800)653-2726 North America, (508)535-8500, FAX (508)535-8545. **727**

BUSINESS WHO'S WHO OF AUSTRALIA, THE. (AT/0068-4503). Riddell Information Services Pty Limited, PO Box 3942, Sydney New South Wales, 2001 Australia. **Tel** 11 61 23682100, FAX 11 61 23682150, telex 126736. **727**

BUSINESS YELLOW PAGES OF AMERICA ON CD-ROM. (CN). Innotech Inc, 2001 Sheppard Avenue East 118, North York, Ontario M2J 4Z7 Canada. **Tel** (416)492-3838. **654**

BUTLLETI OFICIAL DEL PARLAMENT DE CATALUNYA. (SP). Servei de Publicacions del Parlament de Catalunya, Palau del Parlament Parc de la Ciutadella, Barcelona 08003 Catalonia Spain. **Tel** (93)300-6413, FAX (93)300-8962, telex 97-684. **4635**

C-LECT. (US). Chronicle Guidance Publications Inc., PO Box 1190, Moravia NY 13118. **Tel** (315)497-0330. **1813**

C LIBRARY. CD-ROM. (US). Alde Publishing, PO Box 39326, Minneapolis MN 55396. **Tel** (612)474-3755. **1276**

C.U.S.I.P. DIRECTORY. CORPORATE DIRECTORY. (US/0091-3804). Standard & Poor's Corporation, 25 Broadway, New York NY 10004. **Tel** (212)208-8775. **893**

C USER'S GROUP LIBRARY DIRECTORY, THE. (US). C Users' Group, 1601 West 23rd Street, Suite 200, Lawrence KS 66046. **Tel** (913)841-1631, FAX (913)841-2624. **1278**

C USERS JOURNAL, THE. (US/0898-9788). R & D Publications, 1601 West 23rd Street, Suite 200, Lawrence KS 66046. **Tel** (913)841-1631, FAX (913)841-2624. **1278**

C2C ABSTRACTS JAPAN. ANALYTICAL CHEMISTRY. (US/1049-1260). SCAN C2C Inc, Attn Carol G Heffernan Marketing Director, 500 E Street Southwest, Suite 800, 8th Floor, Washington DC 20024. **Tel** (202)863-3850, (800)525-3865, FAX (202)863-3855. **996**

C2C ABSTRACTS JAPAN. CERAMICS. (US/1049-1252). SCAN C2C Inc, Attn Carol G Heffernan Marketing Director, 500 E Street Southwest, Suite 800, 8th Floor, Washington DC 20024. **Tel** (202)863-3850, (800)525-3865, FAX (202)863-3855. **2595**

C2C ABSTRACTS JAPAN. CHEMICAL ENGINEERING. (US/1049-1279). SCAN C2C Inc, Attn Carol G Heffernan Marketing Director, 500 E Street Southwest, Suite 800, 8th Floor, Washington DC 20024. **Tel** (202)863-3850, (800)525-3865, FAX (202)863-3855. **996**

C2C ABSTRACTS JAPAN. CRYSTALLOGRAPHY. (US/1049-1287). SCAN C2C Inc, Attn Carol G Heffernan Marketing Director, 500 E Street Southwest, Suite 800, 8th Floor, Washington DC 20024. **Tel** (202)863-3850, (800)525-3865, FAX (202)863-3855. **996**

C2C ABSTRACTS JAPAN. HYDROCARBONS. (US/1049-1295). SCAN C2C Inc, Attn Carol G Heffernan Marketing Director, 500 E Street Southwest, Suite 800, 8th Floor, Washington DC 20024. **Tel** (202)863-3850, (800)525-3865, FAX (202)863-3855. **996**

C2C ABSTRACTS JAPAN. INORGANIC CHEMISTRY. (US/1049-1309). SCAN C2C Inc, Attn Carol G Heffernan Marketing Director, 500 E Street Southwest, Suite 800, 8th Floor, Washington DC 20024. **Tel** (202)863-3850, (800)525-3865, FAX (202)863-3855. **996**

C2C ABSTRACTS JAPAN. MATERIALS SCIENCES. (US/1049-1317). SCAN C2C Inc, Attn Carol G Heffernan Marketing Director, 500 E Street Southwest, Suite 800, 8th Floor, Washington DC 20024. **Tel** (202)863-3850, (800)525-3865, FAX (202)863-3855. **5174**

C2C ABSTRACTS JAPAN. METALS. (US/1049-1384). SCAN C2C Inc, Attn Carol G Heffernan Marketing Director, 500 E Street Southwest, Suite 800, 8th Floor, Washington DC 20024. **Tel** (202)863-3850, (800)525-3865, FAX (202)863-3855. **4025**

C2C ABSTRACTS JAPAN. ORGANIC CHEMISTRY. (US/1049-1325). SCAN C2C Inc, Attn Carol G Heffernan Marketing Director, 500 E Street Southwest, Suite 800, 8th Floor, Washington DC 20024. **Tel** (202)863-3850, (800)525-3865, FAX (202)863-3855. **1040**

C2C ABSTRACTS JAPAN. PHYSICAL CHEMISTRY. (US/1049-1333). SCAN C2C Inc, Attn Carol G Heffernan Marketing Director, 500 E Street Southwest, Suite 800, 8th Floor, Washington DC 20024. **Tel** (202)863-3850, (800)525-3865, FAX (202)863-3855. **996**

C2C ABSTRACTS JAPAN. PLASTICS. (US/1049-1341). SCAN C2C Inc, Attn Carol G Heffernan Marketing Director, 500 E Street Southwest, Suite 800, 8th Floor, Washington DC 20024. **Tel** (202)863-3850, (800)525-3865, FAX (202)863-3855. **4461**

C2C ABSTRACTS JAPAN. POLYMER CHEMISTRY. (US/1049-135X). SCAN C2C Inc, Attn Carol G Heffernan Marketing Director, 500 E Street Southwest, Suite 800, 8th Floor, Washington DC 20024. **Tel** (202)863-3850, (800)525-3865, FAX (202)863-3855. **996**

C2C ABSTRACTS JAPAN. SURFACE CHEMISTRY. (US/1049-1368). SCAN C2C Inc, Attn Carol G Heffernan Marketing Director, 500 E Street Southwest, Suite 800, 8th Floor, Washington DC 20024. **Tel** (202)863-3850, (800)525-3865, FAX (202)863-3855. **997**

C2C ABSTRACTS JAPAN. TEXTILES. (US/1049-1376). SCAN C2C Inc, Attn Carol G Heffernan Marketing Director, 500 E Street Southwest, Suite 800, 8th Floor, Washington DC 20024. **Tel** (202)863-3850, (800)525-3865, FAX (202)863-3855. **5360**

C2C CURRENTS JAPAN. CHEMISTRY. (US/1049-1228). SCAN C2C Inc, Attn Carol G Heffernan Marketing Director, 500 E Street Southwest, Suite 800, 8th Floor, Washington DC 20024. **Tel** (202)863-3850, (800)525-3865, FAX (202)863-3855. **964**

C2C CURRENTS JAPAN. COMPUTERS. (US/1049-1244). SCAN C2C Inc, Attn Carol G Heffernan Marketing Director, 500 E Street Southwest, Suite 800, 8th Floor, Washington DC 20024. **Tel** (202)863-3850, (800)525-3865, FAX (202)863-3855. **1172**

C2C CURRENTS JAPAN. ELECTRONICS. (US/1049-1236). SCAN C2C Inc, Attn Carol G Heffernan Marketing Director, 500 E Street Southwest, Suite 800, 8th Floor, Washington DC 20024. **Tel** (202)863-3850, (800)525-3865, FAX (202)863-3855. **2037**

C2C CURRENTS JAPAN. MATERIALS. (US/1049-121X). SCAN C2C Inc, Attn Carol G Heffernan Marketing Director, 500 E Street Southwest, Suite 800, 8th Floor, Washington DC 20024. **Tel** (202)863-3850, (800)525-3865, FAX (202)863-3855. **654**

C3I FORECAST. (US). Forecast International / DMS Inc., 22 Commerce Road, Newtown CT 06470. **Tel** (203)426-0800, FAX (203)426-1964, telex 467615. **4038**

CA QUICK SEARCH [COMPUTER FILE]. (US). American Concrete Institute, PO Box 19150, Detroit MI 48219. **Tel** (313)532-2600. **2002**

CAB ABSTRACTS ON CD-ROM [COMPUTER FILE]. (US). CAB International Centre, Wallingford, Oxon OX10 8DE United Kingdom. **Tel** 44 491 832111, FAX 44 491 833508, telex 847964 (COMAGG G). **70**

CAD/CAM ABSTRACTS. (US/0882-1437). Techgnosis Ltd., Blade House, Battersea Road, Cheshire SK4 3EA England. **Tel** 011 44 61 442 2639, FAX 011 44 61 443 1162. **1231**

CADSCAN. (UK). SCAN Journals, 42 Weymouth Street, London W1N 3LQ England. **Tel** 071-499-8425, FAX 071-4931555, telex 261286. **3999**

CALCIFIED TISSUE ABSTRACTS. (UK/0008-0586). Cambridge Scientific Abstracts, 7200 Wisconsin Avenue, #601, Bethesda MD 20814-4823. **Tel** (301)961-6750, (800)843-7751, FAX (301)961-6720. **3655**

CALIFORNIA BANKRUPTCY JOURNAL. (US/1047-0743). California Bankruptcy Forum, 1278 Glenneyre 101, Laguna Beach CA 92651. **Tel** (714)363-6643. **782**

... CALIFORNIA MUSIC DIRECTORY, THE. (US). Music Industry Resources, PO Box 190, San Anselmo CA 94960. **Tel** (415)457-0215. **4107**

CALLALOO. (US/0161-2492). Johns Hopkins University Press, 2715 North Charles Street, Baltimore MD 21218-4319. **Tel** (410)516-6987, FAX (410)516-6968. **3371**

CAMBRIDGE SCIENTIFIC BIOCHEMISTRY ABSTRACTS: PART 1 BIOLOGICAL MEMBRANES. (US/8756-7504). Cambridge Scientific Abstracts, 7200 Wisconsin Avenue, #601, Bethesda MD 20814-4823. **Tel** (301)961-6750, (800)843-7751, FAX (301)961-6720. **484**

CAMBRIDGE SCIENTIFIC BIOCHEMISTRY ABSTRACTS: PART 2 NUCLEIC ACIDS. (US/8756-7512). Cambridge Scientific Abstracts, 7200 Wisconsin Avenue, #601, Bethesda MD 20814-4823. **Tel** (301)961-6750, (800)843-7751, FAX (301)961-6720. **477**

CAMBRIDGE SCIENTIFIC BIOCHEMISTRY ABSTRACTS: PART 3 AMINO-ACIDS, PEPTIDES & PROTEINS. (US/8756-7520). Cambridge Scientific Abstracts, 7200 Wisconsin Avenue, #601, Bethesda MD 20814-4823. **Tel** (301)961-6750, (800)843-7751, FAX (301)961-6720. **484**

CAMPING MAGAZINE, THE. (US/0740-4131). American Camping Association, 5000 State Road 67 North, Martinsville IN 46151-7902. **Tel** (317)342-8456, (800)428-2267, FAX (317)342-2065. **4870**

CANADA-UNITED STATES LAW JOURNAL. (US/0163-6391). Case Western Reserve University / School of Law, 11075 East Boulevard, Cleveland OH 44106. **Tel** (216)368-3304, FAX (216)368-6144. **3125**

CANADIAN EDUCATION INDEX. (CN/0008-3453). Micromedia Limited, 20 Victoria Street, Toronto Ontario M5C 2N8 Canada. **Tel** (416)362-5211, (800)387-2689, FAX (416)362-6161, telex 06524668. **1793**

CANADIAN LAW LIST (1951). (CN/0084-8573). Canada Law Book Inc., 240 Edward Street, Aurora Ontario L4G 3S9 Canada. **Tel** (800)263-3269, (905)841-6472, FAX (905)841-5085. **3139**

CANADIAN PERIODICAL INDEX (1964). (CN/0008-4719). Globe & Mail, 444 Front Street West, Toronto Ontario M5V 2S9 Canada. **Tel** (416)585-5000, FAX (416)585-5249. **412**

CANADIAN YEARBOOK OF INTERNATIONAL LAW. (CN/0069-0058). University of British Columbia Press, 6344 Memorial Road, Vancouver British Columbia V6T 1Z2 Canada. **Tel** (604)228-3259, FAX (604)228-6083. **3125**

CANCER (CD-ROM ED.). (US/1045-7410). Creative Multimedia Corporation, 513 Northwest Avenue, Suite 400, Portland OR 97209. **Tel** (503)241-4351. **3810**

CAREER OPPORTUNITIES. CD-ROM. (US). Quanta Press, Inc., 1313 Fifth Street Southeast, Suite 208C, Minneapolis MN 55414. **Tel** (612)379-3956, FAX (612)623-4570. **4202**

CASE WESTERN RESERVE LAW REVIEW. (US/0008-7262). Case Western Reserve University / School of Law, 11075 East Boulevard, Cleveland OH 44106. **Tel** (216)368-3304, FAX (216)368-6144. **2949**

CATALOGER'S DESKTOP. (US). Library of Congress / Cataloging Distribution Service, Washington DC 20541-5017. **Tel** (800)255-3666, (202)707-6100, FAX (202)707-1334. **412**

CATALOGO DEI LIBRI IN COMMERCIO: AUTORI. (IT). Editrice Bibliografica, Viale Vittoria Veneto 24, 20124 Milan Italy. **Tel** 011 39 2 29006965, FAX 011 39 2 654624. **412**

CATALOGO DEI LIBRI IN COMMERCIO: SOGGETTI. (IT). Editrice Bibliografica, Viale Vittoria Veneto 24, 20124 Milan Italy. **Tel** 011 39 2 29006965, FAX 011 39 2 654624. **412**

CATALOGO DEI LIBRI IN COMMERCIO: TITOLI. (IT). Editrice Bibliografica, Viale Vittoria Veneto 24, 20124 Milan Italy. **Tel** 011 39 2 29006965, FAX 011 39 2 654624. **412**

CATALOGUE AFNOR. (FR/0750-7046). Afnor Norex, Tour Europe Cedex 7, 92049 Paris la Defense France. **Tel** 011 33 1 42915555, FAX 011 33 1 42915656. **4030**

CATALOGUE OF BRITISH OFFICIAL PUBLICATIONS NOT PUBLISHED BY HMSO. (UK/0260-5619). Chadwyck-Healey Limited, The Quorum Barnwell Road, Cambridge CB5 8SW England. **Tel** 011 44 223 215512, telex 9312102281 CH G. **412**

CATALOGUE OF UNITED KINGDOM OFFICIAL PUBLICATIONS [COMPUTER FILE] : UKOP. (UK). Chadwyck-Healey Limited, The Quorum Barnwell Road, Cambridge CB5 8SW England. **Tel** 011 44 223 215512, telex 9312102281 CH G. **4637**

CATCHWORD

Serials available on CD-ROM

CATCHWORD AND TRADE NAME INDEX : CATNI. (UK). Bowker Saur Ltd., A Reed Reference Publishing Company, Part of Reed International PLC, 59-60 Grosvenor Street, London W1X 9DA England. Tel 011 44 71 4935841, FAX 011 44 71 4991590. **5174**

CATHOLIC WORLD (1989), THE. (US/1042-3494). Paulist Press, 997 McArthur Boulevard, Mahwah NJ 07430. Tel (201)825-7300, FAX (201)825-8345. **5027**

CD BOOK. (GW). Wer Liefert Was GmbH, Normannenweg 18 20, 20537 Hamburg Germany. Tel 011 49 40 2515080. **949**

CD COREWORKS. CD-ROM. (US). Roth Publishing Inc, PO Box 406, Great Neck NY 11022. Tel (516)466-3676, (800)899-7684, FAX (516)829-7746. **3373**

CD-DIS (ARLINGTON, VA.). (US/1061-6691). LTS Corporation, 1500 Wilson Blvd., Suite 1010, Arlington VA 22209-2404. **2908**

CD MARKETING. (GW). Wer Liefert Was GmbH, Normannenweg 18 20, 20537 Hamburg Germany. Tel 011 49 40 2515080. **922**

CD-ROM DEVELOPERS LAB. CD-ROM. (US). Software Mart Incorporated, 3933 Steck Street, Suite B115, Austin TX 78759. Tel (512)346-7887. **1276**

CD-ROM DIRECTORY ON DISC, THE. (US/1062-6891). Task Force / England, Pro Libra Ltd, 22 Peters Lane, London EC1M 6DS England. Tel 011 44 71 2515522. **1276**

CD-ROM DIRECTORY, THE. (UK). Task Force Pro Libra Ltd, 22 Peters Lane, London EC1M 6DS England. Tel 01-251-5522, FAX 01-251-8318. **1174**

CD-ROM ENDUSER. (US/1042-8623). Helgerson Associates, 6609 Rosecraft Place, Falls Church VA 22043. Tel (703)237-0682, FAX (703)532-5447. **1174**

CD-ROM HANDBOOK. (US/1059-5260). EBSCO Publishing / Boston, 83 Pine Street, Peabody MA 01960. Tel (800)653-2726 North America, (508)535-8500, FAX (508)535-8545. **3201**

CD-ROM LIBRARIAN. (US/0893-9934). Mecklermedia Corporation, 11 Ferry Lane West, Westport CT 06880. Tel (203)226-6967, (800)632-5537, FAX (203)454-5840. **1174**

CD-ROM SOURCEDISC. (US). Helgerson Associates, 6609 Rosecraft Place, Falls Church VA 22043. Tel (703)237-0682, FAX (703)532-5447. **413**

CD-ROM SOURCEDISC [COMPUTER FILE], THE. (US). Helgerson Associates, 6609 Rosecraft Place, Falls Church VA 22043. Tel (703)237-0682, FAX (703)532-5447. **1276**

CD-ROMS IN PRINT (CD-ROM VERSION). (US/1052-2638). Mecklermedia Corporation, 11 Ferry Lane West, Westport CT 06880. Tel (203)226-6967, (800)632-5537, FAX (203)454-5840. **1276**

CD WORLDLIBRARY : THE INTERACTIVE BIBLICAL LIBRARY. CD-ROM. (US). CDWord Library Inc, PO Box 803133, Dallas TX 75380-3133. Tel (214)770-2414, FAX (214)770-2345. **4943**

CDMARC BIBLIOGRAPHIC. (US/1054-3996). Library of Congress / Cataloging Distribution Service, Washington DC 20541-5017. Tel (800)255-3666, (202)707-6100, FAX (202)707-1334. **413**

CDMARC NAMES. (US/1041-2964). Library of Congress / Cataloging Distribution Service, Washington DC 20541-5017. Tel (800)255-3666, (202)707-6100, FAX (202)707-1334. **1174**

CDMARC SERIALS. (US/1063-8784). Library of Congress / Cataloging Distribution Service, Washington DC 20541-5017. Tel (800)255-3666, (202)707-6100, FAX (202)707-1334. **3201**

CDMARC SUBJECTS. (US/1041-2956). Library of Congress / Cataloging Distribution Service, Washington DC 20541-5017. Tel (800)255-3666, (202)707-6100, FAX (202)707-1334. **3201**

CDMARC SUBJECTS. (US/1041-2956). Library of Congress / Cataloging Distribution Service, Washington DC 20541-5017. Tel (800)255-3666, (202)707-6100, FAX (202)707-1334. **3201**

CDP FILE [COMPUTER FILE] / NATIONAL CENTER FOR CHRONIC DISEASE PREVENTION AND HEALTH PROMOTION. (US). Technical Information Services Branch, National Center for Chronic Disease Prevention and Health Promotion, 1600 Clifton Road, Rhodes Building-Mail Stop K-13, Atlanta GA 30333. **4771**

CERAMIC ABSTRACTS. (US/0095-9960). American Ceramic Society, 735 Ceramic Place, Westerville OH 43081-8720. Tel (614)890-4700, (614)794-5890, FAX (614)899-6109. **2595**

CERAMIC ABSTRACTS CD-ROM. (US/1056-3490). American Ceramic Society, 735 Ceramic Place, Westerville OH 43081-8720. Tel (614)890-4700, (614)794-5890, FAX (614)899-6109. **2587**

CHEMICAL AGE OF INDIA. (II/0009-2320). Technical Press Publications, 5-1 Convent Street, Colaba, Bombay 400 039 India. Tel 2021156, 2021446, 2026361, 3479 CHEM IN, telex 11-3479 CHEM IN. **968**

CHEMISTRY CITATION INDEX. (US/1057-6088). Institute for Scientific Information, 3501 Market Street, Philadelphia PA 19104. Tel (215)386-0100, (800)523-1850, FAX (215)386-6362, telex 84-5305. **1011**

CHEMORECEPTION ABSTRACTS. (US/0300-1261). Cambridge Scientific Abstracts, 7200 Wisconsin Avenue, #601, Bethesda MD 20814-4823. Tel (301)961-6750, (800)843-7751, FAX (301)961-6720. **477**

CHICAGO JOURNAL OF THEORETICAL COMPUTER SCIENCE. (US). Massachusetts Institute of Technology (MIT) Press, 55 Hayward Street, Cambridge MA 02142-1399. Tel (617)253-2889, (617)625-8481, FAX (617)258-6779. **1174**

CHICAGO-KENT LAW REVIEW. (US/0009-3599). Chicago Kent College of Law, 565 West Adams Street, Chicago IL 60661. Tel (312)906-5190, FAX (312)906-5280. **2949**

CHICAGO TRIBUNE INDEX. (US/0731-9045). **5814**

CHICANO DATABASE. (US/1056-2516). Chicano Studies Library Publications, University of California, 3404 Dwinelle Hall, Berkeley CA 94720. Tel (510)642-3859, FAX (510)642-6456. **2258**

CHICANO DATABASE ON CD-ROM. (US/1056-2516). Chicano Studies Library Publications, University of California, 3404 Dwinelle Hall, Berkeley CA 94720. Tel (510)642-3859, FAX (510)642-6456. **2258**

CHICANO INDEX, THE. (US/1044-3487). Chicano Studies Library, University of California at Berkeley, 510 Barrows Hall #2570, Berkeley CA 94720. Tel (510)642-3859. **2635**

CHILDREN'S BOOKS IN PRINT (NEW YORK). (US/0069-3480). R R Bowker, A Reed Reference Publishing Company, Part of Reed International PLC, PO Box 31, 121 Chanlon Drive, New Providence NJ 07974. Tel (908)464-6800, (800)521-8110, FAX (908)665-6688, telex 138-755. **1072**

CHILDREN'S BOOKS IN PRINT. SUBJECT GUIDE. (US). R R Bowker, A Reed Reference Publishing Company, Part of Reed International PLC, PO Box 31, 121 Chanlon Drive, New Providence NJ 07974. Tel (908)464-6800, (800)521-8110, FAX (908)665-6688, telex 138-755. **3458**

CHINESE SCIENCE BULLETIN. (CC/1001-6538). Science Press, 16 Donghuangchenggen North Street, Beijing 100707, People's Republic of China. Tel 011 86 1 4019821, 011 86 1 4010642, FAX 011 86 1 4012180, 011 86 1 4019810, telex 210147. **5094**

CHING FENG (ENGLISH EDITION). (HK/0009-4668). Christian Study Centre on China Religion and Culture, Sixth Floor Kiu Kin Mansion, 566 Nathan Road, Kowloon Hong Kong. Tel 011 852 3 7703310, FAX 011 852 3 7826869. **4943**

CHRISTIAN BRETHREN REVIEW : THE JOURNAL OF THE CHRISTIAN BRETHREN RESEARCH FELLOWSHIP. (UK/0306-7467). Paternoster Press, A division of Send the Light Ltd., PO Box 300, Kingstown Broadway, Cumbria CA3 0QS England. Tel 011 44 228 512512, FAX 011 44 228 514949. **4944**

CHRISTIAN HISTORY (WORCESTER, PA.). (US/0891-9666). Christianity Today Inc., 465 Gundersen Drive, Carol Stream IL 60188. Tel (708)260-6200. **4945**

CHRISTIAN SCIENCE MONITOR (1983), THE. (US/0882-7729). Christian Science Publishing Society, One Norway Street, Boston MA 02115. Tel (617)450-2678, (617)450-2504. **5688**

CHRONICLE OF LATIN AMERICAN ECONOMIC AFFAIRS. (US/1054-8874). University of New Mexico / Latin American Institute, Latin America Data Base, 801 Yale NE, Albuquerque NM 87131-1016. Tel (505)277-6839, FAX (505)277-5989. **1469**

CHUAN KUO HSIN SHU MU. (CC/0578-073X). **4821**

CIA WORLD FACTBOOK. CD-ROM. (US). Quanta Press, Inc., 1313 Fifth Street Southeast, Suite 208C, Minneapolis MN 55414. Tel (612)379-3956, FAX (612)623-4570. **4468**

CIFAR'S GLOBAL COMPANY HANDBOOK. (US/1060-8710). CIFAR, 3490 US Route 1, Princeton NJ 08540. Tel (609)520-9333, FAX (609)520-0905. **657**

CIJE ON DISC. (US/1073-1113). Oryx Press, 4041 North Central Avenue, #700, Phoenix AZ 85012-3397. Tel (800)279-ORYX, (602)265-2651, FAX (602)265-6250, (800)279-4663, (800)279-6799. **1793**

CIMARRON REVIEW. (US/0009-6849). Cimarron Review, 205 Morrill Hall, Oklahoma State University, Stillwater OK 74078-0135. Tel (405)744-9476, FAX (405)744-6326. **3461**

CINAHL (PEABODY, MASS.). (US). EBSCO Publishing / Boston, 83 Pine Street, Peabody MA 01960. Tel (800)653-2726 North America, (508)535-8500, FAX (508)535-8545. **3655**

CINE BULLES. (CN/0820-8921). Association des Cinemas Paralleles du Quebec, 4545 Pierre de Coubertin CP 1000 Succursale M, Montreal Quebec H1V 3R2 Canada. Tel (514)252-3021, FAX (514)251-8038, telex 95-829647. **4065**

CIS INDEX TO PUBLICATIONS OF THE UNITED STATES CONGRESS. (US/0007-8514). Congressional Information Service Inc, 4520 East-West Highway, Suite 800, Bethesda MD 20814-3389. Tel (800)638-8380, (301)654-1550, FAX (301)654-4033, telex 292386 CIS UR. **4697**

CITAS LATINOAMERICANAS EN CIENCIAS SOCIALES Y HUMANIDADES : CLASE. (MX/0185-0903). Centro de Informacion Cientifica y Humanistica, Apartado 70 392, Mexico 20 DF Mexico. Tel 011 52 5 5480208, 011 52 5 6223964. **5195**

CITIS CD-ROM. (IE). CITIS Ltd, 2 Rosemount Terrace, Blackrock Dublin Ireland. Tel 3531-886227, FAX 3531-885971, telex 30259 MSCH ET. **607**

CIVIL AIRCRAFT FORECAST. (US). Forecast International / DMS Inc., 22 Commerce Road, Newtown CT 06470. Tel (203)426-0800, FAX (203)426-1964, telex 467615. **16**

CLASSICA ET MEDIAEVALIA. (DK). Museum Tusculanum Press, University of Copenhagen, Njalsgade 94, DK-2300 Copenhagen D Denmark. Tel 011 45 31542211. **1075**

CLIMATE DYNAMICS. (GW/0930-7575). Springer-Verlag GmbH & Company KG, Heidelberger Platz 3, D 14197 Berlin Germany. Tel 011 49 30 8207223, FAX 011 49 30 8214091, telex 183 319 SPBLN D. **1421**

CLINICAL AND DIAGNOSTIC LABORATORY IMMUNOLOGY (CD-ROM). (US/1071-4138). American Society for Microbiology, 1325 Massachusetts Avenue Northwest, Washington DC 20005-4171. Tel (202)737-3600, FAX (202)737-0367. **3667**

CLINICAL AND DIAGNOSTIC LABORATORY IMMUNOLOGY (PRINT). (US/1071-412X). American Society for Microbiology, 1325 Massachusetts Avenue Northwest, Washington DC 20005-4171. Tel (202)737-3600, FAX (202)737-0367. **3667**

CLINICAL LABORATORY PRODUCT COMPARISON SYSTEM. (US). ECRI Emergency Care Research Institute, 5200 Butler Pike, Plymouth Meeting PA 19462. Tel (215)825-6000, FAX (215)834-1275, telex 510-660-8023. **3565**

CLINICAL MICROBIOLOGY REVIEWS. (US/0893-8512). American Society for Microbiology, 1325 Massachusetts Avenue Northwest, Washington DC 20005-4171. Tel (202)737-3600, FAX (202)737-0367. **561**

CLINMED-CD. (US). Silverplatter Information Inc., 100 River Ridge Drive, Norwood MA 02062. Tel (800)343-0064, (617)769-2599, FAX (617)235-1715. **3567**

CLOTHING AND TEXTILE ARTS INDEX, THE. (US/0887-2937). Clothing & Textile Arts Index, PO Box 1300, Monument CO 80132. Tel (719)488-3716. **1083**

COATES ART REVIEW: IMPRESSIONISM. CD-ROM. (US). Quanta Press, Inc., 1313 Fifth Street Southeast, Suite 208C, Minneapolis MN 55414. Tel (612)379-3956, FAX (612)623-4570. **347**

CODE OF FEDERAL REGULATIONS. (US). Superintendent of Documents, US Government Printing Office, Washington DC 20402. Tel (202)275-3328, FAX (202)786-2377. **4639**

COLLECTIVE CATALOGUE BELGIUM : CCB. CD-ROM. (BE). Brepols NV, Steenwes Op Tielen 68, B-2300 Turnhout Belgium. Tel 011 32 14 402500, FAX 011 32 14 428919. **413**

COLLEGE ADMISSIONS INDEX OF MAJORS & SPORTS. (US). Wintergreen Orchard House Inc, 29 Cherokee Street, New Orleans LA 70118. Tel 800 321-9479, FAX (504)866-8710. **1855**

COLLEGE LITERATURE. (US/0093-3139). College Literature, 544 New Main, West Chester University, West Chester PA 19383. Tel (215)436-2901, FAX (215)436-3540. **3376**

COMMUNICATION ABSTRACTS. (US/0162-2811). SAGE Periodical Press, 2455 Teller Road, Thousand Oaks CA 91320. Tel (805)499-0721, FAX (805)499-0871, telex 100799. **1124**

COMMUNICATIONS REGULATION. (US). Pike & Fischer Inc., 4600 East-West Highway, Suite 200, Bethesda MD 20814-1438. Tel (301)654-6262, FAX (301)654-6297. **1152**

COMPACT CAMBRIDGE LIFE SCIENCES COLLECTION [COMPUTER FILE]. (US). Cambridge Scientific Abstracts, 7200 Wisconsin Avenue, #601, Bethesda MD 20814-4823. Tel (301)961-6750, (800)843-7751, FAX (301)961-6720. **5095**

COMPACT CAMBRIDGE MEDLINE [COMPUTER FILE]. (US). Cambridge Scientific Abstracts, 7200 Wisconsin Avenue, #601, Bethesda MD 20814-4823. Tel (301)961-6750, (800)843-7751, FAX (301)961-6720. **3567**

COMPACT D/SEC. (US/1062-8525). Disclosure Incorporated, 5161 River Road, Bethesda MD 20816. Tel (800)638-8241. **658**

COMPANIES INTERNATIONAL [COMPUTER FILE]. (US). Gale Research Inc., 835 Penobscot Building, 645 Griswold Street, Detroit MI 48226. Tel (800)877-GALE, (313)961-2242, FAX (313)961-6083, (800)414-5043, telex TWX 810-221-7086. **658**

COMPENDEX PLUS. (US/1063-8709). Dialog Information Services, 3460 Hillview Avenue, Palo Alto CA 94304. Tel (415)858-4240, (800)334-2564. **2003**

COMPLETE DIRECTORY OF LARGE PRINT BOOKS & SERIALS, THE. (US/0000-1120). R R Bowker, A Reed Reference Publishing Company, Part of Reed International PLC, PO Box 31, 121 Chanlon Drive, New Providence NJ 07974. Tel (908)464-6800, (800)521-8110, FAX (908)665-6688, telex 138-755. **4828**

COMPREHENSIVE MEDLINE/EBSCO CD-ROM. (US/1040-4074). National Library of Medicine, 8600 Rockville Pike, Bethesda MD 20894. Tel (301)496-6308. **3567**

COMPUTER & CONTROL ABSTRACTS. (UK/0036-8113). Institution of Electrical Engineers / IEE, Michael Faraday House, Six Hills Way, Stevenage Herts SG1 2AY UK. Tel 011 44 438 313311, FAX 011 44 438 742840, telex 825578 IEESTV G. **1208**

COMPUTER REVIEW. (US/0093-416X). Computer Review, 19 Pleasant Street, Gloucester MA 01930. Tel (508)283-2100. **1264**

COMPUTER SELECT. (US/1062-8509). Computer Library, One Park Avenue, Fifth Floor, c/o Patrick Falco, New York NY 10016. Tel (212)503-4409, FAX (212)503-4414. **1284**

COMPUTING ARCHIVE. (US/1053-7856). ACM Association for Computing Machinery, 1515 Broadway, 17th Floor, New York NY 10036. Tel (212)869-7440, FAX (212)869-0481. **1180**

CONCORDIA JOURNAL. (US/0145-7233). Concordia Seminary, 801 de Mun Avenue, St Louis MO 63105. Tel (314)721-5934. **4949**

CONCRETE ABSTRACTS. (US/0045-8007). American Concrete Institute, PO Box 19150, Detroit MI 48219. Tel (313)532-2600. **2003**

CONGRESSIONAL MASTERFILE 2. (US/1064-4679). Congressional Information Service Inc, 4520 East-West Highway, Suite 800, Bethesda MD 20814-3389. Tel (202)638-8380, (301)654-1550, FAX (301)654-4033, telex 292386 CIS UR. **2955**

CONGRESSIONAL RECORD [COMPUTER FILE] : PROCEEDINGS AND DEBATES OF THE ... CONGRESS. (US). Superintendent of Documents, US Government Printing Office, Washington DC 20402. Tel (202)275-3328, FAX (202)786-2377. **2955**

CONGRESSIONAL STAFF DIRECTORY. (US/0589-3178). Staff Directories Ltd., PO Box 62, Mount Vernon VA 22121. Tel (703)739-0900, FAX (703)739-0234. **4640**

CONGRESSIONAL STAFF DIRECTORY. ADVANCE LOCATOR FOR CAPITOL HILL. (US/0069-8938). Staff Directories Ltd., PO Box 62, Mount Vernon VA 22121. Tel (703)739-0900, FAX (703)739-0234. **4640**

CONNECTIONS (PROVIDENCE, R.I.). (US/1051-6700). The Company of Science & Art Inc., 14 Imperial Place, Suite 203, Providence RI 02903. **1276**

CONSOLIDATED INDEX OF ARMY PUBLICATIONS AND BLANK FORMS [MICROFORM]. (US). US Department of Defense Department of the Army, The Pentagon, SAPA-CR, Room 3E718, Washington DC 20310. Tel (703)695-0363, FAX (703)693-5737. **4040**

CONSOLIDATED TREATIES & INTERNATIONAL AGREEMENTS. CURRENT DOCUMENT SERVICE, EUROPEAN COMMUNITY. (US/1059-8561). Oceana Publications, Inc., 75 Main Street, Dobbs Ferry NY 10522. Tel (914)693-1320, FAX (914)693-0402. **4519**

CONSTRUCTION INDEX. (US/0892-2047). ArchiText, 410 South Michigan Avenue, Suite 1008, Chicago IL 60605. Tel (312)939-3202, FAX (312)939-1020. **632**

CONSU/STATS I. CD-ROM. (US). Hopkins Technology, 421 Hazel Lane, Suite 120, Hopkins MN 55343. Tel (612)931-9376, FAX (612)931-9377. **1294**

CONSUMER HEALTH & NUTRITION INDEX. (US/0883-1963). Oryx Press, 4041 North Central Avenue, #700, Phoenix AZ 85012-3397. Tel (800)279-ORYX, (602)265-2651, FAX (602)265-6250, (800)279-4663, (800)279-6799. **4200**

CONSUMER REFERENCE DISC. (US/1053-1424). National Information Services Corp, 3100 St Paul Street, Wyman Towers, Suite 6, Baltimore MD 21218. Tel (410)243-0797, FAX (410)243-0982. **1295**

CONSUMER REPORTS. (US/0010-7174). Consumers Union, 101 Truman Avenue, Yonkers NY 10703. Tel (800)288-7898, (914)378-2000, FAX (914)378-2900. **1295**

CONSUMER REPORTS ON CD-ROM (ADVANCED USER'S ED.). (US/1053-1416). Consumer Reports Books, 9180 Le Saint Drive, Fairfield OH 45014. Tel (800)272-0722. **1471**

CONSUMER REPORTS ON CD-ROM (BEGINNER'S ED.). (US/1053-1408). Consumer Reports Books, 9180 Le Saint Drive, Fairfield OH 45014. Tel (800)272-0722. **1471**

CONSUMERS INDEX TO PRODUCT EVALUATIONS AND INFORMATION SOURCES. (US/0094-0534). Pierian Press, PO Box 1808, Ann Arbor MI 48106. Tel (313)434-5530, (800)678-2435, FAX (313)434-6409. **1300**

CONTEMPORARY AUTHORS. (US/0010-7468). Gale Research Inc., 835 Penobscot Building, 645 Griswold Street, Detroit MI 48226. Tel (800)877-GALE, (313)961-2242, FAX (313)961-6083, (800)414-5043, telex TWX 810-221-7086. **431**

CONTEMPORARY POLICY ISSUES. (US/0735-0007). Allen Press Inc., 810 East 10th Street, PO Box 1897, Lawrence KS 66044-8897. Tel (913)843-1221, (800)627-0629, FAX (913)843-1274. **1471**

CORE MEDLINE/EBSCO CD-ROM. (US/1040-4066). EBSCO Publishing / Boston, 83 Pine Street, Peabody MA 01960. Tel (800)653-2726 North America, (508)535-8500, FAX (508)535-8545. **3569**

CORPORATE DATABASE [COMPUTER FILE] / DATEXT. (US). Datext, Inc., 444 Washington Street, Woburn MA 01801. **661**

CORPORATE DIRECTORY OF U.S. PUBLIC COMPANIES, THE. (US/1059-7964). Walker's Western Research, 1650 Borel Place, Suite 130, San Mateo CA 94402. Tel (800)258-5737, (415)341-1110, FAX (415)341-2351. **661**

CORPORATE FINANCE BLUEBOOK, THE. (US/0740-2546). National Register Publishing Company Inc., PO Box 31, 121 Chanlon Road, New Providence NJ 07974. Tel (800)521-8110, (800)323-6772, FAX (908)665-6688. **784**

CORPORATE FINANCING WEEK - INSTITUTIONAL INVESTOR (FIRM). (US/1064-1912). Institutional Investor Inc., 488 Madison Avenue, New York NY 10022. Tel (212)303-3234, (212)303-3233, FAX (212)303-3353. **785**

CORPORATE TECHNOLOGY DIRECTORY. (US/0887-1930). Corporate Technology Information Services Inc, 12 Alfred Street, Suite 200, Woburn MA 01801-9998. Tel (617)932-3939, (800)333-8036, FAX (617)932-6335, telex 497-2961 CRPTECH. **3477**

CORROSION ABSTRACTS. (US/0010-9339). National Association of Corrosion Engineers, 1440 South Creek Drive, Houston TX 77084. Tel (713)492-0535, FAX (713)492-8254, telex 792310 NACE HOU. **2003**

COTTON AND TROPICAL FIBRES ABSTRACTS BIBLIOGRAPHY. (UK). CAB International Centre, Wallingford, Oxon OX10 8DE United Kingdom. Tel 44 491 832111, FAX 44 491 833508, telex 847964 (COMAGG G). **152**

COUNTRY PROFILE. SENEGAL/ THE ECONOMIST INTELLIGENCE UNIT. (UK). The Economist Intelligence Unit, 40 Duke Street, London W1A 1DW England. Tel 011 44 71 8301000. **1553**

COUNTRY PROFILE. THE GAMBIA, GUINEA-BISSAU, CAPE VERDE. (UK/0968-2422). The Economist Intelligence Unit, 40 Duke Street, London W1A 1DW England. Tel 011 44 71 8301000. **1554**

COUNTY AND CITY COMPENDIUM. CD-ROM. (US). Slater Hall Information Products, 1301 Pennsylvania Avenue Northwest, Washington DC 20004. Tel (202)393-2666. **4551**

COUNTY AND CITY DATA BOOK. (US/0082-9455). Superintendent of Documents, US Government Printing Office, Washington DC 20402. Tel (202)275-3328, FAX (202)786-2377. **2840**

COUNTY & CITY DATA BOOK (CD-ROM ED.). (US/1057-8781). US Department of Commerce, 14th Street & Constitution Avenue NW, Washington DC 20230. Tel (202)482-2000, FAX (202)482-3772. **5326**

COUNTY AND CITY EXTRA. (US/1059-9096). Bernan Associates, 4611-F Assembly Drive, Lanham MD 20706-4391. Tel (301)459-7666, (800)274-4447 US, (800)233-0504 CANADA, FAX (301)459-0056, telex 7108260418. **5326**

COUNTY AND CITY STATISTICS ANNUAL CD-ROM. (US). Slater Hall Information Products, 1301 Pennsylvania Avenue Northwest, Washington DC 20004. Tel (202)393-2666. **5326**

COUNTY AND CITY STATISTICS CD-ROM. (US). Slater Hall Information Products, 1301 Pennsylvania Avenue Northwest, Washington DC 20004. Tel (202)393-2666. **2840**

COUNTY BUSINESS PATTERNS [COMPUTER FILE]. (US). US Department of Commerce / Bureau of the Census, Data User Services Division, Customer Services, Washington DC 20233-0800. Tel (301)763-4100. **1554**

COUNTY-CITY PLUS. CD-ROM. (US). Slater Hall Information Products, 1301 Pennsylvania Avenue Northwest, Washington DC 20004. Tel (202)393-2666. **4551**

CRIMINAL JUSTICE ABSTRACTS. (US/0146-9177). Willow Tree Press, PO Box 249, Monsey NY 10952. Tel (914)354-9139, FAX (914)362-8376. **3080**

CRITICAL CARE MEDICINE. (US/0090-3493). Williams & Wilkins Company, 428 East Preston Street, Baltimore MD 21202-3993. Tel (410)528-4000, (800)638-6423, FAX (410)528-8596, telex 87669. **3723**

CROP PHYSIOLOGY ABSTRACTS. (UK/0306-7556). CAB International Centre, Wallingford, Oxon OX10 8DE United Kingdom. Tel 44 491 832111, FAX 44 491 833508, telex 847964 (COMAGG G). **152**

CROSS CURRENTS. (US/0011-1953). Cross Currents, College of New Rochelle, New Rochelle NY 10805. Tel (914)654-5425, FAX (914)654-5554. **4951**

CSA NEUROSCIENCES ABSTRACTS. (US/0141-7711). Cambridge Scientific Abstracts, 7200 Wisconsin Avenue, #601, Bethesda MD 20814-4823. Tel (301)961-6750, (800)843-7751, FAX (301)961-6720. **3656**

CTI PLUS [COMPUTER FILE]. (UK). Bowker Saur Ltd., A Reed Reference Publishing Company, Part of Reed International PLC, 59-60 Grosvenor Street, London WIX 9DA England. Tel 011 44 71 4935841, FAX 011 44 71 4991590. **5174**

CUMULATIVE BOOK INDEX. CD-ROM. (US/0011-300X). H W Wilson Company, 950 University Avenue, Bronx NY 10452. Tel (800)367-6770, (718)588-8400, FAX (718)590-1617, telex 4990003 HWILSON. **3458**

CUMULATIVE BOOK INDEX, THE. (US/0011-300X). H W Wilson Company, 950 University Avenue, Bronx NY 10452. Tel (800)367-6770, (718)588-8400, FAX (718)590-1617, telex 4990003 HWILSON. **3458**

CUMULATIVE INDEX TO NURSING & ALLIED HEALTH LITERATURE. (US/0146-5554). CINAHL Information Systems, 1509 Wilson Terrace, Glendale CA 91209. Tel (818)409-8005. **3656**

CURRENT AIDS LITERATURE. (UK/0952-8075). CAB International Centre, Wallingford, Oxon OX10 8DE United Kingdom. Tel 44 491 832111, FAX 44 491 833508, telex 847964 (COMAGG G). **3668**

CURRENT

Serials available on CD-ROM

CURRENT ANTARCTIC LITERATURE. (US/0096-879X). National Science Foundation, 1800 G Street Northwest, Washington DC 20550. **Tel** (202)357-9859, (202)357-9498. **2559**

CURRENT CONTENTS. AGRICULTURE, BIOLOGY, & ENVIRONMENTAL SCIENCES. (US/0090-0508). Institute for Scientific Information, 3501 Market Street, Philadelphia PA 19104. **Tel** (215)386-0100, (800)523-1850, FAX (215)386-6362, telex 84-5305. **152**

CURRENT CONTENTS. AGRICULTURE, BIOLOGY & ENVIRONMENTAL SCIENCES (CD-ROM VERSION). (US/1073-1245). Institute for Scientific Information, 3501 Market Street, Philadelphia PA 19104. **Tel** (215)386-0100, (800)523-1850, FAX (215)386-6362, telex 84-5305. **152**

CURRENT CONTENTS. CLINICAL MEDICINE. (US/0891-3358). Institute for Scientific Information, 3501 Market Street, Philadelphia PA 19104. **Tel** (215)386-0100, (800)523-1850, FAX (215)386-6362, telex 84-5305. **3656**

CURRENT CONTENTS. CLINICAL MEDICINE (CD-ROM VERSION). (US/1073-1237). Institute for Scientific Information, 3501 Market Street, Philadelphia PA 19104. **Tel** (215)386-0100, (800)523-1850, FAX (215)386-6362, telex 84-5305. **3656**

CURRENT CONTENTS. LIFE SCIENCES. (US/0011-3409). Institute for Scientific Information, 3501 Market Street, Philadelphia PA 19104. **Tel** (215)386-0100, (800)523-1850, FAX (215)386-6362, telex 84-5305. **5174**

CURRENT CONTENTS. LIFE SCIENCES (CD-ROM VERSION). (US/1073-1229). Institute for Scientific Information, 3501 Market Street, Philadelphia PA 19104. **Tel** (215)386-0100, (800)523-1850, FAX (215)386-6362, telex 84-5305. **5174**

CURRENT CONTENTS ON DISKETTE. AGRICULTURE, BIOLOGY & ENVIRONMENTAL SCIENCES. (US/1062-3167). Institute for Scientific Information, 3501 Market Street, Philadelphia PA 19104. **Tel** (215)386-0100, (800)523-1850, FAX (215)386-6362, telex 84-5305. **152**

CURRENT CONTENTS ON DISKETTE. CLINICAL MEDICINE. (US/1062-3159). Institute for Scientific Information, 3501 Market Street, Philadelphia PA 19104. **Tel** (215)386-0100, (800)523-1850, FAX (215)386-6362, telex 84-5305. **3656**

CURRENT CONTENTS ON DISKETTE. LIFE SCIENCES. J600. (US/1062-3078). Institute for Scientific Information, 3501 Market Street, Philadelphia PA 19104. **Tel** (215)386-0100, (800)523-1850, FAX (215)386-6362, telex 84-5305. **5174**

CURRENT CONTENTS ON DISKETTE. LIFE SCIENCES. J1200. (US/1062-3027). Institute for Scientific Information, 3501 Market Street, Philadelphia PA 19104. **Tel** (215)386-0100, (800)523-1850, FAX (215)386-6362, telex 84-5305. **5174**

CURRENT CONTENTS ON DISKETTE. PHYSICAL, CHEMICAL & EARTH SCIENCES. (US/1062-1180). Institute for Scientific Information, 3501 Market Street, Philadelphia PA 19104. **Tel** (215)386-0100, (800)523-1850, FAX (215)386-6362, telex 84-5305. **1362**

CURRENT CONTENTS ON DISKETTE WITH ABSTRACTS. AGRICULTURE, BIOLOGY & ENVIRONMENTAL SCIENCES. (US/1062-3124). Institute for Scientific Information, 3501 Market Street, Philadelphia PA 19104. **Tel** (215)386-0100, (800)523-1850, FAX (215)386-6362, telex 84-5305. **152**

CURRENT CONTENTS ON DISKETTE WITH ABSTRACTS. CLINICAL MEDICINE. (US/1062-3116). Institute for Scientific Information, 3501 Market Street, Philadelphia PA 19104. **Tel** (215)386-0100, (800)523-1850, FAX (215)386-6362, telex 84-5305. **3656**

CURRENT CONTENTS ON DISKETTE WITH ABSTRACTS. LIFE SCIENCES. (US/1062-3108). Institute for Scientific Information, 3501 Market Street, Philadelphia PA 19104. **Tel** (215)386-0100, (800)523-1850, FAX (215)386-6362, telex 84-5305. **5174**

CURRENT CONTENTS ON DISKETTE WITH ABSTRACTS. PHYSICAL, CHEMICAL & EARTH SCIENCES. (US/1062-3094). Institute for Scientific Information, 3501 Market Street, Philadelphia PA 19104. **Tel** (215)386-0100, (800)523-1850, FAX (215)386-6362, telex 84-5305. **1362**

CURRENT CONTENTS. PHYSICAL, CHEMICAL & EARTH SCIENCES. (US/0163-2574). Institute for Scientific Information, 3501 Market Street, Philadelphia PA 19104. **Tel** (215)386-0100, (800)523-1850, FAX (215)386-6362, telex 84-5305. **1362**

CURRENT CONTENTS. PHYSICAL, CHEMICAL & EARTH SCIENCES (CD-ROM VERSION). (US/1073-1253). Institute for Scientific Information, 3501 Market Street, Philadelphia PA 19104. **Tel** (215)386-0100, (800)523-1850, FAX (215)386-6362, telex 84-5305. **1362**

CURRENT HISTORY (1941). (US/0011-3530). Current History Inc., 4225 Main Street, Philadelphia PA 19127. **Tel** (215)482-4464, FAX (215)482-9197. **2614**

CURRENT INDEX TO JOURNALS IN EDUCATION. (US/0011-3565). Oryx Press, 4041 North Central Avenue, #700, Phoenix AZ 85012-3397. **Tel** (800)279-ORYX, (602)265-2651, FAX (602)265-6250, (800)279-4663, (800)279-6799. **1794**

CURRENT INDUSTRIAL REPORTS. M22P, CONSUMPTION ON THE COTTON SYSTEM AND STOCKS [COMPUTER FILE]. (US). US Department of Commerce / Bureau of the Census, Data User Services Division, Customer Services, Washington DC 20233-0800. **Tel** (301)763-4100. **170**

CURRENT MATHEMATICAL PUBLICATIONS. (US/0361-4794). American Mathematical Society, PO Box 6248, Providence RI 02940-6248. **Tel** (800)321-4267, (401)455-4000, FAX (401)331-3842, telex 797192. **3542**

CURRENT POPULATION SURVEY ... ANNUAL DEMOGRAPHIC FILES [COMPUTER FILE]. (US). US Department of Commerce / Bureau of the Census, Data User Services Division, Customer Services, Washington DC 20233-0800. **Tel** (301)763-4100. **1662**

CURRENT RESEARCH IN LIBRARY & INFORMATION SCIENCE. (UK/0263-9254). Bowker Saur Ltd., A Reed Reference Publishing Company, Part of Reed International PLC, 59-60 Grosvenor Street, London WIX 9DA England. **Tel** 011 44 71 4935841, FAX 011 44 71 4991590. **3205**

CURRENT TECHNOLOGY INDEX : CTI. (UK/0260-6593). Bowker Saur Ltd., A Reed Reference Publishing Company, Part of Reed International PLC, 59-60 Grosvenor Street, London WIX 9DA England. **Tel** 011 44 71 4935841, FAX 011 44 71 4991590. **5174**

CURRICULUM INQUIRY. (US/0362-6784). Blackwell Publishers, 238 Main Street, Cambridge MA 02142. **Tel** (617)547-7110, (800)835-6770, FAX (617)547-0789. **1892**

DACHAUER HEFTE. (GW/0257-9472). Dachauer Hefte, Alte Roemerstrasse 75, D 85221 Dachau Germany. **Tel** 011 49 8131 1741. **2685**

DAILY COURT REVIEW. (US/0740-1949). Daily Court Review, PO Box 1889, Houston TX 77251. **Tel** (713)528-5437, (713)869-5434, FAX (713)869-8887. **2958**

DAILY REPORT. CENTRAL EURASIA. INDEX. (US/1062-9939). Newsbank Inc, 58 Pine Street, New Canaan CT 06840. **Tel** (800)243-7694, (800)762-8182, FAX (203)966-6254. **1130**

DAILY REPORT. EAST ASIA. INDEX. (US/1045-2192). Newsbank Inc, 58 Pine Street, New Canaan CT 06840. **Tel** (800)243-7694, (800)762-8182, FAX (203)966-6254. **1130**

DAILY REPORT, EASTERN EUROPE. INDEX. (US/0731-4116). Newsbank Inc, 58 Pine Street, New Canaan CT 06840. **Tel** (800)243-7694, (800)762-8182, FAX (203)966-6254. **1131**

DAILY REPORT: LATIN AMERICA, INDEX. (US/0278-1360). Newsbank Inc, 58 Pine Street, New Canaan CT 06840. **Tel** (800)243-7694, (800)762-8182, FAX (203)966-6254. **1131**

DAILY REPORT. NEAR EAST & SOUTH ASIA. INDEX. (US/1046-0691). Newsbank Inc, 58 Pine Street, New Canaan CT 06840. **Tel** (800)243-7694, (800)762-8182, FAX (203)966-6254. **1131**

DAILY REPORT. SUB-SAHARAN AFRICA. INDEX (1989). (US/1046-0713). Newsbank Inc, 58 Pine Street, New Canaan CT 06840. **Tel** (800)243-7694, (800)762-8182, FAX (203)966-6254. **1131**

DAILY REPORT. WEST EUROPE. INDEX / FOREIGN BROADCAST INFORMATION SERVICE. (US). Newsbank Inc, 58 Pine Street, New Canaan CT 06840. **Tel** (800)243-7694, (800)762-8182, FAX (203)966-6254. **1131**

DAIRY SCIENCE ABSTRACTS. (UK/0011-5681). CAB International Centre, Wallingford, Oxon OX10 8DE United Kingdom. **Tel** 44 491 832111, FAX 44 491 833508, telex 847964 (COMAGG G). **153**

DALIBRARY. (US/1053-7848). ACM Association for Computing Machinery, 1515 Broadway, 17th Floor, New York NY 10036. **Tel** (212)869-7440, FAX (212)869-0481. **1233**

DANISH YEARBOOK OF PHILOSOPHY. (DK/0070-2749). Museum Tusculanum Press, University of Copenhagen, Njalsgade 94, DK-2300 Copenhagen D Denmark. **Tel** 011 45 31542211. **4344**

DATAPRO COMPETITIVE EDGE IN COMMUNICATIONS, THE. (US/1052-6226). Datapro Information Services Group, 600 Delran Parkway, Delran NJ 08075. **Tel** (609)764-0100, (800)328-2776, FAX (609)764-8953. **1109**

DATAPRO SOFTWARE FINDER (COMPLETE ED.). (US/1052-195X). Datapro Information Services Group, 600 Delran Parkway, Delran NJ 08075. **Tel** (609)764-0100, (800)328-2776, FAX (609)764-8953. **1285**

DATAPRO SOFTWARE FINDER (MICROCOMPUTER ED.). (US/1052-1941). Datapro Information Services Group, 600 Delran Parkway, Delran NJ 08075. **Tel** (609)764-0100, (800)328-2776, FAX (609)764-8953. **1285**

DATAPRO SOFTWARE FINDER (MID-RANGE/MAINFRAME ED.). (US/1052-1968). Datapro Information Services Group, 600 Delran Parkway, Delran NJ 08075. **Tel** (609)764-0100, (800)328-2776, FAX (609)764-8953. **1285**

DAVISON'S TEXTILE "BLUE BOOK". (US/0070-2951). Davison Publishing Company, PO Box 477, Ridgewood NJ 07451. **Tel** (201)445-3135, FAX (201)445-4397. **5350**

DEALMAKERS (BELLE MEAD, N.J.), THE. (US/1055-0771). Dealmakers, PO Box 2630, Mercerville NJ 08690. **Tel** (609)587-6200, FAX (609)587-3511. **4836**

DECISIONES DEL TRIBUNAL SUPREMO DE PUERTO RICO [COMPUTER FILE]. (PR). Compact Disc Technologies Corp., 421 Munoz Rivera Avenue, Midtown Plaza, Suite 106, Hato Rey Puerto Rico 00918. **2959**

DEFENSE & AEROSPACE COMPANIES. (US). Forecast International / DMS Inc., 22 Commerce Road, Newtown CT 06470. **Tel** (203)426-0800, FAX (203)426-1964, telex 467615. **4041**

DEFENSE CONTRACTING AGENCY AUDIT MANUAL. (US). EZ - Far Systems, 360 Wire Road, York PA 17402. **Tel** 1-800-388-1415, FAX (717)975-2813. **4642**

DEFENSE CONTRACTING AGENCY AUDIT MANUAL / DISKETTE. (US). EZ - Far Systems, 360 Wire Road, York PA 17402. **Tel** 1-800-388-1415, FAX (717)975-2813. **4041**

DEFENSE COUNSEL JOURNAL. (US/0895-0016). International Association of Defense Counsel, 20 North Wacker Drive/Suite 3100, Chicago IL 60606. **Tel** (312)368-1494, FAX (312)368-1854. **3089**

DELAWARE BUSINESS DIRECTORY. (US/1048-7085). American Business Directory, 5711 South 86th Circle, Omaha NE 68127. **Tel** (402)593-4600, FAX (402)331-5481. **665**

DEPARTMENT OF THE NAVY SUPPLEMENT / DISKETTE. (US). EZ - Far Systems, 360 Wire Road, York PA 17402. **Tel** 1-800-388-1415, FAX (717)975-2813. **4176**

DEVELOPMENT. SUPPLEMENT. (UK). The Company of Biologists Limited, Bidder Building, 140 Cowley Road, Cambridge CB4 4DL England. **Tel** 011 44 223 426164, FAX 011 44 223 423353. **541**

DIALOG ONDISC. ERIC [COMPUTER FILE]. (US). Dialog Information Services, 3460 Hillview Avenue, Palo Alto CA 94304. **Tel** (415)858-4240, (800)334-2564. **1735**

DIALOG ONDISC. PHILOSOPHER'S INDEX [COMPUTER FILE]. (US). Dialog Information Services, 3460 Hillview Avenue, Palo Alto CA 94304. **Tel** (415)858-4240, (800)334-2564. **4345**

DIARI DE SESSIONS DEL PARLAMENT DE CATALUNYA. (NL). Servei de Publicacions del Parlament de Catalunya, Palau del Parlament Parc de la Ciutadella, Barcelona 08003 Catalonia Spain. **Tel** (93)300-6413, FAX (93)300-8962, telex 97-684. **4471**

DICTIONNAIRE VIDAL. (FR/0419-1153). Office Vulgarisation Pharmaceutiq, 11 rue Quentin Bauchart, 75384 Paris Cedex 08 France. **Tel** 011 33 1 4723 90 91, FAX 011 33 1 4720 72 89. **4299**

DIRECTORY, OCCUPATIONAL SAFETY AND HEALTH LEGISLATION IN CANADA. (CN/0703-6426). Labour Canada / Labour Standards National Headquarters, Ottawa Ontario K1A OJ2 Canada. **Tel** (819)997-3920. **2961**

DIRECTORY OF AMERICAN RESEARCH AND TECHNOLOGY. (US/0886-0076). R R Bowker, A Reed Reference Publishing Company, Part of Reed International PLC, PO Box 31, 121 Chanlon Drive, New Providence NJ 07974. **Tel** (908)464-6800, (800)521-8110, FAX (908)665-6688, telex 138-755. **5174**

DIRECTORY OF CORPORATE AFFILIATIONS / INTERNATIONAL. (US). National Register Publishing Company Inc., PO Box 31, 121 Chanlon Road, New Providence NJ 07974. **Tel** (800)521-8110, (800)323-6772, FAX (908)665-6688. **666**

DIRECTORY OF CORPORATE AFFILIATIONS / U.S. PRIVATE. (US). National Register Publishing Company Inc., PO Box 31, 121 Chanlon Road, New Providence NJ 07974. **Tel** (800)521-8110, (800)323-6772, FAX (908)665-6688. **666**

DIRECTORY OF CORPORATE AFFILIATIONS / U.S. PUBLIC. (US). National Register Publishing Company Inc., PO Box 31, 121 Chanlon Road, New Providence NJ 07974. **Tel** (800)521-8110, (800)323-6772, FAX (908)665-6688. **666**

DIRECTORY OF LIBRARY & INFORMATION PROFESSIONALS. (US/0894-7031). Gale Research Inc., 835 Penobscot Building, 645 Griswold Street, Detroit MI 48226. **Tel** (800)877-GALE, (313)961-2242, FAX (313)961-6083, (800)414-5043, telex TWX 810-221-7086. **3207**

DIRECTORY OF PHYSICIANS IN THE UNITED STATES / AMERICAN MEDICAL ASSOCIATION. (US). American Medical Association, 515 North State Street, Chicago IL 60610. **Tel** (312)464-5000, (800)262-2350, FAX (312)464-5831. **1925**

DIRECTORY OF RESEARCH GRANTS. (US/0146-7336). Oryx Press, 4041 North Central Avenue, #700, Phoenix AZ 85012-3397. **Tel** (800)279-ORYX, (602)265-2651, FAX (602)265-6250, (800)279-4663, (800)279-6799. **1821**

DIRECTORY. POSTAL CODE. (CN/0835-4693). National Philatelic Centre, Canada Postal Corporation, Station 1, Antigonish Nova Scotia B2G 2R8, Canada. **Tel** (902)863-6550, FAX (902)863-6796. **1144**

DISC. (US/1052-4053). Helgerson Associates, 6609 Rosecraft Place, Falls Church VA 22043. **Tel** (703)237-0682, FAX (703)532-5447. **1183**

DISCOVERING AUTHORS. (US/1066-7792). Gale Research Inc., 835 Penobscot Building, 645 Griswold Street, Detroit MI 48226. **Tel** (800)877-GALE, (313)961-2242, FAX (313)961-6083, (800)414-5043, telex TWX 810-221-7086. **3381**

DISSERTATION ABSTRACTS INTERNATIONAL. (US/0419-4217). University Microfilms International, 300 North Zeeb Road, Ann Arbor MI 48106-1346. **Tel** (313)761-4700, (800)521-0600 Exts. 2490, 2491, FAX (313)973-1540. **415**

DISSERTATION ABSTRACTS INTERNATIONAL. A, THE HUMANITIES AND SOCIAL SCIENCES. B, THE SCIENCES AND ENGINEERING. CUMULATED AUTHOR INDEX (MICROFORM). (US). University Microfilms International, 300 North Zeeb Road, Ann Arbor MI 48106-1346. **Tel** (313)761-4700, (800)521-0600 Exts. 2490, 2491, FAX (313)973-1540. **5227**

DISSERTATION ABSTRACTS INTERNATIONAL. C, WORLDWIDE. (US/1042-7279). University Microfilms International, 300 North Zeeb Road, Ann Arbor MI 48106-1346. **Tel** (313)761-4700, (800)521-0600 Exts. 2490, 2491, FAX (313)973-1540. **1821**

DISSERTATION ABSTRACTS ONDISC [COMPUTER FILE]. (US). University Microfilms International, 300 North Zeeb Road, Ann Arbor MI 48106-1346. **Tel** (313)761-4700, (800)521-0600 Exts. 2490, 2491, FAX (313)973-1540. **415**

DMSP SSM/I BRIGHTNESS TEMPERATURE GRIDS. POLAR REGIONS [COMPUTER FILE] / NATIONAL SNOW AND ICE DATA CENTER. (US). National Snow and Ice Data Center, Cooperative Institute for Research in Environmental Sciences, University of Colorado, Boulder CO 80309-0449. **4434**

DOCPAL RESUMENES SOBRE POBLACION EN AMERICA LATINA. (CL/0378-5378). Centro Latinoamericano Demografia, Casilla 91, Santiago Chile. **Tel** 011 56 2 2085051, FAX 011 56 2 480252, telex 340295 UNSTGO CK. **4552**

DOMESTIC CARS SERVICE & REPAIR. (US/1041-4290). Mitchell International Inc, PO Box 26260, San Diego CA 92126-0260. **Tel** (619)578-6550, (800)648-8010, FAX (619)578-4752. **5413**

DRUG LAUNCHES. (UK). IMS World Publications Ltd, 7 Harwodd Avenue, london NW1 6JB England. **Tel** 011 44 71 393 5000, FAX 011 44 393 5900. **4300**

DTI QA REGISTER. (UK/0958-8574). Her Majesty's Stationery Office, 51 Nine Elms Lane, London SW8 5DR England. **Tel** 011 44 71 873 8459, 011 44 71 873 8499, FAX 011 44 71 873 8499, 011 44 71 873 8456, telex 297138. **1605**

E.I.T.D. ELECTRONIC INDUSTRY TELEPHONE DIRECTORY. (US/0422-9053). Harris Publishing Company, 2057-2 Aurora Road, Twinsburg OH 44087. **Tel** (800)888-5900, (216)425-9000, FAX (216)425-7150, telex 510 601 1740. **1605**

EARLY MUSIC NEWS. (UK). Early Music News, Sutton House 2-4 Homerton High, London E9 6JQ England. **Tel** 011 44 71 727 6339. **4116**

EARTH SCIENCES (DUBLIN, OHIO). (US/0899-5168). OCLC Asia Pacific Services, 6565 Frantz Road, Dublin OH 43017. **Tel** (800)848-5878, (614)764-6394 or 6000, FAX (614)764-6096. **1355**

EBSCO CD-ROM HANDBOOK. CD-ROM. (US). EBSCO Publishing / Boston, 83 Pine Street, Peabody MA 01960. **Tel** (800)653-2726 North America, (508)535-8500, FAX (508)535-8545. **3208**

ECCTIS 2000 : THE UK COURSES INFORMATION SERVICE ON CD-ROM. (UK). ECCTIS 2000 Ltd, Fulton House Jessop Avenue, Cheltenham Gloucestershire GL50 3SH England. **Tel** 011 44 242 518724, FAX 011 44 242 225914. **1822**

ECOLOGY ABSTRACTS. (US/0143-3296). Cambridge Scientific Abstracts, 7200 Wisconsin Avenue, #601, Bethesda MD 20814-4823. **Tel** (301)961-6750, (800)843-7751, FAX (301)961-6720. **2184**

ECON/STATS I. CD-ROM. (US). Hopkins Technology, 421 Hazel Lane, Suite 120, Hopkins MN 55343. **Tel** (612)931-9376, FAX (612)931-9377. **1531**

ECONLIT [COMPUTER FILE]. (US). Silverplatter Information Inc., 100 River Ridge Lane, Norwood MA 02062. **Tel** (800)343-0064, (617)769-2599, FAX (617)235-1715. **1531**

ECONOMIC CENSUS. 1987. CD-ROM. (US). US Department of Commerce / Bureau of the Census, Data User Services Division, Customer Services, Washington DC 20233-0800. **Tel** (301)763-4100. **671**

ECONOMIC INQUIRY. (US/0095-2583). Western Economic Association. **1483**

EDP WEEKLY. (US). Computer Age Publications, 3918 Prosperity Avenue/Suite 318, Fairfax VA 22031-3300. **Tel** (703)573-8400, FAX (703)573-8594. **1237**

EDUCATION AUTHORITIES DIRECTORY AND ANNUAL, THE. (UK/0070-9131). School Government Publishing Company Ltd., Darby House Bletchingley Road, Merstham Redhill RH1 3DN England. **Tel** 011 44 737 642223, FAX 011 44 737 644283. **1862**

EDUCATION DIGEST, THE. (US/0013-127X). Prakken Publications Inc., 275 Metty Drive, PO Box 8623, Ann Arbor MI 48107. **Tel** (313)769-1211, (800)530-9673, FAX (313)769-8383. **1739**

EDUCATION INDEX. (US/0013-1385). H W Wilson Company, 950 University Avenue, Bronx NY 10452. **Tel** (800)367-6770, (718)588-8400, FAX (718)590-1617, telex 4990003 HWILSON. **1794**

EDUCATION INDEX. CD-ROM. (US/0013-1385). H W Wilson Company, 950 University Avenue, Bronx NY 10452. **Tel** (800)367-6770, (718)588-8400, FAX (718)590-1617, telex 4990003 HWILSON. **1794**

EDUCATION LIBRARY [COMPUTER FILE]. (US). OCLC Asia Pacific Services, 6565 Frantz Road, Dublin OH 43017. **Tel** (800)848-5878, (614)764-6394 or 6000, FAX (614)764-6096. **1740**

EDUCATION MATERIALS IN LIBRARIES. (US/0895-5514). OCLC Asia Pacific Services, 6565 Frantz Road, Dublin OH 43017. **Tel** (800)848-5878, (614)764-6394 or 6000, FAX (614)764-6096. **3209**

EI PAGE ONE [COMPUTER FILE]. (US). Engineering Information Inc., Castle Point on the Hudson, Hoboken NJ 07030. **Tel** (800)221-1044, (201)216-8500, FAX (201)216-8526, telex 4990438. **2003**

EINKAUFS-1X1 DER DEUTSCHEN INDUSTRIE. (GW/0343-5881). Deutscher Adressbuch-Verlag fur Wirtschaft und Verkehr GmbH, Dav-Verlagshaus, Arheilger Weg 17, D 64380 Rossdorf Germany. **Tel** 06154 699500, FAX 06154 6995490, telex 4191324 DAV D. **832**

EL-HI TEXTBOOKS AND SERIALS IN PRINT. (US/0000-0825). R R Bowker, A Reed Reference Publishing Company, Part of Reed International PLC, PO Box 31, 121 Chanlon Drive, New Providence NJ 07974. **Tel** (908)464-6800, (800)521-8110, FAX (908)665-6688, telex 138-755. **1794**

ELECTRE BIBLIO FRENCH BOOKS IN PRINT. CD-ROM. (FR). Cercle de la Librairie, 35 rue Gregoire de Tours, F-75279 Paris Cedex 06 France. **Tel** 011 33 1 43291000, FAX 011 33 1 43296895, telex LIFRAN 270 838. **415**

ELECTRICAL & ELECTRONICS ABSTRACTS. (UK/0036-8105). Institution of Electrical Engineers / IEE, Michael Faraday House, Six Hills Way, Stevenage Herts SG1 2AY UK. **Tel** 011 44 438 313311, FAX 011 44 438 742840, telex 825578 IEESTV G. **2003**

ELECTRICAL COMPONENT LOCATOR. DOMESTIC CARS, LIGHT TRUCKS & VANS, IMPORTED CARS & TRUCKS. (US/0743-6076). Mitchell International Inc, PO Box 26260, San Diego CA 92126-0260. **Tel** (619)578-6550, (800)648-8010, FAX (619)578-4752. **5414**

ELECTRICITY JOURNAL, THE. (US/1040-6190). The Electricity Journal, 1501 Western Avenue, Suite 100, Seattle WA 98101. **Tel** (206)382-0195, FAX (206)382-0098. **4761**

ELECTRONIC REPRESENTATIVES DIRECTORY. (US/0887-4336). Harris Publishing Company, 2057-2 Aurora Road, Twinsburg OH 44087. **Tel** (800)888-5900, (216)425-9000, FAX (216)425-7150, telex 510 601 1740. **2048**

ELECTRONIC SOURCE BOOK FOR SOUTHERN CALIFORNIA, THE. (US/8755-1527). Paramount Publishing Inc, 13422 Weymouth Street, Westminister CA 92683. **Tel** (714)897-9576, FAX (714)893-0820. **2048**

ELECTRONIC SWEET'S. (US/1062-9580). McGraw-Hill Inc. Construction Information Services Group, Sweet's Group, 1221 Avenue of the Americas, New York NY 10020. **614**

ELECTRONIC SYSTEMS FORECAST. (US). Forecast International / DMS Inc., 22 Commerce Road, Newtown CT 06470. **Tel** (203)426-0800, FAX (203)426-1964, telex 467615. **2048**

ELECTRONIC WARFARE FORECAST. (US). Forecast International / DMS Inc., 22 Commerce Road, Newtown CT 06470. **Tel** (203)426-0800, FAX (203)426-1964, telex 467615. **4043**

ELECTRONICS MANUFACTURERS DIRECTORY. (US/1060-2100). Harris Publishing Company, 2057-2 Aurora Road, Twinsburg OH 44087. **Tel** (800)888-5900, (216)425-9000, FAX (216)425-7150, telex 510 601 1740. **3478**

ELECTRONICS SOURCE BOOK FOR SOUTH ATLANTIC, THE. (US). Paramount Publishing Inc, 13422 Weymouth Street, Westminister CA 92683. **Tel** (714)897-9576, FAX (714)893-0820. **2050**

ELECTRONICS SOURCE BOOK. SOUTHWEST, THE. (US). Paramount Publishing Inc, 13422 Weymouth Street, Westminister CA 92683. **Tel** (714)897-9576, FAX (714)893-0820. **2050**

ELEMENTARY SCHOOL LIBRARY COLLECTION, THE. (US). Brodart Inc., 500 Arch Street, Williamsport PA 17705. **Tel** (800)233-8467 Ext. 572, FAX (717)326-1479. **3209**

EMC TECHNOLOGY. (US/1055-6230). Don White Consultants, Inc., Route 3, Box 2000 D, Gainesville VA 22065. **Tel** (703)347-0030, FAX (703)347-5813. **2053**

EMMY. (US/0164-3495). Emmy Magazine, 5220 Lankerhim Blvd, North Hollywood CA 91601. **Tel** (818)754-2800, FAX (818)761-2827. **1131**

ENA'S NURSING SCAN IN EMERGENCY CARE. (US/1056-7062). NURSECOM Inc., 1211 Locust Street, Philadelphia PA 19107. **Tel** (215)545-7222, (800)242-6757, FAX (215)545-8107. **3855**

ENCYCLOPEDIA OF ASSOCIATIONS. (US/0071-0202). Gale Research Inc., 835 Penobscot Building, 645 Griswold Street, Detroit MI 48226. **Tel** (800)877-GALE, (313)961-2242, (313)961-6083, (800)414-5043, telex TWX 810-221-7086. **1925**

ENCYCLOPEDIA OF ASSOCIATIONS CD-ROM. (US/1070-2318). Gale Research Inc., 835 Penobscot Building, 645 Griswold Street, Detroit MI 48226. **Tel** (800)877-GALE, (313)961-2242, (313)961-6083, (800)414-5043, telex TWX 810-221-7086. **1925**

ENERGY ANALYST (SILVER SPRING, MD.). (US/1045-5728). Quick Source Inc., 700 Roeder Road, Silver Spring MD 20910. **1938**

ENERGY INFORMATION ABSTRACTS. (US/0147-6521). R R Bowker, A Reed Reference Publishing Company, Part of Reed International PLC, PO Box 31, 121 Chanlon Drive, New Providence NJ 07974. **Tel** (908)464-6800, (800)521-8110, FAX (908)665-6688, telex 138-755. **1962**

ENERGY LIBRARY. (US/1049-7420). OCLC Asia Pacific Services, 6565 Frantz Road, Dublin OH 43017. **Tel** (800)848-5878, (614)764-6394 or 6000, FAX (614)764-6096. **1940**

ENGINEERED

Serials available on CD-ROM

ENGINEERED MATERIALS ABSTRACTS. (US/0951-9998). American Society for Metals International, c/o Deborah Barthelmes, Materials Park OH 44073-0002. **Tel** (216)338-5151, FAX (216)338-4634, telex 980-619. **2004**

ENGINEERING INDEX ANNUAL. (US/0360-8557). Engineering Information Inc., Castle Point on the Hudson, Hoboken NJ 07030. **Tel** (800)221-1044, (201)216-8500, FAX (201)216-8526, telex 4990438. **2004**

ENGINEERING INDEX MONTHLY. (US/0742-1974). Engineering Information Inc., Castle Point on the Hudson, Hoboken NJ 07030. **Tel** (800)221-1044, (201)216-8500, FAX (201)216-8526, telex 4990438. **2004**

ENGINEERING RESEARCH CENTRES : A WORLD DIRECTORY OF ORGANIZATIONS & PROGRAMMES. (UK). Longman Group Ltd., Fourth Avenue, Longman House, Harlow Essex CM19 5SR England. **Tel** 011 44 279 429655, FAX 011 44 279 431059, telex 81259. **1974**

ENTERPRISE DSI INFODISK. (US). Faulkner Technical Reports, 7905 Browning Road, Suite 114, Pennsauken NJ 08109. **Tel** (800)843-0460. **1184**

ENTOMOLOGY ABSTRACTS. (US/0013-8924). Cambridge Scientific Abstracts, 7200 Wisconsin Avenue, #601, Bethesda MD 20814-4823. **Tel** (301)961-6750, (800)843-7751, FAX (301)961-6720. **5604**

ENVIRO/ENERGYLINE ABSTRACTS PLUS. (US/1076-6464). R R Bowker, A Reed Reference Publishing Company, Part of Reed International PLC, PO Box 31, 121 Chanlon Drive, New Providence NJ 07974. **Tel** (908)464-6800, (800)521-8110, FAX (908)665-6688, telex 138-755. **2184**

ENVIRONMENT ABSTRACTS. (US/0093-3287). Congressional Information Service Inc, 4520 East-West Highway, Suite 800, Bethesda MD 20814-3389. **Tel** (800)638-8380, (301)654-1550, FAX (301)654-4033, telex 292386 CIS UR. **2184**

ENVIRONMENT ABSTRACTS ANNUAL. (US/0000-1198). Congressional Information Service Inc, 4520 East-West Highway, Suite 800, Bethesda MD 20814-3389. **Tel** (800)638-8380, (301)654-1550, FAX (301)654-4033, telex 292386 CIS UR. **2184**

ENVIRONMENT ABSTRACTS [COMPUTER FILE]. (US). Congressional Information Service Inc, 4520 East-West Highway, Suite 800, Bethesda MD 20814-3389. **Tel** (800)638-8380, (301)654-1550, FAX (301)654-4033, telex 292386 CIS UR. **2184**

ENVIRONMENT & ECOLOGY. (II/0970-0420). Prof Qrt, No H-2 Ground Floor, Kalyani 741235 West Bengal India. **454**

ENVIRONMENT LIBRARY. (US/1049-7404). Silverplatter Information Inc, 100 River Ridge Drive, Norwood MA 02062. **Tel** (800)343-0064, (617)769-2599, FAX (617)235-1715. **2165**

ENVIRONMENTAL ACTION (WASHINGTON, D.C.). (US/0013-922X). Environmental Action, 6930 Carroll Avenue, Suite 600, Takoma Park MD 20912. **Tel** (301)891-1100, FAX (301)891-2218. **2166**

ENVIRONMENTAL PERIODICALS BIBLIOGRAPHY. (US/0145-3815). International Academy at Santa Barbara, 800 Garden Street, Suite D, Santa Barbara CA 93101. **Tel** (805)965-5010, FAX (805)965-6071. **2184**

ENVIRONMENTAL PERIODICALS BIBLIOGRAPHY ON CD-ROM. (US/1053-1440). International Academy at Santa Barbara, 800 Garden Street, Suite D, Santa Barbara CA 93101. **Tel** (805)965-5010, FAX (805)965-6071. **2184**

EQUIPMENT FORECAST, AN. (US). Forecast International / DMS Inc., 22 Commerce Road, Newtown CT 06470. **Tel** (203)426-0800, FAX (203)426-1964, telex 467615. **4043**

ERIC (BOSTON, MASS.). (US/1062-5577). Silverplatter Information Inc., 100 River Ridge Drive, Norwood MA 02062. **Tel** (800)343-0064, (617)769-2599, FAX (617)235-1715. **1745**

ERIC (DUBLIN, OHIO). (US/0894-3699). OCLC Asia Pacific Services, 6565 Frantz Road, Dublin OH 43017. **Tel** (800)848-5878, (614)764-6394 or 6000, FAX (614)764-6096. **1745**

ERIC (PEABODY, MASS.). (US/1065-6537). EBSCO Publishing / Boston, 83 Pine Street, Peabody MA 01960. **Tel** (800)653-2726 North America, (508)535-8500, FAX (508)535-8545. **1745**

ESSAY AND GENERAL LITERATURE INDEX. (US/0014-083X). H W Wilson Company, 950 University Avenue, Bronx NY 10452. **Tel** (800)367-6770, (718)588-8400, FAX (718)590-1617, telex 4990003 HWILSON. **3458**

ESSAY AND GENERAL LITERATURE INDEX. CD-ROM. (US/0014-083X). H W Wilson Company, 950 University Avenue, Bronx NY 10452. **Tel** (800)367-6770, (718)588-8400, FAX (718)590-1617, telex 4990003 HWILSON. **3458**

ESSAYS IN LITERATURE. (US/0094-5404). Western Illinois University, 114 Simpkins Hall, Macomb IL 61455. **Tel** (309) 298-2212, FAX (309) 298-2289. **3342**

ETHNIC NEWS WATCH [COMPUTER FILE]. (US). Softline Information Inc, PO Box 16845, Stamford CT 06905. **2260**

ETHNIC NEWSWATCH [COMPUTER FILE]. (US). Softline Information Inc, PO Box 16845, Stamford CT 06905. **2260**

EUDISED R & D BULLETIN. (FR). K.G. Saur Verlag KG, A Reed Reference Publishing Company, Part of Reed International PLC, Ortlerstrasse 8, D 81373 Munich Germany. **Tel** 011 49 89 769020, FAX 011 49 89 76902150, telex 5212067-SAUR-D. **1745**

EUROCAT - COMPLETE CATALOGUE OF EC PUBLICATIONS AND DOCUMENTS. (UK). Chadwyck-Healey Limited, The Quorum Barnwell Road, Cambridge CB5 8SW England. **Tel** 011 44 223 215512, telex 9312102281 CH G. **4814**

EUROCAT [COMPUTER FILE]. (LU/1021-7789). ELLIS Publications, PO Box 1059, 6201 BB Maastricht Netherlands. **Tel** 011 31 04457 2275, FAX 011 31 04457 2148. **416**

EUROP PRODUCTION. (GW). ABC Publishing Group, POB 100262, D-64202 Darmstadt Germany. **Tel** 011 49 6151 38920. **1634**

EUROPEAN HANDBOOK. (UK/0966-4858). Extel Financial Ltd, Fitzroy House, 13-17 Epworth Street, London EC2A 4DL England. **Tel** 071 825 8000, FAX (0)71 251-2725, telex 884319 EXTELX G. **673**

EUROPEAN PHARMACOPOEIA. (FR). **4303**

EXCERPTA MEDICA. SECTION 1. ANATOMY, ANTHROPOLOGY, EMBRYOLOGY AND HISTOLOGY. (NE/0014-4053). Excerpta Medica Publishing Group, PO Box 548, 1000 AM Amsterdam Netherlands. **Tel** 011 31 20 5803243. **3657**

EXCERPTA MEDICA. SECTION 2A. PHYSIOLOGY. (NE/0367-1089). Excerpta Medica Publishing Group, PO Box 548, 1000 AM Amsterdam Netherlands. **Tel** 011 31 20 5803243. **478**

EXCERPTA MEDICA. SECTION 3. ENDOCRINOLOGY. (NE/0014-407X). Excerpta Medica Publishing Group, PO Box 548, 1000 AM Amsterdam Netherlands. **Tel** 011 31 20 5803243. **3657**

EXCERPTA MEDICA. SECTION 4. MICROBIOLOGY, BACTERIOLOGY, MYCOLOGY, PARASITOLOGY, AND VIROLOGY. (NE). Excerpta Medica Publishing Group, PO Box 548, 1000 AM Amsterdam Netherlands. **Tel** 011 31 20 5803243. **3657**

EXCERPTA MEDICA. SECTION 5. GENERAL PATHOLOGY AND PATHOLOGICAL ANATOMY. (NE/0014-4096). Excerpta Medica Publishing Group, PO Box 548, 1000 AM Amsterdam Netherlands. **Tel** 011 31 20 5803243. **3657**

EXCERPTA MEDICA. SECTION 6. INTERNAL MEDICINE. (NE/0014-410X). Excerpta Medica Publishing Group, PO Box 548, 1000 AM Amsterdam Netherlands. **Tel** 011 31 20 5803243. **3657**

EXCERPTA MEDICA. SECTION 7. PEDIATRICS AND PEDIATRIC SURGERY. (NE/0373-6512). Excerpta Medica Publishing Group, PO Box 548, 1000 AM Amsterdam Netherlands. **Tel** 011 31 20 5803243. **3657**

EXCERPTA MEDICA. SECTION 8. NEUROLOGY AND NEUROSURGERY. (NE/0014-4126). Excerpta Medica Publishing Group, PO Box 548, 1000 AM Amsterdam Netherlands. **Tel** 011 31 20 5803243. **3657**

EXCERPTA MEDICA. SECTION 9. SURGERY. (NE/0014-4134). Excerpta Medica Publishing Group, PO Box 548, 1000 AM Amsterdam Netherlands. **Tel** 011 31 20 5803243. **3657**

EXCERPTA MEDICA. SECTION 10. OBSTETRICS AND GYNECOLOGY. (NE/0014-4142). Excerpta Medica Publishing Group, PO Box 548, 1000 AM Amsterdam Netherlands. **Tel** 011 31 20 5803243. **3657**

EXCERPTA MEDICA. SECTION 11. OTO-, RHINO-, LARYNGOLOGY. (NE/0014-4150). Excerpta Medica Publishing Group, PO Box 548, 1000 AM Amsterdam Netherlands. **Tel** 011 31 20 5803243. **3888**

EXCERPTA MEDICA. SECTION 12. OPHTHALMOLOGY. (NE/0014-4169). Excerpta Medica Publishing Group, PO Box 548, 1000 AM Amsterdam Netherlands. **Tel** 011 31 20 5803243. **3658**

EXCERPTA MEDICA. SECTION 13. DERMATOLOGY AND VENEREOLOGY. (NE/0014-4177). Excerpta Medica Publishing Group, PO Box 548, 1000 AM Amsterdam Netherlands. **Tel** 011 31 20 5803243. **3658**

EXCERPTA MEDICA. SECTION 14. RADIOLOGY. (NE/0014-4185). Excerpta Medica Publishing Group, PO Box 548, 1000 AM Amsterdam Netherlands. **Tel** 011 31 20 5803243. **3658**

EXCERPTA MEDICA. SECTION 16. CANCER. (NE/0014-4207). Excerpta Medica Publishing Group, PO Box 548, 1000 AM Amsterdam Netherlands. **Tel** 011 31 20 5803243. **3658**

EXCERPTA MEDICA. SECTION 17. PUBLIC HEALTH, SOCIAL MEDICINE AND EPIDEMIOLOGY. (NE). Excerpta Medica Publishing Group, PO Box 548, 1000 AM Amsterdam Netherlands. **Tel** 011 31 20 5803243. **3658**

EXCERPTA MEDICA. SECTION 18. CARDIOVASCULAR DISEASES AND CARDIOVASCULAR SURGERY. (NE/0014-4223). Excerpta Medica Publishing Group, PO Box 548, 1000 AM Amsterdam Netherlands. **Tel** 011 31 20 5803243. **3658**

EXCERPTA MEDICA. SECTION 19. REHABILITATION AND PHYSICAL MEDICINE. (NE/0014-4231). Excerpta Medica Publishing Group, PO Box 548, 1000 AM Amsterdam Netherlands. **Tel** 011 31 20 5803243. **3658**

EXCERPTA MEDICA. SECTION 20. GERONTOLOGY AND GERIATRICS. (NE/0014-424X). Excerpta Medica Publishing Group, PO Box 548, 1000 AM Amsterdam Netherlands. **Tel** 011 31 20 5803243. **3658**

EXCERPTA MEDICA. SECTION 21. DEVELOPMENTAL BIOLOGY AND TERATOLOGY. (NE/0014-4258). Excerpta Medica Publishing Group, PO Box 548, 1000 AM Amsterdam Netherlands. **Tel** 011 31 20 5803243. **3658**

EXCERPTA MEDICA. SECTION 22. HUMAN GENETICS. (NE/0014-4266). Excerpta Medica Publishing Group, PO Box 548, 1000 AM Amsterdam Netherlands. **Tel** 011 31 20 5803243. **3658**

EXCERPTA MEDICA. SECTION 23. NUCLEAR MEDICINE. (NE/0014-4274). Excerpta Medica Publishing Group, PO Box 548, 1000 AM Amsterdam Netherlands. **Tel** 011 31 20 5803243. **3658**

EXCERPTA MEDICA. SECTION 24. ANESTHESIOLOGY. (NE/0014-4282). Excerpta Medica Publishing Group, PO Box 548, 1000 AM Amsterdam Netherlands. **Tel** 011 31 20 5803243. **3658**

EXCERPTA MEDICA. SECTION 25. HEMATOLOGY. (NE/0014-4290). Excerpta Medica Publishing Group, PO Box 548, 1000 AM Amsterdam Netherlands. **Tel** 011 31 20 5803243. **3658**

EXCERPTA MEDICA. SECTION 26. IMMUNOLOGY, SEROLOGY AND TRANSPLANTATION. (NE/0014-4304). Excerpta Medica Publishing Group, PO Box 548, 1000 AM Amsterdam Netherlands. **Tel** 011 31 20 5803243. **3658**

EXCERPTA MEDICA. SECTION 27. BIOPHYSICS, BIOENGINEERING AND MEDICAL INSTRUMENTATION. (NE/0014-4312). Excerpta Medica Publishing Group, PO Box 548, 1000 AM Amsterdam Netherlands. **Tel** 011 31 20 5803243. **3658**

EXCERPTA MEDICA. SECTION 28. UROLOGY AND NEPHROLOGY. (NE/0014-4320). Excerpta Medica Publishing Group, PO Box 548, 1000 AM Amsterdam Netherlands. **Tel** 011 31 20 5803243. **3658**

EXCERPTA MEDICA. SECTION 29. CLINICAL BIOCHEMISTRY. (NE/0300-5372). Excerpta Medica Publishing Group, PO Box 548, 1000 AM Amsterdam Netherlands. **Tel** 011 31 20 5803243. **478**

EXCERPTA MEDICA. SECTION 30. CLINICAL AND EXPERIMENTAL PHARMACOLOGY. (NE). Excerpta Medica Publishing Group, PO Box 548, 1000 AM Amsterdam Netherlands. **Tel** 011 31 20 5803243. **3658**

EXCERPTA MEDICA. SECTION 32. PSYCHIATRY. (NE/0014-4363). Excerpta Medica Publishing Group, PO Box 548, 1000 AM Amsterdam Netherlands. **Tel** 011 31 20 5803243. **3659**

EXCERPTA MEDICA. SECTION 35. OCCUPATIONAL HEALTH AND INDUSTRIAL MEDICINE. (NE/0014-4398). Excerpta Medica Publishing Group, PO Box 548, 1000 AM Amsterdam Netherlands. **Tel** 011 31 20 5803243. **2872**

EXCERPTA MEDICA. SECTION 36. HEALTH POLICY, ECONOMICS, AND MANAGEMENT. (NE). Excerpta Medica Publishing Group, PO Box 548, 1000 AM Amsterdam Netherlands. **Tel** 011 31 20 5803243. **3659**

EXCERPTA MEDICA. SECTION 37. DRUG LITERATURE INDEX. (NE/0167-9171). Excerpta Medica Publishing Group, PO Box 548, 1000 AM Amsterdam Netherlands. **Tel** 011 31 20 5803243. **3659**

EXCERPTA MEDICA. SECTION 38. ADVERSE REACTIONS TITLES. (NE/0167-9090). Excerpta Medica Publishing Group, PO Box 548, 1000 AM Amsterdam Netherlands. **Tel** 011 31 20 5803243. **3659**

EXCERPTA MEDICA. SECTION 40. DRUG DEPENDENCE, ALCOHOL ABUSE, AND ALCOHOLISM. (NE/0304-4041). Excerpta Medica Publishing Group, PO Box 548, 1000 AM Amsterdam Netherlands. **Tel** 011 31 20 5803243. **3659**

EXCERPTA MEDICA. SECTION 46. ENVIRONMENTAL HEALTH AND POLLUTION CONTROL. (NE/0300-5194). Excerpta Medica Publishing Group, PO Box 548, 1000 AM Amsterdam Netherlands. **Tel** 011 31 20 5803243. **3659**

EXCERPTA MEDICA. SECTION 49. FORENSIC SCIENCE ABSTRACTS. (NE/0031-0743). Excerpta Medica Publishing Group, PO Box 548, 1000 AM Amsterdam Netherlands. **Tel** 011 31 20 5803243. **3740**

EXCERPTA MEDICA. SECTION 50. EPILEPSY ABSTRACTS. (NE/0303-8459). Excerpta Medica Publishing Group, PO Box 548, 1000 AM Amsterdam Netherlands. **Tel** 011 31 20 5803243. **3659**

EXCERPTA MEDICA. SECTION 52. TOXICOLOGY. (NE/0167-8353). Excerpta Medica Publishing Group, PO Box 548, 1000 AM Amsterdam Netherlands. **Tel** 011 31 20 5803243. **3659**

EXCERPTA MEDICA. SECTION 65. CANCER IMMUNOLOGY. LITERATURE INDEX. (NE/0304-3789). Excerpta Medica Publishing Group, PO Box 548, 1000 AM Amsterdam Netherlands. **Tel** 011 31 20 5803243. **3659**

EXPANDED ACADEMIC INDEX [COMPUTER FILE]. (US). Information Access Company, 362 Lakeside Drive, Foster City CA 94404. **Tel** (800)227-8431. **2496**

FACTS ON FILE. (US/0014-6641). Facts on File Publications, 460 Park Avenue South, New York NY 10016. **Tel** (212)683-2244, (800)322-8755, FAX (212)683-3633, telex 238 552 FACTS UR. **2616**

FACTS ON FILE NEWS DIGEST CD-ROM. (US/1062-9572). Facts on File Publications, 460 Park Avenue South, New York NY 10016. **Tel** (212)683-2244, (800)322-8755, FAX (212)683-3633, telex 238 552 FACTS UR. **2487**

FAMILYSEARCH. INTERNATIONAL GENEALOGICAL INDEX. BRITISH ISLES. (US/1063-4711). The Church of Jesus Christ of Latter-Day Saints, Genealogical Department, 50 East North Temple Street, Salt Lake City UT 84150. **2447**

FAMILYSEARCH. INTERNATIONAL GENEALOGICAL INDEX. DENMARK. (US/1063-4738). The Church of Jesus Christ of Latter-Day Saints, Genealogical Department, 50 East North Temple Street, Salt Lake City UT 84150. **2448**

FAMILYSEARCH. INTERNATIONAL GENEALOGICAL INDEX. U.S. AND CANADA. (US/1063-4703). The Church of Jesus Christ of Latter-Day Saints, Genealogical Department, 50 East North Temple Street, Salt Lake City UT 84150. **2448**

FAMILYSEARCH. INTERNATIONAL GENEALOGICAL INDEX. WALES. (US/1063-472X). The Church of Jesus Christ of Latter-Day Saints, Genealogical Department, 50 East North Temple Street, Salt Lake City UT 84150. **2448**

F&S INDEX PLUS TEXT. INTERNATIONAL. (US/1065-5956). Predicasts Inc., A Ziff Communications Company, 11001 Cedar Avenue, Cleveland OH 44106. **Tel** (800)321-6388, (216)795-3000, FAX (216)229-9944, telex 985 604. **729**

F&S INDEX PLUS TEXT. UNITED STATES. (US/1065-5964). Predicasts Inc., A Ziff Communications Company, 11001 Cedar Avenue, Cleveland OH 44106. **Tel** (800)321-6388, (216)795-3000, FAX (216)229-9944, telex 985 604. **729**

FAULKNER CLIENT SERVER INFODISK. (US). Faulkner Technical Reports, 7905 Browning Road, Suite 114, Pennsauken NJ 08109. **Tel** (800)843-0460. **1184**

FAULKNER COMMUNICATIONS INFODISK CD ROM. (US). Faulkner Technical Reports, 7905 Browning Road, Suite 114, Pennsauken NJ 08109. **Tel** (800)843-0460. **1111**

FAULKNER COMPUTER AND COMMUNICATIONS LIBRARY. (US). Faulkner Technical Reports, 7905 Browning Road, Suite 114, Pennsauken NJ 08109. **Tel** (800)843-0460. **1184**

FAULKNER DATAWORLD INFODISC. (US). Faulkner Technical Reports, 7905 Browning Road, Suite 114, Pennsauken NJ 08109. **Tel** (800)843-0460. **1184**

FAULKNER MICRODATA INFODISK. (US). Faulkner Technical Reports, 7905 Browning Road, Suite 114, Pennsauken NJ 08109. **Tel** (800)843-0460. **1185**

FEDERAL AQUISITION REGULATIONS / DISKETTE. (US). EZ - Far Systems, 360 Wire Road, York PA 17402. **Tel** 1-800-388-1415, FAX (717)975-2813. **4647**

FEDERAL INFORMATION RESOURCES MANAGEMENT REGULATION AND BULLETINS THROUGH TRANSMITTAL CIRCULAR. (US/1068-7386). Superintendent of Documents, US Government Printing Office, Washington DC 20402. **Tel** (202)275-3328, FAX (202)786-2377. **4648**

FEDERAL PROPERTY MANAGEMENT REGULATIONS / DISKETTE. (US). EZ - Far Systems, 360 Wire Road, York PA 17402. **Tel** 1-800-388-1415, FAX (717)975-2813. **4648**

FEDERAL REGISTER. (US/0097-6326). Superintendent of Documents, US Government Printing Office, Washington DC 20402. **Tel** (202)275-3328, FAX (202)786-2377. **2969**

FEDERAL STAFF DIRECTORY. (US/0735-3324). Staff Directories Ltd., PO Box 62, Mount Vernon VA 22121. **Tel** (703)739-0900, FAX (703)739-0234. **4648**

FEDERAL TAX COORDINATOR 2D. (US/0738-8632). Research Institute of America, 117 East Stevens Avenue, Valhalla NY 10595. **Tel** (800)431-9025. **4724**

FEDSTAT (ALEXANDRIA, VA.). (US/1063-0961). US Statistics Inc, PO Box 816, Alexandria VA 22313. **Tel** (703)979-9699, FAX (703)548-4585. **4553**

FERC DATA ON CD-ROM. (US). OPRI, PO Box 1433, Manhattan Beach CA 90266. **Tel** (310)372-0722, FAX (310)374-0259. **1944**

FIELD CROP ABSTRACTS. (UK/0015-069X). CAB International Centre, Wallingford, Oxon OX10 8DE United Kingdom. **Tel** 44 491 832111, FAX 44 491 833508, telex 847964 (COMAGG G). **153**

FILM & VIDEO FINDER. (US/0898-1582). Plexus Publishing Inc., 143 Old Marlton Pike, Medford NJ 08055. **Tel** (609)654-6500, FAX (609)654-4309. **4069**

FINANCIEEL EKONOMISCHE TIJD, DE. (BE/0772-0890). Uitgeversbedrijf Tijd NV, Franklin Building, Posthoflei 3, 2600 Berchem Antwerp Belgium. **Tel** 011 32 3 2860301. **1491**

FIRST PLACE [COMPUTER FILE]. (US). Automated Catalogue Services, Inc., 487 Devon Park Drive, Suite 215, Wayne PA 19087. **Tel** (215)687-7500. **2335**

FISH & FISHERIES WORLDWIDE. (US/1069-9309). National Information Services Corp, 3100 St Paul Street, Wyman Towers, Suite 6, Baltimore MD 21218. **Tel** (410)243-0797, FAX (410)243-0982. **2301**

FISHERIES REVIEW (FORT COLLINS, COLO.). (US/1042-6299). US Fish and Wildlife Service, 1201 Oak Ridge Drive, Suite 200, Fort Collins CO 80525-5589. **Tel** (303)223-9709. **2317**

FLORIDA BUSINESS DIRECTORY. (US/1048-7093). American Business Directory, 5711 South 86th Circle, Omaha NE 68127. **Tel** (402)593-4600, FAX (402)331-5481. **676**

FOOD ANALYST. CD-ROM. (US). Hopkins Technology, 421 Hazel Lane, Suite 120, Hopkins MN 55343. **Tel** (612)931-9376, FAX (612)931-9377. **4191**

FOOD ANALYST PLUS. CD-ROM. (US). Hopkins Technology, 421 Hazel Lane, Suite 120, Hopkins MN 55343. **Tel** (612)931-9376, FAX (612)931-9377. **4191**

FOOD SCIENCE AND TECHNOLOGY ABSTRACTS. (UK/0015-6574). International Food Information Service, c/o H Brookes, Lane End House, Shinfield, Reading Berkshire RG9 2BB England. **Tel** 011/44/734/883895, telex 847204. **2362**

FOOD TRADE REVIEW. (UK/0015-6671). Food Trade Press Ltd, Station House, Hortons Way, Westerham Kent TN16 1BZ England. **Tel** 011 44 689 50551, 011 44 689 53070, FAX 011 44 689 561285. **2340**

FOODS INTELLIGENCE ON COMPACT DISC. (US/1063-4169). Silverplatter Information Inc., 100 River Ridge Drive, Norwood MA 02062. **Tel** (800)343-0064, (617)769-2599, FAX (617)235-1715. **2362**

FOREIGN MILITARY MARKETS, ASIA & PACIFIC RIM. (US). Forecast International / DMS Inc., 22 Commerce Road, Newtown CT 06470. **Tel** (203)426-0800, FAX (203)426-1964, telex 467615. **4044**

FOREIGN MILITARY MARKETS, LATIN AMERICA & CARIBBEAN BASIN. (US). Forecast International / DMS Inc., 22 Commerce Road, Newtown CT 06470. **Tel** (203)426-0800, FAX (203)426-1964, telex 467615. **4044**

FOREIGN MILITARY MARKETS, MIDDLE EAST & AFRICA. (US). Forecast International / DMS Inc., 22 Commerce Road, Newtown CT 06470. **Tel** (203)426-0800, FAX (203)426-1964, telex 467615. **4044**

FOREIGN MILITARY MARKETS, NATO & EUROPE. (US). Forecast International / DMS Inc., 22 Commerce Road, Newtown CT 06470. **Tel** (203)426-0800, FAX (203)426-1964, telex 467615. **4044**

FOREIGN POLICY. (US/0015-7228). Foreign Policy, 2400 N Street NW, Suite 700, Washington DC 20037. **Tel** (202)862-7940, FAX (202)862-2610. **4522**

FOREST INDUSTRIES (SAN FRANCISCO, CALIF.). (US/0015-7430). Miller Freeman Inc., 600 Harrison Street, San Francisco CA 94107. **Tel** (415)905-2337, FAX (415)905-2240, telex 278273. **2400**

FOREST PRODUCTS ABSTRACTS. (UK/0140-4784). CAB International Centre, Wallingford, Oxon OX10 8DE United Kingdom. **Tel** 44 491 832111, FAX 44 491 833508, telex 847964 (COMAGG G). **2399**

FORESTRY ABSTRACTS. (UK/0015-7538). CAB International Centre, Wallingford, Oxon OX10 8DE United Kingdom. **Tel** 44 491 832111, FAX 44 491 833508, telex 847964 (COMAGG G). **2399**

FORTHCOMING BOOKS. (US/0015-8119). R R Bowker, A Reed Reference Publishing Company, Part of Reed International PLC, PO Box 31, 121 Chanlon Drive, New Providence NJ 07974. **Tel** (908)464-6800, (800)521-8110, FAX (908)665-6688, telex 138-755. **416**

FORUM FOR APPLIED RESEARCH AND PUBLIC POLICY. (US/0887-8218). Executive Sciences Institute, 1005 Mississippi Avenue, PO Box 4318, Davenport IA 52808-4318. **Tel** (319)324-4463, FAX (319)322-3725. **1944**

FRANCIS. 617, ECODOC / RESEAU D'INFORMATION EN ECONOMIE GENERALE. (FR/1157-383X). CNRS / Institut d'Information Scientifique et Technique, (Centre National de la Recherche Scientifique), 15 Quai Anatole France, Paris 75700 France. **Tel** 011 33 1 47531515, telex 299 356 F. **1491**

FRANCIS BIBLIOGRAPHIE GEOGRAPHIQUE INTERNATIONALE. 531. (FR/1157-3805). CNRS / Institut d'Information Scientifique et Technique, (Centre National de la Recherche Scientifique), 15 Quai Anatole France, Paris 75700 France. **Tel** 011 33 1 47531515, telex 299 356 F. **2561**

FRANCIS BULLETIN SIGNALETIQUE. 519, PHILOSOPHIE. (FR/1157-3694). CNRS / Institut d'Information Scientifique et Technique, (Centre National de la Recherche Scientifique), 15 Quai Anatole France, Paris 75700 France. **Tel** 011 33 1 47531515, telex 299 356 F. **4347**

FRANCIS BULLETIN SIGNALETIQUE. 520, SCIENCES DE L'EDUCATION. (FR/1157-3708). CNRS / Institut d'Information Scientifique et Technique, (Centre National de la Recherche Scientifique), 15 Quai Anatole France, Paris 75700 France. **Tel** 011 33 1 47531515, telex 299 356 F. **1747**

FRANCIS BULLETIN SIGNALETIQUE. 521, SOCIOLOGIE. (FR/1157-3716). CNRS / Institut d'Information Scientifique et Technique, (Centre National de la Recherche Scientifique), 15 Quai Anatole France, Paris 75700 France. **Tel** 011 33 1 47531515, telex 299 356 F. **5245**

FRANCIS BULLETIN SIGNALETIQUE. 522, HISTOIRE DES SCIENCES ET DES TECHNIQUES. (FR/1157-3724). CNRS / Institut d'Information Scientifique et Technique, (Centre National de la Recherche Scientifique), 15 Quai Anatole France, Paris 75700 France. **Tel** 011 33 1 47531515, telex 299 356 F. **5106**

FRANCIS

Serials available on CD-ROM

FRANCIS BULLETIN SIGNALETIQUE. 523, HISTOIRE ET SCIENCES DE LA LITTERATURE. (FR/1157-3732). CNRS / Institut d'Information Scientifique et Technique, (Centre National de la Recherche Scientifique), 15 Quai Anatole France, Paris 75700 France. **Tel** 011 33 1 47531515, telex 299 356 F. **3389**

FRANCIS BULLETIN SIGNALETIQUE. 524, SCIENCES DU LANGAGE. (FR/1157-3740). CNRS / Institut d'Information Scientifique et Technique, (Centre National de la Recherche Scientifique), 15 Quai Anatole France, Paris 75700 France. **Tel** 011 33 1 47531515, telex 299 356 F. **3282**

FRANCIS BULLETIN SIGNALETIQUE. 525, PREHISTOIRE ET PROTOHISTOIRE. (FR/1157-3759). CNRS / Institut d'Information Scientifique et Technique, (Centre National de la Recherche Scientifique), 15 Quai Anatole France, Paris 75700 France. **Tel** 011 33 1 47531515, telex 299 356 F. **236**

FRANCIS BULLETIN SIGNALETIQUE. 526, ART ET ARCHEOLOGIE. (FR/1157-3767). CNRS / Institut d'Information Scientifique et Technique, (Centre National de la Recherche Scientifique), 15 Quai Anatole France, Paris 75700 France. **Tel** 011 33 1 47531515, telex 299 356 F. **268**

FRANCIS BULLETIN SIGNALETIQUE. 527, HISTOIRE ET SCIENCES DES RELIGIONS. (FR/1157-3775). CNRS / Institut d'Information Scientifique et Technique, (Centre National de la Recherche Scientifique), 15 Quai Anatole France, Paris 75700 France. **Tel** 011 33 1 47531515, telex 299 356 F. **4959**

FRANCIS BULLETIN SIGNALETIQUE. 528, BIBLIOGRAPHIE INTERNATIONALE DE SCIENCE ADMINISTRATIVE. (FR/1157-3783). CNRS / Institut d'Information Scientifique et Technique, (Centre National de la Recherche Scientifique), 15 Quai Anatole France, Paris 75700 France. **Tel** 011 33 1 47531515, telex 299 356 F. **868**

FRANCIS BULLETIN SIGNALETIQUE. 529, ETHNOLOGIE. (FR/1157-3791). CNRS / Institut d'Information Scientifique et Technique, (Centre National de la Recherche Scientifique), 15 Quai Anatole France, Paris 75700 France. **Tel** 011 33 1 47531515, telex 299 356 F. **236**

FRAZEE FORUM. (US). Frazee Forum, PO Box 187, Frazee MN 56544. **Tel** (218)334-3566. **5696**

FRONT PAGE NEWS PLUS BUSINESS. (US/1059-5937). Buckmaster Publishing - Virginia, Route 4, Box 1630, Mineral VA 23117. **Tel** (703)894-5777. **2920**

FULL PAGES IMAGES. (US). Artbeats, PO Box 20083, San Bernardino CA 92404. **Tel** (714)881-1200. **1286**

FULL SPECTRUM. CD-ROM. (US). Alde Publishing, PO Box 39326, Minneapolis MN 55396. **Tel** (612)474-3755. **1233**

GALE DIRECTORY OF DATABASES. (US/1066-8934). Gale Research Inc., 835 Penobscot Building, 645 Griswold Street, Detroit MI 48226. **Tel** (800)877-GALE, (313)961-2242, FAX (313)961-6083, (800)414-5043, telex TWX 810-221-7086. **1237**

GALE GLOBAL ACCESS. ASSOCIATIONS. (US/1065-5050). Silverplatter Information Inc., 100 River Ridge Drive, Norwood MA 02062. **Tel** (800)343-0064, (617)769-2599, FAX (617)235-1715. **5231**

GALE'S LITERARY INDEX. (US/1066-7709). Gale Research Inc., 835 Penobscot Building, 645 Griswold Street, Detroit MI 48226. **Tel** (800)877-GALE, (313)961-2242, FAX (313)961-6083, (800)414-5043, telex TWX 810-221-7086. **3389**

GAS & LIQUID CHROMATOGRAPHY LITERATURE, ABSTRACTS & INDEX. (US/1059-3160). Preston Publications Inc., 7800 Merrimac Avenue, PO Box 48312, Niles IL 60714. **Tel** (708)965-0566, FAX (708)965-7639, telex 910-223-1780 PRESTON NILE. **1011**

GAS TURBINE FORECAST. (US). Forecast International / DMS Inc., 22 Commerce Road, Newtown CT 06470. **Tel** (203)426-0800, FAX (203)426-1964, telex 467615. **2114**

GEFAHRGUT - DANGEROUS GOODS CD-ROM. (GW). Springer-Verlag GmbH & Company KG, Heidelberger Platz 3, D 14197 Berlin Germany. **Tel** 011 49 30 8207223, FAX 011 49 30 8214091, telex 183 319 SPBLN D. **2862**

GENERAL BUSINESSFILE [COMPUTER FILE]. (US). Information Access Company, 362 Lakeside Drive, Foster City CA 94404. **Tel** (800)227-8431. **730**

GENERAL PERIODICALS INDEX [COMPUTER FILE]. (US). Information Access Company, 362 Lakeside Drive, Foster City CA 94404. **Tel** (800)227-8431. **2496**

GENERAL PERIODICALS ONDISC (RESEARCH 1 ED.). (US/1064-8380). University Microfilms International, 300 North Zeeb Road, Ann Arbor MI 48106-1346. **Tel** (313)761-4700, (800)521-0600 Exts. 2490, 2491, FAX (313)973-1540. **2496**

GENERAL SCIENCE INDEX. (US/0162-1963). H W Wilson Company, 950 University Avenue, Bronx NY 10452. **Tel** (800)367-6770, (718)588-8400, FAX (718)590-1617, telex 4990003 HWILSON. **5175**

GENERAL SCIENCE INDEX. CD-ROM. (US/0162-1963). H W Wilson Company, 950 University Avenue, Bronx NY 10452. **Tel** (800)367-6770, (718)588-8400, FAX (718)590-1617, telex 4990003 HWILSON. **5107**

GENERAL SCIENCE SOURCE. (US/1073-1954). EBSCO Publishing / Boston, 83 Pine Street, Peabody MA 01960. **Tel** (800)653-2726 North America, (508)535-8500, FAX (508)535-8545. **5175**

GENETICS ABSTRACTS. (US/0016-674X). Cambridge Scientific Abstracts, 7200 Wisconsin Avenue, #601, Bethesda MD 20814-4823. **Tel** (301)961-6750, (800)843-7751, FAX (301)961-6720. **478**

GEOARCHAEOLOGY. (US/0883-6353). John Wiley & Sons, Inc., 605 Third Avenue, New York NY 10158-0012. **Tel** (212)850-6000, (212)850-6645, FAX (212)850-6088, telex 12-7063. **269**

GEOARCHIVE ON CD-ROM. (US/1070-6046). Geosystems Inc., PO Box 40, Didcot, Oxon OX11 9BX England. **Tel** 011 44 235 813913. **1376**

GEOBASE. (UK). Elsevier Geo Abstracts, An Imprint of Elsevier Science Ltd., The Boulevard, Langford Lane, Kidlington, Oxford OX5 1GB United Kingdom. **Tel** 011 44 865 843000, 011 44 865 843699, FAX 011 44 865 843010. **2561**

GEOGRAPHICAL JOURNAL, THE. (UK/0016-7398). Royal Geographical Society / England, 1 Kensington Gore, London SW7 2AR England. **Tel** 011 44 71 589 5466, FAX 011 44 71 584 4447, telex 933669. **2563**

GEOLOGICAL SOCIETY OF AMERICA BULLETIN. (US/0016-7606). Geological Society of America, PO Box 9140, 3300 Penrose Place, Boulder CO 80301. **Tel** (303)447-2020, (800)472-1988, FAX (303)447-1133. **1378**

GEOREF (CD-ROM). (US/0197-7482). Silverplatter Information Inc., 100 River Ridge Drive, Norwood MA 02062. **Tel** (800)343-0064, (617)769-2599, FAX (617)235-1715. **1363**

GEORGIA BUSINESS DIRECTORY. (US/1048-7220). American Business Directory, 5711 South 86th Circle, Omaha NE 68127. **Tel** (402)593-4600, FAX (402)331-5481. **677**

GEOSCIENCE DOCUMENTATION. (UK/0016-8483). Geosystems Inc., PO Box 40, Didcot, Oxon OX11 9BX England. **Tel** 011 44 235 813913. **1363**

GIURISPRUDENZA : BANCA DATI LAVORO SU CD-ROM. (IT). IPSOA Editore SRL, Casella Postale 12055, Mastrangelo, 20120 Milan Italy. **Tel** 011 39 2 82476248. **2974**

GIURISPRUDENZA PREVIDENZIALE : BANCA DATI LAVORO SU CD-ROM. (IT). IPSOA Editore SRL, Casella Postale 12055, Mastrangelo, 20120 Milan Italy. **Tel** 011 39 2 82476248. **2974**

GLOBE AND MAIL, THE. (CN/0319-0714). Globe & Mail, 444 Front Street West, Toronto Ontario M5V 2S9 Canada. **Tel** (416)585-5000, FAX (416)585-5249. **5785**

GORDON'S PRINT PRICE ANNUAL. (US/0160-6298). Gordon & Lawrence Art Reference Inc., 1840 8th Street South, Naples FL 33940. **Tel** (813)434-6842. **378**

GOVERNMENT COMPUTER NEWS. (US/0738-4300). Cahners Publishing Company, 249 West 17th Street, New York NY 10011. **Tel** (212)645-0067, FAX (212)242-6987. **4651**

GOVERNMENT DISC. 1, US FEDERAL GOVERNMENT [COMPUTER FILE], THE. (US/1053-282X). Highlighted Data Inc., 6628 Medhill Place, Falls Church VA 22043. **Tel** (703)516-9211. **4651**

GOVERNMENT DOCUMENTS CATALOG SUBSCRIPTION SERVICE [COMPUTER FILE]. (US). Auto Graphics Inc., 3201 Temple Avenue, Pomona CA 91768. **Tel** (800)776-6939. **4651**

GPO MONTHLY CATALOG [COMPUTER FILE]. (US). OCLC Asia Pacific Services, 6565 Frantz Road, Dublin OH 43017. **Tel** (800)848-5878, (614)764-6394 or 6000, FAX (614)764-6096. **4698**

GRASSLANDS AND FORAGE ABSTRACTS. (UK/1350-9837). CAB International Centre, Wallingford, Oxon OX10 8DE United Kingdom. **Tel** 44 491 832111, FAX 44 491 833508, telex 847964 (COMAGG G). **153**

GUIDE TO NEW AUSTRALIAN BOOKS. (AT/1035-5391). D. W. Thorpe, A Reed Reference Publishing Company, A Subsidiary of Reed International Books Australia, 18 Salmon Street, Port Melbourne, Victoria 3207 Australia. **Tel** 011 61 3 6451511, FAX 011 61 3 6453981, telex 39476. **3392**

GUIDELINES. (AT/0156-6717). Bibliographic Services Pty.Ltd., PO Box 2, Mt. Waverly Victoria 3149 Australia. **Tel** 011 61 03 8073442, FAX 011 61 03 8072073. **3258**

GUINNESS DISC OF RECORDS [COMPUTER FILE], THE. (US). Comptons Newmedia, 722 Genevieve, Suite M, Solana Beach CA 92075. **Tel** (800)532-3766, (415)597-5555. **1926**

HAIYANG XUEBAO (ENGLISH ED.). (CC/0253-505X). China Ocean Press, 1 Fuxingmenwai Street, Beijing 100860, People's Republic of China. **Tel** 011 86 1 8532211 ext. 5913. **1449**

HANDBUCH DER GROSSUNTERNEHMEN. (GW/0073-0068). Verlag Hoppenstedt & Company, Postfach 100139, D 64201 Darmstadt Germany. **Tel** 011 49 6151 380436. **1493**

HARRIS GEORGIA MANUFACTURERS DIRECTORY. (US/1065-4755). Harris Publishing Company, 2057-2 Aurora Road, Twinsburg OH 44087. **Tel** (800)888-5900, (216)425-9000, FAX (216)425-7150, telex 510 601 1740. **3480**

HARRIS ILLINOIS INDUSTRIAL DIRECTORY. (US/0734-3256). Harris Publishing Company, 2057-2 Aurora Road, Twinsburg OH 44087. **Tel** (800)888-5900, (216)425-9000, FAX (216)425-7150, telex 510 601 1740. **1608**

HARRIS INDIANA INDUSTRIAL DIRECTORY. (US/0888-8175). Harris Publishing Company, 2057-2 Aurora Road, Twinsburg OH 44087. **Tel** (800)888-5900, (216)425-9000, FAX (216)425-7150, telex 510 601 1740. **1608**

HARRIS KENTUCKY INDUSTRIAL DIRECTORY. (US/0887-4255). Harris Publishing Company, 2057-2 Aurora Road, Twinsburg OH 44087. **Tel** (800)888-5900, (216)425-9000, FAX (216)425-7150, telex 510 601 1740. **1608**

HARRIS MANUFACTURERS DIRECTORY (NATIONAL ED.). (US/1061-2076). Harris Publishing Company, 2057-2 Aurora Road, Twinsburg OH 44087. **Tel** (800)888-5900, (216)425-9000, FAX (216)425-7150, telex 510 601 1740. **3480**

HARRIS MANUFACTURERS DIRECTORY (NORTHEAST ED.). (US/1061-2041). Harris Publishing Company, 2057-2 Aurora Road, Twinsburg OH 44087. **Tel** (800)888-5900, (216)425-9000, FAX (216)425-7150, telex 510 601 1740. **3480**

HARRIS MANUFACTURERS DIRECTORY (SOUTHEAST ED.). (US/1061-2033). Harris Publishing Company, 2057-2 Aurora Road, Twinsburg OH 44087. **Tel** (800)888-5900, (216)425-9000, FAX (216)425-7150, telex 510 601 1740. **3480**

HARRIS MANUFACTURERS DIRECTORY (SOUTHWEST ED.), THE. (US/1061-2068). Harris Publishing Company, 2057-2 Aurora Road, Twinsburg OH 44087. **Tel** (800)888-5900, (216)425-9000, FAX (216)425-7150, telex 510 601 1740. **3480**

HARRIS MANUFACTURERS DIRECTORY (WEST & SOUTHWEST ED.). (US/1061-205X). Harris Publishing Company, 2057-2 Aurora Road, Twinsburg OH 44087. **Tel** (800)888-5900, (216)425-9000, FAX (216)425-7150, telex 510 601 1740. **3480**

HARRIS MARYLAND MANUFACTURERS DIRECTORY. (US/1065-7231). Harris Publishing Company, 2057-2 Aurora Road, Twinsburg OH 44087. **Tel** (800)888-5900, (216)425-9000, FAX (216)425-7150, telex 510 601 1740. **3480**

HARRIS MICHIGAN INDUSTRIAL DIRECTORY (TWINSBURG, OHIO: 1984). (US/0888-8167). Harris Publishing Company, 2057-2 Aurora Road, Twinsburg OH 44087. **Tel** (800)888-5900, (216)425-9000, FAX (216)425-7150, telex 510 601 1740. **1608**

HARRIS NORTH CAROLINA MANUFACTURERS DIRECTORY. (US/1065-4720). Harris Publishing Company, 2057-2 Aurora Road, Twinsburg OH 44087. **Tel** (800)888-5900, (216)425-9000, FAX (216)425-7150, telex 510 601 1740. **3480**

HARRIS OHIO INDUSTRIAL DIRECTORY. (US/0888-8140). Harris Publishing Company, 2057-2 Aurora Road, Twinsburg OH 44087. **Tel** (800)888-5900, (216)425-9000, FAX (216)425-7150, telex 510 601 1740. **1608**

HARRIS PENNSYLVANIA INDUSTRIAL DIRECTORY. (US/0734-8541). Harris Publishing Company, 2057-2 Aurora Road, Twinsburg OH 44087. **Tel** (800)888-5900, (216)425-9000, FAX (216)425-7150, telex 510 601 1740. **1608**

HARRIS SOUTH CAROLINA MANUFACTURERS DIRECTORY. (US/1065-4747). Harris Publishing Company, 2057-2 Aurora Road, Twinsburg OH 44087. **Tel** (800)888-5900, (216)425-9000, FAX (216)425-7150, telex 510 601 1740. **3480**

HARRIS WEST VIRGINIA MANUFACTURING DIRECTORY. (US/0887-4247). Harris Publishing Company, 2057-2 Aurora Road, Twinsburg OH 44087. **Tel** (800)888-5900, (216)425-9000, FAX (216)425-7150, telex 510 601 1740. **3480**

HARVARD HEALTH LETTER. (US/1052-1577). Harvard Medical School, 164 Longwood Avenue, 1st Floor, Boston MA 02115. **Tel** (617)432-1485, FAX (617)432-1506. **3580**

HARVARD INTERNATIONAL REVIEW. (US/0739-1854). Harvard International Review, PO Box 401, Cambridge MA 02138. **Tel** (617)495-9607, FAX (617)496-4472. **4523**

HARVARD LAW REVIEW. (US/0017-811X). Harvard Law Review Association, Gannett House, Cambridge MA 02138. **Tel** (617)495-4650. **2977**

HASTINGS COMMUNICATIONS AND ENTERTAINMENT LAW JOURNAL (COMM/ENT). (US/1061-6578). Hastings College of Law, 200 McAllister Street, San Francisco CA 94102. **Tel** (415)565-4816, (415)565-4738, FAX (415)565-4814. **2977**

HASTINGS CONSTITUTIONAL LAW QUARTERLY. (US/0094-5617). Hastings College of Law, 200 McAllister Street, San Francisco CA 94102. Tel (415)565-4816, (415)565-4738, FAX (415)565-4814. 3093

HASTINGS INTERNATIONAL AND COMPARATIVE LAW REVIEW. (US/0149-9246). Hastings College of Law, 200 McAllister Street, San Francisco CA 94102. **Tel** (415)565-4816, (415)565-4738, FAX (415)565-4814. **3129**

HASTINGS LAW JOURNAL. (US/0017-8322). Hastings College of Law, 200 McAllister Street, San Francisco CA 94102. **Tel** (415)565-4816, (415)565-4738, FAX (415)565-4814. **2977**

HASTINGS WOMEN'S LAW JOURNAL. (US/1061-0901). Hastings College of Law, 200 McAllister Street, San Francisco CA 94102. **Tel** (415)565-4816, (415)565-4738, FAX (415)565-4814. **2977**

HAWAII BUSINESS DIRECTORY. (US). Hawaii Business Directory Inc., 1164 Bishop Street, Suite 907, Honolulu HI 96813. **Tel** (808)526-2287. **679**

HEALTH & MEDICAL CARE DIRECTORY. (US/1046-8900). Business Yellow Pages, PO Box 2010, Niagara Falls NY 14302. **Tel** (716)282-2209. **3780**

HEALTH & MEDICAL CARE DIRECTORY ON CD-ROM. (US). Innotech Inc, 2001 Sheppard Avenue East 118, North York, Ontario M2J 4Z7 Canada. **Tel** (416)492-3838. **3780**

HEALTH AND SAFETY SCIENCE ABSTRACTS. (US/0892-9351). Cambridge Scientific Abstracts, 7200 Wisconsin Avenue, #601, Bethesda MD 20814-4823. **Tel** (301)961-6750, (800)843-7751, FAX (301)961-6720. **4810**

HEALTH DEVICES ALERTS. (US/0163-0458). ECRI Emergency Care Research Institute, 5200 Butler Pike, Plymouth Meeting PA 19462. **Tel** (215)825-6000, FAX (215)834-1275, telex 510-660-8023. **3659**

HEALTH INDEX [COMPUTER FILE]. (US). Information Access Company, 362 Lakeside Drive, Foster City CA 94404. **Tel** (800)227-8431. **2602**

HEALTH MATRIX. (US/0748-383X). Case Western Reserve University School of Law, 11075 East Boulevard, Cleveland OH 44106. **Tel** (216)368-3304, FAX (216)368-6144. **3740**

HEALTH PLANNING AND ADMINISTRATION. (US/1065-0679). EBSCO Publishing / Boston, 83 Pine Street, Peabody MA 01960. **Tel** (800)653-2726 North America, (508)535-8500, FAX (508)535-8545. **3659**

HEALTH PLANNING AND ADMINISTRATION DATABASE (HEALTH). (US). American Hospital Association, 840 North Lake Shore Drive, Chicago IL 60611. **Tel** (312)280-6000, (800)242-2626. **3781**

HEALTH REFERENCE CENTER [COMPUTER FILE]. (US). Information Access Company, 362 Lakeside Drive, Foster City CA 94404. **Tel** (800)227-8431. **3659**

HEALTH SOURCE (PEABODY, MASS.). (US/1063-9810). EBSCO Publishing / Boston, 83 Pine Street, Peabody MA 01960. **Tel** (800)653-2726 North America, (508)535-8500, FAX (508)535-8545. **2602**

HEALTHPLAN / NATIONAL LIBRARY OF MEDICINE / [COMPUTER FILE]. (US). Silverplatter Information Inc., 100 River Ridge Drive, Norwood MA 02062. **Tel** (800)343-0064, (617)769-2599, FAX (617)235-1715. **3583**

HEIN'S U.S. TREATY INDEX ON CD-ROM [COMPUTER FILE]. (US). William S. Hein & Company Inc., 1285 Main Street, Buffalo NY 14209. **Tel** (716)882-2600, (800)828-7571, FAX (716)883-8100, telex 91-209 WM S HEIN BUF. **4523**

HELMINTHOLOGICAL ABSTRACTS. (UK/0957-6789). CAB International Centre, Wallingford, Oxon OX10 8DE United Kingdom. **Tel** 44 491 832111, FAX 44 491 833508, telex 847964 (COMAGG G). **5604**

HEP HIGHER EDUCATION DIRECTORY, THE. (US/0736-0797). Higher Education Publications Inc., 6400 Arlington Boulevard, Suite 648, Falls Church VA 22042. **Tel** (703)532-2300, FAX (703)532-2305. **1827**

HERBAGE ABSTRACTS. (UK/0018-0602). CAB International Centre, Wallingford, Oxon OX10 8DE United Kingdom. **Tel** 44 491 832111, FAX 44 491 833508, telex 847964 (COMAGG G). **154**

HEWLETT-PACKARD JOURNAL. (US/0018-1153). Hewlett Packard, 1000 Northeast Circle Boulevard, Corvallis OR 97330. **Tel** (503)757-2000. **1186**

HIGH RELIABILITY ELECTRONIC COMPONENTS. (US/0899-8531). DATA Business Publishing, PO Box 6510, 15 Inverness Way East, Englewood CO 80155. **Tel** (800)447-4666, (303)799-0381, FAX (303)799-4082. **2056**

HIGH TEMPERATURE. (US/0018-151X). Plenum Press, 233 Spring Street, New York NY 10013-1578. **Tel** (212)620-8000, (800)221-9369, FAX (212)463-0742, (212)807-1047, telex 23/421139. **4431**

HILITES DATABASE [ONLINE DATABASE]. (US). Ergosyst Associates Inc, 123 West Eighth Street, Suite 1012, Lawrence KS 66044-2605. **Tel** (913)842-7334, FAX (913)842-7348. **1209**

HISPANIC AMERICAN PERIODICALS INDEX (LOS ANGELES, CALIF.). (US/0270-8558). Regents of the University of California at Los Angeles, 405 Hilgard Avenue, Los Angeles CA 90024-1447. **Tel** (310)825-6634. **2496**

HISTORICAL ABSTRACTS ON DISC [COMPUTER FILE]. (US/1074-7869). ABC Clio Press, PO Box 1911, 130 Cremona, Santa Barbara CA 93117. **Tel** (805)968-1911, (800)422-2546, FAX (805)685-9685. **2618**

HISTORICAL ABSTRACTS. PART A, MODERN HISTORY ABSTRACTS. (US/0363-2717). ABC Clio Press, PO Box 1911, 130 Cremona, Santa Barbara CA 93117. **Tel** (805)968-1911, (800)422-2546, FAX (805)685-9685. **2635**

HISTORICAL ABSTRACTS. PART B, TWENTIETH CENTURY ABSTRACTS. (US/0363-2725). ABC Clio Press, PO Box 1911, 130 Cremona, Santa Barbara CA 93117. **Tel** (805)968-1911, (800)422-2546, FAX (805)685-9685. **2635**

HISTORY SOURCE. (US/1063-9799). EBSCO Publishing / Boston, 83 Pine Street, Peabody MA 01960. **Tel** (800)653-2726 North America, (508)535-8500, FAX (508)535-8545. **2635**

HMC&M, HAZARDOUS MATERIAL CONTROL & MANAGEMENT [COMPUTER FILE] : HMIS, HAZARDOUS MATERIALS INFORMATION SYSTEM. (US). US Department of Defense, The Pentagon, Washington DC 20301. **Tel** (703)545-6700. **2232**

HMC&M [COMPUTER FILE] : HAZARDOUS MATERIAL CONTROL & MANAGEMENT ; HMIS : HAZARDOUS MATERIAL INFORMATION SYSTEM / DEPT. OF DEFENSE. (US). Superintendent of Documents, US Government Printing Office, Washington DC 20402. **Tel** (202)275-3328, FAX (202)786-2377. **2232**

HORN BOOK MAGAZINE (1945), THE. (US/0018-5078). The Horn Book Inc, 11 Beacon Street, Suite 1000, Boston MA 02108-3704. **Tel** (617)227-1555, (800)325-1170, FAX (617)523-0299. **1064**

HORTICULTURAL ABSTRACTS. (UK/0018-5280). CAB International Centre, Wallingford, Oxon OX10 8DE United Kingdom. **Tel** 44 491 832111, FAX 44 491 833508, telex 847964 (COMAGG G). **2434**

HOSPITAL LITERATURE INDEX. (US/0018-5736). American Hospital Association, 840 North Lake Shore Drive, Chicago IL 60611. **Tel** (312)280-6000, (800)242-2626. **3659**

HUMAN ANTIBODIES AND HYBRIDOMAS. (US/0956-960X). Forefront Publishing USA, 24 Glen Hill Road, Wilton CT 06897. **Tel** (203)221-9949, FAX (203)834-0940. **457**

HUMAN GENOME ABSTRACTS. (US/1045-4470). Cambridge Scientific Abstracts, 7200 Wisconsin Avenue, #601, Bethesda MD 20814-4823. **Tel** (301)961-6750, (800)843-7751, FAX (301)961-6720. **478**

HUMANE MEDICINE. (CN/0828-7090). Canadian Medical Association, 1867 Alta Vista Drive, Ottawa Ontario K1G 3Y6 Canada. **Tel** (613)731-9331 ext. 2028, FAX (613)731-4797. **3585**

HUMANITIES INDEX. (US/0095-5981). H W Wilson Company, 950 University Avenue, Bronx NY 10452. **Tel** (800)367-6770, (718)588-8400, FAX (718)590-1617, telex 4990003 HWILSON. **2857**

HUMANITIES INDEX. CD-ROM. (US/0095-5981). H W Wilson Company, 950 University Avenue, Bronx NY 10452. **Tel** (800)367-6770, (718)588-8400, FAX (718)590-1617, telex 4990003 HWILSON. **2847**

HUMANITIES INDEX (CD-ROM ED.). (US/1063-3294). H W Wilson Company, 950 University Avenue, Bronx NY 10452. **Tel** (800)367-6770, (718)588-8400, FAX (718)590-1617, telex 4990003 HWILSON. **2857**

HUMANITIES SOURCE. (US/1073-1962). EBSCO Publishing / Boston, 83 Pine Street, Peabody MA 01960. **Tel** (800)653-2726 North America, (508)535-8500, FAX (508)535-8545. **2857**

HYDRODATA [COMPUTER FILE]. (US). US Geological Survey / Denver, PO Box 25286, Denver CO 80225. **Tel** (303)493-8401. **1414**

HYPATIA (EDWARDSVILLE, ILL.). (US/0887-5367). Indiana University Press, 601 North Morton Street, Bloomington IN 47404. **Tel** (812)855-3830, (800)842-6796. **5558**

IC MASTER. (US/0894-6809). Hearst Business Communications, 1790 Broadway, New York NY 10019. **Tel** (212)969-7500, FAX (212)969-7564. **2057**

IDAHO MANUFACTURING DIRECTORY. (US/1057-347X). Center for Business Development & Research, University of Idaho, Moscow ID 83843. **Tel** (208)885-6611. **3480**

IDENTIDEX. CD-ROM. (US). Micromedex Inc, 600 Grant Street, Denver CO 80203. **Tel** (303)831-1400, FAX (303)837-1717. **3981**

IDIS. (US/0891-8511). Iowa Drug Information Service, The University of Iowa, 100 Oakdale Campus, N330 OH, Iowa City IA 52242-5000. **Tel** (319)335-4800, (800)525-4347, FAX (319)335-4077. **4307**

IDIS SYSTEM / CD-ROM. (US). Iowa Drug Information Service, The University of Iowa, 100 Oakdale Campus, N330 OH, Iowa City IA 52242-5000. **Tel** (319)335-4800, (800)525-4347, FAX (319)335-4077. **4334**

ILLINOIS HISTORICAL JOURNAL. (US/0748-8149). Illinois State Historical Society, 1 Old Capitol Plaza, Springfield IL 62701. **Tel** (217)782-8160, FAX (217)524-8042. **2738**

IMAGING SOLUTIONS INFODISK. (US). Faulkner Technical Reports, 7905 Browning Road, Suite 114, Pennsauken NJ 08109. **Tel** (800)843-0460. **1187**

IMMIGRATION BRIEFINGS. (US/0897-6708). Federal Publications Inc, 1120 20th Street Northwest, Washington DC 20036. **Tel** (202)337-7000, (800)922-4330, FAX (202)659-2233. **2980**

IMMUNOLOGY ABSTRACTS. (US/0307-112X). Cambridge Scientific Abstracts, 7200 Wisconsin Avenue, #601, Bethesda MD 20814-4823. **Tel** (301)961-6750, (800)843-7751, FAX (301)961-6720. **3660**

INDEPENDENT (LONDON, ENGLAND). (UK). Newspaper Publishing PLC, 40 City Road, London EC1Y 2DB England. **Tel** 011 44 71 9561689, 011 44 71 2531222. **5812**

INDEX MEDICUS (1960). (US/0019-3879). Superintendent of Documents, US Government Printing Office, Washington DC 20402. **Tel** (202)275-3328, FAX (202)786-2377. **3660**

INDEX

Serials available on CD-ROM

INDEX MEDICUS LATINO-AMERICANO. (BL/0100-4743). Organizacao Pan American da Saude, rua Botucatu 862, 04023 Sao Paulo SP Brazil. **Tel** (011)549-2611, telex 11 22143. **3586**

INDEX OF ECONOMIC ARTICLES IN JOURNALS AND COLLECTIVE VOLUMES. (US/0536-647X). American Economic Association / Tennessee, 2014 Broadway, Suite 305, Nashville TN 37203-2418. **Tel** (615)322-2595. **1533**

INDEX TO BOOK REVIEWS IN RELIGION. (US/0887-1574). American Theological Library Association, 820 Church Street, 3rd Floor, Evanston IL 60201. **Tel** (708)869-7788, FAX (708)869-8513. **5012**

INDEX TO DENTAL LITERATURE. (US/0019-3992). American Dental Association, 211 East Chicago Avenue, Chicago IL 60611. **Tel** (312)440-2867, (312)440-2500, FAX (312)440-3542. **1338**

INDEX TO IEEE PUBLICATIONS. (US/0099-1368). IEEE, Institution of Electrical and Electronics Engineers, Inc., 345 East 47th Street, New York NY 10017-2394. **Tel** (908)981-1393, FAX (908)981-9667. **2004**

INDEX TO INTERNATIONAL STATISTICS. (US/0737-4461). Congressional Information Service Inc, 4520 East-West Highway, Suite 800, Bethesda MD 20814-3389. **Tel** (800)638-8380, (301)654-1550, FAX (301)654-4033, telex 292386 CIS UR. **5328**

INDEX TO LEGAL PERIODICALS. (US/0019-4077). H W Wilson Company, 950 University Avenue, Bronx NY 10452. **Tel** (800)367-6770, (718)588-8400, FAX (718)590-1617, telex 4990003 HWILSON. **3081**

INDEX TO LEGAL PERIODICALS. CD-ROM. (US/0019-4077). H W Wilson Company, 950 University Avenue, Bronx NY 10452. **Tel** (800)367-6770, (718)588-8400, FAX (718)590-1617, telex 4990003 HWILSON. **3081**

INDEX TO PHILIPPINE PERIODICALS. (PH/0073-599X). University of the Philippines Library, Diliman Quezon Philippines. **2496**

INDEX TO THESES WITH ABSTRACTS ACCEPTED FOR HIGHER DEGREES BY THE UNIVERSITIES OF GREAT BRITAIN AND IRELAND AND THE COUNCIL FOR NATIONAL ACADEMIC AWARDS. (UK/0073-6066). ASLIB, Information House, 20-24 Old Street, London EC1V 9AP England. **Tel** 011 44 71 253 4488, FAX 011 44 71 430 0514, telex 23667 AJLIB G. **1830**

INDEX TO UNITED NATIONS DOCUMENTS AND PUBLICATIONS [COMPUTER FILE]. (US). Newsbank Inc, 58 Pine Street, New Canaan CT 06840. **Tel** (800)243-7694, (800)762-8182, FAX (203)966-6254. **417**

INDEX VETERINARIUS. (UK/0019-4123). CAB International Centre, Wallingford, Oxon OX10 8DE United Kingdom. **Tel** 44 491 832111, FAX 44 491 833508, telex 847964 (COMAGG G). **5528**

INDIAN JOURNAL OF PHARMACOLOGY. (II/0253-7613). Department Pharmacology & Therapy, Pondicherry 605 006 India. **Tel** 11 91 413 36380 ext 201, FAX 11 91 413 38132. **4307**

INDIANA BUSINESS DIRECTORY. (US/1048-7255). American Business Directory, 5711 South 86th Circle, Omaha NE 68127. **Tel** (402)593-4600, FAX (402)331-5481. **682**

INDICE DE LA LITERATURA DENTAL PERIODICA EN CASTELLANO. (AG/0325-0679). Association of Odontologia of Argentina, Junin 959, Buenos Aires Argentina. **Tel** 011 54 1 961 6062 6141. **1324**

INDICE ESPANOL DE CIENCIA Y TECNOLOGIA. (SP/0210-9409). Instituto de Informacion y Documentacion, Cientifica (CINDOC), Joaquin Costa, 22, 28002 Madrid Spain. **Tel** 011 34 1 563-5482 87, FAX (91)564 26 44, telex 22628 CIDMD E. **5112**

INDICE ESPANOL DE CIENCIAS SOCIALES. SERIE A, PSICOLOGIA Y CIENCIAS DE LA EDUCACION. (SP/0213-019X). Consejo Superior Investigacion Cientificas (CSIC), Vitruvio 8, 28006 Madrid Spain. **Tel** 011 34 1 5612833, FAX 011 34 1 4113077, telex 42182. **5203**

INDICE ESPANOL DE CIENCIAS SOCIALES. SERIE C, DERECHO. (SP). Consejo Superior Investigacion Cientificas (CSIC), Vitruvio 8, 28006 Madrid Spain. **Tel** 011 34 1 5612833, FAX 011 34 1 4113077, telex 42182. **3081**

INDICE MEDICO ESPANOL. (SP). Centro Documentacion Informati Biomedica, Avd Blasco Ibanez 17, 46010 Valencia Spain. **Tel** 011 34 6 3610373, 3692466, FAX 011 34 6 3613975. **3660**

INFECTION AND IMMUNITY. (US/0019-9567). American Society for Microbiology, 1325 Massachusetts Avenue Northwest, Washington DC 20005-4171. **Tel** (202)737-3600, FAX (202)737-0367. **563**

INFORMATION INTELLIGENCE, ONLINE LIBRARIES, AND MICROCOMPUTERS. (US/0737-7770). Information Intelligence Inc., PO Box 31098, Phoenix AZ 85046. **Tel** (602)996-2283, (800)228-9982. **3216**

INFORMATION INTELLIGENCE ONLINE NEWSLETTER. (US/0194-0694). Information Intelligence Inc., PO Box 31098, Phoenix AZ 85046. **Tel** (602)996-2283, (800)228-9982. **1274**

INFORMATION SCIENCE ABSTRACTS. (US/0020-0239). Plenum Press, 233 Spring Street, New York NY 10013-1578. **Tel** (212)620-8000, (800)221-9369, FAX (212)463-0742, (212)807-1047, telex 23/421139. **3258**

INIS ATOMINDEX [MICROFORM]. (AU). International Atomic Energy Agency / IAEA, Wagramerstrasse 5, PO Box 100, A-1400 Vienna Austria. **Tel** 011 43 1 2360 ext. 2530, FAX 011 43 1 234564. **4426**

INPHARMA WEEKLY. (NZ/0156-2703). ADIS International Ltd, 41 Centorian Drive, Private Bag 65901, Mairangi Bay, Auckland 10 New Zealand. **Tel** 011 64 9 4798100, FAX 011 64 9 4791418. **4308**

INSIGHT INTO AMERICAN LIFE & OPINIONS REVEALED BY POLLS & SURVEYS. (US/1057-0845). ORS Pub, 1342 Timberlane Road, Suite 201A, Tallahassee FL 32312. **2739**

INSIGHT ON THE NEWS (WASHINGTON, D.C.). (US/1051-4880). Insight Magazine, PO Box 91022, Washington DC 20090. **Tel** (202)269-5365, FAX (202)526-3497. **4477**

INSOURCE CUSTOM SERVICE (CD-ROM). (US). NILS Publishing Company, 21625 Prairie Street, PO Box 2507, Chatsworth CA 91311. **Tel** (818)998-8830, (800)423-5910, FAX (818)718-8482. **2882**

INSPEC ONDISC. (US/1063-7060). University Microfilms International, 300 North Zeeb Road, Ann Arbor MI 48106-1346. **Tel** (313)761-4700, (800)521-0600 Exts. 2490, 2491, FAX (313)973-1540. **2065**

INSPEC [ONLINE DATABASE]. (UK). Institution of Electrical Engineers / IEE, Michael Faraday House, Six Hills Way, Stevenage Herts SG1 2AY UK. **Tel** 011 44 438 313311, FAX 011 44 438 742840, telex 825578 IEESTV G. **2004**

INSTANT BACKGROUND. (US). Radio Advertising Bureau, 304 Park Avenue South, New York NY 10010. **Tel** (212)387-2100, FAX (212)254-8713. **1133**

INSTITUTIONAL INVESTOR (INTERNATIONAL ED.). (US/0192-5660). Institutional Investor Inc., 488 Madison Avenue, New York NY 10022. **Tel** (212)303-3234, (212)303-3233, FAX (212)303-3353. **901**

INSTITUTIONAL INVESTOR (U.S. ED.). (US/0020-3580). Institutional Investor Inc., 488 Madison Avenue, New York NY 10022. **Tel** (212)303-3234, (212)303-3233, FAX (212)303-3353. **901**

INTERNAL AUDITOR, THE. (US/0020-5745). Institute of Internal Auditors / Orlando, Florida, PO Box 140099, Orlando FL 32889. **Tel** (407)830-7600, FAX (407)831-5171, telex 567443. **745**

INTERNATIONAL ABC AEROSPACE DIRECTORY. (UK/0074-1116). Jane's Information Group, Sentinel House, 163 Brighton Road, Coulsdon Surrey CR3 2NX England. **Tel** 011 44 81 763 1030, FAX 011 44 81 763 1006. **24**

INTERNATIONAL AEROSPACE ABSTRACTS. (US/0020-5842). American Institute of Aeronautics & Astronautics / New York, 85 John Street, 4th Floor, New York NY 10038. **Tel** (212)349-1120. **41**

INTERNATIONAL BOOKS IN PRINT. (GW/0170-9348). KG Saur Inc., PO Box 31, New Providence NJ 07974. **Tel** (800)521-8110, (908)665-3576, FAX (908)771-7792. **4821**

INTERNATIONAL BUILDING SCIENCE & STRUCTURAL ABSTRACTS. (IE/0791-492X). CITIS Ltd, 2 Rosemount Terrace, Blackrock Dublin Ireland. **Tel** 3531-886227, FAX 3531-885971, telex 30259 MSCH ET. **617**

INTERNATIONAL CIVIL ENGINEERING ABSTRACTS. (IE/0332-4095). CITIS Ltd, 2 Rosemount Terrace, Blackrock Dublin Ireland. **Tel** 3531-886227, FAX 3531-885971, telex 30259 MSCH ET. **2005**

INTERNATIONAL CONGRESS SERIES. (NE/0531-5131). Elsevier Science Publishers BV, PO Box 211, 1000 AE Amsterdam Netherlands. **Tel** 011 31 20 5803642, FAX 011 31 20 5862696, telex 15682. **3588**

INTERNATIONAL DEFENSE DIRECTORY. (UK/0256-7822). Jane's Information Group, Sentinel House, 163 Brighton Road, Coulsdon Surrey CR3 2NX England. **Tel** 011 44 81 763 1030, FAX 011 44 81 763 1006. **4046**

INTERNATIONAL DIRECTORY OF DISCONTINUED ICS AND DISCRETE SEMICONDUCTORS. (US/0887-008X). DATA Business Publishing, PO Box 6510, 15 Inverness Way East, Englewood CO 80155. **Tel** (800)447-4666, (303)799-0381, FAX (303)799-4082. **2066**

INTERNATIONAL ECONOMIC INSIGHTS. (US/1050-8481). Institute for International Economics, 11 Dupont Circle, 6th Floor, Washington DC 20036. **Tel** (202)328-0583, FAX (202)328-5432. **1636**

INTERNATIONAL FILMARCHIVE CD-ROM. / FIAF. (UK). FIAF / International Federation of Film Archives, 6 Nottingham Street, London W1M 3RB England. **Tel** 011 44 71 2240991. **4072**

INTERNATIONAL FINANCIAL STATISTICS COMPUTER FILE / INTERNATIONAL MONETARY FUND. (US). International Monetary Fund, 700 19th Street Northwest, Publishing Unit, Washington DC 20431. **Tel** (202)623-7430, FAX (202)623-7201. **792**

INTERNATIONAL INSTITUTE OF MANAGEMENT DATABASES PLUS. (UK/0967-652X). Bowker Saur Ltd., A Reed Reference Publishing Company, Part of Reed International PLC, 59-60 Grosvenor Street, London WIX 9DA England. **Tel** 011 44 71 4935841, FAX 011 44 71 4991590. **871**

INTERNATIONAL JOURNAL OF SYSTEMATIC BACTERIOLOGY. (US/0020-7713). American Society for Microbiology, 1325 Massachusetts Avenue Northwest, Washington DC 20005-4171. **Tel** (202)737-3600, FAX (202)737-0367. **564**

INTERNATIONAL LITERARY MARKET PLACE. (US/0074-6827). R R Bowker, A Reed Reference Publishing Company, Part of Reed International PLC, PO Box 31, 121 Chanlon Drive, New Providence NJ 07974. **Tel** (908)464-6800, (800)521-8110, FAX (908)665-6688, telex 138-755. **4821**

INTERNATIONAL NEWS ON FATS, OILS AND RELATED MATERIALS. (US/0897-8026). American Oil Chemists Society, PO Box 3489, Champaign IL 61826-3489. **Tel** (217)359-2344, FAX (217)351-8091, telex 4938651 AOCS UI. **1025**

INTERNATIONAL NURSING INDEX. (US/0020-8124). American Journal of Nursing Company, 555 West 57th Street, New York NY 10019-2961. **Tel** (212)582-8820, FAX (212)586-5462. **3660**

INTERNATIONAL PACKAGING ABSTRACTS. (UK/0260-7409). Pira International, Randalls Road, Leatherhead, Surrey KT22 7RU England. **Tel** 011 44 372 376161, FAX 011 44 372 377526. **4222**

INTERNATIONAL PHARMACEUTICAL ABSTRACTS. (US/0020-8264). American Society of Hospital Pharmacists, 7272 Wisconsin Avenue, Bethesda MD 20814. **Tel** (301)657-3000, (301)657-4383, FAX (301)652-8278. **4334**

INTERNATIONAL PHILOSOPHICAL QUARTERLY. (US/0019-0365). International Philosophical Quarterly, Fordham University, Bronx NY 10458. **Tel** (718)817-4776, FAX (718)817-4785. **4349**

INTERNATIONAL TELEX-DIRECTORY ITD. (GW). Telcom, Postfach 40 06 39, W-5000 Koln 40 Germany. **Tel** (02234)40040, FAX (02234)4004-38, telex 8881686 DAMED. **1158**

INTERNATIONAL WILDLIFE. (US/0020-9112). National Wildlife Federation / Virginia, 8925 Leesburg Pike, Vienna VA 22184. **Tel** (703)790-4000, (800)822-9919, FAX (703)442-7332. **2195**

INTERNATIONALE BIBLIOGRAPHIE DER REZENSIONEN WISSENSCHAFTLICHER LITERATUR. (GW/0020-918X). Zeller Verlag GmbH & Co., Postfac 1949, Jahnstrasse 15, D 49009 Osnabrueck Germany. **Tel** 011 49 541 404590, FAX 011 49 541 41255. **3357**

INTERNATIONALE BIBLIOGRAPHIE DER ZEITSCHRIFTENLITERATUR AUS ALLEN GEBIETEN DES WISSENS. (GW). Zeller Verlag GmbH & Co., Postfac 1949, Jahnstrasse 15, D 49009 Osnabrueck Germany. **Tel** 011 49 541 404590, FAX 011 49 541 41255. **3357**

INTERPRETER RELEASES. (US). Federal Publications Inc, 1120 20th Street Northwest, Washington DC 20036. **Tel** (202)337-7000, (800)922-4330, FAX (202)659-2233. **2984**

IOWA BUSINESS DIRECTORY. (US/1048-7263). American Business Directory, 5711 South 86th Circle, Omaha NE 68127. **Tel** (402)593-4600, FAX (402)331-5481. **684**

IOWA DRUG INFORMATION SERVICE. (US). Iowa Drug Information Service, The University of Iowa, 100 Oakdale Campus, N330 OH, Iowa City IA 52242-5000. Tel (319)335-4800, (800)525-4347, FAX (319)335-4077. **4334**

IRISH JOURNAL OF PSYCHOLOGICAL MEDICINE. (IE/0790-9667). Irish Institute of Psychological Medicine, St. Brendans Hospital, PO Box 418, Dublin 7 Ireland. Tel 011 353 88 578406, FAX 011 353 1 2800504. **3927**

ISSN COMPACT. (FR/1018-4783). ISSN International Centre, 20 rue Bachaumont, F-75002 Paris France. Tel 011 33 1 42367381, FAX 011 33 1 40263243, telex SERIALS 219847F. **3219**

J + W TELEFAX INTERNATIONAL. (GW). Telex-Verlag Jaeger+Waldmann GmbH, PO Box 111454, D-64229 Darmstadt Germany. Tel 011 49 6151 33020, FAX 011 49 6151 330250, telex 419389 TLX D. **1158**

J + W TRAVEL INTERNATIONAL. (GW). Telex-Verlag Jaeger+Waldmann GmbH, PO Box 111454, D-64229 Darmstadt Germany. Tel 011 49 6151 33020, FAX 011 49 6151 330250, telex 419389 TLX D. **5481**

JAHRESSCHAU DER DEUTSCHEN INDUSTRIE. DIE ELEKTRO-INDUSTRIE, ELEKTRONIK UND IHRE HELFER. (GW). Industrieschau Verlagsgesellschaft MBH, PO Box 4034, Berliner Allee 8, W-6000 Darmstadt Germany. Tel (06151)33411, FAX (06151)33164, telex 419257. **2067**

JANE'S A F V SYSTEMS. (UK). Jane's Information Group, Sentinel House, 163 Brighton Road, Coulsdon Surrey CR3 2NX England. Tel 011 44 81 763 1030, FAX 011 44 81 763 1006. **4046**

JANE'S ALL THE WORLD'S AIRCRAFT (LONDON, ENGLAND). (UK/0075-3017). Jane's Information Group, Sentinel House, 163 Brighton Road, Coulsdon Surrey CR3 2NX England. Tel 011 44 81 763 1030, FAX 011 44 81 763 1006. **4046**

JANE'S ARMOURED FIGHTING VEHICLE RETROFIT SYSTEMS. (UK). Jane's Information Group, Sentinel House, 163 Brighton Road, Coulsdon Surrey CR3 2NX England. Tel 011 44 81 763 1030, FAX 011 44 81 763 1006. **4046**

JANE'S AVIONICS. (UK). Jane's Information Group, Sentinel House, 163 Brighton Road, Coulsdon Surrey CR3 2NX England. Tel 011 44 81 763 1030, FAX 011 44 81 763 1006. **4047**

JANE'S BATTLEFIELD SURVEILLANCE SYSTEMS. (UK). Jane's Information Group, Sentinel House, 163 Brighton Road, Coulsdon Surrey CR3 2NX England. Tel 011 44 81 763 1030, FAX 011 44 81 763 1006. **4047**

JANE'S C31 SYSTEMS. (UK). Jane's Information Group, Sentinel House, 163 Brighton Road, Coulsdon Surrey CR3 2NX England. Tel 011 44 81 763 1030, FAX 011 44 81 763 1006. **4047**

JANE'S FIGHTING SHIPS. (UK/0075-3025). Jane's Information Group, Sentinel House, 163 Brighton Road, Coulsdon Surrey CR3 2NX England. Tel 011 44 81 763 1030, FAX 011 44 81 763 1006. **4177**

JANE'S HIGH-SPEED MARINE CRAFT. (UK/0960-7994). Jane's Information Group, Sentinel House, 163 Brighton Road, Coulsdon Surrey CR3 2NX England. Tel 011 44 81 763 1030, FAX 011 44 81 763 1006. **4047**

JANE'S INFANTRY WEAPONS. (UK). Jane's Information Group, Sentinel House, 163 Brighton Road, Coulsdon Surrey CR3 2NX England. Tel 011 44 81 763 1030, FAX 011 44 81 763 1006. **4047**

JANE'S LAND-BASED AIR DEFENCE. (UK). Jane's Information Group, Sentinel House, 163 Brighton Road, Coulsdon Surrey CR3 2NX England. Tel 011 44 81 763 1030, FAX 011 44 81 763 1006. **4047**

JANE'S MILITARY COMMUNICATIONS. (UK/0144-0004). Jane's Information Group, Sentinel House, 163 Brighton Road, Coulsdon Surrey CR3 2NX England. Tel 011 44 81 763 1030, FAX 011 44 81 763 1006. **4047**

JANE'S MILITARY TRAINING SYSTEMS. (UK). Jane's Information Group, Sentinel House, 163 Brighton Road, Coulsdon Surrey CR3 2NX England. Tel 011 44 81 763 1030, FAX 011 44 81 763 1006. **4047**

JANE'S MILITARY VEHICLES AND LOGISTICS. (UK). Jane's Information Group, Sentinel House, 163 Brighton Road, Coulsdon Surrey CR3 2NX England. Tel 011 44 81 763 1030, FAX 011 44 81 763 1006. **4047**

JANE'S NAVAL WEAPON SYSTEMS. (UK). Jane's Information Group, Sentinel House, 163 Brighton Road, Coulsdon Surrey CR3 2NX England. Tel 011 44 81 763 1030, FAX 011 44 81 763 1006. **4047**

JANE'S NBC PROTECTION EQUIPMENT. (UK). Jane's Information Group, Sentinel House, 163 Brighton Road, Coulsdon Surrey CR3 2NX England. Tel 011 44 81 763 1030, FAX 011 44 81 763 1006. **4047**

JANE'S RADAR AND ELECTRONIC WARFARE SYSTEMS. (US). Jane's Information Group, Sentinel House, 163 Brighton Road, Coulsdon Surrey CR3 2NX England. Tel 011 44 81 763 1030, FAX 011 44 81 763 1006. **4047**

JANE'S SECURITY AND CO-IN EQUIPMENT. (UK). Jane's Information Group, Sentinel House, 163 Brighton Road, Coulsdon Surrey CR3 2NX England. Tel 011 44 81 763 1030, FAX 011 44 81 763 1006. **4047**

JANE'S UNDERWATER WARFARE SYSTEMS. (UK). Jane's Information Group, Sentinel House, 163 Brighton Road, Coulsdon Surrey CR3 2NX England. Tel 011 44 81 763 1030, FAX 011 44 81 763 1006. **4047**

JEWISH CHRONICLE (LONDON, ENGLAND : 1845). (UK/0021-633X). Jewish Chronicle / London, 25 Furnival Street, London EC4A 1JT England. Tel 011/44/71/4059252, FAX 011/44/71/4059040, telex 94011415. **5048**

JOURNAL OF ADVANCED ZOOLOGY. (II/0253-7214). Association for the Advancement of Zoology, 2 Zahid Building Golghar, Gorakhpur-273 001 India. Tel 336925. **5587**

JOURNAL OF ADVERTISING. (US/0091-3367). University of Houston / Journal of Advertising, College of Business, Houston TX 77204. Tel (713)749-6671, FAX (713)749-6895. **761**

JOURNAL OF AEROSPACE ENGINEERING. (US/0893-1321). American Society of Civil Engineers / ASCE, 345 East 47th Street, New York NY 10017-2398. Tel (212)705-7179, FAX (212)705-7300, telex 422847 ASCE UI. **25**

JOURNAL OF AMERICAN CULTURE. (US/0191-1813). Popular Press Journals Area, Bowling Green State University, Bowling Green OH 43403. Tel (419)372-7866, (419)372-7865. **2740**

JOURNAL OF ARCHITECTURAL ENGINEERING. (US/1076-0431). American Society of Civil Engineers / ASCE, 345 East 47th Street, New York NY 10017-2398. Tel (212)705-7179, FAX (212)705-7300, telex 422847 ASCE UI. **2025**

JOURNAL OF BACTERIOLOGY. (US/0021-9193). American Society for Microbiology, 1325 Massachusetts Avenue Northwest, Washington DC 20005-4171. Tel (202)737-3600, FAX (202)737-0367. **564**

JOURNAL OF BIOLOGICAL CHEMISTRY, THE. (US/0021-9258). American Society for Biochemistry and Molecular Biology, 9650 Rockville Pike, Bethesda MD 20814. Tel (301)530-7150, FAX (301)571-1824. **489**

JOURNAL OF BONE AND JOINT SURGERY (COMPUTER FILE), THE. (US/1058-2436). Journal of Bone and Joint Surgery, 20 Pickering Street, Needham MA 02192-3157. Tel (617)449-9738, FAX (617)449-9742. **3966**

JOURNAL OF BUSINESS FORECASTING METHODS & SYSTEMS, THE. (US/0278-6087). Graceway Publishing Company, PO Box 159 Station C, Flushing NY 11367. Tel (718)463-3914, FAX (718)544-9086. **1592**

JOURNAL OF CLINICAL MICROBIOLOGY. (US/0095-1137). American Society for Microbiology, 1325 Massachusetts Avenue Northwest, Washington DC 20005-4171. Tel (202)737-3600, FAX (202)737-0367. **565**

JOURNAL OF COLD REGIONS ENGINEERING. (US/0887-381X). American Society of Civil Engineers / ASCE, 345 East 47th Street, New York NY 10017-2398. Tel (212)705-7179, FAX (212)705-7300, telex 422847 ASCE UI. **2025**

JOURNAL OF COMMONWEALTH LITERATURE. (UK/0021-9894). Bowker Saur Ltd., A Reed Reference Publishing Company, Part of Reed International PLC, 59-60 Grosvenor Street, London WIX 9DA England. Tel 011 44 71 4935841, FAX 011 44 71 4991590. **3399**

JOURNAL OF COMPUTING IN CIVIL ENGINEERING. (US/0887-3801). American Society of Civil Engineers / ASCE, 345 East 47th Street, New York NY 10017-2398. Tel (212)705-7179, FAX (212)705-7300, telex 422847 ASCE UI. **2025**

JOURNAL OF CONSTRUCTION ENGINEERING AND MANAGEMENT. (US/0733-9364). American Society of Civil Engineers / ASCE, 345 East 47th Street, New York NY 10017-2398. Tel (212)705-7179, FAX (212)705-7300, telex 422847 ASCE UI. **2025**

JOURNAL OF CONSUMER RESEARCH, THE. (US/0093-5301). University of Chicago Press / Journals Division, PO Box 37005, 5720 South Woodlawn, Chicago IL 60637. Tel (312)753-3347, FAX (312)753-0811. **927**

JOURNAL OF CORPORATE MANAGEMENT, THE. (AT/1038-2410). Institute Corporate Managers, Secretaries and Administrators Ltd., GPO Box 1594, Sydney NSW 2001 Australia. Tel 011 61 02 2235744, FAX 011 61 02 2327174. **3101**

JOURNAL OF DEVELOPMENT STUDIES, THE. (UK/0022-0388). Frank Cass & Company Ltd, Newbury House, 890-900 Eastern Avenue, Newbury Park, Ilford, Essex IG2 7HH United Kingdom. Tel 011 44 81 599 8866, FAX 011 44 81 599 0984, telex 897719. **1569**

JOURNAL OF ECONOMIC LITERATURE. (US/0022-0515). American Economic Association / Tennessee, 2014 Broadway, Suite 305, Nashville TN 37203-2418. Tel (615)322-2595. **1535**

JOURNAL OF ENERGY ENGINEERING. (US/0733-9402). American Society of Civil Engineers / ASCE, 345 East 47th Street, New York NY 10017-2398. Tel (212)705-7179, FAX (212)705-7300, telex 422847 ASCE UI. **2118**

JOURNAL OF ENGINEERING MECHANICS. (US/0733-9399). American Society of Civil Engineers / ASCE, 345 East 47th Street, New York NY 10017-2398. Tel (212)705-7179, FAX (212)705-7300, telex 422847 ASCE UI. **2118**

JOURNAL OF ENVIRONMENTAL ENGINEERING (NEW YORK N.Y.). (US/0733-9372). American Society of Civil Engineers / ASCE, 345 East 47th Street, New York NY 10017-2398. Tel (212)705-7179, FAX (212)705-7300, telex 422847 ASCE UI. **2233**

JOURNAL OF ENVIRONMENTAL HEALTH. (US/0022-0892). National Environmental Health Association, 720 South Colorado Boulevard, Suite 970, Denver CO 80222-1904. Tel (303)756-9090, FAX (303)691-9490. **2175**

JOURNAL OF EVOLUTIONARY PSYCHOLOGY. (US/0737-4828). Institute of Evolutionary Psychology, 5117 Forbes Avenue, Pittsburgh PA 15213. Tel (412)621-7057. **3399**

JOURNAL OF FILM AND VIDEO. (US/0742-4671). Journal Film and Video, Georgia State University, Department of Communication, Atlanta GA 30303. Tel (404)651-3200, FAX (404)651-1409. **4073**

JOURNAL OF FINANCIAL MANAGEMENT AND ANALYSIS. (II/0970-4205). Om Sai Ram Center for Financial Management Research and Training, 15 Prakash Co-Op Housing Society, Bombay 400 054 India. Tel 11 91 22 6121715. **794**

JOURNAL OF FORENSIC ECONOMICS. (US/0898-5510). National Association of Forensic Economists, PO Box 30067, Kansas City MO 64112. Tel (816)235-2833, FAX (816)235-5263. **1499**

JOURNAL OF GEOTECHNICAL ENGINEERING. (US/0733-9410). American Society of Civil Engineers / ASCE, 345 East 47th Street, New York NY 10017-2398. Tel (212)705-7179, FAX (212)705-7300, telex 422847 ASCE UI. **1385**

JOURNAL OF HIGHER EDUCATION (COLUMBUS), THE. (US/0022-1546). Ohio State University Press, 1070 Carmack Road, 180 Pressey Hall, Columbus OH 43210. Tel (614)292-6930, (614)292-1407, FAX (614)292-2065. **1833**

JOURNAL OF HYDRAULIC ENGINEERING (NEW YORK, N.Y.). (US/0733-9429). American Society of Civil Engineers / ASCE, 345 East 47th Street, New York NY 10017-2398. Tel (212)705-7179, FAX (212)705-7300, telex 422847 ASCE UI. **2092**

JOURNAL OF INFRASTRUCTURE SYSTEMS. (US/1076-0342). American Society of Civil Engineers / ASCE, 345 East 47th Street, New York NY 10017-2398. Tel (212)705-7179, FAX (212)705-7300, telex 422847 ASCE UI. **2025**

JOURNAL OF IRRIGATION AND DRAINAGE ENGINEERING. (US/0733-9437). American Society of Civil Engineers / ASCE, 345 East 47th Street, New York NY 10017-2398. Tel (212)705-7179, FAX (212)705-7300, telex 422847 ASCE UI. **2092**

JOURNAL OF LEGAL EDUCATION. (US/0022-2208). Case Western Reserve University / School of Law, 11075 East Boulevard, Cleveland OH 44106. Tel (216)368-3304, FAX (216)368-6144. **2988**

JOURNAL OF LONG TERM CARE ADMINISTRATION, THE. (US/0093-4445). American College of Health Care Administrators, 325 South Patrick Street, Alexandria VA 22314. Tel (703)549-5822, (703)739-7913, FAX (703)739-7901. **3787**

JOURNAL
Serials available on CD-ROM

JOURNAL OF MANAGEMENT IN ENGINEERING. (US/0742-597X). American Society of Civil Engineers / ASCE, 345 East 47th Street, New York NY 10017-2398. **Tel** (212)705-7179, FAX (212)705-7300, telex 422847 ASCE UI. **1983**

JOURNAL OF MATERIALS IN CIVIL ENGINEERING. (US/0899-1561). American Society of Civil Engineers / ASCE, 345 East 47th Street, New York NY 10017-2398. **Tel** (212)705-7179, FAX (212)705-7300, telex 422847 ASCE UI. **2025**

JOURNAL OF MATERIALS SCIENCE. (UK/0022-2461). Chapman & Hall, 2-6 Boundary Row, London SE1 8HN England. **Tel** 011 44 71 865 0066, FAX 011 44 71 522 9623, telex 290164 Chapmag. **4006**

JOURNAL OF MEDICAL ENTOMOLOGY. (US/0022-2585). Entomological Society of America, 9301 Annapolis Road, Suite 300, Lanham MD 20706. **Tel** (301)731-4535, FAX (301)731-4538. **5611**

JOURNAL OF MEDITERRANEAN STUDIES. (MM/1016-3476). Mediterranean Institute, University of Malta, Msida Malta. **Tel** 011 356 333903-6 331734, FAX 011 356 336450. **2848**

JOURNAL OF MONEY, CREDIT, AND BANKING. (US/0022-2879). Ohio State University Press, 1070 Carmack Road, 180 Pressey Hall, Columbus OH 43210. **Tel** (614)292-6930, (614)292-1407, FAX (614)292-2065. **795**

JOURNAL OF OCCUPATIONAL AND ORGANIZATIONAL PSYCHOLOGY. (UK/0963-1798). British Psychological Society, St. Andrews House, 48 Princess Road, Leicester LE1 7DR England. **Tel** 011 44 533 549568. **4598**

JOURNAL OF PERFORMANCE OF CONSTRUCTED FACILITIES. (US/0887-3828). American Society of Civil Engineers / ASCE, 345 East 47th Street, New York NY 10017-2398. **Tel** (212)705-7179, FAX (212)705-7300, telex 422847 ASCE UI. **2025**

JOURNAL OF POPULATION ECONOMICS. (GW/0933-1433). Springer-Verlag GmbH & Company KG, Heidelberger Platz 3, D 14197 Berlin Germany. **Tel** 011 49 30 8207223, FAX 011 49 30 8214091, telex 183 319 SPBLN D. **4554**

JOURNAL OF PORTFOLIO MANAGEMENT. (US/0095-4918). Institutional Investor Inc., 488 Madison Avenue, New York NY 10022. **Tel** (212)303-3234, (212)303-3233, FAX (212)303-3353. **904**

JOURNAL OF PROFESSIONAL ISSUES IN ENGINEERING EDUCATION AND PRACTICE. (US/1052-3928). American Society of Civil Engineers / ASCE, 345 East 47th Street, New York NY 10017-2398. **Tel** (212)705-7179, FAX (212)705-7300, telex 422847 ASCE UI. **2026**

JOURNAL OF RESEARCH IN RURAL EDUCATION. (US/1062-4228). University of Maine / Shiblis Hall, 5766 Shiblis Hall, Orono ME 04469-5766. **Tel** (207)581-2493, FAX (207)581-2423. **1758**

JOURNAL OF ROMAN STUDIES, THE. (UK/0075-4358). Society for Promotion of Roman Studies, 31-34 Gordon Square, London WC1H 0PP England. **Tel** 011 44 71 3878157. **1078**

JOURNAL OF SHELLFISH RESEARCH. (US/0730-8000). Sheridan Press, PO Box 465, Hanover PA 17331. **Tel** (800)352-2210, (717)632-3535, FAX (717)633-8900. **2307**

JOURNAL OF STRUCTURAL ENGINEERING (NEW YORK, N.Y.). (US/0733-9445). American Society of Civil Engineers / ASCE, 345 East 47th Street, New York NY 10017-2398. **Tel** (212)705-7179, FAX (212)705-7300, telex 422847 ASCE UI. **2026**

JOURNAL OF SURVEYING ENGINEERING. (US/0733-9453). American Society of Civil Engineers / ASCE, 345 East 47th Street, New York NY 10017-2398. **Tel** (212)705-7179, FAX (212)705-7300, telex 422847 ASCE UI. **2026**

JOURNAL OF TECHNOLOGY TRANSFER, THE. (US/0892-9912). Technology Transfer Society, 611 North Capitol Avenue, Indianapolis IN 46204. **Tel** (317)262-5022. **5120**

JOURNAL OF THE AMERICAN BOARD OF FAMILY PRACTICE, THE. (US/0893-8652). American Board of Family Practice / Waltham, PO Box 9085, Waltham MA 02254. **Tel** (617)893-3800, (800)843-6356, FAX (617)893-0413, telex 510607779 NEJM BOS. **3738**

JOURNAL OF THE ANCIENT NEAR EASTERN SOCIETY, THE. (US/0897-6074). Jewish Theological Seminary, 3080 Broadway, New York NY 10027. **Tel** (212)678-8856. **2621**

JOURNAL OF THE NEW YORK STATE NURSES ASSOCIATION, THE. (US/0028-7644). New York State Nurses Association, 2113 Western Avenue, Guilderland NY 12084. **Tel** (518)456-5371, FAX (518)456-0697. **3860**

JOURNAL OF TRANSPORTATION ENGINEERING. (US/0733-947X). American Society of Civil Engineers / ASCE, 345 East 47th Street, New York NY 10017-2398. **Tel** (212)705-7179, FAX (212)705-7300, telex 422847 ASCE UI. **2026**

JOURNAL OF TRAUMA, THE. (US/0022-5282). Williams & Wilkins Company, 428 East Preston Street, Baltimore MD 21202-3993. **Tel** (410)528-4000, (800)638-6423, FAX (410)528-8596, telex 87669. **3969**

JOURNAL OF URBAN PLANNING AND DEVELOPMENT. (US/0733-9488). American Society of Civil Engineers / ASCE, 345 East 47th Street, New York NY 10017-2398. **Tel** (212)705-7179, FAX (212)705-7300, telex 422847 ASCE UI. **2026**

JOURNAL OF VIROLOGY. (US/0022-538X). American Society for Microbiology, 1325 Massachusetts Avenue Northwest, Washington DC 20005-4171. **Tel** (202)737-3600, FAX (202)737-0367. **566**

JOURNAL OF WATER RESOURCES PLANNING AND MANAGEMENT. (US/0733-9496). American Society of Civil Engineers / ASCE, 345 East 47th Street, New York NY 10017-2398. **Tel** (212)705-7179, FAX (212)705-7300, telex 422847 ASCE UI. **5535**

JOURNAL OF WATERWAY, PORT, COASTAL, AND OCEAN ENGINEERING. (US/0733-950X). American Society of Civil Engineers / ASCE, 345 East 47th Street, New York NY 10017-2398. **Tel** (212)705-7179, FAX (212)705-7300, telex 422847 ASCE UI. **2092**

JUDICIAL STAFF DIRECTORY. (US). Staff Directories Ltd., PO Box 62, Mount Vernon VA 22121. **Tel** (703)739-0900, FAX (703)739-0234. **3141**

JUNIOR SEARCH. [COMPUTER FILE]. (US). EBSCO Publishing / Boston, 83 Pine Street, Peabody MA 01960. **Tel** (800)653-2726 North America, (508)535-8500, FAX (508)535-8545. **1759**

JUSTICE QUARTERLY. (US/0741-8825). Academy of Criminal Justice Sciences, Northern Kentucky University, 402 Nunn Hall, Highland Heights KY 41099. **Tel** (606)572-5634. **3168**

JUSTIS [COMPUTER FILE] : CELEX, OFFICIAL LEGAL DATABASE OF THE EUROPEAN COMMUNITIES. (UK). Context Limited, Tranley House, Tranley Mews Fleet, London NW3 2QW England. **Tel** 44 71 267 7055. **2992**

KANSAS CITY BUSINESS JOURNAL. (US/0734-2748). Kansas City Business Journal, 324 East 11th Street, Suite 800, Kansas City MO 64106. **Tel** (816)421-5900, FAX (816)472-4010. **688**

KARTOFFELBAU. (GW/0022-9156). Verlag TH Mann OHG, Postfach 200254, W 45837 Gelsenkirchen Germany. **Tel** 011 49 209 9304184. **177**

KENTUCKY BUSINESS DIRECTORY. (US/1048-728X). American Business Directory, 5711 South 86th Circle, Omaha NE 68127. **Tel** (402)593-4600, FAX (402)331-5481. **688**

KEY ABSTRACTS. MACHINE VISION. (UK/0952-7052). Institution of Electrical Engineers / IEE, Michael Faraday House, Six Hills Way, Stevenage Herts SG1 2AY UK. **Tel** 011 44 438 313311, FAX 011 44 438 742840, telex 825578 IEESTV G. **1209**

KING'S COALSTATS. MONTHLY COAL GUIDE. MINE PRICE REPORT. (US/1050-1509). King Publishing Company, PO Box 52210, Knoxville TN 37950. **Tel** (615)584-6294, FAX (615)558-6101, telex 705286. **2142**

KNJIZNICA. (XV/0023-2424). Zveza Bibliotekarskih Drustev Slovenije, Turjaska 1, Ljubljana, Slovenia. **Tel** 061 150 131. **3221**

KOMPASS; MANUEL D'INFORMATIONS SUR L'ECONOMIE DE LA BELGIQUE ET DU GRAND-DUCHE DE LUXEMBOURG. (BE/0075-6636). Reed Information Services Ltd., Windsor Court, East Grinstead House, East Grinstead RH19 1BR England. **Tel** 011 44 342 326972, FAX 011 44 342 327100, telex 95127 INFSER G. **1502**

KOMPASS-SVERIGE. (SW). Kompass Sweden, Saltmaetargatan 8, Box 3223, Stockholm 10364 Sweden. **1615**

KURSBUCH - DEUTSCHE BUNDESBAHN. (GW). DBAG, Geschaeftsbereich, Fernverkehr, Kaiserstrasse 3, D 55116 Mainz Germany. **Tel** 061 31 15 54 18, FAX 061 31 15 57 65. **5432**

LAKE LILLIAN CRIER. (US). Lake Lillian Crier, PO Box 98, Lake Lillian MN 56253. **5696**

LANCET (BRITISH EDITION). (UK/0140-6736). Lancet Ltd, 46 Bedford Square, London WC1B 3SL England. **Tel** 011 44 1 436 4981, FAX (617)868-7738. **3603**

LANCET (NORTH AMERICAN EDITION), THE. (US/0099-5355). The Lancet, 655 Avenue of the Americas, 5th Floor, New York NY 10010. **Tel** (212)633-3800, FAX (212)633-3850. **3603**

LAND & SEA-BASED ELECTRONICS FORECAST. (US). Forecast International / DMS Inc., 22 Commerce Road, Newtown CT 06470. **Tel** (203)426-0800, FAX (203)426-1964, telex 467615. **2070**

LANGUAGES OF THE WORLD. CD-ROM. (US). National Textbook Company, 4255 West Touhy Avenue, Lincolnwood IL 60646. **Tel** (708)679-5500, (800)323-4900, FAX (708)679-2494, telex TWX 9102230736. **3296**

LATIN AMERICAN RESEARCH REVIEW. (US/0023-8791). Latin American Institute, University of New Mexico, 801 Yale Northeast, Albuquerque NM 87131. **Tel** (505)277-5985, FAX (505)277-5989. **2743**

LEADERSHIP DIRECTORIES ON CD-ROM. (US/1075-3869). Chadwyck Healey / Virginia, 1101 King Street, Alexandria VA 22314. **Tel** (800)752-0515 ext. 1000, FAX (703)683-7589. **689**

LEATHERNECK. (US/0023-981X). Marine Corps Association Inc, Box 1775, Quantico VA 22134. **Tel** (703)640-6161, (800)336-0291, FAX (703)640-0823. **4049**

LEGALTRAC [COMPUTER FILE]. (US). Information Access Company, 362 Lakeside Drive, Foster City CA 94404. **Tel** (800)227-8431. **3082**

LIBERTAS MATHEMATICA. (US/0278-5307). American Romanian Academy, Math Department, University of Texas Arlington, Arlington TX 76019. **Tel** (817)261-1179, (817)273-3261, FAX (817)794-5802. **3517**

LIBRARY & INFORMATION SCIENCE ABSTRACTS. (UK/0024-2179). Bowker Saur Ltd., A Reed Reference Publishing Company, Part of Reed International PLC, 59-60 Grosvenor Street, London WIX 9DA England. **Tel** 011 44 71 4935841, FAX 011 44 71 4991590. **3258**

LIBRARY HI TECH. (US/0737-8831). Pierian Press, PO Box 1808, Ann Arbor MI 48106. **Tel** (313)434-5530, (800)678-2435, FAX (313)434-6409. **3225**

LIBRARY LITERATURE. (US/0024-2373). H W Wilson Company, 950 University Avenue, Bronx NY 10452. **Tel** (800)367-6770, (718)588-8400, FAX (718)590-1617, telex 4990003 HWILSON. **3258**

LIBRARY LITERATURE [COMPUTER FILE]. (US). H W Wilson Company, 950 University Avenue, Bronx NY 10452. **Tel** (800)367-6770, (718)588-8400, FAX (718)590-1617, telex 4990003 HWILSON. **3259**

LIBROS EN VENTA EN HISPANOAMERICA Y ESPANA. (PR/0075-918X). Melcher Ediciones, Apartado 6000, San Juan PR 00906. **Tel** (809)723-0162, (809)724-1352, FAX (809)724-2886, telex 724-1352. **419**

LIBROS ESPANOLES EN VENTA, ISBN. (SP). Celesa, Calle Justiniano 9, 28004 Madrid Spain. **Tel** 011 34 1 4101101, 011 34 1 4101736. **419**

LILACS ON CD-ROM. (US). Bireme Latin America & CARI Center, Lilacs CD-ROM, Rua Botucatu 862, 04023 Sao Paulo SP Brazil. **Tel** 011 55 11 5492611. **3660**

LINGUISTICS AND LANGUAGE BEHAVIOR ABSTRACTS. (US/0888-8027). Sociological Abstracts, PO Box 22206, San Diego CA 92192-0206. **Tel** (619)695-8803, FAX (619)695-0416. **3336**

LISA PLUS [COMPUTER FILE]. (UK/0966-8799). Bowker Saur Ltd., A Reed Reference Publishing Company, Part of Reed International PLC, 59-60 Grosvenor Street, London WIX 9DA England. **Tel** 011 44 71 4935841, FAX 011 44 71 4991590. **3259**

LITERARY MARKET PLACE (1988). (US/0000-1155). R R Bowker, A Reed Reference Publishing Company, Part of Reed International PLC, PO Box 31, 121 Chanlon Drive, New Providence NJ 07974. **Tel** (908)464-6800, (800)521-8110, FAX (908)665-6688, telex 138-755. **4821**

LLOYD'S LIST. (UK). Lloyd's of London Press Ltd, Sheepen Place, Colchester, Essex, CO3 3LP England. **Tel** 011 44 206 772113, US: (212)529-9500, US: (800)955-6937, FAX 011 44 206 772880, US: (212)529-9826, telex 987321 LLOYDS G. **5451**

LONGMAN WORLD ENERGY CD-ROM. (UK). Longman Group Ltd., Fourth Avenue, Longman House, Harlow Essex CM19 5SR England. **Tel** 011 44 279 429655, FAX 011 44 279 431059, telex 81259. **1949**

LOOK JAPAN. (JA/0456-5339). Look Japan Publishing Pte Ltd, 24 Raffles Place #25-01 Clifford Center, Singapore 0104 Singapore. **Tel** 011 65 5330333. **2506**

LOS ANGELES TIMES, THE. (US/0458-3035). Los Angeles Times, Times Mirror Square, Los Angeles CA 90053. **Tel** (714)237-5000, (800)528-4637. **5636**

LOTUS ONE SOURCE. CD/CORPORATE. U.S. PUBLIC COS. (US/1060-2178). Lotus Development Corporation, CD-ROM Information Services, 55 Cambridge Parkway, Cambridge MA 02142. **691**

LUCKNOW LIBRARIAN. (II/0024-7219). Uttar Pradesh Library Association, Lucknow Branch, UP Library Association, PO Box 446, Lucknow 226 001 India. **3229**

M + A MESSEPLANER FUR MESSEN UND AUSSTELLUNGEN INTERNATIONAL. (GW). M + A Verlag fuer Messen, Ausstellungen und Kongresse GmbH, Postfach 101528, D 60015 Frankfurt Germany. **Tel** 011 49 69 759502, FAX 011 49 69 75951280, telex 841-411699. **929**

MACADEMIC. CD-ROM. (US). Quantum Leap Technologies, 1399 Southeast 9th Avenue, Suite 4, Hialeah FL 33010-5999. **Tel** (305)885-9985, (800)762-2877, FAX (305)762-9986. **1224**

MACTUTOR. (US/8756-8810). Xplain Corporation, PO Box 250055, Los Angeles CA 90025. **Tel** (310)575-4343, FAX (310)575-0925. **1280**

MACTUTOR COMPANION SOURCE CODE DISKS. (US). Xplain Corporation, PO Box 250055, Los Angeles CA 90025. **Tel** (310)575-4343, FAX (310)575-0925. **1280**

MACWORLD (SAN FRANCISCO, CALIF.). (US/0741-8647). PCW Communications Inc., 501 Second Street, San Francisco CA 94107. **Tel** (415)243-0500, (415)978-3146. **1268**

MADE IN THE USA. (US). National Press Books / Maryland, 7200 Wisconsin Avenue, Suite 212, Bethesda MD 20814. **Tel** (301)657-1616. **1298**

MAGAZINE ARTICLE SUMMARIES (CD-ROM ED.). (US/1041-1151). EBSCO Publishing / Boston, 83 Pine Street, Peabody MA 01960. **Tel** (800)653-2726 North America, (508)535-8500, FAX (508)535-8545. **2497**

MAGAZINE ARTICLE SUMMARIES FULL TEXT ELITE. (US/1060-6769). EBSCO Publishing / Boston, 83 Pine Street, Peabody MA 01960. **Tel** (800)653-2726 North America, (508)535-8500, FAX (508)535-8545. **2497**

MAGAZINE ARTICLE SUMMARIES FULL TEXT SELECT. (US/1058-0255). EBSCO Publishing / Boston, 83 Pine Street, Peabody MA 01960. **Tel** (800)653-2726 North America, (508)535-8500, FAX (508)535-8545. **2497**

MAGAZINE ARTICLE SUMMARIES (PRINT ED.). (US/0895-3376). EBSCO Publishing / Boston, 83 Pine Street, Peabody MA 01960. **Tel** (800)653-2726 North America, (508)535-8500, FAX (508)535-8545. **2497**

MAGAZINE ASAP PLUS [COMPUTER FILE]. (US). Information Access Company, 362 Lakeside Drive, Foster City CA 94404. **Tel** (800)227-8431. **2497**

MAGAZINE ASAP SELECT [COMPUTER FILE]. (US). Information Access Company, 362 Lakeside Drive, Foster City CA 94404. **Tel** (800)227-8431. **2497**

MAGAZINE EXPRESS [COMPUTER FILE]. (US). University Microfilms International, 300 North Zeeb Road, Ann Arbor MI 48106-1346. **Tel** (313)761-4700, (800)521-0600 Exts. 2490, 2491, FAX (313)973-1540. **2497**

MAGAZINE INDEX PLUS [COMPUTER FILE]. (US). Information Access Company, 362 Lakeside Drive, Foster City CA 94404. **Tel** (800)227-8431. **2497**

MAGAZINE INDEX SELECT [COMPUTER FILE]. (US). Information Access Company, 362 Lakeside Drive, Foster City CA 94404. **Tel** (800)227-8431. **2497**

MAGAZINE INDEX, THE. (US). Information Access Company, 362 Lakeside Drive, Foster City CA 94404. **Tel** (800)227-8431. **2497**

MAGAZINE RACK [COMPUTER FILE]. (US). Information Access Company, 362 Lakeside Drive, Foster City CA 94404. **Tel** (800)227-8431. **3229**

MAGAZINE SEARCH. (US/1071-2739). EBSCO Publishing / Boston, 83 Pine Street, Peabody MA 01960. **Tel** (800)653-2726 North America, (508)535-8500, FAX (508)535-8545. **2497**

MAGILL'S SURVEY OF CINEMA. (US/1065-6553). EBSCO Publishing / Boston, 83 Pine Street, Peabody MA 01960. **Tel** (800)653-2726 North America, (508)535-8500, FAX (508)535-8545. **4074**

MAINE BUSINESS DIRECTORY. (US/1048-7115). American Business Directory, 5711 South 86th Circle, Omaha NE 68127. **Tel** (402)593-4600, FAX (402)331-5481. **691**

MAIZE ABSTRACTS. (UK/0267-2987). CAB International Centre, Wallingford, Oxon OX10 8DE United Kingdom. **Tel** 44 491 832111, FAX 44 491 833508, telex 847964 (COMAGG G). **154**

MAMMALS : A MULTIMEDIA ENCYCLOPEDIA. (US). National Geographic Society, 11555 Darnestown, Gaithersburg MD 20878. **Tel** (202)857-7000, (800)638-4077, FAX (202)429-5727, telex 64194 NATGEO. **5591**

MANAGE. (US/0025-1623). National Management Association, 2210 Arbor Boulevard, Dayton OH 45439. **Tel** (513)294-0421, FAX (513)294-2374. **876**

MANAGEMENT AND MARKETING ABSTRACTS. (UK/0308-2172). Pira International, Randalls Road, Leatherhead, Surrey KT22 7RU England. **Tel** 011 44 372 376161, FAX 011 44 372 377526. **731**

MARINE CORPS GAZETTE. (US/0025-3170). Marine Corps Association Inc, Box 1775, Quantico VA 22134. **Tel** (703)640-6161, (800)336-0291, FAX (703)640-0823. **4049**

MARINE TECHNOLOGY SOCIETY JOURNAL. (US/0025-3324). Marine Technology Society, 1828 L Street Northwest, Suite 906, Washington DC 20036. **Tel** (202)775-5966, FAX (202)429-9417. **1452**

MARKETING + DISTRIBUTION ABSTRACTS. (UK). Anbar Publications Ltd, Circle House South, Box 23, Wembley HA9 8DJ England. **Tel** 011 44 81 902 4489. **731**

MARTINDALE-HUBBELL LAW DIRECTORY (PRINT). (US/0191-0221). Martindale-Hubbell, A Reed Reference Publishing Company, Part of Reed International PLC, 121 Chanlon Road, New Providence NJ 07974. **Tel** (800)526-4902, (908)464-6800, FAX (908)464-3553, telex 138755. **3006**

MARYLAND BUSINESS DIRECTORY. (US/1048-7123). American Business Directory, 5711 South 86th Circle, Omaha NE 68127. **Tel** (402)593-4600, FAX (402)331-5481. **692**

MASSACHUSETTS ADMINISTRATIVE LAW LIBRARY ON CD-ROM [COMPUTER FILE] / SOCIAL LAW LIBRARY. (US). The Social Law Library, 1200 Court House, Boston MA 02108. **Tel** (617)720-0294, FAX (617)523-2458. **3007**

MASSACHUSETTS BUSINESS DIRECTORY (OMAHA, NEB.). (US/1048-7131). American Business Directory, 5711 South 86th Circle, Omaha NE 68127. **Tel** (402)593-4600, FAX (402)331-5481. **692**

MASTERPLOTS II. (US). EBSCO Publishing / Boston, 83 Pine Street, Peabody MA 01960. **Tel** (800)653-2726 North America, (508)535-8500, FAX (508)535-8545. **3410**

MATERIALS SCIENCE CITATION INDEX. (US/1062-5496). Institute for Scientific Information, 3501 Market Street, Philadelphia PA 19104. **Tel** (215)386-0100, (800)523-1850, FAX (215)386-6362, telex 84-5305. **5127**

MATHEMATICAL REVIEWS. (US/0025-5629). American Mathematical Society, PO Box 6248, Providence RI 02940-6248. **Tel** (800)321-4267, (401)455-4000, FAX (401)331-3842, telex 797192. **3542**

MATHEMATICS TEACHER, THE. (US/0025-5769). National Council of Teachers of Mathematics, 1906 Association Drive, Reston VA 22091. **Tel** (703)620-9840, FAX (703)476-2970. **3521**

MATHSCI DISC [COMPUTER FILE]. (US). Silverplatter Information Inc., 100 River Ridge Drive, Norwood MA 02062. **Tel** (800)343-0064, (617)769-2599, FAX (617)235-1715. **3522**

MAXWELL COMPACT LIBRARIES. AIDS. (US/1061-5458). Macmillan New Media, 124 Mt. Auburn Street, Cambridge MA 02138. **Tel** (617)661-2955, (800)342-1338, FAX (617)868-7738. **3674**

MEDICAL & PHARMACEUTICAL BIOTECHNOLOGY ABSTRACTS. (US/1063-1178). Cambridge Scientific Abstracts, 7200 Wisconsin Avenue, #601, Bethesda MD 20814-4823. **Tel** (301)961-6750, (800)843-7751, FAX (301)961-6720. **3660**

MEDICAL WASTE MONITOR. (US/1058-2711). MedX, Inc., PO Box 025499, Miami FL 33102-5499. **Tel** (800)527-0666, (305)885-4004, FAX ((305)888-9637. **3612**

MEDLINE KNOWLEDGE FINDER. / MODEL UM-11. (US). Aries Systems Corporation, 200 Sutton Street, North Andover MA 01845. **Tel** (508)975-7570, FAX (508)975-3811. **3615**

MEDLINE KNOWLEDGE FINDER. UM-5. (US). Aries Systems Corporation, 200 Sutton Street, North Andover MA 01845. **Tel** (508)975-7570, FAX (508)975-3811. **3615**

MEDLINE [COMPUTER FILE]. (US). Silverplatter Information Inc., 100 River Ridge Drive, Norwood MA 02062. **Tel** (800)343-0064, (617)769-2599, FAX (617)235-1715. **3615**

MEMBERSHIP DIRECTORY / NATIONAL ASSOCIATION OF BUSINESS ECONOMISTS. (US). NABE / National Association of Business Economists, 1233 20th Street NW Suite 505, Washington DC 20036. **Tel** (202)463-6223. **1504**

MEMOIRES VIVES (MONTREAL). (CN/1188-8296). Goupe PGV Diffusion Archeologie, 5846 Cartier, Montreal, Quebec, H2G 2V2 Canada. **Tel** (514)277-5812, FAX (514)277-5812. **274**

MERCER LAW REVIEW. (US/0025-987X). Mercer University / School of Law, School of Law, Macon GA 31207. **Tel** (912)752-2622, FAX (912)752-2259. **3009**

METALS ABSTRACTS. (UK/0026-0924). American Society for Metals International, c/o Deborah Barthelmes, Materials Park OH 44073-0002. **Tel** (216)338-5151, FAX (216)338-4634, telex 980-619. **4026**

METALWORKING MACHINERY. (US/0885-3827). US Department of Commerce / Bureau of the Census, Data User Services Division, Customer Services, Washington DC 20233-0800. **Tel** (301)763-4100. **4012**

METEOROLOGICAL AND GEOASTROPHYSICAL ABSTRACTS. (US/0026-1130). American Meteorological Society, 45 Beacon Street, Boston MA 02108. **Tel** (617)227-2425. **1363**

METEOROLOGICAL & GEOASTROPHYSICAL ABSTRACTS. (US/1066-2707). American Meteorological Society, 45 Beacon Street, Boston MA 02108. **Tel** (617)227-2425. **1363**

MICHIGAN CITIZEN. (US/1072-2041). Michigan Citizen, PO Box 03560, Highland Park MI 48203. **Tel** (313)869-0033, FAX (313)869-0430. **5693**

MICROBIOLOGICAL REVIEWS. (US/0146-0749). American Society for Microbiology, 1325 Massachusetts Avenue Northwest, Washington DC 20005-4171. **Tel** (202)737-3600, FAX (202)737-0367. **567**

MICROBIOLOGY ABSTRACTS. SECTION A : INDUSTRIAL & APPLIED MICROBIOLOGY. (US/0300-838X). Cambridge Scientific Abstracts, 7200 Wisconsin Avenue, #601, Bethesda MD 20814-4823. **Tel** (301)961-6750, (800)843-7751, FAX (301)961-6720. **478**

MICROBIOLOGY ABSTRACTS. SECTION B, BACTERIOLOGY. (US/0300-8398). Cambridge Scientific Abstracts, 7200 Wisconsin Avenue, #601, Bethesda MD 20814-4823. **Tel** (301)961-6750, (800)843-7751, FAX (301)961-6720. **478**

MICROBIOLOGY ABSTRACTS. SECTION C, ALGOLOGY, MYCOLOGY & PROTOZOOLOGY. (US/0301-2328). Cambridge Scientific Abstracts, 7200 Wisconsin Avenue, #601, Bethesda MD 20814-4823. **Tel** (301)961-6750, (800)843-7751, FAX (301)961-6720. **478**

MICROCOMPUTER INDEX. (US/8756-7040). Learned Information Inc., 143 Old Marlton Pike, Medford NJ 08055-8750. **Tel** (609)654-6266, FAX (609)654-4309. **1209**

MIDDLE EAST DIARY. CD-ROM. (US). Quanta Press, Inc., 1313 Fifth Street Southeast, Suite 208C, Minneapolis MN 55414. **Tel** (612)379-3956, FAX (612)623-4570. **4528**

MIDDLE SEARCH. (US/1071-2755). EBSCO Publishing / Boston, 83 Pine Street, Peabody MA 01960. **Tel** (800)653-2726 North America, (508)535-8500, FAX (508)535-8545. **1795**

MILITARY

Serials available on CD-ROM

MILITARY AIRCRAFT FORECAST. (US). Forecast International / DMS Inc., 22 Commerce Road, Newtown CT 06470. **Tel** (203)426-0800, FAX (203)426-1964, telex 467615. **4050**

MILITARY VEHICLES FORECAST. (US). Forecast International / DMS Inc., 22 Commerce Road, Newtown CT 06470. **Tel** (203)426-0800, FAX (203)426-1964, telex 467615. **4051**

MILLARD COUNTY GAZETTE, THE. (US). Millard County Gazette, PO Box 908, Fillmore UT 84631. **Tel** (801)743-6983. **5757**

MILLION DOLLAR DIRECTORY. (US/0070-7619). Dun & Bradstreet Information Services, 3 Sylvan Way, Parsippany NJ 07054. **Tel** (201)605-6000, (800)526-0651. **1505**

MISSILE FORECAST. (US). Forecast International / DMS Inc., 22 Commerce Road, Newtown CT 06470. **Tel** (203)426-0800, FAX (203)426-1964, telex 467615. **4051**

MISSISSIPPI BUSINESS DIRECTORY. (US/1046-056X). American Business Directory, 5711 South 86th Circle, Omaha NE 68127. **Tel** (402)593-4600, FAX (402)331-5481. **695**

MISSOURI DIRECTORY OF MANUFACTURERS (1988). (US/0895-2469). Harris Publishing Company, 2057-2 Aurora Road, Twinsburg OH 44087. **Tel** (800)888-5900, (216)425-9000, FAX (216)425-7150, telex 510 601 1740. **3484**

MLA INTERNATIONAL BIBLIOGRAPHY. (US/1063-3316). H W Wilson Company, 950 University Avenue, Bronx NY 10452. **Tel** (800)367-6770, (718)588-8400, FAX (718)590-1617, telex 4990003 HWILSON. **3303**

MLA INTERNATIONAL BIBLIOGRAPHY OF BOOKS AND ARTICLES ON THE MODERN LANGUAGES AND LITERATURES (COMPLETE ED.). (US/0024-8215). Modern Language Association of America, 10 Astor Place, New York NY 10003-6981. **Tel** (212)614-6382, FAX (212)477-9863. **3336**

MLA INTERNATIONAL BIBLIOGRAPHY OF BOOKS AND ARTICLES ON THE MODERN LANGUAGES AND LITERATURES (OPTION C). (US/0740-8722). Modern Language Association of America, 10 Astor Place, New York NY 10003-6981. **Tel** (212)614-6382, FAX (212)477-9863. **3303**

MOLECULAR AND CELLULAR BIOLOGY. (US/0270-7306). American Society for Microbiology, 1325 Massachusetts Avenue Northwest, Washington DC 20005-4171. **Tel** (202)737-3600, FAX (202)737-0367. **568**

MONARCH NOTES. CD-ROM. (US). Bureau of Electronic Publishing Inc., 141 New Road, Parsippany NJ 07054. **Tel** (201)808-2700, FAX (201)808-2676. **3413**

MONEY DIGEST (BATH). (CN/0833-3432). Investors Association of Canada, 26 Soho Street, Suite 380, Toronto Ontario M5T 1Z7 Canada. **Tel** (416)340-1723. **907**

MONTANA CODE ANNOTATED STATUTES TEXT. (US). Montana Legislative Council, State Capitol/Room 138, Helena MT 59620-1706. **Tel** (406)444-3064, FAX (406)444-3036. **3012**

MORBIDITY AND MORTALITY WEEKLY REPORT. (US/0149-2195). MMS Publications, CSPO Box 9120, Waltham MA 02254. **Tel** (800)843-6356. **4792**

MORNINGSTAR MUTUAL FUNDS ONDISC. (US/1059-1427). Morningstar Inc, 225 West Wacker Drive, Chicago IL 60606. **Tel** (312)696-6000, (800)876-5005. **908**

MOTORCYCLIST'S POST, THE. (US/0164-9256). Motorcyclist Post, PO Box 154, Rochdale MA 01542. **Tel** (617)885-5221. **5387**

MS-DOS COLLECTION. (US/1051-8592). Selectware Technologies Inc, 29200 Vassar, Suite 200, Livonia MI 48152. **1288**

MSA PROFILE. (US/1043-8629). Woods & Poole Economics Inc., 1794 Columbia Road Northwest, Suite 4, Washington DC 20009. **Tel** (202)332-7111, FAX (202)332-6466. **1506**

MULTI-BIBLE IBM. CD-ROM. (US). Innotech Inc, 2001 Sheppard Avenue East 118, North York, Ontario M2J 4Z7 Canada. **Tel** (416)492-3838. **4979**

MULTI MEDIA BIRDS OF AMERICA. CD-ROM. (US). Creative Multimedia Corporation, 513 Northwest Avenue, Suite 400, Portland OR 97209. **Tel** (503)241-4351. **5618**

MULTIMEDIA AUDUBONS BIRDS. (US). Creative Multimedia Corporation, 513 Northwest Avenue, Suite 400, Portland OR 97209. **Tel** (503)241-4351. **5618**

MULTIMEDIA WORLD FACTBOOK. CD-ROM. (US). Bureau of Electronic Publishing Inc., 141 New Road, Parsippany NJ 07054. **Tel** (201)808-2700, (201)808-2676. **4482**

MUNDO HISPANICO (ATLANTA, GA.). (US/1051-4147). Mundo Hispanico, PO Box 13808, Station K, Atlanta GA 30324. **Tel** (404)881-0441, FAX (404)881-6085. **5654**

MUSE, MUSIC SEARCH. (US/1054-2639). National Information Services Corp, 3100 St Paul Street, Wyman Towers, Suite 6, Baltimore MD 21218. **Tel** (410)243-0797, FAX (410)243-0982. **4132**

MUSIC BUSINESS DIRECTORY. (US/0747-6655). Music Business Directory, 1100 16th Avenue South, Nashville TN 37212. **4133**

MUSIC CATALOG. [COMPUTER FILE]. (US). Library of Congress / Cataloging Distribution Service, Washington DC 20541-5017. **Tel** (800)255-3666, (202)707-6100, FAX (202)707-1334. **420**

MUSIC INDEX ON CD-ROM, THE. (US/1066-1514). Chadwyck-Healey Limited, The Quorum Barnwell Road, Cambridge CB5 8SW England. **Tel** 011 44 223 215512, telex 9312102281 CH G. **4134**

MUSIC LIBRARY. MUSICAL SOUND RECORDINGS. (US/1048-2741). OCLC Asia Pacific Services, 6565 Frantz Road, Dublin OH 43017. **Tel** (800)848-5878, (614)764-6394 or 6000, FAX (614)764-6096. **5317**

... MUSIC RADIO DIRECTORY, THE. (US). Music Industry Resources, PO Box 190, San Anselmo CA 94960. **Tel** (415)457-0215. **4134**

MUSLIM WORLD (HARTFORD), THE. (US/0027-4909). Hartford Seminary, 77 Sherman Street, Hartford CT 06105. **Tel** (203)232-4451, FAX (203)231-0648. **5044**

MUZE / EBSCO CD-ROM. (US). EBSCO Publishing / Boston, 83 Pine Street, Peabody MA 01960. **Tel** (800)653-2726 North America, (508)535-8500, FAX (508)535-8545. **4139**

NATASHA. [CD-ROM]. (US). Sociometrics Corporation, 170 State Street, Suite 260, Los Altos CA 94022. **Tel** (415)949-3282. **3765**

NATIONAL DIRECTORY OF ADDRESSES AND TELEPHONE NUMBERS (MARINA DEL REY, CALIF.), THE. (US/1043-4143). Xiphias, Helms Hall, 8758 Venice Boulevard, Los Angeles CA 90034. **Tel** (310)841-2790, FAX (310)841-2559. **1118**

NATIONAL DIRECTORY OF ADDRESSES AND TELEPHONE NUMBERS (NEW YORK, N.Y.), THE. (US/0740-7203). Omnigraphics Inc., 2500 Penobscot Building, 25th Floor, Detroit MI 48226. **Tel** (313)961-1340, (800)234-1340, FAX (313)961-1383. **697**

NATIONAL ECONOMIC, SOCIAL, & ENVIRONMENTAL DATA BANK [COMPUTER FILE] : NESE DB / U.S. DEPT. OF COMMERCE. (US). National Technical Information Service - NTIS, Room 2027S, 5285 Port Royal Road, Springfield VA 22161. **Tel** (703)487-4630, (703)487-4660, (703)487-4650, FAX (703)321-8547, telex 89-9405. **2178**

NATIONAL HEALTH INTERVIEW SURVEY [COMPUTER FILE] / U.S. DEPARTMENT OF HEALTH AND HUMAN SERVICES, PUBLIC HEALTH SERVICE, CENTERS FOR DISEASE CONTROL. (US). National Center for Health Statistics, 6525 Belcrest Road, Hyattsville MD 20782. **Tel** (301)436-8500. **4792**

NATIONAL LONGITUDINAL SURVEY OF YOUTH, THE. (US/1060-4960). Ohio State University / Human Resource Research, Center for Human Resource Research, Columbus OH 43210. **5252**

NATIONAL METEOROLOGICAL CENTER GRIDPOINT DATA SET, VERSION II. CD-ROM. (US). University of Washington Department of Atmospheric Sciences, Mail Stop AK-40, Seattle WA 98195. **Tel** (206)543-0448, FAX (206)543-0308. **1432**

NATIONAL NEWSPAPER INDEX. (US/0273-3676). Information Access Company, 362 Lakeside Drive, Foster City CA 94404. **Tel** (800)227-8431. **5814**

NATIONAL NEWSPAPER INDEX (MONTHLY). (US). Information Access Company, 362 Lakeside Drive, Foster City CA 94404. **Tel** (800)227-8431. **5814**

NATIONAL REGISTER OF HISTORIC PLACES INDEX ON CD-ROM. (US). Wayzata Technolog Inc., PO Box 807, Grand Rapids MN 55744. **Tel** (218)326-0597, (800)735-7321. **2747**

NATIONAL TRADE DATA BANK, THE. (US/1064-9913). National Technical Information Service - NTIS, Room 2027S, 5285 Port Royal Road, Springfield VA 22161. **Tel** (703)487-4630, (703)487-4660, (703)487-4650, FAX (703)321-8547, telex 89-9405. **847**

NATURAL GAS ANNUAL. (US/0736-9808). National Energy Information Center, Energy Information Administration, Forrestal Building, Room 1F-048, Washington DC 20585. **Tel** (202)586-8800. **4265**

NATURAL RESOURCES (COLLEGE PARK, MD.). (US/1043-7460). **2199**

NATURAL RESOURCES METABASE. (US/1053-1394). National Information Services Corp, 3100 St Paul Street, Wyman Towers, Suite 6, Baltimore MD 21218. **Tel** (410)243-0797, FAX (410)243-0982. **2199**

NEMATOLOGICAL ABSTRACTS. (UK/0957-6797). CAB International Centre, Wallingford, Oxon OX10 8DE United Kingdom. **Tel** 44 491 832111, FAX 44 491 833508, telex 847964 (COMAGG G). **478**

NEUROSCIENCE CITATION INDEX. (US/1057-6096). Institute for Scientific Information, 3501 Market Street, Philadelphia PA 19104. **Tel** (215)386-0100, (800)523-1850, FAX (215)386-6362, telex 84-5305. **3842**

NEW ELECTRONIC ENCYCLOPEDIA. [COMPUTER FILE], THE. (US). Grolier Electronic Publishing, Sherman Turnpike, Danbury CT 06816. **Tel** (203)797-3500, FAX (203)797-3835. **1927**

NEW ENGLAND JOURNAL OF MEDICINE, THE. (US/0028-4793). New England Journal of Medicine, 1440 Main Street, Waltham MA 02154-1649. **Tel** (617)893-3800, (800)843-6356, FAX (617)647-5785, telex 5106015660 NEJM BOS UQ. **3620**

NEW ENGLAND LAW LIBRARY CONSORTIUM UNION CATALOG. CD-ROM. (US). New England Law Library Consortium, Langdell Hall, Cambridge MA 02138. **Tel** (617)495-9918. **3015**

NEW JERSEY BUSINESS DIRECTORY. (US/1048-7158). American Business Directory, 5711 South 86th Circle, Omaha NE 68127. **Tel** (402)593-4600, FAX (402)331-5481. **698**

NEW MEXICO HISTORICAL REVIEW. (US/0028-6206). University of New Mexico, 1013 Mesa Vista Hall, Albuquerque NM 87131-1186. **Tel** (505)277-5839, FAX (505)277-6023. **2748**

NEWSBANK ELECTRONIC INFORMATION SYSTEM [COMPUTER FILE]. (US). Newsbank Inc, 58 Pine Street, New Canaan CT 06840. **Tel** (800)243-7694, (800)762-8182, FAX (203)966-6254. **1197**

NEWSBANK REFERENCE SERVICE COMPUTER FILE. (US). Newsbank Inc, 58 Pine Street, New Canaan CT 06840. **Tel** (800)243-7694, (800)762-8182, FAX (203)966-6254. **1197**

NEWSBYTES : NEWS NETWORK. (US). Metatec Discovery Systems, 7001 Discovery Boulevard, Dublin OH 43017. **Tel** (614)766-3101, (800)637-3472. **1243**

NEWSLETTER - AMERICAN ASSOCIATION OF BIBLE COLLEGES. (US/0736-2595). American Association of Bible Colleges, PO Box 1523, Fayetteville AR 72702. **Tel** (501)521-8164, FAX (501)521-9202. **4981**

NEWSLETTER - FAIRFAX GENEALOGICAL SOCIETY (FAIRFAX COUNTY, VA.). (US/0895-2078). Fairfax Genealogical Society, PO Box 2290, Merrifield VA 22116. **Tel** (703)978-3773. **2463**

NEWSPAPER ABSTRACTS. (US). University Microfilms International, 300 North Zeeb Road, Ann Arbor MI 48106-1346. **Tel** (313)761-4700, (800)521-0600 Exts. 2490, 2491, FAX (313)973-1540. **5814**

NEWSPAPER ABSTRACTS ONDISC. (US/1064-993X). University Microfilms International, 300 North Zeeb Road, Ann Arbor MI 48106-1346. **Tel** (313)761-4700, (800)521-0600 Exts. 2490, 2491, FAX (313)973-1540. **5814**

NEWSPAPER & PERIODICAL ABSTRACTS [ONLINE DATABASE]. (US). University Microfilms International, 300 North Zeeb Road, Ann Arbor MI 48106-1346. **Tel** (313)761-4700, (800)521-0600 Exts. 2490, 2491, FAX (313)973-1540. **5814**

NONWOVENS ABSTRACTS. (UK/9036-1234). Pira International, Randalls Road, Leatherhead, Surrey KT22 7RU England. **Tel** 011 44 372 376161, FAX 011 44 372 377526. **5360**

NORMATIVA TECNICA. (IT.). Schedario Tecnico Editore Spa, Via Cavour 100, 12011 Borgo S Dalmazzo Italy. **Tel** 011 39 171 262296, FAX 011 39 171 262357. **5134**

NORTH AMERICA INDIANS. CD-ROM. (US). Quanta Press, Inc., 1313 Fifth Street Southeast, Suite 208C, Minneapolis MN 55414. **Tel** (612)379-3956, FAX (612)623-4570. **2750**

NORTH DAKOTA LAW REVIEW. (US/0029-2745). University of North Dakota, Grand Forks ND 58202. **Tel** (701)777-2941. **3018**

Serials available on CD-ROM

NOTISUR (ALBUQUERQUE, N.M.). (US/1060-4189). University of New Mexico / Latin American Institute, Latin America Data Base, 801 Yale NE, Albuquerque NM 87131-1016. **Tel** (505)277-6839, FAX (505)277-5989. **4530**

NTIS BIBLIOGRAPHIC DATABASE. (US/1064-0479). National Technical Information Service - NTIS, Room 2027S, 5285 Port Royal Road, Springfield VA 22161. **Tel** (703)487-4630, (703)487-4660, (703)487-4650, FAX (703)321-8547, telex 89-9405. **5175**

NTIS (DUBLIN, OHIO). (US/0897-3474). OCLC Asia Pacific Services, 6565 Frantz Road, Dublin OH 43017. **Tel** (800)848-5878, (614)764-6394 or 6000, FAX (614)764-6096. **421**

NUCLEOTECNICA. (CL/0716-0054). Comis Chilena Energia Nuclear, Amunategui 95, Casilla 188-D, Santiago Chile. **Tel** 011 56 2 6990070, FAX 011 56 2 713121, telex 340465. **2157**

NURSING & ALLIED HEALTH CINAHL CAMBRIDGE. CD-ROM. (US). Cambridge Scientific Abstracts, 7200 Wisconsin Avenue, #601, Bethesda MD 20814-4823. **Tel** (301)961-6750, (800)843-7751, FAX (301)961-6720. **3661**

NURSING & ALLIED HEALTH (CINAHL)-CD [COMPUTER FILE]. (US). Silverplatter Information Inc., 100 River Ridge Drive, Norwood MA 02062. **Tel** (800)343-0064, (617)769-2599, FAX (617)235-1715. **3661**

NURSING FORUM (HILLSDALE). (US/0029-6473). NURSECOM Inc., 1211 Locust Street, Philadelphia PA 19107. **Tel** (215)545-7222, (800)242-6757, FAX (215)545-8107. **3864**

NURSING SCAN IN ADMINISTRATION. (US/1056-3091). NURSECOM Inc., 1211 Locust Street, Philadelphia PA 19107. **Tel** (215)545-7222, (800)242-6757, FAX (215)545-8107. **3865**

NURSING SCAN IN RESEARCH. (US/0897-5647). NURSECOM Inc., 1211 Locust Street, Philadelphia PA 19107. **Tel** (215)545-7222, (800)242-6757, FAX (215)545-8107. **3865**

NUTRITION ABSTRACTS AND REVIEWS. SERIES A: HUMAN & EXPERIMENTAL. (UK/0309-1295). CAB International Centre, Wallingford, Oxon OX10 8DE United Kingdom. **Tel** 44 491 832111, FAX 44 491 833508, telex 847964 (COMAGG G). **4201**

NUTRITION ABSTRACTS AND REVIEWS. SERIES B. LIVESTOCK FEEDS AND FEEDING. (UK/0309-135X). CAB International Centre, Wallingford, Oxon OX10 8DE United Kingdom. **Tel** 44 491 832111, FAX 44 491 833508, telex 847964 (COMAGG G). **155**

OAG TRAVEL DISC [CD ROM]. (UK). Reed Travel Group / England, World Timetable Center, Church Street, Dunstable, Bedfordshire LU5 4HB England. **Tel** 011 44 582 600111, FAX 011 44 582 695348. **5487**

OCLC/AMIGOS COLLECTION ANALYSIS CD. (US/1044-4858). OCLC Asia Pacific Services, 6565 Frantz Road, Dublin OH 43017. **Tel** (800)848-5878, (614)764-6394 or 6000, FAX (614)764-6096. **3238**

OFFICE SYSTEMS RESEARCH JOURNAL. (US/0737-8998). Computer Information Systems, Southwest Missouri State University, 901 South National Avenue, Springfield MO 65804-0089. **Tel** (417)836-5616, FAX (417)836-6337. **700**

OFFICIAL AMERICAN BOARD OF MEDICAL SPECIALTIES (ABMS) DIRECTORY OF BOARD CERTIFIED MEDICAL SPECIALISTS, THE. (US/0000-1406). Marquis Who's Who, A Reed Reference Publishing Company, Part of Reed International PLC, 121 Chanlon Road, New Providence NJ 07974. **Tel** (908)464-6800, (800)521-8110, FAX (908)665-6688, telex 138 755. **3623**

OJCD. (NE). ELLIS Publications, PO Box 1059, 6201 BB Maastricht Netherlands. **Tel** 011 31 04457 2275, FAX 011 31 04457 2148. **3022**

OJINDEX. (NE). ELLIS Publications, PO Box 1059, 6201 BB Maastricht Netherlands. **Tel** 011 31 04457 2275, FAX 011 31 04457 2148. **421**

ONCODISC (PHILADELPHIA, PA.). (US/0897-5639). J.B. Lippincott Company, 227 East Washington Square, Philadelphia PA 19106-3780. **Tel** (215)238-4200 or 4454, FAX (215)238-4227. **3821**

ONCOGENES AND GROWTH FACTORS ABSTRACTS. (US/1043-8963). Cambridge Scientific Abstracts, 7200 Wisconsin Avenue, #601, Bethesda MD 20814-4823. **Tel** (301)961-6750, (800)843-7751, FAX (301)961-6720. **3661**

ONLINE HOTLINE NEWS SERVICE. (US/1040-6646). Information Intelligence Inc., PO Box 31098, Phoenix AZ 85046. **Tel** (602)996-2283, (800)228-9982. **1197**

ONS NURSING SCAN IN ONCOLOGY. (US/1062-5720). NURSECOM Inc., 1211 Locust Street, Philadelphia PA 19107. **Tel** (215)545-7222, (800)242-6757, FAX (215)545-8107. **3866**

ORANGE COUNTY BUSINESS JOURNAL (NEWPORT BEACH, CALIF.). (US/1051-7480). Orange County Business Journal, 4590 MacArthur Boulevard, Suite 100, Newport Beach CA 92660. **Tel** (714)833-8373. **701**

ORDNANCE & MUNITIONS FORECAST. (US). Forecast International / DMS Inc., 22 Commerce Road, Newtown CT 06470. **Tel** (203)426-0800, FAX (203)426-1964, telex 467615. **4053**

ORNAMENTAL HORTICULTURE. (UK/0305-4934). CAB International Centre, Wallingford, Oxon OX10 8DE United Kingdom. **Tel** 44 491 832111, FAX 44 491 833508, telex 847964 (COMAGG G). **2434**

ORTHOPEDIC SURGERY. (NE/0014-4371). Excerpta Medica Publishing Group, PO Box 548, 1000 AM Amsterdam Netherlands. **Tel** 011 31 20 5803243. **3661**

OSHA CD-ROM. (US/1065-9277). Superintendent of Documents, US Government Printing Office, Washington DC 20402. **Tel** (202)275-3328, FAX (202)786-2377. **2867**

OTTAWA LAW REVIEW. (CN/0048-2331). Ottawa Law Review for Canada, University of Ottawa, Law Faculty, 57 Louis Pasteur, Ottawa ONT K1N 6N5 Canada. **Tel** (613)564-4060, (613)564-7195, FAX (613)564-9800. **3024**

OUR EARTH. (US). National Geographic Society, 11555 Darnestown, Gaithersburg MD 20878. **Tel** (202)857-7000, (800)638-4077, FAX (202)429-5727, telex 64194 NATGEO. **1928**

OUTSTATE BUSINESS. (US/1064-3621). Harbor House Publishers, 221 Water Street, Boyne City MI 49712. **Tel** (616)582-2814, FAX (615)582-3392. **702**

PAIS INTERNATIONAL. (US/1064-4660). Silverplatter Information Inc., 100 River Ridge Drive, Norwood MA 02062. **Tel** (800)343-0064, (617)769-2599, FAX (617)235-1715. **1511**

PAIS INTERNATIONAL IN PRINT. (US/1051-4015). Public Affairs Information Service Inc., 521 West 43rd Street, Fifth Floor, New York NY 10036. **Tel** (212)736-6629, (800)288-7247, FAX (212)643-2848. **5227**

PAIS ON CD-ROM [COMPUTER FILE]. (US). Public Affairs Information Service Inc., 521 West 43rd Street, Fifth Floor, New York NY 10036. **Tel** (212)736-6629, (800)288-7247, FAX (212)643-2848. **5227**

PAIS (PEABODY, MASS.). (US/1072-0103). EBSCO Publishing / Boston, 83 Pine Street, Peabody MA 01960. **Tel** (800)653-2726 North America, (508)535-8500, FAX (508)535-8545. **5227**

PAKISTAN JOURNAL OF OTOLARYNGOLOGY. (PK/0257-4985). Pakistan Journal of Otolaryngology, Anklesaria Nursing Home, Garden Road, Karachi Pakistan. **Tel** 011 92 21 4971762, 011 92 21 4971763, FAX 011 92 21 4971763. **3890**

PANEL STUDY OF INCOME DYNAMICS. (US/1060-4952). University of Michigan Survey Research Center, PO Box 1248, Ann Arbor MI 48106. **Tel** (313)936-0099. **1511**

PAPERBOUND BOOKS IN PRINT. (US/0031-1235). R R Bowker, A Reed Reference Publishing Company, Part of Reed International PLC, PO Box 31, 121 Chanlon Drive, New Providence NJ 07974. **Tel** (908)464-6800, (800)521-8110, FAX (908)665-6688, telex 138-755. **4822**

PASCAL. F 10, MECANIQUE, ACOUSTIQUE ET TRANSFERT DE CHALEUR. (FR/1146-5107). Institut de l'Information Scientique et Technique (INIST), 2 Allee du Parc de Brabois, 54514 Vandoeuvre Nancy Cedex France. **Tel** 011 33 83 504600, FAX 011 33 83 504650. **4453**

PATENTIMAGES (NEW HAVEN, CONN.). (US/1064-2692). MicroPatent, 250 Dodge Avenue, New Haven CT 06511. **Tel** (800)648-6787, (203)466-5055. **1307**

PC COMPUTER MAINTENANCE ANNUAL. (US/1045-5701). Champions Management Support Services, 128-B Meadowlake Drive, Downingtown PA 19335. **Tel** (908)276-3477, FAX (301)604-9248. **1270**

PC GUIDE USA. CD-ROM. (US). Macguide Magazine Inc, 444 17th Street, Suite 200, Denver CO 80217. **1198**

PC MAGAZINE (NEW YORK, N.Y.). (US/0888-8507). Ziff-Davis, One Park Avenue, 5th Floor, New York NY 10016. **Tel** (212)503-3500, (609)786-8230. **1271**

PC USER (LONDON, ENGLAND). (UK/0263-5720). EMAP Business & Computer Publishing Ltd., 1 Lincoln Court 1 Lincoln Road, Peterborough PE1 2RP England. **Tel** 011/44/733/68900, FAX 011/44/733/349290. **1271**

PEACE RESEARCH ABSTRACTS. CD-ROM. (CN). Peace Research Institute, 25 Dundana Avenue, Dundas Ontario L9H 4E5 Canada. **Tel** (416)628-2356, FAX (416)628-1830. **4531**

PEDIATRIC INFECTIOUS DISEASE JOURNAL, THE. (US/0891-3668). Williams & Wilkins Company, 428 East Preston Street, Baltimore MD 21202-3993. **Tel** (410)528-4000, (800)638-6423, FAX (410)528-8596, telex 87669. **3908**

PEDIATRICS (EVANSTON). (US/0031-4005). American Academy of Pediatrics, 141 Northwest Point Boulevard, Elk Grove Village IL 60009-0927. **Tel** (708)981-7903, FAX (708)228-5088. **3910**

PERIODICA. (MX/0185-1004). Centro de Informacion Cientifica y Humanistica, Apartado 70 392, Mexico 20 DF Mexico. **Tel** 011 52 5 5480208, 011 52 5 6223964. **5175**

PERIODICALS SCANNED AND ABSTRACTED. LIFE SCIENCES COLLECTION. (US/0891-3889). Cambridge Scientific Abstracts, 7200 Wisconsin Avenue, #601, Bethesda MD 20814-4823. **Tel** (301)961-6750, (800)843-7751, FAX (301)961-6720. **5175**

PERSONAL MEDICAL ADVISOR. (US/1065-0687). EBSCO Publishing / Boston, 83 Pine Street, Peabody MA 01960. **Tel** (800)653-2726 North America, (508)535-8500, FAX (508)535-8545. **3626**

PERSONNEL + TRAINING ABSTRACTS. (UK/0305-067X). MCB University Press, 60 62 Toller Lane, Bradford West Yorkshire BD8 9BX England. **Tel** 011 44 274 499821, FAX 011 44 274 547143, telex 51317 MCBUNI G. **732**

PERSPECTIVES IN PSYCHIATRIC CARE. (US/0031-5990). NURSECOM Inc., 1211 Locust Street, Philadelphia PA 19107. **Tel** (215)545-7222, (800)242-6757, FAX (215)545-8107. **3866**

PERSPECTIVES ON SCIENCE AND CHRISTIAN FAITH. (US/0892-2675). American Scientific Affiliation, PO Box 668, Ipswich MA 01938. **Tel** (508)356-5656. **4986**

PEST-BANK [COMPUTER FILE]. (US). Silverplatter Information Inc., 100 River Ridge Drive, Norwood MA 02062. **Tel** (800)343-0064, (617)769-2599, FAX (617)235-1715. **4246**

PETERSON'S ANNUAL GUIDES TO GRADUATE STUDY. BOOK 1, PETERSON'S GUIDE TO GRADUATE AND PROFESSIONAL PROGRAMS. (US/0894-9344). Peterson's Guides, 202 Carnegie Center, Department 2342, Princeton NJ 08543. **Tel** (800)338-3282, FAX (609)452-0966. **1840**

PETERSON'S ANNUAL GUIDES TO GRADUATE STUDY. BOOK 3, PETERSON'S GUIDE TO GRADUATE PROGRAMS IN THE BIOLOGICAL AND AGRICULTURAL SCIENCES. (US/0894-9360). Peterson's Guides, 202 Carnegie Center, Department 2342, Princeton NJ 08543. **Tel** (800)338-3282, FAX (609)452-0966. **1840**

PETERSON'S ANNUAL GUIDES TO GRADUATE STUDY. BOOK 4, PETERSON'S GUIDE TO GRADUATE PROGRAMS IN THE PHYSICAL SCIENCES AND MATHEMATICS. (US/0894-9379). Peterson's Guides, 202 Carnegie Center, Department 2342, Princeton NJ 08543. **Tel** (800)338-3282, FAX (609)452-0966. **1840**

PETERSON'S GRADLINE [COMPUTER FILE]. (US). Silverplatter Information Inc., 100 River Ridge Drive, Norwood MA 02062. **Tel** (800)343-0064, (617)769-2599, FAX (617)235-1715. **1840**

PETERSON'S GUIDE TO GRADUATE PROGRAMS IN ENGINEERING AND APPLIED SCIENCES. (US/0894-9387). Peterson's Guides, 202 Carnegie Center, Department 2342, Princeton NJ 08543. **Tel** (800)338-3282, FAX (609)452-0966. **1841**

PETERSON'S GUIDE TO GRADUATE PROGRAMS IN THE HUMANITIES AND SOCIAL SCIENCES. (US/0894-9352). Peterson's Guides, 202 Carnegie Center, Department 2342, Princeton NJ 08543. **Tel** (800)338-3282, FAX (609)452-0966. **1841**

PETROLEUM

Serials available on CD-ROM

PETROLEUM ABSTRACTS (TULSA, OKLA.). (US/0031-6423). Petroleum Abstracts, University of Tulsa, Information Services Division, 600 South College Avenue, Harwell Hall 101, Tulsa OK 74104-3189. Tel (800)247-8678, (918)631-2297, FAX (918)599-9361, telex 49 7543. **4284**

PHARMACEUTICAL COMPANY PROFILES. (UK). IMS World Publications Ltd, 7 Harwodd Avenue, london NW1 6JB England. Tel 011 44 71 393 5000, FAX 011 44 393 5900. **4320**

PHILOSOPHER'S INDEX. (US/0031-7993). Philosophy Documentation Center, Bowling Green State University, Bowling Green OH 43403-0189. Tel (419)372-2419, (800)444-2419, FAX (419)372-6987. **4365**

PHONEDISC CALIFORNIA. CD-ROM. (US). Digital Directory Assistance, 6931 Arlington Road, Suite 405, Bethesda MD 20814. Tel (800)284-8353, (301)657-8548. **1161**

PHONEDISC EASTERN EDITION. CD-ROM. (US). Digital Directory Assistance, 6931 Arlington Road, Suite 405, Bethesda MD 20814. Tel (800)284-8353, (301)657-8548. **1161**

PHONEDISC USA RESIDENTIAL (EASTERN & WESTERN EDITIONS). (US). Digital Directory Assistance, 6931 Arlington Road, Suite 405, Bethesda MD 20814. Tel (800)284-8353, (301)657-8548. **1161**

PHONEDISC USA WESTERN EDITION. CD-ROM. (US). Digital Directory Assistance, 6931 Arlington Road, Suite 405, Bethesda MD 20814. Tel (800)284-8353, (301)657-8548. **1161**

PHOTOGRAMMETRIC ENGINEERING AND REMOTE SENSING. (US/0099-1112). American Society for Photogrammetry and Remote Sensing / Maryland, 5410 Grosvenor Lane, Suite 210, Bethesda MD 20814-2160. Tel (301)493-0290, FAX (301)493-0208. **1990**

PHYSICIANS' DESK REFERENCE (COMPACT DISK ED.). (US/1046-2694). Medical Economics Data, Five Paragon Drive, PO Box 27, Montvale NJ 07645. Tel (800)442-6657, (201)358-7200. **4324**

PHYSICIANS' DESK REFERENCE (PRINT ED.). (US/0093-4461). Medical Economics Data, Five Paragon Drive, PO Box 27, Montvale NJ 07645. Tel (800)442-6657, (201)358-7200. **4325**

PHYSICIANS' GENRX. (US). Denniston Publishing Inc., 111 East Putnam Avenue, Riverside CT 06878. Tel (203)698-2500. **4325**

PHYSICIAN'S MEDLINE PLUS. (US/1065-6545). EBSCO Publishing / Boston, 83 Pine Street, Peabody MA 01960. Tel (800)653-2726 North America, (508)535-8500, FAX (508)535-8545. **3661**

PICKUP. (UK). ECCTIS, Fulton House, Jessop Avenue, Cheltenham GL50 3SH England. **1773**

PICTURE ATLAS OF THE WORLD. (US). National Geographic Society, 11555 Darnestown, Gaithersburg MD 20878. Tel (202)857-7000, (800)638-4077, FAX (202)429-5727, telex 64194 NATGEO. **1928**

PIG NEWS AND INFORMATION. (UK/0143-9014). CAB International Centre, Wallingford, Oxon OX10 8DE United Kingdom. Tel 44 491 832111, FAX 44 491 833508, telex 847964 (COMAGG G). **155**

PIK. PRAXIS DER INFORMATIONSVERARBEITUNG UND KOMMUNIKATION. (GW/0930-5157). K.G. Saur Verlag KG, A Reed Reference Publishing Company, Part of Reed International PLC, Ortlerstrasse 8, D 81373 Munich Germany. Tel 011 49 89 769020, FAX 011 49 89 76902150, telex 5212067-SAUR-D. **1199**

PILGRIMAGE. (US/0361-0802). Pilgrimage Press, 427 Lakeshore Drive, Atlanta GA 30307. Tel (404)377-1088. **4608**

PITTSBURGH BUSINESS TIMES-JOURNAL. (US/0883-7910). Pittsburgh Business Weekly Co, 2313 East Carson St, Suite 200, Pittsburgh PA 15203. Tel (412)481-6397, FAX (412)481-9956. **703**

PLACE-NAME-INDEX [COMPUTER FILE]. (US). Buckmaster Publishing - Virginia, Route 4, Box 1630, Mineral VA 23117. Tel (703)894-5777. **2572**

PLANT BREEDING ABSTRACTS. (UK/0032-0803). CAB International Centre, Wallingford, Oxon OX10 8DE United Kingdom. Tel 44 491 832111, FAX 44 491 833508, telex 847964 (COMAGG G). **155**

PLANT DOCTOR. CD-ROM. (US). Quanta Press, Inc., 1313 Fifth Street Southeast, Suite 208C, Minneapolis MN 55414. Tel (612)379-3956, FAX (612)623-4570. **2427**

PLANT GENETIC RESOURCES ABSTRACTS. (UK/0966-0100). CAB International Centre, Wallingford, Oxon OX10 8DE United Kingdom. Tel 44 491 832111, FAX 44 491 833508, telex 847964 (COMAGG G). **479**

PLANT GROWTH REGULATOR ABSTRACTS. (UK/0305-9154). CAB International Centre, Wallingford, Oxon OX10 8DE United Kingdom. Tel 44 491 832111, FAX 44 491 833508, telex 847964 (COMAGG G). **155**

PLASTIC SURGERY. (NE/0014-438X). Elsevier Science Publishers BV, PO Box 211, 1000 AE Amsterdam Netherlands. Tel 011 31 20 5803642, FAX 011 31 20 5862696, telex 15682. **3972**

PLOUGHSHARES. (US/0048-4474). Ploughshares, Emerson College, 100 Beacon Street, Boston MA 02116. Tel (617)926-9875, (617)578-8753. **3424**

POCKET PDR [COMPUTER FILE]. (US/1055-0178). Medical Economics Data, Five Paragon Drive, PO Box 27, Montvale NJ 07645. Tel (800)442-6657, (201)358-7200. **3628**

POEM FINDER ON DISC. (US/1063-1666). Roth Publishing Inc, PO Box 406, Great Neck NY 11022. Tel (516)466-3676, (800)899-7684, FAX (516)829-7746. **3468**

POET LORE. (US/0032-1966). The Writers Center, 7815 Old Georgetown Road, Bethesda MD 20814. Tel (301)654-8664. **3468**

... POLITICAL RISK YEARBOOK. MIDDLE EAST & NORTH AFRICA, THE. (US/0897-8530). Political Risk Services, 6320 Fly Road, Suite 102, PO Box 248, East Syracuse NY 13057-0248. Tel (315)431-0511, FAX (315)431-0200. **4489**

... POLITICAL RISK YEARBOOK. NORTH & CENTRAL AMERICA, THE. (US/0897-8557). Political Risk Services, 6320 Fly Road, Suite 102, PO Box 248, East Syracuse NY 13057-0248. Tel (315)431-0511, FAX (315)431-0200. **4489**

... POLITICAL RISK YEARBOOK. SOUTH AMERICA, THE. (US/0897-8549). Political Risk Services, 6320 Fly Road, Suite 102, PO Box 248, East Syracuse NY 13057-0248. Tel (315)431-0511, FAX (315)431-0200. **4489**

POLITICAL SCIENCE QUARTERLY. (US/0032-3195). Academy of Political Science, 475 Riverside Drive/Suite 1274, New York NY 10115-1274. Tel (212)870-2500, FAX (212)870-2202. **4490**

POLLUTION ABSTRACTS WITH INDEXES. (US/0032-3624). Cambridge Scientific Abstracts, 7200 Wisconsin Avenue, #601, Bethesda MD 20814-4823. Tel (301)961-6750, (800)843-7751, FAX (301)961-6720. **2185**

POLP ASIST [COMPUTER FILE]. (US). US Department of Commerce / Patent and Trademark Office, 211 Crystal Drive, Suite 700, Arlington VA 20002. Tel (703)305-4537, FAX (703)305-6369. **1308**

POLTOX [COMPUTER FILE]. (US). Silverplatter Information Inc., 100 River Ridge Drive, Norwood MA 02062. Tel (800)343-0064, (617)769-2599, FAX (617)235-1715. **2239**

POPULATION STATISTICS. CD-ROM. (US). Slater Hall Information Products, 1301 Pennsylvania Avenue Northwest, Washington DC 20004. Tel (202)393-2666. **4558**

POSTHARVEST NEWS AND INFORMATION. (UK/0957-7505). CAB International Centre, Wallingford, Oxon OX10 8DE United Kingdom. Tel 44 491 832111, FAX 44 491 833508, telex 847964 (COMAGG G). **155**

POTATO ABSTRACTS. (UK/0308-7344). CAB International Centre, Wallingford, Oxon OX10 8DE United Kingdom. Tel 44 491 832111, FAX 44 491 833508, telex 847964 (COMAGG G). **156**

POULTRY ABSTRACTS. (UK/0306-1582). CAB International Centre, Wallingford, Oxon OX10 8DE United Kingdom. Tel 44 491 832111, FAX 44 491 833508, telex 847964 (COMAGG G). **156**

POWDER DIFFRACTION FILE ALPHABETICAL INDEX : INORGANIC COMPOUNDS. (US). Joint Committee on Powder Diffraction Standards / JCPDS, International Centre for Diffraction Data, 12 Campus Boulevard, Newton Square PA 19073. Tel (610)325-9810, FAX (610)325-9823, telex 847170. **1037**

POWDER DIFFRACTION FILE SEARCH MANUAL, HANAWALT METHOD: INORGANIC. (US/0092-1319). Joint Committee on Powder Diffraction Standards / JCPDS, International Centre for Diffraction Data, 12 Campus Boulevard, Newton Square PA 19073. Tel (610)325-9810, FAX (610)325-9823, telex 847170. **1037**

POWDER DIFFRACTION FILE SEARCH MANUAL : ORGANIC. (US/0092-0576). Joint Committee on Powder Diffraction Standards / JCPDS, International Centre for Diffraction Data, 12 Campus Boulevard, Newton Square PA 19073. Tel (610)325-9810, FAX (610)325-9823, telex 847170. **1046**

PREDICASTS F&S INDEX. UNITED STATES ANNUAL EDITION. (US/0277-9676). Predicasts Inc., A Ziff Communications Company, 11001 Cedar Avenue, Cleveland OH 44106. Tel (800)321-6388, (216)795-3000, FAX (216)229-9944, telex 985 604. **422**

PRESIDENTS : IT ALL STARTED WITH GEORGE. (US). National Geographic Society, 11555 Darnestown, Gaithersburg MD 20878. Tel (202)857-7000, (800)638-4077, FAX (202)429-5727, telex 64194 NATGEO. **2755**

PRIMARY SEARCH. (US/1065-2485). EBSCO Publishing / Boston, 83 Pine Street, Peabody MA 01960. Tel (800)653-2726 North America, (508)535-8500, FAX (508)535-8545. **1796**

PRINTING ABSTRACTS. (UK/0031-109X). Pira International, Randalls Road, Leatherhead, Surrey KT22 7RU England. Tel 011 44 372 376161, FAX 011 44 372 377526. **4570**

PRIVACY JOURNAL. (US/0145-7659). Privacy Journal, PO Box 28577, Providence RI 02908. Tel (401)274-7861. **1227**

PROBABILITY AND STOCHASTIC PROCESSES. (GW/0720-2628). Fachinformationszentrum, Karlsruhe Franklinstr, 11 ABT Berlin, D-10587 Berlin Germany. Tel 011 49 30 2611585, or 2611586, FAX 011 49 30 2628069. **3527**

PROCEEDINGS OF THE SOUTH CAROLINA HISTORICAL ASSOCIATION, THE. (US/0361-6207). South Carolina Historical Association, c/o Dr. William S. Brockington, University of South Carolina-Aiken, 171 University Parkway, Aiken SC 29801. Tel (803)641-3223. **2755**

PROGRAMMERS ROM. CD-ROM. (US). Quanta Press, Inc., 1313 Fifth Street Southeast, Suite 208C, Minneapolis MN 55414. Tel (612)379-3956, FAX (612)623-4570. **1281**

PROTEIN SCIENCE : A PUBLICATION OF THE PROTEIN SOCIETY. (US/0961-8368). Cambridge University Press / New York, 40 West 20th Street, New York NY 10011-4211. Tel (212)924-3900, (800)221-4512. **493**

PROTOZOOLOGICAL ABSTRACTS. (UK/0309-1287). CAB International Centre, Wallingford, Oxon OX10 8DE United Kingdom. Tel 44 491 832111, FAX 44 491 833508, telex 847964 (COMAGG G). **5604**

PSYCHOLOGICAL ABSTRACTS. (US/0033-2887). American Psychological Association, 750 First Street Northeast, Washington DC 20002. Tel (800)374-2721, (202)336-5600, (subscriptions - (202)336-5600. **4623**

PSYCHOLOGICAL RECORD, THE. (US/0033-2933). Kenyon College, c/o Charles E. Rice, Gambier OH 43022. Tel (614)427-5377, FAX (614)427-4950. **4611**

PSYCINFO. (US). American Psychological Association, 750 First Street Northeast, Washington DC 20002. Tel (800)374-2721, (202)336-5600, (subscriptions - (202)336-5600. **4623**

PSYCLIT DATABASE. (US). Silverplatter Information Inc., 100 River Ridge Drive, Norwood MA 02062. Tel (800)343-0064, (617)769-2599, FAX (617)235-1715. **4623**

PUBLICATIONS OF THE US GEOLOGICAL SURVEY. CD-ROM. (US). American Geological Institute, 4220 King Street, Alexandria VA 22302. Tel (703)379-2480, FAX (703)379-7563. **1359**

PUBLIQUE ARTE. CD-ROM. (US). Quanta Press, Inc., 1313 Fifth Street Southeast, Suite 208C, Minneapolis MN 55414. Tel (612)379-3956, FAX (612)623-4570. **381**

PUBLISHERS, DISTRIBUTORS, & WHOLESALERS OF THE UNITED STATES. (US/0000-0671). R R Bowker, A Reed Reference Publishing Company, Part of Reed International PLC, PO Box 31, 121 Chanlon Drive, New Providence NJ 07974. Tel (908)464-6800, (800)521-8110, FAX (908)665-6688, telex 138-755. **4822**

PUBLISHERS WEEKLY. (US/0000-0019). Cahners Publishing Company, 249 West 17th Street, New York NY 10011. Tel (212)645-0067, FAX (212)242-6987. **4831**

QADMONIOT. (IS/0033-4839). Israel Exploration Society, 5 Avida Street, 91070 Jerusalem Israel. Tel 011 972 2 227991. **279**

RADAR FORECAST. (US). Forecast International / DMS Inc., 22 Commerce Road, Newtown CT 06470. **Tel** (203)426-0800, FAX (203)426-1964, telex 467615. **4054**

R&D FOCUS. (UK). IMS World Publications Ltd, 7 Harwodd Avenue, london NW1 6JB England. **Tel** 011 44 71 393 5000, FAX 011 44 393 5900. **4327**

RAPRA ABSTRACTS. (UK/0033-6750). RAPRA Technology Ltd., Shawbury Shrewsbury, Shropshire SY4 4NR England. **Tel** 011 44 939 250383, FAX 011 44 939 251118, telex 35134 RAPRA G. **5078**

RATIONELLES BURO + I.E. UND EDV. (GW). Basten GmbH, Schlossparkstrasse 6, W-5100 Aachen Germany. **Tel** 0241/17011, FAX 0241/172501, telex IS 832563. **706**

RBBS-PC IN A BOX. CD-ROM. (US). Quanta Press, Inc., 1313 Fifth Street Southeast, Suite 208C, Minneapolis MN 55414. **Tel** (612)379-3956, FAX (612)623-4570. **1289**

REACTIONS WEEKLY. (NZ/0114-9954). ADIS International Ltd, 41 Centorian Drive, Private Bag 65901, Mairangi Bay, Auckland 10 New Zealand. **Tel** 011 64 9 4798100, FAX 011 64 9 4791418. **4327**

READERS' GUIDE ABSTRACTS. CD-ROM. (US/0899-1553). H W Wilson Company, 950 University Avenue, Bronx NY 10452. **Tel** (800)367-6770, (718)588-8400, FAX (718)590-1617, telex 4990003 HWILSON. **2497**

READERS' GUIDE ABSTRACTS SELECT EDITION. (US). H W Wilson Company, 950 University Avenue, Bronx NY 10452. **Tel** (800)367-6770, (718)588-8400, FAX (718)590-1617, telex 4990003 HWILSON. **2497**

READERS' GUIDE TO PERIODICAL LITERATURE. (US/0034-0464). H W Wilson Company, 950 University Avenue, Bronx NY 10452. **Tel** (800)367-6770, (718)588-8400, FAX (718)590-1617, telex 4990003 HWILSON. **2497**

REALSCAN. BROWARD COUNTY. (US/1053-8917). LaserScan Systems, Inc., 5310 NW 33 Avenue, Suite 115, Ft Lauderdale FL 33309. **4845**

REALSCAN. DADE COUNTY. (US/1053-8925). LaserScan Systems, Inc., 5310 NW 33 Avenue, Suite 115, Ft Lauderdale FL 33309. **4845**

REALSCAN. PALM BEACH COUNTY [COMPUTER FILE] : REAL ESTATE MARKET INFORMATION SYSTEMS. (US/1056-8344). LaserScan Systems, Inc., 5310 NW 33 Avenue, Suite 115, Ft Lauderdale FL 33309. **4845**

REGISTRE DE L'ISDS (ED. SUR MICROFICHE). (FR/0257-2222). ISSN International Centre, 20 rue Bachaumont, F-75002 Paris France. **Tel** 011 33 1 42367381, FAX 011 33 1 40263243, telex SERIALS 219847F. **4819**

REGISTRY OF TOXIC EFFECTS OF CHEMICAL SUBSTANCES [MICROFORM]. (US/0361-2546). Superintendent of Documents, US Government Printing Office, Washington DC 20402. **Tel** (202)275-3328, FAX (202)786-2377. **3983**

REIS [COMPUTER FILE] : REGIONAL ECONOMIC INFORMATION SYSTEM. (US). Bureau of Economic Analysis, US Department of Commerce, 1401 K Street Northwest, Washington DC 20230. **Tel** (202)523-0777. **1516**

RELIGION INDEX ONE. PERIODICALS. (US/0149-8428). American Theological Library Association, 820 Church Street, 3rd Floor, Evanston IL 60201. **Tel** (708)869-7788, FAX (708)869-8513. **5013**

RELIGION INDEX TWO : MULTI-AUTHOR WORKS. (US/0149-8436). American Theological Library Association, 820 Church Street, 3rd Floor, Evanston IL 60201. **Tel** (708)869-7788, FAX (708)869-8513. **4991**

RELIGION INDEXES [COMPUTER FILE]. (US). American Theological Library Association, 820 Church Street, 3rd Floor, Evanston IL 60201. **Tel** (708)869-7788, FAX (708)869-8513. **5013**

RELIGIOUS AND THEOLOGICAL ABSTRACTS. (US/0034-4044). Religious & Theological Abstracts Inc., PO Box 215, 121 South College Street, Myerstown PA 17067. **Tel** (717)866-6734, FAX (717)866-6734. **5013**

REPERTORIO 4 CODICI TRIBUTARI. (IT). IPSOA Editore SRL, Casella Postale 12055, Mastrangelo, 20120 Milan Italy. **Tel** 011 39 2 82476248. **4744**

RESEARCH IN MINISTRY. (US). American Theological Library Association, 820 Church Street, 3rd Floor, Evanston IL 60201. **Tel** (708)869-7788, FAX (708)869-8513. **4992**

RESOURCE/ONE ONDISC [COMPUTER FILE]. (US). University Microfilms International, 300 North Zeeb Road, Ann Arbor MI 48106-1346. **Tel** (313)761-4700, (800)521-0600 Exts. 2490, 2491, FAX (313)973-1540. **2497**

RESOURCES IN EDUCATION. (US/0098-0897). Superintendent of Documents, US Government Printing Office, Washington DC 20402. **Tel** (202)275-3328, FAX (202)786-2377. **1779**

REVIEW : LATIN AMERICAN LITERATURE AND ARTS. (US). The Americas Society, 680 Park Avenue, New York NY 10021. **Tel** (212)249-8950, FAX (212)248-5868. **329**

REVIEW OF AGRICULTURAL ENTOMOLOGY. (UK/0957-6762). CAB International Centre, Wallingford, Oxon OX10 8DE United Kingdom. **Tel** 44 491 832111, FAX 44 491 833508, telex 847964 (COMAGG G). **5604**

REVIEW OF MEDICAL AND VETERINARY ENTOMOLOGY. (UK/0957-6770). CAB International Centre, Wallingford, Oxon OX10 8DE United Kingdom. **Tel** 44 491 832111, FAX 44 491 833508, telex 847964 (COMAGG G). **5604**

REVIEW OF MEDICAL AND VETERINARY MYCOLOGY. (UK/0034-6624). CAB International Centre, Wallingford, Oxon OX10 8DE United Kingdom. **Tel** 44 491 832111, FAX 44 491 833508, telex 847964 (COMAGG G). **5528**

REVIEW OF PLANT PATHOLOGY. (UK/0034-6438). CAB International Centre, Wallingford, Oxon OX10 8DE United Kingdom. **Tel** 44 491 832111, FAX 44 491 833508, telex 847964 (COMAGG G). **479**

REVIEW OF RESEARCH IN DEVELOPMENTAL EDUCATION. (US/0894-3907). National Center for Developmental Education, Appalachian State University, Boone NC 28608. **Tel** (704)262-2876, FAX (704)262-2128. **1780**

REVISTA MEXICANA DE ANESTESIOLOGIA Y REANIMACION. (MX/0185-1012). Societe Mexico de Anestesiologia AC, Insurgentes Sur #636 Desp 502, 03100 Mexico DF Mexico. **Tel** 011 52 6691659, 011 52 6691457, FAX 011 52 6691659. **3684**

REVUE ANDRE MALRAUX. (CN/0839-458X). University of Alberta / Romance Languages, Department of Romance Languages, Edmonton Alberta T6G 2E6 Canada. **Tel** (403)492-2003, (403)439-9393. **3351**

REVUE DE DROIT PENAL ET DE CRIMINOLOGIE. (BE). Editions la Charte Sa, Rue Guimard 19, B 1040 Brussels Belgium. **Tel** 011 32 50 331235, FAX 011 32 50 343768. **3175**

RHODE ISLAND BUSINESS DIRECTORY. (US/1048-7166). American Business Directory, 5711 South 86th Circle, Omaha NE 68127. **Tel** (402)593-4600, FAX (402)331-5481. **708**

RICE ABSTRACTS. (UK/0141-0164). CAB International Centre, Wallingford, Oxon OX10 8DE United Kingdom. **Tel** 44 491 832111, FAX 44 491 833508, telex 847964 (COMAGG G). **1012**

RIGHT STUFFED. CD-ROM, THE. (US). Quantum Leap Technologies, 1399 Southeast 9th Avenue, Suite 4, Hialeah FL 33010-5999. **Tel** (305)885-9985, (800)762-2877, FAX (305)762-9986. **1289**

RISK (CONCORD, N.H.). (US/1073-8673). Franklin Pierce Law Center, 2 White Street, Concord NH 03301. **Tel** (603)228-1541, FAX (603)224-3342, (603)228-0388. **5148**

ROBOTICS ABSTRACTS. (US/0000-1139). R R Bowker, A Reed Reference Publishing Company, Part of Reed International PLC, PO Box 31, 121 Chanlon Drive, New Providence NJ 07974. **Tel** (908)464-6800, (800)521-8110, FAX (908)665-6688, telex 138-755. **1209**

RURAL DEVELOPMENT ABSTRACTS / [PREPARED BY THE COMMONWEALTH BUREAU OF AGRICULTURAL ECONOMICS]. (UK/0140-4768). CAB International Centre, Wallingford, Oxon OX10 8DE United Kingdom. **Tel** 44 491 832111, FAX 44 491 833508, telex 847964 (COMAGG G). **2840**

RURAL LIVING (A&N ELECTRIC COOPERATIVE ED.). (US/1054-4801). Virginia, Maryland & Delaware Association of Electric Cooperatives, 4201 Dominion Boulevard Suite 101, Glen Allen VA 23060. **Tel** (804)346-3344, FAX (804)346-3448. **131**

SAFETY AND HEALTH AT WORK : ILO-CIS BULLETIN. (SZ/1010-7053). International Labour Office - ILO, Publications Sales Service, CH-1211 Geneva 22 Switzerland. **Tel** 011 41 22 7996111. **2872**

SAM-CD : SCIENTIFIC AMERICAN MEDICINE ON CD-ROM. (US). Scientific American Medicine, 415 Madison Avenue, New York NY 10017. **Tel** (212)754-0550, (800)333-1199. **3638**

SCAD+CD. (NE). ELLIS Publications, PO Box 1059, 6201 BB Maastricht Netherlands. **Tel** 011 31 04457 2275, FAX 011 31 04457 2148. **424**

SCHOOLMATCH [COMPUTER FILE]. (US). OCLC Asia Pacific Services, 6565 Frantz Road, Dublin OH 43017. **Tel** (800)848-5878, (614)764-6394 or 6000, FAX (614)764-6096. **1782**

SCIENCE CITATION INDEX (COMPACT DISC ED.). (US/1044-6052). Institute for Scientific Information, 3501 Market Street, Philadelphia PA 19104. **Tel** (215)386-0100, (800)523-1850, FAX (215)386-6362, telex 84-5305. **5176**

SCIENCE CITATION INDEX WITH ABSTRACTS. (US/1061-1290). Institute for Scientific Information, 3501 Market Street, Philadelphia PA 19104. **Tel** (215)386-0100, (800)523-1850, FAX (215)386-6362, telex 84-5305. **5176**

SCIENTIFIC AMERICAN MEDICINE. (US/0194-9063). Scientific American Medicine, 415 Madison Avenue, New York NY 10017. **Tel** (212)754-0550, (800)333-1199. **3639**

SCIENTIFIC AND TECHNICAL BOOKS AND SERIALS IN PRINT. (US/0000-054X). R R Bowker, A Reed Reference Publishing Company, Part of Reed International Publishing PLC, PO Box 31, 121 Chanlon Drive, New Providence NJ 07974. **Tel** (908)464-6800, (800)521-8110, FAX (908)665-6688, telex 138-755. **5176**

SCIMP SELECTIVE CO-OPERATIVE INDEX OF MANAGEMENT PERIODICALS. (FI/0782-2979). Helsinki School of Economics, Runeberginkatu 22 24 SCIMP, 00100 Helsinki Finland. **Tel** 358 0 43131. **733**

SCITECH REFERENCE PLUS. (US/1063-8717). R R Bowker Electronic Publishing, A Reed Reference Publishing Company, Part of Reed International PLC, 121 Chanlon Drive, New Providence NJ 07974. **Tel** (800)323-3288. **5176**

SEALS OF THE U.S. GOVERNMENT. CD-ROM. (US). Quanta Press, Inc., 1313 Fifth Street Southeast, Suite 208C, Minneapolis MN 55414. **Tel** (612)379-3956, FAX (612)623-4570. **382**

SEAWAY REVIEW. (US/0037-0487). Harbor House Publishers, 221 Water Street, Boyne City MI 49712. **Tel** (616)582-2814, FAX (615)582-3392. **5456**

SEED ABSTRACTS. (UK/0141-0180). CAB International Centre, Wallingford, Oxon OX10 8DE United Kingdom. **Tel** 44 491 832111, FAX 44 491 833508, telex 847964 (COMAGG G). **156**

SERIALS DIRECTORY (BIRMINGHAM, ALA. PRINT ED.), THE. (US/0886-4179). EBSCO Publishing / Birmingham, The Serials Directory, PO Box 1943, Birmingham AL 35201-1943. **Tel** editorial inquiries (205)980-2773, toll-free US (800)826-3024, FAX (205)995-1582. **3249**

SERIALS DIRECTORY / EBSCO CD-ROM, THE. (US). EBSCO Publishing / Birmingham, The Serials Directory, PO Box 1943, Birmingham AL 35201-1943. **Tel** editorial inquiries (205)980-2773, toll-free US (800)826-3024, FAX (205)995-1582. **3249**

SHAREWARE GRAB-BAG [COMPUTER FILE]. (US). Alde Publishing, PO Box 39326, Minneapolis MN 55396. **Tel** (612)474-3755. **1290**

SHEPARD'S CALIFORNIA CITATIONS (1919). (US/0730-3661). Shepards McGraw-Hill Inc, 555 Middle Creek Parkway, PO Box 35300, Colorado Springs CO 80935-3530. **Tel** (719)488-3000, (800)458-8811, FAX (800)525-0053. **3049**

SHEPARD'S GEORGIA CITATIONS. (US/0730-3742). Shepards McGraw-Hill Inc, 555 Middle Creek Parkway, PO Box 35300, Colorado Springs CO 80935-3530. **Tel** (719)488-3000, (800)458-8811, FAX (800)525-0053. **3050**

SHEPARD'S ILLINOIS CITATIONS. (US/0730-3904). Shepards McGraw-Hill Inc, 555 Middle Creek Parkway, PO Box 35300, Colorado Springs CO 80935-3530. **Tel** (719)488-3000, (800)458-8811, FAX (800)525-0053. **3050**

SHEPARD'S MASSACHUSETTS CITATIONS. (US/0730-4064). Shepards McGraw-Hill Inc, 555 Middle Creek Parkway, PO Box 35300, Colorado Springs CO 80935-3530. **Tel** (719)488-3000, (800)458-8811, FAX (800)525-0053. **3051**

SHEPARD'S TEXAS CITATIONS. (US/0730-4463). Shepards McGraw-Hill Inc, 555 Middle Creek Parkway, PO Box 35300, Colorado Springs CO 80935-3530. **Tel** (719)488-3000, (800)458-8811, FAX (800)525-0053. **3054**

SHERLOCK

Serials available on CD-ROM

SHERLOCK HOLMES. CD-ROM. (US). Creative Multimedia Corporation, 513 Northwest Avenue, Suite 400, Portland OR 97209. Tel (503)241-4351. **3436**

SIERRA. (US/0161-7362). Sierra, 730 Polk Street, San Francisco CA 94109. Tel (415)923-5656. **2205**

SIGN LANGUAGE STUDIES. (US/0302-1475). Linstok Press, 4020 Blackburn Lane, Burtonsville MD 20866. Tel (301)421-0268, FAX (301)421-0270. **3321**

SLAVIC AND EAST EUROPEAN JOURNAL. (US/0037-6752). ATSEEL / Department of Russian and Slavic Languages, University of Arizona, Modern Languages 340, Tucson AZ 85721. Tel (602)621-9766, FAX (602)621-9765. **3321**

SOCIAL ISSUES RESOURCES SERIES. (US/0740-3127). Social Issues Resources Series Inc, PO Box 2348, Boca Raton FL 33427. Tel (800)327-0513, (407)994-0079. **5308**

SOCIAL PLANNING, POLICY & DEVELOPMENT ABSTRACTS. (US/1042-8380). Sociological Abstracts, PO Box 22206, San Diego CA 92192-0206. Tel (619)695-8803, FAX (619)695-0416. **5266**

SOCIAL RESEARCH METHODOLOGY ABSTRACTS. (NE/0167-8477). Erasmus University / SRM-Documentation Centre, Postbus 1738 Kamer BT 13, 3000 DR Rotterdam, The Netherlands. Tel 010 4081198, FAX 010 4529510. **5227**

SOCIAL SCIENCE SOURCE. (US/1063-9802). EBSCO Publishing / Boston, 83 Pine Street, Peabody MA 01960. Tel (800)653-2726 North America, (508)535-8500, FAX (508)535-8545. **5227**

SOCIAL SCIENCES CITATION INDEX (COMPACT DISC ED.). (US/1044-6044). Institute for Scientific Information, 3501 Market Street, Philadelphia PA 19104. Tel (215)386-0100, (800)523-1850, FAX (215)386-6362, telex 84-5305. **5221**

SOCIAL SCIENCES CITATION INDEX (PRINT ED.). (US/0091-3707). Institute for Scientific Information, 3501 Market Street, Philadelphia PA 19104. Tel (215)386-0100, (800)523-1850, FAX (215)386-6362, telex 84-5305. **5228**

SOCIAL SCIENCES CITATION INDEX WITH ABSTRACTS. (US/1061-1282). Institute for Scientific Information, 3501 Market Street, Philadelphia PA 19104. Tel (215)386-0100, (800)523-1850, FAX (215)386-6362, telex 84-5305. **5221**

SOCIAL SCIENCES INDEX. (US/0094-4920). H W Wilson Company, 950 University Avenue, Bronx NY 10452. Tel (800)367-6770, (718)588-8400, FAX (718)590-1617, telex 4990003 HWILSON. **5228**

SOCIAL SCIENCES INDEX (CD-ROM ED.). (US/1063-3308). H W Wilson Company, 950 University Avenue, Bronx NY 10452. Tel (800)367-6770, (718)588-8400, FAX (718)590-1617, telex 4990003 HWILSON. **5228**

SOCIOFILE DATABASE [COMPUTER FILE], THE. (US). Silverplatter Information Inc., 100 River Ridge Drive, Norwood MA 02062. Tel (800)343-0064, (617)769-2599, FAX (617)235-1715. **5260**

SOCIOLOGICAL ABSTRACTS. (US/0038-0202). Sociological Abstracts, PO Box 22206, San Diego CA 92192-0206. Tel (619)695-8803, FAX (619)695-0416. **5267**

SOCIOLOGY (OXFORD). (UK/0038-0385). British Sociological Association, 351 Station Road, Dorridge-Solihull, West Midlands B93 8EY England. Tel 011 44 564 7724021. **5262**

SOFT-LETTER. (US/0882-3499). Soft-Letter, 17 Main Street, Watertown MA 02172. Tel (617)924-3944, FAX (617)924-7288. **1290**

SOFTWARE ABSTRACTS FOR ENGINEERS : SAFE. (IE/0790-150X). CITIS Ltd, 2 Rosemount Terrace, Blackrock Dublin Ireland. Tel 3531-886227, FAX 3531-885971, telex 30259 MSCH ET. **1210**

SOFTWARE USERS YEAR BOOK CD-ROM. (UK). VNU Business Publications BV, 32-34 Broadwick Street, London W1A 2HG England. Tel 011 44 71 439 4242 ext. 2222, FAX 011 44 71 437 9638, telex 23918 VNU G, 8952440. **1291**

SOILS AND FERTILIZERS. (UK/0038-0792). CAB International Centre, Wallingford, Oxon OX10 8DE United Kingdom. Tel 44 491 832111, FAX 44 491 833508, telex 847964 (COMAGG G). **156**

SOUND CREATIVE. CD ROM. (FR). CDR Informatique, BP 32, 91470 Limours France. Tel 011 33 1 64912676. **5319**

SOUTH AFRICAN TAX CASES, INCLUDING DECISIONS OF THE SUPREME COURT OF SOUTH AFRICA, THE HIGH COURT OF ZIMBABWE AND THE SPECIAL COURTS FOR HEARING INCOME TAX APPEALS. (SA/0038-2752). Juta Subscription Services, PO Box 14373, Kenwyn 7790 South Africa. Tel 011 27 21 7975101, FAX (021)761-5010, telex 523072 SA. **3056**

SOUTH CAROLINA BUSINESS DIRECTORY. (US/1046-0934). American Business Directory, 5711 South 86th Circle, Omaha NE 68127. Tel (402)593-4600, FAX (402)331-5481. **712**

SOUTHERN CALIFORNIA BUSINESS DIRECTORY. (US/1061-2181). American Business Directory, 5711 South 86th Circle, Omaha NE 68127. Tel (402)593-4600, FAX (402)331-5481. **712**

SOUTHWEST REVIEW. (US/0038-4712). Southwest Review, Southern Methodist University, 307 Fondren Library West, Dallas TX 75275. Tel (214)768-1036, (214)768-1037, FAX (214)768-1408. **3353**

SOYABEAN ABSTRACTS. (UK/0141-0172). CAB International Centre, Wallingford, Oxon OX10 8DE United Kingdom. Tel 44 491 832111, FAX 44 491 833508, telex 847964 (COMAGG G). **156**

SPACE SYSTEMS FORECAST. (US). Forecast International / DMS Inc., 22 Commerce Road, Newtown CT 06470. Tel (203)426-0800, FAX (203)426-1964, telex 467615. **4057**

SPORT DISCUS [COMPUTER FILE]. (US). Silverplatter Information Inc., 100 River Ridge Drive, Norwood MA 02062. Tel (800)343-0064, (617)769-2599, FAX (617)235-1715. **1797**

SPORTING NEWS BASEBALL GUIDE AND REGISTER. CD-ROM. (US). Quanta Press, Inc., 1313 Fifth Street Southeast, Suite 208C, Minneapolis MN 55414. Tel (612)379-3956, FAX (612)623-4570. **4921**

SPORTSEARCH. (US/0882-553X). Sport Information Resource Centre, 1600 promenade James Naismith Drive, Gloucester Ontario K1B 5N4 Canada. Tel (613)748-5658, FAX (613)748-5701, telex 053-3660 Sportrec Ott. **4856**

SPOTLIGHT. ACTRESSES. (UK/0308-9827). Spotlight / London, 7 Leicester Place, London WC2H 7BP England. Tel 011 44 1 437 7631, FAX 011 44 1 437 5881. **388**

STANDARD & POOR'S CORPORATION RECORDS. CURRENT NEWS EDITION. (US/0196-4674). Standard & Poor's Corporation, 25 Broadway, New York NY 10004. Tel (212)208-8775. **915**

STANDARD DIRECTORY OF ADVERTISERS (GEOGRAPHICAL ED.). (US/0081-4229). National Register Publishing Company Inc., PO Box 31, 121 Chanlon Road, New Providence NJ 07974. Tel (800)521-8110, (800)323-6772, FAX (908)665-6688. **766**

STANDARD DIRECTORY OF ADVERTISING AGENCIES. (US/0085-6614). National Register Publishing Company Inc., PO Box 31, 121 Chanlon Road, New Providence NJ 07974. Tel (800)521-8110, (800)323-6772, FAX (908)665-6688. **766**

STANDARD DIRECTORY OF INTERNATIONAL ADVERTISERS & AGENCIES. (US). National Register Publishing Company Inc., PO Box 31, 121 Chanlon Road, New Providence NJ 07974. Tel (800)521-8110, (800)323-6772, FAX (908)665-6688. **766**

STANDARD PERIODICAL DIRECTORY, THE. (US/0085-6630). Oxbridge Communications Inc., 150 5th Avenue, Room 302, New York NY 10011. Tel (212)741-0231, FAX (212)633-2938. **3251**

STAT BANK [COMPUTER FILE]. (US). Newsbank Inc, 58 Pine Street, New Canaan CT 06840. Tel (800)243-7694, (800)762-8182, FAX (203)966-6254. **5339**

STATISTICAL MASTERFILE [COMPUTER FILE]. (US). Congressional Information Service Inc, 4520 East-West Highway, Suite 800, Bethesda MD 20814-3389. Tel (800)638-8380, (301)654-1550, FAX (301)654-4033, telex 292386 CIS UR. **5340**

STEELS ALERT. (US/1048-0307). American Society for Metals International, c/o Deborah Barthelmes, Materials Park OH 44073-0002. Tel (216)338-5151, FAX (216)338-4634, telex 980-619. **4021**

SUGAR INDUSTRY ABSTRACTS / [CAB INTERNATIONAL, BUREAU OF HORTICULTURE AND PLANTATION CROPS IN ASSOCIATION WITH TATE & LYLE PLC]. (UK/0957-5022). CAB International Centre, Wallingford, Oxon OX10 8DE United Kingdom. Tel 44 491 832111, FAX 44 491 833508, telex 847964 (COMAGG G). **157**

TAX EXECUTIVE, THE. (US/0040-0025). Tax Executives Institute Inc, 1001 Pennsylvania Avenue Northwest, Suite 320, Washington DC 20004-2505. Tel (202)638-5601, FAX (202)638-5607. **4752**

TEBIWA. (US/0040-0823). Idaho Museum of Natural History, Campus Box 8096, Idaho State University, Pocatello ID 83209. Tel (208)236-3410, FAX (208)236-4000. **4172**

TECH STREET JOURNAL. (US/0889-6461). Tech Street Journal, 238 Littleton Road, Westford MA 01886. Tel (508)692-2290, FAX (508)692-4760. **5162**

TECHNICAL COMMUNICATION QUARTERLY. (US/1057-2252). Association of Teachers of Technical Writing, University of Minnesota, 202 Haecker Hall, St Paul MN 55108. Tel (612)624-9729, FAX (612)624-3617. **1122**

TELEXPORT : LES EXPORTATEURS ET IMPORTATEURS FRANCAIS. (FR). Chambre de Commerce et Industrie de Paris, CEDIP, 201 avenue Jean Lolive, 93507 Pantin Cedex-France. Tel 33 1 47631415, FAX 33 1 42679969. **853**

TENNESSEE HISTORICAL QUARTERLY. (US/0040-3261). Tennessee Historical Society, War Memorial Building, Nashville TN 37219. Tel (615)741-8934. **2762**

TESTO UNICO IMPOSTE DIRETTE. (IT). IPSOA Editore SRL, Casella Postale 12055, Mastrangelo, 20120 Milan Italy. Tel 011 39 2 82476248. **3063**

TEXAS BUSINESS DIRECTORY. (US/1053-6698). American Business Directory, 5711 South 86th Circle, Omaha NE 68127. Tel (402)593-4600, FAX (402)331-5481. **715**

TEXTILE TECHNOLOGY DIGEST. (US/0040-5191). Institute of Textile Technology, 2551 Ivy Road, Charlottesville VA 22903-4641. Tel (804)296-5511, FAX (804)977-5400. **5360**

TGA-PC (ARLINGTON, VA.). (US/1047-045X). The Grant Advisor, PO Box 520, Linden VA 22642. Tel (703)636-1529, FAX (703)636-7313. **1850**

THAI JOURNAL OF AGRICULTURAL SCIENCE. (TH/0049-3589). Agricultural Science Society of Thailand, 196 Phahonyothin Road, Bangkok 10900 Thailand. **141**

THOMAS REGISTER OF AMERICAN MANUFACTURERS AND THOMAS REGISTER CATALOG FILE. (US/0362-7721). Thomas Publishing Company, One Penn Plaza, 250 West 34th Street, New York NY 10119. Tel (210)290-7277. **3489**

THORPE ROM. (US). J. Whitaker & Sons Ltd, 12 Dyott Street, London WC1A 1DF England. Tel 011 44 71 8368911, FAX 011 44 71 836 2909. **3253**

TIJDSCHRIFT VOOR BESTUURSWETENCHAPPEN EN PUBLEKRECHT. (BE/0040-7437). Tijdschrift Voor Bestuursweten, G Mercatorlaan 28, B 1780 Wenmel Belgium. Tel 011 32 2 2694109, FAX 011 32 2 2701319. **3064**

TIME TABLE OF HISTORY. BUSINESS, POLITICS, AND MEDIA. (US/1054-5042). Xiphias, Helms Hall, 8758 Venice Boulevard, Los Angeles CA 90034. Tel (310)841-2790, FAX (310)841-2559. **2631**

TIME TABLE OF HISTORY. SCIENCE AND INNOVATION. (US/1041-2891). Xiphias, Helms Hall, 8758 Venice Boulevard, Los Angeles CA 90034. Tel (310)841-2790, FAX (310)841-2559. **715**

TIMES (LONDON, ENGLAND: 1788). (UK/0140-0460). News International Newspapers Ltd., PO Box 495 Virginia Street, London E1 9XU England. Tel 011 44 71 7823000. **5813**

TOM GENERAL INDEX. (US). Information Access Company, 362 Lakeside Drive, Foster City CA 94404. Tel (800)227-8431. **2497**

TORONTO STAR. (CN/0319-0781). Toronto Star Newspapers Ltd., 1 Yonge Street, Toronto Ontario M5E 1E6 Canada. Tel (416)367-2138. **5796**

TORONTO SUN. MICROFORM, THE. (CN/0837-3175). Toronto Sun, 333 King Street East, Toronto Ontario M5A 3X5 Canada. Tel (416)868-2257. **5796**

TOXICOLOGY ABSTRACTS. (US/0140-5365). Cambridge Scientific Abstracts, 7200 Wisconsin Avenue, #601, Bethesda MD 20814-4823. Tel (301)961-6750, (800)843-7751, FAX (301)961-6720. **3662**

TRANSLATION (NEW YORK). (US/0093-9307). Translation Center, 412 Dodge, Columbia University, New York NY 10027. Tel (212)854-4500, FAX (212)749-0397. **3447**

TROPAG & RURAL [COMPUTER FILE]. (US). Silverplatter Information Inc., 100 River Ridge Drive, Norwood MA 02062. Tel (800)343-0064, (617)769-2599, FAX (617)235-1715. **142**

U.S. DEFENSE BUDGET FORECAST. (US). Forecast International / DMS Inc., 22 Commerce Road, Newtown CT 06470. Tel (203)426-0800, FAX (203)426-1964, telex 467615. **4059**

U.S. EXPORTS OF MERCHANDISE. (US/1057-8773). US Department of Commerce / Bureau of the Census, Data User Services Division, Customer Services, Washington DC 20233-0800. Tel (301)763-4100. **855**

U.S. IMPORTS OF MERCHANDISE. (US/1057-8765). US Department of Commerce / Bureau of the Census, Data User Services Division, Customer Services, Washington DC 20233-0800. Tel (301)763-4100. **855**

UIT HET NIEUWS GLICHT : KNIPSELKRANT. (NE). Nederlandse Kankerbestrijding, Tavm Nijland Sophialaan 8, 1075 BR Amsterdam Netherlands. Tel 011 31 20 6644044. **3716**

ULRICH'S INTERNATIONAL PERIODICALS DIRECTORY. (US/0000-0175). R R Bowker, A Reed Reference Publishing Company, Part of Reed International PLC, PO Box 31, 121 Chanlon Drive, New Providence NJ 07974. Tel (908)464-6800, (800)521-8110, FAX (908)665-6688, telex 138-755. **3254**

ULRICH'S PLUS. (US/1068-0500). R R Bowker Electronic Publishing, A Reed Reference Publishing Company, Part of Reed International PLC, 121 Chanlon Drive, New Providence NJ 07974. Tel (800)323-3288. **3254**

ULRICH'S UPDATE. (US/0000-1074). R R Bowker, A Reed Reference Publishing Company, Part of Reed International PLC, PO Box 31, 121 Chanlon Drive, New Providence NJ 07974. Tel (908)464-6800, (800)521-8110, FAX (908)665-6688, telex 138-755. **3254**

UMI ABI/INFORM--BUSINESS PERIODICALS ONDISC. (US/1064-5381). University Microfilms International, 300 North Zeeb Road, Ann Arbor MI 48106-1346. Tel (313)761-4700, (800)521-0600 Exts. 2490, 2491, FAX (313)973-1540. **734**

UNIDOS : JOURNAL OF OPPORTUNITY. (US). Unidos, 378 Ballena Drive, Diamond Bar CA 91765. Tel (909)396-5935. **717**

UNIQUE (EAST HANOVER, N.J.). (US/0736-4083). TPCI, 13 Moresby Drive, Xanata Ontario K2M 2A2 Can. Tel (613)592-6625, FAX (613)592-8125. **1244**

UNIVERSITY PRESS BOOK NEWS. (US/1040-8991). Book News Inc, 5600 NE Hassalo Street, Portland OR 97213. Tel (503)281-9230. **427**

UNMANNED VEHICLE FORECAST. (US). Forecast International / DMS Inc., 22 Commerce Road, Newtown CT 06470. Tel (203)426-0800, FAX (203)426-1964, telex 467615. **4060**

US HISTORY ON CD-ROM. (US). Bureau of Electronic Publishing Inc., 141 New Road, Parsippany NJ 07054. Tel (201)808-2700, FAX (201)808-2676. **2764**

USA COUNTIES [COMPUTER FILE]. (US). US Department of Commerce / Bureau of the Census, Data User Services Division, Customer Services, Washington DC 20233-0800. Tel (301)763-4100. **2578**

USA STATE FACTBOOK. CD-ROM. (US). Quanta Press, Inc., 1313 Fifth Street Southeast, Suite 208C, Minneapolis MN 55414. Tel (612)379-3956, FAX (612)623-4570. **5345**

USA WARS: CIVIL WAR. CD-ROM. (US). Quanta Press, Inc., 1313 Fifth Street Southeast, Suite 208C, Minneapolis MN 55414. Tel (612)379-3956, FAX (612)623-4570. **4499**

USA WARS: KOREA. CD-ROM. (US). Quanta Press, Inc., 1313 Fifth Street Southeast, Suite 208C, Minneapolis MN 55414. Tel (612)379-3956, FAX (612)623-4570. **4060**

USA WARS: VIETNAM. CD-ROM. (US). Quanta Press, Inc., 1313 Fifth Street Southeast, Suite 208C, Minneapolis MN 55414. Tel (612)379-3956, FAX (612)623-4570. **4060**

VARIETY'S VIDEO DIRECTORY PLUS. (US/1066-8810). R R Bowker Electronic Publishing, A Reed Reference Publishing Company, Part of Reed International PLC, 121 Chanlon Drive, New Providence NJ 07974. Tel (800)323-3288. **4377**

VERMONT BUSINESS DIRECTORY. (US/1048-7174). American Business Directory, 5711 South 86th Circle, Omaha NE 68127. Tel (402)593-4600, FAX (402)331-5481. **718**

VETERINARY BULLETIN (LONDON). (UK/0042-4854). CAB International Centre, Wallingford, Oxon OX10 8DE United Kingdom. Tel 44 491 832111, FAX 44 491 833508, telex 847964 (COMAGG G). **5528**

VIDEO AND FILM CATALOGUE. (CN). National Film Board of Canada, PO Box 6100 Station A, Montreal Quebec H3C 3H5 Canada. Tel (514)283-9427, FAX (514)283-7564. **4079**

VIRGINIA DISC [COMPUTER FILE]. (US). Virginia Polytechnic Institute and State University, 617 North Main Street, Blacksburg VA 24060. Tel (313)764-4392. **1206**

VIRGINIA INDUSTRIAL DIRECTORY. (US/0882-3219). Harris Publishing Company, 2057-2 Aurora Road, Twinsburg OH 44087. Tel (800)888-5900, (216)425-9000, FAX (216)425-7150, telex 510 601 1740. **1631**

VIRGINIA MEDICAL QUARTERLY : VMQ. (US/1052-4231). Medical Society of Virginia, 4205 Dover Road, Richmond VA 23221. Tel (804)353-2721, FAX (804)355-6189. **3650**

VIROLOGY & AIDS ABSTRACTS. (US/0896-5919). Cambridge Scientific Abstracts, 7200 Wisconsin Avenue, #601, Bethesda MD 20814-4823. Tel (301)961-6750, (800)843-7751, FAX (301)961-6720. **3662**

VIROLOGY (NEW YORK, N.Y.). (US/0042-6822). Academic Press, Inc., 6277 Sea Harbor Drive, Orlando FL 32887. Tel (800)543-9534, (407)345-4100, FAX (407)363-9661. **570**

VISITANTE DOMINICAL, EL. (US/0194-9160). El Visitante, PO Box 1130, San Antonio TX 78294. Tel (512)736-1685. **5038**

VOCATIONAL SEARCH. (US/1071-2747). EBSCO Publishing / Boston, 83 Pine Street, Peabody MA 01960. Tel (800)653-2726 North America, (508)535-8500, FAX (508)535-8545. **1798**

WALL STREET JOURNAL ONDISC COMPUTER FILE, THE. (US). University Microfilms International, 300 North Zeeb Road, Ann Arbor MI 48106-1346. Tel (313)761-4700, (800)521-0600 Exts. 2490, 2491, FAX (313)973-1540. **718**

WARD'S BUSINESS DIRECTORY OF U.S. PRIVATE AND PUBLIC COMPANIES. (US/1048-8707). Gale Research Inc., 835 Penobscot Building, 645 Griswold Street, Detroit MI 48226. Tel (800)877-GALE, (313)961-2242, FAX (313)961-6083, (800)414-5043, telex TWX 810-221-7086. **718**

WARRIOR (SHEARWATER). 1978. (CN/0707-8056). The Shearwater Warrior, PO Box 190, Shearwater Nova Scotia B0J 3A0 Canada. Tel FAX 463-5111. **4060**

WARSHIPS FORECAST. (US). Forecast International / DMS Inc., 22 Commerce Road, Newtown CT 06470. Tel (203)426-0800, FAX (203)426-1964, telex 467615. **4061**

WATER RESOURCES ABSTRACTS (COLLEGE PARK, MD.). (US/1040-9009). National Information Services Corp, 3100 St Paul Street, Wyman Towers, Suite 6, Baltimore MD 21218. Tel (410)243-0797, FAX (410)243-0982. **5544**

WATER RESOURCES ABSTRACTS. VOLUME 1. (US/1053-5624). National Information Services Corp, 3100 St Paul Street, Wyman Towers, Suite 6, Baltimore MD 21218. Tel (410)243-0797, FAX (410)243-0982. **5544**

WATER RESOURCES ABSTRACTS [COMPUTER FILE]. (US). OCLC Asia Pacific Services, 6565 Frantz Road, Dublin OH 43017. Tel (614)848-5878, (614)764-6394 or 6000, FAX (614)764-6096. **5544**

WEBSTERS NINTH NEW COLLEGIATE DICTIONARY. CD-ROM. (US). Highlighted Data Inc., 6628 Medhill Place, Falls Church VA 22043. Tel (703)516-9211. **1930**

WEED ABSTRACTS. (UK/0043-1729). CAB International Centre, Wallingford, Oxon OX10 8DE United Kingdom. Tel 44 491 832111, FAX 44 491 833508, telex 847964 (COMAGG G). **157**

WER LIEFERT WAS? CD-ROM. (GW). Wer Liefert Was GmbH, Normannenweg 18 20, 20537 Hamburg Germany. Tel 011 49 40 2515080. **938**

WEST INDIAN MEDICAL JOURNAL, THE. (JM/0043-3144). West Indian Medical Journal, Faculty of Medical Sciences, University of West Indies, Mona Kingston 7 Jamaica. Tel (809)927-1214, FAX (809)927-2556. **3650**

WHEAT, BARLEY AND TRITICALE ABSTRACTS. (UK/0265-7880). CAB International Centre, Wallingford, Oxon OX10 8DE United Kingdom. Tel 44 491 832111, FAX 44 491 833508, telex 847964 (COMAGG G). **157**

WHITAKER'S BOOKBANK CD-ROM SERVICE. (UK/0951-8711). J. Whitaker & Sons Ltd, 12 Dyott Street, London WC1A 1DF England. Tel 011 44 71 8368911, FAX 011 44 71 836 2909. **3256**

WHITAKER'S BOOKS IN PRINT. (UK/0953-0398). J. Whitaker & Sons Ltd, 12 Dyott Street, London WC1A 1DF England. Tel 011 44 71 8368911, FAX 011 44 71 836 2909. **427**

WHO'S WHO ELECTRONICS BUYERS GUIDE (MIDWESTERN ED.). (US/1066-7601). Harris Publishing Company, 2057-2 Aurora Road, Twinsburg OH 44087. Tel (800)888-5900, (216)425-9000, FAX (216)425-7150, telex 510 601 1740. **2086**

WHO'S WHO ELECTRONICS BUYERS GUIDE (NORTHEASTERN ED.). (US/1066-761X). Harris Publishing Company, 2057-2 Aurora Road, Twinsburg OH 44087. Tel (800)888-5900, (216)425-9000, FAX (216)425-7150, telex 510 601 1740. **2086**

WHO'S WHO ELECTRONICS BUYERS GUIDE (SOUTHEASTERN ED.). (US/1066-7628). Harris Publishing Company, 2057-2 Aurora Road, Twinsburg OH 44087. Tel (800)888-5900, (216)425-9000, FAX (216)425-7150, telex 510 601 1740. **2086**

WHO'S WHO ELECTRONICS BUYERS GUIDE (SOUTHWESTERN ED.). (US/1066-7644). Harris Publishing Company, 2057-2 Aurora Road, Twinsburg OH 44087. Tel (800)888-5900, (216)425-9000, FAX (216)425-7150, telex 510 601 1740. **2086**

WHO'S WHO IN AMERICA. (US/0083-9396). Marquis Who's Who, A Reed Reference Publishing Company, Part of Reed International PLC, 121 Chanlon Road, New Providence NJ 07974. Tel (908)464-6800, (800)521-8110, FAX (908)665-6688, telex 138 755. **436**

WHO'S WHO IN AMERICAN EDUCATION (OWINGS MILLS, MD.). (US/1046-7203). Marquis Who's Who, A Reed Reference Publishing Company, Part of Reed International PLC, 121 Chanlon Road, New Providence NJ 07974. Tel (908)464-6800, (800)521-8110, FAX (908)665-6688, telex 138 755. **1791**

WHO'S WHO IN AMERICAN LAW. (US/0162-7880). Marquis Who's Who, A Reed Reference Publishing Company, Part of Reed International PLC, 121 Chanlon Road, New Providence NJ 07974. Tel (908)464-6800, (800)521-8110, FAX (908)665-6688, telex 138 755. **3075**

WHO'S WHO IN ENTERTAINMENT. (US/1044-0887). Marquis Who's Who, A Reed Reference Publishing Company, Part of Reed International PLC, 121 Chanlon Road, New Providence NJ 07974. Tel (908)464-6800, (800)521-8110, FAX (908)665-6688, telex 138 755. **335**

WHO'S WHO IN FINANCE AND INDUSTRY. (US/0083-9523). Marquis Who's Who, A Reed Reference Publishing Company, Part of Reed International PLC, 121 Chanlon Road, New Providence NJ 07974. Tel (908)464-6800, (800)521-8110, FAX (908)665-6688, telex 138 755. **720**

WHO'S WHO IN RELIGION. (US/0160-3728). Marquis Who's Who, A Reed Reference Publishing Company, Part of Reed International PLC, 121 Chanlon Road, New Providence NJ 07974. Tel (908)464-6800, (800)521-8110, FAX (908)665-6688, telex 138 755. **5009**

WHO'S WHO IN SCIENCE AND ENGINEERING. (US/1063-5599). Marquis Who's Who, A Reed Reference Publishing Company, Part of Reed International PLC, 121 Chanlon Road, New Providence NJ 07974. Tel (908)464-6800, (800)521-8110, FAX (908)665-6688, telex 138 755. **5169**

WHO'S WHO IN THE EAST. (US/0083-9760). Marquis Who's Who, A Reed Reference Publishing Company, Part of Reed International PLC, 121 Chanlon Road, New Providence NJ 07974. Tel (908)464-6800, (800)521-8110, FAX (908)665-6688, telex 138 755. **438**

WHO'S WHO IN THE MIDWEST. (US/0083-9787). Marquis Who's Who, A Reed Reference Publishing Company, Part of Reed International PLC, 121 Chanlon Road, New Providence NJ 07974. Tel (908)464-6800, (800)521-8110, FAX (908)665-6688, telex 138 755. **438**

WHO'S WHO IN THE SOUTH AND SOUTHWEST. (US/0083-9809). Marquis Who's Who, A Reed Reference Publishing Company, Part of Reed International PLC, 121 Chanlon Road, New Providence NJ 07974. Tel (908)464-6800, (800)521-8110, FAX (908)665-6688, telex 138 755. **438**

WHO'S WHO IN THE WEST (1971). (US/0896-7709). Marquis Who's Who, A Reed Reference Publishing Company, Part of Reed International PLC, 121 Chanlon Road, New Providence NJ 07974. Tel (908)464-6800, (800)521-8110, FAX (908)665-6688, telex 138 755. **438**

WHO'S

Serials available on CD-ROM

WHO'S WHO IN THE WORLD. (US/0083-9825). Marquis Who's Who, A Reed Reference Publishing Company, Part of Reed International PLC, 121 Chanlon Road, New Providence NJ 07974. Tel (908)464-6800, (800)521-8110, FAX (908)665-6688, telex 138 755. **438**

WHO'S WHO OF AMERICAN WOMEN. (US/0083-9841). Marquis Who's Who, A Reed Reference Publishing Company, Part of Reed International PLC, 121 Chanlon Road, New Providence NJ 07974. Tel (908)464-6800, (800)521-8110, FAX (908)665-6688, telex 138 755. **438**

WHO'S WHO OF EMERGING LEADERS IN AMERICA. (US/0895-965X). Marquis Who's Who, A Reed Reference Publishing Company, Part of Reed International PLC, 121 Chanlon Road, New Providence NJ 07974. Tel (908)464-6800, (800)521-8110, FAX (908)665-6688, telex 138 755. **439**

WILDLIFE & FISH WORLDWIDE. VOLUME 1. (US/1046-6479). National Information Services Corp, 3100 St Paul Street, Wyman Towers, Suite 6, Baltimore MD 21218. Tel (410)243-0797, FAX (410)243-0982. **2209**

WILDLIFE REVIEW & FISHERIES REVIEW. (US/1070-499X). National Information Services Corp, 3100 St Paul Street, Wyman Towers, Suite 6, Baltimore MD 21218. Tel (410)243-0797, FAX (410)243-0982. **2209**

WILDLIFE REVIEW (FORT COLLINS). (US/0043-5511). US Fish and Wildlife Service, 1201 Oak Ridge Drive, Suite 200, Fort Collins CO 80525-5589. Tel (303)223-9709. **2185**

WILDLIFE WORLDWIDE. (US/1070-5007). National Information Services Corp, 3100 St Paul Street, Wyman Towers, Suite 6, Baltimore MD 21218. Tel (410)243-0797, FAX (410)243-0982. **2210**

WILSON BUSINESS ABSTRACTS. (US/1057-6533). H W Wilson Company, 950 University Avenue, Bronx NY 10452. Tel (800)367-6770, (718)588-8400, FAX (718)590-1617, telex 4990003 HWILSON. **735**

WINE ON LINE. (US/1053-4776). Enterprises Publishing, 400 East 59th Street, Suite 9F, New York NY 10022. Tel (212)755-4363, FAX (212)755-4365. **2372**

WOMEN IN MANAGEMENT REVIEW. (UK/0964-9425). MCB University Press, 60 62 Toller Lane, Bradford West Yorkshire BD8 9BX England. Tel 011 44 274 499821, FAX 011 44 274 547143, telex 51317 MCBUNI G. **735**

WOMEN, WATER AND SANITATION. (US/1053-1432). National Information Services Corp, 3100 St Paul Street, Wyman Towers, Suite 6, Baltimore MD 21218. Tel (410)243-0797, FAX (410)243-0982. **2248**

WORLD AGRICULTURAL ECONOMICS AND RURAL SOCIOLOGY ABSTRACTS. (UK/0043-8219). CAB International Centre, Wallingford, Oxon OX10 8DE United Kingdom. Tel 44 491 832111, FAX 44 491 833508, telex 847964 (COMAGG G). **157**

WORLD AVIATION DIRECTORY. (US/0043-826X). McGraw Hill Publishing Company, Inc., 1221 Avenue of the Americas, New York NY 10020. Tel (212)512-6410, (800)525-5003, FAX (212)512-6111. **40**

WORLD BUSINESS DIRECTORY (DETROIT, MICH.). (US/1062-1172). Gale Research Inc., 835 Penobscot Building, 645 Griswold Street, Detroit MI 48226. Tel (800)877-GALE, (313)961-2242, FAX (313)961-6083, (800)414-5043, telex TWX 810-221-7086. **723**

WORLD DRUG MARKET ANNUAL. (UK). IMS World Publications Ltd, 7 Harwodd Avenue, london NW1 6JB England. Tel 011 44 71 393 5000, FAX 011 44 393 5900. **4333**

WORLD FACTBOOK (WASHINGTON, D.C.). (US/0277-1527). National Technical Information Service - NTIS, Room 2027S, 5285 Port Royal Road, Springfield VA 22161. Tel (703)487-4630, (703)487-4660, (703)487-4650, FAX (703)321-8547, telex 89-9405. **2579**

WORLD OF ANIMALS. (US). National Geographic Society, 11555 Darnestown, Gaithersburg MD 20878. Tel (202)857-7000, (800)638-4077, FAX (202)429-5727, telex 64194 NATGEO. **5600**

WORLD PUBLISHING MONITOR. (UK/0960-653X). Pira International, Randalls Road, Leatherhead, Surrey KT22 7RU England. Tel 011 44 372 376161, FAX 011 44 372 377526. **4822**

WORLD TELECOMMUNICATIONS MARKETFILE SERVICES. (UK). Telecom Information Services Ltd, Argyle Circus #3, Bognor Regis, West Sussex PO21 1DS England. Tel 011 44 243 842 082, FAX 011 44 243 842 083. **1169**

WORLD WEATHERDISC. CD-ROM. (US). WeatherDisc Associates, 4584 Northeast 89th, Seattle WA 98115. Tel (206)524-4314. **1437**

YEAR BOOK OF CARDIOLOGY, THE. (US/0145-4145). Mosby Year Book Inc., 11830 Westline Industrial Drive, St Louis MO 63146. Tel (800)325-4177, (314)872-8370, FAX (314)432-1380, telex 44-2402. **3711**

YEAR BOOK OF CRITICAL CARE MEDICINE, THE. (US/0734-3299). Mosby Year Book Inc., 11830 Westline Industrial Drive, St Louis MO 63146. Tel (800)325-4177, (314)872-8370, FAX (314)432-1380, telex 44-2402. **3652**

YEAR BOOK OF ONCOLOGY. (US/1040-1741). Mosby Year Book Inc., 11830 Westline Industrial Drive, St Louis MO 63146. Tel (800)325-4177, (314)872-8370, FAX (314)432-1380, telex 44-2402. **3825**

YEARBOOK OF INTERNATIONAL ORGANIZATIONS. (BE/0084-3814). K.G. Saur Verlag KG, A Reed Reference Publishing Company, Part of Reed International PLC, Ortlerstrasse 8, D 81373 Munich Germany. Tel 011 49 89 769020, FAX 011 49 89 76902150, telex 5212067-SAUR-D. **1930**

ZASSHI SHINBUN SOKATAROGU. PERIODICALS IN PRINT. (JA). Media Research Center Inc, Irimajir Building 6-40 Shin-Ogawa, Hinjuku-ku Tokyo 160 Japan. Tel 81-03-267-6551, FAX 81-03-267-550. **5805**

ZEITUNGS-INDEX. (GW/0340-0107). K.G. Saur Verlag KG, A Reed Reference Publishing Company, Part of Reed International PLC, Ortlerstrasse 8, D 81373 Munich Germany. Tel 011 49 89 769020, FAX 011 49 89 76902150, telex 5212067-SAUR-D. **5802**

ZENTRALBLATT FUER MATHEMATIK UND IHRE GRENZGEBIETE. (GW/0044-4235). Springer-Verlag GmbH & Company KG, Heidelberger Platz 3, D 14197 Berlin Germany. Tel 011 49 30 8207223, FAX 011 49 30 8214091, telex 183 319 SPBLN D. **3543**

ZOOLOGICAL RECORD ON CD. (US/1072-1983). BioSciences Information Service, Biological Abstracts / BIOSIS, 2100 Arch Street, Philadelphia PA 19103-1399. Tel (800)523-4806 US, (215)587-4800 Pennsylvania and worldwide, FAX (215)587-2016, telex 831739. **5604**

Serials available Online

The following index lists all serials in the Directory that are available online. The country code and ISSN are provided when available. As well as the publisher name, address, and telephone/fax numbers. The page number, which prints in bold, refers you to the complete serial listing in Volume I, II or III of the Directory.

3D LONDON. (UK/0953-2331). EMAP Business Publishing Ltd, 258 Field End Road, Ferrari House, Ruislip Middlesex HA4 9UY England. **Tel** 44 81 8684499. **1169**

68 MICRO JOURNAL. (US/0194-5025). 68 Micro Journal, 5900 Cassandea Smith Road, Hixson TN 37343. **Tel** (615)842-4601. **1265**

800 900 REVIEW. (US). Opus Research Incorporated, 345 Chenery Street, San Francisco CA 94131. **Tel** (800)428-6787, (415)239-0244, FAX (415)239-6932. **1148**

1001 HOME IDEAS. (US/0278-0844). Family Media Inc, 3 Park Avenue, New York NY 10016. **2898**

A-E BUSINESS REVIEW. (US). A-E Business Review, PO Box 4808, Cave Creek AZ 85331. **Tel** (602)258-2117, FAX (602)488-0311. **286**

AACN NURSING SCAN IN CRITICAL CARE. (US/1055-8349). NURSECOM Inc., 1211 Locust Street, Philadelphia PA 19107. **Tel** (215)545-7222, (800)242-6757, FAX (215)545-8107. **3849**

AB BOOKMAN'S WEEKLY. (US/0001-0340). AB Bookmans Publications Inc, PO Box AB, Clifton NJ 07015. **Tel** (201)772-0020, FAX (201)772-9281. **4822**

ABA BANKING JOURNAL. (US/0194-5947). Simmons Boardman Publishing Corporation / New York, 345 Hudson Street, New York NY 10014. **Tel** (402)346-4740. **768**

ABACUS (SYDNEY). (AT/0001-3072). Basil Blackwell Publishers Ltd, 108 Cowley Road, Oxford 0X4 1JF England. **Tel** 011 44 865 791100, FAX 011 44 865 791347, telex 837022 OXBOOK G. **735**

ABBEY NEWSLETTER, THE. (US/0276-8291). Abbey Publications, 7105 Geneva Drive, Austin TX 78723. **Tel** (512)929-3992, FAX (515)929-3995. **2478**

ABHANDLUNGEN DER SENCKENBERGISCHEN NATURFORSCHENDEN GESELLSCHAFT. (GW/0365-7000). Senckenberg Naturforschende, Gesellschaft, Senckenberganlage 25, W-6000 Frankfurt Germany. **Tel** 011 49 069 75421, FAX 069-746238. **4161**

ABI/INFORM GLOBAL EDITION [COMPUTER FILE]. (US). University Microfilms International, 300 North Zeeb Road, Ann Arbor MI 48106-1346. **Tel** (313)761-4700, (800)521-0600 Exts. 2490, 2491, FAX (313)973-1540. **725**

ABI/INFORM ONDISC. (US/1062-5127). University Microfilms International, 300 North Zeeb Road, Ann Arbor MI 48106-1346. **Tel** (313)761-4700, (800)521-0600 Exts. 2490, 2491, FAX (313)973-1540. **725**

ABI/INFORM ONDISC: EXPRESS EDITION [COMPUTER FILE]. (US). University Microfilms International, 300 North Zeeb Road, Ann Arbor MI 48106-1346. **Tel** (313)761-4700, (800)521-0600 Exts. 2490, 2491, FAX (313)973-1540. **725**

ABI-TECHNIK. (GW/0720-6763). Verlag Karlheinz Holz, Rheingaustr 85, Postfach 3329, D-65023 Wiesbaden Germany. **Tel** 011 49 611 9450751, FAX 011 49 611 261124. **3186**

ABITARE. (IT/0001-3218). Editrice Abitare Segesta Spa, Corso Monforte 15, 20122 Milan Italy. **Tel** 011 39 2 76090214, FAX 0039 2 791904, telex 315302 ABIT I. **287**

ABN CORRESPONDENCE. (GW/0001-0545). AntiBolshevik Bloc of Nations, Zeppelinstrabe 67, W 8000 Munich 80 Germany. **Tel** 011 49 89 482532, FAX 011 49 89 486519. **4514**

ABN ECONOMIC REVIEW. (NE/0169-5363). Algemene Bank Nederland NV, PO Box 669, Econ Res Dept 2D 40, 1000 EG Amsterdam Netherlands. **Tel** 011 31 20 299111. **768**

ABR-NAHRAIN. (NE/0065-0382). Editions Peeters SA, Bondgenotenlaan 153, BP 41, B-3000 Leuven Belgium. **Tel** 32 16 235170, FAX 32 16 228500, telex 65987 PUL B. **5013**

ABRASIVE ENGINEERING SOCIETY MAGAZINE. (US/0195-0932). Meadowlark Technical Services, 108 Elliot Drive, Butler PA 16001. **Tel** (412)282-6210. **2109**

ABRIDGED READERS' GUIDE TO PERIODICAL LITERATURE. (US/0001-334X). H W Wilson Company, 950 University Avenue, Bronx NY 10452. **Tel** (800)367-6770, (718)588-8400, FAX (718)590-1617, telex 4990003 HWILSON. **2496**

ABSTRACT BULLETIN OF THE INSTITUTE OF PAPER CHEMISTRY. (US). Institute of Paper Chemistry, 575 Fourteenth Street NW, Atlanta GA 30318-5403. **Tel** (404)853-9500, FAX (404)853-9510. **4240**

ABSTRACT BULLETIN OF THE INSTITUTE OF PAPER SCIENCE AND TECHNOLOGY. (US/1047-2088). Institute of Paper Science and Technology, 500 10th Street Northwest, Atlanta GA 30318. **Tel** (404)853-9500, FAX (404)853-9510. **4240**

ABSTRACTS IN BIOCOMMERCE. (UK/0263-6778). Biocommerce Data Ltd, 95 High Street, Slough Berks SL1 1DH United Kingdom. **Tel** 011 44 753-511777, FAX 011 44 753 512239. **3654**

ABSTRACTS OF WORKING PAPERS IN ECONOMICS : THE OFFICIAL JOURNAL OF THE AWPE DATABASE. (US/0951-0079). Cambridge University Press / New York, 40 West 20th Street, New York NY 10011-4211. **Tel** (212)924-3900, (800)221-4512. **1459**

ABU TECHNICAL REVIEW. (MY/0126-6209). Asia Pacific Broadcasting Union, PO Box 1164, 59700 Kuala Lumpur Malaysia. **Tel** 11 60 3 2823108, FAX 11 60 3 2822592, telex MA 32227. **1125**

ACADEMIC AND LIBRARY COMPUTING. (US/1055-4769). Mecklermedia Corporation, 11 Ferry Lane West, Westport CT 06880. **Tel** (203)226-6967, (800)632-5537, FAX (203)454-5840. **1265**

ACADEMY OF MANAGEMENT JOURNAL. (US/0001-4273). Academy of Management, Academy of Management Publications, PO Box 209, Ada OH 45810. **Tel** (419)772-1953, FAX (419)772-1954. **858**

ACADEMY OF MANAGEMENT REVIEW, THE. (US/0363-7425). Academy of Management, Academy of Management Publications, PO Box 209, Ada OH 45810. **Tel** (419)772-1953, FAX (419)772-1954. **859**

ACCA DOCKET. (US/0895-9544). American Corporate Counsel Association, 1225 Connecticut Avenue Northwest, Suite 302, Washington DC 20036. **Tel** (202)296-4523, (202)296-4522, FAX (202)331-7454. **3094**

ACCESS REPORTS. (US/0364-7625). Access Reports Inc, 1624 Dogwood Lane, Lynchburg VA 24503. **Tel** (804)384-5334, FAX (804)846-6928. **4461**

ACCESS (SYRACUSE). (US/0095-5698). John Gordon Burke Publisher Inc., PO Box 1492, Evanston IL 60204. **Tel** (708)866-8625, FAX (708)866-8625. **2496**

ACCOUNTANCY AGE. (UK/0001-4672). VNU Business Publications BV, 32-34 Broadwick Street, London W1A 2HG England. **Tel** 011 44 71 439 4242 ext. 2222, FAX 011 44 71 437 9638, telex 23918 VNU G, 8952440. **735**

ACCOUNTANCY IRELAND. (IE/0001-4699). Institute of Chartered Accountants in Ireland, Chartered Accountants House, 87-89 Pembroke Road, Dublin 4 Ireland. **Tel** 6680400, FAX 6680842, telex 30567. **735**

ACCOUNTANCY (LONDON). (UK/0001-4664). Institute of Chartered Accountants, 399 Silbury Boulevard, Central Milton, Keynes Bucks MK9 2HL England. **Tel** 011 41 71 920 8100, telex 727530. **735**

ACCOUNTANT (AMSTERDAM). (NE/0001-4729). Nederlands Inst Van Reg Accountant, PO Box 7984, 1008 AD Amsterdam Netherlands. **Tel** 011 31 20 6464046. **735**

ACCOUNTANT (LONDON). (UK/0001-4710). Lafferty Publications Ltd. / Dublin, Tower Ida Centre Pearse St., Dublin 2 Ireland. **Tel** 011 353 1 6718022, FAX 01-718520. **735**

ACCOUNTANTS' JOURNAL. (PH/0001-4753). Philippines Institute of Accountants, PO Box 1440, Manila Philippines. **735**

ACCOUNTANTS' JOURNAL (WELLINGTON). (NZ/0001-4745). New Zealand Society of Accountants, PO Box 11342, Wellington New Zealand. **Tel** 001 64 4 4738544, FAX 001 64 4 726282. **735**

ACCOUNTANTS' LIABILITY. (US/8756-6257). Practising Law Institute, 810 Seventh Avenue, New York NY 10019-5818. **Tel** (212)765-5700, FAX (212)581-4670 general correspondence, (212)265-4742 orders and billing inquiries. **736**

ACCOUNTANT'S MAGAZINE, THE. (UK/0001-4761). Institute of Chartered Accountants, 399 Silbury Boulevard, Central Milton, Keynes Bucks MK9 2HL England. **Tel** 011 41 71 920 8100, telex 727530. **736**

ACCOUNTING
Serials available Online

ACCOUNTING AND BUSINESS RESEARCH. (UK/0001-4788). Institute of Chartered Accountants, 399 Silbury Boulevard, Central Milton, Keynes Bucks MK9 2HL England. **Tel** 011 41 71 920 8100, telex 727530. **736**

ACCOUNTING AND TAX DATABASE [ONLINE DATABASE]. (US). University Microfilms International, 300 North Zeeb Road, Ann Arbor MI 48106-1346. **Tel** (313)761-4700, (800)521-0600 Exts. 2490, 2491, FAX (313)973-1540. **725**

ACCOUNTING AND TAX INDEX. (US/1063-0287). University Microfilms International, 300 North Zeeb Road, Ann Arbor MI 48106-1346. **Tel** (313)761-4700, (800)521-0600 Exts. 2490, 2491, FAX (313)973-1540. **725**

ACCOUNTING HISTORIANS JOURNAL, THE. (US/0148-4184). Academy Accounting Historian, University of Arkansas, Building 204, Fayetteville AR 72701. **Tel** (501)575-6125. **737**

ACCOUNTING HORIZONS. (US/0888-7993). American Accounting Association, 5717 Bessie Drive, Sarasota FL 34233-2399. **Tel** (813)921-7747, FAX (813)923-4093. **737**

ACCOUNTING JOURNAL (NEW YORK), THE. (US/0198-7283). Northeast Regional Group of the American Accounting Association, PO Box 1761, Grand Central Station, New York NY 10017. **737**

ACCOUNTING, ORGANIZATIONS AND SOCIETY. (UK/0361-3682). Pergamon Press, An Imprint of Elsevier Science Ltd., The Boulevard, Langford Lane, Kidlington, Oxford OX5 1GB United Kingdom. **Tel** 011 44 865 843000, 011 44 865 843699, FAX 011 44 865 843010. **737**

ACCOUNTING REVIEW, THE. (US/0001-4826). American Accounting Association, 5717 Bessie Drive, Sarasota FL 34233-2399. **Tel** (813)921-7747, FAX (813)923-4093. **737**

ACCOUNTING TODAY. (US/1044-5714). Faulkner & Gray Inc., 11 Penn Plaza, 17th Floor, New York NY 10001. **Tel** (212)967-7000, (800)535-8403. **738**

ACE INTERNATIONAL. ENGLISH EDITION. (US/0148-8856). ACE Publishing Ltd, 20 Atwood Street, Newburyport MA 01950. **Tel** (617)46500206. **5315**

ACHIEVEMENT (LONDON. 1969). (UK/0001-4907). World Trade Magazines Ltd, World Trade House, 49 Dartford Road, Sevenoaks Kent TN13 3TE England. **Tel** (0732)458144, FAX (0732)456295, telex 95130WASEVG. **1596**

ACM TRANSACTIONS ON GRAPHICS. (US/0730-0301). ACM Association for Computing Machinery, 1515 Broadway, 17th Floor, New York NY 10036. **Tel** (212)869-7440, FAX (212)869-0481. **1231**

ACQUISITION/DIVESTITURE WEEKLY REPORT. (US/0279-4160). Acquisition/Divestiture Weekly Report, 5290 Overpass Road, Santa Barbara CA 93111. **Tel** (805)964-7841. **636**

ACROSS THE BOARD. (US/0147-1554). Conference Board, 845 Third Avenue, New York NY 10022. **Tel** (212)759-0900 ext. 582, (800)872-6273, FAX (212)980-7014. **636**

ACTA BIOTECHNOLOGICA. (GW/0138-4988). Akademie-Verlag GmbH, Muehlenstrasse 33 34, D 13162 Berlin Germany. **Tel** 011 49 30 47889300, FAX 011 49 30 47889357. **3685**

ACTA CIENTIFICA VENEZOLANA. (VE/0001-5504). Acta Cientifica Venezolana, Apartado Postal 47286, Caracas 1041 Venezuela. **Tel** (02)752-1002, 751-1420. **5080**

ACTA OECONOMICA. (HU/0001-6373). Akademiai Kiado, Publishing House of the Hungarian Academy of Sciences, Prielle Kornelia u. 19-35, H-1117 Budapest Hungary. **Tel** 011 36 1 1811991, FAX 011 36 1 1811991, telex 22-6228 AKNYO H. **1460**

ACTA POLITICA. (NE/0001-6810). Uitgeverij Boom, Postbus 400, 7940 AK Meppel Netherlands. **Tel** 011 31 20 5220 57012, FAX 011 31 20 5220 54452, telex 42829. **4461**

ACTUALIDAD ECONOMICA. (SP/0001-7655). Recoletos Compania Editorial, Recoletos No. 1 2DA Planta, 28001 Madrid Spain. **Tel** 34 1 3370158, 34 1 3370518. **1544**

ADA IC NEWSLETTER. (US/1064-1505). Ada Information Clearinghouse, c/o IIT Research Institute, PO Box 46593, Washington DC 20050-6593. **Tel** (703)635-1477, (800)232-4211, FAX (703)685-7019. **1278**

ADDICTION & RECOVERY. (US/1052-4614). Medquest Communications Inc., 629 Euclid Avenue, Suite 500, Cleveland OH 44114. **Tel** (216)522-9700. **1338**

ADDICTION LETTER, THE. (US/8756-405X). Manisses Communications Group Inc., PO Box 3357, Providence RI 02906-0757. **Tel** (401)831-6020, (800)333-7771, FAX (401)861-6370. **1338**

ADHESIVES ABSTRACTS. (UK/0891-7760). RAPRA Technology Ltd., Shawbury Shrewsbury, Shropshire SY4 4NR England. **Tel** 011 44 939 250383, FAX 011 44 939 251118, telex 35134 RAPRA G. **1049**

ADHESIVES AGE. (US/0001-821X). Argus Business, 6151 Powers Ferry Road, Atlanta GA 30339. **Tel** (404)995-2500, (800)233-3359. **2007**

ADMINISTRATIVE SCIENCE QUARTERLY. (US/0001-8392). Administrative Science Quarterly, 425 Caldwell Hall, Cornell University, Ithaca NY 14853. **Tel** (607)255-5581, FAX (607)255-7524, telex WUI 6713054. **4624**

ADOPTION HELPER. (CN/1181-845X). Adoption Helper, 189 Springdale Boulevard, Toronto Ontario M4C 1Z6 Canada. **Tel** (416)463-9412, FAX (416)463-9412. **5270**

ADVANCED CERAMICS REPORT. (NE/0268-9847). Elsevier Advanced Technology, An Imprint of Elsevier Science Ltd., The Boulevard, Langford Lane, Kidlington, Oxford OX5 1GB United Kingdom. **Tel** 011 44 865 843000, 011 44 865 843699, FAX 011 44 865 843010. **2585**

ADVANCED COATINGS & SURFACE TECHNOLOGY. (US/0896-422X). Technical Insights Inc., PO Box 1304, Fort Lee NJ 07024-9967. **Tel** (201)568-4744, FAX (201)568-8247, telex 425900 SWIFT UI. **1020**

ADVANCED COMPOSITES BULLETIN. (UK). Elsevier Advanced Technology, An Imprint of Elsevier Science Ltd., The Boulevard, Langford Lane, Kidlington, Oxford OX5 1GB United Kingdom. **Tel** 011 44 865 843000, 011 44 865 843699, FAX 011 44 865 843010. **4453**

ADVANCED MANUFACTURING TECHNOLOGY. (US/0885-5684). Technical Insights Inc., PO Box 1304, Fort Lee NJ 07024-9967. **Tel** (201)568-4744, FAX (201)568-8247, telex 425900 SWIFT UI. **1217**

ADVANCED METALS TECHNOLOGY. (UK/0957-9729). Elsevier Science Publishers Ltd, Crown House, Linton Road, Barking Essex IG11 8JU England. **Tel** 011 44 81 5947272, FAX 081-594-5942, telex 896950. **3997**

ADVANCED MILITARY COMPUTING. (US/0884-9471). Pasha Publications Inc., 1616 North Fort Myer Drive, Suite 1000, Arlington VA 22209. **Tel** (800)424-2908, (703)528-1244, FAX (703)528-3742, (703)528-1253. **1210**

ADVANCED OFFICE TECHNOLOGIES REPORT. (US/1054-1462). Telecommunications Reports, 1333 H Street Northwest, 11th Floor, West Tower, Washington DC 20005. **Tel** (202)842-0520, (800)622-7237, FAX (202)842-3047. **1170**

ADVANCED RECOVERY WEEK. (US/1050-1347). Pasha Publications Inc., 1616 North Fort Myer Drive, Suite 1000, Arlington VA 22209. **Tel** (800)424-2908, (703)528-1244, FAX (703)528-3742, (703)528-1253. **4249**

ADVANCED WIRELESS COMMUNICATIONS. (US/1058-7713). Telecom Publishing Group, 1101 King Street, Suite 444, Alexandria VA 22314. **Tel** (703)683-4100, (800)327-7205, FAX (703)739-6490. **1103**

ADVERTISING AGE. (US/0001-8899). Crain Communications Inc., 1400 Woodbridge, Detroit MI 48207. **Tel** (313)446-6000, (800)992-9970. **754**

ADWEEK (EASTERN ED.). (US/0199-2864). ASM Communications, Adweek, 1515 Broadway, New York NY 10036. **Tel** (212)536-5350. **755**

ADWEEK (NEW ENGLAND ED.). (US/0888-0840). Billboard Publications Inc., 1515 Broadway Billboard, New York NY 10036. **Tel** (212)764-7300, FAX (305)755-7048, telex WU TWX 710-581-6279. **755**

ADWEEK SPECIAL REPORT. (US/0895-3848). ASM Communications, Adweek, 1515 Broadway, New York NY 10036. **Tel** (212)536-5350. **755**

ADWEEK. WESTERN ADVERTISING NEWS. (US/0199-4743). ASM Communications, Adweek, 1515 Broadway, New York NY 10036. **Tel** (212)536-5350. **755**

AEROSPACE AMERICA. (US/0740-722X). American Institute of Aeronautics & Astronautics, 370 l'Enfant Promenade Southwest, Washington DC 20024-2518. **Tel** (202)646-7400, FAX (202)646-7508, telex 204792 AIAA UR. **5**

AEROSPACE DAILY. (US/0193-4546). McGraw Hill Publishing Company, Inc., 1221 Avenue of the Americas, New York NY 10020. **Tel** (212)512-6410, (800)525-5003, FAX (212)512-6111. **5**

AEROSPACE ENGINEERING (WARRENDALE, PA.). (US/0736-2536). Society of Automotive Engineers, 400 Commonwealth Drive, Warrendale PA 15096. **Tel** (412)776-4841, (412)772-7106, FAX (412)776-5760. **5**

AEROSPACE FINANCIAL NEWS. (US/1057-0950). Phillips Business Information, Inc., 1201 Seven Locks Road, Potomac MD 20854. **Tel** (301)424-3338, (800)777-5006, FAX (301)309-3847. **5**

AEROSPACE INTELLIGENCE. (US/1041-7419). Jane's Information Group, Sentinel House, 163 Brighton Road, Coulsdon Surrey CR3 2NX England. **Tel** 011 44 81 763 1030, FAX 011 44 81 763 1006. **5**

AEROSPACE PROPULSION (WASHINGTON, D.C. 1990). (US/1050-5245). McGraw Hill Publishing Company, Inc., 1221 Avenue of the Americas, New York NY 10020. **Tel** (212)512-6410, (800)525-5003, FAX (212)512-6111. **5**

AESIS QUARTERLY. (AT/0313-704x). Australian Mineral Foundation, The Director, 63 Conyngham Street, Glenside South Australia 5065 Australia. **Tel** 011 61 8 3790444, FAX 011 61 8 794634, telex AA 87437 AMFINC. **1361**

AFFLUENT MARKETS ALERT. (US/1041-7508). EPM Communications Inc., 488 East 18th Street, Brooklyn NY 11226. **Tel** (718)469-9330, FAX (718)469-7124. **859**

AFRICA ANALYSIS. (UK/0950-902X). Africa Analysis Ltd, Suite 71 Ludgate House, 107 111 Fleet Street, London EC41 2AB England. **Tel** 011 44 71 353 1117, FAX 011 44 71 353 1516. **1460**

AFRICA NEWS (DURHAM). (US/0191-6521). Africa News Service Inc, PO Box 3851, Durham NC 27702. **Tel** (919)286-0747, telex 3772229. **4514**

AFRICAN BUSINESS. (UK/0141-3929). IC Publications Ltd., 7 Coldbath Square, London EC1R 4LQ England. **Tel** 011 44 71 713-7711, FAX 011 44 71 713-7898, telex 8811757. **637**

AFTENPOSTEN. (NO). Aftenposten, Postboks 1178 Sentrum, 0107 Oslo 1 Norway. **Tel** 011 47 2 863000. **5807**

AFTERMARKET BUSINESS. (US/0892-1121). Advanstar Communications Inc., 131 West First Street, Duluth MN 55802. **Tel** (218)723-9477, (800)346-0085. **637**

AGBIOTECH NEWS AND INFORMATION. (UK/0954-9897). CAB International Centre, Wallingford, Oxon OX10 8DE United Kingdom. **Tel** 44 491 832111, FAX 44 491 833508, telex 847964 (COMAGG G). **149**

AGEXPORTER (WASHINGTON, D.C.). (US/1047-4781). Superintendent of Documents, US Government Printing Office, Washington DC 20402. **Tel** (202)275-3328, FAX (202)786-2377. **45**

AGRA EUROPE (BRITISH EDITION). (UK/0002-1024). Agra Europe London Limited, 25 Frant Road, Tunbridge Wells, Kent TN2 5JT England. **Tel** 011 44 892 533813. **46**

AGRA EUROPE. MILK PRODUCTS. (UK/0950-3730). Agra Europe London Limited, 25 Frant Road, Tunbridge Wells, Kent TN2 5JT England. **Tel** 011 44 892 533813. **191**

AGRA EUROPE. POTATO MARKETS. (UK/0141-2221). Agra Europe London Limited, 25 Frant Road, Tunbridge Wells, Kent TN2 5JT England. **Tel** 011 44 892 533813. **46**

AGRA EUROPE. PRESERVED MILK. (UK/0141-223X). Agra Europe London Limited, 25 Frant Road, Tunbridge Wells, Kent TN2 5JT England. **Tel** 011 44 892 533813. **191**

AGRI MARKETING. (US/0002-1180). Century Communications Inc, 6201 Howard Street, Niles IL 60714-3435. **Tel** (708)647-1200, FAX (708)647-7055. **47**

AGRIBUSINESS WORLDWIDE. (US/0199-1671). Keller Publishing Corporation, 150 Great Neck Road, Great Neck NY 11021. **Tel** (516)829-9210, FAX (516)829-5414, telex 221574 KELLE. **48**

AGRICULTURAL & ENVIRONMENTAL BIOTECHNOLOGY ABSTRACTS. (US/1063-1151). Cambridge Scientific Abstracts, 7200 Wisconsin Avenue, #601, Bethesda MD 20814-4823. **Tel** (301)961-6750, (800)843-7751, FAX (301)961-6720. **150**

AGRICULTURAL ENGINEERING ABSTRACTS. (UK/0308-8863). CAB International Centre, Wallingford, Oxon OX10 8DE United Kingdom. **Tel** 44 491 832111, FAX 44 491 833508, telex 847964 (COMAGG G). **150**

AGRICULTURAL SUPPLY INDUSTRY. (UK/0140-4822). PJB Publications, 18-20 Hill Rise, Richmond Surrey TW10 6UA England. **Tel** 011 44 81 948 3262. **158**

AGROCHEMICALS HANDBOOK. (UK). Royal Society of Chemistry, Thomas Graham House, Science Park, Cambridge CB4 4WF England. **Tel** 011 44 223 420066, FAX 011 44 223 423429, telex 818293 ROYAL. **960**

AGROFORESTRY ABSTRACTS. (UK/0952-1453). CAB International Centre, Wallingford, Oxon OX10 8DE United Kingdom. **Tel** 44 491 832111, FAX 44 491 833508, telex 847964 (COMAGG G). **2398**

AGROW. (UK/0268-313X). PJB Publications, 18-20 Hill Rise, Richmond Surrey TW10 6UA England. **Tel** 011 44 81 948 3262. **57**

Serials Online Index

AHFS DRUG INFORMATION. (US/1063-8792). American Society of Hospital Pharmacists, 7272 Wisconsin Avenue, Bethesda MD 20814. **Tel** (301)657-3000, (301)657-4383, FAX (301)652-8278. **4290**

AI EXPERT. (US/0888-3785). Miller Freeman Inc., 600 Harrison Street, San Francisco CA 94107. **Tel** (415)905-2337, FAX (415)905-2240, telex 278273. **1210**

AIDS ALERT. (US/0887-0292). American Health Consultants, 3525 Piedmont Road, Suite 400, Atlanta GA 30305. **Tel** (800)688-2421, (404)262-7436. **3663**

AIDS THERAPIES. (US). CW Henderson, PO Box 5528, Atlanta GA 30307-0528. **Tel** (404)377-8895, FAX (404)378-5411. **3664**

AIDS WEEKLY. (US/1069-1456). CW Henderson, PO Box 5528, Atlanta GA 30307-0528. **Tel** (404)377-8895, FAX (404)378-5411. **3665**

AIR CARGO WORLD. (US/0745-5100). Argus Business, 6151 Powers Ferry Road, Atlanta GA 30339. **Tel** (404)995-2500, (800)233-3359. **5375**

AIR CONDITIONING, HEATING & REFRIGERATION NEWS. (US/0002-2276). Business News Publishing Company, 755 West Big Beaver Road, Suite 1000, Troy MI 48084. **Tel** (810)362-3700, FAX (810)362-0317, telex 230295. **2602**

AIR POWER HISTORY. (US/1044-016X). Air Power History, Virginia Military Institute, Lexington VA 24450. **Tel** (703)464-7468, FAX (703)464-5229. **8**

AIR SAFETY WEEK. (US/1044-727X). Phillips Business Information, Inc., 1201 Seven Locks Road, Potomac MD 20854. **Tel** (301)424-3338, (800)777-5006, FAX (301)309-3847. **8**

AIR TRANSPORT WORLD. (US/0002-2543). Penton Publishing, 1100 Superior Avenue, Cleveland OH 44114-2543. **Tel** (216)696-7000, FAX (216)696-0836. **8**

AIR UNIVERSITY LIBRARY INDEX TO MILITARY PERIODICALS. (US/0002-2586). Air University Library/LSP, Maxwell Air Force Base, Montgomery AL 36112-5564. **4061**

AIR/WATER POLLUTION REPORT. (US/0002-2608). Business Publishers Inc., 951 Pershing Drive, Silver Spring MD 20910-4464. **Tel** (301)587-6300, (800)274-0122, FAX (301)585-9075. **2159**

AIRCRAFT VALUE NEWSLETTER. (US/1065-8688). Phillips Business Information, Inc., 1201 Seven Locks Road, Potomac MD 20854. **Tel** (301)424-3338, (800)777-5006, FAX (301)309-3847. **9**

AIRLINE FINANCIAL NEWS. (US/1040-5410). Phillips Business Information, Inc., 1201 Seven Locks Road, Potomac MD 20854. **Tel** (301)424-3338, (800)777-5006, FAX (301)309-3847. **10**

AIRPORTS (WASHINGTON, D.C.). (US/1044-9469). McGraw Hill Publishing Company, Inc., 1221 Avenue of the Americas, New York NY 10020. **Tel** (212)512-6410, (800)525-5003, FAX (212)512-6111. **11**

AKRON BUSINESS AND ECONOMIC REVIEW. (US/0044-7048). University of Akron / Akron, 302 East Buchtel 107 Kolbe Hall, Akron OH 44325. **Tel** (216)375-7045. **637**

ALA WASHINGTON NEWSLETTER. (US/0001-1746). American Library Association Washington Newsletter, 110 Maryland Avenue NE, Washington DC 20002. **Tel** (202)547-4440, FAX (202)547-7363. **3188**

ALASKA BUSINESS MONTHLY. (US/8756-4092). Alaska Business Monthly, PO Box 24-1288, Anchorage AK 99524-1288. **Tel** (907)276-4373, FAX (907)279-2900. **637**

ALBERTA SASKATCHEWAN MANITOBA CRIMINAL DECISIONS. (CN/0715-3155). Western Legal Publications Ltd., 301 One Alexander Street, Vancouver BC V6A 1B2 Canada. **Tel** (800)663-0422, (604)687-5671, FAX (604)687-2796. **3104**

ALCOHOL HEALTH AND RESEARCH WORLD. (US/0090-838X). Superintendent of Documents, US Government Printing Office, Washington DC 20402. **Tel** (202)275-3328, FAX (202)786-2377. **1339**

ALISA. AUSTRALIAN LIBRARY AND INFORMATION SCIENCE ABSTRACTS. (AT/0810-9265). Library Publications / University of South Australia, Holbrook Road, Underdale SA 5032 Australia. **Tel** 011 61 8 3026258. **3257**

ALLEGHENY BUSINESS NEWS. (US). Associated Business Publishing, 471 Lincoln Avenue, Suite 300, Pittsburgh PA 15202. **Tel** (412)734-2300. **637**

ALLIANCE ALERT. CHEMICALS/MATERIALS/AGRICULTURE. (US/1053-0673). Securities Data Company, 40 West 57th Street, 11th Floor, New York NY 10019. **Tel** (212)765-5311. **1020**

ALLIANCE ALERT. COMMUNICATIONS. (US/1053-0657). Securities Data Company, 40 West 57th Street, 11th Floor, New York NY 10019. **Tel** (212)765-5311. **1104**

ALLIANCE ALERT. ELECTRONICS/COMPUTER HARDWARE/INDUSTRIAL AUTOMATION. (US/1050-0367). Securities Data Company, 40 West 57th Street, 11th Floor, New York NY 10019. **Tel** (212)765-5311. **1235**

ALLIANCE ALERT. MEDICAL/HEALTH. (US/1053-0649). Securities Data Company, 40 West 57th Street, 11th Floor, New York NY 10019. **Tel** (212)765-5311. **3775**

ALLIANCE ALERT. SOFTWARE/INFORMATION SERVICES. (US/1053-0665). Securities Data Company, 40 West 57th Street, 11th Floor, New York NY 10019. **Tel** (212)765-5311. **1235**

ALMANAC OF FAMOUS PEOPLE. (US/1040-127X). Gale Research Inc., 835 Penobscot Building, 645 Griswold Street, Detroit MI 48226. **Tel** (800)877-GALE, (313)961-2242, FAX (313)961-6083, (800)414-5043, telex TWX 810-221-7086. **429**

ALTERNATIVE ENERGY DIGESTS. (US/1050-3145). International Academy at Santa Barbara, 800 Garden Street, Suite D, Santa Barbara CA 93101. **Tel** (805)965-5010, FAX (805)965-6071. **1931**

ALUMINIUM TODAY. (UK/0955-8209). Argus Press Group, Queensway House, 2 Queensway Redhill, Surrey RH1 1QS England. **Tel** 011 44 737 768611, 011 44 737 761685, FAX 011 44 737 760510, telex 948669 TOPJNL G. **2100**

AMERICA, HISTORY AND LIFE (SANTA BARBARA, CALIF. : 1989). (US/0002-7065). ABC Clio Press, PO Box 1911, 130 Cremona, Santa Barbara CA 93117. **Tel** (805)968-1911, (800)422-2546, FAX (805)685-9685. **2634**

AMERICAN AGENT & BROKER. (US/0002-7200). American Agent & Broker, 408 Olive Street, St. Louis MO 63102. **Tel** (314)421-5445. **2873**

AMERICAN ARCHIVIST, THE. (US/0360-9081). Society of American Archivists, 600 South Federal, Suite 504, Chicago IL 60605. **Tel** (312)922-0140, FAX (312)347-1452. **2478**

AMERICAN ART / NATIONAL MUSEUM OF AMERICAN ART, SMITHSONIAN INSTITUTION. (US). National Museum of American Art, 8th G Street NW, Washington DC 20560. **Tel** (202)357-2725. **336**

AMERICAN BANKER. (US/0002-7561). American Banker, Concourse Level, 1 State Street Plaza, New York NY 10004. **Tel** (212)803-8200, (800)221-1809. **769**

AMERICAN CITY & COUNTY, THE. (US/0149-337X). Argus Business, 6151 Powers Ferry Road, Atlanta GA 30339. **Tel** (404)995-2500, (800)233-3359. **5238**

AMERICAN DEMOGRAPHICS. (US/0163-4089). American Demographics / New York, PO Box 68, Ithaca NY 14851. **Tel** (607)273-6343, (800)828-1133. **4549**

AMERICAN DOCTORAL DISSERTATIONS. (US/0065-809X). University Microfilms International, 300 North Zeeb Road, Ann Arbor MI 48106-1346. **Tel** (313)761-4700, (800)521-0600 Exts. 2490, 2491, FAX (313)973-1540. **1808**

AMERICAN FAMILY PHYSICIAN (1970). (US/0002-838X). American Academy of Family Physicians, 8880 Ward Parkway, Kansas City MO 64114. **Tel** (816)333-9700 ext. 1142, FAX (816)333-0303. **3736**

AMERICAN FAMILY PHYSICIAN. [CD-ROM]. (US). Creative Multimedia Corporation, 513 Northwest Avenue, Suite 400, Portland OR 97209. **Tel** (503)241-4351. **3736**

AMERICAN FOLK MUSIC AND FOLKLORE RECORDINGS. (US/0748-5905). American Folklife Center, Library of Congress, Washington DC 20540. **Tel** (202)707-6590, FAX (202)707-2076. **4099**

AMERICAN FORESTS. (US/0002-8541). American Forestry Association, PO Box 2000, Washington DC 20013. **Tel** (202)667-3300. **2374**

AMERICAN HERITAGE. (US/0002-8738). American Heritage, Forbes Building, 60 Fifth Avenue, New York NY 10011. **Tel** (212)206-5512, (212)620-1804. **2718**

AMERICAN JOURNAL OF DISEASES OF CHILDREN (1960). (US/0002-922X). American Medical Association, 515 North State Street, Chicago IL 60610. **Tel** (312)464-5000, (800)262-2350, FAX (312)464-5831. **3899**

AMERICAN JOURNAL OF HOSPITAL PHARMACY. (US/0002-9289). American Society of Hospital Pharmacists, 7272 Wisconsin Avenue, Bethesda MD 20814. **Tel** (301)657-3000, (301)657-4383, FAX (301)652-8278. **4290**

AMERICAN JOURNAL OF TRIAL ADVOCACY, THE. (US/0160-0281). Cumberland School of Law, 800 Lakeshore Drive, Room 305D, Birmingham AL 35229. **Tel** (205)870-2959. **2932**

AMERICAN LIBRARY DIRECTORY. (US/0065-910X). R R Bowker, A Reed Reference Publishing Company, Part of Reed International PLC, PO Box 31, 121 Chanlon Drive, New Providence NJ 07974. **Tel** (908)464-6800, (800)521-8110, FAX (908)665-6688, telex 138-755. **3257**

AMERICAN MACHINIST (1988). (US/1041-7958). Penton Publishing, 1100 Superior Avenue, Cleveland OH 44114-2543. **Tel** (216)696-7000, FAX (216)696-0836. **2109**

AMERICAN MARKETPLACE. (US/0276-2900). Business Publishers Inc., 951 Pershing Drive, Silver Spring MD 20910-4464. **Tel** (301)587-6300, (800)274-0122, FAX (301)585-9075. **1293**

AMERICAN MEN & WOMEN OF SCIENCE. (US/0000-1287). R R Bowker, A Reed Reference Publishing Company, Part of Reed International PLC, PO Box 31, 121 Chanlon Drive, New Providence NJ 07974. **Tel** (908)464-6800, (800)521-8110, FAX (908)665-6688, telex 138-755. **5173**

AMERICAN MEN AND WOMEN OF SCIENCE: BIOLOGY. (US/0146-0048). R R Bowker, A Reed Reference Publishing Company, Part of Reed International PLC, PO Box 31, 121 Chanlon Drive, New Providence NJ 07974. **Tel** (908)464-6800, (800)521-8110, FAX (908)665-6688, telex 138-755. **5173**

AMERICAN MEN AND WOMEN OF SCIENCE: CHEMISTRY. (US/0146-0056). R R Bowker, A Reed Reference Publishing Company, Part of Reed International PLC, PO Box 31, 121 Chanlon Drive, New Providence NJ 07974. **Tel** (908)464-6800, (800)521-8110, FAX (908)665-6688, telex 138-755. **5173**

AMERICAN MEN AND WOMEN OF SCIENCE: CONSULTANTS. (US/0146-0064). R R Bowker, A Reed Reference Publishing Company, Part of Reed International PLC, PO Box 31, 121 Chanlon Drive, New Providence NJ 07974. **Tel** (908)464-6800, (800)521-8110, FAX (908)665-6688, telex 138-755. **5173**

AMERICAN MEN AND WOMEN OF SCIENCE: ECONOMICS. (US/0094-5315). R R Bowker, A Reed Reference Publishing Company, Part of Reed International PLC, PO Box 31, 121 Chanlon Drive, New Providence NJ 07974. **Tel** (908)464-6800, (800)521-8110, FAX (908)665-6688, telex 138-755. **5173**

AMERICAN MEN AND WOMEN OF SCIENCE: MEDICAL AND HEALTH SCIENCES. (US/0145-9996). R R Bowker, A Reed Reference Publishing Company, Part of Reed International PLC, PO Box 31, 121 Chanlon Drive, New Providence NJ 07974. **Tel** (908)464-6800, (800)521-8110, FAX (908)665-6688, telex 138-755. **5173**

AMERICAN MEN AND WOMEN OF SCIENCE: PHYSICS, ASTRONOMY, MATHEMATICS, STATISTICS, AND COMPUTER SCIENCE. (US/0146-003X). R R Bowker, A Reed Reference Publishing Company, Part of Reed International PLC, PO Box 31, 121 Chanlon Drive, New Providence NJ 07974. **Tel** (908)464-6800, (800)521-8110, FAX (908)665-6688, telex 138-755. **5173**

AMERICAN REHABILITATION. (US/0362-4048). Superintendent of Documents, US Government Printing Office, Washington DC 20402. **Tel** (202)275-3328, FAX (202)786-2377. **5271**

AMERICAN REVIEW OF PUBLIC ADMINISTRATION. (US/0275-0740). L P Cookingham, Institute of Public Affairs, Henry W Block School of Business and Publ Admin, University of Missouri-Kansas City, Kansas City MO 64110. **Tel** (816)276-2342, (816)235-2894, FAX (816)235-2312. **4625**

AMERICAN SALESMAN, THE. (US/0003-0902). National Research Bureau Inc. / Iowa, 200 North Fourth, PO Box 1, Burlington IA 52601. **Tel** (319)752-5415, FAX (319)752-3421. **859**

AMUSEMENT BUSINESS. (US/0003-2344). Billboard Publications Inc., 1515 Broadway Billboard, New York NY 10036. **Tel** (212)764-7300, FAX (305)755-7048, telex WU TWX 710-581-6279. **4856**

ANALYST (LONDON). (UK/0003-2654). Royal Society of Chemistry, Thomas Graham House, Science Park, Cambridge CB4 4WF England. **Tel** 011 44 223 420066, FAX 011 44 223 423429, telex 818293 ROYAL. **1012**

ANGLICAN JOURNAL. (CN/0847-978X). Anglican Journal, 600 Jarvis Street, Toronto Ontario M4Y 2J6 Canada. **Tel** (416)924-9192, FAX (416)924-4452. **4934**

ANIMAL BEHAVIOR ABSTRACTS. (US/0301-8695). Cambridge Scientific Abstracts, 7200 Wisconsin Avenue, #601, Bethesda MD 20814-4823. **Tel** (301)961-6750, (800)843-7751, FAX (301)961-6720. **5604**

ANIMAL BREEDING ABSTRACTS. (UK/0003-3499). CAB International Centre, Wallingford, Oxon OX10 8DE United Kingdom. **Tel** 44 491 832111, FAX 44 491 833508, telex 847964 (COMAGG G). **151**

ANIMALS
Serials available Online

ANIMALS AGENDA. (US/0892-8819). Animal Rights Network, 456 Monroe Turnpike, PO Box 1242, Darien CT 06820. **Tel** (203)452-0446, (800)825-0061, FAX (203)452-9543. **225**

ANNISTON STAR, THE. (US). Anniston Star, PO Box 189, Anniston AL 36202-0189. **Tel** (205)236-1551, FAX (205)231-0027. **5625**

ANNUAIRE. (FR). Orsay, Institut de Physique Nucleaire, Orsay 91406 France. **Tel** 69417305, FAX 69416470, telex IPNORS 692 006 F. **4445**

ANNUAL REVIEW OF BANKING LAW. (US/0739-2451). Butterworth Heinemann / Woburn, MA, 225 Wildwood Avenue, Unit B, Woburn MA 01801. **Tel** (800)366-2665, FAX (617)928-2620, telex 880052. **3084**

ANNUAL SURVEY OF AMERICAN LAW. (US/0066-4413). New York University School of Law, 110 West Third Street, New York NY 10012. **Tel** (212)998-6540, (212)998-6560, FAX (212)995-4032. **2935**

ANNUAL SURVEY OF COLORADO LAW. (US/0160-5658). Continuing Legal Education in Colorado, 600 17th Street/Suite 520, South Denver CO 80202. **Tel** (303)753-3351. **2935**

ANTIOCH REVIEW, THE. (US/0003-5769). Antioch Review, PO Box 148, Yellow Springs OH 45387. **Tel** (513)767-6389. **3337**

ANTITRUST & TRADE REGULATION REPORT. (US/0003-6021). Bureau of National Affairs Inc., 9435 Key West Avenue, Rockville MD 20850. **Tel** (800)372-1033, (301)258-1033, FAX (301)948-5823. **3095**

ANTITRUST BULLETIN. (US/0003-603X). Federal Legal Publications Inc, 157 Chambers Street, New York NY 10007. **Tel** (212)619-4949, FAX (212)608-3141. **3095**

ANTITRUST FREEDOM OF INFORMATION LOG. (US/0891-8546). Washington Regulatory Reporting Association, PO Box 356, Basye VA 22810. **Tel** (703)856-2216. **3095**

ANTITRUST LAW JOURNAL. (US/0003-6056). American Bar Association, 750 North Lake Shore Drive, Chicago IL 60611. **Tel** (312)988-5522, (312)988-5241, FAX (312)988-5528, telex 270593. **3096**

ANTIVIRAL AGENTS BULLETIN. (US/0897-9871). Biotechnology Information Institute, 1700 Rockville Pike, Suite 400, Rockville MD 20852. **Tel** (301)424-0255, FAX (301)424-0257. **3551**

APCO BULLETIN, THE. (US/0001-2165). Association of Public Safety Communications Officers, 2040 S Ridgewood Ave, Suite 104, South Daytona FL 32119-2257. **Tel** (904)322-2500. **4767**

APF REPORTER. (US/0193-4562). Alicia Patterson Foundation, 1001 Pennsylvania Avenue, Suite 1250, Washington DC 20004. **Tel** (202)393-5995. **2917**

API. ARCHITECTURAL PERIODICALS INDEX. (UK/0266-4380). RIBA Publications Ltd, Finsbury Mission, Moreland Street, London EC1V 8B8 England. **Tel** 011 44 71 2510791. **311**

APIBIZ [ONLINE DATABASE]. (US). American Petroleum Institute, 275 Seventh Avenue, New York NY 10001. **Tel** (212)366-4040, FAX (212)366-4298. **4283**

APICULTURAL ABSTRACTS. (UK/0003-648X). International Bee Research Association, 18 North Road, Cardiff CF1 3DY United Kingdom. **Tel** 011 44 1 372409, FAX 011 44 1 665522, telex 23152. **5604**

APILIT [ONLINE DATABASE]. (US). American Petroleum Institute, 275 Seventh Avenue, New York NY 10001. **Tel** (212)366-4040, FAX (212)366-4298. **4283**

APPAREL INDUSTRY MAGAZINE. (US/0192-1878). Shore Communications Inc., 6255 Barfield Road, Suite 200, Atlanta GA 30328. **Tel** (404)252-8831, ((800)241-9034, FAX (404)252-4436. **1081**

APPLIED GENETICS NEWS. (US/0271-7107). Business Communications Inc., 25 Van Zant Street, Suite 13, Norwalk CT 06855. **Tel** (203)853-4266. **542**

APPLIED SCIENCE & TECHNOLOGY INDEX. (US/0003-6986). H W Wilson Company, 950 University Avenue, Bronx NY 10452. **Tel** (800)367-6770, (718)588-8400, FAX (718)590-1617, telex 4990003 HWILSON. **5173**

APPLIED SCIENCE & TECHNOLOGY INDEX (CD-ROM ED.). (US/1063-8695). H W Wilson Company, 950 University Avenue, Bronx NY 10452. **Tel** (800)367-6770, (718)588-8400, FAX (718)590-1617, telex 4990003 HWILSON. **5173**

AQUALINE ABSTRACTS. (UK/0263-5534). Water Research Centre, WRC PLC Frankland Road, Blagrove Swindon SN5 8YF England. **Tel** 011 44 793 511711, FAX 011 44 793 511712, telex 449541. **2002**

AQUATIC SCIENCES & FISHERIES ABSTRACTS (CD-ROM ED.). (US/1064-0460). Cambridge Scientific Abstracts, 7200 Wisconsin Avenue, #601, Bethesda MD 20814-4823. **Tel** (301)961-6750, (800)843-7751, FAX (301)961-6720. **2316**

AQUATIC SCIENCES AND FISHERIES ABSTRACTS. PART 1 : BIOLOGICAL SCIENCES AND LIVING RESOURCES. (US/0140-5373). Cambridge Scientific Abstracts, 7200 Wisconsin Avenue, #601, Bethesda MD 20814-4823. **Tel** (301)961-6750, (800)843-7751, FAX (301)961-6720. **2316**

AQUATIC SCIENCES AND FISHERIES ABSTRACTS. PART 2 : OCEAN TECHNOLOGY, POLICY AND NON-LIVING RESOURCES. (US/0140-5381). Cambridge Scientific Abstracts, 7200 Wisconsin Avenue, #601, Bethesda MD 20814-4823. **Tel** (301)961-6750, (800)843-7751, FAX (301)961-6720. **2316**

AQUATIC SCIENCES AND FISHERIES ABSTRACTS. PART 3 : AQUATIC POLLUTION AND ENVIRONMENTAL QUALITY. (US/1045-6031). Cambridge Scientific Abstracts, 7200 Wisconsin Avenue, #601, Bethesda MD 20814-4823. **Tel** (301)961-6750, (800)843-7751, FAX (301)961-6720. **2317**

ARANCEL DE ADUANAS (TARIC) UPDATES. (SP). Editorial Castro Sa, Lira 1, 1RA Derecha, 28007 Madrid Spain. **Tel** 011 34 1 4093190. **823**

ARCHIVES OF DERMATOLOGY. (US/0003-987X). American Medical Association, 515 North State Street, Chicago IL 60610. **Tel** (312)464-5000, (800)262-2350, FAX (312)464-5831. **3718**

ARCHIVES OF ENVIRONMENTAL HEALTH. (US/0003-9896). Heldref Publications, 1319 Eighteenth Street Northwest, Washington DC 20036-1802. **Tel** (202)296-6267, (800)365-9753, FAX (202)296-5149. **4767**

ARCHIVES OF GENERAL PSYCHIATRY. (US/0003-990X). American Medical Association, 515 North State Street, Chicago IL 60610. **Tel** (312)464-5000, (800)262-2350, FAX (312)464-5831. **3921**

ARCHIVES OF INTERNAL MEDICINE (1960). (US/0003-9926). American Medical Association, 515 North State Street, Chicago IL 60610. **Tel** (312)464-5000, (800)262-2350, FAX (312)464-5831. **3795**

ARCHIVES OF NEUROLOGY (CHICAGO). (US/0003-9942). American Medical Association, 515 North State Street, Chicago IL 60610. **Tel** (312)464-5000, (800)262-2350, FAX (312)464-5831. **3827**

ARCHIVES OF OPHTHALMOLOGY. (US/0003-9950). American Medical Association, 515 North State Street, Chicago IL 60610. **Tel** (312)464-5000, (800)262-2350, FAX (312)464-5831. **3872**

ARCHIVES OF OTOLARYNGOLOGY-HEAD & NECK SURGERY. (US/0886-4470). American Medical Association, 515 North State Street, Chicago IL 60610. **Tel** (312)464-5000, (800)262-2350, FAX (312)464-5831. **3886**

ARCHIVES OF PATHOLOGY & LABORATORY MEDICINE. (US/0003-9985). College of American Pathologists, Q Probes Department, 325 Waukegan Road, Northfield IL 60093. **Tel** (708)446-8800, FAX (708)446-8807. **3893**

ARCHIVES OF SURGERY (CHICAGO. 1960). (US/0004-0010). American Medical Association, 515 North State Street, Chicago IL 60610. **Tel** (312)464-5000, (800)262-2350, FAX (312)464-5831. **3959**

ARIZONA BUSINESS. (US/0093-0717). Arizona State University / Center for Business Research, College of Business-NBJ, Box 874406, Tempe AZ 85287-4406. **Tel** (602)965-3961, FAX (602)965-5458. **1463**

ARIZONA BUSINESS GAZETTE. (US/0273-6950). Phoenix Newspapers Inc., 120 East Van Buren Street, Phoenix AZ 85001. **Tel** (602)271-8503, (602)271-8000. **639**

ARIZONA DAILY STAR. (US/0888-546X). Tucson Citizen, 4850 South Park Avenue, PO Box 26887, Tucson AZ 85726. **Tel** (602)573-4511, (800)695-4492. **5629**

ARIZONA LAW REVIEW. (US/0004-153X). Arizona Law Review, University of Arizona, College of Law, Tucson AZ 85721. **Tel** (602)621-1764. **2937**

ARIZONA REPUBLIC. (US/0892-8711). Phoenix Newspapers Inc., 120 East Van Buren Street, Phoenix AZ 85001. **Tel** (602)271-8503, (602)271-8000. **5629**

ARKANSAS BUSINESS. (US/1053-6582). Arkansas Business, PO Box 3686, Little Rock AR 72203. **Tel** (501)372-1443, FAX (501)375-3623. **639**

ARKANSAS DAILY LEGISLATIVE DIGEST. (US). Arkansas Legislative Digest Inc, 1401 West 6th Street, Little Rock AR 72201-2901. **Tel** (501)376-2843, FAX (501)374-9256. **4630**

ARMADA INTERNATIONAL. (SZ/0252-9793). Armada International, PO Box 139, Ch 8035 Zurich Switzerland. **Tel** 011 41 1 3631126, 011 41 1 3631171, FAX 011 41 1 3619502, telex 815132. **4035**

ART CALENDAR (GREAT FALLS, VA.). (US/0893-3901). Art Calendar, PO Box 199, Upper Fairmount MD 21867. **Tel** (410)651-9150, FAX (410)651-5313. **338**

ART INDEX. (US/0004-3222). H W Wilson Company, 950 University Avenue, Bronx NY 10452. **Tel** (800)367-6770, (718)588-8400, FAX (718)590-1617, telex 4990003 HWILSON. **334**

ART INDEX. CD-ROM. (US/0004-3222). H W Wilson Company, 950 University Avenue, Bronx NY 10452. **Tel** (800)367-6770, (718)588-8400, FAX (718)590-1617, telex 4990003 HWILSON. **334**

ARTBIBLIOGRAPHIES MODERN. (UK/0300-466X). ABC Clio Press, PO Box 1911, 130 Cremona, Santa Barbara CA 93117. **Tel** (805)968-1911, (800)422-2546, FAX (805)685-9685. **334**

ARTS & HUMANITIES CITATION INDEX (PRINT ED.). (US/0162-8445). Institute for Scientific Information, 3501 Market Street, Philadelphia PA 19104. **Tel** (215)386-0100, (800)523-1850, FAX (215)386-6362, telex 84-5305. **2857**

ARTSPEAK (NEW YORK, N.Y.). (US/1065-1543). Art Liaison Inc., 245 8th Avenue, Suite 285, New York NY 10011. **Tel** (212)924-6531. **342**

ASAHI SHIMBUN JAPAN ACCESS. (JA/0917-0332). Asahi Shimbun International Inc., 757 Third Avenue, New York NY 10017. **Tel** (800)666-0170. **2501**

ASAIO JOURNAL (1992). (US/1058-2916). J.B. Lippincott Company, 227 East Washington Square, Philadelphia PA 19106-3780. **Tel** (215)238-4200 or 4454, FAX (215)238-4227. **3960**

ASBESTOS ABATEMENT REPORT. (US/0893-858X). Business Publishers Inc., 951 Pershing Drive, Silver Spring MD 20910-4464. **Tel** (301)587-6300, (800)274-0122, FAX (301)585-9075. **4767**

ASBESTOS CONTROL REPORT. (US/0893-4533). Business Publishers Inc., 951 Pershing Drive, Silver Spring MD 20910-4464. **Tel** (301)587-6300, (800)274-0122, FAX (301)585-9075. **2224**

ASCE ANNUAL COMBINED INDEX. (US/0742-1753). American Society of Civil Engineers / ASCE, 345 East 47th Street, New York NY 10017-2398. **Tel** (212)705-7179, FAX (212)705-7300, telex 422847 ASCE UI. **2002**

ASCE PUBLICATIONS INFORMATION. (US/0734-1962). American Society of Civil Engineers / ASCE, 345 East 47th Street, New York NY 10017-2398. **Tel** (212)705-7179, FAX (212)705-7300, telex 422847 ASCE UI. **2002**

ASFA AQUACULTURE ABSTRACTS. (US/0739-814X). Cambridge Scientific Abstracts, 7200 Wisconsin Avenue, #601, Bethesda MD 20814-4823. **Tel** (301)961-6750, (800)843-7751, FAX (301)961-6720. **2296**

ASFA MARINE BIOTECHNOLOGY ABSTRACTS. (US/1054-2027). Cambridge Scientific Abstracts, 7200 Wisconsin Avenue, #601, Bethesda MD 20814-4823. **Tel** (301)961-6750, (800)843-7751, FAX (301)961-6720. **553**

ASIA PACIFIC JOURNAL OF MANAGEMENT. (SI/0217-4561). University of Singapore / Faculty of Business Administration, 10 Kent Ridge, Singapore 0511 Singapore. **Tel** 011 65 7723101, FAX 011 65 7792621 3571, telex 33943. **860**

ASIAN WALL STREET JOURNAL. WEEKLY, THE. (US/0191-0132). Dow Jones and Company Inc, 200 Burnett Road, Chicopee MA 01021. **Tel** (413)592-7761, (800)568-7625. **1547**

ASIANWEEK. (US/0195-2056). Asian Week, 811 Sacramento Street, San Francisco CA 94108. **Tel** (415)397-0220, FAX (415)397-7258. **5633**

ASSEMBLIES OF GOD HERITAGE. (US/0896-4394). Assemblies of God Archives, 1445 Boonville Avenue, Springfield MO 65802-1894. **Tel** (417)862-2781, (417)862-1447, FAX (417)862-8558. **4936**

ASSET FINANCE & LEASING DIGEST. (UK). Euromoney Publications PLC, Nestor House, Playhouse Yard, London EC4Z 5EX England. **Tel** 011 44 71 779 8888, FAX 011 44 71 779 8617, telex 290700 EUROMON G. **773**

ASSIA. APPLIED SOCIAL SCIENCES INDEX & ABSTRACTS. (UK/0950-2238). Bowker Saur Ltd., A Reed Reference Publishing Company, Part of Reed International PLC, 59-60 Grosvenor Street, London WIX 9DA England. **Tel** 011 44 71 4935841, FAX 011 44 71 4991590. **5226**

ASSIA PLUS [COMPUTER FILE]. (UK). Bowker Saur Ltd., A Reed Reference Publishing Company, Part of Reed International PLC, 59-60 Grosvenor Street, London WIX 9DA England. **Tel** 011 44 71 4935841, FAX 011 44 71 4991590. **5226**

ATLANTA BUSINESS CHRONICLE. (US/0164-8071). Atlanta Business Chronicle, 1801 Peachtree Street, Suite 150, Atlanta GA 30309. **Tel** (404)249-1010, FAX (404)249-1048. **640**

Serials Online Index

ATLANTA CONSTITUTION (ATLANTA, GA. : 1897). (US). Atlanta Journal Constitution, PO Box 4689, Atlanta GA 30302. **Tel** (404)526-5151, (800)944-7363. **5652**

ATLANTA JOURNAL, THE ATLANTA CONSTITUTION INDEX (ANNUAL). (US/0731-9029). University Microfilms International, 300 North Zeeb Road, Ann Arbor MI 48106-1346. **Tel** (313)761-4700, (800)521-0600 Exts. 2490, 2491, FAX (313)973-1540. **2528**

ATLANTIC ECONOMIC JOURNAL. (US/0197-4254). Atlantic Economic Society, Southern Illinois University, Campus Box 1101, Edwardsville IL 62026-1101. **Tel** (618)692-2291, FAX (618)692-3400. **1464**

ATLANTIC TRADE REPORT & GLOBAL DEFENSE INDUSTRY. (US/1053-2404). Bergerac International, Route 1 Box 309, Gainesville VA 22065. **4037**

ATTORNEY-CPA, THE. (US/0571-8279). American Association of Attorney-Certified Public Accountants Inc., 24196 Alicia Parkway, Suite K, Mission Viejo CA 92691. **Tel** (714)768-0336, FAX (714)768-7062. **2938**

AUDIO WEEK. (US/1044-7601). Warren Publishing, Inc., 2115 Ward Court NW, Washington DC 20037. **Tel** (202)872-9200, FAX (202)293-3435. **5315**

AUDIOTEX NOW. (US). Opus Research Incorporated, 345 Chenery Street, San Francisco CA 94131. **Tel** (800)428-6787, (415)239-0244, FAX (415)239-6932. **1150**

AUDIOTEX UPDATE. (US/1045-5795). Worldwide Videotex, PO Box 3273, Boynton Beach FL 33424-3273. **Tel** (407)738-2276, FAX (407)738-2275. **1282**

AUDUBON. (US/0097-7136). National Audubon Society, 700 Broadway, New York NY 10003. **Tel** (212)979-3117. **2187**

AUSTIN BUSINESS JOURNAL. (US/0892-869X). Austin Business Journal, D Vedder, 1301 South Capital of Texas #200C, Austin TX 78746. **Tel** (512)328-0180, FAX (512)338-7304. **641**

AUSTRALIAN ACCOUNTANT, THE. (AT/0004-8631). Australian Society of Certified Practising Accountants, 170 Queen Street, Melbourne Victoria 3000 Australia. **Tel** 011 61 3 6069606, FAX 011 61 3 6708901, telex 32283-ASAML. **739**

AUSTRALIAN FINANCIAL REVIEW, THE. (AT). John Fairfax & Sons Ltd, GPO Box 506, Sydney NSW 2001 Australia. **Tel** 011 61 2 2822833, FAX 011 61 2 2822424, telex 23425. **773**

AUSTRALIAN TAX FORUM. (AT/0812-695X). The Australian Tax Research Foundation, 8th Level, 17 Castlereagh Street, Sydney NSW 2000, Australia. **Tel** 61 2 2324044, FAX 61 2 2216310. **4712**

AUSTRALIAN TAX REVIEW. (AT/0311-094X). The Law Book Company Limited, 44-50 Waterloo Road, North Ryde New South Wales, 2113 Australia. **Tel** 011 61 2 8870177, FAX 011 61 2 8887240, telex ASBOOK 27445. **2939**

AUSTRIA TODAY. (AU/0304-8713). Austria Today, PO Box 47, Schweizertor A 1014, Vienna Austria. **Tel** 11 43 222 5872184, FAX 11 43 222 566159. **2513**

AUTO AGE (VAN NUYS, CALIF.). (US/0894-1270). MacLean Hunter Publishing Corporation / Chicago, IL, 29 North Wacker Drive, Chicago IL 60606-3298. **Tel** (312)726-2802, FAX (312)726-3091. **5404**

AUTO MARKET REPORT. (AT/1035-1051). Autospec Pty. Ltd., PO Box 143, Caulfield East Victoria 3145 Australia. **Tel** 011 61 3 5721858, FAX 011 61 3 5717427. **5405**

AUTOMATED MANUFACTURING STRATEGY. (NE/0951-7162). Elsevier Science Publishers BV, PO Box 211, 1000 AE Amsterdam Netherlands. **Tel** 011 31 20 5803642, FAX 011 31 20 5862696, telex 15682. **1217**

AUTOMATIC MERCHANDISER. (US/1061-1797). Johnson Hill Press Inc., (A division of PTN Publishing Co.), 1233 Janesville Avenue, PO Box 803, Fort Atkinson WI 53538-0803. **Tel** (414)563-6388, FAX (414)563-1704. **2328**

AUTOMOTIVE ENGINEERING. (US/0098-2571). Society of Automotive Engineers, 400 Commonwealth Drive, Warrendale PA 15096. **Tel** (412)776-4841, (412)772-7106, FAX (412)776-5760. **2110**

AUTOMOTIVE NEWS. (US/0005-1551). Crain Communications Inc., 1400 Woodbridge, Detroit MI 48207. **Tel** (313)446-6000, (800)992-9970. **5406**

AUTOMOTIVE NEWS. MARKET DATA BOOK. (US). Crain Communications Inc., 1400 Woodbridge, Detroit MI 48207. **Tel** (313)446-6000, (800)992-9970. **5407**

AUTOMOTIVE PARTS INTERNATIONAL. (US/0896-3614). International Trade Services, PO Box 50120, Washington DC 20004. **Tel** (202)857-8454. **5407**

AUTOPARTS REPORT, THE. (US/1045-1978). Automotive Parts International, PO Box 5950, Bethesda MD 20824. **Tel** (202)857-8454. **5407**

AUTOWEEK. (US/0192-9674). Crain Communications Inc., 1400 Woodbridge, Detroit MI 48207. **Tel** (313)446-6000, (800)992-9970. **5407**

AVANCES EN INVESTIGACION AGROPECUARIA. (MX/0188-7890). AgroSystems Editing, Universidad de Colima, Justo Sierra 592, Colima 28010 Colima Mexico. **Tel** 331 4 11 33, FAX 331 2 75 81. **64**

AVIATION DAILY. (US/0193-4597). McGraw Hill Publishing Company, Inc., 1221 Avenue of the Americas, New York NY 10020. **Tel** (212)512-6410, (800)525-5003, FAX (212)512-6111. **13**

AVIATION WEEK & SPACE TECHNOLOGY. (US/0005-2175). McGraw Hill Publishing Company, Inc., 1221 Avenue of the Americas, New York NY 10020. **Tel** (212)512-6410, (800)525-5003, FAX (212)512-6111. **14**

AZIONE NONVIOLENTA. (IT). Azione Nonviolenta, Via Spagna 8, 37123 Verona Italy. **Tel** 011 39 45 8009803, FAX 011 39 45 8009212. **1072**

BACK STAGE. (US/0005-3635). Back Stage Publications Inc, 330 West 42nd Street, New York NY 10036. **Tel** (212)947-0020. **4064**

BACKPACKER. (US/0277-867X). Rodale Press Inc., 400 South 10th Street, Emmaus PA 18098. **Tel** (215)967-5171, (800)666-2503. **4869**

BAKERY NEWSLETTER. (US/1049-3174). Cahners Publishing Company, 249 West 17th Street, New York NY 10011. **Tel** (212)645-0067, FAX (212)242-6987. **2328**

BALTIMORE BUSINESS JOURNAL. (US/0747-1823). Baltimore Business Journal, 117 Water Street, 9th Floor, Baltimore MD 21202. **Tel** (410)576-1161. **641**

BANGKOK POST, THE. (TH). Post Publishing Company Ltd., 136 Na Ranong Road, Klong Toey 10110 Bangkok, Thailand. **Tel** 011 66 2 2403700. **5811**

BANK AUTOMATION NEWS. (US). Phillips Business Information, Inc., 1201 Seven Locks Road, Potomac MD 20854. **Tel** (301)424-3338, (800)777-5006, FAX (301)309-3847. **1218**

BANK LOAN REPORT. (US). Investment Dealers Digest Inc., Two World Trade Center, 18th Floor, New York NY 10048. **Tel** (212)227-1200, FAX (212)432-1039. **775**

BANK NETWORK NEWS. (US). Faulkner & Gray Inc., 11 Penn Plaza, 17th Floor, New York NY 10001. **Tel** (212)967-7000, (800)535-8403. **775**

BANK SYSTEMS + TECHNOLOGY. (US/1045-9472). Miller Freeman Inc., 600 Harrison Street, San Francisco CA 94107. **Tel** (415)905-2337, FAX (415)905-2240, telex 278273. **776**

BANK TECHNOLOGY NEWS. (US/1060-3506). Faulkner & Gray Inc., 11 Penn Plaza, 17th Floor, New York NY 10001. **Tel** (212)967-7000, (800)535-8403. **776**

BANKING LAW REVIEW. (US/0898-7998). Faulkner & Gray Inc., 11 Penn Plaza, 17th Floor, New York NY 10001. **Tel** (212)967-7000, (800)535-8403. **3085**

BAPTIST PRESS. (US). Southern Baptist Convention, 901 Commerce, Suite 750, Nashville TN 37203. **Tel** (615)244-2355, FAX (615)742-8919. **5056**

BATTERY AND EV TECHNOLOGY NEWS. (US). Business Communications Inc., 25 Van Zant Street, Suite 13, Norwalk CT 06855. **Tel** (203)853-4266. **5087**

BBI NEWSLETTER, THE. (US/1049-4316). American Health Consultants, 3525 Piedmont Road, Suite 400, Atlanta GA 30305. **Tel** (800)688-2421, (404)262-7436. **642**

BBS CALLERS DIGEST. (US/1055-2812). Callers Digest, PO Box 416, Mt Laurel NJ 08054. **1274**

BC BUSINESS. (CN/0829-481X). Canada Wide Magazines Ltd, 401 4180 Lougheed Highway, Burnaby BC V5C 6A7 Canada. **Tel** (604)299-7311, FAX (604)299-9188. **642**

BC OUTDOORS. (CN/0045-3013). Special Interest Publications / Canada, 1132 Hamilton Street/Suite 202, Vancouver BC V6B 2S2 Canada. **Tel** (604)687-1581, FAX (604)687-1925. **4869**

BEAUTIFUL BRITISH COLUMBIA. (CN/0005-7460). Beautiful British Columbia, 929 Ellery Street, Victoria British Columbia, V9A 7B4 Canada. **Tel** (604)384-5456, (800)663-7611, FAX (604)384-2812. **5462**

BEAUTY COUNTER LONDON. (UK/0960-3751). Benn Publications Ltd., Sovereign Way, Tonbridge TNQ 1RW England. **Tel** 011 44 732 364422, FAX 011 44 732 361534, telex 0732 95132 BENTON G. **402**

BEHAVIORAL SCIENCES & THE LAW. (UK/0735-3936). John Wiley & Sons Ltd., Baffins Lane, Chichester West Sussex PO19 1UD England. **Tel** 0243 779777, FAX 0243 776128 BTG:JWP001, telex 86290 WIBOOKG. **2940**

BELFAST TELEGRAPH [MICROFORM]. (UK/0307-5664). Belfast Telegraph Newspapers Ltd., 124 Royal Ave, Belfast BT1 1EB Northern Ireland. **Tel** 011 44 321242, telex BELFAST 74269. **5811**

BENEFITS QUARTERLY. (US/8756-1263). International Society of Certified Employee Benefit Specialists, PO Box 209, Brookfield WI 53005. **Tel** (414)786-8771, FAX (414)786-6647. **1655**

BEREAVEMENT & LOSS RESOURCES. (US/1071-7366). Rivendell Resources, PO Box 3272, Ann Arbor MI 48106-3272. **Tel** (313)761-1960. **4577**

BEST'S REVIEW. (LIFE-HEALTH INSURANCE EDITION). (US/0005-9706). AM Best Company, Ambest Road, Oldwick NJ 08858. **Tel** (908)439-2200 ext. 5653, telex 837744. **2876**

BEST'S REVIEW (PROPERTY/CASUALTY INSURANCE ED.). (US/0161-7745). AM Best Company, Ambest Road, Oldwick NJ 08858. **Tel** (908)439-2200 ext. 5653, telex 837744. **2876**

BETTER HOMES AND GARDENS. (US/0006-0151). Meredith Corporation, Locust at 17th, Des Moines IA 50309. **Tel** (515)284-3000. **2788**

BETTER NUTRITION FOR TODAY'S LIVING. (US). Argus Business, 6151 Powers Ferry Road, Atlanta GA 30339. **Tel** (404)995-2500, (800)233-3359. **4188**

BEVERAGE INDUSTRY. (US/0148-6187). Stagnito Publishing Company, 1935 Sherner Road, Suite 100, Northbrook IL 60062. **Tel** (708)205-5660, FAX (708)205-5680. **2364**

BEVERAGE WORLD. (US/0098-2318). Keller Publishing Corporation, 150 Great Neck Road, Great Neck NY 11021. **Tel** (516)829-9210, FAX (516)829-5414, telex 221574 KELLE. **2364**

BIBLIO-JEUNES; NIVEAUX PRESCOLAIRE ET ELEMENTAIRE: SUPPLEMENT. (CN/0701-5542). Services Documentaires Multimedia Inc, 75 rue de Port-Royal, Suite 300, Montreal Quebec H3L 3T1 Canada. **Tel** (514)382-0895, FAX (514)384-9139. **408**

BIBLIOGRAPHIC INDEX. (US/0006-1255). H W Wilson Company, 950 University Avenue, Bronx NY 10452. **Tel** (800)367-6770, (718)588-8400, FAX (718)590-1617, telex 4990003 HWILSON. **3457**

BIBLIOGRAPHY AND INDEX OF GEOLOGY. (US/0098-2784). American Geological Institute, 4220 King Street, Alexandria VA 22302. **Tel** (703)379-2480, FAX (703)379-7563. **1361**

BIBLIOGRAPHY OF ECONOMIC GEOLOGY. (UK/0016-7053). Geosystems Inc., PO Box 40, Didcot, Oxon OX11 9BX England. **Tel** 011 44 235 813913. **1361**

BICYCLING. (US/0006-2073). Rodale Press Inc., 400 South 10th Street, Emmaus PA 18098. **Tel** (215)967-5171, (800)666-2503. **428**

BILLINGS GAZETTE (BILLINGS, MONT. : DAILY : 1914). (US). The Billings Gazette, PO Box 36300, Billings MT 59107. **Tel** (406)657-1200, (800)669-6397, FAX (406)657-1345. **5705**

BIO-BASE. (US/0742-2318). Gale Research Inc., 835 Penobscot Building, 645 Griswold Street, Detroit MI 48226. **Tel** (800)877-GALE, (313)961-2242, FAX (313)961-6083, (800)414-5043, telex TWX 810-221-7086. **430**

BIO/TECHNOLOGY (NEW YORK, N.Y. 1983). (US/0733-222X). Nature Publishing Company, 65 Bleecker Street, 12th Floor, New York NY 10012. **Tel** (212)477-9600, (800)524-0328, FAX (212)477-8020. **5088**

BIOCONTROL NEWS AND INFORMATION. (UK/0143-1404). CAB International Centre, Wallingford, Oxon OX10 8DE United Kingdom. **Tel** 44 491 832111, FAX 44 491 833508, telex 847964 (COMAGG G). **151**

BIOCYCLE. (US/0276-5055). The JG Press Inc, 419 State Avenue, Emmaus PA 18049. **Tel** (215)967-4135. **2225**

BIODETERIORATION ABSTRACTS. (UK/0951-0621). CAB International Centre, Wallingford, Oxon OX10 8DE United Kingdom. **Tel** 44 491 832111, FAX 44 491 833508, telex 847964 (COMAGG G). **2183**

BIOGRAPHY AND GENEALOGY MASTER INDEX. (US/0730-1316). Gale Research Inc., 835 Penobscot Building, 645 Griswold Street, Detroit MI 48226. **Tel** (800)877-GALE, (313)961-2242, FAX (313)961-6083, (800)414-5043, telex TWX 810-221-7086. **430**

BIOGRAPHY INDEX. (US/0006-3053). H W Wilson Company, 950 University Avenue, Bronx NY 10452. **Tel** (800)367-6770, (718)588-8400, FAX (718)590-1617, telex 4990003 HWILSON. **439**

BIOGRAPHY
Serials available Online

BIOGRAPHY INDEX (CD-ROM ED.). (US/1063-3286). H W Wilson Company, 950 University Avenue, Bronx NY 10452. **Tel** (800)367-6770, (718)588-8400, FAX (718)590-1617, telex 4990003 HWILSON. **439**

BIOLOGICAL ABSTRACTS. (US/0006-3169). BioSciences Information Service, Biological Abstracts / BIOSIS, 2100 Arch Street, Philadelphia PA 19103-1399. **Tel** (800)523-4806 US, (215)587-4800 Pennsylvania and worldwide, FAX (215)587-2016, telex 831739. **477**

BIOLOGICAL ABSTRACTS ON COMPACT DISC. (US/1058-4129). BioSciences Information Service, Biological Abstracts / BIOSIS, 2100 Arch Street, Philadelphia PA 19103-1399. **Tel** (800)523-4806 US, (215)587-4800 Pennsylvania and worldwide, FAX (215)587-2016, telex 831739. **477**

BIOLOGICAL ABSTRACTS / RRM. (US/0192-6985). BioSciences Information Service, Biological Abstracts / BIOSIS, 2100 Arch Street, Philadelphia PA 19103-1399. **Tel** (800)523-4806 US, (215)587-4800 Pennsylvania and worldwide, FAX (215)587-2016, telex 831739. **477**

BIOLOGICAL ABSTRACTS / RRM ON COMPACT DISC. (US/1058-4137). BioSciences Information Service, Biological Abstracts / BIOSIS, 2100 Arch Street, Philadelphia PA 19103-1399. **Tel** (800)523-4806 US, (215)587-4800 Pennsylvania and worldwide, FAX (215)587-2016, telex 831739. **444**

BIOLOGICAL & AGRICULTURAL INDEX. (US/0006-3177). H W Wilson Company, 950 University Avenue, Bronx NY 10452. **Tel** (800)367-6770, (718)588-8400, FAX (718)590-1617, telex 4990003 HWILSON. **477**

BIOMEDICAL MARKET NEWSLETTER. (US). Biomedical Market Newsletter, 3237 Idaho Place, Costa Mesa CA 92626. **Tel** (714)434-9500, (800)875-8181. **3687**

BIOMEDICAL MATERIALS. (UK/0955-7717). Elsevier Advanced Technology, An Imprint of Elsevier Science Ltd., The Boulevard, Langford Lane, Kidlington, Oxford OX5 1GB United Kingdom. **Tel** 011 44 865 843000, 011 44 865 843699, FAX 011 44 865 843010. **3556**

BIOSCAN. (US/0887-6207). Oryx Press, 4041 North Central Avenue, #700, Phoenix AZ 85012-3397. **Tel** (800)279-ORYX, (602)265-2651, FAX (602)265-6250, (800)279-4663, (800)279-6799. **3687**

BIOSCIENCE. (US/0006-3568). American Institute of Biological Sciences, 730 11th Street Northwest, Washington DC 20001-4521. **Tel** (202)628-1500, (202)628-1509, FAX (202)628-1500, telex 209061 AIBS UR. **448**

BIOTECH BUSINESS. (US/0899-5702). Worldwide Videotex, PO Box 3273, Boynton Beach FL 33424-3273. **Tel** (407)738-2276, FAX (407)738-2275. **3687**

BIOTECH PATENT NEWS. (US/0898-2813). Biotech Patent News, PO Box 4482, Metuchen NJ 08840. **Tel** (908)549-1356, FAX (908)549-1356. **3688**

BIOTECHNOLOGY BUSINESS NEWS / FINANCIAL TIMES. (UK). Financial Times Business Information Ltd., Tower House, Southampton Street, London WC2E 7HA England. **Tel** 011 44 71 353 1040. **3688**

BIOTECHNOLOGY INVESTMENT OPPORTUNITIES. (US/0277-9773). High Tech Publishing Company, 10 Ridge Road, PO Box 1923, Brattleboro VT 05301. **Tel** (802)254-3539. **3689**

BIOTECHNOLOGY NEWSWATCH. (US). McGraw Hill Publishing Company, Inc., 1221 Avenue of the Americas, New York NY 10020. **Tel** (212)512-6410, (800)525-5003, FAX (212)512-6111. **3689**

BIOTECHNOLOGY RESEARCH ABSTRACTS. (US/0733-5709). Cambridge Scientific Abstracts, 7200 Wisconsin Avenue, #601, Bethesda MD 20814-4823. **Tel** (301)961-6750, (800)843-7751, FAX (301)961-6720. **3655**

BIRMINGHAM BUSINESS JOURNAL. (US/0889-2237). Birmingham Business Journal, 2101 Magnolia S/Suite 400, Birmingham AL 35205. **Tel** (205)322-0000, FAX (205)322-0040. **643**

BLACK ENTERPRISE. (US/0006-4165). Earl G. Graves Publishing Company, 130 Fifth Avenue, New York NY 10011. **Tel** (212)242-8000, FAX (212)989-8410. **643**

BMT ABSTRACTS : BRITISH MARITIME TECHNOLOGY ABSTRACTS. (UK/0268-9650). BMT Northumbria House Davy Bank, Wallsend, Wallsend Tyne and Wear NE28 6UY England. **Tel** 011 44 91 262 5242, FAX 011 44 91 263 8754, telex 53476. **4185**

BNA CALIFORNIA ENVIRONMENT REPORTER. (US/1052-813X). Bureau of National Affairs Inc., 9435 Key West Avenue, Rockville MD 20850. **Tel** (800)372-1033, (301)258-1033, FAX (301)948-5823. **3110**

BNA PENSION & BENEFITS REPORTER. (US/1069-5117). Bureau of National Affairs Inc., 9435 Key West Avenue, Rockville MD 20850. **Tel** (800)372-1033, (301)258-1033, FAX (301)948-5823. **1655**

BOATING INDUSTRY, THE. (US/0006-5404). Argus Business, 6151 Powers Ferry Road, Atlanta GA 30339. **Tel** (404)995-2500, (800)233-3359. **592**

BOATING WORLD. (US/1059-5155). Billian Publishing Inc., 2100 Powers Ferry Road, Atlanta GA 30339. **Tel** (404)955-5656, FAX (404)952-0669. **592**

BOC WEEK. (US). Capitol Publications, 1101 King Street, Suite 444, Alexandria VA 22314. **Tel** (703)683-4100, (800)655-5597. **1150**

BOCOEX INDEX, THE. (US/1047-496X). The Boston Computer Exchange, Box 1177, Boston MA 02103. **1172**

BOND BUYER (NEW YORK, N.Y. 1982), THE. (US/0732-0469). American Banker, Concourse Level, 1 State Street Plaza, New York NY 10004. **Tel** (212)803-8200, (800)221-1809. **892**

BOOK REPORT. (UK). Euromonitor Publications Ltd., 87-88 Turnmill Street, London EC1M 5QU England. **Tel** 011 44 71 2518024, FAX 011 44 71 6083149, telex 21120. **921**

BOOK REVIEW DIGEST. (US/0006-7326). H W Wilson Company, 950 University Avenue, Bronx NY 10452. **Tel** (800)367-6770, (718)588-8400, FAX (718)590-1617, telex 4990003 HWILSON. **3356**

BOOK REVIEW DIGEST. CD-ROM. (US/0006-7326). H W Wilson Company, 950 University Avenue, Bronx NY 10452. **Tel** (800)367-6770, (718)588-8400, FAX (718)590-1617, telex 4990003 HWILSON. **4821**

BOOK REVIEW INDEX. (US/0524-0581). Gale Research Inc., 835 Penobscot Building, 645 Griswold Street, Detroit MI 48226. **Tel** (800)877-GALE, (313)961-2242, FAX (313)961-6083, (800)414-5043, telex TWX 810-221-7086. **4821**

BOOKS IN PRINT (NEW YORK). (US/0068-0214). R R Bowker, A Reed Reference Publishing Company, Part of Reed International PLC, PO Box 31, 121 Chanlon Drive, New Providence NJ 07974. **Tel** (908)464-6800, (800)521-8110, FAX (908)665-6688, telex 138-755. **411**

BOOKS IN PRINT PLUS. (US/1062-5100). R R Bowker, A Reed Reference Publishing Company, Part of Reed International PLC, PO Box 31, 121 Chanlon Drive, New Providence NJ 07974. **Tel** (908)464-6800, (800)521-8110, FAX (908)665-6688, telex 138-755. **411**

BOOKS IN PRINT SUPPLEMENT. (US/0000-0310). R R Bowker, A Reed Reference Publishing Company, Part of Reed International PLC, PO Box 31, 121 Chanlon Drive, New Providence NJ 07974. **Tel** (908)464-6800, (800)521-8110, FAX (908)665-6688, telex 138-755. **411**

BOOKS IN SERIES. (US/0000-0906). R R Bowker, A Reed Reference Publishing Company, Part of Reed International PLC, PO Box 31, 121 Chanlon Drive, New Providence NJ 07974. **Tel** (908)464-6800, (800)521-8110, FAX (908)665-6688, telex 138-755. **4826**

BOSTON BAR JOURNAL. (US/0524-1111). Boston Bar Association, 16 Beacon Street, Boston MA 02108. **Tel** (617)742-0615, FAX (617)523-0127. **2943**

BOSTON BUSINESS JOURNAL, THE. (US/0746-4975). MCP Inc., 5500 Wayzata Boulevard/Suite 800, Minneapolis MN 55416. **Tel** (612)591-2700, FAX (612)591-2639. **644**

BOSTON COLLEGE THIRD WORLD LAW JOURNAL. (US/0276-3583). Boston College Law School, 885 Centre Street, Newton Centre MA 02159. **Tel** (617)552-8550, FAX (617)552-2615. **3125**

BOSTON GLOBE, THE. (US/0743-1791). Globe Newspaper Company, PO Box 2378, Boston MA 02107. **Tel** (617)929-2720. **5687**

BOSTON HERALD (1982), THE. (US/0738-5854). Boston Herald, PO Box 2096, One Herald Square, Boston MA 02106. **Tel** (617)426-3000, FAX (617)482-3507. **5688**

BOTTOMLINE. (US/0361-4662). 1119 Keystone Way, Carmel IN 46032. **1256**

BOULDER COUNTY BUSINESS REPORT. (US). Boulder County Business Report, 4885 Riverbend Road, Boulder CO 80301. **Tel** (303)440-4950. **644**

BOWNE DIGEST FOR CORPORATE & SECURITIES LAWYERS. (US/0896-906X). Brumberg Publications, 124 Harvard Street, Suite 3, Brookline MA 02146-6432. **Tel** (617)734-1979. **3079**

BOXBOARD CONTAINERS. (US/0006-8497). MacLean Hunter Publishing Corporation / Chicago, IL, 29 North Wacker Drive, Chicago IL 60606-3298. **Tel** (312)726-2802, FAX (312)726-3091. **4218**

BOXOFFICE. (US/0006-8527). Boxoffice, 1800 North Highland Avenue/Suite 710, Hollywood CA 90028. **Tel** (310)465-1186, FAX (213)465-5049. **4064**

BOYS' LIFE. (US/0006-8608). Boys' Life, 1325 Walnut Hill Lane, Irving TX 75062. **Tel** (214)580-2088. **1060**

BP&R BRITISH PLASTICS AND RUBBER. (UK/0307-6164). MCM Publishing Ltd, 37 Nelson Road, Caterham, Surrey CR3 5PP England. **Tel** 011 44 883 347059, FAX 011 44 81 675 8046. **4454**

BRANDS AND THEIR COMPANIES. (US/1047-6407). Gale Research Inc., 835 Penobscot Building, 645 Griswold Street, Detroit MI 48226. **Tel** (800)877-GALE, (313)961-2242, FAX (313)961-6083, (800)414-5043, telex TWX 810-221-7086. **1302**

BRAZIL SERVICE. (US/0889-1761). International Reports Inc., 11300 Rockville Pike 1100, Rockville MD 20852. **Tel** (212)685-6900, FAX (212)685-8566, telex 233139 RPTUR. **1465**

BRITISH EDUCATION INDEX. (UK/0007-0637). University of Leeds, Publications Office, Leeds LS2 9JT England. **Tel** 011 44 113 2335524, telex 556473. **1793**

BROADBAND NETWORKING NEWS. (US/1059-0544). Phillips Business Information, Inc., 1201 Seven Locks Road, Potomac MD 20854. **Tel** (301)424-3338, (800)777-5006, FAX (301)309-3847. **1127**

BROADCASTING (WASHINGTON, D.C. 1957). (US/0007-2028). Cahners Publishing Company, 249 West 17th Street, New York NY 10011. **Tel** (212)645-0067, FAX (212)242-6987. **1128**

BROOKINGS REVIEW, THE. (US/0745-1253). Brookings Institution, 1775 Massachusetts Avenue Northwest, Washington DC 20036-2188. **Tel** (202)797-6255, (800)275-1447. **5193**

BROWN UNIVERSITY CHILD AND ADOLESCENT BEHAVIOR LETTER, THE. (US/1058-1073). Manisses Communications Group Inc., PO Box 3357, Providence RI 02906-0757. **Tel** (401)831-6020, (800)333-7771, FAX (401)861-6370. **4578**

BROWN UNIVERSITY DIGEST OF ADDICTION THEORY AND APPLICATION. (US/1040-6328). Manisses Communications Group Inc., PO Box 3357, Providence RI 02906-0757. **Tel** (401)831-6020, (800)333-7771, FAX (401)861-6370. **1341**

BROWN UNIVERSITY LONG TERM CARE QUALITY LETTER. (US). Manisses Communications Group Inc., PO Box 3357, Providence RI 02906-0757. **Tel** (401)831-6020, (800)333-7771, FAX (401)861-6370. **4769**

BRUNSWICK BUSINESS JOURNAL, THE. (CN/0829-5239). The Brunswick Business Journal, 140 Baig Boulevard, Moncton NB E1E 1C8 Canada. **Tel** (506)857-9696, FAX (506)859-7395. **644**

BRYN MAWR CLASSICAL REVIEW. (US/1055-7660). Bryn Mawr Commentaries, Bryn Mawr College, Thomas Library, Bryn Mawr PA 19010. **Tel** (215)526-5384, FAX (215)526-7475. **1075**

BT CATALYST. (US/1040-9416). North Carolina Biotechnology Center, PO Box 13547, Research Triangle Park NC 27709-3547. **3690**

BUC ... NEW BOAT PRICE GUIDE. (US/0195-346X). BUC International Corporation, 1314 Northeast, 17th Court, Fort Lauderdale FL 33305. **Tel** (305)565-6715, (8000327-6929, FAX (305)561-3095. **592**

BUC USED BOAT PRICE GUIDE. (US/0735-973X). BUC International Corporation, 1314 Northeast, 17th Court, Fort Lauderdale FL 33305. **Tel** (305)565-6715, (8000327-6929, FAX (305)561-3095. **592**

BUFFALO NEWS, THE. (US/0745-2691). Buffalo Evening News, 1 News Plaza, PO Box 100, Buffalo NY 14240. **Tel** 800 777-8640 ext. 4530, FAX (716)856-5150, telex 916430. **5714**

BUILDING DESIGN. (UK/0007-3423). Morgan Grampian, 40 Beresford Street Woolwich, London SE18 6BQ England. **Tel** 011 44 81 855 7777, FAX 011 44 81 855 5548, telex 896238. **294**

BUILDING DESIGN & CONSTRUCTION. (US/0007-3407). Cahners Publishing Company, 249 West 17th Street, New York NY 10011. **Tel** (212)645-0067, FAX (212)242-6987. **294**

BUILDING SUPPLY & HOME CENTERS. (US/0890-9008). Cahners Publishing Company, 249 West 17th Street, New York NY 10011. **Tel** (212)645-0067, FAX (212)242-6987. **604**

BUILDINGS (CEDAR RAPIDS. 1947). (US/0007-3725). Stamats Communications Inc., 427 Sixth Avenue Southeast, Cedar Rapids IA 52406. **Tel** (319)364-6167, FAX (319)365-5421. **605**

BULLETIN / CSD. (SA). Center for Science & Development, PO Box 270, 0001 Pretoria South Africa. **Tel** 011 27 12 2022724, FAX 011 27 12 2022892. **5193**

BULLETIN DES AGRICULTEURS. (CN/0007-4446). Le Bulletin des Agriculteurs, 75 rue de Port Royal Bur 200, Montreal Quebec H3L 3T1 Canada. **Tel** (514)382-4350, FAX (514)382-4356. **69**

Serials Online Index

BULLETIN DU MUSEE BASQUE. (FR). Societe des Amis Musee Basque, 1 rue Marengo, 64100 Bayonne France. **Tel** 011 33 59 590898. **2681**

BULLETIN / INSTITUTE FOR ANTIQUITY AND CHRISTIANITY. (US/0739-0459). Institute Antiquity and Christianity, Claremont Graduate School, Claremont CA 91711. **Tel** (714)621-8066, FAX (714)621-8390. **4941**

BULLETIN OF ECONOMIC RESEARCH. (UK/0307-3378). Basil Blackwell Publishers Ltd, 108 Cowley Road, Oxford 0X4 1JF England. **Tel** 011 44 865 791100, FAX 011 44 865 791347, telex 837022 OXBOOK G. **1590**

BULLETIN OF THE GENERAL THEOLOGICAL CENTER OF MAINE. (US/1052-8202). Bangor Theological Seminary, 159 State Street, Portland ME 04101. **Tel** (207)874-2214. **4941**

BULLETIN OF THE PAN AMERICAN HEALTH ORGANIZATION. (US/0301-5750). Pan American Health Organization, 525 23rd Street Northwest, Office District Sales, Washington DC 20037. **Tel** (202)293-8130, FAX (202)338-0869. **4769**

BULLETIN OF THE WORLD HEALTH ORGANIZATION. (SZ/0042-9686). World Health Organization, Distribution and Sales, 20 Avenue Appia, CH-1211 Geneva 27 Switzerland. **Tel** 011 41 22 7912111, FAX 011 41 22 7880401. **3560**

BULLETIN OFFICIEL DE LA PROPRIETE INDUSTRIELLE BREVETS D'INVENTION ABREGES ET LISTES. (FR/0750-7674). Imprimerie Nationale / France, BP 514, 59505 Douai Cedex France. **Tel** 011 33 27 937090. **1310**

BULLETIN - PHILADELPHIA MUSEUM OF ART. (US/0031-7314). Philadelphia Museum of Art, Publications Department, 2525 Pennsylvania Avenue, Philadelphia PA 19130. **Tel** (215)235-8711, FAX (215)235-8715. **345**

BURLINGTON COUNTY TIMES (WILLINGBORO, N.J.). (US). Burlington County Times, Route 130, Willingboro NJ 08046. **Tel** (609)871-8001. **5709**

BUSINESS AMERICA. (US/0190-6275). Superintendent of Documents, US Government Printing Office, Washington DC 20402. **Tel** (202)275-3328, FAX (202)786-2377. **825**

BUSINESS AND COMMERCIAL AVIATION. (US/0191-4642). McGraw Hill Publishing Company, Inc., 1221 Avenue of the Americas, New York NY 10020. **Tel** (212)512-6410, (800)525-5003, FAX (212)512-6111. **15**

BUSINESS AND HEALTH. (US/0739-9413). Medical Economics Publishing, Five Paragon Drive, Second Floor, Montvale NJ 07645. **Tel** (800)432-4570, (201)358-2210. **645**

BUSINESS AND SOCIETY REVIEW (1974). (US/0045-3609). Business & Society Review, 200 West 57th Street, New York NY 10019. **Tel** (212)399-1088. **645**

BUSINESS AND THE ENVIRONMENT. (US/1052-7206). Cutter Information Corporation, 37 Broadway, Arlington MA 02174-5539. **Tel** (617)648-8700, (800)964-5118, FAX (617)648-8707, (617)648-1950, telex 650 100 9891. **2162**

BUSINESS ASIA. (HK/0572-7545). The Economist Intelligence Unit, 40 Duke Street, London W1A 1DW England. **Tel** 011 44 71 8301000. **646**

BUSINESS ATLANTA. (US/0192-0855). Argus Business, 6151 Powers Ferry Road, Atlanta GA 30339. **Tel** (404)995-2500, (800)233-3359. **646**

BUSINESS COMMUNICATIONS REVIEW. (US/0162-3885). BCR Enterprises Inc., 950 York Road, Suite 203, Hinsdale IL 60521. **Tel** (800)227-1234, (708)986-1432. **646**

BUSINESS CREDIT. (US/0897-0181). National Association of Credit Management, 8815 Centre Park Drive, Suite 200, Columbia MD 21045-2158. **Tel** (410)740-5560, FAX (410)740-5574. **781**

BUSINESS DATELINE. (US). University Microfilms International, 300 North Zeeb Road, Ann Arbor MI 48106-1346. **Tel** (313)761-4700, (800)521-0600 Exts. 2490, 2491, FAX (313)973-1540. **727**

BUSINESS EASTERN EUROPE. (UK). The Economist Intelligence Unit, 40 Duke Street, London W1A 1DW England. **Tel** 011 44 71 8301000. **647**

BUSINESS FIRST (BUFFALO, N.Y.). (US/0749-9418). Business First / Buffalo, 472 Delaware Avenue, Buffalo NY 14202. **Tel** (716)882-6200, FAX (716)882-3020. **648**

BUSINESS FIRST (COLUMBUS, OHIO). (US/0748-6146). Business First of Columbus Inc, 471 East Broad Street, Suite 1500, Columbus OH 43216. **Tel** (614)461-4040, FAX (614)461-5480. **648**

BUSINESS FIRST (LOUISVILLE, KY.). (US/0748-6138). Business First / Kentucky, PO Box 249, Louisville KY 40201. **Tel** (502)583-1731. **648**

BUSINESS FOR CENTRAL NEW JERSEY. (US/1042-8704). Snowden Publications Inc, PO Box 201, Princeton NJ 08542. **Tel** (201)329-0003, FAX (201)329-0252. **862**

BUSINESS HISTORY. (UK/0007-6791). Frank Cass & Company Ltd, Newbury House, 890-900 Eastern Avenue, Newbury Park, Ilford, Essex IG2 7HH United Kingdom. **Tel** 011 44 81 599 8866, FAX 011 44 81 599 0984, telex 897719. **648**

BUSINESS HISTORY REVIEW. (US/0007-6805). Business History Review, Harvard Business School Publishing, Soldiers Field, Boston MA 02163. **Tel** (617)495-6154, FAX (617)496-8066. **648**

BUSINESS HISTORY REVIEW. (US/0007-6805). Harvard Business School, 325 Baker Library, Soldiers Field Road, Boston MA 02163. **Tel** (617)495-6154, FAX (617)495-6001. **648**

BUSINESS INFORMATION ALERT. (US/1042-0746). Alert Publications Inc, 399 West Fullerton Parkway, Chicago IL 60614. **Tel** (312)525-7594, FAX (312)525-7015. **3199**

BUSINESS INSURANCE. (US/0007-6864). Crain Communications Inc., 1400 Woodbridge, Detroit MI 48207. **Tel** (313)446-6000, (800)992-9970. **2877**

BUSINESS JOURNAL (CHARLOTTE, N.C.). (US/0887-5588). The Business Journal / North Carolina, 128 South Tryon Street, Suite 2250, Charlotte NC 28202-6001. **Tel** (704)347-2340. **649**

BUSINESS JOURNAL OF NEW JERSEY (JAMESBURG, N.J : 1985). (US/0889-3403). Micromedia, 55 Park Place, Morristown NJ 07963. **Tel** (201)644-5554. **649**

BUSINESS JOURNAL OF UPPER EAST TENNESSEE AND SOUTHWEST VIRGINIA. (US/1040-6360). The Business Journal, PO Box 643, Blountville TN 37617. **Tel** (615)232-7111. **650**

BUSINESS JOURNAL (PHOENIX, ARIZ.), THE. (US/0895-1632). American City Business Journal, PO Box 16718, Phoenix AZ 85011. **Tel** (602)230-8400, FAX (602)230-0955. **650**

BUSINESS JOURNAL (PORTLAND, OR.), THE. (US/0742-6550). The Business Journal / Oregon, PO Box 14490, Portland OR 97214. **Tel** (503)274-8733, FAX (503)227-2650. **650**

BUSINESS JOURNAL (SACRAMENTO, CALIF.). (US/8756-5897). Business Journal / Sacramento, 1401 21st Street, Sacramento CA 95814. **Tel** (916)447-7661, FAX (916)447-2243. **650**

BUSINESS KOREA. (KO). Business Korea Ltd, Hanam Building/Suite 808, Yoido-dong, Yongdungpo-gu, Seoul 150 Korea. **650**

BUSINESS LATIN AMERICA. (UK/0007-6880). The Economist Intelligence Unit, 40 Duke Street, London W1A 1DW England. **Tel** 011 44 71 8301000. **650**

BUSINESS LAW BRIEF. (UK). Financial Times England, 8 16 Great New Street, London EC4A 3BN England. **Tel** 011 44 71 353 0305, 353 1040, FAX 011 44 353 0846. **3096**

BUSINESS MARKETING. (US/0745-5933). Crain Communications Inc., 1400 Woodbridge, Detroit MI 48207. **Tel** (313)446-6000, (800)992-9970. **922**

BUSINESS NEWS, SAN DIEGO. (US/0738-6869). Business News, 4350 Lajolla Village Drive, San Diego CA 92122. **Tel** (619)565-2636. **651**

BUSINESS ORGANIZATIONS, AGENCIES, AND PUBLICATIONS DIRECTORY. (US/0888-1413). Gale Research Inc., 835 Penobscot Building, 645 Griswold Street, Detroit MI 48226. **Tel** (800)877-GALE, (313)961-2242, FAX (313)961-6083, (800)414-5043, telex TWX 810-221-7086. **651**

BUSINESS PERIODICALS INDEX. (US/0007-6961). H W Wilson Company, 950 University Avenue, Bronx NY 10452. **Tel** (800)367-6770, (718)588-8400, FAX (718)590-1617, telex 4990003 HWILSON. **727**

BUSINESS PERIODICALS INDEX. CD-ROM. (US/0007-6961). H W Wilson Company, 950 University Avenue, Bronx NY 10452. **Tel** (800)367-6770, (718)588-8400, FAX (718)590-1617, telex 4990003 HWILSON. **727**

BUSINESS PERSPECTIVES (MEMPHIS, TENN.). (US/0896-3703). Bureau of Business and Economic Research / Tennessee, Memphis State University, Fogelman College, Memphis TN 38152. **Tel** (901)678-2281, FAX (901)678-2281. **651**

BUSINESS PUBLISHER. (US). JK Publisher, PO Box 71020, Milwaukee WI 53211. **Tel** (414)332-1625, FAX (414)962-0084. **4812**

BUSINESS REVIEW (MONTREAL). (CN/0005-531X). Bank of Montreal, PO Box 6002, Montreal Quebec H3C 3B1 Canada. **652**

BUSINESS REVIEW WEEKLY : BRW. (AT/0727-758X). Business Review Weekly, 469 La Trobe Street, Melbourne VIC 3001 Australia. **Tel** 011 61 3 6033888, FAX 011 61 3 6704328. **652**

BUSINESS TIMES (EAST HARTFORD, CONN.), THE. (US/0744-172X). MacClaren Press, 315 Peck Street, New Haven CT 06513. **Tel** (203)782-1420. **653**

BUSINESS TODAY. (US/0007-7100). Federation for Student Communication, Princeton University, 305 Aaron Burr Hall, Princeton NJ 08544. **Tel** (609)258-1111, FAX (609)921-3710. **653**

BUSINESS TRAVEL NEWS. (US/8750-3670). Miller Freeman Inc., 600 Harrison Street, San Francisco CA 94107. **Tel** (415)905-2337, FAX (415)905-2240, telex 278273. **653**

BUSINESS WORCESTER. (US/0738-8977). Worcester Business Journal, 172 Shrewsbury Street, Worcester MA 01604. **Tel** (508)755-8004. **654**

BUSINESSWEST (SPRINGFIELD, MASS.). (US/1049-9822). BusinessWest, 625 Front Street, Chicopee MA 01013. **Tel** (413)598-8600. **654**

BUTLLETI OFICIAL DEL PARLAMENT DE CATALUNYA. (SP). Servei de Publicacions del Parlament de Catalunya, Palau del Parlament Parc de la Ciutadella, Barcelona 08003 Catalonia Spain. **Tel** (93)300-6413, FAX (93)300-8962, telex 97-684. **4635**

BUYOUTS (WELLESLEY HILLS, MASS.). (US/1040-0990). Securities Data Company, 40 West 57th Street, 11th Floor, New York NY 10019. **Tel** (212)765-5311. **654**

BYGGREFERAT. (SW/0345-1941). Byggdok, Haelsingegatan 47, S 113 31 Stockholm Sweden. **Tel** 011 46 8 340170, FAX 011 46 8 324859. **294**

BYTE. (US/0360-5280). McGraw Hill Publishing Company, Inc., 1221 Avenue of the Americas, New York NY 10020. **Tel** (212)512-6410, (800)525-5003, FAX (212)512-6111. **1273**

BYTE BUYER, THE. (US/0889-8200). PO Box 83086, San Diego CA 92138. **Tel** (619)573-0315. **1172**

C USERS JOURNAL, THE. (US/0898-9788). R & D Publications, 1601 West 23rd Street, Suite 200, Lawrence KS 66046. **Tel** (913)841-1631, FAX (913)841-2624. **1278**

C2C ABSTRACTS JAPAN. ANALYTICAL CHEMISTRY. (US/1049-1260). SCAN C2C Inc, Attn Carol G Heffernan Marketing Director, 500 E Street Southwest, Suite 800, 8th Floor, Washington DC 20024. **Tel** (202)863-3850, (800)525-3865, FAX (202)863-3855. **996**

C2C ABSTRACTS JAPAN. CERAMICS. (US/1049-1252). SCAN C2C Inc, Attn Carol G Heffernan Marketing Director, 500 E Street Southwest, Suite 800, 8th Floor, Washington DC 20024. **Tel** (202)863-3850, (800)525-3865, FAX (202)863-3855. **2595**

C2C ABSTRACTS JAPAN. CHEMICAL ENGINEERING. (US/1049-1279). SCAN C2C Inc, Attn Carol G Heffernan Marketing Director, 500 E Street Southwest, Suite 800, 8th Floor, Washington DC 20024. **Tel** (202)863-3850, (800)525-3865, FAX (202)863-3855. **996**

C2C ABSTRACTS JAPAN. CRYSTALLOGRAPHY. (US/1049-1287). SCAN C2C Inc, Attn Carol G Heffernan Marketing Director, 500 E Street Southwest, Suite 800, 8th Floor, Washington DC 20024. **Tel** (202)863-3850, (800)525-3865, FAX (202)863-3855. **996**

C2C ABSTRACTS JAPAN. HYDROCARBONS. (US/1049-1295). SCAN C2C Inc, Attn Carol G Heffernan Marketing Director, 500 E Street Southwest, Suite 800, 8th Floor, Washington DC 20024. **Tel** (202)863-3850, (800)525-3865, FAX (202)863-3855. **996**

C2C ABSTRACTS JAPAN. INORGANIC CHEMISTRY. (US/1049-1309). SCAN C2C Inc, Attn Carol G Heffernan Marketing Director, 500 E Street Southwest, Suite 800, 8th Floor, Washington DC 20024. **Tel** (202)863-3850, (800)525-3865, FAX (202)863-3855. **996**

C2C ABSTRACTS JAPAN. MATERIALS SCIENCES. (US/1049-1317). SCAN C2C Inc, Attn Carol G Heffernan Marketing Director, 500 E Street Southwest, Suite 800, 8th Floor, Washington DC 20024. **Tel** (202)863-3850, (800)525-3865, FAX (202)863-3855. **5174**

C2C ABSTRACTS JAPAN. METALS. (US/1049-1384). SCAN C2C Inc, Attn Carol G Heffernan Marketing Director, 500 E Street Southwest, Suite 800, 8th Floor, Washington DC 20024. **Tel** (202)863-3850, (800)525-3865, FAX (202)863-3855. **4025**

C2C ABSTRACTS JAPAN. ORGANIC CHEMISTRY. (US/1049-1325). SCAN C2C Inc, Attn Carol G Heffernan Marketing Director, 500 E Street Southwest, Suite 800, 8th Floor, Washington DC 20024. **Tel** (202)863-3850, (800)525-3865, FAX (202)863-3855. **1040**

C2C Serials available Online

C2C ABSTRACTS JAPAN. PHYSICAL CHEMISTRY. (US/1049-1333). SCAN C2C Inc, Attn Carol G Heffernan Marketing Director, 500 E Street Southwest, Suite 800, 8th Floor, Washington DC 20024. **Tel** (202)863-3850, (800)525-3865, FAX (202)863-3855. **996**

C2C ABSTRACTS JAPAN. PLASTICS. (US/1049-1341). SCAN C2C Inc, Attn Carol G Heffernan Marketing Director, 500 E Street Southwest, Suite 800, 8th Floor, Washington DC 20024. **Tel** (202)863-3850, (800)525-3865, FAX (202)863-3855. **4461**

C2C ABSTRACTS JAPAN. POLYMER CHEMISTRY. (US/1049-135X). SCAN C2C Inc, Attn Carol G Heffernan Marketing Director, 500 E Street Southwest, Suite 800, 8th Floor, Washington DC 20024. **Tel** (202)863-3850, (800)525-3865, FAX (202)863-3855. **996**

C2C ABSTRACTS JAPAN. SURFACE CHEMISTRY. (US/1049-1368). SCAN C2C Inc, Attn Carol G Heffernan Marketing Director, 500 E Street Southwest, Suite 800, 8th Floor, Washington DC 20024. **Tel** (202)863-3850, (800)525-3865, FAX (202)863-3855. **997**

C2C ABSTRACTS JAPAN. TEXTILES. (US/1049-1376). SCAN C2C Inc, Attn Carol G Heffernan Marketing Director, 500 E Street Southwest, Suite 800, 8th Floor, Washington DC 20024. **Tel** (202)863-3850, (800)525-3865, FAX (202)863-3855. **5360**

C2C CURRENTS JAPAN. CHEMISTRY. (US/1049-1228). SCAN C2C Inc, Attn Carol G Heffernan Marketing Director, 500 E Street Southwest, Suite 800, 8th Floor, Washington DC 20024. **Tel** (202)863-3850, (800)525-3865, FAX (202)863-3855. **964**

C2C CURRENTS JAPAN. COMPUTERS. (US/1049-1244). SCAN C2C Inc, Attn Carol G Heffernan Marketing Director, 500 E Street Southwest, Suite 800, 8th Floor, Washington DC 20024. **Tel** (202)863-3850, (800)525-3865, FAX (202)863-3855. **1172**

C2C CURRENTS JAPAN. ELECTRONICS. (US/1049-1236). SCAN C2C Inc, Attn Carol G Heffernan Marketing Director, 500 E Street Southwest, Suite 800, 8th Floor, Washington DC 20024. **Tel** (202)863-3850, (800)525-3865, FAX (202)863-3855. **2037**

C2C CURRENTS JAPAN. MANUFACTURING. (US/1051-7545). SCAN C2C Inc, Attn Carol G Heffernan Marketing Director, 500 E Street Southwest, Suite 800, 8th Floor, Washington DC 20024. **Tel** (202)863-3850, (800)525-3865, FAX (202)863-3855. **3476**

C2C CURRENTS JAPAN. MATERIALS. (US/1049-121X). SCAN C2C Inc, Attn Carol G Heffernan Marketing Director, 500 E Street Southwest, Suite 800, 8th Floor, Washington DC 20024. **Tel** (202)863-3850, (800)525-3865, FAX (202)863-3855. **654**

C3I REPORT. (US/0889-4728). Pasha Publications Inc., 1616 North Fort Myer Drive, Suite 1000, Arlington VA 22209. **Tel** (800)424-2908, (703)528-1244, FAX (703)528-3742, (703)528-1253. **4038**

CADCAM LONDON. (UK/0963-5750). EMAP Readerlink, Audit House, 260 Field End Road, Ruislip Middlesex HA4 9LT England. **Tel** 011 44 081 868 4499, FAX 011 44 081 429 3117. **1231**

CADENCE UNIVERSE PERFORMANCE REPORT. (US). CDA Investment Technologies, 1355 Piccard Drive, Rockville MD 20850. **Tel** (301)974-9600, (800)232-2285, FAX (301)590-1389. **893**

CALCIFIED TISSUE ABSTRACTS. (UK/0008-0586). Cambridge Scientific Abstracts, 7200 Wisconsin Avenue, #601, Bethesda MD 20814-4823. **Tel** (301)961-6750, (800)843-7751, FAX (301)961-6720. **3655**

CALGARY HERALD. (CN/0828-1815). Southam Inc. / Attention: Mail Subscriptions, Box 2400 Station M, Calgary Alberta T2P 0W8 Canada. **Tel** (403)235-7100, (403)235-0121, FAX (403)235-8675. **5781**

CALIFORNIA BANKRUPTCY JOURNAL. (US/1047-0743). California Bankruptcy Forum, 1278 Glenneyre 101, Laguna Beach CA 92651. **Tel** (714)363-6643. **782**

CALIFORNIA BUSINESS. (US/0008-0926). CABCO, 1427 Bay Street, Suite 200, San Francisco CA 94123. **Tel** (415)776-9966, FAX (415)776-1472. **654**

CALIFORNIA LABOR LETTER. (US). California Labor Letter, PO Box 3651, Manhattan Beach CA 90266. **Tel** (310)798-3868, FAX (310)798-3872. **1658**

CALIFORNIA MANAGEMENT REVIEW. (US/0008-1256). California Management Review, 350 Barrows Hall, University of California, Berkeley CA 94720. **Tel** (510)642-7159, FAX (510)642-2826. **862**

CALIFORNIA PUBLIC FINANCE. (US). American Banker, Concourse Level, 1 State Street Plaza, New York NY 10004. **Tel** (212)803-8200, (800)221-1809. **4716**

CALIFORNIA WESTERN INTERNATIONAL LAW JOURNAL. (US/0886-3210). California Western School of Law, 225 Cedar Street, San Diego CA 92101. **Tel** (619)239-0391, (800)225-4252, FAX (619)696-9999. **3125**

CALIFORNIA WESTERN LAW REVIEW. (US/0008-1639). California Western School of Law, 225 Cedar Street, San Diego CA 92101. **Tel** (619)239-0391, (800)225-4252, FAX (619)696-9999. **2947**

CAMBRIDGE SCIENTIFIC BIOCHEMISTRY ABSTRACTS: PART 1 BIOLOGICAL MEMBRANES. (US/8756-7504). Cambridge Scientific Abstracts, 7200 Wisconsin Avenue, #601, Bethesda MD 20814-4823. **Tel** (301)961-6750, (800)843-7751, FAX (301)961-6720. **484**

CAMBRIDGE SCIENTIFIC BIOCHEMISTRY ABSTRACTS: PART 2 NUCLEIC ACIDS. (US/8756-7512). Cambridge Scientific Abstracts, 7200 Wisconsin Avenue, #601, Bethesda MD 20814-4823. **Tel** (301)961-6750, (800)843-7751, FAX (301)961-6720. **477**

CAMBRIDGE SCIENTIFIC BIOCHEMISTRY ABSTRACTS: PART 3 AMINO-ACIDS, PEPTIDES & PROTEINS. (US/8756-7520). Cambridge Scientific Abstracts, 7200 Wisconsin Avenue, #601, Bethesda MD 20814-4823. **Tel** (301)961-6750, (800)843-7751, FAX (301)961-6720. **484**

CANADA-UNITED STATES LAW JOURNAL. (US/0163-6391). Case Western Reserve University / School of Law, 11075 East Boulevard, Cleveland OH 44106. **Tel** (216)368-3304, FAX (216)368-6144. **3125**

CANADIAN BANKER (1983). (CN/0822-6830). Canadian Bankers' Association, 199 Bay Street, Suite 3000 COM CT W, Toronto Ontario M5L 1G2 Canada. **Tel** (416)362-6092, FAX (416)362-7705, telex 0623402. **782**

CANADIAN BUSINESS CONDITIONS. (CN/0383-9893). Canadian Imperial Bank of Commerce Economic Division, Commerce Court North, 7th Floor, Toronto Ontario M5L 1A2 Canada. **Tel** (416)980-2211, (416)980-3721. **655**

CANADIAN BUSINESS REVIEW, THE. (CN/0317-4026). Conference Board of Canada, 255 Smyth Road, Ottawa Ontario K1H 8M7 Canada. **Tel** (613)526-3280, FAX (613)526-4857, telex 053-3034. **1467**

CANADIAN CHEMICAL NEWS. (CN/0823-5228). Chemical Institute of Canada, 130 Slater Street/Suite 550, Ottawa Ontario K1P 6E2 Canada. **Tel** (613)232-6252, FAX (613)232-5862. **1021**

CANADIAN DATASYSTEMS. (CN/0008-3364). MacLean Hunter Ltd. Business Publishers / Canada, Box 9100, Station A, Toronto ONT M5W 1A5 Canada. **Tel** (416)946-8420, (800)567-0444. **1256**

CANADIAN DIMENSION. (CN/0008-3402). Canadian Dimension, 228 Notre Dame Avenue, Suite 707, Winnipeg Manitoba R3B 1N7 Canada. **Tel** (204)957-1519, FAX (204)943-4617. **4467**

CANADIAN ELECTRONICS (WILLOWDALE). (CN/1187-6026). Action Communications Inc, 135 Spy Ct, Markham Ontario L3R 5H6 Canada. **Tel** (416)477-3222. **2038**

CANADIAN MACHINERY AND METALWORKING. (CN/0008-4379). MacLean Hunter Ltd. Business Publishers / Canada, Box 9100, Station A, Toronto ONT M5W 1A5 Canada. **Tel** (416)946-8420, (800)567-0444. **2111**

CANADIAN MANAGER. (CN/0045-5156). Canadian Institute of Management, 2175 Sheppard Avenue E/Suite 110, Willowdale Ontario M2J 1W8 Canada. **Tel** (416)493-0155, 800 387-5774, FAX (416)491-1670. **863**

CANADIAN MINING JOURNAL. (CN/0008-4492). Southam Information and Technology Group Inc., 1450 Don Mills Road, Don Mills Ontario M3B 2X7 Canada. **Tel** (416)445-6641, (800)668-2374, FAX (416)442-2261. **2136**

CANADIAN OCCUPATIONAL HEALTH & SAFETY NEWS. (CN/0709-5252). Southam Information and Technology Group Inc., 1450 Don Mills Road, Don Mills Ontario M3B 2X7 Canada. **Tel** (416)445-6641, (800)668-2374, FAX (416)442-2261. **2860**

CANADIAN PACKAGING. (CN/0008-4654). MacLean Hunter Ltd. Business Publishers / Canada, Box 9100, Station A, Toronto ONT M5W 1A5 Canada. **Tel** (416)946-8420, (800)567-0444. **4218**

CANADIAN PAPERMAKER. (CN/1191-887X). MacLean Hunter Ltd. Business Publishers / Canada, Box 9100, Station A, Toronto ONT M5W 1A5 Canada. **Tel** (416)946-8420, (800)567-0444. **4233**

CANADIAN PERIODICAL INDEX (1964). (CN/0008-4719). Globe & Mail, 444 Front Street West, Toronto Ontario M5V 2S9 Canada. **Tel** (416)585-5000, FAX (416)585-5249. **412**

CANADIAN PLASTICS. (CN/0008-4778). Southam Information and Technology Group Inc., 1450 Don Mills Road, Don Mills Ontario M3B 2X7 Canada. **Tel** (416)445-6641, (800)668-2374, FAX (416)442-2261. **4454**

CANCER NEWS (NEW YORK, N.Y.). (US/0008-5464). American Cancer Society Institute Activities, 1599 Clifton Road Northeast, Atlanta GA 30329. **3812**

CANCER VICTORS JOURNAL. (US/0891-0766). International Association of Cancer Victims and Friends, 515 West Sycamore, El Secundo CA 90245. **Tel** (310)822-5032, (310)822-5132. **3813**

CANDLE COMPUTER REPORT. (US/1071-2976). Candle Corporation, 2425 Olympic Boulevard, Santa Monica CA 90404. **Tel** (310)829-5800, FAX (310)582-4233. **1173**

CANDY INDUSTRY (1982). (US/0745-1032). Advanstar Communications Inc., 131 West First Street, Duluth MN 55802. **Tel** (218)723-9477, (800)346-0085. **2330**

CANDY MARKETER (1985). (US/0886-3741). Advanstar Communications Inc., 131 West First Street, Duluth MN 55802. **Tel** (218)723-9477, (800)346-0085. **2330**

CAP WEEKLY. (UK/0953-5594). Agra Europe London Limited, 25 Frant Road, Tunbridge Wells, Kent TN2 5JT England. **Tel** 011 44 892 533813. **72**

CAPACITY MANAGEMENT REVIEW. (US/1049-2194). Institute for Computer Capacity Management, PO Box 82847, Phoenix AZ 85071. **Tel** (602)997-7374, FAX (602)861-2587. **1173**

CAPITAL DISTRICT BUSINESS REVIEW. (US/0747-3699). Capital District Business Review, PO Box 15081, Albany NY 12212. **Tel** (518)437-9855. **655**

CAR AND DRIVER. (US/0008-6002). Hachette Magazines Inc., 1633 Broadway, New York NY 10019. **Tel** (212)767-6000. **5408**

CARD NEWS. (US/0894-0797). Phillips Business Information, Inc., 1201 Seven Locks Road, Potomac MD 20854. **Tel** (301)424-3338, (800)777-5006, FAX (301)309-3847. **782**

CARDFAX. (US). Faulkner & Gray Inc., 11 Penn Plaza, 17th Floor, New York NY 10001. **Tel** (212)967-7000, (800)535-8403. **1601**

CARIBBEAN BUSINESS. (US/0194-8326). Casiano Communications, PO Box 12130, Loiza St. Station, San Juan Puerto Rico 00914. **Tel** (809)728-3000. **655**

CARIBBEAN UPDATE. (US/8756-324X). Mexico Business Monthly, 52 Maples Avenue, Department M, Maplewood NJ 07040. **Tel** (201)762-1565, (800)766-3949, FAX (201)762-9585. **655**

CARPET & FLOORCOVERINGS REVIEW. (UK/0263-4236). Benn Publications Ltd., Sovereign Way, Tonbridge TNQ 1RW England. **Tel** 011 44 732 364422, FAX 011 44 732 361534, telex 0732 95132 BENTON G. **5348**

CASE WESTERN RESERVE LAW REVIEW. (US/0008-7262). Case Western Reserve University / School of Law, 11075 East Boulevard, Cleveland OH 44106. **Tel** (216)368-3304, FAX (216)368-6144. **2949**

CATALOG AGE. (US/0740-3119). Cowles Business Media Inc., 6 River Bend Center, 911 Hope Street, Stamford CT 06907. **Tel** (203)358-9900, (800)775-3777, FAX (203)357-9014. **757**

CATALOGO DEI LIBRI IN COMMERCIO: AUTORI. (IT). Editrice Bibliografica, Viale Vittoria Veneto 24, 20124 Milan Italy. **Tel** 011 39 2 29006965, FAX 011 39 2 654624. **412**

CATALOGO DEI LIBRI IN COMMERCIO: SOGGETTI. (IT). Editrice Bibliografica, Viale Vittoria Veneto 24, 20124 Milan Italy. **Tel** 011 39 2 29006965, FAX 011 39 2 654624. **412**

CATALOGO DEI LIBRI IN COMMERCIO: TITOLI. (IT). Editrice Bibliografica, Viale Vittoria Veneto 24, 20124 Milan Italy. **Tel** 011 39 2 29006965, FAX 011 39 2 654624. **412**

CATHOLIC TRENDS. (US). Catholic News Service, 3211 4th Street Northeast, Washington DC 20017. **Tel** (202)541-3289, (202)541-3250, FAX (202)541-3255, telex 892589. **5026**

CD COMPUTING NEWS. (US/0893-4843). Worldwide Videotex, PO Box 3273, Boynton Beach FL 33424-3273. **Tel** (407)738-2276, FAX (407)738-2275. **1276**

CD-ROM DATABASES. (US). Worldwide Videotex, PO Box 3273, Boynton Beach FL 33424-3273. **Tel** (407)738-2276, FAX (407)738-2275. **1276**

CD-ROM LIBRARIAN. (US/0893-9934). Mecklermedia Corporation, 11 Ferry Lane West, Westport CT 06880. **Tel** (203)226-6967, (800)632-5537, FAX (203)454-5840. **1174**

CD-ROM PROFESSIONAL. (US/1049-0833). Online Inc., 462 Danbury Road, Wilton CT 06897. **Tel** (203)761-1466, (800)248-8466, FAX (203)761-1444. **1276**

CDROM DATABASES. (US/0897-3296). Worldwide Videotex, PO Box 3273, Boynton Beach FL 33424-3273. **Tel** (407)738-2276, FAX (407)738-2275. **1174**

Serials Online Index

Serials available Online COMMON

CELLULAR BUSINESS. (US/0741-6520). Intertec Publishing Corporation, 9800 Metcalf, Overland Park KS 66212. **Tel** (913)341-1300. **1151**

CELLULAR MARKETING. (US/0890-2402). Argus Business, 6151 Powers Ferry Road, Atlanta GA 30339. **Tel** (404)995-2500, (800)233-3359. **922**

CELLULAR SALES & MARKETING. (US/0892-2683). Creative Communications, PO Box 1519-EBS, Herndon VA 22070. **Tel** (710)742-9696. **1151**

CENTRAL AMERICA UPDATE. (CN/0823-7689). Latin American Working Group, 603 Parliament Street, Toronto Ontario M4X 1P9 Canada. **Tel** (416)966-4773, FAX (416)921-0071. **4467**

CENTRAL AMERICA UPDATE (ALBUQUERQUE, N.M.). (US). University of New Mexico / Latin American Institute, Latin America Data Base, 801 Yale NE, Albuquerque NM 87131-1016. **Tel** (505)277-6839, FAX (505)277-5989. **4467**

CENTRAL AMERICA UPDATE (ALBUQUERQUE, N.M.). (US/1054-8882). University of New Mexico / Latin American Institute, Latin America Data Base, 801 Yale NE, Albuquerque NM 87131-1016. **Tel** (505)277-6839, FAX (505)277-5989. **4467**

CENTRAL PENN BUSINESS JOURNAL. (US/1058-3599). CPNC Inc., 1500 North 2nd Street, Harrisburg PA 17102. **656**

CERAMIC ABSTRACTS. (US/0095-9960). American Ceramic Society, 735 Ceramic Place, Westerville OH 43081-8720. **Tel** (614)890-4700, (614)794-5890, FAX (614)899-6109. **2595**

CERAMIC ABSTRACTS CD-ROM. (US/1056-3490). American Ceramic Society, 735 Ceramic Place, Westerville OH 43081-8720. **Tel** (614)890-4700, (614)794-5890, FAX (614)899-6109. **2587**

CERAMIC INDUSTRY. (US/0009-0220). Business News Publishing Company, 755 West Big Beaver Road, Suite 1000, Troy MI 48084. **Tel** (810)362-3700, FAX (810)362-0317, telex 230295. **2587**

CHAIN DRUG REVIEW. (US/0164-9914). Racher Press, 220 Fifth Avenue, New York NY 10001. **Tel** (212)213-6000, FAX (212)213-6106. **656**

CHEESE MARKET NEWS. (US/0891-1509). Cahners Publishing Company, 249 West 17th Street, New York NY 10011. **Tel** (212)645-0067, FAX (212)242-6987. **192**

CHEM SOURCES INTERNATIONAL. (US). Chemical Sources International, Inc., PO Box 1824, Clemson SC 29633. **Tel** (803)646-7840, FAX (803)646-9938. **1021**

CHEMICAL ABSTRACTS. (US/0009-2258). Chemical Abstracts Service, (Subsidiary of The American Chemical Society), 2540 Olentangy River Road, PO Box 3012, Columbus OH 43210-0012. **Tel** (614)447-3731, (800)753-4227, FAX (614)447-3751. **1011**

CHEMICAL BUSINESS. (US/0731-8774). Schnell Publishing Company Inc., 80 Broad Street, New York NY 10004. **Tel** (212)248-4177, telex 226113 CMR UR. **968**

CHEMICAL BUSINESS BULLETINS. (UK). Royal Society of Chemistry, Thomas Graham House, Science Park, Cambridge CB4 4WF England. **Tel** 011 44 223 420066, FAX 011 44 223 423429, telex 818293 ROYAL. **727**

CHEMICAL BUSINESS UPDATE. (UK/0950-6144). Royal Society of Chemistry, Thomas Graham House, Science Park, Cambridge CB4 4WF England. **Tel** 011 44 223 420066, FAX 011 44 223 423429, telex 818293 ROYAL. **1011**

CHEMICAL HAZARDS IN INDUSTRY. (UK/0265-5721). Royal Society of Chemistry, Thomas Graham House, Science Park, Cambridge CB4 4WF England. **Tel** 011 44 223 420066, FAX 011 44 223 423429, telex 818293 ROYAL. **2872**

CHEMICAL MARKETING REPORTER. (US/0090-0907). Schnell Publishing Company Inc., 80 Broad Street, New York NY 10004. **Tel** (212)248-4177, telex 226113 CMR UR. **968**

CHEMICAL MONITOR, THE. (US/1049-1015). Chemical Monitor, Box 314, Lindenhurst NY 11757. **Tel** (516)669-8147. **1022**

CHEMICAL WEEK. (US/0009-272X). Chemical Week Association, 888 Seventh Avenue, 26th Floor, New York NY 10106. **Tel** (212)621-4900. **1022**

CHEMISTRY AND INDUSTRY (LONDON). (UK/0009-3068). Society of Chemical Industry, 14-15 Belgrave Square, London SW1X 8PS England. **Tel** 11 44 71 235 3681, FAX 11 44 71 235 9410. **970**

CHEMORECEPTION ABSTRACTS. (US/0300-1261). Cambridge Scientific Abstracts, 7200 Wisconsin Avenue, #601, Bethesda MD 20814-4823. **Tel** (301)961-6750, (800)843-7751, FAX (301)961-6720. **477**

CHICAGO TRIBUNE (CHICAGO, ILL. : 1963). (US). Chicago Tribune, 777 West Chicago Avenue, Department 300, Chicago IL 60610. **Tel** (312)222-5350. **5659**

CHICAGO TRIBUNE INDEX. (US/0731-9045). **5814**

CHIEF INFORMATION OFFICER JOURNAL. (US/0899-0182). Faulkner & Gray Inc., 11 Penn Plaza, 17th Floor, New York NY 10001. **Tel** (212)967-7000, (800)535-8403. **1174**

CHILD HEALTH ALERT. (US/1064-4849). Child Health Alert, PO Box 338, Newton Highlands MA 02161. **Tel** (617)239-1762, (800)238-6658. **4771**

CHILDREN TODAY. (US/0361-4336). Superintendent of Documents, US Government Printing Office, Washington DC 20402. **Tel** (202)275-3328, FAX (202)786-2377. **5278**

CHILDREN'S BUSINESS. (US/0884-2280). Fairchild Publications Inc, 7 West 34th Street, 4th Floor, New York NY 10001-8191. **Tel** (212)630-4000. **1083**

CHINA BUSINESS REVIEW, THE. (US/0163-7169). The China Business Review, 1818 North Street Northwest, Suite 500, Washington DC 20036. **Tel** (202)429-0340. **657**

CHRISTIAN SCIENCE MONITOR (1983), THE. (US/0882-7729). Christian Science Publishing Society, One Norway Street, Boston MA 02115. **Tel** (617)450-2678, (617)450-2504. **5688**

CHRONICLE OF LATIN AMERICAN ECONOMIC AFFAIRS. (US/1054-8874). University of New Mexico / Latin American Institute, Latin America Data Base, 801 Yale NE, Albuquerque NM 87131-1016. **Tel** (505)277-6839, FAX (505)277-5989. **1469**

CHRONOLOG (PALO ALTO, CALIF.). (US/0163-3732). Dialog Information Services, 3460 Hillview Avenue, Palo Alto CA 94304. **Tel** (415)858-4240, (800)334-2564. **3202**

CHUAN KUO HSIN SHU MU. (CC/0578-073X). **4821**

CIENCIA DA INFORMACAO. (BL/0100-1965). IBICT, SCN-Quadra 2 Bloco K, 70710 Brasilia DF Brazil. **Tel** 011 55 61 3214888, telex (061)2481. **3202**

CIM STRATEGIES. (US/0748-9250). Cutter Information Corporation, 37 Broadway, Arlington MA 02174-5539. **Tel** (617)648-8700, (800)964-5118, FAX (617)648-8707, (617)648-1950, telex 650 100 9891. **3476**

CIMARRON REVIEW. (US/0009-6849). Cimarron Review, 205 Morrill Hall, Oklahoma State University, Stillwater OK 74078-0135. **Tel** (405)744-9476, FAX (405)744-6326. **3461**

CINCINNATI BUSINESS COURIER. (US/0882-8881). Cincinnati Business Courier, 35 East 7th Street, Suite 700, Cincinnati OH 45202. **Tel** (513)621-6665. **657**

CINCINNATI ENQUIRER (CINCINNATI, OHIO : 1872). (US). Cincinnati Enquirer, 312 Elm Street, Cincinnati OH 45202. **Tel** (513)721-2700, (800)876-4500. **5727**

CINCINNATI POST (CINCINNATI, OHIO : 1974). (US). Cincinnati Enquirer, 312 Elm Street, Cincinnati OH 45202. **Tel** (513)721-2700, (800)876-4500. **5727**

CIRCOLAZIONE STRADALE. (IT/1120-4141). Egaf Edizioni SAS, Via F Guarini 2, 47100 Forli Italy. **Tel** 011 39 543 782278, FAX 011 39 543 782255. **5379**

CIRCULAR - CENTRAL BUREAU FOR ASTRONOMICAL TELEGRAMS, INTERNATIONAL ASTRONOMICAL UNION. (US/0081-0304). Central Bureau for Astronomical Telegrams, Smith Astrophysical Observatory, 60 Garden Street, Cambridge MA 02138. **Tel** (617)495-7244, (617)495-7440, (617)495-7444. **394**

CIS INDEX TO PUBLICATIONS OF THE UNITED STATES CONGRESS. (US/0007-8514). Congressional Information Service Inc, 4520 East-West Highway, Suite 800, Bethesda MD 20814-3389. **Tel** (800)638-8380, (301)654-1550, FAX (301)654-4033, telex 292386 CIS UR. **4697**

CITY & STATE (CHICAGO, ILL.). (US/0885-940X). Crain Communications Inc., 1400 Woodbridge, Detroit MI 48207. **Tel** (313)446-6000, (800)992-9970. **4717**

CLASS/BRAND QTR$. (US/8756-1212). Leading National Advertisers Inc, 136 Madison Avenue, New York NY 10016. **Tel** (212)725-2700, (800)562-3282. **757**

CLEARINGHOUSE REVIEW. (US/0009-868X). National Clearinghouse for Legal Services, 205 West Monroe Street 2nd Floor, Chicago IL 60606. **Tel** (312)263-3830. **3179**

CLIMATE DYNAMICS. (GW/0930-7575). Springer-Verlag GmbH & Company KG, Heidelberger Platz 3, D 14197 Berlin Germany. **Tel** 011 49 30 8207223, FAX 011 49 30 8214091, telex 183 319 SPBLN D. **1421**

CLINICAL DIABETES. (US/0891-8929). American Diabetes Association, National Service Center, 1660 Duke Street, Alexandria VA 22314. **Tel** (703)549-1500, (800)232-3472, FAX (703)836-2464. **3726**

CLUB MANAGEMENT. (US/0009-9589). Finan Publishing Company, 8730 Big Bend Boulevard, St Louis MO 63119. **Tel** (314)961-6644. **5230**

CMA : THE MANAGEMENT ACCOUNTING MAGAZINE. (CN/0831-3881). Society of Management Accountants of Canada, 120 King Street West, Suite 850, Hamilton Ontario L8N 3C3 Canada. **Tel** (416)525-4100, FAX (416)525-4533. **741**

COAL ABSTRACTS. (UK/0309-4979). IEA Coal Research, 10-18 Putney Hill, Gemini House, London SW15 6AA England. **Tel** 011 44 81 780 2111, FAX 011 44 81 780 1746, telex 917624. **1961**

COAL & SYNFUELS TECHNOLOGY. (US/0883-9735). Pasha Publications Inc., 1616 North Fort Myer Drive, Suite 1000, Arlington VA 22209. **Tel** (800)424-2908, (703)528-1244, FAX (703)528-3742, (703)528-1253. **1023**

COAL OUTLOOK. (US/0162-2714). Pasha Publications Inc., 1616 North Fort Myer Drive, Suite 1000, Arlington VA 22209. **Tel** (800)424-2908, (703)528-1244, FAX (703)528-3742, (703)528-1253. **1935**

COAL WEEK. (US/0149-578X). McGraw Hill Publishing Company, Inc., 1221 Avenue of the Americas, New York NY 10020. **Tel** (212)512-6410, (800)525-5003, FAX (212)512-6111. **2137**

COAL WEEK INTERNATIONAL. (US/0272-0205). McGraw Hill Publishing Company, Inc., 1221 Avenue of the Americas, New York NY 10020. **Tel** (212)512-6410, (800)525-5003, FAX (212)512-6111. **1439**

COAST BUSINESS. (US/1060-3417). Coast Business, Markham Hotel Building, Suite 900, Gulfport MS 39501. **657**

COLE PAPERS, THE. (US/1062-6727). Cole Group, 2590 Greenwich, Suite 9, San Francisco CA 94123. **Tel** (415)673-2424, FAX (415)673-2449. **2918**

COLLEGE BROADCASTER. (US/1055-0461). National Association of College Broadcast, 71 George Street, Providence RI 02912. **Tel** (401)863-2225, FAX (401)863-2221. **1130**

COLORADO BUSINESS MAGAZINE : CBM. (US/0898-6363). Wiesner Publishing, 7009 South Potomac Street, Englewood CO 80112. **Tel** (303)397-7600, (800)945-0973, FAX (303)397-7619. **658**

COLORADO HIGH TECHNOLOGY DIRECTORY. (US/0883-8208). Leading Edge Communications, 1121 Old Siskiyou Highway, Ashland OR 97520. **Tel** (503)482-4990. **5095**

COLUMBIA JOURNAL OF WORLD BUSINESS, THE. (US/0022-5428). JAI Press Inc., 55 Old Post Road, Suite 2, PO Box 1678, Greenwich CT 06836-1678. **Tel** (203)661-7602, FAX (203)661-0792. **658**

COLUMBUS DISPATCH, THE. (US). Dispatch Printing Company, 34 South Third Street, Columbus OH 43215. **Tel** (614)461-5000. **5727**

COMMERCE BUSINESS DAILY. (US/0095-3423). US Department of Commerce, 14th Street & Constitution Avenue NW, Washington DC 20230. **Tel** (202)482-2000, FAX (202)482-3772. **949**

COMMERCIAL AIRCRAFT FLEETS. (US/0270-5249). Avmark Inc / Montana, Lewis & Clark Trail, Lolo MT 59847. **Tel** (406)273-2580, FAX (406)273-6779. **16**

COMMERCIAL BANKING PRODUCTS SURVEY. BUSINESS CHEQUE ACCOUNTS. (AT/1038-6505). Horan Wall & Walker Pty Ltd, 15-19 Prospect Street, POB 8, Surry Hills New South Wales 2010 Australia. **Tel** 02 331 6600, FAX 02 380 5533. **783**

COMMERCIAL BANKING PRODUCTS SURVEY. COMMERCIAL LOANS. (AT/1038-6491). Horan Wall & Walker Pty Ltd, 15-19 Prospect Street, POB 8, Surry Hills New South Wales 2010 Australia. **Tel** 02 331 6600, FAX 02 380 5533. **783**

COMMERCIAL LENDING NEWSLETTER. (US). Robert Morris Associates, One Liberty Plaza, 1650 Market Street, Philadelphia PA 19103. **Tel** (215)851-9118, (215)851-0585, FAX (215)851-9206. **783**

COMMERCIAL LENDING REVIEW. (US/0886-8204). Institutional Investor Inc., 488 Madison Avenue, New York NY 10022. **Tel** (212)303-3234, (212)303-3233, FAX (212)303-3353. **783**

COMMLAW CONSPECTUS. (US/1068-5871). Columbus School of Law, Catholic University of America, Washington DC 20064. **Tel** (202)319-5144. **2953**

COMMON CARRIER WEEK. (US/0743-4812). Warren Publishing, Inc., 2115 Ward Court NW, Washington DC 20037. **Tel** (202)872-9200, FAX (202)293-3435. **1151**

COMMON CAUSE MAGAZINE. (US/0884-6537). Common Cause, PO Box 220, Washington DC 20044. **Tel** (202)736-5790. **4469**

Serials Online Index

COMMONWEAL. (US/0010-3330). Commonweal, 15 Dutch Street, 5th Floor, New York NY 10038. **Tel** (212)732-0800. **2531**

COMMUNICATION TECHNOLOGY IMPACT. (UK/0142-5854). Elsevier Science Publishers Ltd, Crown House, Linton Road, Barking Essex IG11 8JU England. **Tel** 011 44 81 5947272, FAX 081-594-5942, telex 896950. **1152**

COMMUNICATION WORLD (SAN FRANCISCO, CALIF.). (US/0744-7612). International Association of Business Communicators, One Hallidie Plaza, Suite 600, San Francisco CA 94102. **Tel** (415)433-3400, FAX (415)362-8762. **1107**

COMMUNICATIONS DAILY. (US/0277-0679). Warren Publishing, Inc., 2115 Ward Court NW, Washington DC 20037. **Tel** (202)872-9200, FAX (202)293-3435. **1152**

COMMUNICATIONS INTERNATIONAL. (UK/0305-2109). EMAP Readerlink, Audit House, 260 Field End Road, Ruislip Middlesex HA4 9LT England. **Tel** 011 44 081 868 4499, FAX 011 44 081 429 3117. **1152**

COMMUNICATIONS NEWS (GENEVA, ILL.). (US/0010-3632). Nelson Publishing, 2504 North Tamiami Trail, Nokomis FL 34275. **Tel** (813)966-9521, FAX (813)966-2590. **1108**

COMMUNICATIONS OF THE ACM. (US/0001-0782). ACM Association for Computing Machinery, 1515 Broadway, 17th Floor, New York NY 10036. **Tel** (212)869-7440, FAX (212)869-0481. **1175**

COMMUNICATIONSWEEK INTERNATIONAL. (US/1042-6086). CMP Publications Inc., c/o B. Werner, One Jericho Plaza, Wing A, 2nd Floor, Jericho NY 11753. **Tel** (516)733-6700. **1108**

COMMUNICATIONSWEEK (MANHASSET, N.Y.). (US/0746-8121). CMP Publications Inc., c/o B. Werner, One Jericho Plaza, Wing A, 2nd Floor, Jericho NY 11753. **Tel** (516)733-6700. **1152**

COMMUNITY PHARMACY LONDON. (UK/0960-376X). Benn Publications Ltd., Sovereign Way, Tonbridge TNQ 1RW England. **Tel** 011 44 732 364422, FAX 011 44 732 361534, telex 0732 95132 BENTON G. **4297**

COMMUTER AIR INTERNATIONAL. (US/1054-7436). Argus Business, 6151 Powers Ferry Road, Atlanta GA 30339. **Tel** (404)995-2500, (800)233-3359. **5380**

COMPANIES AND THEIR BRANDS. (US/1047-6393). Gale Research Inc., 835 Penobscot Building, 645 Griswold Street, Detroit MI 48226. **Tel** (800)877-GALE, (313)961-2242, FAX (313)961-6083, (800)414-5043, telex TWX 810-221-7086. **1303**

COMPANIES HOUSE DIRECTORY OF COMPANIES. MICROFICHE. (UK). Companies House Directory Services, Rm G.16, Crown Way, Cardiff CF2 3UZ Wales. **Tel** 0222 380142, FAX 0222 380679. **658**

COMPENDEX PLUS. (US/1063-8709). Dialog Information Services, 3460 Hillview Avenue, Palo Alto CA 94304. **Tel** (415)858-4240, (800)334-2564. **2003**

COMPENSATION AND BENEFITS REVIEW. (US/0886-3687). American Management Association, 135 West 50th Street, New York NY 10020-1201. **Tel** (212)586-8100, (212)903-8375 (periodicals), FAX (212)903-8168, (212)903-8083 (periodicals). **1660**

COMPILATION OF STATE AND FEDERAL PRIVACY LAWS. (US/0882-9136). Privacy Journal, PO Box 28577, Providence RI 02908. **Tel** (401)274-7861. **2954**

COMPLETE DIRECTORY OF LARGE PRINT BOOKS & SERIALS, THE. (US/0000-1120). R R Bowker, A Reed Reference Publishing Company, Part of Reed International PLC, PO Box 31, 121 Chanlon Drive, New Providence NJ 07974. **Tel** (908)464-6800, (800)521-8110, FAX (908)665-6688, telex 138-755. **4828**

COMPLIANCE ENGINEERING. (US/0898-3577). Compliance Engineering, 629 Massachusetts Avenue, Boxborough MA 01719. **Tel** (508)264-4208, FAX (508)635-9407. **1152**

COMPOSITES & ADHESIVES NEWSLETTER, THE. (US/0888-1227). T/C Press, PO Box 36006, Los Angeles CA 90036-0006. **Tel** (213)938-6923, FAX (213)938-6923. **1023**

COMPOSITES INDUSTRY MONTHLY. (US/1058-904X). Composite Market Reports Inc., 7670 Opportunity Road, Suite 250, San Diego CA 92111. **Tel** (619)560-1085. **1969**

COMPUMATH CITATION INDEX : CMCI. (US/0730-6199). Institute for Scientific Information, 3501 Market Street, Philadelphia PA 19104. **Tel** (215)386-0100, (800)523-1850, FAX (215)386-6362, telex 84-5305. **3542**

COMPUTE (GREENSBORO). (US/0194-357X). General Media Publishing Company, 1965 Broadway, New York NY 10023. **Tel** (212)496-6100. **1266**

COMPUTER-AIDED ENGINEERING. (US/0733-3536). Penton Publishing, 1100 Superior Avenue, Cleveland OH 44114-2543. **Tel** (216)696-7000, FAX (216)696-0836. **1228**

COMPUTER AIDED SELLING. (US/8756-8780). Denali Group Inc, 2815 NW Pine Cone Drive/Suite 100, Issaquah WA 98027. **Tel** (206)392-3514, FAX (206)391-7982. **659**

COMPUTER & CONTROL ABSTRACTS. (UK/0036-8113). Institution of Electrical Engineers / IEE, Michael Faraday House, Six Hills Way, Stevenage Herts SG1 2AY UK. **Tel** 011 44 438 313311, FAX 011 44 438 742840, telex 825578 IEESTV G. **1208**

COMPUTER AND INFORMATION SYSTEMS ABSTRACTS JOURNAL. (US/0191-9776). Cambridge Scientific Abstracts, 7200 Wisconsin Avenue, #601, Bethesda MD 20814-4823. **Tel** (301)961-6750, (800)843-7751, FAX (301)961-6720. **1208**

COMPUTER ASAP [ONLINE DATABASE]. (US). Information Access Company, 362 Lakeside Drive, Foster City CA 94404. **Tel** (800)227-8431. **1208**

COMPUTER AUDIT UPDATE. (UK/0960-2593). Elsevier Advanced Technology, An Imprint of Elsevier Science Ltd., The Boulevard, Langford Lane, Kidlington, Oxford OX5 1GB United Kingdom. **Tel** 011 44 865 843000, 011 44 865 843699, FAX 011 44 865 843010. **1256**

COMPUTER CONFERENCE ANALYSIS NEWSLETTER, THE. (US/1071-2216). Guidelines / Pennsylvania, 2512 Deep Creek Road, Perkiomenville PA 18074. **Tel** (215)234-4449. **1236**

COMPUTER DATABASE [ONLINE DATABASE]. (US). Information Access Company, 362 Lakeside Drive, Foster City CA 94404. **Tel** (800)227-8431. **1208**

COMPUTER DEALER NEWS (1990). (CN/1184-2369). Plesman Publications Ltd, 2005 Sheppard Avenue East, 4th Floor, Willowdale Ontario M2J 5B1 Canada. **Tel** (416)497-9562, FAX (416)497-9427, telex 06-986125. **1236**

COMPUTER DESIGN (WINCHESTER). (US/0010-4566). PennWell Publishing Company, 1421 South Sheridan, PO Box 1260, Tulsa OK 74101. **Tel** (918)835-3161, (800)331-4463, FAX (918)831-9497. **1176**

COMPUTER GRAPHICS WORLD. (US/0271-4159). PennWell Publishing Company, 1421 South Sheridan, PO Box 1260, Tulsa OK 74101. **Tel** (918)835-3161, (800)331-4463, FAX (918)831-9497. **1232**

COMPUTER LANGUAGE. (US/0749-2839). Miller Freeman Inc., 600 Harrison Street, San Francisco CA 94107. **Tel** (415)905-2337, FAX (415)905-2240, telex 278273. **1218**

COMPUTER PICTURES. (US/0883-5683). Knowledge Industry Publications Inc, 701 Westchester Avenue, White Plains NY 10604. **Tel** (914)328-9157, (800)800-5474, FAX (914)328-9093. **1232**

COMPUTER PROTOCOLS. (US/0899-126X). WV Publishing Company, PO Box 138, Babson Park, Boston MA 02157. **1177**

COMPUTER REPORT & THE PC STREET PRICE INDEX. (US/1063-8369). Metro Computing, PO Box 1430, Cherry Hill NJ 08034. **Tel** (609)784-8866, FAX (609)784-9814. **1246**

COMPUTER RESELLER NEWS. (US/0893-8377). CMP Publications Inc., c/o B. Werner, One Jericho Plaza, Wing A, 2nd Floor, Jericho NY 11753. **Tel** (516)733-6700. **1244**

COMPUTER RETAIL WEEK. (US/1066-7598). CMP Publications Inc., c/o B. Werner, One Jericho Plaza, Wing A, 2nd Floor, Jericho NY 11753. **Tel** (516)733-6700. **1244**

COMPUTER SCIENCE SYLLABUS. (US/1065-2078). Syllabus Press, 1307 South Mary Avenue, Suite 218, Sunnydale CA 94087-0716. **Tel** (408)773-0670, FAX (408)746-2711. **1177**

COMPUTER SECURITY JOURNAL. (US/0277-0865). Miller Freeman Inc., 600 Harrison Street, San Francisco CA 94107. **Tel** (415)905-2337, FAX (415)905-2240, telex 278273. **1226**

COMPUTER SHOPPER. (US/0886-0556). Ziff-Davis, One Park Avenue, 5th Floor, New York NY 10016. **Tel** (212)503-3500, (609)786-8230. **1244**

COMPUTER + SOFTWARE NEWS. (US/0745-5291). Lebhar Friedman Inc., 3922 Coconut Palm Drive, Tampa FL 33619. **Tel** (800)927-9292, (813)664-6707. **1245**

COMPUTER TALK. (UK). Reed Business Publishing / West Sussex, England, Perrymount Road, Haywards Heath, West Sussex RH16 3DH England. **Tel** 011 44 81 6523500. **1178**

COMPUTER WEEKLY. (UK/0010-4787). Reed Business Publishing / West Sussex, England, Perrymount Road, Haywards Heath, West Sussex RH16 3DH England. **Tel** 011 44 81 6523500. **1178**

COMPUTER WORKSTATIONS. (US/0899-9783). WV Publishing Company, PO Box 138, Babson Park, Boston MA 02157. **1241**

COMPUTERS IN HEALTHCARE. (US/0745-1075). Argus Business, 6151 Powers Ferry Road, Atlanta GA 30339. **Tel** (404)995-2500, (800)233-3359. **1179**

COMPUTERS IN LIBRARIES. (US/1041-7915). Mecklermedia Corporation, 11 Ferry Lane West, Westport CT 06880. **Tel** (203)226-6967, (800)632-5537, FAX (203)454-5840. **3203**

COMPUTERWORLD. (US/0010-4841). CW Communications, 375 Cochituate Road, Box 9171, Framingham MA 01701. **Tel** (508)879-0700. **1236**

COMPUTING CANADA. (CN/0319-0161). Plesman Publications Ltd, 2005 Sheppard Avenue East, 4th Floor, Willowdale Ontario M2J 5B1 Canada. **Tel** (416)497-9562, FAX (416)497-9427, telex 06-986125. **1257**

CONCRETE PRODUCTS (1975). (US/0010-5368). MacLean Hunter Publishing Corporation / Chicago, IL, 29 North Wacker Drive, Chicago IL 60606-3298. **Tel** (312)726-2802, FAX (312)726-3091. **608**

CONFERENCE PAPERS ANNUAL INDEX. (US/0194-0546). Cambridge Scientific Abstracts, 7200 Wisconsin Avenue, #601, Bethesda MD 20814-4823. **Tel** (301)961-6750, (800)843-7751, FAX (301)961-6720. **5096**

CONFERENCE PAPERS INDEX. (US/0162-704X). Cambridge Scientific Abstracts, 7200 Wisconsin Avenue, #601, Bethesda MD 20814-4823. **Tel** (301)961-6750, (800)843-7751, FAX (301)961-6720. **5096**

CONFIDENTIAL REPORT FOR ATTORNEYS. (US/0890-3034). Neubauer & Association Inc., PO Box 1476, Oceanside CA 92051. **Tel** (619)721-3622, FAX (619)721-3683. **2955**

CONNECTICUT CPA QUARTERLY. (US/0884-2817). Connecticut Society of Certified Public Accountants, 179 Allyn Street, Hartford CT 06103. **Tel** (203)525-1153. **741**

CONSERLINE (WASHINGTON, D.C.). (US/1072-611X). OCLC Asia Pacific Services, 6565 Frantz Road, Dublin OH 43017. **Tel** (800)848-5878, (614)764-6394 or 6000, FAX (614)764-6096. **3204**

CONSOLIDATED RETURNS TAX REPORT. (US/1047-8949). Faulkner & Gray Inc., 11 Penn Plaza, 17th Floor, New York NY 10001. **Tel** (212)967-7000, (800)535-8403. **2955**

CONSTRUCTION EQUIPMENT (1970). (US/0192-3978). Cahners Publishing Company, 249 West 17th Street, New York NY 10011. **Tel** (212)645-0067, FAX (212)242-6987. **609**

CONSTRUCTION INDEX. (US/0892-2047). ArchiText, 410 South Michigan Avenue, Suite 1008, Chicago IL 60605. **Tel** (312)939-3202, FAX (312)939-1020. **632**

CONSTRUCTION NEWS (LITTLE ROCK). (US/0160-5607). Construction News / Little Rock, Arkansas, 10825 Financial Center Parkway 133, Little Rock AR 72211. **Tel** (501)376-1931. **610**

CONSTRUCTION REVIEW. (US/0010-6917). Superintendent of Documents, US Government Printing Office, Washington DC 20402. **Tel** (202)275-3328, FAX (202)786-2377. **610**

CONSTRUCTIONAL REVIEW. (AT/0010-695X). Cement and Concrete Association of Australia, PO Box 1889, 25 Berry Street, North Sydney New South Wales, 2059 Australia. **Tel** (02)923-1244, FAX 02 923 1925, telex 75575. **611**

CONSULTANT (HACKENSACK). (US/0010-7069). Cliggott Publishing Company, 55 Holly Hill Lane, Box 4010, Greenwich CT 06830. **Tel** (203)661-0600, (212)993-0440. **3568**

CONSULTANTS AND CONSULTING ORGANIZATIONS DIRECTORY. (US/0196-1292). Gale Research Inc., 835 Penobscot Building, 645 Griswold Street, Detroit MI 48226. **Tel** (800)877-GALE, (313)961-2242, FAX (313)961-6083, (800)414-5043, telex TWX 810-221-7086. **659**

CONSULTANTS NEWS. (US/0045-8201). Kennedy Publications, Templeton Road, Fitzwilliam NH 03447. **Tel** (603)585-6544, (800)531-0007, FAX (603)585-9555. **659**

CONSUMER REPORTS. (US/0010-7174). Consumers Union, 101 Truman Avenue, Yonkers NY 10703. **Tel** (800)288-7898, (914)378-2000, FAX (914)378-2900. **1295**

CONSUMER REPORTS HEALTH LETTER. (US/1044-3193). Consumer Reports Health Letter, 101 Truman Avenue, Yonkers NY 80322-2148. **Tel** (800)288-7898. **4772**

CONSUMER REPORTS ON HEALTH. (US/1058-0832). Consumers Union, 101 Truman Avenue, Yonkers NY 10703. **Tel** (800)288-7898, (914)378-2000, FAX (914)378-2900. **1295**

CONSUMER REPORTS TRAVEL LETTER. (US/0887-8439). Consumers Union, 101 Truman Avenue, Yonkers NY 10703. **Tel** (800)288-7898, (914)378-2000, FAX (914)378-2900. **1295**

CONSUMERS DIGEST (CHICAGO, ILL.). (US/0010-7182). Consumers Digest, 5705 North Lincoln Avenue, Chicago IL 60659. **Tel** (312)275-3590, FAX (312)275-7273. **1296**

CONSUMERS INDEX TO PRODUCT EVALUATIONS AND INFORMATION SOURCES. (US/0094-0534). Pierian Press, PO Box 1808, Ann Arbor MI 48106. **Tel** (313)434-5530, (800)678-2435, FAX (313)434-6409. **1300**

CONSUMERS' RESEARCH MAGAZINE. (US/0095-2222). Consumers Research Magazine, 800 Maryland Avenue Northeast, Washington DC 20002. **Tel** (202)546-1713. **1296**

CONTACT - ASSOCIATION DE SPINA-BIFIDA ET D'HYDROCEPHALIE DU QUEBEC. (CN/1195-6925). Spinda-Bifida Association of Quebec, 5757 Avenue of Decelles, Suite 425, Montreal Quebec H3S 2C3 Canada. **Tel** (514)340-9019, FAX (514)340-9109. **4335**

CONTAINER NEWS. (US/0010-7360). Argus Business, 6151 Powers Ferry Road, Atlanta GA 30339. **Tel** (404)995-2500, (800)233-3359. **5380**

CONTEMPORARY BLACK BIOGRAPHY. (US/1058-1316). Gale Research Inc., 835 Penobscot Building, 645 Griswold Street, Detroit MI 48226. **Tel** (800)877-GALE, (313)961-2242, FAX (313)961-6083, (800)414-5043, telex TWX 810-221-7086. **2259**

CONTEMPORARY MUSICIANS. (US/1044-2197). Gale Research Inc., 835 Penobscot Building, 645 Griswold Street, Detroit MI 48226. **Tel** (800)877-GALE, (313)961-2242, FAX (313)961-6083, (800)414-5043, telex TWX 810-221-7086. **4111**

CONTINUOUS IMPROVEMENT. (US/1071-2240). Solutions Specialists, 8460 Dygert Drive, Alto MI 49302. **Tel** (616)891-9114, FAX (616)891-9114. **3477**

CONTRACTING INTELLIGENCE. (US/1041-7427). Jane's Information Group, Sentinel House, 163 Brighton Road, Coulsdon Surrey CR3 2NX England. **Tel** 011 44 81 763 1030, FAX 011 44 81 763 1006. **4640**

CONTROL & INSTRUMENTATION. (UK/0010-8022). Morgan Grampian, 40 Beresford Street Woolwich, London SE18 6BQ England. **Tel** 011 44 81 855 7777, FAX 011 44 81 855 5548, telex 896238. **1219**

CONVENIENCE STORE. (UK). William Reed Ltd, Broadfield Park, Crawley, West Sussex RH11 9RJ England. **Tel** 011 44 293 613400, FAX 0293-613156. **953**

COOK COUNTY JURY VERDICT REPORTER. (US). Cook County Jury Verdict, 415 North State Street, Chicago IL 60610. **Tel** (312)644-7800. **3089**

CORBEL FORMS MANUAL. (US). Corbel & Company, 1660 Prudential Drive, Jacksonville FL 32207. **Tel** (904)399-5888, FAX (904)399-5551. **5178**

CORNELL HOTEL AND RESTAURANT ADMINISTRATION QUARTERLY, THE. (US/0010-8804). Elsevier Science Publishing Company Inc, Madison Square Station, PO Box 882, New York NY 10159-0882. **Tel** (212)633-3950, FAX (212)633-3990. **2804**

CORPORATE BOARD, THE. (US/0746-8652). Vanguard Publications, 6604 West Saginaw Highway, Lansing MI 48917. **Tel** (517)321-0667, FAX (517)321-1015. **661**

CORPORATE CLEVELAND. (US/1055-5978). Business Journal Publishing Company, 1720 Euclid Avenue, Third Floor, Cleveland OH 44115. **Tel** (216)621-1644. **661**

CORPORATE CONTROLLER. (US/0899-0174). Faulkner & Gray Inc., 11 Penn Plaza, 17th Floor, New York NY 10001. **Tel** (212)967-7000, (800)535-8403. **661**

CORPORATE DETROIT. (US/1062-368X). Corporate Detroit, 3031 West Grand Boulevard, Suite 624, Detroit MI 48202. **Tel** (313)872-6000. **661**

CORPORATE EFT REPORT. (US/0272-0299). Phillips Business Information, Inc., 1201 Seven Locks Road, Potomac MD 20854. **Tel** (301)424-3338, (800)777-5006, FAX (301)309-3847. **784**

CORPORATE GROWTH REPORT, THE. (US/1050-320X). Quality Services Company, 5290 Overpass Road, Santa Barbara CA 93111. **Tel** (805)964-7841, FAX (805)964-1073. **661**

CORPORATE JOBS OUTLOOK!. (US/0892-5232). Corporate Jobs Outlook, PO Box 100, Boerne TX 78006-0100. **Tel** (210)755-8810, FAX (210)755-2410. **4203**

CORPORATE LEGAL TIMES. (US). Giant Steps Publishing Corporation, 222 Merchandise Mart Plaza, Suite 1513, Chicago IL 60654. **Tel** (312)644-4378. **3099**

CORPORATE REPORT MINNESOTA. (US/0279-5299). MCP Inc., 5500 Wayzata Boulevard/Suite 800, Minneapolis MN 55416. **Tel** (612)591-2700, FAX (612)591-2639. **662**

CORPORATE REPORT WISCONSIN. (US/0890-4278). Corporate Report Wisconsin, PO Box 878, Menommomee Falls WI 53052. **Tel** (414) 255-9077, FAX (414)255-3388. **662**

CORPORATE TAXATION. (US/0898-798X). Faulkner & Gray Inc., 11 Penn Plaza, 17th Floor, New York NY 10001. **Tel** (212)967-7000, (800)535-8403. **785**

CORPORATE TECHNOLOGY DIRECTORY. (US/0887-1930). Corporate Technology Information Services Inc, 12 Alfred Street, Suite 200, Woburn MA 01801-9998. **Tel** (617)932-3939, (800)333-8036, FAX (617)932-6335, telex 497-2961 CRPTECH. **3477**

COSMETIC INSIDER'S REPORT. (US/0275-4681). Advanstar Communications Inc., 131 West First Street, Duluth MN 55802. **Tel** (218)723-9477, (800)346-0085. **403**

COSMETIC WORLD NEWS. (UK/0305-0319). Cosmetic World News, 130 Wigmore Street, London W1H 0AT England. **Tel** 011 44 71 4866757, FAX 011 44 71 4875436. **403**

COSMETICS AND TOILETRIES. (US/0361-4387). Allured Publishing Corporation, 362 South Schmale Road, Carol Stream IL 60188-2787. **Tel** (708)653-2155, FAX (708)653-2192. **403**

COSMETICS & TOILETRIES & HOUSEHOLD PRODUCTS MARKETING NEWS IN JAPAN. (JA). Pacific Research Consulting, 18 2 Shikahama 4 Chome, Adachi Ku Tokyo 123 Japan. **Tel** 011 81 3 3899 9953. **403**

COSMETICS AND TOILETRIES MANUFACTURERS AND SUPPLIERS. (UK). Morgan Grampian, 40 Beresford Street Woolwich, London SE18 6BQ England. **Tel** 011 44 81 855 7777, FAX 011 44 81 855 5548, telex 896238. **403**

COSMETICS INTERNATIONAL. (UK). Cosmetics Communications Ltd, 162/168 Regent Street, 332 Linen Hl, London W1R 5TB England. **Tel** 011 44 71 434 1530, FAX 071 4370915, telex 262433 3441. **403**

COSMIC SOFTWARE CATALOG. (US/1043-9935). COSMIC/The University of Georgia, 382 East Broad Street, Athens GA 30602. **Tel** (706)542-3265, FAX (706)542-4807. **1228**

COSMOPOLITAN (1952). (US/0010-9541). The Hearst Corporation, 250 West 55th Street, New York NY 10019. **Tel** (212)649-4014. **5554**

COST ENGINEERING (MORGANTOWN. 1980). (US/0274-9696). American Association of Cost Engineers, PO Box 1557, Morgantown WV 26507. **Tel** (304)296-8444, (800)858-2678, FAX (304)291-5728, telex 887612 AACE MORG UD. **1969**

COTTON AND TROPICAL FIBRES ABSTRACTS BIBLIOGRAPHY. (UK). CAB International Centre, Wallingford, Oxon OX10 8DE United Kingdom. **Tel** 44 491 832111, FAX 44 491 833508, telex 847964 (COMAGG G). **152**

COTTON, WORLD MARKETS & TRADE / UNITED STATES DEPARTMENT OF AGRICULTURE, FOREIGN AGRICULTURAL SERVICE. (US). US Department of Agriculture / Foreign Agricultural Service, 14th Street & Independence Avenue Southwest, Washington DC 20250. **Tel** (202)720-9445, FAX (202)720-7729. **77**

COUNTRY PROFILE. SENEGAL/ THE ECONOMIST INTELLIGENCE UNIT. (UK). The Economist Intelligence Unit, 40 Duke Street, London W1A 1DW England. **Tel** 011 44 71 8301000. **1553**

COUNTRY PROFILE. THE GAMBIA, GUINEA-BISSAU, CAPE VERDE. (UK/0968-2422). The Economist Intelligence Unit, 40 Duke Street, London W1A 1DW England. **Tel** 011 44 71 8301000. **1554**

COUNTY BUSINESS PATTERNS [COMPUTER FILE]. (US). US Department of Commerce / Bureau of the Census, Data User Services Division, Customer Services, Washington DC 20233-0800. **Tel** (301)763-4100. **1554**

COURIER NEWS. (US/0746-9527). Blytheville Courier News, Box 1108, Blytheville AR 72316-1108. **Tel** (501)763-4461, FAX (501)763-6874. **5631**

COURIER PLUS. (US). University Microfilms International, 300 North Zeeb Road, Ann Arbor MI 48106-1346. **Tel** (313)761-4700, (800)521-0600 Exts. 2490, 2491, FAX (313)973-1540. **1924**

CPCU JOURNAL. (US/0162-2706). Society of Chartered Property and Casual Underwriters, Kahler Hall, Providence Road CB#9, Malvern PA 19355. **Tel** (215)251-2743. **2878**

CPI PURCHASING. (US/0746-9012). Cahners Publishing Company, 249 West 17th Street, New York NY 10011. **Tel** (212)645-0067, FAX (212)242-6987. **1023**

CRAIN'S CHICAGO BUSINESS. (US/0149-6956). Crain Communications Inc., 1400 Woodbridge, Detroit MI 48207. **Tel** (313)446-6000, (800)992-9970. **662**

CRAIN'S CLEVELAND BUSINESS. (US/0197-2375). Crain Communications Inc., 1400 Woodbridge, Detroit MI 48207. **Tel** (313)446-6000, (800)992-9970. **663**

CRAIN'S DETROIT BUSINESS. (US/0882-1992). Crain Communications Inc., 1400 Woodbridge, Detroit MI 48207. **Tel** (313)446-6000, (800)992-9970. **663**

CRAIN'S NEW YORK BUSINESS. (US/8756-789X). Crain Communications Inc., 1400 Woodbridge, Detroit MI 48207. **Tel** (313)446-6000, (800)992-9970. **1478**

CREATIVE REVIEW (LONDON, ENGLAND). (UK). Centaur Communications Ltd., St Giles House, 50 Poland Street, London W1V 4AX England. **Tel** 011 44 71 439 4222, FAX 011 44 71 734 6748, telex 261352. **922**

CREATIVITY. (US/0097-6075). Art Direction Book Company, 10 East 39th Street/6th Floor, New York NY 10016. **Tel** (212)889-6500. **758**

CREDIT CARD MANAGEMENT. (US/0896-9329). Faulkner & Gray Inc., 11 Penn Plaza, 17th Floor, New York NY 10001. **Tel** (212)967-7000, (800)535-8403. **785**

CREDIT CARD MANAGEMENT EUROPE. (US). Faulkner & Gray Inc., 11 Penn Plaza, 17th Floor, New York NY 10001. **Tel** (212)967-7000, (800)535-8403. **785**

CREDIT CARD NEWS. (US). Faulkner & Gray Inc., 11 Penn Plaza, 17th Floor, New York NY 10001. **Tel** (212)967-7000, (800)535-8403. **785**

CREDIT RISK MANAGEMENT REPORT. (US/1054-5069). Phillips Business Information, Inc., 1201 Seven Locks Road, Potomac MD 20854. **Tel** (301)424-3338, (800)777-5006, FAX (301)309-3847. **785**

CREDIT UNION EXECUTIVE (MADISON, WIS. 1989). (US/1053-6744). Credit Union National Association, PO Box 431, Madison WI 53701. **Tel** (608)231-4088, (800)356-9655, FAX (608)231-4370. **786**

CREDIT WORLD, THE. (US/0011-1074). International Credit Association, PO Box 27357, St Louis MO 63141. **Tel** (314)991-3030, FAX (314)991-3029. **786**

CRIMINAL JUSTICE ABSTRACTS. (US/0146-9177). Willow Tree Press, PO Box 249, Monsey NY 10952. **Tel** (914)354-9139, FAX (914)362-8376. **3080**

CRIMINAL LAW FORUM. (US/1046-8374). Rutgers University School of Law, 5th and Penn Streets, Camden NJ 08102. **Tel** (609)964-9101, FAX (609)757-6487. **3106**

CROP PHYSIOLOGY ABSTRACTS. (UK/0306-7556). CAB International Centre, Wallingford, Oxon OX10 8DE United Kingdom. **Tel** 44 491 832111, FAX 44 491 833508, telex 847964 (COMAGG G). **152**

CROSSE CITY BUSINESS, LA. (US). **663**

CRSP DAILY EXCESS RETURNS FILE. (US/1052-3456). University of Chicago CRSP, 1101 East 58th Street, Graduate School of Business, Chicago IL 60637. **895**

CSA NEUROSCIENCES ABSTRACTS. (US/0141-7711). Cambridge Scientific Abstracts, 7200 Wisconsin Avenue, #601, Bethesda MD 20814-4823. **Tel** (301)961-6750, (800)843-7751, FAX (301)961-6720. **3656**

CSD BULLETIN. (SA). Center for Science & Development, PO Box 270, 0001 Pretoria South Africa. **Tel** 011 27 12 2022724, FAX 011 27 12 2022892. **5197**

CTDNEWS (PHILADELPHIA, PA.). (US/1062-6743). CTDnews Inc., PO Box 239, 410 Lancaster Avenue, Haverford PA 19041. **Tel** (610)896-2770, FAX (800)554-4283. **3569**

CUMULATIVE BOOK INDEX. CD-ROM. (US/0011-300X). H W Wilson Company, 950 University Avenue, Bronx NY 10452. **Tel** (800)367-6770, (718)588-8400, FAX (718)590-1617, telex 4990003 HWILSON. **3458**

CUMULATIVE BOOK INDEX, THE. (US/0011-300X). H W Wilson Company, 950 University Avenue, Bronx NY 10452. **Tel** (800)367-6770, (718)588-8400, FAX (718)590-1617, telex 4990003 HWILSON. **3458**

CUMULATIVE INDEX TO NURSING & ALLIED HEALTH LITERATURE. (US/0146-5554). CINAHL Information Systems, 1509 Wilson Terrace, Glendale CA 91209. **Tel** (818)409-8005. **3656**

CURRENCY CONFIDENTIAL. (UK/0141-1047). IBC Publishing, 57-61 Mortimer St., London W1N 7TD England. **Tel** 011 44 71 637 4383, FAX 011 44 71 636 6314. **786**

CURRENCY

Serials available Online

Serials Online Index

CURRENCY QUARTERLY. (UK). IBC Publishing, 57-61 Mortimer St., London W1N 7TD England. **Tel** 011 44 71 637 4383, FAX 011 44 71 636 6314. **786**

CURRENT ADVANCES IN PROTEIN BIOCHEMISTRY. (UK/0965-0504). Elsevier Geo Abstracts, An Imprint of Elsevier Science Ltd., The Boulevard, Langford Lane, Kidlington, Oxford OX5 1GB United Kingdom. **Tel** 011 44 865 843000, 011 44 865 843699, FAX 011 44 865 843010. **478**

CURRENT AIDS LITERATURE. (UK/0952-8075). CAB International Centre, Wallingford, Oxon OX10 8DE United Kingdom. **Tel** 44 491 832111, FAX 44 491 833508, telex 847964 (COMAGG G). **3668**

CURRENT AWARENESS IN BIOLOGICAL SCIENCES. (UK/0733-4443). Elsevier Geo Abstracts, An Imprint of Elsevier Science Ltd., The Boulevard, Langford Lane, Kidlington, Oxford OX5 1GB United Kingdom. **Tel** 011 44 865 843000, 011 44 865 843699, FAX 011 44 865 843010. **478**

CURRENT BIOTECHNOLOGY. (UK/0960-5037). Royal Society of Chemistry, Thomas Graham House, Science Park, Cambridge CB4 4WF England. **Tel** 011 44 223 420066, FAX 011 44 223 423429, telex 818293 ROYAL. **3656**

CURRENT BUSINESS REPORTS. ADVANCE MONTHLY RETAIL SALES. (US/0190-5988). US Department of Commerce / Bureau of the Census, Data User Services Division, Customer Services, Washington DC 20233-0800. **Tel** (301)763-4100. **953**

CURRENT CONTENTS. AGRICULTURE, BIOLOGY, & ENVIRONMENTAL SCIENCES. (US/0090-0508). Institute for Scientific Information, 3501 Market Street, Philadelphia PA 19104. **Tel** (215)386-0100, (800)523-1850, FAX (215)386-6362, telex 84-5305. **152**

CURRENT CONTENTS. AGRICULTURE, BIOLOGY & ENVIRONMENTAL SCIENCES (CD-ROM VERSION). (US/1073-1245). Institute for Scientific Information, 3501 Market Street, Philadelphia PA 19104. **Tel** (215)386-0100, (800)523-1850, FAX (215)386-6362, telex 84-5305. **152**

CURRENT CONTENTS. ARTS & HUMANITIES. (US/0163-3155). Institute for Scientific Information, 3501 Market Street, Philadelphia PA 19104. **Tel** (215)386-0100, (800)523-1850, FAX (215)386-6362, telex 84-5305. **334**

CURRENT CONTENTS. CLINICAL MEDICINE. (US/0891-3358). Institute for Scientific Information, 3501 Market Street, Philadelphia PA 19104. **Tel** (215)386-0100, (800)523-1850, FAX (215)386-6362, telex 84-5305. **3656**

CURRENT CONTENTS. CLINICAL MEDICINE (CD-ROM VERSION). (US/1073-1237). Institute for Scientific Information, 3501 Market Street, Philadelphia PA 19104. **Tel** (215)386-0100, (800)523-1850, FAX (215)386-6362, telex 84-5305. **3656**

CURRENT CONTENTS. ENGINEERING, TECHNOLOGY & APPLIED SCIENCES. (US/0095-7917). Institute for Scientific Information, 3501 Market Street, Philadelphia PA 19104. **Tel** (215)386-0100, (800)523-1850, FAX (215)386-6362, telex 84-5305. **2003**

CURRENT CONTENTS. LIFE SCIENCES. (US/0011-3409). Institute for Scientific Information, 3501 Market Street, Philadelphia PA 19104. **Tel** (215)386-0100, (800)523-1850, FAX (215)386-6362, telex 84-5305. **5174**

CURRENT CONTENTS. LIFE SCIENCES (CD-ROM VERSION). (US/1073-1229). Institute for Scientific Information, 3501 Market Street, Philadelphia PA 19104. **Tel** (215)386-0100, (800)523-1850, FAX (215)386-6362, telex 84-5305. **5174**

CURRENT CONTENTS ON DISKETTE. AGRICULTURE, BIOLOGY & ENVIRONMENTAL SCIENCES. (US/1062-3167). Institute for Scientific Information, 3501 Market Street, Philadelphia PA 19104. **Tel** (215)386-0100, (800)523-1850, FAX (215)386-6362, telex 84-5305. **152**

CURRENT CONTENTS ON DISKETTE. CLINICAL MEDICINE. (US/1062-3159). Institute for Scientific Information, 3501 Market Street, Philadelphia PA 19104. **Tel** (215)386-0100, (800)523-1850, FAX (215)386-6362, telex 84-5305. **3656**

CURRENT CONTENTS ON DISKETTE. LIFE SCIENCES. J600. (US/1062-3078). Institute for Scientific Information, 3501 Market Street, Philadelphia PA 19104. **Tel** (215)386-0100, (800)523-1850, FAX (215)386-6362, telex 84-5305. **5174**

CURRENT CONTENTS ON DISKETTE. LIFE SCIENCES. J1200. (US/1062-3027). Institute for Scientific Information, 3501 Market Street, Philadelphia PA 19104. **Tel** (215)386-0100, (800)523-1850, FAX (215)386-6362, telex 84-5305. **5174**

CURRENT CONTENTS ON DISKETTE. PHYSICAL, CHEMICAL & EARTH SCIENCES. (US/1062-1180). Institute for Scientific Information, 3501 Market Street, Philadelphia PA 19104. **Tel** (215)386-0100, (800)523-1850, FAX (215)386-6362, telex 84-5305. **1362**

CURRENT CONTENTS ON DISKETTE WITH ABSTRACTS. AGRICULTURE, BIOLOGY & ENVIRONMENTAL SCIENCES. (US/1062-3124). Institute for Scientific Information, 3501 Market Street, Philadelphia PA 19104. **Tel** (215)386-0100, (800)523-1850, FAX (215)386-6362, telex 84-5305. **152**

CURRENT CONTENTS ON DISKETTE WITH ABSTRACTS. CLINICAL MEDICINE. (US/1062-3116). Institute for Scientific Information, 3501 Market Street, Philadelphia PA 19104. **Tel** (215)386-0100, (800)523-1850, FAX (215)386-6362, telex 84-5305. **3656**

CURRENT CONTENTS ON DISKETTE WITH ABSTRACTS. LIFE SCIENCES. (US/1062-3108). Institute for Scientific Information, 3501 Market Street, Philadelphia PA 19104. **Tel** (215)386-0100, (800)523-1850, FAX (215)386-6362, telex 84-5305. **5174**

CURRENT CONTENTS ON DISKETTE WITH ABSTRACTS. PHYSICAL, CHEMICAL & EARTH SCIENCES. (US/1062-3094). Institute for Scientific Information, 3501 Market Street, Philadelphia PA 19104. **Tel** (215)386-0100, (800)523-1850, FAX (215)386-6362, telex 84-5305. **1362**

CURRENT CONTENTS. PHYSICAL, CHEMICAL & EARTH SCIENCES. (US/0163-2574). Institute for Scientific Information, 3501 Market Street, Philadelphia PA 19104. **Tel** (215)386-0100, (800)523-1850, FAX (215)386-6362, telex 84-5305. **1362**

CURRENT CONTENTS. PHYSICAL, CHEMICAL & EARTH SCIENCES (CD-ROM VERSION). (US/1073-1253). Institute for Scientific Information, 3501 Market Street, Philadelphia PA 19104. **Tel** (215)386-0100, (800)523-1850, FAX (215)386-6362, telex 84-5305. **1362**

CURRENT CONTENTS SEARCH. (US). Institute for Scientific Information, 3501 Market Street, Philadelphia PA 19104. **Tel** (215)386-0100, (800)523-1850, FAX (215)386-6362, telex 84-5305. **2487**

CURRENT CONTENTS. SOCIAL & BEHAVIORAL SCIENCES. (US/0092-6361). Institute for Scientific Information, 3501 Market Street, Philadelphia PA 19104. **Tel** (215)386-0100, (800)523-1850, FAX (215)386-6362, telex 84-5305. **5227**

CURRENT DIGEST OF THE POST-SOVIET PRESS, THE. (US/1067-7542). Current Digest of the Soviet Press, 3857 North High Street, Columbus OH 43214. **Tel** (614)292-4234, FAX (614)267-6310. **4502**

CURRENT DIGEST OF THE SOVIET PRESS, THE. (US/0011-3425). Current Digest of the Soviet Press, 3857 North High Street, Columbus OH 43214. **Tel** (614)292-4234, FAX (614)267-6310. **4470**

CURRENT HEALTH 2. (US/0163-156X). Weekly Reader Corporation, 3001 Cindel Drive, Delran NJ 08370. **Tel** (609)786-1000, (800)446-3355, FAX (609)786-3360. **4772**

CURRENT INDEX TO JOURNALS IN EDUCATION. (US/0011-3565). Oryx Press, 4041 North Central Avenue, #700, Phoenix AZ 85012-3397. **Tel** (800)279-ORYX, (602)265-2651, FAX (602)265-6250, (800)279-4663, (800)279-6799. **1794**

CURRENT INDEX TO STATISTICS. (US/0364-1228). Institute of Mathematical Statistics, 3401 Investment Boulevard, Suite 7, Hayward CA 94545-3819. **Tel** (510)783-8141, FAX (510)783-4131. **3542**

CURRENT OPINION IN CELL BIOLOGY. (US/0955-0674). Current Science, 20 North 3rd Street, Philadelphia PA 19106. **Tel** (215)574-2266, (800)552-5866, FAX (215)574-2270. **535**

CURRENT RESEARCH IN LIBRARY & INFORMATION SCIENCE. (UK/0263-9254). Bowker Saur Ltd., A Reed Reference Publishing Company, Part of Reed International PLC, 59-60 Grosvenor Street, London WIX 9DA England. **Tel** 011 44 71 4935841, FAX 011 44 71 4991590. **3205**

CURRENT TECHNOLOGY INDEX : CTI. (UK/0260-6593). Bowker Saur Ltd., A Reed Reference Publishing Company, Part of Reed International PLC, 59-60 Grosvenor Street, London WIX 9DA England. **Tel** 011 44 71 4935841, FAX 011 44 71 4991590. **5174**

CUSTOM BUILDER. (US/0895-2493). Willows Publishing Group, 38 Lafayette Street, PO Box 998, Yarmouth ME 04096-0998. **Tel** (207)846-0970, FAX (207)846-1561. **612**

CUSTOMS RECORD. (US/1063-7443). International Business Reports, PO Box 1009, Falls Church VA 22041. **Tel** (703)998-2927, FAX (703)998-0019. **3126**

CYPRUS REVIEW, THE. (CY/1015-2881). Intercollege, PO Box 4005, Nicosia, Cyprus. **Tel** 011-357-2-456892, 011-357-2-456813, 456208, FAX 011-357-2-456704, telex 4969 INTERCOL CY. **4471**

DACHAUER HEFTE. (GW/0257-9472). Dachauer Hefte, Alte Roemerstrasse 75, D 85221 Dachau Germany. **Tel** 011 49 8131 1741. **2685**

DAILY HAMPSHIRE GAZETTE. (US/0739-3504). H. S. Gere & Sons Inc, 115 Conz Street, Northampton MA 01060. **Tel** (413)584-5000, FAX (413)585-5222. **5688**

DAILY MAIL (LONDON, ENGLAND). (UK). Mail Newspapers, Carmelite House, London EC4Y 0JA England. **5812**

DAILY POST (LIVERPOOL, ENG. : 1978). (UK). The Liverpool Daily Post and Echo Ltd, PO Box 48 Old Hall Street, Liverpool L69 3EB England. **5812**

DAILY RATES UPDATE. (AT). Horan Wall & Walker Pty Ltd, 15-19 Prospect Street, POB 8, Surry Hills New South Wales 2010 Australia. **Tel** 02 331 6600, FAX 02 380 5533. **787**

DAILY RECORD (PARSIPPANY, N.J.). (US). Daily Record / Parsippany, 629 Parsippany Road, Parsippany NJ 07054. **Tel** (201)428-6200, FAX (201)428-7280. **5710**

DAIRY FOODS. (US/0888-0050). Cahners Publishing Company, 249 West 17th Street, New York NY 10011. **Tel** (212)645-0067, FAX (212)242-6987. **193**

DAIRY FOODS NEWSLETTER. (US/1057-2619). Cahners Publishing Company, 249 West 17th Street, New York NY 10011. **Tel** (212)645-0067, FAX (212)242-6987. **193**

DAIRY INDUSTRIES INTERNATIONAL. (UK/0308-8197). Wilmington Publishing Ltd., PO Box 200, Field End Road, Ruislip Middx HA4 OSY England. **Tel** 011 44 81 841 3970, FAX 011 44 81 841 9676. **193**

DAIRY SCIENCE ABSTRACTS. (UK/0011-5681). CAB International Centre, Wallingford, Oxon OX10 8DE United Kingdom. **Tel** 44 491 832111, FAX 44 491 833508, telex 847964 (COMAGG G). **153**

DALLAS BUSINESS JOURNAL. (US/0899-4129). Dallas Business Journal, 4131 North Central Expressway, Suite 310, Dallas TX 75204. **Tel** (214)520-1010, FAX (214)522-5606. **664**

DATA BASED ADVISOR. (US/0740-5200). Data Based Solutions Inc, 4010 Morena Boulevard, Suite 200, San Diego CA 92117. **Tel** (619)483-6400, (800)336-6060, FAX (619)483-9851. **1253**

DATA BROADCASTING REPORT. (US/0882-5726). Waters Information Services, PO Box 2248, Binghamton NY 13902-2248. **Tel** (607)770-8535, FAX (607)798-1692. **1131**

DATA CHANNELS. (US/0093-7290). Phillips Business Information, Inc., 1201 Seven Locks Road, Potomac MD 20854. **Tel** (301)424-3338, (800)777-5006, FAX (301)309-3847. **1257**

DATA COMMUNICATIONS. (US/0363-6399). McGraw Hill Publishing Company, Inc., 1221 Avenue of the Americas, New York NY 10020. **Tel** (212)512-6410, (800)525-5003, FAX (212)512-6111. **1241**

DATA INFORMER, THE. (US). Information USA, PO Box E, Kensington MD 20895. **Tel** (301)924-0556, (800)955-7693, FAX (301)946-3004. **3205**

DATA STORAGE REPORT. (NE). Jonas Press Publishing Company, 53 Park Belmont Place, San Jose CA 95136-2506. **Tel** (408)629-8249, FAX (408)629-8249. **1181**

DATABASE SEARCHER. (US/0891-6713). Mecklermedia Corporation, 11 Ferry Lane West, Westport CT 06880. **Tel** (203)226-6967, (800)632-5537, FAX (203)454-5840. **1253**

DATABASE (WESTON). (US/0162-4105). Online Inc., 462 Danbury Road, Wilton CT 06897. **Tel** (203)761-1466, (800)248-8466, FAX (203)761-1444. **1253**

DATALINK. (UK). VNU Business Publications BV, 32-34 Broadwick Street, London W1A 2HG England. **Tel** 011 44 71 439 4242 ext. 2222, FAX 011 44 71 437 9638, telex 23918 VNU G, 8952440. **664**

DATAMATION. (US/0011-6963). Cahners Publishing Company, 249 West 17th Street, New York NY 10011. **Tel** (212)645-0067, FAX (212)242-6987. **1258**

DATATRENDS REPORT ON DEC AND IBM, THE. (US). DataTrends Publications, 895 Harrison Street SE, Suite B, Leesburg VA 22075. **Tel** (703)779-0574, (800)766-8130, FAX (703)779-2267. **1181**

DAYTON DAILY NEWS (DAYTON, OHIO : 1987). (US/0897-0920). Dayton Newspapers Inc, 45 South Ludlow Street, Dayton OH 45402. **Tel** (513)225-2135. **5728**

DAYTON-SPRINGFIELD BUSINESS LIFE. (US). Ohio Communications Corp., 6159 Far Hills Avenue, Centreville OH 45459. **Tel** (513)435-7273. **664**

DBMS (REDWOOD CITY, CALIF.). (US/1041-5173). Miller Freeman Inc., 600 Harrison Street, San Francisco CA 94107. **Tel** (415)905-2337, FAX (415)905-2240, telex 278273. **1254**

DBS NEWS. (US/0733-9739). Phillips Business Information, Inc., 1201 Seven Locks Road, Potomac MD 20854. **Tel** (301)424-3338, (800)777-5006, FAX (301)309-3847. **1153**

DEALERSCOPE MERCHANDISING. (US/0888-4501). North American Publishing Company, 401 North Broad Street, Philadelphia PA 19108. **Tel** (215)238-5300, (800)777-8074, FAX (215)238-5283. **953**

DEALING WITH TECHNOLOGY. (UK). Waters Information Services, PO Box 2248, Binghamton NY 13902-2248. **Tel** (607)770-8535, FAX (607)798-1692. **5099**

DEALMAKERS (BELLE MEAD, N.J.), THE. (US/1055-0771). Dealmakers, PO Box 2630, Mercerville NJ 08690. **Tel** (609)587-6200, FAX (609)587-3511. **4836**

DEBATES AND PROCEEDINGS - LEGISLATIVE ASSEMBLY OF MANITOBA. (CN/0542-5492). Queens Printer Statutory Publishing, 200 Vaughn Street, Winnipeg Manitoba R3C 1T5 Canada. **Tel** (204)945-3102. **4641**

DEC PROFESSIONAL, THE. (US/0744-9216). Professional Press Inc, 101 Witmer Road, Horsham PA 19044. **Tel** (215)957-1500, FAX (215)957-1050. **1246**

DEC USER. (UK/0263-6530). EMAP Readerlink, Audit House, 260 Field End Road, Ruislip Middlesex HA4 9LT England. **Tel** 011 44 081 868 4499, FAX 011 44 081 429 3117. **1182**

DEFENSE & AEROSPACE ELECTRONICS. (US/1056-747X). Pasha Publications Inc, 1616 North Fort Myer Drive, Suite 1000, Arlington VA 22209. **Tel** (800)424-2908, (703)528-1244, FAX (703)528-3742, (703)528-1253. **2040**

DEFENSE CLEANUP. (US/1052-0635). Pasha Publications Inc, 1616 North Fort Myer Drive, Suite 1000, Arlington VA 22209. **Tel** (800)424-2908, (703)528-1244, FAX (703)528-3742, (703)528-1253. **2227**

DEFENSE DAILY. (US/0889-0404). Phillips Business Information, Inc., 1201 Seven Locks Road, Potomac MD 20854. **Tel** (301)424-3338, (800)777-5006, FAX (301)309-3847. **4041**

DEFENSE ELECTRONICS. (US/0278-3479). Argus Business, 6151 Powers Ferry Road, Atlanta GA 30339. **Tel** (404)995-2500, (800)233-3359. **2040**

DEFENSE MARKETING INTERNATIONAL. (US/1044-3975). Phillips Business Information, Inc., 1201 Seven Locks Road, Potomac MD 20854. **Tel** (301)424-3338, (800)777-5006, FAX (301)309-3847. **4041**

DEFENSE TECHNOLOGY BUSINESS. (US/1048-4612). Pasha Publications Inc., 1616 North Fort Myer Drive, Suite 1000, Arlington VA 22209. **Tel** (800)424-2908, (703)528-1244, FAX (703)528-3742, (703)528-1253. **4042**

DEFENSE WEEK. (US/0273-3188). King Publishing Group, 627 National Press Building, Washington DC 20045. **Tel** (202)638-4260, FAX (202)662-9744. **4042**

DELAWARE BUSINESS REVIEW. (US/1061-4605). Delaware Business Review, PO Box 3350, Wilmington DE 19804. **Tel** (302)998-9580, FAX (302)998-1276. **665**

DELAWARE JOURNAL OF CORPORATE LAW, THE. (US/0364-9490). Widener University School of Law, 3800 Vartan Way, Harrisburg PA 17110. **Tel** (717)541-3965, FAX (717)541-3966. **3099**

DENTAL ECONOMICS (PITTSBURGH. 1968). (US/0011-8583). PennWell Publishing Company, 1421 South Sheridan, PO Box 1260, Tulsa OK 74101. **Tel** (918)835-3161, (800)331-4463, FAX (918)831-9497. **1320**

DENVER BUSINESS. (US/0746-2964). Tall Oaks Publishing Inc, PO Box 621669, 60 Golden Eagle Lane, Littleton CO 80127. **Tel** (303)973-6600, (800)662-1660, FAX (303)973-5327. **665**

DENVER BUSINESS JOURNAL, THE. (US/0893-7745). Denver Business Journal, 1700 Broadway Suite 515, Denver CO 80290. **Tel** (303)837-3500, FAX (303)433-4718. **665**

DENVER POST (1901). (US). Denver Post, 1560 Broadway, Denver CO 80202. **Tel** (303)832-3232, (800)543-5543. **5642**

DEPAUL BUSINESS LAW JOURNAL. (US/1049-6122). DePaul Business Law Journal, DePaul University, Room 500, Chicago IL 60614. **Tel** (312)362-6178. **3099**

DERMATOLOGY TIMES. (US/0196-6197). Advanstar Communications Inc., 131 West First Street, Duluth MN 55802. **Tel** (218)723-9477, (800)346-0085. **3719**

DESCANT (TORONTO). (CN/0382-909X). Descant, PO Box 314 Station P, Toronto Ontario M5S 2S8 Canada. **Tel** (416)603-0223. **3380**

DESIGN WEEK. (UK/0950-3676). Centaur Communications Ltd., St Giles House, 50 Poland Street, London W1V 4AX England. **Tel** 011 44 71 439 4222, FAX 011 44 71 734 6748, telex 261352. **2899**

DETROIT FREE PRESS (DETROIT, MICH., 1858). (US/1055-2758). Detroit Newspapers, 615 West LaFayette Boulevard, Detroit MI 48226. **Tel** (313)222-6400, (313)222-2419. **5691**

DETROIT NEWS (DETROIT, MICH.), THE. (US/1055-2715). Detroit Newspapers, 615 West LaFayette Boulevard, Detroit MI 48226. **Tel** (313)222-6400, (313)222-2419. **5691**

DEVELOPMENT COMMUNICATION REPORT. (US/0192-1312). Clearinghouse Development Communication, 1815 North Fort Myer Drive, 6th Floor, Arlington VA 22209. **Tel** (703)527-5546, FAX (703)527-4661. **1110**

DEVICES & DIAGNOSTICS LETTER. (US/0098-7573). Washington Business Information Inc., 1117 North 19th Street, Suite 200, Arlington VA 22209. **Tel** (703)247-3433, (800)426-0416, FAX (703)247-3421. **3571**

DG REVIEW. (US/1050-9127). Data Base Publications, 9390 Research Blvd, Ste 11 300, Austin TX 78759. **Tel** (512)343-9066, FAX (512)345-1935. **1182**

DIABETES FORECAST. (US/0095-8301). American Diabetes Association, National Service Center, 1660 Duke Street, Alexandria VA 22314. **Tel** (703)549-1500, (800)232-3472, FAX (703)836-2464. **3727**

DIARI DE SESSIONS DEL PARLAMENT DE CATALUNYA. (NL). Servei de Publicacions del Parlament de Catalunya, Palau del Parlament Parc de la Ciutadella, Barcelona 08003 Catalonia Spain. **Tel** (93)300-6413, FAX (93)300-8962, telex 97-684. **4471**

DICTIONARY OF ORGANIC COMPOUNDS. (US). Routledge Chapman & Hall Inc, 29 West 35th Street, New York NY 10001. **Tel** (212)244-3336, (212)244-6412. **1041**

DIESEL PROGRESS ENGINES & DRIVES. (US/1040-8878). Diesel & Gas Turbine Publishers, 13555 Bishops Court, Brookfield WI 53005. **Tel** (414)784-9177, (800)558-4322, FAX (414)784-8133, telex 275398 DIESL UR. **2112**

DIGITAL MEDIA. (US/1056-7038). Seybold Publications Inc., 428 West Baltimore Pike, PO Box 644, Media PA 19063. **Tel** (610)565-2480, (800)325-3830, FAX (610)565-4659, or 3261, telex 4991494. **2113**

DIGITAL NEWS & REVIEW. (US/1065-7452). Cahners Publishing Company, 249 West 17th Street, New York NY 10011. **Tel** (212)645-0067, FAX (212)242-6987. **1246**

DIGITAL REVIEW (NEW YORK, N.Y.). (US/0739-4314). Cahners Publishing Company, 249 West 17th Street, New York NY 10011. **Tel** (212)645-0067, FAX (212)242-6987. **1267**

DIOGENES (ENGLISH ED.). (IT/0392-1921). Carfax Publishing Company, PO Box 25 Abingdon, Oxfordshire OX14 3UE England. **Tel** 011 44 235 555335, FAX (0279)31067, telex 817484. **4345**

DIRECT ACCESS (CALGARY). (CN/0843-5979). Technical Research Center, 1201 5th Street SW, Suite 200, Calgary Alberta T2R 0V6 Canada. **Tel** (403)262-9445, FAX (403)262-4539. **4386**

DIRECT MARKETING. (US/0012-3188). Hoke Communications Inc, 224 7th Street, Garden City NY 11530. **Tel** (516)746-6700, (800)229-6700. **923**

DIRECT MARKETING INTERNATIONAL. (UK). Detailextra Limited, 3 Bridgefoot, Market Deeping, Peterborough PE6 8AA England. **Tel** 011 44 778 380065, FAX 011 44 778 380075. **923**

DIRECTORIES IN PRINT. (US/0899-353X). Gale Research Inc., 835 Penobscot building, 645 Griswold Street, Detroit MI 48226. **Tel** (800)877-GALE, (313)961-2242, FAX (313)961-6083, (800)414-5043, telex TWX 810-221-7086. **415**

DIRECTORS & BOARDS. (US/0364-9156). Investment Dealers Digest Inc., Two World Trade Center, 18th Floor, New York NY 10048. **Tel** (212)227-1200, FAX (212)432-1039. **865**

DIRECTORY AND INDEX OF STANDARDS. (CN). Standards Council of Canada, 45 O'Conner Street, Suite 1200, Ottawa Ontario K1P 6N7 Canada. **Tel** (613)238-3222, (800)267-8220, FAX (613)995-4564, telex 053-4403. **4030**

DIRECTORY OF ASSOCIATIONS IN CANADA. (CN/0316-0734). Micromedia Limited, 20 Victoria Street, Toronto Ontario M5C 2N8 Canada. **Tel** (416)362-5211, (800)387-2689, FAX (416)362-6161, telex 06524668. **5230**

DIRECTORY OF COMMUNITY SERVICES IN METROPOLITAN TORONTO. (CN/0315-0631). Community Information Center of Metropolitan Toronto, 590 Jarvis Street 5th Floor, Toronto Ontario M4Y 2J4 Canada. **Tel** (416)392-4575. **5282**

DIRECTORY OF CORPORATE AFFILIATIONS / INTERNATIONAL. (US). National Register Publishing Company Inc., PO Box 31, 121 Chanlon Road, New Providence NJ 07974. **Tel** (800)521-8110, (800)323-6772, FAX (908)665-6688. **666**

DIRECTORY OF CORPORATE AFFILIATIONS / U.S. PRIVATE. (US). National Register Publishing Company Inc., PO Box 31, 121 Chanlon Road, New Providence NJ 07974. **Tel** (800)521-8110, (800)323-6772, FAX (908)665-6688. **666**

DIRECTORY OF CORPORATE AFFILIATIONS / U.S. PUBLIC. (US). National Register Publishing Company Inc., PO Box 31, 121 Chanlon Road, New Providence NJ 07974. **Tel** (800)521-8110, (800)323-6772, FAX (908)665-6688. **666**

DIRECTORY OF SCIENTIFIC RESEARCH INSTITUTIONS IN INDIA, THE. (II/0419-3482). INSDOC, 14 Satsang Vihar Marg, New Delhi 110067 India. **Tel** 011 91 11 6863617, FAX 665837, telex 031-73099. **5100**

DIRECTORY OF SOUTH AFRICAN ASSOCIATIONS. (SA). Directory of South African Associations, PO Box 395, Pretoria 0001 South Africa. **Tel** 27-12-8414408, FAX 27-12-862869. **1925**

DIRTY LINEN. (US/1047-4315). Dirty Linen, PO Box 66600, Baltimore MD 21239-6600. **Tel** (410)583-7973, FAX (410)337-6735. **4115**

DISCOUNT MERCHANDISER, THE. (US/0012-3579). Sterling Macfadden, 233 Park Avenue South, New York NY 10003. **Tel** (212)979-4800. **954**

DISCOUNT STORE NEWS. (US/0012-3587). Lebhar Friedman Inc., 3922 Coconut Palm Drive, Tampa FL 33619. **Tel** (800)927-9292, (813)664-6707. **954**

DISCOVER (CHICAGO, ILL.). (US/0274-7529). Walt Disney Publishing Inc., 500 South Buena Vista Street, Burbank CA 91521. **Tel** (818)567-5661. **5101**

DIVERSITY & DIVISION. (US/1064-7430). Madison Center for Educational Affairs, 1155 15th Street, Suite 712, Washington DC 20005. **Tel** (800)225-2862, (202)838-1801. **5244**

DIY WEEK. (UK). Benn Business Information Service Ltd, Riverbank House, Angel Lane, Tonbridge Kent TN9 1SE England. **Tel** 011 44 732 362666, FAX 011 44 732 770483, telex 95454 BBIS. **2811**

DLA BULLETIN (OAKLAND, CALIF.). (US/0272-037X). DLA Bulletin, University of California, Division of Library Automation, Office of the President, 300 Lakeside Drive/Floor 8, Oakland CA 94612-3550. **Tel** (510)987-0564. **3208**

DO-IT-YOURSELF RETAILING. (US/0889-2989). National Retailing Hardware Association, 5822 West 74th Street, Indianapolis IN 46278. **Tel** (317)297-1190. **2811**

DOCUMENT IMAGE AUTOMATION UPDATE. (US/1054-9706). Mecklermedia Corporation, 11 Ferry Lane West, Westport CT 06880. **Tel** (203)226-6967, (800)632-5537, FAX (203)454-5840. **1277**

DOING BUSINESS IN EASTERN EUROPE. (US). Price Waterhouse & Company, 1177 Avenue of the Americas, New York NY 10020. **Tel** (212)596-7000. **667**

DOKUMENTE (KOLN). (GW/0012-5172). **5198**

DOLLARS & SENSE (SOMERVILLE, MASS.). (US/0012-5245). Dollars & Sense, 1 Summer Street, Somerville MA 02143. **Tel** (617)628-8411, FAX (617)628-2025. **1480**

DONOGHUE'S MONEYLETTER. (US/0197-7083). IBC Donoghue Organization, 290 Eliot Street, Ashland MA 01721. **Tel** (800)343-5413, (508)881-2800. **897**

DOORS AND HARDWARE. (US/0361-5294). Doors & Hardware, 14170 Newbrook Drive, Chantilly VA 22021. **Tel** (703)222-2010, FAX (703)222-2410. **613**

DR. DOBB'S JOURNAL (1989). (US/1044-789X). Miller Freeman Inc., 600 Harrison Street, San Francisco CA 94107. **Tel** (415)905-2337, FAX (415)905-2240, telex 278273. **1267**

DRAKE LAW REVIEW. (US/0012-5938). Drake Law Review, Drake University Law School, Des Moines IA 50311. **Tel** (515)271-2930. **2964**

DRUG & COSMETIC INDUSTRY. (US/0012-6527). Advanstar Communications Inc., 131 West First Street, Duluth MN 55802. **Tel** (218)723-9477, (800)346-0085. **4299**

DRUG STORE NEWS. (US/0191-7587). Lebhar Friedman Inc., 3922 Coconut Palm Drive, Tampa FL 33619. **Tel** (800)927-9292, (813)664-6707. **4301**

DRUG TOPICS. (US/0012-6616). Medical Economics Publishing, Five Paragon Drive, Second Floor, Montvale NJ 07645. **Tel** (800)432-4570, (201)358-2210. **4301**

DRUGS OF THE FUTURE. (SP/0377-8282). Prous Science Publishers, Apartado de Correos 540, 08080 Barcelona Spain. **Tel** 011 34 3 4592220, FAX 011 34 3 4581535. **4302**

E&P Serials available Online

E&P ENVIRONMENT. (US/1054-6464). Pasha Publications Inc., 1616 North Fort Myer Drive, Suite 1000, Arlington VA 22209. **Tel** (800)424-2908, (703)528-1244, FAX (703)528-3742, (703)528-1253. **1439**

EARLY MUSIC NEWS. (UK). Early Music News, Sutton House 2-4 Homerton High, London E9 6JQ England. **Tel** 011 44 71 727 6339. **4116**

EARTH SCIENCE OPPORTUNITIES. (US/1058-0425). Patcong Press, 2089 Route 9, Cape May Court House NJ 08210. **Tel** (609)624-0608. **1354**

EAST ASIAN BUSINESS INTELLIGENCE. (US/0888-580X). International Executive Reports, 717 D Street NW/Suite 300, Washington DC 20004-2807. **Tel** (202)628-6900, FAX (202)628 6618, telex 440462 MEER UI. **923**

EAST ASIAN EXECUTIVE REPORTS. (US/0272-1589). International Executive Reports, 717 D Street NW/Suite 300, Washington DC 20004-2807. **Tel** (202)628-6900, FAX (202)628 6618, telex 440462 MEER UI. **3099**

EAST EUROPEAN MARKETS. (UK/0262-0456). Financial Times England, 8 16 Great New Street, London EC4A 3BN England. **Tel** 011 44 71 353 0305, 353 1040, FAX 011 44 353 0846. **897**

EASTERN EUROPEAN & SOVIET TELECOM REPORT. (US/1054-6499). International Technology Consultants, 1724 Kalorama Road, Suite 210, Washington DC 20009. **Tel** (202)234-2138, FAX (202)483-7922. **1154**

EASTERN EUROPEAN ENERGY REPORT. (US/1054-1608). Strategic Marketing Communications, 550 North Maple Avenue, Ridgewood NJ 07450. **Tel** (201)444-1061, (800)443-4188, FAX (201)444-9171. **1937**

EBONY. (US/0012-9011). Johnson Publishing Company / Illinois, 820 South Michigan Avenue, Chicago IL 60605. **Tel** (312)322-9200, (800)272-6602. **2259**

EBRI ISSUE BRIEF. (US/0887-137X). Employee Benefit Research Institute, 2121 K Street Northwest, Suite 600, Washington DC 20037. **Tel** (202)659-0670, FAX (202)775-6312. **1664**

EC ENERGY MONTHLY. (UK/0957-3666). Financial Times Business Information Ltd., Tower House, Southampton Street, London WC2E 7HA England. **Tel** 011 44 71 353 1040. **1937**

ECOLOGY ABSTRACTS. (US/0143-3296). Cambridge Scientific Abstracts, 7200 Wisconsin Avenue, #601, Bethesda MD 20814-4823. **Tel** (301)961-6750, (800)843-7751, FAX (301)961-6720. **2184**

ECONLIT [COMPUTER FILE]. (US). Silverplatter Information Inc., 100 River Ridge Drive, Norwood MA 02062. **Tel** (800)343-0064, (617)769-2599, FAX (617)235-1715. **1531**

ECONOMIC GEOGRAPHY. (US/0013-0095). Clark University, C/O M. J. Beckett, 950 Main Street, Economics Geography Department, Worcester MA 01610. **Tel** (617)793-7311, FAX (508)793-8881. **1483**

ECONOMIC INQUIRY. (US/0095-2583). Western Economic Association. **1483**

ECONOSCOPE. (CN/0712-2012). Royal Bank of Canada, 200 Bay Street, 18th Floor South Tower, Toronto ONT M5J 2J5 Canada. **Tel** (416)974-7242. **1487**

ECOTASS (ENGLISH EDITION). (SZ/0733-5989). Pergamon Press Inc., 660 White Plains Road, Tarrytown NY 10591-5153. **Tel** (914)524-9200, FAX (914)333-2444, telex 13-7328. **1487**

EDELL HEALTH LETTER, THE. (US/0896-6613). Edell Health Letter, 301 Howard Street/ 18th Floor, San Francisco CA 94105. **Tel** (415)512-9100, FAX (415)512-9600. **3573**

EDGE (HACKETTSTOWN, N.J.). (US/1063-8431). Edge Publishing, PO Box 471, Hackettstown NJ 07840. **Tel** (908)852-7217. **1241**

EDGE (MORRISTOWN, N.J.). (US/0890-9563). Vintage Systems Corporation, 103 Washington Street/Suite 378, Morristown NJ 07960. **1154**

EDI IN FINANCE. (UK/0960-4634). Elsevier Science Publishers Ltd, Crown House, Linton Road, Barking Essex IG11 8JU England. **Tel** 011 44 81 5947272, FAX 081-594-5942, telex 896950. **5102**

EDI NEWS. (US/0894-9212). Phillips Business Information, Inc., 1201 Seven Locks Road, Potomac MD 20854. **Tel** (301)424-3338, (800)777-5006, FAX (301)309-3847. **1183**

EDI UPDATE LONDON. (UK/0954-6154). Eurostudy Publishing Co. Ltd., 36 38 Willesden Lane, London N26 7SW England. **Tel** 011 44 71 6374383. **4721**

EDITOR & PUBLISHER. (US/0013-094X). Editor & Publisher Company, 11 West 19th Street, New York NY 10011. **Tel** (212)675-4380. **4814**

EDITORS ONLY. (US/0735-8490). Editors Only, PO Box 17108, Fountain AZ 85269. **Tel** (602)837-6492, FAX (602)837-6872. **2919**

EDN. (US/0012-7515). Cahners Publishing Company, 249 West 17th Street, New York NY 10011. **Tel** (212)645-0067, FAX (212)242-6987. **2042**

EDP WEEKLY. (US). Computer Age Publications, 3918 Prosperity Avenue/Suite 310, Fairfax VA 22031-3300. **Tel** (703)573-8400, FAX (703)573-8594. **1237**

EDUCACION MEDICA Y SALUD. (US/0013-1091). Pan American Health Organization, 525 23rd Street Northwest, Office District Sales, Washington DC 20037. **Tel** (202)293-8130, FAX (202)338-0869. **3573**

EDUCATION INDEX. (US/0013-1385). H W Wilson Company, 950 University Avenue, Bronx NY 10452. **Tel** (800)367-6770, (718)588-8400, FAX (718)590-1617, telex 4990003 HWILSON. **1794**

EDUCATION INDEX. CD-ROM. (US/0013-1385). H W Wilson Company, 950 University Avenue, Bronx NY 10452. **Tel** (800)367-6770, (718)588-8400, FAX (718)590-1617, telex 4990003 HWILSON. **1794**

EDUCATION TECHNOLOGY NEWS. (US/1061-5008). Business Publishers Inc., 951 Pershing Drive, Silver Spring MD 20910-4464. **Tel** (301)587-6300, (800)274-0122, FAX (301)585-9075. **1223**

EDUCATIONAL HORIZONS. (US/0013-175X). Pi Lambda Theta, 4101 East Third Street, Bloomington IN 47407. **Tel** (812)339-3411, FAX (812)339-3462. **1741**

EDUCATIONAL RESEARCH IN AUSTRIA. (AU). Bundesministerium fur Unterricht und Kunst, Minoritemplatz 5, 1014 Vienna Austria. **Tel** 1 53120 3520, FAX 1 53120 3535. **1742**

EDUCOM REVIEW. (US/1045-9146). EDUCOM, 1112 16th Street Northwest, Washington DC 20036. **Tel** (202)872-4200, FAX (202)872-4318. **1822**

EGYPTIAN GAZETTE, THE. (UA). United Distribution Company, 21 Kasr El Nil Street, Cairo Egypt. **5800**

ELECTRIC LIGHT & POWER. (US/0013-4120). PennWell Publishing Company, 1421 South Sheridan, PO Box 1260, Tulsa OK 74101. **Tel** (918)835-3161, (800)331-4463, FAX (918)831-9497. **2043**

ELECTRIC UTILITY WEEK. (US/0736-413X). McGraw Hill Publishing Company, Inc., 1221 Avenue of the Americas, New York NY 10020. **Tel** (212)512-6410, (800)525-5003, FAX (212)512-6111. **2044**

ELECTRIC VEHICLE PROGRESS. (US/0190-4175). Alexander Research & Communications, Inc, 215 Park Avenue South, Suite 1301, New York NY 10003. **Tel** (212)228-0246, FAX (212)228-0376. **2044**

ELECTRICAL CONSTRUCTION AND MAINTENANCE. (US/0013-4260). Intertec Publishing Corporation, 9800 Metcalf, Overland Park KS 66212. **Tel** (913)341-1300. **2044**

ELECTRICAL MARKETING. (US/0149-5771). Intertec Publishing Corporation, 9800 Metcalf, Overland Park KS 66212. **Tel** (913)341-1300. **2045**

ELECTRICAL WORLD. (US/0013-4457). McGraw Hill Publishing Company, Inc., 1221 Avenue of the Americas, New York NY 10020. **Tel** (212)512-6410, (800)525-5003, FAX (212)512-6111. **2045**

ELECTRICITY JOURNAL, THE. (US/1040-6190). The Electricity Journal, 1501 Western Avenue, Suite 100, Seattle WA 98101. **Tel** (206)382-0195, FAX (206)382-0098. **4761**

ELECTRO MANUFACTURING. (US/1041-052X). WV Publishing Company, PO Box 138, Babson Park, Boston MA 02157. **3478**

ELECTRONIC BULLETIN BOARD. (US). New Jersey Department of Labor & Industry, Labor Market & Demographic, CN 388, Trenton NJ 08625. **Tel** (609)984-2595. **1559**

ELECTRONIC BUSINESS. (US/0163-6197). Cahners Publishing Company, 249 West 17th Street, New York NY 10011. **Tel** (212)645-0067, FAX (212)242-6987. **2046**

ELECTRONIC BUYERS' NEWS. (US/0164-6362). CMP Publications Inc., c/o B. Werner, One Jericho Plaza, Wing A, 2nd Floor, Jericho NY 11753. **Tel** (516)733-6700. **2046**

ELECTRONIC CHEMICALS NEWS. (US/0886-5671). Chemical Week Association, 888 Seventh Avenue, 26th Floor, New York NY 10106. **Tel** (212)621-4900. **2047**

ELECTRONIC DESIGN. (US/0013-4872). Penton Publishing, 1100 Superior Avenue, Cleveland OH 44114-2543. **Tel** (216)696-7000, FAX (216)696-0836. **2047**

ELECTRONIC ENGINEERING. (UK/0013-4902). Morgan Grampian, 40 Beresford Street Woolwich, London SE18 6BQ England. **Tel** 011 44 81 855 7777, FAX 011 44 81 855 5548, telex 896238. **2047**

ELECTRONIC ENGINEERING TIMES. (US/0192-1541). CMP Publications Inc., c/o B. Werner, One Jericho Plaza, Wing A, 2nd Floor, Jericho NY 11753. **Tel** (516)733-6700. **2047**

ELECTRONIC IMAGING REPORT. (US/1057-0942). Phillips Business Information, Inc., 1201 Seven Locks Road, Potomac MD 20854. **Tel** (301)424-3338, (800)777-5006, FAX (301)309-3847. **1183**

ELECTRONIC LEARNING. (US/0278-3258). Scholastic Inc, 730 Broadway, New York NY 10003. **Tel** (416)883-5300, FAX (212)505-3653. **1223**

ELECTRONIC MATERIALS TECHNOLOGY NEWS. (US/1045-0955). Business Communications Inc., 25 Van Zant Street, Suite 13, Norwalk CT 06855. **Tel** (203)853-4266. **2047**

ELECTRONIC MEDIA. (US/0745-0311). Crain Communications Inc., 1400 Woodbridge, Detroit MI 48207. **Tel** (313)446-6000, (800)992-9970. **1131**

ELECTRONIC MESSAGING NEWS. (US/1044-9892). Phillips Business Information, Inc., 1201 Seven Locks Road, Potomac MD 20854. **Tel** (301)424-3338, (800)777-5006, FAX (301)309-3847. **1110**

ELECTRONIC NEWS (1991). (US/1061-6624). IDG Communications / New York, 488 Madison Avenue, 6th Floor, New York NY 10022. **Tel** (212)909-5900. **2047**

ELECTRONIC SERVICES UPDATE. (US). International Data Corporation, 5 Speen Street, PO Box 9015, Framingham MA 01701. **Tel** (508)872-8200, (508)935-4443. **2048**

ELECTRONICS AND COMMUNICATIONS ABSTRACTS JOURNAL (RIVERDALE, MD.). (US/0361-3313). Cambridge Scientific Abstracts, 7200 Wisconsin Avenue, #601, Bethesda MD 20814-4823. **Tel** (301)961-6750, (800)843-7751, FAX (301)961-6720. **2003**

ELECTRONICS LETTERS. (UK/0013-5194). Institution of Electrical Engineers / IEE, Michael Faraday House, Six Hills Way, Stevenage Herts SG1 2AY UK. **Tel** 011 44 438 313311, FAX 011 44 438 742840, telex 825578 IEESTV G. **2049**

ELECTRONICS WEEKLY. (UK/0013-5224). Reed Business Publishing / West Sussex, England, Perrymount Road, Haywards Heath, West Sussex RH16 3DH England. **Tel** 011 44 81 6523500. **2050**

ELKHART TRUTH, THE. (US/0746-7516). Truth Publishing Company Inc., 421 South Second Street, Elkhart IN 46516. **Tel** (219)294-1661. **5663**

ELLIPSE. (CN/0046-1830). University de Sherbrooke/ CP 10/FAC, Des Lettres et Sciences Humaines, Quebec Quebec J1K 2R1 Canada. **Tel** (819)821-7277, FAX (819)821-7238. **3384**

EMBASE [ONLINE DATABASE]. (NE). Excerpta Medica / Electronic Publishing Division, Molenwerf 1, 1014 AG Amsterdam, PO Box 2227, 1000 CE Amsterdam, The Netherlands. **Tel** 020 5803201, FAX 020 5803214, telex 18582. **3657**

EMMY. (US/0164-3495). Emmy Magazine, 5220 Lankerhim Blvd, North Hollywood CA 91601. **Tel** (818)754-2800, FAX (818)761-2827. **1131**

EMPLOYEE RELATIONS. (UK/0142-5455). MCB University Press, 60 62 Toller Lane, Bradford West Yorkshire BD8 9BX England. **Tel** 011 44 274 499821, FAX 011 44 274 547143, telex 51317 MCBUNI G. **940**

EMPLOYEE RELATIONS LAW JOURNAL. (US/0098-8898). John Wiley & Sons, Inc., 605 Third Avenue, New York NY 10158-0012. **Tel** (212)850-6000, (212)850-6645, FAX (212)850-6088, telex 12-7063. **3146**

EMPLOYMENT RELATIONS TODAY. (US/0745-7790). John Wiley & Sons, Inc., 605 Third Avenue, New York NY 10158-0012. **Tel** (212)850-6000, (212)850-6645, FAX (212)850-6088, telex 12-7063. **1667**

EMR ON-LINE. (US). American Health Consultants, 3525 Piedmont Road, Suite 400, Atlanta GA 30305. **Tel** (800)688-2421, (404)262-7436. **3724**

EN ROUTE TECHNOLOGY. (US/1057-5618). Telecom Publishing Group, 1101 King Street, Suite 444, Alexandria VA 22314. **Tel** (703)683-4100, (800)327-7205, FAX (703)739-6490. **1184**

ENA'S NURSING SCAN IN EMERGENCY CARE. (US/1056-7062). NURSECOM Inc., 1211 Locust Street, Philadelphia PA 19107. **Tel** (215)545-7222, (800)242-6757, FAX (215)545-8107. **3855**

Serials Online Index

ENCYCLOPEDIA OF ASSOCIATIONS. (US/0071-0202). Gale Research Inc., 835 Penobscot Building, 645 Griswold Street, Detroit MI 48226. **Tel** (800)877-GALE, (313)961-2242, FAX (313)961-6083, (800)414-5043, telex TWX 810-221-7086. **1925**

ENERGY ALERT (TORONTO). (CN/0835-5266). Energy Educators of Ontario, 517 College Street, Suite 406, Toronto ONT M6G 4A2 Canada. **Tel** (416)323-9216, FAX (416)323-0689. **1938**

ENERGY ANALECTS. (CN/0315-1654). C.O. Nickle Publications, 999 8th Street Southwest, Suite 300, Calgary, Alberta T2R 1N7 Canada. **Tel** (403)244-6111. **1938**

ENERGY & ENVIRONMENT. (UK/0958-305X). Multi Science Publ Co Ltd, 107 High Street, Brentwood, Essex CM14 4RX England. **Tel** 011 44 277 244632. **1939**

ENERGY BOOKS QUARTERLY. (US/0892-5461). International Academy at Santa Barbara, 800 Garden Street, Suite D, Santa Barbara CA 93101. **Tel** (805)965-5010, FAX (805)965-6071. **1962**

ENERGY CONSERVATION NEWS. (US/0161-6595). Business Communications Inc., 25 Van Zant Street, Suite 13, Norwalk CT 06855. **Tel** (203)853-4266. **1939**

ENERGY DAILY, THE. (US/0364-5274). King Publishing Group, 627 National Press Building, Washington DC 20045. **Tel** (202)638-4260, FAX (202)662-9744. **1939**

ENERGY, ECONOMICS AND CLIMATE CHANGE. (US/1059-5813). Cutter Information Corporation, 37 Broadway, Arlington MA 02174-5539. **Tel** (617)648-8700, (800)964-5118, FAX (617)648-8707, (617)648-1950, telex 650 100 9891. **1940**

ENERGY INFORMATION ABSTRACTS. (US/0147-6521). R R Bowker, A Reed Reference Publishing Company, Part of Reed International PLC, PO Box 31, 121 Chanlon Drive, New Providence NJ 07974. **Tel** (908)464-6800, (800)521-8110, FAX (908)665-6688, telex 138-755. **1962**

ENERGY INFORMATION ABSTRACTS ANNUAL. (US/0739-3679). R R Bowker, A Reed Reference Publishing Company, Part of Reed International PLC, PO Box 31, 121 Chanlon Drive, New Providence NJ 07974. **Tel** (908)464-6800, (800)521-8110, FAX (908)665-6688, telex 138-755. **1962**

ENERGY REPORT (ARLINGTON, VA.). (US/0888-8183). Pasha Publications Inc., 1616 North Fort Myer Drive, Suite 1000, Arlington VA 22209. **Tel** (800)424-2908, (703)528-1244, FAX (703)528-3742, (703)528-1253. **1941**

ENERGY STATISTICS (CHICAGO, ILL.). (US/0739-3075). Institute of Gas Technology, 3424 South State Street, Chicago IL 60616. **Tel** (312)949-3970, (312)949-3650, FAX (312)949-3776, telex 25-6189. **1962**

ENERGY USER NEWS. (US/0162-9131). Chilton Company, 201 King of Prussia Road, Radnor PA 19089. **Tel** (610)964-4122, (800)695-1214, FAX (610)964-4978, telex 6851035 CHILTON UW. **1942**

ENGINEERED MATERIALS ABSTRACTS. (US/0951-9998). American Society for Metals International, c/o Deborah Barthelmes, Materials Park OH 44073-0002. **Tel** (216)338-5151, FAX (216)338-4634, telex 980-619. **2004**

ENGINEERING AND MINING JOURNAL (1926). (US/0095-8948). MacLean Hunter Publishing Corporation / Chicago, IL, 29 North Wacker Drive, Chicago IL 60606-3298. **Tel** (312)726-2802, FAX (312)726-3091. **2138**

ENGINEERING DIMENSIONS. (CN/0820-8190). Association of Professional Engineers of Ontario, 1155 Yonge Street, Toronto Ontario M4T 2Y5 Canada. **Tel** (416)961-1100, FAX (416)961-1499. **1972**

ENGINEERING ECONOMIST, THE. (US/0013-791X). Institute of Industrial Engineers, 25 Technology Park-Atlanta, Norcross GA 30092. **Tel** (404)449-0460, FAX (404)263-8532. **1973**

ENGINEERING LASERS. (UK). Argus Press Group, Queensway House, 2 Queensway Redhill, Surrey RH1 1QS England. **Tel** 011 44 737 768611, 011 44 737 761685, FAX 011 44 737 760510, telex 948669 TOPJNL G. **1973**

ENHANCED ENERGY RECOVERY NEWS. (US/0271-7085). Business Communications Inc., 25 Van Zant Street, Suite 13, Norwalk CT 06855. **Tel** (203)853-4266. **1943**

ENTERTAINMENT MARKETING LETTER. (US/1048-5112). EPM Communications Inc., 488 East 18th Street, Brooklyn NY 11226. **Tel** (718)469-9330, FAX (718)469-7124. **924**

ENTERTAINMENT WEEKLY. (US/1049-0434). Time Inc. / New York, Time & Life Building, Rockefeller Center, New York NY 10020. **385**

ENTOMOLOGY ABSTRACTS. (US/0013-8924). Cambridge Scientific Abstracts, 7200 Wisconsin Avenue, #601, Bethesda MD 20814-4823. **Tel** (301)961-6750, (800)843-7751, FAX (301)961-6720. **5604**

ENVIRONMENT ABSTRACTS. (US/0093-3287). Congressional Information Service Inc, 4520 East-West Highway, Suite 800, Bethesda MD 20814-3389. **Tel** (800)638-8380, (301)654-1550, FAX (301)654-4033, telex 292386 CIS UR. **2184**

ENVIRONMENT ABSTRACTS ANNUAL. (US/0000-1198). Congressional Information Service Inc, 4520 East-West Highway, Suite 800, Bethesda MD 20814-3389. **Tel** (800)638-8380, (301)654-1550, FAX (301)654-4033, telex 292386 CIS UR. **2184**

ENVIRONMENT TODAY. (US/1054-7517). Enterprise Communications Inc, 1165 Northchase Parkway, Suite 350, Marietta GA 30067. **Tel** (404)988-9558, FAX (404)859-9166. **2166**

ENVIRONMENT WATCH. EAST EUROPE, RUSSIA & EURASIA. (US/1063-5955). Cutter Information Corporation, 37 Broadway, Arlington MA 02174-5539. **Tel** (617)648-8700, (800)964-5118, FAX (617)648-8707, (617)648-1950, telex 650 100 9891. **2166**

ENVIRONMENT WATCH. LATIN AMERICA. (US/1060-1414). Cutter Information Corporation, 37 Broadway, Arlington MA 02174-5539. **Tel** (617)648-8700, (800)964-5118, FAX (617)648-8707, (617)648-1950, telex 650 100 9891. **672**

ENVIRONMENT WATCH. WESTERN EUROPE. (US/1066-6001). Cutter Information Corporation, 37 Broadway, Arlington MA 02174-5539. **Tel** (617)648-8700, (800)964-5118, FAX (617)648-8707, (617)648-1950, telex 650 100 9891. **672**

ENVIRONMENT WEEK. (US/1041-8105). King Publishing Group, 627 National Press Building, Washington DC 20045. **Tel** (202)638-4260, FAX (202)662-9744. **2166**

ENVIRONMENTAL BUSINESS JOURNAL. (US/1045-8611). Enviroquest Business International, PO Box 371769, San Diego CA 92137. **Tel** (619)295-7685, FAX (619)295-5743. **2166**

ENVIRONMENTAL ISSUES REPORT. (US/1061-3935). Capitol Reports, 1500 W.L. El Camino Avenue, Suite 216, Sacramento CA 95833. **Tel** (916)920-9094. **2168**

ENVIRONMENTAL LAW (PORTLAND, ORE.). (US/0046-2276). Northwestern School of Law, 10015 Southwest, Terwilliger Boulevard, Portland OR 97219. **Tel** (503)244-1181 Ext. 700, FAX (503)246-8542. **3111**

ENVIRONMENTAL NUTRITION. (US/0893-4452). R.L. Polk, 521 Fifth Avenue, 11th Floor, New York NY 10175. **Tel** (212)986-0555. **4190**

ENVIRONMENTAL PERIODICALS BIBLIOGRAPHY. (US/0145-3815). International Academy at Santa Barbara, 800 Garden Street, Suite D, Santa Barbara CA 93101. **Tel** (805)965-5010, FAX (805)965-6071. **2184**

EP NEWS SERVICE. (US/8750-7064). EP News Service, 1619 Portland Avenue South, Minneapolis MN 55404. **Tel** (612)339-9579, FAX (612)339-6973. **4956**

EPIEGRAM (1988). (US/1046-1493). Sterling Harbor Press Inc., PO Box 28, Greenport NY 11944. **Tel** (516)323-1355, (516)765-2378, FAX (516)323-1355, (516)765-2544. **1241**

EPIPHANY. (US). Epiphany Journal, PO Box 2250, South Portland ME 04116. **Tel** (207)767-1889. **4956**

EQUAL OPPORTUNITIES INTERNATIONAL. (UK/0261-0159). MCB University Press, 60 62 Toller Lane, Bradford West Yorkshire BD8 9BX England. **Tel** 011 44 274 499821, FAX 011 44 274 547143, telex 51317 MCBUNI G. **1667**

ERDOL & KOHLE, ERDGAS, PETROCHEMIE. (GW/0014-0058). VCH Gesellschaft GmbH, Postfach 101161, D 69451 Weinheim Germany. **Tel** 011 49 6201 606459, FAX 011 49 6201 606184. **4255**

ESPIAL CANADIAN DATA BASE DIRECTORY, THE. (CN/0834-3888). Espial Productions Ltd., 85 Roe Avenue, Toronto Ontario M5M 2H6 Canada. **Tel** (416)485-8063. **1259**

ESSAY AND GENERAL LITERATURE INDEX. (US/0014-083X). H W Wilson Company, 950 University Avenue, Bronx NY 10452. **Tel** (800)367-6770, (718)588-8400, FAX (718)590-1617, telex 4990003 HWILSON. **3458**

ESSAY AND GENERAL LITERATURE INDEX. CD-ROM. (US/0014-083X). H W Wilson Company, 950 University Avenue, Bronx NY 10452. **Tel** (800)367-6770, (718)588-8400, FAX (718)590-1617, telex 4990003 HWILSON. **3458**

ESTATES GAZETTE. DIGEST OF LAND AND PROPERTY CASES. (UK). Estates Gazette Ltd, 151 Wardour Street, London W1V 4BN England. **Tel** 011 44 71 437 0141. **2967**

EUROBUSINESS (LONDON). (UK/0953-0711). Transnational Business Magazines Limited, Stratton House, Stratton Street, London W1X 5FE England. **Tel** 011 44 71 4097009, FAX 011 44 71 4093006. **673**

EUROFOOD. (UK/0955-5404). Agra Europe London Limited, 25 Frant Road, Tunbridge Wells, Kent TN2 5JT England. **Tel** 011 44 892 533813. **2334**

EUROMARKETING : THE WEEKLY EUROPEAN NEWS BULLETIN FROM ADVERTISING AGE. (UK/0952-3820). Crain Communications Ltd., 75-77 Cowcross Street, Cowcross Court, London EC1M 6BP England. **Tel** 011 44 71 6082774. **759**

EUROPE 92 (PORT WASHINGTON, N.Y.). (US/1065-1055). Europe 92, 37 Richards Road, Port Washington NY 11050. **2967**

EUROPE 2000 YEOVIL. (UK/0959-9584). Europe 2000 Ltd., 7A Westminster Street Yeovil, Somerset BA20 1AF England. **Tel** 011 44 935 29489. **2687**

EUROPE ENERGY. (BE). Europe Information Service, rue de Geneve 6, 1140 Brussels Belgium. **Tel** 011 32 2 242 6020, FAX 011 32 2 242 9549. **1944**

EUROPE ENVIRONMENT. (BE/0778-7928). Europe Information Service, rue de Geneve 6, 1140 Brussels Belgium. **Tel** 011 32 2 242 6020, FAX 011 32 2 242 9549. **2171**

EUROPEAN ADHESIVES AND SEALANTS. (UK/0264-9047). Argus Press Group, Queensway House, 2 Queensway Redhill, Surrey RH1 1QS England. **Tel** 011 44 737 768611, 011 44 737 761685, FAX 011 44 737 760510, telex 948669 TOPJNL G. **4223**

EUROPEAN COMMUNITY (SYRACUSE, N.Y.), THE. (US/1045-3857). Political Risk Services, 6320 Fly Road, Suite 102, PO Box 248, East Syracuse NY 13057-0248. **Tel** (315)431-0511, FAX (315)431-0200. **1489**

EUROPEAN COSMETIC MARKETS. (UK). Nicholas Hall & Company, 35 Alexandra Street, Southend-on-Sea, Essex SS1 1BW England. **Tel** 011 44 702 433422, FAX 011 44 702 430787. **404**

EUROPEAN DIRECTORY OF AGROCHEMICAL PRODUCTS. (UK). Royal Society of Chemistry, Thomas Graham House, Science Park, Cambridge CB4 4WF England. **Tel** 011 44 223 420066, FAX 011 44 223 423429, telex 818293 ROYAL. **4245**

EUROPEAN ENERGY REPORT. (UK). Financial Times Business Information Ltd., Tower House, Southampton Street, London WC2E 7HA England. **Tel** 011 44 71 353 1040. **1944**

EUROPEAN JOURNAL OF MARKETING. (UK/0309-0566). MCB University Press, 60 62 Toller Lane, Bradford West Yorkshire BD8 9BX England. **Tel** 011 44 274 499821, FAX 011 44 274 547143, telex 51317 MCBUNI G. **924**

EUROPEAN MANAGEMENT JOURNAL. (UK/0263-2373). Pergamon Press, An Imprint of Elsevier Science Ltd., The Boulevard, Langford Lane, Kidlington, Oxford OX5 1GB United Kingdom. **Tel** 011 44 865 843000, 011 44 865 843699, FAX 011 44 865 843010. **867**

EUROPEAN POLYMERS PAINT COLOUR JOURNAL. (UK/0963-8474). Argus Press Group, Queensway House, 2 Queensway Redhill, Surrey RH1 1QS England. **Tel** 011 44 737 768611, 011 44 737 761685, FAX 011 44 737 760510, telex 948669 TOPJNL G. **4223**

EUROPEAN POWER NEWS. (UK/0261-8214). Argus Press Group, Queensway House, 2 Queensway Redhill, Surrey RH1 1QS England. **Tel** 011 44 737 768611, 011 44 737 761685, FAX 011 44 737 760510, telex 948669 TOPJNL G. **1944**

EUROPEAN RUBBER JOURNAL (LONDON, ENGLAND : 1982). (UK/0266-4151). Crain Communications Ltd., 75-77 Cowcross Street, Cowcross Court, London EC1M 6BP England. **Tel** 011 44 71 6082774. **5075**

EUROPEAN VENTURE CAPITAL JOURNAL : EUROPEAN VCJ. (UK/0954-1675). Venture Economics Ltd, Quadrange 180, Wardourst Street, London W1A 4YG England. **Tel** 011 44 71 434 0411. **1490**

EVANS-NOVAK POLITICAL REPORT. (US/0014-3650). Phillips Business Information, Inc., 1201 Seven Locks Road, Potomac MD 20854. **Tel** (301)424-3338, (800)777-5006, FAX (301)309-3847. **4473**

EXCEPTIONAL CHILD EDUCATION RESOURCES. (US/0160-4309). Council for Exceptional Children, 1920 Association Drive, Reston VA 22091. **Tel** (703)620-3660, FAX (703)264-9494. **1795**

EXCEPTIONAL CHILDREN. (US/0014-4029). Council for Exceptional Children, 1920 Association Drive, Reston VA 22091. **Tel** (703)620-3660, FAX (703)264-9494. **1878**

EXCEPTIONAL PARENT, THE. (US/0046-9157). Exceptional Parent, 120 State Street, Hackensack NJ 07601. **Tel** (201)489-0871. **2278**

EXCHANGE Serials available Online

Serials Online Index

EXCHANGE LILYFIELD. (AT/1033-2014). Stuart Corner and Associates, Freepost 13, PO Box 13, Rozelle NSW 2039 Australia. **Tel** 011 61 02 555 7377, FAX 011 61 02 818 2294. **673**

EXE. (UK/0268-6872). Process Communications Ltd, 10 Barley Mow Passage, Chiswich London W4 4BR England. **Tel** 081 994 6477, FAX 081 994 1533, telex 8811418 SPACES G. **1184**

EXECUTIVE ACCOUNTANT. (UK). Association of Cost & Executive Accounts, 141 149 Fonthill Road/ Tower House, London N4 3HF England. **Tel** 011 44 1 2723925, telex 21610. **743**

EXECUTIVE EXCELLENCE. (US/8756-2308). Stephen Covy and Associates, 3507 North University Avenue, Suite 100, Provo UT 84604. **Tel** (800)331-7716. **867**

EXECUTIVE FEMALE, THE. (US/0199-2880). National Association for Female Executives, 127 West 24th Street, 4th Floor, New York NY 10011. **Tel** (212)477-2200. **867**

EXECUTIVE HEALTH'S GOOD HEALTH REPORT. (US/1071-8680). Executive Health Report, 383 Route 46 West, Fairfield NJ 07004-2402. **Tel** (919)929-7519, FAX (919)929-2458. **2597**

EXECUTIVE HOUSEKEEPING TODAY. (US/0738-6583). National Executive Housekeepers Assn, 1001 Eastwind Drive, Suite 301, Westerville OH 43081. **Tel** (614)895-7166, FAX (614)895-1248. **2790**

EXECUTIVE REPORT (PITTSBURGH, PA.). (US/0279-1382). Executive Report, Three Gateway Center/Fifth Floor, Pittsburgh PA 15222. **Tel** (412)471-4585, FAX (412)644-3006. **674**

EXECUTIVE SPEAKER, THE. (US/0271-3659). The Executive Speaker Company, PO Box 292437, Dayton OH 45429. **Tel** (513)294-8493, FAX (513)294-6044. **867**

EXPORT CONTROL NEWS. (US/0896-0682). Export Control News, 1920 North Street NW, Suite 600, Washington DC 20036. **Tel** (202)463-1250, FAX (202)429-9812, telex 650 3140 383. **834**

EXPORT TIMES (NEW DELHI), THE. (II/0257-8018). S S Gandhi, 221 3 Deendayal Upadhyaya Marg, New Delhi 110002 India. **Tel** 331-7491. **834**

EXTRA PHARMACOPOEIA, THE. (UK). Pharmaceutical Press, 1 Lambeth High Street, London SE1 7JN England. **Tel** 011 44 71 735 9141, FAX 011 44 71 735 7629, telex 265871, (MONREF G). **4304**

F.C.C. WEEK. (US/0738-5714). Dawson-Butwick Publishers, 1300 North 17th Street 1600, Arlington VA 22209. **1111**

FACILITIES DESIGN & MANAGEMENT. (US/0279-4438). Miller Freeman Inc., 600 Harrison Street, San Francisco CA 94107. **Tel** (415)905-2337, FAX (415)905-2240, telex 278273. **2900**

FACTS ON FILE. (US/0014-6641). Facts on File Publications, 460 Park Avenue South, New York NY 10016. **Tel** (212)683-2244, (800)322-8755, FAX (212)683-3633, telex 238 552 FACTS UR. **2616**

FACTSHEET FIVE. (US/0890-6823). Factsheet 5, PO Box 170099, San Francisco CA 94117. **Tel** (415)621-1781. **385**

FAIRFIELD COUNTY BUSINESS JOURNAL. (US/0898-9818). Westfair Communications Inc., 22 Sawmill River Road, Hawthorne NY 10532. **Tel** (914)347-5200, FAX (914)327-5576. **674**

FAITH AND FREEDOM OXFORD. (UK/0014-701X). Manchester College, Mansfield Road, % P B Godfrey, Oxford OX1 3TD, England. **Tel** 11 44 81 393-9122, FAX 11 44 81 393-9122. **4958**

FAMILY HANDYMAN, THE. (US/0014-7230). R D Publications, 28 West 23rd Street, New York NY 10010. **Tel** (800)365-5005, (212)366-8630. **2790**

FARMACEUTSKI GLASNIK. (CI/0014-8202). Hrvatsko Farmaceutsko Drustvo, Masarykova 2, 41000 Zagreb Croatia. **Tel** 011 385 41 427944, FAX 011 385 41 431301. **4304**

FAYETTEVILLE OBSERVER-TIMES, THE. (US/1052-9829). Fayetteville Observer-Times, PO Box 849, Fayetteville NC 28302. **Tel** (919)323-4848. **5723**

FBN (SPARTA, N.J.). (US/1059-2393). Parker and Associates Food Industry Consultants, 66 Woodport Road, Sparta NJ 07871. **2335**

FDA CONSUMER. (US/0362-1332). Superintendent of Documents, US Government Printing Office, Washington DC 20402. **Tel** (202)275-3328, FAX (202)786-2377. **4647**

FDA ENFORCEMENT REPORT. (US/1057-9397). Superintendent of Documents, US Government Printing Office, Washington DC 20402. **Tel** (202)275-3328, FAX (202)786-2377. **1344**

FDA MEDICAL BULLETIN. (US/1063-8067). US Food and Drug Administration / FDA, 5600 Fishers Lane, Room 14-71, Rockville MD 20857. **Tel** (301)443-2410, FAX (301)443-0755. **4305**

FEDERAL & STATE INSURANCE WEEK. (US). JR Publishing Inc., PO Box 6654, McLean VA 22106. **Tel** (703)532-2235. **2880**

FEDERAL BAR NEWS & JOURNAL. (US/0279-4691). Federal Bar Association, 1815 H Street Northwest, Suite 408, Washington DC 20006. **Tel** (202)638-0252, FAX (202)775-0295. **2969**

FEDERAL REGISTER. (US/0097-6326). Superintendent of Documents, US Government Printing Office, Washington DC 20402. **Tel** (202)275-3328, FAX (202)786-2377. **2969**

FERTILIZER INTERNATIONAL. (UK/0015-0304). British Sulphur Corporation Ltd, 31 Mount Pleasant, London WC1X 0AD England. **Tel** 011 44 71 8375600, FAX 011 44 71 8370292, telex 918918 SULFEX G. **87**

FIBER OPTICS NEWS. (US/8756-2049). Phillips Business Information, Inc., 1201 Seven Locks Road, Potomac MD 20854. **Tel** (301)424-3338, (800)777-5006, FAX (301)309-3847. **4434**

FIELD CROP ABSTRACTS. (UK/0015-069X). CAB International Centre, Wallingford, Oxon OX10 8DE United Kingdom. **Tel** 44 491 832111, FAX 44 491 833508, telex 847964 (COMAGG G). **153**

FILM/VIDEO CANADIANA. (CN/0836-1002). National Film Board of Canada, PO Box 6100 Station A, Montreal Quebec H3C 3H5 Canada. **Tel** (514)283-9427, FAX (514)283-7564. **4070**

FINANCE & TREASURY. (US/1070-9215). The Economist Intelligence Unit / New York, 111 West 57th Street, New York NY 10019. **Tel** (800)938-4685, (212)554-0600. **898**

FINANCIAL ANALYSTS JOURNAL, THE. (US/0015-198X). Association for Investment Management Research, PO Box 7947, Charlottesville VA 22906. **Tel** (804)980-3647. **898**

FINANCIAL MARKET TRENDS. (FR/0378-651X). OECD Publications and Information Center, 2 rue Andre-Pascal, 75775 Paris Cedex 16 France. **Tel** 011 33 1 45248167, US:(202)785-6323, FAX 011 33 1 45248500, 45248176, telex 620 160 OCDE. **1491**

FINANCIAL POST, THE. (CN/0015-2021). Financial Post Company Ltd., 333 King Street East, Toronto Ontario M5A 4N2, Canada. **Tel** (416)350-6500, FAX (416)350-6501. **898**

FINANCIAL TECHNOLOGY INTERNATIONAL BULLETIN. (UK/0265-1661). IBC Publishing, 57-61 Mortimer St., London W1N 7TD England. **Tel** 011 44 71 637 4383, FAX 011 44 71 636 6314. **5105**

FINANCIAL WORLD. (US/0015-2064). Financial World, 1328 Broadway, 3rd Floor, New York NY 10001. **Tel** (212)594-5030, FAX (212)629-0021. **898**

FINDEX. (US/0273-4125). Cambridge Information Group Directories Inc, 1200 Quince Orchard Boulevard, Gaithersburg MD 20878. **Tel** (301)590-2300, (800)638-8094, FAX (301)990-8378. **924**

FINNISH TRADE REVIEW. (FI/0015-2463). Finnish Foreign Trade Association, PO Box 908, Arkadiankatu 4-6 BSF, 00101 Helsinki 10 Finland. **Tel** 011 358 0 69591, FAX 011 358 0 694-0028, telex 121696. **835**

FISCAL NOTES. (US). **744**

FISH FARM NEWS, THE. (CN/1180-5633). Fish Farm News, RR 4 Site 465 C-37, Courtenay British Columbia V9N 7J3 Canada. **Tel** (604)338-2455, FAX (604)338-2466. **2301**

FISH FARMING INTERNATIONAL. (UK/0262-0820). EMAP Heighway, Meed House, 21 John Street, London WC1N 2BP England. **Tel** 44 71 4045513, FAX 881 3483, telex 44 71 831 9362. **2301**

FLAME RETARDANCY NEWS. (US/1058-0948). Business Communications Inc., 25 Van Zant Street, Suite 13, Norwalk CT 06855. **Tel** (203)853-4266. **2290**

FLEET EQUIPMENT. (US/0747-2544). Maple Publishing, 134 West Slade, Palatine IL 60067. **Tel** (708)359-6100, FAX (708)359-6420. **5382**

FLIGHT INTERNATIONAL. (UK/0015-3710). Reed Business Publishing / West Sussex, England, Perrymount Road, Haywards Heath, West Sussex RH16 3DH England. **Tel** 011 44 81 6523500. **20**

FLOOR COVERING BUSINESS. (US/1041-2506). International Thomson Retail Press Inc, 345 Park Avenue South, New York NY 10010. **Tel** (212)887-8400. **2905**

FLOORING (NEW YORK, N.Y.). (US/0162-881X). Leo Douglas Publications, 9609 Gayton Road, Suite 100, Richmond VA 23233. **Tel** (804)741-6704. **615**

FLORA ONLINE. (US/0892-9106). Shaun Hardy, Buffalo Museum of Science, Buffalo NY 14211. **511**

FLORIDA ADMINISTRATIVE LAW REPORTS. (US/0194-4800). Florida Administrative Law Reports, PO Box 385, Gainesville FL 32602. **Tel** (904)375-8036. **3093**

FLORIDA TREND. (US/0015-4326). Florida Trend, PO Box 611, St Petersburg FL 33731. **Tel** (813)821-5800, FAX (813)822-5083. **1561**

FLOWER AND GARDEN (KANSAS CITY, MO. : 1982). (US/0891-9534). KC Publishing Inc., 700 West 47th Street, Suite 310, Kansas City MO 64112. **Tel** (816)531-5730, (800)444-0801. **2414**

FLUID ABSTRACTS. CIVIL ENGINEERING. (UK/0962-7170). Elsevier Geo Abstracts, An Imprint of Elsevier Science Ltd., The Boulevard, Langford Lane, Kidlington, Oxford OX5 1GB United Kingdom. **Tel** 011 44 865 843000, 011 44 865 843699, FAX 011 44 865 843010. **2004**

FLUID ABSTRACTS. PROCESS ENGINEERING. (UK/0962-7162). Elsevier Geo Abstracts, An Imprint of Elsevier Science Ltd., The Boulevard, Langford Lane, Kidlington, Oxford OX5 1GB United Kingdom. **Tel** 011 44 865 843000, 011 44 865 843699, FAX 011 44 865 843010. **2004**

FLUID POWER ABSTRACTS. (UK/0015-4644). BHR Group Ltd Brit Hydrom. Research, Cranfield, Bedford MK43 0AJ England. **Tel** 011 44 243 750422, FAX 011 44 243 750074, telex 825059. **2089**

FLUIDEX [ONLINE DATABASE]. (UK). Elsevier Geo Abstracts, An Imprint of Elsevier Science Ltd., The Boulevard, Langford Lane, Kidlington, Oxford OX5 1GB United Kingdom. **Tel** 011 44 865 843000, 011 44 865 843699, FAX 011 44 865 843010. **2004**

FOLIO : THE MAGAZINE FOR MAGAZINE MANAGEMENT. (US/0046-4333). Cowles Business Media Inc., 6 River Bend Center, 911 Hope Street, Stamford CT 06907. **Tel** (203)358-9900, (800)775-3777, FAX (203)357-9014. **4815**

FOLIO'S PUBLISHING NEWS. (US/1053-4563). Cowles Business Media Inc., 6 River Bend Center, 911 Hope Street, Stamford CT 06907. **Tel** (203)358-9900, (800)775-3777, FAX (203)357-9014. **4815**

FOOD & BEVERAGE MARKETING. (US/0731-3799). Charleson Publishing Company, 505 8th Avenue, New York NY 10018. **Tel** (212) 695-0704. **2336**

FOOD & DRINK DAILY. (US). King Publishing Group, 627 National Press Building, Washington DC 20045. **Tel** (202)638-4260, FAX (202)662-9744. **2336**

FOOD & DRUG LETTER, THE. (US/0362-6466). Washington Business Information Inc., 1117 North 19th Street, Suite 200, Arlington VA 22209. **Tel** (703)247-3433, (800)426-0416, FAX (703)247-3421. **2336**

FOOD AND DRUG PACKAGING. (US/0015-6272). Advanstar Communications Inc., 131 West First Street, Duluth MN 55802. **Tel** (218)723-9477, (800)346-0085. **4219**

FOOD CHANNEL, THE. (US/1062-8665). Noble Communications, PO Box 9011, Springfield MO 65890. **Tel** (417)882-5050, ext. 431, FAX (312)644-0493. **2336**

FOOD CHEMICAL NEWS. (US/0015-6337). Food Chemical News Inc, 1101 Pennsylvania Avenue Southeast, Washington DC 20003. **Tel** (202)544-1980, FAX (202)546-3890. **1024**

FOOD, COSMETICS AND DRUG PACKAGING 1986. (UK/0951-4554). Elsevier Advanced Technology, An Imprint of Elsevier Science Ltd., The Boulevard, Langford Lane, Kidlington, Oxford OX5 1GB United Kingdom. **Tel** 011 44 865 843000, 011 44 865 843699, FAX 011 44 865 843010. **4219**

FOOD MANUFACTURE. (UK/0015-6477). Morgan Grampian, 40 Beresford Street Woolwich, London SE18 6BQ England. **Tel** 011 44 81 855 7777, FAX 011 44 81 855 5548, telex 896238. **2338**

FOOD MANUFACTURE INTERNATIONAL. (UK/0267-1506). Morgan Grampian, 40 Beresford Street Woolwich, London SE18 6BQ England. **Tel** 011 44 81 855 7777, FAX 011 44 81 855 5548, telex 896238. **2338**

FOOD MARKETING BRIEFS. (US/0896-4203). Newsletters Inc., PO Box 2730, Bethesda MD 20827. **Tel** (301)469-8507, FAX (301)469-7271. **2338**

FOOD REVIEW. (SA/0257-8867). National Publishing Pty Ltd, 155 2nd Avenue Kenilworth 7700, PO Box 2271, Clareinch 7740 South Africa. **Tel** (021)61-1140, FAX (021)611389, telex 9555542+. **2339**

FOOD TRADE REVIEW. (UK/0015-6671). Food Trade Press Ltd, Station House, Hortons Way, Westerham Kent TN16 1BZ England. **Tel** 011 44 689 50551, 011 44 689 53070, FAX 011 44 689 561285. **2340**

FOODS ADLIBRA (1975). (US/0146-9304). Foods Adlibra Publications, 9000 Plymouth Avenue North, Minneapolis MN 55427. **Tel** (612)540-2720, FAX (612)540-3166, telex 882122. **2362**

FOOTWEAR NEWS. (US/0162-914X). Fairchild Publications Inc, 7 West 34th Street, 4th Floor, New York NY 10001-8191. **Tel** (212)630-4000. **1084**

FOOTWEAR NEWS MAGAZINE. (US/0888-2053). Fairchild Publications Inc, 7 West 34th Street, 4th Floor, New York NY 10001-8191. **Tel** (212)630-4000. **1084**

FOR YOUR INFORMATION (NEW YORK, N. Y.). (US/0890-2992). New York Foundation for Arts, 5 Beekham Street, Suite 600, New York NY 10038. **Tel** (212)233-3900, FAX (212)791-1813. **320**

FORBES. (US/0015-6914). Forbes Magazine, 60 Fifth Avenue, New York NY 10011. **Tel** (212)620-2200, (800)825-0061. **676**

FORENSIC DRUG ABUSE ADVISOR, THE. (US/1048-8731). Forensic Drug Abuse Advisor Inc, PO Box 5139, Berkeley CA 94705. **Tel** (510)339-6420, FAX (510)339-6540. **1344**

FORESIGHT (RESTON, VA.). (US/1063-8407). Marek Enterprise Inc., 800 Third Street, Herndon VA 22070. **Tel** (800)575-2735, FAX (703)709-6328. **676**

FOREST INDUSTRIES (SAN FRANCISCO, CALIF.). (US/0015-7430). Miller Freeman Inc., 600 Harrison Street, San Francisco CA 94107. **Tel** (415)905-2337, FAX (415)905-2240, telex 278273. **2400**

FOREST PRODUCTS ABSTRACTS. (UK/0140-4784). CAB International Centre, Wallingford, Oxon OX10 8DE United Kingdom. **Tel** 44 491 832111, FAX 44 491 833508, telex 847964 (COMAGG G). **2399**

FORESTRY ABSTRACTS. (UK/0015-7538). CAB International Centre, Wallingford, Oxon OX10 8DE United Kingdom. **Tel** 44 491 832111, FAX 44 491 833508, telex 847964 (COMAGG G). **2399**

FORSCHUNGSDOKUMENTATION RAUMORDNUNG, STADEBAU, WOHNUNGSWESEN. (GW). Bundesforschungsanstalt fur Landeskunde und Raumordnung, Informationszentrum Raum und Bau der Fraunhofer-Gesellschaft, Nobelstrasse 12, 7000 Stuttgart 80 Germany. **Tel** (0711)68 68-500. **2823**

FORTUNE. (US/0015-8259). Time Inc. / New York, Time & Life Building, Rockefeller Center, New York NY 10020. **676**

FOUNDATION DIRECTORY, THE. (US/0071-8092). Foundation Center, 79 Fifth Avenue, Department EN, New York NY 10003. **Tel** (212)620-4230, (800)424-9836, FAX (212)807-3677. **4336**

FOUNDRY MANAGEMENT & TECHNOLOGY. (US/0360-8999). Penton Publishing, 1100 Superior Avenue, Cleveland OH 44114-2543. **Tel** (216)696-7000, FAX (216)696-0836. **4002**

FRANCHISING WORLD. (US/1041-7311). International Franchise Association, 1350 New York Avenue Northwest, Suite 900, Washington DC 20005. **Tel** (202)628-8000, telex 323175. **677**

FRAZEE FORUM. (US). Frazee Forum, PO Box 187, Frazee MN 56544. **Tel** (218)334-3566. **5696**

FREE TRADE ADVISORY : THE BIWEEKLY ADVISORY ON HOW THE NORTH AMERICAN FREE TRADE TALKS WILL AFFECT YOUR BUSINESS AND INVESTMENTS IN MEXICO. (US/1058-5745). International Reports Inc, 114 East 32nd Street, Suite 602, New York NY 10016-5506. **Tel** (212)685-6900, FAX (212) 685-8566, telex 233139 RPTUR. **837**

FRESNO BEE, THE. (US/0889-6070). McClatchy Newspapers, PO Box 11016, Fresno CA 93786. **Tel** (209)441-6396. **5635**

FROHLINGER'S MARKETING REPORT. (US/1057-5316). Marketing Strategist Inc, 2060 Holland Way, Merrick NY 11566. **Tel** (516)867-7253, (800)962-7558. **924**

FROZEN FOOD AGE. (US/0016-2191). Frozen Food Age Publishing Corporation, Four Stamford Forum, Stamford CT 06901. **Tel** (203)325-3500. **2341**

FTC FREEDOM OF INFORMATION LOG. (US/0161-7036). Washington Regulatory Reporting Association, PO Box 356, Basye VA 22810. **Tel** (703)856-2216. **837**

FTC : WATCH. (US/0196-0016). Washington Regulatory Reporting Association, PO Box 356, Basye VA 22810. **Tel** (703)856-2216. **2972**

FULLTEXT SOURCES ONLINE. (US/1040-8258). Bibliodata, PO Box 61, Needham Heights MA 02194. **Tel** (617)444-1154, FAX (617)449-4584. **3211**

FUND RAISING MANAGEMENT. (US/0016-268X). Hoke Communications Inc, 224 7th Street, Garden City NY 11530. **Tel** (516)746-6700, (800)229-6700. **868**

FUSION POWER REPORT. (US/0276-2919). Business Publishers Inc., 951 Pershing Drive, Silver Spring MD 20910-4464. **Tel** (301)587-6300, (800)274-0122, FAX (301)585-9075. **1945**

FW FINANCIAL WORLD. (US). Financial World, 1328 Broadway, 3rd Floor, New York NY 10001. **Tel** (212)594-5030, FAX (212)629-0021. **899**

FX WEEK. (US/1050-0782). Waters Information Services, PO Box 2248, Binghamton NY 13902-2248. **Tel** (607)770-8535, FAX (607)798-1692. **677**

GALE DIRECTORY OF DATABASES. (US/1066-8934). Gale Research Inc., 835 Penobscot Building, 645 Griswold Street, Detroit MI 48226. **Tel** (800)877-GALE, (313)961-2242, FAX (313)961-6083, (800)414-5043, telex TWX 810-221-7086. **1237**

GALE DIRECTORY OF PUBLICATIONS AND BROADCAST MEDIA. (US/1048-7972). Gale Research Inc., 835 Penobscot Building, 645 Griswold Street, Detroit MI 48226. **Tel** (800)877-GALE, (313)961-2242, FAX (313)961-6083, (800)414-5043, telex TWX 810-221-7086. **1132**

GAO JOURNAL. (US). US General Accounting Office / District of Columbia, 441 G Street NW, Room 4528, Washington DC 20548. **Tel** (202)275-2812. **744**

GAS DAILY. (US/0885-5935). Pasha Publications Inc., 1616 North Fort Myer Drive, Suite 1000, Arlington VA 22209. **Tel** (800)424-2908, (703)528-1244, FAX (703)528-3742, (703)528-1253. **4257**

GAS ENERGY REVIEW. (US/8756-5471). American Gas Association / Virginia, 1515 Wilson Boulevard, Arlington VA 22209. **Tel** (703)841-8400, (703)841-8559, FAX (703)841-8697. **4257**

GAS WORLD (LONDON, ENGLAND : 1974). (UK/0308-7654). Benn Business Information Service Ltd, Riverbank House, Angel Lane, Tonbridge Kent TN9 1SE England. **Tel** 011 44 732 362666, FAX 011 44 732 770483, telex 95454 BBIS. **4258**

GDI IMPULS. (SZ). Gottlieb Duttweiler-Institut, CH-8803 Ruschlikon Switzerland. **Tel** 011 41 1 7246111, FAX 011 41 1 7246262, telex 826 510. **5200**

GENERAL PERIODICALS ONDISC (RESEARCH 1 ED.). (US/1064-8380). University Microfilms International, 300 North Zeeb Road, Ann Arbor MI 48106-1346. **Tel** (313)761-4700, (800)521-0600 Exts. 2490, 2491, FAX (313)973-1540. **2496**

GENERAL SCIENCE INDEX. (US/0162-1963). H W Wilson Company, 950 University Avenue, Bronx NY 10452. **Tel** (800)367-6770, (718)588-8400, FAX (718)590-1617, telex 4990003 HWILSON. **5175**

GENERAL SCIENCE INDEX. CD-ROM. (US/0162-1963). H W Wilson Company, 950 University Avenue, Bronx NY 10452. **Tel** (800)367-6770, (718)588-8400, FAX (718)590-1617, telex 4990003 HWILSON. **5107**

GENETIC TECHNOLOGY NEWS. (US/0272-9032). Technical Insights Inc., PO Box 1304, Fort Lee NJ 07024-9967. **Tel** (201)568-4744, FAX (201)568-8247, telex 425900 SWIFT UI. **5107**

GENETICS ABSTRACTS. (US/0016-674X). Cambridge Scientific Abstracts, 7200 Wisconsin Avenue, #601, Bethesda MD 20814-4823. **Tel** (301)961-6750, (800)843-7751, FAX (301)961-6720. **478**

GEOARCHIVE ON CD-ROM. (US/1070-6046). Geosystems Inc., PO Box 40, Didcot, Oxon OX11 9BX England. **Tel** 011 44 235 813913. **1376**

GEOBASE. (UK). Elsevier Geo Abstracts, An Imprint of Elsevier Science Ltd., The Boulevard, Langford Lane, Kidlington, Oxford OX5 1GB United Kingdom. **Tel** 011 44 865 843000, 011 44 865 843699, FAX 011 44 865 843010. **2561**

GEOGRAPHICAL ABSTRACTS. HUMAN GEOGRAPHY. (UK/0953-9611). Elsevier Geo Abstracts, An Imprint of Elsevier Science Ltd., The Boulevard, Langford Lane, Kidlington, Oxford OX5 1GB United Kingdom. **Tel** 011 44 865 843000, 011 44 865 843699, FAX 011 44 865 843010. **2580**

GEOGRAPHICAL ABSTRACTS : PHYSICAL GEOGRAPHY. (UK/0954-0504). Elsevier Geo Abstracts, An Imprint of Elsevier Science Ltd., The Boulevard, Langford Lane, Kidlington, Oxford OX5 1GB United Kingdom. **Tel** 011 44 865 843000, 011 44 865 843699, FAX 011 44 865 843010. **2580**

GEOLOGICAL ABSTRACTS. (UK/0954-0512). Elsevier Geo Abstracts, An Imprint of Elsevier Science Ltd., The Boulevard, Langford Lane, Kidlington, Oxford OX5 1GB United Kingdom. **Tel** 011 44 865 843000, 011 44 865 843699, FAX 011 44 865 843010. **1362**

GEOREF (CD-ROM). (US/0197-7482). Silverplatter Information Inc., 100 River Ridge Drive, Norwood MA 02062. **Tel** (800)343-0064, (617)769-2599, FAX (617)235-1715. **1363**

GEORGETOWN LAW JOURNAL, THE. (US/0016-8092). Georgetown University Law Center, 600 New Jersey Avenue NW, Washington DC 20009. **Tel** (202)662-9468, FAX (202)662-9444. **2974**

GEORGIA TREND. (US/0882-5971). Williams Communication, 1770 Indian Trail Road, Suite 350, Norcross GA 30093. **Tel** (404)806-6700. **1492**

GEOSCIENCE DOCUMENTATION. (UK/0016-8483). Geosystems Inc., PO Box 40, Didcot, Oxon OX11 9BX England. **Tel** 011 44 235 813913. **1363**

GEYER'S OFFICE DEALER. (US/0746-8997). Geyer-McAllister Publications Inc, 51 Madison Avenue, New York NY 10010. **Tel** (212)689-4411. **4211**

GIFTS & DECORATIVE ACCESSORIES. (US/0016-9889). Geyer-McAllister Publications Inc, 51 Madison Avenue, New York NY 10010. **Tel** (212)689-4411. **2584**

GLASS INTERNATIONAL. (UK/0143-7836). Argus Press Group, Queensway House, 2 Queensway Redhill, Surrey RH1 1QS England. **Tel** 011 44 737 768611, 011 44 737 761685, FAX 011 44 737 760510, telex 948669 TOPJNL G. **2590**

GLOBAL COMMUNICATIONS. (US/0195-2250). Cardiff Publishing Company, 6300 South Syracuse Way, Suite 650, Englewood CO 80111. **Tel** (303)220-0600, telex 450726. **1112**

GLOBAL ENVIRONMENTAL CHANGE REPORT. (US/1049-9083). Cutter Information Corporation, 37 Broadway, Arlington MA 02174-5539. **Tel** (617)648-8700, (800)964-5118, FAX (617)648-8707, (617)648-1950, telex 650 100 9891. **2216**

GLOBAL INVESTOR. (UK/0951-3604). Euromoney Publications PLC, Nestor House, Playhouse Yard, London EC4Z 5EX England. **Tel** 011 44 71 779 8888, FAX 011 44 71 779 8617, telex 290700 EUROMON G. **899**

GLOBAL MONEY MANAGEMENT. (US). Institutional Investor Inc., 488 Madison Avenue, New York NY 10022. **Tel** (212)303-3234, (212)303-3233, FAX (212)303-3353. **789**

GLOBAL OIL STOCKS & BALANCES. (US). Petroleum Intelligence Weekly, 575 Broadway, 4th Floor, New York NY 10012-3230. **Tel** (212)941-5500, FAX (212)941-5509, telex 62371 PETROIN. **4259**

GLOBAL TELECOM REPORT. (US/1059-4485). Phillips Business Information, Inc., 1201 Seven Locks Road, Potomac MD 20854. **Tel** (301)424-3338, (800)777-5006, FAX (301)309-3847. **1156**

GMP LETTER, THE. (US/0196-626X). Washington Business Information Inc., 1117 North 19th Street, Suite 200, Arlington VA 22209. **Tel** (703)247-3433, (800)426-0416, FAX (703)247-3421. **3479**

GOING PUBLIC. (US/0882-9489). Dealers Digest Inc, Two World Trade Center/18th Floor, New York NY 10048. **Tel** (212)227-1200. **789**

GOLF PRO. (US/1072-1274). Fairchild Publications Inc, 7 West 34th Street, 4th Floor, New York NY 10001-8191. **Tel** (212)630-4000. **4897**

GOOD HOUSEKEEPING (U.S. ED.). (US/0017-209X). The Hearst Corporation, 250 West 55th Street, New York NY 10019. **Tel** (212)649-4014. **2790**

GORMAN'S NEW PRODUCT NEWS. (US/1048-020X). Trend Publishing Inc, 625 North Michigan Avenue, Suite 2500, Chicago IL 60611-3109. **Tel** (312)654-2300, FAX (312)654-2323. **678**

GOVERNMENT COMPUTER NEWS. (US/0738-4300). Cahners Publishing Company, 249 West 17th Street, New York NY 10011. **Tel** (212)645-0067, FAX (212)242-6987. **4651**

GOVERNMENT PRODUCT NEWS. (US/0017-2642). Penton Publishing, 1100 Superior Avenue, Cleveland OH 44114-2543. **Tel** (216)696-7000, FAX (216)696-0836. **950**

GOVERNMENTS OF AUSTRALIA. (AT). International Public Relations Pty Ltd., 33 Walsh Street, West Melbourne Victoria 3003 Australia. **Tel** 011 61 03 329 9333, FAX 011 61 03 329 7996. **4652**

GOWER FEDERAL SERVICE: MINING. (US). Rocky Mountain Mineral Law Foundation, Porter Administration Building, 7039 East 18th Avenue, Denver CO 80220. **Tel** (303)321-8100, FAX (303)321-7657. **2975**

GOWER FEDERAL SERVICE - MISCELLANEOUS LANDS DECISIONS SERVICE. (US). Rocky Mountain Mineral Law Foundation, Porter Administration Building, 7039 East 18th Avenue, Denver CO 80220. **Tel** (303)321-8100, FAX (303)321-7657. **2975**

GOWER FEDERAL SERVICE ROYALTY VALUATION AND MANAGEMENT. (US). Rocky Mountain Mineral Law Foundation, Porter Administration Building, 7039 East 18th Avenue, Denver CO 80220. **Tel** (303)321-8100, FAX (303)321-7657. **1440**

GOWER — Serials available Online

GOWER FEDERAL SERVICES PLAN. (US). Rocky Mountain Mineral Law Foundation, Porter Administration Building, 7039 East 18th Avenue, Denver CO 80220. Tel (303)321-8100, FAX (303)321-7657. **4838**

GPS REPORT. (US/1056-7127). Phillips Business Information, Inc., 1201 Seven Locks Road, Potomac MD 20854. Tel (301)424-3338, (800)777-5006, FAX (301)309-3847. **1156**

GRAND RAPIDS BUSINESS JOURNAL. (US/1045-4055). Grand Rapids Business Journal, 40 Pearl Street NW/Suite 1040, Grand Rapids MI 49503. Tel (616)459-4545. **678**

GRASSLANDS AND FORAGE ABSTRACTS. (UK/1350-9837). CAB International Centre, Wallingford, Oxon OX10 8DE United Kingdom. Tel 44 491 832111, FAX 44 491 833508, telex 847964 (COMAGG G). **153**

GREAT LAKES REPORTER, THE. (US/0748-9544). Center for Great Lakes Studies, 35 East Wacker Drive, Suite 1870, Chicago IL 60601. Tel (312)263-0785. **2172**

GREATER BATON ROUGE BUSINESS REPORT, THE. (US/0747-4652). Baton Rouge Business Report, PO Box 1949, Baton Rouge LA 70821. **678**

GREATER CINCINNATI BUSINESS RECORD, THE. (US/1044-9264). Greater Cincinnati Business Record, 36 East 7th Street, Suite 1500, Cincinnati OH 45202. Tel (513)421-9300. **678**

GREATER LANSING BUSINESS MONTHLY. (US). Greater Lansing Business Monthly, 300 South Washington Square, Suite 580, Lansing MI 48933. Tel (517)487-1714, FAX (517)487-9597. **678**

GREEN MARKETALERT. (US/1052-1755). MarketAlert Publications, 345 Wood Creek Road, Bethlehem CT 06751. **2173**

GREEN MARKETING REPORT. (US/1051-7316). Business Publishers Inc., 951 Pershing Drive, Silver Spring MD 20910-4464. Tel (301)587-6300, (800)274-0122, FAX (301)585-9075. **925**

GREEN MARKETS. (US/0149-5569). Pike & Fischer Inc., 4600 East-West Highway, Suite 200, Bethesda MD 20814-1438. Tel (301)654-6262, FAX (301)654-6297. **90**

GREENHOUSE EFFECT REPORT. (US/1042-5039). Business Publishers Inc., 951 Pershing Drive, Silver Spring MD 20910-4464. Tel (301)587-6300, (800)274-0122, FAX (301)585-9075. **2230**

GREENSBORO NEWS & RECORD. (US/0747-1858). Greensboro News & Record Inc, PO Box 20848, Mail Subscriptions Department, Greensboro NC 27401. Tel (910)274-5280 or, 800 553-6880. **5723**

GREENWEEK. (AT/1034-5876). Greenweek, PO Box 1982, Southport QLD 4215 Australia. Tel 011 60 75 328333, FAX 011 60 75 918206. **2194**

GREETINGS MAGAZINE. (US/1064-2048). MacKay Publishing Corporation, 309 Fifth Avenue, New York NY 10016. Tel (212)679-6677, FAX (212)679-6374. **2584**

GROCER. MONTHLY SUPPLEMENT, THE. (UK). William Reed Ltd, Broadfield Park, Crawley, West Sussex RH11 9RJ England. Tel 011 44 293 613400, FAX 0293-613156. **2342**

GROCERY MARKETING. (US/0888-0360). Trend Publishing Inc, 625 North Michigan Avenue, Suite 2500, Chicago IL 60611-3109. Tel (312)654-2300, FAX (312)654-2323. **2343**

GROUNDWATER MONITOR. (US/0882-6188). Business Publishers Inc., 951 Pershing Drive, Silver Spring MD 20910-4464. Tel (301)587-6300, (800)274-0122, FAX (301)585-9075. **1414**

GUARDIAN (LONDON). (UK/0261-3077). The Guardian, 164 Deansgate, Manchester M60 2RR England. Tel 011 44 61 8327200. **5812**

GUNS & AMMO. (US/0017-5684). Petersen Publishing Company, 6420 Wilshire Bouldevard, Los Angeles CA 90048. Tel (213)782-2485. **4897**

HABS. HOUSING ABSTRACTS. (UK/0952-8156). London Research Centre, 81 Black Prince Road, London SE1 7SZ England. Tel 011 44 71 627 9666, FAX 011 44 71 627 9674. **2823**

HARPER'S BAZAAR. (US/0017-7873). The Hearst Corporation, 250 West 55th Street, New York NY 10019. Tel (212)649-4014. **1085**

HARRIS COUNTY REAL ESTATE REPORT. (US). Revac Publications, 11777 Katy Freeway, Suite 500, Houston TX 77079. Tel (713)496-2388. **4838**

HARVARD BUSINESS REVIEW. (US/0017-8012). Harvard Business Review, Soldiers Field, Boston MA 02163. Tel (617)495-6801, (800)274-3214. **679**

HARVARD HEALTH LETTER. (US/1052-1577). Harvard Medical School, 164 Longwood Avenue, 1st Floor, Boston MA 02115. Tel (617)432-1485, FAX (617)432-1506. **3580**

HARVARD JOURNAL OF LAW & PUBLIC POLICY. (US/0193-4872). Harvard Law School, Publications Center, Cambridge MA 02138. Tel (617)495-7984, (617)495-3694. **2976**

HASTINGS CENTER REPORT, THE. (US/0093-0334). The Hastings Center, 255 Elm Road, Briarcliff Manor NY 10510-9974. Tel (914)762-8500, FAX (914)762-2124. **3580**

HASTINGS COMMUNICATIONS AND ENTERTAINMENT LAW JOURNAL (COMM/ENT). (US/1061-6578). Hastings College of Law, 200 McAllister Street, San Francisco CA 94102. Tel (415)565-4816, (415)565-4738, FAX (415)565-4814. **2977**

HASTINGS CONSTITUTIONAL LAW QUARTERLY. (US/0094-5617). Hastings College of Law, 200 McAllister Street, San Francisco CA 94102. Tel (415)565-4816, (415)565-4738, FAX (415)565-4814. **3093**

HASTINGS INTERNATIONAL AND COMPARATIVE LAW REVIEW. (US/0149-9246). Hastings College of Law, 200 McAllister Street, San Francisco CA 94102. Tel (415)565-4816, (415)565-4738, FAX (415)565-4814. **3129**

HASTINGS LAW JOURNAL. (US/0017-8322). Hastings College of Law, 200 McAllister Street, San Francisco CA 94102. Tel (415)565-4816, (415)565-4738, FAX (415)565-4814. **2977**

HASTINGS WOMEN'S LAW JOURNAL. (US/1061-0901). Hastings College of Law, 200 McAllister Street, San Francisco CA 94102. Tel (415)565-4816, (415)565-4738, FAX (415)565-4814. **2977**

HAWAII BUSINESS. (US/0440-5056). Hawaii Business Publishing Corporation, PO Box 913, Honolulu HI 96808. Tel (808)946-3978. **679**

HAWAII INVESTOR. (US/0745-7073). Honolulu Publishing Company Ltd, 36 Merchant Street, Honolulu HI 96813. Tel (800)272-5245, (808)524-7400. **4838**

HAZARDOUS WASTE BUSINESS. (US/0897-2699). McGraw Hill Publishing Company, Inc., 1221 Avenue of the Americas, New York NY 10020. Tel (212)512-6410, (800)525-5003, FAX (212)512-6111. **2231**

HAZARDOUS WASTE NEWS. (US/0275-374X). Business Publishers Inc., 951 Pershing Drive, Silver Spring MD 20910-4464. Tel (301)587-6300, (800)274-0122, FAX (301)585-9075. **2231**

HAZMAT TRANSPORT NEWS. (US). Business Publishers Inc., 951 Pershing Drive, Silver Spring MD 20910-4464. Tel (301)587-6300, (800)274-0122, FAX (301)585-9075. **2232**

HDTV NEWSLETTER. (US/0892-5771). Advanced Television Publishing, 753 East Fall Creek Road, Alsea OR 97324. Tel (503)487-4186, FAX (503)222-2341. **1132**

HDTV REPORT. (US/1055-9280). Phillips Business Information, Inc., 1201 Seven Locks Road, Potomac MD 20854. Tel (301)424-3338, (800)777-5006, FAX (301)309-3847. **1132**

HEALTH AND SAFETY SCIENCE ABSTRACTS. (US/0892-9351). Cambridge Scientific Abstracts, 7200 Wisconsin Avenue, #601, Bethesda MD 20814-4823. Tel (301)961-6750, (800)843-7751, FAX (301)961-6720. **4810**

HEALTH BUSINESS. (US/1062-6107). Faulkner & Gray Inc., 11 Penn Plaza, 17th Floor, New York NY 10001. Tel (212)967-7000, (800)535-8403. **925**

HEALTH CARE COMPETITION WEEK. (US/0886-2095). Capitol Publications, 1101 King Street, Suite 444, Alexandria VA 22314. Tel (703)683-4100, (800)655-5597. **4778**

HEALTH CARE FINANCING REVIEW. (US/0195-8631). Superintendent of Documents, US Government Printing Office, Washington DC 20402. Tel (202)275-3328, FAX (202)786-2377. **2897**

HEALTH CARE MANAGEMENT REVIEW. (US/0361-6274). Aspen Publishers Inc., 7201 McKinney Circle, Frederick MD 21701. Tel (800)234-1660, (301)698-7100, FAX (301)251-5784, telex 5106014543. **3781**

HEALTH CARE STRATEGIC MANAGEMENT. (US/0742-1478). Business Word Inc., 5350 South Roslyn Street, Suite 400, Englewood CA 80111-2125. Tel (303)290-8500, FAX (303)290-9025. **3781**

HEALTH DEVICES ALERTS. (US/0163-0458). ECRI Emergency Care Research Institute, 5200 Butler Pike, Plymouth Meeting PA 19462. Tel (215)825-6000, FAX (215)834-1275, telex 510-660-8023. **3659**

HEALTH FACTS. (US/0738-811X). Center for Medical Consumers, 237 Thompson Street, New York NY 10012. Tel (212)674-7105, FAX (212)674-7100. **4779**

HEALTH INDUSTRY TODAY. (US/0745-4678). Business Word Inc., 5350 South Roslyn Street, Suite 400, Englewood CA 80111-2125. Tel (303)290-8500, FAX (303)290-9025. **3581**

HEALTH LAWYER, THE. (US/0736-3443). American Bar Association, 750 North Lake Shore Drive, Chicago IL 60611. Tel (312)988-5522, (312)988-5241, FAX (312)988-5528, telex 270593. **2978**

HEALTH LEGISLATION AND REGULATION. (US/0899-8965). Faulkner & Gray Inc., 11 Penn Plaza, 17th Floor, New York NY 10001. Tel (212)967-7000, (800)535-8403. **2978**

HEALTH MANAGEMENT TECHNOLOGY. (US/1074-4770). Argus Business, 6151 Powers Ferry Road, Atlanta GA 30339. Tel (404)995-2500, (800)233-3359. **3582**

HEALTH MANAGER'S UPDATE. (US/0894-4679). McGraw Hill Healthcare Information Center, 1120 Vermont Avenue NW/Suite 1200, Washington DC 20005. Tel (202)686-7900. **4780**

HEALTH MATRIX. (US/0748-383X). Case Western Reserve University School of Law, 11075 East Boulevard, Cleveland OH 44106. Tel (216)368-3304, FAX (216)368-6144. **3740**

HEALTH NEWS & REVIEW. (US/1056-1900). Keats Publishing, PO Box 876, New Canaan CT 06840. Tel (203)966-8721, FAX (203)972-3991. **4191**

HEALTH PERIODICALS DATABASE [ONLINE DATABASE]. (US). Information Access Company, 362 Lakeside Drive, Foster City CA 94404. Tel (800)227-8431. **2602**

HEALTH PLANNING AND ADMINISTRATION DATABASE (HEALTH). (US). American Hospital Association, 840 North Lake Shore Drive, Chicago IL 60611. Tel (312)280-6000, (800)242-2626. **3781**

HEALTH SYSTEMS REVIEW. (US/1055-7466). Federation of American Health Systems, 1405 North Pierce, Suite 311, Little Rock AR 72207. Tel (501)661-9555, FAX (501)663-4903. **3782**

HEALTH TIPS. (US). California Medical Association, PO Box 7690, San Franciso CA 94120-5179. Tel (415)541-0900, FAX (415)882-5116. **4781**

HEALTHCARE EXECUTIVE. (US/0883-5381). American College of Healthcare Executives, 840 North Lake Shore Drive, c/o J. Flory, Chicago IL 60611. Tel (312)943-0544 ext. 3000, FAX (312)943-3791. **3782**

HEALTHCARE FINANCIAL MANAGEMENT. (US/0735-0732). HFMA - Healthcare Financial Management Association, 2 Westbrook Corporation Center, Suite 700, Westchester IL 60154-5700. Tel (708)531-9600, (800)252-4362. **3782**

HEALTHCARE FORUM JOURNAL, THE. (US/0899-9287). Healthcare Forum Journal, 830 Market Street/8th Floor, San Francisco CA 92102. Tel (415)421-8810, FAX (415)421-8837. **3583**

HEALTHCARE PR NEWS. (US/1068-0403). Phillips Business Information, Inc., 1201 Seven Locks Road, Potomac MD 20854. Tel (301)424-3338, (800)777-5006, FAX (301)309-3847. **3782**

HEALTHCARE TECHNOLOGY BUSINESS OPPORTUNITIES. (US/1049-4499). American Health Consultants, 3525 Piedmont Road, Suite 400, Atlanta GA 30305. Tel (800)688-2421, (404)262-7436. **3583**

HEALTHWEEK. (US/0890-2259). Hutchins & Associates, 1865 East Valley Parkway/Suite 206, Escondido CA 92027. **4782**

HEARTCARE. (US). Heartcorps Inc., 5655 Lindero Canyon Road, Suite 701, Westlake Village CA 91362. **3705**

HEATING, PIPING, AND AIR CONDITIONING. (US/0017-940X). Penton Publishing, 1100 Superior Avenue, Cleveland OH 44114-2543. Tel (216)696-7000, FAX (216)696-0836. **2605**

HELICOPTER NEWS. (US/0363-8227). Phillips Business Information, Inc., 1201 Seven Locks Road, Potomac MD 20854. Tel (301)424-3338, (800)777-5006, FAX (301)309-3847. **23**

HELMINTHOLOGICAL ABSTRACTS. (UK/0957-6789). CAB International Centre, Wallingford, Oxon OX10 8DE United Kingdom. Tel 44 491 832111, FAX 44 491 833508, telex 847964 (COMAGG G). **5604**

HERB IRELAND'S SALES PROSPECTOR. CALIFORNIA, ARIZONA, NEVADA AND HAWAII. (US/0270-8833). Westgate Publishing Co., 635 Madison Avenue, 4th Floor, New York NY 10022. Tel (212)715-8652. **925**

HERB IRELAND'S SALES PROSPECTOR. CANADA. (US/0270-8817). MacLean Hunter Publishing Corporation / Chicago, IL, 29 North Wacker Drive, Chicago IL 60606-3298. Tel (312)726-2802, FAX (312)726-3091. **616**

HERB IRELAND'S SALES PROSPECTOR. COLORADO, IDAHO, MONTANA, OREGON, UTAH, WASHINGTON, WYOMING AND ALASKA. (US/0270-8825). Prospector Research Service Inc, PO Box 518, 751 Main Street, Waltham MA 02154. **Tel** (617)899-1271. **925**

HERB IRELAND'S SALES PROSPECTOR. GEORGIA, FLORIDA, ALABAMA AND NORTH AND SOUTH CAROLINA. (US/0270-8752). Prospector Research Service Inc, PO Box 518, 751 Main Street, Waltham MA 02154. **Tel** (617)899-1271. **925**

HERB IRELAND'S SALES PROSPECTOR. ILLINOIS AND INDIANA. (US/0270-8736). Prospector Research Service Inc, PO Box 518, 751 Main Street, Waltham MA 02154. **Tel** (617)899-1271. **925**

HERB IRELAND'S SALES PROSPECTOR. LOUISIANA, MISSISSIPPI, ARKANSAS, OKLAHOMA, KENTUCKY AND TENNESSEE. (US/0270-8779). Prospector Research Services Inc, PO Box 518, 751 Main Street, Waltham MA 02154. **925**

HERB IRELAND'S SALES PROSPECTOR. MARYLAND, VIRGINIA, WEST VIRGINIA, NORTH AND SOUTH CAROLINA, AND DISTRICT OF COLUMBIA. (US/0270-8760). Prospector Research Service Inc, PO Box 518, 751 Main Street, Waltham MA 02154. **Tel** (617)899-1271. **925**

HERB IRELAND'S SALES PROSPECTOR. MISSOURI, KANSAS, IOWA AND NEBRASKA. (US/0270-8795). Prospector Research Service Inc, PO Box 518, 751 Main Street, Waltham MA 02154. **Tel** (617)899-1271. **925**

HERB IRELAND'S SALES PROSPECTOR. NEW ENGLAND. (US/0270-8698). Prospector Research Service Inc, PO Box 518, 751 Main Street, Waltham MA 02154. **Tel** (617)899-1271. **925**

HERB IRELAND'S SALES PROSPECTOR. NEW YORK, NEW JERSEY AND SOUTHERN CONNECTICUT. (US/0270-8701). Prospector Research Services Inc, PO Box 518, 751 Main Street, Waltham MA 02154. **925**

HERB IRELAND'S SALES PROSPECTOR. OHIO AND MICHIGAN. (US/0270-8728). Prospector Research Service Inc, PO Box 518, 751 Main Street, Waltham MA 02154. **Tel** (617)899-1271. **925**

HERB IRELAND'S SALES PROSPECTOR. PENNSYLVANIA, DELAWARE AND SOUTHERN NEW JERSEY. (US/0270-871X). Prospector Research Services Inc, PO Box 518, 751 Main Street, Waltham MA 02154. **925**

HERB IRELAND'S SALES PROSPECTOR. TEXAS, OKLAHOMA AND NEW MEXICO. (US/0270-8787). Prospector Research Service Inc, PO Box 518, 751 Main Street, Waltham MA 02154. **Tel** (617)899-1271. **925**

HERB IRELAND'S SALES PROSPECTOR. WISCONSIN, MINNESOTA, IOWA, NORTH AND SOUTH DAKOTA. (US/0270-8809). Prospector Research Service Inc, PO Box 518, 751 Main Street, Waltham MA 02154. **Tel** (617)899-1271. **925**

HERBAGE ABSTRACTS. (UK/0018-0602). CAB International Centre, Wallingford, Oxon OX10 8DE United Kingdom. **Tel** 44 491 832111, FAX 44 491 833508, telex 847964 (COMAGG G). **154**

HEWLETT-PACKARD JOURNAL. (US/0018-1153). Hewlett Packard, 1000 Northeast Circle Boulevard, Corvallis OR 97330. **Tel** (503)757-2000. **1186**

HFD. (US/0746-7885). Fairchild Publications Inc, 7 West 34th Street, 4th Floor, New York NY 10001-8191. **Tel** (212)630-4000. **2906**

HIGH PERFORMANCE PLASTICS. (UK/0264-7753). Elsevier Advanced Technology, An Imprint of Elsevier Science Ltd., The Boulevard, Langford Lane, Kidlington, Oxford OX5 1GB United Kingdom. **Tel** 011 44 865 843000, 011 44 865 843699, FAX 011 44 865 843010. **4455**

HIGH PERFORMANCE TEXTILES. (UK/0144-5871). Elsevier Advanced Technology, An Imprint of Elsevier Science Ltd., The Boulevard, Langford Lane, Kidlington, Oxford OX5 1GB United Kingdom. **Tel** 011 44 865 843000, 011 44 865 843699, FAX 011 44 865 843010. **5351**

HIGH TECH CERAMICS NEWS. (US/1045-2397). Business Communications Inc., 25 Van Zant Street, Suite 13, Norwalk CT 06855. **Tel** (203)853-4266. **2590**

HIGH-TECH MATERIALS ALERT. (US/0741-0808). Technical Insights Inc., PO Box 1304, Fort Lee NJ 07024-9967. **Tel** (201)568-4744, FAX (201)568-8247, telex 425900 SWIFT UI. **1977**

HIGH TECH SEPARATIONS NEWS. (US/1046-039X). Business Communications Inc., 25 Van Zant Street, Suite 13, Norwalk CT 06855. **Tel** (203)853-4266. **1015**

HILITES DATABASE [ONLINE DATABASE]. (US). Ergosyst Associates Inc, 123 West Eighth Street, Suite 1012, Lawrence KS 66044-2605. **Tel** (913)842-7334, FAX (913)842-7348. **1209**

HISPANIC AMERICAN PERIODICALS INDEX (LOS ANGELES, CALIF.). (US/0270-8558). Regents of the University of California at Los Angeles, 405 Hilgard Avenue, Los Angeles CA 90024-1447. **Tel** (310)825-6634. **2496**

HISTORICAL ABSTRACTS. PART A, MODERN HISTORY ABSTRACTS. (US/0363-2717). ABC Clio Press, PO Box 1911, 130 Cremona, Santa Barbara CA 93117. **Tel** (805)968-1911, (800)422-2546, FAX (805)685-9685. **2635**

HISTORICAL ABSTRACTS. PART B, TWENTIETH CENTURY ABSTRACTS. (US/0363-2725). ABC Clio Press, PO Box 1911, 130 Cremona, Santa Barbara CA 93117. **Tel** (805)968-1911, (800)422-2546, FAX (805)685-9685. **2635**

HOLLYWOOD REPORTER, THE. (US/0018-3660). Hollywood Reporter, 5055 Wilshire Boulevard, 6th Floor, Los Angeles CA 90036. **Tel** (213)525-2000. **4072**

HOME BUSINESS ADVOCATE, THE. (CN/0832-8595). Alternate Press, 272 Highway 5, Rural Route 1, St. George Ontario N0E 1N0 Canada. **Tel** (519)448-4001, FAX (519)448-4001. **680**

HOME FASHIONS MAGAZINE. (US/0896-7962). Fairchild Publications Inc, 7 West 34th Street, 4th Floor, New York NY 10001-8191. **Tel** (212)630-4000. **2900**

HOME OFFICE COMPUTING. (US/0899-7373). Scholastic Inc., 2931 East McCarty Street, PO Box 3710, Jefferson City MO 65102-9957. **Tel** (314)636-5271, (800)631-1586. **1267**

HOME POWER. (US/1050-2416). Home Power, PO Box 520, Ashland OR 97520. **Tel** (916)475-3179, FAX (916)475-3179. **1946**

HONGKONGIANA. (HK). Hong Kong Polytechnic Library, Hong Kong Polytechnic Hung Hom, Kowloon Hong Kong. **Tel** (852) 7666854, FAX (852) 7658274, telex 38964 POLYX HX. **2504**

HONOLULU ADVERTISER, THE. (US/1072-7191). Hawaii Newspaper Agency Inc. / Department of Circulation, PO Box 3350, Honolulu HI 96801. **Tel** (808)525-8000, (808)525-7657, FAX (808)525-7423. **5656**

HONOLULU STAR-BULLETIN. (US). Hawaii Newspaper Agency Inc. / Department of Circulation, PO Box 3350, Honolulu HI 96801. **Tel** (808)525-8000, (808)525-7657, FAX (808)525-7423. **5656**

HORN BOOK MAGAZINE (1945), THE. (US/0018-5078). The Horn Book Inc, 11 Beacon Street, Suite 1000, Boston MA 02108-3704. **Tel** (617)227-1555, (800)325-1170, FAX (617)523-0299. **1064**

HORTICULTURAL ABSTRACTS. (UK/0018-5280). CAB International Centre, Wallingford, Oxon OX10 8DE United Kingdom. **Tel** 44 491 832111, FAX 44 491 833508, telex 847964 (COMAGG G). **2434**

HOSPITAL & HEALTH SERVICES ADMINISTRATION. (US/8750-3735). American College of Healthcare Executives, 840 North Lake Shore Drive, c/o J. Flory, Chicago IL 60611. **Tel** (312)943-0544 ext. 3000, FAX (312)943-3791. **3783**

HOSPITAL LITERATURE INDEX. (US/0018-5736). American Hospital Association, 840 North Lake Shore Drive, Chicago IL 60611. **Tel** (312)280-6000, (800)242-2626. **3659**

HOSPITAL MATERIALS MANAGEMENT. (US/0888-3068). Business Word Inc., 5350 South Roslyn Street, Suite 400, Englewood CA 80111-2125. **Tel** (303)290-8500, FAX (303)290-9025. **3784**

HOT ROD. (US/0018-6031). Petersen Publishing Company, 6420 Wilshire Boulevard, Los Angeles CA 90048. **Tel** (213)782-2485. **5416**

HOTEL & MOTEL MANAGEMENT. (US/0018-6082). Advanstar Communications Inc., 131 West First Street, Duluth MN 55802. **Tel** (218)723-9477, (800)346-0085. **2806**

HOTLINE, THE. (US). The American Political Network, 282 North Washington Street, Falls Church VA 22046. **Tel** (703)237-5130, FAX (703)237-5142. **4476**

HOUSE BEAUTIFUL. (US/0018-6422). The Hearst Corporation, 250 West 55th Street, New York NY 10019. **Tel** (212)649-4014. **300**

HOUSTON POST (1932). (US/1060-3484). The Houston Post, PO Box 4747, Houston TX 77210. **Tel** (713)840-6790, (800)877-1887. **5751**

HOWARD LAW JOURNAL. (US/0018-6813). Editorial and General Offices, Howard University, School of Law, 2900 Van Ness Street, Washington DC 20008. **Tel** (202)686-6570. **2979**

HP PROFESSIONAL. (US/0896-145X). Professional Press Inc, 101 Witmer Road, Horsham PA 19044. **Tel** (215)957-1500, FAX (215)957-1050. **1186**

HTFS DIGEST (1987). (UK/0952-2654). Heat Transfer and Fluid Flow Service, Harwell Laboratory Building 392 #7, Oxfordshire OX11 0RA England. **Tel** 011 44 235 432908, FAX 011 44 235 831981, telex 83135. **2004**

HUMAN ANTIBODIES AND HYBRIDOMAS. (US/0956-960X). Forefront Publishing USA, 24 Glen Hill Road, Wilton CT 06897. **Tel** (203)221-9949, FAX (203)834-0940. **457**

HUMAN GENOME ABSTRACTS. (US/1045-4470). Cambridge Scientific Abstracts, 7200 Wisconsin Avenue, #601, Bethesda MD 20814-4823. **Tel** (301)961-6750, (800)843-7751, FAX (301)961-6720. **478**

HUMAN RESOURCE PLANNING. (US/0199-8986). Human Resource Planning Society, 41 East 42nd Street, Suite 1509, New York NY 10017. **Tel** (212)490-6387, FAX (212)682-6851. **942**

HUMANITIES INDEX. (US/0095-5981). H W Wilson Company, 950 University Avenue, Bronx NY 10452. **Tel** (800)367-6770, (718)588-8400, FAX (718)590-1617, telex 4990003 HWILSON. **2857**

HUMANITIES INDEX. CD-ROM. (US/0095-5981). H W Wilson Company, 950 University Avenue, Bronx NY 10452. **Tel** (800)367-6770, (718)588-8400, FAX (718)590-1617, telex 4990003 HWILSON. **2847**

HUMANITIES INDEX (CD-ROM ED.). (US/1063-3294). H W Wilson Company, 950 University Avenue, Bronx NY 10452. **Tel** (800)367-6770, (718)588-8400, FAX (718)590-1617, telex 4990003 HWILSON. **2857**

HYDRAULICS & PNEUMATICS. (US/0018-814X). Penton Publishing, 1100 Superior Avenue, Cleveland OH 44114-2543. **Tel** (216)696-7000, FAX (216)696-0836. **2090**

IBM SYSTEMS JOURNAL. (US/0018-8670). IBM Corporate Technical Publications, PO Box 218, Yorktown Heights NY 10598. **Tel** (914)241-4184. **1259**

IDAHO BUSINESS REVIEW, THE. (US/8750-4022). Idaho Business Review, PO Box 7193, Boise ID 83707. **Tel** (208)336-3768. **681**

IDC JAPAN REPORT. (US). International Data Corporation, 5 Speen Street, PO Box 9015, Framingham MA 01701. **Tel** (508)872-8200, (508)935-4443. **1609**

IDIS. (US/0891-8511). Iowa Drug Information Service, The University of Iowa, 100 Oakdale Campus, N330 OH, Iowa City IA 52242-5000. **Tel** (319)335-4800, (800)525-4347, FAX (319)335-4077. **4307**

IDIS SYSTEM / CD-ROM. (US). Iowa Drug Information Service, The University of Iowa, 100 Oakdale Campus, N330 OH, Iowa City IA 52242-5000. **Tel** (319)335-4800, (800)525-4347, FAX (319)335-4077. **4334**

IDP REPORT. (US/0197-0178). Simba Information Inc., 213 Danbury Road, Wilton CT 06897-7430. **Tel** (203)834-0033 ext. 133, FAX (203)884-1771. **1254**

IFW. INTERNATIONAL FREIGHTING WEEKLY. (UK/0032-5007). Maclean Hunter Canada / Montreal, 1001 bvd. de Maisonneuve W., Montreal, Quebec H3A 3E1 Canada. **Tel** 514-845-5141, FAX 514-845-4302, telex 055-60604. **5383**

ILLINOIS BUSINESS REVIEW. (US/0019-1922). Bureau of Economic and Business Research / Illinois, 428 Commerce West, 1206 South 6th Street, Champaign IL 61820. **Tel** (217)333-2332, FAX (217)244-3118. **681**

ILLINOIS HISTORICAL JOURNAL. (US/0748-8149). Illinois State Historical Society, 1 Old Capitol Plaza, Springfield IL 62701. **Tel** (217)782-8160, FAX (217)524-8042. **2738**

ILLINOIS PUBLIC EMPLOYEE RELATIONS REPORT / INSTITUTE OF LABOR AND INDUSTRIAL RELATIONS, UNIVERSITY OF ILLINOIS AT URBANA-CHAMPAIGN, THE. (US). Chicago Kent College of Law, 565 West Adams Street, Chicago IL 60661. **Tel** (312)906-5190, FAX (312)906-5280. **4655**

IMAGING ABSTRACTS. (US/0896-100X). Pira International, Randalls Road, Leatherhead, Surrey KT22 7RU England. **Tel** 011 44 372 376161, FAX 011 44 372 377526. **4378**

IMAGING NEWS (ALEXANDRIA, VA.). (US/1058-7705). Telecom Publishing Group, 1101 King Street, Suite 444, Alexandria VA 22314. **Tel** (703)683-4100, (800)327-7205, FAX (703)739-6490. **1113**

IMAGING UPDATE. (US/0889-9142). Imaging Update, PO Box 2287, Fair Oaks CA 95628. **Tel** (916)966-6024. **4565**

IMF SURVEY. (US/0047-083X). International Monetary Fund, 700 19th Street Northwest, Publishing Unit, Washington DC 20431. **Tel** (202)623-7430, FAX (202)623-7201. **790**

IMMUNOLOGY ABSTRACTS. (US/0307-112X). Cambridge Scientific Abstracts, 7200 Wisconsin Avenue, #601, Bethesda MD 20814-4823. **Tel** (301)961-6750, (800)843-7751, FAX (301)961-6720. **3660**

IMPLEMENT & TRACTOR. (US/0019-2953). Farm Press Publishers Inc, PO Box 1420, Clarksdale MS 38614. **Tel** (601)624-8503. **159**

IMPRIMIS. (US/0277-8432). Hillsdale College / Imprimis, 33 East College Street, Hillsdale MI 49242. **Tel** (517)437-7341. **1494**

IMPROVED RECOVERY WEEK. (US/1061-3692). Pasha Publications Inc., 1616 North Fort Myer Drive, Suite 1000, Arlington VA 22209. **Tel** (800)424-2908, (703)528-1244, FAX (703)528-3742, (703)528-1253. **1609**

INC. (BOSTON, MASS.). (US/0162-8968). Inc. Publishing Corporation, 38 Commercial Wharf, Boston MA 02110. **Tel** (617)248-8000. **681**

INDEPENDENT LIVING (1989). (US/1048-3772). Equal Opportunity Publications Inc, 150 Motor Parkway Suite 420, Hauppage NY 11788. **Tel** (516)273-0066, FAX (516)273-8936. **4389**

INDEPENDENT POWER REPORT. (US/1049-0744). McGraw Hill Publishing Company, Inc., 1221 Avenue of the Americas, New York NY 10020. **Tel** (212)512-6410, (800)525-5003, FAX (212)512-6111. **2064**

INDEX MEDICUS LATINO-AMERICANO. (BL/0100-4743). Organizacao Pan American da Saude, rua Botucatu 862, 04023 Sao Paulo SP Brazil. **Tel** (011)549-2611, telex 11 22143. **3586**

INDEX OF ECONOMIC ARTICLES IN JOURNALS AND COLLECTIVE VOLUMES. (US/0536-647X). American Economic Association / Tennessee, 2014 Broadway, Suite 305, Nashville TN 37203-2418. **Tel** (615)322-2595. **1533**

INDEX ON CENSORSHIP. (UK/0306-4220). Writers and Scholars International, Queen Victoria Street, London EC4N 4SS England. **Tel** 011 44 71 3296434, FAX 011 44 71 3296461. **3344**

INDEX TO BOOK REVIEWS IN RELIGION. (US/0887-1574). American Theological Library Association, 820 Church Street, 3rd Floor, Evanston IL 60201. **Tel** (708)869-7788, FAX (708)869-8513. **5012**

INDEX TO CANADIAN LEGAL LITERATURE (LIBRARY ED.). (CN/0832-9257). Carswell Publications, 2330 Midland Avenue, Agincourt Ontario M1S 1P7 Canada. **Tel** (416)291-8421. **3081**

INDEX TO IEEE PUBLICATIONS. (US/0099-1368). IEEE, Institution of Electrical and Electronics Engineers, Inc., 345 East 47th Street, New York NY 10017-2394. **Tel** (908)981-1393, FAX (908)981-9667. **2004**

INDEX TO LEGAL PERIODICALS. (US/0019-4077). H W Wilson Company, 950 University Avenue, Bronx NY 10452. **Tel** (800)367-6770, (718)588-8400, FAX (718)590-1617, telex 4990003 HWILSON. **3081**

INDEX TO LEGAL PERIODICALS. CD-ROM. (US/0019-4077). H W Wilson Company, 950 University Avenue, Bronx NY 10452. **Tel** (800)367-6770, (718)588-8400, FAX (718)590-1617, telex 4990003 HWILSON. **3081**

INDEX TO THE SPORTING NEWS. (US/1041-2859). John Gordon Burke Publisher Inc., PO Box 1492, Evanston IL 60204. **Tel** (708)866-8625, FAX (708)866-8625. **4899**

INDEX VETERINARIUS. (UK/0019-4123). CAB International Centre, Wallingford, Oxon OX10 8DE United Kingdom. **Tel** 44 491 832111, FAX 44 491 833508, telex 847964 (COMAGG G). **5528**

INDIANA BUSINESS MAGAZINE. (US/1060-4154). Curtis Magazine Group Inc., 1200 Waterway Boulevard, Indianapolis IN 46202. **Tel** (317)692-1200, FAX (317)692-4250. **682**

INDIANA BUSINESS REVIEW. (US/0019-6541). Indiana University Business Research Center, Graduate School of Business, Bloomington IN 47405. **Tel** (812)855-5507, FAX (812)855-7763. **1495**

INDIANAPOLIS BUSINESS JOURNAL. (US/0274-4929). IBJ Corporation, 431 North Pennsylvania Street, Indianapolis IN 46204. **Tel** (317)634-6200, FAX (317)263-5060. **682**

INDIVIDUAL WITH DISABILITIES EDUCATION LAW REPORT. (US/1055-520X). LRP Publications, 747 Dresher Road, PO Box 980, Horsham PA 19044-0980. **Tel** (800)341-7874, (215)784-0860, FAX (215)784-9639, (215)784-0870. **2982**

INDONESIAN COMMERCIAL NEWSLETTERS. (IO/0377-0001). PT Data Consult Inc, PO Box 108, Ing Jakarta 13041, Indonesia. **Tel** 11 62 21 3904711, telex 44328 PIOLA JKT. **1495**

INDUSTRIAL BIOPROCESSING. (US/1056-7194). Technical Insights Inc., PO Box 1304, Fort Lee NJ 07024-9967. **Tel** (201)568-4744, FAX (201)568-8247, telex 425900 SWIFT UI. **1946**

INDUSTRIAL COMMUNICATIONS. (US/0737-0415). Phillips Business Information, Inc., 1201 Seven Locks Road, Potomac MD 20854. **Tel** (301)424-3338, (800)777-5006, FAX (301)309-3847. **1113**

INDUSTRIAL DISTRIBUTION. (US/0019-8153). Cahners Publishing Company, 249 West 17th Street, New York NY 10011. **Tel** (212)645-0067, FAX (212)242-6987. **926**

INDUSTRIAL ENERGY BULLETIN. (US/0894-5764). McGraw Hill Publishing Company, Inc., 1221 Avenue of the Americas, New York NY 10020. **Tel** (212)512-6410, (800)525-5003, FAX (212)512-6111. **1610**

INDUSTRIAL FINISHING (WHEATON). (US/0019-8323). Chilton Company, 201 King of Prussia Road, Radnor PA 19089. **Tel** (610)964-4122, (800)695-1214, FAX (610)964-4978, telex 6851035 CHILTON UW. **4224**

INDUSTRIAL HEALTH & HAZARDS UPDATE. (US/0890-3018). Merton Allen Associates, PO Box 15640, Plantation FL 33318-5640. **2863**

INDUSTRIAL MANAGEMENT & DATA SYSTEMS. (UK/0263-5577). MCB University Press, 60 62 Toller Lane, Bradford West Yorkshire BD8 9BX England. **Tel** 011 44 274 499821, FAX 011 44 274 547143, telex 51317 MCBUNI G. **1259**

INDUSTRIAL SPECIALTIES NEWS. (CN/0835-5134). Blendon Information Services, 126 Willowdale Avenue, Suite 1, Willowdale ONT M2N 442 Canada. **Tel** (416)223-5397, FAX (416)225-9297. **4455**

INDUSTRIES IN TRANSITION. (US). Business Communications Inc., 25 Van Zant Street, Suite 13, Norwalk CT 06855. **Tel** (203)853-4266. **682**

INFOMAT INTERNATIONAL BUSINESS [ONLINE DATABASE]. (US). Predicasts Inc., A Ziff Communications Company, 11001 Cedar Avenue, Cleveland OH 44106. **Tel** (800)321-6388, (216)795-3000, FAX (216)229-9944, telex 985 604. **730**

INFORMATION ADVISOR, THE. (US/1050-1576). Find/SVP, 625 Avenue of Americas, New York NY 10011. **Tel** (212)645-4500. **682**

INFORMATION INTELLIGENCE, ONLINE LIBRARIES, AND MICROCOMPUTERS. (US/0737-7770). Information Intelligence Inc., PO Box 31098, Phoenix AZ 85046. **Tel** (602)996-2283, (800)228-9982. **3216**

INFORMATION INTELLIGENCE ONLINE NEWSLETTER. (US/0194-0694). Information Intelligence Inc., PO Box 31098, Phoenix AZ 85046. **Tel** (602)996-2283, (800)228-9982. **1274**

INFORMATION NETWORKS. (US/1073-8126). Telecom Publishing Group, 1101 King Street, Suite 444, Alexandria VA 22314. **Tel** (703)683-4100, (800)327-7205, FAX (703)739-6490. **1113**

INFORMATION SCIENCE ABSTRACTS. (US/0020-0239). Plenum Press, 233 Spring Street, New York NY 10013-1578. **Tel** (212)620-8000, (800)221-9369, FAX (212)463-0742, (212)807-1047, telex 23/421139. **3258**

INFORMATION TODAY. (US/8755-6286). Learned Information Inc., 143 Old Marlton Pike, Medford NJ 08055-8750. **Tel** (609)654-6266, FAX (609)654-4309. **3217**

INFOWORLD. (US/0199-6649). InfoWorld, 155 Bovet Road, Suite 800, San Mateo CA 94402. **Tel** (800)227-8365, (415)572-7341, (415)312-0691, FAX (415)328-1049, (415)312-0547, telex MNPK 176072. **1268**

INNOVATOR'S DIGEST. (US/0890-300X). Infoteam Inc., PO Box 15640, Plantation FL 33318. **Tel** (305)473-9560. **5114**

INSIDE DOT & TRANSPORTATION WEEK. (US/1050-818X). King Publishing Group, 627 National Press Building, Washington DC 20045. **Tel** (202)638-4260, FAX (202)662-9744. **5384**

INSIDE ENERGY/WITH FEDERAL LANDS. (US). McGraw Hill Publishing Company, Inc., 1221 Avenue of the Americas, New York NY 10020. **Tel** (212)512-6410, (800)525-5003, FAX (212)512-6111. **1947**

INSIDE F.E.R.C. (US/0163-948X). McGraw Hill Publishing Company, Inc., 1221 Avenue of the Americas, New York NY 10020. **Tel** (212)512-6410, (800)525-5003, FAX (212)512-6111. **1947**

INSIDE IVHS. (US/1054-2647). Waters Information Services, PO Box 2248, Binghamton NY 13902-2248. **Tel** (607)770-8535, FAX (607)798-1692. **5384**

INSIDE MARKET DATA. (US/1047-2908). Waters Information Services, PO Box 2248, Binghamton NY 13902-2248. **Tel** (607)770-8535, FAX (607)798-1692. **926**

INSIDE MEDIA (STAMFORD, CONN.). (US/1046-5316). Cowles Business Media Inc., 6 River Bend Center, 911 Hope Street, Stamford CT 06907. **Tel** (203)358-9900, (800)775-3777, FAX (203)357-9014. **760**

INSIDE MS. (US/0739-9774). National Multiple Sclerosis Society, 6100 Building Estgate Center, Suite 4800, Chattanooga TN 37411. **Tel** (615)954-9700. **3834**

INSIDE N.R.C. (US/0194-0252). McGraw Hill Publishing Company, Inc., 1221 Avenue of the Americas, New York NY 10020. **Tel** (212)512-6410, (800)525-5003, FAX (212)512-6111. **1947**

INSIDE R & D : THE WEEKLY REPORT ON TECHNICAL INNOVATION. (US/0300-757X). Technical Insights Inc., PO Box 1304, Fort Lee NJ 07024-9967. **Tel** (201)568-4744, FAX (201)568-8247, telex 425900 SWIFT UI. **1025**

INSPEC [ONLINE DATABASE]. (UK). Institution of Electrical Engineers / IEE, Michael Faraday House, Six Hills Way, Stevenage Herts SG1 2AY UK. **Tel** 011 44 438 313311, FAX 011 44 438 742840, telex 825578 IEESTV G. **2004**

INSTITUTIONAL DISTRIBUTION. (US/0020-3572). Bill Communications Inc., 355 Park Avenue South, New York NY 10010-1789. **Tel** (800)821-6897, (212)592-6262, FAX (212)592-6209. **2344**

INSURANCE BROKERS' MONTHLY AND INSURANCE ADVISER. (UK/0260-2385). Insurance Publishing & Printing Co., 7 Stourbridge Road Lye, Stourbridge, West Midlands DY9 7DG England. **Tel** 011 44 384 895228, FAX 011 44 384 893666. **2883**

INSURANCE PERIODICALS INDEX. (US/0074-073X). NILS Publishing Company, 21625 Prairie Street, PO Box 2507, Chatsworth CA 91311. **Tel** (818)998-8830, (800)423-5910, FAX (818)718-8482. **2897**

INSURANCE SYSTEMS BULLETIN. (UK/0268-1935). IBC Publishing, 57-61 Mortimer St., London W1N 7TD England. **Tel** 011 44 71 637 4383, FAX 011 44 71 636 6314. **2884**

INTEGRATED CIRCUITS INTERNATIONAL. (UK/0263-6522). Elsevier Advanced Technology, An Imprint of Elsevier Science Ltd., The Boulevard, Langford Lane, Kidlington, Oxford OX5 1GB United Kingdom. **Tel** 011 44 865 843000, 011 44 865 843699, FAX 011 44 865 843010. **2065**

INTEGRATED WASTE MANAGEMENT. (US/1049-1562). McGraw Hill Publishing Company, Inc., 1221 Avenue of the Americas, New York NY 10020. **Tel** (212)512-6410, (800)525-5003, FAX (212)512-6111. **2233**

INTELLIGENCER JOURNAL. (US/0889-4140). Lancaster Newspapers Inc, 8 West King Street, PO Box 1328, Lancaster PA 17603. **Tel** (717)291-8611. **5737**

INTELLIGENT NETWORK NEWS. (US/1042-6930). Telecom Publishing Group, 1101 King Street, Suite 444, Alexandria VA 22314. **Tel** (703)683-4100, (800)327-7205, FAX (703)739-6490. **1113**

INTELLIGENT SOFTWARE STRATEGIES. (US/1052-7214). Cutter Information Corporation, 37 Broadway, Arlington MA 02174-5539. **Tel** (617)648-8700, (800)964-5118, FAX (617)648-8707, (617)648-1950, telex 650 100 9891. **1287**

INTELLIGENT SYSTEMS REPORT. (US/1054-8696). ISR: Intelligent Systems Report, 2555 Cumberland Parkway/Suite 299, Atlanta GA 30339-3908. **Tel** (404)434-2187, FAX (404)432-6969. **1213**

INTER ALIA (RENO). (US/0092-6086). State Bar of Nevada, 1325 Airmotive Way, Suite 140, Reno NV 89502. **Tel** (702)329-4100, FAX (702)329-0522. **2983**

INTER-AMERICAN TRADE AND INVESTMENT LAW. (US/1078-2028). National Law Center for Inter-American Free Trade, 255 West Alameda, City Hall, 7th Floor East, PO Box 27210, Tucson AZ 85726-7210. **Tel** (800)529-3463, FAX (602)792-8185. **840**

INTERAMERICAN OPPORTUNITIES BRIEFING. (US/1055-9299). IFF International Freedom Foundation, 150 Regent Street, Suite 500, Ches House, London W1R 5FA England. **Tel** 32 2 646 6561, FAX 32 2 646 6598, . **683**

INTERAVIA, AEROSPACE WORLD : BUSINESS & TECHNOLOGY. (SZ). Aerospace Media Publishing SA, 29 Route de l'Aeroport, Box 437, 1215 Geneva 15 Switzerland. **Tel** 011 41 22 7882788, FAX 011 41 22 7882726. **24**

INTERCORP. (US/8750-2550). Commercial News and Media Corporation, PO Box 4430, Stamford CT 06907. **683**

INTERIM CASE CITATIONS TO THE RESTATEMENTS OF THE LAW. (US/0895-2523). American Law Institute, 4025 Chestnut Street, Philadelphia PA 19104-3099. **Tel** (215)243-1661, (800)253-6397, FAX (215)243-1664. **2983**

INTERNAL AUDITOR, THE. (US/0020-5745). Institute of Internal Auditors / Orlando, Florida, PO Box 140099, Orlando FL 32889. **Tel** (407)830-7600, FAX (407)831-5171, telex 567443. **745**

INTERNATIONAL BUILDING SERVICES ABSTRACTS. (UK/0140-4237). Building Services Research and Information Association, Old Bracknell Lane West, Bracknell Berkshire RG12 7AH England. **Tel** 011 44 344 426511, FAX 011 44 344 487575, telex 848288. **617**

INTERNATIONAL COAL REPORT. (UK/0260-4299). Financial Times England, 8 16 Great New Street, London EC4A 3BN England. **Tel** 011 44 71 353 0305, 353 1040, FAX 011 44 353 0846. **1947**

INTERNATIONAL DEFENSE INTELLIGENCE. (US/1041-746X). Jane's Information Group, Sentinel House, 163 Brighton Road, Coulsdon Surrey CR3 2NX England. **Tel** 011 44 81 763 1030, FAX 011 44 81 763 1006. **4046**

INTERNATIONAL DEFENSE REVIEW. (SZ/0020-6512). Jane's Information Group, Sentinel House, 163 Brighton Road, Coulsdon Surrey CR3 2NX England. **Tel** 011 44 81 763 1030, FAX 011 44 81 763 1006. **4046**

INTERNATIONAL GAS TECHNOLOGY HIGHLIGHTS. (US/0276-4040). Institute of Gas Technology, 3424 South State Street, Chicago IL 60616. **Tel** (312)949-3970, (312)949-3650, FAX (312)949-3776, telex 25-6189. **4261**

INTERNATIONAL INSURANCE MONITOR. (US/0020-6997). Chase Communications Group, 2535 Beechwood Avenue, PO Box 9001, Mt Vernon NY 10552. **Tel** (914)699-2020. **2884**

INTERNATIONAL JOURNAL OF BANK MARKETING. (UK/0265-2323). MCB University Press, 60 62 Toller Lane, Bradford West Yorkshire BD8 9BX England. **Tel** 011 44 274 499821, FAX 011 44 274 547143, telex 51317 MCBUNI G. **792**

INTERNATIONAL JOURNAL OF GOVERNMENT AUDITING. (CN/0047-0724). International Journal of Government Auditing, PO Box 50009, Washington DC 20004. **Tel** (202)275-4707, FAX (202)275-4021, telex 7108229273. **4732**

INTERNATIONAL JOURNAL OF MANPOWER. (UK/0143-7720). MCB University Press, 60 62 Toller Lane, Bradford West Yorkshire BD8 9BX England. **Tel** 011 44 274 499821, FAX 011 44 274 547143, telex 51317 MCBUNI G. **1680**

INTERNATIONAL JOURNAL OF OPERATIONS & PRODUCTION MANAGEMENT. (UK/0144-3577). MCB University Press, 60 62 Toller Lane, Bradford West Yorkshire BD8 9BX England. **Tel** 011 44 274 499821, FAX 011 44 274 547143, telex 51317 MCBUNI G. **871**

INTERNATIONAL JOURNAL OF PHYSICAL DISTRIBUTION & LOGISTICS MANAGEMENT. (UK/0960-0035). MCB University Press, 60 62 Toller Lane, Bradford West Yorkshire BD8 9BX England. **Tel** 011 44 274 499821, FAX 011 44 274 547143, telex 51317 MCBUNI G. **871**

INTERNATIONAL JOURNAL OF PURCHASING AND MATERIALS MANAGEMENT. (US/1055-6001). National Association Purchasing Management Inc., PO Box 22160, Tempe AZ 85285. **Tel** (602)752-6276, (800)888-6276, FAX (602)752-7890. **950**

INTERNATIONAL JOURNAL OF RETAIL & DISTRIBUTION MANAGEMENT. (UK/0959-0552). MCB University Press, 60 62 Toller Lane, Bradford West Yorkshire BD8 9BX England. **Tel** 011 44 274 499821, FAX 011 44 274 547143, telex 51317 MCBUNI G. **955**

INTERNATIONAL JOURNAL OF SOCIAL ECONOMICS. (UK/0306-8293). MCB University Press, 60 62 Toller Lane, Bradford West Yorkshire BD8 9BX England. **Tel** 011 44 274 499821, FAX 011 44 274 547143, telex 51317 MCBUNI G. **1496**

INTERNATIONAL JOURNAL OF SOCIOLOGY & SOCIAL POLICY, THE. (UK/0144-333X). MCB University Press, 60 62 Toller Lane, Bradford West Yorkshire BD8 9BX England. **Tel** 011 44 274 499821, FAX 011 44 274 547143, telex 51317 MCBUNI G. **5248**

INTERNATIONAL LABOUR REVIEW. (SZ/0020-7780). International Labour Office - ILO, Publications Sales Service, CH-1211 Geneva 22 Switzerland. **Tel** 011 41 22 7996111. **1680**

INTERNATIONAL LEGAL PERSPECTIVES. (US). Northwestern School of Law, 10015 Southwest, Terwilliger Boulevard, Portland OR 97219. **Tel** (503)244-1181 Ext. 700, FAX (503)246-8542. **3130**

INTERNATIONAL MARKET ALERT. (US/1051-8061). International Reports Inc., 11300 Rockville Pike 1100, Rockville MD 20852. **Tel** (212)685-6900, FAX (212)685-8566, telex 233139 RPTUR. **841**

INTERNATIONAL MARKETING REVIEW. (UK/0265-1335). MCB University Press, 60 62 Toller Lane, Bradford West Yorkshire BD8 9BX England. **Tel** 011 44 274 499821, FAX 011 44 274 547143, telex 51317 MCBUNI G. **926**

INTERNATIONAL MEDICAL TRIBUNE SYNDICATE. (US/1040-7588). Ira Weinstein MD, 257 Park Avenue South, New York NY 10010. **Tel** (212)674-8500, FAX (212)529-8490, telex 147103 IMTS. **3589**

INTERNATIONAL MILLING FLOUR & FEED. (UK). Turret Group, 177 Hagden Lane, Watford Herts WD1 8LN United Kingdom. **Tel** 011 44 923 228577, FAX 011 44 923 221346. **202**

INTERNATIONAL NEW PRODUCT NEWSLETTER. (US/1046-7211). International New Product Newsletter, PO Box 1146, Marblehead MA 01945. **Tel** (508)741-0224, FAX (508)741-0224. **5115**

INTERNATIONAL PACKAGING ABSTRACTS. (UK/0260-7409). Pira International, Randalls Road, Leatherhead, Surrey KT22 7RU England. **Tel** 011 44 372 376161, FAX 011 44 372 377526. **4222**

INTERNATIONAL PHARMACEUTICAL ABSTRACTS. (US/0020-8264). American Society of Hospital Pharmacists, 7272 Wisconsin Avenue, Bethesda MD 20814. **Tel** (301)657-3000, (301)657-4383, FAX (301)652-8278. **4334**

INTERNATIONAL PRODUCT ALERT. (US). Marketing Intelligence Service Ltd, 6473D Route 64, Naples NY 14512. **Tel** (716)374-6326, (800)836-5710, FAX (714)374-5217, telex 469979. **2345**

INTERNATIONAL RESEARCH CENTERS DIRECTORY. (US/0278-2713). Gale Research Inc., 835 Penobscot Building, 645 Griswold Street, Detroit MI 48226. **Tel** (800)877-GALE, (313)961-2242, FAX (313)961-6083, (800)414-5043, telex TWX 810-221-7086. **5115**

INTERNATIONAL SMALL BUSINESS JOURNAL. (UK/0266-2426). Woodcock Publications Ltd, PO Box 1, Macclesfield Cheshire, SK10 4YQ England. **Tel** 0625-828712, FAX 0625-532644. **684**

INTERNATIONAL SOLAR ENERGY INTELLIGENCE REPORT. (US/1045-6325). Business Publishers Inc., 951 Pershing Drive, Silver Spring MD 20910-4464. **Tel** (301)587-6300, (800)274-0122, FAX (301)585-9075. **1948**

INTERNATIONAL TAX REPORT, THE. (UK/0300-1628). IBC Publishing, 57-61 Mortimer St., London W1N 7TD England. **Tel** 011 44 71 637 4383, FAX 011 44 71 636 6314. **902**

INTERNATIONAL TRADE FINANCE. (UK). Financial Times England, 8 16 Great New Street, London EC4A 3BN England. **Tel** 011 44 71 353 0305, 353 1040, FAX 011 44 353 0846. **841**

INTERNATIONAL TRAVEL NEWS (SACRAMENTO, CALIF.). (US/0191-8761). MHR Publishing Corporated, 2122 28th Street, Sacramento CA 95818. **Tel** (916)457-8990 (800)366-9192. **5481**

INTERNATIONALE BIBLIOGRAPHIE DER REZENSIONEN WISSENSCHAFTLICHER LITERATUR. (GW/0020-918X). Zeller Verlag GmbH & Co., Postfac 1949, Jahnstrasse 15, D 49009 Osnabrueck Germany. **Tel** 011 49 541 404590, FAX 011 49 541 41255. **3357**

INTERNATIONALE BIBLIOGRAPHIE DER ZEITSCHRIFTENLITERATUR AUS ALLEN GEBIETEN DES WISSENS. (GW). Zeller Verlag GmbH & Co., Postfac 1949, Jahnstrasse 15, D 49009 Osnabrueck Germany. **Tel** 011 49 541 404590, FAX 011 49 541 41255. **3357**

INTERNATIONALE JAHRESBIBLIOGRAPHIE DER FESTSCHRIFTEN : IJBF. (GW). Zeller Verlag GmbH & Co., Postfac 1949, Jahnstrasse 15, D 49009 Osnabrueck Germany. **Tel** 011 49 541 404590, FAX 011 49 541 41255. **417**

INTERNATIONALE JAHRESBIBLIOGRAPHIE DER KONGRESSBERICHTE. (GW/0933-1905). Zeller Verlag GmbH & Co., Postfac 1949, Jahnstrasse 15, D 49009 Osnabrueck Germany. **Tel** 011 49 541 404590, FAX 011 49 541 41255. **417**

INVESTEXT. (US). Technical Data International, 11 Farnsworth Street, Boston MA 02210. **684**

INVESTING, LICENSING AND TRADING CONDITIONS ABROAD. (US/0021-003X). The Economist Intelligence Unit / New York, 111 West 57th Street, New York NY 10019. **Tel** (800)938-4685, (212)554-0600. **684**

INVESTMENT MANAGEMENT TECHNOLOGY. (US/1057-5626). Waters Information Services, PO Box 2248, Binghamton NY 13902-2248. **Tel** (607)770-8535, FAX (607)798-1692. **903**

INVESTOR'S DAILY. (US). Investors Daily, PO Box 25000, Los Angeles CA 90025. **Tel** (310)207-1832. **903**

IOWA DRUG INFORMATION SERVICE. (US). Iowa Drug Information Service, The University of Iowa, 100 Oakdale Campus, N330 OH, Iowa City IA 52242-5000. **Tel** (319)335-4800, (800)525-4347, FAX (319)335-4077. **4334**

ISDN NEWS. (US/0899-9554). Phillips Business Information, Inc., 1201 Seven Locks Road, Potomac MD 20854. **Tel** (301)424-3338, (800)777-5006, FAX (301)309-3847. **1114**

ISMEC, MECHANICAL ENGINEERING ABSTRACTS. (US/0896-7113). Cambridge Scientific Abstracts, 7200 Wisconsin Avenue, #601, Bethesda MD 20814-4823. **Tel** (301)961-6750, (800)843-7751, FAX (301)961-6720. **2005**

ISRAEL BUSINESS TODAY. (US). Israel Business Today, 350 5th Avenue, Suite 1901, New York NY 10118. **Tel** (212)967-6675. **1497**

ISRAEL HIGH TECH REPORT. (US). Israel Publications, 47 Byron Place, Scarsdale NY 10583. **Tel** (914) 723-8321, telex 33511. **5116**

ISSUES IN LAW & MEDICINE. (US/8756-8160). Issues in Law and Medicine, PO Box 1586, Terre Haute IN 47808. **Tel** (812)232-0103, FAX (812)232-0103. **2985**

ISTP SEARCH. (US). Institute for Scientific Information, 3501 Market Street, Philadelphia PA 19104. **Tel** (215)386-0100, (800)523-1850, FAX (215)386-6362, telex 84-5305. **5117**

ITALIA OGGI. (IT). **5804**

ITEM PROCESSING REPORT. (US/1048-5120). Phillips Business Information, Inc., 1201 Seven Locks Road, Potomac MD 20854. **Tel** (301)424-3338, (800)777-5006, FAX (301)309-3847. **793**

JACKSONVILLE BUSINESS JOURNAL. (US/0885-453X). Jacksonville Business Journal, 1200 Gulflife, Suite 501, Jacksonville FL 32207. **Tel** (904)396-3502, FAX (904)396-5706. **685**

JAMA : THE JOURNAL OF THE AMERICAN MEDICAL ASSOCIATION. (US/0098-7484). American Medical Association, 515 North State Street, Chicago IL 60610. **Tel** (312)464-5000, (800)262-2350, FAX (312)464-5831. **3591**

JANE'S DEFENCE WEEKLY. (UK/0265-3818). Jane's Information Group, Sentinel House, 163 Brighton Road, Coulsdon Surrey CR3 2NX England. **Tel** 011 44 81 763 1030, FAX 011 44 81 763 1006. **4047**

JANE'S INTELLIGENCE REVIEW. (UK/1350-6226). Jane's Information Group, Sentinel House, 163 Brighton Road, Coulsdon Surrey CR3 2NX England. **Tel** 011 44 81 763 1030, FAX 011 44 81 763 1006. **4047**

JAPANESE INVESTMENT IN U.S. REAL ESTATE REVIEW. WESTERN REGION. (US/0898-9761). Mead Ventures Inc, PO Box 44952, Phoenix AZ 85064. **Tel** (602)234-0044, FAX (602)234-0076. **4839**

JAPANESE NEW MATERIALS IACA SERIES. ADVANCED ALLOYS & METALS. (SP). Newmedia International Japan, AV Infanta Carlota 123 5 A, 08029 Barcelona Spain. **Tel** 011 34 3 4195690, FAX 414 42 13. **3482**

JAPANESE NEW MATERIALS IACA SERIES. ADVANCED PLASTICS. (SP). Newmedia International Japan, AV Infanta Carlota 123 5 A, 08029 Barcelona Spain. **Tel** 011 34 3 4195690, FAX 414 42 13. **4455**

JAPANESE NEW MATERIALS IACA SERIES. ELECTRONIC MATERIALS. (SP). Newmedia International Japan, AV Infanta Carlota 123 5 A, 08029 Barcelona Spain. **Tel** 011 34 3 4195690, FAX 414 42 13. **2068**

JAPANESE NEW MATERIALS IACA SERIES. HIGH-PERFORMANCE CERAMICS. (SP). Newmedia International Japan, AV Infanta Carlota 123 5 A, 08029 Barcelona Spain. **Tel** 011 34 3 4195690, FAX 414 42 13. **2591**

JCT, JOURNAL OF COATINGS TECHNOLOGY. (US/0361-8773). Federation of Society Coatings Technology, 492 Norristown Road, Blue Bell PA 19422. **Tel** (215)940-0777. **4224**

JET CARGO NEWS. (US/0021-6003). Hagall Publishing Co., PO Box 920952 #398, Houston TX 77292. **Tel** (713)681-4760, FAX (713)682-3871. **5385**

JET FUEL INTELLIGENCE. (US). Petroleum Intelligence Weekly, 575 Broadway, 4th Floor, New York NY 10012-3230. **Tel** (212)941-5500, FAX (212)941-5509, telex 62371 PETROIN. **4262**

JEWISH BIBLE QUARTERLY, THE. (IS/0792-3910). Jewish Bible Quarterly, PO Box 29002, Jerusalem Israel. **Tel** 011 972 2 759146, FAX 011 972 2 759144. **5017**

JOB FUTURES. (CN/0833-7195). Employment and Immigration Canada, 3rd Floor/Room 358, 305 Rideau Street, Ottawa Ontario K1A 0J9 Canada. **Tel** (819)994-6509. **4205**

JOURNAL DES DEBATS. INDEX. (CN). Assemblee Nationale Ministere Financiere, 5 Place Quebec Bureau 195, Quebec QUE G1R 5P3 Canada. **Tel** (418)643-2754. **2986**

JOURNAL Serials available Online

Serials Online Index

JOURNAL / FLORIDA ENGINEERING SOCIETY. (US/0015-4032). Florida Engineering Society, PO Box 750, Tallahassee FL 32302. **Tel** (904)224-7121, FAX (904)222-4349. **1981**

JOURNAL / FORT SMITH HISTORICAL SOCIETY, THE. (US/0736-4261). Fort Smith Historical Society, 61 South 8th Street, Fort Smith Public Library, Fort Smith AR 72901. **Tel** (501)783-0229, FAX (501)782-8571. **2740**

JOURNAL / INSTITUTE OF MUSLIM MINORITY AFFAIRS. (UK/0266-6952). Institute of Muslim Minority Affairs, 46 Goodge Street/1st Floor, London W1P 1FJ United Kingdom. **Tel** 11 44 71 636 6740, FAX 11 44 71 255 1473, telex 296182. **2265**

JOURNAL OF ASIAN BUSINESS. (US/1068-0055). Association for Asian Studies Inc., University of Michigan, 1 Lane Hall, Ann Arbor MI 48109. **Tel** (313)665-2490, FAX (313)665-3801. **685**

JOURNAL OF BANK ACCOUNTING & AUDITING, THE. (US/0895-853X). Faulkner & Gray Inc., 11 Penn Plaza, 17th Floor, New York NY 10001. **Tel** (212)967-7000, (800)535-8403. **793**

JOURNAL OF BANK COST & MANAGEMENT ACCOUNTING, THE. (US/1070-941X). NABCA - National Association of Bank Cost and Management Accounting, PO Box 458, Northbrook IL 60065-0458. **Tel** (708)272-4233, FAX (708)272-6445. **746**

JOURNAL OF BANK TAXATION, THE. (US/0895-4720). Warren Gorham & Lamont Inc., Park Square Building, 31 St. James Avenue, Boston MA 02116-4112. **Tel** (617)423-2020, (800)950-1207, FAX (617)423-2026. **793**

JOURNAL OF BUSINESS & INDUSTRIAL MARKETING, THE. (US/0885-8624). MCB University Press, 60 62 Toller Lane, Bradford West Yorkshire BD8 9BX England. **Tel** 011 44 274 499821, FAX 011 44 274 547143, telex 51317 MCBUNI G. **927**

JOURNAL OF BUSINESS ETHICS. (NE/0167-4544). Kluwer Academic Publishers, Postbus 322, 3300 AH Dordrecht, The Netherlands. **Tel** 011 (31) 78 524400, FAX 011 31 78 183273, telex 20083. **2251**

JOURNAL OF CALIFORNIA TAXATION, THE. (US/1046-400X). Faulkner & Gray Inc., 11 Penn Plaza, 17th Floor, New York NY 10001. **Tel** (212)967-7000, (800)535-8403. **2987**

JOURNAL OF CASH MANAGEMENT. (US/0731-1281). Treasury Management Association, PO Box 64714S, Baltimore MD 21264. **Tel** (301)907-2862. **873**

JOURNAL OF CLINICAL INVESTIGATION, THE. (US/0021-9738). Rockefeller University Press, 222 East 70th Street, New York NY 10021. **Tel** (212)327-8572, FAX (212)327-7944. **3594**

JOURNAL OF COMMERCIAL LENDING, THE. (US/1062-6271). Robert Morris Associates, One Liberty Plaza, 1650 Market Street, Philadelphia PA 19103. **Tel** (215)851-9118, (215)851-0585, FAX (215)851-9206. **793**

JOURNAL OF CONTEMPORARY HEALTH LAW AND POLICY, THE. (US/0882-1046). Catholic University of America / Columbus School of Law, Washington DC 20064. **Tel** (202)319-5732, FAX (202)319-4313. **2987**

JOURNAL OF CORPORATE MANAGEMENT, THE. (AT/1038-2410). Institute Corporate Managers, Secretaries and Administrators Ltd., GPO Box 1594, Sydney NSW 2001 Australia. **Tel** 011 61 02 2235744, FAX 011 61 02 2327174. **3101**

JOURNAL OF ECONOMIC LITERATURE. (US/0022-0515). American Economic Association / Tennessee, 2014 Broadway, Suite 305, Nashville TN 37203-2418. **Tel** (615)322-2595. **1535**

JOURNAL OF ELECTRONIC DEFENSE. (US/0192-429X). Horizon House, 685 Canton Street, Norwood MA 02062. **Tel** (617)365-4595. **4048**

JOURNAL OF ENERGY AND DEVELOPMENT, THE. (US/0361-4476). ICEED, 909 14th Street, Suite 201, Boulder CO 80302. **Tel** (303)492-7667, (303)541-9504, FAX (303)442-5042. **1948**

JOURNAL OF EUROPEAN INDUSTRIAL TRAINING. (UK/0309-0590). MCB University Press, 60 62 Toller Lane, Bradford West Yorkshire BD8 9BX England. **Tel** 011 44 274 499821, FAX 011 44 274 547143, telex 51317 MCBUNI G. **873**

JOURNAL OF FILM AND VIDEO. (US/0742-4671). Journal Film and Video, Georgia State University, Department of Communication, Atlanta GA 30303. **Tel** (404)651-3200, FAX (404)651-1409. **4073**

JOURNAL OF FINANCIAL MANAGEMENT AND ANALYSIS. (II/0970-4205). Om Sai Ram Center for Financial Management Research and Training, 15 Prakash Co-Op Housing Society, Bombay 400 054 India. **Tel** 11 91 22 6121715. **794**

JOURNAL OF HEALTH CARE MARKETING. (US/0737-3252). American Marketing Association, 250 South Wacker Drive, Suite 200, Chicago IL 60606-5819. **Tel** (312)648-0536, FAX (312)993-7542. **927**

JOURNAL OF INSURANCE REGULATION. (US/0736-248X). National Association of Insurance Commissioners, PO Box 263, Department 42, Kansas City MO 64193. **Tel** (816)842-3600, (816)374-7259, FAX (816)471-7004. **2885**

JOURNAL OF INTERNATIONAL BUSINESS STUDIES. (CN/0047-2506). Western Business School, University of Western Ontario, London, Ontario N6A 3K7 Canada. **Tel** (519)661-4031, FAX (519)661-3700. **687**

JOURNAL OF LEGAL EDUCATION. (US/0022-2208). Case Western Reserve University / School of Law, 11075 East Boulevard, Cleveland OH 44106. **Tel** (216)368-3304, FAX (216)368-6144. **2988**

JOURNAL OF LONG TERM CARE ADMINISTRATION, THE. (US/0093-4445). American College of Health Care Administrators, 325 South Patrick Street, Alexandria VA 22314. **Tel** (703)549-5822, (703)739-7913, FAX (703)739-7901. **3787**

JOURNAL OF MANAGEMENT CONSULTING (AMSTERDAM). (US/0168-7778). Journal of Management Consulting, 858 Longview Road, Burlingame CA 94010-6974. **Tel** (415)342-5259, FAX (415)344-5005. **873**

JOURNAL OF MANAGEMENT INFORMATION SYSTEMS. (US/0742-1222). M. E. Sharpe Inc., 80 Business Park Drive, Armonk NY 10504. **Tel** (914)273-1800, (800)541-6563, FAX (914)273-2106. **3220**

JOURNAL OF MANAGERIAL PSYCHOLOGY. (UK/0268-3946). MCB University Press, 60 62 Toller Lane, Bradford West Yorkshire BD8 9BX England. **Tel** 011 44 274 499821, FAX 011 44 274 547143, telex 51317 MCBUNI G. **4598**

JOURNAL OF MANUAL & MANIPULATIVE THERAPY, THE. (US/1066-9817). Journal of Manual Manipulative Therapy, PO Box 713, Forest Grove OR 97116. **Tel** (503)359-2322, FAX (503)359-3542. **3882**

JOURNAL OF MATERIALS CHEMISTRY. (UK/0959-9428). Royal Society of Chemistry, Thomas Graham House, Science Park, Cambridge CB4 4WF England. **Tel** 011 44 223 420066, FAX 011 44 223 423429, telex 818293 ROYAL. **981**

JOURNAL OF MEDITERRANEAN STUDIES. (MM/1016-3476). Mediterranean Institute, University of Malta, Msida Malta. **Tel** 011 356 333903-6 331734, FAX 011 356 336450. **2848**

JOURNAL OF MONEY, CREDIT, AND BANKING. (US/0022-2879). Ohio State University Press, 1070 Carmack Road, 180 Pressey Hall, Columbus OH 43210. **Tel** (614)292-6930, (614)292-1407, FAX (614)292-2065. **795**

JOURNAL OF MORMON HISTORY. (US/0094-7342). Mormon History Association, PO Box 7010 University Station, Provo UT 84602. **Tel** (801)378-4048. **4969**

JOURNAL OF OCCUPATIONAL AND ORGANIZATIONAL PSYCHOLOGY. (UK/0963-1798). British Psychological Society, St. Andrews House, 48 Princess Road, Leicester LE1 7DR England. **Tel** 011 44 533 549568. **4598**

JOURNAL OF PERSONAL SELLING & SALES MANAGEMENT, THE. (US/0885-3134). Journal of Personal Selling, 155 E Capitol Drive, Hartland WI 53029. **Tel** (414)367-5600. **928**

JOURNAL OF POPULATION ECONOMICS. (GW/0933-1433). Springer-Verlag GmbH & Company KG, Heidelberger Platz 3, D 14197 Berlin Germany. **Tel** 011 49 30 8207223, FAX 011 49 30 8214091, telex 183 319 SPBLN D. **4554**

JOURNAL OF PSYCHOLOGY AND THEOLOGY. (US/0091-6471). Rosemead Graduate School of Psychology, Biola University, 13800 Biola Avenue, La Mirada CA 90639. **Tel** (310)903-4727, FAX (310)903-4748. **4600**

JOURNAL OF PUBLIC POLICY & MARKETING. (US/0743-9156). American Marketing Association, 250 South Wacker Drive, Suite 200, Chicago IL 60606-5819. **Tel** (312)648-0536, FAX (312)993-7542. **929**

JOURNAL OF RETAIL BANKING. (US/0195-2064). American Banker, Concourse Level, 1 State Street Plaza, New York NY 10004. **Tel** (212)803-8200, (800)221-1809. **795**

JOURNAL OF RISK AND INSURANCE, THE. (US/0022-4367). American Risk Insurance Association, California State University, School of Business Administration, Sacramento CA 95819-6088. **Tel** (916)278-6609, (916)278-7386, FAX (916)278-5437. **2885**

JOURNAL OF SMALL BUSINESS MANAGEMENT. (US/0047-2778). International Council for Small Business, Bureau of Business Research, West Virginia University, PO Box 6025, Morgantown WV 26506-6025. **Tel** (304)293-7534, FAX (304)293-7061. **874**

JOURNAL OF SYSTEMS MANAGEMENT. (US/0022-4839). Association for Systems Management, 1433 West Bagley Road, PO Box 38370, Cleveland OH 44138-0370. **Tel** (216)243-6900, (216)243-6902, FAX (216)234-2930. **687**

JOURNAL OF TAXATION OF ESTATES & TRUSTS, THE. (US/1044-9418). Faulkner & Gray Inc., 11 Penn Plaza, 17th Floor, New York NY 10001. **Tel** (212)967-7000, (800)535-8403. **3118**

JOURNAL OF TAXATION OF EXEMPT ORGANIZATIONS, THE. (US/1043-0539). Warren Gorham & Lamont Inc., Park Square Building, 31 St. James Avenue, Boston MA 02116-4112. **Tel** (617)423-2020, (800)950-1207, FAX (617)423-2026. **4735**

JOURNAL OF TAXATION OF S CORPORATIONS, THE. (US/1040-502X). Faulkner & Gray Inc., 11 Penn Plaza, 17th Floor, New York NY 10001. **Tel** (212)967-7000, (800)535-8403. **795**

JOURNAL OF THE AMERICAN COLLEGE OF CARDIOLOGY. (US/0735-1097). Elsevier Science Publishing Company Inc, Madison Square Station, PO Box 882, New York NY 10159-0882. **Tel** (212)633-3950, FAX (212)633-3990. **3707**

JOURNAL OF THE ANCIENT NEAR EASTERN SOCIETY, THE. (US/0897-6074). Jewish Theological Seminary, 3080 Broadway, New York NY 10027. **Tel** (212)678-8856. **2621**

JOURNAL OF THE COPYRIGHT SOCIETY OF THE U.S.A. (US/0886-3520). Fred B. Rothman & Company, 10368 West Centennial Road, Littleton CO 80127. **Tel** (800)457-1986, (303)979-5657, FAX (303)978-1457, telex 87669. **1305**

JOURNAL OF THE DENTAL ASSOCIATION OF THAILAND, THE. (TH/0045-9917). Dental Association of Thailand, PO Box 355, Samsaen Nai Phyatha, Bangkok 10400 Thailand. **Tel** 011 66 2 5394748. **1328**

JOURNAL OF THE INTERNATIONAL ACADEMY OF HOSPITALITY RESEARCH, THE. (US/1052-6099). Scholarly Communications Projects, University Libraries, Virginia Tech, PO Box 90001, Blacksburg VA 24062. **Tel** (703)231-4922, FAX (703)231-3694. **1501**

JOURNAL WATCH. (US/0896-7210). New England Journal of Medicine, 1440 Main Street, Waltham MA 02154-1649. **Tel** (617)893-3800, (800)843-6356, FAX (617)647-5785, telex 5106015660 NEJM BOS UQ. **3660**

JUDICIAL CONDUCT REPORTER. (US/0193-7367). American Judicature Society, 25 East Washington Street, Suite 1600, Chicago IL 60602. **Tel** (312)558-6900, FAX (312)558-9175. **3141**

JUST-IN-TIME & QUICK RESPONSE NEWS. (US/1061-6888). Phillips Business Information, Inc., 1201 Seven Locks Road, Potomac MD 20854. **Tel** (301)424-3338, (800)777-5006, FAX (301)309-3847. **843**

JUSTICE QUARTERLY. (US/0741-8825). Academy of Criminal Justice Sciences, Northern Kentucky University, 402 Nunn Hall, Highland Heights KY 41099. **Tel** (606)572-5634. **3168**

KANKAKEE DAILY JOURNAL. (US). Kankakee Daily Journal, 8 Dearborn Square, Kankakee IL 60901. **Tel** (815)937-3322. **5660**

KANSAS BUSINESS NEWS. (US/0199-3607). Chuck Henry Publications Inc, PO Box 490, Augusta KS 67010-0490. **Tel** (316)775-3201. **688**

KANSAS CITY BUSINESS JOURNAL. (US/0734-2748). Kansas City Business Journal, 324 East 11th Street, Suite 800, Kansas City MO 64106. **Tel** (816)421-5900, FAX (816)472-4010. **688**

KENOSHA NEWS. (US/0749-713X). Kenosha News Publishing Corporation, 715 58th Street, Kenosha WI 53141. **Tel** (414)657-1000. **5768**

KENTUCKY POST (CONVINGTON KY. : 1974). (US). Cincinnati Enquirer, 312 Elm Street, Cincinnati OH 45202. **Tel** (513)721-2700, (800)876-4500. **5729**

KEY BRITISH ENTERPRISES : KBE / COMPILED AND PUBLISHED BY PUBLICATIONS DIVISION, DUN & BRADSTREET LIMITED. (UK/0142-5048). Dun & Bradstreet Information Services, 3 Sylvan Way, Parsippany NJ 07054. **Tel** (201)605-6000, (800)526-0651. **688**

KIDSNET (WASHINGTON, D.C.). (US/1064-1114). Kidsnet Clearinghouse, 6856 Eastern Avenue Northwest, Suite 208, Washington DC 20012. **Tel** (202)291-1400, FAX 9202)882-7315. **1134**

KIPLINGER'S PERSONAL FINANCE MAGAZINE. (US/1056-697X). Kiplinger Washington Editors, 1729 H Street Northwest, Washington DC 20006. **Tel** (202)887-6400, (800)544-0155, FAX (202)331-1206. **795**

KOMMUNAL LITTERATUR. (SW/0023-3056). Bibliotekstjanst AB, Box 200, S-221 00 Lund Sweden. **Tel** 011 46 46 180000. **4698**

KOMPASS-SVERIGE. (SW). Kompass Sweden, Saltmaetargatan 8, Box 3223, Stockholm 10364 Sweden. **1615**

KOSMORAMA. (DK/0023-4222). Det Danske Filmmuseum, Store Sondervoldstraede, 1419 Copenhagen Denmark. **Tel** 011 41 31 576500, FAX 011 41 31 541312, telex 31465. **4073**

LABORATORY HAZARDS BULLETIN. (UK/0261-2917). Royal Society of Chemistry, Thomas Graham House, Science Park, Cambridge CB4 4WF England. **Tel** 011 44 223 420066, FAX 011 44 223 423429, telex 818293 ROYAL. **2872**

LABORDOC [ONLINE DATABASE]. (SZ). International Labour Office - ILO, Publications Sales Service, CH-1211 Geneva 22 Switzerland. **Tel** 011 41 22 7996111. **1535**

LADIES' HOME JOURNAL. (US/0023-7124). Meredith Corporation, Locust at 17th, Des Moines IA 50309. **Tel** (515)284-3000. **5560**

LAFAYETTE BUSINESS DIGEST. (US/1048-2822). Laurendeau Communications, PO Box 587, Lafayette IN 47902. **Tel** (317)742-6918, (800)521-0600, FAX (317)423-8134. **689**

LAGNIAPPE LETTER. (US/1040-3175). Latin American Information Services Inc., 159 West 53rd Street, Suite 28B, New York NY 10019-6050. **Tel** (212)765-5520, FAX (212)765-2927. **1637**

LAGNIAPPE QUARTERLY MONITOR. (US/1040-3183). Latin American Information Services Inc., 159 West 53rd Street, Suite 28B, New York NY 10019-6050. **Tel** (212)765-5520, FAX (212)765-2927. **1615**

LAKE LILLIAN CRIER. (US). Lake Lillian Crier, PO Box 98, Lake Lillian MN 56253. **5696**

LAN COMPUTING. (US/1055-1808). Professional Press Inc, 101 Witmer Road, Horsham PA 19044. **Tel** (215)957-1500, FAX (215)957-1050. **1193**

LAN MAGAZINE. (NE). LAN Magazine BV, Spaarne 55, 2011 CE Haarlem Netherlands. **Tel** 023-366814, FAX 023-360724. **1242**

LAN TECHNOLOGY. (US/1042-4695). M & T Publishing Inc., 411 Borel Avenue, Suite 100, San Mateo CA 94402. **Tel** (415)358-9500, FAX (415)358-9732. **1242**

LAN TIMES. (US/1040-5917). McGraw Hill Publishing Company, Inc., 1221 Avenue of the Americas, New York NY 10020. **Tel** (212)512-6410, (800)525-5003, FAX (212)512-6111. **1242**

LANCASTER NEW ERA. (US). Lancaster Newspapers Inc, 8 West King Street, PO Box 1328, Lancaster PA 17603. **Tel** (717)291-8611. **5737**

LAND ECONOMICS. (US/0023-7639). University of Wisconsin Press, Journal Division, 114 North Murray Street, Madison WI 53715. **Tel** (608)262-4952, FAX (608)262-8909. **103**

LAND MOBILE RADIO NEWS. (US/1070-6593). Phillips Business Information, Inc., 1201 Seven Locks Road, Potomac MD 20854. **Tel** (301)424-3338, (800)777-5006, FAX (301)309-3847. **1134**

LANE REPORT, THE. (US/1063-925X). Lane Communications Group, 269 West Main Street, Lexington KY 40507. **Tel** (606)244-3522, FAX (606)244-3544. **689**

LAS VEGAS BUSINESS PRESS. (US/1071-2186). Las Vegas Business Press, 5300 West Sahara, Suite 101, Las Vegas NV 89102. **Tel** (702)871-6780. **5708**

LASER FOCUS WORLD. (US/1043-8092). PennWell Publishing Company, 1421 South Sheridan, PO Box 1260, Tulsa OK 74101. **Tel** (918)835-3161, (800)331-4463, FAX (918)831-9497. **4437**

LASER REPORT. (US/0023-8600). PennWell Publishing Company, Ten Tara Boulevard 5th Floor, Nashua NH 03062-2801. **Tel** (603)891-0123, (603)891-9177, FAX (603)891-0624, (603)891-0574. **4437**

LASERS & OPTRONICS. (US/0892-9947). Cahners Publishing Company, 249 West 17th Street, New York NY 10011. **Tel** (212)645-0067, FAX (212)242-6987. **4438**

LATIN AMERICA REGIONAL REPORTS. ANDEAN GROUP. (UK/0143-5248). Lettres UK Ltd, 61 Old Street, London EC1V 9HX England. **Tel** 011 44 71 251-0012, FAX 011 44 71 253-8193. **1572**

LATIN AMERICA REGIONAL REPORTS. MEXICO & CENTRAL AMERICA. (UK/0143-5264). Lettres UK Ltd, 61 Old Street, London EC1V 9HX England. **Tel** 011 44 71 251-0012, FAX 011 44 71 253-8193. **1572**

LATIN AMERICAN TELECOM REPORT. (US/1062-3884). International Technology Consultants, 1724 Kalorama Road, Suite 210, Washington DC 20009. **Tel** (202)234-2138, FAX (202)483-7922. **1115**

LATIN AMERICAN WEEKLY REPORT. (UK/0143-5280). Lettres UK Ltd, 61 Old Street, London EC1V 9HX England. **Tel** 011 44 71 251-0012, FAX 011 44 71 253-8193. **2489**

LAW & BUSINESS DIRECTORY OF BANKRUPTCY ATTORNEYS. (US/1064-0371). Prentice-Hall Law and Business, 270 Sylvan Avenue, Englewood Cliffs NJ 07632. **Tel** (800)223-0231, (201)894-8538, FAX (201)894-8666. **3087**

LAW OFFICE TECHNOLOGY REVIEW. (US/1047-6482). Law Office Technology Review, PO Box 2577, Homewood IL 60430. **Tel** (708)957-3322. **1193**

LAWYERS' LIABILITY REVIEW. (US/0896-7075). Timeline Publishing Company, PO Box 1435, Bellvue WA 98009. **Tel** (800)444-7714 or (206)462-7714, FAX (206)462-0411. **2998**

LDC DEBT REPORT. (US). American Banker, Concourse Level, 1 State Street Plaza, New York NY 10004. **Tel** (212)803-8200, (800)221-1809. **796**

LEAD AND ZINC STATISTICS. (UK/0023-9577). International Lead and Zinc Study Group, Metro House, 58 St. James Street, London SW1A 1LD England. **Tel** 011 44 71 4999373, FAX 011 44 71 4933725, telex 299819 ILZSG G. **4025**

LEADER-TELEGRAM. (US/0891-0227). Leader Telegram, PO Box 570, Eau Claire WI 54702. **Tel** (715)833-9254, FAX (715)833-9244. **5768**

LEADERSHIP & ORGANIZATION DEVELOPMENT JOURNAL. (UK/0143-7739). MCB University Press, 60 62 Toller Lane, Bradford West Yorkshire BD8 9BX England. **Tel** 011 44 274 499821, FAX 011 44 274 547143, telex 51317 MCBUNI G. **875**

LEDGER-STAR. (US/0889-6135). Virginian Pilot and Ledger Star, PO Box 2160, 150 West Brambleton, Norfolk VA 23510. **Tel** (804)446-2000. **5759**

LEGAL INFORMATION ALERT. (US/0883-1297). Alert Publications Inc, 399 West Fullerton Parkway, Chicago IL 60614. **Tel** (312)525-7594, FAX (312)525-7015. **3081**

LEGAL RESOURCE INDEX. (US/0272-9296). Information Access Company, 362 Lakeside Drive, Foster City CA 94404. **Tel** (800)227-8431. **3082**

LEGAL WRITING : THE JOURNAL OF THE LEGAL WRITING INSTITUTE. (US). Seattle University / Law Review, 950 Broadway Plaza, Tacoma WA 98402-4470. **Tel** (206)591-2995, FAX (206)591-6313. **3001**

LEXINGTON HERALD-LEADER. (US/0745-4260). Lexington Herald-Leader Company, 100 Midland Avenue, Lexington KY 40508. **Tel** (606)231-3100. **5681**

LIBRARY & INFORMATION SCIENCE ABSTRACTS. (UK/0024-2179). Bowker Saur Ltd., A Reed Reference Publishing Company, Part of Reed International PLC, 59-60 Grosvenor Street, London WIX 9DA England. **Tel** 011 44 71 4935841, FAX 011 44 71 4991590. **3258**

LIBRARY HI TECH. (US/0737-8831). Pierian Press, PO Box 1808, Ann Arbor MI 48106. **Tel** (313)434-5530, (800)678-2435, FAX (313)434-6409. **3225**

LIBRARY LITERATURE. (US/0024-2373). H W Wilson Company, 950 University Avenue, Bronx NY 10452. **Tel** (800)367-6770, (718)588-8400, FAX (718)590-1617, telex 4990003 HWILSON. **3258**

LIBRARY MANAGEMENT (MCB PUBLICATIONS (FIRM). (UK/0143-5124). MCB University Press, 60 62 Toller Lane, Bradford West Yorkshire BD8 9BX England. **Tel** 011 44 274 499821, FAX 011 44 274 547143, telex 51317 MCBUNI G. **3226**

LIBRARY RESOURCES & TECHNICAL SERVICES. (US/0024-2527). American Library Association, 50 East Huron Street, Chicago IL 60611. **Tel** (312)944-6780, (800)545-2433, FAX (312)944-2641. **3227**

LIBRARY SOFTWARE REVIEW. (US/0742-5759). SAGE Periodical Press, 2455 Teller Road, Thousand Oaks CA 91320. **Tel** (805)499-0721, FAX (805)499-0871, telex 100799. **1288**

LICENSING LETTER, THE. (US/8755-6235). New Market Enterprises, PO Box 1665, Scottsdale AZ 85252-1665. **Tel** (602)948-1527. **929**

LIFE ASSOCIATION NEWS. (US/0024-3078). National Association of Life Underwriters, 1922 F Street NW, Washington DC 20006. **Tel** (202)331-6070, FAX (202)835-9608. **2886**

LIGHT LIST. (US/0565-1557). US Department of Transportation / Coast Guard, 2100 Second Street Southwest, Washington DC 20953-0001. **Tel** (202)267-2229. **4178**

LINGUISTICS AND LANGUAGE BEHAVIOR ABSTRACTS. (US/0888-8027). Sociological Abstracts, PO Box 22206, San Diego CA 92192-0206. **Tel** (619)695-8803, FAX (619)695-0416. **3336**

LINK-UP (MINNEAPOLIS, MINN. 1983). (US/0739-988X). Learned Information Inc., 143 Old Marlton Pike, Medford NJ 08055-8750. **Tel** (609)654-6266, FAX (609)654-4309. **1242**

LITERATURE ABSTRACTS. CATALYSTS & CATALYSIS. (US/1065-0539). American Petroleum Institute, 275 Seventh Avenue, New York NY 10001. **Tel** (212)366-4040, FAX (212)366-4298. **4284**

LITERATURE ABSTRACTS. HEALTH & ENVIRONMENT. (US/1065-0490). American Petroleum Institute, 275 Seventh Avenue, New York NY 10001. **Tel** (212)366-4040, FAX (212)366-4298. **2184**

LITERATURE ABSTRACTS. PETROLEUM REFINING & PETROCHEMICALS. (US/1065-0512). American Petroleum Institute, 275 Seventh Avenue, New York NY 10001. **Tel** (212)366-4040, FAX (212)366-4298. **4284**

LITERATURE ABSTRACTS. PETROLEUM SUBSTITUTES. (US/1065-0504). American Petroleum Institute, 275 Seventh Avenue, New York NY 10001. **Tel** (212)366-4040, FAX (212)366-4298. **4284**

LITERATURE ABSTRACTS. TRANSPORTATION & STORAGE. (US/1065-0520). American Petroleum Institute, 275 Seventh Avenue, New York NY 10001. **Tel** (212)366-4040, FAX (212)366-4298. **4284**

LITERATURE & PATENT ABSTRACTS. OILFIELD CHEMICALS. (US/1065-0547). American Petroleum Institute, 275 Seventh Avenue, New York NY 10001. **Tel** (212)366-4040, FAX (212)366-4298. **4284**

LIVERPOOL ECHO. (UK). The Liverpool Daily Post and Echo Ltd, PO Box 48 Old Hall Street, Liverpool L69 3EB England. **5812**

LLOYDS BANK ANNUAL REVIEW. (UK/0953-5004). Pinter Publishers, 25 Floral Street, London WC2 9DS England. **Tel** 44 71 240 9233, FAX 01 379 5553. **1572**

LLOYD'S SHIPPING INDEX. (UK/0144-4549). Lloyd's of London Press Ltd, Sheepen Place, Colchester, Essex, CO3 3LP England. **Tel** 011 44 206 772113, US: (212)529-9500, US: (800)955-6937, FAX 011 44 206 772880, US: (212)529-9826, telex 987321 LLOYDS G. **5452**

LLOYD'S VOYAGE RECORD. (UK/0144-4557). Lloyd's of London Press Ltd, Sheepen Place, Colchester, Essex, CO3 3LP England. **Tel** 011 44 206 772113, US: (212)529-9500, US: (800)955-6937, FAX 011 44 206 772880, US: (212)529-9826, telex 987321 LLOYDS G. **5452**

LNG OBSERVER, THE. (US/1053-6949). Institute of Gas Technology, 3424 South State Street, Chicago IL 60616. **Tel** (312)949-3970, (312)949-3650, FAX (312)949-3776, telex 25-6189. **4263**

LODGING HOSPITALITY. (US/0148-0766). Penton Publishing, 1100 Superior Avenue, Cleveland OH 44114-2543. **Tel** (216)696-7000, FAX (216)696-0836. **2807**

LOGISTICS AND TRANSPORTATION REVIEW, THE. (CN/0047-4991). University of British Columbia Faculty Commerce Business Administration, 1924 West Mall, Room 100, Vancouver British Columbia V6T 1Z2 Canada. **Tel** (604)822-4977, FAX (604)822-8521. **5386**

LONDON BUSINESS MONTHLY MAGAZINE. (CN/0820-5698). Bowes Publishers, PO Box 7400 Station E, London Ontario N5Y 4X3 Canada. **Tel** (519)472-7601, FAX (519)473-2256. **690**

LONDON MAGAZINE (LONDON, ONT.). (CN/0711-6233). London Magazine, 231 Dundas Street, Suite 203, London, ONT N6A 1H1 Canada. **Tel** (519)679-4901, FAX (519)434-7842. **2537**

LONG-DISTANCE LETTER, THE. (US/0740-6851). Phillips Business Information, Inc., 1201 Seven Locks Road, Potomac MD 20854. **Tel** (301)424-3338, (800)777-5006, FAX (301)309-3847. **1159**

LONG TERM CARE MANAGEMENT. (US/0743-1422). Faulkner & Gray Inc., 11 Penn Plaza, 17th Floor, New York NY 10001. **Tel** (212)967-7000, (800)535-8403. **3605**

LOS ANGELES BUSINESS JOURNAL. (US/0194-2603). Los Angeles Business Journal, PO Box 469016, Escondido CA 90246. **Tel** (213)549-5225, (800)255-3302. **690**

LOS ANGELES TIMES, THE. (US/0458-3035). Los Angeles Times, Times Mirror Square, Los Angeles CA 90053. **Tel** (714)237-5000, (800)528-4637. **5636**

LOUISIANA INDUSTRY ENVIRONMENTAL ALERT. (US/1055-257X). Environmental Compliance Reporter, 3154-B College Drive, Suite 522, Baton Rouge LA 70808. **Tel** (504)383-3937. **2177**

LOUISVILLE. (US/0024-6948). Louisville Magazine, 1 Riverfront Plaza, Suite 604, Louisville KY 40202. **Tel** (502)625-0100. **2537**

MACHINE DESIGN. (US/0024-9114). Penton Publishing, 1100 Superior Avenue, Cleveland OH 44114-2543. **Tel** (216)696-7000, FAX (216)696-0836. **2120**

MACINTOSH TIPS & TRICKS (PRINT). (US/1070-6720). Giles Road Press, PO Box 212, Harrington Park NJ 07640-0212. **Tel** (201)767-7001, FAX (201)767-7457. **1194**

MACLEAN'S. (CN/0024-9262). MacLean Hunter Publ. Limited / Toronto, 777 Bay Street, 8th Floor Agency Control, Toronto Ontario M5W 1A7 Canada. **Tel** (416)596-5000, (800)268-6811, FAX (416)596-5526. **2489**

MACON TELEGRAPH. (US/1054-2485). Macon Telegraph Publishing Company, 120 Broadway, Macon GA 31213. **Tel** (912)744-4200. **5654**

MACUSER (NEW YORK, N.Y.). (US/0884-0997). Ziff-Davis, One Park Avenue, 5th Floor, New York NY 10016. **Tel** (212)503-3500, (609)786-8230. **1268**

MACWEEK. (US/0892-8118). Ziff-Davis, One Park Avenue, 5th Floor, New York NY 10016. **Tel** (212)503-3500, (609)786-8230. **1238**

MACWORLD (SAN FRANCISCO, CALIF.). (US/0741-8647). PCW Communications Inc., 501 Second Street, San Francisco CA 94107. **Tel** (415)243-0500, (415)978-3146. **1268**

MAGAZINE INDEX, THE. (US). Information Access Company, 362 Lakeside Drive, Foster City CA 94404. **Tel** (800)227-8431. **2497**

MAGICAL BLEND (1989). (US/1073-5879). Magical Blend, PO Box 600, Chico CA 95927. **Tel** (415)673-1001, (916)893-9037. **4242**

MAGICAL BLEND MAGAZINE. (US/1040-4287). Magical Blend, PO Box 600, Chico CA 95927. **Tel** (415)673-1001, (916)893-9037. **4242**

MAGILL'S CINEMA ANNUAL. (US/0739-2141). Salem Press Inc, 580 Sylvan Avenue, Englewood Cliffs NJ 07632. **Tel** (201)871-3700, (800)221-1592, FAX (201)871-8668, telex 138881. **4074**

MAGILL'S SURVEY OF CINEMA. (US/1065-6553). EBSCO Publishing / Boston, 83 Pine Street, Peabody MA 01960. **Tel** (800)653-2726 North America, (508)535-8500, FAX (508)535-8545. **4074**

MAIL ON SUNDAY. (UK/0263-8878). Hart Mailing Services, 18 Hillside Avenue, Purley, Surrey CR8 2DP England. **Tel** 011 44 81 7630140. **5812**

MAINSTREAM NEWS. (US/1046-6355). Mainstream Center Clarke, 48 Round Hill Road, Northhampton MA 01060. **Tel** (413)582-1121, FAX (413)586-6654. **4391**

MAINSTREAM (SACRAMENTO, CALIF.). (US/0891-088X). Animal Protection Institute of America, PO Box 22505, Sacramento CA 95822. **Tel** (916)731-5521. **226**

MAIZE ABSTRACTS. (UK/0267-2987). CAB International Centre, Wallingford, Oxon OX10 8DE United Kingdom. **Tel** 44 491 832111, FAX 44 491 833508, telex 847964 (COMAGG G). **154**

MANAGED CARE LAW OUTLOOK. (US/1042-4091). Capitol Publications, 1101 King Street, Suite 444, Alexandria VA 22314. **Tel** (703)683-4100, (800)655-5597. **3006**

MANAGED CARE OUTLOOK. (US/0896-6567). Capitol Publications, 1101 King Street, Suite 444, Alexandria VA 22314. **Tel** (703)683-4100, (800)655-5597. **3788**

MANAGED CARE WEEK. (US/1056-7461). Atlantic Information Services Inc., 1050 17th Street Northwest, Suite 480, Washington DC 20036. **Tel** (202)775-9008, (800)521-4323, FAX (202)331-9542. **3788**

MANAGED HEALTHCARE NEWS. (US/1060-1392). Advanstar Communications Inc., 131 West First Street, Duluth MN 55802. **Tel** (218)723-9477, (800)346-0085. **4789**

MANAGEMENT AND MARKETING ABSTRACTS. (UK/0308-2172). Pira International, Randalls Road, Leatherhead, Surrey KT22 7RU England. **Tel** 011 44 372 376161, FAX 011 44 372 377526. **731**

MANAGEMENT CONTENTS [ONLINE DATABASE]. (US). Information Access Company, 362 Lakeside Drive, Foster City CA 94404. **Tel** (800)227-8431. **731**

MANAGEMENT DECISION. (UK/0025-1747). MCB University Press, 60 62 Toller Lane, Bradford West Yorkshire BD8 9BX England. **Tel** 011 44 274 499821, FAX 011 44 274 547143, telex 51317 MCBUNI G. **877**

MANAGEMENT EDUCATION AND DEVELOPMENT. (UK/0047-5688). Management Education & Development, University of Lancaster, Center for the Study of Mgt Learning, Lancaster LA1 4YX England. **Tel** 011 44 524 65201 Ext 4011. **1617**

MANAGEMENT INFORMATION SYSTEMS QUARTERLY. (US/0276-7783). MIS Quarterly, 271 19th Avenue South, MIS Research Center, Minneapolis MN 55455. **Tel** (612)624-7083, (612)624-2035, FAX (612)626-1316. **1194**

MANAGEMENT TODAY. (UK/0025-1925). Haymarket Publishing Ltd., 12 14 Ansdell Street, London W8 5TR England. **Tel** 011 44 483 733800, FAX 011 44 483 776573. **878**

MANAGERIAL LAW. (UK/0309-0558). MCB University Press, 60 62 Toller Lane, Bradford West Yorkshire BD8 9BX England. **Tel** 011 44 274 499821, FAX 011 44 274 547143, telex 51317 MCBUNI G. **3151**

MANITOBA BUSINESS. (CN/0709-2423). Canada Wide Magazines Ltd, 401 4180 Lougheed Highway, Burnaby BC V5C 6A7 Canada. **Tel** (604)299-7311, FAX (604)299-9188. **691**

MANUFACTURING AUTOMATION. (US/1060-2712). Vital Information Publications, 321 Carrera Drive, Mill Valley CA 94941. **Tel** (415)389-8671, (415)345-7018, FAX (415)389-8671, (415)345-7018. **3483**

MANUFACTURING CHEMIST (LONDON: 1981). (UK/0262-4230). Morgan Grampian, 40 Beresford Street Woolwich, London SE18 6BQ England. **Tel** 011 44 81 855 7777, FAX 011 44 81 855 5548, telex 896238. **985**

MANUFACTURING SYSTEMS. (US/0748-948X). Chilton Company, 201 King of Prussia Road, Radnor PA 19089. **Tel** (610)964-4122, (800)695-1214, FAX (610)964-4978, telex 6851035 CHILTON UW. **1617**

MARIETTA DAILY JOURNAL (MARIETTA, GA.), THE. (US/8750-4618). Marietta Daily Journal, 580 Fairground Street, Box 449, Marietta GA 30060. **Tel** (404)428-9411. **5654**

MARINE FISHERIES REVIEW. (US/0090-1830). Superintendent of Documents, US Government Printing Office, Washington DC 20402. **Tel** (202)275-3328, FAX (202)786-2377. **2308**

MARINE TECHNOLOGY SOCIETY JOURNAL. (US/0025-3324). Marine Technology Society, 1828 L Street Northwest, Suite 906, Washington DC 20036. **Tel** (202)775-5966, FAX (202)429-9417. **1452**

MARITIME INFORMATION REVIEW. (NE/0920-1610). Netherlands Maritime Information Center, CMO PO Box 21873, 3000AW Rotterdam Netherlands. **Tel** 011 31 10 4130960, FAX 011 31 10 4112857, telex 26585. **3181**

MARKET. ASIA PACIFIC. (US/1059-275X). W-Two Publications Ltd, 202 The Commons, Suite 401, Ithaca NY 14850. **Tel** (607)277-0934, FAX (607)277-0935. **930**

MARKET--EUROPE. (US/1050-9410). W-Two Publications Ltd, 202 The Commons, Suite 401, Ithaca NY 14850. **Tel** (607)277-0934, FAX (607)277-0935. **845**

MARKET LETTER. (UK/0951-3175). Marketletter Publications Ltd, 54-55 Wilton Road, London SW1V 1DE England. **Tel** 011 44 71 8287272, FAX 011 44 71 8280415. **4314**

MARKET RESEARCH EUROPE. (UK/0308-3446). Euromonitor Publications Ltd., 87-88 Turnmill Street, London EC1M 5QU England. **Tel** 011 44 71 2518024, FAX 011 44 71 6083149, telex 21120. **731**

MARKET SHARE REPORTER. (US/1052-9578). Gale Research Inc., 835 Penobscot Building, 645 Griswold Street, Detroit MI 48226. **Tel** (800)877-GALE, (313)961-2242, FAX (313)961-6083, (800)414-5043, telex TWX 810-221-7086. **930**

MARKETING AND ADVERTISING REFERENCE SERVICE [ONLINE DATABASE]. (US). Predicasts Inc., A Ziff Communications Company, 11001 Cedar Avenue, Cleveland OH 44106. **Tel** (800)321-6388, (216)795-3000, FAX (216)229-9944, telex 985 604. **731**

MARKETING COMPUTERS. (US/0895-5697). Billboard Publications Inc., 1515 Broadway Billboard, New York NY 10036. **Tel** (212)764-7300, FAX (305)755-7048, telex WU TWX 710-581-6279. **1194**

MARKETING INTELLIGENCE & PLANNING. (UK/0263-4503). MCB University Press, 60 62 Toller Lane, Bradford West Yorkshire BD8 9BX England. **Tel** 011 44 274 499821, FAX 011 44 274 547143, telex 51317 MCBUNI G. **931**

MARKETING TO WOMEN (1989). (US/1047-1677). About Women Inc. Publications, 33 Broad Street, Boston MA 02109. **Tel** (617)723-4337, FAX (617)723-7107. **5561**

MARKETLETTER (MARKET ED.). (UK/0891-589X). Marketletter Publications Ltd, 54-55 Wilton Road, London SW1V 1DE England. **Tel** 011 44 71 8287272, FAX 011 44 71 8280415. **2435**

MARTINDALE-HUBBELL LAW DIRECTORY (PRINT). (US/0191-0221). Martindale-Hubbell, A Reed Reference Publishing Company, Part of Reed International PLC, 121 Chanlon Road, New Providence NJ 07974. **Tel** (800)526-4902, (908)464-6800, FAX (908)464-3553, telex 138755. **3006**

MARYLAND BUSINESS & LIVING. (US/0747-0320). Philos Publications, 7 Church Lane/Suite 16, Baltimore MD 21208. **692**

MASS HIGH TECH. (US/8750-2100). Mass High Tech, 500 West Cummings Park, Suite 3500, Woburn MA 01801. **Tel** (617)935-1100. **5127**

MASS SPECTROMETRY BULLETIN. (UK/0025-4738). Royal Society of Chemistry, Thomas Graham House, Science Park, Cambridge CB4 4WF England. **Tel** 011 44 223 420066, FAX 011 44 223 423429, telex 818293 ROYAL. **1011**

MASS TRANSIT (WASHINGTON, D.C.). (US/0364-3484). PTN Publishing Company, 445 Broad Hollow Road, Melville NY 11747. **Tel** (516)845-2700, FAX (516)845-7109. **5386**

MASSACHUSETTS CPA REVIEW. (US/0025-4770). MSCPA: Massachusettes Society of Certified Public Accountants, 105 Chauncy Street/10th Floor, Boston MA 02111-1742. **Tel** (617)556-4000, (800)392-6145, FAX (617)556-4126. **748**

MATHEMATICA IN EDUCATION. (US/1065-2965). Springer-Verlag New York Inc., 175 5th Avenue, New York NY 10010. **Tel** (212)460-1500, telex 232 235 SPB UR. **1763**

MATHEMATICAL REVIEWS. (US/0025-5629). American Mathematical Society, PO Box 6248, Providence RI 02940-6248. **Tel** (800)321-4267, (401)455-4000, FAX (401)331-3842, telex 797192. **3542**

MATRIX (LENNOXVILLE). (CN/0318-3610). Linda Leith, CP 100St Anne de Bellevue, Quebec H9X 3L4 Canada. **Tel** (514)426-8654, FAX (514)426-8658. **3410**

MATRIX NEWS. (US/1059-0749). Matrix Information and Directory Services, 1106 Clayton Lane, Suite 500W, Austin TX 78723. **Tel** (512)451-7602, FAX (512)450-1436. **1242**

MECHANICAL ENGINEERING ABSTRACTS. (US/1063-7311). Cambridge Scientific Abstracts, 7200 Wisconsin Avenue, #601, Bethesda MD 20814-4823. **Tel** (301)961-6750, (800)843-7751, FAX (301)961-6720. **2006**

MED AD NEWS. (US/1067-733X). Engel Communication Inc, 820 Bear Tavern Road, West Trenton NJ 08628. **Tel** (609)530-0044, FAX (609)530-0207. **4314**

MEDIA INDUSTRY NEWSLETTER. (US/0024-9793). Phillips Business Information, Inc., 1201 Seven Locks Road, Potomac MD 20854. **Tel** (301)424-3338, (800)777-5006, FAX (301)309-3847. **1116**

MEDIAWEEK (NEW YORK, N.Y.). (US/1055-176X). EMAP Readerlink, Audit House, 260 Field End Road, Ruislip Middlesex HA4 9LT England. **Tel** 011 44 081 868 4499, FAX 011 44 081 429 3117. **933**

MEDICAL ADVERTISING NEWS. (US/0745-0907). Engel Communication Inc, 820 Bear Tavern Road, West Trenton NJ 08628. **Tel** (609)530-0044, FAX (609)530-0207. **762**

MEDICAL & PHARMACEUTICAL BIOTECHNOLOGY ABSTRACTS. (US/1063-1178). Cambridge Scientific Abstracts, 7200 Wisconsin Avenue, #601, Bethesda MD 20814-4823. **Tel** (301)961-6750, (800)843-7751, FAX (301)961-6720. **3660**

MEDICAL ECONOMICS. (US/0025-7206). Medical Economics Publishing, Five Paragon Drive, Second Floor, Montvale NJ 07645. **Tel** (800)432-4570, (201)358-2210. **3608**

MEDICAL MARKETING & MEDIA. (US/0025-7354). CPS Communications Inc, 7200 West Camino Road, Suite 215, Boca Raton FL 33433. **Tel** (407)368-9301, FAX (407)368-7870. **933**

MEDICAL RESEARCH FUNDING NEWS. (US/1052-9152). Faulkner & Gray Inc., 11 Penn Plaza, 17th Floor, New York NY 10001. **Tel** (212)967-7000, (800)535-8403. **3611**

MEDICAL SCIENCE RESEARCH. (UK/0269-8951). Chapman & Hall, 2-6 Boundary Row, London SE1 8HN England. **Tel** 011 44 71 865 0066, FAX 011 44 71 522 9623, telex 290164 Chapmag. **3611**

MEDICAL TEXTILES. (NE/0266-2078). Elsevier Advanced Technology, An Imprint of Elsevier Science Ltd., The Boulevard, Langford Lane, Kidlington, Oxford OX5 1GB United Kingdom. **Tel** 011 44 865 843000, 011 44 865 843699, FAX 011 44 865 843010. **3612**

MEDICAL WASTE NEWS. (US/1048-4493). Business Publishers Inc., 951 Pershing Drive, Silver Spring MD 20910-4464. **Tel** (301)587-6300, (800)274-0122, FAX (301)585-9075. **3612**

MEDICAL WORLD NEWS. (US/0025-763X). Miller Freeman Inc., 600 Harrison Street, San Francisco CA 94107. **Tel** (415)905-2337, FAX (415)905-2240, telex 278273. **3612**

MEDICINAL & AROMATIC PLANTS ABSTRACTS. (II/0250-4367). Publications & Information Directorate, CSIR, Dr. K.S. Krishnan Marg, New Delhi-110012, India. **Tel** 5726014, FAX 5731353, telex 031-77271 PID IN. **517**

MEETINGS AND CONVENTIONS. (US/0025-8652). Cahners Publishing Company, 249 West 17th Street, New York NY 10011. **Tel** (212)645-0067, FAX (212)242-6987. **692**

MEMBRANE & SEPARATION TECHNOLOGY NEWS. (US/0737-8483). Business Communications Inc., 25 Van Zant Street, Suite 13, Norwalk CT 06855. **Tel** (203)853-4266. **985**

MEMPHIS BUSINESS JOURNAL. (US/0747-167X). Mid South Communications, 88 Union/Suite 105, Memphis TN 38103-5195. **Tel** (901)526-2007. **693**

MERCER BUSINESS : A PUBLICATION OF MERCER COUNTY CHAMBER. (US/0194-9101). Mercer County Chamber of Commerce, PO Box 8307, 2550 Kuser Road, Trenton NJ 08650. **Tel** (609)586-2056, FAX (609)586-8052. **693**

MERGERS AND ACQUISITIONS IN CANADA (RICHMOND HILL, ONT.). (CN/0843-5421). Crosbie and Company, 1 First Canadian Place, 9th Place, Toronto ONT M5X 1A4 Canada. **Tel** (416)362-7726, FAX (416)362-3447. **693**

MERGERS & ACQUISITIONS REPORT. (US). Investment Dealers Digest Inc., Two World Trade Center, 18th Floor, New York NY 10048. **Tel** (212)227-1200, FAX (212)432-1039. **693**

MERRILL'S ILLINOIS LEGAL TIMES. (US/1063-3014). Illinois Legal Times, 222 Merchandise Mart Place, Suite 1513, Chicago IL 60654. **Tel** (312)644-4378, FAX (312)644-0765. **3009**

MESA TRIBUNE. (US). Cox Arizona Publications, PO Box 1547, Mesa AZ 85211. **Tel** (602)898-6500. **5630**

MESSENGER INQUIRER. (US). Owensboro Publishing Company, PO Box 1480, Owensboro KY 42302. **Tel** (502)926-0123. **5681**

METALS ABSTRACTS. (UK/0026-0924). American Society for Metals International, c/o Deborah Barthelmes, Materials Park OH 44073-0002. **Tel** (216)338-5151, FAX (216)338-4634, telex 980-619. **4026**

METALS INDUSTRY NEWS. (UK/0265-8321). Argus Press Group, Queensway House, 2 Queensway Redhill, Surrey RH1 1QS England. **Tel** 011 44 737 768611, 011 44 737 761685, FAX 011 44 737 760510, telex 948669 TOPJNL G. **4011**

METALS WEEK. (US/0026-0975). McGraw Hill Publishing Company, Inc., 1221 Avenue of the Americas, New York NY 10020. **Tel** (212)512-6410, (800)525-5003, FAX (212)512-6111. **4011**

METROPOLITAN HOME. (US/0273-2858). Hachette Magazines Inc., 1633 Broadway, New York NY 10019. **Tel** (212)767-6000. **2902**

METROPOLITAN TORONTO BUSINESS JOURNAL, THE. (CN/0709-003X). Board of Trade of Metropolitan Toronto, PO Box 60, 1 First Canadian Place, Toronto Ontario M5X 1C1 Canada. **Tel** (416)366-6811, (416)366-7139, FAX (416)366-5620. **693**

MEXICO BUSINESS MONTHLY. (US/1054-2663). Mexico Business Monthly, 52 Maples Avenue, Department M, Maplewood NJ 07040. **Tel** (201)762-1565, (800)766-3949, FAX (201)762-9585. **906**

MEXICO DESCONOCIDO. (MX). Editorial Jilguero SA, Monte Pelvoux 110 Primer Piso, Chapultepec Mexico DFCP 11000. **Tel** 011 52 5404040, 011 52 2026585. **5484**

MEXICO SERVICE. (US/1044-6303). United Communications Group, 11300 Rockville Pike, Suite 1100, Rockville MD 20852. **Tel** (301)816-8950 ext. 223, FAX (301)816-8945. **2512**

MEYLER'S SIDE EFFECTS OF DRUGS. (NE/0376-7396). Elsevier Science Publishers BV, PO Box 211, 1000 AE Amsterdam Netherlands. **Tel** 011 31 20 5803642, FAX 011 31 20 5862696, telex 15682. **4315**

MIAMI HERALD (MIAMI, FLA.). (US/0898-865X). Miami Herald Publishing Company, 1 Herald Plaza, Miami FL 33132. **Tel** (305)350-2111, (800)825-6245. **5650**

MIAMI REVIEW. (US/0888-0263). American Lawyer Media, L.P., 600 3rd Avenue, New York NY 10016. **Tel** (212)973-2800. **5718**

MICHIGAN CITIZEN. (US/1072-2041). Michigan Citizen, PO Box 03560, Highland Park MI 48203. **Tel** (313)869-0033, FAX (313)869-0430. **5693**

MICHIGAN CPA, THE. (US/0026-2064). Michigan Association of Certified Public Accountants, PO Box 9054, Farmington Hills MI 48333. **Tel** (313)855-2288, FAX (313)855-9122. **748**

MICHIGAN LAW REVIEW. (US/0026-2234). Michigan Law Review Association, Hutchins Hall, Ann Arbor MI 48109. **Tel** (313)763-5870, FAX (313)764-8309. **3009**

MICHIGAN MANUFACTURERS DIRECTORY. (US/0736-2889). Manufacturers News Inc., 1633 Central Street, Evanston IL 60201-1569. **Tel** (708)864-7000, FAX (708)332-1100. **3484**

MICROBIOLOGY ABSTRACTS. SECTION A : INDUSTRIAL & APPLIED MICROBIOLOGY. (US/0300-838X). Cambridge Scientific Abstracts, 7200 Wisconsin Avenue, #601, Bethesda MD 20814-4823. **Tel** (301)961-6750, (800)843-7751, FAX (301)961-6720. **478**

MICROBIOLOGY ABSTRACTS. SECTION B, BACTERIOLOGY. (US/0300-8398). Cambridge Scientific Abstracts, 7200 Wisconsin Avenue, #601, Bethesda MD 20814-4823. **Tel** (301)961-6750, (800)843-7751, FAX (301)961-6720. **478**

MICROBIOLOGY ABSTRACTS. SECTION C, ALGOLOGY, MYCOLOGY & PROTOZOOLOGY. (US/0301-2328). Cambridge Scientific Abstracts, 7200 Wisconsin Avenue, #601, Bethesda MD 20814-4823. **Tel** (301)961-6750, (800)843-7751, FAX (301)961-6720. **478**

MICROCELL REPORT. (US/1048-6976). Microcell Report, 150 West 22nd Street, Suite 1000, New York NY 10011. **Tel** (800)883-8989 or (212)366-9788, FAX (212)366-9798. **1160**

MICROCOMPUTER INDEX. (US/8756-7040). Learned Information Inc., 143 Old Marlton Pike, Medford NJ 08055-8750. **Tel** (609)654-6266, FAX (609)654-4309. **1209**

MICROPROCESSOR REPORT. (US/0899-9341). MicroDesign Resources Inc., 874 Gravenstein Highway South, Suite 14, Sebastopol CA 95472. **Tel** (707)823-4004, (800)527-0288, FAX (707)823-0504. **1270**

MICROSOFT SYSTEMS JOURNAL. (US/0889-9932). Miller Freeman Inc., 600 Harrison Street, San Francisco CA 94107. **Tel** (415)905-2337, FAX (415)905-2240, telex 278273. **1288**

MICROWAVES & RF. (US/0745-2993). Penton Publishing, 1100 Superior Avenue, Cleveland OH 44114-2543. **Tel** (216)696-7000, FAX (216)696-0836. **4438**

MID AMERICA FARMER GROWER, THE. (US/1040-1423). SJS Publishing Company, PO Box 323, Perryville MO 63775. **Tel** (314)547-2244, FAX (314)547-5663. **108**

MID-ATLANTIC JOURNAL OF BUSINESS, THE. (US/0732-9334). Stillman School of Business, Seton Hall/University South Orange Avenue, South Orange NJ 07070. **Tel** (201)761-9251. **694**

MIDDLE EAST BUSINESS INTELLIGENCE. (US/0731-6305). International Executive Reports, 717 D Street NW/Suite 300, Washington DC 20004-2807. **Tel** (202)628-6900, FAX (202)628 6618, telex 440462 MEER UI. **933**

MIDDLE EAST EXECUTIVE REPORTS. (US/0271-0498). International Executive Reports, 717 D Street NW/Suite 300, Washington DC 20004-2807. **Tel** (202)628-6900, FAX (202)628 6618, telex 440462 MEER UI. **3132**

MIDDLE EAST (LONDON, ENGLAND : 1985). (UK/0305-0734). IC Publications Ltd., 7 Coldbath Square, London EC1R 4LQ England. **Tel** 011 44 71 713-7711, FAX 011 44 71 713-7898, telex 8811757. **1505**

MIDEAST MARKETS. (UK/0098-6461). Financial Times Business Information Ltd., Tower House, Southampton Street, London WC2E 7HA England. **Tel** 011 44 71 353 1040. **846**

MIDRANGE SYSTEMS. (US/1041-8237). Professional Press Inc, 101 Witmer Road, Horsham PA 19044. **Tel** (215)957-1500, FAX (215)957-1050. **1274**

MIDWEST REAL ESTATE NEWS. (US/0893-2719). Argus Business, 6151 Powers Ferry Road, Atlanta GA 30339. **Tel** (404)995-2500, (800)233-3359. **4841**

MILBANK QUARTERLY, THE. (US/0887-378X). Blackwell Publishers, 238 Main Street, Cambridge MA 02142. **Tel** (617)547-7110, (800)835-6770, FAX (617)547-0789. **4791**

MILITARY & COMMERCIAL FIBER BUSINESS. (US/1051-2470). Phillips Business Information, Inc., 1201 Seven Locks Road, Potomac MD 20854. **Tel** (301)424-3338, (800)777-5006, FAX (301)309-3847. **4438**

MILITARY ROBOTICS. (US/0896-0348). L & B Ltd, 19 Rock Creek Church Road NW, Washington DC 20011. **Tel** (202)723-1600, FAX (202)726-2979. **1215**

MILITARY SPACE. (US/0743-7897). Pasha Publications Inc., 1616 North Fort Myer Drive, Suite 1000, Arlington VA 22209. **Tel** (800)424-2908, (703)528-1244, FAX (703)528-3742, (703)528-1253. **28**

MILLING AND BAKING NEWS. (US/0091-4843). Sosland Publishing Company / Missouri, 4800 Main Street, Suite 100, Kansas City MO 64112. **Tel** (816)756-1000, FAX (816)756-0494, telex 820182. **202**

MINE REGULATION REPORTER. (US/1040-8223). Pasha Publications Inc., 1616 North Fort Myer Drive, Suite 1000, Arlington VA 22209. **Tel** (800)424-2908, (703)528-1244, FAX (703)528-3742, (703)528-1253. **3010**

MINERALOGICAL ABSTRACTS. (UK/0026-4601). Mineralogical Society of Great Britain, 41 Queen's Gate, Kensington London SW7 5HR England. **Tel** 011 44 71 584 7516, FAX 011 44 71 823 8021. **1363**

MINING MAGAZINE (LONDON). (UK/0308-6631). Mining Journal Ltd., 60 Worship Street, London EC2A 2HD England. **Tel** 011 44 071 377 2020, FAX 071 247 4100, telex 8952809 MINING G. **2146**

MINNEAPOLIS/ST. PAUL CITYBUSINESS. (US/0883-3044). MCP Inc., 5500 Wayzata Boulevard/Suite 800, Minneapolis MN 55416. **Tel** (612)591-2700, FAX (612)591-2639. **695**

MINNESOTA BUSINESS JOURNAL. (US/0192-5504). Dorn Communications, 15 5th Street/Suite 900, Minneapolis MN 55402. **Tel** (612)835-6855. **695**

MINORITY MARKETS ALERT. (US/1041-7524). EPM Communications Inc., 488 East 18th Street, Brooklyn NY 11226. **Tel** (718)469-9330, FAX (718)469-7124. **906**

MINPROC : MINERAL PROCESSING ABSTRACTS. (CN/0828-8461). Canada Center Mineral & Energy Technology, 555 Booth Street, Ottawa ONT K1A OG1 Canada. **Tel** (613)992-8837, FAX (613)952-2587. **2006**

MISSISSIPPI BUSINESS JOURNAL, THE. (US/0195-0002). Mississippi Business Journal, PO Box 4566, Jackson MS 39216. **Tel** (601)352-9035. **695**

MISSISSIPPI QUARTERLY, THE. (US/0026-637X). Mississippi State University / The Mississippi Quarterly, Box 5272, Mississippi State MS 39762. **Tel** (601)325-3069, FAX (601)325-3299, telex 785045. **2850**

MISSOURI REVIEW, THE. (US/0191-1961). University of Missouri - Columbia, 1507 Hillcrest Hall, Columbia MO 65211. **Tel** (314)882-4474, FAX (314)884-4671. **3412**

MLA INTERNATIONAL BIBLIOGRAPHY. (US/1063-3316). H W Wilson Company, 950 University Avenue, Bronx NY 10452. **Tel** (800)367-6770, (718)588-8400, FAX (718)590-1617, telex 4990003 HWILSON. **3303**

MLA INTERNATIONAL BIBLIOGRAPHY OF BOOKS AND ARTICLES ON THE MODERN LANGUAGES AND LITERATURES (COMPLETE ED.). (US/0024-8215). Modern Language Association of America, 10 Astor Place, New York NY 10003-6981. **Tel** (212)614-6382, FAX (212)477-9863. **3336**

MLA INTERNATIONAL BIBLIOGRAPHY OF BOOKS AND ARTICLES ON THE MODERN LANGUAGES AND LITERATURES (OPTION C). (US/0740-8722). Modern Language Association of America, 10 Astor Place, New York NY 10003-6981. **Tel** (212)614-6382, FAX (212)477-9863. **3303**

MLO, MEDICAL LABORATORY OBSERVER. (US/0580-7247). Medical Economics Publishing, Five Paragon Drive, Second Floor, Montvale NJ 07645. **Tel** (800)432-4570, (201)358-2210. **3617**

MOBILE DATA REPORT. (US/1040-7022). Telecom Publishing Group, 1101 King Street, Suite 444, Alexandria VA 22314. **Tel** (703)683-4100, (800)327-7205, FAX (703)739-6490. **1242**

MOBILE PHONE NEWS. (US/0737-5077). Phillips Business Information, Inc., 1201 Seven Locks Road, Potomac MD 20854. **Tel** (301)424-3338, (800)777-5006, FAX (301)309-3847. **1160**

MOBILE SATELLITE NEWS (POTOMAC, MD.). (US/1046-5286). Phillips Business Information, Inc., 1201 Seven Locks Road, Potomac MD 20854. **Tel** (301)424-3338, (800)777-5006, FAX (301)309-3847. **1160**

MOBILE SATELLITE REPORTS. (US/1046-6061). Warren Publishing, Inc., 2115 Ward Court NW, Washington DC 20037. **Tel** (202)872-9200, FAX (202)293-3435. **1160**

MODERN BREWERY AGE. (US/0026-7538). Business Journals Inc, PO Box 5550, Norwalk CT 06856. **Tel** (203)853-6015, FAX (203)852-8175, telex 353706. **2369**

MODERN — Serials available Online

MODERN BRIDE. (US/0026-7546). Cahners Publishing Company, 249 West 17th Street, New York NY 10011. Tel (212)645-0067, FAX (212)242-6987. **2283**

MODERN CASTING. (US/0026-7562). American Foundrymen's Society, 505 State Street, Des Plaines IL 60016-2277. Tel (708)824-0181, (800)537-4237, FAX (708)824-7848. **4012**

MODERN MACHINE SHOP. (US/0026-8003). Gardner Publications Inc, 6600 Clough Pike, Cincinnati OH 45244. Tel (513)231-8020, (513)231-2818, telex 214132. **2122**

MODERN MATERIALS HANDLING. (US/0026-8038). Cahners Publishing Company, 249 West 17th Street, New York NY 10011. Tel (212)645-0067, FAX (212)242-6987. **3484**

MODERN MATURITY. (US/0026-8046). AARP - American Association of Retired Persons, PO Box 199, Long Beach CA 90801. Tel (310)496-2277. **5180**

MODERN OFFICE TECHNOLOGY. (US/0746-3839). Penton Publishing, 1100 Superior Avenue, Cleveland OH 44114-2543. Tel (216)696-7000, FAX (216)696-0836. **4212**

MODERN PAINT AND COATINGS. (US/0098-7786). Argus Business, 6151 Powers Ferry Road, Atlanta GA 30339. Tel (404)995-2500, (800)233-3359. **4224**

MODERN PLASTICS. (US/0026-8275). McGraw Hill Publishing Company, Inc., 1221 Avenue of the Americas, New York NY 10020. Tel (212)512-6410, (800)525-5003, FAX (212)512-6111. **4456**

MODERN POWER SYSTEMS. (UK/0260-7840). Wilmington Publishing Ltd., PO Box 200, Field End Road, Ruislip Middx HA4 OSY England. Tel 011 44 81 841 3970, FAX 011 44 81 841 9676. **1950**

MODERN TIRE DEALER. (US/0026-8496). Bill Communications Inc., 355 Park Avenue South, New York NY 10010-1789. Tel (800)821-6897, (212)592-6262, FAX (212)592-6209. **5419**

MONDO, IL. (IT/0391-6855). RCS Rizzoli Periodici, Via A Rizzoli 2, 20132 Milan Italy. Tel 011 39 2 27200720. **2519**

MONEY (CHICAGO, ILL.). (US/0149-4953). Time Inc. / New York, Time & Life Building, Rockefeller Center, New York NY 10020. **906**

MONEY DIGEST (BATH). (CN/0833-3432). Investors Association of Canada, 26 Soho Street, Suite 380, Toronto Ontario M5T 1Z7 Canada. Tel (416)340-1723. **907**

MONEY LAUNDERING ALERT. (US/1046-3070). Money Laundering Alert, PO Box 011390, Miami FL 33101. Tel (305)530-1652, (800)232-3652, FAX (305)530-9434. **3087**

MONEY MARKETING. (UK). Centaur Communications Ltd., St Giles House, 50 Poland Street, London W1V 4AX England. Tel 011 44 71 439 4222, FAX 011 44 71 734 6748, telex 261352. **907**

MONITORING REPORT, THE. (US). British Broadcasting Corporation, Caversham Park, Reading RG4 8TZ England. Tel 011 44 734 472742, FAX 011 44 734 463823, telex 848318. **1135**

MONTANA CODE ANNOTATED STATUTES TEXT. (US). Montana Legislative Council, State Capitol/Room 138, Helena MT 59620-1706. Tel (406)444-3064, FAX (406)444-3036. **3012**

MONTANA LAW REVIEW. (US/0026-9972). University of Montana / School of Law, Missoula MT 59812. Tel (406)243-2023, FAX (406)243-2576. **3012**

MONTHLY LABOR REVIEW. (US/0098-1818). Superintendent of Documents, US Government Printing Office, Washington DC 20402. Tel (202)275-3328, FAX (202)786-2377. **1691**

MONTHLY REVIEW (NEW YORK. 1949). (US/0027-0520). Monthly Review Foundation Inc., 122 West 27th Street/10th Floor, New York NY 10001. Tel (212)691-2555. **4543**

MORBIDITY AND MORTALITY WEEKLY REPORT. (US/0149-2195). MMS Publications, CSPO Box 9120, Waltham MA 02254. Tel (800)843-6356. **4792**

MORGAN REPORT ON DIRECTORY PUBLISHING. (US/0890-9512). Morgan-Rand Publications Inc., 1800 Byberry Road 800, Huntingdon Valley PA 19006. Tel (215)938-5511, FAX (215)988-0402. **4817**

MORNING ADVERTISER. (UK). Morning Advertiser, Elvian House, Nixey Chose, Slough SL1 1NQ England. Tel 011 44 753 811911. **5812**

MORTGAGE BACKED SECURITIES LETTER. (US). Investment Dealers Digest Inc., Two World Trade Center, 18th Floor, New York NY 10048. Tel (212)227-1200, FAX (212)432-1039. **800**

MORTGAGE BANKING. (US/0730-0212). Mortgage Bankers Association of America, Department 0021, Washington DC 20073-0021. Tel (202)861-6992. **800**

MORTGAGE MARKETPLACE, THE. (US/0744-3927). American Banker, Concourse Level, 1 State Street Plaza, New York NY 10004. Tel (212)803-8200, (800)221-1809. **800**

MOSCOW NEWS. (RU/0027-1306). Moscow News, 16-2 Tverckaya Ulitsa, Moscow Russia. Tel 7095-209-1984, FAX 7095-209-0267. **5809**

MOTHERING. (US/0733-3013). Mothering Publishing Inc, PO Box 1690, Santa Fe NM 87504. Tel (505)984-8116, FAX (505)986-8335. **2283**

MOTOR REPORT INTERNATIONAL. (UK/0306-6274). Circlemartin Ltd, PO Box 87, Dorking Surrey, RH4 2YS England. Tel 011 44 1 949 3302. **5420**

MOTOR TREND. (US/0027-2094). Petersen Publishing Company, 6420 Wilshire Boulevard, Los Angeles CA 90048. Tel (213)782-2485. **5420**

MOTORCYCLIST'S POST, THE. (US/0164-9256). Motorcyclist Post, PO Box 154, Rochdale MA 01542. Tel (617)885-5221. **5387**

MOUTH. (US/1071-5657). Free Hand Press, Inc., 61 Brighton Street, Rochester NY 14607. Tel (716)473-6764, FAX (716)442-2916. **4391**

MULTICHANNEL NEWS. (US/0276-8593). Chilton, 825 7th Avenue, New York NY 10019. Tel (212)887-8560. **1135**

MULTIMEDIA & VIDEODISC MONITOR. (US/1054-7258). Future Systems Inc, PO Box 26, Falls Church VA 22046. Tel (703)241-1799, (703)532-0529, FAX (703)532-0529, telex 4996279. **1619**

MULTIMEDIA COMPUTING & PRESENTATIONS. (US/1051-953X). Multimedia Computing Corporations, 3501 Ryder Street, Santa Clara CA 95051. **908**

MULTIMEDIA WEEK. (US/1064-6639). Phillips Business Information, Inc., 1201 Seven Locks Road, Potomac MD 20854. Tel (301)424-3338, (800)777-5006, FAX (301)309-3847. **1118**

MULTINATIONAL SERVICE. (INT/1021-4186). Europe Information Service, rue de Geneve 6, 1140 Brussels Belgium. Tel 011 32 2 242 6020, FAX 011 32 2 242 9549. **846**

MUSIC & MEDIA. (NE). Billboard Publications Inc., 1515 Broadway Billboard, New York NY 10036. Tel (212)764-7300, FAX (305)755-7048, telex WU TWX 710-581-6279. **4133**

MUSIC TRADES. (US/0027-4488). Music Trades Corporation, PO Box 432, 80 West Street, Englewood NJ 07631. **4135**

MUSIC WEEK (1983). (UK/0265-1548). Link House Magazines Ltd., Link House, Dingwall Avenue, Croydon Surrey CR9 2TA England. Tel 011 44 81 686 2599, FAX 011 44 81 760 5154, telex 947709. **4135**

N.S.W. MASTER PLUMBER. (AT/0819-1824). Master Plumber & Mechanical Contractors, 121-125 Bland Street, Ashfield NSW 2131 Australia. Tel 011 61 2 7977055, 008 42 4181, FAX 011 61 2 7995841. **2607**

NASHVILLE BUSINESS AND LIFESTYLES. (US/1052-4215). Southeast Magazines Inc, PO Box 24649, 545 Mainstream Road, Suite 101, Nashville TN 37228. Tel (615)242-6992, FAX (615)242-2248. **2490**

NASHVILLE BUSINESS JOURNAL. (US/0889-2873). Nashville Business Journal Inc, 1 Church Street, Nashville TN 37201. Tel (615)254-9154, FAX (615)256-9080. **696**

NATIONAL BUSINESS REVIEW. (NZ/0110-6813). Fourth Estate Holding Ltd, PO Box 145, Auckland 1000 New Zealand. Tel 011 64 9 3071629, FAX 011 64 09 379060. **697**

NATIONAL CATHOLIC REPORTER. (US/0027-8939). National Catholic Reporter Publishing Company, PO Box 419281, 115 East Armour Boulevard, Kansas City MO 64141-6281. Tel (816)531-0538, (800)444-8910, (800)333-7373, FAX (816)531-7466. **5033**

NATIONAL DIRECTORY OF LAW ENFORCEMENT ADMINISTRATORS, CORRECTIONAL INSTITUTIONS, AND RELATED GOVERNMENTAL AGENCIES. (US/1066-5595). National Police Chief and Sheriffs, PO Box 365, Stevens Point WI 54481. Tel (715)345-2772. **3170**

NATIONAL FISHERMAN. (US/0027-9250). Journal Publications, 120 Tillson Avenue, Suite 201, Rockland ME 04841. Tel (207)594-6222, FAX (207)594-8978. **2309**

NATIONAL FORUM (ANN ARBOR). (US/0162-1831). National Forum / Phi Kappa Phi, 129 Quad Center, Auburn University, Auburn AL 36849-5306. Tel (205)844-5200, FAX (205)844-5994. **1836**

NATIONAL HOME CENTER NEWS. (US/0192-6772). Lebhar Friedman Inc., 3922 Coconut Palm Drive, Tampa FL 33619. Tel (800)927-9292, (813)664-6707. **2792**

NATIONAL INSTITUTE ECONOMIC REVIEW. (UK/0027-9501). National Institute for Economic and Social Research / London, 2 Dean Trench Street, Smith Square, London SW1P 3HE England. Tel 011 44 71 222 7665, FAX 011 44 71 222 1435. **1507**

NATIONAL JOURNAL (1975). (US/0360-4217). National Journal Inc., 1501 M Street Northwest, Suite 300, Washington DC 20005. Tel (800)356-4838, (202)739-8541, (800)424-2921. **4483**

NATIONAL MINORITY POLITICS. (US/1057-1655). Richberg Communications Inc., 5757 Westheimer, Suite 3-296, Houston TX 77057. Tel (713)444-4265, FAX (713)583-9534. **2268**

NATIONAL MORTGAGE NEWS. (US/1050-3331). National Thrift News Inc, 212 West 35th Street, 13th Floor, New York NY 10001. Tel (212)563-4008, FAX (212)564-8879. **801**

NATIONAL NEWSPAPER INDEX. (US/0273-3676). Information Access Company, 362 Lakeside Drive, Foster City CA 94404. Tel (800)227-8431. **5814**

NATIONAL NEWSPAPER INDEX (MONTHLY). (US). Information Access Company, 362 Lakeside Drive, Foster City CA 94404. Tel (800)227-8431. **5814**

NATIONAL PETROLEUM NEWS. (US/0149-5267). Hunter Publishing Company Inc., 25 Northwest Point Boulevard, Suite 800, Elk Grove Village IL 60007-1036. Tel (708)427-9512, FAX (708)427-2097. **4265**

NATIONAL PRODUCTIVITY REVIEW. (US/0277-8556). John Wiley & Sons, Inc., 605 Third Avenue, New York NY 10158-0012. Tel (212)850-6000, (212)850-6645, FAX (212)850-6088, telex 12-7063. **880**

NATIONAL PUBLIC ACCOUNTANT (1957), THE. (US/0027-9978). National Society of Public Accountants, 1010 North Fairfax Street, Alexandria VA 22314. Tel (703)549-6400. **748**

NATIONAL REAL ESTATE INVESTOR. (US/0027-9994). Argus Business, 6151 Powers Ferry Road, Atlanta GA 30339. Tel (404)995-2500, (800)233-3359. **909**

NATIONAL REPORT COMPUTERS AND HEALTH. (US/0273-4974). United Communications Group, 11300 Rockville Pike, Suite 1100, Rockville MD 20852. Tel (301)816-8950 ext. 223, FAX (301)816-8945. **1196**

NATIONAL REVIEW (NEW YORK). (US/0028-0038). National Review Inc., 150 East 35th Street, New York NY 10016. Tel (212)679-7330. **4483**

NATIONAL TAX JOURNAL. (US/0028-0283). National Tax Association - Tax Institute of America, 5310 East Main Street, Suite 104, Columbus OH 43213. Tel (614)864-1221, FAX (614)864-1375. **4738**

NATIONAL TRAINING INDEX. (UK). Graduate Group Limited, 25 / 6 Poland Street, First Floor, London W1V 3DB England. Tel 011 44 71 2872172, FAX 011 44 71 4941268. **1766**

NATION'S BUSINESS. (US/0028-047X). Nation's Business, 1615 H Street Northwest, Washington DC 20062. Tel (202)463-5650. **697**

NATION'S CITIES WEEKLY. (US/0164-5935). National League of Cities, 1301 Pennsylvania Avenue Northwest, Washington DC 20004. Tel (202)626-3040, FAX (202)626-3043. **4668**

NATION'S HEALTH (1971), THE. (US/0028-0496). American Public Health Association, 1015 15th Street Northwest, Washington DC 20005. Tel (202)789-5666. **4792**

NATION'S RESTAURANT NEWS. (US/0028-0518). Lebhar Friedman Inc., 3922 Coconut Palm Drive, Tampa FL 33619. Tel (800)927-9292, (813)664-6707. **5072**

NATURAL GAS WEEK. (US/8756-3037). The Oil Daily, 1401 New York Avenue Northwest, Suite 500, Washington DC 20005-2150. Tel (800)621-0050, (800)368-5803, (202)662-0700, FAX (202)662-0739, telex 89472. **4266**

NATURAL HEALTH. (US/1067-9588). Natural Health, PO Box 1200, Brookline Village MA 02147. Tel (617)232-1000, (800)666-8576. **2600**

NATURAL LIFE (UNIONVILLE. 1991). (CN/0701-8002). Alternate Press, 272 Highway 5, Rural Route 1, St. George Ontario N0E 1N0 Canada. Tel (519)448-4001, FAX (519)448-4001. **2600**

NAVY INTERNATIONAL. (UK/0144-3194). Maritime World Ltd, 114 South Street, Dorking Surrey RH4 2EZ England. Tel 011 44 306 631442, FAX 011 44 306 631226, telex 859424 INTLX G. **4180**

NAVY NEWS & UNDERSEA TECHNOLOGY. (US/8756-1700). Pasha Publications Inc, 1616 North Fort Myer Drive, Suite 1000, Arlington VA 22209. Tel (800)424-2908, (703)528-1244, FAX (703)528-3742, (703)528-1253. **4180**

NBER REPORTER. (US/0276-119X). National Bureau of Economic Research, 1050 Massachusetts Avenue, Cambridge MA 02138. Tel (617)868-3900, FAX (617)868-2742. **1507**

NCAHF NEWSLETTER. (US/0890-3417). National Council Against Health Fraud, PO Box 1276, Loma Linda CA 92354. **Tel** (909)824-4690, FAX (909)824-4838. **1298**

NDT UPDATE. (US/1063-3588). NDT Update, PO Box 6273, FDR Station, New York NY 10150. **Tel** (718)706-1007. **4052**

NEA TODAY. (US/0734-7219). National Education Association, 1201 16th Street Northwest, Washington DC 20036. **Tel** (202)822-7802. **1767**

NEBRASKA LAW REVIEW. (US/0047-9209). University of Nebraska / College of Law, Lincoln NE 68583-0903. **Tel** (402)472-1267. **3014**

NEDERLANDSE CHEMISCHE INDUSTRIE. (NE/0470-6021). Haagse Druk-En Uitg Mij, Postbus 30111, 2500 GC Den Haag Netherlands. **Tel** 070-209233, 31320. **987**

NEMATOLOGICAL ABSTRACTS. (UK/0957-6797). CAB International Centre, Wallingford, Oxon OX10 8DE United Kingdom. **Tel** 44 491 832111, FAX 44 491 833508, telex 847964 (COMAGG G). **478**

NETLINE. (US/0892-9467). Telecommunications Reports, 1333 H Street Northwest, 11th Floor, West Tower, Washington DC 20005. **Tel** (202)842-0520, (800)622-7237, FAX (202)842-3047. **1196**

NETWORK MANAGEMENT SYSTEMS & STRATEGIES. (US/1043-1217). DataTrends Publications, 895 Harrison Street SE, Suite B, Leesburg VA 22075. **Tel** (703)779-0574, (800)766-8130, FAX (703)779-2267. **1243**

NETWORK MONITOR. (UK/0953-8402). Elsevier Science Publishers Ltd, Crown House, Linton Road, Barking Essex IG11 8JU England. **Tel** 011 44 81 5947272, FAX 081-594-5942, telex 896950. **1196**

NETWORK WORLD. (US/0887-7661). Network World, Box 9172, Framingham MA 01701. **Tel** (800)622-1108. **1243**

NETWORKING MANAGEMENT. (US/1052-049X). PennWell Publishing Company, 1421 South Sheridan, PO Box 1260, Tulsa OK 74101. **Tel** (918)835-3161, (800)331-4463, FAX (918)831-9497. **1243**

NEUE POLITISCHE LITERATUR. (GW/0028-3320). Verlag Peter Lang GmbH, Eschborner Landstrasse 42-50, D 60489 Frankfurt Germany. **Tel** 011 49 69 7807050. **5210**

NEVADA LAWYER. (US/1068-882X). State Bar of Nevada, 1325 Airmotive Way, Suite 140, Reno NV 89502. **Tel** (702)329-4100, FAX (702)329-0522. **3015**

NEVADA REVIEW OF BUSINESS & ECONOMICS. (US/0148-5881). Bureau of Business & Economic Research / Nevada, University of Nevada, Business Building/Room 415, Reno NV 89557. **Tel** (702)784-6877. **698**

NEW ACCOUNTANT. (US/0882-8067). New Accountant Company, 36 Railroad Avenue, Glen Head NY 11545. **Tel** (516)759-3484. **749**

NEW ENGLAND BUSINESS. (US/0164-3533). New England Business, 20 Park Plaza, Suite 1120, Boston MA 02116. **Tel** (617)426-6677, FAX (617)426-1122. **698**

NEW ENGLAND ECONOMIC INDICATORS. (US/0548-4448). Federal Reserve Bank of Boston, 600 Atlantic Avenue, Research Library D, Boston MA 02106. **Tel** (617)973-3397, (617)973-3403. **1536**

NEW ENGLAND JOURNAL OF MEDICINE, THE. (US/0028-4793). New England Journal of Medicine, 1440 Main Street, Waltham MA 02154-1649. **Tel** (617)893-3800, (800)843-6356, FAX (617)647-5785, telex 5106015660 NEJM BOS UQ. **3620**

NEW ENGLAND LAW REVIEW. (US/0028-4823). New England Law Review, 154 Stuart Street, Boston MA 02116. **Tel** (617)451-0010 ext 237-294-311, FAX (617)422-7385. **3015**

NEW ENGLAND REAL ESTATE NEWS. (US/1042-9689). Argus Business, 6151 Powers Ferry Road, Atlanta GA 30339. **Tel** (404)995-2500, (800)233-3359. **4842**

NEW HAMPSHIRE BUSINESS REVIEW. (US/0164-8152). New Hampshire Business Review, 150 Dow Street, Manchester NH 03101. **Tel** (603)624-1442. **698**

NEW HAVEN REGISTER, THE. (US). New Haven Register Inc, 40 Sargent Drive, New Haven CT 06511. **Tel** (203)789-5200. **5646**

NEW JERSEY BUSINESS. (US/0028-5560). New Jersey Business & Industry Association, 310 Pasaic Avenue, Fairfield NJ 07006. **Tel** (201)882-5004, FAX (201)882-4648. **698**

NEW JERSEY INDUSTRY ENVIRONMENTAL ALERT. (US/1055-2588). Environmental Compliance Reporter, 3154-B College Drive, Suite 522, Baton Rouge LA 70808. **Tel** (504)383-3937. **2178**

NEW JERSEY SUCCESS. (US/0886-9995). 55 Park Place, PO Box 915, Morristown NJ 07963. **698**

NEW LEADER (NEW YORK, N.Y.), THE. (US/0028-6044). American Labor Conference on International Affairs, 275 Seventh Avenue/17th Floor, New York NY 10001. **Tel** (212)807-8240, FAX (212)727-2229. **4543**

NEW MATERIALS/JAPAN. (UK/0265-3443). Elsevier Advanced Technology, An Imprint of Elsevier Science Ltd., The Boulevard, Langford Lane, Kidlington, Oxford OX5 1GB United Kingdom. **Tel** 011 44 865 843000, 011 44 865 843699, FAX 011 44 865 843010. **2107**

NEW MATERIALS KOREA. (NE/0952-6196). Newmedia International Japan, AV Infanta Carlota 123 5 A, 08029 Barcelona Spain. **Tel** 011 34 3 4195690, FAX 414 42 13. **2107**

NEW MEDIA MARKETS. (UK). Financial Times Business Information Ltd., Tower House, Southampton Street, London WC2E 7HA England. **Tel** 011 44 71 353 1040. **934**

NEW MEXICO BUSINESS JOURNAL. (US/0164-6796). New Mexico Business Journal, PO Box 30550, Albuquerque NM 87190. **Tel** (505)889-2911, FAX (505)889-0822. **698**

NEW MIAMI. (US/1059-4140). New Miami The Business of South Florida, 444 Brickell Avenue, Suite 250, Miami FL 33131. **Tel** (305)372-5000. **698**

NEW ORLEANS CITIBUSINESS. (US/0279-4527). Louisiana Business Publishers, 111 Veterans Memorial Boulevard, Suite 1810, Metairie LA 70005. **Tel** (504)834-9292. **698**

NEW REPUBLIC (NEW YORK, N.Y.). (US/0028-6583). New Republic, 1220 19th Street Northwest, Washington DC 20036. **Tel** (202)331-7494. **2851**

NEW STATESMAN & SOCIETY. (UK/0954-2361). Statesman and Nation Publishing Company, 38 Kingsland Road, Foundation House, London E2 8DQ England. **Tel** 011 44 71 739 1737. **5210**

NEW TECHNOLOGY WEEK. (US/0894-0789). King Publishing Group, 627 National Press Building, Washington DC 20045. **Tel** (202)638-4260, FAX (202)662-9744. **5133**

NEW TRADE NAMES IN THE RUBBER AND PLASTICS INDUSTRIES. (UK/0747-4954). RAPRA Technology Ltd., Shawbury Shrewsbury, Shropshire SY4 4NR England. **Tel** 011 44 939 250383, FAX 011 44 939 251118, telex 35134 RAPRA G. **5076**

NEW YORK CITY POETRY CALENDAR. (US/1071-1686). New York City Poetry Calendar, 60 East 4th Street, Apartment 21, New York NY 10003. **Tel** (212)475-7110. **3466**

NEW ZEALAND HERALD, THE. (NZ/0112-8787). Wilson & Horton Ltd, PO Box 32, Auckland New Zealand. **Tel** 011/64/9/795050, FAX 011/64/9/3660146. **5807**

NEWS & OBSERVER (RALEIGH, N.C. : 1894). (US). Raleigh News & Observer, PO Box 191, Raleigh NC 27602. **Tel** (919)829-4700. **5724**

NEWS & RECORD (GREENSBORO, N.C.). (US/1072-0065). Greensboro News & Record Inc, PO Box 20848, Mail Subscriptions Department, Greensboro NC 27401. **Tel** (910)274-5280 or, 800 553-6880. **5724**

NEWS FROM WITHIN. (IS). Alternative Information Center, PO Box 31417, Jerusalem Israel. **Tel** 011 00972 2 241159, 011 00972 2 253151, FAX 011 00972 2 253151. **2770**

NEWS LIBRARY NEWS. (US/1047-417X). Advocate Library, PO Box 588, Baton Rouge LA 70821. **Tel** (504)388-0327. **3234**

NEWSBYTES : NEWS NETWORK. (US). Metatec Discovery Systems, 7001 Discovery Boulevard, Dublin OH 43017. **Tel** (614)766-3101, (800)637-3472. **1243**

NEWSLETTER - CANADIAN EDUCATION ASSOCIATION. (CN/0008-3445). Canadian Education Association, 252 Bloor Street West, Suite 8-200, Toronto Ontario M5S 1V5 Canada. **Tel** (416)924-7721, FAX (416)924-3188. **1867**

NEWSLETTER ON SERIALS PRICING ISSUES. (US/1046-3410). Marcia Tuttle, CB #3938 Davis Library, University of North Carolina at Chapel Hill, Chapel Hill NC 27599. **Tel** (919)962-1067. **3236**

NEWSLETTER - PEOPLE'S MEDICAL SOCIETY (U.S.). (US/0736-4873). People's Medical Society, 462 Walnut Street, Allentown PA 18102. **Tel** (610)770-1670. **3621**

NEWSLETTERS IN PRINT. (US/0899-0425). Gale Research Inc., 835 Penobscot Building, 645 Griswold Street, Detroit MI 48226. **Tel** (800)877-GALE, (313)961-2242, FAX (313)961-6083, (800)414-5043, telex TWX 810-221-7086. **4817**

NEWSMAKERS (DETROIT, MICH.). (US/0899-0417). Gale Research Inc., 835 Penobscot Building, 645 Griswold Street, Detroit MI 48226. **Tel** (800)877-GALE, (313)961-2242, FAX (313)961-6083, (800)414-5043, telex TWX 810-221-7086. **434**

NEWSNET ACTION LETTER. (US/0888-8698). NewsNet Inc, 945 Haverford Road, Bryn Mawr PA 19010. **Tel** (800)345-1301, (215)527-8030. **3236**

NEWSPAPER ABSTRACTS. (US). University Microfilms International, 300 North Zeeb Road, Ann Arbor MI 48106-1346. **Tel** (313)761-4700, (800)521-0600 Exts. 2490, 2491, FAX (313)973-1540. **5814**

NEWSPAPER ABSTRACTS ONDISC. (US/1064-993X). University Microfilms International, 300 North Zeeb Road, Ann Arbor MI 48106-1346. **Tel** (313)761-4700, (800)521-0600 Exts. 2490, 2491, FAX (313)973-1540. **5814**

NEWSPAPER & PERIODICAL ABSTRACTS [ONLINE DATABASE]. (US). University Microfilms International, 300 North Zeeb Road, Ann Arbor MI 48106-1346. **Tel** (313)761-4700, (800)521-0600 Exts. 2490, 2491, FAX (313)973-1540. **5814**

NIHON KESSHO GAKKAI SHI. (JA/0369-4585). Nihon Kessho Gakkai, (Crystallographic Soc. of Japan), Nihon Gakkai Jimu Senta, 4-16, Yayoi 2 Chome, Bunkyoku, Tokyoto 113, Japan. **1033**

NIKKEI SANGYO SHIMBUN. (JA). Nihon Keizai Shimbun Inc., 9-5 Otemachi 1 Chome, Chiyoda-Ku Tokyo 100 Japan. **Tel** 011 81 3 32700251. **5805**

NIKKEI WEEKLY. (JA). Nihon Keizai Shimbun Inc., 9-5 Otemachi 1 Chome, Chiyoda-Ku Tokyo 100 Japan. **Tel** 011 81 3 32700251. **1638**

NITROGEN. (UK/0029-0777). British Sulphur Corporation Ltd, 31 Mount Pleasant, London WC1X 0AD England. **Tel** 011 44 71 8375600, FAX 011 44 71 8370292, telex 918918 SULFEX G. **987**

NON-FOODS MERCHANDISING. (US/0029-103X). Network Publishing Company, 298 5th Avenue 7th Floor, New York NY 10001. **Tel** (212)563-5301. **2351**

NONPROFIT TIMES, THE. (US/0896-5048). The Nonprofit Times, 190 Tamarack Circle, Skillman NJ 08558. **Tel** (609)921-1251, FAX (609)921-6226. **880**

NONPROFIT WORLD. (US). Society for Nonprofit Organization, 6314 Odana Road/Suite 1, c/o K. Burnham, Madison WI 53719. **Tel** (608)274-9777, (800)424-7367, FAX (608)274-9978. **5299**

NONVIOLENCE TODAY. (AT/1031-6434). Editorial Collective, PO Box 5292, West End 4101 Australia. **Tel** 011 61 07 366 2660, FAX 011 61 07 366 3653. **4484**

NONVIOLENT ACTIVIST, THE. (US/8755-7428). Nonviolent Activist, 339 Lafayette Street, New York NY 10012. **Tel** (212)228-0450, FAX (212)228-6193. **3133**

NONWOVENS ABSTRACTS. (UK/9036-1234). Pira International, Randalls Road, Leatherhead, Surrey KT22 7RU England. **Tel** 011 44 372 376161, FAX 011 44 372 377526. **5360**

NONWOVENS INDUSTRY. (US/0163-4429). Rodman Publications Corporation, 17 S Franklin Turnpike, PO Box 555, Ramsey NJ 07446. **Tel** (201)825-2552, FAX (201)825-0553. **1620**

NORTH AMERICAN REPORT ON FREE TRADE. (US). American Banker, Concourse Level, 1 State Street Plaza, New York NY 10004. **Tel** (212)803-8200, (800)221-1809. **847**

NORTHEAST PENNSYLVANIA BUSINESS JOURNAL. (US). **699**

NORTHERN MINER, THE. (CN/0029-3164). Southam Information and Technology Group Inc., 1450 Don Mills Road, Don Mills Ontario M3B 2X7 Canada. **Tel** (416)445-6641, (800)668-2374, FAX (416)442-2261. **2147**

NORTHERN ONTARIO BUSINESS. (CN/0710-2755). Northern Ontario Business, 158 Elgin Street South, Sudbury Ontario P3E 3N5 Canada. **Tel** (705)673-5705, FAX (705)673-9542. **700**

NORTHWESTERN JOURNAL OF INTERNATIONAL LAW & BUSINESS. (US/0196-3228). Northwestern University School of Law, 357 East Chicago Avenue, Chicago IL 60611-3069. **Tel** (312)503-8467, FAX (312)503-0132. **3102**

NORWICH BULLETIN. (US). Norwich Bulletin, 66 Franklin Street, Norwich CT 06360. **Tel** (203)887-9211. **5646**

NOTISUR. (AG). INCASUR, Alberti 36, 1082-Buenos Aires, Argentina. **1695**

NOTISUR (ALBUQUERQUE, N.M.). (US/1060-4189). University of New Mexico / Latin American Institute, Latin America Data Base, 801 Yale NE, Albuquerque NM 87131-1016. **Tel** (505)277-6839, FAX (505)277-5989. **4530**

NTIS ALERT. FOREIGN TECHNOLOGY. (US). National Technical Information Service - NTIS, Room 2027S, 5285 Port Royal Road, Springfield VA 22161. **Tel** (703)487-4630, (703)487-4660, (703)487-4650, FAX (703)321-8547, telex 89-9405. **5135**

NTIS — Serials available Online

NTIS BIBLIOGRAPHIC DATABASE. (US/1064-0479). National Technical Information Service - NTIS, Room 2027S, 5285 Port Royal Road, Springfield VA 22161. **Tel** (703)487-4630, (703)487-4660, (703)487-4650, FAX (703)321-8547, telex 89-9405. **5175**

NUCLEAR MONITOR, THE. (US/0889-3411). Nuclear Information Monitor, 1424 16th Street Northwest, Suite 601, Washington DC 20036. **Tel** (202)328-0002, FAX (202)462-2183. **4449**

NUCLEAR WASTE NEWS (SILVER SPRING, MD.). (US/0276-2897). Business Publishers Inc., 951 Pershing Drive, Silver Spring MD 20910-4464. **Tel** (301)587-6300, (800)274-0122, FAX (301)585-9075. **2237**

NUCLEARFUEL. (US/0149-3574). McGraw Hill Publishing Company, Inc., 1221 Avenue of the Americas, New York NY 10020. **Tel** (212)512-6410, (800)525-5003, FAX (212)512-6111. **2157**

NUCLEONICS WEEK. (US/0048-105X). McGraw Hill Publishing Company, Inc., 1221 Avenue of the Americas, New York NY 10020. **Tel** (212)512-6410, (800)525-5003, FAX (212)512-6111. **1952**

NURSING FORUM (HILLSDALE). (US/0029-6473). NURSECOM Inc., 1211 Locust Street, Philadelphia PA 19107. **Tel** (215)545-7222, (800)242-6757, FAX (215)545-8107. **3864**

NURSING MANAGEMENT. (US/0744-6314). Springhouse Corporation, 1111 Bethlehem Pike, Springhouse PA 19477. **Tel** (215)646-8700. **3864**

NURSING SCAN IN ADMINISTRATION. (US/1056-3091). NURSECOM Inc., 1211 Locust Street, Philadelphia PA 19107. **Tel** (215)545-7222, (800)242-6757, FAX (215)545-8107. **3865**

NURSING SCAN IN RESEARCH. (US/0897-5647). NURSECOM Inc., 1211 Locust Street, Philadelphia PA 19107. **Tel** (215)545-7222, (800)242-6757, FAX (215)545-8107. **3865**

NUTRITION ABSTRACTS AND REVIEWS. SERIES A: HUMAN & EXPERIMENTAL. (UK/0309-1295). CAB International Centre, Wallingford, Oxon OX10 8DE United Kingdom. **Tel** 44 491 832111, FAX 44 491 833508, telex 847964 (COMAGG G). **4201**

NUTRITION ABSTRACTS AND REVIEWS. SERIES B. LIVESTOCK FEEDS AND FEEDING. (UK/0309-135X). CAB International Centre, Wallingford, Oxon OX10 8DE United Kingdom. **Tel** 44 491 832111, FAX 44 491 833508, telex 847964 (COMAGG G). **155**

NUTRITION ACTION HEALTH LETTER. (US/0885-7792). Center for Science in the Public Interest, 1875 Conn Avenue NW, Suite 300, Washington DC 20009. **Tel** (202)332-9110. **4195**

NUTRITION FORUM (PHILADELPHIA, PA.). (US/0748-8165). Nutrition Forum, c/o D. Xu & J. Raso, PO Box 747924, Rego Park NY 11374. **Tel** (718)275-0414, FAX (718)997-8227. **4196**

NUTRITION HEALTH REVIEW. (US/0164-7202). Vegetus Publications, 171 Madison Avenue, New York NY 10016. **Tel** (212)679-3590, FAX (212)679-3597. **4196**

NUTRITION RESEARCH NEWSLETTER. (US/0736-0037). Lyda Associates, Inc., PO Box 700, Palisades NY 10964. **Tel** (914)359-8282, FAX (914)359-1229. **4201**

NUTRITION TODAY (ANNAPOLIS). (US/0029-666X). Williams & Wilkins Company, 428 East Preston Street, Baltimore MD 21202-3993. **Tel** (410)528-4000, (800)638-6423, FAX (410)528-8596, telex 87669. **4197**

OAG TRAVEL PLANNER (EUROPEAN ED.). (US/1075-1548). Official Airline Guides / Illinois, 2000 Clearwater Drive, Oak Brook IL 60521. **Tel** (800)323-3537, FAX (312)574-6091, telex 210144 OAGO UR. **2808**

OAKLAND BUSINESS MONTHLY. (US/8750-0981). Oakland Business Monthly, 7196 Cooley Lake Road, Union Lake MI 48085. **Tel** (313)360-6397. **700**

OAKLAND PRESS. (US). Oakland Press, PO Box 436009, Pontiac MI 48343. **Tel** (313)332-8181. **5693**

OCCUPATIONAL HAZARDS. (US/0029-7909). Penton Publishing, 1100 Superior Avenue, Cleveland OH 44114-2543. **Tel** (216)696-7000, FAX (216)696-0836. **2866**

OCCUPATIONAL HEALTH AND SAFETY LETTER. (US/0196-058X). Business Publishers Inc., 951 Pershing Drive, Silver Spring MD 20910-4464. **Tel** (301)587-6300, (800)274-0122, FAX (301)585-9075. **2866**

OCCUPATIONAL OUTLOOK QUARTERLY. (US/0199-4786). Superintendent of Documents, US Government Printing Office, Washington DC 20402. **Tel** (202)275-3328, FAX (202)786-2377. **1699**

OCEAN INDUSTRY. (US/0029-8026). Ocean Industry, PO Box 2608, Houston TX 77252. **Tel** (713)529-4301, FAX (713)520-4433, telex 287330 GULF UR. **4267**

OCEAN STATE BUSINESS. (US/0741-9929). Ocean State Business, 4 Davol Square, Providence RI 02903. **700**

OCEANIC ABSTRACTS (BETHESDA, MD.). (US/0748-1489). Cambridge Scientific Abstracts, 7200 Wisconsin Avenue, #601, Bethesda MD 20814-4823. **Tel** (301)961-6750, (800)843-7751, FAX (301)961-6720. **1363**

OECD. ECONOMIC OUTLOOK. (FR/0474-5574). OECD Publications and Information Center, 2 rue Andre-Pascal, 75775 Paris Cedex 16 France. **Tel** 011 33 1 45248167, US:(202)785-6323, FAX 011 33 1 45248500, 45248176, telex 620 160 OCDE. **1509**

OECD ECONOMIC STUDIES. (FR/0255-0822). OECD Publications and Information Center, 2 rue Andre-Pascal, 75775 Paris Cedex 16 France. **Tel** 011 33 1 45248167, US:(202)785-6323, FAX 011 33 1 45248500, 45248176, telex 620 160 OCDE. **1576**

OECD ECONOMIC SURVEYS. (FR/0376-6438). OECD Publications and Information Center, 2 rue Andre-Pascal, 75775 Paris Cedex 16 France. **Tel** 011 33 1 45248167, US:(202)785-6323, FAX 011 33 1 45248500, 45248176, telex 620 160 OCDE. **1509**

OECD OBSERVER. (FR/0029-7054). OECD Publications and Information Center, 2 rue Andre-Pascal, 75775 Paris Cedex 16 France. **Tel** 011 33 1 45248167, US:(202)785-6323, FAX 011 33 1 45248500, 45248176, telex 620 160 OCDE. **1510**

OEM DESIGN. (UK/0306-0381). Wilmington Publishing Ltd., PO Box 200, Field End Road, Ruislip Middx HA4 OSY England. **Tel** 011 44 81 841 3970, FAX 011 44 81 841 9676. **3485**

OFF-ROAD (LOS ANGELES). (US/0363-1745). Argus Publishers Corporation, 12100 Wilshire Boulevard, Suite 250, Los Angeles CA 90025. **Tel** (310)820-3601, FAX (310)207-9388. **5422**

OFFICE EQUIPMENT NEWS. (UK/0030-0187). AGB Business Publs Ltd, Audit House, Field End Road, Ruislip Middlesex HA4 9LT England. **Tel** 011 44 81 868 4499. **4213**

OHIO ARCHAEOLOGIST. (US/0048-153X). Archaeological Society of Ohio, 5210 Coonpath Road, Pleasantville OH 43148. **Tel** (800)736-7815. **277**

OHIO CPA JOURNAL, THE. (US/0749-8284). Ohio Society of Certified Public Accountants, PO Box 1810, Metro Place South, Dublin OH 43017. **Tel** (614)764-2727, FAX (614)764-2727. **749**

OHIO INDUSTRY ENVIRONMENTAL ADVISOR. (US). Environmental Compliance Reporter, 3154-B College Drive, Suite 522, Baton Rouge LA 70808. **Tel** (504)383-3937. **2179**

OHIO REPORT (COLUMBUS, OHIO). (US/1063-990X). Gongwer News Service, 175 South 3rd Street, #230, Columbus OH 43215. **Tel** (614)221-1992, FAX (614)221-0678, (614)221-7844. **4671**

OIL & GAS INVESTOR. (US/0744-5881). Hart Publications Inc, 1900 Grant Street, Suite 400, Denver CO 80203. **Tel** (303)837-1917, (800)832-1917, FAX (303)837-8585. **4268**

OIL DAILY, THE. (US/0030-1434). The Oil Daily, 1401 New York Avenue Northwest, Suite 500, Washington DC 20005-2150. **Tel** (800)621-0050, (800)368-5803, (202)662-0700, FAX (202)662-0739, telex 89472. **4269**

OIL EXPRESS. (US/0195-0576). United Communications Group, 11300 Rockville Pike, Suite 1100, Rockville MD 20852. **Tel** (301)816-8950 ext. 223, FAX (301)816-8945. **4269**

OIL PRICE INFORMATION SERVICE. (US/0279-7801). United Communications Group, 11300 Rockville Pike, Suite 1100, Rockville MD 20852. **Tel** (301)816-8950 ext. 223, FAX (301)816-8945. **4270**

OIL SPILL INTELLIGENCE REPORT. (US/0195-3524). Cutter Information Corporation, 37 Broadway, Arlington MA 02174-5539. **Tel** (617)648-8700, (800)964-5118, FAX (617)648-8707, (617)648-1950, telex 650 100 9891. **4270**

OIL SPILL U.S. LAW REPORT. (US/1055-9175). Cutter Information Corporation, 37 Broadway, Arlington MA 02174-5539. **Tel** (617)648-8700, (800)964-5118, FAX (617)648-8707, (617)648-1950, telex 650 100 9891. **3022**

OILWEEK. (CN/0030-1515). MacLean Hunter Ltd. Business Publishers / Canada, Box 9100, Station A, Toronto ONT M5W 1A5 Canada. **Tel** (416)946-8420, (800)567-0444. **4270**

OLD WORLD ARCHAEOLOGY NEWSLETTER. (US/0732-1635). Wesleyan University Department of Classics, Middletown CT 06459. **Tel** (203)347-9211 ext. 2804, FAX (203)343-3903. **277**

OMNI (NEW YORK, N.Y.). (US/0149-8711). General Media Publishing Company, 1965 Broadway, New York NY 10023. **Tel** (212)496-6100. **2542**

ONCOGENES AND GROWTH FACTORS ABSTRACTS. (US/1043-8963). Cambridge Scientific Abstracts, 7200 Wisconsin Avenue, #601, Bethesda MD 20814-4823. **Tel** (301)961-6750, (800)843-7751, FAX (301)961-6720. **3661**

ONE TO ONE. (US/0739-5442). CreeYadio Service, Box 9787, Fresno CA 93794. **Tel** (209)226-0558. **1135**

ONLINE JOURNAL OF CURRENT CLINICAL TRIALS, THE. (US/1059-2725). American Association for the Advancement of Science, 1333 H Street Northwest, Washington DC 20005. **Tel** (202)326-6400, (203)326-6417, (202)326-6430, FAX (202)842-1065. **3624**

ONLINE (WESTON, CONN.). (US/0146-5422). Online Inc., 462 Danbury Road, Wilton CT 06897. **Tel** (203)761-1466, (800)248-8466, FAX (203)761-1444. **1275**

ONLY THE BEST. (US/1053-4326). Education News Service / California, PO Box 1789, Carmichael CA 95609. **Tel** (800)521-8110, (212)337-6934 NEW YORK, ALASKA AND HAWAII, (800)537-8416 CANADA, FAX (212)227-7157, telex 127703. **1224**

ONS NURSING SCAN IN ONCOLOGY. (US/1062-5720). NURSECOM Inc., 1211 Locust Street, Philadelphia PA 19107. **Tel** (215)545-7222, (800)242-6757, FAX (215)545-8107. **3866**

ONZE VOGELS. (NE). Nederlandse Bond van Vogelliefhebbers, Postbox 74, 4600 AB Bergen, Op Zoom, Netherlands. **Tel** 31-1640-35007, FAX 31-1640-39020. **5619**

OPEN SYSTEMS COMMUNICATION. (US/0741-2851). Phillips Business Information, Inc., 1201 Seven Locks Road, Potomac MD 20854. **Tel** (301)424-3338, (800)777-5006, FAX (301)309-3847. **1243**

OPEN SYSTEMS REPORT. (US/1052-701X). Phillips Business Information, Inc., 1201 Seven Locks Road, Potomac MD 20854. **Tel** (301)424-3338, (800)777-5006, FAX (301)309-3847. **1243**

OPEN SYSTEMS TODAY. (US/1061-0839). CMP Publications Inc., c/o B. Werner, One Jericho Plaza, Wing A, 2nd Floor, Jericho NY 11753. **Tel** (516)733-6700. **1248**

OPERA CANADA. (CN/0030-3577). Opera Canada, 366 Adelaide Street East, Suite 433 Toronto, Ontario M5A 3X9 Canada. **Tel** (416)363-0395, FAX (416)363-0396. **4143**

OPERA NEWS. (US/0030-3607). Metropolitan Opera Guild Inc., 70 Lincoln Center Plaza, New York NY 10023. **Tel** (212)769-7080. **4143**

OPHTHALMOLOGY TIMES. (US/0193-032X). Advanstar Communications Inc., 131 West First Street, Duluth MN 55802. **Tel** (218)723-9477, (800)346-0085. **3878**

OPTICAL MATERIALS AND ENGINEERING NEWS. (US). Business Communications Inc., 25 Van Zant Street, Suite 13, Norwalk CT 06855. **Tel** (203)853-4266. **4439**

OPTICAL MEMORY NEWS. (US/0741-5869). Phillips Business Information, Inc., 1201 Seven Locks Road, Potomac MD 20854. **Tel** (301)424-3338, (800)777-5006, FAX (301)309-3847. **1277**

ORANGE COUNTY BUSINESS JOURNAL (NEWPORT BEACH, CALIF.). (US/1051-7480). Orange County Business Journal, 4590 MacArthur Boulevard, Suite 100, Newport Beach CA 92660. **Tel** (714)833-8373. **701**

OREGON BUSINESS. (US/0279-8190). Oregon Business Magazine, 921 Southwest Morrison Street, Suite 407, Portland OR 97205-2722. **Tel** (503)223-0304. **701**

OREGON LAW REVIEW. (US/0196-2043). University of Oregon / Law, 201 Law Center, Eugene OR 97403. **Tel** (503)346-3881, 346-3844, FAX (503)346-1564. **3023**

OREGONIAN (PORTLAND, OR. 1937), THE. (US/8750-1317). Oregonian Publishing Company, 1320 South West Broadway, Portland OR 97201. **Tel** (503)221-8109. **5734**

ORGANIZATIONAL DYNAMICS. (US/0090-2616). American Management Association, 135 West 50th Street, New York NY 10020-1201. **Tel** (212)586-8100, (212)903-8375 (periodicals), FAX (212)903-8168, (212)903-8083 (periodicals). **881**

ORIGINS RESEARCH. (US/0748-9919). Access Research Network, PO Box 38069, Colorado Springs CO 80937. **Tel** (719)633-1772. **4354**

ORIGINS (WASHINGTON). (US/0093-609X). Catholic News Service, 3211 4th Street Northeast, Washington DC 20017. **Tel** (202)541-3289, (202)541-3250, FAX (202)541-3255, telex 892589. **5033**

ORLANDO BUSINESS JOURNAL. (US/8750-8656). Orlando Business Journal, 315 East Robinson Street, Suite 250, Orlando FL 32801. **Tel** (407)649-8470, FAX (407)649-8469. **702**

ORLANDO SENTINEL, THE. (US/0744-6055). Orlando Sentinel, PO Box 2833, Orlando FL 32802. **Tel** (407)420-5000, FAX (407)420-5765. **5650**

ORNAMENTAL HORTICULTURE. (UK/0305-4934). CAB International Centre, Wallingford, Oxon OX10 8DE United Kingdom. **Tel** 44 491 832111, FAX 44 491 833508, telex 847964 (COMAGG G). **2434**

OSI PRODUCT & EQUIPMENT NEWS. (US/0898-0489). DataTrends Publications, 895 Harrison Street SE, Suite B, Leesburg VA 22075. **Tel** (703)779-0574, (800)766-8130, FAX (703)779-2267. **1198**

OSTOMY QUARTERLY. (US/0030-6517). United Ostomy Association Inc, 36 Executive Park/#120, Irvine CA 92714-6744. **Tel** (714)660-8624, FAX (714)660-9262. **3971**

OTC NEWS & MARKET REPORT. (UK/0956-2559). Nicholas Hall & Company, 35 Alexandra Street, Southend-on-Sea, Essex SS1 1BW England. **Tel** 011 44 702 433422, FAX 011 44 702 430787. **4318**

OTHER FRONT, THE. (IS). Alternative Information Center, PO Box 31417, Jerusalem Israel. **Tel** 011 00972 2 241159, 011 00972 2 253151, FAX 011 00972 2 253151. **2770**

OTTAWA LAW REVIEW. (CN/0048-2331). Ottawa Law Review for Canada, University of Ottawa, Law Faculty, 57 Louis Pasteur, Ottawa ONT K1N 6N5 Canada. **Tel** (613)564-4060, (613)564-7195, FAX (613)564-9800. **3024**

OUTDOOR LIFE (NEW YORK, N.Y.). (US/0030-7076). Times Mirror Magazines, Two Park Avenue, New York NY 10016. **Tel** (212)779-5000. **4877**

OUTLOOK ON AT&T. (US/0885-6176). Phillips Business Information, Inc., 1201 Seven Locks Road, Potomac MD 20854. **Tel** (301)424-3338, (800)777-5006, FAX (301)309-3847. **1161**

OUTLOOK (SEATTLE, WASH. : 1983). (US/0737-3732). Program for Appropriate Technology in Health, 4 Nickerson Street, Seattle WA 98109. **Tel** (206)285-3500, FAX (206)285-6619, telex 4740049. **590**

OXFORD BULLETIN OF ECONOMICS AND STATISTICS. (UK/0305-9049). Basil Blackwell Publishers Ltd, 108 Cowley Road, Oxford 0X4 1JF England. **Tel** 011 44 865 791100, FAX 011 44 865 791347, telex 837022 OXBOOK G. **1577**

OXY-FUEL NEWS. (US/1072-8759). Hart Publications Inc, 1900 Grant Street, Suite 400, Denver CO 80203. **Tel** (303)837-1917, (800)832-1917, FAX (303)837-8585. **4271**

P-D NEWS. (US/0478-9997). Publications & Communications, 12416 Hymeadow Drive, Austin TX 78750. **Tel** (512)250-9023, (800)678-9724, FAX (512)331-3900, telex 384303. **944**

PACIFIC BUSINESS NEWS. (US/0030-8552). Crossroads Press Inc., PO Box 833, Honolulu HI 96808. **Tel** (808)521-0021. **5656**

PACKAGING SCIENCE AND TECHNOLOGY ABSTRACTS. (GW/0722-3218). Fraunhofer Institute Lebensmittel-Technologie, Schragenhofstr 35, D-80992 Munich, Germany. **Tel** 011 49 89 14900956, FAX 011 49 89 1400980. **5175**

PACKAGING WEEK. (UK/0267-6117). Benn Publications Ltd., Sovereign Way, Tonbridge TNQ 1RW England. **Tel** 011 44 732 364422, FAX 011 44 732 361534, telex 0732 95132 BENTON G. **4221**

PAINT & INK INTERNATIONAL. (UK/0953-9891). Argus Press Group, Queensway House, 2 Queensway Redhill, Surrey RH1 1QS England. **Tel** 011 44 737 768611, 011 44 737 761685, FAX 011 44 737 760510, telex 948669 TOPJNL G. **4224**

PAIS INTERNATIONAL IN PRINT. (US/1051-4015). Public Affairs Information Service Inc., 521 West 43rd Street, Fifth Floor, New York NY 10036. **Tel** (212)736-6629, (800)288-7247, FAX (212)643-2848. **5227**

PAIS ON CD-ROM [COMPUTER FILE]. (US). Public Affairs Information Service Inc., 521 West 43rd Street, Fifth Floor, New York NY 10036. **Tel** (212)736-6629, (800)288-7247, FAX (212)643-2848. **5227**

PALAESTRA (MACOMB, ILL.). (US/8756-5811). Challenge Publications Ltd, PO Box 508, Macomb IL 61455. **Tel** (309)833-1902. **4392**

PALM BEACH POST, THE. (US). Palm Beach Post, 2751 South Dixie Highway, West Palm Beach FL 33416. **Tel** (407)820-4231. **5650**

PAPER & BOARD ABSTRACTS. (UK/0307-0778). Pira International, Randalls Road, Leatherhead, Surrey KT22 7RU England. **Tel** 011 44 372 376161, FAX 011 44 372 377526. **4240**

PAPERBOARD PACKAGING. (US/0031-1227). Advanstar Communications Inc., 131 West First Street, Duluth MN 55802. **Tel** (218)723-9477, (800)346-0085. **4221**

PAPERBOUND BOOKS IN PRINT. (US/0031-1235). R R Bowker, A Reed Reference Publishing Company, Part of Reed International PLC, PO Box 31, 121 Chanlon Drive, New Providence NJ 07974. **Tel** (908)464-6800, (800)521-8110, FAX (908)665-6688, telex 138-755. **4822**

PAR. PUBLIC ADMINISTRATION REVIEW POPULATION. (US/0033-3352). American Society for Public Administration, 1120 G Street Northwest, Suite 700, Washington DC 20005-3885. **Tel** (202)393-7878, FAX (202)638-4952. **4672**

PARAPLEGIA NEWS. (US/0031-1766). Paralyzed Veterans of America Publications, 2111 East Highland, Suite 180 B, Phoenix AZ 85016. **Tel** (602)246-9426, FAX (602)224-0507. **4392**

PARKERSBURGH NEWS (1916). (US/8750-3956). Parkersburg News, PO Box 1787, Parkersburg WV 26101. **5764**

PARTY & PAPER RETAILER. (US/0899-6008). 4ward Corporation, 70 New Canaan Avenue, Norwalk CT 06850. **Tel** (203)845-8020, FAX (203)845-8022. **956**

PASCAL. F 10, MECANIQUE, ACOUSTIQUE ET TRANSFERT DE CHALEUR. (FR/1146-5107). Institut de l'Information Scientifique et Technique (INIST), 2 Allee du Parc de Brabois, 54514 Vandoeuvre Nancy Cedex France. **Tel** 011 33 83 504600, FAX 011 33 83 504650. **4453**

PATIENT CARE. (US/0031-305X). Medical Economics Publishing, Five Paragon Drive, Second Floor, Montvale NJ 07645. **Tel** (800)432-4570, (201)358-2210. **3738**

PC/COMPUTING (NEW YORK, N.Y.). (US/0899-1847). Ziff-Davis, One Park Avenue, 5th Floor, New York NY 10016. **Tel** (212)503-3500, (609)786-8230. **1270**

PC MAGAZINE (NEW YORK, N.Y.). (US/0888-8507). Ziff-Davis, One Park Avenue, 5th Floor, New York NY 10016. **Tel** (212)503-3500, (609)786-8230. **1271**

PC USER (LONDON, ENGLAND). (UK/0263-5720). EMAP Business & Computer Publishing Ltd., 1 Lincoln Court 1 Lincoln Road, Peterborough PE1 2RP England. **Tel** 011/44/733/68900, FAX 011/44/733/349290. **1271**

PC WEEK (U.S. ED.). (US/0740-1604). Ziff-Davis, One Park Avenue, 5th Floor, New York NY 10016. **Tel** (212)503-3500, (609)786-8230. **1271**

PCN NEWS. (US/1051-3833). Phillips Business Information, Inc., 1201 Seven Locks Road, Potomac MD 20854. **Tel** (301)424-3338, (800)777-5006, FAX (301)309-3847. **1119**

PCS NEWS. (US/1070-6607). Phillips Business Information, Inc., 1201 Seven Locks Road, Potomac MD 20854. **Tel** (301)424-3338, (800)777-5006, FAX (301)309-3847. **1119**

PEACEKEEPING & INTERNATIONAL RELATIONS. (CN/1187-3485). Peacekeeping & International Relations, 76 St Clair Avenue West, Suite 502, Toronto Ontario M4V 1N2 Canada. **Tel** (416)964-6632, FAX (416)964-5833. **4531**

PEDIATRIC REPORT'S CHILD HEALTH NEWSLETTER. (US/1065-1284). IGM Enterprises Inc., 71 Hope Street, Box 155, Providence RI 02906. **Tel** (401)434-7390, FAX (401)435-3634. **3909**

PEDIATRICS FOR PARENTS. (US/0730-6725). Pediatrics for Parents, PO Box 1069, Bangor ME 04402-1069. **Tel** (207)942-7334, FAX (207)947-3134. **3910**

PENNSYLVANIA CPA JOURNAL. (US/0746-1062). Pennsylvania Institute of Certified Public Accountants, 1608 Walnut Street/3rd Floor, Philadelphia PA 19103. **Tel** (215)735-2635, FAX (215)735-3694. **749**

PENNSYLVANIA INDUSTRY ENVIRONMENTAL ADVISOR. (US). Environmental Compliance Reporter, 3154-B College Drive, Suite 522, Baton Rouge LA 70808. **Tel** (504)383-3937. **2179**

PENSION WORLD. (US/0098-1753). Argus Business, 6151 Powers Ferry Road, Atlanta GA 30339. **Tel** (404)995-2500, (800)233-3359. **1701**

PENSIONS & INVESTMENTS (1990). (US/1050-4974). Crain Communications Inc., 1400 Woodbridge, Detroit MI 48207. **Tel** (313)446-6000, (800)992-9970. **911**

PENTON'S CONTROLS & SYSTEMS. (US/1061-0235). Penton Publishing, 1100 Superior Avenue, Cleveland OH 44114-2543. **Tel** (216)696-7000, FAX (216)696-0836. **3486**

PEOPLE (CHICAGO. 1974). (US/0093-7673). Time Inc. / New York, Time & Life Building, Rockefeller Center, New York NY 10020. **2543**

PERCEPTIONS (TOLEDO, OH.). (US/1070-0358). Perceptions, PO Box 2731, Toledo OH 43606-0731. **3423**

PERIODICALS SCANNED AND ABSTRACTED. LIFE SCIENCES COLLECTION. (US/0891-3889). Cambridge Scientific Abstracts, 7200 Wisconsin Avenue, #601, Bethesda MD 20814-4823. **Tel** (301)961-6750, (800)843-7751, FAX (301)961-6720. **5175**

PERSONNEL REVIEW. (UK/0048-3486). MCB University Press, 60 62 Toller Lane, Bradford West Yorkshire BD8 9BX England. **Tel** 011 44 274 499821, FAX 011 44 274 547143, telex 51317 MCBUNI G. **945**

PERSPECTIVES IN PSYCHIATRIC CARE. (US/0031-5990). NURSECOM Inc., 1211 Locust Street, Philadelphia PA 19107. **Tel** (215)545-7222, (800)242-6757, FAX (215)545-8107. **3866**

PERSPECTIVES ON SCIENCE AND CHRISTIAN FAITH. (US/0892-2675). American Scientific Affiliation, PO Box 668, Ipswich MA 01938. **Tel** (508)356-5656. **4986**

PESTDOC. (UK). Derwent Publications Ltd., Derwent House 14, Great Queen Street, London WC2B 5DF England. **Tel** 011 44 71 3442800. **4248**

PESTICIDE & TOXIC CHEMICAL NEWS. (US/0146-0501). Food Chemical News Inc, 1101 Pennsylvania Avenue Southeast, Washington DC 20003. **Tel** (202)544-1980, FAX (202)546-3890. **4246**

PESTICIDE MANUAL, THE. (UK). Royal Society of Chemistry, Thomas Graham House, Science Park, Cambridge CB4 4WF England. **Tel** 011 44 223 420066, FAX 011 44 223 423429, telex 818293 ROYAL. **119**

PETERSEN'S PHOTOGRAPHIC. (US/0199-4913). Petersen Publishing Company, 6420 Wilshire Bouldevard, Los Angeles CA 90048. **Tel** (213)782-2485. **4372**

PETROLEUM ABSTRACTS (TULSA, OKLA.). (US/0031-6423). Petroleum Abstracts, University of Tulsa, Information Services Division, 600 South College Avenue, Harwell Hall 101, Tulsa OK 74104-3189. **Tel** (800)247-8678, (918)631-2297, FAX (918)599-9361, telex 49 7543. **4284**

PETROLEUM/ENERGY BUSINESS NEWS INDEX. (US/0098-7743). American Petroleum Institute, 275 Seventh Avenue, New York NY 10001. **Tel** (212)366-4040, FAX (212)366-4298. **4272**

PETROLEUM INDEPENDENT. (US/0747-2528). Independent Petroleum Association of America, 1101 16th Street NW, Washington DC 20036. **Tel** (201)857-4775. **4272**

PETROLEUM MARKET INTELLIGENCE. (US/1047-630X). Petroleum Intelligence Weekly, 575 Broadway, 4th Floor, New York NY 10012-3230. **Tel** (212)941-5500, FAX (212)941-5509, telex 62371 PETROIN. **4273**

PHARMACEUTICAL BUSINESS NEWS. (UK/0956-0661). Financial Times England, 8 16 Great New Street, London EC4A 3BN England. **Tel** 011 44 71 353 0305, 353 1040, FAX 011 44 353 0846. **4320**

PHARMACEUTICAL MANUFACTURING REVIEW. (UK/0955-3894). Argus Press Group, Queensway House, 2 Queensway Redhill, Surrey RH1 1QS England. **Tel** 011 44 737 768611, 011 44 737 761685, FAX 011 44 737 760510, telex 948669 TOPJNL G. **3486**

PHILADELPHIA BUSINESS JOURNAL. (US/0744-3587). Philadelphia Business Journal, 400 Market Street, Suite 300, Philadelphia PA 19106. **Tel** (215)238-5103. **703**

PHILADELPHIA DAILY NEWS (PHILADELPHIA, PA. : 1925). (US). Philadelphia Newspapers Inc., PO Box 8500 6800, Philadelphia PA 19178. **Tel** (215)854-4790. **5738**

PHILADELPHIA INQUIRER (1969), THE. (US/0885-6613). Philadelphia Newspapers Inc., PO Box 8500 6800, Philadelphia PA 19178. **Tel** (215)854-4790. **5738**

PHOENIX GAZETTE. (US). Phoenix Newspapers Inc., 120 East Van Buren Street, Phoenix AZ 85001. **Tel** (602)271-8503, (602)271-8000. **5630**

PHOSPHORUS AND POTASSIUM. (UK/0031-8426). British Sulphur Corporation Ltd, 31 Mount Pleasant, London WC1X 0AD England. **Tel** 011 44 71 8375600, FAX 011 44 71 8370292, telex 918918 SULFEX G. **988**

PHOTO BUSINESS. (US/0890-8753). Billboard Publications Inc., 1515 Broadway Billboard, New York NY 10036. **Tel** (212)764-7300, FAX (305)755-7048, telex WU TWX 710-581-6279. **4372**

PHOTONICS SPECTRA (PITTSFIELD, MASS. 1982). (US/0731-1230). Laurin Publishing Company Inc, PO Box 4949, Pittsfield MA 01202. **Tel** (413)499-0514, FAX (413)442-3180, telex 232-055 ASAS. **4440**

PHYSICAL

Serials available Online

PHYSICAL THERAPY. (US/0031-9023). American Physical Therapy Association, 1111 North Fairfax Street, Suite 200, Alexandria VA 22314-1488. **Tel** (703)684-2782, FAX (703)684-7343. **4381**

PHYSICIAN AND SPORTSMEDICINE, THE. (US/0091-3847). McGraw Hill Publishing Company, Inc., 1221 Avenue of the Americas, New York NY 10020. **Tel** (212)512-6410, (800)525-5003, FAX (212)512-6111. **3955**

PHYSICIAN EXECUTIVE. (US/0898-2759). American College of Physician Executives, 4890 West Kennedy Boulevard / Suite 200, Tampa FL 33609. **Tel** (813)287-2000, (800)562-8088, FAX (813)287-8993. **3916**

PHYSICIANS' GENRX. (US). Denniston Publishing Inc., 111 East Putnam Avenue, Riverside CT 06878. **Tel** (203)698-2500. **4325**

PIG NEWS AND INFORMATION. (UK/0143-9014). CAB International Centre, Wallingford, Oxon OX10 8DE United Kingdom. **Tel** 44 491 832111, FAX 44 491 833508, telex 847964 (COMAGG G). **155**

PILGRIMAGE. (US/0361-0802). Pilgrimage Press, 427 Lakeshore Drive, Atlanta GA 30307. **Tel** (404)377-1088. **4608**

PIMA MAGAZINE. (US/1046-4352). Paper Industry Management Association, 2400 East Oakton Street, Arlington Heights IL 60005. **Tel** (708)956-0250, FAX (708)956-0520. **4237**

PIMS MEDIA DIRECTORY. (UK/0261-5169). PIMS UK Ltd, Pims House Mildnay Avenue, London N1 4RS England. **Tel** 011 44 71 226 1000. **763**

PIPE LINE INDUSTRY (HOUSTON, TEX.). (US/0032-0145). Gulf Publishing Company / Texas, PO Box 2608, Houston TX 77252. **Tel** (800)231-6275, (713)529-4301, FAX (713)520-4433. **2124**

PIPELINE & GAS JOURNAL. (US/0032-0188). Pipeline and Gas Journal, PO Box 1589, Dallas TX 75221. **Tel** (214)691-3911, FAX (214)987-3940. **4274**

PIPELINE & UTILITIES CONSTRUCTION. (US/0896-1069). Oildom Publ Company, PO Box 219368, Houston TX 77218. **Tel** (713)558-6930, FAX (713)558-7029, telex 203218 ACTH UR. **2124**

PITTSBURGH BUSINESS TIMES-JOURNAL. (US/0883-7910). Pittsburgh Business Weekly Co, 2313 East Carson St, Suite 200, Pittsburgh PA 15203. **Tel** (412)481-6397, FAX (412)481-9956. **703**

PITTSBURGH POST-GAZETTE (PITTSBURGH, PA. 1978). (US/1068-624X). Pittsburgh Post-Gazette, PO Box 566, Pittsburgh PA 15230. **Tel** (412)263-1659. **5738**

PITTSBURGH PRESS, THE. (US). Pittsburgh Post-Gazette, PO Box 566, Pittsburgh PA 15230. **Tel** (412)263-1659. **5738**

PLAIN DEALER (CLEVELAND, OHIO : 1961). (US). Plain Dealer, PO Box 6730 T, Cleveland OH 44101. **Tel** (216)344-4600, FAX (216)694-6369. **5730**

PLANNED SAVINGS. (UK/0032-0668). EMAP Business & Computer Publishing Ltd., 1 Lincoln Court 1 Lincoln Road, Peterborough PE1 2RP England. **Tel** 011/44/733/68900, FAX 011/44/733/349290. **803**

PLANT BREEDING ABSTRACTS. (UK/0032-0803). CAB International Centre, Wallingford, Oxon OX10 8DE United Kingdom. **Tel** 44 491 832111, FAX 44 491 833508, telex 847964 (COMAGG G). **155**

PLANT ENGINEERING. (US/0032-082X). Cahners Publishing Company, 249 West 17th Street, New York NY 10011. **Tel** (212)645-0067, FAX (212)242-6987. **1990**

PLANT GENETIC RESOURCES ABSTRACTS. (UK/0966-0100). CAB International Centre, Wallingford, Oxon OX10 8DE United Kingdom. **Tel** 44 491 832111, FAX 44 491 833508, telex 847964 (COMAGG G). **479**

PLANT GROWTH REGULATOR ABSTRACTS. (UK/0305-9154). CAB International Centre, Wallingford, Oxon OX10 8DE United Kingdom. **Tel** 44 491 832111, FAX 44 491 833508, telex 847964 (COMAGG G). **155**

PLANTS, SITES & PARKS. (US/0191-2933). Billboard Publications Inc., 1515 Broadway Billboard, New York NY 10036. **Tel** (212)764-7300, FAX (305)755-7048, telex WU TWX 710-581-6279. **703**

PLASTICS NEWS (AKRON, OHIO). (US/1042-802X). Crain Communications Inc., 1400 Woodbridge, Detroit MI 48207. **Tel** (313)446-6000, (800)992-9970. **4458**

PLASTICS TECHNOLOGY. (US/0032-1257). Bill Communications Inc., 355 Park Avenue South, New York NY 10010-1789. **Tel** (800)821-6897, (212)592-6262, FAX (212)592-6209. **4458**

PLASTICS WORLD. (US/0032-1273). PTN Publishing Company, 445 Broad Hollow Road, Melville NY 11747. **Tel** (516)845-2700, FAX (516)845-7109. **4458**

PLATT'S OILGRAM NEWS. (US/0163-1284). McGraw Hill Publishing Company, Inc., 1221 Avenue of the Americas, New York NY 10020. **Tel** (212)512-6410, (800)525-5003, FAX (212)512-6111. **4274**

PLATT'S OILGRAM PRICE REPORT. (US/0163-1292). McGraw Hill Publishing Company, Inc., 1221 Avenue of the Americas, New York NY 10020. **Tel** (212)512-6410, (800)525-5003, FAX (212)512-6111. **4275**

PLAYTHINGS. (US/0032-1567). Geyer-McAllister Publications Inc, 51 Madison Avenue, New York NY 10010. **Tel** (212)689-4411. **2585**

PLOUGHSHARES. (US/0048-4474). Ploughshares, Emerson College, 100 Beacon Street, Boston MA 02116. **Tel** (617)926-9875, (617)578-8753. **3424**

POET LORE. (US/0032-1966). The Writers Center, 7815 Old Georgetown Road, Bethesda MD 20814. **Tel** (301)654-8664. **3468**

POLISH AMERICAN JOURNAL (1985 : NATIONAL ED.). (US). Polish American Journal, 1275 Harlem Road, Buffalo NY 14206. **Tel** (716)893-5771, FAX (716)893-5783. **5720**

POLITICAL FINANCE LOBBY REPORTER. (US/0270-353X). Amward Publications, 2000 National Press Building, Washington DC 20045. **Tel** (301)251-9009, FAX (301)251-9058. **4489**

POLLUTION ABSTRACTS WITH INDEXES. (US/0032-3624). Cambridge Scientific Abstracts, 7200 Wisconsin Avenue, #601, Bethesda MD 20814-4823. **Tel** (301)961-6750, (800)843-7751, FAX (301)961-6720. **2185**

POLYMETRIC REPORT (T.S.E. ED.). (CN/0822-6970). Polymetric Report, Box 658 Don Mills, Toronto Ontario M3C 2T6 Canada. **911**

POPULAR MECHANICS (NEW YORK. 1959). (US/0032-4558). The Hearst Corporation, 250 West 55th Street, New York NY 10019. **Tel** (212)649-4014. **5139**

POPULAR PHOTOGRAPHY (1955). (US/0032-4582). Hachette Magazines Inc., 1633 Broadway, New York NY 10019. **Tel** (212)767-6000. **4375**

POPULAR SCIENCE (NEW YORK, N.Y.). (US/0161-7370). Times Mirror Magazines, Two Park Avenue, New York NY 10016. **Tel** (212)779-5000. **5139**

POS NEWS. (US). Faulkner & Gray Inc., 11 Penn Plaza, 17th Floor, New York NY 10001. **Tel** (212)967-7000, (800)535-8403. **803**

POST MAGAZINE. (UK). Buckley Press Ltd, 58 Fleet Street, London EC4Y 1JU England. **Tel** 011 44 71 5833030. **2890**

POSTGRADUATE MEDICINE. (US/0032-5481). McGraw Hill Publishing Company, Inc., 1221 Avenue of the Americas, New York NY 10020. **Tel** (212)512-6410, (800)525-5003, FAX (212)512-6111. **3628**

POSTHARVEST NEWS AND INFORMATION. (UK/0957-7505). CAB International Centre, Wallingford, Oxon OX10 8DE United Kingdom. **Tel** 44 491 832111, FAX 44 491 833508, telex 847964 (COMAGG G). **155**

POTATO ABSTRACTS. (UK/0308-7344). CAB International Centre, Wallingford, Oxon OX10 8DE United Kingdom. **Tel** 44 491 832111, FAX 44 491 833508, telex 847964 (COMAGG G). **156**

POULTRY ABSTRACTS. (UK/0306-1582). CAB International Centre, Wallingford, Oxon OX10 8DE United Kingdom. **Tel** 44 491 832111, FAX 44 491 833508, telex 847964 (COMAGG G). **156**

POWER TRANSMISSION DESIGN. (US/0032-6070). Penton Publishing, 1100 Superior Avenue, Cleveland OH 44114-2543. **Tel** (216)696-7000, FAX (216)696-0836. **2124**

PPO LETTER, THE. (US/1054-2396). Business Information Services Inc., 12811 North Point Lane, Laurel MD 20708. **Tel** (301)604-4001, FAX (301)604-5126. **2890**

PR NEWS. (US). Phillips Business Information, Inc., 1201 Seven Locks Road, Potomac MD 20854. **Tel** (301)424-3338, (800)777-5006, FAX (301)309-3847. **763**

PR WEEK. (UK). Rangenine Ltd, 100 Fleet Street, London EC4Y 1DE England. **Tel** 01-353 9804. **764**

PRACTICAL LAWYER, THE. (US/0032-6429). American Law Institute, 4025 Chestnut Street, Philadelphia PA 19104-3099. **Tel** (215)243-1661, (800)253-6397, FAX (215)243-1664. **3030**

PRECISION TOOLMAKER. (UK/0264-4703). Argus Press Group, Queensway House, 2 Queensway Redhill, Surrey RH1 1QS England. **Tel** 011 44 737 768611, 011 44 737 761685, FAX 011 44 737 760510, telex 948669 TOPJNL G. **2125**

PREGONERO (WASHINGTON, D.C.), EL. (US/8750-9326). El Pregonero, 5001 Eastern Avenue, PO Box 4464, Washington DC 20017. **Tel** (301)853-4504. **5647**

PREPARED FOODS. (US/0747-2536). Cahners Publishing Company, 249 West 17th Street, New York NY 10011. **Tel** (212)645-0067, FAX (212)242-6987. **2353**

PREREFUNDED BOND SERVICE. (US/0737-9595). Kenny Information Systems, 65 Broadway 17th FL, New York NY 10006. **Tel** (212) 770-4500. **803**

PRINTING ABSTRACTS. (UK/0031-109X). Pira International, Randalls Road, Leatherhead, Surrey KT22 7RU England. **Tel** 011 44 372 376161, FAX 011 44 372 377526. **4570**

PRIVATE PLACEMENT REPORTER. (US). American Banker, Concourse Level, 1 State Street Plaza, New York NY 10004. **Tel** (212)803-8200, (800)221-1809. **704**

PROBABILITY AND STOCHASTIC PROCESSES. (GW/0720-2628). Fachinformationszentrum, Karlsruhe Franklinstr, 11 ABT Berlin, D-10587 Berlin Germany. **Tel** 011 49 30 2611585, or 2611586, FAX 011 49 30 2628069. **3527**

PROCEEDINGS OF THE ACADEMY OF POLITICAL SCIENCE. (US). Academy of Political Science, 475 Riverside Drive/Suite 1274, New York NY 10115-1274. **Tel** (212)870-2500, FAX (212)870-2202. **4492**

PROCEEDINGS OF THE ANNUAL MEETING OF THE FLORIDA STATE HORTICULTURAL SOCIETY. (US/0886-7283). Florida State Horticultural Society, PO Box 1146, Lake Alfred FL 33850. **Tel** (813)299-1702, FAX (813)956-5318. **2429**

PROCEEDINGS OF THE SOUTH CAROLINA HISTORICAL ASSOCIATION, THE. (US/0361-6207). South Carolina Historical Association, c/o Dr. William S. Brockington, University of South Carolina-Aiken, 171 University Parkway, Aiken SC 29801. **Tel** (803)641-3223. **2755**

PROCESS AND CHEMICAL ENGINEERING. (UK/0960-5045). Royal Society of Chemistry, Thomas Graham House, Science Park, Cambridge CB4 4WF England. **Tel** 011 44 223 420066, FAX 011 44 223 423429, telex 818293 ROYAL. **2006**

PROCESS INDUSTRIES CANADA. (CN/0826-7243). Southam Information and Technology Group Inc., 1450 Don Mills Road, Don Mills Ontario M3B 2X7 Canada. **Tel** (416)445-6641, (800)668-2374, FAX (416)442-2261. **2016**

PRODUCT ALERT. (US/0740-3801). Marketing Intelligence Service Ltd, 6473D Route 64, Naples NY 14512. **Tel** (716)374-6326, (800)836-5710, FAX (714)374-5217, telex 469979. **2354**

PRODUCT DATA INTERNATIONAL. (US/1050-7043). Warthen Technical Information Services, N5303 Broughton Road, Albany WI 53502-9725. **Tel** (608)862-1702, FAX (608)862-1702. **5142**

PRODUCTIVITY SOFTWARE. (US/1040-1482). Worldwide Videotex, PO Box 3273, Boynton Beach FL 33424-3273. **Tel** (407)738-2276, FAX (407)738-2275. **1289**

PROFESSIONAL BUILDER & REMODELER. (US/1053-6353). Cahners Publishing Company, 249 West 17th Street, New York NY 10011. **Tel** (212)645-0067, FAX (212)242-6987. **624**

PROFESSIONAL SAFETY. (US/0099-0027). American Society of Safety Engineers, 1800 East Oakton Street, Des Plaines IL 60018. **Tel** (312)692-4121. **2868**

PROFIT-BUILDING STRATEGIES FOR BUSINESS OWNERS. (US/0889-9967). The Professional Report, 81 Montgomery Street, Scarsdale NY 10583. **Tel** (914)472-0366. **804**

PROGRESSIVE ARCHITECTURE. (US/0033-0752). Penton Publishing, 1100 Superior Avenue, Cleveland OH 44114-2543. **Tel** (216)696-7000, FAX (216)696-0836. **306**

PROGRESSIVE GROCER, THE. (US/0033-0787). Progressive Grocer, 263 Tresser Boulevard, Stamford CT 06901. **Tel** (203)977-7640. **2354**

PROTOZOOLOGICAL ABSTRACTS. (UK/0309-1287). CAB International Centre, Wallingford, Oxon OX10 8DE United Kingdom. **Tel** 44 491 832111, FAX 44 491 833508, telex 847964 (COMAGG G). **5604**

PROVIDENCE BUSINESS NEWS. (US/0887-8226). Providence Business News, 300 Richmond Street, Providence RI 02903. **Tel** (401)273-2201, FAX (401)274-0670, (401)274-0270. **5741**

PSA JOURNAL. (US/0030-8277). Photographic Society of America, 3000 United Founders Boulevard, Suite 103, Oklahoma City OK 73112. **Tel** (405)843-1437, FAX (405)843-1438. **4376**

PSYCHOLOGICAL ABSTRACTS. (US/0033-2887). American Psychological Association, 750 First Street Northeast, Washington DC 20002. **Tel** (800)374-2721, (202)336-5600, (subscriptions - (202)336-5600. **4623**

PSYCHOLOGICAL RECORD, THE. (US/0033-2933). Kenyon College, c/o Charles E. Rice, Gambier OH 43022. **Tel** (614)427-5377, FAX (614)427-4950. **4611**

PSYCHOLOGY TODAY. (US/0033-3107). Sussex Publishers Inc., 49 East 21st Street, 11th Floor, New York NY 10010. **Tel** (212) 260-7210. **4613**

PSYCINFO. (US). American Psychological Association, 750 First Street Northeast, Washington DC 20002. **Tel** (800)374-2721, (202)336-5600, (subscriptions - (202)336-5600. **4623**

PTS NEWSLETTER DATABASE [ONLINE DATABASE]. (US). Predicasts Inc., A Ziff Communications Company, 11001 Cedar Avenue, Cleveland OH 44106. **Tel** (800)321-6388, (216)795-3000, FAX (216)229-9944, telex 985 604. **732**

PUBLIC BROADCASTING REPORT, THE. (US/0193-3663). Warren Publishing, Inc., 2115 Ward Court NW, Washington DC 20037. **Tel** (202)872-9200, FAX (202)293-3435. **1136**

PUBLIC FINANCE QUARTERLY. (US/0048-5853). SAGE Periodical Press, 2455 Teller Road, Thousand Oaks CA 91320. **Tel** (805)499-0721, FAX (805)499-0871, telex 100799. **4743**

PUBLIC HEALTH REPORTS (1974). (US/0033-3549). Health Resources Administration, Office of the Administrator, DMS Committee Management Branch, 5600 Fishers Lane, Rockville MD 20857. **4797**

PUBLIC HEALTH REPORTS (1974). (US/0033-3549). Superintendent of Documents, US Government Printing Office, Washington DC 20402. **Tel** (202)275-3328, FAX (202)786-2377. **4797**

PUBLIC MONEY & MANAGEMENT. (UK/0954-0962). Basil Blackwell Publishers Ltd, 108 Cowley Road, Oxford 0X4 1JF England. **Tel** 011 44 865 791100, FAX 011 44 865 791347, telex 837022 OXBOOK G. **4743**

PUBLIC PERSONNEL MANAGEMENT. (US/0091-0260). International Personnel Management Association, 1617 Duke Street, Alexandria VA 22314. **Tel** (703)549-7100, FAX (703)684-0948. **946**

PUBLIC PRODUCTIVITY & MANAGEMENT REVIEW. (US/1044-8039). Jossey Bass Inc., 350 Sansome Street, San Francisco CA 94104. **Tel** (415)433-1767, FAX (415)433-0499. **4705**

PUBLIC RELATIONS QUARTERLY. (US/0033-3700). Public Relations Quarterly, PO Box 311, 44 West Market St., Rhinebeck NY 12572. **Tel** (914)876-2081, FAX (914)876-2561. **765**

PUBLIC UTILITIES FORTNIGHTLY. (US/0033-3808). Public Utilities Reports Inc., 2111 Wilson Boulevard, Suite 200, Arlington VA 22201. **Tel** (703)243-7000, (800)368-5001, FAX (703)527-5829. **4762**

PUBLISHERS, DISTRIBUTORS, & WHOLESALERS OF THE UNITED STATES. (US/0000-0671). R R Bowker, A Reed Reference Publishing Company, Part of Reed International PLC, PO Box 31, 121 Chanlon Drive, New Providence NJ 07974. **Tel** (908)464-6800, (800)521-8110, FAX (908)665-6688, telex 138-755. **4822**

PUBLISHERS WEEKLY. (US/0000-0019). Cahners Publishing Company, 249 West 17th Street, New York NY 10011. **Tel** (212)645-0067, FAX (212)242-6987. **4831**

PUGET SOUND BUSINESS JOURNAL. (US/8750-7757). Puget Sound Business Journal, 720 Third Avenue, Suite 800, Seattle WA 98104-2552. **Tel** (206)583-0701, FAX (206)447-8510. **705**

PUGET SOUND COMPUTER USER. (US/0886-8174). Puget Sound Computer User, 3530 Bagley Avenue North, Seattle WA 98103. **Tel** (206)547-4950, FAX (206)547-5355. **1201**

PULP & PAPER. (US/0033-4081). Miller Freeman Inc., 600 Harrison Street, San Francisco CA 94107. **Tel** (415)905-2337, FAX (415)905-2240, telex 278273. **4237**

PULP & PAPER INTERNATIONAL. (US/0033-409X). Miller Freeman Inc., 600 Harrison Street, San Francisco CA 94107. **Tel** (415)905-2337, FAX (415)905-2240, telex 278273. **4238**

PULP & PAPER JOURNAL. (CN/0713-5807). Maclean Hunter Ltd. / UK, Chalk Lane Cockfosters Road, Barnet Herts EN4 0BU England. **Tel** 011 44 81 2423000, FAX 011 44 81 9759753, telex 299072. **4238**

QUARTERLY JOURNAL OF BUSINESS AND ECONOMICS. (US/0747-5535). University of Nebraska / Bureau of Business Research, 200 College Business Administration Building, Lincoln NE 68588-0407. **Tel** (402)472-2334, FAX (402)472-3878. **706**

QUERY. (US). Syllabus Press, 1307 South Mary Avenue, Suite 218, Sunnydale CA 94087-0716. **Tel** (408)773-0670, FAX (408)746-2711. **1249**

QUICK FROZEN FOODS INTERNATIONAL. (US/0033-6416). E W Williams Publications Company, 80 Eighth Avenue, New York NY 10011. **Tel** (212)989-1101, FAX (212)242-5991, telex 427380 QFFI. **2355**

QUINCY HERALD-WHIG, THE. (US/0746-6358). Quincy Herald-Whig, 130 South 5th Street, Quincy IL 62301. **Tel** (217)223-5100. **5661**

RAD! : REVIEW AND DISCUSSION OF ROCK & ROLL CULTURE. (US). Conspiracy M.E.D.I.A., 826 Old Charlotte Pike East, Franklin TN 37064. **Tel** (615)791-1624. **4148**

RAILWAY AGE (BRISTOL). (US/0033-8826). Simmons Boardman Publishing Corporation / New York, 345 Hudson Street, New York NY 10014. **Tel** (402)346-4740. **5435**

RAINBOW (PROSPECT, KY.). (US/0746-4797). Falsoft Inc., PO Box 385, Prospect KY 40059. **Tel** (502)228-4492, FAX (502)228-5121. **1272**

RAM'S HORN (SCOTSBURN). (CN/0827-4053). Ram's Horn, 125 Highfield Road, Toronto Ontario M4L 2V4 Canada. **Tel** (416)469-8414. **124**

READERS' GUIDE ABSTRACTS. CD-ROM. (US/0899-1553). H W Wilson Company, 950 University Avenue, Bronx NY 10452. **Tel** (800)367-6770, (718)588-8400, FAX (718)590-1617, telex 4990003 HWILSON. **2497**

READERS' GUIDE TO PERIODICAL LITERATURE. (US/0034-0464). H W Wilson Company, 950 University Avenue, Bronx NY 10452. **Tel** (800)367-6770, (718)588-8400, FAX (718)590-1617, telex 4990003 HWILSON. **2497**

REAL ESTATE FINANCE. (US/0748-318X). Institutional Investor Inc., 488 Madison Avenue, New York NY 10022. **Tel** (212)303-3234, (212)303-3233, FAX (212)303-3353. **4844**

REAL ESTATE ISSUES. (US/0146-0595). American Society of Real Estate Counselors, 430 North Michigan Avenue, Chicago IL 60611. **Tel** (312)329-8427, FAX (312)329-8881, telex 0253742. **4844**

REAL ESTATE TODAY. (US/0034-0804). National Association of Realtors, 430 North Michigan Avenue, Chicago IL 60611. **Tel** (312)329-8494, (800)874-6500. **4845**

REALTOR NEWS. (US/0279-6309). National Association of Realtors, 430 North Michigan Avenue, Chicago IL 60611. **Tel** (312)329-8494, (800)874-6500. **4846**

RECORD (TORONTO). (CN/0712-8290). David Farrell and Associates, 410 4211 Yonge Street, Toronto Ontario M2P 2A9 Canada. **Tel** (416)221-3366. **4149**

REDBOOK. (US/0034-2106). The Hearst Corporation, 250 West 55th Street, New York NY 10019. **Tel** (212)649-4014. **5565**

REDEMPTION DIGEST AND CORPORATE ACTIONS. (US/1056-506X). Redemption Digest and Corporate Actions, PO Box 2055, Canal Street Station, New York NY 10013. **Tel** (800)879-2663, (212)219-1550, FAX (212)925-0262. **807**

REFRIGERATION SERVICE & CONTRACTING. (US). Business News Publishing Company, 755 West Big Beaver Road, Suite 1000, Troy MI 48084. **Tel** (810)362-3700, FAX (810)362-0317, telex 230295. **2608**

REGIONAL AVIATION WEEKLY. (US/1044-9450). McGraw Hill Publishing Company, Inc., 1221 Avenue of the Americas, New York NY 10020. **Tel** (212)512-6410, (800)525-5003, FAX (212)512-6111. **33**

REGIONAL ECONOMIC PROJECTIONS SERIES. (US/0090-9262). National Planning Association, 1424 16th Street Northwest, Suite 700, Washington DC 20036. **Tel** (202)265-7685. **1516**

REGULATORY UPDATE (PHILADELPHIA, PA.). (US/1065-1896). Regulatory Update, One Franklin Town Boulevard, Philadelphia PA 19103. **Tel** (215)567-7235. **3037**

REHABILITATION INDEX / THE BRITISH LIBRARY, MEDICAL INFORMATION SERVICE. (UK/0955-0984). British Library / Publications Sale Unit, Boston Spa, Wetherby, West Yorkshire LS23 7BQ England. **Tel** 011 44 937 546546 546543, FAX 011 44 937 546333, telex 557381. **4382**

REINSURANCE. (UK/0048-7171). Buckley Press Ltd, 58 Fleet Street, London EC4Y 1JU England. **Tel** 011 44 71 5833030. **2891**

RELEASE 1.0. (US/1047-935X). EDventure Holdings Inc., 104 5th Avenue, 20th Floor, New York NY 10011-6987. **Tel** (212)924-8800. **1239**

RELIGION AND LIFE LETTERS. (US/0730-2363). Spiritual Studies Center, PO Box 1104, Rockville MD 20850. **Tel** (301)963-9243. **4990**

RELIGION INDEX ONE. PERIODICALS. (US/0149-8428). American Theological Library Association, 820 Church Street, 3rd Floor, Evanston IL 60201. **Tel** (708)869-7788, FAX (708)869-8513. **5013**

RELIGION INDEX TWO : MULTI-AUTHOR WORKS. (US/0149-8436). American Theological Library Association, 820 Church Street, 3rd Floor, Evanston IL 60201. **Tel** (708)869-7788, FAX (708)869-8513. **4991**

REMOTE SENSING IN CANADA. (CN). Canada Centre for Remote Sensing, 588 Booth Street, Ottawa ONT K1A OY7 Canada. **Tel** (613)947-1315, FAX (613)943-8828. **5145**

REPORT ON DEFENSE PLANT WASTES. (US/1043-268X). Business Publishers Inc., 951 Pershing Drive, Silver Spring MD 20910-4464. **Tel** (301)587-6300, (800)274-0122, FAX (301)585-9075. **4055**

REPORTS AND TESTIMONY / UNITED STATES GENERAL ACCOUNTING OFFICE, OFFICE OF PUBLIC AFFAIRS. (US). US General Accounting Office / District of Columbia, 441 G Street NW, Room 4528, Washington DC 20548. **Tel** (202)275-2812. **4746**

RESEARCH SERVICES DIRECTORY. (US/0278-1743). Gale Research Inc., 835 Penobscot Building, 645 Griswold Street, Detroit MI 48226. **Tel** (800)877-GALE, (313)961-2242, FAX (313)961-6083, (800)414-5043, telex TWX 810-221-7086. **5147**

RESEARCH TECHNOLOGY MANAGEMENT. (US/0895-6308). Sheridan Press, PO Box 465, Hanover PA 17331. **Tel** (800)352-2210, (717)632-3535, FAX (717)633-8900. **5147**

RESOURCE CENTER BULLETIN. (US). Resource Center, Box 4506, Albuquerque NM 87196. **Tel** (505)842-8288, FAX (505)246-1601. **1779**

RESTAURANT HOSPITALITY. (US/0147-9989). Penton Publishing, 1100 Superior Avenue, Cleveland OH 44114-2543. **Tel** (216)696-7000, FAX (216)696-0836. **5072**

RESTAURANTS & INSTITUTIONS (CHICAGO, ILL.). (US/0273-5520). Cahners Publishing Company, 249 West 17th Street, New York NY 10011. **Tel** (212)645-0067, FAX (212)242-6987. **5073**

RETAIL BANKING PRODUCTS SURVEY. (AT). Horan Wall & Walker Pty Ltd, 15-19 Prospect Street, POB 8, Surry Hills New South Wales 2010 Australia. **Tel** 02 331 6600, FAX 02 380 5533. **809**

RETAIL BANKING PRODUCTS SURVEY. AT CALL DEPOSITS. (AT/1032-870X). Horan Wall & Walker Pty Ltd, 15-19 Prospect Street, POB 8, Surry Hills New South Wales 2010 Australia. **Tel** 02 331 6600, FAX 02 380 5533. **809**

RETAIL BANKING PRODUCTS SURVEY. CONTINUING CREDIT. (AT/1032-8726). Horan Wall & Walker Pty Ltd, 15-19 Prospect Street, POB 8, Surry Hills New South Wales 2010 Australia. **Tel** 02 331 6600, FAX 02 380 5533. **809**

RETAIL BANKING PRODUCTS SURVEY. CREDIT CARDS. (AT/1032-8742). Horan Wall & Walker Pty Ltd, 15-19 Prospect Street, POB 8, Surry Hills New South Wales 2010 Australia. **Tel** 02 331 6600, FAX 02 380 5533. **809**

RETAIL BANKING PRODUCTS SURVEY. TERM DEPOSITS. (AT/1032-8718). Horan Wall & Walker Pty Ltd, 15-19 Prospect Street, POB 8, Surry Hills New South Wales 2010 Australia. **Tel** 02 331 6600, FAX 02 380 5533. **809**

RETAIL BANKING PRODUCTS SURVEY. TERM LOANS. (AT/1032-8734). Horan Wall & Walker Pty Ltd, 15-19 Prospect Street, POB 8, Surry Hills New South Wales 2010 Australia. **Tel** 02 331 6600, FAX 02 380 5533. **809**

REVIEW : LATIN AMERICAN LITERATURE AND ARTS. (US). The Americas Society, 680 Park Avenue, New York NY 10021. **Tel** (212)249-8950, FAX (212)248-5868. **329**

REVIEW OF AGRICULTURAL ENTOMOLOGY. (UK/0957-6762). CAB International Centre, Wallingford, Oxon OX10 8DE United Kingdom. **Tel** 44 491 832111, FAX 44 491 833508, telex 847964 (COMAGG G). **5604**

REVIEW OF MEDICAL AND VETERINARY ENTOMOLOGY. (UK/0957-6770). CAB International Centre, Wallingford, Oxon OX10 8DE United Kingdom. **Tel** 44 491 832111, FAX 44 491 833508, telex 847964 (COMAGG G). **5604**

REVIEW OF MEDICAL AND VETERINARY MYCOLOGY. (UK/0034-6624). CAB International Centre, Wallingford, Oxon OX10 8DE United Kingdom. **Tel** 44 491 832111, FAX 44 491 833508, telex 847964 (COMAGG G). **5528**

REVIEW OF PLANT PATHOLOGY. (UK/0034-6438). CAB International Centre, Wallingford, Oxon OX10 8DE United Kingdom. Tel 44 491 832111, FAX 44 491 833508, telex 847964 (COMAGG G). **479**

REVIEW OF PUBLIC PERSONNEL ADMINISTRATION. (US/0734-371X). University of South Carolina Institute of Public Affairs, Gambrell Hall, Columbia SC 29208. Tel (803)777-8156. **4705**

REVIEW OF SOCIAL ECONOMY. (UK/0034-6764). Routledge, 11 New Fetter Lane, London EC4P 4EE England. Tel 071 583 9855, FAX 071 842 2298. **1581**

REVISTA ARGENTINA DE MICROBIOLOGIA. (AG/0325-7541). Asociacion Argentina de Microbiologia, Bulnes 44PBB, 1176 Buenos Aires Argentina. Tel 011 54 1 982-2220, FAX 011 54 1 982-8557. **569**

REVISTA DE MICROBIOLOGIA. (BL/0001-3714). Society Brasileira Microbioligia, AV Prof Lineu Prestes 1374, 05508 SAO Paulo SP Brazil. Tel 011 55 11 8139647, FAX 011 55 813 9641, telex 1135085. **569**

RICE ABSTRACTS. (UK/0141-0164). CAB International Centre, Wallingford, Oxon OX10 8DE United Kingdom. Tel 44 491 832111, FAX 44 491 833508, telex 847964 (COMAGG G). **1012**

RICHMOND NEWS-LEADER, THE. (US). Richmond Newspapers Inc, PO Box 26551, Richmond VA 23291. Tel (804)649-4181 or, 800 468-3382. **5759**

RICHMOND TIMES-DISPATCH. (US). Richmond Newspapers Inc, PO Box 26551, Richmond VA 23291. Tel (804)649-4181 or, 800 468-3382. **5759**

RILM ABSTRACTS. (US/0033-6955). RILM Abstracts, City University of New York, 33 West 42nd Street, New York NY 10036. Tel (212)642-2709, FAX (212)642-1900. **4160**

RISC MANAGEMENT. (US/1051-1393). Elk Horn Publishing, PO Box 1300, Freedom CA 95019. Tel (408)726-1232. **1202**

RISK MANAGEMENT. (US/0035-5593). Risk and Insurance Management Society, 205 East 42nd Street, New York NY 10164. Tel (212)286-9364. **2892**

RN. (US/0033-7021). Medical Economics Publishing, Five Paragon Drive, Second Floor, Montvale NJ 07645. Tel (800)432-4570, (201)358-2210. **3868**

ROAD AND TRACK. (US/0035-7189). Hachette Magazines Inc., 1633 Broadway, New York NY 10019. Tel (212)767-6000. **5424**

ROANOKE TIMES & WORLD-NEWS. (US). Times World Corporation, PO Box 2491, c/o Karen Walrond, Roanoke VA 24010. Tel (703)981-3100 or, 800 627-2767, FAX (703)981-3365. **5759**

ROBOTICS ABSTRACTS. (US/0000-1139). R R Bowker, A Reed Reference Publishing Company, Part of Reed International PLC, PO Box 31, 121 Chanlon Drive, New Providence NJ 07974. Tel (908)464-6800, (800)521-8110, FAX (908)665-6688, telex 138-755. **1209**

ROBOTICS WORLD. (US/0737-7908). Argus Business, 6151 Powers Ferry Road, Atlanta GA 30339. Tel (404)995-2500, (800)233-3359. **1216**

ROCHESTER BUSINESS JOURNAL (ROCHESTER, N.Y. : 1987). (US/0896-3274). Rochester Business Journal Inc., 55 Saint Paul Street, Rochester NY 14604. Tel (716)546-8303, FAX (716)546-3398. **708**

ROCKY MOUNTAIN HIGH TECHNOLOGY DIRECTORY. (US/0883-8046). Leading Edge Communications, 1121 Old Siskiyou Highway, Ashland OR 97520. Tel (503)482-4990. **5148**

ROCKY MOUNTAIN NEWS (DENVER, COLO. : 1937). (US). Rocky Mountain News, PO Box 719, Circulation Department, Denver CO 80201. Tel (303)892-5310, (303)892-6397. **5644**

ROLLING STONE. (US/0035-791X). Wenner Media Inc., 1290 Avenue of the Americas, 2nd Floor, New York NY 10104. Tel (212)484-1616, FAX (212)759-2966. **4151**

RQ. (US/0033-7072). American Library Association, 50 East Huron Street, Chicago IL 60611. Tel (312)944-6780, (800)545-2433, FAX (312)944-2641. **3247**

RTC PROPERTY DISPOSITION REPORT. (US/1049-7013). DataTrends Publications, 895 Harrison Street SE, Suite B, Leesburg VA 22075. Tel (703)779-0574, (800)766-8130, FAX (703)779-2267. **4847**

RUBBER & PLASTICS NEWS. (US/0300-6123). Crain Communications Inc., 1400 Woodbridge, Detroit MI 48207. Tel (313)446-6000, (800)992-9970. **5077**

RUBBER & PLASTICS NEWS II. (US/0197-2219). Crain Communications Inc., 1400 Woodbridge, Detroit MI 48207. Tel (313)446-6000, (800)992-9970. **5077**

RUBBER WORLD. (US/0035-9572). Rubber World, PO Box 5451, 1867 West Narjet Street, Akron OH 44334-0451. Tel (216)864-2122, FAX (216)864-5298, telex 297690 RWMAG UR. **5078**

RUBY'S PEARLS ELECMAG. (US/1079-6673). Ruby's Pearls, 9832-1 Sandler Road, Jacksonville FL 32222. Tel (904)573-6269, FAX (904)777-6799. **3432**

RURAL DEVELOPMENT ABSTRACTS / [PREPARED BY THE COMMONWEALTH BUREAU OF AGRICULTURAL ECONOMICS]. (UK/0140-4768). CAB International Centre, Wallingford, Oxon OX10 8DE United Kingdom. Tel 44 491 832111, FAX 44 491 833508, telex 847964 (COMAGG G). **2840**

RURAL TELECOMMUNICATIONS. (US/0744-2548). Cooperative Association, 2626 Pennsylvania Avenue Northwest, Washington DC 20037-1695. Tel (202)298-2300, FAX (202)298-2320. **1163**

RUSSIAN AEROSPACE & TECHNOLOGY. (US). Phillips Business Information, Inc., 1201 Seven Locks Road, Potomac MD 20854. Tel (301)424-3338, (800)777-5006, FAX (301)309-3847. **34**

SACRAMENTO BEE, THE. (US/0890-5738). Sacramento Bee, 2100 Q Street, PO Box 15779, Sacramento CA 95852. Tel (916)321-1111, (800)284-3233. **5639**

SAFETY AND HEALTH AT WORK : ILO-CIS BULLETIN. (SZ/1010-7053). International Labour Office - ILO, Publications Sales Service, CH-1211 Geneva 22 Switzerland. Tel 011 41 22 7996111. **2872**

SAINT PAUL PIONEER PRESS (SAINT PAUL, MINN. : 1990 : A.M. ED.). (US/1050-0405). St Paul Pioneer Press Dispatch, 345 Cedar Street, Saint Paul MN 55101. Tel (800)678-7737, (612)222-5011. **5698**

SALES & MARKETING MANAGEMENT. (US/0163-7517). Bill Communications Inc., 355 Park Avenue South, New York NY 10010-1789. Tel (800)821-6897, (212)592-6262, FAX (212)592-6209. **936**

SALES PRO. (US). Marketing Intelligence Service Ltd, 6473D Route 64, Naples NY 14512. Tel (716)374-6326, (800)836-5710, FAX (714)374-5217, telex 469979. **2356**

SAM ADVANCED MANAGEMENT JOURNAL. (US). Society for Advancement of Management, 126 Easr Lee Avenue, Suite 11, Vinton VA 24179. Tel (703)342-5563. **885**

SAN ANTONIO BUSINESS JOURNAL. (US/0895-1551). San Antonio Business Journal, 8200 IH West, Suite 300, San Antonio TX 78230. Tel (512)341-3202, FAX (512)341-3031. **709**

SAN ANTONIO EXECUTIVE. (US). San Antonio Executive, J Gomez, 1603 Babcock, Suite 159, San Antonio TX 78229. Tel (512)341-0110. **709**

SAN ANTONIO LIGHT (SAN ANTONIO, TEX.: 1911). (US). The Light Publications Company, 420 22 Broadway at McCullough, San Antonio TX 78291. Tel (512)271-2700. **5754**

SAN DIEGO BUSINESS JOURNAL. (US/8750-6890). San Diego Business Journal, 4909 Murphy Canyon Road, Suite 20, San Diego CA 92123. Tel (619)277-6359. **709**

SAN DIEGO DAILY TRANSCRIPT. (US). San Diego Daily Transcript, 2131 3rd Avenue, PO Box 85469, San Diego CA 92138. Tel (619)232-4381 Ext. 207. **5639**

SAN FRANCISCO BUSINESS TIMES. (US/0890-0337). San Francisco Business Trends, 275 Battery Street, Suite 940, San Francisco CA 94111. Tel (415)989-2522. **709**

SAN FRANCISCO CHRONICLE. (US). San Francisco Newspaper Agency, 925 Mission Street, San Francisco CA 94103. Tel (415)777-5700, (800)227-4423. **5639**

SAN FRANCISCO EXAMINER, THE. (US). San Francisco Newspaper Agency, 925 Mission Street, San Francisco CA 94103. Tel (415)777-5700, (800)227-4423. **5639**

SAN JOSE MERCURY NEWS. (US/0747-2099). San Jose Mercury News, 750 Ridder Park Drive, San Jose CA 95190. Tel (408)920-5000, (408)920-5609. **5639**

SANDIA SCIENCE NEWS. (US/0276-3672). Sandia Laboratories, Public Information Division 3161, Box 5800, Albuquerque NM 87185. Tel (505)844-7767. **5149**

SARASOTA MAGAZINE. (US/1048-2245). Clubhouse Publishing Inc., 601 South Osprey, Sarasota FL 34236. Tel (813)366-8225, FAX (813)365-7272. **2545**

SASKATCHEWAN BUSINESS. (CN/0709-0854). Sunrise Publication Ltd., 2207 Hanselman Court, Saskatoon Sask S7L 6A8 Canada. Tel (306)244-5668. **709**

SATELLITE COMMUNICATIONS. (US/0147-7439). Cardiff Publishing Company, 6300 South Syracuse Way, Suite 650, Englewood CO 80111. Tel (303)220-0600, telex 450726. **1163**

SATELLITE LEARNING. (US/1054-9935). Enteract Corporation, 1835 Algoa Friendswood Road, Alvin TX 77511. Tel (409)925-3900. **1846**

SATELLITE NEWS. (US/0161-3448). Phillips Business Information, Inc., 1201 Seven Locks Road, Potomac MD 20854. Tel (301)424-3338, (800)777-5006, FAX (301)309-3847. **1163**

SATELLITE TV FINANCE. (UK). Financial Times Business Information Ltd., Tower House, Southampton Street, London WC2E 7HA England. Tel 011 44 71 353 1040. **1138**

SATELLITE WEEK. (US/0193-2861). Warren Publishing, Inc., 2115 Ward Court NW, Washington DC 20037. Tel (202)872-9200, FAX (202)293-3435. **1163**

SATURDAY EVENING POST (1839), THE. (US/0048-9239). Saturday Evening Post Society, 1100 Waterway Boulevard, Indianapolis IN 46202. Tel (317)636-8881, FAX (317)637-0126. **2492**

SAUDI ECONOMIC SURVEY. (SU). Saudi Economic Survey, PO Box 1989, Jeddah 21441 Saudi Arabia. Tel 011 966 2 6514952. **1583**

SAUDI GAZETTE. (SU). Okaz Organization Press Publishers, PO Box 5576, Saud Islam, Jeddah Saudi Arabia. **5810**

SCANDINAVIAN INTERNATIONAL BUSINESS REVIEW. (UK/0962-9262). MCB University Press, 60 62 Toller Lane, Bradford West Yorkshire BD8 9BX England. Tel 011 44 274 499821, FAX 011 44 274 547143, telex 51317 MCBUNI G. **709**

SCANDINAVIAN PERIODICALS INDEX IN ECONOMICS AND BUSINESS : SCANP. (FI). Helsinki School of Economics Library, Uneberginkatu 22-24 Scimp, 00100 Helsinki Finland. Tel 011 358 0 43131, telex 122220 ECON SF. **1538**

SCHOLASTIC UPDATE. (US/0745-7065). Scholastic Inc., 2931 East McCarty Street, PO Box 3710, Jefferson City MO 65102-9957. Tel (314)636-5271, (800)631-1586. **1782**

SCHOOL ARTS. (US/0036-6463). Davis Publications Inc, 50 Portland Street, Worcester MA 01608. Tel (617)754-7201, (800)533-2847, FAX (508)753-3834. **364**

SCIENCE CITATION INDEX (COMPACT DISC ED.). (US/1044-6052). Institute for Scientific Information, 3501 Market Street, Philadelphia PA 19104. Tel (215)386-0100, (800)523-1850, FAX (215)386-6362, telex 84-5305. **5176**

SCIENCE CITATION INDEX WITH ABSTRACTS. (US/1061-1290). Institute for Scientific Information, 3501 Market Street, Philadelphia PA 19104. Tel (215)386-0100, (800)523-1850, FAX (215)386-6362, telex 84-5305. **5176**

SCIENCE OF FOOD AND AGRICULTURE. (US/0738-9310). Council for Agricultural Science and Technology, 4420 West Lincoln Way, Ames IA 50010. Tel (515)292-2125, FAX (515)292-4512. **2356**

SCIENTIFIC AMERICAN. (US/0036-8733). Scientific American Medicine, 415 Madison Avenue, New York NY 10017. Tel (212)754-0550, (800)333-1199. **5155**

SCIENTIFIC AMERICAN MEDICINE. (US/0194-9063). Scientific American Medicine, 415 Madison Avenue, New York NY 10017. Tel (212)754-0550, (800)333-1199. **3639**

SCIMP SELECTIVE CO-OPERATIVE INDEX OF MANAGEMENT PERIODICALS. (FI/0782-2979). Helsinki School of Economics, Runeberginkatu 22 24 SCIMP, 00100 Helsinki Finland. Tel 358 0 43131. **733**

SCISEARCH [ONLINE DATABASE]. (US). Institute for Scientific Information, 3501 Market Street, Philadelphia PA 19104. Tel (215)386-0100, (800)523-1850, FAX (215)386-6362, telex 84-5305. **5176**

SCREEN DIGEST. (UK). Screen Digest, 37 Gower Street, London WC1E 6HH England. Tel 011 44 071 580 2842, FAX 011 44 071 580 0060. **1139**

SCREEN FINANCE. (UK/0965-9587). Financial Times England, 8 16 Great New Street, London EC4A 3BN England. Tel 011 44 71 353 0305, 353 1040, 011 44 353 0846. **4077**

SDI MONITOR. (US/0886-7607). Pasha Publications Inc., 1616 North Fort Myer Drive, Suite 1000, Arlington VA 22209. Tel (800)424-2908, (703)528-1244, FAX (703)528-3742, (703)528-1253. **4056**

SEAFOOD INTERNATIONAL. (UK/0268-1293). EMAP Heighway, Meed House, 21 John Street, London WC1N 2BP England. Tel 44 71 4045513, FAX 881 3483, telex 44 71 831 9362. **2313**

SEATTLE POST-INTELLIGENCER (1921). (US/0745-970X). Seattle Times, PO Box 84647, Seattle WA 98124. Tel (206)464-2121. **5762**

SEATTLE TIMES, THE. (US/0745-9696). Seattle Times, PO Box 84647, Seattle WA 98124. Tel (206)464-2121. **5762**

Serials available Online SOUTHERN

SECOND OPINION (PARK RIDGE, ILL.). (US/0890-1570). Park Ridge Center, 211 East Ontario, Suite 800, Chicago IL 60611. **Tel** (312)266-2222, FAX (312)266-6086. **3640**

SECURED LENDER, THE. (US/0888-255X). Commercial Finance Association, 225 West 34th Street, New York NY 10122. **Tel** (212)594-3490, FAX (212)564-6053. **811**

SECURITIES INTERNATIONAL. (US/0894-2803). McGraw Hill Publishing Company, Inc., 1221 Avenue of the Americas, New York NY 10020. **Tel** (212)512-6410, (800)525-5003, FAX (212)512-6111. **1520**

SECURITIES WEEK. (US/0149-3582). McGraw Hill Publishing Company, Inc., 1221 Avenue of the Americas, New York NY 10020. **Tel** (212)512-6410, (800)525-5003, FAX (212)512-6111. **913**

SECURITY MANAGEMENT (ARLINGTON, VA.). (US/0145-9406). American Society for Industrial Security, 1655 North Fort Myer Drive, Suite 1200, Arlington VA 22209. **Tel** (703)522-5800, FAX (703)522-5226, telex 901892 ASIS AGTN. **885**

SEED ABSTRACTS. (UK/0141-0180). CAB International Centre, Wallingford, Oxon OX10 8DE United Kingdom. **Tel** 44 491 832111, FAX 44 491 833508, telex 847964 (COMAGG G). **156**

SEMICONDUCTOR INDUSTRY AND BUSINESS SURVEY. (US/0730-1014). HTE Research Inc., 400 Oyster Point Boulevard, Suite 220, San Francisco CA 94080. **Tel** (415)871-4377, FAX (415)871-0513. **2080**

SENSOR BUSINESS DIGEST. (US/1060-1902). Vital Information Publications, 321 Carrera Drive, Mill Valley CA 94941. **Tel** (415)389-8671, (415)345-7018, FAX (415)389-8671, (415)345-7018. **3487**

SENSOR REVIEW. (UK/0260-2288). MCB University Press, 60 62 Toller Lane, Bradford West Yorkshire BD8 9BX England. **Tel** 011 44 274 499821, FAX 011 44 274 547143, telex 51317 MCBUNI G. **5157**

SENSOR TECHNOLOGY. (US/8756-4017). Technical Insights Inc., PO Box 1304, Fort Lee NJ 07024-9967. **Tel** (201)568-4744, FAX (201)568-8247, telex 425900 SWIFT UI. **2080**

SETON HALL JOURNAL OF SPORT LAW. (US/1059-4310). Seton Hall University School of Law, One Newark Center, Newark NJ 07102. **Tel** (201)642-8811. **3048**

SEYBOLD REPORT ON DESKTOP PUBLISHING, THE. (US/0736-7260). Seybold Publications Inc., 428 West Baltimore Pike, PO Box 644, Media PA 19063. **Tel** (610)565-2480, (800)325-3830, FAX (610)565-4659, or 3261, telex 4991494. **1263**

SEYBOLD REPORT ON PUBLISHING SYSTEMS, THE. (US/0889-9762). Seybold Publications Inc., 428 West Baltimore Pike, PO Box 644, Media PA 19063. **Tel** (610)565-2480, (800)325-3830, FAX (610)565-4659, or 3261, telex 4991494. **4819**

SHARE INTERNATIONAL. (NE/0169-1341). Share International, PO Box 971, c/o Lynne Girdlestone, North Hollywood CA 91603. **Tel** (818)785-6300, FAX (818)994-0383. **4186**

SHEBOYGAN PRESS (SHEBOYGAN, WIS. : 1924). (US/0749-7121). Sheboygan Press, 626 Center Avenue, Sheboygan WI 53081. **5770**

SHELTERFORCE. (US/0885-9612). National Housing Institute / Shelterforce, 439 Main Street, Orange NJ 07050. **Tel** (201)678-3110, FAX (201)678-0014. **2835**

SHEPARD'S FLORIDA CITATIONS. (US/0730-3718). Shepards McGraw-Hill Inc, 555 Middle Creek Parkway, PO Box 35300, Colorado Springs CO 80935-3530. **Tel** (719)488-3000, (800)458-8811, FAX (800)525-0053. **3050**

SHEPARD'S NEW JERSEY CITATIONS. (US/0730-420X). Shepards McGraw-Hill Inc, 555 Middle Creek Parkway, PO Box 35300, Colorado Springs CO 80935-3530. **Tel** (719)488-3000, (800)458-8811, FAX (800)525-0053. **3052**

SH'MA (PORT WASHINGTON, N.Y.). (US/0049-0385). SH'MA Inc, 99 Park Avenue, Suite S -300, New York NY 10016. **Tel** (212)867-8888, FAX (212)867-8853. **4361**

SHOCK AND VIBRATION DIGEST, THE. (US/0583-1024). The Vibration Institute, 6262 South Kingery Highway, Suite 212, Willowbrook IL 60514. **Tel** (708)654-2254, FAX (708)654-2271, telex (708)654-2271. **2006**

SHOOTING INDUSTRY, THE. (US/0037-4148). Publishers Development Corporation, 591 Camino de La Reina, Suite 200, San Diego CA 92108. **Tel** (619)297-5350, FAX (619)297-5353, telex 695-478. **4917**

SICKNESS & WELLNESS PUBLICATIONS. (US/1041-2832). John Gordon Burke Publisher Inc., PO Box 1492, Evanston IL 60204. **Tel** (708)866-8625, FAX (708)866-8625. **3641**

SIDE EFFECTS OF DRUGS ANNUAL. (NE/0378-6080). Elsevier Science Publishers BV, PO Box 211, 1000 AE Amsterdam Netherlands. **Tel** 011 31 20 5803642, FAX 011 31 20 5862696, telex 15682. **4329**

SITUATION AND OUTLOOK REPORT. FRUIT AND TREE NUTS. (US/1051-7901). Economic Research Service USDA, 341 Victory Drive, Herndon VA 22070. **Tel** (800) 999-6779. **135**

SKI INDUSTRY LETTER, THE. (US/0197-3479). Ski Letter Inc., 115 Lilly Pond Lane, Katonah NY 10536. **Tel** (914)232-5094, FAX (914)232-4499. **4918**

SKIING (NEW YORK, N.Y.). (US/0037-6264). Times Mirror Magazines, Two Park Avenue, New York NY 10016. **Tel** (212)779-5000. **4918**

SKIING TRADE NEWS. (US/0037-6299). Diamandis Communications Inc, 1499 Monrovia Avenue, New Port Beach CA 92663. **Tel** (714)720-5300. **4918**

SKIN DIVER. (US/0037-6345). Petersen Publishing Company, 6420 Wilshire Bouldevard, Los Angeles CA 90048. **Tel** (213)782-2485. **4918**

SLOAN MANAGEMENT REVIEW. (US/0019-848X). Sloan Management Review, MIT E 38 120, 292 Main Street, Cambridge MA 02139. **Tel** (617)253-7170, FAX (617)253-6466. **886**

SLUDGE. (US/0148-4125). Business Publishers Inc., 951 Pershing Drive, Silver Spring MD 20910-4464. **Tel** (301)587-6300, (800)274-0122, FAX (301)585-9075. **2243**

SMALL FLOWS. (US). National Small Flows Clearinghouse, West Virginia University, PO Box 6064, Morgantown WV 26506. **Tel** (800)624-8301. **2243**

SMITHSONIAN. (US/0037-7333). Smithsonian Institution / Washington DC, 420 Lexington Avenue, Suite 1945, New York NY 10170. **Tel** (212)490-1840, (800)533-7901. **4172**

SMOKING AND HEALTH BULLETIN. (US/0081-0363). Technical Information Center, Office on Smoking and Health, Park Building Room 116/5600 Fishers Lane, Rockville MD 20857. **Tel** (301)443-1690. **4803**

SMT TRENDS. (US/0890-7900). Vital Information Publications, 321 Carrera Drive, Mill Valley CA 94941. **Tel** (415)389-8671, (415)345-7018, FAX (415)389-8671, (415)345-7018. **2081**

SNACK FOOD. (US/0037-7406). Stagnito Publishing Company, 1935 Sherner Road, Suite 100, Northbrook IL 60062. **Tel** (708)205-5660, FAX (708)205-5680. **2358**

SOAP, COSMETICS, CHEMICAL SPECIALTIES. (US/0091-1372). PTN Publishing Company, 445 Broad Hollow Road, Melville NY 11747. **Tel** (516)845-2700, FAX (516)845-7109. **1030**

SOCIAL PLANNING, POLICY & DEVELOPMENT ABSTRACTS. (US/1042-8380). Sociological Abstracts, PO Box 22206, San Diego CA 92192-0206. **Tel** (619)695-8803, FAX (619)695-0416. **5266**

SOCIAL RESEARCH METHODOLOGY ABSTRACTS. (NE/0167-8477). Erasmus University / SRM-Documentation Centre, Postbus 1738 Kamer BT 13, 3000 DR Rotterdam, The Netherlands. **Tel** 010 4081198, FAX 010 4529510. **5227**

SOCIAL SCIENCES CITATION INDEX (PRINT ED.). (US/0091-3707). Institute for Scientific Information, 3501 Market Street, Philadelphia PA 19104. **Tel** (215)386-0100, (800)523-1850, FAX (215)386-6362, telex 84-5305. **5228**

SOCIAL SCIENCES INDEX. (US/0094-4920). H W Wilson Company, 950 University Avenue, Bronx NY 10452. **Tel** (800)367-6770, (718)588-8400, FAX (718)590-1617, telex 4990003 HWILSON. **5228**

SOCIAL SCISEARCH. (US). Institute for Scientific Information, 3501 Market Street, Philadelphia PA 19104. **Tel** (215)386-0100, (800)523-1850, FAX (215)386-6362, telex 84-5305. **5221**

SOCIAL SECURITY BULLETIN (WASHINGTON, D.C. : 1938). (US/0037-7910). Superintendent of Documents, US Government Printing Office, Washington DC 20402. **Tel** (202)275-3328, FAX (202)786-2377. **5308**

SOCIAL WORK RESEARCH & ABSTRACTS. (US/0148-0847). National Association of Social Workers, 750 First Street Northeast, Suite 700, Washington DC 20002-4241. **Tel** (800)638-8799, (202)408-8600, FAX (301)587-1321. **5267**

SOCIOLOGICAL ABSTRACTS. (US/0038-0202). Sociological Abstracts, PO Box 22206, San Diego CA 92192-0206. **Tel** (619)695-8803, FAX (619)695-0416. **5267**

SOCIOLOGY (OXFORD). (UK/0038-0385). British Sociological Association, 351 Station Road, Dorridge-Solihull, West Midlands B93 8EY England. **Tel** 011 44 564 7724021. **5262**

SOFT-LETTER. (US/0882-3499). Soft-Letter, 17 Main Street, Watertown MA 02172. **Tel** (617)924-3944, FAX (617)924-7288. **1290**

SOFTWARE ENCYCLOPEDIA, THE. (US/0000-006X). R R Bowker, A Reed Reference Publishing Company, Part of Reed International PLC, PO Box 31, 121 Chanlon Drive, New Providence NJ 07974. **Tel** (908)464-6800, (800)521-8110, FAX (908)665-6688, telex 138-755. **1210**

SOFTWARE MAGAZINE (WESTBOROUGH, MASS.). (US/0897-8085). Sentry Publishing Company, PO Box 542, Winchester MA 01890. **Tel** (508)366-2031. **1290**

SOFWIN REPORTS. (US/1070-101X). Sofwin Publishing Company, 613 Old Farm Road, Columbus OH 43213. **Tel** (614)866-9966, FAX (614)866-9960. **1203**

SOILS AND FERTILIZERS. (UK/0038-0792). CAB International Centre, Wallingford, Oxon OX10 8DE United Kingdom. **Tel** 44 491 832111, FAX 44 491 833508, telex 847964 (COMAGG G). **156**

SOLID STATE AND SUPERCONDUCTIVITY ABSTRACTS. (US/0896-5900). Cambridge Scientific Abstracts, 7200 Wisconsin Avenue, #601, Bethesda MD 20814-4823. **Tel** (301)961-6750, (800)843-7751, FAX (301)961-6720. **4427**

SOLID STATE TECHNOLOGY. (US/0038-111X). PennWell Publishing Company, 1421 South Sheridan, PO Box 1260, Tulsa OK 74101. **Tel** (918)835-3161, (800)331-4463, FAX (918)831-9497. **2081**

SOLID WASTE REPORT. (US/0038-1128). Business Publishers Inc., 951 Pershing Drive, Silver Spring MD 20910-4464. **Tel** (301)587-6300, (800)274-0122, FAX (301)585-9075. **2243**

SOLUTIONS FOR BETTER HEALTH. (US/1050-0219). Haymarket Group Ltd, 45 West 34th Street, New York NY 10001. **Tel** (212)239-0855. **5222**

SOURCEMEX (ALBUQUERQUE, N.M.). (US/1054-8890). Latin American Institute, University of New Mexico, 801 Yale Northeast, Albuquerque NM 87131. **Tel** (505)277-5985, FAX (505)277-5989. **1521**

SOURCEMEX [COMPUTER FILE]. (US/1054-8890). Latin American Institute, University of New Mexico, 801 Yale Northeast, Albuquerque NM 87131. **Tel** (505)277-5985, FAX (505)277-5989. **1521**

SOUTH AFRICAN NATIONAL BIBLIOGRAPHY. (SA/0036-0864). The State Library / Pretoria, PO Box 397, Pretoria South Africa. **Tel** 011 27 12 3861661. **425**

SOUTH BEND TRIBUNE, THE. (US). South Bend Tribune Corporation, 225 West Colfax Avenue, South Bend IN 46626. **Tel** (219)233-6161, FAX (219)239-2642. **5667**

SOUTH CAROLINA BUSINESS JOURNAL. (US/0745-4473). South Carolina Chamber of Commerce, 1201 Main Street, Suite 1810, AT & T Building, Columbia SC 29201. **Tel** (803)799-4601, FAX (803)779-6043. **712**

SOUTH CHINA MORNING POST. (HK). South China Morning Post Ltd., PO Box 47, Tong Chong St., Hong Kong Hong Kong. **Tel** 011 852 5652472, FAX 011 852 5658961. **5802**

SOUTH DAKOTA BUSINESS REVIEW. (US/0038-3260). University of South Dakota Business Research Bureau, 414 East Clark, Vermillion SD 57069. **Tel** (605)677-5287, FAX (605)677-5427. **4748**

SOUTH FLORIDA BUSINESS JOURNAL. (US/0746-2271). South Florida Business Journal, 1050 Lee Wagner Boulevard, Suite 302, Ft. Lauderdale FL 33315. **Tel** (305)359-2100, FAX (305)359-2135. **712**

SOUTHEAST ASIA HIGH TECH REVIEW. (US/0892-1938). Mead Ventures Inc, PO Box 44952, Phoenix AZ 85064. **Tel** (602)234-0044, FAX (602)234-0076. **1627**

SOUTHEAST REAL ESTATE NEWS. (US/0192-1630). Argus Business, 6151 Powers Ferry Road, Atlanta GA 30339. **Tel** (404)995-2500, (800)233-3359. **4847**

SOUTHEASTERN MASSACHUSETTS BUSINESS DIGEST. (US/1040-5380). Southeastern Massachusetts Business Digest Inc, 5 Dover Street/Suite 101, New Bedford MA 02740. **712**

SOUTHERN CALIFORNIA BUSINESS. (US/0038-3880). Los Angeles Area Chamber of Commerce, 404 South Bixel Street, Los Angeles CA 90017. **Tel** (213)629-0671, FAX (213)629-0708. **821**

SOUTHERN NEW JERSEY BUSINESS DIGEST. (US/0892-8835). Southern New Jersey Business Digest, 2449 Golf Road, Philadelphia PA 19131. **712**

SOUTHERN WASTE INFORMATION EXCHANGE CATALOG, THE. (US/0892-5739). Southern Waste Information Exchange, PO Box 960, Tallahassee FL 32302. **Tel** (904)644-5516, FAX (904)574-6704. **2243**

Serials Online Index

SOUTHWEST — Serials available Online

SOUTHWEST JOURNAL OF BUSINESS AND ECONOMICS. (US/8750-4294). Southwest Journal of Business and Economics, Bureau of Business and Economic Research El Paso, El Paso TX 79968-0541. Tel (915)747-5122. **713**

SOUTHWEST REAL ESTATE NEWS. (US/0192-9194). Argus Business, 6151 Powers Ferry Road, Atlanta GA 30339. Tel (404)995-2500, (800)233-3359. **4847**

SOUTHWEST REVIEW. (US/0038-4712). Southwest Review, Southern Methodist University, 307 Fondren Library West, Dallas TX 75275. Tel (214)768-1036, (214)768-1037, FAX (214)768-1408. **3353**

SOVIET AEROSPACE & TECHNOLOGY. (US/1049-5940). Grune & Stratton Inc., 6277 Sea Harbor Drive, Orlando FL 32887. Tel (800)782-4479, (407)345-2567. **5159**

SOVIET AND EASTERN EUROPEAN FOREIGN TRADE. (US/0038-5263). M. E. Sharpe Inc., 80 Business Park Drive, Armonk NY 10504. Tel (914)273-1800, (800)541-6563, FAX (914)273-2106. **1640**

SOVIET PERSPECTIVES. (US/1055-1042). International Freedom Foundation, PO Box 15439, Washington DC 20002. Tel (301)699-0703. **2710**

SOVIET TECHNOLOGY ALERT. (UK/0953-4016). Newmedia International Japan, AV Infanta Carlota 123 5 A, 08029 Barcelona Spain. Tel 011 34 3 4195690, FAX 414 42 13. **5159**

SOYABEAN ABSTRACTS. (UK/0141-0172). CAB International Centre, Wallingford, Oxon OX10 8DE United Kingdom. Tel 44 491 832111, FAX 44 491 833508, telex 847964 (COMAGG G). **156**

SPACE BUSINESS NEWS. (US/0738-9884). Phillips Business Information, Inc., 1201 Seven Locks Road, Potomac MD 20854. Tel (301)424-3338, (800)777-5006, FAX (301)309-3847. **35**

SPACE COMMERCE WEEK. (US). Phillips Business Information, Inc., 1201 Seven Locks Road, Potomac MD 20854. Tel (301)424-3338, (800)777-5006, FAX (301)309-3847. **35**

SPACE EXPLORATION TECHNOLOGY. (US/1052-3383). Phillips Business Information, Inc., 1201 Seven Locks Road, Potomac MD 20854. Tel (301)424-3338, (800)777-5006, FAX (301)309-3847. **35**

SPACE STATION NEWS. (US/0895-8947). Phillips Business Information, Inc., 1201 Seven Locks Road, Potomac MD 20854. Tel (301)424-3338, (800)777-5006, FAX (301)309-3847. **36**

SPARTANBURG HERALD-JOURNAL. (US/0740-4743). Spartanburg Herald-Journal, Circulation Department, PO Box 1657, Spartanburg SC 29304. Tel (803)582-4511. **5743**

SPC. SOAP, PERFUMERY, AND COSMETICS. (UK/0037-749X). Wilmington Publishing Ltd., PO Box 200, Field End Road, Ruislip Middx HA4 0SY England. Tel 011 44 81 841 3970, FAX 011 44 81 841 9676. **405**

SPECIAL DELIVERY (WINNIPEG). (CN/0831-1994). Carleton University / Linguistics, Department of Linguistics, Ottawa Ontario K1S 5B6 Canada. Tel (613)788-2808, (613)788-2340. **3250**

SPECIALTY CHEMICALS (REDHILL). (UK/0262-2262). Argus Press Group, Queensway House, 2 Queensway Redhill, Surrey RH1 1QS England. Tel 011 44 737 768611, 011 44 737 761685, FAX 011 44 737 760510, telex 948669 TOPJNL G. **993**

SPECTRUM 1: STOCK HOLDINGS SURVEY. (US/0091-6854). CDA Investment Technologies, 1355 Piccard Drive, Rockville MD 20850. Tel (301)974-9600, (800)232-2285, FAX (301)590-1389. **914**

SPECTRUM 2: INVESTMENT COMPANY PORTFOLIOS. (US/0091-6862). CDA Investment Technologies, 1355 Piccard Drive, Rockville MD 20850. Tel (301)974-9600, (800)232-2285, FAX (301)590-1389. **914**

SPECTRUM 5. (US). CDA Investment Technologies, 1355 Piccard Drive, Rockville MD 20850. Tel (301)974-9600, (800)232-2285, FAX (301)590-1389. **914**

SPECTRUM 6. (US). CDA Investment Technologies, 1355 Piccard Drive, Rockville MD 20850. Tel (301)974-9600, (800)232-2285, FAX (301)590-1389. **914**

SPEEDNEWS. (US/0271-2598). SPEEDNEWS, 1801 Avenue of the Stars/Suite 210, Los Angeles CA 90067-5902. Tel (310)203-9603, FAX (310)203-9352, telex 292674. **36**

SPIN. (US). American Institute of Physics, 500 Sunnyside Boulevard, Woodbury NY 11797-2999. Tel (516)576-2200, FAX (516)349-7669, telex 960983. **4427**

SPOKESMAN-REVIEW (1894), THE. (US/1064-7317). Cowles Publishing, PO Box 2160, Spokane WA 99210. Tel (509)459-5187. **5762**

SPORT DISCUS [COMPUTER FILE]. (US). Silverplatter Information Inc., 100 River Ridge Drive, Norwood MA 02062. Tel (800)343-0064, (617)769-2599, FAX (617)235-1715. **1797**

SPORT STYLE. (US/0162-2242). Fairchild Publications Inc, 7 West 34th Street, 4th Floor, New York NY 10001-8191. Tel (212)630-4000. **1087**

SPORTS ILLUSTRATED. (US/0038-822X). Time Inc. / New York, Time & Life Building, Rockefeller Center, New York NY 10020. **4922**

ST. JOHN'S JOURNAL OF LEGAL COMMENTARY. (US/1049-0299). St. John's Journal Legal Commentary, St. John's University School of Law, Jamaica NY 11439. Tel (718)990-6688. **3058**

ST. LOUIS BUSINESS JOURNAL. (US/0271-6453). St Louis Business Journal, 612 North 2nd Street, PO Box 647, St Louis MO 63188. Tel (314)421-6200. **713**

ST. LOUIS COMMERCE. (US/0036-293X). Commerce Magazine / St Louis, 100 South 4th Street, Suite 500, St Louis MO 63102. Tel (314)231-5555. **851**

ST. LOUIS POST-DISPATCH. (US). Saint Louis Post-Dispatch, 900 North Tucker Boulevard, St Louis MO 63101. Tel (314)340-8808. **5704**

ST. MARY'S LAW JOURNAL. (US/0581-3441). St. Marys University School of Law, One Camino Santa Maria, San Antonio TX 78228-8604. Tel (210)436-3439, FAX (210)436-3756. **3058**

ST. PETERSBURG TIMES. (US). St. Petersburg Times, PO Box 1121, St Petersburg FL 33731. Tel (813)895-1181, (800)333-7505. **5651**

STAFF PAPERS - INTERNATIONAL MONETARY FUND. (US/0020-8027). International Monetary Fund, 700 19th Street Northwest, Publishing Unit, Washington DC 20431. Tel (202)623-7430, (202)623-7201. **812**

STANDARD & POOR'S CORPORATION RECORDS. CURRENT NEWS EDITION. (US/0196-4674). Standard & Poor's Corporation, 25 Broadway, New York NY 10004. Tel (212)208-8775. **915**

STANDARD & POOR'S EMERGING & SPECIAL SITUATIONS. (US/0882-5440). Standard & Poor's Corporation, 25 Broadway, New York NY 10004. Tel (212)208-8775. **915**

STANDARD-EXAMINER, THE. (US). Ogden Publishing Corporation, PO Box 951, Ogden UT 84404. Tel (801)625-4200, FAX (801)625-4508. **5757**

STANDARD-TIMES (NEW BEDFORD, MASS.), THE. (US/0745-3574). Standard Times Publishing Company Inc, 555 Pleasant Street, PO Box D912, New Bedford MA 02742. Tel (617)997-7411. **5690**

STANZA (MEDFORD, N.J.). (US/1063-8377). Stanza, 22 Ligntning Drive, Medford NJ 08055-9752. **3472**

STAR DATE : THE ASTRONOMY NEWS REPORT / THE UNIVERSITY OF TEXAS AT AUSTIN MCDONALD OBSERVATORY. (US/0889-3098). Star Date/ The Astronomy News, University of Texas/ RLM 15 308, Austin TX 78712. Tel (512)471-5285, (512)471-7756. **400**

STATE (COLUMBIA, S.C. : 1891 : DAILY). (US). The State Record Company Inc., PO Box 1333, Columbia SC 29202. Tel (803)771-6161. **5743**

STATE RECYCLING LAWS UPDATE (QUARTERLY ED.). (US/1070-3217). Raymond Communications, 6429 Auburn Avenue, Riverdale MD 20737. Tel (301)345-4237, FAX (301)345-4768. **2244**

STATE REPORTER. (US). State Reporter Publishing Co., PO Box 749, Helena MT 59624. Tel (406)449-8889. **3059**

STATE REPORTER OF EDUCATION LAW. (US). State Reporter Publishing Co., PO Box 749, Helena MT 59624. Tel (406)449-8889. **1785**

STATE TELEPHONE REGULATION REPORT. (US/0741-8388). Telecom Publishing Group, 1101 King Street, Suite 444, Alexandria VA 22314. Tel (703)683-4100, (800)327-7205, FAX (703)739-6490. **1164**

STEREO REVIEW. (US/0039-1220). Hachette Magazines Inc., 1633 Broadway, New York NY 10019. Tel (212)767-6000. **5319**

STETSON LAW REVIEW. (US/0739-9731). Stetson Law Review, 1401 61st Street South, St Petersburg FL 33707. Tel (813)345-1121 Ext. 257, FAX (813)345-8973. **3059**

STEWART ALSOP'S P.C. LETTER. (US/8756-7822). InfoWorld Editorial Products Group, 155 Bovet Road Suite 800, San Mateo CA 94402. Tel (800)432-2478, FAX (415)312-0547. **1239**

STN (NEW YORK, N.Y.). (US/1061-4524). Times Mirror Magazines, Two Park Avenue, New York NY 10016. Tel (212)779-5000. **4924**

STRATEGIC DEFENSE. (US/0890-7331). Phillips Business Information, Inc., 1201 Seven Locks Road, Potomac MD 20854. Tel (301)424-3338, (800)777-5006, FAX (301)309-3847. **4058**

STRATEGIC INFORMATION ON US AIR TRAVEL. (US). Nationwide Intelligence, Box 1922, Saginaw MI 48605. Tel (517)752-6123, (800)333-4130, FAX (517)752-1605. **5491**

STUART NEWS, THE. (US). Stuart News, PO Box 9009, Stuart FL 33495-9009. Tel (407)287-1550, FAX (407)221-4250. **5651**

STUDIES IN CANADIAN LITERATURE (FREDERICTON, N.B.). (CN/0380-6995). University of New Brunswick Studies in Canadian Literature, Fredericton New Brunswick E3B 5A3 Canada. Tel (506)453-4598, FAX (506)453-4599. **3441**

SUB-SAHARAN MONITOR. (US/1018-1520). International Freedom Foundation, PO Box 15439, Washington DC 20002. Tel (301)699-0703. **1523**

SUCCESSFUL BUSINESS. (US/0161-2042). 13-30 Corporation, 505 Market Street, Knoxville TN 37902. Tel (615)521-0600. **714**

SUCCESSFUL FARMING. (US/0039-4432). Meredith Corporation, Locust at 17th, Des Moines IA 50309. Tel (515)284-3000. **138**

SUGAR INDUSTRY ABSTRACTS / [CAB INTERNATIONAL, BUREAU OF HORTICULTURE AND PLANTATION CROPS IN ASSOCIATION WITH TATE & LYLE PLC]. (UK/0957-5022). CAB International Centre, Wallingford, Oxon OX10 8DE United Kingdom. Tel 44 491 832111, FAX 44 491 833508, telex 847964 (COMAGG G). **157**

SULPHUR. (UK/0039-4890). British Sulphur Corporation Ltd, 31 Mount Pleasant, London WC1X 0AD England. Tel 011 44 71 8375600, FAX 011 44 71 8370292, telex 918918 SULFEX G. **1030**

SUN-SENTINEL (FORT LAUDERDALE, FLA.). (US/0744-8139). News and Sun Sentinel Company, PO Box 14488, Fort Lauderdale FL 33302. Tel (305)356-4000, (305)761-4000, FAX (305)356-4559. **5651**

SUNDAY TELEGRAPH (LONDON, ENGLAND). (UK). Johnsons International Media Services, 43 Millharbour, London E14 9TR England. Tel 011 44 71 538 8288. **5813**

SUNSET (MENLO PARK, CALIF.). (US/0039-5404). Sunset Publishing Corporation, 80 Willow Road, Menlo Park CA 94025. Tel (415)321-3600, (800)777-0117. **2547**

SUPERCONDUCTOR WEEK. (US/0894-7635). Atlantic Information Services Inc., 1050 17th Street Northwest, Suite 480, Washington DC 20036. Tel (202)775-9008, (800)521-4323, FAX (202)331-9542. **1997**

SUPERFUND. (US/0892-2985). Pasha Publications Inc., 1616 North Fort Myer Drive, Suite 1000, Arlington VA 22209. Tel (800)424-2908, (703)528-1244, FAX (703)528-3742, (703)528-1253. **2244**

SUPERMARKET BUSINESS. (US/0196-5700). Howfrey Communication, 1086 Teaneck Road, Teaneck NJ 07666. Tel (210)833-1900. **2359**

SUPERMARKET NEWS. (US/0039-5803). Fairchild Publications Inc, 7 West 34th Street, 4th Floor, New York NY 10001-8191. Tel (212)630-4000. **2359**

SURFACE MODIFICATION TECHNOLOGY NEWS. (US/1058-093X). Business Communications Inc., 25 Van Zant Street, Suite 13, Norwalk CT 06855. Tel (203)853-4266. **1030**

SURVEY OF CURRENT BUSINESS. (US/0039-6222). Superintendent of Documents, US Government Printing Office, Washington DC 20402. Tel (202)275-3328, FAX (202)786-2377. **714**

SVENSKA TIDSKRIFTSARTIKLAR. (SW). Bibliotekstjanst AB, Box 200, S-221 00 Lund Sweden. Tel 011 46 46 180000. **426**

SYLLABUS. (US). Syllabus Press, 1307 South Mary Avenue, Suite 218, Sunnydale CA 94087-0716. Tel (408)773-0670, FAX (408)746-2711. **1225**

SYRACUSE BUSINESS. (US). Schueler Communications Inc., 208 North Townsend Street, Syracuse NY 13203. Tel (315)472-6911. **714**

SYSTEMS & NETWORK INTEGRATION. (US/1060-1384). Systems & Network Integration, PO Box 2030, Manhasset NY 11030-7030. **1291**

SYSTEMS INTEGRATION. (US/1044-4262). Cahners Publishing Company, 249 West 17th Street, New York NY 10011. Tel (212)645-0067, FAX (212)242-6987. **1274**

T.H.E. JOURNAL. SOURCE GUIDE OF HIGH-TECHNOLOGY PRODUCTS FOR EDUCATION. (US/0898-3348). Information Synergy Inc, 150 El Camnio Real, Suite 112, Tustin CA 92680. Tel (714)730-4011. **1225**

TACTICAL TECHNOLOGY. (US/1059-0552). Phillips Business Information, Inc., 1201 Seven Locks Road, Potomac MD 20854. Tel (301)424-3338, (800)777-5006, FAX (301)309-3847. **5161**

TAMPA BAY BUSINESS JOURNAL. (US/0896-467X). Tampa Bay Business Journal, 405 Reo Street/ Suite 210, Tampa FL 33609. Tel (813)289-8225, FAX (813)289-4518. **714**

TAPPING THE NETWORK JOURNAL. (US/1048-5198). Quality Productivity Management Association, 300 North Martingale Road, Suite 230, Schaumberg IL 60173. Tel (708)619-2909. **887**

TAX EXECUTIVE, THE. (US/0040-0025). Tax Executives Institute Inc, 1001 Pennsylvania Avenue Northwest, Suite 320, Washington DC 20004-2505. Tel (202)638-5601, FAX (202)638-5607. **4752**

TAX MANAGEMENT COMPENSATION PLANNING JOURNAL. (US/0747-8607). Tax Management Inc / Washington DC, 1231 25th Street NW, Washington DC 20037. Tel (202)452-4556, (800)372-1033, FAX (202)452-4096, telex 285656 BNAI WSH. **917**

TAX MANAGEMENT ESTATES, GIFTS, AND TRUSTS JOURNAL. (US/0886-3547). Tax Management Inc / Washington DC, 1231 25th Street NW, Washington DC 20037. Tel (202)452-4556, (800)372-1033, FAX (202)452-4096, telex 285656 BNAI WSH. **3119**

TAX MANAGEMENT INTERNATIONAL FORUM, THE. (UK/0143-7941). BNA International Inc., Herron, HSE Dean 10 Farrar Street, 6th Floor, London SW1H 0DL England. Tel (44) 71 222 8831, FAX (44) 71 222 0294, telex 262570 BNA LONG. **4753**

TAX MANAGEMENT INTERNATIONAL JOURNAL. (US/0090-4600). Tax Management Inc / Washington DC, 1231 25th Street NW, Washington DC 20037. Tel (202)452-4556, (800)372-1033, FAX (202)452-4096, telex 285656 BNAI WSH. **887**

TAX MANAGEMENT MEMORANDUM. (US/0148-8295). Bureau of National Affairs Inc., 9435 Key West Avenue, Rockville MD 20850. Tel (800)372-1033, (301)258-1033, FAX (301)948-5823. **4753**

TAX MANAGEMENT REAL ESTATE JOURNAL. (US/8755-0628). Bureau of National Affairs Inc., 9435 Key West Avenue, Rockville MD 20850. Tel (800)372-1033, (301)258-1033, FAX (301)948-5823. **3062**

TAX NEWS SERVICE. (NE/0040-0076). International Bureau of Fiscal Documentation - IBFD Publications, PO Box 20237, 1000 HE Amsterdam The Netherlands. Tel 011 31 20-6267726, FAX 011 31 20-6228658, telex 13217 INTAX NL. **3062**

TAXATION AND MERGERS & ACQUISITIONS. (US/1049-9830). Faulkner & Gray Inc., 11 Penn Plaza, 17th Floor, New York NY 10001. Tel (212)967-7000, (800)535-8403. **4755**

TEA & COFFEE TRADE JOURNAL, THE. (US/0040-0343). Lockwood Trade Journal Co. Inc., 130 West 42nd Street, 22nd Floor, New York NY 10036. Tel (212)391-2060. **2371**

TEBIWA. (US/0040-0823). Idaho Museum of Natural History, Campus Box 8096, Idaho State University, Pocatello ID 83209. Tel (208)236-3410, FAX (208)236-4000. **4172**

TECH-EUROPE. (BE). Europe Information Service, rue de Geneve 6, 1140 Brussels Belgium. Tel 011 32 2 242 6020, FAX 011 32 2 242 9549. **3252**

TECH STREET JOURNAL. (US/0889-6461). Tech Street Journal, 238 Littleton Road, Westford MA 01886. Tel (508)692-2290, FAX (508)692-4760. **5162**

TECHNICAL COMMUNICATION QUARTERLY. (US/1057-2252). Association of Teachers of Technical Writing, University of Minnesota, 202 Haecker Hall, St Paul MN 55108. Tel (612)624-9729, FAX (612)624-3617. **1122**

TECHNICAL COMPUTING. (US/0891-303X). Technical Computing, 9714 South Rice Avenue, Houston TX 77096. Tel (713)774-3942. **1204**

TECHNOLOGY ACCESS REPORT. (US/1050-043X). Univ. R&D Opportunities Inc., 16 Digital Drive, Suite 250, Novato CA 94949. Tel (415)883-7600. **5163**

TECHNOLOGY ALERT (PLANTATION, FLA.). (US/1054-4267). Merton Allen Associates, PO Box 15640, Plantation FL 33318-5640. **5163**

TECHNOLOGY MANAGEMENT ACTION. (US/0886-103X). Technology News Center, A Division of Lynn-Western Newswires, 6810 Butler Valley Road, Korbel CA 95550. Tel (707)668-4027, FAX (707)668-4055. **5164**

TECHNOLOGY RESOURCE GUIDES. (US). Corporate Technology Information Services Inc, 12 Alfred Street, Suite 200, Woburn MA 01801-9998. Tel (617)932-3939, (800)333-8036, FAX (617)932-6335, telex 497-2961 CRPTECH. **5164**

TECHNOLOGY REVIEW. (US/0040-1692). Massachusetts Institute of Technology (MIT), Building W 59, Cambridge MA 02139. Tel (617)253-8291. **5164**

'TEEN. (US/0040-2001). Petersen Publishing Company, 6420 Wilshire Bouldevard, Los Angeles CA 90048. Tel (213)782-2485. **1070**

TELECOM OUTLOOK : THE TELECOMMUNICATIONS & DATA COMMUNICATIONS NEWSLETTER. (US/1045-6562). Market Intelligence Research Company, 2525 Charleston Road, Mountain View CA 94043. Tel (415)961-9000, FAX (415)961-5042. **1164**

TELECOM WORLD. (UK/0963-0597). Just Write Publishing Ltd., PO Box 664 9, Andrewes House, London EC2Y 8EH England. Tel 011 44 71 9200022, FAX 11 44 71 9200041. **1165**

TELECOMMUNICATIONS ALERT. (US/0742-5384). United Communications Group, 11300 Rockville Pike, Suite 1100, Rockville MD 20852. Tel (301)816-8950 ext. 223, FAX (301)816-8945. **1165**

TELECOMMUTING REVIEW. (US/8756-7431). Gil Gordon Associates, 10 Donner Court, Monmouth Junction NJ 08852. Tel (908)329-2266, FAX (908)329-2703. **1166**

TELECONNECT. (US/0740-9354). Telecom Library Inc., 12 West 21st Street, New York NY 10010. Tel (212)691-8215, (800)542-7279. **1166**

TELEMEDIA NEWS AND VIEWS. (US/1071-135X). Opus Research Incorporated, 345 Chenery Street, San Francisco CA 94131. Tel (800)428-6787, (415)239-0244, FAX (415)239-6932. **1167**

TELEPHONE ENGINEER & MANAGEMENT. (US/0040-263X). Advanstar Communications Inc., 131 West First Street, Duluth MN 55802. Tel (218)723-9477, (800)346-0085. **2084**

TELEPHONE NEWS. (US/0271-5430). Phillips Business Information, Inc., 1201 Seven Locks Road, Potomac MD 20854. Tel (301)424-3338, (800)777-5006, FAX (301)309-3847. **1167**

TELEPHONE WEEK. (US/1062-4724). Telecom Publishing Group, 1101 King Street, Suite 444, Alexandria VA 22314. Tel (703)683-4100, (800)327-7205, FAX (703)739-6490. **1167**

TELEPHONY. (US/0040-2656). Intertec Publishing Corporation, 9800 Metcalf, Overland Park KS 66212. Tel (913)341-1300. **1167**

TELEVISUAL. (UK). Centaur Communications Ltd., St Giles House, 50 Poland Street, London W1V 4AX England. Tel 011 44 71 439 4222, FAX 011 44 71 734 6748, telex 261352. **1141**

TEMPLE POLITICAL & CIVIL RIGHTS LAW REVIEW. (US/1062-5887). Temple University School of Law, 1719 North Broad Street, Philadelphia PA 19122. Tel (215)204-1610. **4513**

TEMPTATION OF SAINT ANTHONY, THE. (US/1062-3981). Martin Bormann's Cranial Splints, PO Box 8166, Philadelphia PA 19101-8166. Tel (215)898-0587. **4620**

TERRORIST GROUP PROFILES. (US). Quanta Press, Inc., 1313 Fifth Street Southeast, Suite 208C, Minneapolis MN 55414. Tel (612)379-3956, FAX (612)623-4570. **4536**

TEXAS BANKING. (US/0885-6907). Texas Bankers Association, 203 West 10th Street, Austin TX 78701. Tel (512)472-8388, FAX (512)473-2560. **813**

TEXAS BUSINESS REVIEW. (US/0040-4209). Bureau of Business Research / Texas, University of Texas at Austin, Box 7459, Austin TX 78713. Tel (512)471-1616, FAX (512)471-1063. **1586**

TEXAS INDUSTRY ENVIRONMENTAL ALERT. (US/1055-2561). Environmental Compliance Reporter, 3154-B College Drive, Suite 522, Baton Rouge LA 70808. Tel (504)383-3937. **3116**

TEXAS LABOR MARKET REVIEW / TEXAS EMPLOYMENT COMMISSION. (US). Texas Employment Commission, 101 East 15th Street, Room 208T, Austin TX 78778. Tel (512)463-2619. **937**

TEXTILE TECHNOLOGY DIGEST. (US/0040-5191). Institute of Textile Technology, 2551 Ivy Road, Charlottesville VA 22903-4641. Tel (804)296-5511, FAX (804)977-5400. **5360**

TEXTILE WORLD. (US/0040-5213). MacLean Hunter Publishing Corporation / Chicago, IL, 29 North Wacker Drive, Chicago IL 60606-3298. Tel (312)726-2802, FAX (312)726-3091. **5358**

THEORETICAL CHEMICAL ENGINEERING. (UK/0960-5053). Royal Society of Chemistry, Thomas Graham House, Science Park, Cambridge CB4 4WF England. Tel 011 44 223 420066, FAX 011 44 223 423429, telex 818293 ROYAL. **2007**

THESAURUS OF ERIC DESCRIPTORS. SUPPLEMENT. (US). Oryx Press, 4041 North Central Avenue, #700, Phoenix AZ 85012-3397. Tel (800)279-ORYX, (602)265-2651, FAX (602)265-6250, (800)279-4663, (800)279-6799. **1929**

THOMSON'S INTERNATIONAL BANKING REGULATOR. (UK/0958-353X). American Banker, Concourse Level, 1 State Street Plaza, New York NY 10004. Tel (212)803-8200, (800)221-1809. **814**

THRIFT REGULATOR. (US). American Banker, Concourse Level, 1 State Street Plaza, New York NY 10004. Tel (212)803-8200, (800)221-1809. **814**

TIJDSCHRIFT VOOR BESTUURSWETENCHAPPEN EN PUBLEKRECHT. (BE/0040-7437). Tijdschrift Voor Bestuursweten, G Mercatorlaan 28, B 1780 Wenmel Belgium. Tel 011 32 2 2694109, FAX 011 32 2 2701319. **3064**

TIN INTERNATIONAL. (UK/0040-795X). MIIDA Limited, PO Box 2137, London NW10 6TN England. Tel 011/44/81/9617487. **2152**

TIRE BUSINESS. (US). Crain Communications Inc., 1400 Woodbridge, Detroit MI 48207. Tel (313)446-6000, (800)992-9970. **5078**

TIRE REVIEW (1966). (US/0040-8085). Babcox Publications Inc., 11 South Ford Street, Akron OH 44304. Tel (216)535-7011. **5078**

TITLE MASTER. (US/0747-6418). American Overseas Book Company, 550 Walnut Street, Norwood NJ 07648. Tel (201)767-7600, (201)784-0263, FAX (201)784-0263, telex 882384. **426**

TOBACCO INTERNATIONAL. (US/0049-3945). Lockwood Trade Journal Co Inc, 130 West 42nd Street 22nd Floor, New York NY 10036. Tel (212)391-2060. **5374**

TODAY'S AQUARIST (DEVON, CONN.). (US/1040-2098). Pisces Publishing Group, 417 Bridgeport Avenue, Devon CT 06460. Tel (203)877-4427, FAX (203)877-1927. **4879**

TOLEDO BUSINESS JOURNAL. (US). Telex Communications Inc., PO Box 1986, Toledo OH 43603. Tel (419)244-8200. **715**

TOOLING & PRODUCTION. (US/0040-9243). Huebcore Communications Inc., 1355 Mendiota Heights, Suite 210, Mendiota Heights MN 55120. Tel (612)686-0303. **2130**

TOP-BUSINESS. (GW). Verlag Moderne Industrie, Justus von Liebigstrasse 1, D 86899 Landsberg Lech Germany. Tel 011 49 8191 125453. **1629**

TORONTO STAR. (CN/0319-0781). Toronto Star Newspapers Ltd., 1 Yonge Street, Toronto Ontario M5E 1E6 Canada. Tel (416)367-2138. **5796**

TOTAL HEALTH. (US/0274-6743). Trio Publications Co, 6001 Topanga Canyon Boulevard, Woodland Hills CA 92367. Tel (818)887-6484. **4805**

TOTAL QUALITY ENVIRONMENTAL MANAGEMENT. (US/1055-7571). John Wiley & Sons, Inc., 605 Third Avenue, New York NY 10158-0012. Tel (212)850-6900, (212)850-6645, FAX (212)850-6088, telex 12-7063. **2182**

TOUR & TRAVEL NEWS. (US/0889-3349). CMP Publications Inc., c/o B. Werner, One Jericho Plaza, Wing A, 2nd Floor, Jericho NY 11753. Tel (516)733-6700. **5492**

TOURO JOURNAL OF TRANSNATIONAL LAW. (US/1046-3445). Touro College Fuchsberg Law Center, 300 Nassau Road, Huntington NY 11743. Tel (516)421-2244. **3136**

TOXIC MATERIALS NEWS. (US/0093-5891). Business Publishers Inc., 951 Pershing Drive, Silver Spring MD 20910-4464. Tel (301)587-6300, (800)274-0122, FAX (301)585-9075. **2245**

TOXIC MATERIALS TRANSPORT. (US/0275-3766). Business Publishers Inc., 951 Pershing Drive, Silver Spring MD 20910-4464. Tel (301)587-6300, (800)274-0122, FAX (301)585-9075. **5394**

TOXICOLOGY ABSTRACTS. (US/0140-5365). Cambridge Scientific Abstracts, 7200 Wisconsin Avenue, #601, Bethesda MD 20814-4823. Tel (301)961-6750, (800)843-7751, FAX (301)961-6720. **3662**

TRADE & INDUSTRY ASAP [ONLINE DATABASE]. (US). Information Access Company, 362 Lakeside Drive, Foster City CA 94404. Tel (800)227-8431. **734**

TRADE & INDUSTRY INDEX [ONLINE DATABASE]. (US). Information Access Company, 362 Lakeside Drive, Foster City CA 94404. Tel (800)227-8431. **854**

TRADEMARK REGISTER OF THE UNITED STATES, THE. (US/0082-5786). Trademark Register, National Press Building 1297, Washington DC 20045. Tel (202)662-1233, FAX (202)347-4408. **1309**

TRADING SYSTEMS TECHNOLOGY. (US/0892-5542). Waters Information Services, PO Box 2248, Binghamton NY 13902-2248. Tel (607)770-8535, FAX (607)798-1692. **1249**

TRAFFIC MANAGEMENT. (US/0041-0691). Cahners Publishing Company, 249 West 17th Street, New York NY 10011. Tel (212)645-0067, FAX (212)242-6987. **5394**

TRAFFIC WORLD, THE. (US/0041-073X). Journal of Commerce Inc, 445 Marshall Street, Phillipsburg NJ 08865. Tel (800)222-0356, (908)859-1300. **5394**

TRAINING Serials available Online

TRAINING AND DEVELOPMENT ALERT. (US/0192-0596). Advanced Personnel Systems, PO Box 1438, Roseville CA 95678. Tel (916)781-2900, FAX (916)781-2901. **947**

TRAINING AND DEVELOPMENT ORGANIZATIONS DIRECTORY. (US/0278-5749). Gale Research Inc., 835 Penobscot Building, 645 Griswold Street, Detroit MI 48226. Tel (800)877-GALE, (313)961-2242, FAX (313)961-6083, (800)414-5043, telex TWX 810-221-7086. **888**

TRANSACTIONS OF THE AMERICAN SOCIETY OF CIVIL ENGINEERS. (US/0066-0604). American Society of Civil Engineers / ASCE, 345 East 47th Street, New York NY 10017-2398. Tel (212)705-7179, FAX (212)705-7300, telex 422847 ASCE UI. **2007**

TRANSMISSION & DISTRIBUTION. (US/0041-1280). Intertec Publishing Corporation, 9800 Metcalf, Overland Park KS 66212. Tel (913)341-1300. **2085**

TRANSPORTATION & DISTRIBUTION. (US/0895-8548). Penton Publishing, 1100 Superior Avenue, Cleveland OH 44114-2543. Tel (216)696-7000, FAX (216)696-0836. **5457**

TRAVEL WEEKLY. (US/0041-2082). Reed Travel Group / New Jersey, 500 Plaza Drive, Secaucus NJ 07096. Tel (201)902-2000, (800)360-0015, FAX (201)319-1628. **5497**

TRC THERMODYMANIC TABLES NON-HYDROCARBONS. (US). TRC - Thermodynamics Research Center Data Distribution, Texas A&M University, Tees Business Office, College Station TX 77843-3124. Tel (409)845-5981, FAX (409)862-2352, telex 510-892-7689 TXINTLPRO COSN. **4432**

TRC THERMODYMANIC TABLES - HYDROCARBONS. (US). TRC - Thermodynamics Research Center Data Distribution, Texas A&M University, Tees Business Office, College Station TX 77843-3124. Tel (409)845-5981, FAX (409)862-2352, telex 510-892-7689 TXINTLPRO COSN. **4432**

TRENTONIAN (TRENTON, N.J.), THE. (US/1064-3567). Trentonian, 600 Perry Street, Trenton NJ 08602. Tel (609)989-7800 ext. 235. **5711**

TRIANGLE BUSINESS. (US/0891-0022). Triangle Business, PO Box 91453, Raleigh NC 27625. **5724**

TRIBUNE BUSINESS WEEKLY. (US/1051-7367). South Bend Tribune Corporation, 225 West Colfax Avenue, South Bend IN 46626. Tel (219)233-6161, FAX (219)239-2642. **716**

TRUSTEE. (US/0041-3674). American Hospital Publishing Inc., (A Subsidiary of the American Hospital Association), PO Box 92683, Chicago IL 60675. Tel (312)440-6836, (800)621-6902, FAX (312)951-8491. **3793**

TRUSTS & ESTATES. (US/0041-3682). Argus Business, 6151 Powers Ferry Road, Atlanta GA 30339. Tel (404)995-2500, (800)233-3359. **3119**

TUCSON CITIZEN (1977). (US/0888-5478). Tucson Citizen, 4850 South Park Avenue, PO Box 26887, Tucson AZ 85726. Tel (602)573-4511, (800)695-4492. **5630**

TUFTS UNIVERSITY DIET & NUTRITION LETTER. (US/0747-4105). W. H. White Publications, Inc., 53 Park Place, 8th Floor, New York NY 10007. Tel (212)608-6515. **4199**

TULSA BUSINESS CHRONICLE. (US/0745-5747). Tulsa Business Chronicle, 315 South Boulder Avenue, Tulsa OK 74103. Tel (918)581-8560. **5733**

TULSA WORLD (TULSA, OKLA.). (US/8750-5959). World Publishing Company / Tulsa, PO Box 1770, 315 South Boulder, Tulsa OK 74102. Tel (918)581-8596, FAX (918)583-3550. **5733**

U.C. DAVIS LAW REVIEW. (US/0197-4564). Regents of the University of California / Law, School of Law, Davis CA 95616. Tel (916)752-2551, FAX (916)752-4704. **3067**

U.S. NEWS & WORLD REPORT. (US/0041-5537). US News & World Report Inc, 2400 N Street Northwest, Washington DC 20037. Tel (202)955-2000. **2494**

U.S. OIL WEEK. (US/0502-9767). Capitol Publications, 1101 King Street, Suite 444, Alexandria VA 22314. Tel (703)683-4100, (800)655-5597. **4281**

U.S. RAIL NEWS. (US/0275-3758). Business Publishers Inc., 951 Pershing Drive, Silver Spring MD 20910-4464. Tel (301)587-6300, (800)274-0122, FAX (301)585-9075. **5437**

UCLA LAW REVIEW. (US/0041-5650). UCLA Law Review, 405 Hilgard Avenue, Los Angeles CA 90024. Tel (310)825-4929, FAX (310)206-6489. **3067**

UK PRESS GAZETTE. (UK). Maclean Hunter Ltd. / UK, Chalk Lane Cockfosters Road, Barnet Herts EN4 0BU England. Tel 011 44 81 2423000, FAX 011 44 81 9759753, telex 299072. **2926**

UK VENTURE CAPITAL JOURNAL. (UK/0265-8364). Venture Economics Ltd, Quadrange 180, Wardourst Street, London W1A 4YG England. Tel 011 44 71 434 0411. **815**

UKRAINE (SYRACUSE, N.Y.). (US/1061-1304). Political Risk Services, 6320 Fly Road, Suite 102, PO Box 248, East Syracuse NY 13057-0248. Tel (315)431-0511, FAX (315)431-0200. **1587**

ULRICH'S INTERNATIONAL PERIODICALS DIRECTORY. (US/0000-0175). R R Bowker, A Reed Reference Publishing Company, Part of Reed International PLC, PO Box 31, 121 Chanlon Drive, New Providence NJ 07974. Tel (908)464-6800, (800)521-8110, FAX (908)665-6688, telex 138-755. **3254**

ULRICH'S PLUS. (US/1068-0500). R R Bowker Electronic Publishing, A Reed Reference Publishing Company, Part of Reed International PLC, 121 Chanlon Drive, New Providence NJ 07974. Tel (800)323-3288. **3254**

ULRICH'S UPDATE. (US/0000-1074). R R Bowker, A Reed Reference Publishing Company, Part of Reed International PLC, PO Box 31, 121 Chanlon Drive, New Providence NJ 07974. Tel (908)464-6800, (800)521-8110, FAX (908)665-6688, telex 138-755. **3254**

UN CHRONICLE. (US/0251-7329). United Nations Publications, 2 United Nations Plaza, Room DC2 0853, Department 007C, New York NY 10017. Tel (212)963-8303, (800)253-9646. **4537**

UNESCO COURIER, THE. (FR/0041-5278). UNESCO / France, 31 rue Francois Bonvin, 75732 Paris Cedex 15 France. Tel 011 33 1 45684564, 011 33 1 45684565, FAX 011 33 1 42733007, telex 204461 Paris. **2856**

UNITED STATES BANKER (COS COB). (US/0148-8848). Kalo Communications Inc., 10 Valley Drive, Greenwich CT 06831. Tel (212)599-3310. **815**

UNITED STATES POLITICAL SCIENCE DOCUMENTS. (US/0148-6063). Mid-Atlantic Technology Applications Center (MTAC), University of Pittsburgh, 823 William Pitt Union, Pittsburgh PA 15260. Tel (412)648-7010, FAX (412)648-7003. **4503**

UNIVERSITY OF CALIFORNIA, BERKELEY, WELLNESS LETTER. (US/0748-9234). Health Letter Associates, 632 Broadway, 11th Floor, New York NY 10012. Tel (212)505-2255 ext. 100. **4806**

UNIVERSITY OF COLORADO LAW REVIEW. (US/0041-9516). University of Colorado Law Review, 290 Fleming Law Building, Campus Box 401, Boulder CO 80309. Tel (303)492-6145, FAX (303)492-1200. **3068**

UNIVERSITY OF FLORIDA JOURNAL OF LAW AND PUBLIC POLICY. (US/1047-8035). Journal of Law and Public Policy, 115 Holland Hall, University of Florida, Gainesville FL 32611. Tel (904)392-7139. **3068**

UNIVERSITY OF SAN FRANCISCO LAW REVIEW. (US/0042-0018). University of San Francisco Law Review, 2130 Fulton Street, San Francisco CA 94117. Tel (415)666-6154, FAX (415)666-6433. **3069**

UNIX NEWS LONDON. (UK/0956-2753). APT Data Services, 12 Sutton Row, 4th Floor, London W1V 5FH England. Tel 011 44 71 5287083, FAX 011 44 71 4391105. **1249**

UNIX REVIEW. (US/0742-3136). Miller Freeman Inc., 600 Harrison Street, San Francisco CA 94107. Tel (415)905-2337, FAX (415)905-2240, telex 278273. **1239**

UNIX TODAY!. (US/1040-5038). CMP Publications Inc., c/o B. Werner, One Jericho Plaza, Wing A, 2nd Floor, Jericho NY 11753. Tel (516)733-6700. **1206**

URBAN AFFAIRS ABSTRACTS. (US/0300-6859). Urban Research Institute, University of Louisville, Louisville KY 40292. Tel (502)588-6626, FAX (502)588-7386. **4701**

URBAN RING EDITION. (US). Cook County Jury Verdict, 415 North State Street, Chicago IL 60610. Tel (312)644-7800. **3091**

URBAN TRANSPORT NEWS. (US/0195-4695). Business Publishers Inc., 951 Pershing Drive, Silver Spring MD 20910-4464. Tel (301)587-6300, (800)274-0122, FAX (301)585-9075. **5399**

URETHANES TECHNOLOGY. (UK/0265-637X). Crain Communications Ltd., 75-77 Cowcross Street, Cowcross Court, London EC1M 6BP England. Tel 011 44 71 6082774. **4460**

UROLOGY TIMES. (US/0093-9722). Advanstar Communications Inc., 131 West First Street, Duluth MN 55802. Tel (218)723-9477, (800)346-0085. **3994**

US DEPARTMENT OF STATE DISPATCH. (US/1051-7693). Superintendent of Documents, US Government Printing Office, Washington DC 20402. Tel (202)275-3328, FAX (202)786-2377. **4692**

VA-NYTT. (SW/0042-1995). Byggdok, Haelsingegatan 47, S 113 31 Stockholm Sweden. Tel 011 46 8 340170, FAX 011 46 8 324859. **2183**

VANDERBILT LAW REVIEW. (US/0042-2533). Vanderbilt Law Review, Vanderbilt University School of Law, Nashville TN 37240. Tel (615)322-4766. **3070**

VARBUSINESS. (US/0894-5802). CMP Publications Inc., c/o B. Werner, One Jericho Plaza, Wing A, 2nd Floor, Jericho NY 11753. Tel (516)733-6700. **1239**

VECKANS AFFARER. (SW/0506-4406). Affars Forlaget, PO Box 3188, S 10363 Stockholm Sweden. Tel 011 46 8 7365600. **717**

VEGETARIAN JOURNAL. (US/0885-7636 #y 0883-1165). The Vegetarian Resource Group, PO Box 1463, Baltimore MD 21203-1463. Tel (410)366-8343. **4200**

VEGETARIAN TIMES. (US/0164-8497). Cowles Magazines, PO Box 8200, Harrisburg PA 17105. Tel (717)657-9555, (800)435-9610. **4200**

VENTURE CAPITAL JOURNAL. (US/0883-2773). Securities Data Company, 40 West 57th Street, 11th Floor, New York NY 10019. Tel (212)765-5311. **919**

VERMONT BUSINESS MAGAZINE. (US/0897-7925). Manning Inc., PO Box 6120, Battleboro VT 05301. Tel (802)257-4100. **718**

VERTICAL FILE INDEX. (US/0042-4439). H W Wilson Company, 950 University Avenue, Bronx NY 10452. Tel (800)367-6770, (718)588-8400, FAX (718)590-1617, telex 4990003 HWILSON. **427**

VETDOC. (UK). Derwent Publications Ltd., Derwent House 14, Great Queen Street, London WC2B 5DF England. Tel 011 44 71 3442800. **5528**

VETERINARY BULLETIN (LONDON). (UK/0042-4854). CAB International Centre, Wallingford, Oxon OX10 8DE United Kingdom. Tel 44 491 832111, FAX 44 491 833508, telex 847964 (COMAGG G). **5528**

VIBE (NEW YORK, N.Y.). (US/1070-4701). Time Publishing Ventures Inc., 205 Lexington Avenue, 3rd Floor, New York NY 10016. Tel (212)522-9180, (800)477-3974, FAX (212)522-4578. **2494**

VIBRANT LIFE. (US/0749-3509). Review and Herald Publishing Association, 55 West Oak Ridge Drive, Hagerstown MD 21740. Tel (301)791-7000 ext. 2534, FAX (301)790-9734. **2601**

VIDEO AGE INTERNATIONAL. (US/0278-5013). TV Trade Media Inc., 216 E 75th Street / Suite 1W, New York NY 10021. Tel (212)288-3933, FAX (212)734-9033, telex 428669. **1142**

VIDEO MARKETING NEWS. (US). Phillips Business Information, Inc., 1201 Seven Locks Road, Potomac MD 20854. Tel (301)424-3338, (800)777-5006, FAX (301)309-3847. **4377**

VIDEO STORE. (US/0195-1750). Advanstar Communications Inc., 131 West First Street, Duluth MN 55802. Tel (218)723-9477, (800)346-0085. **1142**

VIDEO TECHNOLOGY NEWSLETTER. (US/1040-2772). Phillips Business Information, Inc., 1201 Seven Locks Road, Potomac MD 20854. Tel (301)424-3338, (800)777-5006, FAX (301)309-3847. **4378**

VIDEO WEEK. (US/0196-5905). Warren Publishing, Inc., 2115 Ward Court NW, Washington DC 20037. Tel (202)872-9200, FAX (202)293-3435. **1142**

VIDEONEWS INTERNATIONAL (HOLLYWOOD, CALIF.). (US/1044-6354). Phillips Business Information, Inc., 1201 Seven Locks Road, Potomac MD 20854. Tel (301)424-3338, (800)777-5006, FAX (301)309-3847. **1143**

VIETNAM MARKET WATCH. (US/1071-7900). Vietnam Market Resources Inc., 1616 Post Road, Fairfield CT 06430. Tel (203)256-0370, (800)999-8438, FAX (203)256-9790. **718**

VIEW (BEDFORD, N.H.). (US/1070-1362). View, PO Box 10624, Bedford NH 03110. Tel (800)225-8439, FAX (603)472-8860. **735**

VIRGINIA MEDICAL QUARTERLY : VMQ. (US/1052-4231). Medical Society of Virginia, 4205 Dover Road, Richmond VA 23221. Tel (804)353-2721, FAX (804)355-6189. **3650**

VIROLOGY & AIDS ABSTRACTS. (US/0896-5919). Cambridge Scientific Abstracts, 7200 Wisconsin Avenue, #601, Bethesda MD 20814-4823. Tel (301)961-6750, (800)843-7751, FAX (301)961-6720. **3662**

VITIS, VITICULTURE AND ENOLOGY ABSTRACTS. (GW/0175-8292). Vitis / Bundesanstalt fuer Zuechtungsforschung, Forschung Wein/ Geilweilerhof, W 6741 Siebeldingen Germany. Tel 011 49 6345 410. **2362**

VOICE TECHNOLOGY NEWS. (US/1045-1498). Phillips Business Information, Inc., 1201 Seven Locks Road, Potomac MD 20854. Tel (301)424-3338, (800)777-5006, FAX (301)309-3847. **2131**

WALL STREET & TECHNOLOGY. (US/1060-989X). Miller Freeman Inc., 600 Harrison Street, San Francisco CA 94107. **Tel** (415)905-2337, FAX (415)905-2240, telex 278273. **919**

WALL STREET COMPUTER REVIEW. (US/0738-4343). Miller Freeman Inc., 600 Harrison Street, San Francisco CA 94107. **Tel** (415)905-2337, FAX (415)905-2240, telex 278273. **919**

WALL STREET NETWORK NEWS. (US/1063-3839). Waters Information Services, PO Box 2248, Binghamton NY 13902-2248. **Tel** (607)770-8535, FAX (607)798-1692. **1244**

WALL STREET TRANSCRIPT, THE. (US/0043-0102). Wall Street Transcript, 100 Wall Street, New York NY 10005. **Tel** (212)747-9500. **919**

WARD'S AUTO WORLD. (US/0043-0315). Ward's Communications Inc., 3000 Town Center, Suite 2750, Southfield MI 48075. **Tel** (810)357-0800. **5428**

WASHINGTON BEVERAGE INSIGHT. (US/0890-8060). George Wells and Associates, 2942 South Columbus Street, Suite A-2, Arlington VA 22206. **Tel** (703)671-8140. **2372**

WASHINGTON DRUG LETTER (WASHINGTON. 1979). (US/0194-1291). Washington Business Information Inc., 1117 North 19th Street, Suite 200, Arlington VA 22209. **Tel** (703)247-3433, (800)426-0416, FAX (703)247-3421. **4332**

WASHINGTON FEDERAL SCIENCE NEWSLETTER. (US/0740-0535). Washington Federal Science, 1057-B National Press Building, Washington DC 20045. **Tel** (202)393-3640. **5169**

WASHINGTON MONTHLY, THE. (US/0043-0633). The Washington Monthly, 1611 Connecticut Avenue Northwest, Suite 7, Washington DC 20009. **Tel** (202)462-0128, FAX (202)332-8413. **4499**

WASHINGTON REMOTE SENSING LETTER. (US/0739-6538). Washington Remote Sensing Letter, 1057-B National Press Building, Editorial Office, Washington DC 20045. **Tel** (202)393-3640. **1361**

WASHINGTON TIMES (WASHINGTON, D.C. : 1982), THE. (US/0732-8494). The Washington Times Corporation, 3400 New York Avenue Northeast, Washington DC 20002. **Tel** (202)635-4000, (800)822-2822. **5648**

WASTE INFORMATION DIGESTS. (US/1050-3153). International Academy at Santa Barbara, 800 Garden Street, Suite D, Santa Barbara CA 93101. **Tel** (805)965-5010, FAX (805)965-6071. **2246**

WASTE TREATMENT TECHNOLOGY NEWS. (US/0885-0003). Business Communications Inc., 25 Van Zant Street, Suite 13, Norwalk CT 06855. **Tel** (203)853-4266. **2246**

WAUSAU DAILY HERALD. (US/0887-4271). Wausau Daily Herald, PO Box 1286, 800 Scott Street, Wausau WI 54402. **Tel** (715)842-2101 ext. 209, FAX (715)848-9360. **5771**

WEED ABSTRACTS. (UK/0043-1729). CAB International Centre, Wallingford, Oxon OX10 8DE United Kingdom. **Tel** 44 491 832111, FAX 44 491 833508, telex 847964 (COMAGG G). **157**

WEEK IN GERMANY, THE. (US). German Information Center, 950 Third Avenue, New York NY 10022. **Tel** (212)888-9840, FAX (212)752-6691. **719**

WEEKLY JAPAN DIGEST, THE. (US/1060-2259). KA Communications, 5510 Columbia Pike, Suite 207, Arlington VA 22204. **Tel** (703)528-7570, (800)669-7570, FAX (703)528-8123. **4500**

WEEKLY OF BUSINESS AVIATION, THE. (US/0509-9528). McGraw Hill Publishing Company, Inc., 1221 Avenue of the Americas, New York NY 10020. **Tel** (212)512-6410, (800)525-5003, FAX (212)512-6111. **39**

WEEKLY RATES SUMMARY. (AT). Horan Wall & Walker Pty Ltd, 15-19 Prospect Street, POB 8, Surry Hills New South Wales 2010 Australia. **Tel** 02 331 6600, FAX 02 380 5533. **816**

WELDING REVIEW INTERNATIONAL. (UK/0262-642X). Argus Press Group, Queensway House, 2 Queensway Redhill, Surrey RH1 1QS England. **Tel** 011 44 737 768611, 011 44 737 761685, FAX 011 44 737 760510, telex 948669 TOPJNL G. **4029**

WEST VIRGINIA LAW REVIEW. (US/0043-3268). West Virginia Law Review, West Virginia University, College of Law, Morgantown WV 26506. **Tel** (304)293-5306. **3073**

WESTCHESTER COUNTY BUSINESS JOURNAL. (US/1057-686X). Westfair Communications Inc., 22 Sawmill River Road, Hawthorne NY 10532. **Tel** (914)347-5200, FAX (914)327-5576. **719**

WESTERN JOURNAL OF MEDICINE, THE. (US/0093-0415). California Medical Association, PO Box 7690, San Francisco CA 94120-5179. **Tel** (415)541-0900, FAX (415)882-5116. **3650**

WESTERN WEEKLY REPORTS. (CN/0049-7525). Carswell / Canada, 2075 Kennedy Road, Scarborough Ontario M1T 3V4 Canada. **Tel** (416)609-3800, (800)387-5164. **3074**

WESTPREUSSEN-JAHRBUCH. (GW/0511-8484). Westpreussen-Verlag Muenster, Norbertstr. 29,, 4400 Meunster, Germany. **Tel** 0251-523424, FAX 0251-533830. **2715**

WHEAT, BARLEY AND TRITICALE ABSTRACTS. (UK/0265-7880). CAB International Centre, Wallingford, Oxon OX10 8DE United Kingdom. **Tel** 44 491 832111, FAX 44 491 833508, telex 847964 (COMAGG G). **157**

WHEELING NEWS-REGISTER. (US). Ogden Newspaper, 1500 Main Street, Wheeling WV 26004. **Tel** (304)233-0100. **5765**

WHITTIER LAW REVIEW. (US/0195-7643). Whittier College / School of Law, 5353 West Third Street, Los Angeles CA 90020. **Tel** (213)938-3621 Ext. 232. **3075**

WHOLE EARTH REVIEW. (US/0749-5056). Whole Earth Review, 27 Gate Five Road, Sausalito CA 94965. **Tel** (415)332-1716, (800)783-4903, FAX (415)332-3110, (201)627-5872. **2495**

WHO'S WHO AMONG BLACK AMERICANS. (US/0362-5753). Gale Research Inc., 835 Penobscot Building, 645 Griswold Street, Detroit MI 48226. **Tel** (800)877-GALE, (313)961-2242, FAX (313)961-6083, (800)414-5043, telex TWX 810-221-7086. **436**

WHO'S WHO AMONG HISPANIC AMERICANS. (US/1052-7354). Gale Research Inc., 835 Penobscot Building, 645 Griswold Street, Detroit MI 48226. **Tel** (800)877-GALE, (313)961-2242, FAX (313)961-6083, (800)414-5043, telex TWX 810-221-7086. **2275**

WHO'S WHO IN AMERICA. (US/0083-9396). Marquis Who's Who, A Reed Reference Publishing Company, Part of Reed International PLC, 121 Chanlon Road, New Providence NJ 07974. **Tel** (908)464-6800, (800)521-8110, FAX (908)665-6688, telex 138 755. **436**

WHO'S WHO IN AMERICAN ART. (US/0000-0191). R R Bowker, A Reed Reference Publishing Company, Part of Reed International PLC, PO Box 31, 121 Chanlon Drive, New Providence NJ 07974. **Tel** (908)464-6800, (800)521-8110, FAX (908)665-6688, telex 138-755. **335**

WHO'S WHO IN AMERICAN EDUCATION (OWINGS MILLS, MD.). (US/1046-7203). Marquis Who's Who, A Reed Reference Publishing Company, Part of Reed International PLC, 121 Chanlon Road, New Providence NJ 07974. **Tel** (908)464-6800, (800)521-8110, FAX (908)665-6688, telex 138 755. **1791**

WHO'S WHO IN AMERICAN POLITICS. (US/0000-0205). R R Bowker, A Reed Reference Publishing Company, Part of Reed International PLC, PO Box 31, 121 Chanlon Drive, New Providence NJ 07974. **Tel** (908)464-6800, (800)521-8110, FAX (908)665-6688, telex 138-755. **436**

WICHITA BUSINESS JOURNAL. (US/0894-4032). Wichita Business Journal, 110 South Main, Suite 200, Wichita KS 67202. **Tel** (316)267-6406, FAX (316)267-8570. **720**

WICHITA COMMERCE. (US/1048-8782). Mercury Publishing Inc. / Wichita, KS, 2012 East Northern, Wichita KS 67216. **Tel** (316)524-3287. **857**

WICHITA EAGLE (1989), THE. (US/1046-3127). The Wichita Eagle-Beacon, Box 820, Attention: Mail Desk, Wichita KS 67201. **Tel** (800)825-6397. **5679**

WILSON BUSINESS ABSTRACTS. (US/1057-6533). H W Wilson Company, 950 University Avenue, Bronx NY 10452. **Tel** (800)367-6770, (718)588-8400, FAX (718)590-1617, telex 4990003 HWILSON. **735**

WIND ENERGY REPORT. (US/0162-8623). Wind Books, PO Box 4008, St Johnsbury VT 05819. **Tel** (802)748-5148, FAX (802)748-3286. **1960**

WINDOWS SOURCES. (US/1065-9641). Ziff-Davis, One Park Avenue, 5th Floor, New York NY 10016. **Tel** (212)503-3500, (609)786-8230. **1207**

WINDSOR STAR MICROFORM, THE. (CN/0839-2277). Windsor Star Ltd, 167 Ferry Street, Windsor Ontario N9A 4M5 Canada. **Tel** (519)255-5774, FAX (519)255-5515. **5798**

WINE BUSINESS INSIDER. (US/1057-8544). Wine Business Publications, 867 West Napa Street, Sonoma CA 95476. **Tel** (707)939-0822, FAX (707)939-0833. **2372**

WINES AND VINES. (US/0043-583X). Wines & Vines, 1800 Lincoln Avenue, San Rafael CA 94901. **Tel** (415)453-9700, FAX (415)453-2517. **2373**

WINSTON-SALEM JOURNAL. (US). Piedmont Publishing Company, PO Box 3159, Winston-Salem NC 27102-3159. **Tel** (910)727-7456. **5724**

WIRED (SAN FRANCISCO, CALIF.). (US/1059-1028). Wired Ventures Ltd., 544 2nd Street, 3rd Floor, San Francisco CA 94107. **Tel** (415)904-0660, FAX (415)904-0669. **1207**

WOMAN'S DAY. (US/0043-7336). Hachette Magazines Inc., 1633 Broadway, New York NY 10019. **Tel** (212)767-6000. **5569**

WOMEN'S SPORTS AND FITNESS. (US/8750-653X). Sports & Fitness Publishing Group, 2025 Pearl Street, Boulder CO 80302. **Tel** (303)440-5111. **4930**

WOOD BASED PANELS INTERNATIONAL. (UK/0040-7798). Benn Publications Ltd., Sovereign Way, Tonbridge TNQ 1RW England. **Tel** 011 44 732 364422, FAX 011 44 732 361534, telex 0732 95132 BENTON G. **2406**

WORKBENCH. (US/0043-8057). KC Publishing Inc., 700 West 47th Street, Suite 310, Kansas City MO 64112. **Tel** (816)531-5730, (800)444-0801. **635**

WORKING WOMAN. (US/0145-5761). Lang Communications, 230 Park Avenue, New York NY 10169. **Tel** (212)551-9500, FAX (212)599-4597. **5572**

WORLD ACCOUNTING REPORT; A MONTHLY BULLETIN ON DEVELOPMENTS IN INTERNATIONAL ACCOUNTING. (UK). Financial Times England, 8 16 Great New Street, London EC4A 3BN England. **Tel** 011 44 71 353 0305, 353 1040, FAX 011 44 353 0846. **753**

WORLD AGRICULTURAL ECONOMICS AND RURAL SOCIOLOGY ABSTRACTS. (UK/0043-8219). CAB International Centre, Wallingford, Oxon OX10 8DE United Kingdom. **Tel** 44 491 832111, FAX 44 491 833508, telex 847964 (COMAGG G). **157**

WORLD (ASHEVILLE, N.C.). (US/0888-157X). God's World Publications, Box 2330, Asheville NC 28802. **Tel** (704)253-8063, (800)951-5437. **2550**

WORLD BANK WATCH, THE. (US/1054-4313). American Banker, Concourse Level, 1 State Street Plaza, New York NY 10004. **Tel** (212)803-8200, (800)221-1809. **816**

WORLD CEMENT. (UK/0263-6050). Palladian Publications Ltd, The Old Forge, Surrey GU8 6DD England. **Tel** 011 44 252 703900. **631**

WORLD CERAMICS ABSTRACTS. (UK/0957-8897). Ceram Research Ltd., Queens Road, Penkhull, Stoke-On-Trent ST4 7LQ England. **Tel** 011 44 782 45431, FAX 011 44 782 412331. **2595**

WORLD COTTON SITUATION. (US). Department of Agriculture / Foreign Agricultural Service, 14th Street and Independence Avenue SW, Washington DC 20250-1000. **Tel** (202)720-3935, FAX (202)720-7729. **147**

WORLD GAS INTELLIGENCE : PIW'S GAS MARKET REPORT. (US). Petroleum Intelligence Weekly, 575 Broadway, 4th Floor, New York NY 10012-3230. **Tel** (212)941-5500, FAX (212)941-5509, telex 62371 PETROIN. **4282**

WORLD HEALTH. (SZ/0043-8502). World Health Organization, Distribution and Sales, 20 Avenue Appia, CH-1211 Geneva 27 Switzerland. **Tel** 011 41 22 7912111, FAX 011 41 22 7880401. **4808**

WORLD INSURANCE REPORT CORPORATE. (UK/0955-4823). Financial Times Business Information Ltd., Tower House, Southampton Street, London WC2E 7HA England. **Tel** 011 44 71 353 1040. **2896**

WORLD PUBLISHING MONITOR. (UK/0960-653X). Pira International, Randalls Road, Leatherhead, Surrey KT22 7RU England. **Tel** 011 44 372 376161, FAX 011 44 372 377526. **4822**

WORLD SURFACE COATINGS ABSTRACTS. (UK/0043-9088). The Paint Research Association, 8 Waldegrave Road, Teddington, Middlesex TW11 8LD England. **Tel** 11 44 81 977 4427, FAX 11 44 81 943 4705, telex 928720. **4226**

WORLD TAX REPORT. (UK). Financial Times Business Information Ltd., Tower House, Southampton Street, London WC2E 7HA England. **Tel** 011 44 71 353 1040. **4759**

WORLD TEXTILE ABSTRACTS. (UK/0043-9118). Elsevier Geo Abstracts, An Imprint of Elsevier Science Ltd., The Boulevard, Langford Lane, Kidlington, Oxford OX5 1GB United Kingdom. **Tel** 011 44 865 843000, 011 44 865 843699, FAX 011 44 865 843010. **5361**

WORLD TEXTILES. (UK). Elsevier Geo Abstracts, An Imprint of Elsevier Science Ltd., The Boulevard, Langford Lane, Kidlington, Oxford OX5 1GB United Kingdom. **Tel** 011 44 865 843000, 011 44 865 843699, FAX 011 44 865 843010. **5360**

WORLD TOBACCO. (UK/0043-9126). Argus Press Group, Queensway House, 2 Queensway Redhill, Surrey RH1 1QS England. **Tel** 011 44 737 768611, 011 44 737 761685, FAX 011 44 737 760510, telex 948669 TOPJNL G. **5374**

WORLD TRIBUNE. (US/0049-8165). World Tribune Press, PO Box 1427, Santa Monica CA 90406. **Tel** (310)451-8811. **4378**

WORLD

WORLD TUNNELLING & SUBSURFACE EXCAVATION. (UK). Mining Journal Ltd., 60 Worship Street, London EC2A 2HD England. **Tel** 011 44 071 377 2020, FAX 071 247 4100, telex 8952809 MINING G. **2153**

WORLD WASTES. (US/1064-8429). Argus Business, 6151 Powers Ferry Road, Atlanta GA 30339. **Tel** (404)995-2500, (800)233-3359. **2248**

WORLD WOOD. (US/0043-9258). Miller Freeman Inc., 600 Harrison Street, San Francisco CA 94107. **Tel** (415)905-2337, FAX (415)905-2240, telex 278273. **2406**

WORLDWIDE BROCHURES (PRINT ED.). (US/1053-9158). Travel Companions International, Inc., 1227 Kenneth Street, Detroit Lakes MN 56501. **Tel** (218)847-1694, (800)852-6752, FAX (218)847-7090. **5500**

WORLDWIDE FINANCIAL REGULATIONS. (UK). The Economist Intelligence Unit / New York, 111 West 57th Street, New York NY 10019. **Tel** (800)938-4685, (212)554-0600. **1641**

WWD. (US/0149-5380). Fairchild Publications Inc, 7 West 34th Street, 4th Floor, New York NY 10001-8191. **Tel** (212)630-4000. **1088**

YACHTING (NEW YORK, N.Y.). (US/0043-9940). Times Mirror Magazines, Two Park Avenue, New York NY 10016. **Tel** (212)779-5000. **597**

YALE ALUMNI MAGAZINE (1984). (US/8750-409X). Yale Alumni Publications Inc., 149 York Street, PO Box 1905, New Haven CT 06509. **Tel** (203)432-0645, FAX (203)432-0651. **1103**

YALE JOURNAL ON REGULATION. (US/0741-9457). Yale Law School, PO Box 208215, New Haven CT 06520. **Tel** (203)432-7652, FAX (203)432-2592. **3076**

YALE LAW JOURNAL, THE. (US/0044-0094). Yale Law Journal, 401 A Yale Station, New Haven CT 06520. **Tel** (203)432-1622, FAX (203)432-2592. **3077**

YOMIURI SHIMBUN (NEW YORK, N.Y.). (US/0890-8710). Yomuiri America, 19600 Magellin Drive, Torrance CA 90502. **Tel** (213)352-3900. **5641**

YOUTH MARKETS ALERT. (US/1041-7516). EPM Communications Inc., 488 East 18th Street, Brooklyn NY 11226. **Tel** (718)469-9330, FAX (718)469-7124. **938**

ZENTRALBLATT FUER MATHEMATIK UND IHRE GRENZGEBIETE. (GW/0044-4235). Springer-Verlag GmbH & Company KG, Heidelberger Platz 3, D 14197 Berlin Germany. **Tel** 011 49 30 8207223, FAX 011 49 30 8214091, telex 183 319 SPBLN D. **3543**

ZOOLOGICAL RECORD (LONDON). (UK/0144-3607). BioSciences Information Service, Biological Abstracts / BIOSIS, 2100 Arch Street, Philadelphia PA 19103-1399. **Tel** (800)523-4806 US, (215)587-4800 Pennsylvania and worldwide, FAX (215)587-2016, telex 831739. **5604**

ZOOLOGICAL RECORD ON CD. (US/1072-1983). BioSciences Information Service, Biological Abstracts / BIOSIS, 2100 Arch Street, Philadelphia PA 19103-1399. **Tel** (800)523-4806 US, (215)587-4800 Pennsylvania and worldwide, FAX (215)587-2016, telex 831739. **5604**

Serials Containing Book Reviews

The following index lists, in alphabetical order, all serials in the Directory that contain book reviews. The country of publication, ISSN, and book review quantity per issue or year are provided, when available. The page number in bold refers you to the complete serial listing in the Directory.

1/1 (SAN FRANCISCO, CALIF.). (US/8756-7717). **4098**

2 D DRAMA, DANCE. (UK/0261-6939). **383**

3 R, ROHRE, ROHRLEITUNGSBAU, ROHRLEITUNGSTRANSPORT. (GW/0340-3386). **2096**

4-H SOUNDER. (US/0740-848X). **1059**

9-1-1 MAGAZINE. (US/1040-7316). **Qty:** 30. **1103**

13TH MOON. (US/0094-3320). **Qty:** 3-5. **3357**

13TH STREET JOURNAL, THE. (US/1041-3111). **311**

19TH CENTURY MUSIC. (US/0148-2076). **4098**

20 DE MAYO. (US/0164-5234). **Qty:** 10. **5631**

24 IMAGES. (CN/0707-9389). **4062**

24HOURS (SANTA MONICA, CALIF.). (US/1047-451X). **2526**

50 PLUS (DURHAM, ONT.). (CN/0840-5395). **5177**

68 MICRO JOURNAL. (US/0194-5025). **1265**

1000 UND 1 BUCH. (AU). **1059**

1001 & 1 BUCH. (AU). **Qty:** 60. **3186**

1199 NEWS. (US/0012-6535). **1642**

A A R N NEWSLETTER. (CN/0001-0197). **Qty:** 4-6. **3849**

A.D.P.H.S.O. (FR/0339-8854). **Qty:** 4. **3775**

A-E BUSINESS REVIEW. (US). **Qty:** 2-4. **286**

A-E-C AUTOMATION NEWSLETTER. (US/0277-1659). **Qty:** 12. **286**

A.G.T. DOKUMENTATION. (GW). **2034**

A.I.I. JOURNAL. (AT/0314-8580). **2872**

A IDEIA. (PO). **4539**

A L'AUTRE, UNE. (CN/0824-8230). **3755**

A.M. AMMINISTRAZIONE & MANAGEMENT. (IT/1121-0788). **4623**

A.M.E. CHURCH REVIEW, THE. (US/0360-3725). **Qty:** 4-6. **4931**

A. MAGAZINE. (US/1070-9401). **Qty:** 20. **2253**

A.N.A. AUDIOLOGIA PROTESICA. (SP). **3885**

A.P.C. REVIEW. (AT/0313-380X). **1720**

A RAYONS OUVERTS. (CN/0835-8672). **3186**

A + T. (AT). **335**

A TO Z OF WHO IS WHO IN AUSTRALIA'S HISTORY, THE. (AT). **2668**

A.U.M.L.A. (AT/0001-2793). **3260**

A.W.R. BULLETIN. (AU/0001-2947). **5269**

A-Z OF UK MARKETING DATA, THE. (UK). **920**

AA FILES. (UK/0261-6823). **Qty:** 6. **287**

AAA, ARBEITEN AUS ANGLISTIK UND AMERIKANISTIK. (AU/0171-5410). **3260**

AAHS JOURNAL. (US/0882-9365). **3**

AAHS NEWSLETTER. (US/0300-6875). **3**

AAII JOURNAL, THE. (US/0192-3315). **890**

AANA JOURNAL. (US/0094-6354). **3849**

AAOHN NEWS / AMERICAN ASSOCIATION OF OCCUPATIONAL HEALTH NURSES, INC. (US/0746-620X). **3850**

AAPG BULLETIN. (US/0149-1423). **4248**

AAPG EXPLORER. (US/0195-2986). **1364**

AAR STUDIES IN RELIGION. (US/0145-2789). **4931**

AARDRIJKSKUNDE, DE. (BE). **2553**

AAS MICROFICHE SERIES. (US/0065-7417). **3**

AB (BRESCIA). (IT/0393-3369). **2159**

ABA/BNA LAWYERS' MANUAL ON PROFESSIONAL CONDUCT. CURRENT REPORTS. (US/0740-4050). **2926**

ABA JOURNAL. (US/0747-0088). **2926**

ABA JUVENILE & CHILD WELFARE LAW REPORTER. (US/0887-896X). **3119**

ABBEY CHRONICLE. (UK/0957-1248). **Qty:** 2 - 20. **3457**

ABBEY NEWSLETTER, THE. (US/0276-8291). **2478**

ABC AND D. ARCHITECT BUILDER CONTRACTOR AND DEVELOPER. (UK/0966-9647). **287**

ABC DER DEUTSCHEN WIRTSCHAFT. CD-ROM. (GW). **1596**

ABC TODAY. (US/1062-3698). **597**

ABEILLE DE FRANCE ET L'APICULTEUR, L'. (FR/0373-4625). **42**

ABERDEEN TIMES, THE. (US). **5674**

ABERDEEN UNIVERSITY REVIEW. (UK/0001-320X). **Qty:** 4-5. **1088**

ABHANDLUNGEN AUS DEM GEBIETE DER AUGENHEILKUNDE. (GW/0567-4921). **3871**

ABHANDLUNGEN - BAYERISCHE AKADEMIE DER WISSENSCHAFTEN, PHILOSOPHISCH-HISTORISCHE KLASSE. (GW). **1073**

ABHANDLUNGEN DER AKADEMIE DER WISSENSCHAFTEN IN GOTTINGEN. PHILOLOGISCH-HISTORISCHE KLASSE. (GW/0930-4304). **1073**

ABHANDLUNGEN DER GEOLOGISCHEN BUNDESANSTALT. (AU/0378-0864). **Qty:** 10. **1364**

ABHANDLUNGEN UND MATERIALIEN ZUR PUBLIZISTIK. (GW/0065-0323). **2609**

ABHATH. (MR). **5189**

ABHINAYA. (II). **3357**

ABILENE REFLECTOR-CHRONICLE. (US/0890-345X). **5668**

ABILITIES (CALGARY). (CN/0845-4469). **Qty:** 1-2. **4382**

ABILITY AND ENTERPRISE. (CN/0832-7890). **Qty:** 20 /yr. **5269**

ABIRA DIGEST. (US/0196-0652). **429**

ABITARE CON ARTE. (IT/1120-6772). **2898**

ABMS DIRECTORY OF CERTIFIED DERMATOLOGISTS. (US/0884-1489). **3717**

ABMS DIRECTORY OF CERTIFIED NEUROLOGICAL SURGEONS. (US/0882-2832). **3957**

ABMS DIRECTORY OF CERTIFIED OBSTETRICIANS AND GYNECOLOGISTS. (US/0884-1535). **3755**

ABMS DIRECTORY OF CERTIFIED UROLOGISTS. (US/0742-0374). **3987**

ABN CORRESPONDENCE. (GW/0001-0545). **4514**

ABNF JOURNAL, THE. (US/1046-7041). **Qty:** 6-8. **3850**

ABORIGINAL CHILD AT SCHOOL, THE. (AT). **1874**

ABORIGINAL HISTORY. (AT/0314-8769). **227**

ABORIGINAL LAW BULLETIN. (AT). **Qty:** 6-12. **2926**

ABORIGINAL NEWS (CANBERRA). (AT/0310-723X). **2253**

ABORIGINAL SCIENCE FICTION. (US/0895-3198). **Qty:** 60. **3357**

ABORTION RESEARCH NOTES. (US/0361-1116). **587**

ABOVE & BEYOND. (CN/0843-7815). **Qty:** 8. **2553**

ABR-NAHRAIN. (NE/0065-0382). **5013**

ABRIDGED CATHOLIC PERIODICAL AND LITERATURE INDEX, THE. (US/0737-3457). **5012**

ABSTRACT BULLETIN OF THE INSTITUTE OF PAPER CHEMISTRY. (US). **4240**

ABSTRACT REVIEW IN SCIENCE EXTENSION. (HU/0238-6178). **5079**

ABSTRACTA IRANICA. (IR/0240-8910). **406**

ABSTRACTS IN HUMAN-COMPUTER INTERACTION. (US/1042-0193). **1208**

ABSTRACTS IN MARYLAND ARCHEOLOGY. (US/0743-4251). **253**

ABSTRACTS OF AIT REPORTS AND PUBLICATIONS ON ENERGY. (TH/0857-6181). **1961**

ABSTRACTS OF SOVIET AND EAST EUROPEAN EMIGRE PERIODICAL LITERATURE. (US/0738-2707). **2513**

ABSTRACTS ON HYGIENE AND COMMUNICABLE DISEASES. (UK/0260-5511). **4809**

ABSTRACTS ON TROPICAL AGRICULTURE. (NE/0304-5951). **149**

ABU TECHNICAL REVIEW. (MY/0126-6209). **1125**

ABYA YALA NEWS. (US/1071-3182). **Qty: varies. 2253**

ACA NEWS (EDMONTON). (CN/0826-497X). **5177**

ACADEME (WASHINGTON. 1979). (US/0190-2946). **1806**

ACADEMIC AND LIBRARY COMPUTING. (US/1055-4769). **1265**

ACADEMIC LIBRARY BOOK REVIEW. (US/0894-993X). **4822**

ACADEMIC MEDICINE. (US/1040-2446). **1806**

ACADEMIC QUESTIONS. (US/0895-4852). **1807**

ACADEMIE ROYALE DES SCIENCES D'OUTRE-MER. CLASSE DES SCIENCES TECHNIQUES. (BE/0373-7063). **1722**

ACADEMY ACCENTS. (US/1071-376X). **Qty: 4. 4931**

ACADEMY BOOKMAN, THE. (US/0001-4249). **3654**

ACADEMY FORUM (NEW YORK), THE. (US/0192-1088). **3918**

ACADEMY OF MANAGEMENT REVIEW, THE. (US/0363-7425). **859**

ACADIAN GENEALOGY EXCHANGE. (US/0199-9591). **Qty: 15. 2436**

ACADIAN LETTERS. (CN/0705-5560). **958**

ACADIANA PROFILE. (US/0001-4397). **2254**

ACAROLOGIA. (FR/0044-586X). **5573**

ACCA DOCKET. (US/0895-9544). **3094**

ACCENT ON WORSHIP. (US/0276-2358). **4931**

ACCENT/REVIEWS. (US/0277-9102). **4931**

ACCESS BY DESIGN. (UK/0959-1591). **Qty: 6. 287**

ACCESS (SYRACUSE). (US/0095-5698). **2496**

ACCESS TO ENERGY. (US/0890-8265). **1930**

ACCESS USA NEWS. (US/1069-6784). **4383**

ACCESS (VICTORIA, AUSTRALIA). (AT/1030-0155). **1802**

ACCIAIO. (IT). **4461**

ACCIAIO INOSSIDABILE, L'. (IT/0515-2291). **3996**

ACCIDENT PREVENTION. (CN/0044-5878). **Qty: 4. 2858**

ACCIDENT PREVENTION MAGAZINE. (CN). **2858**

ACCION. (PY). **5189**

ACCORD (CALGARY). (CN/0226-7845). **2254**

ACCOUNTANCY IRELAND. (IE/0001-4699). **Qty: 12-20. 735**

ACCOUNTANCY (LONDON). (UK/0001-4664). **735**

ACCOUNTANCY SA. (SA/0258-7254). **735**

ACCOUNTANT (NAIROBI), THE. (KE/1010-4135). **735**

ACCOUNTANTS' JOURNAL. (PH/0001-4753). **735**

ACCOUNTANTS' JOURNAL (WELLINGTON). (NZ/0001-4745). **735**

ACCOUNTANT'S MAGAZINE, THE. (UK/0001-4761). **736**

ACCOUNTING AND FINANCE. (AT/0110-5159). **736**

ACCOUNTING AND FINANCE PARKVILLE. (AT/0810-5391). **Qty: varies. 736**

ACCOUNTING HISTORIANS JOURNAL, THE. (US/0148-4184). **737**

ACCOUNTING HISTORIANS NOTEBOOK, THE. (US/1075-1416). **737**

ACCOUNTING PRINCIPLES AND PRACTICES IN CANADA AND THE UNITED STATES OF AMERICA. (CN/0824-300X). **737**

ACCOUNTING WORLD. (UK/0953-2579). **Qty: 60. 738**

ACCREDITATION. (US/0099-0256). **1807**

ACCREDITED INSTITUTIONS OF POSTSECONDARY EDUCATION, PROGRAMS, CANDIDATES. (US/0270-1715). **1807**

ACE BULLETIN (LONDON, ENGLAND). (UK). **1722**

ACHAB ROMA. (IT/1120-849X). **3357**

ACHIEVEMENT (LONDON. 1969). (UK/0001-4907). **1596**

ACHPER NATIONAL JOURNAL, THE. (AT). **2595**

ACHTZEHNTE JAHRHUNDERT, DAS. (GW). **2672**

ACIS : JOURNAL OF THE ASSOCIATION FOR CONTEMPORARY IBERIAN STUDIES. (UK/0955-4270). **3260**

ACKNOWLEDGE : THE WINDOW LETTER. (US/1043-0768). **1283**

ACLU NEWS. (US). **Qty: 2-4. 4503**

ACORN JOURNAL. (AT/1031-1017). **Qty: 3-4. 3850**

ACORN JOURNAL : OFFICIAL JOURNAL OF THE AUSTRALIAN CONFEDERATION OF OPERATING ROOM NURSES. (AT/0156-3491). **3850**

ACORN (PLATTEVILLE), THE. (US/0274-8762). **1887**

ACOUSTICS LETTERS. (UK/0140-1599). **4461**

ACQUISITION/DIVESTITURE WEEKLY REPORT. (US/0279-4160). **636**

ACQUISITIONS LIBRARIAN, THE. (US/0896-3576). **3187**

ACROSS THE BOARD. (US/0147-1554). **636**

ACSM BULLETIN. (US/0747-9417). **2580**

ACT (NEW YORK, N.Y.), THE. (US/0885-6702). **335**

ACT (WHITING). (US/0001-5083). **4931**

ACTA ADRIATICA. (CI/0001-5113). **552**

ACTA ALIMENTARIA (BUDAPEST). (HU/0139-3006). **2325**

ACTA ANAESTHESIOLOGICA BELGICA. (BE/0001-5164). **3680**

ACTA ANAESTHESIOLOGICA ITALICA. (IT/0374-4965). **3680**

ACTA ANTIQUA ACADEMIAE SCIENTIARUM HUNGARICAE. (HU/0044-5975). **3261**

ACTA APPLICANDAE MATHEMATICAE. (NE/0167-8019). **3490**

ACTA ARCHAEOLOGICA ACADEMIAE SCIENTIARUM HUNGARICAE. (HU/0001-5210). **253**

ACTA BALTICA. (GW/0567-7289). **Qty: 3-5. 2672**

ACTA BELGICA HISTORIAE MEDICINAE : OFFICIAL JOURNAL OF THE BELGIAN ASSOCIATION FOR THE HISTORY OF MEDICINE. (BE). **Qty: 100. 3544**

ACTA BIO-MEDICA DE L'ATENEO PARMENSE. (IT/0392-4203). **3544**

ACTA BIOTECHNOLOGICA. (GW/0138-4988). **3685**

ACTA BIOTHEORETICA. (NE/0001-5342). **440**

ACTA BOTANICA INDICA. (II/0379-508X). **497**

ACTA BOTANICA ISLANDICA. (IC/0374-5066). **497**

ACTA BOTANICA NEERLANDICA. (NE/0044-5983). **497**

ACTA CARDIOLOGICA. (BE/0001-5385). **3697**

ACTA CARDIOLOGICA MEDITERRANEA. (IT/0392-9698). **3697**

ACTA CHIRURGICA AUSTRIACA. (AU/0001-544X). **3957**

ACTA CHIRURGICA BELGICA. (BE/0001-5458). **3957**

ACTA CHIRURGICA CATALONIAE. (SP/0211-660X). **3957**

ACTA CHIRURGICA ITALICA. (IT/0001-5466). **3957**

ACTA CIENCIA INDICA. CHEMISTRY. (II/0253-7338). **959**

ACTA CIENCIA INDICA. MATHEMATICS. (II/0970-0455). **3490**

ACTA CIENCIA INDICA. PHYSICS. (II/0253-732X). **4395**

ACTA CIENTIFICA VENEZOLANA. (VE/0001-5504). **5080**

ACTA CYBERNETICA. (HU/0324-721X). **1250**

ACTA CYTOLOGICA. (US/0001-5547). **531**

ACTA ENTOMOLOGICA BOHEMOSLOVACA. (CS/0001-5601). **5604**

ACTA ENTOMOLOGICA CHILENA. (CL/0716-5072). **5604**

ACTA FARMACEUTICA BONAERENSE. (AG/0326-2383). **4288**

ACTA GASTROENTEROLOGICA LATINOAMERICANA. (AG/0300-9033). **3794**

ACTA GEOGRAPHICA SINICA. (CC/0375-5444). **2553**

ACTA GEOLOGICA TAIWANICA. (CH/0065-1265). **1364**

ACTA HAEMATOLOGICA. (SZ/0001-5792). **3769**

ACTA HISTOCHEMICA. (GW/0065-1281). **531**

ACTA HISTORICA ACADEMIAE SCIENTIARUM HUNGARICAE. (HU/0001-5849). **2672**

ACTA HISTORICA ET ARCHAEOLOGICA MEDIAEVALIA. (SP). **253**

ACTA HOSPITALIA. (BE/0044-6009). **Qty: 50-60. 3775**

ACTA LITERARIA. (CL/0716-0909). **3337**

ACTA MATHEMATICA HUNGARICA. (HU/0236-5294). **3490**

ACTA MATHEMATICAE APPLICATAE SINICA. (CH/0168-9673). **3490**

ACTA MEDICA AUSTRIACA. (AU/0303-8173). **3794**

ACTA MEDICA AUXOLOGICA. (IT/0001-6004). **3544**

ACTA MEDICA (MEXICO). (MX/0001-5997). **3544**

ACTA MEDICA PHILIPPINA. (PH/0001-6071). **3544**

ACTA MICROBIOLOGICA HUNGARICA. (HU/0231-4622). **558**

ACTA MORPHOLOGICA HUNGARICA. (HU/0236-5391). **3545**

ACTA MOZARTIANA. (GW/0001-6233). **4098**

ACTA MUSICOLOGICA. (GW/0001-6241). **4098**

ACTA NATURALIA DE L'ATENEO PARMENSE. (IT/0392-419X). **5080**

ACTA NEUROCHIRURGICA. (AU/0001-6268). **3957**

ACTA NEUROLOGICA. (IT/0001-6276). **3825**

ACTA NEUROLOGICA BELGICA. (BE/0300-9009). **3825**

ACTA NEUROLOGICA SCANDINAVICA. (DK/0001-6314). **3825**

ACTA NEUROPATHOLOGICA. (GW/0001-6322). **3892**

ACTA OBSTETRICIA ET GYNECOLOGICA SCANDINAVICA. (SW/0001-6349). **3756**

ACTA ODONTOLOGICA SCANDINAVICA. (NO/0001-6357). **1315**

ACTA OPHTHALMOLOGICA. (DK/0001-639X). **3545**

ACTA ORIENTALIA ACADEMIAE SCIENTIARUM HUNGARICAE. (HU/0001-6446). **2644**

ACTA ORIENTALIA (KBENHAVN). (DK/0001-6438). **3261**

ACTA PAEDIATRICA HUNGARICA. (HU/0231-441X). **3899**

ACTA PAEDIATRICA LATINA. (IT/0365-5504). **3899**

ACTA PEDIATRICA ESPANOLA. (SP). **3899**

ACTA PHARMACEUTICA FENNICA. (FI/0356-3456). **4288**

ACTA PHONIATRICA LATINA. (IT/0392-3088). **3885**

ACTA PHYTOMEDICA. (GW/0065-1567). **497**

ACTA POLITICA. (NE/0001-6810). **4461**

ACTA PSIQUIATRICA Y PSICOLOGICA DE AMERICA LATINA. (AG/0001-6896). **Qty: 40. 3918**

ACTA PSYCHIATRICA BELGICA. (BE/0300-8967). **3919**

ACTA PSYCHIATRICA SCANDINAVICA. (DK/0001-690X). **3919**

ACTA RADIOLOGICA (STOCKHOLM, SWEDEN : 1987). (SW/0284-1851). **3938**

ACTA SLAVICA IAPONICA. (JA/0288-3503). **2672**

ACTA SOCIETATIS ZOOLOGICAE BOHEMOSLOVACAE. (XR/0862-5247). **5573**

ACTA SOCIOLOGICA. (DK/0001-6993). **5237**

ACTA STEREOLOGICA. (XV/0351-580X). **3491**

ACTA STOMATOLOGICA BELGICA. (BE/0001-7000). **1315**

ACTA TECHNICA / ACADEMIAE SCIENTIARUM HUNGARICAE. (HU/0001-7035). **5080**

ACTA THEOLOGICA DANICA. (NE/0065-1672). **4931**

ACTA TROPICA. (SZ/0001-706X). **3985**

ACTA UROLOGICA BELGICA. (BE/0001-7183). **3987**

ACTA ZOOLOGICA MEXICANA. (MX/0065-1737). **5573**

ACTA ZOOLOGICA (STOCKHOLM). (SW/0001-7272). **5574**

ACTAC. (AT). **1125**

ACTAS DE CULTURA Y ENSAYOS FOTOGRAFICOS F/8. (SP). **4366**

ACTES. / ASSOCIATION CANADIENNE DE LINGUISTIQUE APPLIQUEE. (CN). **3261**

ACTES DE LECTURE, LES. (FR/0758-1475). **Qty:** 4. **1722**

ACTINOMYCETES (1982), THE. (IT/0732-0574). **558**

ACTION. (UK). **4932**

ACTION COMMERCIALE, MANUELS. (FR/1142-7086). **920**

ACTION FOR CANADA'S CHILDREN. (CN/0229-2653). **1059**

ACTION FRANCAISE HEBDO, L'. (FR/1166-3286). **4461**

ACTION INFORMATION. (US). **4932**

ACTION INFORMATIQUE. (CN/0844-0883). **1235**

ACTION NATIONALE. (CN/0001-7469). **2526**

ACTION NETWORK. (AT/1032-9005). **5178**

ACTION POETIQUE. (FR). **3459**

ACTION VETERINAIRE, L'. (FR/0001-7523). **5501**

ACTION (WINNIPEG). (CN/0701-1547). **5550**

ACTIVE AND PASSIVE ELECTRONIC COMPONENTS. (US/0882-7516). **2034**

ACTIVE (BELCONNEN). (AT/1031-282X). **4881**

ACTIVE LIVING (TORONTO). (CN/1188-620X). **Qty:** varies. **2595**

ACTIVITE CINEMATOGRAPHIQUE FRANCAISE . / CNC, CENTRE NATIONAL DE LA CINEMATOGRAPHIE, L'. (FR/0397-8435). **4062**

ACTIVITE DES COURS ET TRIBUNAUX. STATISTIQUES DIVERSES. (BE). **3078**

ACTIVITIES, ADAPTATION & AGING. (US/0192-4788). **3748**

ACTS FACTS. (US/1070-9274). **Qty:** 2-3. **2858**

ACTUALIDAD BIBLIOGRAFICA DE FILOSOFIA Y TEOLOGIA. (SP/0211-4143). **4339**

ACTUALIDAD CIVIL. (SP/0213-7100). **3088**

ACTUALIDAD CIVIL. LEGISLACION. (SP/1130-7390). **3088**

ACTUALIDAD FINANCIERA. (SP/0213-6929). **2927**

ACTUALIDAD LABORAL LEGISLACION. (SP). **2927**

ACTUALIDAD PASTORAL. (AG). **Qty:** 20. **5022**

ACTUALIDAD PENAL. (SP/0213-6562). **2927**

ACTUALIDAD TRIBUTARIA. (SP). **2927**

ACTUALIDAD TRIBUTARIA LEGISLACION. (SP). **2927**

ACTUALIDAD Y DERECHO. (SP). **2927**

ACTUALITE CHIMIQUE, L'. (FR/0151-9093). **959**

ACTUALITE DIOCESAINE. (CN/0823-552X). **4932**

ACTUALITE ECONOMIQUE. (CN/0001-771X). **1589**

ACTUALITE IMMOBILIERE. (CN/0701-0516). **4833**

ACTUALITE (MONTREAL. 1976). (CN/0383-8714). **2513**

ACTUALITE RELIGIEUSE DANS LE MONDE (1983). (FR/0757-3529). **4932**

ACTUALITE VIE. (CN/0714-8828). **Qty:** occasionally. **2248**

ACTUALITES (PARIS). (FR/0183-5017). **821**

ACTUARY. (US/0001-7825). **2872**

ACTUEL CIDJ. (FR/0337-9566). **2484**

ACUCAA BULLETIN. (US). **383**

ACUPUNCTURE & ELECTRO-THERAPEUTICS RESEARCH. (UK/0360-1293). **3545**

ACUSTICA. (GW/0001-7884). **4452**

AD 2000. (AT/1031-8453). **Qty:** 35. **4932**

AD ASTRA (WASHINGTON, D.C.). (US/1041-102X). **3**

AD BUSINESS REPORT. (US/1061-1371). **753**

AD CYCLE NEWSLETTER. (AT). **1170**

AD : REVISTA INTERNACIONAL DE DECORACION, DISENO Y ARQUITECTURA. (SP). **2898**

AD VANTAGE (CANOGA PARK, CALIF.). (US/0886-6813). **753**

ADA IC NEWSLETTER. (US/1064-1505). **Qty:** 1-2. **1278**

ADAIR COUNTY REVIEW. (US/1063-9926). **2436**

ADAMS ADDENDA. (US/0739-0076). **Qty:** 4. **2436**

ADAPTED PHYSICAL ACTIVITY QUARTERLY. (US/0736-5829). **1854**

ADB QUARTERLY REVIEW. (PH/0115-074X). **768**

ADB REVIEW / ASIAN DEVELOPMENT BANK. (PH). **768**

ADC TIMES. (US/0749-2642). **2254**

ADDICTION. (UK/0965-2140). **1338**

ADDICTION LETTER, THE. (US/8756-405X). **1338**

ADDVANTAGE. (US/0149-4082). **4881**

ADE BULLETIN. (US/0001-0898). **Qty:** 9. **3261**

ADELAIDE REVIEW. (AT/0815-5992). **Qty:** 50. **312**

ADEM. (BE/0001-8171). **4098**

ADEPT REPORT, THE. (US/1053-2668). **1315**

ADFL BULLETIN. (US/0148-7639). **Qty:** 6. **3261**

ADHAESION. (GW/0001-8198). **1049**

ADHD NEWSLETTER. (US). **4571**

ADHESIVES AGE. (US/0001-821X). **2007**

ADHESIVES & SEALANTS NEWSLETTER. (US/0890-0884). **1049**

ADICCIONES PALMA DE MALLORCA. (SP/0214-4840). **1338**

ADIRONDAC. (US/0001-8236). **Qty:** 12. **4868**

ADIRONDACK DAILY ENTERPRISE. (US). **5707**

ADIRONDACK LIFE. (US/0001-8252). **2526**

ADJUNCT INFO. (US/1063-861X). **Qty:** 4. **1089**

ADLER MUSEUM BULLETIN. (SA). **4083**

ADLER (WIEN). (AU/0001-8260). **Qty:** 40. **2436**

ADMAP : THE JOURNAL OF ADVERTISING MEDIA ANALYSIS AND PLANNING. (UK). **Qty:** not fixed. **754**

ADMINISTRATION & MANAGEMENT SPECIAL INTEREST SECTION NEWSLETTER. (US/8756-629X). **859**

ADMINISTRATION (DUBLIN). (IE/0001-8325). **4624**

ADMINISTRATION ET GESTION. (CN/0704-9765). **4624**

ADMINISTRATION IN SOCIAL WORK. (US/0364-3107). **5270**

ADMINISTRATION PARIS. 1962. (FR/0223-5439). **4461**

ADMINISTRATION PUBLIQUE. (BE). **3091**

ADMINISTRATIVE ACTION. (US/0892-0923). **1807**

ADMINISTRATIVE SCIENCE QUARTERLY. (US/0001-8392). **4624**

ADOLESCENCE. (US/0001-8449). **1059**

ADOLESCENT MEDICINE (GLENVIEW). (US/0044-6335). **3899**

ADOPTED CHILD. (US/0745-3167). **Qty:** 1/yr. **2276**

ADOPTION & FOSTERING. (UK/0308-5759). **5270**

ADOPTION HELPER. (CN/1181-845X). **Qty:** 4. **5270**

ADOPTIVE FAMILIES. (US/1076-1020). **Qty:** 18-24. **5270**

ADRIFT. (US/0736-4970). **3358**

ADRIS NEWSLETTER. (US/0300-7022). **Qty:** 175 per year. **4932**

ADULT AND CONTINUING EDUCATION TODAY. (US/0001-8473). **1799**

ADULT BASIC EDUCATION (ATHENS, GA.). (US/1052-231X). **1799**

ADULT BIBLE STUDIES. (US/0149-8347). **5014**

ADULT EDUCATION QUARTERLY (AMERICAN ASSOCIATION FOR ADULT AND CONTINUING EDUCATION). (US/0741-7136). **1799**

ADULT FAITH RESOURCES NETWORKER. (US/0898-9729). **Qty:** (6-10). **4932**

ADULT VIDEO NEWS. (US/0883-7090). **4366**

ADULTS LEARNING. (UK/0955-2308). **1799**

ADVANCE (SPRINGFIELD). (US/0001-8589). **5054**

ADVANCED BATTERY TECHNOLOGY. (US/0001-8627). **Qty:** 6 per year. **2034**

ADVANCED MATERIALS (METUCHEN, N.J.). (US/0734-7146). **Qty:** 12-15. **2100**

ADVANCES. (US/0741-9783). **3546**

ADVANCES IN BRYOLOGY. (GW/0253-6226). **498**

ADVANCES IN CEMENT RESEARCH. (UK/0951-7197). **598**

ADVANCES IN CHROMATOGRAPHY (NEW YORK, N.Y.). (US/0065-2415). **1038**

ADVANCES IN COLLOID AND INTERFACE SCIENCE. (NE/0001-8686). **1049**

ADVANCES IN DESCRIPTIVE PSYCHOLOGY. (US/0276-9913). **4571**

ADVANCES IN NEUROIMMUNOLOGY. (UK/0960-5428). **3826**

ADVANCES IN ODONATOLOGY : PROCEEDINGS OF THE ... INTERNATIONAL SYMPOSIUM OF ODONATOLOGY. (NE). **5574**

ADVANCES IN WATER RESOURCES. (UK/0309-1708). **5528**

ADVANCES. THE JOURNAL OF MIND BODY HEALTH. (US). **Qty:** varies. **3546**

ADVENT CHRISTIAN WITNESS (1983), THE. (US/0741-4307). **5054**

ADVENTIST HERITAGE. (US/0360-389X). **Qty:** 2-5. **5054**

ADVERTISER (NEW MILFORD, CONN.). (US/0746-7605). **5644**

ADVERTISING AGE. (US/0001-8899). **754**

ADVERTISING LAW ANTHOLOGY. (US/0093-1985). **Qty:** 2. **2928**

ADVISER (WOLVERHAMPTON). (UK/0950-5458). **1293**

ADVISING QUARTERLY, THE. (US/0895-1101). **Qty:** varies. **1722**

ADVISOR (CHAMPAIGN, ILL.), THE. (US/0736-0436). **1722**

ADVOCATE (BATON ROUGE, LA.), THE. (US/1061-3978). **Qty:** 1,000 per year. **5683**

ADVOCATE (BOISE, IDAHO), THE. (US/0515-4987). **Qty:** 6. **2928**

ADVOCATE (DENVER, COLO.). (US/1040-2225). **4285**

ADVOCATE (LOS ANGELES, CALIF.), THE. (US/0001-8996). **2793**

ADVOCATE (MUNCIE, IND.), THE. (US/0279-7097). **Qty:** varies. **5228**

ADVOCATE (NEW YORK, N.Y.), THE. (US/0001-9003). **2254**

ADVOCATE (STAMFORD, CONN.), THE. (US/0279-5167). **5644**

ADVOCATE, THE. (US). **5656**

ADVOCATE (TORONTO. 1976). (CN/0229-5407). **4383**

ADVOCATE (VANCOUVER). (CN/0044-6416). **2928**

ADVOCATE'S ADVOCATE. (US). **2928**

ADVOKATEN (STOCKHOLM). (SW/0281-3505). **2928**

ADWEEK (EASTERN ED.). (US/0199-2864). **755**

ADWEEK. WESTERN ADVERTISING NEWS. (US/0199-4743). **755**

ADYAR LIBRARY BULLETIN, THE. (II/0001-902X). **5041**

AEB, ANALYTICAL & ENUMERATIVE BIBLIOGRAPHY. (US/0161-0376). **Qty:** 45. **3457**

AED (LONDON, ENGLAND). (UK/0144-8234). **1544**

AEG NEWS. (US/0899-5788). **Qty:** varies. **2018**

AEGEAN REVIEW. (US/0891-7213). **3358**

AEGIS (WASHINGTON, D.C.). (US/0883-0029). **4503**

AERIAL APPLICATOR, FARM, FOREST AND FIRE. (US). **158**

AERO REVUE. (SZ/0001-9186). **4**

AEROESPACIO (BUENOS AIRES, ARGENTINA). (AG). **Qty:** 10. **4**

AEROKURIER. (GW/0341-1281). **4**

AERONAUTICA & DIFESA. (IT/0394-820X). **4**

AERONAUTICAL JOURNAL, THE. (UK/0001-9240). **4**

AERONAUTIQUE ET L'ASTRONAUTIQUE, L'. (FR/0001-9275). **4**

AEROSOL SCIENCE AND TECHNOLOGY. (US/0278-6826). **1020**

AEROSPACE ENGINEERING (WARRENDALE, PA.). (US/0736-2536). **5**

AEROSPACE (LONDON, 1974). (UK/0305-0831). **5**

AEROSTATION (ALEXANDRIA, VA.). (US/0741-5974). **Qty:** 4-8. **6**

AESCLEPIUS (MARTINEZ, CALIF.). (US/1067-8646). **287**

AESE BLUELINE. (US/0846-7390). **Qty:** 4. **1351**

AETEI JOURNAL. (II). **Qty:** 12-15. **4932**

AETHLON (SAN DIEGO, CALIF.). (US/1048-3756). **4882**

AEU. ARCHIV. FUER ELEKTRONIK UND UBERTRAGUNGSTECHNIK. (GW/0001-1096). **1148**

AF, ARTE FOTOGRAFICO. (SP/0514-9193). **4366**

AFA WATCHBIRD, THE. (US/0199-543X). **4285**

AFAQ ARABIYAH. (IQ). **312**

AFAS QUARTERLY OF THE AUTOMOTIVE FINE ARTS SOCIETY. (US/0899-9171). **5403**

AFER. (KE/0250-4650). **4932**

AFERS INTERNACIONALS. (SP/0212-1786). **4461**

AFFAIRE DE COEUR. (US/0739-3881). **5073**

AFFIRMATIONS. (US/0162-8038). **4932**

AFGHAN HOUND REVIEW, THE. (US/8750-9776). **Qty:** 2-3. **4285**

AFGHANICA : THE AFGHANISTAN STUDIES NEWSLETTER. (UK). **Qty:** 2-3. **2841**

AFGHANISTAN FORUM. (US/0889-2148). **2484**

AFGHANISTAN REPORT. (PK). **4514**

AFGHANISTAN STUDIES JOURNAL. (US/1046-9834). **Qty:** 1-2 per year. **2501**

AFINIDAD. (SP/0001-9704). **960**

AFKAR INQUIRY. (UK/0267-842X). **4932**

AFRAID (ANAHEIM, CALIF.). (US/1050-0448). **Qty:** 60. **1596**

AFRICA DEVELOPMENT. (SG/0378-3006). **1544**

AFRICA FORUM. (UK/0961-1142). **2501**

AFRICA HEALTH. (UK/0141-9536). **3547**

AFRICA INSIDER. (US/0748-4356). **Qty:** 10. **4462**

AFRICA NEWS (DURHAM). (US/0191-6521). **Qty:** in every issue. **4514**

AFRICA NOW. (UK). **2497**

AFRICA QUARTERLY. (II/0001-9828). **Qty:** 1200/yr. **2636**

AFRICA REPORT. (US/0001-9836). **2636**

AFRICA (ROME, ITALY). (IT/0001-9747). **2636**

AFRICA THEOLOGICAL JOURNAL. (TZ/0253-9322). **4933**

AFRICA TODAY. (US/0001-9887). **Qty:** 40. **4462**

AFRICAN ADMINISTRATIVE STUDIES. (MR/0007-9588). **4625**

AFRICAN AFFAIRS (LONDON). (UK/0001-9909). **4462**

AFRICAN AMERICAN REVIEW. (US/1062-4783). **3358**

AFRICAN ARCHAEOLOGICAL REVIEW, THE. (UK/0263-0338). **253**

AFRICAN ARTS. (US/0001-9933). **312**

AFRICAN BOOK PUBLISHING RECORD, THE. (UK/0306-0322). **4811**

AFRICAN BUSINESS. (UK/0141-3929). **637**

AFRICAN CHRISTIAN STUDIES: THE JOURNAL OF THE FACULTY OF THEOLOGY OF THE CATHOLIC HIGHER INSTITUTE OF EASTERN AFRICA, NAIROBI. (KE). **4933**

AFRICAN COMMENTARY. (US/1045-2303). **2497**

AFRICAN COMMUNIST. (UK/0001-9976). **4539**

AFRICAN ECONOMIC HISTORY. (US/0145-2258). **1544**

AFRICAN ENTOMOLOGY. (SA/1021-3589). **Qty:** 10. **5605**

AFRICAN ENVIRONMENT. (SG/1010-5522). **2159**

AFRICAN HERALD, THE. (US/1069-8205). **Qty:** 4. **5746**

AFRICAN JOURNAL OF ECOLOGY. (UK/0141-6707). **2211**

AFRICAN JOURNAL OF SOCIOLOGY. (KE/1010-4127). **5238**

AFRICAN LAW BIBLIOGRAPHY. (BE). **2928**

AFRICAN MUSIC. (SA/0065-4019). **4098**

AFRICAN NOTES. (NR/0002-0087). **2254**

AFRICAN RED FAMILY. (UK). **4539**

AFRICAN RESEARCH & DOCUMENTATION. (UK/0305-862X). **3188**

AFRICAN REVIEW (DAR ES SALAAM, TANZANIA). (TZ/0002-0117). **5189**

AFRICAN SOCIAL STUDIES FORUM. (KE). **5189**

AFRICAN STATISTICAL YEARBOOK. ANNUAIRE STATISTIQUE POUR L'AFRIQUE. (ET). **5320**

AFRICAN STUDIES BY SOVIET SCHOLARS. (RU). **4539**

AFRICAN STUDIES (JOHANNESBURG). (SA/0002-0184). **227**

AFRICAN STUDIES REVIEW. (US/0002-0206). **2498**

AFRICAN TECHNOLOGY FORUM. (US/1050-0014). **Qty:** 8. **5081**

AFRICAN TIMES (LONDON, ENGLAND : 1984). (UK). **2484**

AFRICAN URBAN QUARTERLY. (US/0747-6108). **2813**

AFRICAN URBAN STUDIES (EAST LANSING, MICH.). (US/0736-6760). **2813**

AFRICAN WILDLIFE UPDATE. (US/1058-9805). **Qty:** 6. **4868**

AFRICAN WOMAN. (UK/0953-9816). **5550**

AFRICAN WORLD NEWS, THE. (US/0747-8879). **2498**

AFRICANA NOTES AND NEWS. (SA/0002-032X). **2498**

AFRICANA RESEARCH BULLETIN. (SL/0259-9651). **5189**

AFRICANUS. (SA). **4462**

AFRIKA JAHRBUCH. (GW). **4462**

AFRIKA-POST. (GW/0002-0389). **4515**

AFRIKA UND UBERSEE. (GW/0002-0427). **3262**

AFRIKASPECTRUM. (GW/0002-0397). **5189**

AFRIQUE AGRICULTURE. (FR/0337-9515). **45**

AFRIQUE ET L'ASIE MODERNES, L'. (FR/0399-0370). **2637**

AFRIQUE HISTOIRE U.S. (US/0741-2592). **2637**

AFRIQUE MEDECINE ET SANTE. (FR). **4763**

AFRO-AMERICANS IN NEW YORK LIFE AND HISTORY. (US/0364-2437). **Qty:** 6 per year. **2254**

AFRO-ASIAN JOURNAL OF NEMATOLOGY. (UK/0963-6420). **Qty:** 1. **5574**

AFRO-HISPANIC REVIEW. (US/0278-8969). **3262**

AFRO SCHOLAR NEWSLETTER. (US/0894-0762). **5189**

AFRO TIMES (BROOKLYN, N.Y.). (US/1044-7199). **5713**

AFSM INTERNATIONAL. (US/1049-2135). **1235**

AFTERIMAGE. (US/0300-7472). **4366**

AFTERLOSS (RANCHO MIRAGE, CALIF.). (US/1044-0534). **4572**

AFTERMATH. (US/0737-1381). **4856**

AFZ. ALLGEMEINE FISCHWIRTSCHAFTSZEITUNG. (GW/0001-1258). **2293**

AG ALERT. (US/0161-5408). **45**

AGACCESS. (US/8756-7733). **45**

AGADA. (US/0740-2392). **5045**

AGAINST THE CURRENT. (US/0739-4853). **Qty:** 10-15. **4462**

AGAINST THE GRAIN (CHARLESTON, S.C.). (US/1043-2094). **Qty:** 5-15. **3188**

AGAPE MAGAZINE. (BE). **4933**

AGATE. ALBERTA GIFTED AND TALENTED EDUCATION. (CN/0833-0603). **1874**

AGBIOTECH NEWS AND INFORMATION. (UK/0954-9897). **149**

AGE AND AGEING. (UK/0002-0729). **3748**

AGE & NUTRITION. (FR). **4186**

AGE OF JOHNSON, THE. (US/0884-5816). **3358**

AGE (OMAHA). (US/0161-9152). **Qty:** Varies. **3748**

AGEING AND SOCIETY. (UK/0144-686X). **3748**

AGEING INTERNATIONAL. (US/0163-5158). **5270**

AGENCY SALES. (US/0749-2332). **921**

AGENDA. (US). **2917**

AGENDA, L'. (IT). **Qty:** 8-10. **3547**

AGENDA (LONDON). (UK/0002-0796). **3459**

AGENDA PARKVILLE. (AT/1033-1115). **Qty:** 5. **312**

AGENTS AND ACTIONS. (SZ/0065-4299). **4289**

AGENZIA VIAGGI. (IT). **5460**

AGGRESSIVE BEHAVIOR. (US/0096-140X). **4572**

AGID NEWS. (TH). **1351**

AGING. (UK/0268-1544). **3749**

AGING NETWORK NEWS. (US/0742-3438). **5178**

AGIR (MONTREAL). (CN/0847-9798). **Qty:** 1-2. **3123**

AGNI (BOSTON, MASS.). (US/1046-218X). **Qty:** 10. **3358**

AGON. (UY). **3358**

AGORA, PAPELES DE FILOSOFIA. (SP). **4339**

AGORA PARIS. 1986. (FR/0984-4783). **2249**

AGORA (RALEIGH, N.C.). (US/0891-3293). **1089**

AGORA (TOKYO JAPAN : 1972). (JA). **5550**

AGRARBERICHTERSTATTUNG. HEFT 4, VIEHHALTUNG. (GW). **149**

AGRARISCHE RUNDSCHAU. (AU/0002-0710). **46**

AGRARRECHT. (GW/0340-840X). **2928**

AGRARTECHNIK INTERNATIONAL. (GW). **158**

AGRARWIRTSCHAFT. (GW/0002-1121). **637**

AGREKON. (SA/0303-1853). **46**

AGRI-BOOK MAGAZINE. TOP CROP MANAGER. (CN). **47**

AGRI FINANCE. (US/0002-1164). **768**

AGRI MARKETING. (US/0002-1180). **47**

AGRI-SERVICE INTERNATIONAL. (BE/1021-4240). **47**

AGRI-TIMES NORTHWEST. (US/0887-2910). **48**

AGRIBIOLOGICAL RESEARCH. (GW/0938-0337). **48**

AGRICOMP. (US). **48**

AGRICONTACT ED. FRANCAISE. (BE/0770-285X). **Qty:** 150. **48**

AGRICULTURA (MADRID, SPAIN). (SP/0002-1334). **49**

AGRICULTURA TECNICA. (CL/0365-2807). **49**

AGRICULTURAL AND VETERINARY CHEMICALS. (UK/0567-431X). **960**

AGRICULTURAL AVIATION (WASHINGTON, D.C.). (US/0745-4864). **6**

AGRICULTURAL BANKER. (II). **769**

AGRICULTURAL CREDIT LETTER, THE. (US/0887-7521). **1460**

AGRICULTURAL EDUCATION MAGAZINE, THE. (US/0732-4677). **50**

AGRICULTURAL ENGINEER, THE. (UK/0308-5732). **50**

AGRICULTURAL ENGINEERING. (US/0002-1458). **1964**

AGRICULTURAL ENGINEERING ABSTRACTS. (UK/0308-8863). **150**

AGRICULTURAL ENGINEERING AUSTRALIA. (AT/0044-6807). **50**

AGRICULTURAL HISTORY. (US/0002-1482). **50**

AGRICULTURAL HISTORY REVIEW, THE. (UK/0002-1490). **50**

AGRICULTURAL LIBRARIES INFORMATION NOTES. (US/0095-2699). **3188**

AGRICULTURAL PROGRESS. (UK/0065-4493). **51**

AGRICULTURAL SITUATION IN INDIA. (II/0002-1679). **52**

AGRICULTURAL SYSTEMS. (UK/0308-521X). **52**

AGRICULTURE AND HUMAN VALUES. (US/0889-048X). **Qty:** 10/yr. **53**

AGRICULTURE ET DEVELOPPEMENT. (FR). **Qty:** 4. **53**

AGRICULTURE INTERNATIONAL. (UK/0269-2457). **54**

AGRICULTURE (MONTREAL). (CN/0002-1687). **54**

AGRISCIENCE (OTTAWA). (CN/0840-8289). **54**

AGRITROP [ENGLSIH ED.]. (FR). **54**

AGRO SUR. (CL/0304-8802). **55**

AGROCHIMICA. (IT/0002-1857). **55**

AGROCIENCIA. (MX/0568-3025). **55**

AGROFORESTRY SYSTEMS. (NE/0167-4366). **2211**

AGROKEMIA ES TALAJTAN. (HU/0002-1873). **56**

AGRONOMIA TROPICAL. (VE/0002-192X). **56**

AGRONOMIE. (FR/0249-5627). **56**

AGRONOMY NEWS. (US/0568-3106). **162**

AGROPECUARIA CATARINENSE. (BL/0103-0779). **Qty:** 4/yr. **56**

AGROTECHNOLOGY TRANSFER. (US/0883-8631). **57**

AGROW. (UK/0268-313X). **57**

AHFAD JOURNAL, THE. (SJ/0255-4070). **Qty: 8-10.** **5550**

AI DIRECTORY. (US/1050-7965). **Qty: 8-15.** **1210**

AI MAGAZINE. (US/0738-4602). **Qty: 8-15.** **1211**

AI TODAY. (US/0893-6552). **1211**

AI TRENDS (MONTHLY). (US/8756-7687). **1211**

AIBC BULLETIN. (US/1040-6018). **1419**

AICHE JOURNAL. (US/0001-1541). **2007**

AIDA PARKER NEWSLETTER. (SA). **Qty: varies.** **4515**

AIDS ACTION. (UK/0953-0096). **3663**

AIDS ANALYSIS AFRICA. (SA/1016-4731). **3663**

AIDS & PUBLIC POLICY JOURNAL. (US/0887-3852). **3663**

AIDS & SOCIETY. (US/1055-0380). **3663**

AIDS BULLETIN TYGERBERG. (SA/1019-8334). **Qty: 4.** **3711**

AIDS CARE. (UK/0954-0121). **3663**

AIDS EDUCATION. (US/0895-8882). **3663**

AIDS EDUCATION AND PREVENTION. (US/0899-9546). **4764**

AIDS UPDATE (RESTON, VA.). (US/1042-4784). **3665**

AIGA JOURNAL OF GRAPHIC DESIGN. (US/0736-5322). **376**

AIM FOR RACIAL HARMONY & PEACE. (US/0194-2069). **5238**

AIMER ET SERVIR. (FR). **3547**

AIPE FACILITIES. (US/1054-7541). **1964**

AIR AND BUSINESS TRAVEL NEWS TRAVEL INDUSTRY DIRECTORY. (UK). **Qty: 20.** **5460**

AIR AND SPACE LAW. (NE). **6**

AIR & SPACE SMITHSONIAN. (US/0886-2257). **6**

AIR CARGO WORLD. (US/0745-5100). **5375**

AIR CONDITIONING, HEATING & REFRIGERATION NEWS. (US/0002-2276). **2602**

AIR FAN. (FR/0223-0038). **4033**

AIR FORCE MAGAZINE. (US/0730-6784). **4034**

AIR FORCE TIMES. (US/0002-2403). **4034**

AIR FORCES MONTHLY. (UK). **7**

AIR INTERNATIONAL. (UK/0306-5634). **7**

AIR LINE PILOT. (US/0002-242X). **7**

AIR NAVIGATION PLAN, CARRIBBEAN AND SOUTH AMERICAN REGIONS / PLAN DE NAVIGATION AERIENNE, REGIONS CARAIBES ET AMERIQUE DU SUD. PLAN DE NAVEGACION AEREA, REGIONES DEL CARIBE Y DE SUDAMERICA. (CN). **7**

AIR PICTORIAL. (UK/0002-2462). **8**

AIR POWER HISTORY. (US/1044-016X). **Qty: 50.** **8**

AIR PROGRESS. (US/0002-2500). **8**

AIR UNIVERSITY LIBRARY INDEX TO MILITARY PERIODICALS. (US/0002-2586). **4061**

AIRFAIR. (US/0044-7005). **Qty: 1-10.** **5460**

AIRFINANCE JOURNAL. (UK/0143-2257). **9**

AIRFORCE. (CN/0704-6804). **Qty: 20.** **9**

AIRPOST JOURNAL, THE. (US/0739-0939). **1144**

AIRPOWER JOURNAL. (US/0897-0823). **4034**

AISLE VIEW : THE NEWSLETTER OF TIPS, TACTICS AND HOW-TO'S FOR SMALL EXHIBITORS. (US). **921**

AIT. ARCHITEKTUR, INNENARCHITEKTUR, TECHNISCHER AUSBAU. (GW/0173-8046). **287**

AITIA. (US/0731-5880). **4339**

AITIM : BOLETIN DE INFORMACION TECNICA / ASOCIACION DE INVESTIGACION TECNICA DE LAS INDUSTRIAS DE LA MADERNA Y CORCHO. (PO). **2374**

AJAKIRI. (CN/0384-8469). **2254**

AJIA KEIZAI. (JA/0002-2942). **1461**

AJL NEWSLETTER. (US/0747-6175). **3188**

AJR INFORMATION. (UK). **4515**

AJS REVIEW. (US/0364-0094). **5045**

AKADEMIAJ STUDOJ. (CN/0824-3050). **3262**

AKIKI, THE. (US/0091-1607). **2436**

AKRON BUGLE. (US). **5713**

AKTIENGESELLSCHAFT, DIE. (GW/0002-3752). **1596**

AKTUELLE SKATTETALL. (NO/0332-8422). **4708**

AKUSTICESKIJ ZURNAL. (RU/0320-7919). **4452**

AKWE:KON JOURNAL. (US). **Qty: varies.** **2717**

AKWESASNE NOTES. (US/0002-3949). **5268**

AL-AALAM. (UK). **2501**

AL-AMN WA-AL-HAYAH. (SU). **3156**

AL-BALAGH. (KU). **5041**

AL-BAYADIR AL-SIYASI. (IS). **2525**

AL-DARAH. (SU). **2645**

AL-DIRASAT AL-ISLAMIYAH. (PK/0002-399X). **5041**

AL-FIHRIST. (LE). **407**

AL-HILAL. (CN). **2767**

AL-'ILM WA-AL-TIKNULUGIYA. (LE/1013-2392). **5082**

AL-IQTISADI AL-KUWAYTI. (KU). **1528**

AL-JAWHARAH. (QA). **5550**

AL-KITAB AL-MAGHRIBI / TUSDIRUHA AL-JAMIYAH AL-MAGHRIBIYAH LIL-TALIF WA-AL-TARJAMAH WA-AL-NASHR. (MR). **407**

AL-KJHALI AL-IQTISADI. (KU). **637**

AL-MAJALLAH AL-ARABIYAH LIL-DIRASAT AL-LUGHAWIYAH. (SJ). **3262**

AL-MASKUKAT. (IQ). **2779**

AL-MAWQIF AL-ADABI. (SY). **3358**

AL-MUJTAMA AL-MADANI WA-AL-TAHAWWUL AL-DIMUQRATI FI AL-WATAN AL-ARABI. (UA). **4625**

AL-MUSAFIR AL-ARABI. (UK/0267-0194). **5460**

AL-MUSTAHLIK. (JO). **1293**

AL-MUSTAQBAL. (US/0153-3401). **2525**

AL-NAHDAH. (MY/0127-2284). **5041**

AL-NASHIR AL-ARABI. (LY). **4811**

AL-QANTARA (MADRID). (SP/0211-3589). **2672**

AL-RAID / YUSDIRUHA AL-MARKAZ AL-ISLAMI FI AKHIN (MASJID BILAL) WA-ITTIHAD AL-TALABAH AL-MUSLIMIN FI URUBBA. (GW). **5041**

AL-RIYADAH WA-AL-SHABAB. (TS). **4882**

AL-SHARQ. (SU). **2767**

AL-TAMWIL WA-AL-TANMIYAH. (US/0250-7455). **4708**

AL-TAWTHIQ AL-ILAMI / TASDURU AN MARKAZ AL-TAWTHIQ AL-ILAMI LI-DUWAL AL-KHALIJ AL-ARABI. (IQ). **3188**

AL-THAQAFAH AL-AJNABIYAH. (IQ). **3359**

AL-TIJARAH. (TS). **1545**

AL-YARMUK. (JO). **2484**

AL-ZIMAM WA-AL-MISAHAT AL-MUNZARIAH FI JUMHURIYAT MISR AL-ARABIYAH / AL-JIHAZ AL-MARKAZI LIL-TABIAH AL-AMMAH WA-AL-IHSA. (UA). **1461**

ALA BULLETIN : A PUBLICATION OF THE AFRICAN LITERATURE ASSOCIATION. (CN/0146-4965). **3359**

ALABAMA ARCHITECTURE. (US). **287**

ALABAMA BAPTIST HISTORIAN, THE. (US/0002-4147). **5054**

ALABAMA BAPTIST, THE. (US/0738-7741). **5625**

ALABAMA FAMILY HISTORY AND GENEALOGY NEWS (1984). (US). **2436**

ALABAMA JOURNAL, THE. (US/0745-323X). **5625**

ALABAMA LAW REVIEW. (US/0002-4279). **2929**

ALABAMA LAWYER, THE. (US/0002-4287). **2929**

ALABAMA LITERARY REVIEW. (US/0890-1554). **Qty: 10 per year.** **3359**

ALABAMA MEDICINE. (US/0738-4947). **3547**

ALABAMA MUNICIPAL JOURNAL, THE. (US/0002-4309). **Qty: 1-2.** **4625**

ALABAMA PURCHASOR. (US/0002-4325). **948**

ALABAMA REVIEW, THE. (US/0002-4341). **2718**

ALADDIN'S WINDOW. (US/1070-6836). **3994**

ALALUZ. (US/0044-7064). **3359**

ALAM AL-ISTITHMAR AL-ARABI. ARAB BUSINESS REPORT. (NE). **1545**

ALAM SEKITAR. (MY/0126-7280). **2223**

ALAM TUB AL-ASSNAN. (GW). **1315**

ALAMANCE GENEALOGIST. (US). **Qty: 12.** **2436**

ALASKA ALMANAC : FACTS ABOUT ALASKA, THE. (US). **2527**

ALASKA (ANCHORAGE, ALASKA). (US/0002-4562). **4868**

ALASKA FISHERMAN'S JOURNAL. (US/0164-8330). **2293**

ALASKA HISTORY (ANCHORAGE, ALASKA). (US/0890-6149). **2718**

ALASKA LAND & HOME MAGAZINE. (US). **2484**

ALASKA LAW REVIEW. (US/0883-0568). **2929**

ALASKA MEDICINE. (US/0002-4538). **3547**

ALASKA PETROLEUM & INDUSTRIAL DIRECTORY. (US/0065-5813). **4249**

ALASKA QUARTERLY REVIEW. (US/0737-268X). **3359**

ALASKAN EPIPHANY. (US/0742-7735). **Qty: 1-5.** **5054**

ALASKA'S INSIDE PASSAGE TRAVELER : SEE MORE, SPEND LESS!. (US/1046-5871). **5460**

ALAUDA. (FR/0002-4619). **Qty: 4.** **5614**

ALBA DE AMERICA. (US/0888-3181). **3359**

ALBA : REVISTA DE POESIA. (SP). **3459**

ALBANIAN CATHOLIC BULLETIN. (US/0272-7250). **5022**

ALBANY DAILY HERALD (ALBANY, GA.). (US). **5652**

ALBANY LAW REVIEW. (US/0002-4678). **2929**

ALBANY STATE COLLEGE JOURNAL OF ARTS AND SCIENCES. (US/0199-9826). **1808**

ALBERTA ARCHAEOLOGICAL REVIEW, THE. (CN/0701-1776). **Qty: varies.** **253**

ALBERTA BUSINESS WHO'S WHO & DIRECTORY. (CN/0827-5750). **429**

ALBERTA (EDMONTON). (CN/0843-9931). **312**

ALBERTA FAMILY HISTORIES SOCIETY QUARTERLY. (CN/0228-9288). **2436**

ALBERTA HISTORY. (CN/0316-1552). **2718**

ALBERTA JOURNAL OF EDUCATIONAL RESEARCH. (CN/0002-4805). **1723**

ALBERTA LAW REVIEW. (CN/0002-4821). **2929**

ALBERTA LEGAL TELEPHONE DIRECTORY. (CN/0823-2350). **3138**

ALBERTA MODERN LANGUAGE JOURNAL. (CN/0318-5176). **3263**

ALBERTA PERSPECTIVE. (CN/0713-8067). **5271**

ALBERTA REPORT. (CN/0225-0519). **2527**

ALBERTA SCIENCE EDUCATION JOURNAL. (CN/0701-1024). **5082**

ALBERTA WILD ROSE QUARTER HORSE JOURNAL. (CN/0227-0579). **2796**

ALBION. (UK). **4563**

ALBION (BOONE). (US/0095-1390). **Qty: 200-250 per year.** **2672**

ALBUM NETWORK, THE. (US/0739-1641). **4099**

ALCOHOL (FAYETTEVILLE, N.Y.). (US/0741-8329). **1339**

ALCOHOLIC BEVERAGE EXECUTIVES' NEWSLETTER INTERNATIONAL. (US/0889-3519). **2363**

ALCOHOLISM TREATMENT QUARTERLY. (US/0734-7324). **1340**

ALCOLOGIA. (IT/0394-9826). **1340**

ALCOOL OU SANTE PARIS. (FR/0002-5054). **1340**

ALCUIN. (UK). **5055**

ALDRICHIMICA ACTA. (US/0002-5100). **960**

ALDRING OG ELDRE. (NO/0801-9991). **5178**

ALE SEFER. (IS). **5045**

ALEPH (MANIZALES, COLOMBIA). (CK/0120-0216). **3359**

ALERGIA (MEXICO). (MX/0002-5151). **3665**

ALEXANDER PARIS REPORT, THE. (US/0747-7813). **890**

ALEXANDRIA DAILY TOWN TALK, THE. (US). **5683**

ALEXANDRIA ECHO PRESS. (US). **5694**

ALEXANOR. (FR/0002-5208). **5574**

ALFA. (BL/0002-5216). **3359**

ALFA OWNER. (US/0364-930X). **5403**

ALFOLD. (HU/0401-3174). **3359**

ALFRED HITCHCOCK'S MYSTERY MAGAZINE. (US/0002-5224). **5074**

ALFRED SUN, THE. (US). **5713**

ALGEMEEN NEDERLANDS TIJDSCHRIFT VOOR WIJSBEGEERTE. (NE/0002-5275). **4340**

ALGEMEINER JOURNAL, DER. (US). **5713**

ALGONQUIAN AND IROQUOIAN LINGUISTICS. (CN/0711-382X). **3263**

ALI-ABA CLE REVIEW. (US/0044-7560). Qty: 6 per year. **1808**

ALI ANTICHE. (IT/0394-6185). Qty: 20. **11**

ALI REPORTER, THE. (US/0164-5757). **2931**

ALIGARH JOURNAL OF ENGLISH STUDIES, THE. (II/0258-0365). **3359**

ALIMENTA. (SZ/0002-5402). **2326**

ALIMENTALEX (MADRID). (SP/0214-803X). **2326**

ALIMENTARIA. (SP/0300-5755). **4764**

ALIMENTAZIONE, NUTRIZIONE, METABOLISMO (1979). (IT/0392-7512). **4187**

ALIRAN MONTHLY. (MY/0127-5127). **5190**

ALISO. (US/0065-6275). **498**

ALIVE (VANCOUVER). (CN/0228-586X). **4187**

ALKALINE PAPER ADVOCATE. (US/0897-2524). **4232**

ALKALMAZOTT MATEMATIKAI LAPEK. (HU/0133-3399). **3492**

ALL-CANADA WEEKLY SUMMARIES. (CN/0705-1360). **3088**

ALLAM- ES JOGTUDOMANY. (HU/0002-564X). **2931**

ALLAMI GAZDASAG. (HU/0587-4815). **57**

ALLATTANI KOEZLEMENYEK. (HU/0002-5658). **5574**

ALLE HENS. (NE/0002-5674). **4174**

ALLEGORICA. (US/0363-2377). **3359**

ALLEGRO (NEW YORK, N.Y.). (US/0002-5704). **4099**

ALLERGIE UND IMMUNOLOGIE. (GW/0323-4398). **3665**

ALLERGOLOGIA ET IMMUNOPATHOLOGIA. (SP/0301-0546). **3665**

ALLERGOLOGIE. (GW/0344-5062). **3665**

ALLERGY ALERT. (CN/0824-1333). **3665**

ALLES UBER WEIN. (GW/0175-8314). Qty: 60. **2363**

ALLGEMEINE FORST UND JAGDZEITUNG. (GW/0002-5852). **2374**

ALLGEMEINE SCHWEIZERISCHE MILITARZEITSCHRIFT. (SZ). **4034**

ALLGEMEINE ZEITSCHRIFT FUER PHILOSOPHIE. (GW). **4340**

ALLIANCE. (IE). **5803**

ALLIANCE LIFE. (US/1040-6794). Qty: 2. **4933**

ALLIANCE REVIEW (ALLIANCE, OHIO : 1924). (US). **5726**

ALLIANZ REPORT. (GW/0943-4569). **2109**

ALLIED HEALTH EDUCATION NEWSLETTER. (US). **3548**

ALLTAG, DER. (SZ). **2513**

ALLUMINIO E LEGHE. (IT). **3997**

ALMANAC OF FAMOUS PEOPLE. (US/1040-127X). **429**

ALMANAC OF THE 50 STATES. (US/0887-0519). **1923**

ALMANACH MODERNE. (CN/0315-2898). **2484**

ALMANACH POPULAIRE CATHOLIQUE. (CN/0821-4034). **5023**

ALMANAKH PANORAMA. (US/0889-0730). Qty: 5-6. **5632**

AL'MANAKH VYDAVNYTSTVA "TRYZUB". (CN/0824-5908). **4812**

ALMANAQUE PUERTORRIQUENO. (PR). **2527**

ALMOST FREE RECIPES AND COOKBOOKS UPDATES. (US/0736-170X). **2788**

ALOE. (SA). **498**

ALOHA (HONOLULU). (US/0147-5436). **5460**

ALPES, LES. (SZ). **5461**

ALPHA BEAT SOUP. (CN/0838-391X). **3359**

ALPHA OMEGAN. (US/0002-6417). **1315**

ALPHABET : THE JOURNAL OF THE FRIENDS OF CALLIGRAPHY. (US). Qty: 3. **369**

ALPINE AVALANCHE. (US). Qty: 40. **5746**

ALPINE JOURNAL, THE. (UK/0065-6569). **4868**

ALPINE SKIING COMPETITION GUIDE. WESTERN/ROCKY EDITION. (US/0733-9348). **4882**

ALTA DIRECCION. (SP/0002-6549). **1596**

ALTADENA REVIEW, THE. (US/0162-8208). **3337**

ALTAMONT ENTERPRISE (1983), THE. (US/0890-6025). **5713**

ALTERNATE ROUTES. (CN/0702-8865). **5238**

ALTERNATIVE AQUACULTURE NETWORK. (US/8755-7894). Qty: 1-4. **552**

ALTERNATIVE ENERGY RETAILER. (US/0273-8163). **1931**

ALTERNATIVE MEDIA. (US/0730-1766). **4463**

ALTERNATIVE (MONTREAL, QUEBEC). (CN/0843-0586). **1643**

ALTERNATIVES ECONOMIQUES DIJON. (FR/0247-3739). **1589**

ALTERNATIVES (INGRAM, TEX.). (US/0893-5025). **2595**

ALTERNATIVES (PETERBOROUGH). (CN/0002-6638). Qty: 40. **2159**

ALTERNATIVES TO THE HIGH COST OF LITIGATION. (US/0736-3613). **3095**

ALUMINIUM (DUSSELDORF). (GW/0002-6689). **3997**

ALUMINIUM INDUSTRY. (UK/0268-5280). **3997**

ALUMNAE DIRECTORY OF SWEET BRIAR COLLEGE. (US). Qty: only books by alumnae. **1096**

ALUMNAE MAGAZINE - SWEET BRIAR COLLEGE. (US/0039-7342). Qty: 1-5. **1808**

ALUMNI DIRECTORY - UNIVERSITY OF VIRGINIA. ALUMNI ASSOCIATION. (US/0738-3762). **1100**

ALUMNI MAGAZINE (MORGANTOWN, W. VA.). (US). **1100**

ALUMNINEWS - CARLETON UNIVERSITY. (CN/0226-5389). **1101**

ALWAYS JUKIN'. (US/0896-9345). Qty: 6. **4099**

ALYTES. (FR/0753-4973). **5574**

AM-POL EAGLE. (US/0276-1904). **5713**

AMA. AGRICULTURAL MECHANIZATION IN ASIA, AFRICA AND LATIN AMERICA. (JA/0084-5841). **158**

AMATEUR ENTOMOLOGIST : THE JOURNAL OF THE AMATEUR ENTOMOLOGISTS' SOCIETY, THE. (UK). **5605**

AMATEUR TELEVISION QUARTERLY. (US/1042-198X). Qty: 4-10. **1148**

AMATEUR WINE MAKER. (UK/0002-6883). **2363**

AMATEUR WRESTLING NEWS. (US/0569-1796). **4882**

AMAZING COMPUTING. (US/0886-9480). **1264**

AMAZONIA PERUANA. (PE/0252-886X). **2718**

AMBASSADOR REPORT. (US/0882-2123). **4933**

AMBC NEWS. (US/1064-1599). Qty: 3 or 4. **205**

AMBIENTE. (IT). **2211**

AMBIENTE CUCINA, L'. (IT/0392-5730). **2898**

AMBIENTE E SICUREZZA SUL LAVORO. (IT/0393-7054). **2858**

AMBIENTE RISORSE SALUTE. (IT/0393-0521). **2160**

AMBIENTE SALUTE TERRITORIO. (IT). Qty: 12. **2211**

AMBIT. (UK/0002-6972). **3459**

AMBIX. (UK/0002-6980). **960**

AMBULATORY RECORD MONITOR. (US/1057-753X). Qty: 4. **3776**

AMC JOURNAL. (US/0891-6209). **2133**

AMCHAM BUSINESS JOURNAL. (PH). Qty: 12. **818**

AMEGHINIANA. (AG/0002-7014). **4226**

AMENAGEMENT ET NATURE. (FR/0044-7463). Qty: 6. **2186**

AMERASIA JOURNAL. (US/0044-7471). **2254**

AMERICA INDIGENA. (MX/0185-1179). **227**

AMERICA (NEW YORK, N.Y. 1909). (US/0002-7049). **5023**

AMERICA OGGI. (US/1042-6965). Qty: 50. **5709**

AMERICAN AGENT & BROKER. (US/0002-7200). **2873**

AMERICAN AMATEUR JOURNALIST, THE. (US/1046-0470). **2770**

AMERICAN ANNALS OF THE DEAF (WASHINGTON, D.C. 1886). (US/0002-726X). **4383**

AMERICAN ANTHROPOLOGIST. (US/0002-7294). **227**

AMERICAN ANTHROPOLOGIST [MICROFORM]. (US/0002-7294). **227**

AMERICAN ANTIQUITY; A QUARTERLY REVIEW OF AMERICAN ARCHAEOLOGY. (US/0002-7316). **253**

AMERICAN-ARAB AFFAIRS. (US/0731-6763). **4515**

AMERICAN ARCHEOLOGY. (US/0740-8358). **254**

AMERICAN ARCHIVIST, THE. (US/0360-9081). **2478**

AMERICAN ART JOURNAL, THE. (US/0002-7359). **336**

AMERICAN ASIAN REVIEW, THE. (US/0737-6650). **2645**

AMERICAN ASTROLOGY. (US/0002-7529). **389**

AMERICAN ATHEIST, THE. (US/0516-9623). **4933**

AMERICAN BABY. (US/0044-7544). **2276**

AMERICAN BABY'S CHILDBIRTH EDUCATOR. (US/0279-490X). **3756**

AMERICAN BANKER. (US/0002-7561). **769**

AMERICAN BANKRUPTCY LAW JOURNAL, THE. (US/0027-9048). **3084**

AMERICAN BAPTIST QUARTERLY. (US/0745-3698). **5055**

AMERICAN BAPTIST WOMAN, THE. (US/0191-0183). **5055**

AMERICAN BEE JOURNAL. (US/0002-7626). **58**

AMERICAN BICYCLIST AND MOTORCYCLIST. (US/0002-7677). **427**

AMERICAN BIOLOGY TEACHER, THE. (US/0002-7685). **441**

AMERICAN BIRDS. (US/0004-7686). Qty: 2 per year. **5614**

AMERICAN BOOK COLLECTOR (1980). (US/0196-5654). **2770**

AMERICAN BOOK REVIEW, THE. (US/0149-9408). **3337**

AMERICAN BREWER (HAYWARD, CALIF.). (US/1055-470X). Qty: (8-10). **2363**

AMERICAN BUDDHIST NEWSLETTER, THE. (US/0747-900X). **5020**

AMERICAN BUILDING CONTRACTOR, THE. (US/0740-3607). **598**

AMERICAN BUNGALOW. (US/1055-0674). Qty: 4. **598**

AMERICAN BUSINESS LAW JOURNAL. (US/0002-7766). **3095**

AMERICAN BUSINESS REVIEW. (US/0743-2348). **859**

AMERICAN BUSINESS TREND SYNOPSIS, THE. (US/8756-3053). **638**

AMERICAN CAGE-BIRD MAGAZINE. (US/0002-7782). **4285**

AMERICAN CAMELLIA YEARBOOK, THE. (US/0065-762X). **2408**

AMERICAN-CANADIAN GENEALOGIST. (US/1076-3902). Qty: 5 to 10. **2436**

AMERICAN CATHOLIC PHILOSOPHICAL QUARTERLY. (US/1051-3558). Qty: Varies. **4340**

AMERICAN CERAMIC CIRCLE JOURNAL. (US/0899-806X). **2586**

AMERICAN CERAMIC SOCIETY BULLETIN. (US/0002-7812). **2586**

AMERICAN CERAMICS. (US/0278-9507). **2586**

AMERICAN CHIROPRACTOR, THE. (US/0194-6536). **4379**

AMERICAN CLINICAL LABORATORY. (US/1041-3235). **3548**

AMERICAN COLLECTOR'S JOURNAL, THE. (US/0164-7008). **248**

AMERICAN COMPUTER LAW DIGEST. (US/8755-1675). **2932**

AMERICAN CONCHOLOGIST. (US/1072-2440). Qty: 12. **5574**

AMERICAN CURRENTS. (US/1070-7352). Qty: 8. **2294**

AMERICAN DANCE GUILD NEWSLETTER. (US/0300-7448). Qty: 1. **1310**

AMERICAN DEMOGRAPHICS. (US/0163-4089). **4549**

AMERICAN DROP-SHIPPERS DIRECTORY. (US/0065-8103). **822**

AMERICAN DYESTUFF REPORTER. (US/0002-8266). **5347**

AMERICAN ECONOMIST (NEW YORK, N.Y. 1960), THE. (US/0569-4345). **1461**

AMERICAN ENTOMOLOGIST (LANHAM, MD.). (US/1046-2821). **5605**

AMERICAN ETHNOLOGIST. (US/0094-0496). **228**

AMERICAN FAMILY PHYSICIAN (1970). (US/0002-838X). **3736**

AMERICAN FENCING. (US/0002-8436). **4882**

AMERICAN FERN JOURNAL. (US/0002-8444). **498**

AMERICAN FIELD. (US/0002-8452). **4868**

AMERICAN FILM. (US/0361-4751). **4063**

AMERICAN FIREWORKS NEWS. (US/8755-3163). **2007**

AMERICAN FITNESS. (US/0893-5238). **2595**

AMERICAN FLY FISHER, THE. (US/0884-3562). **2294**

AMERICAN FOLKLORE SOCIETY NEWSLETTER, THE. (US/0745-5178). **2318**

AMERICAN FORESTS. (US/0002-8541). **2374**

AMERICAN GENEALOGIST (DES MOINES). (US/0002-8592). **2437**

AMERICAN GINSENG TRENDS. (US/1047-7527). **1596**

AMERICAN GO JOURNAL, THE. (US/0148-0243). **4856**

AMERICAN HANDGUNNER, THE. (US/0145-4250). **4882**

AMERICAN HARMONICA ASSOCIATES NEWSLETTER. (US/1050-7493). **Qty:** 4. **4099**

AMERICAN HARP JOURNAL, THE. (US/0002-869X). **4099**

AMERICAN HERITAGE. (US/0002-8738). **2718**

AMERICAN HISTORICAL REVIEW. (US/0002-8762). **2609**

AMERICAN HISTORY ILLUSTRATED. (US/0002-8770). **2719**

AMERICAN HOCKEY MAGAZINE. (US/8756-3789). **4882**

AMERICAN HOMEOPATHY (1984). (US/0747-606X). **3774**

AMERICAN HORTICULTURIST (ALEXANDRIA). (US/0096-4417). **2408**

AMERICAN HORTICULTURIST NEWS. (US). **2408**

AMERICAN ILLUSTRATION SHOWCASE. (US/0278-8128). **376**

AMERICAN IMAGO. (US/0065-860X). **4572**

AMERICAN INDIAN ART MAGAZINE. (US/0192-9968). **336**

AMERICAN INDIAN CULTURE AND RESEARCH JOURNAL. (US/0161-6463). **2254**

AMERICAN INDIAN LAW REVIEW. (US/0094-002X). **Qty:** 1. **2932**

AMERICAN INDIAN QUARTERLY. (US/0095-182X). **2255**

AMERICAN INDUSTRIAL HYGIENE ASSOCIATION JOURNAL. (US/0002-8894). **2858**

AMERICAN INDUSTRY. (US/0002-8908). **859**

AMERICAN INVENTOR (BLOOMINGTON, IND.). (US/1042-1890). **5082**

AMERICAN JAILS. (US/1056-0319). **3156**

AMERICAN JEWELRY MANUFACTURER. (US/0193-0931). **2913**

AMERICAN JEWISH ARCHIVES. (US/0002-905X). **2255**

AMERICAN JEWISH HISTORY. (US/0164-0178). **2255**

AMERICAN JEWISH WORLD, THE. (US/0002-9084). **Qty:** 26. **5045**

AMERICAN JOURNAL (NEW YORK). (US/0092-119X). **Qty:** 4. **2527**

AMERICAN JOURNAL OF ACUPUNCTURE. (US/0091-3960). **3548**

AMERICAN JOURNAL OF AGRICULTURAL ECONOMICS. (US/0002-9092). **58**

AMERICAN JOURNAL OF ARCHAEOLOGY. (US/0002-9114). **254**

AMERICAN JOURNAL OF ART THERAPY. (US/0007-4764). **336**

AMERICAN JOURNAL OF CARDIAC IMAGING. (US/0887-7971). **3698**

AMERICAN JOURNAL OF CASE MANAGEMENT, THE. (US/1051-8967). **5190**

AMERICAN JOURNAL OF CHINESE MEDICINE, THE. (US/0192-415X). **3548**

AMERICAN JOURNAL OF CLINICAL HYPNOSIS, THE. (US/0002-9157). **2857**

AMERICAN JOURNAL OF CLINICAL NUTRITION, THE. (US/0002-9165). **4187**

AMERICAN JOURNAL OF CLINICAL PATHOLOGY. (US/0002-9173). **3892**

AMERICAN JOURNAL OF COSMETIC SURGERY, THE. (US/0748-8068). **3958**

AMERICAN JOURNAL OF CRIMINAL JUSTICE : AJCJ. (US/1066-2316). **Qty:** 6-10. **3156**

AMERICAN JOURNAL OF CRIMINAL LAW. (US/0092-2315). **3105**

AMERICAN JOURNAL OF DENTISTRY. (US/0894-8275). **Qty:** 4-8. **1315**

AMERICAN JOURNAL OF DISEASES OF CHILDREN (1960). (US/0002-922X). **3899**

AMERICAN JOURNAL OF DRUG AND ALCOHOL ABUSE, THE. (US/0095-2990). **1340**

AMERICAN JOURNAL OF EEG TECHNOLOGY, THE. (US/0002-9238). **3827**

AMERICAN JOURNAL OF EMERGENCY MEDICINE, THE. (US/0735-6757). **3723**

AMERICAN JOURNAL OF ENOLOGY AND VITICULTURE. (US/0002-9254). **2363**

AMERICAN JOURNAL OF FAMILY LAW. (US/0891-6330). **3119**

AMERICAN JOURNAL OF FAMILY THERAPY, THE. (US/0192-6187). **4573**

AMERICAN JOURNAL OF FORENSIC MEDICINE AND PATHOLOGY, THE. (US/0195-7910). **3739**

AMERICAN JOURNAL OF FORENSIC PSYCHIATRY, THE. (US/0163-1942). **3919**

AMERICAN JOURNAL OF FORENSIC PSYCHOLOGY, THE. (US/0733-1290). **3739**

AMERICAN JOURNAL OF GERIATRIC PSYCHIATRY, THE. (US/1064-7481). **3749**

AMERICAN JOURNAL OF GERMANIC LINGUISTICS AND LITERATURES. (US/1040-8207). **3263**

AMERICAN JOURNAL OF HEALTH PROMOTION. (US/0890-1171). **Qty:** 12. **4764**

AMERICAN JOURNAL OF HOSPICE AND PALLIATIVE CARE, THE. (US/1049-9091). **Qty:** 12/yr. **5271**

AMERICAN JOURNAL OF HOSPITAL PHARMACY. (US/0002-9289). **4290**

AMERICAN JOURNAL OF INFECTION CONTROL. (US/0196-6553). **3734**

AMERICAN JOURNAL OF INTERNATIONAL LAW, THE. (US/0002-9300). **3123**

AMERICAN JOURNAL OF ISLAMIC SOCIAL SCIENCES, THE. (US/0887-7653). **5190**

AMERICAN JOURNAL OF JURISPRUDENCE (NOTRE DAME), THE. (US/0065-8995). **Qty:** 4-5. **2932**

AMERICAN JOURNAL OF LAW & MEDICINE. (US/0098-8588). **2932**

AMERICAN JOURNAL OF LEGAL HISTORY, THE. (US/0002-9319). **2932**

AMERICAN JOURNAL OF MATHEMATICAL AND MANAGEMENT SCIENCES. (US/0196-6324). **Qty:** 2. **3492**

AMERICAN JOURNAL OF MEDICAL GENETICS. (US/0148-7299). **542**

AMERICAN JOURNAL OF OCCUPATIONAL THERAPY, THE. (US/0272-9490). **1874**

AMERICAN JOURNAL OF OPHTHALMOLOGY. (US/0002-9394). **3871**

AMERICAN JOURNAL OF ORTHODONTICS AND DENTOFACIAL ORTHOPEDICS. (US/0889-5406). **1315**

AMERICAN JOURNAL OF ORTHOPSYCHIATRY. (US/0002-9432). **3919**

AMERICAN JOURNAL OF OTOLARYNGOLOGY. (US/0196-0709). **3885**

AMERICAN JOURNAL OF OTOLOGY (NEW YORK, N.Y.), THE. (US/0192-9763). **3886**

AMERICAN JOURNAL OF PAIN MANAGEMENT. (US/1059-1494). **3548**

AMERICAN JOURNAL OF PERINATOLOGY. (US/0735-1631). **3756**

AMERICAN JOURNAL OF PHARMACEUTICAL EDUCATION. (US/0002-9459). **4290**

AMERICAN JOURNAL OF PHILOLOGY. (US/0002-9475). **1073**

AMERICAN JOURNAL OF PHYSICS. (US/0002-9505). **4396**

AMERICAN JOURNAL OF PREVENTIVE MEDICINE. (US/0749-3797). **3549**

AMERICAN JOURNAL OF PRIMATOLOGY. (US/0275-2565). **5574**

AMERICAN JOURNAL OF PSYCHIATRY, THE. (US/0002-953X). **3920**

AMERICAN JOURNAL OF PSYCHOLOGY, THE. (US/0002-9556). **4573**

AMERICAN JOURNAL OF PUBLIC HEALTH (1971). (US/0090-0036). **4764**

AMERICAN JOURNAL OF SEMIOTICS. (US/0277-7126). **3263**

AMERICAN JOURNAL OF SOCIAL PSYCHIATRY, THE. (US/0277-8173). **3920**

AMERICAN JOURNAL OF SPORTS MEDICINE, THE. (US/0363-5465). **3953**

AMERICAN JOURNAL OF TRIAL ADVOCACY, THE. (US/0160-0281). **2932**

AMERICAN JOURNAL OF TROPICAL MEDICINE AND HYGIENE, THE. (US/0002-9637). **3985**

AMERICAN JOURNALISM. (US/0882-1127). **Qty:** 60-80 per year. **2917**

AMERICAN KITE. (US/1045-3598). **4882**

AMERICAN LABOR (WASHINGTON, D.C.). (US/0889-0609). **1643**

AMERICAN LABORATORY (FAIRFIELD). (US/0044-7749). **960**

AMERICAN LAWYER (NEW YORK. 1979), THE. (US/0162-3397). **2933**

AMERICAN LEGION FIRING LINE, THE. (US). **4539**

AMERICAN LIBRARIES (CHICAGO, ILL.). (US/0002-9769). **3189**

AMERICAN LITERARY HISTORY. (US/0896-7148). **3360**

AMERICAN LITERARY REALISM, 1870-1910. (US/0002-9823). **3337**

AMERICAN LITERATURE. (US/0002-9831). **3360**

AMERICAN LUTHERIE. (US/1041-7176). **4099**

AMERICAN MARKETING ASSOCIATION INTERNATIONAL MEMBERSHIP DIRECTORY AND MARKETING SERVICES GUIDE. (US). **921**

AMERICAN MEDICAL WRITERS ASSOCIATION AMWA JOURNAL. (US). **3549**

AMERICAN MIDDLE SCHOOL EDUCATION. (US/0889-552X). **1860**

AMERICAN MINERALOGIST, THE. (US/0003-004X). **1437**

AMERICAN MODELER (RALEIGH, N.C.). (US/1061-9399). **2771**

AMERICAN MUSEUM NOVITATES. (US/0003-0082). **5574**

AMERICAN MUSIC (CHAMPAIGN, ILL.). (US/0734-4392). **4099**

AMERICAN MUSIC TEACHER, THE. (US/0003-0112). **4099**

AMERICAN NEPTUNE, THE. (US/0003-0155). **4174**

AMERICAN NURSERYMAN. (US/0003-0198). **2408**

AMERICAN ORCHID SOCIETY BULLETIN. (US/0003-0252). **Qty:** 6-12. **2408**

AMERICAN ORGANIST (1979), THE. (US/0164-3150). **4099**

AMERICAN PAINT & COATINGS JOURNAL. (US/0098-5430). **4222**

AMERICAN PAINT & COATINGS JOURNAL. CONVENTION DAILY. (US/0097-4749). **4222**

AMERICAN PAINTING CONTRACTOR. (US/0003-0325). **4222**

AMERICAN PERIODICALS : A JOURNAL OF HISTORY, CRITICISM, AND BIBLIOGRAPHY. (US/1054-7479). **Qty:** 6-10. **4812**

AMERICAN PHARMACY. (US/0160-3450). **4290**

AMERICAN PHILATELIST, THE. (US/0003-0473). **2784**

AMERICAN PHOTO. (US/1046-8986). **4366**

AMERICAN PHOTOGRAPHY SHOWCASE. (US/0278-8314). **4366**

AMERICAN PIGEON JOURNAL. (US/0003-0511). **5574**

AMERICAN POETRY REVIEW, THE. (US/0360-3709). **3460**

AMERICAN POLITICAL SCIENCE REVIEW, THE. (US/0003-0554). **4463**

AMERICAN POSTAL WORKER, THE. (US/0044-7811). **1643**

AMERICAN POTATO JOURNAL. (US/0003-0589). **162**

AMERICAN PREMIERE. (US/0279-0041). **4063**

AMERICAN PRESBYTERIANS. (US/0886-5159). **5055**

AMERICAN

AMERICAN PRINTER (1982). (US/0744-6616). **4563**

AMERICAN PROGRAMMER. (US/1048-5600). **1284**

AMERICAN PURPOSE. (US/0891-446X). **4515**

AMERICAN QUARTERLY. (US/0003-0678). **2719**

AMERICAN QUILTER. (US/8756-6591). **5182**

AMERICAN RABBI (CANOGA PARK, LOS ANGELES, CALIF.), THE. (US/0164-3916). **Qty:** 12-15. **5045**

AMERICAN RECORD GUIDE. (US/0003-0716). **5315**

AMERICAN RECORDER, THE. (US/0003-0724). **4099**

AMERICAN REFERENCE BOOKS ANNUAL. (US/0065-9959). **1923**

AMERICAN REVENUER, THE. (US/0163-1608). **2784**

AMERICAN REVIEW OF CANADIAN STUDIES, THE. (US/0272-2011). **2719**

AMERICAN REVIEW OF INTERNATIONAL ARBITRATION, THE. (US/1050-4109). **2933**

AMERICAN REVIEW OF POLITICS. (US). **Qty:** 25-30. **4463**

AMERICAN REVIEW OF RESPIRATORY DISEASE, THE. (US/0003-0805). **3948**

AMERICAN SAILOR. (US/0279-9553). **591**

AMERICAN SCHOLAR, THE. (US/0003-0937). **2484**

AMERICAN SCHOOL BOARD JOURNAL, THE. (US/0003-0953). **1860**

AMERICAN SCIENTIST. (US/0003-0996). **5082**

AMERICAN SECONDARY EDUCATION. (US/0003-1003). **Qty:** varies. **1724**

AMERICAN SERIES IN MATHEMATICAL AND MANAGEMENT SCIENCES. (US/0883-6221). **3492**

AMERICAN SERIES OF FOREIGN PENAL CODES. (US). **3105**

AMERICAN SHOEMAKING. (US/0003-1038). **3183**

AMERICAN SHOTGUNNER, THE. (US/0162-153X). **4883**

AMERICAN SHOWCASE. ILLUSTRATION. (US). **376**

AMERICAN SHOWCASE OF ILLUSTRATION AND PHOTOGRAPHY. (US/0278-8683). **4366**

AMERICAN SKATING WORLD. (US/0744-1363). **Qty:** 8. **4883**

AMERICAN SOCIOLOGICAL REVIEW. (US/0003-1224). **5238**

AMERICAN SONGWRITER. (US/0896-8993). **Qty:** 12. **4099**

AMERICAN SPACEMODELLING. (US/0883-0991). **2771**

AMERICAN SPECTATOR (ARLINGTON, VA.), THE. (US/0148-8414). **3337**

AMERICAN SPEECH. (US/0003-1283). **3263**

AMERICAN SQUARE DANCE. (US/0091-3383). **1310**

AMERICAN STRING TEACHER. (US/0003-1313). **4100**

AMERICAN STUDIES IN PAPYROLOGY. (US/0569-8642). **1074**

AMERICAN STUDIES IN SCANDINAVIA. (NO/0044-8060). **2719**

AMERICAN STUDIES INTERNATIONAL. (US/0883-105X). **2719**

AMERICAN STUDIES (LAWRENCE). (US/0026-3079). **Qty:** 30-70 per year. **2719**

AMERICAN SURVIVAL GUIDE. (US/8750-5878). **2527**

AMERICAN SUZUKI JOURNAL. (US/0193-5372). **Qty:** 1-4. **4100**

AMERICAN THEATRE. (US/8750-3255). **5361**

AMERICAN THEOSOPHIST, THE. (US/0003-1402). **4934**

AMERICAN TOOL, DIE & STAMPING NEWS. (US/0192-5709). **3475**

AMERICAN TURF MONTHLY. (US/0003-1445). **2796**

AMERICAN UNIVERSITY LAW REVIEW, THE. (US/0003-1453). **2933**

AMERICAN UNIVERSITY STUDIES. SERIES XXII, LATIN AMERICAN STUDIES. (US/0895-0490). **2719**

AMERICAN URBAN GUIDENOTES : THE NEWSLETTER OF GUIDEBOOKS. (US). **5461**

AMERICAN VOICE (LOUISVILLE, KY.), THE. (US/0884-4356). **3360**

AMERICAN WEATHER OBSERVER. (US/8755-9552). **1419**

AMERICAN WHITEWATER. (US/0300-7626). **4883**

AMERICAN WOMAN (NEW YORK, N.Y. 1991). (US/1054-9595). **5550**

AMERICAN WORKER, THE. (US/1047-7136). **1643**

AMERICAN ZOOLOGIST. (US/0003-1569). **5574**

AMERICANA. (US/0090-9114). **2527**

AMERICANS BEFORE COLUMBUS. (US/0066-121X). **2720**

AMERICA'S CORPORATE FAMILIES. (US/0890-6645). **638**

AMERICAS (ENGLISH EDITION). (US/0379-0940). **2551**

AMERICA'S FUTURE FOOD TRENDS. (US). **2326**

AMERICA'S FUTURE (NEW ROCHELLE, N.Y.). (US/0003-1593). **Qty:** 12. **4463**

AMERICAS REVIEW (HOUSTON, TEX.). (US/1042-6213). **Qty:** 12. **3360**

AMERICA'S TEXTILES INTERNATIONAL. (US/0890-9970). **5347**

AMERICAS (WASHINGTON. 1944), THE. (US/0003-1615). **2720**

AMERIKA WOCHE. (US/0745-6557). **5658**

AMERIKAI MAGYAR SZO. (US/0194-7990). **5713**

AMERIKAN UUTISET. (US/0745-9971). **Qty:** 10. **5647**

AMERIKASTUDIEN. (GW/0340-2827). **Qty:** 50. **2720**

AMERINDIA. (FR/0221-8852). **3263**

AMERRIKUA! (SCHUYLER FALLS, N.Y.). (US/1043-7029). **Qty:** 4-6. **2255**

AMICA NEWS BULLETIN, THE. (US/1043-5379). **4100**

AMICUS JOURNAL, THE. (US/0276-7201). **2186**

AMIGO (MONTREAL). (CN/0318-5729). **4934**

AMINA. (FR). **5550**

AMMINISTRAZIONE E POLITICA. (IT/0392-579X). **Qty:** 10. **4463**

AMMONITE. (UK/0951-2500). **Qty:** 12. **3360**

AMMONITE GILLINGHAM, DORSET. (UK/0951-2500). **Qty:** 12. **2318**

AMNESTY ACTION / AI, USA. (US). **4503**

AMOEBA AMSTERDAM. 1976. (NE/0926-3543). **4161**

AMON HEN. (UK). **3360**

AMPERSAND (SAN FRANCISCO, CALIF.), THE. (US/0740-5804). **Qty:** 8. **4563**

AMPHIBIA-REPTILIA. (GW/0173-5373). **5575**

AMPLEFORTH JOURNAL, THE. (UK/0003-2018). **5023**

AMSTERDAM STUDIES IN THE THEORY AND HISTORY OF LINGUISTIC SCIENCE. SERIES IV, CURRENT ISSUES IN LINGUISTIC THEORY. (NE/0304-0763). **3264**

AMSTERDAMER BEITRAEGE ZUR ALTEREN GERMANISTIK. (NE). **3264**

AMUSEMENT PARK GUIDEBOOK. (US). **4848**

AMUSEMENT PARK JOURNAL. (US/0271-7999). **4857**

AN COSANTOIR. (IE). **4040**

AN-HUI SHIH TA HSUEH PAO. (CC). **2841**

ANACRUSIS. (CN/0826-7464). **4100**

ANADARKO DAILY NEWS, THE. (US/0744-1398). **Qty:** 8-10. **5731**

ANAESTHESIA. (UK/0003-2409). **3680**

ANAESTHESIA AND INTENSIVE CARE. (AT/0310-057X). **3680**

ANAIS BRASILEIROS DE DERMATOLOGIA. (BL/0365-0596). **3717**

ANAIS DO INSTITUTO DE HIGIENE E MEDICINA TROPICAL. (PO/0303-7762). **3549**

ANAIS (LOS ANGELES, CALIF.). (US/8755-3910). **3361**

ANALE DE ISTORIE. (RM/1010-5506). **4625**

ANALECTA AUGUSTINIANA. (IT). **5023**

ANALECTA BOLLANDIANA. (BE/0003-2468). **Qty:** 60. **4934**

ANALECTA CISTERCIENSIA. (IT/0003-2476). **5023**

ANALECTA GREGORIANA. (IT/0066-1376). **4934**

ANALECTA TERTII ORDINIS REGULARIS SANCTI FRANCISCI. (IT). **5023**

ANALELE UNIVERSITATI DIN GALATI. FASCICULA II - MATEMATICA, FIZICA, MECANICA TEORETICA. (RM). **3492**

ANALELE UNIVERSITATII DIN GALATI. FASCICULA I, STIINTE SOCIALE SI UMANISTE. (RM/1015-9606). **5190**

ANALELE UNIVERSITATII DIN GALATI.FASCICULA VII, TEHNICA PISCICOLA. (RM). **2294**

ANALELE UNIVERSITATII DIN TIMISOARA. STIINTE SOCIALE SI ECONOMICE. (RM). **5190**

ANALES. (SP/0034-0618). **4290**

ANALES CERVANTINOS. (SP/0569-9878). **3361**

ANALES DE CIENCIAS - UNIVERSIDAD DE MURCIA. (SP/0213-5469). **960**

ANALES DE LA ACADEMIA DE GEOGRAFIA E HISTORIA DE GUATEMALA. (GT/0252-337X). **228**

ANALES DE LA FUNDACION JUAN MARCH. (SP/0532-8500). **4334**

ANALES DE LA LITERATURA ESPANOLA CONTEMPORANEA. (US/0272-1635). **3361**

ANALES DE LITERATURA HISPANOAMERICANA. (SP). **3361**

ANALES DE PEDAGOGIA. (SP/0212-8322). **1724**

ANALES DE VETERINARIA DE MURCIA. (SP/0213-5434). **5502**

ANALES DEL CARIBE. (CU/1017-8937). **Qty:** 3-4. **2841**

ANALES DEL INSTITUTO DE BIOLOGIA, UNIVERSIDAD NACIONAL AUTONOMA DE MEXICO. SERIE BOTANICA. (MX/0374-5511). **498**

ANALES DEL INSTITUTO DE BIOLOGIA, UNIVERSIDAD NACIONAL AUTONOMA DE MEXICO. SERIE ZOOLOGIA. (MX/0368-8720). **5575**

ANALES DEL INSTITUTO DE INVESTIGACIONES ESTETICAS. (MX/0185-1276). **336**

ANALES DEL INSTITUTO DE INVESTIGACIONES MARINAS DE PUNTA DE BETIN. (CK/0120-3959). **552**

ANALES DEL INSTITUTO DE LA PATAGONIA. SERIE CIENCIAS NATURALES. (CL/0716-6486). **4161**

ANALES DEL INSTITUTO DE LA PATAGONIA. SERIE CIENCIAS SOCIALES. (CL/0716-6478). **5190**

ANALES ESPANOLES DE PEDIATRIA. (SP/0302-4342). **3900**

ANALES GALDOSIANOS. (US/0569-9924). **3337**

ANALES OTORRINOLARINGOLOGICOS IBERO-AMERICANOS. (SP/0303-8874). **3886**

ANALISE PSICOLOGICA. (PO/0870-8231). **4573**

ANALISE SOCIAL. (PO/0003-2573). **5239**

ANALISIS ESTADISTICO, URUGUAY: IMPORTACION - EXPORTACION. (UY). **822**

ANALISIS FILOSOFICO. (AG/0326-1301). **4340**

ANALISIS FINANCIERO. (SP). **770**

ANALUSIS. (FR/0365-4877). **1012**

ANALYSE. (NE/0166-7688). **3549**

ANALYSES DE LA S.E.D.E.I.S. (FR/0399-1245). **1461**

ANALYSIS MATHEMATICA (BUDAPEST). (HU/0133-3852). **3493**

ANALYSIS (NEW YORK (N.Y.). (US/0003-2638). **4340**

ANALYSIS OF CLASS 1 RAILROADS. (US). **5400**

ANALYST (LONDON). (UK/0003-2654). **1012**

ANALYSTE (MONTREAL, QUEBEC). (CN/0715-7649). **2527**

ANALYTIC TEACHING. (US/0890-5118). **Qty:** 6. **4340**

ANALYTICAL ABSTRACTS. (UK/0003-2689). **996**

ANALYTICAL AND QUANTITATIVE CYTOLOGY AND HISTOLOGY. (US/0884-6812). **531**

ANALYTICAL CHEMISTRY (WASHINGTON). (US/0003-2700). **1013**

ANALYTICAL INSTRUMENT INDUSTRY REPORT. (UK/0265-3435). **Qty:** varies. **1597**

ANAMNESES VILLEJUIF. (FR/1166-9829). **Qty:** 1-2. **2610**

ANAP. (CU). **58**

ANARCHY. (UK/0003-2751). **4539**

ANARE NEWS (AUSTRALIAN NATIONAL ANTARCTIC RESEARCH EXPEDITIONS). (AT). **5082**

ANATOMIA, HISTOLOGIA, EMBRYOLOGIA. (GW/0340-2096). **5502**

ANATOMISCHER ANZEIGER. (GW/0003-2786). **3678**

ANCESTOR. (AT/0044-8222). **2437**

ANCESTOR HUNT. (US/0736-9115). **Qty:** 4. **2437**

ANCESTORS WEST. (US/0734-4988). **Qty:** 4. **2437**

ANCESTRY. (US). **Qty:** 8. **2437**

ANCESTRY NEWSLETTER. (US/0749-5927). **2437**

ANCETRE (QUEBEC). (CN/0316-0513). **2437**

ANCHORAGE TIMES. (US). **5628**

ANCIENT CONTROVERSY. (US/1042-2471). **4515**

ANCIENT MESOAMERICA. (UK). **254**

ANCIENT PHILOSOPHY (PITTSBURGH, PA.). (US/0740-2007). **Qty:** 50. **4340**

ANCIENT WORLD, THE. (US/0160-9645). **Qty:** 4-12. **254**

AND. JOURNAL OF ART AND ART EDUCATION. (UK/0266-6057). **Qty:** 4. **336**

ANDALUCIA ECONOMICA. (SP/1130-4413). **1462**

ANDEAN REPORT, THE. (PE/0251-2491). **1545**

ANDERSON REPORT, THE. (US/0197-7040). **1231**

ANDERSON'S CAMPGROUND DIRECTORY. (US/0163-268X). **4869**

ANDHRA AGRICULTURAL JOURNAL, THE. (II/0003-2956). **58**

ANDRADE : REVISTA TRIMESTRAL DE POESIA. (SP). **3361**

ANDREWS UNIVERSITY SEMINARY STUDIES. (US/0003-2980). **Qty:** 40. **4934**

ANDREWSREPORT (INDIANAPOLIS, IND.). (US/0892-0850). **4834**

ANDROLOGIA (BERLIN, WEST). (GW/0303-4569). **3549**

ANEKS. (UK/0345-0295). **2673**

ANELLO CHE NON TIENE, L'. (US/0899-5273). **Qty:** 10. **3361**

ANESTESIA E RIANIMAZIONE. (IT/0570-0760). **3681**

ANESTEZIOLOGIJA I REANIMATOLOGIJA. (RU/0201-7563). **3681**

ANESTHESIA AND ANALGESIA. (US/0003-2999). **3681**

ANESTHESIA PROGRESS. (US/0003-3006). **1316**

ANESTHESIOLOGY (PHILADELPHIA). (US/0003-3022). **3681**

ANESTHESIOLOGY REVIEW. (US/0093-4437). **3681**

ANGELICUM. (IT/0003-3081). **4340**

ANGELOS (HALIFAX). (CN/0710-0612). **4934**

ANGESTELLTEN MAGAZIN. (GW/0341-017X). **1643**

ANGEWANDTE BOTANIK. (GW/0066-1759). **499**

ANGEWANDTE PARASITOLOGIE. (GW/0003-3162). **5575**

ANGIOLOGIA. (SP/0003-3170). **3698**

ANGLE DROIT PARIS. (FR/1156-4148). **2933**

ANGLES (VANCOUVER). (CN/0824-2100). **2793**

ANGLIA : ZEITSCHRIFT FUER ENGLISCHE PHILOLOGIE. (GW). **3264**

ANGLICAN DIGEST, THE. (US/0003-3278). **5055**

ANGLICAN JOURNAL. (CN/0847-978X). **4934**

ANGLICAN, THE. (CN/0517-7731). **5055**

ANGLICAN THEOLOGICAL REVIEW. (US/0003-3286). **4934**

ANGLO-AMERICAN LAW REVIEW, THE. (UK/0308-6569). **2933**

ANGLO AMERICAN TRADE DIRECTORY. (UK/0066-1813). **Qty:** 3. **822**

ANGLO-SOVIET JOURNAL, THE. (UK/0044-8265). **2673**

ANGLOFILE. (US). **2484**

ANGOLITE. (US/0402-4249). **3156**

ANGUILLA CONSOLIDATED INDEX OF STATUTES AND SUBSIDIARY LEGISLATION TO ... . (BB). **3123**

ANIMA (CHAMBERSBURG). (US/0097-1146). **4185**

ANIMAL BEHAVIOR ABSTRACTS. (US/0301-8695). **5604**

ANIMAL BEHAVIOR CONSULTANT NEWSLETTER. (US). **225**

ANIMAL BEHAVIOUR. (UK/0003-3472). **5575**

ANIMAL FINDERS' GUIDE. (US). **Qty:** varies. **4285**

ANIMAL KEEPERS' FORUM. (US/0164-9531). **Qty:** 15-20. **5575**

ANIMAL LIBERATION ACTION. (AT/0816-486X). **225**

ANIMAL ORGANIZATIONS & SERVICES DIRECTORY. (US/0748-5069). **225**

ANIMAL PEOPLE. (US/1071-0035). **Qty:** 36. **225**

ANIMAL PRODUCTION. (UK/0003-3561). **205**

ANIMAL TECHNOLOGY. (UK/0264-4754). **5503**

ANIMAL WELFARE. (UK/0962-7286). **225**

ANIMAL WELFARE INSTITUTE QUARTERLY, THE. (US/0743-0841). **Qty:** varies. **225**

ANIMALS AGENDA. (US/0892-8819). **Qty:** 40 per year. **225**

ANIMALS (BOSTON). (US/0030-6835). **225**

ANIMALS' VOICE (CHICO, CALIF.), THE. (US/0889-6712). **225**

ANIMATION JOURNAL. (US/1061-0308). **Qty:** 4. **4063**

ANIMATION MAGAZINE. (US/1041-617X). **Qty:** 5. **4063**

ANIMATO! (CAMBRIDGE, MASS.). (US/1042-539X). **Qty:** 5-10. **4063**

ANIMATOR ST. ALBANS. (UK/0964-5586). **4063**

ANN ARBOR NEWS, THE. (US). **5690**

ANNALES AEQUATORIA. (CG/0254-4296). **228**

ANNALES ARCHEOLOGIQUES ARABES SYRIENNES. (SY/0570-1554). **254**

ANNALES BENJAMIN CONSTANT. (SZ/0263-7383). **3361**

ANNALES DE BIOLOGIE CLINIQUE (PARIS). (FR/0003-3898). **3892**

ANNALES DE BOURGOGNE. (FR/0003-3901). **2674**

ANNALES DE BRETAGNE ET DES PAYS DE L'OUEST. (FR/0399-0826). **2674**

ANNALES DE CARDIOLOGIE ET D'ANGEIOLOGIE. (FR/0003-3928). **3698**

ANNALES DE CHIRURGIE. (FR/0003-3944). **3958**

ANNALES DE DEMOGRAPHIE HISTORIQUE. (FR/0066-2062). **4549**

ANNALES DE GEMBLOUX. (BE/0303-9099). **59**

ANNALES DE GENETIQUE. (FR/0003-3995). **542**

ANNALES DE GEOGRAPHIE. (FR/0003-4010). **2553**

ANNALES DE L'A C F A S. (CN/0066-8842). **5083**

ANNALES DE LA RECHERCHE URBAINE, LES. (FR/0180-930X). **5239**

ANNALES DE LA SOCIETE GEOLOGIQUE DE BELGIQUE. (BE/0037-9395). **1365**

ANNALES DE LA SOCIETE GEOLOGIQUE DU NORD. (FR/0767-7367). **1365**

ANNALES DE LA SOCIETE JEAN-JACQUES ROUSSEAU. (SZ/0259-6563). **3361**

ANNALES DE L'EST. (FR/0365-2017). **2674**

ANNALES DE L'I.H.P. PHYSIQUE THEORIQUE. (FR/0246-0211). **4396**

ANNALES DE L'I.H.P. PROBABILITES ET STATISTIQUES. (FR/0246-0203). **3493**

ANNALES DE L'UNIVERSITE D'ABIDJAN. SERIE G : GEOGRAPHIE. (IV/0302-0924). **2554**

ANNALES DE NORMANDIE. (FR/0003-4134). **2674**

ANNALES DE PEDIATRIE (PARIS). (FR/0066-2097). **3900**

ANNALES DE PHYSIQUE (PARIS). (FR/0003-4169). **4397**

ANNALES DE RADIOLOGIE. (FR/0003-4185). **3938**

ANNALES DE RECHERCHES VETERINAIRES. (FR/0003-4193). **5503**

ANNALES DES MINES DE BELGIQUE. (BE/0003-4290). **2133**

ANNALES DES SCIENCES FORESTIERES. (FR/0003-4312). **2374**

ANNALES DES SCIENCES NATURELLES. ZOOLOGIE ET BIOLOGIE ANIMALE. (FR/0003-4339). **5575**

ANNALES DES TELECOMMUNICATIONS. (FR/0003-4347). **1148**

ANNALES D'UROLOGIE. (FR/0003-4401). **3988**

ANNALES MEDICALES DE NANCY ET DE L'EST. (FR/0221-3796). **3550**

ANNALES PADEREWSKI. (SZ). **4100**

ANNALES - SOCIETE D'ARCHEOLOGIE D'HISTOIRE ET DE FOLKLORE DE NIVELLES ET DU BRABANT WALLON. (BE). **2674**

ANNALES THEOLOGICI. (IT/0394-8226). **Qty:** 45. **4934**

ANNALES UNIVERSITATIS SARAVIENSIS. REIHE : MATHEMATISCH-NATURWISSENSCHAFTLICHE FAKULTAT. (GW/0080-5165). **4162**

ANNALES UNIVERSITATIS SCIENTIARUM BUDAPESTINENSIS DE ROLANDO EOTVOS NOMINATAE. SECTIO COMPUTATORICA. (HU/0138-9491). **3493**

ANNALES UNIVERSITATIS SCIENTIARUM BUDAPESTINENSIS DE ROLANDO EOTVOS NOMINATAE. SECTIO HISTORICA. (HU/0524-8981). **2841**

ANNALI DELLA FONDAZIONE LUIGI EINAUDI. (IT/0531-9870). **5190**

ANNALI DI MICROBIOLOGIA ED ENZIMOLOGIA. (IT/0003-4649). **Qty:** 10. **558**

ANNALI D'ITALIANISTICA. (US/0741-7527). **3362**

ANNALI (ISTITUTO UNIVERSITARIO ORIENTALE (NAPLES, ITALY)). (IT). **3265**

ANNALI ITALIANI DI CHIRURGIA. (IT/0003-469X). **3959**

ANNALI ITALIANI DI MEDICINA INTERNA : ORGANO UFFICIALE DELLA SOCIETA ITALIANA DI MEDICINA INTERNA. (IT/0393-9340). **Qty:** 15. **3794**

ANNALS OF AGRICULTURAL RESEARCH. (II/0970-3179). **59**

ANNALS OF AIR AND SPACE LAW. (CN/0701-158X). **3123**

ANNALS OF ALLERGY. (US/0003-4738). **3666**

ANNALS OF APPLIED BIOLOGY. (UK/0003-4746). **442**

ANNALS OF ARID ZONE. (II/0570-1791). **Qty:** 1000. **162**

ANNALS OF BALLOON HISTORY AND MUSEOLOGY. (US). **11**

ANNALS OF BEHAVIORAL MEDICINE. (US/0883-6612). **3654**

ANNALS OF BOTANY. (UK/0305-7364). **499**

ANNALS OF CLINICAL AND LABORATORY SCIENCE. (US/0091-7370). **3893**

ANNALS OF CLINICAL BIOCHEMISTRY. (UK/0004-5632). **480**

ANNALS OF CLINICAL PSYCHIATRY. (US/1040-1237). **3920**

ANNALS OF DENTISTRY. (US/0003-4770). **1316**

ANNALS OF EARTH. (US/1070-9983). **1351**

ANNALS OF EMERGENCY MEDICINE. (US/0196-0644). **3723**

ANNALS OF HUMAN GENETICS. (UK/0003-4800). **542**

ANNALS OF INTERNAL MEDICINE. (US/0003-4819). **3794**

ANNALS OF IOWA. (US/0003-4827). **Qty:** 70-80. **2720**

ANNALS OF LIBRARY SCIENCE AND DOCUMENTATION. (II/0003-4835). **3190**

ANNALS OF NEUROLOGY. (US/0364-5134). **3827**

ANNALS OF OPHTHALMOLOGY (BIRMINGHAM). (US/0003-4886). **3872**

ANNALS OF OTOLOGY, RHINOLOGY & LARYNGOLOGY, THE. (US/0003-4894). **3886**

ANNALS OF PAEDIATRIC SURGERY. (II/0970-2121). **3900**

ANNALS OF PLASTIC SURGERY. (US/0148-7043). **3959**

ANNALS OF PROBABILITY, THE. (US/0091-1798). **3494**

ANNALS OF REGIONAL SCIENCE, THE. (GW/0570-1864). **2814**

ANNALS OF SAUDI MEDICINE. (SU/0256-4947). **3550**

ANNALS OF SCIENCE. (UK/0003-3790). **5083**

ANNALS OF STATISTICS, THE. (US/0090-5364). **5321**

ANNALS OF THE ACADEMY OF MEDICINE, SINGAPORE. (SI/0304-4602). **3550**

ANNALS OF THE ASSOCIATION OF AMERICAN GEOGRAPHERS. (US/0004-5608). **2554**

ANNALS OF THE BHANDARKAR ORIENTAL RESEARCH INSTITUTE. (II/0378-1143). **3265**

ANNALS OF THE CARNEGIE MUSEUM. (US/0097-4463). **Qty:** varies. **4162**

ANNALS OF THE MISSOURI BOTANICAL GARDEN. (US/0026-6493). **499**

ANNALS OF THE ROYAL COLLEGE OF PHYSICIANS AND SURGEONS OF CANADA. (CN/0035-8800). **Qty:** 80. **3913**

ANNALS OF THE ROYAL COLLEGE OF SURGEONS OF ENGLAND. (UK/0035-8843). **3959**

ANNALS OF THE UKRAINIAN ACADEMY OF ARTS AND SCIENCES IN THE UNITED STATES. (US/0503-1001). **2842**

ANNALS OF THORACIC SURGERY, THE. (US/0003-4975). **3959**

ANNALS OF TOURISM RESEARCH. (US/0160-7383). **5191**

ANNALS OF WYOMING. (US/0003-4991). **2720**

ANNAPOLITAN (ANNAPOLIS, MD.). (US/0899-2320). **2528**

ANNEE BATEAUX (ENGLISH ED.). (FR). **591**

ANNEE SOCIOLOGIQUE (1940/48). (FR/0066-2399). **5239**

ANNISTON STAR, THE. (US). **5625**

ANNUAIRE ADMINISTRATIF ET JUDICIAIRE DE BELGIQUE. ADMINISTRATIEF EN GERECHTELIJK JAARBOEK VOOR BELGIE. (BE/0066-2461). **4626**

ANNUAIRE DE L'ARMEMENT A LA PECHE. (FR/0066-2623). **2294**

ANNUAIRE DE L'AUDIOVISUEL DE LA COMMUNAUTE FRANCAISE. (BE). **1148**

ANNUAIRE DES COMMUNAUTES EUROPEENNES ET DES AUTRES ORGANISATIONS EUROPEENNES. (BE/0771-7962). **4515**

ANNUAIRE DES STATISTIQUES DU COMMERCE EXTERIEUR (KINSHASA). (CG/0304-5692). **5321**

ANNUAIRE DU CINEMA QUEBECOIS. (CN/0849-5726). **4063**

ANNUAIRE DU MARKETING. (FR). **921**

ANNUAIRE DU PAPIER, L'. (FR/0337-4971). **4232**

ANNUAIRE INTERNATIONAL DES VENTES. (FR). **336**

ANNUAIRE STATISTIQUE DE LA BELGIQUE. (BE/0066-3646). **5321**

ANNUAIRE STATISTIQUE DE L'ALGERIE. (AE). **5321**

ANNUAIRE STATISTIQUE DE POCHE - INSTITUT NATIONAL DE STATISTIQUE. (BE/0067-5431). **5321**

ANNUAIRE SUISSE DU MONDE ET DES AFFAIRES. (SZ). **429**

ANNUAL ABSTRACTS OF STATISTICS - CENTRAL OFFICE OF STATISTICS (VALLETTA). (MM/0256-8047). **5321**

ANNUAL AREA LABOR REVIEW. (US/0149-3779). **1644**

ANNUAL - CANADIAN GLADIOLUS SOCIETY. (CN/0319-1915). **2409**

ANNUAL EDITION: NOTICES TO MARINERS. (CN). **4174**

ANNUAL EXHIBITION OF THE CANADIAN SOCIETY OF PAINTERS IN WATER COLOUR. (CN/0318-4978). **336**

ANNUAL FORUM PROCEEDINGS - AMERICAN HELICOPTER SOCIETY. (US/0733-4249). **11**

ANNUAL GENERAL MEETING / DEVON AND CORNWALL RECORD SOCIETY. (UK). **5228**

ANNUAL INSTITUTE FOR CORPORATE COUNSEL. (US/0195-3680). **3095**

ANNUAL INSTITUTE OF EMPLOYMENT LAW. (US/0743-4146). **3144**

ANNUAL LAW SCHOOL SUMMER SCHOOL PROGRAMS AT HOME AND ABROAD. (US). **2934**

ANNUAL OF ARMENIAN LINGUISTICS. (US/0271-9800). **3265**

ANNUAL OF PSYCHOANALYSIS, THE. (US/0092-5055). **3920**

ANNUAL OF THE AMERICAN SCHOOLS OF ORIENTAL RESEARCH, THE. (US/0066-0035). **255**

ANNUAL REPORT - CENTER FOR RESEARCH IN WATER RESOURCES, THE UNIVERSITY OF TEXAS AT AUSTIN. (US/0276-0177). **5529**

ANNUAL REPORT / DELAWARE RIVER BASIN COMMISSION. (US/0418-5455). **5529**

ANNUAL REPORT FOR THE YEAR ENDED ... / EMPLOYMENT APPEALS TRIBUNAL. (IE). **3144**

ANNUAL REPORT - HUNTINGTON LIBRARY, ART GALLERY, BOTANICAL GARDENS. (US/0363-3306). **3190**

ANNUAL REPORT - INDONESIAN NATIONAL SCIENTIFIC DOCUMENTATION CENTER. (IO). **5084**

ANNUAL REPORT, INFORMATION COMMISSIONER. (CN/0826-9904). **4627**

ANNUAL REPORT (MEDIEVAL SETTLEMENT RESEARCH GROUP). (UK). **2675**

ANNUAL REPORT - NATIONAL TRUST OF AUSTRALIA, W.A. (AT). **4628**

ANNUAL REPORT OF THE ACTIVITIES OF THE ALABAMA DEPT. OF PUBLIC HEALTH. (US). **4766**

ANNUAL REPORT OF THE DIRECTOR, HOUSING DEVELOPMENT AND MANAGEMENT DEPARTMENT FOR THE YEAR.../CITY COUNCIL OF NAIROBI. (KE). **2814**

ANNUAL REPORT - RESOURCES FOR THE FUTURE. (US/0486-5561). **2187**

ANNUAL REPORT - THE RAILWAY & LOCOMOTIVE HISTORICAL SOCIETY, INC. (US/0483-9005). **Qty:** 30. **5429**

ANNUAL REPORT - UNITED PLANTING ASSOCIATION OF MALAYSIA. (MY/0304-8349). **61**

ANNUAL REPORT / VICTORIAN MINISTRY OF IMMIGRATION & ETHNIC AFFAIRS. (AT). **1918**

ANNUAL REPORT - YORK GEORGIAN SOCIETY. (UK/0959-3640). **Qty:** 1-2. **5228**

ANNUAL REPORTS FOR THE YEARS ... / REPUBLIC OF ZAMBIA, MINISTRY OF LABOUR AND SOCIAL SERVICES, INDUSTRIAL RELATIONS COURT. (ZA). **3144**

ANNUAL REPORTS OF THE NATIONAL COLLEGIATE ATHLETIC ASSOCIATION. (US/0077-3794). **4883**

ANNUAL SYMPOSIUM ON FOUNDATIONS OF COMPUTER SCIENCE. (US). **1250**

ANNUAL TECHNICAL REPORT / UNITED STATES DEPARTMENT OF AGRICULTURE, SOIL CONSERVATION SERVICE, BISMARCK PLANT MATERIALS CENTER. (US). **5084**

ANNUAL VOLUME / THE OLD WATER-COLOUR SOCIETY'S CLUB. (UK/0958-8825). **337**

ANNUARIO NAZIONALE DELL ENERGIA E DELL AMBIENTE. (IT). **1932**

ANNUARIO SEAT. VOL. D, EDILIZIA. (IT). **598**

ANNUARIO SEAT. VOL. F, ABBIGLIAMENTO ED ESTETICA. (IT). **1081**

ANNUARIO SEAT. VOL. G, P.TURISMO E TEMPO LIBERO. (IT). **5461**

ANNUARIO SEAT. VOL. H, AGRICOLTURA ED ALIMENTAZIONE. (IT). **62**

ANNUARIO SEAT. VOL. I, TRASPORTI, CARTOTECNICA ED EDITORIA. (IT). **1598**

ANNUARIUM HISTORIAE CONCILIORUM. (GW/0003-5157). **2610**

ANOTHER CHICAGO MAGAZINE. (US/0272-4359). **Qty:** 20. **3362**

ANQ (LEXINGTON, KY.). (US/0895-769X). **Qty:** 29. **3362**

ANSEARCHIN' NEWS. (US/0003-5246). **2437**

ANTARCTIC. (NZ/0003-5327). **Qty:** 6. **1351**

ANTARES LA VALETTE. (FR/0751-7580). **3362**

ANTENNA. (UK/0140-1890). **5576**

ANTHOLOGY OF MAGAZINE VERSE AND YEARBOOK OF AMERICAN POETRY (1980). (US/0196-2221). **3460**

ANTHOS; GARTEN- UND LANDSCHAFTSGESTALTUNG. (SZ/0003-5424). **2409**

ANTHROPOLGISCHE VERKENNINGEN. (NE). **Qty:** 40. **228**

ANTHROPOLOGICA (OTTAWA). (CN/0003-5459). **228**

ANTHROPOLOGICAL FORUM. (AT/0066-4677). **229**

ANTHROPOLOGICAL LINGUISTICS. (US/0003-5483). **Qty:** 40. **229**

ANTHROPOLOGICAL QUARTERLY. (US/0003-5491). **229**

ANTHROPOLOGIE ET SOCIETES. (CN/0702-8997). **229**

ANTHROPOLOGIE (PARIS). (FR/0003-5521). **229**

ANTHROPOLOGISCHER ANZEIGER. (GW/0003-5548). **229**

ANTHROPOLOGY & EDUCATION QUARTERLY. (US/0161-7761). **230**

ANTHROPOLOGY AND HUMANISM. (US). **230**

ANTHROPOLOGY AND HUMANISM QUARTERLY. (US/0193-5615). **230**

ANTHROPOLOGY OF WORK REVIEW. (US/0883-024X). **230**

ANTHROPOS. (GR). **230**

ANTHROPOS (BARCELONA, SPAIN). (SP/0211-5611). **2842**

ANTHROPOS FRIBOURG. (SZ/0257-9774). **230**

ANTHROPOZOOLOGICA PARIS. (FR/0761-3032). **5576**

ANTHROZOOS. (US/0892-7936). **5576**

ANTI. (GR). **4515**

ANTI-CANCER DRUGS. (UK/0959-4973). **3979**

ANTICANCER RESEARCH. (GR/0250-7005). **3809**

ANTICHITA VIVA. (IT/0003-5645). **Qty:** 8. **337**

ANTIEK. (NE/0003-5653). **337**

ANTIFURTO. (IT/0391-6227). **5176**

ANTIGONISH REVIEW, THE. (CN/0003-5661). **Qty:** 12. **3337**

ANTIGUA & BARBUDA CONSOLIDATED INDEX TO STATUTES AND SUBSIDIARY LEGISLATION TO ... . (BB). **3123**

ANTINCENDIO (1979). (IT/0393-7089). **2288**

ANTIOCH REVIEW, THE. (US/0003-5769). **3337**

ANTIPODAS : JOURNAL OF HISPANIC STUDIES OF THE UNIVERSITY OF AUCKLAND. (NZ/0113-2415). **3362**

ANTIPODES (BROOKLYN, NEW YORK, N.Y.). (US/0893-5580). **Qty:** 50. **3362**

ANTIQUA (ARCHEOCLUB D'ITALIA). (IT). **255**

ANTIQUARIAN BOOK MONTHLY. (UK). **Qty:** 40-50. **4823**

ANTIQUARIAN BOOK MONTHLY REVIEW. (UK/0306-7475). **4823**

ANTIQUARIAN HOROLOGY AND THE PROCEEDINGS OF THE ANTIQUARIAN HOROLOGICAL SOCIETY. (UK/0003-5785). **2916**

ANTIQUARIES JOURNAL. (UK/0003-5815). **255**

ANTIQUE AIRPLANE DIGEST. (US). **12**

ANTIQUE AUTOMOBILE, THE. (US/0003-5831). **5404**

ANTIQUE BOTTLE & GLASS COLLECTOR. (US/8750-1481). **248**

ANTIQUE COLLECTOR, THE. (UK/0003-5858). **249**

ANTIQUE GAZETTE. (US). **249**

ANTIQUE MAPS, SEA CHARTS, CITY VIEWS, CELESTIAL CHARTS & BATTLE PLANS. (US/0749-4971). **2554**

ANTIQUE PHONOGRAPH MONTHLY, THE. (US/0361-2147). **249**

ANTIQUE POWER MAGAZINE. (US/1042-7392). **Qty:** 6. **249**

ANTIQUE REVIEW. (US/0883-833X). **Qty:** 70-100. **249**

ANTIQUE SHOWCASE. (CN/0713-6315). **249**

ANTIQUE TOY WORLD. (US/0742-0420). **2583**

ANTIQUE TRADER ANTIQUES & COLLECTIBLES PRICE GUIDE, THE. (US/0882-6897). **249**

ANTIQUE TRADER WEEKLY, THE. (US/0161-8342). **249**

ANTIQUES & COLLECTIBLES (GREENVALE, N.Y.). (US/0274-6085). **249**

ANTIQUES & COLLECTING HOBBIES. (US/0884-6294). **249**

ANTIQUES & FINE ART. (US/0886-7208). **249**

ANTIQUES AND THE ARTS WEEKLY. (US). **249**

ANTIQUITE CLASSIQUE, L'. (BE/0770-2817). **1074**

ANTIQUITY. (UK/0003-598X). **255**

ANTISEPTIC, THE. (II/0003-5998). **3551**

ANTITRUST ADVISOR. (US). **3095**

ANTITRUST BULLETIN. (US/0003-603X). **3095**

ANTONIANUM. (IT/0003-6064). **4935**

ANTROPOLOGICA. (VE/0003-6110). **231**

ANTWERP BEE-ARGUS, THE. (US). **Qty:** 6. **5726**

ANTWERP FACETS. (BE/0777-0626). **2913**

ANUARIO DE DERECHO INTERNACIONAL. (SP/0212-0747). **3124**

ANUARIO DE ESTUDIOS MEDIEVALES. (SP/0066-5061). **2675**

ANUARIO DE LA RELOJERIA PARA ESPANA E HISPANOAMERICA. (SP). **2916**

ANUARIO DE LINGUISTICA HISPANICA. (SP/0213-053X). **3266**

ANUARIO DE PSICOLOGIA. (SP). **4574**

ANUARIO DENTAL ESPANOL Y PORTUGUES. (SP). **1316**

ANUARIO ESPANOL DE ACEITES Y GRASAS E INDUSTRIAS AUXILIARES. (SP). **1598**

ANUARIO ESPANOL DE JOYERIA Y RELOJERIA. (SP). **2913**

ANUARIO ESPANOL DE LAS ARTES GRAFICAS. (SP). **4563**

ANUARIO ESPANOL DE PARA-FARMACIA. (SP). **4292**

ANUARIO ESPANOL Y PORTUGUES DE ANALITICA. (SP). **3551**

ANUARIO ESPANOL Y PORTUGUES DE OPTICA Y AUDIOMETRIA. (SP). **4215**

ANUARIO ESTATISTICO DO ESTADO DE SAO PAULO. (BL/0100-8730). **5322**

ANUARIO IEHS. (AG/0326-9671). **2721**

ANUARIO JURIDICO. (MX/0185-3295). **2935**

ANUARUL INSTITUTULUI DE GEOLOGIE SI GEOFIZICA. (RM/0250-2933). **1365**

ANUNCIOS MADRID. (SP/0214-4905). **921**

ANVIL (NOTTINGHAM, NOTTINGHAMSHIRE). (UK). **4935**

ANVIL'S RING, THE. (US/0889-177X). **3998**

ANXIETY (NEW YORK, N.Y.) (US/1070-9797). **4574**

ANZEIGER DER ORNITHOLOGISCHE GESELLSCHAFT IN BAYERN. (GW/0030-5715). **5614**

ANZEIGER FUER SCHADLINGSKUNDE, PFLANZENSCHUTZ, UMWELTSCHUTZ. (GW/0340-7330). **4244**

ANZEIGER FUER SLAVISCHE PHILOLOGIE. (AU/0066-5282). **3266**

AONTAS NEWSLETTER. (IE/1805-1157). **1799**

AOPA PILOT, THE. (US/0001-2084). **12**

AORN JOURNAL. (US/0001-2092). **3851**

AOSTRA JOURNAL OF RESEARCH. (CN). **4250**

APA NEWSLETTERS ON THE BLACK EXPERIENCE, COMPUTER USE, FEMINISM, LAW, MEDICINE, TEACHING. (US/1067-9464). **Qty:** varies. **4341**

APAGAY (MONTREAL). (CN/0382-9251). **Qty:** varies. **5780**

APALACHEE QUARTERLY, THE. (US/0890-6408). **3362**

APARTMENT AGE. (US/0192-0030). **2815**

APARTMENT MANAGEMENT NEWSLETTER. (US/0744-9143). **4834**

APEIRON (CLAYTON). (CN/0003-6390). **1074**

APERTURE (MILLERTON, N.Y.). (US/0003-6420). **4366**

APEX OF THE M. (US/1072-9232). **Qty:** 2. **3460**

APHA NEWSLETTER : A PUBLICATION OF THE AMERICAN PRINTING HISTORY ASSOCIATION, THE. (US). **4563**

APICOLTORE MODERNO, L'. (IT/0518-1259). **5605**

APICULTURAL ABSTRACTS. (UK/0003-648X). **5604**

APIDOLOGIE. (FR/0044-8435). **5576**

APLUS. (BE). **288**

APMA NEWS. (US/8750-2585). **3917**

APO PRODUCTIVITY JOURNAL. (JA/0919-0589). **Qty:** 10. **62**

APOLLINARIS; COMMENTARIUS IURIDICO-CANONICUS. (IT). **2936**

APOLLO (LONDON. 1925). (UK/0003-6536). **337**

APORTES. (CR). **2511**

APORTES MATEMATICOS / UNIVERSIDAD DE TARAPACA, FACULTAD DE CIENCIAS, DEPARTAMENTO DE MATEMATICAS. (CL). **3494**

APOTHEKENHELFERIN, DIE. (GW). **4292**

APOTHEKER-ZEITUNG STUTTGART. (GW/0178-4862). **4292**

APPALACHIA (BOSTON). (US/0003-6587). **4869**

APPALACHIAN FAMILIES. (US/1041-8466). **2437**

APPALACHIAN HERITAGE. (US/0363-2318). **3362**

APPALACHIAN JOURNAL. (US/0090-3779). **Qty:** 20-30 /yr. **2721**

APPALACHIAN READER, THE. (US/1043-2809). **Qty:** 4. **5273**

APPALACHIAN ROOTS. (US/0888-6814). **Qty:** 50. **2437**

APPALACHIAN TRAILWAY NEWS. (US/0003-6641). **4869**

APPALOOSA JOURNAL. (US/0892-385X). **Qty:** 2-3. **2797**

APPAREL INTERNATIONAL. (UK/0263-1008). **1081**

APPETITE. (UK/0195-6663). **4187**

APPLAUSE THEATRE BOOK REVIEW & CATALOG, THE. (US). **383**

APPLELAND BULLETIN, THE. (US/0736-0800). **2437**

APPLESEED QUARTERLY. (CN/1183-3785). **Qty:** 4. **3363**

APPLIANCE SERVICE NEWS. (US/0003-6803). **2810**

APPLICABLE ANALYSIS. (US/0003-6811). **3494**

APPLICANDO. (IT). **1171**

APPLICATION OF COMPUTERS AND OPERATIONS RESEARCH IN THE MINERAL INDUSTRY / SPONSORED BY COLORADO SCHOOL OF MINES. (US/0741-0603). **1171**

APPLIED ACOUSTICS. (UK/0003-682X). **2097**

APPLIED AND THEORETICAL ELECTROPHORESIS. (UK/0954-6642). **1013**

APPLIED ARTIFICIAL INTELLIGENCE. (US/0883-9514). **1211**

APPLIED BIOCHEMISTRY AND BIOTECHNOLOGY. (US). **3685**

APPLIED CATALYSIS. B : ENVIRONMENTAL. (NE/0926-3373). **2161**

APPLIED COGNITIVE PSYCHOLOGY. (UK/0888-4080). **4574**

APPLIED ECONOMICS. (UK/0003-6846). **1463**

APPLIED ENERGY. (UK/0306-2619). **1932**

APPLIED ERGONOMICS. (UK/0003-6870). **1965**

APPLIED GENETICS NEWS. (US/0271-7107). **542**

APPLIED HEALTH PHYSICS ABSTRACTS AND NOTES. (UK/0305-7615). **4433**

APPLIED HYDROGEOLOGY: INTERNATIONAL JOURNAL FOR HYDROGEOLOGISTS. (GW). **1366**

APPLIED LINGUISTICS. (UK/0142-6001). **3266**

APPLIED MAGNETIC RESONANCE. (RU/0937-9347). **4397**

APPLIED MATHEMATICAL MODELLING. (UK/0307-904X). **3495**

APPLIED MECHANICS REVIEWS. (US/0003-6900). **2002**

APPLIED OCEAN RESEARCH. (UK/0141-1187). **1446**

APPLIED ORGANOMETALLIC CHEMISTRY. (UK/0268-2605). **961**

APPLIED PSYCHOLINGUISTICS. (UK/0142-7164). **3266**

APPLIED PSYCHOLOGICAL MEASUREMENT. (US/0146-6216). **4574**

APPLIED RADIOLOGY (1976). (US/0160-9963). **3939**

APPLIED SOLAR ENERGY. (US/0003-701X). **1932**

APPLIED SPECTROSCOPY. (US/0003-7028). **4433**

APPLIED SPECTROSCOPY REVIEWS (SOFTCOVER ED.). (US/0570-4928). **1013**

APPLIED STATISTICS. (UK/0035-9254). **5322**

APPRAISAL. (US/0003-7052). **5085**

APPRAISAL JOURNAL, THE. (US/0003-7087). **Qty:** 12-15/yr. **4834**

APPRAISERS' INFORMATION EXCHANGE, THE. (US/8755-4348). **4834**

APPRENTICE (OTTAWA). (CN/0706-7399). **4857**

APPROPRIATE TECHNOLOGY. (UK/0305-0920). **5085**

APPUNTI DEL CIRCOLO CULTURALE G GHISLANDI. (IT). **Qty:** 4/y. **3337**

APRES-DEMAIN. (FR/0003-7176). **4464**

APT FOR LIBRARIES. (US/1062-0664). **Qty:** 200. **3191**

APUA NEWSLETTER. (UK). **62**

APUNTES. (CL). **3363**

APUNTES (DALLAS, TEX.). (US/0279-9804). **4935**

AQUA FENNICA. (FI/0356-7133). **1412**

AQUA (LONDON). (UK/0003-7214). **5530**

AQUACULTURAL ENGINEERING. (UK/0144-8609). **2295**

AQUACULTURE EUROPE. (BE). **Qty:** 20. **552**

AQUACULTURE IRELAND. (IE/0790-0929). **Qty:** 6. **2295**

AQUACULTURE MAGAZINE. (US/0199-1388). **2295**

AQUAPHYTE. (US/0893-7702). **500**

AQUARAMA. (FR/0151-6981). **4285**

AQUARIUM. (US). **Qty:** varies. **553**

AQUATIC INSECTS. (NE/0165-0424). **5605**

AQUATIC MAMMALS. (UK/0167-5427). **Qty:** 6. **5576**

AQUATICS INTERNATIONAL. (US/1058-7039). **4883**

AQUELARRE (VANCOUVER). (CN/0843-7920). **5551**

AQUI MAGAZINE. (US). **2484**

AQUILON (YELLOWKNIFE). (CN/0834-1443). **Qty:** 2. **3266**

AQUINAS. (IT/0003-7362). **4341**

AQUINAS JOURNAL. (CE). **5191**

AR FALZ. (FR/0755-883X). **3363**

ARAB STUDIES QUARTERLY. (US/0271-3519). **2645**

ARABESQUE (NEW YORK, N.Y.). (US/0148-5865). **4100**

ARABIAN COMPUTER NEWS. (UK/0950-5075). **1235**

ARABIAN HORSE EXPRESS. (US/0194-6803). **Qty:** 12. **2797**

ARABIAN HORSE WORLD. (US/0003-7494). **2797**

ARABIC SCIENCES AND PHILOSOPHY : A HISTORICAL JOURNAL. (UK/0957-4239). **5085**

ARABICA. (NE/0570-5398). **2767**

ARANCEL ADUANERO DE CHILE. (CL). **823**

ARARAT (NEW YORK). (US/0003-7583). **3363**

ARBA SICULA. (US/0271-0730). **3363**

ARBEIDERVERN. (NO/0332-7124). **2859**

ARBEIT UND BERUF. (GW). **4630**

ARBEITNEHMER. (GW). **1651**

ARBEITS- UND SOZIALSTATISTIK. (GW). **1529**

ARBEITS- UND SOZIALSTATISTIK. HAUPTERGEBNISSE / DER BUNDESMINISTER FUR ARBEIT UND SOZIALORDNUNG. (GW/0341-7840). **1651**

ARBEITS- UND SOZIALSTATISTIKEN. (GW). **1529**

ARBEITSBLATTER FUER RESTAURATOREN. (GW/0066-5738). **256**

ARBEITSKRAEFTE IN DEN LANDWIRTSCHAFTLICHEN BETRIEBEN. (GW). **62**

ARBEITSMEDIZIN, SOZIALMEDIZIN, PRAVENTIVMEDIZIN. (GW/0300-581X). **2859**

ARBEITSRECHT DER GEGENWART, DAS. (GW/0066-586X). **3144**

ARBEITSSCHUTZ, ARBEITSHYGIENE. (GW/0138-1555). **2859**

ARBETARHISTORIA : MEDDELANDE FRAN ARBETARRORELSENS ARKIV OCH BIBLIOTEK. (SW/0281-7446). **Qty:** 8-10. **1651**

ARBITRATION AND DISPUTE RESOLUTION LAW JOURNAL, THE. (UK/0965-7053). **3124**

ARBITRATION IN THE SCHOOLS. (US/0003-7885). **1726**

ARBITRATION INTERNATIONAL. (UK/0957-0411). **3124**

ARBITRATION JOURNAL, THE. (US/0003-7893). **2936**

ARBITRIUM : ZEITSCHRIFT FUER REZENSIONEN ZUR GERMANISTISCHEN LITERATURWISSENSCHAFT. (GW). **3337**

ARBORESCENCES (PARIS). (FR/0767-337X). **Qty:** 6. **2375**

ARBORETUM LEAVES. (US/0518-2662). **500**

ARBORICULTURAL JOURNAL, THE. (UK/0307-1375). **2375**

ARBORICULTURE FRUITIERE, L'. (FR/0003-794X). **163**

ARC (MONTREAL). (CN/0229-2807). **Qty:** 12-20/yr. **5055**

ARC NEWS (REDLANDS, CALIF.). (US/1064-6108). **Qty:** 4. **1284**

ARC (OTTAWA). (CN/0705-6397). **Qty:** 4-8. **3460**

ARCADE

ARCADE (SEATTLE, WASH.). (US). 288

ARCADIA. (GW/0003-7982). 3363

ARCHAEOASTRONOMY. (UK/0142-7253). 256

ARCHAEOASTRONOMY (COLLEGE PARK). (US/0190-9940). 256

ARCHAEOLOGIA CANTIANA. (UK/0066-5894). 256

ARCHAEOLOGIA ZAMBIANA. (ZA). Qty: 1. 256

ARCHAEOLOGICAL COMPUTING NEWSLETTER. (UK/0952-3332). 256

ARCHAEOLOGICAL JOURNAL, THE. (UK/0066-5983). 256

ARCHAEOLOGICAL NEWS. (US/0194-3413). 257

ARCHAEOLOGICAL REVIEW FROM CAMBRIDGE. (UK/0261-4332). 257

ARCHAEOLOGICAL SERIES (TUCSON). (US/0196-5409). 257

ARCHAEOLOGY. (US/0003-8113). 257

ARCHAEOLOGY IN OCEANIA. (AT/0728-4896). Qty: 20. 257

ARCHAIOLOGIA. (GR). 258

ARCHE (1957). (FR/0518-2840). 5046

ARCHEOLOGICKE ROZHLEDY. (XR/0044-8605). 259

ARCHEOMATERIALS. (US/0891-2920). 259

ARCHERY ACTION WITH OUTDOOR CONNECTIONS. (AT/1037-6720). Qty: varies. 4884

ARCHFACTS. (NZ/0303-7940). 2479

ARCHIMAG VINCENNES. (FR/0769-0975). 2479

ARCHIMEDE. (IT/0003-8369). 3495

ARCHIPEL PARIS. (FR/0044-8613). 2501

ARCHIPELAG : A. (GW). 4540

ARCHITECT. (NE/0044-8621). 288

ARCHITECT & SURVEYOR. (UK/0308-8596). 288

ARCHITECT, W.A. : THE OFFICIAL JOURNAL OF THE ROYAL AUSTRALIAN INSTITUTE OF ARCHITECTS, W.A. CHAPTER, THE. (AT/0003-8393). Qty: 3. 288

ARCHITECTS INDIA. (II/0970-6852). 288

ARCHITECTS' JOURNAL (LONDON). (UK/0003-8466). 288

ARCHITECTS TRADE JOURNAL. (II/0304-8594). 288

ARCHITECTURA. (GW/0044-863X). 288

ARCHITECTURAL DESIGN. (UK/0003-8504). 288

ARCHITECTURAL HISTORY. (UK/0066-622X). 289

ARCHITECTURAL LIGHTING. (US/0894-0436). 289

ARCHITECTURAL MONOGRAPHS. (UK/0141-2191). 289

ARCHITECTURAL PSYCHOLOGY NEWSLETTER. (UK). 4575

ARCHITECTURAL SCIENCE REVIEW. (AT/0003-8628). 289

ARCHITECTURE & COMPORTEMENT. (SZ/0379-8585). 289

ARCHITECTURE AUSTRALIA. (AT/0003-8725). 289

ARCHITECTURE CALIFORNIA. (US/0738-1131). 290

ARCHITECTURE CONCEPT. (CN/0003-8687). 290

ARCHITECTURE D'AUJOURD'HUI, L'. (BE/0003-8695). 290

ARCHITECTURE MINNESOTA. (US/0149-9106). Qty: 20. 290

ARCHITECTURE NEW JERSEY. (US/0003-8733). 290

ARCHITECTURE NEW ZEALAND. (NZ/0113-4566). 290

ARCHITECTURE TODAY. (UK/0958-6407). Qty: 10. 290

ARCHITECTUUR, BONWEN. (NE/0169-4421). 290

ARCHITEKT (STUTTGART), DER. (GW/0003-875X). 290

ARCHITEKTONIKA THEMATA. (GR/0066-6262). 290

ARCHITEKTUR AKTUELL FACH-JOURNAL. (AU/0570-6602). 290

ARCHITEKTURA A URBANIZMUS. (XO/0044-4680). 291

ARCHITETTURA, STORIA E DOCUMENTI : RIVISTA SEMESTRALE DI STORIA DELL'ARCHITETTURA DEL CENTRO DI STUDI STORICO-ARCHIVISTICI PER LA STORIA DELL'ARTE E DELL'ARCHITETTURA MEDIOEVALE E MODERNA. (IT). 291

ARCHIV DES OFFENTLICHEN RECHTS. (GW/0003-8911). 3092

ARCHIV DES VOLKERRECHTS. (GW/0003-892X). 3124

ARCHIV FUER DIE CIVILISTISCHE PRAXIS. (GW/0003-8997). 3088

ARCHIV FUER FISCHEREIWISSENSCHAFT. (GW/0003-9063). 2296

ARCHIV FUER HYDROBIOLOGIE. (GW/0003-9136). 5530

ARCHIV FUER HYDROBIOLOGIE. SUPPLEMENTBAND, ALGOLOGICAL STUDIES. (GW/0342-1120). 442

ARCHIV FUER KATHOLISCHES KIRCHENRECHT. (GW/0003-9160). 2936

ARCHIV FUER KOMMUNALWISSENSCHAFTEN. (GW/0003-9209). 4630

ARCHIV FUER KRIMINOLOGIE. (GW/0003-9225). 3158

ARCHIV FUER ORIENTFORSCHUNG. (AU/0066-6440). 3266

ARCHIV FUER PHYTOPATHOLOGIE UND PFLANZENSCHUTZ. (GW/0323-5408). 500

ARCHIV FUER PROTISTENKUNDE. (GW/0003-9365). 5576

ARCHIV FUER RECHTS- UND SOZIALPHILOSOPHIE. (GW/0001-2343). 2936

ARCHIV FUER REFORMATIONSGESCHICHTE. BEIHEFT, LITERATURBERICHT. (GW/0341-8375). 2676

ARCHIV FUER SOZIALGESCHICHTE. (GW/0066-6505). 2676

ARCHIV FUER VOLKERKUNDE. (AU/0066-6513). 231

ARCHIV FUR DAS STUDIUM DER NEUEREN SPRACHEN UND LITERATUREN (1961). (GW/0003-8970). 3266

ARCHIV FUR SIPPENFORSCHUNG UND ALLE VERWANDTEN GEBIETE. (GW/0003-9403). 2437

ARCHIVAL INFORMER, THE. (US/8756-9663). 2479

ARCHIVAL ISSUES : JOURNAL OF THE MIDWEST ARCHIVES CONFERENCE. (US/1067-4993). 2479

ARCHIVAR, DER. (GW/0003-9500). 2479

ARCHIVARIA. (CN/0318-6954). Qty: 20. 2479

ARCHIVE OF AUSTRALIAN JUDAICA HOLDINGS TO ... . (AT). 2479

ARCHIVES AND MANUSCRIPTS. (AT/0157-6895). 2479

ARCHIVES & MUSEUM INFORMATICS. (US/1042-1467). 1217

ARCHIVES D'ANATOMIE ET DE CYTOLOGIE PATHOLOGIQUES. (FR/0395-501X). 3678

ARCHIVES DE L'ART FRANCAIS. (FR). 337

ARCHIVES DE L'INSTITUT PASTEUR DE MADAGASCAR. (MG/0020-2495). 3666

ARCHIVES DE PHILOSOPHIE. (FR/0003-9632). 4341

ARCHIVES DE SCIENCES SOCIALES DES RELIGIONS. (FR/0335-5985). 4935

ARCHIVES ET BIBLIOTHEQUES DE BELGIQUE. (BE/0003-9748). 2479

ARCHIVES FRANCAISES DE PEDIATRIE. (FR/0003-9764). 3900

ARCHIVES INFORMATION CIRCULAR. (US/0093-9056). 2479

ARCHIVES ITALIENNES DE BIOLOGIE. (IT/0003-9829). 442

ARCHIVES (LONDON). (UK/0003-9535). 2479

ARCHIVES OF ANDROLOGY. (UK/0148-5016). 3678

ARCHIVES OF COMPLEX ENVIRONMENTAL STUDIES : ACES. (FI/0787-0396). 2161

ARCHIVES OF DERMATOLOGY. (US/0003-987X). 3718

ARCHIVES OF GYNECOLOGY AND OBSTETRICS. (GW/0932-0067). 3757

ARCHIVES OF HISTOLOGY AND CYTOLOGY. (JA/0914-9465). 532

ARCHIVES OF NATURAL HISTORY. (UK/0260-9541). Qty: 8. 4162

ARCHIVES OF NEUROLOGY (CHICAGO). (US/0003-9942). 3827

ARCHIVES OF OPHTHALMOLOGY. (US/0003-9950). 3872

ARCHIVES OF ORAL BIOLOGY. (UK/0003-9969). 1316

ARCHIVES OF PATHOLOGY & LABORATORY MEDICINE. (US/0003-9985). 3893

ARCHIVES OF PHYSICAL MEDICINE AND REHABILITATION. (US/0003-9993). 4379

ARCHIVES OF PSYCHIATRIC NURSING. (US/0883-9417). 3851

ARCHIVES OF TOXICOLOGY. (GW/0340-5761). 3979

ARCHIVES OF VIROLOGY. (AU/0304-8608). 560

ARCHIVI & COMPUTER. (IT/1121-2462). Qty: varies. 1171

ARCHIVIO DI ORTOPEDIA E REUMATOLOGIA. (IT/0390-7368). 3803

ARCHIVIO GLOTTOLOGICO ITALIANO. (IT/0004-0207). 3266

ARCHIVIO ITALIANO DI ANATOMIA E DI EMBRIOLOGIA. (IT/0004-0223). 3678

ARCHIVIO PER L'ALTO ADIGE. (IT/0392-1050). 2255

ARCHIVIO PER L'ANTROPOLOGIA E LA ETNOLOGIA. (IT/0373-3009). 231

ARCHIVIO PUTTI DI CHIRURGIA DEGLI ORGANI DI MOVIMENTO. (IT/0066-670X). 3960

ARCHIVIO SICILIANO DI MEDICINA E CHIRURGIA. 1, ACTA CHIRURGICA MEDITERRANEA. (IT). 3960

ARCHIVIO SICILIANO DI MEDICINA E CHIRURGIA. 5, ACTA PEDIATRICA MEDITERRANEA. (IT/0393-6392). 3900

ARCHIVIO STORICO LODIGIANO. (IT/0004-0347). 2611

ARCHIVIO VENETO, A CURA DELLA R. DEPUTAZIONE DI STORIA PATRIA PER LE VENEZIE. (IT). 2676

ARCHIVO ESPANOL DE ARTE. (SP/0004-0428). 337

ARCHIVO IBERO-AMERICANO. (SP/0004-0452). 2721

ARCHIVO TEOLOGICO GRANADINO. (SP/0210-1629). 5023

ARCHIVOS DE BIOLOGIA Y MEDICINA EXPERIMENTALES. (CL/0004-0533). 442

ARCHIVOS DE BRONCONEUMOLOGIA. (SP/0300-2896). 3948

ARCHIVOS DE CRIMINOLOGIA, NEUROPSIQUIATRIA Y DISCIPLINAS CONEXAS. (EC). 3158

ARCHIVOS DE MEDICINA DEL DEPORTE : PUBLICACION DE LA FEDERACION ESPANOLA DE MEDICINA DEL DEPORTE / FEMEDE. (SP/0212-8799). 3953

ARCHIVOS ESPANOLES DE UROLOGIA. (SP/0004-0614). 3988

ARCHIVOS LATINOAMERICANOS DE NUTRICION. (VE/0004-0622). Qty: 6/yr. 4187

ARCHIVUM FRANCISCANUM HISTORICUM. (IT/0004-0665). 5024

ARCHIVUM HISTORICUM SOCIETATIS IESU. (VC/0037-8887). 5024

ARCHOLOGIAI ERTESITO. (HU/0003-8032). Qty: 20. 259

ARCHTYPE (TORONTO). (CN/0712-1873). 4383

ARCO. (CK/0570-7293). 2842

ARCO ADVERTISER, THE. (US/0890-1511). 5656

ARCTIC. (CN/0004-0843). Qty: 30/yr. 2555

ARCTIC AND ALPINE RESEARCH. (US/0004-0851). 2555

ARCTIC MEDICAL RESEARCH. (FI/0782-226X). 3552

ARCTIC SOUNDER, THE. (US/0897-9502). 5628

ARDELL WELLNESS REPORT, THE. (US/0882-0171). Qty: 6. 4767

AREA (MILAN, ITALY). (IT/0394-0055). 291

AREA NEWS, THE. (US). 5658

AREE. ANNUAL REVIEW OF ENVIRONMENTAL EDUCATION. (UK/0953-0428). Qty: 4. 2161

AREITO. (US/0360-0467). 2255

ARENA. (AT/0004-0932). 4464

ARENA JOURNAL. (AT). Qty: 2. 4540

ARENA MAGAZINE. (AT/1039-1010). Qty: 6. 4540

AREOPAGUS : A LIVING ENCOUNTER WITH TODAY'S RELIGIOUS WORLD. (HK). Qty: 5-10. 4936

ARGOMENTI DI CARDIOLOGIA. (IT/1120-8635). 3699

ARGOS. (AG). 3266

ARGUMENT, DAS. (GW/0004-1157). 4341

ARGUMENTATION AND ADVOCACY. (US/1051-1431). Qty: varies. 1104

ARGUMENTS & FACTS INTERNATIONAL. (UK/0957-0020). Qty: 24. 639

ARGUS-CHAMPION, THE. (US). Qty: 10. 5708

ARGUS (MICROFICHE). (SA). **5810**

ARGUS (SAN FRANCISCO). (US/0194-8172). **3872**

ARHIV PATOLOGIJ. (RU/0004-1955). **3893**

ARHIV ZA HIGIJENU RADA I TOKSIKOLOGIJU. (CR/0004-1254). **Qty: 25-30. 2859**

ARIEL. (CN/0004-1327). **3363**

ARIEL (ENGLISH EDITION). (IS/0004-1343). **3363**

ARIES / ASSOCIATION POUR LA RECHERCHE ET L'INFORMATION SUR L'ESOTERISME. (FR/0752-2452). **4240**

ARION / BOSTON UNIVERSITY. (US). **Qty: 18. 3363**

ARISTOS. (US/0737-0407). **313**

ARITHMETIC TEACHER, THE. (US/0004-136X). **3496**

ARIZONA ANTHROPOLOGIST. (US/1062-1601). **Qty: 2 per issue. 231**

ARIZONA ATTORNEY. (US/1040-4090). **2936**

ARIZONA BUSINESS GAZETTE. (US/0273-6950). **639**

ARIZONA ENGLISH BULLETIN. (US/0004-1483). **3267**

ARIZONA GEOLOGY. (US/1045-4802). **1366**

ARIZONA HIGHWAYS. (US/0004-1521). **5461**

ARIZONA HUNTER & ANGLER. (US/0888-840X). **Qty: 6-12. 4884**

ARIZONA JOURNAL OF INTERNATIONAL AND COMPARATIVE LAW. (US/0743-6963). **3124**

ARIZONA LIVING. (US/0279-6376). **2528**

ARIZONA MOBILE CITIZEN. (US/0004-1564). **2815**

ARIZONA MUSIC NEWS. (US/0518-6129). **4101**

ARIZONA NURSE. (US/0004-1599). **3851**

ARIZONA PHARMACIST, THE. (US/0004-1602). **4292**

ARIZONA QUARTERLY, THE. (US/0004-1610). **Qty: 2. 3363**

ARIZONA REPUBLIC. (US/0892-8711). **5629**

ARIZONA SENIOR WORLD, THE. (US/0270-0425). **Qty: 24. 5629**

ARIZONA SILVER BELT. (US). **5629**

ARIZONA STATE LAW JOURNAL. (US/0164-4297). **Qty: 0-4. 2937**

ARIZONA THOROUGHBRED, THE. (US/0091-4401). **2797**

ARK. (UK). **226**

ARKANSAS AMATEUR, THE. (US/0518-6617). **259**

ARKANSAS BANKER, THE. (US/0004-1726). **773**

ARKANSAS CITY TRAVELER (ARKANSAS CITY, KAN. : 1970). (US/0888-8485). **5674**

ARKANSAS EDUCATOR. (US/0161-7753). **1888**

ARKANSAS EPISCOPALIAN, THE. (US/0890-5258). **5055**

ARKANSAS FAMILY HISTORIAN, THE. (US/0571-0472). **2438**

ARKANSAS HISTORICAL QUARTERLY, THE. (US/0004-1823). **Qty: 40. 2721**

ARKANSAS LAWYER. (US/0571-0502). **2937**

ARKANSAS LIBRARIES. (US/0004-184X). **3191**

ARKANSAS WILDLIFE. (US/1063-0953). **Qty: varies. 2187**

ARKITEKTEN. (DK/0004-198X). **291**

ARKIV FOR NORDISK FILOLOGI. (SW/0066-7668). **3267**

ARL ANNUAL SALARY SURVEY. (US/0361-5669). **1654**

ARLINGTON CATHOLIC HERALD. (US/0361-3712). **5024**

ARLIS/ANZ NEWS. (AT/0157-4043). **408**

ARMCHAIR DETECTIVE, THE. (US/0004-217X). **3363**

ARMED FORCES. (SA). **4035**

ARMED FORCES AND SOCIETY. (US/0095-327X). **4035**

ARMEES D'AUJOURD'HUI. (FR). **4036**

ARMEMENT. (FR). **4036**

ARMENIAN CAUSE, THE. (CN/0826-2667). **2645**

ARMENIAN MIRROR-SPECTATOR, THE. (US/0004-234X). **5687**

ARMENIAN REVIEW, THE. (US/0004-2366). **Qty: 40. 2501**

ARMENIAN WEEKLY, THE. (US/0004-2374). **5687**

ARMOR. (US/0004-2420). **4036**

ARMS COLLECTING. (CN/0380-982X). **2771**

ARMS CONTROL (LONDON, ENGLAND). (UK/0144-0381). **4036**

ARMS CONTROL TODAY. (US/0196-125X). **Qty: 8-10. 3124**

ARMS REGISTER. (US). **755**

ARMSTRONG CHRONICLES. (US/0898-1329). **2438**

ARMY COMMUNICATOR, THE. (US/0362-5745). **4036**

ARMY HISTORY. (US). **4036**

ARMY LOGISTICIAN. (US/0004-2528). **4036**

ARMY MOTORS. (US/0195-5632). **Qty: 4-8. 4036**

ARMY QUARTERLY AND DEFENCE JOURNAL, THE. (UK/0004-2552). **4036**

ARMY RESERVE MAGAZINE. (US/0004-2579). **4036**

ARMY TIMES. (US/0004-2595). **4037**

ARMY (WASHINGTON. 1956). (US/0004-2455). **4037**

AROIDEANA. (US/0197-4033). **2409**

AROUND EUROPE. (BE). **2513**

AROUND THE BEND (RICHMOND, TEX.). (US/0749-517X). **2438**

ARQ : ARCHITECTURE/QUEBEC. (CN/0710-1163). **292**

ARQUITECTURA VIVA. (SP/0214-1256). **292**

ARQUITETURA DO BRASIL : AB. (BL). **292**

ARQUIVOS DE GASTROENTEROLOGIA. (BL/0004-2803). **Qty: 12-15. 3743**

ARRIS (ATLANTA, GA.). (US/1048-5945). **Qty: varies. 292**

ARS CERAMICA. (US/1043-3317). **2586**

ARS MEDICI, MONATSSCHRIFT FUER ALLGEMEINMEDIZIN. (SZ/0004-2897). **3552**

ARS MUSICA DENVER. (US/1058-7500). **Qty: 2. 4101**

ARS NOVA. (SA). **4101**

ARS ORIENTALIS. (US/0571-1371). **337**

ARSC JOURNAL. (US). **Qty: 18. 5315**

ARSIS. (FI/0780-9859). **313**

ARSREDOVISNING / NOBELSTIFTELSEN. (SW). **3144**

ARSSKRIFT - DANSK GEOLOGISK FORENING. (DK). **1366**

ART & ANTIQUES. (US/0195-8208). **337**

ART & AUCTION (NEW YORK, N.Y.). (US/0197-1093). **250**

ART AND AUSTRALIA. (AT/0004-301X). **338**

ART & CRAFT. (UK). **370**

ART & CRAFTS CATALYST. (US). **370**

ART & DESIGN / ARCHITECTURAL DESIGN PUBLICATIONS. (UK/0267-3991). **338**

ART & DESIGN NEWS. (US/1055-2286). **376**

ART AND POETRY TODAY. (II). **338**

ART & TEXT. (AT/0727-1182). **338**

ART AT AUCTION IN AMERICA. (US/1046-4999). **338**

ART BUSINESS NEWS. (US/0273-5652). **338**

ART CALENDAR (GREAT FALLS, VA.). (US/0893-3901). **338**

ART CRITICISM. (US/0195-4148). **338**

ART CULINAIRE (ATLANTA, GA.). (US/0892-1024). **Qty: 3-4. 2788**

ART, DESIGN, ARCHITECTURE : ADA. (SA). **Qty: 4. 338**

ART DOCUMENTATION. (US/0730-7187). **3192**

ART E DOSSIER. (IT/0394-0179). **338**

ART EDUCATION (RESTON). (US/0004-3125). **338**

ART ET METIERS DU LIVRE. (FR). **4823**

ART HISTORY. (UK/0141-6790). **339**

ART IN AMERICA (1939). (US/0004-3214). **339**

ART INDEX. CD-ROM. (US/0004-3222). **334**

ART ISSUES. (US/1046-8471). **Qty: 1-2. 339**

ART JOURNAL (NEW YORK. 1960). (US/0004-3249). **339**

ART LIBRARIES JOURNAL. (UK/0307-4722). **3192**

ART MONTHLY. (UK/0142-6702). **339**

ART MUSCLE. (US). **313**

ART NEW ENGLAND. (US/0274-7073). **Qty: 10. 339**

ART NEW ZEALAND. (NZ/0110-1102). **339**

ART NEWSPAPER. (IT/0960-6556). **Qty: 100/yr. 339**

ART OF EATING, THE. (US/0895-6200). **Qty: 12. 2327**

ART PAPERS. (US/0278-1441). **Qty: 8. 340**

ART POST, THE. (CN/0829-0784). **340**

ART PRESS (PARIS, FRANCE : 1981). (FR/0245-5676). **313**

ART REFERENCE SERVICES QUARTERLY. (US/1050-2548). **340**

ART SALES INDEX (WEYBRIDGE, SURREY : 1985). (UK). **340**

ART SCHOOL MAGAZINE. (NE). **376**

ART-TALK. (US/0741-496X). **340**

ART THERAPY: JOURNAL OF THE AMERICAN ART THERAPY ASSOCIATION. (US/0742-1656). **Qty: 8-12. 4575**

ART TIMES (SAUGERTIES, N.Y.). (US/0891-9070). **Qty: 50. 340**

ART TO SCIENCE IN TISSUE CULTURE. (US). **443**

ART/WORLD (NEW YORK. 1976). (US/0194-1070). **340**

ARTE CRISTIANA. (IT/0004-3400). **340**

ARTE, DE. (SA). **340**

ARTE ESPANOL. (SP). **340**

ARTE FACTUM (ANTWERPEN). (BE/0771-761X). **340**

ARTE IN. (IT). **Qty: 15. 341**

ARTE MEDIEVALE. (IT/0393-7267). **341**

ARTE NAIVE. (IT/0390-1319). **341**

ARTEFACT, THE. (AT/0044-9075). **260**

ARTERY. (US/0098-6127). **3795**

ARTESANIA Y FOLKLORE DE VENEZUELA. (VE). **314**

ARTESANIAS DE AMERICA. (EC). **341**

ARTFORUM INTERNATIONAL. (US). **341**

ARTFUL DODGE. (US/0196-691X). **3363**

ARTHRITIS AND RHEUMATISM. (US/0004-3591). **3803**

ARTHUR GRAPHIC-CLARION, THE. (US). **5658**

ARTI MUSICES. (CI/0587-5455). **4101**

ARTIBUS ASIAE. (SZ/0004-3648). **341**

ARTIBUS ASIAE. SUPPLEMENTUM. (SZ). **341**

ARTICHOKE (CALGARY). (CN/0847-3277). **Qty: 8. 341**

ARTIFACT, THE. (US/0004-3680). **260**

ARTIFICIAL INTELLIGENCE ABSTRACTS. (US/0882-1410). **1208**

ARTIFICIAL INTELLIGENCE AND LAW. (NE/0924-8463). **1211**

ARTIFICIAL INTELLIGENCE IN MEDICINE. (NE/0933-3657). **1211**

ARTILLERYMAN, THE. (US/0884-4747). **4037**

ARTINF. (AG). **341**

ARTIS. (GW/0004-3842). **370**

ARTIST (CALCUTTA). (II/0304-8640). **314**

ARTIST (LONDON. 1931). (UK/0004-3877). **341**

ARTIST'S AND ILLUSTRATOR'S MAGAZINE. (UK/0269-4697). **Qty: 120. 341**

ARTIST'S MAGAZINE, THE. (US/0741-3351). **314**

ARTIST'S MARKET (1979). (US/0161-0546). **376**

ARTLINK. (AT/0727-1239). **342**

ARTNEWSLETTER, THE. (US/0145-7241). **342**

ARTPAPER. (US/0739-8646). **342**

ARTS AND ACTIVITIES. (US/0004-3931). **314**

ARTS AND CRAFTS QUARTERLY MAGAZINE. (US). **Qty: 6. 370**

ARTS & METIERS. (FR/0004-4008). **5086**

ARTS & THE ISLAMIC WORLD. (UK). **314**

ARTS + ARCHITECTURE. (US/0730-9481). **314**

ARTS ASIATIQUES (PARIS). (FR/0004-3958). **342**

ARTS D'AFRIQUE NOIRE. (FR/0337-1603). **Qty: 4. 314**

ARTS — Book Review Index

ARTS EDUCATION REVIEW OF BOOKS, THE. (US/0889-2172). **315**

ARTS EDUCATION : THE MAGAZINE OF THE NATIONAL FOUNDATION FOR ARTS EDUCATION. (UK). **315**

ARTS IN PSYCHOTHERAPY, THE. (US/0197-4556). **3921**

ARTS INDIANA. (US/0897-859X). **Qty: 4-6. 315**

ARTS JOURNAL (ASHEVILLE, N.C.), THE. (US/0739-8662). **315**

ARTS MAGAZINE (NEW YORK). (US/0004-4059). **342**

ARTS MANAGEMENT. (US/0004-4067). **315**

ARTS PATRONAGE SERIES. (US/0066-8168). **315**

ARTS QUARTERLY (NEW ORLEANS, LA. 1978). (US/0740-9214). **342**

ARTS REVIEW. (UK/0004-4091). **315**

ARTS REVIEW YEAR BOOK. (UK). **342**

ARTS / THE ARTS IN RELIGIOUS & THEOLOGICAL STUDIES. (US). **315**

ARTSATLANTIC. (CN/0704-7916). **315**

ARTSOURCE (RENAISSANCE, CALIF.). (US/1064-6620). **Qty: 3. 315**

ARTSPACE. (US/0193-6956). **Qty: 1/yr. 342**

ARTSPEAK (NEW YORK, N.Y.). (US/1065-1543). **Qty: 5. 342**

ARTWORLD EUROPE. (US/1062-8312). **Qty: 10. 342**

ARZNEIMITTEL FORSCHUNG. (GW/0004-4172). **4292**

ARZTLICHE PRAXIS. (GW/0001-9534). **3553**

AS-SARQ AL-AWSAT. (UK/0265-5772). **5811**

ASA NEWSLETTER - APPLIED SCIENCE AND ANALYSIS, INC, THE. (US/1057-9419). **Qty: 24. 4037**

ASB BULLETIN, THE. (US/0001-2386). **Qty: 8-10. 443**

ASBURY PARK PRESS. (US). **5709**

ASBURY THEOLOGICAL JOURNAL, THE. (US). **Qty: 10. 4936**

ASCA NEWSLETTER (FORT LAUDERDALE, FLA.). (US/0747-6000). **4884**

ASCENT. (CN/0707-5588). **1933**

ASCENT (KOOTENAY BAY). (CN/0315-8179). **4936**

ASCI JOURNAL OF MANAGEMENT. (II/0257-8069). **860**

ASEA YONGU. (KO/0021-9126). **2645**

ASEAN BRIEFING. (US). **1547**

ASEAN ECONOMIC BULLETIN. (SI/0217-4472). **1463**

ASEAN FOOD JOURNAL. (MY/0127-7324). **Qty: 12. 2327**

ASFA MARINE BIOTECHNOLOGY ABSTRACTS. (US/1054-2027). **553**

ASH SMOKING AND HEALTH REVIEW. (US/1048-907X). **4767**

ASHA (ROCKVILLE, MD.). (US/0001-2475). **1875**

ASHLAND THEOLOGICAL JOURNAL. (US/1044-6494). **Qty: 35. 4936**

ASHMOLEAN, THE. (UK). **Qty: 2-3. 4084**

ASHRAE HANDBOOK. REFRIGERATION SYSTEMS AND APPLICATIONS. (US). **2603**

ASHRAE JOURNAL. (US/0001-2491). **2603**

ASHTON GAZETTE, THE. (US). **5658**

ASHTREE ECHO. (US/0004-4377). **2438**

ASIA COMPUTER WEEKLY. (SI/0129-5896). **1235**

ASIA JOURNAL OF THEOLOGY. (SI/0218-0812). **4936**

ASIA LETTER, THE. (US/0004-4466). **1463**

ASIA-OCEANIA JOURNAL OF OBSTETRICS AND GYNAECOLOGY. (JA/0389-2328). **3757**

ASIA-PACIFIC AGRIBUSINESS REPORT. (US). **63**

ASIA PACIFIC JOURNAL OF HUMAN RESOURCES. (AT/1038-4111). **Qty: 18. 938**

ASIA PACIFIC JOURNAL OF MANAGEMENT. (SI/0217-4561). **860**

ASIA-PACIFIC JOURNAL OF PUBLIC HEALTH : ASIA-PACIFIC ACADEMIC CONSORTIUM FOR PUBLIC HEALTH. (TH/1010-5395). **4767**

ASIA-PACIFIC POPULATION JOURNAL. (TH/0259-238X). **4549**

ASIA PACIFIC TRAVEL. (US/1045-3881). **5461**

ASIA THEOLOGICAL NEWS. (CH). **4936**

ASIA TRAVEL TRADE. (HK). **5462**

ASIAN AFFAIRS. (BG). **4516**

ASIAN AFFAIRS (LONDON). (UK/0306-8374). **2646**

ASIAN AFFAIRS (NEW YORK). (US/0092-7678). **4516**

ASIAN ALMANAC. (SI/0004-4520). **2646**

ASIAN AMERICAN AND PACIFIC ISLANDER JOURNAL OF HEALTH. (US/1072-0367). **Qty: 4. 4768**

ASIAN AMERICAN NEWS (HOUSTON, TEX.). (US/1070-3969). **2255**

ASIAN AMERICAN POLICY REVIEW. (US/1062-1830). **Qty: 1-2. 2255**

ASIAN AND AFRICAN LINGUISTIC STUDIES. (XR). **3267**

ASIAN AND AFRICAN STUDIES (BRATISLAVA, CZECHOSLOVAKIA). (XO/0571-2742). **2646**

ASIAN AND AFRICAN STUDIES (JERUSALEM). (IS/0066-8281). **Qty: 10. 2638**

ASIAN AND PACIFIC MIGRATION JOURNAL : APMJ. (PH). **Qty: 16-20. 1918**

ASIAN AQUACULTURE. (PH/0115-4974). **Qty: 3. 2296**

ASIAN ARCHITECT AND CONTRACTOR. (HK). **292**

ASIAN ART NEWS. (HK). **Qty: various. 2501**

ASIAN COMMUNICATIONS. (UK/0952-7516). **1149**

ASIAN CULTURE QUARTERLY. (CH/0378-8911). **2646**

ASIAN DEFENCE JOURNAL. (MY/0126-6403). **4037**

ASIAN ECONOMIC AND SOCIAL REVIEW, THE. (II/0970-6305). **1547**

ASIAN ECONOMIC JOURNAL : JOURNAL OF THE EAST ASIAN ECONOMIC ASSOCIATION. (HK/1351-3958). **1633**

ASIAN ENVIRONMENT. (PH/0116-2993). **2161**

ASIAN HOSPITAL. (HK/1011-596X). **3777**

ASIAN HOTEL AND CATERING TIMES. (HK). **2804**

ASIAN JOURNAL OF PHILOSOPHY, THE. (CC). **Qty: 10. 4341**

ASIAN JOURNAL OF PUBLIC ADMINISTRATION / YA-CHOU KUNG KUNG HSING CHENG HSUEH / UNIVERSITY OF HONG KONG, THE. (HK). **4630**

ASIAN LIVESTOCK : MONTHLY PUBLICATION OF THE ANIMAL PRODUCTION AND HEALTH COMMISSION FOR ASIA, THE FAR EAST AND THE SOUTH-WEST PACIFIC. (TH). **206**

ASIAN MIGRANT. (PH). **Qty: 16. 1918**

ASIAN MUSIC. (US/0044-9202). **Qty: 10-20. 4101**

ASIAN-PACIFIC ECONOMIC LITERATURE. (UK/0818-9935). **Qty: 60 year. 1530**

ASIAN PACIFIC JOURNAL OF ALLERGY AND IMMUNOLOGY. (TH/0125-877X). **3666**

ASIAN PERSPECTIVE. (KO). **4516**

ASIAN PERSPECTIVES (HONOLULU). (US/0066-8435). **260**

ASIAN PROFILE. (HK/0304-8675). **Qty: 10. 5192**

ASIAN SECURITY. (JA). **4516**

ASIAN SHIPPING. (HK). **5447**

ASIAN STUDIES. (PH/0004-4679). **2501**

ASIAN STUDIES (CALCUTTA, INDIA). (II). **2501**

ASIAN STUDIES REVIEW. (AT/1035-7823). **2646**

ASIAN SURVEY. (US/0004-4687). **5192**

ASIAN THEATRE JOURNAL. (US/0742-5457). **383**

ASIAN THOUGHT & SOCIETY. (US/0361-3968). **4540**

ASIAN TIMES. (UK/0264-8490). **2485**

ASIAN WALL STREET JOURNAL. WEEKLY, THE. (US/0191-0132). **1547**

ASIANWEEK. (US/0195-2056). **Qty: 51. 5633**

ASIATIC HERPETOLOGICAL RESEARCH. (US/1051-3825). **5577**

ASIATISCHE STUDIEN. (SZ/0004-4717). **2646**

ASIAWEEK. (HK). **2501**

ASIE DU SUD-EST ET MONDE INSULINDIEN. (FR/0395-2681). **2646**

ASIEN. (GW/0721-5231). **2501**

ASK (BETHESDA, MD.). (US/0731-2350). **5086**

ASKOV AMERICAN. (US). **Qty: 5. 5694**

ASL. (AT/1034-9154). **3192**

ASLIB INFORMATION (LONDON, ENGLAND : 1973). (UK/0305-0033). **3192**

ASM NEWS. (US/0044-7897). **560**

ASME BOILER AND PRESSURE VESSEL CODE. (US/0517-5321). **2110**

ASOCIACION TECNICA ESPANOLA DEL PRETENSADO. (SP). **2018**

ASPAREZ. (US/0004-4229). **5633**

ASPECTS DE LA FRANCE. (FR). **4464**

ASPECTS OF EDUCATION : JOURNAL OF THE INSTITUTE OF EDUCATION, THE UNIVERSITY OF HULL. (UK/0066-8672). **1726**

ASPEN DAILY NEWS. (US). **Qty: 1-2. 5641**

ASPIRE (NASHVILLE, TENN.). (US/1076-5778). **2596**

ASPR NEWSLETTER. (US). **4240**

ASR NEWS : AUTOMATIC SPEECH RECOGNITON NEWS. (US/1051-4163). **Qty: 3-4. 1104**

ASSEMBLIES OF GOD EDUCATOR. (US/0196-9560). **1726**

ASSEMBLIES OF GOD HERITAGE. (US/0896-4394). **Qty: 10. 4936**

ASSEMBLY. (US). **5024**

ASSEMBLY AUTOMATION. (UK/0144-5154). **1217**

ASSERTIVE UTILIZATION MANAGEMENT REPORT, THE. (US/1064-4962). **Qty: 1-2. 3553**

ASSESSMENT AND EVALUATION IN HIGHER EDUCATION. (UK/0260-2938). **1810**

ASSESSMENT AND VALUATION LEGAL REPORTER. (US/0090-6352). **4711**

ASSESSMENT DIGEST. (US/0731-0277). **4711**

ASSESSMENT UPDATE. (US/1041-6099). **1810**

ASSET FINANCE & LEASING DIGEST. (UK). **773**

ASSICURAZIONE; QUINDICINALE DI TECHNICA, CRONACA E GIURISPRUDENZA ASSICURATIVA. (IT/0004-5098). **2874**

ASSIG NEWSLETTER. (AT/1030-3812). **3192**

ASSINEWS. (IT). **2874**

ASSISTANT LIBRARIAN. (UK/0004-5152). **3192**

ASSISTIVE TECHNOLOGY. (US/1040-0435). **4384**

ASSOCIATE REFORMED PRESBYTERIAN, THE. (US/0362-0816). **Qty: 15-20. 5055**

ASSOCIATION & SOCIETY MANAGER. (US/0004-5292). **860**

ASSOCIATION EXECUTIVE COMPENSATION STUDY. (US/0273-0367). **640**

ASSOCIATION LAW AND POLICY. (US). **Qty: 4-5/yr. 2937**

ASSOCIATION MANAGEMENT. (US). **860**

ASSOCIATION MANAGEMENT. (US/0004-5578). **640**

ASSOCIATION TRENDS. (US/0196-1942). **640**

ASSOCIATIONS REPORT. (US/0744-1088). **860**

ASSURANCES. (CN/0004-6027). **2874**

ASTC NEWSLETTER. (US/0895-7371). **Qty: 6-10/ yr. 5086**

ASTHMA UPDATE. (US/8756-4734). **3948**

ASTHMA WELFARER. (AT). **3948**

ASTIN BULLETIN. (UK/0515-0361). **2874**

ASTM GEOTECHNICAL TESTING JOURNAL. (US/0149-6115). **1965**

ASTORIA SOUTH FULTON ARGUS, THE. (US). **5658**

ASTRO INVESTOR. (US). **891**

ASTRO-NEWS (BATON ROUGE, LA.). (US/0743-4227). **390**

ASTROGRAPH (ARLINGTON), THE. (US/0094-1417). **391**

ASTROLOGICAL MAGAZINE, THE. (II/0004-6140). **390**

ASTROLOGICAL REVIEW, THE. (US/0044-9784). **390**

ASTROLOGY QUARTERLY. (UK). **Qty: 4. 390**

ASTRONOMIE. (FR). **392**

ASTRONOMIE MAGAZINE, L'. (FR). **Qty: 10. 392**

ASTRONOMIE-QUEBEC. (CN). **Qty: 10. 392**

ASTRONOMY AND ASTROPHYSICS MONTHLY INDEX. (US/0147-4669). **392**

ASTRONOMY & ASTROPHYSICS. SUPPLEMENT SERIES. (FR/0365-0138). **392**

ASTRONOMY (MILWAUKEE). (US/0091-6358). **393**

ASTROPHYSICAL LETTERS AND COMMUNICATIONS. (US/0888-6512). **393**

ASTROPHYSICS AND SPACE SCIENCE. (NE/0004-640X). **393**

ASTUTE INVESTOR (KINGSTON, TENN.), THE. (US/0736-7643). **Qty:** 2-4. **891**

ASWLC. (US/0162-5934). **1126**

AT EASE. (US/0190-4280). **4936**

AT RANDOM. (US/1062-0036). **4812**

AT THE LIBRARY. (CN/0702-7559). **3192**

AT-THE-PARK (CHICAGO, ILL.). (US/1048-9118). **4857**

AT WORK (SAN FRANCISCO, CALIF.). (US/1061-9925). **Qty:** 20-30. **4201**

ATA JOURNAL. ASIA THEOLOGICAL ASSOCIATION. INDIA. (II). **Qty:** 8. **4936**

ATA NEWS. (II). **Qty:** 8. **4936**

ATALA. (US/0160-5674). **5605**

ATALANTA (MUNCHEN). (GW/0171-0079). **5605**

ATALAYA CULTURAL : REVISTA DE POESIA, ARTE Y LITERATURA. (SP). **3460**

ATARI MAGAZINE. (FR/0992-2016). **1264**

ATARISTE. (CN/0847-5644). **1265**

ATCHISON COUNTY MAIL, THE. (US). **5699**

ATCP. (MX). **4232**

ATE NEWS LETTER. (US/0001-2718). **1888**

ATEISMO E DIALOGO. (VC). **4936**

ATEMWEGS- UND LUNGENKRANKHEITEN. (GW/0341-3055). **3948**

ATENCION MEDICA. (MX/0185-6235). **3553**

ATENEA (CONCEPCION, CHILE: 1972). (CL/0004-6507). **2611**

ATENEO VENETO : REVISTA DI SCIENZE, LETTERE ED ARTI. (IT/0004-6558). **315**

ATHENIAN (ATHENS, GREECE). (GR). **Qty:** 8-10. **3267**

ATHENS DAILY NEWS, ATHENS BANNER-HERALD. (US/0898-3712). **Qty:** 15. **5652**

ATHENS MAGAZINE (ATHENS, GA. 1989). (US/1053-623X). **Qty:** 6. **2528**

ATHENS OBSERVER, THE. (US/0744-4001). **5652**

ATHLETIC ADMINISTRATION. (US/0044-9873). **Qty:** 12-18. **1855**

ATHLETICS COACH. (UK/0267-0267). **4884**

ATHLETICS (TORONTO. 1981). (CN/0229-4966). **4884**

ATHOL DAILY NEWS. (US). **5687**

ATIRA TECHNICAL DIGEST. (II/0378-8148). **5348**

ATLA : ALTERNATIVES TO LABORATORY ANIMALS. (UK/0261-1929). **Qty:** 20. **3979**

ATLAL. (SU). **260**

ATLANTA BUSINESS CHRONICLE. (US/0164-8071). **640**

ATLANTA BUSINESS MAKERS & SHAKERS SERIES. (US/1054-5182). **Qty:** 2/yr. **640**

ATLANTA DAILY WORLD. (US). **2255**

ATLANTA HISTORY. (US/0896-3975). **Qty:** 30. **2722**

ATLANTA JEWISH TIMES, THE. (US/0892-3345). **Qty:** 12. **5652**

ATLANTA LAW LIBRARIES ASSOCIATION NEWSLETTER. (US). **2937**

ATLANTA SINGLES. (US/0897-4608). **2485**

ATLANTA SMALL BUSINESS MONTHLY, THE. (US). **640**

ATLANTA VOICE, THE. (US). **Qty:** 10. **5652**

ATLANTIC BAPTIST, THE. (CN/0004-6752). **5055**

ATLANTIC (BOSTON, MASS. : 1981), THE. (US/0276-9077). **2528**

ATLANTIC BUSINESS REPORT. (CN/1192-0203). **641**

ATLANTIC CHARISMATIC. (CN/0821-6479). **5024**

ATLANTIC COASTAL KAYAKER. (US). **Qty:** varies. **4884**

ATLANTIC CONTROL STATES BEVERAGE JOURNAL. (US/0044-9881). **5070**

ATLANTIC ECONOMIC JOURNAL. (US/0197-4254). **1464**

ATLANTIC FIREFIGHTER. (CN/0838-679X). **2288**

ATLANTIC GEOLOGY. (CN/0843-5561). **1366**

ATLANTIC PROVINCES BOOK REVIEW, THE. (CN/0316-5981). **3337**

ATLANTIC REPORT (HALIFAX, N.S.). (CN/0004-6841). **1547**

ATLANTIC SALMON JOURNAL, THE. (CN/0044-992X). **2296**

ATLANTIDE-REPORT: SCIENTIFIC RESULTS OF THE DANISH EXPEDITION TO THE COASTS OF TROPICAL WEST AFRICA, 1945-1946. (DK). **553**

ATLANTIS (WOLFVILLE). (CN/0702-7818). **5551**

ATLETICA : RIVISTA MENSILE DELLA FIDAL. (IT). **4884**

ATMOSPHERE-OCEAN. (CN/0705-5900). **1420**

ATOMIC ENERGY NEWSLETTER. (US). **2154**

ATOMIZATION AND SPRAYS. (US/1044-5110). **2008**

ATOMWIRTSCHAFT, ATOMTECHNIK. (GW/0365-8414). **2154**

ATOSSEMENT VOTRE. (CN/0826-5321). **2296**

ATRIAL NATRIURETIC FACTORS. (UK/0268-1641). **3699**

ATRIUM (LONDON). (UK/0951-8088). **292**

ATS FOCUS. (AT/0727-3096). **Qty:** 3-4. **5086**

ATTAKAPAS GAZETTE. (US/0571-8236). **2722**

ATTI DELLA FONDAZIONE GIORGIO RONCHI (1976). (IT/0391-2051). **4433**

ATTI E MEMORIE DELLA SOCIETA ISTRIANA DI ARCHEOLOGIA E STORIA PATRIA. (IT). **Qty:** 5. **260**

ATTITUDE (BROOKLYN (NEW YORK, N.Y.)). (US/0882-3472). **1310**

ATTITUDES & ARABESQUES. (US/0889-8847). **1310**

ATTORNEY-CPA, THE. (US/0571-8279). **Qty:** varies. **2938**

ATTORNEY FEE AWARDS REPORTER. (US/0732-7552). **2938**

ATTORNEYS MARKETING REPORT. (US/0745-1369). **2938**

ATV NEWS. (US/0744-7809). **4080**

ATV SPORTS. (US/0892-3183). **4884**

ATWOOD HERALD, THE. (US). **5658**

ATZ. AUTOMOBILTECHNISCHE ZEITSCHRIFT. (GW/0001-2785). **5404**

AU FIL DES EVENEMENTS. (CN/0225-1965). **1726**

AU FIL DU BOIS. (CN/0383-0047). **2399**

AU NATUREL (MONTREAL). (CN/0715-4690). **4768**

AU "PAYS" DE MATANE. (CN/0836-3102). **2722**

AUBURN CITIZEN. (US). **5658**

AUBURN JOURNAL. (US). **Qty:** 52. **5633**

AUCKLAND UNIVERSITY LAW REVIEW. (NZ/0067-0510). **Qty:** varies. **3089**

AUDECIBEL. (US/0004-7473). **Qty:** 10. **4384**

AUDIBLE (TORONTO). (CN/0710-2038). **4884**

AUDIO AMATEUR. (US/0004-7546). **5315**

AUDIO (DURANGO, COLO.). (US/0883-8437). **5315**

AUDIO VISUAL. (UK/0305-2249). **1104**

AUDIOFILE (PORTLAND, ME.). (US/1063-0244). **Qty:** 550. **1104**

AUDIOLOGISCHE AKUSTIK. AUDIOLOGICAL ACOUSTICS. (GW/0172-8261). **4384**

AUDIOTEX NEWS. (US/1063-1348). **Qty:** 2. **1149**

AUDIOTEX UPDATE. (US/1045-5795). **1282**

AUDIOVISUAL LIBRARIAN, THE. (UK/0302-3451). **3192**

AUDUBON NATURALIST NEWS : A PUBLICATION OF THE AUDUBON NATURALIST SOCIETY OF THE CENTRAL ATLANTIC STATES. (US/0888-6555). **4162**

AUFBAU (NEW YORK, N.Y.). (US/0004-7813). **5713**

AUFBEREITUNGS-TECHNIK. (GW/0004-783X). **2134**

AUGENOPTIKER, DER. (GW/0004-7929). **3872**

AUGUSTA MELBOURNE. (AT/1033-8934). **Qty:** 6. **293**

AUGUSTINIAN STUDIES. (US/0094-5323). **5024**

AUGUSTINIANA. (BE/0004-8003). **Qty:** 2. **2611**

AUGUSTINIANUM. (IT/0004-8011). **4342**

AUGUSTINUS. (SP/0004-802X). **4937**

AUJOURD'HUI CREDO. (CN/0383-2554). **4937**

AULA ORIENTALIS. (SP/0212-5730). **2646**

AUNT EDNA'S READING LIST. (US). **5551**

AURA (FORT WORTH, TEX.). (US/1054-5441). **2528**

AUREALIS MT. WAVERLEY. (AT/1035-1205). **Qty:** 2-3. **3364**

AUSLEGUNG. (US/0733-4311). **4342**

AUSSENDIENST-INFORMATIONEN. TRAININGSKURS FUR SYSTEMATISCHES VERKAUFEN. (GW/0933-8357). **2874**

AUSSENPOLITIK. (GW/0004-8194). **4516**

AUSSENPOLITIK (ENGLISH EDITION). (GW/0587-3835). **4516**

AUSSENWIRTSCHAFT: ZEITSCHRIFT FUER INTERNATIONALE WIRTSCHAFTSBEZIEHUNGEN. (SZ/0004-8216). **4516**

AUSTIN CHRONICLE (SCOTTSBURG, IND.), THE. (US/0740-4581). **5746**

AUSTIN CHRONICLE, THE. (US/1074-0740). **2528**

AUSTIN GENEALOGICAL SOCIETY : [QUARTERLY]. (US). **Qty:** 10. **2438**

AUSTIN HOMES & GARDENS. (US/0199-1531). **2898**

AUSTRALASIAN BEEKEEPER, THE. (AT/0004-8313). **63**

AUSTRALASIAN BIOTECHNOLOGY. (AT/1036-7128). **Qty:** 10. **3685**

AUSTRALASIAN BUS AND COACH. (AT). **5377**

AUSTRALASIAN CATHOLIC RECORD, THE. (AT/0727-3215). **5024**

AUSTRALASIAN DRAMA STUDIES. (AT/0810-4123). **5361**

AUSTRALASIAN FURNISHING TRADE JOURNAL. (AT). **2898**

AUSTRALASIAN HEALTH AND HEALING. (AT/0812-3896). **Qty:** 4. **2596**

AUSTRALASIAN JOURNAL OF AMERICAN STUDIES : AJAS. (AT/0705-7113). **2722**

AUSTRALASIAN JOURNAL OF DERMATOLOGY, THE. (AT/0004-8380). **3718**

AUSTRALASIAN JOURNAL OF PHILOSOPHY. (AT/0004-8402). **4342**

AUSTRALASIAN JOURNAL OF SPECIAL EDUCATION. (AT/1030-0112). **Qty:** 12. **1875**

AUSTRALASIAN PHYSICAL & ENGINEERING SCIENCES IN MEDICINE. (AT/0158-9938). **3685**

AUSTRALASIAN PLANT PATHOLOGY. (AT/0815-3191). **500**

AUSTRALASIAN PUBLIC LIBRARIES AND INFORMATION SERVICES. (AT/1030-5033). **3193**

AUSTRALASIAN RADIOLOGY. (AT/0004-8461). **3939**

AUSTRALASIAN SHIPPING RECORD. (AT). **5447**

AUSTRALASIAN SHIPS & PORTS. (AT/1032-3449). **5447**

AUSTRALASIAN STAMP CATALOGUE. (AT). **2784**

AUSTRALASIAN TEXTILES. (AT/0725-086X). **5348**

AUSTRALIA AND NEW ZEALAND JOURNAL OF DEVELOPMENTAL DISABILITIES. (AT/0726-3864). **4384**

AUSTRALIA DEPARTMENT OF PRIMARY INDUSTRIES AND ENERGY BASIC FISH STATISTICS. (AT). **2297**

AUSTRALIAN ABORIGINAL STUDIES (CANBERRA, A.C.T. : 1983). (AT/0729-4352). **2668**

AUSTRALIAN ACADEMIC AND RESEARCH LIBRARIES. (AT/0004-8623). **3193**

AUSTRALIAN ACCOUNTANT, THE. (AT/0004-8631). **Qty:** 1-2. **739**

AUSTRALIAN & NEW ZEALAND JOURNAL OF CRIMINOLOGY, THE. (AT/0004-8658). **3158**

AUSTRALIAN AND NEW ZEALAND JOURNAL OF MEDICINE. (AT/0004-8291). **3795**

AUSTRALIAN

AUSTRALIAN AND NEW ZEALAND JOURNAL OF OBSTETRICS AND GYNAECOLOGY. (AT/0004-8666). **3757**

AUSTRALIAN AND NEW ZEALAND JOURNAL OF OPHTHALMOLOGY. (AT/0814-9763). **3872**

AUSTRALIAN AND NEW ZEALAND JOURNAL OF PSYCHIATRY. (AT/0004-8674). **3921**

AUSTRALIAN & NEW ZEALAND JOURNAL OF SERIALS LIBRARIANSHIP. (US/0898-3283). **3193**

AUSTRALIAN AND NEW ZEALAND JOURNAL OF SOCIOLOGY, THE. (AT/0004-8690). **5240**

AUSTRALIAN AND NEW ZEALAND JOURNAL OF SURGERY. (AT/0004-8682). **3960**

AUSTRALIAN & NEW ZEALAND PHYSICIST : A PUBLICATION OF THE AUSTRALIAN INSTITUTE OF PHYSICS & THE NEW ZEALAND INSTITUTE OF PHYSICS, THE. (AT/1036-3831). Qty: 170. **4398**

AUSTRALIAN & NEW ZEALAND STUDIES IN CANADA. (CN/0843-5049). **3364**

AUSTRALIAN & NEW ZEALAND THEATRE RECORD : ANZTR. (AT). **5361**

AUSTRALIAN AND NEW ZEALAND WINE INDUSTRY JOURNAL. (AT). **2363**

AUSTRALIAN ANTIQUE BOTTLE COLLECTOR. (AT). **250**

AUSTRALIAN ARCHAEOLOGY. (AT/0312-2417). **260**

AUSTRALIAN AUTHOR, THE. (AT/0045-026X). **3364**

AUSTRALIAN AUTISM REVIEW. (AT/0312-8857). **4575**

AUSTRALIAN BANKER. (AT/0814-2912). **773**

AUSTRALIAN BAR REVIEW. (AT/0814-8589). **2938**

AUSTRALIAN BEE JOURNAL. (AT/0045-0294). **63**

AUSTRALIAN BIBLICAL REVIEW. (AT/0045-0308). Qty: 20. **5014**

AUSTRALIAN BIRD WATCHER. (AT/0045-0316). **5615**

AUSTRALIAN BIRDKEEPER. (AT/1030-8954). Qty: 12. **5615**

AUSTRALIAN BIRDS : JOURNAL OF THE N. S. W. FIELD ORNITHOLOGISTS CLUB. (AT/0311-8150). **5615**

AUSTRALIAN BOOK COLLECTOR. (AT/1034-0785). Qty: 20. **4823**

AUSTRALIAN BUILDING, CONSTRUCTION AND HOUSING. (AT/1032-240X). Qty: 10. **599**

AUSTRALIAN-CANADIAN STUDIES. (AT/0810-1906). Qty: varies. **2722**

AUSTRALIAN CHRISTIAN. (AT/0004-8852). Qty: 70-100. **4937**

AUSTRALIAN CITRUS NEWS. (AT/0004-8283). Qty: 1-2. **2328**

AUSTRALIAN CLAY JOURNAL AND CERAMIC NEWS. (AT/1035-4611). Qty: varies. **2586**

AUSTRALIAN CLINICAL REVIEW. (AT/0726-3139). **3554**

AUSTRALIAN COLLEGE OF MIDWIVES INCORPORATED JOURNAL. (AT/1031-170X). **3554**

AUSTRALIAN COMMUNICATION REVIEW. (AT/0726-3252). **1104**

AUSTRALIAN COMPUTER JOURNAL, THE. (AT/0004-8917). **1256**

AUSTRALIAN CORPORATE TREASURE. (AT). **641**

AUSTRALIAN COTTON GROWER. (AT/0159-1290). **164**

AUSTRALIAN CRITICAL CARE : OFFICIAL JOURNAL OF THE CONFEDERATION OF AUSTRALIAN CRITICAL CARE NURSES. (AT/1036-7314). **3851**

AUSTRALIAN CYCLIST. (AT). Qty: 6. **428**

AUSTRALIAN DEER. (AT). **2187**

AUSTRALIAN DEFENCE FORCE JOURNAL : JOURNAL OF THE AUSTRALIAN PROFESSION OF ARMS. (AT/0314-1039). **4037**

AUSTRALIAN DENTAL JOURNAL. (AT/0045-0421). **1317**

AUSTRALIAN DOLL DIRECTORY. (AT/0816-3294). **2771**

AUSTRALIAN ECONOMIC HISTORY REVIEW. (AT/0004-8992). **1547**

AUSTRALIAN EDUCATION DIRECTORY / DEPT. OF EDUCATION AND YOUTH AFFAIRS. (AT/0811-3165). **1726**

AUSTRALIAN ENTOMOLOGICAL MAGAZINE. (AT/0311-1881). **5605**

AUSTRALIAN ENTOMOLOGIST, THE. (AT/1320-6133). Qty: 4-8. **5605**

AUSTRALIAN EQUINE VETERINARIAN. (AT/1032-6626). **2797**

AUSTRALIAN EVANGEL. (AT/0812-4353). **4937**

AUSTRALIAN EXPATRIATE, THE. (US/1064-010X). Qty: 12-14. **2668**

AUSTRALIAN FAMILY MELBOURNE. (AT/0811-3661). Qty: 2. **2276**

AUSTRALIAN FAMILY PHYSICIAN. (AT/0300-8495). **3737**

AUSTRALIAN FARM MANAGER, THE. (AT/1035-1914). **64**

AUSTRALIAN FARMERS' AND DEALERS' JOURNAL. (AT/1036-4242). Qty: 4. **158**

AUSTRALIAN FEMINIST STUDIES. (AT/0816-4649). **5551**

AUSTRALIAN FINANCIAL REVIEW, THE. (AT). **773**

AUSTRALIAN FISHERIES. (AT/0004-9115). Qty: varies. **2297**

AUSTRALIAN FOLKLORE. (AT/0819-0852). **2318**

AUSTRALIAN FORESTRY. (AT/0004-9158). **2375**

AUSTRALIAN FRIEND (SYDNEY, N.S.W.). (AT). **4937**

AUSTRALIAN GARDEN HISTORY. (AT/1033-3673). **2409**

AUSTRALIAN GEM & TREASURE HUNTER. (AT/0159-6322). **4869**

AUSTRALIAN GEMMOLOGIST. (AT/0004-9174). **2913**

AUSTRALIAN GEOGRAPHER. (AT/0004-9182). **2555**

AUSTRALIAN GEOGRAPHICAL STUDIES. (AT/0004-9190). **2555**

AUSTRALIAN GLIDING. (AT). **12**

AUSTRALIAN GLIDING YEAR BOOK. (AT). **4885**

AUSTRALIAN GOAT WORLD, THE. (AT). **206**

AUSTRALIAN GRAIN. (AT). **164**

AUSTRALIAN GRAPEGROWER AND WINEMAKER. (AT/0727-3606). **2363**

AUSTRALIAN HAND WEAVER AND SPINNER / HAND WEAVERS AND SPINNERS GUILD OF NEW SOUTH WALES, THE. (AT). Qty: 2. **5183**

AUSTRALIAN HEALTH REVIEW. (AT/0156-5788). **3777**

AUSTRALIAN HISTORICAL STUDIES. (AT/1031-461X). **2668**

AUSTRALIAN HISTORY TEACHER. (AT/0312-2530). **1888**

AUSTRALIAN HUMANIST, THE. (AT/0004-9328). Qty: 3. **2842**

AUSTRALIAN JEWISH DEMOCRAT. (AT). **5046**

AUSTRALIAN JOURNAL OF ADVANCED NURSING. (AT/0813-0531). **3852**

AUSTRALIAN JOURNAL OF AGRICULTURAL ECONOMICS, THE. (AT/0004-9395). **64**

AUSTRALIAN JOURNAL OF ANTHROPOLOGY, THE. (AT/1035-8811). Qty: each issue. **231**

AUSTRALIAN JOURNAL OF ART. (AT/0314-6464). **343**

AUSTRALIAN JOURNAL OF CHINESE AFFAIRS, THE. (AT/0156-7365). **2501**

AUSTRALIAN JOURNAL OF CLINICAL AND EXPERIMENTAL HYPNOSIS. (AT/0156-0417). **2857**

AUSTRALIAN JOURNAL OF CLINICAL HYPNOTHERAPY AND HYPNOSIS, THE. (AT/0810-0713). **2857**

AUSTRALIAN JOURNAL OF COMMUNICATION. (AT/0811-6202). **1104**

AUSTRALIAN JOURNAL OF DAIRY TECHNOLOGY, THE. (AT/0004-9433). **192**

AUSTRALIAN JOURNAL OF EARLY CHILDHOOD. (AT/0312-5033). **1802**

AUSTRALIAN JOURNAL OF ECOLOGY. (AT/0307-692X). **2211**

AUSTRALIAN JOURNAL OF EDUCATION, THE. (AT/0004-9441). **1726**

AUSTRALIAN JOURNAL OF EDUCATIONAL TECHNOLOGY. (AT/0814-673X). Qty: 3. **1810**

AUSTRALIAN JOURNAL OF FORENSIC SCIENCES, THE. (AT/0045-0618). Qty: 4-11. **3740**

AUSTRALIAN JOURNAL OF FRENCH STUDIES. (AT/0004-9468). Qty: 5. **3364**

AUSTRALIAN JOURNAL OF GEODESY, PHOTOGRAMMETRY, AND SURVEYING. (AT/0159-8910). Qty: varies. **2018**

AUSTRALIAN JOURNAL OF HISTORICAL ARCHAEOLOGY, THE. (AT/0810-1868). **260**

AUSTRALIAN JOURNAL OF HOSPITAL PHARMACY. (AT/0310-6810). Qty: 15. **4293**

AUSTRALIAN JOURNAL OF HUMAN COMMUNICATION DISORDERS. (AT/0310-6853). **4384**

AUSTRALIAN JOURNAL OF INFOMATION SYSTEMS, THE. (AT/1039-7841). Qty: 3. **1727**

AUSTRALIAN JOURNAL OF INTERNATIONAL AFFAIRS. (AT/1035-7718). Qty: 2. **4516**

AUSTRALIAN JOURNAL OF JEWISH STUDIES. (AT/1037-0838). **2256**

AUSTRALIAN JOURNAL OF LABOUR LAW. (AT/1030-7222). **3144**

AUSTRALIAN JOURNAL OF LAW AND SOCIETY. (AT/0729-3356). **2938**

AUSTRALIAN JOURNAL OF LINGUISTICS. (AT/0726-8602). **3267**

AUSTRALIAN JOURNAL OF LITURGY. (AT/1030-617X). **4937**

AUSTRALIAN JOURNAL OF MANAGEMENT. (AT/0312-8962). **860**

AUSTRALIAN JOURNAL OF MARRIAGE & FAMILY. (AT/1034-652X). **2276**

AUSTRALIAN JOURNAL OF MEDICAL SCIENCE. (AT/1038-1643). Qty: 30. **3554**

AUSTRALIAN JOURNAL OF MUSIC THERAPY, THE. (AT/1036-9457). **3554**

AUSTRALIAN JOURNAL OF NUTRITION AND DIETETICS. (AT/1032-1322). Qty: varies. **4187**

AUSTRALIAN JOURNAL OF PHYSIOTHERAPY, THE. (AT/0004-9514). **4379**

AUSTRALIAN JOURNAL OF POLITICAL SCIENCE. (AT/1036-1146). Qty: 120. **4464**

AUSTRALIAN JOURNAL OF POLITICS AND HISTORY, THE. (AT/0004-9522). **4464**

AUSTRALIAN JOURNAL OF PSYCHOLOGY. (AT/0004-9530). **4575**

AUSTRALIAN JOURNAL OF PSYCHOTHERAPY. (AT/0728-6155). **4575**

AUSTRALIAN JOURNAL OF PUBLIC ADMINISTRATION. (AT/0313-6647). **4631**

AUSTRALIAN JOURNAL OF PUBLIC HEALTH. (AT/1035-7319). **4768**

AUSTRALIAN JOURNAL OF REMEDIAL EDUCATION. (AT/0726-5115). Qty: 30. **1727**

AUSTRALIAN JOURNAL OF SCIENCE AND MEDICINE IN SPORT. (AT). **3953**

AUSTRALIAN JOURNAL OF SOCIAL ISSUES, THE. (AT/0157-6321). **5274**

AUSTRALIAN JOURNAL OF SOIL AND WATER CONSERVATION. (AT/1032-2426). Qty: 6. **5530**

AUSTRALIAN JOURNAL OF STATISTICS. (AT/0004-9581). **5322**

AUSTRALIAN JOURNAL OF TEACHER EDUCATION, THE. (AT/0313-5373). **1888**

AUSTRALIAN JOURNAL ON AGEING. (AT/0726-4240). **3749**

AUSTRALIAN JOURNALISM REVIEW : AJR. (AT/0810-2686). **2917**

AUSTRALIAN LAW JOURNAL, THE. (AT/0004-9611). **2938**

AUSTRALIAN LAW LIBRARIAN. (AT/1039-6616). **2939**

AUSTRALIAN LAW NEWS. (AT). **2939**

AUSTRALIAN LEFT REVIEW. (AT/0004-9638). Qty: 40. **4465**

AUSTRALIAN LIBRARY JOURNAL, THE. (AT/0004-9670). **3193**

AUSTRALIAN LIBRARY REVIEW. (AT/1034-8042). Qty: 600. **3193**

AUSTRALIAN LITERARY STUDIES. (AT/0004-9697). **3338**

AUSTRALIAN LITHOGRAPHER, PRINTER AND PACKAGER, THE. (AT). **4563**

AUSTRALIAN MACHINERY AND PRODUCTION ENGINEERING. (AT/0004-9719). **2110**

AUSTRALIAN MAMMALOGY. (AT/0310-0049). **5577**

AUSTRALIAN MARINE SCIENCE BULLETIN. (AT/0157-6429). Qty: 8. **553**

AUSTRALIAN MATHEMATICS TEACHER, THE. (AT/0045-0685). **3496**

AUSTRALIAN MEAT INDUSTRY BULLETIN, THE. (AT/0156-2681). **206**

AUSTRALIAN MEDICAL RECORD JOURNAL / MEDICAL RECORD ASSOCIATION OF AUSTRALIA. (AT/0817-3907). **3777**

AUSTRALIAN METEOROLOGICAL MAGAZINE. (AT/0004-9743). **1420**

AUSTRALIAN MINING. (AT/0004-976X). **2134**

AUSTRALIAN MOTHER AND BABY. (AT/1031-4830). **Qty:** varies. **2277**

AUSTRALIAN NATURAL HISTORY. (AT/0004-9840). **4162**

AUSTRALIAN NURSES' JOURNAL. (AT/0045-0758). **3852**

AUSTRALIAN OCCUPATIONAL THERAPY JOURNAL. (AT/0045-0766). **Qty:** 10. **1875**

AUSTRALIAN ORCHID REVIEW. (AT/0045-0782). **2409**

AUSTRALIAN ORTHOPTIC JOURNAL. (AT/0814-0936). **3872**

AUSTRALIAN PARAPSYCHOLOGICAL REVIEW. (AT/1035-9621). **Qty:** 20. **4240**

AUSTRALIAN PARKS AND RECREATION. (AT/0311-8223). **4706**

AUSTRALIAN PHARMACIST / PHARMACEUTICAL SOCIETY OF AUSTRALIA. (AT/0728-4632). **Qty:** 3-4. **4293**

AUSTRALIAN PIPELINER. (AT/0310-1258). **4251**

AUSTRALIAN PLANNER : JOURNAL OF THE ROYAL AUSTRALIAN PLANNING INSTITUTE. (AT/0729-3682). **2815**

AUSTRALIAN PODIATRIST. (AT/0311-3612). **3917**

AUSTRALIAN POLICE JOURNAL. (AT/0005-0024). **3158**

AUSTRALIAN POLL DORSET JOURNAL. (AT). **206**

AUSTRALIAN PRESBYTERIAN LIFE. (AT). **5055**

AUSTRALIAN PRESCRIBER. (AT/0312-8008). **Qty:** 1. **3554**

AUSTRALIAN PRIVATE DOCTOR : THE JOURNAL OF PRIVATE DOCTORS OF AUSTRALIA. (AT). **Qty:** 4. **3554**

AUSTRALIAN PROSTHODONTIC JOURNAL. (AT/0819-0887). **Qty:** 4-6. **1317**

AUSTRALIAN PSYCHOLOGIST. (AT/0005-0067). **4575**

AUSTRALIAN PURCHASING AND SUPPLY (WATERLOO). (AT/1035-0357). **Qty:** 6-12. **949**

AUSTRALIAN QUARTERLY. (AT/0005-0091). **2668**

AUSTRALIAN RECORD AND MUSIC REVIEW. (AT/1033-1352). **4101**

AUSTRALIAN REFRIGERATION, AIR CONDITIONING AND HEATING. (AT). **2603**

AUSTRALIAN RELIGION STUDIES REVIEW. (AT/1031-2943). **Qty:** 15. **4937**

AUSTRALIAN REVIEW OF APPLIED LINGUISTICS. (AT/0155-0640). **Qty:** 8-10. **3267**

AUSTRALIAN ROAD AND TRACK. (AT/1036-3254). **Qty:** varies. **5404**

AUSTRALIAN SCIENCE TEACHERS' JOURNAL, THE. (AT/0045-0855). **5087**

AUSTRALIAN SEA HERITAGE. (AT/0813-0523). **Qty:** 16. **2611**

AUSTRALIAN SHELL NEWS. (AT/0310-1304). **5577**

AUSTRALIAN SHOPFITTING TRADE JOURNAL. (AT). **4210**

AUSTRALIAN SKIING. (AT). **Qty:** 3. **4848**

AUSTRALIAN SOCIAL WORK. (AT/0312-407X). **5274**

AUSTRALIAN SOCIETY. (AT/0729-8595). **2510**

AUSTRALIAN SOCIETY OF INDEXERS NEWSLETTER. (AT/0314-3767). **Qty:** varies. **3193**

AUSTRALIAN STRING TEACHER. (AT/0312-9950). **4101**

AUSTRALIAN SUGAR CRAFT. (AT/1033-6656). **Qty:** 3-4. **2328**

AUSTRALIAN SURVEYOR. (AT/0005-0326). **Qty:** varies. **2019**

AUSTRALIAN SYSTEMATIC BOTANY SOCIETY NEWSLETTER. (AT/1034-1218). **Qty:** 4-8. **501**

AUSTRALIAN TABLE TENNIS. (AT/0814-3668). **4885**

AUSTRALIAN TAFE TEACHER. (AT/0815-3701). **1911**

AUSTRALIAN TAX REVIEW. (AT/0311-094X). **2939**

AUSTRALIAN TEACHER OF THE DEAF. (AT/0005-0334). **1875**

AUSTRALIAN TEACHER, THE. (AT). **1888**

AUSTRALIAN UNIVERSITIES' REVIEW, THE. (AT). **1810**

AUSTRALIAN VETERINARY JOURNAL. (AT/0005-0423). **5505**

AUSTRALIAN VETERINARY PRACTITIONER. (AT/0310-138X). **5505**

AUSTRALIAN WELDING JOURNAL. (AT/0005-0431). **4026**

AUSTRALIAN WELDING RESEARCH. (AT/0045-0960). **4026**

AUSTRALIAN WOMEN'S BOOK REVIEW. (AT/1033-9434). **Qty:** 70. **5551**

AUSTRALIAN YEAR BOOK OF INTERNATIONAL LAW, THE. (AT/0084-7658). **Qty:** 10. **3124**

AUSTRALIAN ZOOLOGIST, THE. (AT/0067-2238). **5577**

AUSTRALIANA. (AT). **2510**

AUSTRALIA'S MINING MONTHLY. (AT). **2134**

AUSTRALIA'S TOP 500 COMPANIES. (AT/0817-3192). **Qty:** 1/year. **726**

AUSTRIA TODAY. (AU/0304-8713). **Qty:** 6-15/yr. **2513**

AUSTRIAN HISTORY YEARBOOK. (US/0067-2378). **2677**

AUSTRIAN STUDIES. (UK/1350-7532). **Qty:** 10/y. **3364**

AUT AUT. (IT/0005-0601). **4342**

AUTHENTIK AUTHENTIK IN ENGLISH. (IE/0791-0797). **3267**

AUTHOR (LONDON. 1949). (UK/0005-0628). **Qty:** 6. **3364**

AUTHOR SERIES. (US/0567-1744). **2722**

AUTISM RESEARCH REVIEW INTERNATIONAL, THE. (US/0893-8474). **Qty:** 4-5. **4575**

AUTO INDUSTRY AUSTRALIA. (AT). **Qty:** 15-20 per year. **5404**

AUTO LAUNDRY NEWS. (US/0005-0776). **5404**

AUTO MERCHANDISING NEWS. (US/0192-186X). **Qty:** 6. **641**

AUTO RACING DIGEST. (US/0090-8029). **4885**

AUTOGRAPH COLLECTOR. (US/1071-3425). **Qty:** 12. **2438**

AUTOHARPOHOLIC, THE. (US/0736-3796). **4101**

AUTOIMMUNE DISEASES. (UK/0142-8365). **3667**

AUTOMATED BUILDER. (US/0899-5540). **2815**

AUTOMATIC CONTROL AND COMPUTER SCIENCES. (US/0146-4116). **1217**

AUTOMATIC MACHINING. (US/0005-1071). **2110**

AUTOMATICA E INSTRUMENTACION. (SP/0213-3113). **1217**

AUTOMATION AND CONTROL. (NZ/0110-6295). **1217**

AUTOMATIZALAS. (HU/0133-1620). **1218**

AUTOMAZIONE NAVALE, L'. (IT/0392-2294). **591**

AUTOMOBIL-INDUSTRIE. (GW/0005-1306). **5405**

AUTOMOBILE ABSTRACTS (NUNEATON. 1975). (UK/0309-0817). **5405**

AUTOMOBILE ALMANAC. (US/0067-2513). **5405**

AUTOMOBILE INTERNATIONAL. (US/0099-2615). **5405**

AUTOMOBILE, L'. (FR). **5405**

AUTOMOTIVE ENGINEER. (UK/0307-6490). **5406**

AUTOMOTIVE ENGINEERING. (US/0098-2571). **2110**

AUTOREVISTA. (SP/0005-1961). **5407**

AUTOSPORT (TEDDINGTON). (UK/0269-946X). **Qty:** 52. **5407**

AUTRE PAROLE, L'. (CN/0228-4146). **4937**

AUTRES TEMPS. (FR). **Qty:** 4. **4937**

AV KOMMUNIKACIO. (HU/0237-9740). **1104**

AV MAGAZINE, THE. (US/0274-7774). **Qty:** 5. **226**

AVALOKA. (US/0890-5541). **Qty:** 10. **4937**

AVALON HILL GENERAL. (US/0888-1081). **Qty:** 6. **4857**

AVANCES EN ALIMENTACION Y MEJORA ANIMAL. (SP). **206**

AVANCES EN INVESTIGACION AGROPECUARIA. (MX/0188-7890). **64**

AVANCES EN PSICOLOGIA CLINICA LATINOAMERICANA. (CK/0120-3797). **4575**

AVANT GARDENER, THE. (US/0005-1926). **Qty:** 25. **2410**

AVANT-SCENE DU CINEMA, L'. (FR/0045-1150). **4064**

AVE: LE MAGAZINE FREUDIEN, L'. (FR). **Qty:** 4. **4575**

AVENIR MONTREAL. 1991. (CN/1187-6611). **1464**

AVES. (BE/0005-1993). **5615**

AVIAN DISEASES. (US/0005-2086). **5505**

AVIAN PATHOLOGY. (UK/0307-9457). **5505**

AVIASTRO (1984). (BE/0772-876X). **Qty:** 15. **12**

AVIATION DESIGN THIAIS. (FR/0997-3753). **13**

AVIATION DIGEST. (US/0884-4755). **13**

AVIATION MEDICINE (BANGALORE). (II/0250-5045). **3554**

AVIATION MONTHLY. (US/0145-1014). **13**

AVIATION NEWS. (UK). **Qty:** 150. **13**

AVIATION QUARTERLY. (US/0360-8670). **13**

AVIATION REPORTS. CIVIL AND/OR MILITARY. (UK/0005-2159). **14**

AVIATION SPACE AND ENVIRONMENTAL MEDICINE. (US/0095-6562). **3554**

AVIAZIONE. (IT/0391-7738). **14**

AVICULTURAL BULLETIN. (US/0567-2856). **5615**

AVICULTURAL JOURNAL, THE. (CN/0317-5650). **5615**

AVICULTURAL MAGAZINE, THE. (UK/0005-2256). **5615**

AVIONICS (POTOMAC, MD.). (US/0273-7639). **14**

AVKO NEWSLETTER. (US). **1875**

AVOTAYNU. (US/0882-6501). **Qty:** 12. **2438**

AVTOMATIKA I TELEMEHANIKA. (RU/0005-2310). **2110**

AVTOMATIKA I VYCISLITEL'NAYA TEHNIKA (RIGA). (LV/0132-4160). **1218**

AVTOMATIKA (KIEV). (UN/0572-2691). **1218**

AWARDS FOR FIRST DEGREE STUDY AT COMMONWEALTH UNIVERSITIES. (UK). **Qty:** 20. **1810**

AWARDS FOR POSTGRADUATE STUDY AT COMMONWEALTH UNIVERSITIES. (UK/0960-7986). **Qty:** 20. **1811**

AWARDS FOR UNIVERSITY ADMINISTRATORS AND LIBRARIANS. (UK). **Qty:** 20. **1727**

AWARDS FOR UNIVERSITY TEACHERS AND RESEARCH WORKERS. (UK/0964-2706). **Qty:** 20. **1727**

AWAZ (TORONTO). (CN/0715-4135). **5780**

AWC NEWS/FORUM. (US/0193-0850). **4160**

AWIS MAGAZINE. (US/1057-5839). **Qty:** 6. **5087**

AWP NEWSLETTER (NORFOLK). (US/0194-6498). **3365**

AXIOS (LOS ANGELES, CALIF.). (US/0278-551X). **3338**

AXIS: ACADEMIC COMPUTING & INFORMATION SYSTEMS. (UK/1352-8971). **1246**

AYRSHIRE CATTLE SOCIETY'S JOURNAL, THE. (UK/0005-2442). **207**

AZALEA CITY NEWS & REVIEW. (US/0744-5318). **5625**

AZANIA. (KE/0067-270X). **Qty:** 10. **260**

AZIENDA PUBBLICA TEORIA E PROBLEMI DI MANAGEMENT. (IT). **4632**

AZIONE NONVIOLENTA. (IT). **1072**

B & D HEIR LINES. (CN/1192-1137). **Qty:** 3 or more. **2438**

B.C.H.S. SLICKENS / BUTTE COUNTY HISTORICAL SOCIETY. (US). **2722**

B.C. HISTORICAL NEWS. (CN/0045-2963). **Qty:** (12-15). **2722**

B. C. JOURNAL OF SPECIAL EDUCATION. (CN/0704-7509). **1875**

B.C. NATURALIST. (CN/0228-8842). **2187**

B. C. PEACE NEWS. (CN/0708-0859). **4516**

B.C. PROFESSIONAL ENGINEER. ANNUAL DIRECTORY NUMBER, THE. (CN). **1966**

B.T.O. NEWS. (UK/0005-3392). **5615**

B70. (DK/0905-4650). **3193**

BABEL. (AT/0005-3503). **3267**

BABY CONNECTION, THE. (US/0894-3990). **1727**

BACA. (IO/0125-9008). **3193**

BACH-JAHRBUCH. (GW/0084-7682). **4101**

BACK FORTY (ALEXANDRIA, VA.), THE. (US/1049-3972). **Qty:** 20. **2188**

BACK OF THE YARDS JOURNAL. (US). **5658**

BACK STAGE. (US/0005-3635). **4064**

BACK STAGE. TV FILM & TAPE PRODUCTION DIRECTORY. (US/0734-9777). **1126**

BACKER UND KONDITOR. (GW/0005-383X). **2328**

BACKGROUNDER / AUSTRALIA, DEPARTMENT OF FOREIGN AFFAIRS AND TRADE. (AT). **4632**

BACKHOME (MOUNTAIN HOME, N.C.). (US/1051-323X) **Qty:** 12. **2528**

BACKSTRETCH, THE. (US/0005-366X). **Qty:** 60/year. **2797**

BACKTRACKER, THE. (US/0094-6915). **2438**

BACKWOODS. (US/1042-7732). **64**

BACKWOODS HOME MAGAZINE. (US/1050-9712). **Qty:** 12. **2485**

BACONIANA. (UK). **430**

BAD ATTITUDE. (US/0896-9531). **Qty:** 10-12. **2793**

BADEN-WURTTEMBERG. (GW/0404-6307). **2677**

BADGER COMMON TATER, THE. (US/0271-5864). **164**

BADGER HERALD. (US/0045-1304). **1089**

BADGER SPORTSMAN. (US/0005-3775). **4869**

BADMINTON NOW. (UK). **4886**

BAGNO OGGI E DOMANI, IL. (IT). **2898**

BAHAMIAN REVIEW. (BF/0005-397X). **2528**

BAHASA DAN SASTRA. (IO). **3267**

BAILAMME. (IT). **4937**

BAKER STREET JOURNAL, THE. (US/0005-4070). **3365**

BAKER'S DIGEST. (US/0191-6114). **2328**

BAKERS JOURNAL. (CN/0005-4097). **2328**

BAKERS' REVIEW (WATFORD). (UK/0005-4100). **2328**

BAKO MAGAZINE. (GW). **3475**

BAKUNIN (DAVIS, CALIF.). (US/1052-3154). **Qty:** 15. **3338**

BALANCE LONDON. (UK/0005-4216). **3555**

BALANCO FINANCEIRO. (BL). **773**

BALDWIN LEDGER, THE. (US/0745-9335). **Qty:** 40-50. **5674**

BALE CATALOGUE OF ISRAEL POSTAGE STAMPS / COMPILED AND PUBLISHED BY MICHAEL H. BALE. (UK). **2784**

BALKAN STUDIES. (GR/0005-4313). **2677**

BALKANMEDIA. (BU/0861-5047). **Qty:** 12-15. **1104**

BALLET REVIEW. (US/0522-0653). **1310**

BALLETT INTERNATIONAL. (GW/0722-6268). **1310**

BALLOON LIFE. (US/0887-6061). **Qty:** 12. **4886**

BALLOT ACCESS NEWS. (US/1043-6898). **Qty:** 1. **4465**

BALLROOM DANCING TIMES, THE. (UK). **1311**

BALLROOM REVIEW, THE. (US/1072-5156). **1311**

BALLS AND BURLAPS. (US/0404-6927). **2410**

BALTIC OBSERVER : NEWS FROM ESTONIA, LATVIA, AND LITHUANIA, THE. (LV). **5806**

BALTIMORE COUNTY HERITAGE PUBLICATION, A. (US/0270-0344). **2722**

'BAMA. (US/0195-0975). **4886**

BAMBOO RIDGE. (US/0733-0308). **Qty:** 1. **3365**

BANAS. (BL/0005-4585). **773**

BANCA, BORSA E TITOLI DI CREDITO. (IT). **773**

BANCAMATICA. (IT/0393-7062). **774**

BANCHE E BANCHIERI. (IT/0390-1378). **774**

BANCNI VESTNIK. (XV/0005-4631). **774**

BAND INTERNATIONAL : THE JOURNAL OF THE INTERNATIONAL MILITARY MUSIC SOCIETY. (UK). **4102**

BAND NEWS. (AT). **4102**

BANDER BLECHE ROHRE. (GW/0005-3848). **3475**

BANDWAGON (COLUMBUS, OHIO : 1957). (US/0005-4968). **4857**

BANGLADESH MEDICAL JOURNAL. (BG/0301-035X). **3555**

BANGLADESH OBSERVER, THE. (BG). **5778**

BANJO NEWSLETTER. (US/0190-1559). **Qty:** 5-8. **4102**

BANK ACCOUNTING & FINANCE. (US/0894-3958). **774**

BANK MARKETING. (US/0888-3149). **775**

BANK NEWS. (US/0005-5123). **775**

BANK NOTE REPORTER. (US/0164-0828). **2780**

BANK OPERATIONS BULLETIN. (US). **775**

BANK PERSONNEL NEWS. (US/0272-3271). **775**

BANK PROTECTION BULLETIN. (US/0091-0392). **775**

BANKERS DIGEST (DALLAS, TEX.). (US/0005-5425). **Qty:** varies. **776**

BANKERS MONTHLY. (US/0005-5476). **776**

BANKING ABSTRACTS. (IT). **777**

BANKING & FINANCE LAW REVIEW. (CN/0832-8722). **3085**

BANKING AUTOMATION BULLETIN FOR EUROPE. (UK/1351-5543). **Qty:** 10. **777**

BANKING LAW ANTHOLOGY. (US/0737-2159). **3085**

BANKING LAW REVIEW. (US/0898-7998). **3085**

BANKING SAFETY DIGEST. (US). **Qty:** 2. **777**

BANKING WORLD. (UK/0737-6413). **777**

BANNER OF TRUTH, THE. (US/0408-4748). **4937**

BANQUE DES MOTS (PARIS). (FR/0067-3951). **3268**

BANQUIER (MONTREAL). (CN/0822-6849). **778**

BAPTIST BIBLE TRIBUNE. (US/0745-5836). **Qty:** 50-100. **5056**

BAPTIST BULLETIN, THE. (US/0005-5689). **5056**

BAPTIST CHALLENGE, THE. (US/8756-9612). **5056**

BAPTIST HISTORY AND HERITAGE. (US/0005-5719). **5056**

BAPTIST LEADER (PHILADELPHIA). (US/0005-5727). **Qty:** 4. **4938**

BAPTIST PEACEMAKER. (US/0735-5815). **5056**

BAPTIST PROGRESS. (US/0005-5751). **5056**

BAPTIST QUARTERLY (LONDON). (UK/0005-576X). **5056**

BAPTIST RECORD (JACKSON, MISS.), THE. (US/0005-5778). **Qty:** 50. **5056**

BAPTIST REVIEW OF THEOLOGY, THE. (CN/1192-4241). **Qty:** 40. **4938**

BAPTIST STANDARD. (US). **5056**

BAPTIST TIMES. (UK/0005-5786). **5056**

BAPTIST TRUE UNION. (US/0883-7864). **5056**

BAPTIST TRUMPET (LITTLE ROCK, ARK.). (US/0888-9074). **5056**

BAPTIST WORLD (WASHINGTON, D.C.). (US/0005-5808). **5056**

BAPTISTS TODAY. (US/1072-7787). **Qty:** 12. **4938**

BAR: BEVERAGE ALCOHOL REPORTER. (CN/0006-0348). **2364**

BAR EXAMINER, THE. (US/0005-5824). **2940**

BARBADOS CONSOLIDATED INDEX TO STATUTES AND SUBSIDIARY LEGISLATION TO ... . (BB). **3124**

BARBOUR COMPENDIUM. BUILDING PRODUCTS. (UK/0260-9169). **Qty:** 2-3. **599**

BAREEL. (BE/0773-5618). **1918**

BARKER, THE. (US/1043-0849). **5505**

BARNARD'S RETAIL MARKETING REPORT. (US/0882-6218). **Qty:** 2. **861**

BARNES ASSOCIATES NATIONAL FUND RAISER. (US/0272-0825). **Qty:** 2-3. **4334**

BARNESVILLE RECORD-REVIEW, THE. (US). **5694**

BARNHART DICTIONARY COMPANION, THE. (US/0736-1122). **Qty:** 12. **1923**

BARNSTABLE PATRIOT. (US/0744-7221). **Qty:** 5. **5687**

BARNSTORMER (FORT WAYNE, IND.), THE. (US/1062-7413). **Qty:** 20 per year. **14**

BARRE GAZETTE (BARRE, MASS. : 1839). (US). **5687**

BARRISTER (PHILADELPHIA, PA.), THE. (US/0739-2494). **Qty:** 4. **2940**

BARRON'S (CHICOPEE, MASS.). (US/1077-8039). **642**

BARRON'S NATIONAL BUSINESS AND FINANCIAL WEEKLY. (US/0005-6073). **642**

BARR'S POST CARD NEWS. (US/0744-4540). **1144**

BARRY COUNTY ADVERTISER. (US/0194-1542). **5702**

BARTENDER. (US/0199-8404). **Qty:** 15. **2364**

BARTONIA. (US/0198-7356). **501**

BASE (BERKELEY, CALIF.). (US/0732-7706). **5087**

BASEBALL BULLETIN. (US/0199-0128). **4886**

BASEBALL CARD NEWS. (US/0746-7966). **2771**

BASEBALL CARDS. (US/8750-5851). **2771**

BASEBALL DIGEST. (US/0005-609X). **4886**

BASEBALL HOBBY NEWS. (US/0199-946X). **2771**

BASEBALL RESEARCH JOURNAL. (US/0734-6891). **4886**

BASEBALL'S FORGOTTEN HEROES. (US). **430**

BASEHOR SENTINEL. (US). **5674**

BASELINE LONDON. (UK/0954-9226). **Qty:** 12-15. **4564**

BASENJI, THE. (US/0094-9744). **4285**

BASES PARIS. (FR/0765-1325). **Qty:** 20. **1274**

BASIC AND APPLIED MYOLOGY : BAM. (IT/1120-9992). **Qty:** 2. **3803**

BASIC DATA ON SEALANTS IN SELECTED EUROPEAN COUNTRIES. (UK). **3475**

BASIC EDUCATION (WASHINGTON, D.C.). (US/0196-4984). **1727**

BASILISCO (OVIEDO, SPAIN). (SP/0210-0088). **4342**

BASIS. (IO/0005-6138). **2647**

BASKET BITS. (US). **370**

BASKETBALL DIGEST. (US/0098-5988). **4886**

BASKETBALL TIMES. (US/0744-2866). **4887**

BASKETMAKER (WESTLAND, MICH.). (US/0897-3458). **370**

BASTERIA. (NE/0005-6219). **Qty:** 5. **5577**

BAT RESEARCH NEWS. (US/0005-6227). **5577**

BATCHELDER REVIEW. (US/0897-7429). **2438**

BATH & KITCHEN MARKETER. (CN/0225-9206). **2898**

BATON ROUGE, LE. (US). **Qty:** 16. **2438**

BATTALION (COLLEGE STATION, TEX. 1893), THE. (US/1055-4726). **Qty:** 10. **1089**

BATTELLE TODAY. (US/0145-8477). **5087**

BATTERY MAN. (US/0005-6359). **1933**

BAUDETTE REGION, THE. (US). **Qty:** 3-10. **5694**

BAUEN FUER DIE LANDWIRTSCHAFT (ZEITSCHRIFT). (GW/0171-7952). **600**

BAUEN MIT HOLZ. (GW/0005-6545). **600**

BAUEN + [I.E. UND] FERTIGHAUS. (GW). **600**

BAUINGENIEUR, DER. (GW/0005-6650). **2019**

BAUMEISTER. (GW/0005-674X). **293**

BAUVERWALTUNG. (GW/0005-6847). **4632**

BAUWIRTSCHAFT (HAUPTVERBAND DER DEUTSCHEN BAUINDUSTRIE). (GW/0341-3810). **600**

BAXTER BULLETIN. (US/0745-7707). **5631**

BAXTER SPRINGS CITIZEN. (US/0455-6000). **Qty:** 15-20. **5674**

BAY STATE BANNER. (US). **5687**

BAY STATE HISTORY. (US). **2722**

BAY VOICE, THE. (US/8750-7188). **5691**

BAYERISCHE BLATTER FUER VOLKSKUNDE. (GW/0720-8006). **Qty:** 5-10. **231**

BAYERISCHES LANDWIRTSCHAFTLICHES JAHRBUCH. (GW/0375-8621). **65**

BAYERNMETALL. (GW). **3998**

BAYLOR BUSINESS REVIEW. (US/0739-1072). **642**

BAYLOR COUNTY BANNER, THE. (US). **5747**

BAYLOR LAW REVIEW. (US/0005-7274). **2940**

BAYRUT TAYMZ. (US/0888-6016). **5633**

BAYVIEWS (OAKLAND, CALIF.). (US/1045-6724). **Qty: 2400. 3193**

BBL. BIBLIOTEKSBLADET. (SW/0006-1867). **3193**

BBS CALLERS DIGEST. (US/1055-2812). **1274**

BC MOUNTAINEER, THE. (CN/0045-2998). **4869**

BC OUTDOORS. (CN/0045-3013). **4869**

BC STUDIES. (CN/0005-2949). **2722**

BCA NEWS (NEW YORK, N.Y.). (US/0005-2841). **642**

BCG NEWSLETTER BOLTON. (UK/0144-588X). **4084**

BCPC MONOGRAPH. (UK). **Qty: 10. 164**

BCS UPDATE. (US/1041-4770). **1171**

BEACHES LEADER, THE. (US/1059-647X). **Qty: 6. 5649**

BEACON-FORUM. (US). **5668**

BEACON (LONDON, ENGLAND). (UK/0005-7339). **4342**

BEACON (TORONTO. 1970). (CN/0382-6384). **4938**

BEAGLE : OCCASIONAL PAPERS OF THE TERRITORY MUSEUM OF ARTS AND SCIENCES, THE. (AT/0811-3653). **2843**

BEALOIDEAS. (IE/0332-270X). **2318**

BEAR FACTS REVIEW. (AT). **2583**

BEAR NEWS. (US/0885-615X). **2188**

BEAUFORT MAGAZINE. (US). **Qty: 2-3. 2528**

BEAUTIFUL GLASS FOR HOME & OFFICE. (US/1043-5468). **2586**

BEAUTY AGE. (US/0887-414X). **402**

BEAUTY COUNTER LONDON. (UK/0960-3751). **Qty: varies. 402**

BEAUX ARTS MAGAZINE. (FR/0757-2271). **343**

BEAVER, THE. (CN/0005-7517). **2722**

BECKETT CIRCLE, THE. (US/0732-2224). **Qty: 4. 3365**

BEDFORDSHIRE FAMILY HISTORY SOCIETY JOURNAL. (UK). **2438**

BEDFORDSHIRE MAGAZINE, THE. (UK/0005-7592). **2678**

BEE CULTURE. (US/1071-3190). **Qty: 12-15. 65**

BEE WORLD. (UK/0005-772X). **5577**

BEECHER CITY JOURNAL. (US/1066-7970). **5658**

BEEDAUDJIMOWIN. (CN). **2256**

BEELDENAAR, DE. (NE). **2780**

BE'EMET?!. (IS/0334-973X). **1060**

BEER WHOLESALER. (US/0005-7770). **2364**

BEETHOVEN NEWSLETTER, THE. (US/0898-6185). **4102**

BEFFROI. (CN/0832-9966). **3365**

BEGINNINGS : THE OFFICIAL NEWSLETTER OF THE AMERICAN HOLISTIC NURSES' ASSOCIATION. (US/1071-2984). **Qty: 6. 3852**

BEHAVIOR ANALYSIS DIGEST. (US/1052-0082). **Qty: 3. 4576**

BEHAVIOR ANALYST, THE. (US/0738-6729). **4576**

BEHAVIOR AND SOCIAL ISSUES. (US/1064-9506). **4576**

BEHAVIOR THERAPIST, THE. (US/0278-8403). **4576**

BEHAVIOR THERAPY. (US/0005-7894). **4576**

BEHAVIORAL & SOCIAL SCIENCES LIBRARIAN. (US/0163-9269). **3193**

BEHAVIORAL SCIENCES NEWSLETTER. (US/0361-4646). **4577**

BEHAVIOUR CHANGE. (AT/0813-4839). **4577**

BEHAVIOURAL NEUROLOGY. (UK/0953-4180). **3828**

BEHAVIOURAL PHARMACOLOGY. (UK/0955-8810). **4293**

BEIHEFT ZUM BULLETIN JUGEND + LITERATUR. (GW/0172-0910). **3365**

BEIJING REVIEW. (CC/1000-9140). **4465**

BEIJING REVIEW (NORTH AMERICAN EDITION). (CC). **4465**

BEING WELL. (US/1064-1424). **Qty: 4-6. 3555**

BEIRUT REVIEW, THE. (LE/1019-0732). **Qty: 6. 4516**

BEITRAEGE ZUR ALGEBRA UND GEOMETRIE. (GW). **3497**

BEITRAEGE ZUR GESCHICHTE DER ARBEITERBEWEGUNG (BERLIN, DDR). (GW/0005-8068). **2678**

BEITRAEGE ZUR GESCHICHTE DER DEUTSCHEN SPRACHE UND LITERATUR (TUEBINGEN). (GW/0005-8076). **3268**

BEITRAEGE ZUR HOCHSCHULFORSCHUNG. (GW/0171-645X). **1811**

BEITRAEGE ZUR NAMENFORSCHUNG. (GW/0005-8114). **2438**

BEITRAEGE ZUR NATURKUNDE NIEDERSACHSENS. (GW/0340-4277). **4162**

BEITRAEGE ZUR REGIONALEN GEOLOGIE DER ERDE. (GW/0522-7038). **1366**

BEITRAEGE ZUR UMWELTGESTALTUNG. (GW). **2225**

BEITRAEGE ZUR UR- UND FRUEHGESCHICHTE DER BEZIRKE ROSTOCK, SCHWERIN UND NEUBRANDENBURG. (GW). **261**

BEKESI ELET. (HU/0522-7232). **5087**

BELFAST TELEGRAPH [MICROFORM]. (UK/0307-5664). **5811**

BELGIAN JOURNAL OF ZOOLOGY. (BE/0777-6276). **5577**

BELGISCH TIJDSCHRIFT VOOR SOCIALE ZEKERHEID. (BE/0775-0234). **5274**

BELGISCH TIJDSCHRIFT VOOR TANDHEELKUNDE. (BE/0775-0285). **1317**

BELGISCHE TUINBOUW. INTERNATIONALE EDITIE, DE. (BE/0005-8483). **2410**

BELIZE CONSOLIDATED INDEX OF STATUTES AND SUBSIDIARY LEGISLATION TO ... . (US). **3124**

BELIZEAN STUDIES. (BH/0250-6831). **2723**

BELLE PLAINE NEWS. (US). **5674**

BELLES LETTRES (ARLINGTON, VA.). (US/0884-2957). **Qty: 300. 3366**

BELLETEN. (TU/0041-4255). **2611**

BELLEVILLE POST. (US). **5709**

BELLEVILLE TIMES NEWS, THE. (US). **5709**

BELLINGHAM REVIEW, THE. (US/0734-2934). **3366**

BELL'S ALASKA, YUKON & BRITISH COLUMBIA TRAVEL GUIDE. (US/1054-5034). **5462**

BELOIT POETRY JOURNAL, THE. (US/0005-8661). **Qty: 35. 3460**

BENCH AND BAR OF MINNESOTA, THE. (US/0276-1505). **Qty: 60. 2941**

BENCH SHEET, THE. (US/0737-4186). **1013**

BENCHMARKS (DENTON, TEX.). (US/1066-0380). **1171**

BEND OF THE RIVER. (US/1063-9241). **Qty: 12. 4162**

BENDEL LIBRARY JOURNAL. (NR/0331-555X). **3194**

BENEDICTINA. (IT/0392-0356). **4938**

BENEDICTINES. (US/0005-8726). **5024**

BENEFITS & COMPENSATION INTERNATIONAL. (UK/0268-764X). **2875**

BENEFITS CANADA. (CN/0703-7732). **938**

BENSON TRACE, THE. (US/0734-0214). **2439**

BENT OF TAU BETA PI, THE. (US/0005-884X). **1966**

BENTON NEWS, THE. (US). **5658**

BEQUADRO. (IT). **4102**

BEREAVEMENT & LOSS RESOURCES. (US/1071-7366). **Qty: 20. 4577**

BEREAVEMENT CARE. (UK/0268-2621). **Qty: 16. 5274**

BEREAVEMENT (CARMEL, IND.). (US/0897-9588). **Qty: 6. 4577**

BERGBAU (HATTINGEN). (GW/0342-5681). **2135**

BERGBAU UND VERARBEITENDES GEWERBE. (GW). **2135**

BERGSMANNEN. (SW/0284-0448). **Qty: 6/yr. 2135**

BERICHTE DER BAYERISCHEN BOTANISCHEN GESELLSCHAFT ZUR ERFORSCHUNG DER HEIMISCHEN FLORA. (GW/0373-7640). **501**

BERICHTE DER BUNSENGESELLSCHAFT FUER PHYSIKALISCHE CHEMIE. (GW/0005-9021). **1050**

BERICHTE DER NATURFORSCHENDEN GESELLSCHAFT ZU FREIBURG I. BR. (GW/0028-0917). **5088**

BERICHTE GYNAKOLOGIE, GEBURTSHILFE. (GW/0722-9852). **3757**

BERICHTE PATHOLOGIE. (GW/0722-9674). **3893**

BERICHTE UBER LANDWIRTSCHAFT. (GW/0005-9080). **65**

BERKELEY JOURNAL OF EMPLOYMENT AND LABOR LAW. (US/1067-7666). **3144**

BERKELEY JOURNAL OF SOCIOLOGY. (US/0067-5830). **Qty: 6 per year. 5240**

BERKELEY MONTHLY, THE. (US/0191-7080). **3338**

BERKELEY PLANNING JOURNAL. (US/1047-5192). **Qty: varies. 2816**

BERKELEY WOMEN'S LAW JOURNAL. (US/0882-4312). **2941**

BERKSHIRE GENEALOGIST, THE. (US/0887-0713). **Qty: 12. 2439**

BERLINER ARZTEBLATT. (GW/0172-8490). **3555**

BERLINER JOURNAL FUER SOZIOLOGIE. (GW). **Qty: 12. 5240**

BERLINER THEOLOGISCHE ZEITSCHRIFT : THEOLOGIA VIATORUM NEUE FOLGE : HALBJAHRESSCHRIFT FUER THEOLOGIE IN DER KIRCHE. (GW/0724-6137). **4938**

BERLINER UND MUNCHENER TIERARZTLICHE WOCHENSCHRIFT. (GW/0005-9366). **5505**

BERMUDA JOURNAL OF ARCHAEOLOGY AND MARITIME HISTORY. (BM/1013-431X). **261**

BERYTUS; ARCHAEOLOGICAL STUDIES. (LE/0067-6195). **261**

BESCHAFTIGUNGSTHERAPIE UND REHABILITATION. (GW/0340-529X). **1875**

BESSATSU SEIKEI GEKA. (JA/0287-1645). **3960**

BEST FESTIVALS OF NORTH AMERICA. (US/0882-4193). **383**

BEST RECIPES. (US/0897-0386). **2328**

BESTE UIT READER'S DIGEST, HET. (NE/0005-9692). **2513**

BET. (UK). **Qty: 18. 642**

BETH MIKRA : KETAV-ET SHEL HA-HEVRAH LE-HEKER HA-MIKRA BE-YISRAEL. (IS/0005-979X). **5046**

BETHANY REPUBLICAN-CLIPPER. (US). **Qty: 20. 5702**

BETON I ZHELEZOBETON. (RU/0005-9889). **600**

BETON : REVUE DU BETON PREFABRIQUE. (BE). **601**

BETTER CROPS WITH PLANT FOOD. (US/0006-0089). **164**

BETTER HEARING. (AT). **Qty: 6. 4384**

BETTER HOMES AND GARDENS DECORATING IDEAS. (US). **2899**

BETTER INVESTING. (US/0006-016X). **892**

BETTER RADIO AND TELEVISION. (US). **1127**

BETWEEN THE LINES (WASHINGTON, D.C.). (US/1049-4421). **4465**

BETWEEN THE SPECIES : A JOURNAL OF ETHICS. (US). **2249**

BETWEEN US. (US/0714-4601). **1811**

BEVERAGE ALCOHOL MARKET REPORT. (US/0736-220X). **2364**

BEVERAGE WORLD. (US/0098-2318). **2364**

BEVERAGE WORLD INTERNATIONAL. (US). **2364**

BEVERLY HILLS COURIER, THE. (US/0892-645X). **Qty: 10-12. 5633**

BEYOND APARTHEID. (NE/0923-4284). **1464**

BEYOND BORDERS. (US/1065-2426). **1655**

BEYOND GERMANNA. (US/1073-838X). **Qty: 6. 2439**

BHARATIYA NEPALI VANMAYA. (II). **3268**

BHARATIYA VIDYA. (II/0378-1984). **2647**

BHASHA. (II/0523-1418). **3268**

BHASHA ANI JIVANA : MARATHI-ABHYASA-PARISHAD-PATRIKA. (II). **3268**

BHAVAN'S JOURNAL. (II/0006-0518). **4342**

BI-STATE REPORTER. (US/0745-4813). **5658**

BI-YEAF. (IS/0302-8194). **14**

BIA BULLETIN. (UK). **443**

BIANNUAL NEWSLETTER OF THE CONFERENCE GROUP ON ITALIAN POLITICS & SOCIETY, THE. (US/1077-9043). **4516**

BIAS JOURNAL. (UK). **1599**

BIB-KRANT LEUVEN. (BE/0776-068X). **3194**

BIBBIA E ORIENTE. (IT/0006-0585). **5014**

BIBEL UND GEMEINDE. (GW/0006-0615). **5014**

BIBEL UND KIRCHE. (GW/0006-0623). **5014**

BIBEL UND LITURGIE. (AU/0006-064X). **5014**

BIBLE BHASHYAM (ENGLISH ED.). (II/0970-2288). **5014**

BIBLE COLLECTORS' WORLD. (US/0883-9204). **Qty: 25. 5014**

BIBLE LANDS. (UK/0006-0763). **5014**

BIBLE LEAGUE QUARTERLY. (UK). **Qty: 6. 5014**

BIBLE-SCIENCE NEWSLETTER. (US/0164-5587). **5014**

BIBLE TODAY, THE. (US/0006-0836). **5015**

BIBLE TRANSLATOR, THE. (UK/0260-0935). **5015**

BIBLICA. (IT/0006-0887). **5015**

BIBLICAL ARCHAEOLOGIST, THE. (US/0006-0895). **261**

BIBLICAL BULLETIN. (US/0749-9280). **5015**

BIBLICAL EVANGELIST, THE. (US/0740-7998). **4938**

BIBLICAL ILLUSTRATOR. (US/0195-1351). **4938**

BIBLICAL POLEMICS. (IS/0792-4739). **4939**

BIBLICAL THEOLOGY BULLETIN. (US/0146-1079). **5015**

BIBLICUM. (SW). **4939**

BIBLIOGRAFIA FILOSOFICA MEXICANA. (MX/0185-240X). **4365**

BIBLIOGRAFIA ITALIANA DI IDRAULICA. (IT/0006-1042). **2087**

BIBLIOGRAPHIE ANNUELLE DE L'HISTOIRE DE FRANCE DU CINQUIEME SIECLE A 1958. (FR). **2634**

BIBLIOGRAPHIE DE LA PHILOSOPHIE. (FR/0006-1352). **4365**

BIBLIOGRAPHIE DER PFLANZENSCHUTZLITERATUR. (GW/0006-1387). **2434**

BIBLIOGRAPHIE INTERNATIONALE DE LA DEMOGRAPHIE HISTORIQUE. (BE/0255-0849). **4561**

BIBLIOGRAPHIE ZUR SYMBOLIK, IKONOGRAPHIE UND MYTHOLOGIE. (GW/0067-706X). **4939**

BIBLIOGRAPHIEN ZUR DEUTSCHEN LITERATUR DES MITTELALTERS. (GW/0523-2767). **3457**

BIBLIOGRAPHY AND INDEX OF GEOLOGY. (US/0098-2784). **1361**

BIBLIOGRAPHY. BOOKS FOR CHILDREN. (US/0147-250X). **1072**

BIBLIOGRAPHY OF AGRICULTURE : ANNUAL CUMULATION. (US/0364-829X). **66**

BIBLIOGRAPHY OF MODERN HEBREW LITERATURE IN TRANSLATION / BY ISAAC GOLDBERG. (IS/0334-309X). **3366**

BIBLIOGRAPHY OF NOISE, A. (US/0092-5756). **2161**

BIBLIOGRAPHY OF REPRODUCTION. (UK/0006-1565). **477**

BIBLIOGRAPHY OF THE SUMMER INSTITUTE OF LINGUISTICS, AUSTRALIAN ABORIGINES BRANCH UP TO ... / COMPILED BY SANDRA RAY. (AT). **3336**

BIBLIOGRAPHY SERIES - NORMAN PATERSON SCHOOL OF INTERNATIONAL AFFAIRS (CARLETON UNIVERSITY). (CN/0383-2848). **4501**

BIBLIONEWS AND AUSTRALIAN NOTES AND QUERIES. (AT/0045-1940). **4824**

BIBLIOTHECA BOTANICA. (GW/0067-7892). **502**

BIBLIOTHECA HUMANISTICA ET REFORMATORICA. (NE). **1074**

BIBLIOTHECA LICHENOLOGICA. (GW). **502**

BIBLIOTHECA MYCOLOGIA. (GW). **443**

BIBLIOTHECA ORIENTALIS. (NE/0006-1913). **2647**

BIBLIOTHECA SACRA (1864). (US/0006-1921). **4939**

BIBLIOTHECK. (UK/0006-193X). **410**

BIBLIOTHEEK EN SAMENLEVING. (NE/0165-1048). **3195**

BIBLIOTHEK. (GW/0341-4183). **3195**

BIBLIOTHEKAR. (GW/0006-1964). **3195**

BIBLIOTHEKSDIENST. (GW/0006-1972). **3195**

BIBLIOTHEKSFORUM BAYERN. (GW/0340-000X). **3195**

BIBLIOTHEQUE DE L'ECOLE DES CHARTES. (FR/0343-6237). **3195**

BIBLIOTHEQUE D'HUMANISME ET RENAISSANCE. (SZ/0006-1999). **2611**

BIBLOS. (PO/0870-4112). **3195**

BICYCLE FORUM. (US/0193-8177). **428**

BICYCLE USA. (US/0747-0371). **428**

BICYCLING. (US/0006-2073). **428**

BIENNIAL REPORT OF EXAMINING AND LICENSING BOARDS / MINNESOTA BOARD OF PSYCHOLOGY. (US). **4577**

BIFOCAL. (US/0888-1537). **3179**

BIG BEAUTIFUL WOMAN. (US/0192-5938). **1082**

BIG BEND REGISTER. (US/0736-7074). **2439**

BIG REEL, THE. (US/0744-723X). **Qty: 6. 4064**

BIG RIVER. (US/1070-8340). **Qty: 4. 2297**

BIG SPRING HERALD. (US/0746-6811). **5747**

BIJDRAGEN EN MEDEDELINGEN BETREFFENDE DE GESCHIEDENIS DER NEDERLANDEN. (NE/0165-0505). **2678**

BIJDRAGEN TIJDSCHRIFT VOOR FILOSOFIE EN THEOLOGIE. (NE). **Qty: 26. 4342**

BIJDRAGEN TOT DE DIERKUNDE. (NE/0067-8546). **5578**

BIJDRAGEN TOT DE TAAL-, LAND- EN VOLKENKUNDE. (NE/0006-2294). **232**

BIKE TECH. (US/0734-5992). **428**

BIKORET U-FARSHANUT. (IS). **3338**

BILAKABIDE : REVISTA DE POESIA. (SP). **3460**

BILANZ. (SZ). **1464**

BILDGEBUNG (BASEL). (SZ/1012-5655). **3939**

BILDUNG UND WISSENSCHAFT. (GW/0177-4212). **5088**

BILINGUAL FAMILY NEWSLETTER, THE. (UK/0952-4096). **2277**

BILINGUAL REVIEW. (US/0094-5366). **Qty: 9. 3269**

BILL-DALE MARCINKO'S AFTA. (US/0193-7782). **3338**

BILLIARDS DIGEST. (US/0164-761X). **4857**

BILLIKEN. (AG). **1060**

BILLINGS GAZETTE (BILLINGS, MONT. : DAILY : 1914). (US). **5705**

BILLINGSLEY YESTERDAY & TODAY. (US/0899-1707). **2439**

BILTEN ZA HEMATOLOGIJU I TRANSFUZIJU. (YU/0350-2023). **3770**

BIMCO BULLETIN. (DK/0901-814X). **5447**

BINARY. (UK/0266-304X). **560**

BINARY COMPUTING IN MICROBIOLOGY. (US/0266-304X). **560**

BINDEREPORT. (GW/0342-3573). **4824**

BINDTEKEN. (BE/0772-2125). **5268**

BINGO. (FR/0523-6207). **2498**

BINNENGEWASSER. (GW/0067-8643). **1352**

BINOCULAR VISION & EYE MUSCLE SURGERY QUARTERLY. (US). **Qty: 4-6. 3872**

BIO-DYNAMICS. (US/0006-2863). **66**

BIO-ELECTRONICS & BIOSENSORS. (UK/0952-0384). **443**

BIO-SCIENCE RESEARCH BULLETIN. (II/0970-0889). **444**

BIO/TECHNOLOGY (NEW YORK, N.Y. 1983). (US/0733-222X). **5088**

BIOACOUSTICS (BERKHAMSTED). (UK/0952-4622). **5578**

BIOCATALYSIS. (SZ/0886-4454). **480**

BIOCHEMICAL JOURNAL (LONDON. 1984). (UK/0264-6021). **481**

BIOCHEMICAL SOCIETY TRANSACTIONS. (UK/0300-5127). **481**

BIOCHEMIE UND PHYSIOLOGIE DER PFLANZEN. (GW/0015-3796). **502**

BIOCHEMIST LONDON. (UK/0954-982X). **Qty: 25+. 481**

BIOCHEMISTRY (EASTON). (US/0006-2960). **482**

BIOCHIMICA CLINICA. (IT/0393-0564). **482**

BIOCYCLE. (US/0276-5055). **2225**

BIODEGRADATION (DORDRECHT). (NE/0923-9820). **2225**

BIODETERIORATION ABSTRACTS. (UK/0951-0621). **2183**

BIOENERGETIC ANALYSIS. (US/0743-4804). **3921**

BIOENGINEERING NEWS. (US/0275-4207). **444**

BIOESSAYS. (UK/0265-9247). **532**

BIOETHICS FORUM. (US/1065-7274). **Qty: 1-4. 2249**

BIOFACTORS (OXFORD). (UK/0951-6433). **483**

BIOGRAPHICAL DIRECTORY / AMERICAN POLITICAL SCIENCE ASSOCIATION. (US). **430**

BIOGRAPHY (HONOLULU). (US/0162-4962). **430**

BIOINFORMATION MANAGER. (GW). **444**

BIOLOGIA & CLINICA HEMATOLOGICA. (SP/0210-895X). **3770**

BIOLOGIA (BUDAPEST). (HU/0133-3844). **444**

BIOLOGIA (LAHORE). (PK/0006-3096). **444**

BIOLOGIA MORA (VLADIVOSTOK). (RU/0134-3475). **553**

BIOLOGIA PLANTARUM. (XR/0006-3134). **502**

BIOLOGICAL ABSTRACTS / RRM. (US/0192-6985). **477**

BIOLOGICAL AGRICULTURE & HORTICULTURE. (UK/0144-8765). **66**

BIOLOGICAL CONSERVATION. (UK/0006-3207). **2188**

BIOLOGICAL JOURNAL OF THE LINNEAN SOCIETY. (UK/0024-4066). **445**

BIOLOGICAL MASS SPECTROMETRY. (UK/1052-9306). **1013**

BIOLOGICAL MEMOIRS. (II/0379-8097). **445**

BIOLOGICAL NOTES (COLUMBUS). (US/0078-3986). **445**

BIOLOGICAL RHYTHMS. (UK/0142-8004). **578**

BIOLOGICAL THERAPY. (US/0733-2661). **3774**

BIOLOGICAL TRACE ELEMENT RESEARCH. (US/0163-4984). **483**

BIOLOGICALS. (UK/1045-1056). **445**

BIOLOGICKE LISTY. (XR/0366-0486). **446**

BIOLOGICO, O. (BL/0366-0567). **446**

BIOLOGISCHE ABHANDLUNGEN. (GW/0006-3282). **446**

BIOLOGIST (LONDON). (UK/0006-3347). **446**

BIOLOGUE (WATERLOO). (CN/0840-8548). **446**

BIOLOGY & PHILOSOPHY. (NE/0169-3867). **446**

BIOLOGY DIGEST. (US/0095-2958). **477**

BIOLOGY INTERNATIONAL. (FR/0253-2069). **447**

BIOLOGY INTERNATIONAL. SPECIAL ISSUES : THE NEWS MAGAZINE OF THE INTERNATIONAL UNION OF BIOLOGICAL SCIENCES (IUBS). (FR). **447**

BIOLOGY OF THE CELL. (FR/0248-4900). **532**

BIOMASS BULLETIN. (UK/0262-7183). **1933**

BIOMEDICA BIOCHIMICA ACTA. (GW/0232-766X). **447**

BIOMEDICAL ETHICS REVIEWS. (US/0742-1796). **3556**

BIOMEDICAL INSTRUMENTATION & TECHNOLOGY. (US/0899-8205). **3687**

BIOMEDICAL LETTERS. (UK/0961-088X). **3556**

BIOMEDICAL SAFETY & STANDARDS. (US). **3557**

BIOMEDICAL TECHNOLOGY INFORMATION SERVICE. (US/0147-2682). **3687**

BIOMETRICS. (US/0006-341X). **5323**

BIOMETRIE-PRAXIMETRIE. (BE/0006-3436). **477**

BIOMIMETICS (NEW YORK, N.Y.). (US/1059-0153). **1966**

BIOPHARM (EUGENE, OR.). (US/1040-8304). **4293**

BIOPHARMACEUTICS & DRUG DISPOSITION. (UK/0142-2782). **4293**

BIOS (MADISON, N.J.). (US/0005-3155). **477**

BIOS (PARIS). (FR/0366-2284). **2364**

BIOSCIENCE. (US/0006-3568). **448**

BIOSCIENCE REPORTS. (US/0144-8463). **532**

BIOSTATISTICA (DAVENPORT, IOWA). (US/1041-7648). **477**

BIOTEC (STUTTGART). (GW/0931-1408). **Qty: 15-20/yr. 3687**

BIOTEC WURZBURG. (GW). **448**

BIOTECH BUSINESS. (US/0899-5702). **Qty:** 12. **3687**

BIOTECH KNOWLEDGE SOURCES. (UK/0953-2226). **3688**

BIOTECH PRODUCTS INTERNATIONAL. (BE/1016-6505). **5088**

BIOTECHNOLOGIE. (NE). **448**

BIOTECHNOLOGY LAW REPORT. (US/0730-031X). **3689**

BIOTECHNOLOGY (NEW YORK, N.Y. : 1983). (US/0275-7559). **3689**

BIOTECHNOLOGY NEWS. (US/0273-3226). **3689**

BIOTECHNOLOGY RESEARCH ABSTRACTS. (US/0733-5709). **3655**

BIOTECHNOLOGY TECHNIQUES. (UK/0951-208X). **3689**

BIP. BULLETIN DE L'INDUSTRIE PETROLIERE. (FR/0300-4554). **4252**

BIRD OBSERVER (BELMONT, MASS.). (US/0893-4630). **5615**

BIRD STUDY. (UK/0006-3657). **5615**

BIRD WATCHER'S DIGEST. (US/0164-3037). **Qty:** 50. **5615**

BIRD WORLD (NORTH HOLLYWOOD). (US/0199-5979). **5615**

BIRDING. (US/0161-1836). **5578**

BIRDING IN SOUTHERN AFRICA. (SA/0006-5838). **5616**

BIRKNER. (GW). **4232**

BIRMINGHAM POETRY REVIEW. (US/1047-2258). **Qty:** 3-6. **3460**

BIRMINGHAM POST-HERALD. (US/1040-1571). **5625**

BIRMINGHAM TIMES, THE. (US). **Qty:** 25 per year. **2256**

BIRTH (BERKELEY, CALIF.). (US/0730-7659). **3757**

BIRTH DEFECTS ORIGINAL ARTICLE SERIES. (US/0547-6844). **3757**

BIRTH GAZETTE, THE. (US/0890-3255). **3757**

BIRTH TRAUMA. (US/0892-7227). **2942**

BIT. (IT). **1172**

BIT FIRENZE. (IT/0394-3666). **3196**

BIT (NORDISK TIDSKRIFT FOR INFORMATIONSBEHANDLING). (DK/0006-3835). **1172**

BITAON LAMOREH LEARVIT. (IS). **1728**

BITS AND PIECES (NEWCASTLE). (US/0006-3894). **861**

BITUMEN. (GW/0006-3916). **2019**

BITZARON. (US/0006-3932). **5046**

BJULETEN' - KOMITETU UKRAJINCIV KANADY. (CN/0503-1036). **2723**

BLACK AND RED. (US). **1089**

BLACK BEAR. (US/8756-0666). **3367**

BLACK COLLEGIAN (NEW ORLEANS), THE. (US/0192-3757). **1811**

BLACK ELEGANCE. (US/0885-9647). **2529**

BLACK EMPLOYMENT & EDUCATION. (US/1053-704X). **Qty:** 20. **643**

BLACK ENTERPRISE. (US/0006-4165). **643**

BLACK FAMILY. (US/0279-0718). **2256**

BLACK FILM REVIEW. (US/0887-5723). **4064**

BLACK HILLS NUGGETS. (US/0523-7203). **2439**

BLACK ISSUES IN HIGHER EDUCATION. (US/0742-0277). **1812**

BLACK MALE/FEMALE RELATIONSHIPS. (US/0740-2163). **5240**

BLACK MARIA. (US/0045-222X). **3367**

BLACK MASKS. (US/0887-7580). **Qty:** 1-2. **5362**

BLACK ORPHEUS. (NR/0067-9100). **3367**

BLACK RESOURCE GUIDE, THE. (US/0882-0643). **2257**

BLACK SCHOLAR, THE. (US/0006-4246). **2257**

BLACK VOICE NEWS, THE. (US). **Qty:** 12-25. **2257**

BLACK WARRIOR REVIEW, THE. (US/0193-6301). **Qty:** 4-8. **3338**

BLACK WRITER MAGAZINE, THE. (US). **3367**

BLACKSHEAR TIMES, THE. (US/0746-9330). **5652**

BLAIR'S GUIDE VICTORIA. (AT/0810-9567). **5465**

BLAKE. (US/0160-628X). **Qty:** 12-20/yr. **316**

BLAST MANUKA. (AT/0819-0739). **2510**

BLATTER FUER DEUTSCHE LANDESGESCHICHTE. (GW/0006-4408). **2611**

BLATTER FUER WURTTEMBERGISCHE KIRCHENGESCHICHTE. (GW/0341-9479). **4939**

BLAUE JUNGS. (GW). **4175**

BLIKI : TIMARIT UN FUGLA. (IC). **Qty:** 1-3. **4163**

BLIMP. (AU). **4064**

BLIND ALLEYS. (US/0737-9269). **3460**

BLIND (AMSTERDAM, NETHERLANDS). (NE). **344**

BLISSFIELD ADVANCE. (US). **5691**

BLITZ LONDON. (UK/0263-2543). **316**

BLK (LOS ANGELES, CALIF.). (US/1043-0075). **Qty:** 36. **2793**

BLM. BONNIERS LITTERARA MAGASIN. (SW/0005-3198). **3367**

BLOEM & BLAD. (NE). **2434**

BLOOD COAGULATION & FIBRINOLYSIS : AN INTERNATIONAL JOURNAL IN HAEMOSTASIS AND THROMBOSIS. (UK/0957-5235). **3795**

BLOOD-HORSE, THE. (US/0006-4998). **2797**

BLOODLINES :. (US/0890-8923). **4286**

BLOOMSBURY REVIEW, THE. (US/0276-1564). **3338**

BLOUNT JOURNAL, THE. (US/1056-6252). **2439**

BLOWING ROCKET, THE. (US/1071-0574). **Qty:** unlimited. **5722**

BLUE & GRAY MAGAZINE. (US/0741-2207). **Qty:** 50 or more per year. **2723**

BLUE BOOK OF PHOTOGRAPHY PRICES. (US/0738-8322). **4367**

BLUE BOOK. OFFICIAL LAWN MOWER TRADE-IN GUIDE. (US). **2410**

BLUE GRASS ROOTS. (US/0278-8071). **2439**

BLUE GUITAR, THE. (IT). **3367**

BLUE JAY. (CN/0006-5099). **4163**

BLUE JAY NEWS. (CN/0822-9988). **4163**

BLUE LINE MAGAZINE. (CN/0847-8538). **3158**

BLUE MOUNTAIN HERITAGE. (US/0743-183X). **2439**

BLUE RIBBON HOME PLANS. (US/0899-4382). **2899**

BLUE RIBBON, THE. (US). **2797**

BLUE RIBBON WORD-FINDS. (US/0194-312X). **4858**

BLUE RIDGE COUNTRY. (US/1041-3456). **Qty:** 4. **2529**

BLUEFIELD DAILY TELEGRAPH. (US). **5763**

BLUEGRASS-BUEHNE. (GW/0936-2479). **Qty:** 6 per year. **4104**

BLUEGRASS UNLIMITED. (US/0006-5137). **Qty:** 30. **4104**

BLUELINE (POTSDAM, N.Y.). (US/0198-9901). **Qty:** 5. **3367**

BLUEPRINT (LONDON. 1983). (UK/0268-4926). **Qty:** 30 per year. **293**

BLUEPRINTS - NATIONAL BUILDING MUSEUM (U.S.). (US/0742-0552). **293**

BLUES ACCESS. (US/1066-4068). **Qty:** 10. **4104**

BLUES & SOUL. (UK). **4104**

BLUES LIFE. (AU/0250-4421). **4104**

BLUES LIFE JOURNAL. (AU/0250-4421). **4104**

BLUES UNLIMITED. (UK/0006-5153). **4104**

BLUMEN EINZELHANDEL. (GW). **2434**

BLYTTIA. (NO/0006-5269). **502**

BMT ABSTRACTS : BRITISH MARITIME TECHNOLOGY ABSTRACTS. (UK/0268-9650). **4185**

... BMUG NEWSLETTER, THE. (US/0899-1014). **1172**

BN. (FI/0784-7726). **Qty:** 20. **4104**

BNAC COMMUNICATOR. (US/1051-208X). **1105**

B'NAI B'RITH INTERNATIONAL JEWISH MONTHLY, THE. (US/0279-3415). **5046**

BNF NUTRITION BULLETIN. (UK/0141-9684). **4188**

BOARD MANUFACTURE AND PROCESSING. (UK/0306-4123). **2399**

BOAT AND MOTOR DEALER. (US/0006-5366). **591**

BOATING NEWS (VANCOUVER). (CN/0700-7388). **592**

BODENKULTUR (1964). (AU/0006-5471). **67**

BODY, MIND, SPIRIT. (US/0895-7657). **4185**

BOER EN DE TUINDER, DE. (BE). **67**

BOGENS VERDEN. (DK/0006-5692). **3196**

BOGG (ARLINGTON, VA.). (US/0882-648X). **Qty:** 50-100. **3368**

BOGONG. (AT/0159-6586). **Qty:** 16. **2188**

BOHEMIA. (CU/0523-8579). **2485**

BOHEMIA (MUNCHEN). (GW/0523-8587). **2678**

BOIS NATIONAL (EDITION VERTE), LE. (FR). **2376**

BOISE (ADA COUNTY, IDAHO) CITY DIRECTORY. (US). **2556**

BOISSIERA. (SZ/0373-2975). **502**

BOITE A NOUVELLES. (CN/1180-6761). **5780**

BOK OG BIBLIOTEK. (NO/0006-5811). **3257**

BOK OG SAMFUNN (OSLO, NORWAY : 1981). (NO). **4824**

BOKIN BOBAI : NIHON BOKIN BOBAI GAKKAI SHI. (JA/0385-5201). **4294**

BOKVAENNEN. (SW/0006-5846). **3368**

BOLETIM / CEHILA. (BL). **2723**

BOLETIM - COIMBRA. UNIVERSIDADE. CENTRO DE ESTUDOS GEOGRAFICOS. (PO/0587-6060). **1074**

BOLETIM DA SOCIEDADE BROTERIANA. (PO/0081-0657). **502**

BOLETIM DE CIENCIAS SOCIAIS. (BL). **5193**

BOLETIM DE CONJUNTURA. (BL). **1548**

BOLETIM DE GEOGRAFIA TEORETICA. (BL). **2556**

BOLETIM DE INDUSTRIA ANIMAL. (BL/0067-9615). **207**

BOLETIM DO CENTRO DE DOCUMENTACAO 25 DE ABRIL. (PO/0871-3643). **5193**

BOLETIM DO INSTITUTO DE PESCA. (BL/0046-9939). **2297**

BOLETIM PAULISTA DE GEOGRAFIA. (BL/0006-6079). **2556**

BOLETIM / UNIVERSIDADE ESTADUAL DE LONDRINA, CCH, CENTRO DE LETRAS E CIENCIAS HUMANAS. (BL). **5193**

BOLETIN ANGLOHISPANO. (US/0731-8111). **2942**

BOLETIN ANUARIO - BANCO CENTRAL DEL ECUADOR. (EC). **5323**

BOLETIN BOTANICO LATINOAMERICANO. (US). **Qty:** 1-2. **502**

BOLETIN / CEHILA. (CK). **4939**

BOLETIN / CENTRO DE ESTUDIOS MONETARIOS LATINOAMERICANOS. (MX). **779**

BOLETIN CHILENO DE PARASITOLOGIA. (CL/0365-9402). **449**

BOLETIN - COMISION DE INTEGRACION ELECTRICA REGIONAL. (UY). **4633**

BOLETIN DE ANTROPOLOGIA. (CK/0120-2510). **232**

BOLETIN DE ESTUDIOS ECONOMICOS. (SP/0006-6249). **1465**

BOLETIN DE ESTUDIOS MEDICOS Y BIOLOGICOS. (MX/0067-9666). **449**

BOLETIN DE LA ACADEMIA COLOMBIANA. (CK/0001-3773). **Qty:** 4. **2513**

BOLETIN DE LA ACADEMIE HONDURENA DE LA LENGUA. (HO/0065-0471). **3269**

BOLETIN DE LA ASOCIACION ESPANOLA DE ORIENTALISTAS. (SP/0571-3692). **2647**

BOLETIN DE LA CAMARA DE CUENTAS Y DEL TRIBUNAL SUPERIOR ADMINISTRATIVO. (DR). **4713**

BOLETIN DE LA ESCUELA DE CIENCIAS ANTROPOLOGICAS DE LA UNIVERSIDAD DE YUCATAN. (MX). **232**

BOLETIN DE LA OFICINA SANITARIA PANAMERICANA. (US/0030-0632). **4769**

BOLETIN DE LA SOCIEDAD CHILENA DE QUIMICA. (CL/0366-1644). **962**

BOLETIN DE LA SOCIEDAD GEOGRAFICA DE LIMA. (PE/0037-8585). **2556**

BOLETIN DE LA SOCIEDAD QUIMICA DEL PERU. (PE/0037-8623). **962**

BOLETIN DE LIMA. (PE/0253-0015). **5193**

BOLETIN DE LITERATURA MEDIEVAL. (SP). **3368**

BOLETIN DE PSICOLOGIA. (CU/0253-5742). **4577**

BOLETIN DEL CENTRO DE ESTUDIOS GENEALOGICOS DE CORDOBA. (AG). **2439**

BOLETIN DEL INSTITUTO AMERICANO DE ESTUDIOS VASCOS. (AG/0020-3637). **3269**

BOLETIN DEL INSTITUTO GEMOLOGICO ESPANOL. (SP/0210-7228). **2913**

BOLETIN DEL MUSEO DE CIENCIAS NATURALES Y ANTROPOLOGICAS JUAN CORNELIO MOYANO. (AG/0326-1484). **262**

BOLETIN DEL SISTEMA ESTATAL DE DOCUMENTACION DEL ESTADO DE MEXICO. (MX/0188-4492). **4633**

BOLETIN ECONOMICO DE LA CONSTRUCCION 1956. (SP/0210-1947). **601**

BOLETIN MEDICO DEL HOSPITAL INFANTIL DE MEXICO (SPANISH EDITION). (MX/0539-6115). **3901**

BOLETIN MEXICANO DE DERECHO COMPARADO. (MX/0041-8633). **3124**

BOLETIN SEMESTRAL - COLEGIO DE MEXICO. (MX/0543-7369). **1089**

BOLI YU TANGCI. (CC/1000-2871). **2586**

BOLLETTINO DEL LAVORO E DEI TRIBUTI. (IT/0394-6592). **Qty:** 2-3. **3144**

BOLLETTINO DELLA DEPUTAZIONE DI STORIA PATRIA PER L'UMBRIA. (IT/0300-4422). **4633**

BOLLETTINO DELLA DOMUS MAZZINIANA. (IT/0012-5385). **2679**

BOLLETTINO DELLA DOXA. (IT). **5240**

BOLLETTINO DELLA SOCIETA DI STUDI VALDESI. (IT/0037-8739). **4939**

BOLLETTINO DELLA SOCIETA ENTOMOLOGICA ITALIANA. (IT/0373-3491). **5606**

BOLLETTINO DELLA SOCIETA GEOGRAFICA ITALIANA. (IT/0037-8755). **2556**

BOLLETTINO DELLA SOCIETA ITALIANA DI TOPOGRAFIA E FOTOGRAMMETRIA. (IT/0392-4424). **2556**

BOLLETTINO DELL'ISTITUTO STORICO ARTISTICO ORVIETANO. (IT/0391-8211). **2612**

BOLLETTINO DI GEODESIA E SCIENZE AFFINI. (IT/0006-6710). **1352**

BOLLETTINO DI GEOFISICA TEORICA ED APPLICATA. (IT/0006-6729). **1403**

BOLLETTINO DI OCEANOLOGIA TEORICA ED APPLICATA. (IT/0393-196X). **1447**

BOLLETTINO DI OCULISTICA. (IT/0006-677X). **3872**

BOLLETTINO DI PSICOLOGIA APPLICATA. (IT/0006-6761). **4577**

BOLLETTINO DI STORIA DELLE SCIENZE MATEMATICHE. (IT/0392-4432). **3497**

BOLLETTINO DI STUDI LATINI. (IT/0006-6583). **3270**

BOLLETTINO DI ZOOLOGIA. (IT/0373-4137). **5578**

BOLLETTINO MALACOLOGICO. (IT/0394-7149). **5578**

BOLLETTINO PER LE FARMACODIPENDENZE E L'ALCOOLISMO. (IT/0392-3126). **1341**

BOLLETTINO STORICO-BIBLIOGRAFICO SUBALPINO. (IT/0391-6715). **Qty:** Varies. **2679**

BOLLETTINO UFFICIALE REGIONE : EMILIA ROMAGNA - PART III. (IT). **Qty:** 1. **4633**

BOLLETTINO UFFICIALE REGIONE : UMBRIA. PART 1 & 2. (IT). **4633**

BOLLETTINO UFFICIALE REGIONE : UMBRIA. PART 4. (IT). **4633**

BOND LAW REVIEW. (AT/1033-4505). **2943**

BOND MANAGEMENT REVIEW. (AT/1036-1456). **861**

BONE MARROW TRANSPLANTATION (BASINGSTOKE). (UK/0268-3369). **3558**

BONJOUR CHEZ-NOUS. (CN/0383-7866). **5780**

BONNER COUNTY DAILY BEE. (US/1047-6822). **5656**

BONNER ZOOLOGISCHE BEITRAEGE. (GW/0006-7172). **5578**

BONNERS FERRY HERALD. (US/1064-9298). **5656**

BONNYVILLE NOUVELLE. (CN/0710-3905). **4887**

BONSAI CLUBS INTERNATIONAL. (US/0744-3277). **2410**

BONSAI : JOURNAL OF THE AMERICAN BONSAI SOCIETY. (US). **2410**

BONSAI MAGAZINE. (US/1068-6193). **2410**

BOOK - AMERICAN ANTIQUARIAN SOCIETY, THE. (US/0740-8439). **4824**

BOOK COLLECTOR, THE. (UK/0006-7237). **4824**

BOOK FORUM. (US/0094-9426). **3338**

BOOK MARKETING UPDATE. (US/0891-8813). **Qty:** 50. **4824**

BOOK NEWSLETTER (MINNEAPOLIS, MINN.). (US/1043-352X). **3338**

BOOK PRODUCTION (BENN PUBLICATIONS LTD.). (UK). **4825**

BOOK REPORT (COLUMBUS, OHIO). (US/0731-4388). **3196**

BOOK REVIEW DIGEST. CD-ROM. (US/0006-7326). **4821**

BOOK REVIEW, THE. (II). **4825**

BOOK TALK (ALBUQUERQUE). (US/0145-627X). **Qty:** 125. **4825**

BOOKBIRD. (DK/0006-7377). **3368**

BOOKMARK (MOSCOW, IDAHO), THE. (US/0735-0295). **3197**

BOOKMARK, THE. (US/0006-7407). **3197**

BOOKMARK (VANCOUVER). (CN/0381-6028). **3197**

BOOKPLATES IN THE NEWS. (US/0045-2521). **2771**

BOOKPRESS, THE. (US). **4825**

BOOKS ABOUT BIRDS. (US). **5616**

BOOKS AND PERIODICALS ONLINE. (US/0951-838X). **3257**

BOOKS & RELIGION. (US/0890-0841). **4939**

BOOKS BY BLACK WOMEN. (US/1040-0362). **4825**

BOOKS FOR YOUR CHILDREN. (UK/0006-7482). **Qty:** 200. **3338**

BOOKS FROM ISRAEL. (IS/0578-932X). **4825**

BOOKS IN ARMENIAN. (CN/0705-8209). **4825**

BOOKS IN CANADA. (CN/0045-2564). **4825**

BOOKS IN DUTCH (1980). (CN/0713-4533). **4825**

BOOKS IN FINNISH (1980). (CN/0714-2382). **4825**

BOOKS IN HUNGARIAN (1980). (CN/0714-2544). **4826**

BOOKS IN LITHUANIAN. (CN/0705-8225). **4826**

BOOKS IN MARATHI. (CN/0317-2406). **4826**

BOOKS IN PERSIAN (1980). (CN/0227-2741). **4826**

BOOKS IN POLISH (1980). (CN/0714-2773). **4826**

BOOKS IN PRINT WITH BOOK REVIEWS PLUS [COMPUTER FILE]. (US). **3197**

BOOKS IN SCOTLAND. (UK/0143-1285). **4826**

BOOKS IRELAND. (IE/0376-6039). **4812**

BOOKS--NOTED FOR YOU. (CN/0829-4976). **4821**

BOOKS OF THE SOUTHWEST. (US/0006-7520). **Qty:** 700-1,000 per year. **3457**

BOOKSELLER (LONDON). (UK/0006-7539). **4821**

BOOKSTORE JOURNAL. (US/0006-7563). **4939**

BOOKTALK. (UK/0307-854X). **Qty:** 300. **4826**

BOOKWAYS (AUSTIN, TEX.). (US/1057-6355). **Qty:** 50-70. **4827**

BOOKWOMAN, THE. (US/0163-1128). **4827**

BOOMBAH HERALD. (US/8755-5832). **Qty:** 1. **4104**

BOOTBLACK (BOYNTON BEACH, FLA.). (US/1040-7405). **3368**

BORDER CROSSINGS (WINNIPEG, MAN.). (CN/0831-2559). **316**

BORDER/LINES. (CN/0826-967X). **4185**

BORDERLANDS (AUSTIN, TEX.). (US/1065-0342). **3460**

BORTHWICK PAPERS / UNIVERSITY OF YORK, BORTHWICK INSTITUTE OF HISTORICAL RESEARCH. (UK/0524-0913). **2679**

BOSTON COLLEGE INTERNATIONAL AND COMPARATIVE LAW REVIEW. (US/0277-5778). **3125**

BOSTON COLLEGE THIRD WORLD LAW JOURNAL. (US/0276-3583). **3125**

BOSTON JEWISH TIMES, THE. (US/8750-1961). **5688**

BOSTON MYCOLOGICAL CLUB BULLETIN. (US/0270-4633). **574**

BOSTON ORGAN CLUB NEWSLETTER, THE. (US/0524-1170). **4104**

BOSTON PARENTS' PAPER, THE. (US/1059-1710). **Qty:** 12. **2277**

BOSTON PHOENIX, THE. (US/0163-3015). **5688**

BOSTON REVIEW (CAMBRIDGE, MASS. : 1982). (US/0734-2306). **Qty:** 30. **3368**

BOSTON ROCK. (US/0889-230X). **4104**

BOSTON UNIVERSITY INTERNATIONAL LAW JOURNAL. (US/0737-8947). **3125**

BOSTON UNIVERSITY LAW REVIEW. (US/0006-8047). **2943**

BOSTONIA (BOSTON, MASS. 1986). (US/1067-2834). **Qty:** 6-10. **3368**

BOTANICA MARINA. (GW/0006-8055). **503**

BOTANICA (NEW DELHI, INDIA). (II/0045-2629). **503**

BOTANISCHE JAHRBUCHER FUER SYSTEMATIK, PFLANZENGESCHICHTE UND PFLANZENGEOGRAPHIE. (GW/0006-8152). **503**

BOTE, DER. (GW). **3338**

BOTH SIDES NOW. (US). **4940**

BOTHALIA. (SA/0006-8241). **504**

BOTSWANA NOTES AND RECORDS. (BS/0525-5090). **2498**

BOTTOM LINE (CHARLESTON, S.C.), THE. (US/0279-1889). **739**

BOTTOM LINE (NEW YORK, N.Y.), THE. (US/0888-045X). **3197**

BOUCHERIE FRANCAISE, LA. (FR). **2329**

BOUNDARY 2. (US/0190-3659). **3368**

BOUNDARY ELEMENTS ABSTRACTS AND NEWSLETTER. (UK/0957-2902). **1966**

BOUNDARY-LAYER METEOROLOGY. (NE/0006-8314). **1421**

BOUNDARY WATERS JOURNAL, THE. (US/0899-2681). **2188**

BOUT DE PAPIER. (CN/0833-9864). **Qty:** 20. **2485**

BOUT DE PAPIER. (CN/0833-9864). **Qty:** 15. **4517**

BOUW. (NE/0366-2330). **601**

BOUWKRONIEK : WEEKBLAD VOOR DE BOUW EN INDUSTRIE. (BE). **601**

BOVINE PRACTITIONER, THE. (US/0524-1685). **5506**

BOWBENDER MAGAZINE. (CN/0827-2638). **4888**

BOWLING DIGEST. (US/8750-3603). **4888**

BOWMAN'S ACCOUNTING REPORT. (US/0897-3482). **Qty:** 5. **739**

BOWNE DIGEST FOR CORPORATE & SECURITIES LAWYERS. (US/0896-906X). **3079**

BOXING MONTHLY. (UK/0956-098X). **Qty:** 15. **4888**

BOXOFFICE. (US/0006-8527). **4064**

BRABANTSE LEEUW, DE. (NE). **2439**

BRABY'S CAPE PROVINCE DIRECTORY. (SA). **5500**

BRADFORD JOURNAL (BRADFORD, PA. : 1973). (US). **Qty:** 4. **5735**

BRAIDWOOD INDEX, THE. (US). **5658**

BRAILLE MONITOR, THE. (US/0006-8829). **4384**

BRAIN. (UK/0006-8950). **3828**

BRAIN AND COGNITION. (US/0278-2626). **4577**

BRAIN AND LANGUAGE. (US/0093-934X). **3828**

BRAIN, BEHAVIOR AND EVOLUTION. (SZ/0006-8977). **3828**

BRAIN RESEARCH BULLETIN. (US/0361-9230). **3829**

BRAINERD DISPATCH. (US). **5694**

BRAKE & FRONT END. (US/0193-726X). **5408**

BRANCH NOTES / WATERLOO-WELLINGTON BRANCH, ONTARIO GENEALOGICAL SOCIETY. (CN/0383-7505). **2439**

BRANCHES & TWIGS : NEWSLETTER OF GENEALOGICAL SOCIETY OF VERMONT. (US/0742-9851). **Qty:** 24. **2440**

BRANDWACHT. (GW/0006-9116). **2288**

BRANDWEEK (NEW YORK, N.Y.). (US/1064-4318). **756**

BRANGUS JOURNAL. (US/0006-9132). **207**

BRANNTWEINWIRTSCHAFT, DIE. (GW). **2365**

BRASIL FLORESTAL. (BL/0045-270X). **2376**

BRASIL PORTO ALEGRE. (BL/0103-751X). **Qty:** 10. **3369**

BRASILIANS, THE. (US/0741-0298). **Qty:** 20 per year. **2724**

BRASS BULLETIN. (SZ/0303-3848). **4105**

BRASS RESEARCH SERIES. (US/0363-454X). **4105**

BRATSTVO (TORONTO). (CN/0006-9264). **5229**

BRAUNKOHLE (DUSSELDORF. 1972). (GW/0341-1060). **1934**

BRAUWELT (1978). (GW/0724-696X). **2329**

BRAUWELT INTERNATIONAL. (GW/0934-9340). **2365**

BRAXTON CITIZEN'S NEWS. (US). **5763**

BRAZIL. (US). **3338**

BRAZIL TIMES, THE. (US). Qty: 50. **5663**

BRAZILIAN BIBLE QUARTERLY. (BL). Qty: 200. **4940**

BRAZILIAN GAZETTE, THE. (UK/0307-160X). **2485**

BRAZORIA COUNTY NEWS, THE. (US). **5747**

BREAKING THE SILENCE (OTTAWA, ONT.). (CN/0713-4266). **5552**

BREAKTHROUGH (ATLANTA, GA.). (US/0885-8578). Qty: 1-2/yr. **2771**

BREAKTHROUGH (EAST ORANGE, N.J.). (US/0889-3942). **1728**

BREAKTHROUGH (HAMMOND, LA.). (US/1056-0130). **2771**

BREAKTHROUGH (SAN FRANCISCO, CALIF.). (US). **4465**

BRECHA (MONTEVIDEO, URUGUAY). (UY). **2917**

BRECHT YEARBOOK, THE. (US/0734-8665). **3369**

BREEDER AND FEEDER. (CN/0712-5291). **207**

BRETHREN IN CHRIST HISTORY AND LIFE. (US/1071-4200). Qty: 12-20. **5057**

BRETHREN LIFE AND THOUGHT. (US/0006-9663). **4940**

BREWER (LONDON). (UK/0006-9736). **2365**

BREWERS BULLETIN, THE. (US/0006-9701). **2365**

BREWERS' GUARDIAN. (UK/0006-9728). **2365**

BREWING INDUSTRY NEWS, THE. (US/0273-5768). **2365**

BRIAR PATCH. (CN/0703-8968). Qty: 20. **5193**

BRICK. (CN/0382-8565). Qty: 10. **3338**

BRICK BULLETIN. (UK/0307-9325). **602**

BRICKER BRANCHES. (US/0897-7879). **2440**

BRIDE OF CHRIST, THE. (US/0197-3045). Qty: 6-8. **5057**

BRIDGE (HONG KONG). (HK/1018-8983). **4940**

BRIDGE (OAK PARK, MICH.), THE. (US/1052-1569). Qty: 3 - 4. **3369**

BRIDGE RIVER LILLOOET NEWS. (CN). Qty: 1. **5781**

BRIDGE (SALEM, OR.), THE. (US/0741-1200). **2724**

BRIDGE, THE. (UK). **4858**

BRIDGE TODAY!. (US/1043-6383). **4858**

BRIDGE WORLD, THE. (US/0006-9876). **4858**

BRIDGEPORT LEADER. (US). **5658**

BRIDGES (SEATTLE, WASH.). (US/1046-8358). Qty: (6-8). **5552**

BRIDGETON EVENING NEWS. (US). **5709**

BRIDGING THE GAP (LANCASTER). (CN/0840-7738). Qty: varies. **2440**

BRIEFING. (TU). **4466**

BRIGHAM YOUNG UNIVERSITY STUDIES (1984). (US/0007-0106). **4940**

BRIO (UNITED KINGDOM BRANCH, INTERNATIONAL ASSOCIATION OF MUSIC LIBRARIES). (UK/0007-0173). **4105**

BRISTOL BAYTIMES. (US). **5628**

BRITANNIA (SOCIETY FOR THE PROMOTION OF ROMAN STUDIES). (UK/0068-113X). Qty: 25. **1075**

BRITANNIA (TORONTO). (CN/0823-7743). **2514**

BRITANNICA BOOK OF THE YEAR. (US/0068-1156). Qty: 100-125. **1923**

BRITISH ACCOUNTING REVIEW, THE. (UK/0890-8389). **740**

BRITISH ARCHAEOLOGICAL BIBLIOGRAPHY. (UK/0964-7104). **286**

BRITISH ARCHER, THE. (UK/0007-0289). **4888**

BRITISH BANDSMAN. (UK). **4105**

BRITISH BEE JOURNAL. (UK/0007-0327). **5578**

BRITISH BIRDS. (UK/0007-0335). **5616**

BRITISH BULLETIN OF PUBLICATIONS ON LATIN AMERICA, THE CARIBBEAN, PORTUGAL AND SPAIN / CANNING HOUSE, HISPANIC AAN LUSO-BRAZILIAN COUNCIL. (UK/0268-2400). **4827**

BRITISH CERAMIC REVIEW. (UK/0306-7076). **2586**

BRITISH CHESS MAGAZINE, THE. (UK/0007-0440). **4858**

BRITISH COLUMBIA GENEALOGIST, THE. (CN/0315-3835). **2440**

BRITISH COLUMBIA MEDICAL JOURNAL. (CN/0007-0556). Qty: 88. **3558**

BRITISH CORROSION JOURNAL. (UK/0007-0599). **2008**

BRITISH DEAF NEWS. (UK/0007-0602). **4385**

BRITISH DENTAL SURGERY ASSISTANT. (UK/0007-0629). **1317**

BRITISH DIGEST ILLUSTRATED. (US/0196-7517). **2514**

BRITISH EDUCATIONAL RESEARCH JOURNAL. (UK/0141-1926). **1728**

BRITISH FOOD JOURNAL (1966). (UK/0007-070X). **2329**

BRITISH GEOLOGIST. (UK). **1368**

BRITISH HOTELIER & RESTAURATEUR : OFFICIAL MAGAZINE OF THE BRITISH HOTELS, RESTAURANTS & CATERERS ASSOCIATION. (UK). **2804**

BRITISH JOURNAL FOR EIGHTEENTH-CENTURY STUDIES, THE. (UK/0141-867X). **3369**

BRITISH JOURNAL FOR THE HISTORY OF PHILOSOPHY. (UK/0960-8788). Qty: 16. **4342**

BRITISH JOURNAL FOR THE HISTORY OF SCIENCE, THE. (UK/0007-0874). **5089**

BRITISH JOURNAL FOR THE PHILOSOPHY OF SCIENCE, THE. (UK/0007-0882). **5089**

BRITISH JOURNAL OF ACADEMIC LIBRARIANSHIP. (UK/0269-0497). **3197**

BRITISH JOURNAL OF ACUPUNCTURE. (UK/0143-4977). **3558**

BRITISH JOURNAL OF AESTHETICS. (UK/0007-0904). **344**

BRITISH JOURNAL OF AUDIOLOGY. (UK/0300-5364). **3887**

BRITISH JOURNAL OF CANADIAN STUDIES. (UK/0269-9222). **2724**

BRITISH JOURNAL OF CLINICAL PRACTICE, THE. (UK/0007-0947). **3558**

BRITISH JOURNAL OF CLINICAL PSYCHOLOGY, THE. (UK/0144-6657). **4578**

BRITISH JOURNAL OF CRIMINOLOGY, DELINQUENCY AND DEVIANT SOCIAL BEHAVIOR, THE. (UK/0007-0955). **3158**

BRITISH JOURNAL OF DERMATOLOGY (1951). (UK/0007-0963). **3718**

BRITISH JOURNAL OF DEVELOPMENTAL PSYCHOLOGY, THE. (UK/0261-510X). **4578**

BRITISH JOURNAL OF DISORDERS OF COMMUNICATION. MONOGRAPH. (UK). **4385**

BRITISH JOURNAL OF EDUCATION AND WORK. (UK). **1728**

BRITISH JOURNAL OF EDUCATIONAL PSYCHOLOGY, THE. (UK/0007-0998). **4578**

BRITISH JOURNAL OF EDUCATIONAL STUDIES. (UK/0007-1005). **1728**

BRITISH JOURNAL OF EDUCATIONAL TECHNOLOGY. (UK/0007-1013). **1889**

BRITISH JOURNAL OF GUIDANCE & COUNSELLING. (UK/0306-9885). **1911**

BRITISH JOURNAL OF INDUSTRIAL RELATIONS. (UK/0007-1080). **1656**

BRITISH JOURNAL OF MATHEMATICAL & STATISTICAL PSYCHOLOGY, THE. (UK/0007-1102). **4622**

BRITISH JOURNAL OF MEDICAL PSYCHOLOGY. (UK/0007-1129). **4578**

BRITISH JOURNAL OF MENTAL SUBNORMALITY. (UK/0374-633X). **1876**

BRITISH JOURNAL OF MIDDLE EASTERN STUDIES. (UK). **2768**

BRITISH JOURNAL OF NON-DESTRUCTIVE TESTING. (UK/0007-1137). **2101**

BRITISH JOURNAL OF OBSTETRICS AND GYNAECOLOGY. (UK/0306-5456). **3758**

BRITISH JOURNAL OF OCCUPATIONAL THERAPY, THE. (UK/0308-0226). **1876**

BRITISH JOURNAL OF OPHTHALMOLOGY. (UK/0007-1161). **3872**

BRITISH JOURNAL OF ORTHODONTICS. (UK/0301-228X). **1317**

BRITISH JOURNAL OF PHOTOGRAPHY. (UK/0007-1196). **4367**

BRITISH JOURNAL OF PHYSICAL EDUCATION. (UK/0144-3569). **1855**

BRITISH JOURNAL OF PHYTOTHERAPY, THE. (UK/0959-6879). Qty: 1-2. **504**

BRITISH JOURNAL OF PLASTIC SURGERY. (UK/0007-1226). **3961**

BRITISH JOURNAL OF PODIATRIC MEDICINE & SURGERY. (UK/0955-8160). **3917**

BRITISH JOURNAL OF PROJECTIVE PSYCHOLOGY. (UK). **4578**

BRITISH JOURNAL OF PSYCHIATRY, THE. (UK/0007-1250). **3922**

BRITISH JOURNAL OF PSYCHOLOGY (1955). (UK/0007-1269). **4578**

BRITISH JOURNAL OF RADIOLOGY, THE. (UK/0007-1285). **3939**

BRITISH JOURNAL OF RELIGIOUS EDUCATION. (UK/0141-6200). **4940**

BRITISH JOURNAL OF RHEUMATOLOGY. (UK/0263-7103). **3803**

BRITISH JOURNAL OF SEXUAL MEDICINE. (UK/0301-5572). **3559**

BRITISH JOURNAL OF SOCIAL PSYCHOLOGY, THE. (UK/0144-6665). **4578**

BRITISH JOURNAL OF SOCIAL WORK, THE. (UK/0045-3102). **5275**

BRITISH JOURNAL OF SOCIOLOGY OF EDUCATION. (UK/0142-5692). **5241**

BRITISH JOURNAL OF SOCIOLOGY, THE. (UK/0007-1315). **5240**

BRITISH JOURNAL OF SPORTS MEDICINE. (UK/0306-3674). **3953**

BRITISH JOURNAL OF SURGERY. (UK/0007-1323). **3961**

BRITISH JOURNAL OF UROLOGY. (UK/0007-1331). **3988**

BRITISH JOURNAL OF VISUAL IMPAIRMENT, THE. (UK/0264-6196). **4385**

BRITISH MEDICAL BULLETIN. (UK/0007-1420). **3559**

BRITISH MUSEUM MAGAZINE. (UK/0965-8297). Qty: 10. **4085**

BRITISH MUSEUM MAGAZINE : JOURNAL OF THE BRITISH MUSEUM SOCIETY. (UK). Qty: 10/year. **4085**

BRITISH ORTHOPTIC JOURNAL. (UK/0068-2314). **3873**

BRITISH POULTRY SCIENCE. (UK/0007-1668). **207**

BRITISH PRINTER, THE. (UK/0007-1684). **4564**

BRITISH REVIEW OF ECONOMIC ISSUES. (UK/0141-4739). Qty: 20. **1465**

BRITISH SUGAR BEET REVIEW. (UK/0007-1854). **165**

BRITISH TRAVEL LETTER. (US/1041-4010). Qty: 10. **5465**

BRITISH VETERINARY JOURNAL, THE. (UK/0007-1935). **5506**

BRITISH VIRGIN ISLANDS CONSOLIDATED INDEX OF STATUTES AND SUBSIDIARY LEGISLATION TO ... . (BB). **3125**

BRITISH WILDLIFE. (UK). **4869**

BRITISH YEAR BOOK OF INTERNATIONAL LAW, THE. (UK/0068-2691). **3125**

BRITTONIA. (US/0007-196X). **504**

BRMNA JOURNAL. (CN/0229-0553). **5430**

BRNO STUDIES IN ENGLISH. (XR/0524-6881). **3270**

BROADCAST EQUIPMENT BUYERS GUIDE (SHAWNEE MISSION, KAN.). (US/0882-5688). **1127**

BROADCAST FINANCIAL JOURNAL. (US/0161-9063). **1127**

BROADCAST SYSTEMS ENGINEERING. (UK/0267-565X). **1128**

BROADCASTER (TORONTO). (CN/0008-3038). **1128**

BROADSIDE (NEW YORK, N.Y. : 1940). (US/0068-2748). **5362**

BROADSIDE (NEW YORK, N.Y. 1962). (US/0740-7955). **4105**

BROKEN BENCH REVIEW. (US/0739-652X). **3085**

BRONTE NEWSLETTER. (US/0737-6340). **3369**

BRONTE SOCIETY PUBLICATIONS. TRANSACTIONS. (UK/0309-7765). **3369**

BRONX COUNTY HISTORICAL SOCIETY JOURNAL, THE. (US/0007-2249). **2724**

BRONX TIMES REPORTER. (US/8750-4499). **Qty: 6. 5714**

BROOKGREEN JOURNAL. (US/0884-8815). **345**

BROOKLYN JOURNAL OF INTERNATIONAL LAW. (US/0740-4824). **3125**

BROOKLYN LAW REVIEW. (US/0007-2362). **2944**

BROOKS' STANDARD RATE BOOK, THE. (US/0193-2314). **1656**

BROOM, BRUSH & MOP. (US/0890-2933). **1600**

BROOMSTICK. (US/0883-9611). **5552**

BROT & BACKWAREN. (GW/0172-8180). **Qty: 30. 2329**

BROTHERHOOD ACTION. (AT/0300-4678). **5229**

BROWBEAT. (US/1075-0371). **Qty: 5-10. 4105**

BROWN UNIVERSITY STD UPDATE, THE. (US/0898-8323). **4769**

BROWNING SOCIETY NOTES. (UK/0950-6349). **3369**

BROWN'S BUSINESS REPORTER. (US/1066-2421). **Qty: 9. 644**

BROWN'S NAUTICAL ALMANAC. (UK/0068-290X). **4175**

BROWNSTONER, THE. (US/0883-962X). **293**

BRUG, DE. (NE). **5806**

BRUNSWICK BUSINESS JOURNAL, THE. (CN/0829-5239). **Qty: varies. 644**

BRUNSWICK NEWS, THE. (US). **5652**

BRUSHWARE (WASHINGTON, D.C.). (US/0007-2710). **2810**

BRYGMESTEREN. (DK/0007-2737). **2365**

BRYN MAWR CLASSICAL REVIEW. (US/1055-7660). **Qty: 100. 1075**

BRYNWT WSTYH HBRTYT. (IS/0334-4525). **5275**

BRYOLOGIST, THE. (US/0007-2745). **504**

BUC ... NEW BOAT PRICE GUIDE. (US/0195-346X). **592**

BUC USED BOAT PRICE GUIDE. (US/0735-973X). **592**

BUCH DER ZEIT. (GW/0007-2761). **4812**

BUCH UND BIBLIOTHEK. (GW/0340-0301). **3197**

BUCKEYE REVIEW. (US/0045-3285). **2257**

BUCKEYE VALLEY NEWS. (US). **5629**

BUCKLEY-LITTLE CATALOGUE OF BOOKS AVAILABLE FROM AUTHORS, THE. (US/0749-615X). **411**

BUCKSKIN BULLETIN. (US/0045-3307). **2724**

BUDAPEST REVIEW OF BOOKS. (HU/1215-735X). **4827**

BUDDHIST-CHRISTIAN STUDIES. (US/0882-0945). **5020**

BUDDHIST STUDIES. (II). **5020**

BUDDY (DALLAS, TEX.). (US/0192-9097). **4105**

BUDESHTE. (FR). **2514**

BUDGET (SUGARCREEK, OHIO : 1928). (US). **5727**

BUECHERSCHIFF; DIE DEUTSCHE BUECHERZEITUNG. (GW/0007-3059). **4827**

BUENASALUD (ED. NACIONAL). (PR/1053-5543). **2596**

BUFFALO BULLETIN, THE. (US). **Qty: 6-12. 5765**

BUFFALO (CUSTER). (US/0196-9137). **208**

BUFFALO LAW REVIEW. (US/0023-9356). **2944**

BUFFALO NEWS, THE. (US/0745-2691). **5714**

BUGLE. (US/0889-6445). **2189**

BUHL HERALD, THE. (US). **5656**

BUILD; JOURNAL OF THE INDUSTRY. (IE/0007-3229). **602**

BUILDING AND CONSTRUCTION LAW. (AT/0815-6050). **602**

BUILDING AND CONSTRUCTION TRADES TODAY. (CN/1186-1398). **602**

BUILDING ECONOMIC ALTERNATIVES. (US/0885-9930). **1465**

BUILDING ECONOMIST, THE. (AT/0007-3431). **603**

BUILDING ENGINEER. (UK). **Qty: 50. 603**

BUILDING (LONDON. ENGLAND). (UK/0007-3318). **603**

BUILDING OKLAHOMA (OKLAHOMA CITY, OKLA. 1989). (US/1071-2879). **603**

BUILDING PERMITS, ANNUAL SUMMARY. (CN/0575-7975). **632**

BUILDING PRODUCTS DIGEST. (US/0742-5694). **2399**

BUILDING SCIENCES. (US). **604**

BUILDING SERVICES CONTRACTOR. (US/0007-3644). **604**

BUILDING SERVICES ENGINEERING RESEARCH & TECHNOLOGY. (UK/0143-6244). **604**

BUILDING SERVICES : THE CIBSE JOURNAL. (UK). **604**

BUILDING STANDARDS. (US/0270-1197). **604**

BUILDINGS ENERGY TECHNOLOGY. (US/0891-3730). **1934**

BUILT ENVIRONMENT (LONDON, 1978). (UK/0263-7960). **Qty: 15. 2816**

BU$INESS OF HERBS, THE. (US/0736-9050). **2411**

BUKKU ENDO TSUSHIN. (JA). **3369**

BUKU SAKU STATISTIK INDONESIA. (IO). **5324**

BULETIN PERSATUAN GEOLOGI MALAYSIA. (MY/0126-6187). **1368**

BULETINUL INSTITUTULUI DE PETROL SI GAZE. (RM/0376-4516). **4252**

BULGARIAN CO-OPERATIVE REVIEW. (BU). **1541**

BULGARIAN HISTORICAL REVIEW. (BU/0324-0207). **2680**

BULGARIAN JOURNAL OF PHYSICS. (BU/0323-9217). **4398**

BULGARSKI KNIGOPIS. (BU). **4821**

BULGARSKO MUZIKOZNANIE (SOFIA, BULGARIA : 1979). (BU/0204-823X). **4105**

BULK SOLIDS HANDLING. (GW/0173-9980). **1967**

BULL & BEAR. (US/0319-1362). **Qty: 12-15. 893**

BULL AND BRANCH : NEWSLETTER OF THE FRIENDS OF THE DARD HUNTER PAPER MUSEUM. (US). **Qty: 2/year. 4232**

BULLETIN. (FR). **5229**

BULLETIN. (CN). **411**

BULLETIN. (US). **Qty: 6. 2411**

BULLETIN. (FR). **1352**

BULLETIN. (US). **1890**

BULLETIN. (US/0469-9076). **1294**

BULLETIN. (BE). **Qty: 150. 1600**

BULLETIN ADMINISTRATIF DES ASSURANCES. (FR). **2944**

BULLETIN (ALABAMA MUSEUM OF NATURAL HISTORY). (US/0196-1039). **4163**

BULLETIN - ALBERT HOFMANN FOUNDATION. (US/1068-4409). **Qty: 8. 4578**

BULLETIN (ALBERTA TEACHERS' ASSOCIATION. SCIENCE COUNCIL). (CN/0820-7941). **5090**

BULLETIN / AMERICAN ACADEMY OF ORTHOPAEDIC SURGEONS. (US/1049-9741). **3880**

BULLETIN / AMERICAN ASSOCIATION FOR THE HISTORY OF NURSING. (US/0898-6622). **Qty: 2-4. 3852**

BULLETIN - AMERICAN ORCHID SOCIETY. (US). **2411**

BULLETIN / AMERICAN SUNBATHING ASSOCIATION, THE. (US/0279-8158). **4849**

BULLETIN - AMIS DE GUSTAVE COURBET. (FR/0983-3943). **345**

BULLETIN (AMNESTY INTERNATIONAL. CANADIAN SECTION-ENGLISH-SPEAKING). (CN/0831-9227). **4504**

BULLETIN AMQ. (CN/0316-8832). **3497**

BULLETIN ANALYTIQUE - CIE. (FR/0243-5314). **2329**

BULLETIN & I.E. ET ANNALES DE LA SOCIETE ROYALE BELGE D'ENTOMOLOGIE. (BE/0374-6038). **5579**

BULLETIN ANTIEKE BESCHAVING : BABESCH. (NE/0165-9367). **2612**

BULLETIN ASPEA. (SZ). **1934**

BULLETIN - ASSOCIATION CANADIENNE POUR L'AVANCEMENT DES ETUDES NEERLANDAISES. (CN/0823-9487). **2680**

BULLETIN - ASSOCIATION DES MEDECINS DE LANGUE FRANCAISE DU CANADA (1977). (CN/0702-7656). **3559**

BULLETIN - ASSOCIATION FOR PSYCHOANALYTIC MEDICINE. (US/0004-542X). **3922**

BULLETIN (ASSOCIATION FOR THE BIBLIOGRAPHY OF HISTORY (U.S.)). (US/0892-4600). **2635**

BULLETIN - ASSOCIATION FOR THE STUDY OF CANADIAN RADIO AND TELEVISION. (CN/0709-0676). **1128**

BULLETIN - ASSOCIATION OF ENGINEERING GEOLOGISTS. (US/0004-5691). **Qty: varies. 1368**

BULLETIN - ASSOCIATION POUR L'ETUDE TAXONOMIQUE DE LA FLORE D'AFRIQUE TROPICALE. (NE). **504**

BULLETIN BAKHTINE, LE. (CN/0821-6886). **3338**

BULLETIN / BIBLIOGRAPHICAL SOCIETY OF AUSTRALIA AND NEW ZEALAND. (AT/0084-7852). **Qty: 12. 3198**

BULLETIN BIBLIOGRAPHIQUE DE DOCUMENTATION TECHNIQUE / GROUPEMENT DE DOCUMENTATION DES INDUSTRIES EXTRACTIVES. (FR/0395-7322). **411**

BULLETIN BIBLIOGRAPHIQUE - INSTITUT NATIONALE DE LA STATISTIQUE ET DES ETUDES ECONOMIQUES. (FR/0020-2398). **1530**

BULLETIN BIBLIOGRAPHIQUE SPELEOLOGIQUE. (SZ/0253-8296). **5173**

BULLETIN - BISMUTH INSTITUTE. (BE/0379-0401). **3999**

BULLETIN - CALCUTTA STATISTICAL ASSOCIATION. (II/0008-0683). **5324**

BULLETIN - CALIFORNIA WATER POLLUTION CONTROL ASSOCIATION. (US/0008-1620). **2225**

BULLETIN - CANADIAN ASSOCIATION FOR UNIVERSITY CONTINUING EDUCATION. (CN/0823-1168). **1812**

BULLETIN - CANADIAN BOTANICAL ASSOCIATION. (CN/0008-3046). **504**

BULLETIN - CANADIAN COMMISSION FOR UNESCO. (CN/0008-4557). **5193**

BULLETIN - CANADIAN SOCIETY FOR MESOPOTAMIAN STUDIES. (CN/0844-3416). **262**

BULLETIN - CANADIAN SOCIETY OF ZOOLOGISTS. (CN/0319-6674). **5579**

BULLETIN / CANADIAN WATER AND WASTEWATER ASSOCIATION. (CN/0836-0278). **5531**

BULLETIN (CATHOLIC CHURCH. PONTIFICIUM CONSILIUM PRO DIALOGO INTER RELIGIONES). (IT). **5024**

BULLETIN - CAVE EXPLORATION GROUP OF EAST AFRICA. (KE/1013-784X). **1403**

BULLETIN / CEA. (CN). **1729**

BULLETIN - CHINESE HISTORICAL SOCIETY OF AMERICA. (US/0577-9065). **2724**

BULLETIN - COASTAL SOCIETY. (US/0277-8815). **1352**

BULLETIN / COLONIAL WATERBIRD SOCIETY. (US). **5616**

BULLETIN - COUNCIL FOR RESEARCH IN MUSIC EDUCATION. (US/0010-9894). **4105**

BULLETIN CRITIQUE DU LIVRE FRANCAIS. (FR/0007-4209). **3338**

BULLETIN / CSD. (SA). **5193**

BULLETIN DE DROIT IMMOBILIER. (CN/0829-1802). **2944**

BULLETIN DE LA BANQUE NATIONALE DE BELGIQUE. (BE/0005-5611). **780**

BULLETIN DE L'A.I.M. (FR/0007-4314). **4940**

BULLETIN DE LA SOCIETE ARCHEOLOGIQUE ET HISTORIQUE DU LIMOUSIN. (FR/0184-7651). **Qty: 1. 263**

BULLETIN DE LA SOCIETE ARCHEOLOGIQUE ET HISTORIQUE DU LIMOUSIN. (FR). **Qty: 1. 263**

BULLETIN DE LA SOCIETE BELGE DE GEOLOGIE. (BE/0379-1807). **Qty: 15/yr. 1368**

BULLETIN DE LA SOCIETE BELGE D'ETUDES GEOGRAPHIQUES. (BE/0037-8925). **2556**

BULLETIN DE LA SOCIETE BOTANIQUE DE FRANCE. ACTUALITES BOTANIQUES. (FR/0181-1789). **504**

BULLETIN DE LA SOCIETE DE L'HISTOIRE DU PROTESTANTISME FRANCAIS (1981). (FR/0037-9050). **5057**

BULLETIN DE LA SOCIETE DES ETUDES OCEANIENNES (POLYNESIE ORIENTALE). (FP). **2669**

BULLETIN DE LA SOCIETE ENTOMOLOGIQUE DE FRANCE. (FR/0037-928X). **5606**

BULLETIN DE LA SOCIETE HISTORIQUE ET FOLKLORIQUE FRANCAISE. (US). **2318**

BULLETIN DE LA SOCIETE MEDICALE D'AFRIQUE NOIRE DE LANGUE FRANCAISE. (SG/0049-1101). **3559**

BULLETIN DE LA SOCIETE PAUL CLAUDEL. (FR/0037-9506). **3369**

BULLETIN DE LA SOCIETE SCIENTIFIQUE HISTORIQUE ET ARCHEOLOGIQUE DE LA CORREZE. (FR). **263**

BULLETIN DE LA SOCIETE THEOPHILE GAUTIER. (FR/0221-7945). **3369**

BULLETIN DE LA SOCIETE ZOOLOGIQUE DE FRANCE. (FR/0037-962X). **5579**

BULLETIN DE L'ACADEMIE VETERINAIRE DE FRANCE. (FR/0001-4192). **5506**

BULLETIN DE L'ACHETEUR, LE. (FR/0757-2859). **Qty:** 4. **294**

BULLETIN DE L'ASSOCIATION DES PROFESSEURS DE MATHEMATIQUES ET L'ENSEIGNEMENT PUBLIC. (FR). **Qty:** 5. **3498**

BULLETIN DE L'ASSOCIATION INTERNATIONALE POUR L'HISTOIRE DU VERRE. (BE). **2586**

BULLETIN DE L'ENTRAIDE MISSIONNAIRE. (CN/0382-9472). **4941**

BULLETIN DE LIAISON DE DEMOGRAPHIE AFRICAINE. (CM/1013-1396). **4550**

BULLETIN DE LIAISON DES LABORATOIRES DES PONTS ET CHAUSSEES. (FR/0458-5860). **1967**

BULLETIN DE L'INSTITUT DE GEOLOGIE DU BASSIN D'AQUITAINE. (FR/0524-0832). **1369**

BULLETIN DE L'INSTITUT FRANCAIS D'ETUDES ANDINES. (PE/0303-7495). **2724**

BULLETIN DE L'INSTITUT PASTEUR. (FR/0020-2452). **3667**

BULLETIN DE L'OIV. (FR/0029-7127). **Qty:** 6. **69**

BULLETIN DE L'UNION DES PHYSICIENS. (FR/0366-3876). **4399**

BULLETIN DE L'UNION INTERNATIONALE CONTRE LA TUBERCULOSE ET LES MALADIES RESPIRATOIRES. (FR/1011-7903). **3949**

BULLETIN DE NOUVELLES - PRESSE ETUDIANTE DU QUEBEC. (CN/0228-1252). **1089**

BULLETIN DE PSYCHOLOGIE. (FR/0007-4403). **4578**

BULLETIN DE PSYCHOLOGIE SCOLAIRE ET D'ORIENTATION. (BE/0007-4411). **4578**

BULLETIN DES ARRETS DE LA COUR DE CASSATION. (FR). **2944**

BULLETIN DES BIBLIOTHEQUES DE FRANCE. (FR/0006-2006). **3198**

BULLETIN DES ETUDES AFRICAINES. (FR/0249-728X). **2498**

BULLETIN DES ETUDES VALERYENNES. (FR/0335-508X). **Qty:** 3. **3369**

BULLETIN DES RECHERCHES AGRONOMIQUES DE GEMBLOUX. (BE/0435-2033). **69**

BULLETIN DES SEANCES - ACADEMIE ROYALE DES SCIENCES D'OUTRE-MER. (BE/0001-4176). **5091**

BULLETIN DES SOCIETES CHIMIQUES BELGES. (BE/0037-9646). **963**

BULLETIN D'ETUDES KARAITES. (FR). **5046**

BULLETIN D'INFORMATION - COMITE EURO-INTERNATIONAL DU BETON. (FR/0378-9489). **Qty:** 5-6. **605**

BULLETIN D'INFORMATION TOXICOLOGIQUE. (CN/0829-5557). **3979**

BULLETIN D'INFORMATION - URSI. (BE/0041-543X). **1128**

BULLETIN D'INFORMATIONS DE L'ASSOCIATION DES BIBLIOTHECAIRES FRANCAIS. (FR/0004-5365). **3198**

BULLETIN D'INFORMATIONS SCIENTIFIQUES - INSTITUT PASTEUR. (FR/1144-3464). **5091**

BULLETIN DU CENTRE GENEVOIS D'ANTHROPOLOGIE / MUSEE D'ETHNOGRAPHIE, DEPARTEMENT D'ANTHROPOLOGIE. (BE/0777-5466). **232**

BULLETIN DU GROUPEMENT D'INFORMATIONS MUTUELLES AMPERE. (SZ/0434-6971). **4399**

BULLETIN DU JARDIN BOTANIQUE NATIONAL DE BELGIQUE. (BE/0524-7837). **504**

BULLETIN DU MUSEE BASQUE. (FR). **Qty:** 1. **2681**

BULLETIN DU MUSEUM NATIONAL D'HISTOIRE NATURELLE. SECTION B : ADANSONIA, BOTANIQUE, PHYTOCHIMIE. (FR/0240-8937). **504**

BULLETIN DU STATEC / SERVICE CENTRAL DE LA STATISTIQUE ET DES ETUDES ECONOMIQUES. (LU/0076-1583). **1530**

BULLETIN - ENTOMOLOGICAL SOCIETY OF CANADA. (CN/0071-0741). **5579**

BULLETIN ET MEMOIRES DE L'ACADEMIE ROYALE DE MEDECINE DE BELGIQUE. (BE/0377-8231). **3560**

BULLETIN FOR INTERNATIONAL FISCAL DOCUMENTATION. (NE/0007-4624). **4715**

BULLETIN FRANCAIS DE LA PECHE ET DE LA PISCICULTURE. (FR/0767-2861). **2298**

BULLETIN / GDR COMMITTEE FOR HUMAN RIGHTS. (GW). **4505**

BULLETIN / GENEALOGICAL FORUM OF OREGON, INC. (US). **2440**

BULLETIN - GENETICS SOCIETY OF CANADA. (CN/0316-4357). **543**

BULLETIN GEODESIQUE. (FR/0007-4632). **1403**

BULLETIN / GEOTHERMAL RESOURCES COUNCIL. (US/0160-7782). **1934**

BULLETIN - GREATER ST. LOUIS DENTAL SOCIETY. (US/0360-2575). **1318**

BULLETIN - HYMN SOCIETY OF GREAT BRITAIN AND IRELAND. (UK/0018-828X). **4106**

BULLETIN - ILLINOIS GEOGRAPHICAL SOCIETY. (US/0019-2031). **2557**

BULLETIN - INDIAN GEOLOGISTS' ASSOCIATION. (II/0379-5098). **1369**

BULLETIN / INSTITUTE FOR ANTIQUITY AND CHRISTIANITY. (US/0739-0459). **Qty:** varies. **4941**

BULLETIN / INSTITUTE FOR THEOLOGICAL ENCOUNTER WITH SCIENCE AND TECHNOLOGY. (US/1073-5976). **4941**

BULLETIN - INSTITUTE OF CLASSICAL STUDIES. (UK/0076-0730). **1075**

BULLETIN - INSTITUTE OF MATHEMATICAL STATISTICS. (US/0146-3942). **5324**

BULLETIN - INSTITUTE OF MATHEMATICS AND ITS APPLICATIONS. (UK/0950-5628). **3498**

BULLETIN (INTERNATIONAL ASSOCIATION OF LIGHTHOUSE AUTHORITIES). (FR/0379-2811). **4175**

BULLETIN - INTERNATIONAL ASSOCIATION OF ORIENTALIST LIBRARIANS. (US/0161-7397). **3198**

BULLETIN / INTERNATIONAL OLD LACERS. (US). **5348**

BULLETIN - KANSAS ORNITHOLOGICAL SOCIETY. (US/0022-8729). **5616**

BULLETIN - KING COUNTY MEDICAL SOCIETY, THE. (US/0023-1592). **3913**

BULLETIN / MAINE ARCHAEOLOGICAL SOCIETY. (US/0542-1292). **263**

BULLETIN / MANITOBA NATURALISTS SOCIETY. (CN/0823-2911). **4164**

BULLETIN MATCH. (CN/0229-5814). **5552**

BULLETIN MENSUEL DE LA SOCIETE LINNEENNE DE LYON. (FR/0366-1326). **4164**

BULLETIN - MICROSCOPICAL SOCIETY OF CANADA. (CN/0383-1825). **572**

BULLETIN MONUMENTAL. (FR/0007-473X). **Qty:** 4 per year. **345**

BULLETIN - NATIONAL TROPICAL BOTANICAL GARDEN. (US/1057-3968). **Qty:** 4. **505**

BULLETIN - NEW MEXICO BUREAU OF MINES & MINERAL RESOURCES. (US/0096-4581). **2135**

BULLETIN (NEW SERIES) OF THE AMERICAN MATHEMATICAL SOCIETY. (US/0273-0979). **3498**

BULLETIN OEPP. (FR/0250-8052). **165**

BULLETIN OF ANIMAL HEALTH AND PRODUCTION IN AFRICA. (KE/0378-9721). **208**

BULLETIN OF ASIAN GEOGRAPHY. (US/0732-2186). **2557**

BULLETIN OF CANADIAN PETROLEUM GEOLOGY. (CN/0007-4802). **4252**

BULLETIN OF CONCERNED ASIAN SCHOLARS. (US/0007-4810). **2647**

BULLETIN OF EASTERN CARIBBEAN AFFAIRS. (BB). **2511**

BULLETIN OF ECONOMIC RESEARCH. (UK/0307-3378). **1590**

BULLETIN OF ELECTROCHEMISTRY. (II/0256-1654). **1034**

BULLETIN OF GRAIN TECHNOLOGY. (II/0007-4896). **200**

BULLETIN OF HISPANIC STUDIES. (UK/0007-490X). **3271**

BULLETIN OF HISTORICAL RESEARCH IN MUSIC EDUCATION, THE. (US/0739-5639). **Qty:** 5-6. **4106**

BULLETIN OF INDONESIAN ECONOMIC STUDIES. (AT/0007-4918). **1466**

BULLETIN OF JUDAEO-GREEK STUDIES. (UK/0954-1179). **5046**

BULLETIN OF MARINE SCIENCE. (US/0007-4977). **1447**

BULLETIN OF MOLECULAR BIOLOGY AND MEDICINE. (IT/0391-481X). **560**

BULLETIN OF NUMBER THEORY AND RELATED TOPICS. BOLETIN DE TEORIA DE NUMEROS Y TEMAS CONEXOS. (AG). **3498**

BULLETIN OF PEACE PROPOSALS. (NO/0007-5035). **4466**

BULLETIN OF PHYSICAL EDUCATION. (UK/0521-0011). **1855**

BULLETIN OF PURE & APPLIED SCIENCES. SEC. D, PHYSICS. (II). **4399**

BULLETIN OF PURE & APPLIED SCIENCES. SEC. E, MATHEMATICS. (II/0970-6577). **3498**

BULLETIN OF PURE & APPLIED SCIENCES. SECTION A, ANIMAL SCIENCE. (II/0970-0765). **5579**

BULLETIN OF PURE & APPLIED SCIENCES. SECTION B, PLANT SCIENCES. (II). **505**

BULLETIN OF SCIENCE, TECHNOLOGY & SOCIETY. (US/0270-4676). **Qty:** 6. **5091**

BULLETIN OF TANZANIAN AFFAIRS. (UK/0952-2948). **2638**

BULLETIN OF THE ABERDEEN UNIVERSITY AFRICAN STUDIES GROUP. (UK/0001-3196). **2638**

BULLETIN OF THE AMATEUR ENTOMOLOGISTS' SOCIETY, THE. (UK/0266-836X). **5606**

BULLETIN OF THE AMERICAN ACADEMY OF PSYCHIATRY AND THE LAW. (US/0091-634X). **3922**

BULLETIN OF THE AMERICAN DAHLIA SOCIETY, INC. (US/0002-8150). **2411**

BULLETIN OF THE AMERICAN HISTORICAL COLLECTION. (PH). **2725**

BULLETIN OF THE AMERICAN HISTORICAL COLLECTION. (PH/0115-3226). **2647**

BULLETIN OF THE AMERICAN METEOROLOGICAL SOCIETY. (US/0003-0007). **1421**

BULLETIN OF THE AMERICAN ROCK GARDEN SOCIETY. (US/0003-0864). **Qty:** 10. **2411**

BULLETIN OF THE AMERICAN SCHOOLS OF ORIENTAL RESEARCH. (US/0003-097X). **264**

BULLETIN OF THE AMERICAN SOCIETY FOR INFORMATION SCIENCE. (US/0095-4403). **3198**

BULLETIN OF THE AMERICAN SOCIETY OF NEWSPAPER EDITORS, THE. (US/0003-1178). **2917**

BULLETIN OF THE ANNA FREUD CENTRE. (UK/0267-3061). **3922**

BULLETIN OF THE ARCHAEOLOGICAL SOCIETY OF CONNECTICUT. (US/0739-5612). **264**

BULLETIN OF THE ARCHAEOLOGICAL SOCIETY OF NEW JERSEY. (US/0196-8319). **264**

BULLETIN OF THE ASIA INSTITUTE. (US/0890-4464). **2647**

BULLETIN OF THE ASSOCIATION FOR BUSINESS COMMUNICATION, THE. (US/8756-1972). **862**

BULLETIN OF THE ASSOCIATION OF BRITISH THEOLOGICAL AND PHILOSOPHICAL LIBRARIES. (UK/0305-781X). **3198**

BULLETIN OF THE ASSOCIATION OF COLLEGE UNIONS-INTERNATIONAL, THE. (US/0004-5659). **Qty:** 1-2. **1861**

BULLETIN OF THE ASTRONOMICAL SOCIETY OF INDIA. (II/0304-9523). **394**

BULLETIN OF THE ATOMIC SCIENTISTS. (US/0096-3402). **5091**

BULLETIN OF THE AUSTRALIAN LITTORAL SOCIETY. (AT/0157-308X). **Qty:** 2-3. **2189**

BULLETIN OF THE AUSTRALIAN MATHEMATICAL SOCIETY. (AT/0004-9727). **3498**

BULLETIN OF THE AUSTRALIAN METEOROLOGICAL AND OCEANOGRAPHIC SOCIETY. (AT/1035-6576). **Qty:** 4. **1421**

BULLETIN OF THE AUSTRALIAN SOCIETY OF LEGAL PHILOSOPHY. (AT/0726-5239). **2945**

BULLETIN OF THE BRITISH ORNITHOLOGIST'S CLUB. (UK/0007-1595). **5616**

BULLETIN OF THE CALCUTTA MATHEMATICAL SOCIETY. (II/0008-0659). **3498**

BULLETIN OF THE CONGREGATIONAL LIBRARY. (US/0010-5821). **3198**

BULLETIN OF THE DEPARTMENT OF INTERNATIONAL AFFAIRS, AFL-CIO, THE. (US/0890-6165). **4517**

BULLETIN

Book Review Index

BULLETIN OF THE EVANGELICAL PHILOSOPHICAL SOCIETY. (US). 4343

BULLETIN OF THE FACULTY OF SCIENCE, IBARAKI UNIVERSITY. SERIES A : MATHEMATICS. (JA). 3498

BULLETIN OF THE FRIENDS OF JADE, THE. (US/0261-7080). 370

BULLETIN OF THE GENERAL THEOLOGICAL CENTER OF MAINE. (US/1052-8202). Qty: 75. 4941

BULLETIN OF THE GLOUCESTER COUNTY HISTORICAL SOCIETY. (US/0887-5413). 2725

BULLETIN OF THE HEGEL SOCIETY OF GREAT BRITAIN, THE. (UK/0263-5232). Qty: 20. 4343

BULLETIN OF THE HENRY MARTYN INSTITUTE OF ISLAMIC STUDIES (HYDERABAD, INDIA). (II). 5042

BULLETIN OF THE HISTORY OF DENTISTRY. (US/0007-5132). 1318

BULLETIN OF THE HISTORY OF MEDICINE. (US/0007-5140). 3560

BULLETIN OF THE INSTITUTE FOR CONTINUING DENTAL EDUCATION OF THE QUEENS COUNTY DENTAL SOCIETY. (US/0739-1773). 1318

BULLETIN OF THE INSTITUTE OF ARCHAEOLOGY / UNIVERSITY OF LONDON, INSTITUTE OF ARCHAEOLOGY. (UK/0076-0722). 264

BULLETIN OF THE INSTITUTE OF EARTH SCIENCES, ACADEMIA SINICA. (CH/0258-0314). 1352

BULLETIN OF THE INSTITUTE OF MARITIME AND TROPICAL MEDICINE IN GDYNIA. (PL/0324-8542). 3985

BULLETIN OF THE INSTITUTION OF ENGINEERS (INDIA). (II/0020-3343). 2037

BULLETIN OF THE INTERNATIONAL ASSOCIATION OF ENGINEERING GEOLOGY. (GW/0074-1612). 2019

BULLETIN OF THE INTERNATIONAL CENTRE FOR HEAT AND MASS TRANSFER. (US/0888-6911). 2111

BULLETIN OF THE INTERNATIONAL GROUP FOR THE STUDY OF MIMOSOIDEAE. (FR). 2411

BULLETIN OF THE INTERNATIONAL ORGANIZATION FOR SEPTUAGINT AND COGNITE STUDIES. (US/0145-3890). 5046

BULLETIN OF THE JEWISH HISTORICAL SOCIETY OF ENGLAND. (UK). 5046

BULLETIN OF THE KOREAN CHEMICAL SOCIETY. (KO/0253-2964). 963

BULLETIN OF THE LONDON MATHEMATICAL SOCIETY, THE. (UK/0024-6093). 3498

BULLETIN OF THE MARX MEMORIAL LIBRARY - LONDON. (UK). 4540

BULLETIN OF THE MARYLAND HERPETOLOGICAL SOCIETY. (US/0025-4231). Qty: 1-6. 5579

BULLETIN OF THE MASSACHUSETTS ARCHAEOLOGICAL SOCIETY. (US/0148-1886). Qty: 6-7. 264

BULLETIN OF THE MEDICAL LIBRARY ASSOCIATION. (US/0025-7338). 3198

BULLETIN OF THE MENNINGER CLINIC. (US/0025-9284). 3922

BULLETIN OF THE NATIONAL GUILD OF CATHOLIC PSYCHIATRISTS, INC, THE. (US/0547-7115). 3922

BULLETIN OF THE NEEDLE AND BOBBIN CLUB, THE. (US/0273-0197). 5183

BULLETIN OF THE NEW YORK ACADEMY OF MEDICINE (1925). (US/0028-7091). 3560

BULLETIN OF THE NEW ZEALAND NATIONAL SOCIETY FOR EARTHQUAKE ENGINEERING. (NZ/0110-0718). 2019

BULLETIN OF THE OHIO BIOLOGICAL SURVEY. (US/0078-3994). 450

BULLETIN OF THE PAN AMERICAN HEALTH ORGANIZATION. (US/0301-5750). 4769

BULLETIN OF THE PHILADELPHIA HERPETOLOGICAL SOCIETY. (US/0553-9587). 5579

BULLETIN OF THE SCHOOL OF ORIENTAL AND AFRICAN STUDIES. (UK/0041-977X). 3271

BULLETIN OF THE SCIENCE FICTION WRITERS OF AMERICA. (US/0192-2424). 3370

BULLETIN OF THE SEISMOLOGICAL SOCIETY OF AMERICA. (US/0037-1106). 1403

BULLETIN OF THE SOCIETY OF VECTOR ECOLOGISTS. (US/0146-6429). 2212

BULLETIN OF THE SOUTHERN CALIFORNIA PALEONTOLOGICAL SOCIETY. (US/0160-4937). 4226

BULLETIN OF THE TEXAS ARCHEOLOGICAL SOCIETY. (US/0082-2930). 264

BULLETIN OF THE TEXAS ORNITHOLOGICAL SOCIETY. (US/0040-4543). 5616

BULLETIN OF THE TORREY BOTANICAL CLUB, THE. (US/0040-9618). 505

BULLETIN OF THE UNESCO REGIONAL OFFICE OF SCIENCE AND TECHNOLOGY FOR AFRICA. (KE/0304-9590). 5091

BULLETIN - OFFICE INTERNATIONAL DES EPIZOOTIES (PARIS). (FR/0300-9823). 5506

BULLETIN - ORNITHOLOGICAL SOCIETY OF THE MIDDLE EAST. (UK). 5616

BULLETIN / PACIFIC SEABIRD GROUP. (US/0740-3771). 5616

BULLETIN PERTAMINA. (IO). 4252

BULLETIN / POLISH GENEALOGICAL SOCIETY, CALIFORNIA. (US/1056-568X). 2441

BULLETIN / PRINTING HISTORICAL SOCIETY. (UK/0144-7505). 4564

BULLETIN - PROFESSIONAL CORPORATION OF PHYSICIANS OF QUEBEC. (CN/0315-2979). Qty: 28. 3561

BULLETIN - ROYAL SOCIETY OF NEW ZEALAND. (NZ/0370-6559). 5091

BULLETIN / SASKATCHEWAN CHORAL FEDERATION. (CN/0838-6730). 4106

BULLETIN - SASKATCHEWAN GENEALOGICAL SOCIETY. (CN/0048-9182). 2441

BULLETIN - SEATTLE GENEALOGICAL SOCIETY. (US/0559-2526). Qty: 100+. 2441

BULLETIN SIGNALETIQUE DES TELECOMMUNICATIONS. (FR/0007-5302). 1150

BULLETIN - SOCIETE BOTANIQUE DU QUEBEC. (CN/0228-975X). 505

BULLETIN - SOCIETE CHATEAUBRIAND. (FR/0081-0754). 3370

BULLETIN - SOCIETE DES AMIS DU JARDIN VAN DEN HENDE INC. (CN/0711-6446). 2411

BULLETIN (SOCIETE D'ETUDES HISTORIQUES DE LA NOUVELLE CALEDONIE). (NL). 2669

BULLETIN - SOCIETE FRANCAISE DE PHOTOGRAMMETRIE ET DE TELEDETECTION. (FR/0244-6014). 4367

BULLETIN / SOCIETE INTERNATIONALE D'ETUDES YOURCENARIENNES. (FR/0987-7940). 3370

BULLETIN - SOCIETY FOR SPANISH AND PORTUGUESE HISTORICAL STUDIES (U.S.). (US/0739-1824). Qty: 5. 2681

BULLETIN - SOCIETY OF WETLAND SCIENTISTS (U.S.). (US/0732-9393). 450

BULLETIN - SOMERSET INDUSTRIAL ARCHAEOLOGICAL SOCIETY. (UK/0954-7029). Qty: 2. 265

BULLETIN / SOUTHERN CALIFORNIA ACADEMY OF SCIENCES. (US/0038-3872). 5092

BULLETIN - SPECIAL LIBRARIES ASSOCIATION. EDUCATION DIVISION. (US/1052-9454). 3198

BULLETIN - SPECIAL LIBRARIES ASSOCIATION. GEOGRAPHY AND MAP DIVISION. (US/0036-1607). Qty: 35. 2557

BULLETIN - STATE BANK OF PAKISTAN. (PK/0039-0011). 781

BULLETIN TECHNIQUE DU MACHINISME ET DE L'EQUIPMENT AGRICOLES. (FR). 158

BULLETIN / THE JAPANESE AMERICAN LIBRARY. (US/0893-8601). 2257

BULLETIN / THE NATIONAL EATING DISORDER INFORMATION CENTRE. (CN/0836-6845). 3829

BULLETIN (TOY TRAIN OPERATING SOCIETY : 1973). (US). 2772

BULLETIN TRIMESTRIEL DE LA FONDATION AUSCHWITZ. (BE/0772-6961). 2681

BULLETIN TRIMESTRIEL DE LA SOCIETE BELGE DE PHOTOGRAMMETRIE-TELEDETECTION ET CARTOGRAPHIE. (BE). Qty: 2. 4367

BULLETIN - U.S. COAST GUARD ACADEMY ALUMNI ASSOCIATION. (US/0191-9814). 1101

BULLETIN - UK CENTRE FOR ECONOMIC AND ENVIRONMENTAL DEVELOPMENT. (UK/0268-7402). Qty: 4/year. 1466

BULLETIN - UNITED BIBLE SOCIETIES. (UK/0041-719X). 5015

BULLETIN VAN HET RYKSMUSEUM. (NE/0165-9510). 4086

BULLETIN - WORKERS LEAGUE (U.S.). CENTRAL COMMITTEE. (US/0279-0165). 4540

BULLETIN - YAKIMA VALLEY GENEALOGICAL SOCIETY. (US/0513-6776). Qty: as received. 2441

BULLETIN / YORKSHIRE NATURALISTS' UNION. (UK/0265-6833). 4164

BULLETINS ET MEMOIRES (SOCIETE ARCHEOLOGIQUE ET HISTORIQUE DE LA CHARENTE : 1983). (FR/0397-579X). 2681

BULLETINS OF THE GEOLOGICAL SURVEY OF INDIA. SERIES A : ECONOMIC GEOLOGY. (II/0536-8782). 1371

BULLETTINO DELL'ISTITUTO STORICO ITALIANO PER IL MEDIO EVO E ARCHIVIO MURATORIANO. (IT). 2681

BULLISIANA. (CN/0705-9108). 394

BULWARK, THE. (UK/0045-3536). 5057

BUMMEI JIHYO. (JA). 5229

BUNDESBAUBLATT. (GW/0007-5884). 2816

BUNDESGESUNDHEITSBLATT. (GW/0007-5914). 4770

BUNGEI KENKYU. (JA). 3370

BUNKER BANNER / BUNKER FAMILY ASSOCIATION OF AMERICA. (US). 2441

BUNSEKI. (JA). 1014

BUOYANT FLIGHT. (US/0361-5065). Qty: 12. 15

BURGENSE. (SP/0521-8195). 4941

BURIED HISTORY. (AT/0007-6260). Qty: 5. 265

BURIED TREASURES. (US/0882-5653). 2441

BURLINGTON MAGAZINE. (UK/0007-6287). 346

BURNETT FAMILY NEWSLETTER. (US/0730-4978). 2441

BUS RIDE. (US/0192-8902). 5378

BUS RIDE: BUS INDUSTRY DIRECTORY. (US/0363-3764). 5378

BUS VERKEHR. (GW). 5378

BUS WORLD. (US/0162-9689). Qty: varies. 5378

BUSES SHEPPERTON. (UK/0007-6392). 5378

BUSH FIRE BULLETIN. (AT). 2288

BUSH-MEETING DUTCH, THE. (US/1071-0523). 4941

BUSHWHACKER MUSINGS : VERNON COUNTY HISTORICAL SOCIETY NEWSLETTER. (US/1070-8243). Qty: few. 2725

BUSINESS & ACQUISITION NEWSLETTER. (US/0738-7253). 645

BUSINESS AND FINANCE. (IE/0007-6473). 781

BUSINESS AND MANAGEMENT EDITIONS: BMB. (BE). 862

BUSINESS AND SOCIETY. (US/0007-6503). 645

BUSINESS AND THE MEDIA. (US/0270-3572). 1105

BUSINESS ARCHIVES. (UK/0007-6538). Qty: 5-10. 3199

BUSINESS BOOK REVIEW. (US/0741-8132). Qty: 50-60. 646

BUSINESS COMMUNICATIONS REVIEW. (US/0162-3885). 646

BUSINESS COUNCIL BULLETIN. (AT/0814-4273). 646

BUSINESS DIRECTIONS. (AT/1031-2315). Qty: 8. 647

BUSINESS DYNAMICS (100 MILE HOUSE). (CN/0831-7291). 647

BUSINESS ECONOMICS (CLEVELAND, OHIO). (US/0007-666X). 1466

BUSINESS EDUCATION TODAY. (UK). 1729

BUSINESS EDUCATION TODAY. (UK/0951-1512). 647

BUSINESS ETHICS (MADISON, WIS.). (US/0894-6582). Qty: 54. 2249

BUSINESS ETHICS RESOURCE. (US/1064-0223). Qty: 3-4. 648

BUSINESS FIRMS DIRECTORY OF THE DELAWARE VALLEY. (US/0091-2581). 648

BUSINESS FIRST (COLUMBUS, OHIO). (US/0748-6146). 648

BUSINESS FORUM (LOS ANGELES, CALIF.). (US/0733-2408). 648

BUSINESS HISTORY. (UK/0007-6791). 648

BUSINESS HISTORY REVIEW. (US/0007-6805). Qty: 125. 648

BUSINESS HISTORY REVIEW. (US/0007-6805). 648

BUSINESS IN BROWARD. (US). 1466

BUSINESS IN PALM BEACH COUNTY. (US). 649

BUSINESS INDIA. (II/0254-5268). **649**

BUSINESS INFORMATION ALERT. (US/1042-0746). **3199**

BUSINESS INFORMATION REVIEW. (UK/0266-3821). **3199**

BUSINESS INSIGHT. (US/1056-6244). **649**

BUSINESS INSURANCE. (US/0007-6864). **2877**

BUSINESS JOURNAL OF UPPER EAST TENNESSEE AND SOUTHWEST VIRGINIA. (US/1040-6360). **650**

BUSINESS LAW BRIEF. (UK). **3096**

BUSINESS LAW REVIEW. (UK). **3096**

BUSINESS LAWYER, THE. (US/0007-6899). **3097**

BUSINESS LIBRARY NEWSLETTER. (US/0191-4006). **3199**

BUSINESS (LUXEMBOURG). (LU). **650**

BUSINESS MARKETING. (US/0745-5933). **922**

BUSINESS MEXICO. (MX/0187-1455). **650**

BUSINESS PERIODICALS INDEX. CD-ROM. (US/0007-6961). **727**

BUSINESS RADIO. (US/0746-8911). **1150**

BUSINESS RECORD (DES MOINES, IOWA). (US/0746-410X). **652**

BUSINESS REVIEW WEEKLY : BRW. (AT/0727-758X). **652**

BUSINESS SPAIN. (UK). **652**

BUSINESS TELECOMMUNICATIONS DIRECTORY. (US/1041-6137). **1150**

BUSINESS TOKYO. (JA/0914-0026). **653**

BUSINESS WHO'S WHO PRODUCTS AND TRADENAMES GUIDE. (AT/1031-1343). **Qty:** 1/year. **727**

BUSINESSGRAM (TAMPA, FLA.). (US/1064-2412). **654**

BUSINESSWEST (SPRINGFIELD, MASS.). (US/1049-9822). **654**

BUSS. (US/0193-6832). **1265**

BUTCHER & PROCESSOR. (UK/0268-1781). **2329**

BUTTERWORTHS CURRENT LAW. (NZ/0110-070X). **3125**

BUTTERWORTHS LAW DIGEST MALAYSIA, SINGAPORE AND BRUNEI. (SI/0951-5720). **2945**

BUVAR. (HU/0007-7356). **450**

BUY BOOKS WHERE, SELL BOOKS WHERE. (US/0732-6599). **4812**

BUYER (MONITOR PRESS). (UK). **949**

BUYER'S GUIDE TO MEDICAL TOYS & BOOKS FOR TODDLERS THROUGH TEENS. (US/1040-7065). **2583**

BUYER'S GUIDE TO REACTIVE CURE SYSTEMS, UV-IR-EB. (US). **1021**

BUYING FOR LIBRARIES. (UK). **3199**

BUZANTINA (THESSALONIKE). (GR/1105-0772). **2682**

BUZZ (THUNDER BAY). (CN/0701-2837). **4941**

BUZZWORM (BOULDER, COLO.). (US/0898-2996). **2189**

BVDA JOURNAL : BRITISH VETERINARY DENTAL ASSOCIATION. (UK). **5507**

BWR TWRH. (IS/0333-6298). **5046**

BYGGEKUNST. (NO/0007-7518). **294**

BYGGREFERAT. (SW/0345-1941). **294**

BYPLAN. (DK/0007-7658). **2816**

BYRON JOURNAL. (UK/0301-7257). **3339**

BYTE. (US/0360-5280). **1273**

BYTOWN TIMES. (CN/0712-2799). **2916**

BYZANTINE STUDIES. (US/0095-4608). **2682**

C.A.R.E. PACKAGE, THE. (US/1064-2609). **Qty:** 50. **3370**

C/A/S/E OUTLOOK. (US/0895-2108). **Qty:** 6-10 / year. **1172**

C & L APPLICATIONS. (UK/0957-4085). **3199**

C.F.O. JOURNAL. (US/0362-9902). **5616**

C.F.P. CHAUD FROID PLOMBERIE. (FR/0750-1552). **2604**

C I E N, CANADIAN INDUSTRIAL EQUIPMENT NEWS. (CN/0319-5902). **3476**

C I M REPORTER. (CN/0701-0710). **2136**

C.J. THE AMERICAS. (US/0896-9922). **3159**

C L I C 'S LEGAL MATERIALS LETTER. (CN/0704-0393). **2945**

C-MAGAZIN. (GW/0935-0373). **4941**

C MAGAZINE (1992). (CN/1193-8625). **Qty:** varies. **317**

C P H A HEALTH DIGEST. (CN/0703-5624). **4770**

C S S E NEWS. (CN/0382-8018). **1730**

C (TORONTO. 1987). (CN/0838-0392). **346**

C USERS JOURNAL, THE. (US/0898-9788). **Qty:** 12-24. **1278**

C1 MOLECULE CHEMISTRY. (SZ/0275-7567). **1035**

CA CRAFT CONNECTION, THE. (US/1042-6280). **370**

CA MAGAZINE. (CN/0317-6878). **740**

CA SELECTS: ACID RAIN & ACID AIR. (US/0885-0097). **997**

CA SELECTS: CERAMIC MATERIALS (PATENTS). (US/0885-0100). **999**

CA SELECTS. CHEMICAL VAPOR DEPOSITION. (US/0885-0119). **999**

CA SELECTS: COLOR SCIENCE. (US/0885-0127). **1000**

CA SELECTS: CONDUCTIVE POLYMERS. (US/0885-0135). **1000**

CA SELECTS: CONTROLLED RELEASE TECHNOLOGY. (US/0740-0748). **1000**

CA SELECTS: CORROSION. (US/0146-4434). **1000**

CA SELECTS: ELECTRICALLY CONDUCTIVE ORGANICS. (US/0885-0143). **1001**

CA SELECTS: ELECTRONIC CHEMICALS & MATERIALS. (US/0885-0151). **1001**

CA SELECTS: HEAT-RESISTANT & ABLATIVE POLYMERS. (US/0162-7821). **1003**

CA SELECTS: LASER-INDUCED CHEMICAL REACTIONS. (US/0885-0178). **1004**

CA SELECTS: ORGANIC OPTICAL MATERIALS. (US/0885-0186). **1006**

CA SELECTS: ORGANIC REACTION MECHANISMS. (US/0162-7848). **1006**

CA SELECTS: ORGANOPHOSPHORUS CHEMISTRY. (US/0162-783X). **1006**

CA SELECTS: PHASE TRANSFER CATALYSIS. (US/0885-0194). **1007**

CA SELECTS: PHOTOCHEMICAL ORGANIC SYNTHESIS. (US/0885-0208). **1007**

CA SELECTS: PHOTORESISTS. (US/0885-0216). **1007**

CA SELECTS: POLYMERIZATION KINETICS & PROCESS CONTROL. (US/0885-0224). **1008**

CA SELECTS: SPECTROCHEMICAL ANALYSIS. (US/0885-0232). **1009**

CA SELECTS: THERMOCHEMISTRY. (US/0162-7864). **1010**

CAAT TRACKS. (CN/0829-254X). **3199**

CABLE COMMUNICATIONS MAGAZINE. (CN/0318-0069). **1128**

CABLE GUIDE. (US/0191-4871). **1129**

CABLE WEEK. ORANGE-SEMINOLE-OSEOLA ED. (US/0744-2327). **1129**

CABLE WORLD. (US/1042-7228). **1150**

CAC NEWS - CHICAGO ARTISTS' COALITION. (US/0890-5908). **Qty:** 5. **346**

CACD JOURNAL. (US/1052-3103). **5276**

CACHE REGISTER, THE. (US/0731-079X). **1236**

CACTUS AND SUCCULENT JOURNAL WOOLLAHRA. (AT/0526-7196). **2411**

CAD CAM. (UK). **1231**

CAD/CAM ABSTRACTS. (US/0882-1437). **1231**

CAD/CAM DIGEST. (UK/0263-6190). **1231**

CAD USER. (UK/0959-6259). **1222**

CADDET NEWSLETTER. (NE). **1934**

CADENCE. (US/0162-6973). **4106**

CADENCE (AUSTIN, TEX.). (US/0887-9141). **1173**

CADERNO DE PESQUISAS TRIBUTARIAS. (BL). **2946**

CADMOS. (SW). **2682**

CADSCAN. (UK). **3999**

CADUCEUS (SPRINGFIELD, ILL.). (US/0882-6447). **3561**

CAFE, CACAO, THE. (FR/0007-9510). **165**

CAFE SOLO. (US/0007-9537). **3461**

CAHIER - SOCIETE D'HISTOIRE DES PAYS-D'EN-HAUT (1989). (CN/0846-5312). **Qty:** 4. **2612**

CAHIERS AFRICAINS D'ADMINISTRATION PUBLIQUE. (MR/0007-9588). **4635**

CAHIERS BERNARD LAZARE. (FR). **5046**

CAHIERS D'ANTHROPOLOGIE ET BIOMETRIE HUMAINE. (FR/0758-2714). **233**

CAHIERS DE CIVILISATION MEDIEVALE. (FR/0007-9731). **2682**

CAHIERS DE DROIT (QUEBEC). (CN/0007-974X). **2946**

CAHIERS DE GEOGRAPHIE DU QUEBEC. (CN/0007-9766). **2557**

CAHIERS DE LA CINEMATHEQUE, LES. (FR/0764-8499). **4064**

CAHIERS DE LA FONDATION, LES. (FR/0983-1851). **654**

CAHIERS DE LA NOUVELLE, LES. (FR/0294-0442). **3371**

CAHIERS DE L'ANALYSE DES DONNEES, LES. (FR/0339-3097). **5324**

CAHIERS DE LEXICOLOGIE. (FR/0007-9871). **3271**

CAHIERS DE LINGUISTIQUE. ASIE ORIENTALE. (FR/0153-3320). **3271**

CAHIERS DE L'INSTITUT DE LINGUISTIQUE DE LOUVAIN. (BE/0771-6524). **3271**

CAHIERS DE LITTERATURE ORALE. (FR/0396-891X). **2318**

CAHIERS DE MEDECINE DU TRAVAIL. (BE/0376-7639). **3561**

CAHIERS DE NUTRITION ET DE DIETETIQUE. (FR/0007-9960). **4188**

CAHIERS DE SOCIOLOGIE ECONOMIQUE ET CULTURELLE, ETHNOPSYCHOLOGIE. (FR/0761-9871). **5241**

CAHIERS DE SPIRITUALITE IGNATIENNE. (CN/0705-8942). **4941**

CAHIERS DE TOPOLOGIE ET GEOMETRIE DIFFERENTIELLE CATEGORIQUES. (FR). **Qty:** Irregular. **3499**

CAHIERS DES AMERIQUES LATINES (PARIS, FRANCE : 1985). (FR). **2725**

CAHIERS DES NATURALISTES. (FR/0008-0039). **Qty:** 4/yr. **5194**

CAHIERS DES RELIGIONS AFRICAINES. (CG/0008-0047). **4942**

CAHIERS D'ETUDES CATHARES. (FR/0008-0063). **4942**

CAHIERS D'HISTOIRE. (FR/0008-008X). **2612**

CAHIERS D'HISTOIRE DE DEUX-MONTAGNES. (CN/0226-7063). **2725**

CAHIERS D'HISTOIRE DE L'INSTITUT DE RECHERCHES MARXISTES. (FR/0221-5047). **2682**

CAHIERS D'HISTOIRE (MONTREAL). (CN/0712-2330). **Qty:** 40. **2613**

CAHIERS D'HISTOIRE (QUEBEC). (CN/0704-6952). **2725**

CAHIERS D'OUTRE-MER. (FR/0373-5834). **2557**

CAHIERS DU CENTRE D'ETUDES DE L'ASIE DE L'EST. (CN/0839-4555). **Qty:** 2. **2844**

CAHIERS DU CENTRE SCIENTIFIQUE ET TECHNIQUE DU BATIMENT. (FR/0008-9850). **5092**

CAHIERS DU CINEMA. (FR/0008-011X). **4064**

CAHIERS DU CREDIT MUTUEL. (FR/0395-8175). **781**

CAHIERS DU CRIC. (FR/0762-6193). **3371**

CAHIERS DU LACITO PARIS. (FR/0994-7736). **3272**

CAHIERS DU MONDE RUSSE ET SOVIETIQUE. (FR/0008-0160). **2682**

CAHIERS ECONOMIQUES. (BE). **1530**

CAHIERS ECONOMIQUES ET MONETAIRES. (FR/0396-4701). **781**

CAHIERS ECONOMIQUES ET SOCIAUX (KINSHASA). (CG/0008-0209). **1550**

CAHIERS ELISABETHAINES. (FR/0184-7678). **3339**

CAHIERS ETHNOLOGIQUES. (FR/0249-5635). **Qty:** 2. **233**

CAHIERS FRANCO-CANADIENS DE LOUEST. (CN/0843-9559). **3272**

CAHIERS INTERNATIONAUX D'HISTOIRE ECONOMIQUE ET SOCIALE. (SZ/1010-3643). **1550**

CAHIERS IVOIRIENS DE RECHERCHE LINGUISTIQUE / INSTITUT DE LINGUISTIQUE APPLIQUU.N.A.C.I-ABIDJAN. (IV/0252-9386). **3272**

CAHIERS JEAN GIRAUDOUX. (FR/0150-6943). **3371**

CAHIERS LINGUISTIQUES D'OTTAWA. (CN/0315-3967). **3272**

CAHIERS NATURALISTES, LES. (FR/0008-0365). **Qty:** 1. **3371**

CAHIERS PAUL-LOUIS COURIER. (FR/0084-8239). **3371**

CAHIERS

CAHIERS PEDAGOGIQUES (FEDERATION DES CERCLES DE RECHERCHE ET D'ACTION PEDAGOGIQUES (FRANCE)). (FR). **1730**

CAHIERS RATIONALISTES, LES. (FR). **5092**

CAHIERS SAINT DOMINIQUE. (FR). **Qty:** 4. **5025**

CAHIERS SAINT-SIMON. (FR/0409-8846). **2613**

CAHIERS SIMONE WEIL. (FR/0181-1126). **4343**

CAHIERS STAELIENS. (FR/0575-1276). **3339**

CAHS JOURNAL, THE. (CN/0007-7771). **Qty:** 12. **15**

CAIRO PAPERS IN SOCIAL SCIENCE. (UA). **5194**

CAJANUS. (JM/0376-7655). **4188**

CAKALELE (HONOLULU, HAWAII). (US/1053-2285). **2647**

CALCIFIED TISSUE ABSTRACTS. (UK/0008-0586). **3655**

CALCUTTA LAW JOURNAL. (II). **2946**

CALDWELL COUNTY GENEALOGICAL SOCIETY, INC. (US/0747-4849). **2441**

CALDWELL MESSENGER (CALDWELL, KAN. 1942), THE. (US/0897-4551). **Qty:** 3-4. **5674**

CALICO JOURNAL. (US/0742-7778). **1222**

CALIFORNIA ANGLER. (US/8750-8907). **2298**

CALIFORNIA ARTS ADVOCATE. (US). **317**

CALIFORNIA BOWLING NEWS. (US/0008-0918). **4889**

CALIFORNIA BUILDER. (US/0527-2009). **606**

CALIFORNIA CABLETTER. (US/0740-0527). **1150**

CALIFORNIA COUNTY FACT BOOK. (US/0590-0158). **2557**

CALIFORNIA DUI REPORT. (US/0892-9033). **3105**

CALIFORNIA FISH AND GAME. (US/0008-1078). **Qty:** 2-6. **2189**

CALIFORNIA GARDEN. (US/0008-1116). **Qty:** 45. **2411**

CALIFORNIA GEOGRAPHER, THE. (US/0575-5700). **2557**

CALIFORNIA GEOLOGY. (US/0026-4555). **Qty:** 35. **1371**

CALIFORNIA HEALTH LAW REPORT. (US). **2946**

CALIFORNIA HISTORIAN. (US/0575-5751). **Qty:** 20-24. **2725**

CALIFORNIA HISTORY ACTION. (US/0882-357X). **2725**

CALIFORNIA HISTORY (SAN FRANCISCO). (US/0162-2897). **2726**

CALIFORNIA HORSE REVIEW. (US/0091-441X). **2797**

CALIFORNIA HORSEMAN'S NEWS. (US/0273-8287). **2797**

CALIFORNIA JAZZ NOW. (US/1067-5213). **Qty:** 11. **4106**

CALIFORNIA JOURNAL. (US/0008-1205). **4466**

CALIFORNIA LAWYER. (US/0279-4063). **Qty:** 30. **2946**

CALIFORNIA LIBRARIES. (US/1056-1528). **3199**

CALIFORNIA MANAGEMENT REVIEW. (US/0008-1256). **862**

CALIFORNIA MONTHLY. (US/0008-1302). **Qty:** 5-6. **1090**

CALIFORNIA MUNICIPAL BOND ADVISOR. (US/0749-2375). **893**

CALIFORNIA NURSE. (US/0008-1310). **3852**

CALIFORNIA PARALEGAL MAGAZINE. (US/1040-2640). **2946**

CALIFORNIA PARKS & RECREATION. (US/0733-5326). **4706**

CALIFORNIA PEACE OFFICER, THE. (US/0199-7025). **Qty:** 4-8. **3159**

CALIFORNIA PRISONER, THE. (US/0884-0075). **3159**

CALIFORNIA PRIVATE SCHOOL DIRECTORY. (US/0098-5147). **1730**

CALIFORNIA PSYCHOLOGIST, THE. (US/0890-0302). **4579**

CALIFORNIA PUBLIC EMPLOYEE RELATIONS : CPER SERIES. (US/0194-3073). **1658**

CALIFORNIA SALES GUIDE TO HIGH-TECH COMPANIES. (US/1041-0260). **5092**

CALIFORNIA SCHOOL LAW DIGEST. (US/0094-2057). **2946**

CALIFORNIA SENIOR CITIZEN. (US/0748-5727). **Qty:** 4. **5633**

CALIFORNIA SOCIOLOGIST. (US/0162-8712). **5241**

CALIFORNIA SOUTHERN BAPTIST, THE. (US/0008-1558). **5057**

CALIFORNIA STAATS-ZEITUNG. (US/0890-1473). **5633**

CALIFORNIA TAX LAWYER. (US). **Qty:** 3. **4716**

CALIFORNIA TECH, THE. (US/0008-1582). **1090**

CALIFORNIA TOMATO GROWER, THE. (US/0527-3277). **166**

CALIFORNIA UNION LIST OF PERIODICALS. (US/0095-8034). **412**

CALIFORNIA WESTERN INTERNATIONAL LAW JOURNAL. (US/0886-3210). **3125**

CALIFORNIA WESTERN LAW REVIEW. (US/0008-1639). **2947**

CALIFORNIA WOMAN, THE. (US/0008-1663). **5552**

CALIFORNIANS (SAN FRANCISCO, CALIF.), THE. (US/0745-5895). **Qty:** 60. **2726**

CALIOPE Y POLIMNIA : REVISTA DE POESIA Y CUENTOS. (SP). **3461**

CALIPER (TORONTO). (CN/0045-4001). **4385**

CALL-A.P.P.L.E. (US/8755-4909). **1265**

CALL BOARD (SAN FRANCISCO, CALIF.). (US/1064-0703). **Qty:** 10-15 / year. **5362**

CALL OF THE PLATEAU. (US/0575-6383). **2726**

CALL SHEET / SCREEN ACTORS GUILD. (US). **4064**

CALLAHAN COUNTY STAR. (US). **5747**

CALLALOO. (US/0161-2492). **3371**

CALLBOARD. (CN). **5362**

CALLIGRAPH. (US/0749-954X). **377**

CALLIGRAPHY REVIEW (NORMAN, OKLA.). (US/0895-7819). **Qty:** 6-8. **377**

CALVACADE OF ACTS & ATTRACTIONS. (US). **384**

CALVARY BAPTIST THEOLOGICAL JOURNAL. (US/8756-0429). **5057**

CALVERT CO. MARYLAND GENEALOGY NEWSLETTER. (US/0895-8939). **2441**

CALVIN THEOLOGICAL JOURNAL. (US/0008-1795). **4942**

CALVINIST CONTACT. (CN/0410-3882). **5057**

CALYPSO LOG (LOS ANGELES, CALIF.). (US/8756-6354). **1447**

CALYX (CORVALLIS). (US/0147-1627). **Qty:** 30. **3371**

CALZADO Y TENERIA. (MX). **1082**

CAM MAGAZINE. (US/0883-7880). **606**

CAMBRIA. (UK/0306-9796). **2557**

CAMBRIAN LAW REVIEW, THE. (UK/0084-8328). **Qty:** 10. **2947**

CAMBRIAN MEDIEVAL CELTIC STUDIES. (UK). **3272**

CAMBRIDGE ANTHROPOLOGY. (UK). **233**

CAMBRIDGE LAW JOURNAL, THE. (UK/0008-1973). **2947**

CAMBRIDGE MEDIEVAL CELTIC STUDIES. (UK/0260-5600). **3272**

CAMBRIDGE QUARTERLY. (UK/0008-199X). **3339**

CAMBRIDGE REPORT ON CORPORATE MERGERS AND CORPORATE POLICY, THE. (US/0273-6357). **782**

CAMBRIDGE REVIEW OF INTERNATIONAL AFFAIRS. (UK/0955-7571). **4467**

CAMBRIDGE REVIEW, THE. (UK/0008-2007). **1090**

CAMBRIDGE SCIENTIFIC BIOCHEMISTRY ABSTRACTS: PART 3 AMINO-ACIDS, PEPTIDES & PROTEINS. (US/8756-7520). **484**

CAMELLIA JOURNAL, THE. (US/0008-204X). **2411**

CAMERA (DURANGO, COLO.). (US/0883-489X). **4368**

CAMERA OBSCURA (BERKELEY). (US/0270-5346). **4065**

CAMERART. (JA/0008-2082). **4368**

CAMERART PHOTO TRADE DIRECTORY. (JA). **4368**

CAMERAWORK. (US). **4368**

CAMERON HERALD (CAMERON, TEX.). (US). **5747**

CAMPAIGN AUSTRALIA. (AT). **Qty:** 12. **2793**

CAMPBELL RIVER UPPER ISLANDER, THE. (CN/0318-9538). **5781**

CAMPESINO, EL. (CL). **71**

CAMPING AND RV MAGAZINE. (US/0896-5706). **Qty:** 30-40. **4849**

CAMPING CANADA. (CN/0384-9856). **4870**

CAMPING MAGAZINE, THE. (US/0740-4131). **4870**

CAMPING TRAILER & TRAVEL TRAILER TRADE-IN-GUIDE. (US/0736-1939). **5378**

CAMPUS ACTIVITIES PROGRAMMING. (US/0746-2328). **1813**

CAMPUS ECOLOGIST, THE. (US/0889-7344). **2212**

CAMPUS-FREE COLLEGE DEGREES. (US/1043-2086). **Qty:** varies. **1813**

CAMPUS LIFE (WHEATON, ILL.). (US/0008-2538). **1061**

CAMPUS OUTREACH. (US/1046-6975). **1813**

CAMPUS REPORT (STANFORD). (US/0049-2108). **1090**

CAMPUS SAFETY REPORT NEWSLETTER. (US/0885-3398). **4770**

CAMPUS SECURITY REPORT. (US/1055-4319). **Qty:** 12. **4770**

CAMPUS WATCH. (US/1050-5644). **1814**

CANADA JOURNAL (DEUTSCHE AUSG.). (CN/0829-0814). **Qty:** 8. **654**

CANADA LUTHERAN (NATIONAL ED.). (CN/0832-0179). **Qty:** 8-15. **5057**

CANADA QUILTS. (CN/0381-7369). **5183**

CANADA YEARBOOK. (CN/0068-8142). **1923**

CANADA'S WHO'S WHO OF THE POULTRY INDUSTRY. (CN/0068-8134). **431**

CANADIAN ACOUSTICS. (CN/0711-6659). **2162**

CANADIAN AERONAUTICS AND SPACE JOURNAL. (CN/0008-2821). **15**

CANADIAN AIRCRAFT OPERATOR, THE. (CN/0008-2848). **15**

CANADIAN ALPINE JOURNAL, THE. (CN/0068-8207). **4870**

CANADIAN AMATEUR (1987). (CN/0834-3977). **2037**

CANADIAN-AMERICAN SLAVIC STUDIES. (US/0090-8290). **2683**

CANADIAN AND INTERNATIONAL EDUCATION. (CN/0315-1409). **Qty:** 6. **1730**

CANADIAN APPRAISER, THE. (CN/0827-2697). **4835**

CANADIAN ASSOCIATION OF PHYSICAL ANTHROPOLOGY NEWSLETTER. (CN). **233**

CANADIAN ASSOCIATION OF RADIOLOGISTS JOURNAL. (CN/0846-5371). **3939**

CANADIAN AUTHOR (1992). (CN/1193-9974). **3372**

CANADIAN AUTHOR & BOOKMAN. (CN/0008-2937). **3372**

CANADIAN AVIATION NEWS (1984). (CN/0829-2132). **Qty:** 2-6/yr. **15**

CANADIAN BANKER (1983). (CN/0822-6830). **782**

CANADIAN BAPTIST, THE. (CN/0008-2988). **Qty:** 15. **4942**

CANADIAN BAR REVIEW. REVUE DU BARREAU CANADIEN, THE. (CN/0008-3003). **2947**

CANADIAN BAR REVIEW, THE. (CN/0008-3003). **3125**

CANADIAN BEEKEEPING. (CN/0576-4688). **72**

CANADIAN BIOTECH NEWS. (CN/1188-455X). **Qty:** 50. **3690**

CANADIAN BOOK REVIEW ANNUAL. (CN/0383-770X). **3339**

CANADIAN BUSINESS REVIEW, THE. (CN/0317-4026). **1467**

CANADIAN C.S. LEWIS JOURNAL, THE. (CN/0711-2173). **3372**

CANADIAN CAVER, THE. (CN/0833-0948). **4870**

CANADIAN CD-ROM NEWS. (CN/0848-8649). **1173**

CANADIAN CHILDREN'S LITERATURE. (CN/0319-0080). **Qty:** 120. **3372**

CANADIAN CIVIL ENGINEER. (CN/0825-7515). **2020**

CANADIAN COIN NEWS. (CN/0702-3162). **2780**

CANADIAN CORPORATE COUNSEL. (CN/1188-2026). **655**

CANADIAN CRIMINAL CASES (BOUND CUMULATION). (CN/0008-3348). **3105**

CANADIAN CRITICAL CARE NURSING JOURNAL. (CN/0826-6778). **3852**

CANADIAN DEFENCE QUARTERLY (TORONTO). (CN/0315-3495). **4038**

CANADIAN DIMENSION. (CN/0008-3402). **Qty:** 5. **4467**

CANADIAN DISCIPLE. (CN/0008-3410). **Qty:** varies. **4942**

CANADIAN EDUCATION INDEX. (CN/0008-3453). **1793**

CANADIAN EMERGENCY NEWS. (CN/0847-947X). **Qty: varies. 4770**

CANADIAN ENTOMOLOGIST, THE. (CN/0008-347X). **5606**

CANADIAN ETHNIC STUDIES. (CN/0008-3496). **2257**

CANADIAN FACILITY MANAGEMENT & DESIGN. (CN/1193-7505). **863**

CANADIAN FAMILY LAW QUARTERLY. (CN/0832-6983). **3119**

CANADIAN FAMILY PHYSICIAN. (CN/0008-350X). **3737**

CANADIAN FLIGHT. (CN/0008-3577). **16**

CANADIAN FOLK MUSIC BULLETIN. (CN/0829-5344). **4107**

CANADIAN FOLK MUSIC JOURNAL. (CN/0318-2568). **4107**

CANADIAN FORUM. (CN/0008-3631). **Qty: 40. 3339**

CANADIAN FUNERAL DIRECTOR. (CN/0319-3225). **2406**

CANADIAN FUNERAL NEWS. (CN/0382-5876). **2406**

CANADIAN GEMMOLOGIST. (CN/0226-7446). **Qty: 4. 2913**

CANADIAN GENERAL AVIATION NEWS. (CN/0226-5648). **16**

CANADIAN GEOGRAPHER. (CN/0008-3658). **2558**

CANADIAN GEOGRAPHIC. (CN/0706-2168). **2558**

CANADIAN GEOTECHNICAL JOURNAL. (CN/0008-3674). **1352**

CANADIAN GUIDER. (CN/0300-435X). **1730**

CANADIAN HAIRDRESSER. (CN/0008-3720). **402**

CANADIAN HIGHWAY CARRIERS GUIDE. (CN/0702-8733). **5378**

CANADIAN HISTORICAL REVIEW. (CN/0008-3755). **2726**

CANADIAN HOME ECONOMICS JOURNAL. (CN/0008-3763). **Qty: 4 per year. 2789**

CANADIAN HORSEMAN (GUELPH). (CN/0840-6200). **Qty: varies. 2797**

CANADIAN HOSPITAL DIRECTORY. (CN/0068-8932). **3777**

CANADIAN HOUSE AND HOME. (CN/0826-7642). **Qty: 24-40 approx. 2904**

CANADIAN HOUSING. (CN/0826-7278). **Qty: 2. 2817**

CANADIAN HR REPORTER. (CN/0838-228X). **939**

CANADIAN HUMAN RIGHT REPORTER. (CN/0226-2177). **4505**

CANADIAN INDEPENDENT ADJUSTER, THE. (CN/0008-3828). **2877**

CANADIAN INDIA STAR, THE. (CN/0319-8715). **2648**

CANADIAN INSURANCE. (CN/0008-3879). **2877**

CANADIAN INSURANCE LAW REVIEW. (CN/0836-0456). **2948**

CANADIAN INVESTMENT REVIEW. (CN/0840-6863). **894**

CANADIAN JEWISH NEWS MONTREAL ED. (CN). **5046**

CANADIAN JOURNAL OF ADMINISTRATIVE LAW & PRACTICE. (CN/0835-6742). **3092**

CANADIAN JOURNAL OF AFRICAN STUDIES. (CN/0008-3968). **2638**

CANADIAN JOURNAL OF AGRICULTURAL ECONOMICS. (CN/0008-3976). **72**

CANADIAN JOURNAL OF ANAESTHESIA. (CN/0832-610X). **3682**

CANADIAN JOURNAL OF APPLIED SPECTROSCOPY. (CN/1183-7306). **4434**

CANADIAN JOURNAL OF ARCHAEOLOGY. (CN/0705-2006). **Qty: 5-6. 265**

CANADIAN JOURNAL OF BEHAVIOURAL SCIENCE. (CN/0008-400X). **4579**

CANADIAN JOURNAL OF CARDIOVASCULAR NURSING. (CN/0843-6096). **3700**

CANADIAN JOURNAL OF CIVIL ENGINEERING. (CN/0315-1468). **2020**

CANADIAN JOURNAL OF COMMUNICATION. (CN/0705-3657). **1105**

CANADIAN JOURNAL OF COMMUNITY MENTAL HEALTH. (CN/0713-3936). **5276**

CANADIAN JOURNAL OF CRIMINOLOGY. (CN/0704-9722). **3159**

CANADIAN JOURNAL OF EARLY CHILDHOOD EDUCATION. (CN/0226-7071). **1803**

CANADIAN JOURNAL OF EDUCATION. (CN/0380-2361). **1730**

CANADIAN JOURNAL OF EDUCATIONAL COMMUNICATION. (CN/0710-4340). **Qty: 6/year. 1105**

CANADIAN JOURNAL OF FAMILY LAW. (CN/0704-1225). **3120**

CANADIAN JOURNAL OF FISHERIES AND AQUATIC SCIENCES. (CN/0706-652X). **2298**

CANADIAN JOURNAL OF GASTROENTEROLOGY, THE. (CN/0835-7900). **3743**

CANADIAN JOURNAL OF HERBALISM. (CN/0848-9629). **Qty: 12. 2412**

CANADIAN JOURNAL OF HISTORY. (CN/0008-4107). **Qty: 12. 2613**

CANADIAN JOURNAL OF HISTORY OF SPORT. (CN/0712-9815). **4889**

CANADIAN JOURNAL OF HUMAN SEXUALITY, THE. (CN/1188-4517). **5187**

CANADIAN JOURNAL OF INFORMATION SCIENCE. (CN/0380-9218). **3199**

CANADIAN JOURNAL OF INSURANCE LAW. (CN/0822-109X). **2948**

CANADIAN JOURNAL OF IRISH STUDIES, THE. (CN/0703-1459). **Qty: 20. 3372**

CANADIAN JOURNAL OF ITALIAN STUDIES. (CN/0705-3002). **3372**

CANADIAN JOURNAL OF LATIN AMERICAN AND CARIBBEAN STUDIES. (CN/0826-3663). **2726**

CANADIAN JOURNAL OF LAW AND JURISPRUDENCE, THE. (CN/0841-8209). **2948**

CANADIAN JOURNAL OF LAW AND SOCIETY. (CN/0829-3201). **2948**

CANADIAN JOURNAL OF LIFE INSURANCE. (CN/0706-5582). **2877**

CANADIAN JOURNAL OF LINGUISTICS. (CN/0008-4131). **3272**

CANADIAN JOURNAL OF MARKETING RESEARCH. (CN/0829-4836). **922**

CANADIAN JOURNAL OF MEDICAL RADIATION TECHNOLOGY. (CN/0820-5930). **3939**

CANADIAN JOURNAL OF MEDICAL TECHNOLOGY. (CN/0008-4158). **3562**

CANADIAN JOURNAL OF NATIVE EDUCATION. (CN/0710-1481). **1730**

CANADIAN JOURNAL OF NETHERLANDIC STUDIES. (CN/0225-0500). **2683**

CANADIAN JOURNAL OF NURSING ADMINISTRATION. (CN/0838-2948). **3852**

CANADIAN JOURNAL OF NURSING RESEARCH, THE. (CN/0844-5621). **Qty: varies. 3852**

CANADIAN JOURNAL OF OCCUPATIONAL THERAPY (1939). (CN/0008-4174). **3922**

CANADIAN JOURNAL OF OPHTHALMOLOGY. (CN/0008-4182). **3873**

CANADIAN JOURNAL OF OPTOMETRY. (CN/0045-5075). **4215**

CANADIAN JOURNAL OF PHILOSOPHY. (CN/0045-5091). **4343**

CANADIAN JOURNAL OF POLITICAL SCIENCE. (CN/0008-4239). **4467**

CANADIAN JOURNAL OF PROGRAM EVALUATION, THE. (CN/0834-1516). **4636**

CANADIAN JOURNAL OF PSYCHIATRY. (CN/0706-7437). **3923**

CANADIAN JOURNAL OF PSYCHOLOGY. (CN/0008-4255). **4579**

CANADIAN JOURNAL OF PUBLIC HEALTH. (CN/0008-4263). **4770**

CANADIAN JOURNAL OF REGIONAL SCIENCE, THE. (CN/0705-4580). **Qty: approx. 6/year; English and French. 2817**

CANADIAN JOURNAL OF REHABILITATION. (CN/0828-0827). **4379**

CANADIAN JOURNAL OF REMOTE SENSING. (CN/0703-8992). **16**

CANADIAN JOURNAL OF RESEARCH IN EARLY CHILDHOOD EDUCATION, THE. (CN/0827-0899). **1803**

CANADIAN JOURNAL OF SCHOOL PSYCHOLOGY. (CN/0829-5735). **Qty: 4. 1730**

CANADIAN JOURNAL OF SOCIOLOGY. (CN/0318-6431). **5241**

CANADIAN JOURNAL OF SPECIAL EDUCATION. (CN/0827-3391). **1876**

CANADIAN JOURNAL OF SPORT SCIENCES. (US/0833-1235). **3953**

CANADIAN JOURNAL OF SURGERY. (CN/0008-428X). **3961**

CANADIAN JOURNAL OF URBAN RESEARCH. (CN/1188-3774). **2817**

CANADIAN JOURNAL OF VETERINARY RESEARCH. (CN/0830-9000). **5507**

CANADIAN JOURNAL OF WOMEN AND THE LAW. (CN/0832-8781). **2948**

CANADIAN JOURNAL ON AGING. (CN/0714-9808). **3750**

CANADIAN LACEMAKER GAZETTE. (CN/0824-1856). **5183**

CANADIAN LAW LIBRARIES. (CN/1180-176X). **Qty: 25-30. 2948**

CANADIAN LAWYER. (CN/0703-2129). **2948**

CANADIAN LIBRARY JOURNAL. (CN/0008-4352). **3200**

CANADIAN LITERATURE. (CN/0008-4360). **3372**

CANADIAN MACHINERY AND METALWORKING. (CN/0008-4379). **2111**

CANADIAN MANAGER. (CN/0045-5156). **863**

CANADIAN MINES HANDBOOK. (CN/0068-9289). **2136**

CANADIAN MINING JOURNAL. (CN/0008-4492). **2136**

CANADIAN MODERN LANGUAGE REVIEW, THE. (CN/0008-4506). **3272**

CANADIAN MONEYSAVER. (CN/0713-3286). **Qty: 22. 894**

CANADIAN MUSIC EDUCATOR, THE. (CN/0008-4549). **4107**

CANADIAN MUSICIAN. (CN/0708-9635). **4107**

CANADIAN MUSLIM, THE. (CN/0707-2945). **5042**

CANADIAN NATIVE LAW REPORTER. (CN/0225-2279). **Qty: infrequent. 2948**

CANADIAN NEWS INDEX (TORONTO). (CN/0225-7459). **5781**

CANADIAN NUMISMATIC JOURNAL, THE. (CN/0008-4573). **2780**

CANADIAN NURSE (1924). (CN/0008-4581). **3852**

CANADIAN OCCUPATIONAL HEALTH & SAFETY NEWS. (CN/0709-5252). **2860**

CANADIAN OCCUPATIONAL SAFETY AND HEALTH LAW MONTHLY REPORT. (CN/0825-608X). **2948**

CANADIAN ONCOLOGY NURSING JOURNAL. (CN/1181-912X). **Qty: 4-6. 3853**

CANADIAN ONCOLOGY NURSING JOURNAL. (CN/1181-912X). **Qty: 4-6. 3853**

CANADIAN ORCHESTRAS AND YOUTH ORCHESTRAS DIRECTORY. (CN/1189-9956). **4107**

CANADIAN ORCHID JOURNAL, THE. (CN/0824-1554). **2412**

CANADIAN PARLIAMENTARY GUIDE. (CN/0315-6168). **4636**

CANADIAN PARLIAMENTARY REVIEW. (CN/0229-2548). **4636**

CANADIAN PATENT REPORTER. (CN/0008-4689). **1302**

CANADIAN PHILATELIST. (CN/0045-5253). **2784**

CANADIAN PLAINS BULLETIN. (CN/0316-0343). **2726**

CANADIAN POETRY (LONDON, ONT.). (CN/0704-5646). **3461**

CANADIAN POLICE CHIEF NEWSLETTER. (CN/0713-4517). **3159**

CANADIAN PSYCHOLOGY. (CN/0708-5591). **4579**

CANADIAN PUBLIC ADMINISTRATION. (CN/0008-4840). **4636**

CANADIAN PUBLIC POLICY. (CN/0317-0861). **Qty: 4. 1468**

CANADIAN RAIL. (CN/0008-4875). **5430**

CANADIAN RAILWAY MODELLER. (CN/0849-2964). **5430**

CANADIAN REFERENCE DIRECTORY ON BUSINESS PLANNING AND FUNDING. (CN). **655**

CANADIAN REVIEW OF AMERICAN STUDIES. (CN/0007-7720). **2530**

CANADIAN REVIEW OF ART EDUCATION, RESEARCH AND ISSUES. (CN/0706-8107). **346**

CANADIAN REVIEW OF SOCIAL POLICY (1987). (CN/0836-303X). **5276**

CANADIAN REVIEW OF SOCIOLOGY AND ANTHROPOLOGY, THE. (CN/0008-4948). **233**

CANADIAN REVIEW OF STUDIES IN NATIONALISM. (CN/0317-7904). **2635**

CANADIAN SCENE (TORONTO. 1951). (CN/0319-6577). **2530**

CANADIAN SCHOOL EXECUTIVE (1982). (CN/0228-0914). **1861**

CANADIAN SCIENCE (DOWNSVIEW, ONT.). (CN/0712-4848). **5092**

CANADIAN SECURITY. (CN/0709-3403). **Qty: varies. 5176**

CANADIAN SLAVONIC PAPERS. (CN/0008-5006). **3272**

CANADIAN SOCIAL WORK REVIEW. (CN/0820-909X). **5276**

CANADIAN SOCIETY OF FORENSIC SCIENCE JOURNAL. (CN/0008-5030). **3740**

CANADIAN SPECTROSCOPIC NEWS (1972). (CN/0381-5447). **4434**

CANADIAN SPEECHES, ISSUES OF THE DAY. (CN/1191-0860). **1105**

CANADIAN STAMP NEWS. (CN/0702-3154). **2784**

CANADIAN STUDIES IN POPULATION. (CN/0380-1489). **4550**

CANADIAN THEATRE REVIEW. (CN/0315-0836). **5362**

CANADIAN THEOSOPHIST, THE. (CN/0045-544X). **4942**

CANADIAN TOKEN, THE. (CN/0703-895X). **2772**

CANADIAN TREASURER. (CN/0845-7328). **655**

CANADIAN ULTRALIGHT NEWS. (CN/0821-6673). **16**

CANADIAN UNIVERSITY MUSIC REVIEW. (CN/0710-0353). **4107**

CANADIAN (VERNON, B.C.). (CN/0836-3196). **655**

CANADIAN VET SUPPLIES. (CN/0825-754X). **5507**

CANADIAN VOCATIONAL JOURNAL. (CN/0045-5520). Qty: 4. **1911**

CANADIAN WATER RESOURCES JOURNAL. (CN/0701-1784). **5531**

CANADIAN WEST (1985). (CN/0829-5026). **2726**

CANADIAN WOMEN'S STUDIES. (CN/0713-3235). Qty: varies. **5553**

CANADIAN WORKSHOP. (CN/0704-0717). **633**

CANADIAN WORLD FEDERALIST (1975). (CN/0382-8662). Qty: 3. **3125**

CANADIAN WRITER'S JOURNAL. (CN/0827-293X). Qty: 8-10. **3372**

CANADIAN YEARBOOK OF INTERNATIONAL LAW. (CN/0069-0058). **3125**

CANADIANA GERMANICA. (CN/0703-1599). **2683**

CANADO-AMERICAIN, LE. (US/0576-6478). **2530**

CANAL & RIVERBOAT. (UK/0141-2302). **4870**

CANBERRA ANTHROPOLOGY. (AT/0314-9099). **233**

CANBERRA HISTORICAL JOURNAL. (AT/0313-5977). Qty: 1,000. **2669**

CANCER BIOCHEMISTRY BIOPHYSICS. (US/0305-7232). **3810**

CANCER CAUSES & CONTROL : CCC. (UK/0957-5243). **3810**

CANCER FORUM. (AT/0311-306X). **3811**

CANCER INVESTIGATION. (US/0735-7907). **3811**

CANCER LETTER, THE. (US/0096-3917). **3811**

CANCER SURVEYS. (US/0261-2429). **3812**

CANELOBRE. (SP). **317**

CANMORE LEADER. (CN/0824-3646). **5781**

CANOE AND KAYAK RACING NEWS. (US). **592**

CANOE (CAMDEN, ME.). (US/0360-7496). **592**

CANTERAS Y EXPLOTACIONES. (SP/0008-5677). **2111**

CANTIGUEIROS (LEXINGTON, KY.). (US/0898-8463). **3372**

CANTRILL'S FILMNOTES. (AT/0158-4154). Qty: 20. **4065**

CANYON COURIER WEEKENDER, THE. (US/0192-0197). **5642**

CANYON ECHO. (US/0164-7024). Qty: 4-6. **2530**

CANYON LEGACY. (US/0897-3423). Qty: 16-20. **2613**

CANYON NEWS (CANYON, TEX. : 1926). (US). Qty: 5. **5748**

CAO TIMES. (US/0146-3365). **390**

CAPACITOR INDUSTRY NEWSLETTER : BIMONTHLY NEWS FOR THE FILM CAPACITOR TRADE AND ALLIED DIELECTRIC MARKETS. (US/1056-6813). **1600**

CAPE BRETON'S MAGAZINE. (CN/0319-4639). **2726**

CAPE COD LIFE. (US/0199-7238). Qty: 2. **2530**

CAPE LIBRARIAN, THE. (SA/0008-5790). **3200**

CAPITAL & CLASS. (UK/0309-8168). **1590**

CAPITAL BAPTIST. (US/0528-0559). **5057**

CAPITAL ENERGY LETTER. (US/0195-5292). **1935**

CAPITAL PUNISHMENT (PLANO, TEX.). (US). **3160**

CAPITAL (RHINEBECK, N.Y.), THE. (US/0885-4718). **2441**

CAPITAL SPORTS FOCUS. (US/1041-5742). **4889**

CAPITAL TIMES, THE. (US/0749-4068). **5766**

CAPSULE. (US). Qty: 6. **5178**

CAR AND DRIVER ROAD TEST ANNUAL. (US/8755-626X). **5409**

CAR COLLECTOR & CAR CLASSICS MAGAZINE. (US/1057-4441). **5409**

CAR-DEL SCRIBE. (US/0008-6029). **2441**

CAR MODELER. (US/1048-6194). Qty: 6-8. **2772**

CARAVAN BUSINESS. (UK/0268-5558). **5466**

CARBOHYDRATE POLYMERS. (UK/0144-8617). **1040**

CARBOHYDRATE RESEARCH. (NE/0008-6215). **1040**

CARBONATES AND EVAPORITES. (US/0891-2556). **1371**

CARCINOGENESIS (NEW YORK). (US/0143-3334). **3814**

CARDINAL NEWS, THE. (US). **5580**

CARDIOLOGIA (ROMA). (IT/0393-1978). **3700**

CARDIOLOGY IN PRACTICE. (UK/0262-5547). **3701**

CARDIOLOGY IN THE YOUNG. (US/1047-9511). Qty: 8. **3701**

CARDIOLOGY MANAGEMENT. (US/0892-9327). **3701**

CARDIOMYOLOGY. (IT/0394-073X). **450**

CARDIOPULMONARY PHYSICAL THERAPY JOURNAL. (US). **4379**

CARDIOSCIENCE. (IT/1015-5007). **3701**

CARDIOVASCULAR AND INTERVENTIONAL RADIOLOGY. (US/0174-1551). **3939**

CARDIOVASCULAR DRUGS AND THERAPY. (US/0920-3206). **3701**

CARDIOVASCULAR PHARMACOLOGY. (UK/0263-7243). **3701**

CARDIOVASCULAR REVIEWS & REPORTS. (US/0197-3118). **3702**

CARDOZO ARTS & ENTERTAINMENT LAW JOURNAL. (US/0736-7694). **2948**

CARDOZO LAW REVIEW. (US/0270-5192). Qty: 5. **2948**

CARDOZO STUDIES IN LAW AND LITERATURE. (US/1043-1500). **2948**

CARDS INTERNATIONAL. (US/0956-5558). **655**

CAREER CENTER BULLETIN, THE. (US). **4201**

CAREER DEVELOPMENT FOR EXCEPTIONAL INDIVIDUALS. (US/0885-7288). **1911**

CAREER EDUCATION AND GUIDANCE. (UK/0954-3732). **1730**

CAREER EDUCATION NEWS : CENTRAL NEWS SERVICE FOR THE WORLDS OF WORK AND LEARNING. (US). **4202**

CAREER FOCUS FOR TODAY'S RISING BLACK PROFESSIONAL. (US/1049-9954). **4202**

CAREER FOCUS FOR TODAY'S RISING HISPANIC PROFESSIONAL. (US/1049-9946). **4202**

CAREER FUTURES. (US/1045-4314). Qty: 4-6 per year. **4202**

CAREER INFO CUS. (CN/1182-9192). Qty: 12. **1911**

CAREER OPPORTUNITIES NEWS. (US/0739-5043). **4202**

CAREER PATHFINDER, THE. (US/0885-7547). **4202**

CAREERS & COLLEGES. (US/1065-9935). Qty: 20. **4202**

CAREERS & THE DISABLED. (US/1056-277X). **4202**

CAREFREE ENTERPRISE. (US/0738-9604). Qty: 4. **2530**

CARETAKER GAZETTE, THE. (US/1074-3642). Qty: 6. **4203**

CARGO SYSTEMS INTERNATIONAL. (UK/0306-0985). **5379**

CARGOWORLD. (GW/0172-9314). Qty: 10. **5448**

CARIB. (JM). **3372**

CARIB BASIN TRADE UPDATE. (US/0888-1065). **1601**

CARIBBEAN AFFAIRS. (TR/1011-5765). Qty: 6. **2511**

CARIBBEAN/AMERICAN DIRECTORY. (US/0275-2883). **655**

CARIBBEAN BUSINESS. (US/0194-8326). **655**

CARIBBEAN CONTACT. (TR) **4942**

CARIBBEAN DATELINE. (US). Qty: 15. **894**

CARIBBEAN FLITE GUIDE. (US). **16**

CARIBBEAN GEOGRAPHY. (JM/0252-9939). **2558**

CARIBBEAN HANDBOOK, THE. (AQ). Qty: 25. **5466**

CARIBBEAN JOURNAL OF EDUCATION. (JM/0376-7701). **1730**

CARIBBEAN LAW AND BUSINESS. (BB/1013-9230). **3097**

CARIBBEAN QUARTERLY. (JM/0254-8038). **2486**

CARIBBEAN REVIEW. (US/0008-6525). **4467**

CARIBBEAN SHIPPING : THE JOURNAL OF THE CARIBBEAN SHIPPING ASSOCIATION. (JM) **5448**

CARIBBEAN TRAVEL AND LIFE. (US/1052-1011). Qty: Varies. **5466**

CARIBBEAN UPDATE. (US/8756-324X). **655**

CARIBBEAN WRITER, THE. (VI/0893-1550). Qty: 10. **3373**

CARICOM BULLETIN. (GY). **1550**

CARICOM PERSPECTIVE. (GY). **2551**

CARILLON NEWS. (US/0730-5001). **4107**

CARING FOR ANIMALS (OTTAWA, ONT.). (CN/0825-1711). **226**

CARITAS (FREIBURG IM BREISGAU). (GW/0008-6614). **4334**

CARLETON INTERNATIONAL STUDIES. (CN/0702-8334). **4517**

CARLETON UNIVERSITY STUDENT JOURNAL OF PHILOSOPHY, THE. (CN/0317-073X). **4343**

CARLSONREPORT. (US/0889-2288). Qty: 12. **952**

CARLYLE STUDIES ANNUAL. (US/1074-2670). **3373**

CARMEL PINE CONE AND CARMEL VALLEY OUTLOOK, THE. (US). Qty: 25. **5633**

CARMELUS. (IT/0008-6673). **5025**

CARNIVOROUS PLANT NEWSLETTER. (US/0190-9215). **506**

CAROLINA CHEMTIPS. (US/0748-0466). **966**

CAROLINA CHRISTIAN. (US/0008-672X). Qty: 15-20. **4942**

CAROLINA COUNTRY. (US/0008-6746). **1541**

CAROLINA GARDENER. (US/1063-7451). Qty: 12-15. **2412**

CAROLINA QUARTERLY. (US/0008-6797). Qty: 9. **3373**

CAROLINAS GENEALOGICAL SOCIETY BULLETIN, THE. (US/0363-440X). **2441**

CAROLINIAN (RALEIGH), THE. (US/0045-5873). **5722**

CAROUSEL NEWS & TRADER, THE. (US/0892-9769). **250**

CARP. CANADIAN ASSOCIATION OF RETIRED PERSONS. (CN/1193-8544). **5178**

CARPATHO-RUSYN AMERICAN. (US/0749-9213). **2258**

CARRIAGE JOURNAL, THE. (US/0008-6916). Qty: 10-12. **2772**

CARRIAGE TRADE (SARNIA, ONT.). (CN/0831-2907). **5348**

CARROLL CABLES. (US/0892-2152). **2442**

CARROLL COUNTY GENEALOGICAL QUARTERLY. (US/0734-5682). **2442**

CARROLL TODAY NEWS. (US). **5669**

CARROUSEL ART. (US/0740-0780). **250**

CARS & PARTS. (US/0008-6975). **5409**

CARSON VALLEY CHRONICLE. (US). Qty: 12. **5707**

CARTA AL EJECUTIVO ANDINO. (PE). **1633**

CARTA DE CLACSO. (AG). **5194**

CARTACTUAL. (HU/0008-7009). **2558**

CARTE ITALIANE. (US/0737-9412). **3373**

CARTELLINA, LA. (IT/1120-4621). Qty: 15-20. **4108**

CARTOGRAPHIC JOURNAL, THE. (UK/0008-7041). **2581**

CARTOGRAPHICA (1980). (CN/0317-7173). Qty: 30. **2581**

CARTOGRAPHY. (AT/0069-0805). **2581**

CARTOGRAPHY AND GEOGRAPHIC INFORMATION SYSTEMS. (US/1050-9844). **2581**

CARTOMANIA. (US/0894-2595). **Qty:** 5-10/yr. **2558**

CARTONNAGES EMBALLAGES MODERNES. (FR). **4218**

CARTOUCHE ENGLISH EDITION (CALGARY). (CN/1183-2045). **2581**

CARTOUCHE FRENCH EDITION (CALGARY). (CN/1183-2045). **2581**

CAS JOURNAL. (US/1053-7694). **Qty:** 2. **4108**

CASA DEL TIEMPO. (MX/0185-4275). **2511**

CASA STILE. (IT/0390-1513). **2583**

CASA TESSIL REPORTER. (IT/0394-882X). **5348**

CASA VOGUE. (IT/0008-7173). **2899**

CASAULT FOL. (CN/0820-7402). **5781**

CASCADE CAVER, THE. (US/0008-7211). **1403**

CASCADE COURIER, THE. (US). **5705**

CASCADES EAST. (US/0194-8954). **4870**

CASE ANALYSIS IN SOCIAL SCIENCE IN SOCIAL THERAPY. (US/0149-6948). **5241**

CASE REGISTER. (US/0272-2119). **949**

CASE TRENDS. (US/1046-5944). **1227**

CASE UPDATE. (US/0749-7709). **2949**

CASE WESTERN RESERVE JOURNAL OF INTERNATIONAL LAW. (US/0008-7254). **3125**

CASHTON RECORD. (US). **5766**

CASINO CHRONICLE. (US/0889-9797). **Qty:** (12-20). **2804**

CASINO EXPLORER. (US). **4858**

CASINOS : THE INTERNATIONAL CASINO GUIDE. (US/1040-9920). **4858**

CASOPIS PRO MINERALOGII A GEOLOGII. (XR/0008-7378). **1371**

CASOPIS PRO MODERNI FILOLOGII / CESKOSLOVENSKA AKADEMIE VED. (NE/0862-8459). **3273**

CASS COUNTY CONNECTIONS. (US/1074-5742). **2442**

CASS COUNTY GENEALOGICAL SOCIETY QUARTERLY. (US). **2442**

CASSAVA NEWSLETTER. (CK/0120-1824). **Qty:** 6-12 per year. **166**

CASSIOPEIA (VICTORIA). (CN/0715-4747). **394**

CAST METALS. (UK/0953-4962). **Qty:** 12. **3999**

CASTANEA. (US/0008-7475). **Qty:** 4. **506**

CASTING WORLD. (US/0887-9060). **3999**

CASTINGS. (AT/0008-7521). **3999**

CASTRO, EL. (SP). **3461**

CASTRUM PEREGRINI. (NE/0008-7556). **3373**

CAT FANCY (SAN JUAN CAPISTRANO, CALIF.). (US/0892-6514). **4286**

CAT NEWS. (SZ). **2189**

CATALAN REVIEW. (SP/0213-5949). **Qty:** 10 to 12. **2258**

CATALOG OF COPYRIGHT ENTRIES. FOURTH SERIES. PART 3. PERFORMING ARTS. (US/0163-7312). **1302**

CATALOGING & CLASSIFICATION QUARTERLY. (US/0163-9374). **3200**

CATALOGING SERVICE BULLETIN. (US/0160-8029). **3200**

CATALOGO GENERAL - FONDO DE CULTURA ECONOMICA, MEXICO. (MX). **1531**

CATALOGUE & INDEX. (UK/0008-7629). **3200**

CATALOGUE DE LA PRODUCTION CINEMATOGRAPHIQUE FRANCAISE. (FR/0224-7518). **4065**

CATALOGUE DE LIVRES AU FORMAT DE POCHE. (FR/0769-1696). **412**

CATALOGUE - FUNNEL. (CN/0826-2861). **4065**

CATALOGUE OF CONODONTS. (GW). **4226**

CATALYSIS REVIEWS : SCIENCE AND ENGINEERING. (US/0161-4940). **2009**

CATALYST (ATLANTA, GA.). (US/0896-7423). **3373**

CATALYST / CITIZENS FOR PUBLIC JUSTICE. (CN/0824-2062). **Qty:** 10. **4467**

CATALYST (GOROKA, PAPUA NEW GUINEA). (PP/0253-2921). **2669**

CATALYST (MENLO PARK, CALIF.), THE. (US/0897-3318). **Qty:** 4. **1876**

CATALYST (MONTPELIER, VT.). (US/0742-6534). **Qty:** 8-10/yr. **1468**

CATALYSTS IN CHEMISTRY. (UK/0309-5770). **967**

CATASTROPHISM AND ANCIENT HISTORY. (US/0733-8058). **Qty:** 4. **2613**

CATECHIST. (US/0008-7726). **5025**

CATENA (GIESSEN). (GW/0341-8162). **166**

CATERING & HEALTH. (UK/0267-3851). **2330**

CATHEDRAL AGE. (US/0008-7874). **294**

CATHOLIC ADVANCE, THE. (US/0008-7904). **5025**

CATHOLIC ANCESTOR. (UK). **Qty:** 10. **2442**

CATHOLIC ARCHIVES : THE JOURNAL OF THE CATHOLIC ARCHIVES SOCIETY. (UK/0261-4316). **5025**

CATHOLIC CHRONICLE, THE. (US/0008-7971). **5025**

CATHOLIC EXPONENT, THE. (US/0162-7031). **5025**

CATHOLIC FREE PRESS, THE. (US/0008-8056). **Qty:** 1 /wk. **5026**

CATHOLIC GAZETTE. (UK/0008-8064). **5026**

CATHOLIC HERALD. (UK/0008-8072). **5026**

CATHOLIC HERALD (SACRAMENTO, CALIF.). (US/0746-4185). **5026**

CATHOLIC HISTORICAL REVIEW, THE. (US/0008-8080). **5026**

CATHOLIC JOURNALIST. (US/0008-8129). **2918**

CATHOLIC LIBRARY WORLD, THE. (US/0008-820X). **3201**

CATHOLIC MEDICAL QUARTERLY : JOURNAL OF THE GUILD OF CATHOLIC DOCTORS. (UK/0008-8226). **3562**

CATHOLIC MESSENGER. (US/0008-8234). **5026**

CATHOLIC NEW TIMES. (CN/0701-0788). **Qty:** 22. **5026**

CATHOLIC REGISTER, THE. (CN/0383-1620). **5026**

CATHOLIC SENTINEL - CATHOLIC CHURCH. DIOCESE OF BAKER (OR.). (US/0162-0363). **Qty:** 52. **5026**

CATHOLIC SINGLES. (US/0886-8190). **5242**

CATHOLIC STANDARD (WASHINGTON, D.C.). (US/0411-2741). **5026**

CATHOLIC SUN (SYRACUSE, N.Y.), THE. (US/0744-267X). **5026**

CATHOLIC TELEGRAPH. (US). **Qty:** 51 per year. **5727**

CATHOLIC TIMES (COLUMBUS, OHIO), THE. (US/0745-6050). **Qty:** 50. **5026**

CATHOLIC TIMES (MONTREAL). (CN/0703-1521). **5026**

CATHOLIC TRANSCRIPT, THE. (US). **Qty:** 25. **5645**

CATHOLIC TWIN CIRCLE. (US/0273-6136). **5026**

CATHOLIC UNIVERSE-BULLETIN, THE. (US/0162-7023). **5027**

CATHOLIC UNIVERSITY LAW REVIEW (1975). (US/0008-8390). **Qty:** 1-4. **2949**

CATHOLIC VOICE (OAKLAND, CALIF.), THE. (US/0279-0645). **Qty:** 12+. **5027**

CATHOLIC WORLD (1989), THE. (US/1042-3494). **5027**

CATHOLIC WORLD REPORT, THE. (US/1058-8159). **5027**

CATHOLIC YOUTH MINISTRY. (US/0277-8165). **5027**

CATHOLICA (MUNSTER). (GW/0008-8501). **5027**

CATO POLICY REPORT. (US/0743-605X). **1468**

CATS MAGAZINE. (US/0008-8544). **4286**

CATTLEMAN. (US/0008-8552). **209**

CAUSE/EFFECT. (US/0164-534X). **1814**

CAUT BULLETIN. (CN/0834-9614). **Qty:** 20-30. **1814**

CAVALRY JOURNAL, THE. (US/1074-0252). **2613**

CAVE SCIENCE (1982). (UK/0263-760X). **1404**

CAVES & CAVING. (UK/0142-1832). **1371**

CAYMAN ISLANDS CONSOLIDATED INDEX OF STATUTES AND SUBSIDIARY LEGISLATION TO ... . (BB). **3126**

CAZENOVIA REPUBLICAN. (US). **5714**

CBA RECORD. (US/0892-1822). **2949**

CBE VIEWS. (US/0164-5609). **Qty:** 6-10. **451**

CBMR DIGEST. (US/1043-1241). **4108**

CC AI. (BE/0773-4182). **1212**

CCA NEWS / CHRISTIAN CONFERENCE OF ASIA. (SI/0129-9891). **4943**

CCCO NEWS NOTES. (US/0008-5952). **4039**

CCLM NEWSLETTER. (US/0273-3315). **3373**

CD COMPUTING NEWS. (US/0893-4843). **Qty:** 12. **1276**

CD-ROM DATABASES. (US). **Qty:** 12. **1276**

CD-ROM DIRECTORY, THE. (UK). **1174**

CD-ROM ENDUSER. (US/1042-8623). **1174**

CD ROM INTERNATIONAL. (FR). **1276**

CD-ROM LIBRARIAN. (US/0893-9934). **1174**

CD-ROM NEWSLETTER ALTON. (UK/0954-3600). **1276**

CD-ROM PROFESSIONAL. (US/1049-0833). **Qty:** 36. **1276**

CDR IN. (DK). **1468**

CDS REVIEW. (US/0091-1666). **1318**

CE.D.R.E.S. DOCUMENTI. (IT). **1531**

CEA ADVISOR. (US/0007-8050). **1731**

CEA CRITIC. (US/0007-8069). **3373**

CEA FORUM. (US/0007-8034). **3273**

CEDAR TREE, THE. (US/0738-1905). **2442**

CEE NEWS. (US/1045-2710). **2038**

CEI. (UK). **1151**

CELESTINESCA. (US/0147-3085). **Qty:** 4-8. **3373**

CELL AND CHROMOSOME RESEARCH. (II/0254-2935). **533**

CELL BIOCHEMISTRY AND FUNCTION. (UK/0263-6484). **484**

CELL BIOLOGY AND TOXICOLOGY (PRINCETON SCIENTIFIC PUBLISHERS). (NE/0742-2091). **533**

CELL BIOLOGY INTERNATIONAL. (UK/1065-6995). **533**

CELL BIOPHYSICS. (US/0163-4992). **495**

CELL (CAMBRIDGE). (US/0092-8674). **533**

CELL CONTACT PHENOMENA. (UK/0142-8039). **533**

CELL CYCLE. (UK/0263-7251). **533**

CELL DIFFERENTIATION SHEFFIELD. (UK/0263-726X). **533**

CELL MEMBRANES. (UK/0142-8047). **533**

CELL MOTILITY AND THE CYTOSKELETON. (US/0886-1544). **533**

CELL NUCLEUS. (UK/0141-299X). **534**

CELL TRANSFORMATION. (UK/0142-8063). **534**

CELLE NEWSLETTER. (US/0743-4979). **2442**

CELLULAR BUSINESS. (US/0741-6520). **1151**

CELLULAR POLYMERS. (UK/0262-4893). **4454**

CELLULAR SALES & MARKETING. (US/0892-2683). **Qty:** 1-2. **1151**

CELSIUS. (AT). **2604**

CELULOZA SI HIRTIE (BUCHAREST, ROMANIA : 1986). (RM). **4233**

CEMENT, CONCRETE AND AGGREGATES. (US/0149-6123). **606**

CENCRASTUS. (UK). **317**

CENIMM; CENTRO NACIONAL DE INVESTIGACIONES METALURGICAS. (SP). **4000**

CENSO DO CALCADO RS / ASSOCIACAO COMERCIAL E INDUSTRIAL DE NOVO HAMBURGO. (BL). **1082**

CENTENNIAL STATE LIBRARIES. (US/0887-1116). **3201**

CENTER FOR STRATEGIC AND INTERNATIONAL STUDIES, GEORGETOWN UNIVERSITY, THE. (US/0272-2429). **4517**

CENTER PAPER (PRINCETON, N.J.). (US/0513-1529). **4551**

CENTER QUARTERLY. (US/0890-4634). **Qty:** Varies. **4368**

CENTER STAGE (NEW YORK). (US). **5362**

CENTRAL AFRICAN CHAMBER OF COMMERCE AND INDUSTRY DIRECTORY. (CM). **818**

CENTRAL AFRICAN JOURNAL OF MEDICINE. (RH/0008-9176). **3562**

CENTRAL

CENTRAL ALABAMA GENEALOGICAL SOCIETY : NEWSLETTER. (US) **2442**

CENTRAL AMERICA REPORT. (US). **4517**

CENTRAL AMERICA REPORT. (UK/0267-4130). **Qty:** 12. **4505**

CENTRAL & INNER ASIAN STUDIES. (US/0893-2301). **2648**

CENTRAL ASIATIC JOURNAL. (GW/0008-9192). **2648**

CENTRAL BANKING. (UK/0960-6319). **Qty:** varies. **782**

CENTRAL EUROPEAN HISTORY. (US/0008-9389). **2683**

CENTRAL FLORIDA MAGAZINE. (US/8750-2852). **2530**

CENTRAL IDAHO STAR-NEWS, THE. (US/0747-248X). **5656**

CENTRAL IDAHO STAR-NEWS, THE. (US). **5656**

CENTRAL ILLINOIS GENEALOGICAL QUARTERLY. (US/0577-0807). **Qty:** 20-25. **2442**

CENTRAL KENTUCKY NEWS-JOURNAL. (US). **5680**

CENTRAL MONTANA WAGON TRAILS. (US/0883-9603). **2442**

CENTRAL NEVADA'S GLORIOUS PAST. (US/0882-8792). **2727**

CENTRAL NORTH CAROLINA JOURNAL. (US/1050-1339). **2530**

CENTRAL RAILWAY CHRONICLE. (US/0008-9532). **5430**

CENTRAL STATE BUSINESS REVIEW. (US/8756-4521). **656**

CENTRAL STATES ARCHAEOLOGICAL JOURNAL. (US/0008-9559). **265**

CENTRAL VIRGINIA HERITAGE. (US/1043-4895). **Qty:** 50. **2442**

CENTRE SCIENTIFIQUE ET TECHNIQUE DE LA CONSTRUCTION. (BE/0770-7274). **Qty:** 2. **607**

CENTZONTLE : REVISTA DE LA SOCIEDAD MEXICANA DE ORNITOLOGIA. (MX). **5580**

CEPA NEWSLETTER. (US/8756-0550). **1231**

CERAMIC ABSTRACTS. (US/0095-9960). **2595**

CERAMIC ARTS & CRAFTS. (US/0009-0190). **2587**

CERAMIC REVIEW. (UK/0144-1825). **2587**

CERAMIC SCOPE. (US/0009-0247). **2587**

CERAMIC STUDY GROUP NEWSLETTER. (AT). **Qty:** 20. **2772**

CERAMICA INFORMAZIONE. (IT/0009-0271). **2587**

CERAMICA MADRID. (SP/0210-010X). **2587**

CERAMICA PER L'EDILIZIA INTERNATIONAL. (IT). **2587**

CERAMICA (SAO PAULO). (BL/0366-6913). **Qty:** 4. **2587**

CERAMICS INTERNATIONAL. (IT/0272-8842). **2588**

CERAMICS MONTHLY. (US/0009-0328). **2588**

CERAMICS PADDINGTON. (AT/1035-1841). **2588**

CERAMIQUE MODERNE, LA. (FR/0009-0336). **2588**

CERAMURGIA. (IT/0045-6152). **2588**

CEREAL FOODS WORLD. (US/0146-6283). **2331**

CEREAL RESEARCH COMMUNICATIONS. (HU/0133-3720). **200**

CEREBRAL CORTEX (NEW YORK, N.Y. 1991). (US/1047-3211). **3829**

CEREDIGION. (UK/0069-2263). **2683**

CERN COURIER. (SZ/0304-288X). **4446**

CERTIFIED ACCOUNTANT. (IE/0306-2406). **Qty:** 15-20. **740**

CERTIFIED ENGINEERING TECHNICIAN. (US/0746-6641). **Qty:** varies. **1968**

CERVANTES (GAINESVILLE, FLA.). (US/0277-6995). **Qty:** 450. **431**

CERVANTES : REVISTA DE POESIA E INFORMACION CULTURAL. (SP) **3461**

CESKOSLOVENSKA FARMACIE. (XR/0009-0530). **4296**

CESKOSLOVENSKA FYSIOLOGIE. (XR/0009-0557). **579**

CESKOSLOVENSKA PSYCHOLOGIE. (XR/0009-062X). **4580**

CESKOSLOVENSKY ARCHITEKT. (XR/0009-0697). **295**

CESKOSLOVENSKY CASOPIS PRO FYSIKU. (XR/0009-0700). **4399**

CESSNA OWNER MAGAZINE, THE. (US/0745-3523). **16**

CEW, CHEMICAL ENGINEERING WORLD. (II/0009-2517). **Qty:** 36-48. **2009**

CEYLON MEDICAL JOURNAL. (CE/0009-0875). **3562**

CFE BATIMENT. (FR). **2038**

CFE INDUSTRIE. (FR/1146-1497). **2038**

CFI, CERAMIC FORUM INTERNATIONAL. (GW/0173-9913). **2588**

CGA MAGAZINE. (CN/0318-742X). **740**

CGST JOURNAL. (HK). **4943**

CHAIN MERCHANDISER. (US/0009-0921). **952**

CHAIN-REACTION (CARLTON, VIC.). (AT/0312-1372). **2189**

CHAKRA. (US). **3373**

CHALLENGE. (US). **5553**

CHALLENGE (CARTHAGE, ILL.). (US/0745-6298). **1877**

CHALLENGE IN EDUCATIONAL ADMINISTRATION. (CN/0045-625X). **1861**

CHALLENGE (WASHINGTON, D.C. 1989). (US/1062-1849). **Qty:** 12. **4943**

CHALLENGE (WHITE PLAINS). (US/0577-5132). **1469**

CHALLENGER (BUFFALO, N.Y.), THE. (US/1040-8886). **5714**

CHALLENGER (NORTH VANCOUVER). (CN/0824-8427). **1731**

CHALLENGES OF THE CHANGING ECONOMY OF NEW YORK CITY. (US). **1469**

CHAMBER OF MINES JOURNAL. (RH/0009-1162). **2136**

CHAMBEREXECUTIVE. (US/0884-8114). **819**

CHAMP CHANNELS. (US/0747-9840). **5580**

CHAMPAIGN COUNTY GENEALOGICAL SOCIETY QUARTERLY. (US/0277-2086). **2442**

CHANGE (NEW ROCHELLE, N.Y.). (US/0009-1383). **1814**

CHANGING MEDICAL MARKETS. (US/1070-6771). **922**

CHANGING MEN (MADISON, WIS.). (US/0889-7174). **Qty:** 28. **3994**

CHANGING SCHOOLS (MUNCIE, IND. (US/0738-9418). **1731**

CHANGING WORK (NEW HAVEN, CONN.). (US/0883-1416). **1659**

CHANOYU QUARTERLY (KYOTO, JAPAN : 1976). (JA). **5268**

CHAOS NETWORK, THE. (US/1070-8146). **5242**

CHAPEL HILL NEWSPAPER, THE. (US). **5723**

CHAPTER ONE. (US/0895-3384). **1814**

CHARIOTEER, THE. (US/0577-5574). **3374**

CHARISMA AND CHRISTIAN LIFE. (US/0895-156X). **4943**

CHARITIES USA. (US/0364-0760). **5277**

CHARITON REVIEW, THE. (US/0098-9452). **3374**

CHARITY LONDON. 1983. (UK/0265-5209). **4335**

CHARLES BELL JOURNAL, THE. (UK). **3778**

CHARLES LAMB BULLETIN, THE. (UK/0308-0951). **3339**

CHARLESTON DAILY MAIL (CHARLESTON, W.VA. : 1920). (US). **5763**

CHARLESTON MAGAZINE, THE. (UK/0963-4770). **Qty:** 6. **3374**

CHARLOTTESVILLE ALBEMARLE OBSERVER. (US/0882-9322). **5758**

CHART AND QUILL. (US/0737-2655). **2442**

CHART MAGAZINE. (CN). **Qty:** 12. **4109**

CHARTER (SYDNEY, AUSTRALIA). (AT). **Qty:** 6. **740**

CHARTERED ACCOUNTANT, THE. (II/0009-188X). **740**

CHARTERED BUILDER. (AT/0311-1903). **607**

CHARTERED BUILDER (ASCOT, 1989). (UK/0957-8773). **Qty:** 30. **607**

CHARTERED QUANTITY SURVEYOR. (UK/0142-5196). **2020**

CHARTERED SECRETARY (NEW DELHI). (II/0376-7868). **863**

CHARTERED SURVEYOR : BUILDING AND QUANTITY SURVEYING QUARTERLY. (UK). **607**

CHARTERED SURVEYOR WEEKLY. (UK/0264-049X). **4835**

CHASQUI (WILLIAMSBURG, VA.). (US/0145-8973). **Qty:** 40. **3374**

CHASSE MAREE. (FR). **Qty:** 20. **233**

CHAT (TRYON), THE. (US/0009-1987). **5580**

CHATELAINE (EDITION FRANCAISE). (CN/0317-2635). **5553**

CHATELAINE (TORONTO, ONT.: 1928). (CN/0009-1995). **5553**

CHATHAM COURIER, THE ROUGH NOTES, THE. (US/1064-4644). **5714**

CHATHAM HOUSE PAPERS. (UK/0143-5795). **4517**

CHATTAHOOCHEE REVIEW, THE. (US/0741-9155). **3339**

CHATTANOOGA FREE PRESS. (US). **5744**

CHAUFFAGE, VENTILATION, CONDITIONNEMENT. (FR/0009-2029). **2604**

CHE-CHIANG HSUEH KAN. ZHEJIANGXUEKAN CHE-CHIANG SHENG SHE HUI KO HSUEH YEN CHIU SO. (CC). **5195**

CHE-CHIANG TA HSUEH HSUEH PAO. (CC). **5093**

CHEER NEWS TODAY. (US/0893-8091). **4889**

CHEESE REPORTER. (US/0009-2142). **192**

CHELYS (VIOLA DA GAMBA SOCIETY). (UK/0952-8407). **4109**

CHEM 13 NEWS. CHEM 12 NEWS. (CN/0703-1157). **Qty:** 5. **967**

CHEM-FACTS: AMMONIA. (UK). **967**

CHEM-FACTS: BELGIUM. (UK). **967**

CHEM-FACTS: CANADA. (UK). **967**

CHEM-FACTS: FEDERAL REPUBLIC OF GERMANY. (UK). **967**

CHEM-FACTS: FRANCE. (UK). **967**

CHEM-FACTS: ITALY. (UK). **967**

CHEM-FACTS: JAPAN. (UK). **967**

CHEM-FACTS METHANOL. (UK). **967**

CHEM-FACTS: NETHERLANDS. (UK). **967**

CHEM-FACTS: POLYETHYLENE. (UK). **967**

CHEM-FACTS: POLYPROPYLENE. (UK). **967**

CHEM-FACTS: SPAIN. (UK). **967**

CHEM-FACTS: UNITED KINGDOM. (UK). **967**

CHEMICAL ABSTRACTS. (US/0009-2258). **1011**

CHEMICAL AGE OF INDIA. (II/0009-2320). **Qty:** 12. **968**

CHEMICAL & ENGINEERING NEWS. (US/0009-2347). **1022**

CHEMICAL BUSINESS. (II/0970-3136). **2009**

CHEMICAL DESIGN AUTOMATION NEWS. (US/0886-6716). **968**

CHEMICAL ENGINEERING EDUCATION. (US/0009-2479). **2009**

CHEMICAL FORMULARY; A COLLECTION OF VALUABLE, TIMELY, PRACTICAL COMMERCIAL FORMULAE AND RECIPES FOR MAKING THOUSANDS OF PRODUCTS IN MANY FIELDS OF INDUSTRY, THE. (US). **1022**

CHEMICAL INDUSTRY NOTES. (US/0045-639X). **1011**

CHEMICAL INFORMATION BULLETIN. (US/0364-1910). **968**

CHEMICAL INSIGHT. (UK/0045-6403). **1022**

CHEMICAL MARKETING REPORTER. (US/0090-0907). **968**

CHEMICAL MATTERS. (UK). **Qty:** 5-6. **1022**

CHEMICAL PACKAGING REVIEW, THE. (US/1054-5131). **2162**

CHEMICAL REVIEWS. (US/0009-2665). **969**

CHEMICAL SPECIATION AND BIOAVAILABILITY. (UK/0954-2299). **2162**

CHEMICAL WEEKLY. (II/0045-6500). **Qty:** 52. **969**

CHEMICKE LISTY. (XR/0009-2770). **969**

CHEMIE DER ERDE. (GW/0009-2819). **1438**

CHEMIE MAGAZINE : MAANDBLAD VAN DE VLAAMSE CHEMISCHE VERENIGING. (BE). **969**

CHEMIE, MIKROBIOLOGIE, TECHNOLOGIE DER LEBENSMITTEL. (GW/0366-7154). **2331**

CHEMIE-TECHNIK. (GW/0340-9961). **2010**

CHEMISCHE INDUSTRIE (DUSSELDORF). (GW/0009-2959). **970**

CHEMIST & DRUGGIST. (UK/0009-3033). **4296**

CHEMIST (NEW YORK), THE. (US/0009-3025). **970**

CHEMISTRY AND INDUSTRY (LONDON). (UK/0009-3068). **970**

CHEMISTRY IN AUSTRALIA. (AT/0314-4240). **970**

CHEMISTRY IN BRITAIN. (UK/0009-3106). **970**

CHEMISTRY IN NEW ZEALAND. (NZ/0110-5566). **971**

CHEMISTRY INTERNATIONAL. (UK/0193-6484). **971**

CHEMOMETRICS AND INTELLIGENT LABORATORY SYSTEMS : LABORATORY INFORMATION MANAGEMENT. (NE/0925-5281). **1014**

CHEMORECEPTION ABSTRACTS. (US/0300-1261). **477**

CHEMOSPHERE (OXFORD). (UK/0045-6535). **2226**

CHEMTECH. (US/0009-2703). **1022**

CHENEY SENTINEL, THE. (US). **5674**

CHEROKEE COUNTY HERALD, THE. (US). **5625**

CHEROKEE FAMILY RESEARCHER. (US). **2443**

CHEROKEE ONE FEATHER, THE. (US/0890-4448). **2258**

CHESAPEAKE BAY MAGAZINE. (US/0045-656X). **593**

CHESOPIEAN, THE. (US/0009-3300). **Qty:** 8-10. **265**

CHESS. (UK/0009-3319). **4858**

CHESS COLLECTOR. (UK). **Qty:** 2-4. **4858**

CHESS CORRESPONDENT, THE. (US/0009-3327). **4858**

CHESS HORIZONS. (US/0147-2569). **Qty:** 10. **4858**

CHESS IN INDIANA. (US/1044-8888). **4858**

CHESS LIFE (1980). (US/0197-260X). **4858**

CHEST. (US/0012-3692). **3702**

CHESTER COUNTY LAW REPORTER. (US). **2949**

CHESTER COUNTY PRESS. (US). **Qty:** 6. **5735**

CHESTERTON REVIEW, THE. (CN/0317-0500). **3374**

CHEVRON WORLD. (US/0148-3102). **4253**

CHICAGO CRUSADER, THE. (US). **5658**

CHICAGO DEFENDER (1973). (US/0745-7014). **Qty:** 12 per year. **5659**

CHICAGO GENEALOGIST. (US/0009-3556). **Qty:** 11. **2443**

CHICAGO HISTORY. (US/0272-8540). **Qty:** 1 extended review each year. **2727**

CHICAGO-KENT LAW REVIEW. (US/0009-3599). **2949**

CHICAGO LAWYER. (US/0199-8374). **2950**

CHICAGO MEDICINE. (US/0009-3637). **Qty:** 72. **3563**

CHICAGO REVIEW. (US/0009-3696). **Qty:** 12. **3374**

CHICAGO SHORELAND NEWS, THE. (US). **5659**

CHICAGO SOURCEBOOK. (US/1078-5949). **757**

CHICAGO TALENT SOURCEBOOK. (US/0734-6662). **757**

CHICAGO THEOLOGICAL SEMINARY REGISTER, THE. (US/0739-5124). **4943**

CHICAGO TIMES MAGAZINE. (US/0894-5640). **2530**

CHICAGO TRIBUNE (CHICAGO, ILL. : 1963). (US). **5659**

CHICANO-LATINO LAW REVIEW. (US/1061-8899). **Qty:** 2-6. **2950**

CHICO ENTERPRISE-RECORD. (US/0746-5548). **5633**

CHICOREL INDEX SERIES. (US/0590-983X). **2844**

CHICOREL INDEX TO SHORT STORIES IN ANTHOLOGIES AND COLLECTIONS. (US/0149-4503). **3374**

CHIEF EXECUTIVE (NEW YORK, N.Y. 1977). (US/0160-4724). **863**

CHIEF INFORMATION OFFICER JOURNAL. (US/0899-0182). **1174**

CHIEFTAIN (IROQUOIS). (CN/0821-7696). **5782**

CHIEN CHU SHIH (TAIPEI, TAIWAN). (CH). **295**

CHIH WU SHENG LI HSUEH TUNG HSUN. (CC/0412-0914). **506**

CHIH WU YEN CHIU. (CC). **506**

CHIKASUI GAKKAI SHI. (JA/0913-4182). **1413**

CHIKUSAN NO KENKYU. ANIMAL HUSBANDRY. (JA). **5507**

CHILD AND FAMILY. (US/0009-3882). **2277**

CHILD & FAMILY BEHAVIOR THERAPY. (US/0731-7107). **4580**

CHILD AND MAN. (UK/0009-3890). **Qty:** 20. **1731**

CHILD & YOUTH SERVICES. (US/0145-935X). **5278**

CHILD CARE, HEALTH AND DEVELOPMENT. (UK/0305-1862). **3901**

CHILD CARE INFORMATION EXCHANGE. (US/0164-8527). **Qty:** varies. **5278**

CHILD CARE WORKER, THE. (SA/0258-8927). **5242**

CHILD DEVELOPMENT ABSTRACTS AND BIBLIOGRAPHY. (US/0009-3939). **3655**

CHILD EDUCATION. (UK/0009-3947). **1890**

CHILD LANGUAGE TEACHING AND THERAPY. (UK/0265-6590). **1877**

CHILD LIFE (INDIANAPOLIS, IND. 1922). (US/0009-3971). **1061**

CHILD (NEW YORK, N.Y.). (US/0894-7988). **2277**

CHILD PROTECTION REPORT. (US/0147-1260). **4771**

CHILD PSYCHIATRY AND HUMAN DEVELOPMENT. (US/0009-398X). **3923**

CHILD PSYCHIATRY QUARTERLY. (II/0009-3998). **3901**

CHILD SAFETY NEWS. (AT). **Qty:** 10. **4771**

CHILD SAFETY REVIEW. (UK/0957-4107). **Qty:** 15-20. **4771**

CHILD STUDY JOURNAL. (US/0009-4005). **4580**

CHILD SUPPORT REPORT. (US/0884-8076). **3120**

CHILD WELFARE. (US/0009-4021). **5278**

CHILDHOOD EDUCATION. (US/0009-4056). **1803**

CHILDREN & TEENS TODAY. (US/0882-942X). **5278**

CHILDREN AND WAR. (UK/0956-3113). **5195**

CHILDREN IN HOSPITAL. (AT/0814-9127). **Qty:** varies. **4580**

CHILDREN'S ADVOCATE, THE. (US/0739-425X). **Qty:** 6. **5279**

CHILDREN'S ALBUM, THE. (US/0749-8659). **1061**

CHILDREN'S BOOK BAG, THE. (US/1064-0541). **3374**

CHILDREN'S BOOK REVIEW SERVICE. (US/0090-7987). **3339**

CHILDREN'S FOCUS. (US/0893-486X). **1061**

CHILDREN'S FOLKLORE REVIEW, THE. (US/0739-5558). **2318**

CHILDREN'S HEALTH CARE. (US/0273-9615). **3901**

CHILDREN'S LITERATURE ASSOCIATION QUARTERLY. (US/0885-0429). **3340**

CHILDREN'S MINISTRY. (US/1054-1144). **Qty:** 20-30. **4943**

CHILDREN'S WORLD (BOSTON, MASS.). (US/0895-2221). **1877**

CHILDSCOPE. (US/0882-6390). **3902**

CHILEANS, THE. (UK). **506**

CHILTON'S I&CS. (US/0746-2395). **1968**

CHILTON'S REVIEW OF OPTOMETRY. (US/0147-7633). **4215**

CHIMIE NOUVELLE. (BE/0771-730X). **972**

CHINA AGRIBUSINESS REPORT. (HK). **73**

CHINA AND OURSELVES. (CN/0828-1602). **4943**

CHINA-BRITAIN TRADE REVIEW. (UK/0952-9756). **Qty:** 25. **827**

CHINA BUSINESS & TRADE. (US/0731-7700). **Qty:** 5 per year. **827**

CHINA BUSINESS REVIEW, THE. (US/0163-7169). **Qty:** 3. **657**

CHINA EXCHANGE NEWS. (US/0272-0086). **5195**

CHINA FACTS & FIGURES ANNUAL. (US/0190-602X). **2502**

CHINA INFORMATION. (NE/0920-203X). **4468**

CHINA LETTER. (US/0529-3189). **657**

CHINA MARKET. (HK). **1633**

CHINA NOTES. (US/0009-4412). **4943**

CHINA NOW. (UK/0045-6764). **Qty:** 20. **2502**

CHINA PRAYER LETTER. (HK). **5058**

CHINA QUARTERLY (LONDON). (UK/0305-7410). **2648**

CHINA REPORT (NEW DELHI). (II/0009-4455). **2648**

CHINA RIGHTS FORUM. (US/1068-4166). **Qty:** 4-10. **4505**

CHINA STUDY JOURNAL. (UK/0956-4314). **4943**

CHINA UPDATE (OUD-HEVERLEE, BELGIUM). (BE). **2502**

CHINESE AMERICAN FORUM. (US/0895-4690). **1731**

CHINESE ANNALS OF MATHEMATICS. SER. B. (CC/0252-9599). **3500**

CHINESE CULTURE. (CH/0009-4544). **3374**

CHINESE ECONOMIC STUDIES. (US/0009-4552). **1469**

CHINESE EDUCATION. (US/0009-4560). **1731**

CHINESE HISTORIANS. (US/1043-643X). **Qty:** 10-15. **2649**

CHINESE JOURNAL OF ACOUSTICS. (CC). **4452**

CHINESE JOURNAL OF BOTANY. (CC/1001-0718). **506**

CHINESE LAW AND GOVERNMENT. (US/0009-4609). **2950**

CHINESE LITERATURE (MADISON). (US/0161-9705). **3375**

CHINESE MUSIC. (US/0192-3749). **4109**

CHINESE STUDIES IN PHILOSOPHY. (US/0023-8627). **4343**

CHINESE THEOLOGICAL REVIEW. (US/0896-7660). **4943**

CHINESE YEARBOOK OF INTERNATIONAL LAW AND AFFAIRS. (US/0731-0854). **3126**

CHING FENG (ENGLISH EDITION). (HK/0009-4668). **4943**

CHIP CHATS. (US/0577-9294). **633**

CHIP'S CLOSET CLEANER. (US/1064-9719). **2530**

CHIRIBOTAN. (JA/0577-9316). **Qty:** 6. **5094**

CHIRICU (BLOOMINGTON, IND. : 1981). (US/0277-7223). **Qty:** 1-2. **2613**

CHIRIHAK. (KO). **2558**

CHIROPODY REVIEW. (UK/0009-4714). **Qty:** 6. **3917**

CHIROPRACTIC JOURNAL OF AUSTRALIA. (AT/1036-0913). **4379**

CHIROPRACTIC PRODUCTS. (US/1041-2360). **3563**

CHIROPRACTIC REPORT, THE. (CN/0836-1444). **Qty:** 1-2. **4380**

CHIRURGIA. (IT/0394-9508). **3961**

CHIRURGIA DEGLI ORGANI DI MOVIMENTO. (IT/0009-4749). **3961**

CHIRURGIA GASTROENTEROLOGICA. (IT/0009-4765). **3743**

CHIRURGIA ITALIANA. (IT/0009-4773). **3962**

CHISHOLM TRAIL, THE. (US). **2443**

CHITARRE. (IT). **4109**

CHITTENANGO, BRIDGEPORT TIMES. (US). **5715**

CHOCOLATE NEWS. (UK). **2331**

CHOCOLATE SINGLES. (US/0882-4460). **2258**

CHOCOLATIER. (US/0887-591X). **2331**

CHOCTAW ADVOCATE, THE. (US). **5625**

CHOCTAW COMMUNITY NEWS. (US). **5700**

CHOICE. (US/0009-4978). **3201**

CHOICE INDIA. (II). **5195**

CHOICES (EVANSTON, ILL.). (US/0735-6358). **1062**

CHOIX : DOCUMENTATION AUDIOVISUELLE. (CN/0706-2257). **1891**

CHOIX : DOCUMENTATION IMPRIMEE. (CN/0706-2249). **3201**

CHOLESTEROL AND LIPOPROTEINS. (UK/0964-7597). **485**

CHORAL JOURNAL, THE. (US/0009-5028). **4109**

CHORUS! (DULUTH, GA.). (US/1044-7857). **4109**

CHORUS (HALIFAX). (CN/0821-1108). **4109**

CHOSON ILBO (MIJU PAN). (US/0743-7056). **Qty:** 306. **5715**

CHRIST TO THE WORLD. (IT/0011-1465). **4943**

CHRISTIAN ACTIVITIES CALENDAR (MIDDLE ATLANTIC ED.). (US/0883-4210). **4944**

CHRISTIAN

CHRISTIAN BEGINNINGS. (US/1058-8558). **4944**

CHRISTIAN CENTURY (1902), THE. (US/0009-5281). **4944**

CHRISTIAN CHALLENGE, THE. (US/0890-6793). Qty: rarely. **5058**

CHRISTIAN COMMUNITY (COLUMBUS), THE. (US/0145-3297). **4944**

CHRISTIAN COMMUNITY : THE MAGAZINE OF THE NATIONAL CENTRE FOR CHRISTIAN COMMUNITIES AND NETWORKS. (UK). **4944**

CHRISTIAN COUNSELING TODAY. (US/1076-9668). Qty: 12. **4944**

CHRISTIAN COURIER. (CN/1192-3415). Qty: 40. **5058**

CHRISTIAN EDUCATION DIGEST. (US/8756-1751). **4944**

CHRISTIAN EDUCATION JOURNAL. (US/0739-8913). Qty: 3 per year. **4944**

CHRISTIAN EDUCATORS JOURNAL. (US). **4944**

CHRISTIAN HERALD. (US/0009-5354). **431**

CHRISTIAN HERALD WORTHING. (UK/0953-4385). Qty: 350. **5058**

CHRISTIAN HOME AND SCHOOL. (US). Qty: Lori Feonstra. **2278**

CHRISTIAN INDEX, THE. (US). Qty: varies. **5058**

CHRISTIAN JOURNAL (FORT WORTH, TEX.). (US/1056-3644). Qty: 6-10. **4945**

CHRISTIAN LEADER (HILLSBORO). (US/0009-5419). **5058**

CHRISTIAN LIBRARIAN (CEDARVILLE, OHIO), THE. (US/0412-3131). **3202**

CHRISTIAN LIFE COMMUNITIES HARVEST. (US/0739-6422). Qty: 20-25. **4945**

CHRISTIAN MEDICAL & DENTAL SOCIETY JOURNAL. (US). Qty: 4. **3563**

CHRISTIAN MESSENGER. (GH/0009-5478). **4945**

CHRISTIAN MINISTRY, THE. (US/0033-4138). **4945**

CHRISTIAN MUSIC. (UK). **4109**

CHRISTIAN NEW AGE QUARTERLY. (US/0899-7292). **4945**

CHRISTIAN NEWS (NEW HAVEN, MO.). (US/0009-5516). Qty: 250. **4945**

CHRISTIAN OBSERVER (MANASSAS, VA.). (US/0899-2584). **4945**

CHRISTIAN PARAPSYCHOLOGIST, THE. (UK/0308-6194). **4241**

CHRISTIAN RENEWAL. (CN/0820-7593). Qty: 25-40. **4945**

CHRISTIAN RESEARCH JOURNAL. (US). Qty: 8-12. **4945**

CHRISTIAN RETAILING. (US/0892-0281). **952**

CHRISTIAN SCHOLAR'S REVIEW. (US/0017-2251). **4946**

CHRISTIAN SCIENCE MONITOR (1983), THE. (US/0882-7729). **5688**

CHRISTIAN SOCIAL ACTION (WASHINGTON, D.C.). (US/0897-0459). **4946**

CHRISTIAN STANDARD. (US/0009-5656). **4946**

CHRISTIAN STATESMAN. (US/0009-5664). Qty: (6-8). **4946**

CHRISTIAN VISION. (CN/0843-7602). **3375**

CHRISTIAN WEEK. (CN/0835-412X). **4946**

CHRISTIANISME AU VINGTIEME SIECLE, LE. (FR/0009-5729). **4946**

CHRISTIANITY AND CRISIS. (US/0009-5745). **4946**

CHRISTIANITY & LITERATURE. (US/0148-3331). Qty: 80. **3375**

CHRISTIANITY TODAY (WASHINGTON). (US/0009-5753). **4946**

CHRISTIAN'S EXPOSITOR. (US/1073-2209). Qty: 10. **4946**

CHRISTIANS WRITING. (AT/0729-4042). Qty: 20. **3375**

CHRISTOPHER STREET. (US/0146-7921). **2793**

CHROMIUM REVIEW. (SA/0256-0038). **4000**

CHRONIC DISEASES IN CANADA. (CN/0228-8699). **3563**

CHRONIC PAIN LETTER. (US). **3564**

CHRONICA (DAVIS). (US/0009-5931). **3375**

CHRONICLE. (US). **5695**

CHRONICLE (BARTON, VT.). (US/0746-438X). Qty: 6. **5757**

CHRONICLE CAREER INDEX. (US/0276-0355). **4203**

CHRONICLE OF HIGHER EDUCATION, THE. (US/0009-5982). **1815**

CHRONICLE OF PHILANTHROPY, THE. (US/1040-676X). **4335**

CHRONICLE OF THE HORSE, THE. (US/0009-5990). **2798**

CHRONICLE OF THE U.S. CLASSIC POSTAL ISSUES, THE. (US/0009-6008). **2784**

CHRONICLE (OMAHA, NEB.), THE. (US/0030-2201). **4188**

CHRONICLE SUMMARY REPORT. (US/0193-1601). **1815**

CHRONICLE, THE. (US). Qty: 6. **5230**

CHRONICLE TWO-YEAR COLLEGE DATABOOK. (US/0191-3662). **1815**

CHRONICLE VOCATIONAL SCHOOL MANUAL. (US/0276-0371). **1912**

CHRONICLES OF OKLAHOMA. (US/0009-6024). **2728**

CHRONICLES (PHILADELPHIA, PA.). (US/0893-2921). **2443**

CHRONICLES (ROCKFORD, ILL.). (US/0887-5731). **2844**

CHRONIQUE DE LA RECHERCHE MINIERE. (FR/0182-564X). **1371**

CHRONIQUE DE L'U.G.G.I. (FR/0047-1259). **1404**

CHRONIQUE D'EGYPTE. (BE/0009-6067). **265**

CHRONIQUE FEMINISTE. (BE). **5553**

CHRONIQUE JUDICIAIRE D'HAITI, LA. (HT). **3126**

CHRONIQUES ITALIENNES. (FR/0766-4257). **3273**

CHRONOBIOLOGIA. (IT/0390-0037). **3795**

CHRONOSTRATIGRAPHIE UND NEOSTRATOTYPEN. (GW/0578-0578). **1353**

CHRYSALIS (NEW YORK, N.Y.). (US/0888-9384). Qty: 12 or more. **4343**

CHULPAN MUNHWA. (KO/0009-6245). **4828**

CHUNG-HUA CH'I KUAN I CHIH TSA CHIH. (CC/0254-1785). **3564**

CHUNG-HUA MIN KUO CHI CHI SHE PEI HSUAN LU. (CH). **2111**

CHUNG-HUA PI FU KO TSA CHIH. (CC/0412-4030). **3718**

CHUNG-KUO HAI YUN. (HK). **5448**

CHUNG-KUO SHU-HUA. (HK/0529-6463). **377**

CHUNG-KUO TA LU YEN CHIU (KUO LI CHENG CHIH TA HSUEH. KUO CHI KUAN HSI YEN CHIU CHUNG HSIN). (CH). **4518**

CHUNG-SHAN TA HSUEH HSUEH PAO. CHE HSUEH SHE HUI KO HSUEH PAN. (CC/0412-443X). **5195**

CHUNG YANG MIN TSU HSUEH YUAN HSUEH PAO / ZHONGYANG MINZU XUEYUAN XUEBAO. (CC). **2258**

CHURCH ADVOCATE (FINDLAY, OHIO), THE. (US/0009-630X). **4947**

CHURCH AND SOCIETY (NEW YORK). (US/0037-7805). **4947**

CHURCH AND STATE. (US/0009-6334). Qty: varies. **4468**

CHURCH & SYNAGOGUE LIBRARIES. (US/0009-6342). Qty: varies. **3202**

CHURCH GROWTH DIGEST. (UK/0268-7658). Qty: 40. **4947**

CHURCH GROWTH TODAY. (US). **4947**

CHURCH HERITAGE. (AT/0156-224X). Qty: 6-8. **4947**

CHURCH HISTORY. (US/0009-6407). **4947**

CHURCH MANAGEMENT. (US/0009-6431). Qty: 50 per year. **4947**

CHURCH MUSIC QUARTERLY. (UK/0307-6334). **4109**

CHURCH MUSIC REPORT : TCMR, THE. (US/1071-9903). Qty: 12. **4109**

CHURCH MUSICIAN, THE. (US/0009-6466). **4109**

CHURCH (NEW YORK, N.Y.). (US/0883-5667). **4947**

CHURCH OBSERVER. (UK/0009-6482). **4947**

CHURCH OF ENGLAND NEWSPAPER : CEN. (UK/0964-816X). **2514**

CHURCH OF GOD MISSIONS. (US/0009-6504). **4947**

CHURCH RECREATION MAGAZINE. (US/0162-4652). **4849**

CHURCH RESOURCE DIRECTORY. (US). **4947**

CHURCH SECRETARY'S SWAP SHOP, THE. (US/0738-6885). **4948**

CHURCH TEACHERS. (US/0164-6451). **4948**

CHURCH TIMES, THE. (US). **4948**

CHURCH WORLD. (US/0009-6601). **5027**

CHURCHMAN (LONDON. 1879). (UK/0009-661X). **4948**

CIAT INTERNATIONAL. (CK). Qty: 10. **74**

CICINDELA. (US/0590-6334). **5580**

CIEL ET TERRE. (BE/0009-6709). **394**

CIENCIA DA INFORMACAO. (BL/0100-1965). **3202**

CIENCIA HOJE : REVISAT DE DIVULGACAO CIENTIFICA DA SOCIEDADE BRASILEIRA PARA O PROGRESSO DA CIENCIA. (BL/0101-8515). **5094**

CIENCIA (MEXICO CITY, MEXICO). (MX/0185-075X). **5094**

CIENCIA PEDIATRIKA (MADRID, SPAIN : 1986). (SP). **3902**

CIENCIA TOMISTA. (SP/0210-0398). **5027**

CIENCIA Y DESARROLLO. (MX/0185-0008). **5094**

CIENTIFICA (JABOTICABAL). (BL/0100-0039). **5507**

CIERVO, EL. (SP/0045-6896). **4948**

CIFRAS. (CK/0120-5331). **5799**

CIM BULLETIN. (CN/0317-0926). **2136**

CIM-MANAGEMENT. (GW/0179-2679). **1174**

CIMAISE. (FR/0009-6830). **347**

CIMARRON REVIEW. (US/0009-6849). Qty: 8. **3461**

CIMBEBASIA : JOURNAL OF THE STATE MUSEUM, WINDHOEK. (SX/1012-4926). **5095**

CIMENTS, BETONS, PLATRES, CHAUX. (FR/0397-006X). Qty: 3/yr. **607**

CINCINNATI ENQUIRER (CINCINNATI, OHIO : 1872). (US). **5727**

CINE & MEDIA. (BE/1016-9660). **1106**

CINE BULLES. (CN/0820-8921). Qty: 20. **4065**

CINE CUBANO. (CU/0009-6946). **4065**

CINE-FICHES DE GRAND ANGLE, LES. (BE/0773-2279). **4065**

CINEASTE (NEW YORK, N.Y.). (US/0009-7004). **4066**

CINEFAN. (US/0095-1447). **4066**

CINEFEX. (US/0198-1056). **4066**

CINEFOCUS. (US/1059-0900). Qty: 3. **4066**

CINEFORUM. (IT/0009-7039). **4066**

CINEMA D'OGGI. (IT/0392-9981). **4066**

CINEMA E CINEMA. (IT). **4066**

CINEMA IN INDIA. (II). **4066**

CINEMA NUOVO. (IT/0009-711X). Qty: 10/yr. **4066**

CINEMA PAPERS. (AT/0311-3639). Qty: 6. **4066**

CINEMA TECHNOLOGY. (UK). Qty: 3-4. **4066**

CINEMA (ZURICH, SWITZERLAND). (SZ/1010-3627). **4066**

CINEMACABRE. (US/0198-1064). **4066**

CINEMAGIC (NEW YORK, N.Y.). (US/0090-3000). **4067**

CINEMAS (MONTREAL). (CN/1181-6945). Qty: 10. **4067**

CINEVUE. (US/0895-805X). **4368**

CIRCA (BELFAST, NORTHERN IRELAND). (UK/0263-9475). Qty: 4-6. **347**

CIRCAEA : BULLETIN OF THE ASSOCIATION FOR ENVIRONMENTAL ARCHAEOLOGY. (UK/0268-425X). Qty: varies. **266**

CIRCUIT (MONTREAL). (CN/0821-1876). **3273**

CIRCUIT NEWS. (US/1058-9317). **2038**

CIRCUIT RIDER (NASHVILLE), THE. (US/0146-9924). **5058**

CIRCUIT RIDER (SPRINGFIELD, ILL.), THE. (US/0741-8264). **2443**

CIRCUIT WORLD. (UK/0305-6120). **2038**

CIRCULATION (NEW YORK, N.Y.). (US/0009-7322). **3702**

CIRCULATION RESEARCH. (US/0009-7330). **3702**

CIRCULO - CIRCULO DE CULTURA PANAMERICANO. (US/0009-7349). Qty: 15. **3376**

CIRCUS REPORT, THE. (US/0889-5996). **4849**

CIRP ANNALS. (SZ/0007-8506). **2111**

CIRUGIA DEL URUGUAY. (UY/0009-7381). **3962**

CIRUGIA PLASTICA IBERO-LATINOAMERICANA. (SP/0376-7892). **3962**

CISEM INFORMAZIONI. (IT). **1732**

CISSNA PARK NEWS, THE. (US). **Qty: 15. 5659**

CISTERCIAN STUDIES QUARTERLY. (US/1062-6549). **5027**

CITE (HOUSTON, TEX.). (US/8755-0415). **295**

CITEAUX, COMMENTARII CISTERCIENSES. (BE/0774-4919). **Qty: approx. 20. 5027**

CITES NOUVELLES. (CN/0319-5198). **5782**

CITIES & VILLAGES. (US/0009-7535). **4638**

CITIES (LONDON, ENGLAND). (UK/0264-2751). **2817**

CITIZEN ADVOCACY FORUM. (US/1071-2321). **Qty: 1-2. 5279**

CITIZEN PARTICIPATION (MEDFORD). (US/0198-8468). **4468**

CITIZENS' GUIDE TO LOCAL GOVERNMENT (OLYMPIA, WASH.). (US). **4638**

CITRUS AND SUB-TROPICAL FRUIT JOURNAL, THE. (SA/0257-2095). **167**

CITTA DI VITA. (IT/0009-7632). **4948**

CITY & COUNTRY CLUB LIFE. (US/0897-4926). **2530**

CITY & TOWN (NORTH LITTLE ROCK, ARK.). (US/0193-8371). **4638**

CITY HALL DIGEST. (US/0190-0005). **Qty: 36. 4638**

CITY JOURNAL (NEW YORK, N.Y.), THE. (US/1060-8540). **Qty: 4. 4468**

CITY LIGHTS REVIEW. (US/1045-1943). **3376**

CITY LIMITS. (US/0199-0330). **2818**

CITY OF LONDON LAW REVIEW. (UK/0306-9788). **2950**

CITY OF LOS ANGELES PLANNING AND ZONING CODE : CHAPTER 1 OF THE LOS ANGELES MUNICIPAL CODE. (US). **2818**

CITY PAPER. (US/0195-0843). **5686**

CITY SUN, THE. (US/8750-2720). **Qty: 6. 5715**

CIUDAD DE DIOS, LA. (SP/0009-7756). **4948**

CIVIC AFFAIRS. (II/0009-7772). **4638**

CIVIC PUBLIC WORKS. (CN/0829-772X). **4760**

CIVIL AFFAIRS JOURNAL AND NEWSLETTER. (US/0045-7035). **4638**

CIVIL AVIATION TRAINING : CAT. (UK/0960-9024). **16**

CIVIL ENGINEER IN SOUTH AFRICA, THE. (SA/0009-7845). **2020**

CIVIL ENGINEERING SURVEYOR. (UK/0266-139X). **2021**

CIVIL ENGINEERING SYSTEMS. (UK/0263-0257). **2021**

CIVIL JUSTICE QUARTERLY. (UK/0261-9261). **3089**

CIVIL PROTECTION. (UK/0961-2564). **Qty: 2-3. 1072**

CIVIL RIGHTS & CIVIL LIBERTIES LITIGATION : A GUIDE TO [SECTION SYMBOL] 1983 / SHELDON H. NAHMOD. (US). **4506**

CIVIL WAR HISTORY. (US/0009-8078). **2728**

CIVIL WAR NEWS, THE. (US/1053-1181). **Qty: 150. 2728**

CIVIL WAR REGIMENTS. (US/1055-3266). **Qty: 32. 2728**

CIVIL WAR ROUND TABLE DIGEST. (US/0009-8086). **2728**

CIVIL WAR TOKEN JOURNAL, THE. (US). **2780**

CIVILIAN-BASED DEFENSE. (US/0886-6015). **Qty: 2. 4039**

CIVILISATIONS. (BE/0009-8140). **5242**

CIVILTA CATTOLICA, LA. (IT/0009-8167). **5027**

CIVILTA CLASSICA E CRISTIANA. (IT/0392-8632). **3273**

CIVIS MUNDI. (NE/0030-3283). **4540**

CIVITAS. REVISTA ESPANOLA DE DERECHO DEL TRABAJO. (SP/0212-6095). **2951**

CJ INTERNATIONAL. (US/0882-0244). **3160**

CLA JOURNAL. (US/0007-8549). **3273**

CLADISTICS. (US/0748-3007). **451**

CLAIMS (SEATTLE, WASH.). (US/0895-7991). **2878**

CLAIRLIEU : TIJDSCHRIFT GEWIJD ANN DE GESCHIEDENIS DER KRUISHEREN. (BE). **2683**

CLAIRON (MONTREAL). (CN/0710-099X). **5016**

CLAN DIGGER. (US/8755-3635). **2443**

CLANDIGGER (EDMONTON). (CN/0226-2436). **2443**

CLAO JOURNAL, THE. (US/0733-8902). **3873**

CLARIN : REVISTA DE CULTURA. (SP). **3461**

CLARINET (POCATELLO, IDAHO), THE. (US/0361-5553). **4110**

CLARION-LEDGER, THE. (US/0744-9526). **5700**

CLARION (NEW YORK. 1972). (US/0191-8079). **1815**

CLARISWORKS JOURNAL. (US/1059-6542). **1174**

CLARK CLARION, THE. (US/0883-2692). **2443**

CLARKSVILLE TIMES, THE. (US/1040-2489). **Qty: 6. 5748**

CLASS ACT. (US). **Qty: 2-3. 1732**

CLASS (NEW YORK, N.Y.). (US/0747-3826). **Qty: 40-50. 2486**

CLASS RACEHORSES OF AUSTRALIA AND NEW ZEALAND. (AT/0814-2513). **2798**

CLASSIC AND SPORTSCAR. (UK). **Qty: 24. 5411**

CLASSIC IMAGES. (US/0275-8423). **Qty: 150. 4067**

CLASSIC TOY TRAINS. (US/0895-0997). **2772**

CLASSICAL AND MODERN LITERATURE. (US/0197-2227). **1075**

CLASSICAL ANTIQUITY. (US/0278-6656). **1075**

CLASSICAL BULLETIN (ST. LOUIS, MO.), THE. (US/0009-8337). **Qty: 25. 1075**

CLASSICAL JOURNAL (CLASSICAL ASSOCIATION OF THE MIDDLE WEST AND SOUTH), THE. (US/0009-8353). **1075**

CLASSICAL MUSIC. (UK). **4110**

CLASSICAL OUTLOOK, THE. (US/0009-8361). **1075**

CLASSICAL REVIEW. (UK/0009-840X). **1076**

CLASSICAL WORLD, THE. (US/0009-8418). **Qty: 200-250. 1076**

CLASSMATE. (CN/0315-906X). **Qty: 6-10. 1732**

CLAUDEL STUDIES. (US/0090-1237). **3376**

CLAVIER. (US/0009-854X). **4110**

CLAY COUNTY FREE PRESS. (US). **5763**

CLAY MINERALS. (UK/0009-8558). **1438**

CLAY TIMES-JOURNAL, THE. (US/1053-9123). **5625**

CLAYS AND CLAY MINERALS. (US/0009-8604). **1438**

CLAYTON-FILLMORE REPORT, THE. (US/1047-6083). **Qty: 12/yr. 4835**

CLE JOURNAL AND REGISTER, THE. (US). **Qty: unlimited. 2951**

CLEAN AIR. (UK/0300-5143). **2226**

CLEAN YIELD, THE. (US/0882-3820). **895**

CLEANING AND RESTORATION. (US/0886-9901). **5349**

CLEARING HOUSE (MENASHA, WIS.). (US/0009-8655). **1732**

CLEARINGHOUSE REVIEW. (US/0009-868X). **3179**

CLEARY NEWS. (US/0883-7716). **2443**

CLEBURNE COUNTY HISTORICAL SOCIETY JOURNAL. (US/0740-5987). **2728**

CLEBURNE NEWS (HEFLIN, ALA.). (US). **5626**

CLEF, LA. (CN). **2951**

CLEM LABINE'S TRADITIONAL BUILDING. (US/0898-0284). **Qty: 18. 295**

CLEMENTS' ENCYCLOPEDIA OF WORLD GOVERNMENTS. BIANNUAL SUPPLEMENT. (US/0733-0286). **4468**

CLENEXCHANGE (MILFORD, OHIO : 1984). (US). **3202**

CLEVELAND ADVOCATE (CLEVELAND, TEX.), THE. (US/0746-7125). **5748**

CLEVELAND ENGINEERING. (US/0009-8809). **1968**

CLEVELAND MAGAZINE. (US/0160-8533). **Qty: 12. 2486**

CLIENT COUNSELING UPDATE : CCU. (US/0276-752X). **2951**

CLIMATIC CHANGE. (NE/0165-0009). **1422**

CLIMATOLOGICAL BULLETIN (MONTREAL). (CN/0541-6256). **1422**

CLIMBING (ASPEN, COLO.). (US/0045-7159). **4871**

CLINICA CHIMICA ACTA. (NE/0009-8981). **972**

CLINICA DIETOLOGICA, LA. (IT/0392-7318). **4188**

CLINICA E INVESTIGACION EN GINECOLOGIA Y OBSTETRICIA. (SP/0210-573X). **3758**

CLINICA E LABORATORIO (ROMA). (IT/0391-2035). **3565**

CLINICA EUROPEA. (IT/0009-9007). **3565**

CLINICA Y ANALISIS GRUPAL. (SP/0210-0657). **4581**

CLINICAL AND EXPERIMENTAL DERMATOLOGY. (UK/0307-6938). **3718**

CLINICAL AND EXPERIMENTAL HYPERTENSION. PART A, THEORY AND PRACTICE. (US/0730-0077). **3703**

CLINICAL AND EXPERIMENTAL HYPERTENSION. PART B, HYPERTENSION IN PREGNANCY. (US/0730-0085). **3758**

CLINICAL & EXPERIMENTAL METASTASIS. (UK/0262-0898). **3815**

CLINICAL AND EXPERIMENTAL OBSTETRICS & GYNECOLOGY. (IT/0390-6663). **3758**

CLINICAL AND EXPERIMENTAL OPTOMETRY. (AT/0816-4622). **4215**

CLINICAL AND EXPERIMENTAL RHEUMATOLOGY. (IT/0392-856X). **3565**

CLINICAL AND INVESTIGATIVE MEDICINE. (UK/0147-958X). **3565**

CLINICAL AND LABORATORY HAEMATOLOGY. (UK/0141-9854). **3771**

CLINICAL AUTONOMIC RESEARCH : OFFICIAL JOURNAL OF THE CLINICAL AUTONOMIC RESEARCH SOCIETY. (UK/0959-9851). **3565**

CLINICAL BIOFEEDBACK AND HEALTH. (CN/0827-1038). **4581**

CLINICAL CARDIOLOGY (MAHWAH, N.J.). (US/0160-9289). **3703**

CLINICAL CONNECTION, THE. (US/0890-409X). **Qty: 4. 4385**

CLINICAL CYTOGENETICS. (UK/0260-5872). **535**

CLINICAL ECOLOGY. (US/0735-9306). **3565**

CLINICAL ENDOCRINOLOGY (OXFORD). (UK/0300-0664). **3727**

CLINICAL GENETICS. (DK/0009-9163). **543**

CLINICAL GERONTOLOGIST. (US/0731-7115). **3750**

CLINICAL HEMORHEOLOGY. (US/0271-5198). **3771**

CLINICAL INTENSIVE CARE : INTERNATIONAL JOURNAL OF CRITICAL & CORONARY CARE MEDICINE. (UK/0956-3075). **3703**

CLINICAL LAB LETTER. (US/0197-8454). **3893**

CLINICAL LABORATORY SCIENCE. (US/0894-959X). **3566**

CLINICAL NEPHROLOGY. (GW/0301-0430). **3989**

CLINICAL NEUROLOGY AND NEUROSURGERY. (NE/0303-8467). **3830**

CLINICAL NEUROPATHOLOGY. (GW/0722-5091). **3894**

CLINICAL NUCLEAR MEDICINE. (US/0363-9762). **3847**

CLINICAL NURSING RESEARCH. (US/1054-7738). **3853**

CLINICAL NUTRITION. (UK/0261-5614). **4188**

CLINICAL OTOLARYNGOLOGY AND ALLIED SCIENCES. (UK/0307-7772). **3887**

CLINICAL PHARMACOKINETICS. (US/0312-5963). **4296**

CLINICAL PHARMACY. (US/0278-2677). **4297**

CLINICAL PSYCHIATRY NEWS. (US/0270-6644). **3923**

CLINICAL PSYCHOLOGY REVIEW. (US/0272-7358). **4581**

CLINICAL RADIOLOGY. (UK/0009-9260). **3940**

CLINICAL SCIENCE (1979). (UK/0143-5221). **485**

CLINICAL SOCIOLOGY REVIEW. (US/0730-840X). **5242**

CLINICAL SPORTS MEDICINE. (UK/0953-9875). **3953**

CLINICAL SUPERVISOR, THE. (US/0732-5223). **4581**

CLINICIAN'S RESEARCH DIGEST. (US/8756-3207). **4581**

CLINIQUE OPHTALMOLOGIQUE PARIS, LA. (FR/0009-9368). **3873**

CLINTON COUNTY NEWS. (US). **Qty: 15. 5659**

CLINTON DAILY ITEM. (US). **5688**

CLIO (FORT WAYNE, IND.). (US/0884-2043). **3376**

CLIO MEDICA. (NE/0366-676X). **3567**

CLIO (SANTO DOMINGO). (DR/0009-9376). **2844**

CLIS OBSERVER. (II/0970-0943). **3202**

CLOCKMAKER (HINCKLEY). (UK/0961-5032). **2772**

CLOCKWATCH REVIEW. (US/0740-9311). Qty: 6-8. **317**

CLOTH DOLL, THE. (US/8755-2655). **371**

CLOVIS NEWS-JOURNAL. (US). **5712**

CLUB INFORMATIONS NANTERRE. (FR/1161-1804). **1968**

CLUES (BOWLING GREEN, OHIO). (US/0742-4248). **5074**

CLUMBER SPANIEL CORRESPONDENCE. (AT). Qty: 6-12. **4286**

CMAJ. CANADIAN MEDICAL ASSOCIATION JOURNAL. (CN/0820-3946). **3567**

CMEA NEWS. (US/0007-8638). **4110**

CMM, CONFECTIONERY MANUFACTURE AND MARKETING. (UK/0007-8654). **3477**

CMN. COMMON MARKET NEWS. (UK/0300-4406). **1470**

CMN OFFICE MACHINE NEWS. (US/0889-5880). **4211**

CN LINES. (US/1061-9739). **5430**

CO-EXISTENCE (DORDRECHT). (NE/0587-5994). **4518**

CO-OPERATIVE ASSOCIATIONS IN NOVA SCOTIA. (CN/0318-3955). **1541**

COACHES' CORNER, THE. (US). **2918**

COACHING DIRECTOR. (AT/0814-7752). **4890**

COACHING VOLLEYBALL. (US/0894-4237). Qty: 2-3. **4890**

COACHING WOMEN'S BASKETBALL. (US/0894-4245). **4890**

COAL (CHICAGO, ILL. : 1988). (US/1040-7820). **2137**

COAL PEOPLE. (US/0748-6073). **2728**

COAL PREPARATION (NEW YORK, N.Y.). (US/0734-9343). **2137**

COAL TRANSPORTATION REPORT. (US/0732-8397). **5379**

COALFIELD PROGRESS, THE. (US/0889-3330). **5758**

COALITION CLOSE-UP. (US/0730-1251). **4518**

COALTRANS INTERNATIONAL. (UK). Qty: 16. **2137**

COALTRANS WORCESTER PARK. (UK/0269-381X). **1935**

COAST WATCH. (US/0194-5742). Qty: 6. **1448**

COASTAL CRUISING. (US/0897-750X). Qty: 3-6. **4890**

COASTAL MANAGEMENT. (US/0892-0753). **2190**

COASTAL OBSERVER (PAWLEYS ISLAND, S.C.). (US/8750-3425). Qty: 6-8 per year. **5742**

COASTAL RESEARCH. (US/0271-5376). **1353**

COASTAL ZONE MANAGEMENT. (US/0045-723X). **4253**

COASTGUARD. (UK). **4175**

COAT OF ARMS, THE. (UK/0010-003X). **2443**

COATINGS. (CN/0225-6363). **4223**

COATNEY/COURTNEY EXCHANGE. (US). **2443**

COBBLESTONE. (US/0199-5197). **1062**

COCHRANE TIMES. (CN/0319-745X). **5782**

COCKRELL CONNECTION, THE. (US/0891-5296). **2443**

COCONUT STATISTICS / COMPILED AND EXPANDED BY UCAP RESEARCH DEPARTMENT. (PH). **152**

COCOS : JOURNAL OF THE COCONUT RESEARCH INSTITUTE OF SRI LANKA. (CE/0255-4100). **167**

CODA MAGAZINE. (CN/0820-926X). **4110**

CODESRIA BULLETIN. (SG/0850-8712). Qty: 4. **5195**

CODY ENTERPRISE, THE. (US/0747-2498). Qty: 2. **5772**

COFFEE & COCOA INTERNATIONAL. (UK/0262-5938). **2366**

COFFEY COUNTY TODAY. (US/0745-838X). Qty: 10. **5675**

COFFEY COUSINS' CLEARINGHOUSE. (US/0749-758X). **2443**

COGENERATION & RESOURCE RECOVERY. (US). **1935**

COGENERATION JOURNAL, THE. (US/0883-5985). **4400**

COGNITION & EMOTION. (UK/0269-9931). **4581**

COGNITION (SCARBOROUGH). (CN/0227-0781). **167**

COGNITIVE DEVELOPMENT. (US/0885-2014). **4581**

COGNITIVE SCIENCE. (US/0364-0213). **1212**

COGNIZER REPORT. (US/1057-8374). **1175**

COGNIZER REPORT. (US). **1212**

COI. COUNTERTRADE AND OFFSET INTELLIGENCE. (UK/0950-916X). Qty: (3-4). **827**

COIFFURE DE PARIS, LA. (FR). **402**

COIN MAGAZINE. (US). **2780**

COIN SLOT (LUZERNE, PA.), THE. (US/0745-8533). **250**

COIN WORLD. (US/0010-0447). **2780**

COINAGE. (US/0010-0455). **2780**

COINS (IOLA, WIS.). (US/0010-0471). **2780**

COLADA. (SP/0010-0544). **4000**

COLD REGIONS SCIENCE AND TECHNOLOGY. (NE/0165-232X). **1968**

COLE CHRONICLE. (US/0887-1264). **2443**

COLE PAPERS, THE. (US/1062-6727). Qty: 3-5. **2918**

COLECCION ESTUDIOS CIEPLAN. (CL/0716-0631). **1552**

COLECCION JUVENIL MC. (SP). **2278**

COLEMAN COUNTY CHRONICLE. (US). Qty: 2. **5748**

COLLABORATION (HIGH FALLS). (US/0164-1522). **4344**

COLLECTANEA FRANCISCANA. (IT/0010-0749). Qty: 200-250. **5027**

COLLECTED LETTERS / CORRESPONDENCE SOCIETY OF SURGEONS. (US/0162-6477). **3962**

COLLECTED LETTERS OF THE INTERNATIONAL CORRESPONDENCE SOCIETY OF OBSTETRICIANS, GYNECOLOGISTS. (US/0443-9058). **3759**

COLLECTIBLE AUTOMOBILE. (US/0742-812X). **5411**

COLLECTIBLE NEWSPAPERS. (US/1076-4356). Qty: 3. **2772**

COLLECTION AGENCY REPORT. (US/1052-4029). Qty: 4 /yr. **658**

COLLECTION BUILDING. (US/0160-4953). **3202**

COLLECTION FORUM (OTTAWA). (CN/0831-4985). **4165**

COLLECTION MANAGEMENT. (US/0146-2679). **3202**

COLLECTION ORGANISATION PEDAGOGIQUE. (CN/0820-7860). **1861**

COLLECTIONS (COLUMBIA, S.C.). (US/1046-2252). **4087**

COLLECTIONS FOR A HISTORY OF STAFFORDSHIRE. (UK). **2684**

COLLECTOR CAR NEWS. (US/0888-1944). **2772**

COLLECTORS JOURNAL (VINTON). (US/0164-6915). **5669**

COLLECTORS' SHOWCASE (SAN DIEGO, CALIF.). (US/0744-5989). **250**

COLLEGE AND JUNIOR TENNIS. (US/0279-1153). **4890**

COLLEGE & RESEARCH LIBRARIES. (US/0010-0870). **3203**

COLLEGE AND UNIVERSITY. (US/0010-0889). **1816**

COLLEGE BAND DIRECTORS NATIONAL ASSOCIATION JOURNAL. (US/0742-8480). **4110**

COLLEGE BOARD REVIEW, THE. (US/0010-0951). **1816**

COLLEGE BOUND (EVANSTON, ILL.). (US/1068-7912). Qty: 50. **1816**

COLLEGE BROADCASTER. (US/1055-0461). Qty: 4. **1130**

COLLEGE COMPOSITION AND COMMUNICATION. (US/0010-096X). **1816**

COLLEGE ENGLISH. (US/0010-0994). **3274**

COLLEGE FINANCIAL AID STRATEGIES. (US). **1816**

COLLEGE HOCKEY. (US/1061-6357). **4890**

COLLEGE LITERATURE. (US/0093-3139). Qty: 30/yr. **3376**

COLLEGE MATHEMATICS JOURNAL, THE. (US/0746-8342). **3500**

COLLEGE MUSIC SYMPOSIUM. (US/0069-5696). Qty: 6 per year. **4110**

COLLEGE STUDENT AFFAIRS JOURNAL, THE. (US/0888-210X). Qty: varies. **1817**

COLLEGE STUDENT JOURNAL. (US/0146-3934). **1817**

COLLEGIATE BASEBALL. (US/0530-9751). Qty: 5-10. **4890**

COLLEGIATE MICROCOMPUTER. (US/0731-4213). **1266**

COLLEGIATE TRENDS (RIDGEWOOD, N.J.). (US/1065-0296). Qty: 12. **1817**

COLLETTIVITA CONVIVENZE. (IT/1120-639X). **4771**

COLLIE REVIEW. (US/0744-0731). **4286**

COLLIN CHRONICLES. (US/1060-0949). **2443**

COLLISION. (US/0739-7437). Qty: 20 or more per year. **5411**

COLLOID AND POLYMER SCIENCE. (GW/0303-402X). **1050**

COLLOQUIUM. (AT/0588-3237). **4948**

COLONIAL LATIN AMERICAN HISTORICAL REVIEW. (US/1063-5769). Qty: 28 minimum. **2728**

COLONIAL WATERBIRDS. (US/0738-6028). **5617**

COLONIAL WILLIAMSBURG ARCHAEOLOGICAL SERIES. (US/0069-5971). **266**

COLOQUIO/CIENCIAS. (PO/0870-7650). **5095**

COLOQUIO : LETRAS. (PO/0010-1451). **3376**

COLORADO BANKRUPTCY COURT REPORTER, THE. (US/1048-3683). **2952**

COLORADO ENGINEER, THE. (US/0010-1583). **1968**

COLORADO ENVIRONMENTAL REPORT, THE. (US/0891-3463). **2190**

COLORADO FIELD ORNITHOLOGISTS' JOURNAL. (US/1066-7342). **5617**

COLORADO GENEALOGIST, THE. (US/0010-1613). **2443**

COLORADO GREEN. (US/0195-0045). **2412**

COLORADO HERITAGE. (US/0272-9377). **2729**

COLORADO LABOR ADVOCATE. (US/0190-8235). **5642**

COLORADO LAWYER. (US/0363-7867). Qty: 2-4. **2952**

COLORADO LIBRARIES. (US/0147-9733). Qty: 25. **3203**

COLORADO MEDICINE (1980). (US/0199-7343). Qty: 1-3. **3567**

COLORADO NURSE (1985). (US/8750-846X). **3854**

COLORADO OUTDOORS. (US/0010-1699). Qty: 2-3. **2190**

COLORADO PROSPECTOR. (US/0010-1702). **2729**

COLORADO REVIEW (1985). (US/1046-3348). **3340**

COLORADO WOMAN. (US/1042-9549). Qty: 25. **5553**

COLORBAT LAB PRO. (US/1055-0704). Qty: Varies. **347**

COLOURAGE. (II/0010-1826). **5349**

COLTON CLARION. (US/0896-9590). **2443**

COLUMBAN MISSION. (US/0095-4438). **4948**

COLUMBIA BUSINESS LAW REVIEW. (US/0898-0721). **3097**

COLUMBIA DAILY SPECTATOR. (US). **1090**

COLUMBIA FLIER. (US/0192-7841). **5686**

COLUMBIA HUMAN RIGHTS LAW REVIEW. (US/0090-7944). **4506**

COLUMBIA JOURNAL OF ENVIRONMENTAL LAW. (US/0098-4582). **3110**

COLUMBIA JOURNAL OF LAW AND SOCIAL PROBLEMS. (US/0010-1923). **2953**

COLUMBIA JOURNAL OF TRANSNATIONAL LAW. (US/0010-1931). **3126**

COLUMBIA JOURNAL OF WORLD BUSINESS, THE. (US/0022-5428). **658**

COLUMBIA LAW REVIEW. (US/0010-1958). **2953**

COLUMBIA MISSOURIAN. (US/0747-1874). Qty: 312. **5703**

COLUMBIA (NEW HAVEN). (US/0010-1869). **5028**

COLUMBIA (NEW YORK, N.Y. 1978). (US/0162-3893). **1090**

COLUMBIA NEWS-TIMES, THE. (US/1053-7511). Qty: 10. **5653**

COLUMBIA (RHINEBECK, N.Y.), THE. (US/8755-2914). **2443**

COLUMBIA SPECTATOR. (US). **5715**

COLUMBIANA. (US/0893-276X). **2531**

COLUMBUS TIMES, THE. (US). **Qty:** 30 per year. **5653**

COLUSA COUNTY SUN HERALD. (US/0897-8743). **Qty:** 156. **5634**

COM-AND, COMPUTER AUDIT NEWS DEVELOPMENTS. (US/0738-4270). **741**

COMBAT NATURE PERIGUEUX. (FR/0184-7473). **Qty:** 4. **2163**

COMBINED INDEX FOR THE JOURNALS SULPHUR, NITROGEN AND PHOSPHORUS & POTASSIUM. (UK). **1023**

COMBROAD. (UK/0951-0826). **1130**

COMBUSTION SCIENCE AND TECHNOLOGY. (US/0010-2202). **1051**

COME-ALL-YE (HATBORO, PA.). (US/0736-6132). **2319**

COMENTARIOS BIBLIOGRAFICOS AMERICANOS. (UY/0301-6579). **3340**

COMIC TALE EASY READER. (US/0748-2264). **1062**

COMICS JOURNAL, THE. (US/0194-7869). **377**

COMITATUS. (US/0069-6412). **3377**

COMITE INTERNATIONAL DES POIDS ET MESURES, COMITE CONSULTATIF D'ELECTRICITE. RAPPORT. (FR). **4030**

COMLA NEWSLETTER. (JM/0378-1070). **3203**

COMMAND (DENVER, COLO.). (US/0010-2474). **Qty:** 4-8. **4039**

COMMENTAIRE (JULLIARD). (FR/0180-8214). **Qty:** 4. **3377**

COMMENTARY (NEW YORK). (US/0010-2601). **5047**

COMMENTS FROM THE FRIENDS. (US/1063-7575). **Qty:** 4. **4949**

COMMENTS ON ASTROPHYSICS. (US/0146-2970). **394**

COMMENTS ON ATOMIC AND MOLECULAR PHYSICS. (UK/0010-2687). **4446**

COMMENTS ON MODERN CHEMISTRY. PART A, COMMENTS ON INORGANIC CHEMISTRY. (UK/0260-3594). **1036**

COMMENTS ON PLASMA PHYSICS AND CONTROLLED FUSION. (US/0374-2806). **4400**

COMMERCE INTERNATIONAL. (UK/0010-2733). **828**

COMMERCIAL AGRICULTURE IN ZIMBABWE. (RH). **75**

COMMERCIAL AND INDUSTRIAL FLOORSPACE STATISTICS, WALES. (UK/0262-5334). **5325**

COMMERCIAL APPEAL, THE. (US/0745-4856). **5744**

COMMERCIAL FISHING. (UK/0143-652X). **2299**

COMMERCIAL LENDING NEWSLETTER. (US). **783**

COMMERCIAL LENDING REVIEW. (US/0886-8204). **783**

COMMERCIAL RECORD (SOUTH WINDSOR, CT.), THE. (US/0010-3098). **4836**

COMMITTEE ON EAST ASIAN LIBRARIES BULLETIN. (US/0148-6225). **3203**

COMMLAW CONSPECTUS. (US/1068-5871). **2953**

COMMODITIES LAW LETTER. (US/0277-2930). **2953**

COMMON BOUNDARY, THE. (US/0885-8500). **4582**

COMMON FOCUS. (US). **4582**

COMMON GROUND. (UK/0010-325X). **4949**

COMMON GROUND (CHARLOTTETOWN). (CN/0715-478X). **Qty:** 4-6. **5553**

COMMON GROUND (VANCOUVER). (CN/0824-0698). **3774**

COMMON LIVES, LESBIAN LIVES. (US/0891-6969). **2794**

COMMON MARKET LAW REVIEW. (NE/0165-0750). **2953**

COMMON SENSE ECONOMICS. (CN/0319-7549). **1470**

COMMON SENSE ON ENERGY AND OUR ENVIRONMENT. (US/1052-6331). **Qty:** 5-10. **1935**

COMMON SENSE PEST CONTROL QUARTERLY. (US/8756-7881). **4244**

COMMONWEAL. (US/0010-3330). **2531**

COMMONWEALTH. (FR/0395-6989). **3377**

COMMONWEALTH CURRENTS. (UK/0141-8513). **2908**

COMMONWEALTH ESSAYS & STUDIES. (FR). **3377**

COMMONWEALTH FORESTRY HANDBOOK, THE. (UK). **2377**

COMMONWEALTH FORESTRY REVIEW, THE. (UK/0010-3381). **2399**

COMMONWEALTH-JOURNAL (SOMERSET, KY.), THE. (US/0899-1839). **5680**

COMMONWEALTH LAW BULLETIN. (UK/0305-0718). **Qty:** 4. **2953**

COMMONWEALTH NOVEL IN ENGLISH. (US/0732-6734). **Qty:** 1-2. **3340**

COMMONWEALTH OF DOMINICA CONSOLIDATED INDEX OF STATUTES AND SUBSIDIARY LEGISLATION TO ... . (BB). **3126**

COMMONWEALTH UNIVERSITIES YEARBOOK. (UK/0069-7745). **1817**

COMMUNAL SOCIETIES. (US/0739-1250). **5242**

COMMUNAUTE CHRETIENNE. (CN/0010-3454). **4949**

COMMUNICATIE. (BE/0771-7342). **1106**

COMMUNICATIO. (SA). **1106**

COMMUNICATIO SOCIALIS YEARBOOK. (II/0970-0382). **4949**

COMMUNICATION BOOKNOTES. (US/0748-657X). **1125**

COMMUNICATION BRIEFINGS. (US/0730-7799). **757**

COMMUNICATION - CANADIAN CO-ORDINATING COUNCIL ON DEAFNESS. (CN/0228-5401). **4385**

COMMUNICATION EDUCATION. (US/0363-4523). **1106**

COMMUNICATION ET INFORMATION. (CN/0382-7798). **1106**

COMMUNICATION - INTERNATIONAL SKATING UNION. (SZ). **4891**

COMMUNICATION LONDON. 1967. (UK/0045-7663). **3923**

COMMUNICATION MONOGRAPHS. (US/0363-7751). **1107**

COMMUNICATION OUTLOOK. (US/0161-4126). **1107**

COMMUNICATION RESEARCH REPORTS. (US/0882-4096). **1107**

COMMUNICATION RESEARCH TRENDS. (US/0144-4646). **1107**

COMMUNICATION THEORY. (US/1050-3293). **1107**

COMMUNICATION WORLD (SAN FRANCISCO, CALIF.). (US/0744-7612). **Qty:** 11. **1107**

COMMUNICATIONES ARCHEOLOGICAE HUNGARIAE. (HU). **Qty:** 8. **266**

COMMUNICATIONS & COGNITION. (BE/0378-0880). **1108**

COMMUNICATIONS & STRATEGIES MONTPELLIER. (FR/1157-8637). **1175**

COMMUNICATIONS FROM THE INTERNATIONAL BRECHT SOCIETY. (US/0740-8943). **3377**

COMMUNICATIONS IN ALGEBRA. (US/0092-7872). **3500**

COMMUNICATIONS IN APPLIED NUMERICAL METHODS. (UK/0748-8025). **3500**

COMMUNICATIONS IN LABORATORY MEDICINE. (UK/0267-3320). **3567**

COMMUNICATIONS IN PARTIAL DIFFERENTIAL EQUATIONS. (US/0360-5302). **3501**

COMMUNICATIONS IN SOIL SCIENCE AND PLANT ANALYSIS. (US/0010-3624). **167**

COMMUNICATIONS IN STATISTICS : SIMULATION AND COMPUTATION. (US/0361-0918). **1282**

COMMUNICATIONS IN STATISTICS : STOCHASTIC MODELS. (US/0882-0287). **5325**

COMMUNICATIONS IN STATISTICS : THEORY AND METHODS. (US/0361-0926). **3501**

COMMUNICATIONS OF THE DUBLIN INSTITUTE FOR ADVANCED STUDIES. SERIES D. GEOPHYSICAL BULLETIN. (IE/0070-7422). **1404**

COMMUNICATOR'S JOURNAL. (US/0737-3244). **1108**

COMMUNIO (SPOKANE, WASH.). (US/0094-2065). **Qty:** 1-2. **4949**

COMMUNION. (FR/0042-370X). **5028**

COMMUNION ET DIACONIE WATTRELOS. (FR/0224-0254). **4949**

COMMUNIQUE / CANADIAN COMMUNICATION ASSOCIATION. (CN/0821-4379). **1108**

COMMUNIQUE - CHILDREN'S AID SOCIETY OF OTTAWA. (CN/0319-7468). **5279**

COMMUNIQUE HEBROMADAIRE (INSTITUT NATIONAL DE STATISTIQUE (BELGIUM) : 1982). (BE/0771-0410). **5325**

COMMUNIQUE / HUMAN FACTORS ASSOCIATION OF CANADA. (CN/0712-936X). **2860**

COMMUNIQUE (KENT). (US/0164-775X). **4582**

COMMUNIQUE - LEARNING DISABILITIES ASSOCIATION OF ONTARIO. (CN/0843-2236). **1877**

COMMUNIQUE / NATIONAL ASSOCIATION FOR GIFTED CHILDREN. (US/0884-3643). **1877**

COMMUNIQUE NATIONAL DE LA SCRP. (CN/0710-071X). **757**

COMMUNIQUE / ORDER OF THE INDIAN WARS. (US). **2729**

COMMUNIQUE - SOCIETY FOR INTERCULTURAL EDUCATION, TRAINING AND RESEARCH. (US/0276-1386). **1733**

COMMUNISME (PARIS, FRANCE : 1982). (FR/0751-3496). **4540**

COMMUNITIES (LOUISA). (US/0199-9346). **Qty:** 6. **2818**

COMMUNITY ALTERNATIVES. (US/1052-7656). **5279**

COMMUNITY & JUNIOR COLLEGE LIBRARIES. (US/0276-3915). **3203**

COMMUNITY ANIMAL CONTROL. (US/0278-2863). **226**

COMMUNITY CABLE LETTER. (US/1074-3936). **1152**

COMMUNITY CHANGE. (US/0896-9159). **Qty:** 4. **2818**

COMMUNITY COLLEGE JOURNALIST : OFFICIAL PUBLICATION OF THE COMMUNITY COLLEGE JOURNALISM ASSOCIATION. (US). **2918**

COMMUNITY COLLEGE REVIEW. (US/0091-5521). **1817**

COMMUNITY COLLEGE WEEK. (US/1041-5726). **1817**

COMMUNITY DENTISTRY AND ORAL EPIDEMIOLOGY. (DK/0301-5661). **1319**

COMMUNITY DEVELOPMENT JOURNAL. (UK/0010-3802). **5242**

COMMUNITY ECONOMICS (GREENFIELD, MASS.). (US/1045-4322). **Qty:** 3-5. **2818**

COMMUNITY EDUCATION JOURNAL. (US/0045-7736). **Qty:** varies. **1733**

COMMUNITY HEALTH FUNDING REPORT. (US/1052-6552). **5280**

COMMUNITY HERALD (MONONA, WIS.), THE. (US/0745-6646). **5766**

COMMUNITY JOBS. (US/0195-1157). **Qty:** 12. **1660**

COMMUNITY/JUNIOR COLLEGE. (US/0277-6774). **1817**

COMMUNITY NEWS (BROWNS MILLS, N.J.), THE. (US/0745-8150). **5709**

COMMUNITY QUARTERLY. (AT/0814-401X). **Qty:** 6. **2818**

COMMUNITY RADIO NEWS. (US). **Qty:** 5 - 8. **1130**

COMMUNITY RELATIONS REPORT (BARTLESVILLE, OKLA.), THE. (US/0736-7147). **Qty:** 4/yr. **757**

COMMUNITY REVIEW (NEW BRUNSWICK). (US/0163-8475). **1818**

COMMUNITY SERVICE BUSINESS. (US/0747-6086). **5196**

COMMUNITY SERVICE NEWSLETTER. (US/0277-6189). **2818**

COMMUNITY, TECHNICAL, AND JUNIOR COLLEGE JOURNAL. (US/0884-7169). **1818**

COMMUTER (COLLEGE PARK, MD.), THE. (US/0734-3817). **5380**

COMPACT CAMBRIDGE MEDLINE [COMPUTER FILE]. (US). **3567**

COMPANIES HOLDING BOILER AND PRESSURE VESSEL CERTIFICATES OF AUTHORIZATION FOR USE OF CODE SYMBOL STAMPS. (US/0148-6594). **2112**

COMPANIES HOLDING NUCLEAR CERTIFICATES OF AUTHORIZATION. (US/0272-6777). **2154**

COMPANION (TORONTO). (CN/0010-3985). **5028**

COMPANY LAW DIGEST (NEW DELHI, INDIA). (II). **3098**

COMPANY LAW JOURNAL (NEW DELHI, INDIA). (II). **3098**

COMPANY SECRETARY'S REVIEW. (UK/0309-703X). **3098**

COMPARABLE WORTH PROJECT NEWSLETTER. (US/0278-4122). **658**

COMPARATIST, THE. (US/0195-7678). **3377**

COMPARATIVE AND INTERNATIONAL LAW JOURNAL OF SOUTHERN AFRICA, THE. (SA/0010-4051). **3126**

COMPARATIVE BIOCHEMISTRY AND PHYSIOLOGY. A, COMPARATIVE PHYSIOLOGY. (UK/0300-9629). **579**

COMPARATIVE BIOCHEMISTRY AND PHYSIOLOGY. B, COMPARATIVE BIOCHEMISTRY. (UK/0305-0491). **486**

COMPARATIVE CIVILIZATIONS REVIEW. (US/0733-4540). **5196**

COMPARATIVE DRAMA. (US/0010-4078). **5363**

COMPARATIVE ECONOMIC STUDIES. (US/0888-7233). **Qty:** 18. **1470**

COMPARATIVE JURIDICAL REVIEW. (US/0069-7893). **2954**

COMPARATIVE LABOR LAW JOURNAL. (US/1043-5255). **3145**

COMPARATIVE LITERATURE. (US/0010-4124). **3377**

COMPARATIVE LITERATURE STUDIES (URBANA). (US/0010-4132). **3377**

COMPARATIVE PHYSIOLOGY AND ECOLOGY. (II/0379-0436). **579**

COMPARATIVE POLITICAL STUDIES. (US/0010-4140). **4469**

COMPARATIVE ROMANCE LINGUISTICS NEWSLETTER. (US/0010-4167). **3274**

COMPARATIVE STATE POLITICS. (US/1047-1006). **Qty:** 3. **4469**

COMPARATIVE STRATEGY. (US/0149-5933). **4518**

COMPARATIVE STUDIES IN SOCIETY AND HISTORY. (UK/0010-4175). **5196**

COMPARE. (UK/0305-7925). **1891**

COMPASS. (UK). **4469**

COMPASS & TAPE. (US/1074-5696). **Qty:** 1-2. **2581**

COMPEL. (IE/0332-1649). **2039**

COMPENDIUM NEWSLETTER, THE. (US/0198-9103). **2190**

COMPENSATION AND BENEFITS REVIEW. (US/0886-3687). **1660**

COMPETITION ANGLER. (US/1047-1669). **4871**

COMPETITIONS (LOUISVILLE, KY.). (US/1058-6539). **Qty:** 1-2. **295**

COMPETITIVE ADVANCES. MATERIALS AND PROCESSES. (US). **5095**

COMPETITIVE INTELLIGENCE REVIEW. (US/1058-0247). **659**

COMPILATION OF STATE AND FEDERAL PRIVACY LAWS. (US/0882-9136). **2954**

COMPILER, THE. (US/1059-6569). **3160**

COMPLEAT GOLFER. (SA/1015-8014). **4891**

COMPLEAT MOTHER, THE. (CN/0829-8564). **Qty:** 8-10. **3759**

COMPLEMENTARY MEDICINE INDEX : CURRENT AWARENESS TOPICS SERVICES. (UK/0950-6667). **3567**

COMPLETE INTELLIGENCE DIGEST SERVICE. (UK). **4469**

COMPLEX VARIABLES THEORY AND APPLICATION. (US/0278-1077). **3501**

COMPLICATIONS IN ORTHOPEDICS. (US/0887-1736). **3881**

COMPOSER/USA. (US). **4111**

COMPOSITE POLYMERS. (UK/0952-6919). **4454**

COMPOSITE STRUCTURES. (UK/0263-8223). **2101**

COMPOSITES. (UK/0010-4361). **2101**

COMPOSITES & ADHESIVES NEWSLETTER, THE. (US/0888-1227). **1023**

COMPOSITES SCIENCE AND TECHNOLOGY. (UK/0266-3538). **2101**

COMPOSITION CHRONICLE. (US/0897-263X). **Qty:** 9 per year. **3377**

COMPOSITION STUDIES : FRESHMAN ENGLISH NEWS. (US). **Qty:** 20-40 per year. **3274**

COMPREHENSIVE DISSERTATION INDEX. (US). **3567**

COMPREHENSIVE THERAPY. (US/0098-8243). **3567**

COMPTES RENDUS DE L'ACADEMIE D'AGRICULTURE DE FRANCE. (FR/0989-6988). **Qty:** 1. **76**

COMPTES RENDUS DE THERAPEUTIQUE ET DE PHARMACOLOGIE CLINIQUE. (FR/0293-9908). **Qty:** 11. **4297**

COMPUTATIONAL COMPLEXITY. (SZ/1016-3328). **3501**

COMPUTATIONAL LINGUISTICS (ASSOCIATION FOR COMPUTATIONAL LINGUISTICS). (US/0891-2017). **1175**

COMPUTE (GREENSBORO). (US/0194-357X). **1266**

COMPUTER AIDED DESIGN. (UK/0010-4485). **1231**

COMPUTER AIDED DESIGN REPORT. (US/0276-749X). **1232**

COMPUTER AIDED SELLING. (US/8756-8780). **Qty:** 6-10/yr. **659**

COMPUTER & ELECTRONICS GRADUATE, THE. (US/0882-200X). **4203**

COMPUTER AND INFORMATION SYSTEMS ABSTRACTS JOURNAL. (US/0191-9776). **1208**

COMPUTER APPLICATIONS IN THE BIOSCIENCES. (UK/0266-7061). **1176**

COMPUTER BOOK REVIEW. (US/0737-0334). **1176**

COMPUTER BUYER'S GUIDE AND HANDBOOK. (US/0738-9213). **1266**

COMPUTER COMMUNICATIONS. (UK/0140-3664). **1240**

COMPUTER DATA STORAGE NEWSLETTER. (FR/0988-3452). **Qty:** 12. **1276**

COMPUTER DISPLAY REVIEW, THE. (US/0010-4582). **1264**

COMPUTER EDUCATION. (UK/0010-4590). **Qty:** 20/yr. **1222**

COMPUTER GRAPHICS FORUM : A JOURNAL OF THE EUROPEAN ASSOCIATION FOR COMPUTER GRAPHICS. (NE/0167-7055). **1232**

COMPUTER GRAPHICS WORLD. (US/0271-4159). **1232**

COMPUTER-INTEGRATED MANUFACTURING SYSTEMS. (UK/0951-5240). **1228**

COMPUTER JOURNAL. (UK/0010-4620). **1176**

COMPUTER JOURNAL (KALISPELL, MONT.). (US/0748-9331). **1177**

COMPUTER LAW AND SECURITY REPORT, THE. (UK). **1225**

COMPUTER/LAW JOURNAL. (US/0164-8756). **2954**

COMPUTER LAW REPORTER. (US/0739-7771). **2954**

COMPUTER LAWYER, THE. (US/0742-1192). **2955**

COMPUTER LITERACY NEWSLETTER. (US). **Qty:** 12. **1177**

COMPUTER LIVING, NEW YORK. (US/8750-4375). **1177**

COMPUTER (LONG BEACH, CALIF.). (US/0018-9162). **1266**

COMPUTER MARKETING NEWSLETTER, THE. (US/0886-7194). **Qty:** varies. **1244**

COMPUTER MUSIC JOURNAL. (US/0148-9267). **1240**

COMPUTER PAPER (BRITISH COLUMBIA ED.). (CN/0840-3929). **1177**

COMPUTER PERIPHERALS REVIEW. (US/0149-5054). **1264**

COMPUTER POST. (CN/1194-305X). **Qty:** 5. **1177**

COMPUTER PRODUCT NEWS. (BE). **1244**

COMPUTER PUBLICITY NEWS. (US/0276-9972). **758**

COMPUTER REVIEW. (US/0093-416X). **1264**

COMPUTER SECURITY, AUDITING AND CONTROLS. (US/0738-4262). **1226**

COMPUTER SECURITY DIGEST. (US/0882-1453). **1226**

COMPUTER SPEECH & LANGUAGE. (UK/0885-2308). **3274**

COMPUTER SWEDEN. (SW/0280-9982). **1178**

COMPUTER SYSTEMS SCIENCE AND ENGINEERING. (UK/0267-6192). **1228**

COMPUTER USERS' YEAR BOOK. (UK/0268-6821). **1245**

COMPUTERITER. (US/8756-7911). **1266**

COMPUTERIZED DRAFTING AND DESIGN NEWSLETTER. (US/0748-660X). **1232**

COMPUTERS AND COMPOSITION. (US/8755-4615). **Qty:** 3. **1222**

COMPUTERS AND ELECTRONICS IN AGRICULTURE. (NE/0168-1699). **76**

COMPUTERS AND LAW SYDNEY. (AT/0811-7225). **Qty:** 12. **1178**

COMPUTERS & MATHEMATICS WITH APPLICATIONS (1987). (UK/0898-1221). **1179**

COMPUTERS & MINING. (US/1068-4425). **Qty:** varies. **2138**

COMPUTERS AND PEOPLE. (US/0361-1442). **1218**

COMPUTERS & SECURITY. (UK/0167-4048). **1226**

COMPUTERS & STRUCTURES. (UK/0045-7949). **1228**

COMPUTERS IN CARDIOLOGY. (US/0276-6574). **3703**

COMPUTERS IN EDUCATION JOURNAL. (US/1069-3769). **1179**

COMPUTERS IN EDUCATION (TORONTO, ONT.). (CN/0823-9940). **1222**

COMPUTERS IN GENEALOGY. (UK/0263-3248). **1266**

COMPUTERS IN HUMAN SERVICES. (US/0740-445X). **1179**

COMPUTERS IN LIBRARIES. (US/1041-7915). **3203**

COMPUTERS IN NURSING. (US/0736-8593). **3854**

COMPUTERS IN THE SCHOOLS. (US/0738-0569). **1222**

COMPUTING CANADA. (CN/0319-0161). **1257**

COMPUTING NEWS / YORK UNIVERSITY. (CN/0226-9201). **1180**

COMPUTING NOW!. (CN/0823-6437). **1273**

COMPUTING RESOURCES FOR THE PROFESSIONAL. (US/0276-5756). **659**

COMPUTING TEACHER, THE. (US/0278-9175). **1222**

COMPUTING TODAY (LONDON). (UK/0142-7210). **1266**

COMSTOCK'S. (US). **659**

COMUNI D'ITALIA. (IT/0394-8277). **4640**

COMUNICACION PSIQUIATRICA. (SP/0210-1424). **3923**

COMUNICACION Y SOCIEDAD. (SP/0214-0039). **1109**

COMUNICACIONES. (CU). **1109**

COMUNICACIONES (CORAL GABLES, FLA.). (US/0748-3104). **1152**

COMUNIMEF. (MX). **784**

COMUNIUNEA ROMANEASCA. (US/0197-1441). **3377**

CON TEXT MAGAZINE. (BE). **1083**

CONCEPT NEWS. (II/0970-6437). **5196**

CONCEPTS IN MAGNETIC RESONANCE. (US/1043-7347). **Qty:** 1-4. **4443**

CONCERN (REGINA). (CN/0836-7310). **Qty:** 6/year. **3854**

CONCERTINA & SQUEEZEBOX. (US). **4111**

CONCH REVIEW OF BOOKS, THE. (US/0092-7708). **3340**

CONCHO RIVER REVIEW. (US/1048-9568). **Qty:** 10. **3377**

CONCORD BUSINESS. (US). **659**

CONCORDIA HISTORICAL INSTITUTE QUARTERLY. (US/0010-5260). **Qty:** 10. **5058**

CONCORDIA JOURNAL. (US/0145-7233). **4949**

CONCORDIA THEOLOGICAL QUARTERLY. (US/0038-8610). **Qty:** varies. **4949**

CONCOURS MEDICAL. (FR/0010-5309). **3568**

CONCRETE ABSTRACTS. (US/0045-8007). **2003**

CONCRETE INTERNATIONAL. (US/0162-4075). **608**

CONCRETE (LONDON). (UK/0010-5317). **2021**

CONCRETE PLANT AND PRODUCTION. (UK/0264-0236). **608**

CONDITION MONITORING AND DIAGNOSTIC TECHNOLOGY. (UK). **1969**

CONDIZIONAMENTO DELL'ARIA, RISCALDAMENTO, REFRIGERAZIONE. (IT/0373-7772). **2604**

CONDOR (LOS ANGELES, CALIF.), THE. (US/0010-5422). **5617**

CONFECTIONERY PRODUCTION. (UK/0010-5473). **2332**

CONFEDERATE CHRONICLES OF TENNESSEE. (US/0895-9455). **2729**

CONFEDERATE HISTORICAL INSTITUTE JOURNAL. (US/0734-3671). **2614**

CONFEDERATE VETERAN (MURFREESBORO, TENN.). (US/0890-2216). **Qty:** 36. **2729**

CONFIDENCIAL ECONOMICO NORDESTE. (BL). **1470**

CONFLICT INTERNATIONAL. (UK/0963-1674). **4518**

CONFLICT QUARTERLY. (CN/0227-1311). **4518**

CONFLICT STUDIES. (UK/0069-8792). **4518**

CONFRONTATION/CHANGE LITERARY REVIEW. (US/0363-9460). **5196**

CONFRONTATION (SOUTHAMPTON, N.Y.). (US/0010-5716). **Qty:** 40. **3377**

CONFRONTI. (IT). **4950**

CONGENITAL ANOMALIES. (JA/0914-3505). **Qty:** varies. **543**

CONGREGATIONALIST (BELOIT), THE. (US/0010-5856). **4950**

CONGRES ARCHEOLOGIQUE DE FRANCE. (FR/0069-8881). **266**

CONGRESS & THE PRESIDENCY. (US/0734-3469). **4469**

CONGRESS MONTHLY (1985). (US/0887-0764). **2258**

CONGRESS PUBLICATIONS. (SZ). **2021**

CONGRESSIONAL STAFF DIRECTORY. ADVANCE LOCATOR FOR CAPITOL HILL. (US/0069-8938). **4640**

CONJUNCTIONS (NEW YORK, N.Y.). (US/0278-2324). **3340**

CONNAISSANCE DES ARTS, PLAISIR DE FRANCE. (FR/0395-5907). **348**

CONNAISSANCEG DES PERES DE L'EGGLISE. (FR). **4950**

CONNECT (ANN ARBOR, MICH.). (US/1070-0994). **1180**

CONNECT (BRATTLEBORO, VT.). (US/1041-682X). **1733**

CONNECT. BRUNSWICK. (AT/0158-4995). **1733**

CONNECT (SUISUN, CALIF.). (US/0896-0666). **3203**

CONNECTICUT ANCESTRY. (US/0197-2103). **2444**

CONNECTICUT ANTIQUARIAN, THE. (US/0010-6054). **2729**

CONNECTICUT BAR JOURNAL. (US/0010-6070). **2955**

CONNECTICUT ENGLISH JOURNAL. (US/0893-0376). **1891**

CONNECTICUT HISTORICAL SOCIETY BULLETIN, THE. (US/0885-4831). **Qty:** 10. **2729**

CONNECTICUT INSURANCE LAW REVIEW, THE. (US/0742-924X). **2955**

CONNECTICUT JOURNAL OF INTERNATIONAL LAW. (US/0897-1218). **3126**

CONNECTICUT LAW REVIEW. (US/0010-6151). **2955**

CONNECTICUT LAW TRIBUNE, THE. (US/0198-0289). **2955**

CONNECTICUT MEDICINE. (US/0010-6178). **3568**

CONNECTICUT NUTMEGGER, THE. (US/0045-8120). **2444**

CONNECTICUT TECHNOLOGY DIRECTORY. (US/1046-9672). **5096**

CONNECTION TECHNOLOGY. (US/8756-4076). **5096**

CONNECTIONS (FULLERTON, CALIF.). (US/0894-170X). **1180**

CONNECTIONS (MINNEAPOLIS, MINN. 1993). (US/1070-8154). **4386**

CONNECTIONS (NEW YORK, N.Y.). (US/0272-6513). **1062**

CONNECTIONS (POINTE CLAIRE). (CN/0707-7130). **2444**

CONNECTIONS (TORONTO). (CN/0226-1766). **5242**

CONNERSVILLE NEWS-EXAMINER. (US). **5663**

CONNEXIONS (CUPERTINO, CALIF.). (US/0894-5926). **1241**

CONNOLLY REPORT, THE. (CN/0823-6216). **895**

CONRAD GREBEL REVIEW, THE. (CN/0829-044X). **4950**

CONRADIAN : THE JOURNAL OF THE JOSEPH CONRAD SOCIETY (U.K.), THE. (UK). **Qty:** 4. **3378**

CONRADIANA. (US/0010-6356). **431**

CONSCIENCE CANADA NEWSLETTER. (CN/0823-8669). **4718**

CONSCIENCE ET LIBERTE. (SZ). **4950**

CONSCIENCE (WASHINGTON, D.C.). (US/0740-6835). **Qty:** 6. **588**

CONSCIOUSNESS. (AT). **4241**

CONSCIOUSNESS AND COGNITION. (US/1053-8100). **4582**

CONSENSUS (BROOKLYN). (US/0090-0842). **659**

CONSENSUS (WINNIPEG). (CN/0317-1493). **Qty:** 40. **4950**

CONSER TABLES. (US/0190-3608). **3204**

CONSERVATION ADMINISTRATION NEWS. (US/0192-2912). **3204**

CONSERVATION BIOLOGY. (US/0888-8892). **2190**

CONSERVATIONEWS. (US). **Qty:** 4-10. **4828**

CONSERVATIONIST, THE. (US/0010-650X). **2190**

CONSERVATIVE JUDAISM. (US/0010-6542). **Qty:** 15. **5047**

CONSERVATIVE NEWSLINE. (UK). **4469**

CONSERVATIVE REVIEW (WASHINGTON, D.C.). (US/1047-5990). **Qty:** 12-15. **1471**

CONSORT (DOLMETSCH FOUNDATION), THE. (UK/0268-9111). **Qty:** 15. **4111**

CONSORT (HALIFAX). (CN/0823-8278). **4111**

CONSTITUTIONAL AND PARLIAMENTARY INFORMATION. (SZ/0010-6623). **3092**

CONSTITUTIONAL COMMENTARY. (US/0742-7115). **3092**

CONSTITUTIONAL FORUM. (CN/0847-3889). **3092**

CONSTITUTIONAL POLITICAL ECONOMY. (US/1043-4062). **Qty:** 15. **3092**

CONSTRUCT IN STEEL. (AT/1030-2581). **Qty:** varies. **608**

CONSTRUCTION COMPUTING. (UK/0264-6854). **1180**

CONSTRUCTION EQUIPMENT, OPERATION AND MAINTENANCE. (US/0010-6771). **609**

CONSTRUCTION LAW LETTER. (CN/0827-3480). **2956**

CONSTRUCTION MANAGEMENT AND ECONOMICS. (UK/0144-6193). **610**

CONSTRUCTION NEWS (LITTLE ROCK). (US/0160-5607). **610**

CONSTRUCTION SPECIFIER, THE. (US/0010-6925). **610**

CONSTRUCTIONAL REVIEW. (AT/0010-695X). **611**

CONSTRUCTIS. (UK). **611**

CONSTRUCTIVE CITIZEN PARTICIPATION. (CN/0319-2385). **Qty:** 100. **5242**

CONSTRUCTOR (WASHINGTON). (US/0162-6191). **611**

CONSULTANT - ASSOCIATION OF CONSULTING FORESTERS OF AMERICA, THE. (US/0010-7085). **Qty:** 4. **2378**

CONSULTANT PRACTICE. (US/0748-1837). **864**

CONSULTANT, THE. (US). **2378**

CONSULTANTS NEWS. (US/0045-8201). **659**

CONSULTING OPPORTUNITIES JOURNAL. (US/0273-4613). **659**

CONSULTING-SPECIFYING ENGINEER. (US/0892-5046). **2097**

CONSUMER AFFAIRS LETTER, THE. (US/0270-0999). **1294**

CONSUMER ALERT. (US). **1294**

CONSUMER ALERT COMMENTS. (US/0740-4964). **1294**

CONSUMER BUYING GUIDE (SKOKIE, ILL.). (US). **1294**

CONSUMER CURRENTS. (MY/0128-1143). **Qty:** 40. **1294**

CONSUMER HEALTH & NUTRITION INDEX. (US/0883-1963). **4200**

CONSUMER PHARMACIST, THE. (US/0738-0615). **4298**

CONSUMERS INDEX TO PRODUCT EVALUATIONS AND INFORMATION SOURCES. (US/0094-0534). **1300**

CONSUMERS' RESEARCH MAGAZINE. (US/0095-2222). **1296**

CONSUMING PASSIONS. (US/0741-7748). **4189**

CONTACT. (CN). **5096**

CONTACT. (UK). **4386**

CONTACT. (UK/0573-777X). **4950**

CONTACT : A BI-MONTHLY PUBLICATION OF THE CHRISTIAN MEDICAL COMMISSION, WORLD COUNCIL OF CHURCHES. (SZ). **3568**

CONTACT - ASSOCIATION CANADIENNE DES PROFESSIONNELS DE LA VENTE. (CN/1193-7521). **Qty:** varies. **659**

CONTACT - CANADIAN ELECTROACOUSTIC COMMUNITY. (CN/0838-3340). **Qty:** 10. **2039**

CONTACT - CANADIAN PROFESSIONAL SALES ASSOCIATION. (CN/1193-7513). **Qty:** varies. **659**

CONTACT DERMATITIS. (DK/0105-1873). **3718**

CONTACT (DON MILLS). (CN/0703-119X). **Qty:** 2-4. **4836**

CONTACT II. (US/0197-6796). **3461**

CONTACT LENS JOURNAL. (US/0096-2716). **3873**

CONTACT LENS JOURNAL (THORNTON HEATH, SURREY), THE. (UK/0306-9575). **4215**

CONTACT-LINSE, DIE. (GW). **4215**

CONTACT - NATIONAL ASSOCIATION OF FREE WILL BAPTISTS. (US/0573-7796). **Qty:** 12. **5058**

CONTACT QUARTERLY. (US/0198-9634). **1311**

CONTACT (TORONTO. 1972). (CN/0319-7379). **4386**

CONTACT - UNIVERSITE SIMON FRASER. FACULTE D'EDUCATION. (CN/0714-3192). **3275**

CONTACTS; REVUE FRANCAISE DE L'ORTHODOXIE. (FR/0045-8325). **4950**

CONTADURIA UNIVERSIDAD DE ANTIOQUIA. (CK/0120-4203). **741**

CONTAGIOUS MAGAZINE. (AT). **1062**

CONTAINERISATION INTERNATIONAL WORLD DIRECTORY OF LINER SHIPPING AGENTS. (UK/0951-5879). **829**

CONTAMINACION AMBIENTAL. (CK). **2226**

CONTAMINATION CONTROL ABSTRACTS. (UK/0952-1542). **2183**

CONTEMPORARY ACCOUNTING RESEARCH. (CN/0823-9150). **742**

CONTEMPORARY APPROACHES TO IBSEN : PROCEEDINGS OF THE INTERNATIONAL IBSEN SEMINARY. (NO). **3340**

CONTEMPORARY CHRISTIAN MUSIC (1986). (US/1049-3379). **4111**

CONTEMPORARY DRUG PROBLEMS. (US/0091-4509). **1342**

CONTEMPORARY EDUCATION. (US/0010-7476). **Qty:** 16. **1891**

CONTEMPORARY EUROPEAN HISTORY. (UK/0960-7773). **2684**

CONTEMPORARY FRENCH CIVILIZATION. (US/0147-9156). **2684**

CONTEMPORARY GERMAN PHILOSOPHY. (US/0740-719X). **4344**

CONTEMPORARY HYPNOSIS : THE JOURNAL OF THE BRITISH SOCIETY OF EXPERIMENTAL AND CLINICAL HYPNOSIS. (UK/0960-5290). **2857**

CONTEMPORARY ISSUES IN CLINICAL NUTRITION. (US/0736-4369). **4189**

CONTEMPORARY ISSUES IN SMALL ANIMAL PRACTICE. (US/0891-9747). **5508**

CONTEMPORARY JEWRY. (US/0147-1694). **Qty:** 10-15. **2259**

CONTEMPORARY MUSIC REVIEW. (UK/0749-4467). **4111**

CONTEMPORARY NURSE : A JOURNAL FOR THE AUSTRALIAN NURSING PROFESSION. (AT/1037-6178). **3854**

CONTEMPORARY PACIFIC, THE. (US/1043-898X). **2510**

CONTEMPORARY PHILOSOPHY (BOULDER, COLO.). (US/0732-4944). **4344**

CONTEMPORARY PSYCHOLOGY. (US/0010-7549). **4582**

CONTEMPORARY RECORD : THE JOURNAL OF THE INSTITUTE OF CONTEMPORARY BRITISH HISTORY. (UK/0950-9224). **2684**

CONTEMPCRARY REVIEW (LONDON, ENGLAND). (UK/0010-7565). **2486**

CONTEMPORARY SOCIOLOGY (WASHINGTON). (US/0094-3061). **5243**

CONTEMPORARY SOUTHEAST ASIA. (SI/0129-797X). **2649**

CONTEMPORARY SSOCIAL PSYCHOLOGY. (US/1041-3030). **Qty:** 5 per year. **4582**

CONTEMPORARY TIMES. (US/1071-2917). **Qty:** 2-3. **864**

CONTEMPORARY VERSE TWO. (CN/0831-9502). **3461**

CONTEMPORARY WALES : AN ANNUAL REVIEW OF ECONOMIC AND SOCIAL RESEARCH. (UK/0951-4937). **1471**

CONTENT FOR CANADIAN JOURNALISTS (1984). (CN/0045-835X). **2918**

CONTINENT CENDRARS. (SZ). **3378**

CONTINENTAL COMMENTS. (US/0573-8164). **5412**

CONTINENTAL FRANCHISE REVIEW. (US/0045-8376). **660**

CONTINENTAL MODELLER. (UK/0955-1298). **2773**

CONTINGENCIES (WASHINGTON, D.C.). (US/1048-9851). **Qty:** 10-12/yr. **2878**

CONTINGENCY PLANNING & RECOVERY JOURNAL : CPR-J. (US/0899-4595). **1226**

CONTINUING CARE RESOURCES. (CN/0824-1384). **Qty:** 3-4. **3778**

CONTINUING EDUCATION (TORONTO). (CN/0318-5141). **4298**

CONTINUING HIGHER EDUCATION REVIEW. (US/0893-0384). **1818**

CONTINUITE. (CN/0714-9476). **348**

CONTINUITY. (US/0277-1446). **2614**

CONTINUO. (CN/0705-6656). **Qty:** 60 /yr. **4111**

CONTINUO (BRISBANE, QLD.). (AT/0310-6802). **4112**

CONTINUOUS IMPROVEMENT. (US/1071-2240). **Qty:** 4. **3477**

CONTINUOUS JOURNEY. (US/1065-3406). **864**

CONTRA MUNDUM. (US/1070-9495). **Qty:** 35. **4950**

CONTRABAND. (US/0888-7586). **Qty:** 5. **5683**

CONTRADDIZIONE, LA. (IT). **4470**

CONTREE / RAAD VIR GEESTESWETENSKAPLIKE NAVORSING, INSTITUUT VIR GESKIEDENISNAVORSING, AFDELING STREEKGESKIEDENIS. (SA/0379-9867). **2638**

CONTRETEMPS (MONTREAL). (CN/0829-240X). **2212**

CONTRIBUTIONS IN BLACK STUDIES. (US/0196-9099). **2845**

CONTRIBUTIONS IN ETHNIC STUDIES. (US/0196-7088). **2259**

CONTRIBUTIONS IN MILITARY STUDIES. (US/0883-6884). **4040**

CONTRIBUTIONS SERIES - AMERICAN ASSOCIATION OF STRATIGRAPHIC PALYNOLOGISTS. (US/0160-8843). **1372**

CONTRIBUTIONS TO ATMOSPHERIC PHYSICS. (GW/0303-4186). **1424**

CONTRIBUTIONS TO GEOLOGY (LARAMIE). (US/0010-7980). **1372**

CONTRIBUTIONS TO LIBRARY SCIENCE. BIBLIOTEEKUNDIGE HYDRAES. (SA). **3204**

CONTRIBUTIONS TO POLITICAL ECONOMY. (UK/0277-5921). **1590**

CONTRIBUTIONS TO THE STUDY OF CHILDHOOD AND YOUTH. (US/0273-124X). **4583**

CONTRIBUTIONS TO THE STUDY OF MASS MEDIA AND COMMUNICATIONS. (US/0732-4456). **1109**

CONTRIBUTIONS TO THE STUDY OF RELIGION. (US/0196-7053). **4950**

CONTROL AND COMPUTERS. (US/0730-9538). **1219**

CONTROL & INSTRUMENTATION. (UK/0010-8022). **1219**

CONTROL ENGINEERING. (US/0010-8049). **1219**

CONTROL THEORY AND ADVANCED TECHNOLOGY. (JA/0911-0704). **Qty:** 1-2. **1180**

CONTROLLED CLINICAL TRIALS. (US/0197-2456). **3568**

CONTROLLER. (SZ/0010-8073). **17**

CONTROLLERS MAGAZINE. (NE). **660**

CONTROSPAZIO. (IT). **296**

CONVEYANCER AND PROPERTY LAWYER, THE. (UK/0010-8200). **2956**

COOKING LIGHT (SOUTHERN LIVING, INC.). (US/0886-4446). **4189**

COOK'S ILLUSTRATED. (US/1068-2821). **Qty:** 12. **2789**

COOKSTOVE NEWS. (US/0882-3561). **5097**

COOPERATION AND CONFLICT. (NO/0010-8367). **4470**

COOPERATIVE ACCOUNTANT, THE. (US/0010-8391). **742**

COOPERATIVE ADVERTISING PLANS FOR YELLOW PAGES. (US/0883-4857). **758**

COOPERATIVE TECHNOLOGY RD&D REPORT. (US/1062-5399). **Qty:** 2. **5097**

COOPERAZIONE EDUCATIVA. (IT). **1733**

COPEIA. (US/0045-8511). **5581**

COPENHAGEN PAPERS IN EAST AND SOUTHEAST ASIAN STUDIES. (DK/0903-2703). **5243**

COPPER STATE BULLETIN. (US/0098-4841). **Qty:** 20. **2444**

COPY EDITOR. (US/1049-3190). **4813**

COPYRIGHT BULLETIN : QUARTERLY REVIEW / UNESCO. (FR/0010-8634). **1303**

COPYRIGHT (GENEVA). (SZ/0010-8626). **1303**

CORD. COCONUT RESEARCH & DEVELOPMENT. (IO/0215-1162). **168**

CORD (ST. BONAVENTURE, N.Y.), THE. (US/0010-8685). **5028**

CORDAGE NEWS. (US/1063-746X). **5349**

CORDIALITY. (US). **2486**

CORDOVA TIMES, THE. (US/1048-8766). **5629**

CORE (NORTH YORK). (CN/1183-1944). **1818**

CORE TEACHER. (US/0045-8538). **1891**

CORELLA. (AT/0155-0438). **Qty:** 4. **5617**

CORINTHIAN HORSE SPORT. (CN/0829-2930). **Qty:** varies. **2798**

CORMORANT NEWS BULLETIN, THE. (US/0045-8554). **5412**

CORMOSEA BULLETIN. (US/0734-449X). **3204**

CORNELL ALUMNI NEWS. (US/1058-3467). **1101**

CORNELL DAILY SUN. (US). **5715**

CORNELL ENGINEER, THE. (US/0010-8790). **1969**

CORNELL INTERNATIONAL LAW JOURNAL. (US/0010-8812). **3126**

CORNELL LAW REVIEW. (US/0010-8847). **2956**

CORNELL VETERINARIAN. SUPPLEMENT. (US/0589-7432). **5508**

CORNELL VETERINARIAN, THE. (US/0010-8901). **5508**

CORNERSTONE (CHICAGO, ILL.). (US/0275-2743). **4950**

CORNSILK. (US/0731-8375). **2444**

CORNSTALK GAZETTE. (AT/0818-7339). **384**

CORONA (BOZEMAN). (US/0270-6687). **3378**

CORONARY CLUB BULLETIN, THE. (US/8755-5271). **3703**

CORONICA, LA. (US/0193-3892). **3275**

CORPORATE BOARD, THE. (US/0746-8652). **Qty:** 30 per year. **661**

CORPORATE CONDUCT QUARTERLY. (US/1061-8775). **2957**

CORPORATE CONSUMER FORUM TRENDLETTER. (US). **Qty:** 4. **2789**

CORPORATE CONTROLLER. (US/0899-0174). **661**

CORPORATE ETHICS MONITOR, THE. (CN/0841-1956). **661**

CORPORATE EXAMINER, THE. (US/0361-2309). **661**

CORPORATE FINANCE BLUEBOOK, THE. (US/0740-2546). **784**

CORPORATE FINANCE SOURCEBOOK, THE. (US/0163-3031). **785**

CORPORATE GIVING WATCH. (US/0747-8003). **5280**

CORPORATE GROWTH REPORT, THE. (US/1050-320X). **661**

CORPORATE LEGAL TIMES. (US). **3099**

CORPORATE MEETINGS AND INCENTIVES. (US/0745-1636). **5467**

CORPORATE REPORT MINNESOTA. (US/0279-5299). **662**

CORPORATE SHOWCASE. (US/0742-9975). **377**

CORPORATE TECHNOLOGY DIRECTORY. (US/0887-1930). **3477**

CORPUS CHRISTI CALLER-TIMES. (US/0894-5365). **5748**

CORPUS OF EARLY KEYBOARD MUSIC. (GW/0070-0371). **4112**

CORRECTIONS DIGEST. (US). **3161**

CORRECTIONS TODAY. (US/0190-2563). **Qty:** 30-40. **3161**

CORRELATION. (UK/0260-8790). **390**

CORRESPONDENCE CHESS. (UK). **4859**

CORRIERE EUROPEO. (IT). **1634**

CORRIERE TERMO IDRO SANITARIO, IL. (IT/0393-9723). **2604**

CORROSION AUSTRALASIA. (AT/0155-6002). **2011**

CORROSION PREVENTION AND CONTROL. (UK/0010-9371). **2011**

CORROSION PREVENTION/INHIBITION DIGEST. (US/0364-3301). **2011**

CORROSION Y PROTECCION. (SP/0045-8678). **2012**

CORYELL NEWSLETTER. (US/0883-7600). **2444**

COSMEP NEWSLETTER (1981). (US/1064-4482). **Qty:** 20. **4813**

COSMETIC NEWS : CN. (IT). **Qty:** 6-12. **403**

COSMETIC WORLD. (US/0589-8447). **403**

COSMETIC WORLD NEWS. (UK/0305-0319). **403**

COSMETICS AND TOILETRIES. (US/0361-4387). **403**

COSMETICS & TOILETRIES. (IT). **403**

COSMOPOLITAN (1952). (US/0010-9541). **5554**

COSMOPOLITAN CONTACT. (US/0010-955X). **4541**

COST ENGINEER. (UK/0010-9606). **864**

COST ENGINEERING (MORGANTOWN. 1980). (US/0274-9696). **1969**

COSTRUIRE IN LATERIZIO. (IT/0394-1590). **296**

COSTRUZIONI. (IT/0010-9665). **611**

COSTUME. (UK/0590-8876). **1083**

COTON ET FIBRES TROPICALES. (FR/0010-9711). **2413**

COTTAGE CONNECTION, THE. (US). **662**

COTTONWOOD CHRONICLE. (US). **5656**

COTTONWOOD (LAWRENCE, KAN.). (US/0147-149X). **Qty:** 12. **3378**

COULICOU. (CN/0822-7098). **1062**

COUNCIL COLUMNS / COUNCIL ON FOUNDATIONS. (US). **Qty:** 15. **4335**

COUNCIL OF GENEALOGY COLUMNISTS NEWSLETTER. (US/1046-641X). **Qty:** 350. **2444**

COUNCIL SPOTLIGHT BOOKNOTES. (US/0740-1183). **4502**

COUNSEL : THE JOURNAL OF THE BAR OF ENGLAND & WALES. (UK/0268-3784). **2957**

COUNSELING AND HUMAN DEVELOPMENT. (US/0193-7375). **5281**

COUNSELING CLIENTS IN THE ENTERTAINMENT INDUSTRY. (US/0271-2385). **2957**

COUNSELING INTERVIEWER, THE. (US/0160-6794). **4583**

COUNSELOR PREPARATION. (US/0271-5368). **1877**

COUNTDOWN (ATHENS, OHIO). (US/0746-8830). **Qty:** 6-12. **17**

COUNTDOWN / JUVENILE DIABETES FOUNDATION INTERNATIONAL. (US/1070-9282). **3727**

COUNTED THREAD. (US/0164-3460). **5183**

COUNTER-TERRORISM. (US/0887-6398). **5196**

COUNTERPOINT (WASHINGTON, D.C.). (US/1053-1386). **1877**

COUNTERTERRORISM & SECURITY REPORT. (US/1064-9093). **4519**

COUNTRY LIFE IN BRITISH COLUMBIA. (CN/0011-0183). **77**

COUNTRY MUSIC. (US/0090-4007). **4112**

COUNTRY MUSIC NEWS (OTTAWA). (CN/0714-8356). **4112**

COUNTRY MUSIC PEOPLE. (UK/0591-2237). **4112**

COUNTRY MUSIC ROUND UP. (UK/0140-5721). **4112**

COUNTRY SHOPPER, THE. (US/0192-1126). **5715**

COUNTRY-SIDE. (UK/0011-023X). **2213**

COUNTRY TIMES (THORNHILL). (CN/0821-7971). **4112**

COUNTRY (TORONTO). (CN/1180-8047). **Qty:** 12/year. **4112**

COUNTRYMAN, THE. (UK/0011-0272). **2514**

COUNTRYSIDE AND SMALL STOCK JOURNAL (1985). (US/8750-7595). **209**

COUNTY LINE. (US/0888-2851). **Qty:** 4. **2444**

COUNTY LINE (PANAMA CITY, FLA.), THE. (US/0888-2851). **Qty:** 4. **2444**

COUP D'OEIL GRANDVILLIERS. (FR/0987-0113). **Qty:** 6. **3874**

COUP D'OEIL SUR L'HALTEROPHILIE. (CN/0227-6909). **4891**

COURANT (MONTREAL). (CN/0712-4570). **4871**

COURANTS PARIS. 1990. (FR/1146-5786). **5532**

COURIER. AFRICA-CARIBBEAN-PACIFIC-EUROPEAN COMMUNITIES, THE. (CY/1013-7335). **1554**

COURIER (BROCKTON, MASS.), THE. (US/1062-8371). **Qty:** 20. **4859**

COURIER (CANADA. CANADIAN FORCES BASE (COLD LAKE, ALTA.)). (CN/0045-8872). **5782**

COURIER (MIDDLETOWN, N.J.), THE. (US/0891-7272). **5709**

COURIER OF HISTORICAL EVENTS. (US). **Qty:** 4. **2614**

COURRIER AUSTRALIEN. (AT/0011-0442). **Qty:** 4. **2486**

COURRIER DE GAND, LE. (BE/0770-9021). **5778**

COURRIER DE LA MONETIQUE ET DE LA CARTE A MEMOIRE, LE. (FR/0757-8768). **830**

COURRIER DE LA NATURE, LE. (FR). **2191**

COURRIER DES PAYS DE L'EST. (FR/0590-0239). **1478**

COURRIER FRONTENAC. (CN/0704-0474). **5782**

COURSES ET ELEVAGE. (FR). **4891**

COURT REVIEW. (US/0011-0647). **Qty:** 1-2. **3140**

COUSINS ET COUSINES. (US/0740-3046). **2444**

COVENANT COMPANION. (US/0011-0671). **5058**

COVENANT DISCIPLESHIP QUARTERLY. (US/1052-3790). **Qty:** 1. **4951**

COVENANT QUARTERLY, THE. (US/0361-0934). **4951**

COVENANTER WITNESS. (US/0749-4319). **4951**

COVERED BRIDGE TOPICS. (US). **2022**

COVERTACTION INFORMATION BULLETIN. (US/0275-309X). **4519**

COVINGTON LEADER, THE. (US). **Qty:** 8. **5745**

COYUNTURA ANDINA. (CK). **1554**

CPA COMPUTER REPORT. (US/0745-1342). **742**

CPA DIGEST. (US/0741-3610). **742**

CPA MARKETING REPORT. (US/0279-1021). **922**

CPA PERSONNEL REPORT. (US/0745-0877). **939**

CPA PROFIT REPORT. (US/1047-5834). **742**

CPA SOFTWARE NEWS, THE. (US/1068-8285). **Qty:** 2-6. **662**

CPCU JOURNAL. (US/0162-2706). **2878**

CPJ : CANADIAN PHARMACEUTICAL JOURNAL. (CN/0828-6914). **4298**

CPRS NATIONAL NEWSLETTER. (CN/0710-0701). **758**

CPU NEWS : JOURNAL OF THE COMMONWEALTH PRESS UNION. (UK). **Qty:** 4/5. **2918**

CPU : QUARTERLY OF THE COMMONWEALTH PRESS UNION. (UK). **2918**

CQ-DL. (GW). **1109**

CRAB, THE. (US/0300-7561). **3204**

CRAFT & NEEDLEWORK AGE. (US/0887-9818). **5183**

CRAFT CONNECTION. (US/1067-8328). **371**

CRAFT CONTACTS (1983). (CN/0823-2148). **371**

CRAFT DIGEST. (US). **Qty:** 30-40. **2773**

CRAFT FACTOR. (CN/0228-7498). **371**

CRAFT RANGE. (US/0199-5200). **371**

CRAFT SHOW DIGEST. (US/0882-7486). **371**

CRAFT SUPPLY DIRECTORY. (US). **2584**

CRAFTNEWS (TORONTO). (CN/0319-7832). **371**

CRAFTS (CRAFTS ADVISORY COMMITTEE). (UK/0306-610X). **371**

CRAFTS 'N THINGS. (US/0146-6607). **371**

CRAFTS (PEORIA, ILL.). (US/0148-9267). **371**

CRAFTS REPORT, THE. (US/0160-7650). **Qty:** 30. **372**

CRAG AND CANYON. (CN/0701-3558). **4871**

CRAIG-LINKS. (US). **2444**

CRANBERRIES (PORTLAND). (US/0011-0787). **168**

CRANE NEWS (CRANE, TEX. : 1945)-. (US). **Qty:** 12. **5748**

CRANFORD CHRONICLE (1979). (US). **5709**

CRANSTON HERALD. (US). **5741**

CRAZYHORSE (LITTLE ROCK, ARK.). (US/0011-0841). **Qty:** 2/yr. **3462**

CREAM CITY REVIEW. (US/0884-3457). **Qty:** 10. **3340**

CREATING EXCELLENCE. (US/1045-7011). **663**

CREATION/EVOLUTION. (US/0738-6001). **543**

CREATION MAGAZINE. (FR/0765-9911). **758**

CREATION RESEARCH QUARTERLY. (US/0092-9166). **Qty:** 12-20. **5097**

CREATION SCIENCE DIALOGUE. (CN/0229-253X). **5097**

CREATION SOCIAL SCIENCE AND HUMANITIES QUARTERLY. (US/0740-3399). **Qty:** 6-8 per year. **5196**

CREATION SPIRITUALITY. (US/1053-9891). **Qty:** 20. **4951**

CREATIVE. (US/0737-5883). **758**

CREATIVE BLACK BOOK (PORTFOLIO ED.), THE. (US/0740-283X). **758**

CREATIVE BLACK BOOK (PRODUCER'S ED.), THE. (US/0889-6372). **758**

CREATIVE BLACK BOOK, THE. (US/0738-9000). **758**

CREATIVE CAMERA. (UK/0011-0876). **4368**

CREATIVE CHILD AND ADULT QUARTERLY, THE. (US/0884-4291). **1877**

CREATIVE FORUM. (II). **3378**

CREATIVE KIDS. (US/0892-9599). **1062**

CREATIVE LOAFING (1978). (US/0889-8685). **5653**

CREATIVE NURSING. (US). **Qty:** 5-10. **3854**

CREATIVE OHIO. (US/0741-6504). **372**

CREATIVE REAL ESTATE MAGAZINE. (US/0194-7222). **4836**

CREATIVE TRAINING TECHNIQUES. (US/1053-170X). **939**

CREATIVE TRANSFORMATION. (US/1062-4708). **Qty:** 8. **4951**

CREATIVE WOMAN (PARK FOREST SOUTH, ILL.), THE. (US/0736-4733). **5554**

CREATIVITY AND INNOVATION MANAGEMENT. (UK/0963-1690). **Qty:** 25 /year. **864**

CREATIVITY RESEARCH JOURNAL. (US/1040-0419). **5196**

CREATOR (WICHITA, KAN.). (US/1045-0815). **Qty:** 25. **4113**

CREDIT CARD MANAGEMENT. (US/0896-9329). **785**

CREDIT MANAGEMENT. (UK/0265-2099). **Qty:** 6. **785**

CREDIT MANUAL OF COMMERCIAL LAWS. (US/0070-1467). **Qty:** 1. **3099**

CREDIT UNION MANAGEMENT. (US/0273-9267). **786**

CREDIT UNION REPORT. (US/0894-752X). **786**

CREDIT WORLD, THE. (US/0011-1074). **Qty:** 6. **786**

CREDO. (NO). **4951**

CREEPING BENT. (US/8756-0291). **3462**

CREIGHTON LAW REVIEW. (US/0011-1155). **2957**

CRESCENDO & JAZZ MUSIC. (UK/0962-7472). **Qty:** varies. **4113**

CRESCENT INTERNATIONAL. (CN/0705-3754). **4470**

CRESSET (VALPARAISO), THE. (US/0011-1198). **Qty:** 25. **3340**

CREWE, BURKEVILLE JOURNAL, THE. (US/8755-9463). **5758**

CRIME CONTROL DIGEST. (US/0011-1295). **3161**

CRIMINAL APPEAL REPORTS (SENTENCING), THE. (UK/0144-3321). **3105**

CRIMINAL DEFENSE NEWSLETTER. (US/0731-082X). **3105**

CRIMINAL JUSTICE ABSTRACTS. (US/0146-9177). **3080**

CRIMINAL JUSTICE ETHICS. (US/0731-129X). **Qty:** 2-4. **2249**

CRIMINAL JUSTICE HISTORY. (US/0194-0953). **3162**

CRIMINAL JUSTICE JOURNAL (SAN DIEGO, CALIF.). (US/0145-4226). **3162**

CRIMINAL JUSTICE POLICY REVIEW. (US/0887-4034). **Qty:** 4-8. **3162**

CRIMINAL JUSTICE REVIEW (ATLANTA, GA.). (US/0734-0168). **3162**

CRIMINAL LAW FORUM. (US/1046-8374). **3106**

CRIMINAL LAW REVIEW (LONDON, ENGLAND). (UK/0011-135X). **3106**

CRIMINOLOGIST, THE. (UK/0011-1376). **3163**

CRIMINOLOGY (BEVERLY HILLS). (US/0011-1384). **3163**

CRISIS (NEW YORK, N.Y.), THE. (US/0011-1422). **2259**

CRISIS (NOTRE DAME, IND.). (US). **5028**

CRISIS (TORONTO). (CN/0227-5910). **4583**

CRISTALLO / CENTRO DI CULTURA DELL'ALTO ADIGE, IL. (IT/0011-1449). **3340**

CRISTIANESIMO NELLA STORIA. (IT/0393-3598). **4951**

CRISWELL THEOLOGICAL REVIEW. (US/0892-5712). **4951**

CRITERIO. (AG/0011-1473). **5028**

CRITICA HISPANICA. (US/0278-7261). **3275**

CRITICA (LA JOLLA, CALIF.). (US/8755-3325). **5243**

CRITICA LETTERARIA. (IT/0390-0142). **3378**

CRITICA; REVISTA HISPANOAMERICANA DE FILOSOFIA. (MX/0011-1503). **Qty:** 8. **4344**

CRITICA SOCIOLOGICA, LA. (IT/0011-1546). **5243**

CRITICAL ARTS. (SA/0256-0046). **1109**

CRITICAL CARE NURSE. (US/0279-5442). **3854**

CRITICAL DIGEST. (US/0045-9070). **5363**

CRITICAL MASS (HALIFAX). (CN/1180-193X). **Qty:** 3-6. **3462**

CRITICAL MATRIX. (US/1066-288X). **Qty:** 2. **5554**

CRITICAL PUBLIC HEALTH. (UK/0958-1596). **4772**

CRITICAL QUARTERLY, THE. (UK/0011-1562). **3379**

CRITICAL REVIEW (NEW YORK, N.Y.). (US/0891-3811). **Qty:** 12. **4470**

CRITICAL REVIEWS IN ORAL BIOLOGY AND MEDICINE. (US/1045-4411). **1319**

CRITICAL SOCIOLOGY. (US/0896-9205). **5243**

CRITICAL STUDIES IN MASS COMMUNICATION. (US/0739-3180). **1109**

CRITICAL TEXTS. (US/0730-2304). **3341**

CRITICISM (DETROIT). (US/0011-1589). **2845**

CRITICON. (FR). **3379**

CRITIQUE - BOLINGBROKE SOCIETY. (US/0011-1619). **3341**

CRITIQUE COMMUNISTE. (FR). **4541**

CROC. (CN/0226-6083). **3379**

CROISSANCE. (FR). **4519**

CRONACHE FARMACEUTICHE. (IT/0011-1783). **4298**

CROP PROTECTION (GUILDFORD, SURREY). (UK/0261-2194). **169**

CROP REPORT / ALBERTA WHEAT POOL. (CN). **169**

CROSBYTON REVIEW, THE. (US). **Qty:** varies. **5748**

CROSS-CULTURAL PSYCHOLOGY BULLETIN. (CN/0710-068X). **4583**

CROSS CURRENT. (UK/0260-6313). **1734**

CROSS CURRENTS. (US/0011-1953). **Qty:** 35. **4951**

CROSS POINT. (US/1064-4490). **Qty:** 10-12. **4951**

CROSSCURRENTS (NEW BRUNSWICK, N.J.). (US/1053-9778). **234**

CROSSCURRENTS (SASKATOON). (CN/0704-6588). **318**

CROSSOSOMA. (US/0891-9100). **Qty:** 3-5. **507**

CROSSROAD TRAILS. (US/0735-6196). **2444**

CROSSROADS (DE KALB, ILL.). (US/0741-2037). **2503**

CROSSROADS (OAKLAND, CALIF.). (US/1051-0575). **Qty:** 10. **4470**

CROSSROADS (SHOAL LAKE, MAN.). (CN). **5783**

CROSSROADS (SPRINGDALE, ARK.). (US/1044-5544). **5281**

CROSSSTITCH SAMPLER. (US/1054-1551). **5183**

CROSSTALK AND ANGLICAN JOURNAL EPISCOPAL. (CN/0845-4795). **5058**

CROSSTIES. (US/0097-4536). **2378**

CROSSWORLD (LONDON, ONT.). (CN/0225-3992). **2908**

CROWLEY POST-SIGNAL, THE. (US). **Qty:** 12. **5683**

CROWN JEWELS OF THE WIRE. (US/0884-7983). **1153**

CRS PUBLICATIONS' CAREER OPPORTUNITY INDEX (EAST-SOUTH-CENTRAL). (US/0897-909X). **4203**

CRS PUBLICATIONS' CAREER OPPORTUNITY INDEX (WESTERN). (US/0898-218X). **4203**

CRUCIBLE. (UK/0011-2100). **4951**

CRUCIBLE (TORONTO). (CN/0381-8047). **5097**

CRUISE INDUSTRY NEWS QUARTERLY, THE. (US/0893-1240). **5467**

CRUISING AROUND THE WORLD. (US/0744-6004). **5467**

CRUISING WORLD. (US/0098-3519). **593**

CRUX MATHEMATICORUM. (CN/0705-0348). **Qty:** (varies per year). **3502**

CRUX OF THE NEWS. (US/0591-2296). **4952**

CRUX (PRETORIA). (SA/0250-0035). **3275**

CRYO LETTERS. (UK/0143-2044). **Qty: 6. 452**

CRYOGENICS (GUILFORD). (UK/0011-2275). **4401**

CRYPTOGAMIC BOTANY. (GW/0935-2147). **507**

CRYPTOGAMIE. ALGOLOGIE. (FR/0181-1568). **Qty: 4. 452**

CRYPTOGAMIE. BRYOLOGIE, LICHENOLOGIE. (FR/0181-1576). **Qty: 4. 507**

CRYPTOGAMIE. MYCOLOGIE (1979). (FR/0181-1584). **Qty: 4. 507**

CRYPTOLOGIA. (US/0161-1194). **1226**

CRYPTOSYSTEMS JOURNAL. (US/0899-8159). **1181**

CRYPTOZOOLOGY. (US/0736-7023). **5581**

CSAS NEWSLETTER. (CN/0714-8240). **209**

CSD BULLETIN. (SA). **5197**

CSG BACKGROUNDER / COUNCIL OF STATE GOVERNMENTS. (US). **4641**

CSP. CRITICAL SOCIAL POLICY. (UK/0261-0183). **4541**

CT INFOS PARIS. (FR/1165-4651). **2332**

CTA ACTION (1986). (US/0896-7326). **1862**

CTC BULLETIN : OCCASIONAL BULLETIN OF THE COMMISSION ON THEOLOGICAL CONCERNS, CHRISTIAN CONFERENCE OF ASIA. (SI). **4952**

CTDNEWS (PHILADELPHIA, PA.). (US/1062-6743). **3569**

CTNS BULLETIN. (US/0889-8243). **Qty: 25-30. 5098**

CTOSIAN. (US). **1245**

CUADERNOS AMERICANOS. (MX/0011-2356). **2730**

CUADERNOS DE ECONOMIA (SANTIAGO). (CL/0716-0046). **1478**

CUADERNOS DE ECONOMIA SOCIAL. (AG/0325-9757). **1478**

CUADERNOS DE FILOSOFIA. (CL). **4344**

CUADERNOS DE INVESTIGACION FILOLOGICA. (SP/0211-0547). **3276**

CUADERNOS DE MARCHA. (UY). **2551**

CUADERNOS DE TEOLOGIA. (AG). **4952**

CUADERNOS DE TRADUCCION E INTERPRETACION. (SP/0212-0550). **3276**

CUADERNOS DEL CENDES. (VE). **1478**

CUADERNOS DEL TERCER MUNDO. (UY). **1554**

CUADERNOS PARA INVESTIGACION DE LA LITERATURA HISPANICA. (SP/0210-0061). **3379**

CUB CLUES. (US/0889-437X). **17**

CUBA BUSINESS. (UK/0951-4708). **Qty: 6. 663**

CUBA UPDATE. (US/0196-0830). **4541**

CUBAN JOURNAL OF AGRICULTURAL SCIENCE. (CU/0253-5815). **77**

CUBAN STUDIES. (US/0361-4441). **2730**

CUE SHEET, THE. (US/0888-9015). **4113**

CUED SPEECH ANNUAL. (US/1041-6226). **3276**

CUED SPEECH CENTER LINES. (US/1041-6196). **4386**

CUISINE AUCKLAND. (NZ/0113-1206). **Qty: 30. 2789**

CUKORIPAR. (US). **2332**

CULTIC STUDIES JOURNAL. (US/0748-6499). **5243**

CULTIVADOR MODERNO, EL. (SP). **77**

CULTIVAR. (FR/0045-9216). **170**

CULTURA E FE. (BL). **4952**

CULTURA, LA. (IT). **2845**

CULTURA LUDENS. (US/0882-3049). **5197**

CULTURAL FUTURES RESEARCH. (US/0748-772X). **234**

CULTURAL INFORMATION SERVICE. (US/0097-952X). **4952**

CULTURAL VISTAS. (US/1048-8650). **Qty: 12. 2845**

CULTURE & TRADITION. (CN/0701-0184). **2319**

CULTURE, MEDICINE AND PSYCHIATRY. (NE/0165-005X). **3924**

CUMBERLAND FLAG, THE. (US/0011-2968). **4952**

CUMBERLAND LAW REVIEW. (US/0360-8298). **2957**

CUMBERLAND LAWYER, THE. (US/0590-3378). **2957**

CUMBERLAND PRESBYTERIAN, THE. (US/0011-2976). **5058**

CUMBRIA. (UK/0590-3394). **2514**

CUMHURIYET. (TU). **5811**

CUNICULTURAL. (SP/0210-1912). **210**

CUOIO, PELLI, MATERIE CONCIANTI. (IT/0011-3034). **Qty: 10. 3183**

CUPA JOURNAL (WASHINGTON, D.C. 1987). (US/1046-9508). **939**

CUPA NEWS (WASHINGTON D.C. : 1987). (US/0892-7855). **1819**

CURARE. (GW/0344-8622). **3924**

CURRENCY FORECASTERS DIGEST. (US). **Qty: 12/yr. 1478**

CURRENT ADVANCES IN CLINICAL CHEMISTRY. (UK/0885-1980). **1011**

CURRENT AFFAIRS BULLETIN. (AT/0011-3182). **4470**

CURRENT ARCHAEOLOGY. (UK/0011-3212). **266**

CURRENT AUSTRALIAN AND NEW ZEALAND LEGAL LITERATURE INDEX. (AT). **2957**

CURRENT AWARENESS IN PARTICLE TECHNOLOGY / PUBLISHED AND COMPILED BY: PARTICLE SCIENCE AND TECHNOLOGY INFORMATION SERVICE, UNIVERSITY OF TECHNOLOGY, LOUGHBOROUGH, GREAT BRITAIN. (UK/0376-4842). **5098**

CURRENT BIBLIOGRAPHY ON AFRICAN AFFAIRS, A. (US/0011-3255). **2635**

CURRENT CENTRAL LEGISLATION. (II). **2957**

CURRENT COINS OF THE WORLD. (US/0070-1882). **2781**

CURRENT EYE RESEARCH. (UK/0271-3683). **3874**

CURRENT GENETICS. (GW/0172-8083). **544**

CURRENT GEOGRAPHICAL PUBLICATIONS. (US/0011-3514). **2580**

CURRENT HISTORY (1941). (US/0011-3530). **2614**

CURRENT INDEX TO JOURNALS IN EDUCATION. (US/0011-3565). **1794**

CURRENT INDEX TO JOURNALS IN EDUCATION. SEMIANNUAL CUMULATION. (US). **1734**

CURRENT ISSUES IN MIDDLE LEVEL EDUCATION. (US/1059-7107). **Qty: 1-2. 1734**

CURRENT LITERATURE IN FAMILY PLANNING. (US/0092-6000). **2287**

CURRENT MUSICOLOGY. (US/0011-3735). **4113**

CURRENT (NEW YORK). (US/0011-3131). **2487**

CURRENT NOTES. (US/8750-1937). **Qty: 2. 1181**

CURRENT OPINION IN THERAPEUTIC PATENTS. (UK). **1303**

CURRENT POPULATION REPORTS. SERIES P-60, CONSUMER INCOME. (US/0730-4803). **1478**

CURRENT PUBLICATIONS IN LEGAL AND RELATED FIELDS. (US/0011-3859). **3080**

CURRENT SCIENCE. (II/0011-3891). **5098**

CURRENT SOCIOLOGY (PARIS, FRANCE). (UK/0011-3921). **5244**

CURRENT SURGERY. (US/0149-7944). **3963**

CURRENT TOPICS IN HUMAN INTELLIGENCE. (US/8755-0040). **4584**

CURRENT TOPICS IN RESEARCH ON SYNAPSES. (US/0747-5454). **580**

CURRENT WORLD AFFAIRS. (US/1050-4850). **Qty: 100. 4040**

CURRENTLY (TORONTO). (CN/0384-9627). **4087**

CURRENTS IN THEOLOGY AND MISSION. (US/0098-2113). **4952**

CURRENTS (TORONTO). (CN/0715-7045). **5244**

CURRENTS (WASHINGTON, D.C. 1983). (US/0748-478X). **1819**

CURRICULUM AND TEACHING. (AT/0726-416X). **1734**

CURRICULUM PERSPECTIVES. (AT/0159-7868). **1892**

CURRICULUM PRODUCT NEWS : CPN. (US/1063-3375). **1892**

CURRICULUM REVIEW. (US/0147-2453). **1892**

CUSHING CITIZEN, THE. (US). **Qty: 6. 5731**

CUSO FORUM (OTTAWA, ONT. : 1980). (CN/0823-5740). **1634**

CUSSCO NEWSLETTER. (CN/0823-3918). **4773**

CUSTOM CHEMICAL SYNTHESIS SERVICES IN OTHER EUROPEAN COUNTRIES. (UK). **974**

CUSTOS. (SA). **4706**

CUTBANK. (US/0734-9963). **Qty: 2-4. 3379**

CUTTING TOOL ENGINEERING. (US/0011-4189). **4000**

CUTTINGTON RESEARCH JOURNAL. (LB). **3341**

CVETOVODSTVO. (RU/0041-4905). **2413**

CWA NEWS. (US/0007-9227). **1662**

CYBEREDGE JOURNAL. (US/1061-3099). **Qty: 10-15. 1181**

CYBERNETICA. (BE/0011-4227). **1250**

CYBERNETICS AND SYSTEMS. (US/0196-9722). **1250**

CYBIUM. (FR/0399-0974). **Qty: 4. 2299**

CYCLE NEWS EAST. (US/0274-7502). **428**

CYCLE TOURING & CAMPAIGNING. (UK). **428**

CYCLES (PITTSBURGH). (US/0011-4294). **5098**

CYCLIC AMP (SHEFFIELD, ENGLAND). (UK/0142-8055). **486**

CYCLING U.S.A. (US/0274-4813). **Qty: 1-2. 428**

CYCLING WORLD. (UK/0143-0238). **Qty: 4. 4892**

CYCLODEXTRIN NEWS. (HU/0951-256X). **1041**

CYNEGETICUS. (US/0160-2543). **4892**

CYPRUS JOURNAL OF ECONOMICS, THE. (CY/1013-3224). **1479**

CYPRUS REVIEW, THE. (CY/1015-2881). **Qty: 6-8. 4471**

CYPRUS REVIEW, THE. (CY). **5197**

CYRILLOMETHODIANUM. (GR). **2614**

CYTOPATHOLOGY (OXFORD). (UK/0956-5507). **535**

CYTOTECHNOLOGY (DORDRECHT). (NE/0920-9069). **535**

CZECHOSLOVAK AND CENTRAL EUROPEAN JOURNAL. (US/1056-005X). **Qty: 10. 2685**

CZECHOSLOVAK ECONOMIC PAPERS. (CS/0590-5001). **1479**

CZECHOSLOVAK INDUSTRIAL DESIGN. (XR). **2097**

D (DALLAS. 1978). (US/0164-8292). **2532**

D.H. LAWRENCE REVIEW, THE. (US/0011-4936). **Qty: 25. 3341**

D-J-M ENZYME REPORT. (US/0731-4027). **453**

D.O., DIARIO OFICIAL, ESTADO DO RIO DE JANEIRO. PARTE III. (BL). **2958**

D'A PALMA DE MALLORCA. (SP/1130-3794). **296**

DAAT. (IS/0334-2336). **5047**

DACHAUER HEFTER. (GW/0934-361X). **2685**

DACHDECKER-HANDWERK, DAS. (GW/0012-124X). **612**

DAFFODIL JOURNAL, THE. (US/0011-5290). **2413**

DAFTAR PENERBITAN PENERBITAN BIRO PUSAT STATISTIK. (IO). **5326**

DAILY ASTORIAN, THE. (US/0739-5078). **Qty: 25. 5733**

DAILY CALIFORNIAN. (US/1050-2300). **5634**

DAILY CHIEF-UNION, THE. (US). **5727**

DAILY CITIZEN, THE. (US). **Qty: 52. 5631**

DAILY COMMERCE. (US/0279-4195). **830**

DAILY COURT REVIEW. (US/0740-1949). **2958**

DAILY DEMOCRAT. DAVIS EDITION. (US). **5634**

DAILY DEMOCRAT (WOODLAND, CALIF.). (US/0747-1890). **5634**

DAILY DUNKLIN DEMOCRAT, THE. (US/1047-7160). **Qty: 12. 5703**

DAILY EASTERN NEWS, THE. (US/0894-1599). **1091**

DAILY HAMPSHIRE GAZETTE. (US/0739-3504). **5688**

DAILY HERALD (PROVO, UTAH. 1939), THE. (US/0891-2777). **Qty: 10-20. 5756**

DAILY HOME. (US/1059-6461). **5626**

DAILY JAPAN DIGEST, THE. (US/1060-2240). **Qty: 20/yr. 4471**

DAILY JOURNAL, THE. (US). **Qty: 25. 5695**

DAILY MAIL BOOK OF HOME PLANS. (UK). **296**

DAILY MESSENGER (UNION CITY, TENN.). (US/0745-5534). **5745**

DAILY MOUNTAIN EAGLE. (US/0893-0759). **5626**

DAILY NEWS HALIFAX-DARTMOUTH EDITION. (CN/0715-4321). **5783**

DAILY NEWS LEADER, THE. (US/0747-2501). **5758**

DAILY PRESS (1988). (US/1042-8496). **Qty:** varies. **5634**

DAILY PRESS (ESCANABA, MICH.). (US). **5691**

DAILY RECORD (PARSIPPANY, N.J.). (US). **5710**

DAILY RECORDER, THE. (US/0197-8055). **Qty:** 5-7. **2958**

DAILY REGISTER (PORTAGE, WIS.). (US/0747-2927). **Qty:** 12. **5766**

DAILY REPORTER, THE. (US). **5675**

DAILY REVIEW, THE. (US). **5634**

DAILY SOUTHERNER. (US). **5723**

DAILY STAR (ONEONTA, NEW YORK). (US). **5715**

DAILY TELEGRAM, THE. (US). **5766**

DAILY TIMES. (NR) **5807**

DAILY TIMES-NEWS, THE. (US). **Qty:** 60. **5723**

DAILY TIMES (PRIMOS, PA.). (US). **5736**

DAILY TIMES (SALISBURY, MD.). (US). **5686**

DAILY TIMES, THE. (US). **5772**

DAILY TRIBUNE NEWS (CARTERSVILLE, GA.), THE. (US/1049-6750). **5653**

DAILY WORLD (HELENA, ARK.), THE. (US/8750-5274). **Qty:** 20. **5631**

DAIRY EXPORTER. (NZ/0111-915X). **193**

DAIRY GOAT JOURNAL. (US/0011-5592). **193**

DAIRY INDUSTRIES INTERNATIONAL. (UK/0308-8197). **193**

DAIRY INDUSTRY NEWSLETTER. (UK/0956-8131). **Qty:** 1-2. **193**

DAIRYMAN (ARMADALE), THE. (AT). **194**

DAIRYMEN'S DIGEST. NORTH CENTRAL REGION EDITION. (US/0745-9033). **194**

DAKOTA COUNTY GENEALOGIST, THE. (US/1044-6524). **Qty:** (2). **2444**

DAKOTA OUTDOORS. (US/1041-1968). **Qty:** 12. **4871**

DALE NEWS, THE. (US). **Qty:** 10/year. **5663**

DALHOUSIE FRENCH STUDIES. (CN/0711-8813). **3379**

DALHOUSIE GAZETTE, THE. (CN/0011-5819). **1091**

DALHOUSIE JOURNAL OF LEGAL STUDIES. (CN/1188-4258). **Qty:** 6-10. **2959**

DALHOUSIE REVIEW, THE. (CN/0011-5827). **Qty:** 40. **3380**

DALLAS OBSERVER. (US/0732-0299). **384**

DALLAS POST TRIBUNE, THE. (US/0746-7303). **5749**

DALLAS WEEKLY, THE. (US/0885-1271). **5749**

DAN CHUA. (US/0747-2315). **Qty:** 4,000. **5028**

DANCE AND DANCERS. (UK/0011-5983). **1311**

DANCE AUSTRALIA. (AT). **1311**

DANCE CONNECTION. (CN/0838-1313). **Qty:** 5. **1311**

DANCE IN CANADA. (CN/0317-9737). **1312**

DANCE MATTERS. (UK). **1312**

DANCE (NEW YORK, N.Y. 1988). (US/0894-4849). **1312**

DANCE NOW. (UK/0966-6346). **Qty:** 12. **1312**

DANCE RESEARCH. (UK/0264-2875). **1312**

DANCE RESEARCH JOURNAL. (US/0149-7677). **1312**

DANCE TEACHER NOW. (US/0199-1795). **1312**

DANCE THEATRE JOURNAL. (UK/0264-9160). **Qty:** Varies. **1312**

DANCEVIEW. (US). **Qty:** 16-20. **1312**

DANCING TIMES. (UK/0011-605X). **1312**

DANCING USA. (US/1053-5454). **Qty:** 6. **1313**

DANCSCENE. (US/0745-3949). **1313**

DANDELION. (CN/0383-9575). **Qty:** 8. **3380**

DANGEROUS GOODS : NEWSLETTER. (CN/0710-0914). **Qty:** occasionally. **5380**

DANSALAN QUARTERLY. (PH). **2650**

DANSER. (FR/0755-7639). **1313**

DANSK AUDIOLOGOPDI. (DK/0105-7200). **Qty:** 20. **3887**

DANSK ORNITHOLOGISK FORENINGS TIDSSKRIFT. (DK/0011-6394). **5617**

DANSK TEOLOGISK TIDSSKRIFT. (DK/0105-3191). **4952**

DANSK UDSYN. (DK/0106-4622). **2685**

DANSKE MALERMESTRE. (DK/0905-6440). **4223**

DANSKE STUDIER. (DK/0106-4525). **3341**

DANVILLE NEWS (DANVILLE, PA.). (US). **5736**

DANVILLE REGISTER, THE. (US/0744-3242). **Qty:** 52. **5758**

DAPHNIS. (SZ/0300-693X). **3380**

DARI DE SEAMA ALE SEDINTELOR - INSTITUL DE GEOLOGIE SI GEOFIZICA. 4, STRATIGRAFIE. (RM/0254-7309). **1373**

DARI DE SEAMA ALE SEDINTELOR - INSTITUL DE GEOLOGIE SI GEOFIZICA. 5. TECTONICA SI GEOLOGIE REGIONALA. (RM/0253-1798). **1373**

DARIEN NEWS, THE. (US). **Qty:** 3-4. **5653**

DARK SHADOWS ANNOUNCEMENT, THE. (US). **1131**

DARKNERVE. (US). **4241**

DARSHANA INTERNATIONAL. (II/0011-6734). **4344**

DARTMOUTH ALUMNI MAGAZINE. (US). **1101**

DARTMOUTH COLLEGE LIBRARY BULLETIN. (US/0011-6750). **Qty:** 2. **3205**

DARTMOUTH REVIEW, THE. (US). **1091**

DARTS WORLD. (UK/0140-6000). **4892**

DARWINIANA. (AG/0011-6793). **Qty:** 2-3. **508**

DASEIN. (US/0011-6807). **318**

DATA ARCHIVE BULLETIN / SSRC. (UK/0307-1391). **2481**

DATA BASE. (US/0095-0033). **1257**

DATA BASED ADVISOR. (US/0740-5200). **1253**

DATA/COMM INDUSTRY REPORT. (US/0149-9556). **1257**

DATA EXTRACT. (AT). **Qty:** 24. **2510**

DATA JURIDICA. (NE). **2959**

DATA PROCESSING. (UK/0011-684X). **1257**

DATA PROCESSING & COMMUNICATIONS SECURITY. (US/0749-1484). **1257**

DATA PROCESSING AUDITING REPORT. (US/0735-3863). **3571**

DATA RESOURCE MANAGEMENT. (US/1053-5594). **Qty:** 4. **865**

DATA SECURITY LETTER. (US/1065-9986). **Qty:** 3-4. **1181**

DATABASE AND NETWORK JOURNAL. (UK/0265-4490). **1253**

DATABASE CANADA. (CN/0840-7797). **1253**

DATABASE PROGRAMMING & DESIGN. (US/0895-4518). **1253**

DATABASE SEARCHER. (US/0891-6713). **1253**

DATABASE (WESTON). (US/0162-4105). **Qty:** (3/4 per issue). **1253**

DATAMATION. (US/0011-6963). **1258**

DATAPRO REPORTS ON MINICOMPUTERS. (US/0275-0813). **1274**

DATAPRO REPORTS ON OFFICE AUTOMATION. (US). **1258**

DATEK IMAGING SUPPLIES MONTHLY, THE. (US/1050-6993). **4564**

DATEN DES GESUNDHEITSWESENS. (GW/0172-3723). **Qty:** 12. **4809**

DATENSCHUTZ UND DATENSICHERUNG. (GW). **2959**

DATUTOP, DEPARTMENT OF ARCHITECTURE, TAMPERE UNIVERSITY OF TECHNOLOGY OCCASIONAL PAPERS. (FI/0359-7105). **296**

DATZ : AQUARIEN TERRARIEN. (GW/0941-8393). **2773**

DAUGHTERS OF SARAH. (US/0739-1749). **4952**

DAVID Y GOLIATH : BOLETIN CLACSO. (AG/0325-0431). **2551**

DAVIESS COUNTY HISTORICAL QUARTERLY, THE. (US/0882-2395). **2730**

DAWN. (PK). **2503**

DAWSON AND HIND. (CN/0703-6507). **4087**

DAYANANDA SANDESA. (II). **4952**

DAYTON DAILY NEWS (DAYTON, OHIO : 1987). (US/0897-0920). **5728**

DAYTON REVIEW (DAYTON, IOWA). (US). **Qty:** 12. **5669**

DAZE INC, THE. (US/0895-3961). **2588**

DB. DEUTSCHE BAUZEITUNG (1981). (GW/0721-1902). **296**

DBZ. DEUTSCHE BRIEFMARKEN-ZEITUNG. (GW/0931-4393). **2773**

DDZ. DER DEUTSCHE ZOLLBEAMTE. (GW). **4719**

DE HAEN NEW PRODUCT SURVEY. (US). **4299**

DE PAUL LAW REVIEW. (US/0011-7188). **Qty:** 0-1. **2959**

DE PERE JOURNAL. (US/0748-6219). **Qty:** 1-2. **5766**

DEAF LIFE. (US/0898-719X). **Qty:** 6-12. **4386**

DEAF USA. (US/0898-5480). **Qty:** 12/yr. **4386**

DEALMAKERS (BELLE MEAD, N.J.), THE. (US/1055-0771). **4836**

DEAN BURGON NEWS, THE. (US). **5230**

DEATH STUDIES. (US/0748-1187). **4584**

DEATH VALLEY GATEWAY GAZETTE. (US/0746-7419). **5707**

DEBATE (LIMA, PERU). (PE). **4471**

DEBATES AND PROCEEDINGS - LEGISLATIVE ASSEMBLY OF MANITOBA. (CN/0542-5492). **4641**

DEBATES EN SOCIOLOGIA. (PE). **5244**

DEC PROFESSIONAL, THE. (US/0744-9216). **1246**

DECANTER (LONDON. 1985). (UK/0954-4240). **2366**

DECCAN GEOGRAPHER. (II/0011-7269). **Qty:** 6. **2559**

DECEMBER ROSE. (US/0748-1195). **5178**

DECHEMA CORROSION HANDBOOK. (UK). **2012**

DECIDUOUS FRUIT GROWER, THE. (SA/0302-7074). **2413**

DECISION (CANADIAN ED.). (CN/0820-9057). **4952**

DECISION LINE. (US/0732-6823). **664**

DECISIONS MEDIAS. (FR/1165-8606). **1109**

DECKS AWASH. (CN/0317-7076). **Qty:** 3. **2487**

DECORATION CHEZ-SOI. (CN/0705-1093). **2899**

DECORATIVE ARTS DIGEST. (US/0888-076X). **372**

DECORATIVE ARTS SOCIETY NEWSLETTER, THE. (US/0884-4011). **372**

DECORATIVE RUG, THE. (US/1045-8816). **2904**

DECOY MAGAZINE. (US/1055-0364). **Qty:** 6. **2773**

DED BRIEF. (GW). **Qty:** 6-8. **2908**

DEEP SKY. (US/0735-3073). **395**

DEEP SOUTH GENEALOGICAL QUARTERLY. (US/0418-4904). **2445**

DEER AND DEER HUNTING. (US/0164-7318). **4871**

DEER FARMER, THE. (NZ/0110-7992). **210**

DEER PARK BROADCASTER. (US). **Qty:** 2/year. **5749**

DEFECT ACTION SHEETS. (UK). **612**

DEFENCE (ETON). (UK/0142-6184). **4040**

DEFENCE INDUSTRY AND AEROSPACE REPORT. (AT/1033-2898). **Qty:** 1-2. **4040**

DEFENCE JOURNAL. (PK). **4040**

DEFENDER NORTH MELBOURNE. (AT/0811-6407). **Qty:** approx. 20/year. **3179**

DEFENDERS. (US/0162-6337). **2191**

DEFENSA MADRID. (SP/0211-3732). **17**

DEFENSE ACQUISITION REPORT. (US/1072-2386). **Qty:** 6. **4040**

DEFENSE & ECONOMY : WORLD REPORT AND SURVEY. (US/0364-9008). **4519**

DEFENSE COUNSEL JOURNAL. (US/0895-0016). **Qty:** 12. **3089**

DEFENSE

DEFENSE LATIN AMERICA. (UK/0261-233X). **4041**

DEFENSE LAW JOURNAL. (US/0011-7587). **2959**

DEFENSE MEDIA REVIEW. (US/0893-0619). **4041**

DEFENSE MONITOR, THE. (US/0195-6450). **4041**

DEFENSE NATIONALE. (FR/0336-1489). **4041**

DEFENSE NEWS (SPRINGFIELD, VA.). (US/0884-139X). **4041**

DEFENSE TRANSPORTATION JOURNAL. (US/0011-7625). **Qty:** 15-20. **4042**

DEFENSE WEEK. (US/0273-3188). **4042**

DEFENSOR CHIEFTAIN. (US/0011-7633). **Qty:** 6 per year. **5712**

DEFINED PROVIDENCE. (US/1066-2197). **3462**

DEGRE SECOND. (US/0148-561X). **3341**

DEGRES. (BE/0376-8163). **3276**

DEHAEN'S NEW PRODUCT SURVEY. MONTHLY SUPPLEMENT. (US). **4299**

DEJINY VED A TECHNIKY. (XR/0300-4414). **5099**

DELAWARE BUSINESS REVIEW. (US/1061-4605). **665**

DELAWARE CONSERVATIONIST. (GW/0045-9852). **2191**

DELAWARE GAZETTE (DELAWARE, OHIO 1932), THE. (US/1064-2013). **Qty:** 5-6/yr. **5728**

DELAWARE JOURNAL OF CORPORATE LAW, THE. (US/0364-9490). **3099**

DELAWARE LAWYER. (US/0735-6595). **2959**

DELAWARE MEDICAL JOURNAL. (US/0011-7781). **Qty:** 4. **3571**

DELAWARE VALLEY RAIL PASSENGER, THE. (US) **Qty:** varies. **5431**

DELAY LETTER, THE. (US/1064-6531). **923**

DELFINO ROMA, IL. (IT/1121-0311). **Qty:** 70/yr. **2487**

DELHI LAW REVIEW. (II). **2959**

DELO (BEOGRAD). (YU/0011-7935). **3380**

DELPHIN. (GW). **318**

DELTA KAPPA GAMMA BULLETIN, THE. (US/0011-8044). **1734**

DELTA OPTIMIST, THE. (CN/0710-1422). **5783**

DELTA (PALMERSTON NORTH). (NZ/0419-9855). **1735**

DELTION AUTOKINETISTIKES NOMOTHESIAS KAI NOMOLOGIAS. (GR). **2959**

DEMING HEADLIGHT (1956). (US/0738-8349). **5712**

DEMOCRAT-LEADER (FAYETTE, MO.). (US/0746-9934). **5703**

DEMOCRAT-REPORTER, THE. (US). **5626**

DEMOCRATIC JOURNALIST, THE. (XR/0011-8214). **2918**

DEMOCRATIC LEFT. (US/0164-3207). **Qty:** 1. **4471**

DEMOGRAFIE. (XR/0011-8265). **4551**

DENEUVE (SAN FRANCISCO, CALIF.). (US/1062-6247). **Qty:** 30-40. **2794**

DENISON REVIEW, THE. (US). **5669**

DENPUN KAGAKU. (JA/0021-5406). **2333**

DENTAL COMPUTER NEWSLETTER. (US/0738-9744). **Qty:** 20. **1320**

DENTAL-ECHO. (GW/0011-8575). **1320**

DENTAL ECONOMICS (PITTSBURGH. 1968). (US/0011-8583). **1320**

DENTAL HYGIENE NEWS (ROCHESTER, N.Y.). (US/0882-9543). **1321**

DENTAL LAB PRODUCTS. (US/0146-9738). **1321**

DENTAL-LABOR. LABORATOIRE DENTAIRE. DENTAL LABORATORY, DAS. (GW). **1321**

DENTAL MATERIALS. (DK/0109-5641). **1321**

DENTAL OUTLOOK, THE. (AT/0418-694X). **1321**

DENTAL PRACTICE (EWELL). (UK/0011-8710). **1321**

DENTAL PRODUCTS REPORT. (US/0011-8737). **1321**

DENTAL TECHNICIAN. (UK/0011-8796). **1321**

DENTAL UPDATE. (UK/0305-5000). **1321**

DENTEKSA. (SA/0259-563X). **1322**

DENTIST (WACO, TEX.). (US/0887-5669). **1322**

DENTISTRY (CHICAGO, ILL.). (US/0277-3635). **Qty:** 12. **1322**

DENTISTRY TODAY. (US/8750-2186). **1322**

DENTO MAXILLO FACIAL RADIOLOGY. (UK/0250-832X). **1322**

DENTON RECORD-CHRONICLE. (US). **5749**

DENVER QUARTERLY. (US/0011-8869). **Qty:** 4. **3380**

DENVER WESTERNERS ROUNDUP, THE. (US/0278-7970). **Qty:** 40-50. **2730**

DEO. (UK). **4114**

DEPARTMENT CHAIR, THE. (US/1049-3255). **Qty:** 4-8. **1862**

DEQUINCY NEWS, THE. (US). **Qty:** 20. **5683**

DERECHO Y REFORMA AGRARIA; REVISTA. (VE/0304-2820). **2960**

DERMATOLOGISCHE MONATSSCHRIFT. (GW/0011-9083). **3719**

DERMATOLOGY IN PRACTICE (LONDON). (UK/0262-5504). **3719**

DERMATOSEN IN BERUF UND UMWELT. (GW/0343-2432). **3720**

DERMO TIME. (IT). **3720**

DESALINATION. (NE/0011-9164). **5532**

DESARROLLO INDOAMERICANO. (CK/0418-7547). **2730**

DESARROLLO NACIONAL. (US/0279-2958). **5099**

DESCENDER, THE. (US/0420-0063). **2445**

DESCENT (SYDNEY). (AT/0084-9731). **Qty:** 25,000. **2445**

DESCENT WELLS. (UK/0046-0036). **1373**

DESERET NEWS (SALT LAKE CITY, UTAH : 1964). (US/0745-4724). **5756**

DESERT CALL / SPIRITUAL LIFE INSTITUTE. (US/0011-9229). **4953**

DESERT LIFE. (US). **Qty:** 5. **4871**

DESERT PLANTS. (US/0734-3434). **508**

DESIGN. (II/0011-9261). **296**

DESIGN AND CONTROL OF CONCRETE MIXTURES. (US/0190-6755). **612**

DESIGN BOOK REVIEW. (US/0737-5344). **296**

DESIGN DK. (DK). **Qty:** 3-4. **297**

DESIGN ENGINEERING (LONDON, ENGLAND). (UK/0308-8448). **1970**

DESIGN FOR ARTS IN EDUCATION. (US/0732-0973). **318**

DESIGN ISSUES. (US/0747-9360). **297**

DESIGN (LONDON). (UK/0011-9245). **2097**

DESIGN MANAGEMENT JOURNAL. (US/1045-7194). **Qty:** 12-16. **1970**

DESIGN METHODS. (US/1067-9359). **Qty:** 1-5. **297**

DESIGN PRODUCTS & APPLICATIONS. (UK). **2097**

DESIGN SOLUTIONS. (US/0277-3538). **297**

DESIGN STUDIES. (UK/0142-694X). **2097**

DESIGN SYSTEMS STRATEGIES. (US/0895-6790). **1233**

DESIGN TECHNOLOGY TEACHING. (UK). **372**

DESIGN WORLD. (AT/0810-6029). **297**

DESIGNERS DIGEST MAGAZINE. (GW). **378**

DESIGNERS' JOURNAL. (UK/0264-8148). **297**

DESIGNERS WEST. (US/0192-1487). **2900**

DESIGNINK. (AU/1035-0500). **297**

DESKTOP MAGAZINE. (AT/1037-7603). **1233**

DESKTOP PUBLISHER. (US). **1263**

DESOTO COUNTY TRIBUNE, THE. (US). **Qty:** 52. **5700**

DETAIL (MUNCHEN). (GW/0011-9571). **297**

DETAILS (NEW YORK, N.Y.). (US/0740-4921). **3995**

DETENTION REPORTER. (US/0742-552X). **3163**

DETROIT COLLEGE OF LAW ALUMNI NEWS. (US). **1101**

DETROIT COLLEGE OF LAW REVIEW. (US/0099-135X). **2960**

DETROIT FREE PRESS (DETROIT, MICH., 1858). (US/1055-2758). **Qty:** 100. **5691**

DETROIT LABOR NEWS. (US/1072-1525). **Qty:** 3/year. **1662**

DETROIT LEGAL NEWS (DAILY ED.). (US/0739-9480). **Qty:** 20. **2960**

DETROIT MARINE HISTORIAN. (US). **Qty:** varies. **5448**

DETROIT NEWS (DETROIT, MICH.), THE. (US/1055-2715). **5691**

DETROITER, THE. (US/0011-9709). **819**

DEUTSCH - BRASILIANISCHE HEFTE. CADERNOS GERMANO - BRASILEIROS. (GW). **2551**

DEUTSCHAMERIKANER (CHICAGO), DER. (US/0273-5261). **2532**

DEUTSCHE ARCHITEKTUR. (GE/0011-9865). **311**

DEUTSCHE BUHNE, DIE. (GW). **5363**

DEUTSCHE GEWAESSERKUNDLICHE MITTEILUNGEN. (GW/0012-0235). **5532**

DEUTSCHE HEBE- UND FORDERTECHNIK. (GW/0012-0278). **5099**

DEUTSCHE HYDROGRAPHISCHE ZEITSCHRIFT. (GW/0012-0308). **1354**

DEUTSCHE JUGEND. (GW/0012-0332). **5282**

DEUTSCHE KRANKENPFLEGEZEITSCHRIFT. (GW/0012-074X). **3855**

DEUTSCHE KUNST UND DENKMALPFLEGE. (GW/0012-0375). **297**

DEUTSCHE LEBENSMITTEL-RUNDSCHAU. (GW/0012-0413). **2333**

DEUTSCHE MILCHWIRTSCHAFT (HILDESHEIM). (GW/0012-0480). **194**

DEUTSCHE OPTIKERZEITUNG. (GW/0344-7103). **3874**

DEUTSCHE RICHTERZEITUNG. (GW). **2960**

DEUTSCHE SCHRIFT, DIE. (GW). **3276**

DEUTSCHE SCHWARZBUNTE. (GW/0343-3145). **210**

DEUTSCHE SPRACHE. (GW/0340-9341). **3276**

DEUTSCHE STOMATOLOGIE. (GW/0863-4904). **1322**

DEUTSCHE STUDIEN (SCHLOSS BLECKEDE). (GW/0012-0812). **2515**

DEUTSCHE UNIVERSITATSZEITUNG. (GW). **1820**

DEUTSCHE ZAHNAERZTLICHE ZEITSCHRIFT. (GW/0012-1029). **1322**

DEUTSCHE ZEITSCHRIFT FUER MUND-, KIEFER- UND GESICHTS- CHIRURGIE. (GW/0343-3137). **3963**

DEUTSCHE ZEITSCHRIFT FUER ONKOLOGIE. (GW/0931-0037). **3816**

DEUTSCHE ZEITSCHRIFT FUER SPORTMEDIZIN. (GW/0344-5925). **3954**

DEUTSCHER GARTENBAU. (GW). **2413**

DEUTSCHES ALLGEMEINES SONNTAGSBLATT. (GW). **5801**

DEUTSCHES ARZTEBLATT. (GW/0012-1207). **3571**

DEUTSCHES TIERARZTEBLATT. (GW/0340-1898). **5508**

DEUTSCHES VERWALTUNGSBLATT. (GW/0012-1363). **2960**

DEUTSCHLAND ARCHIV. (GW/0012-1428). **4471**

DEVELOPING COUNTRY COURIER, THE. (US/0160-8037). **4471**

DEVELOPMENT (CAMBRIDGE). (UK/0950-1991). **541**

DEVELOPMENT COMMUNICATION REPORT. (US/0192-1312). **1110**

DEVELOPMENT FORUM - UNITED NATIONS. (US/0251-6632). **1479**

DEVELOPMENT IN PRACTICE. (UK/0961-4524). **Qty:** approx. 60 per year. **2909**

DEVELOPMENT JOURNAL (LONDON). (UK/0957-4115). **4642**

DEVELOPMENT POLICY AND ADMINISTRATION REVIEW. (II). **4642**

DEVELOPMENT POLICY REVIEW. (UK/0950-6764). **2909**

DEVELOPMENT SOUTHERN AFRICA (SANDTON, SOUTH AFRICA). (SA). **2909**

DEVELOPMENTAL DISABILITIES BULLETIN. (CN/1184-0412). **4386**

DEVELOPMENTAL GENETICS. (US/0192-253X). **544**

DEVELOPMENTAL MEDICINE & CHILD NEUROLOGY. (UK/0012-1622). **3657**

DEVELOPMENTS (EDMONTON). (CN/0714-1017). **1342**

DEVENIR. (SZ). **3571**

DEVIANCE ET SOCIETE. (SZ/0378-7931). **4584**

DEVIANT BEHAVIOR. (US/0163-9625). **4584**

DEVON & CORNWALL NOTES & QUERIES. (UK/0012-1681). **2685**

DEWAN MASYARAKAT. (MY). **5198**

DEWITT COUNTY GENEALOGICAL QUARTERLY. (US/0890-4456). **2445**

DGA NEWS. (US/1075-6116). **Qty:** 15-20. **4067**

DHZ MARKT. (NE). **2811**

DIABETES CARE. (US/0149-5992). **3727**

DIABETES DATELINE : THE NDIC BULLETIN. (US). **3727**

DIABETES EDUCATOR, THE. (US/0145-7217). **3727**

DIABETES IN THE NEWS (1987). (US/0893-5939). **3728**

DIABETES SELF-MANAGEMENT. (US/0741-6253). **3728**

DIABETES SPECTRUM. (US/1040-9165). **3728**

DIABETIC MEDICINE. (UK/0742-3071). **3728**

DIABETIC TRAVELER, THE. (US/0899-2398). **Qty:** 4-6. **5468**

DIACHRONICA. (GW/0176-4225). **Qty:** 8. **3277**

DIACRITICS. (US/0300-7162). **3341**

DIAGNOSTIC ENGINEERING : NEWSLETTER OF THE INSTITUTION OF DIAGNOSTIC ENGINEERS. (UK/0269-0225). **Qty:** 20-30. **1970**

DIAGNOSTIC MICROBIOLOGY AND INFECTIOUS DISEASE. (US/0732-8893). **562**

DIAGRAMMES. (FR/0224-3911). **Qty:** 4. **3503**

DIAKONEO (NEW ORLEANS, LA.). (US/1070-7875). **Qty:** 3-4. **4953**

DIAKONIA (MAINZ, GERMANY : 1972). (GW/0341-9592). **4953**

DIAKRISIS. (GW/0174-5506). **Qty:** 8. **4953**

DIALECTICA. (SZ/0012-2017). **4345**

DIALECTICAL ANTHROPOLOGY. (NE/0304-4092). **235**

DIALOG (EDMONTON). (CN/0842-8336). **Qty:** 2. **4386**

DIALOG (ST. PAUL). (US/0012-2033). **Qty:** 16. **4953**

DIALOGO ECUMENICO. (SP/0210-2870). **4953**

DIALOGO FILOSOFICO. (SP/0213-1196). **4345**

DIALOGO SOCIAL. (PN/0046-0206). **2614**

DIALOGOS. (PR/0012-2122). **4345**

DIALOGUE & ALLIANCE. (US/0891-5881). **Qty:** 30. **4953**

DIALOGUE - ANGLICAN CHURCH OF CANADA. DIOCESE OF ONTARIO. (CN/1184-6283). **Qty:** varies. **4953**

DIALOGUE (BRAILLE ED.). (US/1069-6865). **Qty:** 2. **4386**

DIALOGUE - CANADIAN PHILOSOPHICAL ASSOCIATION. (CN/0012-2173). **4345**

DIALOGUE (CASSETTE ED.). (US/1069-6873). **Qty:** 2. **4386**

DIALOGUE (COLOMBO, SRI LANKA). (CE/0012-2181). **5021**

DIALOGUE IMMERSION. (CN/0824-4189). **3277**

DIALOGUE IN INSTRUMENTAL MUSIC EDUCATION. (US/0147-7544). **4114**

DIALOGUE : JOURNAL OF ADDIS ABABA UNIVERSITY MAIN CAMPUS TEACHERS ASSOCIATION. (US). **Qty:** 4. **1820**

DIALOGUE (LARGE PRINT ED.). (US/1069-6857). **Qty:** 2. **4386**

DIALOGUE (LOS ANGELES). (US/0012-2157). **Qty:** 22. **5059**

DIALOGUE (MILWAUKEE, WIS.). (US/0012-2246). **4345**

DIALYSIS & TRANSPLANTATION. (US/0090-2934). **3571**

DIAMOND DEPOSITIONS, SCIENCE AND TECHNOLOGY. (US/1051-9084). **1023**

DIAMOND INSIGHT. (US/0954-5581). **Qty:** 2-3. **2914**

DIAMOND INTERNATIONAL. (UK/0957-0446). **Qty:** 1 or 2. **2914**

DIAMOND NEWS & S.A. JEWELLER. (SA). **2914**

DIAMOND REGISTRY BULLETIN, THE. (US/0199-9753). **2914**

DIAMOND TRAIL NEWS. (US). **5669**

DIAMOND WORLD. (II). **Qty:** 3-4. **2914**

DIAMOND WORLD REVIEW. (IS). **2914**

DIAMONDBACK, THE. (US). **Qty:** 20. **5686**

DIANDU YU HUANBAO. (CC/1000-4742). **2041**

DIANOIA (CAMROSE). (CN/1192-1854). **Qty:** 1-2. **1820**

DIAPASON (CHICAGO), THE. (US/0012-2378). **4114**

DIARIO LAS AMERICAS. (US/0744-3234). **5649**

DIARIST'S JOURNAL. (US). **3381**

DICK VINOCUR'S FOOTPRINTS. (US/1063-9276). **Qty:** 6. **4564**

DICKENS QUARTERLY. (US/0742-5473). **3381**

DICKENS STUDIES ANNUAL. (US/0084-9812). **3381**

DICKENSIAN, THE. (UK/0012-2440). **Qty:** 12-20. **3381**

DICKENSON STAR, THE. (US/0746-584X). **5758**

DICKINSON LAW REVIEW. (US/0012-2459). **2960**

DICKINSON PRESS (DICKINSON, N.D. 1942), THE. (US/1049-6718). **5725**

DICKINSON STUDIES. (US/0164-1492). **Qty:** 6. **3462**

DICTA / NEWSLETTER FOR ATTORNEYS OF SAN DIEGO COUNTY. (US/0417-4569). **Qty:** varies. **2960**

DICTIONARIES. (US/0197-6745). **3277**

DICTIONARY OF LITERARY BIOGRAPHY. (US). **3381**

DIDAKTIEF. (NE). **1735**

DIDASCALIA (ROSARIO, SANTA FE, ARGENTINA). (AG). **5028**

DIDASKALIA (LISBOA). (PO/0253-1674). **4953**

DIDASKALIA (OTTERBURNE). (CN/0847-1266). **4953**

DIDEROT STUDIES. (SZ/0070-4806). **3381**

DIE CASTING MANAGEMENT. (US/0745-449X). **3477**

DIECIOCHO. (US/0163-0415). **3381**

DIELECTRICS & EI NEWS BULLETIN. (SW). **2041**

DIETETIQUE (MONTREAL). (CN/0701-1350). **4190**

DIETSCHE WARANDE EN BELFORT. (BE/0012-2645). **3381**

DIFESA PENALE, LA. (IT). **3106**

DIFFUSION DES PROGRAMMES AUDIOVISUELS, LA. (BE). **4368**

DIGEST BUSINESS & LAW JOURNAL. (CN/0315-811X). **3099**

DIGEST OF CHIROPRACTIC ECONOMICS, THE. (US/0415-8407). **3572**

DIGEST OF INFORMATION ON FUSES PROTECTIVE AND SWITCHING DEVICES. (UK). **2041**

DIGEST OF INVESTMENT ADVICES, THE. (US/0012-2742). **896**

DIGEST OF REPORT - TRANSPORT AND ROAD RESEARCH LABORATORY. (UK/0269-8196). **5440**

DIGEST - UNIVERSITY OF PENNSYLVANIA. DEPT. OF FOLKLORE AND FOLKLIFE, THE. (US/0737-7703). **2333**

DIKAIO KAI POLITIKE (THESSALONIKE, GREECE : 1982). (GR). **3127**

DIKTA. (US/0363-5414). **Qty:** 2/year. **3206**

DILIMAN REVIEW, THE. (PH/0012-2858). **5198**

DIME NOVEL ROUND-UP (1953). (US/0012-2874). **3381**

DIMENSIONAL STONE. (US/0883-0258). **613**

DIMENSIONS ECONOMIQUES DE LA BOURGOGNE. (FR). **5227**

DIMENSIONS (LITTLE ROCK, ARK. 1973). (US/0160-6425). **1892**

DIMENSIONS (MONTREAL). (CN/0709-2334). **1735**

DIMENSIONS (NEW YORK, N.Y.). (US/0882-1240). **Qty:** 30. **2685**

DIMENSIONS OF CRITICAL CARE NURSING. (US/0730-4625). **3855**

DIMENSIONS OF EARLY CHILDHOOD. (US/0160-6425). **1803**

DIONISO. (IT). **5363**

DIONYSOS (SUPERIOR, WISC.). (US/1044-4149). **Qty:** 12-15. **1342**

DIOTIMA. (GR/1010-7363). **4345**

DIPLOMAT (LONDON, ENGLAND), THE. (UK). **4520**

DIPLOMES - UNIVERSITE DE MONTREAL. (CN/0228-9636). **1820**

DIPPY. DIRECT INPUT PHOTOTYPESETTING NEWSLETTER. (US). **4564**

DIQIU HUAXUE. (CC/0379-1726). **1373**

DIRASAT KURDIYAH. (FR/0765-1074). **2768**

DIRECT MARKETING NEWS (MARKHAM). (CN/1187-7111). **Qty:** 5-10. **923**

DIRECTION. (US/0092-7449). **5381**

DIRECTION ET GESTION DES ENTREPRISES. (FR/0012-320X). **Qty:** 6. **665**

DIRECTION (WINNIPEG). (US/0384-8515). **Qty:** 12-15. **4953**

DIRECTIONS AT RIDER COLLEGE. (US/0279-408X). **1101**

DIRECTIONS (AUSTIN, TEX.). (US/0742-678X). **1237**

DIRECTIONS IN GOVERNMENT. (AT/1030-391X). **Qty:** 8-12. **4472**

DIRECTIONS (NEW YORK, N.Y. : 1985). (US/0883-9727). **923**

DIRECTIONS SUVA. (FJ/1011-5846). **Qty:** 2. **3206**

DIRECTOR (LONDON. 1935). (UK/0012-3242). **666**

DIRECTOR (MADISON, WIS.), THE. (US/0199-3186). **2407**

DIRECTOR, THE. (II/0012-3250). **665**

DIRECTORSHIP (WESTPORT). (US/0193-4279). **Qty:** 40. **865**

DIRECTORY. (US/0543-2774). **3206**

DIRECTORY / AMERICAN CHAMBER OF COMMERCE IN ITALY. (IT). **819**

DIRECTORY / AMERICAN COUNCIL OF INDEPENDENT LABORATORIES, INC. (US). **5100**

DIRECTORY - BRITISH COLUMBIA MOTOR TRANSPORT ASSOCIATION. (CN/0714-8658). **5381**

DIRECTORY FOR EXCEPTIONAL CHILDREN, THE. (US/0070-5012). **1877**

DIRECTORY : JUVENILE AND ADULT CORRECTIONAL DEPARTMENTS, INSTITUTIONS, AGENCIES AND PAROLING AUTHORITIES, UNITED STATES AND CANADA. (US). **3163**

DIRECTORY OF ASSOCIATIONS IN CANADA. (CN/0316-0734). **5230**

DIRECTORY OF BOOK, CATALOG, AND MAGAZINE PRINTERS. (US/0895-139X). **4564**

DIRECTORY OF CANADIAN ORCHESTRAS AND YOUTH ORCHESTRAS / ANNUAIRE CANADIEN DES ORCHESTRES ET ORCHESTRES DES JEUNES. (CN/0705-6249). **4114**

DIRECTORY OF ENVIRONMENTAL ORGANIZATIONS (LOS ANGELES). (US/0270-1111). **2213**

DIRECTORY OF EUROPEAN RETAILERS. (UK). **953**

DIRECTORY OF EXECUTIVE RECRUITERS (STANDARD ED.). (US/0090-6484). **940**

DIRECTORY OF FLORIDA INDUSTRIES. (US). **923**

DIRECTORY OF FOREST INDUSTRIES IN MALAYSIA. (MY). **2400**

DIRECTORY OF FREE PROGRAMS, PERFORMING TALENT AND ATTRACTIONS, THE. (US/0736-7759). **384**

DIRECTORY OF GERIATRIC PUBLICATIONS, THE. (US/0745-). **3750**

DIRECTORY OF HIGHER EDUCATION COURSES. (AT). **Qty:** 3. **1821**

DIRECTORY OF HOSPITALS IN INDIA. (II). **3779**

DIRECTORY OF IOWA MUNICIPALITIES. (US/0363-1842). **4643**

DIRECTORY OF MAILING LIST COMPANIES. (US). **666**

DIRECTORY OF MANAGEMENT CONSULTANTS. (US/0743-6890). **865**

DIRECTORY OF MEMBER AGENCIES IN THE UNITED STATES AND CANADA. (US/1045-1684). **5283**

DIRECTORY OF MICHIGAN MUNICIPAL OFFICIALS. (US/0148-7442). **Qty:** 20. **4643**

DIRECTORY OF MULTIMEDIA EQUIPMENT, SOFTWARE, AND SERVICES / ICIA. (US). **1153**

DIRECTORY OF OBSOLETE SECURITIES. (US/0085-0551). **896**

DIRECTORY OF PROFESSIONAL GENEALOGISTS. (US/1055-6710). **Qty:** 50-75. **2445**

DIRECTORY OF PROFESSIONAL GENEALOGISTS AND RELATED SERVICES. (US/0272-3387). **Qty:** 50-75. **2445**

DIRECTORY OF RECOGNIZED ACCREDITING BODIES. (US). **1821**

DIRECTORY

DIRECTORY OF SCIENTIFIC & TECHNICAL ASSOCIATIONS IN ISRAEL. (IS/0334-2824). **5100**

DIRECTORY OF SOURCES FOR EDITORS, REPORTERS & RESEARCHERS, THE. (CN/1197-5148). **2919**

DIRECTORY OF SOUTHEAST ASIAN ACADEMIC & SPECIAL LIBRARIES. (TH). **3208**

DIRECTORY OF TELEFACSIMILE SITES IN NORTH AMERICAN LIBRARIES. (US/1049-7218). **1153**

DIRECTORY OF TEXAS FOUNDATIONS. (US). **4335**

DIRECTORY - PARENT COOPERATIVE PRESCHOOLS INTERNATIONAL. (CN). **1803**

DIRECTORY / SPECTROSCOPY SOCIETY OF CANADA. (CN/0709-8448). **4401**

DIRECTORY / TOY TRAIN OPERATING SOCIETY. (US/0732-9873). **2584**

DIREZIONE DEL PERSONALE. (IT). **940**

DIRIGENTE RURAL, O. (BL/0012-3374). **79**

DIRITTO AEREO. (IT/0012-3390). **2962**

DIRITTO DEL LAVORO. (IT/0012-3404). **3146**

DIRITTO DELLE RADIODIFFUSIONI E DELLE TELECOMUNICAZIONI, IL. (IT). **2962**

DIRITTO DELL'ECONOMIA, IL. (IT). **2962**

DIRITTO DI AUTORE, IL. (IT/0012-3420). **1304**

DIRITTO DI FAMIGLIA E DELLE PERSONE. (IT). **3120**

DIRITTO ECCLESIASTICO E RASSEGNA DI DIRITTO MATRIMONIALE, IL. (IT/0012-3455). **2963**

DIRT RIDER. (US/0735-4355). **4081**

DIRTY LINEN. (US/1047-4315). Qty: 15. **4115**

DIS COLLECTOR (CHESWOLD, DEL. : 1981). (US/0731-843X). **4115**

DISABILITY AND REHABILITATION. (UK/0963-8288). **4387**

DISABILITY ISSUES. (US/1063-9373). Qty: 10. **4387**

DISABILITY RAG, THE. (US/0749-8586). Qty: 3-4. **4387**

DISABLED OUTDOORS. (US). **4387**

DISABLED OUTDOORS MAGAZINE. (US/1067-098X). **4387**

DISASTER PREPAREDNESS IN THE AMERICAS. AMERICAN SANITARY BUREAU. (US/0251-4494). Qty: 12. **4773**

DISASTERS. (UK/0361-3666). **5284**

DISC. (US/1052-4053). **1183**

DISC SPORTS. (US/0747-9956). **4893**

DISCERNER. (US/0416-0274). **4954**

DISCERNING TRAVELER, THE. (US/0898-6231). Qty: 36. **5468**

DISCIPLE (ST. LOUIS, MO.). (US/0092-8372). **5059**

DISCIPLESHIP JOURNAL. (US/0273-5865). **4954**

DISCIPLIANA (1960). (US/0732-9881). **4954**

DISCIPULOS RESPONSABLES. (US/1052-3804). Qty: 1. **4954**

DISCLOSURE RECORD. (US/0094-2561). **788**

DISCOURSE. (UK/0159-6306). **1736**

DISCOURSE PROCESSES. (US/0163-853X). **3277**

DISCOVERY AND INNOVATION. (KE/1015-079X). **5101**

DISCOVERY (VANCOUVER. 1972). (CN/0319-8480). **2191**

DISCOVERY (VICTORIA). (CN/0822-5796). **4087**

DISCURSO. (PY/0737-8742). **3381**

DISCURSO LITERARIO. (PY/0737-8742). **3382**

DISEASE INFORMATION. (FR/1012-5329). **5509**

DISEASES OF THE COLON & RECTUM. (US/0012-3706). **3744**

DISEGNO MAGAZINE. (IT). **1233**

DISKUSSION DEUTSCH. (GW/0342-1589). **3277**

DISNEY CHANNEL MAGAZINE, THE. (US/0747-4644). **1131**

DISP. (SZ). **2022**

DISPATCH-NEWS, THE. (US). **5742**

DISPENSING OPTICS. (UK/0954-3201). **4215**

DISPLAY. (DK/0107-7481). **1241**

DISPLAY & DESIGN IDEAS. (US/1049-9172). **759**

DISPLAYS. (UK/0141-9382). **1228**

DISPOSABLES AND NONWOVENS. (UK/0012-3811). **5350**

DISPOSITIO. (US/0734-0591). Qty: 4-8. **3382**

DISPUTE RESOLUTION FORUM. (US). **2963**

DISSENT (NEW YORK). (US/0012-3846). **4541**

DISTANCE EDUCATION. (AT/0158-7919). Qty: 24 per year. **1736**

DISTANCE EDUCATION AND TECHNOLOGY NEWSLETTER. (US/1064-2439). Qty: 12-18. **1736**

DISTANT CROSSROADS. (US). **2445**

DISTRICT COUNCIL JOURNAL. (US/0748-1179). **4645**

DIVER. (UK). **4893**

DIVER MAGAZINE. (CN/0706-5132). **4893**

DIVER (PORTLAND CONN.), THE. (US/0273-8589). Qty: 2. **4893**

DIVERSION (TITUSVILLE). (US/0363-4825). **4850**

DIVERSITY & DIVISION. (US/1064-7430). Qty: 12. **5244**

DIVINE LIFE, THE. (II). **4185**

DIX-NEUVIEME SIECLE : BULLETIN DE LA SOCIETE DES ETUDES ROMANTIQUES. (FR). **3382**

DIZHEN DIZHI. (CC/0253-4967). **1404**

DK NEWSLETTER. (II). **415**

DM NEWS. (US/0194-3588). **923**

DMT. DANSK MUSIK TIDSSKRIFT. (DK/0106-5629). Qty: 5-10. **4115**

DNA PROBES. (UK/0266-6308). **453**

DNA REPORTER. (US). Qty: 4. **3855**

DOAR, HA-. (US/0017-6524). **5047**

DOCK AND HARBOUR AUTHORITY. (UK/0012-4419). **5449**

DOCKLANDS NEWS. (UK/0264-9691). **667**

DOCTRINA PENAL. (AG). **3107**

DOCTRINE AND LIFE. (IE/0012-446X). **4954**

DOCUMENTA OPHTHALMOLOGICA. (NE/0012-4486). **3874**

DOCUMENTAIRE EN EUROPE, LE. (BE). **4068**

DOCUMENTALISTE (PARIS). (FR/0012-4508). **3208**

DOCUMENTARY EDITING. (US/0196-7134). Qty: 15. **2919**

DOCUMENTATION CATHOLIQUE, LA. (FR/0012-4613). **5028**

DOCUMENTATION ET BIBLIOTHEQUES. (CN/0315-2340). **3208**

DOCUMENTATION-REFUGIES. (FR/0984-8541). **4472**

DOCUMENTATION TOURISTIQUE. (FR). **5468**

DOCUMENTS D'ANALISI GEOGRAFICA / [PUBLICACIONS DEL DEPARTAMENT DE GEOGRAFIA, UNIVERSITAT AUTONOMA DE BARCELONA]. (SP/0212-1573). **2560**

DODD DIGGINGS. (US/0736-2854). **2445**

DOD'S REPORT. (UK/0956-0580). **1605**

DOE HET VEILIG. (BE/0773-6231). **2861**

DOG FANCY (LOS ANGELES, CALIF.). (US/0892-6522). **4286**

DOG RIVER REVIEW. (US/0749-260X). **3382**

DOG WATCH, THE. (AT). **4176**

DOG WORLD. (US/0012-4893). **4286**

DOGS IN CANADA. (CN/0012-4915). **4286**

DOHNER FAMILY NEWSLETTER. (US/0736-2412). **2445**

DOKUMENTATION FUER UMWELTSCHUTZ UND LANDESPFLEGE. (GW/0026-6957). **2191**

DOKUMENTATIONSDIENST LATEINAMERIKA. AUSGEWAHLTE NEUERE LITERATUR. (GW/0342-037X). **5198**

DOLL CASTLE NEWS. (US/0363-7972). **372**

DOLL DESIGNS. (US/1050-4796). **372**

DOLL READER. (US/0744-0901). **2584**

DOLL TALK FOR COLLECTORS. (US/0012-5229). **2773**

DOLL TIMES. (US). **2584**

DOLLAR$ENSE (LOS ANGELES). (US/0194-8490). **1296**

DOLLARS & SENSE (SOMERVILLE, MASS.). (US/0012-5245). Qty: 10. **1480**

DOLLARS & SENSE (WASHINGTON, D.C. 1979). (US/0745-9092). Qty: 5. **4720**

DOLOR. (SP/0214-0659). **3573**

DOLPHIN LOG. (US/8756-6362). **1448**

DOMES (MILWAUKEE, WIS.). (US/1060-4367). Qty: 60/year. **2768**

DOMINION LAW REPORTS. (CN/0012-5350). **3089**

DOMUS. (IT/0012-5377). **2900**

DONKEY DIGEST. (AT/1031-6280). **5582**

DONNEES STATISTIQUES DU LIMOUSIN. (FR/0395-8280). **5326**

DONOGHUE'S MONEYLETTER. (US/0197-7083). **897**

DONT ACTE. (CN/0381-1875). **669**

DORCHESTER COUNTY GENEALOGICAL MAGAZINE, THE. (US/8755-2353). **2445**

DORIS LESSING NEWSLETTER. (US/0882-486X). Qty: Varies. **3382**

DORM. (US/0743-2860). **1091**

DOROT. (US/0886-2796). **2445**

DOS INTERNATIONAL. (GW/0933-1557). **1183**

DOSHISHA AMERIKA KENKYU. (JA/0420-0918). **2615**

DOSSIER. L'UFFICIO TECNICO. (IT/0394-8315). **298**

DOSSIERS DE L'OUTRE-MER : BULLETIN D'INFORMATION DU CENADDOM, LES. (FR/0337-4084). **1556**

DOSTOEVSKY STUDIES : JOURNAL OF THE INTERNATIONAL DOSTOEVSKY SOCIETY. (AU/1013-2309). **3382**

DOTOKU TO KYOIKU. (JA). **1737**

DOUBLE FEATURE (LETHBRIDGE). (CN/0824-278X). **2278**

DOUBLE-GUN JOURNAL, THE. (US/1050-2262). Qty: 4-8. **4893**

DOUBLE LIAISON. (FR/0012-5709). **4223**

DOUBLE LIAISON-CHIMIE DES PEINTURES. (FR/0012-5709). **4223**

DOUBLE REED, THE. (US/0741-7659). **4115**

DOUGHTY TREE, THE. (US/0897-3350). **2446**

DOUGLAS DAILY DISPATCH. (US). **5630**

DOUGLAS ENTERPRISE, THE. (US). **5653**

DOWN BEAT. (US/0012-5768). **4115**

DOWN EAST. (US/0012-5776). **5468**

DOWN SYNDROME NEWS / THE NEWSLETTER OF THE NATIONAL DOWN SYNDROME CONGRESS. (US/0161-0716). **544**

DOWN THE ROAD. (US/1072-4656). **4203**

DOWN TO EARTH. (US/0012-5792). **80**

DOWN UNDER QUILTS. (AT/1033-4513). Qty: 45. **5183**

DOWNEAST ANCESTRY. (US/0891-0960). **2446**

DOWN'S SYNDROME. (US/0149-7162). **544**

DOWNS SYNDROME ASSOCIATION OF NEW SOUTH WALES NEWSLETTER. (AT). Qty: 4. **4387**

DOWNSIDE REVIEW, THE. (UK/0012-5806). **3382**

DOWNTOWN NEWS. (US). **5634**

DP, DANSK PRESSE. (DK). **2515**

DR. FOX'S NEW HEALTH JOURNAL. (US/1043-8165). **4774**

DR : THE FASHION BUSINESS. (UK). **1083**

DRAFT HORSE JOURNAL, THE. (US/0012-5865). Qty: 2. **2798**

DRAGON (LAKE GENEVA, WIS.). (US/0279-6848). **4860**

DRAGONFLY (PORTLAND). (US/0364-359X). **3382**

DRAKE UPDATE. (US). **1091**

DRAMA. (UK/0012-5946). **5363**

DRAMA BROADSHEET. (UK/0261-1651). Qty: 6. **5363**

DRAMA-LOGUE. (US/0272-2720). **5364**

DRAMA/THEATRE TEACHER, THE. (US/1046-5022). **5364**

DRAMATHERAPY (NEWSLETTER). (UK). **5364**

DRAMATHERAPY : THE JOURNAL OF THE BRITISH ASSOCIATION OF DRAMATHERAPY. (UK). Qty: 2 or 3. **5364**

DRAMATISTS GUILD QUARTERLY, THE. (US/0012-6004). **5364**

DRAUDZES VESTIS. (CN/0701-0214). **4954**

DRAUGAS. (US). **5659**

DRAWING (NEW YORK, N.Y. 1979). (US/0191-6963). **349**

DREISER STUDIES. (US/0896-6362). **3382**

DRESDEN ENTERPRISE AND SHARON TRIBUNE. (US). **5745**

DRESS. (US/0361-2112). **1083**

DRESSAGE & CT. (US/0147-796X). **2798**

DREW GATEWAY, THE. (US/0012-6152). **4954**

DREXEL INSULATION REPORT. (US). **Qty:** 4. **613**

DRIEMAANDELIJKSE BLADEN. (NE). **3278**

DRILLING NEWS. (UK/0955-7369). **4255**

DRINKING AND DRUG PRACTICES SURVEYOR, THE. (US/0363-0811). **1343**

DRINKING WATER & BACKFLOW PREVENTION. (US/1055-2782). **5533**

DRIPPING SPRINGS DISPATCH, THE. (US/0746-603X). **5749**

DRIVER/EDUCATION (TORONTO). (CN/1183-7314). **Qty:** 5-10. **5413**

DRIVER (MIAMI, FLA.). (US/1062-9394). **Qty:** 8. **4893**

DRIVERS AND CONTROLS. (UK/0950-5490). **Qty:** 4. **1971**

DROIT ET AFFAIRES INTERNATIONAL. (FR/0184-5926). **2964**

DRUCKINDUSTRIE (ST. GALLEN). (SZ/0046-0737). **4564**

DRUCKWELT. (GW/0012-6519). **4564**

DRUG ABUSE UPDATE. (US/0739-6562). **1343**

DRUG AND CHEMICAL TOXICOLOGY (NEW YORK, N.Y. 1978). (US/0148-0545). **3980**

DRUG AND THERAPEUTICS BULLETIN. (UK/0012-6543). **4299**

DRUG DEVELOPMENT AND INDUSTRIAL PHARMACY. (US/0363-9045). **4300**

DRUG DEVELOPMENT RESEARCH. (US/0272-4391). **4300**

DRUG LAW REPORT. (US/0734-6166). **2964**

DRUG NEWS & PERSPECTIVES. (SP/0214-0934). **4301**

DRUG TARGETING. (UK/0952-0317). **4301**

DRUG THERAPY TOPICS. (US/0882-6684). **4301**

DRUG TOPICS REDBOOK UPDATE. (US/0731-8596). **4301**

DRUGLINK INFORMATION LETTER. (UK/0305-4349). **1343**

DRUGS AND DRUG ABUSE EDUCATION NEWSLETTER, (1982). (US/0744-2823). **1344**

DRUGS & SOCIETY (NEW YORK, N.Y.). (US/8756-8233). **1344**

DRUGS MADE IN GERMANY. (GW/0012-6683). **4302**

DRUM. EAST AFRICAN EDITION. (KE/0419-7690). **2278**

DRUMMER (SAN FRANCISCO, CALIF.). (US/1055-7415). **2794**

DRVNA INDUSTRIJA. (CI/0012-6772). **2400**

DRYCLEANER NEWS. (US/0012-6802). **5350**

DSM LETTER. (US). **2042**

DTW. DEUTSCHE TIERAERZTLICHE WOCHENSCHRIFT. (GW/0341-6593). **5509**

DU. (SZ/0012-6837). **2515**

DUCKS UNLIMITED. (US/0012-6950). **2191**

DUKE LAW JOURNAL. (US/0012-7086). **2964**

DUKE MATHEMATICAL JOURNAL. (US/0012-7094). **3504**

DULCIMER PLAYER NEWS, THE. (US/0098-3527). **Qty:** 6 /year. **4115**

DULUTH BUDGETEER, THE. (US). **5695**

DUNE BUGGIES AND HOT VWS. (US/0012-7132). **5413**

DUNGEON MASTER. (US). **2794**

DUN'S BUSINESS RANKINGS. (US/0734-2845). **669**

DUN'S CENSUS OF AMERICAN BUSINESS. (US/0196-8610). **728**

DUN'S INDUSTRIAL GUIDE, THE METALWORKING DIRECTORY. (US/0278-8799). **4001**

DUN'S LATIN AMERICA'S TOP 25,000. (US/0742-9649). **669**

DURANGO HERALD, THE. (US). **5642**

DURHAM ARCHAEOLOGICAL JOURNAL. (UK/0265-8038). **267**

DURHAM UNIVERSITY JOURNAL, THE. (UK/0012-7280). **1822**

DUTCH HARBOR FISHERMAN. (US). **5629**

DUTCHESS, THE. (US/0735-6242). **2446**

DVADTSAT DVA. (IS). **3382**

DVW HESSEN MITTEILUNGEN. (GW/0173-6280). **2022**

DVZ DEUTSCHE VERKEHRS-ZEITUNG. (GW/0342-166X). **5381**

DW DOKUMENTATION WASSER. (GW/0012-5156). **5533**

DWB. (BE/0012-2645). **3383**

DWF. (IT). **Qty:** 15-20. **5554**

DWI JOURNAL. (US/0889-0234). **2965**

DWJ, DEUTSCHES WAFFEN-JOURNAL. (GW). **Qty:** 80-100. **4893**

DX MAGAZINE, THE. (US/1043-4208). **1154**

DX NEWS. (US/0737-1659). **2773**

DYES AND PIGMENTS. (UK/0143-7208). **4223**

DYNAMIC BUSINESS : A PUBLICATION OF THE SMALLER MANUFACTURER'S COUNCIL. (US/0279-4039). **Qty:** varies. **670**

DYNAMIC (NEW YORK, N.Y.). (US/0741-0263). **4472**

DYNAMIC SYSTEMS AND APPLICATIONS. (US/1056-2176). **3504**

DYNAMICS. (BE). **670**

DYNAMISCHE PSYCHIATRIE. (GW/0012-740X). **3924**

DZIENNIK ZWIAZKOWY. (US/0742-6615). **Qty:** 10-20. **5660**

E & MJ INTERNATIONAL DIRECTORY OF MINING. (US). **2138**

E I C, ELECTRONIQUE, INDUSTRIELLE & COMMERCIALE. (CN/0226-7748). **2056**

E (NORWALK, CONN.). (US/1046-8021). **Qty:** varies. **2164**

EAA EXPERIMENTER. (US/0894-1289). **18**

EACROTANAL INFORMATION. (TZ). **235**

EAF JOURNAL. (CN/0831-3318). **1862**

EAGLE (CAMBRIDGE, N.Y.), THE. (US/0745-9831). **Qty:** 3. **5716**

EAGLE, THE. (US). **3163**

EAGLET, THE. (US/0732-1007). **2446**

EANHS BULLETIN. (KE/0374-7387). **4165**

EAR (NEW YORK, N.Y.). (US/0893-9500). **4115**

EARLY AMERICAN LITERATURE. (US/0012-8163). **3341**

EARLY CHILD DEVELOPMENT AND CARE. (UK/0300-4430). **2278**

EARLY CHILDHOOD EDUCATION. (CN/0012-8171). **1737**

EARLY CHILDHOOD NEWS. (US). **1803**

EARLY CHILDHOOD RESEARCH QUARTERLY. (US/0885-2006). **1803**

EARLY CHINA. (US/0362-5028). **2650**

EARLY DRAMA, ART, AND MUSIC MONOGRAPH SERIES. (US). **319**

EARLY DRAMA, ART, AND MUSIC REVIEW, THE. (US/1048-9401). **319**

EARLY INTERVENTION. (US/1058-8396). **Qty:** 12. **5284**

EARLY KEYBOARD JOURNAL. (US/0899-8132). **Qty:** 5-10. **4116**

EARLY KEYBOARD STUDIES NEWSLETTER. (US/0882-0201). **4116**

EARLY MUSIC. (UK/0306-1078). **4116**

EARLY MUSIC HISTORY. (UK/0261-1279). **4116**

EARNSHAW'S INFANTS-GIRLS-BOYS WEAR REVIEW. (US/0161-2786). **1083**

EARTH FIRST! (1991). (US/1055-8411). **Qty:** 8. **2164**

EARTH GARDEN. (AT/0310-222x). **Qty:** 20. **5244**

EARTH ISLAND JOURNAL. (US/1041-0406). **2164**

EARTH, MOON, AND PLANETS. (NE/0167-9295). **395**

EARTH SCIENCE BULLETIN. (US/0012-8236). **1354**

EARTH SCIENCES HISTORY. (US/0736-623X). **1355**

EARTH SURFACE PROCESSES AND LANDFORMS. (UK/0197-9337). **1374**

EARTH (WAUKESHA, WIS.). (US/1056-148X). **1355**

EARTHCARE NORTHWEST. (US/0732-684X). **Qty:** 4. **2192**

EARTHKEEPER MAGAZINE. (CN/1181-7828). **Qty:** 20. **2164**

EARTHQUAKE SPECTRA. (US/8755-2930). **2022**

EARTHWORD. (US). **Qty:** 3. **2164**

EAST AFRICAN AGRICULTURAL AND FORESTRY JOURNAL. (KE/0012-8325). **80**

EAST AFRICAN MEDICAL JOURNAL, THE. (KE/0012-835X). **3573**

EAST ASIA (FRANKFURT AM MAIN, GERMANY). (GW/0723-8398). **1556**

EAST ASIA SERIES. (US/0066-0957). **2503**

EAST ASIAN EXECUTIVE REPORTS. (US/0272-1589). **3099**

EAST ASIAN PASTORAL REVIEW. (PH/0116-0257). **4954**

EAST CAROLINA UNIVERSITY PUBLICATIONS IN HISTORY. (US/0070-8089). **2615**

EAST CENTRAL EUROPE. (US/0094-3037). **2846**

EAST COAST ANGLER. (US/0899-0506). **2300**

EAST COUNTY CHRONICLE. (US). **5656**

EAST EUROPEAN MARKETS. (UK/0262-0456). **897**

EAST EUROPEAN QUARTERLY. (US/0012-8449). **2686**

EAST EUROPEAN STATISTICS SERVICE. (BE). **1531**

EAST HAMPTON STAR, THE. (US). **Qty:** 52. **5716**

EAST KENTUCKIAN, THE. (US/0424-107X). **2446**

EAST LONDON RECORD. (UK/0141-6286). **2686**

EAST MIDLAND ARCHAEOLOGICAL BULLETIN. (UK). **267**

EAST MIDLAND GEOGRAPHER. (UK/0012-8481). **2560**

EAST TENNESSEE ROOTS. (US/0885-4025). **2446**

EAST TEXAS BANNER. (US). **Qty:** 4. **5749**

EAST TEXAS FAMILY RECORDS. (US/0272-4405). **2446**

EAST TEXAS HISTORICAL JOURNAL. (US/0424-1444). **Qty:** 30 - 50. **2732**

EAST/WEST BUSINESS & TRADE. (US/1065-6790). **Qty:** 5 per year. **832**

EAST/WEST EDUCATION. (US/0899-0247). **Qty:** 25/year. **1737**

EAST WEST FORTNIGHTLY BULLETIN. (BE/0012-8570). **1634**

EASTERN AFRICA ECONOMIC REVIEW. (KE/1011-4750). **1480**

EASTERN ANTHROPOLOGIST, THE. (II/0012-8686). **235**

EASTERN BASKETBALL. (US/0195-0223). **4893**

EASTERN DAILY PRESS. (UK/0307-0956). **Qty:** 400. **5812**

EASTERN ECONOMIC JOURNAL. (US/0094-5056). **1480**

EASTERN EUROPEAN ECONOMICS. (US/0012-8775). **1481**

EASTERN GAZETTE (1985), THE. (US/8750-961X). **Qty:** 5. **5685**

EASTERN GREAT LAKES SALES GUIDE TO HIGH-TECH COMPANIES. (US/1040-0559). **5102**

EASTERN ITASCAN, THE. (US). **5695**

EASTERN JOURNAL OF PRACTICAL THEOLOGY. (CN). **5059**

EASTERN PHARMACIST. (II/0012-8872). **4302**

EASTERN TRAVEL SALES GUIDE. (US/0739-4780). **5468**

EASTERN WORKER. (PK/0012-8953). **1664**

EASTLAND TELEGRAM (EASTLAND, TEX. : 1953). (US). **Qty:** 12 per year. **5749**

EASTMAN NOTES. (US/0147-345X). **4116**

EASTSIDE PARENT. (US/1065-2655). **2278**

EASTSIDE SUN. (US). **5634**

EASY LIVING GUIDE : THE ORIGINAL GUIDE FOR THE COMMUNITIES OF NEW WESTMINSTER, COQUITLAM, PORT MOODY, BURNABY. (CN/0821-7394). **2487**

EASY READER. (US/0194-6412). **5634**

EATERN AIZONA COURIER. (US). 5630

EATON COUNTY QUEST. (US). **Qty:** 4. 2446

EAU, L'INDUSTRIE, LES NUISANCES, L'. (FR/0755-5016). 2227

EAU VIVE, L'. (CN/0046-1016). **Qty:** 40. 5783

EAWARUDO. (JA). 18

EBONY JR. (US/0091-8660). 1063

ECCLESIA MADRID. (SP/0012-9038). 5029

ECCLESIA ORANS. (IT/1010-3872). 4954

ECD. ENERGY CONSERVATION DIGEST. (US/0270-823X). 1937

ECHEC +. (CN/0825-0049). 4860

ECHO. (SZ/0012-9143). 1893

ECHO DES BOIS, L'. (BE). 2400

ECHO DES RECHERCHES, L'. (FR/0012-9283). 1154

ECHO-X. (CN/0820-6295). 3941

ECHOCARDIOGRAPHY (MOUNT KISCO, N.Y.). (US/0742-2822). 3704

ECHOS DU MONDE CLASSIQUE. (CN/0012-9356). 267

ECLECTIC THEOSOPHIST, THE. (US/0890-8117). 4955

ECLIPSE-NEWS-REVIEW, THE. (US). 5670

ECN. EUROPEAN CHEMICAL NEWS. (UK/0014-2875). 974

ECO ALERT / CONSERVATION COUNCIL. (CN/0833-448X). 2192

ECO E NOTIZIARIO DELL ECOLOGIA. (IT). 2213

ECO/LOG WEEK. (CN/0315-0380). 2227

ECO LOGIC. (US). **Qty:** 2. 2213

ECOLE. (IT). 2213

ECOLOGIA MEDITERRANEA. (FR/0153-8756). 2213

ECOLOGICAL ENTOMOLOGY. (UK/0307-6946). 5607

ECOLOGICAL ILLNESS LAW REPORT. (US/8755-9013). 3110

ECOLOGICAL SOCIETY OF AUSTRALIA BULLETIN. (AT). **Qty:** 6. 2214

ECOLOGIST (1979). (UK/0261-3131). 2214

ECOLOGY AND FARMING : INTERNATIONAL IFOAM MAGAZINE. (GW). 81

ECOLOGY LAW QUARTERLY. (US/0046-1121). 3110

ECOLOGY OF FOOD AND NUTRITION. (US/0367-0244). 4190

ECOLOGY (TEMPE). (US/0012-9658). 2214

ECONEWS (ARCATA, CALIF.). (US/0885-7237). **Qty:** 6. 2192

ECONOMETRIC INVESTING. (US/8756-4602). 897

ECONOMETRIC REVIEWS. (US/0747-4938). 1481

ECONOMETRIC THEORY. (US/0266-4666). 1591

ECONOMIA & LAVORO (1967). (IT/0012-978X). 1481

ECONOMIA AZIENDALE : FOUR MONTHLY REVIEW OF THE ACCADEMIA ITALIANA DI ECONOMIA AZIENDALE. (IT). 1591

ECONOMIA DELLE FONTI DI ENERGIA. (IT). 1937

ECONOMIA INTERNAZIONALE. (IT/0012-981X). 1634

ECONOMIA (LISBOA). (PO/0870-3531). 1481

ECONOMIC AFFAIRS (CALCUTTA). (II/0424-2513). 1482

ECONOMIC AFFAIRS (LONDON, ENGLAND). (UK/0265-0665). 1482

ECONOMIC ANALYSIS AND POLICY. (AT/0313-5926). 1591

ECONOMIC AND INDUSTRIAL DEMOCRACY. (UK/0143-831X). 1664

ECONOMIC AWARENESS. (UK/0953-4997). 1482

ECONOMIC BOTANY. (US/0013-0001). 508

ECONOMIC DEVELOPER. (US/1041-9969). **Qty:** 12. 1482

ECONOMIC EDUCATION BULLETIN (GREAT BARRINGTON). (US/0424-2769). 789

ECONOMIC GEOGRAPHY. (US/0013-0095). 1483

ECONOMIC HISTORY REVIEW, THE. (UK/0013-0117). 1557

ECONOMIC JOURNAL (LONDON). (UK/0013-0133). 1483

ECONOMIC MODELLING. (UK/0264-9993). 1591

ECONOMIC PLANNING IN FREE SOCIETIES. (CN/1191-3576). 81

ECONOMIC PLANNING JOURNAL IN FREE SOCIETIES FOR AGRICULTURE AND RELATED INDUSTRIES. (CN/1191-3576). 81

ECONOMIC QUALITY CONTROL. (GW/0940-5151). 1484

ECONOMIC RECORD, THE. (AT/0013-0249). 1484

ECONOMIC REPORT (ALBUQUERQUE, N.M.), THE. (US/0738-7210). 1484

ECONOMIC REVIEW (COLOMBO). (CE/0259-9775). 1484

ECONOMIC STUDIES (CALCUTTA, INDIA). (II/0013-0362). **Qty:** 12-15/yr. 1558

ECONOMIC SYSTEMS RESEARCH. (UK/0953-5314). 1485

ECONOMIC THEORY. (GW/0938-2259). 1591

ECONOMIC TIMES. (UK). 671

ECONOMIC TRENDS (NEW DELHI). (II/0014-9470). 1591

ECONOMIC WORLD (LOS ANGELES). (US/0164-3525). 1486

ECONOMICA (LONDON). (UK/0013-0427). 1486

ECONOMICS AND PHILOSOPHY. (UK/0266-2671). 1486

ECONOMICS & POLITICS (OXFORD, ENGLAND). (UK/0954-1985). 1486

ECONOMICS CLASSICS - OLD AND RARE BOOKS ON ECONOMICS. (US). 1486

ECONOMICS (LONDON). (UK/0300-4287). 1486

ECONOMICS OF EDUCATION REVIEW. (US/0272-7757). 1737

ECONOMICS OF PLANNING. (NE/0013-0451). 1558

ECONOMIE AND GESTION AGRO-ALIMENTAIRE. (FR/0981-8715). 81

ECONOMIE APPLIQUEE. (SZ/0013-0494). 1591

ECONOMIE ET HUMANISME. (FR/0245-9132). 1634

ECONOMIE ET STATISTIQUE. (FR/0336-1454). 1532

ECONOMIA INTERNAZIONALE.

ECONOMIE FAMILIALE HOME ECONOMICS, L'. (FR/0397-8389). **Qty:** 4. 2789

ECONOMIE FAMILIALE, L'. (FR). 2789

ECONOMIE, L'. (FR/0013-0478). 1558

ECONOMIES ET SOCIETES. (FR/0013-0567). 1487

ECONOMISCH EN SOCIAAL TIJDSCHRIFT. (BE/0013-0575). **Qty:** 120. 671

ECONOMY AND SOCIETY. (UK/0308-5147). 5199

ECOS. (UK/0143-9073). 2192

ECOSSISTEMA / FACULDADE DE AGRONOMIA E ZOOTECNIA "MANOEL CARLOS GONCALVES.". (BL/0100-4107). 81

ECRITIQUE (IOWA CITY, IOWA). (US/1061-1479). 3383

ECRITS SUR LE CINEMA (SUPPLEMENT). (CN/0822-6350). 4068

ECRITURE FRANCAISE DANS LE MONDE. (CN/0228-7951). 3383

ECUMENE. (UK/0967-4608). **Qty:** 40. 2560

ECUMENICAL REVIEW, THE. (SZ/0013-0796). 4955

ECUMENICAL TRENDS. (US/0360-9073). 4955

ECUMENISM. (CN/0383-431X). 4955

EDDA. (NO/0013-0818). 3341

EDEBIYAT (PHILADELPHIA, PA.). (SZ/0364-6505). 3383

EDGEWATER TRIBUNE. (US/0745-774X). 5642

EDI FORUM. (US/1048-3047). **Qty:** 5-10/yr. 671

EDI NEWS. (US/0894-9212). 1183

EDI RESEARCH AUSTRALIA. (AT/1034-8360). **Qty:** 4. 1183

EDI UPDATE LONDON. (UK/0954-6154). **Qty:** 10-20. 4721

EDI WORLD. (US/1055-0399). 2042

EDIFICACION CRISTIANA. (SP). 4955

EDIOS. (CN/0707-2287). 4345

EDITING HISTORY. (US/0883-3532). 4814

EDITIO. (GW/0931-3079). 3341

EDITOR & PUBLISHER. (US). 924

EDITOR, EL. (US). 5749

EDITORIAL EYE, THE. (US/0193-7383). **Qty:** 1. 4814

EDITOR'S DIGEST. (US). 4814

EDITOR'S FORUM (KANSAS CITY, MO.). (US/0746-3014). **Qty:** 4. 2919

EDITORS ONLY. (US/0735-8490). **Qty:** 2. 2919

EDIZIONI PER LA CONSERVAZIONE. (IT/1120-1819). **Qty:** 25-30. 4828

EDMOND EVENING SUN, THE. (US). **Qty:** 20. 5731

EDMONTON AUTISM SOCIETY UPDATE. (CN). **Qty:** 6. 3831

EDP AUDITOR JOURNAL, THE. (US/0885-0445). 1258

EDP WEEKLY. (US). **Qty:** 10. 1237

EDPACS. (US/0736-6981). 1226

EDUCA. (UK/0141-8459). 1912

EDUCACION MEDICA Y SALUD. (US/0013-1091). 3573

EDUCADORES; REVISTA LATINOAMERICANA DE EDUCACION. (AG/0422-6399). 1794

EDUCARE (PRETORIA). (SA/0256-8829). 1738

EDUCATED TRAVELER, THE. (US/1052-0597). **Qty:** 30. 5469

EDUCATING ABLE LEARNERS, DISCOVERING & NURTURING TALENT. (US/0896-9574). 1878

EDUCATING AT-RISK YOUTH. (US/1040-0729). 5284

EDUCATION 3-13. (UK/0300-4279). 1804

EDUCATION & AGEING. (UK). 3750

EDUCATION AND SOCIETY (MELBOURNE). (AT/0726-2655). **Qty:** 18. 1738

EDUCATION & TRAINING (BRADFORD). (UK/0040-0912). 1912

EDUCATION & TREATMENT OF CHILDREN. (US/0748-8491). **Qty:** 10-15. 1893

EDUCATION BIBLIOGRAPHY. (PP). 1794

EDUCATION CANADA. (CN/0013-1253). **Qty:** 20-40. 1738

EDUCATION (CHULA VISTA). (US/0013-1172). 1738

EDUCATION DIGEST, THE. (US/0013-127X). 1739

EDUCATION (EDINBURGH). (UK/0013-1164). 1863

EDUCATION ENFANTINE, L'. (FR/0013-1288). 1739

EDUCATION FOR LIBRARY AND INFORMATION SERVICES, AUSTRALIA. (AT). **Qty:** 6-10. 3209

EDUCATION FORUM (TORONTO, 1988). (CN/0840-9269). **Qty:** 6. 1893

EDUCATION IN KENYA. (KE). 1739

EDUCATION INDEX. (US/0013-1385). 1794

EDUCATION INDEX. CD-ROM. (US/0013-1385). 1794

EDUCATION LAW JOURNAL. (CN/0838-2875). 2965

EDUCATION LIBRARIES. (US/0148-1061). 3209

EDUCATION LIBRARIES JOURNAL. (UK/0957-9575). 3209

EDUCATION LINKS. (AT/0814-6802). 1740

EDUCATION QUARTERLY, THE. (II/0013-1482). 1740

EDUCATION, RESEARCH AND PERSPECTIVES. (AT/0311-2543). 1822

EDUCATION TODAY. (UK/0013-1547). 1740

EDUCATION U.S.A. (US/0013-1571). 1741

EDUCATION WEEK. (US/0277-4232). 1741

EDUCATION WITH PRODUCTION. (BS). 1741

EDUCATIONAL ADMINISTRATION AND POLICY REVIEW. (AT). 1863

EDUCATIONAL ADMINISTRATION QUARTERLY. (US/0013-161X). 1863

EDUCATIONAL AND PSYCHOLOGICAL MEASUREMENT. (US/1013-1644). 4585

EDUCATIONAL & TRAINING TECHNOLOGY INTERNATIONAL : ETTI. (UK/0954-7304). 1741

EDUCATIONAL CHANGE. (US/0748-0806). 1741

EDUCATIONAL COMPUTING AND TECHNOLOGY. (UK). 1223

EDUCATIONAL CONSIDERATIONS. (US/0146-9282). **Qty:** 4-8. 1913

EDUCATIONAL FORUM (WEST LAFAYETTE, IND.), THE. (US/0013-1725). 1741

EDUCATIONAL FOUNDATIONS (ANN ARBOR, MICH.). (US/1047-8248). **1741**

EDUCATIONAL FREEDOM. (US/0013-1741). **2965**

EDUCATIONAL GERONTOLOGY. (US/0360-1277). **1800**

EDUCATIONAL HORIZONS. (US/0013-175X). **Qty:** 16. **1741**

EDUCATIONAL MANAGEMENT & ADMINISTRATION : JOURNAL OF THE BRITISH EDUCATIONAL MANAGEMENT AND ADMINISTRATION SOCIETY. (UK/0263-211X). **1863**

EDUCATIONAL MEDIA AND TECHNOLOGY YEARBOOK. (US/8755-2094). **1893**

EDUCATIONAL OASIS. (US/0892-2853). **1893**

EDUCATIONAL PHILOSOPHY AND THEORY. (AT/0013-1857). **1893**

EDUCATIONAL PLANNING. (US/0315-9388). **1742**

EDUCATIONAL POLICY (LOS ALTOS, CALIF.). (US/0895-9048). **1742**

EDUCATIONAL PSYCHOLOGY IN PRACTICE. (UK/0266-7363). **4586**

EDUCATIONAL RESEARCH QUARTERLY. (US/0196-5042). **1742**

EDUCATIONAL RESEARCH (WINDSOR). (UK/0013-1881). **1742**

EDUCATIONAL RESEARCHER (WASHINGTON, D.C. : 1972). (US/0013-189X). **1742**

EDUCATIONAL REVIEW (BIRMINGHAM). (UK/0013-1911). **1742**

EDUCATIONAL STUDIES. (UK/0305-5698). **1743**

EDUCATIONAL STUDIES (AMES). (US/0013-1946). **Qty:** 100. **1743**

EDUCATIONAL STUDIES IN MATHEMATICS. (NE/0013-1954). **1743**

EDUCATIONAL TECHNOLOGY. (US/0013-1962). **1893**

EDUCATIONAL TECHNOLOGY RESEARCH AND DEVELOPMENT. (US/1042-1629). **1743**

EDUCATIONAL THEORY. (US/0013-2004). **Qty:** varies. **1743**

EDUCATORE. (IT). **Qty:** 20/yr. **1743**

EDUCATORS GRADE GUIDE TO FREE TEACHING AIDS. (US/0070-9387). **1893**

EDUCATORS GUIDE TO FREE GUIDANCE MATERIALS. (US/0070-9417). **1913**

EDUCATORS GUIDE TO FREE HEALTH, PHYSICAL EDUCATION AND RECREATION MATERIALS. (US). **1855**

EDUCATORS GUIDE TO FREE HOME ECONOMICS AND CONSUMER EDUCATION MATERIALS. (US). **2789**

EDUCATORS GUIDE TO FREE SCIENCE MATERIALS / COMPILED AND EDITED BY MARY H. SATERSTROM. (US/0070-9425). **1894**

EDUCATORS INDEX OF FREE MATERIALS. (US). **1743**

EDUCATOR'S INTERNATIONAL GUIDE TO FREE & LOW COST HEALTH AUDIO-VISUAL TEACHING AIDS. (US). **4774**

EDUCAZIONE SANITARIA E PROMOZIONE DELLA SALUTE. (IT). **4774**

EDUCOM REVIEW. (US/1045-9146). **Qty:** 15-20. **1822**

EDUTECH REPORT, THE. (US/0883-1327). **1223**

EEO TRENDS AND ISSUES. (US/0740-204X). **Qty:** 10. **1664**

EESTI HAAL. (UK). **5812**

EFFECTIVE SCHOOL PRACTICES. (US/1068-7378). **1894**

EFFECTIVE SPECIAL SERVICES MANAGEMENT. (US/0890-4790). **866**

EFRYDIAU ATHRONYDDOL. (UK). **4345**

EFTHINI. (GR). **2515**

EGALITE (MONCTON). (CN/0226-6873). **4472**

EGE COGRAFYA DERGISI / [EGE UNIVERSITESI, EDEBIYAT FAKULTESI, COGRAFYA BOLUMU]. (TU). **2560**

EGESZSEGNEVELES. EDUCATIO SANITARIA. (HU). **4774**

EGLISE CANADIENNE, L'. (CN/0013-2322). **4955**

EGLISE ET THEOLOGIE. (CN/0013-2349). **4955**

EGO KIDS MAGAZINE. (CN). **1083**

EGREGIOUS STEAMBOAT JOURNAL, THE. (US/1058-3556). **Qty:** 15-25. **4176**

EGRETTA : VOGELKUNDLICHE NACHRICHTEN AUS OSTERREICH. (AU/0013-2373). **Qty:** 8-10. **4165**

EGYPTIAN JOURNAL OF DAIRY SCIENCE. (UA/0378-2700). **2334**

EIGHTEENTH-CENTURY FICTION (DOWNSVIEW, ONT.). (CN/0840-6286). **3383**

EIGHTEENTH CENTURY (LUBBOCK), THE. (US/0193-5380). **2686**

EIGHTEENTH-CENTURY STUDIES. (US/0013-2586). **319**

EIGHTEENTH CENTURY, THE. (US/0161-0996). **2635**

EIGSE. (IE/0013-2608). **3278**

EIGSE CHEOL TIRE. (IE/0332-298X). **4160**

EINTRACHT HARMONY. (US). **2515**

EIRE-IRELAND (ST. PAUL). (US/0013-2683). **3341**

EIRENE; STUDIA GRAECA ET LATINA. (XR/0046-1628). **1076**

EISEI DOBUTSU. (JA/0424-7086). **5607**

EISENBAHNINGENIEUR, DER. (GW/0013-2810). **5431**

EISMA 'S VAKPERS. (NE/0920-2099). **4223**

EISZEITALTER UND GEGENWART. (GW/0424-7116). **1374**

EJHP, EUROPEAN JOURNAL OF HOSPITAL PHARMACY. (GW/0992-4663). **4302**

EKATA. (CN/0715-3902). **2532**

EKKLESIA KAI THEOLOGIA : EKKLESIASTIKE KAI THEOLOGIKE EPETERIS TES HIERAS ARCHIEPISKOPES THYATEIRON KAI MEGALES VRETANNIAS. (GR). **5039**

EKLITRA / ASSOCIATION CULTURELLE PICARDE. (FR/0424-7175). **2515**

EKONOMICKO-MATEMATICKY OBZOR. (CS/0013-3027). **1591**

EKONOMICKY CASOPIS. (XO/0013-3035). **1488**

EKONOMIKA PRACE. (XO). **1488**

EKONOMSKA POLITIKA. (YU/0013-3248). **Qty:** 100. **671**

EKSPOR (INDONESIA. BIRO PUSAT STATISTIK). (IO). **832**

EL DORADO GAZETTE, GEORGETOWN GAZETTE & TOWN CRIER. (US/8750-6289). **Qty:** 12. **5634**

EL-E-PHANT. (US). **3383**

EL SOL (SALINAS, CALIF.). (US/1064-1998). **Qty:** 10. **5635**

ELAEIS. (MY/0128-1828). **Qty:** 2. **5102**

ELASTOMERS. (US). **4455**

ELBERT ROGERS' WASHINGTON STATE SCORE. (US/0736-881X). **2532**

ELBERTON STAR, THE. (US). **Qty:** 50. **5653**

ELDERSONG. (US). **4116**

ELECTION ADMINISTRATION REPORTS. (US/0145-8124). **4472**

ELECTRE BIBLIO FRENCH BOOKS IN PRINT. CD-ROM. (FR). **415**

ELECTRIC CONSUMER. (US/0745-4651). **1937**

ELECTRIC LINES. (US/0895-2116). **2043**

ELECTRIC MACHINES AND POWER SYSTEMS. (US/0731-356X). **2043**

ELECTRIC PROPULSION. (CN/0831-6899). **2044**

ELECTRIC VEHICLE DEVELOPMENTS. (UK/0141-9811). **5381**

ELECTRICAL APPARATUS. (US/0190-1370). **2044**

ELECTRICAL EQUIPMENT LONDON. (UK/0013-4317). **2045**

ELECTRICAL INDIA. (II/0013-435X). **2045**

ELECTRICAL MANUFACTURING (LIBERTYVILLE, ILL.). (US/0895-3716). **3478**

ELECTRICAL WORLD. (US/0013-4457). **2045**

ELECTRICITY JOURNAL, THE. (US/1040-6190). **Qty:** 3. **4761**

ELECTROMAGNETIC NEWS REPORT. (US/0270-4935). **2046**

ELECTROMAGNETICS. (US/0272-6343). **2046**

ELECTROMYOGRAPHY AND CLINICAL NEUROPHYSIOLOGY. (BE/0301-150X). **3796**

ELECTRON SPIN RESONANCE. (UK/0305-9758). **1015**

ELECTRON (WILLOUGHBY, OHIO), THE. (US/0740-1922). **Qty:** 2-3. **5728**

ELECTRONIC APPLICATION NEWS. (II/0013-4813). **2046**

ELECTRONIC ATLAS NEWSLETTER, THE. (US/1053-0924). **1183**

ELECTRONIC GREEN JOURNAL. (US/1076-7975). **2165**

ELECTRONIC MAIL & MICRO SYSTEMS. (US/8756-2537). **1154**

ELECTRONIC MARKET TRENDS. (US/0886-8506). **2047**

ELECTRONIC MEDIA. (US/0745-0311). **1131**

ELECTRONIC MODELING. (US/0275-9136). **2047**

ELECTRONIC PHOTOGRAPHY NEWS. (US/0896-0976). **Qty:** 5-6. **4369**

ELECTRONIC PRODUCTS (1981). (US/0013-4953). **2048**

ELECTRONIC PUBLIC INFORMATION NEWSLETTER. (US/1057-834X). **4645**

ELECTRONIC SERVICING & TECHNOLOGY. (US/0278-9922). **2048**

ELECTRONIC SHOPPING NEWS. (US/0893-0333). **1154**

ELECTRONIC TECHNOLOGY (LONDON). (UK/0141-061X). **2048**

ELECTRONIC TRADER. (UK). **2048**

ELECTRONICS AND COMMUNICATIONS ABSTRACTS JOURNAL (RIVERDALE, MD.). (US/0361-3313). **2003**

ELECTRONICS INFORMATION & PLANNING. (II/0304-9876). **2049**

ELECTRONICS MANUFACTURE & TEST. (UK/0265-301X). **2049**

ELECTRONICS TIMES. (UK). **2050**

ELECTRONICS TODAY INTERNATIONAL. (UK/0811-0727). **2050**

ELECTRONIQUE EUROPE 2000 PARIS. (FR/0994-1894). **2050**

ELEKTOR AACHEN. (GW/0932-5468). **2051**

ELEKTOR ELECTRONICS. (UK/0268-4519). **2051**

ELEKTRICESTVO. (RU/0013-5380). **2051**

ELEKTRICHESKIE STANTSII. (RU/0201-4564). **2051**

ELEKTRISCHE BAHNEN. (GW/0013-5437). **5431**

ELEKTRISCHE ENERGIE-TECHNIK. (GW/0170-2033). **1937**

ELEKTROMEISTER + DEUTSCHES ELEKTROHANDWERK. (GW/0012-1258). **2051**

ELEKTRONIKAI ES HRADASTECHNIKAI SZAKIRODALMI TAJEKOZTATO. (HU/0231-066X). **2052**

ELEKTROTECHNICKY CASOPIS. (XO/0013-578X). **2052**

ELEKTROTEHNIKA (ZAGREB). (CI/0013-5844). **2052**

ELEKTROWARME INTERNATIONAL. EDITION A : ELEKTOWARME IM TECHNISCHEN AUSBAU. (GW/0174-6189). **2604**

ELEKTROWARME INTERNATIONAL. EDITION B : INDUSTRIELLE ELEKTROWARME. (GW/0340-3521). **2605**

ELEKTUUR. (NE/0013-5895). **Qty:** 10. **2052**

ELEMENTARY SCHOOL LIBRARY COLLECTION, THE. (US). **3209**

ELEMENTARY TEACHERS' GUIDE TO FREE CURRICULUM MATERIALS. (US/0070-9980). **1894**

ELEPAIO. (US/0013-6069). **2192**

ELEPHANT (DETROIT, MICH.). (US/0737-108X). **5582**

ELETTRONICA E TELECOMUNICAZIONI. (IT/0013-6123). **2052**

ELEUTHERIA (OTTAWA). (CN/0843-8064). **Qty:** 2-3. **4345**

ELEVAGE INSEMINATION. (FR/0422-9703). **210**

ELEVATOR WORLD. (US/0013-6158). **2113**

ELEVATORI MODERNI : SOLLEVAMENTO E TRASPORTO A FUNE. (IT/1121-7995). **Qty:** 10. **5381**

ELEX. (NE). **Qty:** 5. **2053**

ELF (TONAWANDA, N.Y.). (US/1054-3376). **Qty:** 5-10. **3341**

ELGAR SOCIETY JOURNAL, THE. (UK). **5230**

ELH. (US/0013-8304). **3342**

ELITES AFRICAINES, LES. (FR). **432**

ELIZABETHAN REVIEW, THE. (US/1066-7059). **Qty:** 12. **3384**

ELK CITY DAILY NEWS, THE. (US). **5732**

ELKHART TRUTH, THE. (US/0746-7516). **5663**

ELKHORN INDEPENDENT (ELKHORN, WIS. : 1892). (US). **5767**

ELKO INDEPENDENT (1915). (US). **5707**

ELKS MAGAZINE, THE. (US/0013-6263). **5231**

ELLE. (NE). 5554

ELLE (NEW YORK, N.Y.). (US/0888-0808). 5555

ELLENIKA NEA (LONDON, ONT.). (CN/0821-7270). 5784

ELLENIKE KTENIATRIKE. (GR/0018-0068). 5509

ELLENOKANADIKA CHRONIKA. (CN/0820-7801). 5784

ELLIS COUNTY STAR, THE. (US). 5675

ELLIS COUSINS NEWSLETTER, THE. (US/0740-1477). 2446

ELLSWORTH AMERICAN. (US). Qty: 52. 5685

ELMONT HERALD. (US/1070-7328). 5716

ELOIZES. (CN/0228-0124). 3384

ELT JOURNAL. (UK/0951-0893). 3278

ELTEKNIK MED AKTUELL ELEKTRONIK. (SW/0346-6310). 2053

ELVIS COSTELLO INFORMATION SERVICE. (NE). 4116

ELVIS MONTHLY. (UK/0013-6484). 4116

ELY ECHO. (US/0746-7087). 5695

EMA, ELEKTRISCHE MASCHINEN. (GW). 2053

EMAJL-KERAMIKA-STAKLO. (CI/0350-3607). 2588

EMBROIDERY. (UK/0013-6611). 5184

EMC. EDUCATIONAL MEDIA SPECIAL INTEREST COUNCIL. (CN/0824-782X). 3209

EMC TECHNOLOGY. (US/1055-6230). 2053

EMC TECHNOLOGY ... ANTHOLOGY. (US/0748-108X). 2053

EMERALD CITY COMIX AND STORIES. (US/1042-9166). 3384

EMERGENCIAS. (SP). 3724

EMERGENCY. (US/0162-5942). 4774

EMERGENCY LIBRARIAN. (US/0315-8888). 3209

EMERGENCY MANAGEMENT TODAY : AN INFORMATION SERVICE OF EMERGENCY MANAGEMENT INFORMATION SERVICES. (US/0747-9085). Qty: 15-20. 1073

EMERGENCY MEDICAL UPDATE. (US/1064-5934). Qty: 4. 3724

EMERGENCY PREPAREDNESS DIGEST. (CN/0837-5771). 1073

EMERITA. (SP/0013-6662). 1076

EMF KEEPTRACK. (US/1059-6631). Qty: 3. 2966

EMI. EDUCATIONAL MEDIA INTERNATIONAL. (UK/0952-3987). 1894

EMIE BULLETIN. (US/0737-9021). Qty: 5. 3209

EMMA. (GW). 5555

EMMANUEL (NEW YORK, N.Y.). (US/0013-6719). 4955

EMMY. (US/0164-3495). 1131

EMOTIONAL FIRST AID. (US/0739-828X). 4586

EMPIRE STATE MASON. (US/0013-6794). 5231

EMPIRE STATE SURVEYOR. (US). Qty: rarely. 2023

EMPIRISCHE PADAGOGIK. (GW/0931-5020). Qty: 4-6. 1744

EMPLOYEE ASSISTANCE PROGRAM MANAGEMENT LETTER. (US/0896-0941). 866

EMPLOYEE ASSISTANCE QUARTERLY. (US/0749-0003). 2861

EMPLOYEE BENEFIT NOTES. (US/0887-1388). 1665

EMPLOYEE BENEFIT PLAN REVIEW. (US/0013-6808). 2879

EMPLOYEE BENEFITS. (US/0194-3499). 1665

EMPLOYEE COMMUNICATION. (US/0885-7202). Qty: 2-10. 1110

EMPLOYEE COUNSELLING TODAY. (UK/0933-8217). 4586

EMPLOYEE OWNERSHIP REPORT, THE. (US/0899-8833). 671

EMPLOYEE RELATIONS. (UK/0142-5455). 940

EMPLOYEE RELATIONS LAW JOURNAL. (US/0098-8898). 3146

EMPLOYEE RELATIONS REPORT (RICHMOND, VA.). (US/0735-4738). 1665

EMPLOYEE SERVICES MANAGEMENT. (US/0744-3676). 940

EMPLOYEE TESTING & THE LAW. (US/0889-5422). 3147

EMPLOYERS NEGOTIATING SERVICE. (US/0898-2139). 4646

EMPLOYMENT AND TRAINING REPORTER. (US/0146-9673). Qty: 35-50. 4204

EMS COMMUNICATOR. (US/0275-0716). 3724

EMS LEADER, THE. (US/0897-0297). 3724

EN PASSANT, POETRY. (US/0271-5023). 3468

ENBI TO PORIMA. (JA/0367-021X). 4455

ENCEPHALE. (FR/0013-7006). 3832

ENCHANTMENT. (US/0046-1946). 2533

ENCLITIC. (US/0193-5798). 3342

ENCOMIA. (US/0363-4841). Qty: 6-8. 3342

ENCORE. (US/0071-0164). 5364

ENCOUNTER (INDIANAPOLIS). (US/0013-7081). Qty: Approx 10 in each issue. 4956

ENCOUNTERS (ST. PAUL, MINN.). (US/0273-5717). 5102

ENCUENTRO. (NQ). 2732

ENCYCLOPEDIA OF ARBITRATION LAW. (UK). 3180

END PAPERS. (UK/0262-7922). 4473

ENDANGERED SPECIES UPDATE. (US). Qty: 10. 2192

ENDOCRINE RESEARCH. (US/0743-5800). 3729

ENDOCURIETHERAPY / HYPERTHERMIA ONCOLOGY. (US/8756-1689). 3816

ENDOMETRIOSIS ASSOCIATION NEWSLETTER. (US/0897-1870). 3760

ENDOSCOPY REVIEW. (US/8756-968X). 3744

ENDOTHELIUM. (UK/0957-3518). 454

ENERGIA NUCLEAR E AGRICULTURA. (BL/0100-3593). 2154

ENERGIE ALTERNATIVE HTE. (IT/0391-5360). 5103

ENERGIE DIALOG. (GW). 1938

ENERGY ALERT (TORONTO). (CN/0835-5266). 1938

ENERGY & EDUCATION. (US/0891-0979). 1939

ENERGY & FUELS. (US/0887-0624). 1939

ENERGY BOOKS QUARTERLY. (US/0892-5461). 1962

ENERGY CONSERVATION NEWS. (US/0161-6595). 1939

ENERGY DAILY, THE. (US/0364-5274). 1939

ENERGY DEVELOPMENTS. (GW/0342-5665). 1940

ENERGY DIGEST. (UK/0367-1119). 1940

ENERGY ECONOMICS. (UK/0140-9883). 1940

ENERGY ECONOMIST. (UK/0262-7108). 1940

ENERGY ENGINEERING : JOURNAL OF THE ASSOCIATION OF ENERGY ENGINEERS. (US/0199-8595). 1940

ENERGY EXPLORATION & EXPLOITATION. (UK/0144-5987). 1940

ENERGY INFORMER. (US). Qty: 12. 1940

ENERGY JOURNAL (CAMBRIDGE, MASS.). (US/0195-6574). 1940

ENERGY LAW JOURNAL. (US/0270-9163). Qty: 1-2. 2966

ENERGY MANAGEMENT TECHNOLOGY. (US/0745-984X). 5103

ENERGY NEWSBRIEF, THE. (US/1059-289X). Qty: 1-2. 1941

ENERGY POLICY. (UK/0301-4215). 1941

ENERGY PROCESSING CANADA. (CN/0319-5759). 1941

ENERGY REVIEW (SANTA BARBARA). (US/0094-8063). 1942

ENERGY SOURCES. (US/0090-8312). 1942

ENERGY (STAMFORD, CONN. 1975). (US/0149-9386). 1942

ENERGY STUDIES REVIEW. (CN/0843-4379). 1942

ENERGY TODAY. (US/0093-500X). 1942

ENERGY UNLIMITED. (US/0279-621X). 1942

ENERGY USER NEWS. (US/0162-9131). 1942

ENERGY UTILITIES. (UK/0959-0196). Qty: 25. 1488

ENERGY WORLD. (UK/0307-7942). Qty: 30. 1943

ENERPRESSE. (FR/0153-9442). 1943

ENFANCE MAJUSCULE PARIS. (FR/1164-8589). Qty: 6/year. 3164

ENFANT D'ABORD, L'. (FR/0399-4988). 3903

ENFERMERA AL DIA. (MX/0185-0970). 3855

ENFO. (US/0276-9956). 2165

ENFOQUES EN ATENCION PRIMARIA. (CL/0716-2774). 3574

ENGEKIGAKU / HENSHU WASEDA DAIGKU ENGEKI GAKKAI. (JA). 5364

ENGINEER OF CALIFORNIA. (US/0277-1233). 1972

ENGINEERED SYSTEMS. (US/0891-9976). 2113

ENGINEERING ANALYSIS WITH BOUNDARY ELEMENTS. (UK/0955-7997). 1972

ENGINEERING & SCIENCE. (US/0013-7812). 1972

ENGINEERING AND TECHNOLOGY DEGREES. (US/0071-0393). 1972

ENGINEERING AUTOMATION REPORT. (US). Qty: 12-16. 1219

ENGINEERING AUTOMATION REPORT. (US/1065-6952). Qty: 12. 1972

ENGINEERING DESIGNER. (UK/0013-7898). 2098

ENGINEERING DIMENSIONS. (CN/0820-8190). Qty: 6. 1972

ENGINEERING IN MINIATURE. (UK/0955-7644). 2773

ENGINEERING MANPOWER BULLETIN. (US/0013-8037). 1973

ENGINEERING OPTIMIZATION. (UK/0305-215X). 1973

ENGINEERING PLASTICS. (UK/0952-6900). 4455

ENGINEERING SERVICES MANAGEMENT. (UK/0951-7871). 1974

ENGINEERING STRUCTURES. (UK/0141-0296). 2023

ENGINEERING WORLD (LONDON, ENGLAND). (UK). 1974

ENGINEERS AND ENGINES MAGAZINE. (US/0013-8142). 158

ENGINEERS AUSTRALIA. (AT/1032-1195). 1974

ENGLISCH AMERIKANISCHE STUDIEN. (GW/0172-1992). 3384

ENGLISH AND AMERICAN STUDIES IN GERMAN; SUMMARIES OF THESES AND MONOGRAPHS. (GW). 3278

ENGLISH DANCE AND SONG. (UK/0013-8231). 384

ENGLISH EDUCATION. (US/0007-8204). 1894

ENGLISH FOR SPECIFIC PURPOSES (NEW YORK, N.Y.). (US/0889-4906). 3278

ENGLISH HISTORICAL REVIEW, THE. (UK/0013-8266). 2615

ENGLISH IN AFRICA. (SA/0376-8902). 3384

ENGLISH IN AUSTRALIA. (AT/0155-2147). 3279

ENGLISH JOURNAL. (US/0013-8274). 1894

ENGLISH LANGUAGE NOTES. (US/0013-8282). Qty: 16. 3342

ENGLISH LITERATURE IN TRANSITION, 1880-1920. (US/0013-8339). 3342

ENGLISH (LONDON). (UK/0013-8215). 3384

ENGLISH QUARTERLY, THE. (CN/0013-8355). 1894

ENGLISH RECORD, THE. (US/0013-8363). 1744

ENGLISH STUDIES. (NE/0013-838X). 3384

ENGLISH WESTERNERS' TALLY SHEET. (UK/0013-841X). 2732

ENGLISH WORLD-WIDE. (NE/0172-8865). 3279

ENLIGHTENMENT AND DISSENT. (UK/0262-7612). 4473

ENNIS DAILY NEWS, THE. (US/8755-9056). 5749

ENQUETE SOCIO-ECONOMIQUE. (BE). 4562

ENRICH!. (US). 671

ENSAYOS ECONOMICOS. (AG/0325-3937). 1591

ENSEIGNANTS (MONTREAL). (CN/0046-2101). 1744

ENSEIGNEMENT DU RUSSE, L'. (FR/0300-2608). 3279

ENSEIGNEMENT ET LA PEDAGOGIE EN ROUMANIE, L'. (RM). 1744

ENSEIGNEMENT MATHEMATIQUE. (FR/0013-8584). 3505

ENSEIGNEMENT PHILOSOPHIQUE, L'. (FR/0986-1653). 4365

ENSEMBLE. (CN/0842-8409). 4956

ENSEMBLE. (US). 384

ENSIGN (SAN MATEO, CALIF.), THE. (US/0744-3129). Qty: approx. 24/year. **593**

ENTERPRISE LEDGER (ENTERPRISE, ALA. : 1977). (US). Qty: 1-5. **5626**

ENTERPRISE (VANCOUVER). (CN/0319-8626). **1542**

ENTERTAINMENT AND SPORTS LAWYER : PUBLICATION OF THE FORUM COMMITTEE ON THE ENTERTAINMENT AND SPORTS INDUSTRIES, THE. (US/0732-1880). **2966**

ENTERTAINMENT LAW REPORTER. (US/0270-3831). **2966**

ENTERTAINMENT MAGAZINE, THE. (US/0883-1890). **4850**

ENTOMOLOGIA EXPERIMENTALIS ET APPLICATA. (NE/0013-8703). **5607**

ENTOMOLOGICA FENNICA. (FI/0785-8760). **5607**

ENTOMOLOGICA SCANDINAVICA. (DK/0013-8711). **5607**

ENTOMOLOGICAL NEWS. (US/0013-872X). **5607**

ENTOMOLOGISCHE ABHANDLUNGEN. (GW/0373-8981). **5607**

ENTOMOLOGISKE MEDDELELSER. (DK/0013-8851). **5608**

ENTOMOLOGISTE, L'. (FR/0013-8886). **5608**

ENTOMOLOGIST'S GAZETTE. (UK/0013-8894). Qty: 20. **5608**

ENTOMOLOGIST'S MONTHLY MAGAZINE, THE. (UK/0013-8908). Qty: 16. **5608**

ENTOMOLOGIST'S RECORD AND JOURNAL OF VARIATION, THE. (UK/0013-8916). Qty: 6. **5582**

ENTOMON. (II/0377-9335). Qty: 500. **5608**

ENTOPATH NEWS, THE. (UK). Qty: varies. **2378**

ENTOURAGE (DOWNSVIEW, ONT.). (CN/0829-8815). Qty: 5. **5284**

ENTREPRENEUR (SANTA MONICA, CALIF.). (US/0163-3341). **672**

ENTREPRENEURIAL MANAGER'S NEWSLETTER. (US/0272-0396). **672**

ENTREPRENEURSHIP AND REGIONAL DEVELOPMENT. (UK/0898-5626). **672**

ENTREPRISE 1951, L'. (BE/0777-6357). **2605**

ENTREPRISE ET L'HOMME. (BE). Qty: 6. **2249**

ENTROPIE. (FR/0013-9084). **1975**

ENVIROLINE (CALGARY). (CN/0847-4524). Qty: 50. **2165**

ENVIROLINE (FINDLAY, OHIO). (US/1072-2416). Qty: 2. **2165**

ENVIROLINE USER'S MANUAL. (US/0270-0751). **2228**

ENVIRONMENT & INDUSTRY DIGEST. (UK/0958-2126). **2192**

ENVIRONMENT & PLANNING A. (UK/0308-518X). **2821**

ENVIRONMENT AND PLANNING. B, PLANNING & DESIGN. (UK/0265-8135). **2821**

ENVIRONMENT AND PLANNING. C, GOVERNMENT & POLICY. (UK/0263-774X). **4646**

ENVIRONMENT AND PLANNING. D, SOCIETY & SPACE. (UK/0263-7758). **5199**

ENVIRONMENT BUSINESS. (UK/0959-7042). **2165**

ENVIRONMENT INSTITUTE OF AUSTRALIA NEWSLETTER. (AT/1030-1429). **2165**

ENVIRONMENT INTERNATIONAL. (UK/0160-4120). **2165**

ENVIRONMENT PROTECTION ENGINEERING. (PL/0324-8828). **2166**

ENVIRONMENT VIEWS. (CN/0701-9637). **2166**

ENVIRONMENTAL ACTION (WASHINGTON, D.C.). (US/0013-922X). Qty: 8. **2166**

ENVIRONMENTAL AND PLANNING LAW JOURNAL. (AT/0813-300X). **3111**

ENVIRONMENTAL AND URBAN ISSUES. (US/1044-033X). **2821**

ENVIRONMENTAL BIOLOGY OF FISHES. (NE/0378-1909). **2300**

ENVIRONMENTAL BUILDING NEWS : A NEWSLETTER ON ENVIRONMENTALLY SUSTAINABLE DESIGN & CONSTRUCTION. (US/1062-3957). Qty: 15. **614**

ENVIRONMENTAL CARCINOGENESIS REVIEWS. (US/0882-8164). **3816**

ENVIRONMENTAL CONTROL NEWS FOR SOUTHERN INDUSTRY. (US/0013-9238). **2167**

ENVIRONMENTAL DIGEST (OWEN SOUND). (CN/1183-8795). Qty: 5-6. **2228**

ENVIRONMENTAL EDUCATION AND INFORMATION. (UK/0144-9281). Qty: 35. **2167**

ENVIRONMENTAL ENGINEERING (BURY SAINT EDMUNDS, ENG. : 1988). (UK/0954-5824). **1975**

ENVIRONMENTAL ETHICS. (US/0163-4275). **2167**

ENVIRONMENTAL FORUM (WASHINGTON, D.C.), THE. (US/0731-5732). **3111**

ENVIRONMENTAL GEOCHEMISTRY AND HEALTH. (UK/0269-4042). **2167**

ENVIRONMENTAL HEALTH LETTER. (US/0196-0598). **2228**

ENVIRONMENTAL HEALTH (LONDON). (UK/0013-9270). **2822**

ENVIRONMENTAL HEALTH REVIEW. (CN/0319-6771). **4774**

ENVIRONMENTAL HISTORY REVIEW : EHR. (US/1053-4180). **2228**

ENVIRONMENTAL IMPACT. (UK). **2167**

ENVIRONMENTAL LAW ANTHOLOGY. (US/1054-8297). Qty: 1. **3111**

ENVIRONMENTAL LAW NEWSLETTER. (US/0163-545X). **3111**

ENVIRONMENTAL LAW (PORTLAND, ORE.). (US/0046-2276). Qty: varies. **3111**

ENVIRONMENTAL LAW SECTION JOURNAL. (US/8756-9280). **3111**

ENVIRONMENTAL LAW (WASHINGTON D.C.). (US/0748-8769). **3112**

ENVIRONMENTAL LIABILITY REPORT, THE. (US/1043-2698). **2168**

ENVIRONMENTAL MONITORING AND ASSESSMENT. (NE/0167-6369). **2168**

ENVIRONMENTAL NUTRITION. (US/0893-4452). **4190**

ENVIRONMENTAL POLICY REVIEW. (IS/0792-0032). **2168**

ENVIRONMENTAL POLLUTION (1987). (UK/0269-7491). **2229**

ENVIRONMENTAL PROFESSIONAL, THE. (US/0191-5398). **2169**

ENVIRONMENTAL PROGRESS. (US/0278-4491). **2229**

ENVIRONMENTAL PROTECTION : THE LEGAL FRAMEWORK / FRANK F. SKILLERN. (US). **3112**

ENVIRONMENTAL RESEARCH (NEW YORK, N.Y.). (US/0013-9351). **2169**

ENVIRONMENTAL SCIENCE & ENGINEERING (AURORA). (CN/0835-605X). **1975**

ENVIRONMENTAL SCIENCE & TECHNOLOGY. (US/0013-936X). **2169**

ENVIRONMENTAL SOFTWARE. (UK/0266-9838). **2170**

ENVIRONMENTAL SOFTWARE REPORT. (US/1043-2884). Qty: 6. **2170**

ENVIRONMENTAL SPECTRUM. (US/0013-9386). **2170**

ENVIRONMENTALIST, THE. (UK/0251-1088). **2193**

ENVIRONMENTS. (CN/0711-6780). **2822**

ENVIRONNEMENT. (BE). **2171**

ENVOI. (UK/0013-9394). **3462**

ENVOI (MONTREAL). (CN/0823-1834). **4894**

EOS (WASHINGTON, D.C.). (US/0096-3941). **1404**

EPA WATCH. (US/1065-920X). Qty: 2. **2171**

EPE. (UK/0963-5920). **2053**

EPETERIS. (CY/0071-0954). **2650**

EPHEMERIDES MARIOLOGICAE. (SP/0425-1466). **4956**

EPHEMERIDES THEOLOGICAE LOVANIENSES. (BE/0013-9513). **4956**

EPHEMERIS HELLENON NOMIKON. (GR). **2967**

EPI NEWSLETTER. (US/0251-4710). **3713**

EPIDEMIOLOGIA E PSICHIATRIA SOCIALE. (IT/1121-189X). **3734**

EPIDEMIOLOGICAL BULLETIN - PAN AMERICAN HEALTH ORGANIZATION. (US/0256-1859). **3734**

EPIDEMIOLOGY MONITOR, THE. (US/0744-0898). **4775**

EPIEGRAM (1988). (US/1046-1493). **1241**

EPILOGE. (GR). **1560**

EPILOGUE (HALIFAX, N.S.). (CN/0836-088X). Qty: 20-30. **3209**

EPIPHANY. (US). Qty: 15. **4956**

EPISCOPAL NEWS, THE. (US/0195-0681). **4956**

EPISCOPAL WOMEN'S HISTORY PROJECT, THE. (US/0749-9574). **5059**

EPISODES. (CN/0705-3797). Qty: 12. **1375**

EPISTEME NS : REVISTA DEL INSTITUTE DE FILOSOFIA. (VE). **4345**

EPISTEMOLOGIA. (IT). **5103**

EPISTOLODIDAKTIKA. (UK). **1744**

EPOPTEIA. (GR). Qty: 20. **4345**

EPTA BULLETIN. (BE). Qty: 10-12. **5059**

EQUAL MEANS. (US/1059-164X). **5555**

EQUAL OPPORTUNITIES INTERNATIONAL. (UK/0261-0159). **1667**

EQUAL OPPORTUNITY. (US/0071-1039). **1822**

EQUAL TIME (MENTOR, OHIO). (US/1063-0589). Qty: 10. **5555**

EQUESTRIAN TRAILS. (US/0013-9831). **2798**

EQUINE PRACTICE. (US/0162-8941). **2798**

EQUINE VETERINARY JOURNAL. (UK/0425-1644). **5509**

EQUINEWS. (CN/0828-864X). **2799**

EQUINOX (CAMDEN EAST). (CN/0710-9911). **2560**

EQUIPMENT JOURNAL. (CN/0710-2720). Qty: 17. **2114**

EQUITY AND CHOICE. (US/0882-3863). **1744**

EQUIVALENCIAS. (SP). **3462**

ERA, ELEKTRICITETENS RATIONELLA ANVANDNING. (SW). **2054**

ERASMUS IN ENGLISH. (CN/0071-1063). **4346**

ERASMUS OF ROTTERDAM SOCIETY YEARBOOK. (US/0276-2854). Qty: 3-6. **1076**

ERBA D'ARNO. (IT). Qty: 15. **319**

ERBA D'ARNO. (IT/0394-5618). **2615**

ERBE UND AUFTRAG (BEURON). (GW/0013-9963). **5029**

ERDE. (GW/0013-9998). Qty: 30. **2560**

ERDKUNDE. (GW/0014-0015). **1375**

ERDOGAZDASAG ES FAIPAR. (HU/0014-0066). **2400**

ERDOL, ERDGAS, KOHLE. (GW/0179-3187). **4255**

ERDOL-INFORMATIONSDIENST. (GW/0343-6705). **672**

ERFAHRUNGSHEILKUNDE. (GW/0014-0082). **3575**

ERFRISCHUNGSGETRANK, DAS. (GW/0342-2232). **2367**

ERGANZUNGSHEFT ZU PETERMANNS GEOGRAPHSCHISCHEN MITTEILUNGEN. (GW). **2560**

ERGO-MED. (GW/0170-2327). **3575**

ERGODIC THEORY AND DYNAMICAL SYSTEMS. (UK/0143-3857). **3505**

ERGONOMICS ABSTRACTS. (UK/0046-2446). **1209**

ERGONOMICS IN DESIGN. (US/1064-8046). Qty: 20-30. **1975**

ERIA, EL. (SP). **3385**

ERIE DAILY TIMES, THE. (US). **5736**

ERIGENIA. (US/8755-2000). **509**

ERKENNTNIS. (NE/0165-0106). **4346**

ERLANGER BEITRAEGE ZUR SPRACH UND KUNSTWISSENSCHAFT. (GW/0425-2268). **1076**

ERN. EXECUTIVE RECRUITER NEWS. (US/0271-0781). **940**

ERNAHRUNG (VIENNA, AUSTRIA). (AU/0250-1554). Qty: 40-70. **4190**

ERNAHRUNGSWIRTSCHAFT. (GW). **2334**

ERROR TRENDS. (US). **2781**

ERSKINE ECHO, THE. (US). Qty: 10. **5695**

ERWACHSENENBILDUNG IN OESTERREICH. (AU). **1800**

ERWERBSOBSTBAU. (GW/0014-0309). **170**

ERYTHROCYTES. (UK/0268-808X). **536**

ERZIEHUNG UND WISSENSCHAFT. (GW/0342-0671). **1745**

ESCALE (QUEBEC). (CN/0822-4056). **4176**

ESCAP AGRICULTURE DIVISION, ARSAP/FADINAP, REGIONAL INFORMATION SUPPORT SERVICE (RISS). (TH/0252-354X). **153**

ESCRIBANO, EL. (US/0014-0376). **2732**

ESCRITOS. (CK). **2846**

ESPACE GEOGRAPHIQUE. (FR/0046-2497). **2560**

ESPACES ET SOCIETES. (FR/0014-0481). **298**

ESPANOL EN AUSTRALIA. (AT). **Qty:** 50. **3279**

ESPERANTO. (NE/0014-0635). **Qty:** 60/year. **3279**

ESPERIENZE LETTERARIE. (IT/0392-3495). **3385**

ESPIONAGE MAGAZINE. (US/8756-8535). **5074**

ESPIRITU. (SP/0014-0716). **4346**

ESPRIT CREATEUR, L'. (US/0014-0767). **3342**

ESPRIT DE CORPS, CANADIAN MILITARY THEN & NOW. (CN/1194-2266). **Qty:** 24-30. **4043**

ESQ. (US/0093-8297). **3385**

ESSAY AND GENERAL LITERATURE INDEX. (US/0014-083X) **3458**

ESSAY AND GENERAL LITERATURE INDEX. CD-ROM. (US/0014-083X). **3458**

ESSAYS AND MONOGRAPHS IN COLORADO HISTORY. (US/0899-0409). **2732**

ESSAYS AND STUDIES (LONDON, ENGLAND : 1950). (UK/0071-1357). **3385**

ESSAYS IN ARTS AND SCIENCES. (US/0361-5634). **Qty:** 1. **2846**

ESSAYS IN CRITICISM. (UK/0014-0856). **3385**

ESSAYS IN GRAHAM GREENE. (US/0738-0763). **3385**

ESSAYS IN POETICS. (UK/0308-888X). **3385**

ESSAYS IN THEATRE. (CN/0821-4425). **Qty:** approx. 12/year. **5364**

ESSAYS ON CANADIAN WRITING. (CN/0316-0300). **3385**

ESSECOME. (IT/0394-8625). **3164**

ESSENTIAL GUIDE TO PRESCRIPTION DRUGS, THE. (US/0894-7058). **4303**

ESSEX ARCHAEOLOGY AND HISTORY : THE TRANSACTIONS OF THE ESSEX ARCHAEOLOGICAL SOCIETY. (UK/0308-3462). **Qty:** 5. **2686**

ESSEX FAMILY HISTORIAN, THE. (UK/0140-7503). **2446**

ESSEX INSTITUTE HISTORICAL COLLECTIONS. (US). **2732**

ESSEX SUCCULENT REVIEW. (UK). **2414**

EST EUROPEEN, L'. (FR/0014-1097). **2686**

EST MEDECINE. (FR/0248-9643). **3575**

EST-OVEST. (IT/0046-256X). **4473**

ESTADISTICA ESPANOLA. (SP/0014-1151). **5327**

ESTADO DA PARAIBA, ANUARIO ESTATISTICO. (BL). **5327**

ESTES TRAILS. (US/0737-481X). **2446**

ESTIMATE, THE. (US/1043-1667). **4520**

ESTRATEGIA ECONOMICA Y FINANCIERA. (CK/0121-4802). **1489**

ESTRENO. (US/0097-8663). **Qty:** 30. **5364**

ESTUAIRE. (CN/0700-365X). **Qty:** 50-75/yr. **3462**

ESTUARIES. (US/0160-8347). **554**

ESTUDIOS DE ASIA & AFRICA. (MX/0185-0164). **2503**

ESTUDIOS DEL DESARROLLO. (INT/1013-4069). **5199**

ESTUDIOS ECLESIASTICOS. (SP/0210-1610). **5029**

ESTUDIOS FILOLOGICOS. (CL/0071-1713). **3280**

ESTUDIOS FILOSOFICOS. (VE). **4346**

ESTUDIOS FRANCISCANOS. (SP). **5327**

ESTUDIOS - INSTITUTO DE ESTUDIO ECONOMICOS SOBRE LA REALIDAD ARGENTINA Y LATINOAMERICANA. (AG/0325-6928). **1489**

ESTUDIOS INTERNACIONALES. (CL/0716-0240). **4473**

ESTUDIOS MADRID. (SP/0210-0525). **3385**

ESTUDIOS PARAGUAYOS. (PY/0251-2483). **2732**

ESTUDIOS SOCIALES (SANTIAGO, CHILE). (CL/0716-0321). **Qty:** 4. **5199**

ESTUDIOS TERRITORIALES. (SP/0211-6871). **2822**

ESWAU HUPPEDAY. (US/0747-5810). **2446**

ETA SIGMA GAMMAN, THE. (US/8756-5943). **4775**

ETC. (US/0014-164X). **3280**

ETCETERA. (US). **250**

ETHICAL MANAGEMENT. (US/1058-6571). **Qty:** 12. **2249**

ETHICS & POLICY. (US/1065-0113). **Qty:** 4. **2250**

ETHICS IN-SERVICE. (CN/0824-5622). **2250**

ETHICS RESOURCE CENTER REPORT. (US/0748-5344). **2250**

ETHIKOS. (US/0895-5026). **Qty:** 6/yr. **2250**

ETHIOPIAN MEDICAL JOURNAL. (ET/0014-1755). **Qty:** 2. **3575**

ETHIOPIAN REVIEW. (US/1056-2354). **Qty:** 12. **2639**

ETHNIC AND RACIAL STUDIES. (UK/0141-9870). **2260**

ETHNIC FORUM. (US/0278-9078). **2260**

ETHNIC GROUPS. (US/0308-6860). **2260**

ETHNIC REPORTER (CLAREMONT, CALIF.), THE. (US/0893-7362). **2260**

ETHNIC WOMAN, THE. (US/0897-4683). **2260**

ETHNICITY AND PUBLIC POLICY SERIES. (US). **2260**

ETHNOARTS INDEX. (US/0893-0120). **Qty:** 10-12. **334**

ETHNOGRAPHIE, L'. (FR). **235**

ETHNOHISTORY. (US/0014-1801). **2261**

ETHNOLOGIA FENNICA. (FI/0355-1776). **235**

ETHNOLOGIA SCANDINAVICA. (SW/0348-9698). **Qty:** 30. **2319**

ETHNOMUSICOLOGY. (US/0014-1836). **4117**

ETHNOS. (SW/0014-1844). **236**

ETHOLOGY. (GW/0179-1613). **5583**

ETHOS. (US/0091-2131). **4586**

ETNOS (LUBLIN, POLAND). (PL). **4956**

ETOILE DU MATIN. (CN/0712-2667). **5016**

ETR. (GW/0013-2845). **5431**

ETTELAAT. (IR). **5803**

ETUDES ANGLAISES. (FR/0014-195X). **3342**

ETUDES BALKANIQUES. (BU/0324-1645). **2687**

ETUDES CANADIENNES. (FR/0153-1700). **Qty:** 1. **2732**

ETUDES CELTIQUES. (FR/0373-1928). **3336**

ETUDES CLASSIQUES (NAMUR, BELGIUM). (BE/0014-200X). **Qty:** 150. **1076**

ETUDES DE LETTRES. (SZ/0014-2026). **3385**

ETUDES DE LINGUISTIQUE APPLIQUEE. (FR/0071-190X). **3280**

ETUDES ET MEMOIRES. (FR/0078-9585). **5469**

ETUDES ET STATISTIQUES - BANQUE DES ETATS DE L'AFRIQUE CENTRALE. (CM/0014-2069). **728**

ETUDES FINNO-OUGRIENNES. (FR). **3280**

ETUDES GERMANIQUES. (FR/0014-2115). **3280**

ETUDES INTERNATIONALES (QUEBEC). (CN/0014-2123). **4521**

ETUDES INUIT. (CN/0701-1008). **236**

ETUDES IRLANDAISES. (FR/0183-973X). **2687**

ETUDES LITTERAIRES (UNIVERSITE LAVAL). (CN/0014-214X). **3386**

ETUDES QUATERNAIRES LANGUEDOCIENNES. (FR). **4227**

ETUDES STATISTIQUES (BRUSSELS, BELGIUM). (BE/0522-7585). **5327**

ETUDES THEOLOGIQUES ET RELIGIEUSES. (FR/0014-2239). **4956**

ETUDES TSIGANES. (FR/0014-2247). **4553**

EUDISED R & D BULLETIN. (FR). **1745**

EUDORA WELTY NEWSLETTER. (US/0146-7220). **3386**

EUGENE O'NEILL REVIEW, THE. (US/1040-9483). **3386**

EULAR BULLETIN. MONOGRAPH SERIES. (SZ/0253-0333). **3804**

EUNTES DOCETE. (IT). **4956**

EUPHORBIA JOURNAL, THE. (US/0737-8823). **2414**

EUPHORIA ET CACOPHORIA. (JA). **3720**

EURAIL GUIDE. (US/0085-0330). **5431**

EURASIAN STUDIES YEARBOOK. (US). **Qty:** 40. **3386**

EUREKA (BECKENHAM). (UK/0261-2097). **2098**

EUREKA SENTINEL (EUREKA, NEV. : 1902). (US). **5707**

EURO PRINTER. (GW/0938-1236). **4564**

EUROFACH ELECTRONICA. (SP/0211-2973). **2054**

EUROFRUIT. (UK). **2414**

EUROIL. (NO/0802-9474). **4255**

EUROPA-ARCHIV. (GW/0014-2476). **4521**

EUROPA DELLA CEE. (IT). **1634**

EUROPA DOMANI. (IT/0390-2102). **Qty:** 4-5. **833**

EUROPA E LA CEE, L'. (IT). **4521**

EUROPA ETHNICA. (AU/0014-2492). **2261**

EUROPAEISCHE GRUNDRECHTE - ZEITSCHRIFT. (GW/0341-9800). **4507**

EUROPAEISCHE RUNDSCHAU. (AU/0304-2782). **4521**

EUROPAISCHE INTEGRATION AUSWAHLBIBLIOGRAPHIE. (GW). **4473**

EUROPAISCHE ZEITUNG. (GW). **4473**

EUROPAMARKT : MILCH. (GW). **194**

EUROPE. (FR/0014-2751). **Qty:** 8. **3342**

EUROPE EN FORMATION, L'. (FR/0014-2808). **4521**

EUROPE ENERGY. (BE). **1944**

EUROPE ENVIRONMENT. (BE/0778-7928). **2171**

EUROPE PLURILINGUE. (FR/1161-8884). **Qty:** 2. **2487**

EUROPEAN ACCESS. (UK/0264-7362). **4473**

EUROPEAN ACCOUNTING REVIEW. (UK/0963-8180). **743**

EUROPEAN APPLIED RESEARCH REPORTS. ENVIRONMENT AND NATURAL RESOURCES SECTION. (UK/0272-4626). **2171**

EUROPEAN APPLIED RESEARCH REPORTS. NUCLEAR SCIENCE AND TECHNOLOGY SECTION. (SZ/0379-4229). **2155**

EUROPEAN BUREAU OF ADULT EDUCATION NEWSLETTER. (NE). **1745**

EUROPEAN BUSINESS INTELLIGENCE BRIEFING. (UK/0957-0039). **673**

EUROPEAN BUSINESS LAW REVIEW. (UK/0959-6941). **3099**

EUROPEAN COMPANIES. (UK/0071-2582). **673**

EUROPEAN COMPANION, THE. (UK). **Qty:** 6-10. **4521**

EUROPEAN CONSORTIUM FOR POLITICAL RESEARCH NEWS. (UK). **4473**

EUROPEAN EARTHQUAKE ENGINEERING. (IT/0394-5103). **2023**

EUROPEAN ENVIRONMENTAL LAW REVIEW. (UK/0966-1646). **3112**

EUROPEAN ENVIRONMENTAL YEARBOOK. (UK). **2171**

EUROPEAN HEART JOURNAL. (UK/0195-668X). **3704**

EUROPEAN INDUSTRIAL RELATIONS REVIEW. (UK/0309-7234). **1668**

EUROPEAN INFORMATION SERVICE. (UK/0261-2747). **2516**

EUROPEAN INTELLECTUAL PROPERTY REVIEW. (UK/0142-0461). **1304**

EUROPEAN JOURNAL OF CELL BIOLOGY. (GW/0171-9335). **536**

EUROPEAN JOURNAL OF CHIROPRACTIC. (UK/0263-9114). **3575**

EUROPEAN JOURNAL OF CLINICAL NUTRITION. (UK/0954-3007). **4190**

EUROPEAN JOURNAL OF CLINICAL PHARMACOLOGY. (GW/0031-6970). **4303**

EUROPEAN JOURNAL OF COGNITIVE PSYCHOLOGY, THE. (UK/0954-1446). **4586**

EUROPEAN JOURNAL OF COMMUNICATION (LONDON). (UK/0267-3231). **1111**

EUROPEAN JOURNAL OF DEVELOPMENT RESEARCH, THE. (UK/0957-8811). **2909**

EUROPEAN JOURNAL OF DISORDERS OF COMMUNICATION. (UK/0963-7273). **Qty:** 25. **1111**

EUROPEAN JOURNAL OF EDUCATION. (UK/0141-8211). **1745**

EUROPEAN JOURNAL OF ENGINEERING EDUCATION. (UK/0304-3797). **1975**

EUROPEAN JOURNAL OF EPIDEMIOLOGY. (IT/0393-2990). **3735**

EUROPEAN JOURNAL OF FOREST PATHOLOGY. (GW/0300-1237). **2379**

EUROPEAN JOURNAL OF GYNAECOLOGICAL ONCOLOGY. (IT/0392-2936). **3817**

EUROPEAN JOURNAL OF HAEMATOLOGY. (DK/0902-4441). **3771**

EUROPEAN JOURNAL OF IMPLANT AND REFRACTIVE SURGERY, THE. (FR/0955-3681). **3874**

EUROPEAN JOURNAL OF INFORMATION SYSTEMS. (UK/0960-085X). **1184**

EUROPEAN JOURNAL OF INTERCULTURAL STUDIES. (UK/0952-391X). **2261**

EUROPEAN JOURNAL OF INTERNATIONAL AFFAIRS, THE. (IT/0394-6444). **4473**

EUROPEAN JOURNAL OF MECHANICAL ENGINEERING. (BE/0777-2734). **2114**

EUROPEAN JOURNAL OF MEDICINAL CHEMISTRY. (FR/0223-5234). **3575**

EUROPEAN JOURNAL OF MEDICINE. (FR/1165-0478). **Qty:** 12. **3575**

EUROPEAN JOURNAL OF MINERALOGY (STUTTGART). (GW/0935-1221). **1439**

EUROPEAN JOURNAL OF ORIENTAL MEDICINE. (UK). **Qty:** 12. **3575**

EUROPEAN JOURNAL OF ORTHODONTICS. (UK/0141-5387). **1323**

EUROPEAN JOURNAL OF PERSONALITY. (UK/0890-2070). **4587**

EUROPEAN JOURNAL OF POLITICAL RESEARCH. (NE/0304-4130). **4473**

EUROPEAN JOURNAL OF PROTISTOLOGY. (GW/0932-4739). **562**

EUROPEAN JOURNAL OF PSYCHIATRY, THE. (SP/0213-6163). **3925**

EUROPEAN JOURNAL OF PSYCHOLOGY OF EDUCATION. (PO/0256-2928). **1878**

EUROPEAN JOURNAL OF RHEUMATOLOGY AND INFLAMMATION (ENGLISH EDITION). (UK/0140-1610). **3804**

EUROPEAN JOURNAL OF SERIALS LIBRARIANSHIP. (US/1048-5287). **3209**

EUROPEAN JOURNAL OF SURGERY, THE. (SW/1102-4151). **3964**

EUROPEAN JUDAISM. (UK/0014-3006). **5047**

EUROPEAN MAC PROFESSIONAL. (SP). **1237**

EUROPEAN MANAGEMENT JOURNAL. (UK/0263-2373). **867**

EUROPEAN MEDIA BULLETIN. (UK/0962-8312). **1132**

EUROPEAN MICROSCOPY AND ANALYSIS. (UK/0958-1952). **Qty:** varies. **572**

EUROPEAN MICROSCOPY & ANALYSIS. (UK). **572**

EUROPEAN OFFSHORE PETROLEUM NEWSLETTER. (NO/0332-5210). **4256**

EUROPEAN PACKAGING MAGAZINE (HEUSENSTAMM, GERMANY). (GW). **Qty:** 4. **4219**

EUROPEAN POWER NEWS. (UK/0261-8214). **1944**

EUROPEAN REPORT. (BE). **1635**

EUROPEAN RESPIRATORY REVIEW : AN OFFICIAL JOURNAL OF THE EUROPEAN RESPIRATORY SOCIETY. (DK/0905-9180). **3949**

EUROPEAN REVIEW OF AGRICULTURAL ECONOMICS. (NE/0165-1587). **82**

EUROPEAN REVIEW OF NATIVE AMERICAN STUDIES. (GW/0238-1486). **Qty:** 20. **2261**

EUROPEAN ROMANTIC REVIEW. (US/1050-9585). **Qty:** 10. **3386**

EUROPEAN RUBBER DIRECTORY. (UK/0306-414X). **5075**

EUROPEAN RUBBER JOURNAL (LONDON, ENGLAND : 1982). (UK/0266-4151). **5075**

EUROPEAN SCIENCE EDITING : BULLETIN OF THE EUROPEAN ASSOCIATION OF SCIENCE EDITORS. (UK/0309-4715). **Qty:** 1-9. **4815**

EUROPEAN SECURITY STUDIES. (UK). **4043**

EUROPEAN SOCIOLOGICAL REVIEW. (UK/0266-7215). **5245**

EUROPEAN STUDIES NEWSLETTER. (US/0046-2802). **2687**

EUROPEAN TAXATION. (NE/0014-3138). **4722**

EUROPEAN TAXATION. SUPPLEMENTARY SERVICE. (NE/0531-4577). **4722**

EUROPEAN TRANSPORT LAW. (BE/0014-3154). **2967**

EUROPEAN WATER POLLUTION CONTROL : OFFICIAL PUBLICATION OF THE EUROPEAN WATER POLLUTION CONTROL ASSOCIATION (EWPCA). (NE/0925-5060). **5533**

EUROSLOT OLDHAM. (UK/0966-0259). **Qty:** 12/yr. **4860**

EUSKAL HERRIKO POETAK. (SP). **3386**

EVALUATION & RESEARCH IN EDUCATION. (UK/0950-0790). **1745**

EVALUATION ENGINEERING. (US/0149-0370). **2054**

EVALUATOR (RIVER FOREST, ILL.). (US/8756-775X). **320**

EVANGELICAL BAPTIST. (CN/0014-3324). **5059**

EVANGELICAL BEACON, THE. (US/0014-3332). **4957**

EVANGELICAL FRIEND. (US/0014-3340). **4957**

EVANGELICAL JOURNAL. (US/0741-1758). **Qty:** 15-20/yr. **4957**

EVANGELICAL LIBRARY BULLETIN. (UK). **3209**

EVANGELICAL MISSIONS QUARTERLY. (US/0014-3359). **Qty:** 32. **4957**

EVANGELICAL QUARTERLY. (UK/0014-3367). **4957**

EVANGELICAL REVIEW OF THEOLOGY. (II/0144-8153). **4957**

EVANGELICAL STUDIES BULLETIN. (US/0890-703X). **Qty:** 2-3. **4957**

EVANGELICAL TIMES. (UK). **5060**

EVANGELIKALE MISSIOLOGIE. (GW/0177-8706). **Qty:** 20. **4957**

EVANGELISCHE ERZIEHER, DER. (GW/0014-3413). **4957**

EVANGELISCHE KOMMENTARE. (GW/0300-4236). **4957**

EVANGELISCHE THEOLOGIE. (GW/0014-3502). **4957**

EVANGELISM (MEQUON, WIS.). (US/0890-667X). **Qty:** 4. **4957**

EVANGELIST (ALBANY, N.Y.), THE. (US/0738-8489). **Qty:** 5. **5029**

EVANGELIUM / GOSPEL / EUAGGELION. (GW). **4957**

EVANGELIUM UND WISSENSCHAFT. (GW/0934-0769). **Qty:** 10-20. **4957**

EVANGELIZING TODAY'S CHILD. (US/0891-3846). **Qty:** 20/yr. **4958**

EVANSIA. (US/0747-9859). **509**

EVANSVILLE PRESS. (US/0896-6249). **5664**

EVELYN WAUGH NEWSLETTER AND STUDIES. (US/1058-8272). **Qty:** 3-4. **432**

EVENING CHRONICLE (OLDHAM). (UK/0968-3623). **Qty:** 250+. **5812**

EVENING JOURNAL (LUBBOCK, TEX.). (US/0745-547X). **5749**

EVENING NEWS (HARRISBURG, PA.), THE. (US/0887-7939). **5736**

EVENING NEWS (JEFFERSONVILLE, IND. : 1924). (US). **Qty:** 52. **5664**

EVENING NEWS (NORWICH. 1991). (UK/0964-4946). **5812**

EVENING TELEGRAM (HERKIMER, N.Y.). (US). **Qty:** 12. **5716**

EVENING TIMES. (US). **Qty:** 5/year. **5631**

EVENT (NEW WESTMINSTER). (CN/0315-3770). **Qty:** 3. **3386**

EVERGREEN CHRONICLES, THE. (US/1043-3333). **Qty:** 5. **2794**

EVERYBODY'S MONEY. (US/0423-8710). **1296**

EVERYONE'S BACKYARD. (US/0749-3940). **2171**

EVERYTHING NATURAL. (US/0889-8421). **2790**

EVOLUTION PSYCHIATRIQUE, L'. (FR/0014-3855). **3925**

EVOLUTIONARY THEORY & REVIEW. (US). **Qty:** 100. **236**

EVOLUTIONARY TRENDS IN PLANTS. (UK/1011-3258). **Qty:** 10. **509**

EWGS BULLETIN. (US/0738-5234). **2446**

EWING EXCHANGE. (US/0892-2144). **2446**

EX LIBRIS (PORTSMOUTH, N.H.). (US/1042-6647). **3386**

EX TEMPORE. (CN/0276-6795). **4117**

EXCALIBUR (DOWNSVIEW, ONT.). (CN/0823-1915). **5784**

EXCEL (SAN FRANCISCO, CALIF.). (US/0893-5017). **5200**

EXCEPTIONAL CHILDREN. (US/0014-4029). **1878**

EXCEPTIONAL HUMAN EXPERIENCE. (US/1053-4768). **Qty:** 120. **4243**

EXCEPTIONAL PARENT, THE. (US/0046-9157). **2278**

EXCERPTA BOTANICA. SECTIO A. TAXONOMICA ET CHOROLOGICA. (GW/0014-4037). **509**

EXCERPTA INFORMATICA. (NE/0169-5509). **1219**

EXCESS EXPRESS. (US/0740-1388). **2879**

EXCHANGE. (NE/0166-2740). **Qty:** 20. **4958**

EXCHANGE (PROVO). (US/0146-4000). **1091**

EXE. (UK/0268-6872). **Qty:** 22. **1184**

EXECUTIVE : AN ACADEMY OF MANAGEMENT PUBLICATION, THE. (US). **867**

EXECUTIVE COMMUNICATIONS. (US/0892-3299). **1111**

EXECUTIVE DEVELOPMENT. (UK). **867**

EXECUTIVE EDGE. (US/1048-2954). **2597**

EXECUTIVE EDUCATOR, THE. (US/0161-9500). **1863**

EXECUTIVE EXCELLENCE. (US/8756-2308). **867**

EXECUTIVE HOUSEKEEPING TODAY. (US/0738-6583). **Qty:** 4. **2790**

EXECUTIVE INTELLIGENCE REVIEW. (US/0273-6314). **Qty:** 10. **1490**

EXECUTIVE REPORT ON MANAGED CARE, THE. (US/0898-9753). **940**

EXECUTIVE SECRETARY BRADFORD. (UK/0955-6230). **Qty:** 4. **4204**

EXECUTIVE SYSTEMS INTERNATIONAL NEWSLETTER. (UK/0968-8803). **Qty:** 10. **674**

EXERCISE PHYSIOLOGY (NEW YORK, N.Y.). (US/0748-3155). **3954**

EXERCISE STANDARDS & MALPRACTICE REPORTER, THE. (US/0891-0278). **2968**

EXETER. (US/0195-0207). **1091**

EXETER NEWS-LETTER (1867), THE. (US/0886-3962). **5708**

EXHIBIT BUILDER SOURCE BOOK DIRECTORY. (US). **674**

EXHIBIT REVIEW, THE. (US/1046-2872). **Qty:** 10-12. **759**

EXPERIENTIAL EDUCATION. (US/0739-2338). **1746**

EXPERIMENT. (US/0014-4770). **3463**

EXPERIMENTAL AGING RESEARCH. (US/0361-073X). **3750**

EXPERIMENTAL AGRICULTURE. (UK/0014-4797). **82**

EXPERIMENTAL HEAT TRANSFER. (UK/0891-6152). **4430**

EXPERIMENTAL LUNG RESEARCH. (US/0190-2148). **3949**

EXPERIMENTAL PATHOLOGY (1981). (GW/0232-1513). **3894**

EXPERIMENTAL PHYSIOLOGY. (UK/0958-0670). **580**

EXPERIMENTAL ROCKET FLYER. (US/1062-8576). **18**

EXPERIMENTAL TECHNIQUES (WESTPORT, CONN.). (US/0732-8818). **2114**

EXPERIMENTAL THERMAL AND FLUID SCIENCE. (US/0894-1777). **4427**

EXPERT AND THE LAW, THE. (US/0737-8726). **2968**

EXPERT SYSTEMS FOR INFORMATION MANAGEMENT. (UK/0953-5551). **1212**

EXPERT WITNESS JOURNAL. (US/0277-0555). **2968**

EXPLICATOR, THE. (US/0014-4940). **3386**

EXPLORATION GEOPHYSICS. (US/0071-3473). **1405**

EXPLORATION GEOPHYSICS (MELBOURNE). (AT/0812-3985). **Qty:** 1-2. **4402**

EXPLORATION INTERNATIONAL NEWS. (UK/0960-9989). **4256**

EXPLORATION (SANTA FE, N.M.). (US/0277-089X). **236**

EXPLORATIONS (DAYTON, OHIO). (US/0889-8693). **Qty:** 29. **4958**

EXPLORATIONS IN ETHNIC STUDIES. (US/0730-904X). **2261**

EXPLORATIONS IN KNOWLEDGE. (UK/0261-1376). **Qty:** 20+. **4346**

EXPLORATIONS IN SIGHTS AND SOUNDS. (US/0733-3323). **2261**

EXPLORE (LAWRENCE, KAN.). (US/0741-8493). **1823**

EXPLORER NEWS. (US/0895-8521). **2560**

EXPLORER, THE. (US/0014-5009). **4165**

EXPLORERS JOURNAL. (US/0014-5025). **5104**

EXPLORING B. (US/0162-4431). **5060**

EXPLOSIVES AND PYROTECHNICS. (US/0014-505X). **Qty:** 2. **2012**

EXPO (WAUCONDA, ILL.). (US/1046-3925). **867**

EXPONENT II. (US). **Qty:** 4. **4958**

EXPORT GAZETTE. (II). **834**

EXPORT GRAFICAS USA. (US/0741-7160). **378**

EXPORT HANDBOOK SYDNEY. (AT/0312-3774). **674**

EXPORT (NEW YORK, N.Y.). (US/0014-519X). **2811**

EXPORT POLYGRAPH INTERNATIONAL. (GW/0344-2039). **378**

EXPORT SALES AND MARKETING MANUAL. (US/1054-8327). **834**

EXPORT TIMES (NEW DELHI), THE. (II/0257-8018). **834**

EXPORTADOR, EL. (US/0279-456X). **835**

EXPOSITIONES MATHEMATICAE. (GW/0723-0869). **3505**

EXPOSITORY TIMES, THE. (UK/0014-5246). **5016**

EXQUISITE CORPSE. (US/0740-7823). **Qty:** 12-16. **3463**

EXTRACELLULAR MATRIX. (UK/0268-1617). **536**

EXTRACTA ORTHOPAEDICA. (GW/0344-5046). **3881**

EXTRACTA UROLOGICA. (GW/0344-5038). **3990**

EXTRAPOLATION. (US/0014-5483). **3342**

EXTRUSION COMMUNIQUE. (UK/0958-0549). **Qty:** 4. **2334**

EYE : THE INTERNATIONAL REVIEW OF GRAPHIC DESIGN. (UK/0960-779X). **378**

EYELINE. (AT). **Qty:** 1 per issue. **373**

F.A.R.O.G. FORUM JOURNAL BILINGUE. (US/0741-577X). **Qty:** 5 or 6. **5200**

F.A.S. PUBLIC INTEREST REPORT. (US/0092-9824). **5104**

F.I.B.A. RULES CASEBOOK. (CN/0712-5585). **4894**

F.I.D. NEWS BULLETIN. (NE/0014-5874). **3210**

F.O.C. REVIEW. (US/1041-8164). **3387**

F. SCOTT FITZGERALD SOCIETY NEWSLETTER. (US). **Qty:** 3-4. **3387**

F.Y.E.O. (US/0738-4203). **4044**

FABIAN REVIEW. (UK). **Qty:** 6. **4541**

FABIAN TRACT. (UK/0307-7535). **4474**

FABIS. (SY/0255-6448). **171**

FABRERIES. (CN/0318-6725). **5608**

FABRICATIONS : THE JOURNAL OF THE SOCIETY OF ARCHITECTURAL HISTORIANS, AUSTRALIA & NEW ZEALAND. (AT/1033-1867). **298**

FABRIK OG BOLIG. (DK/0106-3324). **2688**

FABRIMETAL. (BE/0377-9084). **3478**

FABULA. (GW/0014-6242). **2319**

FACE AU RISQUE. (FR/0014-6269). **5200**

FACE (MALIBU, CALIF.). (US/1064-7953). **2533**

FACE (SAO PAULO, BRAZIL). (BL/0103-1562). **3281**

FACES ROCKS. (US/0882-2921). **4117**

FACET TALK. (AT/1035-0977). **2773**

FACETS FEATURES. (US/0736-3745). **4068**

FACHBERICHTE HUTTENPRAXIS METALLWEITERVERARBEITUNG. (GW/0340-8043). **4001**

FACHSPRACHE. (AU/0251-1207). **3281**

FACIAL ORTHOPEDICS AND TEMPOROMANDIBULAR ARTHROLOGY. (US/0749-0399). **3881**

FACIAL PLASTIC SURGERY. (US/0736-6825). **3964**

FACILITIES DESIGN & MANAGEMENT. (US/0279-4438). **2900**

FACILITIES MANAGER : THE OFFICIAL PUBLICATION OF THE ASSOCIATION OF PHYSICAL PLANT ADMINISTRATORS OF UNIVERSITIES AND COLLEGES. (US/0882-7249). **867**

FACILITIES PLANNING NEWS. (US/1045-7089). **Qty:** 3-4. **298**

FACILITY MANAGEMENT JOURNAL : A PUBLICATION OF THE INTERNATIONAL FACILITY MANAGEMENT ASSOCIATION. (US/1059-3667). **Qty:** 12/yr. **867**

FACT BOOK : TABLES AND CHARTS ON THE NEW YORK METROPOLITAN REGION. (US). **5327**

FACT SHEET - FOOD ANIMAL CONCERNS TRUST. (US/0882-3022). **226**

FACTS FOR YOU. (II). **1561**

FACTS (SEATTLE, WASH. : 1962). (US/0427-8879). **5760**

FACTSHEET FIVE. (US/0890-6823). **Qty:** 100. **385**

FACTUM. (SZ). **Qty:** 12. **5060**

FACTUM : BOLETIN OFICIAL DEL COLEGIO DE ABOGADOS DE PUERTO RICO. (PR). **2968**

FAENZA. (IT/0014-679X). **Qty:** Various. **2589**

FAIR EMPLOYMENT COMPLIANCE. (US/0885-7172). **Qty:** 2-12. **3148**

FAIRBANKS DAILY NEWS-MINER. (US/8750-5495). **Qty:** 52. **5629**

FAIRCHILD TROPICAL GARDEN BULLETIN. (US/0014-6943). **2414**

FAIRFAX JOURNAL (SPRINGFIELD. 1980), THE. (US/0273-6403). **5758**

FAIRPLAY WORLD PORTS DIRECTORY. (UK/0261-2356). **5449**

FAIRPRESS. (US/0192-3110). **5645**

FAIRSHARE. (US/0273-3560). **3120**

FAIRTEST EXAMINER, THE. (US/0898-2511). **Qty:** 8-10. **1746**

FAITH. (US). **5016**

FAITH AND FELLOWSHIP. (US). **Qty:** 25. **5060**

FAITH & FORM. (US/0014-7001). **298**

FAITH AND FREEDOM OXFORD. (UK/0014-701X). **4958**

FAITH AND MISSION. (US/0740-0659). **4958**

FAITH AND PHILOSOPHY : JOURNAL OF THE SOCIETY OF CHRISTIAN PHILOSOPHERS. (US/0739-7046). **4346**

FAITH & REASON. (US/0098-5449). **Qty:** 2. **4958**

FAITH TODAY (TORONTO). (CN/0706-7003). **4958**

FAITH TODAY (WILLOWDALE). (CN/0832-1191). **4958**

FAIZULISLAM. (PK). **5285**

FAJR (JERUSALEM). (IS). **2503**

FAMILIA. (SA/0014-7117). **2447**

FAMILIES IN SOCIETY. (US/1044-3894). **5285**

FAMILIES OF WYOMING CO., WV. (US/0890-0353). **2447**

FAMILIES OF YANCEY COUNTY, NC. (US/0890-0361). **2447**

FAMILJA KANA. (MM). **Qty:** 11. **2279**

FAMILY ADVOCATE. (US/0163-710X). **3120**

FAMILY AFFAIRS. (US). **Qty:** 1-4. **2279**

FAMILY AND CONCILIATION COURTS REVIEW. (US/1047-5699). **3120**

FAMILY ASSOCIATION NEWSLETTER, DRODDY, DRODY, DRAWDY & VARIANTS, THE. (US/0749-4505). **2447**

FAMILY (BOSTON, MASS.), THE. (US/0899-1529). **5029**

FAMILY BUSINESS REVIEW. (US/0894-4865). **674**

FAMILY CONNECTIONS. (CN/1195-9428). **Qty:** 10. **2279**

FAMILY FINDINGS. (US/0533-0939). **2447**

FAMILY HISTORY. (UK/0014-7265). **2447**

FAMILY HISTORY CAPERS. (US/0742-1419). **2447**

FAMILY HISTORY FOR BEGINNERS. (AT/0815-3922). **2447**

FAMILY LAW (CHICHESTER). (UK/0014-7281). **3120**

FAMILY LAW QUARTERLY. (US/0014-729X). **3120**

FAMILY LAW REVIEW. (US/0149-1431). **3120**

FAMILY LIFE. (CN/0014-7303). **Qty:** 11. **2279**

FAMILY LIFE. (UK). **2279**

FAMILY LIFE EDUCATOR. (US/0732-9962). **2279**

FAMILY LIFE MATTERS. (US/1064-6167). **Qty:** 1/2. **2279**

FAMILY MEDICINE. (US/0742-3225). **Qty:** 10. **3737**

FAMILY PHYSICIAN (KUALA LUMPUR, MALAYSIA). (MY). **3737**

FAMILY PLANNING PERSPECTIVES. (US/0014-7354). **588**

FAMILY PLANNING TODAY. (UK/0309-1112). **589**

FAMILY PRACTICE. (UK/0263-2136). **3737**

FAMILY PRACTICE RECERTIFICATION. (US/0163-6642). **3737**

FAMILY PROCESS. (US/0014-7370). **2279**

FAMILY RECORDS TODAY. (US/0736-1858). **Qty:** 150-200. **2447**

FAMILY RELATIONS. (US/0197-6664). **2279**

FAMILY ROOTS : JOURNAL OF THE FAMILY ROOTS FAMILY HISTORY SOCIETY. EASTBOURNE AND DISTRICT. (UK). **2447**

FAMILY SNOOP. (US). **Qty:** 3-4. **2447**

FAMILY SYSTEMS MEDICINE. (US/0736-1718). **3737**

FAMILY TREE MAGAZINE. (UK/0267-1131). **2447**

FAMILY TREE TALK. (US/0747-9441). **2447**

FAMUAN (TALLAHASSEE, FLA.), THE. (US/1063-9942). **Qty:** varies. **5649**

FANFARE (TENAFLY, N.J.). (US/0148-9364). **4117**

FANG YEN. (CC). **3281**

FANGORIA. (US/0164-2111). **4068**

FANTASY & SCIENCE FICTION. (US/0024-984X). **3387**

FANTASY BOOK. (US/0277-0717). **3387**

FANTASY COMMENTATOR. (US/1051-5011). **3387**

FAR EASTERN AFFAIRS. (RU). **1561**

FARBE. (GW/0014-7680). **1024**

FARBE + I.E. UND LACK ADRESSBUCH MIT BEZUGSQUELLENNACHWEIS. (GW). **4223**

FARBE + LACK. (GW/0014-7699). **4223**

FARM BUILDING PROGRESS. (UK/0309-4111). **Qty:** Varies. **158**

FARM BUILDINGS AND ENGINEERING : JOURNAL OF THE FARM BUILDINGS INFORMATION CENTRE AND THE FARM BUILDINGS ASSOCIATION. (UK/0265-5373). **614**

FARM DEVELOPMENT REVIEW. (UK). **84**

FARM JOURNAL (PHILADELPHIA. 1956). (US/0014-8008). **85**

FARM MANAGEMENT (KENILWORTH). (UK/0014-8059). **Qty:** 4. **85**

FARM NEWS OF ERIE AND WYOMING COUNTIES. (US). **85**

FARM REVIEW (JOLIET, ILL.). (US). **85**

FARMACEUTISCH TIJDSCHRIFT VOOR BELGIE. (BE/0369-9714). **4304**

FARMACEUTSKI GLASNIK. (CI/0014-8202). **4304**

FARMACEVTISK REVY. (SW/0014-8210). **4304**

FARMACI. (IT). **4304**

FARMACOTERAPIA MADRID. (SP/0214-8935). **4305**

FARMERS' ADVANCE, THE. (US/0745-211X). **5692**

FARMER'S DIGEST. (US/0046-3337). **85**

FARMING FORUM. (AT). **86**

FARMING NEWS. (UK). **86**

FARMING TODAY (NAIROBI, KENYA). (KE). **86**

FARO DEL POETA : REVISTA TRIMESTRAL DE POESIA. (SP). **3463**

FARR FOOTNOTES. (US/0897-778X). **2448**

FASEB JOURNAL, THE. (US/0892-6638). **455**

FASHIONEWS (BURLINGAME, CALIF.). (US/0892-5216). **1084**

FAST FOLK MUSICAL MAGAZINE. (US/8755-9137). **4117**

FATE (MARION). (US/0014-8776). **4241**

FATIGUE & FRACTURE OF ENGINEERING MATERIALS & STRUCTURES. (UK/8756-758X). **2102**

FAULKNER & GRAY'S BANKRUPTCY LAW REVIEW. (US/1043-0547). **2968**

FAULKNER FACTS AND FIDDLINGS. (US/0430-1188). **2733**

FAULKNER NEWSLETTER AND YOKNAPATAWPHA REVIEW, THE. (US/0733-6357). **Qty:** 6. **432**

FAUNA D'ITALIA. (IT/0430-1226). **5583**

FAUNA (OSLO). (NO/0014-8881). **5583**

FAUQUIER TIMES-DEMOCRAT. (US/1050-7655). **5758**

FAYETTE ADVERTISER, THE. (US/0746-9942). **5703**

FAYETTE CONNECTION, THE. (US/0739-8093). **2448**

FAYETTE FACTS. (US/0737-1012). **2448**

FAYETTE FALCON, THE. (US). **Qty:** 10-12/yr. **5745**

FCX CAROLINA COOPERATOR. (US/0195-3346). **86**

FDC REPORTS. PRESCRIPTION AND OTC PHARMACEUTICALS. MID-WEEK REPORT. (US/0734-6506). **4305**

FDGB REVIEW. (GW/0323-7028). **1669**

FED IN PRINT: ECONOMICS AND BANKING TOPICS. (US). **Qty:** 8. **729**

FEDERAL ACQUISITION REPORT. (US/8755-9285). **4647**

FEDERAL BAR NEWS & JOURNAL. (US/0279-4691). **Qty:** 20-25. **2969**

FEDERAL COMPUTER MARKET REPORT. (US/1042-721X). **1237**

FEDERAL EMPLOYEES ALMANAC. (US/0071-4127). **4702**

FEDERAL JOBS DIGEST. (US/0739-1684). **4204**

FEDERAL LABOR RELATIONS REPORTER. (US/0199-4883). **1669**

FEDERAL MANAGERS QUARTERLY. (US/0893-8415). **868**

FEDERAL MERIT SYSTEMS REPORTER. (US/0746-035X). **4702**

FEDERAL PROBATION. (US/0014-9128). **3164**

FEDERAL TIMES. (US/0014-9233). **4703**

FEDERAL VETERINARIAN, THE. (US/0164-6257). **Qty:** 10/yr. **5510**

FEDERALIST (WASHINGTON, D.C.: 1980), THE. (US/0736-8151). **Qty:** 2. **2733**

FEDERATION NEWS / FEDERATION OF NOVA SCOTIAN HERITAGE. (CN/1197-5334). **2733**

FEDNEWS, THE. (US/0430-2761). **1669**

FEED COMPOUNDER. (UK/0950-771X). **200**

FEED MANAGEMENT. (US/0014-956X). **201**

FEEDBACK PAPERS. (GW). **1240**

FEEDS & FEEDING. (UK/0961-978X). **201**

FEITEN. (BE). **4649**

FELD WALD WASSER. SCHWEIZERISCHE JAGDZEITUNG. (SZ/0014-9756). **4871**

FELIX RAVENNA. (IT/0391-7517). **268**

FELLOWSHIP (NEW YORK). (US/0014-9810). **4521**

FELL'S INTERNATIONAL COIN BOOK. (US/0430-2958). **2781**

FEMALE BODYBUILDING AND WEIGHT TRAINING. (US/0888-4102). **2597**

FEMINIE. (CN). **Qty:** 24. **5555**

FEMINISM & PSYCHOLOGY. (UK/0959-3535). **5555**

FEMINISMS (COLUMBUS, OHIO). (US/1041-1801). **5556**

FEMINIST BOOKSTORE NEWS. (US/0741-6555). **5556**

FEMINIST COLLECTIONS (MADISON, WIS.). (US/0742-7441). **5556**

FEMINIST, DER. (GW/0179-8367). **5556**

FEMINIST ISSUES. (US/0270-6679). **5556**

FEMINIST REVIEW. (UK/0141-7789). **5556**

FEMINIST STUDIES. (US/0046-3663). **5556**

FEMINIST TEACHER. (US/0882-4843). **Qty:** 3-6 per year. **1894**

FEMMES D'ACTION. (CN/0226-9902). **5556**

FEMS MICROBIOLOGY. (NE/0921-8254). **562**

FEN. FINITE ELEMENT NEWS. (UK/0309-6688). **5105**

FERDINAND NEWS, THE. (US). **Qty:** 10. **5664**

FERGUSON FILES. (US/1040-2276). **2448**

FERGUSON'S SRI LANKA DIRECTORY. (CE). **2503**

FERN GAZETTE, THE. (UK/0308-0838). **510**

FERNBANK QUARTERLY. (US/0742-650X). **5105**

FERNSEH- UND KINOTECHNIK. (GW/0015-0142). **4068**

FERRARI WORLD. (UK/0958-7462). **5415**

FERROELECTRICS. (US/0015-0193). **4402**

FERROELECTRICS. LETTERS SECTION. (US/0731-5171). **2054**

FERTIGUNGSTECHNIK UND BETRIEB. (GW/0015-024X). **2114**

FERTILISER NEWS. (II/0015-0266). **87**

FERTILITY AND STERILITY. (US/0015-0282). **3576**

FERTILIZER TECHNOLOGY. (US/0378-0430). **171**

FESPP NEWSLETTER. (DK). **Qty:** 2-4. **580**

FESTIVAL QUARTERLY. (US/8750-3530). **4959**

FETUS (NASHVILLE, TENN.), THE. (US/1057-137X). **Qty:** 6. **3761**

FEU ET LUMIERE SAINT-BROLADRE. (FR/0760-5099). **5029**

FEUERVERZINKEN. (GW). **4002**

F+I-BAU. (GW/0340-2967). **615**

F+I-BAU BAUEN MIT SYSTEMEN. (GW). **615**

FIBER AND INTEGRATED OPTICS. (US/0146-8030). **4434**

FIBEROPTIC PRODUCT NEWS. (US/0890-653X). **1155**

FIBERSCOPE. (US/0198-8387). **5351**

FIBERWORKS QUARTERLY. (US/8756-7121). **Qty:** 25. **5351**

FIBRE BOX HANDBOOK. (US/0196-7215). **4219**

FIBULA. (NE/0015-5676). **Qty:** 15/yr. **2616**

FICTION FOCUS. (AT/0819-5358). **3387**

FICTION INTERNATIONAL. (US/0092-1912). **Qty:** 1-2. **3387**

FIDDLEHEAD, THE. (CN/0015-0630). **3387**

FIELD NOTES - ARKANSAS ARCHEOLOGICAL SOCIETY. (US/0015-0711). **Qty:** 8-10/yr. **268**

FIELD (OBERLIN, OHIO). (US/0015-0657). **3463**

FIELD STUDIES. (UK/0428-304X). **4165**

FIELD TRIP GUIDEBOOK (COLUMBIA). (US/0197-0976). **1375**

FIELDIANA. BOTANY. (US/0015-0746). **510**

FIELDIANA : GEOLOGY. (US/0096-2651). **1375**

FIELDIANA : ZOOLOGY. (US/0015-0754). **5583**

FIFTH COLUMN. (CN/0229-7094). **298**

FIFTH ESTATE. (US/0015-0800). **Qty:** 10. **4541**

FIFTY-FIVE PLUS (BATTERSEA). (CN/0840-4496). **Qty:** 12-18. **5179**

FIFTY SOMETHING. (AT). **5179**

FIGHT DIRECTOR, THE. (UK). **5364**

FIGHT RACISM, FIGHT IMPERIALISM!: ANTI-IMPERIALIST BULLETIN OF THE REVOLUTIONARY COMMUNIST GROUP. (UK/0143-5426). **Qty:** 15. **4474**

FIGHTING WOMAN NEWS. (US/0146-8812). **2597**

FIJI LIBRARY ASSOCIATION NEWSLETTER. (FJ). **3210**

FIJI REPUBLIC GAZETTE. (FJ). **5800**

FIJI TIMES, THE. (FJ). **5800**

FIKR O NAZAR. (PK/0430-4055). **5042**

FILIPINAS (SAN FRANCISCO, CALIF.). (US/1063-4630). **2261**

FILM & HISTORY (NEWARK, N.J.). (US/0360-3695). **Qty:** 10. **4069**

FILM AND TELEVISION TECHNICIAN. (UK). **4069**

FILM & VIDEO FINDER. (US/0898-1582). **4069**

FILM COMMENT. (US/0015-119X). **4069**

FILM CRITICISM. (US/0163-5069). **Qty:** 10. **4069**

FILM CULTURE. (US/0015-1211). **4069**

FILM DIRECTIONS. (IE). **4069**

FILM DOPE. (UK/0305-1706). **4069**

FILM EN TELEVISIE EN VIDEO. (BE). **Qty:** 10. **4069**

FILM INDEX. (AT). **Qty:** 4. **4070**

FILM JOURNAL (HOLLINS), THE. (US/0046-3787). **4070**

FILM QUARTERLY. (US/0015-1386). **4070**

FILM REVIEW (ENGLAND). (UK). **Qty:** 120. **4070**

FILM UND FARBE. (GW/0934-0378). **4070**

FILM/VIDEO CANADIANA. (CN/0836-1002). **4070**

FILMFAUST. (GW). **4070**

FILMFAX. (US/0895-0393). **4070**

FILMHAFTET : TIDSKRIFT OM FILM OCH TV. (SW/0345-3057). **Qty:** 20-30. **4070**

FILMKUNST. (AU/0015-1599). **4071**

FILMS IN REVIEW. (US/0015-1688). **4071**

FILOLOGIA E CRITICA (SALERNO EDITRICE). (IT/0391-2493). **3387**

FILOLOGIAI KOZLONY. (HU/0015-1785). **3281**

FILOSOFIA. (IT/0015-1823). **4346**

FILOSOFIA (ATHENAI). (GR/1105-2120). **4346**

FILOSOFIA OGGI. (IT). **4346**

FILOZOFIA (BRATISLAVA). (XO/0046-385X). **4347**

FILOZOFICKY CASOPIS (USTAV PRO FILOZOFII A SOCIOLOGII CSAV). (XR/0015-1831). **4347**

FILSON CLUB HISTORY QUARTERLY, THE. (US/0015-1874). **Qty:** 25-30. **2733**

FILTRATION & SEPARATION. (UK/0015-1882). **2012**

FINAL FRONTIER. (US/0899-4161). **20**

FINANCE & DEVELOPMENT. (US/0015-1947). **1635**

FINANCIAL ANALYSTS JOURNAL, THE. (US/0015-198X). **898**

FINANCIAL COUNSELING AND PLANNING. (US/1052-3073). **Qty:** 1-3. **898**

FINANCIAL TECHNOLOGY INTERNATIONAL BULLETIN. (UK/0265-1661). **Qty:** 10-20. **5105**

FINANCIAL TIMES (LONDON ED.). (UK/0307-1766). **5812**

FINANCIAL TIMES NORTH SEA LETTER AND EUROPEAN OFFSHORE NEWS. (UK/0950-1037). **1944**

FINANCIAL WOMAN TODAY. (US/1059-3950). **5556**

FINANCIEEL OVERHEIDSMANAGEMENT. (NE/0922-1026). **4649**

FINANZ-RUNDSCHAU. (GW/0340-9007). **4726**

FINANZARCHIV. (GW/0015-2218). **4726**

FINCASTLE HERALD, THE. (US/8750-7323). **5758**

FINE ART & AUCTION REVIEW. (CN/0833-0891). **350**

FINE GARDENING. (US/0896-6281). **2414**

FINE HOMEBUILDING. (US/0273-1398). **615**

FINE MADNESS. (US/0737-4704). **3388**

FINE PRINT (SAN FRANCISCO). (US/0361-3801). **4565**

FINE TOOL JOURNAL, THE. (US/0745-6824). **Qty:** 40. **250**

FINE WOODWORKING. (US/0361-3453). **634**

FINESCALE MODELER. (US/0277-979X). **2773**

FINEST HOUR. (US/0882-3715). **2688**

FINISHERS' MANAGEMENT. (US/0015-2358). **868**

FINISHING. (UK/0264-2506). **4224**

FINNAM NEWSLETTER / FINNISH-AMERICAN HISTORICAL SOCIETY OF THE WEST. (US). **2261**

FINNISH AMERICANA. (US/0162-5462). **2733**

FIRE & MOVEMENT. (US/0147-0051). **Qty:** 2-4. **4861**

FIRE & SECURITY PROTECTION. (UK). **5177**

FIRE APPARATUS JOURNAL. (US/0885-8837). **Qty:** 6. **2289**

FIRE CHIEF. (US/0015-2552). **2289**

FIRE CONTROL DIGEST. (US/0889-5740). **2289**

FIRE ENGINEERING. (US/0015-2587). **2289**

FIRE ENGINEERS JOURNAL. (UK/0143-5337). **2289**

FIRE INTERNATIONAL. (UK/0015-2609). **2289**

FIRE PREVENTION (LONDON, 1971). (UK/0309-6866). **2289**

FIRE PROTECTION CONTRACTOR, THE. (US/1043-2485). **2289**

FIRE PROTECTION HANDBOOK. (US/0734-5984). **2289**

FIRE SURVEYOR. (UK/0262-7981). **2290**

FIRE TECHNOLOGY. (US/0015-2684). **2290**

FIRE (TUNBRIDGE WELLS). (UK/0142-2510). **2290**

FIREHEART (MAYNARD, MASS.). (US/1046-6029). **4185**

FIREHOUSE. (US/0145-4064). **2290**

FIREMAN MELBOURNE, THE. (AT/0812-0056). **2290**

FIRESIDE CHATS. (US/0015-2714). **2785**

FIREWATCH

FIREWATCH / NAFED. (US). **2290**

FIREWEED. (CN/0706-3857). **Qty:** infrequently. **5556**

FIREWEED : A FEMINIST QUARTERLY. (CN/0383-7912). **5557**

FIREWORKS BUSINESS. (US/8755-4372). **675**

FIRST AIDER. (US). **3954**

FIRST BREAK. (UK/0263-5046). **1405**

FIRST CHOICE CANADA. (CN/0820-8859). **Qty:** 6. **5382**

FIRST DAYS. (US/0428-4836). **2785**

FIRST DROP / COASTER NEWS. (UK). **Qty:** unlimited. **4861**

FIRST HAND. (US/0744-6349). **2794**

FIRST LANGUAGE. (UK/0142-7237). **3281**

FIRST PERSPECTIVE. (CN). **Qty:** 24 per year. **2261**

FIRST READING. (CN/0824-197X). **5245**

FIRST STEPS ON THE LADDER OF LEARNING. (AT). **1804**

FIRST THINGS (NEW YORK, N.Y.). (US/1047-5141). **4959**

FIRSTS (LOS ANGELES, CALIF.). (US/1066-5471). **Qty:** 24. **4821**

FISCAL LETTER, THE. (US/0197-288X). **4726**

FISCH UND FANG. (GW/0015-2838). **4894**

FISCHWAID (1982). (GW/0722-706X). **2301**

FISH CULTURIST, THE. (US/0015-2919). **2301**

FISH FARM NEWS, THE. (CN/1180-5633). **2301**

FISH FARMING INTERNATIONAL. (UK/0262-0820). **2301**

FISH SNIFFER (NORTHERN CALIFORNIA-NEVADA ED.), THE. (US/0747-3397). **5635**

FISH SUPPLIES INTERNATIONAL : PROCESSING & MARKETING NEWS. (CN/0229-1924). **2301**

FISHERIES (BETHESDA). (US/0363-2415). **2302**

FISHERIES ECONOMICS NEWSLETTER. (UK/0309-4294). **2317**

FISHERIES PRODUCT NEWS. (US/1047-2525). **2302**

FISHERMAN (NEW JERSEY, DELAWARE BAY ED.), THE. (US/1040-0117). **4894**

FISHERMAN, THE. (CN/0015-2986). **2302**

FISHERMEN'S NEWS, THE. (US/0015-2994). **2303**

FISHING BOAT WORLD. (HK/1033-1247). **Qty:** 40. **2303**

FISHING FACTS (SOUTHERN ED.). (US/0899-9589). **2303**

FISHING NEWS INTERNATIONAL. (UK/0015-3044). **2303**

FISHING WORLD. (US/0015-3079). **2303**

FISICA E TECNOLOGIA. (IT/0391-9757). **5105**

FISK(E) FAMILY ASSOCIATION : NEWSLETTER. (US). **2448**

FIT THIRD AGE. (CN/0827-3103). **3751**

FITNESS BULLETIN, THE. (CN/0820-6163). **2597**

FITNESS MANAGEMENT (SOLANA BEACH, CALIF.). (US/0882-0481). **2597**

FITOPATOLOGIA. (PE/0430-6155). **Qty:** 4. **510**

FITOPATOLOGIA BRASILEIRA. (BL/0100-4158). **172**

FITOTERAPIA. (IT/0367-326X). **510**

FIVE OWLS, THE. (US/0892-6735). **1063**

FIVE STONES, THE. (US/1064-136X). **Qty:** varies. **5060**

FIZIKO-MATEMATICHESKO SPISANIE. (BU/0015-3265). **4403**

FIZIOLOGIIA RASTENII. (RU/0015-3303). **510**

FLAG BULLETIN, THE. (US/0015-3370). **2616**

FLAGSCAN. (CN/0833-1510). **Qty:** 12-16. **2448**

FLAME (SEATTLE, WASH.). (US). **Qty:** 4. **5557**

FLAMING CRESCENT, THE. (US). **4474**

FLANNERY O'CONNOR BULLETIN. (US/0091-4924). **Qty:** 2. **432**

FLARE (TORONTO). (CN/0708-4927). **5557**

FLASH ART (INTERNATIONAL EDITION). (IT/0394-1493). **350**

FLASHBACK (FAYETTEVILLE, ARK.). (US/0428-5573). **Qty:** 2+ /year. **2733**

FLAT EARTH NEWS. (US/8756-0313). **1405**

FLATBUSH GUIDE, THE. (US). **5470**

FLAVOUR AND FRAGRANCE JOURNAL. (UK/0882-5734). **2335**

FLEETLINE. (AT/0312-4681). **Qty:** 6. **5382**

FLEISCHEREI. (GW/0015-3613). **2335**

FLESNEWS. (US/1064-3540). **1804**

FLETCHER FORUM OF WORLD AFFAIRS, THE. (US/1046-1868). **4521**

FLETCHER-O'LEARY PERIODICAL, THE. (CN/0715-4518). **2448**

FLEXPACK MATERIALS & MARKETS BULLETIN. (UK). **4219**

FLIGHT INTERNATIONAL DIRECTORY. PART 1, UNITED KINGDOM. (UK). **Qty:** 20. **21**

FLIGHT INTERNATIONAL DIRECTORY. PART II, MAINLAND EUROPE AND IRELAND. (UK). **Qty:** 20. **21**

FLIGHT REPORTS. (US/0194-9039). **21**

FLIGHT SAFETY BULLETIN. (CN/0826-032X). **21**

FLINDERS JOURNAL OF HISTORY AND POLITICS. (AT/0726-7215). **4474**

FLINT JOURNAL (1935). (US). **5692**

FLOATING. (US). **4850**

FLOODTIDE. (US). **4959**

FLORA-LINE, THE. (US/1062-855X). **Qty:** (unlimited). **2435**

FLORA (LONDON). (UK/0306-882X). **2435**

FLORA. MORPHOLOGIE, GEOBOTANIK, OKOLOGIE. (GW/0367-2530). **2216**

FLORA NEOTROPICA. (US/0071-5794). **510**

FLORA OF BANGLADESH. (BG). **511**

FLORA OG FAUNA. (DK/0015-3818). **5584**

FLORIDA ANTHROPOLOGIST, THE. (US/0015-3893). **236**

FLORIDA ARCHITECT. (US/0015-3907). **298**

FLORIDA BAPTIST WITNESS / ORGAN OF THE FLORIDA BAPTIST STATE CONVENTION. (US). **5060**

FLORIDA BAR JOURNAL, THE. (US/0015-3915). **2970**

FLORIDA BUSINESS PUBLICATIONS INDEX. (US/0191-183X). **676**

FLORIDA BUSINESS SOUTHWEST. (US/1047-6105). **676**

FLORIDA CATHOLIC, THE. (US/0746-4584). **5029**

FLORIDA CONTRACTOR. (US/0046-4112). **2605**

FLORIDA EDUCATION. (US/0015-4016). **1747**

FLORIDA ENTOMOLOGIST, THE. (US/0015-4040). **5608**

FLORIDA ENVIRONMENTS. (US/0894-9743). **2172**

FLORIDA FIELD NATURALIST. (US/0738-999X). **5584**

FLORIDA FLAMBEAU, THE. (US). **5649**

FLORIDA FUNDING. (US/0887-3038). **Qty:** 12. **868**

FLORIDA GARDENER, THE. (US/0426-5750). **2414**

FLORIDA GENEALOGIST, THE. (US/0161-4932). **Qty:** 30. **2448**

FLORIDA GEOGRAPHER, THE. (US/0739-0041). **2560**

FLORIDA GROCER. (US/0191-586X). **2335**

FLORIDA HISTORICAL QUARTERLY, THE. (US/0015-4113). **Qty:** 80. **2733**

FLORIDA HOTEL & MOTEL JOURNAL. (US/8750-6807). **2805**

FLORIDA JOURNAL OF ANTHROPOLOGY, THE. (US/0164-1662). **236**

FLORIDA LAW REVIEW. (US/1045-4241). **Qty:** 1. **2971**

FLORIDA LIVING. (US/0888-9600). **Qty:** 12. **2533**

FLORIDA MANUFACTURERS REGISTER. (US/0882-9438). **3479**

FLORIDA NURSE, THE. (US/0015-4199). **3856**

FLORIDA READING QUARTERLY, THE. (US/0015-4261). **1747**

FLORIDA RETIREMENT LIVING. (US/0160-5739). **Qty:** 6. **5179**

FLORIDA REVIEW (ORLANDO, FLA.), THE. (US/0742-2466). **Qty:** 6 - 10. **3463**

FLORIDA SCIENTIST. (US/0098-4590). **5105**

FLORIDA STAR (JACKSONVILLE, FLA. : 1951), THE. (US/0740-798X). **Qty:** varies. **2616**

FLORIDA STATE UNIVERSITY LAW REVIEW. (US/0096-3070). **Qty:** 1. **2971**

FLORIDA TAX REVIEW. (US). **Qty:** one /issue. **2971**

FLORIDA TIMES-UNION (JACKSONVILLE, FLA. : 1910). (US/0740-2325). **5649**

FLORIDA TOURISM INDUSTRY REPORT. (US/0889-0099). **5470**

FLORIDA TRUCK NEWS. (US/0015-4334). **Qty:** 2. **5382**

FLORIDA VOCATIONAL JOURNAL. (US/0145-9376). **1913**

FLORIDA WATER RESOURCES JOURNAL. (US/0896-1794). **5533**

FLORIDA WILDLIFE. (US/0015-4369). **2194**

FLORIDAGRICULTURE (GAINESVILLE, FLA.). (US/0015-3869). **Qty:** 2-3. **87**

FLORISSANT VALLEY REPORTER, THE. (US). **5703**

FLORIST (GUNZBURG, GERMANY). (GW/0015-4393). **2435**

FLORIST TRADE MAGAZINE. (UK/0015-4415). **2435**

FLORTECNICA. (IT). **Qty:** 15-20. **2414**

FLOWER AND GARDEN (KANSAS CITY, MO. : 1982). (US/0891-9534). **2414**

FLOWER NEWS : THE FLORAL INDUSTRY'S NATIONAL WEEKLY. (US/0015-4490). **2414**

FLOWER OF THE FOREST BLACK GENEALOGICAL JOURNAL. (US/0738-159X). **2448**

FLOWERS&. (US/0199-4751). **2435**

FLUE. (US/0731-2636). **320**

FLUG REVUE. (GW/0015-4547). **21**

FLUID PHASE EQUILIBRIA. (NE/0378-3812). **1052**

FLUID POWER ABSTRACTS. (UK/0015-4644). **2089**

FLUID SEALING ABSTRACTS. (UK/0015-4660). **2089**

FLUORIDE. (US/0015-4725). **487**

FLUSSIGES OBST. (GW/0015-4539). **2335**

FLY FISHERMAN. (US/0015-4741). **2304**

FLY ROD & REEL. (US/1045-0149). **Qty:** 6. **2304**

FLYFISHING. (US/0744-7191). **Qty:** varies. **2304**

FLYING MODELS. (US/0015-4849). **2773**

FLYING NEEDLE, THE. (US/0270-2959). **5184**

FLYING REVIEW. (US/0274-5798). **Qty:** 12. **21**

FLYING SAUCER REVIEW. (UK/0015-4881). **21**

FLYPAPER (CALGARY). (CN/0317-2481). **4895**

FNP NEWSLETTER : FOOD, NUTRITION AND HEALTH. (US/0160-8053). **4191**

FNP NEWSLETTER, FOOD PACKAGING AND LABELING. (US/0194-2980). **4219**

FOCAL POINT (ENGLEWOOD, COLO.). (US/0279-8840). **5060**

FOCUS (AUSTIN, TEX. 1985). (US/0883-8194). **1247**

FOCUS (AUSTIN, TEX. 1989). (US/1041-2549). **1185**

FOCUS (BURBANK, CALIF.). (US/1054-4208). **4241**

FOCUS : CHICAGO. (US/0362-0905). **4071**

FOCUS (CHICAGO. 1977). (US/0148-026X). **2971**

FOCUS, FIBRE OPTIC COMMUNICATION & USER SYSTEMS. (UK/0959-0188). **Qty:** 4. **1155**

FOCUS - JOINT CENTER FOR POLITICAL STUDIES. (US/0740-0195). **2261**

FOCUS, LIBRARY SERVICE TO OLDER ADULTS, PEOPLE WITH DISABILITIES. (US/0740-4956). **Qty:** 8. **3211**

FOCUS (MADISON). (US/0195-5705). **1491**

FOCUS (NEW YORK, N.Y. 1950). (US/0015-5004). **2561**

FOCUS ON ASIAN STUDIES. (US/0046-4295). **2651**

FOCUS ON CRITICAL CARE. (US/0736-3605). **3856**

FOCUS ON DENTAL COMPUTERS. (US/0748-1810). **1323**

FOCUS ON EXCEPTIONAL CHILDREN. (US/0015-511X). **1879**

FOCUS ON GENDER. (0968-2864). **5557**

FOCUS ON INTERNATIONAL & COMPARATIVE LIBRARIANSHIP. (UK/0305-8468). **3211**

FOCUS ON LEARNING PROBLEMS IN MATHEMATICS. (US/0272-8893). **1879**

FOCUS ON MISSIONS; OCCASIONAL NEWS SUPPLEMENT FOR MISSIONARIES. (US). **4959**

FOCUS ON SECURITY. (US/1071-9997). **Qty:** 1-4. **3211**

FOCUS ON SURGICAL EDUCATION. (US/0742-9819). **3965**

FOCUS (SAN FRANCISCO, CALIF.). (US/1047-0719). **3669**

FOELDRAJZI ERTESITO. (HU/0015-5403). **2561**

FOERDERN UND HEBEN. (GW/0373-6482). **2114**

FOGLI DI COLLEGAMENTO DELLA L O C. (IT). **Qty:** 4-5. **4521**

FOGLIO TORINO, IL. (IT/0393-7380). **4365**

FOI ET LA VIE, LA. (FR/0015-5357). **Qty:** 5. **4959**

FOKUS PA FAMILIEN. (NO/0332-5415). **2280**

FOLDING KAYAKER. (US/1056-2273). **Qty:** 3. **4895**

FOLDRAJZI KOZLEMENYEK. (HU/0015-5411). **2561**

FOLIA ENTOMOLOGICA MEXICANA. (MX/0430-8603). **5609**

FOLIA GEOBOTANICA & PHYTOTAXONOMICA. (XR/0015-5551). **511**

FOLIA HEREDITARIA ET PATHOLOGICA. (IT/0015-5578). **545**

FOLIA PARASITOLOGICA / CZECHOSLOVAK ACADEMY OF SCIENCE. (XR/0015-5683). **5584**

FOLIA VETERINARIA. (XO/0015-5748). **5510**

FOLIA ZOOLOGICA (BRNO). (XR/0139-7893). **5584**

FOLIO (BROCKPORT, N.Y.). (US/0882-3030). **3388**

FOLIO (LOUISVILLE, KY.). (US/0741-1537). **Qty:** 2. **5060**

FOLIO (SAINT LOUIS, MO.). (US/0896-3096). **Qty:** 10. **2733**

FOLK ART FINDER. (US/0738-8357). **Qty:** varies. **350**

FOLK ART MESSENGER. (US/1043-5026). **Qty:** 4. **350**

FOLK DIRECTORY, THE. (UK/0430-876X). **5231**

FOLK HARP JOURNAL. (US/0094-8934). **Qty:** 5. **4118**

FOLK (KBENHAVN). (DK/0085-0756). **236**

FOLK LIFE. (UK/0430-8778). **2319**

FOLK MUSIC JOURNAL. (UK/0531-9684). **4118**

FOLK NEWS (WASHINGTON, D.C.). (US). **4118**

FOLK OG FORSKNING / UDG. AF UNIVERSTETSFORENINGEN FOR DET SYDLIGE OG VESTLIGE JYLLAND. (DK/0105-712X). **2846**

FOLK ROOTS. (UK/0951-1326). **Qty:** 6. **4118**

FOLKLOR ARCHIVUM. (HU). **2319**

FOLKLORE AND MYTHOLOGY STUDIES (LOS ANGELES, CALIF. : 1977). (US/0162-6280). **2320**

FOLKLORE BRABANCON. (BE/0015-590X). **2320**

FOLKLORE (CALCUTTA). (II/0015-5896). **2320**

FOLKLORE DE FRANCE. (FR/0015-5918). **Qty:** 4. **2320**

FOLKLORE FORUM. (US/0015-5926). **Qty:** 15-20. **2320**

FOLKLORE (LONDON). (UK/0015-587X). **Qty:** 12 - 15. **2320**

FOLKLORE (MOOSE JAW). (CN/0824-3085). **2320**

FOLKLORE SUISSE. (SZ/0015-5969). **2320**

FOLKLORE WOMEN'S COMMUNICATION. (US/0160-9831). **2320**

FOLKNIK, THE. (US/0146-9169). **4118**

FOLLETOS MUNDO CRISTIANO. (SP). **2280**

FOLLIA DI NEW YORK. (US/0015-6000). **2846**

FONDERIE, FONDEUR D'AUJOURD'HUI. (FR/0249-3136). **4002**

FONTANE BLATTER. (GW/0015-6175). **3388**

FONTES ARTIS MUSICAE. (SZ/0015-6191). **4118**

FONTI ORALI-STUDI E RICERCHE. (IT). **2688**

FOOD AND CHEMICAL TOXICOLOGY. (UK/0278-6915). **3980**

FOOD & FIBER LETTER, THE. (US/0739-6791). **Qty:** 20. **2336**

FOOD AND NUTRITION BULLETIN. (JA/0379-5721). **4191**

FOOD & SERVICE / TEXAS RESTAURANT ASSOCIATION. (US/0891-0154). **2336**

FOOD AUSTRALIA : OFFICIAL JOURNAL OF CAFTA AND AIFST. (AT/1032-5298). **2336**

FOOD BIOTECHNOLOGY. (US/0890-5436). **3692**

FOOD CHEMISTRY. (UK/0308-8146). **1024**

FOOD CONTROL. (UK). **2336**

FOOD DISTRIBUTION MAGAZINE : FDM. (US/1048-8197). **2337**

FOOD HISTORY NEWS. (US/1067-1951). **Qty:** 12. **2337**

FOOD INDUSTRIES OF SOUTH AFRICA. (SA/0015-6450). **2337**

FOOD INSTITUTE REPORT, THE. (US/0745-4503). **2337**

FOOD MAGAZINE LONDON. 1988. (UK/0953-5047). **2338**

FOOD MANAGEMENT AMERSFOORT. (NE/0168-325X). **2338**

FOOD MARKETING & TECHNOLOGY. (GW/0932-2744). **2338**

FOOD MARKETS IN REVIEW. (US). **2338**

FOOD MICROBIOLOGY. (UK/0740-0020). **563**

FOOD POLICY. (UK/0306-9192). **2339**

FOOD PROCESSING (BROMLEY, LONDON, ENGLAND). (UK/0264-9462). **2339**

FOOD PROCESSOR. (AT). **2339**

FOOD PRODUCTION MANAGEMENT. (US/0191-6181). **2339**

FOOD SCIENCE & TECHNOLOGY TODAY. (UK/0950-9623). **Qty:** 4. **2340**

FOOD TECHNOLOGY (CHICAGO). (US/0015-6639). **2340**

FOOD TRADE REVIEW. (UK/0015-6671). **Qty:** 120. **2340**

FOODTALK (SAN FRANCISCO, CALIF.). (US/1065-0067). **Qty:** 10-12. **4191**

FOOKIEN TIMES PHILIPPINES YEARBOOK, THE. (PH). **2651**

FOOT WORSHIP NEWS. (US). **5268**

FOOTBALL DIGEST. (US/0015-6760). **4895**

FOOTHILLS SENTINEL. (US/8750-3026). **5630**

FOOTHILLS TRADER. (US/0191-7463). **5645**

FOOTLOOSE LIBRARIAN, THE. (US/0733-3196). **5474**

FOOTNOTES (RESTON, VA.). (US/8755-9048). **4895**

FOOTPRINTS. (UK). **Qty:** 10. **2448**

FOOTPRINTS (FORT WORTH). (US/0426-8261). **2448**

FOOTWORK. (US/0743-2259). **2846**

FOR PARENTS. (US/0277-612X). **2280**

FORDHAM INTERNATIONAL LAW JOURNAL. (US/0747-9395). **3128**

FORDHAM LAW REVIEW. (US/0015-704X). **2971**

FORDYCE LETTER, THE. (US/0733-0324). **Qty:** 3. **1675**

FOREFRONT CO. (US). **Qty:** 4-6. **4959**

FOREIGN INTELLIGENCE LITERARY SCENE. (US/0749-9132). **Qty:** up to 20/yr. **4522**

FOREIGN INVESTMENT IN THE US. (UK/0958-3076). **899**

FOREIGN LODGING LIST. (US). **2805**

FOREIGN POLICY BULLETIN (WASHINGTON, D.C.). (US/1052-7036). **Qty:** 25. **4522**

FOREIGN SERVICE JOURNAL. (US/0146-3543). **4522**

FOREIGN TAX LAW BI-WEEKLY BULLETIN. (US/0095-7291). **3128**

FOREIGN TRADE BULLETIN. (II/0015-7317). **836**

FORENSIC ACCOUNTING REVIEW. (US/8756-8888). **3100**

FORENSIC DRUG ABUSE ADVISOR, THE. (US/1048-8731). **Qty:** Varies. **1344**

FORENSIC OF PI KAPPA DELTA, THE. (US/0015-735X). **Qty:** 5-10. **1111**

FORENSIC REPORTS. (US/0888-692X). **3740**

FORESIGHT (EDMONTON). (CN/0711-3927). **Qty:** 10. **5179**

FORESKRIFTER OM STATLIG TJANSTEPENSIONERING / STATENS ARBETSGIVARVERK. (SW/0348-1115). **1675**

FOREST AND BIRD. (NZ). **4165**

FOREST & CONSERVATION HISTORY. (US/1046-7009). **Qty:** 60 /yr. **2379**

FOREST NOTES. (US/0015-7457). **2380**

FOREST PLANNING-CANADA. (CN/0832-1655). **2380**

FOREST SCIENCE. (US/0015-749X). **2381**

FOREST SCIENCE. MONOGRAPH. (US/0071-7568). **2381**

FOREST TIMES. (CN/0706-7747). **2381**

FORESTRY AND BRITISH TIMBER. (UK). **2400**

FORESTRY CHRONICLE, THE. (CN/0015-7546). **2381**

FORESTRY (LONDON). (UK/0015-752X). **2382**

FORESTRY ON THE HILL. (CN/1185-9598). **2382**

FORET CONSERVATION. (CN/0380-321X). **2382**

FORET PRIVEE (1977), LA. (FR/0153-0216). **Qty:** 5-6. **2382**

FORET WALLONE. (BE). **2382**

FORM. (SW/0015-766X). **2900**

FORM FUNCTION FINLAND. (FI/0358-8904). **Qty:** 10. **2098**

FORM (SEEHEIM-JUGENHEIM, WEST GERMANY). (GW/0015-7678). **2098**

FORMAT (ST. CHARLES). (US/0190-678X). **350**

FORMATION EMPLOI. (FR). **1675**

FORMAZIONE PSICHIATRICA : PERIODICO TRIMESTRALE A CURA DELLA CLINICA PSICHIATRICA DELL'UNIVERSITA DI CATANIA. (IT). **3925**

FORME E LA STORIA, LE. (IT). **3388**

FORMULA. (IT). **Qty:** 20. **4474**

FORNERI, IL. (CN/0713-0627). **3282**

FORO AMMINISTRATIVO (ANNUAL). (IT). **3093**

FORO INTERNACIONAL. (MX/0185-013X). **4474**

FORO ITALIANO, IL. (IT/0015-783X). **2972**

FORSCHUNGS- UND SITZUNGSBERICHTE. (GW/0515-9083). **2823**

FORSCHUNGSDOKUMENTATION RAUMORDNUNG, STADEBAU, WOHNUNGSWESEN. (GW). **2823**

FORSCHUNGSFORDERUNGEN UND FORSCHUNGSAUFTRAGE. (AU). **5106**

FORSTLICHE UMSCHAU. (GW/0015-7988). **2383**

FORSTWISSENSCHAFTLICHES CENTRALBLATT. (GW/0015-8003). **2383**

FORSYTH COUNTY GENEALOGICAL SOCIETY JOURNAL, THE. (US/0741-8159). **Qty:** 12. **2448**

FORT MCMURRAY TODAY. (CN/0316-7542). **5784**

FORT MILL TIMES. (US). **Qty:** 12. **5742**

FORT RILEY POST, THE. (US). **Qty:** 1-2. **5675**

FORTNIGHT (BELFAST). (IE/0046-4694). **3343**

FORTRAN JOURNAL. (US/1060-0221). **Qty:** 6. **1185**

FORTSCHRITTE DER KIEFERORTHOPAEDIE. (GW/0015-816X). **1323**

FORTSCHRITTE DER MEDIZIN. (GW/0015-8178). **3577**

FORTSCHRITTE DER PFLANZENZUCHTUNG. (GW/0301-2727). **172**

FORTSCHRITTLICHE LANDWIRT, DER. (AU). **Qty:** 50. **88**

FORUM. (US). **Qty:** 4. **4959**

FORUM (BONNER, MONT.). (US/0883-4970). **5016**

FORUM / CONFERENCE OF DEFENCE ASSOCIATIONS. (CN/0848-8886). **Qty:** 18. **4044**

FORUM - COUNCIL OF EUROPE. (FR/0252-0958). **2516**

FORUM DER LETTEREN. (NE/0015-8496). **3388**

FORUM (DON MILLS). (CN/0380-3147). **2881**

FORUM FOR EKONOMI OCH TEKNIK. (FI/0533-070X). **5106**

FORUM FOR MODERN LANGUAGE STUDIES. (UK/0015-8518). **3282**

FORUM

FORUM FOR PROMOTING 3-19 COMPREHENSIVE EDUCATION. (UK/0963-8253). Qty: 20. **1747**

FORUM FOR SOCIAL ECONOMICS, THE. (US/0736-0932). Qty: varies. **1491**

FORUM HOMOSEXUALITAT UND LITERATUR. (GW/0931-4091). Qty: 10. **3388**

FORUM ITALICUM. (US/0014-5858). **3388**

FORUM LINGUISTICUM. (US/0163-0768). **3282**

FORUM MUSIKBIBLIOTHEK. (GW/0173-5187). **3211**

FORUM (NORTH HOLLYWOOD). (US/0164-6931). Qty: 4. **3107**

FORUM OF EDUCATION, THE. (AT/0015-8542). **1824**

FORUM (REGINA, SASK.). (CN/0831-3016). **3211**

FORUM (SCRANTON, PA.). (US/0015-8399). **2516**

FORUM, STADTE, HYGIENE. (GW/0342-202X). **2194**

FORUM WARE. (GW/0340-7705). Qty: 20. **2194**

FOSTERLETTER. (CN/0701-3418). **2280**

FOSTER'S BOTANICAL & HERB REVIEWS. (US/1047-000X). **2415**

FOTOGESCHICHTE. (GW/0720-5260). **4369**

FOTOHANDEL. (NE). **4369**

FOTOINTERPRETACJA W GEOGRAFII. (PL/0071-8076). **2561**

FOUNDATION DRILLING. (US/0274-5186). **615**

FOUNDATION NEWS. (US/0015-8976). **4336**

FOUNDATION ONE. (US/0272-5622). **4776**

FOUNDATIONS (ST. ALBANS, HERTS). (UK). Qty: 5. **5060**

FOUNDRYMAN, THE. (UK/0007-0718). Qty: 15. **4002**

FOUR CORNERS ADVISOR, THE. (US/0162-6647). **1491**

FOUR DIRECTIONS (TELLICO PLAINS, TENN.), THE. (US/1070-7549). Qty: 4 or more. **3388**

FOUR QUARTERS. (US/0015-9107). **3388**

FOUR SEASONS, THE. (US/0532-3215). **511**

FOURSQUARE WORLD ADVANCE. (US/0015-9182). **4959**

FOX FAMILY FACTS. (US/1044-9809). **2449**

FOX (NEW YORK, N.Y. 1984). (US/1041-9470). **3995**

FRA FYSIKKENS VERDEN. (NO/0015-9247). **4403**

FRACASTORO, IL. (IT/0015-9271). **3577**

FRAME NEWS. (UK/0268-4306). Qty: 6-10. **226**

FRAMERS FORUM. (US). **1185**

FRANCE AMERIQUE (NEW YORK, N.Y.). (US/0747-2757). Qty: 12 per year. **5716**

FRANCE ... SPECIALIZED CATALOGUE OF ARTIST PROOFS, DE LUXE SHEETS, IMPERFORATES, COLOR ESSAYS, FIRST DAY COVERS, COLLECTIVE PROOFS, PRINTERS INSPECTION PROOFS, ILLUSTRATIONS. (US/0197-7202). **2785**

FRANCE TODAY (SAN FRANCISCO, CALIF. 1987). (US/0895-3651). Qty: 10. **2688**

FRANCHISE LEGAL DIGEST. (US/0739-8239). **3100**

FRANCHISE MAGAZINE. (UK/0268-8395). **677**

FRANCISCAN, THE. (UK). **5029**

FRANCOFONIA. (IT). Qty: 12/yr. **3389**

FRANCOPHONIE RUGBY. (UK/0957-1744). **3282**

FRANK LLOYD WRIGHT QUARTERLY. (US). Qty: 8-10. **299**

FRANKFURTER ALLGEMEINE. (GW/0174-4909). **5801**

FRANKLIN ADVOCATE, THE. (US). **5700**

FRANKLIN CHALLENGER. (US/8750-7390). Qty: 2. **5664**

FRANKLIN COUNTY HISTORICAL REVIEW, THE. (US/0046-4651). **2734**

FRANSE NEDERLANDEN: JAARBOEK. LES PAYS-BAS FRANCAIS: ANNALES, DE. (BE). **2688**

FRATERNAL HERALD. (US/0006-9256). **5231**

FRATERNITY NEWS - FRATERNITY FOR CANADIAN ASTROLOGERS. (CN/0710-510X). **390**

FRAUEN UND FILM. (GW). **4071**

FREDDO. (IT/0016-0296). **2605**

FREDERICK FINDINGS. (US/0899-4188). **2449**

FREE ASSOCIATIONS. (UK/0267-0887). **3925**

FREE CHINA JOURNAL, THE. (CH). **5798**

FREE CHURCH CHRONICLE. (UK/0016-0326). **4960**

FREE FLIGHT (OTTAWA ONT.). (CN/0827-2557). **4895**

FREE INQUIRY (BUFFALO). (US/0272-0701). **4347**

FREE LANCE STAR, THE. (US). Qty: 52. **5758**

FREE RADICAL RESEARCH COMMUNICATIONS. (SZ/8755-0199). **1052**

FREE SPIRIT (MIAMI, FLA.). (US/1062-8134). Qty: 12-15. **4388**

FREE SPIRIT (MINNEAPOLIS, MINN.). (US/0895-2256). **1063**

FREE TRADE LAW REPORTER. (CN). **2972**

FREE VENICE BEACHHEAD. (US/0884-9641). **5635**

FREEDOM MAGAZINE. (US). **2533**

FREEDOM SOCIALIST, THE. (US/0272-4367). **4542**

FREELANCE (REGINA). (CN/0705-1379). **3389**

FREELANCE WRITER'S REPORT. (US/0731-549X). Qty: 50. **2920**

FREEMAN (IRVINGTON-ON-HUDSON, N.Y.), THE. (US/0016-0652). **1592**

FREER PRESS, THE. (US). **5750**

FREETHINKER, THE. (UK/0016-0687). **4347**

FREETHOUGHT HISTORY. (US/1071-7269). **4347**

FREETHOUGHT TODAY. (US/0882-8512). **4960**

FREIBURGER ZEITSCHRIFT FUER PHILOSOPHIE UND THEOLOGIE. (SZ/0016-0725). **4347**

FREIGHT MANAGEMENT. (UK/0016-0873). **5383**

FREIGHT NEWS EXPRESS. (UK). **5383**

FREIGHTER, THE. (CN/0820-5280). Qty: 6. **5784**

FREIGHTER TRAVEL NEWS. (US/0016-089X). Qty: 2-4. **837**

FREMONT COUNTY NOSTALGIA NEWS. (US/8756-8446). Qty: (varies). **2449**

FREMONTIA (SACRAMENTO, CALIF.). (US/0092-1793). **511**

FRENCH FORUM. (US/0098-9355). **3343**

FRENCH POLITICS AND SOCIETY. (US/0882-1267). Qty: 40-50. **4474**

FRENCH REVIEW, THE. (US/0016-111X). **3283**

FRENCH STUDIES. (UK/0016-1128). **3343**

FRENCH STUDIES IN SOUTHERN AFRICA. (SA/0259-0247). **3389**

FRESHWATER. (CN/0834-4302). **4176**

FRESHWATER BIOLOGY. (UK/0046-5070). **456**

FRESHWATER FISHING AUSTRALIA. (AT/1032-125X). **2304**

FRESNO BEE, THE. (US/0889-6070). **5635**

FRIEDENSWARTE, DIE. (SZ/0340-0255). **3128**

FRIEND (SALT LAKE CITY), THE. (US/0009-4102). **4960**

FRIENDLY LETTER, A. (US/0739-5418). **5060**

FRIENDLY WOMAN, THE. (US/0740-5618). **5557**

FRIENDLY WORD, THE. (IE/0790-3642). **5060**

FRIENDS JOURNAL. (US/0016-1322). **4960**

FRIENDS OF FINANCIAL HISTORY. (US/0278-8861). Qty: 5. **899**

FRIENDS OF KEBYAR. (US/0890-9717). **299**

FRIGHTEN THE HORSES. (US/1072-5644). Qty: 5-10. **5187**

FRISKO. (US). **2533**

FROHLINGER'S MARKETING REPORT. (US/1057-5316). **924**

FROM THE BROTHERS GRIMM. (US/1070-8898). Qty: 2. **2320**

FRONIMO; RIVISTA TRIMESTRALE DI CHITARRA E LIUTO, IL. (IT). **4118**

FRONT LINE SUPERVISOR'S BULLETIN. (US). **941**

FRONT PAGE DETECTIVE. (US/0016-2043). Qty: varies. **5074**

FRONTIER CHRONICLES. (US/1050-3560). Qty: 24. **2616**

FRONTIERS (BOULDER). (US/0160-9009). **5557**

FRONTIERS OF MEDICAL AND BIOLOGICAL ENGINEERING. (NE/0921-3775). **3692**

FROZEN FOOD REPORT. (US/0192-0367). **2342**

FRUIT AND VEGETABLE TRUCK RATE REPORT / UNITED STATES DEPARTMENT OF AGRICULTURE, AGRICULTURAL MARKETING SERVICE, FRUIT AND VEGETABLE MARKET NEWS SERVICE. (US). **837**

FRUIT BELGE, LE. (BE/0016-2248). **2415**

FRUIT COUNTRY. (US). **89**

FRUIT GARDENER, THE. (US/1049-4545). Qty: 6. **2415**

FRUIT GROWER MAIDSTONE. (UK/0953-2188). **172**

FRUIT VARIETIES JOURNAL. (US/0091-3642). **2415**

FRUITS. (FR/0016-2299). **2415**

FRUITS & LEGUMES. (FR/0754-0698). Qty: 1. **2342**

FT SYSTEMS. (US/0740-4980). **1254**

FTC : WATCH. (US/0196-0016). **2972**

FU JEN STUDIES : LITERATURE & LINGUISTICS. (CH/1015-0021). Qty: 1. **3283**

FUEL OIL NEWS. (US/0016-2396). **4256**

FUEL PROCESSING TECHNOLOGY. (NE/0378-3820). **1025**

FULDAER HOCHSCHULSCHRIFTEN / HERAUSGEGEBEN VON DER THEOLOGISCHEN FAKULTAT FULDA. (GW). **4960**

FULL-COURT PRESS, THE. (US/0892-5364). **5696**

FULL CRY (SEDALIA). (US/0016-2620). Qty: 3-4. **4872**

FULLTEXT SOURCES ONLINE. (US/1040-8258). **3211**

FULTON COUNTY IMAGES. (US/1070-7735). Qty: 3-4. **2616**

FULTON COUNTY NEWS (MCCONNELLSBURG, PA.). (US). **5736**

FULTON-HICKMAN GENEALOGICAL JOURNAL. (US/1065-0164). **2449**

FULTON SUN, THE. (US/8750-6696). **5703**

FUNCTION. (AT/0313-6825). Qty: 5. **3506**

FUNCTIONAL ORTHODONTIST, THE. (US/8756-3150). **1324**

FUNCTIONS. (CN/0821-2708). **3506**

FUND RAISING MANAGEMENT. (US/0016-268X). **868**

FUNDAMENTAL AND APPLIED TOXICOLOGY. (US/0272-0590). **3980**

FUNDAMENTAL & CLINICAL PHARMACOLOGY. (FR/0767-3981). **4305**

FUNDAMENTALS OF COSMIC PHYSICS. (US/0094-5846). **395**

FUNDBERICHTE AUS BADEN-WURTTEMBERG. (GW). **268**

FUNDBERICHTE AUS OSTERREICH. (AU). **268**

FUNK-TECHNIK. AUSGABE ZV (MUNCHEN). (GW/0342-0426). **1156**

FUNKSCHAU. (GW/0016-2841). **2055**

FUNKTIONSKRANKHEITEN DES BEWEGUNGSAPPARATES. (GW/0258-2015). **3804**

FUR AGE WEEKLY. (US/0016-2884). **3184**

FURIOUS FICTIONS. (US/1065-7983). **3389**

FURMAN STUDIES. (US/0190-4701). **2846**

FURNISHING FLOORS. DOMESTIC AND CONTRACT. (AT/0816-5947). **2905**

FURNITURE HISTORY. (UK/0016-3058). **2905**

FURROW, THE. (IE/0016-3120). **5029**

FUSE MAGAZINE. (CN/0838-603X). Qty: 15. **320**

FUSION ASIA. (II/0970-0080). **2504**

FUSION FACTS (SALT LAKE CITY, UTAH). (US/1051-8738). Qty: 8. **1945**

FUSION MAGAZINE. (CN/0832-9656). Qty: few. **2589**

FUSION WILMINGTON, DEL. (US/0016-3155). **2589**

FUTRAL, FUTRELL, FUTRELLE AND RELATED FAMILIES, WATKINS, CLIFFORD, WOOD. (US/0734-080X). **2449**

FUTURA. (IE/0016-3252). **1084**

FUTURE HEALTH. (CN/0225-395X). **Qty:** approx. 2/yr. **3577**

FUTURE (NEW DELHI, INDIA). (II/0252-1873). **2280**

FUTURE REFLECTIONS. (US/0883-3419). **4388**

FUTURE SURVEY. (US/0190-3241). **1533**

FUTURE SURVEY ANNUAL. (US/0273-0138). **5107**

FUTURES INDUSTRY'S MANAGED ACCOUNT REPORTS. (US/0197-5382). **899**

FUTURES INTERNATIONAL LAW LETTER. (US). **2973**

FUTURES (LONDON). (UK/0016-3287). **1492**

FUTURES RESEARCH QUARTERLY. (US/8755-3317). **5107**

FUTURIBLES (PARIS). (FR/0337-307X). **5246**

FUTURICS. (US/0164-1220). **Qty:** 2-10. **5107**

FUTURIST, THE. (US/0016-3317). **5107**

FV. FOTO-VIDEO ACTUALIDAD. (SP/0214-2244). **4369**

FWP JOURNAL. (SA/0015-9026). **4027**

G.A.S. LITES. (US/0882-8377). **2449**

G. GESCHICHTE MIT PFIFF. (GW/0173-539X). **Qty:** 40/year. **2616**

GABONAIPAR. (HU/0133-0918). **201**

GACETA ARQUEOLOGICA ANDINA. (PE/0254-8240). **268**

GACETA POETICA : REVISTA TRIMESTRAL DE POESIA. (SP). **3463**

GAELIC GLEANINGS. (US/0882-2166). **2449**

GAFFNEY LEDGER, THE. (US/0748-934X). **5742**

GAIAN SCIENCE FOR GEOPHYSIOLOGY RESEARCHERS & TEACHERS. (US/1051-6689). **Qty:** 12. **1405**

GAIRM. (UK/0016-3929). **3343**

GAKKAI SENTA NEWS. (JA). **5107**

GALACTIC CENTRAL BIBLIOGRAPHIES FOR THE AVID READER. (US/1049-6386). **416**

GALAKSIJA. (YU/0350-123X). **5107**

GALAXIA 71 [I.E. SETENTA Y UNO]. (VE). **320**

GALLATIN TRAILS. (US/0883-1920). **2449**

GALLAUDET TODAY. (US/0016-4089). **1879**

GALLERIES. (UK/0265-7511). **4088**

GALLERY (NEW YORK, N.Y.). (US/0195-072X). **3995**

GALLERY OF FINE HOME PLANS. (US/0899-4404). **299**

GALLIMAUFRY. (US/0161-2549). **3389**

GALPAGUCCHA. (II). **3283**

GALVANOTECNICA & NUOVE FINITURE. (IT/1120-6454). **487**

GAM ON YACHTING. (CN/0016-4259). **Qty:** 8. **593**

GAMA NEWS JOURNAL. (US/1058-0808). **2881**

GAMBLING / INFORMATION AIDS. (US). **3165**

GAMC NEWS. (US/0743-7307). **868**

GAME BIRD BULLETIN. (US). **2194**

GAMUT (TORONTO). (CN/0713-3545). **321**

GANG JOURNAL, THE. (US/1061-5326). **3165**

GANITA. (II/0046-5402). **Qty:** 1. **3506**

GARBAGE (BROOKLYN, NEW YORK, N.Y.). (US/1044-3061). **2194**

GARBO. (SP). **2517**

GARDEN CITY TELEGRAM (GARDEN CITY, KAN. : 1953). (US). **5675**

GARDEN CLIPPINGS. (CN/0318-7705). **2415**

GARDEN DESIGN. (US/0733-4923). **2415**

GARDEN HISTORY. (UK/0307-1243). **2415**

GARDEN RAILWAYS. (US/0747-0622). **5431**

GARDEN WRITERS NEWSLETTER. (US). **2415**

GARDENING IN ALBERTA. (CN/1188-2972). **Qty:** 3. **2416**

GARDENS' BULLETIN, SINGAPORE, THE. (SI/0374-7859). **89**

GARTENBAU- UND FELDGEMUSE- ANBAUERHEBUNG / BEARBEITET IM OSTERREICHISCHEN STATISTISCHEN ZENTRALAMT. (AU). **2434**

GARTENPRAXIS. (GW/0341-2105). **Qty:** 3. **2416**

GAS ABSTRACTS. (US/0016-4844). **4283**

GAS ENGINE MAGAZINE. (US/0435-1304). **250**

GAS (MUNCHEN). (GW/0343-2092). **4257**

GAS SEPARATION & PURIFICATION. (UK/0950-4214). **4258**

GAS WARME INTERNATIONAL. (GW/0020-9384). **4258**

GAS WORLD (LONDON, ENGLAND : 1974). (UK/0308-7654). **4258**

GASKELL SOCIETY JOURNAL, THE. (UK/0951-7200). **3389**

GASKIYA TA FI KWABO. (NR). **5807**

GASLIGHT (CLEVELAND, MINN.). (US/1062-015X). **Qty:** 6. **3389**

GASTRIC SECRETION. (UK/0142-8098). **3744**

GASTROENTEROLOGY & ENDOSCOPY NEWS. (US/0883-8348). **3745**

GASTROENTEROLOGY (NEW YORK, N.Y. 1943). (US/0016-5085). **3745**

GASTROPODIA. (US/0435-1363). **5584**

GATELODGE : THE PRISON OFFICERS' MAGAZINE. (UK). **3165**

GATES GAZETTE. (US/0897-7798). **2449**

GATEWAY HERITAGE. (US/0198-9375). **2734**

GATEWAY: THE JOURNAL OF THE BELL COUNTY HISTORICAL SOCIETY. (US). **2734**

GATFWORLD (PITTSBURGH, PA.). (US/1048-0293). **378**

GATHERING. (CN/0823-1869). **Qty:** 3. **4960**

GATHERING GIBSONS. (US/0893-3162). **2449**

GATHERING OF THE TRIBES, A. (US/1058-9112). **3390**

GATO TUERTO, EL. (US/8755-3651). **3390**

GAUGE RAIL-ROADING, O. (US/1062-1482). **2773**

GAUHATI LAW REPORTS. (II). **2973**

GAVEA-BROWN. (US/0276-7910). **3390**

GAY AIRLINE & TRAVEL CLUB NEWSLETTER, THE. (US). **2794**

GAZ D'AUJOURD'HUI. (FR/0016-5328). **Qty:** 3-4. **4259**

GAZETTE - AUSTRALIAN MATHEMATICAL SOCIETY. (AT/0311-0729). **3506**

GAZETTE - CANADIAN FORCES BASE GAGETOWN (1981). (CN/0713-391X). **4044**

GAZETTE (CEDAR RAPIDS, IOWA), THE. (US/1066-0291). **5670**

GAZETTE DE L'HOTEL DROUOT, LA. (FR). **321**

GAZETTE DES ARCHIVES, LA. (FR/0016-5522). **2481**

GAZETTE DES FEMMES, LA. (CN/0704-4550). **5557**

GAZETTE LEADER. (US). **Qty:** 12. **5710**

GB+GW; GARTNERBORSE UND GARTENWELT. (GW/0342-4731). **2416**

GC/MS UPDATE. PART A ENVIRONMENTAL. (UK/0962-9327). **Qty:** 25. **2172**

GDG REPORT, THE. (US/0883-3087). **3165**

GDR BULLETIN: NEWSLETTER FOR LITERATURE AND CULTURE IN THE GERMAN DEMOCRATIC REPUBLIC. (US). **Qty:** 25. **3283**

GE RI CO NEWS : BOLLETINO DI INFORMAZIONE E INNOVAZIONE RICERCA TECNOLOGICA. (IT). **5107**

GEFAEHRLICHE LADUNG. (GW/0016-5808). **5383**

GEGENWART. (SZ/0016-5867). **4960**

GEGENWARTSKUNDE. (GW/0016-5875). **5200**

GEIJUTSU SHINCHO. (JA). **351**

GEIST UND LEBEN (WURZBURG). (GW/0016-5921). **3390**

GEIST (VANCOUVER). (CN/1181-6554). **3390**

GEITEHOUDER, DE. (NE). **211**

GEMATOLOGIYA I TRANSFUZIOLOGIYA. (RU). **3771**

GEMEENTE. (BE). **4650**

GEMEINDEVERZEICHNIS FUER NIEDERSACHSEN. (GW). **2823**

GEMMA : REVISTA INTERNACIONAL DE LITERATURA. (SP). **3390**

GEMS & GEMOLOGY (GEMOLOGICAL INSTITUTE OF AMERICA : 1967). (US/0016-626X). **1439**

GEMS OF POETRY AND PROSE. (CN/0834-1737). **3390**

GEMSTONE PRICE REPORT. (BE). **2914**

GEMSTONE REGISTRY BULLETIN, THE. (US/0882-6269). **2914**

GEN, GASTROENTEROLOGIA, ENDOCRINOLOGIA I NUTRICION. (VE/0016-3503). **3746**

GENDAI KAGAKU. CHEMISTRY TODAY. (JA). **976**

GENDAI KORIA. (JA). **2651**

GENDER & HISTORY. (UK/0953-5233). **5557**

GENDER & SOCIETY. (US/0891-2432). **5200**

GENDERS (AUSTIN, TEX.). (US/0894-9832). **2846**

GENEAGRAM. (US/8756-7989). **2449**

GENEALOGICAL AIDS BULLETIN (1978). (US/0738-5226). **Qty:** Varies. **2449**

GENEALOGICAL AND HISTORICAL MAGAZINE OF THE SOUTH, THE. (US/0743-5843). **2449**

GENEALOGICAL CLEARINGHOUSE QUARTERLY, THE. (US/0882-0422). **2449**

GENEALOGICAL COMPUTER PIONEER. (US/0735-0287). **2449**

GENEALOGICAL GOLDMINE. (US/0738-3770). **Qty:** 12. **2450**

GENEALOGICAL JOURNAL (LEXINGTON, N.C.), THE. (US/0731-9606). **2450**

GENEALOGICAL JOURNAL (SALT LAKE CITY, UTAH). (US/0146-2229). **Qty:** 4y. **2450**

GENEALOGICAL RECORD (HOUSTON, TEX.), THE. (US/0433-3209). **2450**

GENEALOGICAL TIPS. (US/0433-3233). **2450**

GENEALOGIES BOURBONNAISES ET DU CENTRE / CERCLE GENEALOGIQUE ET HERALDIQUE DU BOURBONNAIS. (FR/0223-7237). **2450**

GENEALOGIST (MANCHESTER, N.H.), THE. (US/0196-4259). **2450**

GENEALOGIST (NEW YORK), THE. (US/0197-1468). **Qty:** 15-20. **2450**

GENEALOGISTS' MAGAZINE : OFFICIAL ORGAN OF THE SOCIETY OF GENEALOGISTS, THE. (UK/0016-6391). **2450**

GENEESKUNDE EN SPORT. (NE/0016-6448). **3954**

GENERAL AVIATION NEWS. (US/0191-927X). **22**

GENERAL AVIATION NEWS AND FLYER. (US/1052-9136). **22**

GENERAL DENTISTRY. (US/0363-6771). **1324**

GENERAL HOSPITAL PSYCHIATRY. (US/0163-8343). **3925**

GENERAL MUSIC JOURNAL. (US/8755-5905). **4119**

GENERAL PRACTITIONER. (UK/0046-5607). **3737**

GENERAL SCIENCE INDEX. (US/0162-1963). **5175**

GENERAL SCIENCE INDEX. CD-ROM. (US/0162-1963). **5107**

GENERATIONS (SAN FRANCISCO, CALIF.). (US/0738-7806). **5179**

GENERATIONS (WINNIPEG). (CN/0226-6105). **Qty:** 20-50. **2451**

GENESIS 2. (US/0016-6669). **5047**

GENESIS (WASHINGTON, D.C.). (US/0744-0596). **3761**

GENETIC ENGINEER & BIOTECHNOLOGIST, THE. (UK/0959-020X). **3692**

GENETIC ENGINEERING LETTER. (US/0276-1882). **545**

GENETIC ENGINEERING NEWS. (US/0270-6377). **545**

GENETIC EPISTEMOLOGIST, THE. (GW/0740-9583). **546**

GENETIC RESOURCES AND CROP EVOLUTION. (NE/0925-9864). **511**

GENETICA. (NE/0016-6707). **546**

GENETICAL RESEARCH. (UK/0016-6723). **546**

GENETICS ABSTRACTS. (US/0016-674X). **478**

GENETIKA. (RU/0016-6758). **546**

GENETIKA I SELEKTSIYA. (BU/0016-6766). **2416**

GENEVE-AFRIQUE. (SZ/0016-6774). **5246**

GENEWATCH. (US/0740-9737). **Qty:** varies. **3692**

GENIE

GENIE LOGICIEL & SYSTEMES EXPERTS. (FR/1166-4738). **1286**

GENIE, THE. (US/0534-0020). **2451**

GENII. (US/0016-6855). **4862**

GENITOURINARY MEDICINE. (UK/0266-4348). **4776**

GENRE (NORMAN, OKLA.). (US/0016-6928). **3343**

GENTE. (MX). **2488**

GENUINE CORVETTE BLACK BOOK, THE. (US). **5415**

GENUS. (IT/0016-6987). **4553**

GEO PLEIN-AIR. (CN/1194-5303). Qty: 20. **4896**

GEO2. (US/0735-0511). Qty: varies. **1376**

GEOARCHAEOLOGY. (US/0883-6353). **269**

GEOBIOS (JODHPUR). (II/0251-1223). **456**

GEOBIOS (LYON, FRANCE). (FR/0016-6995). Qty: 6. **4227**

GEOBIOS NEW REPORTS. (II). **456**

GEOCARTO INTERNATIONAL. (HK/1010-6049). **2561**

GEOCHRONIQUE. (FR/0292-8477). **1376**

GEODESIA. (NE). **2561**

GEODEZIA ES KARTOGRAFIA. (HU/0016-7118). **2581**

GEODRILLING. (UK/0268-0165). **1405**

GEODYNAMICS SERIES. (US/0277-6669). **1376**

GEOFISICA INTERNACIONAL : REVISTA DE LA UNION GEOFISICA MEXICANA AUSPICIADA POR EL INSTITUTO DE GEOFISICA DE LA UNIVERSIDAD NACIONAL AUTONOMA DE MEXICO. (MX/0016-7169). **4404**

GEOFIZICHESKII ZHURNAL. (UN/0203-3100). **1405**

GEOFIZIKA ZAGREB. (CI/0352-3659). **1405**

GEOGRAFFITY (BLACKSBURG, VA.). (US/1063-9837). **2517**

GEOGRAFIA. (BL). **2561**

GEOGRAFICKY CASOPIS. GEOGRAFICHESKII ZHURNAL. GEOGRAPHICAL REVIEW. GEOGRAPHISCHE ZEITSCHRIFT. REVUE DE GEOGRAPHIE. (XO/0016-7193). **2562**

GEOGRAFISKA ANNALER. SERIES B, HUMAN GEOGRAPHY. (NO/0435-3684). **2823**

GEOGRAPHIA. (PL). **2562**

GEOGRAPHICA (KUALA LUMPUR). (MY/0126-6101). **2562**

GEOGRAPHICAL ABSTRACTS. HUMAN GEOGRAPHY. (UK/0953-9611). **2580**

GEOGRAPHICAL ABSTRACTS : PHYSICAL GEOGRAPHY. (UK/0954-0504). **2580**

GEOGRAPHICAL ANALYSIS. (US/0016-7363). **2562**

GEOGRAPHICAL JOURNAL, THE. (UK/0016-7398). **2563**

GEOGRAPHICAL PAPERS. DEPARTMENT OF GEOGRAPHY, UNIVERSITY OF READING. (UK/0305-5914). **2563**

GEOGRAPHICAL PERSPECTIVES. (US/0199-994X). **2563**

GEOGRAPHICAL REVIEW. (US/0016-7428). **2563**

GEOGRAPHICAL REVIEW OF INDIA. (II). **2563**

GEOGRAPHICAL : THE MONTHLY MAGAZINE OF THE ROYAL GEOGRAPHICAL SOCIETY. (UK). **2563**

GEOGRAPHIE PHYSIQUE ET QUATERNAIRE. (CN/0705-7199). **2563**

GEOGRAPHISCHE RUNDSCHAU. (GW/0016-7460). **2564**

GEOGRAPHISCHES JAHRBUCH. (GW). **2564**

GEOGRAPHISCHES JAHRBUCH BURGENLAND. (AU). **2564**

GEOGRAPHY. (UK/0016-7487). **2564**

GEOGRAPHY BULLETIN. (AT). **2564**

GEOGRAPHY RESEARCH FORUM. (US/0333-5275). Qty: 10. **2564**

GEOJOURNAL. (GE/0343-2521). **2564**

GEOLIT. (GW). **2564**

GEOLOGICAL ABSTRACTS. (UK/0954-0512). **1362**

GEOLOGICAL MAGAZINE. (UK/0016-7568). **1378**

GEOLOGICAL NEWSLETTER (PORTLAND). (US/0270-5451). Qty: 3-4. **1378**

GEOLOGICAL REPORT (TORONTO). (CN/0472-9889). **1378**

GEOLOGICKY ZBORNIK / GEOLOGICA CARPATHICA. (XO/0016-7738). **1379**

GEOLOGIE EN MIJNBOUW. (NE/0016-7746). **1379**

GEOLOGIJA RUDNYH MESTOROZDENIJ. (RU/0016-7770). **2139**

GEOLOGISCHES JAHRBUCH, REIHE F : BODENKUNDE. (GW/0341-6445). **1379**

GEOLOGUES. (FR/0016-7916). **1380**

GEOLOGY (BOULDER). (US/0091-7613). **1380**

GEOLOGY STUDIES. (US/0068-1016). **1380**

GEOMAGNETIZM I AERONOMIJA. (RU/0016-7940). **4443**

GEOMETRIC AND FUNCTIONAL ANALYSIS : GAFA. (SZ/1016-443X). **3507**

GEOMICROBIOLOGY JOURNAL. (US/0149-0451). **563**

GEOMUNDO. (PN/0256-7253). **2564**

GEOPHYSICAL AND ASTROPHYSICAL FLUID DYNAMICS. (US/0309-1929). **1405**

GEOPHYSICAL JOURNAL. (US/0275-9128). **1405**

GEOPHYSICAL MONOGRAPH. (US/0065-8448). **1406**

GEOPHYSICAL PROSPECTING. (NE/0016-8025). **1406**

GEOPHYSICAL RESEARCH LETTERS. (US/0094-8276). **1406**

GEOPHYSICS. (US/0016-8033). **1406**

GEOPOLITIQUE. (FR/0752-1693). **4522**

GEORGE HERBERT JOURNAL. (US/0161-7435). Qty: 8-12. **3390**

GEORGE MASON UNIVERSITY LAW REVIEW. (US/0741-8736). **2973**

GEORGE SAND STUDIES. (US/0897-0483). **3343**

GEORGE WASHINGTON JOURNAL OF INTERNATIONAL LAW AND ECONOMICS, THE. (US/0748-4305). Qty: Approx. 6. **3128**

GEORGE WASHINGTON JOURNAL OF INTERNATIONAL LAW AND ECONOMICS, THE. (US). **3128**

GEORGE WASHINGTON LAW REVIEW, THE. (US/0016-8076). **2973**

GEORGE WRIGHT FORUM, THE. (US/0732-4715). Qty: 1-2. **2194**

GEORGETOWN CURRENT. (US). **5647**

GEORGETOWN LAW JOURNAL, THE. (US/0016-8092). **2974**

GEORGETOWN MEDICAL BULLETIN. (US/0016-8106). **3780**

GEORGETOWN (WASHINGTON, D.C. : 1987). (US/0895-1624). **1091**

GEORGETOWNER, THE. (US/0730-9082). **2534**

GEORGIA BULLETIN. (US). **5030**

GEORGIA GENEALOGICAL MAGAZINE. (US/0435-5393). **2451**

GEORGIA HISTORICAL QUARTERLY, THE. (US/0016-8297). Qty: 4. **2734**

GEORGIA JOURNAL (ATHENS, GA.). (US/0746-5963). **2534**

GEORGIA JOURNAL OF SCIENCE. (US/0147-9369). Qty: 4/yr. **5107**

GEORGIA LAW REVIEW (ATHENS, GA.: 1966). (US/0016-8300). **2974**

GEORGIA LIBRARIAN, THE. (US/0016-8319). Qty: 30-40. **3212**

GEORGIA LIVING. (US/1049-6432). **2488**

GEORGIA MUSIC NEWS. (US/0046-5798). **4119**

GEORGIA REVIEW, THE. (US/0016-8386). **3390**

GEORGIA STATE UNIVERSITY LAW REVIEW. (US/8755-6847). **2974**

GEORGIA VETERINARIAN, THE. (US/0886-5760). **5510**

GEORGIA WILDLIFE. (US/0164-8608). **2194**

GEORGIAN ANNUAL. (US). **4241**

GEOSCIENCE CANADA. (CN/0315-0941). **1380**

GEOSCIENTIST. (UK/0961-5628). **1380**

GEOSUR / [ASOCIACION SUDAMERICANA DE ESTUDIOS GEOPOLITICOS E INTERNACIONALES]. (UY). **4522**

GEOTECHNICAL ABSTRACTS. (US/0016-8491). **1363**

GEOTECHNICAL ENGINEERING. (TH/0046-5828). **2023**

GEOTECHNICAL FABRICS REPORT. (US/0882-4983). **5351**

GEOTECHNICAL NEWS. (CN/0823-650X). Qty: 3-5. **1381**

GEOTECHNIK. (GW/0172-6145). Qty: 4. **2023**

GEOTECHNIQUE. (UK/0016-8505). **2023**

GEOTEKTONIKA. (RU/0016-853X). **1381**

GEOTHERMAL HOT LINE. (US/0735-0503). **1945**

GEOTHERMAL REPORT. (US/0733-9100). **1945**

GEOTIMES. (US/0016-8556). **1381**

GERANIUMS AROUND THE WORLD. (US/0016-8599). Qty: 1. **2416**

GEREFORMEERD THEOLOGISCH TIJDSCHRIFT. (NE/0016-8610). **4960**

GERFAUT, LE. (BE/0251-1193). **5617**

GERIATRIC NURSING (NEW YORK). (US/0197-4572). **3856**

GERMAN BRIEF. (GW). **1492**

GERMAN CONNECTION, THE. (US/8755-1756). **2451**

GERMAN GENEALOGICAL DIGEST. (US). **2451**

GERMAN HISTORY : THE JOURNAL OF THE GERMAN HISTORY SOCIETY. (UK/0266-3554). **2689**

GERMAN JOURNAL OF PSYCHOLOGY, THE. (GW/0705-5870). **4587**

GERMAN POLITICS AND SOCIETY. (US/1045-0300). Qty: 30-35/ yr. **5200**

GERMAN QUARTERLY, THE. (US/0016-8831). **3390**

GERMAN STUDIES REVIEW. (US/0149-7952). **2689**

GERMAN TEACHING. (UK/0953-4822). **3283**

GERMANIC NOTES AND REVIEWS. (US). **2846**

GERMANIC REVIEW, THE. (US/0016-8890). **3343**

GERMANISCH-ROMANISCHE MONATSSCHRIFT. (GW/0016-8904). **3283**

GERMANISTIK (TUEBINGEN). (GW/0016-8912). **3336**

GERMANISTISCHE ABHANDLUNGEN (STUTTGART). (GW/0435-5903). **3284**

GERMANISTISCHE MITTEILUNGEN. (BE/0771-3703). **3284**

GERMANO-SLAVICA. (CN/0317-4956). **3391**

GERMANTOWN CRIER. (US/0742-6631). **2734**

GERMINATION. (CN/0704-6286). **3463**

GERODONTOLOGY. (US/0734-0664). **3751**

GERONTOLOGIST, THE. (US/0016-9013). **3751**

GERONTOLOGY & GERIATRICS EDUCATION. (US/0270-1960). **3752**

GERONTOLOGY SPECIAL INTEREST SECTION NEWSLETTER. (US/0279-4101). **3752**

GESAR. (US/0738-2294). **5021**

GESCHICHTE. (SZ). **2616**

GESELLSCHAFT UND POLITIK. (AU/0016-9099). **5201**

GESHER (WORLD JEWISH CONGRESS. ISRAEL EXECUTIVE). (IS/0435-8406). Qty: 100/yr. **5047**

GESTALT JOURNAL, THE. (US/0190-0412). **4588**

GESTION 2000. (BE/0773-0543). **868**

GESTION (LAVAL). (CN/0701-0028). Qty: 6-8. **868**

GESTIONESCUOLA. (IT/0393-5523). Qty: 12. **869**

GESTOS (IRVINE, CALIF.). (US/1040-483X). **5364**

GESUNDE PFLANZEN. (GW/0367-4223). **2230**

GET READY SHEET, THE. (US/0148-7566). **3212**

GET RICH NEWS. (US). **677**

GETTING READY. (US/1064-0827). **1063**

GETTYSBURG REVIEW (1988). (US/0898-4557). Qty: 20. **3391**

GEWERKSCHAFTLICHE RUNDSCHAU. (SZ). **1676**

GIA QUARTERLY. (US/1070-7794). Qty: 4. **4119**

GIAIDS. GIORNALE ITALIANO DELL' AIDS. (IT/1120-7892). **3669**

GIATROS DERMATOLOGIE. (GW/0932-8661). **3720**

GIATROS HNO. (GW/0930-8318). **3888**

GIATROSERTHOPAEDIE. (GW/0930-8326). **3881**

GIATROSGYNAKOLOGIE. (GW/0177-9109). **3761**

GOVERNMENTS

GIATROSPAEDIATRIE. (GW/0177-9095). **3903**

GIATROSUROLOGIE. (GW/0178-7527). **3990**

GIBBONS STAMP MONTHLY. (UK). **Qty:** 50-100 per year. **2785**

GIBIER, FAUNE SAUVAGE. (FR/0761-9243). **2216**

GIDROLIZNAIA I LESOKHIMICHESKAILA PROMYSHLENNOST. (RU/0016-9706). **2401**

GIDS OP MAATSCHAPPELIJK GEBIED. (BE/0378-4657). **Qty:** 80. **5286**

GIESSEREI. (GW/0016-9765). **4003**

GIFTED CHILD QUARTERLY, THE. (US/0016-9862). **1879**

GIFTED CHILD TODAY, THE. (US/0892-9580). **1063**

GIFTED CHILDREN MONTHLY. (US/8750-684X). **1879**

GIFTED EDUCATION INTERNATIONAL. (UK/0261-4294). **1879**

GIFTED EDUCATION PRESS QUARTERLY. (US/1064-0053). **1879**

GIGUERERIE (EDITION FRANCAISE). (CN/0713-3162). **2451**

GILCREASE MAGAZINE OF AMERICAN HISTORY AND ART, THE. (US/0730-5036). **4088**

GILGAMESH. (IQ). **321**

GIMTOJI KALBA. (LI). **Qty:** 8-10/yr. **1112**

GINECOLOGIA Y OBSTETRICIA DE MEXICO. (MX/0300-9041). **3761**

GIORNALE DEGLI ECONOMISTI E ANNALI DI ECONOMIA. (IT/0017-0097). **1492**

GIORNALE DELL' INSTALLATORE ELETTRICO, IL. (IT/0392-3630). **2056**

GIORNALE DELL' OFFICINA. (IT/0017-0240). **2115**

GIORNALE DELLA LIBRERIA. (IT). **4815**

GIORNALE DELLA SUBFORNITURA, IL. (IT/0392-3622). **1607**

GIORNALE DELL'ARTE (TURIN, ITALY). (IT/0394-0543). **321**

GIORNALE DELL'INGEGNERE, IL. (IT). **1976**

GIORNALE DELL'INSTALLATORE TELEFONICO, IL. (IT/1120-219X). **1976**

GIORNALE DI ANESTESIA STOMATOLOGICA. (IT/0391-5670). **1324**

GIORNALE DI EMODINAMICA. (IT/0392-7679). **3704**

GIORNALE DI GEOLOGIA. (IT/0017-0291). **1381**

GIORNALE DI MALATTIE INFETTIVE E PARASSITARIE. (IT/0017-0321). **4777**

GIORNALE DI MEDICINA MILITARE. (IT/0017-0364). **3578**

GIORNALE DI METAFISICA. (IT). **4347**

GIORNALE ITALIANO DELLE MALATTIE DEL TORACE. (IT/0017-0437). **3949**

GIORNALE ITALIANO DI CARDIOLOGIA. (IT/0046-5968). **3705**

GIORNALE ITALIANO DI CHIMICA CLINICA. (IT/0392-2227). **976**

GIORNALE ITALIANO DI DERMATOLOGIA E VENEREOLOGIA. (IT/0392-0488). **3720**

GIORNALE ITALIANO DI ONCOLOGIA. (IT/0392-128X). **3817**

GIORNALE ITALIANO DI OSTETRICIA E GINECOLOGIA. (IT/0391-9013). **3761**

GIORNALE STORICO DELLA LUNIGIANA. (IT/0017-050X). **269**

GIORNALE STORICO DI PSICOLOGIA DINAMICA. (IT/0391-2515). **4588**

GIORNALINO (NEW YORK, N.Y.), IL. (US/0434-0299). **1748**

GIRARD PRESS, THE. (US). **5675**

GIRL GROUPS GAZETTE, THE. (US). **4119**

GISSING JOURNAL, THE. (UK). **3391**

GISTER EN VANDAG. (SA). **Qty:** 2. **1895**

GIURISPRUDENZA COSTITUZIONALE. (IT/0436-0222). **3093**

GIVING USA UPDATE. (US/0899-3793). **4336**

GLACIOLOGICAL DATA. (US/0149-1776). **1413**

GLADIATOR SPORTS MAGAZINE. (US). **4896**

GLAS UND RAHMEN. (GW/0036-3065). **2589**

GLASFORUM. (GW/0017-0852). **2589**

GLASGOW ARCHAEOLOGICAL JOURNAL. (UK). **269**

GLASGOW NATURALIST. (UK/0373-241X). **4165**

GLASNIK SLOVENSKEGA ETNOLOSKEGA DRUSTVA. (XV/0351-2908). **237**

GLASS ART (BROOMFIELD, COLO.). (US/1068-2147). **2589**

GLASS ART MAGAZINE (BROOMFIELD, COLO.). (US/0886-8131). **2589**

GLASS ART SOCIETY PHOTOGRAPHIC DIRECTORY. (US/0740-8889). **2589**

GLASS COLLECTOR'S DIGEST. (US/0893-8660). **2589**

GLASS INDUSTRY, THE. (US/0017-1026). **2590**

GLASS INTERNATIONAL. (UK/0143-7836). **2590**

GLASS NEWS. (US/0890-3743). **2590**

GLASS ON METAL. THE ENAMELISTS' NEWSLETTER. (US). **2590**

GLASS (REDHILL). (UK/0017-0984). **2590**

GLASS TECHNOLOGY. (UK/0017-1050). **2590**

GLASTECHNISCHE BERICHTE. (GW/0017-1085). **2590**

GLASTEKNISK TIDSKRIFT. (SW/0017-1093). **2590**

GLAUCOMA (MIAMI). (US/0164-4645). **3875**

GLAZED EXPRESSIONS. (UK/0261-0329). **Qty:** 4 or 5. **299**

GLEANER INDEX / NATIONAL LIBRARY OF JAMAICA, THE. (JM/0259-0336). **5805**

GLEANINGS IN BEE CULTURE. (US/0017-114X). **5585**

GLEANINGS (KEOKUK). (US). **2451**

GLEN RIDGE PAPER. (US). **5710**

GLENDIVE RANGER-REVIEW. (US). **5705**

GLENWOOD POST. (US). **Qty:** 6-12. **5643**

GLIDER RIDER'S ULTRALIGHT FLYING. (US/0883-7937). **22**

GLIM NEWSLETTER, THE. (UK). **5328**

GLITCHES (BEND, ORE.). (US/0732-667X). **1233**

GLOBAL AFFAIRS. (US/0886-6198). **4522**

GLOBAL CHURCH GROWTH. (US/0731-1125). **Qty:** 12. **4960**

GLOBAL CITY REVIEW. (US/1068-0586). **3343**

GLOBAL JOURNAL ON CRIME AND CRIMINAL LAW. (NE/0928-9313). **3165**

GLOBAL JUSTICE. (US/1060-0884). **Qty:** 3-6. **4523**

GLOBAL RISK ASSESSMENTS: ISSUES, CONCEPTS, AND APPLICATIONS. (US/0739-4640). **900**

GLOBAL TAPESTRY. (UK). **3463**

GLOBAL TECTONICS AND METALLOGENY. (GW/0163-3171). **1356**

GLOBE AND LAUREL. (UK/0017-1204). **4044**

GLOBEHOPPER. (CN/0711-7108). **5478**

GLORY OF INDIA. (II). **2504**

GLOUCESTERSHIRE FAMILY HISTORY SOCIETY JOURNAL. (UK/0143-0513). **Qty:** 10. **2451**

GLOXINIAN, THE. (US/0017-1352). **512**

GLYCOBIOLOGY (OXFORD). (UK/0959-6658). **487**

GNOSIS (MONTREAL). (CN/0316-618X). **Qty:** varies. **4347**

GNOSIS (SAN FRANCISCO, CALIF.). (US/0894-6159). **Qty:** 50-60. **4960**

GNOSTICA. (US/0145-885X). **4241**

GNSI NEWSLETTER. (US/0199-5464). **5108**

GOAT VETERINARY SOCIETY JOURNAL. (UK). **5510**

GODS REVIVALIST AND BIBLE ADVOCATE. (US/0745-0788). **5016**

GOD'S SPECIAL PEOPLE. (US/0896-2413). **4960**

GOD'S WORD TODAY. (US/0199-3429). **Qty:** 3. **5016**

GOETHE YEARBOOK. (US/0734-3329). **432**

GOING DOWN SWINGING. (AT/0157-3950). **Qty:** 10-20/year. **3391**

GOINGSNAKE MESSENGER, THE. (US). **Qty:** 20. **2735**

GOLD COAST GAZETTE (SEA CLIFF, N.Y.). (US/1065-1748). **Qty:** 12. **5716**

GOLD + SILBER, UHREN + SCHMUCK. (GW/0017-1573). **2914**

GOLDEN GATE UNIVERSITY LAW REVIEW. (US/0363-0307). **2975**

GOLDEN ROOTS OF THE MOTHER LODE. NEWSLETTER. (US/8755-5697). **2451**

GOLDEN ROOTS OF THE MOTHER LODE, THE. (US/8755-3023). **2451**

GOLDEN YEARS MAGAZINE. (US). **5179**

GOLDENE KEYT, DI. (IS). **3391**

GOLDENSEAL. (US/0099-0159). **2320**

GOLDFINCH, THE. (US/0278-0208). **Qty:** 12. **1063**

GOLF JOURNAL. (US/0017-1794). **4896**

GOLF NEWS MAGAZINE. (US). **4896**

GOLF REPORTER, THE. (US/0745-7502). **4897**

GOLF WORLD. (US/0017-1891). **4897**

GOLFSHOP OPERATIONS. (US/0017-1824). **924**

GOLFWEEK. (US/0890-3514). **4897**

GOLOS INSTYTUTU. (CN/0318-0042). **2262**

GONGYE WEISHENGWU. (CC/1001-6678). **563**

GONZAGA LAW REVIEW. (US/0046-6115). **2975**

GOOD APPLE NEWSPAPER, THE. (US/0884-688X). **1895**

GOOD FRUIT & VEGETABLES. (AT). **2417**

GOOD HEALTH (DON MILLS). (CN/0229-5903). **1297**

GOOD-NEWS-LETTER. (CN/0713-3677). **4961**

GOOD NEWS LETTER (WASHINGTON, D.C.), THE. (US/0738-6419). **Qty:** 3. **5030**

GOOD NEWS (WILMORE). (US/0436-1563). **5060**

GOOD TIMES (GREENVILLE, NY.). (US/0191-4995). **2534**

GOODING COUNTY LEADER. (US). **5656**

GOODWIN NEWS, THE. (US/0892-1423). **2451**

GORDIAN (1948). (GW/0017-2243). **2342**

GORDON JOURNAL. (US). **Qty:** 6. **5706**

GORDON'S PRINT PRICE ANNUAL. (US/0160-6298). **Qty:** 4. **378**

GORGET ET SASH : JOURNAL OF THE EARLY MODERN WARFARE SOCIETY. (US/0892-466X). **4044**

GOSPEL HERALD BEAMSVILLE. (CN/0829-4666). **Qty:** 30-40. **4961**

GOSPEL STANDARD, OR, FEEBLE CHRISTIAN'S SUPPORT, THE. (UK). **Qty:** 25. **4961**

GOSPEL TIDINGS (OMAHA, NEB.). (US/0745-7618). **5060**

GOSPEL WITNESS (TORONTO. 196?). (CN/0828-1769). **4961**

GOTTINGISCHE GELEHRTE ANZEIGEN. (GW/0017-1549). **2847**

GOURD, THE. (US/0888-5672). **90**

GOURGUES REPORT, THE. (US/0743-5185). **900**

GOVERNANCE (OXFORD). (UK/0952-1895). **4651**

GOVERNING (WASHINGTON, D.C.). (US/0894-3842). **4475**

GOVERNMENT ACCOUNTANTS JOURNAL, THE. (US/0883-1483). **744**

GOVERNMENT AND OPPOSITION (LONDON). (UK/0017-257X). **4475**

GOVERNMENT & POLITICS ALERT. (US/1054-5859). **Qty:** 240. **4651**

GOVERNMENT BUSINESS WORLD REPORT. (US/0017-2588). **678**

GOVERNMENT EXECUTIVE. (US/0017-2626). **4651**

GOVERNMENT FINANCE REVIEW. (US/0883-7856). **4728**

GOVERNMENT MICROCOMPUTER LETTER. (US/0882-6587). **Qty:** 3-5. **1267**

GOVERNMENT PRODUCTIVITY NEWS. (US/0896-0674). **4652**

GOVERNMENT PUBLICATIONS REVIEW (1982). (US/0277-9390). **3212**

GOVERNMENT REFERENCE BOOKS. (US/0072-5188). **4652**

GOVERNMENTS OF ALABAMA. (US/0883-3753). **4728**

GOVERNMENTS OF ARKANSAS. (US/0883-3761). **4728**

GOVERNMENTS OF GEORGIA. (US/0883-3818). **4728**

GOVERNMENTS OF ILLINOIS. (US/0883-3826). **4728**

GOVERNMENTS OF INDIANA. (US/0883-3834). **4728**

GOVERNMENTS

GOVERNMENTS OF IOWA. (US/0883-3842). **4728**

GOVERNMENTS OF KANSAS. (US/0883-3850). **4728**

GOWER FEDERAL SERVICE: MINING. (US). **Qty:** 1-3/year. **2975**

GOYA. (SP/0017-2715). **351**

GQ. (US/0016-6979). **3995**

GQ (UK EDITION). (UK/0954-8750). **Qty:** 48. **3995**

GRACE THEOLOGICAL JOURNAL. (US/0198-666X). **4961**

GRADHIVA. (FR/0764-8928). **237**

GRADIVA. (US/0363-8057). **3343**

GRADUATE FACULTY PHILOSOPHY JOURNAL. (US/0093-4240). **4347**

GRADUATE FORUM (MINDANAO STATE UNIVERSITY. UNIVERSITY RESEARCH CENTER). (PH). **2504**

GRADUATE OUTLOOK. (AT/0314-0679). **Qty:** 2. **1826**

GRADUATE SCHOOL RESEARCH JOURNAL : A PUBLICATION OF GRADUATE SCHOOL OF BUSINESS ADMINISTRATION AND GRADUATE SCHOOL OF EDUCATION. (PH/0030-7858). **1826**

GRAFISCH NIEUWS. (BE/0773-591X). **4815**

GRAFISKT FORUM. (SW). **378**

GRAIL (WATERLOO). (CN/0828-4083). **4961**

GRAINEWS. (CN/0229-8090). **173**

GRAINGER SOCIETY JOURNAL, THE. (UK/0141-5085). **4119**

GRAMOPHONE INCLUDING COMPACT DISC NEWS AND REVIEWS. (UK/0017-310X). **5316**

GRAND RIVER VALLEY REVIEW, THE. (US/0739-084X). **2735**

GRAND SLAM (OTTAWA). (CN/0701-0745). **4897**

GRAND STREET. (US/0734-5496). **3391**

GRAND TIMES. (US/1068-1345). **Qty:** 18. **5179**

GRAND VALLEY STAR AND VIDETTE. (CN/0834-616X). **5785**

GRANGE NEWS, THE. (US/0043-0587). **90**

GRANI. (GW/0017-3185). **2517**

GRANMA (DAILY EDITION, SPANISH). (CU/0017-3223). **5799**

GRANMA INTERNATIONAL. (CU/0864-4624). **5799**

GRANT ADVISOR, THE. (US/0740-5383). **Qty:** 6-10/yr. **1826**

GRANVILLE SENTINEL (GRANVILLE, N.Y. : 1885). (US). **Qty:** 6. **5716**

GRAPHIC ARTS PRODUCT NEWS (CHICAGO). (US/0274-5976). **379**

GRAPHIC COMMUNICATIONS WORLD. (US/0884-6901). **4565**

GRAPHIC DESIGN, USA. (US). **379**

GRAPHIC MONTHLY, THE. (CN/0227-2806). **4565**

GRAPHICUS. (IT/0017-3436). **2488**

GRAPHIS. (SZ/0017-3452). **379**

GRAPHISCHE KUNST. (GW). **379**

GRASAS Y ACEITES (SEVILLA). (SP/0017-3495). **488**

GRASS AND FORAGE SCIENCE. (UK/0142-5242). **90**

GRASS ROOTS CAMPAIGNING. (US). **4475**

GRASS ROOTS SHEPPARTON. (AT/0310-2890). **Qty:** 18. **90**

GRASSROOTS CATALOG. (US). **2452**

GRASSROOTS DEVELOPMENT. (US/0733-6608). **2910**

GRASSROOTS ECONOMIC ORGANIZING NEWSLETTER. (US/1071-0590). **Qty:** 5-10. **1592**

GRASSROOTS EDITOR. (US/0017-3541). **2920**

GRASSROOTS FOR HIGH RISQUE LIBRARIANS. (US/0889-5198). **Qty:** 5. **3212**

GRASSROOTS FUNDRAISING JOURNAL. (US/0740-4832). **Qty:** 4. **4337**

GRASSROOTS (MADISON). (US/0361-1515). **1344**

GRAY AREAS. (US/1062-5712). **Qty:** varies. **2534**

GRAY'S SPORTING JOURNAL. (US/0273-6691). **4873**

GRAZER BEITRAEGE. (AU/0376-5253). **3284**

GRAZER BEITRAEGE. SUPPLEMENTBAND. (AU). **269**

GREAT BASIN NATURALIST, THE. (US/0017-3614). **4165**

GREAT BEND TRIBUNE (1972). (US/0891-7078). **Qty:** 5. **5676**

GREAT CIRCLE. (AT/0156-8698). **Qty:** 24. **4176**

GREAT EXPEDITIONS. (US/0706-7682). **5478**

GREAT LAKES ENTOMOLOGIST, THE. (US/0090-0222). **5609**

GREAT LAKES FISHERMAN. (CN/0847-0685). **Qty:** 12. **2304**

GREAT LAKES FISHERMAN (COLUMBUS, OHIO). (US/0194-5564). **2304**

GREAT LAKES LOG. (US/1067-4144). **5449**

GREAT LAKES WETLANDS. (US/1062-5356). **2216**

GREAT OUTDOORS. (SA). **2194**

GREAT PLAINS QUARTERLY. (US/0275-7664). **2735**

GREAT PLAINS RESEARCH. (US/1052-5165). **Qty:** 20-25. **4166**

GREAT PLAINS SOCIOLOGIST, THE. (US/0896-0054). **Qty:** 10. **5246**

GREAT RIVER REVIEW. (US/0160-2144). **Qty:** 12. **3392**

GREATER GREENWOOD BUSINESS JOURNAL, THE. (US). **Qty:** 12. **678**

GREATER LANSING BUSINESS MONTHLY. (US). **678**

GREATER LLANO ESTACADO SOUTHEAST HERITAGE, THE. (US/0145-8825). **2735**

GREATER LOS ANGELES PUBLIC SERVICE GUIDE. (US). **4653**

GREATER PHOENIX JEWISH NEWS. (US/0747-444X). **5047**

GREATER WINNIPEG BUSINESS. (CN/0830-8535). **678**

GREECE & ROME. (UK/0017-3835). **1077**

GREEK ACCENT. (US/0279-1234). **2689**

GREEK ORTHODOX THEOLOGICAL REVIEW, THE. (US/0017-3894). **Qty:** 50/year. **4961**

GREEK REVIEW OF SOCIAL RESEARCH. (GR). **5201**

GREEKAMERICAN, THE. (US/0890-0035). **2262**

GREEN. (CN/0823-6380). **4897**

GREEN BOOK BUYERS' GUIDE FOR GARDEN MERCHANDISE. (US/0147-3891). **2417**

GREEN BUSINESS LETTER, THE. (US/1056-490X). **2172**

GREEN CAR JOURNAL. (US/1059-6143). **5415**

GREEN EGG. (US/1066-7385). **Qty:** 30-40. **4241**

GREEN LIBRARY JOURNAL (BERKELEY, CALIF. 1992). (US/1059-0838). **2173**

GREEN REVOLUTION (YORK, PA.). (US/0017-3983). **Qty:** 1. **4542**

GREEN TEACHER (TORONTO). (CN/1192-1285). **2173**

GREEN THUMB NEWS. (US/0749-2138). **2417**

GREENE COUNTY DEMOCRAT (EUTAW, ALA.), THE. (US/0889-518X). **Qty:** 12. **5626**

GREENE COUNTY INDEPENDENT. (US). **5626**

GREENE GENES. (US/0898-9974). **Qty:** 20+. **2452**

GREENER MANAGEMENT INTERNATIONAL. (UK). **2173**

GREENFIELD QUARTERLY. (US/0883-170X). **2452**

GREENHOUSE MANAGER. (US/0744-8988). **2417**

GREENMASTER. (CN/0380-3333). **4897**

GREENPEACE BUSINESS. (UK/0962-9467). **2173**

GREENPOINT GAZETTE. (US). **Qty:** 10. **5717**

GREEN'S MAGAZINE. (CN/0824-2992). **Qty:** 2-4. **3392**

GREENSBORO WATCHMAN. (US). **5626**

GREENSBURG DAILY NEWS. (US). **5664**

GREENSWARD. (UK/0017-4092). **90**

GREENWEEK. (AT/1034-5876). **2194**

GREENWICH MAGAZINE. (US/1051-0745). **Qty:** 5. **2488**

GREENWOOD AND SOUTHSIDE CHALLENGER, THE. (US/1068-6673). **Qty:** 2. **5664**

GREENWOOD ENCYCLOPEDIA OF BLACK MUSIC, THE. (US/0272-0264). **4119**

GREENWOOD GAZETTE, THE. (US). **Qty:** 12. **5664**

GREGORIOS O PALAMAS. (GR/1011-3010). **4961**

GREGORIUSBLAD. (NE). **4119**

GRENADA CONSOLIDATED INDEX OF STATUTES AND SUBSIDIARY LEGISLATION TO ... . (US). **3081**

GRIDIRON COACH. (US/1071-1902). **Qty:** 1. **4897**

GRIFFITH OBSERVER. (US/0195-3982). **395**

GRIOT (HOUSTON, TEX.), THE. (US/0737-0873). **Qty:** 2/yr. **2735**

GRIPE/ GROUP FOR RESEARCH IN PATHOLOGY EDUCATION. (US). **Qty:** varies. **3894**

GRIT AND STEEL. (US/0017-4297). **Qty:** n. **4873**

GRNLAND (1953). (DK/0017-4556). **4553**

GROCERS' REVIEW. (NZ/0113-1850). **Qty:** 10. **2342**

GROENTEN EN FRUIT : G & F. (NE/0017-4491). **2417**

GRONDBOOR EN HAMER. (NE/0017-4505). **1381**

GROTIANA (1980). (NE). **3128**

GROUND ENGINEERING. (UK/0017-4653). **2024**

GROUND WATER. (US/0017-467X). **1413**

GROUND WATER AGE. (US/0046-645X). **5533**

GROUNDS MAINTENANCE. (US/0017-4688). **2417**

GROUNDSMAN. (UK/0017-4696). **2418**

GROUNDSWELL. (US/0162-7899). **2155**

GROUP ANALYSIS. (UK/0533-3164). **3926**

GROUP (LOVELAND, COLO.). (US/0163-8971). **Qty:** 20-30. **1064**

GROUP (NEW YORK. 1977). (US/0362-4021). **4588**

GROUP PRACTICE JOURNAL. (US/0199-5103). **Qty:** 2. **3780**

GROUP RESEARCH REPORT. (US/0017-4742). **Qty:** 10-12. **4475**

GROUP'S JR. HIGH MINISTRY. (US/0884-0504). **1064**

GROWER. (UK/0017-4785). **2418**

GROWING EDGE (CORVALLIS, OR.), THE. (US/1043-2906). **2418**

GROWING WITHOUT SCHOOLING. (US/0745-5305). **Qty:** 20-30. **1895**

GROWTH AND CHANGE. (US/0017-4815). **2823**

GROWTH, DEVELOPMENT, AND AGING. (US/1041-1232). **Qty:** 0-1. **456**

GROWTH GENETICS & HORMONES. (US/0898-6630). **3903**

GROWTH (PRETORIA, SOUTH AFRICA). (SA). **1564**

GRUNDLAGEN DER GERMANISTIK. (GW/0533-3350). **3284**

GRUNDTVIG STUDIER. (DK/0107-4164). **4961**

GSA TODAY. (US/1052-5173). **1381**

GTEC NEWS. (CN/0833-0611). **1879**

GUAM BUSINESS NEWS. (GU/1045-053X). **678**

GUANGARA LIBERTARIA. (US/0890-0280). **2617**

GUARDIAN (LONDON). (UK/0261-3077). **5812**

GUARDIAN (NEW YORK, N.Y.), THE. (US/0017-5021). **2920**

GUARDIAN - WRIGHT STATE'S STUDENT NEWSPAPER. (US). **5728**

GUARDMOUNT. (US/0883-0843). **3182**

GUERNSEY EVENING PRESS AND STAR. (UK). **5812**

GUERRES MONDIALES ET CONFLITS CONTEMPORAINS. (FR). **4045**

GUGONG XUESHU JIKAN. (CH/1011-9094). **351**

GUIA DE CONCURSOS : REVISTA DE INFORMACION CULTURAL Y LITERARIA. (SP). **3392**

GUIA DE LA INDUSTRIA ALIMENTARIA. (MX). **2343**

GUIA, EL. (SP). **321**

GUIDE DE LA MUSIQUE, LE. (BE). **4119**

GUIDE DE L'AUDIOVISUEL EUROPEEN, LE. (FR). **4071**

GUIDE DU PRODUCTEUR DE DISQUES, LE. (BE). **5317**

GUIDE TO AMERICAN DIRECTORIES. (US/0533-5248). **1926**

GUIDE TO AMERICAN EDUCATIONAL DIRECTORIES. (US/0072-8225). **1748**

GUIDE TO ELECTRONICS INDUSTRY IN INDIA. (II/0376-5229). **2056**

GUIDE TO FLORIDA RETIREMENT LIVING. (US/0889-051X). **5179**

GUIDE TO GEORGIA. (US/0434-8877). Qty: 12/yr. **5479**

GUIDE TO INDIAN PERIODICAL LITERATURE. (II/0017-5285). **416**

GUIDE TO JEWISH EUROPE. (US). **5479**

GUIDE TO JEWISH ITALY. (US). **5479**

GUIDE TO MICROFORMS IN PRINT. AUTHOR, TITLE. (GW/0164-0747). **416**

GUIDE TO NEW INDUSTRIAL POLICY OF GOVERNMENT OF INDIA. (II). **1608**

GUIDE TO PORT ENTRY. (UK). **5449**

GUIDE TO REAL ESTATE AND MORTGAGE BANKING SOFTWARE. (US). Qty: 10. **1286**

GUIDE TO SPRINGFIELD. (US). **2534**

GUIDE TO SUMMER CAMPS AND SUMMER SCHOOLS, THE. (US/0072-8705). **4850**

GUIDE TO THE AMERICAN LEFT (KANSAS CITY, MO. 1984). (US/0894-4547). **4502**

GUIDE TO THE ANTIQUE SHOPS OF BRITAIN. (UK). **250**

GUIDE TO THE CANADIAN FINANCIAL SERVICES INDUSTRY. (CN/0827-0864). **789**

GUIDE TO THE HOUSE OF COMMONS. (UK). **4475**

GUIDE TO THE MOTOR INDUSTRY OF JAPAN. (JA). **5415**

GUIDE (TORONTO). (CN/0533-5051). Qty: 1-3. **1676**

GUIDEBOOK - WEST TEXAS GEOLOGICAL SOCIETY. (US/0510-1387). **1382**

GUIDELINES FOR TODAY. (US/0891-1452). **4961**

GUIDEPOST (WASHINGTON, D.C.). (US/0017-5323). **4588**

GUIDES TO CONTEMPORARY ISSUES. (US). **2488**

GUILD (NEW YORK, N.Y.). (US/0885-3975). **373**

GUILD NOTES. (US/0148-0588). **4508**

GUILD OF BOOK WORKERS JOURNAL. (US/0434-9245). **4828**

GUION. (CK). **2488**

GUITAR CANADA. (CN/0830-8721). **4120**

GUITAR INTERNATIONAL. (UK). **4120**

GUITAR REVIEW, THE. (US/0017-5471). **4120**

GUJARAT STATISTICAL REVIEW. (II/0379-3419). **3542**

GUJARATA SAMSODHANA MANDALANUM TRAIMASIKA. (II). **2504**

GULDEN PASSER, DE. (BE). Qty: 1. **4570**

GULF COAST HISTORICAL REVIEW. (US/0892-9025). Qty: 30-40. **2735**

GULF COUNTY BREEZE. (US). **5649**

GULLET. (UK/0952-0643). **3579**

GULLIVER (BARI, ITALY). (IT). **1112**

GUMMI BEREIFUNG. (GW). **5075**

GUMMI, FASERN, KUNSTSTOFFE. (GW/0176-1625). **5076**

GUN DOG. (US/0279-5086). **4873**

GUN REPORT. (US/0017-5617). Qty: 12. **250**

GUN WORLD. (US/0017-5641). **4897**

GUNNER. (UK). Qty: 30. **4045**

GUNS CONTROL. (US). **3165**

GUNS REVIEW. (UK). **4897**

GUNZO. (JA). **3392**

GUOJI RIBAO. (US/0741-126X). Qty: 12. **5635**

GURNEE PRESS. (US/0745-810X). **5660**

GURU NANAK JOURNAL OF SOCIOLOGY. (II/0970-0242). **5246**

GUYANA CONSOLIDATED INDEX TO STATUTES AND SUBSIDIARY LEGISLATION TO 1ST JAN. .... . (US). **3081**

GUYANA LIBRARY ASSOCIATION BULLETIN. (GY). **3212**

GWIAZDA POLARNA. (US/0740-5944). Qty: 25. **5767**

GYMNASIUM (HEIDELBERG). (GW/0342-5231). **1077**

GYOSEI KANRI KENKYU. (JA). **4653**

GZ : GOLDSCHMIEDE UND UHRMACHER ZEITUNG. (GW). **2914**

H. G. WELLS NEWSLETTER, THE. (UK/0306-5480). **3392**

H + G ZEITSCHRIFT FUER HAUTKRANKHEITEN. (GW/0301-0481). **3720**

HA-SHILTH-SA. (CN/0715-4143). **5785**

HA'ARETZ. (IS). **5804**

HABITAT (FALMOUTH, ME.). (US/0739-2052). **2194**

HABITAT (LONDON). (UK/0028-9043). **2194**

HABITAT (MELBOURNE). (AT/0310-2939). **2194**

HABITAT NEWS. (KE/0251-7205). **2823**

HACK'D (WOODBRIDGE, VA.). (US/1055-033X). **4081**

HACTION. (CN/0714-7066). **5287**

HADASSAH MAGAZINE. (US/0017-6516). **5048**

HAEGI. (KO). **4176**

HAEMATOLOGIA. (HU/0017-6559). **3797**

HAEMATOLOGICA (ROMA). (IT/0390-6078). **3772**

HAEMOSTASEOLOGIE. (GW/0720-9355). **3580**

HAEUSER. (GW/0724-6528). **299**

HAFTEN FOR KRITISKA STUDIER. (SW/0345-4789). **4475**

HAIYANG YUYE. (CC/1004-2490). **2305**

HALF MOON BAY REVIEW AND PESCADERO PEBBLE. (US). **5635**

HALI. (UK/0142-0798). **5351**

HALIKSAI : U.N.M. CONTRIBUTIONS TO ANTHROPOLOGY. (US). **237**

HALLE YEARBOOK. (UK). **4120**

HALLEL CAPPOQUIN. (IE/0791-1513). Qty: 10-12. **5030**

HALSTAD VALLEY JOURNAL. (US). **5696**

HALVE MAEN, DE. (US/0017-6834). **2452**

HAMBROOK HERALD, THE. (CN/0821-5472). **2452**

HAMDARD ISLAMICUS. (PK/0250-7196). **5042**

HAMERSKY & ALLIED FAMILIES NEWSLETTER. (US/0882-4150). **2452**

HAMILTON LAWYER. (CN/1188-4827). Qty: 5-10. **2976**

HAMLET STUDIES. (II/0256-2480). Qty: 6. **3392**

HAMLINE LAW REVIEW. (US/0198-7364). **2976**

HAMMER & DOLLY. (US/1064-4822). **5416**

HAMMOND VINDICATOR, THE. (US). **5684**

HAN-GUK SUSAN HAKHOIJI. (KO/0374-8111). **2305**

HAN HSUEH YEN CHIU TUNG HSUN. (CH). **2504**

HANCOCK COUNTY COURIER (NEW CUMBERLAND, W. VA. : 1943). (US). Qty: 24. **5764**

HAND PAPERMAKING. (US/0887-1418). Qty: 4-6. **4234**

HANDBOOK - INTERNATIONAL CHAMBER OF COMMERCE. (FR/0378-049X). **820**

HANDBOOK OF CERTIFICATION/LICENSURE REQUIREMENTS FOR SCHOOL PSYCHOLOGISTS, THE. (US). **4588**

HANDBOOK OF OPTICAL MEMORY SYSTEMS & UPDATES. (US). **1185**

HANDBOOK OF PRIVATE SCHOOLS, THE. (US/0072-9884). **1749**

HANDBUCH DER DATENBANKEN FUER NATURWISSENSCHAFT, TECHNIK, PATENTE. (GW/0936-1375). **1185**

HANDBUCH DER PFLANZENANATOMIE. (GW). **512**

HANDCHIRURGIE, MIKROCHIRURGIE, PLASTISCHE CHIRURGIE. (GW/0722-1819). **3965**

HANDGUNNER. (UK/0260-8693). Qty: 6. **4898**

HANDLOADER. (US/0017-7393). **4898**

HANDMADE (ASHEVILLE, N.C.). (US/0275-9640). **5184**

HANDWOVEN. (US/0198-8212). **5351**

HANDY APPRAISAL CHART. (US/0891-2254). **616**

HANG GLIDING. (US/0895-433X). **4898**

HANG KUNG HSUEH PAO. (CC). **22**

HANGUK KIDIKKYO CHANGNOHOE HOEBO. (KO). **5061**

HANGUK KWA KUKCHE CHONGCHI. (KO). **4523**

HAN'GUK NONGHWA HAKHOE CHI. (KO/0368-2897). **91**

HANSA. (GW/0017-7504). **4177**

HANZAIGAKU ZASSHI. (JA/0302-0029). **3740**

HARAMBEE. (US). Qty: 1. **2262**

HARAS AL-WATANI (RIYADH, SAUDI ARABIA). (SU). **2504**

HARBOUR & SHIPPING. (CN/0017-7636). **5450**

HARBOUR, HARBOR, HARBER, AND WITT, WHITT, WHIT FAMILY ASSOCIATION BULLETIN. (US/0731-6968). **2452**

HARDIN COUNTY HISTORICAL QUARTERLY. (US/8755-6073). **2735**

HARDWICK GAZETTE, THE. (US/0744-5512). **5757**

HARLEY WOMEN. (US/0893-6447). Qty: 0-2. **4851**

HARPER'S (NEW YORK, N.Y.). (US/0017-789X). **3343**

HARPIES & QUINES. (UK/0966-2995). Qty: 30. **5558**

HARRIS INDIANA INDUSTRIAL DIRECTORY. (US/0888-8175). **1608**

HARRISON INDEPENDENT. (US/0892-4163). **5717**

HARRISONBURG DAILY NEWS RECORD. (US). Qty: 40. **5758**

HARROWSMITH (CANADIAN ED.). (CN/0381-6885). **2534**

HARRY BROWNE'S SPECIAL REPORTS. (US). **900**

HART BULLETIN. (NE/0301-8202). **3705**

HARTLEPOOL MAIL. (UK). **5812**

HARVARD ADVOCATE (CAMBRIDGE, MASS.), THE. (US/0017-8004). **3393**

HARVARD BUSINESS SCHOOL BULLETIN. (US/0017-8020). **679**

HARVARD CIVIL RIGHTS-CIVIL LIBERTIES LAW REVIEW. (US/0017-8039). **4508**

HARVARD CRIMSON, THE. (US). **5688**

HARVARD DIVINITY BULLETIN. (US/0017-8047). **4962**

HARVARD EDUCATIONAL REVIEW. (US/0017-8055). **1749**

HARVARD HUMAN RIGHTS JOURNAL. (US/1057-5057). **4508**

HARVARD INDEPENDENT, THE. (US). **1092**

HARVARD INTERNATIONAL LAW JOURNAL. (US/0017-8063). **3128**

HARVARD INTERNATIONAL REVIEW. (US/0739-1854). Qty: 8. **4523**

HARVARD JOURNAL OF ASIATIC STUDIES. (US/0073-0548). Qty: 15. **2652**

HARVARD JOURNAL OF LAW & PUBLIC POLICY. (US/0193-4872). Qty: 2. **2976**

HARVARD JOURNAL ON LEGISLATION. (US/0017-808X). **2977**

HARVARD LAW RECORD. (US/0017-8101). **2977**

HARVARD LAW REVIEW. (US/0017-811X). **2977**

HARVARD MAGAZINE. (US/0095-2427). **1092**

HARVARD MEDICAL ALUMNI BULLETIN. (US/0191-7757). **1102**

HARVARD POLITICAL REVIEW. (US/0090-1032). **4475**

HARVARD REVIEW. (US). Qty: 130. **3393**

HARVARD SEMITIC MONOGRAPHS. (US/0073-0637). **5016**

HARVARD UKRAINIAN STUDIES. (US/0363-5570). **2690**

HARVARD WOMEN'S LAW JOURNAL. (US/0270-1456). **2977**

HARVEST (PORT MORESBY). (PP/0378-8865). **91**

HARVESTER, THE. (UK/0017-8217). **5017**

HASKELL COUNTY MONITOR-CHIEF, THE. (US). Qty: 5-10. **5676**

HASSADEH. (IS/0017-8314). **91**

HASSELBLAD FORUM. (SW/0282-5449). **4370**

HASTINGS CENTER REPORT, THE. (US/0093-0334). **3580**

HASTINGS COMMUNICATIONS AND ENTERTAINMENT LAW JOURNAL (COMM/ENT). (US/1061-6578). Qty: 1-3 per year. **2977**

HASTINGS CONSTITUTIONAL LAW QUARTERLY. (US/0094-5617). Qty: 1-3 per year. **3093**

HASTINGS HERALD (SPOKANE, WASH.). (US/0898-543X). **2452**

HASTINGS INTERNATIONAL AND COMPARATIVE LAW REVIEW. (US/0149-9246). Qty: 1-3. **3129**

HASTINGS LAW JOURNAL. (US/0017-8322). **Qty:** 1-3. **2977**

HASTINGS WOMEN'S LAW JOURNAL. (US/1061-0901). **Qty:** 102 per year. **2977**

HATTIESBURG AMERICAN. (US). **5700**

HAUSFRAU, MONATSSCHRIFT FUR DIE FRAUENWELT AMERIKAS, DIE. (US/0017-842X). **2517**

HAUSTECHNISCHE RUNDSCHAU. (GW/0017-8438). **616**

HAUSWIRTSCHAFT UND WISSENSCHAFT. (GW/0017-8454). **2790**

HAUTARZT. (GW/0017-8470). **3720**

HAVANA HERALD. (US). **Qty:** 10. **5649**

HAWAII BAR JOURNAL MICROFORM. (US). **2977**

HAWAII BUSINESS DIRECTORY. (US). **679**

HAWAII HERALD (1969). (US/8750-913X). **2262**

HAWAII MEDICAL JOURNAL (1962). (US/0017-8594). **Qty:** 2-3. **3581**

HAWAII REVIEW. (US/0093-9625). **3393**

HAWAII, THE BIG ISLAND UPDATE. (US/1042-8046). **5479**

HAWAIIAN JOURNAL OF HISTORY, THE. (US/0440-5145). **2669**

HAWAIIAN SHELL NEWS. (US/0017-8624). **1449**

HAWK EYE, THE. (US). **5670**

HAWK : THE INDEPENDENT JOURNAL OF THE ROYAL AIR STAFF COLLEGE. (UK). **Qty:** apporx. 6. **22**

HAY DRAMAGITAKAN HANDES. (US/0884-0180). **2781**

HAYES DRUGGIST DIRECTORY. (US). **4306**

HAYES HISTORICAL JOURNAL: A JOURNAL OF THE GILDED AGE. (US/0364-5924). **Qty:** 8. **2736**

HAZ-MAT TECHNOLOGY. (US/0888-6849). **4777**

HAZARD HERALD-VOICE. (US). **5681**

HAZARD PREVENTION. (US/0743-8826). **2862**

HAZARD TIMES, THE. (US/0883-752X). **5681**

HAZARDOUS CARGO BULLETIN. (UK/0143-6864). **5450**

HAZARDS. (UK/0267-7296). **2862**

HAZARD'S PAVILION. (US/0892-6913). **4121**

HAZMAT WORLD. (US/0898-5685). **2232**

HB. HOOSIER BANKER. (US/0018-473X). **790**

HE HUAXUE YU FANGSHE HUAXUE. (CC/0253-9950). **976**

HEAD INJURY UPDATE. (US/0887-1779). **Qty:** 12. **3965**

HEAD OFFICE AT HOME. (CN/1183-6709). **679**

HEADACHE. (US/0017-8748). **3833**

HEADACHE QUARTERLY. (US/1059-7565). **3833**

HEADLINES. (UK/0957-8714). **Qty:** 6 per issue. **1864**

HEAD'S LETTER, THE. (US/1044-6389). **Qty:** varies. **1750**

HEALDSBURG TRIBUNE-ENTERPRISE AND SCIMITAR. (US/0017-8810). **5635**

HEALING HAND, THE. (UK). **Qty:** 2-3. **4962**

HEALING (SACRAMENTO, CALIF.). (US/1064-4237). **4777**

HEALTH AFFAIRS (MILLWOOD, VA.). (US/0278-2715). **4777**

HEALTH AND HYGIENE (LONDON). (UK/0140-2986). **Qty:** 20-25. **4777**

HEALTH & NUTRITION UPDATE. (CN/0831-8530). **4191**

HEALTH AND POPULATION. PERSPECTIVES AND ISSUES. (SZ/0253-6803). **4777**

HEALTH & SAFETY AT WORK (CROYDON). (UK/0141-8246). **2862**

HEALTH AND SAFETY COMMISSION NEWSLETTER. (UK). **Qty:** 60. **4777**

HEALTH & SAFETY MONITOR. (UK/0140-8534). **2862**

HEALTH & SOCIAL WORK. (US/0360-7283). **5287**

HEALTH BULLETIN (EDINBURGH). (UK/0374-8014). **4778**

HEALTH CARE FINANCING REVIEW. (US/0195-8631). **2897**

HEALTH CARE FOR WOMEN INTERNATIONAL. (US/0739-9332). **3762**

HEALTH CARE LABOR MANUAL. (US/0095-3792). **1676**

HEALTH CARE MANAGEMENT REVIEW. (US/0361-6274). **3781**

HEALTH CARE PARLIAMENTARY MONITOR. (UK). **3581**

HEALTH CARE STRATEGIC MANAGEMENT. (US/0742-1478). **3781**

HEALTH CARE SUPERVISOR, THE. (US/0731-3381). **3781**

HEALTH CITY SUN. (US). **Qty:** 20. **5712**

HEALTH CONSCIOUSNESS (OVIEDO, FLA.). (US/0895-9986). **Qty:** 30-40. **4779**

HEALTH DEVICES. (US/0046-7022). **3581**

HEALTH ECONOMICS. (US/1057-9230). **4779**

HEALTH EDUCATION JOURNAL, THE. (UK/0017-8969). **2598**

HEALTH EDUCATION RESEARCH. (UK/0268-1153). **4779**

HEALTH ESTATE JOURNAL : JOURNAL OF THE INSTITUTE OF HOSPITAL ENGINEERING. (UK/0957-7742). **3781**

HEALTH FACILITIES ENERGY REPORT. (US/0272-8443). **1946**

HEALTH FACT NEWS. (US/0279-5639). **2598**

HEALTH FACTS. (US/0738-811X). **Qty:** on occasion. **4779**

HEALTH FOODS BUSINESS. (US/0149-9602). **2343**

HEALTH FOR THE MILLIONS. (II/0970-8685). **4779**

HEALTH FORUM. (AT/1030-6072). **Qty:** 20. **4779**

HEALTH FUNDS DEVELOPMENT LETTER. (US/0193-7928). **3581**

HEALTH INFORMATION AND LIBRARIES. (HU/0864-991X). **3213**

HEALTH MANAGEMENT QUARTERLY. (US/0891-3250). **3781**

HEALTH MARKETING QUARTERLY. (US/0735-9683). **3582**

HEALTH NEWS & REVIEW. (US/1056-1900). **4191**

HEALTH/PAC BULLETIN. (US/0017-9051). **4780**

HEALTH POLICY AND PLANNING. (UK/0268-1080). **4780**

HEALTH PROGRESS (SAINT LOUIS, MO.). (US/0882-1577). **3781**

HEALTH PROMOTION INTERNATIONAL. (UK/0957-4824). **4781**

HEALTH PROMOTION JOURNAL OF AUSTRALIA. (AT/1036-1073). **3582**

HEALTH PROMOTION PRACTITIONER. (US/1060-5517). **Qty:** 12. **4781**

HEALTH SCIENCE (1985). (US/0883-8216). **4781**

HEALTH SERVICE JOURNAL, THE. (UK/0952-2271). **4781**

HEALTH SERVICES INTERNATIONAL. (UK/1011-5153). **4781**

HEALTH SERVICES MANAGEMENT. (UK/0953-8534). **3781**

HEALTH SERVICES MANAGEMENT RESEARCH : AN OFFICIAL JOURNAL OF THE ASSOCIATION OF UNIVERSITY PROGRAMS IN HEALTH ADMINISTRATION. (UK/0951-4848). **3781**

HEALTH VALUES. (US/0147-0353). **Qty:** 18 /yr. **4782**

HEALTH VISITOR : THE JOURNAL OF THE HEALTH VISITORS' ASSOCIATION. (UK/0017-9140). **3856**

HEALTH WORLD. (US/0888-7330). **4782**

HEALTH YOURSELF. (AT). **Qty:** 2-6. **2598**

HEALTHCARE COMMUNITY RELATIONS & MARKETING LETTER. (US/0894-9980). **3583**

HEALTHCARE FINANCIAL MANAGEMENT. (US/0735-0732). **3782**

HEALTHCARE INFORMATICS. (US/1050-9135). **3782**

HEALTHCARE INFORMATION MANAGEMENT. (US). **3782**

HEALTHCARE MARKETING ABSTRACTS. (US/0891-5016). **925**

HEALTHLINES (ANN ARBOR, MICH.). (US/8756-453X). **Qty:** 12. **4782**

HEALTHLINES (WACO, TEX.). (US/1048-5562). **Qty:** 5. **4782**

HEALTHSHARING. (CN/0226-1510). **Qty:** 4-6. **4782**

HEALTHSPAN. (US/0883-0452). **3740**

HEALTHY HORIZONS. (CN/0823-7352). **2343**

HEARING HEALTH. (US/0888-2517). **Qty:** 2-3. **1297**

HEARING INSTRUMENTS. (US/0092-4466). **3888**

HEARING JOURNAL, THE. (US/0745-7472). **3888**

HEARING REHABILITATION QUARTERLY. (US/0360-9278). **4388**

HEART & LUNG. (US/0147-9563). **3856**

HEART LONDON. 1987. (UK/0953-0495). **3705**

HEART OF TEXAS RECORDS. (US/0093-9854). **2452**

HEARTLAND BOATING. (US/1042-1009). **Qty:** 6. **593**

HEAT TRANSFER ENGINEERING. (US/0145-7632). **2012**

HEAT TREATMENT OF METALS. (UK/0305-4829). **4003**

HEATHER SOCIETY BULLETIN, THE. (UK). **5231**

HEAVY HORSE WORLD. (UK/0951-2640). **Qty:** 8. **2799**

HEAVY METAL. (US/0885-7822). **3393**

HEBREW STUDIES. (US/0146-4094). **Qty:** 30-50. **5048**

HECATE. (AT/0311-4198). **Qty:** 2-10. **5558**

HEENSCHUT. (NE/0017-9515). **Qty:** 30-40. **299**

HEILIGER DIENST. (AU/0017-9620). **4962**

HEILPADAGOGISCHE FORSCHUNG. (GW). **1750**

HEIMEN. (NO/0017-9841). **2690**

HEIR-LINES (LAKE ORION, MICH.). (US/0739-6082). **Qty:** 5-6. **2452**

HEISEY NEWS. (US/0731-8014). **2590**

HEJNA. (US/0748-7568). **2262**

HELGOLAENDER MEERESUNTERSUCHUNGEN. (GW/0174-3597). **554**

HELICOPTER NEWS. (US/0363-8227). **23**

HELICOPTER WORLD (LONDON. 1982). (UK/0262-0448). **23**

HELICOPTERS. (CN/0227-3160). **23**

HELICTITE. (AT/0017-9973). **5109**

HELIKON. (HU/0017-999X). **3393**

HELINIUM. (BE/0018-0009). **2690**

HELIOS (LUBBOCK). (US/0160-0923). **1077**

HELMANTICA. (SP/0018-0114). **1077**

HELPER (AMERICAN SOCIAL HEALTH ASSOCIATION). (US). **4782**

HELR. THE HARVARD ENVIRONMENTAL LAW REVIEW. (US/0147-8257). **3113**

HELSINGIN SANOMAT. (FI/0355-2047). **5800**

HELVETICA CHIRURGICA ACTA. (SZ/0018-0181). **3903**

HEMATOLOGICAL ONCOLOGY. (UK/0278-0232). **3772**

HEMET NEWS, THE. (US). **5635**

HEMINGWAY REVIEW, THE. (US/0276-3362). **3344**

HEMISPHERE (MIAMI, FLA.). (US/0898-3038). **4475**

HEMOGLOBIN. (US/0363-0269). **3797**

HEMOPHILIA ONTARIO. (CN/0822-5974). **3772**

HEMPSTEAD TRAILS. (US). **2453**

HENCEFORTH. (US/0895-7622). **Qty:** 5-10. **4962**

HENCKEL GENEALOGICAL BULLETIN. (US/0739-6341). **2453**

HENDERSON HOME NEWS. (US). **5707**

HENRY JAMES REVIEW, THE. (US/0273-0340). **3344**

HEP HIGHER EDUCATION DIRECTORY, THE. (US/0736-0797). **1827**

HEPATOLOGY. (GW/0171-6123). **3797**

HER WORLD ANNUAL. (SI). **5558**

HERALD AND TRIBUNE (JONESBORO, TENN. : 1869). (US). **Qty:** 5. **5745**

HERALD-CHRONICLE (WINCHESTER, TENN.), THE. (US/0893-3707). **Qty:** 12. **5745**

HERALD-CITIZEN (COOKEVILLE, TENN.). (US/8750-5541). **Qty:** 50. **5745**

HERALD-COASTER, THE. (US). **5750**

HERALD (CONROE, TEX.), THE. (US/0730-6520). **2453**

HERALD-DISPATCH (LOS ANGELES, CALIF. : 1981). (US/8750-2038). **5635**

HERALD OF LIBRARY SCIENCE. (II/0018-0521). **Qty:** 22. **3213**

HERALD (RINCON, GA.), THE. (US/0899-627X). **Qty:** 5. **5654**

HERALD-STANDARD (UNIONTOWN, PA. : 1980). (US). **Qty:** 4. **5736**

HERALD-STAR, THE. (US/0890-8656). **5728**

HERALD, THE. (PK). **2504**

HERALD, THE. (US). **5645**

HERALD, THE. (US). **Qty:** 15. **5660**

HERALDRY IN CANADA. (CN/0441-6619). **2453**

HERALDRY, THE ARMIGER'S NEWS. (US). **2453**

HERANCA JUDAICA. (BL). **5048**

HERB QUARTERLY, THE. (US/0163-9900). **Qty:** 20. **2418**

HERB, SPICE, AND MEDICINAL PLANT DIGEST, THE. (US/1048-3160). **Qty:** 4-5. **2418**

HERBALGRAM (AUSTIN, TEX.). (US/0899-5648). **512**

HERBARIUM NEWS. (US/0731-7824). **512**

HERBERTIA (1984). (US/8756-9418). **2418**

HERD BOOK - BRITISH GOAT SOCIETY. (UK). **195**

HEREDITY. (UK/0018-067X). **547**

HERITAGE (AUSTIN, TEX.). (US/1047-5613). **2736**

HERITAGE (CARSON, CALIF.). (US/0895-0792). **2262**

HERITAGE OUTLOOK. (UK/0261-1988). **300**

HERITAGE REVIEW. (US/0162-8267). **2690**

HERITAGE SCOTLAND : THE MAGAZINE OF THE NATIONAL TRUST FOR SCOTLAND. (UK/0264-9144). **2690**

HERITAGE SEEKERS. (CN/0707-0780). **Qty:** varies. **2453**

HERIZONS. (CN/0711-7485). **Qty:** 20. **5558**

HERMATHENA. (IE/0018-0750). **4348**

HERMES AMERICANUS. (US/0741-1286). **3285**

HERODOTE. (FR/0338-487X). **2565**

HERPETOFAUNA. (AT). **5585**

HERPETOFAUNA NEWS. (UK/0269-8498). **5585**

HERPETOLOGICA. (US/0018-0831). **5585**

HERPETOLOGICAL JOURNAL, THE. (UK/0268-0130). **5585**

HERPETOLOGICAL REVIEW. (US/0018-084X). **5585**

HERPETOLOGY (PASADENA). (US/0441-666X). **5585**

HERS NEWSLETTER. (US/0892-628X). **3762**

HERTFORDSHIRE PEOPLE. (UK/0309-913X). **2453**

HERVORMDE TEOLOGIESE STUDIES. (SA). **4962**

HERVORMER, DIE. (SA). **4962**

HETEROFONIA. (MX/0018-1137). **4121**

HETI VILAGGAZDASAG : HVG. (HU/0139-1682). **1635**

HEURISTICS (ROCKVILLE, MD.). (US/1040-6433). **Qty:** 4. **1229**

HEVRAH U-REVAHAH. (IS). **5287**

HEYTHROP JOURNAL. (UK/0018-1196). **5030**

HI-RISE. (CN/0715-5948). **2534**

HIBALLER FOREST MAGAZINE. (CN/0708-2169). **2384**

HIBOU (ST-LAMBERT). (CN/0709-9177). **1064**

HIDDEN VALLEY JOURNAL. (US/0741-4773). **2453**

HIDUP. (IO/0377-9610). **5030**

HIGDON FAMILY NEWSLETTER. (US/0739-3199). **2453**

HIGH COLOR. (US/1060-5282). **Qty:** 120. **1233**

HIGH COUNTRY NEWS. (US/0191-5657). **2195**

HIGH FLIGHT. (CN/0708-4331). **23**

HIGH FRONTIER NEWSWATCH. (US/0892-5674). **Qty:** 4. **4045**

HIGH INTEGRITY SYSTEMS. (UK/0967-2648). **1247**

HIGH PERFORMANCE (LOS ANGELES). (US/0160-9769). **385**

HIGH PERFORMANCE REVIEW. (US/0277-1357). **5317**

HIGH PLAINS APPLIED ANTHROPOLOGIST. (US/0882-4894). **237**

HIGH PLAINS LITERARY REVIEW. (US/0888-4153). **Qty:** 6. **3344**

HIGH ROLLER. (US/0197-6044). **3213**

HIGH SCOPE RESOURCE. (US/0887-2007). **1750**

HIGH TEMPERATURE SCIENCE. (US/0018-1536). **1052**

HIGH TEMPERATURES - HIGH PRESSURES. (UK/0018-1544). **4431**

HIGH TIMBER TIMES. (US). **5643**

HIGH VOLUME PRINTING. (US/0737-1020). **4565**

HIGHER EDUCATION. (NE/0018-1560). **1828**

HIGHER EDUCATION DIRECTORY. (US/0740-9230). **1828**

HIGHER EDUCATION IN EUROPE. (RM/0379-7724). **1828**

HIGHER EDUCATION MANAGEMENT (PARIS, FRANCE). (FR/1013-851X). **1828**

HIGHER EDUCATION POLICY. (UK/0952-8733). **1828**

HIGHER EDUCATION RESEARCH AND DEVELOPMENT. (AT/0729-4360). **1828**

HIGHER EDUCATION REVIEW. (UK/0018-1609). **1828**

HIGHLAND HERITAGE. (CN/0707-2554). **2453**

HIGHLANDER (BARRINGTON), THE. (US/0161-5378). **Qty:** 10 per year. **2262**

HIGHLANDER, THE. (US). **5750**

HIGHLANDS PRESS. (US). **5650**

HIGHLIGHT QUEBEC. (CN/0825-4850). **4963**

HIGHWAY & VEHICLE SAFETY REPORT. (US/0161-0325). **5440**

HIKAKU TOSHISHI KENKYU. (JA). **2824**

HILBORN FAMILY JOURNAL. (CN/0707-3836). **2453**

HILLSBORO ARGUS (HILLSBORO, OR.). (US/8750-5479). **Qty:** 5. **5733**

HIMALAYAN INSTITUTE QUARTERLY GUIDE TO PROGRAMS AND OTHER OFFERINGS. (US/0891-6144). **4348**

HIMALAYAN JOURNAL, THE. (II). **4873**

HIMALAYAN PLANT JOURNAL. (II). **2418**

HIMALAYAN RESEARCH BULLETIN. (US/0891-4834). **5652**

HIMICESKIE VOLOKNA. (RU/0023-1118). **4455**

HINDU-CHRISTIAN STUDIES BULLETIN. (CN/0844-4587). **Qty:** 8-15. **5041**

HINDU (MADRAS, INDIA : DAILY). (II). **5803**

HINDUSTAN ANTIBIOTICS BULLETIN. (II/0018-1935). **4306**

HINDUSTAN YEAR-BOOK AND WHO'S WHO. (II/0970-1168). **5012**

HIRAM POETRY REVIEW, THE. (US/0018-2036). **3464**

HIRURGIJA (MOSKVA). (RU/0023-1207). **3965**

HIS DOMINION (REGINA). (CN/0229-7175). **4963**

HISLA. (PE). **1565**

HISPALIS MEDICA. (SP/0018-2125). **3584**

HISPAMERICA (COLLEGE PARK). (US/0363-0471). **3394**

HISPANIA. (US/0018-2133). **3285**

HISPANIA (MADRID). (SP/0018-2141). **2690**

HISPANIA SACRA. (SP/0018-215X). **5030**

HISPANIC AMERICAN ARTS. (UY/0738-5625). **321**

HISPANIC AMERICAN HISTORICAL REVIEW, THE. (US/0018-2168). **2262**

HISPANIC AMERICAN PERIODICALS INDEX (LOS ANGELES, CALIF.). (US/0270-8558). **2496**

HISPANIC BOOKS BULLETIN. (US/0894-2358). **4828**

HISPANIC BUSINESS. (US/0199-0349). **679**

HISPANIC JOURNAL. (US/0271-0986). **3394**

HISPANIC JOURNAL OF BEHAVIORAL SCIENCES. (US/0739-9863). **2262**

HISPANIC LINGUISTICS. (US/0742-5287). **3285**

HISPANIC LINK. (US). **2262**

HISPANIC LINK WEEKLY REPORT. (US). **Qty:** 50. **2262**

HISPANIC REVIEW. (US/0018-2176). **3285**

HISPANIC TIMES MAGAZINE. (US/0892-1369). **4204**

HISPANIC (WASHINGTON, D.C.). (US/0898-3097). **2262**

HISPANO NEWS, EL. (US). **Qty:** 20. **2263**

HISPANOFILA. (US/0018-2206). **3394**

HISTOCHEMICAL JOURNAL. (UK/0018-2214). **536**

HISTOIRE DE L'EDUCATION. (FR/0221-6280). **1750**

HISTOIRE DES SCIENCES MEDICALES. (FR/0440-8888). **3584**

HISTOIRE, L'. (FR/0182-2411). **2617**

HISTOIRE SOCIALE. (CN/0018-2257). **Qty:** 65. **5201**

HISTOPATHOLOGY. (UK/0309-0167). **3894**

HISTORIA CRITICA (BOGOTA, COLOMBIA). (CK). **Qty:** 6. **2736**

HISTORIA MEDICINAE VETERINARIAE. (DK/0105-1423). **5511**

HISTORIA MEXICANA. (MX/0185-0172). **2736**

HISTORIA, QUESTOES & DEBATES. (BL/0100-6932). **2736**

HISTORIA (SANTIAGO). (CL/0073-2435). **2736**

HISTORIA (THREE RIVERS). (SA/0018-229X). **Qty:** 20. **2640**

HISTORIA Y CULTURA (LIMA). (PE/0073-2486). **2617**

HISTORIAN (KINGSTON), THE. (US/0018-2370). **2618**

HISTORIC BRASS SOCIETY JOURNAL. (US/1045-4616). **Qty:** 10-20. **4121**

HISTORIC BRASS SOCIETY NEWSLETTER. (US/1045-4594). **Qty:** 10-20. **4121**

HISTORIC CLAY TOBACCO PIPE STUDIES. (US/0747-8801). **269**

HISTORIC HOUSES, CASTLES, AND GARDENS IN GREAT BRITAIN AND IRELAND. (UK/0073-2567). **2691**

HISTORICA (CESKOSLOVENSKA AKADEMIE VED. SEKCE HISTORICKA). (XR/0440-9205). **2691**

HISTORICA (LIMA). (PE/0252-8894). **2737**

HISTORICAL ARCHAEOLOGY. (US/0440-9213). **269**

HISTORICAL GENEALOGICAL MAGAZINE SPECIALIZING IN CLINTON AND BOONE COUNTIES. (US/1064-041X). **Qty:** 1-2. **2453**

HISTORICAL GEOGRAPHY. (US). **2565**

HISTORICAL JOURNAL (CAMBRIDGE, CAMBRIDGESHIRE). (UK/0018-246X). **2618**

HISTORICAL JOURNAL OF FILM, RADIO, AND TELEVISION. (UK/0143-9685). **4071**

HISTORICAL JOURNAL OF MASSACHUSETTS. (US/0276-8313). **2737**

HISTORICAL METALLURGY. (UK/0142-3304). **4003**

HISTORICAL METHODS. (US/0161-5440). **5201**

HISTORICAL NEW HAMPSHIRE. (US/0018-2508). **2737**

HISTORICAL NEWS. (NZ/0439-2345). **2618**

HISTORICAL PERFORMANCE. (US/0898-8587). **4121**

HISTORICAL REVIEW. (NZ/0018-2516). **Qty:** varies. **2669**

HISTORICAL REVIEW OF BERKS COUNTY. (US/0018-2524). **2737**

HISTORICAL SOCIAL RESEARCH (KOLN). (GW/0172-6404). **5246**

HISTORICAL STUDIES IN EDUCATION. (CN/0843-5057). **Qty:** 80. **1750**

HISTORICAL STUDIES IN THE PHYSICAL AND BIOLOGICAL SCIENCES. (US/0890-9997). **4404**

HISTORICKY CASOPIS. (XO/0018-2575). **2691**

HISTORIE; JYSKE SAMLINGER. (DK). **2691**

HISTORIGRAM. (CN/0821-1469). **Qty:** 2. **2737**

HISTORISCH GEOGRAFISCH TIJDSCHRIFT. (NE/0167-9775). **Qty:** 20-25. **2565**

HISTORISCH-POLITISCHE BUCH, DAS. (GW/0018-2605). **2618**

HISTORISCHE ZEITSCHRIFT. (GW/0018-2613). **2619**

HISTORISCHE ZEITSCHRIFT. SONDERHEFT. (GW/0440-971X). **2619**

HISTORISCHES JAHRBUCH. (GW/0018-2621). **2619**

HISTORISCHES JAHRBUCH DER STADT LINZ. (AU/0440-9736). **2691**

HISTORISK TIDSKRIFT FOR FINLAND. (FI/0046-7596). **2691**

HISTORISK TIDSKRIFT (STOCKHOLM). (SW/0345-469X). **Qty:** 50. **2691**

HISTORISK TIDSSKRIFT. (NO/0018-263x). **2691**

HISTORISK TIDSSKRIFT. (DK). **2691**

HISTORY AND ANTHROPOLOGY. (SZ/0275-7206). **237**

HISTORY & COMPUTING. (UK/0957-0144). **1186**

HISTORY AND TECHNOLOGY. (SZ/0734-1512). **5110**

HISTORY AND THEORY. (US/0018-2656). **2635**

HISTORY IN AFRICA. (US/0361-5413). **2640**

HISTORY (LONDON). (UK/0018-2648). **2619**

HISTORY MICROCOMPUTER REVIEW. (US/0887-1078). **2619**

HISTORY OF ECONOMIC THOUGHT NEWSLETTER. (UK/0440-9884). **Qty:** 15. **1592**

HISTORY OF EDUCATION QUARTERLY. (US/0018-2680). **1750**

HISTORY OF EDUCATION SOCIETY BULLETIN. (UK/0018-2699). **1750**

HISTORY OF HIGHER EDUCATION ANNUAL. (US/0737-2698). **1829**

HISTORY OF PHILOSOPHY QUARTERLY. (US/0740-0675). **4348**

HISTORY OF POLITICAL ECONOMY. (US/0018-2702). **1565**

HISTORY OF POLITICAL THOUGHT. (UK/0143-781X). **4476**

HISTORY OF RELIGIONS. (US/0018-2710). **4963**

HISTORY OF SCIENCE. (UK/0073-2753). **5110**

HISTORY OF THE GENEVA BIBLE. (UK). **5017**

HISTORY OF UNIVERSITIES. (UK/0144-5138). **1829**

HISTORY OF WOMEN RELIGIOUS NEWS AND NOTES. (US/1054-545X). **Qty:** varies. **4963**

HISTORY TEACHER (LONG BEACH, CALIF.), THE. (US/0018-2745). **1896**

HISTORY TODAY. (UK/0018-2753). **2619**

HISTORY (WASHINGTON). (US/0361-2759). **2619**

HISTORY WORKSHOP. (UK/0309-2984). **2619**

HITCHCOCK ANNUAL. (US/1062-5518). **4072**

HITOTSUBASHI RONSO. (JA/0018-2818). **5201**

HLABC FORUM. (CN/0826-0125). **3213**

HLI REPORT. (US/0899-2673). **2280**

HMO PRACTICE. (US/0891-6624). **Qty:** 12. **5287**

HOBBES STUDIES. (NE/0921-5891). **4348**

HOBBY GREENHOUSE. (US/1040-6212). **Qty:** 20. **2418**

HOBBY MERCHANDISER (NEW YORK, N.Y.). (US/0744-1738). **2774**

HOCKEY DIGEST (EVANSTON, ILL.). (US/0046-7693). **4899**

HOCKEY NEWS, THE. (CN/0018-3016). **4899**

HOFSTRA ENVIRONMENTAL LAW DIGEST. (US/0882-6765). **3113**

HOFSTRA LAW REVIEW. (US/0091-4029). **2978**

HOGAKU. (US/0886-1862). **4121**

HOHLE, DIE. (AU/0018-3091). **1356**

HOKHMAH. (SZ/0379-7465). **5061**

HOKUBEI HOCHI. (US/8756-6451). **Qty:** 60. **5761**

HOLDSWORTH LAW REVIEW / UNIVERSITY OF BIRMINGHAM. (UK). **2979**

HOLE. (CN/1180-1670). **3394**

HOLISTIC EDUCATION REVIEW. (US/0898-0926). **1751**

HOLISTIC MASSAGE. (US/0748-6855). **2598**

HOLISTIC MEDICINE (SEATTLE, WASH.). (US/0898-6029). **3584**

HOLLAND HERALD. (NE). **2517**

HOLLAND SENTINEL (1977), THE. (US/1050-4044). **Qty:** varies. **5692**

HOLLANDSE KRANT. (CN/0837-1342). **Qty:** 6. **2263**

HOLLINS CRITIC, THE. (US/0018-3644). **3344**

HOLLYWOOD MAGAZINE. (US/1045-361X). **2488**

HOLOCENE (SEVENOAKS). (UK/0959-6836). **1382**

HOLOGRAPHICS INTERNATIONAL. (UK/0951-3914). **4434**

HOLSTON PASTFINDER. (US/0887-3135). **Qty:** 8. **2453**

HOLY LAND. (US). **4963**

HOLZ ALS ROH- UND WERKSTOFF. (GW/0018-3768). **2401**

HOLZ-KUNSTSTOFF. (GW). **2401**

HOLZ-ZENTRALBLATT. (GW/0018-3792). **2384**

HOLZFORSCHUNG. (GW/0018-3830). **2401**

HOLZFORSCHUNG UND HOLZVERWERTUNG. (AU/0018-3849). **2401**

HOLZZUCHT, DIE. (GW/0437-7168). **2384**

HOME-BASED & SMALL BUSINESS NETWORK. (US/1067-7739). **Qty:** 4. **680**

HOME BUSINESS ADVOCATE, THE. (CN/0832-8595). **Qty:** 20/yr. **680**

HOME CARE TODAY. (CN/0847-2378). **5288**

HOME ECONOMICS. (UK). **2791**

HOME ECONOMIST, THE. (UK). **2791**

HOME ENERGY (BERKELEY, CALIF.). (US/0896-9442). **Qty:** 1-6. **1946**

HOME FURNISHINGS EXECUTIVE (GREENSBORO, N.C.). (US/1073-5585). **2906**

HOME HEALTH CARE SERVICES QUARTERLY. (US/0162-1424). **5288**

HOME HEALTH JOURNAL. (US/0734-7588). **3584**

HOME HEALTHCARE NURSE. (US/0884-741X). **3856**

HOME LIFE (NASHVILLE). (US/0018-4071). **5061**

HOME PLANET NEWS. (US/0273-303X). **Qty:** 16-44. **3394**

HOME PLANS GUIDE. (US/0899-4374). **300**

HOME PLANS TO BUILD. (US/0899-4366). **300**

HOME POWER. (US/1050-2416). **Qty:** 4-6. **1946**

HOME SCHOOL RESEARCHER. (US/1054-8033). **1751**

HOME SHOP MACHINIST, THE. (US/0744-6640). **2115**

HOMECARE (LOS ANGELES, CALIF.). (US/0882-2700). **5288**

HOMEHEALTH MAGAZINE. (US/0883-0835). **4783**

HOMEMAKER OF THE NATIONAL EXTENSION HOMEMAKERS COUNCIL, THE. (US/0146-9487). **2791**

HOMEOWNER, THE. (US/0747-3176). **616**

HOMESTEAD (KENTVILLE). (CN/0712-6476). **5786**

HOMETOWN PRESS. (US/1064-1742). **2534**

HOMILETIC. (US/0738-0534). **Qty:** 50-75/yr. **4963**

HOMILETIC & PASTORAL REVIEW. (US/0018-4268). **5030**

HOMILETICS (NORTH CANTON, OHIO). (US/1040-6255). **4963**

HOMINES. (PR/0252-8908). **5201**

HOMME. (FR/0439-4216). **237**

HOMO. (GW/0018-442X). **237**

HONDURAS ROTARIA. (HO). **680**

HONDURAS UPDATE. (US/0741-8167). **2512**

HONEY HOLE. (US/0895-4046). **Qty:** 1. **4899**

HONG KONG GOVERNMENT GAZETTE, THE. (HK). **4654**

HONG KONG JOURNAL OF BUSINESS MANAGEMENT. (HK). **Qty:** 1. **869**

HONG KONG MONTHLY DIGEST OF STATISTICS. (HK/0300-418X). **4698**

HONOLULU STAR-BULLETIN. (US). **Qty:** 50-75. **5656**

HONOLULU WEEKLY. (US/1057-414X). **Qty:** 10. **5656**

HOOF BEATS (COLUMBUS, OHIO). (US/0018-4683). **2799**

HOOFBEATS. (AT/0811-8698). **Qty:** Varies. **2799**

HOOFPRINTS FROM THE YELLOWSTONE CORRAL OF THE WESTERNERS. (US/0742-7727). **2738**

HOOK (BONITA, CALIF.), THE. (US/0736-9220). **4177**

HOOKER'S ICONES PLANTARIUM. (UK). **513**

HOOKUP. (US). **2305**

HOOSHARAR. (US/0018-4721). **2263**

HOOSIER JOURNAL OF ANCESTRY, THE. (US/0147-1228). **2454**

HOOSIER OUTDOORS. (US/0018-4780). **4873**

HOPKINS QUARTERLY. (CN/0094-9086). **3344**

HOPSCOTCH (SARATOGA SPRINGS, N.Y.). (US/1044-0488). **1064**

HORA DE POESIA. (SP/0212-9442). **3464**

HORECO. (SP). **5071**

HOREN : JUNGER LITERATURKREIS, DIE. (GW/0018-4942). **3394**

HORIZONS (GAMBRILLS, MD.). (US/1064-6434). **4388**

HORIZONS IN BIBLICAL THEOLOGY. (US/0195-9085). **5017**

HORIZONS (OAKVILLE). (CN/0712-6077). **4963**

HORIZONS SF. (CN/0229-1215). **3394**

HORIZONS (VILLANOVA). (US/0360-9669). **4963**

HORMONE RESEARCH. (SZ/0301-0163). **3730**

HORN BOOK GUIDE TO CHILDREN'S AND YOUNG ADULT BOOKS, THE. (US/1044-405X). **1064**

HORN BOOK MAGAZINE (1945), THE. (US/0018-5078). **1064**

HORN CALL, THE. (US/0046-7928). **4121**

HORN OF AFRICA. (US/0161-4703). **2640**

HORNBILL. (II). **457**

HORNERO, EL. (AG/0073-3407). **5586**

HORNS OF PLENTY, MALCOLM COWLEY AND HIS GENERATION. (US/0896-9965). **3394**

HOROLOGICAL JOURNAL. (UK/0018-5108). **2916**

HOROLOGICAL TIMES. (US/0145-9546). **2916**

HORROR SHOW, THE. (US/0748-2914). **3394**

HORS CADRE. (FR/0755-0863). **4072**

HORSE & RIDER. (US/0018-5159). **2799**

HORSE AND RIDER (LONDON, ENGLAND). (UK). **2799**

HORSE PLAY. (US/0092-6353). **2799**

HORSE TIMES. (US/0744-4257). **2799**

HORSE WORLD. (US/0018-5191). **2800**

HORSEMEN'S JOURNAL, THE. (US/0018-5256). **2800**

HORSEMEN'S YANKEE PEDLAR. (US/0199-6436). **2800**

HORSEPOWER (AURORA). (CN/0840-6715). **Qty:** varies. **2800**

HORTICULTURAL NEWS (NEW BRUNSWICK, N.J.). (US/0886-5779). **2419**

HORTICULTURE. (US/0018-5329). **2419**

HORTICULTURE IN NEW ZEALAND : JOURNAL OF THE ROYAL NEW ZEALAND INSTITUTE OF HORTICULTURE. (NZ/1170-1803). **2419**

HORTICULTURE REVIEW. (CN/0823-8472). **2419**

HORTICULTURIST/ INSTITUTE OF HORTICULTURE, THE. (UK/0964-8992). **Qty:** 20. **2419**

HORTIDEAS. (US/0742-8219). **Qty:** 30/per yr. **2419**

HORTSCIENCE. (US/0018-5345). **2419**

HORTUS (FARNHAM). (UK/0950-1657). **Qty:** 1-20. **2419**

HOSPICE JOURNAL, THE. (US/0742-969X). **5288**

HOSPICE LETTER. (US/0193-6816). **3783**

HOSPITAL 2000. (SP/0214-2422). **300**

HOSPITAL & COMMUNITY PSYCHIATRY. (US/0022-1597). **3926**

HOSPITAL & HEALTH SERVICES ADMINISTRATION. (US/8750-3735). **3783**

HOSPITAL & HEALTHCARE AUSTRALIA. (AT/0813-7471). **3783**

HOSPITAL CONTRACTS MANUAL. (US/0734-0028). **2979**

HOSPITAL EDITORS' IDEA EXCHANGE. (US/1046-1647). **Qty:** 4/yr. **1112**

HOSPITAL, EL. (US/0018-5485). **3783**

HOSPITAL FUND RAISING NEWSLETTER. (US/0193-9939). **3784**

HOSPITAL GIFT SHOP MANAGEMENT. (US/0738-7946). **869**

HOSPITAL MANAGEMENT REVIEW. (US/0737-903X). **3659**

HOSPITAL MATERIALS MANAGEMENT. (US/0888-3068). **3784**

HOSPITAL MATERIALS MANAGEMENT NEWS. (US/0749-6672). **3784**

HOSPITAL SECURITY AND SAFETY MANAGEMENT. (US/0745-1148). **3785**

HOSPITAL TOPICS. (US/0018-5868). **3785**

HOSPITALITY & TOURISM EDUCATOR. (US). **2806**

HOSPITALITY LAW. (US/0889-5414). **2979**

HOSPITALS & HEALTH SERVICES YEARBOOK AUSTRALIA. (AT). **3786**

HOT FLASH: A NEWSLETTER FOR MIDLIFE AND OLDER WOMEN. (US). **5558**

HOT LINE CONSTRUCTION EQUIPMENT MONTHLY UPDATE. (US/1047-4382). **616**

HOT SHOE INTERNATIONAL. (UK/0959-6933). **4370**

HOTEL & CATERING REVIEW (BLACKROCK, DUBLIN). (US/0332-4400). **2806**

HOTEL/MOTEL SECURITY AND SAFETY MANAGEMENT. (US/8750-5126). **Qty:** 12 per year. **2806**

HOTEL RESTAURANT. (GW). **5071**

HOTEL UPDATE NEWSLETTER. (US). **2806**

HOTELS (NEWTON, MASS.). (US/1047-2975). **2807**

HOUILLE BLANCHE, LA. (FR/0018-6368). **2090**

HOUNDS AND HUNTING. (US/0018-6384). **4286**

HOUSE & GARDEN (NEW YORK). (US/0018-6406). **2901**

HOUSE MAGAZINE. (UK/0309-0426). **4476**

HOUSE PRICES. (UK/0263-3639). **4838**

HOUSEMENDING NOTEBOOK. (US/1054-6421). **616**

HOUSEPLANT MAGAZINE. (US/1061-4079). **Qty:** 12. **2420**

HOUSING & PLANNING REVIEW. (UK/0018-6589). **2824**

HOUSING NEW JERSEY. (US/1071-2585). **Qty:** 3-4. **2824**

HOUSING REVIEW (LONDON). (UK/0018-6651). **2825**

HOUSING STUDIES. (UK/0267-3037). **2825**

HOUSMAN SOCIETY JOURNAL. (UK/0305-926X). **3394**

HOUSTON BUSINESS JOURNAL. (US/0277-4976). **680**

HOUSTON JOURNAL OF INTERNATIONAL LAW. (US/0194-1879). **3129**

HOUSTON LAWYER. (US/0439-660X). **Qty:** 20-30. **2979**

HOUSTON MONTHLY. (US/0272-8060). **2535**

HOUSTON REVIEW, THE. (US/0272-4030). **2738**

HOUSTON SUN, THE. (US/1071-2941). **5751**

HOUSTONIAN (HUNTSVILLE, TEX.). (US). **5751**

HOW TO DOUBLE YOUR INCOME. (US/0277-0334). **404**

HOW TO FIND INFORMATION ABOUT COMPANIES. (US/0278-372X). **680**

HOWARD JOURNAL OF COMMUNICATIONS, THE. (US/1064-6175). **Qty:** 8. **1112**

HOWARD LAW JOURNAL. (US/0018-6813). **2979**

HOWARD WAY LETTER, THE. (US/0891-8244). **869**

HOWE ENTERPRISE, THE. (US). **Qty:** varies. **5751**

HPV NEWS (INDIANAPOLIS, IND.). (US/0898-6894). **1977**

HR/PC. (US/0884-9129). **941**

HRPLANNING NEWSLETTER, THE. (US/0733-0332). **Qty:** 10. **941**

HRVATSKA KRSCANSKA BIBLIOGRAFIJA. (CI). **5012**

HSIN HUA WEN CHAI. (CC). **2504**

HSUEH PAO. CHE HSUEH SHE HUI KO HSUEH PAN. (CC). **5202**

HSUEH PAO (WU-HAN KUNG HSUEH YUAN). (CC). **5111**

HUAXUE SHIJI. (CH/0258-3283). **5365**

HUDEBNI VEDA. (XR/0018-7003). **4121**

HUDSON REVIEW, THE. (US/0018-702X). **322**

HUDSON VALLEY. (US/0191-9288). **2535**

HUDSON VALLEY GREEN TIMES. (US/0888-661X). **Qty:** 2-4. **2173**

HUDSON VALLEY REGIONAL REVIEW, THE. (US/0742-2075). **Qty:** 8. **2847**

HUDSON'S WASHINGTON NEWS MEDIA CONTACTS DIRECTORY. (US/0441-389X). **2920**

HUGHSTON HEALTH ALERT. (US/1070-7778). **Qty:** 1. **3954**

HUISARTS NU : MAANDBLAD VAN DE WETENSCHAPPELIJKE VERENIGING DER VLAAMSE HUISARTSEN : HANU. (BE/0775-0501). **3738**

HUMAN BIOLOGY. (US/0018-7143). **457**

HUMAN DEVELOPMENT. (SZ/0018-716X). **4588**

HUMAN DEVELOPMENT (NEW YORK). (US/0197-3096). **4589**

HUMAN ECOLOGIST, THE. (US/8755-7878). **5202**

HUMAN ETHOLOGY NEWSLETTER. (US/0739-2036). **Qty:** 12. **237**

HUMAN EVENTS (WASHINGTON). (US/0018-7194). **4476**

HUMAN EVOLUTION. (IT/0393-9375). **237**

HUMAN MOSAIC. (US/0018-7240). **Qty:** 8. **5247**

HUMAN ORGANIZATION. (US/0018-7259). **237**

HUMAN PATHOLOGY. (US/0046-8177). **3895**

HUMAN RESOURCE DEVELOPMENT QUARTERLY. (US/1044-8004). **941**

HUMAN RESOURCE EXECUTIVE. (US/1040-0443). **941**

HUMAN RESOURCE MANAGEMENT. (SA/1010-8092). **Qty:** 15. **941**

HUMAN RESOURCE MANAGEMENT NEWS. (US). **942**

HUMAN RESOURCES ABSTRACTS. (US/0099-2453). **1533**

HUMAN RESOURCES NEWS. (AT). **Qty:** 6-8. **942**

HUMAN RESOURCES PROFESSIONAL (NEW YORK, N.Y.), THE. (US/1040-5232). **942**

HUMAN RIGHTS (CHICAGO, ILL.). (US/0046-8185). **2979**

HUMAN RIGHTS INTERNET REPORTER. (US/0275-049X). **4502**

HUMAN RIGHTS (MONTREAL). (CN/0711-2122). **4509**

HUMAN RIGHTS QUARTERLY. (US/0275-0392). **4509**

HUMAN SERVICES IN THE RURAL ENVIRONMENT. (US/0193-9009). **5288**

HUMAN STRESS. (US/0885-1174). **4589**

HUMAN SYSTEMS MANAGEMENT. (NE/0167-2533). **5111**

HUMANIST (BUFFALO, N.Y.), THE. (US/0018-7399). **4348**

HUMANIST IN CANADA. (CN). **Qty:** 16-20. **4348**

HUMANISTIC JUDAISM. (US/0441-4195). **5048**

HUMANISTIC PSYCHOLOGIST, THE. (US/0887-3267). **Qty:** 12-18. **4589**

HUMANITAS (BRESCIA, ITALY). (IT). **4348**

HUMANITIES EDUCATION. (US/0882-5475). **2847**

HUMANITY & SOCIETY. (US/0160-5976). **Qty:** 4 per year. **5247**

HUMBOLDT JOURNAL OF SOCIAL RELATIONS. (US/0160-4341). **Qty:** 10-15. **5202**

HUMBOLDT SPANISCHE AUSGABE. (GW/0018-7615). **2847**

HUMBOLDT SUN. (US). **5707**

HUME STUDIES. (US/0319-7336). **4348**

HUMPTY DUMPTY'S MAGAZINE. (US/0273-7590). **1064**

HUNGARIAN HERITAGE REVIEW. (US/0889-2695). **2263**

HUNGARIAN LIBRARY AND INFORMATION SCIENCE ABSTRACTS. (HU/0046-8304). **3258**

HUNGARIAN STUDIES NEWSLETTER. (US/0194-164X). **2692**

HUNGARIAN STUDIES REVIEW. (CN/0713-8083). **2692**

HUNGER NOTES. (US). **Qty:** 3-4. **5288**

HUNGER NOTES. (US/0740-1116). **2910**

HUNGRY MIND REVIEW. (US/0887-5499). **Qty:** 250. **4829**

HUNT. (US). **4873**

HUNTIA. (US/0073-4071). **513**

HUNTINGTON LIBRARY QUARTERLY, THE. (US/0018-7895). **352**

HUNTSVILLE TIMES, THE. (US). **5627**

HURRICANE ALICE. (US/0882-7907). **Qty:** 10-12/year. **5558**

HUSSERL STUDIES. (NE/0167-9848). **4348**

HUSTLER (COLUMBUS). (US/0149-4635). **3995**

HWAHAK KYOYUK. CHEMICAL EDUCATION. (KO/0304-5277). **977**

HYBRID CIRCUIT TECHNOLOGY. (US/0747-1599). **5111**

HYBRID CIRCUITS : JOURNAL OF THE INTERNATIONAL SOCIETY FOR HYBRID MICROELECTRONICS-UK / INTERNATIONAL SOCIETY FOR HYBRID ELECTRONICS, UNITED KINGDOM. (UK/0265-3028). **2056**

HYBRIDOMA. (US/0272-457X). **3670**

HYDROBIOLOGIA. (NE/0018-8158). **457**

HYDROBIOLOGICAL BULLETIN. (NE/0165-1404). **457**

HYDROBIOLOGICAL STUDIES. (XR/0577-3644). **1414**

HYDROGEN LETTER, THE. (US/1057-0713). **977**

HYDROGRAPHIC JOURNAL. (UK/0309-7846). **1414**

HYDROLOGICAL PROCESSES. (UK/0885-6087). **1414**

HYDROLOGICAL SCIENCES JOURNAL. (UK/0262-6667). **1415**

HYDROMETALLURGY. (NE/0304-386X). **4003**

HYGIE. (FR/0751-7149). **4783**

HYGIENE + MEDIZIN. (GW/0172-3790). **3585**

HYMN, THE. (US/0018-8271). **4121**

HYMNOLOGISKE MEDDELELSER. (DK/0106-4940). **4121**

HYPERLINK MAGAZINE. (US/1045-4624). **1186**

HYPERTENSION (DALLAS, TEX. 1979). (US/0194-911X). **3705**

HYPNOSIS REPORTS. (US/0882-6072). **2858**

HYPNOTHERAPY TODAY. (US/0882-8652). **2858**

HYSTERIA (KITCHENER). (CN/0229-5385). **5558**

I & P. (FR). **4523**

I.C.I.D. BULLETIN. (II/0300-2810). **2090**

I C O M NEWS. (FR/0018-8999). **4089**

I CARE. (IT/0394-817X). **3585**

I.D. CHECKING GUIDE. (US/1041-5793). **4655**

I.D.E.E (BRIGHAM). (CN/1192-7755). **Qty:** 12. **5289**

I-D MAGAZINE. (UK). **Qty:** 100/yr. **1064**

I D R C REPORTS. (CN/0315-9981). **2910**

I/O NEWS. (US/0274-9998). **1267**

I.S.C.A. QUARTERLY, THE. (US/0741-2940). **Qty:** 2-3. **380**

I YUAN TO YING. (CC). **322**

IA. INGEGNERIA AMBIENTALE. (IT/0394-5871). **2232**

IA, THE JOURNAL OF THE SOCIETY FOR INDUSTRIAL ARCHEOLOGY. (US/0160-1040). **269**

IAAH NEWSLETTER. (AT/0819-9558). **4783**

IACD QUARTERLY. (US/8756-2189). **4589**

IACEE NEWSLETTER. (FI/0786-9916). **Qty:** 50-60. **1977**

IAHPER JOURNAL, THE. (US). **1855**

IAJRC JOURNAL. (US/0098-9487). **4122**

IALL JOURNAL OF LANGUAGE LEARNING TECHNOLOGIES, THE. (US/1050-0049). **Qty:** 3. **3286**

IASLIC BULLETIN. (II/0018-8441). **3214**

IASP NEWSLETTER (INTERNATIONAL ASSOCIATION OF SCHOLARLY PUBLISHERS). (NO/0333-3620). **4815**

IAWA BULLETIN. NEW SERIES. (NE). **2401**

IBERIAN STUDIES. (UK/0307-3262). **2517**

IBERO-AMERIKANISCHES ARCHIV. (GW/0340-3068). **2738**

IBEROAMERICANA. (GW/0342-1864). **2738**

IBFAN NEWS. (US/0889-4000). **5289**

IBM SYSTEMS JOURNAL. (US/0018-8670). **1259**

IBSEN NEWS AND COMMENT : NEWSLETTER OF THE IBSEN SOCIETY OF AMERICA. (US). **3344**

ICA INFORMATION. (IS/0334-6056). **4655**

ICAME JOURNAL / INTERNATIONAL COMPUTER ARCHIVE OF MODERN ENGLISH. (NO/0801-5775). **3286**

ICARBS. (US/0360-8409). **3214**

ICASALS PUBLICATION. (US/0538-5318). **2565**

ICC BUSINESS WORLD : MAGAZINE OF THE INTERNATIONAL CHAMBER OF COMMERCE. (FR). **820**

ICC INTERNATIONAL COURT OF ARBITRATION BULLETIN, THE. (FR/1017-284X). **3129**

ICE RIVER. (US/1043-7010). **3395**

ICELAND REVIEW (REYKJAVIK, ICELAND : 1984). (IC/0019-1094). **2692**

ICELANDIC CANADIAN. (CN/0046-8452). **Qty:** 8-12. **2263**

ICHTHYOLOGICAL EXPLORATION OF FRESHWATERS. (GW/0936-9902). **2305**

ICLAS NEWS. (FI/1018-4635). **Qty:** 10. **5111**

ICMM NEWS. (US/0883-1343). **4089**

ICO. (SW/0106-1348). **352**

ICO. INTELLIGENCE ARTIFICIELLE ET SCIENCES COGNITIVES AU QUEBEC. (CN/1189-6078). **Qty:** 3. **5111**

ICP INFORMATION NEWSLETTER. (US/0161-6951). **1015**

ICSSR JOURNAL OF ABSTRACTS AND REVIEWS : ECONOMICS. (II). **1533**

ICSSR JOURNAL OF ABSTRACTS AND REVIEWS: GEOGRAPHY. (II). **2565**

ICSSR JOURNAL OF ABSTRACTS AND REVIEWS : POLITICAL SCIENCE. (II/0250-9660). **4476**

ICSSR JOURNAL OF ABSTRACTS AND REVIEWS. SOCIOLOGY AND SOCIAL ANTHROPOLOGY / INDIAN COUNCIL OF SOCIAL SCIENCE RESEARCH. (II). **5202**

ICSSR NEWSLETTER. (II/0018-9049). **5202**

ICUIS BIBLIOGRAPHY SERIES. (US/0161-5483). **5012**

ICUIS METRO-MINISTRY NEWS : THE INTERDENOMINATIONAL NEWSLETTER OF THE INSTITUTE ON THE CHURCH IN URBAN INDUSTRIAL SOCIETY. (US). **4964**

ID SYSTEMS. (US/0892-676X). **5111**

IDAHO ARCHAEOLOGIST. (US/0893-2271). **270**

IDAHO ENTERPRISE, THE. (US). **5656**

IDAHO FRUIT TREE CENSUS / U.S. DEPARTMENT OF AGRICULTURE, ECONOMICS AND STATISTICS SERVICE AND IDAHO DEPARTMENT OF AGRICULTURE. (US). **2420**

IDAHO GENEALOGICAL SOCIETY QUARTERLY. (US/0445-2127). **2454**

IDAHO LIBRARIAN, THE. (US/0019-1213). **Qty:** 5-10. **3214**

IDAHO MOUNTAIN EXPRESS. (US/0279-8964). **5656**

IDAHO PRESS-TRIBUNE. (US). **5657**

IDAHO STATE JOURNAL. (US). **5657**

IDEA. (JA/0019-1299). **380**

IDEA (ROME). (IT/0019-1280). **Qty:** 30. **2620**

IDEA SPEKTRUM. (GW). **4964**

IDEA TODAY. (US/1040-8126). **1313**

IDEAS AND DEBATES : A JOURNAL OF ART WRITING. (CN). **352**

IDEAS EN ARTE Y TECNOLOGIA / UNIVERSIDAD DE BELGRANO. (AG/0326-3878). **300**

IDEAS EN CIENCIAS SOCIALES / UNIVERSIDAD DE BELGRANO. (AG/0326-386X). **5202**

IDESIA. (CL/0073-4675). **2195**

IDF BULLETIN. (US/0306-4980). **3731**

IDIOM 23. (AT/1032-1640). **3395**

IDIS. (US/0891-8511). **4307**

IDIS-LITERATURLISTE. SOZIALMEDIZIN / IDIS. (GW/0932-5034). **4783**

IDIS-LITERATURLISTE. SUCHTINFORMATION / IDIS. (GW/0932-4240). **1345**

IDISHER KEMFER. (US/1050-5296). **2504**

IDLER (TORONTO). (CN/0828-1289). **2535**

IDOJARAS (BUDAPEST 1897). (HU/0367-7443). **1426**

IDR. INDUSTRIAL DIAMOND REVIEW. (UK/0019-8145). **2115**

IE, INVESTMENT EXECUTIVE. (CN/0840-9137). **900**

IEE PROCEEDINGS. PART H, MICROWAVES, ANTENNAS, AND PROPAGATION. (UK/0950-107X). **2058**

IEE PRODUCTRONIC. (GW). **2058**

IEEE COMMUNICATIONS MAGAZINE. (US/0163-6804). **1157**

IEEE COMPUTER GRAPHICS AND APPLICATIONS. (US/0272-1716). **1233**

IEEE EXPERT. (US/0885-9000). **1229**

IEEE MICRO. (US/0272-1732). **1267**

IEEE SIGNAL PROCESSING MAGAZINE. (US/1053-5888). **2060**

IEEE SOFTWARE. (US/0740-7459). **1286**

IFCO NEWS. (US/1065-1675). **4964**

IFDA DOSSIER / INTERNATIONAL FOUNDATION FOR DEVELOPMENT ALTERNATIVES. (SZ). **4523**

IFES REVIEW. (UK/1010-8734). **4964**

IFLA JOURNAL. (GW/0340-0352). **3214**

IFO SCHNELLDIENST. (GW/0018-974X). **681**

IFO-STUDIEN. (GW/0018-9731). **1494**

IFOAM BULLETIN. (US/0195-0304). **94**

IGIENE E SANITA PUBBLICA. (IT/0019-1639). **4783**

IGIENE MODERNA. (IT/0019-1655). **4783**

IGLU. INSTITUTO DE GESTION Y LIDERAZGO UNIVERSITARIO. (CN/1183-5052). **1829**

IGLU. INSTITUTO DE GESTION Y LIDERAZGO UNIVERSITARIO. (CN/1183-5052). **1829**

IIC DOCUMENT SERVICE. (US/0738-7938). **1113**

IIC; INTERNATIONAL REVIEW OF INDUSTRIAL AND COPYRIGHT LAW. (GW/0018-9855). **1304**

IIPS NEWSLETTER. (II). **4553**

IJDL. INTERNATIONAL JOURNAL OF DRAVIDIAN LINGUISTICS. (II/0378-2484). **3286**

ILEIA NEWSLETTER. (NE/0920-8771). **174**

ILGA PINK BOOK. (NE). **2794**

ILIFF REVIEW, THE. (US/0019-1795). **4964**

ILL. IA. MO. SEARCHER, THE. (US/0737-5239). **2454**

ILLIANA GENEALOGIST. (US/0019-1809). **2454**

ILLINOIAN-STAR DAILY. (US). **5660**

ILLINOIS AGRI-NEWS. (US/0194-7443). **94**

ILLINOIS ARCHITECTURE REFERENCE DIRECTORY, THE. (US/0747-6345). **300**

ILLINOIS AUDUBON. (US/1061-9801). **4166**

ILLINOIS AVIATION (SPRINGFIELD, ILL. : 1979). (US/0276-640X). **23**

ILLINOIS BAPTIST. (US/0019-1868). **5061**

ILLINOIS BAR JOURNAL. (US/0019-1876). **2980**

ILLINOIS HISTORICAL JOURNAL. (US/0748-8149). **Qty:** 100. **2738**

ILLINOIS ISSUES. (US/0738-9663). **4476**

ILLINOIS JOURNAL OF HEALTH, PHYSICAL EDUCATION, RECREATION, AND DANCE. (US/1062-2764). **Qty:** varies. **1751**

ILLINOIS MAGAZINE. (US/0747-9794). **2738**

ILLINOIS MANUFACTURERS DIRECTORY. (US/0160-3302). **3480**

ILLINOIS MASTER PLUMBER. (US/0019-2112). **2606**

ILLINOIS PARKS & RECREATION. (US/0019-2155). **4706**

ILLINOIS PHARMACIST (1979). (US/0195-2099). **4307**

ILLINOIS PSYCHOLOGIST : NEWSLETTER OF THE ILLINOIS PSYCHOLOGICAL ASSOCIATION. (US/0019-2198). **4589**

ILLINOIS REVIEW, THE. (US/1067-4128). **3344**

ILLINOIS SCHOOL BOARD JOURNAL. (US/0019-221X). **1864**

ILLINOIS SCHOOL RESEARCH AND DEVELOPMENT. (US/0163-822X). **1751**

ILLINOIS SCHOOLS JOURNAL. (US/0019-2236). **1896**

ILLINOIS SERVICES DIRECTORY. (US/0092-3818). **1609**

ILLINOIS STATE GENEALOGICAL SOCIETY QUARTERLY. (US/0046-8622). **2454**

ILLINOIS TIMES. (US/0199-7823). **Qty:** 12. **5660**

ILLINOIS WILDLIFE. (US/0019-2317). **Qty:** 4. **2195**

ILLINOIS WRITERS REVIEW. (US/0733-9526). **Qty:** (15-20). **3344**

ILLNESS CRISIS & LOSS. (US/1054-1373). **Qty:** 8. **2251**

ILLUSTRATED LONDON NEWS, THE. (UK/0019-2422). **2517**

ILLUSTRATION 63. I.E. DREIUNDSECHZIG. (GW/0019-2457). **380**

ILLUSTRATOR, THE. (US/0019-2465). **380**

ILMU MASYARAKAT : TERBITAN PERSATUAN SAINS SOSIAL MALAYSIA. (MY). **5203**

ILP MAGAZINE. (UK/0951-2187). **1677**

IMA BULLETIN : THE NEWSLETTER OF THE INTERNATIONAL MIDI ASSOCIATION, THE. (US). **1247**

IMAGE AND VISION COMPUTING. (UK/0262-8856). **1233**

IMAGE FILE. (US/1046-6614). **Qty:** 2. **4089**

IMAGE (ST. LOUIS, MO.). (US/0748-1780). **3395**

IMAGE TECHNOLOGY (LONDON). (UK/0950-2114). **4072**

IMAGE--THE JOURNAL OF NURSING SCHOLARSHIP. (US/0743-5150). **3857**

IMAGE (VANCOUVER). (CN/0383-9710). **3586**

IMAGEN (SAN JUAN, P.R.). (PR/0890-6548). **2488**

IMAGES (NELSON). (CN/0384-5990). **5558**

IMAGINATION, COGNITION AND PERSONALITY. (US/0276-2366). **4589**

IMAGINE (BOSTON, MASS.). (US/0747-489X). **3464**

IMAGINE (MONTREAL). (CN/0709-8855). **Qty:** 50. **3395**

IMAGING SERVICE BUREAU NEWS. (US/1055-8098). **Qty:** 5. **1609**

IMAGING UPDATE. (US/0889-9142). **4565**

IMAGO MUNDI (LYMPNE). (UK/0308-5694). **Qty:** 20. **2582**

IMANUEL. (IS/0302-8127). **5048**

IMFAMA. (SA/0019-2724). **Qty:** 6. **4389**

IMM ABSTRACTS. (UK/0019-0020). **4003**

IMMAGINE RIFLESSA, L'. (IT). **3395**

IMME BOLETIN TECNICO. (VE/0376-723X). **2024**

IMMIGRANTS & MINORITIES. (UK/0261-9288). **1919**

IMMIGRATION DIGEST. (US/0899-5400). **2454**

IMMIGRATION LAW REPORT. (US/0731-5767). **2980**

IMMOBILIEN-BERATER. (GW/0934-5693). **4839**

IMMUNOBIOLOGY (1979). (GW/0171-2985). **3670**

IMMUNOHEMATOLOGY. (US/0894-203X). **Qty:** 1. **3772**

IMMUNOLOGICAL INVESTIGATIONS. (US/0882-0139). **3671**

IMMUNOLOGY. (UK/0019-2805). **3671**

IMMUNOLOGY ABSTRACTS. (US/0307-112X). **3660**

IMMUNOLOGY & ALLERGY PRACTICE. (US/0194-7508). **3671**

IMMUNOLOGY AND INFECTIOUS DISEASES. (UK/0959-4957). **3671**

IMMUNOLOGY TODAY (AMSTERDAM. REGULAR ED.). (UK/0167-5699). **3671**

IMMUNOLOGY TRIBUNE. (US/0271-3284). **3672**

IMMUNOPHARMACOLOGY. (US/0162-3109). **3672**

IMP, INDUSTRIAL MODELS & PATTERNS. (US/0146-0161). **3481**

IMPACT ASSESSMENT BULLETIN. (US/0734-9165). **Qty:** 12-15/yr. **2173**

IMPACT INTERNATIONAL. (UK/0046-8703). **4523**

IMPACT JOURNAL. (US/0162-1300). **4655**

IMPACT (MANILA). (PH/0300-4155). **Qty:** 15. **5203**

IMPACT PUMP NEWS & PATENTS. (US/1056-1536). **2115**

IMPACT SINGAPORE. (SI/0129-2862). **Qty:** 6. **4964**

IMPACT SYDNEY, 1986. (AT/1030-3847). **3113**

IMPACT VALVE NEWS & PATENTS. (US/1056-1544). **2115**

IMPERIAL QUARTERLY MAGAZINE. (CN/1188-0066). **2517**

IMPERIAL VALLEY PRESS. (US). **5635**

IMPIANTISTICA ITALIANA. (IT/0394-1582). **617**

IMPOR MENURUT JENIS BARANG DAN NEGERI ASAL. (IO). **839**

IMPORTWEEK. (CN/0702-8385). **839**

IMPOSTE LAVORO PREVIDENZA. (IT). **Qty:** 2-3. **1677**

IMPRESA. (IT/0035-6816). **1609**

IMPREVUE (MONTPELLIER). (FR/0242-5149). **3395**

IMPRINT (NEW YORK, N.Y. : 1976). (US/0277-7061). **380**

IMPRINT (NEW YORK, NEW YORK). (US/0019-3062). **3857**

IMPRINT (WATERLOO). (CN/0706-7380). **1829**

IMPROVISOR. (US/0892-1911). **Qty:** 2. **4122**

IMSA JOURNAL. (US/1064-2560). **5441**

IN BUSINESS. (US/0190-2458). **2232**

IN CONTEXT (SEQUIM, WASH.). (US/0741-6180). **4349**

IN DANCE. (US/0883-9956). **1313**

IN DEFENSE OF THE ALIEN. (US/0275-634X). **1919**

IN DIE SKRIFLIG. (SA/1018-6441). **Qty:** 25. **4964**

IN-FISHERMAN, THE. (US/0276-9905). **Qty:** 15. **2305**

IN GEARDAGUM : ESSAYS ON OLD ENGLISH LANGUAGE AND LITERATURE. (US). **3286**

IN JOPLIN METROPOLITAN. (US/0743-1503). **5480**

IN OTHER WORDS NUNAWADING. (AT/1036-1421). **Qty:** Varies. **3286**

IN SITU. (US/0146-2520). **1440**

IN THEORY ONLY. (US/0360-4365). **4122**

IN THESE TIMES. (US/0160-5992). **5203**

IN TRANSIT (WASHINGTON). (US/0019-3291). **5384**

IN UNITY. (AT/0442-3844). **4964**

INA NEWSLETTER. (UK/0255-013X). **4227**

INA NEWSLETTER / INTERNATIONAL NANNOPLANKTON ASSOCIATION. (NE). **4231**

INC HEBDO CONSOMMATEURS ACTUALITES. (FR/1145-0673). **1297**

INCHIESTA. (IT). **Qty:** 10/year. **5247**

INCIDENTS OF THE WAR. (US). **4370**

INCIPIT. (AG/0326-0941). **3395**

INCITE (SYDNEY). (AT/0158-0876). **3214**

INDAGINI E QUADERNI. (IT). **3344**

INDEPENDENCE. (AT). **Qty:** 8-10. **1751**

INDEPENDENT (ELMIRA). (CN/0833-8019). **Qty:** varies. **5786**

INDEPENDENT LIVING. (AT/0815-2276). **4389**

INDEPENDENT (LONDON, ENGLAND). (UK). **5812**

INDEPENDENT METHODIST BULLETIN, THE. (US/0744-4087). **5061**

INDEPENDENT MONTHLY, THE. (AT/1033-9957). **Qty:** 30-40. **4476**

INDEPENDENT (NEW YORK, N.Y. : 1978). (US/0731-5198). **Qty:** 1-2. **4072**

INDEPENDENT PRESS (BLOOMFIELD, N.J.). (US/0747-4075). **5710**

INDEPENDENT REPUBLICAN. (US/8750-2364). **Qty:** 4-5/yr. **4476**

INDEPENDENT REPUBLICAN, 1812. (US). **Qty:** 3 or 4. **2488**

INDEPENDENT SCHOLAR, THE. (US/1066-5633). **Qty:** 3. **1829**

INDEPENDENT SCHOOL (BOSTON, MASS.). (US/0145-9635). **1751**

INDEPENDENT SENIOR, THE. (CN/0847-5288). **Qty:** 6. **5179**

INDEPENDENT SHAVIAN, THE. (US/0019-3763). **3396**

INDEPENDENT TEACHER FORTITUDE VALLEY. (AT/1033-2464). **Qty:** 2. **1896**

INDEX INDIA. (II/0019-3844). **417**

INDEX INDO-ASIATICUS. (II/0019-3852). **2653**

INDEX INTERNATIONALIS INDICUS. (II). **5021**

INDEX OF ISLAMIC LITERATURE. (UK). **3458**

INDEX ON CENSORSHIP. (UK/0306-4220). **3344**

INDEX TO AMERICAN REFERENCE BOOKS ANNUAL. (US/0192-6969). **1926**

INDEX TO BLACK PERIODICALS. (US/0899-6253). **2276**

INDEX TO BOOK REVIEWS IN RELIGION. (US/0887-1574). **5012**

INDEX TO CANADIAN LEGAL LITERATURE (LIBRARY ED.). (CN/0832-9257). **3081**

INDEX TO FREE PERIODICALS. (US/0147-5630). **2496**

INDEX TO INDIAN LEGAL PERIODICALS. (II/0019-4034). **2981**

INDEX TO JEWISH PERIODICALS. (US/0019-4050). **5013**

INDEX TO PHILIPPINE PERIODICALS. (PH/0073-599X). **2496**

INDEXER. (UK/0019-4131). **3215**

INDIA ABROAD. (US/0046-8932). **2263**

INDIA CALLING. (II). **1133**

INDIA CURRENTS. (US/0896-095X). **2488**

INDIA INTERNATIONAL CENTRE QUARTERLY. (II/0376-9771). **2653**

INDIA LEATHER & LEATHER PRODUCTS DIRECTORY. (II/0376-978X). **3184**

INDIA MAGAZINE OF HER PEOPLE AND CULTURE, THE. (II). **2263**

INDIA TODAY. (II). **2504**

INDIA-WEST. (US/0883-721X). **5636**

INDIA WHO'S WHO. (II/0073-6244). **Qty:** 5000. **433**

INDIAN ANTHROPOLOGIST. (II). **238**

INDIAN-ARTIFACT MAGAZINE. (US/0736-265X). **Qty:** 6-10/yr. **270**

INDIAN BAR REVIEW. (II). **2981**

INDIAN BEE JOURNAL. (II/0019-4425). **94**

INDIAN BOOK INDUSTRY. (II/0019-4433). **4829**

INDIAN BOOK REVIEW. (II). **4829**

INDIAN CERAMICS. (II/0019-4492). **2591**

INDIAN CHEMICAL ENGINEER. (II/0019-4506). **2013**

INDIAN CHURCH HISTORY REVIEW. (II/0019-4530). **4964**

INDIAN COFFEE. (II/0019-4549). **174**

INDIAN CONCRETE JOURNAL, THE. (II/0019-4565). **Qty:** 25. **617**

INDIAN DAIRYMAN. (II/0019-4603). **195**

INDIAN EDUCATIONAL REVIEW. (II/0019-4700). **1752**

INDIAN ENERGY AND POWER UPDATE. (II). **1946**

INDIAN EXPORT TRADE JOURNAL, THE. (II/0019-4735). **4523**

INDIAN FARMING. (II/0019-4786). **94**

INDIAN FOOD PACKER. (II/0019-4808). **2344**

INDIAN FORESTER, THE. (II/0019-4816). **2384**

INDIAN GEOGRAPHICAL JOURNAL, THE. (II/0019-4824). **2566**

INDIAN HIGHWAYS. (II/0376-7256). **5441**

INDIAN HISTORICAL REVIEW, THE. (II/0376-9836). **2653**

INDIAN HORIZONS. (II/0378-2964). **2848**

INDIAN HORTICULTURE. (II/0019-4875). **2420**

INDIAN JOURNAL OF ADULT EDUCATION. (US/0019-5006). **1801**

INDIAN JOURNAL OF AGRICULTURAL ECONOMICS, THE. (II/0019-5014). **94**

INDIAN JOURNAL OF AGRICULTURAL RESEARCH. (II/0367-8245). **95**

INDIAN JOURNAL OF AGRICULTURAL SCIENCES, THE. (II/0019-5022). **95**

INDIAN JOURNAL OF AMERICAN STUDIES. (II/0019-5030). **2738**

INDIAN JOURNAL OF ANIMAL HEALTH. (II/0019-5057). **5511**

INDIAN JOURNAL OF BEHAVIOUR. (II/0970-0897). **4589**

INDIAN JOURNAL OF BOTANY. (II/0250-829X). **513**

INDIAN JOURNAL OF CANCER. (II/0019-509X). **3818**

INDIAN JOURNAL OF CHEST DISEASES & ALLIED SCIENCES, THE. (II/0377-9343). **Qty:** 12. **3706**

INDIAN JOURNAL OF CLINICAL PSYCHOLOGY. (II/0303-2582). **4589**

INDIAN JOURNAL OF CRIMINOLOGY. (II/0376-9844). **3166**

INDIAN JOURNAL OF CRIMINOLOGY & CRIMINALISTICS, THE. (II/0970-4345). **3166**

INDIAN JOURNAL OF CRYOGENICS. (II/0379-0479). **4405**

INDIAN JOURNAL OF DAIRY SCIENCE. (II/0019-5146). **195**

INDIAN JOURNAL OF DERMATOLOGY. (II/0019-5154). **3720**

INDIAN JOURNAL OF DERMATOLOGY, VENEREOLOGY AND LEPROLOGY. (II/0378-6323). **Qty:** 6-10. **3720**

INDIAN JOURNAL OF ECONOMICS. (II/0019-5170). **1494**

INDIAN JOURNAL OF ENVIRONMENTAL HEALTH. (II/0367-827X). **2174**

INDIAN JOURNAL OF ENVIRONMENTAL PROTECTION. (II/0253-7141). **2174**

INDIAN JOURNAL OF EXPERIMENTAL BIOLOGY. (II/0019-5189). **458**

INDIAN JOURNAL OF FORESTRY. (II/0250-524X). **2384**

INDIAN JOURNAL OF GASTROENTEROLOGY. (II/0254-8860). **3746**

INDIAN JOURNAL OF HEREDITY. (II/0374-826X). **548**

INDIAN JOURNAL OF HOSPITAL PHARMACY. (II/0019-526X). **4307**

INDIAN JOURNAL OF INDUSTRIAL RELATIONS. (II/0019-5286). **681**

INDIAN JOURNAL OF LEPROSY. (II/0254-9395). **4784**

INDIAN JOURNAL OF MARINE SCIENCES. (II/0379-5136). **1450**

INDIAN JOURNAL OF MECHANICS AND MATHEMATICS. (II/0537-2038). **3508**

INDIAN JOURNAL OF MEDICAL RESEARCH. SECTION A, INFECTIOUS DISEASES. (II/0970-955X). **3586**

INDIAN JOURNAL OF MEDICAL RESEARCH. SECTION B, BIOMEDICAL RESEARCH OTHER THAN INFECTIOUS DISEASES. (II/0970-9568). **3586**

INDIAN JOURNAL OF MEDICAL SCIENCES. (II/0019-5359). **3586**

INDIAN JOURNAL OF MYCOLOGY AND PLANT PATHOLOGY. (II/0303-4097). **575**

INDIAN JOURNAL OF NUTRITION AND DIETETICS, THE. (II/0022-3174). **4192**

INDIAN JOURNAL OF OPHTHALMOLOGY. (II/0301-4738). **3875**

INDIAN JOURNAL OF OTOLARYNGOLOGY. (II/0019-5421). **3888**

INDIAN JOURNAL OF PATHOLOGY & MICROBIOLOGY. (II/0377-4929). **3895**

INDIAN JOURNAL OF PEDIATRICS. (II/0019-5456). **3904**

INDIAN JOURNAL OF PHARMACEUTICAL SCIENCES. (II/0250-474X). **4307**

INDIAN JOURNAL OF PHARMACOLOGY. (II/0253-7613). **Qty:** 6-8. **4307**

INDIAN JOURNAL OF PHYSICAL ANTHROPOLOGY AND HUMAN GENETICS. (II/0378-8156). **548**

INDIAN JOURNAL OF PHYSICS AND PROCEEDINGS OF THE INDIAN ASSOCIATION FOR THE CULTIVATION OF SCIENCE. (II/0019-5480). **Qty:** 550. **5112**

INDIAN JOURNAL OF PHYSIOLOGY AND PHARMACOLOGY. (II/0019-5499). **581**

INDIAN JOURNAL OF PLANT PHYSIOLOGY. (II/0019-5502). **513**

INDIAN JOURNAL OF PLANT PROTECTION. (II/0253-4355). **513**

INDIAN JOURNAL OF POLITICS. (II/0303-9951). **4476**

INDIAN JOURNAL OF PSYCHIATRIC SOCIAL WORK. (II/0302-1610). **5289**

INDIAN JOURNAL OF PUBLIC ADMINISTRATION, THE. (II/0019-5561). **4656**

INDIAN JOURNAL OF PUBLIC HEALTH. (II/0019-557X). **4784**

INDIAN JOURNAL OF REGIONAL SCIENCE. (II/0046-9017). **2825**

INDIAN JOURNAL OF SOCIAL RESEARCH. (II/0019-5626). **5203**

INDIAN JOURNAL OF SOCIAL WORK, THE. (II/0019-5634). **5289**

INDIAN JOURNAL OF TECHNOLOGY. (II/0019-5669). **5112**

INDIAN JOURNAL OF THEORETICAL PHYSICS. (II/0019-5693). **4405**

INDIAN JOURNAL OF VETERINARY MEDICINE. (II/0970-051X). **Qty:** 1. **5512**

INDIAN JUDGMENT REPORTER : IJR. (II). **2981**

INDIAN MINING & ENGINEERING JOURNAL, THE. (II/0019-5944). **2140**

INDIAN PEDIATRICS. (II/0019-6061). **3904**

INDIAN PHILOSOPHICAL QUARTERLY. (II/0376-415X). **4349**

INDIAN PRACTITIONER. (II/0019-6169). **3587**

INDIAN PSYCHOLOGICAL ABSTRACTS. (II). **4589**

INDIAN PSYCHOLOGICAL REVIEW. (II/0019-6215). **4589**

INDIAN PSYCHOLOGIST. (II/0970-2520). **4589**

INDIAN REVIEW OF LIFE SCIENCES. (II/0253-4436). **458**

INDIAN SCHOLAR. (II). **3344**

INDIAN SCIENCE INDEX. (II). **5112**

INDIAN SHIPPING. (II/0970-4299). **5450**

INDIAN SPICES. (II/0019-6401). **840**

INDIAN SUGAR. (II/0019-6428). **2344**

INDIAN THEOLOGICAL STUDIES. (II/0253-620X). **Qty:** 1,000. **4964**

INDIAN TRADER, THE. (US/0046-9076). **2738**

INDIAN VETERINARY JOURNAL, THE. (II/0019-6479). **5512**

INDIANA AUDUBON QUARTERLY. (US/0019-6525). **Qty:** 100-200. **5617**

INDIANA CRIMINAL LAW REVIEW. (US). **3107**

INDIANA ENGLISH. (US/1070-9371). **Qty:** 1-2/year. **3286**

INDIANA LAW JOURNAL (BLOOMINGTON). (US/0019-6665). **Qty:** 0-2. **2982**

INDIANA LAW REVIEW. (US/0090-4198). **2982**

INDIANA MAGAZINE OF HISTORY. (US/0019-6673). **2739**

INDIANA MUSICATOR. (US/0273-9933). **4122**

INDIANA QUERIES. (US/1044-694X). **2454**

INDIANA REGISTER. (US/0193-1520). **Qty:** 12/y. **2982**

INDIANA REVIEW. (US/0738-386X). **Qty:** 15-20. **3344**

INDIANA STATE BOARD OF HEALTH BULLETIN, THE. (US/0019-6754). **4784**

INDIANA THEORY REVIEW. (US/0271-8022). **Qty:** 3-4. **4122**

INDIANA UNIVERSITY URALIC AND ALTAIC SERIES. (US/0893-2913). **3287**

INDIANAPOLIS MONTHLY. (US/0899-0328). **2535**

INDICA. (II/0019-686X). **Qty:** 5. **2653**

INDICADORES DE COYUNTURA. (AG/0537-3468). **1534**

INDICATOR (NANAIMO). (CN/0381-0917). **4848**

INDICE GENERAL DE PUBLICACIONES PERIODICAS CUBANAS. (CU). **5203**

INDICE PENALE, L'. (IT/0019-7084). **3107**

INDIGENOUS WOMAN. (US/1070-1400). **2264**

INDIKATOR EKONOMI. (IO). **1567**

INDIKATOR KESEJAHTERAAN RAKYAT / WELFARE INDICATORS. (IO). **5289**

INDIKATOR PEMBANGUNAN INDUSTRI PERTANIAN. (IO). **95**

INDIVIDUAL PSYCHOLOGY. (US/0277-7010). **4590**

INDIVIDUAL PSYCHOLOGY REPORTER. (US/0888-4595). **4590**

INDO-IRANIAN JOURNAL. (NE/0019-7246). **4349**

INDOCHINA CHRONOLOGY. (US/0897-4519). **2653**

INDONESIA CIRCLE : [JOURNAL]. (UK/0306-2848). **2505**

INDONESIA (ITHACA). (US/0019-7289). **2654**

INDONESIAN IMPORTERS. (IO). **840**

INDONESIAN QUARTERLY, THE. (IO). **2654**

INDOOR AIR BULLETIN. (US/1055-5242). **Qty:** unlimited. **2174**

INDOOR AIR QUALITY UPDATE. (US/1040-5313). **2606**

INDRAMA. (II). **2505**

INDUSTRIA AZUCARERA, LA. (AG/0325-0326). **95**

INDUSTRIA CARNICA LATINOAMERICANA, LA. (AG/0325-3414). **213**

INDUSTRIA CONSERVE. (IT/0019-7483). **2344**

INDUSTRIA DEL LEGNO & DEL MOBILE, L'. (IT/0392-9086). **634**

INDUSTRIA DEL MOBILE, L'. (IT). **634**

INDUSTRIA DELLA CARTA. (IT/0019-7548). **4234**

INDUSTRIA DELLA GOMMA, L'. (IT/0019-7556). **5076**

INDUSTRIA HOTELERA EN ESPANA. (SP). **2807**

INDUSTRIA LEMNULUI (BUCHAREST, ROMANIA : 1986). (RM). **2384**

INDUSTRIA SACCARIFERA ITALIANA. (IT/0019-7734). **2344**

INDUSTRIA Y QUIMICA. (AG). **978**

INDUSTRIAL AND COMMERCIAL TRAINING. (UK/0019-7858). **942**

INDUSTRIAL AND CORPORATE CHANGE. (UK/0960-6491). **1610**

INDUSTRIAL & ENGINEERING CHEMISTRY RESEARCH. (US/0888-5885). **2013**

INDUSTRIAL AND TRADE DIRECTORY. (KE). **840**

INDUSTRIAL ARCHAEOLOGY REVIEW. (UK/0309-0728). **270**

INDUSTRIAL ARCHAEOLOGY (TAVISTOCK). (UK/0019-7971). **270**

INDUSTRIAL CERAMICS. (IT). **2591**

INDUSTRIAL CONTROLS INTELLIGENCE & THE PLC INSIDER'S NEWSLETTER. (US/1074-0511). **Qty:** 2-3. **1188**

INDUSTRIAL CORROSION. (UK/0265-0584). **Qty:** 1. **2102**

INDUSTRIAL CORROSION ABSTRACTS. (UK/0955-7040). **2013**

INDUSTRIAL ENGINEERING (NORCROSS, GA.). (US/0019-8234). **2098**

INDUSTRIAL FABRIC PRODUCTS REVIEW. (US/0019-8307). **5352**

INDUSTRIAL FINISHING (WHEATON). (US/0019-8323). **4224**

INDUSTRIAL FIRE WORLD. (US/0749-890X). **2291**

INDUSTRIAL GROUPINGS IN JAPAN. (JA). **682**

INDUSTRIAL HEATING. (US/0019-8374). **4431**

INDUSTRIAL HYGIENE DIGEST. (US/0019-8382). **2872**

INDUSTRIAL HYGIENE NEWS (PITTSBURGH). (US/0147-5401). **2863**

INDUSTRIAL LUBRICATION AND TRIBOLOGY. (UK/0036-8792). **3481**

INDUSTRIAL MANAGEMENT & DATA SYSTEMS. (UK/0263-5577). **1259**

INDUSTRIAL MANAGEMENT (DES PLAINES). (US/0019-8471). **1610**

INDUSTRIAL MATHEMATICS. (US/0019-8528). **3509**

INDUSTRIAL METROLOGY. (NE/0921-5956). **4030**

INDUSTRIAL MINERALS. (UK/0019-8544). **1440**

INDUSTRIAL NEWS (IAEGER, W.VA.). (US). **Qty:** 20. **5764**

INDUSTRIAL PROPERTY. (SZ/0019-8625). **1304**

INDUSTRIAL PSYCHOLOGY. (SA/0258-5200). **Qty:** 3. **4590**

INDUSTRIAL PURCHASING AGENT. (US/0019-8641). **950**

INDUSTRIAL REHABILITATION QUARTERLY. (US). **1611**

INDUSTRIAL RELATIONS & MANAGEMENT LETTER. (AT). **1678**

INDUSTRIAL RELATIONS JOURNAL (KARACHI, PAKISTAN). (PK). **Qty:** 4200. **1678**

INDUSTRIAL RELATIONS JOURNAL (LONDON, ENGLAND). (UK/0019-8692). **1678**

INDUSTRIAL RELATIONS LAW JOURNAL. (US/0145-188X). **3149**

INDUSTRIAL RELATIONS LEGAL INFORMATION BULLETIN. (UK). **3149**

INDUSTRIAL RELATIONS RESEARCH ASSOCIATION SERIES NEWSLETTER. (US/0749-2162). **1678**

INDUSTRIAL RESEARCHER. (II). **901**

INDUSTRIAL ROBOT, THE. (UK/0143-991X). **1219**

INDUSTRIE ALIMENTARI (PINEROLO). (IT/0019-901X). **2344**

INDUSTRIE-ANZEIGER. (GW/0019-9036). **617**

INDUSTRIE CERAMIQUE, L'. (FR/0019-9044). **Qty:** 3/yr. **2591**

INDUSTRIE DELLE BEVANDE. (IT/0390-0541). **2367**

INDUSTRIE LACKIER BETRIEB. (GW/0019-9109). **4224**

INDUSTRIE SENEGALAISE, L'. (SG). **1611**

INDUSTRIE SERVICE. (GW). **3481**

INDUSTRIE TEXTILE (PARIS). (FR/0019-9176). **5352**

INDUSTRIEBAU HANNOVER. (GW/0935-2023). **617**

INDUSTRIELLE OBST- UND GEMUESEVERWERTUNG, DIE. (GW/0367-939X). **2344**

INDUSTRIES DES CEREALES. (FR/0245-4505). **202**

INDUSTRISTATISTIK. (DK/0070-3532). **1534**

INDUSTRY AND DEVELOPMENT. GLOBAL REPORT / UNITED NATIONS INDUSTRIAL DEVELOPMENT ORGANIZATION. (US). **1611**

INDUSTRY AND ENVIRONMENT (ENGLISH EDITION). (FR/0378-9993). **2863**

INDUSTRY & HIGHER EDUCATION. (UK/0950-4222). **1611**

INDUSTRY INTERNATIONAL. (US/0276-7317). **682**

INDUSTRY REVIEW. (US). **5360**

INDY CAR RACING MAGAZINE. (US/1071-1759). **Qty:** 10. **4900**

INFANCIA Y APRENDIZAJE. (SP/0210-3702). **4590**

INFANT BEHAVIOR & DEVELOPMENT. (US/0163-6383). **4590**

INFANT MENTAL HEALTH JOURNAL. (US/0163-9641). **4590**

INFANTRY. (US/0019-9532). **4046**

INFECTION. (GW/0300-8126). **Qty:** 6. **3714**

INFECTION AND IMMUNITY. (US/0019-9567). **563**

INFECTIOUS DISEASE PRACTICE. (US/0162-6493). **3587**

INFERTILITY. (US/0160-7626). **3762**

INFINITY LIMITED. (US/1050-7280). **Qty:** 1-2. **3396**

INFO DGA. (FR). **682**

INFO FRANCHISE NEWSLETTER, THE. (US/0147-5924). **840**

INFO-INFOGETTABLE. (GW). **1064**

INFO JOURNAL / INTERNATIONAL FORTEAN ORGANIZATION. (US/0019-0144). **Qty:** 20. **4241**

INFOBRAZIL / CENTER OF BRAZILIAN STUDIES. (US/0736-8666). **1567**

INFOCUS (PORTLAND, OR.). (US/1040-2179). **870**

INFOFISH INTERNATIONAL. (MY/0127-2012). **Qty:** 50-60 copies. **2305**

INFOR MARECHALERIE. (BE/0774-4323). **3396**

INFORM (SILVER SPRING, MD.). (US/0892-3876). **4370**

INFORMACION SISTEMATICA. (MX/0185-2973). **5806**

INFORMACIONES Y MEMORIAS DE LA SOCIEDAD DE INGENIEROS DEL PERU. (PE). **1978**

INFORMAL LOGIC (WINDSOR, ONT.). (CN/0824-2577). **4349**

INFORMATEUR CATHOLIQUE (1985). (CN/0833-9228). **4964**

INFORMATIK-SPEKTRUM. (GW/0170-6012). **1259**

INFORMATION AGE. (UK/0261-4103). **1226**

INFORMATION AND COMPUTATION. (US/0890-5401). **1219**

INFORMATION & I.E. E DOCUMENTAZIONE. (IT/0390-2439). **1260**

INFORMATION AND LIBRARY MANAGER. (UK/0260-6879). **3215**

INFORMATION & MANAGEMENT. (NE/0378-7206). **1254**

INFORMATION AND REFERRAL. (US/0278-2383). **5289**

INFORMATION AND SOCIETY. (AT/1033-6273). **5247**

INFORMATION AND SOFTWARE TECHNOLOGY. (UK/0950-5849). **1260**

INFORMATION BULLETIN - CHILDREN'S COURT OF NEW SOUTH WALES. (AT/1031-6590). **2982**

INFORMATION BULLETIN / COMISION DE DERECHOS HUMANOS DE GUATEMALA, USA. (US). **4509**

INFORMATION BULLETIN (ROMANIAN-AMERICAN HERITAGE CENTER (U.S.). (US/0748-6502). **2739**

INFORMATION BULLETIN / WESTERN ASSOCIATION OF MAP LIBRARIES. (US/0049-7282). **3215**

INFORMATION - CANADIAN ASSOCIATION OF SOCIAL WORKERS. (CN/0315-3150). **5289**

INFORMATION CARDIOLOGIQUE, L'. (FR/0220-2476). **3706**

INFORMATION DEVELOPMENT. (UK/0266-6669). **3215**

INFORMATION EAUX. (FR/0012-9003). **5534**

INFORMATION GRAMMATICALE (PARIS), L'. (FR/0222-9838). **Qty:** 4/yr. **3287**

INFORMATION HOTLINE. (US/0360-5817). **3216**

INFORMATION INTELLIGENCE, ONLINE LIBRARIES, AND MICROCOMPUTERS. (US/0737-7770). **3216**

INFORMATION INTELLIGENCE ONLINE NEWSLETTER. (US/0194-0694). **1274**

INFORMATION - LUTHERAN WORLD FEDERATION NEWS SERVICE. (SZ). **5061**

INFORMATION MANAGEMENT & TECHNOLOGY. (UK). **Qty:** 9-10. **3258**

INFORMATION MANAGEMENT BULLETIN. (US/1046-9303). **Qty:** 2-3. **1188**

INFORMATION PROCHE-ORIENT. (CN/0711-2157). **2654**

INFORMATION RESEARCH NEWS. (UK/0959-8928). **3216**

INFORMATION RESOURCES MANAGEMENT JOURNAL. (US/1040-1628). **Qty:** 4. **3216**

INFORMATION RETRIEVAL & LIBRARY AUTOMATION. (US/0020-0220). **1275**

INFORMATION SEARCHER. (US/1055-3916). **Qty:** 4. **1752**

INFORMATION SERVICE NEWS AND ABSTRACTS / ADVISORY, CONCILIATION AND ARBITRATION SERVICE, WORK RESEARCH UNIT. (UK/0951-0524). **942**

INFORMATION SOCIETY, THE. (US/0197-2243). **3216**

INFORMATION SOURCES. (US/0734-9637). **3216**

INFORMATION STANDARDS QUARTERLY. (US/1041-0031). **3217**

INFORMATION STRATEGY. (US/0743-8613). **Qty:** (up to 4). **870**

INFORMATION SYSTEMS MANAGEMENT. (US/1058-0530). **Qty:** (published in each issue). **870**

INFORMATION SYSTEMS SECURITY. (US/1065-898X). **Qty:** 12. **1226**

INFORMATION TECHNOLOGY & LEARNING. (UK/0952-7923). **1286**

INFORMATION TECHNOLOGY NEWSLETTER (HARRISBURG, PA.). (US/1057-7939). **Qty:** 2. **3217**

INFORMATION TODAY. (US/8755-6286). **3217**

INFORMATIONS MONDIALES - UNDA. (BE/0258-9494). **1133**

INFORMATIONSDIENST SUDLICHES AFRIKA. (GW/0721-5088). **4477**

INFORMATIONWEEK (MANHASSET, N.Y.). (US/8750-6874). **1260**

INFORMATIQUE ET BUREAUTIQUE : L'HEBDO ROMAND DE L'INFORMATIQUE. (SZ). **1229**

INFORMATIQUE ET SCIENCES JURIDIQUES. (FR). **1226**

INFORMATIQUE PROFESSIONNELLE, L'. (FR/0750-1080). **1260**

INFORMATIVO. (BL/0524-2932). **5203**

INFORMATIVO CLAT. (VE). **1679**

INFORMATIVO LEGAL RODRIGO. (PE). **2982**

INFORMATORE AGRARIO, L'. (IT). **96**

INFORMATORE SCOLASTICO. (IT). **1092**

INFORMAZIONE CARDIOLOGICA. (IT). **Qty:** 6. **3706**

INFORME LATNOAMERICANO. (UK/0263-5372). **2489**

INFORMED. BLUE BANNER EDITION. (US/0730-6628). **4308**

INFORMER. (IT). **2517**

INFORMER (RALEIGH), THE. (US/0195-4318). **3217**

INFOS PARIS. (FR/0758-5373). **Qty:** 10. **96**

INGEGNERIA ALIMENTARE. LE CONSERVE ANIMALI. (IT/0394-588X). **Qty:** 20/yr. **2344**

INGENIERIA HIDRAULICA (LA HABANA). (CU/0253-0678). **2091**

INGENIEUR (DEN HAAG). (NE/0020-1146). **1978**

INGLESIDE INDEX, THE. (US). **5751**

INITIATIVE EUROPE MONITOR. (UK/0955-1697). **682**

INITIATIVES IN POPULATION. (PH/0115-2181). **4553**

INJURY. (UK/0020-1383). **3587**

INK & GALL. (US/0894-0479). **353**

INKSTONE. (CN/0714-2870). **3464**

INLAND ARCHITECT. (US/0020-1472). **Qty:** 10. **301**

INLAND EMPIRE MAGAZINE. (US/0199-5073). **Qty:** 50. **682**

INLAND RIVER GUIDE. (US/0198-859X). **5450**

INLAND SEAS. (US/0020-1537). **Qty:** 20. **2739**

INN BUSINESS (ESSEX, ONT.). (CN/0821-7610). **2807**

INNER HORIZONS. (US/0897-229X). **Qty:** (approx. 50-70). **5030**

INNER WOMAN. (US/1049-9709). **5559**

INNES REVIEW, THE. (UK/0020-157X). **5030**

INNOTECH JOURNAL. (PH). **1752**

INNOTECH NEWSLETTER. (PH). **1752**

INNOVATING (RENSSELAERVILLE, N.Y.). (US/1053-2587). **Qty:** 8. **870**

INNOVATION AND TECHNOLOGY TRANSFER/ DG XIII. (LU/0255-0806). **5114**

INNOVATION (MCLEAN, VA.). (US/0731-2334). **2099**

INNOVATIONS & RESEARCH IN CLINICAL SERVICES, COMMUNITY SUPPORT, AND REHABILITATION. (US/1062-7553). **Qty:** 12. **3926**

INNOVATIVE PACKAGING PARIS. (FR/0988-6249). **4219**

INORGANIC CHEMISTRY. (US/0020-1669). **1036**

INPSIDER (ATLANTA, GA.), THE. (US/1068-5340). **Qty:** 80. **4241**

INPUT. (CN/0706-151X). **3217**

INQUIRER, THE. (UK/0020-1723). **4965**

INQUIRY (OSLO). (NO/0020-174X). **4349**

INSCAPE LONDON. (UK/0264-7141). **353**

INSCRIPTIONS (STEVENS POINT, WIS.). (US/0882-2883). **Qty:** when received. **2454**

INSECT WORLD (LANSING, MICH.). (US/1043-6057). **1064**

INSECTA MUNDI. (US/0749-6737). **Qty:** 8-10. **5609**

INSEGNARE ALL' HANDICAPPATO. (IT/0393-8859). **1880**

INSERVICE (SYRACUSE, N.Y.). (US/0732-3808). **1864**

INSIDE ARTS. (US/1069-2029). **Qty:** 6-8. **385**

INSIDE BLUEGRASS. (US/0891-0537). **4122**

INSIDE CHICAGO. (US). **5480**

INSIDE COLLECTOR, THE. (US/1052-861X). **251**

INSIDE IRELAND. (IE/0332-2483). **2518**

INSIDE MS. (US/0739-9774). **3834**

INSIDE RADIO. (US/0731-9312). **1133**

INSIDE SPORTS. (US/0195-3478). **4900**

INSIDE THE AUBURN TIGERS (AUBURN, ALA.). (US/0279-2273). **4900**

INSIDE THE LEADING MAIL ORDER HOUSES. (US/0743-2895). **760**

INSIDE TRACK (HAMMONTON, N.J.). (US/1052-1607). **Qty:** 8. **4851**

INSIDER, THE. (BU/0861-3117). **Qty:** 12/yr. **2518**

INSIEME. (IT/0020-1871). **683**

INSIGHT (AKRON, OHIO). (US). **3217**

INSIGHT (BOSTON, MASS.). (US/0742-5244). **Qty:** 4/yr. **3396**

INSIGHT LAGOS. 1987. (NR/0794-7968). **4965**

INSIGHT (NORTHAMPTON). (UK/1354-2575). **2102**

INSIGHT ON COLLECTABLES (1987). (CN/0836-5873). **251**

INSIGHT (SAN FRANSISCO, CALIF.). (US/1060-135X). **Qty:** 2-4. **3857**

INSIGHTS INTO CHRISTIAN EDUCATION. (US/8756-3347). **4965**

INSIGHTS INTO OPEN EDUCATION/ UNIVERSITY OF NORTH DAKOTA. (US/0740-5596). **1896**

INSOLVENCY INTELLIGENCE. (UK/0950-2645). **2983**

INSPEC TOPICS. T0740. SEMICONDUCTOR LASERS. (UK). **Qty:** varies. **2065**

INSPIRATION (PITTSBURGH, PA.). (US/1065-8092). **Qty:** 3. **4965**

INSPIRED. (US). **301**

INSTALADOR, EL. (SP). **2065**

INSTALLATORE ITALIANO. (IT/0020-2118). **2606**

INSTAURATION. (US/0277-2302). **Qty:** 5. **4477**

INSTITUTE FOR MATH MANIA PRESENTS WONDERFUL IDEAS, THE. (US/1058-0573). **Qty:** 2-3. **3509**

INSTITUTE OF CRIMINOLOGY & FORENSIC SCIENCES BULLETIN. (US/0739-8514). **3166**

INSTITUTION OF MINING AND METALLURGY. TRANSACTIONS. SECTION B : APPLIED EARTH SCIENCES. (UK/0371-7453). **2140**

INSTITUTION OF MINING AND METALLURGY. TRANSACTIONS. SECTION C : MINERAL PROCESSING AND EXTRACTIVE METALLURGY. (UK/0371-9553). **4004**

INSTITUTIONAL DISTRIBUTION. (US/0020-3572). **2344**

INSTRUCTIONAL DEVELOPMENT AT WATERLOO. (CN/0228-2313). **1896**

INSTRUMENTALIST, THE. (US/0020-4331). **4122**

INSTRUMENTENBAU ZEITSCHRIFT, MUSIK INTERNATIONAL : IZ. (GW/0934-3962). **4122**

INSTRUMENTENBAUREPORT. (GW/0936-014X). **4123**

INSULATION GUIDE. (US/0737-2817). **1947**

INSULIN AND GLUCAGON. (UK/0142-8144). **3731**

INSURANCE ADVOCATE. (US/0020-4587). **2882**

INSURANCE ALMANAC (ENGLEWOOD. 1933), THE. (US/0074-0675). **2882**

INSURANCE AND EMPLOYEE BENEFITS LITERATURE. (US/0735-3944). **2883**

INSURANCE BROKERS' MONTHLY AND INSURANCE ADVISER. (UK/0260-2385). **Qty:** 10. **2883**

INSURANCE ECONOMICS SURVEYS. (US/0020-4668). **2883**

INSURANCE FORUM, THE. (US/0095-2923). **2883**

INSURANCE LAW ANTHOLOGY. (US/0892-4422). **2983**

INSURANCE LAW JOURNAL (SYDNEY, N.S.W.). (AT/1030-2379). **2883**

INSURANCE LAW MONTHLY. (UK). **2883**

INSURANCE MARKETING INSIDER. (US/1040-6867). **2884**

INSURANCE RECORD OF AUSTRALIA & NEW ZEALAND, THE. (AT). **2884**

INSURANCE SYSTEMS BULLETIN. (UK/0268-1935). **Qty:** 10-20. **2884**

INTEGRACION LATINOAMERICANA. (AG). **1635**

INTEGRAL YOGA. (US/0161-1380). **4965**

INTEGRATED MANUFACTURING SYSTEMS. (UK/0957-6061). **2116**

INTEGRATION (AMSTERDAM). (NE/0167-9260). **2066**

INTELLECTUAL ACTIVIST, THE. (US/0730-2355). **4477**

INTELLECTUAL PROPERTY JOURNAL. (CN/0824-7064). **1305**

INTELLECTUAL PROPERTY LAW (CHUR, SWITZERLAND). (UK/0892-2365). **1305**

INTELLECTUAL PROPERTY NEWSLETTER. (UK). **1305**

INTELLIGENCE DIGEST. (UK/0020-4900). **1496**

INTELLIGENCE (NEW YORK, N.Y. 1984). (US/1042-4296). **Qty:** 12. **1189**

INTELLIGENCE (NORWOOD). (US/0160-2896). **4590**

INTELLIGENCER (WHEELING, W.VA.) (US). **Qty:** 150-200. **5764**

INTELLIGENT SYSTEMS REPORT. (US/1054-8696). **Qty:** 12. **1213**

INTENSIVBEHANDLUNG. (GW/0341-3063). **3588**

INTENSIVE CARE WORLD (BALDOCK). (UK/0266-7037). **3588**

INTENSIVE THERAPY AND CLINICAL MONITORING. (UK). **3588**

INTER ALIA (RENO). (US/0092-6086). **Qty:** 12 per year. **2983**

INTER-AMERICAN ARBITRATION. (CN/0715-4771). **2983**

INTER-AMERICAN MUSIC REVIEW. (US/0195-6655). **4123**

INTER CDI ETAMPES. (FR/0242-2999). **Qty:** 6. **683**

INTER-CITY EXPRESS (OAKLAND, CALIF.). (US/0274-7464). **5636**

INTER DEPENDENT, THE. (US/0094-5072). **Qty:** 12. **4524**

INTER ECONOMICS. (GW/0020-5346). **1636**

INTER-MECANIQUE DU BATIMENT. (CN/0831-411X). **617**

INTER-PARLIAMENTARY BULLETIN. (SZ/0020-5079). **4524**

INTER-SOCIETY COLOR COUNCIL NEWS. (US/0731-2911). **5114**

INTERACTING WITH COMPUTERS. (UK/0953-5438). **1189**

INTERACTION - CANADIAN CHILD DAY CARE FEDERATION. (CN/0835-5819). **Qty:** 16. **5290**

INTERACTION (CANBERRA, A.C.T.). (AT/0818-6286). **1880**

INTERACTION (WASHINGTON, D.C. : 1981). (US/8756-6281). **2195**

INTERACTIVE LEARNING INTERNATIONAL. (UK/0748-5743). **1223**

INTERACTIVE VIDEO. (US/0743-4537). **1133**

INTERAMERICANA (RIO PIEDRAS, P.R.). (PR/8750-5428). **5808**

INTERAVIA (ENGLISH ED.). (UK/0020-5168). **24**

INTERBEHAVIORIST, THE. (US/8755-612X). **4590**

INTERCERAM. (GW/0020-5214). **2591**

INTERCHAMBER. (ET). **841**

INTERCHANGE - SCHOOL OF BUSINESS AND ECONOMICS. WILFRID LAURIER UNIVERSITY. (CN/0823-9851). **683**

INTERCHANGE SYDNEY. (AT/0814-4834). **Qty:** 4-5. **1801**

INTERCHANGE (SYDNEY, AUSTRALIA). (AT). **5017**

INTERCHANGE (TORONTO. 1984). (CN/0826-4805). **1753**

INTERCOLLEGIATE REVIEW, THE. (US/0020-5249). **1831**

INTERCOM (LETCHWORTH DEVELOPMENTAL SERVICES). (US). **1753**

INTERCONTINENTAL ADVANCED MANAGEMENT REPORT, THE. (US/0739-313X). **871**

INTERCULTURAL HORIZONS. (CN/0827-1550). **5247**

INTERCULTURE. (CN/0828-797X). **4965**

INTERCULTURE (MONTREAL. ED. FRANCAISE). (CN/0712-1571). **4965**

INTERDISCIPLINARY SCIENCE REVIEWS : ISR. (UK/0308-0188). **5114**

INTERFACE. (US/0163-6626). **1223**

INTERFACE (AMSTERDAM). (NE/0303-3902). **4123**

INTERFACE (CHICAGO). (US/0270-6717). **3217**

INTERFACE (MONTREAL. 1984). (CN/0826-4864). **Qty:** 5. **5114**

INTERFACE (SOCIETY FOR ENVIRONMENTAL GEOCHEMISTRY AND HEALTH). (US/0161-0120). **2233**

INTERFAITH WOMEN'S NEWS & NETWORK. (US/0892-6719). **5559**

INTERIGHTS BULLETIN. (UK/0268-3709). **Qty:** 8. **4509**

INTERIOR CONSTRUCTION. (US/0888-0387). **617**

INTERIOR DECORATORS' HANDBOOK. (US/0733-8511). **2901**

INTERIOR LANDSCAPE INDUSTRY. (US/0742-1648). **2420**

INTERIORSCAPE. (US/0744-8635). **2420**

INTERLAKEN REVIEW, THE. (US). **Qty:** 3. **5717**

INTERMEDIA (LONDON). (UK/0309-118X). **1157**

INTERMEDIAIR BELGIE. (BE). **1567**

INTERMEDIAIRE DES GENEALOGISTES. (BE/0020-5621). **2454**

INTERMODAL ASIA. (HK). **5450**

INTERMOUNTAIN CATHOLIC. (US/0273-6187). **4965**

INTERMOUNTAIN JEWISH NEWS. (US/0047-0511). **5643**

INTERNAL AUDITOR, THE. (US/0020-5745). **745**

INTERNAL MEDICINE NEWS & CARDIOLOGY NEWS. (US/0274-5542). **3746**

INTERNAMERICA (NEEDHAM, MASS.). (US/1061-7337). **Qty:** 3-4. **1680**

INTERNASJONAL POLITIKK (OSLO, NORWAY). (NO/0020-577X). **4524**

INTERNATIONAL ACCOUNTING BULLETIN. (UK/0265-0223). **745**

INTERNATIONAL AFFAIRS BULLETIN. (SA/0258-7270). **4524**

INTERNATIONAL AFFAIRS (LONDON). (UK/0020-5850). **4524**

INTERNATIONAL AFFAIRS STUDIES. (PL/0867-4493). **4524**

INTERNATIONAL AGRICULTURAL DEVELOPMENT (CROWBOROUGH, EAST SUSSEX). (UK/0261-4413). **96**

INTERNATIONAL AND COMPARATIVE LAW QUARTERLY, THE. (UK/0020-5893). **3129**

INTERNATIONAL ANNUAL JOURNAL OF ARTS, SCIENCES, ENGINEERING, AGRICULTURE, AND TECHNOLOGY. (US/0749-0682). **5114**

INTERNATIONAL ARBITRATION REPORT. (US/0886-0114). **3129**

INTERNATIONAL ASSOCIATION OF PANORAMIC PHOTOGRAPHERS :. (US/1063-7478). **4370**

INTERNATIONAL AUCTION RECORDS. (US/0074-1922). **353**

INTERNATIONAL AUTHORS AND WRITERS WHO'S WHO, THE. (UK/0143-8263). **433**

INTERNATIONAL AVIATION MECHANICS JOURNAL. (US/0045-1193). **24**

INTERNATIONAL BIBLIOGRAPHY OF STUDIES ON ALCOHOL. (US). **1350**

INTERNATIONAL BLOOD/PLASMA NEWS. (US/0742-7719). **3772**

INTERNATIONAL BONSAI. (US/0198-9561). **2420**

INTERNATIONAL BOTTLER AND PACKER, THE. (UK/0020-6199). **4219**

INTERNATIONAL BRAIN DOMINANCE REVIEW. (US/1046-5448). **Qty:** 2. **4590**

INTERNATIONAL BUILDING SERVICES ABSTRACTS. (UK/0140-4237). **617**

INTERNATIONAL BULK JOURNAL : IBJ. (UK/0260-1087). **5384**

INTERNATIONAL BULLETIN OF LAW & MENTAL HEALTH. (CN/0843-4964). **2983**

INTERNATIONAL BULLETIN OF MISSIONARY RESEARCH. (US/0272-6122). **4965**

INTERNATIONAL BUSINESS LAWYER. (UK/0309-7676). **3129**

INTERNATIONAL CD-ROM REPORT, THE. (CN/0847-0456). **1189**

INTERNATIONAL CHEMICAL ENGINEERING. (US/0020-6318). **2013**

INTERNATIONAL CHILDREN'S RIGHTS MONITOR. (SZ/0259-3696). **Qty:** 25. **4477**

INTERNATIONAL CHORAL BULLETIN. (US/0896-0968). **Qty:** 4-6. **4123**

INTERNATIONAL CLASSIFICATION. (GW/0340-0050). **3218**

INTERNATIONAL CLINICAL NUTRITION REVIEW. (AT/0813-9008). **Qty:** 4-5/yr. **4192**

INTERNATIONAL CLINICAL PSYCHOPHARMACOLOGY. (UK/0268-1315). **4308**

INTERNATIONAL COAL LETTER. (BE). **2140**

INTERNATIONAL COAL REPORT. (UK/0260-4299). **1947**

INTERNATIONAL COMET QUARTERLY, THE. (US/0736-6922). **395**

INTERNATIONAL COMMUNICATIONS REPORT. (UK). **1157**

INTERNATIONAL COMPUTER LAW ADVISER. (US/0893-2859). **1189**

INTERNATIONAL CONFERENCE ON THE PHYSICS OF SEMICONDUCTORS : PROCEEDINGS. (SI). **4405**

INTERNATIONAL CONSTRUCTION LAW REVIEW, THE. (UK/0265-1416). **3129**

INTERNATIONAL CONTRIBUTIONS TO LABOUR STUDIES. (UK/1052-9187). **1680**

INTERNATIONAL DENDROLOGY SOCIETY YEARBOOK. (UK/0307-322X). **514**

INTERNATIONAL DENTAL JOURNAL. (UK/0020-6539). **1325**

INTERNATIONAL DEVELOPMENT ABSTRACTS. (UK/0262-0855). **2913**

INTERNATIONAL DIRECTORY OF BOOK COLLECTORS. (UK). **4829**

INTERNATIONAL DIRECTORY OF RESOURCES FOR ARTISANS, THE. (US/0898-1094). **373**

INTERNATIONAL DOCUMENTARY. (US/0742-5333). **Qty:** 5-10. **4072**

INTERNATIONAL DOCUMENTS REVIEW. (US/1054-4933). **Qty:** 46. **4524**

INTERNATIONAL DOMOTIQUE NEWS PARIS. (FR/1148-3555). **5115**

INTERNATIONAL DREDGING REVIEW. (US/0737-8181). **1979**

INTERNATIONAL DRUG REPORT. (US/0148-4648). **3166**

INTERNATIONAL DRUG THERAPY NEWSLETTER. (US/0020-6571). **4308**

INTERNATIONAL ECONOMY, THE. (US/0898-4336). **1636**

INTERNATIONAL EDUCATION. (US/0160-5429). **1753**

INTERNATIONAL EDUCATOR (WASHINGTON, D.C.). (US/1059-4221). **Qty:** 2 - 3. **1753**

INTERNATIONAL ELECTROCHEMICAL PROGRESS. (US/0741-1413). **978**

INTERNATIONAL EMPLOYMENT GAZETTE. (US/1058-0506). **Qty:** varies. **4205**

INTERNATIONAL ENCYCLOPEDIA OF COMPOSITES. (GW). **1979**

INTERNATIONAL ENDODONTIC JOURNAL. (UK/0143-2885). **1325**

INTERNATIONAL ENVIRONMENT & SAFETY. (UK/0141-4836). **2174**

INTERNATIONAL ENVIRONMENTAL AFFAIRS. (US/1041-4665). **2195**

INTERNATIONAL EXAMINER (SEATTLE, WASH. 1973). (US/1065-1500). **Qty:** 20-50. **2654**

INTERNATIONAL EXECUTIVE. (US/0020-6652). **4502**

INTERNATIONAL FAMILY PLANNING PERSPECTIVES. (US/0190-3187). **2281**

INTERNATIONAL FELLOWSHIP NEWSLETTER, THE. (US). **4965**

INTERNATIONAL FIBER JOURNAL. (US/1049-801X). **5352**

INTERNATIONAL FICTION REVIEW. (CN/0315-4149). **3396**

INTERNATIONAL FINANCE SECTION PUBLICATIONS. (US). **1496**

INTERNATIONAL FINANCIAL LAW REVIEW. (UK/0262-6969). **3100**

INTERNATIONAL FIRE PHOTOGRAPHERS ASSOCIATION : NEWSLETTER : IFPA. (US). **4371**

INTERNATIONAL FOOD INGREDIENT. (NE/0924-5863). **2345**

INTERNATIONAL FORUM FOR LOGOTHERAPY, THE. (US/0191-3379). **4349**

INTERNATIONAL FORUM ON INFORMATION AND DOCUMENTATION. (NE/0304-9701). **3218**

INTERNATIONAL FREEDOM FOUNDATION. (SA/0897-5086). **1636**

INTERNATIONAL FRUIT WORLD. (SZ/0250-944X). **2345**

INTERNATIONAL GYMNAST (1986). (US/0891-6616). **4900**

INTERNATIONAL HAIR ROUTE. (CN/0820-6880). **3720**

INTERNATIONAL HEPATOLOGY COMMUNICATIONS. (NE/0928-4346). **3797**

INTERNATIONAL HISTORY REVIEW, THE. (CN/0707-5332). **2620**

INTERNATIONAL HUMANIST. (NE). **4349**

INTERNATIONAL INFORMATION, COMMUNICATION & EDUCATION. (II/0970-1850). **Qty:** 25. **3218**

INTERNATIONAL INSURANCE MONITOR. (US/0020-6997). **2884**

INTERNATIONAL INTERACTIONS. (UK/0305-0629). **4524**

INTERNATIONAL INVENTION REGISTER. (US/8755-9609). **1305**

INTERNATIONAL JOURNAL. (CN/0020-7020). **2692**

INTERNATIONAL JOURNAL FOR DEVELOPMENT TECHNOLOGY. (UK). **5115**

INTERNATIONAL JOURNAL FOR HOUSING SCIENCE AND ITS APPLICATIONS. (US/0146-6518). **2825**

INTERNATIONAL JOURNAL FOR NUMERICAL METHODS IN FLUIDS. (UK/0271-2091). **2091**

INTERNATIONAL JOURNAL FOR VITAMIN AND NUTRITION RESEARCH (SUPPLEMENT). (SZ/0300-9831). **4192**

INTERNATIONAL JOURNAL OF ADHESION AND ADHESIVES. (UK/0143-7496). **1053**

INTERNATIONAL JOURNAL OF ADOLESCENCE AND YOUTH. (UK/0267-3843). **2281**

INTERNATIONAL JOURNAL OF ADVERTISING. (UK/0265-0487). **760**

INTERNATIONAL JOURNAL OF AFRICAN HISTORICAL STUDIES, THE. (US/0361-7882). **2640**

INTERNATIONAL JOURNAL OF AGING & HUMAN DEVELOPMENT, THE. (US/0091-4150). **5247**

INTERNATIONAL JOURNAL OF AMBIENT ENERGY. (UK/0143-0750). **1947**

INTERNATIONAL JOURNAL OF ANDROLOGY. (UK/0105-6263). **3588**

INTERNATIONAL JOURNAL OF ANGIOLOGY, THE. (US/1061-1711). **3706**

INTERNATIONAL JOURNAL OF ARTIFICIAL ORGANS, THE. (IT/0391-3988). **3798**

INTERNATIONAL JOURNAL OF BIOCHEMISTRY, THE. (UK/0020-711X). **488**

INTERNATIONAL JOURNAL OF BIOLOGICAL MARKERS, THE. (IT/0393-6155). **3818**

INTERNATIONAL JOURNAL OF BIOMETEOROLOGY. (NE/0020-7128). **1426**

INTERNATIONAL JOURNAL OF BIOSOCIAL AND MEDICAL RESEARCH. (US/1044-811X). **5248**

INTERNATIONAL JOURNAL OF CANCER. (US/0020-7136). **3818**

INTERNATIONAL JOURNAL OF CARDIAC IMAGING. (US/0167-9899). **3706**

INTERNATIONAL JOURNAL OF CAREER MANAGEMENT, THE. (HK/0955-6214). **4205**

INTERNATIONAL

INTERNATIONAL JOURNAL OF CHILDBIRTH EDUCATION, THE. (US/0887-8625). **3762**

INTERNATIONAL JOURNAL OF CHILDREN'S RIGHTS, THE. (NE/0927-5568). **3121**

INTERNATIONAL JOURNAL OF CLINICAL AND EXPERIMENTAL HYPNOSIS, THE. (US/0020-7144). **2858**

INTERNATIONAL JOURNAL OF CLINICAL MONITORING AND COMPUTING. (NE/0167-9945). **1190**

INTERNATIONAL JOURNAL OF CLINICAL NEUROPSYCHOLOGY, THE. (US/0749-8470). **4591**

INTERNATIONAL JOURNAL OF CLINICAL PHARMACOLOGY, THERAPY AND TOXICOLOGY (1980). (GW/0174-4879). **4308**

INTERNATIONAL JOURNAL OF CLOTHING SCIENCE AND TECHNOLOGY. (UK/0955-6222). **1085**

INTERNATIONAL JOURNAL OF COGNITIVE EDUCATION & MEDIATED LEARNING. (UK/0957-4964). **1753**

INTERNATIONAL JOURNAL OF COMPARATIVE AND APPLIED CRIMINAL JUSTICE. (US/0192-4036). **3166**

INTERNATIONAL JOURNAL OF COMPUTER APPLICATIONS IN TECHNOLOGY. (SZ/0952-8091). **1190**

INTERNATIONAL JOURNAL OF COMPUTER SYSTEMS SCIENCE & ENGINEERING. (UK). **Qty:** 8. **1190**

INTERNATIONAL JOURNAL OF CONSTRUCTION MAINTENANCE & REPAIR, THE. (UK/0959-5090). **618**

INTERNATIONAL JOURNAL OF CONTINUING ENGINEERING EDUCATION. (SZ/0957-4344). **1979**

INTERNATIONAL JOURNAL OF COSMETIC SCIENCE. (UK/0142-5463). **404**

INTERNATIONAL JOURNAL OF DERMATOLOGY. (US/0011-9059). **3721**

INTERNATIONAL JOURNAL OF DEVELOPMENT BANKING : IJDB. (II). **792**

INTERNATIONAL JOURNAL OF EARLY CHILDHOOD. (CN/0020-7187). **Qty:** 4. **1753**

INTERNATIONAL JOURNAL OF ECOLOGY AND ENVIRONMENTAL SCIENCES. (II/0377-015X). **2217**

INTERNATIONAL JOURNAL OF EDUCOLOGY. (AT/0818-0563). **1754**

INTERNATIONAL JOURNAL OF ELECTRICAL ENGINEERING EDUCATION. (UK/0020-7209). **2066**

INTERNATIONAL JOURNAL OF ELECTRICAL POWER & ENERGY SYSTEMS. (UK/0142-0615). **2066**

INTERNATIONAL JOURNAL OF ENERGY SYSTEMS. (US/0226-1472). **1947**

INTERNATIONAL JOURNAL OF ENGINEERING EDUCATION, THE. (GW). **1980**

INTERNATIONAL JOURNAL OF ENVIRONMENTAL ANALYTICAL CHEMISTRY. (US/0306-7319). **1015**

INTERNATIONAL JOURNAL OF EPIDEMIOLOGY. (UK/0300-5771). **3735**

INTERNATIONAL JOURNAL OF FATIGUE. (UK/0142-1123). **2102**

INTERNATIONAL JOURNAL OF FOOD MICROBIOLOGY. (NE/0168-1605). **2345**

INTERNATIONAL JOURNAL OF FOOD SCIENCE AND TECHNOLOGY. (UK/0950-5423). **2345**

INTERNATIONAL JOURNAL OF FRONTIER MISSIONS. (US/0743-2429). **Qty:** 2-3 per year. **4965**

INTERNATIONAL JOURNAL OF FUSION ENERGY. (US/0146-4981). **495**

INTERNATIONAL JOURNAL OF GENERAL SYSTEMS. (US/0308-1079). **1247**

INTERNATIONAL JOURNAL OF GOVERNMENT AUDITING. (CN/0047-0724). **4732**

INTERNATIONAL JOURNAL OF GROUP PSYCHOTHERAPY, THE. (US/0020-7284). **3927**

INTERNATIONAL JOURNAL OF HEALTH PLANNING & MANAGEMENT, THE. (UK/0749-6753). **4785**

INTERNATIONAL JOURNAL OF HEALTH SCIENCES. (NE/0924-2287). **4785**

INTERNATIONAL JOURNAL OF HUMAN-COMPUTER INTERACTION. (US/1044-7318). **1220**

INTERNATIONAL JOURNAL OF HUMANITIES AND PEACE, THE. (US/1042-4032). **Qty:** 5-6. **2848**

INTERNATIONAL JOURNAL OF INSTRUCTIONAL MEDIA. (US/0092-1815). **1897**

INTERNATIONAL JOURNAL OF LAW AND THE FAMILY. (UK/0950-4109). **3121**

INTERNATIONAL JOURNAL OF LEGAL INFORMATION. (US/0731-1265). **Qty:** more than 100. **3218**

INTERNATIONAL JOURNAL OF LEPROSY AND OTHER MYCOBACTERIAL DISEASES. (US/0148-916X). **4785**

INTERNATIONAL JOURNAL OF LEXICOGRAPHY. (UK/0950-3846). **3287**

INTERNATIONAL JOURNAL OF MARITIME HISTORY. (CN/0843-8714). **4177**

INTERNATIONAL JOURNAL OF MATERIALS & PRODUCT TECHNOLOGY. (SZ/0268-1900). **1980**

INTERNATIONAL JOURNAL OF MECHANICAL ENGINEERING EDUCATION, THE. (UK/0306-4190). **2116**

INTERNATIONAL JOURNAL OF MEDICAL MICROBIOLOGY AND HYGIENE ABSTRACTS OF MICROBIOLOGY, VIROLOGY, PARASITOLOGY, PREVENTIVE MEDICINE AND ENVIRONMENTAL HYGIENE. (GW/0937-1591). **564**

INTERNATIONAL JOURNAL OF MENTAL HEALTH. (US/0020-7411). **3927**

INTERNATIONAL JOURNAL OF MICROCIRCULATION: CLINICAL AND EXPERIMENTAL. (NE/0167-6865). **3798**

INTERNATIONAL JOURNAL OF MIDDLE EAST STUDIES. (UK/0020-7438). **2768**

INTERNATIONAL JOURNAL OF MINI & MICROCOMPUTERS. (US/0702-0481). **1274**

INTERNATIONAL JOURNAL OF MODELLING & SIMULATION. (US/0228-6203). **1282**

INTERNATIONAL JOURNAL OF MORAL AND SOCIAL STUDIES. (UK/0267-9655). **2251**

INTERNATIONAL JOURNAL OF MUSIC EDUCATION / INTERNATIONAL SOCIETY FOR MUSIC EDUCATION. (UK). **4123**

INTERNATIONAL JOURNAL OF NUMERICAL METHODS FOR HEAT & FLUID FLOW. (UK/0961-5539). **Qty:** 12-15. **1980**

INTERNATIONAL JOURNAL OF OBSTETRIC ANESTHESIA. (UK/0959-289X). **3763**

INTERNATIONAL JOURNAL OF OFFENDER THERAPY AND COMPARATIVE CRIMINOLOGY. (US/0306-624X). **3166**

INTERNATIONAL JOURNAL OF ONCOLOGY. (GR/1019-6439). **3818**

INTERNATIONAL JOURNAL OF OPERATIONS & PRODUCTION MANAGEMENT. (UK/0144-3577). **871**

INTERNATIONAL JOURNAL OF OPTOELECTRONICS. (UK/0952-5432). **4435**

INTERNATIONAL JOURNAL OF ORAL AND MAXILLOFACIAL SURGERY. (DK/0901-5027). **3966**

INTERNATIONAL JOURNAL OF ORGANIZATIONAL ANALYSIS. (US/1055-3185). **684**

INTERNATIONAL JOURNAL OF OROFACIAL MYOLOGY, THE. (US/0735-0120). **1325**

INTERNATIONAL JOURNAL OF ORTHODONTICS. (US/0020-7500). **1325**

INTERNATIONAL JOURNAL OF PEPTIDE AND PROTEIN RESEARCH. (DK/0367-8377). **1042**

INTERNATIONAL JOURNAL OF PHARMACEUTICAL TECHNOLOGY & PRODUCT MANUFACTURE. (UK/0260-6267). **4308**

INTERNATIONAL JOURNAL OF PHARMACY PRACTICE. (UK/0961-7671). **4309**

INTERNATIONAL JOURNAL OF POLITICAL ECONOMY. (US/0891-1916). **4477**

INTERNATIONAL JOURNAL OF POLITICS, CULTURE, AND SOCIETY. (US/0891-4486). **5248**

INTERNATIONAL JOURNAL OF POLYMERIC MATERIALS. (US/0091-4037). **978**

INTERNATIONAL JOURNAL OF PRESSURE VESSELS AND PIPING, THE. (UK/0308-0161). **2116**

INTERNATIONAL JOURNAL OF PROJECT MANAGEMENT. (UK/0263-7863). **1980**

INTERNATIONAL JOURNAL OF PSYCHO-ANALYSIS, THE. (UK/0020-7578). **4591**

INTERNATIONAL JOURNAL OF PSYCHOSOMATICS. (US/0884-8297). **3589**

INTERNATIONAL JOURNAL OF PUBLIC ADMINISTRATION. (US/0190-0692). **4657**

INTERNATIONAL JOURNAL OF PURCHASING AND MATERIALS MANAGEMENT. (US/1055-6001). **Qty:** 2/yr. **950**

INTERNATIONAL JOURNAL OF QUALITATIVE STUDIES IN EDUCATION : QSE. (UK/0951-8398). **1754**

INTERNATIONAL JOURNAL OF REFRACTORY METALS & HARD MATERIALS. (UK/0263-4368). **4004**

INTERNATIONAL JOURNAL OF REFRIGERATION. (UK/0140-7007). **2606**

INTERNATIONAL JOURNAL OF REHABILITATION RESEARCH. (GW/0342-5282). **4389**

INTERNATIONAL JOURNAL OF REMOTE SENSING. (UK/0143-1161). **1980**

INTERNATIONAL JOURNAL OF RESEARCH AND ENGINEERING (POSTAL APPLICATION). (US/1043-7134). **1145**

INTERNATIONAL JOURNAL OF ROBOTICS & AUTOMATION. (US/0826-8185). **1213**

INTERNATIONAL JOURNAL OF SATELLITE COMMUNICATIONS. (UK/0737-2884). **1158**

INTERNATIONAL JOURNAL OF SCIENCE AND TECHNOLOGY. (US/0891-5083). **Qty:** 1. **5115**

INTERNATIONAL JOURNAL OF SCIENCE EDUCATION. (UK/0950-0693). **5115**

INTERNATIONAL JOURNAL OF SLAVIC LINGUISTICS AND POETICS. (US/0538-8228). **3287**

INTERNATIONAL JOURNAL OF SOCIAL PSYCHIATRY, THE. (UK/0020-7640). **Qty:** 16-20. **3927**

INTERNATIONAL JOURNAL OF SOCIOLOGY. (US/0020-7659). **5248**

INTERNATIONAL JOURNAL OF SOCIOLOGY & SOCIAL POLICY, THE. (UK/0144-333X). **5248**

INTERNATIONAL JOURNAL OF SOLAR ENERGY. (SZ/0142-5919). **1948**

INTERNATIONAL JOURNAL OF SPORT BIOMECHANICS. (US/0740-2082). **495**

INTERNATIONAL JOURNAL OF SPORT NUTRITION. (US/1050-1606). **4192**

INTERNATIONAL JOURNAL OF SPORT PSYCHOLOGY. (IT/0047-0767). **4900**

INTERNATIONAL JOURNAL OF SUPERCOMPUTER APPLICATIONS, THE. (US/0890-2720). **1287**

INTERNATIONAL JOURNAL OF TECHNOLOGY MANAGEMENT. (SZ/0267-5730). **5115**

INTERNATIONAL JOURNAL OF THE ADDICTIONS. (US/0020-773X). **1345**

INTERNATIONAL JOURNAL OF THE SOCIOLOGY OF LANGUAGE. (NE/0165-2516). **3287**

INTERNATIONAL JOURNAL OF THE SOCIOLOGY OF LAW. (UK/0194-6595). **2984**

INTERNATIONAL JOURNAL OF THERAPEUTIC COMMUNITIES. (UK/0196-1365). **3589**

INTERNATIONAL JOURNAL OF TRANSLATION. (II). **3288**

INTERNATIONAL JOURNAL OF TROPICAL AGRICULTURE. (II/0254-8755). **97**

INTERNATIONAL JOURNAL OF TROPICAL PLANT DISEASES. (II/0254-0126). **514**

INTERNATIONAL JOURNAL OF TURBO & JET-ENGINES. (IS/0334-0082). **24**

INTERNATIONAL JOURNAL OF TURKISH STUDIES. (US/0272-7919). **2692**

INTERNATIONAL JOURNAL OF URBAN AND REGIONAL RESEARCH. (UK/0309-1317). **2825**

INTERNATIONAL JOURNAL OF VEHICLE DESIGN. (SZ/0143-3369). **5417**

INTERNATIONAL JOURNAL OF WATER RESOURCES DEVELOPMENT. (UK/0790-0627). **5534**

INTERNATIONAL JOURNAL OF WILDLAND FIRE, THE. (US/1049-8001). **2291**

INTERNATIONAL JOURNAL OF WINE MARKETING. (HK/0954-7541). **2368**

INTERNATIONAL JOURNAL ON DRUG POLICY, THE. (UK/0955-3959). **1345**

INTERNATIONAL JOURNAL ON GROUP RIGHTS. (NE/0927-5908). **3130**

INTERNATIONAL JOURNAL ON POLICY AND INFORMATION. (US/0251-1266). **5204**

INTERNATIONAL

INTERNATIONAL JOURNAL ON THE UNITY OF THE SCIENCES. (US/0896-2294). **5115**

INTERNATIONAL JOURNAL ON WORLD PEACE. (US/0742-3640). **4524**

INTERNATIONAL LABMATE. (UK/0143-5140). **1015**

INTERNATIONAL LABOR AND WORKING CLASS HISTORY. (US/0147-5479). **1680**

INTERNATIONAL LAW PRACTICUM. (US/1041-3405). **3130**

INTERNATIONAL LAWYER, THE. (US/0020-7810). **3130**

INTERNATIONAL LAWYERS' NEWSLETTER. (US/0738-9728). **3130**

INTERNATIONAL LEGAL PERSPECTIVES. (US). **Qty:** 2. **3130**

INTERNATIONAL LEGAL PRACTITIONER. (UK/0309-7684). **3130**

INTERNATIONAL LIBRARY MOVEMENT. (II/0970-0048). **3218**

INTERNATIONAL LICENSING DIRECTORY, THE. (UK). **1305**

INTERNATIONAL LICHENOLOGICAL NEWSLETTER. (GW/0731-2830). **514**

INTERNATIONAL LIVING (WASHINGTON, D.C.). (US/0277-2442). **5481**

INTERNATIONAL MARINE BUSINESS JOURNAL. (US). **593**

INTERNATIONAL MARKETING REVIEW. (UK/0265-1335). **926**

INTERNATIONAL MARXIST REVIEW : IMR / ORGAN OF THE REVOLUTIONARY MARXIST TENDENCY OF THE FOURTH INTERNATIONAL. (UK). **4477**

INTERNATIONAL MEDIA GUIDE. EDITION, BUSINESS/PROFESSIONAL PUBLICATIONS, EUROPE. (US/0730-5273). **761**

INTERNATIONAL MEDIA GUIDE. EDITION, BUSINESS/PROFESSIONAL PUBLICATIONS, MIDDLE EAST/AFRICA. (US). **761**

INTERNATIONAL MIGRATION (GENEVA, SWITZERLAND). (SZ/0020-7985). **1919**

INTERNATIONAL MIGRATION REVIEW : IMR. (US/0197-9183). **1919**

INTERNATIONAL NETWORKS. (US/0739-9898). **1158**

INTERNATIONAL NEWS ON FATS, OILS AND RELATED MATERIALS. (US/0897-8026). **1025**

INTERNATIONAL NURSING REVIEW (LONDON, ENGLAND). (SZ/0020-8132). **3857**

INTERNATIONAL OBSERVER (WASHINGTON, D.C.). (US/1061-0324). **2620**

INTERNATIONAL OLD LACERS INC., BULLETIN. (US/0740-6746). **Qty:** 20. **5352**

INTERNATIONAL OLYMPIC LIFTER. (US/0739-5396). **Qty:** 4-6. **4901**

INTERNATIONAL OPHTHALMOLOGY. (NE/0165-5701). **3875**

INTERNATIONAL ORGANIZATION. (US/0020-8183). **4525**

INTERNATIONAL PACKAGING ABSTRACTS. (UK/0260-7409). **4222**

INTERNATIONAL PAF USERS GROUP SOFTWARE. (US). **Qty:** 2. **1190**

INTERNATIONAL PARALLELS. (US/1055-3649). **841**

INTERNATIONAL PEAT JOURNAL. (FI/0782-7784). **1948**

INTERNATIONAL PENTECOSTAL HOLINESS ADVOCATE, THE. (US/0145-6970). **Qty:** 16-18. **5061**

INTERNATIONAL PERMACULTURE SPECIES YEARBOOK, THE. (US/0896-5781). **2217**

INTERNATIONAL PEST CONTROL. (UK/0020-8256). **4245**

INTERNATIONAL PHARMACEUTICAL ABSTRACTS. (US/0020-8264). **4334**

INTERNATIONAL PHILOSOPHICAL QUARTERLY. (US/0019-0365). **Qty:** 40. **4349**

INTERNATIONAL POETRY REVIEW (GREENSBORO). (US/0145-0786). **3344**

INTERNATIONAL POLYMER PROCESSING. (GW/0930-777X). **4455**

INTERNATIONAL POPULAR BRIDGE MONTHLY. (UK/0951-1555). **4851**

INTERNATIONAL PRESS JOURNAL. (CN). **2920**

INTERNATIONAL PROBLEMS. (IS/0020-840X). **Qty:** 40. **4525**

INTERNATIONAL PSYCHOLOGIST. (US/0047-116X). **4591**

INTERNATIONAL PUBLIC RELATIONS REVIEW. (UK/0269-0357). **Qty:** 10. **761**

INTERNATIONAL QUARTERLY OF COMMUNITY HEALTH EDUCATION. (US/0272-684X). **4785**

INTERNATIONAL QUARTERLY OF ENTOMOLOGY. (TU/0256-6672). **5610**

INTERNATIONAL QUARTERLY (TALLAHASS., FLA.). (US/1060-6084). **Qty:** 2 per issue. **3396**

INTERNATIONAL RAILWAY JOURNAL AND RAPID TRANSIT REVIEW. (UK/0744-5326). **5432**

INTERNATIONAL RAILWAY TRAVELER, THE. (US/0891-7655). **5432**

INTERNATIONAL REAL ESTATE JOURNAL. (US/8755-6138). **4839**

INTERNATIONAL REHABILITATION REVIEW. (US/0020-8477). **4389**

INTERNATIONAL RELATIONS (LONDON). (UK/0047-1178). **4525**

INTERNATIONAL REVIEW FOR THE SOCIOLOGY OF SPORT. (GW/0074-7769). **4901**

INTERNATIONAL REVIEW OF ADMINISTRATIVE SCIENCES. (BE/0020-8523). **4657**

INTERNATIONAL REVIEW OF AFRICAN AMERICAN ART, THE. (US/1045-0920). **353**

INTERNATIONAL REVIEW OF MISSIONS. (SZ/0020-8582). **4966**

INTERNATIONAL REVIEW OF NEUROBIOLOGY. (US/0074-7742). **459**

INTERNATIONAL REVIEW OF SOCIAL HISTORY. (NE/0020-8590). **5248**

INTERNATIONAL REVIEW OF SOCIOLOGY OF EDUCATION. (AT/0726-4178). **5248**

INTERNATIONAL REVIEW OF THE RED CROSS. (SZ/0020-8604). **Qty:** 15. **5290**

INTERNATIONAL RICE RESEARCH NEWSLETTER. (PH/0115-0944). **Qty:** 4. **174**

INTERNATIONAL RICE RESEARCH NOTES. (PH). **Qty:** 4. **175**

INTERNATIONAL ROUND TABLE, THE. (US). **841**

INTERNATIONAL SAUDI-REPORT. (UK/0265-5799). **2505**

INTERNATIONAL SCHOOLS JOURNAL, THE. (UK). **1754**

INTERNATIONAL SEMIOTIC SPECTRUM. (CN/0825-0456). **2848**

INTERNATIONAL SMALL BUSINESS JOURNAL. (UK/0266-2426). **684**

INTERNATIONAL SOCIAL SCIENCE REVIEW. (US/0278-2308). **5204**

INTERNATIONAL SOCIAL SECURITY REVIEW (ENGLISH EDITION). (SZ/0020-871X). **5290**

INTERNATIONAL SOCIAL WORK. (UK/0020-8728). **5290**

INTERNATIONAL SOCIETY OF BASSISTS. (US/0892-0532). **4123**

INTERNATIONAL STUDIES IN PHILOSOPHY. (US/0270-5664). **4349**

INTERNATIONAL SUGAR JOURNAL. (UK/0020-8841). **2345**

INTERNATIONAL TAX ADVISOR, THE. (NE/0920-315X). **2984**

INTERNATIONAL TAX & BUSINESS LAWYER. (US/0741-4269). **3131**

INTERNATIONAL TAX REPORT, THE. (UK/0300-1628). **902**

INTERNATIONAL TELEVISION & VIDEO ALMANAC. (US/0895-2213). **1133**

INTERNATIONAL TEXTILES. (NE/0020-8914). **5352**

INTERNATIONAL THIRD WORLD STUDIES JOURNAL & REVIEW. (US/1041-3944). **4526**

INTERNATIONAL TRADE FORUM. (SZ/0020-8957). **926**

INTERNATIONAL TRADE JOURNAL, THE. (US/0885-3908). **841**

INTERNATIONAL TRAVEL NEWS (SACRAMENTO, CALIF.). (US/0191-8761). **5481**

INTERNATIONAL TREE CROPS JOURNAL, THE. (UK/0143-5698). **2385**

INTERNATIONAL TROMBONE ASSOCIATION SERIES. (US/0363-5708). **4123**

INTERNATIONAL TV & VIDEO GUIDE. (UK). **1133**

INTERNATIONAL UNDERSTANDING AT SCHOOL. (FR). **1897**

INTERNATIONAL UROLOGY AND NEPHROLOGY. (HU/0301-1623). **3990**

INTERNATIONAL VISITOR. (US/1058-5575). **Qty:** 3. **5481**

INTERNATIONAL WATER REPORT. (US/0893-8776). **2233**

INTERNATIONAL WHO'S WHO IN MUSIC AND MUSICIANS' DIRECTORY. (UK/0307-2894). **433**

INTERNATIONAL YEARBOOK OF EDUCATIONAL AND TRAINING TECHNOLOGY. (UK). **1897**

INTERNATIONAL ZOO-NEWS. (UK/0020-9155). **5586**

INTERNATIONALE BIBLIOGRAPHIE DER REZENSIONEN WISSENSCHAFTLICHER LITERATUR. (GW/0020-918X). **3357**

INTERNATIONALE BIBLIOGRAPHIE DER ZEITSCHRIFTENLITERATUR AUS ALLEN GEBIETEN DES WISSENS. (GW). **3357**

INTERNATIONALE JAHRESBIBLIOGRAPHIE DER FESTSCHRIFTEN : IJBF. (GW). **417**

INTERNATIONALE JAHRESBIBLIOGRAPHIE DER KONGRESSBERICHTE. (GW/0933-1905). **417**

INTERNATIONALE KATHOLISCHE ZEITSCHRIFT. (GW/0341-8693). **5030**

INTERNATIONALE KIRCHLICHE ZEITSCHRIFT. (SZ/0020-9252). **4966**

INTERNATIONALE MATHEMATISCHE NACHRICHTEN. (AU). **3510**

INTERNATIONALES ARCHIV FUER SOZIALGESCHICHTE DER DEUTSCHEN LITERATUR. (GW/0340-4528). **3397**

INTERNATIONALES ASIEN FORUM. (GW/0020-9449). **5204**

INTERNATIONALES SAUNA-ARCHIV. (GW/0178-7764). **2599**

INTERNATIONALES VERKEHRSWESEN. (GW/0020-9511). **5384**

INTERNISTISCHE PRAXIS. (GW/0020-9570). **3590**

INTERNSHIPS. (US/0272-5460). **4205**

INTERP CENTRAL CLEARINGHOUSE NEWSLETTER. (US/0890-1538). **4205**

INTERPLASTICS (MILANO). (IT/0392-3800). **4455**

INTERPRES. (IT). **3397**

INTERPRETATION (RICHMOND). (US/0020-9643). **4966**

INTERPRETATION (THE HAGUE). (US/0020-9635). **4478**

INTERPRETE, L'. (SZ/0047-1291). **3288**

INTERRACE (SCHENECTADY, N.Y.). (US/1047-5370). **Qty:** 5-9. **2264**

INTERRACIAL BOOKS FOR CHILDREN BULLETIN. (US/0146-5562). **1065**

INTERSCAMBIO. (IT/0394-087X). **1497**

INTERSCHOLASTIC ATHLETIC ADMINISTRATION. (US/0097-871X). **Qty:** 4. **4901**

INTERSECTIONS. (US/0095-6945). **5249**

INTERSEZIONI. (IT). **2848**

INTERSTATE. (US/0363-9991). **3397**

INTERTAX. (NE/0165-2826). **4733**

INTERVAL (SAN DIEGO, CALIF.). (US/0276-3052). **4123**

INTERVALLE. (GW). **4123**

INTERVENANT. (CN/0823-213X). **Qty:** 10. **1345**

INTERVENOR : NEWSLETTER OF THE CANADIAN ENVIRONMENTAL LAW ASSOCIATION. (CN/0820-3458). **Qty:** 6/yr. **3113**

INTERVENTION. (CN/0047-1321). **5290**

INTERVENTION (QUEBEC). (CN/0705-1972). **2535**

INTERVENTIONS ECONOMIQUES POUR UNE ALTERNATIVE SOCIALE. (CN/0715-3570). **1497**

INTERVENTIONS SONORES. (CN/1181-7739). **Qty:** 12. **4124**

INTI (PROVIDENCE, R.I.). (US/0732-6750). **Qty:** 10. **3397**

INTIMATE FASHION NEWS. (US/1061-5792). **Qty:** 2-3. **1085**

INUIT ART ENTHUSIASTS NEWSLETTER, THE. (CN/0824-0639). **353**

INUIT ART QUARTERLY. (CN/0831-6708). **353**

INUKTITUT (ENGLISH AND INUIT EDITION). (CN/0020-9872). **Qty:** 2. **2264**

INVENTORS' DIGEST (COLORADO SPRINGS, COLO.). (US/0883-9859). **Qty:** 6-12. **5116**

INVENTORS' VOICE. (US/0748-7851). **5116**

INVERT MAGAZINE. (UK/0957-3828). **429**

INVERTEBRATE REPRODUCTION & DEVELOPMENT. (IS/0792-4259). **5586**

INVESTAMERICA (SAN FRANCISCO, CALIF.). (US/1040-2934). **902**

INVESTIGACION AGRARIA. ECONOMIA. (SP/0213-635X). **97**

INVESTIGACION AGRARIA. PRODUCCION Y PROTECCION VEGETALES. (SP/0213-5000). **175**

INVESTIGACION AGRARIA. PRODUCCION Y SANIDAD ANIMALES. (SP/0213-5035). **213**

INVESTIGACION Y TECNICA DEL PAPEL. (SP/0368-0789). **4234**

INVESTIGATING. (AT/0815-9602). **5116**

INVESTIGATOR. (AT/0021-0013). **2669**

INVESTMENT ADVISOR (SHREWSBURY, N.J.). (US/1069-1731). Qty: 6. **902**

INVESTMENT BULLETIN. (US/0401-8680). **902**

INVESTMENT DEALERS' DIGEST, THE. (US/0021-0080). **793**

INVESTOR RELATIONS NEWSLETTER. (US). **903**

INVESTOR, U.S.A. (US/0739-8026). **903**

INVESTOR'S DAILY. (US). **903**

INVESTOR'S YEARBOOK. (US/0741-9813). **903**

INVIRONMENT (BUFFALO GROVE, ILL.). (US/1059-4078). Qty: 4. **2175**

INVIVO. (CN/0836-3838). **459**

INVOLVEMENT & PARTICIPATION / IPA. (UK). **872**

INVOLVEMENT : THE JOURNAL OF THE INVOLVEMENT & PARTICIPATION ASSOCIATION. (UK). **872**

INWARD LIGHT. (US/0021-0250). **4966**

IO, MANAGEMENT-ZEITSCHRIFT INDUSTRIELLE ORGANISATION. (SZ/0019-9281). **872**

IOLA HERALD, THE. (US/0886-8360). **5768**

IOP NEWSLETTER. (US/1016-4928). **514**

IOWA ARCHITECT. (US/0021-0439). Qty: 10-20. **301**

IOWA BIRD LIFE. (US/0021-0455). Qty: varies. **5617**

IOWA CONSERVATIONIST. (US/0021-0471). **2195**

IOWA DENTAL JOURNAL, THE. (US/0021-0498). **1325**

IOWA INTERLINK. (US/1050-2270). **4657**

IOWA MANUFACTURERS REGISTER. (US/0737-7940). **3481**

IOWA MEDICINE. (US/0746-8709). **3590**

IOWA MUNICIPALITIES. (US/0021-0595). **4657**

IOWA QUERIES. (US/1044-6931). **2454**

IOWA REVIEW, THE. (US/0021-065X). **3397**

IOWA SCIENCE TEACHERS' JOURNAL. (US/0021-0676). **5116**

IOWA STATE UNIVERSITY VETERINARIAN. (US/0099-5851). **5512**

IOWA WOMAN. (US/0271-8227). Qty: 20. **5559**

IP MARK. (SP). **684**

IPA REVIEW (1986). (AT/1030-4177). **4733**

IPADE ALAGBARA. (US/0883-6620). **5268**

IPEF, INSTITUTO DE PESQUISAS E ESTUDOS FLORESTAIS. (BL/0100-4557). **2385**

IPI DATA SERVICE. MIDDLE EAST. (US). **4261**

IPM PRACTITIONER, THE. (US/0738-968X). **4245**

IPN-BLATTER. (GW/0179-5775). Qty: 16. **1755**

IPPF OPEN FILE. (UK). Qty: 300. **589**

IPTC NEWS. (UK/1012-8719). **1158**

IQBAL REVIEW. (PK/0021-0773). **3397**

IRAL, INTERNATIONAL REVIEW OF APPLIED LINGUISTICS IN LANGUAGE TEACHING. (GW/0019-042X). **3288**

IRAN NAMEH. BUNYAD-I MUTALAAT-I IRAN. (US/0892-4147). Qty: 8-10. **2654**

IRAN TIMES, THE. (US). Qty: 45050. **5647**

IRANIAN STUDIES. (US/0021-0862). **2768**

IRANIAN WOMEN QUARTERLY. (CN). **5559**

IRANIYAN (TORONTO). (CN/0832-2007). Qty: 12. **5786**

IRANSHINASI (BETHESDA, MD.). (US/1051-5364). **3397**

IRE EMPLOYMENT LAW : THE INTERNATIONAL NEWSLETTER ON ENGAGEMENTS AND DISMISSALS. (BE). **3150**

IRE JOURNAL, THE. (US/0164-7016). Qty: 8. **2921**

IRELAND : A PARLIAMENTARY DIRECTORY. (IE). **4658**

IRELAND OF THE WELCOMES. (IE/0021-0943). **2518**

IRELAND TODAY. (IE/0332-0103). **5481**

IRENIKON. (BE/0021-0978). **4966**

IRIS (CHARLOTTESVILLE, VA.). (US/0896-1301). **5204**

IRIS (MONTPELLIER). (FR/0291-2066). Qty: 1. **3397**

IRISH AMERICA. (US/0884-4240). **2739**

IRISH ANCESTOR, THE. (IE/0047-1437). **2454**

IRISH ASTRONOMICAL JOURNAL, THE. (UK/0021-1052). **396**

IRISH BAPTIST HISTORICAL SOCIETY JOURNAL. (IE/0075-0727). **5061**

IRISH BIBLICAL STUDIES. (IE/0268-6112). Qty: 20. **5017**

IRISH BIOTECH NEWS. (IE/0790-1747). **459**

IRISH BIRDS. (IE/0332-0111). Qty: 2-10. **5617**

IRISH ECHO. (US/0192-1215). **2264**

IRISH ECONOMIC AND SOCIAL HISTORY. (IE/0332-4893). **2692**

IRISH EDITION. (US/1063-7532). Qty: 50. **2264**

IRISH FARMER'S JOURNAL. (IE). **97**

IRISH FORESTRY. (IE/0021-1192). **2385**

IRISH GENEALOGIST. (UK/0306-8358). **2454**

IRISH GENEALOGY DIGEST. (US/8756-1484). **2454**

IRISH GEOGRAPHY. (IE/0075-0778). **2566**

IRISH HERITAGE LINKS. (UK/0957-0837). **2454**

IRISH HISTORICAL STUDIES. (IE/0021-1214). **2692**

IRISH JOURNAL OF EDUCATION, THE. (IE/0021-1257). **1755**

IRISH JOURNAL OF MEDICAL SCIENCE. (IE/0021-1265). **3590**

IRISH JOURNAL OF PSYCHOLOGICAL MEDICINE. (IE/0790-9667). **3927**

IRISH JOURNAL OF PSYCHOLOGY, THE. (IE/0303-3910). **4592**

IRISH JURIST, THE. (IE/0021-1273). **2985**

IRISH LITERARY SUPPLEMENT. (US/0733-3390). **3397**

IRISH MEDICAL JOURNAL. (IE/0332-3102). Qty: 6. **3590**

IRISH NATURALISTS' JOURNAL, THE. (UK/0021-1311). **4166**

IRISH NEWS AND BELFAST MORNING NEWS, THE. (IE). **5803**

IRISH QUERIES. (US/1044-6923). **2454**

IRISH REVIEW (CORK, IRELAND). (IE/0790-7850). Qty: 30. **2518**

IRISH SLAVONIC STUDIES. (UK/0260-2067). Qty: 30-40. **2692**

IRISH SWORD, THE. (IE/0021-1389). **2693**

IRISH UNIVERSITY REVIEW. (IE/0021-1427). **3344**

IRISH VETERINARY JOURNAL. (IE/0368-0762). **5512**

IRISH VETERINARY NEWS. (IE). **5512**

IRISH VOICE (NEW YORK, N.Y.). (US/0895-4534). Qty: 52 per year. **5717**

IRODALOMTORTENETI KOZLEMENYEK. (HU/0021-1486). **3458**

IRON AND STEEL ENGINEER. (US/0021-1559). **4004**

IRON AND STEEL INDUSTRY. ANNUAL STATISTICS FOR THE UNITED KINGDOM. (UK/0572-709X). **1612**

IRON & STEELMAKER. (US/0275-8687). **4005**

IRON-MEN ALBUM MAGAZNE. (US). **2117**

IRONMAKING & STEELMAKING. (UK/0301-9233). **4005**

IRPI. INTERNATIONAL REINFORCED PLASTICS INDUSTRY. (UK/0261-5487). Qty: 6. **4455**

IRRICAB. (IS/0376-5083). **175**

IRRIGATION AND POWER. (II/0367-9993). **2091**

IRRIGATION FARMER, THE. (AT). **175**

IRRINEWS. (IS/0304-3606). **175**

IRSST / IRSST, INSTITUT DE RECHERCHE EN SANTE ET EN SECURITE DU TRAVAIL DU QUEBEC, L'. (CN/0822-2754). **2864**

IS AUDIT & CONTROL JOURNAL. (US/1076-4100). **1260**

ISA TRANSACTIONS. (US/0019-0578). **5116**

ISAAS NEWSLETTER / INDIAN SOCIETY FOR AFRO-ASIAN STUDIES. (II). **4526**

ISIE. (US/0894-928X). Qty: 4. **5290**

ISIS. (US/0021-1753). **5116**

ISIS MAGAZINE : MAGAZINE OF THE INDEPENDENT SCHOOLS INFORMATION SERVICE, THE. (UK). Qty: 9. **1755**

ISKCON WORLD REVIEW, THE. (US/0748-2280). **4966**

ISKUSSTVO. (RU/0021-177X). **353**

ISLA (MANGILAO, GUAM). (GU/1054-9390). Qty: 10. **238**

ISLAMIC AFFAIRS. (US/0748-0482). **5043**

ISLAMIC QUARTERLY, THE. (UK/0021-1842). **4966**

ISLAMIC STUDIES. (PK/0578-8072). Qty: 4. **5043**

ISLAMOCHRISTIANA. ISLAMIYAT MASIHIYAT. (IT). **4966**

ISLAND. (AT/1035-3127). **3397**

ISLAND GROWER, THE. (CN/0827-2824). Qty: 5-10. **2420**

ISLAND (LANTZVILLE). (CN/0227-0773). **3464**

ISLAND MAGAZINE, THE. (CN/0384-8175). **2739**

ISLAND (OAKLAND, CALIF.). (US/0894-3494). **2693**

ISLAND PACKET, THE. (US/0746-4886). **5742**

ISLAND PARENT MAGAZINE. (CN/0838-5505). **2281**

ISLAND PROPERTIES REPORT. QUARTERLY REPORT. (US/0882-1887). **4839**

ISLAND. SANDY BAY. (AT/1035-3127). **3397**

ISLANDER, THE. (US). Qty: 52. **5654**

ISLANDS (SANTA BARBARA, CALIF.). (US/0745-7847). **5481**

ISLANDWIDE RUNNER. (US/0740-6266). **4901**

ISM. INFORMATION SECURITY MONITOR. (UK/0950-7388). Qty: 5. **1227**

ISMEC, MECHANICAL ENGINEERING ABSTRACTS. (US/0896-7113). **2005**

ISOKINETICS AND EXERCISE SCIENCE. (US). **2599**

ISOTECH JOURNAL OF THERMOMETRY. (US). **5116**

ISOZYMES. (US/0160-3787). **488**

ISPT JOURNAL OF RESEARCH. (II). **4592**

ISRAEL ENVIRONMENT BULLETIN. (IS/0334-3804). **2175**

ISRAEL EXPLORATION JOURNAL. (IS/0021-2059). **270**

ISRAEL HORIZONS. (US/0021-2083). **5048**

ISRAEL JOURNAL OF BOTANY. (IS/0021-213X). **514**

ISRAEL JOURNAL OF MEDICAL SCIENCES. (IS/0021-2180). **3590**

ISRAEL JOURNAL OF PLANT SCIENCES. (IS/0792-9978). **514**

ISRAEL JOURNAL OF PSYCHIATRY AND RELATED SCIENCES, THE. (IS/0333-7308). **3927**

ISRAEL JOURNAL OF VETERINARY MEDICINE. (IS/0334-9152). Qty: 4-6. **5512**

ISRAEL JOURNAL OF ZOOLOGY. (IS/0021-2210). **5587**

ISRAEL LAW REVIEW. (IS/0021-2237). Qty: 4-8. **2985**

ISRAEL NUMISMATIC JOURNAL. (IS/0021-2288). **2781**

ISRAEL SOCIAL SCIENCE RESEARCH. (IS). Qty: 2-8. **5205**

ISRAELI FOREIGN AFFAIRS. (US/0883-9832). **4526**

ISRAELI JOURNAL OF AQUACULTURE, BAMIDGEH. (IS/0792-156X). **2306**

ISS DIRECTORY OF OVERSEAS SCHOOLS. (US/0732-7862). **1755**

ISSLEDOVANIE ZEMLI IZ KOSMOSA. (SZ/0275-911X). **1981**

ISSO NEWSLETTER, THE. (US/1064-4393). Qty: 2/yr. **25**

ISSUE PAPER / U.S. COMMITTEE FOR REFUGEES. (US/0882-9276). **1919**

ISSUES & OBSERVATIONS. (US/1065-464X). Qty: 2. **872**

ISSUES & STUDIES. (CH/1013-2511). **4526**

ISSUES & VIEWS. (US/1041-3839). Qty: 4. **2264**

ISSUES, EVENTS & IDEAS. (CN/0704-6936). **1804**

ISSUES IN CHILD ABUSE ACCUSATIONS. (US/1043-8823). Qty: 75. **5291**

ISSUES IN COMPREHENSIVE PEDIATRIC NURSING. (US/0146-0862). **3857**

ISSUES

ISSUES IN INTEGRATIVE STUDIES. (US). **1755**

ISSUES IN LAW & MEDICINE. (US/8756-8160). Qty: 15-20. **2985**

ISSUES IN MENTAL HEALTH NURSING. (US/0161-2840). **3858**

ISSUES IN SCIENCE AND TECHNOLOGY. (US/0748-5492). **5116**

ISSUES IN SOCIAL WORK EDUCATION / ASSOCIATION OF TEACHERS IN SOCIAL WORK EDUCATION. (UK/0261-4154). **5291**

ISSUES IN WRITING. (US/0897-0696). Qty: 10. **2921**

ISTF NEWS. (US/0276-2056). **2385**

ISTF NOTICIAS. (US/0743-5991). Qty: 8. **2385**

ISTMO. (MX/0021-261X). **5249**

ISURI : DO. HARISIMHA GAURA VISVAVIDYALAYA, SAGARA KE HINDI-VIBHAGA KE ANTARGATA KRIYASILA BUNDELI-PITHA KA AYOJANA. (II). **3288**

IT LINK. (UK/0954-2612). **3219**

IT TRAINING. (UK/0954-7940). **1223**

ITALIA CONTEMPORANEA. (IT/0392-3568). **2693**

ITALIA GRAFICA, L'. (IT/0021-2784). **4566**

ITALIAN-AMERICAN BUSINESS. (IT). **1636**

ITALIAN AMERICANA. (US/0096-8846). Qty: 25-35/yr. **2264**

ITALIAN CARS. (UK/0960-3204). **5417**

ITALIAN GENEALOGIST. (US/0884-9080). **2455**

ITALIAN GENERAL REVIEW OF DERMATOLOGY. (IT/0021-292X). **3721**

ITALIAN GREYHOUND, THE. (US/0735-8504). **4286**

ITALIAN JOURNAL OF BIOCHEMISTRY. (IT/0021-2938). **488**

ITALIAN JOURNAL OF GASTROENTEROLOGY, THE. (IT/0392-0623). **3746**

ITALIAN JOURNAL OF ORTHOPAEDICS AND TRAUMATOLOGY. (IT/0390-5489). **3882**

ITALIAN JOURNAL OF SURGICAL SCIENCES, THE. (US/0392-3525). **3966**

ITALIAN QUARTERLY. (US/0021-2954). **2693**

ITALIAN QUERIES. (US/0897-7410). **2455**

ITALIAN TRIBUNE NEWS. (US). Qty: 25. **5710**

ITALIANA VITA. (CN/0700-3234). **2693**

ITALIENISCH. (GW/0171-4996). **3288**

ITALIQUES / UNIVERSITE DE LA SORBONNE NOUVELLE (PARIS III), U.E.R. D'ITALIEN ET ROUMAIN, CENTRE DE RECHERCHES SUR L'ITALIE MODERNE ET CONTEMPORAINE. (FR/0751-2163). **3397**

ITAWAMBA SETTLERS. (US/0737-7932). Qty: 5-6. **2455**

ITC COMMUNICATOR. (US/0885-8063). **1114**

ITC JOURNAL, THE. (NE/0303-2434). **1356**

ITE JOURNAL. (US/0162-8178). **5384**

ITEM. (SP/0214-0349). **3219**

ITEM, THE. (US). Qty: 12. **5742**

ITEMS - SOCIAL SCIENCE RESEARCH COUNCIL (U.S.). (US/0049-0903). **5205**

ITG JOURNAL. (US/0363-2849). **4124**

ITI. INTERNATIONAL TELECOMMUNICATIONS INTELLIGENCE. (UK/0268-9960). **1158**

ITL. INSTITUUT VOOR TOEGEPASTE LINGUISTIK. (BE/0019-0829). **3288**

ITPI JOURNAL. (II). **2825**

IT'S HAPPENING. (US/0098-7549). **1880**

IUCN BULLETIN. (SZ/0020-9058). **2196**

IUDAU. (UY). **2985**

IUFRO NEWS. (AU/0256-5145). **2402**

IUGOSLAVICA PHYSIOLOGICA ET PHARMOCOLOGICA ACTA. (YU/0021-3225). **581**

IUS CANONICUM. (SP/0021-325X). **2985**

IUSTITIA (BLOOMINGTON). (IT/0092-3524). **2985**

IVY JOURNAL. (US/0882-4142). **514**

IWK INTERNATIONALE WISSENSCHAFTLICHE KORRESPONDENZ ZUR GESCHICHTE DER DEUTSCHEN ARBEITERBEWEGUNG. (GW/0046-8428). Qty: 200. **1681**

IWSS. (US). **2420**

IZARD COUNTY HISTORIAN, THE. (US/0164-7539). **2739**

J. IIC-CG : JOURNAL OF THE INTERNATIONAL INSTITUTE FOR CONSERVATION, CANADIAN GROUP. (CN/0381-0402). **353**

J P 4. (IT/0394-3437). **25**

JAARBOEK (VLAAMS INSTITUUT VOOR AMERIKAANSE KULTUREN). (BE). **270**

JABBERWOCKY. (UK/0305-8182). **3398**

JACA : JOURNAL OF THE ASSOCIATION FOR COMMUNICATION ADMINISTRATION. (US/0360-0939). Qty: 3-4. **1114**

JACK-PINE WARBLER. (US). Qty: 6. **5617**

JACKSON ADVOCATE. (US/0047-1704). Qty: 52. **5700**

JACKSON COUNTY PILOT. (US). **5696**

JACKSON HERALD. (US). **5654**

JACKSON HOLE GUIDE, THE. (US). Qty: 6. **5772**

JACKSONVILLE NEWS (JACKSONVILLE, ALA.). (US). Qty: 12. **5627**

JACKSONVILLE PATRIOT. (US/1064-7260). Qty: 12. **5631**

JACT REVIEW. (UK/0268-0181). Qty: 50. **1077**

JAEGER'S INTERTRAVEL. (GW). **5481**

JAHRBUCH DES ARCHIVS DER DEUTSCHEN JUGENDBEWEGUNG. (GW/0587-5277). **5249**

JAHRBUCH DES FREIEN DEUTSCHEN HOCHSTIFTS. (GW/0071-9463). **3398**

JAHRBUCH DES HISTORISCHEN VEREINS DILLINGEN AN DER DONAU. (GW). Qty: 5-10. **2693**

JAHRBUCH DES VEREINS ZUM SCHUTZ DER BERGWELT. (GW/0171-4694). **2196**

JAHRBUCH DES WIENER GOETHE-VEREINS. (AU). Qty: 10-15. **3398**

JAHRBUCH - DEUTSCHE SHAKESPEARE-GESELLSCHAFT WEST. (GW/0070-4326). **3398**

JAHRBUCH FUER ANTIKE UND CHRISTENTUM. (GW/0075-2541). **4967**

JAHRBUCH FUER FINNISCH-DEUTSCHE LITERATURBEZIEHUNGEN. (FI/0781-3619). **3398**

JAHRBUCH FUER INTERNATIONALE GERMANISTIK. (GW/0449-5233). **3289**

JAHRBUCH FUER LITURGIK UND HYMNOLOGIE. (GW/0075-2681). **4124**

JAHRBUCH FUER VOLKSLIEDFORSCHUNG. (GW/0075-2789). **4124**

JAHRBUCH / GESELLSCHAFT FUER DIE GESCHICHTE UND BIBLIOGRAPHIE DES BRAUWESENS E.V. (GW/0072-422X). **2368**

JAHRBUCHER FUER GESCHICHTE OSTEUROPAS. (PL/0021-4019). **2694**

JAHRESBERICHT (AKADEMIE FUR RAUMFORSCHUNG UND LANDESPLANUNG (GERMANY)). (GW/0515-9091). **2825**

JAHRESBERICHT DER DEUTSCHEN MATHEMATIKER-VEREINIGUNG. (GW/0012-0456). **3511**

JAHRESBERICHT DER GEWERBEAUFSICHT. (GW). **2864**

JAHRESBERICHT DES HISTORISCHEN VEREINS FUER STRAUBING UND UMGEBUNG. (GW). **2694**

JAHRESBERICHT - GESELLSCHAFT FUER STRAHLEN- UND UMWELTFORSCHUNG MHB MUNCHEN. (GW/0721-930X). **460**

JAHRESBERICHTE UND MITTEILUNGEN DES OBERRHEINISCHEN GEOLOGISCHEN VEREINES. (GW/0078-2947). **1384**

JAHRESSCHRIFT FUER MITTELDEUTSCHE VORGESCHICHTE. (GW/0075-2932). **271**

JAHRESSCHRIFT / SALZBURGER MUSEUM CAROLINO AUGUSTEUM. (AU/0558-3438). Qty: 2-4. **4089**

JAHRESSTATISTIK DES AUSSENHANDELS DER SCHWEIZ. STATISTIQUE ANNUELLE DU COMMERCE EXTERIEUR DE LA SUISSE. (SZ). **730**

JAHRESTAGUNG KERNTECHNIK. (GW/0720-9207). **2156**

JAMA FORUM, THE. (JA/0286-5971). **5417**

JAMA : THE JOURNAL OF THE AMERICAN MEDICAL ASSOCIATION. (US/0098-7484). **3591**

JAMAICA CONSOLIDATED INDEX OF STATUTES AND SUBSIDIARY LEGISLATION TO ... . (BB). **3131**

JAMAICA JOURNAL. (JM/0021-4124). **2536**

JAMAICAN HISTORICAL REVIEW, THE. (JM/1010-6367). **2740**

JAMES BURNSIDE BULLETIN OF RESEARCH, THE. (US/1046-2279). **2740**

JAMES DICKEY NEWSLETTER. (US/0749-0291). **3464**

JAMES JOYCE LITERARY SUPPLEMENT. (US/0899-3114). **3345**

JAMES JOYCE QUARTERLY. (US/0021-4183). **3345**

JAMES WHITE REVIEW, THE. (US/0891-5393). Qty: 25/yr. **3345**

JANE'S A F V SYSTEMS. (US). **4046**

JANE'S ALL THE WORLD'S AIRCRAFT (LONDON, ENGLAND). (UK/0075-3017). **4046**

JANE'S ARMOURED FIGHTING VEHICLE RETROFIT SYSTEMS. (UK). **4046**

JANE'S DEFENCE WEEKLY. (UK/0265-3818). **4047**

JANE'S RADAR AND ELECTRONIC WARFARE SYSTEMS. (US). **4047**

JANG. (II). **5803**

JAPAN CHRISTIAN ACTIVITY NEWS. (JA/0021-4353). **4967**

JAPAN ECONOMIC DAILY. (US/0734-0575). **1498**

JAPAN FOUNDATION NEWSLETTER, THE. (JA/0385-2318). Qty: 20. **5249**

JAPAN HARVEST. (JA/0021-440X). **4967**

JAPAN LETTER. (US/0446-6241). **2654**

JAPAN MISSIONARY BULLETIN, THE. (JA/0021-4531). **4967**

JAPAN NOTEBOOK. (US/1053-4997). Qty: 15-20. **2654**

JAPANESE AMERICAN VERNACULAR NEWSPAPERS, ABSTRACT-INDEX. (US/0893-8598). **3219**

JAPANESE CIRCULATION JOURNAL. (JA/0047-1828). **3706**

JAPANESE ECONOMIC STUDIES. (US/0021-4841). **1569**

JAPANESE JOURNAL OF RELIGIOUS STUDIES. (JA/0304-1042). Qty: 12-16. **4967**

JAPANESE JOURNAL OF THORACIC SURGERY. (JA). **3949**

JAPANESE PHILATELY. (US/0146-0994). **2785**

JAPANESE PRESS, THE. (JA). **5805**

JAPANESE RELIGIONS. (JA/0448-8954). Qty: 3-5. **4967**

JAPANESE SLAVIC AND EAST EUROPEAN STUDIES. (JA/0389-1186). **2694**

JAPANINFO. (GW/0931-3230). Qty: 10. **685**

JAPOS BULLETIN. (US/0278-436X). **2785**

JAQUE. (SP). **4862**

JARDINS DE FRANCE PARIS. (FR/0021-5481). Qty: 10. **2421**

JASNA NEWS. (US/0892-8665). **3398**

JASO : JOURNAL OF THE ANTHROPOLOGICAL SOCIETY OF OXFORD. (UK/0044-8370). **238**

JASPER COUNTY GLEANER, THE. (US/0749-8314). **2455**

JASPER JOURNAL, THE. (US). **5745**

JASSA. (AT/0313-5934). Qty: 8. **793**

JAUNA GAITA. (CN/0448-9179). **2848**

JAZYKOVEDNY CASOPIS. (XO/0021-5597). **3289**

JAZZ EDUCATORS JOURNAL. (US/0730-9791). **4124**

JAZZ FORUM. (US/0021-5635). **4124**

JAZZ JOURNAL INTERNATIONAL. (UK/0140-2285). **4125**

JAZZ-PODIUM. (GW/0021-5686). **4125**

JAZZ REPORT (TORONTO). (CN/0843-3151). Qty: 8. **4125**

JAZZ SCENE, LA. (US). Qty: 15. **4125**

JAZZ TIMES (WASHINGTON). (US/0272-572X). **4125**

JAZZ WORLD (NEW YORK, N.Y. 1984). (US/0749-4564). **4125**

JAZZFREUND (MENDEN), DER. (GW/0021-5724). **4125**

JAZZIZ (GAINESVILLE, FLA.). (US/0741-5885). **4125**

JBI ABSTRACTS. (JM). **1363**

JBI JOURNAL, THE. (JM). **1613**

JBSP. JOURNAL OF THE BRITISH SOCIETY FOR PHENOMENOLOGY. (UK/0007-1773). **4350**

JCT, AN INTERDISCIPLINARY JOURNAL OF CURRICULUM STUDIES. (US/1057-896X). **1897**

JCT, JOURNAL OF COATINGS TECHNOLOGY. (US/0361-8773). **4224**

JE ME SOUVIENS. (US/0195-7384). **2455**

JE TAI TI LI. (CC). **2567**

JEAN RHYS REVIEW. (US/0889-759X). **3399**

JEEVADHARA (ENGLISH ED.). (II/0970-1125). **4967**

JEFFERSON. (SW/0345-5653). **4125**

JEI. JOURNAL OF ECONOMIC ISSUES. (US/0021-3624). **1592**

JELENKOR. (HU/0447-6425). **3399**

JEMS. (US/0197-2510). **3724**

JEN KOU HSUEH KAN / KUO LI TAI-WAN TA HSUEH. (CH). **4554**

JEN MIN JIH PAO SO YIN. (CC). **5798**

JEN WEN TSA CHIH RENWEN ZAZHI. (CC). **2505**

JERSEY WOMAN. (US/0197-4610). **5559**

JERUSALEM JOURNAL OF INTERNATIONAL RELATIONS, THE. (US/0363-2865). **4526**

JESUS PARIS. 1973. (FR/1154-7138). Qty: 4. **4967**

JET. (US/0021-5996). **2265**

JET. JOURNAL OF EDUCATION FOR TEACHING. (UK/0260-7476). **1897**

JEU. (CN/0382-0335). **5365**

JEWELLERY INTERNATIONAL. (UK/0961-4559). Qty: 1 or 2. **2914**

JEWISH ADVOCATE, THE. (US). Qty: 12. **2265**

JEWISH AFFAIRS. (SA). **5048**

JEWISH BIBLE QUARTERLY, THE. (IS/0792-3910). Qty: 6. **5017**

JEWISH BOOK NEWS. (US/8755-299X). **5048**

JEWISH CURRENTS. (US/0021-6399). **5048**

JEWISH EDUCATION. (US/0021-6429). **5049**

JEWISH FOLKLORE AND ETHNOLOGY REVIEW. (US/0890-9113). **2321**

JEWISH FRONTIER. (US/0021-6453). **2265**

JEWISH HISTORICAL STUDIES : TRANSACTIONS OF THE JEWISH HISTORICAL SOCIETY OF ENGLAND. (UK). **5049**

JEWISH JOURNAL OF GREATER LOS ANGELES, THE. (US/0888-0468). Qty: 24. **5049**

JEWISH JOURNAL OF SOCIOLOGY, THE. (UK/0021-6534). **5249**

JEWISH NEWS OF GREATER PHOENIX. (US/1070-5848). **5630**

JEWISH NEWS (RICHMOND, VA.), THE. (US/0744-6632). **5049**

JEWISH OBSERVER, THE. (US/0021-6615). **5049**

JEWISH PRESS (BROOKLYN), THE. (US/0021-6674). **2265**

JEWISH QUARTERLY REVIEW (PHILADELPHIA, PA.). (US/0021-6682). Qty: 40-50. **5049**

JEWISH QUARTERLY, THE. (UK/0449-010X). **5049**

JEWISH SOCIAL STUDIES. (US/0021-6704). **5049**

JEWISH SOCIAL WORK FORUM, THE. (US/0021-6712). **5291**

JEWISH SPECTATOR. (US/0021-6720). **5049**

JEWISH STANDARD (TORONTO). (CN/0021-6739). **5049**

JEWISH STAR (CALGARY). (CN/0228-2283). **5787**

JEWISH STAR (EDMONTON EDITION). (CN/0228-6017). **5787**

JEWISH TELEVIMAGE REPORT. (US/1056-3342). **5049**

JEWISH TIMES. (US). **5737**

JEWISH TRANSCRIPT, THE. (US/0021-678X). **2265**

JEWISH VEGETARIANS OF NORTH AMERICA : NEWSLETTER. (US/0883-1904). Qty: 4. **4192**

JEWISH VETERAN, THE. (US/0047-2018). **2265**

JEWISH VOICE, THE. (US/0021-6828). **5049**

JEWISH WEEKLY NEWS. (US/0021-6860). **2265**

JEWISH WESTERN BULLETIN. (CN/0021-6879). **5787**

JEWISH WORLD (ALBANY), THE. (US/0199-4441). **2265**

JIB GEMS. (CN/0839-105X). **4089**

JICARILLA CHIEFTAIN. (US/0021-695X). **2265**

JIHAD (TEHRAN, IRAN). (IR). **2505**

JIJNASA (CALCUTTA, INDIA). (II). **2654**

JIKKEN DOBUTSU. (JA/0007-5124). **3592**

JIKKEN SHAKAI SHINRIGAKU KENKYU. (JA/0387-7973). **4592**

JIM RENNIE'S SPORTS LETTER. (CN/0712-2632). **4901**

JIM TAYLOR'S CURRENTS. (CN/0828-9662). **4967**

JING BAO JOURNAL. (US). **4047**

JINSHAN SHIBAO. (US/0746-5432). Qty: 2. **5636**

JMR, JOURNAL OF MARKETING RESEARCH. (US/0022-2437). **927**

JMR. JOURNAL OF MOLECULAR RECOGNITION. (UK/0952-3499). **460**

JNMM : JOURNAL OF THE INSTITUTE OF NUCLEAR MATERIALS MANAGEMENT. (US/0893-6188). **2156**

JOB INFORMATION LETTER. (US/8756-1670). **4205**

JOB PROSPECTS AUSTRALIA. (AT/1031-0894). Qty: 4. **4205**

JOBSON'S MINING YEAR BOOK. (AT/0075-3777). **2141**

JOERNAAL VIR EIETYDSE : GESKIEDENIS EN INTERNASIONALE VERHOUDINGE. (SA). **2620**

JOHN DONNE JOURNAL. (US/0738-9655). **3345**

JOHN KETTLE'S FUTURELETTER. (CN/0712-8177). **685**

JOHN MARSHALL LAW REVIEW, THE. (US/0270-854X). **2986**

JOHN TWIGG'S REPORT ON B.C. (CN/0838-1542). Qty: 3. **1498**

JOHN WHITMER HISTORICAL ASSOCIATION JOURNAL, THE. (US/0739-7852). **5061**

JOHNSON JOURNAL. (US/8755-1721). **2455**

JOHNSONIAN NEWS LETTER. (US/0021-728X). **3399**

JOHO SHORI KENKYU. (JA/0388-5038). **1213**

JOJOBA HAPPENINGS. (US/0746-3766). **98**

JOKESMITH, THE. (US/0749-4351). Qty: 6-8. **1114**

JOKULL. (IC/0449-0576). **1415**

JONATHAN (MONTREAL). (CN/0711-026X). **5049**

JONESREPORT. (US/0889-485X) **927**

JONG HOLLAND. (NE/0168-9193). Qty: 8. **354**

JOPLIN GLOBE. (US). **5703**

JORDEMODERN. (SW/0021-7468). Qty: 10. **3763**

JORNAL BRASILEIRO DE PSIQUIATRIA. (BL/0047-2085). **3928**

JORNAL BRASILEIRO DE UROLOGIA. (BL/0100-0519). **3990**

JORNAL PORTUGUES (SAN PABLO, CALIF.). (US/8756-2200). Qty: 20 per year. **5636**

JOSEPH CONRAD TODAY. (US/0162-413X). **433**

JOSLIN'S JAZZ JOURNAL. (US/0735-1585). **4125**

JOUETS (MONTREAL. 1976). (CN/0707-5081). **2584**

JOURNAAL / UITGAVE STICHTING VOOR CULTURELE SAMENWERKING (STICUSA). (NE). **2694**

JOURNAL - ADDICTION RESEARCH FOUNDATION, THE. (CN/0044-6203). **4786**

JOURNAL-ADVOCATE. (US). **5643**

JOURNAL (AMERICAN ACADEMY OF GNATHOLOGIC ORTHOPEDICS). (US/0886-1064). **1325**

JOURNAL - AMERICAN CIVIL LIBERTIES UNION FOUNDATION. NATIONAL PRISON PROJECT. (US/0748-2655). Qty: 1. **3167**

JOURNAL / AMERICAN RHODODENDRON SOCIETY. (US/0745-7839). **2421**

JOURNAL - AMERICAN WINE SOCIETY. (US/0364-698X). **2368**

JOURNAL AND REPORT OF PROCEEDINGS - PERMANENT WAY INSTITUTION. (UK/0031-5524). **2025**

JOURNAL - ARCHIVES OF AMERICAN ART. (US/0003-9853). **354**

JOURNAL BELGE DE RADIOLOGIE (1924). (BE/0021-7646). **3942**

JOURNAL-BULLETIN RHODE ISLAND ALMANAC. (US/0364-2909). **2536**

JOURNAL / CALIFORNIA RARE FRUIT GROWERS. (US/0894-8445). **98**

JOURNAL / CALIFORNIA TRADITIONAL MUSIC SOCIETY. (US/1053-3664). Qty: 6-12. **2321**

JOURNAL (CAMP VERDE, ARIZ.), THE. (US/0744-3285). **5630**

JOURNAL - CANADIAN DENTAL ASSOCIATION. (CN/0709-8936). Qty: 36/yr. **1325**

JOURNAL - CANADIAN ORAL HISTORY ASSOCIATION. (CN/0383-6894). **2740**

JOURNAL / CHARTERED INSURANCE INSTITUTE, THE. (UK). Qty: 3-6 per year. **2885**

JOURNAL - COLLEGE OF MEDICINE, THE OHIO STATE UNIVERSITY. (US/0030-1132). **3592**

JOURNAL - COLORADO DENTAL ASSOCIATION. (US/0010-1559). **1326**

JOURNAL - CONNECTICUT STATE DENTAL ASSOCIATION, THE. (US/0010-6232). **1326**

JOURNAL / CORNWALL FAMILY HISTORY SOCIETY. (UK/0141-7614). **2455**

JOURNAL / CROHN'S AND COLITIS FOUNDATION OF CANADA, THE. (CN/1197-4982). Qty: 3-4. **3746**

JOURNAL D'AGRICULTURE TRADITIONNELLE ET DE BOTANIQUE APPLIQUEE. (FR/0183-5173). **98**

JOURNAL DE CORNWALL, LE. (CN/0704-0660). **5787**

JOURNAL DE DROIT FISCAL. (BE). **2986**

JOURNAL DE LA SOCIETE DES AMERICANISTES. (FR/0037-9174). Qty: 1. **271**

JOURNAL DE L'IMMERSION, LE. (CN/0833-1812). **3289**

JOURNAL DE MEDECINE DE LYON. (FR/0021-7883). **3592**

JOURNAL DE MUSIQUE ANCIENNE. (CN/0838-9349). **4125**

JOURNAL DE PHARMACIE CLINIQUE. (FR/0291-1981). **4310**

JOURNAL DE PSYCHANALYSE DE L'ENFANT. (FR). **3928**

JOURNAL DE RECHERCHE OCEANOGRAPHIQUE. (FR/0397-5347). Qty: 2. **1450**

JOURNAL DENTAIRE DU QUEBEC. (CN). **1326**

JOURNAL DENTAIRE DU QUEBEC. (CN). **1326**

JOURNAL DES AFRICANISTES. (FR/0399-0346). **238**

JOURNAL DES DEBATS (QUEBEC). (CN/0709-3632). **4478**

JOURNAL DES INGENIEURS (BRUSSELS, BELGIUM : 1984). (BE/0021-8065). **1981**

JOURNAL DES JUGES DE PAIX ET DE POLICE. (BE). **2986**

JOURNAL DES TRIBUNAUX DU TRAVAIL. (BE). **3150**

JOURNAL D'OUTREMONT, LE. (CN/0824-1317). **2536**

JOURNAL DU DROIT INTERNATIONAL. (FR/0021-8170). **3131**

JOURNAL / FLINTSHIRE HISTORICAL SOCIETY. (UK). **2694**

JOURNAL - FLORIDA GENEALOGICAL SOCIETY (1978). (US/0735-6420). **2455**

JOURNAL FOR ANTHROPOSOPHY. (US/0021-8235). **4967**

JOURNAL FOR CHRISTIAN STUDIES, A. (US/0889-5848). Qty: 2/yr. **4967**

JOURNAL FOR CONTEMPORARY HISTORY / JOERNAAL VIR EIETYDSE GESKIEDENIS. (SA). **4526**

JOURNAL FOR HIGHER EDUCATION MANAGEMENT. (US). Qty: 6-8/yr. **1832**

JOURNAL FOR PEACE & JUSTICE STUDIES. (US). **4526**

JOURNAL FOR QUALITY AND PARTICIPATION, THE. (US/1040-9602). **1681**

JOURNAL FOR RESEARCH IN MATHEMATICS EDUCATION. (US/0021-8251). **3511**

JOURNAL FOR THE ANTHROPOLOGICAL STUDY OF HUMAN MOVEMENT AT NEW YORK UNIVERSITY. (US/0891-7124). Qty: 4. **238**

JOURNAL FOR THE CALLIGRAPHIC ARTS. (US). **380**

JOURNAL FOR THE EDUCATION OF THE GIFTED. (US/0162-3532). **1880**

JOURNAL FOR THE HISTORY OF ARABIC SCIENCE. (SY/0379-2927). **5118**

JOURNAL FOR THE HISTORY OF ASTRONOMY. (UK/0021-8286). **396**

JOURNAL FOR THE SCIENTIFIC STUDY OF RELIGION. (US/0021-8294). **4967**

JOURNAL

JOURNAL FOR THE STUDY OF RELIGION. (SA/1011-7601). **4967**

JOURNAL FOR THE STUDY OF THE NEW TESTAMENT. (UK/0142-064X). **5017**

JOURNAL FOR THE STUDY OF THE OLD TESTAMENT. (UK/0309-0892). **5017**

JOURNAL FOR THE THEORY OF SOCIAL BEHAVIOUR. (UK/0021-8308). **4593**

JOURNAL - FORENSIC SCIENCE SOCIETY. (UK/0015-7368). **3741**

JOURNAL / FORT SMITH HISTORICAL SOCIETY, THE. (US/0736-4261). **2740**

JOURNAL FRANCAIS D'AMERIQUE. (US/0195-2889). Qty: 20. **5636**

JOURNAL FROM THE RADICAL REFORMATION, A. (US/1058-3084). Qty: 8-12. **4968**

JOURNAL FUER BETRIEBSWIRTSCHAFT. (AU/0344-9327). Qty: 20-30. **685**

JOURNAL FUER ORNITHOLOGIE. (GW/0021-8375). **5618**

JOURNAL - GALPIN SOCIETY. (UK/0072-0127). Qty: varies. **4125**

JOURNAL-GAZETTE (FORT WAYNE, IND.), THE. (US/0734-3701). **5665**

JOURNAL / GERMAN-TEXAN HERITAGE SOCIETY, THE. (US). Qty: 3-5. **2455**

JOURNAL / GLASS ART SOCIETY. (US/0278-9426). **2591**

JOURNAL-HERALD (WHITE HAVEN, PA.). (US). **5737**

JOURNAL - HISTORICAL FIREARMS SOCIETY OF SOUTH AFRICA. (SA). **251**

JOURNAL / HOUSTON ARCHEOLOGICAL SOCIETY. (US/8756-8071). **271**

JOURNAL / INSTITUTE OF MUSLIM MINORITY AFFAIRS. (UK/0266-6952). **2265**

JOURNAL - INTERNATIONAL CHINESE SNUFF BOTTLE SOCIETY. (US/0734-5534). **251**

JOURNAL INTERNATIONAL DES SCIENCES DE LA VIGNE ET DU VIN. (FR/1151-0985). **175**

JOURNAL - JAPANESE ASSOCIATION OF GROUNDWATER HYDROLOGY. (JA). **1415**

JOURNAL - KEMENTERIAN PELAJARAN MALAYSIA. (MY/0126-7957). **1756**

JOURNAL - NEW ZEALAND DIETETIC ASSOCIATION. (NZ/0110-635X). Qty: 4. **4192**

JOURNAL OF ABSTRACTS (AND ARTICLES) IN INTERNATIONAL EDUCATION. (US/1064-0746). Qty: 2. **1795**

JOURNAL OF ACADEMIC LIBRARIANSHIP. (US/0099-1333). **3219**

JOURNAL OF ACCESS STUDIES / FORUM FOR ACCESS STUDIES. (UK/0269-2562). **1801**

JOURNAL OF ACCOUNTANCY. (US/0021-8448). **746**

JOURNAL OF ACCOUNTING & ECONOMICS. (NE/0165-4101). **746**

JOURNAL OF ACCOUNTING EDUCATION. (US/0748-5751). **746**

JOURNAL OF ACOUSTIC EMISSION. (US/0730-0050). **1981**

JOURNAL OF ADHESION SCIENCE AND TECHNOLOGY. (NE/0169-4243). **1053**

JOURNAL OF ADHESION, THE. (UK/0021-8464). **1053**

JOURNAL OF ADOLESCENT CHEMICAL DEPENDENCY. (US/0896-7768). **1345**

JOURNAL OF ADULT EDUCATION. (US/0090-4244). **1801**

JOURNAL OF ADVANCED COMPOSITION. (US/0731-6755). Qty: 30. **3289**

JOURNAL OF ADVANCED NURSING. (UK/0309-2402). **3858**

JOURNAL OF ADVANCED ZOOLOGY. (II/0253-7214). **5587**

JOURNAL OF ADVANCES IN HEALTH AND NURSING CARE. (UK/0960-9857). **3858**

JOURNAL OF ADVENTIST EDUCATION, THE. (US/0021-8480). **1897**

JOURNAL OF ADVERTISING. (US/0091-3367). **761**

JOURNAL OF AESTHETIC EDUCATION, THE. (US/0021-8510). **2848**

JOURNAL OF AESTHETICS AND ART CRITICISM, THE. (US/0021-8529). **354**

JOURNAL OF AFRICAN EARTH SCIENCES (AND THE MIDDLE EAST). (UK/0899-5362). **1384**

JOURNAL OF AFRICAN ECONOMIES. (UK/0963-8024). **1637**

JOURNAL OF AFRICAN HISTORY. (UK/0021-8537). **2640**

JOURNAL OF AFRICAN LANGUAGES AND LINGUISTICS. (NE/0167-6164). **3289**

JOURNAL OF AFRICAN LAW. (UK/0021-8553). **2986**

JOURNAL OF AFRICAN ZOOLOGY. (BE/0776-7943). **5587**

JOURNAL OF AGING & SOCIAL POLICY. (US/0895-9420). **5179**

JOURNAL OF AGRICULTURAL & ENVIRONMENTAL ETHICS. (CN/1187-7863). **2251**

JOURNAL OF AGRICULTURAL AND FOOD CHEMISTRY. (US/0021-8561). **99**

JOURNAL OF AGRICULTURAL & FOOD INFORMATION. (US/1049-6505). **99**

JOURNAL OF AGRICULTURAL ECONOMICS. (UK/0021-857X). **99**

JOURNAL OF AGRICULTURAL RESEARCH (LAHORE). (PK/0368-1157). **175**

JOURNAL OF AGRICULTURAL SCIENCE, THE. (UK/0021-8596). **99**

JOURNAL OF AIR LAW AND COMMERCE, THE. (US/0021-8642). **2987**

JOURNAL OF AIR TRAFFIC CONTROL, THE. (US/0021-8650). **25**

JOURNAL OF ALLIED HEALTH. (US/0090-7421). **3593**

JOURNAL OF ALTERNATIVE AND COMPLEMENTARY MEDICINE. (UK/0959-9886). Qty: 36. **3593**

JOURNAL OF AMBULATORY CARE MANAGEMENT, THE. (US/0148-9917). **3786**

JOURNAL OF AMBULATORY CARE MARKETING. (US/0886-9723). **3725**

JOURNAL OF AMERICAN COLLEGE HEALTH. (US/0744-8481). **3593**

JOURNAL OF AMERICAN CULTURE. (US/0191-1813). **2740**

JOURNAL OF AMERICAN ETHNIC HISTORY. (US/0278-5927). **2265**

JOURNAL OF AMERICAN FOLKLORE. (US/0021-8715). **2321**

JOURNAL OF AMERICAN HISTORY, THE. (US/0021-8723). **2740**

JOURNAL OF AMERICAN INDIAN FAMILY RESEARCH, THE. (US/0730-6148). **2455**

JOURNAL OF AMERICAN ORGANBUILDING. (US/1048-2482). Qty: 2. **4125**

JOURNAL OF AMERICAN STUDIES. (UK/0021-8758). **2740**

JOURNAL OF ANALYTICAL AND APPLIED PYROLYSIS. (NE/0165-2370). **1016**

JOURNAL OF ANALYTICAL PSYCHOLOGY. (UK/0021-8774). **4593**

JOURNAL OF ANALYTICAL TOXICOLOGY. (US/0146-4760). **3981**

JOURNAL OF ANATOMY. (UK/0021-8782). **3679**

JOURNAL OF ANIMAL ECOLOGY, THE. (UK/0021-8790). **5587**

JOURNAL OF ANIMAL MORPHOLOGY AND PHYSIOLOGY, THE. (II/0021-8804). **5587**

JOURNAL OF ANTHROPOLOGICAL RESEARCH. (US/0091-7710). **238**

JOURNAL OF ANTHROPOSOPHIC MEDICINE. (US/1067-4640). **3593**

JOURNAL OF APHIDOLOGY. (II/0970-3810). **5610**

JOURNAL OF APPLIED AQUACULTURE. (US/1045-4438). **2306**

JOURNAL OF APPLIED BEHAVIOR ANALYSIS. (US/0021-8855). **4593**

JOURNAL OF APPLIED BUSINESS RESEARCH. (US/0892-7626). Qty: 5. **685**

JOURNAL OF APPLIED COMMUNICATION RESEARCH : JACR. (US/0090-9882). **1114**

JOURNAL OF APPLIED COSMETOLOGY. (IT/0392-8543). **3721**

JOURNAL OF APPLIED CRYSTALLOGRAPHY. (DK/0021-8898). **1032**

JOURNAL OF APPLIED DEVELOPMENTAL PSYCHOLOGY. (US/0193-3973). **4593**

JOURNAL OF APPLIED ECOLOGY, THE. (UK/0021-8901). **2217**

JOURNAL OF APPLIED ELECTROCHEMISTRY. (UK/0021-891X). **1034**

JOURNAL OF APPLIED FIRE SCIENCE. (US/1044-4300). **2291**

JOURNAL OF APPLIED GERONTOLOGY. (US/0733-4648). **3753**

JOURNAL OF APPLIED ICHTHYOLOGY. (GW/0175-8659). **2306**

JOURNAL OF APPLIED MANUFACTURING SYSTEMS, THE. (US/0899-0956). Qty: 2-4. **1613**

JOURNAL OF APPLIED MEDICINE. (II/0377-0400). **3593**

JOURNAL OF APPLIED NUTRITION, THE. (US/0021-8960). **4192**

JOURNAL OF APPLIED PHYSIOLOGY (1985). (US/8750-7587). **581**

JOURNAL OF APPLIED POULTRY RESEARCH. (US/1056-6171). **213**

JOURNAL OF APPLIED RECREATION RESEARCH. (CN/0843-9117). **4851**

JOURNAL OF APPLIED REHABILITATION COUNSELING. (US/0047-2220). **1880**

JOURNAL OF APPLIED SEED PRODUCTION. (US/8755-8750). Qty: 1 per year. **175**

JOURNAL OF APPLIED SOCIAL SCIENCES, THE. (US/0146-4310). Qty: 7. **5291**

JOURNAL OF APPLIED SOCIOLOGY - SOCIETY FOR APPLIED SOCIOLOGY (U.S.). (US/0749-0232). **5249**

JOURNAL OF AQUACULTURE IN THE TROPICS. (II/0970-0846). **2306**

JOURNAL OF AQUARICULTURE & AQUATIC SCIENCES. (US/0733-2076). **460**

JOURNAL OF AQUATIC FOOD PRODUCTS TECHNOLOGY. (US/1049-8850). **2306**

JOURNAL OF ARAB AFFAIRS. (US/0275-3588). **4527**

JOURNAL OF ARACHNOLOGY, THE. (US/0161-8202). **5587**

JOURNAL OF ARBORICULTURE. (US/0278-5226). **2421**

JOURNAL OF ARID ENVIRONMENTS. (UK/0140-1963). **1357**

JOURNAL OF ARIZONA HISTORY, THE. (US/0021-9053). **2740**

JOURNAL OF ARTHROPLASTY, THE. (US/0883-5403). **3966**

JOURNAL OF ARTIFICIAL INTELLIGENCE IN EDUCATION. (US/1043-1020). **1213**

JOURNAL OF ARTS & IDEAS. (II/0970-5309). **323**

JOURNAL OF ARTS MANAGEMENT AND LAW, THE. (US/0733-5113). **386**

JOURNAL OF ASIAN BUSINESS. (US/1068-0055). **685**

JOURNAL OF ASIAN CULTURE. (US/0162-6795). **2505**

JOURNAL OF ASIAN HISTORY. (GW/0021-910X). **2655**

JOURNAL OF ASIAN MARTIAL ARTS. (US/1057-8358). Qty: 18/year. **2599**

JOURNAL OF ASIAN PACIFIC COMMUNICATION. (UK/0957-6851). **1114**

JOURNAL OF ASIAN STUDIES, THE. (US/0021-9118). **2655**

JOURNAL OF ASSOCIATION OF EXPLORATION GEOPHYSICISTS. (II/0257-1412). **1407**

JOURNAL OF ASTHMA, THE. (US/0277-0903). **3950**

JOURNAL OF ATMOSPHERIC CHEMISTRY. (NE/0167-7764). **1426**

JOURNAL OF AUDIOLOGICAL MEDICINE. (UK/0963-7133). **3889**

JOURNAL OF AUDIOVISUAL MEDIA IN MEDICINE, THE. (UK/0140-511X). **3593**

JOURNAL OF AUSTRALIAN POLITICAL ECONOMY, THE. (AT/0156-5826). **1498**

JOURNAL OF AUSTRALIAN STUDIES. (AT/0314-769X). **2669**

JOURNAL OF AUTOMATED REASONING. (NE/0168-7433). **1220**

JOURNAL OF AUTOMATIC CHEMISTRY, THE. (UK/0142-0453). **1016**

JOURNAL OF AVIAN BIOLOGY. (DK/0908-8857). **5618**

JOURNAL OF BAHA'I STUDIES. (CN/0838-0430). **4968**

JOURNAL OF BALTIC STUDIES. (US/0162-9778). **2694**

JOURNAL OF BANK ACCOUNTING & AUDITING, THE. (US/0895-853X). **793**

JOURNAL OF BANK TAXATION, THE. (US/0895-4720). **793**

JOURNAL OF BANKING AND FINANCE LAW AND PRACTICE. (AT/1034-3040). **793**

JOURNAL OF BASQUE STUDIES. (US/0747-6256). **2694**

JOURNAL OF BECKETT STUDIES. (US). Qty: 8-10. **3399**

JOURNAL OF BEHAVIORAL DECISION MAKING. (UK/0894-3257). **4594**

JOURNAL OF BIBLICAL COUNSELING, THE. (US/1063-2166). Qty: 6-10. **4968**

JOURNAL OF BIBLICAL ETHICS IN MEDICINE. (US/1050-3404). Qty: 3/yr. **2251**

JOURNAL OF BIOCHEMICAL AND BIOPHYSICAL METHODS. (NE/0165-022X). **489**

JOURNAL OF BIOGEOGRAPHY. (UK/0305-0270). **2567**

JOURNAL OF BIOLOGICAL CURATION. (UK/0958-7608). **4090**

JOURNAL OF BIOLOGICAL EDUCATION. (UK/0021-9266). **460**

JOURNAL OF BIOLOGICAL PHOTOGRAPHY. (US/0274-497X). **460**

JOURNAL OF BIOLOGICAL PHYSICS. (NE/0092-0606). **495**

JOURNAL OF BIOMECHANICAL ENGINEERING. (US/0148-0731). **3694**

JOURNAL OF BIOMEDICAL ENGINEERING. (UK/0141-5425). **3694**

JOURNAL OF BIOMOLECULAR STRUCTURE & DYNAMICS. (US/0739-1102). **461**

JOURNAL OF BIOSOCIAL SCIENCE. (UK/0021-9320). **5205**

JOURNAL OF BLACK PSYCHOLOGY, THE. (US/0095-7984). **4594**

JOURNAL OF BONE AND JOINT SURGERY. AMERICAN VOLUME (PRINT ED.). (US/0021-9355). **3882**

JOURNAL OF BORDERLANDS STUDIES. (US/0886-5655). Qty: (10). **2740**

JOURNAL OF BRITISH MUSIC THERAPY. (UK/0951-5038). **4125**

JOURNAL OF BROADCASTING & ELECTRONIC MEDIA. (US/0883-8151). **1134**

JOURNAL OF BRYOLOGY. (UK/0373-6687). **515**

JOURNAL OF BURN CARE & REHABILITATION, THE. (US/0273-8481). **3594**

JOURNAL OF BUSINESS ADMINISTRATION (VANCOUVER). (CN/0021-941X). **686**

JOURNAL OF BUSINESS & FINANCE LIBRARIANSHIP. (US/0896-3568). **3219**

JOURNAL OF BUSINESS & INDUSTRIAL MARKETING, THE. (US/0885-8624). **927**

JOURNAL OF BUSINESS AND SOCIAL STUDIES, THE. (NR/0021-9428). **686**

JOURNAL OF BUSINESS COMMUNICATION (1973). (US/0021-9436). **1114**

JOURNAL OF BUSINESS ETHICS. (NE/0167-4544). **2251**

JOURNAL OF BUSINESS FORECASTING METHODS & SYSTEMS, THE. (US/0278-6087). **1592**

JOURNAL OF BUSINESS LAW, THE. (UK/0021-9460). **3101**

JOURNAL OF BUSINESS (SINGAPORE). (SI/0377-0419). **686**

JOURNAL OF C LANGUAGE TRANSLATION, THE. (US/1042-5721). Qty: 1. **1279**

JOURNAL OF CALIFORNIA AND GREAT BASIN ANTHROPOLOGY. (US/0191-3557). Qty: varies. **238**

JOURNAL OF CALIFORNIA TAXATION, THE. (US/1046-400X). **2987**

JOURNAL OF CANADIAN ART HISTORY. (CN/0315-4297). **323**

JOURNAL OF CANADIAN PETROLEUM TECHNOLOGY, THE. (CN/0021-9487). **4262**

JOURNAL OF CANADIAN POETRY. (CN/0705-1328). **3464**

JOURNAL OF CANADIAN STUDIES. (CN/0021-9495). Qty: 8-10. **2740**

JOURNAL OF CANCER CARE. (UK/0960-9768). **3819**

JOURNAL OF CANCER EDUCATION, THE. (US/0885-8195). **3819**

JOURNAL OF CARBOHYDRATE CHEMISTRY. (US/0732-8303). **1042**

JOURNAL OF CARDIAC SURGERY. (US/0886-0440). **3966**

JOURNAL OF CARDIOPULMONARY REHABILITATION. (US/0883-9212). **3706**

JOURNAL OF CARDIOVASCULAR ELECTROPHYSIOLOGY. (US/1045-3873). **3707**

JOURNAL OF CAREER PLANNING & EMPLOYMENT. (US/0884-5352). **4206**

JOURNAL OF CARIBBEAN HISTORY, THE. (BB/0047-2263). **2741**

JOURNAL OF CARIBBEAN STUDIES. (US/0190-2008). **2741**

JOURNAL OF CASE MANAGEMENT. (US/1061-3706). Qty: 6-12. **3787**

JOURNAL OF CELL SCIENCE. (UK/0021-9533). **537**

JOURNAL OF CENTRAL ASIA. (PK). **2655**

JOURNAL OF CEPHALOPOD BIOLOGY. (US/0843-6150). Qty: 2-5. **461**

JOURNAL OF CHEMICAL AND ENGINEERING DATA. (US/0021-9568). **2014**

JOURNAL OF CHEMICAL DEPENDENCY TREATMENT. (US/0885-4734). **1345**

JOURNAL OF CHEMICAL EDUCATION. (US/0021-9584). **980**

JOURNAL OF CHEMICAL INFORMATION AND COMPUTER SCIENCES. (US/0095-2338). **980**

JOURNAL OF CHEMICAL NEUROANATOMY. (UK/0891-0618). **3834**

JOURNAL OF CHEMICAL TECHNOLOGY AND BIOTECHNOLOGY (1986). (UK/0268-2575). **1026**

JOURNAL OF CHILD AND ADOLESCENT PSYCHIATRIC AND MENTAL HEALTH NURSING. (US/0897-9685). Qty: 12/yr. **3928**

JOURNAL OF CHILD AND ADOLESCENT PSYCHOTHERAPY. (US/0748-8793). **4594**

JOURNAL OF CHILD AND YOUTH CARE. (CN/0840-982X). **5291**

JOURNAL OF CHILD NEUROLOGY. (US/0883-0738). **3904**

JOURNAL OF CHILD PSYCHOTHERAPY. (UK/0075-417X). Qty: 6-10. **3928**

JOURNAL OF CHILD SEXUAL ABUSE. (US/1053-8712). **5291**

JOURNAL OF CHILDHOOD COMMUNICATION DISORDERS. (US/0735-3170). **1880**

JOURNAL OF CHINESE LINGUISTICS. (US/0091-3723). **3289**

JOURNAL OF CHINESE MEDICINE, THE. (UK/0143-8042). **3594**

JOURNAL OF CHINESE PHILOSOPHY. (US/0301-8121). **4350**

JOURNAL OF CHINESE RELIGIONS. (US/0737-769X). **4968**

JOURNAL OF CHINESE STUDIES (ALBUQUERQUE, N.M.). (US/0742-5929). **2505**

JOURNAL OF CHIROPRACTIC. (US/0744-9984). **3594**

JOURNAL OF CHIROPRACTIC EDUCATION, THE. (US/1042-5055). Qty: 1-2. **3805**

JOURNAL OF CHRISTIAN EDUCATION. (AT/0021-9657). **4968**

JOURNAL OF CHRISTIAN HEALING, THE. (US/0738-2944). **4968**

JOURNAL OF CHRISTIAN JURISPRUDENCE. (US/0741-6075). **2987**

JOURNAL OF CHRISTIAN NURSING. (US/0743-2550). **3858**

JOURNAL OF CHRISTIAN RECONSTRUCTION, THE. (US/0360-1420). **4968**

JOURNAL OF CHROMATOGRAPHIC SCIENCE. (US/0021-9665). **1016**

JOURNAL OF CHURCH AND STATE. (US/0021-969X). Qty: 100-125. **4478**

JOURNAL OF CIVIL DEFENSE. (US/0740-5537). Qty: 30. **1073**

JOURNAL OF CLASSROOM INTERACTION, THE. (US/0749-4025). **1756**

JOURNAL OF CLEAN TECHNOLOGY AND ENVIRONMENTAL SCIENCES. (US/1052-1062). **2175**

JOURNAL OF CLINICAL AND EXPERIMENTAL GERONTOLOGY. (US/0192-1193). **3753**

JOURNAL OF CLINICAL AND EXPERIMENTAL NEUROPSYCHOLOGY. (NE/0168-8634). **3834**

JOURNAL OF CLINICAL & LABORATORY IMMUNOLOGY. (UK/0141-2760). **3673**

JOURNAL OF CLINICAL ANESTHESIA. (US/0952-8180). **3683**

JOURNAL OF CLINICAL COMPUTING. (US/0090-1091). **3787**

JOURNAL OF CLINICAL ENGINEERING. (US/0363-8855). **3694**

JOURNAL OF CLINICAL ETHICS, THE. (US/1046-7890). **2251**

JOURNAL OF CLINICAL HEMATOLOGY AND ONCOLOGY. (US/0162-9360). **3772**

JOURNAL OF CLINICAL IMMUNOASSAY. (US/0736-4393). **3673**

JOURNAL OF CLINICAL ORTHODONTICS. (US/0022-3875). **1326**

JOURNAL OF CLINICAL PERIODONTOLOGY. (DK/0303-6979). **1326**

JOURNAL OF CLINICAL PHARMACY AND THERAPEUTICS. (UK/0269-4727). **4310**

JOURNAL OF CLINICAL PSYCHIATRY, THE. (US/0160-6689). **3928**

JOURNAL OF CLINICAL PSYCHOANALYSIS. (US). **3928**

JOURNAL OF CLINICAL PSYCHOLOGY. (US/0021-9762). **4595**

JOURNAL OF CLINICAL PSYCHOPHARMACOLOGY. (US/0271-0749). **4310**

JOURNAL OF COAL QUALITY, THE. (US/0732-8087). **1948**

JOURNAL OF COASTAL RESEARCH. (US/0749-0208). **1357**

JOURNAL OF COFFEE RESEARCH. (II/0374-8537). **176**

JOURNAL OF COGNITIVE PSYCHOTHERAPY, THE. (US/0889-8391). **4595**

JOURNAL OF COLLEGE ADMISSIONS, THE. (US/0734-6670). **1832**

JOURNAL OF COLLEGE & UNIVERSITY FOODSERVICE. (US/1053-8739). **2345**

JOURNAL OF COLLEGE AND UNIVERSITY LAW, THE. (US/0093-8688). **2987**

JOURNAL OF COLLEGE AND UNIVERSITY STUDENT HOUSING, THE. (US/0161-827X). Qty: 2/yr. **1832**

JOURNAL OF COLLEGE MANAGEMENT. (UK). **1832**

JOURNAL OF COLLEGE SCIENCE TEACHING. (US/0047-231X). **5118**

JOURNAL OF COLLEGE STUDENT PSYCHOTHERAPY. (US/8756-8225). **4595**

JOURNAL OF COLLOID AND INTERFACE SCIENCE. (US/0021-9797). **1054**

JOURNAL OF COMMON MARKET STUDIES. (UK/0021-9886). **1569**

JOURNAL OF COMMONWEALTH & COMPARATIVE POLITICS, THE. (UK/0306-3631). **4478**

JOURNAL OF COMMONWEALTH LITERATURE. (UK/0021-9894). **3399**

JOURNAL OF COMMUNICATION. (US/0021-9916). **1114**

JOURNAL OF COMMUNICATION AND RELIGION, THE. (US/0894-2838). **4968**

JOURNAL OF COMMUNICATION THERAPY. (US/0734-4368). **4595**

JOURNAL OF COMMUNITY PSYCHOLOGY. (US/0090-4392). **4595**

JOURNAL OF COMPARATIVE FAMILY STUDIES. (CN/0047-2328). **2281**

JOURNAL OF COMPARATIVE LITERATURE & AESTHETICS. (II/0252-8169). **354**

JOURNAL OF COMPREHENSIVE HEALTH IN SOUTH AFRICA. (SA). **4786**

JOURNAL OF COMPUTER-BASED INSTRUCTION. (US/0098-597X). **1223**

JOURNAL OF COMPUTER INFORMATION SYSTEMS, THE. (US/0887-4417). **1260**

JOURNAL OF COMPUTERS IN MATHEMATICS AND SCIENCE TEACHING, THE. (US/0731-9258). **1224**

JOURNAL OF COMPUTING & SOCIETY. (US/1044-0755). **5205**

JOURNAL OF COMPUTING IN CHILDHOOD EDUCATION. (US/1043-1055). **1224**

JOURNAL OF COMPUTING IN HIGHER EDUCATION. (US/1042-1726). **1832**

JOURNAL OF CONCHOLOGY. (UK/0022-0019). **5587**

JOURNAL OF CONSTRUCTIONAL STEEL RESEARCH. (UK/0143-974X). **618**

JOURNAL OF CONSUMER AFFAIRS, THE. (US/0022-0078). **1297**

JOURNAL OF CONSUMER POLICY. (NE/0168-7034). **1297**

JOURNAL OF CONSUMER STUDIES AND HOME ECONOMICS. (UK/0309-3891). **1298**

JOURNAL OF CONTEMPLATIVE PSYCHOTHERAPY. (US/0894-8577). **3928**

JOURNAL OF CONTEMPORARY AFRICAN STUDIES : JCAS. (SA/0258-9001). **2848**

JOURNAL OF CONTEMPORARY ASIA. (UK/0047-2336). **2655**

JOURNAL OF CONTEMPORARY CRIMINAL JUSTICE. (US/1043-9862). **3167**

JOURNAL — Book Review Index

JOURNAL OF CONTEMPORARY HEALTH LAW AND POLICY, THE. (US/0882-1046). **2987**

JOURNAL OF CONTEMPORARY HISTORY. (UK/0022-0094). **2621**

JOURNAL OF CONTEMPORARY LAW. (US/0097-9937). **2987**

JOURNAL OF CONTINUING EDUCATION IN THE HEALTH PROFESSIONS, THE. (CN/0894-1912). **Qty: 12. 3594**

JOURNAL OF CONTINUING HIGHER EDUCATION, THE. (US/0737-7363). **1832**

JOURNAL OF CONTINUING SOCIAL WORK EDUCATION. (US/0276-0878). **1756**

JOURNAL OF CONTRACT LAW. (AT/1030-7230). **2987**

JOURNAL OF CORPORATE MANAGEMENT, THE. (AT/1038-2410). **3101**

JOURNAL OF CORPORATION LAW, THE. (US/0360-795X). **3101**

JOURNAL OF COST MANAGEMENT FOR THE MANUFACTURING INDUSTRY. (US/0899-5141). **873**

JOURNAL OF COUNTRY MUSIC, THE. (US/0092-0517). **4126**

JOURNAL OF COUPLES THERAPY. (US/0897-4446). **2281**

JOURNAL OF CRANIOFACIAL GENETICS AND DEVELOPMENTAL BIOLOGY. (DK/0270-4145). **3805**

JOURNAL OF CRIME & JUSTICE. (US/0735-648X). **3167**

JOURNAL OF CRIMINAL JUSTICE EDUCATION. (US/1051-1253). **3167**

JOURNAL OF CRIMINAL LAW & CRIMINOLOGY. (US/0091-4169). **3107**

JOURNAL OF CRITICAL ANALYSIS, THE. (US/0022-0213). **1756**

JOURNAL OF CRITICAL ILLNESS, THE. (US/1040-0257). **3595**

JOURNAL OF CROATIAN STUDIES. (US/0075-4218). **3289**

JOURNAL OF CROSS-CULTURAL GERONTOLOGY. (NE/0169-3816). **3753**

JOURNAL OF CRUSTACEAN BIOLOGY. (US/0278-0372). **555**

JOURNAL OF CULINARY PRACTICE. (US/1052-9241). **2346**

JOURNAL OF CULTURAL DIVERSITY. (US/1071-5568). **Qty: 1-2. 5206**

JOURNAL OF CULTURAL ECONOMICS. (NE/0885-2545). **323**

JOURNAL OF CULTURAL GEOGRAPHY. (US/0887-3631). **2567**

JOURNAL OF CUNEIFORM STUDIES. (US/0022-0256). **3290**

JOURNAL OF CURRENT LASER ABSTRACTS. (CN/0022-0264). **4426**

JOURNAL OF DANISH ARCHAEOLOGY. (DK/0108-464X). **271**

JOURNAL OF DATA & COMPUTER COMMUNICATIONS. (US/1054-089X). **1260**

JOURNAL OF DATABASE MANAGEMENT. (US/1063-8016). **Qty: 4. 1254**

JOURNAL OF DEMOCRACY. (US/1045-5736). **4478**

JOURNAL OF DENTAL EDUCATION. (US/0022-0337). **1326**

JOURNAL OF DENTAL HYGIENE. (US/1043-254X). **1326**

JOURNAL OF DENTISTRY. (UK/0300-5712). **1326**

JOURNAL OF DENTISTRY FOR CHILDREN. (US/0022-0353). **1326**

JOURNAL OF DEPRESSION & STRESS. (US). **3928**

JOURNAL OF DERMATOLOGIC SURGERY AND ONCOLOGY, THE. (US/0148-0812). **3967**

JOURNAL OF DERMATOLOGICAL TREATMENT, THE. (UK/0954-6634). **3721**

JOURNAL OF DESIGN HISTORY. (UK/0952-4649). **2099**

JOURNAL OF DEVELOPING AREAS, THE. (US/0022-037X). **Qty: 80. 2910**

JOURNAL OF DEVELOPMENT COMMUNICATION, THE. (MY/0128-3863). **1114**

JOURNAL OF DEVELOPMENT ECONOMICS. (NE/0304-3878). **1569**

JOURNAL OF DEVELOPMENT STUDIES, THE. (UK/0022-0388). **1569**

JOURNAL OF DEVELOPMENTAL PHYSIOLOGY. (UK/0141-9846). **3763**

JOURNAL OF DHARMA. (II/0253-7222). **Qty: 50/year. 4968**

JOURNAL OF DISABILITY POLICY STUDIES, THE. (US/1044-2073). **4389**

JOURNAL OF DISPERSION SCIENCE AND TECHNOLOGY. (US/0193-2691). **4428**

JOURNAL OF DISTANCE EDUCATION / REVUE DE L'ENSEIGNEMENT A DISTANCE. (CN/0830-0445). **1756**

JOURNAL OF DIVORCE & REMARRIAGE. (US/1050-2556). **2281**

JOURNAL OF DOCUMENT AND TEXT MANAGEMENT. (UK). **1192**

JOURNAL OF DOCUMENTATION. (UK/0022-0418). **3219**

JOURNAL OF DRUG ISSUES. (US/0022-0426). **1346**

JOURNAL OF DYNAMIC SYSTEMS, MEASUREMENT, AND CONTROL. (US/0022-0434). **1982**

JOURNAL OF EARLY ADOLESCENCE, THE. (US/0272-4316). **4596**

JOURNAL OF EARLY SOUTHERN DECORATIVE ARTS. (US/0098-9266). **Qty: occasional. 373**

JOURNAL OF EAST TENNESSEE HISTORY. (US). **Qty: 5. 2741**

JOURNAL OF EAST TENNESSEE HISTORY, THE. (US/1058-2126). **Qty: 1. 2741**

JOURNAL OF EAST-WEST BUSINESS. (US/1066-9868). **686**

JOURNAL OF EASTERN AFRICAN RESEARCH & DEVELOPMENT. (KE/0251-0405). **2640**

JOURNAL OF ECCLESIASTICAL HISTORY, THE. (UK/0022-0469). **4968**

JOURNAL OF ECOLOGY, THE. (UK/0022-0477). **515**

JOURNAL OF ECONOMIC AND SOCIAL INTELLIGENCE. (UK). **5206**

JOURNAL OF ECONOMIC AND TAXONOMIC BOTANY. (II/0250-9768). **515**

JOURNAL OF ECONOMIC BEHAVIOR & ORGANIZATION. (NE/0167-2681). **1498**

JOURNAL OF ECONOMIC COOPERATION AMONG ISLAMIC COUNTRIES. (TU). **1498**

JOURNAL OF ECONOMIC DYNAMICS & CONTROL. (NE/0165-1889). **1499**

JOURNAL OF ECONOMIC EDUCATION, THE. (US/0022-0485). **1499**

JOURNAL OF ECONOMIC HISTORY, THE. (US/0022-0507). **1569**

JOURNAL OF ECONOMIC LITERATURE. (US/0022-0515). **1535**

JOURNAL OF ECONOMIC PSYCHOLOGY. (NE/0167-4870). **1593**

JOURNAL OF ECONOMIC STUDIES (BRADFORD). (UK/0144-3585). **1499**

JOURNAL OF ECONOMIC SURVEYS. (UK/0950-0804). **1570**

JOURNAL OF ECUMENICAL STUDIES. (US/0022-0558). **Qty: 200. 4968**

JOURNAL OF EDUCATION (BOSTON, MASS.). (US/0022-0574). **1756**

JOURNAL OF EDUCATION FINANCE. (US/0098-9495). **1865**

JOURNAL OF EDUCATION FOR BUSINESS. (US/0883-2323). **687**

JOURNAL OF EDUCATION FOR LIBRARY AND INFORMATION SCIENCE. (US/0748-5786). **3220**

JOURNAL OF EDUCATIONAL ADMINISTRATION AND HISTORY. (UK/0022-0620). **Qty: 80. 1865**

JOURNAL OF EDUCATIONAL ADMINISTRATION, THE. (AT/0022-0639). **1865**

JOURNAL OF EDUCATIONAL COMPUTING RESEARCH. (US/0735-6331). **1224**

JOURNAL OF EDUCATIONAL GERONTOLOGY. (UK/0268-9987). **3753**

JOURNAL OF EDUCATIONAL ISSUES OF LANGUAGE MINORITY STUDENTS. (US). **1757**

JOURNAL OF EDUCATIONAL MEASUREMENT. (US/0022-0655). **1757**

JOURNAL OF EDUCATIONAL PUBLIC RELATIONS. (US/0741-3653). **Qty: 30-40. 1757**

JOURNAL OF EDUCATIONAL RESEARCH (WASHINGTON, D.C.), THE. (US/0022-0671). **1757**

JOURNAL OF EDUCATIONAL TECHNOLOGY SYSTEMS. (US/0047-2395). **1224**

JOURNAL OF EDUCATIONAL TELEVISION. (UK/0260-7417). **1757**

JOURNAL OF EDUCATIONAL THOUGHT. (CN/0022-0701). **1757**

JOURNAL OF EGYPTIAN ARCHAEOLOGY, THE. (UK/0075-4234). **271**

JOURNAL OF ELDER ABUSE & NEGLECT. (US/0894-6566). **5291**

JOURNAL OF ELECTROCARDIOLOGY. (US/0022-0736). **3707**

JOURNAL OF ELECTRONIC DEFENSE. (US/0192-429X). **4048**

JOURNAL OF ELECTRONIC ENGINEERING : JEE. (JA/0385-4507). **2068**

JOURNAL OF ELECTRONIC PACKAGING. (US/1043-7398). **2069**

JOURNAL OF ELECTROPHYSIOLOGICAL TECHNOLOGY. (UK/0307-5095). **3595**

JOURNAL OF ELECTROPHYSIOLOGY. (US/0892-1059). **2069**

JOURNAL OF ELECTROSTATICS. (NE/0304-3886). **2069**

JOURNAL OF EMERGENCY NURSING. (US/0099-1767). **3858**

JOURNAL OF EMOTIONAL AND BEHAVIORAL PROBLEMS. (US/1064-7023). **4596**

JOURNAL OF END USER COMPUTING. (US/1063-2239). **Qty: 4. 1192**

JOURNAL OF ENDOCRINOLOGICAL INVESTIGATION. (IT/0391-4097). **3731**

JOURNAL OF ENDOCRINOLOGY, THE. (UK/0022-0795). **3731**

JOURNAL OF ENERGY AND DEVELOPMENT, THE. (US/0361-4476). **1948**

JOURNAL OF ENERGY & NATURAL RESOURCES LAW. (UK/0264-6811). **2987**

JOURNAL OF ENERGY ENGINEERING. (US/0733-9402). **2118**

JOURNAL OF ENERGY, HEAT AND MASS TRANSFER. (II/0970-9991). **4431**

JOURNAL OF ENERGY, NATURAL RESOURCES & ENVIRONMENTAL LAW. (US/1053-377X). **3113**

JOURNAL OF ENGINEERING FOR INDUSTRY. (US/0022-0817). **1982**

JOURNAL OF ENGINEERING MATERIALS AND TECHNOLOGY. (US/0094-4289). **2118**

JOURNAL OF ENGLISH AND GERMANIC PHILOLOGY, THE. (US/0363-6941). **3290**

JOURNAL OF ENGLISH LINGUISTICS. (US/0075-4242). **3290**

JOURNAL OF ENTOMOLOGICAL RESEARCH. (II/0378-9519). **5587**

JOURNAL OF ENVIRONMENT & DEVELOPMENT, THE. (US/1070-4965). **1499**

JOURNAL OF ENVIRONMENTAL BIOLOGY. (II/0254-8704). **2233**

JOURNAL OF ENVIRONMENTAL ENGINEERING (NEW YORK N.Y.). (US/0733-9372). **2233**

JOURNAL OF ENVIRONMENTAL HYDROLOGY. (US/1058-3912). **1416**

JOURNAL OF ENVIRONMENTAL LAW. (UK/0952-8873). **3113**

JOURNAL OF ENVIRONMENTAL LAW AND LITIGATION. (US/1049-0280). **3113**

JOURNAL OF ENVIRONMENTAL PATHOLOGY, TOXICOLOGY AND ONCOLOGY. (US/0731-8898). **3819**

JOURNAL OF ENVIRONMENTAL SCIENCE AND HEALTH. PART A, ENVIRONMENTAL SCIENCE AND ENGINEERING. (US/0360-1226). **1982**

JOURNAL OF ENVIRONMENTAL SCIENCE AND HEALTH. PART B, PESTICIDES, FOOD CONTAMINANTS, AND AGRICULTURAL WASTES. (US/0360-1234). **2176**

JOURNAL OF ENZYME INHIBITION. (SZ/8755-5093). **461**

JOURNAL OF EPILEPSY. (US/0896-6974). **3835**

JOURNAL OF EQUINE VETERINARY SCIENCE. (US/0737-0806). **2800**

JOURNAL OF ERIE STUDIES. (US/0090-1938). **Qty: 2-4. 2741**

JOURNAL OF ESSENTIAL OIL RESEARCH, THE. (US/1041-2905). **1026**

JOURNAL OF ETHIOPIAN STUDIES. (ET/0304-2243). **2640**

JOURNAL OF ETHNIC STUDIES, THE. (US/0091-3219). **2266**

JOURNAL OF ETHNOBIOLOGY. (US/0278-0771). **238**

JOURNAL OF ETHNOPHARMACOLOGY. (SZ/0378-8741). **4311**

JOURNAL OF EURO MARKETING. (US/1049-6483). **927**

JOURNAL OF EUROPEAN BUSINESS, THE. (US/1044-002X). **1613**

JOURNAL OF EUROPEAN ECONOMIC HISTORY, THE. (IT/0391-5115). **1570**

JOURNAL OF EUROPEAN INDUSTRIAL TRAINING. (UK/0309-0590). **873**

JOURNAL OF EUROPEAN STUDIES. (UK/0047-2441). **2694**

JOURNAL OF EVOLUTIONARY BIOLOGY. (SZ/1010-061X). **548**

JOURNAL OF EVOLUTIONARY ECONOMICS. (GW/0936-9937). **1593**

JOURNAL OF EVOLUTIONARY PSYCHOLOGY. (US/0737-4828). **3399**

JOURNAL OF EXPERIENTIAL EDUCATION, THE. (US/1053-8259). **Qty: 3-5. 1880**

JOURNAL OF EXPERIMENTAL & CLINICAL CANCER RESEARCH : CR. (IT/0392-9078). **3819**

JOURNAL OF EXPERIMENTAL BIOLOGY. (UK/0022-0949). **582**

JOURNAL OF EXPERIMENTAL BOTANY. (UK/0022-0957). **515**

JOURNAL OF EXPERIMENTAL EDUCATION, THE. (US/0022-0973). **1898**

JOURNAL OF EXPLOSIVES ENGINEERING, THE. (US/0889-0668). **1982**

JOURNAL OF EXPOSURE ANALYSIS AND ENVIRONMENTAL EPIDEMIOLOGY. (US/1053-4245). **2176**

JOURNAL OF EXTENSION. (US/0022-0140). **1914**

JOURNAL OF EXTRA-CORPOREAL TECHNOLOGY, THE. (US/0022-1058). **Qty: 4-8. 3772**

JOURNAL OF FAMILY PRACTICE, THE. (US/0094-3509). **3738**

JOURNAL OF FAMILY PSYCHOTHERAPY. (US/0897-5353). **2282**

JOURNAL OF FAMILY WELFARE, THE. (II/0022-1074). **589**

JOURNAL OF FEMINIST FAMILY THERAPY. (US/0895-2833). **2282**

JOURNAL OF FEMINIST STUDIES IN RELIGION. (US/8755-4178). **4969**

JOURNAL OF FERROCEMENT. (TH/0125-1759). **632**

JOURNAL OF FIELD ARCHAEOLOGY. (US/0093-4690). **271**

JOURNAL OF FILM AND VIDEO. (US/0742-4671). **Qty: 4-6. 4073**

JOURNAL OF FINANCIAL MANAGEMENT AND ANALYSIS. (II/0970-4205). **794**

JOURNAL OF FIRE PROTECTION ENGINEERING. (US/1042-3915). **2291**

JOURNAL OF FISH BIOLOGY. (UK/0022-1112). **2306**

JOURNAL OF FISH DISEASES. (UK/0140-7775). **2306**

JOURNAL OF FLUID CONTROL, THE. (US/8755-8564). **2091**

JOURNAL OF FLUID MECHANICS. (UK/0022-1120). **2091**

JOURNAL OF FLUIDS ENGINEERING. (US/0098-2202). **2092**

JOURNAL OF FLUORINE CHEMISTRY. (SZ/0022-1139). **981**

JOURNAL OF FOETAL MEDICINE. (IT/0392-9507). **3763**

JOURNAL OF FOLKLORE RESEARCH. (US/0737-7037). **2321**

JOURNAL OF FOOD BIOCHEMISTRY. (US/0145-8884). **2346**

JOURNAL OF FOOD DISTRIBUTION RESEARCH. (US/0047-245X). **Qty: 300. 2346**

JOURNAL OF FOOD ENGINEERING. (UK/0260-8774). **2346**

JOURNAL OF FOOD PROCESS ENGINEERING. (US/0145-8876). **2346**

JOURNAL OF FOOD PROCESSING AND PRESERVATION. (US/0145-8892). **2346**

JOURNAL OF FOOD PRODUCTS MARKETING. (US/1045-4446). **2346**

JOURNAL OF FOOD QUALITY. (US/0146-9428). **2346**

JOURNAL OF FOOD SAFETY. (US/0149-6085). **2346**

JOURNAL OF FOOD SCIENCE AND TECHNOLOGY. (II/0022-1155). **4193**

JOURNAL OF FOODSERVICE SYSTEMS. (US/0196-4283). **2347**

JOURNAL OF FORAMINIFERAL RESEARCH. (US/0096-1191). **5588**

JOURNAL OF FOREIGN EXCHANGE AND INTERNATIONAL FINANCE. (II). **794**

JOURNAL OF FORENSIC ECONOMICS. (US/0898-5510). **Qty: 2. 1499**

JOURNAL OF FORENSIC IDENTIFICATION. (US/0895-173X). **3741**

JOURNAL OF FORESTRY. (US/0022-1201). **2385**

JOURNAL OF FORTH APPLICATION AND RESEARCH, THE. (US/0738-2022). **1279**

JOURNAL OF FUNCTIONAL PROGRAMMING. (UK/0956-7968). **1279**

JOURNAL OF FURTHER AND HIGHER EDUCATION. (UK/0309-877X). **1832**

JOURNAL OF GASTRONOMY, THE. (US/0747-7368). **2347**

JOURNAL OF GAY & LESBIAN PSYCHOTHERAPY. (US/0891-7140). **2794**

JOURNAL OF GAY & LESBIAN SOCIAL SERVICES. (US/1053-8720). **2794**

JOURNAL OF GEM INDUSTRY. (II/0022-1244). **Qty: 3-4. 2915**

JOURNAL OF GEMMOLOGY AND PROCEEDINGS OF THE GEMMOLOGICAL ASSOCIATION OF GREAT BRITAIN. (UK/0022-1252). **Qty: 4. 1440**

JOURNAL OF GENERAL EDUCATION (UNIVERSITY PARK, PA.), THE. (US/0021-3667). **1757**

JOURNAL OF GENERAL INTERNAL MEDICINE. (US/0884-8734). **3798**

JOURNAL OF GENERAL ORTHODONTICS. (US/1048-1990). **Qty: 2. 1327**

JOURNAL OF GENERAL PSYCHOLOGY, THE. (US/0022-1309). **4597**

JOURNAL OF GEOGRAPHY (HOUSTON). (US/0022-1341). **2567**

JOURNAL OF GEOGRAPHY IN HIGHER EDUCATION. (UK/0309-8265). **2567**

JOURNAL OF GEOLOGICAL EDUCATION. (US/0022-1368). **1384**

JOURNAL OF GEOMAGNETISM AND GEOELECTRICITY. (JA/0022-1392). **1407**

JOURNAL OF GERIATRIC DRUG THERAPY. (US/8756-4629). **3753**

JOURNAL OF GERIATRIC PSYCHIATRY AND NEUROLOGY. (US/0891-9887). **3753**

JOURNAL OF GERONTOLOGICAL NURSING. (US/0098-9134). **3858**

JOURNAL OF GERONTOLOGICAL SOCIAL WORK. (US/0163-4372). **5292**

JOURNAL OF GERONTOLOGY (KIRKWOOD). (US/0022-1422). **3753**

JOURNAL OF GLOBAL BUSINESS (HARRISONBURG, VA.). (US/1053-7287). **687**

JOURNAL OF GLOBAL INFORMATION MANAGEMENT. (US/1062-7375). **Qty: 4. 3220**

JOURNAL OF GLOBAL MARKETING. (US/0891-1762). **927**

JOURNAL OF GREAT LAKES RESEARCH. (US/0380-1330). **1416**

JOURNAL OF GYNECOLOGIC SURGERY. (US/1042-4067). **3763**

JOURNAL OF HAND SURGERY (ST. LOUIS, MO.), THE. (US/0363-5023). **3967**

JOURNAL OF HAND THERAPY. (US/0894-1130). **4380**

JOURNAL OF HAZARDOUS MATERIALS. (NE/0304-3894). **2234**

JOURNAL OF HEAD & NECK PATHOLOGY. (BE/0770-9471). **3595**

JOURNAL OF HEAD TRAUMA REHABILITATION, THE. (US/0885-9701). **4380**

JOURNAL OF HEALTH AND HUMAN RESOURCES ADMINISTRATION. (US/0160-4198). **5292**

JOURNAL OF HEALTH & SOCIAL POLICY. (US/0897-7186). **5292**

JOURNAL OF HEALTH CARE CHAPLAINCY. (US/0885-4726). **4969**

JOURNAL OF HEALTH CARE FOR THE POOR AND UNDERSERVED. (US/1049-2089). **4786**

JOURNAL OF HEALTH CARE MARKETING. (US/0737-3252). **927**

JOURNAL OF HEALTH EDUCATION. ASSOCIATION FOR THE ADVANCEMENT OF HEALTH EDUCATION. (US/1055-6699). **4786**

JOURNAL OF HEALTH OCCUPATIONS EDUCATION. (US/0890-6874). **3595**

JOURNAL OF HEALTH POLITICS, POLICY AND LAW. (US/0361-6878). **2987**

JOURNAL OF HEALTHCARE MATERIAL MANAGEMENT. (US/0889-2482). **3787**

JOURNAL OF HEALTHCARE PROTECTION MANAGEMENT. (US/0891-7930). **3787**

JOURNAL OF HEAT TREATING. (US/0190-9177). **4006**

JOURNAL OF HELLENIC STUDIES. (UK/0075-4269). **1078**

JOURNAL OF HELMINTHOLOGY. (UK/0022-149X). **5588**

JOURNAL OF HERBS, SPICES & MEDICINAL PLANTS. (US/1049-6475). **2421**

JOURNAL OF HEREDITY, THE. (US/0022-1503). **548**

JOURNAL OF HETEROCYCLIC CHEMISTRY. (US/0022-152X). **1042**

JOURNAL OF HIGH RESOLUTION CHROMATOGRAPHY : HRC. (GW/0935-6304). **1017**

JOURNAL OF HIGHER EDUCATION. (AT/1034-3350). **1898**

JOURNAL OF HIMALAYAN STUDIES & REGIONAL DEVELOPMENT. (II). **2218**

JOURNAL OF HISPANIC PHILOLOGY. (US/0147-5460). **3290**

JOURNAL OF HISTORICAL GEOGRAPHY. (UK/0305-7488). **2567**

JOURNAL OF HISTORICAL RESEARCH. (II/0022-1562). **2655**

JOURNAL OF HISTORICAL REVIEW, THE. (US/0195-6752). **2621**

JOURNAL OF HISTORICAL SOCIOLOGY. (UK/0952-1909). **5249**

JOURNAL OF HISTORY AND POLITICS. (US/0228-6939). **2621**

JOURNAL OF HISTOTECHNOLOGY. (US/0147-8885). **538**

JOURNAL OF HOME ECONOMICS (WASHINGTON). (US/0022-1570). **2791**

JOURNAL OF HOMOSEXUALITY. (US/0091-8369). **2795**

JOURNAL OF HOSPITAL INFECTION, THE. (US/0195-6701). **3714**

JOURNAL OF HOSPITAL MARKETING. (US/0883-7570). **3787**

JOURNAL OF HOSPITALITY & LEISURE MARKETING. (US/1050-7051). **4851**

JOURNAL OF HOUSING FOR THE ELDERLY. (US/0276-3893). **2826**

JOURNAL OF HUMAN HYPERTENSION. (UK/0950-9240). **3707**

JOURNAL OF HUMAN JUSTICE, THE. (CN/0847-2971). **2987**

JOURNAL OF HUMAN LACTATION. (US/0890-3344). **3763**

JOURNAL OF HUMAN NUTRITION AND DIETETICS. (UK/0952-3871). **4193**

JOURNAL OF HUMAN RESOURCES, THE. (US/0022-166X). **1914**

JOURNAL OF HUMANISTIC EDUCATION. (US/0890-0493). **1898**

JOURNAL OF HUMANITIES (ZOMBA, MALAWI). (MW). **2848**

JOURNAL OF HYDRAULIC RESEARCH. (NE/0022-1686). **2092**

JOURNAL OF HYDROLOGY, NEW ZEALAND. (NZ/0022-1708). **1416**

JOURNAL OF HYPERBARIC MEDICINE. (US/0884-1225). **3595**

JOURNAL OF IMMUNOASSAY. (US/0197-1522). **3673**

JOURNAL OF IMPERIAL AND COMMONWEALTH HISTORY, THE. (UK/0308-6534). **2695**

JOURNAL OF INDIAN COUNCIL OF PHILOSOPHICAL RESEARCH. (II). **4350**

JOURNAL OF INDIAN EDUCATION. (II/0377-0435). **1757**

JOURNAL OF INDIAN PHILOSOPHY. (NE/0022-1791). **4350**

JOURNAL OF INDIAN WRITING IN ENGLISH, THE. (II/0302-1319). **3400**

JOURNAL OF INDIGENOUS STUDIES, THE. (CN/0838-4711). **2741**

JOURNAL OF INDO-EUROPEAN STUDIES, THE. (US/0092-2323). **3290**

JOURNAL OF INDUSTRIAL IRRADIATION TECHNOLOGY. (US/0735-7923). **981**

JOURNAL OF INDUSTRIAL RELATIONS, THE. (AT/0022-1856). **1682**

JOURNAL OF INDUSTRIAL TEACHER EDUCATION. (US/0022-1864). **1914**

JOURNAL OF INDUSTRIAL TECHNOLOGY / THE NATIONAL ASSOCIATION OF INDUSTRIAL TECHNOLOGY. (US/0882-6404). **Qty: 2. 5118**

JOURNAL OF INFECTION, THE. (UK/0163-4453). **3714**

JOURNAL OF INFERENTIAL AND DEDUCTIVE BIOLOGY. (US/0883-1378). **461**

JOURNAL OF INFORMATION ETHICS. (US/1061-9321). **2251**

JOURNAL OF INFORMATION NETWORKING. (UK/0966-9248). **1242**

JOURNAL OF INFORMATION TECHNOLOGY MANAGEMENT. (US/1042-1319). **Qty: 8. 873**

JOURNAL OF INHERITED METABOLIC DISEASE. (UK/0141-8955). **3798**

JOURNAL OF INORGANIC AND ORGANOMETALLIC POLYMERS. (US/1053-0495). **981**

JOURNAL OF INSTITUTE OF ECONOMIC RESEARCH. (II/0020-2851). **1570**

JOURNAL OF INSTITUTIONAL AND THEORETICAL ECONOMICS : JITE. (GW/0932-4569). **5206**

JOURNAL OF INSTRUCTIONAL PSYCHOLOGY. (US/0094-1956). **4597**

JOURNAL OF INSURANCE MEDICINE (NEW YORK, N.Y.). (US/0743-6661). **2885**

JOURNAL OF INTENSIVE ENGLISH STUDIES. (US/0899-885X). **3290**

JOURNAL OF INTERCULTURAL STUDIES. (AT/0725-6868). **1919**

JOURNAL OF INTERCULTURAL STUDIES (HIRAKATA, OSAKA). (JA/0388-0508). **239**

JOURNAL OF INTERDISCIPLINARY CYCLE RESEARCH. (NE/0022-1945). **461**

JOURNAL OF INTERDISCIPLINARY HISTORY, THE. (US/0022-1953). **2621**

JOURNAL OF INTERDISCIPLINARY LITERARY STUDIES. (NE/1044-8985). **Qty: 6. 3400**

JOURNAL OF INTERDISCIPLINARY STUDIES. (US/0890-0132). **Qty: 10-12 per year. 4969**

JOURNAL OF INTERFERON RESEARCH. (US/0197-8357). **565**

JOURNAL OF INTERGROUP RELATIONS. (US/0047-2492). **5250**

JOURNAL OF INTERIOR DESIGN EDUCATION AND RESEARCH. (US/0147-0418). **2901**

JOURNAL OF INTERLIBRARY LOAN & INFORMATION SUPPLY. (US/1042-4458). **3220**

JOURNAL OF INTERMOUNTAIN ARCHEOLOGY. (US/0738-2030). **271**

JOURNAL OF INTERNATIONAL AND COMPARATIVE SOCIAL WELFARE. (US/0898-5847). **5292**

JOURNAL OF INTERNATIONAL BANKING LAW. (UK/0267-937X). **3087**

JOURNAL OF INTERNATIONAL BUSINESS STUDIES. (CN/0047-2506). **687**

JOURNAL OF INTERNATIONAL CONSUMER MARKETING. (US/0896-1530). **928**

JOURNAL OF INTERNATIONAL FINANCIAL MARKETS, INSTITUTIONS & MONEY. (US/1042-4431). **1637**

JOURNAL OF INTERNATIONAL FOOD & AGRIBUSINESS MARKETING. (US/0897-4438). **2347**

JOURNAL OF INTERNATIONAL MARKETING AND MARKETING RESEARCH. (UK). **Qty: 100. 928**

JOURNAL OF INTERNATIONAL MARKETING (EAST LANSING, MICH.). (US/1069-031X). **928**

JOURNAL OF INTERNATIONAL TRADE AND ECONOMIC DEVELOPMENT. (UK/0963-8199). **1637**

JOURNAL OF INTERVENTIONAL CARDIOLOGY. (US/0896-4327). **3707**

JOURNAL OF INTRAVENOUS NURSING. (US/0896-5846). **3858**

JOURNAL OF INTRAVENOUS THERAPY (LOS ANGELES). (US/0194-1658). **3595**

JOURNAL OF INVESTIGATIVE SURGERY. (US/0894-1939). **3967**

JOURNAL OF INVITATIONAL THEORY AND PRACTICE. (US/1060-6041). **Qty: 1-2. 1898**

JOURNAL OF IRISH ARCHAEOLOGY, THE. (IE/0268-537X). **271**

JOURNAL OF IRREPRODUCIBLE RESULTS, THE. (US/0022-2038). **5118**

JOURNAL OF ISLAMIC BANKING & FINANCE : QUARTERLY PUBLICATION OF THE INTERNATIONAL ASSOCIATION OF ISLAMIC BANKS, KARACHI (ASIAN REGION). (PK). **795**

JOURNAL OF ITALIAN FOOD & WINE. (US/1073-3124). **Qty: 12-18. 2347**

JOURNAL OF JAPANESE LINGUISTICS. (JA). **Qty: 1. 3290**

JOURNAL OF JAPANESE STUDIES, THE. (US/0095-6848). **Qty: 35-50. 2655**

JOURNAL OF JAPANESE TRADE & INDUSTRY. (JA/0285-9556). **687**

JOURNAL OF JEWISH COMMUNAL SERVICE. (US/0022-2089). **2266**

JOURNAL OF JEWISH EDUCATION. (US). **5050**

JOURNAL OF JEWISH MUSIC AND LITURGY. (US/0197-0100). **4126**

JOURNAL OF JEWISH STUDIES, THE. (UK/0022-2097). **Qty: 40. 5050**

JOURNAL OF JUVENILE LAW. (US/0160-2098). **3121**

JOURNAL OF KNOT THEORY AND ITS RAMIFICATIONS. (SI/0218-2165). **3513**

JOURNAL OF KOREAN STUDIES (SEATTLE, WASH. : 1979), THE. (US/0731-1613). **2655**

JOURNAL OF LABOR RESEARCH. (US/0195-3613). **Qty: 12 per year. 1682**

JOURNAL OF LANGUAGE AND SOCIAL PSYCHOLOGY. (US/0261-927X). **3290**

JOURNAL OF LANGUAGE FOR INTERNATIONAL BUSINESS, THE. (US/8755-0504). **3290**

JOURNAL OF LATIN AMERICAN STUDIES. (UK/0022-216X). **2741**

JOURNAL OF LAW AND COMMERCE, THE. (US/0733-2491). **2988**

JOURNAL OF LAW & EDUCATION. (US/0275-6072). **1865**

JOURNAL OF LAW AND ETHICS IN DENTISTRY. (US/0894-8879). **1327**

JOURNAL OF LAW AND INFORMATION SCIENCE. (AT/0729-1485). **Qty: varies. 2988**

JOURNAL OF LAW & POLITICS. (US/0749-2227). **2988**

JOURNAL OF LAW AND RELIGION, THE. (US/0748-0814). **Qty: varies. 2988**

JOURNAL OF LAW AND SOCIETY. (UK/0263-323X). **2988**

JOURNAL OF LEARNING DISABILITIES. (US/0022-2194). **1880**

JOURNAL OF LEARNING SKILLS, THE. (US/0740-5715). **1757**

JOURNAL OF LEGAL ASPECTS OF SPORT. (US/1072-0316). **2988**

JOURNAL OF LEGAL EDUCATION. (US/0022-2208). **Qty: 4. 2988**

JOURNAL OF LEGAL HISTORY, THE. (UK/0144-0365). **2988**

JOURNAL OF LEGAL MEDICINE (CHICAGO. 1979), THE. (US/0194-7648). **3741**

JOURNAL OF LEGAL STUDIES EDUCATION, THE. (US/0896-5811). **2988**

JOURNAL OF LEGISLATION. (US/0146-9584). **2989**

JOURNAL OF LIBERTARIAN STUDIES, THE. (US/0363-2873). **5206**

JOURNAL OF LIBRARY ADMINISTRATION. (US/0193-0826). **3220**

JOURNAL OF LIBRARY AND INFORMATION SCIENCE (DELHI). (II/0970-714X). **3220**

JOURNAL OF LIGHT CONSTRUCTION (NEW ENGLAND ED), THE. (US/1050-2610). **Qty: 12. 618**

JOURNAL OF LINGUISTICS. (UK/0022-2267). **3290**

JOURNAL OF LIQUID CHROMATOGRAPHY. (US/0148-3919). **1017**

JOURNAL OF LITERARY SEMANTICS. (NE/0341-7638). **Qty: 10. 3290**

JOURNAL OF LITERARY STUDIES (PRETORIA, SOUTH AFRICA). (SA/0256-4718). **3345**

JOURNAL OF LONG TERM CARE ADMINISTRATION, THE. (US/0093-4445). **Qty: 12-15. 3787**

JOURNAL OF LOSS PREVENTION IN THE PROCESS INDUSTRIES. (UK/0950-4230). **2099**

JOURNAL OF MACROMARKETING. (US/0276-1467). **928**

JOURNAL OF MACROMOLECULAR SCIENCE. REVIEWS IN MACROMOLECULAR CHEMISTRY. (US/0022-2356). **1042**

JOURNAL OF MAHARASHTRA AGRICULTURAL UNIVERSITIES. (II/0378-2395). **176**

JOURNAL OF MAMMALOGY. (US/0022-2372). **5588**

JOURNAL OF MANAGEMENT. (US/0149-2063). **873**

JOURNAL OF MANAGEMENT CONSULTING (AMSTERDAM). (US/0168-7778). **Qty: 8-10. 873**

JOURNAL OF MANAGEMENT IN MEDICINE. (UK/0268-9235). **3596**

JOURNAL OF MANAGEMENT STUDIES, THE. (UK/0022-2380). **874**

JOURNAL OF MANAGEMENT SYSTEMS, THE. (US/1041-2808). **Qty: 8. 943**

JOURNAL OF MANUFACTURING SYSTEMS. (US/0278-6125). **3482**

JOURNAL OF MARITAL AND FAMILY THERAPY. (US/0194-472X). **2282**

JOURNAL OF MARKETING. (US/0022-2429). **928**

JOURNAL OF MARKETING CHANNELS. (US/1046-669X). **928**

JOURNAL OF MARKETING EDUCATION. (US/0273-4753). **928**

JOURNAL OF MARKETING FOR HIGHER EDUCATION. (US/0884-1241). **1833**

JOURNAL OF MARKETING FOR MENTAL HEALTH. (US/0883-7589). **4787**

JOURNAL OF MARKETING MANAGEMENT. (UK/0267-257X). **928**

JOURNAL OF MARRIAGE AND THE FAMILY. (US/0022-2445). **2282**

JOURNAL OF MASS MEDIA ETHICS. (US/0890-0523). **2251**

JOURNAL OF MATERIALS CHEMISTRY. (UK/0959-9428). **981**

JOURNAL OF MATERIALS EDUCATION, THE. (US/0738-7989). **Qty: 12. 2103**

JOURNAL OF MATERIALS RESEARCH. (US/0884-2914). **2103**

JOURNAL OF MATHEMATICAL AND PHYSICAL SCIENCES. (II/0047-2557). **3513**

JOURNAL OF MATHEMATICAL BEHAVIOR, THE. (US/0732-3123). **3513**

JOURNAL OF MATHEMATICAL PSYCHOLOGY. (US/0022-2496). **4598**

JOURNAL OF MATHEMATICAL SOCIOLOGY, THE. (US/0022-250X). **5250**

JOURNAL OF MAYAN LINGUISTICS. (US/0195-475X). **3291**

JOURNAL OF MEDIA ECONOMICS. (US/0899-7764). **Qty: 4. 1115**

JOURNAL OF MEDICAL ENTOMOLOGY. (US/0022-2585). **5611**

JOURNAL OF MEDICAL PRIMATOLOGY. (SZ/0047-2565). **5513**

JOURNAL OF MEDICINAL CHEMISTRY. (US/0022-2623). **490**

JOURNAL OF MEDICINE AND PHILOSOPHY, THE. (NE/0360-5310). **3596**

JOURNAL OF MEDICINE (WESTBURY). (US/0025-7850). **3596**

JOURNAL OF MEDIEVAL AND RENAISSANCE STUDIES, THE. (US/0047-2573). **2695**

JOURNAL OF MEDITERRANEAN STUDIES. (MM/1016-3476). **Qty: 15-20. 2848**

JOURNAL OF MEMBRANE SCIENCE. (NE/0376-7388). **5119**

JOURNAL OF MENNONITE STUDIES. (CN/0824-5053). **4969**

JOURNAL OF MEN'S STUDIES, THE. (US/1060-8265). **Qty: 20-30. 3995**

JOURNAL OF MENTAL HEALTH ADMINISTRATION. (US/0092-8623). **5292**

JOURNAL OF METEOROLOGY. (UK/0307-5966). **Qty: 25. 1426**

JOURNAL OF MICROCOLUMN SEPARATIONS, THE. (US/1040-7685). **981**

JOURNAL OF MICROCOMPUTER SYSTEMS MANAGEMENT. (US/1043-6464). **1192**

JOURNAL OF MICROSCOPY (OXFORD). (UK/0022-2720). **572**

JOURNAL OF MICROWAVE POWER AND ELECTROMAGNETIC ENERGY, THE. (US/0832-7823). **2069**

JOURNAL OF MIDDLE ATLANTIC ARCHAEOLOGY. (US/0883-9697). **271**

JOURNAL OF MILITARY AVIATION. (US/1057-8307). **Qty: 18. 26**

JOURNAL OF MILITARY HISTORY, THE. (US/0899-3718). **Qty: 120. 4048**

JOURNAL OF MIND AND BEHAVIOR, THE. (US/0271-0137). **4598**

JOURNAL OF MINES, METALS & FUELS. (II/0022-2755). **2141**

JOURNAL OF MINISTRY IN ADDICTION & RECOVERY. (US/1053-8755). **1346**

JOURNAL OF MINORITY AGING, THE. (US/0742-6291). **5180**

JOURNAL OF MISSISSIPPI HISTORY, THE. (US/0022-2771). **Qty: 50. 2741**

JOURNAL OF MODERN AFRICAN STUDIES, THE. (UK/0022-278X). **2640**

JOURNAL OF MODERN GREEK STUDIES. (US/0738-1727). **2695**

JOURNAL OF MODERN HELLENISM. (US/0743-7749). **Qty: 10/year. 2266**

JOURNAL OF MODERN KOREAN STUDIES, THE. (US/8756-2235). **2655**

JOURNAL OF MODERN LITERATURE. (US/0022-281X). **3345**

JOURNAL OF MOLECULAR AND CELLULAR CARDIOLOGY. (UK/0022-2828). **3707**

JOURNAL OF MOLECULAR GRAPHICS. (UK/0263-7855). **1234**

JOURNAL OF MOLECULAR STRUCTURE. (NE/0022-2860). **1054**

JOURNAL OF MOLLUSCAN STUDIES. (UK/0260-1230). **5588**

JOURNAL OF MONEY, CREDIT, AND BANKING. (US/0022-2879). **795**

JOURNAL OF MORAL EDUCATION. (UK/0305-7240). **1758**

JOURNAL OF MOTOR BEHAVIOR. (US/0022-2895). **583**

JOURNAL OF MOTOR VEHICLE LAW. (CN/0840-7754). **2989**

JOURNAL OF MULTICULTURAL SOCIAL WORK. (US/1042-8224). **5292**

JOURNAL OF MULTILINGUAL AND MULTICULTURAL DEVELOPMENT. (UK/0143-4632). **3291**

JOURNAL OF MULTINATIONAL FINANCIAL MANAGEMENT. (US/1042-444X). **1637**

JOURNAL OF MUSCLE RESEARCH AND CELL MOTILITY. (UK/0142-4319). **538**

JOURNAL OF MUSIC THEORY PEDAGOGY, THE. (US/0891-7639). **Qty:** 2-4. **4126**

JOURNAL OF MUSIC THERAPY. (US/0022-2917). **4126**

JOURNAL OF MUSICOLOGICAL RESEARCH, THE. (US/0141-1896). **4126**

JOURNAL OF MUSICOLOGY (ST. JOSEPH, MICH.), THE. (US/0277-9269). **4126**

JOURNAL OF NARRATIVE TECHNIQUE, THE. (US/0022-2925). **Qty:** 3. **3400**

JOURNAL OF NATURAL PRODUCTS. (US/0163-3864). **1043**

JOURNAL OF NATURAL TOXINS. (US/1058-8108). **4311**

JOURNAL OF NAVAJO EDUCATION. (US/1042-3265). **Qty:** 10. **1758**

JOURNAL OF NAVIGATION, THE. (UK/0373-4633). **4177**

JOURNAL OF NEAR INFRARED SPECTROSCOPY. (UK). **4436**

JOURNAL OF NEGRO EDUCATION, THE. (US/0022-2984). **1758**

JOURNAL OF NEUROCYTOLOGY. (UK/0300-4864). **538**

JOURNAL OF NEUROIMMUNOLOGY. (NE/0165-5728). **3836**

JOURNAL OF NEUROLOGIC REHABILITATION. (US/0888-4390). **3836**

JOURNAL OF NEUROLOGICAL & ORTHOPAEDIC MEDICINE & SURGERY, THE. (US/0890-6599). **3967**

JOURNAL OF NEUROPATHOLOGY AND EXPERIMENTAL NEUROLOGY. (US/0022-3069). **3836**

JOURNAL OF NEUROSCIENCE METHODS. (NE/0165-0270). **3837**

JOURNAL OF NEUROSCIENCE NURSING, THE. (US/0888-0395). **3859**

JOURNAL OF NEUROSCIENCE RESEARCH. (US/0360-4012). **3837**

JOURNAL OF NEW GENERATION COMPUTER SYSTEMS. (GW/0863-0445). **1192**

JOURNAL OF NEW JERSEY POETS. (US/0363-4205). **Qty:** 2-4 per year. **3464**

JOURNAL OF NEWSPAPER AND PERIODICAL HISTORY. (UK/0265-5942). **2921**

JOURNAL OF NON-EQUILIBRIUM THERMODYNAMICS. (GW/0340-0204). **4431**

JOURNAL OF NONLINEAR BIOLOGY. (US/1047-1200). **495**

JOURNAL OF NONPROFIT & PUBLIC SECTOR MARKETING. (US/1049-5142). **928**

JOURNAL OF NORTHERN LUZON. (PH/0115-2408). **1758**

JOURNAL OF NUCLEAR AGRICULTURE AND BIOLOGY. (II/0379-5489). **100**

JOURNAL OF NUCLEAR MATERIALS. (NE/0022-3115). **2156**

JOURNAL OF NUCLEAR MEDICINE (1978), THE. (US/0161-5505). **3848**

JOURNAL OF NUCLEAR MEDICINE TECHNOLOGY. (US/0091-4916). **3848**

JOURNAL OF NURSE-MIDWIFERY. (US/0091-2182). **3859**

JOURNAL OF NURSING EDUCATION, THE. (US/0148-4834). **3859**

JOURNAL OF NURSING JOCULARITY. (US/1055-3088). **Qty:** 8. **3859**

JOURNAL OF NUTRITION EDUCATION. (US/0022-3182). **4193**

JOURNAL OF NUTRITION FOR THE ELDERLY. (US/0163-9366). **4193**

JOURNAL OF NUTRITION IN RECIPE & MENU DEVELOPMENT. (US/1055-1379). **4193**

JOURNAL OF NUTRITIONAL IMMUNOLOGY. (US/1049-5150). **4193**

JOURNAL OF OBJECTIVE STUDIES. (II). **5043**

JOURNAL OF OBSTETRICS AND GYNAECOLOGY. (UK/0144-3615). **3763**

JOURNAL OF OCCUPATIONAL AND ORGANIZATIONAL PSYCHOLOGY. (UK/0963-1798). **Qty:** (8-12). **4598**

JOURNAL OF OCCUPATIONAL MEDICINE AND TOXICOLOGY. (US/1054-044X). **3981**

JOURNAL OF OCULAR PHARMACOLOGY. (US/8756-3320). **3876**

JOURNAL OF OFFENDER MONITORING. (US/1043-500X). **3167**

JOURNAL OF OFFENDER REHABILITATION. (US/1050-9674). **3167**

JOURNAL OF OFFICIAL STATISTICS. (SW/0282-423X). **5329**

JOURNAL OF OMAN STUDIES, THE. (MK/0378-8180). **2655**

JOURNAL OF ONE-DAY SURGERY. (UK/0963-5386). **3968**

JOURNAL OF ONE-NAME STUDIES, THE. (UK/0262-4842). **2455**

JOURNAL OF OPHTHALMIC NURSING & TECHNOLOGY. (US/0744-7132). **3859**

JOURNAL OF OPTIMAL NUTRITION, THE. (US/1061-2130). **4193**

JOURNAL OF OPTOMETRIC EDUCATION. (US/0098-6917). **4216**

JOURNAL OF OPTOMETRIC VISION DEVELOPMENT (1976). (US/0149-886X). **4216**

JOURNAL OF ORAL AND MAXILLOFACIAL SURGERY. (US/0278-2391). **3968**

JOURNAL OF ORGANIZATIONAL BEHAVIOR MANAGEMENT. (US/0160-8061). **4599**

JOURNAL OF ORGONOMY, THE. (US/0022-3298). **3596**

JOURNAL OF ORIENTAL RESEARCH, MADRAS, THE. (II/0022-3301). **3291**

JOURNAL OF ORIENTAL STUDIES (HONG KONG). (HK/0022-331X). **2655**

JOURNAL OF ORTHOMOLECULAR MEDICINE. (CN/0834-4825). **3929**

JOURNAL OF ORTHOPAEDIC RHEUMATOLOGY. (UK/0951-9580). **3882**

JOURNAL OF ORTHOPAEDIC SURGICAL TECHNIQUES, THE. (UK/0334-0236). **3882**

JOURNAL OF OTOLARYNGOLOGY. SUPPLEMENT, THE. (CN/0707-7270). **3889**

JOURNAL OF OTOLARYNGOLOGY, THE. (CN/0381-6605). **3889**

JOURNAL OF PACIFIC HISTORY, THE. (AT/0022-3344). **2669**

JOURNAL OF PAEDIATRICS, OBSTETRICS, AND GYNAECOLOGY. (HK/1012-8875). **3905**

JOURNAL OF PAIN AND SYMPTOM MANAGEMENT. (US/0885-3924). **3596**

JOURNAL OF PALEONTOLOGY. (US/0022-3360). **4227**

JOURNAL OF PALESTINE STUDIES. (US/0377-919X). **2655**

JOURNAL OF PALLIATIVE CARE. (CN/0825-8597). **Qty:** 10-15. **5292**

JOURNAL OF PAN AFRICAN STUDIES, THE. (US/0888-6601). **5206**

JOURNAL OF PARAMETRICS. (US/1015-7891). **747**

JOURNAL OF PARAPSYCHOLOGY, THE. (US/0022-3387). **4241**

JOURNAL OF PARENTERAL SCIENCE AND TECHNOLOGY. (US/0279-7976). **4311**

JOURNAL OF PARK AND RECREATION ADMINISTRATION. (US/0735-1968). **4706**

JOURNAL OF PASTORAL CARE, THE. (US/0022-3409). **Qty:** 25. **4969**

JOURNAL OF PASTORAL COUNSELING, THE. (US/0449-508X). **4969**

JOURNAL OF PASTORAL PRACTICE, THE. (US/0196-9072). **5017**

JOURNAL OF PASTORAL PSYCHOTHERAPY. (US/0886-5477). **4599**

JOURNAL OF PASTORAL THEOLOGY. (US/1064-9867). **4969**

JOURNAL OF PATHOLOGY. (UK/0022-3417). **3895**

JOURNAL OF PEACE RESEARCH. (NO/0022-3433). **4527**

JOURNAL OF PEASANT STUDIES, THE. (UK/0306-6150). **5250**

JOURNAL OF PEDIATRIC & PERINATAL NUTRITION. (US/8756-6206). **3905**

JOURNAL OF PEDIATRIC ENDOCRINOLOGY, THE. (UK/0334-018X). **3905**

JOURNAL OF PEDIATRIC HEALTH CARE. (US/0891-5245). **3905**

JOURNAL OF PEDIATRIC OPHTHALMOLOGY AND STRABISMUS. (US/0191-3913). **3905**

JOURNAL OF PEDIATRICS, THE. (US/0022-3476). **3905**

JOURNAL OF PENSION PLANNING AND COMPLIANCE. (US/0148-2181). **904**

JOURNAL OF PENTECOSTAL THEOLOGY. (UK/0966-7369). **5062**

JOURNAL OF PERINATAL & NEONATAL NURSING, THE. (US/0893-2190). **3859**

JOURNAL OF PERINATAL EDUCATION, THE. (US/1058-1243). **Qty:** 4. **3764**

JOURNAL OF PERSONAL SELLING & SALES MANAGEMENT, THE. (US/0885-3134). **928**

JOURNAL OF PERSONALITY. (US/0022-3506). **4599**

JOURNAL OF PERSONALITY ASSESSMENT. (US/0022-3891). **4599**

JOURNAL OF PERSONALITY DISORDERS. (US/0885-579X). **4599**

JOURNAL OF PESTICIDE REFORM. (US/0893-357X). **Qty:** 8. **4245**

JOURNAL OF PETROLEUM GEOLOGY. (UK/0141-6421). **4262**

JOURNAL OF PETROLEUM SCIENCE & ENGINEERING. (NE/0920-4105). **4262**

JOURNAL OF PETROLEUM TECHNOLOGY. (US/0149-2136). **4262**

JOURNAL OF PETROLOGY. (UK/0022-3530). **1458**

JOURNAL OF PHARMACEUTICAL CARE IN PAIN & SYMPTOM CONTROL. (US/1056-4950). **4311**

JOURNAL OF PHARMACEUTICAL MARKETING & MANAGEMENT. (US/0883-7597). **4311**

JOURNAL OF PHARMACEUTICAL SCIENCES. (US/0022-3549). **4312**

JOURNAL OF PHARMACOEPIDEMIOLOGY. (US/0896-6966). **3596**

JOURNAL OF PHARMACY TEACHING. (US/1044-0054). **4312**

JOURNAL OF PHARMACY TECHNOLOGY, THE. (US/8755-1225). **4313**

JOURNAL OF PHENOMENOLOGICAL PSYCHOLOGY. (US/0047-2662). **4599**

JOURNAL OF PHILOSOPHY OF EDUCATION. (UK/0309-8249). **1898**

JOURNAL OF PHILOSOPHY, THE. (US/0022-362X). **4350**

JOURNAL OF PHOTOGRAPHIC SCIENCE, THE. (UK/0022-3638). **4371**

JOURNAL OF PHYSICAL EDUCATION, RECREATION & DANCE. (US/0730-3084). **1856**

JOURNAL OF PLANNING EDUCATION AND RESEARCH. (US/0739-456X). **Qty:** 25. **2826**

JOURNAL OF PLANT ANATOMY AND MORPHOLOGY. (II/0256-436X). **515**

JOURNAL OF PLANT PHYSIOLOGY. (GW/0176-1617). **516**

JOURNAL OF PLANTATION CROPS. (II/0304-5242). **176**

JOURNAL OF PLASMA PHYSICS. (UK/0022-3778). **4410**

JOURNAL OF POLICE AND CRIMINAL PSYCHOLOGY. (US/0882-0783). **Qty:** 1-2. **3167**

JOURNAL OF POLICY ANALYSIS AND MANAGEMENT. (US/0276-8739). **4479**

JOURNAL OF POLITICS, THE. (US/0022-3816). **4479**

JOURNAL OF POLYGRAPH SCIENCE, THE. (US/0893-4827). **3167**

JOURNAL OF POLYMER ENGINEERING. (IS/0334-6447). **2104**

JOURNAL OF POPULAR CULTURE. (US/0022-3840). **2741**

JOURNAL OF POPULAR LITERATURE. (US/0897-3075). **3400**

JOURNAL OF POST KEYNESIAN ECONOMICS. (US/0160-3477). **1593**

JOURNAL OF POSTGRADUATE MEDICINE (BOMBAY). (II/0022-3859). **3597**

JOURNAL OF POWDER & BULK SOLIDS TECHNOLOGY. (UK/0147-698X). **2014**

JOURNAL OF PRACTICAL APPLICATIONS OF SPACE. (US/1046-8757). **Qty:** 1-10. **26**

JOURNAL OF PRACTICAL APPROACHES TO DEVELOPMENTAL HANDICAP. (CN/0707-7807). **4390**

JOURNAL OF PRACTICAL NURSING, THE. (US/0022-3867). **3860**

JOURNAL OF PRE-RAPHAELITE STUDIES (1992), THE. (US/1060-149X). **2848**

JOURNAL OF PREHISTORIC RELIGION. (SW/0283-8486). **4969**

JOURNAL OF PRESSURE VESSEL TECHNOLOGY. (US/0094-9930). **2118**

JOURNAL OF PRISONERS ON PRISONS. (CN/0838-164X). **3167**

JOURNAL OF PROBATION AND PAROLE : THE JOURNAL OF THE NEW YORK STATE PROBATION OFFICERS ASSOCIATION. (US/0278-1042). **Qty: 2-5. 3167**

JOURNAL OF PROCESS CONTROL. (UK/0959-1524). **3482**

JOURNAL OF PROFESSIONAL SERVICES MARKETING. (US/0748-4623). **929**

JOURNAL OF PROGRESSIVE HUMAN SERVICES. (US/1042-8232). **5292**

JOURNAL OF PROMOTION MANAGEMENT. (US/1049-6491). **874**

JOURNAL OF PROPERTY RESEARCH. (UK/0959-9916). **4839**

JOURNAL OF PROPERTY VALUATION & INVESTMENT. (UK/0960-2712). **4839**

JOURNAL OF PROSTHETIC DENTISTRY, THE. (US/0022-3913). **1327**

JOURNAL OF PROSTHETICS AND ORTHOTICS. (US/1040-8800). **Qty: 10-20. 3597**

JOURNAL OF PROTECTIVE COATINGS & LININGS. (US/8755-1985). **5119**

JOURNAL OF PROTOZOOLOGY, THE. (US/0022-3921). **5588**

JOURNAL OF PSYCHIATRY & NEUROSCIENCE. (CN/1180-4882). **3929**

JOURNAL OF PSYCHOACTIVE DRUGS. (US/0279-1072). **1346**

JOURNAL OF PSYCHOHISTORY, THE. (US/0145-3378). **4599**

JOURNAL OF PSYCHOLOGICAL RESEARCHES. (II/0022-3972). **4600**

JOURNAL OF PSYCHOLOGY AND CHRISTIANITY. (US/0733-4273). **4969**

JOURNAL OF PSYCHOLOGY & HUMAN SEXUALITY. (US/0890-7064). **4600**

JOURNAL OF PSYCHOLOGY AND JUDAISM. (US/0700-9801). **4600**

JOURNAL OF PSYCHOLOGY AND THEOLOGY. (US/0091-6471). **4600**

JOURNAL OF PSYCHOPHARMACOLOGY (OXFORD, ENGLAND). (UK/0269-8811). **4313**

JOURNAL OF PSYCHOPHYSIOLOGY. (UK/0269-8803). **4600**

JOURNAL OF PSYCHOSOCIAL NURSING AND MENTAL HEALTH SERVICES. (US/0279-3695). **3860**

JOURNAL OF PSYCHOSOCIAL ONCOLOGY. (US/0734-7332). **3819**

JOURNAL OF PSYCHOTHERAPY PRACTICE AND RESEARCH, THE. (US/1055-050X). **3929**

JOURNAL OF PUBLIC ADMINISTRATION RESEARCH AND THEORY. (US/1053-1858). **4659**

JOURNAL OF PUBLIC HEALTH DENTISTRY. (US/0022-4006). **Qty: varies. 1328**

JOURNAL OF PUBLIC HEALTH POLICY. (US/0197-5897). **4787**

JOURNAL OF PUBLIC POLICY. (UK/0143-814X). **4479**

JOURNAL OF PURE AND APPLIED SCIENCES (ANKARA). (TU/0022-4057). **5119**

JOURNAL OF QUANTITATIVE ANTHROPOLOGY. (NE/0922-2995). **239**

JOURNAL OF QUESTIONED DOCUMENT EXAMINATION. (US/1061-3455). **Qty: 2 / year. 3167**

JOURNAL OF RADIOLOGICAL PROTECTION. (UK/0952-4746). **4436**

JOURNAL OF RANGE MANAGEMENT. (US/0022-409X). **100**

JOURNAL OF RAPTOR RESEARCH, THE. (US/0892-1016). **5588**

JOURNAL OF READING BEHAVIOR. (US/0022-4111). **1758**

JOURNAL OF REAL ESTATE FINANCE AND ECONOMICS, THE. (US/0895-5638). **4839**

JOURNAL OF RECEPTOR RESEARCH. (US/0197-5110). **538**

JOURNAL OF RECONSTRUCTIVE MICROSURGERY. (US/0743-684X). **3968**

JOURNAL OF RECREATIONAL MATHEMATICS. (US/0022-412X). **3514**

JOURNAL OF REFUGEE STUDIES. (UK/0951-6328). **1919**

JOURNAL OF REGRESSION THERAPY, THE. (US/1054-0830). **4600**

JOURNAL OF REGULATORY ECONOMICS. (US/0922-680X). **843**

JOURNAL OF REHABILITATION. (US/0022-4154). **5292**

JOURNAL OF REHABILITATION ADMINISTRATION. (US/0148-3846). **4390**

JOURNAL OF REHABILITATION IN ASIA, THE. (II/0022-4162). **4380**

JOURNAL OF RELIGION AND PSYCHICAL RESEARCH, THE. (US/0731-2148). **Qty: 20-30. 4969**

JOURNAL OF RELIGION AND THE APPLIED BEHAVIORAL SCIENCES. (US/0275-1402). **4970**

JOURNAL OF RELIGION IN AFRICA. (NE/0022-4200). **4970**

JOURNAL OF RELIGION IN DISABILITY & REHABILITATION. (US/1059-9258). **4970**

JOURNAL OF RELIGION IN PSYCHOTHERAPY. (US/1045-5876). **3929**

JOURNAL OF RELIGIOUS & THEOLOGICAL INFORMATION. (US/1047-7845). **3220**

JOURNAL OF RELIGIOUS ETHICS, THE. (US/0384-9694). **2251**

JOURNAL OF RELIGIOUS GERONTOLOGY. (US/1050-2289). **5180**

JOURNAL OF RELIGIOUS HISTORY, THE. (AT/0022-4227). **4970**

JOURNAL OF RELIGIOUS STUDIES. (II/0047-2735). **4970**

JOURNAL OF RELIGIOUS THOUGHT, THE. (US/0022-4235). **4970**

JOURNAL OF REPRODUCTION & FERTILITY. (UK/0022-4251). **3597**

JOURNAL OF REPRODUCTIVE AND INFANT PSYCHOLOGY. (UK/0264-6838). **Qty: 5-10. 3764**

JOURNAL OF REPRODUCTIVE MEDICINE. (US/0024-7758). **3764**

JOURNAL OF RESEARCH IN PHARMACEUTICAL ECONOMICS. (US/0896-6621). **4313**

JOURNAL OF RESEARCH IN RURAL EDUCATION. (US/1062-4228). **1758**

JOURNAL OF RESEARCH ON CHRISTIAN EDUCATION. (US/1065-6219). **Qty: 6. 4970**

JOURNAL OF RESEARCH ON COMPUTING IN EDUCATION. (US/0888-6504). **1224**

JOURNAL OF RESEARCH ON THE LEPIDOPTERA, THE. (US/0022-4324). **5611**

JOURNAL OF RETAILING. (US/0022-4359). **955**

JOURNAL OF RHEUMATOLOGY, THE. (CN/0315-162X). **3805**

JOURNAL OF RITUAL STUDIES. (US/0890-1112). **4970**

JOURNAL OF ROMAN ARCHAEOLOGY. (US/1047-7594). **271**

JOURNAL OF ROMAN STUDIES, THE. (UK/0075-4358). **Qty: 80/yr. 1078**

JOURNAL OF RURAL AND SMALL SCHOOLS. (US/0890-9520). **1758**

JOURNAL OF RURAL COMMUNITY PSYCHOLOGY. (US/0276-2285). **Qty: 1. 4601**

JOURNAL OF RURAL COOPERATION. (IS/0377-7480). **1542**

JOURNAL OF RURAL DEVELOPMENT (HYDERABAD, INDIA). (II/0970-3357). **5206**

JOURNAL OF RURAL HEALTH, THE. (US/0890-765X). **4787**

JOURNAL OF SAN DIEGO HISTORY, THE. (US/0022-4383). **2742**

JOURNAL OF SCHOOL HEALTH, THE. (US/0022-4391). **4787**

JOURNAL OF SCHOOL PSYCHOLOGY. (US/0022-4405). **4601**

JOURNAL OF SCIENCE AND MATHEMATICS EDUCATION IN SOUTHEAST ASIA. (MY/0126-7663). **1758**

JOURNAL OF SCIENTIFIC AND APPLIED PHOTOGRAPHY AND CINEMATOGRAPHY. (US). **4371**

JOURNAL OF SCOUTING HISTORY. (US). **Qty: 2/yr. 5232**

JOURNAL OF SECURITY ADMINISTRATION. (US/0195-9425). **3168**

JOURNAL OF SEDIMENTARY PETROLOGY. (US/0022-4472). **1458**

JOURNAL OF SEDIMENTARY RESEARCH. SECTION A, SEDIMENTARY PETROLOGY AND PROCESSES. (US/1073-130X). **1459**

JOURNAL OF SEDIMENTARY RESEARCH. SECTION B, STRATIGRAPHY AND GLOBAL STUDIES. (US/1073-1318). **1459**

JOURNAL OF SEMANTICS (NIJMEGEN). (NE/0167-5133). **3291**

JOURNAL OF SEMI-CUSTOM ICS. (UK/0264-3375). **2069**

JOURNAL OF SEMITIC STUDIES. (UK/0022-4480). **2266**

JOURNAL OF SERVICES MARKETING, THE. (US/0887-6045). **929**

JOURNAL OF SEX & MARITAL THERAPY. (US/0092-623X). **5187**

JOURNAL OF SEX EDUCATION AND THERAPY. (US/0161-4576). **5187**

JOURNAL OF SEX RESEARCH, THE. (US/0022-4499). **5187**

JOURNAL OF SEXUAL HEALTH. (UK/0963-6757). **Qty: 6 - 10. 5187**

JOURNAL OF SHELLFISH RESEARCH. (US/0730-8000). **2307**

JOURNAL OF SIKH STUDIES. (II/0379-8194). **4970**

JOURNAL OF SLAVIC LINGUISTICS. (US/1068-2090). **Qty: 2-3. 3292**

JOURNAL OF SMALL ANIMAL PRACTICE, THE. (UK/0022-4510). **5513**

JOURNAL OF SMALL BUSINESS MANAGEMENT. (US/0047-2778). **874**

JOURNAL OF SMOKING-RELATED DISORDERS, THE. (UK/0959-2431). **3981**

JOURNAL OF SOCIAL AND ADMINISTRATIVE PHARMACY : JSAP. (SW/0281-0662). **4313**

JOURNAL OF SOCIAL AND CLINICAL PSYCHOLOGY. (US/0736-7236). **4601**

JOURNAL OF SOCIAL AND PERSONAL RELATIONSHIPS. (UK/0265-4075). **4601**

JOURNAL OF SOCIAL DEVELOPMENT IN AFRICA. (RH). **Qty: 16. 5206**

JOURNAL OF SOCIAL POLICY. (UK/0047-2794). **5293**

JOURNAL OF SOCIAL PSYCHOLOGY, THE. (US/0022-4545). **4601**

JOURNAL OF SOCIAL RESEARCH (RANCHI). (II/0449-315X). **239**

JOURNAL OF SOCIAL SCIENCE. (MW). **5207**

JOURNAL OF SOCIAL SERVICE RESEARCH. (US/0148-8376). **5293**

JOURNAL OF SOCIAL STUDIES RESEARCH. (US/0885-985X). **5207**

JOURNAL OF SOCIAL STUDIES, THE. (BG). **Qty: 3-4. 5207**

JOURNAL OF SOCIAL WORK & HUMAN SEXUALITY. (US/0276-3850). **5293**

JOURNAL OF SOCIAL WORK EDUCATION. (US/1043-7797). **5293**

JOURNAL OF SOCIAL WORK PRACTICE. (UK/0265-0533). **5293**

JOURNAL OF SOCIOLOGICAL STUDIES, THE. (II). **5250**

JOURNAL OF SOCIOLOGY AND SOCIAL WELFARE. (US/0191-5096). **5293**

JOURNAL OF SOIL AND WATER CONSERVATION. (US/0022-4561). **2196**

JOURNAL OF SOLAR ENERGY ENGINEERING. (US/0199-6231). **1949**

JOURNAL OF SOUTH ASIAN AND MIDDLE EASTERN STUDIES. (US/0149-1784). **2769**

JOURNAL OF SOUTH ASIAN LITERATURE. (US/0091-5637). **3400**

JOURNAL OF SOUTHEAST ASIAN STUDIES (SINGAPORE). (SI/0022-4634). **2655**

JOURNAL OF SOUTHERN AFRICAN STUDIES. (UK/0305-7070). **2641**

JOURNAL OF SOUTHERN HISTORY, THE. (US/0022-4642). **2742**

JOURNAL OF SOUTHWEST GEORGIA HISTORY, THE. (US/0739-1943). **2742**

JOURNAL OF SOVIET MILITARY STUDIES, THE. (US/0954-254X). **4048**

JOURNAL OF SOVIET NATIONALITIES. (US/1043-7916). **2266**

JOURNAL OF SPACE LAW. (US/0095-7577). **2989**

JOURNAL OF SPECIAL EDUCATION, THE. (US/0022-4669). **1881**

JOURNAL OF SPECULATIVE PHILOSOPHY, THE. (US/0891-625X). **4351**

JOURNAL OF SPEECH-LANGUAGE PATHOLOGY AND AUDIOLOGY. (CN/0848-1970). **Qty: 20-24. 4390**

JOURNAL OF SPELEAN HISTORY, THE. (US/0022-4693). **1357**

JOURNAL OF SPORT AND SOCIAL ISSUES. (US/0193-7235). **5250**

JOURNAL OF SPORT BEHAVIOR. (US/0162-7341). **Qty: 2 per year. 4902**

JOURNAL OF SPORT HISTORY. (US/0094-1700). **4902**

JOURNAL OF SPORT MANAGEMENT. (US/0888-4773). **4902**

JOURNAL OF SPORTS MEDICINE AND PHYSICAL FITNESS. (IT/0022-4707). **3954**

JOURNAL OF SPORTS PHILATELY. (US/0447-953X). **2785**

JOURNAL OF SPORTS SCIENCES. (UK/0264-0414). **4902**

JOURNAL OF STAFF DEVELOPMENT, THE. (US/0276-928X). **1801**

JOURNAL OF STAFF, PROGRAM & ORGANIZATION DEVELOPMENT, THE. (US/0736-7627). **1898**

JOURNAL OF STAINED GLASS : THE JOURNAL OF THE BRITISH SOCIETY OF MASTER GLASS PAINTERS, THE. (UK). **2591**

JOURNAL OF STATISTICAL COMPUTATION AND SIMULATION. (US/0094-9655). **1282**

JOURNAL OF STATISTICAL RESEARCH - UNIVERSITY OF DACCA. INSTITUTE OF STATISTICAL RESEARCH AND TRAINING. (BG/0256-422X). **5329**

JOURNAL OF STRAIN ANALYSIS FOR ENGINEERING DESIGN, THE. (UK/0309-3247). **2118**

JOURNAL OF STRATEGIC AND SYSTEMIC THERAPIES, THE. (CN/0711-5075). **3929**

JOURNAL OF STRATEGIC STUDIES, THE. (UK/0140-2390). **4048**

JOURNAL OF STRENGTH AND CONDITIONING RESEARCH. (US/1064-8011). **4902**

JOURNAL OF STROKE AND CEREBROVASCULAR DISEASES. (US/1052-3057). **3837**

JOURNAL OF STRUCTURAL ENGINEERING. (II/0970-0137). **2026**

JOURNAL OF STRUCTURAL LEARNING. (US/0022-4774). **1758**

JOURNAL OF STUDENT FINANCIAL AID, THE. (US/0884-9153). **1758**

JOURNAL OF STUDIES ON ALCOHOL. (US/0096-882X). **1346**

JOURNAL OF SUBSTANCE ABUSE. (US/0899-3289). **1346**

JOURNAL OF SUNG-YUAN STUDIES. (US/1059-3152). **Qty:** 4-5. **2505**

JOURNAL OF SUPERVISION AND TRAINING IN MINISTRY. (US/0160-7774). **Qty:** 10. **4970**

JOURNAL OF SURGICAL ONCOLOGY. (US/0022-4790). **3820**

JOURNAL OF SURVEYING ENGINEERING. (US/0733-9453). **2026**

JOURNAL OF SUSTAINABLE AGRICULTURE. (US/1044-0046). **100**

JOURNAL OF SYMBOLIC LOGIC, THE. (US/0022-4812). **3515**

JOURNAL OF SYNAGOGUE MUSIC. (US/0449-5128). **4126**

JOURNAL OF SYSTEMS MANAGEMENT. (US/0022-4839). **687**

JOURNAL OF TAMIL STUDIES. (II/0022-4855). **2849**

JOURNAL OF TAXATION OF ESTATES & TRUSTS, THE. (US/1044-9418). **3118**

JOURNAL OF TAXATION OF EXEMPT ORGANIZATIONS, THE. (US/1043-0539). **4735**

JOURNAL OF TAXATION OF S CORPORATIONS, THE. (US/1040-502X). **795**

JOURNAL OF TEACHER EDUCATION. (US/0022-4871). **1865**

JOURNAL OF TEACHING IN INTERNATIONAL BUSINESS. (US/0897-5930). **688**

JOURNAL OF TEACHING IN PHYSICAL EDUCATION. (US/0273-5024). **1856**

JOURNAL OF TEACHING IN SOCIAL WORK. (US/0884-1233). **5293**

JOURNAL OF TEACHING WRITING. (US/0735-1259). **Qty:** 4. **3292**

JOURNAL OF TECHNOLOGY EDUCATION. (US/1045-1064). **5120**

JOURNAL OF TECHNOLOGY TRANSFER, THE. (US/0892-9912). **Qty:** 4. **5120**

JOURNAL OF TEXAS CATHOLIC HISTORY AND CULTURE / TEXAS CATHOLIC HISTORICAL SOCIETY, THE. (US/1048-2431). **Qty:** 20. **5031**

JOURNAL OF TEXTURE STUDIES. (US/0022-4901). **2347**

JOURNAL OF THE ACADEMY OF MARKETING SCIENCE. (US/0092-0703). **929**

JOURNAL OF THE AERONAUTICAL SOCIETY OF INDIA, THE. (II/0001-9267). **26**

JOURNAL OF THE AFRO-AMERICAN HISTORICAL AND GENEALOGICAL SOCIETY. (US/0272-1937). **2455**

JOURNAL OF THE ALABAMA ACADEMY OF SCIENCE, THE. (US/0002-4112). **5120**

JOURNAL OF THE ALABAMA DENTAL ASSOCIATION, THE. (US/0002-4198). **Qty:** 6-10 per year. **1328**

JOURNAL OF THE ALLEGHENIES. (US/0276-7449). **2742**

JOURNAL OF THE AMERICAN ACADEMY OF DERMATOLOGY. (US/0190-9622). **3721**

JOURNAL OF THE AMERICAN ACADEMY OF PHYSICIAN ASSISTANTS. (US/0893-7400). **3597**

JOURNAL OF THE AMERICAN ACADEMY OF RELIGION. (US/0002-7189). **4970**

JOURNAL OF THE AMERICAN ANALGESIA SOCIETY. (US/0002-7243). **3597**

JOURNAL OF THE AMERICAN ASSOCIATION OF VARIABLE STAR OBSERVERS, THE. (US/0271-9053). **396**

JOURNAL OF THE AMERICAN BOARD OF FAMILY PRACTICE, THE. (US/0893-8652). **3738**

JOURNAL OF THE AMERICAN CHAMBER OF COMMERCE IN JAPAN / ACCJ, THE. (JA/0002-7847). **820**

JOURNAL OF THE AMERICAN CHEMICAL SOCIETY. (US/0002-7863). **982**

JOURNAL OF THE AMERICAN COLLEGE OF CARDIOLOGY. (US/0735-1097). **3707**

JOURNAL OF THE AMERICAN COLLEGE OF TOXICOLOGY. (US/0730-0913). **3982**

JOURNAL OF THE AMERICAN DIETETIC ASSOCIATION. (US/0002-8223). **4194**

JOURNAL OF THE AMERICAN GERIATRICS SOCIETY. (US/0002-8614). **3753**

JOURNAL OF THE AMERICAN HELICOPTER SOCIETY. (US/0002-8711). **26**

JOURNAL OF THE AMERICAN HISTORICAL SOCIETY OF GERMANS FROM RUSSIA. (US/0162-8283). **2695**

JOURNAL OF THE AMERICAN INSTITUTE FOR CONSERVATION. (US/0197-1360). **323**

JOURNAL OF THE AMERICAN INSTITUTE OF HOMEOPATHY. (US/0002-8967). **3775**

JOURNAL OF THE AMERICAN KILLIFISH ASSOCIATION, THE. (US/0002-967X). **2307**

JOURNAL OF THE AMERICAN LISZT SOCIETY. (US/0147-4413). **4126**

JOURNAL OF THE AMERICAN MEDICAL WOMEN'S ASSOCIATION (1972). (US/0098-8421). **3597**

JOURNAL OF THE AMERICAN MOSQUITO CONTROL ASSOCIATION. (US/8756-971X). **4245**

JOURNAL OF THE AMERICAN MUSICAL INSTRUMENT SOCIETY. (US/0362-3300). **4126**

JOURNAL OF THE AMERICAN MUSICOLOGICAL SOCIETY. (US/0003-0139). **4126**

JOURNAL OF THE AMERICAN OPTOMETRIC ASSOCIATION. (US/0003-0244). **Qty:** 30-40 per year. **4216**

JOURNAL OF THE AMERICAN ORIENTAL SOCIETY. (US/0003-0279). **3292**

JOURNAL OF THE AMERICAN OSTEOPATHIC ASSOCIATION, THE. (US/0098-6151). **3598**

JOURNAL OF THE AMERICAN PLANNING ASSOCIATION. (US/0194-4363). **2826**

JOURNAL OF THE AMERICAN PODIATRIC MEDICAL ASSOCIATION. (US/8750-7315). **3918**

JOURNAL OF THE AMERICAN PSYCHOANALYTIC ASSOCIATION. (US/0003-0651). **4601**

JOURNAL OF THE AMERICAN ROMANIAN ACADEMY OF ARTS AND SCIENCES. (US/0896-1018). **2518**

JOURNAL OF THE AMERICAN SOCIETY FOR INFORMATION SCIENCE. (US/0002-8231). **3220**

JOURNAL OF THE AMERICAN SOCIETY FOR PSYCHICAL RESEARCH (1932). (US/0003-1070). **4242**

JOURNAL OF THE AMERICAN SOCIETY OF BREWING CHEMISTS. (US/0361-0470). **982**

JOURNAL OF THE AMERICAN STATISTICAL ASSOCIATION. (US/0162-1459). **5329**

JOURNAL OF THE AMERICAN STUDIES ASSOCIATION OF TEXAS. (US/0587-5064). **Qty:** 25. **2742**

JOURNAL OF THE AMERICAN TAXATION ASSOCIATION, THE. (US/0198-9073). **4735**

JOURNAL OF THE AMERICAN VETERINARY MEDICAL ASSOCIATION. (US/0003-1488). **5513**

JOURNAL OF THE ANATOMICAL SOCIETY OF INDIA. (II/0003-2778). **3679**

JOURNAL OF THE ARIZONA-NEVADA ACADEMY OF SCIENCE. (US/0193-8509). **Qty:** 4-5. **1357**

JOURNAL OF THE ASSOCIATION FOR PERSONS WITH SEVERE HANDICAPS, THE. (US/0749-1425). **1881**

JOURNAL OF THE ASSOCIATION OF CHILDREN'S PROSTHETIC-ORTHOTIC CLINICS. (US/0884-8424). **3883**

JOURNAL OF THE ASSOCIATION OF NURSES IN AIDS CARE, THE. (US/1055-3290). **Qty:** 5-10. **3860**

JOURNAL OF THE ASSOCIATION OF PHYSICIANS OF INDIA. (II). **3799**

JOURNAL OF THE ASSOCIATION OF SURVEYORS OF PAPUA NEW GUINEA, THE. (PP). **2026**

JOURNAL OF THE ASTRONAUTICAL SCIENCES, THE. (US/0021-9142). **26**

JOURNAL OF THE ATMOSPHERIC SCIENCES. (US/0022-4928). **1427**

JOURNAL OF THE AUSTRALIAN CATHOLIC HISTORICAL SOCIETY. (AT/0084-7259). **5031**

JOURNAL OF THE AUSTRALIAN ENTOMOLOGICAL SOCIETY. (AT/0004-9050). **5588**

JOURNAL OF THE AUSTRALIAN MATHEMATICAL SOCIETY. SERIES A : PURE MATHEMATICS AND STATISTICS. (AT/0263-6115). **3515**

JOURNAL OF THE AUSTRALIAN MATHEMATICAL SOCIETY. SERIES B : APPLIED MATHEMATICS, THE. (AT/0334-2700). **3515**

JOURNAL OF THE AUSTRALIAN NAVAL INSTITUTE. (AT/0312-5807). **4178**

JOURNAL OF THE AUSTRALIAN WAR MEMORIAL. (AT/0729-6274). **4048**

JOURNAL OF THE BOMBAY NATURAL HISTORY SOCIETY. (II/0006-6982). **4166**

JOURNAL OF THE BRITISH ARCHAEOLOGICAL ASSOCIATION. (UK/0068-1288). **272**

JOURNAL OF THE BRITISH ASSOCIATION FOR IMMEDIATE CARE, THE. (UK). **3725**

JOURNAL OF THE BRITISH ASSOCIATION OF TEACHERS OF THE DEAF, THE. (UK/0266-4062). **1881**

JOURNAL OF THE BRITISH ASTRONOMICAL ASSOCIATION. (UK/0007-0297). **396**

JOURNAL OF THE BRITISH CONTACT LENS ASSOCIATION. (UK/0141-7037). **3876**

JOURNAL OF THE BROMELIAD SOCIETY. (US/0090-8738). **Qty:** 6. **516**

JOURNAL OF THE CAMBRIDGESHIRE FAMILY HISTORY SOCIETY. (UK/0309-5800). **Qty:** 40. **2455**

JOURNAL OF THE CANADIAN ATHLETIC THERAPISTS ASSOCIATION, THE. (CN/0225-9877). **3954**

JOURNAL OF THE CANADIAN CHIROPRACTIC ASSOCIATION, THE. (CN/0008-3194). **3805**

JOURNAL OF THE CANADIAN CHURCH HISTORICAL SOCIETY. (CN/0008-3208). **4970**

JOURNAL OF THE CHEMICAL SOCIETY, CHEMICAL COMMUNICATIONS. (UK/0022-4936). **982**

JOURNAL OF THE CHINESE LANGUAGE TEACHERS ASSOCIATION. (US/0009-4595). **3292**

JOURNAL OF THE CHRISTIAN MEDICAL FELLOWSHIP. (UK). **4970**

JOURNAL OF THE CLAN CAMPBELL SOCIETY (UNITED STATES OF AMERICA). (US/0731-955X). **2455**

JOURNAL OF THE COMMUNITY DEVELOPMENT SOCIETY. (US/0010-3829). **5250**

JOURNAL OF THE CONDUCTORS' GUILD. (US/0734-1032). **Qty:** 10-12. **4127**

JOURNAL OF THE CORK HISTORICAL AND ARCHAEOLOGICAL SOCIETY. (IE/0010-8731). **2695**

JOURNAL OF THE COUNTY LOUTH ARCHAEOLOGICAL AND HISTORICAL SOCIETY. (IE/0070-1327). **272**

JOURNAL OF THE DAGUERREIAN SOCIETY. (US). **Qty:** 4-5. **4371**

JOURNAL OF THE DEPARTMENT OF ENGLISH (UNIVERSITY OF CALCUTTA. DEPT. OF ENGLISH). (II). **3400**

JOURNAL OF THE EARLY REPUBLIC. (US/0275-1275). **2742**

JOURNAL OF THE ELECTROCHEMICAL SOCIETY OF INDIA. (II/0013-466X). **1026**

JOURNAL OF THE ENTOMOLOGICAL SOCIETY OF SOUTHERN AFRICA. (SA/0013-8789). **Qty:** 4/yr. **5589**

JOURNAL OF THE EUROPEAN ASSOCIATION OF MARINE SCIENCES AND TECHNIQUES. (NE/0924-7963). **1450**

JOURNAL OF THE EXPERIMENTAL ANALYSIS OF BEHAVIOR. (US/0022-5002). **4601**

JOURNAL OF THE FLORIDA MEDICAL ASSOCIATION (1974). (US/0015-4148). Qty: 6-10 per year. **3598**

JOURNAL OF THE FLUORESCENT MINERAL SOCIETY. (US/0160-0958). **1440**

JOURNAL OF THE GEOGRAPHICAL ASSOCIATION OF TANZANIA. (TZ/0016-738X). **2567**

JOURNAL OF THE GEOLOGICAL SOCIETY OF INDIA. (II/0016-7622). Qty: 20. **1385**

JOURNAL OF THE GEOLOGICAL SOCIETY OF IRAQ. (IQ/0533-8301). **1385**

JOURNAL OF THE GLASS ASSOCIATION, THE. (UK). **2592**

JOURNAL OF THE GREATER HOUSTON DENTAL SOCIETY, THE. (US/1062-0265). Qty: 10. **1328**

JOURNAL OF THE GYPSY LORE SOCIETY. (US/0017-6087). Qty: 5. **2321**

JOURNAL OF THE HELLENIC DIASPORA. (US/0364-2976). **2695**

JOURNAL OF THE HERPETOLOGICAL ASSOCIATION OF AFRICA. (SA/0441-6651). **5589**

JOURNAL OF THE HISTORICAL SOCIETY OF SOUTH AUSTRALIA. (AT/0312-9640). **2669**

JOURNAL OF THE HISTORY OF BIOLOGY. (NE/0022-5010). **462**

JOURNAL OF THE HISTORY OF IDEAS. (US/0022-5037). **4351**

JOURNAL OF THE HISTORY OF MEDICINE AND ALLIED SCIENCES. (US/0022-5045). **3598**

JOURNAL OF THE HISTORY OF PHILOSOPHY. (US/0022-5053). **4351**

JOURNAL OF THE HISTORY OF THE BEHAVIORAL SCIENCES. (US/0022-5061). **4601**

JOURNAL OF THE HISTORY OF THE NEUROSCIENCES. (UK/0964-704X). **490**

JOURNAL OF THE HONG KONG ARCHAEOLOGICAL SOCIETY. (HK). **272**

JOURNAL OF THE HONG KONG BRANCH OF THE ROYAL ASIATIC SOCIETY. (HK/0085-5774). **5232**

JOURNAL OF THE IDAHO ACADEMY OF SCIENCE. (US/0536-3012). **5120**

JOURNAL OF THE IES. (US/1052-2883). **2176**

JOURNAL OF THE INDIAN ACADEMY OF FORENSIC SCIENCES. (II/0579-4749). **3741**

JOURNAL OF THE INDIAN ACADEMY OF MATHEMATICS, THE. (II/0970-5120). **3515**

JOURNAL OF THE INDIAN ACADEMY OF PHILOSOPHY, THE. (II/0019-4271). **4351**

JOURNAL OF THE INDIAN CHEMICAL SOCIETY. (II/0019-4522). **982**

JOURNAL OF THE INDIAN DENTAL ASSOCIATION. (II/0019-4611). **1328**

JOURNAL OF THE INDIAN INSTITUTE OF ARCHITECTS. (II/0019-4913). **302**

JOURNAL OF THE INDIAN INSTITUTE OF SCIENCE. (II/0019-4964). **5120**

JOURNAL OF THE INDIAN MUSICOLOGICAL SOCIETY. (II/0251-012X). **4127**

JOURNAL OF THE INDIAN SOCIETY OF AGRICULTURAL STATISTICS. (II/0019-6363). **154**

JOURNAL OF THE INDIAN SOCIETY OF ORIENTAL ART. (II/0970-6070). **354**

JOURNAL OF THE INDIAN SOCIETY OF SOIL SCIENCE. (II/0019-638X). **177**

JOURNAL OF THE INDIAN STATISTICAL ASSOCIATION. (II/0537-2585). **5330**

JOURNAL OF THE INSTITUTE OF HEALTH EDUCATION. (UK/0307-3289). **4787**

JOURNAL OF THE INSTITUTE OF MINE SURVEYORS OF SOUTH AFRICA. (SA/0020-2983). **2142**

JOURNAL OF THE INSTITUTE OF WOOD SCIENCE. (UK/0020-3203). **2402**

JOURNAL OF THE INSTITUTION OF CHEMISTS, CALCUTTA. (II/0020-3254). **983**

JOURNAL OF THE INTERDENOMINATIONAL THEOLOGICAL CENTER, THE. (US/0092-6558). **4971**

JOURNAL OF THE INTERNATIONAL ASSOCIATION OF BUDDHIST STUDIES, THE. (US/0193-600X). **5021**

JOURNAL OF THE INTERNATIONAL PHONETIC ASSOCIATION. (UK/0025-1003). **3292**

JOURNAL OF THE IOWA ACADEMY OF SCIENCE, THE. (US/0896-8381). **5121**

JOURNAL OF THE IOWA ARCHEOLOGICAL SOCIETY. (US/0535-5729). Qty: 1. **272**

JOURNAL OF THE IRISH COLLEGES OF PHYSICIANS AND SURGEONS. (IE/0374-8405). **3598**

JOURNAL OF THE IRISH DENTAL ASSOCIATION, THE. (IE/0021-1133). **1328**

JOURNAL OF THE IRISH FAMILY HISTORY SOCIETY. (IE/0790-7060). **2455**

JOURNAL OF THE IRISH SOCIETY FOR LABOUR LAW. (IE/0790-0473). **3150**

JOURNAL OF THE JAPANESE AND INTERNATIONAL ECONOMIES. (US/0889-1583). **1637**

JOURNAL OF THE JOHANNES SCHWALM HISTORICAL ASSOCIATION, INC. (US/8755-3805). **2742**

JOURNAL OF THE KAFKA SOCIETY OF AMERICA. (US/0894-6388). **3345**

JOURNAL OF THE KANSAS BAR ASSOCIATION, THE. (US/0022-8486). **2989**

JOURNAL OF THE KENTUCKY MEDICAL ASSOCIATION, THE. (US/0023-0294). **3598**

JOURNAL OF THE KOREAN INSTITUTE OF SURFACE ENGINEERING. (KO). **1983**

JOURNAL OF THE LANCASTER COUNTY HISTORICAL SOCIETY. (US/0023-7477). **2742**

JOURNAL OF THE LAW SOCIETY OF SCOTLAND, THE. (UK/0458-8711). Qty: 80. **2989**

JOURNAL OF THE LEPIDOPTERISTS' SOCIETY. (US/0024-0966). **5589**

JOURNAL OF THE LINCOLN ASSASSINATION. (US). Qty: 3. **2742**

JOURNAL OF THE LINGUISTIC ASSOCIATION OF NIGERIA : JOLAN. (NR/0189-5680). **3292**

JOURNAL OF THE LONDON MATHEMATICAL SOCIETY. (UK/0024-6107). **3515**

JOURNAL OF THE LOUISIANA STATE MEDICAL SOCIETY, THE. (US/0024-6921). Qty: 1-2/yr. **3599**

JOURNAL OF THE MALACOLOGICAL SOCIETY OF AUSTRALIA. (AT/0085-2988). **5589**

JOURNAL OF THE MALAYSIAN BRANCH OF THE ROYAL ASIATIC SOCIETY. (SI/0126-7353). **2656**

JOURNAL OF THE MAMMILLARIA SOCIETY, THE. (UK/0464-8072). **516**

JOURNAL OF THE MARINE BIOLOGICAL ASSOCIATION OF INDIA. (II/0025-3146). **555**

JOURNAL OF THE MARINE BIOLOGICAL ASSOCIATION OF THE UNITED KINGDOM. (UK/0025-3154). **555**

JOURNAL OF THE MARKET RESEARCH SOCIETY. (UK/0025-3618). **929**

JOURNAL OF THE MASSACHUSETTS DENTAL SOCIETY. (US/0025-4800). Qty: 4. **1328**

JOURNAL OF THE MEDICAL ASSOCIATION OF GEORGIA. (US/0025-7028). **3599**

JOURNAL OF THE MICHIGAN DENTAL ASSOCIATION, THE. (US/0026-2102). **1328**

JOURNAL OF THE MIDWEST MODERN LANGUAGE ASSOCIATION, THE. (US/0742-5562). **3292**

JOURNAL OF THE MINNESOTA ACADEMY OF SCIENCE. (US/0026-539X). **5121**

JOURNAL OF THE MUHYIDDIN IBN ARABI SOCIETY. (UK/0266-2183). **5043**

JOURNAL OF THE MUSIC ACADEMY, MADRAS, THE. (II). **4127**

JOURNAL OF THE N.J. ASSOCIATION OF OSTEOPATHIC PHYSICIANS AND SURGEONS, THE. (US/0892-0249). **3599**

JOURNAL OF THE NATIONAL AGRICULTURAL SOCIETY OF CEYLON. (CE/0547-3616). **101**

JOURNAL OF THE NATIONAL ASSOCIATION OF ADMINISTRATIVE LAW JUDGES. (US/0735-0821). **3093**

JOURNAL OF THE NATIONAL ASSOCIATION OF DOCUMENT EXAMINERS. (US/8755-1020). **3168**

JOURNAL OF THE NATIONAL BUILDINGS ORGANISATION. (II/0027-8815). **618**

JOURNAL OF THE NATIONAL MEDICAL ASSOCIATION. (US/0027-9684). **3599**

JOURNAL OF THE NEW ENGLAND WATER WORKS ASSOCIATION. (US/0028-4939). **4761**

JOURNAL OF THE NEW JERSEY DENTAL ASSOCIATION. (US/0093-7347). **1328**

JOURNAL OF THE NEW YORK ENTOMOLOGICAL SOCIETY. (US/0028-7199). **5589**

JOURNAL OF THE NEW YORK STATE NURSES ASSOCIATION, THE. (US/0028-7644). Qty: 4-6/yr. **3860**

JOURNAL OF THE NEW ZEALAND SOCIETY OF PERIODONTOLOGY. (NZ/0111-1485). **1328**

JOURNAL OF THE NORTH AMERICAN BENTHOLOGICAL SOCIETY. (US/0887-3593). **2218**

JOURNAL OF THE NORTH-EAST INDIA COUNCIL FOR SOCIAL SCIENCE RESEARCH, THE. (II). **5207**

JOURNAL OF THE NORTH MIDDLESEX FAMILY HISTORY SOCIETY. (UK/0141-9544). **2456**

JOURNAL OF THE OPERATIONAL RESEARCH SOCIETY, THE. (UK/0160-5682). **3515**

JOURNAL OF THE ORDERS AND MEDALS SOCIETY OF AMERICA, THE. (US). **2781**

JOURNAL OF THE ORIENTAL INSTITUTE, M.S. UNIVERSITY OF BARODA. (II/0030-5324). **2505**

JOURNAL OF THE ORIENTAL SOCIETY OF AUSTRALIA, THE. (AT/0030-5340). **2656**

JOURNAL OF THE PAKISTAN HISTORICAL SOCIETY. (PK/0030-9796). **2656**

JOURNAL OF THE PAKISTAN MEDICAL ASSOCIATION. (PK/0030-9982). **3599**

JOURNAL OF THE PALAEONTOLOGICAL SOCIETY OF INDIA. (II/0552-9360). **4227**

JOURNAL OF THE PATENT AND TRADEMARK OFFICE SOCIETY. (US/0882-9098). **1305**

JOURNAL OF THE PHILOSOPHY OF SPORT. (US/0094-8705). **4902**

JOURNAL OF THE PLAYING-CARD SOCIETY. (UK/0305-2133). **4862**

JOURNAL OF THE POLYNESIAN SOCIETY. (NZ/0032-4000). **3292**

JOURNAL OF THE PRINT WORLD. (US/0737-7436). Qty: 4-6. **4566**

JOURNAL OF THE RESEARCH SOCIETY OF PAKISTAN. (PK/0034-5431). **5207**

JOURNAL OF THE ROCKY MOUNTAIN MEDIEVAL AND RENAISSANCE ASSOCIATION. (US/0195-8453). **2621**

JOURNAL OF THE ROYAL ARMY MEDICAL CORPS. (UK/0035-8665). **3599**

JOURNAL OF THE ROYAL ARTILLERY, THE. (UK). **4048**

JOURNAL OF THE ROYAL ASIATIC SOCIETY OF GREAT BRITAIN & IRELAND. (UK/0035-869X). **2769**

JOURNAL OF THE ROYAL ASTRONOMICAL SOCIETY OF CANADA, THE. (CN/0035-872X). **396**

JOURNAL OF THE ROYAL AUSTRALIAN HISTORICAL SOCIETY. (AT/0035-8762). **2670**

JOURNAL OF THE ROYAL COLLEGE OF PHYSICIANS OF LONDON. (UK/0035-8819). Qty: (25-30). **3599**

JOURNAL OF THE ROYAL COLLEGE OF SURGEONS OF EDINBURGH. (UK/0035-8835). **3968**

JOURNAL OF THE ROYAL MUSICAL ASSOCIATION. (UK/0269-0403). **4127**

JOURNAL OF THE ROYAL NAVAL MEDICAL SERVICE. (UK/0035-9033). **3599**

JOURNAL OF THE ROYAL SOCIETY OF ANTIQUARIES OF IRELAND, THE. (IE/0035-9106). Qty: varies. **2695**

JOURNAL OF THE ROYAL SOCIETY OF HEALTH. (UK/0264-0325). **4787**

JOURNAL OF THE ROYAL SOCIETY OF MEDICINE. (UK/0141-0768). **3599**

JOURNAL OF THE ROYAL SOCIETY OF NEW ZEALAND. (NZ/0303-6758). **5121**

JOURNAL OF THE ROYAL STATISTICAL SOCIETY. SERIES A (GENERAL). (UK/0035-9238). **5330**

JOURNAL OF THE ROYAL STATISTICAL SOCIETY. SERIES A: (STATISTICS IN SOCIETY). (UK). **5330**

JOURNAL OF THE SAN JUAN ISLANDS. (US/0734-3809). **5761**

JOURNAL OF THE SIAM SOCIETY, THE. (TH). **2656**

JOURNAL OF THE SOCIETY FOR ACCELERATIVE LEARNING AND TEACHING, THE. (US/0273-2459). **1881**

JOURNAL OF THE SOCIETY FOR ARMENIAN STUDIES. (US/0747-9301). **2656**

JOURNAL OF THE SOCIETY FOR ARMY HISTORICAL RESEARCH. (UK/0037-9700). **Qty:** 16. **4048**

JOURNAL OF THE SOCIETY FOR ITALIC HANDWRITING, THE. (UK/0037-9743). **380**

JOURNAL OF THE SOCIETY FOR PSYCHICAL RESEARCH. (UK/0037-9751). **Qty:** 10-12. **4242**

JOURNAL OF THE SOCIETY FOR UNDERWATER TECHNOLOGY. (UK/0141-0814). **1450**

JOURNAL OF THE SOCIETY OF ARCHER-ANTIQUARIES. (UK/0560-6152). **4902**

JOURNAL OF THE SOCIETY OF ARCHITECTURAL HISTORIANS. (US/0037-9808). **302**

JOURNAL OF THE SOCIETY OF COSMETIC CHEMISTS. (US/0037-9832). **1026**

JOURNAL OF THE SOCIETY OF DAIRY TECHNOLOGY. (UK/0037-9840). **196**

JOURNAL OF THE SOCIETY OF DYERS AND COLOURISTS. (UK/0037-9859). **1026**

JOURNAL OF THE SOCIETY OF LEATHER TECHNOLOGISTS AND CHEMISTS. (UK/0144-0322). **Qty:** 3-4. **3184**

JOURNAL OF THE SOUTH AFRICAN INSTITUTE OF MINING & METALLURGY. (SA/0038-223X). **2142**

JOURNAL OF THE SOUTH AFRICAN VETERINARY ASSOCIATION. (SA/0301-0732). **5513**

JOURNAL OF THE SOUTH CAROLINA BAPTIST HISTORICAL SOCIETY. (US/0146-0196). **5062**

JOURNAL OF THE SOUTH SEAS SOCIETY. (SI). **2656**

JOURNAL OF THE SOUTHERN CALIFORNIA DENTAL HYGIENISTS' ASSOCIATION. (US/0038-3899). **1329**

JOURNAL OF THE SOUTHERN ORTHOPAEDIC ASSOCIATION. (US/1059-1052). **3883**

JOURNAL OF THE SOUTHWEST. (US/0894-8410). **Qty:** 40. **2742**

JOURNAL OF THE SRI LANKA BRANCH OF THE ROYAL ASIATIC SOCIETY. (CE/1013-9818). **2656**

JOURNAL OF THE UNITED SERVICE INSTITUTION OF INDIA, THE. (II/0041-770X). **4048**

JOURNAL OF THE VIOLIN SOCIETY OF AMERICA. (US/0148-6845). **Qty:** varies. **4127**

JOURNAL OF THE WALTER ROTH MUSEUM OF ARCHAEOLOGY AND ANTHROPOLOGY. (GY). **239**

JOURNAL OF THE WASHINGTON ACADEMY OF SCIENCES. (US/0043-0439). **5122**

JOURNAL OF THE WEST. (US/0022-5169). **Qty:** 200. **2742**

JOURNAL OF THE WESTERN PACIFIC ORTHOPAEDIC ASSOCIATION, THE. (HK/0043-4019). **3883**

JOURNAL OF THE WESTERN SOCIETY OF PERIODONTOLOGY / PERIODONTAL ABSTRACTS, THE. (US/0148-4893). **1329**

JOURNAL OF THE WILLIAM MORRIS SOCIETY, THE. (UK/0084-0254). **373**

JOURNAL OF THE WORLD AQUACULTURE SOCIETY. (US/0893-8849). **2307**

JOURNAL OF THE WRITERS GUILD OF AMERICA. WEST. (US/1055-1948). **3400**

JOURNAL OF THE YUGOSLAV FOREIGN TRADE. (YU/0022-5452). **4527**

JOURNAL OF THE ZOOLOGICAL SOCIETY OF INDIA. (II/0049-8769). **5589**

JOURNAL OF THEOLOGICAL STUDIES. (UK/0022-5185). **4971**

JOURNAL OF THEOLOGY. (US/0361-1906). **Qty:** 12 per year. **4971**

JOURNAL OF THEOLOGY FOR SOUTHERN AFRICA. (SA/0047-2867). **4971**

JOURNAL OF THERMAL STRESSES. (UK/0149-5739). **2119**

JOURNAL OF THETA ALPHA KAPPA. (US/8756-4785). **4971**

JOURNAL OF THIRD WORLD SPECTRUM. (US/1072-5040). **4527**

JOURNAL OF THIRD WORLD STUDIES. (US/8755-3449). **1637**

JOURNAL OF THOUGHT. (US/0022-5231). **1759**

JOURNAL OF TISSUE CULTURE METHODS. (NE/0271-8057). **538**

JOURNAL OF TISSUE VIABILITY. (UK/0965-206X). **Qty:** varies. **538**

JOURNAL OF TOXICOLOGY AND ENVIRONMENTAL HEALTH. (US/0098-4108). **3982**

JOURNAL OF TOXICOLOGY. CLINICAL TOXICOLOGY. (US/0731-3810). **3982**

JOURNAL OF TOXICOLOGY. CUTANEOUS AND OCULAR TOXICOLOGY. (US). **3982**

JOURNAL OF TOXICOLOGY. TOXIN REVIEWS. (US/0731-3837). **3982**

JOURNAL OF TRACE AND MICROPROBE TECHNIQUES. (US/0733-4680). **1017**

JOURNAL OF TRACE ELEMENTS AND ELECTROLYTES IN HEALTH AND DISEASE. (GW/0931-2838). **3600**

JOURNAL OF TRADITIONAL ACUPUNCTURE, THE. (US/0270-661X). **3600**

JOURNAL OF TRADITIONAL CHINESE MEDICINE. (CC/0254-6272). **3600**

JOURNAL OF TRANSLATION AND TEXTLINGUISTICS. (US/1055-4513). **3292**

JOURNAL OF TRANSPERSONAL PSYCHOLOGY, THE. (US/0022-524X). **4602**

JOURNAL OF TRANSPORT ECONOMICS AND POLICY. (UK/0022-5258). **5385**

JOURNAL OF TRANSPORT HISTORY, THE. (UK/0022-5266). **5385**

JOURNAL OF TRANSPORTATION ENGINEERING. (US/0733-947X). **2026**

JOURNAL OF TRAUMATIC STRESS. (US/0894-9867). **4602**

JOURNAL OF TRAVEL AND TOURISM MARKETING. (US/1054-8408). **5482**

JOURNAL OF TRAVEL RESEARCH. (US/0047-2875). **5482**

JOURNAL OF TREE FRUIT PRODUCTION. (US/1055-1387). **177**

JOURNAL OF TREE SCIENCES. (II). **2386**

JOURNAL OF TROPICAL ECOLOGY. (UK/0266-4674). **2218**

JOURNAL OF TROPICAL FOREST SCIENCE. (MY/0128-1283). **2386**

JOURNAL OF TROPICAL MEDICINE AND HYGIENE. (UK/0022-5304). **3986**

JOURNAL OF TROPICAL PEDIATRICS (1980). (UK/0142-6338). **3905**

JOURNAL OF TURFGRASS MANAGEMENT. (US/1070-437X). **2422**

JOURNAL OF UFO STUDIES, THE. (US/0730-5478). **26**

JOURNAL OF UKRAINIAN GRADUATE STUDIES. (CN/0701-1792). **2695**

JOURNAL OF UKRAINIAN STUDIES. (CN/0228-1635). **2849**

JOURNAL OF ULTRASOUND IN MEDICINE. (US/0278-4297). **3943**

JOURNAL OF UNCONVENTIONAL HISTORY. (US). **Qty:** 6-10 per year. **2621**

JOURNAL OF UNDERGRADUATE RESEARCH IN PHYSICS, THE. (US/0731-3764). **Qty:** 2. **4410**

JOURNAL OF URBAN AFFAIRS. (US/0735-2166). **2826**

JOURNAL OF URBAN AND CULTURAL STUDIES. (US/1054-1802). **Qty:** 6. **1759**

JOURNAL OF URBAN PLANNING AND DEVELOPMENT. (US/0733-9488). **2026**

JOURNAL OF UROLOGICAL NURSING. (US/0738-7350). **Qty:** 1-4 per year. **3991**

JOURNAL OF VAISNAVA STUDIES, THE. (US/1062-1237). **Qty:** 12. **4971**

JOURNAL OF VASCULAR AND INTERVENTIONAL RADIOLOGY. (US/1051-0443). **3943**

JOURNAL OF VASCULAR SURGERY. (US/0741-5214). **3969**

JOURNAL OF VEGETABLE CROP PRODUCTION. (US/1049-6467). **177**

JOURNAL OF VEGETATION SCIENCE. (SW/1100-9233). **Qty:** 100. **516**

JOURNAL OF VERTEBRATE PALEONTOLOGY. (US/0272-4634). **4227**

JOURNAL OF VETERINARY PHARMACOLOGY AND THERAPEUTICS. (UK/0140-7783). **5514**

JOURNAL OF VISION REHABILITATION (LINCOLN, NEB.). (US/1041-0384). **3876**

JOURNAL OF VISUAL IMPAIRMENT & BLINDNESS. (US/0145-482X). **4390**

JOURNAL OF VISUAL LITERACY. (US/1051-144X). **3292**

JOURNAL OF VOLUNTEER ADMINISTRATION, THE. (US/0733-6535). **5293**

JOURNAL OF WATER BORNE COATINGS. (US/0163-4526). **4224**

JOURNAL OF WATER RESOURCES. (IQ/0255-0148). **5535**

JOURNAL OF WATER RESOURCES PLANNING AND MANAGEMENT. (US/0733-9496). **5535**

JOURNAL OF WATERWAY, PORT, COASTAL, AND OCEAN ENGINEERING. (US/0733-950X). **2092**

JOURNAL OF WEST AFRICAN LANGUAGES, THE. (UK/0022-5401). **3292**

JOURNAL OF WEST INDIAN LITERATURE. (BB/0258-8501). **Qty:** 6-8. **3400**

JOURNAL OF WILDLIFE DISEASES. (US/0090-3558). **5514**

JOURNAL OF WILDLIFE REHABILITATION. (US/1071-2232). **2196**

JOURNAL OF WIND ENGINEERING AND INDUSTRIAL AERODYNAMICS. (NE/0167-6105). **1983**

JOURNAL OF WOMEN & AGING. (US/0895-2841). **5559**

JOURNAL OF WOMEN AND RELIGION. (US/0888-5621). **4971**

JOURNAL OF WOMEN'S HEALTH. (US/1059-7115). **3600**

JOURNAL OF WOMEN'S HISTORY. (US/1042-7961). **5559**

JOURNAL OF WOMEN'S MINISTRIES. (US/1064-1084). **4971**

JOURNAL OF WOOD CHEMISTRY AND TECHNOLOGY. (US/0277-3813). **1055**

JOURNAL OF WORLD FOREST RESOURCE MANAGEMENT. (UK/0261-4286). **2386**

JOURNAL OF WORLD HISTORY. (US/1045-6007). **Qty:** 15-20. **2621**

JOURNAL OF ZOO AND WILDLIFE MEDICINE : OFFICIAL PUBLICATION OF THE AMERICAN ASSOCIATION OF ZOO VETERINARIANS. (US/1042-7260). **5514**

JOURNAL (OGDENSBURG, N.Y.), THE. (US/0893-5149). **Qty:** 5. **5717**

JOURNAL - OKLAHOMA STATE MEDICAL ASSOCIATION. (US/0030-1876). **3601**

JOURNAL - ONTARIO ASSOCIATION OF CHILDREN'S AID SOCIETIES. (CN/0030-283X). **5293**

JOURNAL - ONTARIO OCCUPATIONAL HEALTH NURSES ASSOCIATION. (CN/0828-542X). **Qty:** 1-3. **3860**

JOURNAL-OPINION. (US/0746-1674). **Qty:** 12. **5757**

JOURNAL / RHODE ISLAND BAR ASSOCIATION. (US/1073-8800). **Qty:** 4. **2990**

JOURNAL (SANGEET RESEARCH ACADEMY (CALCUTTA, INDIA)). (II). **4127**

JOURNAL - SEATTLE-KING COUNTY DENTAL SOCIETY. (US). **1329**

JOURNAL - SINGAPORE COMPUTER SOCIETY. (SI). **1261**

JOURNAL STAR, THE. (US). **5660**

JOURNAL - TEXAS SOCIETY FOR ELECTRON MICROSCOPY. (US/0196-5662). **572**

JOURNAL / THE CANADIAN FOUNDATION FOR ILEITIS AND COLITIS. (CN/0827-4681). **Qty:** 3-4. **3747**

JOURNAL : THE LITERARY MAGAZINE OF THE OHIO STATE UNIVERSITY, THE. (US/1045-084X). **Qty:** 1-4. **3400**

JOURNAL - TIMBER DEVELOPMENT ASSOCIATION OF INDIA. (II/0377-936X). **2402**

JOURNAL - UNITED REFORMED CHURCH HISTORY SOCIETY. (UK/0049-5433). **5062**

JOURNAL - WESTERN NEW YORK GENEALOGICAL SOCIETY. (US/0890-6858). **2456**

JOURNAL - WORLD PHEASANT ASSOCIATION. (UK). **2196**

JOURNALEN SYKEPLEIEN. (NO). **3860**

JOURNALISM HISTORY. (US/0094-7679). **Qty:** 50. **2921**

JOURNALIST. (UK/0022-5541). **2921**

JOURNALIST (EDMONTON). (CN/0823-1672). **1092**

JOURNEY (LYNCHBURG, VA.). (US/0887-8854). **4971**

JOURNEYMEN (CANDIA, N.H.). (US/1061-8538). **Qty:** 12 /yr. **3995**

JOY OF HERBS, THE. (US/1040-8134). **2422**

JOYAS & JOYEROS. (SP/0213-120X). **2915**

JOYFUL WOMAN MAGAZINE, THE. (US/0885-8004). **Qty:** 6. **5559**

JPC. JOURNAL OF PLANAR CHROMATOGRAPHY, MODERN TLC. (GW/0933-4173). **983**

JPMS; JOURNAL OF POLITICAL & MILITARY SOCIOLOGY. (US/0047-2697). **5250**

JR. HIGH MINISTRY. (US/1055-1409). Qty: 10-20. **4971**

JSAE REVIEW. (JA/0389-4304). **5418**

JTA DAILY NEWS BULLETIN. (US/0021-3772). **5050**

JTA WEEKLY NEWS DIGEST. (US/0021-6763). **2266**

JUDAICA. (SZ/0022-572X). **5050**

JUDAICA BOOK NEWS. (US/0022-5754). **5013**

JUDAISM. (US/0022-5762). **5050**

JUDICATURE. (US/0022-5800). Qty: 12. **2990**

JUDICIAL CONDUCT REPORTER. (US/0193-7367). **3141**

JUDICIAL STAFF DIRECTORY. (US). **3141**

JUDO. (UK/0022-5819). **2599**

JUGENDWOHL. (GW/0022-5975). **1065**

JUKE BLUES. (UK). Qty: 17. **4127**

JUMP CUT. (US/0146-5546). Qty: 1-4. **1115**

JUNEAU EMPIRE. (US). **5629**

JUNGE KIRCHE; EINE ZEITSCHRIFT EUROPAISCHER CHRISTEN. (GW/0022-6319). **4971**

JUNIOR BOOKSHELF. (UK/0022-6505). **1072**

JUNIOR HIGH MAGAZINE ABSTRACTS. (US/1045-5493). **1795**

JUNIOR SCHOLASTIC. (US/0022-6688). **1065**

JURIDICA. (MX). **2990**

JURIS. (US/0022-6807). **2990**

JURISPRUDENCE DU PORT D'ANVERS. (BE). **3181**

JURIST (WASHINGTON), THE. (US/0022-6858). **5031**

JURISTENZEITUNG. (GW/0022-6882). **2991**

JUS GENTIUM. (IT/0022-6963). **3131**

JUSER (LOS ANGELES, CALIF.). (US/0888-9007). **2769**

JUSSENS VENNER. (NO/0022-6971). **2991**

JUST B'TWX US. (US/0075-4587). **3221**

JUST CAUSE. (CN/0824-281X). **2991**

JUST COMPENSATION. (US/0738-6494). **2991**

JUSTICE FOR CHILDREN. (US/0888-9120). **3121**

JUSTICE (NEW YORK, N.Y. 1919). (US/0022-7013). Qty: 1-2. **1682**

JUSTICE OF THE PEACE (CHICHESTER). (UK/0141-5859). **2991**

JUSTICE PROFESSIONAL, THE. (US/0888-4315). **2991**

JUSTICE QUARTERLY. (US/0741-8825). **3168**

JUSTICE SYSTEM JOURNAL, THE. (US/0098-261X). **3141**

JUVENILE AND FAMILY COURT NEWSLETTER. (US/0162-9859). **3121**

JUVENILE JUSTICE DIGEST. (US/0094-2413). **3168**

JUVENILE LAW REPORTS. (US/0276-9603). **3121**

K.A.R.D. FILES DYE DATA, THE. (US/0899-1723). **2456**

K.A.R.D. FILES PRESENTS ABSHIRE ABSTRACTS, THE. (US/0899-1685). **2456**

K.A.R.D. FILES PRESENTS BLAKELEY BANDWAGON, THE. (US/0899-1715). **2456**

K.A.R.D. FILES PRESENTS LUTTRELL LINEAGES & DATA, THE. (US/0899-1731). **2456**

K.A.R.D. FILES PRESENTS RAMBO REFERENCES, THE. (US/0899-174X). **2456**

K & I.E. EN C. KUNST EN CULTUUR. (BE/0022-7277). **323**

K & K. (DK). Qty: 8-10. **3401**

KADAMBINI. (II). **3401**

KAEHYOK SINANG. (KO). **4971**

KAHPER JOURNAL (RICHMOND, KY.). (US/0022-7269). **1856**

KAHTOU. (CN/0827-2077). **2536**

KAILASH. (NP/0377-7499). **239**

KAINDL-ARCHIV : MITTEILUNGEN DER RAIMUND FRIEDRICH KAINDL GESELLSCHAFT. (GW). **3708**

KAIROS (OAKLAND, CALIF.). (US/0277-710X). **3345**

KAIROS; ZEITSCHRIFT FUER RELIGIONSWISSENSCHAFT UND THEOLOGIE. (AU/0022-7757). **4971**

KAJIAN MALAYSIA : JOURNAL OF MALAYSIAN STUDIES. (MY/0127-4082). **2656**

KALAVRITT / KALAVRTTA. (II). **355**

KALEIDOSCOPE / A SPECTRUM OF ARTICLES FOCUSING ON FAMILIES. (US). **2282**

KALEIDOSCOPE (AKRON, OHIO), THE. (US/0748-8742). Qty: 2. **3401**

KALENDAR HOLOSU SPASYTELJA. (CN/0381-5110). **5039**

KALENDAR SVITLA. (CN/0380-0962). **5031**

KALENDARZ DZIENNIKA POLSKIEGO. (UK). **196**

KALENDER FUER DEN BIOGARTEN. (GW/0931-380X). **462**

KALKI (ORADELL). (US/0022-7994). **3345**

KALLIOPE. (US/0735-7885). Qty: 6-10 per year. **323**

KALONA NEWS, THE. (US). Qty: 2. **5671**

KALORI; JOURNAL OF THE MUSEUMS ASSOCIATION OF AUSTRALIA. (AT/0047-312X). **4090**

KALTE UND KLIMATECHNIK. (GW/0343-2246). **2606**

KAMERA UND SCHULE. (GW/0022-8109). **4371**

KAN-SU CHIAO YU. (CH). **1759**

KANADA KURIER (ALBERTA AUSG.). (CN/0712-8878). **5787**

KANADA KURIER (AUSGABE FUER BRITISH COLUMBIA). (CN/0712-8886). **5787**

KANADA KURIER (MANITOBA AUSG.). (CN/0712-8894). **5787**

KANADA KURIER (MONTREAL AUSG.). (CN/0712-8908). **5787**

KANADA KURIER (ONTARIO AUSGABE). (CN/0712-8916). **5787**

KANADA KURIER (OTTAWA AUSG.). (CN/0712-8924). **5787**

KANADA KURIER (SASKATCHEWAN AUSG.). (CN/0712-8932). **5787**

KANADA KURIER (TORONTO AUSGABE). (CN/0712-8940). **5788**

KANADSKE LISTY (TORONTO. 1973). (CN/0449-7368). **5788**

KANAWA MAGAZINE FOR RECREATIONAL PADDLING IN CANADA. (CN/1189-5152). Qty: 6-8. **4874**

KANE'S BEVERAGE WEEK. (US/0882-2573). **2368**

KANG SHENG SU. (CC/0254-6116). **4313**

KANSANTALOUDELLINEN AIKAKAUSKIRJA. (FI/0022-8427). **1501**

KANSAS ANTHROPOLOGIST, THE. (US/1069-0379). Qty: 2. **239**

KANSAS BUSINESS NEWS. (US/0199-3607). **688**

KANSAS CITY GENEALOGIST, THE. (US/0451-3991). Qty: 4. **2456**

KANSAS CITY GRAIN MARKET REVIEW. (US/0738-7296). **1501**

KANSAS ENGLISH. (US/0739-0157). **1899**

KANSAS GEOGRAPHER, THE. (US). **2567**

KANSAS HISTORY. (US/0149-9114). **2743**

KANSAS KIN. (US/0451-4084). **2456**

KANSAS MUSIC REVIEW. (US/0022-8702). **4127**

KANSAS RESTAURANT. (US/0022-8753). **5071**

KANSAS SCHOOL NATURALIST. (US/0022-877X). **1899**

KANSAS WILDLIFE & PARKS. (US/0898-6975). **2197**

KANSAS WORKS. (US). Qty: 12. **5676**

KANT-STUDIEN. (GW/0022-8877). **4351**

KANTOOR EN EFFICIENCY. (NE). **4212**

KAO KU JEN LEI HSUEH KAN / KUO LI TAIWAN TA HSUEH. (CH/0077-5843). **240**

KAPPA DELTA PI RECORD. (US/0022-8958). **1759**

KARATE AND ORIENTAL ARTS. (UK). **4902**

KARATE, KUNG-FU ILLUSTRATED. (US/0888-031X). **4902**

KARD FILES ADAMSON ANCESTRY, THE. (US/0899-1693). **2456**

KARDIOLOGIJA. (RU/0022-9040). **3708**

KARNTNER SCHULVERSUCHSINFORMATIONEN. (AU). Qty: 2. **1759**

KARTER NEWS. (US/0096-3216). **4903**

KARTHAGO. (FR/0453-3429). **272**

KARTING. (UK/0022-913X). Qty: 1. **4903**

KARTOFEL I OVOSHCHI. (RU/0022-9148). **177**

KASARINLAN. (PH/0116-0923). **2656**

KASHRUS MAGAZINE. (US/1074-3502). Qty: 3. **2347**

KATAHDIN TIMES. (US/1064-0657). **5685**

KATES KIN. (US/0741-2045). **2456**

KATHMANDU REVIEW. (NP). **1501**

KATORIKKU KENKYU. (JA). **5031**

KAUAI UPDATE, THE. (US/0898-1418). **5482**

KAUFMAN KOUNTY KONNECTIONS. (US/0884-7525). Qty: 25. **2456**

KAVAKA. (II/0379-5179). **575**

KAWASAKI MEDICAL JOURNAL. (JA/0385-0234). **3601**

KEA NEWS. (US/0164-3959). **1759**

KEADAAN ANGKATEN KERJA DI INDONESIA : ANGKA SEMENTARA. (IO). **1682**

KEATS-SHELLEY JOURNAL. (US/0453-4387). **3401**

KEATS-SHELLEY REVIEW. (UK). **3401**

KEEP THE FAITH. (US). **4971**

KEEPER'S LOG. (US/0883-0061). Qty: 4-5. **2026**

KEEPER'S VOICE. (US/0274-4872). **3168**

KEEPING UP. (US/0890-1422). **5207**

KEHRWIEDER. (GW/0176-473X). **5451**

KEIKINZOKU KOGYO TOKEI NEMPO. (JA). **4025**

KELLY'S POST OFFICE LONDON BUSINESS DIRECTORY. (UK/0266-3791). **688**

KELTICA. (US/0192-1207). **2696**

KEMBLE OCCASIONAL, THE. (US/0453-4867). **4566**

KEMIA. (FI/0355-1628). **1027**

KEMIAI KOEZLEMENYEK. (HU/0022-9814). **983**

KEMIJA U INDUSTRIJI. (CI/0022-9830). **983**

KENDRICK GAZETTE, THE. (US). **5657**

KENNEL REVIEW. (US/0164-4289). **4287**

KENNIS EN METHODE. (NE/0165-1773). **4351**

KENT FAMILY HISTORY SOCIETY JOURNAL. (UK/0305-9359). **2456**

KENT RECUSANT HISTORY. (UK/0044-4018). **5031**

KENTUCKY AFIELD. (US/1059-9177). Qty: 5. **4874**

KENTUCKY ALUMNUS. (US/0732-6297). **1102**

KENTUCKY BENCH & BAR. (US/0164-9345). **2992**

KENTUCKY BUSINESS DIRECTORY. (US/1048-728X). **688**

KENTUCKY COLLEGES AND UNIVERSITIES : DEGREES CONFERRED. (US/0145-9120). **1833**

KENTUCKY HAPPY HUNTING GROUND. (US/0023-0235). **4874**

KENTUCKY JOURNAL (LEXINGTON, KY.). (US/1063-9357). Qty: 20. **2536**

KENTUCKY JOURNAL OF COMMERCE AND INDUSTRY, THE. (US/0279-5388). **843**

KENTUCKY LAW JOURNAL. (US/0023-026X). **2992**

KENTUCKY LIBRARIES. (US/0732-5452). **3221**

KENTUCKY MANUFACTURERS REGISTER. (US/0741-9031). **3482**

KENTUCKY PHARMACIST, THE. (US/0194-567X). **4313**

KENTUCKY POETRY REVIEW. (US/0889-647X). **3345**

KENTUCKY QUERIES. (US/0899-1359). **2456**

KENTUCKY WARBLER, THE. (US/0160-5070). **5618**

KENYA PAST AND PRESENT. (KE/0257-8301). **2641**

KENYON REVIEW, THE. (US/0163-075X). **3345**

KEPADATAN PERUSAHAAN INDUSTRI DAN TENAGA KERJA DI SEKTOR INDUSTRI TERHADAP JUMLAH PENDUDUK DI TIAP-TIAP PROPINSI, KABUPATEN, KOTA MADYA. (IO). **1682**

KERALA SOCIOLOGIST. (II). **5250**

KERAMISCHE ZEITSCHRIFT. (GW/0023-0561). **2592**

KERAULOPHON, THE. (US/0735-8660). **4127**

KERK EN THEOLOGIE. (NE/0450-1489). **4972**

KERN-GEN, THE. (US/0453-7637). **2456**

KERNOS. (BE). **4972**

KERNTECHNIK (1987). (GW/0932-3902). **2156**

KERSHNER KINFOLK. (US/0736-0886). **2456**

KERUX. (US/0888-3513). **4972**

KERYGMA (OTTAWA). (CN/0023-0693). **4972**

KERYGMA UND DOGMA. BEIHEFT. (GW/0453-7726). **4972**

KEY ABSTRACTS. ADVANCED MATERIALS. (UK/0950-4753). **2005**

KEY BRITISH ENTERPRISES : KBE / COMPILED AND PUBLISHED BY PUBLICATIONS DIVISION, DUN & BRADSTREET LIMITED. (UK/0142-5048). **688**

KEY BUSINESS RATIOS. (US/0708-1553). **731**

KEY (GOREVILLE). (US/0160-8932). **929**

KEY NOTES MUSICAL LIFE IN THE NETHERLANDS. (NE). **4127**

KEY REPORTER, THE. (US/0023-0804). **1092**

KEY VIVE. (AT/0310-8260). **4127**

KEY WEST CITIZEN, THE. (US). **Qty: 12-14. 5650**

KEYBOARD (CUPERTINO, CALIF.). (US/0730-0158). **4128**

KEYSTONE FOLKLORE. (US/0149-8444). **2321**

KEYSTONE (PITTSBURGH, PA. 1968), THE. (US/0744-4036). **5432**

KHIMICHESKAIA FIZIKA. (US/0733-2831). **1055**

KHOLODILNAIA TEKHNIKA. (RU). **2606**

KIBBUTZ TRENDS. (IS/5792-7290). **4542**

KICK IT OVER. (CN/0823-6526). **Qty: 6-10. 4542**

KID PROOF. (CN/0843-0284). **1065**

KIDS, KIDS, KIDZ MAGAZINE. (US). **2282**

KIDS TORONTO. (CN/0826-9696). **4851**

KIDSPORTS (ARLINGTON, VA.). (US/1054-7002). **1065**

KIDSPRINT TIMES. (US/1065-3872). **1804**

KIELER MEERESFORSCHUNGEN. SONDERHEFT. (GW/0172-7893). **555**

KIKAIKA NOGYO. (JA). **159**

KIKAN ANIMA. (JA). **4167**

KILLSHOT. (CN/0711-7094). **4862**

KIN KOLLECTING. (US/1069-207X). **2457**

KINAADMAN. WISDOM. (PH). **2656**

KINCARDINE INDEPENDENT, THE. (CN/0834-6674). **5788**

KINDAI CHUGOKU KENKYU IHO / HENSHUSHA, TOYO BUNKO KINDAI CHUGOKU KENKYU IINKAI. (JA). **2657**

KINDRED SPIRIT. (US). **Qty: 3. 4972**

KINESIOLOGY AND MEDICINE FOR DANCE. (US/1058-7438). **Qty: 7-8. 1313**

KINESIS (CARBONDALE, ILL.). (US/0023-1568). **4351**

KINESIS (VANCOUVER). (CN/0317-9095). **5560**

KINFOLKS (LAKE CHARLES, LA.). (US/0742-7654). **Qty: approx. 20. 2457**

KINGSTON THIS WEEK. (CN/0712-9068). **5788**

KINISTINO POST [MICROFORM], THE. (CN). **5788**

KINSHIP KRONICLE. (US/0882-9802). **Qty: 4+. 2457**

KIPLING JOURNAL. (UK/0023-1738). **Qty: 12-16. 3402**

KIPLINGER'S PERSONAL FINANCE MAGAZINE. (US/1056-697X). **795**

KIPU. (EC). **5250**

KIRCHENMUSIKER, DER. (GW/0023-1819). **4128**

KIRKE OG KULTUR. (NO/0023-186X). **4972**

KIRKIA. (RH). **516**

KIRYAT SEFER. (IS/0023-1851). **5050**

KISWAHILI. (TZ/0856-048X). **3293**

KITABAT. (BA). **3402**

KITELINES. (US/0192-3439). **Qty: 12-16. 4851**

KITH 'N KIN (FREMONT, OHIO). (US/1053-5837). **Qty: rarely. 2457**

KITPLANES. (US/0891-1851). **27**

KIVA (TUSCON, ARIZ.), THE. (US/0023-1940). **Qty: 10. 272**

KJEMI. (NO/0023-1983). **1027**

KLANSMAN, THE. (US/0749-0763). **2266**

KLASGIDS. (SA/1010-3465). **3293**

KLEIO. (SA/0023-2084). **2641**

KLERONOMIA : PERIODIKON DEMODIEUMA TOU PATRIARCHIKOU HIDRYMATOS PATERIKON MELETON. (GR). **4972**

KLINICESKAJA MEDICINA. (RU/0023-2149). **3602**

KLINISCHES LABOR. (GW/0941-2131). **Qty: approx. 30/year. 5123**

KNIFE WORLD. (US/0276-9042). **Qty: 8. 2774**

KNIGHT LETTER (FORT WORTH, TEX.). (US/0454-8973). **2457**

KNIT & CHAT. (CN/0711-639X). **5184**

KNITTING INTERNATIONAL. (UK/0266-8394). **5353**

KNITTING TIMES. (US/0023-2300). **5184**

KNJIZNICA. (XV/0023-2424). **3221**

KNOWLEDGE-BASED SYSTEMS (GUILDFORD, SURREY). (UK/0950-7051). **1193**

KNOWLEDGE ENGINEERING REVIEW, THE. (UK/0269-8889). **1214**

KNOWLEDGE (FORT WORTH, TEX.). (US/0738-8640). **3345**

KNOWLEDGE MATTERS. (US/0886-4063). **4351**

KNOX COUNTY DAILY NEWS (BICKNELL, IND. : 1991). (US/1060-6173). **5665**

KOBE GAKUIN KEIZAIGAKU RONSHU. (JA). **1502**

KOBRIN LETTER, THE. (US/0271-1990). **Qty: varies. 3345**

KODALY ENVOY. (US). **Qty: 4/yr. 1899**

KODIKAS. (GW/0171-0834). **3293**

KOEDOE. (SA/0075-6458). **5589**

KOEPEL VIJF. (BE/0771-7172). **1760**

KOERS. (SA/0023-270X). **Qty: 4. 4351**

KOGNITIONSWISSENSCHAFT. (GW/0938-7986). **4602**

KOINONIA (PRINCETON, N.J.). (US/1047-1057). **Qty: 20-30. 4972**

KOKS I HIMIJA. (RU/0023-2815). **1044**

KOKUGAKUIN DAIGAKU NIHON BUNKA KENKYUJO HO. (JA). **4972**

KOKUSAI KANKEI-GAKU KENKYU. (JA). **4527**

KOLNER DOMBLATT. (GW/0450-6413). **302**

KOLNER ZEITSCHRIFT FUER SOZIOLOGIE UND SOZIALPSYCHOLOGIE. (GW/0023-2653). **5251**

KOMBA. (KE). **5590**

KOMMUNIKATION. (SZ). **1159**

KOMPASS; AUSTRALIA. (AT). **731**

KONOMISKE ANALYSER. (NO). **1502**

KONSTHISTORISK TIDSKRIFT. (SW/0023-3609). **355**

KONTANT (BERLIN, GERMANY). (GW). **1066**

KONTINENT. (GW). **2518**

KONTINENT (BERLIN, GERMANY). (GW/0176-4179). **4480**

KONYVTARI FIGYELO. (HU/0023-3773). **3222**

KOOKS MAGAZINE. (US/1045-103X). **4242**

KOREA BUSINESS WORLD. (KO). **689**

KOREA HERALD, THE. (KO). **5805**

KOREA NEWSREVIEW. (US/0146-9657). **2506**

KOREA OBSERVER. (KO). **Qty: 4. 2849**

KOREA/UPDATE. (US). **4510**

KOREAN BUSINESS REVIEW. (KO). **689**

KOREAN CULTURE (LOS ANGELES). (US/0270-1618). **2657**

KOREAN JOURNAL OF BIOCHEMISTRY. (KO/0378-8512). **490**

KOREAN STUDIES. (US/0145-840X). **2657**

KOREANA. (KO). **355**

KORNYEZETVEDELMI SZAKIRODALMI TAJEKOZTATO. (HU/0231-0716). **2218**

KORTARS. (HU/0023-415X). **3402**

KOSHER GOURMET MAGAZINE, THE. (US/0888-4811). **2791**

KOSMETIK INTERNATIONAL. (GW). **404**

KOSMORAMA. (DK/0023-4222). **4073**

KOSMOS + OEKUMENE. (NE). **4972**

KOSMOS (STUTTGART). (GW/0023-4230). **5124**

KOSMOS (TORRANCE, CALIF.). (US/0278-8101). **390**

KOUNTRY KORRAL MAGAZINE. (SW). **4128**

KOVOVE MATERIALY. (XO/0023-432X). **4007**

KOZGAZDASAGI SZEMLE. (HU/0023-4346). **689**

KOZUTI KOZLEKEDESI SZAKIRODALMI TAJEKOZTATO. (HU/0231-0724). **5441**

KRAFTFUTTER. (GW/0023-4427). **202**

KRANKENDIENST. (GW/0023-4486). **3602**

KRANKENHAUS-HYGIENE + INFEKTIONSVERHUTUNG. (GW/0720-3373). **4788**

KRANKENHAUSPHARMAZIE. (GW/0173-7597). **4313**

KRANKENHAUSUMSCHAU. (GW/0023-4508). **3787**

KRANKENPFLEGE. (SZ/0253-0465). **3861**

KRANKENVERSICHERUNG (BERLIN), DIE. (GW/0301-4835). **2886**

KREFELD IMMIGRANTS AND THEIR DESCENDANTS. (US/0883-7961). **2457**

KREISFREIE STADTE UND LANDKREISE IN ZAHLEN. (GW). **5330**

KRIEG UND LITERATUR. (GW/0935-9060). **2696**

KRIMINALISTIK. (GW/0023-4699). **3168**

KRIMINALSOZIOLOGISCHE BIBLIOGRAPHIE. (AU). **3168**

KRISIS (INTERNATIONAL CIRCLE FOR RESEARCH IN PHILOSOPHY). (US/0894-5233). **4351**

KRITERION. (BL/0100-512X). **Qty: 10. 4351**

KRITIKON LITTERARUM. (GW). **3293**

KRMIVA. (CI/0023-4850). **103**

KRONIKA (TORONTO). (CN/0704-4380). **2536**

KRONOS. (US/0361-6584). **2622**

KRYTYKA. (PL/0867-5244). **2696**

KSU ECONOMIC AND BUSINESS REVIEW. (JA/0387-2955). **1571**

KUANG-TUNG HUA YUAN CHI KAN. (CH). **355**

KUANGCHUANG DIZHI. (CC/0258-7106). **1441**

KUANGYE GONGCHENG. (CC/0253-6099). **2143**

KUCHE. (GW/0344-4376). **Qty: 20. 2348**

KUENSTLERGILDE; EIN MITTEILUNGSBLATT FUER UNSERE MITGLIEDER, DIE. (GW). **355**

KUKILA. (IO/0126-9223). **5618**

KULTUR CHRONIK. (GW/0724-343X). **Qty: 20. 323**

KULTURA I ZHIZN. (RU/0023-5199). **4528**

KULTURA (PARIS). (FR/0023-5148). **3403**

KULTURA SLOVA. (XO/0023-5202). **3293**

KULTUURLEVEN. (BE/0023-5288). **Qty: 8. 5251**

KUNA-MELBA NEWS. (US). **5657**

KUNAPIPI. (DK/0106-5734). **Qty: occasionally. 3403**

KUNST IN HESSEN UND AM MITTELRHEIN. (GW/0452-8514). **356**

KUNST OG KULTUR. (NO/0023-5415). **373**

KUNST UND KIRCHE. (AU/0023-5431). **356**

KUNSTHANDEL, DER. (GW/0023-5504). **356**

KUNSTSTOFF-JOURNAL. (GW/0047-3766). **4456**

KUPRIAKAI SPOUDAI. (CY/0081-1580). **2696**

KURIER (ORANGE, VA), DER. (US/1059-9762). **2457**

KURT WEILL NEWSLETTER. (US/0899-6407). **4128**

KURZBERICHT UBER LATEINAMERIKA. (GW). **Qty: 3. 1502**

KW MAGAZINE. (CN/0822-8140). **2536**

KWARTALNIK HISTORII I TEORII RUCHU ZAWODOWEGO. (PL/0860-9357). **1683**

KYBERNETES. (UK/0368-492X). **1252**

KYBERNETIKA. (XR/0023-5954). **1252**

KYKLOS. (SZ/0023-5962). **5208**

KYONGYONG NONJIP (SOUL TAEHAKKYO. KYONGYONG YONGUSO). (KO/0023-369X). **1615**

KYRIAKATIKA NEA. (US/0746-4479). **5689**

KYRKOHISTORISK AARSSKRIFT. (SW/0085-2619). **4972**

KYUSHU SHINKEI SEISHIN IGAKU. (JA/0023-6144). **3930**

L. A. ARCHITECT. (US/0885-7377). **302**

L.A.S.I.E. (AT/0047-3774). **3222**

L.A. WEEKLY. (US/0192-1940). **5636**

L.C. CLASSIFICATION: ADDITIONS AND CHANGES. (US/0041-7912). **3222**

LA FERIA NEWS, THE. (US). Qty: 12. **5751**

LA PORTE HERALD-ARGUS, THE. (US). **5665**

LA RECORD. (UK). **3222**

LA YOUTH. (US). Qty: 4. **1066**

LABOR AND EMPLOYMENT LAW ANTHOLOGY. (US). **3150**

LABOR & INVESTMENTS. (US/0279-0467). **1683**

LABOR ARBITRATION IN GOVERNMENT. (US/0047-3839). **3150**

LABOR ARBITRATION INFORMATION SYSTEM. (US/0744-5253). **3150**

LABOR HISTORY. (US/0023-656X). Qty: 60-70. **1683**

LABOR HOSPITALARIA. (SP/0211-8262). Qty: 4-6. **3787**

LABOR NOTES (DETROIT, MICH.). (US/0275-4452). **1684**

LABOR PAGE, THE. (US/8755-1284). **1685**

LABOR RESEARCH REVIEW. (US/0885-4238). **1685**

LABOR STUDIES JOURNAL. (US/0160-449X). **1685**

LABOR WORLD, THE. (US/0023-6667). **1685**

LABORATORIO 2000. (IT/1120-8376). **984**

LABORATORIUM PRAKTIJK. (NE). **463**

LABORATORIUMSMEDIZIN. (GW/0342-3026). **3603**

LABORATORY AND RESEARCH METHODS IN BIOLOGY AND MEDICINE. (US/0160-8584). **463**

LABORATORY ANIMALS (LONDON). (UK/0023-6772). **5515**

LABORATORY EQUIPMENT DIGEST. (UK/0023-6829). **5125**

LABORATORY MEDICINE. (US/0007-5027). **3603**

LABORATORY MICROCOMPUTER. (UK/0262-2955). **1268**

LABORATORY NEWS. (UK/0266-7169). Qty: 20. **463**

LABORATORY PRIMATE NEWSLETTER. (US/0023-6861). **5515**

LABORATORY PRODUCT NEWS. (CN/0047-3855). **5125**

LABORATORY ROBOTICS AND AUTOMATION. (US/0895-7533). **1214**

LABOUR CAPITAL AND SOCIETY. (CN/0706-1706). **1685**

LABOUR EDUCATION. (SZ/0378-5467). **1685**

LABOUR FORCE / DEPARTMENT OF STATISTICS, THE. (JM). **1686**

LABOUR (HALIFAX). (CN/0700-3862). **1686**

LABOUR (HALIFAX). (CN/0700-3862). Qty: 70. **1686**

LABOUR HISTORY (CANBERRA). (AT/0023-6942). **1686**

LABOUR NETWORK. (AT). Qty: 3-4. **1686**

LABOUR NEWS & GRAPHICS. (CN/0832-6223). **1686**

LABOUR RESEARCH (LONDON). (UK/0023-7000). **1686**

LABYRINTH (WATERLOO). (CN/0318-8450). **1078**

LABYRINTHOS. (IT/0393-0807). **356**

LACERTA. (NE/0023-7051). **5590**

LACIO DROM : RIVISTA BIMESTRALE DI STUDI ZINGARI. (IT/0394-2791). Qty: 30. **2321**

LACMA PHYSICIAN. (US/0162-7163). **3914**

LACTATION REVIEW, THE. (US/0362-3173). **3764**

LADDER (WASHINGTON, D.C.), THE. (US/0882-1828). Qty: 2. **3294**

LADENBAU. (SZ/0458-6123). **302**

LADY. (UK/0023-7167). Qty: 12. **2518**

LADY'S CIRCLE. (US/0023-7191). **5560**

LADY'S CIRCLE PATCHWORK QUILTS. (US/0731-9916). **5184**

LAFAYETTE COUNTY HERITAGE NEWS. (US/1064-5527). Qty: 1 or 2. **2457**

LAG & [I.E. OCH] AVTAL. (SW). **3151**

LAI NOTES / THE UNIVERSITY OF NEW MEXICO LATIN AMERICAN INSTITUTE. (US). **1833**

LAKARTIDNINGEN. (SW/0023-7205). **3603**

LAKE ALFRED PRESS. (US). Qty: 25. **5650**

LAKE CHARLES AMERICAN-PRESS. (US/0739-1196). **5684**

LAKE CITIES SUN, THE. (US). **5751**

LAKE LOG CHIPS. (US/0270-5680). **844**

LAKE NEWS, THE. (US/8750-3689). **5681**

LAKE PLACID NEWS. (US). **5717**

LAKE SUPERIOR MAGAZINE. (US/0890-3050). **2537**

LAKELAND BOATING (1982). (US/0744-9194). **594**

LAKEVILLE JOURNAL, THE. (US). **5645**

LAKOTA TIMES, THE. (US/0744-2238). **5744**

LAM-MISPAHA. (US/0894-9816). **5050**

LAMAR DAILY NEWS AND HOLLY CHIEFTAIN, THE. (US). **5643**

LAMAR DEMOCRAT. (US/0745-9300). Qty: 1 or 2. **5703**

LAMAR JOURNAL OF THE HUMANITIES. (US/0275-410X). **2849**

LAMBDA BOOK REPORT. (US/1048-9487). Qty: 420. **2795**

LAMB'S PASTURES. (US/0883-7708). **2457**

LAMIERA. (IT/0391-5891). **4007**

LAMP, THE. (AT/0047-3936). **3861**

LAMPAS. (NE/0165-8204). **3294**

LAMPASAS DISPATCH RECORD. (US/8750-1759). **5751**

LAN MAGAZINE. (NE). **1242**

LANCASTER COUNTY CONNECTIONS. (US/0748-1071). **2457**

LANCET (NORTH AMERICAN EDITION), THE. (US/0099-5355). **3603**

LAND AND HUMAN SETTLEMENTS. (CN/0715-3023). **2910**

LAND AND MINERALS SURVEYING. (UK/0265-4210). **2027**

LAND & WATER INTERNATIONAL. (NE/0023-7604). **2093**

LAND COMPENSATION REPORTS. (CN/0380-4208). **2993**

LAND JUGEND. (AU). **103**

LAND REFORM, LAND SETTLEMENT AND COOPERATIVES. (IT/0251-1894). **1542**

LAND- UND FORSTWIRTSCHAFLICHE BETRIEB, DER. (AU). **2386**

LAND USE LAW & ZONING DIGEST. (US/0094-7598). **2993**

LAND USE POLICY. (UK/0264-8377). **1502**

LANDBOUWMECHANISATIE. (NE/0023-7795). **159**

LANDBOUWTIJDSCHRIFT (1988). (BE/0776-2143). **104**

LANDFALL. (NZ/0023-7930). **3403**

LANDINSPEKTREN; TIDSSKRIFT FOR OPMALINGSOG MATRIKELVAESEN. (DK/0105-4570). **2027**

LANDMARK (CALGARY). (CN/0843-459X). **2422**

LANDMARKS OBSERVER. (US/0272-1384). **2743**

LANDMARKS (SEATTLE, WASH.). (US/0734-4007). **2743**

LANDSCAPE ARCHITECT & SPECIFIER NEWS. (US/1060-9962). **2422**

LANDSCAPE ARCHITECTURAL REVIEW. (CN/0228-6963). **2422**

LANDSCAPE AUSTRALIA. (AT/0310-9011). **2423**

LANDSCAPE (BERKELEY, CALIF.). (US/0023-8023). **2568**

LANDSCAPE DESIGN. (UK/0020-2908). **2423**

LANDSCAPE HISTORY. (UK/0143-3768). Qty: 40. **2423**

LANDSCAPE RESEARCH. (UK/0142-6397). Qty: 30. **2423**

LANDSCAPE, THE. (NZ/0110-1439). **2422**

LANDSCAPE TRADES. (CN/0225-6398). **2423**

LANDSCHAFTSARCHITEKTUR. (GW/0323-3162). **2423**

LANDSCOPE. (AT/0815-4465). Qty: 4. **2197**

LANDSTINGENS PLANER. (SW) **5294**

LANDTECHNIK, DIE. (GW/0023-8082). **159**

LANDWIRTSCHAFTLICHES WOCHENBLATT FUR WESTFALEN UND LIPPE. (GW). **104**

LANDWORKER, THE. (UK). **1687**

LANE COUNTY HISTORIAN. (US/0458-7227). **2743**

LANG VAN. (CN/0832-1922). **2489**

LANGAGE ET L'HOMME, LE. (BE/0458-7251). **3294**

LANGAGE ET SOCIETE. (FR/0181-4095). **3294**

LANGMUIR. (US/0743-7463). **1055**

LANGSTON HUGHES REVIEW, THE. (US/0737-0555). **3345**

LANGUAGE AND EDUCATION. (UK/0950-0782). **3294**

LANGUAGE AND LEARNING. (UK). **1899**

LANGUAGE AND LITERATURE (SAN ANTONIO, TEX.). (US/1057-6037). **3294**

LANGUAGE AND SOCIETY. (CN/0709-7751). Qty: 2 per year. **3295**

LANGUAGE AND SPEECH. (UK/0023-8309). **3295**

LANGUAGE AND STYLE. (US/0023-8317). **3295**

LANGUAGE ARTS. (US/0360-9170). **1804**

LANGUAGE ASSOCIATION BULLETIN. (US/0889-6917). **1899**

LANGUAGE (BALTIMORE). (US/0097-8507). **3295**

LANGUAGE, CULTURE, AND CURRICULUM. (UK/0790-8318). **3295**

LANGUAGE IN SOCIETY. (UK/0047-4045). **3295**

LANGUAGE INTERNATIONAL. (NE/0923-182X). **3295**

LANGUAGE LEARNING. (US/0023-8333). **3295**

LANGUAGE LEARNING JOURNAL : THE JOURNAL OF THE ASSOCIATION OF LANGUAGE LEARNING. (UK/0957-1736). **3295**

LANGUAGE PROBLEMS & LANGUAGE PLANNING. (US/0272-2690). **3295**

LANGUAGE SCIENCES (OXFORD). (UK/0388-0001). **3295**

LANGUAGE TEACHER / JAPAN ASSOCIATION OF LANGUAGE TEACHERS, THE. (JA/0289-7938). Qty: 60. **3296**

LANGUAGE TESTING. (UK/0265-5322). **3296**

LANGUAGE TRAINING. (UK). **689**

LANGUAGES OF DESIGN. (NE/0927-3034). **3296**

LANGUES ET LINGUISTIQUE. (CN/0226-7144). Qty: 5. **3296**

LANGUES MODERNES, LES. (FR/0023-8376). **3296**

LANGUES ORIENTALES ANCIENNES PHILOLOGIE ET LINGUISTIQUE. (BE/0987-7738). **3296**

LANSING METROPOLITAN QUARTERLY. (US). **2622**

LANSING STATE JOURNAL. (US/0274-9742). Qty: 52. **5692**

LANTERN. (SA/0023-8422). **2499**

LANTERN'S CORE, THE. (US/0047-4053). **3222**

LANTMANNEN. (SW). **104**

LANTZVILLE LOG, THE. (CN/0710-5487). **5788**

LAOGRAPHIA. (GR/1010-7266). **2321**

LAPIDARY JOURNAL, THE. (US/0023-8457). **2915**

LAPIS (MUNCHEN). (GW/0342-2933). **1357**

LAPIZ : REVISTA MENSUAL DE ARTE. (SP/0212-1700). **356**

LAPORAN TAHUNAN PUSAT DOKUMENTASI ILMIAH NASIONAL. (IO). **396**

LAPURAN TAHUNAN SURUHANJAYA PERKHIDMATAN AWAM NEGERI SABAH. (MY). **4661**

LARAMIE DAILY BOOMERANG (LARAMIE, WYO. : 1957). (US). **5772**

LARGE ANIMAL VETERINARY REPORT. (US/1069-1774). **5515**

LARGO CONSUMO. (IT). **929**

LARUE COUNTY HERALD NEWS, THE. (US). **5681**

LARYNGOSCOPE. SUPPLEMENT, THE. (US). **3889**

LARYNGOSCOPE, THE. (US/0023-852X). **3889**

LAS CRUCES BULLETIN. (US/0885-8527). **5814**

LAS VEGAS OPTIC. (US). **5712**

LAS VEGAS REVIEW-JOURNAL. (US). **5707**

LASER AND PARTICLE BEAMS. (UK/0263-0346). **4437**

LASER CHEMISTRY. (SZ/0278-6273). **984**

LASER UND OPTOELEKTRONIK. (GW/0722-9003). **4411**

LASERS & OPTRONICS. (US/0892-9947). **4438**

LATE IMPERIAL CHINA. (US/0884-3236). **2658**

LATERANUM. (VC/1010-7215). **4972**

LATHAM LETTER, THE. (US/0740-5820). **2177**

LATIN AMERICA EVANGELIST. (US). **4973**

LATIN AMERICAN APPLIED RESEARCH / PESQUISA APLICADA LATINO AMERICANA / INVESTIGACION APLICADA LATINOAMERICANA. (AG/0327-0793). **2014**

LATIN AMERICAN INDEX. (US/0090-9416). **Qty:** 5 per year. **4480**

LATIN AMERICAN INDIAN LITERATURES JOURNAL. (US/0888-5613). **Qty:** 10-15. **3403**

LATIN AMERICAN JEWISH STUDIES NEWSLETTER (1983). (US/0738-1379). **Qty:** 10. **5050**

LATIN AMERICAN LITERARY REVIEW. (US/0047-4134). **3345**

LATIN AMERICAN MINING LETTER. (UK/0267-5099). **2143**

LATIN AMERICAN PERSPECTIVES. (US/0094-582X). **4542**

LATIN AMERICAN RESEARCH REVIEW. (US/0023-8791). **Qty:** 25-35. **2743**

LATIN AMERICAN THEATRE REVIEW. (US/0023-8813). **5365**

LATIN AMERICAN TRAVEL & PAN AMERICAN HIGHWAY GUIDE. (US/0075-8159). **5482**

LATINAMERICA PRESS. (PE). **2744**

LATINAMERICAN FORESTRY BIBLIOGRAPHY / INSTITUTO FORESTAL LATINOAMERICANO. (VE/0798-1945). **2386**

LATINITAS. (VC/0023-883X). **3296**

LATOHATAR. (HU). **3346**

LATOMUS. (BE/0023-8856). **3404**

LAUGHING BEAR NEWSLETTER. (US/1056-0327). **4816**

LAUREL MESSENGER. (US/0023-8988). **2744**

LAUREL OUTLOOK. (US). **Qty:** 25 per year. **5705**

LAURENTIANUM. (IT/0023-902X). **5031**

LAVAL THEOLOGIQUE ET PHILOSOPHIQUE. (CN/0023-9054). **4973**

LAVORO E PREVIDENZA OGGI. (IT/0390-251X). **3151**

LAW & INEQUALITY. (US/0737-089X). **2994**

LAW & JUSTICE. (UK/0269-817X). **2994**

LAW AND ORDER. (US/0023-9194). **3168**

LAW AND PHILOSOPHY. (NE/0167-5249). **2994**

LAW & SOCIETY REVIEW. (US/0023-9216). **2994**

LAW CALENDAR. (AT). **2995**

LAW COMPUTERS AND ARTIFICIAL INTELLIGENCE. (UK). **1214**

LAW ENFORCEMENT INTELLIGENCE ANALYSIS DIGEST. (US/0895-3945). **3168**

LAW ENFORCEMENT NEWS. (US/0364-1724). **Qty:** 22. **3169**

LAW IN CONTEXT (BUNDOORA, VIC.). (AT/0811-5796). **2995**

LAW INSTITUTE JOURNAL. (AT/0023-9267). **Qty:** 200. **2995**

LAW LIBRARIAN (LONDON). (UK/0023-9275). **3222**

LAW LIBRARY JOURNAL. (US/0023-9283). **3222**

LAW, MEDICINE & HEALTH CARE. (US/0277-8459). **2995**

LAW NOW. (CN/0841-2626). **Qty:** Varies. **2995**

LAW OF THE HANDICAPPED : REPORTER AND COMMENTATOR, THE. (US/0733-6233). **2996**

LAW OFFICE ADMINISTRATOR. (US/1071-7242). **Qty:** 2-3. **875**

LAW OFFICE GUIDE IN COMPUTERS. (US/0739-5132). **2996**

LAW OFFICE MANAGEMENT JOURNAL. (CN/0843-7076). **2996**

LAW OFFICE TECHNOLOGY REVIEW. (US/1047-6482). **1193**

LAW REVIEW JOURNAL. (US/0734-1938). **2996**

LAW SCHOOL ADMINISTRATOR'S JOURNAL. (US/0741-1170). **2996**

LAW SCHOOL JOURNAL. (US/0737-2590). **2996**

LAW SOCIETY JOURNAL (SYDNEY, N.S.W. : 1982). (AT). **2997**

LAW SOCIETY'S GAZETTE. (UK/0262-1495). **2997**

LAW TALK (WELLINGTON, N.Z.). (NZ). **2997**

LAW TEACHER'S JOURNAL. (US/0741-1197). **2997**

LAWN & GARDEN TRADE. (CN/0705-212X). **2423**

LAWRENCE COUNTY ADVOCATE. (US/0883-6531). **Qty:** 20. **5745**

LAWYER HIRING & TRAINING REPORT. (US/0739-1706). **2997**

LAWYER'S ALERT. (US/0278-9817). **2998**

LAWYERS IN EUROPE. (UK/0959-0889). **3132**

LAWYER'S PC, THE. (US/0740-0942). **2998**

LAWYERS WEEKLY (SCARBOROUGH). (CN/0830-0151). **2998**

LBL RESEARCH REVIEW. (US/0882-1305). **4448**

LC & YOU. (US/8755-4313). **404**

LC GC. (US/0888-9090). **984**

LC GC INTERNATIONAL. (US/0895-5441). **984**

LC-MS UPDATE. (UK/0964-1645). **Qty:** 25/year. **5125**

LCOMM NEWS / LIBRARY COUNCIL OF METROPOLITAN MILWAUKEE. (US). **3222**

LDA JOURNAL. (US/0092-4458). **1329**

LEABHARLANN, AN. (IE/0023-9542). **3223**

LEAD BELLY LETTER. (US/1056-5329). **Qty:** 4-5. **4128**

LEADER (ANDERSON, IND.). (US/1055-2626). **Qty:** 7. **4973**

LEADER (OTTAWA. 1976). (CN/0711-5377). **4851**

LEADER (POINT PLEASANT BEACH, N.J.). (US/0745-6816). **Qty:** 4-6 per year. **5710**

LEADER (RESEARCH TRIANGLE PARK, N.C.), THE. (US/0195-0622). **5723**

LEADER-TELEGRAM. (US/0891-0227). **Qty:** 150. **5768**

LEADER-VINDICATOR, THE. (US). **5737**

LEADERS MAGAZINE (LEXINGTON). (US/0023-9631). **2886**

LEADER'S PRODUCT LIABILITY LAW AND STRATEGY. (US/0733-513X). **2999**

LEADERSHIP & ORGANIZATION DEVELOPMENT JOURNAL. (UK/0143-7739). **875**

LEADERSHIP (CAROL STREAM). (US/0199-7661). **4973**

LEADERSHIP (WASHINGTON). (US/0195-9204). **875**

LEADING EDGE (PROVO, UTAH), THE. (US/1049-5983). **Qty:** 15. **3404**

LEAFLET, THE. (US/0023-964X). **1761**

LEAGUE BULLETIN. (US). **2744**

LEARNING AND INDIVIDUAL DIFFERENCES. (US/1041-6080). **1761**

LEARNING LETTER. (US). **Qty:** 8. **1761**

LEARNING (PALO ALTO, CALIF.). (US/0090-3167). **1900**

LEATHER CONSERVATION NEWS. (US/0898-0128). **Qty:** Varies. **3185**

LEATHER MANUFACTURER, THE. (US/0023-9763). **3185**

LEATHER SCIENCE (MADRAS). (II/0023-9771). **3185**

LEATHERNECK. (US/0023-981X). **4049**

LEAVEN (FRANKLIN PARK, ILL.). (US/8750-2011). **2282**

LEBANON NEWS (WASHINGTON, D.C. 1978). (US/0742-9665). **2489**

LEBEN UND UMWELT. (GW/0303-4283). **463**

LEBENDE SPRACHEN. (GW/0023-9909). **3297**

LEBENDIGE SEELSORGE. (GW). **4973**

LEBENSBILDER AUS SCHWABEN UND FRANKEN. (GW). **433**

LEBENSMITTEL TECHNOLOGIE. (SZ). **2348**

LEBENSMITTEL- UND BIOTECHNOLOGIE. (AU/0254-9298). **2348**

LEBENSMITTEL-WISSENSCHAFT + I.E. UND TECHNOLOGIE. (UK/0023-6438). **2348**

LEBENSMITTELTECHNIK. (GW/0047-4290). **Qty:** 25. **2348**

LEBER, MAGEN, DARM. (GW/0300-8622). **3747**

L'ECOUTE, A. (CN/0700-3900). **4128**

LECTINS SHEFFIELD. (UK/0143-4217). **490**

LECTOR (BERKELEY, CALIF.). (US/0732-8001). **3346**

LECTURAS DE HISTORIA DEL ARTE. (SP). **357**

LEDER. (GW/0024-0176). **3185**

LEEDS STUDIES IN ENGLISH. (UK/0075-8566). **3297**

LEETOWN NEWS. (US). **5671**

LEFT BUSINESS OBSERVER. (US/1042-0134). **Qty:** 3. **1503**

LEFT CURVE. (US/0160-1857). **4480**

LEGACY (AMHERST, MASS.). (US/0748-4321). **3404**

LEGACY (FORT COLLINS, COLO.). (US/1052-3774). **4706**

LEGAL ACTION. (UK/0266-3953). **Qty:** 7-10. **2999**

LEGAL ALERT. (CN/0712-841X). **3101**

LEGAL ASPECTS OF MEDICAL PRACTICE. (US/0190-2350). **2999**

LEGAL BIBLIOGRAPHY JOURNAL. (US/0741-1189). **3081**

LEGAL BUSINESS. (UK/0958-4609). **2999**

LEGAL EXECUTIVE, THE. (UK/0024-0362). **2999**

LEGAL HISTORY. (II/0377-0907). **2999**

LEGAL INFORMATION ALERT. (US/0883-1297). **3081**

LEGAL INTELLIGENCER, THE. (US/0277-495X). **2999**

LEGAL INVESTIGATOR, THE. (US/0741-417X). **3000**

LEGAL REFERENCE SERVICES QUARTERLY. (US/0270-319X). **3000**

LEGAL RESEARCH JOURNAL. (US/0146-0382). **3000**

LEGAL RESEARCH UPDATE. (CN/0835-6009). **Qty:** 4. **3000**

LEGAL TIMES. (US/0732-7536). **3001**

LEGAL VIDEO REVIEW. (US/0898-9427). **3001**

LEGAL WRITING JOURNAL. (US/0732-4529). **3001**

LEGAL WRITING : THE JOURNAL OF THE LEGAL WRITING INSTITUTE. (US). **Qty:** 1. **3001**

LEGGERE. (IT). **Qty:** 150. **3404**

LEGGERE DONNA. (IT). **5560**

LEGION. (CN/0024-0435). **4049**

LEGISLATIVE MANUAL - GENERAL ASSEMBLY OF SOUTH CAROLINA. (US/0362-272X). **4661**

LEGISLATIVE REPORTING SERVICE / COMMERCE CLEARING HOUSE. (US). **4661**

LEGISLATIVE STUDIES QUARTERLY. (US/0362-9805). **4480**

LEGNO, IL. (IT). **844**

LEGON OBSERVER, THE. (GH/0024-0540). **2641**

LEICA-FOTOGRAFIE. (GW/0024-0621). **4371**

LEICA FOTOGRAFIE INTERNATIONAL. (GW/0937-3977). **4371**

LEICHHARDT HISTORICAL JOURNAL. (AT). **2670**

LEIDSE GERMANISTISCHE EN ANGLISTISCHE REEKS. (NE/0458-9971). **3404**

LEIDSE ROMANTISCHE REEKS. (NE/0075-8647). **3404**

LEISURE BEVERAGE INSIDER NEWSLETTER. (US/1040-3736). **2369**

LEISURE INDUSTRY REPORT. (US). **4851**

LEISURE INFORMATION QUARTERLY / NEW YORK UNIVERSITY, SCHOOL OF EDUCATION, HEALTH, NURSING AND ARTS PROFESSIONS, DEPT. OF RECREATION, LEISURE STUDIES, PHYSICAL EDUCATION & SPORT. (US). **4851**

LEISURE LINES (SACRAMENTO, CALIF.). (US/0733-5377). **4706**

LEISURE PAINTER AND CRAFTSMAN. (UK). **4224**

LEISURE SCIENCES. (US/0149-0400). 5208

LEISURE STUDIES. (UK/0261-4367). 4852

LEISURE WHEELS. (CN/0709-7093). 5385

LEMEL. (AT/0729-5898). 2915

LEMKIVSCINA. (US/0888-2436). 2696

LEMOUZI. (FR/0024-0761). Qty: 3-4. 2321

LENGAS. (FR/0153-0313). Qty: 2. 3297

LENGUAJES. (AG). 3297

LENGUAS MODERNAS (SANTIAGO). (CL/0716-0542). 3297

LEOPOLDIANUM. (BL/0101-9635). Qty: 6. 1834

LEPROSY REVIEW. (UK/0305-7518). Qty: 3/yr. 3604

LESBIAN AND GAY STUDIES NEWSLETTER : LGSN. (CN/1064-5950). 2795

LESBIAN CONTRADICTION. (US/1064-4776). Qty: 8. 2795

LESBIAN NEWS (CANOGA PARK, CALIF.), THE. (US/0739-1803). 2795

LESHONENU. (IS/0024-1091). 3297

LESHONENU LA-AM. (IS). 3297

LESNICTVI. (XR/0024-1105). 2387

LESNOE KHOZAJSTVO (MOSKVA). (RU/0024-1113). 2387

LESSING YEARBOOK. (US/0075-8833). 3346

LETHAIA. (NO/0024-1164). 4227

LETRAS DE BUENOS AIRES. (AG/0326-2928). 3404

LETRAS DE HOJE. (BL/0101-3335). 3297

LETRAS FEMENINAS. (US/0277-4356). Qty: (12-16). 3404

LETRAS PENINSULARES. (US/0897-7542). Qty: 25-40. 3404

LET'S DANCE. (US/0024-1253). Qty: occasionally. 1313

LET'S HALT AWHILE IN GREAT BRITAIN. (UK). 2807

LET'S LIVE. (US/0024-1288). 4194

LET'S PLAY HOCKEY. (US/0889-4795). Qty: 2. 4903

LETTER EXCHANGE, THE. (US/0882-3804). 3404

LETTER (HOUSTON, TEX.). (US/0899-3017). 875

LETTERS AND NOTICES. (UK). 4973

LETTORE DI PROVINCIA, IL. (IT/0024-1350). 3405

LETTRE ADA, LA. (FR). 1280

LETTRE AFRIQUE EXPANSION, LA. (FR/0996-9888). Qty: 10. 4480

LETTRE DE LA SURETE DE FONCTIONNEMENT, LA. (FR). 1616

LETTRE DE L'EDI PARIS, LA. (FR/1145-9646). 1115

LETTRE DE L'OIV. (FR). 105

LETTRE DE TELETEL, LA. (FR/0766-5385). 1115

LETTRE MENSUELLE DE FRANCE PHARMACIE LABORATOIRES, LA. (FR/1145-4881). 4314

LETTRE TOURISTIQUE PARIS, LA. (FR/1146-1918). Qty: 4. 5483

LETTRES QUEBECOISES. (CN/0382-084X). 3405

LETTRES ROMANES / UNIVERSITE CATHOLIQUE DE LOUVAIN, LES. (BE). 3405

LETTURE. (IT/0024-144X). Qty: 350. 5365

LEUVENSE BIJDRAGEN. (BE/0024-1482). Qty: 50. 3297

LEVANT (LONDON). (UK/0075-8914). Qty: varies. 273

LEVELTARI KOEZLEMENYEK. (HU/0024-1512). 2622

LEVENDE NATUUR, DE. (NE/0024-1520). Qty: 6. 2197

LEVENDE TALEN. (NE/0024-1539). 3297

LEVIATHAN (DUSSELDORF). (GW/0340-0425). 5208

LEWISTON MORNING TRIBUNE. (US/0892-2586). 5657

LEXINGTON THEOLOGICAL QUARTERLY. (US/0024-1628). 4973

LEXIS. (PE/0254-9239). 3297

LEYTE-SAMAR STUDIES. (PH/0024-1679). 2658

LHAT BULLETIN. (US). 302

LI GUIDE TO DINING & WINING NEWSLETTER. (US/1070-9940). Qty: 12. 2348

LIAISON ENERGIE FRANCOPHONIE. (CN/0840-7827). Qty: 10. 1949

LIAISON - INTERGOVERNMENTAL COMMITTEE ON URBAN AND REGIONAL RESEARCH. (CN/0843-5278). Qty: 30. 2827

LIAISON (THEATRE-ACTION). (CN/0227-227X). Qty: 25-30. 5365

LIAISONS (MONTREAL). (CN/0707-7726). 3297

LIANHE ZAO BOA. (SI). Qty: 520 /year. 5810

LIBER ANNUUS - STUDIUM BIBLICUM FRANCISCANUM. (IS). 5017

LIBERAL EDUCATION (WASHINGTON, D.C.). (US/0024-1822). 1834

LIBERATION (MILTON. 1984). (CN/0829-0954). 4973

LIBERATOR (1988), THE. (US/1040-3760). 5251

LIBERIA-FORUM. (GW/0179-4515). 2641

LIBERTARIAN DIGEST, THE. (US/0272-5959). 4480

LIBERTAS. (GW/0341-9762). 4480

LIBERTAS MATHEMATICA. (US/0278-5307). Qty: 10. 3517

LIBERTE (BRUSSELS, BELGIUM). (BE). Qty: 4. 2911

LIBERTE (MONTREAL). (CN/0024-2020). Qty: 20. 3465

LIBERTY BELL (REEDY, W. VA.). (US/0145-7667). 4481

LIBERTY GAZETTE (LIBERTY, TEX.). (US). Qty: 4/year. 5752

LIBERTY (PORT TOWNSEND, WASH.). (US/0894-1408). 4481

LIBRARIANS COLLECTION LETTER. (US/1063-5386). Qty: 3-6. 3223

LIBRARIAN'S WORLD. (US/0739-0297). 3223

LIBRARIES & CULTURE. (US/0894-8631). 4829

LIBRARY. (UK/0024-2160). Qty: varies. 418

LIBRARY & ARCHIVAL SECURITY. (US/0196-0075). 3224

LIBRARY AND INFORMATION NEWS. (UK/0269-8161). 3224

LIBRARY AND INFORMATION RESEARCH NEWS. (UK/0141-6561). 3224

LIBRARY & INFORMATION SCIENCE RESEARCH. (US/0740-8188). 3224

LIBRARY BINDINGS (WEYBURN). (CN/0228-541X). 3224

LIBRARY BULLETIN (INSTITUTE OF SOUTHEAST ASIAN STUDIES). (SI/0073-9723). 3225

LIBRARY CURRENTS. (US/0741-4188). 3225

LIBRARY HI TECH. (US/0737-8831). Qty: 25. 3225

LIBRARY HI TECH NEWS. (US/0741-9058). 3225

LIBRARY HISTORY. (UK/0024-2306). 3225

LIBRARY JOURNAL (1976). (US/0363-0277). 3225

LIBRARY MANAGEMENT QUARTERLY. (US). 3226

LIBRARY MONITOR. (UK/0957-2791). 3226

LIBRARY OF CONGRESS INFORMATION BULLETIN. (US/0041-7904). 3226

LIBRARY OUTREACH REPORTER. (US/0895-1179). 3226

LIBRARY PERSONNEL NEWS. (US/0891-2742). 943

LIBRARY PR NEWS. (US/0164-9566). 3226

LIBRARY PROGRESS (INTERNATIONAL). (II/0970-1052). 3226

LIBRARY REVIEW (GLASGOW). (UK/0024-2535). 3227

LIBRARY SOFTWARE REVIEW. (US/0742-5759). 1288

LIBRARY TALK. (US/1043-237X). 3227

LIBRARY WORK. (UK/0953-9638). 3228

LIBRESENS PARIS. (FR/1157-7452). Qty: 10. 5062

LIBRI (KBENHAVN). (DK/0024-2667). 3228

LIBROS EN VENTA EN HISPANOAMERICA Y ESPANA. (PR/0075-918X). 419

LIBYA ANTIQUA / KINGDOM OF LIBYA, MINISTRY OF NATIONAL ECONOMY. (LY/0459-2980). 273

LIBYAN STUDIES : ANNUAL REPORT OF THE SOCIETY FOR LIBYAN STUDIES. (UK). 2641

LICENSED BEVERAGE JOURNAL. (US/0024-2764). 2369

LICENSING JOURNAL, THE. (US/1040-4023). Qty: 60. 1616

LICENSING LETTER, THE. (US/8755-6235). 929

LICENSING REVIEW. (UK/0959-8421). 3003

LIDE A ZEME. (XR/0024-2896). 2568

LIEN HORTICOLE. (FR/0293-6852). 2424

LIETUVIU DIENOS. (US/0024-2950). 2267

LIFE & PEACE REVIEW. (SW/0284-0200). 4973

LIFE AND WORK. (UK/0024-306X). 5062

LIFE ASSOCIATION NEWS. (US/0024-3078). 2886

LIFE CHEMISTRY REPORTS. (US/0278-6281). 490

LIFE FORUM. (PH). 5031

LIFE INSURANCE SELLING. (US/0024-3140). 2887

LIFE SCIENCE LAB PRODUCTS. (US/1056-0866). 463

LIFE SUPPORT SYSTEMS. (UK/0261-989X). 3604

LIFELINER. (US/0047-4630). 2458

LIFEPRINTS. (US). Qty: 2. 4390

LIFTOFF (GRAND RAPIDS, MICH.). (US/1060-7692). 27

LIGAND QUARTERLY NOTIZIE TECHNICHE. (IT). Qty: 5/yr. 3604

LIGEIA. (FR/0989-6023). 324

LIGHT AND LIFE (WINONA LAKE). (US/0024-3299). 5062

LIGHT AVIATION. (UK). 27

LIGHT (CHICAGO, ILL.). (US/1064-8186). Qty: 4-8. 3405

LIGHT METALS (NEW YORK). (US/0147-0809). 4007

LIGHT (NASHVILLE, TENN.). (US). 4973

LIGHT OF CONSCIOUSNESS. (US/1040-7448). 4973

LIGHT OF LIFE. (II/0970-2571). Qty: 11. 4974

LIGHTBEARER. (UK). 5062

LIGHTHOUSE (UNIVERSITY PARK, PA.), THE. (US/1070-6690). 4128

LIGHTING DESIGN & APPLICATION. (US/0360-6325). Qty: 10. 2070

LIGHTING DIMENSIONS. (US/0191-541X). 4074

LIGHTING JOURNAL (RUGBY, WARWICKSHIRE). (UK). 2071

LIGHTING RESEARCH & TECHNOLOGY. (UK/0024-3426). 2071

LIGHTING + SOUND INTERNATIONAL. (UK/0268-7429). 5126

LIGHTWAVE. (US/0741-5834). 4438

LIGHTWORKS. (US/0161-4223). 357

LIGUORIAN. (US/0024-3450). 5031

LILITH (NEW YORK). (US/0146-2334). 5050

LIMA TIMES. (PE). 2552

LIMNOLOGY AND OCEANOGRAPHY. (US/0024-3590). 1451

LIMOUSIN LEADER, THE. (CN/0381-5552). 214

LINACRE QUARTERLY, THE. (US/0024-3639). 2252

LINCOLN COUNTY JOURNAL. (US). 5657

LINCOLN COUNTY RECORD (PIOCHE, NEV. : 1968). (US/8755-3260). Qty: 12. 5707

LINCOLN HERALD. (US/0024-3671). Qty: 30. 2744

LINCOLN JOURNAL (LINCOLN, NEB.). (US/1054-7983). 5706

LINCOLN LAW REVIEW (SAN FRANCISCO, CALIF.). (US/0024-368X). 3003

LINCOLN REVIEW. (US/0192-5083). Qty: 30. 2744

LINDA HALL LIBRARY MISCELLANY. (US/0273-0227). 3228

LINDEN LANE MAGAZINE. (US/0736-1084). Qty: 30. 324

LINEA D'OMBRA. (IT). 3405

LINEA EDP. (IT). 1193

LINEAGE (COMMACK, N.Y.). (US/0899-1871). Qty: 2. 2458

LINEAGRAFICA. (IT/0024-3744). 380

LINEAPELLE. (IT). 3185

LINEAR AND MULTILINEAR ALGEBRA. (US/0308-1087). 3517

LINES OF DESCENT. (CN). 2458

LINES REVIEW. (UK/0459-4541). 3346

LINGUA FRANCA : THE REVIEW OF ACADEMIC LIFE. (US/1051-3310). 1834

LINGUE DEL MONDO. (IT) 3298

LINGUIST (LONDON, ENGLAND : 1986). (UK/0268-5965). 3298

LINGUISTIC ANALYSIS. (US/0098-9053). Qty: 3-5 per year. 3298

LINGUISTICA ANTVERPIENSIA. (BE/0304-2294). 3299

LINGUISTICA ATLANTICA : JOURNAL OF THE ATLANTIC PROVINCES LINGUISTIC ASSOCATION. (CN). 3299

LINGUISTICA Y LITERATURA : REVISTA DEL DEPARTAMENTO DE ESPANOL. (CK/0120-5587). 3299

LINGUISTICS. (NE/0024-3949). 3299

LINGUISTICS AND LANGUAGE BEHAVIOR ABSTRACTS. (US/0888-8027). 3336

LINGUISTICS AND PHILOSOPHY. (NE/0165-0157). 3299

LININGTON LINEUP. (US/8756-5609). 3405

LINK. (II/0459-469X). 2506

LINK LINE. (US/0735-8407). 1761

LINK (NEW YORK), THE. (US/0024-4007). 2658

LINK-UP (MINNEAPOLIS, MINN. 1983). (US/0739-988X). 1242

LINK (WINNIPEG. 1974). (CN/0380-299X). 2658

LINK (WOODLAND HILLS). (US). 3837

LINKS : SOZIALISTISCHE ZEITUNG. (GW/0024-404X). Qty: 6 per year. 4543

LINNEANA BELGICA. (BE/0024-4090). Qty: 10. 463

LINN'S STAMP NEWS. (US/0161-6234). 2785

LINQ. (AT). Qty: 10-12/yr. 3405

LINSCOTT'S DIRECTORY OF IMMUNOLOGICAL AND BIOLOGICAL REAGENTS. (US/0740-7394). 3674

LINTUMIES / SUOMEN LINTUTIETEELLINEN YHDISTYS. (FI/0357-3524). 5618

LION AND THE UNICORN (BROOKLYN), THE. (US/0147-2593). 3346

LIP (LANCASTER, PA.). (US/0744-3722). 3346

LIP SERVICE. (US/0893-620X). 4129

LIPOSOMES. (UK/0264-9659). 490

LIQUOR STORE MONTHLY. (SA). 2369

LIRE, BULLETIN DE LA SOCIETE BIBLIOGRAPHIQUE ET ORGANE DU BUREAU D'INFORMATIONS BIBLIOGRAPHIQUES.... (FR). Qty: 120. 419

LISAN AL-ARAB. (CN/0833-3858). 5788

LIST OF CURRENT PERIODICAL PUBLICATIONS IN ETHIOPIA. (ET/0459-5009). 2635

LISTE DES TRAVAUX ARACHNOLOGIQUES PARUS EN ... OU ACTUELLEMENT SOUS PRESSE. (FR). 5590

LISTE OFFICIELLE DES NAVIRES DE MER BELGES ET DE LA FLOTTE DE LA FORCE NAVALE. (BE). 5451

LISTEN (FRANKFURT AM MAIN, GERMANY). (GW/0179-7417). 3346

LISTEN (MOUNTAIN VIEW, CALIF.). (US/0024-435X). 1346

LISTENING (RIVER FOREST). (US/0024-4414). 4974

LISTENING (WASHINGTON). (US/0196-7258). 4390

LISZT SOCIETY JOURNAL, THE. (UK). 4129

LITCHFIELD COUNTY TIMES, THE. (US/0744-6705). 5645

LITE FLYER. (US/1043-4968). 27

LITERACY (TORONTO). (CN/0700-5369). 1881

LITERARY AND LINGUISTIC COMPUTING. (UK/0268-1145). 1193

LITERARY CRITERION, THE. (II/0024-452X). Qty: 20. 3406

LITERARY ENDEAVOUR, THE. (II/0255-2779). 3406

LITERARY HALF-YEARLY, THE. (II/0024-4554). 3406

LITERARY MAGAZINE REVIEW. (US/0732-6637). 3346

LITERARY ONOMASTICS STUDIES. (US/0160-8703). 3406

LITERARY READER. (II). 3406

LITERARY RESEARCH. (US/0891-6365). 3406

LITERARY REVIEW (EDINBURGH). (UK/0144-4360). 3346

LITERARY REVIEW OF CANADA, THE. (CN/1188-7494). Qty: 75. 3406

LITERARY REVIEW (TEANECK), THE. (US/0024-4589). 3406

LITERARY SKETCHES. (US/0024-4597). Qty: 4-6. 3406

LITERAT, DER. (GW/0024-4627). 3406

LITERATUR FUER LESER. (GW/0343-1657). 3406

LITERATUR IN WISSENSCHAFT UND UNTERRICHT : LWU. (GW/0024-4643). Qty: 20/yr. 3406

LITERATURA (BUDAPEST). (HU/0133-2368). 3406

LITERATURE AND BELIEF. (US/0732-1929). 3407

LITERATURE & HISTORY. (UK/0306-1973). 3407

LITERATURE AND MEDICINE. (US/0278-9671). 3605

LITERATURE AND PSYCHOLOGY. (US/0024-4759). 3407

LITERATURE & THEOLOGY. (UK/0269-1205). 3407

LITERATURE FILM QUARTERLY. (US/0090-4260). Qty: 4. 4074

LITERATURE SCAN. ANESTHESIOLOGY. (US/0892-2438). 3683

LITERATURE SCAN. TRANSPLANTATION. (US/0883-8410). 3969

LITERATURINFORMATION TERRITORIALFORSCHUNG, TERRITORIALPLANUNG. (GW). 2568

LITERATURNAIA ROSSIIA : EZHENEDELNIK PRAVLENIIA SOIUZA PISATELEI RSFSR I PRAVLENIIA MOSKOVSKOGO OTDELENIIA SOIUZA PISATELEIA RSFSR. (RU). 3346

LITHIC TECHNOLOGY. (US/0197-7261). 273

LITHIUM (EDINBURGH). (UK/0954-1381). 4314

LITIGATION (CHICHESTER, ENGLAND). (UK/0263-2160). 3003

LITORAL. (SP). 3407

LITTEREALITE. (CN/0843-4182). 3408

LITUANUS. (US/0024-5089). Qty: 7. 2697

LITURGICAL MINISTRY. (US/1059-7786). 4974

LITURGISCHES JAHRBUCH. (GW/0024-5100). 4974

LIVE ANIMAL TRADE & TRANSPORT MAGAZINE. (US/1043-1039). Qty: 8/yr. 226

LIVE LINES. (NZ). 2071

LIVE OAK (OAKLAND, CALIF. 1982), THE. (US/0897-9839). Qty: 3-6. 2458

LIVER (COPENHAGEN). (DK/0106-9543). 3799

LIVERPOOL CLASSICAL MONTHLY : LCM. (UK/0309-3700). 251

LIVERPOOL FAMILY HISTORIAN. (UK/0260-759X). 2458

LIVERPOOL LAW REVIEW, THE. (UK/0144-932X). 3003

LIVESTOCK MARKET DIGEST. (US/0024-5208). 214

LIVESTOCK WEEKLY (SAN ANGELO). (US/0162-5047). Qty: 5. 215

LIVING BLUES. (US/0024-5232). 4129

LIVING CHURCH (1942), THE. (US/0024-5240). 4974

LIVING EARTH (BRISTOL). (UK/0954-1098). Qty: 20. 105

LIVING (HOUSTON, ED.). (US/0741-5486). 4840

LIVING IN SOUTH CAROLINA. (US/0047-486X). Qty: 10-15. 1298

LIVING LIGHT, THE. (US/0024-5275). 5031

LIVING MARXISM. (UK/0955-2448). 4543

LIVING MUSEUM, THE. (US/0024-5283). 4090

LIVING MUSIC. (US/8755-092X). Qty: 1. 4129

LIVING ORTHODOXY. (US/0279-8433). 5039

LIVING PRAYER. (US/0890-5568). 4974

LIVING PULPIT, THE. (US/1059-2733). Qty: 20. 4974

LIVING WITH TEENAGERS. (US/0162-4261). 2283

LIVING WORLD (LOS ANGELES, CALIF.). (US/0896-2154). Qty: 4. 2252

LLA BULLETIN. (US/0196-3023). 3228

LLEN CYMRU. (UK/0076-0188). 3346

LLETRA DE CANVI. (SP). 3408

LLEWELLYN'S NEW WORLDS OF MIND AND SPIRIT. (US). Qty: 50. 4242

LLOYD'S AVIATION LAW. (US). 3181

LLOYD'S LIST. (UK). 5451

LLOYD'S LOADING LIST. (UK). 5386

LLOYD'S MARITIME AND COMMERCIAL LAW QUARTERLY. (UK/0306-2945). 3181

LLOYD'S MARITIME ASIA. (HK/0217-1120). 5451

LLOYD'S PROFESSIONAL LIABILITY TODAY. (UK/0268-9669). 3004

LLOYD'S SHIPBUILDING REVIEW. (UK). 5452

LO-BLADET. (DK/0105-032X). 1688

LOBBY DIGEST & PUBLIC AFFAIRS MONTHLY, THE. (CN/1193-4034). Qty: 12. 4662

LOCAL ECONOMY. (UK/0269-0942). 1573

LOCAL GOVERNMENT IN SOUTHERN AFRICA. (SA/1015-0048). 4662

LOCAL GOVERNMENT POLICY MAKING. (UK/0264-2050). 4663

LOCAL GOVERNMENT REVIEW. (UK). 4663

LOCAL GOVERNMENT STUDIES. (UK/0300-3930). 876

LOCAL HISTORIAN (COLUMBUS, OHIO). (US/0893-3340). 2744

LOCAL HISTORIAN (LONDON. 1968). (UK/0024-5585). Qty: 50. 2697

LOCAL HISTORY. (US/0266-2698). Qty: 300. 2697

LOCAL POPULATION STUDIES. (UK/0143-2974). 4554

LOCAL TRANSPORT TODAY. (UK/0962-6220). 5386

LOCKE NEWSLETTER, THE. (UK/0307-2606). Qty: 4/year. 4352

LOCUS (CAMBRIDGE, MASS.). (US/0047-4959). 3408

LOCUS (DENTON, TEX.). (US/0898-8056). Qty: 50. 2744

LOEX NEWS. (US/0739-0386). 3228

LOFTY TIMES. (US). 3465

LOG (HAYES), THE. (UK/0024-5798). 28

LOG OF MYSTIC SEAPORT, THE. (US/0024-5828). 2744

LOG TRAIN, THE. (US/0743-281X). 5432

LOGBUCH, DAS. (GW/0175-7601). 2774

LOGGER (VANCOUVER). (CN/1193-5855). 2402

LOGIA (FORT WAYNE, INDIANA). (US/1064-0398). Qty: 20. 4974

LOGISTICA MANAGEMENT. (IT/1120-3587). 876

LOGISTICS AND TRANSPORTATION REVIEW, THE. (CN/0047-4991). 5386

LOGISTICS SPECTRUM. (US/0024-5852). 5126

LOGOPEDIE EN FONIATRIE. (NE/0166-252X). 4391

LOGOS. (UK/0957-9656). 4830

LOHN + GEHALT. (GW/0172-9047). 690

LOIS DU QUEBEC. (CN/0318-4447). 3004

L'OISEAU MAGAZINE : REVUE DE LA LIGUE FRANCAISE POUR LA PROTECTION DES OISEAUX. (FR/0297-5785). Qty: 50. 5618

LOISIR ET SOCIETE. (CN/0705-3436). 4852

LOK-MAGAZIN. (GW). 5432

LOLLIPOPS. (US/0890-3557). 1900

LONDON ARCHAEOLOGIST, THE. (UK/0024-5984). Qty: varies. 273

LONDON CORN CIRCULAR, THE. (UK). 202

LONDON JOURNAL, THE. (UK/0305-8034). 2697

LONDON LOG. (UK). 5483

LONDON MAGAZINE. (UK/0024-6085). 3408

LONDON MAGAZINE (LONDON, ONT.). (CN/0711-6233). Qty: 6-12. 2537

LONDON MARKET NEWSLETTER. (UK/0265-8356). 2887

LONDON PHILATELIST, THE. (UK). 2785

LONDON REVIEW OF BOOKS, THE. (UK/0260-9592). 3346

LONDON THEATRE NEWS. (US/1064-0312). Qty: 4. 5365

LONE STAR HORSE REPORT. (US/0892-6271). 2800

LONE STAR HUMOR DIGEST, THE. (US/8756-7369). 4863

LONE STAR SIERRAN. (US/0195-1955). Qty: 1. 2177

LONERGAN STUDIES NEWSLETTER. (CN/0828-184X). 4974

LONG ISLAND HISTORICAL JOURNAL, THE. (US/0898-7084). **Qty:** 12. **2744**

LONG ISLAND JEWISH WEEK, THE. (US/0745-5607). **5051**

LONG ISLAND JEWISH WORLD. (US/0199-2899). **2267**

LONG ISLAND POETRY COLLECTIVE NEWSLETTER, THE. (US). **3465**

LONG ISLAND'S NIGHTLIFE MAGAZINE. (US/0744-7590). **4852**

LONG POND REVIEW. (US/8756-5099). **3408**

LONG TERM CARE MANAGEMENT. (US/0743-1422). **3605**

LOOK AT FINLAND. (FI/0024-6379). **2519**

LOOK BACK AT BOB DYLAN. (US/1049-4340). **4129**

LOOKOUT (NEW YORK), THE. (US/0024-6425). **Qty:** 1-2. **5295**

LOOKOUT, THE. (US). **4974**

LOOKOUT, THE. (SP). **2519**

LOON, THE. (US/0024-645X). **5618**

LOOSE CHANGE. (US/0278-4114). **2774**

LORE AND LANGUAGE. (UK/0307-7144). **2322**

LORE (MILWAUKEE, WIS.). (US/0276-475X). **4090**

LOS ALTOS TOWN CRIER. (US/8750-4588). **Qty:** 50. **5636**

LOS ANGELES. (US/0024-6522). **2537**

LOS ANGELES LAWYER. (US/0162-2900). **3004**

LOS ANGELES TIMES, THE. (US/0458-3035). **5636**

LOSS, GRIEF & CARE. (US/8756-4610). **4603**

LOSS PREVENTION. (UK/0097-2312). **2014**

LOST GENERATION JOURNAL. (US/0091-2948). **3408**

LOST IN CANADA?. (US/0362-4293). **Qty:** varies. **2458**

LOST TREASURE. (US/0195-2692). **5074**

LOT OF BUNKUM. YEARBOOK, A. (US/0882-2425). **2458**

LOT'S WIFE (MICROFICHE). (AT). **5777**

LOTTA CONTRO LA TUBERCOLOSI E LE MALATTIE POLMONARI SOCIALI. (IT/0368-7546). **3950**

LOTUS (CAMBRIDGE, MASS.). (US/8756-7334). **1288**

LOTUS (MUSKOGEE, ILL.). (US/1056-3954). **4603**

LOTUS NEWSLETTER. (US/0316-0106). **105**

LOUISBURG HERALD, THE. (US/8750-6378). **Qty:** 52. **5677**

LOUISIANA ARCHAEOLOGY. (US/1071-7358). **273**

LOUISIANA EDUCATION RESEARCH JOURNAL. (US/0740-5235). **Qty:** 5. **1762**

LOUISIANA GENEALOGICAL REGISTER, THE. (US/0148-7655). **2458**

LOUISIANA HISTORY. (US/0024-6816). **2745**

LOUISIANA LAW REVIEW. (US/0024-6859). **3004**

LOUISIANA OUT-OF-DOORS. (US/0738-8098). **Qty:** Varies. **4874**

LOUISIANA WEEKLY, THE. (US). **Qty:** 3 to 4. **5684**

LOUISVILLE. (US/0024-6948). **2537**

LOUISVILLE LAW EXAMINER. (US/0890-8605). **3004**

LOUVAIN BREWING LETTERS. (BE/0777-8805). **2369**

LOUVAIN STUDIES. (BE/0024-6964). **4974**

LOV OG RETT. (NO/0024-6980). **3004**

LOVECRAFT STUDIES. (US/0899-8361). **Qty:** 5-10. **3409**

LOVELAND DAILY REPORTER-HERALD. (US). **5643**

LOWDOWN 1982. (AT/0158-099X). **Qty:** 24. **386**

LOYALIST GAZETTE, THE. (CN/0047-5149). **2745**

LOYOLA LAW REVIEW. (US/0192-9720). **3004**

LOYOLA OF LOS ANGELES INTERNATIONAL AND COMPARATIVE LAW JOURNAL. (US/0277-5417). **3132**

LOYOLA OF LOS ANGELES LAW REVIEW. (US/0147-9857). **3004**

LOYOLA UNIVERSITY OF CHICAGO LAW JOURNAL. (US/0024-7081). **3005**

LP GAS REVIEW. (UK). **4263**

LRA'S ECONOMIC NOTES. (US/0895-5220). **1688**

LUBRICATION ENGINEERING. (US/0024-7154). **2120**

LUCARNE. (CN/0711-3285). **302**

LUCAS. (AT/1030-4428). **4975**

LUCEAFARUL. (US). **3346**

LUCHA STRUGGLE. (US/0885-4378). **5208**

LUCKNOW LAW TIMES. (II). **3005**

LUCRARI STIINTIFICE, INSTITUL AGRONOMIC "N. BALCESCU," BUCURESTI, SERIA D, ZOOTEHNIE. (RM/0374-8898). **5590**

LUCRURI NOI SI VECHI. (US/8756-8012). **4975**

LUDOWICI NEWS, THE. (US). **5654**

LUFT- UND RAUMFAHRT. (GW/0173-6264). **28**

LUFTWAFFEN-FORUM. (GW). **28**

LUMEN VITAE. (BE/0024-7324). **4975**

LUMIERE ET VIE. (FR/0024-7359). **4975**

LUNDIAN : AN INTERNATIONAL MAGAZINE, THE. (SW). **2519**

LUQMAN. (IR). **5043**

LURELU. (CN/0705-6567). **Qty:** 200. **1066**

LUSAKA PROVINCE ANNUAL REPORT FOR THE YEAR ... / REPUBLIC OF ZAMBIA, OFFICE OF THE PRIME MINISTER. (ZA). **4663**

LUSO-BRAZILIAN REVIEW. (US/0024-7413). **1078**

LUSOAMERICANO (NEWARK, N.J.). (US/0898-9052). **Qty:** 12. **5710**

LUSTRUM. (GW/0024-7421). **1078**

LUTHERAN AMBASSADOR, THE. (US/0746-3413). **5062**

LUTHERAN EDUCATION. (US/0024-7448). **5063**

LUTHERAN JOURNAL, THE. (US/0360-6945). **5063**

LUTHERAN LAYMAN, THE. (US/0024-7464). **Qty:** varies. **4975**

LUTHERAN LIBRARIES. (US/0024-7472). **3229**

LUTHERAN PARTNERS. (US/0885-9922). **5063**

LUTHERAN SENTINEL. (US/0024-7510). **5063**

LUTHERAN SPOKESMAN. (US/0024-7537). **5063**

LUTHERAN SYNOD QUARTERLY, THE. (US/0360-9685). **5063**

LUTHERAN, THE. (AT). **5062**

LUTHERAN THEOLOGICAL JOURNAL. (AT/0024-7553). **5063**

LUTHERAN VISTAS. (US). **5063**

LUTHERISCHE THEOLOGIE UND KIRCHE. (GW). **4975**

LUTHERJAHRBUCH. (GW/0342-0914). **4975**

LUTRA. (NE/0024-7634). **5590**

LUX; LA REVUE DE L'ECLAIRAGE. (FR/0024-7669). **2071**

LVNW NIEUWS. (NE). **5295**

LYCHNOS: LARDOMSHISTORISKA SAMFUNDETS ARSBOK. (SW/0076-1648). **5126**

LYMPHOCYTES SHEFFIELD. (UK/0142-8179). **490**

LYNN/LINN LINEAGE QUARTERLY. (US/0892-418X). **2459**

M & A JAPAN. (UK). **797**

M.C.G.S. REPORTER. (US/0740-1531). **Qty:** 4. **2459**

M/C HEALTH AND FITNESS NEWSLETTER. (AT). **4789**

M/E/A/N/I/N/G (NEW YORK, N.Y.). (US/1040-8576). **Qty:** 10. **324**

M. MACINTOSH MAGAZINE. (IT/1120-8465). **1264**

M.O.C.A. BULLETIN. (AT/0819-9000). **357**

MAANDELIJKSE MEDEDELINGEN - INSPECTIE VOOR HET BRANDWEERWEZEN. (NE). **619**

MAARAKENNUS JA KULJETUS. (FI). **2027**

MAARAV. (US/0149-5712). **3300**

MAAS JOURNAL OF ISLAMIC SCIENCE. (II/0970-1672). **5043**

MAB 'S-GRAVENHAGE. (NE/0924-6304). **747**

MAC/CHICAGO (CHICAGO, ILL.). (US/1045-5825). **1193**

MAC HOME JOURNAL. (US). **1268**

MACCHINE. (IT/0024-8959). **2120**

MACEDONIAN REVIEW. (XN/0350-3089). **2849**

MACHIAVELLI STUDIES. (US/1049-9776). **Qty:** 3. **3409**

MACHINE INTELLIGENCE NEWS. (UK/0267-0429). **1215**

MACHINE KNITTING MONTHLY. (UK/0269-9761). **5184**

MACHINE-MEDIATED LEARNING. (US/0732-6718). **1224**

MACHINE OUTIL. (FR/0024-9149). **2120**

MACHINE VISION AND APPLICATIONS. (US/0932-8092). **1252**

MACHINERY AND PRODUCTION ENGINEERING. (UK/0024-919X). **2120**

MACHINISME AGRICOLE TROPICAL. (FR/0242-2565). **159**

MACHINIST, THE. (US/0047-5378). **Qty:** 3. **1688**

MACINTOSH DISCOUNT REPORTER NEWSLETTER, THE. (US/1048-3535). **1194**

MACINTOUCH. (US/0887-9648). **1194**

MACKNIT. (US/0886-1188). **5184**

MACLEAN'S. (CN/0024-9262). **2489**

MACON MAGAZINE. (US). **Qty:** 6. **2537**

MACON TELEGRAPH. (US/1054-2485). **Qty:** 6-12. **5654**

MACROMOLECULES. (US/0024-9297). **1044**

MACTUTOR. (US/8756-8810). **1280**

MACTUTOR COMPANION SOURCE CODE DISKS. (US). **1280**

MACUSER LONDON. (UK/0269-3275). **1268**

MACWEEK. (US/0892-8118). **1238**

MACWORLD (LONDON). (UK/0957-2341). **1194**

MADDEN FAMILY NEWSLETTER. (US/0883-556X). **2459**

MADEMOISELLE (NEW YORK, N.Y. 1935). (US/0024-9394). **5560**

MADILL RECORD, THE. (US). **5732**

MADISON AVENUE HANDBOOK, THE. (US/0076-2148). **762**

MADISON CO. MUSINGS. (US/1071-1937). **Qty:** 12. **2459**

MADISON COUNTY RECORD. (US/0889-4205). **5627**

MADISON MAGAZINE. (US/0192-7442). **2537**

MADOQUA (WINDHOEK. 1975). (SX/1011-5498). **4167**

MADRONO. (US/0024-9637). **517**

MAGAZIN FUER AMERIKANISTIK. (GW/0170-2513). **2745**

MAGAZINE - ALABAMA GENEALOGICAL SOCIETY, INC. (US/0568-806X). **2459**

MAGAZINE & BOOKSELLER. (US/0744-3102). **4816**

MAGAZINE ARTICLE SUMMARIES (CD-ROM ED.). (US/1041-1151). **2497**

MAGAZINE DESIGN & PRODUCTION. (US/0882-049X). **2922**

MAGAZINE FOR CHRISTIAN YOUTH, THE. (US/8756-4564). **4975**

MAGAZINE / HUXFORD GENEALOGICAL SOCIETY, INC. (US/0747-8445). **2459**

MAGAZINE LITTERAIRE. (FR/0024-9807). **3409**

MAGAZINE OF CONCRETE RESEARCH. (UK/0024-9831). **2027**

MAGAZINE OF HISTORY. (US/0882-228X). **2622**

MAGAZINE OF SPECULATIVE POETRY, THE. (US/8755-8785). **3465**

MAGAZINE OF VIRGINIA GENEALOGY. (US/0743-8095). **2459**

MAGHREB QUARTERLY. (UK/0961-9836). **1573**

MAGHREB REPORT. (US/1071-7579). **Qty:** 5. **2499**

MAGHREB REVIEW, THE. (UK/0309-457X). **2641**

MAGICAL BLEND (1989). (US/1073-5879). **4242**

MAGICAL BLEND MAGAZINE. (US/1040-4287). **Qty:** 100. **4242**

MAGILL. (IE/0332-1754). **2519**

MAGISTRA. (CN). **Qty:** 10. **5031**

MAGISTRATE, THE. (UK). **3169**

MAGNESIUM RESEARCH : OFFICIAL ORGAN OF THE INTERNATIONAL SOCIETY FOR THE DEVELOPMENT OF RESEARCH ON MAGNESIUM. (UK/0953-1424). **3605**

MAGNETIC RESONANCE IN CHEMISTRY : MRC. (UK/0749-1581). **1044**

MAGNETIC RESONANCE REVIEW. (US/0097-7330). **4444**

MAGNETIC SEPARATION NEWS. (US/0731-3632). **4444**

MAGNETOHYDRODYNAMICS (NEW YORK, N.Y. 1989). (US/0891-9801). **2071**

MAGNOLIA (HAMMOND, LA.). (US/0738-3053). **Qty:** Occasionally. **5233**

MAGNOLIA (WINSTON-SALEM, N.C.). (US/1054-9153). **Qty:** 4. **2424**

MAGYAR ALLATORVOSOK LAPJA. (HU/0025-004X). **5516**

MAGYAR ALUMINUM. (HU/0025-0058). **4008**

MAGYAR GEOFIZIKA. (HU/0025-0120). **1408**

MAGYAR GRAFIKA. (HU/0479-480X). **380**

MAGYAR NAPTAR (NEW YORK). (US/0094-1484). **2489**

MAGYAR NYELVOR. (HU/0025-0236). **3300**

MAGYAR PEDAGOGIA. (HU/0025-0260). **1762**

MAGYAR PSZICHOLOGIAI SZEMLE. (HU/0025-0279). **4603**

MAGYAR TUDOMANY. (HU/0025-0325). **5126**

MAHA BODHI, THE. (II/0025-0406). **5021**

MAHARASHTRA TAIMSA VARSHIKA. (II). **2506**

MAHASAGAR. (II/0542-0938). **1451**

MAHD BULLETIN. (US/1064-5608). **Qty:** 1 or 2. **3229**

MAIA. (IT/0025-0538). **1078**

MAIL ORDER BUSINESS DIRECTORY : A COMPLETE GUIDE TO THE MAIL ORDER MARKET. (US/0085-2953). **691**

MAILBOX NEWS. (US/0889-4884). **2791**

MAILING LIST TIDBITS. (US). **Qty:** 20/yr. **929**

MAIN. (US/0147-1201). **4186**

MAIN GROUP METAL CHEMISTRY. (UK/0334-7575). **4008**

MAIN SHEET. (US/0025-0600). **594**

MAINE ANTIQUE DIGEST. (US/0147-0639). **251**

MAINE HISTORICAL SOCIETY QUARTERLY. (US/0163-1152). **2745**

MAINE NATURALIST (STEUBEN, ME.). (US/1063-3626). **Qty:** 60. **4167**

MAINE ORGANIC FARMER & GARDENER, THE. (US/0891-9194). **106**

MAINE (ORONO, ME.). (US). **1102**

MAINE REGISTER, STATE YEAR-BOOK AND LEGISLATIVE MANUAL. (US/0145-9597). **4663**

MAINE SPORTSMAN, THE. (US/0199-0365). **4904**

MAINE TIMES. (US/0025-0783). **5685**

MAINE UNITED METHODIST, THE. (US/0745-0273). **5063**

MAINLINES (INDIANAPOLIS, IND.). (US/0278-9450). **Qty:** 1. **3861**

MAINSTREAM (SACRAMENTO, CALIF.). (US/0891-088X). **Qty:** 1-2. **226**

MAINSTREAM (SAN DIEGO, CALIF.). (US/0278-8225). **Qty:** 6. **4391**

MAINTENANCE FARNHAM. (UK/0953-2110). **1985**

MAINTENANCE SUPPLIES. (US/0025-0929). **2236**

MAINTENANCE TECHNOLOGY. (US/0899-5729). **619**

MAINZER REIHE, DIE. (GW/0076-2784). **3465**

MAIRENA (RIO PIEDRAS, SAN JUAN, P.R.). (PR/1050-835X). **3465**

MAJALAH DEMOGRAFI INDONESIA. (IO/0126-0251). **4554**

MAJALAH FAKULTAS HUKUM UNIVERSITAS AIRLANGGA. (IO). **3005**

MAJALAH PEMBINAAN BAHASA INDONESIA. (IO/0126-4737). **3300**

MAJALLAH. (SY). **3300**

MAJALLAH-I FIZIK. (IR). **4411**

MAJALLAH-I ZABANSHINASI. (IR/0259-9082). **3301**

MAJALLAT AL-BUHUTH ABTARIKHIYAH. (LY). **2641**

MAJALLAT AL-TAWTHIQ AL-TARBAWI. (SU). **1762**

MAJALLAT DIRASAT AL-KHALIJ WA-AL-JAZIRAH AL-ARABIYAH. (KU). **2769**

MAJOR COMPANIES OF EUROPE. (UK). **691**

MAJOR COMPANIES OF NIGERIA. (UK). **844**

MAKAI. (US/0745-2896). **1451**

MAKEDONIKA (THESSALONIKA). (GR/0076-289X). **Qty:** 4-5. **2850**

MAKEDONSKA TRIBUNA. (US/0024-9009). **5665**

MAKERERE ADULT EDUCATION JOURNAL. (UG). **1801**

MAKING WAVES (PORT ALBERNI). (CN/1192-2427). **Qty:** 2. **1504**

MAKTABA. (KE/0253-5971). **3229**

MAKTABAT AL-IDARAH. (SU). **3229**

MAL SORI. (KO). **3301**

MALACOLOGICAL REVIEW. (US/0076-3004). **5590**

MALACOLOGY DATA NET. (US/0892-6506). **5590**

MALADIES CHRONIQUES AU CANADA. (CN/0228-8702). **3606**

MALAHAT REVIEW, THE. (CN/0025-1216). **3409**

MALAKOLOGISCHE ABHANDLUNGEN. (GW/0070-7260). **5590**

MALAWIAN GEOGRAPHER, THE. (MW/1010-5549). **2568**

MALAWIAN WRITERS SERIES. (MW). **3409**

MALAYALAM LITERARY SURVEY. (II). **3465**

MALAYAN LAW JOURNAL (BILINGUAL ED.). (SI/0025-1283). **3005**

MALAYAN NATURE JOURNAL, THE. (MY/0025-1291). **4167**

MALAYSIAN APPLIED BIOLOGY. (MY/0126-8643). **463**

MALAYSIAN BUSINESS. (MY). **691**

MALAYSIAN JOURNAL OF PATHOLOGY, THE. (MY/0126-8635). **3896**

MALAYSIAN JOURNAL OF TROPICAL GEOGRAPHY. (MY/0127-1474). **2568**

MALCOLM LOWRY REVIEW, THE. (CN/0828-5020). **Qty:** varies. **3347**

MALEDICTA. (US/0363-3659). **Qty:** 40. **3301**

MALEDICTA PRESS PUBLICATIONS. (US/0363-9037). **3301**

MALIBU SURFSIDE NEWS, THE. (US/0191-7307). **5636**

MALINI. (US/0737-8688). **2267**

MALL OG MINNE. (NO/0024-855X). **3301**

MALLAS JA OLUT. (FI/0356-3014). **2369**

MALLET, THE. (US/0162-8879). **634**

MALLORN. (UK/0308-6674). **3409**

MALPRACTICE PREVENTION REPORTER. (US/0739-6031). **Qty:** 1-2. **3005**

MALPRACTICE REPORTER. ANESTHESIOLOGY, THE. (US/0738-1018). **3005**

MALPRACTICE REPORTER. HOSPITALS, THE. (US/0738-1956). **3005**

MALT NEWSLETTER. (CN/0710-3417). **3229**

MALTESE DIRECTORY : CANADA, UNITED STATES. (CN/0317-6983). **2745**

MALVERN DAILY RECORD. (US). **Qty:** 4. **5631**

MALVERN LEADER (MALVERN, IOWA : 1883). (US). **5671**

MAMMAL REVIEW. (UK/0305-1838). **5590**

MAMMARY GLAND. (UK/0964-7600). **464**

MAMMOTH TRUMPET. (US/8755-6898). **273**

MAN AT ARMS. (US/0191-3522). **Qty:** 6/yr. **4049**

MAN! (AUSTIN, TEX.). (US/1056-5175). **3995**

MAN-ENVIRONMENT SYSTEMS. (US/0025-1550). **303**

MAN IN INDIA. (II/0025-1569). **240**

MAN IN THE NORTHEAST. (US/0191-4138). **240**

MAN (LONDON). (UK/0025-1496). **Qty:** 60/yr. **240**

MAN-MADE TEXTILES IN INDIA. (II/0377-7537). **Qty:** 12. **5354**

MANA. (FJ). **3409**

MANA (ALEXANDRIA, VA.). (US/0464-8145). **2519**

MANAB MON. (II/0025-1615). **4603**

MANAGE. (US/0025-1623). **876**

MANAGEMENT ACCOUNTANT, THE. (II/0025-1674). **747**

MANAGEMENT ACCOUNTING (LONDON). (UK/0025-1682). **747**

MANAGEMENT ACCOUNTING (NEW YORK, N.Y.). (US/0025-1690). **747**

MANAGEMENT AND MARKETING ABSTRACTS. (UK/0308-2172). **731**

MANAGEMENT COMMUNICATION QUARTERLY. (US/0893-3189). **1115**

MANAGEMENT DAN USAHAWAN INDONESIA. (IO/0302-9859). **876**

MANAGEMENT EDUCATION AND DEVELOPMENT. (UK/0047-5688). **1617**

MANAGEMENT IN GOVERNMENT. (II/0047-570X). **4664**

MANAGEMENT INTERNATIONAL REVIEW. (GW/0025-181X). **877**

MANAGEMENT NEWS : THE NEWSPAPER OF THE BRITISH INSTITUTE OF MANAGEMENT. (UK/0025-1844). **877**

MANAGEMENT QUARTERLY. (US/0025-1860). **877**

MANAGEMENT REVIEW. (US). **878**

MANAGEMENT TODAY. (UK/0025-1925). **878**

MANAGER'S MAGAZINE. (US/0025-1968). **2887**

MANAGING DIVERSITY. (US). **Qty:** 12. **1689**

MANAGING END-USER COMPUTING. (US/1048-6933). **Qty:** (up to 12). **1268**

MANAGING (PITTSBURGH). (US/0162-3346). **878**

MANAR AL-ISLAM. (TS). **5043**

MANASABHARATI : SRI RAMACARITAMANASA CATUSSATABDI SAMAROHA SAMITI, MADHYAPRADESA, BHOPALA KI MASIKA MUKHAPATRIKA. (II). **3409**

MANCUNION : THE OFFICIAL NEWSPAPER OF MANCHESTER UNIVERSITY STUDENTS UNION. (UK). **1093**

M&R. MARINE AND RECREATION NEWS. (US/0025-312X). **594**

MANEDSSTATISTIKK OVER UTENRIKSHANDELEN. (NO/0332-6403). **1536**

MANGAJIN (ATLANTA, GA.). (US/1051-8177). **Qty:** 2. **380**

MANHATTAN MEDICINE. (US/0744-4966). **3606**

MANHATTAN REVIEW (NEW YORK, N.Y. : 1980), THE. (US/0275-6889). **3465**

MANITOBA ARCHAEOLOGICAL QUARTERLY. (CN/0705-2669). **273**

MANITOBA HISTORY. (CN/0226-5044). **2745**

MANITOBA LAW JOURNAL (1966). (CN/0076-3861). **3006**

MANITOBA MEDICINE. (CN/0832-6096). **3606**

MANITOBA PSYCHOLOGIST. (CN/0711-1533). **4603**

MANITOBAN. (CN). **5789**

MANITOULIN EXPOSITOR. (CN/0834-6682). **Qty:** 10-15. **5789**

MANKIND QUARTERLY. (US/0025-2344). **240**

MANLEY FAMILY NEWSLETTER. (US/0883-7805). **2459**

MANNERING REPORT, THE. (US). **Qty:** 6. **5208**

MANNING TIMES, THE. (US). **Qty:** 5. **5742**

MANOA. (US/1045-7909). **3347**

MANORAMA YEAR BOOK. (II/0542-5778). **1927**

MANPOWER DOCUMENTATION. (II/0047-5793). **1689**

MANPOWER JOURNAL. (II/0542-5808). **1689**

MANTHANA. (II). **2506**

MANUAL. NEW YORK BUILDING LAWS. (US). **3006**

MANUFACTURING AUTOMATION. (US/1060-2712). **Qty:** 2-3/year. **3483**

MANUFACTURING CHEMIST (LONDON: 1981). (UK/0262-4230). **985**

MANUFACTURING CLOTHIER (LONDON). (UK/0025-2565). **1085**

MANUFACTURING SYSTEMS. (US/0748-948X). **1617**

MANUSCRIPTA (ST. LOUIS, MO.). (US/0025-2603). **Qty:** 15. **2850**

MANUSCRIPTS FOR TUBA SERIES. (US/0363-6585). **4130**

MANUSCRITOS POETICOS. (SP). **3465**

MANUSHI. (II/0257-7305). **5560**

MANUTENCION Y ALMACENAJE. (SP/0025-2646). **5127**

MANUTENZIONE : TECNICA E MANAGEMENT. (IT). **Qty:** 20. **5127**

MANY CORNERS. (US). **3347**

MANY PATHS. (US). **Qty:** varies. **4975**

MANY VOICES. (US/1042-2277). **Qty:** 12-15. **4603**

MAP COLLECTOR, THE. (UK/0140-427X). **Qty:** 4. **2582**

MAPICS THE MAGAZINE. (US/0891-7973). **Qty:** 2-3 per year. **879**

MAPLINE. (US/0196-0881). **2582**

MAPLINE. SPECIAL NUMBER. (US). **2582**

MAPPE, DIE. (GW/0025-2697). **2902**

MAPPING AWARENESS. (UK/0954-7126). **1194**

MAPPING AWARENESS & GIS EUROPE. (UK/0954-712636). **1242**

MAR Y PESCA. (CU/0025-2735). **2308**

MARCHE MONDIAL DE L'AUDIOVISUEL, LE. (BE). **4371**

MARCHE ROMANE. (BE/0542-6669). **3301**

MARCHES TROPICAUX ET MEDITERRANEENS. (FR/0025-2859). **845**

MARFA INDEPENDENT AND THE BIG BEND SENTINEL, THE. (US/0747-119X). **5752**

MARGARETOLOGIST, THE. (US/0892-1989). **2915**

MARGIN. (II/0025-2921). **1573**

MARGIN (COLORADO SPRINGS, COLO.), THE. (US/0887-851X). **1504**

MARICHEM. (UK/0264-2697). **5386**

MARIN COUNTY COURT REPORTER. (US/0745-8959). **3006**

MARIN INDEPENDENT JOURNAL. (US/0891-5164). **5637**

MARINE BEHAVIOUR AND PHYSIOLOGY. (US/0091-181X). **583**

MARINE CORPS GAZETTE. (US/0025-3170). **4049**

MARINE DIGEST AND TRANSPORTATION NEWS. (US/1059-2970). **Qty:** 1-2. **845**

MARINE DOCK AGE. (US). **594**

MARINE ECOLOGY (BERLIN, WEST). (GW/0173-9565). **2218**

MARINE ENGINEERING DIGEST. (CN/0824-734X). **1986**

MARINE ENVIRONMENTAL RESEARCH. (UK/0141-1136). **2177**

MARINE FISH MANAGEMENT. (US/0195-4555). **2308**

MARINE FISH MONTHLY. (US/1045-3555). **Qty:** 3. **2308**

MARINE FISHERIES REVIEW. (US/0090-1830). **2308**

MARINE GEODESY. (US/0149-0419). **1358**

MARINE GEOPHYSICAL RESEARCHES. (NE/0025-3235). **1451**

MARINE GEOTECHNOLOGY. (US/0360-8867). **1451**

MARINE INSURANCE INTERNATIONAL. (UK/0268-1927). **2887**

MARINE MAMMAL NEWS. (US). **5591**

MARINE NEWS. (UK). **5452**

MARINE ORNITHOLOGY. (SA). **5618**

MARINE POLICY. (UK/0308-597X). **1452**

MARINE STORES INTERNATIONAL. (UK). **1617**

MARINE STRUCTURES. (UK/0951-8339). **4179**

MARINE TECHNOLOGY SOCIETY JOURNAL. (US/0025-3324). **1452**

MARINE TRADES (1978). (CN/0705-8993). **845**

MARINER (VANCOUVER, B.C.). (CN/0829-545X). **5452**

MARINER'S MIRROR. (UK/0025-3359). **4179**

MARIPOSA FOLK FESTIVAL. (CN/0712-6263). **4130**

MARITIME ANTHROPOLOGICAL STUDIES : MAST. (NE/0922-1476). **241**

MARITIME DEFENCE. (UK/0950-558X). **Qty:** 2. **4179**

MARITIME INFORMATION REVIEW. (NE/0920-1610). **Qty:** 15. **3181**

MARITIME PATROL AVIATION. (CN). **Qty:** 6. **28**

MARITIME POLICY AND MANAGEMENT. (UK/0308-8839). **5452**

MARITIME WORKER. (AT). **1690**

MARJORIE KINNAN RAWLINGS JOURNAL OF FLORIDA LITERATURE, THE. (US/1060-3409). **3410**

MARK. (FI). **930**

MARK TWAIN SOCIETY BULLETIN. (US/0272-6378). **Qty:** 1. **3410**

MARKET. ASIA PACIFIC. (US/1059-275X). **Qty:** 12. **930**

MARKET LETTER. (UK/0951-3175). **4314**

MARKET WATCH (NEW YORK, N.Y.). (US/0277-9277). **2369**

MARKETING HIGHER EDUCATION. (US/0896-7156). **931**

MARKETING LIBRARY SERVICES. (US/0896-3908). **3230**

MARKETING NEWS. (US/0025-3790). **931**

MARKETING RESEARCH (CHICAGO, ILL.). (US/1040-8460). **932**

MARKETING TECHNOLOGY. (US/8756-2855). **Qty:** 5. **932**

MARKETING (TORONTO). (CN/0025-3642). **932**

MARKETING TREASURES. (US/0895-1799). **932**

MARKT, DER. (AU). **933**

MARKWICK MIDDEN. (CN/0821-3275). **2459**

MARLBORO HERALD-ADVOCATE. (US). **5743**

MARMAC GUIDE TO PHILADELPHIA, A. (US/0736-8127). **5483**

MARQUEE (WASHINGTON, D.C.). (US). **5365**

MARQUETTE LAW REVIEW. (US/0025-3987). **3006**

MARRIAGE & FAMILY REVIEW. (US/0149-4929). **2283**

MARRIAGE PARTNERSHIP. (US/0897-5469). **4975**

MARS DAILY SENTINEL, LE. (US). **5671**

MARSHALL COUNTY HISTORICAL QUARTERLY. (US/0738-7571). **2745**

MARSHALL ISLANDS JOURNAL (1980). (XE/0892-2098). **5806**

MARSHFIELD MAIL, THE. (US). **Qty:** 52. **5704**

MART JOURNAL. (CN/0711-7922). **1763**

MART (MONTREAL). (CN/0319-2709). **2121**

MARTHA'S KIDLIT NEWSLETTER. (US/1045-4292). **Qty:** 6. **1066**

MARTHA'S VINEYARD TIMES, THE. (US/8750-1449). **Qty:** 6. **5689**

MARTYRDOM AND RESISTANCE. (US/0892-1571). **2267**

MARXISM TODAY. (UK/0025-4118). **2519**

MARXIST REVIEW. LONDON. (UK/0965-9749). **Qty:** approx. 35. **4543**

MARXISTISCHE BLATTER. (GW/0542-7770). **4543**

MARYKNOLL. (US/0025-4142). **Qty:** 11. **5032**

MARYLAND AND DELAWARE GENEALOGIST, THE. (US/0025-4150). **2459**

MARYLAND ARCHEOLOGY. (US/0148-6012). **273**

MARYLAND BIRDLIFE. (US/0147-9725). **Qty:** 5-10. **5618**

MARYLAND ENTOMOLOGIST. (US/0275-8652). **5591**

MARYLAND GRAPEVINE, THE. (US/1052-6161). **178**

MARYLAND HISTORIAN, THE. (US/0025-424X). **Qty:** 10-12. **2622**

MARYLAND HISTORICAL MAGAZINE. (US/0025-4258). **2745**

MARYLAND LAW REVIEW (1936). (US/0025-4282). **3006**

MARYLAND MAGAZINE (1988). (US/1040-7936). **Qty:** 6 /yr. **2745**

MARYLAND MEDICAL JOURNAL (1985). (US/0886-0572). **Qty:** 10-12. **3606**

MARYLAND NATURALIST, THE. (US/0096-4158). **Qty:** 1-6. **4167**

MARYLAND NURSE, THE. (US/0047-6080). **Qty:** 8. **3861**

MARYLAND PROSECUTOR, THE. (US/0748-2957). **3108**

MARYLAND REGISTER. (US/0360-2834). **3007**

MAS (NEW YORK, N.Y.). (US/1046-5634). **2267**

MASABEY 'ENWS. (IS/0792-0970). **1690**

MASCHINE, DIE. (GW/0340-5737). **2121**

MASCHINENBAU. (SZ). **2121**

MASCHINENSCHADEN, DER. (GW/0025-4517). **2121**

MASON COUNTY GENEALOGICAL SOCIETY NEWSLETTER, THE. (US/0885-4459). **Qty:** 20. **2459**

MASONRY SOCIETY JOURNAL, THE. (US/0741-1294). **Qty:** 2-10. **620**

MASS HIGH TECH. (US/8750-2100). **5127**

MASS MEDIA : RIVISTA BIMESTRALE DELLA COMUNICAZIONE. (IT). **Qty:** 50. **1116**

MASSACHUSETTS DAILY COLLEGIAN, THE. (US/0890-0434). **5689**

MASSACHUSETTS DISCRIMINATION LAW REPORTER. (US/0199-5235). **3007**

MASSACHUSETTS MUSIC NEWS. (US/0147-2550). **Qty:** 6800. **4130**

MASSACHUSETTS NURSE, THE. (US/0163-0784). **3861**

MASSACHUSETTS POLITICAL ALMANAC, THE. (US/0277-1314). **4664**

MASSACHUSETTS QUERIES. (US/0897-7739). **2459**

MASSACHUSETTS REVIEW, THE. (US/0025-4878). **2850**

MASSACHUSETTS WILDLIFE. (US/0025-4924). **2198**

MASSAGE (DAVIS, CALIF.). (US/1057-378X). **Qty:** 18. **2599**

MAST. MANITOBA ASSOCIATION OF SCHOOL TRUSTEES. (CN/0381-9531). **4664**

MASTER DRAWINGS. (US/0025-5025). **380**

MASTER SERMON SERIES. (US/0362-0808). **4976**

MASTHEAD, THE. (US/0025-5122). **2922**

MATATU. (NE/0932-9714). **3410**

MATCH (MULHEIM). (GW/0340-6253). **985**

MATEKON. (US/0025-1127). **1504**

MATEMAATTISTEN AINEIDEN AIKAKAUSKIRJA. (FI/0025-5149). **3517**

MATEMATIKAI LAPOK. (HU/0025-519X). **3518**

MATERIAL CULTURE. (US/0883-3680). **Qty:** 3-5. **241**

MATERIAL UND ORGANISMEN; BEIHEFT. (GW/0025-5270). **1017**

MATERIALI E STRUTTURE. (IT). **303**

MATERIALIEN ZUR POLITISCHEN BILDUNG. (GW/0340-0476). **4481**

MATERIALS & DESIGN. (UK/0264-1275). **2104**

MATERIALS AUSTRALIA. (AT/1037-7107). **Qty:** 4. **4008**

MATERIALS EDGE. (UK/0952-5211). **4008**

MATERIALS ENGINEERING. (US/0025-5319). **2105**

MATERIALS EVALUATION. (US/0025-5327). **2105**

MATERIALS FORUM. (AT/0883-2900). **1986**

MATERIALS INFORMATION ENGINEERED MATERIALS SEARCH-IN-PRINT SERIES. (US). **2105**

MATERIALS MANAGEMENT AND DISTRIBUTION. (CN/0025-5343). **1618**

MATERIALS PERFORMANCE. (US/0094-1492). **2105**

MATERIALS SCIENCE AND TECHNOLOGY. (UK/0267-0836). **2105**

MATERIAUX ET ORGANISMES. (GW/0543-0119). **464**

MATERIAUX ET TECHNIQUES. (FR/0032-6895). **2106**

MATERNAL & CHILD HEALTH (RICHMOND, SURREY). (UK/0262-0200). **3738**

MATERNAL-CHILD NURSING JOURNAL. (US/0090-0702). **3861**

MATH NOTEBOOK. (US/0272-8885). **1882**

MATHEMATICA IN EDUCATION. (US/1065-2965). **Qty:** 4. **1763**

MATHEMATICAL BIOSCIENCES. (US/0025-5564). **464**

MATHEMATICAL GAZETTE. (UK/0025-5572). **3519**

MATHEMATICAL REPORTS (CHUR, SWITZERLAND). (SZ/0275-7214). **3520**

MATHEMATICAL REVIEWS. (US/0025-5629). **3542**

MATHEMATICAL SCIENTIST. (AT/0312-3685). **3520**

MATHEMATICAL SOCIAL SCIENCES. (NE/0165-4896). **5208**

MATHEMATICAL SPECTRUM. (UK/0025-5653). **3520**

MATHEMATICAL SYSTEMS IN ECONOMICS. (GW/0344-3302). **3520**

MATHEMATICS AND COMPUTER EDUCATION. (US/0730-8639). **3520**

MATHEMATICS AND COMPUTERS IN SIMULATION. (NE/0378-4754). **1282**

MATHEMATICS IN SCHOOL. (UK/0305-7259). **3520**

MATHEMATICS MAGAZINE. (US/0025-570X). **3521**

MATHEMATICS OF COMPUTATION. (US/0025-5718). **3521**

MATHEMATICS STUDENT (AHMEDABAD), THE. (II/0025-5742). **3521**

MATHEMATICS TEACHER, THE. (US/0025-5769). **3521**

MATHEMATICS TEACHING. (UK/0025-5785). **3521**

MATILDA ZIEGLER MAGAZINE FOR THE BLIND. (US/0025-5955). **4391**

MATRIART (TORONTO). (CN/1182-6169). **358**

MATRIMONIAL STRATEGIST, THE. (US/0736-4881). **3121**

MATRIX : A REVIEW FOR PRINTERS AND BIBLIOPHILES. (UK/0261-3093). **334**

MATRIX (LENNOXVILLE). (CN/0318-3610). **Qty:** 30-40. **3410**

MATRIX NEWS. (US/1059-0749). **Qty:** 8-10. **1242**

MATSYA. (II/0253-9314). **2308**

MATURE HEALTH. (US/0891-9232). **4789**

MATURE LIVING (NASHVILLE). (US/0162-427X). **5180**

MATURE MARKET REPORT. (US/0894-2609). **933**

MATURE TRAVELER. (US/1043-2280). **Qty:** 5-6. **5484**

MAUI UPDATE, THE. (US/0895-9390). **5484**

MAVERICK GUIDE TO NEW ZEALAND, THE. (US/0278-5501). **5484**

MAYBERRY GAZETTE, THE. (US/1043-2639). **1134**

MAYDICA. (IT/0025-6153). **107**

MAYFLOWER DESCENDANT : A MAGAZINE OF PILGRIM GENEALOGY AND HISTORY, THE. (US/8756-3959). **2459**

MAYGAMV. (II). **3301**

MAYO CLINIC PROCEEDINGS. (US/0025-6196). **3799**

MAYVILLE MONITOR. (US). **5692**

MBB : BELASTINGBESCHOUWINGEN. (NE/0005-8335). **4737**

MBEA TODAY. (US/0892-9831). **1763**

MC : THE MODERN CHURCHMAN. (UK/0025-7597). **4976**

MCCORMICK MESSENGER. (US). **Qty:** 50. **5743**

MCDONALD QUARTERLY. (CN/1183-8329). **5295**

MCFARLAND COMMUNITY LIFE. (US/0883-6566). **5769**

MCGILL JOURNAL OF EDUCATION. (CN/0024-9033). **Qty:** 10-15. **1763**

MCGILL LAW JOURNAL. (CN/0024-9041). **3132**

MCGRAW-HILL'S HEALTH BUSINESS. (US/0888-9805). **4790**

MCHENRY COUNTY ILLINOIS CONNECTION QUARTERLY. (US/0885-8314). **2460**

MCINTOSH TIMES, THE. (US). **5697**

MCKEAN COUNTY MINER (SMETHPORT, PA. : 1974). (US). **Qty:** 2. **5737**

MCKINNEY MAZE, THE. (US/0736-2420). **2460**

MCLEAN PROVIDENCE JOURNAL AND FAIRFAX HERALD, THE. (US). **Qty:** 5. **5759**

MCM. (IT/0393-8190). **Qty:** 6-7/yr. **324**

MCMAHON HEAVY CONSTRUCTION COST GUIDE. (US/1050-270X). **2027**

MCN, THE AMERICAN JOURNAL OF MATERNAL CHILD NURSING. (US/0361-929X). **3861**

MDA NEWSMAGAZINE / MUSCULAR DYSTROPHY ASSOCIATION. (US/8750-2321). **3806**

MDE. MANAGERIAL AND DECISION ECONOMICS. (UK/0143-6570). **1504**

MDI MANAGEMENT JOURNAL. (II/0970-6623). **692**

MEALEY'S LITIGATION REPORT. TOBACCO. (US/0886-0122). **3007**

MEALEY'S LITIGATION REPORTS. BAD FAITH. (US/0893-1011). **3007**

MEANJIN (PARKVILLE, VIC.). (AT/0815-953X). **3410**

MEANS CONCRETE COST DATA. (US/1075-0533). **620**

MEANS CONSTRUCTION COST INDEXES. (US/0361-9591). **620**

MEANS ELECTRICAL COST DATA. (US/0748-7002). **620**

MEANS HISTORICAL COST INDEXES. (US/0277-8610). **620**

MEANS SQUARE FOOT COSTS : RESIDENTIAL, COMMERCIAL, INDUSTRIAL, INSTITUTIONAL. (US/0732-815X). **621**

MEASUREMENT AND EVALUATION IN COUNSELING AND DEVELOPMENT. (US/0748-1756). **1763**

MEASUREMENT SCIENCE & TECHNOLOGY. (UK/0957-0233). **4412**

MEASUREMENTS & CONTROL. (US/0148-0057). **5127**

MEAT SCIENCE. (UK/0309-1740). **215**

MECCANICA (MILAN). (NE/0025-6455). **4428**

MECHANICAL ENGINEERING BULLETIN. (II/0379-5527). **2121**

MECHANICAL ENGINEERING (NEW YORK, N.Y. 1919). (US/0025-6501). **2122**

MECHANICAL INCORPORATED ENGINEER. (UK/0954-6529). **Qty:** Varies. **2122**

MECHANICAL MUSIC. (US/1045-795X). **4130**

MEDAL LONDON. (UK/0263-7707). **2781**

MEDAL NEWS HINDHEAD. 1989. (UK/0958-4986). **2781**

MEDDELELSER OM GRNLAND. BIOSCIENCE. (DK/0106-1054). **464**

MEDDELELSER OM GRNLAND. GEOSCIENCE. (DK/0106-1046). **1358**

MEDDELELSER OM GRNLAND. MAN & SOCIETY. (DK/0106-1062). **2519**

MEDECIN BIOPATHOLOGISTE PARIS, LE. (FR/0999-6338). **3607**

MEDECIN DU QUEBEC. (CN/0025-6692). **Qty:** 50. **3607**

MEDECINE DU SPORT. (FR/0025-6722). **3955**

MEDECINE ET ARMEES. (FR/0300-4937). **4049**

MEDECINE TROPICALE. (FR/0025-682X). **Qty:** 4/yr. **3986**

MEDEDELINGEN VAN DE WERKGROEP VOOR TERTIAIRE EN KWARTAIRE GEOLOGIE. (NE/0165-280X). **1387**

MEDELLIN. (CK). **5032**

MEDIA AND METHODS. (US/0025-6897). **1900**

MEDIA ASIA. (SI/0129-6612). **1116**

MEDIA BOX. (BE). **4852**

MEDIA, CULTURE & SOCIETY. (UK/0163-4437). **5251**

MEDIA CULTURE REVIEW. (US). **Qty:** 3. **1116**

MEDIA DEVELOPMENT. (UK). **1116**

MEDIA FORUM. (IT/0394-9575). **762**

MEDIA GENERAL INDUSTRISCOPE. (US). **906**

MEDIA GUIDE INTERNATIONAL. EDITION : BUSINESS/PROFESSIONAL PUBLICATIONS. (US/0164-1743). **762**

MEDIA INFORMATION AUSTRALIA. (AT/0312-9616). **1116**

MEDIA JAYA. (IO). **1574**

MEDIA LETTER (CORAL GABLES, FLA.). (US/1054-6952). **Qty:** 6. **845**

MEDIA PEOPLE (N.S.W./A.C.T. ED.). (AT/0815-5615). **1125**

MEDIA PROFILES. THE CAREER DEVELOPMENT EDITION. (US/0740-1906). **944**

MEDIA PROFILES. THE HEALTH SCIENCES EDITION. (US/0740-1892). **4790**

MEDIA REPORT TO WOMEN. (US/0145-9651). **1117**

MEDIA SELECTION. (GW/0934-4217). **692**

MEDIA SPECTRUM. (US/0731-3675). **Qty:** 10-12. **3230**

MEDIAEVAL SCANDINAVIA SUPPLEMENTS. (DK/0106-102X). **2697**

MEDIAFILE. (US/0885-4610). **2922**

MEDIAPLUSNEWS. (IT/1120-1932). **692**

MEDIASPOUVOIRS. (FR/0762-5642). **Qty:** 4. **1117**

MEDICAL ABBREVIATIONS - 8600 CONVENIENCES AT THE EXPENSE OF COMMUNICATIONS AND SAFETY. (US). **3607**

MEDICAL ABSTRACTS NEWSLETTER. (US/0730-7810). **Qty:** 2-3. **3660**

MEDICAL & BIOLOGICAL ENGINEERING & COMPUTING. (UK/0140-0118). **3695**

MEDICAL ANTHROPOLOGY QUARTERLY. (US/0745-5194). **241**

MEDICAL AUDIT NEWS. (UK/0959-2903). **748**

MEDICAL CARE REVIEW. (US/0025-7087). **3608**

MEDICAL DECISION MAKING. (US/0272-989X). **1215**

MEDICAL DEVICE APPROVAL LETTER. (US/1060-8338). **Qty:** 2-3. **3608**

MEDICAL EDUCATION. (UK/0308-0110). **3609**

MEDICAL ELECTRONICS (PITTSBURGH, PA.). (US/0149-9734). **3609**

MEDICAL GROUP MANAGEMENT JOURNAL. (US/0899-8949). **3609**

MEDICAL HISTORY. (UK/0025-7273). **3609**

MEDICAL HUMANITIES REVIEW. (US/0892-2772). **Qty:** 40. **3609**

MEDICAL HYPNOANALYSIS JOURNAL. (US/0894-5098). **Qty:** 8. **4603**

MEDICAL IMAGING AND MONITORING. (AT). **3609**

MEDICAL JOURNAL OF AUSTRALIA. (AT/0025-729X). **3610**

MEDICAL JOURNAL - UNIVERSITY OF TORONTO. (CN/0833-2207). **3610**

MEDICAL LABORATORY SCIENCES. (UK/0308-3616). **3610**

MEDICAL LAW REPORTS. (UK/0957-9346). **3008**

MEDICAL LIABILITY MONITOR. (US/0732-9636). **3008**

MEDICAL MALPRACTICE DEFENSE REPORTER, THE. (US/0893-8229). **3008**

MEDICAL MALPRACTICE PREVENTION. (US/0885-744X). **3008**

MEDICAL-MORAL NEWSLETTER, THE. (US/0025-7397). **3610**

MEDICAL OFFICE MANAGER. (US/1052-4894). **Qty:** 2 or 3. **3788**

MEDICAL PROBLEMS OF PERFORMING ARTISTS. (US/0885-1158). **3611**

MEDICAL PROGRESS (HONG KONG). (HK/0377-9963). **4315**

MEDICAL PROGRESS THROUGH TECHNOLOGY. (NE/0047-6552). **3695**

MEDICAL REFERENCE SERVICES QUARTERLY. (US/0276-3869). **3230**

MEDICAL RESEARCH FUNDING BULLETIN. (US). **3611**

MEDICAL SCIENCE RESEARCH. (UK/0269-8951). **3611**

MEDICAL TEACHER. (UK/0142-159X). **3611**

MEDICAL TECHNOLOGIST AND SCIENTIST, THE. (UK/0309-2666). **3612**

MEDICAL TRIBUNE (1980). (US/0279-9340). **3612**

MEDICAL WORLD NEWS. (US/0025-763X). **3612**

MEDICINA & HISTORIA. (SP/0300-8169). **3612**

MEDICINA (BUENOS AIRES). (AG/0025-7680). **Qty:** 26. **3613**

MEDICINA CLINICA. (SP/0025-7753). **3613**

MEDICINA DE REHABILITACION. (SP/0214-8714). **4381**

MEDICINA DELLO SPORT. (IT). **3955**

MEDICINA E INFORMATICA. (IT/1120-3773). **3613**

MEDICINAL & AROMATIC PLANTS ABSTRACTS. (II/0250-4367). **517**

MEDICINE AND LAW. (GW/0723-1393). **3742**

MEDICINE DIGEST. (UK). **3613**

MEDICINE INTERNATIONAL. THE MONTHLY ADD-ON JOURNAL. UK EDITION. (UK/0144-0403). **3613**

MEDICINE, SCIENCE, AND THE LAW. (UK/0025-8024). **Qty:** 10. **3742**

MEDICINSKAJA RADIOLOGIJA. (RU/0025-8334). **3943**

MEDICINSKAJA SESTRA. (RU/0025-8342). **3861**

MEDICINSKI PREGLED. (YU/0025-8105). **3614**

MEDICINSKI RAZGLEDI. (XV/0025-8121). **3614**

MEDIEN + ERZIEHUNG. (GW/0341-6860). **1117**

MEDIEN KONKRET. (GW/0931-9808). **1117**

MEDIEVAL ARCHAEOLOGY. (UK/0076-6097). **274**

MEDIEVAL CERAMICS. (UK). **2592**

MEDIEVAL ENCOUNTERS. (NE/1380-7854). **2623**

MEDIEVAL PROSOPOGRAPHY. (US/0198-9405). **2698**

MEDIOEVO LATINO. (IT). **2635**

MEDIOS AUDIO-VISUALES. (SP). **4074**

MEDISCH CONTACT. (NE). **3614**

MEDISTAT / WORLD MEDICAL MARKET ANALYSIS. (UK). 3614

MEDITERRANEAN HISTORICAL REVIEW. (UK). 2698

MEDITERRANEAN LANGUAGE REVIEW. (GW/0724-7567). 3301

MEDITERRANEE MEDICALE. (FR/0302-9263). 3614

MEDITSINSKAIA POMOSHCH / MEDICAL CARE / MINISTERSTVO ZDRAVOOKHRANENIA RF. (RU/0869-7760). 3614

MEDIUM AEVUM. (UK/0025-8385). 3301

MEDIUM (FRANKFURT). (GW/0025-8350). 1117

MEDIZIN, GESELLSCHAFT, UND GESCHICHTE : JAHRBUCH DES INSTITUTS FUER GESCHICHTE DER MEDIZIN DER ROBERT BOSCH STIFTUNG. (GW/0939-351X). Qty: 4-6/yr. 3615

MEDIZIN UND GESELLSCHAFT. (GW/0323-6153). 3615

MEDIZINISCHE MONATSSCHRIFT FUER PHARMAZEUTEN. (GW/0342-9601). 4315

MEDIZINISCHE MONATSSCHRIFT (STUTTGART). (GW/0025-8474). 3615

MEDIZINTECHNIK (STUTTGART). (GW/0344-9416). 3615

MEDWAY VALLEY NEWS (1978). (CN/0711-1754). 2198

MEEKER HERALD, THE. (US). Qty: varies. 5643

MEER & YACHTEN. (FR). 594

MEERESFORSCHUNG. (GW/0341-6836). 1452

MEETING PLANNERS ALERT. (US/0743-3832). 944

MEETINGS MONTHLY, NEWS BULLETIN. (CN/0841-9663). 5484

MEETINGS (NEW YORK, N.Y. 1980). (US/8755-1810). 3230

MEGAFON. (AG). 3410

MEIE ELU OUR LIFE. (CN/0047-665X). Qty: 10. 5789

MEIERIPOSTEN. (NO/0025-8776). 196

MEJ : MEDIA EDUCATION JOURNAL. (UK). 1763

MEKEEL'S WEEKLY STAMP NEWS. (US). 2785

MELA NOTES. (US/0364-2410). 3230

MELANESIAN JOURNAL OF THEOLOGY : JOURNAL OF THE MELANESIAN ASSOCIATION OF THEOLOGICAL SCHOOLS. (PP). 4976

MELANGES DE SCIENCE RELIGIEUSE. (FR/0025-8911). 4976

MELANGES - INSTITUT DOMINICAIN D'ETUDES ORIENTALES DU CAIRE. (UA/0575-1330). 3302

MELBOURNE JOURNAL OF POLITICS. (AT/0085-3224). Qty: 5. 4481

MELBURNER BLETER. (AT). Qty: 3. 3410

MELITA THEOLOGICA. (MM/1012-9588). 4976

MELPOMENE (MINNEAPOLIS, MINN.). (US/1043-8734). 5561

MELTING POT, THE. (US). 2460

MELTON JOURNAL, THE. (US/0891-7116). 1763

MELUS. (US/0163-755X). 3410

MELUSINE. (FR). Qty: 5. 325

MELVILLE SOCIETY EXTRACTS. (US/0193-8991). Qty: 4. 3411

MELYEPITESI ES VIZEPITESI SZAKIRODALMI TAJEKOZTATO. (HU/0231-0732). 2027

MEMBERS DIRECTORY / THE INSTITUTION OF ENVIRONMENTAL HEALTH OFFICERS. (UK/0264-5947). 4790

MEMBERSHIP DIRECTORY / EL PASO COUNTY HISTORICAL SOCIETY. (US). 2746

MEMBERSHIP DIRECTORY / MARYLAND GENEALOGICAL SOCIETY. (US/1056-0394). 2460

MEMBERSHIP DIRECTORY / NATIONAL ASSOCIATION OF BUSINESS ECONOMISTS. (US). Qty: 4/yr. 1504

MEMBERSHIP DIRECTORY - NATIONAL SOCIETY FOR PERFORMANCE AND INSTRUCTION. (US/0730-7675). 1224

MEMBERSHIP LIST - CANADIAN ASSOCIATION OF MUSIC LIBRARIES (1984). (CN/0828-7007). 3231

MEMBERSHIP LIST - THE GALPIN SOCIETY. (UK). Qty: varies. 4130

MEMBRANE BIOCHEMISTRY. (US/0149-046X). 490

MEMBRANE PROTEINS (NEW YORK, N.Y.). (US/0161-2883). 464

MEMBRANE TECHNOLOGY. (UK/0958-2118). 3695

MEMO (QUEBEC. (CN/0848-0877). 693

MEMO: TO THE PRESIDENT. (US/0047-6692). 1835

MEMOIR (ANTHROPOLOGICAL SURVEY OF INDIA). (II/0536-6712). 241

MEMOIR - NEW MEXICO BUREAU OF MINES & MINERAL RESOURCES. (US/0548-5975). 2143

MEMOIRE DE TRAME. (FR/0987-3090). 3231

MEMOIRES DE BIOSPEOLOGIE. (FR/0184-0266). 464

MEMOIRES DE LA SOCIETE GENEALOGIQUE CANADIENNE-FRANCAISE. (CN/0037-9387). 2460

MEMOIRES DE LA SOCIETE GEOLOGIQUE DU NORD. (FR/0767-7375). 1358

MEMOIRES ET DOCUMENTS (FRANCE. SERVICE DE DOCUMENTATION ET DE CARTOGRAPHIE GEOGRAPHIQUES). (FR). 2569

MEMOIRES VIVES (MONTREAL). (CN/1188-8296). Qty: 3. 274

MEMOIRS OF THE CONNECTICUT ACADEMY OF ARTS AND SCIENCES. (US/0069-8970). 2850

MEMOIRS OF THE ZOOLOGICAL SURVEY OF INDIA. (II). 5591

MEMORANDUM - AMERICAN NEWSPAPER PUBLISHERS ASSOCIATION. (US/0270-9864). 4816

MEMORIA (TURIN, ITALY). (IT/0392-4564). 2623

MEMORIAS DA SOCIEDADE BROTERIANA. (PO/0081-0665). 518

MEMORIE DELLA SOCIETA ENTOMOLOGICA ITALIANA. (IT/0037-8747). 5612

MEMORIE DOMENICANE (PISTOIA : 1970). (IT). 2698

MEMORY LANE (LEIGH-ON-SEA, ESSEX). (UK/0266-8033). 4130

MEMOS (SPRINGFIELD, MO.). (US/0885-7776). 4976

MEMPHIS BUSINESS JOURNAL. (US/0747-167X). 693

MEN OF ACHIEVEMENT. (UK/0306-3666). 433

MENDOCINO BEACON, THE. (US). 5637

MENNESKER OG RETTIGHETER. (NO/0800-0735). 4510

MENNOGESPRACH (WATERLOO). (CN/0824-5673). 5063

MENNONITE (1936), THE. (US/0025-9330). 5063

MENNONITE BRETHREN HERALD. (CN/0025-9349). Qty: 50. 5063

MENNONITE FAMILY HISTORY. (US/0730-5214). 2460

MENNONITE HISTORIAN. (CN/0700-8066). 5064

MENNONITE HISTORICAL BULLETIN. (US/0025-9357). Qty: 16/yr. 5064

MENNONITE LIFE. (US/0025-9365). Qty: 20. 5064

MENNONITE QUARTERLY REVIEW, THE. (US/0025-9373). Qty: 40-45. 5064

MENNONITE REPORTER. (CN/0380-0121). Qty: 20-30. 5789

MENNONITE WEEKLY REVIEW. (US/0889-2156). Qty: 50. 5677

MENNONITISCHE POST. (CN/0705-4041). Qty: 2-5. 5064

MENS & MELODIE. (NE/0025-9462). 4131

MEN'S WEAR OF CANADA. (CN/0025-9535). 1086

MENSA BULLETIN. (US/0025-9543). 5233

MENSAJE (SANTIAGO, CHILE). (CL/0025-956X). 4976

MENSAJERO (SAN FRANCISCO, CALIF.), EL. (US/1040-5712). Qty: 3. 2746

MENSALOHA. (US/8750-4529). 4603

MENSCH & BUERO. (GW/0933-8241). 4212

MENSCH + RECHT : QUARTALSZEITSCHRIFT DER SCHWEIZERISCHEN GESELLSCHAFT FUR DIE EUROPAISCHE MENSCHENRECHTSKONVENTION (SGEMKO) / HERAUSGEBERIN SGEMKO. (SZ). 4510

MENSCH UND BUERO. (GW/0933-8241). 4212

MENTAL AND PHYSICAL DISABILITY LAW REPORTER. (US/0883-7902). 3009

MENTAL HANDICAP : JOURNAL OF THE BRITISH INSTITUTE OF MENTAL HANDICAP. (UK/0261-9997). 5296

MENTAL HEALTH IN AUSTRALIA (1973). (AT/0310-5776). 4790

MENTAL HEALTH SPECIAL INTEREST SECTION NEWSLETTER. (US/0279-4136). 4790

MENTAL RETARDATION (WASHINGTON). (US/0047-6765). 1882

MENTALITIES. (NZ/0111-8854). Qty: 25. 4604

MENTOR (SINGAPORE). (SI). 1763

MENTORING INTERNATIONAL. (CN/0843-5405). 4604

MER & BATEAUX PARIS. (FR/0999-7148). 594

MER. MARINE ENGINEERS REVIEW. (UK/0047-5955). 1987

MER (TOKYO, JAPAN). (JA/0503-1540). 1452

MERCADO. (AG/0325-0687). 1574

MERCED SUN-STAR. (US). 5637

MERCHANT MAGAZINE, THE. (US/0739-9723). 2402

MERCIAN GEOLOGIST. (UK/0025-990X). Qty: 12. 1387

MERCURY (POTTSTOWN, PA.). (US). 5737

MERCURY (SAN FRANCISCO). (US/0047-6773). 397

MERIDIAN (BUNDOORA, VIC.). (AT/0728-5914). 3347

MERIDIAN - MAP & GEOGRAPHY ROUND TABLE (AMERICAN LIBRARY ASSOCIATION). (US/1040-7421). 2582

MERLYN'S PEN. (US/0882-2050). 1066

MERRILL LYNCH EUROMONEY DIRECTORY, THE. (UK). 798

MERRILL-PALMER QUARTERLY (1960). (US/0272-930X). 4604

MERTON SEASONAL OF BELLARMINE COLLEGE, THE. (US/0899-4927). 2490

MESOAMERICA (ANTIGUA, GUATEMALA). (GT/0252-9963). 2746

MESOAMERICA (INSTITUTE FOR CENTRAL AMERICAN STUDIES (COSTA RICA)). (CR). 2512

MESOLITHIC MISCELLANY. (US/0259-3548). 274

MESQUITE MESSENGER. (US). Qty: 12 or more. 2402

MESSAGE (1993). (US/1071-5215). 5043

MESSAGE (NASHVILLE, TENN.). (US/0026-0231). 5064

MESSENGER (FORT DODGE, IOWA), THE. (US/0740-6991). 5671

MESSENGER (MADISON, N.C.). (US/0892-1814). 5723

MESSENGER (SCARBOROUGH). (CN/0228-2828). 5789

MESSIANIC OUTREACH, THE. (US/0278-2782). Qty: 2. 5051

MESSING ABOUT IN BOATS. (US). Qty: varies. 4904

MESTER (LOS ANGELES). (US/0160-2764). Qty: 2. 3411

META (MONTREAL). (CN/0026-0452). 3302

METABOLIC, PEDIATRIC AND SYSTEMIC OPHTHALMOLOGY (1985). (US/0882-889X). Qty: 30. 3876

METAL FINISHING. (US/0026-0576). 4009

METAL POWDER REPORT. (UK/0026-0657). 4009

METALL (BERLIN). (GW/0026-0746). 4009

METALLBEWERKING. (NE). 4009

METALLI. (IT). 4009

METALLOBERFLACHE. (GW/0026-0797). 4009

METALLOFIZIKA (KIEV). (UN/0204-3580). 4009

METALLOVEDENIE I TERMICESKAJA OBRABOTKA (KALININ). (RU/0026-0819). 4009

METALLURG. (RU/0026-0827). 4010

METALLURGICAL TRANSACTIONS. B, PROCESS METALLURGY. (US/0360-2141). 4010

METALSMITH. (US/0270-1146). Qty: 4. 374

METALURGIA (SAO PAULO). (BL/0026-0983). 4011

METALURGIA Y ELECTRICIDAD. (SP/0026-0991). 4011

METAPHILOSOPHY. (UK/0026-1068). 4352

METAPHYSICAL REVIEW, THE. (AT/0814-8805). 3411

METASCIENCE. (AT/0815-0796). Qty: 70/year. 5128

METEOR NEWS. (US/0146-9959). Qty: 5. 397

METEORITICS. (US/0026-1114). **Qty:** 24. **1387**

METEOROLOGICAL MAGAZINE. (UK/0026-1149). **1430**

METEOROLOGIE, LA. (FR/0026-1181). **1431**

METHOD (LOS ANGELES, CALIF.). (US/0736-7392). **4353**

METHODIST HISTORY. (US/0026-1238). **Qty:** 15-20. **5064**

METHODIST RECORDER. (UK). **5064**

METHODOLOGY AND SCIENCE. (NE/0543-6095). **5209**

METHODS AND FINDINGS IN EXPERIMENTAL AND CLINICAL PHARMACOLOGY. (SP/0379-0355). **4315**

METHODS OF INFORMATION IN MEDICINE. (GW/0026-1270). **3616**

METLFAX. (US/0026-1297). **4012**

METMENYS. (US/0543-615X). **3411**

METRIC TODAY. (US/1050-5628). **Qty:** (6 per year). **4031**

METRIKA. (GW/0026-1335). **3523**

METRO (SAN JOSE, CALIF.). (US/0882-4290). **2538**

METRO SPORTS MAGAZINE. (US). **Qty:** 10. **4904**

METRO TIMES (DETROIT, MICH.), THE. (US/0746-4045). **Qty:** 25. **5692**

METROLOGIA. (GW/0026-1394). **4031**

METRON. (IT/0026-1424). **5332**

METROPARKS EMERALD NECKLACE. (US). **Qty:** 4. **4874**

METROPOLIS (PARIS). (FR/0223-5633). **2828**

METROPOLITAN ALMANAC (1989). (US/1045-5108). **2538**

METROPOLITAN HOME. (US/0273-2858). **2902**

METU KALENDORIUS - PRISIKELIMO PARAPIJA, EKONOMINE SEKCIJA. (CN/0380-1373). **2490**

METUCHEN, EDISON REVIEW. (US/0747-2390). **5710**

MEXICAN STUDIES. (US/0742-9797). **1505**

MEXICO DESCONOCIDO. (MX). **Qty:** 2. **5484**

MEXICO LEDGER. (US). **5704**

MEXICO NOW : A MONTHLY REPORT FROM SOUTH OF THE BORDER. (MX). **5484**

MEXICO REPORT (EL PASO, TEX.). (US/0277-0946). **1574**

MEXLETTER. (MX/0026-1858). **798**

MIAMI MEDICINE : THE OFFICIAL PUBLICATION OF THE DADE COUNTY MEDICAL ASSOCIATION. (US). **3616**

MIAMI MENSUAL. (US/0273-9372). **2538**

MIAMI TODAY. (US/0889-2296). **Qty:** 50. **5650**

MIBI-FNIM. (IS). **4543**

MICHIANA SEARCHER. (US/0736-5004). **2460**

MICHIGAN ACADEMICIAN. (US/0026-2005). **Qty:** 8-12. **2850**

MICHIGAN ALUMNUS. (US/0746-2565). **1102**

MICHIGAN BAR JOURNAL, THE. (US/0164-3576). **3009**

MICHIGAN BEVERAGE NEWS. (US/0026-2021). **2369**

MICHIGAN BOTANIST. (US/0026-203X). **518**

MICHIGAN CHRISTIAN ADVOCATE. (US/0026-2072). **4977**

MICHIGAN CHRONICLE, THE. (US). **5692**

MICHIGAN CITIZEN. (US/1072-2041). **Qty:** 40. **5693**

MICHIGAN DAILY, THE. (US/0745-967X). **5693**

MICHIGAN DISCUSSIONS IN ANTHROPOLOGY. (US/0193-7804). **241**

MICHIGAN FOUNDATION DIRECTORY. (US/0362-1561). **4338**

MICHIGAN GERMANIC STUDIES. (US/0098-8030). **Qty:** 16. **3302**

MICHIGAN GOLFER. (US). **Qty:** 1. **4904**

MICHIGAN GOLFER. (US/1071-2313). **4904**

MICHIGAN HISTORICAL REVIEW, THE. (US/0890-1686). **Qty:** 50. **2746**

MICHIGAN HISTORY. (US/0026-2196). **2746**

MICHIGAN HOSPITALS. (US/0026-220X). **3789**

MICHIGAN JOURNAL OF POLITICAL SCIENCE. (US/0733-4486). **4481**

MICHIGAN LAW REVIEW. (US/0026-2234). **Qty:** 6. **3009**

MICHIGAN LIVING. (US/0735-1798). **5484**

MICHIGAN MIDDLE SCHOOL JOURNAL. (US/0270-6571). **1764**

MICHIGAN MUNICIPAL REVIEW. (US/0026-2331). **Qty:** 50. **4665**

MICHIGAN OUT-OF-DOORS. (US/0026-2382). **Qty:** 12. **2198**

MICHIGAN QUARTERLY REVIEW. (US/0026-2420). **Qty:** varies. **3347**

MICHIGAN ROMANCE STUDIES. (US/0270-3629). **3302**

MICHIGAN RUNNER, THE. (US/0279-1773). **4904**

MICHIGAN SLAVIC MATERIALS. (US/0543-9930). **3302**

MICHIGAN THEOLOGICAL JOURNAL. (US/1048-2709). **Qty:** 10. **4977**

MICHIGANA. (US/0462-372X). **2460**

MICKLE STREET REVIEW, THE. (US/0194-1313). **3411**

MICRO ECONOMICS / THE BOSTON COMPUTER SOCIETY. (US/0883-4296). **694**

MICRO MONEY. (US/0742-9398). **1269**

MICRO SOFTWARE MARKETING. (US/0738-6354). **1288**

MICROBIAL ECOLOGY IN HEALTH AND DISEASE. (UK/0891-060X). **3616**

MICROBIOLOGICAL UPDATE, THE. (US/0889-3381). **567**

MICROCOMPUTER APPLICATIONS (ANAHEIM). (US/0820-0750). **1269**

MICROCOMPUTER INDEX. (US/8756-7040). **1209**

MICROCOMPUTER REVIEW. (US/8755-7525). **1269**

MICROCOMPUTERS FOR INFORMATION MANAGEMENT. (US/0742-2342). **1269**

MICROELECTRONICS. (UK/0026-2692). **2072**

MICROELECTRONICS AND RELIABILITY. (UK/0026-2714). **2072**

MICROFORM MARKET PLACE. (US/0362-0999). **4822**

MICROGRAPHICS AND OPTICAL STORAGE EQUIPMENT REVIEW. (US/0882-3294). **1277**

MICROGRAPHICS NEWSLETTER. (US/0883-9808). **1195**

MICROINFO (TORONTO). (CN/0826-2705). **1269**

MICROMATH : A JOURNAL OF THE ASSOCIATION OF TEACHERS OF MATHEMATICS. (UK/0267-5501). **3523**

MICRON AND MICROSCOPICA ACTA. (UK/0739-6260). **573**

MICRONESICA. (GU/0026-279X). **4167**

MICROPALEONTOLOGY. (US/0026-2803). **4228**

MICROPOROUS MATERIALS. (NE/0927-6513). **Qty:** 15/yr. **986**

MICROPROCESSING AND MICROPROGRAMMING. (NE/0165-6074). **Qty:** 10. **1269**

MICROPROCESSORS AND MICROSYSTEMS. (UK/0141-9331). **1230**

MICROSCOPE (LONDON). (US/0026-282X). **573**

MICROSCOPE TECHNOLOGY & NEWS. (US/1041-0716). **Qty:** 10. **573**

MICROSCOPY. (UK/0026-2838). **573**

MICROSCOPY SOCIETY OF AMERICA BULLETIN. (US/1062-9785). **Qty:** 15-20. **573**

MICROSTATION MANAGER. (US/1057-9567). **1195**

MICROTECNIC. (SZ/0026-2854). **4031**

MICROWAVE JOURNAL (EURO-GLOBAL ED.). (US/0192-6217). **2072**

MID-AMERICA (CHICAGO). (US/0026-2927). **5032**

MID-AMERICA COMMERCE & INDUSTRY. (US/0193-2047). **950**

MID-AMERICA FOLKLORE. (US/0275-6013). **2322**

MID-AMERICA THEOLOGICAL JOURNAL. (US/0734-9882). **4977**

MID-AMERICAN JOURNAL OF BUSINESS. (US/0895-1772). **Qty:** 3. **694**

MID-AMERICAN REVIEW. (US/0747-8895). **Qty:** 10-20. **3411**

MID-AMERICAN REVIEW OF SOCIOLOGY. (US/0732-913X). **5252**

MID-ATLANTIC COUNTRY. (US/0888-1022). **2538**

MID-ATLANTIC JOURNAL OF BUSINESS, THE. (US/0732-9334). **694**

MID-ATLANTIC SALES GUIDE TO HIGH-TECH COMPANIES. (US/1040-0575). **5128**

MID-ATLANTIC THOROUGHBRED. (US/1056-3245). **2800**

MID-CONTINENT BOTTLER. (US/0026-2978). **2369**

MID-NORTH MONITOR, THE. (CN/0227-3853). **5789**

MID-STREAM (INDIANAPOLIS). (US/0544-0653). **Qty:** 50. **4977**

MID WEEK PETROLEUM ARGUS. (UK). **4264**

MID-WEST CONTRACTOR. (US/0026-3044). **621**

MIDDEN, THE. (CN/0047-7222). **274**

MIDDLE EAST, ABSTRACTS AND INDEX. (US/0162-766X). **2635**

MIDDLE EAST & SOUTH ASIA FOLKLORE BULLETIN, THE. (US/1074-0244). **Qty:** 15. **2322**

MIDDLE EAST CIVIL AVIATION. (US/1054-9838). **Qty:** 12. **28**

MIDDLE EAST ECONOMIC SURVEY. (CY/0544-0424). **4264**

MIDDLE EAST EXECUTIVE REPORTS. (US/0271-0498). **3132**

MIDDLE EAST FOCUS. (CN/0705-8594). **4528**

MIDDLE EAST INDUSTRY & TRANSPORT. (UK/0261-1473). **5387**

MIDDLE EAST INSIGHT. (US/0731-9371). **4482**

MIDDLE EAST INTERNATIONAL. (UK/0047-7249). **4528**

MIDDLE EAST JOURNAL OF ANESTHESIOLOGY. (LE/0544-0440). **3683**

MIDDLE EAST JOURNAL, THE. (US/0026-3141). **2635**

MIDDLE EAST (LONDON, ENGLAND : 1985). (UK/0305-0734). **Qty:** 12-24. **1505**

MIDDLE EAST MILITARY BALANCE / JAFFEE CENTER FOR STRATEGIC STUDIES, THE. (IS). **Qty:** 30/yr. **4049**

MIDDLE EAST POLICY. (US/1061-1924). **Qty:** various. **4528**

MIDDLE EAST REPORT (NEW YORK, N.Y. : 1988). (US/0899-2851). **2526**

MIDDLE EAST STUDIES ASSOCIATION BULLETIN. (US/0026-3184). **2769**

MIDDLE EASTERN STUDIES. (UK/0026-3206). **2769**

MIDDLE SCHOOL JOURNAL. (US/0094-0771). **1764**

MIDDLEBURY COLLEGE MAGAZINE. (US/0745-2454). **1093**

MIDDLETOWN NEWS (MIDDLETOWN, IND. : 1913). (US). **Qty:** 2. **5665**

MIDEAST MARKETS. (UK/0098-6461). **846**

MIDGETS & MINI-SPRINTS RACING NEWS. (US/0889-5279). **4904**

MIDLAND ANCESTOR : JOURNAL OF THE BIRMINGHAM AND MIDLAND SOCIETY FOR GENEALOGY AND HERALDRY, THE. (UK/0307-2851). **Qty:** 40-50. **2460**

MIDLAND HISTORY. (UK/0047-729X). **2698**

MIDLIFE WOMAN. (US/1061-348X). **Qty:** 24. **5561**

MIDSTREAM (NEW YORK). (US/0026-332X). **5051**

MIDWEST FLYER MAGAZINE. (US/0273-7515). **Qty:** 6. **28**

MIDWEST HISTORICAL AND GENEALOGICAL REGISTER. (US/0271-8685). **2460**

MIDWEST POETRY REVIEW. (US/0745-8738). **Qty:** 4. **3466**

MIDWEST QUARTERLY (PITTSBURG), THE. (US/0026-3451). **Qty:** 8 or more per year. **2538**

MIDWEST RACING NEWS. (US/0047-732X). **4904**

MIDWEST REVIEW (WAYNE, NEB. : 1975). (US/0740-3208). **2746**

MIDWESTERN DENTIST. (US/0026-3478). **1330**

MIDWIFERY TODAY. (US/0891-7701). **3765**

MIDWIFERY TODAY AND CHILDBIRTH EDUCATION. (US). **Qty:** 25-35. **3765**

MIDWIVES CHRONICLE AND NURSING NOTES. (UK/0026-3524). **3765**

MIGRANT, THE. (US/0026-3575). **5618**

MIGRATION (BERLIN, WEST). (GW/0721-2887). **1920**

MIGRATION TODAY. (SZ/0544-1188). **1920**

MIGRATION WORLD MAGAZINE. (US/1058-5095). **Qty:** 5. **1920**

MIGRATIONS SANTE. (FR/0335-7198). **4791**

MIJU HAN'GUK ILBO. (US/1041-7281). **5647**

MIKE SHAYNE MYSTERY MAGAZINE. (US/0026-3621). **5074**

MIKROELEKTRONIK. (GW). **2072**

MIKROKOSMOS (STUTTGART). (GW/0026-3680). **573**

MILANO FINANZA : MF. (IT). **798**

MILCH PRAXIX UND RINDERMAST, DIE. (GW/0343-0200). **215**

MILCHWISSENSCHAFT. (GW/0026-3788). **196**

MILESTONES. (US). **3789**

MILIEU MAGAZINE ALPHEN AAN DEN RIJN. (NE/0924-6282). **2177**

MILITAIRE SPECTATOR, DE. (NE). **4050**

MILITANT (NEW YORK, N.Y. 1941), THE. (US/0026-3885). **5718**

MILITARY & POLICE UNIFORM ASSOCIATION NEWSLETTER, THE. (US/1072-8112). **2795**

MILITARY CHAPLAIN, THE. (US/0026-3958). **4050**

MILITARY CHAPLAINS' REVIEW. (US/0360-9693). **4050**

MILITARY HISTORY JOURNAL. (SA/0026-4016). **4050**

MILITARY HISTORY OF THE SOUTHWEST. (US/0898-8064). Qty: 40/yr. **4050**

MILITARY HISTORY OF THE WEST. (US/1071-2011). Qty: 50. **4050**

MILITARY LIFESTYLE (UNITED STATES EDITION). (US/0885-8403). Qty: 1. **4051**

MILITARY LIVING. (US/0740-5065). **4051**

MILITARY LIVING'S R & R REPORT. (US/0740-5073). **4051**

MILITARY MEDICINE. (US/0026-4075). **3617**

MILITARY MICROWAVES ANNUAL CONFERENCE PROCEEDINGS. (UK). **4051**

MILITARY MODELLING. (UK/0026-4083). **2774**

MILITARY POLICE (1987). (US/0895-4208). **3169**

MILITARY REVIEW. (US/0026-4148). **4051**

MILITARY ROBOTICS. (US/0896-0348). **1215**

MILITARY (SACRAMENTO, CALIF.). (US/1046-2511). Qty: 30-50. **4051**

MILITARY VEHICLES. (US/0893-3863). **4051**

MILK INDUSTRY. (UK/0026-4172). **196**

MILK PRODUCER. (UK/0026-4180). **197**

MILL HUNK HERALD, THE. (US). **3466**

MILLARD COUNTY GAZETTE, THE. (US). **5757**

MILLENNIUM. (UK/0305-8298). **4529**

MILLENNIUM FILM JOURNAL. (US/1064-5586). Qty: 2. **4074**

MILLER COMPREHENSIVE GOVERNMENTAL GAAP GUIDE. (US/0891-6918). **748**

MILLER COMPREHENSIVE GOVERNMENTAL GAAP GUIDE UPDATE SERVICE. (US). **748**

MILLIMETRO, IL. (IT/0392-5498). **2922**

MILLTOWN STUDIES. (IE/0332-1428). **4977**

MILNE'S POULTRY DIGEST. (AT/1032-3767). **215**

MILTON QUARTERLY. (US/0026-4326). Qty: 10-15/yr. **3347**

MILWAUKEE COURIER. (US/0026-4350). Qty: 52. **5769**

MILWAUKEE PROFESSIONAL NURSE. (US/0026-4369). **3861**

MILWAUKEE READER. (US/0026-4377). **4830**

MIMAR (SINGAPORE). (SI/0129-8372). **303**

MIMS INDIA. (II/0970-1036). **4316**

MIN FAX. (US/1047-1359). **2828**

MIND. (UK/0026-4423). **4353**

MIND & LANGUAGE. (UK/0268-1064). **3302**

MIND BODY HEALTH DIGEST. (US/0898-3127). **3799**

MIND, THE MEETINGS INDEX. SERIES SEMT, SCIENCE, ENGINEERING, MEDICINE, TECHNOLOGY. (US/0739-5914). **5175**

MINDSZENTY REPORT, THE. (US/0026-4474). **4977**

MINE AND QUARRY. (UK/0369-1632). **2144**

MINERACAO METALURGIA (1968). (BL/0100-6908). **4012**

MINERAL & ENERGY INFORMATION SOURCES. (US). **2144**

MINERAL INFORMATION SOURCES. (US/0749-9876). **1358**

MINERAL PLANNING. (UK/0267-1409). **1441**

MINERAL PROCESSING AND EXTRACTIVE METALLURGY REVIEW. (UK/0882-7508). **2144**

MINERALOGICAL ABSTRACTS. (UK/0026-4601). **1363**

MINERALOGICAL MAGAZINE. (UK/0026-461X). **1441**

MINERALOGICAL RECORD, THE. (UK/0026-4628). **1441**

MINERALOLTECHNIK. (GW/0341-1893). **1442**

MINERALS & METALLURGICAL PROCESSING. (US/0747-9182). **4012**

MINERALS ENGINEERING. (UK/0892-6875). **2144**

MINERALS EXPLORATION ALERT. (US/0730-6474). **1442**

MINERAUX ET FOSSILES, LE GUIDE DU COLLECTIONNEUR. (FR/0335-6566). **1358**

MINER'S NEWS. (US/0890-6157). Qty: 10. **2145**

MINERVA ANESTESIOLOGICA. (IT/0375-9393). **3683**

MINERVA (ARLINGTON, VA.). (US/0736-718X). **4051**

MINERVA CARDIOANGIOLOGICA. (IT/0026-4725). **3708**

MINERVA CHIRURGICA. (IT/0026-4733). **3970**

MINERVA GINECOLOGICA. (IT/0026-4784). **3765**

MINERVA (LONDON). (UK/0026-4695). Qty: 12. **5129**

MINERVA MEDICA. (IT/0026-4806). **3799**

MINERVA MEDICOLEGALE : ORGANO UFFICIALE DELLA SOCIETA ITALIANA DI MMEDICINA LEGALE E DELLE ASSICURAZIONI. (IT/0026-4849). **3742**

MINERVA OFTALMOLOGICA. (IT/0026-4903). **3876**

MINERVA ORTOPEDICA E TRAUMATOLOGICA. (IT). **3883**

MINERVA PEDIATRICA. (IT/0026-4946). **3906**

MINERVA PSICHIATRICA. (IT/0391-1772). **3931**

MINERVA STOMATOLOGICA. (IT/0026-4970). **1330**

MINERVA UROLOGICA E NEFROLOGICA. (IT/0393-2249). **3991**

MINES DIRECTORY. (US/0197-9965). **2145**

MINES MAGAZINE. (US/0096-4859). Qty: 4. **1442**

MING STUDIES. (US/0147-037X). **2658**

MINIATURE QUILTS. (US/1065-0245). Qty: 6. **5185**

MINIATURE WARGAMES. (UK). Qty: 70. **2774**

MINIATURES DEALER (CLIFTON, VA. : 1985). (US/0882-9187). **2774**

MINIATURES SHOWCASE. (US/0896-7288). **2775**

MINING ENGINEER (LONDON). (UK/0026-5179). **2145**

MINING ENGINEERING. (US/0026-5187). **2145**

MINING EXPLORATION AND DEVELOPMENT REVIEW, BRITISH COLUMBIA AND YUKON TERRITORY. (CN/0318-1766). **2145**

MINING JOURNAL (LONDON. 1908). (UK/0026-5225). **2146**

MINING MAGAZINE (LONDON). (UK/0308-6631). **2146**

MINING MIRROR. (US). **2146**

MINING SURVEY (JOHANNESBURG). (SA/0026-5268). **2146**

MINING TECHNOLOGY (MANCHESTER). (UK/0026-5276). **2146**

MINISTRIES TODAY. (US/0891-5725). **4977**

MINISTRY CURRENTS. (US/1069-1766). Qty: 32. **4977**

MINISTRY (WASHINGTON, D.C.). (US/0026-5314). **4977**

MINNESOTA ARCHAEOLOGIST, THE. (US/0026-5403). **275**

MINNESOTA CALLS. (US). **2539**

MINNESOTA CITIES. (US/0148-8546). **4665**

MINNESOTA DAILY, THE. (US). Qty: 75. **5697**

MINNESOTA ENGLISH JOURNAL. (US). Qty: 4/year. **1900**

MINNESOTA FIRE CHIEF. (US/0026-5470). **2291**

MINNESOTA FLYER. (US/0889-4809). Qty: 3. **28**

MINNESOTA GENEALOGIST. (US/0581-0086). Qty: 15. **2460**

MINNESOTA HISTORY. (US/0026-5497). Qty: 20-25. **2746**

MINNESOTA HORTICULTURIST, THE. (US/0026-5500). **2424**

MINNESOTA MANUFACTURERS REGISTER. (US/0738-1514). **3484**

MINNESOTA MEDICINE. (US/0026-556X). **3617**

MINNESOTA MONTHLY (COLLEGEVILLE, MINN.). (US/0739-8700). **2539**

MINNESOTA REVIEW (NEW YORK, N.Y.). (US/0026-5667). Qty: 25. **3347**

MINNESOTA VOLUNTEER, THE. (US/0196-593X). **2198**

MINORITIES & WOMEN IN BUSINESS. (US/1053-2749). Qty: 1-4. **5561**

MINORITIES IN BUSINESS INSIDER. (US/1050-3463). **1690**

MINORITY BUSINESS ENTREPRENEUR. (US/1048-0919). **695**

MINORITY BUSINESS NEWS U.S.A. (US). Qty: 6. **695**

MINORITY ENGINEER : ME, THE. (US/0884-1829). **1988**

MINORITY ENTRPRENEUR. A CLEARINGHOUSE FOR BUSINESS DEVELOPMENT. (US). **695**

MINORITY NURSE NEWSLETTER. (US/1071-9946). Qty: 6-10. **3861**

MINOSEG ES MEGBIZHATOSAG. (HU/0580-4485). **4220**

MINOT DAILY NEWS, THE. (US/0885-3053). **5726**

MINUTES / OCIC. (BE/0771-0461). Qty: 20-40. **4074**

MINWA NO TECHO. (JA). **2322**

MIORITA. (US/0110-0068). **2699**

MIRABELLA (NEW YORK, N.Y.). (US/1044-5153). **5561**

MIRACLES MAGAZINE. (US/1061-3927). **4977**

MIRROR (DAWSON CREEK). (CN/0712-1105). **5790**

MIRROR (LONDON, ONT.). (CN/0711-5911). **1093**

MIRROR MONTREAL. 1990. (CN/1182-5812). Qty: 51. **2539**

MIRROR NEWS. (US/0191-4677). **3484**

MIRRORS : INTERNATIONAL HAIKU FORUM. (US). Qty: 20-30/year. **3466**

MISA DOMINICAL CASTILIAN. (SP). **4977**

MISA DOMINICAL CATALONIAN. (SP). **4977**

MISCELLANEA FRANCESCANA. (IT). **5032**

MISCELLANEA MUSICOLOGICA (ADELAIDE). (AT/0076-9355). **4131**

MISCELLANEOUS SERIES - NEW ZEALAND GEOGRAPHICAL SOCIETY. (NZ/0078-0022). **2569**

MISHPACHA (VIENNA, VA.). (US/1050-9348). Qty: each issue. **5051**

MISION (BUENOS AIRES, ARGENTINA). (AG). **4977**

MISSIOLOGY. (US/0091-8296). **4977**

MISSION. (DK). **4978**

MISSION AND MINISTRY. (US/1058-0565). **5064**

MISSION (DEPARTEMENT EVANGELIQUE FRANCAIS D'ACTION APOSTOLIQUE). (FR/0760-2626). Qty: 5. **5064**

MISSION-FOCUS. (US/0164-4696). **5064**

MISSION FRONTIERS. (US/0889-9436). **4978**

MISSION: JOURNAL OF MISSION STUDIES. (CN/1198-0400). **4978**

MISSION (QUEBEC). (CN/0708-9813). **5032**

MISSION STUDIES. (NE/0168-9789). **4978**

MISSIONALIA. (SA/0256-9507). Qty: 45. **5013**

MISSIONARY TIDINGS (WINONA LAKE, IND.). (US/1043-0725). Qty: 50. **4978**

MISSISSIPPI ARCHAEOLOGY. (US/0738-775X). **275**

MISSISSIPPI BANKER, THE. (US/0026-6159). **799**

MISSISSIPPI BUSINESS JOURNAL, THE. (US/0195-0002). **695**

MISSISSIPPI COLLEGE LAW REVIEW. (US/0277-1152). **3010**

MISSISSIPPI DENTAL ASSOCIATION JOURNAL. (US/0098-4329). **1330**

MISSISSIPPI FOLKLORE REGISTER. (US/0026-6248). **2322**

MISSISSIPPI GEOLOGY. (US/0275-8555). **1388**

MISSISSIPPI (JACKSON, MISS. 1982). (US/0747-1602). **2539**

MISSISSIPPI LAW JOURNAL. (US/0026-6280). **3011**

MISSISSIPPI LAW JOURNAL. CUMULATIVE TEN-YEAR INDEX FOR VOLUMES 41-50. (US). **3011**

MISSISSIPPI LIBRARIES. (US/0194-388X). **Qty: 12. 3231**

MISSISSIPPI MAGAZINE (JACKSON). (US/0199-5677). **Qty: 6. 2539**

MISSISSIPPI MUNICIPALITIES. (US/0026-6337). **4666**

MISSISSIPPI QUARTERLY, THE. (US/0026-637X). **2850**

MISSISSIPPI RAG, THE. (US/0742-4612). **Qty: 24. 4131**

MISSISSIPPI RN, THE. (US/0026-6388). **3861**

MISSOULIAN (MISSOULA, MONT. 1961). (US/0746-4495). **5693**

MISSOURI ARCHAEOLOGICAL SOCIETY QUARTERLY. (US/0743-7641). **Qty: 4-8. 275**

MISSOURI BOTANICAL GARDEN BULLETIN. (US/0026-6507). **518**

MISSOURI FOLKLORE SOCIETY JOURNAL. (US/0731-2946). **2322**

MISSOURI HISTORICAL REVIEW. (US/0026-6582). **Qty: 16. 2747**

MISSOURI LAW REVIEW. (US/0026-6604). **3011**

MISSOURI LIBRARIES. (US/0899-6458). **3231**

MISSOURI MUNICIPAL REVIEW. (US/0026-6647). **4666**

MISSOURI QUERIES. (US/1041-6552). **2461**

MISSOURI REVIEW, THE. (US/0191-1961). **3412**

MISSOURI STATE GENEALOGICAL ASSOCIATION JOURNAL. (US/0747-5667). **2461**

MISSOURI TEAMSTER. (US/0026-6728). **1691**

MISSOURI WILDLIFE. (US). **2218**

MISTLETOE LEAVES. (US). **2747**

MITTEILUNGEN AUS DER ARBEITSMARKT- UND BERUFSFORSCHUNG. (GW/0340-3254). **1691**

MITTEILUNGEN DER ANTHROPOLOGISCHEN GESELLSCHAFT IN WIEN. (AU/0066-4693). **241**

MITTEILUNGEN DER GEOGRAPHISCHEN GESELLSCHAFT IN MUNCHEN. (GW/0072-0941). **2569**

MITTEILUNGEN DER KARL-MAY-GESELLSCHAFT. (GW/0941-7842). **3412**

MITTEILUNGEN DER OSTERREICHISCHEN GEOGRAPHISCHEN GESELLSCHAFT. (AU). **2569**

MITTEILUNGEN DER OSTERREICHISCHEN GEOLOGISCHEN GESELLSCHAFT. (AU/0378-8199). **1388**

MITTEILUNGEN DER SCHWEIZERISCHEN ENTOMOLOGISCHEN GESELLSCHAFT. (SZ/0036-7575). **5612**

MITTEILUNGEN DES DEUTSCHEN GERMANISTENVERBANDES. (GW/0418-9426). **1764**

MITTEILUNGEN DES OSTERREICHISCHEN STAATSARCHIVS. (AU). **2482**

MITTEILUNGEN DES SUDETENDEUTSCHEN ARCHIVS. (GW). **2699**

MITTEILUNGEN DES VEREINS DEUTSCHER EMAILFACHLEUTE E.V. UND DES DEUTSCHEN EMAIL ZENTRUSM E.V. (GW/0723-886X). **2592**

MITTEILUNGEN FUER DIE VIEH- UND FLEISCHWIRTSCHAFT. (GW). **216**

MITTEILUNGEN KLOSTERNEUBURG : REBE UND WEIN, OBSTBAU UND FRUCHTEVERWERTUNG. (AU/0007-5922). **2369**

MITTEILUNGEN - PTB. (GW/0030-834X). **5129**

MITTEILUNGEN UND FORSCHUNGSBEITRAGE DER CUSANUS-GESELLSCHAFT. (GW/0590-451X). **4353**

MITTEILUNGSBLATT DER ARBEITSGEMEINSCHAFT KATHOLISCH-THEOLOGISCHER BIBLIOTHEKEN, AKTHB. (GW/0177-8358). **Qty: 10. 3231**

MITTEILUNGSBLATT - VERBAND DER BIBLIOTHEKEN DES LANDES NORDRHEIN WESTFALEN. (GW/0042-3629). **3232**

MITTELLATEINISCHES JAHRBUCH. (GW/0076-9762). **3302**

MITTELMAN LETTER, THE. (US/0739-0963). **1330**

MIZUNAMI-SHI KASEKI HAKUBUTSUKAN KENKYU HOKOKU. (JA/0385-0900). **4228**

MJP. MONTREAL JOURNAL OF POETICS. (CN/0823-1605). **3466**

ML NEWSLETTER. (AT). **3303**

MLA JOB INFORMATION LIST. ENGLISH ED. (US). **4206**

MLJEKARSTVO. (CI/0026-704X). **197**

MM. (DK/0105-6972). **4131**

MMR, MINERALS & METALS REVIEW. (II/0378-6366). **4012**

MOBILE & HOLIDAY HOMES. (UK). **2828**

MOBILE BEACON & ALABAMA CITIZEN, THE. (US). **5627**

MOBILE TELECOMMUNICATIONS NEWS. (UK/0267-1255). **1160**

MOBILIA (AMSTERDAM). (NE/0165-5302). **Qty: 5-10/yr. 2906**

MOBILITY (WASHINGTON). (US/0195-8194). **695**

MOCI; MONITEUR DU COMMERCE INTERNATIONAL, LE. (FR/0026-9719). **3011**

MODASPORT VACANZE. (IT). **Qty: 4. 1086**

MODEL AUTO REVIEW. (UK/0267-2715). **2775**

MODEL AVIATION CANADA. (CN/0317-7831). **28**

MODEL BOATS. (UK/0144-2910). **594**

MODEL RAILROADER. (US/0026-7341). **2775**

MODEL RETAILER (CLIFTON, VA.). (US/0191-6904). **2775**

MODEL SHIP BUILDER. (US/0199-7068). **Qty: 20. 4179**

MODEL SHIPWRIGHT. (UK). **Qty: varies. 2775**

MODELTEC. (US/0742-7107). **5129**

MODERN AGE (CHICAGO). (US/0026-7457). **2539**

MODERN AGING RESEARCH. (US/0275-360X). **3754**

MODERN & CONTEMPORARY FRANCE. (UK/0963-9489). **5209**

MODERN APPLICATIONS NEWS. (US/0277-9951). **4012**

MODERN ATHLETE AND COACH. (AT). **4905**

MODERN AUSTRIAN LITERATURE. (US/0026-7503). **3412**

MODERN BREWERY AGE. (US/0026-7538). **2369**

MODERN BREWERY AGE BLUE BOOK. (US). **2369**

MODERN CASTING. (US/0026-7562). **4012**

MODERN CHURCHMAN, THE. (UK/0026-7597). **4978**

MODERN DRAMA. (CN/0026-7694). **5366**

MODERN DRUMMER. (US/0194-4533). **4131**

MODERN FICTION STUDIES. (US/0026-7724). **3347**

MODERN FOOD SERVICE NEWS. (US/0888-7829). **5072**

MODERN GREEK SOCIETY. (US/0147-0779). **5209**

MODERN GREEK STUDIES YEARBOOK. (US/0884-8432). **Qty: 30-40. 2699**

MODERN HAIKU. (US/0026-7821). **Qty: 35. 3466**

MODERN HEBREW LITERATURE. (IS/0334-4266). **3412**

MODERN JEWISH STUDIES ANNUAL. (US/0270-9406). **3412**

MODERN JUDAISM. (US/0276-1114). **5051**

MODERN LANGUAGE JOURNAL (BOULDER, COLO.), THE. (US/0026-7902). **3303**

MODERN LANGUAGE QUARTERLY (SEATTLE). (US/0026-7929). **3347**

MODERN LANGUAGE STUDIES. (US/0047-7729). **3303**

MODERN LAW REVIEW. (UK/0026-7961). **3011**

MODERN LITURGY. (US/0363-504X). **4978**

MODERN LOGIC. (US/1047-5982). **Qty: 20-25. 3523**

MODERN MACHINE SHOP. (US/0026-8003). **2122**

MODERN MATURITY (NRTA ED.). (US/0747-6302). **5180**

MODERN MEDICINE (NEDERLANDSE ED.). (NE/0929-0141). **3617**

MODERN PAINTERS (LONDON, ENGLAND). (UK/0953-6698). **358**

MODERN PLASTICS. (US/0026-8275). **4456**

MODERN POWER SYSTEMS. (UK/0260-7840). **1950**

MODERN PSYCHOANALYSIS. (US/0361-5227). **Qty: 10-15. 4604**

MODERN RAILWAYS. (UK/0026-8356). **5433**

MODERN SCHOOLMAN, THE. (US/0026-8402). **4353**

MODERN SCIENCE AND VEDIC SCIENCE. (US/0891-5989). **4186**

MODERNA SPRAK. (SW/0026-8577). **3303**

MODERNE MATHEMATIK IN ELEMENTARER DARSTELLUNG. (GW). **3523**

MODESTO BEE, THE. (US). **5637**

MODO DESIGN MAGAZINE. (IT/0391-3635). **2902**

MODSPIL. (DK/0105-9238). **4131**

MODULAR HI-FI COMPONENTS SERVICE DATA. (US/0730-1197). **2073**

MODULUS. (US/0191-4022). **303**

MOEBIUS. (CN/0225-1582). **3412**

MOHAVE COUNTY MINER (KINGMAN, ARIZ. : 1931). (US). **Qty: 6-8. 5630**

MOHAWK, THE. (US/0740-9699). **2461**

MOLE. (CN/0827-2387). **4131**

MOLECULAR AND CHEMICAL NEUROPATHOLOGY. (US/1044-7393). **3838**

MOLECULAR BIOLOGY REPORTS. (NE/0301-4851). **465**

MOLECULAR BIOTHERAPY. (US/0952-8172). **465**

MOLECULAR MEMBRANE BIOLOGY. (US/0968-7688). **491**

MOLEKULIARNAIA SPEKTROSKOPIIA. (RU). **4438**

MOLINI D'ITALIA. (IT/0026-9018). **Qty: 30. 202**

MOLODA UKRAINA. (CN/0026-9042). **2519**

MOLTEN SALTS BULLETIN. (FR). **1442**

MOM ... GUESS WHAT ... !. (US). **2795**

MOMENT (NEW YORK). (US/0099-0280). **5051**

MOMENTUM (WASHINGTON). (US/0026-914X). **4978**

MONAHANS NEWS (MONAHANS, TEX. : 1931). (US). **5752**

MONARCHY CANADA. (CN/0319-4019). **Qty: 25-30 per year. 4482**

MONASH PAPERS ON SOUTHEAST ASIA. (AT). **2659**

MONASH UNIVERSITY LAW REVIEW. (AT/0311-3140). **Qty: 2. 3011**

MONASTIC STUDIES. (CN/0026-9190). **5032**

MONATSHEFTE FUER VETERINAERMEDIZIN. (GW/0026-9263). **5516**

MONATSSCHRIFT FUER DEUTSCHES RECHT. (GW/0340-1812). **3011**

MONATSSCHRIFT FUER KRIMINOLOGIE UND STRAFRECHTSREFORM. (GW/0026-9301). **3169**

MONDAY DEVELOPMENTS. (US/1043-8157). **Qty: 50. 5296**

MONDAY MAGAZINE (1983). (CN/0832-4719). **Qty: 10. 696**

MONDAY MORNING (INDIANAPOLIS, IND.). (US/0360-6171). **5065**

MONDAY REPORT (TALLAHASSEE, FLA.), THE. (US/0733-9089). **1866**

MONDE A BICYCLETTE, LE. (CN/0823-5570). **429**

MONDE ALPHABETIQUE / LE REGROUPEMENT DES GROUPES POPULAIRES EN ALPHABETISATION DU QUEBEC, LE. (CN/1183-515X). **1764**

MONDE ALPIN ET RHODANIEN, LE. (FR). **5269**

MONDE DU ROCK. (CN/0823-0498). **4132**

MONDE ET LES MINERAUX, LE. (FR/0153-9167). **1442**

MONDE JUIF, LE. (FR/0026-9425). **2699**

MONDE JURIDIQUE, LE. (CN/0828-4989). **3011**

MONDES EN DEVELOPPEMENT. (FR/0302-3052). **1505**

MONDES ET CULTURES : COMPTES RENDUS TRIMESTRIELS DES SEANCES DE L'ACADEMIE DES SCIENCES D'OUTRE-MER. (FR/0221-0436). **5129**

MONDO APERTO. (IT/0026-9492). **1638**

MONDO BANCARIO. (IT/0026-9506). **799**

MONDO CINESE. (IT/0390-2811). **2507**

MONDO DEL LATTE, IL. (IT/0368-9123). **197**

MONDO E MISSIONE. (IT/0026-6094). **5032**

MONDO GIUDIZIARIO, IL. (IT). **Qty:** 30. **3011**

MONDO LADINO : BOLLETTINO DELL'ISTITUTO CULTURALE LADINO. (IT). **3304**

MONETARIA. (MX/0185-1136). **799**

MONEY AFFAIRS / CEMLA, CENTRE FOR LATIN AMERICAN MONETARY STUDIES. (MX). **1506**

MONEY DIGEST (BATH). (CN/0833-3432). **Qty:** 12. **907**

MONGOLIA SOCIETY NEWSLETTER (1985), THE. (US/0894-6523). **2659**

MONGOLIA SOCIETY OCCASIONAL PAPERS, THE. (US/0077-0396). **2659**

MONGOLIA SOCIETY SPECIAL PAPERS, THE. (US/0896-0925). **2659**

MONGOLIAN STUDIES. (US/0190-3667). **2659**

MONIST, THE. (US/0026-9662). **4353**

MONITEUR ARCHITECTURE AMC, LE. (FR/0998-4194). **303**

MONITOR. (US). **Qty:** 3-4. **2865**

MONITOR. (AT). **2073**

MONITOR (TRENTON, N.J.), THE. (US/0746-8350). **5710**

MONITORING TIMES. (US/0889-5341). **1135**

MONK (SAN FRANCISCO, CALIF.). (US/0899-6059). **4604**

MONOCLONAL ANTIBODIES. (UK/0261-4960). **3675**

MONOGRAPH: LEGAL AND ADMINISTRATIVE SERIES. (SZ). **3011**

MONOGRAPH (MAXWELL GRADUATE SCHOOL OF CITIZENSHIP AND PUBLIC AFFAIRS. METROPOLITAN STUDIES PROGRAM). (US/0738-3207). **4666**

MONOGRAPH / ONTARIO ASSOCIATION GEOGRAPHIC ENVIRONMENTAL EDUCATION, THE. (CN/0048-1793). **2569**

MONOGRAPH SERIES. (AT). **Qty:** 4. **2147**

MONOGRAPH SERIES - FACULTY OF COMMERCE AND BUSINESS ADMINISTRATION, UNIVERSITY OF BRITISH COLUMBIA. (CN/0572-6972). **696**

MONOGRAPH SERIES ON MINERAL DEPOSITS. (GW/0341-6356). **1442**

MONOGRAPH SERIES (UNIVERSITY OF CALIFORNIA, SAN DIEGO. CENTER FOR U.S.-MEXICAN STUDIES). (US). **2747**

MONOGRAPHIEN ZUR PHILOSOPHISCHEN FORSCHUNG. (GW). **4353**

MONOGRAPHS. (US). **29**

MONOGRAPHS OF THE HEBREW UNION COLLEGE. (US/0190-5627). **5051**

MONROE COUNTY GENEALOGICAL SOCIETY NEWS. (US/0893-5718). **2461**

MONROE EVENING TIMES (MONROE, WIS. 1898). (US/1068-5820). **Qty:** 12. **5769**

MONTAGNE ET ALPINISME, LA. (FR/0047-7923). **4875**

MONTAGUE'S MODERN BOTTLE IDENTIFICATION AND PRICE GUIDE. (US/0192-3900). **2592**

MONTANA. (US/0026-9891). **2747**

MONTANA OIL JOURNAL (1953). (US/0047-794X). **4264**

MONTANA OUTDOORS. (US/0027-0016). **4875**

MONTEREY LIFE. (US/0274-8770). **2539**

MONTESSORI NEWS / IMS. (US/0889-6720). **1765**

MONTESSORI OBSERVER / IMS, THE. (US/0889-5643). **1765**

MONTGOMERY ADVERTISER (1987), THE. (US/0892-4457). **5627**

MONTGOMERY COUNTY GENEALOGICAL SOCIETY QUARTERLY. (US/1041-777X). **2461**

MONTH AT UNESCO, THE. (FR/1014-9759). **4979**

MONTH (LONDON. 1882), THE. (UK/0027-0172). **4979**

MONTHLY COMMENTARY ON INDIAN ECONOMIC CONDITIONS. (II/0027-030X). **Qty:** 1-2. **1574**

MONTHLY INDICATORS OF CURRENT ECONOMIC SITUATION OF BANGLADESH. (BG). **1575**

MONTHLY INFORMATION REVIEW - BANQUE MAROCAINE DU COMMERCE EXTERIEUR. (MR/0851-0202). **846**

MONTHLY LABOR REVIEW. (US/0098-1818). **1691**

MONTHLY NEWSLETTER - INDIAN INVESTMENT CENTRE. (II/0019-4999). **907**

MONTHLY NOTES OF THE ASTRONOMICAL SOCIETY OF SOUTHERN AFRICA. (SA/0024-8266). **397**

MONTHLY OIL REPORT. (UK). **4264**

MONTHLY PUBLIC OPINION SURVEYS. (II). **Qty:** 1-2. **4482**

MONTHLY PUBLIC OPINION SURVEYS. (II/0537-1848). **2526**

MONTHLY RECORD OF THE FREE CHURCH OF SCOTLAND, THE. (UK). **5065**

MONTHLY REVIEW (NEW YORK. 1949). (US/0027-0520). **4543**

MONTHLY STATISTICAL BULLETIN. (MW). **5333**

MONTHLY STATISTICAL REPORT - AMERICAN PETROLEUM INSTITUTE. STATISTICS DEPT. (US). **4284**

MONTHLY WEATHER REVIEW. NORTHERN TERRITORY / COMMONWEALTH OF AUSTRALIA, BUREAU OF METEOROLOGY, DEPARTMENT OF THE INTERIOR. (AT). **1432**

MONTREAL CE MOIS-CI. (CN/0316-8530). **4852**

MONTREAL CUISINE. (CN/0823-2857). **5072**

MONTSERRAT CONSOLIDATED INDEX OF STATUTES AND SUBSIDIARY LEGISLATION TO 1ST JANUARY ... . (BB). **3132**

MONUMENTA ARCHAEOLOGICA (LOS ANGELES). (US/0363-7565). **275**

MONUMENTA GERMANIAE HISTORICA. (GW). **2699**

MONUMENTA MUSICAE SVECICAE / SVENSKA SAMFUNDET FOR MUSIKFORSKNING. (SW/0077-1473). **4132**

MONUMENTA NIPPONICA. (JA/0027-0741). **Qty:** 60. **2659**

MONUMENTA NIPPONICA MONOGRAPHS. (JA). **2507**

MONUMENTA SERICA. (GW/0254-9948). **2623**

MONUMENTS HISTORIQUES (1980). (FR/0242-830X). **304**

MOODY COURIER, THE. (US). **Qty:** 10. **5752**

MOODY STREET IRREGULARS. (US/0196-2604). **Qty:** 5-10. **3413**

MOOREA : THE JOURNAL OF THE IRISH GARDEN PLANT SOCIETY. (IE/0332-4273). **2424**

MOOREANA : JOURNAL OF THE PALMETUM. (AT/1037-1842). **Qty:** 3. **518**

MOP : GEBAEUDEUNTERHALT & REINIGUNG. (SZ). **621**

MORAL EDUCATION FORUM. (US/0163-6480). **1765**

MORALITY IN MEDIA INC. NEWSLETTER. (US/0027-1004). **3170**

MORAROJI KENKYU. (JA). **2252**

MORAVIAN (1989), THE. (US/1041-0961). **Qty:** 6-8. **4979**

MOREANA. (FR/0047-8105). **Qty:** 3. **3413**

MORICHES BAY TIDE. (US). **5718**

MORNING NEWS (BLACKFOOT, IDAHO), THE. (US/0893-3812). **Qty:** 1 per month. **5657**

MORNING NEWS (ERIE, PA.). (US). **Qty:** 20. **5737**

MORNING NEWS TRIBUNE. (US/1042-3621). **5761**

MORNING STAR, THE. (UK). **5812**

MOROCCO COURIER, THE. (US/1060-5231). **5665**

MORRELL, MORRILL FAMILIES ASSOCIATION NEWSLETTER. (US/0889-7247). **2461**

MORTGAGE BANKING. (US/0730-0212). **800**

MORTON TRIBUNE. (US). **Qty:** 10. **5752**

MORTUARY MANAGEMENT. (US/0027-1268). **2407**

MOSCOSOA : CONTRIBUCIONES CIENTIFICAS DEL JARDIN BOTANICO NACIONAL "DR. RAFAEL M. MOSCOSO". (DR/0254-6442). **518**

MOSCOW NEWS. (RU/0027-1306). **5809**

MOSELLA. (FR). **2569**

MOSKVA. (RU/0131-2332). **3413**

MOSQUITO SYSTEMATICS. (US/0091-3669). **2177**

MOSSBAUER EFFECT REFERENCE AND DATA JOURNAL. (US/0163-9587). **4426**

MOSSBAUER HANDBOOK. (US/0272-2755). **1012**

MOTHER & CHILD (LAHORE). (PK/0379-2617). **2283**

MOTHERING. (US/0733-3013). **2283**

MOTHEROOT JOURNAL. (US/0739-5272). **4830**

MOTIF (COLUMBUS, OHIO). (US/0278-2286). **2322**

MOTOR. (NE). **4082**

MOTOR COACH AGE. (US/0739-117X). **5387**

MOTOR INDUSTRY JOURNAL. (AT/0729-0799). **5420**

MOTOR ITALIA. (IT). **5420**

MOTORCYCLE DRAG RACING. (US/0883-7228). **Qty:** 2. **4082**

MOTORCYCLE INDUSTRY MAGAZINE : MI. (US/0884-626X). **4082**

MOTORCYCLE TOURING. (US/1041-5734). **5485**

MOTORCYCLIST'S POST, THE. (US/0164-9256). **5387**

MOTORIK. (GW/0170-5792). **4792**

MOTORSPORTS MARKETING NEWS. (US). **Qty:** 12. **762**

MOTS. (FR/0243-6450). **4482**

MOULTRIE COUNTY HERITAGE. (US/8756-0836). **2461**

MOUNTAIN ADVOCATE (BARBOURVILLE, KY.). (US). **Qty:** 5. **5681**

MOUNTAIN CITIZEN. (US). **2490**

MOUNTAIN EMPIRE GENEALOGICAL QUARTERLY, THE. (US/0882-4266). **2461**

MOUNTAIN RECORD. (US/0896-8942). **5021**

MOUNTAIN RESEARCH AND DEVELOPMENT. (US/0276-4741). **241**

MOUNTAINEER (SEATTLE, WASH.). (US/0027-2620). **Qty:** 3-4. **4875**

MOUTH. (US/1071-5657). **4391**

MOUVEMENT SOCIAL, LE. (FR/0027-2671). **2623**

MOUVEMENTS. (CN/0823-5651). **1691**

MOVEMENT AND DANCE : MAGAZINE OF THE LABAN GUILD. (UK). **Qty:** 4. **1314**

MOVEMENT THEATRE QUARTERLY. (US/1065-1519). **Qty:** 4-5. **5366**

MOVIE COLLECTOR'S WORLD. (US/8750-5401). **Qty:** 100. **2775**

MOVIE (LONDON). (UK/0027-268X). **4075**

MOVIE/TV MARKETING. (JA). **933**

MOVIELINE (LOS ANGELES, CALIF.). (US/1055-0917). **Qty:** 11 per year. **4075**

MOVIMENTO. (IT). **4604**

MOVING FORWARD : THE NATIONAL NEWSPAPER FOR PEOPLE WITH DISABILITIES. (US/1056-7240). **4391**

MOVING IMAGE REVIEW. (US/0897-0769). **4075**

MOVING OUT. (US). **3413**

MOVOZNAVSTVO (KIEV). (RU/0027-2833). **3304**

MOYEN FRANCAIS. (CN/0226-0174). **Qty:** 15. **3413**

MOZNAYIM. (IS/0027-2892). **3413**

MPG SPIEGEL. (GW/0341-7727). **5130**

MPLA NEWSLETTER (1975). (US/0145-6180). **3232**

MR. COGITO. (US/0740-1205). **Qty:** 1-3. **3466**

MRAX INFORMATION. (BE/0024-8320). **Qty:** 5-6. **5209**

MRS BULLETIN. (US/0883-7694). **2107**

MS BIBLIOTEKSNYT. (DK). **4529**

MS CANADA. (CN/0315-1131). **Qty:** 1-2. **3838**

MS QUARTERLY REPORT. (US/0738-3967). **3838**

MS. TREE. (US/0826-2586). **5074**

MSOS JOURNAL. (CN/0831-3040). **Qty:** 15. **5180**

MSRRT NEWSLETTER. (US). **3232**

MT. STERLING ADVOCATE, THE. (US). **5681**

MTA. PEDIATRIA. (SP/0210-8135). **3906**

MUCCHIO SELVAGGIO, IL. (IT). **4132**

MUEHLE + MISCHFUTTERTECHNIK, DIE. (GW/0027-2949). **203**

MUEMLEKVEDELEM. (HU/0541-2439). **275**

MUENCHENER THEOLOGISCHE ZEITSCHRIFT. (GW/0580-1400). **5032**

MUFON UFO JOURNAL, THE. (US/0270-6822). **29**

MUGENDAI. (JA). **2851**

MUIR'S ORIGINAL LOG HOME GUIDE FOR BUILDERS AND BUYERS. (US/0844-3459). **621**

MUJTAMA AL-BATRUL. (TS). **4265**

MULBERRY PRESS. (US). Qty: 20. **5650**

MULIKA. (TZ). **3413**

MULLENS ADVOCATE, THE. (US/1064-6132). Qty: 6. **5764**

MULLMAGAZIN. (GW/0934-3482). Qty: 5. **2236**

MULTI MEDIA BIRDS OF AMERICA. CD-ROM. (US). **5618**

MULTI-MEDIA COMPUTING. (NE/0923-8182). **1196**

MULTICHANNEL NEWS. (US/0276-8593). **1135**

MULTICULTURAL EDUCATION ABSTRACTS. (UK/0260-9770). **1795**

MULTICULTURAL EDUCATION JOURNAL. (CN/0823-6283). **1765**

MULTICULTURAL EDUCATION REVIEW. (AT/1033-6281). **1765**

MULTICULTURAL REVIEW. (US/1058-9236). **2268**

MULTIHULL INTERNATIONAL. (UK). **1988**

MULTIHULLS. (US/0749-4122). **4905**

MULTIMIND. (UK). **1901**

MULTINATIONAL EMPLOYER. (UK/0953-7929). Qty: 10-15. **944**

MULTINATIONAL EXECUTIVE TRAVEL COMPANION. (US/0093-7487). Qty: 4-8. **5485**

MULTINATIONAL MONITOR. (US/0197-4637). **846**

MULTISTATE TAX ANALYST. (US/0892-4678). **4738**

MULTISTATE TAX COMMISSION REVIEW. (US). **4738**

MULTIVARIATE EXPERIMENTAL CLINICAL RESEARCH. (US/0147-3964). **4605**

MUNCHNER ZEITSCHRIFT FUER BALKANKUNDE. (GW/0170-8929). **2699**

MUNDO CRISTIANO. (SP/0027-3252). **5032**

MUNDO EJECUTIVO. (MX). Qty: 36. **800**

MUNDO FINANCIERO. (SP/0300-3884). **1506**

MUNDO HISPANICO (ATLANTA, GA.). (US/1051-4147). **5654**

MUNDO NUEVO. (VE/0379-6922). **4529**

MUNICIPAL FINANCE JOURNAL. (US/0199-6134). **4738**

MUNICIPAL REVIEW & AMA NEWS. (UK/0027-3562). **4667**

MUNICIPAL WORLD. (CN/0027-3589). **879**

MUNICIPALITY (1916), THE. (US/0027-3597). **4667**

MUNSTER (MUNCHEN), DAS. (GW/0027-299X). Qty: 20. **359**

MUNSTERS & THE ADDAMS FAMILY REUNION, THE. (US). **1135**

MUNZEN REVUE. (SZ). **2782**

MURRAY LEDGER & TIMES, THE. (US). **5681**

MUSCOGIANA (COLUMBUS, GA.). (US/1042-3419). **2461**

MUSE. ARTS AND ENTERTAINMENT IN CANBERRA. (AT/0158-9571). Qty: varies. **359**

MUSE (OTTAWA). (CN/0820-0165). **4091**

MUSEES. (CN/0706-098X). Qty: 24. **4091**

MUSEES ET COLLETIONS PUBLIQUES DE FRANCE. (FR/0027-383X). Qty: 4. **4091**

MUSEON, LE. (BE/0771-6494). **420**

MUSEUM (BRAUNSCHWEIG). (GW/0341-8634). **4092**

MUSEUM HELVETICUM. (SZ/0027-4054). **275**

MUSEUM NEWS (WASHINGTON). (US/0027-4089). **4092**

MUSEUM OF CALIFORNIA, THE. (US). Qty: 4. **4092**

MUSEUMS AND ART GALLERIES IN GREAT BRITAIN AND IRELAND. (UK/0141-6723). **4093**

MUSEUMS JOURNAL. (UK/0027-416X). **4093**

MUSEUMSKUNDE. (GW/0027-4178). **4093**

MUSHING (ESTER, ALASKA). (US/0895-9668). Qty: 4. **4905**

MUSHIR (RAWALPINDI, PAKISTAN). (PK). Qty: varies. **4979**

MUSHROOM (MOSCOW, IDAHO). (US/0740-8161). **575**

MUSIC ANALYSIS. (UK). **4132**

MUSIC & AUTOMATA. (UK/0262-8260). **4132**

MUSIC & LETTERS. (UK/0027-4224). **4132**

MUSIC AND LITURGY. (UK/0305-4438). Qty: 15/yr. **4133**

MUSIC AND THE TEACHER. (AT/0047-8431). Qty: 12. **4133**

MUSIC BOX, THE. (UK). **4133**

MUSIC CLUBS MAGAZINE (1963). (US/0161-2654). **4133**

MUSIC EDUCATORS JOURNAL. (US/0027-4321). **4133**

MUSIC FOR THE LOVE OF IT. (US/0898-8757). Qty: 3-4. **4133**

MUSIC FROM CHINA NEWSLETTER. (US/1071-2801). Qty: 2. **4133**

MUSIC HALL. (UK). **4133**

MUSIC-IN-PRINT SERIES. (US/0146-7883). **4133**

MUSIC LEADER, THE. (US/0027-4372). **4134**

MUSIC NEWS FROM PRAGUE. (XR/0027-4410). **4134**

MUSIC OF THE SPHERES. (US/0892-2721). **4186**

MUSIC PERCEPTION. (US/0730-7829). **4134**

MUSIC REFERENCE SERVICES QUARTERLY. (US/1058-8167). **4134**

MUSIC RESEARCHER'S EXCHANGE, THE. (US/0271-5163). **4134**

MUSIC REVELATION. (US/0882-8229). Qty: varies. **4134**

MUSIC REVIEW, THE. (UK/0027-4445). **4134**

MUSIC ROW. (US/0745-5054). **4135**

MUSIC SCENE (DIETIKON, SWITZERLAND). (SZ). **4135**

MUSIC TEACHER. (UK/0027-4461). **4135**

MUSIC TECHNOLOGY (ELY). (UK/0957-6606). **4135**

MUSIC THEORY SPECTRUM. (US/0195-6167). **4135**

MUSICA. (IT). **4135**

MUSICA DISCIPLINA. (IT/0077-2461). **4135**

MUSICA DOMANI : ORGANO DELLA SOCIETA ITALIANA PER L'EDUCAZIONE MUSICALE. (IT/0391-4380). Qty: 10. **4135**

MUSICA JUDAICA. (US/0147-7536). **4136**

MUSICA (ROME, ITALY : 1985). (IT). **4136**

MUSICAE SACRAE MINISTERIUM (ROME). (IT). **4136**

MUSICAL AMERICA (1987). (US/1042-3443). **4136**

MUSICAL OPINION. (UK/0027-4623). Qty: 25-30. **4136**

MUSICAL QUARTERLY, THE. (US/0027-4631). **4136**

MUSICAL TIMES (LONDON, ENGLAND : 1957). (UK/0027-4666). **4136**

MUSICIAN (GLOUCESTER, MASS.). (US/0733-5253). **4137**

MUSICK. (CN/0226-8620). **4137**

MUSICOLOGICAL STUDIES & DOCUMENTS. (GW/0077-2496). **4137**

MUSICOLOGY AUSTRALIA. (AT/0814-5857). **4137**

MUSICWORKS. (CN/0225-686X). **4137**

MUSIK IN BAYERN : HALBJAHRESSCHRIFT DER GESELLSCHAFT FUER BAYERISCHE MUSIKGESCHICHTE E.V. (GW). **4137**

MUSIK UND BILDUNG. (GW/0027-4747). **4138**

MUSIK UND GOTTESDIENST. (SZ/1015-6798). **4138**

MUSIK UND KIRCHE. (GW/0027-4771). **4138**

MUSIKFORSCHUNG. (GW/0027-4801). **4138**

MUSIKINSTRUMENT, DAS. (GW/0027-4828). **4138**

MUSIKREVY. (SW/0027-4844). **4138**

MUSIKTHEORIE. (GW/0177-4182). **4138**

MUSIKTHERAPEUTISCHE UMSCHAU. (GW/0172-5505). **4138**

MUSIKWISSENSCHAFTLICHE STUDIENBIBLIOTHEK. (GW). **4138**

MUSIL-FORUM. (GW). **3414**

MUSK-OX, THE. (CN/0077-2542). **2569**

MUSKOGEE DAILY PHOENIX AND TIMES-DEMOCRAT. (US). **5732**

MUSKY HUNTER MAGAZINE. (US/1041-6366). Qty: 30. **4875**

MUSLIM EDUCATION QUARTERLY. (UK/0267-615X). **1765**

MUSLIM JOURNAL. (US/0883-816X). **5044**

MUSLIM SCIENTIST. (US/0148-0995). **5210**

MUSLIM WORLD BOOK REVIEW, THE. (UK/0260-3063). **5044**

MUSLIM WORLD (HARTFORD), THE. (US/0027-4909). **5044**

MUSLIM WORLD LEAGUE JOURNAL, THE. (SU). **5044**

MUSTANG!. (US/1043-2590). **2801**

MUSTANG TIMES. (US/0744-2572). **5421**

MUSU ZINIOS. (US). **4979**

MUTABLE DILEMMA, THE. (US/0892-5429). **4242**

MUTAGENESIS. (UK/0267-8357). **549**

MUTANTIA : ZONA DE LUCIDEZ IMPLACABLE. (AG). **5252**

MUTATION BREEDING NEWSLETTER. (AU). **110**

MUTTERSPRACHE (WIESBADEN). (GW/0027-514X). Qty: 40. **3304**

MUTUAL AID. (US/0734-9998). **4792**

MUTUAL FUND FACT BOOK. (US/0077-2550). **908**

MUTUAL FUNDS MAGAZINE. (US). **909**

MUVESZETTORTENETI ERTESITO. (HU/0027-5247). **325**

MUZIEK & DANS. (NE/0166-0535). **4139**

MUZSIKA. (HU/0027-5336). **4139**

MUZZLE BLASTS. (US). **4905**

MUZZLELOADER, THE. (US/0274-5720). Qty: 18. **4905**

MVS UPDATE. (UK). **1280**

MY FRIEND. (US/0164-3568). **1066**

MYCOLOGIA. (US/0027-5514). **575**

MYCOLOGICAL RESEARCH. (UK/0953-7562). **575**

MYCOLOGIST, THE. (UK/0269-915X). **576**

MYCOLOGY SERIES. (US/0730-9597). **576**

MYCOTAXON. (US/0093-4666). **518**

MYCOTOXIN RESEARCH. (GW/0178-7888). **519**

MYOTIS. (GW/0580-3896). **5592**

MYRTLE BEACH JOURNAL, THE. (US/0745-8584). **5637**

MYSTERY NEWS. (US/0734-9076). Qty: 420. **3348**

MYSTERY READERS JOURNAL. (US/1043-3473). **3414**

MYSTERY REVIEW, THE. (CN/1192-8700). Qty: 12. **3414**

MYSTICS QUARTERLY (IOWA CITY, IOWA). (US/0742-5503). **3414**

MYSTIQUE (TORONTO). (CN/0710-1988). **5188**

MYTHLORE. (US/0146-9339). **3414**

MYTHPRINT. (US/0146-9347). **3414**

N.A.C.W.P.I JOURNAL. (US/0027-576X). Qty: 4. **4139**

N.A.V.A. NEWS. (US). **2623**

N & M. NATUR OG MILJ. (NO/0802-4618). **2198**

N. B. NATURALIST. (CN/0047-9551). **4168**

N.C. ... ANNUAL REPORT OF HAZARDOUS WASTE GENERATED, STORED, TREATED OR DISPOSED. (US). **2237**

N.P.N. MEDECINE. (FR/0248-9635). **3618**

N.R.S., LA NOUVELLE REVUE SOCIALISTE. (FR). **4543**

N.Y. HABITAT. (US/0745-0893). **4841**

NAAMAT. (IS). **5562**

NAAMKUNDE. (NE/0167-5257). **3304**

NAATI NEWS. (AT/1031-5411). **3304**

NAAWP NEWS : PUBLICATION OF THE NATIONAL ASSOCIATION FOR THE ADVANCEMENT OF WHITE PEOPLE. (US). **5684**

NABE NEWS (CLEVELAND, OHIO). (US/0745-3205). **1506**

NACADA JOURNAL / NATIONAL ACADEMIC ADVISING ASSOCIATION. (US/0271-9517). **1836**

NACHRICHTEN AUS DEM OFFENTLICHEN VERMESSUNGSDIENST NORDRHEIN-WESTFALEN. (GW). Qty: 5. **2027**

NACHRICHTEN AUS NIEDERSACHSENS URGESCHICHTE. (GW). **275**

NACHRICHTEN DER GESELLSCHAFT FUER NATUR- UND VOLKERKUNDE OSTASIENS/HAMBURG. (GW/0016-9080). **2623**

NACHRICHTEN DER NIEDERSACHSISCHEN VERMESSUNGS- UND KATASTERVERWALTUNG. (GW). **2582**

NACHRICHTEN FUER DOKUMENTATION. (GW/0027-7436). **3232**

NACHRICHTENDIENST. (GW/0012-1185). Qty: 20. **5297**

NACOI FORUM. (CN/0708-5249). **2268**

NACTA JOURNAL. (US/0149-4910). **110**

NAE WASHINGTON INSIGHT (NEWSLETTER ED.). (US/0199-3038). **4979**

NAEA NEWS. (US/0160-6395). **359**

NAFTILIAKI. (GR). **5453**

NAGA, THE ICLARM QUARTERLY. (PH/0116-290X). **2308**

NAGOYA MEDICAL JOURNAL. (JA/0027-7649). **3618**

NAHNU AL-ARAB. (UA). **2507**

NAHRO ROSTER. (US/0363-6453). **2829**

NAIKA. (JA/0547-1729). **3800**

NAMAH-I DANISHKADAH-I DAMPIZISHKI. (IR/0042-0123). **5516**

NAMES. (US/0027-7738). Qty: 6-8. **2461**

NAMIBIA ABSTRACTS. (ZA). **4482**

NAMIBIANA. (SX/0259-2010). **2642**

NAN KAI SHIH HSUEH / NAN KAI TA HSUEH LI SHIH HSI HSUEH SHU WEI YUAN HUI. (CC). **2623**

NANJING HANGKONG XUEYUAN XUEBAO. (CC/1000-1956). **29**

NANNY TIMES. (US). **2283**

NANTUCKET JOURNAL (NANTUCKET, MASS. 1987). (US/1056-2265). Qty: 3. **2747**

NANZAN REVIEW OF AMERICAN STUDIES : A JOURNAL OF CENTER FOR AMERICAN STUDIES, NANZAN UNIVERSITY. (JA). **5210**

NAOS (ENGLISH ED.). (US/0889-342X). Qty: 20. **3304**

NAPA COUNTY RECORD AND NAPA VALLEY NEWS. (US/0744-6942). Qty: 13. **5637**

NAPSAC NEWS. (US/0192-1223). **589**

NARC OFFICER, THE. (US/0889-7794). **3170**

NARF LEGAL REVIEW, THE. (US/0739-862X). **3013**

NAROD POLSKI. (US/0027-7894). **5032**

NARODNA TVORCHIST TA ETNOGRAFIIA. (UN/0130-6936). **374**

NARODNO ZEMEDELSKO ZNAME. (US/8755-9706). **4482**

NARROW GAUGE AND SHORT LINE GAZETTE. (US/0148-2122). Qty: 15. **5433**

NASA TECH BRIEFS (WASHINGTON, D.C. 1976). (US/0145-319X). **5130**

NASE DEJINY. (US/0745-239X). **2461**

NASE REC. (XR/0027-8203). **3305**

NASE RODINA (SAINT PAUL, MINN.). (US/1045-8190). Qty: 8. **2461**

NASFAA NEWSLETTER. (US/0882-4630). **1866**

NASH & CIBINIC REPORT, THE. (US/0891-9291). **4668**

NASH NOTATIONS. (US/8756-4726). **2461**

NASHR-I DANISH. (IR/0259-9090). **5044**

NASHRAT MAHAD SHUUN AL-AQALLIYAT AL-MUSLIMAH, JAMIAT AL-MALIK ABD AL-AZIZ BI-JIDDAH. (SU). **5044**

NASHUA REPORTER AND WEEKLY NASHUA POST, THE. (US). **5672**

NASHVILLE BUSINESS JOURNAL. (US/0889-2873). Qty: 10. **696**

NASSA NEWS. (US/8756-0925). **325**

NASSAUISCHE ANNALEN. (GW/0077-2887). **2700**

NASTAWGAN. (CN/0828-1327). Qty: 12. **594**

NATAT'S REPORTER. (US/0735-9691). Qty: 10. **4668**

NATCHEZ TRACE TRAVELER. (US/0738-985X). **2461**

NATCHITOCHES GENEALOGIST, THE. (US/0742-5872). **2461**

NATHANIEL HAWTHORNE REVIEW : THE OFFICIAL PUBLICATION OF THE NATHANIEL HAWTHORNE SOCIETY, THE. (US/0890-4197). Qty: 4. **3348**

NATION (NEW YORK, N.Y.), THE. (US/0027-8378). **3348**

NATIONAL ACADEMY SCIENCE LETTERS. (II/0250-541X). **5130**

NATIONAL AQUATICS JOURNAL. (US). **4906**

NATIONAL ASSOCIATION FOR OLMSTED PARKS. (US/0895-819X). **4707**

NATIONAL ASSOCIATION OF CONSUMER AGENCY ADMINISTRATORS NEWS. (US/0270-2835). **1298**

NATIONAL ASSOCIATION OF HOME AND WORKSHOP WRITERS NEWSLETTER. (US). Qty: 5. **634**

NATIONAL BANKING LAW REVIEW. (CN/0822-1081). **3087**

NATIONAL BANKRUPTCY REPORTER. (US/0275-0252). **3087**

NATIONAL BAR ASSOCIATION MAGAZINE. (US/0741-0115). **3013**

NATIONAL BAR BULLETIN, THE. (US). **3013**

NATIONAL BLACK LAW JOURNAL. (US/0896-0194). **3013**

NATIONAL BUILDER (LONDON). (UK/0027-8807). **621**

NATIONAL BULLETIN OF LITURGY. (CN/0084-8425). **4980**

NATIONAL BUS TRADER. (US/0194-939X). Qty: 1-2. **5388**

NATIONAL BUSINESS REVIEW. (NZ/0110-6813). **697**

NATIONAL BUTTON BULLETIN, THE. (US/0027-884X). **2775**

NATIONAL CATHOLIC REGISTER. (US/0027-8920). **5032**

NATIONAL CATHOLIC REPORTER. (US/0027-8939). **5033**

NATIONAL CHRISTIAN REPORTER, THE. (US/0279-8913). **4980**

NATIONAL CIVIC REVIEW. (US/0027-9013). **4668**

NATIONAL CULINARY REVIEW, THE. (US/0747-7716). Qty: 6-12. **2350**

NATIONAL DEFENSE (WASHINGTON). (US/0092-1491). **4052**

NATIONAL DENTAL ASSOCIATION JOURNAL. (US/1050-530X). **1330**

NATIONAL DIRECTORY OF AIDS CARE. (US). **4792**

NATIONAL DIRECTORY OF BULLETIN BOARD SYSTEMS. (US/0884-9536). **1196**

NATIONAL DIRECTORY OF LOCAL RESEARCHERS. (US/0742-9045). **2462**

NATIONAL DIRECTORY OF WOMEN-OWNED BUSINESS FIRMS. (US/0886-389X). **697**

NATIONAL DRAGSTER. (US/0466-2199). **4906**

NATIONAL EDUCATOR, THE. (US/0739-1617). Qty: 12. **5637**

NATIONAL EMPLOYMENT LISTING SERVICE FOR HUMAN SERVICES. (US/0194-0775). **1692**

NATIONAL ENGINEER, THE. (US/0027-9218). **1988**

NATIONAL ENVIRONMENTAL ENFORCEMENT JOURNAL. (US). **3114**

NATIONAL FIRE & ARSON REPORT, THE. (US/1064-4814). **3170**

NATIONAL FISHERMAN. (US/0027-9250). **2309**

NATIONAL FLUORIDATION NEWS. (US/0027-9269). **3982**

NATIONAL FORENSIC JOURNAL. (US/0749-1042). **3742**

NATIONAL FORUM (ANN ARBOR). (US/0162-1831). Qty: 16-20. **1836**

NATIONAL FORUM OF APPLIED EDUCATIONAL RESEARCH JOURNAL. (US/0895-3880). **1867**

NATIONAL FORUM OF EDUCATIONAL ADMINISTRATION AND SUPERVISION JOURNAL. (US/0888-8132). **1766**

NATIONAL FORUM OF SPECIAL EDUCATION JOURNAL. (US/1043-2167). Qty: 12,000. **1882**

NATIONAL GALLERY TECHNICAL BULLETIN. (UK/0140-7430). **359**

NATIONAL GENEALOGICAL SOCIETY QUARTERLY. (US/0027-934X). **2462**

NATIONAL GEOGRAPHICAL JOURNAL OF INDIA, THE. (II/0027-9374). Qty: 20-25. **2570**

NATIONAL GREENHOUSE GARDENER. (US/0883-8313). **2425**

NATIONAL GUARD ALMANAC. (US/0363-8618). **4052**

NATIONAL HISPANIC JOURNAL. (US/0734-9920). **2268**

NATIONAL HIV/AIDS LEGAL LINK NEWSLETTER. (AT/1037-6615). **3013**

NATIONAL INSOLVENCY REVIEW. (CN/0822-2584). **3087**

NATIONAL INSTITUTE OF ARTS AND LETTERS, AMERICAN ACADEMY OF ARTS AND LETTERS. (US). **325**

NATIONAL INTEREST, THE. (US/0884-9382). **4529**

NATIONAL JAIL AND ADULT DETENTION DIRECTORY. (US/0192-8228). **3170**

NATIONAL JEWISH POST & OPINION (INDIANAPOLIS, INC. : 1984). (US/0888-0379). Qty: 10. **5665**

NATIONAL JOB MARKET. (US/0747-4296). **4206**

NATIONAL JOURNAL OF SOCIOLOGY. (US/0892-4287). Qty: approx. 4. **5252**

NATIONAL KNIFE MAGAZINE, THE. (US/1051-4600). **2775**

NATIONAL LIBRARIAN : THE NLA NEWSLETTER. (US/0191-359X). **3233**

NATIONAL MINORITY POLITICS. (US/1057-1655). Qty: 6. **2268**

NATIONAL MONTHLY CONDOMINIUM EXECUTIVE REPORT. (US/0739-5647). **4841**

NATIONAL MOTORIST. (US/0279-3083). Qty: 10. **5485**

NATIONAL NETWORK NEWS. (CN/1181-8107). Qty: varies. **4052**

NATIONAL NEWS - NATIONAL PENSIONERS AND SENIOR CITIZENS FEDERATION. (CN/0849-2115). **5180**

NATIONAL NEWSLETTER - ASSOCIATION OF PART-TIME PROFESSIONALS (U.S.). (US/0739-2931). **4206**

NATIONAL NEWSPAPER ASSOCIATION DIRECTORY. (US/0147-7528). **4817**

NATIONAL NOTARY, THE. (US/0894-7872). **4668**

NATIONAL NOW TIMES. (US/0149-4740). **5582**

NATIONAL ON-CAMPUS REPORT. (US/0300-6646). **1836**

NATIONAL (OTTAWA). (CN/0315-2286). **3013**

NATIONAL (OTTAWA. 1978). (CN/0709-1370). Qty: 2 or 3. **1882**

NATIONAL PACKING NEWS. (US/1073-6948). **2351**

NATIONAL PALACE MUSEUM BULLETIN. (CH/0027-9846). **4093**

NATIONAL PARALEGAL REPORTER. (US/1058-482X). **3014**

NATIONAL PARK GUIDE (NEW YORK, N.Y.). (US/0734-7960). **4707**

NATIONAL PARKS JOURNAL. (AT/0047-9012). Qty: 12. **2198**

NATIONAL PARKS (WASHINGTON, D.C.). (US/0276-8186). **4707**

NATIONAL PASTIME, THE. (US/0734-6905). **4906**

NATIONAL PETROLEUM NEWS. (US/0149-5267). **4265**

NATIONAL POLITICAL SCIENCE REVIEW. (US/0896-629X). **4483**

NATIONAL PRISON PROJECT JOURNAL, THE. (US/1076-769X). Qty: 1. **3170**

NATIONAL PRODUCTIVITY REVIEW. (US/0277-8556). **880**

NATIONAL PUBLIC ACCOUNTANT (1957), THE. (US/0027-9978). **748**

NATIONAL RADIO PUBLICITY DIRECTORY. (US/0276-4520). **1135**

NATIONAL RAILWAYS OF ZIMBABWE. (RH). **5433**

NATIONAL REPORT FOR TRAINING AND DEVELOPMENT. (US/0749-9884). **880**

NATIONAL REVIEW (NEW YORK). (US/0028-0038). **4483**

NATIONAL RIGHT TO LIFE NEWS. (US/0164-7415). **589**

NATIONAL SERVICE NEWSLETTER. (US/1059-4922). **5297**

NATIONAL SPEED SPORT NEWS. (US/0028-0208). **4906**

NATIONAL SQUARE DANCE DIRECTORY. (US/0196-0040). **1314**

NATIONAL STAMPAGRAPHIC. (US/0747-5527). Qty: 2-3. **381**

NATIONAL STOCK DOG MAGAZINE. (US/0028-0267). **4287**

NATIONAL STRENGTH & CONDITIONING ASSOCIATION JOURNAL. (US/0744-0049). **1857**

NATIONAL TECHNICAL INSTITUTIE FOR THE DEAF FOCUS. (US/0739-9278). **Qty:** 2. **4391**

NATIONAL TOMBSTONE EPITAPH, THE. (US/0890-068X). **2747**

NATIONAL TRIAL LAWYER (FLORIDA ED.). (US/1066-7733). **3014**

NATIONAL TRIAL LAWYER (NATIONAL ED.). (US/1049-684X). **3014**

NATIONAL TRIAL LAWYER (NEW YORK ED.). (US/1060-9210). **3014**

NATIONAL UTILITY CONTRACTOR, THE. (US/0192-0359). **622**

NATIONAL VANGUARD. (US/0897-4012). **5252**

NATIONAL WEATHER DIGEST. (US/0271-1052). **1432**

NATIONAL WETLANDS NEWSLETTER. (US/0164-0712). **3114**

NATIONAL WOMEN'S HEALTH REPORT. (US/0741-9147). **Qty:** 12/yr. **4792**

NATIONAL WOODLANDS. (US/0279-9812). **2388**

NATIONALITIES PAPERS. (US/0090-5992). **2268**

NATIONS AND NATIONALISM. (UK/1354-5078). **4483**

NATION'S BUSINESS. (US/0028-047X). **697**

NATION'S CITIES WEEKLY. (US/0164-5935). **Qty:** varies. **4668**

NATION'S HEALTH (1971), THE. (US/0028-0496). **4792**

NATIVE NEVADAN, THE. (US/0028-0534). **2539**

NATIVE PEOPLES. (US/0895-7606). **Qty:** 10. **2747**

NATIVE STUDIES REVIEW. (CN/0831-585X). **2268**

NATIVE VOICE. (CN/0028-0542). **Qty:** 5. **2539**

NATO MUTUAL SUPPORT ACT, AS AMENDED (ACQUISITION AND CROSS SERVICING AGREEMENTS WITH NATO ALLIES AND OTHER COUNTRIES); REPORT OF AGREEMENTS AND TRANSACTIONS / DEPARTMENT OF DEFENSE. (US). **Qty:** 4. **4052**

NATUR + I.E. UND RECHT. (GW). **3114**

NATUR-UND GANZHEITSMEDIZIN : NGM. (GW/0934-7909). **3619**

NATUR UND LAND. (AU/0028-0607). **2178**

NATUR UND MUSEUM (FRANKFURT AM MAIN : 1962). (GW/0028-1301). **4168**

NATURA. (NE/0028-0631). **4168**

NATURA & MED. (GW/0931-1513). **3775**

NATURAL AREAS JOURNAL. (US/0885-8608). **Qty:** 6-16. **2199**

NATURAL FOODS MERCHANDISER. (US/0164-338X). **2351**

NATURAL GAS WEEK. (US/8756-3037). **4266**

NATURAL HAZARDS OBSERVER. (US/0193-8355). **1358**

NATURAL HISTORY. (US/0028-0712). **4168**

NATURAL HISTORY BOOK REVIEWS. (UK). **4174**

NATURAL LANGUAGE AND LINGUISTIC THEORY. (NE/0167-806X). **3305**

NATURAL LIFE MAGAZINE. (CN/0830-0887). **4194**

NATURAL LIFE (UNIONVILLE. 1991). (CN/0701-8002). **Qty:** 50. **2600**

NATURAL RESOURCES FORUM. (NE/0165-0203). **2199**

NATURAL RESOURCES FORUM LIBRARY. (NE/0167-4110). **2199**

NATURAL RESOURCES JOURNAL. (US/0028-0739). **3115**

NATURAL STONE DIRECTORY : DIMENSION STONE SOURCES FOR BRITAIN AND IRELAND. (UK). **Qty:** 10-20. **622**

NATURALEZA Y GRACIA. (SP/0470-3790). **4980**

NATURALIST (LEEDS). (UK/0028-0771). **4168**

NATURALIST REVIEW. (US/0888-6547). **2199**

NATURALIST (TRINIDAD AND TOBAGO). (TR). **4168**

NATURALISTE CANADIEN, LE. (CN/0028-0798). **2219**

NATURE CANADA. (CN/0374-9894). **2199**

NATURE (LONDON). (UK/0028-0836). **5131**

NATURE NORTHWEST. (CN/0836-4702). **4169**

NATURE NOTEBOOK. (US). **466**

NATURE, SOCIETY, AND THOUGHT. (US/0890-6130). **Qty:** 10. **5210**

NATURE SOCIETY NEWS. (US/0890-3735). **Qty:** 12-24. **5592**

NATUREN. (NO/0028-0887). **5131**

NATUREN. (NO). **5131**

NATURENS VERDEN. (DK/0028-0895). **5131**

NATUROPATHIC PHYSICIAN / THE AMERICAN ASSOCIATION OF NATUROPATHIC PHYSICIANS, THE. (US). **Qty:** 8-12. **3619**

NATURWISSENSCHAFTEN, DIE. (GW/0028-1042). **5131**

NATUUR EN TECHNIEK. (NE/0028-1093). **5131**

NATUURHISTORISCH MAANBLAD : ORGAAN VAN HET NATUURHISTORISCH GENOOTSCHAP IN LIMBURG. (NE). **4169**

NATUURWETENSCHAPPELIJK TIJDSCHRIFT. (BE/0770-1748). **4169**

NAUTICA. (IT/0392-369X). **4179**

NAUTICAL BRASS, ETC. (US). **Qty:** 12. **4179**

NAUTICAL MAGAZINE. (UK/0028-1336). **4179**

NAUTICAL RESEARCH JOURNAL. (US/0738-7245). **4179**

NAVA NEWS / NORTH AMERICAN VEXILLOLOGICAL ASSOCIATION. (US/1053-3338). **Qty:** varies. **2623**

NAVAJO NATION MESSENGER, THE. (US). **5712**

NAVAL AFFAIRS. (US/0028-1409). **4179**

NAVAL ARCHITECT, THE. (UK/0306-0209). **5453**

NAVAL HISTORY. (US/1042-1920). **4180**

NAVAL LAW REVIEW. (US/1049-0272). **3183**

NAVAL REVIEW. (UK). **Qty:** 50. **4180**

NAVAL STORES REVIEW (1979). (US/0164-4580). **2403**

NAVAL WAR COLLEGE REVIEW. (US/0028-1484). **4180**

NAVALAKATHA. (II/0028-1492). **3414**

NAVIGATION (PARIS). (FR/0028-1530). **4180**

NAVIGATION (WASHINGTON). (US/0028-1522). **4180**

NAVIRES, PORTS & CHANTIERS. (FR/0028-159X). **4180**

NAVY INTERNATIONAL. (UK/0144-3194). **4180**

NAVY NEWS. (US/0028-1670). **5759**

NAVY TIMES. (US/0028-1697). **4180**

NAZARETH (COMBERMERE). (CN/1183-1863). **Qty:** 10-12. **5033**

NCAA BASKETBALL. (US/0276-1017). **4906**

NCAA FOOTBALL RULES AND INTERPRETATIONS. (US/0736-5160). **4906**

NCAA MEN'S WATER POLO RULES. (US/0734-0508). **4907**

NCAA NEWS, THE. (US/0027-6170). **4907**

NCAHF NEWSLETTER. (US/0890-3417). **1298**

NCBA COOPERATIVE BUSINESS JOURNAL. (US/1065-7207). **697**

NCEOA JOURNAL. (US/0889-8405). **1766**

NCGR JOURNAL. (US). **390**

NCJW JOURNAL. (US/0161-2115). **2268**

NCPHS NEWSLETTER. (US/1054-9188). **1146**

NCSA NEWSLETTER. (CN/0824-4820). **5297**

NCVO NEWS. (UK/0955-2170). **Qty:** 200-300. **5297**

NDAA BULLETIN / NATIONAL DISTRICT ATTORNEYS ASSOCIATION. (US). **3108**

NEAR EAST ARCHAEOLOGICAL SOCIETY BULLETIN. (US/0739-0068). **Qty:** 5-10. **275**

NEAR NORTH NEWS. (US/0028-1778). **Qty:** 15. **5661**

NEARA JOURNAL. (US/0149-2551). **Qty:** 3. **2748**

NEAS. NEWSLETTER OF ENGINEERING ANALYSIS SOFTWARE. (US/0739-697X). **1988**

NEBRASKA ANCESTREE. (US/0270-4463). **2462**

NEBRASKA BIRD REVIEW, THE. (US/0028-1816). **Qty:** 1-2. **5592**

NEBRASKA CATTLEMAN. (US/1062-8274). **216**

NEBRASKA HISTORY. (US/0028-1859). **2748**

NEBRASKA LAW REVIEW. (US/0047-9209). **3014**

NEBRASKA LIBRARY ASSOCIATION QUARTERLY. (US/0028-1883). **3233**

NEBRASKA NURSE. (US/0028-1921). **3862**

NEBRASKA RESOURCES. (US). **2200**

NEBRASKA SPEECH AND HEARING JOURNAL. (US/0470-570X). **4391**

NEBRASKALAND. (US/0028-1964). **4852**

NED. GEREF. TEOLOGIESE TYDSKRIF. (SA/0378-9888). **Qty:** 30. **4980**

NEDERLANDS BOSBOUW TIJDSCHRIFT. (NE/0369-3651). **2389**

NEDERLANDS INTERNATIONAAL PRIVATRECHT : REPERTORIUM OP VERDRAGENRECHT, WETGEVING, RECHTSPRAAK EN LITERATUUR. (NE/0167-7594). **3014**

NEDERLANDS THEOLOGISCH TIJDSCHRIFT. (NE/0028-212X). **4980**

NEDERLANDS TIJDSCHRIFT VOOR FOTONICA. (NE/0925-5338). **4413**

NEDERLANDS TIJDSCHRIFT VOOR NATUURKUNDE (AMSTERDAM. 1991). (NE/0926-4264). **5132**

NEDERLANDS TIJDSCHRIFT VOOR TANDHEELKUNDE. (NE/0028-2200). **1330**

NEDERLANDS VAN NU. (BE/0771-5080). **3305**

NEDERLANDSCH ARCHIEVENBLAD. (NE/0028-2049). **2482**

NEDERLANDSE BOEK. (NE/0166-0586). **3348**

NEEDLE ARTS. (US). **5185**

NEEDLEPOINT PLUS. (US/1040-5518). **5185**

NEGATIVE CAPABILITY. (US/0277-5166). **3414**

NEGRO EDUCATIONAL REVIEW, THE. (US/0548-1457). **1767**

NEGRO HISTORY BULLETIN. (US/0028-2529). **2748**

NEHW HEALTH WATCH. (US/8756-0356). **3862**

NEIGHBORHOOD WORKS, THE. (US/0193-791X). **2829**

NEIL SPERRY'S GARDENS. (US/1061-3994). **2425**

NEMA NEWS. (US). **4093**

NEMATROPICA. (US/0099-5444). **5592**

NENKAN NIHON NO IRASUTORESHON. (JA). **381**

NEOLOGY / EDMONTON SCIENCE FICTION AND COMIC ARTS SOCIETY. (CN/0228-913X). **3415**

NEONATAL NETWORK. (US/0730-0832). **3906**

NEONATOLOGY LETTER. (US/0747-6132). **3765**

NEOPHILOLOGUS. (NE/0028-2677). **3305**

NEPTUNIA. (FR). **4181**

NEPTUNUS. (BE). **4181**

NERVE CELL BIOLOGY / UNIVERSITY OF SHEFFIELD BIOMEDICAL INFORMATION SERVICE. (UK/0142-8225). **466**

NERVENARZT. (GW/0028-2804). **3839**

NERVENHEILKUNDE. (GW/0722-1541). **3839**

NERVLINE. A MICROCOMPUTER INFORMATION RETRIEVAL SYSTEM IN THE CLINICAL NEUROSCIENCES. (US). **3839**

NERVURE PARIS. (FR/0988-4068). **Qty:** 9. **3931**

NESHOBA DEMOCRAT, THE. (US). **5701**

NET RESULTS. (US/0270-4900). **Qty:** 30. **4980**

NETBALL MAGAZINE. (UK/0959-1117). **Qty:** 3. **4907**

NETHERLANDS INTERNATIONAL LAW REVIEW. (NE/0165-070X). **3133**

NETHERLANDS JOURNAL OF PLANT PATHOLOGY. (NE/0028-2944). **519**

NETHERLANDS JOURNAL OF ZOOLOGY. (NE/0028-2960). **5592**

NETSUSOKUTEI. (JA/0386-2615). **987**

NETWORK ADMINISTRATOR. (US/1073-1164). **Qty:** 2-4. **1243**

NETWORK COMPUTING. (UK/0966-7873). **1243**

NETWORK (MELBOURNE (VIC). (AT/0159-7302). **Qty:** 4. **5433**

NETWORK NEWS (BLUFFTON, OHIO). (US/0745-418X). **5065**

NETWORK NEWS - NATIONAL WOMEN'S HEALTH NETWORK (U.S.). (US/8755-867X). **4793**

NETWORK (SALT LAKE CITY, UTAH). (US/0890-3530). **Qty:** 10-12. **5562**

NETWORKER (ASHEVILLE, N.C.), THE. (US/1070-762X). **Qty:** 12. **4186**

NEU. (IT). **3839**

NEUE ARBEITERPRESSE. (GW). **1693**

NEUE CHINA, DAS. (GW). **2660**

NEUE DENKSCHRIFTEN DES NATURHISTORISCHEN MUSEUMS IN WIEN. (AU). **4228**

NEUE FREIE ZEITUNG. (AU). **2520**

NEUE GERMANISTIK. (US/0730-1359). **3415**

NEUE HOCHSCHULE, DIE. (GW). **1914**

NEUE KERAMIK. (GW/0933-2367). **3466**

NEUE ORDNUNG, DIE. (GW). **4980**

NEUE POLITISCHE LITERATUR. (GW/0028-3320). **5210**

NEUE TECHNIK. (SZ/0028-3398). **5132**

NEUE ZEITSCHRIFT FUER MISSIONSWISSENSCHAFT. NOUVELLE REVUE DE SCIENCE MISSIONAIRE. (SZ/0028-3495). **4980**

NEUEREN SPRACHEN, DIE. (GW/0342-3816). **3305**

NEUES GLAS. (GW/0723-2454). **2592**

NEUES JAHRBUCH FUER GEOLOGIE UND PALAONTOLOGIE. ABHANDLUNGEN. (GW/0077-7749). **1389**

NEUES JAHRBUCH FUER GEOLOGIE UND PALAONTOLOGIE. MONATSHEFTE. (GW/0028-3630). **1389**

NEUES JAHRBUCH FUER MINERALOGIE. ABHANDLUNGEN. (GW/0077-7757). **1443**

NEUES JAHRBUCH FUER MINERALOGIE. MONATSHEFTE. (GW/0028-3649). **1443**

NEUPHILOLOGISCHE MITTEILUNGEN. (FI/0028-3754). **3305**

NEURAL COMPUTATION. (US/0899-7667). **1215**

NEURAL NETWORKS TODAY. (US). **1215**

NEURAL, PARALLEL AND SCIENTIFIC COMPUTATIONS. (US/1061-5369). **Qty:** 15. **1197**

NEURO-CHIRURGIE. (FR/0028-3770). **3839**

NEURO-OPHTHALMOLOGY (AMSTERDAM : AEOLUS PRESS. 1980). (NE/0165-8107). **3876**

NEUROBIOLOGIA (RECIFE). (BL/0028-3800). **3839**

NEUROBIOLOGY OF AGING. (US/0197-4580). **3839**

NEUROCOMPUTERS. (US/0893-1585). **1197**

NEUROCOMPUTING (AMSTERDAM). (NE/0925-2312). **1215**

NEUROHYPOPHYSIAL HORMONES. (UK/0143-4276). **3732**

NEUROLAW LETTER, THE. (US/1058-4706). **Qty:** 10. **3015**

NEUROLOGIA CROATICA : GLASILO UDRUZENJA NEUROLOGA JUGOSLAVIJE, OFFICIAL JOURNAL OF YUGOSLAV NEUROLOGICAL ASSOCIATION. (CI/0353-8842). **Qty:** 20. **3840**

NEUROLOGIA EN COLOMBIA. (CK/0120-1034). **3840**

NEUROLOGIA PSICHIATRIA SCIENZE UMANE. (IT). **3931**

NEUROLOGICAL RESEARCH (NEW YORK). (UK/0161-6412). **3840**

NEUROLOGY AND NEUROBIOLOGY. (US/0736-4563). **3841**

NEUROLOGY, INDIA. (II/0028-3886). **Qty:** 2-5. **3841**

NEUROPATHOLOGY AND APPLIED NEUROBIOLOGY. (UK/0305-1846). **3896**

NEUROPEPTIDES (EDINBURGH). (UK/0143-4179). **3841**

NEUROPEPTIDES (SHEFFIELD). (UK/0142-8233). **3841**

NEUROPHYSIOLOGIE CLINIQUE. (NE/0987-7053). **3841**

NEUROREHABILITATION (READING, MASS.). (US/1053-8135). **3842**

NEUROREPORT. (UK/0959-4965). **3842**

NEUROSCIENCE AND BIOBEHAVIORAL REVIEWS. (US/0149-7634). **3842**

NEUROTOXICOLOGY (PARK FOREST SOUTH). (US/0161-813X). **3843**

NEUSPRACHLICHE MITTEILUNGEN AUS WISSENSCHAFT UND PRAXIS : NM. (GW/0028-3983). **1767**

NEVADA APPEAL (CARSON CITY, NEV. : 1968). (US). **Qty:** 12. **5708**

NEVADA HISTORICAL SOCIETY QUARTERLY (1961). (US/0047-9462). **2748**

NEVADA LAWYER. (US/1068-882X). **Qty:** 8-12. **3015**

NEVADA STATISTICAL ABSTRACT. (US). **5334**

NEVADA WAGE SURVEY. (US). **1693**

NEW ACCOUNTANT. (US/0882-8067). **749**

NEW ADVOCATE (BOSTON, MASS.), THE. (US/0895-1381). **3415**

NEW AFRICAN (LONDON. 1978). (UK/0142-9345). **2499**

NEW AGE JOURNAL (1983). (US/0746-3618). **4186**

NEW AGE RETAILER. (US/1042-6566). **4186**

NEW AGE, THE. (US). **2490**

NEW AGE WEEKLY. (II/0047-9500). **4483**

NEW AMBEROLA GRAPHIC, THE. (US/0028-4181). **Qty:** 8-10. **5318**

NEW AMERICAN (BELMONT, MASS.), THE. (US/0885-6540). **4483**

NEW AMERICAN (NEW YORK, N.Y.) (US). **2269**

NEW AMERICAN PRESS, THE. (US/1045-8093). **Qty:** 10. **5650**

NEW AMERICAN WRITING. (US/0893-7842). **3415**

NEW & EMERGING TECHNOLOGY. (US/0882-6382). **5132**

NEW ART EXAMINER. (US/0886-8115). **Qty:** 6 /yr. **359**

NEW BLACKFRIARS. (UK/0028-4289). **4980**

NEW BOOKBINDER, THE. (UK/0261-5363). **Qty:** 3-5. **4830**

NEW BOOKS IN THE COMMUNICATIONS LIBRARY. (US/0734-8142). **1118**

NEW BREED MICROFORM, THE. (US). **2269**

NEW BREWER, THE. (US/0741-0506). **2369**

NEW CANADIAN REVIEW. (CN/0832-932X). **3415**

NEW CAR COST GUIDE. (US/0731-4787). **5421**

NEW CATALYST. (CN/0834-969X). **2540**

NEW CATHOLIC EXPLORER. (US/1044-8322). **5033**

NEW CHOICES FOR THE BEST YEARS. (US/1041-6277). **5180**

NEW CHURCH LIFE. (US/0275-0805). **5065**

NEW CIVIL ENGINEER. (UK/0307-7863). **2027**

NEW COIN POETRY. (SA/0028-4459). **3466**

NEW COLLAGE MAGAZINE. (US/0028-4467). **Qty:** Varies. **3466**

NEW COMMUNITY. (UK/0047-9586). **2269**

NEW CONSUMER. (UK/0958-7349). **Qty:** 12. **1298**

NEW CONTRAST. (SA/1017-5415). **3415**

NEW COVENANT (ANN ARBOR, MICH.). (US/0744-8589). **5033**

NEW CRITERION (NEW YORK, N.Y.), THE. (US/0734-0222). **326**

NEW DANCE REVIEW, THE. (US/1040-8908). **Qty:** 1-2. **1314**

NEW DELTA REVIEW. (US/1050-415X). **Qty:** 6. **3415**

NEW DEPARTURES. (UK/0028-4580). **326**

NEW DESIGNS FOR YOUTH DEVELOPMENT. (US/0270-2541). **Qty:** 2-4. **1067**

NEW DIMENSIONS. (US). **1298**

NEW DIRECTIONS FOR WOMEN. (US/0160-1075). **5562**

NEW DIRECTIONS (VANCOUVER. 1985). (CN/0827-6153). **4483**

NEW DOCTOR. (AT/0313-2153). **Qty:** 2. **3916**

NEW DRIVER (HIGHLAND PARK, ILL.). (US/0279-6384). **5421**

NEW EDUCATION (MELBOURNE, VIC.). (AT). **Qty:** 24. **1767**

NEW ELECTRONIC ENCYCLOPEDIA. [COMPUTER FILE], THE. (US). **1927**

NEW ENERGY NEWS. (US/1075-0045). **1951**

NEW ENGLAND ANTIQUES JOURNAL. (US/0897-5795). **251**

NEW ENGLAND BUSINESS. (US/0164-3533). **698**

NEW ENGLAND ENTERTAINMENT DIGEST. (US/0896-1506). **Qty:** 6. **5366**

NEW ENGLAND ENTERTAINMENT DIGEST [MICROFORM]. (US). **5366**

NEW ENGLAND ENVIRONMENTAL NETWORK NEWS. (US/0198-8476). **2178**

NEW ENGLAND FARM BULLETIN & GARDEN GAZETTE. (US). **2425**

NEW ENGLAND GARDENER. (US/0896-8160). **Qty:** 10. **2425**

NEW ENGLAND HISTORICAL AND GENEALOGICAL REGISTER, THE. (US/0028-4785). **2462**

NEW ENGLAND JOURNAL OF BLACK STUDIES. (US/0747-4970). **2269**

NEW ENGLAND JOURNAL OF HISTORY / NEW ENGLAND HISTORY TEACHERS ASSOCIATION, THE. (US). **5210**

NEW ENGLAND JOURNAL OF HUMAN SERVICES. (US/0277-996X). **5298**

NEW ENGLAND JOURNAL OF MEDICINE, THE. (US/0028-4793). **3620**

NEW ENGLAND JOURNAL OF OPTOMETRY. (US/0028-4807). **Qty:** varies. **4216**

NEW ENGLAND JOURNAL OF PUBLIC POLICY. (US/0749-016X). **4668**

NEW ENGLAND JOURNAL ON CRIMINAL AND CIVIL CONFINEMENT. (US/0740-8994). **Qty:** 2-4. **3170**

NEW ENGLAND LAW LIBRARY CONSORTIUM UNION CATALOG. CD-ROM. (US). **3015**

NEW ENGLAND LAW REVIEW. (US/0028-4823). **3015**

NEW ENGLAND PRINTER & PUBLISHER. (US/0162-8771). **4567**

NEW ENGLAND PURCHASER. (US/0028-4858). **950**

NEW ENGLAND QUARTERLY, THE. (US/0028-4866). **2748**

NEW ENGLAND READING ASSOCIATION JOURNAL. (US/0028-4882). **1901**

NEW ENGLAND REVIEW (1990). (US/1053-1297). **3415**

NEW ENGLAND RUNNER. (US/1041-4800). **4907**

NEW ENGLAND SALES GUIDE TO HIGH-TECH COMPANIES. (US/1040-0591). **5132**

NEW ENGLAND SENIOR CITIZEN. (US/0163-2248). **5180**

NEW ENGLAND THEATRE JOURNAL. (US/1050-9720). **Qty:** 10. **5366**

NEW EQUIPMENT DIGEST. (US/0028-4963). **2123**

NEW FARMER AND GROWER. (UK/0952-1402). **111**

NEW FEDERALIST. (US/1043-2264). **Qty:** 10. **4484**

NEW FORMATIONS. (UK/0950-2378). **3348**

NEW FOUNDATION PAPERS. (US/0748-6804). **4981**

NEW FROM EUROPE. (US/0740-3569). **5132**

NEW FROM U.S. (US/0740-3577). **2540**

NEW FRONTIERS IN EDUCATION. (II/0047-9705). **1837**

NEW GERMAN CRITIQUE. (US/0094-033X). **3415**

NEW GERMAN STUDIES. (UK/0307-2770). **3305**

NEW GROUND. (SA/1016-9075). **2178**

NEW GUARD. (US/0028-5137). **4484**

NEW GUN WEEK, THE. (US/0195-1599). **Qty:** 15-20 per year. **4907**

NEW HAMPSHIRE BAR JOURNAL. (US/0548-4928). **3015**

NEW HAMPSHIRE GENEALOGICAL RECORD, THE. (US/1055-0763). **2462**

NEW HAMPSHIRE MAGAZINE (DURHAM). (US/0199-0306). **1093**

NEW HAMPSHIRE PREMIER. (US/1050-5512). **2540**

NEW HAMPSHIRE TOWN & CITY. (US/0545-171X). **4669**

NEW HAVEN REGISTER, THE. (US). **5646**

NEW HEAVEN, NEW EARTH. (US/0896-3150). **5665**

NEW HOLSTEIN REPORTER. (US/0749-6982). **5769**

NEW HORIZON (LONDON, ENGLAND). (UK/0955-095X). **5044**

NEW HORIZONS IN EDUCATION (SYDNEY, N.S.W.). (AT). **1767**

NEW HUMANIST (LONDON, ENGLAND). (UK/0306-512x). **4353**

NEW IN CHESS YEARBOOK. (NE/0168-7697). **4864**

NEW INTERNATIONAL (NEW YORK, N.Y. : 1983). (US/0737-3724). **4543**

NEW INTERNATIONALIST. (UK/0305-9529). **4529**

NEW JERSEY 50 PLUS. (US). **Qty: 24. 5711**

NEW JERSEY BEVERAGE JOURNAL. (US/0028-5552). **2369**

NEW JERSEY BUSINESS SOURCE BOOK, THE. (US/1049-2879). **698**

NEW JERSEY EDUCATION LAW REPORT, THE. (US/0279-8557). **3015**

NEW JERSEY HISTORICAL COMMISSION NEWSLETTER. (US/0047-9772). **Qty: 20-30. 2748**

NEW JERSEY LAWYER (MAGAZINE). (US/0195-0983). **3015**

NEW JERSEY MEDIA GUIDE. (US/1054-5190). **1118**

NEW JERSEY MEDICINE. (US/0885-842X). **3620**

NEW JERSEY NURSE (1978). (US/0196-4895). **3862**

NEW JERSEY OUTDOORS. (US/0028-5889). **2200**

NEW JERSEY PARENT-TEACHER. (US/0028-5897). **Qty: 2. 1867**

NEW JERSEY POLITICAL ALMANAC. (US/8756-2618). **4669**

NEW JERSEY QUERIES. (US/0899-1340). **2462**

NEW JERSEY REALTOR. (US/0028-5919). **4842**

NEW JERSEY REPORTER. (US/0195-3192). **Qty: 3. 4669**

NEW JERSEY REVIEW OF LITERATURE, THE. (US/1073-8576). **Qty: 4. 3415**

NEW JERSEY TRIAL LAWYER, THE. (US/1051-8746). **3015**

NEW JOURNAL (NEW HAVEN, CONN.), THE. (US/0028-6001). **1093**

NEW LANGUAGE PLANNING NEWSLETTER. (II). **Qty: 4. 3305**

NEW LAUREL REVIEW. (US/0145-8388). **3415**

NEW LAW FOR SURVEYORS. (UK/0264-8121). **4842**

NEW LAW JOURNAL, THE. (UK/0306-6479). **3015**

NEW LEADER (NEW YORK, N.Y.), THE. (US/0028-6044). **4543**

NEW LIBRARY SCENE, THE. (US/0735-8571). **3234**

NEW LIBRARY WORLD. (UK/0307-4803). **3234**

NEW LIFE. (AT). **5777**

NEW LITERARY HISTORY. (US/0028-6087). **3348**

NEW LITERATURE REVIEW. (AT/0314-7495). **3348**

NEW LITURGY. BULLETIN OF THE NATIONAL SECRETARIAT, IRISH EPISCOPAL COMMISSION FOR LITURGY. (IE). **5033**

NEW MARITIMES. (CN/0713-4789). **5790**

NEW MENORAH. (US/0883-0215). **4981**

NEW MERCERSBURG REVIEW, THE. (US/0895-7460). **Qty: 2. 4981**

NEW METHODS (SAN FRANCISCO, CALIF.). (US/0277-3015). **5517**

NEW MEXICO ARCHITECTURE. (US/0545-3151). **304**

NEW MEXICO FARM AND RANCH. (US/0028-6192). **Qty: 2. 112**

NEW MEXICO GENEALOGIST. (US). **Qty: 2-6. 2462**

NEW MEXICO HISTORICAL REVIEW. (US/0028-6206). **2748**

NEW MEXICO HUMANITIES REVIEW. (US/0738-9671). **Qty: 20/yr. 2851**

NEW MEXICO JOURNAL OF SCIENCE. (US/0270-3017). **5132**

NEW MEXICO MAGAZINE (SANTA FE, N.M. : 1974). (US/0028-6249). **2540**

NEW MEXICO PROFESSIONAL ENGINEER (1977). (US/0149-1954). **1988**

NEW MEXICO WILDLIFE. (US/0028-6338). **2200**

NEW MYSTERY. (US/1048-8324). **3416**

NEW MYTHS. (US/1055-9868). **3416**

NEW OBSERVATIONS. (US/0737-5387). **3416**

NEW OPTIONS. (US/0890-1619). **4529**

NEW ORDER (LINCOLN, NEB.), THE. (US/0740-3283). **4544**

NEW ORLEANS GENESIS, THE. (US/0548-6424). **Qty: 20. 2462**

NEW ORLEANS MUSIC. (UK/0308-1990). **4140**

NEW OUTLOOK (TEL AVIV). (IS/0028-6427). **4529**

NEW OXFORD REVIEW. (US/0149-4244). **4981**

NEW PACIFIC (SEATTLE, WASH.), THE. (US/1050-3080). **Qty: 4. 2540**

NEW PAGES. (US/0271-8197). **4817**

NEW PATRIOT (CHICAGO, ILL. 1988). (US/0047-9829). **Qty: 10-20. 3348**

NEW PERSPECTIVE (HAMILTON). (CN/0715-4445). **2269**

NEW PERSPECTIVES ON TURKEY. (TU/0896-6346). **5210**

NEW PHILOSOPHY, THE. (US/0028-6443). **4353**

NEW PHYSICIAN. (US/0028-6451). **3620**

NEW PHYTOLOGIST, THE. (UK/0028-646X). **519**

NEW PITTSBURGH COURIER (CITY ED.). (US/1047-8051). **Qty: 12. 5738**

NEW PITTSBURGH COURIER (NATIONAL ED.). (US/1047-806X). **5738**

NEW POLITICAL SCIENCE. (US/0739-3148). **Qty: 6-8 /yr. 4484**

NEW PRODUCT DEVELOPMENT. (US/0733-8252). **934**

NEW RENAISSANCE, THE. (US/0028-6575). **Qty: 2-4. 326**

NEW REPUBLIC (NEW YORK, N.Y.). (US/0028-6583). **2851**

NEW SCHOLAR, THE. (US/0028-6613). **5210**

NEW SOLIDARITY. (US/0028-6737). **2540**

NEW STUDIES IN ATHLETICS. (UK/0961-933X). **Qty: 4. 4907**

NEW TECHNICAL BOOKS. (US/0028-6869). **987**

NEW TECHNOLOGY IN THE HUMAN SERVICES. (UK). **5252**

NEW TECHNOLOGY WEEK. (US/0894-0789). **5133**

NEW TECHNOLOGY, WORK, AND EMPLOYMENT. (UK/0268-1072). **1694**

NEW THOUGHT (SCOTTSDALE, ARIZ.). (US/0146-7832). **4981**

NEW TIMES (PHOENIX, ARIZ.). (US/0279-3962). **5630**

NEW TIMES (SEATTLE, WASH.). (US/1044-2782). **4186**

NEW TIMES : THE JOURNAL OF DEMOCRATIC LEFT. (UK/0960-748X). **5210**

NEW TREND (BALTIMORE, MD.). (US/0732-1848). **4530**

NEW UNIONIST (MINNEAPOLIS, MINN.). (US/1070-7727). **Qty: 3. 1694**

NEW VICO STUDIES. (US/0733-9542). **4353**

NEW VOICES (DIEGO MARTIN, TRINIDAD AND TOBAGO). (TR/0387-4185). **3416**

NEW WAYS (EVANSTON, ILL.). (US). **3931**

NEW WELSH REVIEW, THE. (UK/0954-2116). **Qty: 200. 3416**

NEW WOMAN. (US/0028-6974). **5562**

NEW WORLD (1989), THE. (US/1043-3538). **Qty: 12. 5033**

NEW WORLD OUTLOOK. (US/0043-8812). **Qty: 2-4. 5065**

NEW YORK AFRICAN STUDIES ASSOCIATION NEWSLETTER. (US/0148-7264). **2642**

NEW YORK AMSTERDAM NEWS (1962). (US/1059-1818). **5718**

NEW YORK AUTO REPAIR NEWS. (US/0191-4979). **5421**

NEW YORK BAPTIST, THE. (US/0893-9063). **Qty: 2-4. 4981**

NEW YORK BEACON. (US). **5718**

NEW YORK BUSINESS ENVIRONMENT. (US/1065-1888). **Qty: 4. 3115**

NEW YORK CITY SUBWAY GUIDE. (US). **5485**

NEW YORK CIVIL MOTION CITATOR. (US/1043-0628). **3016**

NEW YORK EDUCATION LAW REPORT. (US/0896-4122). **3016**

NEW YORK FOLKLORE. (US/0361-204X). **Qty: 30. 2323**

NEW YORK GENEALOGICAL AND BIOGRAPHICAL RECORD, THE. (US/0028-7237). **Qty: 120. 2462**

NEW YORK GUARDIAN, THE. (US/1060-0167). **5711**

NEW YORK HERALD TIMES CROSSWORD PUZZLES ONLY. (US/0886-9936). **4864**

NEW YORK HERALD TRIBUNE LARGE PRINT CROSSWORDS. (US/0892-0168). **4864**

NEW YORK INTERNATIONAL LAW REVIEW. (US/1050-9453). **3133**

NEW YORK JEWISH WEEK, THE. (US/0745-5356). **Qty: 26. 2269**

NEW YORK LAW JOURNAL. (US/0028-7326). **3016**

NEW YORK LITERARY FORUM. (US/0149-1040). **3416**

NEW YORK METRO SALES GUIDE TO HIGH-TECH COMPANIES. (US/1040-0583). **5133**

NEW YORK NATIVE. (US/0744-060X). **2795**

NEW YORK OPERA NEWSLETTER, THE. (US/1043-2361). **Qty: 3-4. 386**

NEW YORK REAL ESTATE JOURNAL. (US/1057-2104). **Qty: 3. 4842**

NEW YORK REVIEW OF SCIENCE FICTION, THE. (US/1052-9438). **Qty: 100. 3416**

NEW YORK RUNNING NEWS. (US/0161-7338). **4907**

NEW YORK STATE BANKER, THE. (US/0028-7539). **801**

NEW YORK STATE BAR JOURNAL. (US/0028-7547). **3016**

NEW YORK STATE DENTAL JOURNAL. (US/0028-7571). **Qty: varies. 1330**

NEW YORK STATE GFOA NEWSLETTER. (US/1064-0762). **Qty: 2. 801**

NEW YORK STATE JOURNAL OF MEDICINE. (US/0028-7628). **3621**

NEW YORK STATE QUERIES. (US/1041-6560). **2462**

NEW YORK STYLE & DESIGN. (US). **2540**

NEW YORK TIMES BOOK REVIEW, THE. (US/0028-7806). **3349**

NEW YORK TIMES, THE. (US/0362-4331). **5719**

NEW YORK UNIVERSITY JOURNAL OF INTERNATIONAL LAW & POLITICS. (US/0028-7873). **3133**

NEW YORK UNIVERSITY LAW REVIEW (1950). (US/0028-7881). **3016**

NEW YORK UNIVERSITY REVIEW OF LAW AND SOCIAL CHANGE. (US/0048-7481). **3016**

NEW YORKER (NEW YORK, N.Y. : 1925). (US/0028-792X). **2490**

NEW YORKIN UUTISET. (US/0895-5549). **Qty: varies. 5719**

NEW YOUTH CONNECTIONS. (US/0737-285X). **1067**

NEW ZEALAND ANTARCTIC RECORD. (NZ/0110-5124). **2570**

NEW ZEALAND BEEKEEPER, THE. (NZ). **112**

NEW ZEALAND BOOKS. (NZ/1170-9103). **4831**

NEW ZEALAND BUSINESS WHO'S WHO, THE. (NZ/0071-9571). **699**

NEW ZEALAND CARTOGRAPHY AND GEOGRAPHIC INFORMATION SYSTEMS : THE JOURNAL OF THE NEW ZEALAND CARTOGRAPHIC SOCIETY. (NZ/0110-6007). **2582**

NEW ZEALAND DENTAL JOURNAL. (NZ/0028-8047). **1330**

NEW ZEALAND DISABLED. (NZ). **Qty: at least 6. 4391**

NEW ZEALAND ECONOMIC PAPERS. (NZ/0077-9954). **1507**

NEW ZEALAND ENTOMOLOGIST, THE. (NZ/0077-9962). **5592**

NEW ZEALAND FAMILY PHYSICIAN, THE. (NZ/0110-022X). **3738**

NEW ZEALAND FARMER, THE. (NZ). **112**

NEW ZEALAND FISHERMAN. (NZ/0113-9606). **4908**

NEW ZEALAND FORESTRY. (NZ/0112-9597). **2389**

NEW ZEALAND GEOLOGICAL SURVEY BASIN STUDIES. (NZ). **1389**

NEW ZEALAND GEOLOGICAL SURVEY PALEONTOLOGICAL BULLETIN. (NZ). **1389**

NEW ZEALAND HISTORIC PLACES. (NZ). **Qty: 10/yr. 2670**

NEW ZEALAND HOME AND BUILDING. (NZ/0110-098X). **Qty: 3-5. 2902**

NEW ZEALAND INTERNATIONAL BUSINESS. (NZ/0113-8138). **699**

NEW ZEALAND INTERNATIONAL REVIEW. (NZ/0110-0262). **4530**

NEW ZEALAND JOURNAL OF ADULT LEARNING. (NZ/0112-224X). **1801**

NEW ZEALAND JOURNAL OF AGRICULTURAL RESEARCH. (NZ/0028-8233). **112**

NEW ZEALAND JOURNAL OF BOTANY. (NZ/0028-825X). **519**

NEW ZEALAND JOURNAL OF ECOLOGY. (NZ/0110-6465). **2219**

NEW ZEALAND JOURNAL OF EDUCATIONAL STUDIES. (NZ/0028-8276). **Qty:** 16. **1768**

NEW ZEALAND JOURNAL OF FORESTRY SCIENCE. (NZ/0048-0134). **2389**

NEW ZEALAND JOURNAL OF GEOGRAPHY. (NZ/0028-8292). **2570**

NEW ZEALAND JOURNAL OF GEOLOGY AND GEOPHYSICS. (NZ/0028-8306). **1389**

NEW ZEALAND JOURNAL OF HISTORY, THE. (NZ/0028-8322). **2670**

NEW ZEALAND JOURNAL OF INDUSTRIAL RELATIONS. (NZ/0110-0637). **1694**

NEW ZEALAND JOURNAL OF MARINE AND FRESHWATER RESEARCH. (NZ/0028-8330). **556**

NEW ZEALAND JOURNAL OF MEDICAL LABORATORY SCIENCE. (NZ/1171-0195). **3621**

NEW ZEALAND JOURNAL OF OCCUPATIONAL THERAPY. (NZ/1171-0462). **Qty:** 8/year. **2865**

NEW ZEALAND JOURNAL OF PHYSIOTHERAPY. (NZ/0303-7193). **4381**

NEW ZEALAND JOURNAL OF PSYCHOLOGY (CHRISTCHURCH. 1983). (NZ/0112-109X). **4605**

NEW ZEALAND JOURNAL OF SPORTS MEDICINE, THE. (NZ/0110-6384). **3955**

NEW ZEALAND JOURNAL OF ZOOLOGY. (NZ/0301-4223). **5592**

NEW ZEALAND LAW SOCIETY'S NEWS SHEET, THE. (NZ). **3016**

NEW ZEALAND LIBRARIES. (NZ/0028-8381). **3234**

NEW ZEALAND LISTENER. (NZ). **1135**

NEW ZEALAND LOCAL GOVERNMENT. (NZ). **4669**

NEW ZEALAND MATHEMATICS MAGAZINE, THE. (NZ/0549-0510). **3524**

NEW ZEALAND MEDICAL JOURNAL. (NZ/0028-8446). **3621**

NEW ZEALAND MONTHLY REVIEW 1986. (NZ/0112-9120). **2510**

NEW ZEALAND NATURAL SCIENCES. (NZ/0113-7492). **1358**

NEW ZEALAND NEWS UK. (UK/0028-8500). **5812**

NEW ZEALAND NURSING FORUM. (NZ/0110-7968). **3862**

NEW ZEALAND NURSING JOURNAL, THE. (NZ/0028-8535). **3862**

NEW ZEALAND OUTLOOK. (NZ/0113-1982). **2510**

NEW ZEALAND POPULATION REVIEW. (NZ/0111-199X). **4555**

NEW ZEALAND RAILWAY OBSERVER. (NZ/0028-8624). **Qty:** 12. **5433**

NEW ZEALAND SCIENCE REVIEW. (NZ/0028-8667). **5133**

NEW ZEALAND SLAVONIC JOURNAL. (NZ). **2851**

NEW ZEALAND SPEECH-LANGUAGE THERAPISTS' JOURNAL, THE. (NZ/0110-571X). **3889**

NEW ZEALAND VETERINARY JOURNAL. (NZ/0048-0169). **5517**

NEW ZEALAND WILDLIFE. (NZ/0028-8802). **4875**

NEW ZEALAND WINGS. (NZ/0110-1471). **Qty:** 25/year. **30**

NEW ZEALAND WOOL MARKET REVIEW. (NZ/0113-2792). **5354**

NEWBERG ON CLASS ACTIONS. (US). **3017**

NEWCOMEN BULLETIN / NEWCOMEN SOCIETY FOR THE STUDY OF THE HISTORY OF ENGINEERING AND TECHNOLOGY, THE. (UK) **5133**

NEWCOMERSTOWN NEWS (1953). (US). **5729**

NEWEST REVIEW, THE. (CN). **Qty:** 40. **3349**

NEWFOUNDLAND ANCESTOR. (CN/0838-049X). **2462**

NEWFOUNDLAND & LABRADOR BUSINESS JOURNAL. (CN). **699**

NEWFOUNDLAND HERALD, THE. (CN/0824-3581). **Qty:** 52. **2490**

NEWFOUNDLAND QUARTERLY (1971). (CN/0380-5832). **2748**

NEWFOUNDLAND SOCIAL AND ECONOMIC PAPERS. (CN/0078-0332). **5211**

NEWFOUNDLAND STUDIES. (CN/0823-1737). **Qty:** 6. **2749**

NEWINGTON TOWN CRIER. (US/0745-0796). **5646**

NEWNAN TIMES-HERALD, THE. (US/0883-2536). **Qty:** 52. **5654**

NEWPORT THIS WEEK. (US). **5741**

NEWS & LETTERS. (US/0028-8969). **1508**

NEWS AND NOTES FROM ALL OVER, NEWSLETTER OF THE SOCIETY FOR THE ERADICATION OF TELEVISION. (US). **2490**

NEWS & OBSERVER (RALEIGH, N.C. : 1894). (US). **5724**

NEWS & RECORD. (US/0747-2862). **Qty:** 100. **5759**

NEWS AND ROUND TABLE. (US). **5298**

NEWS & VIEWS - ONTARIO GENEALOGICAL SOCIETY, LEEDS & GRENVILLE BRANCH. (CN/0708-6350). **Qty:** 3. **2462**

NEWS / BECKMAN CENTER FOR THE HISTORY OF CHEMISTRY. (US/1052-0414). **987**

NEWS BULLETIN / MICHIGAN BUSINESS EDUCATION ASSOCIATION. (US/0026-2048). **Qty:** 5. **699**

NEWS BULLETIN OF THE AUSTRALIAN DENTAL ASSOCIATION. (AT/0810-7440). **Qty:** Varies. **1331**

NEWS (CALIFORNIA ASSOCIATION OF COMMUNITY COLLEGES). (US). **1837**

NEWS-CHRONICLE (SHIPPENSBURG, PA.). (US). **Qty:** 26. **5738**

NEWS CIRCLE, THE. (US/0193-1814). **Qty:** 10. **2269**

NEWS-COMMERCIAL, THE. (US). **Qty:** 12. **5701**

NEWS DIGEST INTERNATIONAL. (AT). **2670**

NEWS-EXAMINER, THE. (US). **5657**

NEWS FOR SENIORS. (CN/0710-958X). **5180**

NEWS FROM DBDH. (DK/0904-9681). **2607**

NEWS FROM ICELAND. (IC). **2520**

NEWS FROM NATIVE CALIFORNIA. (US/1040-5437). **Qty:** 15-20. **2749**

NEWS FROM THE NORTHWEST. (US/0747-8739). **2462**

NEWS FROM WITHIN. (IS). **Qty:** 8-10. **2770**

NEWS-GAZETTE (CHAMPAIGN, ILL.). (US/1042-3354). **5661**

NEWS-GRAM - CHRISTIAN BUSINESS MEN OF CANADA. (CN/0710-5770). **4981**

NEWS IBM. (US). **Qty:** 6. **1288**

NEWS JOURNAL - SOCIETY FOR COMMERCIAL ARCHEOLOGY (U.S.). (US/0735-1399). **304**

NEWS JOURNAL (WILMINGTON, DEL.), THE. (US/1042-4121). **5647**

NEWS LETTER - BAR ASSOCIATION OF SRI LANKA. (CE). **3017**

NEWS LETTER - CUMBRIA FAMILY HISTORY SOCIETY. (UK/0140-1912). **Qty:** varies. **2462**

NEWS LETTER / MONTANA GEOLOGICAL SOCIETY. (US). **1389**

NEWS LETTER / POPULATION CENTRE BANGALORE. (II). **590**

NEWS NOTES & DEADLINES. (US). **Qty:** 6. **2922**

NEWS OF LITURGY. (UK). **4981**

NEWS OF NORWAY. (US/0028-9272). **2700**

NEWS OF THE LEPIDOPTERISTS' SOCIETY. (US/0091-1348). **5592**

NEWS - ONTARIO PUBLIC SCHOOL TEACHERS' FEDERATION (1989). (CN/0846-4715). **Qty:** varies. **1768**

NEWS PHOTOGRAPHER. (US/0199-2422). **Qty:** (varies). **4372**

NEWS-RECORD OF MAPLEWOOD AND SOUTH ORANGE. (US). **5711**

NEWS-REVIEW (INYOKERN, CALIF.), THE. (US/0893-9004). **5637**

NEWS / THEATRE ONTARIO. (CN/0821-4476). **5366**

NEWSBOY. (US/0028-9396). **Qty:** 5/year. **3416**

NEWSFLASH / NEW BRUNSWICK TEACHERS' ASSOCIATION. (CN/0715-5484). **1768**

NEWSHEET - COUNCIL FOR ENVIRONMENTAL EDUCATION. (UK/0960-9199). **Qty:** 150. **2178**

NEWSLEAF - ONTARIO GENEALOGICAL SOCIETY. (CN/0380-1616). **2462**

NEWSLETTER - AFRICAN-AMERICAN FAMILY HISTORY ASSOCIATION. (US/0893-4290). **2463**

NEWSLETTER (AMERICAN ACADEMY OF PSYCHIATRY AND THE LAW). (US/0896-5633). **Qty:** varies. **3931**

NEWSLETTER / AMERICAN AEROBICS ASSOCIATION. (US/8755-8742). **2600**

NEWSLETTER / AMERICAN ASSOCIATION OF BOTANICAL GARDENS AND ARBORETA. (US/0569-2423). **519**

NEWSLETTER - AMERICAN ASSOCIATION OF TISSUE BANKS. (US/0270-2673). **3621**

NEWSLETTER - AMERICAN MUSICAL INSTRUMENT SOCIETY. (US/0160-2365). **4140**

NEWSLETTER - AMERICAN RESEARCH CENTER IN EGYPT. (US/0402-0731). **276**

NEWSLETTER - APPALACHIAN CENTER, BEREA COLLEGE. (US). **1093**

NEWSLETTER / ASSOCIATION FOR CANADIAN THEATRE RESEARCH. (CN/1193-7564). **Qty:** 10. **5366**

NEWSLETTER - ASSOCIATION FOR CHINESE MUSIC RESEARCH. (US/1071-0639). **4140**

NEWSLETTER - ASSOCIATION FOR NATIVE DEVELOPMENT IN THE PERFORMING AND VISUAL ARTS. (CN/0316-8409). **326**

NEWSLETTER - ASSOCIATION FOR WOMEN IN MATHEMATICS. (US). **5562**

NEWSLETTER - ASSOCIATION OF SYSTEMATICS COLLECTIONS. (US/0147-7889). **4094**

NEWSLETTER / ATLANTIC CANADA INSTITUTE. (CN/0713-4479). **2541**

NEWSLETTER - AUSTRALIAN AND NEW ZEALAND SOCIETY OF NUCLEAR MEDICINE. (AT/0159-8376). **Qty:** varies. **3848**

NEWSLETTER - AUSTRALIAN ANTHROPOLOGICAL SOCIETY. (AT/0727-3134). **Qty:** approx 20/year. **242**

NEWSLETTER / AUSTRALIAN LAW LIBRARIANS' GROUP. (AT/0311-5984). **3235**

NEWSLETTER / AUSTRALIAN MAP CIRCLE. (AT/0811-9511). **Qty:** 3-4. **2570**

NEWSLETTER - BRITISH COLUMBIA COUNCIL FOR THE FAMILY. (CN/0706-9022). **2284**

NEWSLETTER / CALIFORNIA NATIVE PLANT SOCIETY, BRISTLECONE CHAPTER. (US). **Qty:** 1-2. **519**

NEWSLETTER / CANADIAN ASSOCIATION OF MUSIC LIBRARIES. (CN/0383-1299). **3235**

NEWSLETTER / CANADIAN ASSOCIATION OF RHODES SCHOLARS. (CN/0821-039X). **1837**

NEWSLETTER - CANADIAN ASSOCIATION ON GERONTOLOGY. (CN/0712-676X). **5180**

NEWSLETTER (CANADIAN BOOKBINDERS AND BOOK ARTISTS GUILD). (CN/0822-9538). **4831**

NEWSLETTER - CANADIAN EDUCATION ASSOCIATION. (CN/0008-3445). **1867**

NEWSLETTER - CANADIAN INSTITUTE OF UKRAINIAN STUDIES. (CN/0702-8474). **2700**

NEWSLETTER (CANADIAN MAGAZINE PUBLISHERS ASSOCIATION). (CN/1184-7379). **4817**

NEWSLETTER - CANADIAN PHYSIOTHERAPY ASSOCIATION. SPORTS PHYSIOTHERAPY DIVISION. (CN/0824-2917). **3955**

NEWSLETTER - CANADIAN RESEARCH INSTITUTE FOR THE ADVANCEMENT OF WOMEN. (CN/0229-7256). **5562**

NEWSLETTER - CANADIAN SOCIETY OF ENVIRONMENTAL BIOLOGISTS. (CN/0318-5133). **Qty:** 14. **2200**

NEWSLETTER - CENTER FOR HOLOCAUST STUDIES (BROOKLYN, NEW YORK, N.Y.). (US/0737-8092). **2700**

NEWSLETTER - CENTER FOR MIGRATION STUDIES (U.S.). (US/8756-4467). **1920**

NEWSLETTER (CHINESE AMERICAN LIBRARIANS ASSOCIATION). (US/0736-8887). **3235**

NEWSLETTER - COLCHESTER HISTORICAL SOCIETY. (CN/0821-2430). **2749**

NEWSLETTER / COMMITTEE ON SOCIALIST STUDIES. (CN/0712-5275). **4544**

NEWSLETTER (COMMONWEALTH SCIENCE COUNCIL (GREAT BRITAIN). EARTH SCIENCES PROGRAMME). (UK/0588-7739). **1358**

NEWSLETTER / CONFERENCE GROUP ON ITALIAN POLITICS & SOCIETY. (US/0896-9825). **4530**

NEWSLETTER / COUNCIL OF NOVA SCOTIA ARCHIVES. (CN/0829-7142). **2482**

NEWSLETTER (CRIMINAL LAWYERS' ASSOCIATION (TORONTO, ONT.)). (CN/0715-5980). **3108**

NEWSLETTER - DANISH CENTRE FOR TECHNICAL AIDS FOR REHABILITATION AND EDUCATION. (DK). **1882**

NEWSLETTER, EAST ASIAN ART & ARCHAEOLOGY. (US/8755-4593). **360**

NEWSLETTER (ENABLEMENT INFORMATION SERVICE (BOSTON, MASS.)). (US). **4981**

NEWSLETTER - EUBIOS ETHICS INSTITUTE. (NZ/1170-5485). Qty: 10. **2252**

NEWSLETTER - FAIRFAX GENEALOGICAL SOCIETY (FAIRFAX COUNTY, VA.). (US/0895-2078). Qty: 3. **2463**

NEWSLETTER / FEDERATION OF CATHOLIC PARENT-TEACHER ASSOCIATIONS OF ONTARIO. (CN/0227-6291). **1768**

NEWSLETTER FOR RSEEA. (US/8756-8942). **112**

NEWSLETTER FROM DICK B. ON THE SPIRITUAL ROOTS OF ALCOHOLICS ANONYMOUS, A. (US/1068-302X). **4981**

NEWSLETTER FROM THE COMMISSION FOR SCIENTIFIC RESEARCH IN GREENLAND. (DK/0106-1372). **5133**

NEWSLETTER - FRONTENAC HISTORIC FOUNDATION. (CN/0381-0119). **304**

NEWSLETTER - GENEALOGICAL SOCIETY OF NEW JERSEY. (US). **2463**

NEWSLETTER - GLASGOW & WEST OF SCOTLAND FAMILY HISTORY SOCIETY. (UK/0141-8009). Qty: 18-20/year. **2463**

NEWSLETTER / INDIANA COVERED BRIDGE SOCIETY. (US). **2749**

NEWSLETTER / INNISFIL HISTORICAL SOCIETY. (CN/0713-8806). **2749**

NEWSLETTER - INSTITUTE FOR STUDIES IN AMERICAN MUSIC. (US/0145-8396). **4141**

NEWSLETTER - IOWA ARCHEOLOGICAL SOCIETY. (US/0578-655X). **276**

NEWSLETTER - LEAGUE OF OREGON CITIES (1980). (US/0731-1435). **4669**

NEWSLETTER - LITTLE BIG HORN ASSOCIATES. (US/0459-5866). Qty: 10. **2749**

NEWSLETTER - LONG POINT BIRD OBSERVATORY. (CN/0317-9575). **5618**

NEWSLETTER / MONMOUTH COUNTY HISTORICAL ASSOCIATION. (US/0740-8781). **2750**

NEWSLETTER - MONROE COUNTY HISTORICAL SOCIETY (WIS.). (US/1075-248X). Qty: 12. **2750**

NEWSLETTER - NAFSA: ASSOCIATION OF INTERNATIONAL EDUCATORS (WASHINGTON, D.C.). (US/1067-4780). **1768**

NEWSLETTER / NATIONAL ALOPECIA AREATA FOUNDATION, NAAF. (US/0894-1769). Qty: 5. **3715**

NEWSLETTER / NATIONAL CARTOGRAPHIC INFORMATION CENTER. (US/0364-7064). **2582**

NEWSLETTER - NATIONAL COUNCIL FOR INTERNATIONAL VISITORS. (US/0196-9420). **2911**

NEWSLETTER - NATIONAL COUNCIL FOR THERAPY AND REHABILITATION THROUGH HORTICULTURE (U.S.). (US/0739-1609). **2425**

NEWSLETTER / NATIONAL EARLY AMERICAN GLASS CLUB. (US). **2592**

NEWSLETTER / NEW HAMPSHIRE SOCIETY OF GENEALOGISTS. (US/8755-173X). **2463**

NEWSLETTER - NEW ZEALAND. NATURE CONSERVATION COUNCIL. (NZ/0111-686X). **2200**

NEWSLETTER / NORTH AMERICAN SOCIETY OF OCEANIC HISTORY. (US/1065-2329). **4181**

NEWSLETTER - NOVA SCOTIA BIRD SOCIETY. (CN/0383-9567). **5592**

NEWSLETTER OF SWEDISH BUILDING RESEARCH. (SW). **622**

NEWSLETTER OF THE AFRO-AMERICAN RELIGIOUS HISTORY GROUP OF THE AMERICAN ACADEMY OF RELIGION. (US/0889-6178). **2750**

NEWSLETTER OF THE AMERICAN COMMITTEE TO ADVANCE THE STUDY OF PETROGLYPHS AND PICTOGRAPHS. (US/0278-2871). **242**

NEWSLETTER OF THE AMERICAN HANDEL SOCIETY. (US/0888-8701). **4141**

NEWSLETTER OF THE AMERICAN INSTITUTE OF STRESS, THE. (US/1047-2517). Qty: 12 per year. **3621**

NEWSLETTER OF THE ASSOCIATION OF OFFICIAL SEED ANALYSTS, THE. (US/0004-5764). **112**

NEWSLETTER OF THE AUSTRALIAN ROBOT ASSOCIATION. (AT/0726-3716). Qty: 10. **1220**

NEWSLETTER OF THE CENTER FOR PROCESS STUDIES. (US/0360-618X). **4982**

NEWSLETTER OF THE CPA/SCP SECTION ON WOMEN & PSYCHOLOGY. (CN/0831-9510). **4605**

NEWSLETTER OF THE NEW YORK STATE COUNCIL FOR THE SOCIAL STUDIES, THE. (US). **5211**

NEWSLETTER OF THE NORTH CAROLINA FOLKLORE SOCIETY. (US/0888-6121). **2323**

NEWSLETTER OF THE TEXTILE MUSEUM ASSOCIATION OF SOUTHERN CALIFORNIA. (US). Qty: 4. **5354**

NEWSLETTER OF THE TILES AND ARCHITECTURAL CERAMICS SOCIETY. (UK). Qty: varies. **304**

NEWSLETTER OF THE YELLOWHEAD REGIONAL LIBRARY. (CN/0708-1979). **3235**

NEWSLETTER ON EDUCATION AND TRAINING PROGRAMMES FOR INFORMATION PERSONNEL. (NE). **3236**

NEWSLETTER ON INTELLECTUAL FREEDOM. (US/0028-9485). **3236**

NEWSLETTER / ONTARIO ASSOCIATION OF LIBRARY TECHNICIANS. (CN/0229-2645). **3236**

NEWSLETTER / ONTARIO FORESTRY ASSOCIATION. (CN/0834-2008). Qty: varies. **2389**

NEWSLETTER - PLANETARY ASSOCIATION FOR CLEAN ENERGY. (CN/0708-918X). **1951**

NEWSLETTER / ROSS COUNTY GENEALOGICAL SOCIETY. (US/0740-4395). **2464**

NEWSLETTER-SOCIAL WELFARE HISTORY GROUP. (US/0560-3870). Qty: 1-2. **5299**

NEWSLETTER / SOCIETY FOR ARMENIAN STUDIES. (US/0740-5510). **2660**

NEWSLETTER / SOCIETY OF THE SEVEN SAGES. (CN/0701-9890). **3417**

NEWSLETTER - SOUTH AUSTRALIAN ADVISORY COMMITTEE ON LIBRARY SERVICES TO THE DISABLED. (AT/0810-0926). **3236**

NEWSLETTER - STUDY GROUP ON EIGHTEENTH-CENTURY RUSSIA. (UK/0306-8455). Qty: 5-8. **2700**

NEWSLETTER / SUFFOLK COUNTY ARCHAEOLOGICAL ASSOCIATION. (US). **276**

NEWSLETTER / THE AMERICAN BRAHMS SOCIETY. (US/8756-8357). **4141**

NEWSLETTER / THE CROW WING COUNTY HISTORICAL SOCIETY. (US/0895-0822). Qty: 4. **2750**

NEWSLETTER - THE SOCIETY OF ARCHITECTURAL HISTORIANS. (US/0049-1195). **304**

NEWSLETTER TO MEMBERS OF THE TEXAS BAPTIST HISTORICAL SOCIETY. (US). Qty: 5-10. **2624**

NEWSLETTER - VANCOUVER HISTORICAL SOCIETY (1980). (CN/0823-0161). **2750**

NEWSLETTER / W.H. AUDEN SOCIETY. (UK). **3467**

NEWSLETTER / WEST COAST ENVIRONMENTAL LAW RESEARCH FOUNDATION. (CN/0715-4275). **3115**

NEWSLETTER - WESTERN ASSOCIATION FOR ART CONSERVATION. (US/1052-0066). **326**

NEWSLETTER - WESTMORLAND HISTORICAL SOCIETY. (CN/0382-0831). **2750**

NEWSLETTER - WILLEM MENGELBERG SOCIETY. (US/1051-0788). **4141**

NEWSLETTER-WRITERS GUILD OF AMERICA, WEST. (US/0043-9533). **3417**

NEWSLETTERS ON STRATIGRAPHY. (NE/0078-0421). **1389**

NEWSLINE - MANITOBA LIBRARY ASSOCIATION. (CN/0227-6569). **3236**

NEWSLINE - TRAVEL INDUSTRY ASSOCIATION OF AMERICA. (US/0749-985X). **5486**

NEWSPAPER FINANCIAL EXECUTIVE JOURNAL. (US/0889-4590). **2922**

NEWSPAPER FUND ADVISER UPDATE. (US). Qty: 4y. **5711**

NEWSPAPER RESEARCH JOURNAL. (US/0739-5329). **4817**

NEWSPAPER TECHNIQUES (DARMSTADT, GERMANY). (GW). **4817**

NEWSPEACE. (UK/0048-0304). Qty: 12. **4982**

NEWSTIME (LONDON, ENGLAND). (UK). **4817**

NEWSWATCH (LAGOS). (NR/0189-8892). **2499**

NEWSWEEK (U.S. ED.). (US/0028-9604). **2490**

NEWTON KANSAN (NEWTON, KAN. : 1952). (US). **5677**

NEXUS (HAMILTON, ONT.). (CN/0711-5342). **242**

NFAIS NEWSLETTER. (US/0090-0893). Qty: (varies). **3236**

NHAC VIET. (US/1063-1909). Qty: 10. **4141**

NIAGARA BRUCE TRAIL CLUB. (CN/0706-7429). **4876**

NIBBLE. (US/0734-3795). **1280**

NICARAUAC : REVISTA BIMESTRAL DEL MINISTERIO DE CULTURA. (NQ). **5252**

NICHE (BALTIMORE, MD.). (US/1064-0347). Qty: 12. **955**

NICOLA VALLEY HISTORICAL QUARTERLY. (CN/0708-8132). **2750**

NIEDERDEUTSCHES WORT. (GW/0078-0545). **3306**

NIEDERSAECHSISCHE WIRTSCHAFT. (GW). **1575**

NIEMAN REPORTS. (US/0028-9817). **2923**

NIEREN- UND HOCKDRUCKKRANKHEITEN. (GW/0300-5224). **3622**

NIEUW NEUF. (BE). **305**

NIEUWE WEST-INDISCHE GIDS. (NE/0028-9930). **5211**

NIGERIAN CHRISTIAN, THE. (NR/0029-005X). **4982**

NIGERIAN CURRENT LAW REVIEW : THE JOURNAL OF THE NIGERIAN INSTITUTE OF ADVANCED LEGAL STUDIES. (NR/0189-207X). **3017**

NIGERIAN FIELD. (UK/0029-0076). **4169**

NIGERIAN JOURNAL OF ECONOMIC AND SOCIAL STUDIES, THE. (NR/0029-0092). **1508**

NIGERIAN JOURNAL OF INTERNATIONAL AFFAIRS. (NR/0331-3646). **4530**

NIGERIAN JOURNAL OF NUTRITIONAL SCIENCES. (NR/0189-0913). **4195**

NIGERIAN JOURNAL OF PUBLIC AFFAIRS, THE. (NR). **4669**

NIGERIAN JOURNAL OF THEOLOGY, THE. (NR). **4982**

NIGERIAN LIBRARY AND INFORMATION SCIENCE REVIEW. (NR/0189-4412). **3236**

NIGRIZIA. (IT/0029-0173). Qty: 50. **4982**

NIHON HAKUYO KIKAN GAKKAI SHI. JOURNAL OF THE MARINE ENGINEERING SOCIETY IN JAPAN. (JA). **1989**

NIHON KANGO KYOKAI CHOSA KENKYU HOKOKU. (JA/0911-0844). **3862**

NIHON KAZE KOGAKKAI SHI. (JA). **1989**

NIHON NO SHINGAKU / NIHON KIRISUTOKYO GAKKAI HEN. (JA). **4982**

NIHON PURANKUTON GAKKAI HO. (JA). **556**

NIHON SHOKUHIN KOGYO GAKKAI SHI. (JA/0029-0394). Qty: 30. **2351**

NIHON TOKEI GAKKAISHI (TOKYO. 1970). (JA/0389-5602). **5334**

NIKKEI PASOKON. (JA). **1238**

NIKON WORLD. (US). **4372**

NIMHANS JOURNAL. (II). **3931**

NINETEENTH CENTURY CONTEXTS. (US/0890-5495). **3417**

NINETEENTH-CENTURY FRENCH STUDIES. (US/0146-7891). Qty: 60-80. **3349**

NINETEENTH-CENTURY LITERATURE. (US/0891-9356). **3417**

NINETEENTH CENTURY PROSE. (US/1052-0406). **3417**

NINETEENTH-CENTURY STUDIES (CHARLESTON, S.C.). (US/0893-7931). Qty: 8-12. **3417**

NINETEENTH CENTURY : THE MAGAZINE OF THE VICTORIAN SOCIETY IN AMERICA. (US). **360**

NINETEENTH CENTURY THEATRE. (US/0893-3766). **5367**

NINETY. (FR). **381**

NINNAU : THE NORTH AMERICAN WELSH NEWSLETTER. (US/0890-0485). Qty: 25. **2270**

NIP (CINCINNATI, OHIO. 1993). (US/1074-0791). **2491**

NIR NEWS. (UK/0960-3360). **4413**

NITROGEN FIXING TREE RESEARCH REPORTS : A PUBLICATION OF THE NITROGEN FIXING TREE ASSOCIATION (NFTA). (TH). **2389**

NITTANY GROTTO NEWS. (US/0732-5398). **1358**

NJ AUDUBON. (US/0886-6619). **2200**

NJCM BULLETIN / NEDERLANDS JURISTEN COMITE VOOR DE MENSENRECHTEN. (NE). **4511**

NJEA REVIEW. (US/0027-6758). **1769**

NLADA CORNERSTONE. (US/0739-9111). **3180**

NLGI SPOKESMAN. (US/0027-6782). **2123**

NML TECHNICAL JOURNAL. (II/0027-6839). **4013**

NMR IN BIOMEDICINE. (UK/0952-3480). **3622**

NO-DIG INTERNATIONAL. (UK/0960-4405). **2027**

NO TO SHINKEI. (JA/0006-8969). **3844**

NOAH'S ARK. (US/0892-4945). **Qty:** 10-20. **1067**

NOETIC SCIENCES BULLETIN. (US/0897-1013). **4606**

NOETIC SCIENCES REVIEW. (US/0897-1005). **4606**

NOGYO KISHO. (JA/0021-8588). **1432**

NOISE CONTROL ENGINEERING JOURNAL. (US/0736-2501). **2178**

NOISE NEWS. (US/0146-4809). **2179**

NOISE POLLUTION PUBLICATIONS ABSTRACTS. (US/0733-172X). **2179**

NOK LAPJA. (HU). **5563**

NOLO NEWS. (US/0890-2208). **Qty:** 40. **3017**

NOLOAD FUND X. (US/0194-0104). **910**

NOLPE NOTES. (US/0047-8997). **3017**

NOMA. (NR/0331-6742). **114**

NOMADIC PEOPLES. (CN/0822-7942). **2270**

NOMINA. (UK/0141-6340). **3306**

NOMISMATIKA KHRONIKA. (GR). **Qty:** 2-3 per year. **2782**

NOMOS (FORTALEZA, BRAZIL). (BL). **Qty:** 2. **3018**

NON-CREDIT LEARNING NEWS. (US/0886-0165). **1801**

NON-DESTRUCTIVE TESTING - AUSTRALIA. (AT/0157-6461). **1989**

NONPROFIT INSIGHTS. (US/1056-4594). **4739**

NONPROFIT TIMES, THE. (US/0896-5048). **880**

NONPROFIT WORLD. (US). **Qty:** 6. **5299**

NONVIOLENCE TODAY. (AT/1031-6434). **4484**

NONVIOLENT ACTIVIST, THE. (US/8755-7428). **Qty:** 15. **3133**

NONWOVENS ABSTRACTS. (UK/9036-1234). **5360**

NOR KIANK. (US/0194-0074). **5637**

NORD E SUD. (IT/0029-1188). **2700**

NORD GENEALOGIE. (FR). **Qty:** 6. **2464**

NORD (HEARST). (CN/0382-8883). **5790**

NORDEN (NEW YORK, N.Y.). (US/0895-2612). **5719**

NORDEN; NORD-NORGES LANDBRUKSTIDSSKRIFT. (NO). **114**

NORDEUROPA STUDIEN. (GW). **2700**

NORDIC HYDROLOGY. (DK/0029-1277). **1416**

NORDIC JOURNAL OF BOTANY. (DK/0107-055X). **Qty:** 30. **520**

NORDIC JOURNAL OF LINGUISTICS. (NO/0332-5865). **3306**

NORDIC JOURNAL OF PSYCHIATRY. (NO/0803-9488). **3931**

NORDIC SOUNDS. (DK/0108-2914). **5318**

NORDICOM REVIEW OF NORDIC MASS COMMUNICATION RESEARCH, THE. (SW/0349-6244). **1118**

NORDISK ADMINISTRATIVT TIDSSKRIFT. (DK/0029-1285). **4669**

NORDISK ALKOHOL TIDSKRIFT. (FI/0782-9671). **Qty:** 15. **1347**

NORDISK JUDAISTIK / SCANDINAVIAN JEWISH STUDIES. (SW/0348-1646). **5051**

NORDISK PEDAGOGIK. (DK/0901-8050). **1769**

NORDISK PSYKOLOGI. (DK/0029-1463). **4606**

NORDISK ST-FORUM. (NO/0801-7220). **5211**

NORDISK TIDSKRIFT FOR DOVUNDERVISNINGEN. (SW/0029-1471). **1883**

NORDISK TIDSSKRIFT FOR INTERNATIONAL RET. PUBLIKATIONSSERIE. (DK). **3133**

NORDISK TIDSSKRIFT FOR SPECIALPAEDAGOGIK. (NO/0048-0509). **1883**

NORDSTJERNAN (1991). (US/1059-7670). **5719**

NORFOLK ANCESTOR : JOURNAL OF THE NORFOLK & NORWICH GENEALOGICAL SOCIETY, THE. (UK/0140-5403). **2464**

NORMALISATIE-NIEUWS (DELFT). (NE/0929-2985). **4032**

NORMAS LEGALES. (PE). **3018**

NORMAT. (NO/0801-3500). **3524**

NOROIL. (NO/0332-544X). **4266**

NOROIS. (FR/0029-182X). **Qty:** 4. **2570**

NORSEMAN. (NO/0029-1846). **2520**

NORSK ANTHROPOLOGISK TIDSSKRIFT. (NO/0802-7285). **242**

NORSK FARMACEUTISK TIDSSKRIFT. (DK/0029-1935). **4318**

NORSK FILOSOFISK TIDSSKRIFT. (NO/0029-1943). **4353**

NORSK GEOGRAFISK TIDSSKRIFT. (NO/0029-1951). **2571**

NORSK GEOLOGISK TIDSSKRIFT. (NO/0029-196X). **1390**

NORSK HAGETIDEND. (NO/0029-1986). **2426**

NORSK LANDBRUK. (NO). **114**

NORSK LINGVISTISK TIDSSKRIFT : NLT. (NO/0800-3076). **3306**

NORSK LITTERR ARBOK. (NO/0078-1266). **3418**

NORSK MILITRT TIDSSKRIFT. (NO/0029-2028). **Qty:** 12-15. **4053**

NORSK MUSIKKTIDSSKRIFT. (NO/0332-5482). **4142**

NORSK PEDAGOGISK TIDSKRIFT. (NO). **1769**

NORSK SKOGBRUK. (NO/0029-2087). **2389**

NORSK SLEKTSHISTORISK TIDSSKRIFT. (NO/0029-2141). **2464**

NORSK STATSVITENSKAPELIG TIDSSKRIFT. (NO/0801-1745). **4484**

NORSK TEOLOGISK TIDSSKRIFT. (NO/0029-2176). **4982**

NORSK TIDSSKRIFT FOR MISJON. (NO/0029-2214). **4982**

NORTH AMERICAN HUNTER. (US/0194-4320). **4876**

NORTH CAROLINA BEACON. (US/1064-4830). **Qty:** 52. **5724**

NORTH CAROLINA CENTRAL LAW JOURNAL. (US/0549-7434). **3018**

NORTH CAROLINA CHRISTIAN ADVOCATE. (US/0029-2435). **5724**

NORTH CAROLINA ENGLISH TEACHER. (US/0887-5596). **1901**

NORTH CAROLINA FOLKLORE JOURNAL. (US/0090-5844). **2323**

NORTH CAROLINA GENEALOGICAL SOCIETY JOURNAL, THE. (US/0360-1056). **2464**

NORTH CAROLINA HISTORICAL REVIEW, THE. (US/0029-2494). **2750**

NORTH CAROLINA INDEPENDENT, THE. (US/0737-8254). **Qty:** 50. **5724**

NORTH CAROLINA JOURNAL OF INTERNATIONAL LAW AND COMMERCIAL REGULATION. (US/0743-1759). **3133**

NORTH CAROLINA LAW REVIEW. (US/0029-2524). **3018**

NORTH CAROLINA LIBRARIES. (US/0029-2540). **Qty:** 40. **3237**

NORTH CAROLINA LITERARY REVIEW. (US/1063-0724). **Qty:** 6-10. **3418**

NORTH CAROLINA NATURALIST. (US/1070-468X). **4169**

NORTH CAROLINA QUERIES. (US/0897-7755). **2464**

NORTH CAROLINA STATE BAR QUARTERLY. (US/0164-6850). **3018**

NORTH CENTRAL NORTH DAKOTA GENEALOGICAL RECORD. (US/0736-5667). **2464**

NORTH CENTRAL SALES GUIDE TO HIGH-TECH COMPANIES. (US/1040-0540). **5134**

NORTH COUNTRY ANVIL. (US). **2541**

NORTH DAKOTA HISTORY. (US/0029-2710). **2750**

NORTH DAKOTA LAW REVIEW. (US/0029-2745). **3018**

NORTH DAKOTA MUSIC EDUCATOR. (US/0029-2753). **4142**

NORTH DAKOTA OUTDOORS. (US/0029-2761). **4876**

NORTH DAKOTA QUARTERLY, THE. (US/0029-277X). **Qty:** 20/yr. **2541**

NORTH DAKOTA R E C MAGAZINE. (US). **1542**

NORTH EAST OUT DOORS. (US/0199-8463). **4876**

NORTH IRISH ROOTS. (UK/0264-9217). **Qty:** 6. **2464**

NORTH JERSEY PROSPECTOR, THE. (US/0745-8908). **5711**

NORTH LOUISIANA GENEALOGICAL SOCIETY JOURNAL. (US). **2464**

NORTH QUEENSLAND NATURALIST. (AT/0078-1630). **4169**

NORTH SAN ANTONIO TIMES, THE. (US). **5753**

NORTH SHORE SENTINEL. (CN/0715-5786). **5791**

NORTH STAR BAPTIST. (US/0744-0278). **Qty:** 40. **4982**

NORTH WOODS CALL, THE. (US/0029-2958). **4876**

NORTHAMPTONSHIRE PAST & PRESENT. (UK). **2700**

NORTHEAST. (US/0549-8880). **Qty:** varies. **3418**

NORTHEAST AFRICAN STUDIES. (US/0740-9133). **2500**

NORTHEAST ALABAMA SETTLERS. (US/0742-583X). **2464**

NORTHEAST EQUINE JOURNAL. (US). **2801**

NORTHEAST IMPROVER, THE. (US/0145-9112). **197**

NORTHEAST JOURNAL OF BUSINESS & ECONOMICS, THE. (US/8755-5123). **1508**

NORTHEAST MISSISSIPPI DAILY JOURNAL. (US/0744-5431). **5701**

NORTHEAST MISSISSIPPI HISTORICAL & GENEALOGICAL SOCIETY QUARTERLY, THE. (US/1060-5568). **Qty:** 5. **2464**

NORTHEAST SUN. (US/0738-971X). **1951**

NORTHEASTERN GEOLOGY. (US/0194-1453). **1390**

NORTHERN CALIFORNIA HOME & GARDEN. (US/0898-1191). **2902**

NORTHERN CALIFORNIA MEDICINE. (US). **3623**

NORTHERN CALIFORNIA SUN. (US/8755-8866). **1951**

NORTHERN CATHOLIC HISTORY. (UK/0307-4455). **5033**

NORTHERN HISTORY. (UK/0078-172X). **2624**

NORTHERN ILLINOIS UNIVERSITY LAW REVIEW. (US/0734-1490). **3018**

NORTHERN JOURNAL OF APPLIED FORESTRY. (US/0742-6348). **2389**

NORTHERN KENTUCKY LAW REVIEW. (US/0198-8549). **3018**

NORTHERN LIFE (SUDBURY). (CN/0700-527X). **Qty:** less than 10. **5791**

NORTHERN LIGHTS (CHELMSFORD). (CN/0822-0808). **3467**

NORTHERN LOGGER AND TIMBER PROCESSOR, THE. (US/0029-3156). **2403**

NORTHERN MINER, THE. (CN/0029-3164). **2147**

NORTHERN MOSAIC (THUNDER BAY). (CN/0384-0840). **5791**

NORTHERN MOSIAC (LLOYDMINSTER). (CN/0824-3484). **326**

NORTHERN NEW ENGLAND REVIEW. (US/0190-3012). **3418**

NORTHERN OHIO LIVE. (US/0271-5147). **2541**

NORTHERN ONTARIO BUSINESS. (CN/0710-2755). **700**

NORTHERN PERSPECTIVE. (AT/0314-989X). **Qty:** 15-20. **3418**

NORTHERN RAVEN, THE. (US/0277-0997). **4169**

NORTHERN REVIEW, THE. (US/0894-3362). **326**

NORTHERN REVIEW (WHITEHORSE). (CN). **Qty:** 30. **326**

NORTHERN SCOTLAND. (UK/0306-5278). **Qty:** 12-15. **2700**

NORTHERN VIRGINIAN. (US/0164-6710). **2541**

NORTHERN WOMAN JOURNAL. (CN/0824-4081). **5563**

NORTHGLENN-THORNTON SENTINEL. (US). **Qty:** 25. **5644**

NORTHLAND QUARTERLY, THE. (US/0899-708X). **3418**

NORTHLINE. (CN/0714-475X). **1838**

NORTHROP UNIV. LAW J. AEROSP., BUS. TAX. (US/0887-4301). **3019**

NORTHSHORE CITIZEN (1990). (US/1057-3771). **Qty:** 2-3. **5761**

NORTHUMBERLAND NEWS. (CN/0228-0531). **5791**

NORTHUMBRIANA. (UK). **2520**

NORTHWARD JOURNAL. (CN/0706-0955). **360**

NORTHWEST ARKANSAS TIMES (FAYETTEVILLE, AR.). (US/1066-3355). **5632**

NORTHWEST ARTS. (US/0744-4680). **326**

NORTHWEST BAPTIST WITNESS. (US/0745-2195). **5065**

NORTHWEST BOAT TRAVEL. (US/0192-1169). **594**

NORTHWEST CHESS. (US/0146-6941). **4864**

NORTHWEST ENVIRONMENTAL JOURNAL, THE. (US/0749-7962). **2179**

NORTHWEST ETHNIC NEWS. (US/0894-3109). Qty: 8-14. **2270**

NORTHWEST EXPLORER (YELLOWKNIFE). (CN/0820-6724). **2541**

NORTHWEST FOLKLORE. (US/0029-3369). **2323**

NORTHWEST GEORGIA HISTORICAL & GENEALOGICAL QUARTERLY. (US/0887-588X). Qty: 1-2. **2464**

NORTHWEST MISSOURI GENEALOGY SOCIETY JOURNAL. (US/0741-8248). **2464**

NORTHWEST OHIO QUARTERLY. (US/0029-3407). **2751**

NORTHWEST PALATE, THE. (US/0892-8363). Qty: 12. **2351**

NORTHWEST PARKS & WILDLIFE. (US/1060-4812). Qty: 2 per year. **4169**

NORTHWEST PASSAGES HISTORICAL NEWSLETTER. (US/0885-7628). Qty: 6-10. **2751**

NORTHWEST PUBLIC POWER BULLETIN. (US/1055-6761). **1951**

NORTHWEST REVIEW (EUGENE, OR.). (US/0029-3423). **3349**

NORTHWEST RUNNER. (US/0883-7945). **4908**

NORTHWEST SAILBOARD. (US). **594**

NORTHWEST SAILBOARD. (US/1063-8164). **4908**

NORTHWEST SALES GUIDE TO HIGH-TECH COMPANIES. (US/1040-0516). **5134**

NORTHWEST SCIENCE. (US/0029-344X). **5134**

NORTHWEST TRAIL TRACER. (US/0740-4999). Qty: 4. **2464**

NORTHWESTERN JOURNAL OF INTERNATIONAL LAW & BUSINESS. (US/0196-3228). **3102**

NORTHWESTERN MINDANAO RESEARCH JOURNAL. (PH/0115-2009). **2660**

NORTHWESTERN NATURALIST : A JOURNAL OF VERTEBRATE BIOLOGY. (US/1051-1733). **4169**

NORTHWESTERN UNIVERSITY LAW REVIEW. (US/0029-3571). **3019**

NORTHWESTERNER (LARKSPUR, CALIF.). (US/0894-0800). **5433**

NORTON NOTES. (US/1049-1821). **2284**

NORVEG. (NO/0029-3601). **242**

NORWAY CURRENT, THE. (US/1071-2607). **5693**

NORWEGIAN ARCHAEOLOGICAL REVIEW. (NO/0029-3652). **276**

NOR'WESTING. (US/0739-747X). **594**

NOSTOC MAGAZINE. (US). **3467**

NOTE D'INFORMATION TECHNIQUE - CENTRE SCIENTIFIQUE ET TECHNIQUE DE LA CONSTRUCTION. (FR/0379-6264). Qty: 2. **622**

NOTE ECONOMICHE - MONTE DEI PASCHI DI SIENA. (IT/0391-8289). **1593**

NOTE TRIMESTRIELLE DE CONJONCTURE / STATEC, LUXEMBOURG. (LU). **1508**

NOTEBOOKS FOR STUDY AND RESEARCH - INTERNATIONAL INSTITUTE FOR RESEARCH AND EDUCATION. (FR/0298-7902). **4484**

NOTES AND ABSTRACTS IN AMERICAN AND INTERNATIONAL EDUCATION. (US/0029-3962). **1796**

NOTES AND QUERIES. (UK/0029-3970). **3306**

NOTES & QUERIES FOR SOMERSET AND DORSET. (UK/0029-3989). **2700**

NOTES BIBLIOGRAPHIQUES CARAIBES. (GP/0180-4103). **421**

NOTES DU CENTRE D'ETUDES DU TOURISME, LES. (CN/0229-2718). **5486**

NOTES ET DOCUMENTS (INSTITUT INTERNATIONAL JACQUES MARITAIN). (IT). **4354**

NOTES FROM UNDERGROUND. (US/0550-0974). **5388**

NOTES ON AMERICA'S FOLK ART ENVIRONMENTS. (US). **360**

NOTES ON CONTEMPORARY LITERATURE. (US/0029-4047). **3349**

NOTES ON LINGUISTICS. (US/0736-0673). **3306**

NOTES ON LITERACY. (US/0737-6707). **3307**

NOTES ON MISSISSIPPI WRITERS. (US/0029-4071). **3418**

NOTES ON SCRIPTURE IN USE. (US/0737-2876). **5018**

NOTES ON TIN. (UK/0535-3378). **4014**

NOTFALL-MEDIZIN (ERLANGEN). (GW/0341-2903). **3725**

NOTICIARIO DE HISTORIA AGRARIA. (SP/1132-1261). **115**

NOTICIAS ALIADAS. (PE). Qty: 12. **2512**

NOTICIERO DE LA AMBAC. (MX). **3237**

NOTIZIARIO CHIMICO E FARMACEUTICO. (IT/0550-1156). **988**

NOTIZIARIO DEL CENTRO DI DOCUMENTAZIONE. (IT/0392-4270). **421**

NOTIZIARIO TESSILE ABBIGLIAMENTO. (IT). **5354**

NOTIZIE AIRI. (IT). **5134**

NOTRE-DAME DU CAP. (CN/0700-6500). Qty: 9. **5033**

NOTRE DAME JOURNAL OF FORMAL LOGIC. (US/0029-4527). **4354**

NOTRE DAME LAW REVIEW, THE. (US/0745-3515). **3019**

NOTTINGHAM MEDIEVAL STUDIES. (UK/0078-2122). Qty: 4. **2624**

NOUS. (FR). Qty: 4. **5253**

NOUS (BLOOMINGTON). (US/0029-4624). **4354**

NOUS VOULONS LIRE PESSAC. (FR/0153-9027). **3349**

NOUVEAU BIOLOGISTE, LE. (FR/0181-3684). **467**

NOUVEAU RECUEIL COMPLET DES FABLIAUX. (NE). **3418**

NOUVEAUX CAHIERS, LES. (FR/0550-1350). **5051**

NOUVEL OFFICIEL DE L'AMEUBLEMENT. (FR). **2906**

NOUVELLE REVUE D'ENTOMOLOGIE. (FR/0374-9797). **5612**

NOUVELLE REVUE PEDAGOGIQUE. (FR/0029-4837). **1769**

NOUVELLE REVUE THEOLOGIQUE. (BE/0029-4845). **4982**

NOUVELLE TOUR DE FEU, LA. (FR/0294-4030). **3467**

NOUVELLES ARCHIVES HOSPITALIERES. (FR/0029-4853). **3790**

NOUVELLES DE L'A.Q.T. (CN/0826-2799). **4413**

NOUVELLES DE LA REPUBLIQUE DES LETTRES (NAPLES, ITALY). (IT/0392-2332). **3307**

NOUVELLES DE L'ACADEMIE / ACADEMIE DES SCIENCES, LES. (FR/0246-1226). **5135**

NOUVELLES DE L'ESTAMPE. (FR/0029-4888). Qty: 5. **4567**

NOUVELLES ESTHETIQUES (FRENCH ED.), LES. (FR). **405**

NOUVELLES FISCALES (PARIS), LES. (FR/0399-1636). Qty: 7. **801**

NOUVELLES / LA FEDERATION DES SOCIETES D'HISTOIRE DU QUEBEC. (CN/0829-2612). Qty: 20. **2751**

NOUVELLES, LES. (US/0270-174X). **1306**

NOUVELLES QUESTIONS FEMINISTES. (FR/0248-4951). **5563**

NOUVELLES UNIVERSITAIRES EUROPEENNES. (BE). **1838**

NOUVELLES UNIVERSITAIRES (MONTREAL). (CN/0709-8006). **1695**

NOVA ET VETERA (FRIBOURG). (SZ/0029-5027). **4982**

NOVA HRVATSKA. (UK/0143-3563). **2660**

NOVA LAW REVIEW. (US/1049-0248). **3019**

NOVA MATICA. (YU/0353-8052). **3349**

NOVA SCOTIA CHRISTMAS TREE JOURNAL. (CN/0832-8293). **2390**

NOVA SCOTIA GENEALOGIST, THE. (CN/0714-3672). **2465**

NOVA SCOTIA HISTORICAL REVIEW. (CN/0227-4752). Qty: 20. **2751**

NOVA SCOTIA MEDICAL JOURNAL, THE. (CN/0838-2638). **3623**

NOVASCOPE. (US/0892-5003). **2491**

NOVATEUR, LE. (CN/0825-0596). **1620**

NOVEL. (US/0029-5132). **3349**

NOVENYTERMELES. (HU/0546-8191). **179**

NOVI DNI. (CN/0048-1017). Qty: 24. **2270**

NOVIJ SLAH. (CN/0029-5310). **5791**

NOVOE RUSSKOE SLOVO. (US/0730-8949). **5719**

NOVOS ESTUDOS CEBRAP. (BL/0101-3300). **4485**

NOVUM GEBRAUCHSGRAPHIK. (GW/0302-9794). **381**

NOVYJ MIR. (RU/0130-7673). **3349**

NOVYJ ZURNAL. (US/0029-5337). **2851**

NOW AND THEN (JOHNSON CITY, TENN.). (US/0896-2693). **2751**

NOW DIG THIS. (UK). Qty: 12. **4142**

NOW L.A. / OFFICIAL PUBLICATION OF THE LOS ANGELES CHAPTER, NATIONAL ORGANIZATION FOR WOMEN (NOW). (US/0741-9627). **5563**

NOW (TORONTO. 1981). (CN/0712-1326). Qty: 52. **4853**

NPTA MANAGEMENT NEWS. (US/0739-2214). Qty: 4. **4235**

NRECA--APPA LEGAL REPORTING SERVICE. (US/0362-8833). **3020**

NSOA BULLETIN. (US/0146-9975). **4142**

NSPA WASHINGTON REPORTER, THE. (US/0469-3922). **749**

NSS BULLETIN, THE. (US/0146-9517). Qty: varies. **1359**

NSS NEWS. (US/0027-7010). Qty: 24-30. **1359**

NSUKKA LIBRARY NOTES. (NR/0331-1481). **3237**

NSV REPORT. (US). Qty: 5. **5253**

NTDRA DEALER NEWS. (US/0027-7045). Qty: 3/yr. **5076**

NTIAC NEWSLETTER. (US/0730-8086). **1989**

NTZ : NACHRICTENTECHNISCHE ZEITSCHRIFT. (GW/0027-707X). **1161**

NUCLEAR ENERGY (1978). (UK/0140-4067). **1951**

NUCLEAR ENGINEER, THE. (UK/0262-5091). **2156**

NUCLEAR EUROPE WORLDSCAN. (SZ/1016-5975). **2157**

NUCLEAR LAW BULLETIN. (FR/0304-341X). **3020**

NUCLEAR MEDICINE COMMUNICATIONS. (UK/0143-3636). **3848**

NUCLEAR MONITOR, THE. (US/0889-3411). Qty: 1-5. **4449**

NUCLEAR NEWS (HINSDALE). (US/0029-5574). **2157**

NUCLEAR PLANT JOURNAL. (US/0892-2055). **1952**

NUCLEAR SAFETY. (US/0029-5604). **2157**

NUCLEAR SCIENCE AND ENGINEERING. (US/0029-5639). **2157**

NUCLEAR SCIENCE APPLICATIONS. (SZ/0191-1686). **4449**

NUCLEAR SCIENCE APPLICATIONS. (SZ/0191-1686). **4449**

NUCLEAR TIMES (NEW YORK, N.Y.). (US/0734-5836). **4485**

NUCLEOSIDES & NUCLEOTIDES. (US/0732-8311). **491**

NUCLEOTECNICA. (CL/0716-0054). Qty: 2. **2157**

NUCLEUS (CALCUTTA). (II/0029-568X). Qty: 6-8. **550**

NUDE & NATURAL. (US/1070-9835). **2491**

NUESTRO. (US/0147-3247). **2270**

NUEVA REVISTA DE FILOLOGIA HISPANICA. (MX/0185-0121). **3307**

NUEZ (NEW YORK, N.Y.), LA. (US/0898-1140). **3419**

NUIT BLANCHE. (CN/0823-2490). **3419**

NUMEN (INTERNATIONAL ASSOCIATION FOR THE HISTORY OF RELIGIONS). (NE/0029-5973). **4982**

NUMERICAL FUNCTIONAL ANALYSIS AND OPTIMIZATION. (US/0163-0563). **3525**

NUMERICAL HEAT TRANSFER. PART A, APPLICATIONS. (US/1040-7782). **4432**

NUMERICAL HEAT TRANSFER. PART B, FUNDAMENTALS. (US/1040-7790). **4432**

NUMISMATIC CIRCULAR, THE. (UK). **2782**

NUMISMATIC NEWS (KRAUSE PUBLICATIONS : 1977). (US/0029-604X). **2782**

NUMISMATICA, LA. (IT). **Qty:** 20. **2782**

NUMISMATIST, THE. (US/0029-6090). **2782**

NUNCIUS. (IT). **5135**

NUOVA ANTOLOGIA. (IT/0029-6147). **2491**

NUOVA CORRENTE. (IT/0029-6155). **4354**

NUOVA EUROPA, LA. (IT). **Qty:** 30. **4983**

NUOVA RIVISTA DI NEUROLOGIA. (IT). **3844**

NUOVA RIVISTA MUSICALE ITALIANA. (IT/0029-6228). **4142**

NUOVA RIVISTA STORICA. (IT/0029-6236). **2624**

NUOVO CIMENTO DELLA SOCIETA ITALIANA DI FISICA. SEZIONE B. (IT/0369-4100). **Qty:** 50. **4413**

NUOVO CIMENTO DELLA SOCIETA ITALIANA DI FISICA [SEZIONE] C, IL. (IT/0390-5551). **Qty:** 50. **4413**

NUOVO CIMENTO DELLA SOCIETA ITALIANA DI FISICA, [SEZIONE] D. (IT/0392-6737). **Qty:** 50. **4449**

NUOVO CIMENTO DELLA SOCIETA ITALIANA DI FIZICA. SEZIONE A. (IT/0369-4097). **Qty:** 50. **4449**

NUOVO MEZZOGIORNO. (IT/0029-6376). **1509**

NUOVO OSSERVATORE, IL. (IT). **1509**

NUOVO PAESE. (AT/0311-6166). **Qty:** 6-11. **2701**

NUOVO SAGGIATORE : BOLLETTINO DELLA SOCIETA ITALIANA DI FISICA, IL. (IT). **Qty:** 50. **4413**

NURADEEN. (US/8756-4637). **5044**

NURSCENE. (CN/0382-8476). **Qty:** 2. **3862**

NURSE EDUCATOR. (US/0363-3624). **3863**

NURSE PRACTITIONER, THE. (US/0361-1817). **3863**

NURSE, THE PATIENT & THE LAW, THE. (US/0196-6790). **Qty:** 4. **3020**

NURSERY MANAGER. (US). **2426**

NURSING ADMINISTRATION QUARTERLY. (US/0363-9568). **3863**

NURSING & ALLIED HEALTH CINAHL CAMBRIDGE. CD-ROM. (US). **3661**

NURSING & HEALTH CARE. (US/0276-5284). **3863**

NURSING AND HEALTH SCIENCE EDUCATION REVIEW. (AT/1033-6273). **3863**

NURSING BC. (CN/1185-3638). **Qty:** 3-5. **3863**

NURSING ECONOMIC$. (US/0746-1739). **3864**

NURSING EXECUTIVE (HOSPITAL ED.). (US/8756-7598). **3864**

NURSING FORUM (HILLSDALE). (US/0029-6473). **Qty:** 12. **3864**

NURSING JOURNAL OF INDIA. (II/0029-6503). **3864**

NURSING MATTERS. (US/0272-9512). **3864**

NURSING OUTLOOK. (US/0029-6554). **3865**

NURSING (OXFORD). (UK/0142-0372). **3865**

NURSING RESEARCH ABSTRACTS. (UK/0141-3899). **3865**

NURSING RESEARCH (NEW YORK). (US/0029-6562). **3865**

NURSING RSA. (SA/0258-1647). **3865**

NURSINGWORLD JOURNAL. (US/0745-8630). **Qty:** 8-12. **3866**

NUT EDUCATION REVIEW. (UK/0951-7855). **Qty:** 100. **1769**

NUT KERNEL, THE. (US/0738-596X). **2426**

NUTIDA MUSIK. (SW/0029-6597). **4142**

NUTRITION ACTION HEALTH LETTER. (US/0885-7792). **4195**

NUTRITION AND CANCER. (US/0163-5581). **4195**

NUTRITION & FOOD SCIENCE. (UK/0034-6659). **4195**

NUTRITION AND HEALTH (BERKHAMSTED). (UK/0260-1060). **4195**

NUTRITION & THE M.D. (US/0732-0167). **4196**

NUTRITION (BURBANK, LOS ANGELES COUNTY, CALIF.). (US/0899-9007). **4196**

NUTRITION FORUM (PHILADELPHIA, PA.). (US/0748-8165). **Qty:** 6-10. **4196**

NUTRITION FUNDING REPORT, THE. (US/0892-1474). **4196**

NUTRITION HEALTH REVIEW. (US/0164-7202). **4196**

NUTRITION NEWS (ROSEMONT). (US/0369-6464). **4196**

NUTRITION NOTES. (US). **4196**

NUTRITION RESEARCH (NEW YORK, N.Y.). (US/0271-5317). **4196**

NUTRITION WEEK. (US/0736-0096). **4197**

NUTRITIONAL PERSPECTIVES. (US/0160-3922). **4197**

NUTSHELL NEWS. (US/0164-3290). **374**

NUTSHELL (SNOWMASS VILLAGE, COLO.). (US/0740-7971). **944**

NUTZFAHRZEUG, DAS. (GW). **5388**

NUTZUNGSARTEN DER BODENFLACHEN. (GW). **1509**

NV; NEUE VERPACKUNG. (GW/0341-0390). **4220**

NVB. NOISE & VIBRATION BULLETIN. (UK/0144-7785). **2179**

NVS NIEUWS. (NE). **4794**

NY FOOD LETTER, THE. (US/1065-7967). **2351**

NYA ANTIK & AUKTION. (SW/0346-9212). **251**

NYALA / NATIONAL FAUNA PRESERVATION SOCIETY OF MALAWI. (MW). **2201**

NYAME AKUMA. (CN/0713-5815). **277**

NYCAP NEWS. (US/1070-7336). **2179**

NYELVTUDOMANYI KOEZLEMENYEK. (HU/0029-6791). **3307**

NYLA BULLETIN. (US/0027-7134). **3238**

NYLON HIGHWAY. (US/1071-2615). **1409**

NYPIRG AGENDA. (US/1044-3134). **1298**

NYTT NORSK TIDSSKRIFT. (NO/0800-336X). **4485**

O AGRONOMICO. (BL). **116**

O ARQUEOLOGO PORTUGUES. (PO). **277**

O C P, ON CONTINUING PRACTICE. (CN/0315-1042). **4318**

O.N.E. NEWSLETTER. (CN/0229-1428). **4197**

O.S.B.E.R. OIL SPILL BULLETIN AND ENVIRONMENTAL REVIEW. (UK/0959-9134). **Qty:** 4. **2238**

O SOLO. (BL/0584-0821). **180**

OAHU UPDATE, THE. (US/1042-8038). **5487**

OAK LEAVES (BAY CITY, TEX.). (US/0740-8013). **2465**

OAKES ACORNS. (US/0897-7771). **2465**

OAKLAND POST. (US). **5638**

OAZ, OSTERREICHISCHE APOTHEKER-ZEITUNG. (AU/0253-5238). **4318**

OB. GYN. NEWS. (US/0029-7437). **3766**

OBER INCOME LETTER. (US/0882-6323). **910**

OBERFLACHE - SURFACE. (SZ/0048-1270). **4014**

OBERPFALZ, DIE. (GW/0342-9873). **Qty:** 10-15. **2701**

OBESITY RESEARCH. (US/1071-7323). **3623**

OBIETTIVO MODA. (IT). **1086**

OBION ORIGINS. (US). **2465**

OBITER DICTA (1963). (CN/0029-7585). **3020**

OBJECTOR (SAN FRANCISCO, CALIF.). (US/0279-103X). **3183**

OBJEKTIV HELLERUP. (DK/0107-6329). **4372**

OBSERVATORY, THE. (UK/0029-7704). **397**

OBSERVER (LONDON). (UK/0029-7712). **5813**

OBSERVER (RIO RANCHO, N.M.), THE. (US/1049-7374). **Qty:** 3. **5712**

OBSERVER (ROCKFORD), THE. (US/0029-7739). **Qty:** 6. **5033**

OBSIDIAN II. (US/0888-4412). **3419**

OBST UND GARTEN. (GW/0029-7798). **2426**

OBSTETRICS AND GYNECOLOGY (NEW YORK. 1953). (US/0029-7844). **3766**

OBZORNIK ZA MATEMATIKO IN FIZIKO. (XV/0473-7466). **3525**

OCCASIONAL ESSAYS. (CR). **4983**

OCCASIONAL - NOVA SCOTIA MUSEUM. (CN/0704-5824). **4094**

OCCASIONAL PAPER - MAXWELL GRADUATE SCHOOL OF CITIZENSHIP AND PUBLIC AFFAIRS. METROPOLITAN STUDIES PROGRAM. (US/0732-507X). **4670**

OCCASIONAL PAPERS - BOWDOIN COLLEGE. MUSEUM OF ART. (US/0893-0589). **4094**

OCCASIONAL PAPERS - DEPARTMENT OF HISTORY, ARKANSAS TECH UNIVERSITY. (US). **2624**

OCCASIONAL PAPERS ON ANTIQUITIES. (US/8756-047X). **251**

OCCASIONAL PAPERS ON MOLLUSKS. (US/0073-0807). **5593**

OCCASIONAL PAPERS ON RELIGION IN EASTERN EUROPE. (US/0731-5465). **4983**

OCCASIONAL PAPERS. SOUTH ASIA SERIES. (US/0076-812X). **2661**

OCCASIONAL PUBLICATION - BOREAL INSTITUTE FOR NORTHERN STUDIES. (CN/0068-0303). **2751**

OCCASIONAL STUDIES OF THE ECONOMIC COMMISSION FOR EUROPE. (SZ). **1638**

OCCUPATIONAL AND ENVIRONMENTAL MEDICINE REPORT, THE. (US/0894-2811). **Qty:** 10. **5300**

OCCUPATIONAL BRIEFS / CGP. (US/1064-7333). **4207**

OCCUPATIONAL HAZARDS. (US/0029-7909). **2866**

OCCUPATIONAL HEALTH. (UK/0029-7917). **2866**

OCCUPATIONAL SAFETY & HEALTH (BIRMINGHAM). (UK/0143-5353). **2867**

OCCUPATIONAL THERAPY IN HEALTH CARE. (US/0738-0577). **1883**

OCCUPATIONAL THERAPY IN MENTAL HEALTH. (US/0164-212X). **2867**

OCCUPATIONAL THERAPY INDEX : CURRENT AWARENESS TOPICS SERVICE. (UK/0950-6675). **1883**

OCEAN AIR INTERACTIONS. (US/0743-0876). **1359**

OCEAN AND COASTAL LAW JOURNAL. (US). **3182**

OCEAN CHALLENGE. (UK). **1453**

OCEAN DEVELOPMENT AND INTERNATIONAL LAW. (US/0090-8320). **3182**

OCEAN INDUSTRY. (US/0029-8026). **4267**

OCEAN REALM. (US/0738-9833). **1453**

OCEAN SCIENCE NEWS. (US/0029-8069). **1453**

OCEAN VOICE. (UK/0261-6777). **4181**

OCEANIA. (AT/0029-8077). **Qty:** 50. **2670**

OCEANIC ABSTRACTS (BETHESDA, MD.). (US/0748-1489). **1363**

OCEANIC LINGUISTICS. (US/0029-8115). **3307**

OCEANIS : SERIE DE DOCUMENTS OCEANOGRAPHIQUES. (FR/0182-0745). **1454**

OCEANUS (WOODS HOLE). (US/0029-8182). **1454**

OCLC MICRO. (US/8756-5196). **3238**

OCMW FOCUS. (BE). **2829**

OCONOMOWOC ENTERPRISE, THE. (US). **Qty:** 30-35. **5769**

OCTANE. (CN/0835-1740). **4267**

OCULAR SURGERY NEWS. (US/8750-3085). **3971**

ODENSE UNIVERSITY STUDIES IN ENGLISH. (DK/0078-3293). **3308**

ODESSA RECORD, THE. (US/1062-2934). **5761**

ODONATOLOGICA. (NE/0375-0183). **Qty:** 30. **467**

ODONTO-STOMATOLOGIE TROPICALE. (FR/0251-172X). **1331**

ODTU : GELISME DERGISI. (TU). **1509**

O'DWYER'S DIRECTORY OF PUBLIC RELATIONS FIRMS. (US/0078-3374). **763**

ODYSSEUS (FLUSHING, N.Y.). (US/0883-3664). **5487**

ODYSSEY (PETERBOROUGH, N.H.). (US/0163-0946). **398**

OEBALIA. (IT/0392-6613). **556**

OESTERREICHISCHE WASSERWIRTSCHAFT. (AU/0029-9588). **2094**

OESTERREICHISCHE ZEITSCHRIFT FUER VOLKSKUNDE. (AU/0029-9669). **2323**

OEUVRES ET CRITIQUES. (FR/0338-1900). **3349**

OF A LIKE MIND. (US/0892-5984). **4186**

OF COUNSEL (NEW YORK, N.Y.). (US/0730-3815). **3021**

OFF-LEAD. (US/0094-0186 #y 0094-0816). **4287**

OFF OUR BACKS. (US/0030-0071). **Qty:** 25-30. **5563**

OFF THE SHELF (HUMBLE, TEX.). (US/1059-3993). **Qty: 100. 3420**

OFFENTLICHE ABFALLBESEITIGUNG. (GW). **2238**

OFFENTLICHE DIENST, DER. (AU). **1699**

OFFICE AUTOMATION. (US/0472-6049). **4213**

OFFICE-MANAGEMENT (BADEN-BADEN). (GW/0722-2572). **880**

OFFICE PROFESSIONAL, THE. (US/0739-3156). **Qty: 3/yr. 1118**

OFFICE SYSTEMS ERGONOMICS REPORT. (US/0749-3932). **1989**

OFFICE SYSTEMS (GEORGETOWN, CONN.). (US/8750-3441). **4213**

OFFICE SYSTEMS RESEARCH JOURNAL. (US/0737-8998). **Qty: 2-4. 700**

OFFICER REVIEW. (US/0736-7317). **4053**

OFFICERSFORBUNDSBLADET. (SW). **Qty: 5-10. 4053**

OFFICIAL BOARD MARKETS. (US/0030-0284). **4235**

OFFICIAL CALIFORNIA APARTMENT JOURNAL. (US/0191-6335). **2829**

OFFICIAL DETECTIVE. (US/0894-1211). **Qty: varies. 5074**

OFFICIAL GUIDE TO AMERICAN HISTORIC INNS, THE. (US/1043-1195). **2808**

OFFICIAL HANDBOOK OF THE AAU CODE. (US/0091-3405). **4909**

OFFICIAL HOTEL AND RESORT GUIDE. (US). **2808**

OFFICIAL JOURNAL - ILLINOIS POLICE ASSOCIATION. (US/0019-2171). **3171**

OFFICIAL JOURNAL OF THE INSTITUTE OF LABOUR RELATIONS, UNIVERSITY OF SOUTH AFRICA. (SA/0379-8410). **1699**

OFFICIAL MOTOR CARRIER DIRECTORY. (US/0472-6243). **5388**

OFFICIAL MUSEUM PRODUCTS AND SERVICES DIRECTORY, THE. (US/0276-637X). **4094**

OFFICIAL STAR TREK FAN CLUB OF CANADA. (CN/1192-7445). **5234**

OFFICIAL UNITED STATES TENNIS ASSOCIATION YEARBOOK AND TENNIS GUIDE WITH THE OFFICIAL RULES, THE. (US/0196-5425). **4910**

OFFSHORE (CONROE, TEX.). (US/0030-0608). **4267**

OFFSHORE RESEARCH FOCUS. (UK/0309-4189). **Qty: 12. 4267**

OFFSHORE TAX PLANNING REVIEW. (UK). **4739**

OFFSHORE (WEST NEWTON). (US/0274-9394). **594**

OH CALCUTTA. (II/0377-7596). **2507**

OH&S CANADA. (CN/0827-4576). **2867**

OHIO. (US/0279-3504). **2541**

OHIO ARCHIVIST (1987), THE. (US/1047-5400). **3239**

OHIO CPA JOURNAL, THE. (US/0749-8284). **749**

OHIO HISTORY. (US/0030-0934). **2752**

OHIO HOLSTEIN NEWS. (US/0199-7580). **197**

OHIO JOURNAL OF SCIENCE, THE. (US/0030-0950). **Qty: 20. 5136**

OHIO LIBRARIES (COLUMBUS, OHIO. 1988). (US/1046-4336). **Qty: varies. 3239**

OHIO MEDIA SPECTRUM. (US/0192-6942). **3239**

OHIO MONTHLY RECORD. (US/0163-0008). **3021**

OHIO MOTOR VEHICLE LAWS. (US). **3021**

OHIO NEWS (WOOSTER, OHIO). (US/0899-4862). **197**

OHIO NORTHERN UNIVERSITY LAW REVIEW. (US/0094-534X). **Qty: 4. 3021**

OHIO QUERIES. (US/0897-7747). **2465**

OHIO READING TEACHER. (US/0030-1035). **Qty: 16. 3308**

OHIO REVIEW (ATHENS), THE. (US/0360-1013). **Qty: 6. 3420**

OHIO RUNNER, THE. (US/0279-9634). **4910**

OHIO STATE JOURNAL ON DISPUTE RESOLUTION. (US/1046-4344). **3022**

OHIO STATE LAW JOURNAL. (US/0048-1572). **3022**

OHIO WRITER. (US/0896-5730). **2923**

OHIOANA QUARTERLY. (US/0030-1248). **3420**

OHIOSCAPES NEWSLETTER. (US). **2830**

OHS BULLETIN. (CN/0714-6736). **2541**

OIKOS. (DK/0030-1299). **2220**

OIL & GAS DIRECTORY (HOUSTON, TEX. 1970). (US). **4268**

OIL AND GAS FIELD STUDIES. (US/0161-0961). **4268**

OIL & GAS FINANCE & ACCOUNTANCY. (UK/0902-3752). **Qty: 4-5. 749**

OIL & GAS FINANCE AND ACCOUNTING. (UK/0962-3752). **Qty: 8-9. 749**

OIL & GAS (OXFORD, OXFORDSHIRE). (UK/0263-5070). **3022**

OIL & GAS RUSSIA & POST SOVIET REPUBLICS. HYDROCARBONS BRIEF. (UK/0967-537X). **Qty: 16. 4269**

OIL GAS. (GW/0342-5622). **4269**

OILWEEK. (CN/0030-1515). **4270**

OISEAU ET LA REVUE FRANCAISE D'ORNITHOLOGIE. (FR/0030-1531). **5619**

OJANCANO (CHAPEL HILL, N.C.). (US/0899-983X). **3420**

OJC THE OHIO JEWISH CHRONICLE, THE. (US). **5729**

OKANAGAN HISTORY. (CN/0830-0739). **2752**

OKIKA O HAWAII, NA. (US/0099-8745). **2426**

OKIKE. (NR/0331-0566). **3420**

OKLAHOMA BANKER. (US/0030-1647). **802**

OKLAHOMA BAR JOURNAL, THE. (US/0030-1655). **Qty: 48. 3022**

OKLAHOMA CITY UNIVERSITY LAW REVIEW. (US/0364-9458). **3022**

OKLAHOMA CONSTITUTION, THE. (US/0890-1007). **Qty: 4. 4671**

OKLAHOMA COWMAN. (US/0030-1698). **217**

OKLAHOMA DENTAL ASSOCIATION JOURNAL. (US/0164-9442). **1331**

OKLAHOMA EAGLE, THE. (US/0745-385X). **5732**

OKLAHOMA GENEALOGICAL SOCIETY QUARTERLY. (US/0474-0742). **Qty: 30. 2465**

OKLAHOMA GEOLOGY NOTES. (US/0030-1736). **Qty: 1-2. 1443**

OKLAHOMA HOME & LIFE STYLE. (US/0895-1586). **2542**

OKLAHOMA LAW REVIEW. (US/0030-1752). **Qty: 1. 3022**

OKLAHOMA OBSERVER, THE. (US/0030-1795). **4485**

OKLAHOMA REALTOR. (US/0745-5046). **4842**

OKLAHOMA TODAY. (US/0030-1892). **2542**

OKLAHOMA WOMEN'S FRONT PAGE NEWS. (US/1071-1643). **Qty: 12. 5563**

OKMULGEE COUNTY GENEALOGICAL SOCIETY NEWSLETTER. (US). **Qty: 3-4 per year. 2465**

OKONOMI OG POLITIK. (DK/0030-1906). **1577**

OKUMENISCHE RUNDSCHAU. (GW/0029-8654). **4983**

OLD BOTTLE MAGAZINE. (US/0030-1965). **252**

OLD CAR VALUE GUIDE. (US/0475-1876). **5422**

OLD CARS. (US/0048-1637). **5422**

OLD CARS PRICE GUIDE. (US/0194-6404). **5422**

OLD DOMINION GARDENER. (US/0274-6956). **2426**

OLD-HOUSE JOURNAL, THE. (US/0094-0178). **623**

OLD LADY OF THREADNEEDLE STREET, THE. (UK). **2520**

OLD LAWRENCE REMINISCENCES. (US/1044-1905). **2465**

OLD LYONS RECORDER, THE. (US). **Qty: varies. 5644**

OLD MILL NEWS. (US/0276-3338). **305**

OLD NORTHWEST, THE. (US/0360-5531). **2752**

OLD TESTAMENT ABSTRACTS. (US/0364-8591). **5013**

OLD TESTAMENT ESSAYS. (SA/1010-9919). **5018**

OLD TIME COUNTRY. (US/1044-1042). **4143**

OLD-TIME HERALD. (US/1040-3582). **4143**

OLD TOY SOLDIER. (US/1064-4164). **Qty: 4-5. 2585**

OLD WEST. (US/0030-2058). **2752**

OLD WORLD ARCHAEOLOGY NEWSLETTER. (US/0732-1635). **Qty: 2-3. 277**

OLDE MACHINERY MART. (AT/1031-4555). **2123**

OLDE TIMES. (US/0883-6442). **2752**

OLEAGINEUX. (FR/0030-2082). **117**

OLIFANT. (US/0381-9132). **3420**

OLMSTE(A)D'S GENEALOGY RECORDED. (US/0162-0800). **2465**

O'LOCHLAINNS PERSONAL JOURNAL OF IRISH FAMILIES. (US/1056-0378). **Qty: 40. 2465**

OLS NEWS : THE INDEPENDENT VOICE OF OPEN LEARNING. (UK/0169-9729). **1770**

OLSEN'S AGRIBUSINESS REPORT. (US/0197-9361). **Qty: 12. 117**

OLSEN'S BIOTECHNOLOGY REPORT. (US/0889-616X). **Qty: 12. 3695**

OLYMPIC REVIEW. (SZ/0377-192X). **4910**

OMAHA STAR, THE. (US). **5707**

OMAHA WORLD-HERALD (OMAHA, NB : 1954 : SUNRISE ED.). (US). **5707**

O'MAHONY JOURNAL, THE. (IE). **2465**

OMBUDSMAN OFFICE PROFILES / INTERNATIONAL OMBUDSMAN OFFICE PROFILES. (CN/0714-6132). **3022**

OMEGA (FARMINGDALE). (US/0030-2228). **4606**

OMNI : OPTICAL MEDIA NEWS AND INFORMATION. (UK). **1277**

ON BALANCE (DENVER, COLO.). (US/1062-7049). **Qty: (varies). 4606**

ON CAMPUS (SASKATOON). (CN/0711-3617). **1839**

ON CAMPUS WITH WOMEN. (US/0734-0141). **5563**

ON CUE. (US/1041-6234). **1770**

ON DISENO. (SP). **2902**

ON GUARD (CLEVELAND, TENN.). (US/0738-758X). **4983**

ON GUARD (NEW YORK, N.Y.). (US/1064-007X). **Qty: 1-2. 4053**

ON-LINE REVIEW. (UK/0309-314X). **1275**

ON LOCATION. (US/0149-7014). **4075**

ON ONE WHEEL. (US/0893-4606). **429**

ON OUR BACKS. (US/0890-2224). **Qty: 20-40. 2795**

ON THE ISSUES. (US/0895-6014). **5563**

ON THE LEVEL ASHFIELD. (AT/1036-8124). **Qty: 12. 2600**

ON THE RISK. (US/0885-4416). **Qty: 4. 2889**

ON THE STRATEGY OF INDUSTRIALIZATION IN DEVELOPING COUNTRIES AND THE EXPERIENCES IN THE ECONOMIC AND SOCIAL DEVELOPMENT IN SOCIALIST COUNTRIES. (GW). **1620**

ON TRACK (SANTA ANA, CALIF.). (US/0279-2737). **Qty: 12. 4911**

ONALASKA COMMUNITY LIFE. (US/1053-6906). **Qty: 48. 5769**

ONCOGENES. (UK/0950-0561). **550**

ONCOLOGY. (SZ/0030-2414). **3821**

ONCOLOGY NURSING FORUM. (US/0190-535X). **3866**

ONDE ELECTRIQUE. (FR/0030-2430). **2074**

ONDERNEMEN. (BE/0772-3326). **5065**

ONE CHURCH. (US/0030-2503). **5039**

ONE IN CHRIST. (UK/0030-252X). **4983**

ONE PEACEFUL WORLD. (US). **2220**

ONE-PERSON LIBRARY, THE. (US/0748-8831). **Qty: 12-15. 3239**

ONE TO ONE. (US/0739-5442). **Qty: 5-10. 1135**

ONE, TWO, THREE, FOUR. (US/0889-0536). **4143**

ONE WORLD (GENEVA). (SZ/0303-125X). **4983**

ONKOLOGIE. (SZ/0378-584X). **3822**

ONLINE & CDROM REVIEW : THE INTERNATIONAL JOURNAL OF ONLINE & OPTICAL INFORMATION SYSTEMS. (UK). **1275**

ONLINE (COLOGNE, GERMANY : 1982). (GW). **1197**

ONLINE HOTLINE NEWS SERVICE. (US/1040-6646). **1197**

ONLINE TODAY. (US/0891-4672). **3239**

ONLINE (WESTON, CONN.). (US/0146-5422). **Qty: (3/4 per issue). 1275**

ONOMA. (BE/0078-463X). **3308**

ONOMASTICA CANADIANA. (CN/0078-4656). **Qty: 10-12. 3308**

ONOMASTICKY ZPRAVODAJ CSAV. (XR). **3308**

ONS AMSTERDAM. (NE/0166-1809). **2701**

ONS ERFDEEL. (BE/0030-2651). **327**

ONS GEESTEILJK ERF. (BE/0774-2827). **4983**

ONTARIO AMATEUR WRESTLING ASSOCIATION RESULTS BOOK. (CN/0822-6806). **4911**

ONTARIO ANNUAL PRACTICE (1973). (CN/0318-3556). **3142**

ONTARIO BIRD BANDING. (CN/0475-025X). **5619**

ONTARIO BIRDS. (CN/0822-3890). **5619**

ONTARIO BRANCH NEWS. (CN/0710-345X). **4795**

ONTARIO BUSINESS. (CN/0227-1397). **701**

ONTARIO CONSERVATION NEWS. (CN/0383-6479). **Qty:** 16-20. **2201**

ONTARIO DEMOCRAT, THE. (CN/0827-2247). **4485**

ONTARIO FIELD BIOLOGIST, THE. (CN/0078-4834). **467**

ONTARIO FOLKDANCER. (CN/0384-5052). **1314**

ONTARIO HISTORY. (CN/0030-2953). **2752**

ONTARIO MATHEMATICS GAZETTE. (CN/0030-3011). **3525**

ONTARIO MEDICAL REVIEW. (CN/0030-302X). **3624**

ONTARIO MEDICAL TECHNOLOGIST / ONTARIO SOCIETY OF MEDICAL TECHNOLOGISTS. (CN/0228-877X). **3624**

ONTARIO MUNICIPAL BOARD REPORTS. (CN/0318-7527). **3023**

ONTARIO OUT OF DOORS. (CN/0707-3178). **4876**

ONTARIO PIPELINE. (CN/0380-1624). **5537**

ONTARIO PSYCHOLOGIST, THE. (CN/0030-3054). **4606**

ONTARIO RECYCLING UPDATE. (CN/0823-6143). **2238**

ONTARIO TECHNOLOGIST, THE. (CN/0380-1969). **5136**

ONTARIO VACATION FARMS. (CN/0712-1636). **5487**

ONTARIO WATER SKIER, THE. (CN/0226-5702). **4911**

ONTHEBUS (LOS ANGELES, CALIF.). (US/1043-884X). **Qty:** 40. **3420**

ONTONAGON HERALD. (US). **Qty:** 26. **5693**

ONZE TAAL (AMSTERDAM, NETHERLANDS). (NE). **3308**

ONZE VOGELS. (NE). **5619**

OP CIT. (IT/0030-3305). **Qty:** 15. **361**

OPEC BULLETIN. (AU/0474-6279). **Qty:** 5. **4270**

OPEC REVIEW. (US/0277-0180). **4270**

OPELIKA AUBURN NEWS. (US/1044-7539). **5627**

OPEN DOOR (LEXINGTON, KY.), THE. (US/0732-6319). **1102**

OPEN DOORS (SANTA ANA, CALIF.). (US/8756-5234). **4983**

OPEN EARTH. (UK/0141-3619). **1359**

OPEN HANDS. (US/0888-8833). **Qty:** 3-4. **2795**

OPEN LEARNING. (UK/0268-0513). **1801**

OPEN MINDS. (US/1043-3880). **Qty:** 12/yr. **4606**

OPEN SPACE (OPEN SPACES SOCIETY, GREAT BRITAIN). (UK). **Qty:** 30. **2201**

OPEN WHEEL. (US/0279-0254). **4911**

OPENBAAR KUNSTBEZIT IN VLAANDEREN. (BE). **327**

OPER UND KONZERT (MUNCHEN). (GW/0030-3518). **4143**

OPERA AUSTRALIA. (AT). **4143**

OPERA CANADA. (CN/0030-3577). **Qty:** varies. **4143**

OPERA FANATIC. (US/0891-3757). **4143**

OPERA JOURNAL, THE. (US/0030-3585). **4143**

OPERA (LONDON). (UK/0030-3526). **4143**

OPERA MONTHLY. (US/0897-6554). **4143**

OPERA NEWS. (US/0030-3607). **4143**

OPERA QUARTERLY, THE. (US/0736-0053). **4144**

OPERATING SURVEY OF CANADIAN RETAILING. (CN/0824-6769). **956**

OPERATIONS MANAGEMENT REVIEW. (US/0734-1458). **881**

OPERATIONS OF BANK PEMBANGUNAN INDONESIA. (IO). **802**

OPERATIONS RESEARCH/MANAGEMENT SCIENCE. (US/0030-3658). **1209**

OPERATIONS RESEARCH/MANAGEMENT SCIENCE YEARBOOK. (US/0473-0496). **881**

OPERATIVE DENTISTRY. (US/0361-7734). **1332**

OPERATIVE ORTHOPADIE UND TRAUMATOLOGIE. (GW/0934-6694). **3883**

OPERATORE SANITARIO, L'. (IT/0392-5153). **Qty:** 12-15. **3624**

OPHTHALMIC & PHYSIOLOGICAL OPTICS. (UK/0275-5408). **4216**

OPHTHALMIC LITERATURE. (UK/0030-3720). **3877**

OPHTHALMIC PAEDIATRICS AND GENETICS. (NE/0167-6784). **550**

OPHTHALMIC PRACTICE. (CN/0832-9869). **Qty:** 10-12. **3877**

OPHTHALMIC SURGERY. (US/0022-023X). **3971**

OPHTHALMOLOGICA (BASEL). (SZ/0030-3755). **3877**

OPHTHALMOLOGY (ROCHESTER, MINN.). (US/0161-6420). **3878**

OPINION. (US). **3023**

OPINION DE BAGDAD, L'. (IQ). **4485**

OPINION (LOS ANGELES, CALIF.), LA. (US/0276-590X). **5638**

OPPORTUNITY (CHICAGO, ILL. : 1983). (US/0741-3750). **701**

OPSEARCH. (II/0030-3887). **Qty:** 15. **881**

OPTICA PURA Y APLICADA. (SP/0030-3917). **4439**

OPTICAL AND QUANTUM ELECTRONICS. (UK/0306-8919). **4439**

OPTICAL COMPUTING & PROCESSING. (UK/0954-2264). **1277**

OPTICAL ENGINEERING. (US/0091-3286). **4439**

OPTICAL INDUSTRY & SYSTEMS ENCYCLOPEDIA & DICTIONARY, THE. (US/0191-0639). **4439**

OPTICAL PRISM. (CN/0824-3441). **4216**

OPTICS AND LASER TECHNOLOGY. (UK/0030-3992). **4439**

OPTICS AND PHOTONICS NEWS. (US/1047-6938). **4439**

OPTIK; ZEITSCHRIFT FUER LICHT- UND ELEKTRONENOPTIK. (GW). **4440**

OPTIMIST (ABILENE), THE. (US/0030-4069). **1094**

OPTIMST, THE. (CN/0384-5230). **Qty:** 2-4. **5563**

OPTION FINANCE ED. FRANCAISE. (FR/0989-1900). **Qty:** 2. **802**

OPTION (LOS ANGELES, CALIF.). (US/0882-178X). **4144**

OPTION PAIX. (CN/0823-9703). **4530**

OPTIONS (WAYNE, N.J.). (US/0362-2770). **2270**

OPTOLASER MILANO. (IT/1120-8724). **2074**

OPTOMETRIE. (GW/0030-4123). **4216**

OPTOMETRISTE. (CN/0708-3173). **Qty:** 8. **4216**

OPTOMETRY TODAY. (II). **Qty:** 4. **4217**

OPTOMETRY TODAY (LONDON). (UK/0268-5485). **4217**

OPUS INTERNATIONAL. (FR/0048-2056). **327**

OPUSCULA ARCHAEOLOGICA (ZAGREB, CROATIA). (CI/0473-0992). **277**

OPUSCULA ATHENIENSIA. (SW/0078-5520). **1078**

OR MANAGER. (US/8756-8047). **3866**

ORACION DE LAS HORAS. (SP). **4984**

ORACLE MAGAZINE. (US/1065-3171). **1198**

ORAFO ITALIANO. (IT/0471-7376). **2915**

ORAITA. (IS). **5051**

ORAL HEALTH. (CN/0030-4204). **1332**

ORAL HISTORY ASSOCIATION OF AUSTRALIA JOURNAL. (AT/0158-7366). **Qty:** varies. **2670**

ORAL HISTORY (COLCHESTER). (UK/0143-0955). **2625**

ORAL HISTORY REVIEW, THE. (US/0094-0798). **2625**

ORAL SURGERY, ORAL MEDICINE, ORAL PATHOLOGY. (US/0030-4220). **1332**

ORAL TRADITION. (US/0883-5365). **2323**

ORANA. (AT/0045-6705). **3239**

ORANGE COUNTY GENEALOGICAL SOCIETY. (US/0736-0185). **2465**

ORANGE COUNTY LAWYER. (US/0897-5698). **Qty:** 2. **3023**

ORANGE LEADER (ORANGE, TEX.). (US/0885-8047). **5753**

ORANGEVILLE CITIZEN, THE. (CN/0319-180X). **5792**

ORATORI DEL GIORNO, GLI. (IT/0393-4012). **3023**

ORBIS; BULLETIN INTERNATIONAL DE DOCUMENTATION LINGUISTIQUE. (BE/0030-4379). **Qty:** 15. **3308**

ORBIS LITTERARUM. (DK/0105-7510). **3420**

ORBIS MUSICAE. (IS/0303-3937). **4144**

ORBIS (PHILADELPHIA). (US/0030-4387). **4485**

ORBIS (YOULGREAVE, DERBYSHIRE). (UK/0030-4425). **3467**

ORBIT (AMSTERDAM). (NE/0167-6830). **3878**

ORBIT (TORONTO). (CN/0030-4433). **1902**

ORCHADIAN, THE. (AT/0474-3342). **2426**

ORCHARDIST OF NEW ZEALAND, THE. (NZ/0110-6260). **180**

ORCHESTER, DAS. (GW/0030-4468). **4144**

ORCHID ADVOCATE, THE. (US/0097-9546). **2426**

ORCHID DIGEST, THE. (US/0199-9559). **2426**

ORCHID REVIEW. (UK/0030-4476). **2436**

ORCHIDEE, DIE. (GW/0473-1425). **Qty:** 10-20. **2426**

ORCRIST. (US/0474-3369). **3420**

ORDER (DORDRECHT). (NE/0167-8094). **3526**

OREGON HISTORICAL QUARTERLY. (US/0030-4727). **2752**

OREGON LAW REVIEW. (US/0196-2043). **Qty:** seldom. **3023**

OREGON OPTOMETRY. (US/0274-6549). **4217**

ORFF ECHO, THE. (US/0095-2613). **4144**

ORGAN (ABBOTSFORD). (CN/0703-1254). **3420**

ORGAN (BOURNEMOUTH). (UK/0030-4883). **4144**

ORGAN YEARBOOK, THE. (NE/0920-3192). **4144**

ORGANI DI TRASMISSIONE. (IT). **2123**

ORGANIC FARMER (MONTPELIER, VT.). (US/1063-6803). **Qty:** 8-10. **117**

ORGANIC MASS SPECTROMETRY. (UK/0030-493X). **1018**

ORGANIC PREPARATIONS AND PROCEDURES INTERNATIONAL. (US/0030-4948). **1045**

ORGANISER. (II). **5253**

ORGANISTS' REVIEW. (UK/0048-2161). **4144**

ORGANIZACIJA IN KADRI. (YU/0350-1531). **881**

ORGANIZATION DEVELOPMENT JOURNAL. (US/0889-6402). **Qty:** 4-10. **881**

ORGANIZATION STUDIES. (GW/0170-8406). **5211**

ORGANIZATION TRENDS. (US/0882-5769). **4338**

ORGANIZER MAILING, THE. (US/1063-9233). **Qty:** 10. **4671**

ORGANIZZAZIONE SANITARIA. (IT/0394-283X). **Qty:** 6. **3790**

ORGANO, L'. (IT). **4144**

ORGANO OFICIAL DE LA JUNTA CIVICO-MILITAR CUBANA. (US/0272-4650). **2752**

ORGANOMETALLIC COMPOUNDS. (UK/0030-5138). **1045**

ORGANOMETALLICS. (US/0276-7333). **1045**

ORGEL (AMERSFOORT, NETHERLANDS). (NE). **4144**

ORGUE (PARIS), L'. (FR/0030-5170). **4145**

ORIENS ANTIQUUS. (IT/0030-5189). **2661**

ORIENS EXTREMUS. (GW/0030-5197). **3420**

ORIENT (DEUTSCHES ORIENT-INSTITUT). (GW/0030-5227). **2661**

ORIENTAL ART. (UK/0030-5278). **Qty:** 12. **361**

ORIENTAL INSECTS. (US/0030-5316). **Qty:** 3-4. **5612**

ORIENTALIA CHRISTIANA ANALECTA. (IT). **5039**

ORIENTALIA CHRISTIANA PERIODICA. (IT/0030-5375). **5039**

ORIENTALIA LOVANIENSIA PERIODICA. (BE/0085-4522). **3308**

ORIENTATIONS (HONG KONG). (HK/0030-5448). **2661**

ORIENTATIONS (TORONTO). (CN/0710-2151). **1839**

ORIENTE MODERNO. (IT/0030-5472). **2661**

ORIENTEERING NORTH AMERICA. (US/0886-1080). **Qty:** 2-3. **4911**

ORIENTO. (JA). **2661**

ORIGINAL WNC BUSINESS JOURNAL, THE. (US/1065-027X). **Qty:** 4-6. **701**

ORIGINS (GA.). (US). **2465**

ORIGINS (LOMA LINDA). (US/0093-7495). **Qty:** 4. **5136**

ORIGINS RESEARCH. (US/0748-9919). **4354**

ORION. (IT). **Qty:** 24-30. **4486**

ORION (NEW YORK, N.Y.). (US/1058-3130). **4170**

ORITA. (NR/0030-5596). **4984**

ORKESTER JOURNALEN. (SW/0030-5642). **4145**

ORLANDO SPECTATOR, THE. (US/1070-860X). **Qty:** 3-4. **5650**

ORNAMENTAL/MISCELLANEOUS METAL FABRICATOR. (US/0191-5940). **Qty:** 6. **4014**

ORNIS FENNICA. (FI/0030-5685). **5619**

ORNIS SCANDINAVICA. (NO/0030-5693). **5619**

ORNITHOLOGISCHE BEOBACHTER. (SZ/0030-5707). **5619**

ORNITHOLOGISCHE MITTEILUNGEN. (GW/0030-5723). **5619**

OROMOCTO POST, THE. (CN/0710-5460). **5792**

ORQUIDEA (MEXICO. 1971). (MX/0300-3701). **520**

ORSA JOURNAL ON COMPUTING. (US/0899-1499). **1198**

ORSTOM ACTUALITES. (FR/0758-833X). **Qty:** 20. **5136**

ORTE. (SZ). **3421**

ORTHODONTIC REVIEW. (US/0895-5034). **1332**

ORTHODOX CATHOLIC VOICE, THE. (US). **Qty:** 4-5. **5039**

ORTHODOX HERALD, THE. (US/0744-1495). **5039**

ORTHODOX LIFE. (US/0030-5820). **5040**

ORTHODOX OBSERVER. (US/0731-2547). **4984**

ORTHODOX TRADITION. (US/0742-4019). **4984**

ORTHODOX WORD, THE. (US/0030-5839). **Qty:** 1. **5040**

ORTHODOXIE HEUTE. (GW/0931-0347). **5040**

ORTHOPAEDIC PRODUCT NEWS. (UK/0954-4755). **3883**

ORTHOPAEDIC REVIEW. (US/0094-6591). **3883**

ORTHOPEDIC NURSING / NATIONAL ASSOCIATION OF ORTHOPEDIC NURSES. (US/0744-6020). **3884**

ORTHOPEDICS (THOROFARE). (US/0147-7447). **3884**

ORYX. (UK/0030-6053). **2201**

OS2 PROFESSIONAL. (US/1069-6814). **1289**

OSAGE COUNTY CHRONICLE (BURLINGAME, KAN. : 1983). (US/1040-6077). **5678**

OSCAR ISRAELOWITZ'S GUIDE TO JEWISH NEW YORK CITY. (US). **5269**

OSERS NEWS IN PRINT. (US/0888-5508). **5300**

OSGOOD JOURNAL, THE. (US). **5666**

OSGOODE HALL LAW JOURNAL. (CN). **3023**

OSHKAABEWIS NATIVE JOURNAL. (US/1053-0193). **3421**

OSHKOSH ADVANCE-TITAN. (US/0300-676X). **Qty:** 7. **5769**

OSNABRUCKER LAND HEIMAT-JAHRBUCH. (GW). **2701**

OSPEDALE. (IT/0030-6231). **3790**

OSPEDALI D'ITALIA-CHIRURGIA. (IT/0030-6266). **3971**

OSSERVATORE ROMANO, L'. (VC/0030-6312). **5813**

OSSERVATORIO SUL MERCATO IMMOBILIARE. (IT). **4842**

OSTEOPATHIE : THERAPIES MANUELLES. (FR/0753-6019). **4795**

OSTERREICHISCHE AMTSVORMUND, DER. (AU). **3122**

OSTERREICHISCHE FORSTZEITUNG (1987). (AU). **2390**

OSTERREICHISCHE JURISTEN-ZEITUNG. (AU/0029-9251). **3024**

OSTERREICHISCHE ZEITSCHRIFT FUER POLITIKWISSENSCHAFT. (AU/0378-5149). **4486**

OSTERREICHISCHE ZEITSCHRIFT FUER VERMESSUNGSWESEN UND PHOTOGRAMMETRIE. (GW). **2571**

OSTERREICHISCHES RECHT DER WIRTSCHAFT. (AU). **3024**

OSTERREICHS FISCHEREI. (AU/0029-9987). **Qty:** 30-40. **2310**

OSTEUROPA (STUTTGART). (GW/0030-6428). **4486**

OSTEUROPA WIRTSCHAFT. (GW/0030-6460). **1511**

OSTOMY QUARTERLY. (US/0030-6517). **3971**

OSTRICH. SUPPLEMENT, THE. (SA). **5593**

OSU QUEST. (US/0279-0025). **1839**

OTAR. (NE). **2028**

OTHER ISRAEL : NEWSLETTER OF THE ISRAELI COUNCIL FOR ISRAELI-PALESTINIAN PEACE, THE. (IS/0792-4615). **Qty:** 20. **2270**

OTHER SIDE (SAVANNAH), THE. (US/0145-7675). **4984**

OTIS RUSH. (AT/0819-7288). **Qty:** varies. **327**

OTOLARYNGOLOGY AND HEAD AND NECK SURGERY. (US/0194-5998). **3971**

OTORINOLARINGOLOGIA. (IT/0392-6621). **3890**

OTTAR. (NO/0030-6703). **4170**

OTTAWA ARCHAEOLOGIST, THE. (CN/0702-7974). **277**

OTTAWA BANDING GROUP. (CN/0827-2298). **5619**

OTTAWA BRANCH NEWS - ONTARIO GENEALOGICAL SOCIETY. (CN/0708-5583). **2466**

OTTAWA JEWISH BULLETIN (1993). (CN/1196-1929). **2270**

OTTAWA LAW REVIEW. (CN/0048-2331). **Qty:** 12. **3024**

OTTAWA SUN, THE. (CN/0843-2570). **Qty:** 24. **5792**

OTTERWISE (PORTLAND, ME.). (US/1052-8415). **Qty:** 4. **1067**

OTTO NOVECENTO. (IT). **3421**

OUA/DATA'S ... GUIDE TO CORPORATE GIVING IN MAINE. (US/0883-2730). **4338**

OUDTESTAMENTISCHE STUDIEN. (NE/0169-7226). **5018**

OUR GENERATION (MONTREAL). (CN/0030-686X). **4544**

OUR LADY'S DIGEST. (US/0030-6886). **4984**

OUR LIBRARY PRESENTS ... . (US). **3240**

OUR OWN. (US). **Qty:** 30. **2795**

OUR SUNDAY VISITOR. (US/0030-6967). **5034**

OUR TIMES (TORONTO). (CN/0822-6377). **Qty:** 10. **1700**

OUR WORLD (DAYTONA BEACH, FLA.). (US/1044-6699). **5487**

OURS (MINNEAPOLIS, MINN.). (US/0899-9333). **Qty:** 6. **5300**

OUSLEY NEWSLETTER. (US/0733-6381). **2466**

OUT & ABOUT (NEW HAVEN, CONN.). (US/1066-7776). **Qty:** 6/year. **2795**

OUT AUCKLAND. (NZ/0110-4454). **2795**

OUT/LOOK (SAN FRANCISCO, CALIF.). (US/0896-7733). **2795**

OUT (NEW YORK, N.Y.). (US/1062-7928). **Qty:** 3. **2795**

OUT WEST (SACRAMENTO, CALIF.). (US/0899-1413). **5488**

OUTAOUAIS GENEALOGIQUE. (CN/0707-8137). **2466**

OUTBOUND (WILLOWDALE). (CN/0843-1566). **31**

OUTCROP (DENVER, COLO.). (US/0888-5184). **1390**

OUTDOOR HIGHLIGHTS. (US/0279-8700). **4876**

OUTDOOR INDIANA. (US/0030-7068). **Qty:** 1-3. **4707**

OUTDOOR JOURNAL. (US/0890-7196). **4877**

OUTDOOR OKLAHOMA. (US/0030-7106). **Qty:** 3. **4877**

OUTDOOR SPORTS & RECREATION. (US/0892-8355). **4877**

OUTDOORS ILLUSTRATED. (UK/0962-1016). **Qty:** 10. **4877**

OUTDOORS UNLIMITED. (US/0030-7181). **3421**

OUTDOORS WEST. (US). **4877**

OUTLOOK (GRAND RAPIDS, MICH.), THE. (US/8750-5754). **5065**

OUTLOOK NEW CHURCH. GENERAL CONFERENCE. (UK/0969-1049). **4984**

OUTLOOK (WASHINGTON, D.C. 1989). (US/1044-5706). **5564**

OUTPOST EXCHANGE. (US/0748-8394). **1298**

OUTPUT. (SZ/0303-8351). **1261**

OUTPUT (RICHMOND HILL). (CN/1184-9770). **Qty:** 1-5. **1224**

OUTREACH (CHICAGO). (US/0270-207X). **3725**

OUTSIDE (1980). (US/0278-1433). **4877**

OUTSIDE PLANT. (US/0747-8763). **1119**

OVERHEIDSMANAGEMENT : VAKBLAD VOOR FINANCIEN AUTOMATISERING EN PERSONEEL 7 ORGANISATIE. (NE/0928-8503). **4672**

OVERLAND. (AT/0030-7416). **Qty:** 70. **2511**

OVERLAND JOURNAL. (US/0738-1093). **Qty:** 12 per year. **2752**

OVERSEAS DEVELOPMENT. (UK). **2911**

OVERSEAS JOBS EXPRESS. (UK/0966-7660). **4208**

OVERTONES (LINCOLN, NEB.). (US/0884-920X). **3240**

OVERVIEW (TORONTO). (CN/0700-3617). **4486**

OWL (DON MILLS). (CN/0382-6627). **1067**

OWL OF MINERVA, THE. (US/0030-7580). **Qty:** 12 yr. **4354**

OWNER BUILDER MAGAZINE. (AT/0728-7275). **Qty:** occasionally. **623**

OWNERS AT WORK. (US/1046-5049). **1543**

OWOSSO ARGUS-PRESS, THE. (US). **Qty:** 12. **5693**

OXFORD ART JOURNAL. (UK/0142-6540). **361**

OXFORD BULLETIN OF ECONOMICS AND STATISTICS. (UK/0305-9049). **1577**

OXFORD JOURNAL OF LEGAL STUDIES. (UK/0143-6503). **3024**

OXFORD LITERARY REVIEW, THE. (UK/0305-1498). **3349**

OXFORD POETRY (OXFORD, OXFORDSHIRE). (UK). **3467**

OXFORD REVIEW OF EDUCATION. (UK/0305-4985). **1771**

OXFORD SLAVONIC PAPERS. (UK/0078-7256). **3336**

OXFORD STUDIES IN COMPARATIVE EDUCATION. (UK/0961-2149). **1771**

OXFORDSHIRE FAMILY HISTORIAN, THE. (UK). **2466**

OXIDATION COMMUNICATIONS. (BU/0209-4541). **1045**

OXONIENSIA. (UK). **277**

OXYGEN RADICALS. (UK/0950-057X). **491**

OYO YAKURI. (JA/0300-8533). **4319**

OZ ARTS MAGAZINE. (AT/1037-1311). **327**

OZARKS MOUNTAINEER, THE. (US/0030-7769). **2753**

OZONE NEWS. (US/1065-5905). **Qty:** 1-5. **5212**

OZS, OSTERREICHISCHE ZEITSCHRIFT FUER SOZIOLOGIE. (AU/1011-0070). **Qty:** approx. 20 per year. **5253**

P & S / THE COLLEGE OF PHYSICIANS AND SURGEONS OF COLUMBIA UNIVERSITY. (US/0743-507X). **3625**

P C DISC. (SP). **1198**

P-D NEWS. (US/0478-9997). **944**

P FORM. (US/1067-2222). **Qty:** 4. **361**

P.H.M. - REVUE HORTICOLE. (FR). **2427**

P-O-P TIMES. (US/1040-8169). **763**

PAAC NOTES (CHICAGO, ILL.). (US/1059-7913). **Qty:** 3. **3715**

PACE ENVIRONMENTAL LAW REVIEW. (US/0738-6206). **3115**

PACE LAW REVIEW. (US/0272-2410). **3024**

PACIFIC AFFAIRS. (CN/0030-851X). **Qty:** 60. **4486**

PACIFIC ARTS. (US). **327**

PACIFIC

PACIFIC BOATING ALMANAC. NORTHERN CALIFORNIA & NEVADA. (US/0193-3515). **595**

PACIFIC BOATING ALMANAC. SOUTHERN CALIFORNIA, ARIZONA & BAJA. (US/0193-3507). **595**

PACIFIC CITIZEN, THE. (US/0030-8579). **5638**

PACIFIC COAST NURSERYMAN & GARDEN SUPPLY DEALER. (US/0192-7159). **2427**

PACIFIC CONSERVATION BIOLOGY. (AT/1038-2097). **2201**

PACIFIC DISCOVERY. (US/0030-8641). **Qty:** 8-10. **5137**

PACIFIC HISTORICAL REVIEW. (US/0030-8684). **2753**

PACIFIC ISLANDS MONTHLY. (AT/0030-8722). **2670**

PACIFIC MAGAZINE (HONOLULU, HAWAII). (US/0744-1754). **2511**

PACIFIC MARITIME MAGAZINE. (US/0741-7586). **Qty:** 2. **5453**

PACIFIC NORTHWEST FORUM, THE. (US). **2753**

PACIFIC NORTHWEST INSECT CONTROL HANDBOOK. (US). **4246**

PACIFIC NORTHWEST PLANT DISEASE CONTROL HANDBOOK. (US). **2427**

PACIFIC NORTHWEST QUARTERLY. (US/0030-8803). **Qty:** varies. **2753**

PACIFIC NORTHWEST TRADE DIRECTORY. (US). **848**

PACIFIC PERSPECTIVE. (FJ/0377-2543). **2670**

PACIFIC RAIL NEWS. (US/8750-8486). **5433**

PACIFIC REPORT (RED HILL). (AT/1031-6981). **Qty:** 12. **702**

PACIFIC RESEARCH : A PERIODICAL OF THE PEACE RESEARCH CENTRE, AUSTRALIAN NATIONAL UNIVERSITY. (AT/1031-9379). **Qty:** 20. **4530**

PACIFIC REVIEW (OXFORD, ENGLAND). (UK/0951-2748). **4486**

PACIFIC REVIEW (SAN DIEGO, CALIF.). (US/0739-8360). **Qty:** 3/yr. **3421**

PACIFIC STUDIES. (US/0275-3596). **Qty:** 20. **2670**

PACIFIC SUN. (US/0048-2641). **5638**

PACIFIC TELECOMMUNICATIONS REVIEW. (US/1066-3894). **Qty:** 4. **1119**

PACIFIC THEOLOGICAL REVIEW. (US/0360-1897). **4984**

PACIFIC TRIBUNE (VANCOUVER, B.C.). (CN). **5792**

PACIFIC VIEWPOINT. (NZ/0030-8978). **1577**

PACIFIC WORLD. (NZ/0113-0846). **Qty:** 4. **2201**

PACIFIC YACHTING. (CN/0030-8986). **595**

PACIFICA : AUSTRALIAN THEOLOGICAL STUDIES. (AT). **4984**

PACING AND CLINICAL ELECTROPHYSIOLOGY. (US/0147-8389). **3708**

PACK & PADDLE. (US/1059-4493). **Qty:** 18. **4911**

PACK-O-FUN. (US/0030-901X). **1067**

PACKAGING DESIGN IN JAPAN. (JA). **4220**

PACKAGING NEWS (LONDON). (UK/0030-9133). **4220**

PACKAGING STRATEGIES. (US/8755-6189). **4221**

PACKAGING TRENDS : JAPAN. (JA). **4221**

PACS & LOBBIES. (US/0886-6457). **4511**

PADAGOGIK (WEINHEIM AN DER BERGSTRASSE, GERMANY). (GW/0043-3446). **1771**

PAEDAGOGICA HISTORICA. (BE/0030-9230). **1771**

PAEDAGOGISCHE STUDIEN. (NE/0165-0645). **1771**

PAEDIATRIC ANAESTHESIA. (FR/1155-5645). **3907**

PAEDIATRICA INDONESIANA. (IO/0030-9311). **3907**

PAGE (CHICAGO, ILL.), THE. (US/1056-6023). **Qty:** 10 per year. **1263**

PAGE PEDIGREE. (US/0897-7763). **2466**

PAGEANTRY (ALTAMONTE SPRINGS, FLA.). (US/1075-3133). **Qty:** 4. **2542**

PAGES (CHICAGO, ILL.). (US/0883-6752). **Qty:** 12. **2923**

PAGES (NORTHEAST ED.). (US/0742-4981). **5488**

PAGINAS (CENTRO DE ESTUDIOS Y PUBLICACIONES). (PE). **4985**

PAI BOLETIN INFORMATIVO. (US/0251-4729). **4795**

PAIDEIA. (IT/0030-9435). **421**

PAIDEUMA (ORONO). (US/0090-5674). **434**

PAINT & COATINGS INDUSTRY. (US/0884-3848). **4224**

PAINT & INK INTERNATIONAL. (UK/0953-9891). **4224**

PAINT & RESIN. (UK/0261-5746). **4224**

PAINT CHECK. (US/1059-6313). **4853**

PAINT HORSE JOURNAL (1979). (US/0164-5706). **Qty:** 10-12 per year. **2801**

PAINT TITLES. (UK/0144-4425). **4226**

PAINTBRUSH (LARAMIE). (US/0094-1964). **Qty:** 2-5/yr. **3467**

PAINTED BRIDE QUARTERLY, THE. (US/0362-7969). **Qty:** 4/yr. **3467**

PAINTINDIA. ANNUAL. (II/0030-9540). **4224**

PAINTING & WALLCOVERING CONTRACTOR. (US/0735-9713). **4224**

PAKISTAN ADMINISTRATION : A JOURNAL OF THE PAKISTAN ADMINISTRATIVE STAFF COLLEGE. (PK). **1868**

PAKISTAN & GULF ECONOMIST. (PK). **702**

PAKISTAN DEVELOPMENT REVIEW. (PK/0030-9729). **1511**

PAKISTAN EXPORTS. (PK/0030-977X). **848**

PAKISTAN EXPORTS (KARACHI, PAKISTAN : 1982). (PK). **848**

PAKISTAN HOTEL AND TRAVEL REVIEW. (PK). **2808**

PAKISTAN JOURNAL OF APPLIED ECONOMICS. (PK/0254-9204). **1511**

PAKISTAN JOURNAL OF BOTANY. (PK/0556-3321). **520**

PAKISTAN JOURNAL OF FORESTRY, THE. (PK/0030-9818). **2390**

PAKISTAN JOURNAL OF OTOLARYNGOLOGY. (PK/0257-4985). **3890**

PAKISTAN JOURNAL OF PSYCHOLOGY. (PK/0030-9869). **Qty:** 1,000. **4606**

PAKISTAN JOURNAL OF SCIENTIFIC AND INDUSTRIAL RESEARCH. (PK/0030-9885). **Qty:** 100. **5137**

PAKISTAN JOURNAL OF SCIENTIFIC RESEARCH. (PK/0552-9050). **5137**

PAKISTAN LIBRARY BULLETIN. (PK/0030-9966). **Qty:** 500 per year. **3240**

PAKISTAN PEDIATRIC JOURNAL. (PK). **3907**

PAKISTAN SEAFOOD DIGEST. (PK/1010-3562). **2352**

PAKISTAN SYSTEMATICS. (PK). **520**

PAKISTAN VETERINARY JOURNAL. (PK/0253-8318). **5518**

PAKIZAH INTIRNASHINAL. (CN/0711-4222). **5564**

PALABRA. (SP). **4985**

PALABRA, LA. (US/0277-1535). **3421**

PALABRA Y EL HOMBRE, LA. (MX/0185-5727). **2851**

PALACIO, EL. (US/0031-0158). **2753**

PALAEOBULGARICA. STAROBULGARISTIKA. (BU). **2702**

PALAEONTOGRAPHICA. ABTEILUNG B : PALAEOPHYTOLOGIE. (GW/0375-0299). **4229**

PALAEONTOLOGY. (UK/0031-0239). **4229**

PALAESTRA (MACOMB, ILL.). (US/8756-5811). **4392**

PALAIOS. (US/0883-1351). **4229**

PALATE PLEASERS. (US/0893-0244). **2352**

PALATINE IMMIGRANT, THE. (US/0884-5735). **Qty:** 80. **2466**

PALEOBIOLOGY. (US/0094-8373). **4229**

PALEOPATHOLOGY NEWSLETTER. (US/0148-4737). **Qty:** 70-80. **278**

PALESTINE EXPLORATION QUARTERLY. (UK/0031-0328). **278**

PALESTINE PERSPECTIVES. (US/0163-3716). **4531**

PALESTINE REFUGEES TODAY. (US/0031-0336). **5300**

PALESTINE YEARBOOK OF INTERNATIONAL LAW, THE. (CY). **3133**

PALETTEN. (SW/0031-0352). **361**

PALLIATIVE CARE INDEX. (UK/0961-4591). **3625**

PALM BEACH LIFE. (US/0031-0417). **2542**

PALMETTO (ORLANDO, FLA.), THE. (US/0276-4164). **2427**

PALO ALTO WEEKLY. (US/0199-1159). **Qty:** 12. **5638**

PALOMINO HORSES. (US/0031-045X). **2801**

PALYNOLOGY. (US/0191-6122). **1390**

PALYNOS. (US/0256-1670). **521**

PAMATKY ARCHEOLOGICKE. (XR/0031-0506). **278**

PAMPHLET SERIES - UNIVERSITY OF CALIFORNIA, LOS ANGELES. CHICANO STUDIES CENTER. (US). **2270**

PAMTECO TRACINGS. (US/1047-3173). **2466**

PAN. (MX). **2352**

PAN-AFRICAN SOCIAL SCIENCE REVIEW. (NR/8755-7436). **5212**

PAN-EROTIC REVIEW. (US/0896-2898). **5188**

PAN-PACIFIC ENTOMOLOGIST, THE. (US/0031-0603). **Qty:** 2-4 per year. **5612**

PAN PIPES. (US/0889-7581). **Qty:** varies. **4145**

PANADERIA NOTICIAS. (SP). **2352**

PANAMA CANAL SPILLWAY, THE. (PN/0364-8044). **5454**

PANCREATIC AND SALIVARY SECRETION. (UK/0142-825X). **3732**

PANDORA (DENVER, COLO.). (US/0275-519X). **3422**

PANEL RESOURCE PAPER. (US/0739-2346). **1902**

PANGEA : BULLETIN D'INFORMATION SUR LA COOPERATION GEOLOGIQUE INTERNATIONALE / CENTRE INTERNATIONAL POUR LA FORMATION ET LES ECHANGES GEOLOGIQUES. (FR/0760-1751). **1390**

PANJAB. URDU. (CN/0701-0508). **2753**

PANOLA STORY, THE. (US/0730-1693). **2466**

PANOLA WATCHMAN (CARTHAGE, TEX. : 1873). (US). **5753**

PANOPTICON. (BE). **3171**

PANORAMA. (UK). **Qty:** 6. **4221**

PANORAMA MODA & ABBIGLIAMENTO. (IT). **2491**

PANTHEIST VISION. (US/0742-5368). **4354**

PAPER AGE. (US/0031-1081). **4235**

PAPER & BOARD ABSTRACTS. (UK/0307-0778). **4240**

PAPER CONSERVATION NEWS (LONDON). (UK/0140-1033). **4235**

PAPER CONSERVATOR. (UK/0309-4227). **4235**

PAPER (LONDON). (UK/0306-8234). **4236**

PAPER MONEY. (US/0031-1162). **2783**

PAPER (NEW YORK, N.Y.). (US/0892-3809). **327**

PAPER. SOUTHERN AFRICA. (SA/0254-3494). **4236**

PAPER SUMMARIES - AMERICAN SOCIETY FOR NONDESTRUCTIVE TESTING. (US/0272-4723). **1990**

PAPERI JA PUU. (FI/0031-1243). **4236**

PAPERS. (AT). **3422**

PAPERS AND PROCEEDINGS - TASMANIAN HISTORICAL RESEARCH ASSOCIATION. (AT/0039-9809). **2670**

PAPERS AND STUDIES IN CONTRASTIVE LINGUISTICS. (PL/0137-2459). **3309**

PAPERS IN AUSTRALIAN LINGUISTICS. (AT/0078-9062). **3309**

PAPERS IN PIDGIN AND CREOLE LINGUISTICS. (AT/0811-0026). **3309**

PAPERS OF THE BIBLIOGRAPHICAL SOCIETY OF CANADA. (CN/0067-6896). **422**

PAPERS ON FRENCH SEVENTEENTH CENTURY LITERATURE. (GW/0343-0758). **Qty:** 60 per year. **3422**

PAPERS ON LANGUAGE & LITERATURE. (US/0031-1294). **3422**

PAPERS PRESENTED AT THE SHORT COURSE IN PAINT TECHNOLOGY. (US). **2015**

PAPERS - WEST TENNESSEE HISTORICAL SOCIETY. (US/0361-6215). **2753**

PAPETIER DE FRANCE, LE. (FR). **4236**

PAPIER AUS OESTERREICH. (AU/1011-0186). **4236**

PAPIER, DAS. (GW/0031-1340). **4236**

PAPIER- UND ZELLSTOFF-DIENST. (GW/0171-1458). **4237**

PAPIERE ZUR LINGUISTIK. (GW). **3309**

PAPPUS. (CN/0710-0469). **521**

PAPRIPARI ES NYOMDAIPARI SZAKIRODALMI TAJEKOZTATO. (HU/0231-0740). **4237**

PAPUA NEW GUINEA JOURNAL OF EDUCATION. (PP/0031-1472). **1771**

PAPUA NEW GUINEA MEDICAL JOURNAL. (PP/0031-1480). **3626**

PAPYRUS BODMER. (SZ). **3422**

PAR EXCELLANCE MAGAZINE. (US/0886-4527). **Qty:** 10-12. **4911**

PAR. PUBLIC ADMINISTRATION REVIEW POPULATION. (US/0033-3352). **4672**

PARA-LEGAL UPDATE. (US/0146-2954). **3025**

PARABOLA. (AT). **3526**

PARACHUTE. (CN/0318-7020). **361**

PARACLETE (SPRINGFIELD, MO.). (US/0190-4639). **5065**

PARADOX INFORMANT. (US/1058-7071). **Qty:** 48. **1280**

PARAGLIDE. (US/0745-9688). **4053**

PARAGRAPH (MODERN CRITICAL THEORY GROUP). (UK/0264-8334). **3309**

PARAGRAPH POOLE. (UK/0953-8577). **2851**

PARAGRAPH (STRATFORD). (CN/1182-543X). **Qty:** 100. **3422**

PARALEGAL, THE. (US/0739-3601). **3025**

PARALLELES (UNIVERSITE DE GENEVE. ECOLE DE TRADUCTION ET D'INTERPRETATION). (SZ). **3310**

PARAMETERS (CARLISLE, PA.). (US/0031-1723). **4053**

PARAMETRO; MENSILE INTERNAZIONALE DI ARCHITETTURA & URBANISTICA. (IT). **305**

PARAPLEGIA NEWS. (US/0031-1766). **4392**

PARAPSYCHOLOGY REVIEW. (US/0031-1804). **4242**

PARASITICA. (BE/0031-1812). **521**

PARASITOLOGY. (UK/0031-1820). **492**

PARATUS. (SA). **4053**

PARENT & CHILD. (US/1041-178X). **Qty:** 8. **2284**

PARENT AND PRESCHOOLER : PP. (US/0887-0365). **1771**

PARENT CARE / YOUR CHILD CARE NEWS-LINE. (CN/1195-1893). **Qty:** 6-10. **2284**

PARENTGUIDE NEWS. (US/0896-1468). **2284**

PARENTING (SAN FRANCISCO, CALIF.). (US/0890-247X). **2284**

PARENTS AND CHILDREN TOGETHER. (US/1050-7108). **2284**

PARENTS' PRESS. (US/0889-8863). **Qty:** 5-10. **2285**

PARENT'S SAY. (AT/0818-8114). **1772**

PARENTS SHOPPING GUIDE. (AT/1030-1968). **2285**

PARENTWISE. (UK). **4985**

PARERGON. (AT/0313-6221). **1079**

PARFUMERIE UND KOSMETIK. (GW/0031-1952). **405**

PARIS NEWS, THE. (US/8756-2081). **5753**

PARIS PASSION : THE MAGAZINE OF THE FRENCH CAPITAL. (FR). **2521**

PARIS POST-INTELLIGENCER, THE. (US/0893-3669). **5746**

PARIS REVIEW, THE. (US/0031-2037). **3422**

PARIS SUCCESS. (BE). **Qty:** 2. **1086**

PARISH COMMUNICATION. (US/0279-7828). **4985**

PARK & GROUNDS MANAGEMENT. (US/1057-204X). **4707**

PARK RECORD (1964), THE. (US/0745-9483). **5757**

PARK WORLD. (UK). **3486**

PARKER DIRECTORY OF CALIFORNIA ATTORNEYS. (US/0196-6138). **3025**

PARKER PAPERS. (US/0898-5456). **2466**

PARKING SECURITY REPORT. (US/1052-9985). **4795**

PARKS AND GROUNDS. (SA). **2427**

PARKS & SPORTS GROUNDS. (UK/0031-224X). **Qty:** 12. **5488**

PARKS NEWBURY. (UK/0960-233X). **2202**

PARKWATCH. (AT). **2202**

PARLEMENTS ET FRANCOPHONIE. (FR/0258-4751). **Qty:** 2 or 4. **4486**

PARLIAMENTARIAN. (UK/0031-2282). **4672**

PARLIAMENTARY HISTORY : A YEARBOOK. (UK/0264-2824). **4672**

PARLIAMENTS, ESTATES & REPRESENTATION. (UK/0260-6755). **4487**

PARNASSOS. (GR/0048-301X). **Qty:** 10. **3310**

PARNASSUS : POETRY IN REVIEW. (US/0048-3028). **Qty:** 40 per year. **3467**

PAROLA DEL PASSATO, LA. (IT/0031-2355). **1079**

PAROLES GELEES : UCLA FRENCH STUDIES. (US). **Qty:** 3. **3422**

PARSONS NEWS, THE. (US). **Qty:** 10y. **5678**

PARTICLE ACCELERATORS. (US/0031-2460). **4413**

PARTICULATE SCIENCE AND TECHNOLOGY. (US/0272-6351). **2015**

PARTIE PRENANTE. (FR/0294-0531). **1772**

PARTISAN REVIEW (1936). (US/0031-2525). **4544**

PARTNERS IN PRINT. (CN/1195-4981). **Qty:** 2-3. **881**

PASAA. (TH/0125-2488). **3310**

PASADENA JOURNAL OF BUSINESS. (US/0743-6610). **702**

PASADENA STAR-NEWS. (US/1069-2827). **5638**

PASQUE PETALS. (US/0031-2649). **3467**

PASS IN REVIEW. (US). **4831**

PASSENGER PIGEON, THE. (US/0031-2703). **Qty:** infrequent. **5619**

PASSENGER TRAIN JOURNAL. (US/0160-6913). **5433**

PASSING SHOW (NEW YORK, N.Y.). (US/1061-8112). **5367**

PASSPORT (CHICAGO). (US/0031-272X). **5488**

PASSPORT TO LEGAL UNDERSTANDING. (US/0737-7630). **3025**

PASSWORD (EL PASO). (US/0031-2738). **2753**

PAST & PRESENT. (UK/0031-2746). **2625**

PAST & PRESENT (WATERLOO). (CN/0702-7125). **2852**

PASTICCERIA INTERNAZIONALE. (IT/0392-4718). **2352**

PASTORAL CARE IN EDUCATION. (UK/0264-3944). **1772**

PASTORAL HORIZONS. (AT). **Qty:** 1-2. **5034**

PASTORAL LIFE. (US/0031-2762). **Qty:** 40-50. **4985**

PASTORAL MUSIC. (US/0363-6569). **4145**

PASTORAL MUSIC NOTEBOOK. (US/0145-6636). **Qty:** 10. **4145**

PASTORAL SCIENCES. (CN/0713-3383). **Qty:** 15. **4985**

PASTRYCOOKS AND BAKERS NEWS MONTHLY. (AT/0818-6561). **Qty:** 3-4. **2353**

PASTURAS TROPICALES. (CK/1012-7410). **Qty:** 10. **118**

PATHOLOGY. (AT/0031-3025). **3897**

PATHWAY TO GOD. (II). **4985**

PATHWAYS (HAMILTON). (CN/0840-8114). **Qty:** 6. **2179**

PATHWAYS (MAYNARDVILLE, TENN.). (US/8755-4747). **2753**

PATIENT CARE. (US/0031-305X). **3738**

PATIO. (FR). **4607**

PATOLOGICESKAJA FIZIOLOGIJA I EKSPERIMENTALNAJA TERAPIJA. (RU/0031-2991). **584**

PATRE. (FR). **Qty:** 10/yr. **217**

PATRIDES (TORONTO). (CN/0824-359X). **2270**

PATRIOT (HARRISBURG, PA. : DAILY). (US/1041-4029). **5738**

PATRIOT LEDGER (CITY EDITION), THE. (US). **Qty:** 100/year. **5689**

PATRIOT LEDGER (SOUTH EDITION), THE. (US). **Qty:** 100/year. **5689**

PATRIOT LEDGER (SUBURBAN EDITION), THE. (US). **Qty:** 100/year. **5689**

PATRISTIC AND BYZANTINE REVIEW, THE. (US/0737-738X). **4985**

PATRISTICS. (US/0360-652X). **4985**

PATTERNS OF PREJUDICE. (UK/0031-322X). **2270**

PATTERSON'S ELEMENTARY EDUCATION. (US/1044-1417). **1772**

PATTERSON'S SCHOOLS CLASSIFIED. (US/0553-4054). **1839**

PAUTA. (MX). **4145**

PAW PRINTS. (US/0163-562X). **1067**

PAWN REVIEW, THE. (US/0162-0061). **3422**

PAYROLL EXCHANGE. (US/0194-6196). **1701**

PAYS D'EUROPE OCCIDENTALE EN..., LES. (FR). **2702**

PAZIFISCHE RUNDSCHAU. (CN/0048-3095). **5792**

PC ACTIVE. (NE/0925-5745). **1270**

PC AI. (US/0894-0711). **Qty:** 3-6. **1215**

PC BUSINESS SOFTWARE. (UK/0954-2833). **1270**

PC GRAPHICS & VIDEO. (US/1077-5862). **Qty:** 120. **1234**

PC HOME JOURNAL. (US). **1270**

PC-PRAXIS 1989. (GW/0940-6743). **1199**

PC PUBLISHING. (US/0896-8209). **4818**

PC REPORT. (US). **1271**

PC-SIG MAGAZINE. (US/1042-0681). **Qty:** (unlimited). **1289**

PC TECHNIQUES. (US/1053-6205). **Qty:** 25. **1289**

PC USER (LONDON, ENGLAND). (UK/0263-5720). **1271**

PCA MESSENGER, THE. (US/0191-4162). **Qty:** 11 or more. **4986**

PCR / PRODUCTION AND CASTING REPORT. (UK/0142-632X). **1621**

PCTE NEWSLETTER. (FR). **1199**

PEA RIVER TRAILS. (US/8756-4181). **Qty:** irregularly. **2467**

PEACE AND CHANGE. (US/0149-0508). **4531**

PEACE & DEMOCRACY NEWS. (US/0749-5900). **4531**

PEACE AND FREEDOM. (US/0015-9093). **5564**

PEACE COURIER. (FI/0031-594X). **4531**

PEACE MAGAZINE. (CN/0826-9521). **Qty:** 12. **4531**

PEACE NEWSLETTER (SYRACUSE, N.Y.). (US/0735-4134). **Qty:** 6-8. **4531**

PEACE RESEARCH. (CN/0008-4697). **Qty:** 4. **4531**

PEACE REVIEW (PALO ALTO, CALIF.). (US/1040-2659). **4531**

PEACEKEEPING & INTERNATIONAL RELATIONS. (CN/1187-3485). **Qty:** 6. **4531**

PEACEMAKER, THE. (US/0031-3602). **4487**

PEACEWORK (CAMBRIDGE, MASS.). (US/0748-0725). **4487**

PEACH TIMES. (US/0031-3610). **2427**

PEAK RUNNING PERFORMANCE. (US). **Qty:** 2. **4911**

PEAKE STUDIES. (SZ/1013-1191). **3422**

PEASANT STUDIES. (US/0149-1547). **5212**

PEAT NEWS. (CN/0706-1307). **119**

PECUNIA. BRUXELLES, DE. (BE/1015-6283). **881**

PED FORUM. (US/1046-2082). **4704**

PEDAGOGIA MEDICA. (IT/1120-8627). **3626**

PEDAGOGIKA. (XR/0031-3815). **1772**

PEDIATRE, LE. (FR/0397-9180). **Qty:** 6. **3907**

PEDIATRIA MEDICA E CHIRURGICA, LA. (IT/0391-5387). **3907**

PEDIATRIA MODERNA. (BL/0031-3920). **3907**

PEDIATRIC ANNALS. (US/0090-4481). **3908**

PEDIATRIC DERMATOLOGY. (US/0736-8046). **3908**

PEDIATRIC EMERGENCY & CRITICAL CARE. (US/1059-0870). **Qty:** 2-4. **3908**

PEDIATRIC HEMATOLOGY AND ONCOLOGY. (US/0888-0018). **3773**

PEDIATRIC MENTAL HEALTH. (US/0278-4998). **3909**

PEDIATRIC NEUROLOGY. (US/0887-8994). **3909**

PEDIATRIC NEUROSURGERY. (SZ/1016-2291). **3909**

PEDIATRIC NURSING. (US/0097-9805). **3866**

PEDIATRIC PATHOLOGY. (US/0277-0938). **3897**

PEDIATRIC PRIMARY CARE. (US/1071-5711). **Qty:** 2-4. **3909**

PEDIATRIC RADIOLOGY. (GW/0301-0449). **3944**

PEDIATRIC REVIEWS AND COMMUNICATION. (SZ/0882-9225). **3909**

PEDIATRIC THERAPEUTICS AND TOXICOLOGY. (US/0893-6218). **3909**

PEDIATRICS — Book Review Index

PEDIATRICS FOR PARENTS. (US/0730-6725). **3910**

PEDIATRIE. (FR/0031-4021). **3910**

PEDMED. (SA/1017-1711). **3626**

PEDOBIOLOGIA. (GW/0031-4056). **181**

PEDOLOGIE. (BE/0079-0419). **181**

PEDRALBES. (SP). **2702**

PEEK (65). (US/0739-0653). **1264**

PEGASUS. (UK/0031-4080). **Qty:** 12-20. **4053**

PEGBAR. (CN/0828-9247). **381**

PEGBOARD (MENLO PARK, CALIF.). (US/0892-5763). **1230**

PELITA BPKS. (IO/0126-3692). **5300**

PELIZZA'S POSITIVE PRINCIPLES FOR BETTER LIVING. (US/1070-6674). **4607**

PELLISSIPIAN (CLINTON, TENN.). (US/0736-5594). **Qty:** 5. **2467**

PEMBIMBING PEMBACA. (IO). **3240**

PEMBROKE MAGAZINE, THE. (US/0097-496X). **3423**

PEN-BASED COMPUTING. (US/1054-4011). **1248**

PEN INTERNATIONAL. (UK). **Qty:** 35. **3423**

PENINSULA HERITAGE. (US/0895-8165). **5034**

PENINSULA (SAN MATEO), LA. (US/0197-2197). **2754**

PENN SOUNDS. (US/1046-0292). **Qty:** 3-4. **4145**

PENN STATE HORTICULTURAL REVIEWS. (US). **2427**

PENNSYLVANIA ARCHAEOLOGIST. (US/0031-4358). **278**

PENNSYLVANIA CHIEFS OF POLICE ASSOCIATION BULLETIN. (US/0031-4404). **3171**

PENNSYLVANIA FOLKLIFE. (US/0031-4498). **2754**

PENNSYLVANIA FORESTS. (US/0031-4501). **Qty:** 4. **2390**

PENNSYLVANIA GAME NEWS. (US/0031-451X). **Qty:** 15. **4877**

PENNSYLVANIA GENEALOGICAL MAGAZINE, THE. (US/0882-3685). **2467**

PENNSYLVANIA GEOGRAPHER, THE. (US/0553-5980). **2572**

PENNSYLVANIA GEOLOGY. (US/0048-3214). **1391**

PENNSYLVANIA HERITAGE (1974). (US/0270-7500). **2754**

PENNSYLVANIA HISTORY. (US/0031-4528). **Qty:** 40. **2754**

PENNSYLVANIA HOSPITALS. (US/0744-5636). **3790**

PENNSYLVANIA LAW JOURNAL-REPORTER. (US/0279-8166). **3025**

PENNSYLVANIA MAGAZINE (CAMP HILL, PA.). (US/0744-4230). **Qty:** 30. **5488**

PENNSYLVANIA MAGAZINE OF HISTORY AND BIOGRAPHY, THE. (US/0031-4587). **2754**

PENNSYLVANIA MENNONITE HERITAGE. (US/0148-4036). **2467**

PENNSYLVANIA NURSE, THE. (US/0031-4617). **Qty:** varies. **3866**

PENNSYLVANIA POLICE CRIMINAL LAW BULLETIN, THE. (US/0098-7174). **Qty:** 13. **3171**

PENNSYLVANIA QUERIES. (US/1044-6915). **2467**

PENNSYLVANIA REVIEW (PITTSBURGH, PA.), THE. (US/8756-5668). **Qty:** (4-5 per year). **3423**

PENORRA : REVISTA TRIMESTRAL DE POESIA, LA. (SP). **3468**

PENSACOLA NEWS JOURNAL. (US). **5650**

PENSAMIENTO IBEROAMERICANO. (SP/0212-0208). **1512**

PENSAMIENTO (MADRID). (SP/0031-4749). **4354**

PENSEE CATHOLIQUE, LA. (FR/0031-4781). **5034**

PENSIERO MAZZINIANO, IL. (IT). **Qty:** 30-40. **4487**

PENSION FUNDS AND THEIR ADVISERS. (UK/0140-6647). **911**

PENSION WORLD. (US/0098-1753). **1701**

PENTECOSTAL EVANGEL. (US/0031-4897). **5066**

PENTECOSTAL FREE-WILL BAPTIST MESSENGER. (US/0745-2330). **5066**

PENTECOSTAL MESSENGER, THE. (US/0031-4919). **5066**

PENTECOSTAL MINISTER, THE. (US/0279-7038). **4986**

PENTECOSTAL TESTIMONY, THE. (CN/0031-4927). **Qty:** 3/year. **4986**

PEOPLE & THE PLANET / IPPF, UNFPA, IUCN. (UK/0968-1655). **Qty:** varies. **4556**

PEOPLE (CHICAGO. 1974). (US/0093-7673). **2543**

PEOPLE (ENGLISH ED.). (UK/0301-5645). **590**

PEOPLE (PALO ALTO. 1979), THE. (US/0199-350X). **4544**

PEOPLE POWER. (US/0148-0030). **1298**

PEOPLE'S CULTURE (KANSAS CITY, KAN.). (US/1071-7250). **4544**

PEOPLE'S FOLK DANCE DIRECTORY. (US/0160-5550). **1314**

PEOPLE'S WEEKLY WORLD [MICROFORM]. (US). **Qty:** 10. **5720**

PEOPLE'S WORLD (BERKELEY). (US/0031-5044). **5638**

PEOPLING OF THE BRITISH PERIPHERIES IN THE EIGHTEENTH CENTURY, THE. (AT). **2625**

PEPTIDES (NEW YORK, N.Y, : 1980). (US/0196-9781). **492**

PER LA FILOSOFIA. (IT). **Qty:** 25. **4354**

PERCEPTION (LONDON). (UK/0301-0066). **4607**

PERCEPTION (OTTAWA). (CN/0704-5263). **5301**

PERCEPTIONS (TOLEDO, OH.). (US/1070-0358). **Qty:** 4. **3423**

PERCEPTUAL AND MOTOR SKILLS. (US/0031-5125). **4607**

PERCUSSION INTERNATIONAL AUDIO MAGAZINE. (US/0743-8621). **5318**

PERCUSSIVE NOTES. (US/0553-6502). **4145**

PEREGRINE FUND NEWSLETTER, THE. (US). **2202**

PERFICIT. (SP). **Qty:** 100. **3310**

PERFILES EDUCATIVOS. (MX). **1840**

PERFORMANCE PRACTICE REVIEW. (US/1044-1638). **4145**

PERFORMANCE (VANIER). (CN/0832-8196). **4912**

PERFORMANCES MARSEILLE. (FR/0996-5882). **Qty:** 6/yr. **1773**

PERFORMING ARTS & ENTERTAINMENT IN CANADA. (CN/1185-3433). **387**

PERFORMING ARTS JOURNAL. (US/0735-8393). **387**

PERFORMING ARTS (LOS ANGELES EDITION). (US/0031-5222). **387**

PERFUSION : DURCHBLUTUNGSSTORUNGEN UND ARTERIOSKLEROSE IN KLINIK UND PRAXIS. (GW/0935-0020). **3626**

PERFUSION LIFE. (US/0747-3079). **Qty:** 1-10. **3773**

PERINATAL PRESS. (US/0160-7219). **3766**

PERIOD HOME RENOVATOR BUYER'S GUIDE. (AT/1036-3181). **2907**

PERIODICA MATHEMATICA HUNGARICA. (HU/0031-5303). **3526**

PERIODICA MUSICA. (CN/0822-7594). **4145**

PERIODICA POLYTECHNICA. CIVIL ENGINEERING. (HU/0553-6626). **2028**

PERIODICA POLYTECHNICA: ELECTRICAL ENGINEERING. ELEKTROTECHNIK. (HU/0031-532X). **2075**

PERIODICAL (COUNCIL ON AMERICA'S MILITARY PAST). (US). **4053**

PERIODICOS Y REVISTAS ESPANOLAS E HISPANOAMERICANAS. (SP). **4818**

PERIODICUM BIOLOGORUM. (CI/0031-5362). **468**

PERIOPERATIVE OPTIONS AND OPPORTUNITIES. (US/1070-8979). **Qty:** 2-3. **3626**

PERISTIL (ZAGREB). (CI/0553-6707). **362**

PERKINS JOURNAL. (US/0730-2142). **4986**

PERKINS PRESS. (US/0898-1574). **2467**

PERMACULTURE INTERNATIONAL JOURNAL. (AT/1037-8480). **119**

PERSISTENCE OF VISION. (US). **Qty:** 1-2. **4076**

PERSON-CENTERED REVIEW. (US/0883-2293). **4607**

PERSONA Y DERECHO. (SP/0211-4526). **3090**

PERSONAL COMPOSITION REPORT, THE. (US). **4567**

PERSONAL COMPUTER REPORT (MINEOLA, N.Y.). (US/0894-3532). **1199**

PERSONAL IDENTIFICATION NEWS. (US/0883-5608). **1227**

PERSONAL IM OEFFENTLICHEN DIENST. (GW). **4699**

PERSONAL INJURY VERDICT SURVEY. ALABAMA EDITION. (US/8755-6413). **3026**

PERSONAL INJURY VERDICT SURVEY. ALASKA EDITION. (US/8755-6618). **3026**

PERSONAL INJURY VERDICT SURVEY. ARIZONA EDITION. (US/8755-6774). **3026**

PERSONAL INJURY VERDICT SURVEY. ARKANSAS EDITION. (US/8755-6782). **3026**

PERSONAL INJURY VERDICT SURVEY. CALIFORNIA EDITION. (US/8755-6790). **3026**

PERSONAL INJURY VERDICT SURVEY. COLORADO EDITION. (US/8755-6731). **3026**

PERSONAL INJURY VERDICT SURVEY. CONNECTICUT EDITION. (US/8755-6596). **3026**

PERSONAL INJURY VERDICT SURVEY. DELAWARE EDITION. (US/8755-6529). **3026**

PERSONAL INJURY VERDICT SURVEY. FLORIDA EDITION. (US/8755-6723). **3026**

PERSONAL INJURY VERDICT SURVEY. GEORGIA EDITION. (US/8755-6758). **3026**

PERSONAL INJURY VERDICT SURVEY. HAWAII EDITION. (US/8755-674X). **3027**

PERSONAL INJURY VERDICT SURVEY. IDAHO EDITION. (US/8755-6693). **3027**

PERSONAL INJURY VERDICT SURVEY. ILLINOIS EDITION. (US/8755-6685). **3027**

PERSONAL INJURY VERDICT SURVEY. INDIANA EDITION. (US/8755-6715). **3027**

PERSONAL INJURY VERDICT SURVEY. IOWA EDITION. (US/8755-6669). **3027**

PERSONAL INJURY VERDICT SURVEY. KANSAS EDITION. (US/8755-6677). **3027**

PERSONAL INJURY VERDICT SURVEY. KENTUCKY EDITION. (US/8755-6707). **3027**

PERSONAL INJURY VERDICT SURVEY. LOUISIANA EDITION. (US/8755-6820). **3027**

PERSONAL INJURY VERDICT SURVEY. MAINE EDITION. (US/8755-6545). **3027**

PERSONAL INJURY VERDICT SURVEY. MARYLAND EDITION. (US/8755-6537). **3027**

PERSONAL INJURY VERDICT SURVEY. MICHIGAN EDITION. (US/8755-6499). **3027**

PERSONAL INJURY VERDICT SURVEY. MISSISSIPPI EDITION. (US/8755-6480). **3027**

PERSONAL INJURY VERDICT SURVEY. MISSOURI EDITION. (US/8755-6472). **3027**

PERSONAL INJURY VERDICT SURVEY. MONTANA EDITION. (US/8755-6464). **3027**

PERSONAL INJURY VERDICT SURVEY. NEBRASKA EDITION. (US/8755-6642). **3027**

PERSONAL INJURY VERDICT SURVEY. NEW HAMPSHIRE EDITION. (US/8755-6391). **3027**

PERSONAL INJURY VERDICT SURVEY. NEW MEXICO EDITION. (US/8755-6375). **3027**

PERSONAL INJURY VERDICT SURVEY. NEW YORK EDITION. (US/8755-6383). **3027**

PERSONAL INJURY VERDICT SURVEY. NORTH CAROLINA EDITION. (US/8755-6359). **3028**

PERSONAL INJURY VERDICT SURVEY. NORTH DAKOTA EDITION. (US/8755-6812). **3028**

PERSONAL INJURY VERDICT SURVEY. OHIO EDITION. (US/8755-6367). **3028**

PERSONAL INJURY VERDICT SURVEY. OKLAHOMA EDITION. (US/8755-6405). **3028**

PERSONAL INJURY VERDICT SURVEY. OREGON EDITION. (US/8755-6766). **3028**

PERSONAL INJURY VERDICT SURVEY. PENNSYLVANIA EDITION. (US/8755-6804). **3028**

PERSONAL INJURY VERDICT SURVEY. SOUTH CAROLINA EDITION. (US/8755-6448). **3028**

PERSONAL INJURY VERDICT SURVEY. SOUTH DAKOTA EDITION. (US/8755-6456). **3028**

PHILOSOPHY

PERSONAL INJURY VERDICT SURVEY. TENNESSEE EDITION. (US/8755-643X). **3028**

PERSONAL INJURY VERDICT SURVEY. TEXAS EDITION. (US/8755-6421). **3028**

PERSONAL INJURY VERDICT SURVEY. UTAH EDITION. (US/8755-6650). **3028**

PERSONAL INJURY VERDICT SURVEY. VERMONT EDITION. (US/8755-6626). **3028**

PERSONAL INJURY VERDICT SURVEY. VIRGINIA EDITION. (US/8755-657X). **3028**

PERSONAL INJURY VERDICT SURVEY. WASHINGTON, D.C. EDITION. (US/8755-6510). **3028**

PERSONAL INJURY VERDICT SURVEY. WASHINGTON EDITION. (US/8755-6553). **3028**

PERSONAL INJURY VERDICT SURVEY. WEST VIRGINIA EDITION. (US/8755-6561). **3028**

PERSONAL INJURY VERDICT SURVEY. WISCONSIN EDITION. (US/8755-660X). **3028**

PERSONAL INJURY VERDICT SURVEY. WYOMING EDITION. (US/8755-6634). **3028**

PERSONAL SELLING POWER. (US/0738-8594). **934**

PERSONALHISTORISK TIDSSKRIFT. (DK/0300-3655). **2467**

PERSONALITY STUDY AND GROUP BEHAVIOUR. (II). **4607**

PERSONHISTORISK TIDSKRIFT. (SW/0031-5699). **434**

PERSONNEL MANAGEMENT ABSTRACTS. (US/0031-577X). **732**

PERSONNEL MANAGEMENT (LONDON. 1969). (UK/0031-5761). **945**

PERSONNEL NEWS. (US). **4704**

PERSONNEL PSYCHOLOGY. (US/0031-5826). **4607**

PERSOON EN GEMEENSCHAP. (BE/0031-5842). **1773**

PERSOONIA. (NE/0031-5850). **576**

PERSPECTIVA MUNDIAL. (US/0164-3169). **1701**

PERSPECTIVA (SOUTH HADLEY, MASS.). (US/1059-0536). **3310**

PERSPECTIVA TEOLOGICA. (BL/0102-4469). **Qty:** 4-5. **4986**

PERSPECTIVE (BOSTON, MASS. 1990). (US/1071-4154). **4531**

PERSPECTIVES : A JOURNAL OF REFORMED THOUGHT. (US). **Qty:** 30/yr. **4986**

PERSPECTIVES AGRICOLES. (FR/0399-8533). **119**

PERSPECTIVES - GERONTOLOGICAL NURSING ASSOCIATION. (CN/0831-7445). **Qty:** 4. **3866**

PERSPECTIVES IN COVENANT EDUCATION. (US/1070-8944). **Qty:** 10-12. **1773**

PERSPECTIVES IN EDUCATION AND DEAFNESS. (US/1051-6204). **4392**

PERSPECTIVES IN PSYCHIATRIC CARE. (US/0031-5990). **Qty:** 12. **3866**

PERSPECTIVES IN RELIGIOUS STUDIES. (US/0093-531X). **4986**

PERSPECTIVES MEDIEVALES. (FR/0338-2338). **Qty:** 1. **3423**

PERSPECTIVES OF NEW MUSIC. (US/0031-6016). **1240**

PERSPECTIVES ON ADDICTIONS NURSING. (US/1057-1639). **Qty:** 8-16. **3867**

PERSPECTIVES ON POLITICAL SCIENCE. (US/1045-7097). **4487**

PERSPECTIVES ON SCIENCE AND CHRISTIAN FAITH. (US/0892-2675). **4986**

PERSPECTIVES ON THE MEDICAL TRANSCRIPTION PROFESSION. (US/1066-3533). **Qty:** 4-6. **3626**

PERSPECTIVES (SASKATOON). (CN/0316-3334). **5212**

PERSPECTIVES (TOLEDO, OHIO). (US/0883-6086). **3350**

PERSPEKTIEF. (NE/0167-9104). **4372**

PERSPEKTIVEN (VIENNA, AUSTRIA). (AU). **623**

PERTANIKA. (MY/0126-6128). **119**

PEST RESISTANCE MANAGEMENT. (US). **4246**

PESTICIDE MANUAL. (UK). **Qty:** 5. **4246**

PESTICIDES TRUST AFFILIATION. (UK). **Qty:** 40 /yr. **4247**

PET DEALER. (US/0553-8572). **4287**

PET DEALER ANNUAL GUIDE. (US/0553-8572). **Qty:** 52/yr. **4287**

PETER DAG INVESTMENT LETTER, THE. (US/0196-9323). **911**

PETERBOROUGH TRANSCRIPT, THE. (US). **Qty:** 12. **5708**

PETERMANNS GEOGRAPHISCHE MITTEILUNGEN. (GW/0031-6229). **Qty:** 100. **2572**

PETERSEN'S PHOTOGRAPHIC. (US/0199-4913). **4372**

PETITS PROPOS CULINAIRES. (UK/0142-4857). **4197**

PETROCOMPANIES. (UK). **1953**

PETROLEUM. (VE). **4272**

PETROLEUM ECONOMIST (ENGLISH EDITION). (UK/0306-395X). **4272**

PETROLEUM ENGINEER INTERNATIONAL. (US/0164-8322). **4272**

PETROLEUM INFORMATION INTERNATIONAL. (US/0730-7632). **4273**

PETROLEUM MANAGEMENT (HOUSTON, TEX.). (US/0884-4550). **4273**

PETROLEUM REVIEW (LONDON. 1978). (UK/0020-3076). **4273**

PETROSTRATEGIES ENGLISH ED. (FR/0298-6027). **1953**

PEUPLE BRETON, LE. (FR/0245-9507). **2271**

PEUPLES DU MONDE. (FR/0555-9952). **4986**

PFLANZENARZT, DER. (AU/0031-6733). **521**

PFLANZENSOZIOLOGIE; EINE REIHE VEGETATIONSKUNDLICHER GEBIETSMONOGRAPHIEN. (GW). **2427**

PHALANX (ALEXANDRIA). (US/0195-1920). **2107**

PHALGU : PHALGU SAHITYA SAMSADARA MUKHAPATRA. (II). **3423**

PHARMA-MARKETING-JOURNAL. (GW/0721-5665). **1512**

PHARMACA. (CI/0031-6857). **4319**

PHARMACEUTICA ACTA HELVETIAE. (SZ/0031-6865). **4319**

PHARMACEUTICAL JOURNAL (1933). (UK/0031-6873). **4320**

PHARMACEUTICAL JOURNAL OF KENYA. (KE/0378-228X). **4320**

PHARMACEUTICAL MARKETING. (UK). **Qty:** 10 or more. **4320**

PHARMACEUTICAL MEDICINE (BASINGSTOKE). (UK/0265-0673). **4320**

PHARMACEUTICAL TECHNOLOGY. (US/0147-8087). **4321**

PHARMACEUTICAL TECHNOLOGY INTERNATIONAL. (US/0164-6826). **4321**

PHARMACEUTICAL TIMES. (UK). **Qty:** 10-15. **4321**

PHARMACEUTIQUES PARIS. (FR/1240-0866). **4321**

PHARMACIE HOSPITALIERE FRANCAISE, LA. (FR/0369-9579). **3791**

PHARMACOLOGY, BIOCHEMISTRY AND BEHAVIOR. (US/0091-3057). **4322**

PHARMACOPSYCHIATRY. (GW/0176-3679). **4323**

PHARMACOTHERAPY. (US/0277-0008). **4323**

PHARMAZEUTISCHE INDUSTRIE, DIE. (GW/0031-711X). **4324**

PHARMAZEUTISCHE ZEITUNG. (GW/0031-7136). **4324**

PHAROS OF ALPHA OMEGA ALPHA-HONOR MEDICAL SOCIETY, THE. (US/0031-7179). **3627**

PHASE. (SP). **5034**

PHASE TRANSITIONS. (US/0141-1594). **4414**

PHELPS COUNTY GENEALOGICAL SOCIETY QUARTERLY. (US/0884-2140). **2467**

PHENIX. (FR/0300-3639). **4864**

PHENOMENOLOGICAL INQUIRY. (US/0885-3886). **Qty:** 5-8. **4355**

PHENOMENOLOGY AND PEDAGOGY. (CN/0820-9189). **4355**

PHENOMENOLOGY & SOCIAL SCIENCE NEWSLETTER. (US). **5212**

PHILADELPHIA ARCHITECT. (US/1071-1651). **Qty:** 12. **306**

PHILADELPHIA CITY PAPER. (US/0733-6349). **5738**

PHILADELPHIA GAY NEWS. (US). **Qty:** 4. **5738**

PHILADELPHIA MAGAZINE (1967). (US/0031-7233). **2543**

PHILADELPHIA NEW OBSERVER, THE. (US/0890-8435). **5738**

PHILATELIC EXPORTER, THE. (UK/0031-7381). **1146**

PHILATELIC JOURNALIST, THE. (US/0048-3710). **2786**

PHILATELIC LITERATURE REVIEW. (US/0270-1707). **2786**

PHILATELIE AU QUEBEC. (CN/0381-7547). **Qty:** 8 to 10. **2786**

PHILATELIST AND PJGB, THE. (UK/0260-6739). **2786**

PHILIPPINE ECONOMIC JOURNAL, THE. (PH/0031-7500). **1512**

PHILIPPINE ENTOMOLOGIST. (PH/0369-9536). **5594**

PHILIPPINE GEOGRAPHICAL JOURNAL. (PH/0031-7551). **2572**

PHILIPPINE JOURNAL OF BIOTECHNOLOGY. (PH/0117-0503). **Qty:** varies. **3695**

PHILIPPINE JOURNAL OF EDUCATION, THE. (PH/0031-7624). **1773**

PHILIPPINE JOURNAL OF LABOR AND INDUSTRIAL RELATIONS. (PH). **1701**

PHILIPPINE JOURNAL OF LINGUISTICS. (PH/0048-3796). **3310**

PHILIPPINE JOURNAL OF NUTRITION. (PH/0031-7640). **4197**

PHILIPPINE JOURNAL OF OPHTHALMOLOGY. (PH/0031-7659). **3878**

PHILIPPINE JOURNAL OF PUBLIC ADMINISTRATION. (PH/0031-7675). **4673**

PHILIPPINE JOURNAL OF SCIENCE, THE. (PH/0031-7683). **5138**

PHILIPPINE JOURNAL OF VETERINARY MEDICINE. (PH/0031-7705). **Qty:** 1. **5518**

PHILIPPINE LAW GAZETTE. (PH/0115-2483). **3142**

PHILIPPINE LAW JOURNAL. (PH/0031-7721). **3029**

PHILIPPINE LETTER, THE. (US/0379-2870). **703**

PHILIPPINE QUARTERLY OF CULTURE AND SOCIETY. (PH/0115-0243). **5253**

PHILIPPINE SOCIOLOGICAL REVIEW. (PH/0031-7810). **5253**

PHILIPPINE STATISTICIAN, THE. (PH/0031-7829). **5336**

PHILIPPINE STUDIES. (PH/0031-7837). **Qty:** 18. **2625**

PHILIPPINE TECHNOLOGY JOURNAL. (PH/0116-7294). **5138**

PHILIPPINIANA SACRA. (PH/0554-0577). **2625**

PHILOLOGICAL QUARTERLY. (US/0031-7977). **3310**

PHILOLOGOS. (GR). **Qty:** 10-20. **1079**

PHILOSOPHER (MONTREAL, QUEBEC). (CN/0827-1887). **4355**

PHILOSOPHER, THE. (UK). **Qty:** 20. **4355**

PHILOSOPHER'S INDEX. (US/0031-7993). **4365**

PHILOSOPHIA MATHEMATICA. (US/0031-8019). **3526**

PHILOSOPHIA NATURALIS. (GW/0031-8027). **4355**

PHILOSOPHIA (RAMAT GAN). (IS/0048-3893). **4355**

PHILOSOPHIA REFORMATA. (NE/0031-8035). **4355**

PHILOSOPHICA. (BE/0379-8402). **4355**

PHILOSOPHICAL BOOKS. (UK/0031-8051). **4355**

PHILOSOPHICAL FORUM, THE. (US/0031-806X). **4355**

PHILOSOPHICAL INVESTIGATIONS. (US/0190-0536). **4355**

PHILOSOPHICAL PAPERS (GRAHAMSTOWN). (SA/0556-8641). **4356**

PHILOSOPHICAL QUARTERLY, THE. (UK/0031-8094). **4356**

PHILOSOPHICAL REVIEW, THE. (US/0031-8108). **4356**

PHILOSOPHICAL STUDIES (DUBLIN, IRELAND). (IE/0554-0739). **4356**

PHILOSOPHIQUES. (CN/0316-2923). **4356**

PHILOSOPHISCHE RUNDSCHAU. (GW/0031-8159). **4356**

PHILOSOPHISCHE RUNDSCHAU. BEIHEFT. (GW/0554-0828). **4356**

PHILOSOPHISCHER LITERATURANZEIGER. (GW/0031-8175). **4356**

PHILOSOPHISCHES JAHRBUCH (FREIBURG). (GW/0031-8183). **4356**

PHILOSOPHY. (UK). **4356**

PHILOSOPHY AND LITERATURE. (US/0190-0013). **4356**

PHILOSOPHY

PHILOSOPHY AND PHENOMENOLOGICAL RESEARCH. (US/0031-8205). **Qty:** 25-30. **4356**

PHILOSOPHY & PUBLIC AFFAIRS. (US/0048-3915). **5212**

PHILOSOPHY AND SOCIAL ACTION. (II/0377-2772). **5253**

PHILOSOPHY & SOCIAL CRITICISM. (US/0191-4537). **4357**

PHILOSOPHY EAST & WEST. (US/0031-8221). **4357**

PHILOSOPHY IN CONTEXT. (US/0742-2733). **4357**

PHILOSOPHY IN SCIENCE. (US/0277-2434). **5138**

PHILOSOPHY (LONDON). (UK/0031-8191). **4357**

PHILOSOPHY OF MUSIC EDUCATION REVIEW. (US/1063-5734). **Qty:** 2. **4146**

PHILOSOPHY OF SCIENCE (EAST LANSING). (US/0031-8248). **5138**

PHILOSOPHY TODAY (CELINA). (US/0031-8256). **4357**

PHLEBOLOGIE UND PROKTOLOGIE. (GW/0340-305X). **3800**

PHLS MICROBIOLOGY DIGEST. (UK/0265-3400). **568**

PHOBLACHT, AN. (IE). **5803**

PHOEBE (ONEONTA, N.Y.). (US/1045-0904). **Qty:** 15-20. **5564**

PHOEBUS. (US/0193-8061). **362**

PHOENIX. (NE). **278**

PHOENIX (MINNEAPOLIS, MINN.), THE. (US/0893-4509). **4608**

PHOENIX RISING (TORONTO, ONT.). (CN/0710-1457). **3932**

PHOENIX (TORONTO). (CN/0031-8299). **Qty:** 50. **1079**

PHOLEOS. (US/0733-8864). **1409**

PHONETICA. (SZ/0031-8388). **3310**

PHOTO COMMUNIQUE. (CN/0708-5435). **4373**

PHOTO - FORUM. (AT). **4373**

PHOTO-LAB-INDEX. (US/0884-9528). **4373**

PHOTO OPPORTUNITY. (US/0899-4587). **882**

PHOTOFINISHING NEWS LETTER. (US/0889-2393). **Qty:** 2-3. **4374**

PHOTOGRAMMETRIC ENGINEERING AND REMOTE SENSING. (US/0099-1112). **1990**

PHOTOGRAMMETRIC RECORD, THE. (UK/0031-868X). **2572**

PHOTOGRAPH COLLECTOR, THE. (US/0271-0838). **4374**

PHOTOGRAPH COLLECTORS' RESOURCE DIRECTORY / THE PHOTOGRAPHIC ARTS CENTER, THE. (US). **4374**

PHOTOGRAPHER'S FORUM. (US/0194-5467). **4374**

PHOTOGRAPHIC CANADIANA. (CN/0704-0024). **4374**

PHOTOGRAPHIC INSIGHT. (US/0898-7572). **4374**

PHOTOGRAPHIC JOURNAL (1956). (UK/0031-8736). **4374**

PHOTOGRAPHICA. (US). **4374**

PHOTOGRAPHIE. (SZ). **4374**

PHOTOGRAPHIES MAGAZINE. (FR/0988-7679). **Qty:** 9/yr. **4374**

PHOTOGRAPHS (NEW YORK, N.Y. : 1982). (US/0740-4158). **4374**

PHOTOGRAPHY IN NEW YORK. (US/1040-0346). **4374**

PHOTOLETTER, THE. (US/0190-1400). **4375**

PHOTONICS SPECTRA (PITTSFIELD, MASS. 1982). (US/0731-1230). **4440**

PHOTOSYNTHESIS RESEARCH. (NE/0166-8595). **521**

PHOTOSYNTHETICA. (NE/0300-3604). **492**

PHOTOVOLTAIC INSIDER'S REPORT. (US/0731-4671). **1953**

PHRONEMA. (AT/0819-4920). **1094**

PHRONESIS. (NE/0031-8868). **4357**

PHRONESIS (HEIDELBERG, GERMANY). (NE/0031-8868). **4357**

PHYCOLOGIA (OXFORD). (UK/0031-8884). **521**

PHYLON (1960). (US/0031-8906). **5213**

PHYSICAL & OCCUPATIONAL THERAPY IN GERIATRICS. (US/0270-3181). **4381**

PHYSICAL & OCCUPATIONAL THERAPY IN PEDIATRICS. (US/0194-2638). **4381**

PHYSICAL DISABILITIES SPECIAL INTEREST SECTION NEWSLETTER. (US/0279-411X). **1883**

PHYSICAL EDUCATION INDEX (CAPE GIRARDEAU). (US/0191-9202). **1796**

PHYSICAL EDUCATION REVIEW. (UK/0140-7708). **1857**

PHYSICAL EDUCATOR, THE. (US/0031-8981). **1857**

PHYSICAL THERAPY. (US/0031-9023). **4381**

PHYSICIAN AND SPORTSMEDICINE, THE. (US/0091-3847). **3955**

PHYSICIAN ASSISTANT (1983). (US/8750-7544). **3627**

PHYSICIAN EXECUTIVE. (US/0898-2759). **3916**

PHYSICIAN EXECUTIVE REVIEW. (US). **Qty:** 2-3. **3916**

PHYSICS AND CHEMISTRY OF GLASSES. (UK/0031-9090). **2593**

PHYSICS AND CHEMISTRY OF LIQUIDS. (US/0031-9104). **1056**

PHYSICS IN CANADA. (CN/0031-9147). **Qty:** 6. **4415**

PHYSICS IN MEDICINE & BIOLOGY. (UK/0031-9155). **479**

PHYSICS OF METALS. (US/0275-9144). **4014**

PHYSICS TEACHER, THE. (US/0031-921X). **1902**

PHYSICS TODAY. (US/0031-9228). **4416**

PHYSIK DATEN. (GW/0344-8401). **4416**

PHYSIOLOGICAL CHEMISTRY AND PHYSICS AND MEDICAL NMR. (US/0748-6642). **469**

PHYSIOLOGICAL ENTOMOLOGY. (UK/0307-6962). **5612**

PHYSIOLOGY CANADA (1983). (CN/0822-9058). **585**

PHYSIOTHERAPY. (UK/0031-9406). **4382**

PHYSIOTHERAPY CANADA. (CN/0300-0508). **3627**

PHYSIOTHERAPY IN SPORT. (UK/0954-0741). **Qty:** 3. **3955**

PHYSIS. SECCIONES A, B Y C. (AG/0326-1441). **5594**

PHYTOLOGIA. (US/0031-9430). **Qty:** 12. **522**

PHYTOLOGIA MEMOIRS. (US). **522**

PHYTOMORPHOLOGY. (II/0031-9449). **522**

PHYTON (BUENOS AIRES). (AG/0031-9457). **522**

PHYTON (HORN). (AU/0079-2047). **522**

PHYTOPROTECTION. (CN/0031-9511). **181**

PI QUALITY. (US). **1199**

PIANO GUILD NOTES. (US/0031-9546). **4146**

PIANO JOURNAL / EUROPEAN PIANO TEACHERS ASSOCIATION. (UK/0267-7253). **4146**

PIANO QUARTERLY, THE. (US/0031-9554). **4146**

PIANO TECHNICIAN'S JOURNAL. (US/0031-9562). **4146**

PICA. (CN/0225-7114). **4170**

PICTON, LE. (FR/0151-6086). **Qty:** 6. **2702**

PICTURE PERFECT. (US/1045-0629). **4375**

PIEDMONT LITERARY REVIEW. (US/0275-357X). **3423**

PIERRE-FORT - PIERRE GENEALOGICAL SOCIETY, THE. (US/0737-7975). **2467**

PIG FARMER, THE. (AT/0031-9740). **217**

PIGMENT & RESIN TECHNOLOGY. (UK/0369-9420). **4225**

PIGS. (NE/0168-9533). **217**

PIK. PRAXIS DER INFORMATIONSVERARBEITUNG UND KOMMUNIKATION. (GW/0930-5157). **1199**

PILGRIMAGE. (US/0361-0802). **4608**

PILOT (BOSTON, MASS.), THE. (US/0744-933X). **31**

PILOT (MONTREAL). (CN/0380-6618). **31**

PINE COUNTY COURIER. (US). **Qty:** 5. **5698**

PINE LOG, THE. (US). **5753**

PINE RIVER JOURNAL. (US). **Qty:** 14. **5698**

PINELLAS COUNTY REVIEW. (US/0746-746X). **Qty:** 4-6 per year. **803**

PING CHUAN TUNG TU. (CC/1000-0240). **1391**

PING PANG SHIH CHIEH. (CC). **4912**

PINHOLE JOURNAL. (US/0885-1476). **4375**

PINTER REVIEW, THE. (US/0895-9706). **3423**

PINTURAS Y ACABADOS INDUSTRIALES. (SP/0031-9953). **4225**

PIONEER (BEMIDJI, MINN.), THE. (US/0899-1812). **Qty:** 6. **5698**

PIONEER BRANCHES. (US). **Qty:** 12. **2467**

PIONEER WAGON, THE. (US/0735-309X). **2467**

PIP COLLEGE "HELPS" NEWSLETTER. (US/0732-5258). **Qty:** 3-5. **1883**

PIPE LINE INDUSTRY (HOUSTON, TEX.). (US/0032-0145). **2124**

PIPELINE & GAS JOURNAL. (US/0032-0188). **4274**

PIPELINES ABSTRACTS : BHRA ABSTRACTS JOURNAL. (UK/0265-3990). **2124**

PIPES & PIPELINES INTERNATIONAL (1965). (UK/0032-020X). **4274**

PITT MAGAZINE. (US). **1102**

PITTSBURGH HISTORY. (US/1069-4706). **Qty:** 40. **2754**

PIXEL (TORONTO). (CN/0835-8095). **1234**

PIZZA TODAY. (US/0743-3115). **2353**

PJG (MIAMI, FLA.). (US/1043-0083). **2427**

PLA BULLETIN. (US/0197-9299). **3241**

PLACENTA (EASTBOURNE). (UK/0143-4004). **539**

PLAIN RAPPER, THE. (US/0032-0412). **5301**

PLAIN TRUTH (PASADENA, CALIF.), THE. (US/0032-0420). **4986**

PLAINDEALER (WICHITA, KAN. 1919), THE. (US/0898-4360). **5678**

PLAINS ANTHROPOLOGIST. (US/0032-0447). **2271**

PLAINSWOMAN. (US/0148-902X). **5564**

PLAN CANADA. (CN/0032-0544). **2830**

PLAN OG ARBEID. (NO/0032-0609). **1702**

PLANET TODAY. (CN/1183-6040). **2179**

PLANETARIAN, THE. (US/0090-3213). **Qty:** 4-8. **398**

PLANETARY REPORT, THE. (US/0736-3680). **Qty:** 6. **398**

PLANNED GIVING TODAY. (US/1052-4770). **Qty:** 6. **4338**

PLANNER (LONDON). (UK/0309-1384). **2830**

PLANNING. (UK). **4673**

PLANNING & ZONING NEWS. (US/0738-114X). **2831**

PLANNING (CHICAGO, ILL. 1969). (US/0001-2610). **2831**

PLANNING FOR HIGHER EDUCATION. (US/0736-0983). **1841**

PLANNING HISTORY. (UK/0959-5805). **2702**

PLANNING HISTORY PRESENT. (US/1071-1953). **Qty:** varies. **2831**

PLANNING NEWS (ALBANY, N.Y.). (US/0885-6737). **2831**

PLANNING NEWS SOUTH MELBOURNE. (AT/0313-3796). **Qty:** few. **2831**

PLANNING PERSPECTIVES : PP. (UK/0266-5433). **2831**

PLANNING PRACTICE + RESEARCH. (UK/0269-7459). **2831**

PLANNING REVIEW. (US/0094-064X). **882**

PLANO STAR COURIER (1986). (US/0895-4305). **5753**

PLANODION. (GR/1105-2473). **Qty:** 10-15. **3424**

PLANT & GARDEN. (CN). **2427**

PLANT BIOTECHNOLOGY. (UK/0260-5902). **523**

PLANT BREEDING. (GW/0179-9541). **523**

PLANT, CELL AND ENVIRONMENT. (UK/0140-7791). **523**

PLANT ENGINEERING. (US/0032-082X). **1990**

PLANT PATHOLOGY. (UK/0032-0862). **524**

PLANT PROTECTION QUARTERLY. (AT/0815-2195). **120**

PLANT VARIETIES & SEEDS. (UK/0952-3863). **2427**

PLANTA MEDICA. (GW/0032-0943). **4325**

PLANTER, THE. (MY/0126-575X). **Qty:** 3800 x 12. **120**

PLANTLINE. (AT/0726-4623). **Qty:** 25. **3486**

PLANTS & GARDENS. (US/0362-5850). **2428**

PLANTS & GARDENS NEWS / BROOKLYN BOTANIC GARDEN. (US). **2428**

PLASMA NEWS REPORT. (US/0892-6352). **Qty:** 6. **1028**

PLASTIC FIGURE AND PLAYSET COLLECTOR. (US). **2585**

PLASTIC NEWS INTERNATIONAL. (AT). **2107**

PLASTICS AND RUBBER INTERNATIONAL. (UK/0309-4561). **4457**

PLASTICS BULLETIN. (BE). **Qty:** 10. **4457**

PLASTICS ENGINEERING. (US/0091-9578). **4458**

PLASTICS NEWS (AKRON, OHIO). (US/1042-802X). **4458**

PLASTICS SOUTHERN AFRICA. (SA/0032-2660). **2107**

PLASTICS TECHNOLOGY. (US/0032-1257). **4458**

PLASTICULTURE. (FR). **4459**

PLASTIZINE. (CN/0715-5719). **381**

PLASTVERARBEITER, DER. (GW/0032-1338). **4459**

PLATE WORLD. (US/0195-5780). **2593**

PLATELETS SHEFFIELD. (UK/0142-8268). **3773**

PLATING AND SURFACE FINISHING. (US/0360-3164). **4225**

PLATINUM METALS REVIEW. (UK/0032-1400). **Qty:** 3-8. **4015**

PLATON. (GR/1105-073X). **Qty:** 1,000. **1079**

PLATTE COUNTY, MISSOURI, HISTORICAL & GENEALOGICAL SOCIETY BULLETIN. (US). **Qty:** 12-16. **2468**

PLAY & CULTURE. (US/0894-4253). **5213**

PLAY AND PARENTING CONNECTIONS. (CN/0835-4014). **3241**

PLAYBACK AND FAST FORWARD. (II). **703**

PLAYERS. (US/0149-466X). **3996**

PLAYGIRL. (US/0032-1494). **5564**

PLAYING-CARD WORLD. (UK/0966-4033). **4865**

PLAYS (BOSTON). (US/0032-1540). **5367**

PLAZA MAYOR. (PE). **2831**

PLC INSIDER'S NEWSLETTER, THE. (US/1040-9718). **Qty:** 3 /yr. **1265**

PLEASURE BOATING. (US/0191-7366). **595**

PLERUS. (PR/0048-4466). **1512**

PLEXUS (OAKLAND, CALIF.). (US/0274-5526). **5564**

PLONGEE. (CN/0228-3530). **Qty:** 20. **4912**

PLOUGH, THE. (US/0740-9125). **4986**

PLOUGHSHARES. (US/0048-4474). **3424**

PLOUGHSHARES MONITOR. (CN/0703-1866). **4532**

PLOWMAN (BROOKLIN). (CN/0840-707X). **3468**

PLUM CREEK ALMANAC. (US/0898-5197). **Qty:** 6-10. **2468**

PLUMBING. (UK/0032-1656). **Qty:** 0-10. **2607**

PLUMBING BUSINESS. (US). **2607**

PLUMBLINE. (US/0741-1421). **1841**

PLURAL SOCIETIES. (NE/0048-4482). **5213**

PLURILINGUA. (BE). **3310**

PLYMOUTH BULLETIN. (US/0032-1737). **5423**

PM NET WORK, THE. (US/1040-8754). **882**

PM PLUS. (UK). **946**

PM. PRAXIS DER MATHEMATIK. (GW/0032-7042). **3527**

PMC. PRACTICE OF MINISTRY IN CANADA. (CN/0825-0391). **Qty:** 14-16. **4986**

PMEA NEWS. (US/0030-8102). **4146**

PMI. POWDER METALLURGY INTERNATIONAL. (GW/0048-5012). **4015**

PN REVIEW (MANCHESTER, GREATER MANCHESTER : 1979). (UK/0144-7076). **3350**

PNCC STUDIES. (US/0734-4570). **4987**

PNEUMA (SPRINGFIELD). (US/0272-0965). **5066**

PNLA QUARTERLY. (US/0030-8188). **3241**

PNPA PRESS. (US/0030-8196). **4818**

POA (1985). (US/0882-9624). **2801**

PODIATRIC PRODUCTS. (US/0890-3972). **3918**

PODIATRY MANAGEMENT. (US/0744-3528). **3918**

POE STUDIES. (US/0090-5224). **434**

POEM. (US/0032-1885). **3468**

POET. (II/0032-194X). **3468**

POET AND CRITIC (AMES, IOWA). (US/0032-1958). **3468**

POET LORE. (US/0032-1966). **Qty:** 10 per year. **3468**

POET (SHREVEPORT, LA.), THE. (US/0748-4062). **Qty:** varies. **3468**

POETICA (MUNCHEN). (NE/0303-4178). **3424**

POETICS JOURNAL. (US/0731-5236). **3350**

POETICS TODAY. (US/0333-5372). **3424**

POETRY & AUDIENCE. (UK/0032-2040). **Qty:** 51. **3469**

POETRY AUSTRALIA. (AT/0032-2059). **3469**

POETRY CANADA REVIEW. (CN/0709-3373). **Qty:** 14. **3350**

POETRY (CHICAGO). (US/0032-2032). **3469**

POETRY DURHAM. (UK). **3469**

POETRY EAST. (US/0197-4009). **3469**

POETRY FLASH. (US/0737-4747). **3469**

POETRY IRELAND REVIEW, THE. (IE/0332-2998). **Qty:** 40-50. **3469**

POETRY NIPPON. (JA/0032-2105). **3469**

POETRY REVIEW (LONDON). (UK/0032-2156). **3350**

POETRY TORONTO. (CN/0381-6591). **3469**

POETRY WALES. (UK/0032-2202). **Qty:** 40. **3469**

POINT SERIES. (PP/0253-2913). **4987**

POINT THEOLOGIQUE, LE. (FR). **4987**

POINT VETERINAIRE, LE. (FR/0335-4997). **5518**

POINTER, THE. (US/0554-4246). **1883**

POKROKY MATEMATIKY, FYSIKY A ASTRONOMIE. (XR/0032-2423). **5138**

POLAR RECORD, THE. (UK/0032-2474). **5138**

POLAR TIMES, THE. (US/0032-2482). **2572**

POLARFORSCHUNG. (GW/0032-2490). **5138**

POLEMIC. (AT). **3029**

POLESTAR. (UK). **Qty:** 4-6. **1774**

POLICE AND LAW ENFORCEMENT. (US/0092-8933). **3171**

POLICE CHIEF, THE. (US/0032-2571). **3171**

POLICE COLLECTORS NEWS. (US/1071-1724). **Qty:** 12. **3172**

POLICE COMPUTER REVIEW. (US/1061-1509). **1289**

POLICE JOURNAL (CHICHESTER). (UK/0032-258X). **3172**

POLICE MARKSMAN, THE. (US/0164-8365). **3172**

POLICE REVIEW (LONDON). (UK/0309-1414). **3172**

POLICE STUDIES. (US/0141-2949). **3172**

POLICY AND POLITICS. (UK/0305-5736). **4487**

POLICY AND RESEARCH REPORT. (US/0741-8485). **5213**

POLICY (CENTRE FOR INDEPENDENT STUDIES (N.S.W.)). (AT/1032-6634). **4487**

POLICY GUIDE OF THE AMERICAN CIVIL LIBERTIES UNION. (US/0275-3170). **4511**

POLICY OPTIONS. (CN/0226-5893). **4488**

POLICY REVIEW (WASHINGTON). (US/0146-5945). **5213**

POLICY STUDIES. (UK/0144-2872). **4488**

POLICY STUDIES JOURNAL. (US/0190-292X). **4488**

POLICY STUDIES REVIEW. (US/0278-4416). **4488**

POLIMERI (ZAGREB). (CI/0351-1871). **4459**

POLIN. (UK/0268-1056). **5052**

POLISH AMERICAN JOURNAL (1985 : NATIONAL ED.). (US). **Qty:** 3. **5720**

POLISH AMERICAN STUDIES (CHICAGO, ILL.). (US/0032-2806). **2754**

POLISH AMERICAN WORLD. (US). **Qty:** 12. **5720**

POLISH FAMILY TREE SURNAMES. (US/0271-2644). **2468**

POLISH GENEALOGICAL SOCIETY NEWSLETTER. (US/0735-9349). **2468**

POLISH HERITAGE. (US/0735-9209). **Qty:** 20-40. **2754**

POLISH JOURNAL OF OCCUPATIONAL MEDICINE AND ENVIRONMENTAL HEALTH. (PL/0867-8383). **Qty:** 4. **3628**

POLISH POLAR RESEARCH. (PL/0138-0338). **5138**

POLISH POLITICAL SCIENCE / POLISH ASSOCIATION OF POLITICAL SCIENCE. (PL/0208-7375). **4488**

POLISH REVIEW (NEW YORK. 1956), THE. (US/0032-2970). **Qty:** 30. **5213**

POLITICA. (DK/0105-0710). **4488**

POLITICAL AFFAIRS. (US/0032-3128). **4488**

POLITICAL FINANCE LOBBY REPORTER. (US/0270-353X). **4489**

POLITICAL HANDBOOK OF THE WORLD (1975). (US/0193-175X). **Qty:** 2. **4489**

POLITICAL RESEARCH QUARTERLY. (US/1065-9129). **4489**

POLITICAL RESOURCE DIRECTORY (NATIONAL ED.). (US/0898-4271). **4489**

POLITICAL SCIENCE. (NZ/0032-3187). **4490**

POLITICAL SCIENCE QUARTERLY. (US/0032-3195). **4490**

POLITICAL SCIENCE REVIEWER, THE. (US/0091-3715). **4490**

POLITICAL STUDIES. (UK/0032-3217). **4490**

POLITICAL WARFARE. (US/1056-3334). **Qty:** 10. **4532**

POLITICS & SOCIETY. (US/0032-3292). **5213**

POLITICS AND SOCIETY IN GERMANY, AUSTRIA, AND SWITZERLAND. (UK/0954-6030). **Qty:** 2. **5254**

POLITICS AND THE INDIVIDUAL. (GW/0939-6071). **4490**

POLITICS AND THE LIFE SCIENCES. (US/0730-9384). **4490**

POLITICS (MANCHESTER (GREATER MANCHESTER)). (UK/0263-3957). **4491**

POLITIK UND KULTUR. (GW). **4491**

POLITIKA EKONOMIE. (XR/0032-3233). **1512**

POLITIKON. (SA/0258-9346). **4491**

POLITIQUE INTERNATIONALE. (FR/0221-2781). **4532**

POLITIQUES ET MANAGEMENT PUBLIC. (FR/0758-1726). **Qty:** 3. **4491**

POLITY. (US/0032-3497). **Qty:** 3. **4491**

POLIZEI, VERKEHR + TECHNIK. (GW). **3172**

POLKA NEWS, THE. (US/0273-6454). **1314**

POLK'S MINNEAPOLIS SUBURBAN CITY DIRECTORY. (US). **2572**

POLLING REPORT, THE. (US/0887-171X). **Qty:** 20. **5254**

POLLUTION ABSTRACTS WITH INDEXES. (US/0032-3624). **2185**

POLLUTION ENGINEERING. (US/0032-3640). **2238**

POLLUTION EQUIPMENT NEWS. (US/0032-3659). **2239**

POLLUTION PREVENTION. (UK). **2239**

POLYGRAPH, DER. (GW/0032-3845). **4567**

POLYGRAPH (LINTHICUM HEIGHTS). (US/0197-7024). **3172**

POLYHEDRON. (UK/0277-5387). **1037**

POLYMER COMPOSITES. (US/0272-8397). **4459**

POLYMER DEGRADATION AND STABILITY. (UK/0141-3910). **988**

POLYMER NETWORKS & BLENDS. (CN/1181-9510). **1046**

POLYMER-PLASTICS TECHNOLOGY AND ENGINEERING (SOFTCOVER ED.). (US/0360-2559). **2015**

POLYMER TESTING. (UK/0142-9418). **4459**

POMONA : NORTH AMERICAN FRUIT EXPLORERS' QUARTERLY. (US/0748-6510). **2428**

POMPANO LEDGER. (US). **5650**

POMPEIIANA NEWSLETTER. (US/0892-5941). **3311**

PONCHATOULA TIMES, THE. (US). **Qty:** 24 per year. **5684**

PONTIAC-OAKLAND COUNTY LEGAL NEWS. (US/0739-0203). **3029**

PONTOTOC COUNTY QUARTERLY, OKLAHOMA. (US). **2468**

POODLE VARIETY. (US/0882-2816). **Qty:** 1. **4287**

POOL & BILLIARD MAGAZINE. (US/1049-2852). **Qty:** 6. **4912**

POOL & SPA MARKETING. (CN/0711-2998). **Qty:** 2. **934**

POOL & SPA NEWS. (US/0194-5351). **703**

POOL & SPA NEWS DIRECTORY ISSUE. (US). **4853**

POOP SHEET, THE. (US/0195-0037). **4912**

POPE COUNTY HISTORICAL ASSOCIATION QUARTERLY. (US). **2754**

POPLINE. (US). **4556**

POPOLI. (IT/0394-4247). **Qty:** 50. **2521**

POPULAR ARCHAEOLOGY. (US/0300-774X). **278**

POPULAR ARCHAEOLOGY. TECHNICAL PUBLICATION. (US). **278**

POPULAR CERAMICS. (US/0032-4477). **2593**

POPULAR COMMUNICATIONS. (US/0733-3315). **1119**

POPULAR CULTURE IN LIBRARIES. (US/1053-8747). **3241**

POPULAR MINING. (US/8756-6257). **Qty:** 4. **2148**

POPULAR MUSIC AND SOCIETY. (US/0300-7766). **4147**

POPULAR MUSIC (CAMBRIDGE UNIVERSITY PRESS). (UK/0261-1430). **4147**

POPULAR PLASTICS & PACKAGING. (II). **4459**

POPULAR WOODWORKING. (US/0884-8823). **2403**

POPULATION. (FR/0032-4663). **4556**

POPULATION AND DEVELOPMENT REVIEW. (US/0098-7921). **4556**

POPULATION EDUCATION IN ASIA AND THE PACIFIC NEWSLETTER. (TH). **4557**

POPULATION ET SOCIETES. (FR/0184-7783). **4557**

POPULATION REVIEW. (US/0032-471X). **4558**

POPULATION STUDIES. (UK/0032-4728). **4558**

POPULATION TIMES, THE. (BG). **590**

POPULATION TODAY. (US/0749-2448). **4558**

PORK CITY PRESS. (US). **5650**

PORK JOURNAL. (AT/1032-3759). **218**

PORT CONSTRUCTION AND OCEAN TECHNOLOGY. (UK/0264-8733). **624**

PORT DOVER MAPLE LEAF. (CN/0834-7166). **Qty:** 6. **5793**

PORT GIBSON REVEILLE (PORT GIBSON, MISS.: 1890). (US). **5701**

PORT OF LONDON. (UK/0030-8064). **5454**

PORT OF TORONTO NEWS. (CN/0477-6410). **5454**

PORT TOWNSEND JEFFERSON COUNTY LEADER, THE. (US/1050-1460). **Qty:** 10. **5762**

PORTABLE 100 (1986). (US/0888-0131). **Qty:** 4-6. **1199**

PORTABLE COMPANION, THE. (US/0732-7501). **1272**

PORTABLE PAPER, THE. (US/0886-9138). **1199**

PORTE & CANCELLI. (IT/1120-2637). **1621**

PORTER'S GUIDE TO CONGRESSIONAL ROLL CALL VOTES. HOUSE. (US/0748-2310). **4674**

PORTER'S GUIDE TO CONGRESSIONAL ROLL CALL VOTES. SENATE. (US/0748-2329). **4491**

PORTLAND OBSERVER. (US). **Qty:** 10. **5734**

PORTLAND PRESS HERALD, THE. (US). **5685**

PORTLAND REV. (1981). (US/0885-7121). **3424**

PORTOLAN / WASHINGTON MAP SOCIETY, THE. (US). **2573**

PORTSMOUTH HERALD, THE. (US/0746-6218). **5709**

PORTUGUESE TIMES (NEW BEDFORD, MASS.). (US/0746-3928). **5689**

PORZELLAN + GLAS : P + G / ORGAN DES BUNDESVERBANDES DES GLAS-, PORZELLAN- UND KERAMIK-EINZELHANDELS. (GW). **2593**

POSEBNA IZDANJA INSTITUTA ZA ZASTITU BILJA. (YU/0408-9952). **525**

POSEV. (GW/0032-5201). **4491**

POSEY COUNTY NEWS & THE TIMES. (US). **5666**

POSITIF. (FR/0048-4911). **4076**

POSITIONS LUTHERIENNES. (FR/0032-5228). **5066**

POSITIVE APPROACH, A. (US/0891-8791). **Qty:** 40. **4392**

POSITIVE ATTITUDE POSTERS. (US). **946**

POSITIVE HEALTH. (UK/0958-5737). **4795**

POSITIVE IMPACT. (US). **Qty:** 12. **704**

POSSIBLES. (CN/0703-7139). **Qty:** 5-6. **5213**

POST-GAZETTE (BOSTON, MASS.). (US/0888-0107). **Qty:** 26. **5689**

POST, KENYA. (KE/0253-5963). **5139**

POST SCRIPT (JACKSONVILLE, FLA.). (US/0277-9897). **Qty:** 3-5. **4076**

POSTA (LAKE OSWEGO, OR.), LA. (US/0885-7385). **2786**

POSTAL HISTORY ANNUAL, THE. (UK). **1146**

POSTAL HISTORY JOURNAL. (US/0032-5341). **1146**

POSTAL STATIONERY. (US/0554-8373). **2786**

POSTCARD CLASSICS. (US/0897-4020). **Qty:** 2. **375**

POSTCARD COLLECTOR. (US/0746-6102). **2777**

POSTGESCHICHTE. (SZ). **2786**

POSTGRADUATE DOCTOR. AFRICA. (UK/0142-7946). **3628**

POSTGRADUATE DOCTOR. MIDDLE EAST EDITION. (UK/0140-7724). **3628**

POSTGRADUATE EDUCATION FOR GENERAL PRACTICE. (UK/0959-4299). **3738**

POSTGRADUATE MEDICAL JOURNAL. (UK/0032-5473). **3628**

POSTGRADUATE MEDICINE. (US/0032-5481). **3628**

POSTHARVEST NEWS AND INFORMATION. (UK/0957-7505). **155**

POSTPRAXIS, DIE. (GW/0554-842X). **1147**

POSTSECONDARY EDUCATION OPPORTUNITY. (US/1068-9818). **1842**

POTASH REVIEW. (SZ/0032-5546). **182**

POTATO EYES. (US/1041-9926). **Qty:** 8. **3424**

POTATO GROWER. (AT/0815-6514). **182**

POTATO RESEARCH. (NE/0014-3065). **182**

POTOMAC ALMANAC. (US/0194-2182). **5687**

POTOMAC APPALACHIAN (MAY 1972). (US/0098-8154). **4877**

POTOMAC BASIN REPORTER. (US). **Qty:** 2-10. **5537**

POTTERY IN AUSTRALIA. (AT/0048-4954). **2593**

POTTERY SOUTHWEST. (US/0738-8020). **2593**

POULTRY PRESS. (US/0032-5783). **218**

POUR. (FR/0245-9442). **5254**

POUR LA SCIENCE. (FR/0153-4092). **5139**

POVERKHNOST. (US/0734-1520). **4417**

POVERTY. (UK/0032-5856). **5301**

POWDER COATINGS. (US/0163-4542). **4225**

POWDER COATINGS BULLETIN. (UK/0140-8445). **4225**

POWDER HANDLING & PROCESSING. (GW/0934-7348). **2148**

POWELL TRIBUNE, THE. (US/0740-1078). **Qty:** 2. **5772**

POWER FARMING MAGAZINE. (AT/0311-1911). **160**

POWER INTERNATIONAL. (UK/0950-1487). **2124**

POWER LINE (WASHINGTON, D.C.), THE. (US/0738-5676). **1953**

POWER TRANSMISSION DESIGN. (US/0032-6070). **2124**

POWERBOAT (VAN NUYS, CALIF.). (US/0032-6089). **Qty:** 1-2 /year. **595**

POWERLIFTING USA. (US/0199-8536). **4913**

POWYS NOTES. (US/1058-7691). **Qty:** 4-6. **3350**

POWYS REVIEW, THE. (UK/0309-1619). **3350**

PPT EXPRESS. (US/1068-8897). **Qty:** varies. **5301**

PR & V : PR EN VOORLICHTING. (NE). **763**

PR REPORTER (EXETER, N.H.). (US/0048-2609). **764**

PRABUDDHA BHARATA. (II/0032-6178). **5041**

PRACE INSTYTUTU TECHNIKI BUDOWLANEJ. (PL/0138-0796). **2028**

PRACHYA PRATIBHA. (II). **2662**

PRACI BHASA-VIJNAN (CALCUTTA). (II/0970-9940). **3311**

PRACTICAL ACCOUNTANT, THE. (US/0032-6321). **749**

PRACTICAL ALLERGY & IMMUNOLOGY. (CN/0831-0998). **3675**

PRACTICAL AQUACULTURE & LAKE MANAGEMENT. (US/1057-218X). **Qty:** 8. **2310**

PRACTICAL DIABETES. (UK/0266-447X). **3732**

PRACTICAL ENDODONTICS. (US/1056-7933). **1333**

PRACTICAL ENGLISH TEACHING. (UK/0260-4752). **1902**

PRACTICAL FARM IDEAS QUARTERLY. (UK/0968-0136). **Qty:** 8. **160**

PRACTICAL GASTROENTEROLOGY. (US/0277-4208). **3747**

PRACTICAL LAWYER, THE. (US/0032-6429). **Qty:** 4 per year. **3030**

PRACTICAL SUPERVISION. (US/0742-7859). **882**

PRACTICAL WINERY/VINEYARD. (US/1057-2694). **2370**

PRACTICE (NEW YORK, N.Y.). (US/0742-9940). **Qty:** 2. **4545**

PRACTICES (CINCINNATI, OHIO). (US/1059-7239). **Qty:** 1. **306**

PRACTICING ANTHROPOLOGY. (US/0888-4552). **243**

PRACTICING ARCHITECT. (US/0888-3424). **306**

PRACTISING MANAGER. (AT/0159-1193). **882**

PRAGMATICS & BEYOND NEW SERIES. (NE/0922-842X). **3311**

PRAGMATICS : QUARTERLY PUBLICATION OF THE INTERNATIONAL PRAGMATICS ASSOCIATION. (BE/1018-2101). **Qty:** 30-40. **3311**

PRAGUE BULLETIN OF MATHEMATICAL LINGUISTICS, THE. (XR/0032-6585). **3311**

PRAHISTORISCHE FORSCHUNGEN / HERAUSGEGEBEN VON DER ANTHROPOLOGISCHEN GESELLSCHAFT IN WIEN. (AU/0032-6534). **243**

PRAIRIE FIRE (WINNIPEG). (CN/0821-1124). **Qty:** 60. **3424**

PRAIRIE FORUM. (CN/0317-6282). **2754**

PRAIRIE JOURNAL OF CANADIAN LITERATURE, THE. (CN/0827-2921). **Qty:** varies. **3424**

PRAIRIE MESSENGER. (CN/0032-664X). **5793**

PRAIRIE NATURALIST, THE. (US/0091-0376). **Qty:** 6-10. **4170**

PRAIRIE SCHOONER. (US/0032-6682). **3424**

PRAIRIELAND PIONEER. (US/0892-6131). **2468**

PRAJNAN. (II/0032-6690). **803**

PRAKTISCH MANAGEMENT. (BE/0772-6856). **Qty:** 2 /year. **882**

PRAKTISCHE SCHADLINGSBEKAMPFER, DER. (GW/0032-6801). **182**

PRAKTISCHE THEOLOGIE. (NE). **4987**

PRAKTISCHE TIERARZT. (GW/0032-681X). **5518**

PRAPARATOR. (GW/0032-6542). **4170**

PRASADA (CALCUTTA, INDIA). (II). **3425**

PRASARA. (II). **1802**

PRASHASNIKA. (II). **4674**

PRATIBHA INDIA. (II). **1842**

PRATICA SOCIALE. (IT). **4608**

PRATIQUE DU SOUDAGE, LA. (BE). **4027**

PRATIQUE LONDON. (UK/0269-1396). **Qty:** 4. **3715**

PRAVNEHISTORICKE STUDIE. (XR/0079-4929). **2703**

PRAVNIK (PRAGUE, CZECHOSLOVAKIA). (XR). **Qty:** 30 per year. **3030**

PRAVOSLAVNAIA RUS. (US/0032-7018). **4987**

PRAVOSLAVNAJA ZIZN. (US/0032-6992). **5040**

PRAXIS DER KLINISCHEN VERHALTENSMEDIZIN UND REHABILITATION. (GW/0933-842X). **3932**

PRAXIS DER PSYCHOMOTORIK. (GW/0170-060X). **1884**

PRAXIS DER PSYCHOTHERAPIE UND PSYCHOSOMATIK. (GW/0171-791X). **4608**

PRAXIS GRUNDSCHULE. (GW/0170-3722). **1094**

PRAXIS: JOURNAL OF POLITICAL SCIENCE. (PH/0116-709X). **4492**

PRAXIS VETERINARIA. (CI/0350-4441). **5518**

PRC NEWSLETTER. (US/8755-3902). **4375**

PRE-LAW JOURNAL. (US/0741-1162). **3030**

PRE- (PRAIRIE VILLAGE, KAN.). (US/1042-0304). **4818**

PREACHER'S MAGAZINE, THE. (US/0162-3982). **4987**

PREACHING (JACKSONVILLE, FLA.). (US/0882-7036). **4987**

PRECIOUS FIBERS. (US/0886-4268). **5355**

PRECISION ENGINEERING. (US/0141-6359). **2125**

PREDICAMENT, THE. (US/0199-0705). **4913**

PREGON DE LA TFP. (AG). Qty: 6. **4987**

PREGONERO (WASHINGTON, D.C.), EL. (US/8750-9326). **5647**

PRENATAL DIAGNOSIS. (UK/0197-3851). **3767**

PRENSA MEDICA ARGENTINA. (AG/0032-745X). **3629**

PRENSA (ORLANDO, FLA.), LA. (US/0888-756X). **5650**

PRENSA SAN DIEGO, LA. (US/0738-9183). Qty: 6. **2271**

PREPARATIVE BIOCHEMISTRY. (US/0032-7484). **492**

PREPODAVANIE ISTORII V SHKOLE. (RU/0132-0696). **2626**

PREPRESS BULLETIN, THE. (US/8750-2224). Qty: 3-4. **5034**

PREPRINTS OF PAPERS PRESENTED AT THE AES CONVENTIONS. (US). **5318**

PRESBYTERIAN HISTORY. (CN/0827-9713). **4987**

PRESBYTERIAN LAYMAN, THE. (US/0555-0572). **5066**

PRESBYTERIAN RECORD (MONTREAL). (CN/0032-7573). **5066**

PRESBYTERIAN SURVEY. (US/0032-759X). Qty: 15. **5066**

PRESBYTERION. (US/0193-6212). **5066**

PRESCHOOL PERSPECTIVES. (US/0748-4054). **1805**

PRESCOTT JOURNAL (PRESCOTT, WIS. : 1930). (US). **5770**

PRESCRIPTION PRODUCTS GUIDE. (AT/0818-4445). **4325**

PRESENCE AFRICAINE (PARIS, FRANCE : 1967). (FR/0032-7638). **2271**

PRESENCE (MONTREAL. 1992). (CN/1188-5580). Qty: 8. **4987**

PRESENTING THE SEASON. (US). **5235**

PRESERVATION LAW REPORTER. (US/0882-715X). **3030**

PRESERVATION REPORT. (US). **2755**

PRESIDENTIAL STUDIES QUARTERLY. (US/0360-4918). **4674**

PRESIDENTS & PRIME MINISTERS. (US/1060-5088). **4492**

PRESLIA. (XR/0032-7786). **525**

PRESQUE ISLE COUNTY ADVANCE. (US). Qty: 10. **5693**

PRESS & SUN-BULLETIN. (US/0886-8816). Qty: 200. **5720**

PRESS DEMOCRAT (SANTA ROSA, CALIF.). (US/0747-220X). **5638**

PRESS FOR CONVERSION. (CN/1183-8892). Qty: 40. **4054**

PRESS INDEPENDENT. (CN/1182-9931). Qty: 12/yr. **2543**

PRESS REVIEW (TORONTO). (CN/0706-9286). **2923**

PRESSE MEDICALE (1983), LA. (FR/0755-4982). **3629**

PRESSE UND SPRACHE. (GW/0935-8064). **2923**

PRESSURE (BETHESDA, MD.). (US/0889-0242). **3629**

PRESTEL DIRECTORY, THE. (UK/0266-0288). **1162**

PRETRE ET PASTEUR. (CN/0383-8307). **4987**

PREVENTION IN HUMAN SERVICES. (US/0270-3114). **4810**

PREVENTIVE LAW REPORTER. (US/0734-1660). Qty: 4. **3030**

PREVIEW. (US/0899-9821). **3241**

PREVIEW (RICHARDSON, TEX.). (US/0892-6468). **387**

PREVUE (READING, PA.). (US/1045-1234). **1119**

PREZZI INFORMATIVI DELL EDILIZIA MATERIALI ED OPERE COMPIUTE : IMPIANTI TECNICI. (IT). **624**

PREZZI INFORMATIVI DELL EDILIZIA MATERIALI ED OPERE COMPIUTE : NUOVE COSTRUZIONI. (IT). **624**

PRIEST, THE. (US/0032-8200). **5034**

PRIESTS & PEOPLE. (UK/0952-6390). **5034**

PRIKLADNAIA MEKHANIKA. (RU). **2125**

PRIMAL INSTITUTE NEWSLETTER, THE. (US/0164-5056). **4608**

PRIMARILY NURSING. (US/0739-4446). Qty: 45. **3867**

PRIMARY EDUCATION AUSTRALIA. (AT/0048-5284). **1805**

PRIMARY GEOGRAPHER. (UK/0956-277X). **2573**

PRIMARY SOURCE (JACKSON, MISS.). (US/0741-6563). **2482**

PRIMARY SOURCES AND ORIGINAL WORKS. (US/1042-8216). **3241**

PRIMARY TEACHING STUDIES. (UK/0268-2176). Qty: 12-15 per year. **1902**

PRIMATE EYE. (UK/0305-8417). Qty: 3. **5594**

PRIME NUMBER. (AT/0816-9349). **3527**

PRIME TIME (NEW YORK). (US/0194-2611). **5181**

PRIME TIMES (MADISON). (US/0195-5934). **5181**

PRIMROSES. (US/0162-6671). **2428**

PRINCE GEORGE'S COUNTY GENEALOGICAL SOCIETY BULLETIN. (US/1052-1380). Qty: 2. **2468**

PRINCETON ALUMNI WEEKLY. (US/0149-9270). Qty: 17. **1102**

PRINCETON RECOLLECTOR. (US/0196-1136). **2755**

PRINCETON SEMINARY BULLETIN, THE. (US/0032-8413). **4987**

PRINCETON STUDIES IN INTERNATIONAL FINANCE. (US/0081-8070). **1639**

PRINCIPAL MATTERS. (AT). Qty: approx. 10 per year. **1868**

PRINSBURG NEWS. (US/8750-0698). **5698**

PRINT BUYING. (UK). **4568**

PRINT COLLECTOR'S NEWSLETTER, THE. (US/0032-8537). **381**

PRINT (NEW YORK). (US/0032-8510). **381**

PRINT QUARTERLY. (UK/0265-8305). **4568**

PRINTED CIRCUIT FABRICATION. (US/0274-8096). **2075**

PRINTER'S NEWS (WELLINGTON). (NZ/0048-5330). **4568**

PRINTING ABSTRACTS. (UK/0031-109X). **4570**

PRINTING HISTORY. (US/0192-9275). **4568**

PRINTING INDUSTRIES. (UK/0307-7195). **4568**

PRINTING JOURNAL. (US/0191-8273). **4568**

PRINTING WORLD. (UK/0032-8715). **4568**

PRIORITIES (VANCOUVER). (CN/0700-6543). Qty: varies. **5564**

PRISCILLA PAPERS. (US/0898-753X). Qty: varies. **4988**

PRISMA. (IO). **1513**

PRISMA LATINOAMERICANO. (CU). **4532**

PRISMET. (NO/0032-8447). **4988**

PRISON SERVICE JOURNAL. (UK/0300-3558). **3173**

PRITEL LIDU : CASOPIS SLEZSKE CIRKVE EVANGELICKE. (XR). **4988**

PRIVACY & AMERICAN BUSINESS. (US/1070-0536). **704**

PRIVACY EN REGISTRATIE. (NE). **4512**

PRIVATE CARRIER. (US/0032-8871). **5389**

PRIVATE EYE WEEKLY. (US). Qty: 12. **2543**

PRIVATE LIBRARY. (UK/0032-8898). **3241**

PRIVATE POST, THE. (UK). **2787**

PRIVATE PRACTICE. (US/0032-891X). **3629**

PRIVATE VARNISH. (US/1047-9473). **5434**

PRIVILEGED TRAVELER, THE. (US/0887-4131). **5489**

PRO BIKE NEWS. (US/1064-2765). Qty: 7. **429**

PRO/E, THE MAGAZINE. (US/1069-6113). **1200**

PRO ECCLESIA (NORTHFIELD, MINN.). (US/1063-8512). **4988**

PRO-LIFE NEWS. (CN/0715-4356). **3767**

PRO REGE. (US/0276-4830). **1842**

PROA. (CK/0032-9150). **306**

PROBABILISTIC ENGINEERING MECHANICS. (UK/0266-8920). **2125**

PROBABILITY AND STOCHASTIC PROCESSES. (GW/0720-2628). **3527**

PROBATE LAW JOURNAL. (US/0737-3112). **3031**

PROBATION AND PAROLE DIRECTORY (COLLEGE PARK, MD.). (US/0732-0965). **3173**

PROBATION AND PAROLE LAW REPORTS. (US/0276-6965). **3173**

PROBATION JOURNAL. (UK). **3173**

PROBE. (US/1062-4155). **5139**

PROBE (LONDON. 1954). (UK/0032-9185). **1333**

PROBLEM OBSERVER. (UK). **4865**

PROBLEME DE INFORMARE SI DOCUMENTARE. (RM/0032-924X). **3242**

PROBLEMES D'AMERIQUE LATINE. (FR/0765-1333). **2512**

PROBLEMI DELLA PEDAGOGIA, I. (IT). **1774**

PROBLEMI DI GESTIONE. (IT). **704**

PROBLEMI NA GEOGRAFIIATA. (BU/0204-7209). **2573**

PROBLEMIST, THE. (UK/0032-9398). Qty: varies. **4865**

PROBLEMS OF COMMUNISM. (UK). **4545**

PROBLEMS OF CULTURE / COMMITTEE FOR CULTURE, RESEARCH INSTITUTE FOR CULTURE AT THE COMMITTEE FOR CULTURE, AND THE BULGARIAN ACADEMY OF SCIENCES. (BU/0204-8620). **5254**

PROBLEMS OF ECONOMICS. (US/0032-9436). **1513**

PROBLEMY DALNEGO VOSTOKA. (RU). **2662**

PROBLEMY PRAWNE HANDLU ZAGRANICZNEGO. (PL). **3134**

PROBLEMY SOTSIALNOI GIGIENY I ISTORIIA MEDITSINY / NII SOTSIALNOI GIGIENY, EKONOMIKI I UPRAVLENIIA ZDRAVOOKHRANENIEM IM N.A. SEMASHKO RAMN, AO ASSOTSIATSIIA 'MEDITSINSKAIA LITERATURA.'. (RU/0869-866X). **4796**

PROBLEMY TUBERKULEZA. (RU/0032-9533). **3951**

PROBUS. (NE/0921-4771). **3312**

PROCEEDINGS - AMERICAN SOCIETY FOR THE ADVANCEMENT ANESTHESIA IN DENTISTRY. (US/0164-1700). **3684**

PROCEEDINGS AND PAPERS OF THE ANNUAL CONFERENCE OF THE CALIFORNIA MOSQUITO AND VECTOR CONTROL ASSOCIATION. (US/0160-6751). **2239**

PROCEEDINGS AND REPORTS - FLORIDA STATE UNIVERSITY, CENTER FOR YUGOSLAV-AMERICAN STUDIES, RESEARCH AND EXCHANGES. (US/0196-9730). **2703**

PROCEEDINGS ... ANNUAL CONFERENCE / AGRONOMY SOCIETY OF NEW ZEALAND. (NZ/0110-6589). **121**

PROCEEDINGS ... ANNUAL CONFERENCE OF THE AMERICAN COUNCIL ON CONSUMER INTERESTS. (US/0275-1356). **1299**

PROCEEDINGS, ANNUAL TECHNICAL MEETING - INSTITUTE OF ENVIRONMENTAL SCIENCES. (US/0361-2007). **5140**

PROCEEDINGS - ASTRONOMICAL SOCIETY OF AUSTRALIA. (AT/0066-9997). **398**

PROCEEDINGS ... CONFERENCE ON GROUND CONTROL IN MINING. (US). **2148**

PROCEEDINGS - INTERNATIONAL COMPUTER SOFTWARE & APPLICATIONS CONFERENCE. (US/0730-3157). **1289**

PROCEEDINGS OF AMERICAN PEANUT RESEARCH AND EDUCATION SOCIETY, INC. (US/0197-9748). **183**

PROCEEDINGS OF ... PAKISTAN CONGRESS OF ZOOLOGY. (PK). **5595**

PROCEEDINGS OF THE ACADEMY OF NATURAL SCIENCES OF PHILADELPHIA. (US/0097-3157). **4170**

PROCEEDINGS

PROCEEDINGS OF THE ACADEMY OF POLITICAL SCIENCE. (US). **4492**

PROCEEDINGS OF THE AMERICAN ETHNOLOGICAL SOCIETY. (US/0731-4108). **243**

PROCEEDINGS OF THE ANNUAL CONFERENCE - CANADIAN COUNCIL ON INTERNATIONAL LAW. (CN/0317-9087). **3134**

PROCEEDINGS OF THE ... ANNUAL CONFERENCE ON TAXATION HELD UNDER THE AUSPICES OF THE NATIONAL TAX ASSOCIATION-TAX INSTITUTE OF AMERICA. (US/1066-8608). **4742**

PROCEEDINGS OF THE ANNUAL CONVENTION - AMERICAN ASSOCIATION OF BOVINE PRACTITIONERS. CONVENTION. (US/0743-0450). **5519**

PROCEEDINGS OF THE ANNUAL MEETING OF THE ENTOMOLOGICAL SOCIETY OF ALBERTA. (CN/0071-0709). **5612**

PROCEEDINGS OF THE AUSTRALIAN PHYSIOLOGICAL AND PHARMACOLOGICAL SOCIETY. (AT/0067-2084). Qty: 4. **585**

PROCEEDINGS OF THE CENTER FOR JEWISH-CHRISTIAN LEARNING. (US/0887-4913). Qty: 1-2. **4988**

PROCEEDINGS OF THE ... CONFERENCE OF THE AUSTRALIAN SOCIETY OF SUGAR CANE TECHNOLOGISTS. (AT/0726-0822). **183**

PROCEEDINGS OF THE CONGRESS OF THE INTERNATIONAL INSTITUTE OF PUBLIC FINANCE. (US/0195-8917). **4742**

PROCEEDINGS OF THE ... CONVENTION. (UK/0143-0610). **3425**

PROCEEDINGS OF THE ENTOMOLOGICAL SOCIETY OF WASHINGTON. (US/0013-8797). Qty: 6-10/yr. **5595**

PROCEEDINGS OF THE GEOLOGISTS' ASSOCIATION. (UK/0016-7878). **1391**

PROCEEDINGS OF THE INSTITUTION OF ELECTRICAL ENGINEERS. (UK/0020-3270). **2077**

PROCEEDINGS OF THE INSTITUTION OF MECHANICAL ENGINEERS. PART I, JOURNAL OF SYSTEMS & CONTROL ENGINEERING. (UK/0959-6518). **2126**

PROCEEDINGS OF THE INTERNATIONAL CONFERENCE ON LASERS. (US/0190-4132). Qty: 2. **5140**

PROCEEDINGS OF THE IRISH BIBLICAL ASSOCIATION. (IE/0332-4427). **5019**

PROCEEDINGS OF THE LEHIGH COUNTY HISTORICAL SOCIETY. (US/0273-2912). **2755**

PROCEEDINGS OF THE MICROSCOPICAL SOCIETY OF CANADA. (CN/0381-1751). **573**

PROCEEDINGS OF THE MUSKEG RESEARCH CONFERENCE. (CN/0541-4393). **2573**

PROCEEDINGS OF THE NEW ZEALAND SOCIETY OF ANIMAL PRODUCTION. (NZ/0370-2731). **219**

PROCEEDINGS OF THE NIPR SYMPOSIUM ON ANTARCTIC METEORITES. (JA/0914-5621). **398**

PROCEEDINGS OF THE ROYAL SOCIETY OF NEW ZEALAND. (NZ/0557-4161). **5141**

PROCEEDINGS OF THE SEMINAR FOR ARABIAN STUDIES. (UK). **2662**

PROCEEDINGS OF THE ... SEMINAR OF CATASTROPHISM AND ANCIENT HISTORY. (US/0890-5592). **2626**

PROCEEDINGS OF THE SOUTH DAKOTA ACADEMY OF SCIENCE. (US/0096-378X). **5142**

PROCEEDINGS OF THE SPECIAL CONVENTION OF THE NATIONAL COLLEGIATE ATHLETIC ASSOCIATION. (US/0094-4459). **4913**

PROCEEDINGS OF THE TECHNOLOGICAL CONFERENCE. (II). **5355**

PROCEEDINGS OF THE UNITARIAN UNIVERSALIST HISTORICAL SOCIETY, THE. (US/0731-4078). **5066**

PROCEEDINGS OF THE VIRGIL SOCIETY. (UK/0083-629X). **5235**

PROCEEDINGS OF THE WESTERN PHARMACOLOGY SOCIETY. (US/0083-8969). Qty: 4 per year. **4326**

PROCEEDINGS - ROYAL MICROSCOPICAL SOCIETY. (UK/0035-9017). **573**

PROCEEDINGS - UNITED STATES NAVAL INSTITUTE. (US/0041-798X). **4182**

PROCEEDINGS - UNIVERSITY OF BRISTOL SPELAEOLOGICAL SOCIETY. (UK/0373-7527). **1409**

PROCESS CONTROL & QUALITY. (US/0924-3089). **2016**

PROCESS ENGINEERING. (UK/0370-1859). **2016**

PROCESS STUDIES. (US/0360-6503). **4358**

PROCESSED WORLD. (US/0735-9381). **3425**

PROCHE-ORIENT CHRETIEN. (IS/0032-9622). Qty: 20. **5040**

PROCLAIM (NASHVILLE). (US/0162-4326). **4988**

PROCOMM ENTERPRISES MAGAZINE. (US/0896-7229). **1162**

PRODUCE BUSINESS. (US/0886-5663). **2354**

PRODUCT DATA INTERNATIONAL. (US/1050-7043). Qty: varies. **5142**

PRODUCT LIABILITY INTERNATIONAL. (UK). **3032**

PRODUCTION. (US/0032-9819). **2126**

PRODUCTION JOURNAL. (UK/0032-9878). **4818**

PRODUCTION OF MILK AND MILK PRODUCTS. (IE/0791-3036). **198**

PRODUCTION PLANNING & CONTROL. (UK/0953-7287). **1622**

PRODUCTIVE AGING NEWS. (US/0887-3798). **5302**

PRODUCTIVITY (STAMFORD, CONN.). (US/0275-8040). **883**

PRODUCTS FINISHING. (US/0032-9940). **3486**

PRODUCTS FINISHING DIRECTORY. (US/0478-4251). **4016**

PROEDUCATION. (US/8756-5188). **1774**

PROFESSION COMPTABLE, LA. (FR/0766-9208). **750**

PROFESSIONAL COMMUNICATOR, THE. (US/0891-1207). Qty: 5/year. **1120**

PROFESSIONAL EDUCATOR, THE. (US/0196-786X). **1903**

PROFESSIONAL ELECTRONICS / THE OFFICIAL JOURNAL OF NESDA AND ISCET. (US). **2077**

PROFESSIONAL ENGINEERING. (UK/0953-6639). **2127**

PROFESSIONAL GENEALOGISTS OF ARKANSAS NEWSLETTER. (US/1040-4430). Qty: 20. **2468**

PROFESSIONAL GEOGRAPHER, THE. (US/0033-0124). **2573**

PROFESSIONAL HOTEL & RESTAURANT INTERIORS. (UK/0959-2687). **2902**

PROFESSIONAL LANDSCAPER. (UK). **2429**

PROFESSIONAL MARKETING REPORT. (US/0160-0362). **935**

PROFESSIONAL MEDICAL ASSISTANT, THE. (US/0033-0140). **3630**

PROFESSIONAL MONITOR / MICHIGAN ASSOCIATION OF THE PROFESSIONS, THE. (US/0744-7817). **3032**

PROFESSIONAL PHOTOGRAPHER (1964), THE. (US/0033-0167). Qty: 12 per year. **4375**

PROFESSIONAL PRINTER. (UK/0308-4205). **4569**

PROFESSIONAL PULIZIE. (IT/1120-8368). **2127**

PROFESSIONAL QUILTER MAGAZINE, THE. (US/0891-5237). **5185**

PROFESSIONAL READING GUIDE FOR EDUCATIONAL ADMINISTRATORS. (AT). Qty: 20. **1869**

PROFESSIONAL RENOVATION. (CN/1182-0470). **2903**

PROFESSIONAL SAFETY. (US/0099-0027). **2868**

PROFESSIONAL SKATER, THE. (US/8750-9369). **4913**

PROFESSIONAL STAINED GLASS. (US/0885-1808). **2593**

PROFESSIONAL SURVEYOR. (US/0278-1425). **2029**

PROFESSIONAL TRANSLATOR & INTERPRETER. (UK/0995-616X). **3312**

PROFESSIONAL UPHOLSTERER, THE. (US/0882-1518). **2903**

PROFESSIONI INFERMIERISTICHE. (IT/0033-0205). **3867**

PROFIL : SOZIALDEMOKRATISCHE ZEITSCHRIFT FUR POLITIK, WIRTSCHAFT UND KULTUR. (SZ/0555-3482). **4545**

PROFIL (VIENNA, AUSTRIA : 1979). (AU). **2521**

PROFILES (SOLANA BEACH, CALIF.). (US/8755-464X). **1272**

PROFITABLE LAWYER, THE. (US/0743-5401). **3032**

PROFITRAVEL. (GW). **705**

PROGENITOR. (AT/0725-914X). **2468**

PROGNOSIS. (XR). Qty: 100 per year. **5799**

PROGRAM (ASLIB). (UK/0033-0337). **3242**

PROGRAM LONDON. 1987. (UK/0952-8865). **1248**

PROGRAMME WITH ABSTRACTS - CANADIAN METEOROLOGICAL AND OCEANOGRAPHIC SOCIETY. (CN/0842-0408). **1455**

PROGRES AGRICOLE ET VITICOLE, LE. (FR/0369-8173). **122**

PROGRESOS DE OBSTETRICIA Y GINECOLOGIA. (SP/0304-5013). **3767**

PROGRESOS EN DIAGNOSTICO PRENATAL. (SP/1130-0523). **3767**

PROGRESS IN HUMAN GEOGRAPHY. (UK/0309-1325). **2573**

PROGRESS IN PAPER RECYCLING. (US/1061-1452). **4237**

PROGRESS IN PHYSICAL GEOGRAPHY. (UK/0309-1333). **2573**

PROGRESS IN RUBBER AND PLASTICS TECHNOLOGY. (UK/0266-7320). **5077**

PROGRESS OF EDUCATION, THE. (II/0033-0663). **1775**

PROGRESS (SEATTLE, WASH.), THE. (US/0739-6023). **5034**

PROGRESSIVE FARMER. (US/0033-0760). **123**

PROGRESSIVE LIBRARIAN. (US/1052-5726). **3242**

PROGRESSIVE (MADISON), THE. (US/0033-0736). **4532**

PROGRESSO MEDICO (ROMA). (IT/0370-1514). **3972**

PROJET. (FR/0033-0884). **1639**

PROLACTIN SHEFFIELD. (UK/0142-8276). **3732**

PROMENY (CZECHOSLOVAK SOCIETY OF ARTS AND SCIENCES IN AMERICA). (US/0033-1058). **2852**

PROMETEO (MILAN, ITALY). (IT). **5214**

PROMETHEUS. (AT/0810-9028). Qty: 40-50 /year. **3242**

PROMISE (REGINA). (CN/0826-533X). **5066**

PROMOTION AND EDUCATION. (FR/0751-7149). **4797**

PROOFTEXTS. (US/0272-9601). **3425**

PROP. 65 NEWS. (US/0895-5042). Qty: 1. **3115**

PROPANE CANADA. (CN/0033-1260). **4275**

PROPELLER (EAST DETROIT). (US/0194-6218). **4913**

PROPERTY DISPOSITION HANDBOOK. (US). **2832**

PROPERTY FINANCE. (UK/0955-8658). **804**

PROPERTY MANAGEMENT. (LONDON). (UK/0263-7472). **4843**

PROPERTY TAX JOURNAL. (US/0731-0285). **4742**

PROPOS DE CUISINE. (CN/0821-1264). **624**

PROSPECTIVE ET SANTE. (FR/0152-2108). **3543**

PROSPECTS (PARIS). (FR/0033-1538). **1775**

PROSPETTIVA. (IT/0394-0802). **362**

PROSPETTIVE PSICOANALITICHE NEL LAVORO ISTITUZIONALE. (IT). **4609**

PROSPICE. (UK/0308-2776). **3426**

PROSTHETICS AND ORTHOTICS INTERNATIONAL. (DK/0309-3646). **4392**

PROTEE. (CN/0300-3523). Qty: 6. **3312**

PROTEIN ABNORMALITIES. (US/0736-4547). **586**

PROTEIN SCIENCE : A PUBLICATION OF THE PROTEIN SOCIETY. (US/0961-8368). Qty: 40-60/yr. **493**

PROTESTANT REFORMED THEOLOGICAL JOURNAL. (US/1070-8138). Qty: 10. **4988**

PROTESTANTESIMO. (IT/0033-1767). **5066**

PROTOTYPE MODELER. (US/0734-1482). **2777**

PROUST RESEARCH ASSOCIATION NEWSLETTER. (US/0048-5659). **3350**

PROUT PRESS (WASHINGTON, D.C.). (US/1045-7585). **5647**

PROVENANCE. (US/0739-4241). **2483**

PROVERBIUM (COLUMBUS, OHIO). (US/0743-782X). Qty: 5-10. **2323**

PROVIDENCE BUSINESS NEWS. (US/0887-8226). Qty: 12. **5741**

PROVIDENCE VISITOR (1984), THE. (US/8750-5452). Qty: 5-6/year. **5741**

PROVIDER (WASHINGTON, D.C.). (US/0888-0352). **5302**

PROVINCIAL NEWSJOURNAL - INFANT DEVELOPMENT PROGRAMMES OF B.C. (CN/0824-9946). **5302**

PROZAH. (IS). **3426**

PRS NEWS. (UK/0309-0019). **5235**

PRUDENTIA. (NZ). **3426**

PRUFROCK JOURNAL, THE. (US/1047-1855). **Qty:** 10. **1884**

PRZEGLAD SPAWALNICTWA. (PL/0033-2364). **5142**

PRZEWALSKI HORSE. (NE/0167-7926). **2801**

PSA JOURNAL. (US/0030-8277). **Qty:** varies. **4376**

PSI CHI NEWSLETTER. (US/0033-2569). **4609**

PSI RESEARCH. (US/0749-2898). **4242**

PSICHIATRIA E PSICOTERAPIA ANALITICA. (IT/0393-9774). **3932**

PSICHIATRIA GENERALE E DELL'ETA EVOLUTIVA. (IT/0555-5299). **3932**

PSICOANALISI CONTRO. (IT/0393-6902). **Qty:** 12-15. **3932**

PSIQUIS. (SP/0210-8348). **3933**

PSSC SOCIAL SCIENCE INFORMATION. (PH). **5214**

PSYCHIATRIC ANNALS. (US/0048-5713). **3933**

PSYCHIATRIC BULLETIN OF THE ROYAL COLLEGE OF PSYCHIATRISTS. (UK/0955-6036). **3933**

PSYCHIATRIC FORUM, THE. (US/0033-2690). **3933**

PSYCHIATRIC HOSPITAL, THE. (US/0885-7717). **3791**

PSYCHIATRIC TIMES, THE. (US/0893-2905). **3933**

PSYCHIATRIE, RECHERCHE ET INTERVENTION EN SANTE MENTALE DE L'ENFANT : P.R.I.S.M.E. (CN/1180-5501). **3934**

PSYCHIATRY IN PRACTICE. (UK/0262-5377). **3934**

PSYCHIATRY (WASHINGTON, D.C.). (US/0033-2747). **3934**

PSYCHIC OBSERVER. (US/0048-573X). **4242**

PSYCHOANALYTIC QUARTERLY, THE. (US/0033-2828). **4610**

PSYCHOBIOLOGY (AUSTIN, TEX.). (US/0889-6313). **4610**

PSYCHOHISTORY REVIEW, THE. (US/0363-891X). **2626**

PSYCHOLOGIA. (JA/0033-2852). **4610**

PSYCHOLOGIA UNIVERSALIS. (GW/0555-5582). **4610**

PSYCHOLOGICA BELGICA. (BE/0033-2879). **4610**

PSYCHOLOGICAL MEDICINE. (UK/0033-2917). **4611**

PSYCHOLOGICAL MEDICINE. MONOGRAPH SUPPLEMENT. (UK/0264-1801). **4611**

PSYCHOLOGICAL PERSPECTIVES. (US/0033-2925). **4611**

PSYCHOLOGICAL RECORD, THE. (US/0033-2933). **Qty:** 5-10. **4611**

PSYCHOLOGICAL REPORTS. (US/0033-2941). **4611**

PSYCHOLOGICAL SCIENCE. (US/0956-7976). **4611**

PSYCHOLOGICAL STUDIES. (II/0033-2968). **4611**

PSYCHOLOGIE & EDUCATION. (FR). **4611**

PSYCHOLOGIE IN ERZIEHUNG UND UNTERRICHT. (GW/0342-183X). **1903**

PSYCHOLOGIES. (FR). **4612**

PSYCHOLOGISCHE BEITRAEGE. (GW/0033-3018). **4612**

PSYCHOLOGISCHE RUNDSCHAU. (GW/0033-3042). **4612**

PSYCHOLOGY AND SOCIOLOGY OF SPORT. (US/0885-7423). **4612**

PSYCHOLOGY IN THE SCHOOLS. (US/0033-3085). **4612**

PSYCHOLOGY (SAVANNAH). (US/0033-3077). **4613**

PSYCHOLOGY TODAY. (US/0033-3107). **4613**

PSYCHOMETRIKA. (US/0033-3123). **4613**

PSYCHOMUSICOLOGY. (US/0275-3987). **4147**

PSYCHOPHYSIOLOGY. (US/0048-5772). **586**

PSYCHOSOCIAL REHABILITATION JOURNAL. (US/0147-5622). **Qty:** 24. **3934**

PSYCHOTHERAPY IN PRIVATE PRACTICE. (US/0731-7158). **4614**

PSYCHOTHERAPY PATIENT, THE. (US/0738-6176). **3935**

PSYCHOTHERAPY RESEARCH. (US/1050-3307). **4614**

PSYCHOTROPES (MONTREAL). (CN/0715-9684). **1348**

PSYCHOTROPICS (RENO, NEV.). (US/0895-5727). **Qty:** 2. **3986**

PSZICHOLOGIA: AZ MTA PSZICHOLOGIAI INTEZETENEK FOLYOIRATA. (HU/0230-0508). **4614**

PTERIDINES. (GW/0933-4807). **5143**

PTIT FOCUS. (TH/0857-7749). **4276**

PTR. PHYTOTHERAPY RESEARCH. (UK/0951-418X). **525**

PUBBLICITA IN ITALIA. (US). **764**

PUBLIC ACCOUNTING REPORT. (US/0161-309X). **750**

PUBLIC ADMINISTRATION (LONDON). (UK/0033-3298). **4704**

PUBLIC ADMINISTRATION QUARTERLY. (US/0734-9149). **4676**

PUBLIC ADMINISTRATION TIMES. (US/0149-8797). **4676**

PUBLIC ART REVIEW. (US/1040-211X). **Qty:** 2-4/yr. **362**

PUBLIC BUDGETING & FINANCE. (US/0275-1100). **4743**

PUBLIC CITIZEN. (US/0738-5927). **1299**

PUBLIC EMPLOYEE RELATIONS LIBRARY. (US). **4705**

PUBLIC ENTERPRISE / INTERNATIONAL CENTER FOR PUBLIC ENTERPRISES IN DEVELOPING COUNTRIES. (YU/0351-3564). **2911**

PUBLIC FINANCE. (NE/0033-3476). **4743**

PUBLIC FUND DIGEST. (US/0736-7848). **4743**

PUBLIC GARDEN, THE. (US/0885-3894). **2429**

PUBLIC HEALTH (LONDON). (UK/0033-3506). **4797**

PUBLIC HISTORIAN, THE. (US/0272-3433). **2626**

PUBLIC INNOVATION ABROAD. (US/0887-4468). **2832**

PUBLIC INTEREST, THE. (US/0033-3557). **5214**

PUBLIC INTERNATIONAL LAW. (GW/0340-7349). **3134**

PUBLIC JUSTICE REPORT. (US/0742-5325). **4676**

PUBLIC LAND LAW REVIEW, THE. (US/0732-0264). **3033**

PUBLIC LIBRARIES. (US/0163-5506). **3243**

PUBLIC LIBRARY JOURNAL. (UK/0268-893X). **3243**

PUBLIC LIBRARY QUARTERLY (NEW YORK, N.Y.). (US/0161-6846). **3243**

PUBLIC MANAGER (POTOMAC, MD.), THE. (US/1061-7639). **4676**

PUBLIC MONEY & MANAGEMENT. (UK/0954-0962). **4743**

PUBLIC PERSPECTIVE, THE. (US/1050-5067). **Qty:** up to 6 per year. **5336**

PUBLIC POLICY AND AGING REPORT, THE. (US/1055-3037). **Qty:** 6. **5181**

PUBLIC POWER. (US/0033-3654). **4762**

PUBLIC RELATIONS. (UK). **764**

PUBLIC RELATIONS ALMANAC FOR EDUCATORS, THE. (US/0273-3757). **764**

PUBLIC RELATIONS CAREER DIRECTORY. (US/0882-8288). **764**

PUBLIC RELATIONS JOURNAL, THE. (US/0033-3670). **764**

PUBLIC RELATIONS QUARTERLY. (US/0033-3700). **765**

PUBLIC RELATIONS REVIEW (RIVERDALE, N.Y.). (US/0363-8111). **765**

PUBLIC RISK. (US/0891-7183). **1514**

PUBLIC SCHOOL FINANCE PROGRAMS OF THE UNITED STATES AND CANADA. (US). **1776**

PUBLIC SECTOR QUALITY REPORT. (US/1067-4489). **Qty:** 6-8. **732**

PUBLIC SERVANT. DIE STAATSAMPTENAAR, THE. (SA/0033-376X). **Qty:** 16. **4677**

PUBLIC TECHNOLOGY. (US/0882-1445). **5143**

PUBLIC UNDERSTANDING OF SCIENCE. (UK/0963-6625). **5143**

PUBLIC UTILITIES LAW ANTHOLOGY. (US/0095-5086). **3033**

PUBLIC WELFARE (WASHINGTON). (US/0033-3816). **5303**

PUBLIC WORKS. (US/0033-3840). **1992**

PUBLICACIONES ESPECIALES - INSTITUTO ESPANOL DE OCEANOGRAFIA. (SP/0214-7378). **1455**

PUBLICATION OF THE KRESS LIBRARY OF BUSINESS AND ECONOMICS. (US/0073-0777). **705**

PUBLICATION - WATER RESOURCES RESEARCH CENTER, UNIVERSITY OF MASSACHUSETTS AT AMHERST. (US/0542-9315). **5538**

PUBLICATIONES MATHEMATICAL (DEBRECEN). (HU/0033-3883). **3529**

PUBLICATIONS. (US). **4148**

PUBLICATIONS. (BE). **279**

PUBLICATIONS IN CONDUCT AND COMMUNICATION. (US/0556-2678). **1094**

PUBLICATIONS OF THE ARKANSAS PHILOLOGICAL ASSOCIATION. (US/0160-3124). **Qty:** 2. **3312**

PUBLICATIONS OF THE INTERNATIONAL BUREAU OF FISCAL DOCUMENTATION. (NE/0074-2112). **750**

PUBLICATIONS OF THE INTERNATIONAL MARITIME ORGANIZATION. (UK). **Qty:** 25. **4182**

PUBLICATIONS OF THE NEBRASKA STATE HISTORICAL SOCIETY. (US/0191-037X). **2755**

PUBLICATIONS OF THE NUTTALL ORNITHOLOGICAL CLUB. (US/0550-4082). **5619**

PUBLICATIONS OF THE PIPE ROLL SOCIETY, THE. (UK). **5235**

PUBLICATIONS (SCOTTISH TEXT SOCIETY). (UK). **Qty:** 3. **3426**

PUBLICATIONS (TOPOR & ASSOCIATES). (US/1063-1771). **Qty:** unlimited. **1843**

PUBLICATIONS UPDATE / THE WORLD BANK. (US). **804**

PUBLICUS (BASEL, SWITZERLAND). (SZ). **4677**

PUBLISHED. (US/0882-7400). **3426**

PUBLISHERS' AUXILIARY. (US/0048-5942). **4818**

PUBLISHER'S MONTHLY. (II). **4818**

PUBLISHERS REPORTS. (UK/0953-7899). **4819**

PUBLISHERS WEEKLY. (US/0000-0019). **4831**

PUBLIUS. (US/0048-5950). **4492**

PUBLIZISTIK. (GW/0033-4006). **2923**

PUCE A L'ORIELLE (MONTREAL). (CN/0824-068X). **1776**

PUCKERBRUSH REVIEW. (US/0890-3433). **Qty:** 10. **3350**

PUDDING MAGAZINE. (US/0196-5913). **3470**

PUERTO DEL SOL. (US/0738-517X). **3426**

PUERTO RICO HEALTH SCIENCES JOURNAL. (PR/0738-0658). **3631**

PUERTO RICO LIVING. (US/0033-4049). **2544**

PULASKI COUNTY JOURNAL. (US). **5666**

PULLER, THE. (US/8750-4219). **160**

PULPIT DIGEST (1978). (US/0160-838X). **4988**

PULSE BEATS ALCOHOL & DRUG ABUSE. (US). **1348**

PULSO DEL PERIODISMO. (US/1051-8126). **Qty:** 4. **2923**

PUMPS AND OTHER FLUIDS MACHINERY ABSTRACTS. (UK/0302-2870). **2127**

PUNCTURE (SAN FRANCISCO, CALIF.). (US/1047-4528). **Qty:** 40. **4148**

PUNDIT. (CN/0712-1318). **Qty:** 6. **3426**

PUNTO. (VE). **307**

PUNTO CRITICO. (MX). **1514**

PUNTO DE VISTA. (AG/0326-3061). **Qty:** 3. **2552**

PUPPETRY JOURNAL, THE. (US/0033-443X). **5367**

PURABHILEKH-PURATATVA : JOURNAL OF THE DIRECTORATE OF ARCHIVES, ARCHAEOLOGY AND MUSEUM, PANAJI-GOA. (II). **279**

PURCHASING & SUPPLY MANAGEMENT / INSTITUTE OF PURCHASING AND SUPPLY. (UK/0309-7242). **951**

PURDUE ALUMNUS, THE. (US/0033-4502). **1102**

PURE AND APPLIED MATHEMATIKA SCIENCES. (II). **3529**

PURE-BRED DOGS, AMERICAN KENNEL GAZETTE. (US/0033-4561). **Qty:** 12. **4287**

PURPAN. (FR/0395-8655). **123**

PUTNAM DEMOCRAT (WINFIELD, W. VA.). (US). Qty: 12. 5764

PV NEWS. (US/0739-4829). 1954

PW PERSONEELSMANAGEMENT. (NE). 705

PYNCHON NOTES. (US/0278-1891). Qty: 6-8. 3426

PYROTECHNICA. (US/0272-6521). 1028

PYTTERSEN'S NEDERLANDSE ALMANAK. (NE). 2521

QADMONIOT. (IS/0033-4839). 279

QINGBAO KEXUE. (CC/1000-8489). 3243

QRQ. (IS/0302-6248). 4843

QST. (US/0033-4812). 1136

QTGO. QUADERNI DI TECNICA E GESTIONE OSPEDALIERA. (IT/1120-7906). 3791

QUADERNI CALABRESI : QUADERNI DEL MEZZOGIORNO E DELLE ISOLE. (IT). 2521

QUADERNI DI ARCHEOLOGIA DELLA LIBIA. (IT/0079-8258). 279

QUADERNI DI STORIA. (IT). Qty: 10/year. 2626

QUADERNI DI TERZO MONDO. (IT/0391-7312). Qty: 20. 4492

QUADERNI D'ITALIANISTICA. (CN/0226-8043). 3426

QUADERNI IBERO-AMERICANI. (IT/0033-4960). 3350

QUADERNI MARCHIGIANI DI MEDICINA. (IT/0392-9620). 3632

QUADERNI MEDIEVALI. (IT). Qty: 10/yr. 2704

QUADERNI SARDI DI ECONOMIA. (IT/0391-8394). 1579

QUADERNI URBINATI DI CULTURA CLASSICA. (IT/0033-4987). 1079

QUADERNO MONTESSORI. (IT). 1884

QUADERNS D'ALLIBERAMENT. (SP/0210-7554). 4493

QUADRANT. (AT/0033-5002). Qty: 100. 2511

QUADRANT (NEW YORK). (US/0033-5010). 4614

QUAERENDO. (NE/0014-9527). 4831

QUAIL UNLIMITED MAGAZINE. (US/0746-2638). 5619

QUAKER HISTORY. (US/0033-5053). Qty: 10. 4989

QUAKER LIFE. (US/0033-5061). Qty: 20. 4989

QUAKER : MONATSHEFTE DER DEUTSCHEN FREUNDE, DER. (GW). 4989

QUAKER MONTHLY. (UK/0033-507X). 4989

QUAKER RELIGIOUS THOUGHT. (US/0033-5088). 5066

QUAKER YEOMEN, THE. (US/0737-8246). 2468

QUALITE (DOLLARD-DES-ORMEAUX). (CN/0226-3432). 883

QUALITE TOTALE. (CN). Qty: 4. 883

QUALITY ABSTRACTS. (US/1071-1945). 883

QUALITY AND RELIABILITY ENGINEERING INTERNATIONAL. (UK/0748-8017). 1992

QUALITY BY DESIGN. (US/0893-360X). Qty: 6-8. 625

QUALITY CARE ADVOCATE. (US/0892-6174). 5303

QUALITY CONTROL AND APPLIED STATISTICS. (US/0033-5207). 5176

QUALITY DIGEST. (US/1049-8699). 1705

QUALITY IN HEALTH CARE : QHC. (UK/0963-8172). 3632

QUALITY PROGRESS. (US/0033-524X). 1993

QUARRY WEST. (US/0736-4628). 3427

QUARTER CIRCLE. (CN/0228-0612). 2801

QUARTERLY - ASSOCIATION OF PROFESSIONAL GENEALOGISTS (U.S.). (US/1056-6732). 2468

QUARTERLY BULLETIN OF THE ALPINE GARDEN SOCIETY. (UK/0002-6476). 2429

QUARTERLY BULLETIN OF THE AMERICAN ASSOCIATION OF TEACHERS OF ESPERANTO. (US/0002-7499). 3313

QUARTERLY BULLETIN OF THE SOUTH AFRICAN LIBRARY. (SA/0038-2418). 3243

QUARTERLY - CANADIAN CAT ASSOCIATION. (CN/0828-4865). 4287

QUARTERLY / CENTRAL GEORGIA GENEALOGICAL SOCIETY, INC. (US/0738-8209). Qty: 10. 2469

QUARTERLY / CHRISTIAN LEGAL SOCIETY. (US/0736-0142). Qty: 12. 3033

QUARTERLY DEC JOURNAL. (US/1063-1216). Qty: 4/yr. 706

QUARTERLY ECONOMIC COMMENTARY. (IE/0376-7191). 1514

QUARTERLY ECONOMIC REVIEW / UGANDA COMMERCIAL BANK. (UG). 1580

QUARTERLY GUIDE TO THE ECONOMY / PREPARED BY RAL MERCHANT BANK LIMITED. (RH). Qty: 4. 1514

QUARTERLY JOURNAL - FLORIDA AGRICULTURAL AND MECHANICAL UNIVERSITY, TALLAHASSEE, THE. (US). 1843

QUARTERLY JOURNAL OF ADMINISTRATION, THE. (NR/0001-8333). 1869

QUARTERLY JOURNAL OF ENGINEERING GEOLOGY, THE. (UK/0481-2085). 2029

QUARTERLY JOURNAL OF FORESTRY. (UK/0033-5568). 2391

QUARTERLY JOURNAL OF IDEOLOGY. (US/0738-9752). Qty: 8-10. 5254

QUARTERLY JOURNAL OF MUSIC TEACHING AND LEARNING, THE. (US/1066-0437). Qty: 2-3. 4148

QUARTERLY JOURNAL OF THE ROYAL METEOROLOGICAL SOCIETY. (UK/0035-9009). 1434

QUARTERLY - MUSEUM OF THE FUR TRADE. (US/0027-4135). 2756

QUARTERLY NEWS-LETTER - BOOK CLUB OF CALIFORNIA. (US/0006-7202). Qty: 3-4. 4831

QUARTERLY NEWSLETTER OF THE LABORATORY OF COMPARATIVE HUMAN COGNITION, THE. (US/0278-4351). 4615

QUARTERLY NEWSLETTER - STANDING COMMITTEE ON ENVIRONMENTAL LAW. (US). 3115

QUARTERLY - NORTHEASTERN NEVADA HISTORICAL SOCIETY. (US/0160-9602). 2756

QUARTERLY OF THE NATIONAL ASSOCIATION FOR OUTLAW AND LAWMAN HISTORY, INC. (US/1071-4189). Qty: 12-15. 2756

QUARTERLY / OLYMPIA GENEALOGICAL SOCIETY. (US). 2469

QUARTERLY - ORANGE COUNTY CALIFORNIA GENEALOGICAL SOCIETY. (US/0030-4263). Qty: 12-20. 2469

QUARTERLY / OREGON GENEALOGICAL SOCIETY. (US/0738-1891). Qty: 12-16. 2469

QUARTERLY - PHI LAMBDA KAPPA MEDICAL FRATERNITY. (US/0739-2079). 3917

QUARTERLY REVIEW OF BIOLOGY, THE. (US/0033-5770). 471

QUARTERLY REVIEW OF FILM AND VIDEO. (SZ/1050-9208). 4076

QUARTERLY REVIEW OF HISTORICAL STUDIES, THE. (II/0033-5800). 2627

QUARTERLY REVIEW OF WINES. (US/0740-1248). Qty: 4. 2370

QUARTERLY REVIEW ON DOUBLESPEAK. (US/0735-5920). 1120

QUARTERLY REVIEW - UNITED METHODIST BOARD OF HIGHER EDUCATION AND MINISTRY (U.S.). (US/0270-9287). 5066

QUARTERLY - THE MUSEUM OF THE FUR TRADE. (US/0027-4135). Qty: 25. 3185

QUARTERLY WEST. (US/0194-4231). 3427

QUARTZ DEVICES DIRECTORY. (US). Qty: 20. 3487

QUATERNAIRE : BULLETIN DE L'ASSOCIATION FRANCAISE POUR L'ETUDE DU QUATERNAIRE : INTERNATIONAL JOURNAL OF THE FRENCH QUATERNARY ASSOCIATION. (FR/1142-2904). Qty: 3. 1393

QUATRE SAISONS DU JARDINAGE, LES. (FR/0242-4959). 2429

QUATRE-TEMPS. (CN/0820-5515). 525

QUE PASA SAN ANTONIO. (US). 5489

QUEBEC A VOTRE PORTEE, LE. (CN/0836-0014). 2756

QUEBEC CHRONICLE-TELEGRAPH. (CN). Qty: 20 per year. 5793

QUEBEC FRANCAIS. (CN/0316-2052). 3427

QUEBEC PHARMACIE (MONTREAL, 1981). (CN/0826-9874). Qty: 5. 4327

QUEBEC SCEPTIQUE. (CN/0843-865X). Qty: 10. 4243

QUEBEC SCIENCE. (CN/0021-6127). 5143

QUEBEC STUDIES. (US/0737-3759). 2756

QUEBEC VERT. (CN/0705-6923). 2202

QUEBEC YACHTIING, VOILE & MOTEUR. (CN/0833-918X). 595

QUEEN OF PEACE WILDERNESS GAZETTE. (US). 4989

QUEEN'S GAZETTE. (CN/0319-2725). 1843

QUEEN'S LAW JOURNAL. (CN/0316-778X). 3033

QUEEN'S PAPERS IN INDUSTRIAL RELATIONS. (CN/0838-6609). 1705

QUEEN'S QUARTERLY. (CN/0033-6041). 5214

QUEENSLAND COUNTRY LIFE. (AT/0033-6084). 124

QUEENSLAND FAMILY HISTORIAN : JOURNAL OF THE QUEENSLAND FAMILY HISTORY SOCIETY, INC. (AT/0811-3394). Qty: 10-15. 2469

QUEENSLAND FRUIT AND VEGETABLE NEWS. (AT/0033-6122). 2429

QUEENSLAND GRAINGROWER, THE. (AT). 203

QUEENSLAND PROPERTY REPORT. (AT). 4843

QUEENSLAND TEACHERS PROFESSIONAL MAGAZINE. (AT/0813-8206). Qty: 1. 1903

QUEL CORPS?. (FR/0337-6338). 1776

QUELLEN UND FORSCHUNGEN AUS ITALIENISCHEN ARCHIVEN UND BIBLIOTHEKEN. (GW/0079-9068). 2627

QUEST : FOR A POSITIVE LIFESTYLE. (US/1064-4059). Qty: 12/year. 2796

QUEST (GRAND RAPIDS, MICH.). (US/1065-7738). Qty: 4-12. 32

QUEST (LUSAKA, ZAMBIA). (ZA/1011-226X). Qty: 10. 4358

QUEST: MANHATTAN PROPERTIES & COUNTRY ESTATES. (UK). 4843

QUEST (NATIONAL ASSOCIATION FOR PHYSICAL EDUCATION IN HIGHER EDUCATION). (US/0033-6297). 3955

QUEST (WHEATON, ILL.), THE. (US/1040-533X). Qty: 24. 4358

QUESTION DE SPIRITUALITE, TRADITION, LITTERATURES. (FR). 4243

QUESTIONS (BIRMINGHAM). (UK/0954-920X). 1903

QUI PARLE. (US/1041-8385). Qty: 4. 2852

QUICK PRINTING. (US/0191-4588). 4569

QUICK TRIPS TRAVEL LETTER. (US/1064-0339). Qty: 36+. 5489

QUICKBORN. (GW). 3313

QUILL AND SCROLL (IOWA CITY). (US/0033-6505). 2923

QUILL (CHICAGO), THE. (US/0033-6475). Qty: 10/yr. 2923

QUILTER'S NEWSLETTER MAGAZINE. (US/0274-712X). 5185

QUIMERA (BARCELONA, SPAIN). (SP/0211-3325). 3351

QUINTO LINGO. (US/0033-6602). 3313

QUIPU. (MX/0185-5093). 5144

QUIRK'S MARKETING RESEARCH REVIEW. (US/0893-7451). Qty: 5. 765

QUMRAN CHRONICLE. (PL/0867-8715). Qty: 5-10. 5019

QUONDAM ET FUTURUS (BIRMINGHAM, ALA.). (US/8755-3627). 3351

QWL NEWS & ABSTRACTS / WORK RESEARCH UNIT. (UK). Qty: 10. 946

R A I F. RESEAU D'ACTION ET D'INFORMATION POUR LES FEMMES. (CN/0705-3762). 5565

R & D MANAGEMENT. (UK/0033-6807). 5144

R.C.M. MAGAZINE. (UK/0033-684X). 4148

R. E. TODAY. (UK). 4989

R.F. DESIGN. (US/0163-321X). 1993

R.I.A. (PARIS, 1977). (FR/0035-4244). 2355

R L S, REGIONAL LANGUAGE STUDIES ... NEWFOUNDLAND. (CN/0079-9335). 3313

R P M WEEKLY. (CN/0033-7064). 4148

RABBINICS TODAY. (US/1066-0585). Qty: 10. 5052

RABELS ZEITSCHRIFT FUER AUSLANDISCHES UND INTERNATIONALES PRIVATRECHT. (GW/0033-7250). 3134

RAC NEWSLETTER. (US/0163-9838). 2006

RAC, REFRIGERATION AND AIR CONDITIONING. (UK). 2607

RACCOON. (US/0148-0162). 3470

RACE & CLASS. (UK/0306-3968). **2271**

RACE RELATIONS SURVEY / SOUTH AFRICAN INSTITUTE OF RACE RELATIONS. (SA). **4493**

RACECAR ENGINEERING. (UK/0961-1096). **Qty:** 6. **5423**

RACING PIGEON BULLETIN. (US/0146-8383). **4914**

RACING PIGEON PICTORIAL. (UK/0033-7404). **4914**

RACING PIGEON, THE. (UK/0033-7390). **4914**

RACING STAR WEEKLY. (US/0033-7439). **2802**

RACONTEUR (BATON ROUGE, LA. ANNUAL ED.), LE. (US/0893-4525). **Qty:** 6-10. **2469**

RAD HARLOW. (UK/0264-6412). **3944**

RAD! : REVIEW AND DISCUSSION OF ROCK & ROLL CULTURE. (US). **Qty:** 12. **4148**

RADDLE MOON. (CN/0826-5909). **Qty:** 4. **3427**

RADIANCE (OAKLAND, CALIF.). (US/0889-9495). **Qty:** 8-10. **405**

RADIATION MEDICINE. (JA/0288-2043). **3944**

RADIATION PROTECTION DOSIMETRY. (UK/0144-8420). **4440**

RADIATION PROTECTION IN AUSTRALIA. (AT/0729-7963). **4798**

RADIATION PROTECTION MANAGEMENT. (US/0740-0640). **2868**

RADICAL AMERICA. (US/0033-7617). **4493**

RADICAL HISTORIANS NEWSLETTER. (US/0730-1812). **Qty:** 3. **2627**

RADICAL HISTORY REVIEW. (US/0163-6545). **4545**

RADICAL PHILOSOPHY. (UK/0300-211X). **4358**

RADICAL TEACHER (CAMBRIDGE). (US/0191-4847). **1776**

RADIO AGE (AUGUSTA, GA.). (US/0892-6360). **1137**

RADIO COMMUNICATION. (UK/0033-7803). **2078**

RADIO CONTROL CAR ACTION. (US/0886-1609). **2777**

RADIO CONTROL MODELS & ELECTRONICS. (UK/0033-7838). **2777**

RADIO IN THE UNITED STATES. (US/0740-2341). **1137**

RADIO MODELLER. (UK/0144-0713). **2777**

RADIOACTIVE WASTE MANAGEMENT AND THE NUCLEAR FUEL CYCLE. (SZ/0739-5876). **2240**

RADIOACTIVE WASTE MANAGEMENT (CHUR, SWITZERLAND : 1981). (SZ/0275-7273). **2240**

RADIOACTIVITY & RADIOCHEMISTRY. (US/1045-845X). **1029**

RADIOCARBON. (US/0033-8222). **Qty:** (2-3). **1393**

RADIOGRAPHER. (AT/0033-8273). **3632**

RADIOLOGIA MEDICA. (IT/0033-8362). **3945**

RADIOLOGIC TECHNOLOGY. (US/0033-8397). **3945**

RADIOLOGY. (US/0033-8419). **3945**

RADIOLOGY & IMAGING LETTER. (US/0741-160X). **3849**

RADIOLOGY MANAGEMENT. (US/0198-7097). **Qty:** 1-2. **3946**

RADIOSCAN MAGAZINE (SPANISH ED.). (US/1050-3641). **1120**

RADIOTEHNIKA (MOSKVA). (RU/0033-8486). **1138**

RADIOTEHNIKA I ELEKTRONIKA. (RU/0033-8494). **2078**

RADIOTHERAPY AND ONCOLOGY. (NE/0167-8140). **3823**

RADIUS (STUTTGART, GERMANY). (GW/0033-8532). **4989**

RADIX (BERKELEY, CALIF.). (US/0275-0147). **4989**

RADON NEWS DIGEST. (US/0896-7180). **2241**

RAFT (CLEVELAND, OHIO). (US/0891-0545). **3314**

RAFU SHIMPO. (US). **5638**

RAG MAG (GOODHUE, MINN.). (US/0742-2768). **Qty:** 2-4. **3427**

RAG TIMES. (US/0090-4570). **4148**

RAGAN REPORT, THE. (US/0197-6060). **706**

RAGGUAGLIO LIBRARIO, IL. (IT/0033-8648). **423**

RAGIUSAN. RASSEGNA GIURIDICA DELLA SANITA. (IT/1120-1762). **3034**

RAICES (MADRID, SPAIN). (SP/0212-6753). **2271**

RAIDA / INSTITUTE FOR WOMEN'S STUDIES IN THE ARAB WORLD, BEIRUT UNIVERSITY COLLEGE. (LE). **5565**

RAIL CLASSICS & RAILWAY QUARTERLY. (US/0743-9075). **5434**

RAIL ENGINEERING INTERNATIONAL (1981). (UK/0141-4615). **5434**

RAIL INTERNATIONAL. (BE/0020-8442). **5434**

RAILFAN & RAILROAD. (US/0163-7266). **5435**

RAILPACE NEWSMAGAZINE. (US/0745-5267). **5435**

RAILROAD MODEL CRAFTSMAN. (US/0033-877X). **2777**

RAILROAD REVENUES, EXPENSES, AND INCOME: CLASS I RAILROADS IN THE UNITED STATES. (US). **5435**

RAILS (WELLINGTON). (NZ/0110-6155). **Qty:** varies. **5435**

RAILWATCH. (UK/0267-5943). **Qty:** 4. **5435**

RAILWAY HISTORY MONOGRAPH, THE. (US/0093-8505). **5436**

RAILWAYS. (SA/0254-2218). **5436**

RAINBOW (PROSPECT, KY.). (US/0746-4797). **1272**

RAINCOAST CHRONICLES. (CN/0315-2804). **2756**

RAINFOREST ACTION NETWORK ALERT & WORLD RAINFOREST REPORT. (US). **Qty:** varies. **2180**

RAJASTHAN BOARD JOURNAL OF EDUCATION. RAJASTHANA BORDA SIKSHANA PATRIKA, THE. (II/0033-9083). **1776**

RAJASTHAN LAW WEEKLY, THE. (II/0377-7723). **3034**

RAKENNUSTUOTANTO. (FI). **625**

RAMPIKE (TORONTO). (CN/0711-7647). **3427**

RAM'S HORN (HANOVER, N.H.), THE. (US/0272-2747). **3314**

RAM'S HORN (SCOTSBURN). (CN/0827-4053). **Qty:** 4. **124**

RAMUS. (AT/0048-671X). **1079**

RAND JOURNAL OF ECONOMICS, THE. (US/0741-6261). **1594**

RAND MCNALLY CAMPGROUND & TRAILER PARK GUIDE, EASTERN. (US/0733-8309). **4708**

RANDAX EDUCATION GUIDE TO COLLEGES SEEKING STUDENTS. (US). **1843**

R&D INNOVATOR. (US/1061-1894). **Qty:** 6-12. **5144**

RANDOL MINING DIRECTORY. (US/1054-027X). **Qty:** 200. **2149**

RANDOM LENGTHS (SAN PEDRO, CALIF.). (US/0891-8627). **Qty:** varies. **5638**

RANGER. (US). **Qty:** 4. **4708**

RANGIFER. (NO/0333-256X). **5596**

RANKIN COUNTY NEWS. (US). **5701**

RAPID COMMUNICATIONS IN MASS SPECTROMETRY. (UK/0951-4198). **1018**

RAPPORT ANNUEL - ONSS. (BE). **5303**

RAPPORT DE RECHERCHE LPC. (FR/0222-8394). **2030**

RAPPORT - GRONLANDS GEOLOGISKE UNDERSOGELSE. (DK/0418-6559). **1393**

RAPPORT (LOS ANGELES, CALIF.). (US/1061-6861). **Qty:** 60. **388**

RAPPORTS HET FRANSE BOEK. (NE). **3427**

RARE BOOKS AND MANUSCRIPTS LIBRARIANSHIP. (US/0884-450X). **3244**

RARE BOOKS NEWSLETTER. (UK). **4832**

RARITAN. (US/0275-1607). **3351**

RASSEGNA CHIMICA. (IT/0033-9334). **990**

RASSEGNA DI CULTURA E VITA SCOLASTICA. (IT). **Qty:** 35. **5214**

RASSEGNA DI MEDICINA SPERIMENTALE. (IT/0033-9555). **586**

RASSEGNA DI SERVIZIO SOCIALE. (IT/0033-9601). **Qty:** 25.yr. **4798**

RASSEGNA DI STATISTICHE DEL LAVORO. (IT/0033-961X). **1537**

RASSEGNA IBERISTICA. (IT/0392-4777). **3428**

RASSEGNA MUSICALE CURCI. (IT/0033-9806). **4148**

RASSEGNA PARLAMENTARE. (IT/0486-0373). **3093**

RASSEGNA SINDACALE. (IT/0033-9849). **1705**

RASSEGNA STORICA DEL RISORGIMENTO. (IT/0033-9873). **2704**

RAT NEWS LETTER. (US/0309-1848). **5519**

RATEL. (UK/0305-1218). **5596**

RATING AND VALUATION REPORTER. (UK). **3034**

RATING APPEALS. (UK). **3034**

RATIO (OXFORD). (UK/0034-0006). **4358**

RAUMFORSCHUNG UND RAUMORDNUNG. (GW/0034-0111). **33**

RAUMPLANUNG, INFORMATIONSHEFTE / EJPD, BUNDESAMT FUR RAUMPLANUNG. (SZ). **2832**

RAW MATERIALS REPORT. (SW/0349-6287). **2203**

RAW VISION. (UK/0955-1182). **Qty:** 12. **363**

RAWLINSONS NEW ZEALAND CONSTRUCTION HANDBOOK. (NZ). **625**

RAYDAN. (YE). **2662**

RAYON JEUNESSE. (CN/0841-758X). **1068**

RAYS. (IT/0390-7740). **3946**

RAZA LAW JOURNAL, LA. (US/8755-8815). **3034**

RAZON Y FE. (SP/0034-0235). **2853**

RC MODELER (1969). (US/0033-6866). **2777**

RCDA (NEW YORK, N.Y.). (US/1061-656X). **4989**

RCDA. RELIGION IN COMMUNIST DOMINATED AREAS. (US/0034-3978). **4546**

RE-NEW (PORT HOPE). (CN/0845-5341). **Qty:** 8-10/yr. **2832**

REACTIONS. (AT/0157-7271). **3632**

READ, AMERICA!. (US/0891-4214). **Qty:** 4-6. **1776**

READ (UKARUMPA, PAPUA NEW GUINEA). (PP). **1884**

READERS' GUIDE ABSTRACTS. CD-ROM. (US/0899-1553). **2497**

READING & WRITING. (NE/0922-4777). **3314**

READING HORIZONS. (US/0034-0502). **Qty:** 20-25. **3314**

READING IMPROVEMENT. (US/0034-0510). **3314**

READING IN A FOREIGN LANGUAGE. (UK/0264-2425). **3314**

READING INSTRUCTION JOURNAL, THE. (US/0275-441X). **Qty:** 3. **1843**

READING MEDIEVAL STUDIES : ANNUAL PROCEEDINGS OF THE GRADUATE CENTRE FOR MEDIEVAL STUDIES IN THE UNIVERSITY OF READING. (UK). **Qty:** 4-6. **2704**

READING PSYCHOLOGY. (UK/0270-2711). **4615**

READING RESEARCH AND INSTRUCTION. (US/0886-0246). **3314**

READING (SUNDERLAND). (UK/0034-0472). **1903**

READING TEACHER, THE. (US/0034-0561). **3314**

READINGS - AMERICAN ORTHOPSYCHIATRIC ASSOCIATION. (US/0886-3784). **3935**

READINGS ON EQUAL EDUCATION. (US/0270-1448). **1884**

REAL ESTATE DIGEST, THE. (US/0882-8733). **4844**

REAL ESTATE INVESTING LETTER. (US). **Qty:** 6. **4844**

REAL ESTATE TODAY. (US/0034-0804). **4845**

REAL LIFE MAGAZINE. (US/0739-196X). **363**

REAL PEOPLE. (US/1040-9335). **2544**

REAL POTTERY. (UK). **2593**

REAL PROPERTY LAW SECTION NEWSLETTER. (US/0147-135X). **4845**

REAL TIME MAGAZINE. (BE/1018-0303). **1221**

REAL WEST. (US/0034-0898). **2756**

REALITES INDUSTRIELLES. (FR). **2149**

REALTOR NEWS. (US/0279-6309). **4846**

REALTY. (US/0481-9004). **4846**

REAPER; NEW ZEALAND'S EVANGELICAL MONTHLY. (NZ/0034-107X). **4989**

REASON. (US/0048-6906). **5214**

REB. REVISTA ECLESIASTICA BRASILEIRA. (BL/0101-8434). **5035**

REBUS, DE. (SA/0250-0329). **3035**

REC NEWSLETTER, THE. (US/0899-014X). **Qty:** very few. **3530**

RECAREERING NEWSLETTER. (US/1068-199X). **4209**

RECENT PUBLICATIONS IN NATURAL HISTORY. (US/0738-0925). **4174**

RECENT TITLES IN LAW FOR THE SUBJECT SPECIALIST. AGRICULTURE, ANIMAL, AND FOOD LAW. (US/0899-0662). **3035**

RECENTI PROGRESSI IN MEDICINA. (IT/0034-1193). **3801**

RECEPTOR (CLIFTON, N.J. JOURNAL). (US/1052-8040). **493**

RECEUIL DES LOIS ET DE LA LEGISLATION FINANCIERE. (FR). **Qty: 12. 4678**

RECHERCHE EN DANSE, LA. (FR/0752-5729). **1314**

RECHERCHE ET INDUSTRIE. (FR/0767-0273). **5145**

RECHERCHE (PARIS. 1970). (FR/0029-5671). **5145**

RECHERCHES AMERINDIENNES AU QUEBEC. (CN/0318-4137). **243**

RECHERCHES DE SCIENCE RELIGIEUSE. (FR/0034-1258). **4989**

RECHERCHES ECONOMIQUES DE LOUVAIN. (BE/0770-4518). **1515**

RECHERCHES FEMINISTES. (CN/0838-4479). **5565**

RECHERCHES SOCIOLOGIQUES. (BE/0303-9625). **Qty: 30. 5215**

RECHT DER DATENVERARBEITUNG : RDV. (GW/0178-8930). **1227**

RECHT DER JUGEND UND DES BILDUNGSWESEN. (GW/0034-1312). **3035**

RECHT DER SCHULE. (AU). **3036**

RECHT DER WIRTSCHAFT, DAS. (GW). **3102**

RECHT IN OST UND WEST. (GW/0486-1485). **3036**

RECHT UND POLITIK. (GW/0344-7871). **3036**

RECHT UND SCHADEN. (GW/0343-9771). **3036**

RECHT ZOLL UND VERFAHREN. (GW) **3134**

RECHTSMEDIZIN BERLIN. (GW/0937-9819). **3742**

RECHTSRHEINISCHES KOLN. (GW/0179-2938). **2704**

RECHTSTHEORIE. (GW/0034-1398). **3036**

RECOMBINANT DNA. (UK/0261-4979). **551**

RECONCILIATION QUARTERLY (NEW MALDEN, SURREY). (UK/0034-1479). **Qty: 12. 4990**

RECONSTRUCTIONIST. (US/0034-1495). **5052**

RECORD COLLECTOR, THE. (UK/0034-155X). **4149**

RECORD COLLECTOR'S MONTHLY. (US/8755-6154). **Qty: 8-20/yr. 2777**

RECORD IN EDUCATIONAL ADMINISTRATION AND SUPERVISION. (US/0739-0580). **1869**

RECORD ROUNDUP (NORTH CAMBRIDGE, MASS.). (US/1071-4170). **Qty: 5-20. 4149**

RECORD (TROY, N.Y.). (US/1053-8976). **5720**

RECORD (WASHINGTON, D.C. : 1975). (US/0145-8566). **3036**

RECORDER (GREENFIELD, MASS.). (US). **5690**

RECORDER MAGAZINE, THE. (UK/0306-4409). **4149**

RECORDER (NEW YORK, N.Y. 1985), THE. (US/0885-7741). **2627**

RECORDER, THE. (UK). **4149**

RECORDER (TORONTO). (CN/0704-7231). **4149**

RECORDS OF EARLY ENGLISH DRAMA. (CN/0700-9283). **Qty: 450. 5367**

RECORDS OF THE AMERICAN CATHOLIC HISTORICAL SOCIETY OF PHILADELPHIA. (US/0002-7790). **5035**

RECORDS OF THE GEOLOGICAL SURVEY OF INDIA. (II/0370-5226). **1393**

RECORDS OF THE SOUTH AUSTRALIAN MUSEUM. (AT/0376-2750). **4095**

RECOUP. (CN/0709-6402). **2241**

RECOVERING LITERATURE. (US/0300-6425). **3351**

RECOVERING (SAN FRANCISCO, CALIF.). (US/0896-2391). **Qty: 12. 1348**

RECREATION EXCHANGE. (AT). **Qty: 4. 4853**

RECREATION EXECUTIVE REPORT. (US/0890-2194). **Qty: 5. 4853**

RECRUITING TRENDS. (US/0034-1827). **706**

RECUEIL DE MEDECINE VETERINAIRE. (FR/0034-1843). **5520**

RECUEIL DES BREVETS D'INVENTION. (BE/0034-1851). **1308**

RECUEIL DES TRAVAUX CHIMIQUES DES PAYS-BAS (1920). (NE/0165-0513). **991**

RECUEIL FISCAL. COURS D'IMPOT. (CN/0712-6573). **750**

RECUEIL FISCAL. PROBLEMES ET SOLUTIONS. (CN/0712-6565). **4744**

RECUPERARE. EDILIZIA DESIGN IMPIANTI. (IT/0392-4599). **307**

RECURRING BIBLIOGRAPHY OF HYPERTENSION. (US/0090-1326). **3710**

RECYCLAGE RECUPERATION PARIS. (FR/1156-962X). **2220**

RECYCLING CANADA. (CN/1183-8809). **Qty: 5-6. 2241**

RED APPLE BULLETIN. (US). **5657**

RED BASS. (US/0883-0126). **329**

RED MENACE. (CN/0711-2270). **4546**

RED NOTEBOOK. COMMUNICATING WITH HEARING PEOPLE, THE. (US). **4393**

RED RIVER VALLEY HERITAGE PRESS, THE. (US/0739-1838). **Qty: 3-4. 2756**

RED TAPE (DETROIT, MICH.). (US/0735-7427). **3244**

RED TIDE NEWSLETTER. (IE/0791-248X). **1455**

RED WING REPUBLICAN EAGLE. (US). **5698**

REDBOOK. (US/0034-2106). **5565**

REDEMPTION DIGEST AND CORPORATE ACTIONS. (US/1056-506X). **807**

REDEN-BERATER, DER. (GW/0932-1543). **1120**

REDNECK REVIEW OF LITERATURE, THE. (US/0887-5715). **Qty: 50. 3428**

REDSTART, THE. (US/0034-2165). **5596**

REDWOOD CITY ALMANAC. (US/0195-0533). **5639**

REDWOOD NEWS. (US). **2404**

REDWOOD RESEARCHER. (US/0890-2968). **2469**

REESE RIVER REVEILLE (AUSTIN, NEV. : 1950). (US). **5708**

REFER. (UK/0144-2384). **3244**

REFERATEBLATT ZUR RAUMENTWICKLUNG. (GW/0341-2512). **4679**

REFERATEORGAN SCHWEISSEN UND VERWANDTE VERFAHREN. (GW/0340-4749). **4027**

REFERATIVNYI ZHURNAL: ELEKTRONIKA. (RU). **2078**

REFERATIVNYI ZHURNAL FARMAKOLOGIYA OBSHCHAYA FARMAKOLOGIYA NERVNOI SISTEMY. (RU/0134-580X). **471**

REFERATIVNYJ ZURNAL - VSESOUZNYJ INSTITUT NAUCNOJ I TEHNICESKOJ INFORMACII. 77, FARMAKOLOGIA EFFEKTORNYH SISTEM, HIMIOTERAPEVTICESKIE SREDSTVA. (RU/0202-5132). **471**

REFEREE (FRANKSVILLE, WIS.). (US/0733-1436). **4914**

REFERENCE AND RESEARCH BOOK NEWS. (US/0887-3763). **3244**

REFERENCE BOOK OF CORPORATE MANAGEMENTS. (US/0735-6498). **884**

REFERENCE BOOK REVIEW, THE. (US/0272-1988). **1928**

REFERENCE LIBRARIAN, THE. (US/0276-3877). **3244**

REFERENCE REVIEWS. (UK/0950-4125). **1928**

REFERENCE SERVICES REVIEW. (US/0090-7324). **1928**

REFERENCES DE LA POSTE PARIS. (FR/0983-1924). **1147**

REFLECTION (NEW HAVEN). (US/0362-0611). **4990**

REFLECTIONS. (AT/0156-7799). **3530**

REFLECTIONS (NORTH BATTLEFORD. 1976). (CN/0384-0697). **3244**

REFLECTIONS ON CANADIAN LITERACY : RCL. (CN/1180-1239). **1884**

REFLECTIONS (TAZEWELL, TENN.). (US/1071-0515). **Qty: 4. 2756**

REFLECTOR (1983), THE. (US/0893-3286). **Qty: 12. 5701**

REFLECTOR (AMARILLO, TEX.), THE. (US/0484-2685). **2469**

REFLETS ET PERSPECTIVES DE LA VIE ECONOMIQUE. (BE/0034-2971). **1639**

REFLEX (SEATTLE, WASH.). (US/1054-3465). **Qty: 4-6. 329**

REFORM. (AT). **3037**

REFORM. (UK/0306-7262). **5067**

REFORM JUDAISM. (US/0482-0819). **5052**

REFORMA NEWSLETTER. (US/0891-8880). **3244**

REFORMATION & REVIVAL JOURNAL. (US/1071-7277). **4990**

REFORMATION REVIEW, THE. (US/0034-303X). **5019**

REFORMATION TODAY. (UK/0034-3048). **4990**

REFORMATUSOK LAPJA. (HU). **5067**

REFORMED LITURGY AND MUSIC. (US/0362-0476). **4990**

REFORMED PERSPECTIVE. (CN/0714-8208). **4990**

REFORMED REVIEW (HOLLAND, MICH.). (US/0034-3064). **Qty: 50. 4990**

REFORMED THEOLOGICAL REVIEW, THE. (AT/0034-3072). **4990**

REFORMED WORLD. (SZ/0034-3056). **4990**

REFRACTORY GIRL. (AT/0310-4168). **5565**

REFRIGERATED TRANSPORTER. (US/0034-3129). **5391**

REFRIGERATION. (US). **2608**

REFUGEE ABSTRACTS : A PUBLICATION OF THE INTERNATIONAL REFUGEE INTEGRATION RESOURCE CENTRE. (SZ/0253-1445). **1921**

REFUGEE UPDATE ENGLISH ED. (CN/0251-6500). **4512**

REFUSE NEWS. (US). **Qty: 6-12. 2241**

REGATTA. (UK). **4914**

REGENERATION. (US/8756-3002). **125**

REGGAE REPORT. (US/1065-3023). **Qty: 2. 4149**

REGINA. (CN/0315-212X). **2544**

REGIONAL DIRECTORY OF MINORITY & WOMEN-OWNED BUSINESS FIRMS (CENTRAL ED.). (US/1047-7799). **706**

REGIONAL DIRECTORY OF MINORITY & WOMEN-OWNED BUSINESS FIRMS. (WESTERN EDITION). (US/0886-3946). **706**

REGIONAL JOURNAL OF SOCIAL ISSUES. (AT/0158-7102). **5255**

REGIONAL PLAN NEWS. (US/0034-3374). **4679**

REGIONAL SCIENCE AND URBAN ECONOMICS. (NE/0166-0462). **2833**

REGIONAL STUDIES. (UK/0034-3404). **5215**

REGISTER (MONTREAL, 1980). (CN/0226-7586). **2627**

REGISTER OF AUSTRALIAN MINING. (AT). **2149**

REGISTER OF THE KENTUCKY HISTORICAL SOCIETY, THE. (US/0023-0243). **2756**

REGISTER OF THE SPENCER MUSEUM OF ART, THE. (US/0733-866X). **4095**

REGISTRY HANDBOOK: NUMBER SECTION. SUPPLEMENT. (US). **991**

REGISTRY OF MEMBERS - CLINICAL SOCIOLOGY ASSOCIATION. (US/0733-0251). **5255**

REGULATED RIVERS. (UK/0886-9375). **1359**

REGULATIONS / INTERNATIONAL SKATING UNION. (SZ). **4914**

REGULATORY AFFAIRS JOURNAL. (UK/0960-7889). **3633**

REHAB & COMMUNITY CARE MANAGEMENT. (CN/1192-2508). **Qty: 8-12. 3633**

REHABILITATION DIGEST. (CN/0048-7139). **4393**

REHABILITATION NURSING. (US/0278-4807). **3868**

REHABILITATION PSYCHOLOGY. (US/0090-5550). **4615**

REICHENBACHIA / STAATLICHES MUSEUM FUER TIERKUNDE IN DRESDEN. (GW/0070-7279). **5613**

REINFORCED PLASTICS (LONDON). (UK/0034-3617). **4460**

REINIGER + WASCHER. (GW/0034-3625). **5355**

REINRAUMTECHNIK. (GW/0931-9190). **5145**

REINSURANCE LAW REPORTS. (UK/0961-7264). **3037**

REITEN UND FAHREN. (GW/0720-5104). **4914**

RELACIONES INTERNACIONALES. (MX/0185-0814). **4533**

RELATIONS INDUSTRIELLES / INDUSTRIAL RELATIONS. (CN/0034-379X). **1706**

RELATIONS INTERNATIONALES. (FR/0335-2013). **Qty:** 4. **4533**

RELATIVELY SPEAKING (EDMONTON). (CN/0701-8878). **2469**

RELAZIONE DEL CONSIGLIO DIRETTIVO ALLA ASSEMBLEA GENERALE DEI SOCI. (IT). **1624**

RELAZIONI INTERNAZIONALI. (IT/0034-3846). **4533**

RELC JOURNAL. (SI/0033-6882). **3315**

RELEASE. (AT/0157-3470). **Qty:** 1 /year. **3174**

RELEASING HORMONES. (UK/0142-8314). **3733**

RELEVE, LA. (RW). **2642**

RELIABILITY REVIEW (MILWAUKEE, WIS.). (US/0277-9633). **Qty:** 3. **1993**

RELIGION & LITERATURE. (US/0888-3769). **4990**

RELIGION & PUBLIC EDUCATION. (US/1056-7224). **1777**

RELIGION AND SOCIETY (BANGALORE, INDIA). (II/0034-3951). **4991**

RELIGION & SOCIETY REPORT, THE. (US/0742-6984). **4991**

RELIGION INDEX ONE. PERIODICALS. (US/0149-8428). **5013**

RELIGION INDEX TWO : MULTI-AUTHOR WORKS. (US/0149-8436). **4991**

RELIGION INDEXES [COMPUTER FILE]. (US). **5013**

RELIGION TEACHER'S JOURNAL. (US/0034-401X). **4991**

RELIGION WATCH. (US/0886-2141). **4991**

RELIGIONEN DER MENSCHHEIT, DIE. (GW/0486-3585). **4991**

RELIGIONSGESCHICHTLICHE VERSUCHE UND VORARBEITEN. (GW). **4991**

RELIGIONSVIDENSKABELIGT TIDSSKRIFT. (DK/0108-1993). **4991**

RELIGIOUS BROADCASTING. (US/0034-4079). **Qty:** 24-30. **1138**

RELIGIOUS EDUCATION. (US/0034-4087). **4991**

RELIGIOUS FREEDOM REPORTER. (US/0275-3529). **3093**

RELIGIOUS HUMANISM. (US/0034-4095). **4992**

RELIGIOUS LIFE (CHICAGO, ILL.). (US/0279-0459). **4992**

RELIGIOUS SOCIALISM. (US/0278-7784). **4992**

RELIGIOUS STUDIES AND THEOLOGY. (CN/0829-2922). **4992**

RELIGIOUS STUDIES REVIEW. (US/0319-485X). **4992**

RELIGIOUS TRADITIONS. (AT/0156-1650). **4992**

RELIX. (US/0146-3489). **4149**

RELOCATABLE BUSINESS. (US/1070-8081). **Qty:** 1 or 2. **706**

RELOCATION / REALTY UPDATE. (US). **Qty:** 1-2. **946**

RELOCATION REPORT, THE. (US/0275-7613). **4846**

REMAINS TO BE FOUND. (US/0738-5889). **2469**

REMEMBER THAT SONG. (US/0889-8790). **4149**

REMINDER. ZONE ONE. BRANDON, GROVELAND, ATLAS AND HADLEY TOWNSHIPS, THE. (US/0194-245X). **5693**

REMINERALIZE THE EARTH. (US/1066-4106). **184**

REMODELING (WASHINGTON, D.C.). (US/0885-8039). **626**

REMOTE SENSING IN CANADA. (CN). **5145**

REMOTE SENSING REVIEWS. (SZ/0275-7257). **1993**

RENAISSANCE AND REFORMATION. (CN/0034-429X). **2705**

RENAISSANCE (ARDMORE, PA.). (US/1072-3625). **Qty:** 4-20. **2271**

RENAISSANCE STUDIES. (UK/0269-1213). **2705**

RENAISSANCE UNIVERSAL JOURNAL. (US/0712-4767). **4533**

RENAL EDUCATOR. (AT/0816-990X). **3992**

RENAL FAILURE. (US/0886-022X). **3992**

RENAL PHYSIOLOGY. (UK/0300-3434). **3993**

RENCONTRE (QUEBEC. EDITION ANGLAISE). (CN/0709-9495). **4679**

RENCONTRE (QUEBEC. EDITION FRANCAISE). (CN/0709-9487). **4679**

RENDEZVOUS (POCATELLO, IDAHO). (US/0034-4400). **3429**

RENDICONTI DEL CIRCOLO MATEMATICO DI PALERMO. (IT/0009-725X). **3531**

RENDICONTI DEL SEMINARIO MATEMATICO. (IT). **3531**

RENEGADE (BLOOMFIELD HILLS). (US). **3429**

RENEWABLE ENERGY BULLETIN. (UK/0306-364X). **1954**

RENEWAL MAGAZINE. (UK). **Qty:** 40/50. **4992**

RENLEIXUE XUEBAO. (CC/1000-3193). **244**

RENNINGER'S ANTIQUE GUIDE. (US). **252**

RENOVATEC BARCELONA. (SP/0214-3127). **626**

RENSSELAER ENGINEER. (US/0034-4508). **1993**

RENTAL RATES COMPILATION. (US/0164-0593). **626**

REPERTOIRE ANALYTIQUE DU BULLETIN JURIDIQUE / UCANSS, UNION DES CAISSES NATIONALES DE SECURITE SOCIALE. (FR). **5304**

REPERTOIRE DES MEMBRES / ORDRE DES AGRONOMES DU QUEBEC. (CN/0822-9430). **125**

REPERTOIRE MENSUEL DU MINISTERE DE L'INTERIEUR. (FR/0240-4729). **4680**

REPERTORIEN ZUR DEUTSCHEN LITERATURGESCHICHTE. (GW/0486-4166). **3429**

REPERTORIO AMERICANO. (CR). **3429**

REPORT. (US/0529-8172). **2833**

REPORT AND STATEMENT OF ACCOUNTS - LIQUOR CONTROL COMMISSION. (AT). **3174**

REPORT - AUDUBON SOCIETY OF RHODE ISLAND. (US/0274-502X). **Qty:** 2. **2203**

REPORT - CENTRAL SOYA, INC., FORT WAYNE IND. (US/0411-4094). **2627**

REPORT - EDUCATION COMMISSION OF THE STATES. (US/0531-8335). **1844**

REPORT - FEDERAL BAR ASSOCIATION. SECTION OF TAXATION. (US/0742-5317). **3037**

REPORT FROM THE CAPITAL. (US/0364-6661). **Qty:** 12/yr. **4992**

REPORT OF PROCEEDINGS OF THE CONGRESS OF THE UNIVERSITIES OF THE COMMONWEALTH. (UK). **1844**

REPORT OF RESEARCH - DIVISION OF FOOD RESEARCH. (AT). **2355**

REPORT OF THE COMMITTEE ON FOREIGN AFFAIRS FOR THE ... SESSION OF THE ... NATIONAL ASSEMBLY APPOINTED ON ... / REPUBLIC OF ZAMBIA. (ZA). **4533**

REPORT OF THE PUBLIC ACCOUNTS COMMITTEE. (ZA). **4746**

REPORT ON GUATEMALA. (US/1043-3856). **Qty:** 1-2. **5215**

REPORT ON PUBLICATIONS OF THE SCHOOL OF INTERNATIONAL AFFAIRS AND THE REGIONAL INSTITUTES. (US/0084-8921). **4533**

REPORT ON THE BACKGROUND, CURRENT PROGRAMMES AND PLANNED DEVELOPMENT OF THE BANGLADESH INSTITUTE OF DEVELOPMENT STUDIES, A. (BG). **5215**

REPORT - ROYAL GREENWICH OBSERVATORY. (UK/0308-3322). **399**

REPORT / THE OHIO GENEALOGICAL SOCIETY. (US). **2470**

REPORTER. (US). **5698**

REPORTER (FOND DU LAC, WIS.), THE. (US/0749-7172). **5770**

REPORTER FOR CONSCIENCE' SAKE, THE. (US/0034-4796). **4055**

REPORTER ON HUMAN REPRODUCTION AND THE LAW. (US/8756-2057). **Qty:** 6. **3038**

REPORTER ON THE LEGAL PROFESSION. (US/8755-7509). **Qty:** 10. **3038**

REPORTER - ONTARIO ENGLISH CATHOLIC TEACHERS' ASSOCIATION. (CN/0384-5648). **Qty:** 5. **1903**

REPORTS AND MEMOIRS. (IT/0577-3199). **280**

REPORTS FROM GENERAL PRACTICE. (UK/0557-3912). **3739**

REPORTS / MINORITY RIGHTS GROUP. (UK/0305-6252). **4512**

REPORTS - NATIONAL CENTER FOR SCIENCE EDUCATION (U.S.). (US/1064-2358). **1778**

REPORTS ON MATHEMATICAL PHYSICS. (PL/0034-4877). **4419**

REPRESENTATIONS (BERKELEY, CALIF.). (US/0734-6018). **2853**

REPRESENTATIVE RESEARCH IN SOCIAL PSYCHOLOGY. (US/0034-4907). **4615**

REPRODUCER, THE. (US/0742-9088). **2777**

REPRODUCTION. (UK/0034-4958). **4569**

REPROGRAF, DER. (GW). **Qty:** 10. **4376**

REPTILE & AMPHIBIAN MAGAZINE. (US/1059-0668). **5596**

REPULESI SZAKIRODALMI TAJEKOZTATO. (HU/0231-3928). **33**

RERIC HOLDINGS LIST : / AN OCCASIONAL PUBLICATION OF RERIC. (TH). **1955**

RERUNS. (US/0278-6397). **1138**

RES PUBLICA. (PL/0860-4592). **2492**

RES PUBLICA LITTERARUM. (IT/0275-4304). **Qty:** 10. **1079**

RESCUE NEWS. (UK/0950-5830). **280**

RESEARCH AND DEVELOPMENT NEWS. (US/0486-476X). **5538**

RESEARCH AND DEVELOPMENT PROGRAMS GUIDE. (US/0163-0202). **4055**

RESEARCH & TEACHING IN DEVELOPMENTAL EDUCATION. (US/1046-3364). **Qty:** 2-3. **1884**

RESEARCH ANIMALS IN CANADA. (CN/0229-1223). **226**

RESEARCH CONTRIBUTIONS OF THE AMERICAN BAR FOUNDATION. (US). **3039**

RESEARCH EVALUATION. (UK/0958-2029). **5146**

RESEARCH FOR DEVELOPMENT : THE JOURNAL OF THE NIGERIAN INSTITUTE OF SOCIAL & ECONOMIC RESEARCH. (NR/0189-0085). **1517**

RESEARCH (GOTTINGEN, GERMANY). (GW/0722-6349). **244**

RESEARCH IN AFRICAN LITERATURES. (US/0034-5210). **3429**

RESEARCH IN EDUCATION (MANCHESTER). (UK/0034-5237). **1779**

RESEARCH IN ENGINEERING DESIGN. (US/0934-9839). **1994**

RESEARCH IN MELANESIA. (PP/0254-0665). **Qty:** 2. **244**

RESEARCH IN PHENOMENOLOGY. (US/0085-5553). **4358**

RESEARCH INTO HIGHER EDUCATION ABSTRACTS. (UK/0034-5326). **1797**

RESEARCH MONOGRAPHS IN BANKING AND FINANCE. (UK/0950-849X). **808**

RESEARCH NEWS - FAMILY HISTORY WORLD. (US/0884-3716). **2470**

RESEARCH NOTES (LIVINGSTONE MUSEUM). (ZA). **4095**

RESEARCH PAMPHLET - FOREST RESEARCH INSTITUTE. (MY). **Qty:** 1-4/yr. **2393**

RESEARCH PAPER - CENTRE FOR URBAN AND COMMUNITY STUDIES. UNIVERSITY OF TORONTO. (CN/0316-0068). **2833**

RESEARCH, POLICY AND PLANNING : THE JOURNAL OF THE SOCIAL SERVICES RESEARCH GROUP. (UK/0264-519X). **5215**

RESEARCH QUARTERLY FOR EXERCISE AND SPORT. (US/0270-1367). **1858**

RESEARCH REPORTS: AMERICAN INSTITUTE FOR ECONOMIC RESEARCH. (US/0034-5407). **1517**

RESEARCH REPORTS / DEPARTMENT OF ANTHROPOLOGY, UNIVERSITY OF MASSACHUSETTS, AMHERST. (US). **244**

RESEARCH REVIEW - INSTITUTE OF AFRICAN STUDIES. (GH/0020-2703). **2643**

RESEARCH STRATEGIES. (US/0734-3310). **3245**

RESENA DE ACTIVIDADES - CENEP. (AG). **4559**

RESERVE FORCES ALMANAC. (US/0363-860X). **4055**

RESIDENT AND STAFF PHYSICIAN. (US/0034-5555). **3634**

RESIDENTIAL TREATMENT FOR CHILDREN & YOUTH. (US/0886-571X). **5306**

RESIST (SOMERVILLE, MASS.). (US/0897-2613). **Qty:** 1-2 per year. **4493**

RESISTANCE NEWS / NATIONAL RESISTANCE COMMITTEE. (US). **4493**

RESISTANCE (VANCOUVER). (CN/0824-586X). **4493**

RESOLUTION. (US/1050-3978). **1201**

RESORT DEVELOPMENT & OPERATION. (US/8750-1252). **Qty:** 2-5. **2809**

RESOURCE — Book Review Index

RESOURCE. (CN/0832-9354). **4992**

RESOURCE DIRECTORY (TORONTO). (US/0822-2479). **2903**

RESOURCE (DON MILLS, ONT.). (CN/0828-9522). **4846**

RESOURCE-MAG. (CN/0712-7243). **2924**

RESOURCE MANAGEMENT AND OPTIMIZATION. (UK/0142-2391). **2204**

RESOURCE (OTTAWA). (CN/0700-5237). **227**

RESOURCE RECYCLING / NORTH AMERICA'S RECYCLING JOURNAL. (US/0744-4710). **Qty:** 50-60. **2242**

RESOURCE RECYCLING'S BOTTLE/CAN RECYCLING UPDATE. (US/1052-4916). **2242**

RESOURCE RICHMOND. (AT/1031-3796). **5777**

RESOURCE SHARING & INFORMATION NETWORKS. (US/0737-7797). **3245**

RESOURCES FOR AMERICAN LITERARY STUDY. (US/0048-7384). **3351**

RESOURCES FOR FEMINIST RESEARCH : RFR. (CN/0707-8412). **5565**

RESOURCES IN AGING. (US/0892-0818). **5306**

RESOURCES IN EDUCATION. ANNUAL CUMULATION. (US/0197-9973). **1797**

RESOURCES POLICY. (UK/0301-4207). **2204**

RESOURCES (WASHINGTON, D.C. 1959). (US/0048-7376). **2204**

RESPIRATORY CARE. (US/0020-1324). **3951**

RESPIRATORY PROTECTION NEWSLETTER. (US/0882-0953). **2869**

RESPONSABILITA CIVILE E PREVIDENZA. (IT). **3039**

RESPONSE (NEW YORK. 1967). (US/0034-5709). **5052**

RESPONSE (SOLANA BEACH, CALIF.). (US/0732-2933). **4799**

RESPONSIVE COMMUNITY, THE. (US/1053-0754). **Qty:** 6-8. **5256**

RESPONSIVE PHILANTHROPY. (US/1065-0008). **Qty:** 4/yr. **4339**

RESSI REVIEW. (US/0199-3534). **4846**

RESSOURCE (OTTAWA). (CN/0700-5245). **227**

RESTAURANT BUSINESS. (US/0097-8043). **5072**

RESTAURANT HOSPITALITY. (US/0147-9989). **5072**

RESTAURANT MANAGEMENT INSIDER. (US/1052-4088). **5072**

RESTAURANT WINE. (US/1040-7030). **5073**

RESTAURATOR. (DK/0034-5806). **2483**

RESTAURO & CITTA. (IT). **308**

RESTORATION & MANAGEMENT NOTES. (US/0733-0707). **2204**

RESTORATION OF LOST OR OBLITERATED CORNERS AND SUBDIVISION OF SECTIONS. (US). **2574**

RESTORATION QUARTERLY. (US/0486-5642). **Qty:** 35-40. **4993**

RESTORATION (TUCSON, ARIZ.). (US/0736-5934). **252**

RESUMENES ANALITICOS EN EDUCACION. (CL/0716-0151). **1797**

RESUMES DE JURISPRUDENCE PENALE DU QUEBEC. (CN/0822-7616). **3083**

RESURGENCE. (UK/0034-5970). **4494**

RESURRECTION PARIS. (FR/0484-5854). **5035**

RETAIL DIRECTORY. (UK). **956**

RETAIL NEWS LETTER ED. FRANCAISE. (FR/1017-785X). **Qty:** 20. **957**

RETAIL NEWS WEST. (US/8750-4286). **957**

RETAIL SECURITY MANAGEMENT LETTER. (US/0883-2234). **3175**

RETAIL SYSTEMS ALERT. (US/0898-8439). **957**

RETAIL WORLD. (AT). **957**

RETHINKING MARXISM. (US/0893-5696). **1594**

RETHINKING SCHOOLS. (US/0895-6855). **Qty:** 2-4. **1779**

RETIRED MILITARY ALMANAC. (US/0149-7197). **4055**

RETIRED OFFICER (ALEXANDRIA, VA.), THE. (US/0034-6160). **4055**

RETIRED OFFICER MAGAZINE (ALEXANDRIA, VA.), THE. (US/1061-3102). **Qty:** 50. **4055**

RETIREMENT LIFESTYLE. (CN/0844-5982). **Qty:** 6-10. **5181**

RETTUNGSDIENST. (GW/0178-2525). **3634**

RETURN TO THE SOURCE. (US/0743-1244). **4993**

REUMATOLOGO : PUBBLICA IL BOLLETTINO DELLA SOCIETA ITALIANA DI REUMATOLOGIA, IL. (IT/0391-8963). **3806**

REUNIONS (MILWAUKEE, WIS.). (US/1046-5235). **2470**

REVIEW AND EXPOSITOR (BERNE). (US/0034-6373). **5067**

REVIEW & PERSPECTIVE / COLLEGE OF BUSINESS AND ECONOMICS, UNIVERSITY OF KENTUCKY. (US). **1581**

REVIEW (CHARLOTTESVILLE). (US/0190-3233). **3351**

REVIEW FOR RELIGIOUS. (US/0034-639X). **5035**

RE:VIEW - FRIENDS OF PHOTOGRAPHY. (US/0891-5326). **4376**

REVIEW JOURNAL OF PHILOSOPHY & SOCIAL SCIENCE. (II/0258-1701). **Qty:** 1-2. **4359**

REVIEW : LATIN AMERICAN LITERATURE AND ARTS. (US). **Qty:** 20-25 per year. **329**

REVIEW OF AFRICAN POLITICAL ECONOMY. (UK/0305-6244). **1581**

REVIEW OF ARCHAEOLOGY, THE. (US/1050-4877). **280**

REVIEW OF BLACK POLITICAL ECONOMY, THE. (US/0034-6446). **1517**

REVIEW OF BOOKS ON THE BOOK OF MORMON. (US/1050-7930). **4993**

REVIEW OF BUSINESS. (US/0034-6454). **Qty:** 3-4. **708**

REVIEW OF CONTEMPORARY FICTION. (US/0276-0045). **3351**

REVIEW OF EDUCATION, THE. (US/0098-5597). **1779**

REVIEW OF ENGLISH STUDIES. (UK/0034-6551). **3429**

REVIEW OF EXISTENTIAL PSYCHOLOGY AND PSYCHIATRY (1972). (US/0361-1531). **4615**

REVIEW OF INTERNATIONAL AFFAIRS. (YU/0486-6096). **4534**

REVIEW OF INTERNATIONAL BROADCASTING. (US/0149-9971). **1138**

REVIEW OF LITIGATION, THE. (US/0734-4015). **3040**

REVIEW OF MARKETING AND AGRICULTURAL ECONOMICS. (AT/0034-6616). **128**

REVIEW OF METAPHYSICS, THE. (US/0034-6632). **Qty:** 120. **4359**

REVIEW OF NATIONAL LITERATURES. (US/0034-6640). **3351**

REVIEW OF POLITICAL ECONOMY. (UK/0953-8259). **4494**

REVIEW OF POLITICS, THE. (US/0034-6705). **Qty:** 50. **4494**

REVIEW OF PROGRESS IN COLORATION AND RELATED TOPICS. (UK/0557-9325). **1029**

REVIEW OF PUBLIC PERSONNEL ADMINISTRATION. (US/0734-371X). **Qty:** 10-12. **4705**

REVIEW OF RADICAL POLITICAL ECONOMICS, THE. (US/0486-6134). **1594**

REVIEW OF RELIGIOUS RESEARCH. (US/0034-673X). **4993**

REVIEW OF SOCIAL ECONOMY. (UK/0034-6764). **1581**

REVIEW OF TEXAS BOOKS. (US/0892-6212). **Qty:** 160 per year. **4832**

REVIEW OF THE RIVER PLATE, THE. (AG/0325-7487). **1581**

REVIEW, THE. (UK/0034-6349). **2892**

REVIEWS IN AMERICAN HISTORY. (US/0048-7511). **2757**

REVIEWS IN ANTHROPOLOGY. (US/0093-8157). **244**

REVIEWS IN CHEMICAL ENGINEERING. (UK/0264-8431). **2017**

REVIEWS IN INORGANIC CHEMISTRY (LONDON, ENGLAND). (UK/0193-4929). **1037**

REVIEWS JOURNAL. (AT/0157-3705). **3351**

REVIEWS ON CARDS. (US). **3246**

REVISTA AEREA. (US/0279-4519). **33**

REVISTA ANDINA. (PE). **5216**

REVISTA ARGENTINA DE CIRUGIA. (AG). **Qty:** 32/yr. **3973**

REVISTA ARGENTINA DE MICOLOGIA : ORGANO DE DIFUSION DE LA SOCIEDAD ARGENTINA DE MICOLOGIA. (AG/0325-4755). **576**

REVISTA ARGENTINA DE POLITICA Y TEORIA. (AG). **4494**

REVISTA ASTRONOMICA. (AG/0374-4272). **399**

REVISTA AVICULTURA. (CU/0257-9162). **220**

REVISTA BIBLICA. (AG/0034-7078). **5019**

REVISTA BRASILEIRA DE ANESTESIOLOGIA. (BL/0034-7094). **3684**

REVISTA BRASILEIRA DE ECONOMIA. (BL/0034-7140). **1518**

REVISTA BRASILEIRA DE ENTOMOLOGIA. (BL/0085-5626). **Qty:** varies. **5613**

REVISTA BRASILEIRA DE ESTUDOS POLITICOS. (BL/0034-7191). **4494**

REVISTA BRASILEIRA DE GENETICA. (BL/0100-8455). **551**

REVISTA BRASILEIRA DE ZOOLOGIA. (BL/0101-8175). **5596**

REVISTA CAFETERA DE COLOMBIA. (CK). **185**

REVISTA CATALANA DE TEOLOGIA. (SP/0210-5551). **4993**

REVISTA CHILENA DE DERECHO. (CL). **3040**

REVISTA CHILENA DE ENTOMOLOGIA. (CL/0034-740X). **5613**

REVISTA CHILENA DE PEDIATRIA. (CL/0370-4106). **3911**

REVISTA COLOMBIANA DE EDUCACION (BOGOTA, COLOMBIA : 1978). (CK). **1780**

REVISTA COLOMBIANA DE OBSTETRICIA Y GINECOLOGIA. (CK/0034-7434). **3768**

REVISTA COSTARRICENSE DE CIENCIAS MEDICAS. (CR/0253-2948). **3635**

REVISTA CRITICA DE CIENCIAS SOCIAIS. (PO). **5216**

REVISTA CUBANA DE CONSTRUCCION NAVAL; REVISTA CIENTIFICO TECNICA. (CU/0864-2621). **5455**

REVISTA CUBANA DE DERECHO. (CU). **3040**

REVISTA CUBANA DE HIGIENE Y EPIDEMIOLOGIA. (CU/0253-1151). **3736**

REVISTA DA ACADEMIA SOBRALENSE DE ESTUDOS E LETRAS. (BL). **2757**

REVISTA DA ESCOLA DE BIBLIOTECONOMIA DA UFMG. (BL/0100-0829). **Qty:** 4. **3246**

REVISTA DA PROCURADORIA GERAL DO ESTADO DE SAO PAULO. (BL). **3040**

REVISTA DA SOCIEDADE BRASILEIRA DE MEDICINA TROPICAL. (BL/0037-8682). **3986**

REVISTA DE ADMINISTRACAO DE EMPRESAS. (BL/0034-7590). **885**

REVISTA DE ADMINISTRACAO MUNICIPAL. (BL). **4683**

REVISTA DE ADMINISTRACAO PUBLICA (RIO DE JANEIRO). (BL/0034-7612). **4683**

REVISTA DE ADMINISTRACION PUBLICA. (MX/0482-5209). **4683**

REVISTA DE ARQUEOLOGIA (RIO DE JANEIRO, BRAZIL). (BL). **280**

REVISTA DE BIOLOGIA TROPICAL. (CR/0034-7744). **3986**

REVISTA DE CHIRURGIE ONCOLOGIE, RADIOLOGIE, O.R.L., OFTALMOLOGIE, STOMATOLOGIE. ONCOLOGIA. (RM/0377-4724). **3823**

REVISTA DE CHIRURGIE, ONCOLOGIE, RADIOLOGIE, O.R.L. OFTALMOLOGIE, STOMATOLOGIE. SERIA : STOMATOLOGIE. (RM/0377-7871). **3635**

REVISTA DE CIENCIA POLITICA (SANTIAGO). (CL/0716-1417). **Qty:** 3 per year. **4494**

REVISTA DE CIENCIAS DE LA EDUCACION. (SP). **1780**

REVISTA DE CIENCIAS SOCIALES (RIO PIEDRAS, P.R.). (PR/0034-7817). **Qty:** 3-6/year. **5216**

REVISTA DE CIENCIAS SOCIALES (SAN JOSE). (CR/0482-5276). **5216**

REVISTA DE CRITICA LITERARIA LATINOAMERICANA. (PE/0252-8843). **3351**

REVISTA DE DERECHO ADMINISTRATIVO. (AG/0327-2265). **3040**

REVISTA DE DERECHO PUERTORRIQUENO. (PR/0034-7930). **3040**

REVISTA DE DIREITO CIVIL. (BL). **3091**

REVISTA DE DIREITO DO TRABALHO (SAO PAULO). (BL/0102-8774). **3153**

REVISTA DE DIVULGACAO CULTURAL / FURB. (BL). **2757**

REVISTA DE EDUCACION. (CL). **1780**

REVISTA DE ESTUDIOS HISPANICOS (RIO PIEDRAS, P.R.). (PR/0378-7974). **3315**

REVISTA DE ESTUDIOS HISPANICOS (UNIVERSITY, AL.). (US/0034-818X). **3315**

REVISTA DE ESTUDIOS HISTORICO-JURIDICOS. (CL/0716-5455). **3041**

REVISTA DE FARMACIA E BIOQUIMICA DA UNIVERSIDADE DE SAO PAULO. (BL/0370-4726). **4328**

REVISTA DE FILOSOFIA. (MX/0185-3481). **4359**

REVISTA DE FILOSOFIA DE LA UNIVERSIDAD DE COSTA RICA. (CR/0034-8252). **4359**

REVISTA DE FOMENTO SOCIAL. (SP/0015-6043). **5216**

REVISTA DE HISTORIA (HEREDIA). (CR/1012-9790). **2758**

REVISTA DE INTERPRETACAO BIBLICA LATINO-AMERICANA : RIBLA. (CR). **5019**

REVISTA DE INVESTIGACION CLINICA. (MX/0034-8376). **3801**

REVISTA DE INVESTIGACIONES MARINAS. (CU/0252-1962). **557**

REVISTA DE LA ASOCIACION ARGENTINA DE MINERALOGIA, PETROLOGIA Y SEDIMENTOLOGIA. (AG/0325-0253). **1395**

REVISTA DE LA ASOCIACION ESPANOLA DE NEUROPSIQUIATRIA. (SP/0211-5735). **3935**

REVISTA DE LA ASOCIACION ODONTOLOGICA ARGENTINA. (AG/0004-4881). **1334**

REVISTA DE LA EDUCACION SUPERIOR. (MX). **1846**

REVISTA DE LA FACULTAD DE DERECHO DE LA UNIVERSIDAD COMPLUTENSE. (SP). **3041**

REVISTA DE LA FACULTAD DE DERECHO DE MEXICO. (MX/0185-1810). **3041**

REVISTA DE LA IMAGEN Y EL SONIDO: EIKONOS. (SP). **4376**

REVISTA DE LA INTEGRACION Y EL DESARROLLO DE CENTROAMERICA. (HO/0252-8762). **1518**

REVISTA DE LA SANIDAD DE LAS FUERZAS POLICIALES. (PE/0254-3435). **3635**

REVISTA DE LA UNION MATEMATICA ARGENTINA (1968). (AG/0041-6932). **3531**

REVISTA DE LETRAS (FORTALEZA). (BL/0101-8051). **3351**

REVISTA DE LITERATURA. (SP/0034-849X). **3459**

REVISTA DE MARINA. (CL/0034-8511). **Qty: 6. 4055**

REVISTA DE MEDICINA DE LA UNIVERSIDAD DE NAVARRA. (SP/0556-6177). **3973**

REVISTA DE METALURGIA (MADRID). (SP/0034-8570). **4018**

REVISTA DE MICROBIOLOGIA. (BL/0001-3714). **Qty: 4. 569**

REVISTA DE MUSICA LATINOAMERICANA. (US/0163-0350). **4149**

REVISTA DE PEDIATRIA PREVENTIVA E SOCIALE. NIPIOLOGIA. (IT/0392-4416). **3911**

REVISTA DE PRE-HISTORIA. (BL). **Qty: 5. 2758**

REVISTA DE PROCESSO. (BL). **3091**

REVISTA DE PSICOANALYSIS. (AG/0034-8740). **4616**

REVISTA DE PSICOLOGIA GENERAL Y APLICADA. (SP/0373-2002). **Qty: 20. 4616**

REVISTA DE SAUDE PUBLICA. (BL/0034-8910). **4799**

REVISTA DE SOLDADURA. (SP/0048-7759). **4027**

REVISTA DEL ARCHIVO HISTORICO DEL GUAYAS. (EC). **2483**

REVISTA DEL DERECHO COMERCIAL Y DE LAS OBLIGACIONES. (AG/0556-6428). **3102**

REVISTA DEL DERECHO INDUSTRIAL. (AG/0326-0763). **3041**

REVISTA DEL INSTITUTO MEXICANO DEL PETROLEO. (MX/0538-1428). **4277**

REVISTA DEL INSTITUTO URUGUAYO DE DERECHO PENAL. (UY). **3108**

REVISTA DEL PENSAMIENTO CENTROAMERICANO. (NQ/0378-3340). **2512**

REVISTA DO COLEGIO BRASILEIRO DE CIRURGIOES. (BL/0100-6991). **3973**

REVISTA DO HOSPITAL DAS CLINICAS. (BL/0041-8781). **3635**

REVISTA DO IRB / INSTITUTO DE RESSEGUROS DO BRASIL. (BL/0019-0446). **2892**

REVISTA ESPANOLA DE ALERGOLOGIA E INMUNOLOGIA CLINICA : ORGANO OFICIAL DE LA SOCIEDAD ESPANOLA DE ALERGOLOGIA E INMUNOLOGIA CLINICA. (SP/0214-1477). **3676**

REVISTA ESPANOLA DE ANESTESIOLOGIA Y REANIMACION. (SP/0034-9356). **3684**

REVISTA ESPANOLA DE ANTROPOLOGIA AMERICANA. (SP/0556-6533). **244**

REVISTA ESPANOLA DE CARDIOLOGIA. (SP/0300-8932). **3710**

REVISTA ESPANOLA DE CIENCIA Y TECNOLOGIA DE ALIMENTOS / EDITADA POR EL CONSEJO SUPERIOR DE INVESTIGACIONES CIENTIFICAS. (SP/1131-799X). **2356**

REVISTA ESPANOLA DE DOCUMENTACION CIENTIFICA. (SP/0210-0614). **3246**

REVISTA ESPANOLA DE ENFERMEDADES DIGESTIVAS. (SP/1130-0108). **3747**

REVISTA ESPANOLA DE GERIATRIA Y GERONTOLOGIA. (SP/0211-139X). **3755**

REVISTA ESPANOLA DE LECHERIA. (SP/0300-5550). **Qty: varies. 198**

REVISTA ESPANOLA DE LINGUISTICA. (SP/0210-1874). **3316**

REVISTA ESPANOLA DE MICROPALEONTOLOGIA. (SP/0556-655X). **4230**

REVISTA EUROPEA DE ESTUDIOS LATINOAMERICANOS Y DEL CARIBE. EUROPEAN REVIEW OF LATIN AMERICAN AND CARIBBEAN STUDIES. (NE/0924-0608). **Qty: 25. 5216**

REVISTA HISPANICA MODERNA. (US/0034-9593). **Qty: 22-40. 3430**

REVISTA IBEROAMERICANA. (US/0034-9631). **3430**

REVISTA INTERAMERICANA DE BIBLIOGRAFIA (1972). (US/0020-4994). **423**

REVISTA INTERAMERICANA DE BIBLIOTECOLOGIA / UNIVERSIDAD DE ANTIOQUIA, ESCUELA INTERAMERICANA DE BIBLIOTECOLOGIA. (CK/0120-0976). **3246**

REVISTA INTERAMERICANA DE DIREITO INTELECTUAL : RIDI. (BL). **1308**

REVISTA INTERAMERICANA DE PSICOLOGIA. (US/0034-9690). **Qty: varies. 4616**

REVISTA INTERNACIONAL DE CIENCIAS SOCIALES. (SP/0379-0762). **5216**

REVISTA INTERNACIONAL DE METODOS NUMERICOS PARA CALCULO Y DISEfNO EN INGENIERIA. (SP/0213-1315). **1994**

REVISTA JAVERIANA (BOGOTA). (CK/0120-3088). **Qty: 10/yr. 2552**

REVISTA JURIDICA DE CATALUNYA. (SP). **3042**

REVISTA JURIDICA DE LA UNIVERSIDAD DE PUERTO RICO. (PR/0886-2516). **Qty: 1 or 2. 3042**

REVISTA JURIDICA DEL PERU. (PE). **3042**

REVISTA LATINOAMERICANA DE ESTUDIOS EDUCATIVOS. (MX/0185-1284). **1780**

REVISTA LATINOAMERICANA DE ESTUDIOS ETNOLINGUISTICOS. (PE). **3316**

REVISTA LATINOAMERICANA DE FILOSOFIA. (AG/0325-0725). **4359**

REVISTA LATINOAMERICANA DE MICROBIOLOGIA (1970). (MX/0187-4640). **Qty: 6 to 10. 569**

REVISTA LATINOAMERICANA DE PATOLOGIA. (VE/0300-9068). **3897**

REVISTA LATINOAMERICANA DE PSICOLOGIA. (CK/0120-0534). **Qty: 10. 4616**

REVISTA LATINOAMERICANA DE QUIMICA. (MX/0370-5943). **1047**

REVISTA MARITIMA BRASILEIRA. (BL/0034-9860). **4182**

REVISTA MEDICA DE CHILE. (CL/0034-9887). **3801**

REVISTA MEDICA DE PANAMA. (PN/0379-1629). **3636**

REVISTA MEXICANA DE ANALISIS DE LA CONDUCTA. (MX). **4616**

REVISTA MEXICANA DE MICOLOGIA. (MX/0187-3180). **576**

REVISTA MEXICANA DE PEDIATRIA. (MX/0035-0052). **3911**

REVISTA MEXICANA DE POLITICA EXTERIOR. (MX/0185-6022). **2758**

REVISTA MUSICAL CHILENA. (CL/0716-2790). **4150**

REVISTA ODONTOLOGICA ECUATORIANA. (EC/0484-8020). **Qty: 4. 1334**

REVISTA ORL. (AG/0326-7067). **3891**

REVISTA PARAGUAYA DE SOCIOLOGIA. (PY/0035-0354). **5216**

REVISTA PAULISTA DE MEDICINA. (BL/0035-0362). **Qty: 4. 3636**

REVISTA PERUANA DE DERECHO DE LA EMPRESA. (PE). **3042**

REVISTA PERUANA DE ENTOMOLOGIA. (PE/0080-2425). **5613**

REVISTA PERUANA DE POBLACION. (PE). **4560**

REVISTA PORTUGUESA DE CIENCIAS VETERINARIAS. (PO/0035-0389). **5520**

REVISTA PORTUGUESA DE ESTOMATOLOGIA E CIRURGIA MAXILO-FACIAL. (PO/0035-0397). **1334**

REVISTA PORTUGUESA DE FILOSOFIA. (PO/0870-5283). **4359**

REVISTA/REVIEW INTERAMERICANA. (PR/0360-7917). **5216**

REVISTA SOBRE RELACIONES INDUSTRIALES Y LABORALES / UNIVERSIDAD CATOLICA ANDRES BELLO. (VE). **1708**

REVISTA TELEGRAFICA ELECTRONICA. (AG/0035-0516). **2079**

REVISTA TEOLOGICA LIMENSE. (PE). **Qty: 30. 5035**

REVISTA TRIBUTARIA. (UY). **3042**

REVISTA UNIVERSIDAD EAFIT. (CK/0120-033X). **4683**

REVISTA URUGUAYA DE CIENCIAS SOCIALES. (UY). **5217**

REVISTA URUGUAYA DE DERECHO PROCESAL. (UY). **3042**

REVISTA URUGUAYA DE ESTUDIOS INTERNACIONALES. (UY). **4534**

REVISTA URUGUAYA DE PSICOANALISIS. (UY/0484-8268). **4616**

REVISTA URUGUAYA DE PSICOLOGIA. (UY). **4616**

REVITALIZED SIGNS. (US). **4616**

REVMEDIA LONDON. (UK/0955-8500). **Qty: Occasionally. 1183**

REVOLUCIONES POR MINUTO : RPM. (SP). **4150**

REVOLUTION (STATEN ISLAND, N.Y.). (US/1059-0927). **Qty: 4. 3868**

REVTECH. (US). **Qty: 6. 1202**

REVUE ACEDA. (CN/0382-7976). **1884**

REVUE ADMINISTRATIVE, LA. (FR/0035-0672). **Qty: 6. 4683**

REVUE AFRICAINE DE THEOLOGIE. (CG/1016-2461). **4993**

REVUE ANDRE MALRAUX. (CN/0839-458X). **3351**

REVUE ARBIDO. (SZ/0258-0772). **3246**

REVUE BELGE D'ARCHEOLOGIE ET D'HISTOIRE DE L'ART. (BE/0035-077X). **330**

REVUE BELGE DE DROIT INTERNATIONAL. (BE/0035-0788). **3135**

REVUE BELGE DE GEOGRAPHIE. (BE/0035-0796). **2575**

REVUE BELGE DE MEDECINE DENTAIRE 1984. (BE/0775-0293). **1334**

REVUE BELGE DE MUSICOLOGIE. (BE/0771-6788). **4150**

REVUE BELGE DE PHILOLOGIE ET D'HISTOIRE. (BE/0035-0818). **3316**

REVUE BELGE DE SECURITE SOCIALE. (BE/0771-1530). **5306**

REVUE BELGE D'HISTOIRE CONTEMPORAINE. (BE). **2706**

REVUE BELGE DU CINEMA. (BE/0774-0115). **Qty: 2-3. 4077**

REVUE BELGE DU FEU. (BE/0771-4033). **2292**

REVUE BENEDICTINE. (BE/0035-0893). **4993**

REVUE BIBLIQUE. (FR/0035-0907). **5019**

REVUE CANADIENNE D'ETUDES CINEMATOGRAPHIQUES. (CN/0847-5911). **Qty: 5-6. 4077**

REVUE CANADIENNE D'ETUDES DU DEVELOPPEMENT. (CN/0225-5189). **Qty: 30. 1639**

REVUE CELFAN. (US/0890-6998). **3430**

REVUE D'ALLEMAGNE. (FR/0035-0974). **Qty: 3/yr. 2706**

REVUE D'AUVERGNE. (FR/0035-1008). **2706**

REVUE DE COMMINGES. (FR/0035-1059). **2706**

REVUE

REVUE DE DROIT CANONIQUE. (FR/0556-7378). **4993**

REVUE DE DROIT COMMERCIAL BELGE. (BE). **3102**

REVUE DE DROIT INTELLECTUAL L'INGENIEUR-CONSEIL. (BE). **1308**

REVUE DE DROIT INTERNATIONAL ET DE DROIT COMPARE. (BE/0775-4663). **3135**

REVUE DE DROIT JUDICIAIRE. (CN/0822-5117). **3091**

REVUE DE DROIT PENAL ET DE CRIMINOLOGIE. (BE). **Qty:** 50. **3175**

REVUE DE DROIT (SHERBROOKE). (CN/0317-9656). **3043**

REVUE DE DROIT SOCIAL. (BE). **3043**

REVUE DE GEOGRAPHIE ALPINE. (FR/0035-1121). **Qty:** 4. **2575**

REVUE DE GEOGRAPHIE DE LYON. (FR/0035-113X). **2575**

REVUE DE GEOGRAPHIE. MADAGASCAR. (MG/0047-5416). **2575**

REVUE DE LA BANQUE, LA. (BE). **810**

REVUE DE LA CERAMIQUE ET DU VERRE, LA. (FR/0294-202X). **Qty:** 20. **2593**

REVUE DE LA CERAMIQUE, LA. (FR) **2593**

REVUE DE LA SOUDURE (BRUXELLES). (BE/0035-127X). **4027**

REVUE DE L'ACLA. (CN/1193-1493). **Qty:** 12. **3316**

REVUE DE L'AGRICULTURE. (BE/0035-1296). **129**

REVUE DE L'ALIMENTATION ANIMALE. (FR/0242-6595). **220**

REVUE DE L'ARBITRAGE. (FR/0556-7440). **3043**

REVUE DE LARYNGOLOGIE, D'OTOLOGIE ET DE RHINOLOGIE. (FR/0035-1334). **3891**

REVUE DE L'EDUCATION PHYSIQUE. (BE). **1858**

REVUE DE L'ENERGIE. (FR/0303-240X). **Qty:** 10. **1956**

REVUE DE L'INSTITUT DE SOCIOLOGIE. (BE/0771-6796). **5217**

REVUE DE LITTERATURE COMPAREE. (FR/0035-1466). **3430**

REVUE DE L'OCEAN INDIEN, ECONOMIE. (MG). **1518**

REVUE DE L'UNIVERSITE DE MONCTON (1976). (CN/0316-6368). **Qty:** 2. **1846**

REVUE DE L'UNIVERSITE SAINTE-ANNE. (CN/0706-8115). **1846**

REVUE DE MATHEMATIQUES SPECIALES. (FR/0035-1504). **3531**

REVUE DE MEDECINE VETERINAIRE. (FR/0035-1555). **5520**

REVUE DE METALLURGIE (PARIS). (FR/0035-1563). **4018**

REVUE DE MICROPALEONTOLOGIE. (FR/0035-1598). **4230**

REVUE DE QUMRAN. (FR/0035-1725). **5052**

REVUE DE SCIENCE CRIMINELLE ET DE DROIT PENAL COMPARE. (FR/0035-1733). **3108**

REVUE DE STATISTIQUE APPLIQUEE. (FR/0035-175X). **5337**

REVUE DE THEOLOGIE ET DE PHILOSOPHIE. (SZ/0035-1784). **4359**

REVUE DE TOURISME. (SZ/0251-3102). **5490**

REVUE D'ECONOMIE INDUSTRIELLE. (FR/0154-3229). **Qty:** 4. **1582**

REVUE D'ECONOMIE REGIONAL ET URBAINE. (FR). **2834**

REVUE DES ARCHEOLOGUES ET HISTORIENS D'ART DE LOUVAIN. (BE/0080-2530). **281**

REVUE DES ECHANGES DE L'ASSOCIATION FRANCOPHONE INTERNATIONALE DES DIRECTEURS D'ETABLISSEMENTS SCOLAIRES, LA. (CN/0822-8329). **1780**

REVUE DES ETUDES ARMENIENNES (PARIS). (FR/0080-2549). **2663**

REVUE DES ETUDES AUGUSTINIENNES. (FR/0035-2012). **4993**

REVUE DES ETUDES BYZANTINES. (FR/0373-5729). **2706**

REVUE DES ETUDES COOPERATIVES MUTUALISTES ET ASSOCIATIVES. (FR). **1543**

REVUE DES ETUDES GEORGIENNES ET CAUCASIENNES. (FR/0373-1537). **3316**

REVUE DES ETUDES ITALIENNES. (FR/0035-2047). **3430**

REVUE DES ETUDES JUIVES. (FR/0484-8616). **5052**

REVUE DES ETUDES SLAVES. (FR/0080-2557). **2706**

REVUE DES LANGUES ROMANES. (FR/0223-3711). **3316**

REVUE DES LIVRES POUR ENFANTS, LA. (FR). **3351**

REVUE DES QUESTIONS SCIENTIFIQUES. (BE/0035-2160). **5148**

REVUE DES SCIENCES DE L'EDUCATION. (CN/0318-479X). **1780**

REVUE DES SCIENCES PHILOSOPHIQUES ET THEOLOGIQUES (PARIS : 1947). (FR/0035-2209). **4359**

REVUE DES SCIENCES RELIGIEUSES. (FR/0035-2217). **Qty:** 4. **4993**

REVUE D'ETUDES COMPARATIVES EST-OUEST. (FR/0338-0599). **4546**

REVUE D'ETUDES PALESTINIENNES. (LE/0252-8290). **4534**

REVUE D'HISTOIRE DE LA MEDECINE HEBRAIQUE. (FR/0035-2330). **3636**

REVUE D'HISTOIRE DE L'AMERIQUE FRANCAISE. (CN/0035-2357). **2758**

REVUE D'HISTOIRE DES SCIENCES. (FR/0151-4105). **5148**

REVUE D'HISTOIRE DIPLOMATIQUE. (FR/0035-2365). **4534**

REVUE D'HISTOIRE DU BAS ST-LAURENT. (CN/0381-8454). **Qty:** 5. **2758**

REVUE D'HISTOIRE DU THEATRE. (FR/0035-2373). **5368**

REVUE D'HISTOIRE ECCLESIASTIQUE. (BE/0035-2381). **5013**

REVUE D'HISTOIRE MAGHREBINE. (TI). **2643**

REVUE D'HISTOIRE MODERNE ET CONTEMPORAINE. (FR/0048-8003). **2628**

REVUE D'INTEGRATION EUROPEENNE. (CN/0703-6337). **Qty:** 15. **4494**

REVUE DIPLOMATIQUE DE L'OCEAN INDIEN. (MG). **4534**

REVUE D'ODONTO-STOMATOLOGIE DU MIDI DE LA FRANCE. (FR/0035-2470). **1334**

REVUE DU BARREAU, LA. (CN/0383-669X). **3043**

REVUE DU BOIS ET DE SES APPLICATIONS. (FR/0373-5133). **2404**

REVUE DU MARCHE COMMUN ET DE L'UNION EUROPEENNE. (FR). **Qty:** 10. **1582**

REVUE DU MARCHE UNIQUE EUROPEEN. (FR/1155-4274). **Qty:** 4. **1639**

REVUE DU MONDE MUSULMAN ET DE LA MEDITERRANEE. (FR/0997-1327). **5044**

REVUE DU NORD. (FR/0035-2624). **2706**

REVUE DU PALAIS DE LA DECOUVERTE. (FR/0339-7521). **Qty:** 6. **5148**

REVUE DU PRACTICIEN, LA. (FR/0035-2640). **3636**

REVUE DU RHUMATISME ET DES MALADIES OSTEO-ARTICULAIRES. (FR/0035-2659). **3806**

REVUE DU TARN. (FR). **2706**

REVUE DU TRESOR, LA. (FR/0035-2713). **751**

REVUE ECONOMIQUE. (FR/0035-2764). **1595**

REVUE ECONOMIQUE ET SOCIALE (LAUSANNE). (SZ/0035-2772). **1595**

REVUE EGYPTIENNE DE DROIT INTERNATIONAL. (UA/0080-259X). **3135**

REVUE FORESTIERE FRANCAISE. (FR/0035-2829). **2394**

REVUE FRANCAISE D'AQUARIOLOGIE, HERPETOLOGIE. (FR/0399-1075). **557**

REVUE FRANCAISE DE GEOTECHNIQUE. (FR/0181-0529). **Qty:** 4. **1395**

REVUE FRANCAISE DE GYNECOLOGIE ET D'OBSTETRIQUE. (FR/0035-290X). **3768**

REVUE FRANCAISE DE PEDAGOGIE. (FR). **1780**

REVUE FRANCAISE DE SCIENCE POLITIQUE. (FR/0035-2950). **4495**

REVUE FRANCAISE DE SOCIOLOGIE. (FR/0035-2969). **5256**

REVUE FRANCAISE D'ETUDES AMERICAINES. (FR/0397-7870). **2759**

REVUE FRANCAISE D'HISTOIRE D'OUTRE-MER. (FR/0300-9513). **Qty:** 4. **2706**

REVUE FRANCAISE DU MARKETING. (FR/0035-3051). **936**

REVUE FRANCOPHONE DE LOUISIANE. (US/0890-9555). **3431**

REVUE FRONTENAC. (CN/0715-9994). **Qty:** 5-10. **3431**

REVUE GENERAL NUCLEAIRE. (FR/0335-5004). **1956**

REVUE GENERALE DE DROIT. (CN/0035-3086). **3043**

REVUE GENERALE DE DROIT INTERNATIONAL PUBLIC. (FR/0373-6156). **3135**

REVUE GENERALE DE L'ELECTRICITE. (FR/0035-3116). **2079**

REVUE GENERALE DE THERMIQUE. (FR/0035-3159). **2128**

REVUE GENERALE DU FROID, LA. (FR/0035-3205). **2608**

REVUE GEOGRAPHIQUE DE L'EST. (FR/0035-3213). **2575**

REVUE GEOGRAPHIQUE DES PYRENEES ET DU SUD-OUEST. (FR/0035-3221). **2575**

REVUE HISTORIQUE. (FR/0035-3264). **2628**

REVUE HISTORIQUE DES ARMEES. (FR/0035-3299). **4056**

REVUE INTERNATIONALE DE CRIMINOLOGIE ET DE POLICE TECHNIQUE. (FR/0035-3329). **3175**

REVUE INTERNATIONALE DE DROIT COMPARE. (FR/0035-3337). **3135**

REVUE INTERNATIONALE DE LA CROIX-ROUGE. (SZ). **Qty:** 12/yr. **2911**

REVUE INTERNATIONALE DE PHILOSOPHIE. (BE/0048-8143). **4359**

REVUE INTERNATIONALE DES SERVICES DE SANTE DES FORCES ARMEES : ORGANE DU COMITE INTERNATIONAL DE MEDECINE ETUDE PHARMACIE MILITAIRES. (BE/0259-8582). **3636**

REVUE INTERNATIONALE DU TRAVAIL. (SZ/0378-5599). **1708**

REVUE INTERNATIONALE P M E. (BE). **708**

REVUE JURIDIQUE DU RWANDA. IGAZETI ISOBANURA AMATEGEKO MU RWANDA. (NR). **3043**

REVUE JURIDIQUE DU ZAIRE; DROIT ECRIT ET DROIT COUTUMIER. (CG). **3043**

REVUE MARITIME 1990, LA. (FR/1146-2132). **4182**

REVUE MEDICALE DE BRUXELLES. (BE/0035-3639). **3636**

REVUE MUSICALE DE SUISSE ROMANDE. (SZ). **4150**

REVUE NOIRE. (FR/1157-4127). **Qty:** 4. **330**

REVUE NOUVELLE, LA. (BE/0035-3809). **2522**

REVUE OFFICIELLE DE LA SOCIETE FRANCAISE D'ORL ET DE PATHOLOGIE CERVICO-FACIALE. (FR/1155-1087). **3891**

REVUE PARLEMENTAIRE CANADIENNE. (CN/0229-2556). **4684**

REVUE PENITENTIAIRE ET DE DROIT PENAL (1940). (FR). **3175**

REVUE PHILOSOPHIQUE DE LA FRANCE ET DE L'ETRANGER. (FR/0035-3833). **4359**

REVUE PHILOSOPHIQUE DE LOUVAIN. (BE/0035-3841). **4360**

REVUE POLYTECHNIQUE. (SZ/0374-4256). **5148**

REVUE PRATIQUE DU FROID ET DU CONDITIONNEMENT DE L'AIR. (FR/0370-6699). **2608**

REVUE PRESCRIRE, LA. (FR/0247-7750). **3637**

REVUE QUART MONDE. (FR). **4512**

REVUE QUEBECOISE DE LINGUISTIQUE THEORIQUE ET APPLIQUEE. (CN/0835-3581). **3317**

REVUE QUEBECOISE DE PSYCHOLOGIE. (CN/0225-9885). **4617**

REVUE ROUMAINE DE MATHEMATIQUES PURES ET APPLIQUEES. (RM/0035-3965). **3531**

REVUE SCHWEIZ. (SZ). **Qty:** 10. **708**

REVUE SUISSE D'AGRICULTURE. (SZ/0375-1325). **130**

REVUE SUISSE DE VITICULTURE, ARBORICULTURE, HORTICULTURE. (SZ/0375-1430). **2430**

REVUE SYNDICALE SUISSE. (SZ/0035-421X). **1708**

REVUE TECHNIQUE MACHINISME AGRICOLE. (FR/0223-0135). **5424**

REVUE THEOLOGIQUE DE LOUVAIN. (BE/0080-2654). **4994**

REVUE THOMISTE. (FR/0035-4295). **4994**

REVUE VOILE QUEBEC, LA. (CN/0820-4969). **595**

RFD (WOLF CREEK). (US/0149-709X). **2796**

RFE. REVISTA FORESTAL ESPANOLA. (SP/1130-958X). **Qty:** 10. **2394**

RG. (CN/0831-375X). **2796**

RHEINISCHE VIERTELJAHRSBLATTER. (GW/0035-4473). **2707**

RHETORIC REVIEW. (US/0735-0198). **Qty:** 12. **3317**

RHETORIC SOCIETY QUARTERLY. (US/0277-3945). **Qty:** 20. **3317**

RHETORICA. (US/0734-8584). **3317**

RHETORIK. (GW/0720-5775). **3317**

RHINOLOGY. (NE/0300-0729). **3891**

RHINOLOGY. SUPPLEMENT. (NE/1013-0047). **3897**

RHODE ISLAND BAR JOURNAL. (US/0556-8595). **Qty:** 4. **3044**

RHODE ISLAND MEDICINE. (US/1061-222X). **Qty:** 4-6. **3637**

RHODE ISLAND QUERIES. (US/0893-181X). **2470**

RHODE ISLAND ROOTS. (US/0730-1235). **2470**

RHODESIANS WORLDWIDE. (UK). **Qty:** 6/year. **2500**

RHODODENDRON, THE. (AT/0485-0637). **2430**

RHODORA. (US/0035-4902). **526**

RIA INTERNATIONAL, REVUE DES INDUSTRIES D'ART EXPORT. (FR). **363**

RIABILITAZIONE E APPRENDIMENTO. (IT/0393-7518). **Qty:** 20. **4382**

RIBOSOMES & TRANSLATION. (UK/0952-0414). **551**

RICARDA HUCH, STUDIEN ZU IHREM LEBEN UND WERK. (GW). **3431**

RICARDIAN. (UK/0048-8267). **5236**

RICE WORLD. (US). **185**

RICE WORLD & SOYBEAN NEWS, THE. (US/0738-5943). **Qty:** 12. **185**

RICERCA E INNOVAZIONE. (IT). **5148**

RICERCHE DI STORIA SOCIALE E RELIGIOSA. (IT). **4994**

RICERCHE ECONOMICHE. (IT/0035-5054). **1518**

RICERCHE PEDAGOGICHE. (IT). **Qty:** 15/16. **1781**

RICERCHE STORICHE SALESIANA / A CURA DELL'ISTITUTO STORICO SALESIANO. (IT). **5035**

RICHFIELD REAPER, THE. (US/0746-6730). **5757**

RICHMOND POST. (US). **5639**

RICHMOND QUARTERLY, THE. (US/0276-6515). **Qty:** (as received). **3431**

RID RIVISTA ITALIANA DIFESA. (IT). **4056**

RIDDELL, RIDDLE, RUDDELL TRAIL, THE. (US/0737-6758). **2470**

RIDIM/RCMI NEWSLETTER. (US/0360-8727). **Qty:** 3-5. **363**

RIDOTTO. (IT). **5368**

RIFLE. (US/0162-3583). **4915**

RIFORMA MEDICA. (IT/0035-5259). **3637**

RIGHT HERE. (US/0895-3139). **2492**

RIGHT OF AESTHETIC REALISM TO BE KNOWN, THE. (US/0882-3731). **4360**

RIGHT OF WAY. (US/0035-5275). **4846**

RIGHTING WORDS. (US/0892-581X). **2924**

RIGHTS (NEW YORK, N.Y. 1953). (US/0035-5283). **Qty:** 1 per year. **4512**

RILCE : REVISTA DE FILOLOGIA HISPANICA. (SP). **3431**

RILM ABSTRACTS. (US/0033-6955). **4160**

RING SYSTEMS HANDBOOK. (US/0742-5996). **1047**

RINSHO HOSHASEN. JAPANESE JOURNAL OF CLINICAL RADIOLOGY. (JA/0009-9252). **3946**

RIO GRANDE HISTORY. (US/0146-1869). **2759**

RIPON COLLEGE MAGAZINE. (US/0300-7928). **1094**

RIPON COLLEGE UPDATE. (US/0744-7450). **1846**

RIPON FORUM. (US/0035-5526). **4495**

RIRON TO HOHO. (JA/0913-1442). **Qty:** 12. **5256**

RISALAT AL-MAKTABAH. (JO). **3247**

RISC USER. (UK/0966-1913). **1202**

RISING STAR (RISING STAR, TEX. : 1965). (US). **5754**

RISK ABSTRACTS. (CN/0824-3336). **4811**

RISK & BENEFITS MANAGEMENT. (US/0893-2654). **2892**

RISK (CONCORD, N.H.). (US/1073-8673). **5148**

RISK, ISSUES IN HEALTH & SAFETY. (US/1047-0484). **4800**

RISK (LONDON. 1987). (UK/0952-8776). **810**

RISK MANAGEMENT FOR EXECUTIVE WOMEN. (US/0732-2666). **2892**

RISK MANAGEMENT REPORTS. (US/0199-6827). **2892**

RISORGIMENTO, IL. (IT/0035-5607). **2707**

RISPARMIO, IL. (IT). **810**

RISTORAZIONE COLLETTIVA. (IT/1120-6039). **2356**

RITTENHOUSE : JOURNAL OF THE AMERICAN SCIENTIFIC INSTRUMENT ENTERPRISE. (US). **Qty:** 4. **2099**

RIVER REPORTER, THE. (US). **5720**

RIVER RUNNER MAGAZINE. (US). **595**

RIVERDALE PRESS, THE. (US). **Qty:** 50. **5720**

RIVERINE GRAZIER, THE. (AT). **Qty:** 6. **5777**

RIVERLANDER. (AT). **5539**

RIVERS (FORT COLLINS, COLO.). (US/0898-8048). **Qty:** 12. **5539**

RIVERTON RANGER, THE. (US). **5772**

RIVISTA AERONAUTICA. (IT). **33**

RIVISTA BIBLICA. (IT/0035-5798). **5019**

RIVISTA DEI COMBUSTIBILI. (IT/0370-5463). **4277**

RIVISTA DEL NUOVO CIMENTO. (IT/0035-5917). **Qty:** 50. **4420**

RIVISTA DELLA SOCIETA ITALIANA DI SCIENZA DELL'ALIMENTAZIONE, LA. (IT/0391-4887). **2356**

RIVISTA DELLA STAZIONE SPERIMENTALE DEL VETRO. (IT). **5148**

RIVISTA DELLE SOCIETA. (IT/0035-6018). **3103**

RIVISTA DELLE TECNOLOGIE TESSILI. (IT/0394-5413). **5355**

RIVISTA DELL'INFERMIERE. (IT). **3792**

RIVISTA D'EUROPA. (IT). **2707**

RIVISTA DI AGRICOLTURA SUBTROPICALE E TROPICALE. (IT/0035-6026). **130**

RIVISTA DI ANTROPOLOGIA. (IT). **245**

RIVISTA DI ARCHEOLOGIA. (IT/0392-0895). **281**

RIVISTA DI BIOLOGIA. (IT/0035-6050). **472**

RIVISTA DI CARDIOLOGIA PREVENTIVA E RIABILITATIVA : ORGANO DELL'ASSOCIAZIONE NAZIONALE DEI CENTRI PER LE MALATTIE CARDIOVASCOLARI. (IT/0393-2028). **3710**

RIVISTA DI DIRITTO INDUSTRIALE. (IT/0035-614X). **1308**

RIVISTA DI DIRITTO INTERNAZIONALE. (IT/0035-6158). **3135**

RIVISTA DI DIRITTO VALUTARIO E DI ECONOMIA INTERNAZIONALE. (IT). **1639**

RIVISTA DI ESTETICA. (IT/0035-6212). **4360**

RIVISTA DI INFORMATICA. (IT/0390-668X). **1202**

RIVISTA DI MATEMATICA PER LE SCIENZE ECONOMICHE E SOCIALI / ASSOCIAZIONE PER LA MATEMATICA APPLICATA ALLE SCIENZE ECONOMICHE E SOCIALI. (IT). **3532**

RIVISTA DI MEDICINA DEL LAVORO ED IGIENE INDUSTRIALE. (IT/0391-2825). **2869**

RIVISTA DI NEUROBIOLOGIA. (IT/0035-6336). **3845**

RIVISTA DI NEURORADIOLOGIA. (IT). **Qty:** 2-4. **3845**

RIVISTA DI PARASSITOLOGIA. (IT/0035-6387). **569**

RIVISTA DI PATOLOGIA NERVOSA E MENTALE. (IT/0035-6433). **3936**

RIVISTA DI PATOLOGIA VEGETALE. (IT/0035-6441). **526**

RIVISTA DI POLITICA ECONOMICA. (IT/0391-6170). **1595**

RIVISTA DI PSICOLOGIA DELL'ARTE. (IT). **330**

RIVISTA DI STORIA DELLA STORIOGRAFIA MODERNA. (IT). **2628**

RIVISTA DI STORIA ECONOMICA. (IT/0393-3415). **1582**

RIVISTA DI STUDI FENICI. (IT). **281**

RIVISTA DI STUDI ITALIANI. (CN/0821-3216). **3431**

RIVISTA DI STUDI LIGURI. (FR/0035-6603). **281**

RIVISTA DI STUDI POLITICI INTERNAZIONALI. (IT/0035-6611). **Qty:** 80. **4534**

RIVISTA DI TEOLOGIA MORALE. (IT). **4994**

RIVISTA GIURUDICA DELLA SCUOLA. (IT/0391-1845). **1870**

RIVISTA INGAUNA E INTEMELIA. (IT). **281**

RIVISTA INTERNAZIONALE DI ECONOMIA DEI TRASPORTI. (IT/0303-5247). **1519**

RIVISTA ITALIANA DEGLI ODONTOTECNICI. (IT/0391-5611). **1335**

RIVISTA ITALIANA DELLA SALDATURA. (IT/0035-6794). **4027**

RIVISTA ITALIANA DELLE SOSTANZE GRASSE. (IT/0035-6808). **1029**

RIVISTA ITALIANA DI CHIRURGIA PLASTICA. (IT/0391-2221). **3974**

RIVISTA ITALIANA DI DIRITTO DEL LAVORO. (IT/0393-2494). **3154**

RIVISTA ITALIANA DI DIRITTO E PROCEDURA PENALE. (IT). **3109**

RIVISTA ITALIANA DI ECONOMIA, DEMOGRAFIA E STATISTICA. (IT/0035-6832). **1519**

RIVISTA ITALIANA DI GEOTECNICA. (IT/0557-1405). **1395**

RIVISTA ITALIANA DI OTORINOLARINGOLOGIA, AUDIOLOGIA E FONIATRIA. (IT/0392-1360). **3891**

RIVISTA ITALIANA DI PALEONTOLOGIA E STRATIGRAFIA. (IT/0035-6883). **Qty:** varies. **4230**

RIVISTA ITALIANA D'IGIENE. (IT/0035-6921). **Qty:** 8. **4800**

RIVISTA LITURGICA. (IT/0035-6956). **5035**

RIVISTA MARITTIMA. (IT/0035-6964). **4182**

RIVISTA MILITARE. (IT/0035-6980). **Qty:** 6. **4056**

RIVISTA SPERIMENTALE DI FRENIATRIA E MEDICINA LEGALE DELLE ALIENAZIONI MENTALI. (IT/0370-7261). **3936**

RIVISTA STORICA DELL'ANTICHITA. (IT/0300-340X). **2628**

RIVISTA STORICA ITALIANA. (IT/0035-7073). **2707**

RIVISTA TRIMESTRALE DI DIRITTO E PROCEDURA CIVILE. (IT). **3045**

RIVISTA TRIMESTRALE DI DIRITTO PUBBLICO. (IT/0557-1464). **3094**

RIV'ON LE-MEHKAR HEVRATI. (IS/0334-4762). **5217**

RLA, REVISTA DE LINGUISTICA TEORICA Y APLICADA. (CL/0033-698X). **Qty:** 2-6. **3317**

RMCLAS REVIEW. (US/0749-9728). **2552**

RMS NEWS. (CN/0824-5665). **2272**

ROAD LAW AND ROAD LAW REPORTS. (UK/1352-0717). **Qty:** 12. **5443**

ROAD TRAFFIC LAW BULLETIN. (UK/0265-7937). **5443**

ROANOKE BEACON, THE. (US). **Qty:** 10. **5724**

ROANOKE TIMES & WORLD-NEWS. (US). **5759**

ROBB REPORT, THE. (US/0279-1447). **2492**

ROBERT FROST REVIEW, THE. (US/1062-6999). **Qty:** 2-3. **3431**

ROBERTS REGISTOR. (US/8756-7741). **2470**

ROBERTSON REPORT. (US/0898-5448). **2470**

ROBESON COUNTY REGISTER, THE. (US/0888-3807). **2470**

ROBINSON JEFFERS NEWSLETTER. (US/0300-7936). **Qty:** 200. **434**

ROBOTICA. (UK/0263-5747). **1216**

ROCAS Y MINERALES. (SP/0378-3316). **2150**

ROCENKA - KRAJSKE KULTURNI STREDISKO V BRNE. (XR). **2707**

ROCHESTER GOLF WEEK & SPORTS LEDGER. (US). **4915**

ROCK & GEM. (US/0048-8453). **1444**

ROCK & ICE. (US/0885-5722). **Qty:** 1 each issue. **4878**

ROCK & ROLL CONFIDENTIAL. (US/0891-9372). **Qty:** 12. **4150**

ROCK CREEK CURRENT, THE. (US/1062-2721). **5647**

ROCK MECHANICS. SUPPLEMENT. (AU/0080-3375). **1994**

ROCKDALE CITIZEN, THE. (US/1050-1401). **Qty:** 10. **5654**

ROCKET (SEATTLE, WA). (US). **Qty:** 24. **4151**

ROCKFORD LABOR NEWS (MICROFICHE). (US). **1708**

ROCKIN' 50'S. (US/0738-7717). **4151**

ROCKS AND MINERALS. (US/0035-7529). **1444**

ROCKY MOUNTAIN CAVING. (US/8756-033X). **Qty:** 4. **1410**

ROCKY MOUNTAIN GARDENER. (US/1054-9552). **Qty:** 20/year. **2430**

ROCKY MOUNTAIN PAY DIRT. (US/0886-0912). **2150**

ROCKY MOUNTAIN REVIEW OF LANGUAGE AND LITERATURE. (US/0361-1299). **Qty:** 40-50. **3431**

ROCKY MOUNTAIN UNION FARMER. (US/0035-7650). **130**

ROD SERLING'S THE TWILIGHT ZONE MAGAZINE. (US/0279-6090). **3431**

RODEO NEWS. (US/0149-6425). **4915**

RODNA GRUDA SLOVENIJA. (XV/0557-2282). **2272**

ROELAND PARK SUN, THE. (US) **5678**

ROEPER REVIEW. (US/0278-3193). **1885**

ROESSLERIA. (BL/0101-7616). **2204**

ROGUE DIGGER. (US/0048-8534). **2470**

ROLLERCOASTER! MAGAZINE. (US/0896-7261). **4865**

ROLLING STONE. (US/0035-791X). **4151**

ROMA. (II). **2628**

ROMANCE PHILOLOGY. (US/0035-8002). **3318**

ROMANCE QUARTERLY. (US/0883-1157). **3318**

ROMANIA. (FR/0035-8029). **3318**

ROMANIC REVIEW. (US/0035-8118). **3431**

ROMANISTISCHE ZEITSCHRIFT FUER LITERATURGESCHICHTE. (GW/0343-379X). **3318**

ROMANTIC MOVEMENT. (US/0557-2738). **3459**

ROMANTIC TIMES. (US/0747-3370). **5074**

ROMANTIST, THE. (US/0161-682X). **3432**

ROND DE TAFEL. (NE/0035-8169). **4994**

RONDOM GEZIN. (BE/0773-4239). **2285**

RONTGENPRAXIS (STUTTGART). (GW/0035-7820). **3946**

ROOF. (UK). **2834**

ROOM OF ONE'S OWN. (CN/0316-1609). **Qty:** 2-4. **3432**

ROOT AND BRANCH. (UK/0306-9958). **2470**

ROOT CELLAR PRESERVES. (US/0748-6251). **2470**

ROOTS & BRANCHES. (US/0893-4150). **2471**

ROOTS AND LEAVES. (US/0748-2485). **Qty:** 1-4. **2471**

ROOTS & SHOOTS QUARTERLY. (US/0738-2391). **2471**

ROOTS DIGEST. (US/8755-8343). **2471**

ROOTS TRACER. (US/0736-802X). **Qty:** (no limit). **2471**

ROSE FAMILY BULLETIN. (US/0748-7827). **2471**

ROSEBUD COUNTY PRESS. (US/8750-2097). **5706**

ROSSICA OLOMUCENSIA. (XR). **3318**

ROSTER / THE BIRMINGHAM GENEALOGICAL SOCIETY, INC. (US/8756-4351). **2471**

ROSTRUM, THE. (US). **Qty:** 2-3. **1121**

ROSWELL DAILY RECORD, THE. (US). **5713**

ROTA-GENE. (US/0730-5168). **2471**

ROTKIN REVIEW, THE. (US/0883-735X). **4376**

ROUND BOBBIN. (US/1076-058X). **5185**

ROUND ROCK LEADER. (US/0164-9124). **5754**

ROUND TABLE, THE. (UK/0035-8533). **4534**

ROUND UP (UNIVERSITY PARK, N.M.). (US/0744-5555). **5713**

ROUNDUP / LOW INCOME HOUSING INFORMATION SERVICE. (US). **2834**

ROUNDUP RECORD-TRIBUNE & WINNETT TIMES. (US/0890-9660). **Qty:** 20. **5706**

ROWAN COUNTY REGISTER. (US/0885-8454). **Qty:** 30. **2471**

ROYAL ASTRONOMICAL SOCIETY OF NEW ZEALAND VARIABLE STAR MONTHLY CIRCULARS M. (NZ). **399**

ROYAL COLLEGE OF MUSIC MAGAZINE. (UK). **4151**

ROYAL ENGINEERS JOURNAL, THE. (UK/0035-8878). **1995**

ROYAL MILITARY POLICE JOURNAL. (UK). **Qty:** varies. **3183**

ROYAL SERVICE. (US/0035-9084). **5067**

ROYALTY DIGEST. (UK/0967-5744). **2522**

RPCV WRITERS & READERS. (US/1062-4694). **3432**

RRT. (CN/0831-2478). **3952**

RS. CUADERNOS DE REALIDADES SOCIALES. (SP/0302-7724). **5256**

RS. RIFIUTI SOLIDI. (IT/0394-5391). **2242**

RSA JOURNAL. (UK). **5149**

RSG. RICHTING SPORT-GERICHT. (NE/0926-7638). **1904**

RSSI. RECHERCHES SEMIOTIQUES. SEMIOTIC INQUIRY. (CN/0229-8651). **3318**

RTW REVIEW. (US/0887-3003). **Qty:** 150. **1087**

RUACH SERIES. (US). **4994**

RUBBER BOARD BULLETIN. (II/0537-0507). **5077**

RUBBER CHEMISTRY AND TECHNOLOGY. (US/0035-9475). **5077**

RUBBER INDIA. (II/0035-9491). **5077**

RUBBER NEWS. (II/0035-9513). **5077**

RUG HOOKING. (US/1045-4373). **Qty:** 3. **375**

RUGBY (NEW YORK). (US/0162-1297). **4915**

RUIMTE VOOR CULTUUR. (BE). **2853**

RUMANIAN REVIEW. (RM/0035-8088). **3352**

RUNDFUNK UND FERNSEHEN. (GW/0035-9874). **1138**

RUNDFUNKTECHNISCHE MITTEILUNGEN. (GW/0035-9890). **1138**

RUNDSCHAU FUER FLEISCHUNTERSUCHUNG UND LEBENSMITTELUBERWACHUNG. (GW/0341-0668). **2356**

RUNDT'S WORLD BUSINESS INTELLIGENCE. (US). **1519**

RUNNER (EDMONTON). (CN/0707-3186). **1858**

RUNNER'S GAZETTE. (US/0199-6983). **4916**

RUNNING. (UK). **4916**

RUNNING & FITNEWS. (US/0898-5162). **2601**

RUNNING RESEARCH NEWS. (US/0887-7033). **4916**

RUNNING TIMES. (US/0147-2968). **4916**

RUNZHEIMER REPORTS ON TRANSPORTATION. (US/0730-8655). **5392**

RURAL AFRICANA. (US/0085-5839). **1582**

RURAL BUILDER. (US/0888-3025). **627**

RURAL BUSINESS MAGAZINE. (AT/1031-3079). **131**

RURAL DELIVERY. (CN/0703-7724). **2544**

RURAL EDUCATOR (FORT COLLINS), THE. (US/0273-446X). **1781**

RURAL HISTORY. (UK/0956-7933). **5256**

RURAL NEW ENGLAND MAGAZINE. (US). **Qty:** 20. **131**

RURAL SOCIOLOGY. (US/0036-0112). **5257**

RURAL TELECOMMUNICATIONS. (US/0744-2548). **1163**

RURAL VOICE (BLYTH). (CN/0700-5385). **Qty:** 5-6. **131**

RUSI JOURNAL / ROYAL UNITED SERVICES INSTITUTE FOR DEFENCE STUDIES, THE. (UK). **4056**

RUSISTIKA : THE RUSSIAN JOURNAL OF THE ASSOCIATION FOR LANGUAGE LEARNING. (UK/0957-1760). **Qty:** varies. **3318**

RUSSELL. (CN/0036-0163). **4360**

RUSSELL'S OFFICIAL NATIONAL MOTOR COACH GUIDE. (US/0036-0171). **5392**

RUSSIA AND HER NEIGHBORS. (US/1066-0127). **5217**

RUSSIAN HISTORY (PITTSBURGH). (US/0094-288X). **2707**

RUSSIAN LINGUISTICS. (NE/0304-3487). **3318**

RUSSIAN ORTHODOX JOURNAL, THE. (US/0036-0317). **5040**

RUSSIAN REVIEW (STANFORD), THE. (US/0036-0341). **2708**

RUSSISTIK. (GW/0935-8072). **3318**

RUSSKAIA RECH. (RU/0036-0368). **3318**

RUSSKII GOLOS (NEW YORK, N.Y.). (US/0036-0406). **2272**

RUSSKOE VOZROZHDENIE. (US/0222-1543). **5040**

RUTGERS COMPUTER & TECHNOLOGY LAW JOURNAL. (US/0735-8938). **1202**

RUTGERS LAW JOURNAL. (US/0277-318X). **3045**

RUTGERS LAW REVIEW. (US/0036-0465). **Qty:** 2-4. **3045**

RUTLAND HISTORICAL SOCIETY QUARTERLY. (US/0748-2493). **Qty:** 1800/yr. **2759**

RUTLAND RECORD. (UK/0260-3322). **2708**

S.A.A.D. DIGEST. (UK/0049-1160). **1335**

S.A. ARGIEFBLAD. (SA/1012-2796). **Qty:** 15. **2483**

S.A.M. ADVANCED MANAGEMENT JOURNAL (1984). (US/0749-7075). **885**

S & L MUSEUM NEWSLETTER. (CN/0715-5034). **4096**

S.C.A.N. : SIMCOE COUNTY ANCESTORS' NEWS. (CN/0823-9533). **2471**

S D ; SPACE DESIGN. (JA/0563-0991). **308**

S/N. SPEECHWRITER'S NEWSLETTER. (US/0272-8079). **1121**

S.S.A. NEWSLETTER : A PUBLICATION OF THE SUDAN STUDIES ASSOCIATION. (US/0899-3785). **2500**

SA JOURNAL OF FOOD SCIENCE AND NUTRITION, THE. (SA/1013-3666). **Qty:** varies. **4199**

SAAGVERKEN. (SW). **2404**

SAAMIS SEEKER. (CN/0229-7205). **2471**

SABER LEER. (SP/0213-6449). **3352**

SABRETACHE. (AT/0486-8013). **4056**

SAC NEWS MONTHLY. (US). **5684**

SACRAMENTAL LIFE. (US/0899-2061). **Qty:** 15. **4995**

SACRAMENTO BEE, THE. (US/0890-5738). **5639**

SACRAMENTO (JONSSON COMMUNICATIONS CORPORATION). (US/0747-8712). **2544**

SACRAMENTO MEDICINE. (US/0886-2826). **3638**

SACRAMENTO NEWS & REVIEW. (US/1065-3287). **Qty:** 26. **2544**

SACRAMENTO OBSERVER, THE. (US/0036-2212). **Qty:** 52. **5639**

SACRED ART JOURNAL. (US/0741-9163). **364**

SACRED MUSIC. (US/0036-2255). **5035**

SADA AL-USBU. (BA). **2508**

SADDLE AND BRIDLE. (US/0036-2271). **2802**

SAE, SAMMLUNG ARBEITSRECHTLICHER ENTSCHEIDUNGEN. (GW). **Qty:** 40-50. **3154**

SAFARI (TUCSON, ARIZ.). (US/0199-5316). **Qty:** 25. **4916**

SAFE JOURNAL. (US/0191-6319). **34**

SAFETY & HEALTH. (US/0891-1797). **2869**

SAFETY AND HEALTH AT WORK : ILO-CIS BULLETIN. (SZ/1010-7053). **2872**

SAFETY & HEALTH PRACTITIONER. (UK/0958-479X). **4800**

SAFETY MANAGEMENT LONDON. (UK). **Qty:** 20. **4801**

SAGA-BOOK. (UK/0305-9219). **Qty:** 10. **3432**

SAGAMIEN. (CN/0226-2169). **2575**

SAGE (ATLANTA, GA.). (US/0741-8639). **5565**

SAGE FAMILY STUDIES ABSTRACTS. (US/0164-0283). **2287**

SAGE PUBLIC ADMINISTRATION ABSTRACTS. (US/0094-6958). **4699**

SAGE URBAN STUDIES ABSTRACTS. (US/0090-5747). **2840**

SAGETRIEB. (US/0735-4665). **3470**

SAGGI NEUROPSICOLOGIA INFANTILE PSICOPEDAGOGIA RIABILITAZIONE. (IT/0390-5179). **4617**

SAGUAROLAND BULLETIN. (US/0275-6919). **527**

SAHIFAT AL-MAKTABAH. (UA). **3247**

SAHITYA SANKETA. (II). **3433**

SAHOVSKI GLASNIK. (CI). **4865**

SAILBOARD RETAILER. (US/1063-8180). **4916**

SAILING. (US/0036-2719). **596**

SAILING CANADA. (CN/0709-4744). **596**

SAINT BARTHOLOMEW'S HOSPITAL JOURNAL. (UK/0036-2778). **Qty:** 16. **3638**

SAINT CHRISTOPHER AND NEVIS CONSOLIDATED INDEX OF STATUTES AND SUBSIDIARY LEGISLATION TO ... . (BB). **3135**

SAINT LOUIS UNIVERSITY LAW JOURNAL. (US/0036-3030). **Qty:** 2-3. **3045**

SAINT LOUIS UNIVERSITY PUBLIC LAW REVIEW. (US/0898-8404). **3045**

SAINT LUCIA CONSOLIDATED INDEX OF STATUTES AND SUBSIDIARY LEGISLATION TO ... . (BB). **3135**

SAINT VINCENT AND THE GRENADINES CONSOLIDATED INDEX OF STATUTES AND SUBSIDIARY LEGISLATION TO ... . (BB). **3135**

SAINTPAULIA INTERNATIONAL NEWS. (US). **2430**

SAINTS HERALD. (US/0036-3251). **Qty:** 6-8 per year. **5067**

SAIPA. (SA/0036-0767). **4684**

SAIS REVIEW (JOHNS HOPKINS UNIVERSITY. SCHOOL OF ADVANCED INTERNATIONAL STUDIES: 1981). (US/0036-0775). **Qty:** 20. **4534**

SAISONS D'ALSACE STRASBOURG. (FR/0048-9018). **2522**

SAL TERRAE. (SP). **4995**

SALALM NEWSLETTER. (US/0098-6275). **3247**

SALAMANDRA (FRANKFURT-AM-MAIN). (GW/0036-3375). **5597**

SALAR. (CN/0827-3472). **2312**

SALES & MARKETING MANAGEMENT. (US/0163-7517). **936**

SALES MANAGER'S BULLETIN. (US/0036-3421). **885**

SALES MOTIVATION (SANTA MONICA, CALIF.). (US/0892-8193). **709**

SALESIANUM. (IT/0036-3502). **5036**

SALESMAN'S GUIDE NATIONWIDE DIRECTORY: MAJOR MASS MARKET MERCHANDISERS (EXCLUSIVE OF NEW YORK METROPOLITAN AREA), THE. (US). **709**

SALINE, THE. (US/0893-3057). **2471**

SALISBURY POST, THE. (US/0747-0738). **5724**

SALISBURY REVIEW, THE. (UK/0265-4881). **Qty:** 30. **3352**

SALLY ANN. (CN/0838-7397). **4995**

SALMAGUNDI (SARATOGA SPRINGS). (US/0036-3529). **2853**

SALMANTICENSIS. (SP/0036-3537). **5036**

SALMON AND TROUT MAGAZINE, THE. (UK/0036-3545). **2312**

SALMON FARMING. (UK/0951-9882). **2312**

SALOME (CHICAGO, ILL.). (US/0749-6435). **1314**

SALT (CHICAGO, ILL.). (US/0883-2587). **4995**

SALT (EDMONTON). (CN/0709-616X). **4995**

SALT LAKE TRIBUNE (SALT LAKE CITY, UTAH : 1890). (US/0746-3502). **5757**

SALUBRITAS (ENGLISH EDITION). (US/0191-5789). **4801**

SALZBURGER JAHRBUCH FUER PHILOSOPHIE. (AU/0080-5696). **4360**

SAMAB. (SA/0370-8314). **4096**

SAMBODHI. (II). **4360**

SAMIKSA. (II/0304-5110). **Qty:** 4. **4617**

SAMISDAT. (US/0226-840X). **3352**

SAMMAMISH VALLEY NEWS. (US). **5762**

SAMMLUNG DER EIDGENOSSISCHEN GESETZE. (SZ). **3045**

SAMMLUNG GEOGRAPHISCHER FUHRER. (GW/0344-6565). **2575**

SAMMLUNG METZLER. (GW/0558-3667). **3433**

SAMS AUTO RADIO SERVICE DATA. (US/0163-3627). **2080**

SAMS TRANSISTOR RADIO. (US). **5149**

SAMSON PERSONAL COMPUTER. (BE). **1290**

SAMTIDEN. (NO/0036-3928). **Qty:** 5-10. **2522**

SAMYA SHAKTI : A JOURNAL OF WOMEN'S STUDIES. (II/0970-5880). **5566**

SAN ANGELO STANDARD-TIMES. (US). **5754**

SAN DIEGO BUSINESS JOURNAL. (US/8750-6890). **709**

SAN DIEGO LAW REVIEW, THE. (US/0036-4037). **3046**

SAN DIEGO MAGAZINE (1949). (US/0036-4045). **2544**

SAN DIEGO PHYSICIAN. (US). **Qty:** 2. **3638**

SAN DIEGO UNION (SAN DIEGO, CALIF. : 1930). (US). **5639**

SAN DIEGO WRITERS MONTHLY. (US/1054-6774). **Qty:** 24. **2924**

SAN FRANCISCO BAY GUARDIAN, THE. (US/0036-4096). **Qty:** 50 per year. **2545**

SAN FRANCISCO BAY TIMES. (US). **5639**

SAN FRANCISCO CHRONICLE. (US). **5639**

SAN FRANCISCO JUNG INSTITUTE LIBRARY JOURNAL, THE. (US/0270-6210). **4617**

SAN FRANCISCO MEDICINE. (US/0361-705X). **3638**

SAN FRANCISCO POST. (US). **5639**

SAN FRANCISCO REVIEW OF BOOKS. (US/0194-0724). **Qty:** 200-300/yr. **330**

SAN JOAQUIN AGRICULTURAL LAW REVIEW. (US/1055-422X). **Qty:** 1. **3046**

SAN JOSE POST-RECORD, THE. (US/0036-4185). **5640**

SAN JUAN RECORD (1953), THE. (US/0894-3273). **Qty:** 3 or 4. **5757**

SAN JUAN STAR, THE. (PR/8750-6122). **5808**

SAN LUIS OBISPO COUNTY GENEALOGICAL SOCIETY, INC. (US/1047-5893). **2471**

SAN LUIS OBISPO COUNTY TELEGRAM-TRIBUNE. (US). **Qty:** 12. **5640**

SANA UPDATE NEWSLETTER. (AT/0811-2711). **4056**

SANCTUARY ASIA. (II). **2204**

SAND MOUNTAIN REPORTER. (US/0890-1724). **5628**

SANDERS COUNTY LEDGER (THOMPSON FALLS, MONT. : 1959). (US). **5706**

SANDLAPPER (1990). (US/1046-3267). **2628**

SANDS AND CORAL. (PH). **3433**

SANGEET NATAK. (II/0036-4339). **4152**

SANITAR UND HEIZUNGSTECHNIK. (GW/0036-4401). **2608**

SANITARY MAINTENANCE. (US/0036-4436). **2242**

SANTA BARBARA NEWS-PRESS (1932). (US). **5640**

SANTA CLARA COMPUTER AND HIGH-TECHNOLOGY LAW JOURNAL. (US/0882-3383). **3046**

SANTA CLARA COUNTY CONNECTIONS. (US/0895-6103). **2471**

SANTA CLARA LAW REVIEW. (US/0146-0315). **Qty:** 4. **3046**

SANTA FE NEW MEXICAN, THE. (US). **5713**

SANTA GERTRUDIS JOURNAL, THE. (US/0036-455X). **221**

SANTE MENTALE AU QUEBEC. (CN/0383-6320). **3936**

SANTIAGO. (CU/0048-9115). **3433**

SANTO, IL. (IT/0391-7819). **Qty:** 40-50. **4995**

SAP, SPECTRA OF ANTHROPOLOGICAL PROGRESS. (II). **245**

SAPERE. (IT/0036-4681). **Qty:** 60/year. **5149**

SAPIENTIA. (AG/0036-4703). **4360**

SAPIENZA. (IT/0036-4711). **4360**

SAR MAGAZINE, THE. (US/0161-0511). **5236**

SARANCE. (EC). **2759**

SARATOGA (RHINEBECK, N.Y.), THE. (US/0740-9702). **2471**

SARCOIDOSIS. (IT/0393-1447). **3638**

SARJANA : JURNAL FAKULTI SASTERA DAN SAINS SOSIAL, UNIVERSITI MALAYA. (MY). **2663**

SARMATIAN REVIEW, THE. (US/1059-5872). **Qty:** 10-15. **2708**

SAS BULLETIN. (US/0899-8922). **Qty:** 5. **282**

SASKATCHEWAN ANGLICAN. (CN/0703-9433). **4995**

SASKATCHEWAN ASSOCIATION OF SOCIAL WORKERS NEWSLETTER. (CN). **Qty:** 6. **5306**

SASKATCHEWAN HISTORY. (CN/0036-4908). **Qty:** 8. **2759**

SASKATCHEWAN LAW REVIEW. (CN/0036-4916). **3046**

SASKATCHEWAN POETRY BOOK. (CN/0080-6560). **3470**

SASKATOON HISTORY REVIEW. (CN/0843-6002). **2759**

SATELLITE COMMUNICATIONS. (US/0147-7439). **1163**

SATELLITE RETAILER. (US/0890-1252). **957**

SATURDAY NIGHT. (CN/0036-4975). **2545**

SAUDI MEDICAL JOURNAL. (SU/0379-5284). **3638**

SAUGETIERKUNDLICHE MITTEILUNGEN. (GW/0036-2344). **472**

SAUL BELLOW JOURNAL. (US/0735-1550). **434**

SAUVEGARDE DE L'ENFANCE. (FR/0036-5041). **5307**

SAVACOU. (JM/0036-5068). **364**

SAVANNAH EVENING PRESS. (US/8750-4685). **5655**

SAVING AND PRESERVING ARTS AND CULTURAL ENVIRONMENTS. (US/0748-8378). **330**

SAVING HEALTH. (UK/0036-5106). **Qty:** 2. **4995**

SAVINGS AND DEVELOPMENT. (IT). **1519**

SAVVY SHOPPER, THE. (US/1057-3275). **5490**

SAWADDI. (TH/0581-8893). **2663**

SAXOPHONE JOURNAL. (US/0276-4768). **4152**

SAYBROOK REVIEW. (US/0740-0853). **4617**

SAYERS REVIEW, THE. (US). **3433**

SBANE ENTERPRISE. (US/8750-3158). **Qty:** 50. **709**

SBORNIK CESKE GEOGRAFICKE SPOLECNOSTI. (XR/1210-115X). **2576**

SBORNIK K DEJINAM 19. A 20. STOLETI. (XR). **2628**

SCAG TELECOMMUNITY. (US/0889-5856). **1163**

SCALA. (GW/0303-4232). **2522**

SCALE AIRCRAFT MODELLING. (UK). **Qty:** 12. **2777**

SCALE CABINETMAKER, THE. (US/0145-8213). **2777**

SCAN NEWSLETTER. (US/0273-3080). **1221**

SCAN (NORTH SYDNEY). (AT/0726-4127). **1904**

SCANDINAVIAN ACTUARIAL JOURNAL. (SW/0346-1238). **2893**

SCANDINAVIAN-CANADIAN STUDIES. (CN/0823-1796). **Qty:** 10-12. **2759**

SCANDINAVIAN DAIRY INFORMATION. (SW/1101-2706). **198**

SCANDINAVIAN DAIRY INFORMATION - SDI. (SW/1101-2706). **198**

SCANDINAVIAN ECONOMIC HISTORY REVIEW, THE. (SW/0358-5522). **1583**

SCANDINAVIAN FOREST ECONOMICS. (FI/0355-032X). **2394**

SCANDINAVIAN JOURNAL OF DEVELOPMENT ALTERNATIVES. (SW/0280-2791). **4535**

SCANDINAVIAN JOURNAL OF ECONOMICS, THE. (UK/0347-0520). **1520**

SCANDINAVIAN JOURNAL OF EDUCATIONAL RESEARCH. (UK/0031-3831). **1781**

SCANDINAVIAN JOURNAL OF INFECTIOUS DISEASES. (NO/0036-5548). **3716**

SCANDINAVIAN JOURNAL OF METALLURGY. (SW/0371-0459). **4018**

SCANDINAVIAN JOURNAL OF NUTRITION NARINGSFORSKNING. (SW/1102-6480). **Qty:** 1-4. **4199**

SCANDINAVIAN JOURNAL OF PSYCHOLOGY. (SW/0036-5564). **4617**

SCANDINAVIAN JOURNAL OF RHEUMATOLOGY. (SW/0300-9742). **3807**

SCANDINAVIAN JOURNAL OF SOCIAL WELFARE. (DK/0907-2055). **5307**

SCANDINAVIAN JOURNAL OF UROLOGY AND NEPHROLOGY. (SW/0036-5599). **3993**

SCANDINAVIAN JOURNAL OF WORK, ENVIRONMENT & HEALTH. (FI/0355-3140). **2870**

SCANDINAVIAN PSYCHOANALYTIC REVIEW, THE. (NO/0106-2301). **4617**

SCANDINAVIAN REVIEW [MICROFORM]. (US). **2272**

SCANDINAVIAN STUDIES: PUBLICATION OF THE SOCIETY FOR THE ADVANCEMENT OF SCANDINAVIAN STUDY. (US/0036-5637). **Qty:** 100-150. **3433**

SCANDINAVICA. (UK/0036-5653). **Qty:** 40. **3433**

SCANNING. (US/0161-0457). **574**

SCANNING MICROSCOPY. (US/0891-7035). **574**

SCARLET & GOLD. (CN/0316-4209). **3176**

SCARSDALE INQUIRER, THE. (US) Qty: 6-8. **5721**

SCENIC TRIPS TO THE GEOLOGIC PAST. (US/0548-5983). **1396**

SCHATZKAMMER DER DEUTSCHEN SPRACHE, DICHTUNG UND GESCHICHTE. (US/0740-1965). **3433**

SCHAULADE, DIE. (GW) **2593**

SCHIFFBAUFORSCHUNG. (GW/0036-6056). **4183**

SCHOHARIE COUNTY HISTORICAL REVIEW. (US/0361-8528). **2759**

SCHOLARLY PUBLISHING. (CN/0036-634X). **4819**

SCHOLASTIC CHOICES. (US/0883-475X). **2792**

SCHOLASTIC COACH. (US/0036-6382). **4917**

SCHOLASTIC COACH AND ATHLETIC DIRECTOR. (US/1077-5625). **4917**

SCHOMBURG CENTER JOURNAL, THE. (US/0883-3400). **2272**

SCHOOL ARTS. (US/0036-6463). **364**

SCHOOL BUSINESS AFFAIRS. (US/0036-651X). **1871**

SCHOOL COUNSELOR, THE. (US/0036-6536). **1885**

SCHOOL EN COMPUTER. (BE). **1224**

SCHOOL EN WET. (NE). **1782**

SCHOOL FOOD SERVICE JOURNAL. (US/0160-6271). **2356**

SCHOOL FOODSERVICE & NUTRITION. (US/1075-3885). **2356**

SCHOOL FOODSERVICE RESEARCH REVIEW. (US/0149-6808). **2356**

SCHOOL LAW REPORTER. (US/1059-4094). **3046**

SCHOOL LIBRARIAN, THE. (UK/0036-6595). **3247**

SCHOOL LIBRARIAN'S WORKSHOP, THE. (US/0271-3667). **3247**

SCHOOL LIBRARIES IN CANADA. (CN/0227-3780). **3248**

SCHOOL LIBRARY JOURNAL (NEW YORK, N.Y.). (US/0362-8930). Qty: 4,000 per year. **3248**

SCHOOL LIBRARY MEDIA ANNUAL. (US/0739-7712). **3248**

SCHOOL LIBRARY MEDIA QUARTERLY. (US/0278-4823). **3248**

SCHOOL MAGAZINE. (AT). **1095**

SCHOOL MUSIC NEWS, THE. (US/0036-6668). **4152**

SCHOOL ORGANISATION & MANAGEMENT ABSTRACTS. (UK/0261-2755). **1797**

SCHOOL PSYCHOLOGY REVIEW. (US/0279-6015). **4618**

SCHOOL SAFETY : NATIONAL SCHOOL SAFETY CENTER NEWSJOURNAL. (US). Qty: 2-3. **1782**

SCHOOL SCIENCE. (II/0036-679X). **5149**

SCHOOL SCIENCE AND MATHEMATICS. (US/0036-6803). **5149**

SCHOOL SCIENCE REVIEW. (UK/0036-6811). **5149**

SCHOOL SECURITY REPORT. (US/1060-426X). Qty: 12. **1871**

SCHOOL SOCIAL WORK JOURNAL. (US/0161-5653). Qty: 4. **1871**

SCHOOLS ABROAD OF INTEREST TO AMERICANS. (US/0899-2002). **1782**

SCHOOLS (OLYMPIA, WASH.). (US). **1847**

SCHRIFTTUM DER AGRARWIRTSCHAFT, DAS. (AU/0036-6986). **132**

SCHUHTECHNIK 1987. (GW/0933-808X). **1087**

SCHULDEN DES LANDES, DER GEMEINDEN, SAMTGEMEINDEN UND LANDKREISE. (GW). **4747**

SCHUTZ SOCIETY REPORTS : NEWSLETTER OF THE AMERICAN HEINRICH SCHUTZ SOCIETY. (US). **4152**

SCHWEISSEN UND SCHNEIDEN. (GW/0036-7184). **4027**

SCHWEIZER ALUMINIUM RUNDSCHAU. (SZ/0036-7257). **4018**

SCHWEIZER INGENIEUR UND ARCHITEKT. (SZ/0251-0960). **1995**

SCHWEIZER LOGISTIK-KATALOG / SWISS LOGISITICS CATALOGUE. (SZ). **1929**

SCHWEIZER MONATSSCHRIFT FUER ZAHNMEDIZIN. (SZ/1011-4203). **1335**

SCHWEIZER SPITAL. (SZ/0304-4432). **3792**

SCHWEIZER VOLKSKUNDE. (SZ/0048-9522). Qty: 10-15. **2324**

SCHWEIZER WAFFEN-MAGAZIN. (SZ/0253-4878). **4056**

SCHWEIZERISCHE APOTHEKER-ZEITUNG. GIORNALE SVIZZERO DI FARMACIA. (SZ/0036-7508). **4329**

SCHWEIZERISCHE MEDIZINISCHE WOCHENSCHRIFT. (SZ/0036-7672). **3639**

SCHWEIZERISCHE RUNDSCHAU FUER MEDIZIN PRAXIS. (SZ/1013-2058). **3801**

SCHWEIZERISCHE ZEITSCHRIFT FUER GESCHICHTE. (SZ/0036-7834). **2708**

SCHWEIZERISCHE ZEITSCHRIFT FUER SPORTMEDIZIN. (SZ/0036-7885). **3955**

SCHWEIZERISCHE ZEITSCHRIFT FUER VOLKSWIRTSCHAFT UND STATISTIK. (SZ/0303-9692). **1538**

SCHWEIZERISCHES ARCHIV FUER VOLKSKUNDE. (SZ/0036-794X). Qty: 40-50. **2324**

SCHWEIZERISCHES IDIOTIKON. WORTERBUCH DER SCHWEIZERDEUTSCHEN SPRACHE. (SZ). **3319**

SCHWENKFELDIAN, THE. (US/0036-8032). **5067**

SCI RECORD BOOK OF TROPHY ANIMALS, THE. (US/0195-7538). **4878**

SCI-TECH NEWS. (US/0036-8059). **3248**

SCIENCE ACTIVITIES. (US/0036-8121). **5150**

SCIENCE AND CHILDREN. (US/0036-8148). **1904**

SCIENCE & CULTURE. (II/0036-8156). **5150**

SCIENCE & GOVERNMENT REPORT. (US/0048-9581). **5150**

SCIENCE AND INDUSTRY. (NE/0925-5842). **5150**

SCIENCE & PUBLIC POLICY. (UK/0302-3427). **4685**

SCIENCE & RELIGION NEWS. (US/1048-8642). Qty: 70. **4995**

SCIENCE AND SOCIETY (NEW YORK, 1936). (US/0036-8237). **5218**

SCIENCE & TECHNOLOGY LIBRARIES (NEW YORK, N.Y.). (US/0194-262X). **3248**

SCIENCE AS CULTURE. (UK/0950-5431). **5151**

SCIENCE BOOKS & FILMS. (US/0098-342X). **5151**

SCIENCE BUDGET. (IE/0332-1126). **5151**

SCIENCE BULLETIN (OTTAWA). (CN/1184-227X). **4495**

SCIENCE ET COMPORTEMENT. (CN/0841-7741). **4618**

SCIENCE ET VIE. (FR/0036-8369). **5151**

SCIENCE FICTION. (AT/0314-6677). Qty: 10-20. **3434**

SCIENCE FICTION AGE (HERNDON, VA.). (US/1065-1829). **3434**

SCIENCE FICTION AND FANTASY BOOK REVIEW INDEX. (US/1046-1922). **3459**

SCIENCE FICTION CHRONICLE. (US/0195-5365). **3434**

SCIENCE FICTION EYE. (US/1071-3018). Qty: 40-60/year. **3434**

SCIENCE-FICTION STUDIES. (CN/0091-7729). **3434**

SCIENCE FOR PEOPLE (LONDON). (UK/0144-8447). **5151**

SCIENCE/HEALTH ABSTRACTS. (US/0890-7110). **5152**

SCIENCE IN NEW GUINEA. (PP/0310-4303). Qty: varies. **5152**

SCIENCE IN PARLIAMENT. (UK/0263-6271). Qty: 5. **5152**

SCIENCE IS ELEMENTARY. (US/1064-7015). **5152**

SCIENCE LINK. (CN/0821-7246). **2924**

SCIENCE NEWS (WASHINGTON). (US/0036-8423). **5152**

SCIENCE OF COMPUTER PROGRAMMING. (NE/0167-6423). **1281**

SCIENCE OF THE TOTAL ENVIRONMENT, THE. (NE/0048-9697). **2181**

SCIENCE OF TSUNAMI HAZARDS. (US/8755-6839). **1456**

SCIENCE REPORTER. (II/0036-8512). Qty: 48. **5153**

SCIENCE SCOPE (WASHINGTON, D.C.). (US/0887-2376). **5153**

SCIENCE TEACHER (WASHINGTON, D.C.), THE. (US/0036-8555). **5153**

SCIENCE, TECHNOLOGY & SOCIETY. (US/0275-8075). Qty: 75-100. **5153**

SCIENCE TODAY. (UK). **5153**

SCIENCE TRENDS. (US/0043-0749). **5153**

SCIENCE (WASHINGTON, D.C.). (US/0036-8075). **5154**

SCIENCES DES ALIMENTS. (FR/0240-8813). **2356**

SCIENCES ET TECHNIQUES DE L'EAU. (CN). **1418**

SCIENCES ET TECHNIQUES EN PERSPECTIVE. (FR/0294-0264). **5154**

SCIENCES GEOLOGIQUES. BULLETIN. (FR/0302-2692). **1396**

SCIENCES (NEW YORK), THE. (US/0036-861X). **5154**

SCIENTIA CANADENSIS. (CN/0829-2507). **5154**

SCIENTIA PAEDAGOGICA EXPERIMENTALIS. (BE/0582-2351). **1783**

SCIENTIA PHARMACEUTICA. (AU/0036-8709). **4329**

SCIENTIFIC AMERICAN. (US/0036-8733). **5155**

SCIENTIFIC SLEUTHING REVIEW. (US/1043-4224). **5155**

SCIENTIFIC WORLD. (UK/0036-8857). **5156**

SCIENTIFUR. (DK/0105-2403). **3186**

SCIENTOMETRICS. (NE/0138-9130). **5156**

SCIFANT. (US/0882-1348). **5074**

SCIMA. (II). **1252**

SCINTILLA (TORONTO). (CN/0824-6009). **3434**

SCIPHERS (COLLEGE STATION, TEX.). (US/1071-4103). **2924**

SCITECH BOOK NEWS. (US/0196-6006). **5156**

SCODA NEWSLETTER : STANDING CONFERENCE ON DRUG ABUSE. (UK). **1349**

SCORE (NASHVILLE, TENN.). (US/1074-5769). Qty: 36. **4152**

SCORE (TORONTO). (CN/0711-3226). Qty: 2-4. **4917**

SCOTLANDS REGIONS. (UK/0305-6562). **4685**

SCOTS LAW TIMES; THE LANDS TRIBUNAL FOR SCOTLAND REPORTS, THE. (UK/0036-908X). **3047**

SCOTS MAGAZINE, THE. (UK). **2522**

SCOTT KING'S DIABETES INTERVIEW. (US/1058-6598). Qty: 3. **3676**

SCOTTISH-AMERICAN GENEALOGIST. (US/0271-5031). **2471**

SCOTTISH BAPTIST MAGAZINE. (UK/0036-9136). **5067**

SCOTTISH BEEKEEPER. (UK/0370-8918). **132**

SCOTTISH BIRDS. (UK/0036-9144). **5620**

SCOTTISH BOOK COLLECTOR. (UK/0954-8769). **4819**

SCOTTISH BUILDING AND CIVIL ENGINEERING YEAR BOOK. (UK/0085-6002). **627**

SCOTTISH BULLETIN OF EVANGELICAL THEOLOGY, THE. (UK/0265-4539). **4995**

SCOTTISH EDUCATIONAL REVIEW. (UK/0141-9072). **1783**

SCOTTISH GENEALOGIST, THE. (UK/0300-337X). Qty: 6. **2472**

SCOTTISH GEOGRAPHICAL MAGAZINE. (UK/0036-9225). **2576**

SCOTTISH HISTORICAL REVIEW, THE. (UK/0036-9241). **2709**

SCOTTISH JOURNAL OF GEOLOGY. (UK/0036-9276). **1396**

SCOTTISH JOURNAL OF PHYSICAL EDUCATION. (UK/0140-2315). **1858**

SCOTTISH JOURNAL OF POLITICAL ECONOMY. (UK/0036-9292). **1595**

SCOTTISH JOURNAL OF RELIGIOUS STUDIES, THE. (UK/0143-8301). Qty: 12. **4995**

SCOTTISH JOURNAL OF THEOLOGY. (UK/0036-9306). **4995**

SCOTTISH LANGUAGE. (UK/0264-0198). **3319**

SCOTTISH LAW GAZETTE, THE. (UK/0036-9314). **3047**

SCOTTISH LIBRARIES (1987). (UK/0950-0189). **3248**

SCOTTISH LITERARY JOURNAL. (UK/0305-0785). **3434**

SCOTTISH LITERARY JOURNAL. THE YEAR'S WORK IN SCOTTISH LITERARY AND LINGUISTIC STUDIES. (UK). **3319**

SCOTTISH PHOTOGRAPHY BULLETIN. (UK/0269-1787). **4376**

SCOTTISH PLANNING LAW & PRACTICE. (UK/0144-8196). **3047**

SCOTTISH RITE JOURNAL. (US/0279-7011). **5236**

SCOTTISH SLAVONIC REVIEW. (UK/0265-3273). **3319**

SCOTTISH STUDIES (EDINBURGH). (UK/0036-9411). **3434**

SCOTTISH TRADITION. (CN/0703-1580). **2545**

SCP JOURNAL. (US/0883-1300). **Qty: varies. 4995**

SCP NEWSLETTER. (US/0883-1319). **4996**

SCRAP PROCESSING AND RECYCLING. (US/0898-0756). **4018**

SCREAMING EAGLE, THE. (US). **4056**

SCREEN. (UK/0036-9543). **4077**

SCREEN ACTOR HOLLYWOOD. (US/0890-5266). **4077**

SCREEN DIGEST. (UK). **1139**

SCREEN PRINTING. (US). **4569**

SCREEN PRINTING TECHNIQUES. (US/0362-160X). **4569**

SCRIBE (VANCOUVER). (CN/0824-6947). **2760**

SCRIBLERIAN AND THE KIT-CATS, THE. (US/0190-731X). **2854**

SCRIP (RICHMOND). (UK/0143-7690). **4329**

SCRIPT (PARIS, 1988). (FR/0993-2097). **Qty: 500-1000. 4077**

SCRIPTA MEDITERRANEA. (CN/0226-8418). **2854**

SCRIPTA THEOLOGICA. (SP/0036-9764). **4996**

SCRIPTURA. (SA/0254-1807). **5019**

SCRIPTURE BULLETIN. (UK/0036-9780). **5019**

SCRIPTWRITERS MARKET. (US/0748-6456). **4077**

SCRIVENER. (CN/0227-5090). **3435**

SCROLL (MALVERNE, N.Y.). (US/0890-524X). **1292**

SCULPTURE REVIEW. (US/0747-5284). **364**

SCUOLA CATTOLICA, LA. (IT/0036-9810). **5036**

SEA BREEZES. (UK/0036-9977). **5455**

SEA CHEST, THE. (US/0582-3471). **2760**

SEA FRONTIERS (1988). (US/0897-2249). **1456**

SEA HERITAGE NEWS. (US/0270-5524). **2545**

SEA HISTORY GAZETTE. (US/0896-1646). **5455**

SEA PEN. (CN/0700-9275). **557**

SEA POWER (1971). (US/0199-1337). **4183**

SEA SWALLOW, THE. (UK). **Qty: 2-3. 5620**

SEA TECHNOLOGY. (US/0093-3651). **1456**

SEA WIND. (CN/1011-1603). **2205**

SEAFARER (LONDON). (UK/0037-007X). **Qty: 200. 4183**

SEAFDEC NEWSLETTER / SOUTHEAST ASIAN FISHERIES DEVELOPMENT CENTER. (TH). **2313**

SEAFOOD BUSINESS (CAMDEN, ME.). (US/0889-3217). **2357**

SEAFOOD INTERNATIONAL. (UK/0268-1293). **2313**

SEAFOOD LEADER. (US/0744-4664). **2313**

SEAMAN, THE. (UK/0037-0142). **1710**

SEAPORT. (US/0743-6246). **Qty: 8-9. 2760**

SEAPORTS AND THE SHIPPING WORLD. (CN/0037-0150). **5455**

SEAPOSTER. (US). **2787**

SEARCH AND RESCUE MAGAZINE. (US/0092-5136). **4802**

SEARCH AND SEIZURE LAW REPORT. (US/0095-1005). **3047**

SEARCH (DUBLIN). (IE/0332-0618). **4996**

SEARCH MAGAZINE (AMHERST). (US/0037-0290). **35**

SEARCH (MIAMI), THE. (US/0272-5827). **2664**

SEARCH (NASHVILLE). (US/0048-9913). **5067**

SEARCH (NILES, ILL.). (US/0277-5727). **2472**

SEARCH (SANTA CLARA, CALIF.). (US/0886-1560). **3248**

SEARCH (SYDNEY). (AT/0004-9549). **5156**

SEARCH YORK. (UK/0958-3467). **5307**

SEARCHERS & RESEARCHERS OF ELLIS COUNTY, TEXAS. (US/0732-2879). **2472**

SEARCHING TOGETHER. (US/0739-2281). **5067**

SEARCHLIGHT (LONDON). (UK/0262-4591). **Qty: 4-6. 5257**

SEARMG NEWSLETTER. (AT/0158-1953). **2854**

SEASONS. (CN/0227-793X). **4171**

SEATTLE HOME AND GARDEN. (US). **2431**

SEATTLE TIMES, THE. (US/0745-9696). **5762**

SEATTLE'S CHILD. (US/1064-4512). **Qty: varies. 2286**

SEAWAYS (1980). (UK/0144-1019). **4183**

SEC REPORT. (US/0885-9078). **4917**

SECHERESSE MONTROUGE. (FR/1147-7806). **1360**

SECHZIG - NA UND ?. (GW). **5181**

SECOL REVIEW, THE. (US/0730-6245). **3320**

SECOND BOAT, THE. (US/0274-6441). **Qty: 6-12. 2472**

SECOND CENTURY (ABILENE, TEX.), THE. (US/0276-7899). **4996**

SECOND LANGUAGE RESEARCH. (UK/0267-6583). **3320**

SECOND OPINION (PARK RIDGE, ILL.). (US/0890-1570). **3640**

SECOND OPINION (SAN FRANCISCO, CALIF.). (US/0748-9528). **4802**

SECOND STONE, THE. (US/1047-3971). **Qty: 6. 2796**

SECONDS (NEW YORK, N.Y.). (US/1052-5025). **4152**

SECRET PARIS. (FR/1163-2747). **Qty: 6. 710**

SECRETARY, THE. (US/0037-0622). **710**

SECTION A - REVUE D'ARCHITECTURE. (CN/0715-9781). **308**

SECURED LENDER, THE. (US/0888-255X). **811**

SECURITE, ENVIRONEMENT. (SZ/1015-6356). **2870**

SECURITE ET MEDECINE DU TRAVAIL. (FR/0755-2386). **Qty: 4. 2870**

SECURITY AFFAIRS. (US/0889-4876). **4535**

SECURITY LETTER. (US/0363-4922). **Qty: 23/yr. 947**

SECURITY MANAGEMENT (ARLINGTON, VA.). (US/0145-9406). **885**

SECURITY TRADERS HANDBOOK. (US/0885-2693). **1520**

SEDIMENTOLOGY. (UK/0037-0746). **1410**

SEDONA RED ROCK NEWS. (US/1044-7555). **5630**

SEE THE MUSIC. (CN/0826-5216). **4152**

SEEDBED. (US/0363-5074). **Qty: varies. 4996**

SEEDHEAD NEWS, THE. (US). **Qty: 5-7. 2431**

SEEDS & SOWERS. (CN/0843-5197). **1905**

SEEDS (DECATUR, GA.). (US/0194-4495). **Qty: 15-20. 2912**

SEFARAD. (SP/0037-0894). **5052**

SEGNO PESCARA. (IT/0391-3910). **330**

SEGURIDAD SOCIAL. (MX/0379-0304). **1710**

SEIDENKI GAKKAI KOEN RONBUNSHU : SEIDENKI GAKKAI ZENKOKU TAIKAI. (JA). **4445**

SEIJI HANDOBUKKU. (JA). **4495**

SEISMOLOGICAL RESEARCH LETTERS. (US/0895-0695). **1397**

SEL & POIVRE. (CN/0714-6116). **5073**

SELECCIONES AVICOLAS. (SP/0582-4818). **221**

SELECT : THE PHOTOGRAPHIC SHOWCASE. (GW). **4376**

SELECTED LIST OF ACQUISITIONS CATALOGED. (US/0537-9342). **3047**

SELECTED MONOGRAPHS ON TAXATION. (NE). **4747**

SELECTED PAPERS FROM THE WEST VIRGINIA SHAKESPEARE AND RENAISSANCE ASSOCIATION. (US/0885-9574). **Qty: 1-3. 3435**

SELECTED REFERENCE. (US). **1626**

SELECTIEF DEN HAAG. 1991. (NE/0926-4183). **5156**

SELECTION DE FILMS POUR LA JEUNESSE. (FR). **1069**

SELECTIONS FROM THE ANNALES, ECONOMIES, SOCIETES, CIVILISATIONS. (US). **5218**

SELEZIONE VETERINARIA. (IT/0037-1521). **5521**

SELF ADHESIVE MATERIALS & MARKETS BULLETIN. (UK). **4222**

SELF PUBLISHING UPDATE. (US/0736-1882). **710**

SELF-REALIZATION. (US/0037-1564). **4360**

SELLERS LETTERS. (US/0740-2740). **2472**

SELLING TO THE OTHER EDUCATIONAL MARKETS. (US/1054-4593). **936**

SEMAINE VETERINAIRE, LA. (FR/0396-5015). **5521**

SEMANA. (IS). **2508**

SEMANA MEDICA (BUENOS AIRES, ARGENTINA : 1894). (AG). **3640**

SEMANTIKOS. (FR/0395-3556). **3320**

SEMENCES ET PROGRES. (FR/0395-8930). **5156**

SEMICONDUCTOR INTERNATIONAL. (US/0163-3767). **2080**

SEMICONDUCTOR WORLD. (JA). **2108**

SEMICONDUCTORS AND INSULATORS. (US/0309-5991). **4421**

SEMINAR (TORONTO). (CN/0037-1939). **3320**

SEMINARIUM. (VC/0582-6314). **5036**

SEMINARS IN COLON & RECTAL SURGERY. (US/1043-1489). **3974**

SEMINARS IN HEARING. (US/0734-0451). **3891**

SEMINARS IN INTERVENTIONAL RADIOLOGY. (US/0739-9529). **3946**

SEMINARS IN LIVER DISEASE. (US/0272-8087). **3801**

SEMINARS IN NEUROLOGY. (US/0271-8235). **3846**

SEMINARS IN REPRODUCTIVE ENDOCRINOLOGY. (US/0734-8630). **3733**

SEMINARS IN RESPIRATORY MEDICINE. (US/0192-9755). **3952**

SEMINARS IN SPEECH AND LANGUAGE. (US/0734-0478). **3320**

SEMINARS IN THROMBOSIS AND HEMOSTASIS. (US/0094-6176). **3774**

SEMINOLE TRIBUNE, THE. (US/0891-8252). **5651**

SEMIOSIS. (GW/0170-219X). **3320**

SEMIOTEXTE (NEW YORK). (US/0093-9579). **5257**

SEMIOTIC REVIEW OF BOOKS. (CN/0847-1622). **Qty: 30. 1121**

SEMIOTICA. (NE/0037-1998). **3320**

SEMPER REFORMANDA. (US/1065-3783). **Qty: 3-6. 4996**

SENIOR DIGEST. (US). **Qty: 100. 5181**

SENIOR MEDIA GUIDE. (US/1050-3803). **936**

SENIOR NEWS. (SA/0037-2234). **Qty: 2. 5181**

SENIOR SCENE. (AT). **5182**

SENIOR WORLD QUARTERLY. (CN/0714-8798). **5182**

SENIORS TODAY. (CN/0715-4046). **Qty: 2-10. 5182**

SENSIBLE SOUND, THE. (US/0199-4654). **5318**

SENSOR BUSINESS DIGEST. (US/1060-1902). **Qty: 3-4/year. 3487**

SENSOR REVIEW. (UK/0260-2288). **5157**

SENSORS (PETERSBOROUGH, N.H.). (US/0746-9462). **1996**

SENTIER CHASSE-PECHE. (CN/0711-7957). **4878**

SENTINEL (CHICAGO, ILL.). (US/0037-2331). **5662**

SENTINEL-RECORD, THE. (US). **5632**

SENTINEL (TORONTO. 1957). (CN/0049-0202). **5067**

SENZA SORDINO. (US). **4152**

SEPARATION AND PURIFICATION METHODS (SOFTCOVER ED.). (US/0360-2540). **1029**

SEPARATION SCIENCE AND TECHNOLOGY. (US/0149-6395). **1029**

SEPARATIONS TECHNOLOGY. (US/0956-9618). **1996**

SEPTS (SAINT PAUL, MINN.), THE. (US/1049-1783). **Qty: 6-10. 2472**

SEQUENCES. (FR/0559-4871). **3471**

SEQUENTIAL ANALYSIS. (US/0747-4946). **3533**

SEQUOIA (SAN FRANCISCO). (US/0199-8153). **Qty: 12-20. 4996**

SER-BULLETIN. (NE/0920-4849). **1710**

SERB WORLD U.S.A. (US/8756-5579). **2760**

SERBIAN STUDIES. (US/0742-3330). **2709**

SERIALS LIBRARIAN, THE. (US/0361-526X). **3249**

SERIALS REVIEW. (US/0098-7913). **3249**

SERIE CIENTIFICA. INSTITUTO ANTARTICO CHILENO. (CL/0073-9871). **1360**

SERIE: PRODUCCION ANIMAL. (SP). **133**

SERIES IN PSYCHOSOCIAL EPIDEMIOLOGY. (US/1044-5633). **3936**

SERIGRAFIA (MILANO, ITALY). (IT). **4569**

SERLIN REPORT ON PARALLEL PROCESSING, THE. (US/0894-2226). **1202**

SERRA D'OR. (SP/0037-2501). **3352**

SERTOMAN. (US/0744-2807). **5307**

SERVAMUS. (SA). **3176**

SERVANT (THREE HILLS). (CN/0848-1741). Qty: 24. **4996**

SERVICE BUSINESS. (US/0736-5764). **710**

SERVICE DEALER'S NEWSLETTER. SDN. (US/0739-6236). **5739**

SERVICE NEWS PARIS. (FR/1144-2433). **886**

SERVICE STATION MANAGEMENT. (US/0488-3896). **5425**

SERVICES MARKETING NEWSLETTER. (US/0891-0952). **886**

SERVIZI SOCIALI. (IT). **4685**

SESAME (MEDFORD, OR.). (US/0883-1467). **4819**

SETON HALL JOURNAL OF SPORT LAW. (US/1059-4310). **3048**

SETON HALL LAW REVIEW. (US/0586-5964). **3048**

SETON HALL LEGISLATIVE JOURNAL. (US/0361-8951). **3048**

SEVENTEENTH-CENTURY FRENCH STUDIES. (UK/0265-1068). **3435**

SEVENTEENTH CENTURY NEWS. (US/0037-3028). **3435**

SEW. (NE). **3136**

SEW IT BEGINS. (CN/0821-4247). **5186**

SEW IT SEAMS. (US/0888-577X). **5186**

SEWANEE REVIEW, THE. (US/0037-3052). **3352**

SEWARD PHOENIX LOG. (US). **5629**

SEX EDUCATION COALITION NEWS. (US/0741-9686). **1783**

SEXTANT (WASHINGTON, D.C.). (US/0731-2180). **1272**

SEXUAL AND MARITAL THERAPY. (UK/0267-4653). **2286**

SEXUAL COERCION & ASSAULT. (US/0884-4372). **5257**

SEYBOLD REPORT ON DESKTOP PUBLISHING, THE. (US/0736-7260). **1263**

SEZ. (US/0190-3640). **3435**

SFI BULLETIN. (US/0085-6592). **4917**

SFINX. (DK/0105-7618). **2629**

SHADES. (CN/0228-3115). **4152**

SHAHID (TEHRAN, IRAN : 1983). (IR). **2493**

SHAIR INTERNATIONAL FORUM. (CN/1185-3158). Qty: 5-6. **2545**

SHAKER MESSENGER, THE. (US/0270-9368). **2760**

SHAKER QUARTERLY, THE. (US/0582-9348). **4997**

SHAKESPEARE BULLETIN. (US/0748-2558). Qty: 25-30. **5368**

SHAKESPEARE IN SOUTHERN AFRICA : JOURNAL OF THE SHAKESPEARE SOCIETY OF SOUTHERN AFRICA. (SA/1011-582X). **5368**

SHAKESPEARE NEWSLETTER, THE. (US/0037-3214). **3352**

SHAKESPEARE ON FILM NEWSLETTER. (US/0739-6570). **3435**

SHAKESPEARE QUARTERLY. (US/0037-3222). **3435**

SHAKESPEARE SURVEY (CAMBRIDGE). (UK/0080-9152). **434**

SHAKHTNYI I KARERNYI TRANSPORT. (RU). **2151**

SHALE SHAKER. (US/0037-3257). **1397**

SHAMAN'S DRUM. (US/0887-8897). **4997**

SHAMROCK TEXAN, THE. (US). **5754**

SHAN CHA. (CC). **3435**

SHAN-HSI SHIH TA HSUEH PAO. CHE HSUEH SHE HUI KO HSUEH PAN. (CC). **5218**

SHANG-HAI CHEN CHIU TSA CHIH. (CC). **3640**

SHANG-HAI WEN HSUEH. (CC). **3436**

SHANTIH. (US/0037-329X). **3436**

SHAONIEN ZHONGGUO (SAN FRANCISCO, CALIF.). (US/0749-7679). **5640**

SHAPE (WOODLAND HILLS, CALIF.). (US/0744-5121). **2601**

SHARE INTERNATIONAL. (NE/0169-1341). **4186**

SHARE (TORONTO). (CN/0709-4647). **5794**

SHAREWARE MAGAZINE. (US/1042-0681). **1202**

SHARING IDEAS. (US/0886-1501). **2545**

SHARING THE PRACTICE. (US/0193-8274). Qty: 50. **4997**

SHARING THE VICTORY. (US/0745-1245). **4917**

SHAVIAN (LONDON). (UK/0037-3346). Qty: 8-10/yr. **3436**

SHAW. (US/0741-5842). **3352**

SHEEP CANADA MAGAZINE. (CN/0702-8881). **221**

SHEEP MAGAZINE. (US/0279-9200). **221**

SHEEP RETURNS. (NZ). **221**

SHEET METAL INDUSTRIES. (UK/0037-3435). **4019**

SHEET MUSIC EXCHANGE, THE. (US/0741-7780). **4152**

SHELBY COUNTY REPORTER (1955). (US/1063-9489). **5628**

SHELBY EXCHANGE. (US). **2472**

SHELLS AND SEA LIFE. (US/0747-6078). **5597**

SHELTER SENSE. (US/0734-3078). **5307**

SHELTERFORCE. (US/0885-9612). Qty: 12-15. **2835**

SHELTIE INTERNATIONAL. (US/0745-2012). Qty: 2. **4288**

SHELTIE PACESETTER. (US/0744-6608). **4288**

SHEM TOV. (US/0843-6924). **2472**

SHENANDOAH. (US/0037-3583). Qty: 4-6. **3436**

SHENATON LE-MIKRA ULE-HEKER HA-MIZRAH HA-KADUM. (IS). **5019**

SHENG LI KO HSUEH CHIN CHAN. (CC/0559-7765). **587**

SHENGWU HUAXUE ZAZHI. (CC/1000-8543). **3696**

SHEPARD'S MANUAL OF FEDERAL PRACTICE / EDITORIAL STAFF, EDITOR IN CHIEF, RUDOLPH W. FISCHER ... [ET AL.]. (US). **3051**

SHEPHERD EXPRESS. (US/1071-5185). Qty: 40. **5770**

SHEPHERD (NEW WASHINGTON, OHIO), THE. (US/8750-7897). Qty: 2. **221**

SHERIDAN PRESS (SHERIDAN, WYO.), THE. (US/1074-682X). **5772**

SHERLOCK HOLMES JOURNAL, THE. (UK/0037-3621). **3436**

SHERLOCKIAN TIDBITS. (US/1040-4937). **3436**

SHERMAN SENTINEL, THE. (US/1071-4480). Qty: 6. **2493**

SHHH. (US/0883-1688). **4393**

SHHH NEWS. (AT/1033-792X). Qty: 6. **4393**

SHIAWASSEE STEPPIN' STONES. (US/0735-8016). **2472**

SHIH CHIEH CHIH SHIH / SHIJIE ZHISHI. (CC). **4535**

SHIH CHIEH CHING CHI (CHUNG-KUO SHIH CHIEH CHING CHI HSUEH HUI). (CC). **1583**

SHIH CHIEH WEN HSUEH. (CC). **3436**

SHIH HSUEH CHING PAO / CHUNG-KUO SHIH HSUEH HUI, CHUNG-KUO LI SHIH HSUEH NIEN CHIEN PIEN CHI PU PIEN. (CC). **2664**

SHIH TZU REPORTER, THE. (US/1040-5801). **4288**

SHIN BOEI RONSHU. (JA). **4057**

SHINGLE, THE. (US/0037-377X). **3055**

SHINING LIGHT. (US). Qty: 6/year. **4997**

SHINING STAR (CARTHAGE, ILL.). (US/0884-5514). **1905**

SHIPBROKER, THE. (UK/0142-6680). **5456**

SHIPCARE & MARITIME MANAGEMENT. (UK/0263-7944). **5456**

SHIPMATE (ANNAPOLIS, MD.). (US/0488-6720). **4183**

SHIPPING & MARINE INDUSTRIES JOURNAL. (II/0970-0285). **5456**

SHIPPING STATISTICS. (GW). **5402**

SHIPS ATLAS, THE. (UK). **5456**

SHIPS MONTHLY. (UK/0037-394X). **4183**

SH'MA (PORT WASHINGTON, N.Y.). (US/0049-0385). **4361**

SHOAL LAKE STAR. (CN). Qty: 4. **5794**

SHOCK AND VIBRATION DIGEST, THE. (US/0583-1024). **2006**

SHOFAR (MELVILLE, N.Y.). (US/0748-9706). Qty: varies. **1069**

SHOFAR (WEST LAFAYETTE, IND.). (US/0882-8539). Qty: 60/yr. **5052**

SHOKURYO KEIZAI HAKUSHO. (JA). **2357**

SHOKURYO SEISAKU KENKYU. (JA/0387-9836). **2357**

SHONI GEKA. (JA/0385-6313). **3911**

SHOOTER'S BIBLE, THE. (US/0080-9365). **4917**

SHOOTING INDUSTRY, THE. (US/0037-4148). **4917**

SHOOTING SPORTS RETAILER. (US/0887-9397). **957**

SHOOTING SPORTSMAN (WILLIAMSPORT, PA.). (US/1050-5717). **4878**

SHOOTING STAR REVIEW. (US/0892-1407). **3436**

SHORT BOOK REVIEWS / INTERNATIONAL STATISTICAL INSTITUTE. (NE). **4822**

SHORT LINE, THE. (US/0199-4050). Qty: 6. **5436**

SHORT STORY (COLUMBIA, S.C.). (US/1052-648X). Qty: 2. **3436**

SHORTHORN, THE. (US/0892-6603). **1095**

SHOSHI SAKUIN TEMBO. (JA). **3249**

SHOW HORSE (BANGOR, ME.). (US/8755-3929). **2802**

SHOW MUSIC. (US/8755-9560). **4153**

SHOWCASE (MINNEAPOLIS). (US/0196-1586). **4153**

SHROPSHIRE FAMILY HISTORY JOURNAL. (UK/0261-135X). **2472**

SHROUD SPECTRUM INTERNATIONAL. (US/0738-6524). **5157**

SHU FA. (CC). **382**

SHUPIHUI. (PE/0254-2021). **2273**

SHUTTERBUG. (US/0895-321X). **4376**

SHUTTLE, SPINDLE & DYEPOT. (US/0049-0423). **375**

SI QUE. (CN/0229-5776). **3436**

SI YU YAN. (CH/0258-8412). **2854**

SIAJ - JOURNAL OF THE SINGAPORE INSTITUTE OF ARCHITECTS. (SI/0049-0520). **308**

SIALIA. (US/0890-7021). **5597**

SIAM NEWS : A PUBLICATION OF SOCIETY FOR INDUSTRIAL AND APPLIED MATHEMATICS. (US). **3535**

SIAM REVIEW. (US/0036-1445). **3535**

SIBBALD GUIDE TO THE TEXAS TOP TWO-FIFTY, THE. (US/0278-3266). **710**

SIBLING INFORMATION NETWORK NEWSLETTER. (US). **2286**

SIC. (VE/0049-0431). **4496**

SICANGU SUN TIMES. (US/1070-7786). **2273**

SICHERHEITSBEAUFTRAGTER. (GW/0300-3337). **3176**

SICHERHEITSINGENIEUR. (GW/0300-3329). **2870**

SICILIA PARRA. (US/8755-6987). **2273**

SIDA, BOTANICAL MISCELLANY. (US/0883-1475). **527**

SIDA, CONTRIBUTIONS TO BOTANY. (US/0036-1488). **527**

SIDA RAPPORT. (SW/0282-6011). **2912**

SIDE-SADDLE NEWS. (US/0744-3056). **2802**

SIDE STREETS OF THE WORLD. (US/0741-7624). **5491**

SIDIC (ENGLISH ED.). (IT). **4997**

SIDNEY ARGUS-HERALD, THE. (US). **5672**

SIECUS REPORT. (US/0091-3995). **5188**

SIEMENS REVIEW. (GW/0302-2528). **2081**

SIERRA. (US/0161-7362). **2205**

SIERRA COUNTY SENTINEL. (US). **5713**

SIERRA HERITAGE. (US/0886-6503). **Qty:** 6-10 per year. **5491**

SIFRUT YELADIM VA-NOAR. (IS/0334-276X). **1069**

SIGHT AND SOUND (LONDON). (UK/0037-4806). **Qty:** 144. **4078**

SIGHTHOUND REVIEW. (US/8750-1953). **4288**

SIGN LANGUAGE STUDIES. (US/0302-1475). **3321**

SIGN WORLD. (UK/0049-0466). **766**

SIGNAL. (US). **3436**

SIGNAL (1950). (US/0037-4938). **1121**

SIGNAL (LISBON, OHIO). (US/0893-4592). **5730**

SIGNAL PROCESSING. (NE/0165-1684). **2081**

SIGNAL PROCESSING. IMAGE COMMUNICATION. (NE/0923-5965). **2081**

SIGNAL TRANSDUCTION & CYCLIC NUCLEOTIDES. (UK/0964-7589). **493**

SIGNAL UND DRAHT. (GW/0037-4997). **5436**

SIGNOS UNIVERSITARIOS : REVISTA DE LA UNIVERSIDAD DEL SALVADOR. (AG). **Qty:** 80. **1847**

SIGNPOST. (UK). **2809**

SIGNUM. (FI/0355-0036). **3249**

SIGUCCS NEWSLETTER. (US/0736-6892). **1244**

SIIRTOLAISUUS / SIIRTOLAISUUSINSTITUUTTI. (FI/0355-3779). **1921**

SIKH COURIER, THE. (UK). **Qty:** 6. **4997**

SIKH REVIEW, THE. (II/0037-5128). **Qty:** 24. **4997**

SIKSI : THE NORDIC ART REVIEW. (FI/0782-7423). **330**

SILENT NEWS. (US/0049-0490). **5721**

SILICATES INDUSTRIELS. (BE/0037-5225). **2594**

SILLIMAN JOURNAL. (PH/0037-5284). **2854**

SILVAE GENETICA. (GW/0037-5349). **528**

SILVER (WHITTIER, CALIF.). (US/0899-6105). **Qty:** 6. **4019**

SILVERFISH REVIEW. (US/0164-1085). **Qty:** varies. **3437**

SIMAN KERIAH. (IS). **3352**

SIMANTIKA. (US/8755-7517). **3437**

SIMIOLUS. (NE/0037-5411). **364**

SIMMENTAL SHIELD. (US/0192-3072). **221**

SIMMONS REVIEW, THE. (US/0049-0512). **1095**

SIMON STEVIN. (BE/0037-5454). **3535**

SIMPLY STATED. (US/0731-2016). **3437**

SIMSBURY NEWS, THE. (US/0891-9542). **5646**

SIMULATION & GAMING. (US/1046-8781). **1283**

SIMULATION/GAMES FOR LEARNING. (UK/0142-9361). **1905**

SIMULATION PRACTICE AND THEORY. (NE/0928-4869). **1244**

SIMULATION (SAN DIEGO, CALIF.). (US/0037-5497). **1283**

SINAI. (IS). **5052**

SING OUT. (US/0037-5624). **Qty:** varies. **4153**

SING OUT EAST DONCASTER. (AT/0818-0555). **4153**

SINGAPORE BUSINESS. (SI/0129-2951). **851**

SINGAPORE JOURNAL OF EDUCATION. (SI/0129-4776). **1784**

SINGAPORE JOURNAL OF OBSTETRICS & GYNAECOLOGY. (SI/0129-3273). **Qty:** 1-2. **3768**

SINGAPORE LAW REVIEW. (SI/0080-9705). **3055**

SINGAPORE STAMP CATALOGUE IN FULL COLOUR. (MY/0127-1563). **2787**

SINGAPORE STATISTICAL NEWS : SSN. (SI/0217-4316). **5338**

SINGENDE KIRCHE. (AU/0037-5721). **4153**

SINGLE ADULT MINISTRY INFORMATION. (US/0887-1167). **4997**

SINGLE HOUND. (US/1044-8934). **3471**

SINGLE LIVING MAGAZINE : AN IOWA PERSPECTIVE. (US). **2493**

SINGLE PARENT, THE. (US/0037-5748). **2286**

SINGLELIFE (MILWAUKEE, WIS.). (US/8756-0380). **Qty:** 6. **2493**

SINGMUL HAKHOE CHI. (KO/0583-421X). **528**

SINISTER WISDOM. (US/0196-1853). **Qty:** 1-6. **2796**

SINO-AMERICAN RELATIONS. (CH). **4535**

SINO-JAPANESE STUDIES. (US). **Qty:** varies. **2664**

SINO-WESTERN CULTURAL RELATIONS JOURNAL. (US/1041-875X). **4535**

SINTESE. (BL/0103-4332). **5219**

SINTEZA. (XV/0049-0601). **Qty:** 6000. **364**

SIPAPU. (US/0037-5837). **Qty:** 10. **3352**

SISKIYOU COUNTY (CA) SERIES. (US/1040-3620). **2545**

SISKIYOU PIONEER IN FOLKLORE, FACT AND FICTION, THE. (US/0196-0725). **2324**

SISMODINAMICA (DURHAM, N.H.). (US/1051-6441). **2031**

SISTEMA (MADRID). (SP/0210-0223). **5219**

SISTEMI INTELLIGENTI. (IT). **1217**

SISTERS TODAY. (US/0037-590X). **5036**

SITE REPORT, THE. (US/0275-1488). **3488**

SITE SELECTION & INDUSTRIAL DEVELOPMENT. (US/1041-3073). **4847**

SITES (NEW YORK, N.Y.). (US/0747-9409). **330**

SITREP. (CN/0316-5620). **4057**

SIXTEENTH CENTURY JOURNAL, THE. (US/0361-0160). **Qty:** 200. **2629**

SIYYON. (IS/0044-4758). **Qty:** 20-25. **5052**

SKAGIT VALLEY HERALD. (US/1071-197X). **Qty:** 12. **5762**

SKANNER, THE. (US). **5734**

SKATTERETT. (NO/0333-2810). **3055**

SKEPTIC (ALTADENA, CALIF.). (US/1063-9330). **Qty:** 30-40. **5158**

SKEPTICAL INQUIRER, THE. (US/0194-6730). **4243**

SKEPTIKER. (GW/0936-9244). **Qty:** 10-20. **4243**

SKI INDUSTRY LETTER, THE. (US/0197-3479). **Qty:** 5-10. **4918**

SKI NAUTIQUE NEWS. (CN/0714-8267). **4918**

SKI RACING. (US/0037-6213). **Qty:** 1-5. **4918**

SKILL (DETROIT, MICH.). (US/0279-2028). **1710**

SKILLINGS' MINING REVIEW. (US/0037-6329). **2151**

SKIN & ALLERGY NEWS. (US/0037-6337). **3722**

SKIN DIVER. (US/0037-6345). **4918**

SKINNED KNUCKLES. (US/0164-3509). **5425**

SKIPPING STONES. (US/0899-529X). **Qty:** 20. **1069**

SKOG & FORSKNING. (SW/1101-9506). **2395**

SKOG INDUSTRI. (NO/0800-8582). **4239**

SKOL VREIZH. (FR/0755-8848). **1784**

SKY AND TELESCOPE. (US/0037-6604). **399**

SKY CALENDAR. (US/0733-6314). **399**

SKYDIVING. (US/0192-7361). **4918**

SKYWAYS. (II). **35**

SKYWAYS (POUGHKEEPSIE, N.Y.). (US/1051-6956). **Qty:** Varies. **35**

SKYWAYS: THE JOURNAL OF THE AIRPLANE 1920-1940. (US). **35**

SL RIVISTA DI ORGANIZZAZIONE. (IT). **1520**

SLAGER. (NE). **2357**

SLAVE RIVER JOURNAL. (CN/0707-4964). **5794**

SLAVIC AND EAST EUROPEAN JOURNAL. (US/0037-6752). **Qty:** 75-100. **3321**

SLAVIC REVIEW. (US/0037-6779). **2854**

SLAVICA SLOVACA. (XO/0037-6787). **3321**

SLAVONIC AND EAST EUROPEAN REVIEW, THE. (US/0037-6795). **2629**

SLB BURIER : NACHRICHTEN AUS DER SACHSISCHEN LANDESBIBLIOTHEK DRESDEN. (GW/0863-0682). **3437**

SLEEP WATCHERS. (US/0748-5352). **3641**

SLEZSKY SBORNIK. (XR/0037-6833). **5258**

SLOAN MANAGEMENT REVIEW. (US/0019-848X). **886**

SLOANE REPORT, THE. (US/0882-5939). **1203**

SLOVAK CATHOLIC FALCON. (US/0897-8107). **5036**

SLOVAK MUSIC. (XO/0862-0407). **4153**

SLOVAK V AMERIKE. (US/0199-6819). **5739**

SLOVAKIA (WEST PATERSON, N.J.). (US/0583-5623). **2709**

SLOVANSKY PREHLED. (XR/0037-6922). **4496**

SLOVENE STUDIES. (US/0193-1075). **2710**

SLOVENIJA (SLOVENSKA IZSELJENSKA MATICA). (XV). **2273**

SLOVENSKA ARCHEOLOGIA. (XO/0037-6949). **282**

SLOVENSKA DRZAVA. (CN/0037-6957). **4496**

SLOVENSKA LITERATURA. (XO/0037-6973). **3437**

SLOVENSKA REC. (XO/0037-6981). **3322**

SLOVENSKE DIVADLO. (XO/0037-699X). **5368**

SLOVENSKY NARODOPIS. (XO/0037-7023). **245**

SLOVO A SLOVESNOST. (GW/0037-7031). **3322**

SLVGS NEWS, THE. (US/0890-1287). **Qty:** 8. **2472**

SLVGS QUERY QUARTERLY, THE. (US/1051-9912). **Qty:** 8. **2472**

SMALL BUSINESS CHRONICLE. (US). **711**

SMALL BUSINESS ECONOMICS. (NE/0921-898X). **1520**

SMALL BUSINESS FORUM. (US/1053-4695). **Qty:** 9. **711**

SMALL BUSINESS IN WESTERN AUSTRALIA. (AT/0817-5764). **Qty:** 8. **711**

SMALL BUSINESS REPORT (MONTEREY, CALIF.). (US/0164-5382). **711**

SMALL BUSINESS START-UP INDEX. (US/1049-9636). **711**

SMALL BUSINESS TODAY. (US). **711**

SMALL COMPUTERS IN THE ARTS NEWS. (US/0748-2043). **330**

SMALL ENTERPRISE DEVELOPMENT. (UK/0957-1329). **711**

SMALL FARMER'S JOURNAL. (US/0743-9989). **135**

SMALL POND MAGAZINE OF LITERATURE, THE. (US/0737-1535). **Qty:** 10-15. **3437**

SMALL PRESS. (US/0000-0485). **Qty:** 640. **4569**

SMALL PRESS BOOK REVIEW, THE. (US/8756-7202). **4832**

SMALL PRESS REVIEW. (US/0037-7228). **Qty:** 100. **3353**

SMALL SIBLINGS. (US/0897-7860). **2472**

SMALL TOWN. (US/0196-1683). **2835**

SMALL TOWN OBSERVER, THE. (US/1061-9933). **2835**

SMALL WARS AND INSURGENCIES. (UK/0959-2318). **4057**

SMALL WORLD (GUILFORD). (US/0037-7260). **2907**

SMARANDACHE FUNCTION JOURNAL. (US/1053-4792). **Qty:** (if they refer to Smarandache function). **3536**

SMART CARD MONTHLY. (US/0893-9462). **1203**

SMART CARDS AND COMMENTS. (US/0882-665X). **Qty:** 6. **1227**

SMENA. (RU). **2523**

SMITH ALUMNAE QUARTERLY. (US). **1103**

SMITH COLLEGE STUDIES IN SOCIAL WORK. (US/0037-7317). **5307**

SMITH PAPERS. (US/0278-3134). **2472**

SMITHSONIAN. (US/0037-7333). **4172**

SMITHSONIAN CONTRIBUTIONS TO THE EARTH SCIENCES. (US/0081-0274). **1360**

SMOKY MOUNTAIN HISTORICAL SOCIETY NEWSLETTER. (US/0884-6111). **2760**

SMPTE JOURNAL (1976). (US/0036-1682). **Qty:** 1/yr. **4078**

SMRC-NEWSLETTER. (US/0584-5025). **2760**

SMT TRENDS. (US/0890-7900). **Qty:** 4/year. **2081**

SNACKS MAGAZINE, THE. (UK). **2358**

SNAKE. (JA/0386-3425). **Qty:** 1-3. **5597**

SNIPS. (US/0037-7457). **Qty:** 24-36 per year. **2608**

SNOWY EGRET. (US/0037-7473). **4172**

SOARING. (US/0037-7503). **35**

SOBORNOST. (UK/0144-8722). **5040**

SOBRE LOS DERIVADOS DE LA CANA DE AZUCAR (HAVANA, CUBA : 1983). (CU). **2358**

SOCCER AMERICA. (US/0163-4070). **4919**

SOCCER DIGEST (EVANSTON). (US/0149-2365). **4919**

SOCCER JOURNAL. (US/0560-3617). **4919**

SOCCER JR. (US/1060-9911). **Qty:** 1-2. **1069**

SOCIAAL BESTEK. (NE). **5258**

SOCIAL ACTION & THE LAW. (US/0272-765X). **3056**

SOCIAL ACTION (NEW DELHI). (II/0037-7627). **Qty:** 50. **5258**

SOCIAL ANARCHISM. (US/0196-4801). **4546**

SOCIAL AND ECONOMIC STUDIES. (JM/0037-7651). **5219**

SOCIAL ANTHROPOLOGY : THE JOURNAL OF THE EUROPEAN ASSOCIATION OF SOCIAL ANTHROPOLOGISTS. (UK/0964-0282). **245**

SOCIAL BEHAVIOR AND PERSONALITY. (NZ/0301-2212). **5258**

SOCIAL BIOLOGY. (US/0037-766X). **551**

SOCIAL CHANGE. (II/0049-0857). **Qty:** 1,200. **5308**

SOCIAL CHANGE AND DEVELOPMENT. (RH). **4546**

SOCIAL CHOICE AND WELFARE. (GW/0176-1714). **5308**

SOCIAL COGNITION. (US/0278-016X). **5258**

SOCIAL CONCEPT. (US/0737-7762). **5219**

SOCIAL DEVELOPMENT ISSUES. (US/0147-1473). **5308**

SOCIAL DYNAMICS. (SA/0253-3952). **5258**

SOCIAL EDUCATION. (US/0037-7724). **5219**

SOCIAL HISTORY (LONDON). (UK/0307-1022). **2630**

SOCIAL HISTORY OF ALCOHOL REVIEW, THE. (US/0887-2783). **1349**

SOCIAL HISTORY OF MEDICINE : THE JOURNAL OF THE SOCIETY FOR THE SOCIAL HISTORY OF MEDICINE. (UK/0951-631X). **3641**

SOCIAL IDENTITIES. (UK/1350-4630). **5259**

SOCIAL INDICATORS NETWORK NEWS. (US/0885-6729). **5219**

SOCIAL INDICATORS RESEARCH. (NE/0303-8300). **5219**

SOCIAL INVENTIONS. (UK/0954-206X). **Qty:** 40. **5259**

SOCIAL JUSTICE REVIEW. (US/0037-7767). **5036**

SOCIAL JUSTICE (SAN FRANCISCO, CALIF.). (US/1043-1578). **3177**

SOCIAL ONCOLOGY NETWORK ... NEWSLETTER. (US/0882-4398). **5259**

SOCIAL POLICY. (US/0037-7783). **5259**

SOCIAL PROBLEMS. (US/0037-7791). **5220**

SOCIAL QUESTIONS BULLETIN (1981). (US/0731-0234). **Qty:** 12. **4997**

SOCIAL SCIENCE & MEDICINE (1982). (US/0277-9536). **5220**

SOCIAL SCIENCE COMPUTER REVIEW. (US/0894-4393). **1272**

SOCIAL SCIENCE HISTORY. (US/0145-5532). **5220**

SOCIAL SCIENCE JOURNAL (FORT COLLINS), THE. (US/0362-3319). **5220**

SOCIAL SCIENCE MONITOR. (US/0195-7791). **5220**

SOCIAL SCIENCE RECORD. (US/0037-7872). **5221**

SOCIAL SCIENCES. (RU/0134-5486). **5221**

SOCIAL SCIENCES IN HEALTH. (UK/1352-4127). **5221**

SOCIAL SCIENCES INDEX. (US/0094-4920). **5228**

SOCIAL SCIENCES (SWINDON, WILTSHIRE, ENGLAND). (UK). **5221**

SOCIAL SCIENTIST (NEW DELHI). (II/0970-0293). **5221**

SOCIAL SERVICES RESEARCH. (UK). **5221**

SOCIAL SERVICES RESEARCH JOURNAL. (UK/0265-6957). **5309**

SOCIAL STUDIES (PHILADELPHIA, PA. : 1953). (US/0037-7996). **5222**

SOCIAL STUDIES REVIEW (MILLBRAE, CALIF.). (US/1056-6325). **5222**

SOCIAL STUDIES REVIEW (NEW YORK, N.Y.). (US/1047-7217). **5222**

SOCIAL SURVEY. (AT/0037-8011). **5259**

SOCIAL TEXT. (US/0164-2472). **5259**

SOCIAL THEORY AND PRACTICE. (US/0037-802X). **Qty:** 3-6. **5222**

SOCIAL THOUGHT (WASHINGTON, D.C.). (US/0099-183X). **4997**

SOCIAL TRENDS. (IT). **5222**

SOCIAL WELFARE. (II/0037-8038). **5309**

SOCIAL WORK AND CHRISTIANITY. (US/0737-5778). **5309**

SOCIAL WORK IN HEALTH CARE. (US/0098-1389). **5309**

SOCIAL WORK (MANILA). (PH/0583-7057). **5309**

SOCIAL WORK (NEW YORK). (US/0037-8046). **5309**

SOCIAL WORK RESEARCH & ABSTRACTS. (US/0148-0847). **5267**

SOCIAL WORK REVIEW (NEWTON, AUCKLAND, N.Z.). (NZ/0111-7351). **Qty:** 15. **5310**

SOCIAL WORK STELLENBOSCH. (SA/0037-8054). **5310**

SOCIAL WORK TODAY. (UK/0037-8070). **5310**

SOCIAL WORK WITH GROUPS (NEW YORK. 1978). (US/0160-9513). **5310**

SOCIAL WORKER. TRAVAILLEUR SOCIAL. (CN/0037-8089). **Qty:** 9. **5310**

SOCIALISM AND DEMOCRACY. (US/0885-4300). **4546**

SOCIALISMO Y PARTICIPACION. (PE). **4546**

SOCIALIST ACTION. (UK). **4547**

SOCIALIST (LOS ANGELES, CALIF.). (US/0884-6154). **4547**

SOCIALIST PERSPECTIVE. (II). **Qty:** 2-4. **4547**

SOCIALIST REVIEW (SAN FRANCISCO). (US/0161-1801). **4547**

SOCIALIST STANDARD. (UK/0037-8259). **4547**

SOCIALIST WORKER. (UK). **Qty:** 50. **1711**

SOCIALIST WORKER (TORONTO). (CN/0836-7094). **Qty:** 12/yr. **4547**

SOCIETA E STORIA. (IT). **2630**

SOCIETY AND NATURE. (US/1062-9599). **Qty:** varies. **2182**

SOCIETY FOR GERMAN-AMERICAN STUDIES NEWSLETTER. (US/0741-5753). **2273**

SOCIETY FOR INDUSTRIAL ARCHEOLOGY NEWSLETTER. (US/0160-1067). **282**

SOCIETY FOR ORGANIC PETROLOGY NEWSLETTER, THE. (US/0743-3816). **1459**

SOCIETY (NEW BRUNSWICK). (US/0147-2011). **5222**

SOCIETY NEWS (BROOMALL, PA.). (US/8756-8861). **4153**

SOCIO-ECONOMIC PLANNING SCIENCES. (US/0038-0121). **1521**

SOCIOBIOLOGY. (US/0361-6525). **5597**

SOCIOCRITICISM. (US/1041-9861). **5260**

SOCIOLINGUISTICA. (GW/0933-1883). **3322**

SOCIOLOGIA. (XO/0049-1225). **5260**

SOCIOLOGIA INTERNATIONALIS. (GW/0038-0164). **5260**

SOCIOLOGIA RURALIS. (NE/0038-0199). **5260**

SOCIOLOGICAL ABSTRACTS. (US/0038-0202). **5267**

SOCIOLOGICAL ANALYSIS. (US/0038-0210). **4998**

SOCIOLOGICAL BULLETIN. (II/0038-0229). **5260**

SOCIOLOGICAL FOCUS (KENT, OHIO). (US/0038-0237). **5260**

SOCIOLOGICAL IMAGINATION. (US/1077-5048). **Qty:** 1-4. **5260**

SOCIOLOGICAL PRACTICE. (US/0163-8505). **5261**

SOCIOLOGICAL REVIEW MONOGRAPH, THE. (UK/0081-1769). **5261**

SOCIOLOGICAL REVIEW, THE. (UK/0038-0261). **5261**

SOCIOLOGICAL SPECTRUM. (US/0273-2173). **5261**

SOCIOLOGICAL VIEWPOINTS. (US/1060-0876). **5261**

SOCIOLOGIE DU TRAVAIL (PARIS). (FR/0038-0296). **1711**

SOCIOLOGIE ET SOCIETES. (CN/0038-030X). **5262**

SOCIOLOGIE ROMANEASCA. (RM). **5262**

SOCIOLOGIJA SELA. (CI/0038-0326). **Qty:** 10. **5262**

SOCIOLOGISCHE GIDS. (BE/0038-0334). **5262**

SOCIOLOGISK FORSKNING. (SW/0038-0342). **5262**

SOCIOLOGY OF EDUCATION ABSTRACTS. (UK/0038-0415). **1797**

SOCIOLOGY OF HEALTH & ILLNESS. (UK/0141-9889). **5262**

SOCIOLOGY OF SPORT JOURNAL. (US/0741-1235). **4919**

SOCIOLOGY (OXFORD). (UK/0038-0385). **Qty:** 200. **5262**

SOCIONOMEN 1987. (SW/0283-1929). **5310**

SODOBNOST. (XV/0038-0482). **2523**

SOFT TECHNOLOGY. (AT/0810-1434). **Qty:** 16-20. **1957**

SOFTWARE DEVELOPER'S MONTHLY. (US). **1290**

SOFTWARE FOR ENGINEERING AND WORKSTATIONS. (UK/0952-8768). **1203**

SOFTWARE INDUSTRY REPORT. (US/1042-7252). **1290**

SOFTWARE MAINTENANCE NEWS. (US/0741-4501). **Qty:** 2. **1291**

SOFTWARE : PRACTICE & EXPERIENCE. (UK/0038-0644). **1291**

SOFTWARE PROCESS, QUALITY & ISO 9000. (US/1070-5457). **Qty:** 20. **1291**

SOFTWARE PROTECTION. (US/0733-1274). **1227**

SOFTWARE TESTING, VERIFICATION & RELIABILITY. (UK/0960-0833). **1291**

SOFTWARE WORLD. (UK/0038-0652). **1291**

SOIL & TILLAGE RESEARCH. (NE/0167-1987). **186**

SOIL DYNAMICS AND EARTHQUAKE ENGINEERING (1984). (UK/0267-7261). **1996**

SOIL MECHANICS SERIES (MONTREAL, QUEBEC). (CN/0541-6329). **2031**

SOIL SCIENCE SOCIETY OF AMERICA JOURNAL. (US/0361-5995). **187**

SOIL TECHNOLOGY. (GW/0933-3630). **187**

SOINS. (SZ). **2912**

SOINS PARIS. (FR/0038-0814). **3869**

SOINS. PSYCHIATRIE. (FR/0241-6972). **3937**

SOJOURNER (CAMBRIDGE). (US/0191-8699). **5566**

SOL DE TEXAS, EL. (US). **Qty:** 6. **5754**

SOL (HOUSTON, TEX.), EL. (US/0891-818X). **5754**

SOL (PHOENIX, ARIZ. : 1939). (US). **5630**

SOL (WINNIPEG). (CN/0709-504X). **Qty:** 6. **1957**

SOLANUS. (UK/0038-0903). **3250**

SOLAR LAW : CUMULATIVE SUPPLEMENT / PRESENT AND FUTURE : WITH PROPOSED FORMS. SANDY F. KRAEMER. (US). **3056**

SOLAR PHYSICS. (NE/0038-0938). **400**

SOLAR PROGRESS. (AT/0729-6436). **Qty:** 8. **1957**

SOLAR TODAY. (US/1042-0630). **1957**

SOLARIS. (CN/0709-8863). **3437**

SOLDAT UND TECHNIK. (GW/0038-0989). **4057**

SOLDERING & SURFACE MOUNT TECHNOLOGY : JOURNAL OF THE SMART (SURFACE MOUNT & RELATED TECHNOLOGIES) GROUP. (UK/0954-0911). **4019**

SOLDIER. (UK). **4057**

SOLDIER OF FORTUNE. (US/0145-6784). **4057**

SOLETTER. (US/0747-623X). **1997**

SOLICITORS' JOURNAL (LONDON, ENGLAND : 1928). (UK/0038-1047). **3056**

SOLID STATE AND SUPERCONDUCTIVITY ABSTRACTS. (US/0896-5900). **4427**

SOLID STATE COMMUNICATIONS. (US/0038-1098). **4421**

SOLID STATE TECHNOLOGY. (US/0038-111X). **2081**

SOLIDARIDAD SAN JUAN, METRO MANILA. (PH/0117-3138). **Qty:** 40 / year. **4496**

SOLIDARITY (DETROIT, MICH.). (US/0164-856X). **1711**

SOLOINTIMO SOLOMARE. (IT). **Qty:** 4. **1087**

SOLPLAN REVIEW. (CN/0828-6574). **2835**

SOMATICS. (US/0147-5231). **4361**

SOMATOTHERAPIES ET SOMATOLOGIE. (FR). **Qty:** 3. **3642**

SOMERSET HERALD (PRINCESS ANNE, MD. : 1985). (US/8756-6397). **Qty:** 12. **5687**

SOMOS (BUENOS AIRES, ARGENTINA). (AG). **2552**

SON, VIDEO MAGAZINE. (FR/0765-3530). **5319**

SONANCES. (CN/0712-2438). **4153**

SONDERHEFT - DEUTSCHE KERAMISCHE GESELLSCHAFT. (GW/0417-2256). **2594**

SONDERPADAGOGIK. (GW). **1885**

SONG NEWS. (CN/0704-5859). **187**

SONG (TORONTO). (CN/0822-4226). **3471**

SONNECK SOCIETY BULLETIN, THE. (US). **4153**

SONORA REVIEW. (US/0275-5203). **Qty:** 1-3. **3353**

SONS OF NORWAY VIKING, THE. (US/0038-1462). **2273**

SONUS. (US/0739-229X). **Qty:** 500. **4153**

SOO, THE. (US/0733-5296). **5436**

SOPHIA. (AT/0038-1527). **Qty:** 3. **4998**

SORONDA. (PG). **Qty:** 2. **2643**

SOROUSH / SURUSH. (IR). **2508**

SORTIE (MONTREAL). (CN/0714-7376). **2796**

SOSIALKONOMEN. (NO). **1595**

SOUDAGE ET TECHNIQUES CONNEXES. (FR/0038-173X). **Qty:** 6/yr. **4027**

SOULE NEWSLETTER. (US/0584-164X). **2473**

SOUND ADVICE. (US/0733-4605). **4847**

SOUND & COMMUNICATIONS. (US/0038-1845). **1122**

SOUND OF VIENNA, THE. (US/0192-5180). **2546**

SOUND POST (GRANITE FALLS, MINN.). (US/0749-0755). **4154**

SOUND WAVES : MONTHLY NEWSLETTER. (US). **252**

SOUNDBOARD. (US/0145-6237). **4154**

SOUNDINGS EAST. (US). **3438**

SOUNDINGS (ESSEX, CONN.). (US). **596**

SOUNDINGS (MILWAUKEE, WIS.). (US/0888-4072). **5457**

SOUNDS AUSTRALIAN : AUSTRALIAN MUSIC CENTRE JOURNAL. (AT/0811-3149). **Qty:** 6. **4154**

SOUNDS OF GOSPEL RECORDINGS. (US). **4998**

SOUNDTRACK. (BE/0771-6303). **5319**

SOUNDTRACK!. (BE). **4078**

SOUNDTRACK (RINGWOOD, N.J.). (US/1042-0649). **5319**

SOURCE (UNITED NATIONS DEVELOPMENT PROGRAMME). (US). **2243**

SOURCE (WINTER PARK, FLA.). (US/0898-8811). **Qty:** (varies). **712**

SOURCES CHRETIENNES. (FR/0750-1978). **5040**

SOURCES ET SUPPLEMENT VIE DOMINICAINE. (SZ). **Qty:** 30. **4998**

SOURCES OF COMPILED LEGISLATIVE HISTORIES. (US/0275-5157). **3083**

SOURCES (TORONTO). (CN/0700-480X). **2924**

SOUROZH. (UK/0950-2742). **Qty:** 10. **4998**

SOUS-TERRE. (CN/0827-9772). **1411**

SOUTH AFRICA INTERNATIONAL. (SA/0015-5055). **2500**

SOUTH AFRICA REPORTER. (US/1053-5497). **851**

SOUTH AFRICAN ARCHAEOLOGICAL BULLETIN, THE. (SA/0038-1969). **282**

SOUTH AFRICAN BUILDER, THE. (SA). **627**

SOUTH AFRICAN FORESTRY JOURNAL. (SA/0038-2167). **2395**

SOUTH AFRICAN GEOGRAPHICAL JOURNAL. (SA/0373-6245). **Qty:** varies. **2576**

SOUTH AFRICAN HISTORICAL JOURNAL. (SA). **Qty:** 50. **2643**

SOUTH AFRICAN JOURNAL OF ANIMAL SCIENCE. (SA/0375-1589). **222**

SOUTH AFRICAN JOURNAL OF BOTANY. (SA/0254-6299). **528**

SOUTH AFRICAN JOURNAL OF BUSINESS MANAGEMENT. (SA). **886**

SOUTH AFRICAN JOURNAL OF CHEMISTRY. (SA/0379-4350). **992**

SOUTH AFRICAN JOURNAL OF ECONOMICS, THE. (SA/0038-2280). **1521**

SOUTH AFRICAN JOURNAL OF LIBRARY AND INFORMATION SCIENCE. (SA/0256-8861). **3250**

SOUTH AFRICAN JOURNAL OF MUSICOLOGY. (SA/0258-509X). **4154**

SOUTH AFRICAN JOURNAL OF PHYSICS. (SA/0379-4377). **4421**

SOUTH AFRICAN JOURNAL OF PHYSIOTHERAPY. (SA/0379-6175). **3642**

SOUTH AFRICAN JOURNAL OF SCIENCE. (SA/0038-2353). **5158**

SOUTH AFRICAN JOURNAL OF SURGERY. (SA/0038-2361). **3975**

SOUTH AFRICAN JOURNAL OF WILDLIFE RESEARCH. (SA/0379-4369). **2205**

SOUTH AFRICAN JOURNAL OF ZOOLOGY. (SA/0254-1858). **5597**

SOUTH AFRICAN JOURNAL ON HUMAN RIGHTS. (SA/0258-7203). **4513**

SOUTH AFRICAN LABOUR BULLETIN. (SA/0377-5429). **1711**

SOUTH AFRICAN MEDICAL JOURNAL. (SA/0038-2469). **3642**

SOUTH AFRICAN MUSIC TEACHER. (SA/0038-2493). **4154**

SOUTH AFRICAN NATIONAL BIBLIOGRAPHY. (SA/0036-0864). **425**

SOUTH AFRICAN OPTOMETRIST, SUID-AFRIKAANSE OOGKUNDIGE, THE. (SA/0378-9411). **4217**

SOUTH AFRICAN ORCHID JOURNAL. SUID-AFRIKAANSE ORGIDEEJOERNAAL. (SA). **2431**

SOUTH AFRICAN OUTLOOK. (SA/0038-2523). **4998**

SOUTH AFRICAN SHIPPING NEWS AND FISHING INDUSTRY REVIEW, THE. (SA/0038-2671). **5457**

SOUTH AFRICAN SUGAR JOURNAL, THE. (SA/0038-2728). **187**

SOUTH AFRICAN SUGAR YEAR BOOK, THE. (SA). **136**

SOUTH AFRICAN THEATRE JOURNAL : SATJ. (SA). **Qty:** 8-10. **5368**

SOUTH AFRICAN YEARBOOK OF INTERNATIONAL LAW. (SA/0379-8895). **3136**

SOUTH AMBOY CITIZEN (SOUTH AMBOY, N.J. 1884), THE. (US/1041-2514). **Qty:** 3. **5711**

SOUTH AMERICAN EXPLORER. (US/0889-7891). **Qty:** 15. **4878**

SOUTH ASIA. (AT/0085-6401). **Qty:** 35. **2664**

SOUTH ASIA BULLETIN. (US/0732-3867). **2665**

SOUTH ASIA IN REVIEW. (US/0889-8650). **2665**

SOUTH ASIA RESEARCH. (UK/0262-7280). **2854**

SOUTH ASIAN ANTHROPOLOGIST. (II/0257-7348). **245**

SOUTH ASIAN STUDIES (JAIPUR). (II/0038-285X). **2665**

SOUTH ATLANTIC QUARTERLY, THE. (US/0038-2876). **2854**

SOUTH ATLANTIC REVIEW. (US/0277-335X). **Qty:** 100. **3322**

SOUTH AUSTRALIAN DAIRY FARMER'S JOURNAL, THE. (AT/0049-1446). **199**

SOUTH AUSTRALIAN GENEALOGIST. (AT/0311-2756). **2473**

SOUTH AUSTRALIAN GEOGRAPHICAL JOURNAL. (AT/1030-0481). **2576**

SOUTH AUSTRALIAN NATURALIST; THE JOURNAL OF THE FIELD NATURALISTS' SECTION OF THE ROYAL SOCIETY OF SOUTH AUSTRALIA. (AT/0038-2965). **Qty:** 2-3. **4172**

SOUTH AUSTRALIAN ORNITHOLOGIST. (AT/0038-2973). **Qty:** 2-3/yr. **5620**

SOUTH AUSTRALIAN SCHOOL POST. (AT). **1784**

SOUTH AUSTRALIAN SCIENCE TEACHERS JOURNAL. (AT). **Qty:** 12. **1905**

SOUTH BEND TRIBUNE, THE. (US). **5667**

SOUTH CAROLINA BUSINESS JOURNAL. (US/0745-4473). **712**

SOUTH CAROLINA HISTORICAL MAGAZINE. (US/0038-3082). **2761**

SOUTH CAROLINA MAGAZINE OF ANCESTRAL RESEARCH, THE. (US/0190-826X). **2473**

SOUTH CAROLINA NURSE, THE. (US/1046-7394). **Qty:** 2-3. **3869**

SOUTH CAROLINA OUT-OF-DOORS. (US/0887-9249). **Qty:** 2. **2205**

SOUTH CAROLINA POLICY FORUM : A REVIEW OF PUBLIC AFFAIRS IN SOUTH CAROLINA, THE. (US). **Qty:** 4. **4686**

SOUTH CAROLINA REVIEW, THE. (US/0038-3163). **3353**

SOUTH CAROLINA WILDLIFE. (US/0038-3198). **2205**

SOUTH CENTRAL REVIEW. (US/0743-6831). **3322**

SOUTH CENTRAL SALES GUIDE TO HIGH-TECH COMPANIES. (US/1040-0532). **5159**

SOUTH DAKOTA ARCHAEOLOGY. (US/0276-5543). **Qty:** 1-2. **282**

SOUTH DAKOTA AUTHORS' CATALOG. (US/0742-8936). **4832**

SOUTH DAKOTA BIRD NOTES. (US/0038-3252). **Qty:** 10. **5620**

SOUTH DAKOTA CHURCHMAN. (US). **4998**

SOUTH DAKOTA CONSERVATION DIGEST. (US/0038-3279). **2205**

SOUTH DAKOTA EPISCOPAL CHURCH NEWS. (US/0746-9276). **4998**

SOUTH DAKOTA HIGH LINER MAGAZINE. (US/1067-4977). **Qty:** 6-12. **2493**

SOUTH DAKOTA HISTORY. (US/0361-8676). **2761**

SOUTH DAKOTA LAW REVIEW. (US/0038-3325). **Qty:** Varies. **3057**

SOUTH DAKOTA MAGAZINE (YANKTON, S.D.). (US/0886-2680). **2546**

SOUTH DAKOTA REVIEW. (US/0038-3368). **3438**

SOUTH EAST ASIAN REVIEW, THE. (II). **2665**

SOUTH EASTERN LATIN AMERICANIST. (US/0049-1527). **2761**

SOUTH FLORIDA PIONEERS. (US/8756-2766). **2473**

SOUTH JERSEY MAGAZINE. (US/0275-4428). **2761**

SOUTH OF THE MOUNTAINS. (US/0489-9563). **2761**

SOUTH PIERCE COUNTY DISPATCH, THE. (US). **5762**

SOUTH SHORE NEWS (WEST HANOVER, MASS.). (US/0192-4869). **Qty:** 6. **5690**

SOUTH SHORE RECORD. (US/0038-352X). **2546**

SOUTH SLAV JOURNAL, THE. (UK). **2710**

SOUTH TEXAS LAW REVIEW. (US/1052-343X). **3057**

SOUTH WHIDBEY RECORD. (US/1064-0622). **Qty:** 6-8. **5762**

SOUTHAMPTON MEDICAL JOURNAL. (UK/0266-0342). **3642**

SOUTHEAST ASIA MICROFILMS NEWSLETTER. (MY). **2483**

SOUTHEAST ASIAN BULLETIN OF MATHEMATICS. (HK/0129-2021). **3536**

SOUTHEAST ASIAN JOURNAL OF SOCIAL SCIENCE. (SI). **5222**

SOUTHEAST ASIAN JOURNAL OF TROPICAL MEDICINE AND PUBLIC HEALTH, THE. (TH/0038-3619). **4803**

SOUTHEAST SALES GUIDE TO HIGH-TECH COMPANIES. (US/1040-0567). **5159**

SOUTHEASTERN ARCHAEOLOGY. (US/0734-578X). **282**

SOUTHEASTERN EUROPE (PITTSBURGH). (US/0094-4467). **2523**

SOUTHEASTERN FRONT. (US). **3438**

SOUTHEASTERN GEOGRAPHER. (US/0038-366X). **2576**

SOUTHEASTERN POLITICAL REVIEW. (US/0730-2177). **4496**

SOUTHERLY. (AT/0038-3732). **3438**

SOUTHERN ACCENTS. (US/0149-516X). **2903**

SOUTHERN AFRICAN JOURNAL OF EPIDEMIOLOGY & INFECTION : OFFICIAL JOURNAL OF THE SEXUALLY TRANSMITTED DISEASES, INFECTIOUS DISEASES, AND EPIDEMIOLOGICAL SOCIETIES OF SOUTHERN AFRICA, THE. (SA). **3716**

SOUTHERN BAPTIST EDUCATOR, THE. (US/0038-3848). **5067**

SOUTHERN BEVERAGE JOURNAL. (US/0193-0613). **2371**

SOUTHERN BUSINESS & ECONOMIC JOURNAL, THE. (US/0743-779X). **Qty:** 10-12. **712**

SOUTHERN CALIFORNIA BEVERAGE BULLETIN. (US/0192-1835). **2371**

SOUTHERN

SOUTHERN CALIFORNIA BUSINESS. (US/0038-3880). **Qty: 2-3. 821**

SOUTHERN CALIFORNIA LAW REVIEW. (US/0038-3910). **3057**

SOUTHERN CALIFORNIA QUARTERLY. (US/0038-3929). **Qty: 15-20. 2761**

SOUTHERN CALIFORNIA SENIOR LIFE. (US). **5182**

SOUTHERN CALIFORNIA WOODWORKER, THE. (US/0898-3550). **635**

SOUTHERN CHANGES. (US/0193-2446). **Qty: 20+. 4513**

SOUTHERN COMMUNICATION JOURNAL, THE. (US/1041-794X). **1122**

SOUTHERN CROSS (SAN DIEGO, CALIF.). (US/0745-0257). **5036**

SOUTHERN ECHOES. (US/0735-6870). **2473**

SOUTHERN ECONOMIC JOURNAL. (US/0038-4038). **1521**

SOUTHERN ECONOMIST. (II/0038-4046). **1521**

SOUTHERN EXPOSURE (DURHAM, N.C.). (US/0146-809X). **2761**

SOUTHERN FOLKLORE. (US/0899-594X). **Qty: 15-20 per year. 2324**

SOUTHERN FRIEND, THE. (US/0743-7439). **5067**

SOUTHERN FUNERAL DIRECTOR. (US/0038-4135). **2407**

SOUTHERN GENEALOGICAL INDEX. (US/8755-1748). **2473**

SOUTHERN GENEALOGIST'S EXCHANGE QUARTERLY, THE. (US/0584-4487). **2473**

SOUTHERN GRAPHICS. (US/0274-774X). **382**

SOUTHERN HERALD (LIBERTY, MISS.), THE. (US/0893-3790). **5701**

SOUTHERN HISTORIAN, THE. (US/0738-5102). **Qty: 70. 2761**

SOUTHERN HISTORY. (UK/0142-4688). **Qty: 20. 2710**

SOUTHERN HOSPITALS. (US/0038-4178). **3792**

SOUTHERN HUMANITIES REVIEW. (US/0038-4186). **Qty: 50-70. 2854**

SOUTHERN ILLINOIS UNIVERSITY LAW JOURNAL. (US/0145-3432). **3057**

SOUTHERN INDIANA GENEALOGICAL SOCIETY QUARTERLY. (US/0747-8453). **2473**

SOUTHERN INSURANCE. (US/0038-4216). **2894**

SOUTHERN JOURNAL OF APPLIED FORESTRY. (US/0148-4419). **2395**

SOUTHERN LIVING. (US/0038-4305). **2546**

SOUTHERN OUTDOORS (MONTGOMERY). (US/0199-3372). **4878**

SOUTHERN PARTISAN, THE. (US/0739-1714). **Qty: 60. 4496**

SOUTHERN PLUMBING, HEATING, COOLING. (US/0038-4461). **2608**

SOUTHERN POETRY REVIEW. (US/0038-447X). **Qty: 6-8. 3471**

SOUTHERN POLITICAL REPORT. (US/0739-3938). **Qty: 1 or 2. 4496**

SOUTHERN QUARTERLY, THE. (US/0038-4496). **Qty: 50. 331**

SOUTHERN QUERIES : THE CONTACT MAGAZINE FOR PEOPLE SEARCHING FOR THEIR SOUTHERN ANCESTORS. (US/1048-8057). **Qty: 18-25. 2473**

SOUTHERN REVIEW (ADELAIDE). (AT/0038-4526). **3353**

SOUTHERN REVIEW (BATON ROUGE), THE. (US/0038-4534). **3438**

SOUTHERN ROOTS AND SHOOTS. (US/0895-2876). **2473**

SOUTHERN SOCIAL STUDIES JOURNAL. (US/1047-7942). **5222**

SOUTHERN STAR. (US). **5628**

SOUTHERN STARS. (NZ/0049-1640). **Qty: 128. 400**

SOUTHERN STUDIES. (US/0735-8342). **2761**

SOUTHERN THEATRE. (US/0584-4738). **5368**

SOUTHERN UNIVERSITY LAW REVIEW. (US/0099-1465). **3057**

SOUTHERN UTAH NEWS. (US/0049-1659). **5757**

SOUTHLAND TIMES. (NZ/0112-9910). **5807**

SOUTHSIDE CHALLENGER, THE. (US). **Qty: 2. 5667**

SOUTHSIDE VIRGINIAN, THE. (US/0736-5683). **2473**

SOUTHWEST DIGEST. (US). **Qty: 45. 5754**

SOUTHWEST INTERNATIONAL WINE & FOOD REVIEW. (US). **2358**

SOUTHWEST JOURNAL OF LINGUISTICS. (US/0737-4143). **Qty: 5. 3322**

SOUTHWEST MUSEUM PAPERS. (US/0076-0994). **4096**

SOUTHWEST PHILOSOPHY REVIEW. (US/0897-2346). **Qty: 5-10/year. 4361**

SOUTHWEST PROFILE. (US/0895-6049). **2546**

SOUTHWEST SALES GUIDE TO HIGH-TECH COMPANIES. (US/1040-0524). **5159**

SOUTHWEST VIRGINIA ENTERPRISE. (US). **5759**

SOUTHWESTERN AMERICAN LITERATURE. (US/0049-1675). **3438**

SOUTHWESTERN ARCHIVIST. (US/1056-1021). **Qty: 2. 3250**

SOUTHWESTERN HISTORICAL QUARTERLY. (US/0038-478X). **2761**

SOUTHWESTERN JOURNAL OF THEOLOGY. (US/0038-4828). **Qty: 150. 5067**

SOUTHWESTERN LORE. (US/0038-4844). **Qty: 12. 282**

SOUTHWESTERN PAY DIRT. (US/0886-0920). **2151**

SOUTHWESTERN UNIVERSITY LAW REVIEW. (US/0886-3296). **3057**

SOUVENANCE ANABAPTISTE. (FR/0769-1734). **4999**

SOUVENIR NAPOLEONIEN, LE. (FR/0246-1919). **2630**

SOUVENIRS & NOVELTIES. (US/0038-4968). **2585**

SOVETSKOE ZDRAVOOKHRANENIE. (RU/0038-5239). **4803**

SOVIET ANALYST. (UK/0049-1713). **4496**

SOVIET AND EASTERN EUROPEAN FOREIGN TRADE. (US/0038-5263). **1640**

SOVIET & EASTERN EUROPEAN REPORT. (UK/0963-7036). **3136**

SOVIET ANTHROPOLOGY AND ARCHAEOLOGY. (US/0038-528X). **245**

SOVIET ARMED FORCES REVIEW ANNUAL. (US/0148-0928). **4057**

SOVIET BUSINESS & TRADE (1982). (US/0731-7727). **851**

SOVIET JOURNAL OF PSYCHOLOGY. (US/0891-2726). **4619**

SOVIET LAW AND GOVERNMENT. (US/0038-5530). **3057**

SOVIET MATERIALS SCIENCE REVIEWS. (US/0888-689X). **2129**

SOVIET REVIEW. (AT/1033-6257). **1522**

SOVIET REVIEW (WHITE PLAINS), THE. (US/0038-5794). **2523**

SOVIET STUDIES. (UK/0038-5859). **4547**

SOVIET STUDIES IN HISTORY. (US/0038-5867). **2710**

SOVIET STUDIES IN PHILOSOPHY. (US/0038-5883). **4361**

SOVREMENNAIA VYSSHAIA SHKOLA. (PL). **1847**

SOYA BLUEBOOK. (US/0275-4509). **Qty: 10 per year. 188**

SOZIAL- UND PRAEVENTIVMEDIZIN. (SZ/0303-8408). **4803**

SOZIALE SICHERHEIT (WIEN). (AU/0038-6065). **5310**

SOZIALVERSICHERUNGS-BERATER. (GW/0936-9198). **5310**

SOZIOLOGISCHE REVUE. (GW/0343-4109). **5263**

SPACE AGE TIMES. (US/0738-0968). **35**

SPACE AND SECURITY NEWS. (US/1071-2569). **35**

SPACE (BEACONSFIELD). (UK/0267-954X). **35**

SPACE LETTER. (US). **Qty: 6. 36**

SPACE NEWS (SPRINGFIELD, VA.). (US/1046-6940). **36**

SPACE RESEARCH IN BULGARIA. (BU/0204-9104). **400**

SPACE SCIENCE REVIEWS. (NE/0038-6308). **400**

SPACE TODAY. (US/0889-6054). **400**

SPANISH STUDIES. (UK). **Qty: approx. 3/year. 2710**

SPANISH TODAY. (US/0049-1802). **3439**

SPANNER. (UK). **Qty: varies. 365**

SPARE RIB. (UK/0306-7971). **5566**

SPARTACIST. (US/0038-6596). **4547**

SPE PRODUCTION ENGINEERING. (US/0885-9221). **4279**

SPEAK UP. (CN/0383-9370). **2762**

SPEAKER BUILDER. (US/0199-7920). **5319**

SPEAKIN' OUT NEWS. (US). **2273**

SPEAQ-OUT. (CN/0229-6535). **Qty: 10-20. 3323**

SPEAR (TORONTO). (CN/0315-0208). **2273**

SPEARHEAD. (UK). **4535**

SPEC-COM. (US/0883-2560). **1139**

SPEC (NEW CARLISLE). (CN/0226-9120). **5795**

SPECCHIO ECONOMICO. (IT). **1522**

SPECIAL CARE IN DENTISTRY. (US/0275-1879). **1335**

SPECIAL CHILDREN (BIRMINGHAM). (UK/0951-6875). **1885**

SPECIAL-INTEREST AUTOS. (US/0049-1845). **5425**

SPECIAL PUBLICATION - CUSHMAN FOUNDATION FOR FORAMINIFERAL RESEARCH. (US/0070-2242). **5597**

SPECIAL PUBLICATION SERIES - PYMATUNING LABORATORY OF ECOLOGY, UNIVERSITY OF PITTSBURGH. (US/0192-5563). **2221**

SPECIAL PUBLICATIONS. (US/0067-6179). **4096**

SPECIAL RECREATION DIGEST. (US/0747-0185). **4854**

SPECIALIST (NEW YORK, N.Y.). (US/0273-9399). **3251**

SPECIALITY PAPER & BOARD MATERIALS & MARKETS BULLETIN. (UK). **4222**

SPECIALTY & CUSTOM DEALER. (US/0193-7278). **5425**

SPECIALTY CHEMICALS (REDHILL). (UK/0262-2262). **993**

SPECIALTY NEWS. (US/0886-2052). **851**

SPECIALTY STORE SERVICE BULLETIN. (US/1052-5564). **958**

SPECIALTY TRAVEL INDEX: THE DIRECTORY TO SPECIAL INTEREST TRAVEL. (US/0889-7085). **5491**

SPECIES (BROOKFIELD). (US/1016-927X). **Qty: 5-8. 2205**

SPECTATOR (LONDON. 1828). (UK/0038-6952). **2523**

SPECTROSCOPY INTERNATIONAL. (US/1040-7669). **993**

SPECTROSCOPY LETTERS. (US/0038-7010). **4442**

SPECTROSCOPY (OTTAWA, ONT.). (CN/0712-4813). **993**

SPECTRUM 5. (US). **914**

SPECTRUM (ST. PAUL, MINN.). (US/0739-2559). **1921**

SPECTRUM (TAKOMA PARK, MD.). (US/0890-0264). **Qty: 3. 4999**

SPECTRUM (TEL AVIV, ISRAEL). (IS/0334-1046). **1711**

SPECULATIONS IN SCIENCE AND TECHNOLOGY. (UK/0155-7785). **5159**

SPECULUM. (US/0038-7134). **2710**

SPEECH AND DRAMA. (UK/0038-7142). **5368**

SPEECH COMMUNICATION. (NE/0167-6393). **1122**

SPEEDHORSE (MONTHLY), THE. (US/0364-9237). **2802**

SPEEDNEWS. (US/0271-2598). **Qty: 2 per week. 36**

SPEEDWAY SCENE. (US/0747-5403). **4920**

SPEEDX. (US/0882-8091). **1122**

SPEEDY BEE. (US/0190-6798). **5598**

SPEKTRUM. (SZ/0038-7274). **3471**

SPELD. (AT). **Qty: 6. 1885**

SPELEO DIGEST. (US/0584-8717). **1411**

SPENSER NEWSLETTER. (US/0038-7347). **3471**

SPICE. (US/0894-6183). **Qty: 5. 4999**

SPICE NEWSLETTER. (II). **2358**

SPIDR NEWS. (US/0888-9325). **Qty: varies. 1711**

SPIEGEL DER LETTEREN. (BE/0038-7479). **3439**

SPIEGEL (HAMBURG), DER. (GW/0038-7452). **2523**

SPIEGEL HISTORIAEL. (NE/0038-7487). **2630**

SPIELRAUM. (GW/0934-4853). **Qty: 30. 2601**

SPIN-OFF (LOVELAND, COLO.). (US/0198-8239). **5356**

SPINNER (NEW BEDFORD, MASS.). (US/0730-2657). **2762**

SPIRIT & LIFE (CLYDE, MO.). (US/0038-7592). **4999**

STATISTICS

SPIRIT (SISTERS, OR.). (US/0885-0291). **4999**

SPIRIT (SOUTH ORANGE). (US/0038-7584). **3471**

SPIRITUAL LIFE (WASHINGTON). (US/0038-7630). **5036**

SPIRITUALITY TODAY. (US/0162-6760). **5036**

SPITBALL. (US/8755-741X). Qty: 40. **3439**

SPIXIANA. (GW/0341-8391). **5598**

SPLITTING HEIRS. (CN). **2473**

SPOKEN ENGLISH. (UK/0038-772X). **3323**

SPOKESMAN (EDMONTON). (CN/0700-5229). **4394**

SPOKESMAN-REVIEW (1894), THE. (US/1064-7317). **5762**

SPOON RIVER POETRY REVIEW. (US). Qty: 4-6. **3471**

SPORT & MEDICINA. (IT/0392-9647). **3956**

SPORT AND SPORT 2. (UK). **4920**

SPORT AVIATION. (US/0038-7835). **4920**

SPORT FLYER. (US/8750-8117). **4920**

SPORT MARKETING QUARTERLY. (US/1061-6934). Qty: 4. **4920**

SPORT (NEW YORK). (US/0038-7797). **4920**

SPORT PSYCHOLOGIST, THE. (US/0888-4781). **4619**

SPORT PSYCHOLOGY TRAINING BULLETIN. (US/1044-3118). Qty: varies. **4921**

SPORT REPORT. (AT). Qty: 4. **4921**

SPORT ROCKETRY. (US/1076-2701). **2778**

SPORT SCENE. (US/0270-1812). **4921**

SPORTING CLASSICS. (US). **4921**

SPORTING NEWS ... BASEBALL YEARBOOK, THE. (US/0275-0732). **4921**

SPORTS. (SI). Qty: 3. **4922**

SPORTS MEDICINE DIGEST. (US/0731-9770). **3956**

SPORTS MEDICINE STANDARDS AND MALPRACTICE REPORTER, THE. (US/1041-696X). **3956**

SPORTS 'N SPOKES. (US/0161-6706). **4923**

SPORTS, PARKS & RECREATION LAW REPORTER, THE. (US/0893-8210). **3058**

SPORTS TURF BULLETIN. (UK/0490-5474). Qty: varies. **4923**

SPORTSMEDICINE DIGEST. (US/0731-9770). **3956**

SPORTUNTERRICHT. (GW/0342-2402). **1858**

SPORTWISSENSCHAFT. (GW). **4923**

SPOT (HOUSTON, TEX.). (US/1049-0450). Qty: 12. **4377**

SPOTLIGHT (INDIANAPOLIS, IND.). (US). **5667**

SPOTLIGHT (WASHINGTON), THE. (US/0191-6270). **5648**

SPRACHDIENST, DER. (GW/0038-8459). **3323**

SPRACHE UND DATENVERARBEITUNG. (GW/0343-5202). **3323**

SPRACHE UND LITERATUR IN WISSENSCHAFT UND UNTERRICHT. (GW/0724-9713). **3323**

SPRACHKUNST. (AU/0038-8483). **3323**

SPRACHREPORT / INSTITUT FUER DEUTSCHE SPRACHE. (GW). **3323**

SPRACHTYPOLOGIE UND UNIVERSALIENFORSCHUNG. (GW/0942-2919). **3323**

SPRACHWISSENSCHAFT. (GW/0344-8169). **3323**

SPRAK NYTT. (NO). **3323**

SPRAKVARD. (SW/0038-8440). **3323**

SPRECHSAAL. (GW/0341-0439). **2594**

SPRING. (US/0362-0522). Qty: 30. **4619**

SPRINGFIELD ADVANCE-PRESS. (US). Qty: 48. **5698**

SPRINGFIELD MAGAZINE. (US/0164-6745). **2546**

SPRINGFIELD MAGAZINE (SPRINGFIELD, MO.). (US/0195-0894). Qty: 12. **2546**

SPRINGHOUSE, THE. (US/0888-3319). **2324**

SPRINGS MAGAZINE (COLORADO SPRINGS, COLO.). (US/0748-6405). Qty: 15. **2546**

SPRINGS VALLEY HERALD. (US). Qty: 1. **5667**

SPRINGVILLE HERALD (SPRINGVILLE, UTAH). (US). **5757**

SPUDMAN. (US/0038-8661). Qty: 1-2/yr. **137**

SPUMS JOURNAL. (AT/0813-1988). **3642**

SPUTNIK (ANGL. JAZ.). (RU/0131-8721). **2523**

SQL FORUM. (US/1068-0950). **1204**

SQUASH NEWS (HOPE VALLEY, R.I.). (US/0164-7148). Qty: 4-6. **4924**

SRASHTA. (II). **3439**

SRI LANKA JOURNAL OF THE HUMANITIES, THE. (CE/0378-486X). **2854**

SRI LANKA VETERINARY JOURNAL : THE OFFICIAL JOURNAL OF THE SRI LANKA VETERINARY ASSOCIATION, THE. (CE). **5522**

SRINAGAR LAW JOURNAL. (II). **3058**

SRPSKA BORBA. (US/0279-1293). **2273**

SSI UPDATE. (US/0898-8242). Qty: 2. **36**

ST. CLOUD STATE UNIVERSITY CHRONICLE. (US/0747-1025). **1095**

ST. CROIX REVIEW, THE. (US/0093-2582). **5223**

ST. GEORGE MAGAZINE. (US/0882-8741). **5491**

ST. JOHNS REVIEW (1981), THE. (US/0277-4720). **1847**

ST. LOUIS BUSINESS JOURNAL. (US/0271-6453). **713**

ST. LOUIS JOURNALISM REVIEW, THE. (US/0036-2972). **2924**

ST. LOUIS METROPOLITAN MEDICINE. (US/0892-1334). **3642**

ST. LOUIS POST-DISPATCH. (US). Qty: 200. **5704**

ST. LOUIS REVIEW. (US/0036-3022). **5036**

ST. LOUIS SENTINEL. (US). Qty: 50. **5704**

ST. LOUIS UNIVERSITY RESEARCH JOURNAL. (PH/0036-3014). **2855**

ST. MARK'S REVIEW. (AT/0036-3103). Qty: 40-50. **4999**

ST. MARY'S LAW JOURNAL. (US/0581-3441). **3058**

ST NEWS. (NE). Qty: 5-20. **1204**

ST. PAUL'S FAMILY MAGAZINE. (US/0896-8276). Qty: 24/yr. **365**

ST. THOMAS'S HOSPITAL GAZETTE (1981). (UK/0263-3507). **3792**

ST. VLADIMIR'S THEOLOGICAL QUARTERLY. (US/0036-3227). **5040**

STAATSCOURANT. (NE/0169-5037). **4687**

STADEN-JAHRBUCH. (BL/0582-1150). Qty: 2-3. **2762**

STADION (COLOGNE, GERMANY). (GW/0172-4029). **4924**

STAFFRIDER SERIES. (SA). **3439**

STAGE AND TELEVISION TODAY, THE. (UK/0038-9099). **5368**

STAGES (NORWOOD, N.J.). (US/1041-6048). **5369**

STAHL UND EISEN. (GW/0340-4803). **4020**

STAINLESS STEEL EUROPE. (NE). **1030**

STAINLESS STEEL INDUSTRY. (UK/0306-2988). **1627**

STAINLESS STEELS DIGEST. (US/0730-8140). **4020**

STAL. (RU/0038-920X). **4020**

STALKER. (US/0882-7311). **2473**

STALLION REGISTER FOR .... (US). **2802**

STAMFORD AMERICAN (STAMFORD, TEX. : 1965). (US). Qty: 10. **5754**

STAMP COLLECTOR. (US/0277-3899). **2787**

STAMP DEALER FORUM. (US/8755-3139). **2787**

STAMP LOVER, THE. (UK/0038-9277). **2787**

STAMP WHOLESALER, THE. (US/0038-9315). **2787**

STAMPA MEDICA. (IT/0038-9323). **3642**

STAMPS (NEW YORK, N.Y. 1932). (US/0038-9358). **2787**

STAND MAGAZINE. (UK/0952-648X). Qty: 8-10. **3439**

STANDARD BEARER (GRAND RAPIDS), THE. (US/0362-4692). **4999**

STANDARD CATALOGUE OF MALAYSIA-SINGAPORE-BRUNEI COINS AND PAPER MONEY. (MY/0126-9682). **2783**

STANDARD (EVANSTON, ILL.), THE. (US/0038-9382). Qty: Varies. **5068**

STANDARD GUIDEBOOK TO THE ISLES OF SCILLY, THE. (UK). **5491**

STANDORTWAHL DER BETRIEBE IN DER BUNDESREPUBLIK DEUTSCHLAND UND BERLIN (WEST) / BUNDESMINISTER FUR ARBEIT UND SOZIALORDNUNG, DIE. (GW). **1585**

STANFORD BUSINESS SCHOOL MAGAZINE. (US/0883-265X). **713**

STANFORD FRENCH REVIEW. (US/0163-657X). **3353**

STANFORD HUMANITIES REVIEW. (US/1048-3721). Qty: 10. **2855**

STANFORD ITALIAN REVIEW. (US/0730-6857). **3353**

STANFORD JOURNAL OF INTERNATIONAL LAW. (US/0731-5082). **3136**

STANFORD LITERATURE REVIEW. (US/0886-666X). **3353**

STANFORD MAGAZINE, THE. (US/0745-3981). **1095**

STANGER REPORT, THE. (US/0195-6620). **916**

STANGER'S INVESTMENT ADVISOR. (US/1052-5912). **916**

STAPLES WORLD. (US). Qty: 6. **5698**

STAR-COURIER, THE. (US). Qty: 26 per year. **5754**

STAR-DEMOCRAT (EASTON, MD.), THE. (US/1065-2345). Qty: 50-75. **5687**

STAR (FRANKFORT, ILL.), THE. (US/0746-5742). **5662**

STAR GUIDE. (US/1060-9997). **2493**

STAR PROGRESS, THE. (US). **5632**

STARS AND STRIPES, THE NATIONAL TRIBUNE, THE. (US/0894-8542). Qty: 75. **4057**

STARS MARIEMBOURG. (BE/0776-0698). **425**

START (SAN FRANCISCO, CALIF.). (US/0889-6216). **1204**

STARTEXT INK. (US/0890-6688). Qty: 12/y. **1122**

STAT (VANCOUVER). (CN/0844-3955). **852**

STATE (CHARLOTTE, N.C.), THE. (US/0038-9994). Qty: 12. **2762**

STATE (COLUMBIA, S.C. : 1891 : DAILY). (US). **5743**

STATE COURT JOURNAL. (US/0145-3076). **3058**

STATE EDUCATION LEADER. (US/0736-7511). **1785**

STATE GOVERNMENT NEWS. (US/0039-0119). **4687**

STATE JOURNAL, THE. (US). **5682**

STATE LIBRARIAN. (UK/0305-9189). **3251**

STATE NEWS. (US). Qty: 180. **5694**

STATE OF HAWAII DATA BOOK. (US/0073-1080). **5339**

STATE POLICY REPORTS. (US/8750-6637). **4688**

STATE RECYCLING LAWS UPDATE (QUARTERLY ED.). (US/1070-3217). Qty: 2. **2244**

STATE REVENUE NEWSLETTER, THE. (US/0883-6760). **2787**

STATEMENT (FORT COLLINS, CO.). (US). **3324**

STATEMENTS (CHICAGO, ILL. 1985). (US/1054-7746). Qty: 3. **309**

STATEN ISLAND HISTORIAN, THE. (US/0039-0232). **2762**

STATEN ISLAND REGISTER. (US/0890-9881). **5721**

STATESMAN JOURNAL. (US/0739-5507). **5734**

STATESMAN (STONY BROOK, N.Y.). (US). **1848**

STATESMAN, THE. (PK/0039-0313). **3353**

STATION RELAY, THE. (US). **5223**

STATISTICA NEERLANDICA. (NE/0039-0402). **5339**

STATISTICAL MASTERFILE [COMPUTER FILE]. (US). **5340**

STATISTICAL PROFILE OF IOWA. (US). **1538**

STATISTICAL SCIENCE. (US/0883-4237). **5340**

STATISTICAL YEARBOOK OF THE SOCIALIST REPUBLIC OF ROMANIA. (RM/0377-5739). **5341**

STATISTICIAN, THE. (UK/0039-0526). **5341**

STATISTICS AND COMPUTING. (UK/0960-3174). **1210**

STATISTICS & DECISIONS. (GW/0721-2631). **5342**

STATISTICS

STATISTICS (BERLIN, DDR). (GW/0233-1888). **3543**

STATISTICS OF PAPER, PAPERBOARD AND WOOD PULP. (US/0731-8863). **4240**

STATISTIK DER ALLGEMEINBILDENDEN SCHULEN IN NIEDERSACHSEN. (GW). **1798**

STATISTIK ENERGI. (IO). **1963**

STATISTIK IN DER RENTENVERSICHERUNG. (GW). **5311**

STATISTIK INDUSTRI KECIL. (IO). **1539**

STATISTIK LINGKUNGAN HIDUP INDONESIA. (IO). **1539**

STATISTIK PENDIDIKAN DILUAR LINGKUNGAN DEPARTEMEN P & K. (IO). **1798**

STATISTIK PENDIDIKAN DILUAR LINGKUNGAN DEPARTEMEN P & K DI-SUMATERA UTARA. (IO). **1798**

STATISTIK PERHUBUNGAN - BIRO PUSAT STATISTIK (LALU LINTAS ANGKUTAN BARANG ANTAR PULAU MENURUT JENIS PELAYARAN). (IO/0216-6909). **5457**

STATISTIK PERKEBUNAN BESAR. (IO). **138**

STATISTIK PERUMAHAN DAN LINGKUNGANNYA. (IO). **2841**

STATISTIQUE CRIMINELLE DE LA BELGIQUE. (BE). **3083**

STATISTIQUE DU TRAFIC INTERNATIONAL DES PORTS, U.E.B.L. / ROYAUME DE BELGIQUE, MINISTERE DES AFFAIRES ECONOMIQUES, INSTITUT NATIONAL DE BELGIQUE. (BE). **5402**

STATISTIQUES & ETUDES : MIDI-PYRENEES. (FR/0396-0099). **5343**

STATISTIQUES DE LA CONSTRUCTION ET DU LOGEMENT. (BE/0772-7712). **633**

STATISTIQUES DEMOGRAPHIQUES. (BE/0067-5490). **4563**

STATISTIQUES DIVERSES. (FR). **3083**

STATISTIQUES DU COMMERCE EXTERIEUR DE L'UNION ECONOMIQUE BELGO-LUXEMBURGEOISE. (BE/0772-6694). **734**

STATISTIQUES DU COMMERCE INTERIEUR ET DES TRANSPORTS / ROYAUME DE BELGIQUE, MINISTERE DES AFFAIRES ECONOMIQUES, INSTITUT NATIONAL DE STATISTIQUE. (BE). **734**

STATISTIQUES FINANCIERES. (BE). **734**

STATISTIQUES INDUSTRIELLES. (BE/0772-7704). **1539**

STATISTIQUES JUDICIAIRES. (BE/0775-311X). **3083**

STATISTISCHE BEIHEFTE ZU DEN MONATSBERICHTEN DER DEUTSCHEN BUNDESBANK. REIHE 4 : SAISONBEREINIGTE WIRTSCHAFTSZAHLEN. (GW/0418-8330). **1539**

STATISTISCHES JAHRBUCH BERLIN. (GW). **5343**

STATISTISK ARBOG. (DK). **5343**

STATISTISK ARBOG FOR NORGE (MICROFICHE). (NO). **5343**

STATISTISK MANEDSHEFTE. (NO/0029-3636). **5344**

STATISZTIKAI SZEMLE. (HU/0039-0690). **1540**

STATSVETENSKAPLIG TIDSKRIFT. (SW/0039-0747). **4497**

STATUS REPORT - INSURANCE INSTITUTE FOR HIGHWAY SAFETY. (US/0018-988X). **5444**

STATUS (SCOTTSDALE). (US/0195-9190). **2082**

STATUTE LAW REVIEW. (UK/0144-3593). **3059**

STAUB, REINHALTUNG DER LUFT. (GW/0039-0771). **2244**

STAVIVO. (XR/0039-0801). **628**

STEAMBOAT BILL (1958). (US/0039-0844). **2762**

STEEL CONSTRUCTION : JOURNAL OF THE AUSTRALIAN INSTITUTE OF STEEL CONSTRUCTION. (AT/0049-2205). **628**

STEEL INDUSTRY UPDATE. (US/1063-4339). Qty: 2. **4020**

STEERING WHEEL (AUSTIN). (US/0039-1298). **5393**

STEINBECK QUARTERLY. (US/0039-100X). **435**

STENDHAL CLUB (GRENOBLE). (FR/0039-1158). **3440**

STEP-BY-STEP GRAPHICS. (US/0886-7682). **382**

STEPPING BACK IN TIME. (US/0894-8313). Qty: 12. **2473**

STEPPKE. (GW/0938-0914). **1069**

STEREO FM RADIO. (AT/0313-0797). **1139**

STERNE UND WELTRAUM. (GW/0039-1263). **400**

STEROID RECEPTORS. (UK/0142-8330). **540**

STEROIDS. (US/0039-128X). **473**

STETSON LAW REVIEW. (US/0739-9731). Qty: varies. **3059**

STEUBEN NEWS. (US). **4513**

STEUER UND WIRTSCHAFT. (GW). **4750**

STEVE WILSON REPORT, THE. (US/1065-0865). **3353**

STEVEN DWORMAN'S INFORMERCIAL MARKETING REPORT. (US/1058-0344). Qty: 4-5. **937**

STILL HERE : JOB/SCHOLARSHIP REFERRAL NEWSLETTER / SCHOOL OF COMMUNICATIONS, HOWARD UNIVERSITY. (US). **1122**

STIRPES. (US/0039-1522). **2473**

STITCH 'N SEW QUILTS. (US/0744-1649). **5186**

STITCHES : THE JOURNAL OF MEDICAL HUMOUR. (CN). Qty: 10. **3643**

STOCK CAR RACING. (US/0734-7340). **4924**

STOCK MARKET MAGAZINE, THE. (US/0039-1638). **916**

STOCKTON RECORD (STOCKTON, CALIF.). (US). **5640**

STOFF MISBRUK : INFORMASJON FRA SENTRALRADET FOR NARKOTIKAPROBLEMER. (NO). **1349**

STOMATOLOGIJA. (RU/0039-1735). **1336**

STOMATOLOSKI GLASNIK SRBIJE. (YU/0039-1743). **1336**

STONE COUNTRY. (US/0146-1397). **3472**

STONE LION REVIEW. (US/0747-6744). **3440**

STONE SOUP (SANTA CRUZ, CALIF.). (US/0094-579X). **1069**

STONEHAM CATALOGUE OF BRITISH STAMPS, THE. (UK/0142-615X). **2787**

STONES & BONES NEWSLETTER. (US/0585-3699). **246**

STOP (BRATISLAVA). (XO/0139-6501). **5426**

STORES. (US/0039-1867). **958**

STORIA DEL PENSIERO ECONOMICO. BOLLETTINO DI INFORMAZIONE. (IT). **1585**

STORIA DELLA STORIOGRAFIA. (IT). **2630**

STORY ART; A MAGAZINE FOR STORYTELLERS. (US/0039-1999). Qty: 4. **3440**

STORYVILLE (CHIGWELL). (UK/0039-2030). **4154**

STOUTONIA, THE. (US). **1095**

STRAD, THE. (UK/0039-2049). **4154**

STRAIN. (UK/0039-2103). **2129**

STRAITS TIMES, THE. (SI). **5810**

STRANA I MIR. (GW). **2523**

STRANGE MAGAZINE. (US/0894-8968). Qty: 12. **2493**

STRANI JEZICI. (CI/0351-0840). **3440**

STRASSE UND AUTOBAHN. (GW/0039-2162). **2031**

STRASSENVERKEHRSUNFAELLE. (GW). **5445**

STRATEGIC HEALTH CARE MARKETING. (US/0749-5153). **3793**

STRATEGIC PLANNING AND ENERGY MANAGEMENT. (US/8750-3204). **1958**

STRATEGIC PLANNING MANAGEMENT. (US/0748-4895). **887**

STRATEGIC REVIEW. (US/0091-6846). **4058**

STRATEGIC REVIEW FOR SOUTHERN AFRICA. (SA). **5223**

STRATEGIES & SOLUTIONS. (US/1067-9537). Qty: 2. **4804**

STRATEGIES (BIRMINGHAM). (UK/0959-8936). **1905**

STRATEGIES DU MANAGEMENT PARIS. (FR/1148-750X). **887**

STRATEGY & TACTICS (CAMBRIA, CALIF.). (US/1040-886X). **4058**

STRATTON MAGAZINE. (US/1064-1629). **4924**

STREET MACHINE (LONDON, ENGLAND). (UK/0143-5949). **5426**

STREET MAGAZINE. (US/0190-1737). **2547**

STREET NEWS. (US). **2547**

STREIT. (GW/0175-4467). Qty: 4-10. **3060**

STRELEC (JERSEY CITY, N.J.). (US/0747-7287). **3440**

STRENGTH AND HEALTH. (US/0039-2308). **2601**

STRICKLAND SCENE. (US/0733-8392). **2474**

STRINGS (SAN ANSELMO, CALIF.). (US/0888-3106). **4155**

STROEZ I FUNKCII NA MOZKA. (BU/0204-4560). **3846**

STROITEL. (RU/0039-2375). **629**

STROJNISKI VESTNIK. (XV/0039-2480). **5160**

STROKE (1970). (US/0039-2499). **3710**

STROKE CONNECTION. (US/1047-014X). Qty: 6. **5312**

STROKING TIMES, THE. (US/8756-0364). **4382**

STROLLING ASTRONOMER, THE. (US/0039-2502). **400**

STROM + SEE. (SZ/0039-2510). **5393**

STROMATA. (AG/0049-2353). **4999**

STRUCTURAL ENGINEERING INTERNATIONAL : JOURNAL OF THE INTERNATIONAL ASSOCIATION FOR BRIDGE AND STRUCTURAL ENGINEERING (IABSE). (SZ/1016-8664). **5393**

STRUCTURAL ENGINEERING REVIEW. (UK/0952-5807). **2031**

STRUCTURAL SURVEY. (US). **629**

STRUCTURES AND ENVIRONMENT HANDBOOK. (US/0149-1245). **629**

STRUCTURIST. (CN/0081-6027). **365**

STRUGGLE : MATHEMATICS FOR LOW ATTAINERS. (UK). **1885**

STRUMENTI MUSICALI. (IT/0392-890X). **4155**

STUART NEWS, THE. (US). Qty: 40. **5651**

STUDENT AID NEWS. (US/0194-2212). **1785**

STUDENT CONTRIBUTION SERIES. (US). **3251**

STUDENT GUIDE TO THE SAT. (US/1043-8378). **1848**

STUDENT HANDBOOK OF INFORMATION ON UNIVERSITY POLICIES AND PRACTICES. (NR). **1848**

STUDENT LEADERSHIP MAGAZINE. (US). Qty: 4-6/year. **1849**

STUDENT PUBLICATION OF THE SCHOOL OF DESIGN. (US/0078-1444). **309**

STUDENT SUCCESS TUTOR DIRECTORY. SARASOTA COUNTY. (US/0899-2355). **1786**

STUDENT VOICE. (US/0039-2804). **1095**

STUDI CATTOLICI. (IT/0039-2901). **5036**

STUDI DI LETTERATURA ISPANO-AMERICANA. (IT/0585-4776). **3440**

STUDI DI TEOLOGIA. (IT). Qty: 60. **4999**

STUDI ECONOMICI E SOCIALI. (IT/0391-8750). **1628**

STUDI ECUMENICI. (IT/0393-3687). Qty: 8-10. **4999**

STUDI ETNO-ANTROPOLOGICI E SOCIOLOGICI / PUBBLICATA SOTTO GLI AUSPICI DEL CONSIGLIO NAZIONALE DELLE RICHERCHE. (IT). **246**

STUDI. FATTI. RICERCHE. (IT/0393-3695). **2493**

STUDI FRANCESI. (IT/0039-2944). **3440**

STUDI GERMANICI. (IT/0039-2952). **3440**

STUDI GORIZIANI. (IT). **2855**

STUDI ITALIANI DI FILOLOGIA CLASSICA. (IT/0039-2987). **1080**

STUDI LINGUISTICI ITALIANI. (IT/0394-3569). **3324**

STUDI PIEMONTESI. (IT). Qty: 120-130/yr. **2711**

STUDI ROMANI. (IT/0039-2995). **2630**

STUDI SENESI NEL CIRCOLO GIURIDICO DELLA R. UNIVERSITA. (IT/0039-3010). **3060**

STUDIA CANONICA. (CN/0039-310X). **5036**

STUDIA CELTICA. (UK/0081-6353). **3324**

STUDIA DIPLOMATICA. (BE/0770-2965). **4497**

STUDIA HIBERNICA. (IE/0081-6477). **3324**

STUDIA IRANICA. (NE/0772-7852). **2665**

STUDIA LEIBNITIANA. (GW/0039-3185). **4361**

STUDIA LINGUISTICA. (SW/0039-3193). **3324**

STUDIA LITURGICA. (NE/0039-3207). **5000**

STUDIA LOGICA. (PL/0039-3215). **4362**

STUDIA MORALIA. (IT/0081-6736). **5000**

STUDIA MUSICOLOGICA NORVEGICA. (NO/0332-5024). **4155**

STUDIA MYSTICA. (US/0161-7222). **3441**

STUDIA NEOPHILOLOGICA. (SW/0039-3274). **3325**

STUDIA PATAVINA. (IT/0039-3304). Qty: 100-120. **5000**

STUDIA PHONETICA POSNANIENSIA. (PL/0861-2085). **3325**

STUDIA PSYCHOLOGICA. (XO) **4619**

STUDIA ROSENTHALIANA. (NE/0039-3347). **2273**

STUDIA SLAVICA ACADEMIAE SCIENTIARUM HUNGARICAE. (HU/0039-3363). **3325**

STUDIA SPINOZANA. (GW). **4362**

STUDIA THEOLOGICA. (NO/0039-338X). **5000**

STUDIEN ZUR UMWELT DES NEUEN TESTAMENTS. (GW/0585-6272). **5000**

STUDIES. (IE/0039-3495). **2523**

STUDIES IN 20TH CENTURY LITERATURE. (US/0145-7888). **3354**

STUDIES IN AMERICAN FICTION. (US/0091-8083). **3354**

STUDIES IN AMERICAN HUMOR. (US/0095-280X). **3441**

STUDIES IN AMERICAN INDIAN LITERATURE. (US). Qty: 20-40. **3441**

STUDIES IN AMERICAN JEWISH LITERATURE (ALBANY, N.Y.). (US/0271-9274). **3441**

STUDIES IN ART EDUCATION. (US/0039-3541). **365**

STUDIES IN BIBLIOGRAPHY AND BOOKLORE. (US/0039-3568). **5013**

STUDIES IN BROWNING AND HIS CIRCLE. (US/0095-4489). **435**

STUDIES IN CENTRAL AND EAST ASIAN RELIGIONS : JOURNAL OF THE SEMINAR FOR BUDDHIST STUDIES, COPENHAGEN & AARHUS. (DK/0904-2431). Qty: 10. **5022**

STUDIES IN CHRISTIAN ETHICS. (UK). **5000**

STUDIES IN COMPARATIVE COMMUNISM. (UK/0039-3592). **4548**

STUDIES IN COMPARATIVE INTERNATIONAL DEVELOPMENT. (US/0039-3606). **5223**

STUDIES IN COMPARATIVE RELIGION. (UK/0039-3622). **5000**

STUDIES IN CONSERVATION. (UK/0039-3630). **366**

STUDIES IN CONTEMPORARY SATIRE. (US/0163-4143). Qty: 2/yr. **3441**

STUDIES IN ECONOMIC ANALYSIS. (US/0198-8263). **1595**

STUDIES IN EDUCATIONAL ADMINISTRATION. (AT). **1872**

STUDIES IN EIGHTEENTH-CENTURY CULTURE. (US/0360-2370). **2631**

STUDIES IN ENGLISH LITERATURE, 1500-1900. (US/0039-3657). **3442**

STUDIES IN FAMILY PLANNING. (US/0039-3665). **591**

STUDIES IN FORMATIVE SPIRITUALITY. (US/0193-2748). Qty: 3-5. **5037**

STUDIES IN HISTORY OF MEDICINE AND SCIENCE. (II). **3643**

STUDIES IN HUMAN RIGHTS. (US/0146-3586). **4513**

STUDIES IN ICONOGRAPHY. (US/0148-1029). **5000**

STUDIES IN LANGUAGE LEARNING. (US/0736-9867). **3326**

STUDIES IN LATIN AMERICAN POPULAR CULTURE. (US/0730-9139). Qty: 10. **331**

STUDIES IN MEDIEVAL AND RENAISSANCE TEACHING. (US/1050-9739). Qty: varies. **2711**

STUDIES IN MODERN EUROPEAN HISTORY AND CULTURE. (US/0098-275X). **2711**

STUDIES IN MUSIC. (AT/0081-8267). **4155**

STUDIES IN PHILOSOPHY AND EDUCATION. (US/0039-3746). **4362**

STUDIES IN POLITICAL ECONOMY. (CN/0707-8552). Qty: varies. **4497**

STUDIES IN POPULAR CULTURE. (US/0888-5753). Qty: varies. **2855**

STUDIES IN RELIGION. (CN/0008-4298). **5001**

STUDIES IN RESOURCE MANAGEMENT. (NZ/0113-0994). **2206**

STUDIES IN ROMANTICISM. (US/0039-3762). **3442**

STUDIES IN SCIENCE EDUCATION. (UK/0305-7267). **5160**

STUDIES IN SCOTTISH LITERATURE. (US/0039-3770). **3354**

STUDIES IN SECOND LANGUAGE ACQUISITION. (US/0272-2631). **3326**

STUDIES IN SHORT FICTION. (US/0039-3789). **3354**

STUDIES IN SIKHISM AND COMPARATIVE RELIGION. (II). **5001**

STUDIES IN SOVIET THOUGHT. (NE/0039-3797). **4362**

STUDIES IN THE AGE OF CHAUCER. (US/0190-2407). **435**

STUDIES IN THE AMERICAN RENAISSANCE. (US/0149-015X). **3354**

STUDIES IN THE DECORATIVE ARTS. (US/1069-8825). Qty: 10. **375**

STUDIES IN THE HUMANITIES. (US). **2855**

STUDIES IN THE LINGUISTIC SCIENCES. (US/0049-2388). **3326**

STUDIES IN THE NOVEL. (US/0039-3827). **3354**

STUDIES IN WESTERN AUSTRALIAN HISTORY. (AT). **2671**

STUDIES IN ZIONISM. (IS/0334-1771). **5053**

STUDIES ON NEOTROPICAL FAUNA AND ENVIRONMENT. (NE/0165-0521). **5598**

STUDIES ON WOMEN ABSTRACTS. (UK/0262-5644). **5572**

STUDIES OVER DE SOCIAAL-ECONOMISCHE GESCHIEDENIS VAN LIMBURG. (NE/0562-4231). **1585**

STUDII SI ARTICOLE DE ISTORIE. (RM/0585-749X). **2711**

STUDII SI CERCETARI DE ANTROPOLOGIE. (RM). **246**

STUDII SI CERCETARI DE BIOCHIMIE. (RM). **493**

STUDII SI MATERIALE DE ISTORIE MEDIE. (RM/0567-6312). **2712**

STUDII SI MATERIALE DE ISTORIE MODERNA. (RM/0567-6320). **2712**

STYLE (FAYETTEVILLE). (US/0039-4238). **3443**

SUB-STANCE. (US/0049-2426). **3443**

SUBSEA ENGINEERING NEWS. (UK/0266-2205). **2095**

SUBSTANCE ABUSE IN SCHOOLS. (US/0895-8874). **1349**

SUBURBAN. COTE DES NEIGES EDITION. (CN/0229-2998). **5795**

SUBURBAN (COTE-SAINT-LUC ED.). (CN/0226-9686). **5795**

SUBURBAN. DOLLARD DES ORMEAUX EDITION. (CN/0229-298X). **5795**

SUBURBAN (LAVAL EDITION). (CN/0229-3048). **2547**

SUBURBAN. NEW BORDEAUX, CARTIERVILLE EDITION. (CN/0229-3013). **5795**

SUBURBAN NEWS (READING), THE. (US/0194-276X). Qty: 10. **5690**

SUBURBAN. NOTRE DAME DE GRACE EDITION. (CN/0229-2971). **5795**

SUBURBAN. ST. LAURENT EDITION. (CN/0229-303X). **5795**

SUBURBAN (WESTMOUNT EDITION). (CN/0229-3005). **5795**

SUCCESSFUL ADVERTISING STRATEGIES. (US/0882-3502). **767**

SUCCESSFUL FUND RAISING. (US/1070-9061). Qty: 1-5. **4339**

SUCCESSFUL HOTEL MARKETER, THE. (US/1040-600X). **2809**

SUCCESSFUL MARKETING TO SENIOR CITIZENS. (US/8755-321X). **937**

SUCCESSFUL SELLING & MANAGING. (AT/1036-1693). **937**

SUCHASNIST. (US/0585-8364). **3443**

SUD; INFORMATION ECONOMIQUE : PROVENCE ALPES COTE D'AZUR. (FR). Qty: 3. **1585**

SUDAN NOTES AND RECORDS. (SJ/0375-2984). **2855**

SUDAN UPDATE. (UK). **2493**

SUDOST EUROPA : [MONATSSCHRIFT DER ABTEILUNG GEGENWARTSFORSCHUNG DES SUDOST-INSTITUTS]. (GW/0722-480X). **5224**

SUDOST-FORSCHUNGEN. (GW/0081-9077). **2712**

SUDOSTDEUTSCHES ARCHIV. (GW/0081-9085). **2712**

SUDOSTEUROPA-MITTEILUNGEN. (GW/0340-174X). **2712**

SUFFOLK TRANSNATIONAL LAW REVIEW. (US/0886-2648). **3136**

SUFFOLK UNIVERSITY LAW REVIEW. (US/0039-4696). **3060**

SUFISM (SAN RAFAEL, CALIF.). (US/0898-3380). Qty: 12. **5001**

SUGAR CANE (1983). (UK/0265-7406). **188**

SUGAR JOURNAL. (US/0039-4734). **188**

SUGAR WORLD. (CN/0229-737X). **2359**

SUGARBEET GROWER, THE. (US/0039-4750). Qty: 2-3. **188**

SUGARLAND. (PH/0039-4777). **188**

SUICIDE & LIFE-THREATENING BEHAVIOR. (US/0363-0234). **4619**

SUID-AFRIKAAN, DIE. (SA/1011-7547). **1523**

SUID-AFRIKAANSE BOSBOUTYDSKRIF. (SA/0038-2167). **2396**

SUID-AFRIKAANSE GEOGRAAF. (SA). **2577**

SUID-AFRIKAANSE TEATERSUSTER. (US). **3870**

SUID-AFRIKAANSE TYDSKRIF VIR APTEEKWESE. (SA/0038-2558). **4330**

SUID-AFRIKAANSE TYDSKRIF VIR NATUURWETENSKAP EN TEGNOLOGIE. (SA/0254-3486). **5160**

SUISAN KAIYO KENKYU. (JA/0916-1562). **2314**

SULFUR LETTERS. (UK/0278-6117). **1038**

SULFUR (PASADENA, CALIF.). (US/0730-305X). Qty: 15. **3443**

SULFUR REPORTS. (SZ/0196-1772). **1038**

SULLIVAN COUNTY DEMOCRAT. (US). Qty: 12. **4497**

SULPHUR IN AGRICULTURE. (US/0160-0680). **188**

SUMLEN. (SW/0346-8119). **4155**

SUMMA MUSICAE MEDII AEVI. (GW/0585-9158). **4155**

SUMMARY OF ACTIVITIES - MENTAL HEALTH LAW PROJECT. (US/0363-2687). **3060**

SUMMER EMPLOYMENT DIRECTORY OF THE UNITED STATES. (US). **1712**

SUMMIT (BIG BEAR LAKE). (US/0039-5056). **4879**

SUMTER COUNTY JOURNAL. (US). **5628**

SUN AT WORK IN EUROPE. (UK/0269-1159). **1958**

SUN (BREMERTON, WASH.), THE. (US/1050-3692). Qty: 45. **5762**

SUN/COAST ARCHITECT/BUILDER. (US/0744-8872). **629**

SUN DANCER REVIEW. (US/1062-6387). Qty: (varies). **3443**

SUN (HUMMELSTOWN, PA.). (US). Qty: 5-10. **5739**

SUN-REPORTER, THE. (US/0890-0930). **5640**

SUN-TIMES (HEBER SPRINGS, ARK.). (US/1050-5105). **5632**

SUNDAY SCHOOL COUNSELOR. (US/0039-5285). **5068**

SUNDAY TELEGRAM, THE. (US). **5685**

SUNDAY TIMES (LONDON, ENGLAND : 1931). (UK). **5813**

SUNDEW GARDENS REPORTS. (US/1052-2247). **4362**

SUNRISE (ALTADENA, CALIF.). (US/0562-6048). Qty: 6-20. **4362**

SUNSET (MENLO PARK, CALIF.). (US/0039-5404). **2547**

SUNSTONE. (US/0363-1370). Qty: 15-20. **5001**

SUNWORLD. (AT/0149-1938). Qty: 4. **1958**

SUOMEN KALASTUSLEHTI. (FI). **2314**

SUOMEN MATKAILU. (FI/0359-0607). **2523**

SUOMEN SHAKKI. (FI). **4924**

SUPER AUTOMOTIVE SERVICE. (US/0896-0437). **5426**

SUPER STOCK & DRAG ILLUSTRATED. (US/0039-5692). **4924**

SUPERCOMPUTER. (NE/0168-7875). **1204**

SUPERCOMPUTING REVIEW. (US/1048-6836). **1204**

SUPERCONDUCTOR INDUSTRY. (US/1042-4105). **5161**

SUPERMAGAZINE D'ARTISANAT LES MOUSTARTS. (CN/0824-6254). **376**

SUPLEMENTO ANTROPOLOGICO - UNIVERSIDAD CATOLICA. (PY/0378-9896). **246**

SUPOSTAVITELNO

SUPOSTAVITELNO EZIKOZNANIE. (BU/0204-8701). **Qty:** 30-60. **3327**

SUPPLEMENT AU BULLETIN ANALYTIQUE PETROLIER. (FR/0249-0420). **4280**

SUPPLEMENTS TO NOVUM TESTAMENTUM. (NE/0167-9732). **5001**

SUPPLEMENTS TO VETUS TESTAMENTUM. (NE/0083-5889). **5001**

SUPPLY LINE. (US/8750-0124). **Qty:** 4-8. **4058**

SUPPORT FOR LEARNING. (UK/0268-2141). **1786**

SUPREME COURT CASES, THE. (II). **3061**

SUR L'EMPREMIER. (CN/0228-9016). **2762**

SUREPAY UPDATE. (US/0195-5225). **813**

SURFACE DESIGN JOURNAL. (US/0197-4483). **Qty:** 4. **5356**

SURFACE ENGINEERING. (UK/0267-0844). **1997**

SURFACE WAVE ABSTRACTS. (UK/0049-2639). **4453**

SURFER. (US/0039-6036). **4924**

SURGERY, GYNECOLOGY & OBSTETRICS. (US/0039-6087). **3975**

SURGERY (OXFORD). (UK/0263-9319). **3975**

SURGICAL NEUROLOGY. (US/0090-3019). **3976**

SURGICAL TECHNOLOGIST, THE. (US/0164-4238). **3644**

SURNAME AND PUBLICATION INDEX. (US/0270-9856). **2474**

SURVEILLANT (WASHINGTON, D.C.). (US/1051-0923). **4058**

SURVEY OF CHAINS AND GROUPS. (CN). **2359**

SURVEY OF OPHTHALMOLOGY. (US/0039-6257). **3879**

SURVEYING AND LAND INFORMATION SYSTEMS. (US/1052-2905). **2583**

SURVEYING TECHNICIAN. (UK/0952-5793). **2032**

SURVEYS IN GEOPHYSICS. (NE/0169-3298). **1411**

SURVEYS IN HIGH ENERGY PHYSICS. (SZ/0142-2413). **4451**

SURVEYS ON MATHEMATICS FOR INDUSTRY. (AU/0938-1953). **1997**

SURVIVAL (LONDON). (UK/0039-6338). **4058**

SURVIVAL : THE INTERNATIONAL NEWSLETTER OF SURVIVAL INTERNATIONAL. (UK). **4513**

SURYA INDIA. (II). **2508**

SUSSEX FAMILY HISTORIAN. (UK). **2474**

SUSTAINABLE FARMING. (CN/1180-1506). **Qty:** 4. **138**

SUVREMENNA ZHURNALISTIKA / [SBZH, NAUCHNO-INFORMATSIONEN TSENTUR]. (BU/0205-1656). **2924**

SVA BULLETIN : OFFIZIELLES ORGAN DER SVA UND DESOAF. (SZ/0036-777X). **4451**

SVENSK BOTANISK TIDSKRIFT. (SW/0039-646X). **528**

SVENSK EXEGETISK ARSBOK. (SW/1100-2298). **5020**

SVENSK FARMACEUTISK TIDSKRIFT. (SW/0039-6524). **4330**

SVENSK MISSIONSTIDSKRIFT. (SW/0346-217X). **5001**

SVENSK PAPPERSTIDNING. (SW/0039-6680). **4239**

SVENSK TEOLOGISK KVARTALSKRIFT. (SW/0039-6761). **5001**

SVENSK TIDSKRIFT. (SW/0039-677X). **3354**

SVENSK TIDSKRIFT FOR MUSIKFORSKNING. (SW/0081-9816). **4155**

SVENSKA TIDNINGSARTIKLAR. (SW/0039-6907). **426**

SVERIGES FRIMARKEN OCH HELSAKER / SVERIGES FILATELIST-FORBUND. (SW/0347-1152). **2787**

SVETSEN. (SW/0039-7091). **4028**

SVOBODA (JERSEY CITY). (US/0274-6964). **5711**

SWAMP GAS JOURNAL, THE. (CN/0707-7106). **37**

SWARA / EAST AFRICAN WILD LIFE SOCIETY. (KE). **5598**

SWEDISH AMERICAN GENEALOGIST. (US/0275-9314). **Qty:** 1-2. **2474**

SWEDISH-AMERICAN HISTORICAL QUARTERLY. (US/0730-028X). **2762**

SWEDISH TOWN AND COUNTRY PLANNING REVIEW, THE. (SW/0032-0560). **Qty:** 6. **2836**

SWEET POTATO. (US/0147-5282). **4155**

SWIM (ARLINGTON, VA.). (US/8755-2027). **4924**

SWIMMING TEACHER. (UK/0306-0403). **Qty:** occassionally. **4925**

SWIMMING TECHNIQUE. (US/0039-7415). **4925**

SWIMMING WORLD AND JUNIOR SWIMMER (1965). (US/0039-7431). **4925**

SWISS AMERICAN REVIEW. (US). **Qty:** 6. **5721**

SWORD OF THE LORD, THE. (US/0039-7547). **5001**

SYCAMORE REVIEW. (US/1043-1497). **Qty:** 6. **3443**

SYDNEY LAW REVIEW, THE. (AT/0082-0512). **3062**

SYDNEY REVIEW 1988. (AT/1032-2892). **Qty:** 40. **331**

SYDNEY'S CHILD. (AT/1034-6384). **Qty:** 11. **2286**

SYGEPLEJERSKEN. (DK/0106-8350). **3870**

SYLLABUS. (US). **3062**

SYLLECTA CLASSICA. (US/1040-3612). **1080**

SYLVATROP. (PH/0115-0022). **2396**

SYMBOLS. (US/0889-7425). **246**

SYMBOLS OF AMERICAN LIBRARIES. (US/0095-0874). **3252**

SYMPOSIUM (SYRACUSE). (US/0039-7709). **3327**

SYNAPSE. (FR/0762-7475). **3846**

SYNAXIS. (CN/0710-1627). **5002**

SYNERGY (DALLAS). (US/0164-8993). **3252**

SYNESIS. (IT). **3444**

SYNOPSES OF THE BRITISH FAUNA. (UK/0082-1101). **5598**

SYNTHESE (DORDRECHT). (NE/0039-7857). **4363**

SYNTHESIS AND REACTIVITY IN INORGANIC AND METAL-ORGANIC CHEMISTRY. (US/0094-5714). **994**

SYNTHETIC COMMUNICATIONS. (US/0039-7911). **1048**

SYNTHETIC CRYSTALS NEWSLETTER. (UK/0309-8133). **Qty:** 6. **1033**

SYRACUSE NEW TIMES. (US/0893-844X). **Qty:** 13. **2493**

SYSDATA. (SZ). **1262**

SYSTEEMTEORETISCH BULLETIN - INTERAKTIE AKADEMIE. (BE/0775-5694). **1886**

SYSTEM (LINKOPING). (UK/0346-251X). **3327**

SYSTEMATIC BOTANY. (US/0363-6445). **Qty:** 6-8. **528**

SYSTEMATIC ENTOMOLOGY. (UK/0307-6970). **5613**

SYSTEMES SOLAIRES. (FR/0295-5873). **1959**

SYSTEMS RESEARCH AND INFORMATION SCIENCE. (US/0882-3014). **3252**

SYSTEMS SCIENCE. (PL/0137-1223). **1249**

SYSTEMS THINKER, THE. (US/1050-2726). **Qty:** 2-4. **887**

SYSTEMS USER. (US/0199-8951). **1262**

SZACHY. (PL). **4866**

SZAZADOK. (HU/0039-8098). **2631**

SZINHAZ. (HU/0039-8136). **5369**

SZOCIOLOGIA (BUDAPEST. 1972). (HU/0133-3461). **5264**

T A S A, TEACHING ATYPICAL STUDENTS IN ALBERTA. (CN/0315-1808). **1886**

T & D. (AT/1037-9687). **887**

T & G RECORD. (UK). **Qty:** 25. **1713**

T.E.C. (PARIS). (FR/0397-6513). **2244**

T.E. NOTES. (US/1054-514X). **Qty:** (20-30). **3354**

T.U.B.A. JOURNAL. (US/0363-4787). **Qty:** 4. **4156**

TAA REPORT. (US/1041-1453). **Qty:** 2. **4832**

TAAL EN TONGVAL. (BE/0039-8691). **3327**

TAAMULI. (TZ). **4497**

TAARS NEWS & NOTES. (US/0740-0241). **284**

TABLE (LONDON. 1953). (UK/0264-7133). **4689**

TABLEAUX DE L'ECONOMIE CALEDONIENNE. (NL). **5344**

TABLET (LONDON), THE. (UK/0039-8837). **5002**

TABLET, THE. (US/0039-8845). **5037**

TABLOID (FAIRFAX, VA.), THE. (US/0279-053X). **4569**

TACT : THE AIR CARGO TARIFF. (NE). **5394**

TACTICAL NOTEBOOK. (US). **Qty:** 50. **4058**

TAFRIJA (TUCKER, GA.). (US/1070-7522). **389**

TAG (STERLING, VA.). (US/1067-9197). **Qty:** 1-3. **1281**

TAGLINE (OLNEY). (UK/0968-0349). **4820**

TAGS. (US). **1786**

TAHQIQAT-I ISLAMI. (II). **5045**

TAI-WAN SHUI LI. (CH). **2244**

TAIDE. (FI/0039-8977). **366**

TAITEEN KESKUSTOIMIKUNNAN TIEDOTUSLEHTI. (FI). **331**

TAITO. (FI/0355-7421). **376**

TAIWAN COMMUNIQUE. (US). **4513**

TAIWAN ENTERPRISE. (CH). **1628**

TAIWAN EXPORTERS GUIDE. (CH). **853**

TAIWAN HAIXIA. (CC/1000-8160). **1457**

TAIWAN STUDIES NEWSLETTER. (US/1048-2342). **2666**

TAIYO CHIKYU KEIHO EISEI CHOSA HOKOKU. (JA). **37**

TAIYO (HEIBONSHA). (JA). **2509**

TAKE FIVE (SASKATOON, SASK.). (CN/0821-0160). **2547**

TAKING CARE. (US). **4804**

TALBOT TIMES. (CN/0827-2816). **2474**

TALEN GRONINGEN. (NE/0922-1166). **3327**

TALENTED. (AT/0815-8150). **Qty:** 5 /year. **1849**

TALES OF THE TWELVE. (CN/0713-3901). **4097**

TALISMAN (HOBOKEN, N.J.). (US/0898-8684). **Qty:** 6. **3472**

TALK (LONDON, ENGLAND). (UK). **1122**

TALKIN' UNION (TAKOMA PARK MD.). (US/0738-7911). **1713**

TALKING LEAF (LOS ANGELES, CALIF. : 1972). (US/0300-6247). **2274**

TALKING LEAVES (WARRENVILLE, ILL.). (US/0894-833X). **Qty:** 4-8. **2206**

TALKS OF POPE JOHN PAUL II. (US). **5037**

TALON (AURORA, COLO.). (US/0892-6476). **Qty:** 4-6. **5598**

TAMARIND PAPERS, THE. (US/0276-3397). **382**

TAMIL EELAM DOCUMENTATION BULLETIN. (CN/0822-2762). **4513**

TAMKANG REVIEW. (CH/0049-2949). **3354**

TAMPA BAY HISTORY. (US/0272-1406). **2762**

TAMPA BAY LIFE (TAMPA, FLA.). (US/1048-0056). **2547**

TANDLAKARTIDNINGEN. (SW/0039-6982). **1336**

TANK. (UK/0039-9418). **4058**

TANTARA. (MG). **2671**

TANTRA (TORREON, N.M.). (US/1064-0584). **Qty:** 12-24. **4363**

TANZANIAN MATHEMATICAL BULLETIN / THE MATHEMATICAL ASSOCIATION OF TANZANIA, THE. (TZ). **3538**

TAR RIVER POETRY. (US/0740-9141). **Qty:** 6. **3472**

TARBIZS. (IS/0334-3650). **5053**

TARBUT (NEW YORK, N.Y. : 1989). (US/0792-5891). **331**

TAREAS. (PN/0494-7061). **5224**

TARGET. (NE/0924-1884). **3327**

TARGET GUN. (UK/0143-8751). **4925**

TARHEEL BANKER, THE. (US/0039-9663). **813**

TARIQ AL-SALAMAH / AL-JAMIYAH AL-URDUNIYAH LIL-WIQAYAH MIN HAWADITH AL-TURUQ. (JO). **5394**

$TARTING $MART. (US/1042-9557). **715**

TAS TOTS. (AT). **1070**

TASMANIAN ANCESTRY. (AT/0159-0677). **Qty:** varies. **2474**

TASPO MAGAZIN. (GW/0177-5014). **2432**

TASTE FULL. (US). **Qty:** 25-30. **2359**

TATE'S EXPORT. (UK). **853**

TATTVALOKAH / TATTVALOKA. (II). **5041**

TAVERNA DE AUERBACH, LA. (IT/0394-3518). **3472**

TAX ADVISER, THE. (US/0039-9957). **4751**

TAX EXECUTIVE, THE. (US/0040-0025). **4752**

TAX EXEMPT NEWS. (US/0194-228X). **4752**

TAX, FINANCIAL AND ESTATE PLANNING FOR THE OWNER OF A CLOSELY-HELD CORPORATION. (US/0194-8822). **3119**

TAX LAW ANTHOLOGY. (US/0892-4430). **3062**

TAX NEWS SERVICE. (NE/0040-0076). **3062**

TAX PLANNING INTERNATIONAL. (UK). **4754**

TAXATION. (UK/0040-0149). **4754**

TAXATION (DON MILLS). (CN/0384-9201). **4755**

TAXATION OF PATENT ROYALTIES, DIVIDENDS, INTEREST IN EUROPE. (NE). **4755**

TAXATION OF PRIVATE INVESTMENT INCOME. (NE). **4755**

TAXIDERMY TODAY. (US/0279-9731). **Qty:** varies. **2778**

TAXON. (GW/0040-0262). **529**

TBC NEWS. (US/1046-8927). **Qty:** 3-4. **4394**

TC. TWIN CITIES. (US/0274-5151). **2547**

TCNN RESEARCH BULLETIN. (NR/0794-7046). **Qty:** 3. **5002**

TE & MS TELECOM ASIA. (HK). **1164**

TE REO. (NZ/0494-8440). **3327**

TEACH (FORT WORTH, TEX.). (US/8755-8769). **5002**

TEACHER EDUCATION. (II/0312-4886). **1905**

TEACHER EDUCATION AND SPECIAL EDUCATION. (US/0888-4064). **1886**

TEACHER EDUCATION QUARTERLY (CLAREMONT, CALIF.). (US/0737-5328). **1906**

TEACHER (HALIFAX). (CN/0382-408X). **1906**

TEACHERS & WRITERS. (US/0739-0084). **3444**

TEACHERS COLLEGE RECORD (1970). (US/0161-4681). **1849**

TEACHERS OF THE WORLD. (GW/0492-4134). **1906**

TEACHING & LEARNING : THE JOURNAL OF NATURAL INQUIRY. (US/0887-9486). **1906**

TEACHING EARTH SCIENCES. (UK/0957-8005). **1360**

TEACHING EDUCATION (COLUMBIA, S.C.). (US/1047-6210). **Qty:** 2 per year. **1906**

TEACHING ELEMENTARY PHYSICAL EDUCATION. (US/1045-4853). **1805**

TEACHING ENGLISH IN THE TWO-YEAR COLLEGE. (US/0098-6291). **1850**

TEACHING ENGLISH TO DEAF AND SECOND-LANGUAGE STUDENTS. (US). **1886**

TEACHING EXCEPTIONAL CHILDREN. (US/0040-0599). **1886**

TEACHING FORUM. (CN/0380-3589). **1850**

TEACHING GEOGRAPHY. (UK). **1907**

TEACHING HISTORY (EMPORIA, KAN.). (US/0730-1383). **2631**

TEACHING HISTORY (LONDON). (UK/0040-0610). **1907**

TEACHING MATHEMATICS. (AT/0313-7767). **Qty:** 15-20 per year. **3538**

TEACHING MATHEMATICS AND ITS APPLICATIONS. (UK/0268-3679). **3538**

TEACHING PHILOSOPHY. (US/0145-5788). **4363**

TEACHING POLITICS. (II). **4498**

TEACHING PRE-K-8. (US/0891-4508). **1805**

TEACHING PUBLIC ADMINISTRATION : TPA. (UK/0144-7394). **4690**

TEACHING SCIENCE. (UK/0028-0763). **5161**

TEACHING SOCIOLOGY. (US/0092-055X). **5264**

TEACHING STATISTICS. (UK/0141-982X). **1798**

TEAM AND TRAIL. (US). **4925**

TEAM MARKETING REPORT. (US). **Qty:** 5-6. **4925**

TECH, THE. (US/0148-9607). **5690**

TECHNI-PORC. (FR/0181-6764). **Qty:** 6. **222**

TECHNICA (BASEL). (BE/0040-0866). **2915**

TECHNICAL AID TO THE DISABLED JOURNAL. (AT/0725-2919). **Qty:** 6-10. **4394**

TECHNICAL ANALYSIS OF STOCKS AND COMMODITIES (JOURNAL). (US/0738-3355). **917**

TECHNICAL COMMUNICATION QUARTERLY. (US/1057-2252). **Qty:** 20. **1122**

TECHNICAL COMPUTING. (US/0891-303X). **1204**

TECHNICAL DIAGNOSTICS AND NONDESTRUCTIVE TESTING. (UK/0955-3835). **1998**

TECHNICAL MONOGRAPH - GREAT BRITAIN. SOIL SURVEY. (UK/0072-7210). **189**

TECHNICAL SERVICES LAW LIBRARIAN. (US/0195-4857). **3252**

TECHNICAL SERVICES QUARTERLY. (US/0731-7131). **3252**

TECHNICAL SOARING. (US/0744-8996). **37**

TECHNICALITIES. (US/0272-0884). **3252**

TECHNICIAN ASSOCIATION NEWS. (US). **2083**

TECHNICIEN DU FILM ET DE LA VIDEO, LA TECHNIQUE, L'EXPLOITATION CINEMAGRAPHIQUE, LE. (FR). **4078**

TECHNICKE PRIUCKY (STATNI VYZKUMNY USTAV PRO STAVBU STROJU). (XR/0231-5297). **2130**

TECHNIK UND GESELLSCHAFT (FRANKFURT AM MAIN, GERMANY). (GW/0723-0664). **5162**

TECHNIKAS APSKATS - LATVIESU INZENIERU APVIENIBA. (CN/0381-5366). **1998**

TECHNIQUE MODERNE, LA. (FR/0040-1250). **5162**

TECHNIQUES & CULTURE. (FR/0248-6016). **5162**

TECHNIQUES, SCIENCES, METHODES : TSM. (FR/0299-7258). **2244**

TECHNISCH-OEKONOMISCHE INFORMATION DER ZIVILEN LUFTFAHRT. (GW). **37**

TECHNISCHE MITTEILUNGEN DER SCHWEIZERISCHEN TELEGRAPHEN- UND TELEPHON-VERWALTUNG. (SZ/0040-1471). **5162**

TECHNISCHE MITTEILUNGEN FUER SAPPEURE, PONTONIERE, UND MINEURE. (SZ). **2032**

TECHNISCHES MESSE : TM. (GW/0171-8096). **4033**

TECHNOLOGIES BANCAIRES. (FR/0765-3069). **813**

TECHNOLOGY & CONSERVATION. (US/0146-1214). **366**

TECHNOLOGY FOR CARDIOLOGY. (US/8756-8586). **3710**

TECHNOLOGY FOR MATERIALS MANAGEMENT. (US/8756-8608). **3644**

TECHNOLOGY FOR RESPIRATORY THERAPY. (US/8756-8616). **3952**

TECHNOLOGY FOR SURGERY. (US/8756-8624). **3976**

TECHNOLOGY FORECASTS AND TECHNOLOGY SURVEYS. (US/0886-0890). **5163**

TECHNOLOGY IRELAND. (IE/0040-1676). **5164**

TECHNOLOGY MANAGEMENT ACTION. (US/0886-103X). **5164**

TECHNOLOGY RESOURCE GUIDES. (US). **5164**

TECHNOLOGY REVIEW. (US/0040-1692). **5164**

TECHNOLOGY TEACHER, THE. (US/0746-3537). **5164**

TECHNOLOGY UPDATE (PALO ALTO, CALIF.). (US/0896-8586). **4394**

TECHNOMETRICS. (US/0040-1706). **5176**

TECHNOSTYLE. (CN/0712-4627). **3444**

TECNICA MOLITORIA. (IT/0040-1862). **204**

TECNICA PESQUERA. (MX). **2314**

TECNICA TEXTIL INTERNACIONAL. (SP/0040-1900). **5356**

TECNOLOGIA ELETTRICHE. INDUSTRIA ITALIANA ELETTROTECNICA ED ELETTRONICA. (IT/0390-6698). **2083**

TECNOLOGIE DEI SERVIZI PUBBLICI. (IT). **4690**

TECNOLOGIE MECCANICHE. (IT/0391-1683). **2130**

TECOLOTE, EL. (US/0741-0034). **2493**

TECTONICS (WASHINGTON, D.C.). (US/0278-7407). **1411**

TEELINE : THE SHORTHAND AND BUSINESS STUDIES MAGAZINE. (UK). **1850**

TEENQUEST. (US/0890-4006). **1070**

TEHNICESKAJA ELEKTRODINAMIKA. (UN/0204-3599). **2084**

TEHNOLOGIJA MESA. (YU/0494-9846). **3488**

TEILHARD REVIEW, THE. (UK/0040-2184). **246**

TEJAS JOURNAL OF AUDIOLOGY AND SPEECH PATHOLOGY. (US/0738-8837). **3891**

TEKAWENNAKE. (CN/0300-3159). **2547**

TEKNOS. (IT). **5165**

TELE-C.L.E.F. (CN/0822-451X). **3063**

TELECOM. (FR). **1164**

TELECOM WORLD. (UK/0963-0597). **1165**

TELECOMMUNICATION JOURNAL (ENGLISH EDITION). (SZ/0497-137X). **1165**

TELECOMMUNICATIONS COUNSELOR. (US/0735-388X). **1165**

TELECOMMUNICATIONS NEWS. (UK/0264-4568). **1165**

TELECOMMUNICATIONS (NORTH AMERICAN EDITION). (US/0278-4831). **1166**

TELECOMMUNICATIONS POLICY. (UK/0308-5961). **1166**

TELECOMMUNICATORS DISPATCH, THE. (US/0887-1647). **1166**

TELECOMMUTING REVIEW. (US/8756-7431). **Qty:** 4. **1166**

TELECONNECT. (US/0740-9354). **1166**

TELEGRAPH HERALD (1935). (US/1041-293X). **Qty:** 2. **5673**

TELEMA (KINSHASA). (CG/1013-7769). **5002**

TELEMANAGEMENT (PICKERING). (CN/0840-5476). **1167**

TELEMARKETING. (US/0730-6156). **1167**

TELEMATICS COMMUNICATIONS QUARTERLY. (US). **Qty:** 1. **1123**

TELESCOPE (DETROIT). (US/0040-2702). **4184**

TELESPAN. (US/0743-2283). **1167**

TELESPECTATEUR, LE. (CN/0712-6891). **1140**

TELEVISION BROADCAST. (US/0898-767X). **1140**

TELEVISION (LONDON). (UK/0308-454X). **1141**

TELEVISION QUARTERLY (BEVERLY HILL). (US/0040-2796). **1141**

TELLURIDE TIMES-JOURNAL, THE. (US). **5644**

TELOS (ST. LOUIS). (US/0090-6514). **5224**

TEMA CELESTE. (IT). **Qty:** varies. **366**

TEMAS DE TRABAJO SOCIAL. (CU/0256-2863). **5312**

TEMAS (NEW YORK, N.Y.). (US/0040-2869). **2493**

TEMENOS. (UK/0262-4524). **332**

TEMPDIGEST (HOUSTON, TEX.). (US/0897-5574). **Qty:** 3-4. **4209**

TEMPLE INTERNATIONAL AND COMPARATIVE LAW JOURNAL. (US/0889-1915). **3136**

TEMPLE LAW REVIEW. (US/0899-8086). **3063**

TEMPLE POLITICAL & CIVIL RIGHTS LAW REVIEW. (US/1062-5887). **Qty:** 2. **4513**

TEMPO. (MZ). **2500**

TEMPO (LONDON). (UK/0040-2982). **4156**

TEMPO MEDICO. (IT). **3645**

TEMPO PRESENTE. (IT). **Qty:** 80. **4498**

TEMPS DE VIVRE (MONTREAL). (CN/0708-7632). **5182**

TEMPS LIBRE (MONTREAL). (CN/0823-5708). **Qty:** 4. **5492**

TEMPTATION OF SAINT ANTHONY, THE. (US/1062-3981). **4620**

TEN.8. (UK/0142-9663). **4377**

TENKI. (JA/0546-0921). **1436**

TENNESSEE ANCESTORS. (US/0882-0635). **Qty:** 5. **2474**

TENNESSEE FOLKLORE SOCIETY BULLETIN. (US/0040-3253). **Qty:** 6-10. **2324**

TENNESSEE JOURNAL OF HEALTH, PHYSICAL EDUCATION, RECREATION, AND DANCE / TENNESSEE ASSOCIATION OF HEALTH, PHYSICAL EDUCATION, RECREATION, AND DANCE. (US/0890-1597). **Qty:** 2-8. **1859**

TENNESSEE

TENNESSEE LAW REVIEW. (US/0040-3288). **3063**

TENNESSEE LIBRARIAN. (US/0162-1564). **3252**

TENNESSEE LINGUISTICS. (US/0740-8021). **3328**

TENNESSEE QUERIES. (US/0898-5472). **2474**

TENNESSEE REGISTER, THE. (US/1041-1569). Qty: 10. **5746**

TENNESSEE VOLUNTEERS MAGAZINE. (US). **1095**

TENNIS LONDON. 1981. (UK/0262-9224). **4925**

TENNIS MAGAZINE. AUSTRALIA. (AT). **4926**

TENNIS WEEK. (US/0194-9098). **4926**

TENNIS WORLD. (UK/0040-3474). **4926**

TENNISPRO. (US). **4926**

TENOLAI. (II). **5176**

TENOR. (II). **3445**

TEOLOGIA Y VIDA. (CL/0049-3449). Qty: 25-30. **5002**

TEOLOGINEN AIKAKAUSKIRJA. TEOLOGISK TIDSKRIFT. (FI/0040-3555). Qty: 160. **5002**

TEPLOENERGETIKA (MOSKVA, 1954). (RU/0040-3636). **2130**

TEPLOFIZIKA VYSOKIKH TEMPERATUR. (RU/0040-3644). **4423**

TER HERKENNING. (NE). **5002**

TERATOLOGY (PHILADELPHIA). (US/0040-3709). **474**

TERESIANUM. (IT). **5003**

TERMNET NEWS : JOURNAL OF THE INTERNATIONAL NETWORK FOR TERMINOLOGY (TERMNET). (AU/0251-5253). **3328**

TERRA ET AQUA. (NE/0376-6411). Qty: 6/yr. **2096**

TERRA GRISCHUNA. (SZ). **2712**

TERRA (LOS ANGELES, CALIF.). (US/0040-3733). **4173**

TERRA NOVA. (UK/0954-4879). **1411**

TERRAE INCOGNITAE. (US/0082-2884). **2577**

TERRE DE CHEZ NOUS. DOSSIER D'INFORMATION TECHNIQUE ET PROFESSIONNELLE, LA. (CN/0823-2784). **141**

TERRE DE CHEZ NOUS (MONTREAL). (CN/0040-3830). **141**

TERREBONNE LIFE LINES. (US/0735-2794). Qty: 15. **2474**

TERRELL TRAILS. (US/0884-2108). **2474**

TERRITOIRES. (FR). **4498**

TERRITORIAL, THE. (US/0890-4235). Qty: 3-4. **2547**

TERROR AUSTRALIS: THE AUSTRALIAN HORROR & FANTASY MAGAZINE. (AT/1031-3001). **3445**

TERTIARY RESEARCH. (NE/0308-9649). **1399**

TERZIARIA. (IT). Qty: 30. **1524**

TERZO MONDO. (IT/0040-392X). Qty: 20. **5264**

TERZOOCCHIO. (IT). Qty: 20. **366**

TESL CANADA JOURNAL. (CN/0826-435X). **3328**

TESL REPORTER. (US/0886-0661). Qty: 4. **1787**

TESOL QUARTERLY. (US/0039-8322). **3328**

TEST. (SZ). **1300**

TEST & MEASUREMENT WORLD. (US/0744-1657). **2084**

TEST (OAKHURST, N.J.). (US/0193-4120). **2130**

TETON. (US/0049-3481). **4879**

TETON VALLEY NEWS. (US/0889-9851). Qty: 10. **5657**

TEX-RAYS : OFFICIAL JOURNAL TEXAS SOCIETY OF RADIOLOGIC TECHNOLOGISTS, INC. (US). **3947**

TEXAS ARCHITECT. (US/0040-4179). **310**

TEXAS BANKING. (US/0885-6907). Qty: 3. **813**

TEXAS BAPTIST HISTORY. (US/0732-4324). **5068**

TEXAS BAR JOURNAL. (US/0040-4187). **3063**

TEXAS BASKETBALL MAGAZINE. (US). **4926**

TEXAS BICYCLIST. (US). **429**

TEXAS BOOKS IN REVIEW. (US/0739-3202). Qty: 125. **4833**

TEXAS CAVER, THE. (US/0040-4233). **1411**

TEXAS CHILD CARE. (US/1049-9466). Qty: 12-16. **1070**

TEXAS CITY SUN. (US). **5755**

TEXAS COACH. (US/0040-4241). **4926**

TEXAS COLLEGE ENGLISH. (US/0889-6011). Qty: varies. **1850**

TEXAS EMS MAGAZINE. (US/1063-8202). **4805**

TEXAS GARDENER (WACO, TX.). (US/0744-0987). **2432**

TEXAS GULF HISTORICAL AND BIOGRAPHICAL RECORD, THE. (US). **2763**

TEXAS HIGHWAYS (AUSTIN, TEX.). (US/0040-4349). **5492**

TEXAS INTERNATIONAL LAW JOURNAL. (US/0163-7479). **3136**

TEXAS JEWISH POST, THE. (US/0040-439X). **5755**

TEXAS JOURNAL OF IDEAS, HISTORY, AND CULTURE. (US/0894-3354). Qty: 10-12. **2855**

TEXAS JOURNAL OF POLITICAL STUDIES. (US/0191-0930). Qty: 20-25. **4498**

TEXAS LAW REVIEW. (US/0040-4411). **3064**

TEXAS LIVESTOCK MARKET NEWS. (US/0199-7041). **222**

TEXAS MANUFACTURERS REGISTER. (US/0743-1163). **3488**

TEXAS OBSERVER, THE. (US). **5755**

TEXAS PRINTER. (US/1043-2302). **4570**

TEXAS REVIEW (HUNTSVILLE, TEX.), THE. (US/0885-2685). **3354**

TEXAS STATE DIRECTORY. (US/0363-7530). **4690**

TEXAS STUDIES IN LITERATURE AND LANGUAGE. (US/0040-4691). **3445**

TEXAS TELLER QUARTERLY NEWSLETTER. (US/0892-5186). Qty: 6. **3445**

TEXAS THOROUGHBRED (WICHITA FALLS, KAN.). (US/0164-6168). **2802**

TEXAS VETERINARIAN. (US/1071-0566). **5522**

TEXAS VETERINARY MEDICAL JOURNAL. (US/0040-4756). **5522**

TEXAS WOMAN (FORT WORTH, TEX.). (US/0279-2443). **5567**

TEXINCON AHMEDABAD. (II/0970-5686). **5357**

TEXT TECHNOLOGY. (US/1053-900X). **1205**

TEXTBOOK NEWS. (US/0733-8228). **1787**

TEXTES - SOCIETE HISTORIQUE DE QUEBEC. (CN/0081-1130). Qty: 3. **2763**

TEXTIL- ES TEXTILRUHAZATI IPARI SZAKIRODALMI TAJEKOZTATO. (HU/0209-9578). **5357**

TEXTIL PRAXIS INTERNATIONAL. (GW/0040-4853). **5357**

TEXTILE ASIA. (HK/0049-3554). **5357**

TEXTILE CHEMIST AND COLORIST. (US/0040-490X). **5357**

TEXTILE DYER & PRINTER. (II/0040-4926). Qty: 26. **5357**

TEXTILE FLAMMABILITY DIGEST. (US/0738-9620). **5357**

TEXTILE INDUSTRY & TRADE JOURNAL. (II/0040-4993). **5358**

TEXTILE MAGAZINE, THE. (II/0040-5078). Qty: 12. **5358**

TEXTILE MANUFATURING. (US/1065-1713). **5358**

TEXTILE RESEARCH JOURNAL. (US/0040-5175). **5358**

TEXTILE TECHNOLOGY DIGEST. (US/0040-5191). **5360**

TEXTILE TRENDS. (II/0040-5205). **5358**

TEXTILE VIEW MAGAZINE. (NE). **5358**

TEXTILES. (UK/0306-0748). **5359**

TEXTILVEREDLUNG. (SZ/0040-5310). **5359**

TEXTRACTS. (US/0495-3789). **5359**

TEXTUAL STUDIES IN CANADA. (CN). Qty: 8-10. **3355**

TEXTURES AND MICROSTRUCTURES. (US/0730-3300). **1033**

TGA-PC (ARLINGTON, VA.). (US/1047-045X). Qty: 6-10/yr. **1850**

THALIA (OTTAWA). (CN/0706-5604). **3445**

THANATOS. (US/0160-8681). Qty: 12-15. **4363**

THEATER. (GW). **5369**

THEATER IN OSTERREICH / WIENER GESELLSCHAFT FUER THEATERFORSCHUNG, INSTITUT FUER THEATERWISSENSCHAFT AN DER UNIVERSITAT WIEN. (AU). **5370**

THEATER (NEW HAVEN, CONN.). (US/0161-0775). **5370**

THEATER RUNDSCHAU. (GW). Qty: 30/year. **5370**

THEATER WEEK. (US/0896-1956). **5370**

THEATERZEITSCHRIFT. (GW/0723-1172). Qty: 10-15. **389**

THEATRE & THERAPY. (UK). **5370**

THEATRE CRAFTS. (US/0040-5469). **5370**

THEATRE CRAFTS DIRECTORY. (US). **5370**

THEATRE CRAFTS INTERNATIONAL. (US/1060-3042). **5370**

THEATRE DIRECTORY OF THE SAN FRANCISCO BAY AREA. (US/0737-0172). **5370**

THEATRE HISTORY IN CANADA. (CN/0226-5761). **5370**

THEATRE HISTORY STUDIES. (US/0733-2033). **5370**

THEATRE INSIGHT. (US). **5370**

THEATRE IRELAND. (IE/0263-6344). **5370**

THEATRE JOURNAL (WASHINGTON, D.C.). (US/0192-2882). **5371**

THEATRE NOTEBOOK. (UK/0040-5523). **5371**

THEATRE ORGAN (1970). (US/0040-5531). Qty: 3. **4156**

THEATRE RECORD. (UK/0962-1792). **5371**

THEATRE RESEARCH IN CANADA. (CN/1196-1198). Qty: 10. **5371**

THEATRE RESEARCH INTERNATIONAL. (UK/0307-8833). **5371**

THEATRE SOUTHWEST. (US/0743-5452). **5371**

THEATRE STUDIES. (US/0362-0964). Qty: 25. **5371**

THEATRE SURVEY. (US/0040-5574). **5371**

THEATRE TIMES. (US/0732-300X). **5371**

THEM DAYS. (CN/0381-6109). **2763**

THEMATA CHOROU + TECHNON. (GR/0074-1191). **310**

THEMELIOS. (UK/0307-8388). **5003**

THEMEN DER PRAKTISCHEN THEOLOGIE, THEOLOGIA PRACTICA. (GW/0720-9525). **5003**

THEMES IN DRAMA. (UK/0263-676X). **389**

THEODORE ROOSEVELT ASSOCIATION JOURNAL. (US/0161-8423). **435**

THEOLOGIAI SZEMLE. (HU/0133-7599). **5003**

THEOLOGICA XAVERIANA. (CK). **5037**

THEOLOGICAL BOOK REVIEW. (UK/0954-2191). **5003**

THEOLOGICAL DIGEST & OUTLOOK. (CN/1184-8901). Qty: 5. **5003**

THEOLOGICAL EDUCATOR, THE. (US/0198-6856). Qty: 75-100. **5003**

THEOLOGICAL REVIEW (BEIRUT, LEBANON). (LE/0379-9557). **5003**

THEOLOGIE DER GEGENWART. (GW). **5003**

THEOLOGISCH-PRAKTISCHE QUARTALSCHRIFT. (AU/0040-5663). **5037**

THEOLOGISCHE BEITRAEGE. (GW/0342-2372). **5003**

THEOLOGISCHE LITERATURZEITUNG. (GW/0040-5671). **5004**

THEOLOGISCHE QUARTALSCHRIFT (MUNCHEN). (GW/0342-1430). Qty: 50. **5004**

THEOLOGISCHE REVUE. (GW/0040-568X). **5004**

THEOLOGISCHE RUNDSCHAU. (GW/0040-5698). **5004**

THEOLOGISCHE ZEITSCHRIFT. (SZ/0040-5701). **5004**

THEOLOGOS, HO. (IT). Qty: 15-20. **5004**

THEOLOGY DIGEST. (US/0040-5728). **5004**

THEOLOGY TODAY (EPHRATA, PA.). (US/0040-5736). **5004**

THEORETICAL AND APPLIED GENETICS. (GW/0040-5752). **551**

THEORETICAL LINGUISTICS. (GW/0301-4428). **3328**

THEORETICAL MEDICINE. (NE/0167-9902). **3645**

THEORIA. (SW/0040-5825). **4363**

THEORIA (PIETERMARITZBURG). (SA/0040-5817). **2855**

THEORIA/PRAXIS: A GRADUATE JOURNAL OF THEORY AND CRITICISM. (CN) **5224**

THEORY AND DECISION. (NE/0040-5833). **4363**

THEORY AND PRACTICE : JOURNAL OF THE MUSIC THEORY SOCIETY OF NEW YORK STATE. (US/0741-6156). **Qty:** 4. **4156**

THEORY & PSYCHOLOGY. (UK/0959-3543). **4620**

THEORY AND RESEARCH IN SOCIAL EDUCATION. (US/0093-3104). **5224**

THEOSOPHICAL HISTORY. (US/0951-497X). **Qty:** 12. **5004**

THEOSOPHICAL MOVEMENT, THE. (II/0040-5884). **5045**

THEOSOPHY. (US/0040-5906). **4363**

THERAPEUTIC DRUG MONITORING. (US/0163-4356). **4330**

THERAPEUTISCHE UMSCHAU. (SZ/0040-5930). **3976**

THERAPIE. (FR/0040-5957). **4330**

THERAPIE DER GEGENWART. (GW/0040-5965). **3645**

THERIOGENOLOGY. (US/0093-691X). **5522**

THERIOS : REVISTA DE MEDICINA VETERINARIA Y PRODUCCION ANIMAL. (AG). **Qty:** 20 per year. **5523**

THERMOLOGY. (US/0882-3758). **3645**

THESAURUS - INSTITUTO CARO Y CUERVO. (CK/0040-604X). **Qty:** 10. **3328**

THESAURUS LINGUAE LATINAE. (GW). **1929**

THESES ZOOLOGICAE. (GW). **5598**

THESIS. (US/0892-2330). **1850**

THESIS ELEVEN. (US/0725-5136). **5264**

THETA (DURHAM). (US/0040-6066). **4243**

THIEF RIVER FALLS TIMES. (US/8750-3883). **5699**

THIN-WALLED STRUCTURES. (UK/0263-8231). **2032**

THINKING. (US/0190-3330). **1907**

THINKING FAMILIES. (US/1046-0845). **1787**

THIRD OPINION. (AT/1030-5467). **2511**

THIRD RAIL (LOS ANGELES, CALIF.). (US/0741-5958). **3446**

THIRD WAY. (UK/0309-3492). **Qty:** 50. **5004**

THIRD WORLD ECONOMICS. (MY/0128-4134). **1524**

THIRD WORLD LIBRARIES. (US/1052-3049). **3253**

THIRD WORLD PLANNING REVIEW. (UK/0142-7849). **2836**

THIRD WORLD QUARTERLY. (UK/0143-6597). **1587**

THIRD WORLD REPORTS. (UK). **2912**

THIRD WORLD RESOURCES. (US/8755-8831). **2912**

THIRD WORLD RESURGENCE. (MY/0128-357X). **2855**

THIS PEOPLE. (US/0273-6527). **5004**

THIS WEEK MAGAZINE (PORTLAND, ORE.). (US/0746-1100). **5734**

THISTLE, THE. (CN). **2493**

THOMAS HARDY YEAR BOOK. (UK/0082-416X). **3446**

THOMAS WOLFE REVIEW, THE. (US/0276-5683). **3446**

THOMIST, THE. (US/0040-6325). **4363**

THORAX. (UK/0040-6376). **3952**

THOREAU SOCIETY BULLETIN, THE. (US/0040-6406). **Qty:** 40. **3446**

THORNY TRAIL, THE. (US/0094-0844). **2475**

THOROUGHBRED OF CALIFORNIA, THE. (US/0049-3821). **2803**

THOROUGHBRED RECORD. FOREIGN STATISTICAL REVIEW, THE. (US). **2803**

THOROUGHBRED TIMES. (US/0887-2244). **2803**

THOUGHT & ACTION (WASHINGTON, D.C.). (US/0748-8475). **1850**

THOUGHT (NEW YORK). (US/0040-6457). **5005**

THREADS MAGAZINE. (US/0882-7370). **5359**

THREADS OF LIFE. (US/0895-8416). **Qty:** 20-30/yr. **2475**

THREEPENNY REVIEW, THE. (US/0275-1410). **3446**

THRESHOLD. (UK/0040-6562). **3446**

THRESHOLDS IN EDUCATION. (US/0196-9641). **1787**

THROMBOSIS AND HAEMOSTASIS. (GW/0340-6245). **3801**

THROMBOSIS RESEARCH. (US/0049-3848). **3710**

THRUST. (US/0190-3381). **1714**

THUNDER BAY MAGAZINE. (CN/0823-6542). **2547**

THURGOOD MARSHALL LAW REVIEW. (US/0749-1646). **3064**

THYMUS. (NE/0165-6090). **3677**

TIBET JOURNAL, THE. (II). **2666**

TIBETAN REVIEW. (II/0040-6708). **2577**

TIBIA. (GW). **4156**

TIDE : TERI INFORMATION DIGEST ON ENERGY. (II/0971-085X). **1959**

TIDEWATER VIRGINIA FAMILIES. (US/1061-8678). **Qty:** 35. **2475**

TIDINGS (LOS ANGELES). (US/0040-6791). **5037**

TIDSKRIFT FOR MEDICINSK OCH TEKNISK FOTOGRAFI. (SW/1100-6323). **4377**

TIDSKRIFT FOR RATTSSOCIOLOGI. (SW). **3064**

TIDSKRIFT I FORTIFIKATION. (SW/0040-6937). **Qty:** 4. **4059**

TIDSSKRIFT FOR DEN NORSKE LAEGEFORENING; TIDSSKRIFT FOR PRAKTISK MEDISIN. THE JOURNAL OF THE NORWEGIAN MEDICAL ASSOCIATION. (NO/0029-2281). **3645**

TIDSSKRIFT FOR RETTSVIDENSKAP. (NO/0040-7143). **3064**

TIDSSKRIFT FOR SAMFUNNSFORSKNING. (NO/0040-716X). **5224**

TIDSSKRIFT FOR TEOLOGI OG KIRKE. (NO/0040-7194). **5005**

TIE REPORT. (NE/0196-254X). **1714**

TIEMPOS MEDICOS DE ESPANA. (SP/0210-9999). **1788**

TIERARZTLICHE PRAXIS. (GW/0303-6286). **5523**

TIERARZTLICHE UMSCHAU. (GW/0049-3864). **5523**

TIETOPALVELU. (FI/0782-825X). **3253**

TIGERPAPER. (TH). **2207**

TIGHTWAD GAZETTE. (US/1065-366X). **Qty:** 2. **2793**

TIJDSCHRIFT RECHTSDOCUMENTATIE. (BE/0771-0704). **3064**

TIJDSCHRIFT VAN DE VERENIGING VOOR NEDERLANDSE MUZIEKGESCHIEDENIS. (NE/0042-3874). **4156**

TIJDSCHRIFT VOOR ALCOHOL, DRUGS EN ANDERE PSYCHOTROPE STOFFEN. (NE/0378-2778). **1349**

TIJDSCHRIFT VOOR ANTILLIAANS RECHT, JUSTICIA / UITGEVER STICHTING TIJDSCHRIFT VOOR ANTILLIAANS RECHT, JUSTICIA. (NA). **3064**

TIJDSCHRIFT VOOR ARBITRAGE. (NE/0167-1359). **3064**

TIJDSCHRIFT VOOR BESTUURSWETENCHAPPEN EN PUBLEKRECHT. (BE/0040-7437). **3064**

TIJDSCHRIFT VOOR BESTUURSWETENSCHAPPEN EN PUBLEKRECHT. (BE). **4690**

TIJDSCHRIFT VOOR CRIMINOLOGIE. (NE/0165-182X). **3178**

TIJDSCHRIFT VOOR DIERGENEESKUNDE. (NE/0040-7453). **5523**

TIJDSCHRIFT VOOR ECONOMIE EN MANAGEMENT. (BE/0772-7674). **1524**

TIJDSCHRIFT VOOR ECONOMISCHE EN SOCIALE GEOGRAFIE : TESG. (NE/0040-747X). **1524**

TIJDSCHRIFT VOOR FAMILIE- EN JEUGDRECHT. (NE). **3122**

TIJDSCHRIFT VOOR GENEESKUNDE. (BE/0371-683X). **Qty:** 150-160/yr. **3802**

TIJDSCHRIFT VOOR GESCHIEDENIS (1920). (NE/0040-7518). **2631**

TIJDSCHRIFT VOOR MARKETING. (NE). **937**

TIJDSCHRIFT VOOR ONDERWIJSRESEARCH. (NE/0166-591X). **5165**

TIJDSCHRIFT VOOR PARAPSYCHOLOGIE. (NE). **4243**

TIJDSCHRIFT VOOR PRIVAATRECHT. (BE). **3091**

TIJDSCHRIFT VOOR PSYCHIATRIE. (NE/0303-7339). **3937**

TIJDSCHRIFT VOOR SEKSUOLOGIE. (NE/0167-5915). **5188**

TIJDSCHRIFT VOOR SOCIAAL WETENSCHAPPELIJK ONDERZOEK VAN DE LANDBOUW. (NE/0921-481X). **Qty:** 20. **141**

TIJDSCHRIFT VOOR SOCIALE WETENSCHAPPEN. (BE/0040-7615). **5224**

TIJDSCHRIFT VOOR THEOLOGIE. (NE/0168-9959). **5005**

TIJDSCHRIFT VOOR VERVOERSWETENSCHAP. (NE/0040-7623). **5394**

TIJDSCHRIFT VOOR WELZIJNSWERK. (BE). **Qty:** 20. **5312**

TIKALIA. (GT). **141**

TIKHOOKEANSKAIA GEOLOGIIA. ENGLISH. (SZ/8755-755X). **1399**

TILBURG FOREIGN LAW REVIEW. (NE/0926-874X). **3064**

TILE & DECORATIVE SURFACES. (US/0192-9550). **2907**

TILLER (ALEXANDRIA, VA.), THE. (US/1068-896X). **4184**

TIMARIT MALS OG MENNINGAR. (IC). **3355**

TIMBER GROWER. (UK/0040-7763). **Qty:** varies. **2396**

TIMBER TRADE REVIEW. (MY). **1629**

TIMBER/WEST. (US/0192-0642). **2405**

TIME & TIDE. (II/0040-7836). **Qty:** 24-30. **4078**

TIME (CHICAGO, ILL.). (US/0040-781X). **2493**

TIMELINE. (US/0748-9579). **2763**

TIMELINES (EUGENE, OR). (US/1074-1593). **2253**

TIMEPIECE. (UK). **2916**

TIMES 1000, THE. (UK). **715**

TIMES-BULLETIN. THE. (US/8750-1503). **5730**

TIMES CLARION (HARLOWTON, MONT.), THE. (US/0889-5627). **Qty:** 10. **5706**

TIMES EDUCATIONAL SUPPLEMENT, THE. (UK/0040-7887). **1788**

TIMES INTERNATIONAL (LAGOS, NIGERIA : 1979). (NR). **2644**

TIMES LEADER (WILKES-BARRE, PA.). (US/0896-4084). **5740**

TIMES OF OMAN. (MK). **5807**

TIMES OF THE AMERICAS, THE. (US/0040-7917). **2552**

TIMES OF TI. (US/0746-0392). **5721**

TIMES-PLAIN DEALER, THE. (US). **Qty:** 2-3. **5673**

TIMES-POST. (US/0746-3901). **5702**

TIMES RECORD (BRUNSWICK, ME), THE. (US/0747-1300). **5685**

TIMES STANDARD, THE. (US). **Qty:** 50. **5640**

TIMES, THE. (US). **Qty:** 12/year. **5655**

TIMES (TRENTON, N.J. PRINCETON METRO ED.), THE. (US/8750-9083). **5711**

TIMES TRIBUNE (CORBIN, KY.). (US). **5682**

TIN AND ITS USES. (UK/0040-7941). **4022**

TIN INTERNATIONAL. (UK/0040-795X). **2152**

TINCTORIA. (IT/0040-7984). **5359**

TINTA (SANTA BARBARA, CALIF.). (US/0739-7003). **3446**

TIROLER HEIMAT. (AU/1013-8919). **2712**

TIRRA LIRRA. (AT/1038-8400). **Qty:** 4-6. **3446**

TISSUE & CELL. (UK/0040-8166). **540**

TISSUE ANTIGENS. (DK/0001-2815). **3802**

TITLE INDEX OF CURRENT REVIEWS. (US/0739-4616). **426**

TIZ. (GW/0722-9488). **2152**

TJFR HEALTH NEWS REPORTER. (US). **Qty:** 12. **3646**

TJI : TOBACCO JOURNAL INTERNATIONAL. (GW/0721-5185). **5373**

TJURUNGA; AN AUSTRALASIAN BENEDICTINE REVIEW. (AT). **5037**

TJUSTBYGDEN. (SW). **2712**

TLC -- FOR PLANTS. (CN/0835-3271). **2432**

TMO UPDATE. (US/0270-0123). **4033**

TMSA AEROSPACE MARKET OUTLOOK. (US/0271-7417). **37**

TOBACCO, WORLD MARKETS & TRADE / UNITED STATES DEPARTMENT OF AGRICULTURE, FOREIGN AGRICULTURAL SERVICE. (US). **5374**

TOCHER; TALES, SONGS, TRADITION. (UK/0049-397X). **4156**

TOCQUEVILLE REVIEW, THE. (US/0730-479X). **5224**

TODAY IN MISSISSIPPI. (US/1052-2433). **2084**

TODAY'S AQUARIST (DEVON, CONN.). (US/1040-2098). **Qty:** Varies. **4879**

TODAY'S CATHOLIC (SAN ANTONIO, TEX.). (US/0745-3612). **5037**

TODAY'S CATHOLIC TEACHER. (US/0040-8441). **1873**

TODAY'S CHEMIST AT WORK. (US/1062-094X). **994**

TODAY'S CHICAGO WOMAN. (US/1071-3786). **5567**

TODAY'S CHIROPRACTIC. (US/0091-2360). **Qty:** 18. **3646**

TODAY'S CHRISTIAN WOMAN. (US/0163-1799). **5005**

TODAY'S FEED LOTTING. (AT/1034-6147). **223**

TODAY'S HEALTH (TORONTO). (CN/0821-6819). **4805**

TODAY'S HEALTHCARE MANAGER. (US/1054-5204). **Qty:** 4-6. **3793**

TODAY'S HERBS. (US). **Qty:** 12. **3775**

TODAY'S MOTOR. (AT/1033-1069). **Qty:** varies. **2130**

TODAY'S PARENT. (CN/0823-9258). **2286**

TODAY'S PARISH. (US/0040-8549). **5005**

TODAY'S REFINERY. (US/1048-0935). **4280**

TODAY'S TRANSPORT INTERNATIONAL. (US/0040-859X). **853**

TODAY'S TRUCKING. (CN/0837-1512). **5394**

TOERTENELMI SZEMLE. (HU/0040-9634). **2631**

TOHOGAKU. (JA/0495-7199). **2666**

TOK BLONG PASIFIK. (CN). **Qty:** varies. **2671**

TOLDOT HA-DOAR SHEL ERETS YISRAEL. (IS). **2787**

TOLE WORLD. (US/0199-4514). **332**

TOLEDO SPORTSMAN, THE. (US/8750-6726). **4926**

TOLL FREE DIGEST. (US/0363-2962). **1168**

TOLLEY'S COMPUTER LAW AND PRACTICE. (UK/0266-4801). **1227**

TON REPORT. (GW). **5319**

TONEEL TEATRAAL. (NE/0040-9170). **389**

TONGA YONGU. (KO). **2666**

TONKAWA NEWS, THE. (US). **Qty:** 12. **5732**

TONOPAH TIMES-BONANZA AND GOLDFIELD NEWS. (US). **5708**

TOOL & ALLOY STEELS. (II/0377-9408). **2130**

TOP 10'S AND TRIVIA OF ROCK & ROLL AND RHYTHM & BLUES. (US). **4156**

TOP AGRAR : DAS MAGAZIN FUR MODERNE LANDWIRTSCHAFT. (GW). **141**

TOPEKA GENEALOGICAL SOCIETY QUARTERLY, THE. (US/0734-8495). **2475**

TOPICAL LAW. (UK/0265-9735). **3065**

TOPICAL LAW REPORTS. (CN). **853**

TOPICAL STUDIES. (US). **2763**

TOPICAL TIME. (US/0040-9332). **Qty:** 20-50. **2788**

TOPICS IN CLINICAL NUTRITION. (US/0883-5691). **4199**

TOPICS IN EARLY CHILDHOOD SPECIAL EDUCATION. (US/0271-1214). **1886**

TOPICS IN GERIATRIC REHABILITATION. (US/0882-7524). **3755**

TOPICS IN HEALTH INFORMATION MANAGEMENT. (US/0270-5230). **3793**

TOPICS IN HOSPITAL PHARMACY MANAGEMENT. (US/0271-1206). **4331**

TOPICS IN LANGUAGE DISORDERS. (US/0271-8294). **3329**

TOPOI. (NE/0167-7411). **4364**

TORONTO IRISH NEWS. (CN/0821-2740). **2763**

TORONTO JOURNAL OF THEOLOGY. (CN/0826-9831). **5005**

TORONTO LIFE. (CN/0049-4194). **2548**

TORONTO REVIEW OF CONTEMPORARY WRITING ABROAD, THE. (CN). **Qty:** 15-20. **3447**

TORONTO SOUTH ASIAN REVIEW, THE. (CN/0714-3508). **3447**

TORRE (RIO PIEDRAS (SAN JUAN), P.R.), LA. (PR/0040-9588). **3447**

TOSCANA QUI. (IT). **Qty:** 3. **332**

TOSHOKAN KYORYOKU TSUSHIN. (JA/0913-8005). **3253**

TOT TALK. (CN/0824-507X). **4805**

TOTAH TRACINGS. (US). **Qty:** 15. **2475**

TOTAL EMPLOYEE INVOLVEMENT. (US/0896-7776). **888**

TOTAL HEALTH. (US/0274-6743). **4805**

TOTAL PRODUCTIVE MAINTENANCE : TPM. (US/1054-1233). **888**

TOTH-MAATIAN REVIEW, THE. (US/0740-7564). **2494**

TOUCHSTONE. (US). **Qty:** 8-10. **5005**

TOUCHSTONE (CHICAGO, ILL. 1986). (US/0897-327X). **5005**

TOUCHSTONE (WINNIPEG. (CN/0827-3200). **5005**

TOUNG PAO. (NE/0082-5433). **2666**

TOURISM MANAGEMENT (1982). (UK/0261-5177). **888**

TOURIST ATTRACTIONS & PARKS. (US/0194-4894). **4855**

TOURISTIC ANALYSIS REVIEW. (FR). **5494**

TOURNAMENTS ILLUMINATED. (US/0732-6645). **2713**

TOURO JOURNAL OF TRANSNATIONAL LAW. (US/1046-3445). **Qty:** 2. **3136**

TOURO LAW REVIEW. (US/8756-7326). **3065**

TOURS ON MOTORCOACH. (CN/0847-9348). **5494**

TOUTE JUSTICE (OTTAWA, ONT.), EN. (CN/0824-2801). **3065**

TOWARD FREEDOM. (US/0040-9898). **4536**

TOWARD FREEDOM (1990). (US/1063-4134). **Qty:** 12 /year. **4536**

TOWARD FREEDOM EUROFILE. (US). **4536**

TOWARDS WHOLENESS. (UK). **5005**

TOWERS CLUB USA NEWSLETTER. (US/0193-4953). **2925**

TOWN & COUNTRY PLANNING. (UK/0040-9960). **4691**

TOWN & VILLAGE. (US/0040-9979). **5721**

TOWN PLANNING REVIEW. (UK/0041-0020). **2837**

TOWNSHIPS SUN, THE. (CN/0316-022X). **Qty:** 12. **5796**

TOWSON STATE JOURNAL OF INTERNATIONAL AFFAIRS. (US/0041-0063). **4536**

TOXIC MATERIALS TRANSPORT. (US/0275-3766). **5394**

TOXIC SUBSTANCES JOURNAL. (US/0199-3178). **2871**

TOXICOLOGIC PATHOLOGY. (US/0192-6233). **3898**

TOXICOLOGICAL AND ENVIRONMENTAL CHEMISTRY. (UK/0277-2248). **3984**

TOXICOLOGY ABSTRACTS. (US/0140-5365). **3662**

TOXICOLOGY AND INDUSTRIAL HEALTH. (US/0748-2337). **3984**

TOXICOLOGY IN VITRO. (UK/0887-2333). **3984**

TPA MESSENGER. (US/0194-9802). **Qty:** 4. **4820**

TPUG MAGAZINE. (CN/0825-0367). **1205**

TR NEWS. (US/0738-6826). **5394**

TRABAJADORES. (CU). **5799**

TRABAJOS DE PREHISTORIA. (SP/0082-5638). **284**

TRAC, TRENDS IN ANALYTICAL CHEMISTRY (PERSONAL EDITION). (NE/0165-9936). **1019**

TRACE (MEXICO CITY, MEXICO). (MX/0185-6286). **5224**

TRACER - OHIO GENEALOGICAL SOCIETY. HAMILTON COUNTY CHAPTER, THE. (US/8756-8462). **2475**

TRACES (MONTREAL). (CN/0841-6397). **1908**

TRACES OF SOUTH CENTRAL KENTUCKY. (US/0882-2158). **2475**

TRACK & FIELD NEWS. (US/0041-0284). **4926**

TRACK & FIELD QUARTERLY REVIEW. (US/0041-0292). **Qty:** 3-4. **4926**

TRACKER, THE. (US/0041-0330). **Qty:** 4-5. **4157**

TRACTEURS & MACHINES AGRICOLES PARIS. (FR/0754-121X). **161**

TRACTION YEARBOOK. (US/0730-5400). **5394**

TRACTRIX. (NE/0924-0829). **5166**

TRADE DIRECTORY. (MM). **854**

TRADE-MARK REPORTER, THE. (US/0041-056X). **1308**

TRADESHOW & EXHIBIT MANAGER. (US/0893-2662). **767**

TRADING CYCLES. (US/0892-3280). **Qty:** 1-2. **917**

TRADING LAW. (UK/0262-9240). **3136**

TRADING LAW AND TRADING LAW REPORTS. (UK/1352-061X). **Qty:** 18. **3104**

TRADISJON. (NO/0332-5997). **2325**

TRADITION MAGAZINE. (FR/0980-8493). **Qty:** 1. **4157**

TRADITION (WALNUT, IOWA). (US/1071-1864). **Qty:** 8-10. **4157**

TRADITIONAL DWELLINGS AND SETTLEMENTS REVIEW. (US/1050-2092). **Qty:** 6-8. **5225**

TRADITIONAL MEDICAL SYSTEMS. (II/0025-7109). **3647**

TRADITIONAL TAEKWON-DO. (US/0745-2365). **4927**

TRADUIRE / SOCIETE FRANCAISE DES TRADUCTEURS. (FR/0395-773X). **3329**

TRAFFIC ENGINEERING & CONTROL. (UK/0041-0683). **5394**

TRAFFIC TOPICS. (US/0735-7613). **5394**

TRAFFIC WORLD, THE. (US/0041-073X). **5394**

TRAI TIM DU'C ME. (US/0744-6128). **5005**

TRAIL AND TIMBERLINE. (US/0041-0756). **Qty:** 12-15. **4879**

TRAIL BREAKERS. (US/0362-0344). **2475**

TRAIL SEEKERS. (US/0739-6643). **2475**

TRAIL TALES. (US). **2475**

TRAILER/BODY BUILD. (US/0041-0772). **5394**

TRAILS (WINDSOR). (CN/1195-4906). **Qty:** 4. **2475**

TRAIN COLLECTORS QUARTERLY, THE. (US/0041-0829). **2778**

TRAINING AND DEVELOPMENT ALERT. (US/0192-0596). **947**

TRAINING AND DEVELOPMENT IN AUSTRALIA. (AT/0310-4664). **716**

TRAINING DIGEST. (UK/0141-7134). **947**

TRAINING MEDIA REVIEW. (US/1072-3188). **Qty:** 10. **1123**

TRAINING (MINNEAPOLIS). (US/0095-5892). **948**

TRAINING OFFICER, THE. (UK/0041-090X). **948**

TRAINING TOMORROW. (UK/0957-0004). **4691**

TRAINS. (US/0041-0934). **5437**

TRAIT D'UNION (ROUYN). (CN/0820-7720). **4691**

TRANET. (US/0739-0971). **2207**

TRANSACTIONAL ANALYSIS JOURNAL. (US/0362-1537). **4620**

TRANSACTIONS - AMERICAN CRYSTALLOGRAPHIC ASSOCIATION. (US/0065-8006). **1033**

TRANSACTIONS - BRISTOL AND GLOUCESTERSHIRE ARCHAEOLOGICAL SOCIETY. (UK/0068-1032). **Qty:** 6. **284**

TRANSACTIONS - INSTITUTE OF BRITISH GEOGRAPHERS (1965). (UK/0020-2754). **2577**

TRANSACTIONS OF THE ANCIENT MONUMENTS SOCIETY. (UK/0951-001X). **366**

TRANSACTIONS OF THE CHARLES S. PIERCE SOCIETY. (US/0009-1774). **4364**

TRANSACTIONS OF THE FACULTY OF ACTUARIES. (UK/0071-3686). **2894**

TRANSACTIONS OF THE HISTORIC SOCIETY OF LANCASHIRE AND CHESHIRE FOR THE YEAR. (UK/0140-332X). **2713**

TRANSACTIONS OF THE HUGUENOT SOCIETY OF SOUTH CAROLINA. (US/0363-3152). **Qty:** 1-5. **5237**

TRANSACTIONS OF THE INDIAN CERAMIC SOCIETY. (II/0371-750X). **2594**

TRANSACTIONS OF THE MONUMENTAL BRASS SOCIETY. (UK/0143-1250). **284**

TRANSACTIONS OF THE ROYAL SOCIETY OF TROPICAL MEDICINE AND HYGIENE. (UK/0035-9203). **3987**

TRANSACTIONS OF THE SAEST. (II/0036-0678). **1035**

TRANSACTIONS OF THE UNITARIAN HISTORICAL SOCIETY. (UK/0082-7800). **Qty:** 5-6. **5068**

TRANSACTIONS OF THE YORKSHIRE DIALECT SOCIETY. (UK/0954-6316). 3329

TRANSACTIONS. SECTION A, MINING INDUSTRY / INSTITUTION OF MINING & METALLURGY. (UK/0371-7844). 2152

TRANSACTIONS - THE SOCIETY OF NAVAL ARCHITECTS AND MARINE ENGINEERS. (US/0081-1661). 4184

TRANSACTIONS. TRAFODION. (UK). Qty: 2. 2484

TRANSACTOR, THE. (CN/0827-2530). 1273

TRANSAFRICA FORUM. (US/0730-8876). 4536

TRANSATLANTIC PERSPECTIVES. (US/0192-477X). 4339

TRANSCRIPT. (US/1040-4848). 1123

TRANSCRIPT, THE. (US). 1123

TRANSCULTURAL PSYCHIATRIC RESEARCH REVIEW. (CN/0041-1108). Qty: 20. 3937

TRANSFORMATION (EXETER). (UK/0265-3788). 5005

TRANSFUSION MEDICINE REVIEWS. (US/0887-7963). 3647

TRANSFUSION (PHILADELPHIA). (US/0041-1132). 3774

TRANSILVANIA. (RM). 2713

TRANSITION. (AT/0157-7344). Qty: varies. 310

TRANSITION (LONDON, ENGLAND). (UK/0267-8950). 1917

TRANSITION (OTTAWA). (CN/0049-4429). Qty: 4. 2286

TRANSITION : THE NEWSLETTER ABOUT REFORMING ECONOMIES / TRANSITION AND MACRO-ADJUSTMENT, COUNTRY ECONOMICS DEPARTMENT, WORLD BANK. (US). 1640

TRANSITIONS ABROAD. (US/1061-2343). 1788

TRANSITIONS (CINCINNATI, OHIO). (US/0278-2804). 5395

TRANSLATION REVIEW. (US/0737-4836). Qty: 12. 3329

TRANSMISSION & DISTRIBUTION. (US/0041-1280). 2085

TRANSMISSION (MONTREAL). (CN/0824-510X). 3329

TRANSNATIONAL ASSOCIATIONS. (BE/0020-6059). 4691

TRANSNATIONAL DATA AND COMMUNICATIONS REPORT. (US/0892-399X). 1168

TRANSNATIONAL PERSPECTIVES. (SZ/0376-6403). 3136

TRANSPACIFIC (VENICE, CALIF.). (US/1047-7977). 2274

TRANSPLANTATION AND IMMUNOLOGY LETTER. (US/0748-1861). 3976

TRANSPORT-ACTION. (CN/0227-3020). 5395

TRANSPORT-DIENST + WIRTSCHAFTS-CORRESPONDENT. (GW). 5395

TRANSPORT ECHO ED. BILINGUE. (BE/0009-6083). 5395

TRANSPORT ENGINEER, THE. (UK/0020-3122). 1999

TRANSPORT HISTORY. (UK/0041-1469). 5395

TRANSPORT (LONDON. 1980). (UK/0144-3453). 5395

TRANSPORT MANAGEMENT; THE BRITISH JOURNAL OF TRADE AND TRANSPORT. (UK/0041-1515). Qty: 6. 5395

TRANSPORT REVIEW. (UK). 5396

TRANSPORT THEORY AND STATISTICAL PHYSICS. (US/0041-1450). 4430

TRANSPORT TOPICS. (US/0041-1558). 5396

TRANSPORTATION (DORDRECHT). (NE/0049-4488). 5396

TRANSPORTATION JOURNAL. (US/0041-1612). 5396

TRANSPORTATION LAW JOURNAL, THE. (US/0049-450X). 3065

TRANSPORTATION PLANNING AND TECHNOLOGY. (US/0308-1060). 5396

TRANSPORTATION SCIENCE. (US/0041-1655). 5397

TRANSPORTATION WORLDWIDE. (US/8750-8397). 854

TRANSPORTS. (FR/0564-1373). Qty: 6. 5397

TRAP & FIELD. (US/0041-1760). 4927

TRAPPER AND PREDATOR CALLER, THE. (US/8750-233X). 3186

TRAPPER (NORTH BATTLEFORD. 1990). (CN/1184-7417). 4879

TRASFUSIONE DEL SANGUE. (IT/0041-1787). 3802

TRATTAMENTI E FINITURA. (IT/0041-1833). 4022

TRAVAIL ET MAITRISE. (FR/0750-8964). 948

TRAVAIL ET METHODES. (FR/0041-185X). 888

TRAVAIL ET SANTE. (CN/0829-0369). 2871

TRAVAIL HUMAIN, LE. (FR/0041-1868). 4620

TRAVAIL SOCIAL ACTUALITES PARIS. (FR/0753-9711). 5313

TRAVAUX DE LINGUISTIQUE. (BE). 3329

TRAVAUX DE L'INSTITUT DE GEOGRAPHIE DE REIMS. (FR/0048-7163). Qty: 20. 2577

TRAVAUX ET DOCUMENTS. (FR/0298-8879). Qty: 4. 4536

TRAVEL 800. (US/0192-155X). 5494

TRAVEL AND DESCRIPTION SERIES. (US). 2763

TRAVEL AUSTRALIA SYDNEY. (AT/0817-2935). 5495

TRAVEL BOOKS WORLDWIDE. (US/1058-7098). Qty: 180. 5495

TRAVEL BUSINESS ANALYST ASIA ED. (HK/1011-7768). Qty: 4. 5495

TRAVEL BUSINESS ANALYST EUROPE ED. (HK/0256-419X). Qty: 3. 5495

TRAVEL CHINA NEWSLETTER. (CN/0834-258X). 5495

TRAVEL HOLIDAY. (US/0199-025X). 5495

TRAVEL MARKETING AND AGENCY MANAGEMENT GUIDELINES. (US/0275-3545). Qty: 3. 5496

TRAVEL PUBLISHING NEWS. (US/1043-6138). 5496

TRAVEL SCOOP. (CN/0822-9228). Qty: 20-30. 5496

TRAVEL SMART. (US/0741-5826). 5496

TRAVEL TIDINGS. (US/0895-4135). 5496

TRAVEL TRENDS IN THE UNITED STATES AND CANADA. (US). 5497

TRAVELIN TALK NEWSLETTER, THE. (US/1052-1615). Qty: 4. 5497

TRAVELLER'S GUIDE TO THE MIDDLE EAST. (UK). 5497

TRAVELORE REPORT, THE. (US/0270-2398). 5497

TRAVELWRITER MARKETLETTER. (US/0738-9094). 2925

TRAVERS LES VIGNES, A. (CN/0824-1465). 2371

TRAVERSO (CLAVERACK, N.Y.). (US/1041-7494). 4157

TRAVESSIA. (BL/0101-9570). 3447

TREASURE CHEST (NEW YORK, N.Y.). (US/0897-814X). 252

TREASURE STATE LINES. (US). 2475

TREASURY MANAGEMENT INTERNATIONAL. (UK/0967-523X). Qty: 1 per year. 814

TREATING ABUSE TODAY. (US/1052-3995). 5313

TREBEDE : REVISTA DE POESIA. (SP). 3472

TREE PHYSIOLOGY. (CN/0829-318X). Qty: 4. 2397

TREE SHAKER / EASTERN KENTUCKY GENEALOGICAL SOCIETY. (US/0893-2069). 2475

TREE TRACERS, THE. (US/0162-1440). 2475

TREES AND NATURAL RESOURCES. (AT/0814-4680). 2207

TREES FROM THE GROVE. (US/1046-6339). 2476

TREESEARCHER, THE. (US). 2476

TREFILE, LE. (GW/0374-2261). 4022

TRELLIS. (CN/0380-1470). 2432

TREND. (XR). 5167

TREND. (II). 2667

TRENDLETTER. (GW/0935-5596). 716

TRENDS AND APPLICATIONS. (US). 1205

TRENDS & WORDS. (IT). 937

TRENDS IN BIOCHEMICAL SCIENCES (AMSTERDAM. REGULAR ED.). (UK/0167-7640). 493

TRENDS IN BIOTECHNOLOGY (PERSONAL EDITION). (NE/0167-7799). 3697

TRENDS IN HEALTH CARE, LAW & ETHICS. (US/1062-5364). Qty: 4-6. 2253

TRENDS IN HOUSING. (US/0300-6026). 2837

TRI-CITY COMPUTING MAGAZINE. (US). Qty: 12. 1205

TRI-CITY GENEALOGICAL SOCIETY BULLETIN, THE. (US/0496-1803). 2476

TRI-CITY REPORTER, THE. (US). 5746

TRI-CITY TRIBUNE. (US). Qty: 12. 5632

TRI-COUNTY GENEALOGY. (US/0896-419X). Qty: 8-10. 2476

TRI-COUNTY SEARCHER, THE. (US/0742-5015). 2476

TRI-STATE PACKET OF THE TRI-STATE GENEALOGICAL SOCIETY, THE. (US/0740-896X). 2476

TRIAL. (US/0041-2538). 3066

TRIAL ADVOCATE QUARTERLY. (US/0743-412X). 3066

TRIAL DIPLOMACY JOURNAL. (US/0160-7308). 3066

TRIANGLE OF MU PHI EPSILON, THE. (US/0041-2600). 4157

TRIATHLON SPORTS. (AT). 4927

TRIBAL TRIBUNE. (US). Qty: 1-2. 5733

TRIBOLOGIE UND SCHMIERUNGSTECHNIK. (GW/0724-3472). 1048

TRIBOLOGY INTERNATIONAL. (UK/0301-679X). 2108

TRIBOMATERIALS NEWS. (US/1063-9195). Qty: 2-4. 4424

TRIBUNA DE NEW YORK & NEW JERSEY, LA. (US). 5712

TRIBUNAUX CORRECTIONNELS, COURS D'APPEL, CONSEILS DE GUERRE ET COUR MILITAIRE. (BE). 3083

TRIBUNE. (UK/0041-2821). 5813

TRIBUNE DE L'ORGUE, LA. (SZ/1013-6835). 4157

TRIBUNE DES INDUSTRIES DE LA LANGUE, LA. (FR/1148-7666). 3330

TRIBUNE PRESS REPORTER. (US). 5771

TRIBUNE-STAR, THE. (US/0745-9599). 5667

TRIBUS. (GW/0082-6413). 247

TRICYCLE (NEW YORK, N.Y.). (US/1055-484X). Qty: 20. 5022

TRIDENT (WASHINGTON, D.C.). (US/0882-1674). 2788

TRIERER THEOLOGISCHE ZEITSCHRIFT. (GW/0041-2945). 5006

TRIERER ZEITSCHRIFT FUER GESCHICHTE UND KUNST DES TRIERER LANDES UND SEINER NACHBARGEBIETE. (GW/0041-2953). Qty: 10. 2713

TRIMESTRE ECONOMICO, EL. (MX/0041-3011). 1640

TRINITY DIGEST. (US). 2925

TRINITY WORLD FORUM. (US). 5068

TRIQUARTERLY / NORTHWESTERN UNIVERSITY. (US/0041-3097). 3447

TRISTANIA. (US/0360-3385). 3448

TRIVIA. (US/0736-928X). Qty: 2-3. 3355

TRO OCH LIV. (SW/0346-2803). Qty: 50-60. 5006

TROIS MOIS DE NOUVEAUTES. (FR/0294-0035). 4833

TROPICAL AGRICULTURE. (UK/0041-3216). Qty: 16-20. 142

TROPICAL AND GEOGRAPHICAL MEDICINE. (NE/0041-3232). 3987

TROPICAL DISEASES BULLETIN. (UK/0041-3240). 3662

TROPICAL DOCTOR. (UK/0049-4755). 3987

TROPICAL ECOLOGY. (II/0564-3295). Qty: 8-15. 2222

TROPICAL FISH HOBBYIST. (US/0041-3259). 2315

TROPICAL GRASSLANDS. (AT/0049-4763). 189

TROPICAL LEPIDOPTERA. (US/1048-8138). Qty: 10. 5614

TROPICAL TIMBERS. (UK/0269-980X). 2399

TROPICAL VETERINARIAN. (NR/0253-4851). Qty: 5. 3987

TROUBADOUR (FREDERICTON). (CN/0713-8113). 4157

TROUBLE AND STRIFE. (UK). Qty: 6-8. 5567

TROUT AND SALMON. (UK/0041-3372). 2315

TRUBUS. (IO/0126-0057). 142

TRUCK CANADA. (CN/0315-5501). 5398

TRUE DETECTIVE. (US/0041-350X). Qty: varies. 5075

TRUE WEST. (US/0041-3615). **2764**

TRULY PORTABLE. (US/0749-5897). **1273**

TRUMANN DEMOCRAT, THE. (US). **Qty: 20. 5632**

TRUMANSBURG FREE PRESS. (US). **Qty: 2-3. 5721**

TRUMPETER (LONDON). (CN/0148-673X). **Qty: 5-10. 2788**

TRUMPETER (VICTORIA). (CN/0832-6193). **Qty: 6-10. 2222**

TRUPPENPRAXIS. (GW). **4059**

TRUST NEWS. (AT). **2207**

TRUSTEE (EDMONTON, ALTA.). (CN/0229-4141). **1873**

TRUSTEESHIP (WASHINGTON, D.C.). (US/1068-1027). **Qty: varies. 1851**

TRUTH AT LAST, THE. (US). **4498**

TRUTH (PHILADELPHIA), THE. (US/0041-3690). **2274**

TRUTH SEEKER (SAN DIEGO, CALIF.), THE. (US/0041-3712). **5006**

TRUXBOOK. (CN/0820-5655). **855**

TRYON DAILY BULLETIN, THE. (US). **5724**

TSITOLOGIIA. (RU/0041-3771). **540**

TSR HOTLINE. (US/8755-4380). **888**

TSUKUBA DAIGAKU TAIIKU KAGAKUKEI KIYO. (JA/0386-7129). **1859**

TTT, INTERDISCIPLINAIR TIJDSCHRIFT VOOR TAAL- & TEKSTWETENSCHAP. (NE/0167-4773). **3330**

TU SHU KUAN HSUEH YU TZU HSUN KO HSUEH. (CH/0363-3640). **3254**

TUBE & PIPE TECHNOLOGY. (UK/0953-2366). **4023**

TUBE SUBSTITUTION HANDBOOK. (US). **2085**

TUCSON CITIZEN (1977). (US/0888-5478). **5630**

TUCSON GUIDE QUARTERLY. (US). **Qty: 3. 2548**

TUDOMANYOS ES MUSZAKI TAJEKOZTATAS. (HU/0041-3917). **3254**

TUDOMANYOS KOZLEMENYEK. (HU). **Qty: 3-4. 1859**

TUESDAY LETTER. (US/0047-8733). **2207**

TUEXEMIA. (GW/0772-494X). **Qty: 30-40. 2222**

TUG LINES. (US/0892-4961). **1281**

TUIN EN LANDSCHAP. (NE). **2432**

TUINBOUW VISIE. (BE/0776-4472). **2432**

TULANE LAW REVIEW. (US/0041-3992). **3066**

TULANE LAWYER. (US). **3066**

TULANE STUDIES IN GEOLOGY AND PALEONTOLOGY. (US/0041-4018). **1400**

TULANE STUDIES IN POLITICAL SCIENCE. (US/0082-6744). **4498**

TULIMULD. (SW/0041-4034). **3448**

TULSA ANNALS. (US/0564-4437). **Qty: 7-8. 2476**

TULSA STUDIES IN WOMEN'S LITERATURE. (US/0732-7730). **3448**

TUMORI. (IT/0300-8916). **3824**

TUNDRA DRUMS, THE. (US). **5629**

TUNDRA TIMES. (US/0049-4801). **Qty: 5-10. 5629**

TUNG WU FA LU HSUEH PAO. (CH). **3067**

TUNNELLING AND UNDERGROUND SPACE TECHNOLOGY. (UK/0886-7798). **2033**

TUNNELS & TUNNELLING. (UK/0041-414X). **2033**

TUNNELS. ET OUVRAGES SOUTERRAINS. (FR). **2033**

TURBOMACHINERY DIGEST. (US). **2131**

TURCICA (PARIS). (BE/0082-6847). **3330**

TURF & RECREATION. (CN/1186-0170). **2433**

TURF AND SPORT DIGEST. (US/0041-4158). **4927**

TURISMO D'ITALIA. (IT). **2809**

TURKEY HUNTER, THE. (US/0896-1786). **4880**

TURKEY MONITOR. (UK/0950-3234). **4757**

TURKEYS. (UK/0041-428X). **223**

TURKISH JOURNAL OF PEDIATRICS, THE. (TU/0041-4301). **3912**

TURKISH STUDIES ASSOCIATION BULLETIN. (US/0275-6048). **3355**

TURKIYE ISTATISTIK YLL. STATISTICAL YEARBOOK OF TURKEY. (TU). **5345**

TURKIYE OZETLI NUFUS BIBLIOGRAFYAS. (TU). **4563**

TURNER STUDIES. (UK/0260-597X). **367**

TURNING POINTS (CHESHIRE). (US/0274-8894). **716**

TURNOUT, THE. (CN/0227-244X). **5437**

TURRIALBA : REVISTA INTERAMERICANO DE CIENCIAS AGRICOLAS. (CR/0041-4360). **143**

TURTLE QUARTERLY. (US/0896-2022). **Qty: 32. 2274**

TUTTITALIA. (UK). **Qty: varies. 3330**

TUTTO SCUOLA. (IT). **1788**

TV EXECUTIVE, THE. (US/0736-2986). **1141**

TVORCHESTVO. (RU/0041-4565). **332**

TVZ : VAKBLAD VOOR DE VERPLEGKUNDIGEN. (NE/0303-6456). **3870**

TWIN CITIES CHRISTIAN, THE. (US/0745-8606). **Qty: 50 /yr. 5006**

TWIN CITIES READER. (US/0193-2802). **2548**

TWIN CITY NEWS (CHATTAHOOCHEE, FLA.). (US/0889-2245). **Qty: 10. 5651**

TWO THIRDS. (CN/0705-3452). **2912**

TWR'S INSIDER REPORT. (US). **Qty: 50. 5567**

TYDSKRIF VAN DIE TANDHEELKUNDIGE VERENIGING VAN SUID AFRIKA. (SA/0011-8516). **1337**

TYDSKRIF VIR DIE SUID-AFRIKAANSE REG. (SA). **3067**

TYDSKRIF VIR LETTERKUNDE. (SA/0041-476X). **2315**

TYDSKRIF VIR REGSWETENSKAP. (SA/0258-252X). **3067**

TYDSKRIF VIR VOLKSKUNDE EN VOLKSTAAL. (SA/0049-4933). **2325**

TYO TERVEYS TURVALLISUUS. (FI/0041-4816). **Qty: 10. 2871**

TYPOGRAFISCHE MONATSBLATTER. (SZ). **4570**

TYPOGRAPHIC : THE JOURNAL OF THE SOCIETY OF TYPOGRAPHIC DESIGNERS. (UK). **4570**

TZ FUER METALLBEARBEITUNG. (GW/0170-9577). **4023**

U.C. DAVIS LAW REVIEW. (US/0197-4564). **Qty: varies. 3067**

U.I.T. JOURNAL. (GW). **4927**

U.K. MAGAZINE. (US/8750-1082). **2524**

U.S.A.N. AND THE U.S.P. DICTIONARY OF DRUG NAMES. (US/0090-6816). **4331**

U.S.A. OIL INDUSTRY DIRECTORY. (US/0082-8599). **4281**

U.S.A. OILFIELD SERVICE, SUPPLY, AND MANUFACTURERS DIRECTORY. (US). **4281**

U.S. AGRICULTURAL POLICY GUIDE. (US/0895-545X). **4691**

U.S. CATHOLIC. (US/0041-7548). **5037**

U.S. CONGRESS HANDBOOK, THE. (US/0196-7614). **4691**

U.S. EMPLOYMENT OPPORTUNITIES. (US/0890-5959). **4209**

U.S. FARM NEWS. (US/0041-7637). **143**

U.S. GLASS, METAL & GLAZING. (US/0041-7661). **2595**

U.S. MEDICINE. (US/0191-6246). **3917**

U.S. RAIL NEWS. (US/0743-7994). **5437**

U.S. / R&D. (US). **5167**

U.S. WATER NEWS. (US/0749-1980). **5541**

U.S. WOMAN ENGINEER. (US/0272-7838). **2000**

U&C UNIFICAZIONE & CERTIFICAZIONE. (IT/0394-9605). **630**

UBERSETZUNGEN, KERNTECHNISCHE REGELN. (GW). **Qty: 1. 2159**

UCLA HISTORICAL JOURNAL. (US/0276-864X). **Qty: 8. 2632**

UCLA JOURNAL OF DANCE ETHNOLOGY. (US/0884-3198). **1314**

UCLA MAGAZINE (1989). (US/1075-2749). **1103**

UCLA PACIFIC BASIN LAW JOURNAL. (US/0884-0768). **3067**

UFAHAMU. (US/0041-5715). **2500**

UFFICIOSTILE. (IT). **310**

UFO TIMES. (UK/0958-4846). **38**

UFONTAS, AS. (BL). **38**

UGOL. (RU/0041-5790). **2152**

UHF. ULTRA HIGH FIDELITY. (CN/0847-1851). **Qty: 3. 5319**

UHREN, JUWELEN, SCHMUCK. (GW). **2916**

UIS BULLETIN. (AU/0254-9824). **1400**

UITP BIBLIO-INDEX. TRANSPORT-VERKEHR. (BE/0041-5146). **5398**

UJ MAGYAR HIREK. (HU/0866-4749). **2524**

UJ TUKOR. (HU). **2524**

UK PESTICIDE GUIDE, THE. (UK/0952-7788). **4248**

UKRAINIAN QUARTERLY, THE. (US/0041-6010). **4498**

UKRAINIAN REPORTER. (UN/0964-4326). **4537**

UKRAINIAN REVIEW (LONDON, ENGLAND). (UK/0041-6029). **4499**

UKRAINIAN WEEKLY, THE. (US/0273-9348). **2274**

UKRAINSKYI FILATELIST / SOIUZ UKRAINSKYKH FILATELISTIV I NUMIZMATYKIV. (US/0198-6252). **2788**

UKRAINSKYI ISTORYK. (US/0041-6061). **2714**

ULASAN GETAH MALAYSIA. (MY/0126-9089). **5078**

ULSTER FOLKLIFE. (NL/0082-7347). **2325**

ULSTER JOURNAL OF ARCHAEOLOGY. (UK/0082-7355). **285**

ULSTER MEDICAL JOURNAL. (UK/0041-6193). **3648**

ULTIMATE ISSUES. (US/0888-3440). **5053**

ULTIMISSIME PELLICCERIA. (IT). **3186**

ULTRAFIT AUSTRALIA. (AT). **Qty: 7. 2601**

ULTRAPURE WATER. (US/0747-8291). **5541**

ULTRASONICS. (UK/0041-624X). **4424**

ULTRASTRUCTURAL PATHOLOGY. (US/0191-3123). **3898**

ULULA. (US/0747-8011). **3449**

ULYSSES NEWS, THE. (US). **5678**

UMAP JOURNAL, THE. (US/0197-3622). **3540**

UMBEN. (PP). **Qty: 1,000. 5264**

UMBRELLA (GLENDALE). (US/0160-0699). **Qty: 100. 367**

UME TRENDS. (US). **3540**

UMSATZSTEUER-RUNDSCHAU (COLOGNE, GERMANY : 1986). (GW/0341-8669). **3067**

UNABASHED LIBRARIAN, THE. (US/0049-514X). **3254**

UNASYLVA. (IT/0041-6436). **2397**

UNB LAW JOURNAL. (CN/0836-6632). **3067**

UNCLASSIFIED (WASHINGTON, D.C.). (US/1062-3450). **Qty: 8-10. 5177**

UNCOVERINGS. (US/0277-0628). **5186**

UNDER AFRIKAS SOL. (DK). **5006**

UNDER WESTERN SKIES. (US/0279-6244). **4079**

UNDERCURRENT (NEW YORK). (US/0192-0871). **Qty: 2. 4927**

UNDERLINE. (US/0276-0398). **310**

UNDERSEA BIOMEDICAL RESEARCH. (US/0093-5387). **3697**

UNDERSTANDING JAPAN. (JA/0041-6576). **2509**

UNDERSTANDING OUR GIFTED. (US/1040-1350). **1886**

UNDERSTANDING PEOPLE. (US). **4621**

UNDERWATER LETTER, THE. (US/0041-6592). **Qty: 6. 1458**

UNDERWATER MEDICINE AND RELATED SCIENCES. (US/0191-2534). **3648**

UNDERWATER NEWS & TECHNOLOGY. (US/1069-6547). **Qty: 20. 1458**

UNDISCOVERED COUNTRIES JOURNAL. (US/1068-3267). **Qty: 12. 3449**

UNDRO NEWS. (SZ/0250-9377). **2912**

UNDZER VEG (TORONTO). (CN/0382-0610). **2274**

UNESCO ADULT EDUCATION INFORMATION NOTES. (FR/0376-4907). **1802**

UNICORN (CARLTON, TAS.). (AT/0311-4775). **1788**

UNIDOS : JOURNAL OF OPPORTUNITY. (US). **717**

UNIE GOODWOOD, DIE. (SA/0259-5591). **Qty: 120. 1908**

UNIFICATION NEWS. (US/1061-0871). **Qty: 12. 5006**

UNIFORM BUILDING CODE. (US). **630**

UNIFORMED SERVICES ALMANAC. (US/0503-1982). **4059**

UNIMA CANADA. (CN/0708-5745). **389**

UNION COUNTY LEADER, THE. (US). Qty: 6. **5713**

UNION DEMOCRACY REVIEW. (US). **1716**

UNION LABOR NEWS (MADISON, WIS.). (US/0041-6924). **1716**

UNION LEADER. (US/0161-9292). **2548**

UNION MEDICALE DU CANADA. (CN/0041-6959). **3648**

UNION POSTALE. (SZ). **1147**

UNION WRITES NEWSLETTER. (US/0748-6839). **1716**

UNIQUE (EAST HANOVER, N.J.). (US/0736-4083). Qty: 5. **1244**

UNISA ENGLISH STUDIES. (SA/0041-5359). **3449**

UNISA PSYCHOLOGIA. (SA). **4621**

UNITARIAN QUEST. (AT). **1071**

UNITARIAN UNIVERSALIST CHRISTIAN, THE. (US/0362-0492). **5068**

UNITAS FRATRUM. (GW/0344-9254). **5068**

UNITE CHRETIENNE. (FR). **5006**

UNITED CHURCH OBSERVER, THE. (CN/0041-7238). **5006**

UNITED DAUGHTERS OF THE CONFEDERACY MAGAZINE. (US). **2764**

UNITED EVANGELICAL. (US/0041-7262). **5040**

UNITED EVANGELICAL ACTION. (US/0041-7270). **5006**

UNITED FLY TYERS' ROUNDTABLE. (US/0747-9832). **2315**

UNITED KINGDOM, THE COMMONWEALTH OF NATIONS, A DIRECTORY OF GOVERNMENTS, THE. (US/0193-4783). **4499**

UNITED METHODIST CHRISTIAN ADVOCATE, THE. (US/8750-7668). Qty: 12/yr. **5068**

UNITED METHODIST REPORTER (DALLAS, TEX.), THE. (US/0737-5581). **5068**

UNITED MINE WORKERS JOURNAL. (US/0041-7327). **1716**

UNITED NATIONS RESOLUTIONS. SERIES 2, RESOLUTIONS AND DECISIONS OF THE SECURITY COUNCIL. (US/0898-2929). **3137**

UNITED RETIREMENT BULLETIN. (US). **5182**

UNITED SENIORS HEALTH REPORT. (US/1043-9250). **5182**

UNITED STATES AIR FORCE ACADEMY JOURNAL OF PROFESSIONAL MILITARY ETHICS. (US/0731-2865). **4059**

UNITED STATES SPACE FOUNDATION PROCEEDINGS. (US). **38**

UNITED STATES TRADE FAIR. (US/0742-3675). **952**

UNITED SYNAGOGUE REVIEW. (US/0041-8153). **5053**

UNIVERS DU FRANCAIS SEVRES, L'. (FR/1018-872X). Qty: 4. **1788**

UNIVERSAL MESSAGE, THE. (PK). **5045**

UNIVERSAL MILITARY ABSTRACTS. (II). Qty: 4-8. **4059**

UNIVERSALIST FRIENDS. (US). **5068**

UNIVERSALIST - QUAKER UNIVERSALIST GROUP. (UK/0267-6648). **5068**

UNIVERSITAS. ENGLISH LANGUAGE EDITION (STUTTGART). (GW/0341-0129). **2856**

UNIVERSITES (MONTREAL). (CN/0226-7454). **1852**

UNIVERSITY ADMINISTRATION. OSMANIA UNIVERSITY. HYDERABAD. (II/0970-9584). **1852**

UNIVERSITY BOOKMAN, THE. (US/0041-9265). **1852**

UNIVERSITY CITY LIGHT. (US/0889-8154). Qty: 12. **5641**

UNIVERSITY DAILY, THE. (US). **5755**

UNIVERSITY OF ARKANSAS AT LITTLE ROCK LAW JOURNAL. (US/0162-8372). **3068**

UNIVERSITY OF BALTIMORE LAW REVIEW. (US/0091-5440). **3068**

UNIVERSITY OF CALIFORNIA, BERKELEY, WELLNESS LETTER. (US/0748-9234). **4806**

UNIVERSITY OF CHICAGO LAW REVIEW, THE. (US/0041-9494). **3068**

UNIVERSITY OF CINCINNATI LAW REVIEW. (US/0009-6881). **3068**

UNIVERSITY OF COLORADO LAW REVIEW. (US/0041-9516). **3068**

UNIVERSITY OF DAYTON LAW REVIEW. (US/0162-9174). **3068**

UNIVERSITY OF EDINBURGH JOURNAL. (UK/0041-9567). **1852**

UNIVERSITY OF FLORIDA JOURNAL OF LAW AND PUBLIC POLICY. (US/1047-8035). Qty: varies. **3068**

UNIVERSITY OF GHANA LAW JOURNAL. (GH/0041-9605). **3068**

UNIVERSITY OF HAWAII LAW REVIEW. (US/0271-9835). **3068**

UNIVERSITY OF MIAMI ENTERTAINMENT & SPORTS LAW REVIEW. (US/1051-2225). **3069**

UNIVERSITY OF MICHIGAN JOURNAL OF LAW REFORM. (US/0363-602X). **3069**

UNIVERSITY OF MISSISSIPPI STUDIES IN ENGLISH, THE. (US/0278-310X). **3449**

UNIVERSITY OF NEW SOUTH WALES LAW JOURNAL, THE. (AT/0313-0096). Qty: 2-3/yr. **3069**

UNIVERSITY OF NOTTINGHAM MONOGRAPHS IN THE HUMANITIES, (UK). **2856**

UNIVERSITY OF PENNSYLVANIA LAW REVIEW. (US/0041-9907). **3069**

UNIVERSITY OF PORTLAND REVIEW. (US/0041-9923). **2548**

UNIVERSITY OF PUGET SOUND LAW REVIEW. (US/0161-0708). **3069**

UNIVERSITY OF RICHMOND LAW REVIEW. (US/0566-2389). **3069**

UNIVERSITY OF SAN FRANCISCO LAW REVIEW. (US/0042-0018). **3069**

UNIVERSITY OF TASMANIA LAW REVIEW. (AT/0082-2108). **3069**

UNIVERSITY OF TOLEDO LAW REVIEW, THE. (US/0042-0190). **3069**

UNIVERSITY OF TORONTO LAW JOURNAL, THE. (CN/0042-0220). **3069**

UNIVERSITY OF WESTERN AUSTRALIA LAW REVIEW. (AT/0042-0328). **3069**

UNIVERSITY OF WINDSOR REVIEW, THE. (CN/0042-0352). **3449**

UNIVERSITY PRESS BOOK NEWS. (US/1040-8991). **427**

UNIVERSITY PUBLISHING. (US/0191-4146). **4833**

UNIVERSO. (IT/0042-0409). **2578**

UNIX/BUSINESS. (UK/0958-6253). **1239**

UNIX NEWS LONDON. (UK/0956-2753). Qty: 60. **1249**

UNLISTED DRUGS. (US/0042-0441). **4331**

UNMUZZLED OX. (US/0049-5557). **3472**

UNSCHEDULED EVENTS. (US/0042-0468). **5264**

UNSER TSAYT. (US/0042-0506). Qty: 4. **2494**

UNSER WALD : ZEITSCHRIFT DER SCHUTZGEMEINSCHAFT DEUTSCHER WALD. (GW). Qty: 30. **2397**

UNSERE JUGEND. (GW/0342-5258). **1789**

UNSERE STIMME. (GW). **3355**

UNTERNEHMUNG. (SZ/0042-059X). **889**

UNTERRICHTSPRAXIS, DIE. (US/0042-062X). **3331**

UNTERRICHTSWISSENSCHAFT. (GW/0340-4099). **1789**

UNVEILING. (US/0747-931X). **3449**

UP-DATE - B.C. NUTRITION COUNCIL. (CN/0823-8332). **4199**

UP HERE : LIFE IN CANADA'S NORTH. (CN). **2548**

UPCHURCH BULLETIN. (US/0270-465X). **2476**

UPDATE & DIALOG. (DK/0906-7272). **5007**

UPDATE / CONGRESSIONAL CAUCUS FOR WOMEN'S ISSUES. (US). **4692**

UPDATE / INTERPRETATION CANADA. (CN/0715-3392). **1789**

UPDATE ON LAW-RELATED EDUCATION. (US/0147-8648). **3070**

UPDATE - UNIVERSITY OF SOUTH CAROLINA. DEPT. OF MUSIC. (US/8755-1233). **4157**

UPDATE USSR. (US/0884-6227). **4499**

UPPER CANADIAN, THE. (CN/0711-0081). Qty: 12. **252**

UPPER COUNTY NEWS-REPORTER, THE. (US). **5657**

UPSHAW FAMILY JOURNAL, THE. (US/0098-8960). **2476**

UPSOUTH (BOWLING GREEN, KY.). (US/1069-8051). **3449**

UQAR-INFORMATION. (CN/0711-2254). **1853**

URAL-ALTAISCHE JAHRBUCHER. (GW/0042-0786). **3331**

URAL-ALTAISCHE JAHRBUCHER (WIESBADEN, GERMANY : 1981). (GW/0042-0786). Qty: 30-40. **3331**

URBAN ACADEMIC LIBRARIAN. (US/0276-9298). **3255**

URBAN AGE, THE. (US). Qty: 20. **2837**

URBAN DESIGN UPDATE: NEWSLETTER OF THE INSTITUTE FOR URBAN DESIGN. (US/0895-8076). **2837**

URBAN EDGE (ENGLISH ED.), THE. (US/0163-6510). **2837**

URBAN HISTORY REVIEW. (CN/0703-0428). **2764**

URBAN INDIA. (II/0970-9045). **2838**

URBAN LAND. (US/0042-0891). **2838**

URBAN LEAGUE REVIEW, THE. (US/0147-1740). **2274**

URBAN OUTLOOK. (US/0732-8265). **2838**

URBAN TRANSPORTATION MONITOR, THE. (US/1040-4880). **5399**

URBAN WILDLIFE MANAGER'S NOTEBOOK. (US/0882-584X). **2208**

URBAN WILDLIFE NEWS. (US/0882-5858). **2222**

URJA. (II/0378-9535). **1960**

URNER BARRY'S MEAT & POULTRY DIRECTORY. (US/0738-6745). **223**

UROLOGIA. (IT/0391-5603). Qty: 20-25. **3993**

UROLOGIC NURSING. (US/1053-816X). **3870**

UROLOGIJA I NEFROLOGIJA. (RU/0042-1154). **3994**

URPE. (US/0743-1694). **1525**

URWAH AL-WUTHQA (GENEVA, SWITZERLAND). (SZ). **5045**

US-CHINA REVIEW. (US/0164-3886). **4537**

US HISTORY ON CD-ROM. (US). **2764**

USA OUTDOORS. (US/0883-6841). **4880**

USA TODAY (INTERNATIONAL ED.). (US/1051-7405). Qty: 80. **5722**

USA TODAY (NEW YORK, N.Y.). (US/0161-7389). **2548**

USCTA NEWS. (US/0744-0103). **2803**

USDF CALENDAR OF COMPETITIONS. (US/0882-5009). **2803**

USE OF ENGLISH, THE. (UK/0042-1243). **1789**

USP DI. ADVICE FOR THE PATIENT. (US/0740-6916). **4331**

USP DI. DRUG INFORMATION FOR THE HEALTH CARE PROVIDER. (US/0740-4174). **4332**

USPEHI FIZICESKIH NAUK. (RU/0042-1294). **4424**

USPEHI SOVREMENNOI BIOLOGII. (RU/0042-1324). **475**

USQR, UNION SEMINARY QUARTERLY REVIEW. (US/0362-1545). **5007**

USSR FACTS & FIGURES ANNUAL. (US/0148-7760). **5345**

USYSA NETWORK. (US). Qty: 4. **4928**

UTAH BIRDS : JOURNAL OF THE UTAH ORNITHOLOGICAL SOCIETY. (US). **5620**

UTAH BUSINESS MAGAZINE. (US). Qty: 8-12/year. **717**

UTAH FISHING. (US/0897-7283). **4880**

UTAH HISTORICAL QUARTERLY. (US/0042-143X). **2764**

UTAH-IDAHO SOUTHERN BAPTIST WITNESS. (US/0746-0228). Qty: 2/yr. **5068**

UTAH LAW REVIEW. (US/0042-1448). **3070**

UTAH LIBRARIES/NEWS. (US). **3255**

UTAH MUSIC EDUCATOR. (US/0502-871X). **4157**

UTBLICK LANDSKAP. (SW). **310**

UTENSIL. (IT/0392-6567). **2131**

UTILITY PURCHASING AND STORES. (US/0042-1588). **952**

UTNE READER, THE. (US/8750-0256). **2549**

UTOPIAN STUDIES. (US/1045-991X). Qty: 40. **4548**

UTUNK : ROMANIA SZOCIALISTA KOZTARSASAG IROSZOVETSEGENEK LAPJA. (RM). **3355**

UTUSAN KONSUMER. (MY/0126-950X). **1300**

UWI STUDENT'S LAW REVIEW. (BB). **3070**

UWLA LAW REVIEW. (US/0899-7446). **3070**

V.S.T — Book Review Index

V.S.T. (FR/0396-8669). **3937**

VA-NYTT. (SW/0042-1995). **2183**

VACCINE. (UK/0264-410X). **3649**

VAJRA BODHI SEA. (US/0507-6986). **5022**

VAJRADHATU SUN, THE. (US/0882-0813). **5022**

VALDEZ VANGUARD. (US). **5629**

VALDOSTA DAILY TIMES, THE. (US). **5655**

VALENCIA FRUITS. (SP). **143**

VALFARDS BULLETINEN / SCB. (SW/0280-1418). **5313**

VALLEY CATHOLIC, THE. (US/8750-6238). **Qty:** 1. **5038**

VALLEY FORGE JOURNAL, THE. (US/0734-5712). **2764**

VALLEY GAZETTE, THE. (US/1056-4853). **5740**

VALLEY LEAVES. (US/0507-6544). **2476**

VALLEY MAGAZINE (GRANADA HILLS, CALIF.). (US/8750-1430). **1300**

VALLEY MAGAZINE (SELINSGROVE, PA.). (US/1046-0454). **5498**

VALLEY NEWS. (US). **5657**

VALLEY NEWS (MONTEBELLO). (CN/0715-4887). **5796**

VALPARAISO UNIVERSITY LAW REVIEW. (US/0042-2363). **Qty:** 1/year. **3070**

VAN VECHTEN REPORT, THE. (US). **937**

VANDANCE (VANCOUVER). (CN/0705-8063). **Qty:** 4. **1314**

VANDERBILT JOURNAL OF TRANSNATIONAL LAW. (US/0090-2594). **3137**

VANDERBILT LAW REVIEW. (US/0042-2533). **3070**

VANDERBILT MAGAZINE. (US). **1103**

VANDERBILT STREET REVIEW. (US/0275-7672). **3450**

VANGUARD (VALPARAISO). (US/0042-2568). **5007**

VAR FAGELVARLD. (SW/0042-2649). **5620**

VAR TRYGGHET. (SW). **5313**

VARIA AEGYPTIACA. (US/0887-4026). **2632**

VARIETY. (US/0042-2738). **4079**

VARLIK. (TU). **3450**

VAROSI KOZLEKEDES. (HU/0133-0314). **Qty:** approx. 10. **5399**

VARSITY (TORONTO). (CN/0042-2789). **1096**

VASA. (SZ/0301-1526). **3802**

VASA STAR, THE. (US/0746-0627). **2274**

VASCULAR MEDICINE REVIEW. (UK/0954-2582). **3802**

VASCULAR REPORTS. (US/0748-8971). **3977**

VASCULUM, THE. (UK/0049-5891). **Qty:** 1-2. **4173**

VASUTI KOZLEKEDESI SZAKIRODALMI TAJEKOZTATO. (HU/0231-0767). **5437**

VAT INTELLIGENCE. (UK/0263-9947). **717**

VDT NEWS. (US/0742-938X). **4806**

VEALER, THE. (US/0749-6664). **2360**

VECTOR (READING). (UK/0505-0448). **3450**

VEDANTA KESARI, THE. (II/0042-2983). **4364**

VEDERE CONTACT INTERNATIONAL. (IT/0392-0453). **4217**

VEDERE INTERNATIONAL. (IT/0302-6256). **4217**

VEDIC LIGHT. (II). **5041**

VEGETARIAN (ALTRINCHAM, CHESHIRE : 1980). (UK/0260-3233). **Qty:** 10. **4200**

VEGETARIAN GOURMET. (US/1065-6340). **2360**

VEGETARIAN JOURNAL. (US/0885-7636 #y 0883-1165). **4200**

VEGETARIAN TIMES. (US/0164-8497). **4200**

VEGETARIAN VOICE. (US/0271-1591). **4806**

VEGETATIO. (NE/0042-3106). **529**

VEGYIPARI SZAKIRODALMI TAJEKOZTATO MUANYAG- ES GUMIIPARI KULONLENYOMATA. (HU/0231-0775). **995**

VEHICLE IDENTIFICATION. (US/8756-940X). **5427**

VEHICLE SYSTEM DYNAMICS. (NE/0042-3114). **2131**

VEHICULES A MOTEUR NEUFS MIS EN CIRCULATION. (BE). **5427**

VEJVISER I STATISTIKKEN. (DK/0109-8314). **5345**

VEKER, DER. (US/8750-8478). **5265**

VELD & FLORA. (SA/0042-3203). **530**

VELDWERK AMSTERDAM. (NE/0922-2782). **2912**

VELIGER, THE. (US/0042-3211). **5599**

VELO-NEWS. (US/0161-1798). **429**

VELTRO, IL. (IT/0042-3254). **2524**

VENDING TIMES. (US/0042-3327). **4214**

VENEREOLOGY : OFFICIAL PUBLICATION OF THE NATIONAL VENEREOLOGY COUNCIL OF AUSTRALIA. (AT). **Qty:** 8. **3716**

VENTURA COUNTY STAR-FREE PRESS. (US). **5641**

VENTURE INWARD / THE MAGAZINE OF THE ASSOCIATION FOR RESEARCH AND ENLIGHTENMENT. (US/0748-3406). **5007**

VENTURE PRODUCT NEWS. (US/0738-7199). **5168**

VENTURES IN RESEARCH. (US/0092-556X). **5168**

VENUS; JAPANESE JOURNAL OF MALACOLOGY. (JA/0042-3580). **5599**

VERA LEX. (US/0893-4851). **Qty:** 10-12. **2253**

VERANDA (ATLANTA, GA.). (US/1040-8150). **2903**

VERBA. (SP). **3331**

VERBATIM. (US/0162-0932). **Qty:** 12+ per year. **3331**

VERBINDING ROTTERDAM. (NE/0922-6540). **1168**

VERBONDSNIEUWS VOOR DE BELGISCHE SIERTEELT. (BE). **2436**

VERDAD (CORPUS CHRISTI, TEX. : 1942). (US). **2275**

VERDE AMBIENTE. (IT). **Qty:** 40. **2222**

VERDI NEWSLETTER. (US/0160-2667). **Qty:** 1-2. **4158**

VEREINTE NATIONEN. (GW/0042-384X). **4537**

VERFASSUNG UND RECHT IN UBERSEE. (GW/0506-7286). **3094**

VERGILIUS (1959). (US/0506-7294). **1080**

VERHANDLUNGEN DER ORNITHOLOGISCHE GESELLSCHAFT IN BAYERN. (GW). **5620**

VERHANDLUNGEN DES HISTORISCHEN VEREINS FUER NIEDERBAYERN. (GW). **Qty:** 5. **2714**

VERITABLE AMIE. (CN/0831-0866). **5567**

VERKAUFSLEITER-SERVICE. (GW/0178-5893). **718**

VERKOPEN! VAKMAGAZINE VOOR COMMERCIELE AKTIE. (NE). **952**

VERKSTADERNA. (SW/0042-4056). **2131**

VERKUNDIGUNG UND FORSCHUNG. (GW/0342-2410). **5007**

VERMESSUNG, PHOTOGRAMMETRIE, KULTURTECHNIK. (SZ/0252-9424). **2000**

VERMONT BAR JOURNAL & LAW DIGEST, THE. (US/0748-4925). **Qty:** 30. **3071**

VERMONT HISTORY. (US/0042-4161). **2764**

VERMONT REGISTERED NURSE. (US/0191-1880). **3870**

VERNACULAR ARCHITECTURE. (UK/0305-5477). **310**

VERNON COUNTY BROADCASTER. (US). **5771**

VEROFFENTLICHUNGEN. (GW). **3071**

VEROFFENTLICHUNGEN DES MUSEUMS FUER UR- UND FRUHGESCHICHTE POTSDAM. (GE/0079-4376). **285**

VERRE (PARIS, FRANCE). (FR/0984-7979). **Qty:** 6. **2595**

VERS UN DEVELOPPEMENT SOLIDAIRE. (SZ). **Qty:** 25. **4537**

VERSAILLES REPUBLICAN (VERSAILLES, IND. : 1893). (US). **5668**

VERSION (SIDNEY, N.S.W.). (AT). **Qty:** 12. **2511**

VERTIFLITE. (US/0042-4455). **39**

VERWALTUNG UND FORTBILDUNG. (GW). **4693**

VERWARMING EN VENTILATIE. (NE/0042-451X). **2608**

VERZEICHNIS DER BERUFSBILDENDEN SCHULEN. (GW). **1917**

VESTNIK DERMATOLOGII I VENEROLOGII. (RU/0042-4609). **3723**

VESTNIK, LE MESSAGER. (FR/0767-7294). **2524**

VESTNIK MOSKOVSKOGO UNIVERSITETA. SERIIA VI, EKONOMIKA. (RU/0130-0105). **1525**

VESTNIK OFTALMOLOGII. (RU/0042-465X). **3879**

VESTNIK OTORINOLARINGOLOGII. (RU/0042-4668). **3891**

VESTNIK (OWINGS MILLS, MD.). (US/1055-2278). **Qty:** 10. **2275**

VESTNIK USTEDNIHO USTAVU GEOLOGICKEHO. (XR/0042-1359). **1401**

VETERA CHRISTIANORUM. (IT/0506-8126). **Qty:** 30. **5020**

VETERINARIA ARGENTINA. (AG/0326-4629). **Qty:** 20 per year. **5523**

VETERINARIA (MEXICO). (MX/0301-5092). **5523**

VETERINARY AND COMPARATIVE ORTHOPAEDICS AND TRAUMATOLOGY. (GW/0932-0814). **5524**

VETERINARY AND HUMAN TOXICOLOGY. (US/0145-6296). **Qty:** 50-60. **5524**

VETERINARY CLINICAL PATHOLOGY. (US/0275-6382). **5525**

VETERINARY HISTORY. (UK/0301-6943). **5525**

VETERINARY MEDICINE (1985). (US/8750-7943). **5526**

VETERINARY PRACTICE. (UK/0042-4897). **5526**

VETERINARY RECORD. (UK/0042-4900). **5526**

VETERINARY REVIEW (SYDNEY, N.S.W.). (AT). **Qty:** 2. **5527**

VETERINARY SURGERY. (US/0161-3499). **5527**

VETERINARY TECHNICIAN. (US/8750-8990). **5527**

VETERINARY TIMES. (UK/1352-9374). **Qty:** varies. **5527**

VETTE VUES MAGAZINE. (US/0279-8476). **5427**

VETUS TESTAMENTUM. (NE/0042-4935). **5020**

VEZETESTUDOMANY. (HU). **Qty:** 6. **718**

VFW, VETERANS OF FOREIGN WARS MAGAZINE. (US/0161-8598). **4060**

VGB-KRAFTWERKSTECHNIK. (GW/0372-5715). **2000**

VIATOR (BERKELEY). (US/0083-5897). **1080**

VIBRATIONS (CLARENDON HILLS, ILL.). (US/1066-8268). **4424**

VICA JOURNAL. (US/1044-0151). **4209**

VICE VERSA (MONTREAL, QUEBEC). (CN/0829-2299). **2549**

VICTOR VALLEY MAGAZINE. (US/0738-8586). **2549**

VICTORIA ADVOCATE (VICTORIA, TEX. : DAILY). (US). **5755**

VICTORIA INSIDER. (CN/0843-4395). **Qty:** 3. **2765**

VICTORIA NATURALIST, THE. (CN/0049-612X). **Qty:** 2. **4173**

VICTORIAN HOMES. (US/0744-415X). **310**

VICTORIAN NATURALIST. (AT/0042-5184). **4173**

VICTORIAN NETBALLER. (AT). **4928**

VICTORIAN ORGAN JOURNAL. (AT/0310-4834). **Qty:** varies. **4158**

VICTORIAN PERIODICALS REVIEW. (US/0709-4698). **3355**

VICTORIAN POETRY. (US/0042-5206). **Qty:** 6. **3450**

VICTORIAN REVIEW. (CN/0848-1512). **3450**

VICTORIAN STUDIES. (US/0042-5222). **3450**

VICTORIAN YEAR-BOOK. (AT/0067-1223). **4701**

VICTORIANS INSTITUTE JOURNAL. (US/0886-3865). **5237**

VICTORY LANE. (US/0887-1426). **Qty:** 10. **4928**

VICTORY MUSIC REVIEW. (US). **4158**

VIDA HISPANICA (1972). (UK/0308-4957). **3332**

VIDA Y PENSAMIENTO. (CR). **5007**

VIDE, LES COUCHES MINCES, LE. (FR/0223-4335). **4424**

VIDEO AGE INTERNATIONAL. (US/0278-5013). **Qty:** 20-25/yr. **1142**

VIDEO & AUDIO REPORT. (NE). **1123**

VIDEO COMPUTING. (US/8756-5250). **1142**

VIDEO GUIDE (VANCOUVER). (CN/0228-6726). **1142**

VIDEO LIBRARIAN, THE. (US/0887-6851). **Qty:** 10 or less. **4377**

VIDEO NETWORKS. (US/0738-7563). **1142**

VIDEO-PRESSE. (CN/0315-3975). **1071**

VIDEO RATING GUIDE FOR LIBRARIES. (US/1045-3393). **3255**

VIDEO TIMES (SKOKIE, ILL.). (US/0742-8111). **4378**

VIDEO WATCHDOG. (US/1070-9991). **Qty:** 6-12 per year. **4079**

VIDEOGRAPHY. (US/0363-1001). **1143**

VIDEOMAKER. (US/0889-4973). **Qty:** 12 per month. **1168**

VIDEOMANIA. (CN/0711-7914). **4867**

VIDEOVISIE. (NE). **1143**

VIDURA. (II). **1123**

VIDYAJYOTI (DELHI). (II/0970-1222). **5038**

VIE CONSACREE. (BE). **5007**

VIE DES ARTS. (CN/0042-5435). **332**

VIE DES COMMUNAUTES RELIGIEUSES. (CN). **5007**

VIE ET MILIEU (1980). (FR/0240-8759). **Qty:** 3-4/yr. **2222**

VIE FRANCAISE (QUEBEC). (CN/0382-0262). **2549**

VIE OBLATE. (CN/0318-9392). **5038**

VIE PEDAGOGIQUE. (CN/0707-2511). **1790**

VIE SOCIALE. (FR/0042-5605). **Qty:** 6. **5225**

VIE WALLONNE. (BE/0042-5648). **2715**

VIER BULLETIN. (AT). **Qty:** 2 to 4. **1790**

VIERTELJAHRES-SCHRIFTENREIHE - OSTERREICHISCHES FORSCHUNGSINSTITUT FUR SPARKASSENWESEN. (AU). **Qty:** 4. **815**

VIERTELJAHRESSCHRIFT FUER HEILPADAGOGIK UND IHRE NACHBARGEBIETE. (SZ/0017-9655). **1790**

VIERTELJAHRSHEFTE FUER ZEITGESCHICHTE. SCHRIFTENREIHE. (GW/0506-9408). **2632**

VIETNAM GENERATION. (US/1042-7597). **Qty:** 50+/yr. **2765**

VIETNAM TODAY. (AT/1030-9985). **4537**

VIETNAM UPDATE. (US/0899-6601). **2632**

VIETNAM WAR NEWSLETTER. (US/0743-2496). **4060**

VIETNAMESE STUDIES. HANOI, VIETNAM (1966). (VM/0085-7823). **2667**

VIEWCAMERA (SACRAMENTO, CALIF.). (US/1066-6958). **4378**

VIEWPOINTS (ATLANTA, GA.). (US/1064-5063). **5069**

VIEWS (BOSTON, MASS.). (US/0743-8044). **4378**

VIGENCIA. (AG). **2856**

VIGIL. (UK/0954-0881). **3451**

VIGILANCE. (FR/0398-9399). **1790**

VIGILIAE CHRISTIANAE. (NE/0042-6032). **3451**

VIJNANA SARASVATI. (II). **3255**

VIKALPA. (II/0256-0909). **889**

VILAG ES NYELV. (HU). **3332**

VILLAGE CRIER (TOMS RIVER, N.J.), THE. (US/1066-1204). **Qty:** 24. **5712**

VILLAGE VOICE (NEW YORK), THE. (US/0042-6180). **2549**

VILLAGER (MISSISSAUGA). (CN/0226-5907). **5797**

VILLAMOSSAG. (HU/0042-6210). **2085**

VILLANOVA LAW REVIEW. (US/0042-6229). **3071**

VILLE PLATTE GAZETTE, THE. (US/8750-6785). **Qty:** 12. **5684**

VIM & VIGOR. (US/0886-6554). **2601**

VINCULOS. (CR/0304-3703). **247**

VINCULUM. (AT/0157-759X). **3540**

VINDUET. (NO/0042-6288). **3451**

VINEYARD GAZETTE, THE. (US). **Qty:** 2-3. **5690**

VINIFERA WINE GROWERS JOURNAL, THE. (US/0095-3563). **190**

VINTAGE AIRPLANE, THE. (US/0091-6943). **39**

VINTAGE FORD, THE. (US/0042-6350). **5427**

VINTAGE JAZZ MART. (UK/0042-6369). **4158**

VINTAGE (NEW YORK, N.Y. 1971). (US/0049-6456). **2360**

VINTAGE TRIUMPH, THE. (US/0147-9695). **5427**

VINUM. (SZ/0177-2570). **Qty:** 1-2. **2372**

VIOLENT KIN!. (US/1064-5071). **Qty:** 12-15. **3178**

VIOLEXCHANGE, THE. (US/0892-5437). **4158**

VIP NEWSLETTER. (US/0738-7091). **4394**

VIP. VAKBLAD VOOR IMAGE PROCESSING. (NE/0926-3241). **1221**

VIRGINIA APPALACHIAN NOTES. (US/0739-3482). **2476**

VIRGINIA BAPTIST REGISTER, THE. (US/0083-6311). **5069**

VIRGINIA BAR ASSOCIATION JOURNAL, THE. (US/0360-3857). **Qty:** (varies). **3071**

VIRGINIA COUNTRY. (US/0734-6603). **2549**

VIRGINIA ENGINEER (1974), THE. (US/0504-4251). **2000**

VIRGINIA ENGLISH BULLETIN. (US/0504-426X). **Qty:** 6-10. **3332**

VIRGINIA FORESTS (1974). (US/0740-011X). **2398**

VIRGINIA GARDENER NEWSLETTER / DEPARTMENT OF HORTICULTURE, COOPERATIVE EXTENSION DIVISION, VIRGINIA TECH. (US). **Qty:** varies. **2433**

VIRGINIA GAZETTE (1930). (US/0049-6480). **5760**

VIRGINIA GENEALOGIST, THE. (US/0300-645X). **Qty:** 75. **2476**

VIRGINIA GEOGRAPHER, THE. (US/0042-6512). **2579**

VIRGINIA INDUSTRIAL DIRECTORY. (US/0882-3219). **1631**

VIRGINIA JOURNAL OF INTERNATIONAL LAW. (US/0042-6571). **3137**

VIRGINIA LAW REVIEW. (US/0042-6601). **3071**

VIRGINIA MAGAZINE OF HISTORY AND BIOGRAPHY, THE. (US/0042-6636). **2765**

VIRGINIA MEDICAL QUARTERLY : VMQ. (US/1052-4231). **Qty:** 6-10. **3650**

VIRGINIA NUMISMATIST, THE. (US). **Qty:** 3-4 per year. **2783**

VIRGINIA NURSE. (US/0270-7780). **3870**

VIRGINIA PHARMACIST, THE. (US/0042-6717). **4332**

VIRGINIA POULTRYMAN, THE. (US/0042-6733). **223**

VIRGINIA QUARTERLY REVIEW, THE. (US/0042-675X). **3355**

VIRGINIA REVIEW. (US/0732-9156). **Qty:** 8-10. **4693**

VIRGINIA SETTLERS (QUARTERLY). (US/0885-2626). **2476**

VIRGINIA TIDEWATER GENEALOGY. (US/0099-2496). **2476**

VIRGINIA TOWN & CITY. (US/0042-6784). **4693**

VIRGINIA UNITED METHODIST ADVOCATE. (US/0891-5598). **5069**

VIRGINIA/WEST VIRGINIA QUERIES. (US/0890-9423). **2476**

VIRGINIA WOOLF MISCELLANY. (US/0736-251X). **3355**

VIRGINIAN (STAUNTON, VA.), THE. (US/0743-4243). **2549**

VIROLOGY & AIDS ABSTRACTS. (US/0896-5919). **3662**

VIRTUAL REALITY REPORT. (US/1052-6242). **1283**

VIRTUE. (US/0164-7288). **5007**

VIRUS GENES. (US/0920-8569). **571**

VISALIA TIMES-DELTA. (US). **Qty:** 20/year. **5641**

VISAO. (BL/0042-6873). **2553**

VISIBILITIES. (US/0892-7375). **2796**

VISIBLE LANGUAGE. (US/0022-2224). **Qty:** 4-6. **4570**

VISION. (UK/0142-8543). **1143**

VISION. (UK). **Qty:** 6. **5568**

VISION. (MX/0042-6911). **3355**

VISION. (US). **Qty:** 30. **5008**

VISION FOR AMERICA'S FUTURE: AN AGENDA FOR THE 1990S, A. (US/1055-9213). **5313**

VISION LETTER, THE. (US/0042-6962). **4499**

VISION (PASADENA, CALIF.). (US/0882-6609). **5008**

VISION RESOURCE UPDATE. (US). **4394**

VISIONS. (US/1043-4194). **2601**

VISIONS-INTERNATIONAL. (US). **Qty:** 30. **3451**

VISIONS MAGAZINE (BOSTON, MASS.). (US/1064-8658). **Qty:** 4. **4378**

VISITANTE DOMINICAL, EL. (US/0194-9160). **5038**

VISITOR BEHAVIOR. (US/0892-4996). **4621**

VISTAZO. (EC). **5800**

VISTI - INSTYTUTU SV. VOLODYMYRA. (CN/0380-0369). **2275**

VISUAL ANTHROPOLOGY (JOURNAL). (UK/0894-9468). **247**

VISUAL ARTS NEWS. (CN/0704-0512). **368**

VISUAL ARTS RESEARCH. (US/0736-0770). **Qty:** (1-2). **368**

VISUAL MERCHANDISING & STORE DESIGN. (US/0745-4295). **958**

VISUAL RESOURCES. (US/0197-3762). **368**

VISUM NIEUWS. (NE/0925-8275). **1853**

VISVA HINDI DARSANA. (II). **3332**

VITA E PENSIERO. (IT/0042-725X). **4364**

VITA E SALUTE. (IT/0042-7268). **Qty:** 30/yr. **2495**

VITA MONASTICA. (IT). **Qty:** 30. **5008**

VITA SOCIALE. (IT/0042-7365). **5038**

VITAE SCHOLASTICAE. (US/0735-1909). **1790**

VITAL CHRISTIANITY (1994). (US/1077-6982). **5008**

VITAL SIGNS (STORRS, CONN.). (US/0749-856X). **4621**

VITAL STATISTICS IN CORRECTIONS. (US). **3084**

VITALITY. (CN/0829-6014). **2602**

VITAMIN CONNECTION. (UK/0957-6436). **4200**

VITIS. (GW/0042-7500). **475**

VITIS, VITICULTURE AND ENOLOGY ABSTRACTS. (GW/0175-8292). **2362**

VITREOUS ENAMELLER. (UK/0042-7519). **2017**

VITRIINI. (FI/0357-749X). **2810**

VIVA. (KE). **5568**

VIVANT UNIVERS. (BE/0042-7527). **2579**

VIVARIUM. (NE/0042-7543). **4364**

VLAAMS DIERGENEESKUNDIG TIJDSCHRIFT. (BE/0303-9021). **5527**

VLAAMSE GIDS, DE. (BE). **2856**

VLAANDEREN. (BE/0042-7683). **332**

VM UPDATE. (UK). **1281**

VOCATIONAL ASPECT OF EDUCATION, THE. (UK/0305-7879). **1917**

VOCATIONAL EDUCATION JOURNAL. (US/0884-8009). **1917**

VOCATIONAL EVALUATION AND WORK ADJUSTMENT BULLETIN. (US/0160-8312). **4395**

VOEDING. (NE/0042-7926). **4200**

VOENNO-ISTORICHESKI SBORNIK. (BU/0204-4080). **4060**

VOGUE (NEW YORK). (US/0042-8000). **5568**

VOICE (EAST LANSING, MICH.). (US/0883-573X). **Qty:** 1-2. **1790**

VOICE M.A.N, THE. (US/0505-8708). **Qty:** 24-30. **2433**

VOICE OF MISSIONS. (US/0042-8175). **5069**

VOICE OF THE DIABETIC. (US/1041-8490). **3733**

VOICE OF THE TURTLE (SAN DIEGO, CALIF.). (US/0739-9324). **5237**

VOICE OF THE WORKING WOMAN, THE. (II). **1717**

VOICE OF UNITED SENIOR CITIZENS OF ONTARIO, INC. (CN/0382-0068). **5182**

VOICE OF YOUTH ADVOCATES. (US/0160-4201). **3451**

VOICE (WESTCHESTER). (US/0049-6669). **5008**

VOICES (AMERICAN ACADEMY OF PSYCHOTHERAPISTS). (US/0042-8272). **3937**

VOICES IN ITALIAN AMERICANA. (US/1048-292X). **Qty:** 14. **3451**

VOICES OF MEXICO. (MX/0186-9418). **2512**

VOICES OF THE AFRICAN DIASPORA. (US/1054-4283). **2275**

VOIE LACTEE. (CN/0710-5479). **Qty:** 5. **3769**

VOIES FERREES. (FR/0249-4914). **857**

VOIR DIRE (MONTREAL). (CN/0826-4503). **Qty:** 6. **4395**

VOIX DES PRAIRIES, LA. (US/0743-1848). **2476**

VOIX SEFARAD. (CN/0704-5352). **Qty:** 5. **2275**

VOLKSKUNDE (1940). (BE/0775-3128). **Qty:** approx. 20-25 per year. **2325**

VOLKSKUNDIG BULLETIN. (NE). **2325**

VOLTA REVIEW, THE. (US/0042-8639). **4395**

VOLUNTAS : INTERNATIONAL JOURNAL OF VOLUNTARY AND NON-PROFIT ORGANISATIONS. (UK/0957-8765). **4339**

VOPROSY IAZYKOZNANIIA. (RU/0373-658X). **3332**

VOPROSY IKHTIOLOGII. (RU/0042-8752). **2315**

VOPROSY ISTORII. (RU/0042-8779). **2633**

VOPROSY MEDICINSKOJ HIMII. (RU/0042-8809). **494**

VORGANGE. (GW/0507-4150). **2524**

VORWARTS (NEW YORK, N.Y.). (US/0746-7869). **5722**

VOTRE SUCCES. (CN/0843-6665). **718**

VOX BENEDICTINA. (CN/0715-8726). **Qty:** 10. **5038**

VOX LATINA. (GW/0172-5300). **3332**

VOX PATRUM. (PL). **5008**

VOX REFORMATA. (AT/0728-0912). **5008**

VOYAGE EN GROUPE. (CN/0711-6136). **5499**

VOYAGER. (US). **5651**

VOYAGER INTERNATIONAL. (US/1040-8541). **2579**

VOYAGEUR (GREEN BAY, WIS.). (US/1062-7634). **Qty:** 15. **2633**

VOZ DE LA CULTURA, LA. (SP). **332**

VOZ DE LA VALDERIA, LA. (SP). **2524**

VOZ, LA. (US). **2495**

VOZ (SEATTLE, WASH.). (US). **2495**

VR. VERMESSUNGSWESEN UND RAUMORDNUNG. (GW/0340-5141). **2579**

VRIJ NEDERLAND : VN. (NE). **2524**

VSAM UPDATE. (UK). **1281**

VSE UPDATE. (UK). **Qty:** 2. **1281**

V+T. VERKEHR UND TECHNIK. (GW/0340-4536). **5399**

VUELTA. (MX/0185-1586). **2512**

VULKANOLOGIIA I SEISMOLOGIA. (US/0742-0463). **1412**

VVS BULLETIN. (NE). **5346**

VYCHODOSLOVENSKY KRAJ V TLACI. (XO). **2636**

VYZVOLNYI SHLIAKH. (UK/0042-9422). **3355**

W. (US/0162-9115). **1088**

W.W. 1 AERO. (US/0736-198X). **Qty:** Varies. **39**

WACO CITIZEN, THE. (US). **Qty:** 104. **5755**

WACO TRIBUNE-HERALD. (US). **5755**

WACONDA ROOTS AND BRANCHES. (US/8755-2167). **2477**

WAFFEN- UND KOSTUMKUNDE. (GW/0042-9945). **252**

WAGE-PRICE LAW & ECONOMICS REVIEW. (US/0361-6665). **1526**

WAGES FOR HOUSEWORK : CAMPAIGN BULLETIN, THE. (CN/0229-1967). **1717**

WAGNER. (UK). **4158**

WAGNER NEWS (LONDON, ENGLAND). (UK/0261-3468). **389**

WAGONER (JOURNAL). (US). **2477**

WAHDAH (CAIRO, EGYPT). (UA). **2667**

WAHKIAKUM COUNTY EAGLE. (US). **5763**

WAHL ZUM NIEDERSACHSISCHEN LANDTAG DER ... . (GW). **4503**

WAKARUSA TRIBUNE, THE. (US). **Qty:** 15. **5668**

WAKE FOREST LAW REVIEW. (US/0043-003X). **3072**

WALKING MAGAZINE, THE. (US/1042-2102). **2602**

WALL PAPER (NEW YORK, N.Y.), THE. (US/0273-6837). **2903**

WALL STREET JOURNAL (EUROPE). (BE/0921-9986). **5778**

WALLACE STEVENS JOURNAL, THE. (US/0148-7132). **Qty:** 10. **3473**

WALLACEANA. (MY). **Qty:** 4. **2222**

WALLEYE. (US/0744-1266). **4880**

WALLS & CEILINGS. (US/0043-0161). **631**

WALT WHITMAN QUARTERLY REVIEW. (US/0737-0679). **3452**

WANDERING VOLHYNIANS. (CN/1180-2901). **2715**

WANGAR. (CN/0712-1865). **5797**

WAR CRY (NEW YORK, N.Y.), THE. (US/0043-0234). **5314**

WAR, LITERATURE, AND THE ARTS. (US/1046-6967). **Qty:** 6. **3452**

WAR RESEARCH INFO SERVICE. (US/1058-823X). **4060**

WARBIRDS. (US/0744-6624). **39**

WARMER BULLETIN. (UK). **Qty:** 12-14/yr. **2245**

WARP AND WEFT (MCMINNVILLE, OR.). (US/0732-6890). **5359**

WARRIOR (SHEARWATER. 1978). (CN/0707-8056). **4060**

WARROAD PIONEER. (US). **Qty:** 10-20. **5699**

WARSHIP INTERNATIONAL. (US/0043-0374). **4185**

WARTA DEMOGRAFI. (IO). **4560**

WARTA GEOLOGI. (MY/0126-5539). **1401**

WARWICK BEACON. (US). **5741**

WAS TUN. (GW/0043-0404). **4499**

WASAFIRI. (UK/0269-0055). **Qty:** 40-45 per year. **3452**

WASCANA REVIEW. (CN/0043-0412). **3452**

WASECA COUNTY NEWS. (US/0745-8177). **Qty:** 3. **5699**

WASHINGTON APPLE PI. (US/1056-7682). **1207**

WASHINGTON BUSINESS JOURNAL. (US/0737-3147). **Qty:** 56. **719**

WASHINGTON COASTAL CURRENTS. (US). **2208**

WASHINGTON COUNSELETTER. (US/0740-8501). **1790**

WASHINGTON CRIME NEWS SERVICES' CORPORATE SECURITY DIGEST. (US/0894-3826). **3178**

WASHINGTON CRIME NEWS SERVICES' NARCOTICS CONTROL DIGEST. (US/0889-5708). **3178**

WASHINGTON CRIMINAL JUSTICE REPORT'S CRIME VICTIMS DIGEST. (US/0884-5107). **3179**

WASHINGTON, D.C. MINI-MICRO COMPUTER REPORT, THE. (US/0363-7905). **1273**

WASHINGTON FEDERAL SCIENCE NEWSLETTER. (US/0740-0535). **Qty:** 50+. **5169**

WASHINGTON INFORMER, THE. (US/0741-9414). **Qty:** 10. **2275**

WASHINGTON INQUIRER. (US/0749-1050). **4538**

WASHINGTON INTERNATIONAL ARTS LETTER. (US/0043-0609). **2856**

WASHINGTON ISLAND OBSERVER. (US). **Qty:** 32. **5771**

WASHINGTON JOURNALISM REVIEW (1983). (US/0741-8876). **2925**

WASHINGTON LAW REVIEW (1967). (US/0043-0617). **3072**

WASHINGTON MONTHLY, THE. (US/0043-0633). **4499**

WASHINGTON NURSE, THE. (US/0734-5666). **3871**

WASHINGTON PARK ARBORETUM BULLETIN. (US/1046-8749). **2433**

WASHINGTON POST BOOK WORLD, THE. (US). **4833**

WASHINGTON POST (WASHINGTON, D.C. : 1974). (US/0190-8286). **5648**

WASHINGTON QUARTERLY, THE. (US/0163-660X). **4538**

WASHINGTON REMOTE SENSING LETTER. (US/0739-6538). **Qty:** 50. **1361**

WASHINGTON REPORT INGAA. (US). **Qty:** 8. **4281**

WASHINGTON REPORT ON AFRICA. (US/0733-8104). **Qty:** 5 per year. **4499**

WASHINGTON REPORT ON LONG TERM CARE. (US/0091-7311). **3793**

WASHINGTON REPORT ON MIDDLE EAST AFFAIRS, THE. (US/8755-4917). **2526**

WASHINGTON REPORT ON THE HEMISPHERE. (US/0275-5599). **Qty:** 24. **2912**

WASHINGTON REVIEW. (US/0163-903X). **Qty:** 9. **333**

WASHINGTON RICELETTER. (US). **2361**

WASHINGTON STATE BAR NEWS. (US/0886-5213). **3073**

WASHINGTON TIMES-HERALD (WASHINGTON, IND.). (US). **5668**

WASHINGTON UNIVERSITY JOURNAL OF URBAN AND CONTEMPORARY LAW. (US/8756-0801). **3073**

WASHINGTON UNIVERSITY LAW QUARTERLY. (US/0043-0862). **3073**

WASHINGTON VIEW. (US/1042-4229). **2549**

WASHINGTONIAN (WASHINGTON, D.C.), THE. (US/0043-0897). **2549**

WASSER-KALENDER (BERLIN). (GW/0511-3520). **5541**

WASSER UND BODEN. (GW/0043-0951). **145**

WASSERVERSORGUNG UND ABWASSERBESEITIGUNG IN DER WIRTSCHAFT. (GW). **5541**

WASTE AGE. (US/0043-1001). **2245**

WASTE BUSINESS WEST. (CN/1185-4731). **2246**

WASTE MANAGEMENT & ENVIRONMENT. (AT). **2246**

WASTE PLANNING. (UK/0965-3147). **2246**

WASTE RECOVERY REPORT. (US/0889-0072). **Qty:** 20-30. **2246**

WASTES MANAGEMENT. (UK). **2246**

WATAUGA DEMOCRAT. (US/0745-1903). **5724**

WATCH & CLOCK REVIEW. (US/0279-6198). **2916**

WATCHING AND WAITING. (UK). **5008**

WATER, AIR, AND SOIL POLLUTION. (NE/0049-6979). **2247**

WATER & WASTEWATER INTERNATIONAL. (US/0891-5385). **5542**

WATER DESALINATION REPORT. (US). **5542**

WATER EQUIPMENT NEWS. (US/0194-1194). **5542**

WATER INTERNATIONAL. (US/0250-8060). **5542**

WATER LAW. (UK/0959-9754). **5543**

WATER NEWS. (US). **5543**

WATER NEWS (CAMBRIDGE). (CN/0821-0233). **5543**

WATER NEWSLETTER. (US/0043-1273). **5543**

WATER REPORTER, THE. (US). **5543**

WATER RESOURCES BULLETIN (URBANA). (US/0043-1370). **5544**

WATER RESOURCES MONOGRAPH. (US/0270-9600). **5547**

WATER RESOURCES RESEARCH. (US/0043-1397). **5547**

WATER S. A. (SA/0378-4738). **5547**

WATER SERVICES. (UK/0301-7028). **2248**

WATER SKIER (WINTER HAVEN), THE. (US/0049-7002). **4928**

WATER WELL JOURNAL. (US/0043-1443). **5548**

WATERBULLETIN. (UK/0262-9909). **5548**

WATERFRONT NEWS. (US/8756-0038). **Qty:** 2. **596**

WATERFRONT WORLD. (US/0733-0677). **2839**

WATERLINES. (UK/0262-8104). **5548**

WATERLOO CHRONICLE. (CN). **5797**

WATERSCHAPSBELANGEN. (NE/0043-1486). **5548**

WATERWHEEL (SILVER SPRING, MD.). (US/0898-6606). **5008**

WATKINS REPORT ON CONSULTANTS' MARKETING STRATEGIES, THE. (US/0894-1041). **889**

WAVELENGTH (NEW ORLEANS, LA.). (US/0741-2460). **4158**

WAVERLY GAZETTE (WAVERLY, KAN. : 1898). (US). **Qty:** 10. **5679**

WAVES (SPRING VALLEY, CALIF.). (US/1055-0348). **2096**

WAWATAY NEWS. (CN/0703-9387). **2275**

WAY OF ST. FRANCIS (1980). (US/0273-8295). **5008**

WAY, THE. (UK/0043-1575). **5008**

WAYNE LAW REVIEW. (US/0043-1621). **Qty:** 1/year. **3073**

WBAI FOLIO. (US). **1143**

WCA NATIONAL UPDATE. (US). **333**

WCCI FORUM. (US/0116-5461). **1908**

WDA JOURNAL. (US/1046-9338). **1337**

WEATHER. (UK/0043-1656). **1436**

WEATHER & CLIMATE REPORT. (US/0730-8256). **1436**

WEATHER AND FORECASTING. (US/0882-8156). **1436**

WEATHERWISE. (US/0043-1672). **1436**

WEB ABBOTSFORD. (AT/1036-3912). **Qty:** 2. **1908**

WEBBER'S. (AT). **Qty:** 4. **3452**

WEBBIA. (IT/0083-7792). **Qty:** 2-4. **530**

WEBER STUDIES. (US/0891-8899). **Qty:** 12-18. **2856**

WEBSTER'S WAGON WHEEL. (US/1067-523X). **2477**

WEEDMAN NEWSLETTER. (US/0883-7791). **2477**

WEEKENDS. (US). **Qty:** 6. **5499**

WEEKLY BULLET, THE. (US/0743-460X). **4929**

WEEKLY BULLETIN - WEEKLY BULLETIN LEATHER SHOE NEWS CO. (US). **3186**

WEEKLY INDIA TRIBUNE. (US/0744-4524). **5662**

WEEKLY INSIDERS TURKEY LETTER. (US/0160-4910). **157**

WEEKLY JAPAN DIGEST, THE. (US/1060-2259). **Qty:** 4-5. **4500**

WEEKLY NEWS (MIAMI, FLA.), THE. (US/0199-4395). **2796**

WEEKLY REGISTER-CALL (CENTRAL CITY, COLO. : 1861). (US). **5644**

WEEKLY REVIEW, THE. (KE). **4538**

WEGEN. (NE/0043-2067). **2033**

WEHRAUSBILDUNG. (GW/0178-3084). **4061**

WEHRMEDIZIN UND WEHRPHARMAZIE. (GW). **4332**

WEHRMEDIZINISCHE MONATSSCHRIFT. (GW/0043-2156). **3650**

WEHRTECHNIK. (GW/0043-2172). **4061**

WEIGHING & MEASUREMENT. (US/0095-537X). **4033**

WEIMARER BEITRAEGE. (GW/0323-4223). **Qty:** 75. **3452**

WEIRD TALES. (US/0898-5073). **3452**

WELCOME HOME. (US/8750-9563). **Qty:** 3-4. **2286**

WELDING AND METAL FABRICATION. (UK/0043-2245). **4028**

WELDING DATA BOOK. (US/0511-4365). **4028**

WELDING DESIGN & FABRICATION. (US/0043-2253). **4028**

WELDING DISTRIBUTOR (1966). (US/0192-7671). **938**

WELDING JOURNAL. (US/0043-2296). **4028**

WELFARE IN AUSTRALIA. (AT/0310-4869). **Qty:** 1. **5314**

WELFARE MANCHESTER. (UK/0269-879X). **5314**

WELFARE RIGHTS BULLETIN. (UK/0263-2098). **5314**

WELFARE TO WORK. (US/1060-5622). **Qty:** 20. **5314**

WELLNESS NEWSLETTER, THE. (US/0740-8498). **2602**

WELLNESS PERSPECTIVES. (US/0748-1764). **Qty:** 1-2. **4807**

WELLSIAN (EDWALTON, NOTTINGHAMSHIRE : 1976). (UK/0263-1776). **3452**

WELSH JOURNAL OF EDUCATION, THE. (UK/0957-297X). **1791**

WELT DES ISLAMS, DIE. (NE/0043-2539). **5045**

WELT DES ORIENTS, DIE. (GW/0043-2547). **3332**

WELTKUNST, DIE. (GW/0043-261X). **368**

WELTMISSION, DIE. (GW/0723-6204). **Qty:** 12-15. **5008**

WELTMISSION (EVANGELISCHES MISSIONSWERK IN DER BUNDESREPUBLIK DEUTSCHLAND UND BERLIN WEST). (GW/0341-082X). **5008**

WELTWIRTSCHAFT (TUBINGEN), DIE. (GW/0043-2652). **1588**

WELTWOCHE, DIE. (SZ). **2525**

WELZYNSWEEKBLAD 1981. (NE/0169-0639). **5314**

WEN HSUEH YUEH PAO (CHANG-SHA SHIH, CHINA). (CC). **3452**

WEN HUI YUEH KAN / WEN HUI YUEH KAN PIEN CHI PU. (CC). **333**

WER IST WER?. (GW). **435**

WERELD EN ZENDING. (NE/0165-988X). **5009**

WERKBLAD NEDERLANDSE DIDACTIEK. (BE). **1791**

WERKSTOFFE, BETRIEBSLEITUNG + TECHNIK. (GW). **2033**

WESCON CONFERENCE RECORD (1979). (US/1044-6036). **2085**

WESLEYAN ADVOCATE, THE. (US/0043-289X). **5069**

WESLEYAN CHRISTIAN ADVOCATE. (US/0190-6097). **5069**

WESLEYAN (MIDDLETOWN). (US/0148-4249). **1103**

WESLEYAN THEOLOGICAL JOURNAL. (US/0092-4245). **5009**

WESLEYAN WORLD. (US/0739-0440). **5009**

WEST AFRICA (LONDON). (UK/0043-2962). **2500**

WEST AFRICAN JOURNAL OF ARCHAEOLOGY. (NR/0083-8160). **285**

WEST AFRICAN JOURNAL OF BIOLOGICAL AND APPLIED CHEMISTRY. (NR/0043-2989). **995**

WEST AFRICAN JOURNAL OF MEDICINE. (NR/0189-160X). **3650**

WEST AFRICAN JOURNAL OF SURGERY. (NR/0331-054X). **3977**

WEST BRANCH. (US/0149-6441). **3452**

WEST EUROPEAN POLITICS. (UK/0140-2382). **4500**

WEST HAWAII TODAY. (US/0744-4591). **5656**

WEST HILLS REVIEW. (US/0890-9024). **3452**

WEST INDIAN LAW JOURNAL. (JM/0253-7370). **3073**

WEST INDIAN MEDICAL JOURNAL, THE. (JM/0043-3144). **3650**

WEST OF ENGLAND MEDICAL JOURNAL. (UK). **3650**

WEST ORANGE TIMES. (US). **Qty:** 200/year. **5651**

WEST TEXAS HISTORICAL ASSOCIATION YEAR BOOK, THE. (US/0886-6155). **2765**

WEST VIRGINIA ADVOCATE, THE. (US/0891-9240). **5765**

WEST VIRGINIA HILLBILLY (RICHWOOD, W.VA. : 1986). (US/0888-0409). **5765**

WEST VIRGINIA HILLS & STREAMS. (US/0279-0580). **2208**

WEST VIRGINIA HISTORY. (US/0043-325X). **2765**

WEST VIRGINIA LAW REVIEW. (US/0043-3268). **3073**

WEST VIRGINIA LIBRARIES. (US/0043-3276). **3256**

WESTBOROUGH NEWS, THE. (US/0893-3782). **Qty:** 3. **5690**

WESTBRIDGE ART MARKET REPORT. (CN/1191-3371). **368**

WESTCHESTER BAR JOURNAL. (US/0746-1844). **3073**

WESTCHESTER FAMILY. (US/1043-6774). **1071**

WESTCHESTER HISTORIAN, THE. (US/0049-7266). **2765**

WESTERLY. (AT/0043-342X). **3452**

WESTERLY SUN, THE. (US/1065-1209). **5741**

WESTERN AMERICAN LITERATURE. (US/0043-3462). **Qty:** 140/year. **3453**

WESTERN & EASTERN TREASURES. (US/0890-0876). **Qty:** 30-50. **4880**

WESTERN ANGLER. (AT/1035-493X). **Qty:** 3. **2316**

WESTERN AUSTRALIA IN BRIEF. (AT/0727-2022). **Qty:** 11. **3073**

WESTERN CANADA OUTDOORS (ALBERTA EDITION). (CN/0836-446X). **2208**

WESTERN CANADA OUTDOORS (SASKATCHEWAN EDITION). (CN/0836-4451). **2208**

WESTERN CANADIAN ANTHROPOLOGIST, THE. (CN/0829-0547). **247**

WESTERN CATHOLIC REPORTER. (CN/0512-5235). **5038**

WESTERN CITY (SACRAMENTO, CALIF. : 1976). (US/0279-5337). **4694**

WESTERN COLLEGE READING & LEARNING ASSOCIATION NEWSLETTER. (US/0746-1305). **1853**

WESTERN EXPRESS. (US/0510-2332). **2788**

WESTERN FARMER AND GRAZIER. WESTERN FARM WEEKLY. (AT). **Qty:** 12. **145**

WESTERN FISHERIES MAGAZINE. (AT/1033-4149). **2316**

WESTERN FOLKLORE. (US/0043-373X). **2325**

WESTERN HISTORICAL QUARTERLY. (US/0043-3810). **Qty:** 42 per year average. **2636**

WESTERN HORSEMAN, THE. (US/0043-3837). **2803**

WESTERN HUMANITIES REVIEW. (US/0043-3845). **3453**

WESTERN ILLINOIS REGIONAL STUDIES. (US/0192-1355). **2766**

WESTERN JOURNAL OF APPLIED FORESTRY. (US/0885-6095). **2398**

WESTERN JOURNAL OF BLACK STUDIES, THE. (US/0197-4327). **2275**

WESTERN KANSAS WORLD. (US). **Qty:** 6. **5679**

WESTERN LEGAL HISTORY. (US/0896-2189). **Qty:** 10-12. **3073**

WESTERN MARYLAND GENEALOGY. (US/0747-7805). **Qty:** 15. **2477**

WESTERN MINING DIRECTORY. (US/0162-9026). **2153**

WESTERN NEW ENGLAND LAW REVIEW. (US/0190-6593). **3073**

WESTERN NEW YORK FAMILY MAGAZINE. (US). **Qty:** 15 per year. **2286**

WESTERN NEWS (LIBBY, MONT.), THE. (US/0745-0362). **5706**

WESTERN OUTDOORS. (US/0043-4000). **4880**

WESTERN PENNSYLVANIA GENEALOGICAL SOCIETY QUARTERLY. (US/0278-7431). **Qty:** 50-60. **2477**

WESTERN PLANNER, THE. (US/0279-0602). **4695**

WESTERN POLITICAL QUARTERLY, THE. (US/0043-4078). **4500**

WESTERN PREHISTORIC RESEARCH ARCHEOLOGICAL MONOGRAPH. (US/0739-1080). **285**

WESTERN PRODUCER. (CN/0043-4094). **146**

WESTERN QUEENS GAZETTE, THE. (US). **Qty:** 20. **5722**

WESTERN RIDER (1987). (CN/0820-571X). **2803**

WESTERN ROOFING INSULATION AND SIDING. (US/0164-5803). **631**

WESTERN SKIER. (CN/1184-2679). **Qty:** varies. **4929**

WESTERN STAR (BESSEMER, ALA.), THE. (US/0889-0080). **Qty:** 12. **5628**

WESTERN STATE UNIVERSITY LAW REVIEW. (US/0362-8892). **Qty:** Approx. 10. **3073**

WESTERN STATES JEWISH HISTORY. (US/0749-5471). **2275**

WESTERN TAX REVIEW. (US/8755-0083). **4758**

WESTERN VIKING. (US). **Qty:** 10-15/year. **2275**

WESTERN WHEEL. (CN/0701-1571). **2550**

WESTERN WILDLANDS. (US/0363-6690). **2208**

WESTFALEN (MUNSTER). (GW/0043-4337). **2715**

WESTFIELD LEADER, THE. (US). **5712**

WESTINDIAN DIGEST. (UK/0143-6619). **2525**

WESTLAKER TIMES, THE. (US/0746-9802). **Qty:** 12 per year. **5731**

WESTMINSTER WINDOW. (US). **Qty:** 25. **5644**

WESTMINSTER THEOLOGICAL JOURNAL, THE. (US/0043-4388). **5009**

WESTON DEMOCRAT, THE. (US). **5765**

WESTWARD INTO NEBRASKA. (US/0738-0380). **Qty:** varies. **2477**

WESTWAYS. (US/0043-4434). **5428**

WETENSCHAP EN SAMENLEVING. (NE/0043-4442). **146**

WETENSCHAPPELIJKE TIJDINGEN. (BE). **2715**

WETLANDS : JOURNAL OF THE COAST AND WETLANDS SOCIETY. (AT). **2511**

WETTBEWERB IN RECHT UND PRAXIS : WRP. (GW/0172-049X). **3104**

WETTER UND LEBEN. (AU/0043-4450). **1437**

WETTERAUER GESCHICHTSBLAETTER. (GW/0509-6213). **2715**

WETUMPKA HERALD, THE. (US). **Qty:** 42. **5628**

WFS QUARTERLY. (US/1071-1767). **2293**

WHALEWATCHER. (US/0273-4419). **5600**

WHAT CAR?. (UK). **5428**

WHAT THEY SAID. (US/0512-5804). **2633**

WHAT'S AHEAD IN HUMAN RESOURCES. (US). **948**

WHAT'S BREWING. (CN/0714-2056). **2372**

WHAT'S NEW IN FARMING. (UK). **146**

WHAT'S NEW IN HOME ECONOMICS. (US/0043-4590). **2793**

WHAT'S ON VIDEO AND CINEMA. (AT). **4378**

WHEAT LIFE. (US/0043-4701). **146**

WHEEL CLICKS. (US/0043-4744). **5438**

WHEELING NEWS-REGISTER. (US). **Qty:** 150-200/year. **5765**

WHEELS OF TIME. (US/0738-565X). **5399**

WHEELWRIGHTINGS. (US/0192-5865). **3453**

WHERE THE TRAILS CROSS. (US/0092-4164). **2477**

WHERE TO EAT IN CANADA. (CN/0315-3088). **5073**

WHICH COMPUTER?. (UK/0140-3435). **1207**

WHICH LONDON SCHOOL?. (UK/0959-7271). **1791**

WHISKEY, WOMEN, AND ... . (US/0091-7664). **4159**

WHISPERING WIND. (US/0300-6565). **Qty:** 18. **2275**

WHISTLE PUNK. (CN/0825-477X). **2398**

WHISTLER QUESTION. (CN/0383-820X). **5797**

WHITE BOOK OF SKI AREAS. U.S. AND CANADA, THE. (US/0163-9684). **4929**

WHITE LIGHT, THE. (US/0742-8820). **4243**

WHITE ROCKER (1990), THE. (US/1049-3387). **5756**

WHITE TOPS, THE. (US/0043-499X). **4867**

WHITE WOLF MAGAZINE. (US/0897-9391). **4867**

WHITEWRIGHT SUN, THE. (US). **Qty:** 12. **5756**

WHITTIER NEWSLETTER. (US/0511-8832). **435**

WHO MAKES MACHINERY IN GERMANY. (GW). **Qty:** 15. **2132**

WHO OWNS WHAT IN WORLD BANKING. (UK). **816**

WHOLE AGAIN RESOURCE GUIDE, THE. (US/0734-9033). **5265**

WHOLE EARTH REVIEW. (US/0749-5056). **Qty:** 250. **2495**

WHOLE LIFE. (US/0888-2061). **4807**

WHOLE LIFE TIMES. (US/0279-5604). **4200**

WHOLESALER (ELMHURST), THE. (US/0032-1680). **2609**

WHO'S MAILING WHAT!. (US/8755-2671). **767**

WHO'S WHO AMONG BLACK AMERICANS. (US/0362-5753). **436**

WHO'S WHO, CHICANO OFFICEHOLDERS. (US/0738-4637). **436**

WHO'S WHO IN INDIAN RELICS. (US/0747-7538). **437**

WHO'S WHO IN INTELLECTUAL PROPERTY. (US/0899-1766). **1309**

WHO'S WHO IN RISK MANAGEMENT. (US). **437**

WHO'S WHO IN THE EMERGENCY & RESCUE SERVICES. (UK). **4807**

WHO'S WHO IN THE FISH INDUSTRY. (US/0270-160X). **2316**

WHO'S WHO IN THE MOTION PICTURE INDUSTRY. (US/0278-6516). **438**

WHO'S WHO IN WESTERN EUROPE. (UK). **438**

WHO'S WHO (LONDON. 1849). (UK/0083-937X). **438**

WIADOMOSCI INSTYTUTU METEOROLOGII I GOSPODARKI WODNEJ. (PL/0208-6263). **1437**

WICAZO SA REVIEW. (US/0749-6427). **2766**

WIDE ANGLE. (US/0160-6840). **4080**

WIDE SMILES. (US/1056-7402). **Qty:** 4-8. **5314**

WIEDZA OBRONNA : DWUMIESIECZNIK TOWARZYSTWA WIEDZY OBRONNEJ. (PL/0209-0031). **4061**

WIENER BEITRAEGE ZUR ENGLISCHEN PHILOLOGIE. (AU/0083-9914). **3333**

WIENER GESCHICHTSBLATTER. (AU/0043-5317). **2716**

WIENER JAHRBUCH FUR PHILOSOPHIE. (AU/0083-999X). **4365**

WIENER MEDIZINISCHE WOCHENSCHRIFT. (AU/0043-5341). **3651**

WIENER SLAVISTISCHES JAHRBUCH. (AU/0084-0041). **3333**

WIENER STUDIEN. (AU/0084-005X). **3333**

WIENER STUDIEN. (AU). **2716**

WIENER TIERARZTLICHE MONATSSCHRIFT. (AU/0043-535X). **5527**

WIENER ZEITSCHRIFT FUER DIE KUNDE DES MORGENLANDES. (AU/0084-0076). **2633**

WILBUR REGISTER, THE. (US). **5763**

WILCOX PROGRESSIVE ERA. (US). **Qty:** 6. **5628**

WILD EARTH. (US/1055-1166). **Qty:** 6-10. **2183**

WILD WEST (LEESBURG, VA.). (US/1046-4638). **2766**

WILDERNESS ALBERTA. (CN/0830-8284). **2209**

WILDERNESS MEDICINE LETTER : THE OFFICIAL NEWSLETTER OF THE WILDERNESS MEDICAL SOCIETY. (US). **3651**

WILDERNESS RECORD. (US/0194-3030). **Qty:** 12. **2209**

WILDERNESS (WASHINGTON, D.C.). (US/0736-6477). **2209**

WILDFLOWER. (CN/0842-5132). **2209**

WILDFLOWER (AUSTIN, TEX. 1984). (US/0898-8803). **Qty:** (6-8). **530**

WILDFLOWER (AUSTIN, TEX. 1988). (US/0896-4858). **Qty:** 6 per year. **530**

WILDFOWL CARVING AND COLLECTING. (US/0886-3407). **Qty:** 3/year. **376**

WILDLIFE ART NEWS. (US/0746-9640). **368**

WILDLIFE AUSTRALIA. (AT/0043-5481). **2209**

WILDLIFE COLLECTABLES JOURNAL, THE. (CN/0827-2409). **2209**

WILDLIFE IN NORTH CAROLINA. (US/0043-549X). **2209**

WILDLIFE JOURNAL. (US/0893-6560). **Qty:** 1. **2209**

WILDLIFE REHABILITATION TODAY. (US/1044-2618). **Qty:** minimum 4/year. **227**

WILKAMITE RECORD, THE. (US). **5702**

WILLDENOWIA. (GW/0511-9618). **530**

WILLIAM AND MARY LAW REVIEW. (US/0043-5589). **3075**

WILLIAM AND MARY QUARTERLY, THE. (US/0043-5597). **2766**

WILLIAM CARLOS WILLIAMS REVIEW. (US/0196-6286). **Qty:** 4-6 per year. **3356**

WILLIAM MITCHELL LAW REVIEW. (US/0270-272X). **3075**

WILLIAMS' FAMILY BULLETIN, THE. (US/0043-5627). **2477**

WILLIAMS NEWS. (US). **Qty:** 10. **5630**

WILLIAMS REPORT. (US/1075-8550). **Qty:** 4. **1124**

WILLIAMSON COUNTY SUN, THE. (US). **Qty:** 5. **5756**

WILLIAMSPORT SUN-GAZETTE. (US/1056-3083). **5740**

WILLOW TRANSFER QUARTERLY. (CN/0826-2098). **2595**

WILLOWS JOURNAL. (US). **5641**

WILMINGTON JOURNAL (WILMINGTON, N.C.), THE. (US/0049-7649). **5724**

WILSHIRE CENTER'S LARCHMONT CHRONICLE. (US/0192-1932). **5641**

WILSON BULLETIN (WILSON ORNITHOLOGICAL SOCIETY), THE. (US/0043-5643). **5621**

WILSON LIBRARY BULLETIN. (US/0043-5651). **3256**

WILSON QUARTERLY (WASHINGTON), THE. (US/0363-3276). **2495**

WILTSHIRE ARCHAEOLOGICAL AND NATURAL HISTORY MAGAZINE (1982). (UK/0262-6608). **285**

WIN NEWS. (US/0145-7985). **5568**

WINCHESTER SUN (WINCHESTER, KY. : 1912). (US). **Qty:** 10-12. **5683**

WIND ENERGY ABSTRACTS. (US/0277-2140). **Qty:** 30+ /yr. **1960**

WIND ENERGY NEWS. (US/0886-2818). **1960**

WIND ENERGY REPORT. (US/0162-8623). **1960**

WIND ENGINEERING. (UK/0309-524X). **1437**

WIND (PIKEVILLE, KY.). (US/0361-2481). **3453**

WINDER NEWS, THE. (US). **Qty:** 4. **5655**

WINDIRECTIONS. (UK/0950-0642). **Qty:** 4. **1960**

WINDLESS ORCHARD, THE. (US/0043-5716). **3473**

WINDMILL HERALD. (CN/0712-6417). **5798**

WINDOW FASHIONS. (US/0886-9669). **2904**

WINDPOWER MONTHLY. (DK/0109-7318). **1960**

WINDS OF CHANGE (BOULDER, COLO.). (US/0888-8612). **Qty:** 4-8. **5169**

WINDSOR REVIEW OF LEGAL AND SOCIAL ISSUES. (CN/0838-3596). **3075**

WINDSOR STAR MICROFORM, THE. (CN/0839-2277). **5798**

WINDSOR THIS MONTH. (CN/0318-2460). **2550**

WINDSOR YEARBOOK OF ACCESS TO JUSTICE, THE. (CN/0710-0841). **3075**

WINDSPEAKER. (CN/0834-177X). **Qty:** 1-2/yr. **5798**

WINDSPORT. (CN/0826-5003). **4929**

WINDSURF MAGAZINE. (UK). **Qty:** 5. **597**

WINDSURFING CALIFORNIA. (US/1063-8172). **4929**

WINE ADVOCATE, THE. (US/0887-8463). **2372**

WINE EAST. (US/0892-662X). **2372**

WINE INVESTOR. EXECUTIVE EDITION, THE. (US/0889-4256). **2372**

WINE NEWS (CORAL GABLES, FLA.), THE. (US/1065-4895). **2372**

WINE NEWS, THE. (US). **Qty:** 12/yr. **2372**

WINE PRODUCTION, AUSTRALIA AND STATES / AUSTRALIAN BUREAU OF STATISTICS. (AT). **2362**

WINE SPECTATOR, THE. (US/0193-497X). **2372**

WINE TIDINGS. (CN/0228-6157). **2372**

WINE WORLD. (US/0199-7483). **2373**

WINES AND VINES. (US/0043-583X). **2373**

WINES & VINES. BUYER'S GUIDE ISSUE. (US/0043-583X). **2373**

WINESBURG EAGLE, THE. (US/0147-3166). **439**

WINESTATE. (AT/0156-6490). **Qty:** 6. **2373**

WING & SHOT. (US/0892-1849). **4880**

WINGS (CALGARY). (CN/0701-1369). **39**

WINGS OF GOLD (PENSACOLA, FLA.). (US/0274-7405). **Qty:** 4. **39**

WINGTIPS (LANSING, N.Y.). (US/8756-4505). **5600**

WINNING (TULSA, OKLA.). (US/0744-2467). **4867**

WINNIPEG SUN (1980). (CN/0711-3773). **5798**

WINONA COURIER. (US). **5699**

WINSTON-SALEM CHRONICLE. (US). **5724**

WINSTON-SALEM JOURNAL. (US). **5724**

WINTER PARK-MAITLAND OBSERVER. (US/1064-3613). **Qty:** 12. **5651**

WIRE INDUSTRY. (UK/0043-6011). **2086**

WIRE (LONDON, ENGLAND). (UK/0952-0686). **4159**

WIRE WORLD INTERNATIONAL. (GW/0043-6046). **2086**

WIRED (SAN FRANCISCO, CALIF.). (US/1059-1028). **Qty:** 40. **1207**

WIREWORLD. (GW/0934-5906). **2001**

WIRTSCHAFT UND GESELLSCHAFT. (AU/0378-5130). **1588**

WIRTSCHAFT UND WETTBEWERB. (GW/0043-6151). **857**

WIRTSCHAFTSEIGENE FUTTER. (GW/0049-7711). **224**

WIRTSCHAFTSINFORMATIK. (GW/0937-6429). **1263**

WIRTSCHAFTSPRUFUNG, DIE. (GW/0043-6313). **753**

WIRTSCHAFTSRECHT. (GW/0512-6320). **Qty:** 50-70. **3104**

WIRTSCHAFTSSCHUTZ + SICHERHEITSTECHNIK. (GW/0173-3303). **3179**

WISCONSERVATION. (US/0164-3649). **2210**

WISCONSIN ARBORIST, THE. (US/0887-8927). **2183**

WISCONSIN ARCHEOLOGIST, THE. (US/0043-6364). **Qty:** varies. **285**

WISCONSIN CHINA SERIES. (US/0084-053X). **3453**

WISCONSIN ENGLISH JOURNAL. (US). **Qty:** 1-3. **3333**

WISCONSIN GOLF. (US/1042-6620). **Qty:** 6 /yr. **4930**

WISCONSIN JEWISH CHRONICLE, THE. (US/0043-6488). **5053**

WISCONSIN LAW REVIEW. (US/0043-650X). **3075**

WISCONSIN LAWYER. (US/1043-0490). **4695**

WISCONSIN LUTHERAN QUARTERLY. (US/0362-5648). **Qty:** 40. **5009**

WISCONSIN MAGAZINE OF HISTORY. (US/0043-6534). **2766**

WISCONSIN NEWMONTH. (US/1059-0935). **2550**

WISCONSIN PHARMACIST, THE. (US/0043-6585). **4332**

WISCONSIN REVIEW (OSHKOSH). (US/0043-6631). **3453**

WISCONSIN SCHOOL MUSICIAN, THE. (US/0043-6658). **4159**

WISCONSIN SILENT SPORTS. (US/0882-9640). **4930**

WISCONSIN SMALL BUSINESS COUNSELOR. (US/0897-5116). **Qty:** 12. **889**

WISCONSIN SOCIOLOGIST, THE. (US/0043-6666). **Qty:** 1-4. **5265**

WISCONSIN TRAILS. (US/0095-4314). **2550**

WISDEN'S CRICKETERS ALMANAC. (UK). **4930**

WISE WOMAN, THE. (US/0883-119X). **5568**

WISENET. (AT/0815-0753). **Qty:** 3-4 per year. **5568**

WISER NOW. (US/1071-2275). **Qty:** 10. **3755**

WISSENSCHAFT UND WELTBILD; ZEITSCHRIFT FUER GRUNDFRAGEN DER FORSCHUNG UND WELTANSCHAUUNG. (AU/0043-6798). **4365**

WISSENSCHAFTLICHE ZEITSCHRIFT. (GW/0040-1528). **2495**

WISSENSCHAFTSRECHT, WISSENSCHAFTSVERWALTUNG, WISSENSCHAFTSFORDERUNG. (GW/0443-6976). **3076**

WISTRA. (GW/0721-6890). **3109**

WITHOUT PREJUDICE. (US/0892-9408). **4514**

WITHOUT PREJUDICE (EDMONTON). (CN/0706-5574). **2896**

WITNESS (AMBLER), THE. (US/0197-8896). **Qty:** 10/year. **5069**

WITTYWORLD. (US/0892-9807). **Qty:** 4 or more. **376**

WITZ (PENNGROVE, CALIF.). (US/1061-4583). **Qty:** 20 per year. **3453**

WIZARD: THE GUIDE TO COMICS. (US). **Qty:** (varies). **2779**

WLN PARTICIPANT. (US/0278-6303). **3256**

WLW JOURNAL. (US/0272-1996). **3256**

WNC BUSINESS JOURNAL. (US/1049-7145). **723**

WOCHENBLATT FUER PAPIERFABRIKATION. (GW/0043-7131). **4240**

WOHNBAUFORSCHUNG IN OSTERREICH. (AU). **Qty:** 20. **2839**

WOLFENBUTTELER NOTIZEN ZUR BUCHGESCHICHTE. (GW/0341-2253). **4833**

WOLFENBUTTELER RENAISSANCE MITTEILUNGEN. (GW/0342-4340). **2716**

WOLGAN KWAHAK. (CH). **5170**

WOLVES AND RELATED CANIDS. (US/0899-9317). **Qty:** 4-6. **5600**

WOMAN ACTIVIST, THE. (US/0049-7770). **4500**

WOMAN ALIVE. (UK/0962-2152). **Qty:** 80. **5009**

WOMAN ENGINEER. (GREENLAWN, N.Y.), THE. (US/0887-2120). **2001**

WOMAN ENGINEER, THE. (UK). **Qty:** varies. **2001**

WOMAN LOCALLY. (US/0163-3244). **5569**

WOMAN WRITER. (AT/0313-6485). **Qty:** 6. **3454**

WOMANIST (OTTAWA). (CN/0849-4975). **Qty:** 10. **5569**

WOMAN'S ART JOURNAL. (US/0270-7993). **Qty:** 34. **368**

WOMAN'S ENTERPRI$E. (US/0898-6126). **5569**

WOMAN'S TOUCH. (US/0190-4620). **5569**

WOMANSPEAK. (AT/0311-8479). **5569**

WOMBAT. (US). **1071**

WOMEN. (UK/0957-4042). **5569**

WOMEN ALIVE. (US/0890-3395). **Qty:** 6/year. **5009**

WOMEN & CRIMINAL JUSTICE. (US/0897-4454). **3179**

WOMEN AND ENVIRONMENTS. (CN/0229-480X). **Qty:** 10. **5569**

WOMEN & HEALTH. (US/0363-0242). **3769**

WOMEN AND LANGUAGE. (US/8755-4550). **Qty:** 6-8. **3333**

WOMEN & PERFORMANCE. (US/0740-770X). **Qty:** 2-6/yr. **5372**

WOMEN & POLITICS. (US/0195-7732). **4500**

WOMEN & THERAPY. (US/0270-3149). **5569**

WOMEN ARTISTS NEWS. (US/0149-7081). **Qty:** 40-50. **333**

WOMEN IN BUSINESS (KANSAS CITY, MO.). (US/0043-7441). **Qty:** 6. **723**

WOMEN IN NATURAL RESOURCES. (US). **5570**

WOMEN IN THE ARTS BULLETIN. (US). **369**

WOMEN LAWYERS' JOURNAL. (US/0043-7468). **3076**

WOMEN LIKE ME. (US/0821-4794). **723**

WOMEN POLICE MAGAZINE. (US). **Qty:** 4/year. **3179**

WOMEN UNLIMITED. (US). **5570**

WOMEN WITH WHEELS. (US/1043-979X). **5428**

WOMEN'S ADVOCATE (NEW YORK, N.Y.). (US). **Qty:** 20. **3122**

WOMEN'S & CHILDREN'S WEAR AND FASHION ACCESSORIES BUYERS. (US/0741-0735). **1088**

WOMEN'S ART MAGAZINE. (UK). **Qty:** Approx. 20. **369**

WOMENS ART REGISTER BULLETIN. (AT). **Qty:** 10-40. **333**

WOMEN'S COACHING CLINIC. (US/0146-1133). **4930**

WOMEN'S CONCERNS. (CN/0827-2263). **5009**

WOMEN'S EDUCATION. (CN/0714-9786). **Qty:** 8. **1791**

WOMENS GLOBAL NETWORK FOR REPRODUCTIVE RIGHTS NEWSLETTER. (NE). **5570**

WOMEN'S HEALTH LETTER. (US/1062-4163). **Qty:** 8/year. **3651**

WOMEN'S LARGE & HALF SIZE SPECIALTY STORES. (US/0743-3972). **1088**

WOMEN'S LEAGUE OUTLOOK. (US/0043-7557). **5053**

WOMEN'S QUARTERLY REVIEW. (US/0882-1135). **5571**

WOMEN'S RECORD, THE. (US/0888-4609). **Qty:** 12. **5571**

WOMEN'S REVIEW OF BOOKS, THE. (US/0738-1433). **3356**

WOMEN'S RIGHTS LAW REPORTER. (US/0085-8269). **3076**

WOMEN'S STUDIES. (US/0049-7878). **5571**

WOMEN'S STUDIES INTERNATIONAL FORUM. (UK/0277-5395). **5571**

WOMEN'S STUDIES JOURNAL. (NZ). **Qty:** 15-20. **5571**

WOMEN'S STUDIES QUARTERLY. (US/0732-1562). **5571**

WOMEN'S TRAVEL CONNECTIONS. (US/0882-8458). **5499**

WOMEN'S TRAVELLER. (US). **5499**

WOMEN'S WORLD (WASHINGTON, D.C.). (US/0043-759X). **5572**

WOMENWISE. (US/0890-9695). **4808**

WOOD AND FIBER SCIENCE. (US/0735-6161). **2406**

WOOD MACHINING NEWS. (US/0743-5231). **Qty:** 6. **2406**

WOOD RIVER JOURNAL. (US). **5658**

WOODALL'S CAMPGROUND DIRECTORY. EASTERN EDITION. (US/0162-7406). **4881**

WOODALL'S CAMPGROUND DIRECTORY. NORTH AMERICAN EDITION. (US/0146-1362). **4881**

WOODALL'S MISSOURI/ARKANSAS CAMPGROUND DIRECTORY. (US/0163-5328). **4881**

WOODENBOAT, THE. (US/0095-067X). **597**

WOODS 'N' WATER. (US/0194-8253). **4881**

WOODSIDE REPORT, THE. (CN/1192-2958). **Qty:** 2-4 per year. **1960**

WOODSMITH. (US/0164-4114). **635**

WOODSTOCK TIMES. (US). **Qty:** 4 times a year. **5722**

WOODVILLE LEADER AND DUNN COUNTY PICTORIAL MESSENGER, THE. (US/0748-6812). **Qty:** 6. **5772**

WOODWORKER (HEMEL HEMPSTEAD. (1910)). (UK/0043-776X). **635**

WOODWORKING INTERNATIONAL. (UK). **635**

WOODWORKING INTERNATIONAL NURNBERG. (GW/0177-7114). **635**

WOODWORKING (MARKHAM). (CN/0838-4185). **2406**

WOOL (PALMERSTON NORTH). (NZ/0110-6015). **5360**

WOOL REPORT NEW ZEALAND. (NZ/0112-6059). **Qty:** 3 per year. **5360**

WOOL TECHNOLOGY AND SHEEP BREEDING. (AT/0043-7875). **224**

WOORD EN DAAD WORD AND ACTION. (SA/0257-8921). **5009**

WORCESTER MAGAZINE (WORCESTER). (US/0191-4960). **4855**

WORD AMONG US, THE. (US/0742-4639). **5038**

WORD AND WAY. (US/0049-7959). **5009**

WORD & WORLD. (US/0275-5270). **5009**

WORD OF MOUTH (SAN ANTONIO, TEX.). (US/1048-3950). **1886**

WORD ON WORSHIP. (US/0888-1316). **5010**

WORD WAYS. (US/0043-7980). **Qty:** 10. **3333**

WORDPERFECTIONIST, THE. (US). **1292**

WORDS BY SPECIALISTS. (US). **Qty:** 2. **1791**

WORDS (WILLOW GROVE). (US/0164-4742). **4214**

WORDSWORTH CIRCLE. (US/0043-8006). **3356**

WORDWATCHING. (US/0731-9290). **1791**

WORK, EMPLOYMENT AND SOCIETY. (UK/0950-0170). **Qty:** 56. **1718**

WORK RELATED ABSTRACTS. (US/0273-3234). **1540**

WORK STUDY. (UK/0043-8022). **889**

WORK TIMES. (US/0736-9166). **723**

WORKAMERICA. (US/0740-4077). **1718**

WORKAMPER NEW$. (US/0895-3678). **Qty:** 6 /year. **1718**

WORKBASKET AND HOME ARTS MAGAZINE, THE. (US/0162-9123). **376**

WORKBENCH. (US/0043-8057). **635**

WORKBOOK, THE. (US/0195-4636). **1300**

WORKER CO-OPS (TORONTO. 1980). (CN/0829-576X). **1543**

WORKERS' ADVOCATE SUPPLEMENT, THE. (US/0882-6366). **Qty:** 3-4. **4500**

WORKER'S ADVOCATE, THE. (US/0276-363X). **Qty:** 3-4. **4548**

WORKERS EDUCATION. (II). **1719**

WORKERS VANGUARD (NEW YORK, N.Y.). (US/0276-0746). **1719**

WORKERS VOICE, THE. (BM). **1719**

WORKFORCE (WASHINGTON, D.C.). (US/1063-4363). **Qty:** 6-8. **1719**

WORKING CLASS, THE. (II). **1719**

WORKING FOR WILDLIFE. (CN/0229-7183). **2210**

WORKING PAPER SERIES - UNIVERSITY OF ARIZONA. MEXICAN AMERICAN STUDIES AND RESEARCH CENTER. (US/0732-7749). **5226**

WORKING PAPERS IN IRISH STUDIES. (US/0732-2674). **2716**

WORKING PAPERS IN LINGUISTICS (SEATTLE, WASH.). (US/0892-8886). **3333**

WORKING TOGETHER (SEATTLE, WASH.). (US/1064-8585). **Qty:** 5. **5314**

WORKS AND DAYS. (US/0886-2060). **Qty:** 4 /year. **333**

WORKSITE WELLNESS WORKS. (US/1053-492X). **Qty:** 4/yr. **4200**

WORLD ACCOUNTING REPORT; A MONTHLY BULLETIN ON DEVELOPMENTS IN INTERNATIONAL ACCOUNTING. (UK). **753**

WORLD ACROBATICS. (AT/1038-6963). **389**

WORLD AFFAIRS (WASHINGTON). (US/0043-8200). **4538**

WORLD AIRNEWS. (SA). **40**

WORLD AIRSHOW NEWS. (US/0888-5265). **Qty:** 6. **40**

WORLD ALMANAC AND BOOK OF FACTS, THE. (US/0084-1382). **1930**

WORLD AMATEUR BOXING MAGAZINE. (GW). **4930**

WORLD & I, THE. (US/0887-9346). **2495**

WORLD ARCHAEOLOGY. (UK/0043-8243). **285**

WORLD AROUND YOU, THE. (US/0199-8293). **4395**

WORLD (ASHEVILLE, N.C.). (US/0888-157X). **Qty:** 40. **2550**

WORLD

WORLD AUTOMOTIVE MARKET, THE. (US). **5428**

WORLD BIRDWATCH : THE NEWSLETTER OF THE INTERNATIONAL COUNCIL FOR BIRD PRESERVATION. (UK). **Qty:** varies. **2210**

WORLD CEMENT. (UK/0263-6050). **631**

WORLD CERAMICS ABSTRACTS. (UK/0957-8897). **2595**

WORLD COGENERATION. (US/1053-5802). **2132**

WORLD CURRENCY YEARBOOK. (US/0743-5363). **816**

WORLD ECONOMY, THE. (UK/0378-5920). **1641**

WORLD EDUCATION NEWS & REVIEWS. (US/0897-6724). **Qty:** 4-10. **1791**

WORLD FAITHS ENCOUNTER. (UK). **5010**

WORLD FISHING. (UK/0043-8480). **2316**

WORLD FOOTWEAR. (US/0894-3079). **1088**

WORLD FUTURES. (US/0260-4027). **4365**

WORLD HIGHWAYS. (US/0043-8529). **5446**

WORLD HOSPITALS. (UK/0512-3135). **3793**

WORLD INSURANCE REPORT. (UK). **2896**

WORLD INTELLECTUAL PROPERTY REPORT. (UK/0952-7613). **1309**

WORLD JOURNAL OF MICROBIOLOGY & BIOTECHNOLOGY. (UK/0959-3993). **571**

WORLD JOURNAL OF PSYCHOSYNTHESIS. (US/0043-860X). **3937**

WORLD JOURNAL OF SURGERY. (US/0364-2313). **3977**

WORLD LEATHER. (US/0894-3087). **3186**

WORLD LEISURE & RECREATION. (US). **4855**

WORLD LITERATURE TODAY. (US/0196-3570). **Qty:** 1,000 per year. **3454**

WORLD LITERATURE WRITTEN IN ENGLISH. (CN/0093-1705). **3356**

WORLD MARKET PERSPECTIVE. (US/0229-4044). **817**

WORLD MUSIC CONNECTIONS. (US/1049-0140). **4159**

WORLD NEUROLOGY. (UK/0899-9465). **3847**

WORLD (NEW YORK, N.Y. : 1967), THE. (US/0043-8154). **3473**

WORLD NEWS. (UK). **Qty:** varies. **1527**

WORLD OF BANKING, THE. (US/0730-8736). **817**

WORLD OF BEER, THE. (IT/1121-158X). **2373**

WORLD OF MUSIC (WILHELMSHAVEN). (SZ/0043-8774). **4159**

WORLD ORDER. (US/0043-8804). **5010**

WORLD PATENT INFORMATION. (UK/0172-2190). **1309**

WORLD PEACE NEWS. (US/0049-8130). **4538**

WORLD PENTECOST. (UK). **5069**

WORLD POLICY GUIDE. (UK). **2896**

WORLD POLITICS. (US/0043-8871). **4538**

WORLD PRESS REVIEW. (US/0195-8895). **4539**

WORLD PROGRESS. (US/0043-8901). **2550**

WORLD PUBLISHING MONITOR. (UK/0960-653X). **4822**

WORLD PUMPS. (UK/0262-1762). **2132**

WORLD RESOURCE REVIEW. (US/1042-8011). **2210**

WORLD RESOURCES. (US/0887-0403). **2210**

WORLD RIVERS REVIEW. (US). **5549**

WORLD SOCCER. (UK). **4930**

WORLD STAINLESS STEEL STATISTICS. (UK). **4026**

WORLD STATUS MAP. (US/0887-9559). **Qty:** 6/yr. **5499**

WORLD TANKER FLEET REVIEW. (UK). **5458**

WORLD TAX REPORT. (UK). **4759**

WORLD TECHNOLOGY PATENT LICENSING GAZETTE. (US/0278-8047). **1310**

WORLD TEXTILE ABSTRACTS. (UK/0043-9118). **5361**

WORLD TOBACCO. (UK/0043-9126). **5374**

WORLD TOBACCO SITUATION / UNITED STATES DEPARTMENT OF AGRICULTURE, FOREIGN AGRICULTURAL SERVICE. (US). **5374**

WORLD TODAY, THE. (UK/0043-9134). **4539**

WORLD TOY NEWS. (UK). **2585**

WORLD TRADE INDEX. (UK). **858**

WORLD TRAVELING. (US/0163-1780). **5500**

WORLD TRIBUNE. (US/0049-8165). **Qty:** 10. **4378**

WORLD VISION. (US). **2913**

WORLD WAR II INVESTIGATOR. (UK/0953-4857). **2633**

WORLDLIT. (CN/0820-6686). **1887**

WORLDRADIO, INC. (US). **1169**

WORLD'S FAIR (CORTE MADERA, CALIF.). (US/0273-480X). **5226**

WORLD'S FAIR, THE. (UK). **4868**

WORLD'S POULTRY SCIENCE JOURNAL. (UK/0043-9339). **224**

WORLDWIDE BROCHURES (PRINT ED.). (US/1053-9158). **5500**

WORLDWIDE BUSINESS PRACTICES REPORT. (US/1069-4447). **724**

WORLDWIDE OFFSHORE CONTRACTORS & EQUIPMENT DIRECTORY. (US/1058-9686). **4285**

WORLDWIDE PETROCHEMICAL DIRECTORY. (US/0084-2583). **4282**

WORLDWIDE PROJECTS. (US/0192-5512). **2001**

WORLDWIDE TRAVEL PLANNER. (US/0890-4766). **5500**

WORMWOOD REVIEW, THE. (US/0043-9401). **Qty:** 60. **3454**

WORSHIP. (US/0043-941X). **5010**

WORSHIP AND ARTS. (US/0890-5754). **5010**

WORSHIP AND PREACHING. (UK/0032-7407). **5010**

WORSHIP WORKS. (US/1051-9653). **5010**

WPA, WRITING PROGRAM ADMINISTRATION. (US/0196-4682). **3454**

WPNR, WEEKBLAD VOOR PRIVAATRECHT, NOTARIAAT EN REGISTRATIE. (NE). **3076**

WRANGELL SENTINEL. (US). **Qty:** 3-4. **5629**

WRANGLER. (US). **2766**

WRAP. (UK). **4808**

WRAP UP (NORWOOD, N.J.). (US/0741-8523). **3652**

WREE-VIEW OF WOMEN FOR RACIAL AND ECONOMIC EQUALITY, THE. (US/0892-3116). **4514**

WRF COMMENT. (CN/0821-1248). **1527**

WRIGHTSVILLE HEADLIGHT, THE. (US/0747-3737). **Qty:** 2-4. **5655**

WRITE NOW!. (US). **3454**

WRITER (BOSTON). (US/0043-9517). **3454**

WRITER'S DIGEST, THE. (US/0043-9525). **3454**

WRITER'S GUIDELINES (PITTSBURG, MO.). (US/1053-1793). **2925**

WRITERS' JOURNAL (SAINT PAUL, MINN.). (US/0891-8759). **3454**

WRITER'S LIFELINE. (CN/0225-610X). **2926**

WRITING CENTER JOURNAL, THE. (US). **1854**

WRITING INSTRUCTOR, THE. (US/0277-7789). **Qty:** 3-6. **3334**

WRITING TEACHER (SAN ANTONIO, TEX.). (US/0894-5837). **1908**

WRITTEN WORD, THE. (US/0738-8004). **1792**

WT. WERKSTATTSTECHNIK. (GW/0340-4544). **2132**

WURTTEMBERGISCHES WOCHENBLATT FUR LANDWIRTSCHAFT. (GW). **147**

WWF NEWS. (SZ/0254-3893). **Qty:** 12. **2210**

WYOMING ARCHAEOLOGIST, THE. (US/0043-9665). **Qty:** 3-4. **285**

WYOMING CATHOLIC REGISTER, THE. (US/0746-5580). **5038**

WYOMING GEO-NOTES. (US/8756-0348). **1401**

WYOMING STOCKMAN FARMER. (US/0043-9800). **147**

WYOMING WOOL GROWER. (US/0043-9827). **224**

XAVIER REVIEW. (US/0887-6681). **Qty:** 2 - 6. **3356**

XIBEI SHI-DI. (CH/1000-4076). **2668**

Y.E.S. QUARTERLY. (US/0884-6677). **Qty:** 8-12. **5600**

YA HOTLINE. (CN/0701-8894). **1071**

YAGL-AMBU; PAPUA NEW GUINEA JOURNAL OF THE SOCIAL SCIENCES AND HUMANITIES. (PP). **5226**

YALE ALUMNI MAGAZINE (1984). (US/8750-409X). **Qty:** 30-35. **1103**

YALE DAILY NEWS. (US/0890-2240). **5647**

YALE JOURNAL OF BIOLOGY AND MEDICINE, THE. (US/0044-0086). **3652**

YALE JOURNAL OF INTERNATIONAL LAW, THE. (US/0889-7743). **Qty:** 8-20 per year. **3138**

YALE JOURNAL OF LAW AND FEMINISM. (US/1043-9366). **3076**

YALE JOURNAL ON REGULATION. (US/0741-9457). **Qty:** 1-2 per year. **3076**

YALE LAW & POLICY REVIEW. (US/0740-8048). **3077**

YALE LAW JOURNAL, THE. (US/0044-0094). **3077**

YALE LAW REPORT. (US/0513-1391). **3077**

YALE REVIEW, THE. (US/0044-0124). **5226**

YALE SCIENTIFIC. (US/0091-0287). **5171**

YALE WEEKLY BULLETIN AND CALENDAR. (US/0740-0233). **1096**

YALOBUSHA PIONEER. (US/0742-7638). **2766**

YANKEE (DUBLIN, N.H.). (US/0044-0191). **2550**

YANKEE HOMES. (US/8756-0259). **4848**

YANKEE HORSETRADER. (US/0192-5210). **2803**

YANKEE OILMAN. (US/0044-0205). **4283**

YAOWU FENXI ZAZHI. (CC/0254-1793). **4333**

YAXKIN. (HO). **Qty:** 2. **248**

YAYA. (CN/0824-1457). **Qty:** 2. **3257**

YEAR BOOK - AMERICAN ACADEMY OF ACTUARIES. (US/0569-2032). **2896**

YEAR BOOK, AUSTRALIA. (AT/0810-8633). **5346**

YEAR BOOK / DUTCHESS COUNTY HISTORICAL SOCIETY. (US/0739-8565). **2766**

YEAR BOOK - FLORIDA GENEALOGICAL SOCIETY, TAMPA, FLA. (US/0428-7282). **2478**

YEAR BOOK - NATIONAL AURICULA & PRIMULA SOCIETY (NORTHERN SECTION). (UK). **148**

YEARBOOK AND PHILATELIC SOCIETIES' DIRECTORY. (UK/0260-1265). **2788**

YEARBOOK : COMMERCIAL ARBITRATION. (NE). **3104**

YEARBOOK - CREDIT UNION NATIONAL ASSOCIATION. (US). **817**

YEARBOOK FOR TRADITIONAL MUSIC. (US/0740-1558). **4159**

YEARBOOK OF COMPARATIVE AND GENERAL LITERATURE. (US/0084-3695). **3356**

YEARBOOK OF FINNISH FOREIGN POLICY. (FI/0355-0079). **4539**

YEARBOOK OF GERMAN-AMERICAN STUDIES. (US/0741-2827). **2766**

YEARBOOK OF LANGLAND STUDIES, THE. (US/0890-2917). **3473**

YEARBOOK OF POPULATION RESEARCH IN FINLAND. (FI/0506-3590). **Qty:** 1-3 per year. **4561**

YEARBOOK OF THE CALIFORNIA AVOCADO SOCIETY. (US/0096-5960). **2434**

YELLOW BRICK ROAD (ROCHESTER, N.Y.). (US/0888-5745). **1071**

YELLOW SILK. (US/0736-9212). **3455**

YELLOWBACK LIBRARY. (US). **3455**

YELLOWED PAGES. (US/1050-7361). **Qty:** 20. **2478**

YELLOWJACKET (QUINCY, ILL.). (US/0277-9668). **2478**

YERUSHOLAYMER ALMANAKH. (IS). **3455**

YES (LONDON, ENGLAND). (UK). **5010**

YESTERYEAR (PRINCETON). (US/0194-9349). **Qty:** 60. **252**

YESTERYEARS. (US/0044-037X). **2478**

YICHUAN. (CC/0253-9772). **552**

YIDDISH. (US/0364-4308). **3455**

YIDDISHKEIT. (IS/0792-044X). **5054**

YIDISHE SHPRAKH. (US/0044-0442). **3334**

YIHUA BAO. (US/0745-2322). **5763**

YO YO TIMES. (US/0897-7704). **1071**

YOGA AND HEALTH. (UK/0953-2161). **4365**

YOGA INTERNATIONAL. (US/1055-7911). **4186**

YOGA JOURNAL. (US/0191-0965). **2602**

YOGA LIFE (1982). (CN/0824-2526). **4365**

YORK COUNTY COAST STAR. (US). **5685**

YORK DAILY RECORD (YORK, PA. : 1973). (US/1043-4313). **5741**

YORK PAPERS IN LINGUISTICS. (UK/0307-3238). **3334**

YORKSHIRE ARCHAEOLOGICAL JOURNAL, THE. (UK/0084-4276). **285**

YOU! (AGOURA HILLS, CALIF.). (US/1064-8682). **5038**

YOUNG CHILDREN. (US/0044-0728). **1806**

YOUNG EAST. (JA/0513-5974). **5022**

YOUNG FASHIONS MAGAZINE. (US/0884-7630). **1088**

YOUNG PEOPLE NOW. (UK). **5314**

YOUNG SOCIALIST (NEW YORK, 1972). (US/0360-0157). **3356**

YOUNG SOLDIER. (AT/0300-3264). **1071**

YOUNG VOICES (OLYMPIA, WASH.). (US/1046-8404). Qty: 10/year. **1072**

YOUR CHURCH. (US/0049-8394). **5010**

YOUR CLASSIC. (UK/0957-6525). **5429**

YOUR COMPUTER CAREER. (US/0884-4615). **4210**

YOUR HEALTH & FITNESS. (US/0279-9324). **4808**

YOUR MORTGAGE MAGAZINE. (AT/1039-0081). Qty: 3. **817**

YOUR NEWS. (CN/0833-2908). Qty: 4-5. **5798**

YOUR SCHOOL & THE LAW. (US/0094-0399). **3077**

YOUTH AND POLICY. (UK/0262-9798). **1072**

YOUTH IN SOCIETY. (UK/0307-1790). **5314**

YOUTH LAW NEWS. (US/0882-8520). Qty: 4/yr. **3122**

YOUTH LEADER (SPRINGFIELD, MO.), THE. (US/0190-4566). Qty: 32/year. **5011**

YOUTH MARKETING REPORT. (US). **938**

YOUTH POLICY. (US). **5314**

YOUTH THEATRE JOURNAL. (US/0892-9092). **5372**

YOUTH UPDATE (REXDALE, ONT.). (CN/0830-9221). **3179**

YOUTHWORKER JOURNAL. (US/0747-3486). **5011**

YU WEN HSUEH HSI (JEN MIN CHIAO YU CHU PAN SHE). (CH). **3334**

YU WEN YUEH KAN. (CH). **3334**

YU YEN CHIAO HSUEH YU YEN CHIU. (CC). **3334**

YUANZIHE WULI. (CC/0253-3790). **4451**

YUGNTRUF. (US/0098-3640). Qty: varies. **3456**

YUKON DATA BOOK. (CN/0829-0652). **2550**

YUKON NEWS (1972). (CN/0318-1952). **5798**

YWN. (IS/0021-3306). **4365**

Z MAGAZINE. (ZA). **2644**

Z MAGAZINE (BOSTON, MASS.). (US/1056-5507). Qty: 20/year. **4501**

Z MISCELLANEOUS. (US/0892-9696). **3456**

ZAC, ZEITSCHRIFT FUER ANTIMIKROBIELLE, ANTINEOPLASTISCHE CHEMOTHERAPIE. (GW/0724-9004). **3652**

ZAHNAERZTLICHE MITTEILUNGEN. (GW/0044-1643). **1337**

ZAHNARZTEBLATT BADEN-WURTTEMBERG. (GW/0340-3017). **1337**

ZAIRE-AFRIQUE. (CG/0251-298X). **2644**

ZAMBEZIA. (RH/0379-0622). **5226**

ZAMBIA INDUSTRIAL CASES REPORTS / REPUBLIC OF ZAMBIA, MINISTRY OF LABOUR AND SOCIAL SERVICES, INDUSTRIAL RELATIONS COURT, THE. (ZA). **3155**

ZAMBIA NURSE (KITWE, ZAMBIA : 1978). (ZA/0044-1740). **3871**

ZAMBIAN GEOGRAPHICAL JOURNAL. (ZA). **2579**

ZAMBIAN ORNITHOLOGICAL SOCIETY NEWSLETTER. (ZA/0378-4533). Qty: 1-2. **5621**

ZAPAD. (CN/0226-3068). **2275**

ZAPAD TODAY. (CN). **2275**

ZAPISKI RUSSKOI AKADEMICHESKOI GRUPPY V SSHA. (US). Qty: 5-6. **1854**

ZASSHI KIJI SAKUIN, JINBUN SHAKAI HEN. (JA). **2857**

ZAVALA COUNTY SENTINEL (LA PRYOR, TEX. : 1913). (US). **5756**

ZAVODSKAJA LABORATORIJA. (RU/0321-4265). **1020**

ZBORNIK FILOZOFICKEJ FAKULTY UNIVERZITY KOMENSKEHO. ETHNOLOGIA SLAVICA. (XO/0083-4106). **248**

ZEITGEMASSE SCHAFHALTUNG : MIT EINEM KAPITEL UBER MILCHSCHAFHALTUNG. (AU). Qty: 70. **199**

ZEITSCHRIFT DER DEUTSCHEN GEMMOLOGISCHEN GESELLSCHAFT. (GW). **2915**

ZEITSCHRIFT DER SAVIGNY-STIFTUNG FUER RECHTSGESCHICHTE. KANONISTISCHE ABTEILUNG. (GW/0323-4142). **3077**

ZEITSCHRIFT DER SAVIGNY-STIFTUNG FUER RECHTSGESCHICHTE. ROMANISTISCHE ABTEILUNG. (AU). **3077**

ZEITSCHRIFT DES AACHENER GESCHICHTSVEREINS. (GW/0065-0137). **2716**

ZEITSCHRIFT DES VEREINS FUER LUBECKISCHE GESCHICHTE UND ALTERTUMSKUNDE. (GW/0083-5609). **2717**

ZEITSCHRIFT FUER ACKER- UND PFLANZENBAU. (GW/0931-2250). **148**

ZEITSCHRIFT FUER ANALYSIS UND IHRE ANWENDUNGEN. (GW/0232-2064). **3541**

ZEITSCHRIFT FUER ANGEWANDTE ENTOMOLOGIE. (GW/0044-2240). **5614**

ZEITSCHRIFT FUER ANGEWANDTE MATHEMATIK UND MECHANIK. (GW/0044-2267). **3541**

ZEITSCHRIFT FUER ARBEITSRECHT UND SOZIALRECHT. (AU/0044-2321). **3155**

ZEITSCHRIFT FUER ARBEITSWISSENSCHAFT. (GW/0340-2444). **1720**

ZEITSCHRIFT FUER ARZTLICHE FORTBILDUNG. (GW/0044-2178). **3739**

ZEITSCHRIFT FUER ASTHETIK UND ALLGEMEINE KUNSTWISSENSCHAFT (BONN, GERMANY). (GW/0044-2186). **369**

ZEITSCHRIFT FUER AUSLAENDISCHES OEFFENTLICHES RECHT UND VOELKERRECHT. (GW/0044-2348). **3138**

ZEITSCHRIFT FUER AUSLANDISCHE LANDWIRTSCHAFT. (GW/0049-8599). **148**

ZEITSCHRIFT FUER BALKANOLOGIE. (GW/0044-2356). **2717**

ZEITSCHRIFT FUER BAYERISCHE KIRCHENGESCHICHTE. (GW). **5070**

ZEITSCHRIFT FUER BERUFS- UND WIRTSCHAFTSPADAGOGIK 1980. (GW/0172-2875). **1918**

ZEITSCHRIFT FUER BEWASSERUNGSWIRTSCHAFT. (GW/0049-8602). **148**

ZEITSCHRIFT FUER CELTISCHE PHILOLOGIE. (GW/0084-5302). **3335**

ZEITSCHRIFT FUER DEN ERDKUNDEUNTERRICHT. (GW/0044-2461). **2579**

ZEITSCHRIFT FUER DEUTSCHE PHILOLOGIE. (GW/0044-2496). **3335**

ZEITSCHRIFT FUER DEUTSCHE PHILOLOGIE. BEIHEFT. (GW). **3335**

ZEITSCHRIFT FUER DEUTSCHES ALTERTUM UND DEUTSCHE LITERATUR. (GW/0044-2518). **3335**

ZEITSCHRIFT FUER DIALEKTOLOGIE UND LINGUISTIK. (GW/0044-1449). **3335**

ZEITSCHRIFT FUER DIE ALTTESTAMENTLICHE WISSENSCHAFT. (GW/0044-2526). **5020**

ZEITSCHRIFT FUER DIE ALTTESTAMENTLICHE WISSENSCHAFT. BEIHEFTE. (GW). **5020**

ZEITSCHRIFT FUER EISENBAHNWESEN UND VERKEHRSTECHNIK. (GW/0373-322X). **5438**

ZEITSCHRIFT FUER ENERGIEWIRTSCHAFT. (GW/0343-5377). **1961**

ZEITSCHRIFT FUER ENTWICKLUNGSPSYCHOLOGIE UND PADAGOGISCHE PSYCHOLOGIE. (GW/0049-8637). **1792**

ZEITSCHRIFT FUER ERKRANKUNGEN DER ATMUNGSORGANE. (GW/0303-657X). **3952**

ZEITSCHRIFT FUER ETHNOLOGIE. (GW/0044-2666). **248**

ZEITSCHRIFT FUER EVANGELISCHES KIRCHENRECHT. (GW/0044-2690). **5070**

ZEITSCHRIFT FUER EXPERIMENTELLE UND ANGEWANDTE PSYCHOLOGIE. (GW/0044-2712). **4622**

ZEITSCHRIFT FUER FLUGWISSENSCHAFTEN UND WELTRAUMFORSCHUNG. (GW/0342-068X). **40**

ZEITSCHRIFT FUER FRANZOSISCHE SPRACHE UND LITERATUR. (GW/0044-2747). **3335**

ZEITSCHRIFT FUER GASTROENTEROLOGIE. (GW/0044-2771). **3748**

ZEITSCHRIFT FUER GEMEINWIRTSCHAFT. (AU). Qty: 15-20. **1589**

ZEITSCHRIFT FUER GEOLOGISCHE WISSENSCHAFTEN. (GW/0303-4534). Qty: 30 per year. **1401**

ZEITSCHRIFT FUER GEOMORPHOLOGIE. (GW/0372-8854). **1401**

ZEITSCHRIFT FUER GERONTOLOGIE. (GW/0044-281X). **3755**

ZEITSCHRIFT FUER GESCHICHTSWISSENSCHAFT. (GW/0044-2828). Qty: 300. **2634**

ZEITSCHRIFT FUER GLETSCHERKUNDE UND GLAZIALGEOLOGIE. (AU/0044-2836). **1401**

ZEITSCHRIFT FUER JAGDWISSENSCHAFT. (GW/0044-2887). **4931**

ZEITSCHRIFT FUER KIRCHENGESCHICHTE. (GW/0044-2925). **5011**

ZEITSCHRIFT FUER KLINISCHE PSYCHOLOGIE. (GW/0084-5345). **4622**

ZEITSCHRIFT FUER KLINISCHE PSYCHOLOGIE, PSYCHOPATHOLOGIE UND PSYCHOTHERAPIE. (GW/0723-6557). **4622**

ZEITSCHRIFT FUER KRISTALLOGRAPHIE. (GW). **1033**

ZEITSCHRIFT FUER KULTURTECHNIK UND LANDENWICKLUNG. (GW/0934-666X). **148**

ZEITSCHRIFT FUER KUNSTGESCHICHTE. (GW/0044-2992). **369**

ZEITSCHRIFT FUER LARMBEKAMPFUNG. (GW/0174-1098). **2248**

ZEITSCHRIFT FUER LUFT- UND WELTRAUMRECHT. (GW/0340-8329). **3078**

ZEITSCHRIFT FUER LYMPHOLOGIE. (GW/0343-8554). **3653**

ZEITSCHRIFT FUER MISSION. (GW). **5011**

ZEITSCHRIFT FUER MORPHOLOGIE UND ANTHROPOLOGIE. (GW/0044-314X). **248**

ZEITSCHRIFT FUER MYKOLOGIE. (GW/0170-110X). **576**

ZEITSCHRIFT FUER OSTFORSCHUNG. (GW/0044-3239). **2717**

ZEITSCHRIFT FUER PAEDAGOGIK. (GW/0044-3247). **1792**

ZEITSCHRIFT FUER PAEDAGOGISCHE PSYCHOLOGIE. (SZ/1010-0652). Qty: 12. **4622**

ZEITSCHRIFT FUER PARAPSYCHOLOGIE UND GRENZGEBIETE DER PSYCHOLOGIE. (GW/0028-3479). **4243**

ZEITSCHRIFT FUER PHILOSOPHISCHE FORSCHUNG. (GW/0044-3301). **4365**

ZEITSCHRIFT FUER POLITIK. (GW/0044-3360). **4501**

ZEITSCHRIFT FUER RELIGIONS- UND GEISTESGESCHICHTE. (GW/0044-3441). **5011**

ZEITSCHRIFT FUER SAUGETIERKUNDE. (GW/0044-3468). **476**

ZEITSCHRIFT FUER SCHWEIZERISCHE ARCHAEOLOGIE UND KUNSTGESCHICHTE. (SZ/0044-3476). **286**

ZEITSCHRIFT FUER SEMIOTIK. (GW/0170-6241). **5172**

ZEITSCHRIFT FUER SLAVISCHE PHILOLOGIE. (GW/0044-3492). **3335**

ZEITSCHRIFT FUER SPIELMUSIK. (GW). **4160**

ZEITSCHRIFT FUER THEOLOGIE UND KIRCHE. (GW/0044-3549). **5011**

ZEITSCHRIFT

ZEITSCHRIFT FUER TIERPHYSIOLOGIE, TIERERNAHRUNG UND FUTTERMITTELKUNDE. (GW/0044-3565). **5600**

ZEITSCHRIFT FUER TRANSPLANTATIONSMEDIZIN. (GW). **3653**

ZEITSCHRIFT FUER UNFALLCHIRURGIE UND VERSICHERUNGSMEDIZIN. (SZ/1017-1584). **3653**

ZEITSCHRIFT FUER UNTERNEHMENSGESCHICHTE. (GW/0342-2852). **725**

ZEITSCHRIFT FUER VERKEHRSWISSENSCHAFT. (GW/0044-3670). **5400**

ZEITSCHRIFT FUER VERMESSUNGSWESEN. ZFV. (GW/0340-4560). **2034**

ZEITSCHRIFT FUER VERWALTUNG. (AU). **3094**

ZEITSCHRIFT FUER WIRTSCHAFTS- UND SOZIALWISSENSCHAFTEN. (GW/0342-1783). **1528**

ZEITSCHRIFT FUER WIRTSCHAFTSGEOGRAPHIE. (GW/0044-3751). **2580**

ZEITSCHRIFT FUER ZIVILPROZESS. (GW/0342-3468). **3078**

ZEITSCHRIFT FUER ZOOLOGISCHE SYSTEMATIK UND EVOLUTIONSFORSCHUNG. (GW/0044-3808). **5600**

ZEITSCHRIFT FUHRUNG + ORGANISATION : ZFO. (GW/0722-7485). **725**

ZEITSCHRIFT FUR GANZHEITSFORSCHUNG. (AU). **Qty:** 20-30. **4365**

ZEITSCHRIFT FUR KULTUR, POLITIK, KIRCHE. (SW). **5070**

ZEITSCHRIFT FUR SCHWEIZERISCHE KIRCHENGESCHICHTE. REVUE D'HISTOIRE ECCLESIASTIQUE SUISSE. (SZ/0044-3484). **5011**

ZEITSCHRIFT FUR TIERZUCHTUNG UND ZUCHTUNGSBIOLOGIE (HAMBURG, GERMANY : 1939). (GW/0044-3581). **224**

ZEITSCHRIFT INTERNE REVISION. (GW/0044-3816). **725**

ZEITSCRHIFT FUR KLINISCHE MEDIZIN (BERLIN, DDR). (GW/0233-1608). **3653**

ZEITUNG FUER KOMMUNALE WIRTSCHAFT. (GW). **Qty:** 20. **4695**

ZEITUNGS-INDEX. (GW/0340-0107). **5802**

ZEITWENDE. (GW/0341-7166). **3356**

ZEMLEDELIE. (RU/0044-3913). **148**

ZENAIR NEWS. (US/0889-4353). **40**

ZENTRALASIATISCHE STUDIEN DES SEMINARS FUER SPRACH- UND KULTURWISSENSCHAFT ZENTRALASIENS DER UNIVERSITAT BONN. (GW/0514-857X). **2668**

ZENTRALBLATT FUER CHIRURGIE. (GW/0044-409X). **3978**

ZENTRALBLATT FUER CHIRURGIE. SONDERBAND. (GW/0044-409X). **3978**

ZENTRALBLATT FUER MIKROBIOLOGIE. (GW/0232-4393). **571**

ZENTRALBLATT FUER NEUROCHIRURGIE. (GW/0044-4251). **3978**

ZENTRALBLATT FUER VETERINARMEDIZIN. REIHE A. (GW/0514-7158). **5528**

ZENTRALBLATT HAUT- UND GESCHLECHTSKRANKHEITEN. (GW/0343-3048). **3723**

ZEOLITES. (US/0144-2449). **1038**

ZERO TO THREE. (US/0736-8038). **3912**

ZESZYTY HISTORYCZNE. (FR/0044-4391). **2717**

ZESZYTY LITERACKIE : ZL. (FR). **3456**

ZETETIC SCHOLAR. (US/0741-6229). **4243**

ZEV, DET, GLASERS ANNALEN, DIE EISENBAHNTECHNIK. (GW/0941-0589). **5438**

ZFA, ZEITSCHRIFT FUER ARBEITSRECHT. (GW). **3156**

ZFBR, ZEITSCHRIFT FUER DEUTSCHES UND INTERNATIONALES BAURECHT. (GW). **3078**

ZHILISHCHNOE STROITELSTVO. (RU/0044-4472). **631**

ZHONGGUO KANGSHENGSU ZAZHI. (CC/1001-8689). **4333**

ZHONGGUO YIYAO GONGYE ZAZHI. (CC/1001-8255). **4334**

ZHONGHUA LILIAO ZAZHI. (CC/0254-1408). **4382**

ZHONGHUA MINGUO XIAOERKE YIXUEHUI ZAZHI. (CH/0001-6578). **Qty:** 6. **3912**

ZHONGHUA WULIYIXUE ZAZHI. (CC/0254-1424). **3654**

ZHONGHUA XUEYEXUE ZAZHI. (CC/0253-2727). **3774**

ZHONGHUA YISHI ZAZHI. (CC/0255-7053). **3654**

ZHONGYANG YANJIUYUAN LISHI YUYAN YANJIUSUO JIKAN. (CH/1012-4195). **2510**

ZHURNAL EVOLIUTSIONNOI BIOKHIMII I FIZIOLOGII. (RU/0044-4529). **494**

ZHURNAL FIZICHESKOI KHIMII. (RU/0044-4537). **1059**

ZHURNAL NAUCHNOI I PRIKLADNOI FOTOGRAFII I KINEMATOGRAFII. (US/0734-1504). **4378**

ZHURNAL VYSSHEI NERVNOI DEIATELNOSTI IMENI I. P. PAVLOVA. (RU/0044-4677). **3847**

ZHURNALIST. (RU/0130-3589). **2926**

ZI INTERNATIONAL. (GW/0341-0552). **631**

ZIEKENHUIS, HET. (NE/0044-4715). **3794**

ZIELSPRACHE DEUTSCH. (GW/0341-5864). **3336**

ZIELSPRACHE ENGLISCH. (GW/0342-6173). **Qty:** 30 per year. **3336**

ZIMBABWE AGRICULTURAL JOURNAL. (RH/1017-5156). **149**

ZIMBABWE AT WORK. (RH). **1632**

ZIMBABWE JOURNAL OF AGRICULTURAL RESEARCH, THE. (RH/0251-1045). **149**

ZIMBABWE LIBRARIAN, THE. (RH/1015-6828). **3257**

ZIMBABWE SCIENCE NEWS, THE. (RH/1016-1503). **5172**

ZIMBABWE VETERINARY JOURNAL. (RH/1016-1511). **5528**

ZINCSCAN. (UK/0950-1592). **4025**

ZINOCYY SVIT. (CN/0513-9856). **5572**

ZINOTAJS. (CN/0227-2423). **2717**

ZIONIST IDEAS. (IS). **5054**

ZION'S HERALD (1975). (US/0098-9282). **5070**

ZIRAN KEXUESHI YANJIU. (CC/1000-0224). **1361**

ZIVILDIENST, DER. (GW). **4696**

ZLR, ZEITSCHRIFT FUER DAS GESAMTE LEBENSMITTELRECHT. (GW/0342-3476). **3078**

ZNAMJA (MOSKVA). (RU/0130-1616). **3356**

ZODAK CENTRE FOR RELIGIOUS RESEARCH PUBLICATIONS. (AT). **Qty:** 20. **5011**

ZODIAQUE. (FR/0044-4952). **369**

ZONING AND PLANNING LAW HANDBOOK. (US/0731-5791). **3078**

ZONING AND PLANNING LAW REPORT. (US/0161-8113). **3078**

ZONING REPORT (MARGATE, FL.), THE. (US/0748-0083). **Qty:** 2-4. **2839**

ZOO ANVERS. (BE/0044-5029). **5601**

ZOO BIOLOGY. (US/0733-3188). **5601**

ZOO GOER, THE. (US/0163-416X). **Qty:** 5. **5601**

ZOOLOGICA. (GW/0044-5088). **5601**

ZOOLOGICA SCRIPTA. (UK/0300-3256). **5601**

ZOOLOGICAL SCIENCE. (JA/0289-0003). **5602**

ZOOLOGISCHE ABHANDLUNGEN / STAATLICHES MUSEUM FUER TIERKUNDE IN DRESDEN. (GW/0375-5231). **5602**

ZOOLOGISCHE DOCUMENTATIE. (BE/0563-1750). **5603**

ZOOLOGISCHE GARTEN; ZEITSCHRIFT FUER DIE GESAMTE TIERGARTNEREI. (GW/0044-5169). **5603**

ZOOLOGISCHE JAHRBUCHER. ABTEILUNG FUER ALLGEMEINE ZOOLOGIE UND PHYSIOLOGIE DER TIERE. (GW/0044-5185). **5603**

ZOOLOGISCHE JAHRBUCHER. ABTEILUNG FUER ANATOMIE UND ONTOGENIE DER TIERE. (GW/0044-5177). **5603**

ZOOLOGISCHE JAHRBUCHER. ABTEILUNG FUER SYSTEMATIK, OKOLOGIE UND GEOGRAPHIE DER TIERE. (GW/0044-5193). **5603**

ZOOLOGISCHE MEDEDELINGEN. (NE/0024-0672). **5603**

ZOONOOZ. (US). **5603**

ZOR. ZEITSCHRIFT FUER OPERATIONS-RESEARCH. (GW/0340-9422). **5173**

ZPA. ZEITSCHRIFT FUER PRAKTISCHE AUGENHEILKUNDE. (GW/0173-2595). **3880**

ZPRAVY - SVU. (US/0036-2050). **2857**

ZUCKER- UND SUSSWAREN WIRTSCHAFT. (GW/0373-0204). **2362**

ZUCKERINDUSTRIE. (GW/0344-8657). **1031**

ZVAIGZNOTA DEBESS. (LV/0135-129X). **401**

ZVAZAJ. (CN/0700-5172). **2767**

ZWEIG LETTER, THE. (US/1068-1310). **Qty:** 8 /yr. **890**

ZWF CIM. (GW/0932-0482). **2132**

ZWR. (GW/0044-166X). **1337**

ZYGON. (UK/0591-2385). **5012**

ZYMURGY. (US/0196-5921). **2373**

ZZAP! 64. (UK/0954-867X). **1245**

Serials Accepting Advertising

The following index lists, in alphabetical order, all active serials in the Directory that accept advertising. The country code, ISSN, publisher address and telephone number, advertising manager and telephone number are provided, when available. The page number in bold refers you to the complete serial listing in Volume I, II or III of the Directory.

1/1 (SAN FRANCISCO, CALIF.). (US/8756-7717). **4098**

2 D DRAMA, DANCE. (UK/0261-6939). **383**

3-2-1 CONTACT. (US/0195-4105). **1059**

3 R, ROHRE, ROHRLEITUNGSBAU, ROHRLEITUNGSTRANSPORT. (GW/0340-3386). **2096**

4-H SOUNDER. (US/0740-848X). **1059**

9-1-1 MAGAZINE. (US/1040-7316). **1103**

13TH MOON. (US/0094-3320). **3357**

13TH STREET JOURNAL, THE. (US/1041-3111). **311**

16 MAGAZINE. (US/0270-899X). **1059**

16 (NEW YORK, N.Y.). (US/1075-3109). **1059**

19TH CENTURY MUSIC. (US/0148-2076). **4098**

20/20. (US/0192-1304). **4214**

20 DE MAYO. (US/0164-5234). **Adv Mgr:** P. Cacheiro. **5631**

24 IMAGES. (CN/0707-9389). **4062**

24HOURS (SANTA MONICA, CALIF.). (US/1047-451X). **2526**

30 JOURS DANS L'EGLISE ET DANS LE MONDE. (FR). **Adv Mgr:** Ehrica Biondi. **5022**

33 METAL PRODUCING. (US/0149-1210). **3996**

50 PLUS (DURHAM, ONT.). (CN/0840-5395). **5177**

68 MICRO JOURNAL. (US/0194-5025). **1265**

100 MILE HOUSE FREE PRESS. (CN/0843-0403). **Adv Mgr:** Terry Gibbons, **Tel** (604)395-2219. **5779**

800 ITALIANO. (IT). **335**

1,000 LARGEST GOVERNMENTS, THE. (US/0883-413X). **4623**

1590 BROADCASTER. (US/0192-8597). **Adv Mgr:** Maurice Parent. **5707**

A A R N NEWSLETTER. (CN/0001-0197). **Adv Mgr:** Jan Henry, **Tel** (403)484-3895. **3849**

A & V, MONOGRAFIAS DE ARQUITECTURA Y VIVIENDA. (SP/0213-487X). **286**

A.D.P.H.S.O. (FR/0339-8854). **3775**

A.G.T. DOKUMENTATION. (GW). **2034**

A.H.E.A. ACTION. (US/0194-7176). **2788**

A.I.I. JOURNAL. (AT/0314-8580). **2872**

A.L.B.A. BOWLS. (US/0001-1754). **4881**

A L'AUTRE, UNE. (CN/0824-8230). **3755**

A.M. AMMINISTRAZIONE & MANAGEMENT. (IT/1121-0788). **4623**

A. MAGAZINE. (US/1070-9401). **Adv Mgr:** Karen Wang. **2253**

A.N.A. AUDIOLOGIA PROTESICA. (SP). **3885**

A P C O PUBLIC SAFETY COMMUNICATIONS. (US). **4763**

A + T. (AT). **335**

A.T.A. JOURNAL. (HK/1015-8138). **Adv Mgr:** Erica Cheng, Esther Chan and Janette Li. **5347**

A TO Z OF WHO IS WHO IN AUSTRALIA'S HISTORY, THE. (AT). **2668**

A.U.M.L.A. (AT/0001-2793). **3260**

A.V. GUIDE. (US/0091-360X). **1887**

A.W.R. BULLETIN. (AU/0001-2947). **5269**

AAA, ARBEITEN AUS ANGLISTIK UND AMERIKANISTIK. (AU/0171-5410). **3260**

AAAD BULLETIN, THE. (US/1071-1414). **4881**

AAASS NEWSLETTER. (US/0883-9549). **2671**

AABB NEWS BRIEFS. (US/8756-6095). **3769**

AACSB NEWSLINE. (US/0360-697X). **Adv Mgr:** Janet Lipkind. **1806**

AAEA NEWSLETTER (AMES, IOWA). (US/0888-9651). **42**

AAHS JOURNAL. (US/0882-9365). **3**

AAHS NEWSLETTER. (US/0300-6875). **3**

AAMI NEWS. (US/0739-0270). **3543**

AANA JOURNAL. (US/0094-6354). **3849**

AAOHN NEWS / AMERICAN ASSOCIATION OF OCCUPATIONAL HEALTH NURSES, INC. (US/0746-620X). **3850**

AAPG BULLETIN. (US/0149-1423). **4248**

AAPG EXPLORER. (US/0195-2986). **1364**

AAR STUDIES IN RELIGION. (US/0145-2789). **4931**

AARCTIMES. (US/0893-8520). **3947**

AARDRIJKSKUNDE, DE. (BE). **2553**

AAS MICROFICHE SERIES. (US/0065-7417). **3**

AATSEEL'S NEWSLETTER / AMERICAN ASSOCIATION OF TEACHERS OF SLAVIC AND EAST EUROPEAN LANGUAGES. (US). **1720**

AAZPA REGIONAL CONFERENCE PROCEEDINGS. (US/0731-0439). **5572**

AB BOOKMAN'S YEARBOOK. (US/0065-0005). **4822**

AB (BRESCIA). (IT/0393-3369). **Adv Mgr:** Matteo Monzagnoli. **2159**

ABA JOURNAL. (US/0747-0088). **2926**

ABACUS (SYDNEY). (AT/0001-3072). **735**

ABBEVILLE HERALD. (US). **5629**

ABBEY. (US). **3357**

ABC AIR TRAVEL ATLAS. (UK). **5459**

ABC AND D. ARCHITECT BUILDER CONTRACTOR AND DEVELOPER. (UK/0966-9647). **Adv Mgr:** Nick Rapley. **287**

ABC DER DEUTSCHEN WIRTSCHAFT. CD-ROM. (GW). **1596**

ABC EXECUTIVE FLIGHT PLANNER EUROPE, MIDDLE EAST, AFRICA. (UK/0959-1389). **5459**

ABC TODAY. (US/1062-3698). **Adv Mgr:** Bob K., **Tel** (703)812-2087. **597**

ABC WORLD AIRWAYS GUIDE, THE. (UK). **5460**

ABD. (US/0001-0502). **3**

ABEILLE. (CN/0821-5111). **5572**

ABEILLE DE FRANCE ET L'APICULTEUR, L'. (FR/0373-4625). **Adv Mgr:** Chong Wing. **42**

ABERDEEN AMERICAN-NEWS. (US/1074-7117). **5743**

ABERDEEN PETROLEUM REPORT. (UK/0263-5054). **4249**

ABERDEEN TIMES, THE. (US). **5674**

ABERNATHY WEEKLY REVIEW, THE. (US/0895-4291). **Adv Mgr:** Judy Luce. **5746**

ABHANDLUNGEN DER AKADEMIE DER WISSENSCHAFTEN IN GOTTINGEN. MATHEMATISCH-PHYSIKALISCHE KLASSE. (GW/0341-9843). **3490**

ABHANDLUNGEN DER GEOLOGISCHEN BUNDESANSTALT. (AU/0378-0864). **1364**

ABHATH. (MR). **5189**

ABI-TECHNIK. (GW/0720-6763). **3186**

ABILENE REFLECTOR-CHRONICLE. (US/0890-345X). **5668**

ABILITIES (CALGARY). (CN/0845-4469). **Adv Mgr Tel** (416)977-5002. **4382**

ABINGTON JOURNAL (CLARKS SUMMIT, PA.). (US). **Adv Mgr:** Ron Bartizek, **Tel** (717)586-7822. **5734**

ABIRA DIGEST. (US/0196-0652). **429**

ABITARE CON ARTE. (IT/1120-6772). **Adv Mgr:** Brivio Givsi. **2898**

ABMS DIRECTORY OF CERTIFIED DERMATOLOGISTS. (US/0884-1489). **3717**

ABMS DIRECTORY OF CERTIFIED NEUROLOGICAL SURGEONS. (US/0882-2832). **3957**

ABMS DIRECTORY OF CERTIFIED OBSTETRICIANS AND GYNECOLOGISTS. (US/0884-1535). **3755**

ABMS DIRECTORY OF CERTIFIED PLASTIC SURGEONS. (US/0749-839X). **3957**

ABMS DIRECTORY OF CERTIFIED UROLOGISTS. (US/0742-0374). **3987**

ABNF JOURNAL, THE. (US/1046-7041). **Adv Mgr Tel** same as publisher. **3850**

ABORIGINAL CHILD AT SCHOOL, THE. (AT). **1874**

ABORIGINAL LAW BULLETIN. (AT). **2926**

ABORIGINAL

Advertising Accepted Index

ABORIGINAL SCIENCE FICTION. (US/0895-3198). **Adv Mgr:** Mary Ryan, **Tel** (617)935-9326. **3357**

ABORTION RESEARCH NOTES. (US/0361-1116). **587**

ABOUT THE HOUSE. (UK/0001-3242). **4098**

ABOVE & BEYOND. (CN/0843-7815). **Adv Mgr:** Dennis Huntley, **Tel** (403)873-2296. **2553**

ABSOLUTE SOUND, THE. (US/0097-1138). **5315**

ABSTRACT REVIEW IN SCIENCE EXTENSION. (HU/0238-6178). **5079**

ABSTRACTA IRANICA. (IR/0240-8910). **406**

ABSTRACTS, ANNUAL MEETING - ASSOCIATION OF AMERICAN GEOGRAPHERS. (US/0197-1700). **2553**

ABSTRACTS IN BIOCOMMERCE. (UK/0263-6778). **3654**

ABSTRACTS IN HUMAN-COMPUTER INTERACTION. (US/1042-0193). **1208**

ABSTRACTS IN MARYLAND ARCHEOLOGY. (US/0743-4251). **253**

ABSTRACTS OF AIT REPORTS AND PUBLICATIONS ON ENERGY. (TH/0857-6181). **1961**

ABSTRACTS OF ENGLISH STUDIES. (US/0001-3560). **3356**

ABSTRACTS OF PAPERS PRESENTED AT THE ... WORLD CONGRESS OF THE INTERNATIONAL POLITICAL SCIENCE ASSOCIATION. (CN/0709-6895). **4514**

ABSTRACTS OF SOVIET AND EAST EUROPEAN EMIGRE PERIODICAL LITERATURE. (US/0738-2707). **2513**

ABSTRACTS ON HYGIENE AND COMMUNICABLE DISEASES. (UK/0260-5511). **4809**

ABSTRACTS ON RURAL DEVELOPMENT IN THE TROPICS. (NE/0169-605X). **5189**

ABSTRACTS ON TROPICAL AGRICULTURE. (NE/0304-5951). **149**

ABSTRACTS WITH PROGRAMS - GEOLOGICAL SOCIETY OF AMERICA. (US/0016-7592). **1364**

ABU TECHNICAL REVIEW. (MY/0126-6209). **1125**

ABYA YALA NEWS. (US/1071-3182). **Adv Mgr:** David Techlon. **2253**

AC. THE ADCRAFTER. (US/0001-8066). **753**

AC/UNU NEWSLETTER / THE AMERICAN COUNCIL FOR THE UNITED NATIONS UNIVERSITY. (US). **1806**

ACA BULLETIN - ASSOCIATION FOR COMMUNICATION ADMINISTRATION. (US/0360-0939). **Adv Mgr:** Ronald Applbaum. **1103**

ACA NEWS (EDMONTON). (CN/0826-497X). **5177**

ACADEME (WASHINGTON. 1979). (US/0190-2946). **1806**

ACADEMIC AND LIBRARY COMPUTING. (US/1055-4769). **1265**

ACADEMIC LIBRARY BOOK REVIEW. (US/0894-993X). **4822**

ACADEMIC MEDICINE. (US/1040-2446). **1806**

ACADEMIC PSYCHIATRY. (US/1042-9670). **3918**

ACADEMIC QUESTIONS. (US/0895-4852). **1807**

ACADEMIE ROYALE DES SCIENCES D'OUTRE-MER. CLASSE DES SCIENCES TECHNIQUES. (BE/0373-7063). **1722**

ACADEMY FORUM (NEW YORK), THE. (US/0192-1088). **3918**

ACADEMY OF MANAGEMENT JOURNAL. (US/0001-4273). **858**

ACADEMY OF MANAGEMENT REVIEW, THE. (US/0363-7425). **859**

ACADIAN GENEALOGY EXCHANGE. (US/0199-9591). **2436**

ACADIAN LETTERS. (CN/0705-5560). **958**

ACADIANA PROFILE. (US/0001-4397). **2254**

ACAFO. (AG). **4366**

ACC BASKETBALL HANDBOOK. (US/0733-0448). **4881**

ACCA DOCKET. (US/0895-9544). **Adv Mgr:** Jeffrey Logel, **Tel** (202)296-4522. **3094**

ACCENT. (US/0192-7507). **2913**

ACCENT/REVIEWS. (US/0277-9102). **4931**

ACCESS BY DESIGN. (UK/0959-1591). **287**

ACCESS (NEW YORK, N.Y. : 1983). (US/0890-4537). **1722**

ACCESS USA NEWS. (US/1069-6784). **Adv Mgr:** Dan Ramage, **Tel** (708)679-1100. **4383**

ACCESS (VICTORIA, AUSTRALIA). (AT/1030-0155). **1802**

ACCIAIO. (IT). **4461**

ACCIDENT PREVENTION. (CN/0044-5878). **2858**

ACCION. (PY). **5189**

ACCORD (CALGARY). (CN/0226-7845). **2254**

ACCOUNTANCY IRELAND. (IE/0001-4699). **735**

ACCOUNTANCY (LONDON). (UK/0001-4664). **735**

ACCOUNTANCY SA. (SA/0258-7254). **735**

ACCOUNTANT (NAIROBI), THE. (KE/1010-4135). **735**

ACCOUNTANTS' JOURNAL. (PH/0001-4753). **735**

ACCOUNTANTS' JOURNAL (WELLINGTON). (NZ/0001-4745). **735**

ACCOUNTANT'S MAGAZINE, THE. (UK/0001-4761). **736**

ACCOUNTING AND BUSINESS RESEARCH. (UK/0001-4788). **736**

ACCOUNTING AND FINANCE. (AT/0110-5159). **736**

ACCOUNTING AND FINANCE PARKVILLE. (AT/0810-5391). **736**

ACCOUNTING EDUCATION NEWS. (US/0882-956X). **736**

ACCOUNTING EDUCATORS' JOURNAL, THE. (US/1041-0392). **736**

ACCOUNTING FORUM (ADELAIDE, S. AUST.). (AT/0155-9982). **737**

ACCOUNTING WORLD. (UK/0953-2579). **738**

ACCT TRUSTEE QUARTERLY. (US/0271-9746). **1807**

ACE BULLETIN (LONDON, ENGLAND). (UK). **1722**

ACHAB ROMA. (IT/1120-849X). **3357**

ACHIEVEMENT (LONDON. 1969). (UK/0001-4907). **1596**

ACHPER NATIONAL JOURNAL, THE. (AT). **2595**

ACHTZEHNTE JAHRHUNDERT, DAS. (GW). **2672**

ACIS : JOURNAL OF THE ASSOCIATION FOR CONTEMPORARY IBERIAN STUDIES. (UK/0955-4270). **3260**

ACJ (PLATTE CITY, MO.). (US/1068-8021). **204**

ACLIS NEWS. (AT/1032-0431). **Adv Mgr:** Gordon Bower, **Tel** 61 6 2621200. **3187**

ACORN JOURNAL. (AT/1031-1017). **3850**

ACORN JOURNAL : OFFICIAL JOURNAL OF THE AUSTRALIAN CONFEDERATION OF OPERATING ROOM NURSES. (AT/0156-3491). **Adv Mgr:** K. Collins, **Tel** 02 212 2780. **3850**

ACOUSTIC GUITAR. (US/1049-9261). **4098**

ACQUISITION/DIVESTITURE WEEKLY REPORT. (US/0279-4160). **636**

ACQUISITIONS LIBRARIAN, THE. (US/0896-3576). **3187**

ACQUISITIONS MONTHLY. (UK). **636**

ACQUISIZIONI FUSIONI CONCORRENZA. (IT). **1596**

ACRES, U.S.A. (US). **43**

ACROSS THE BOARD. (US/0147-1554). **636**

ACS NEWSLETTER / ASSOCIATION FOR CANADIAN STUDIES. (CN/0714-2579). **2526**

AC'S TECH FOR THE COMMODORE AMIGA. (US/1053-7929). **Adv Mgr:** Donna Viveiros. **1170**

ACSM BULLETIN. (US/0747-9417). **2580**

ACSUS MEMBERSHIP DIRECTORY. (US/0892-7111). **2717**

ACT. ADVERTISING/COMMUNICATIONS TIMES. (US/0193-4457). **753**

ACTA AD ARCHAEOLOGIAM ET ARTIUM HISTORIAM PERTINENTIA. (IT/0065-0900). **335**

ACTA ALIMENTARIA (BUDAPEST). (HU/0139-3006). **2325**

ACTA ANAESTHESIOLOGICA BELGICA. (BE/0001-5164). **3680**

ACTA ANAESTHESIOLOGICA ITALICA. (IT/0374-4965). **Adv Mgr:** A. Pagamento. **3680**

ACTA ANATOMICA. (SZ/0001-5180). **3678**

ACTA ANTIQUA ACADEMIAE SCIENTIARUM HUNGARICAE. (HU/0044-5975). **3261**

ACTA APPLICANDAE MATHEMATICAE. (NE/0167-8019). **3490**

ACTA ARCHAEOLOGICA ACADEMIAE SCIENTIARUM HUNGARICAE. (HU/0001-5210). **253**

ACTA AUTOMATICA SINICA / INSTRUMENT SOCIETY OF AMERICA. (US). **2109**

ACTA BELGICA HISTORIAE MEDICINAE : OFFICIAL JOURNAL OF THE BELGIAN ASSOCIATION FOR THE HISTORY OF MEDICINE. (BE). **3544**

ACTA BIOCHIMICA ET BIOPHYSICA HUNGARICA. (HU/0237-6261). **479**

ACTA BIOQUIMICA CLINICA LATINOAMERICANA. (AG/0325-2957). **479**

ACTA BIOTECHNOLOGICA. (GW/0138-4988). **3685**

ACTA BOREALIA. (NO/0800-3831). **1351**

ACTA BOTANICA INDICA. (II/0379-508X). **497**

ACTA BOTANICA ISLANDICA. (IC/0374-5066). **497**

ACTA BOTANICA MALACITANA. (SP/0210-9506). **497**

ACTA BOTANICA SINICA. (US/0095-4195). **497**

ACTA CARDIOLOGICA. (BE/0001-5385). **3697**

ACTA CARDIOLOGICA MEDITERRANEA. (IT/0392-9698). **3697**

ACTA CHIMICA HUNGARICA. (HU/0231-3146). **959**

ACTA CHIRURGICA AUSTRIACA. (AU/0001-544X). **3957**

ACTA CHIRURGICA BELGICA. (BE/0001-5458). **3957**

ACTA CHIRURGICA CATALONIAE. (SP/0211-660X). **3957**

ACTA CHIRURGICA ITALICA. (IT/0001-5466). **Adv Mgr:** A. Pagamento. **3957**

ACTA CIENCIA INDICA. CHEMISTRY. (II/0253-7338). **959**

ACTA CIENCIA INDICA. MATHEMATICS. (II/0970-0455). **3490**

ACTA CIENCIA INDICA. PHYSICS. (II/0253-732X). **4395**

ACTA CIENTIFICA VENEZOLANA. (VE/0001-5504). **5080**

ACTA CYTOLOGICA. (US/0001-5547). **531**

ACTA DERMATO-VENEREOLOGICA. (SW/0001-5555). **3717**

ACTA DIRECTORY. (CN/0848-2497). **5460**

ACTA ECCLESIASTICA SLOVENIAE. (XV/0351-2789). **2672**

ACTA ENTOMOLOGICA CHILENA. (CL/0716-5072). **5604**

ACTA FARMACEUTICA BONAERENSE. (AG/0326-2383). **4288**

ACTA GASTROENTEROLOGICA LATINOAMERICANA. (AG/0300-9033). **3794**

ACTA GEOGRAPHICA SINICA. (CC/0375-5444). **2553**

ACTA HAEMATOLOGICA. (SZ/0001-5792). **3769**

ACTA HISTOCHEMICA. (GW/0065-1281). **531**

ACTA HISTORICA ACADEMIAE SCIENTIARUM HUNGARICAE. (HU/0001-5849). **2672**

ACTA HISTORICA ET ARCHAEOLOGICA MEDIAEVALIA. (SP). **253**

ACTA HOSPITALIA. (BE/0044-6009). **3775**

ACTA HYDROBIOLOGICA SINICA. (CC/0559-9385). **552**

ACTA JUTLANDICA : AARSSKRIFT FOR UNIVERSITETSUNDERVISNINGEN I JYLLAND. (DK/0065-1354). **1807**

ACTA MATHEMATICA HUNGARICA. (HU/0236-5294). **3490**

ACTA MATHEMATICA SINICA. NEW SERIES. (CC/1000-9574). **3490**

ACTA MATHEMATICAE APPLICATAE SINICA. (CH/0168-9673). **3490**

ACTA MECHANICA SINICA. (CC/0567-7718). **4427**

ACTA MEDICA AUSTRIACA. (AU/0303-8173). **3794**

ACTA MEDICA PHILIPPINA. (PH/0001-6071). **3544**

ACTA MICROBIOLOGICA HUNGARICA. (HU/0231-4622). **558**

ACTA MORPHOLOGICA HUNGARICA. (HU/0236-5391). **3545**

ACTA MOZARTIANA. (GW/0001-6233). **4098**

ACTA MUSICOLOGICA. (GW/0001-6241). **4098**

ACTA NEUROLOGICA. (IT/0001-6276). **3825**

Advertising Accepted Index

ACTA NEUROLOGICA BELGICA. (BE/0300-9009). **3825**

ACTA NEUROLOGICA SCANDINAVICA. (DK/0001-6314). **3825**

ACTA OBSTETRICIA ET GYNECOLOGICA SCANDINAVICA. (SW/0001-6349). **3756**

ACTA ODONTOLOGICA SCANDINAVICA. (NO/0001-6357). **1315**

ACTA OECONOMICA. (HU/0001-6373). **1460**

ACTA ONCOLOGICA (STOCKHOLM, SWEDEN). (SW/0284-186X). **3808**

ACTA OPHTHALMOLOGICA. (DK/0001-639X). **3545**

ACTA ORIENTALIA ACADEMIAE SCIENTIARUM HUNGARICAE. (HU/0001-6446). **2644**

ACTA ORTHOPAEDICA SCANDINAVICA. (DK/0001-6470). **3880**

ACTA PAEDIATRICA HUNGARICA. (HU/0231-441X). **3899**

ACTA PAEDIATRICA LATINA. (IT/0365-5504). **Adv Mgr:** Luigi Menozzi. **3899**

ACTA PEDIATRICA ESPANOLA. (SP). **3899**

ACTA PHARMACEUTICA FENNICA. (FI/0356-3456). **4288**

ACTA PHARMACEUTICA TURCICA. (TU/1010-0849). **4289**

ACTA PHONIATRICA LATINA. (IT/0392-3088). **Adv Mgr:** A. Pagamento. **3885**

ACTA PHYTOMEDICA. (GW/0065-1567). **497**

ACTA POLITICA. (NE/0001-6810). **4461**

ACTA PSIQUIATRICA Y PSICOLOGICA DE AMERICA LATINA. (AG/0001-6896). **Adv Mgr:** Ms. Perez-Feinandez, **Tel** 54 1 8545602. **3918**

ACTA PSYCHIATRICA BELGICA. (BE/0300-8967). **3919**

ACTA PSYCHIATRICA SCANDINAVICA. (DK/0001-690X). **3919**

ACTA RADIOLOGICA (STOCKHOLM, SWEDEN : 1987). (SW/0284-1851). **3938**

ACTA SCIENTIARUM MATHEMATICARUM. (HU/0001-6969). **3490**

ACTA SOCIOLOGICA. (DK/0001-6993). **5237**

ACTA STEREOLOGICA. (XV/0351-580X). **3491**

ACTA STOMATOLOGICA BELGICA. (BE/0001-7000). **1315**

ACTA TECHNICA / ACADEMIAE SCIENTIARUM HUNGARICAE. (HU/0001-7035). **5080**

ACTA THEOLOGICA DANICA. (NE/0065-1672). **4931**

ACTA TROPICA. (SZ/0001-706X). **3985**

ACTA UROLOGICA BELGICA. (BE/0001-7183). **3987**

ACTA VETERINARIA (BRNO, CZECHOSLOVAKIA). (CS/0001-7213). **1020**

ACTA ZOOLOGICA MEXICANA. (MX/0065-1737). **5573**

ACTA ZOOLOGICA (STOCKHOLM). (SW/0001-7272). **5574**

ACTAC. (AT). **1125**

ACTAS DE CULTURA Y ENSAYOS FOTOGRAFICOS F/8. (SP). **4366**

ACTAS DE LA FUNDACION PUIGVERT : UROLOGIA, NEFROLOGIA, ANDROLOGIA / INSTITUTO DE UROLOGIA, NEFROLOGIA, ANDROLOGIA, HOSPITAL DE LA SANTA CRUZ Y SAN PABLO. (SP/0213-2885). **3987**

ACTES. / ASSOCIATION CANADIENNE DE LINGUISTIQUE APPLIQUEE. (CN). **3261**

ACTION COMMERCIALE, MANUELS. (FR/1142-7086). **920**

ACTION FOR CANADA'S CHILDREN. (CN/0229-2653). **1059**

ACTION FRANCAISE HEBDO, L'. (FR/1166-3286). **4461**

ACTION IN TEACHER EDUCATION. (US/0162-6620). **1887**

ACTION INFORMATIQUE. (CN/0844-0883). **1235**

ACTION JURIDIQUE CFDT. (FR). **2927**

ACTION NATIONALE. (CN/0001-7469). **2526**

ACTION NETWORK. (AT/1032-9005). **5178**

ACTION POETIQUE. (FR). **3459**

ACTION SPORTS RETAILER (1993). (US/1072-9291). **952**

ACTION VETERINAIRE, L'. (FR/0001-7523). **5501**

ACTION (WINNIPEG). (CN/0701-1547). **5550**

ACTIVE AND PASSIVE ELECTRONIC COMPONENTS. (US/0882-7516). **2034**

ACTIVE LIVING (TORONTO). (CN/1188-620X). **Adv Mgr:** Sharon Doherty, **Tel** (613)264-2722. **2595**

ACTIVIDAD MINERA. (AG/0326-6672). **2132**

ACTIVITE DES COURS ET TRIBUNAUX. STATISTIQUES DIVERSES. (BE). **3078**

ACTIVITIES, ADAPTATION & AGING. (US/0192-4788). **3748**

ACTON FREE PRESS. (CN). **Adv Mgr:** S. Dorsey. **5779**

ACTUALIDAD PASTORAL. (AG). **5022**

ACTUALITE CHIMIQUE, L'. (FR/0151-9093). **959**

ACTUALITE DIOCESAINE. (CN/0823-552X). **4932**

ACTUALITE IMMOBILIERE. (CN/0701-0516). **4833**

ACTUALITE (MONTREAL. 1976). (CN/0383-8714). **2513**

ACTUALITE RELIGIEUSE DANS LE MONDE (1983). (FR/0757-3529). **4932**

ACTUALITES ODONTO-STOMATOLOGIQUES. (FR/0001-7817). **1315**

ACUPUNCTURE & ELECTRO-THERAPEUTICS RESEARCH. (UK/0360-1293). **3545**

ACUSTICA. (GW/0001-7884). **4452**

ACUTE CARE. (SZ/0254-0819). **3850**

AD ASTRA (WASHINGTON, D.C.). (US/1041-102X). **3**

AD-EXPRESS AND DAILY IOWEGIAN AND CITIZEN. (US/0746-1119). **5656**

AD : REVISTA INTERNACIONAL DE DECORACION, DISENO Y ARQUITECTURA. (SP). **2898**

ADA STRATEGIES. (US/0893-0570). **1255**

ADAIR COUNTY FREE PRESS (GREENFIELD, IOWA : 1984). (US). **Adv Mgr:** Kristine Morken-Houl, **Tel** (515)743-6121. **5668**

ADAM FILM WORLD GUIDE. ADAM FILM WORLD DIRECTORY OF ADULT FILMS. (US). **4062**

ADAMS ADDENDA. (US/0739-0076). **2436**

ADAPTED PHYSICAL ACTIVITY QUARTERLY. (US/0736-5829). **1854**

ADAPTIVE BEHAVIOR. (US/1059-7123). **4571**

ADC TIMES. (US/0749-2642). **2254**

ADCA, AMERICAN DIRECTORY OF COLLECTION AGENCIES AND ATTORNEYS. (US/0148-5350). **768**

ADDVANTAGE. (US/0149-4082). **4881**

ADE BULLETIN. (US/0001-0898). **Adv Mgr:** Stephen Olsen, **Tel** (212)614-6317. **3261**

ADEL NEWS TRIBUNE. (US/0746-0716). **Adv Mgr:** Grace Day. **5651**

ADELAIDE LAW REVIEW, THE. (AT/0065-1915). **2927**

ADELAIDE REVIEW. (AT/0815-5992). **Adv Mgr:** Phillip Virgo. **312**

ADEM. (BE/0001-8171). **4098**

ADFL BULLETIN. (US/0148-7639). **3261**

ADHAESION. (GW/0001-8198). **1049**

ADHESIVES AGE. (US/0001-821X). **2007**

ADICCIONES PALMA DE MALLORCA. (SP/0214-4840). **1338**

ADIRONDAC. (US/0001-8236). **4868**

ADIRONDACK DAILY ENTERPRISE. (US). **Adv Mgr:** Catherine Moore. **5707**

ADIRONDACK LIFE. (US/0001-8252). **2526**

ADLER (WIEN). (AU/0001-8260). **2436**

ADMAP : THE JOURNAL OF ADVERTISING MEDIA ANALYSIS AND PLANNING. (UK). **Adv Mgr:** T. Clifton, **Tel** 0491 411000. **754**

ADMINISTRATION (DUBLIN). (IE/0001-8325). **4624**

ADMINISTRATION ET GESTION. (CN/0704-9765). **4624**

ADMINISTRATION IN SOCIAL WORK. (US/0364-3107). **5270**

ADMINISTRATION PARIS. 1962. (FR/0223-5439). **4461**

ADMINISTRATION PUBLIQUE. (BE). **3091**

ADMINISTRATIVE LAW REPORTS. (UK/0957-9710). **Adv Mgr:** Mrs. Curtis. **2927**

ADMINISTRATIVE LAW REPORTS (TORONTO). (CN/0824-2615). **3091**

ADMINISTRATIVE LAW REVIEW. (US/0001-8368). **3092**

ADMINISTRATIVE SCIENCE QUARTERLY. (US/0001-8392). **4624**

ADNEWS (OCT. 13, 1981). (CN/0712-9041). **Adv Mgr:** Rob Bale. **754**

ADOLESCENCE. (US/0001-8449). **1059**

ADOLESCENZA. (IT/1120-3714). **Adv Mgr:** Dott Dalla, **Tel** 06-86207165. **1059**

ADOPTION & FOSTERING. (UK/0308-5759). **5270**

ADOPTIVE FAMILIES. (US/1076-1020). **Adv Mgr:** Sue Slominski, **Tel** (612)535-4829. **5270**

ADRESSBUCH DES DEUTSCHSPRACHIGEN BUCHHANDEL. (GW/0065-2032). **4823**

ADRIFT. (US/0736-4970). **3358**

ADULT AND CONTINUING EDUCATION TODAY. (US/0001-8473). **1799**

ADULT BASIC EDUCATION (ATHENS, GA.). (US/1052-231X). **1799**

ADULT EDUCATION. (US). **1799**

ADVENTURING

ADULT EDUCATION IN FINLAND. (FI/0001-8503). **1799**

ADULT EDUCATION QUARTERLY (AMERICAN ASSOCIATION FOR ADULT AND CONTINUING EDUCATION). (US/0741-7136). **1799**

ADULT VIDEO NEWS. (US/0883-7090). **4366**

ADULTS LEARNING. (UK/0955-2308). **1799**

ADVANCE ACS ABSTRACTS. (US/1068-8382). **Adv Mgr Tel** (203)256-8211. **959**

ADVANCE LEADER, THE. (US). **Adv Mgr:** Mark Caruso. **5734**

ADVANCE OF BUCKS COUNTY, THE. (US). **Adv Mgr:** Jane Parr, **Tel** (215)968-2244. **5734**

ADVANCE-SENTINEL, THE. (US). **Adv Mgr:** Larry Dilbeck. **5744**

ADVANCE (SPRINGFIELD). (US/0001-8589). **5054**

ADVANCE-YEOMAN. (US). **Adv Mgr:** Brian Wyatt, **Tel** (502)442-7389. **5679**

ADVANCE (ZURICH). (CN/0824-6610). **5779**

ADVANCED BATTERY TECHNOLOGY. (US/0001-8627). **Adv Mgr:** R. Morey, **Tel** same as publisher. **2034**

ADVANCED COMPOSITE MATERIALS : THE OFFICIAL JOURNAL OF THE JAPAN SOCIETY OF COMPOSITE MATERIALS. (JA/0924-3046). **2100**

ADVANCED COMPOSITES LETTERS. (UK/0963-6935). **2100**

ADVANCED IMAGING (WOODBURY, N.Y.). (US/1042-0711). **1276**

ADVANCED MATERIALS TECHNOLOGY. (UK/0957-4778). **5080**

ADVANCED PACKAGING. (US/1065-0555). **Adv Mgr:** Jackie Fanella. **2034**

ADVANCED POWDER TECHNOLOGY. (NE/0921-8831). **5080**

ADVANCED TECHNOLOGY IN THE PACIFIC NORTHWEST. (US/8755-7258). **5081**

ADVANCED TECHNOLOGY LIBRARIES. (US/0044-636X). **3187**

ADVANCES IN APPLIED PROBABILITY. (UK/0001-8678). **3491**

ADVANCES IN COLLOID AND INTERFACE SCIENCE. (NE/0001-8686). **1049**

ADVANCES IN FEED TECHNOLOGY. (GW/0936-2975). **199**

ADVANCES IN MODERN ENVIRONMENTAL TOXICOLOGY. (US/0276-5063). **2858**

ADVANCES IN NEUROIMMUNOLOGY. (UK/0960-5428). **3826**

ADVANCES IN ORTHOPAEDIC SURGERY. (US/0738-2278). **3958**

ADVANCES IN PHYSIOLOGY EDUCATION. (US/1043-4046). **577**

ADVANCES IN POLYMER TECHNOLOGY. (US/0730-6679). **4453**

ADVANCES IN THANATOLOGY. (US/0196-1934). **4572**

ADVENTIST HERITAGE. (US/0360-389X). **5054**

ADVENTIST REVIEW (WEEKLY). (US/0161-1119). **5054**

ADVENTIST REVIEW (WEEKLY, SOUTHWESTERN EDITION). (US/0745-6441). **5054**

ADVENTURE WEST. (US). **Adv Mgr:** Rick Yess, **Tel** (702)832-3700. **4868**

ADVENTURING IN CONSERVATION. (CN/0225-6533). **2185**

ADVERTENTIEBLAD — Advertising Accepted Index

ADVERTENTIEBLAD VAN DE REPUBLIEK SURINAME. (SR). **4461**

ADVERTISER-GLEAM, THE. (US). **Adv Mgr:** Don Woodward. **5625**

ADVERTISER (NEW MILFORD, CONN.). (US/0746-7605). **5644**

ADVERTISER, THE. (US). **Adv Mgr:** Karen Strickland. **5734**

ADVERTISING AGE. (US/0001-8899). **754**

ADVERTISING EXPENDITURE IN MAIN MEDIA. (AT/0313-2382). **Adv Mgr:** Mr. Holt, **Tel** 02 439 3750. **1103**

ADVERTIZER-HERALD, THE. (US). **Adv Mgr:** Cindy Wise. **5741**

ADVISER (WOLVERHAMPTON). (UK/0950-5458). **Adv Mgr:** H.A. Horton. **1293**

ADVISING QUARTERLY, THE. (US/0895-1101). **Adv Mgr:** Lia hutton, **Tel** (202)785-0022. **1722**

ADVISOR (CHAMPAIGN, ILL.), THE. (US/0736-0436). **1722**

ADVISOR, THE. (US). **Adv Mgr:** Charles Hixson. **5734**

ADVOCATE (BATON ROUGE, LA.), THE. (US/1061-3978). **Adv Mgr:** Donald R. Stewart. **5683**

ADVOCATE (BOISE, IDAHO), THE. (US/0515-4987). **2928**

ADVOCATE (EDMONTON). (CN/0847-2890). **Adv Mgr:** Gladys, **Tel** (403)421-1167. **5270**

ADVOCATE (INDIANAPOLIS, IND. : 1984). (US). **4503**

ADVOCATE (LOS ANGELES, CALIF.), THE. (US/0001-8996). **2793**

ADVOCATE (NEW YORK, N.Y.), THE. (US/0001-9003). **2254**

ADVOCATE (STAMFORD, CONN.), THE. (US/0279-5167). **5644**

ADVOCATE, THE. (US). **5656**

ADVOCATE (TORONTO. 1976). (CN/0229-5407). **4383**

ADVOCATE (VANCOUVER). (CN/0044-6416). **Adv Mgr:** G. Roberts. **2928**

ADVOKATEN (STOCKHOLM). (SW/0281-3505). **2928**

ADWEEK (EASTERN ED.). (US/0199-2864). **755**

ADWEEK. WESTERN ADVERTISING NEWS. (US/0199-4743). **755**

AEB, ANALYTICAL & ENUMERATIVE BIBLIOGRAPHY. (US/0161-0376). **3457**

AED (LONDON, ENGLAND). (UK/0144-8234). **1544**

AEG NEWS. (US/0899-5788). **Adv Mgr:** K. Rose, **Tel** (617)891-8597. **2018**

AEGEAN REVIEW. (US/0891-7213). **3358**

AEGIS, THE. (US). **Adv Mgr:** Kay Kline, **Tel** (410)838-4409. **5690**

AEGIS (WASHINGTON, D.C.). (US/0883-0029). **4503**

AEJMC NEWS. (US/0747-8909). **2917**

AERIAL APPLICATOR, FARM, FOREST AND FIRE. (US). **158**

AERO REVUE. (SZ/0001-9186). **4**

AEROCOMERCIAL. (AG/0326-1360). **4**

AEROESPACIO (BUENOS AIRES, ARGENTINA). (AG). **Adv Mgr:** Liliana Carlos. **4**

AEROKURIER. (GW/0341-1281). **4**

AERONAUTICA & DIFESA. (IT/0394-820X). **4**

AERONAUTICAL JOURNAL, THE. (UK/0001-9240). **4**

AERONAUTIQUE ET L'ASTRONAUTIQUE, L'. (FR/0001-9275). **4**

AEROSOL SCIENCE AND TECHNOLOGY. (US/0278-6826). **1020**

AEROSPACE AMERICA. (US/0740-722X). **5**

AEROSPACE CONSULTANTS DIRECTORY. (US/0747-8151). **5**

AEROSPACE ENGINEERING (WARRENDALE, PA.). (US/0736-2536). **5**

AEROSPACE (LONDON, 1974). (UK/0305-0831). **5**

AEROSPACE NEWS AND REVIEW. (US). **5**

AEROSTATION (ALEXANDRIA, VA.). (US/0741-5974). **6**

AETEI JOURNAL. (II). **4932**

AETHLON (SAN DIEGO, CALIF.). (US/1048-3756). **Adv Mgr:** J. Duncan, **Tel** (615)929-4339. **4882**

AEU. ARCHIV. FUER ELEKTRONIK UND UBERTRAGUNGSTECHNIK. (GW/0001-1096). **1148**

AEU : JOURNAL OF ASIA ELECTRONICS UNION. (JA/0385-0447). **2034**

AF, ARTE FOTOGRAFICO. (SP/0514-9193). **4366**

AFA WATCHBIRD, THE. (US/0199-543X). **4285**

AFAS QUARTERLY OF THE AUTOMOTIVE FINE ARTS SOCIETY. (US/0899-9171). **5403**

AFERS INTERNACIONALS. (SP/0212-1786). **4461**

AFFAIRE DE COEUR. (US/0739-3881). **5073**

AFFAIRES (MONTREAL. 1981). (CN/0229-3404). **636**

AFFARSVARLDEN (1974). (SW/0345-3766). **1544**

AFFILIA. (US/0886-1099). **5270**

AFFIRMATIONS. (US/0162-8038). **4932**

AFFIRMATIVE ACTION REGISTER. (US/0146-2113). **938**

AFGHAN HOUND REVIEW, THE. (US/8750-9776). **4285**

AFINIDAD. (SP/0001-9704). **960**

AFKAR INQUIRY. (UK/0267-842X). **4932**

AFRAID (ANAHEIM, CALIF.). (US/1050-0448). **1596**

AFRICA DEVELOPMENT. (SG/0378-3006). **1544**

AFRICA FORUM. (UK/0961-1142). **2501**

AFRICA HEALTH. (UK/0141-9536). **3547**

AFRICA INVESTMENT MONITOR. (US/1053-8763). **Adv Mgr:** same as editor. **890**

AFRICA NEWS (DURHAM). (US/0191-6521). **4514**

AFRICA NOW. (UK). **2497**

AFRICA QUARTERLY. (II/0001-9828). **2636**

AFRICA REPORT. (US/0001-9836). **2636**

AFRICA (ROME, ITALY). (IT/0001-9747). **2636**

AFRICA THEOLOGICAL JOURNAL. (TZ/0253-9322). **4933**

AFRICA TODAY. (US/0001-9887). **Adv Mgr:** Erik Hauser. **4462**

AFRICAN ADMINISTRATIVE STUDIES. (MR/0007-9588). **4625**

AFRICAN AFFAIRS (LONDON). (UK/0001-9909). **4462**

AFRICAN AMERICAN REVIEW. (US/1062-4783). **3358**

AFRICAN-AMERICAN TRAVELER, THE. (US/0895-6235). **2553**

AFRICAN ARCHAEOLOGICAL REVIEW, THE. (UK/0263-0338). **253**

AFRICAN ARTS. (US/0001-9933). **312**

AFRICAN BOOK PUBLISHING RECORD, THE. (UK/0306-0322). **4811**

AFRICAN BUSINESS. (UK/0141-3929). **637**

AFRICAN BUSINESS & CHAMBER OF COMMERCE REVIEW. (SA/0250-0817). **Adv Mgr:** Mr. J. Kapp. **817**

AFRICAN COMMENTARY. (US/1045-2303). **2497**

AFRICAN ECONOMIC HISTORY. (US/0145-2258). **1544**

AFRICAN FARMING AND FOOD PROCESSING. (UK). **45**

AFRICAN HERALD, THE. (US/1069-8205). **5746**

AFRICAN JOURNAL OF ECOLOGY. (UK/0141-6707). **2211**

AFRICAN JOURNAL OF SOCIOLOGY. (KE/1010-4127). **5238**

AFRICAN LANGUAGES AND CULTURES. (UK/0954-416X). **3262**

AFRICAN MUSIC. (SA/0065-4019). **4098**

AFRICAN NOTES. (NR/0002-0087). **2254**

AFRICAN RESEARCH & DOCUMENTATION. (UK/0305-862X). **3188**

AFRICAN REVIEW (DAR ES SALAAM, TANZANIA). (TZ/0002-0117). **5189**

AFRICAN SOCIAL STUDIES FORUM. (KE). **5189**

AFRICAN STATISTICAL YEARBOOK. ANNUAIRE STATISTIQUE POUR L'AFRIQUE. (ET). **5320**

AFRICAN STUDIES BY SOVIET SCHOLARS. (RU). **4539**

AFRICAN STUDIES (JOHANNESBURG). (SA/0002-0184). **227**

AFRICAN STUDIES REVIEW. (US/0002-0206). **2498**

AFRICAN TECHNOLOGY FORUM. (US/1050-0014). **Adv Mgr:** K.Wasiyo. **5081**

AFRICAN TIMES (LONDON, ENGLAND : 1984). (UK). **2484**

AFRICAN URBAN QUARTERLY. (US/0747-6108). **2813**

AFRICAN VIOLET MAGAZINE. (US/0002-0265). **Adv Mgr:** D Richardson, **Tel** (410)686-4667. **2408**

AFRICAN WORLD NEWS, THE. (US/0747-8879). **2498**

AFRICANA ANNUAL. (US). **3188**

AFRICANA NOTES AND NEWS. (SA/0002-032X). **2498**

AFRICANA RESEARCH BULLETIN. (SL/0259-9651). **5189**

AFRIKA JAHRBUCH. (GW). **4462**

AFRIKA-POST. (GW/0002-0389). **4515**

AFRIKA UND UBERSEE. (GW/0002-0427). **3262**

AFRIKASPECTRUM. (GW/0002-0397). **5189**

AFRIQUE AGRICULTURE. (FR/0337-9515). **45**

AFRIQUE HISTOIRE U.S. (US/0741-2592). **2637**

AFRIQUE MEDECINE ET SANTE. (FR). **4763**

AFRIQUE MEDICALE. (SG/0002-0516). **3892**

AFRO-AMERICANS IN NEW YORK LIFE AND HISTORY. (US/0364-2437). **2254**

AFRO-ASIAN JOURNAL OF NEMATOLOGY. (UK/0963-6420). **5574**

AFRO-HISPANIC REVIEW. (US/0278-8969). **3262**

AFRO SCHOLAR NEWSLETTER. (US/0894-0762). **5189**

AFRO TIMES (BROOKLYN, N.Y.). (US/1044-7199). **Adv Mgr:** Jean Wells. **5713**

AFSM INTERNATIONAL. (US/1049-2135). **1235**

AFTERMATH. (US/0737-1381). **4856**

AFTON STAR-ENTERPRISE, THE. (US). **Adv Mgr:** Mary Lou Cheers. **5668**

AFZ. ALLGEMEINE FISCHWIRTSCHAFTSZEITUNG. (GW/0001-1258). **2293**

AG ALERT. (US/0161-5408). **45**

AG IMPACT. (US/0196-0857). **45**

AG. REVIEW (PUTNAM, CONN.). (US/0194-6625). **45**

AGAINST THE GRAIN (CHARLESTON, S.C.). (US/1043-2094). **Adv Mgr:** Edna Laughrey. **3188**

AGAPE MAGAZINE. (BE). **4933**

AGE AND AGEING. (UK/0002-0729). **3748**

AGENCY SALES. (US/0749-2332). **921**

AGENDA. (US). **2917**

AGENDA DES FESTIVALS AUDIOVISUELS EN EUROPE, L'. (BE/0777-6268). **5315**

AGENDA, L'. (IT). **Adv Mgr:** Carla Misto. **3547**

AGENDA (LONDON). (UK/0002-0796). **3459**

AGENDA NEW YORK. (US/1045-4969). **5271**

AGENDA PARKVILLE. (AT/1033-1115). **312**

AGENT AMERICA. (CN). **5460**

AGENT & MANAGER. (US/1065-5921). **859**

AGENT CANADA. (CN/0834-0471). **Adv Mgr:** Frank Cumming. **5460**

AGENTS AND ACTIONS. (SZ/0065-4299). **4289**

AGENZIA VIAGGI. (IT). **5460**

AGGIORNAMENTI SOCIALI. (IT/0002-094X). **4933**

AGGRESSIVE BEHAVIOR. (US/0096-140X). **4572**

AGID NEWS. (TH). **1351**

AGING (MILAN, ITALY). (IT/0394-9532). **3749**

AGING NETWORK NEWS. (US/0742-3438). **5178**

AGLOW. (US/0748-6677). **4933**

AGNI (BOSTON, MASS.). (US/1046-218X). **Adv Mgr:** Erin, **Tel** (617)353-7135. **3358**

AGON. (UY). **3358**

AGORA (RALEIGH, N.C.). (US/0891-3293). **1089**

AGORA (TOKYO JAPAN : 1972). (JA). **5550**

AGRARISCH RECHT. (NE/0167-4242). **2928**

AGRARISCHE RUNDSCHAU. (AU/0002-0710). **46**

Advertising Accepted Index   ALABAMA

AGRARTECHNIK INTERNATIONAL. (GW). **158**

AGRARWIRTSCHAFT. (GW/0002-1121). **637**

AGRI-BOOK MAGAZINE. (CN/0705-3878). **47**

AGRI-BOOK MAGAZINE. TOP CROP MANAGER. (CN). **47**

AGRI-EQUIPMENT & CHEMICAL. (US). **158**

AGRI FINANCE. (US/0002-1164). **768**

AGRI MARKETING. (US/0002-1180). **47**

AGRI NEWS. (US/0745-3450). **5694**

AGRI-NEWS (BILLINGS, MONT.). (US). **Adv Mgr:** Donna Owen. **5702**

AGRI-TIMES NORTHWEST. (US/0887-2910). **48**

AGRI VIEW. (US). **Adv Mgr:** Jeffrey Cook. **48**

AGRIBUSINESS (NEW YORK, N.Y.). (US/0742-4477). **48**

AGRIBUSINESS WORLDWIDE. (US). **48**

AGRICOLA VERGEJ. (SP). **48**

AGRICOMP. (US). **48**

AGRICULTURA DE LAS AMERICAS (OVERLAND PARK, KANS.). (US/0002-1350). **48**

AGRICULTURA (MADRID, SPAIN). (SP/0002-1334). **49**

AGRICULTURAL AND VETERINARY CHEMICALS. (UK/0567-431X). **960**

AGRICULTURAL AVIATION (WASHINGTON, D.C.). (US/0745-4864). **6**

AGRICULTURAL BANKER. (II). **769**

AGRICULTURAL ENGINEER, THE. (UK/0308-5732). **50**

AGRICULTURAL ENGINEERING. (US/0002-1458). **1964**

AGRICULTURAL ENGINEERING ABSTRACTS. (UK/0308-8863). **150**

AGRICULTURAL HISTORY. (US/0002-1482). **50**

AGRICULTURAL HISTORY REVIEW, THE. (UK/0002-1490). **50**

AGRICULTURAL PROGRESS. (UK/0065-4493). **51**

AGRICULTURAL SCIENCE IN FINLAND. (FI/0789-600X). **Adv Mgr:** Sari Torkko, **Tel** 358-16-1881. **52**

AGRICULTURAL SCIENCE. MELBOURNE. (AT/1030-4614). **Adv Mgr:** Amanda Davis. **52**

AGRICULTURAL SITUATION IN INDIA. (II/0002-1679). **52**

AGRICULTURAL SYSTEMS. (UK/0308-521X). **52**

AGRICULTURE AND FORESTRY BULLETIN. (CN/0705-3983). **53**

AGRICULTURE AND HUMAN VALUES. (US/0889-048X). **Adv Mgr:** Richard Haynes. **53**

AGRICULTURE ET DEVELOPPEMENT. (FR). **53**

AGRICULTURE INTERNATIONAL. (UK/0269-2457). **54**

AGRICULTURE (MONTREAL). (CN/0002-1687). **54**

AGRICULTURE TEACHERS DIRECTORY. (US). **54**

AGRIPROMO ABIDJAN. (IV/1018-8568). **2813**

AGRISCIENCE (OTTAWA). (CN/0840-8289). **54**

AGRISCIENTIA. (AG). **54**

AGRITROP [ENGLSIH ED.]. (FR). **54**

AGRO SUR. (CL/0304-8802). **55**

AGROCIENCIA. (MX/0568-3025). **55**

AGROFORESTRY SYSTEMS. (NE/0167-4366). **2211**

AGROKEMIA ES TALAJTAN. (HU/0002-1873). **56**

AGROPECUARIA CATARINENSE. (BL/0103-0779). **56**

AGROW. (UK/0268-313X). **57**

AGUA - TECNOLOGIA Y TRATAMIENTO. (AG). **Adv Mgr:** Carlos Gonzalez Acha. **5529**

AGWEEK. (US/0884-6162). **57**

AHA. (US/8755-500X). **Adv Mgr Tel** (212)860-5445. **312**

AHA NEWS (CHICAGO, ILL.). (US/0891-6608). **3775**

AI APPLICATIONS. (US/1051-8266). **1210**

AI DIRECTORY. (US/1050-7965). **Adv Mgr:** Mike Hamilton, **Tel** (415)853-0197. **1210**

AI MAGAZINE. (US/0738-4602). **Adv Mgr:** Mike Hamilton, **Tel** (415)853-0197. **1211**

AI TODAY. (US/0893-6552). **1211**

AICHE JOURNAL. (US/0001-1541). **2007**

AIDS & SOCIETY. (US/1055-0380). **3663**

AIDS CARE. (UK/0954-0121). **3663**

AIDS CLINICAL CARE. (US/1043-1543). **Adv Mgr:** Carolyn Ferris, **Tel** (617)893-3800 Ext 1217. **3711**

AIDS EDUCATION AND PREVENTION. (US/0899-9546). **4764**

AIDS (LONDON). (UK/0269-9370). **3664**

AIDS PATIENT CARE. (US/0893-5068). **3664**

AIDS RESEARCH AND HUMAN RETROVIRUSES. (US/0889-2229). **3664**

AIDS SCAN. (US/1040-6778). **3664**

AIGA JOURNAL OF GRAPHIC DESIGN. (US/0736-5322). **Adv Mgr:** Michelle Kalvert. **376**

AIKEN STANDARD. (US/0893-2557). **Adv Mgr:** Charles O. Grice. **5741**

AIM. AUTOMOTIVE INDUSTRY MATTERS. (AT/0044-5681). **5403**

AIM FOR RACIAL HARMONY & PEACE. (US/0194-2069). **5238**

AIPE FACILITIES. (US/1054-7541). **Adv Mgr:** M. Fening. **1964**

AIR AND BUSINESS TRAVEL NEWS TRAVEL INDUSTRY DIRECTORY. (UK). **5460**

AIR & SPACE SMITHSONIAN. (US/0886-2257). **6**

AIR CARGO WORLD. (US/0745-5100). **5375**

AIR CHARTER GUIDE, THE. (US/0890-2925). **Adv Mgr:** Meara McLaughlin. **5375**

AIR CONDITIONING, HEATING & REFRIGERATION NEWS. (US/0002-2276). **2602**

AIR DISTANCES MANUAL. (UK). **7**

AIR ENTHUSIAST. (UK/0143-5450). **7**

AIR EXTRA. (UK/0307-7411). **7**

AIR FAN. (FR/0223-0038). **4033**

AIR FORCE MAGAZINE. (US/0730-6784). **4034**

AIR FORCE TIMES. (US/0002-2403). **4034**

AIR FORCES MONTHLY. (UK). **7**

AIR INTERNATIONAL. (UK/0306-5634). **7**

AIR LINE PILOT. (US/0002-242X). **7**

AIR NAVIGATION PLAN, CARRIBBEAN AND SOUTH AMERICAN REGIONS / PLAN DE NAVIGATION AERIENNE, REGIONS CARAIBES ET AMERIQUE DU SUD. PLAN DE NAVEGACION AEREA, REGIONES DEL CARIBE Y DE SUDAMERICA. (CN). **7**

AIR PICTORIAL. (UK/0002-2462). **8**

AIR POWER HISTORY. (US/1044-016X). **Adv Mgr:** Jack Neufeld. **8**

AIR PROGRESS. (US/0002-2500). **8**

AIRBRUSH ACTION. (US/1040-8509). **369**

AIRCRAFT MAINTENANCE INTERNATIONAL. (UK/0955-8063). **9**

AIRCRAFT MAINTENANCE TECHNOLOGY. (US/1072-3145). **9**

AIRCRAFT TECHNOLOGY ENGINEERING & MAINTENANCE. (UK/0967-439X). **Adv Mgr:** Lesley White. **1964**

AIRFAIR. (US/0044-7005). **Adv Mgr:** Dawn Silverberg. **5460**

AIRFINANCE ANNUAL. (UK/0266-2132). **9**

AIRFINANCE JOURNAL. (UK/0143-2257). **9**

AIRFORCE. (CN/0704-6804). **Adv Mgr:** D. Slater, **Tel** (613)992-6096. **9**

AIRLINE HANDBOOK. (US/0095-4683). **5460**

AIRLINER PRICE GUIDE OF COMMERCIAL-REGIONAL & COMMUTER AIRCRAFT, THE. (US). **Adv Mgr:** Judy Ellenburg. **10**

AIRLINERS (MIAMI, FLA.). (US/0896-6575). **Adv Mgr:** Pauline. **5460**

AIRPORT ALERT. (UK). **10**

AIRPORT BUSINESS. (US/1072-1797). **637**

AIRPORT FORUM. (GW/0002-2802). **10**

AIRPORT POCKET GUIDE (DOMESTIC ED.). (US/0894-1513). **5460**

AIRPORT SUPPORT. (UK). **10**

AIRPORTS INTERNATIONAL. (UK/0002-2853). **11**

AIRPOST JOURNAL, THE. (US/0739-0939). **Adv Mgr:** S. Solart, **Tel** (215)949-1548. **1144**

AISLE VIEW : THE NEWSLETTER OF TIPS, TACTICS AND HOW-TO'S FOR SMALL EXHIBITORS. (US). **921**

AIT. ARCHITEKTUR, INNENARCHITEKTUR, TECHNISCHER AUSBAU. (GW/0173-8046). **287**

AITIA. (US/0731-5880). **4339**

AITIM : BOLETIN DE INFORMACION TECNICA / ASOCIACION DE INVESTIGACION TECHNICA DE LAS INDUSTRIAS DE LA MADERNA Y CORCHO. (PO). **2374**

AJAKIRI. (CN/0384-8469). **2254**

AJL NEWSLETTER. (US/0747-6175). **3188**

AJR INFORMATION. (UK). **4515**

AJS REVIEW. (US/0364-0094). **5045**

AKRON BUGLE. (US). **5713**

AKTEN ZUR DEUTSCHEN AUSWARTIGEN POLITIK, 1918-1945. SER. E : 1941-1945. (GW). **2609**

AKTIENGESELLSCHAFT, DIE. (GW/0002-3752). **1596**

AKWE:KON JOURNAL. (US). **Adv Mgr:** Jennifer Bedell, **Tel** (607)255-4308. **2717**

AKWESASNE NOTES. (US/0002-3949). **5268**

AL-AALAM. (UK). **2501**

AL-AMN WA-AL-HAYAH. (SU). **3156**

AL-ARABIYYA. (US/0889-8731). **Adv Mgr:** Pil Parkinson. **3262**

AL-BALAGH. (KU). **5041**

AL-DARAH. (SU). **2645**

AL-DIRASAT AL-ISLAMIYAH. (PK/0002-399X). **5041**

AL-FIHRIST. (LE). **407**

AL-HILAL. (CN). **Adv Mgr:** L. Owaisi. **2767**

AL-IDARI. (LE). **1596**

AL-'ILM WA-AL-TIKNULUGIYA. (LE/1013-2392). **5082**

AL-IQTISADI AL-KUWAYTI. (KU). **1528**

AL-JAWHARAH. (QA). **5550**

AL-MAGALLA AL-TIBBIYYA AL-URDUNIYYA. (JO/0446-9283). **3547**

AL-MAJALLAH AL-ARABIYAH LIL-DIRASAT AL-LUGHAWIYAH. (SJ). **3262**

AL-MAWQIF AL-ADABI. (SY). **3358**

AL-MUJTAMA AL-MADANI WA-AL-TAHAWWUL AL-DIMUQRATI FI AL-WATAN AL-ARABI. (UA). **4625**

AL-MUSAFIR AL-ARABI. (UK/0267-0194). **5460**

AL-MUSTAHLIK. (JO). **1293**

AL-MUSTAQBAL. (US/0153-3401). **2525**

AL-NAHDAH. (MY/0127-2284). **5041**

AL-NASHIR AL-ARABI. (LY). **4811**

AL-RIM. (JO). **2185**

AL-RIYADAH WA-AL-SHABAB. (TS). **4882**

AL-SHARQ. (SU). **2767**

AL-TAWTHIQ AL-ILAMI / TASDURU AN MARKAZ AL-TAWTHIQ AL-ILAMI LI-DUWAL AL-KHALIJ AL-ARABI. (IQ). **3188**

AL-THAQAFAH AL-AJNABIYAH. (IQ). **3359**

AL-TIJARAH. (TS). **1545**

AL VOCANTE. (SP). **2872**

AL-YARMUK. (JO). **2484**

ALA BULLETIN : A PUBLICATION OF THE AFRICAN LITERATURE ASSOCIATION. (CN/0146-4965). **3359**

ALA ... WORLDWIDE DIRECTORY & FACT BOOK. (US/0741-076X). **4034**

ALABAMA ARCHITECTURE. (US). **287**

ALABAMA BAPTIST, THE. (US/0738-7741). **Adv Mgr:** Bobbie Maxwell, **Tel** (205)870-4720. **5625**

ALABAMA CATTLEMAN. (US/0516-3889). **204**

ALABAMA ENGINEER, THE. (US/0401-1457). **1964**

ALABAMA FARMER. (US). **57**

ALABAMA FORESTS. (US/0275-6625). **2374**

ALABAMA HERITAGE. (US/0887-493X). **2717**

ALABAMA JOURNAL, THE. (US/0745-323X). **5625**

ALABAMA LAWYER, THE. (US/0002-4287). **2929**

ALABAMA LEGAL DIRECTORY, THE. (US/0145-4390). **2929**

ALABAMA LIBRARIAN, THE. (US/0002-4295). **Adv Mgr Tel** (205)262-5210. **3188**

ALABAMA

ALABAMA LITERARY REVIEW. (US/0890-1554). **Adv Mgr:** Editor. **3359**

ALABAMA MEDICINE. (US/0738-4947). **3547**

ALABAMA MESSENGER, THE. (US/0273-9593). **5625**

ALABAMA MUNICIPAL JOURNAL, THE. (US/0002-4309). **4625**

ALABAMA PEACE OFFICERS' JOURNAL. (US/0279-5175). **3156**

ALABAMA PURCHASOR. (US/0002-4325). **948**

ALABAMA SCHOOL JOURNAL. (US/0002-435X). **1860**

ALABAMA WILDLIFE. (US/0894-8356). **4868**

ALADDIN'S WINDOW. (US/1070-6836). **3994**

ALAM AL-ISTITHMAR AL-ARABI. ARAB BUSINESS REPORT. (NE). **1545**

ALAM SEKITAR. (MY/0126-7280). **2223**

ALAM TUB AL-ASSNAN. (GW). **1315**

ALAMBRE. (GW/0002-4406). **3475**

ALAMEDA TIMES STAR. (US). **Adv Mgr:** Sharon Kinkade. **5632**

ALAMOGORDO DAILY NEWS. (US). **Adv Mgr:** Milly House. **5712**

ALARMES, PROTECTION, SECURITE. (FR/0290-0106). **2858**

ALASKA AIRLINES MAGAZINE. (US). **2527**

ALASKA (ANCHORAGE, ALASKA). (US/0002-4562). **4868**

ALASKA BAPTIST MESSENGER. (US/0194-7834). **5054**

ALASKA BAR RAG, THE. (US/0276-1025). **2929**

ALASKA BUSINESS MONTHLY. (US/8756-4092). **637**

ALASKA DIRECTORY OF ATTORNEYS. (US/0275-1895). **2929**

ALASKA FISHERMAN'S JOURNAL. (US/0164-8330). **2293**

ALASKA HISTORY (ANCHORAGE, ALASKA). (US/0890-6149). **2718**

ALASKA JOURNAL OF COMMERCE & PACIFIC RIM REPORTER. (US/0271-3276). **Adv Mgr:** Joan Ray, **Tel** (907)249-1942. **822**

ALASKA LAND & HOME MAGAZINE. (US). **2484**

ALASKA LAW REVIEW. (US/0883-0568). **2929**

ALASKA MARINE RADIO DIRECTORY. (US/8755-3422). **1148**

ALASKA MEDICINE. (US/0002-4538). **3547**

ALASKA NURSE, THE. (US/0002-4546). **3850**

ALASKA PETROLEUM & INDUSTRIAL DIRECTORY. (US/0065-5813). **4249**

ALASKAMEN USA. (US/1055-2227). **5550**

ALAUDA. (FR/0002-4619). **Adv Mgr:** Brichambaut. **5614**

ALBA DE AMERICA. (US/0888-3181). **3359**

ALBA : REVISTA DE POESIA. (SP). **3459**

ALBANY DAILY HERALD (ALBANY, GA.). (US). **5652**

ALBANY HERALD. (US). **Adv Mgr:** Geneva Thompson. **5765**

ALBANY LAW JOURNAL OF SCIENCE & TECHNOLOGY. (US/1059-4280). **Adv Mgr:** J. Seymalak, **Tel** (518)472-5855. **2929**

ALBANY LAW REVIEW. (US/0002-4678). **2929**

ALBANY NEWS (ALBANY, TEX.). (US). **5746**

ALBANY STATE COLLEGE JOURNAL OF ARTS AND SCIENCES. (US/0199-9826). **1808**

ALBEMARLE MAGAZINE, THE. (US/0273-7841). **Adv Mgr:** William Carden. **2527**

ALBERTA BUSINESS (CALGARY). (CN/0827-2603). **Adv Mgr:** Mark Reis. **637**

ALBERTA BUSINESS WHO'S WHO & DIRECTORY. (CN/0827-5750). **429**

ALBERTA CATHOLIC DIRECTORY. (CN/0316-473X). **5022**

ALBERTA CRAFT MAGAZINE. (CN/0834-910X). **369**

ALBERTA DAIRYMAN. (CN/1194-9589). **191**

ALBERTA DOCTORS' DIGEST, THE. (CN/0833-8477). **3547**

ALBERTA (EDMONTON). (CN/0843-9931). **312**

ALBERTA FAMILY HISTORIES SOCIETY QUARTERLY. (CN/0228-9288). **2436**

ALBERTA LAW REPORTS. (CN/0703-3117). **2929**

ALBERTA LAW REVIEW. (CN/0002-4821). **2929**

ALBERTA LEGAL TELEPHONE DIRECTORY. (CN/0823-2350). **3138**

ALBERTA PAST. (CN). **2718**

ALBERTA PERSPECTIVE. (CN/0713-8067). **5271**

ALBERTA REPORT. (CN/0225-0519). **2527**

ALBERTA WILD ROSE QUARTER HORSE JOURNAL. (CN/0227-0579). **2796**

ALBIA UNION-REPUBLICAN, THE. (US). **Adv Mgr:** Mary Ann Crall. **5668**

ALBION. (UK). **4563**

ALBION (BOONE). (US/0095-1390). **Adv Mgr:** Michael Moore. **2672**

ALBION NEWS, THE. (US). **Adv Mgr:** Peggy Fails, **Tel** (814)756-4133. **5734**

ALBUM DE ORO. (US). **429**

ALBUM (MADRID, SPAIN). (SP). **335**

ALBUM NETWORK, THE. (US/0739-1641). **4099**

ALBUQUERQUE JOURNAL (ALBUQUERQUE, N.M. : 1926). (US). **5712**

ALBUQUERQUE TRIBUNE, THE. (US). **Adv Mgr:** Scott Daskins, **Tel** (505)823-3301. **5712**

ALCOHOL (FAYETTEVILLE, N.Y.). (US/0741-8329). **1339**

ALCOHOLIC BEVERAGE EXECUTIVES' NEWSLETTER INTERNATIONAL. (US/0889-3519). **2363**

ALCOHOLISM : CLINICAL AND EXPERIMENTAL RESEARCH. (US/0145-6008). **1340**

ALCOHOLISM TREATMENT QUARTERLY. (US/0734-7324). **1340**

ALCOLOGIA. (IT/0394-9826). **1340**

ALDRING OG ELDRE. (NO/0801-9991). **5178**

ALDUS MAGAZINE. (US/1046-0616). **1284**

ALEF. (IS/0736-8518). **2254**

ALEPH (MANIZALES, COLOMBIA). (CK/0120-0216). **3359**

ALERGIA (MEXICO). (MX/0002-5151). **3665**

Advertising Accepted Index

ALEXANDER CITY OUTLOOK, THE. (US/0738-5110). **Adv Mgr:** Billy McGhee. **5625**

ALEXANDRIA DAILY TOWN TALK, THE. (US). **Adv Mgr:** Bill Heintzler, **Tel** (318)487-6391. **5683**

ALEXANDRIA ECHO PRESS. (US). **Adv Mgr:** Jody Hanson. **5694**

ALEXANDRIA HERALD (ALEXANDRIA, S.D.). (US). **5743**

ALEXANDRIA PORT GAZETTE PACKET. (US/1066-6273). **Adv Mgr:** Chrissy Wick, **Tel** (703)838-0302. **5758**

ALEXANOR. (FR/0002-5208). **5574**

ALFA. (BL/0002-5216). **3359**

ALFA OWNER. (US/0364-930X). **5403**

ALFRED HITCHCOCK'S MYSTERY MAGAZINE. (US/0002-5224). **5074**

ALFRED SUN, THE. (US). **5713**

ALGEMEEN NEDERLANDS TIJDSCHRIFT VOOR WIJSBEGEERTE. (NE/0002-5275). **4340**

ALGEMEINER JOURNAL, DER. (US). **5713**

ALGOMA RECORD-HERALD. (US). **5765**

ALI-ABA COURSE MATERIALS JOURNAL. (US/0145-6342). **Adv Mgr:** K. Lawner. **2930**

ALI ANTICHE. (IT/0394-6185). **11**

ALIMENTA. (SZ/0002-5402). **2326**

ALIMENTALEX (MADRID). (SP/0214-803X). **2326**

ALIMENTARIA. (SP/0300-5755). **4764**

ALIMENTAZIONE, NUTRIZIONE, METABOLISMO (1979). (IT/0392-7512). **4187**

ALIMENTOS PROCESADOS. (US/0744-625X). **2326**

ALISCOPE. (FR). **225**

ALISO. (US/0065-6275). **498**

ALIVE (VANCOUVER). (CN/0228-586X). **4187**

ALKALINE PAPER ADVOCATE. (US/0897-2524). **4232**

ALKALMAZOTT MATEMATIKAI LAPEK. (HU/0133-3399). **3492**

ALKI. (US/8756-4173). **3189**

ALL ABOUT BLOWOUT. (NO). **4249**

ALL-CANADA WEEKLY SUMMARIES. (CN/0705-1360). **3088**

ALLAM- ES JOGTUDOMANY. (HU/0002-564X). **2931**

ALLE HENS. (NE/0002-5674). **4174**

ALLEGHENY TIMES. (US). **5734**

ALLEGORICA. (US/0363-2377). **3359**

ALLEGRO (NEW YORK, N.Y.). (US/0002-5704). **4099**

ALLERGIE UND IMMUNOLOGIE. (GW/0323-4398). **3665**

ALLERGOLOGIA ET IMMUNOPATHOLOGIA. (SP/0301-0546). **3665**

ALLERGOLOGIE. (GW/0344-5062). **3665**

ALLERGY PROCEEDINGS. (US/1046-9354). **3666**

ALLES UBER WEIN. (GW/0175-8314). **Adv Mgr:** Beata Kratz. **2363**

ALLESTIRE. (IT). **Adv Mgr:** Giorgio Dell'Orto. **287**

ALLGEMEINE FORST UND JAGDZEITUNG. (GW/0002-5852). **2374**

ALLGEMEINE SCHWEIZERISCHE MILITARZEITSCHRIFT. (SZ). **4034**

ALLGEMEINE ZEITSCHRIFT FUER PHILOSOPHIE. (GW). **4340**

ALLIANCE. (IE). **5803**

ALLIANCE LIFE. (US/1040-6794). **Adv Mgr:** Doug Wicks. **4933**

ALLIANCE (MONTREAL. 1969). (CN/0711-6829). **1860**

ALLIANCE REVIEW (ALLIANCE, OHIO : 1924). (US). **Adv Mgr:** Don Watson. **5726**

ALLIED HEALTH TRENDS. (US/0275-7699). **4764**

ALLIED NEWS. (US). **5734**

ALLTAG, DER. (SZ). **2513**

ALLUMINIO E LEGHE. (IT). **3997**

ALMANAC OF SEAPOWER, THE. (US/0736-3559). **4174**

ALMANAC OF THE CANNING, FREEZING, PRESERVING INDUSTRIES, THE. (US/0887-4999). **2362**

ALMANACCO DI FOTOGRAFARE. (IT/0393-9758). **4366**

ALMANACH MODERNE. (CN/0315-2898). **2484**

ALMANACH POLONII. (PL). **2513**

ALMANACH POPULAIRE CATHOLIQUE. (CN/0821-4034). **5023**

ALMANACK FOR THE YEAR OF OUR LORD ... (LONDON, ENGLAND). (UK/0083-9256). **1923**

ALMANAKH PANORAMA. (US/0889-0730). **Adv Mgr:** Angela Nersesian. **5632**

AL'MANAKH VYDAVNYTSTVA "TRYZUB". (CN/0824-5908). **4812**

ALMANAQUE NAUTICO. (SP). **391**

ALMANAQUE PUERTORRIQUENO. (PR). **2527**

ALMOND FACTS. (US/0886-4365). **2408**

ALMOST FREE RECIPES AND COOKBOOKS UPDATES. (US/0736-170X). **2788**

ALOE. (SA). **498**

ALOHA (HONOLULU). (US/0147-5436). **5460**

ALPES, LES. (SZ). **5461**

ALPHA ACTION REPORTER. (CN/0227-0897). **4383**

ALPHA FLIGHT. (US/8750-0558). **4856**

ALPHA OMEGAN. (US/0002-6417). **1315**

ALPINE AVALANCHE. (US). **Adv Mgr:** Lauren Spear. **5746**

ALPINE JOURNAL, THE. (UK/0065-6569). **4868**

ALPINE SKIING COMPETITION GUIDE. WESTERN/ROCKY EDITION. (US/0733-9348). **4882**

ALPINE SUN. (US/8750-8257). **Adv Mgr:** Teresa Harn. **5633**

ALSHP NEWSLETTER. (US). **4290**

ALTA DIRECCION. (SP/0002-6549). **1596**

ALTAMONT ENTERPRISE (1983), THE. (US/0890-6025). **5713**

ALTERNATE ROUTES. (CN/0702-8865). **5238**

ALTERNATIVE ENERGY RETAILER. (US/0273-8163). **1931**

ALTERNATIVE MEDIA. (US/0730-1766). **4463**

ALTERNATIVE (MONTREAL, QUEBEC). (CN/0843-0586). **1643**

ALTERNATIVES (AMSTERDAM). (US/0304-3754). **1545**

ALTERNATIVES ECONOMIQUES DIJON. (FR/0247-3739). **1589**

ALTERNATIVES (PETERBOROUGH). (CN/0002-6638). **Adv Mgr:** M Ruby, **Tel** (519)888-4545. **2159**

ALTRIMEDIA. (IT/0392-5692). **1104**

ALTUS TIMES, THE. (US). **5731**

ALUMI-NEWS. (CN/0705-4157). **598**

ALUMINIUM (DUSSELDORF). (GW/0002-6689). **3997**

ALUMINIUM INDUSTRY. (UK/0268-5280). **3997**

ALUMNI DIRECTORY - UNIVERSITY OF VIRGINIA. ALUMNI ASSOCIATION. (US/0738-3762). **1100**

ALUMNI MAGAZINE (MORGANTOWN, W. VA.). (US). **1100**

ALUMNINEWS - CARLETON UNIVERSITY. (CN/0226-5389). **1101**

ALVA REVIEW-COURIER, THE. (US). **Adv Mgr:** Maggie Yates. **5731**

ALVARADO POST. (US). **5746**

ALWAYS JUKIN'. (US/0896-9345). **Adv Mgr:** Rick. **4099**

ALYTES. (FR/0753-4973). **5574**

AM-FM RADIO GUIDE NEW YORK. (US/0160-8150). **1126**

AM-POL EAGLE. (US/0276-1904). **Adv Mgr:** James Lasky, **Tel** (716)835-9457. **5713**

AMA. AGRICULTURAL MECHANIZATION IN ASIA, AFRICA AND LATIN AMERICA. (JA/0084-5841). **158**

AMADOR LEDGER DISPATCH. (US/1045-8336). **Adv Mgr:** Jerry Behrens. **5633**

AMAR CHITRA KATHA. (II). **1059**

AMATEUR ENTOMOLOGIST : THE JOURNAL OF THE AMATEUR ENTOMOLOGISTS' SOCIETY, THE. (UK). **5605**

AMATEUR TELEVISION QUARTERLY. (US/1042-198X). **Adv Mgr:** Henry Rvh. **1148**

AMATEUR WINE MAKER. (UK/0002-6883). **2363**

AMATEUR WRESTLING NEWS. (US/0569-1796). **Adv Mgr Tel** (405)524-8551. **4882**

AMAZING COMPUTING. (US/0886-9480). **1264**

AMAZING SPIDER-MAN, THE. (US/0274-5232). **4856**

AMBC NEWS. (US/1064-1599). **Adv Mgr:** C. Ehrman, **Tel** (919)542-5704. **205**

AMBIENTE. (IT). **2211**

AMBIENTE CUCINA, L'. (IT/0392-5730). **2898**

AMBIENTE E SICUREZZA SUL LAVORO. (IT/0393-7054). **Adv Mgr:** Davide Carissimi. **2858**

AMBIENTE RISORSE SALUTE. (IT/0393-0521). **Adv Mgr:** F. Fujani. **2160**

AMBIENTE SALUTE TERRITORIO. (IT). **Adv Mgr:** Guido Gnocchi. **2211**

AMBIO. (SW/0044-7447). **2160**

AMBIT. (UK/0002-6972). **3459**

AMBITO FINANCIERO. (AG). **Adv Mgr:** Eduardo Ribas Somar. **638**

AMBIX. (UK/0002-6980). **960**

AMBLER GAZETTE, THE. (US). **Adv Mgr:** Mike Fisher, **Tel** (215)542-0200 ext. 271. **5734**

AMBOY NEWS, THE. (US). **5658**

AMBULANCE WORLD (1986). (AT/0817-4474). **3723**

AMC. ACTA MEDICA COLOMBIANA. (CK/0120-2448). **3794**

AMC. AMERICAN MARITIME CASES. (US/0160-6786). **3180**

AMC JOURNAL. (US/0891-6209). **2133**

AMC NEWSLETTER. (US). **4099**

AMCHAM BUSINESS JOURNAL. (PH). **Adv Mgr:** L. A. Acejas. **818**

AME JOURNAL. (US). **Adv Mgr Tel** (904)934-5000. **11**

AMEGHINIANA. (AG/0002-7014). **4226**

AMENAGEMENT ET NATURE. (FR/0044-7463). **2186**

AMERASIA JOURNAL. (US/0044-7471). **Adv Mgr:** G. Owotsu, **Tel** (310)825-3415. **2254**

AMERICA. (IT). **755**

AMERICA INDIGENA. (MX/0185-1179). **227**

AMERICA (NEW YORK, N.Y. 1909). (US/0002-7049). **5023**

AMERICA OGGI. (US/1042-6965). **Adv Mgr:** Louis d'Alo, **Tel** (201)358-6582. **5709**

AMERICAN AERONAUT. (US/0279-7968). **1643**

AMERICAN AGENT & BROKER. (US/0002-7200). **2873**

AMERICAN AGRICULTURIST (1976). (US/0161-8237). **58**

AMERICAN AMATEUR JOURNALIST, THE. (US/1046-0470). **2770**

AMERICAN ANNALS OF THE DEAF (WASHINGTON, D.C. 1886). (US/0002-726X). **Adv Mgr:** Susan Flanagan, **Tel** (202)651-5340. **4383**

AMERICAN ANTHROPOLOGIST. (US/0002-7294). **227**

AMERICAN ANTIQUITY; A QUARTERLY REVIEW OF AMERICAN ARCHAEOLOGY. (US/0002-7316). **253**

AMERICAN-ARAB AFFAIRS. (US/0731-6763). **4515**

AMERICAN ARCHIVIST, THE. (US/0360-9081). **Adv Mgr:** T Brinati, **Tel** (312)922-0140. **2478**

AMERICAN ART / NATIONAL MUSEUM OF AMERICAN ART, SMITHSONIAN INSTITUTION. (US). **Adv Mgr Tel** (202)357-4647. **336**

AMERICAN ART THERAPY ASSOCIATION NEWSLETTER. (US/1066-4076). **4572**

AMERICAN ARTIST DIRECTORY OF ART SCHOOLS AND WORKSHOPS. (US/0146-9606). **312**

AMERICAN ASIAN REVIEW, THE. (US/0737-6650). **2645**

AMERICAN ASTROLOGY. (US/0002-7529). **389**

AMERICAN ATHEIST, THE. (US/0516-9623). **4933**

AMERICAN BABY. (US/0044-7544). **2276**

AMERICAN BABY'S CHILDBIRTH EDUCATOR. (US/0279-490X). **3756**

AMERICAN BANK ATTORNEYS. (US). **3084**

AMERICAN BANK DIRECTORY. (US/0569-292X). **769**

AMERICAN BANKER. (US/0002-7561). **769**

AMERICAN BEE JOURNAL. (US/0002-7626). **58**

AMERICAN BICYCLIST AND MOTORCYCLIST. (US/0002-7677). **427**

AMERICAN BIOLOGY TEACHER, THE. (US/0002-7685). **441**

AMERICAN BIRDS. (US/0004-7686). **Adv Mgr:** John Gourlay, **Tel** (212)546-9127. **5614**

AMERICAN (BLACKDUCK, MINN.), THE. (US/0747-0363). **Adv Mgr:** Cindy Fisher-Preuett, **Tel** $218)835-4211. **5694**

AMERICAN BOOK COLLECTOR (1980). (US/0196-5654). **2770**

AMERICAN BOOK PRICES CURRENT. (US/0091-9357). **4823**

AMERICAN BOOK REVIEW, THE. (US/0149-9408). **3337**

AMERICAN BOOKSELLER (NEW YORK. 1977). (US/0148-5903). **4823**

AMERICAN BREWER (HAYWARD, CALIF.). (US/1055-470X). **Adv Mgr:** Bill Owens. **2363**

AMERICAN BUDDHIST NEWSLETTER, THE. (US/0747-900X). **5020**

AMERICAN BUILDING CONTRACTOR, THE. (US/0740-3607). **598**

AMERICAN BUNGALOW. (US/1055-0674). **Adv Mgr:** Al Griffin. **598**

AMERICAN BUSINESS IN ARGENTINA ... DIRECTORY. (AG). **Adv Mgr:** Justo Antonio Lofeudo. **638**

AMERICAN BUSINESS LAW JOURNAL. (US/0002-7766). **3095**

AMERICAN BUSINESS REVIEW. (US/0743-2348). **859**

AMERICAN CAGE-BIRD MAGAZINE. (US/0002-7782). **4285**

AMERICAN-CANADIAN GENEALOGIST. (US/1076-3902). **2436**

AMERICAN CATHOLIC PHILOSOPHICAL QUARTERLY. (US/1051-3558). **4340**

AMERICAN CEMENT DIRECTORY, THE. (US). **598**

AMERICAN CERAMIC SOCIETY BULLETIN. (US/0002-7812). **2586**

AMERICAN CERAMICS. (US/0278-9507). **2586**

AMERICAN CHIANINA JOURNAL. (US/0198-8816). **Adv Mgr:** Terry Atchison, **Tel** (816)431-2808. **205**

AMERICAN CHIROPRACTOR, THE. (US/0194-6536). **4379**

AMERICAN CHRISTMAS TREE JOURNAL. (US/0569-3845). **58**

AMERICAN CINEMATOGRAPHER. (US/0002-7928). **4063**

AMERICAN CLEAN CAR. (US/0095-1811). **638**

AMERICAN CLINICAL LABORATORY. (US/1041-3235). **3548**

AMERICAN COLLECTOR'S JOURNAL, THE. (US/0164-7008). **248**

AMERICAN CONCHOLOGIST. (US/1072-2440). **Adv Mgr:** W. Sage. **5574**

AMERICAN COONER. (US/0002-807X). **4882**

AMERICAN COUNTRY COLLECTIBLES. (US). **2770**

AMERICAN CURRENTS. (US/1070-7352). **2294**

AMERICAN DANCE GUILD NEWSLETTER. (US/0300-7448). **1310**

AMERICAN DEMOGRAPHICS. (US/0163-4089). **4549**

AMERICAN DROP-SHIPPERS DIRECTORY. (US/0065-8103). **822**

AMERICAN DRUGGIST (1974). (US/0190-5279). **4290**

AMERICAN DYESTUFF REPORTER. (US/0002-8266). **5347**

AMERICAN EDUCATIONAL RESEARCH JOURNAL. (US/0002-8312). **1723**

AMERICAN ENTERPRISE (WASHINGTON, D.C.), THE. (US/1047-3572). **Adv Mgr:** Ashley Cooper, **Tel** (202)862-5870. **638**

AMERICAN ETHNOLOGIST. (US/0094-0496). **228**

AMERICAN EXPORT REGISTER. (US/0272-1163). **Adv Mgr Tel** (212)629-1130. **822**

AMERICAN FAMILY PHYSICIAN (1970). (US/0002-838X). **3736**

AMERICAN FARRIERS' JOURNAL. (US/0274-6565). **Adv Mgr:** Alice Musser. **2796**

AMERICAN FASTENER JOURNAL. (US/1064-3834). **1596**

AMERICAN FENCING. (US/0002-8436). **4882**

AMERICAN FERN JOURNAL. (US/0002-8444). **498**

AMERICAN FIELD. (US/0002-8452). **4868**

AMERICAN FILM. (US/0361-4751). **4063**

AMERICAN FIRE JOURNAL. (US/0739-3709). **2287**

AMERICAN FIREWORKS NEWS. (US/8755-3163). **2007**

AMERICAN FITNESS. (US/0893-5238). **2595**

AMERICAN FITNESS QUARTERLY. (US/0889-2121). **2596**

AMERICAN FOOD AND AG EXPORTER. (US/1065-3775). **2326**

AMERICAN FORESTS. (US/0002-8541). **2374**

AMERICAN FUCHSIA SOCIETY BULLETIN. (US/0194-3456). **2408**

AMERICAN GINSENG TRENDS. (US/1047-7527). **Adv Mgr:** R. Zunker. **1596**

AMERICAN GLASS REVIEW. (US/0002-8649). **2586**

AMERICAN GO JOURNAL, THE. (US/0148-0243). **4856**

AMERICAN HANDGUNNER, THE. (US/0145-4250). **4882**

AMERICAN HARMONICA ASSOCIATES NEWSLETTER. (US/1050-7493). **Adv Mgr:** Alan Eichler, **Tel** (616)962-2989. **4099**

AMERICAN HARP JOURNAL, THE. (US/0002-869X). **4099**

AMERICAN HEALTH (NEW YORK, N.Y.). (US/0730-7004). **2596**

AMERICAN HEART JOURNAL, THE. (US/0002-8703). **3698**

AMERICAN HERITAGE. (US/0002-8738). **2718**

AMERICAN HIKER. (US/0279-9472). **4868**

AMERICAN HISTORICAL REVIEW. (US/0002-8762). **2609**

AMERICAN HISTORY ILLUSTRATED. (US/0002-8770). **2719**

AMERICAN HOCKEY MAGAZINE. (US/8756-3789). **Adv Mgr:** Jensen, **Tel** (612)522-1200. **4882**

AMERICAN HOLINESS JOURNAL. (US). **4933**

AMERICAN HOME ECONOMICS ASSOCIATION ACTION. (US/0194-7176). **2788**

AMERICAN HOMEOPATHY (1984). (US/0747-606X). **3774**

AMERICAN HORSES IN SPORT. (US/0897-1498). **2796**

AMERICAN HORTICULTURIST (ALEXANDRIA). (US/0096-4417). **2408**

AMERICAN — Advertising Accepted Index

AMERICAN HORTICULTURIST NEWS. (US). **2408**

AMERICAN ILLUSTRATION SHOWCASE. (US/0278-8128). **376**

AMERICAN INDIAN AND ALASKA NATIVE MENTAL HEALTH RESEARCH. (US/0893-5394). **5271**

AMERICAN INDIAN ART MAGAZINE. (US/0192-9968). **336**

AMERICAN INDIAN CULTURE AND RESEARCH JOURNAL. (US/0161-6463). **2254**

AMERICAN INDIAN LAW REVIEW. (US/0094-002X). **Adv Mgr Tel** (405)325-5191. **2932**

AMERICAN INDIAN QUARTERLY. (US/0095-182X). **2255**

AMERICAN INDUSTRIAL HYGIENE ASSOCIATION JOURNAL. (US/0002-8894). **2858**

AMERICAN INDUSTRY. (US/0002-8908). **859**

AMERICAN INVENTOR (BLOOMINGTON, IND.). (US/1042-1890). **5082**

AMERICAN JAILS. (US/1056-0319). **Adv Mgr:** Pat Cain, **Tel** (301)790-3930. **3156**

AMERICAN JEWELRY MANUFACTURER. (US/0193-0931). **2913**

AMERICAN JEWISH HISTORY. (US/0164-0178). **2255**

... AMERICAN-JEWISH MEDIA DIRECTORY, THE. (US/1041-0139). **755**

AMERICAN JEWISH WORLD, THE. (US/0002-9084). **5045**

AMERICAN JOURNAL (NEW YORK). (US/0092-119X). **2527**

AMERICAN JOURNAL OF ACUPUNCTURE. (US/0091-3960). **3548**

AMERICAN JOURNAL OF AGRICULTURAL ECONOMICS. (US/0002-9092). **58**

AMERICAN JOURNAL OF ANCIENT HISTORY. (US/0362-8914). **Adv Mgr:** Wendy Lurie. **1073**

AMERICAN JOURNAL OF ART THERAPY. (US/0007-4764). **336**

AMERICAN JOURNAL OF BOTANY. (US/0002-9122). **498**

AMERICAN JOURNAL OF CARDIAC IMAGING. (US/0887-7971). **3698**

AMERICAN JOURNAL OF CASE MANAGEMENT, THE. (US/1051-8967). **5190**

AMERICAN JOURNAL OF CHINESE MEDICINE, THE. (US/0192-415X). **3548**

AMERICAN JOURNAL OF CLINICAL HYPNOSIS, THE. (US/0002-9157). **2857**

AMERICAN JOURNAL OF CLINICAL NUTRITION, THE. (US/0002-9165). **4187**

AMERICAN JOURNAL OF CLINICAL PATHOLOGY. (US/0002-9173). **3892**

AMERICAN JOURNAL OF COSMETIC SURGERY, THE. (US/0748-8068). **3958**

AMERICAN JOURNAL OF CRITICAL CARE. (US/1062-3264). **3850**

AMERICAN JOURNAL OF DENTISTRY. (US/0894-8275). **1315**

AMERICAN JOURNAL OF DISEASES OF CHILDREN (1960). (US/0002-922X). **3899**

AMERICAN JOURNAL OF DRUG AND ALCOHOL ABUSE, THE. (US/0095-2990). **1340**

AMERICAN JOURNAL OF EEG TECHNOLOGY, THE. (US/0002-9238). **3827**

AMERICAN JOURNAL OF EMERGENCY MEDICINE, THE. (US/0735-6757). **3723**

AMERICAN JOURNAL OF ENOLOGY AND VITICULTURE. (US/0002-9254). **2363**

AMERICAN JOURNAL OF EPIDEMIOLOGY. (US/0002-9262). **3734**

AMERICAN JOURNAL OF FAMILY LAW. (US/0891-6330). **3119**

AMERICAN JOURNAL OF FAMILY THERAPY, THE. (US/0192-6187). **4573**

AMERICAN JOURNAL OF FORENSIC MEDICINE AND PATHOLOGY, THE. (US/0195-7910). **3739**

AMERICAN JOURNAL OF FORENSIC PSYCHIATRY, THE. (US/0163-1942). **3919**

AMERICAN JOURNAL OF FORENSIC PSYCHOLOGY, THE. (US/0733-1290). **3739**

AMERICAN JOURNAL OF GASTROENTEROLOGY, THE. (US/0002-9270). **3743**

AMERICAN JOURNAL OF GERIATRIC PSYCHIATRY, THE. (US/1064-7481). **3749**

AMERICAN JOURNAL OF HEALTH PROMOTION. (US/0890-1171). **Adv Mgr:** David Revels, **Tel** (810)650-9600. **4764**

AMERICAN JOURNAL OF HOSPICE AND PALLIATIVE CARE, THE. (US/1049-9091). **5271**

AMERICAN JOURNAL OF HOSPITAL PHARMACY. (US/0002-9289). **4290**

AMERICAN JOURNAL OF INFECTION CONTROL. (US/0196-6553). **3734**

AMERICAN JOURNAL OF INTERNATIONAL LAW, THE. (US/0002-9300). **3123**

AMERICAN JOURNAL OF ISLAMIC SOCIAL SCIENCES, THE. (US/0887-7653). **5190**

AMERICAN JOURNAL OF JURISPRUDENCE (NOTRE DAME), THE. (US/0065-8995). **Adv Mgr Tel** (219)255-2938. **2932**

AMERICAN JOURNAL OF LEGAL HISTORY, THE. (US/0002-9319). **2932**

AMERICAN JOURNAL OF MATHEMATICAL AND MANAGEMENT SCIENCES. (US/0196-6324). **3492**

AMERICAN JOURNAL OF MATHEMATICS. (US/0002-9327). **3492**

AMERICAN JOURNAL OF MEDICAL GENETICS. (US/0148-7299). **542**

AMERICAN JOURNAL OF NEPHROLOGY. (SZ/0250-8095). **3988**

AMERICAN JOURNAL OF NEURORADIOLOGY. (US/0195-6108). **3827**

AMERICAN JOURNAL OF OBSTETRICS AND GYNECOLOGY. (US/0002-9378). **3756**

AMERICAN JOURNAL OF OCCUPATIONAL THERAPY, THE. (US/0272-9490). **1874**

AMERICAN JOURNAL OF OPHTHALMOLOGY. (US/0002-9394). **3871**

AMERICAN JOURNAL OF ORTHODONTICS AND DENTOFACIAL ORTHOPEDICS. (US/0889-5406). **1315**

AMERICAN JOURNAL OF ORTHOPSYCHIATRY. (US/0002-9432). **3919**

AMERICAN JOURNAL OF OTOLARYNGOLOGY. (US/0196-0709). **3885**

AMERICAN JOURNAL OF OTOLOGY (NEW YORK, N.Y.), THE. (US/0192-9763). **3886**

AMERICAN JOURNAL OF PAIN MANAGEMENT. (US/1059-1494). **Adv Mgr:** D. McCoy, **Tel** (209)946-3145. **3548**

AMERICAN JOURNAL OF PATHOLOGY, THE. (US/0002-9440). **3892**

AMERICAN JOURNAL OF PERINATOLOGY. (US/0735-1631). **3756**

AMERICAN JOURNAL OF PHARMACEUTICAL EDUCATION. (US/0002-9459). **4290**

AMERICAN JOURNAL OF PHILOLOGY. (US/0002-9475). **1073**

AMERICAN JOURNAL OF PHYSICS. (US/0002-9505). **4396**

AMERICAN JOURNAL OF PHYSIOLOGY : CELL PHYSIOLOGY. (US/0363-6143). **577**

AMERICAN JOURNAL OF PHYSIOLOGY : ENDOCRINOLOGY AND METABOLISM. (US/0193-1849). **577**

AMERICAN JOURNAL OF PHYSIOLOGY : GASTROINTESTINAL AND LIVER PHYSIOLOGY. (US/0193-1857). **578**

AMERICAN JOURNAL OF PHYSIOLOGY : HEART AND CIRCULATORY PHYSIOLOGY. (US/0363-6135). **578**

AMERICAN JOURNAL OF PHYSIOLOGY : REGULATORY, INTEGRATIVE AND COMPARATIVE PHYSIOLOGY. (US/0363-6119). **578**

AMERICAN JOURNAL OF PHYSIOLOGY RENAL, FLUID AND ELECTROLYTE PHYSIOLOGY. (US/0363-6127). **578**

AMERICAN JOURNAL OF POLITICAL SCIENCE. (US/0092-5853). **4463**

AMERICAN JOURNAL OF PREVENTIVE MEDICINE. (US/0749-3797). **3549**

AMERICAN JOURNAL OF PSYCHIATRY, THE. (US/0002-953X). **3920**

AMERICAN JOURNAL OF PSYCHOLOGY, THE. (US/0002-9556). **4573**

AMERICAN JOURNAL OF PUBLIC HEALTH (1971). (US/0090-0036). **4764**

AMERICAN JOURNAL OF RHINOLOGY. (US/1050-6586). **3886**

AMERICAN JOURNAL OF ROENTGENOLOGY (1976). (US/0361-803X). **3938**

AMERICAN JOURNAL OF SEMIOTICS. (US/0277-7126). **3263**

AMERICAN JOURNAL OF SOCIAL PSYCHIATRY, THE. (US/0277-8173). **3920**

AMERICAN JOURNAL OF SPORTS MEDICINE, THE. (US/0363-5465). **3953**

AMERICAN JOURNAL OF THEOLOGY & PHILOSOPHY. (US/0194-3448). **4340**

AMERICAN JOURNAL OF TRIAL ADVOCACY, THE. (US/0160-0281). **2932**

AMERICAN JOURNAL OF VETERINARY RESEARCH. (US/0002-9645). **5502**

AMERICAN JOURNAL ON ADDICTIONS, THE. (US/1055-0496). **1340**

AMERICAN JOURNALISM. (US/0882-1127). **Adv Mgr:** Alf Pratte, **Tel** (801)378-2077. **2917**

AMERICAN KENNEL CLUB AWARDS. (US/0888-627X). **4285**

AMERICAN KITE. (US/1045-3598). **4882**

AMERICAN LABOR (WASHINGTON, D.C.). (US/0889-0609). **1643**

AMERICAN LABORATORY (FAIRFIELD). (US/0044-7749). **960**

AMERICAN LANGUAGE JOURNAL, THE. (US/0734-7545). **3263**

AMERICAN LAWYER (NEW YORK. 1979), THE. (US/0162-3397). **2933**

AMERICAN LEGION, THE. (US/0886-1234). **4034**

AMERICAN LIBRARIES (CHICAGO, ILL.). (US/0002-9769). **3189**

AMERICAN LITERARY HISTORY. (US/0896-7148). **3360**

AMERICAN LITERARY REALISM, 1870-1910. (US/0002-9823). **3337**

AMERICAN LITERARY REVIEW. (US/1051-5062). **Adv Mgr:** Rebecca Stephens, **Tel** (817)565-2127. **3360**

AMERICAN LITERATURE. (US/0002-9831). **3360**

AMERICAN LUTHERIE. (US/1041-7176). **4099**

AMERICAN MALACOLOGICAL BULLETIN. (US/0740-2783). **5574**

AMERICAN MARKETING ASSOCIATION INTERNATIONAL MEMBERSHIP DIRECTORY AND MARKETING SERVICES GUIDE. (US). **921**

AMERICAN MATHEMATICAL MONTHLY, THE. (US/0002-9890). **3492**

AMERICAN MEDICAL NEWS. (US/0001-1843). **3549**

AMERICAN MEDICAL WRITERS ASSOCIATION AMWA JOURNAL. (US). **3549**

AMERICAN MIDDLE SCHOOL EDUCATION. (US/0889-552X). **1860**

AMERICAN MODELER (RALEIGH, N.C.). (US/1061-9399). **2771**

AMERICAN MOTOR CARRIER. (US/0003-0066). **5375**

AMERICAN MOTORCYCLIST. (US/0277-9358). **4080**

AMERICAN MUSIC (CHAMPAIGN, ILL.). (US/0734-4392). **4099**

AMERICAN MUSIC TEACHER, THE. (US/0003-0112). **Adv Mgr:** Diane DeVillez. **4099**

AMERICAN NEPTUNE, THE. (US/0003-0155). **4174**

AMERICAN NURSE, THE. (US/0098-1486). **3850**

AMERICAN NURSERYMAN. (US/0003-0198). **2408**

AMERICAN OIL & GAS REPORTER, THE. (US/0145-9198). **Adv Mgr:** Charlie Cookson, **Tel** (316)788-6271. **4249**

AMERICAN OPTOMETRIC ASSOCIATION NEWS. (US/0094-9620). **Adv Mgr Tel** (314)991-4100. **4215**

AMERICAN ORCHID SOCIETY BULLETIN. (US/0003-0252). **2408**

AMERICAN ORGANIST (1979), THE. (US/0164-3150). **4099**

AMERICAN ORTHOPTIC JOURNAL. (US/0065-955X). **Adv Mgr Tel** (608)262-5839. **3871**

AMERICAN OXONIAN, THE. (US/0003-0295). **1808**

AMERICAN PAINT & COATINGS JOURNAL. (US/0098-5430). **4222**

AMERICAN PAINT & COATINGS JOURNAL. CONVENTION DAILY. (US/0097-4749). **4222**

AMERICAN PAINTING CONTRACTOR. (US/0003-0325). **4222**

AMERICAN PAPERMAKER (1991). (US/1056-4772). **Adv Mgr:** Carolyn Benedict, **Tel** (404)325-9153. **4232**

AMERICAN PEONY SOCIETY BULLETIN, THE. (US). **2408**

AMERICAN PERIODICALS : A JOURNAL OF HISTORY, CRITICISM, AND BIBLIOGRAPHY. (US/1054-7479). **Adv Mgr:** Jane Tanner, **Tel** (817)565-2124. **4812**

AMERICAN PHARMACY. (US/0160-3450). **4290**

AMERICAN PHARMACY TECHNICIAN JOURNAL, THE. (US/1060-5576). **4290**

AMERICAN PHILATELIST, THE. (US/0003-0473). **2784**

AMERICAN PHOTO. (US/1046-8986). **Adv Mgr:** Arlene Weinberg. **4366**

AMERICAN PIGEON JOURNAL. (US/0003-0511). **5574**

AMERICAN POETRY REVIEW, THE. (US/0360-3709). **3460**

AMERICAN POLITICAL SCIENCE REVIEW, THE. (US/0003-0554). **4463**

AMERICAN POWER BOAT ASSOCIATION ROSTER. (US/0278-7040). **591**

AMERICAN PREMIERE. (US/0279-0041). **4063**

AMERICAN PRINTER (1982). (US/0744-6616). **4563**

AMERICAN PSYCHOLOGIST, THE. (US/0003-066X). **4573**

AMERICAN QUARTERLY. (US/0003-0678). **2719**

AMERICAN QUILTER. (US/8756-6591). **5182**

AMERICAN RABBI (CANOGA PARK, LOS ANGELES, CALIF.), THE. (US/0164-3916). **5045**

AMERICAN RAILS. (US/8750-5762). **5429**

AMERICAN RECORD GUIDE. (US/0003-0716). **5315**

AMERICAN RECORDER, THE. (US/0003-0724). **4099**

AMERICAN RED ANGUS. (US/0886-4357). **205**

AMERICAN REGISTER OF PRINTING AND GRAPHIC ARTS SERVICES, THE. (US/0276-5519). **4563**

AMERICAN REVENUER, THE. (US/0163-1608). **2784**

AMERICAN REVIEW OF CANADIAN STUDIES, THE. (US/0272-2011). **2719**

AMERICAN REVIEW OF INTERNATIONAL ARBITRATION, THE. (US/1050-4109). **Adv Mgr:** Elisa Varian, **Tel** (914)591-4288. **2933**

AMERICAN REVIEW OF POLITICS. (US). **Adv Mgr:** M. LeDuc, **Tel** (501)450-3412. **4463**

AMERICAN REVIEW OF RESPIRATORY DISEASE, THE. (US/0003-0805). **3948**

AMERICAN ROWING. (US/0888-1154). **4883**

AMERICAN SAILOR. (US/0279-9553). **591**

AMERICAN SALON: OFFICIAL PUBLICATION OF THE NHCA. (US/0741-5737). **402**

AMERICAN SCHOLAR, THE. (US/0003-0937). **2484**

AMERICAN SCHOOL & UNIVERSITY. (US/0003-0945). **1860**

AMERICAN SCHOOL BOARD JOURNAL, THE. (US/0003-0953). **1860**

AMERICAN SCIENTIST. (US/0003-0996). **5082**

AMERICAN SECONDARY EDUCATION. (US/0003-1003). **1724**

AMERICAN SENIOR, THE. (US/1055-8306). **5178**

AMERICAN SERIES IN MATHEMATICAL AND MANAGEMENT SCIENCES. (US/0883-6221). **3492**

AMERICAN SHIPPER (1991). (US/1074-8350). **822**

AMERICAN SHOEMAKING. (US/0003-1038). **3183**

AMERICAN SHOTGUNNER, THE. (US/0162-153X). **4883**

AMERICAN SHOWCASE. ILLUSTRATION. (US). **376**

AMERICAN SKATING WORLD. (US/0744-1363). **Adv Mgr:** P. Weber. **4883**

AMERICAN SONGWRITER. (US/0896-8993). **Adv Mgr:** Rick Hogan, **Tel** (615)244-6065. **4099**

AMERICAN SPACEMODELLING. (US/0883-0991). **2771**

AMERICAN SPECTATOR (ARLINGTON, VA.), THE. (US/0148-8414). **3337**

AMERICAN SQUARE DANCE. (US/0091-3383). **1310**

AMERICAN STATISTICIAN, THE. (US/0003-1305). **5320**

AMERICAN STRING TEACHER. (US/0003-1313). **4100**

AMERICAN STUDIES IN PAPYROLOGY. (US/0569-8642). **1074**

AMERICAN STUDIES IN SCANDINAVIA. (NO/0044-8060). **2719**

AMERICAN STUDIES INTERNATIONAL. (US/0883-105X). **2719**

AMERICAN STUDIES (LAWRENCE). (US/0026-3079). **2719**

AMERICAN SURVIVAL GUIDE. (US/8750-5878). **2527**

AMERICAN SUZUKI JOURNAL. (US/0193-5372). **4100**

AMERICAN SWIMMING COACHES ASSOCIATION WORLD CLINIC YEARBOOK. (US/0747-5853). **4883**

AMERICAN TAXIDERMIST MAGAZINE. (US). **2771**

AMERICAN TEACHER. (US/0003-1380). **1888**

AMERICAN THEATRE. (US/8750-3255). **5361**

AMERICAN TOOL, DIE & STAMPING NEWS. (US/0192-5709). **3475**

AMERICAN TRAPPER. (US/1050-4036). **2186**

AMERICAN TURF MONTHLY. (US/0003-1445). **2796**

AMERICAN UNIVERSITY JOURNAL OF INTERNATIONAL LAW AND POLICY, THE. (US/0888-630X). **3123**

AMERICAN UNIVERSITY LAW REVIEW, THE. (US/0003-1453). **Adv Mgr:** Martine Tavakoli. **2933**

AMERICAN VOICE (LOUISVILLE, KY.), THE. (US/0884-4356). **3360**

AMERICAN WAY (DALLAS, TEX.). (US/0003-1518). **11**

AMERICAN WEATHER OBSERVER. (US/8755-9552). **1419**

AMERICAN WHITEWATER. (US/0300-7626). **4883**

AMERICAN WORKER, THE. (US/1047-7136). **1643**

AMERICAN ZOOLOGIST. (US/0003-1569). **5574**

AMERICANA. (US/0090-9114). **2527**

AMERICANS BEFORE COLUMBUS. (US/0066-121X). **2720**

AMERICAR AUSTRALIA. (AT/1032-6499). **5403**

AMERICAS REVIEW (HOUSTON, TEX.). (US/1042-6213). **Adv Mgr:** M. Tristan, **Tel** (713)741-2841. **5530**

AMERICAS REVIEW / WORLD OF INFORMATION, THE. (UK). **1923**

AMERICA'S TEXTILES INTERNATIONAL. (US/0890-9970). **5347**

AMERICUS TIMES-RECORDER. (US). **Adv Mgr:** Jeff Masters. **5652**

AMERIKA WOCHE. (US/0745-6557). **Adv Mgr:** Rita Hetz. **5658**

AMERIKAI MAGYAR SZO. (US/0194-7990). **5713**

AMERIKAN UUTISET. (US/0745-9971). **5647**

AMERIKASTUDIEN. (GW/0340-2827). **Adv Mgr:** Korkendick, **Tel** 11 49 89 348017. **2720**

AMERRIKUA! (SCHUYLER FALLS, N.Y.). (US/1043-7029). **Adv Mgr:** Donald Papson. **2255**

AMES FORESTER. (US). **2374**

AMI (MISSISSAUGA, ONT.). (CN/0830-8586). **383**

AMICA NEWS BULLETIN, THE. (US/1043-5379). **4100**

AMIGAWORLD TECH JOURNAL, THE. (US/1054-4631). **1264**

AMIGO (MONTREAL). (CN/0318-5729). **4934**

AMINA. (FR). **5550**

AMITYVILLE RECORD, THE. (US) **Adv Mgr:** Alfred James. **5713**

AMMINISTRAZIONE E POLITICA. (IT/0392-579X). **4463**

AMMONITE. (UK/0951-2500). **Adv Mgr:** John H. Greaves. **3360**

AMMONITE GILLINGHAM, DORSET. (UK/0951-2500). **2318**

AMON HEN. (UK). **3360**

AMPHIBIA-REPTILIA. (GW/0173-5373). **5575**

AMPHIBIOUS WARFARE REVIEW. (US/0886-344X). **Adv Mgr:** Carl White. **4034**

AMPHORA. (CN/0003-200X). **4823**

AMPLEFORTH JOURNAL, THE. (UK/0003-2018). **5023**

AMRO. (UK). **Adv Mgr:** (Editor). **3549**

AMSTAT NEWS. (US/0163-9617). **5320**

AMSTERDAMER BEITRAEGE ZUR ALTEREN GERMANISTIK. (NE). **3264**

AMUSEMENT BUSINESS. (US/0003-2344). **4856**

AMUSEMENT PARK JOURNAL. (US/0271-7999). **4857**

AN COSANTOIR. (IE). **4040**

AN-HUI SHIH TA HSUEH PAO. (CC). **2841**

ANACORTES AMERICAN. (US). **Adv Mgr:** James Dean. **5758**

ANACRUSIS. (CN/0826-7464). **4100**

ANADARKO DAILY NEWS, THE. (US/0744-1398). **Adv Mgr:** Vic Brian. **5731**

ANAESTHESIA AND INTENSIVE CARE. (AT/0310-057X). **3680**

ANAESTHESIOLOGICA (OULU). (FI/0358-4836). **3680**

ANAESTHESIST, DER. (GW/0003-2417). **3681**

ANAIS BRASILEIROS DE DERMATOLOGIA. (BL/0365-0596). **3717**

ANAIS DO INSTITUTO DE HIGIENE E MEDICINA TROPICAL. (PO/0303-7762). **3549**

ANALECTA CARTUSIANA. (AU/0253-1593). **4934**

ANALECTA GREGORIANA. (IT/0066-1376). **4934**

ANALELE INSTITUTULUI DE GEODEZIE, FOTOGRAMMETRIE, CARTOGRAFIE SI ORGANIZAREA TERITORIULUI. (RM/0253-1232). **1351**

ANALELE UNIVERSITATI DIN GALATI. FASCICULA II - MATEMATICA, FIZICA, MECANICA TEORETICA. (RM). **3492**

ANALELE UNIVERSITATII DIN GALATI. FASCICULA I, STIINTE SOCIALE SI UMANISTE. (RM/1015-9606). **5190**

ANALELE UNIVERSITATII DIN GALATI.FASCICULA VII, TEHNICA PISCICOLA. (RM). **2294**

ANALES DE LA FACULTAD DE VETERINARIA DE LEON. (SP/0373-1170). **5502**

ANALES DEL CARIBE. (CU/1017-8937). **2841**

ANALES DEL INSTITUTO DE ESTUDIOS MADRILENOS. (SP/0584-6374). **2673**

ANALES ESPANOLES DE PEDIATRIA. (SP/0302-4342). **3900**

ANALES GALDOSIANOS. (US/0569-9924). **3337**

ANALES OTORRINOLARINGOLOGICOS IBERO-AMERICANOS. (SP/0303-8874). **Adv Mgr:** Sr. Javier Moqxo Estton. **3886**

ANALISE PSICOLOGICA. (PO/0870-8231). **4573**

ANALISIS FILOSOFICO. (AG/0326-1301). **4340**

ANALISIS FINANCIERO. (SP). **770**

ANALIZ STILEI ZARUBEZHNOI KHUDOZHESTVENNOI I NAUCHNOI LITERATURY. (RU/0202-2435). **3264**

ANALUSIS. (FR/0365-4877). **1012**

ANALYSE. (NE/0166-7688). **3549**

ANALYSE & KRITIK. (GW/0171-5860). **5190**

ANALYSIS MATHEMATICA (BUDAPEST). (HU/0133-3852). **3493**

ANALYSIS (NEW YORK (N.Y.). (US/0003-2638). **4340**

ANALYSIS OF CLASS 1 RAILROADS. (US). **5400**

ANALYST (LONDON). (UK/0003-2654). **1012**

ANALYST WATCH. (US/1071-2364). **Adv Mgr:** Eden Levinson. **890**

ANALYSTE (MONTREAL, QUEBEC). (CN/0715-7649). **2527**

ANALYTIC TEACHING. (US/0890-5118). **4340**

ANALYTICAL ABSTRACTS. (UK/0003-2689). **996**

ANALYTICAL AND QUANTITATIVE CYTOLOGY AND HISTOLOGY. (US/0884-6812). **531**

ANALYTICAL CHEMISTRY (WASHINGTON). (US/0003-2700). **1013**

ANALYTICAL INSTRUMENT INDUSTRY REPORT. (UK/0265-3435). **1597**

ANALYTICAL SCIENCES : THE INTERNATIONAL JOURNAL OF THE JAPAN SOCIETY FOR ANALYTICAL CHEMISTRY. (JA/0910-6340). **1013**

ANALYTISCHE PSYCHOLOGIE. (SZ/0301-3006). **4573**

ANAMNESES VILLEJUIF. (FR/1166-9829). **2610**

ANAP. (CU). **58**

ANATOLIAN STUDIES. (UK/0066-1546). **254**

ANATOMIA

Advertising Accepted Index

ANATOMIA, HISTOLOGIA, EMBRYOLOGIA. (GW/0340-2096). **5502**

ANATOMICA, PATHOLOGICA, MICROBIOLOGICA. (FI/0358-4895). **3678**

ANATOMICAL RECORD, THE. (US/0003-276X). **3678**

ANATOMISCHER ANZEIGER. (GW/0003-2786). **3678**

ANATOMY AND EMBRYOLOGY. (GW/0340-2061). **3678**

ANCESTOR. (AT/0044-8222). **Adv Mgr:** Julie Taylor, **Tel** 03 6637034. **2437**

ANCESTRY. (US). **Adv Mgr:** Jane Allen. **2437**

ANCESTRY (SALT LAKE CITY, UTAH). (US/1075-475X). **2437**

ANCETRE (QUEBEC). (CN/0316-0513). **2437**

ANCHORAGE TIMES. (US). **5628**

ANCIENT CONTROVERSY. (US/1042-2471). **4515**

ANCIENT MESOAMERICA. (UK). **254**

ANCIENT PHILOSOPHY (PITTSBURGH, PA.). (US/0740-2007). **4340**

ANCIENT TL. (UK/0735-1348). **254**

ANCIENT WORLD, THE. (US/0160-9645). **Adv Mgr:** J. Remer, **Tel** (312)743-1907. **254**

ANDALUCIA ECONOMICA. (SP/1130-4413). **Adv Mgr:** Rosa Mafner, **Tel** 95-446-1775. **1462**

ANDALUSIA STAR-NEWS, THE. (US/0746-2115). **5625**

ANDERSON HERALD-BULLETIN. (US/0893-908X). **Adv Mgr:** Linda Millisor. **5662**

ANDERSON'S CAMPGROUND DIRECTORY. (US/0163-268X). **4869**

ANDHRA AGRICULTURAL JOURNAL, THE. (II/0003-2956). **58**

ANDOVER ADVOCATE, THE. (US/0746-6447). **5674**

ANDRADE : REVISTA TRIMESTRAL DE POESIA. (SP). **3361**

ANDREJ BELYJ SOCIETY NEWSLETTER, THE. (US/0743-2410). **3457**

ANDROLOGIA (BERLIN, WEST). (GW/0303-4569). **3549**

ANEKS. (UK/0345-0295). **2673**

ANELLO CHE NON TIENE, L'. (US/0899-5273). **3361**

ANEP. ANNUAIRE EUROPEEN DE PETROLE. (GW/0342-6947). **4249**

ANESTESIA E RIANIMAZIONE. (IT/0570-0760). **3681**

ANESTHESIA AND ANALGESIA. (US/0003-2999). **3681**

ANESTHESIA PROGRESS. (US/0003-3006). **1316**

ANESTHESIE REANIMATION PRATIQUE PARIS. (FR/0996-8296). **3681**

ANESTHESIOLOGY (PHILADELPHIA). (US/0003-3022). **3681**

ANESTHESIOLOGY REVIEW. (US/0093-4437). **3681**

ANGESTELLTEN MAGAZIN. (GW/0341-017X). **1643**

ANGEWANDTE BOTANIK. (GW/0066-1759). **499**

ANGEWANDTE MAKROMOLEKULARE CHEMIE. (SZ/0003-3146). **4454**

ANGEWANDTE PARASITOLOGIE. (GW/0003-3162). **5575**

ANGIER INDEPENDENT, THE. (US/8750-0221). **5722**

ANGIOLOGIA. (SP/0003-3170). **3698**

ANGLE DROIT PARIS. (FR/1156-4148). **2933**

ANGLES (VANCOUVER). (CN/0824-2100). **2793**

ANGLIA : ZEITSCHRIFT FUER ENGLISCHE PHILOLOGIE. (GW). **3264**

ANGLICAN DIGEST, THE. (US/0003-3278). **5055**

ANGLICAN JOURNAL. (CN/0847-978X). **Adv Mgr:** B. Trotter, **Tel** (416)924-9192. **4934**

ANGLICAN, THE. (CN/0517-7731). **5055**

ANGLICAN THEOLOGICAL REVIEW. (US/0003-3286). **Adv Mgr:** J. Winter, **Tel** (708)864-6024. **4934**

ANGLICAN YEAR BOOK. (CN/0317-8765). **4934**

ANGLO-AMERICAN DIRECTORY OF MEXICO. (MX). **2528**

ANGLO-AMERICAN LAW REVIEW, THE. (UK/0308-6569). **2933**

ANGLO AMERICAN TRADE DIRECTORY. (UK/0066-1813). **Adv Mgr:** Judy Bowyer, **Tel** 44 352 770246. **822**

ANGLO-SOVIET JOURNAL, THE. (UK/0044-8265). **2673**

ANGLOFILE. (US). **2484**

ANGORABOT & SYBOTHAAR -BLAD. (SA/0003-3464). **205**

ANGUILLA CONSOLIDATED INDEX OF STATUTES AND SUBSIDIARY LEGISLATION TO ... . (BB). **3123**

ANGUS JOURNAL. (US/0194-9543). **205**

ANGUS TIMES. (CN/0849-6188). **Adv Mgr:** L Reich. **205**

ANGUS TOPICS. (US/0402-4265). **Adv Mgr:** Ernest Bingham. **205**

ANIMA (CHAMBERSBURG). (US/0097-1146). **4185**

ANIMAL BEHAVIOUR. (UK/0003-3472). **5575**

ANIMAL BREEDING ABSTRACTS. (UK/0003-3499). **151**

ANIMAL FINDERS' GUIDE. (US). **Adv Mgr:** Sharon Hoctor, **Tel** (812)898-2678. **4285**

ANIMAL GENETICS. (UK/0268-9146). **542**

ANIMAL KEEPERS' FORUM. (US/0164-9531). **Adv Mgr:** Susan D. Chan, **Tel** (913)272-5821, Ext. 31. **5575**

ANIMAL LEARNING & BEHAVIOR. (US/0090-4996). **5575**

ANIMAL LIBERATION ACTION. (AT/0816-486X). **Adv Mgr:** T. Poulton, **Tel** 03 818 4925. **225**

ANIMAL ORGANIZATIONS & SERVICES DIRECTORY. (US/0748-5069). **225**

ANIMAL PEOPLE. (US/1071-0035). **225**

ANIMAL PRODUCTION. (UK/0003-3561). **205**

ANIMAL TECHNOLOGY. (UK/0264-4754). **5503**

ANIMALIA (BARCELONA). (SP/0214-3151). **4285**

ANIMALS AGENDA. (US/0892-8819). **Adv Mgr:** David Patrice Greanville, **Tel** (203)452-0446. **225**

ANIMALS' VOICE (CHICO, CALIF.), THE. (US/0889-6712). **225**

ANIMATION MAGAZINE. (US/1041-617X). **4063**

ANIMATO! (CAMBRIDGE, MASS.). (US/1042-539X). **4063**

ANIMATOR ST. ALBANS. (UK/0964-5586). **4063**

ANIMAZIONE SOCIALE. (IT/0392-5870). **Adv Mgr:** Lulena Ortauda, **Tel** 011 814 2748. **5271**

ANN ARBOR NEWS, THE. (US). **5690**

ANN ARBOR OBSERVER. (US/0192-5717). **Adv Mgr:** E. Enos, **Tel** (313)769-3175. **2484**

ANNALAS DALA SOCIETAD RHAETO-ROMANSCHA. NSS. (SZ). **2674**

ANNALES. (TI). **59**

ANNALES BENJAMIN CONSTANT. (SZ/0263-7383). **3361**

ANNALES CHIRURGIAE ET GYNAECOLOGIAE. (FI/0355-9521). **3756**

ANNALES DE BIOCHIMIE CLINIQUE DU QUEBEC. (CN/0709-8502). **480**

ANNALES DE BIOLOGIE CLINIQUE (PARIS). (FR/0003-3898). **3892**

ANNALES DE CARDIOLOGIE ET D'ANGEIOLOGIE. (FR/0003-3928). **3698**

ANNALES DE CHIRURGIE. (FR/0003-3944). **3958**

ANNALES DE GEMBLOUX. (BE/0303-9099). **59**

ANNALES DE L'A C F A S. (CN/0066-8842). **5083**

ANNALES DE LA RECHERCHE URBAINE, LES. (FR/0180-930X). **5239**

ANNALES DE LA SOCIETE ENTOMOLOGIQUE DE FRANCE. (FR/0037-9271). **Adv Mgr:** J. Y. Raspius. **5575**

ANNALES DE LA SOCIETE GEOLOGIQUE DE BELGIQUE. (BE/0037-9395). **1365**

ANNALES DE LA SOCIETE GEOLOGIQUE DU NORD. (FR/0767-7367). **1365**

ANNALES DE L'EST. (FR/0365-2017). **2674**

ANNALES DE L'I.H.P. PHYSIQUE THEORIQUE. (FR/0246-0211). **4396**

ANNALES DE L'I.H.P. PROBABILITES ET STATISTIQUES. (FR/0246-0203). **3493**

ANNALES DE L'INSTITUT FOURIER. (FR/0373-0956). **3493**

ANNALES DE PEDIATRIE (PARIS). (FR/0066-2097). **3900**

ANNALES DE PHYSIQUE (PARIS). (FR/0003-4169). **4397**

ANNALES DE RADIOLOGIE. (FR/0003-4185). **3938**

ANNALES DES MINES DE BELGIQUE. (BE/0003-4290). **2133**

ANNALES DES SCIENCES NATURELLES. ZOOLOGIE ET BIOLOGIE ANIMALE. (FR/0003-4339). **5575**

ANNALES D'UROLOGIE. (FR/0003-4401). **3988**

ANNALES HYDROGRAPHIQUES. (FR/0373-3629). **1412**

ANNALES INTERNATIONALES DE CRIMINOLOGIE. (FR/0003-4452). **3156**

ANNALES MEDICALES DE NANCY ET DE L'EST. (FR/0221-3796). **3550**

ANNALES SCIENTIFIQUES DE L'ECOLE NORMALE SUPERIEURE. (FR/0012-9593). **3493**

ANNALES THEOLOGICI. (IT/0394-8226). **Adv Mgr:** Anbrogio Piras, **Tel** 68802208. **4934**

ANNALES UNIVERSITATIS SARAVIENSIS. REIHE : MATHEMATISCH-NATURWISSENSCHAFTLICHE FAKULTAT. (GW/0080-5165). **4162**

ANNALES UNIVERSITATIS SCIENTIARUM BUDAPENTINENSIS DE ROLANDO EOTVOS NOMINATAE. SECTIO PHILOLOGICA MODERNA. (HU). **3264**

ANNALES UNIVERSITATIS SCIENTIARUM BUDAPESTINENSIS DE ROLANDO EOTVOS NOMINATAE. SECTIO PHILOSOPHICA ET SOCIOLOGICA. (HU/0524-9023). **4341**

ANNALI DELLA FONDAZIONE LUIGI EINAUDI. (IT/0531-9870). **5190**

ANNALI DI OSTETRICIA, GINECOLOGIA, MEDICINA PERINATALE. (IT/0300-0087). **3757**

ANNALI D'ITALIANISTICA. (US/0741-7527). **3362**

ANNALI ITALIANI DI CHIRURGIA. (IT/0003-469X). **3959**

ANNALI ITALIANI DI MEDICINA INTERNA : ORGANO UFFICIALE DELLA SOCIETA ITALIANA DI MEDICINA INTERNA. (IT/0393-9340). **Adv Mgr:** Marine Buongiorno, **Tel** (06)8077011. **3794**

ANNALS OF AGRICULTURAL RESEARCH. (II/0970-3179). **59**

ANNALS OF ALLERGY. (US/0003-4738). **3666**

ANNALS OF APPLIED BIOLOGY. (UK/0003-4746). **442**

ANNALS OF ARID ZONE. (II/0570-1791). **162**

ANNALS OF BEHAVIORAL MEDICINE. (US/0883-6612). **3654**

ANNALS OF CLINICAL AND LABORATORY SCIENCE. (US/0091-7370). **3893**

ANNALS OF CLINICAL BIOCHEMISTRY. (UK/0004-5632). **480**

ANNALS OF CLINICAL PSYCHIATRY. (US/1040-1237). **3920**

ANNALS OF EARTH. (US/1070-9983). **1351**

ANNALS OF EMERGENCY MEDICINE. (US/0196-0644). **3723**

ANNALS OF EPIDEMIOLOGY. (US/1047-2797). **3734**

ANNALS OF HUMAN GENETICS. (UK/0003-4800). **542**

ANNALS OF INTERNAL MEDICINE. (US/0003-4819). **3794**

ANNALS OF LIBRARY SCIENCE AND DOCUMENTATION. (II/0003-4835). **3190**

ANNALS OF MEDICINE (HELSINKI). (FI/0785-3890). **3550**

ANNALS OF NEUROLOGY. (US/0364-5134). **3827**

ANNALS OF NUTRITION & METABOLISM. (SZ/0250-6807). **4187**

ANNALS OF OTOLOGY, RHINOLOGY & LARYNGOLOGY, THE. (US/0003-4894). **3886**

ANNALS OF PAEDIATRIC SURGERY. (II/0970-2121). **3900**

ANNALS OF PLASTIC SURGERY. (US/0148-7043). **3959**

ANNALS OF PROBABILITY, THE. (US/0091-1798). **3494**

ANNALS OF PURE AND APPLIED LOGIC. (NE/0168-0072). **3494**

ANNALS OF SAUDI MEDICINE. (SU/0256-4947). **3550**

ANNALS OF STATISTICS, THE. (US/0090-5364). **5321**

ANNALS OF THE ACADEMY OF MEDICINE, SINGAPORE. (SI/0304-4602). **3550**

ANNALS OF THE ASSOCIATION OF AMERICAN GEOGRAPHERS. (US/0004-5608). **2554**

ANNALS OF THE ENTOMOLOGICAL SOCIETY OF AMERICA. (US/0013-8746). **5605**

ANNALS OF THE ROYAL COLLEGE OF PHYSICIANS AND SURGEONS OF CANADA. (CN/0035-8800). **Adv Mgr:** Maclean Hunter, **Tel** (416)596-5949. **3913**

ANNALS OF THE ROYAL COLLEGE OF SURGEONS OF ENGLAND. (UK/0035-8843). **3959**

ANNALS OF THORACIC SURGERY, THE. (US/0003-4975). **3959**

ANNALS OF TOURISM RESEARCH. (US/0160-7383). **5191**

ANNALS OF TROPICAL PAEDIATRICS. (UK/0272-4936). **3985**

ANNALS OF VASCULAR SURGERY. (US/0890-5096). **3959**

ANNALS OF WARSAW AGRICULTURAL UNIVERSITY, SGGW-AR. ANIMAL SCIENCE. (PL/0208-5739). **205**

ANNALS OF WARSAW AGRICULTURAL UNIVERSITY - SGGW-AR. FORESTRY AND WOOD TECHNOLOGY. (PL/0208-5704). **2374**

ANNAPOLITAN (ANNAPOLIS, MD.). (US/0899-2320). **Adv Mgr:** Susan Fink. **2528**

ANNEE BATEAUX (ENGLISH ED.). (FR). **591**

ANNEE SOCIALE / INSTITUT DE SOCIOLOGIE, UNIVERSITE LIBRE DE BRUXELLES, L'. (BE/0066-2380). **5191**

ANNIE'S CROCHET NEWSLETTER. (US/0745-6360). **5183**

ANNISTON STAR, THE. (US). **Adv Mgr:** Hershel Victory. **5625**

ANNOTATED GUIDE TO WOMEN'S PERIODICALS IN THE U.S. & CANADA, THE. (US/0741-9899). **5550**

ANNUAIRE ABREGE DE STATISTIQUES AGRICOLES, REGION RHONE-ALPES. (FR). **151**

ANNUAIRE ADMINISTRATIF ET JUDICIAIRE DE BELGIQUE. ADMINISTRATIEF EN GERECHTELIJK JAARBOEK VOOR BELGIE. (BE/0066-2461). **4626**

ANNUAIRE - ASSOCIATION DES INSTITUTIONS D'ENSEIGNEMENT SECONDAIRE. (CN/0066-8990). **1724**

ANNUAIRE / ASSOCIATION GENERALE DES HUGIENISTES ET TECHNICIENS MUNICIPAUX. (FR). **4765**

ANNUAIRE CATHOLIQUE DE FRANCE. (FR/0066-2488). **5023**

ANNUAIRE (CONSEIL DE LA COOPERATION DE LA SASKATCHEWAN). (CN/0822-9368). **822**

ANNUAIRE DE L'ADMINISTRATION DES DIRECTIONS REGIONALES DE L'INDUSTRIE ET DE LA RECHERCHE. (FR/1140-7123). **2133**

ANNUAIRE DE L'ARMEMENT A LA PECHE. (FR/0066-2623). **2294**

ANNUAIRE DE L'AUDIOVISUEL DE LA COMMUNAUTE FRANCAISE. (BE). **1148**

ANNUAIRE DE L'EGLISE CATHOLIQUE AU CANADA. (CN/0821-9885). **Adv Mgr:** Raymond Bertrand. **5023**

ANNUAIRE DE L'EGLISE CATHOLIQUE AU CANADA. (CN/0821-9885). **Adv Mgr:** Raymond Bertrand. **5023**

ANNUAIRE DENTAIRE. (FR). **1316**

ANNUAIRE DES BIBLIOTHECAIRES-CONSEILS DU QUEBEC. (CN/0825-3927). **3190**

ANNUAIRE DES COMMUNAUTES EUROPEENNES ET DES AUTRES ORGANISATIONS EUROPEENNES. (BE/0771-7962). **4515**

ANNUAIRE DES FEMMES DE MONTREAL, L'. (CN/0823-0188). **5271**

ANNUAIRE DES MEMBRES DE L'ASSOCIATION DES BIBLIOTHECAIRES FRANCAIS. (FR). **3190**

ANNUAIRE DES STATISTIQUES DU COMMERCE EXTERIEUR (KINSHASA). (CG/0304-5692). **5321**

ANNUAIRE DU CINEMA QUEBECOIS. (CN/0849-5726). **4063**

ANNUAIRE DU MARKETING. (FR). **921**

ANNUAIRE DU PAPIER, L'. (FR/0337-4971). **4232**

ANNUAIRE EGYPTIEN DES ENTREPRISES, DES SERVICES, DE L'INDUSTRIE ET DU COMMERCE EXTERIEUR. (UA). **822**

ANNUAIRE INTERNATIONAL DES VENTES. (FR). **336**

ANNUAIRE STATISTIQUE DE LA BELGIQUE. (BE/0066-3646). **5321**

ANNUAIRE STATISTIQUE DE L'ALGERIE. (AE). **5321**

ANNUAIRE STATISTIQUE DE POCHE - INSTITUT NATIONAL DE STATISTIQUE. (BE/0067-5431). **5321**

ANNUAIRE STATISTIQUE DU MAROC (RABAT, MOROCCO : 1982). (MR). **5321**

ANNUAIRE STATISTIQUE / INSTITUT DE STATISTIQUES ET D'ETUDES ECONOMIQUES DU BURUNDI. (BD). **Adv Mgr:** Jean Paul Nimpagaritse. **1528**

ANNUAIRE SUISSE DU MONDE ET DES AFFAIRES. (SZ). **429**

ANNUAIRE TELEPHONIQUE JUDICIAIRE DU QUEBEC. (CN/0316-6120). **2934**

ANNUAL ABSTRACT OF STATISTICS - NIGERIA. FEDERAL OFFICE OF STATISTICS. (NR/0078-0626). **5321**

ANNUAL AREA LABOR REVIEW. (US/0149-3779). **1644**

ANNUAL BULLETIN OF HISTORICAL LITERATURE. (UK/0066-3832). **2610**

ANNUAL BULLETIN OF STATISTICS. (UK/0305-2370). **2362**

ANNUAL - CANADIAN GLADIOLUS SOCIETY. (CN/0319-1915). **2409**

ANNUAL CONFERENCE OF THE ATLANTIC CANADA ECONOMICS ASSOCIATION. (CN/0319-003X). **1462**

ANNUAL CONFERENCE / THE ONTARIO PETROLEUM INSTITUTE. (CN/0078-5040). **4249**

ANNUAL DIRECTORY / HAWAII STATE BAR ASSOCIATION. (US/0277-0520). **2934**

ANNUAL DRUG DATA REPORT. (SP/0379-4121). **4291**

ANNUAL EDITION: NOTICES TO MARINERS. (CN). **4174**

ANNUAL EXHIBITION OF THE CANADIAN SOCIETY OF PAINTERS IN WATER COLOUR. (CN/0318-4978). **336**

ANNUAL FORUM PROCEEDINGS - AMERICAN HELICOPTER SOCIETY. (US/0733-4249). **11**

ANNUAL INDEX OF FOUNDATION REPORTS / OFFICES OF THE ATTORNEY GENERAL. (US). **4334**

ANNUAL MEETING - INTERNATIONAL OIL SCOUTS ASSOCIATION. (US/0731-9800). **4249**

ANNUAL MEMBERSHIP DIRECTORY - NATIONAL ASSOCIATION OF ADVISORS FOR THE HEALTH PROFESSIONS. (US/1075-6507). **3913**

ANNUAL OF ARMENIAN LINGUISTICS. (US/0271-9800). **3265**

ANNUAL OF CARDIAC SURGERY. (UK/0952-0562). **3959**

ANNUAL OF THE AMERICAN SCHOOLS OF ORIENTAL RESEARCH, THE. (US/0066-0035). **255**

ANNUAL OF THE SOCIETY OF CHRISTIAN ETHICS, THE. (US/0732-4928). **4935**

... ANNUAL OFFICIAL VOLLEYBALL REFERENCE GUIDE OF THE UNITED STATES VOLLEYBALL ASSOCIATION, THE. (US). **4883**

ANNUAL PRICE REVIEW. (US/0270-4188). **Adv Mgr:** Lisa Sharkus, **Tel** (800)932-0617. **60**

ANNUAL REGISTER OF BOOK VALUES. VOYAGES, TRAVEL & EXPLORATION. (UK/0968-7548). **407**

ANNUAL REPORT - AGRICULTURAL RESEARCH DEPARTMENT, PHILIPPINE COCONUT AUTHORITY. (PH). **60**

ANNUAL REPORT AND ACCOUNTS - NATIONAL INSTITUTE FOR PRODUCTIVITY. (TZ). **1597**

ANNUAL REPORT ... ANNUAL MEETING / OREGON HORTICULTURAL SOCIETY. (US/0885-7849). **2409**

ANNUAL REPORT / DELAWARE RIVER BASIN COMMISSION. (US/0418-5455). **5529**

ANNUAL REPORT / EUROPEAN SCIENCE FOUNDATION. (FR). **5084**

ANNUAL REPORT FOR THE YEAR ENDED ... / EMPLOYMENT APPEALS TRIBUNAL. (IE). **3144**

ANNUAL REPORT - HUNTINGTON LIBRARY, ART GALLERY, BOTANICAL GARDENS. (US/0363-3306). **3190**

ANNUAL REPORT - INDONESIAN NATIONAL SCIENTIFIC DOCUMENTATION CENTER. (IO). **5084**

ANNUAL REPORT, INFORMATION COMMISSIONER. (CN/0826-9904). **4627**

ANNUAL REPORT / KENYA TUBERCULOSIS AND RESPIRATORY DISEASES RESEARCH CENTRE. (KE/1015-0072). **3948**

ANNUAL REPORT - MINDOLO ECUMENICAL FOUNDATION. (RH). **4935**

ANNUAL REPORT, MUNICIPAL EDUCATION DEPARTMENT, FOR THE YEAR ... . (KE). **1725**

ANNUAL REPORT - NATIONAL TRUST OF AUSTRALIA, W.A. (AT). **4628**

ANNUAL REPORT / NEW YORK STATE, OFFICE OF ADVOCATE FOR THE DISABLED. (US). **4628**

ANNUAL REPORT OF THE ACTIVITIES OF THE ALABAMA DEPT. OF PUBLIC HEALTH. (US). **4766**

ANNUAL REPORT OF THE BEAN IMPROVEMENT COOPERATIVE. (US/0084-7747). **163**

ANNUAL REPORT OF THE DIRECTOR, HOUSING DEVELOPMENT AND MANAGEMENT DEPARTMENT FOR THE YEAR.../CITY COUNCIL OF NAIROBI. (KE). **2814**

ANNUAL REPORT ON THE RESULTS OF TREATMENT IN GYNECOLOGICAL CANCER. (SW/0348-8799). **3809**

ANNUAL REPORT - THE RAILWAY & LOCOMOTIVE HISTORICAL SOCIETY, INC. (US/0483-9005). **5429**

ANNUAL REPORT - TOWN AND COUNTRY PLANNING ASSOCIATION. (UK/0308-082X). **2815**

ANNUAL REPORT / VICTORIAN MINISTRY OF IMMIGRATION & ETHNIC AFFAIRS. (AT). **1918**

ANNUAL REPORTS FOR THE YEARS ... / REPUBLIC OF ZAMBIA, MINISTRY OF LABOUR AND SOCIAL SERVICES, INDUSTRIAL RELATIONS COURT. (ZA). **3144**

ANNUAL REPORTS OF THE NATIONAL COLLEGIATE ATHLETIC ASSOCIATION. (US/0077-3794). **4883**

ANNUAL REVIEW OF EUROPEAN EXPORT INDUSTRIES : FURNITURE. (GW). **2904**

ANNUAL REVIEW OF WOMEN IN WORLD RELIGIONS, THE. (US/1056-4578). **4935**

ANNUAL REVIEW - THE JUNIOR CHAMBER OF COMMERCE FOR LONDON. (UK/0306-8501). **818**

ANNUAL STATISTICAL BULLETIN - SWAZILAND. CENTRAL STATISTICAL OFFICE. (SQ/0300-2098). **5321**

ANNUAL SURVEY OF AMERICAN LAW. (US/0066-4413). **2935**

ANNUAL TECHNICAL REPORT / UNITED STATES DEPARTMENT OF AGRICULTURE, SOIL CONSERVATION SERVICE, BISMARCK PLANT MATERIALS CENTER. (US). **5084**

ANNUAL VOLUME / THE OLD WATER-COLOUR SOCIETY'S CLUB. (UK/0958-8825). **337**

ANNUARIO DELLE UNIVERSITA DEGLI STUDI IN ITALIA / ISTITUTO NAZIONALE DELL'INFORMAZIONE. (IT/0392-8411). **1810**

ANNUARIO ... DELL'INDUSTRIA ITALIANA DELLA MAGLIERIA E DELLA CALZETTERIA / MAGLIECALZE. (IT). **5347**

ANNUARIO NAZIONALE DELL ENERGIA E DELL AMBIENTE. (IT). **1932**

ANNUARIO SEAT. VOL. A, SIDERURGIA E MECCANICA. (IT). **3998**

ANNUARIO SEAT. VOL. B, ELETTROTECNICA, TERMOTECNICA E ATTREZZATURE INDUSTRIALI. (IT). **5084**

ANNUARIO SEAT. VOL. C, CHIMICA, MATERIE PLASTICHE, MEDICINA. (IT). **961**

ANNUARIO SEAT. VOL. E, ARREDAMENTO. (IT). **2810**

ANNUARIO SEAT. VOL. I, TRASPORTI, CARTOTECNICA ED EDITORIA. (IT). **1598**

ANNUARIO SEAT. VOL. L, CREDITO, ASSICURAZIONI E SERVIZI PER LE AZIENDE. (IT). **772**

ANOKA COUNTY UNION, THE. (US). **Adv Mgr:** Hugh Campbell. **5694**

ANOTHER CHICAGO MAGAZINE. (US/0272-4359). **Adv Mgr:** Sara Skolnik, **Tel** (708)869-3235. **3362**

ANPI MAGAZINE. (BE/0778-7383). **2288**

ANQ (LEXINGTON, KY.). (US/0895-769X). **3362**

ANTARCTIC. (NZ/0003-5327). **1351**

ANTARCTIC AND SOUTHERN OCEANS LAW AND POLICY OCCASIONAL PAPERS. (AT/1034-361X). **Adv Mgr:** David McGuire. **3123**

ANTARES LA VALETTE. (FR/0751-7580). **3362**

ANTELOPE VALLEY PRESS. (US/0744-5830). **5633**

ANTENNA. (UK/0140-1890). **5576**

ANTENNE MARSEILLE, L'. (FR/0395-8582). **5377**

ANTHONY

ANTHONY REPUBLICAN AND THE ANTHONY BULLETIN (ANTHONY, KAN. : 1973). (US). **Adv Mgr:** Jim Dunn. **5674**

ANTHOS; GARTEN- UND LANDSCHAFTSGESTALTUNG. (SZ/0003-5424). **2409**

ANTHROPOLGISCHE VERKENNINGEN. (NE). **Adv Mgr:** M. Brandt, **Tel** 2159-49991. **228**

ANTHROPOLOGICA (OTTAWA). (CN/0003-5459). **228**

ANTHROPOLOGICAL FORUM. (AT/0066-4677). **229**

ANTHROPOLOGICAL INDEX TO CURRENT PERIODICALS IN THE LIBRARY OF THE ROYAL ANTHROPOLOGICAL INSTITUTE. (UK/0003-5467). **248**

ANTHROPOLOGICAL LINGUISTICS. (US/0003-5483). **229**

ANTHROPOLOGICAL QUARTERLY. (US/0003-5491). **229**

ANTHROPOLOGIE ET SOCIETES. (CN/0702-8997). **229**

ANTHROPOLOGISCHER ANZEIGER. (GW/0003-5548). **229**

ANTHROPOLOGY & EDUCATION QUARTERLY. (US/0161-7761). **230**

ANTHROPOLOGY AND HUMANISM. (US). **230**

ANTHROPOLOGY AND HUMANISM QUARTERLY. (US/0193-5615). **230**

ANTHROPOLOGY NEWSLETTER. (US/0098-1605). **230**

ANTHROPOLOGY OF WORK REVIEW. (US/0883-024X). **230**

ANTHROPOLOGY TODAY. (UK/0268-540X). **230**

ANTHROPOS (BARCELONA, SPAIN). (SP/0211-5611). **2842**

ANTHROPOS FRIBOURG. (SZ/0257-9774). **230**

ANTHROPOZOOLOGICA PARIS. (FR/0761-3032). **5576**

ANTHROZOOS. (US/0892-7936). **5576**

ANTI. (GR). **Adv Mgr:** Roumpou, **Tel** 01 72 32 819. **4515**

ANTI-CANCER DRUG DESIGN. (UK/0266-9536). **3809**

ANTI-CANCER DRUGS. (UK/0959-4973). **3979**

ANTICANCER RESEARCH. (GR/0250-7005). **3809**

ANTICHITA VIVA. (IT/0003-5645). **337**

ANTICHTHON. (AT/0066-4774). **1074**

ANTIEK. (NE/0003-5653). **337**

ANTIFURTO. (IT/0391-6227). **Adv Mgr:** Roberto Recalcati. **5176**

ANTIGUA & BARBUDA CONSOLIDATED INDEX TO STATUTES AND SUBSIDIARY LEGISLATION TO ... . (BB). **3123**

ANTIMICROBIAL AGENTS AND CHEMOTHERAPY. (US/0066-4804). **559**

ANTINCENDIO (1979). (IT/0393-7089). **Adv Mgr:** Nunzio Rubino. **2288**

ANTIOCH REVIEW, THE. (US/0003-5769). **3337**

ANTIPODAS : JOURNAL OF HISPANIC STUDIES OF THE UNIVERSITY OF AUCKLAND. (NZ/0113-2415). **3362**

ANTIPODES (BROOKLYN, NEW YORK, N.Y.). (US/0893-5580). **Adv Mgr:** M. Arkin. **3362**

ANTIQUA (ARCHEOCLUB D'ITALIA). (IT). **255**

ANTIQUARIAN BOOK MONTHLY. (UK). **Adv Mgr:** Jan Richford, **Tel** same as publisher. **4823**

Advertising Accepted Index

ANTIQUARIAN BOOK MONTHLY REVIEW. (UK/0306-7475). **4823**

ANTIQUARIAN HOROLOGY AND THE PROCEEDINGS OF THE ANTIQUARIAN HOROLOGICAL SOCIETY. (UK/0003-5785). **2916**

ANTIQUE AIRPLANE DIGEST. (US). **12**

ANTIQUE AUTOMOBILE, THE. (US/0003-5831). **5404**

ANTIQUE BOTTLE & GLASS COLLECTOR. (US/8750-1481). **248**

ANTIQUE CAR TIMES. (US/0164-7237). **Adv Mgr:** B. Gardner, **Tel** (901)424-2809. **248**

ANTIQUE COLLECTING. (UK). **249**

ANTIQUE COLLECTOR, THE. (UK/0003-5858). **249**

ANTIQUE GAZETTE. (US). **249**

ANTIQUE MARKET REPORT. (US/8750-9024). **249**

ANTIQUE PHONOGRAPH MONTHLY, THE. (US/0361-2147). **249**

ANTIQUE POWER MAGAZINE. (US/1042-7392). **249**

ANTIQUE REVIEW. (US/0883-833X). **Adv Mgr:** JoAnne Geiger, **Tel** (614)885-9758. **249**

ANTIQUE SHOWCASE. (CN/0713-6315). **249**

ANTIQUE TOY WORLD. (US/0742-0420). **2583**

ANTIQUE TRADER WEEKLY, THE. (US/0161-8342). **249**

ANTIQUES & COLLECTIBLES (GREENVALE, N.Y.). (US/0274-6085). **249**

ANTIQUES & COLLECTING HOBBIES. (US/0884-6294). **249**

ANTIQUES & FINE ART. (US/0886-7208). **249**

ANTIQUES AND THE ARTS WEEKLY. (US). **249**

ANTIQUITY. (UK/0003-598X). **255**

ANTISEPTIC, THE. (II/0003-5998). **3551**

ANTITRUST ADVISOR. (US). **3095**

ANTITRUST BULLETIN. (US/0003-603X). **3095**

ANTIVIRAL AGENTS BULLETIN. (US/0897-9871). **3551**

ANTONIE VAN LEEUWENHOEK. (NE/0003-6072). **559**

ANTROPOLOGICA. (VE/0003-6110). **231**

ANTWERP BEE-ARGUS, THE. (US). **5726**

ANTWERP FACETS. (BE/0777-0626). **2913**

ANUARIO ANTROPOLOGICO. (BL). **231**

ANUARIO DE DERECHO INTERNACIONAL. (SP/0212-0747). **3124**

ANUARIO DE LA NIEVE. (SP). **4883**

ANUARIO DE LA RELOJERIA PARA ESPANA E HISPANOAMERICA. (SP). **2916**

ANUARIO DE LINGUISTICA HISPANICA. (SP/0213-053X). **3266**

ANUARIO DE PSICOLOGIA. (SP). **4574**

ANUARIO DENTAL ESPANOL Y PORTUGUES. (SP). **1316**

ANUARIO ESPANOL DE JOYERIA Y RELOJERIA. (SP). **2913**

ANUARIO ESPANOL DE LAS ARTES GRAFICAS. (SP). **4563**

ANUARIO ESPANOL DE PARA-FARMACIA. (SP). **4292**

ANUARIO ESPANOL DE SEGUROS. (SP/0211-125X). **891**

ANUARIO ESPANOL Y PORTUGUES DE ANALITICA. (SP). **3551**

ANUARIO ESPANOL Y PORTUGUES DE OPTICA Y AUDIOMETRIA. (SP). **4215**

ANUARIO FINANCIERO DE MEXICO. (MX). **772**

ANUARIO IEHS. (AG/0326-9671). **2721**

ANUARIO JURIDICO. (MX/0185-3295). **2935**

ANUNCIOS MADRID. (SP/0214-4905). **921**

ANVIL (NOTTINGHAM, NOTTINGHAMSHIRE). (UK). **4935**

ANVIL'S RING, THE. (US/0889-177X). **3998**

ANZEIGER DER ORNITHOLOGISCHE GESELLSCHAFT IN BAYERN. (GW/0030-5715). **5614**

ANZEIGER FUER SCHADLINGSKUNDE, PFLANZENSCHUTZ, UMWELTSCHUTZ. (GW/0340-7330). **4244**

ANZEIGER FUER SLAVISCHE PHILOLOGIE. (AU/0066-5282). **3266**

AOPA PILOT, THE. (US/0001-2084). **12**

AORN JOURNAL. (US/0001-2092). **3851**

AOSTRA JOURNAL OF RESEARCH. (CN). **4250**

APA MEMBERSHIP REGISTER. (US/0737-1446). **4574**

APA MONITOR. (US/0001-2114). **4574**

APA NEWSLETTERS ON THE BLACK EXPERIENCE, COMPUTER USE, FEMINISM, LAW, MEDICINE, TEACHING. (US/1067-9464). **Adv Mgr:** Diana Walls, **Tel** (302)831-1112. **4341**

APAGAY (MONTREAL). (CN/0382-9251). **5780**

APALACHEE QUARTERLY, THE. (US/0890-6408). **3362**

APARTMENT AGE. (US/0192-0030). **2815**

APARTMENT MANAGEMENT NEWSLETTER. (US/0744-9143). **4834**

APCA DIRECTORY AND RESOURCE BOOK. (US/0094-9191). **2224**

APCO BULLETIN, THE. (US/0001-2165). **4767**

APEA JOURNAL, THE. (AT/0084-7534). **4250**

APEIRON (CLAYTON). (CN/0003-6390). **1074**

APERTURE (MILLERTON, N.Y.). (US/0003-6420). **4366**

APEX (BRUSSELS). (BE/0773-5251). **5576**

APHA NEWSLETTER : A PUBLICATION OF THE AMERICAN PRINTING HISTORY ASSOCIATION, THE. (US). **4563**

APIACTA. (RM/0003-6455). **62**

APICOLTORE MODERNO, L'. (IT/0518-1259). **5605**

APICULTURAL ABSTRACTS. (UK/0003-648X). **5604**

APIS, THE. (US/0887-7386). **226**

APLA BULLETIN. (CN/0001-2203). **3191**

APLUS. (BE). **288**

APMA NEWS. (US/8750-2585). **3917**

APOCALYPSE. (US). **4857**

APOLLO (LONDON. 1925). (UK/0003-6536). **337**

APORTES. (CR). **2511**

APOTHEKENHELFERIN, DIE. (GW). **4292**

APOTHEKER-JAHRBUCH. (GW/0066-5347). **4292**

APOTHEKER-ZEITUNG STUTTGART. (GW/0178-4862). **4292**

APPALACHIA (BOSTON). (US/0003-6587). **4869**

APPALACHIAN FAMILIES. (US/1041-8466). **2437**

APPALOOSA JOURNAL. (US/0892-385X). **Adv Mgr:** Gretchen Naccarato. **2797**

APPAREL. (NZ). **1081**

APPAREL INDUSTRY MAGAZINE. (US/0192-1878). **1081**

APPAREL INTERNATIONAL. (UK/0263-1008). **1081**

APPAREL NEWS SOUTH. (US/0744-6403). **1081**

APPAREL (SAINTE-ANNE-DE-BELLEVUE). (CN/1196-2283). **Adv Mgr:** Lumina Fillion. **1081**

APPLAUSE THEATRE BOOK REVIEW & CATALOG, THE. (US). **383**

APPLE-WORKS FORUM. (US/0893-4118). **1171**

APPLESEED QUARTERLY. (CN/1183-3785). **3363**

APPLEWOOD TRANSCRIPT. (US). **Adv Mgr:** John Tracy. **5641**

APPLIANCE. (US/0003-6781). **2810**

APPLIANCE MANUFACTURER. (US/0003-679X). **2810**

APPLIANCE SERVICE NEWS. (US/0003-6803). **2810**

APPLICABLE ANALYSIS. (US/0003-6811). **3494**

APPLICANDO. (IT). **1171**

APPLICATION OF COMPUTERS AND OPERATIONS RESEARCH IN THE MINERAL INDUSTRY / SPONSORED BY COLORADO SCHOOL OF MINES. (US/0741-0603). **1171**

APPLICATOR, THE. (US). **Adv Mgr:** Jan Burchett. **599**

APPLIED ACOUSTICS. (UK/0003-682X). **2097**

APPLIED AND ENVIRONMENTAL MICROBIOLOGY. (US/0099-2240). **559**

APPLIED ARTIFICIAL INTELLIGENCE. (US/0883-9514). **1211**

APPLIED ARTS MAGAZINE. (CN). **Adv Mgr:** Brian Patterson. **376**

APPLIED BIOCHEMISTRY AND BIOTECHNOLOGY. (US). **3685**

APPLIED COGNITIVE PSYCHOLOGY. (UK/0888-4080). **4574**

APPLIED CYTOGENETICS. (US/1056-5191). **Adv Mgr:** Leslee, **Tel** (913)541-9077. **542**

APPLIED ECONOMICS. (UK/0003-6846). **1463**

APPLIED ENERGY. (UK/0306-2619). **1932**

APPLIED ERGONOMICS. (UK/0003-6870). **1965**

APPLIED GENETICS NEWS. (US/0271-7107). **542**

APPLIED GEOGRAPHY (SEVENOAKS). (UK/0143-6228). **2554**

APPLIED HEALTH PHYSICS ABSTRACTS AND NOTES. (UK/0305-7615). **4433**

APPLIED HYDROGEOLOGY: INTERNATIONAL JOURNAL FOR HYDROGEOLOGISTS. (GW). **1366**

APPLIED LINGUISTICS. (UK/0142-6001). **3266**

APPLIED MAGNETIC RESONANCE. (RU/0937-9347). **4397**

APPLIED MANAGEMENT NEWSLETTER. (US/0889-8227). **Adv Mgr:** Eric J. Steele. **938**

APPLIED MATHEMATICAL MODELLING. (UK/0307-904X). **3495**

APPLIED MATHEMATICS AND COMPUTATION. (US/0096-3003). **3495**

APPLIED MICROBIOLOGY AND BIOTECHNOLOGY. (GW/0175-7598). **559**

APPLIED MICROWAVE & WIRELESS. (US/1075-0207). **4433**

APPLIED MICROWAVE MAGAZINE. (US/1061-3528). **4433**

APPLIED OCCUPATIONAL AND ENVIRONMENTAL HYGIENE. (US/1047-322X). **2859**

APPLIED OCEAN RESEARCH. (UK/0141-1187). **1446**

APPLIED ORGANOMETALLIC CHEMISTRY. (UK/0268-2605). **961**

APPLIED PHYSICS. A, SOLIDS AND SURFACES. (GW/0721-7250). **4397**

APPLIED PHYSICS. B, PHOTOPHYSICS AND LASER CHEMISTRY. (GW/0721-7269). **4433**

APPLIED PSYCHOLOGICAL MEASUREMENT. (US/0146-6216). **4574**

APPLIED PSYCHOLOGY. (UK/0269-994X). **4574**

APPLIED RADIOLOGY (1976). (US/0160-9963). **3939**

APPLIED SPECTROSCOPY. (US/0003-7028). **4433**

APPLIED SPECTROSCOPY REVIEWS (SOFTCOVER ED.). (US/0570-4928). **1013**

APPLIED STATISTICS. (UK/0035-9254). **5322**

APPRAISAL REVIEW & MORTGAGE UNDERWRITING JOURNAL. (US/1041-1585). **Adv Mgr:** Editor. **4834**

APPRAISERS' INFORMATION EXCHANGE, THE. (US/8755-4348). **4834**

APPRENTICE (OTTAWA). (CN/0706-7399). **4857**

APPROPRIATE TECHNOLOGY. (UK/0305-0920). **5085**

APPUNTI DEL CIRCOLO CULTURALE G GHISLANDI. (IT). **3337**

APRES-DEMAIN. (FR/0003-7176). **4464**

APS OBSERVER. (US/1050-4672). **4575**

APSA DEPARTMENTAL SERVICES PROGRAM, SURVEY OF DEPARTMENTS. (US/0094-7954). **4464**

APSA DIRECTORY OF DEPARTMENT CHAIRPERSONS. (US/0196-5255). **4464**

APSA DIRECTORY OF MEMBERS - AMERICAN POLITICAL SCIENCE ASSOCIATION. (US). **4464**

APUNTES. (CL). **3363**

APUNTES PASTORALES. (CR). **Adv Mgr:** Randall M. Wittig, **Tel** 853919. **4935**

AQUA (LONDON). (UK/0003-7214). **5530**

AQUACULTURAL ENGINEERING. (UK/0144-8609). **2295**

AQUACULTURE EUROPE. (BE). **552**

AQUACULTURE IRELAND. (IE/0790-0929). **2295**

AQUACULTURE MAGAZINE. (US/0199-1388). **2295**

AQUACULTURE MAGAZINE. BUYER'S GUIDE ... AND INDUSTRY DIRECTORY. (US/0898-9540). **2296**

AQUACULTURE NEWS. (US). **Adv Mgr:** David Ryan. **2296**

AQUALINE ABSTRACTS. (UK/0263-5534). **2002**

AQUARAMA. (FR/0151-6981). **Adv Mgr:** A. Saegel. **4285**

AQUARIUM. (US). **Adv Mgr:** Mary Gries, **Tel** (503)588-1815. **553**

AQUATIC INSECTS. (NE/0165-0424). **5605**

AQUATIC LIVING RESOURCES (MONTROUGE). (FR/0990-7440). **2296**

AQUATICS INTERNATIONAL. (US/1058-7039). **4883**

AQUELARRE (VANCOUVER). (CN/0843-7920). **Adv Mgr:** Miram, **Tel** (604)251-6678. **5551**

AQUI MAGAZINE. (US). **2484**

AQUILON (YELLOWKNIFE). (CN/0834-1443). **3266**

ARAB AMERICAN ALMANAC. (US/0742-9576). **2721**

ARAB GULF JOURNAL OF SCIENTIFIC RESEARCH. (SU/1015-4442). **5085**

ARAB NEWS. (SU/0254-833X). **5809**

ARAB OIL & GAS DIRECTORY. (FR/0304-8551). **4250**

ARAB STUDIES QUARTERLY. (US/0271-3519). **2645**

ARAB TRIBUNE, THE. (US). **5625**

ARABESQUE (NEW YORK, N.Y.). (US/0148-5865). **4100**

ARABIAN COMPUTER NEWS. (UK/0950-5075). **1235**

ARABIAN HORSE EXPRESS. (US/0194-6803). **Adv Mgr:** Tammy Gomez, **Tel** 1-800-533-9734. **2797**

ARABIAN HORSE TIMES, THE. (US/0279-8425). **2797**

ARABIAN HORSE WORLD. (US/0003-7494). **2797**

ARABIAN JOURNAL FOR SCIENCE AND ENGINEERING. (UK/0377-9211). **5085**

ARABIAN SYSTEMS GUIDE. (UK). **Adv Mgr:** Damon Thomson, **Tel** 44 462 420 205. **1171**

ARABIC SCIENCES AND PHILOSOPHY : A HISTORICAL JOURNAL. (UK/0957-4239). **5085**

ARABICA. (NE/0570-5398). **2767**

ARABIDOPSIS INFORMATION SERVICE. (GW/0066-5657). **500**

ARABLE FARMING. (UK/0269-6797). **62**

ARACHNOLOGIA : BULLETIN D'INFORMATION ET DE LIAISON DU CENTRE INTERNATIONAL DE DOCUMENTATION ARACHNOLOGIQUE. (FR/0763-1901). **5576**

ARARAT (NEW YORK). (US/0003-7583). **3363**

ARBEIDERVERN. (NO/0332-7124). **2859**

ARBEIT UND BERUF. (GW). **4630**

ARBEITEN ZUR GESCHICHTE DES PIETISMUS. (GW). **4935**

ARBEITEN ZUR KIRCHLICHEN ZEITGESCHICHTE. REIHE B: DARSTELLUNGEN. (GW). **4935**

ARBEITNEHMER. (GW). **1651**

ARBEITS- UND SOZIALSTATISTIK. (GW). **1529**

ARBEITS- UND SOZIALSTATISTIK. HAUPTERGEBNISSE / DER BUNDESMINISTER FUR ARBEIT UND SOZIALORDNUNG. (GW/0341-7840). **1651**

ARBEITS- UND SOZIALSTATISTIKEN. (GW). **1529**

ARBEITSBLATTER FUER RESTAURATOREN. (GW/0066-5738). **256**

ARBEITSMEDIZIN, SOZIALMEDIZIN, PRAVENTIVMEDIZIN. (GW/0300-581X). **2859**

ARBEITSRECHT DER GEGENWART, DAS. (GW/0066-586X). **3144**

ARBEITSSCHUTZ, ARBEITSHYGIENE. (GW/0138-1555). **2859**

ARBETARHISTORIA : MEDDELANDE FRAN ARBETARRORELSENS ARKIV OCH BIBLIOTEK. (SW/0281-7446). **Adv Mgr:** Lars Wessman, **Tel** 46 8 4546500. **1651**

ARBITRATION IN THE SCHOOLS. (US/0003-7885). **1726**

ARBITRATOR BARTON. (AT/0729-7904). **2936**

ARBITRIUM : ZEITSCHRIFT FUER REZENSIONEN ZUR GERMANISTISCHEN LITERATURWISSENSCHAFT. (GW). **3337**

ARBOR AGE. (US/0279-0106). **2375**

ARBORICULTURAL JOURNAL, THE. (UK/0307-1375). **2375**

ARBORICULTURE FRUITIERE, L'. (FR/0003-794X). **163**

ARC (MONTREAL). (CN/0229-2807). **5055**

ARC NEWS (REDLANDS, CALIF.). (US/1064-6108). **Adv Mgr:** Karen Hunter. **1284**

ARC TODAY, THE. (US). **5273**

ARCADE HERALD. (US/0746-102X). **Adv Mgr:** Amy Gordon. **5713**

ARCADE (SEATTLE, WASH.). (US). **288**

ARCADIA. (GW/0003-7982). **3363**

ARCADIA BIBLIOGRAPHICA VIRORUM ERUDITORUM. (GW/0195-7163). **407**

ARCHAEOASTRONOMY. (UK/0142-7253). **256**

ARCHAEOASTRONOMY (COLLEGE PARK). (US/0190-9940). **256**

ARCHAEOLOGIA, OR MISCELLANEOUS TRACTS RELATING TO ANTIQUITY. (UK/0261-3409). **256**

ARCHAEOLOGIA ZAMBIANA. (ZA). **256**

ARCHAEOLOGICAL COMPUTING NEWSLETTER. (UK/0952-3332). **256**

ARCHAEOLOGICAL NEWS. (US/0194-3413). **257**

ARCHAEOLOGICAL SERIES (TUCSON). (US/0196-5409). **257**

ARCHAEOLOGISCHE MITTEILUNGEN AUS IRAN. (US/0066-6033). **257**

ARCHAEOLOGY. (US/0003-8113). **257**

ARCHAEOLOGY IN OCEANIA. (AT/0728-4896). **Adv Mgr:** D. Koller, **Tel** (02)692-2666. **257**

ARCHAEOMETRY. (UK/0003-813X). **257**

ARCHAIOLOGIA. (GR). **258**

ARCHAOLOGIE DER SCHWEIZ. (SZ). **258**

ARCHAOLOGISCHE FORSCHUNGEN. (GW). **258**

ARCHBOLD BUCKEYE. (US). **Adv Mgr:** Mary Huber. **5726**

ARCHE (1957). (FR/0518-2840). **Adv Mgr:** Y Level, **Tel** 46228055. **5046**

ARCHEION : THE NEWSLETTER OF THE STATE ARCHIVES. (AT/0812-6755). **Adv Mgr:** Martyn Killion, **Tel** 011 2 2370126. **2479**

ARCHEOMATERIALS. (US/0891-2920). **259**

ARCHERY ACTION WITH OUTDOOR CONNECTIONS. (AT/1037-6720). **Adv Mgr:** Jo Whitmore, **Tel** 07 2644910. **4884**

ARCHIE AT RIVERDALE HIGH. (US/0746-8660). **4857**

ARCHIE (NEW YORK, N.Y.). (US/0735-6455). **4857**

ARCHIE'S PALS 'N GALS. (US/0745-7774). **4857**

ARCHIFACTS. (NZ/0303-7940). **2479**

ARCHIMAG VINCENNES. (FR/0769-0975). **2479**

ARCHIMEDE. (IT/0003-8369). **3495**

ARCHIPELAG : A. (GW). **4540**

ARCHITECT. (NE/0044-8621). **288**

ARCHITECT & SURVEYOR. (UK/0308-8596). **288**

ARCHITECT DESIGNED HOUSES. (AT/1034-4101). **Adv Mgr:** Carolyn Winton. **288**

ARCHITECT, W.A. : THE OFFICIAL JOURNAL OF THE ROYAL AUSTRALIAN INSTITUTE OF ARCHITECTS, W.A. CHAPTER, THE. (AT/0003-8393). **Adv Mgr:** Brian Wart, **Tel** (09)321-1960. **288**

ARCHITECTI. (PO). **288**

ARCHITECTS' EMPLOYMENT CLEARINGHOUSE. (US). **288**

ARCHITECTS INDIA. (II/0970-6852). **288**

ARCHITECTS' JOURNAL (LONDON). (UK/0003-8466). **288**

ARCHITECTS TRADE JOURNAL. (II/0304-8594). **288**

ARCHITECTURAL DESIGN. (UK/0003-8504). **288**

ARCHITECTURAL DESIGNS. (US/0747-5179). **289**

ARCHITECTURAL LIGHTING. (US/0894-0436). **289**

ARCHITECTURAL MONOGRAPHS. (UK/0141-2191). **289**

ARCHITECTURAL RECORD. (US/0003-858X). **289**

ARCHITECTURAL SCIENCE REVIEW. (AT/0003-8628). **289**

ARCHITECTURE & COMPORTEMENT. (SZ/0379-8585). **289**

ARCHITECTURE AUSTRALIA. (AT/0003-8725). **289**

ARCHITECTURE CONCEPT. (CN/0003-8687). **290**

ARCHITECTURE D'AUJOURD'HUI, L'. (BE/0003-8695). **290**

ARCHITECTURE MINNESOTA. (US/0149-9106). **Adv Mgr:** J. VanDyne, **Tel** (612)338-6763. **290**

ARCHITECTURE NEW JERSEY. (US/0003-8733). **290**

ARCHITECTURE NEW ZEALAND. (NZ/0113-4566). **290**

ARCHITECTURE SA. (SA/0250-054X). **290**

ARCHITECTURE TODAY. (UK/0958-6407). **Adv Mgr:** S. Peters. **290**

ARCHITECTUUR, BONWEN. (NE/0169-4421). **290**

ARCHITEKT (STUTTGART), DER. (GW/0003-875X). **290**

ARCHITEKTONIKA THEMATA. (GR/0066-6262). **290**

ARCHITEKTUR

Advertising Accepted Index

ARCHITEKTUR AKTUELL FACH-JOURNAL. (AU/0570-6602). **290**

ARCHITEKTUR WETTBEWERBE. (GW/0341-2784). **291**

ARCHITEKTURA A URBANIZMUS. (XO/0044-8680). **291**

ARCHITETTURA, STORIA E DOCUMENTI : RIVISTA SEMESTRALE DI STORIA DELL'ARCHITETTURA DEL CENTRO DI STUDI STORICO-ARCHIVISTICI PER LA STORIA DELL'ARTE E DELL'ARCHITETTURA MEDIOEVALE E MODERNA. (IT). **291**

ARCHIV DES OFFENTLICHEN RECHTS. (GW/0003-8911). **3092**

ARCHIV DES VOLKERRECHTS. (GW/0003-892X). **3124**

ARCHIV FUER DIE CIVILISTISCHE PRAXIS. (GW/0003-8997). **3088**

ARCHIV FUER FISCHEREIWISSENSCHAFT. (GW/0003-9063). **2296**

ARCHIV FUER HYDROBIOLOGIE. (GW/0003-9136). **5530**

ARCHIV FUER HYDROBIOLOGIE. SUPPLEMENTBAND, ALGOLOGICAL STUDIES. (GW/0342-1120). **442**

ARCHIV FUER KOMMUNALWISSENSCHAFTEN. (GW/0003-9209). **4630**

ARCHIV FUER KRIMINOLOGIE. (GW/0003-9225). **3158**

ARCHIV FUER MUSIKWISSENSCHAFT. (GW/0003-9292). **4100**

ARCHIV FUER MUSIKWISSENSCHAFT. BEIHEFTE. (GW). **4100**

ARCHIV FUER PROTISTENKUNDE. (GW/0003-9365). **5576**

ARCHIV FUER RECHTS- UND SOZIALPHILOSOPHIE. (GW/0001-2343). **2936**

ARCHIV FUER VOLKERKUNDE. (AU/0066-6513). **231**

ARCHIV FUR DAS STUDIUM DER NEUEREN SPRACHEN UND LITERATUREN (1961). (GW/0003-8970). **3266**

ARCHIV FUER SIPPENFORSCHUNG UND ALLE VERWANDTEN GEBIETE. (GW/0003-9403). **2437**

ARCHIVAL INFORMER, THE. (US/8756-9663). **2479**

ARCHIVAR, DER. (GW/0003-9500). **2479**

ARCHIVES AND MANUSCRIPTS. (AT/0157-6895). **2479**

ARCHIVES D'ANATOMIE ET DE CYTOLOGIE PATHOLOGIQUES. (FR/0395-501X). **3678**

ARCHIVES DE L'ART FRANCAIS. (FR). **337**

ARCHIVES DE L'INSTITUT PASTEUR DE MADAGASCAR. (MG/0020-2495). **3666**

ARCHIVES DE PHILOSOPHIE. (FR/0003-9632). **4341**

ARCHIVES DES MALADIES DU COEUR ET DES VAISSEAUX. (FR/0003-9683). **3699**

ARCHIVES FRANCAISES DE PEDIATRIE. (FR/0003-9764). **3900**

ARCHIVES INFORMATION CIRCULAR. (US/0093-9056). **2479**

ARCHIVES (LONDON). (UK/0003-9535). **2479**

ARCHIVES OF ANDROLOGY. (UK/0148-5016). **3678**

ARCHIVES OF COMPLEX ENVIRONMENTAL STUDIES : ACES. (FI/0787-0396). **2161**

ARCHIVES OF DERMATOLOGY. (US/0003-987X). **3718**

ARCHIVES OF ENVIRONMENTAL HEALTH. (US/0003-9896). **4767**

ARCHIVES OF FAMILY MEDICINE. (US/1063-3987). **3736**

ARCHIVES OF GENERAL PSYCHIATRY. (US/0003-990X). **3921**

ARCHIVES OF GYNECOLOGY AND OBSTETRICS. (GW/0932-0067). **3757**

ARCHIVES OF HISTOLOGY AND CYTOLOGY. (JA/0914-9465). **532**

ARCHIVES OF INTERNAL MEDICINE (1960). (US/0003-9926). **3795**

ARCHIVES OF NATURAL HISTORY. (UK/0260-9541). **4162**

ARCHIVES OF NEUROLOGY (CHICAGO). (US/0003-9942). **3827**

ARCHIVES OF OPHTHALMOLOGY. (US/0003-9950). **3872**

ARCHIVES OF ORAL BIOLOGY. (UK/0003-9969). **1316**

ARCHIVES OF OTOLARYNGOLOGY-HEAD & NECK SURGERY. (US/0886-4470). **3886**

ARCHIVES OF PATHOLOGY & LABORATORY MEDICINE. (US/0003-9985). **3893**

ARCHIVES OF PHYSICAL MEDICINE AND REHABILITATION. (US/0003-9993). **4379**

ARCHIVES OF PSYCHIATRIC NURSING. (US/0883-9417). **3851**

ARCHIVES OF SURGERY (CHICAGO. 1960). (US/0004-0010). **3959**

ARCHIVES OF THE FOUNDATION OF THANATOLOGY (1976). (US/0160-7081). **4341**

ARCHIVI & COMPUTER. (IT/1121-2462). **Adv Mgr:** Cerri Roberto. **1171**

ARCHIVIO DI ORTOPEDIA E REUMATOLOGIA. (IT/0390-7368). **3803**

ARCHIVIO GLOTTOLOGICO ITALIANO. (IT/0004-0207). **3266**

ARCHIVIO ITALIANO DI ANATOMIA E DI EMBRIOLOGIA. (IT/0004-0223). **3678**

ARCHIVIO PER L'ANTROPOLOGIA E LA ETNOLOGIA. (IT/0373-3009). **231**

ARCHIVIO PUTTI DI CHIRURGIA DEGLI ORGANI DI MOVIMENTO. (IT/0066-670X). **3960**

ARCHIVIO SICILIANO DE MEDICINA E CHIRURGIA. 4. ACTA MEDICA MEDITERRANEA. (IT/0393-6384). **3960**

ARCHIVIO SICILIANO DI MEDICINA E CHIRURGIA. 1. ACTA CHIRURGICA MEDITERRANEA. (IT). **3960**

ARCHIVIO SICILIANO DI MEDICINA E CHIRURGIA. 5. ACTA PEDIATRICA MEDITERRANEA. (IT/0393-6392). **3900**

ARCHIVOS DE BIOLOGIA Y MEDICINA EXPERIMENTALES. (CL/0004-0533). **442**

ARCHIVOS DE BRONCONEUMOLOGIA. (SP/0300-2896). **3948**

ARCHIVOS DE FARMACOLOGIA Y TOXICOLOGIA. (SP/0304-8616). **4292**

ARCHIVOS DE MEDICINA DEL DEPORTE : PUBLICACION DE LA FEDERACION ESPANOLA DE MEDICINA DEL DEPORTE / FEMEDE. (SP/0212-8799). **Adv Mgr:** John Ajuria. **3953**

ARCHIVOS DE NEUROBIOLOGIA. (SP/0004-0576). **3827**

ARCHIVOS DE OFTALMOLOGIA DE BUENOS AIRES. (AG/0066-6777). **3872**

ARCHIVOS DEL INSTITUTO DE CARDIOLOGIA DE MEXICO. (MX/0020-3785). **3699**

ARCHIVOS ESPANOLES DE UROLOGIA. (SP/0004-0614). **Adv Mgr Tel** 34 1 319 6001. **3988**

ARCHIVOS LATINOAMERICANOS DE NUTRICION. (VE/0004-0622). **4187**

ARCHTYPE (TORONTO). (CN/0712-1873). **Adv Mgr:** Lynda Nancoo, **Tel** (416)482-8255. **4383**

ARCO ADVERTISER, THE. (US/0890-1511). **Adv Mgr:** Tom Cammack. **5656**

ARCTIC AND ALPINE RESEARCH. (US/0004-0851). **2555**

ARCTIC ANTHROPOLOGY. (US/0066-6939). **Adv Mgr Tel** (608)262-5839. **231**

ARCTIC MEDICAL RESEARCH. (FI/0782-226X). **3552**

ARCTIC SOUNDER, THE. (US/0897-9502). **Adv Mgr:** Doris Anderson, **Tel** (907)442-2716. **5628**

AREA (LONDON 1969). (UK/0004-0894). **2555**

AREA (MILAN, ITALY). (IT/0394-0055). **Adv Mgr:** Givsi Brivio. **291**

AREA NEWS, THE. (US). **5658**

AREE. ANNUAL REVIEW OF ENVIRONMENTAL EDUCATION. (UK/0953-0428). **2161**

AREITO. (US/0360-0467). **2255**

ARENA. (AT/0004-0932). **4464**

ARENA JOURNAL. (AT). **Adv Mgr:** G. Rundle. **4540**

ARENA MAGAZINE. (AT/1039-1010). **Adv Mgr:** G. Rundle. **4540**

ARFFAS VIEWPOINT. (AT). **4035**

ARGOMENTI DI CARDIOLOGIA. (IT/1120-8635). **3699**

ARGOS. (AG). **3266**

ARGUMENT, DAS. (GW/0004-1157). **4341**

ARGUMENTATION AND ADVOCACY. (US/1051-1431). **Adv Mgr Tel** (800)228-5424. **1104**

ARGUMENTS & FACTS INTERNATIONAL. (UK/0957-0020). **639**

ARGUS-CHAMPION, THE. (US). **Adv Mgr:** Robert Shemphe. **5708**

ARGUS (MICROFICHE). (SA). **5810**

ARGUS (MONTREAL). (CN/0315-9930). **3191**

ARGUS (SAN FRANCISCO). (US/0194-8172). **3872**

ARHIV ZA HIGIJENU RADA I TOKSIKOLOGIJU. (CR/0004-1254). **Adv Mgr Tel** 38 41 434188 Ext. 56. **2859**

ARIEL. (CN/0004-1327). **3363**

ARIEL (ENGLISH EDITION). (IS/0004-1343). **3363**

ARION / BOSTON UNIVERSITY. (US). **Adv Mgr:** Julie Seeger. **3363**

ARISTOS. (US/0737-0407). **313**

ARISTOTELES WERKE. (GW). **4341**

ARITHMETIC TEACHER, THE. (US/0004-136X). **3496**

ARIZONA ATTORNEY. (US/1040-4090). **2936**

ARIZONA BAPTIST BEACON (ARIZONA SOUTHERN BAPTIST CONVENTION). (US/1044-0186). **4936**

ARIZONA BEVERAGE ANALYST. (US/0164-6281). **2363**

ARIZONA BEVERAGE GUIDE. (US/0746-1151). **2363**

ARIZONA BUSINESS GAZETTE. (US/0273-6950). **639**

ARIZONA CAPITOL TIMES. (US/0744-7477). **Adv Mgr:** Kathy Borders, **Tel** (602)258-7026. **4630**

ARIZONA CATTLELOG (1985). (US/8750-8281). **206**

ARIZONA GREAT OUTDOORS. (US/1069-0298). **4869**

ARIZONA GROCER. (US/0004-1505). **2327**

ARIZONA HUNTER & ANGLER. (US/0888-840X). **Adv Mgr:** Tom Stiles. **4884**

ARIZONA JOURNAL OF INTERNATIONAL AND COMPARATIVE LAW. (US/0743-6963). **3124**

ARIZONA LIVING. (US/0279-6376). **2528**

ARIZONA MOBILE CITIZEN. (US/0004-1564). **2815**

ARIZONA MUSIC NEWS. (US/0518-6129). **4101**

ARIZONA NURSE. (US/0004-1599). **3851**

ARIZONA PHARMACIST, THE. (US/0004-1602). **4292**

ARIZONA PORTFOLIO, THE. (US/0882-4932). **337**

ARIZONA QUARTERLY, THE. (US/0004-1610). **3363**

ARIZONA REALTOR DIGEST. (US/0199-9206). **4834**

ARIZONA REPUBLIC. (US/0892-8711). **5629**

ARIZONA SENIOR WORLD, THE. (US/0270-0425). **Adv Mgr:** Jamie Hastings. **5629**

ARIZONA SILVER BELT. (US). **5629**

ARIZONA STATE LAW JOURNAL. (US/0164-4297). **2937**

ARIZONA THOROUGHBRED, THE. (US/0091-4401). **2797**

ARIZONA TREND AZ. (US/1046-476X). **2528**

ARK. (UK). **226**

ARKANSAS BANKER, THE. (US/0004-1726). **773**

ARKANSAS BAPTIST (1987). (US/1040-6506). **Adv Mgr:** Nelle O'Bryan. **5055**

ARKANSAS BUSINESS. (US/1053-6582). **Adv Mgr:** Karen Raley, **Tel** (501)372-1443. **639**

ARKANSAS CATTLE BUSINESS. (US/0004-1750). **Adv Mgr Tel** (501)224-2114. **206**

ARKANSAS CITY TRAVELER (ARKANSAS CITY, KAN. : 1970). (US/0888-8485). **5674**

ARKANSAS DENTISTRY. (US/1056-4764). **1316**

ARKANSAS EDUCATOR. (US/0161-7753). **1888**

ARKANSAS GROCER. (US/0004-1815). **2327**

ARKANSAS HISTORICAL QUARTERLY, THE. (US/0004-1823). **2721**

ARKANSAS LAWYER. (US/0571-0502). **2937**

ARKANSAS LIBRARIES. (US/0004-184X). **3191**

ARKANSAS NURSING NEWS. (US). **3851**

ARKANSAS PRESERVATION. (US). **2187**

ARKANSAS STATE DIRECTORY. (US). **4630**

ARKANSAS VALLEY JOURNAL. (US/0004-1890). **63**

ARKITEKTEN. (DK/0004-198X). **291**

ARKITEKTUR DK. (DK/0004-2013). **292**

ARKKITEHTI. (FI/0004-2129). **292**

ARL ANNUAL SALARY SURVEY. (US/0361-5669). **1654**

ARLINGTON CATHOLIC HERALD. (US/0361-3712). **5024**

ARLIS/NA UPDATE. (US/0743-040X). **3192**

ARMADA INTERNATIONAL. (SZ/0252-9793). **4035**

ARMADA TIMES. (US/0890-3751). **Adv Mgr:** Jim Misener, **Tel** (810)784-5551. **5691**

ARMCHAIR DETECTIVE, THE. (US/0004-217X). **3363**

ARMED FORCES. (SA). **4035**

ARMED FORCES AND SOCIETY. (US/0095-327X). **4035**

ARMED FORCES COMPTROLLER, THE. (US/0004-2188). **Adv Mgr:** C. Meek, **Tel** (703)998-4000. **4035**

ARMEES D'AUJOURD'HUI. (FR). **4036**

ARMEMENT. (FR). **4036**

ARMENIAN MIRROR-SPECTATOR, THE. (US/0004-234X). **5687**

ARMENIAN REVIEW, THE. (US/0004-2366). **2501**

ARMENIAN WEEKLY, THE. (US/0004-2374). **5687**

ARMOUR CHRONICLE, THE. (US/8750-2488). **5743**

ARMS COLLECTING. (CN/0380-982X). **2771**

ARMS CONTROL, DISARMAMENT AND INTERNATIONAL SECURITY. (US/0899-6547). **4036**

ARMS CONTROL (LONDON, ENGLAND). (UK/0144-0381). **Adv Mgr:** Anne Kidson. **4036**

ARMS CONTROL TODAY. (US/0196-125X). **Adv Mgr:** Tom Pfieffer. **3124**

ARMSTRONG CHRONICLES. (US/0898-1329). **2438**

ARMSTRONG OIL DIRECTORIES, LOUISIANA, TEXAS GULF COAST, EAST TEXAS, ARK. AND MISS. (US/0273-4931). **4251**

ARMSTRONG OIL DIRECTORIES, ROCKY MOUNTAIN AND CENTRAL UNITED STATES. (US/0273-5229). **4251**

ARMSTRONG OIL DIRECTORIES, TEXAS AND SOUTHEASTERN NEW MEXICO. (US/0277-2280). **4251**

ARMY AVIATION. (US/0004-248X). **12**

ARMY MEDICAL SERVICES MAGAZINE. (UK). **3552**

ARMY MOTORS. (US/0195-5632). **Adv Mgr Tel** (816)737-5111. **4036**

ARMY/NAVY STORE & OUTDOOR MERCHANDISER. (US/0160-7278). **1081**

ARMY QUARTERLY AND DEFENCE JOURNAL, THE. (UK/0004-2552). **4036**

ARMY TIMES. (US/0004-2595). **4037**

AROIDEANA. (US/0197-4033). **2409**

ARQ : ARCHITECTURE/QUEBEC. (CN/0710-1163). **292**

ARQUITECTURA VIVA. (SP/0214-1256). **292**

ARQUITETURA DO BRASIL : AB. (BL). **292**

ARQUIVOS BRASILEIROS DE CARDIOLOGIA. (BL/0066-782X). **3699**

ARQUIVOS DE GASTROENTEROLOGIA. (BL/0004-2803). **Adv Mgr:** Jarbas Antonio de Godoy. **3743**

ARQUIVOS DE NEURO-PSIQUIATRIA. (BL/0004-282X). **Adv Mgr:** Marilia L. Spina Franca. **3827**

ARS CERAMICA. (US/1043-3317). **2586**

ARS MEDICI, MONATSSCHRIFT FUER ALLGEMEINMEDIZIN. (SZ/0004-2897). **3552**

ARS NOVA. (SA). **4101**

ARSC JOURNAL. (US). **Adv Mgr:** Gary Thalheimer. **5315**

ARSREDOVISNING / NOBELSTIFTELSEN. (SW). **3144**

ART & ANTIQUES. (US/0195-8208). **337**

ART & AUCTION (NEW YORK, N.Y.). (US/0197-1093). **250**

ART AND AUSTRALIA. (AT/0004-301X). **338**

ART & CRAFT. (UK). **370**

ART & CRAFTS CATALYST. (US). **370**

ART & DESIGN / ARCHITECTURAL DESIGN PUBLICATIONS. (UK/0267-3991). **338**

ART & DESIGN NEWS. (US/1055-2286). **Adv Mgr:** Jeanne Pulliam. **376**

ART AND POETRY TODAY. (II). **338**

ART & TEXT. (AT/0727-1182). **338**

ART AT AUCTION IN AMERICA. (US/1046-4999). **338**

ART BUSINESS NEWS. (US/0273-5652). **338**

ART BUYER'S HANDBOOK. (GW/0932-3333). **338**

ART CALENDAR (GREAT FALLS, VA.). (US/0893-3901). **338**

ART CULINAIRE (ATLANTA, GA.). (US/0892-1024). **2788**

ART, DESIGN, ARCHITECTURE : ADA. (SA). **Adv Mgr:** Nico Dekker, **Tel** 02 462 2018. **338**

ART DOCUMENTATION. (US/0730-7187). **3192**

ART E DOSSIER. (IT/0394-0179). **338**

ART EDUCATION (RESTON). (US/0004-3125). **338**

ART ET METIERS DU LIVRE. (FR). **4823**

ART HISTORY. (UK/0141-6790). **339**

ART IN AMERICA (1939). (US/0004-3214). **339**

ART INDEX. CD-ROM. (US/0004-3222). **334**

ART ISSUES. (US/1046-8471). **339**

ART JOURNAL (NEW YORK. 1960). (US/0004-3249). **Adv Mgr:** R. Ramirez. **339**

ART LIBRARIES JOURNAL. (UK/0307-4722). **3192**

ART MONTHLY. (UK/0142-6702). **339**

ART MUSCLE. (US). **Adv Mgr:** Angel French. **313**

ART NEW ENGLAND. (US/0274-7073). **Adv Mgr:** C. Errett, **Tel** (617)782-3008. **339**

ART NEW ZEALAND. (NZ/0110-1102). **339**

ART NEWSPAPER. (IT/0960-6556). **Adv Mgr:** L. Comoy. **339**

ART OF THE WEST. (US/1047-4994). **Adv Mgr:** Tim Tierrey. **340**

ART PAPERS. (US/0278-1441). **Adv Mgr:** Ashley Wisner, **Tel** (404)588-1837. **340**

ART POST, THE. (CN/0829-0784). **340**

ART PRESS (PARIS, FRANCE : 1981). (FR/0245-5676). **Adv Mgr:** Amy Pinel. **313**

ART REFERENCE SERVICES QUARTERLY. (US/1050-2548). **340**

ART SALES INDEX (WEYBRIDGE, SURREY : 1985). (UK). **340**

ART SCHOOL MAGAZINE. (NE). **376**

ART-TALK. (US/0741-496X). **340**

ART THERAPY : JOURNAL OF THE AMERICAN ART THERAPY ASSOCIATION. (US/0742-1656). **Adv Mgr:** C. Fryer. **4575**

ART TIMES (SAUGERTIES, N.Y.). (US/0891-9070). **Adv Mgr:** Cornelia, **Tel** (914)246-6944. **340**

ART WORLD. (IT). **340**

ART/WORLD (NEW YORK. 1976). (US/0194-1070). **340**

ARTE CRISTIANA. (IT/0004-3400). **340**

ARTE, DE. (SA). **340**

ARTE ESPANOL. (SP). **340**

ARTE FACTUM (ANTWERPEN). (BE/0771-761X). **Adv Mgr:** D. E. Deyrie. **340**

ARTE IN. (IT). **Adv Mgr:** Matteo Altilia, **Tel** 011 39 02 26144639. **341**

ARTE NAIVE. (IT/0390-1319). **341**

ARTE VENETA : RIVISTA DI STORIA DELL'ARTE. (IT/0392-5234). **341**

ARTEFACT, THE. (AT/0044-9075). **260**

ARTEMIA NEWSLETTER. (BE/0775-454X). **2296**

ARTERE (MONTREAL). (CN/0823-4124). **Adv Mgr:** Michel Lauzier. **3777**

ARTERIOSCLEROSIS AND THROMBOSIS. (US/1049-8834). **3699**

ARTES CONSTRUCTIONUM. (FI/0355-3213). **2018**

ARTESANIA Y FOLKLORE DE VENEZUELA. (VE). **314**

ARTFORUM INTERNATIONAL. (US). **341**

ARTFUL DODGE. (US/0196-691X). **3363**

ARTHRITIS AND RHEUMATISM. (US/0004-3591). **3803**

ARTHRITIS NEWS (TORONTO). (CN/0820-9006). **3803**

ARTHRITIS TODAY. (US/0890-1120). **3803**

ARTHRO EXPRESS. (CN). **Adv Mgr Tel** same as publisher. **3803**

ARTHUR GRAPHIC-CLARION, THE. (US). **Adv Mgr:** Phylis Burkfield. **5658**

ARTI MUSICES. (CI/0587-5455). **4101**

ARTIBUS ASIAE. (SZ/0004-3648). **341**

ARTIBUS ASIAE. SUPPLEMENTUM. (SZ). **341**

ARTIBUS ET HISTORIAE. (AU/0391-9064). **4063**

ARTICHOKE (CALGARY). (CN/0847-3277). **341**

ARTIFICIAL INTELLIGENCE IN MEDICINE. (NE/0933-3657). **1211**

ARTILLERYMAN, THE. (US/0884-4747). **4037**

ARTINF. (AG). **Adv Mgr:** Ines Katzenstein, **Tel** 322 3215 / 804-6129. **341**

ARTIS. (GW/0004-3842). **370**

ARTIST (CALCUTTA). (II/0304-8640). **314**

ARTIST (LONDON. 1931). (UK/0004-3877). **Adv Mgr:** P. Hunter. **341**

ARTIST'S AND ILLUSTRATOR'S MAGAZINE. (UK/0269-4697). **Adv Mgr:** Paul Harris, **Tel** 071 609 2177. **341**

ARTIST'S MAGAZINE, THE. (US/0741-3351). **314**

ARTIST'S MARKET (1979). (US/0161-0546). **376**

ARTLINK. (AT/0727-1239). **Adv Mgr:** S. Britton. **342**

ARTNEWS. (US/0004-3273). **314**

ARTPAPER. (US/0739-8646). **342**

ARTS AND ACTIVITIES. (US/0004-3931). **314**

ARTS AND CRAFTS QUARTERLY MAGAZINE. (US). **370**

ARTS & METIERS. (FR/0004-4008). **5086**

ARTS & SCIENCES JOURNAL. (PH). **314**

ARTS & THE ISLAMIC WORLD. (UK). **314**

ARTS + ARCHITECTURE. (US/0730-9481). **314**

ARTS BEAT (HAMILTON). (CN/0843-2260). **342**

ARTS D'AFRIQUE NOIRE. (FR/0337-1603). **Adv Mgr:** DITO. **314**

ARTS EDUCATION REVIEW OF BOOKS, THE. (US/0889-2172). **315**

ARTS EDUCATION : THE MAGAZINE OF THE NATIONAL FOUNDATION FOR ARTS EDUCATION. (UK). **315**

ARTS IN PSYCHOTHERAPY, THE. (US/0197-4556). **3921**

ARTS INDIANA. (US/0897-859X). **Adv Mgr:** Kay Ivcevich, **Tel** (317)259-1407. **315**

ARTS JOURNAL (ASHEVILLE, N.C.), THE. (US/0739-8662). **315**

ARTS MAGAZINE (NEW YORK). (US/0004-4059). **342**

ARTS QUARTERLY (NEW ORLEANS, LA. 1978). (US/0740-9214). **342**

ARTS REACH. (US/1065-8130). **315**

ARTS REVIEW. (UK/0004-4091). **315**

ARTS REVIEW YEAR BOOK. (UK). **342**

ARTSATLANTIC. (CN/0704-7916). **Adv Mgr:** Lori Devine, **Tel** (902)628-6134. **315**

ARTSCENE (LOS ANGELES, CALIF.). (US/0733-4869). **342**

ARTSEARCH. (US/0730-9023). **383**

ARTSOURCE (RENAISSANCE, CALIF.). (US/1064-6620). **Adv Mgr:** Sarah Meyers. **315**

ARTSPACE. (US/0193-6956). **Adv Mgr:** R Heller. **342**

ARTSPEAK (NEW YORK, N.Y.). (US/1065-1543). **342**

ARTWORLD HOTLINE. (US/1057-5413). **Adv Mgr:** Sarah Meyers. **315**

ARUKORU KENKYU TO YAKUBUTSU IZON. (JA/0389-4118). **1341**

ARVADA JEFFERSON SENTINEL, THE. (US/1060-5207). **5641**

ARZNEIMITTEL FORSCHUNG. (GW/0004-4172). **4292**

ARZTEBLATT BADEN-WURTTEMBERG. (GW/0001-947X). **3553**

ARZTLICHE PRAXIS. (GW/0001-9534). **3553**

AS-SARQ AL-AWSAT. (UK/0265-5772). **5811**

ASA NEWS (LOS ANGELES, CALIF.). (US/0278-2219). **2498**

ASA NEWSLETTER - APPLIED SCIENCE AND ANALYSIS, INC, THE. (US/1057-9419). **4037**

ASAHI EVENING NEWS. (JA/0025-2816). **5805**

ASAIO — Advertising Accepted Index

ASAIO JOURNAL (1992). (US/1058-2916). **Adv Mgr:** Kathleen Phelan, **Tel** (215)238-4492. **3960**

ASB BULLETIN, THE. (US/0001-2386). **443**

ASBESTOS MANAGEMENT SOURCEBOOK. (US/1046-0438). **599**

ASBSD BULLETIN. (US/0001-2408). **1860**

ASBURY PARK PRESS. (US). **5709**

ASC BULLETIN. (US). **532**

ASCA NEWSLETTER (FORT LAUDERDALE, FLA.). (US/0747-6000). **4884**

ASCI JOURNAL OF MANAGEMENT. (II/0257-8069). **860**

ASDA NEWS (1981). (US/0277-3627). **1317**

ASEAN FOOD JOURNAL. (MY/0127-7324). **Adv Mgr:** Dr. Alex Buchanan. **2327**

ASEAN JOURNAL OF CLINICAL SCIENCES. (SI/0129-4881). **3553**

ASHCROFT CACHE CREEK JOURNAL. (CN). **Adv Mgr:** J. Van Allen. **5780**

ASHLEY NEWS OBSERVER, THE. (US). **Adv Mgr:** Charlotte Johnson. **5631**

ASHRAE JOURNAL. (US/0001-2491). **2603**

ASHTON GAZETTE, THE. (US). **5658**

ASIA BUSINESS REPORT. (AT). **639**

ASIA COMPUTER WEEKLY. (SI/0129-5896). **Adv Mgr:** Jeff Chua, **Tel** 294-3366. **1235**

ASIA INSURANCE REVIEW. (SI/0218-2696). **Adv Mgr:** Joanna Org. **2874**

ASIA ... MEASURES & MAGNITUDES. (HK). **773**

ASIA-OCEANIA JOURNAL OF OBSTETRICS AND GYNAECOLOGY. (JA/0389-2328). **3757**

ASIA-PACIFIC AFRICA-MIDDLE EAST PETROLEUM DIRECTORY. (US/0748-4089). **4251**

ASIA PACIFIC HANDBOOK. (UK/0966-0453). **Adv Mgr:** Kevin Brady. **640**

ASIA PACIFIC INTERNATIONAL JOURNAL OF BUSINESS LOGISTICS. (HK/0952-8067). **640**

ASIA PACIFIC INTERNATIONAL MANAGEMENT REVIEW. (HK/0954-2957). **860**

ASIA PACIFIC JOURNAL OF HUMAN RESOURCES. (AT/1038-4111). **Adv Mgr:** Ros Makris. **938**

ASIA-PACIFIC JOURNAL OF PUBLIC HEALTH : ASIA-PACIFIC ACADEMIC CONSORTIUM FOR PUBLIC HEALTH. (TH/1010-5395). **4767**

ASIA PACIFIC PAPERMAKER. (AT/1320-9787). **Adv Mgr:** Jan Henderson. **4232**

ASIA PACIFIC TRAVEL. (US/1045-3881). **5461**

ASIA PULP & PAPER, TECHNOLOGY MARKETS. (JA). **Adv Mgr:** Kei Yuhara. **4232**

ASIA THEOLOGICAL NEWS. (CH). **4936**

ASIA TODAY. (AT/0813-2844). **Adv Mgr:** A.L. Mazey. **640**

ASIA TRAVEL TRADE. (HK). **5462**

ASIA YEARBOOK. (HK). **1547**

ASIAFAB : ASIA FERTILIZER AND AGROCHEMICALS BULLETIN. (UK). **Adv Mgr:** Helen Kelly. **164**

ASIAMAC JOURNAL. (HK/1015-5023). **2110**

ASIAN AFFAIRS. (BG). **4516**

ASIAN AFFAIRS (LONDON). (UK/0306-8374). **2646**

ASIAN AFFAIRS (NEW YORK). (US/0092-7678). **4516**

ASIAN AMERICAN AND PACIFIC ISLANDER JOURNAL OF HEALTH. (US/1072-0367). **4768**

ASIAN AMERICAN POLICY REVIEW. (US/1062-1830). **Adv Mgr:** Grace Kim. **2255**

ASIAN AND AFRICAN STUDIES (JERUSALEM). (IS/0066-8281). **2638**

ASIAN ARCHITECT AND CONTRACTOR. (HK). **Adv Mgr:** Teresa Chan. **292**

ASIAN ART. (US/0894-234X). **343**

ASIAN ART NEWS. (HK). **Adv Mgr:** Amy Schrier. **2501**

ASIAN-AUSTRALASIAN JOURNAL OF ANIMAL SCIENCES. (KO/1011-2367). **Adv Mgr:** Jong K. Ha. **5504**

ASIAN AVIATION. (SI). **Adv Mgr Tel** (65)4747088. **12**

ASIAN BUSINESS. (HK/0254-3729). **Adv Mgr:** Katherina Chan. **640**

ASIAN COMMUNICATIONS. (UK/0952-7516). **1149**

ASIAN COMPUTER MONTHLY. (HK/0254-217X). **1235**

ASIAN DEFENCE JOURNAL. (MY/0126-6403). **4037**

ASIAN ECONOMIC AND SOCIAL REVIEW, THE. (II/0970-6305). **1547**

ASIAN ECONOMIC JOURNAL : JOURNAL OF THE EAST ASIAN ECONOMIC ASSOCIATION. (HK/1351-3958). **Adv Mgr Tel** (852)547-8313. **1633**

ASIAN ECONOMIES. (KO/0304-260X). **1547**

ASIAN ENVIRONMENT. (PH/0116-2993). **2161**

ASIAN HOSPITAL. (HK/1011-596X). **3777**

ASIAN HOTEL AND CATERING TIMES. (HK). **Adv Mgr:** Teresa Chan. **2804**

ASIAN JOURNAL OF PHILOSOPHY, THE. (CC). **4341**

ASIAN JOURNAL OF PUBLIC ADMINISTRATION / YA-CHOU KUNG KUNG HSING CHENG HSUEH / UNIVERSITY OF HONG KONG, THE. (HK). **4630**

ASIAN JOURNAL OF SURGERY. (HK/1015-9584). **3960**

ASIAN-PACIFIC ECONOMIC LITERATURE. (UK/0818-9935). **Adv Mgr:** W. Hacker. **1530**

ASIAN PACIFIC JOURNAL OF ALLERGY AND IMMUNOLOGY. (TH/0125-877X). **3666**

ASIAN PERSPECTIVE. (KO). **Adv Mgr:** J.M. You. **4516**

ASIAN PERSPECTIVES (HONOLULU). (US/0066-8435). **260**

ASIAN PROFILE. (HK/0304-8675). **Adv Mgr:** Winnie Leing. **5192**

ASIAN RECORDER. (II/0004-4644). **2646**

ASIAN SHIPPING. (HK). **5447**

ASIAN SOURCES COMPUTER PRODUCTS. (HK/0254-5586). **1235**

ASIAN SOURCES ELECTRONICS. (HK/0254-1114). **2036**

ASIAN SOURCES HARDWARES FOR WORLD MARKETS. (HK). **1598**

ASIAN SOURCES TIMEPIECES. (HK/0254-1173). **2916**

ASIAN STUDIES (CALCUTTA, INDIA). (II). **2501**

ASIAN STUDIES REVIEW. (AT/1035-7823). **Adv Mgr:** Wendy Miller. **2646**

ASIAN SURVEY. (US/0004-4687). **5192**

ASIAN THEATRE JOURNAL. (US/0742-5457). **383**

ASIAN THOUGHT & SOCIETY. (US/0361-3968). **4540**

ASIAN TIMES. (UK/0264-8490). **2485**

ASIAN VENTURE CAPITAL JOURNAL, THE. (HK/1012-3334). **891**

ASIAN WALL STREET JOURNAL. (HK/0377-9920). **640**

ASIAN WALL STREET JOURNAL. WEEKLY, THE. (US/0191-0132). **1547**

ASIANWEEK. (US/0195-2056). **Adv Mgr:** Jacqueline Rodina. **5633**

ASIATISCHE STUDIEN. (SZ/0004-4717). **2646**

ASIAWEEK. (HK). **2501**

ASIE DU SUD-EST ET MONDE INSULINDIEN. (FR/0395-2681). **2646**

ASIEN. (GW/0721-5231). **2501**

ASKOV AMERICAN. (US). **Adv Mgr:** David Heiller. **5694**

ASL. (AT/1034-9154). **3192**

ASLIB INFORMATION (LONDON, ENGLAND : 1973). (UK/0305-0033). **3192**

ASLIB PROCEEDINGS. (UK/0001-253X). **3192**

ASM NEWS. (US/0044-7897). **560**

ASME BOILER AND PRESSURE VESSEL CODE. (US/0517-5321). **2110**

ASME NEWS (1981). (US/0279-9316). **2110**

ASOCIACION TECNICA ESPANOLA DEL PRETENSADO. (SP). **2018**

ASPAREZ. (US/0004-4229). **Adv Mgr:** Salpi Khouri, **Tel** (818)500-9555. **5633**

ASPE. AGENZIA DI STAMPA SUI PROBLEMI DELL' EMARGINAZIONE. (IT/0394-6479). **Adv Mgr:** Lulena Ortalda, **Tel** 011 8142748. **5240**

ASPECTS DE LA FRANCE. (FR). **4464**

ASPEN DAILY NEWS. (US). **Adv Mgr:** Cassandra Davenport. **5641**

ASPIRE (NASHVILLE, TENN.). (US/1076-5778). **2596**

ASSECURANZ-COMPASS. (AU). **Adv Mgr:** G Vermeirsch, **Tel** 02-345-9070. **2874**

ASSEMBLIES OF GOD HERITAGE. (US/0896-4394). **4936**

ASSESSMENT AND EVALUATION IN HIGHER EDUCATION. (UK/0260-2938). **1810**

ASSESSMENT AND VALUATION LEGAL REPORTER. (US/0090-6352). **4711**

ASSESSMENT DIGEST. (US/0731-0277). **4711**

ASSET FINANCE & LEASING DIGEST. (UK). **773**

ASSET (ST. LOUIS, MO.), THE. (US/0883-7384). **738**

ASSIA, JEWISH MEDICAL ETHICS. (IS/0334-3871). **3553**

ASSICURAZIONE; QUINDICINALE DI TECHNICA, CRONACA E GIURISPRUDENZA ASSICURATIVA. (IT/0004-5098). **2874**

ASSIG NEWSLETTER. (AT/1030-3812). **3192**

ASSINEWS. (IT). **2874**

ASSISTANT LIBRARIAN. (UK/0004-5152). **3192**

ASSOCIATE REFORMED PRESBYTERIAN, THE. (US/0362-0816). **5055**

ASSOCIATION & SOCIETY MANAGER. (US/0004-5292). **860**

ASSOCIATION EXECUTIVE COMPENSATION STUDY. (US/0273-0367). **640**

ASSOCIATION LAW AND POLICY. (US). **Adv Mgr:** R.S. Boege, **Tel** (202)626-2703. **2937**

ASSOCIATION MANAGEMENT. (US). **860**

ASSOCIATION MANAGEMENT. (US/0004-5578). **640**

ASSOCIATION MEETINGS. (US/1042-3141). **756**

ASSOCIATION NEWS - INDUSTRIAL FIRST AID ATTENDANTS ASSOCIATION OF BRITISH COLUMBIA. (CN/0844-0506). **3795**

ASSOCIATION TRENDS. (US/0196-1942). **640**

ASSOCIATIONS REPORT. (US/0744-1088). **860**

ASSUMPTION PIONEER, THE. (US). **5683**

ASSURANCES. (CN/0004-6027). **2874**

ASTHMA WELFARER. (AT). **Adv Mgr:** Dorothy Nardi. **3948**

ASTIN BULLETIN. (UK/0515-0361). **2874**

ASTORIA SOUTH FULTON ARGUS, THE. (US). **Adv Mgr:** Erma Geiman. **5658**

ASTRO AGENTS. (US/1065-7584). **Adv Mgr:** Taaffe O'Connell. **389**

ASTRO CASTER. (US/1065-7533). **Adv Mgr:** Taaffe O'Connell. **390**

ASTROGRAPH (ARLINGTON), THE. (US/0094-1417). **391**

ASTROLOGICAL MAGAZINE, THE. (II/0004-6140). **Adv Mgr:** B. Niranjan Babu. **390**

ASTROLOGICAL REVIEW, THE. (US/0044-9784). **390**

ASTROLOGY QUARTERLY. (UK). **Adv Mgr:** Nicholas Campion. **390**

ASTRONOMIE. (FR). **392**

ASTRONOMIE MAGAZINE, L'. (FR). **392**

ASTRONOMIE-QUEBEC. (CN). **392**

ASTRONOMY & ASTROPHYSICS. SUPPLEMENT SERIES. (FR/0365-0138). **392**

ASTRONOMY (MILWAUKEE). (US/0091-6358). **393**

ASTROPHYSICAL LETTERS AND COMMUNICATIONS. (US/0888-6512). **393**

ASTROPHYSICS AND SPACE SCIENCE. (NE/0004-640X). **393**

ASTRUIM. (NE). **393**

ASWLC. (US/0162-5934). **1126**

ASYMPTOTIC ANALYSIS. (NE/0921-7134). **3496**

AT A DISTANCE. (US). **1726**

AT RANDOM. (US/1062-0036). **4812**

AT-THE-PARK (CHICAGO, ILL.). (US/1048-9118). **4857**

AT WORK (SAN FRANCISCO, CALIF.). (US/1061-9925). **4201**

ATALANTA (MUNCHEN). (GW/0171-0079). **5605**

ATALAYA CULTURAL : REVISTA DE POESIA, ARTE Y LITERATURA. (SP). **3460**

AT&T DATALINE. (US/1041-2530). **1149**

ATARI MAGAZINE. (FR/0992-2016). **1264**

ATARI USER. (UK/0266-545X). **1264**

ATARISTE. (CN/0847-5644). **1265**

ATCHISON COUNTY MAIL, THE. (US). **Adv Mgr:** Bill Farmer. **5699**

ATCP. (MX). **4232**

ATE NEWS LETTER. (US/0001-2718). **1888**

ATEMWEGS- UND LUNGENKRANKHEITEN. (GW/0341-3055). **3948**

ATENCION MEDICA. (MX/0185-6235). **3553**

ATENEA (CONCEPCION, CHILE: 1972). (CL/0004-6507). **2611**

ATHENIAN (ATHENS, GREECE). (GR). **Adv Mgr:** Katia Stamatiadou. **3267**

ATHENS DAILY NEWS, ATHENS BANNER-HERALD. (US/0898-3712). **Adv Mgr:** Frank Moss, **Tel** (706)208-2308. **5652**

ATHENS DAILY REVIEW. (US/1040-6522). **5746**

ATHENS MAGAZINE (ATHENS, GA. 1989). (US/1053-623X). **Adv Mgr:** Kathy Russo, **Tel** (706)208-2329. **2528**

ATHENS OBSERVER, THE. (US/0744-4001). **5652**

ATHLETIC ADMINISTRATION. (US/0044-9873). **Adv Mgr:** Cynthia Klenke, **Tel** (919)489-1916. **1855**

ATHLETIC BUSINESS. (US/0747-315X). **640**

ATHLETIC MANAGEMENT. (US). **Adv Mgr:** Bill Kaprelian, **Tel** (708)584-9289. **4884**

ATHLETICS COACH. (UK/0267-0267). **4884**

ATHLETICS TODAY. (UK/0269-1302). **4884**

ATHLETICS (TORONTO. 1981). (CN/0229-4966). **4884**

ATHLON'S PRO FOOTBALL. (US/0734-2888). **4884**

ATHOL DAILY NEWS. (US). **Adv Mgr:** Bernard Cunningham. **5687**

ATIKOKAN PROGRESS. (CN). **Adv Mgr:** Eve Shine. **5780**

ATLA : ALTERNATIVES TO LABORATORY ANIMALS. (UK/0261-1929). **3979**

ATLAL. (SU). **260**

ATLANTA BUSINESS CHRONICLE. (US/0164-8071). **640**

ATLANTA DAILY WORLD. (US). **Adv Mgr:** J.R. Simmons. **2255**

ATLANTA HISTORY. (US/0896-3975). **2722**

ATLANTA JEWISH TIMES, THE. (US/0892-3345). **Adv Mgr:** Dan Chorgnec, **Tel** (404)352-2400. **5652**

ATLANTA LAKE LIFE. (US). **4848**

ATLANTA LAW LIBRARIES ASSOCIATION NEWSLETTER. (US). **Adv Mgr:** Roger Glenn, **Tel** 800-633-4604 ext. 461. **2937**

ATLANTA SINGLES. (US/0897-4608). **2485**

ATLANTA SMALL BUSINESS MONTHLY, THE. (US). **640**

ATLANTA VOICE, THE. (US). **Adv Mgr:** Malcolm Caldwell, **Tel** (404)524-6426 Ext. 29. **5652**

ATLANTIC. (UK). **823**

ATLANTIC BAPTIST, THE. (CN/0004-6752). **5055**

ATLANTIC (BOSTON, MASS. : 1981), THE. (US/0276-9077). **2528**

ATLANTIC BUSINESS REPORT. (CN/1192-0203). **641**

ATLANTIC CITY MAGAZINE. (US/0194-9993). **Adv Mgr:** Mr. Senoff, **Tel** (609)272-7903. **2485**

ATLANTIC CO-OPERATOR, THE. (CN/0703-5357). **1541**

ATLANTIC COASTAL KAYAKER. (US). **Adv Mgr:** Bob Hicks, **Tel** (508)356-2057. **4884**

ATLANTIC CONSTRUCTION JOURNAL. (CN/0842-9588). **599**

ATLANTIC CONTROL STATES BEVERAGE JOURNAL. (US/0044-9881). **5070**

ATLANTIC CONTROL STATES/WEST VIRGINIA BEVERAGE JOURNAL. (US). **Adv Mgr:** Arnold Lazarus. **2363**

ATLANTIC ECONOMIC JOURNAL. (US/0197-4254). **1464**

ATLANTIC FIREFIGHTER. (CN/0838-679X). **2288**

ATLANTIC FORESTRY JOURNAL. (CN/0832-5502). **2375**

ATLANTIC INSIGHT. (CN/0708-5400). **2485**

ATLANTIC LIFESTYLE BUSINESS. (CN/1184-051X). **Adv Mgr:** Hubert F. Hutton. **641**

ATLANTIC MINING JOURNAL. (CN/0840-6693). **2134**

ATLANTIC MONTHLY (1993), THE. (US/1072-7825). **2485**

ATLANTIC NEWS-TELEGRAPH. (US/8756-6400). **Adv Mgr:** Kim Johnson. **5668**

ATLANTIC PROVINCES BOOK REVIEW, THE. (CN/0316-5981). **3337**

ATLANTIC SALMON JOURNAL, THE. (CN/0044-992X). **2296**

ATLANTIC TRUCKING. (CN/0830-1808). **5377**

ATLANTIDE-REPORT: SCIENTIFIC RESULTS OF THE DANISH EXPEDITION TO THE COASTS OF TROPICAL WEST AFRICA, 1945-1946. (DK). **553**

ATLANTIS (WOLFVILLE). (CN/0702-7818). **5551**

ATLAS (LONDON, ENGLAND : 1985). (UK/0267-484X). **343**

ATLETICA LEGGERA. (IT/0392-2251). **2596**

ATLETICA : RIVISTA MENSILE DELLA FIDAL. (IT). **4884**

ATMOSPHERE-OCEAN. (CN/0705-5900). **1420**

ATOMIZATION AND SPRAYS. (US/1044-5110). **2008**

ATOMWIRTSCHAFT, ATOMTECHNIK. (GW/0365-8414). **2154**

ATOSSEMENT VOTRE. (CN/0826-5321). **2296**

ATRI TURF NOTES. (AT/0729-9397). **Adv Mgr:** same as editor. **2797**

ATRIAL NATRIURETIC FACTORS. (UK/0268-1641). **3699**

ATRIUM (LONDON). (UK/0951-8088). **292**

ATTITUDE (BROOKLYN (NEW YORK, N.Y.)). (US/0882-3472). **1310**

ATTORNEY-CPA, THE. (US/0571-8279). **2938**

ATTORNEY FEE AWARDS REPORTER. (US/0732-7552). **2938**

ATTORNEYS' DIRECTORY OF SAN DIEGO COUNTY. (US/0193-9300). **3078**

ATTORNEYS PERSONNEL REPORT. (US/8750-2763). **2938**

ATTUALITA CINEMATOGRAFICHE. (IT). **4064**

ATTUALITA IN CHIRURGIA. (IT/0390-5527). **3960**

ATV NEWS. (US/0744-7809). **4080**

ATV SPORTS. (US/0892-3183). **4884**

ATWATER SIGNAL. (US). **5633**

ATWOOD HERALD, THE. (US). **5658**

ATZ. AUTOMOBILTECHNISCHE ZEITSCHRIFT. (GW/0001-2785). **5404**

AU COEUR DE L'AFRIQUE. (BD). **4937**

AU FIL DES EVENEMENTS. (CN/0225-1965). **Adv Mgr:** Jean Caughon, **Tel** (418)529-1756. **1726**

AU FIL DU BOIS. (CN/0383-0047). **2399**

AU NATUREL (MONTREAL). (CN/0715-4690). **4768**

AUBURN CITIZEN. (US). **5658**

AUBURN JOURNAL. (US). **Adv Mgr:** Debbie Dragon. **5633**

AUBURN PLAINSMAN, THE. (US/1071-1279). **5625**

AUCKLAND UNIVERSITY LAW REVIEW. (NZ/0067-0510). **3089**

AUDECIBEL. (US/0004-7473). **4384**

AUDIBLE (TORONTO). (CN/0710-2038). **4884**

AUDIO CRITIC, THE. (US/0146-4701). **5315**

AUDIO (DURANGO, COLO.). (US/0883-8437). **5315**

AUDIO VISUAL. (UK/0305-2249). **1104**

AUDIO VISUAL DIRECTORY. (UK/0956-2931). **1126**

AUDIO VISUAL DIRECTORY. (UK). **5315**

AUDIOFILE (PORTLAND, ME.). (US/1063-0244). **Adv Mgr:** Merris Grohman, **Tel** (207)828-3994. **1104**

AUDIOLOGISCHE AKUSTIK. AUDIOLOGICAL ACOUSTICS. (GW/0172-8261). **4384**

AUDIOLOGY. (SZ/0020-6091). **3886**

AUDIOVISUAL LIBRARIAN, THE. (UK/0302-3451). **3192**

AUDIT TUNBRIDGE WELLS. (UK/0961-124X). **641**

AUDITING. (US/0278-0380). **739**

AUDIVIDEO INTERNATIONAL. (US/0362-1162). **5315**

AUDUBON NATURALIST NEWS : A PUBLICATION OF THE AUDUBON NATURALIST SOCIETY OF THE CENTRAL ATLANTIC STATES. (US/0888-6555). **4162**

AUERBACH DATA BASE MANAGEMENT. (US/0735-9977). **Adv Mgr:** Phil Brady, **Tel** (212)971-5120. **1253**

AUFBAU (NEW YORK, N.Y.). (US/0004-7813). **5713**

AUFBEREITUNGS-TECHNIK. (GW/0004-783X). **2134**

AUGENOPTIKER, DER. (GW/0004-7929). **3872**

AUGMENTATIVE AND ALTERNATIVE COMMUNICATION. (US/0743-4618). **1104**

AUGUSTA AREA TIMES. (US/0749-7083). **5765**

AUGUSTA DAILY GAZETTE, THE. (US). **Adv Mgr:** Len Hudson. **5674**

AUGUSTA EAGLE, THE. (US). **5658**

AUGUSTA MELBOURNE. (AT/1033-8934). **Adv Mgr:** Lallum Fraser. **293**

AUJOURD'HUI CREDO. (CN/0383-2554). **Adv Mgr:** G. Gautier. **4937**

AUK, THE. (US/0004-8038). **5615**

AUNT EDNA'S READING LIST. (US). **5551**

AURA (FORT WORTH, TEX.). (US/1054-5441). **Adv Mgr:** Kari Metroka. **2528**

AUREALIS MT. WAVERLEY. (AT/1035-1205). **3364**

AURISA NEWS. (AT/0811-3130). **2815**

AURORA SENTINEL. (US). **Adv Mgr:** Jim Gourley. **5642**

AUSGRABUNGEN UND FUNDE IN WESTFALEN-LIPPE / IM AUFTRAG DES LANDSCHAFTSVERBANDES WESTFALEN-LIPPE HERAUSGEGEBEN VON WESTFALISCHES MUSEUM FUER ARCHAOLOGIE, AMT FUER BODENDENKMALPFLEGE. (GW/0175-6133). **2677**

AUSLEGUNG. (US/0733-4311). **4342**

AUSSENPOLITIK. (GW/0004-8194). **4516**

AUSSENPOLITIK (ENGLISH EDITION). (GW/0587-3835). **4516**

AUSSENWIRTSCHAFT: ZEITSCHRIFT FUER INTERNATIONALE WIRTSCHAFTSBEZIEHUNGEN. (SZ/0004-8216). **4516**

AUSTIN BUSINESS JOURNAL. (US/0892-869X). **Adv Mgr:** Rebecca Melancon. **641**

AUSTIN CHRONICLE (SCOTTSBURG, IND.), THE. (US/0740-4581). **Adv Mgr:** Jerald Corder. **5746**

AUSTIN CHRONICLE, THE. (US/1074-0740). **2528**

AUSTIN HOMES & GARDENS. (US/0199-1531). **2898**

AUSTRALASIAN ANGORA MOHAIR JOURNAL. (AT). **3183**

AUSTRALASIAN BEEKEEPER, THE. (AT/0004-8313). **Adv Mgr:** J. Gardner. **63**

AUSTRALASIAN BIOTECHNOLOGY. (AT/1036-7128). **Adv Mgr:** Gary Dolder. **3685**

AUSTRALASIAN BUS AND COACH. (AT). **5377**

AUSTRALASIAN CATHOLIC RECORD, THE. (AT/0727-3215). **Adv Mgr:** A. Crow, **Tel** 011 61 2 550 9411. **5024**

AUSTRALASIAN DRAMA STUDIES. (AT/0810-4123). **5361**

AUSTRALASIAN FURNISHING TRADE JOURNAL. (AT). **Adv Mgr:** Joanne Royal. **2898**

AUSTRALASIAN HEALTH AND HEALING. (AT/0812-3896). **2596**

AUSTRALASIAN JOURNAL OF AMERICAN STUDIES : AJAS. (AT/0705-7113). **2722**

AUSTRALASIAN JOURNAL OF DERMATOLOGY, THE. (AT/0004-8380). **3718**

AUSTRALASIAN JOURNAL OF PHILOSOPHY. (AT/0004-8402). **4342**

AUSTRALASIAN JOURNAL OF SPECIAL EDUCATION. (AT/1030-0112). **1875**

AUSTRALASIAN PHYSICAL & ENGINEERING SCIENCES IN MEDICINE. (AT/0158-9938). **3685**

AUSTRALASIAN PUBLIC LIBRARIES AND INFORMATION SERVICES. (AT/1030-5033). **3193**

AUSTRALASIAN RADIOLOGY. (AT/0004-8461). **Adv Mgr:** Bloxham Chambers. **3939**

AUSTRALASIAN RELIGION INDEX. (AT/1033-2626). **4937**

AUSTRALASIAN — Advertising Accepted Index

AUSTRALASIAN SHIPS & PORTS. (AT/1032-3449). **5447**

AUSTRALASIAN TEXTILES. (AT/0725-086X). **5348**

AUSTRALIA AND NEW ZEALAND JOURNAL OF DEVELOPMENTAL DISABILITIES. (AT/0726-3864). **4384**

AUSTRALIA DEPARTMENT OF PRIMARY INDUSTRIES AND ENERGY BASIC FISH STATISTICS. (AT). **2297**

AUSTRALIAN ACADEMIC AND RESEARCH LIBRARIES. (AT/0004-8623). **3193**

AUSTRALIAN ACCOUNTANT, THE. (AT/0004-8631). **739**

AUSTRALIAN ACCOUNTING REVIEW. (AT). **739**

AUSTRALIAN AND NEW ZEALAND BIOTECHNOLOGY DIRECTORY. (AT/1032-8068). **3686**

AUSTRALIAN AND NEW ZEALAND CATALOGUE OF NEW FILMS AND VIDEOS, THE. (AT/1035-8005). **4064**

AUSTRALIAN AND NEW ZEALAND JOURNAL OF MEDICINE. (AT/0004-8291). **3795**

AUSTRALIAN AND NEW ZEALAND JOURNAL OF OBSTETRICS AND GYNAECOLOGY. (AT/0004-8666). **3757**

AUSTRALIAN AND NEW ZEALAND JOURNAL OF OPHTHALMOLOGY. (AT/0814-9763). **3872**

AUSTRALIAN AND NEW ZEALAND JOURNAL OF PSYCHIATRY. (AT/0004-8674). **3921**

AUSTRALIAN & NEW ZEALAND JOURNAL OF SERIALS LIBRARIANSHIP. (US/0898-3283). **3193**

AUSTRALIAN AND NEW ZEALAND JOURNAL OF SOCIOLOGY, THE. (AT/0004-8690). **5240**

AUSTRALIAN AND NEW ZEALAND JOURNAL OF SURGERY. (AT/0004-8682). **3960**

AUSTRALIAN & NEW ZEALAND PHYSICIST : A PUBLICATION OF THE AUSTRALIAN INSTITUTE OF PHYSICS & THE NEW ZEALAND INSTITUTE OF PHYSICS, THE. (AT/1036-3831). **4398**

AUSTRALIAN & NEW ZEALAND STUDIES IN CANADA. (CN/0843-5049). **3364**

AUSTRALIAN & NEW ZEALAND THEATRE RECORD : ANZTR. (AT). **5361**

AUSTRALIAN AND NEW ZEALAND WINE INDUSTRY DIRECTORY. (AT/1033-7954). **Adv Mgr:** Paul Clancy. **2363**

AUSTRALIAN AND NEW ZEALAND WINE INDUSTRY JOURNAL. (AT). **2363**

AUSTRALIAN ANTIQUE BOTTLE COLLECTOR. (AT). **250**

AUSTRALIAN ARCHAEOLOGY. (AT/0312-2417). **260**

AUSTRALIAN AUTHOR, THE. (AT/0045-026X). **Adv Mgr:** Ray Koppe, **Tel** 02 3180877. **3364**

AUSTRALIAN AUTISM REVIEW. (AT/0312-8857). **4575**

AUSTRALIAN BANKER. (AT/0814-2912). **773**

AUSTRALIAN BEAUTY COUNTER. (AT/0726-2566). **402**

AUSTRALIAN BEE JOURNAL. (AT/0045-0294). **63**

AUSTRALIAN BIRDKEEPER. (AT/1030-8954). **5615**

AUSTRALIAN BOOK COLLECTOR. (AT/1034-0785). **4823**

AUSTRALIAN BOOKS IN PRINT. (AT). **3193**

AUSTRALIAN BOOKSELLER & PUBLISHER. (AT). **4823**

AUSTRALIAN BUILDING, CONSTRUCTION AND HOUSING. (AT/1032-240X). **Adv Mgr Tel** 818 4111. **599**

AUSTRALIAN-CANADIAN STUDIES. (AT/0810-1906). **2722**

AUSTRALIAN CANEGROWER. (AT/0157-3039). **63**

AUSTRALIAN CHRISTIAN. (AT/0004-8852). **Adv Mgr:** C. Ambrosia. **4937**

AUSTRALIAN CITRUS NEWS. (AT/0004-8283). **Adv Mgr Tel** 11 61 8 2319056. **2328**

AUSTRALIAN CLAY JOURNAL AND CERAMIC NEWS. (AT/1035-4611). **2586**

AUSTRALIAN COAL REPORT. (AT/0157-4566). **Adv Mgr:** Mr. J. Barton, **Tel** 221-8440. **1933**

AUSTRALIAN COLLEGE OF MIDWIVES INCORPORATED JOURNAL. (AT/1031-170X). **3554**

AUSTRALIAN COMMUNICATION REVIEW. (AT/0726-3252). **1104**

AUSTRALIAN COMPUTER JOURNAL, THE. (AT/0004-8917). **1256**

AUSTRALIAN CONCRETE CONSTRUCTION. (AT/1031-3249). **599**

AUSTRALIAN CORPORATE TREASURE. (AT). **641**

AUSTRALIAN COTTON GROWER. (AT/0159-1290). **Adv Mgr:** Brian O'Connell. **164**

AUSTRALIAN CRITICAL CARE : OFFICIAL JOURNAL OF THE CONFEDERATION OF AUSTRALIAN CRITICAL CARE NURSES. (AT/1036-7314). **Adv Mgr:** Jane Perkins. **3851**

AUSTRALIAN CULTURAL HISTORY. (AT/0728-8433). **2668**

AUSTRALIAN CYCLIST. (AT). **Adv Mgr:** David Turner, **Tel** 02 913 1266. **428**

AUSTRALIAN DAIRY FOODS. (AT). **192**

AUSTRALIAN DEER. (AT). **2187**

AUSTRALIAN DEFENCE FORCE JOURNAL : JOURNAL OF THE AUSTRALIAN PROFESSION OF ARMS. (AT/0314-1039). **Adv Mgr:** Irene Coombes, **Tel** 011 06 265 1193. **4037**

AUSTRALIAN DENTAL JOURNAL. (AT/0045-0421). **1317**

AUSTRALIAN DOLL DIRECTORY. (AT/0816-3294). **2771**

AUSTRALIAN DRILLING. (AT/1037-3535). **1966**

AUSTRALIAN ECONOMIC PAPERS. (AT/0004-900X). **1590**

AUSTRALIAN ECONOMIC REVIEW. (AT/0004-9018). **1464**

AUSTRALIAN EDUCATION INDEX. (AT/0004-9026). **1793**

AUSTRALIAN ENTOMOLOGICAL MAGAZINE. (AT/0311-1881). **Adv Mgr:** M. Schneider. **5605**

AUSTRALIAN ENTOMOLOGIST, THE. (AT/1320-6133). **Adv Mgr:** A. P. Mackey. **5605**

AUSTRALIAN EQUINE VETERINARIAN. (AT/1032-6626). **2797**

AUSTRALIAN EVANGEL. (AT/0812-4353). **4937**

AUSTRALIAN EXPATRIATE, THE. (US/1064-010X). **2668**

AUSTRALIAN FAMILY PHYSICIAN. (AT/0300-8495). **3737**

AUSTRALIAN FARM MANAGER, THE. (AT/1035-1914). **64**

AUSTRALIAN FARMERS' AND DEALERS' JOURNAL. (AT/1036-4242). **Adv Mgr:** Garry Kennedy, **Tel** 11 61 3 6576130. **158**

AUSTRALIAN FEMINIST STUDIES. (AT/0816-4649). **5551**

AUSTRALIAN FINANCIAL REVIEW, THE. (AT). **773**

AUSTRALIAN FISHERIES. (AT/0004-9115). **Adv Mgr:** Angela, **Tel** 62 272 5182. **2297**

AUSTRALIAN FOLKLORE. (AT/0819-0852). **2318**

AUSTRALIAN FOREST GROWER. (AT). **2375**

AUSTRALIAN FOREST RESEARCH. (AT/0004-914X). **2375**

AUSTRALIAN GARDEN HISTORY. (AT/1033-3673). **2409**

AUSTRALIAN GAS JOURNAL, THE. (AT/0004-9166). **Adv Mgr:** L. Trimmings, **Tel** (03)544-2233. **4251**

AUSTRALIAN GEM & TREASURE HUNTER. (AT/0159-6322). **4869**

AUSTRALIAN GEMMOLOGIST. (AT/0004-9174). **2913**

AUSTRALIAN GEOGRAPHER. (AT/0004-9182). **2555**

AUSTRALIAN GEOGRAPHICAL STUDIES. (AT/0004-9190). **2555**

AUSTRALIAN GIFTGUIDE. (AT/0312-5327). **Adv Mgr:** Stephanie Goodmanson, **Tel** 011 61 2 8184111. **2583**

AUSTRALIAN GLIDING. (AT). **Adv Mgr:** F. Packerham. **12**

AUSTRALIAN GLIDING YEAR BOOK. (AT). **4885**

AUSTRALIAN GOAT WORLD, THE. (AT). **206**

AUSTRALIAN GRAIN. (AT). **Adv Mgr:** Brian O'Connell. **164**

AUSTRALIAN GRAPEGROWER AND WINEMAKER. (AT/0727-3606). **2363**

AUSTRALIAN GYMNAST. (AT). **4885**

AUSTRALIAN HAND WEAVER AND SPINNER / HAND WEAVERS AND SPINNERS GUILD OF NEW SOUTH WALES, THE. (AT). **5183**

AUSTRALIAN HISTORICAL STUDIES. (AT/1031-461X). **2668**

AUSTRALIAN HISTORY TEACHER. (AT/0312-2530). **1888**

AUSTRALIAN HOSPITAL ENGINEER. (AT/0727-730X). **3777**

AUSTRALIAN HUMANIST, THE. (AT/0004-9328). **Adv Mgr Tel** 03 853 6662. **2842**

AUSTRALIAN INSOLVENCY BULLETIN. (AT/1033-9345). **2938**

AUSTRALIAN JOURNAL OF ADVANCED NURSING. (AT/0813-0531). **3852**

AUSTRALIAN JOURNAL OF AGRICULTURAL ECONOMICS, THE. (AT/0004-9395). **64**

AUSTRALIAN JOURNAL OF AGRICULTURAL RESEARCH. (AT/0004-9409). **64**

AUSTRALIAN JOURNAL OF ANTHROPOLOGY, THE. (AT/1035-8811). **231**

AUSTRALIAN JOURNAL OF ART. (AT/0314-6464). **343**

AUSTRALIAN JOURNAL OF BOTANY. (AT/0067-1924). **501**

AUSTRALIAN JOURNAL OF CHEMISTRY. (AT/0004-9425). **961**

AUSTRALIAN JOURNAL OF CHINESE AFFAIRS, THE. (AT/0156-7365). **2501**

AUSTRALIAN JOURNAL OF CLINICAL HYPNOTHERAPY AND HYPNOSIS, THE. (AT/0810-0713). **Adv Mgr:** Stephen May. **2857**

AUSTRALIAN JOURNAL OF COMMUNICATION. (AT/0811-6202). **1104**

AUSTRALIAN JOURNAL OF DAIRY TECHNOLOGY, THE. (AT/0004-9433). **192**

AUSTRALIAN JOURNAL OF EARLY CHILDHOOD. (AT/0312-5033). **1802**

AUSTRALIAN JOURNAL OF EXPERIMENTAL AGRICULTURE. (AT/0816-1089). **64**

AUSTRALIAN JOURNAL OF FORENSIC SCIENCES, THE. (AT/0045-0618). **Adv Mgr:** John Rowe. **3740**

AUSTRALIAN JOURNAL OF HOSPITAL PHARMACY. (AT/0310-6810). **Adv Mgr:** B Parsons. **4293**

AUSTRALIAN JOURNAL OF HUMAN COMMUNICATION DISORDERS. (AT/0310-6853). **4384**

AUSTRALIAN JOURNAL OF INSTRUMENTATION AND CONTROL. (AT). **1966**

AUSTRALIAN JOURNAL OF INTERNATIONAL AFFAIRS. (AT/1035-7718). **4516**

AUSTRALIAN JOURNAL OF LAW AND SOCIETY. (AT/0729-3356). **2938**

AUSTRALIAN JOURNAL OF LINGUISTICS. (AT/0726-8602). **3267**

AUSTRALIAN JOURNAL OF LITURGY. (AT/1030-617X). **4937**

AUSTRALIAN JOURNAL OF MARINE AND FRESHWATER RESEARCH. (AT/0067-1940). **1446**

AUSTRALIAN JOURNAL OF MARRIAGE & FAMILY. (AT/1034-652X). **2276**

AUSTRALIAN JOURNAL OF MEDICAL SCIENCE. (AT/1038-1643). **Adv Mgr:** B. Walker, **Tel** (07)371-3370. **3554**

AUSTRALIAN JOURNAL OF NUTRITION AND DIETETICS. (AT/1032-1322). **4187**

AUSTRALIAN JOURNAL OF PHARMACY. (AT/0311-8002). **4293**

AUSTRALIAN JOURNAL OF PHYSICS. (AT/0004-9506). **4398**

AUSTRALIAN JOURNAL OF PHYSIOTHERAPY, THE. (AT/0004-9514). **4379**

AUSTRALIAN JOURNAL OF PLANT PHYSIOLOGY. (AT/0310-7841). **501**

AUSTRALIAN JOURNAL OF POLITICAL SCIENCE. (AT/1036-1146). **4464**

AUSTRALIAN JOURNAL OF POLITICS AND HISTORY, THE. (AT/0004-9522). **4464**

AUSTRALIAN JOURNAL OF PSYCHOLOGY. (AT/0004-9530). **4575**

AUSTRALIAN JOURNAL OF PSYCHOTHERAPY. (AT/0728-6155). **4575**

AUSTRALIAN JOURNAL OF PUBLIC ADMINISTRATION. (AT/0313-6647). **4631**

AUSTRALIAN JOURNAL OF PUBLIC HEALTH. (AT/1035-7319). **Adv Mgr:** Rhana Pike. **4768**

AUSTRALIAN JOURNAL OF REMEDIAL EDUCATION. (AT/0726-5115). **1727**

AUSTRALIAN JOURNAL OF SCIENCE AND MEDICINE IN SPORT. (AT). **3953**

AUSTRALIAN JOURNAL OF SOCIAL ISSUES, THE. (AT/0157-6321). **5274**

AUSTRALIAN JOURNAL OF SOIL AND WATER CONSERVATION. (AT/1032-2426). **5530**

AUSTRALIAN JOURNAL OF SOIL RESEARCH. (AT/0004-9573). **164**

AUSTRALIAN JOURNAL OF TEACHER EDUCATION, THE. (AT/0313-5373). **1888**

AUSTRALIAN JOURNAL OF ZOOLOGY. (AT/0004-959X). **5577**

AUSTRALIAN JOURNAL ON AGEING. (AT/0726-4240). **3749**

AUSTRALIAN JOURNALISM REVIEW : AJR. (AT/0810-2686). **2917**

AUSTRALIAN KEY BUSINESS DIRECTORY, THE. (AT). **641**

AUSTRALIAN LAW JOURNAL, THE. (AT/0004-9611). **2938**

AUSTRALIAN LAW LIBRARIAN. (AT/1039-6616). **2939**

AUSTRALIAN LAW NEWS. (AT). **Adv Mgr Tel** 03-6631578. **2939**

AUSTRALIAN LEFT REVIEW. (AT/0004-9638). **Adv Mgr Tel** 5651855. **4465**

AUSTRALIAN LIBRARY JOURNAL, THE. (AT/0004-9670). **3193**

AUSTRALIAN LIBRARY REVIEW. (AT/1034-8042). **Adv Mgr:** S. Miles. **3193**

AUSTRALIAN LITERARY STUDIES. (AT/0004-9697). **3338**

AUSTRALIAN LITHOGRAPHER, PRINTER AND PACKAGER, THE. (AT). **4563**

AUSTRALIAN MACHINERY AND PRODUCTION ENGINEERING. (AT/0004-9719). **2110**

AUSTRALIAN MARINE SCIENCE BULLETIN. (AT/0157-6429). **553**

AUSTRALIAN MATHEMATICS TEACHER, THE. (AT/0045-0685). **Adv Mgr Tel** (08)3630288. **3496**

AUSTRALIAN MEAT INDUSTRY BULLETIN, THE. (AT/0156-2681). **206**

AUSTRALIAN MEDICAL RECORD JOURNAL / MEDICAL RECORD ASSOCIATION OF AUSTRALIA. (AT/0817-3907). **3777**

AUSTRALIAN MEDICINE : NEWSMAGAZINE OF THE AUSTRALIAN MEDICAL ASSOCIATION. (AT). **Adv Mgr:** Julie Taylor. **3554**

AUSTRALIAN MINER, THE. (AT). **2134**

AUSTRALIAN MINING. (AT/0004-976X). **2134**

AUSTRALIAN MOTHER AND BABY. (AT/1031-4830). **2277**

AUSTRALIAN NATURAL HISTORY. (AT/0004-9840). **Adv Mgr:** Mike Field, **Tel** 339-8331. **4162**

AUSTRALIAN NURSES' JOURNAL. (AT/0045-0758). **3852**

AUSTRALIAN NUTGROWER. (AT/0819-7849). **164**

AUSTRALIAN OCCUPATIONAL THERAPY JOURNAL. (AT/0045-0766). **1875**

AUSTRALIAN OFFICIAL JOURNAL OF PATENTS (CANBERRA, A.C.T. : 1987). (AT). **1301**

AUSTRALIAN OIL & GAS DIRECTORY. (AT/0157-728X). **4251**

AUSTRALIAN ORCHID REVIEW. (AT/0045-0782). **2409**

AUSTRALIAN ORTHOPTIC JOURNAL. (AT/0814-0936). **3872**

AUSTRALIAN OUTLOOK. LONDON. (UK/0301-5785). **Adv Mgr:** S. Melvin. **2510**

AUSTRALIAN PACKAGING. (AT/0004-9921). **4218**

AUSTRALIAN PARKS AND RECREATION. (AT/0311-8223). **Adv Mgr:** Eva Smith. **4706**

AUSTRALIAN PHARMACIST / PHARMACEUTICAL SOCIETY OF AUSTRALIA. (AT/0728-4632). **4293**

AUSTRALIAN PIPELINER. (AT/0310-1258). **Adv Mgr:** Claire Bowley. **4251**

AUSTRALIAN PLANNER : JOURNAL OF THE ROYAL AUSTRALIAN PLANNING INSTITUTE. (AT/0729-3682). **2815**

AUSTRALIAN PLANTS. (AT/0005-0008). **2410**

AUSTRALIAN PLUMBING INDUSTRY MAGAZINE. (AT/0817-6337). **2603**

AUSTRALIAN PODIATRIST. (AT/0311-3612). **Adv Mgr:** S. Reardon, **Tel** 03 8829666. **3917**

AUSTRALIAN POLICE JOURNAL. (AT/0005-0024). **3158**

AUSTRALIAN POLL DORSET JOURNAL. (AT). **206**

AUSTRALIAN PRESBYTERIAN LIFE. (AT). **5055**

AUSTRALIAN PRINTER MAGAZINE. (AT). **4563**

AUSTRALIAN PRIVATE DOCTOR : THE JOURNAL OF PRIVATE DOCTORS OF AUSTRALIA. (AT). **Adv Mgr:** Ron Hill, **Tel** (08)212 3551. **3554**

AUSTRALIAN PROFILE. (AT). **Adv Mgr:** Mr. Holt, **Tel** 02 439 3750. **1464**

AUSTRALIAN PROJECT MANAGER. (AT). **861**

AUSTRALIAN PROSTHODONTIC JOURNAL. (AT/0819-0887). **1317**

AUSTRALIAN PSYCHOLOGIST. (AT/0005-0067). **4575**

AUSTRALIAN PURCHASING AND SUPPLY (WATERLOO). (AT/1035-0357). **949**

AUSTRALIAN QUARTER HORSE MAGAZINE. (AT). **Adv Mgr:** Michael Vink. **2797**

AUSTRALIAN QUARTERLY. (AT/0005-0091). **2668**

AUSTRALIAN REFRIGERATION, AIR CONDITIONING AND HEATING. (AT). **2603**

AUSTRALIAN RELIGION STUDIES REVIEW. (AT/1031-2943). **4937**

AUSTRALIAN REVIEW OF APPLIED LINGUISTICS. (AT/0155-0640). **Adv Mgr:** R. Baldauf. **3267**

AUSTRALIAN ROAD AND TRACK. (AT/1036-3254). **Adv Mgr:** D. McLeod, **Tel** same as publisher. **5404**

AUSTRALIAN SCIENCE TEACHERS' JOURNAL, THE. (AT/0045-0855). **5087**

AUSTRALIAN SEA HERITAGE. (AT/0813-0523). **Adv Mgr:** H. Clements, **Tel** (02 2810266. **2611**

AUSTRALIAN SHELL NEWS. (AT/0310-1304). **5577**

AUSTRALIAN SHOPFITTING TRADE JOURNAL. (AT). **4210**

AUSTRALIAN SKIING. (AT). **Adv Mgr:** Stephen Kay. **4848**

AUSTRALIAN SOCIAL WORK. (AT/0312-407X). **5274**

AUSTRALIAN SOCIETY. (AT/0729-8595). **2510**

AUSTRALIAN SOCIETY OF INDEXERS NEWSLETTER. (AT/0314-3767). **3193**

AUSTRALIAN STOCK HORSE JOURNAL. (AT/0817-8550). **2797**

AUSTRALIAN STRING TEACHER. (AT/0312-9950). **4101**

AUSTRALIAN SUGAR CRAFT. (AT/1033-6656). **Adv Mgr:** Maxine Halliday, **Tel** (08)2933367. **2328**

AUSTRALIAN SUGAR YEAR BOOK, THE. (AT/0067-2173). **2328**

AUSTRALIAN SUPER REVIEW. (AT/0819-341X). **773**

AUSTRALIAN SURVEYOR. (AT/0005-0326). **Adv Mgr:** C. Fuller, **Tel** (06)2822282. **2019**

AUSTRALIAN SYSTEMATIC BOTANY. (AT/1030-1887). **501**

AUSTRALIAN SYSTEMATIC BOTANY SOCIETY NEWSLETTER. (AT/1034-1218). **Adv Mgr:** Dr. G. Leach. **501**

AUSTRALIAN TABLE TENNIS. (AT/0814-3668). **4885**

AUSTRALIAN TAFE TEACHER. (AT/0815-3701). **1911**

AUSTRALIAN TAX REVIEW. (AT/0311-094X). **2939**

AUSTRALIAN TEACHER OF THE DEAF. (AT/0005-0334). **1875**

AUSTRALIAN TEACHER, THE. (AT). **1888**

AUSTRALIAN TRANSPORT. (AT/0005-0385). **Adv Mgr:** J Balodis, **Tel** 61 3 5870888. **5377**

AUSTRALIAN UNIVERSITIES' REVIEW, THE. (AT). **1810**

AUSTRALIAN VETERINARY JOURNAL. (AT/0005-0423). **5505**

AUSTRALIAN VETERINARY PRACTITIONER. (AT/0310-138X). **5505**

AUSTRALIAN WELDING JOURNAL. (AT/0005-0431). **4026**

AUSTRALIAN WELDING RESEARCH. (AT/0045-0960). **4026**

AUSTRALIAN WOMEN'S BOOK REVIEW. (AT/1033-9434). **Adv Mgr:** M. Grossman, **Tel** 03 365-2247. **5551**

AUSTRALIAN WORKER : OFFICIAL JOURNAL OF THE AUSTRALIAN WORKERS' UNION, THE. (AT). **1654**

AUSTRALIAN ZOOLOGIST, THE. (AT/0067-2238). **5577**

AUSTRALIANA. (AT). **2510**

AUSTRALIA'S MINING MONTHLY. (AT). **2134**

AUSTRALIA'S TOP 500 COMPANIES. (AT/0817-3192). **Adv Mgr:** Max Cunningham. **726**

AUSTRIA TODAY. (AU/0304-8713). **2513**

AUSTRIACA. (FR/0396-4590). **2677**

AUSTRIAN STUDIES. (UK/1350-7532). **Adv Mgr:** Kathryn MacLean. **3364**

AUTHENTIK AUTHENTIK IN ENGLISH. (IE/0791-0797). **3267**

AUTHOR (LONDON. 1949). (UK/0005-0628). **Adv Mgr:** K. Pool. **3364**

AUTHOR SERIES. (US/0567-1744). **2722**

AUTO INDUSTRY AUSTRALIA. (AT). **Adv Mgr:** Bette Billett, **Tel** 011 61 3 8291156. **5404**

AUTO-JOURNAL (PARIS), L'. (FR/0005-0768). **5404**

AUTO LAUNDRY NEWS. (US/0005-0776). **5404**

AUTO MERCHANDISING NEWS. (US/0192-186X). **Adv Mgr:** Richard Burns. **641**

AUTO MODIFIEE, L'. (CN/0822-1006). **4885**

AUTO RACING DIGEST. (US/0090-8029). **4885**

AUTOCAD USER. (CN). **Adv Mgr:** M. Sean, **Tel** (905)475-4231. **1171**

AUTOGLASS (MCLEAN, VA.). (US/1047-2061). **2586**

AUTOGRAFO : QUADRIMESTRALE DEL CENTRO DI RICERCA SULLA TRADIZIONE MANOSCRITTA DI AUTORI CONTEMPORANEI, UNIVERSITA DI PAVIA. (IT). **3365**

AUTOGRAPH COLLECTOR. (US/1071-3425). **2438**

AUTOHARP QUARTERLY. (US/1071-1619). **Adv Mgr:** Ivan Stiles, **Tel** (215)935-9062. **4101**

AUTOHARPOHOLIC, THE. (US/0736-3796). **4101**

AUTOIMMUNE DISEASES. (UK/0142-8365). **3667**

AUTOMATED BUILDER. (US/0899-5540). **2815**

AUTOMATIC MACHINING. (US/0005-1071). **2110**

AUTOMATIC MERCHANDISER. (US/1061-1797). **2328**

AUTOMATICA E INSTRUMENTACION. (SP/0213-3113). **1217**

AUTOMATION AND CONTROL. (NZ/0110-6295). **1217**

AUTOMATION NEWS (NEW YORK, N.Y.). (US/0736-3737). **1218**

AUTOMATIZALAS. (HU/0133-1620). **1218**

AUTOMAZIONE NAVALE, L'. (IT/0392-2294). **591**

AUTOMOBIL-INDUSTRIE. (GW/0005-1306). **5405**

AUTOMOBILE ABSTRACTS (NUNEATON. 1975). (UK/0309-0817). **5405**

AUTOMOBILE ALMANAC. (US/0067-2513). **5405**

AUTOMOBILE INTERNATIONAL. (US/0099-2615). **5405**

AUTOMOBILE YEAR. (SZ). **5406**

AUTOMOTIVE COOLING JOURNAL : ACJ. (US/0005-1497). **5406**

AUTOMOTIVE ENGINEER. (UK/0307-6490). **5406**

AUTOMOTIVE ENGINEERING. (US/0098-2571). **2110**

AUTOMOTIVE EXECUTIVE (1979). (US/0195-1564). **5406**

AUTOMOTIVE MARKET REPORT. (US/0733-2084). **921**

AUTOMOTIVE NEWS. (US/0005-1551). **5406**

AUTOMOTIVE NEWS. MARKET DATA BOOK. (US). **5407**

AUTOMOTIVE PRODUCTS REPORT. (US/8750-4103). **5407**

AUTOMOTIVE REBUILDER. (US/0567-2317). **5407**

AUTOMOTIVE RETAILER (VANCOUVER). (CN/0005-1578). **Adv Mgr:** Lea Allen. **5407**

AUTOMOTIVE WEEK. (US/0889-3918). **5407**

AUTOREVISTA. (SP/0005-1961). **5407**

AUTOSPORT (TEDDINGTON). (UK/0269-946X). **Adv Mgr:** Matthew Newell, **Tel** (908)665-7811. **5407**

AUTOSTRADE. (IT). **5439**

AUTOWEEK. (US/0192-9674). **5407**

AUTREMENT. SERIE MONDE. (FR). **5192**

AV KOMMUNIKACIO. (HU/0237-9740). **1104**

AVALOKA. (US/0890-5541). **4937**

AVANCES

Advertising Accepted Index

AVANCES EN ALIMENTACION Y MEJORA ANIMAL. (SP). **206**

AVANCES EN CIENCIAS VETERINARIAS. (CL/0716-260X). **5505**

AVANCES EN PSICOLOGIA CLINICA LATINOAMERICANA. (CK/0120-3797). **4575**

AVANT-SCENE DU CINEMA, L'. (FR/0045-1150). **4064**

AVANTGARDE (NEDERLANDSE ED.). (NE/0926-910X). **5551**

AVE: LE MAGAZINE FREUDIEN, L'. (FR). **4575**

AVEC (PENNGROVE, CALIF.). (US/0899-3750). **3365**

AVENEMENT, L'. (SZ). **2485**

AVENGERS, THE. (US/0274-5240). **4857**

AVENIR MONTREAL. 1991. (CN/1187-6611). **1464**

AVENIRS. (FR/0005-1969). **1911**

AVENUE (NEW YORK, N.Y.). (US/0279-1226). **Adv Mgr:** Susan Harris. **2528**

AVES. (BE/0005-1993). **5615**

AVIACAO EM REVISTA. (BL/0102-4876). **Adv Mgr:** Francisco Carlos Alves. **12**

AVIAN DISEASES. (US/0005-2086). **5505**

AVIAN PATHOLOGY. (UK/0307-9457). **5505**

AVIASPORT. (FR/0005-2094). **Adv Mgr:** Gebard Pabot. **4885**

AVIASTRO (1984). (BE/0772-876X). **Adv Mgr:** Johan A Francois, **Tel** 32 2 5373899. **12**

AVIATION DESIGN THIAIS. (FR/0997-3753). **13**

AVIATION DIGEST. (US/0884-4755). **13**

AVIATION EQUIPMENT MAINTENANCE. (US/0745-0214). **13**

AVIATION MEDICINE (BANGALORE). (II/0250-5045). **3554**

AVIATION NEWS. (UK). **Adv Mgr:** Peter Smith. **13**

AVIATION QUARTERLY. (US/0360-8670). **13**

AVIATION REPORT. SYDNEY. (AT/1035-9079). **13**

AVIATION SPACE AND ENVIRONMENTAL MEDICINE. (US/0095-6562). **3554**

AVIATION WEEK & SPACE TECHNOLOGY. (US/0005-2175). **14**

AVIATORS HOT LINE. (US/0195-0347). **14**

AVIAZIONE. (IT/0391-7738). **14**

AVICULTURAL BULLETIN. (US/0567-2856). **5615**

AVICULTURAL JOURNAL, THE. (CN/0317-5650). **5615**

AVICULTURAL MAGAZINE, THE. (UK/0005-2256). **5615**

AVIDEO. (US/0747-1335). **1104**

AVIONICS (POTOMAC, MD.). (US/0273-7639). **14**

AVIRON CANADIEN. (CN/1184-9789). **Adv Mgr:** Barbara Lalonde, **Tel** (613)748-5656. **591**

AVIRON (ED QUEBECOISE). (CN/0821-1477). **5780**

AVKO NEWSLETTER. (US). **1875**

AVMARK AVIATION ECONOMIST. (UK/0961-2513). **Adv Mgr:** Nick Moreno. **14**

AVON NEWS. (US). **Adv Mgr:** Frank Chilinski. **5644**

AVOTAYNU. (US/0882-6501). **2438**

AVPI. AGRICULTURAL AND VETERINARY PRODUCT INDEX. (AT/0816-1623). **Adv Mgr:** G Hand. **64**

AVTOMATIKA I TELEMEHANIKA. (RU/0005-2310). **2110**

AVTOMATIKA (KIEV). (UN/0572-2691). **1218**

AWARDS FOR FIRST DEGREE STUDY AT COMMONWEALTH UNIVERSITIES. (UK). **Adv Mgr:** Sue Kirkland. **1810**

AWARDS FOR POSTGRADUATE STUDY AT COMMONWEALTH UNIVERSITIES. (UK/0960-7986). **Adv Mgr:** Sue Kirkland. **1811**

AWARDS FOR UNIVERSITY ADMINISTRATORS AND LIBRARIANS. (UK). **Adv Mgr:** Sue Kirkland. **1727**

AWARDS FOR UNIVERSITY TEACHERS AND RESEARCH WORKERS. (UK/0964-2706). **Adv Mgr:** Sue Kirkland. **1727**

AWAZ (TORONTO). (CN/0715-4135). **5780**

AWC NEWS/FORUM. (US/0193-0850). **4160**

AWIS MAGAZINE. (US/1057-5839). **Adv Mgr:** Annette Duplinsky. **5087**

AWP NEWSLETTER (NORFOLK). (US/0194-6498). **3365**

AXIS: ACADEMIC COMPUTING & INFORMATION SYSTEMS. (UK/1352-8971). **1246**

AXONE (DARTMOUTH). (CN/0834-7824). **Adv Mgr:** Sera Nicosia, **Tel** (416)547-8822. **3852**

AYRSHIRE CATTLE SOCIETY'S JOURNAL, THE. (UK/0005-2442). **207**

AYRSHIRE DIGEST. (US/0005-2450). **192**

AZALEA CITY NEWS & REVIEW. (US/0744-5318). **5625**

AZIENDA PUBBLICA TEORIA E PROBLEMI DI MANAGEMENT. (IT). **4632**

AZIMUTH. (AT/0728-4586). **Adv Mgr:** R. Phillips. **599**

AZIONE NONVIOLENTA. (IT). **1072**

AZLE NEWS ADVERTISER. (US). **Adv Mgr:** Marie Maxfield. **5746**

AZUR-CAMPING-MAGAZIN. (GW/0935-0454). **4848**

AZURE (TORONTO). (CN/0829-982X). **Adv Mgr:** Sergio Sgaramella. **2898**

B & D HEIR LINES. (CN/1192-1137). **2438**

B. C. CATHOLIC, THE. (CN/0007-0483). **5024**

B.C. CAVER : THE NEWSLETTER OF THE BRITISH COLUMBIA SPELEOLOGICAL FEDERATION. (CN). **1402**

B. C. JOURNAL OF SPECIAL EDUCATION. (CN/0704-7509). **1875**

B.C. NATURALIST. (CN/0228-8842). **2187**

B.C. PROFESSIONAL ENGINEER. ANNUAL DIRECTORY NUMBER, THE. (CN). **Adv Mgr:** Gillian Cobban, **Tel** (604)924-6733. **1966**

B N A TOPICS. (CN/0045-3129). **2784**

B.T.O. NEWS. (UK/0005-3392). **5615**

B70. (DK/0905-4650). **3193**

BA PAPYRUS. (US/1060-4030). **370**

BABEL. (AT/0005-3503). **3267**

BABY CONNECTION, THE. (US/0894-3990). **1727**

BABY TALK (1977). (US/0749-971X). **Adv Mgr:** Merrill Sugarman, **Tel** (212)989-8181. **3900**

BACA. (IO/0125-9008). **3193**

BACK HOME IN KENTUCKY. (US/0199-6290). **Adv Mgr:** Lori Fisher. **2722**

BACK OF THE YARDS JOURNAL. (US). **5658**

BACK STAGE. (US/0005-3635). **4064**

BACK STAGE. TV FILM & TAPE PRODUCTION DIRECTORY. (US/0734-9777). **1126**

BACKER UND KONDITOR. (GW/0005-383X). **2328**

BACKGROUNDER / AUSTRALIA, DEPARTMENT OF FOREIGN AFFAIRS AND TRADE. (AT). **4632**

BACKHOME (MOUNTAIN HOME, N.C.). (US/1051-323X). **Adv Mgr:** W M Janes, **Tel** (704)859-9000. **2528**

BACKSTRETCH, THE. (US/0005-366X). **Adv Mgr:** Shelia Eck, **Tel** (800)325-3487. **2797**

BACKWOODS. (US/1042-7732). **64**

BACKWOODS HOME MAGAZINE. (US/1050-9712). **Adv Mgr:** Jennifer Hoie, **Tel** (503)488-2053. **2485**

BAD ATTITUDE. (US/0896-9531). **Adv Mgr:** J. Sterling. **2793**

BADEN-WURTTEMBERG. (GW/0404-6307). **2677**

BADGER COMMON TATER, THE. (US/0271-5864). **164**

BADGER HERALD. (US/0045-1304). **1089**

BADGER SPORTSMAN. (US/0005-3775). **4869**

BADMINTON MAGAZINE, THE. (US/0747-9069). **4886**

BADMINTON NOW. (UK). **Adv Mgr:** Joanne James, **Tel** 011 44 61 486 6159. **4886**

BADMINTON U S A. (US/0045-1312). **4886**

BAESSLER-ARVHIC. (GW). **231**

BAGNO OGGI E DOMANI, IL. (IT). **2898**

BAHAMAS HANDBOOK AND BUSINESSMAN'S ANNUAL. (BF/0067-2912). **Adv Mgr:** E. D. Hill. **5462**

BAHAMIAN REVIEW. (BF/0005-397X). **2528**

BAILAMME. (IT). **4937**

BAKER & TAYLOR'S SCHOOL SELECTION GUIDE. (US/0732-8052). **1727**

BAKER STREET JOURNAL, THE. (US/0005-4070). **3365**

BAKER'S DIGEST. (US/0191-6114). **2328**

BAKERS JOURNAL. (CN/0005-4097). **Adv Mgr:** Anna Spencer, **Tel** (416)271-1366. **2328**

BAKERS' REVIEW (WATFORD). (UK/0005-4100). **2328**

BAKERY PRODUCTION AND MARKETING. (US/0005-4127). **2328**

BAKING & SNACK SYSTEMS. (US/1040-9254). **2328**

BAKO MAGAZINE. (GW). **3475**

BAKUNIN (DAVIS, CALIF.). (US/1052-3154). **3338**

BALANCE LONDON. (UK/0005-4216). **3555**

BALANCO FINANCEIRO. (BL). **773**

BALDWIN LEDGER, THE. (US/0745-9335). **Adv Mgr:** Christopher Miller, **Tel** (913)594-6424. **5674**

BALKANMEDIA. (BU/0861-5047). **Adv Mgr:** Mr. Stamov. **1104**

BALLARD NEWS-TRIBUNE (SEATTLE, WASH. : 1976). (US). **Adv Mgr:** Lani Doely. **5760**

BALLET-HOO. (CN/0045-1347). **1310**

BALLET REVIEW. (US/0522-0653). **1310**

BALLETT INTERNATIONAL. (GW/0722-6268). **1310**

BALLOON LIFE. (US/0887-6061). **Adv Mgr:** Tom Hamilton. **4886**

BALLOONS TODAY. (US/1049-9970). **Adv Mgr:** Greg Smith. **2528**

BALLROOM DANCING TIMES, THE. (UK). **1311**

BALLROOM REVIEW, THE. (US/1072-5156). **1311**

BALLS AND BURLAPS. (US/0404-6927). **2410**

BALLS AND STRIKES. (US/0199-2406). **4886**

BALTIC ASTRONOMY. (LI). **393**

BALTIC OBSERVER : NEWS FROM ESTONIA, LATVIA, AND LITHUANIA, THE. (LV). **Adv Mgr:** Einars Vitols, **Tel** 371-2-462119. **5806**

BALTIMORE BUSINESS JOURNAL. (US/0747-1823). **Adv Mgr:** Gary Press. **641**

BALTIMORE CHRONICLE. (US). **5685**

BALTIMORE ENGINEER, THE. (US/0005-4496). **1966**

BALTIMORE JEWISH TIMES. (US/0005-450X). **5046**

BALTIMORE MAGAZINE. (US/0005-4453). **Adv Mgr:** Linda Sciuto. **2528**

BALTIMORE MESSENGER (1985), THE. (US/1041-0872). **Adv Mgr:** Mark Iacurra. **5685**

BAM. (US/0194-5793). **Adv Mgr:** Marianne Stone. **4102**

'BAMA. (US/0195-0975). **4886**

BAMBOO RIDGE. (US/0733-0308). **3365**

BAN VIET (1987). (CN/0845-4817). **Adv Mgr:** Nghi Do, **Tel** (416)536-3611. **2256**

BANAS. (BL/0005-4585). **773**

BANCA, BORSA E TITOLI DI CREDITO. (IT). **773**

BANCAMATICA. (IT/0393-7062). **Adv Mgr:** Nicolo de Nicolo. **774**

BANCHE E BANCHIERI. (IT/0390-1378). **774**

BANCNI VESTNIK. (XV/0005-4631). **774**

BAND & FESTIVAL GUIDE. (US/0735-4711). **4102**

BAND INTERNATIONAL : THE JOURNAL OF THE INTERNATIONAL MILITARY MUSIC SOCIETY. (UK). **4102**

BAND NEWS. (AT). **4102**

BANDAOTI XUEBAO. (CC/0253-4177). **2036**

BANDER BLECHE ROHRE. (GW/0005-3848). **3475**

BANDWAGON (COLUMBUS, OHIO : 1957). (US/0005-4968). **4857**

BANGKOK POST, THE. (TH). **5811**

BANGKOK POST WEEKLY REVIEW. (TH). **642**

BANGLADESH MEDICAL JOURNAL. (BG/0301-035X). **3555**

BANGLADESH MEDICAL RESEARCH COUNCIL BULLETIN. (BG/0377-9238). **3555**

BANGLADESH OBSERVER, THE. (BG). **5778**

BANGOR DAILY NEWS. (US/0892-8738). **Adv Mgr:** Wayne A. Lawton, **Tel** (207)990-8261. **5687**

BANJO NEWSLETTER. (US/0190-1559). **4102**

BANK ACCOUNTING & FINANCE. (US/0894-3958). **774**

BANK AND QUOTATION RECORD. (US/0005-5026). **774**

BANK DIRECTOR (BRENTWOOD, TENN.). (US/1070-7611). **774**

BANK MARKETING. (US/0888-3149). **775**

BANK NEWS. (US/0005-5123). **775**

BANK NOTE REPORTER. (US/0164-0828). **2780**

BANK OPERATIONS BULLETIN. (US). **775**

BANK PERSONNEL NEWS. (US/0272-3271). **775**

BANK PROTECTION BULLETIN. (US/0091-0392). **775**

BANK RESOLUTION REPORTER. (US/1056-7232). **Adv Mgr:** Jim Hallander. **776**

BANKER & TRADESMAN. (US/0005-5409). **Adv Mgr:** Jeffery Keller. **4834**

BANKERS' ALMANAC AND YEAR BOOK, THE. (UK). **776**

BANKERS DIGEST (DALLAS, TEX.). (US/0005-5425). **Adv Mgr:** B.J.B. **776**

BANKERS HANDBOOK FOR ASIA. (HK). **776**

BANKERS MAGAZINE (BOSTON), THE. (US/0005-545X). **776**

BANKERS MONTHLY. (US/0005-5476). **776**

BANKING & FINANCE LAW REVIEW. (CN/0832-8722). **3085**

BANKING & FINANCIAL TRAINING. (UK/0265-7988). **777**

BANKING LAW REVIEW. (US/0898-7998). **3085**

BANKING WORLD. (UK/0737-6413). **777**

BANKS & FINANCIAL INSTITUTIONS IN SINGAPORE. (SI). **777**

BANKS IN INSURANCE REPORT. (US/8756-6079). **3085**

BANNER-GAZETTE, THE. (US/0194-3545). **Adv Mgr:** John C. Roberts, **Tel** (812)967-3176. **5662**

BANNER (GRAND RAPIDS), THE. (US/0005-5557). **4937**

BANNER-NEWS, THE. (US). **Adv Mgr:** Susan Carmichael. **5631**

BANNER PRESS NEWSPAPER, THE. (US/0891-1118). **Adv Mgr:** Chad Ferguson. **5747**

BANQUE DES MOTS (PARIS). (FR/0067-3951). **3268**

BANQUE ET INFORMATIQUE. (FR). **778**

BANQUIER (MONTREAL). (CN/0822-6849). **778**

BAPTIST & REFLECTOR. (US). **5055**

BAPTIST BIBLE TRIBUNE. (US/0745-5836). **Adv Mgr:** Michelle Dove. **5056**

BAPTIST BULLETIN, THE. (US/0005-5689). **5056**

BAPTIST CHALLENGE, THE. (US/8756-9612). **5056**

BAPTIST COURIER. (US/0744-6985). **5056**

BAPTIST HERALD, THE. (US/0005-5700). **4938**

BAPTIST LEADER (PHILADELPHIA). (US/0005-5727). **Adv Mgr:** M. Brown, **Tel** (610)768-2151. **4938**

BAPTIST MESSENGER (OKLAHOMA CITY, OKLA.). (US/0744-9518). **5056**

BAPTIST PROGRESS. (US/0005-5751). **5056**

BAPTIST QUARTERLY (LONDON). (UK/0005-576X). **5056**

BAPTIST RECORD (JACKSON, MISS.), THE. (US/0005-5778). **Adv Mgr:** Teresa Dickens. **5056**

BAPTIST STANDARD. (US). **Adv Mgr:** Doug Hylton. **5056**

BAPTIST TIMES. (UK/0005-5786). **5056**

BAPTIST TRUE UNION. (US/0883-7864). **5056**

BAPTIST TRUMPET (LITTLE ROCK, ARK.). (US/0888-9074). **5056**

BAPTIST UNION DIRECTORY, THE. (UK/0302-3184). **5056**

BAPTIST WORLD (WASHINGTON, D.C.). (US/0005-5808). **5056**

BAPTISTS TODAY. (US/1072-7787). **Adv Mgr:** Karen Cheponis, **Tel** (414)377-6822. **4938**

BAR: BEVERAGE ALCOHOL REPORTER. (CN/0006-0348). **2364**

BAR BRIEF (BEVERLY HILLS, CALIF.). (US/0749-0615). **2939**

BAR QUARTERLY. (UK/0307-8647). **4824**

BARBADOS CONSOLIDATED INDEX TO STATUTES AND SUBSIDIARY LEGISLATION TO .... (BB). **3124**

BARBIE (NEW YORK, N.Y. 1984). (US/0743-4898). **Adv Mgr:** Jacob Hill. **1060**

BARBOUR COMPENDIUM. BUILDING PRODUCTS. (UK/0260-9169). **Adv Mgr:** Barry Nutter. **599**

BARCELONA QUIRURGICA. (SP/0304-4475). **3960**

BARKER, THE. (US/1043-0849). **5505**

BARNARD'S RETAIL MARKETING REPORT. (US/0882-6218). **Adv Mgr:** W. Barnard, **Tel** (212)752-9810. **861**

BARNESVILLE RECORD-REVIEW, THE. (US). **5694**

BARNSTABLE PATRIOT. (US/0744-7221). **Adv Mgr:** Lucinda Harrison. **5687**

BARNSTORMER (FORT WAYNE, IND.), THE. (US/1062-7413). **14**

BARRE GAZETTE (BARRE, MASS. : 1839). (US). **5687**

BARRICADA INTERNACIONAL (ENGLISH ED.). (NQ/1013-9567). **2511**

BARRISTER (CHICAGO). (US/0094-5277). **2940**

BARRISTER (PHILADELPHIA, PA.), THE. (US/0739-2494). **Adv Mgr:** Carla Davard. **2940**

BARRON FAMILY NEWSLETTER, THE. (US/0882-8202). **2438**

BARRON'S (CHICOPEE, MASS.). (US/1077-8039). **642**

BARRON'S NATIONAL BUSINESS AND FINANCIAL WEEKLY. (US/0005-6073). **642**

BARR'S POST CARD NEWS. (US/0744-4540). **1144**

BARRY COUNTY ADVERTISER. (US/0194-1542). **5702**

BARTENDER. (US/0199-8404). **Adv Mgr:** Jamie, **Tel** (908)766-6006. **2364**

BARTONIA. (US/0198-7356). **501**

BASE (BERKELEY, CALIF.). (US/0732-7706). **5087**

BASEBALL BULLETIN. (US/0199-0128). **4886**

BASEBALL CARD NEWS. (US/0746-7966). **2771**

BASEBALL CARDS. (US/8750-5851). **2771**

BASEBALL DIGEST. (US/0005-609X). **4886**

BASEBALL HOBBY NEWS. (US/0199-946X). **2771**

BASEBALL (MONTREAL). (CN/0821-4123). **4886**

BASEBALL RESEARCH JOURNAL. (US/0734-6891). **4886**

BASEBALL RULE BOOK. NATIONAL FEDERATION EDITION. (US/0270-1537). **4886**

BASEBALL'S FORGOTTEN HEROES. (US). **430**

BASEHOR SENTINEL. (US). **Adv Mgr:** Angela Skwark. **5674**

BASELINE LONDON. (UK/0954-9226). **Adv Mgr:** M. D. Daines. **4564**

BASENJI, THE. (US/0094-9744). **4285**

BASES PARIS. (FR/0765-1325). **1274**

BASIC AND APPLIED MYOLOGY : BAM. (IT/1120-9992). **Adv Mgr:** G. L. Borgato. **3803**

BASIS. (IO/0005-6138). **2647**

BASKET BITS. (US). **370**

BASKETBALL DIGEST. (US/0098-5988). **4886**

BASKETBALL TIMES. (US/0744-2866). **4887**

BASKETBALL WEEKLY. (US/0005-6170). **Adv Mgr:** K Ballew, **Tel** (313)881-9554. **4887**

BASKETMAKER (WESTLAND, MICH.). (US/0897-3458). **370**

BASS MASTER MAGAZINE. (US/0199-3291). **2297**

BASS (NEW YORK, N.Y.). (US/0742-0609). **2297**

BASSIN'. (US/0884-4739). **2297**

BASTROP ADVERTISER AND COUNTY NEWS, THE. (US). **Adv Mgr:** Steve Taylor. **5747**

BASTROP DAILY ENTERPRISE, THE. (US). **Adv Mgr:** Robert Godfrey. **5683**

BAT RESEARCH NEWS. (US/0005-6227). **5577**

BATESVILLE GUARD. (US). **5631**

BATH & KITCHEN MARKETER. (CN/0225-9206). **2898**

BATH COUNTY NEWS-OUTLOOK. (US). **Adv Mgr:** Margaret Metz. **5679**

BATHROOMS. (UK/0950-0197). **600**

BATON ROUGE DAILY NEWS. (US/1044-3630). **Adv Mgr:** Bill Richard, **Tel** (504)927-6242. **5683**

BATTALION (COLLEGE STATION, TEX. 1893), THE. (US/1055-4726). **Adv Mgr:** Patricia Heck, **Tel** (409)845-2696. **1089**

BATTERIES INTERNATIONAL. (UK/0957-9249). **Adv Mgr:** H. Cullimore, **Tel** 011 44 276 856461. **2036**

BATTERY MAN. (US/0005-6359). **Adv Mgr:** Suzanne Kellerman. **1933**

BATTLE LAKE REVIEW. (US). **5694**

BATTLEFORD TELEGRAPH. (CN/0226-6377). **5780**

BAUDETTE REGION, THE. (US). **Adv Mgr:** John Oren. **5694**

BAUEN FUER DIE LANDWIRTSCHAFT (ZEITSCHRIFT). (GW/0171-7952). **600**

BAUEN MIT HOLZ. (GW/0005-6545). **600**

BAUEN + [I.E. UND] FERTIGHAUS. (GW). **600**

BAUFORUM. (AU). **600**

BAUINGENIEUR, DER. (GW/0005-6650). **2019**

BAUMEISTER. (GW/0005-674X). **293**

BAUVERWALTUNG. (GW/0005-6847). **4632**

BAUWIRTSCHAFT (HAUPTVERBAND DER DEUTSCHEN BAUINDUSTRIE). (GW/0341-3810). **600**

BAUWIRTSCHAFTLICHE INFORMATIONEN / BETRIEBSWIRTSCHAFTLICHES INSTITUT DER WESTDEUTSCHEN BAUINDUSTRIE. (GW/0721-6173). **Adv Mgr:** Elvira Bodenmuller. **600**

BAXTER BULLETIN. (US/0745-7707). **Adv Mgr:** Eddie Majeste. **5631**

BAXTER SPRINGS CITIZEN. (US/0455-6000). **Adv Mgr:** Jeff Nichols. **5674**

BAY & DELTA YACHTSMAN. (US/0191-4731). **591**

BAY AREA GUILD NEWSLETTER. (US). **2940**

BAY STATE BANNER. (US). **5687**

BAY STATE LIBRARIAN. (US/0005-6944). **3193**

BAY VOICE, THE. (US/8750-7188). **5691**

BAYERNMETALL. (GW). **3998**

BAYLOR COUNTY BANNER, THE. (US). **Adv Mgr:** Earl Gwinn. **5747**

BAYLOR LAW REVIEW. (US/0005-7274). **2940**

BAYREUTH. (GW). **2513**

BAYRUT TAYMZ. (US/0888-6016). **Adv Mgr:** Amale Paige, **Tel** (213)469-4354. **5633**

BAYSIDE TIMES. (US). **Adv Mgr:** Howard Swengler. **5714**

BAYSTATE REALTOR. (US/0891-5539). **Adv Mgr:** Bonnie Michaud, **Tel** (508)887-9371. **4834**

BBL. BIBLIOTEKSBLADET. (SW/0006-1867). **3193**

BBS CALLERS DIGEST. (US/1055-2812). **Adv Mgr:** Richard Paquette. **1274**

BC AGRICULTURE. (CN/0847-1444). **65**

BC BUSINESS. (CN/0829-481X). **Adv Mgr:** Tim Kelley. **642**

BC MOUNTAINEER, THE. (CN/0045-2998). **4869**

BC OUTDOORS. (CN/0045-3013). **4869**

BCG NEWSLETTER BOLTON. (UK/0144-588X). **4084**

BCS UPDATE. (US/1041-4770). **1171**

BEACHES LEADER, THE. (US/1059-647X). **Adv Mgr:** Linda Borgstede. **5649**

BEACON (1989), THE. (US/1044-4289). **Adv Mgr:** Martin Hilson. **5709**

BEACON-FORUM. (US). **5668**

BEACON FREE PRESS. (US). **Adv Mgr:** Audrey Morgenstern. **5714**

BEACON (TORONTO. 1970). (CN/0382-6384). **4938**

BEAN HOME NEWSLETTER, THE. (US/0882-4428). **1060**

BEAR FACTS REVIEW. (AT). **2583**

BEATRICE DAILY SUN. (US). **Adv Mgr:** Ron Sohl, **Tel** (402)223-5233. **5706**

BEAUFORT GAZETTE, THE. (US). **Adv Mgr:** Patsey Parker. **5741**

BEAUFORT MAGAZINE. (US). **Adv Mgr:** K. Griffin. **2528**

BEAUTIFUL BRITISH COLUMBIA. (CN/0005-7460). **Adv Mgr:** Key Pacific, **Tel** (604)388-4324. **5462**

BEAUTIFUL GLASS FOR HOME & OFFICE. (US/1043-5468). **2586**

BEAUTY AGE. (US/0887-414X). **402**

BEAUTY CLASSIC. (US/0886-8751). **402**

BEAUTY COUNTER LONDON. (UK/0960-3751). **Adv Mgr:** Liz Barnes, **Tel** 44 71 334 7334. **402**

BEAUX ARTS MAGAZINE. (FR/0757-2271). **343**

BEAVER COUNTY TIMES (SOUTHERN ED.). (US). **Adv Mgr:** Robert Woelfez, **Tel** (412)775-3200. **5734**

BEAVER, THE. (CN/0005-7517). **2722**

BEBIDAS. (US/0005-7533). **2364**

BECKETT BASEBALL CARD MONTHLY. (US/0886-0599). **2771**

BECKETT BASKETBALL MAGAZINE. (US/1055-8179). **2771**

BECKETT CIRCLE, THE. (US/0732-2224). **Adv Mgr:** Frederick N. Smith, **Tel** (704)547-2996. **3365**

BECOIS-VOLANT. (CN/0820-9863). **4887**

BED TIMES. (US/0893-5556). **2904**

BEDFORD BULLETIN (1984). (US/8750-1570). **5758**

BEDFORD COUNTY INQUIRER. (US). **Adv Mgr Tel** (814)623-1151. **5734**

BEDFORD SUN BANNER. (US/0746-262X). **5727**

BEDFORDSHIRE FAMILY HISTORY SOCIETY JOURNAL. (UK). **2438**

BEDFORDSHIRE MAGAZINE, THE. (UK/0005-7592). **2678**

BEE CULTURE. (US/1071-3190). **Adv Mgr:** D. Feagan, **Tel** (216)725-6677 Ext.3220. **65**

BEE, THE. (US). **5765**

BEE WORLD. (UK/0005-772X). **5577**

BEECHER CITY JOURNAL. (US/1066-7970). **5658**

BEEDAUDJIMOWIN. (CN). **2256**

BEEF (ST. PAUL, MINN.). (US/0005-7738). **207**

BEEFMASTER COWMAN, THE. (US/0194-4282). **207**

BEELDENAAR, DE. (NE). **2780**

BEER WHOLESALER. (US/0005-7770). **2364**

BEEVILLE BEE-PICAYUNE. (US/0889-8618). **Adv Mgr:** Dick Carter. **5747**

BEFFROI. (CN/0832-9966). **3365**

BEGINNINGS : THE OFFICIAL NEWSLETTER OF THE AMERICAN HOLISTIC NURSES' ASSOCIATION. (US/1071-2984). **3852**

BEGONIAN, THE. (US/0096-8684). **2410**

BEHAVIOR ANALYST, THE. (US/0738-6729). **4576**

BEHAVIOR RESEARCH METHODS, INSTRUMENTS, & COMPUTERS : A JOURNAL OF THE PSYCHONOMIC SOCIETY, INC. (US/0743-3808). **4576**

BEHAVIOR THERAPIST, THE. (US/0278-8403). **4576**

BEHAVIOR THERAPY. (US/0005-7894). **4576**

BEHAVIORAL & SOCIAL SCIENCES LIBRARIAN. (US/0163-9269). **3193**

BEHAVIORAL DISORDERS. (US/0198-7429). **1875**

BEHAVIORAL ECOLOGY. (US/1045-2249). **2211**

BEHAVIORAL MEDICINE ABSTRACTS. (US/0197-7717). **3654**

BEHAVIORAL MEDICINE (WASHINGTON, D.C.). (US/0896-4289). **3555**

BEHAVIORAL NEUROSCIENCE. (US/0735-7044). **4576**

BEHAVIORAL SCIENCES & THE LAW. (UK/0735-3936). **2940**

BEHAVIOUR CHANGE. (AT/0813-4839). **4577**

BEHAVIOURAL NEUROLOGY. (UK/0953-4180). **3828**

BEHAVIOURAL PHARMACOLOGY. (UK/0955-8810). **4293**

BEHAVORIAL HEALTHCARE TOMORROW. (US/1063-8490). **Adv Mgr:** Nancy E. Bechtel. **4768**

BEIHEFT ZUM BULLETIN JUGEND + LITERATUR. (GW/0172-0910). **3365**

BEIJING REVIEW. (CC/1000-9140). **4465**

BEIJING REVIEW (NORTH AMERICAN EDITION). (CC). **4465**

BEIRUT REVIEW, THE. (LE/1019-0732). **4516**

BEITRAEGE ZUR ALGEBRA UND GEOMETRIE. (GW). **3497**

BEITRAEGE ZUR GESCHICHTE DER DEUTSCHEN SPRACHE UND LITERATUR (TUEBINGEN). (GW/0005-8076). **3268**

BEITRAEGE ZUR HOCHSCHULFORSCHUNG. (GW/0171-645X). **1811**

BEITRAEGE ZUR NAMENFORSCHUNG. (GW/0005-8114). **2438**

BEITRAEGE ZUR NATURKUNDE NIEDERSACHSENS. (GW/0340-4277). **4162**

BEITRAEGE ZUR REGIONALEN GEOLOGIE DER ERDE. (GW/0522-7038). **1366**

BEITRAEGE ZUR UR- UND FRUEHGESCHICHTE DER BEZIRKE ROSTOCK, SCHWERIN UND NEUBRANDENBURG. (GW). **261**

BEITRAEGE ZUR VOGELKUNDE. (GW/0005-8211). **5615**

BEITRAGE ZUR GESCHICHTE DER FDJ. (GW). **5240**

BEKESI ELET. (HU/0522-7232). **5087**

BEL AGE, LE. (CN/0835-8702). **5178**

BELFAST TELEGRAPH [MICROFORM]. (UK/0307-5664). **5811**

BELGIAN BUSINESS. (BE). **642**

BELGIAN JOURNAL OF ZOOLOGY. (BE/0777-6276). **5577**

BELGISCH TIJDSCHRIFT VOOR TANDHEELKUNDE. (BE/0775-0285). **1317**

BELGISCHE FRUITREVUE. (BE/0005-8467). **2328**

BELGISCHE PROTESTANTSE. (BE). **5056**

BELGISCHE TUINBOUW. INTERNATIONALE EDITIE, DE. (BE/0005-8483). **2410**

BELIZE CONSOLIDATED INDEX OF STATUTES AND SUBSIDIARY LEGISLATION TO ... . (US). **3124**

BELIZE TODAY. (BH). **4632**

BELIZEAN STUDIES. (BH/0250-6831). **2723**

BELL TOWER, THE. (US/0092-8666). **Adv Mgr:** Bill Martin, **Tel** (810)349-4494. **4102**

BELLE BANNER, THE. (US). **Adv Mgr:** Ron Lewis. **5702**

BELLE PLAINE NEWS. (US). **Adv Mgr:** Carol Cole. **5674**

BELLEFONTAINE EXAMINER. (US/0747-3273). **Adv Mgr:** Cindy Titus. **5727**

BELLES LETTRES (ARLINGTON, VA.). (US/0884-2957). **Adv Mgr:** J. Mullaney, **Tel** (301)294-0278. **3366**

BELLEVILLE NEWS-DEMOCRAT. (US/8750-1058). **Adv Mgr:** Dave Baur. **5658**

BELLEVILLE POST. (US). **5709**

BELLEVILLE TELESCOPE (BELLEVILLE, KAN. : 1923). (US/0740-0985). **5674**

BELLEVILLE TIMES NEWS, THE. (US). **5709**

BELLEVUE KIRKLAND REDMOND (KING COUNTY WASH.) POLK DIRECTORY. (US). **2556**

BELLEVUE LEADER. (US/0193-0389). **Adv Mgr:** Ron Stadie. **5706**

BELLMORE MERRICK OBSERVER. (US). **Adv Mgr:** Wilma Pokress. **5714**

BELL'S ALASKA, YUKON & BRITISH COLUMBIA TRAVEL GUIDE. (US/1054-5034). **Adv Mgr:** Tim Bell, **Tel** (604)769-3073. **5462**

BELOIT DAILY CALL, THE. (US/8750-1791). **5674**

BELSER KUNSTQUARTAL. (GW). **4084**

BENBROOK NEWS, THE. (US). **5747**

BENCH AND BAR OF MINNESOTA, THE. (US/0276-1505). **Adv Mgr:** Julie A. Schaeffer, **Tel** (612)473-9677. **2941**

BENCHMARK OBAN. (UK/0951-6859). **Adv Mgr:** Anne Creechan. **2111**

BENCHMARK (WASHINGTON, D.C.). (US/0743-0310). **3092**

BEND BULLETIN, THE. (US). **5733**

BEND OF THE RIVER. (US/1063-9241). **Adv Mgr:** Sue Hunter, **Tel** (419)874-7534. **4162**

BENDEL LIBRARY JOURNAL. (NR/0331-555X). **3194**

BENEFITS & COMPENSATION INTERNATIONAL. (UK/0268-764X). **2875**

BENEFITS CANADA. (CN/0703-7732). **938**

BENEFITS LAW JOURNAL. (US/0897-7992). **3144**

BENEFITS NEWS ANALYSIS. (US/0199-3100). **642**

BENSHEIMER HEFTE. (GW/0522-9014). **4938**

BENT COUNTY DEMOCRAT. (US). **5642**

BENT OF TAU BETA PI, THE. (US/0005-884X). **1966**

BENTON COUNTY DAILY RECORD. (US). **5631**

BENTON COURIER, THE. (US). **Adv Mgr:** Rebecca Windburn. **5631**

BENTON NEWS, THE. (US). **Adv Mgr:** Paula Kerkemeyer. **5658**

BEQUADRO. (IT). **4102**

BEREAVEMENT & LOSS RESOURCES. (US/1071-7366). **4577**

BEREAVEMENT CARE. (UK/0268-2621). **Adv Mgr:** P. Scowen. **5274**

BEREAVEMENT (CARMEL, IND.). (US/0897-9588). **Adv Mgr Tel** (719)282-1948. **4577**

BERGBAU (HATTINGEN). (GW/0342-5681). **2135**

BERGSMANNEN. (SW/0284-0448). **Adv Mgr:** L. Eck. **2135**

BERICHTE DER BUNSENGESELLSCHAFT FUER PHYSIKALISCHE CHEMIE. (GW/0005-9021). **1050**

BERICHTE UBER LANDWIRTSCHAFT. (GW/0005-9080). **65**

BERITA BIBLIOGRAFI (JAKARTA, INDONESIA : 1984). (IO/0216-1273). **408**

BERKELEY JOURNAL OF EMPLOYMENT AND LABOR LAW. (US/1067-7666). **3144**

BERKELEY MONTHLY, THE. (US/0191-7080). **3338**

BERKELEY WOMEN'S LAW JOURNAL. (US/0882-4312). **2941**

BERKS COUNTY LAW JOURNAL. (US/8750-3379). **Adv Mgr:** J. Gwinther, **Tel** (610)375-4591. **2941**

BERKSHIRE MAGAZINE. (US/1042-587X). **2723**

BERLIN JOURNAL, THE. (US/8755-4003). **Adv Mgr:** Betty Van Sistine. **5765**

BERLIN REPORTER, THE. (US/1074-3499). **Adv Mgr:** Lucille Jalbert. **5708**

BERLINER ARZTEBLATT. (GW/0172-8490). **Adv Mgr:** Peter Geschlius. **3555**

BERLINER JOURNAL FUER SOZIOLOGIE. (GW). **Adv Mgr:** Axel Mischke, **Tel** (030)2236 377. **5240**

BERLINER THEOLOGISCHE ZEITSCHRIFT : THEOLOGIA VIATORUM NEUE FOLGE : HALBJAHRESSCHRIFT FUER THEOLOGIE IN DER KIRCHE. (GW/0724-6137). **4938**

BERLINER UND MUNCHENER TIERARZTLICHE WOCHENSCHRIFT. (GW/0005-9366). **5505**

BERLINGSKE TIDENDE. (DK). **5799**

BERMUDIAN, THE. (BM). **Adv Mgr:** Ms. Daveby, **Tel** (809)295-7104. **4887**

BERTIE LEDGER-ADVANCE. (US). **Adv Mgr:** Cliff Clark, **Tel** (919)794-3185. **5722**

BERYTUS; ARCHAEOLOGICAL STUDIES. (LE/0067-6195). **261**

BESCHAFTIGUNGSTHERAPIE UND REHABILITATION. (GW/0340-529X). **1875**

BESSATSU SEIKEI GEKA. (JA/0287-1645). **3960**

BESSATSU TAIYO (HEIBONSHA). (JA). **2502**

BEST GUIDE TO AMSTERDAM & BENELUX VENUES (FOR GAY MEN AND LESBIANS). (NE). **5463**

BEST GUIDE TO GREAT BRITAIN (FOR GAY MEN). (NE). **5463**

BEST 'N' MOST IN DFS, THE. (SW/1100-3006). **824**

BEST RECIPES. (US/0897-0386). **2328**

BEST-SELLING HOME PLANS FROM HOME MAGAZINE. (US/0743-2461). **2899**

BESTE AUS READER'S DIGEST, DAS. (GW/0005-9668). **2485**

BESTE UIT READER'S DIGEST, HET. (NE/0005-9692). **2513**

BEST'S SAFETY DIRECTORY. (US/0090-7480). **2859**

BET. (UK). **642**

BETA. (NO/0801-3322). **861**

BETHANY REPUBLICAN-CLIPPER. (US). **Adv Mgr:** Kathy Conger. **5702**

BETHEL HOME NEWS, THE. (US). **Adv Mgr:** Jim DeFillipo. **5645**

BETON : REVUE DU BETON PREFABRIQUE. (BE). **Adv Mgr:** Mrs. M.R. Roisin, **Tel** 32/2-734-7795. **601**

BETRIEBSKRANKENKASSEN. (GW). **2876**

BETTENDORF NEWS. (US). **5668**

BETTER BUILDINGS. (US/0744-530X). **Adv Mgr:** J. Schein, **Tel** same as publisher. **601**

BETTER HEARING. (AT). **Adv Mgr:** Trevor Kingston. **4384**

BETTER HOMES AND GARDENS. (US/0006-0151). **2788**

BETTER HOMES AND GARDENS DECORATING IDEAS. (US). **2899**

BETTER HOMES AND GARDENS HOME PLAN IDEAS. (US). **293**

BETTER HOMES AND GARDENS WOOD. (US/0743-894X). **2904**

BETTER INVESTING. (US/0006-016X). **Adv Mgr:** Martha Stephens. **892**

BETTER RADIO AND TELEVISION. (US). **1127**

BETTER ROADS. (US/0006-0208). **5439**

BETTY AND ME. (US/0006-0267). **4857**

BETTY AND VERONICA COMICS DIGEST MAGAZINE. (US/0886-134X). **4857**

BETWEEN THE LINES (WASHINGTON, D.C.). (US/1049-4421). **4465**

BETWEEN US. (CN/0714-4601). **1811**

BEVERAGE ALCOHOL MARKET REPORT. (US/0736-220X). **2364**

BEVERAGE WORLD. (US/0098-2318). **2364**

BEVERAGE WORLD INTERNATIONAL. (US). **2364**

BEVERAGES. (US/0409-2945). **2364**

BEVERLY HILLS BAR ASSOCIATION JOURNAL. (US/1051-628X). **2941**

BEVERLY HILLS COURIER, THE. (US/0892-645X). **Adv Mgr:** Sande Schwartz. **5633**

BEVERLY REVIEW, THE. (US/0006-0410). **5658**

BEVERLY TIMES, THE. (US). **Adv Mgr:** David Lodge, **Tel** (508)922-1234. **5687**

BEVOLKERUNG IN NORDRHEIN-WESTFALEN, DIE. (GW). **4561**

BEYOND APARTHEID. (NE/0923-4284). **1464**

BEYOND SIGHT. (CN/0712-2446). **4887**

BGS, ZEITSCHRIFT DES BUNDESGRENZSCHUTZES. (GW/0302-9468). **2513**

BHARATIYA NEPALI VANMAYA. (II). **3268**

BHARATIYA VIDYA. (II/0378-1984). **2647**

BHASHA ANI JIVANA : MARATHI-ABHYASA-PARISHAD-PATRIKA. (II). **3268**

BHAVAN'S JOURNAL. (II/0006-0518). **4342**

BI-STATE REPORTER. (US/0745-4813). **5658**

BI-YEAF. (IS/0302-8194). **14**

BIA BULLETIN. (UK). **443**

BIANNUAL NEWSLETTER OF THE CONFERENCE GROUP ON ITALIAN POLITICS & SOCIETY, THE. (US/1077-9043). **4516**

BIB-KRANT LEUVEN. (BE/0776-068X). **3194**

BIBEL UND KIRCHE. (GW/0006-0623). **5014**

BIBLE BHASHYAM (ENGLISH ED.). (II/0970-2288). **5014**

BIBLE COLLECTORS' WORLD. (US/0883-9204). **5014**

BIBLE LANDS. (UK/0006-0763). **5014**

BIBLE PUZZLER. (UK/0965-531X). **Adv Mgr:** Paul Slide. **5056**

BIBLE TODAY, THE. (US/0006-0836). **5015**

BIBLE TRANSLATOR, THE. (UK/0260-0935). **5015**

BIBLICAL ARCHAEOLOGIST, THE. (US/0006-0895). **261**

BIBLICAL EVANGELIST, THE. (US/0740-7998). **4938**

BIBLICAL ILLUSTRATOR. (US/0195-1351). **4938**

BIBLICAL RECORDER. (US/0279-8182). **5057**

BIBLICAL RESEARCH. (US/0067-6535). **Adv Mgr:** C. Katter, **Tel** (312)509-5840. **5015**

BIBLICAL THEOLOGY BULLETIN. (US/0146-1079). **5015**

BIBLIOGRAFIA AGROMETEOROLOGII. (PL/0239-958X). **1420**

BIBLIOGRAFIA FILOSOFICA MEXICANA. (MX/0185-240X). **4365**

BIBLIOGRAFIA GOSPODARKI I INZYNIERII WODNEJ. (PL/0239-622X). **5531**

BIBLIOGRAFIA HYDROLOGII I OCEANOLOGII. (PL/0239-6246). **1412**

BIBLIOGRAFIA METEOROLOGII: POLSKA. (PL/0239-6270). **1421**

BIBLIOGRAPHIE ANNUELLE DE L'HISTOIRE DE FRANCE DU CINQUIEME SIECLE A 1958. (FR). **2634**

BIBLIOGRAPHIE DE LA PHILOSOPHIE. (FR/0006-1352). **4365**

BIBLIOGRAPHIE DER PFLANZENSCHUTZLITERATUR. (GW/0006-1387). **2434**

BIBLIOGRAPHIE JURISTISCHER FESTSCHRIFTEN UND FESTSCHRIFTENBEITRAGE : DEUTSCHLAND, SCHWEIZ, OSTERREICH. (GW). **3079**

BIBLIOGRAPHIEN ZUR DEUTSCHEN LITERATUR DES MITTELALTERS. (GW/0523-2767). **3457**

BIBLIOGRAPHY OF AGRICULTURE : ANNUAL CUMULATION. (US/0364-829X). **66**

BIBLIOGRAPHY OF NOISE, A. (US/0092-5756). **2161**

BIBLIOGRAPHY OF REPRODUCTION. (UK/0006-1565). **477**

BIBLIONEWS AND AUSTRALIAN NOTES AND QUERIES. (AT/0045-1940). **4824**

BIBLIOTHECA BOTANICA. (GW/0067-7892). **502**

BIBLIOTHECA EPHEMERIDUM THEOLOGICARUM LOVANIENSIUM. (BE). **4939**

BIBLIOTHECA MYCOLOGIA. (GW). **443**

BIBLIOTHECK. (UK/0006-193X). **410**

BIBLIOTHEEK EN SAMENLEVING. (NE/0165-1048). **3195**

BIBLIOTHEK. (GW/0341-4183). **3195**

BIBLIOTHEK. (GW). **3457**

BIBLIOTHEKAR. (GW/0006-1964). **3195**

BIBLIOTHEKSDIENST. (GW/0006-1972). **3195**

BIBLIOTHEKSFORUM BAYERN. (GW/0340-000X). **3195**

BIBLIOTHEQUE D'HUMANISME ET RENAISSANCE. (SZ/0006-1999). **2611**

BIBLISCHE ZEITSCHRIFT. (GW/0006-2014). **5015**

BIC US. BUSINESS INDUSTRY COORDINATOR. (US). **643**

BICYCLE BUSINESS JOURNAL. (US/0745-8126). **428**

BICYCLE FORUM. (US/0193-8177). **428**

BICYCLE GUIDE. (US/0889-289X). **428**

BICYCLE USA. (US/0747-0371). **Adv Mgr:** D. Jones. **428**

BICYCLING. (US/0006-2073). **428**

BICYCLING AUSTRALIA. (AT/1034-8085). **428**

BIENNIAL REPORT OF EXAMINING AND LICENSING BOARDS / MINNESOTA BOARD OF PSYCHOLOGY. (US). **4577**

BIG BEAUTIFUL WOMAN. (US/0192-5938). **1082**

BIG BEND REGISTER. (US/0736-7074). **2439**

BIG BOOK OF METALWORKING MACHINERY. (US/0045-1983). **3999**

BIG LAKE WILDCAT, THE. (US). **Adv Mgr:** David Werst. **5747**

BIG REEL, THE. (US/0744-723X). **4064**

BIG SANDY NEWS (LOUISA, KY. : 1974). (US/0891-2327). **5679**

BIG SKY BUSINESS JOURNAL. (US/8756-6567). **Adv Mgr:** Dennis Pyburn. **643**

BIG SPRING HERALD. (US/0746-6811). **Adv Mgr:** Ken Dulaney. **5747**

BIJDRAGEN EN MEDEDELINGEN BETREFFENDE DE GESCHIEDENIS DER NEDERLANDEN. (NE/0165-0505). **2678**

BIKHAMA. (II). **3367**

BILAKABIDE : REVISTA DE POESIA. (SP). **3460**

BILANZ. (SZ). **1464**

BILANZ DER WOHNBEVOELKERUNG IN DEN GEMEINDEN DER SCHWEIZ. (SZ). **4561**

BILDERHEFTE. (GW/0522-9790). **4084**

BILDGEBUNG (BASEL). (SZ/1012-5655). **3939**

BILINGUAL FAMILY NEWSLETTER, THE. (UK/0952-4096). **2277**

BILINGUAL REVIEW. (US/0094-5366). **Adv Mgr:** Theresa Hammon. **3269**

BILL-DALE MARCINKO'S AFTA. (US/0193-7782). **3338**

BILLBOARD (CINCINNATI, OHIO. 1963). (US/0006-2510). **4103**

BILLBOARD INTERNATIONAL TALENT & TOURING DIRECTORY. (US/0732-0124). **4103**

BILLERICA NEWS, THE. (US). **Adv Mgr:** John Vistorino. **5687**

BILLIARDS DIGEST. (US/0164-761X). **4857**

BILLIKEN. (AG). **1060**

BILLINGS GAZETTE (BILLINGS, MONT. : DAILY : 1914). (US). **5705**

BILTEN ZA HEMATOLOGIJU I TRANSFUZIJU. (YU/0350-2023). **3770**

BIMCO BULLETIN. (DK/0901-814X). **5447**

BINARY. (UK/0266-304X). **Adv Mgr:** Evans. **560**

BINDEREPORT. (GW/0342-3573). **4824**

BINDTEKEN. (BE/0772-2125). **5268**

BINGGONG XUEBAO. (CC/1000-1093). **4038**

BINGO. (FR/0523-6207). **2498**

BINNENGEWASSER. (GW/0067-8643). **1352**

BINOCULAR VISION & EYE MUSCLE SURGERY QUARTERLY. (US). **Adv Mgr:** Judy, **Tel** (904)378-1129. **3872**

BINSTED'S DIRECTORY OF FOOD TRADE MARKS AND BRAND NAMES. (UK). **2329**

BIO-DYNAMICS. (US/0006-2863). **66**

BIO-ELECTRONICS & BIOSENSORS. (UK/0952-0384). **443**

BIO-JOULE. (CN/0708-1936). **1933**

BIO-SCIENCE RESEARCH BULLETIN. (II/0970-0889). **444**

BIO/TECHNOLOGY (NEW YORK, N.Y. 1983). (US/0733-222X). **5088**

BIOACOUSTICS (BERKHAMSTED). (UK/0952-4622). **5578**

BIOCATALYSIS. (SZ/0886-4454). **480**

BIOCHEMICAL JOURNAL (LONDON. 1984). (UK/0264-6021). **481**

BIOCHEMICAL SOCIETY SYMPOSIA. (UK/0067-8694). **481**

BIOCHEMICAL SOCIETY TRANSACTIONS. (UK/0300-5127). **481**

BIOCHEMIE UND PHYSIOLOGIE DER PFLANZEN. (GW/0015-3796). **502**

BIOCHEMIST LONDON. (UK/0954-982X). **Adv Mgr:** Samantha Burt, **Tel** 0225 442574. **481**

BIOCHEMISTRY AND CELL BIOLOGY. (CN/0829-8211). **481**

BIOCHEMISTRY (EASTON). (US/0006-2960). **482**

BIOCHEMISTRY INTERNATIONAL. (AT/0158-5231). **482**

BIOCHIMICA CLINICA. (IT/0393-0564). **482**

BIOCHIMICA ET BIOPHYSICA ACTA. (NE/0006-3002). **482**

BIOCHIMICA ET BIOPHYSICA ACTA. BIOMEMBRANES. (NE/0005-2736). **482**

BIOCHIMICA ET BIOPHYSICA ACTA. PROTEIN STRUCTURE AND MOLECULAR ENZYMOLOGY. (NE/0167-4838). **482**

BIOCHROMATOGRAPHY. (US/0888-4404). **482**

BIOCONTROL NEWS AND INFORMATION. (UK/0143-1404). **151**

BIOCYCLE. (US/0276-5055). **2225**

BIODEGRADATION (DORDRECHT). (NE/0923-9820). **2225**

BIODETERIORATION ABSTRACTS. (UK/0951-0621). **2183**

BIOESSAYS. (UK/0265-9247). **532**

BIOFACTORS (OXFORD). (UK/0951-6433). **483**

BIOGENIC AMINES. (UK/0168-8561). **483**

BIOGEOCHEMISTRY. (NE/0168-2563). **2188**

BIOGRAPHICAL DIRECTORY / AMERICAN POLITICAL SCIENCE ASSOCIATION. (US). **430**

BIOGRAPHY (HONOLULU). (US/0162-4962). **430**

BIOINFORMATION MANAGER. (GW). **444**

BIOLOGIA & CLINICA HEMATOLOGICA. (SP/0210-895X). **3770**

BIOLOGIA MORA (VLADIVOSTOK). (RU/0134-3475). **553**

BIOLOGICA — Advertising Accepted Index

BIOLOGICA. (FI). **502**

BIOLOGICAL AGRICULTURE & HORTICULTURE. (UK/0144-8765). **66**

BIOLOGICAL CONSERVATION. (UK/0006-3207). **2188**

BIOLOGICAL MASS SPECTROMETRY. (UK/1052-9306). **1013**

BIOLOGICAL MEMOIRS. (II/0379-8097). **445**

BIOLOGICAL NOTES (COLUMBUS). (US/0078-3986). **445**

BIOLOGICAL PAPERS OF THE UNIVERSITY OF ALASKA. (US/0568-8604). **445**

BIOLOGICAL PSYCHIATRY (1969). (US/0006-3223). **3921**

BIOLOGICAL RHYTHMS. (UK/0142-8004). **578**

BIOLOGICAL THERAPY. (US/0733-2661). **3774**

BIOLOGICAL TRACE ELEMENT RESEARCH. (US/0163-4984). **483**

BIOLOGICO, O. (BL/0366-0567). **446**

BIOLOGISCHE ABHANDLUNGEN. (GW/0006-3282). **446**

BIOLOGIST (LONDON). (UK/0006-3347). **446**

BIOLOGUE (WATERLOO). (CN/0840-8548). **446**

BIOLOGY & PHILOSOPHY. (NE/0169-3867). **446**

BIOLOGY DIGEST. (US/0095-2958). **477**

BIOLOGY INTERNATIONAL. (FR/0253-2069). **447**

BIOLOGY INTERNATIONAL. SPECIAL ISSUES : THE NEWS MAGAZINE OF THE INTERNATIONAL UNION OF BIOLOGICAL SCIENCES (IUBS). (FR). **447**

BIOLOGY OF REPRODUCTION. (US/0006-3363). **578**

BIOLOGY OF THE CELL. (FR/0248-4900). **532**

BIOLOGY OF THE NEONATE. (SZ/0006-3126). **3900**

BIOMATERIALS. (UK/0142-9612). **3556**

BIOMEDICA BIOCHIMICA ACTA. (GW/0232-766X). **447**

BIOMEDICAL INSTRUMENTATION & TECHNOLOGY. (US/0899-8205). **3687**

BIOMEDICAL LETTERS. (UK/0961-088X). **3556**

BIOMEDICAL SAFETY & STANDARDS. (US). **3557**

BIOMETALS. (US/0966-0844). **483**

BIOMETRICS. (US/0006-341X). **5323**

BIOPEOPLE (SAN MATEO, CALIF.). (US/1065-612X). **Adv Mgr:** Bill Stanley, Tel (408)732-2555. **447**

BIOPHARM (EUGENE, OR.). (US/1040-8304). **4293**

BIOPHARMACEUTICS & DRUG DISPOSITION. (UK/0142-2782). **4293**

BIOPOLYMERS. (US/0006-3525). **483**

BIOPROBES (EUGENE, OR.). (US/1064-251X). **5088**

BIOS (MADISON, N.J.). (US/0005-3155). **477**

BIOS (PARIS). (FR/0366-2284). **2364**

BIOSCIENCE. (US/0006-3568). **448**

BIOSCIENCE REPORTS. (US/0144-8463). **532**

BIOTEC (STUTTGART). (GW/0931-1408). **Adv Mgr:** Michele Francaviglia. **3687**

BIOTEC WURZBURG. (GW). **448**

BIOTECH BUYERS' GUIDE. (US/1067-2818). **3687**

BIOTECH KNOWLEDGE SOURCES. (UK/0953-2226). **3688**

BIOTECH PATENT NEWS. (US/0898-2813). **Adv Mgr:** Alicia Parr. **3688**

BIOTECH PRODUCTS INTERNATIONAL. (BE/1016-6505). **5088**

BIOTECHNIQUES. (US/0736-6205). **3557**

BIOTECHNOLOGIE. (NE). **448**

BIOTECHNOLOGY INFORMATION NEWS. (UK/0952-147X). **3689**

BIOTECHNOLOGY LAW REPORT. (US/0730-031X). **3689**

BIOTECHNOLOGY LETTERS. (UK/0141-5492). **3689**

BIOTECHNOLOGY (NEW YORK, N.Y. : 1983). (US/0275-7559). **3689**

BIOTECHNOLOGY NEWS. (US/0273-3226). **3689**

BIOTECHNOLOGY TECHNIQUES. (UK/0951-208X). **3689**

BIOTECHNOLOGY THERAPEUTICS. (US/0898-2848). **3690**

BIOTECNOLOGIA APLICADA : REVISTA DE LA SOCIEDAD IBEROLATINOAMERICANA PARA INVESTIGACIONES SOBRE INTERFERON Y BIOTECNOLOGIA EN SALUD. (CU/0864-4551). **Adv Mgr:** Alfredo Delgado, Tel 21-8854. **3690**

BIOTREATMENT NEWS. (US/1058-0239). **Adv Mgr:** E. Card, Tel same as publisher. **5088**

BIOVENTURE VIEW. (US/0892-1903). **Adv Mgr:** Bill Stanley, Tel (408)732-2555. **448**

BIRD OBSERVER (BELMONT, MASS.). (US/0893-4630). **5615**

BIRD WATCHER'S DIGEST. (US/0164-3037). **Adv Mgr:** A. Thompson, Tel 800-879-2473. **5615**

BIRD WORLD (NORTH HOLLYWOOD). (US/0199-5979). **5615**

BIRDING. (US/0161-1836). **Adv Mgr:** Susanna Lawson, Tel (804)983-3021. **5578**

BIRDING IN SOUTHERN AFRICA. (SA/0006-5838). **5616**

BIRKNER. (GW). **4232**

BIRMINGHAM. (US/0006-369X). **2529**

BIRMINGHAM BUSINESS JOURNAL. (US/0889-2237). **Adv Mgr:** Linda Geldolatt. **643**

BIRMINGHAM NEWS, THE. (US/0899-0050). **Adv Mgr:** Bill Ward. **5625**

BIRMINGHAM POST & MAIL YEAR BOOK AND WHO'S WHO, THE. (UK). **Adv Mgr:** Lorraine Watton. **430**

BIRMINGHAM POST-HERALD. (US/1040-1571). **5625**

BIRMINGHAM TIMES, THE. (US). **Adv Mgr:** Comer Allen, Tel (205)251-5158. **2256**

BIRTH (BERKELEY, CALIF.). (US/0730-7659). **3757**

BIRTH DEFECTS ORIGINAL ARTICLE SERIES. (US/0547-6844). **3757**

BIRTH GAZETTE, THE. (US/0890-3255). **3757**

BIRTH PSYCHOLOGY BULLETIN. (US/0734-3124). **3758**

BIRTH ST. LEONARDS. (AT/1032-9625). **Adv Mgr:** Matthew Chivers, David Knight. **2277**

BISBEE OBSERVER, THE. (US/0895-2450). **Adv Mgr:** Laura Swan. **5629**

BISMARCK TRIBUNE, THE. (US) **Adv Mgr:** Lani Renneau. **5725**

BIT. (IT). **1172**

BIT. (CI). **1256**

BIT FIRENZE. (IT/0394-3666). **3196**

BITACORA. (SP/0212-632X). **591**

BITAMIN (VITAMIN). (JA). **962**

BITE ME. (US). **2485**

BITZARON. (US/0006-3932). **5046**

BIULETYN STATYSTYCZNY. (PL/0006-4025). **5323**

BIWABIK TIMES. (US). **5694**

BLACFAX. (US/0882-6595). **2256**

BLACK AND MAGENTA, THE. (US). **1089**

BLACK AND RED. (US). **1089**

BLACK & WHITE (BIRMINGHAM, ALA.). (US/1064-0134). **Adv Mgr:** Chuck Geiss. **2485**

BLACK BEAR. (US/8756-0666). **3367**

BLACK BELT (BURBANK, CALIF.). (US/0277-3066). **4887**

BLACK COLLEGIAN (NEW ORLEANS), THE. (US/0192-3757). **1811**

BLACK COUNTRY BUSINESS DIRECTORY (SOUTH EDITION). (UK/0957-1035). **Adv Mgr:** Susan Hicks, Tel 0908-614477. **643**

BLACK ELEGANCE. (US/0885-9647). **2529**

BLACK EMPLOYMENT & EDUCATION. (US/1053-704X). **Adv Mgr:** Dennis Matthews, Tel (404)469-5891. **643**

BLACK ENTERPRISE. (US/0006-4165). **Adv Mgr:** Earl G. Graves, Jr., Tel (212)242-8000. **643**

BLACK FAMILY. (US/0279-0718). **2256**

BLACK FILM REVIEW. (US/0887-5723). **4064**

BLACK HEALTH. (US/1042-329X). **4768**

BLACK ISSUES IN HIGHER EDUCATION. (US/0742-0277). **1812**

BLACK MALE/FEMALE RELATIONSHIPS. (US/0740-2163). **5240**

BLACK MARIA. (US/0045-222X). **3367**

BLACK MASKS. (US/0887-7580). **Adv Mgr:** B. Turner. **5362**

BLACK MUSIC RESEARCH JOURNAL. (US/0276-3605). **4103**

BLACK ORPHEUS. (NR/0067-9100). **3367**

BLACK SCHOLAR, THE. (US/0006-4246). **2257**

BLACK VIDEO GUIDE, THE. (US/0882-7532). **4064**

BLACK VOICE NEWS, THE. (US). **2257**

BLACK WARRIOR REVIEW, THE. (US/0193-6301). **Adv Mgr:** Mark Drew. **3338**

BLACK'S OFFICE LEASING GUIDE. CONNECTICUT/NEW YORK SUBURBS. (US). **4210**

BLACK'S OFFICE LEASING GUIDE. HOUSTON OFFICE SPACE MARKET. (US). **4210**

BLACK'S OFFICE LEASING GUIDE. PHILADELPHIA & SUBURBS, SOUTHERN NEW JERSEY, DELAWARE. (US). **4210**

BLACK'S OFFICE LEASING GUIDE. WASHINGTON / BALTIMORE METRO AREA. (US). **4210**

BLACKSHEAR TIMES, THE. (US/0746-9330). **Adv Mgr:** Cheryl Williams. **5652**

BLACKWELL JOURNAL-TRIBUNE. (US). **Adv Mgr:** Lamar Allen. **5731**

BLADE-ATLAS, THE. (US). **Adv Mgr:** Becky Siedenburg, Tel (608)935-2331. **5765**

BLADE-EMPIRE. (US). **Adv Mgr:** Joni Regnier, Tel (913)243-2424. **5674**

BLADE MAGAZINE, THE. (US/0744-6179). **Adv Mgr:** Luci Stone, Tel (615)894-0339. **2771**

BLADE, THE. (US). **5652**

BLAIR PRESS, THE. (US). **Adv Mgr:** Liz Hjornevik. **5765**

BLAIR'S GUIDE VICTORIA. (AT/0810-9567). **5465**

BLAKE. (US/0160-628X). **316**

BLAST MANUKA. (AT/0819-0739). **Adv Mgr:** Bill Tully. **2510**

BLAUE JUNGS. (GW). **4175**

BLIMP. (AU). **4064**

BLIND ALLEYS. (US/0737-9269). **3460**

BLIND (AMSTERDAM, NETHERLANDS). (NE). **344**

BLIND SPOT PHOTOGRAPHY. (US/1068-1647). **Adv Mgr:** Micheal C., Tel (212)633-1317. **4367**

BLISSFIELD ADVANCE. (US). **Adv Mgr:** Paul Heidbreder, Tel (517)486-4290. **5691**

BLITZ CHESS. (US/1053-3087). **4857**

BLITZ LONDON. (UK/0263-2543). **316**

BLK (LOS ANGELES, CALIF.). (US/1043-0075). **Adv Mgr:** Cedric Whitfield, Tel (310)410-0808. **2793**

BLM. BONNIERS LITTERARA MAGASIN. (SW/0005-3198). **3367**

BLOCK (EAST BARNET, HERTFORDSHIRE). (UK/0143-3245). **2513**

BLOEM & BLAD. (NE). **2434**

BLONDE COUNTRY / ANNUAL HEARD REFERENCE ED. (CN/0711-1797). **207**

BLOOD BANK WEEK. (US/0747-2420). **3770**

BLOOD COAGULATION & FIBRINOLYSIS : AN INTERNATIONAL JOURNAL IN HAEMOSTASIS AND THROMBOSIS. (UK/0957-5235). **3795**

BLOOD-HORSE, THE. (US/0006-4998). **2797**

BLOOD PURIFICATION. (SZ/0253-5068). **3770**

BLOOD TRANSFUSION. (UK/0261-4596). **3795**

BLOODLINES :. (US/0890-8923). **Adv Mgr:** T. Birdsong, Tel (616)343-9020. **4286**

BLOOMFIELD JOURNAL, THE. (US/0746-9632). **Adv Mgr:** Frank Chilinski. **5645**

BLOOMSBURY REVIEW, THE. (US/0276-1564). **3338**

BLOUNT COUNTIAN, THE. (US/1056-3288). **Adv Mgr:** Ricky Hicks. **5625**

BLOWING ROCKET, THE. (US/1071-0574). **Adv Mgr:** Jerry Burns. **5722**

BLUE & GRAY MAGAZINE. (US/0741-2207). **Adv Mgr:** Robin Roth, Tel (614)870-1865. **2723**

BLUE BOOK : MEMBERSHIP DIRECTORY & BUYER'S GUIDE. (US). **2329**

BLUE BUFFALO. (CN/0820-8352). **3367**

BLUE JAY. (CN/0006-5099). **4163**

BLUE JAY NEWS. (CN/0822-9988). **4163**

BLUE LINE MAGAZINE. (CN/0847-8538). **3158**

BOOKS

BLUE MOUND LEADER. (US). **Adv Mgr:** Cindy Stuart. **5658**

BLUE MOUNTAIN HERITAGE. (US/0743-183X). **2439**

BLUE RIBBON FILL-IT-INS. (US/0194-3111). **4858**

BLUE RIBBON HOME PLANS. (US/0899-4382). **2899**

BLUE RIBBON, THE. (US). **2797**

BLUE RIBBON WORD-FINDS. (US/0194-312X). **4858**

BLUE RIDGE COUNTRY. (US/1041-3456). **Adv Mgr:** Jo Dietrich. **2529**

BLUE SWAN REVIEW : GUIDE TO WOMEN'S FASHION CATALOGS, THE. (US/1041-3936). **1082**

BLUEFIELD DAILY TELEGRAPH. (US). **Adv Mgr:** Donna Clayton, **Tel** (304)327-2816. **5763**

BLUEGRASS-BUEHNE. (GW/0936-2479). **4104**

BLUEGRASS MUSIC NEWS. (US/0006-5129). **4104**

BLUEGRASS UNLIMITED. (US/0006-5137). **Adv Mgr:** Pat Jeffries, **Tel** (703)349-8181. **4104**

BLUEPRINT (LONDON. 1983). (UK/0268-4926). **Adv Mgr:** R. Leeks, **Tel** 071-486-7419. **293**

BLUES ACCESS. (US/1066-4068). **4104**

BLUES & SOUL. (UK). **4104**

BLUES LIFE. (AU/0250-4421). **4104**

BLUES LIFE JOURNAL. (AU/0250-4421). **Adv Mgr:** Fran. **4104**

BLUES UNLIMITED. (UK/0006-5153). **4104**

BLUFFTON NEWS, THE. (US). **5727**

BLUMEN EINZELHANDEL. (GW). **2434**

BLYTTIA. (NO/0006-5269). **502**

BMCIS BUILDING MAINTENANCE PRICE BOOK. (UK/0261-2933). **601**

BMX PLUS. (US/0195-0320). **428**

BN. (FI/0784-7726). **4104**

B'NAI B'RITH INTERNATIONAL JEWISH MONTHLY, THE. (US/0279-3415). **5046**

BNB NBB COMPTES ANNUELS DES ENTERPRISES BELGES. CD-ROM. (BE). **739**

BOARD MANUFACTURE AND PROCESSING. (UK/0306-4123). **2399**

BOAT AND MOTOR DEALER. (US/0006-5366). **591**

BOAT GUIDE. (CN/0826-2802). **592**

BOAT INTERNATIONAL. (UK/0264-9136). **592**

BOATBUILDER (RIVERSIDE, CONN.). (US/0886-0254). **592**

BOATING INDUSTRY MARINE BUYERS' GUIDE. (US). **592**

BOATING INDUSTRY, THE. (US/0006-5404). **592**

BOATING (NEW YORK, N.Y.). (US/0006-5374). **Adv Mgr:** Peter Beckenbach, **Tel** (212)767-5571. **592**

BOATING NEWS (VANCOUVER). (CN/0700-7388). **592**

BOATING PRODUCT NEWS. (US/0190-4507). **592**

BOATING WORLD. (US/1059-5155). **Adv Mgr:** Jay Perkins, **Tel** same as publisher. **592**

BOB DAMRON'S ADDRESS BOOK. (US). **5187**

BOCA RATON. (US/0740-2856). **2529**

BODENKULTUR (1964). (AU/0006-5471). **67**

BODOBOKA. (NO). **4085**

BODY LEEDS. (UK/0006-5501). **Adv Mgr:** Sally Barlow. **5407**

BODY, MIND, SPIRIT. (US/0895-7657). **Adv Mgr:** Clarke Williams. **4185**

BODY POLITIC XTRA. (CN/0826-0508). **2793**

BOER EN DE TUINDER, DE. (BE). **Adv Mgr:** Van Eylen, **Tel** 016 242246. **67**

BOGENS VERDEN. (DK/0006-5692). **3196**

BOGONG. (AT/0159-6586). **2188**

BOHEMIA. (CU/0523-8579). **2485**

BOICE LYDELL'S SPORT KARATE INTERNATIONAL. (US/1064-6507). **4887**

BOIS NATIONAL (EDITION VERTE), LE. (FR). **Adv Mgr:** J. Andre. **2376**

BOISE (ADA COUNTY, IDAHO) CITY DIRECTORY. (US). **2556**

BOITE A NOUVELLES. (CN/1180-6761). **Adv Mgr:** Suzanne Lacroix, **Tel** (705)232-5222. **5780**

BOK OG BIBLIOTEK. (NO/0006-5811). **3257**

BOK OG SAMFUNN (OSLO, NORWAY : 1981). (NO). **4824**

BOKIN BOBAI : NIHON BOKIN BOBAI GAKKAI SHI. (JA/0385-5201). **4294**

BOKVAENNEN. (SW/0006-5846). **3368**

BOLETIM DE CONJUNTURA. (BL). **1548**

BOLETIM DE INDUSTRIA ANIMAL. (BL/0067-9615). **207**

BOLETIM DE ZOOLOGIA. (BL/0101-3580). **5578**

BOLETIM DO INSTITUTO DE ARQUEOLOGIA BRASILEIRA. (BL). **262**

BOLETIM DO INSTITUTO DE PESQUISAS VETERINARIAS DESIDERIO FINAMOR. (BL). **5506**

BOLETIM FBCN. (BL). **2188**

BOLETIM TRIMESTRAL DE ESTATISTICA (FUNCHAL). (PO/0303-1705). **5323**

BOLETIN ANUARIO - BANCO CENTRAL DEL ECUADOR. (EC). **5323**

BOLETIN BIBLIOGRAFICO (REGIONAL CENTER FOR BOOK PROMOTION IN LATIN AMERICA AND THE CARIBBEAN). (CK/0120-1204). **4824**

BOLETIN / CENTRO DE ESTUDIOS MONETARIOS LATINOAMERICANOS. (MX). **779**

BOLETIN / CIRCA, CENTRO DE INFORMACION Y REFERENCIA SOBRE CENTROAMERICA Y EL CARIBE. (CR). **Adv Mgr:** Ethel Garcia Buchard. **2511**

BOLETIN - COMISION DE INTEGRACION ELECTRICA REGIONAL. (UY). **4633**

BOLETIN DE ANTROPOLOGIA. (CK/0120-2510). **232**

BOLETIN DE ESTUDIOS ECONOMICOS. (SP/0006-6249). **1465**

BOLETIN DE ESTUDIOS MEDICOS Y BIOLOGICOS. (MX/0067-9666). **449**

BOLETIN DE LA ACADEMIE HONDURENA DE LA LENGUA. (HO/0065-0471). **3269**

BOLETIN DE LA ESCUELA DE CIENCIAS ANTROPOLOGICAS DE LA UNIVERSIDAD DE YUCATAN. (MX). **232**

BOLETIN DE LA INSTITUCION LIBRE DE ENSENANZA. (SP). **1728**

BOLETIN DE LA SOCIEDAD CHILENA DE QUIMICA. (CL/0366-1644). **962**

BOLETIN DE LA SOCIEDAD QUIMICA DEL PERU. (PE/0037-8623). **962**

BOLETIN DE LA SOCIEDAD VASCO-NAVARRA DE PEDIATRIA. (SP/0037-8658). **3901**

BOLETIN DE LIMA. (PE/0253-0015). **5193**

BOLETIN DEL CENTRO DE ESTUDIOS GENEALOGICOS DE CORDOBA. (AG). **2439**

BOLETIN DEL INSTITUTO GEMOLOGICO ESPANOL. (SP/0210-7228). **2913**

BOLETIN DEL SISTEMA ESTATAL DE DOCUMENTACION DEL ESTADO DE MEXICO. (MX/0188-4492). **4633**

BOLETIN ECONOMICO DE LA CONSTRUCCION 1956. (SP/0210-1947). **Adv Mgr:** J. L. Balcells Canela. **601**

BOLETIN MEDICO DEL HOSPITAL INFANTIL DE MEXICO (SPANISH EDITION). (MX/0539-6115). **3901**

BOLETIN MEXICANO DE DERECHO COMPARADO. (MX/0041-8633). **3124**

BOLETIN OFICIAL DEL MINISTERIO DE ECONOMIA Y HACIENDA. (SP). **4633**

BOLETIN SEMESTRAL - COLEGIO DE MEXICO. (MX/0543-7369). **1089**

BOLETIN TECNICO - ARPEL. (UY/0253-6005). **4252**

BOLETIN - UNIVERSIDAD DE PANAMA, DIRECCION DE PLANIFICACION UNIVERSITARIA. (PN). **1812**

BOLI YU TANGCI. (CC/1000-2871). **2586**

BOLIVAR COMMERCIAL, THE. (US). **5700**

BOLLETTINO DEI CHIMICI IGIENISTI. PARTE LEGISLATIVA. REPUBBLICA ITALIANA. (IT). **3110**

BOLLETTINO DELLA DOXA. (IT). **5240**

BOLLETTINO DELLA SOCIETA DI STUDI VALDESI. (IT/0037-8739). **4939**

BOLLETTINO DELLA SOCIETA ENTOMOLOGICA ITALIANA. (IT/0373-3491). **5606**

BOLLETTINO DELLA SOCIETA GEOGRAFICA ITALIANA. (IT/0037-8755). **2556**

BOLLETTINO DELLA SOCIETA ITALIANA DI FARMACIA OSPEDALIERA. (IT/0037-8798). **Adv Mgr:** Dott Dalla, **Tel** 06-86207165. **4294**

BOLLETTINO DELLA SOCIETA ITALIANA DI TOPOGRAFIA E FOTOGRAMMETRIA. (IT/0392-4424). **2556**

BOLLETTINO DELL'ISTITUTO STORICO ARTISTICO ORVIETANO. (IT/0391-8211). **2612**

BOLLETTINO DI GEODESIA E SCIENZE AFFINI. (IT/0006-6710). **1352**

BOLLETTINO DI GEOFISICA TEORICA ED APPLICATA. (IT/0006-6729). **1403**

BOLLETTINO DI LEGISLAZIONE TECNICA. (IT/0392-3789). **5089**

BOLLETTINO DI OCULISTICA. (IT/0006-677X). **3872**

BOLLETTINO DI PSICOLOGIA APPLICATA. (IT/0006-6761). **4577**

BOLLETTINO DI ZOOLOGIA. (IT/0373-4137). **5578**

BOLLETTINO ECONOMICO. (IT). **1465**

BOLLETTINO MALACOLOGICO. (IT/0394-7149). **5578**

BOLLETTINO PER LE FARMACODIPENDENZE E L'ALCOOLISMO. (IT/0392-3126). **1341**

BOMB (NEW YORK, N.Y.). (US/0743-3204). **Adv Mgr:** M. Monforton, **Tel** (212)431-3943 Ext. 3. **316**

BOMBAY MARKET. (II). **2502**

BON APPETIT. (US/0006-6990). **2788**

BOND BUYER (NEW YORK, N.Y. 1982), THE. (US/0732-0469). **892**

BOND LAW REVIEW. (AT/1033-4505). **Adv Mgr:** Everett, **Tel** 011 61 75 951060. **2943**

BOND MANAGEMENT REVIEW. (AT/1036-1456). **861**

BONDHOLDER / IFR, THE. (UK/0961-8171). **779**

BONE MARROW TRANSPLANTATION (BASINGSTOKE). (UK/0268-3369). **3558**

BONITA BANNER. (US/0191-5479). **Adv Mgr:** Steve Akers. **5649**

BONJOUR CHEZ-NOUS. (CN/0383-7866). **5780**

BONNER COUNTY DAILY BEE. (US/1047-6822). **Adv Mgr:** James Thompson. **5656**

BONNERS FERRY HERALD. (US/1064-9298). **5656**

BONNYVILLE NOUVELLE. (CN/0710-3905). **Adv Mgr:** Rene VanBrabant, **Tel** (403)826-3876. **4887**

BONSAI CLUBS INTERNATIONAL. (US/0744-3277). **2410**

BONSAI : JOURNAL OF THE AMERICAN BONSAI SOCIETY. (US). **2410**

BONSAI MAGAZINE. (US/1068-6193). **2410**

BONSAI TODAY. (US/1044-2529). **Adv Mgr:** Pat Palmer, **Tel** (508)443-7110. **2410**

BOOK AUCTION RECORDS. (UK/0068-0095). **4824**

BOOK COLLECTOR, THE. (UK/0006-7237). **4824**

BOOK FORUM. (US/0094-9426). **3338**

BOOK MARKETING UPDATE. (US/0891-8813). **Adv Mgr:** Bob Sanny. **4824**

BOOK PRODUCTION (BENN PUBLICATIONS LTD.). (UK). **4825**

BOOK REPORT (COLUMBUS, OHIO). (US/0731-4388). **3196**

BOOK REVIEW, THE. (II). **4825**

BOOK TALK (ALBUQUERQUE). (US/0145-627X). **4825**

BOOKBIRD. (DK/0006-7377). **3368**

BOOKMARK, THE. (US/0006-7407). **3197**

BOOKMARK (VANCOUVER). (CN/0381-6028). **3197**

BOOKPLATES IN THE NEWS. (US/0045-2521). **2771**

BOOKPRESS, THE. (US). **4825**

BOOKS AND PERIODICALS ONLINE. (US/0951-838X). **3257**

BOOKS & RELIGION. (US/0890-0841). **4939**

BOOKS BY BLACK WOMEN. (US/1040-0362). **4825**

BOOKS FOR YOUR CHILDREN. (UK/0006-7482). **Adv Mgr Tel** same as publisher. **3338**

BOOKS FROM ISRAEL. (IS/0578-932X). **4825**

BOOKS IN ARMENIAN. (CN/0705-8209). **4825**

BOOKS IN CANADA. (CN/0045-2564). **4825**

BOOKS IN DUTCH (1980). (CN/0713-4533). **4825**

BOOKS — Advertising Accepted Index

BOOKS IN FINNISH (1980). (CN/0714-2382). **4825**

BOOKS IN HUNGARIAN (1980). (CN/0714-2544). **4826**

BOOKS IN LITHUANIAN. (CN/0705-8225). **4826**

BOOKS IN MARATHI. (CN/0317-2406). **4826**

BOOKS IN PERSIAN (1980). (CN/0227-2741). **4826**

BOOKS IN POLISH (1980). (CN/0714-2773). **4826**

BOOKS IN SCOTLAND. (UK/0143-1285). **4826**

BOOKS IRELAND. (IE/0376-6039). **4812**

BOOKSELLER (LONDON). (UK/0006-7539). **4821**

BOOKSTORE JOURNAL. (US/0006-7563). **4939**

BOOKWAYS (AUSTIN, TEX.). (US/1057-6355). **Adv Mgr:** A. Prewett, **Tel** (512)478-7414. **4827**

BOOKWOMAN, THE. (US/0163-1128). **4827**

BOOMBAH HERALD. (US/8755-5832). **4104**

BOONE COUNTY RECORDER, THE. (US). **Adv Mgr:** Sandra Cupps. **5679**

BOONVILLE HERALD AND ADIRONDACK TOURIST. (US). **Adv Mgr:** Teresa Freeman, **Tel** (315)942-4449. **5714**

BOPUXUE ZAZHI. (CC/1000-4556). **Adv Mgr:** Qianmai Sun. **4434**

BORDER CROSSINGS (WINNIPEG, MAN.). (CN/0831-2559). **316**

BORDER/LINES. (CN/0826-967X). **4185**

BOREALIS (TORONTO). (CN/0840-6189). **4706**

BOREAS. (NO/0300-9483). **1368**

BORSENBLATT FUR DEN DEUTSCHEN BUCHHANDEL. FRANKFURTER AUSGABE. SONDERNUMMER. (GW). **4827**

BORZOI QUARTERLY (WHEAT RIDGE, COLO.), THE. (US/0746-2875). **Adv Mgr:** Cindy Kerstiens. **4286**

BOSTON BAR JOURNAL. (US/0524-1111). **2943**

BOSTON COLLEGE ENVIRONMENTAL AFFAIRS LAW REVIEW. (US/0190-7034). **3110**

BOSTON COLLEGE INTERNATIONAL AND COMPARATIVE LAW REVIEW. (US/0277-5778). **3125**

BOSTON COLLEGE LAW REVIEW. (US/0161-6587). **2943**

BOSTON JEWISH TIMES, THE. (US/8750-1961). **Adv Mgr:** Eleanor Grosser, **Tel** (617)367-9100 ext.36. **5688**

BOSTON PARENTS' PAPER, THE. (US/1059-1710). **Adv Mgr:** Clarke Williams. **2277**

BOSTON PHOENIX, THE. (US/0163-3015). **5688**

BOSTON REVIEW (CAMBRIDGE, MASS. : 1982). (US/0734-2306). **Adv Mgr:** Kim Cooper. **3368**

BOSTON ROCK. (US/0889-230X). **4104**

BOSTON SYMPHONY ORCHESTRA. (US/0006-8020). **Adv Mgr:** Steve Ganak, **Tel** (617)542-6913. **4104**

BOSTON UNIVERSITY INTERNATIONAL LAW JOURNAL. (US/0737-8947). **3125**

BOSTON UNIVERSITY LAW REVIEW. (US/0006-8047). **2943**

BOSTONIA (BOSTON, MASS. 1986). (US/1067-2834). **Adv Mgr:** M. Mediate, **Tel** (617)353-5390. **3368**

BOTANICA MARINA. (GW/0006-8055). **503**

BOTANICA (NEW DELHI, INDIA). (II/0045-2629). **503**

BOTANICAL REVIEW, THE. (US/0006-8101). **503**

BOTANISCHE JAHRBUCHER FUER SYSTEMATIK, PFLANZENGESCHICHTE UND PFLANZENGEOGRAPHIE. (GW/0006-8152). **503**

BOTH SIDES NOW. (US). **4940**

BOTSCHAFT, DIE. (US). **Adv Mgr:** Carla, **Tel** (717)392-1321. **5735**

BOTTIN COMMUNES. (FR). **4634**

BOTTIN MONDAIN; TOUT PARIS, TOUTE LA FRANCE. (FR). **5465**

BOTTLED WATER REPORTER. (US/1046-543X). **2365**

BOTTOM LINE (CHARLESTON, S.C.), THE. (US/0279-1889). **Adv Mgr:** Linda Timmons. **739**

BOTTOM LINE (NEW YORK, N.Y.), THE. (US/0888-045X). **Adv Mgr:** Sue Kurpeski, **Tel** (617)293-2194. **3197**

BOTTOMLINE (WASHINGTON, D.C. : 1983). (US/0740-5464). **779**

BOUCHERIE FRANCAISE, LA. (FR). **2329**

BOULEVARD (NEW YORK, N.Y.). (US/0885-9337). **3368**

BOUNDARY 2. (US/0190-3659). **3368**

BOUNDARY CREEK TIMES, THE. (CN/0822-8671). **5781**

BOUNDARY ELEMENTS ABSTRACTS AND NEWSLETTER. (UK/0957-2902). **1966**

BOUNDARY-LAYER METEOROLOGY. (NE/0006-8314). **1421**

BOUNDARY WATERS JOURNAL, THE. (US/0899-2681). **Adv Mgr:** L. Antonson, **Tel** (218)365-6184. **2188**

BOUT DE PAPIER. (CN/0833-9864). **2485**

BOUT DE PAPIER. (CN/0833-9864). **Adv Mgr:** D. Hulley. **4517**

BOUW. (NE/0366-2330). **601**

BOUWKRONIEK : WEEKBLAD VOOR DE BOUW EN INDUSTRIE. (BE). **Adv Mgr:** Jan Van Hoorick, **Tel** (02)513-82-95. **601**

BOUWWERELD. (NE/0026-5942). **602**

BOVINE PRACTITIONER, THE. (US/0524-1685). **5506**

BOWBENDER MAGAZINE. (CN/0827-2638). **4888**

BOWDLE PIONEER, THE. (US). **5743**

BOWLING DIGEST. (US/8750-3603). **4888**

BOWLING MAGAZINE (1988). (US/1050-5121). **Adv Mgr:** John Dill, **Tel** (612)856-2465. **4888**

BOXING MONTHLY. (UK/0956-098X). **Adv Mgr:** Jo Eady. **4888**

BOXOFFICE. (US/0006-8527). **4064**

BOYERTOWN AREA TIMES, THE. (US). **Adv Mgr:** Jim Davidheiser. **5735**

BOYS' LIFE. (US/0006-8608). **Adv Mgr Tel** (212)532-0985. **1060**

BOZEMAN DAILY CHRONICLE. (US). **Adv Mgr:** Mike Smit. **5705**

BOZJA BESEDA. (CN). **4940**

BOZZE. (IT/0391-6723). **4517**

BP&R BRITISH PLASTICS AND RUBBER. (UK/0307-6164). **4454**

BRABANTSE LEEUW, DE. (NE). **2439**

BRABY'S CAPE PROVINCE DIRECTORY. (SA). **5500**

BRABY'S NATAL DIRECTORY. (SA). **2485**

BRACKEN COUNTY NEWS, THE. (US). **Adv Mgr:** Kathy Bay, **Tel** (606)735-2198. **5679**

BRADENTON HERALD, THE. (US). **Adv Mgr:** Ed Gruwell. **5649**

BRADFORD JOURNAL (BRADFORD, PA. : 1973). (US). **Adv Mgr:** G. Nichols. **5735**

BRADFORD'S DIRECTORY OF MARKETING RESEARCH AGENCIES AND MANAGEMENT CONSULTANTS IN THE UNITED STATES AND THE WORLD. (US/0068-063X). **921**

BRAHMAN JOURNAL, THE. (US/0192-6764). **207**

BRAIDWOOD INDEX, THE. (US). **Adv Mgr:** Pam Divine. **5658**

BRAIN. (UK/0006-8950). **3828**

BRAIN DYSFUNCTION. (SZ/0259-1278). **3828**

BRAIN RESEARCH BULLETIN. (US/0361-9230). **3829**

BRAINERD DISPATCH. (US). **5694**

BRAKE & FRONT END. (US/0193-726X). **5408**

BRANDON NEWS. (US). **Adv Mgr:** Susie Howell. **5649**

BRANDON VALLEY CHALLENGER. (US/0746-8261). **Adv Mgr:** June Ketcham. **5743**

BRANDSTOFFEN BRUSSEL. (BE/0778-5097). **1021**

BRANDVAERN. (DK/0106-6072). **2288**

BRANDWACHT. (GW/0006-9116). **2288**

BRANDWEEK (NEW YORK, N.Y.). (US/1064-4318). **756**

BRANGUS JOURNAL. (US/0006-9132). **207**

BRANNTWEINWIRTSCHAFT, DIE. (GW). **2365**

BRANSON'S COUNTRY REVIEW. (US/1066-4033). **4105**

BRANT NEWS. (CN/0707-7998). **5781**

BRASILIANS, THE. (US/0741-0298). **Adv Mgr:** Jack Donado. **2724**

BRASS BULLETIN. (SZ/0303-3848). **4105**

BRASS RESEARCH SERIES. (US/0363-454X). **4105**

BRATSTVO (TORONTO). (CN/0006-9264). **5229**

BRAUINDUSTRIE. (GW/0341-7115). **2365**

BRAUNKOHLE (DUSSELDORF. 1972). (GW/0341-1060). **1934**

BRAUWELT (1978). (GW/0724-696X). **2329**

BRAUWELT INTERNATIONAL. (GW/0934-9340). **2365**

BRAXTON CITIZEN'S NEWS. (US). **Adv Mgr:** Jeanine Given. **5763**

BRAZIL TIMES, THE. (US). **Adv Mgr:** Larry Knight. **5663**

BRAZILIAN BIBLE QUARTERLY. (BL). **4940**

BRAZILIAN GAZETTE, THE. (UK/0307-160X). **2485**

BRAZILIAN JOURNAL OF MEDICAL AND BIOLOGICAL RESEARCH. (BL/0100-879X). **Adv Mgr:** L. J. Greene, **Tel** (016)633-3825. **3558**

BRAZORIA COUNTY NEWS, THE. (US). **5747**

BRAZOSPORT FACTS, THE. (US/1065-7886). **5747**

BREAKING THE SILENCE (OTTAWA, ONT.). (CN/0713-4266). **5552**

BREAKTHROUGH (ATLANTA, GA.). (US/0885-8578). **2771**

BREAKTHROUGH (HAMMOND, LA.). (US/1056-0130). **2771**

BREAST DISEASES. (US/1043-321X). **3758**

BRECHA (MONTEVIDEO, URUGUAY). (UY). **2917**

BRECKENRIDGE AMERICAN. (US). **Adv Mgr:** David Hall. **5747**

BREEDER AND FEEDER. (CN/0712-5291). **207**

BREESE JOURNAL, THE. (US). **5658**

BREMER COUNTY INDEPENDENT (1959). (US/0899-8698). **Adv Mgr:** Jayne Thomas Hall. **5668**

BRENNSTOFF-WAERME-KRAFT. (GW/0006-9612). **1934**

BRETHREN MISSIONARY HERALD. (US/0161-5238). **Adv Mgr:** Charles Turner, **Tel** (219)267-7158. **4940**

BREWER (LONDON). (UK/0006-9736). **2365**

BREWERS BULLETIN, THE. (US/0006-9701). **2365**

BREWERS' GUARDIAN. (UK/0006-9728). **2365**

BREWING & DISTILLING INTERNATIONAL. (UK/0308-1265). **Adv Mgr:** Kath Adkin, **Tel** 44 283 66784. **2365**

BREWING INDUSTRY NEWS, THE. (US/0273-5768). **2365**

BREWTON STANDARD, THE. (US). **5625**

BRIAR PATCH. (CN/0703-8968). **Adv Mgr:** George Manz. **5193**

BRICK BULLETIN. (UK/0307-9325). **602**

BRICKER BRANCHES. (US/0897-7879). **2440**

BRIDAL APPAREL NEWS. (US). **1082**

BRIDAL GUIDE. (US/0882-7451). **2277**

BRIDE OF CHRIST, THE. (US/0197-3045). **Adv Mgr:** Charles Shoemaker. **5057**

BRIDES AND SETTING UP HOME. (UK/0006-9787). **Adv Mgr:** Helen Fifield, **Tel** 011 44 71 499 9080. **2277**

BRIDGE (HONG KONG). (HK/1018-8983). **4940**

BRIDGE (OAK PARK, MICH.), THE. (US/1052-1569). **3369**

BRIDGE RIVER LILLOOET NEWS. (CN). **Adv Mgr:** J. Wright. **5781**

BRIDGE, THE. (UK). **4858**

BRIDGE TODAY!. (US/1043-6383). **4858**

BRIDGE WORLD, THE. (US/0006-9876). **4858**

BRIDGEPORT INDEX, THE. (US). **Adv Mgr:** Keith Bridwell. **5747**

BRIDGEPORT LEADER. (US). **5658**

BRIDGETON EVENING NEWS. (US). **5709**

BRIDGING THE GAP (LANCASTER). (CN/0840-7738). **Adv Mgr:** Alex W. Fraser. **2440**

BRIEF (CHICAGO. 1980), THE. (US/0273-0995). **2943**

BRIEFING. (TU). **4466**

BRIGHAM YOUNG UNIVERSITY EDUCATION AND LAW JOURNAL. (US). **2943**

BRIGHAM YOUNG UNIVERSITY LAW REVIEW. (US/0360-151X). **Adv Mgr:** Amy, **Tel** (801)378-5677. **2943**

BRIGITTE. (GW). **1082**

BRILLION NEWS, THE. (US/0749-7210). **5765**

BRIO (UNITED KINGDOM BRANCH, INTERNATIONAL ASSOCIATION OF MUSIC LIBRARIES). (UK/0007-0173). **4105**

BRISTOL BAYTIMES. (US). **Adv Mgr:** Tanya Holman, **Tel** (907)842-5572. **5628**

BRISTOL HERALD COURIER, BRISTOL VIRGINIA-TENNESSEAN. (US/8750-6505). **Adv Mgr:** Bill Cummings, **Tel** (703)669-2181. **5758**

BRISTOL PILOT. (US). **Adv Mgr:** Jane Parr, **Tel** (215)968-2244. **5735**

BRITAIN'S COMPUTER INDUSTRY. (UK). **1236**

BRITANNIA (SOCIETY FOR THE PROMOTION OF ROMAN STUDIES). (UK/0068-113X). **Adv Mgr:** H.Cockle. **1075**

BRITANNIA (TORONTO). (CN/0823-7743). **2514**

BRITEQ PRESSE. (CN/0706-1056). **1934**

BRITISH ALTERNATIVE THEATRE DIRECTORY. (UK/0142-5218). **5362**

BRITISH-AMERICAN DEAL REVIEW, THE. (US/1044-2944). **1633**

BRITISH ARCHER, THE. (UK/0007-0289). **4888**

BRITISH BANDSMAN. (UK). **4105**

BRITISH BEE JOURNAL. (UK/0007-0327). **5578**

BRITISH BIRDS. (UK/0007-0335). **Adv Mgr:** S. Barnes, **Tel** 44 621 815085. **5616**

BRITISH CERAMIC REVIEW. (UK/0306-7076). **2586**

BRITISH CHESS MAGAZINE, THE. (UK/0007-0440). **4858**

BRITISH CLOTHING INDUSTRY YEAR BOOK / SPONSORED BY THE CLOTHING EXPORT COUNCIL OF GREAT BRITAIN, THE. (UK). **1082**

BRITISH COLUMBIA & ALBERTA HOME BUSINESS REPORT. (CN/1191-8640). **644**

BRITISH COLUMBIA GENEALOGIST, THE. (CN/0315-3835). **2440**

BRITISH COLUMBIA HOLSTEIN NEWS. (CN/0824-4774). **192**

BRITISH COLUMBIA LAW REPORTS (CALGARY). (CN/0703-3060). **2943**

BRITISH COLUMBIA MEDICAL JOURNAL. (CN/0007-0556). **3558**

BRITISH COLUMBIA'S WEDDING BELLS. (CN/0840-464X). **Adv Mgr:** Alethea Wakefield. **2277**

BRITISH CORROSION JOURNAL. (UK/0007-0599). **2008**

BRITISH DEAF NEWS. (UK/0007-0602). **4385**

BRITISH DENTAL SURGERY ASSISTANT. (UK/0007-0629). **1317**

BRITISH EDUCATIONAL RESEARCH JOURNAL. (UK/0141-1926). **1728**

BRITISH ELECTIONS AND PARTIES YEARBOOK. (UK/0968-2481). **4634**

BRITISH EXPORTS TO NORTH AMERICA. (UK). **825**

BRITISH GEOLOGIST. (UK). **1368**

BRITISH HOMING WORLD. (UK). **5616**

BRITISH HOTELIER & RESTAURATEUR : OFFICIAL MAGAZINE OF THE BRITISH HOTELS, RESTAURANTS & CATERERS ASSOCIATION. (UK). **2804**

BRITISH JOURNAL FOR EIGHTEENTH-CENTURY STUDIES, THE. (UK/0141-867X). **3369**

BRITISH JOURNAL FOR THE HISTORY OF PHILOSOPHY. (UK/0960-8788). **Adv Mgr:** Deborah Mann, **Tel** same as publisher. **4342**

BRITISH JOURNAL FOR THE HISTORY OF SCIENCE, THE. (UK/0007-0874). **5089**

BRITISH JOURNAL FOR THE PHILOSOPHY OF SCIENCE, THE. (UK/0007-0882). **5089**

BRITISH JOURNAL OF ACADEMIC LIBRARIANSHIP. (UK/0269-0497). **3197**

BRITISH JOURNAL OF ACUPUNCTURE. (UK/0143-4977). **3558**

BRITISH JOURNAL OF AESTHETICS. (UK/0007-0904). **344**

BRITISH JOURNAL OF AUDIOLOGY. (UK/0300-5364). **3887**

BRITISH JOURNAL OF CANCER. (UK/0007-0920). **3809**

BRITISH JOURNAL OF CLINICAL PHARMACOLOGY. (UK/0306-5251). **4294**

BRITISH JOURNAL OF CLINICAL PRACTICE, THE. (UK/0007-0947). **3558**

BRITISH JOURNAL OF CLINICAL PSYCHOLOGY, THE. (UK/0144-6657). **4578**

BRITISH JOURNAL OF CRIMINOLOGY, DELINQUENCY AND DEVIANT SOCIAL BEHAVIOR, THE. (UK/0007-0955). **3158**

BRITISH JOURNAL OF DERMATOLOGY (1951). (UK/0007-0963). **3718**

BRITISH JOURNAL OF DEVELOPMENTAL PSYCHOLOGY, THE. (UK/0261-510X). **4578**

BRITISH JOURNAL OF DISORDERS OF COMMUNICATION. MONOGRAPH. (UK). **4385**

BRITISH JOURNAL OF EDUCATION AND WORK. (UK). **1728**

BRITISH JOURNAL OF EDUCATIONAL PSYCHOLOGY, THE. (UK/0007-0998). **4578**

BRITISH JOURNAL OF EDUCATIONAL STUDIES. (UK/0007-1005). **1728**

BRITISH JOURNAL OF GUIDANCE & COUNSELLING. (UK/0306-9885). **1911**

BRITISH JOURNAL OF HEALTHCARE COMPUTING, THE. (UK/0265-5217). **1172**

BRITISH JOURNAL OF HOLOCAUST EDUCATION. (UK/0966-095X). **Adv Mgr:** Anne Kidson. **2679**

BRITISH JOURNAL OF INDUSTRIAL RELATIONS. (UK/0007-1080). **1656**

BRITISH JOURNAL OF MATHEMATICAL & STATISTICAL PSYCHOLOGY, THE. (UK/0007-1102). **4622**

BRITISH JOURNAL OF MEDICAL PSYCHOLOGY. (UK/0007-1129). **4578**

BRITISH JOURNAL OF MENTAL SUBNORMALITY. (UK/0374-633X). **1876**

BRITISH JOURNAL OF MIDDLE EASTERN STUDIES. (UK). **2768**

BRITISH JOURNAL OF NON-DESTRUCTIVE TESTING. (UK/0007-1137). **2101**

BRITISH JOURNAL OF OBSTETRICS AND GYNAECOLOGY. (UK/0306-5456). **3758**

BRITISH JOURNAL OF OCCUPATIONAL THERAPY, THE. (UK/0308-0226). **1876**

BRITISH JOURNAL OF ORTHODONTICS. (UK/0301-228X). **1317**

BRITISH JOURNAL OF PHARMACOLOGY. (UK/0007-1188). **4294**

BRITISH JOURNAL OF PHOTOGRAPHY. (UK/0007-1196). **4367**

BRITISH JOURNAL OF PHYSICAL EDUCATION. (UK/0144-3569). **1855**

BRITISH JOURNAL OF PHYTOTHERAPY, THE. (UK/0959-6879). **504**

BRITISH JOURNAL OF PLASTIC SURGERY. (UK/0007-1226). **3961**

BRITISH JOURNAL OF PODIATRIC MEDICINE & SURGERY. (UK/0955-8160). **3917**

BRITISH JOURNAL OF PROJECTIVE PSYCHOLOGY. (UK). **4578**

BRITISH JOURNAL OF PSYCHIATRY, THE. (UK/0007-1250). **3922**

BRITISH JOURNAL OF PSYCHOLOGY (1955). (UK/0007-1269). **4578**

BRITISH JOURNAL OF RADIOLOGY, THE. (UK/0007-1285). **3939**

BRITISH JOURNAL OF RELIGIOUS EDUCATION. (UK/0141-6200). **4940**

BRITISH JOURNAL OF RHEUMATOLOGY. (UK/0263-7103). **3803**

BRITISH JOURNAL OF SEXUAL MEDICINE. (UK/0301-5572). **3559**

BRITISH JOURNAL OF SOCIAL PSYCHOLOGY, THE. (UK/0144-6665). **4578**

BRITISH JOURNAL OF SOCIAL WORK, THE. (UK/0045-3102). **5275**

BRITISH JOURNAL OF SOCIOLOGY OF EDUCATION. (UK/0142-5692). **5241**

BRITISH JOURNAL OF SOCIOLOGY, THE. (UK/0007-1315). **5240**

BRITISH JOURNAL OF SPORTS MEDICINE. (UK/0306-3674). **3953**

BRITISH JOURNAL OF SURGERY. (UK/0007-1323). **3961**

BRITISH JOURNAL OF THEATRE NURSING : NATNEWS : THE OFFICIAL JOURNAL OF THE NATIONAL ASSOCIATION OF THEATRE NURSES, THE. (UK). **Adv Mgr:** John Matthews, Pam Noble, **Tel** 0831-224771, 062 082 3383. **3852**

BRITISH JOURNAL OF UROLOGY. (UK/0007-1331). **3988**

BRITISH JOURNAL OF VISUAL IMPAIRMENT, THE. (UK/0264-6196). **4385**

BRITISH LIBRARY JOURNAL, THE. (UK/0305-5167). **3197**

BRITISH MEDICAL BULLETIN. (UK/0007-1420). **3559**

BRITISH MEDICAL JOURNAL ED. ESPANOLA. (SP/0213-3954). **3795**

BRITISH MUSEUM MAGAZINE. (UK/0965-8297). **4085**

BRITISH MUSEUM MAGAZINE : JOURNAL OF THE BRITISH MUSEUM SOCIETY. (UK). **4085**

BRITISH MUSIC. (UK/0958-5664). **4105**

BRITISH ORTHOPTIC JOURNAL. (UK/0068-2314). **3873**

BRITISH PERFORMING ARTS YEARBOOK. (UK/0951-5208). **384**

BRITISH PHARMACEUTICAL INDUSTRY. (UK). **4294**

BRITISH POULTRY SCIENCE. (UK/0007-1668). **207**

BRITISH PRINTER, THE. (UK/0007-1684). **4564**

BRITISH REPORTS, TRANSLATIONS AND THESES RECEIVED BY THE BRITISH LIBRARY DOCUMENT SUPPLY CENTRE. (UK/0959-4922). **3197**

BRITISH REVIEW OF ECONOMIC ISSUES. (UK/0141-4739). **Adv Mgr:** Allistair Dawson, **Tel** 011 44 782 412515 ext. 4079. **1465**

BRITISH ROWING ALMANACK AND ARA YEAR BOOK. (UK). **4849**

BRITISH SUGAR BEET REVIEW. (UK/0007-1854). **165**

BRITISH VETERINARY JOURNAL, THE. (UK/0007-1935). **5506**

BRITISH VIRGIN ISLANDS CONSOLIDATED INDEX OF STATUTES AND SUBSIDIARY LEGISLATION TO ... . (BB). **3125**

BRITISH WILDLIFE. (UK). **Adv Mgr:** A.Branson, **Tel** 0256 760663. **4869**

BRITTONIA. (US/0007-196X). **504**

BRMNA JOURNAL. (CN/0229-0553). **5430**

BROAD TOP BULLETIN. (US). **Adv Mgr:** Chris Hodge. **5735**

BROADCAST ENGINEERING NEWS. (AT/0155-3720). **Adv Mgr:** Dion Stead. **1127**

BROADCAST ENGINEERING (OVERLAND PARK). (US/0007-1994). **1127**

BROADCAST EQUIPMENT BUYERS GUIDE (SHAWNEE MISSION, KAN.). (US/0882-5688). **1127**

BROADCAST FINANCIAL JOURNAL. (US/0161-9063). **1127**

BROADCAST HARDWARE INTERNATIONAL. (UK/0269-493X). **1127**

BROADCAST SYSTEMS ENGINEERING. (UK/0267-565X). **1128**

BROADCASTER (TORONTO). (CN/0008-3038). **1128**

BROADCASTING & CABLE INTERNATIONAL. (US). **Adv Mgr:** Randi Schatz, **Tel** (212)337-6944. **1128**

BROADCASTING (WASHINGTON, D.C. 1957). (US/0007-2028). **1128**

BROADSIDE (NEW YORK, N.Y. 1962). (US/0740-7955). **4105**

BROILER INDUSTRY. (US/0007-2176). **207**

BROKEN BENCH REVIEW. (US/0739-652X). **3085**

BROKEN SPOKE, THE. (CN/0045-3226). **5408**

BROKER WORLD. (US/0273-6551). **Adv Mgr:** Robb Edwards. **2876**

BRONX COUNTY HISTORICAL SOCIETY JOURNAL, THE. (US/0007-2249). **2724**

BRONX TIMES REPORTER. (US/8750-4499). **Adv Mgr:** Evelyn Perreira, **Tel** (718)597-1116. **5714**

BROOKE COUNTY REVIEW. (US). **Adv Mgr:** Mary Ann Wilson, **Tel** (304)737-0946. **5763**

BROOKE NEWS. (US). **Adv Mgr:** Mary Ann Wilson, **Tel** (304)737-0946. **5763**

BROOKLINE CITIZEN. (US). **5688**

BROOKLYN ENGINEER, THE. (US/0271-6437). **1966**

BROOKS' STANDARD RATE BOOK, THE. (US/0193-2314). **1656**

BROOKVILLE AMERICAN (BROOKVILLE, IND. : 1873). (US). **Adv Mgr:** Donald G. Siuty. **5663**

BROOKVILLE DEMOCRAT, THE. (US). **Adv Mgr:** Donald Goutz, **Tel** (317)647-4221. **5663**

BROOM — Advertising Accepted Index

BROOM, BRUSH & MOP. (US/0890-2933). **1600**

BROOMFIELD ENTERPRISE. (US). **Adv Mgr Tel** 466-3636. **5642**

BROOMSTICK. (US/0883-9611). **5552**

BROT & BACKWAREN. (GW/0172-8180). **2329**

BROTHERHOOD ACTION. (AT/0300-4678). **5229**

BROWBEAT. (US/1075-0371). **Adv Mgr:** Mike Rizzi. **4105**

BROWN AND WHITE, THE. (US). **Adv Mgr:** Cameron Moltzman, **Tel** (610)758-4184. **1089**

BROWN SWISS BULLETIN, THE. (US/0007-2516). **207**

BROWN UNIVERSITY DIGEST OF ADDICTION THEORY AND APPLICATION. (US/1040-6328). **1341**

BROWNING SOCIETY NOTES. (UK/0950-6349). **3369**

BROWN'S BUSINESS REPORTER. (US/1066-2421). **644**

BROWN'S DIRECTORY OF NORTH AMERICAN AND INTERNATIONAL GAS COMPANIES. (US/0197-8098). **4252**

BROWN'S NAUTICAL ALMANAC. (UK/0068-290X). **Adv Mgr:** D. Provan. **4175**

BROWN'S NAUTICAL ALMANAC; DAILY TIDE TABLES. (UK/0068-290X). **Adv Mgr:** D. Provan. **4175**

BROWNS NEWS/ILLUSTRATED. (US/0278-9973). **4888**

BROWNSTONER, THE. (US/0883-962X). **293**

BROWNSVILLE HERALD (BROWNSVILLE, TEX. : 1910). (US/0894-2064). **Adv Mgr:** Julie Moreno, **Tel** (210)982-6636. **5747**

BROWNSVILLE STATES-GRAPHIC. (US/0893-3839). **Adv Mgr:** M. Arwood. **5744**

BRUCKMANNS PANTHEON. (GW/0720-0056). **345**

BRUG, DE. (NE). **5806**

BRUNSWICK BUSINESS JOURNAL, THE. (CN/0829-5239). **Adv Mgr:** J. Matthews. **644**

BRUNSWICK NEWS, THE. (US). **Adv Mgr:** Ron Walden, **Tel** (912)265-8320. **5652**

BRUSH-MORGAN COUNTY NEWS-TRIBUNE. (US). **5642**

BRUSHWARE (WASHINGTON, D.C.). (US/0007-2710). **Adv Mgr:** C. Wurzer, **Tel** (301)983-1152. **2810**

BRYGMESTEREN. (DK/0007-2737). **2365**

BRYNWT WSTYH HBRTYT. (IS/0334-4525). **5275**

BRYOLOGIST, THE. (US/0007-2745). **504**

BUBBA MAGAZINE. (US/1068-3208). **Adv Mgr:** Logan Ward. **2529**

BUCH DER ZEIT. (GW/0007-2761). **4812**

BUCH UND BIBLIOTHEK. (GW/0340-0301). **3197**

BUCHEREI DES PADIATERS. (GW/0373-3165). **3901**

BUCKER NEWS LETTER, THE. (US/0889-4388). **15**

BUCKEYE OSTEOPATHIC PHYSICIAN. (US/0898-3070). **Adv Mgr:** same as editor. **4294**

BUCKEYE REVIEW. (US/0045-3285). **2257**

BUCKEYE VALLEY NEWS. (US). **Adv Mgr:** Rhoda Sylvester. **5629**

BUCKLEY-LITTLE CATALOGUE OF BOOKS AVAILABLE FROM AUTHORS, THE. (US/0749-615X). **411**

BUCKSKIN BULLETIN. (US/0045-3307). **2724**

BUDDHIST-CHRISTIAN STUDIES. (US/0882-0945). **5020**

BUDDY (DALLAS, TEX.). (US/0192-9097). **4105**

BUDESHTE. (FR). **2514**

BUDGET - LOS ANGELES. (US/0090-242X). **Adv Mgr:** V Baab. **4714**

BUDGET (SUGARCREEK, OHIO : 1928). (US). **Adv Mgr:** Virginia Baab. **5727**

BUDGET TRAVEL IN CANADA (UNITED STATES EDITION). (US). **5465**

BUECHERSCHIFF; DIE DEUTSCHE BUECHERZEITUNG. (GW/0007-3059). **4827**

BUENA SALUD. (US/0896-2642). **4769**

BUENASALUD (ED. NACIONAL). (PR/1053-5543). **Adv Mgr:** Arnaldo Jimenez. **2596**

BUFFALO BULLETIN, THE. (US). **5765**

BUFFALO (CUSTER). (US/0196-9137). **208**

BUFFALO LAW JOURNAL. (US/0197-4955). **2944**

BUFFALO NEWS, THE. (US/0745-2691). **5714**

BUFFALO SPREE. (US/0300-7499). **2529**

BUGLE. (US/0889-6445). **Adv Mgr:** Kathy Jackson, **Tel** (406)523-4595. **2189**

BUHL HERALD, THE. (US). **5656**

BUILD; JOURNAL OF THE INDUSTRY. (IE/0007-3229). **602**

BUILDCORE INDEX. (CN/0227-0595). **602**

BUILDER & CONTRACTOR. (US/0273-7965). **602**

BUILDER/DEALER. (US/0892-824X). **Adv Mgr:** Charles Manciho, **Tel** (814)838-0028. **602**

BUILDER DEVELOPER WEST. (US/0273-6225). **602**

BUILDER DIRECTORY, HONG KONG. (HK). **602**

BUILDER (WASHINGTON, D.C. : 1981). (US/0744-1193). **602**

BUILDERS MERCHANTS JOURNAL (TONBRIDGE AND MALLING, KENT : 1985). (UK/0268-1323). **602**

BUILDING AND CONSTRUCTION TRADES TODAY. (CN/1186-1398). **602**

BUILDING AUTOMATION. (IT). **Adv Mgr:** Pierangela Donina, **Tel** 70602276. **603**

BUILDING CONTROL. (UK/0265-6493). **603**

BUILDING COST FILE. WESTERN EDITION. (US/0194-0295). **603**

BUILDING ECONOMIC ALTERNATIVES. (US/0885-9930). **1465**

BUILDING ECONOMIST, THE. (AT/0007-3431). **603**

BUILDING ENGINEER. (UK). **603**

BUILDING IDEAS (DES MOINES). (US/0093-0938). **294**

BUILDING (LONDON. ENGLAND). (UK/0007-3318). **603**

BUILDING OKLAHOMA (OKLAHOMA CITY, OKLA. 1989). (US/1071-2879). **603**

BUILDING OPERATING MANAGEMENT. (US/0007-3490). **603**

BUILDING PRODUCTS DIGEST. (US/0742-5694). **2399**

BUILDING SERVICES CONTRACTOR. (US/0007-3644). **604**

BUILDING SERVICES : THE CIBSE JOURNAL. (UK). **604**

BUILDING STANDARDS. (US/0270-1197). **604**

BUILDING SUPPLY & HOME CENTERS. (US/0890-9008). **604**

BUILDING SUPPLY HOME CENTERS (MIDWEST ED.). (US/1075-8038). **605**

BUILDING SUPPLY HOME CENTERS (NORTHEAST ED.). (US/1075-802X). **605**

BUILDING SUPPLY HOME CENTERS (SOUTH ED.). (US/1075-8054). **605**

BUILDING SUPPLY HOME CENTERS (WEST ED.). (US/1075-8046). **605**

BUILDING SURVEYOR MELBOURNE. (AT/0728-9820). **Adv Mgr:** D. Wadworth. **605**

BUILDING SYSTEMS BUILDER. (US/1064-5896). **Adv Mgr:** Charles Mancino, **Tel** (814)838-0028. **605**

BUILDINGS (CEDAR RAPIDS. 1947). (US/0007-3725). **605**

BUILDINGS ENERGY TECHNOLOGY. (US/0891-3730). **1934**

BU$INESS OF HERBS, THE. (US/0736-9050). **2411**

BULETIN PERSATUAN GEOLOGI MALAYSIA. (MY/0126-6187). **1368**

BULGARIAN ACADEMIC BOOKS. (BU/0324-0509). **4827**

BULGARIAN CO-OPERATIVE REVIEW. (BU). **1541**

BULGARIAN FILMS. (BU/0204-8884). **4064**

BULGARIAN HISTORICAL REVIEW. (BU/0324-0207). **2680**

BULGARIAN JOURNAL OF PHYSICS. (BU/0323-9217). **4398**

BULGARSKI KNIGOPIS. (BU). **Adv Mgr:** Asen Georgiev, **Tel** 011 359 2 882811 Ext. 376. **4821**

BULGARSKO MUZIKOZNANIE (SOFIA, BULGARIA : 1979). (BU/0204-823X). **4105**

BULK SOLIDS HANDLING. (GW/0173-9980). **1967**

BULL & BEAR. (US/0319-1362). **Adv Mgr Tel** (407)682-6170. **893**

BULLETIN. (US). **2411**

BULLETIN. (II). **4343**

BULLETIN. (US). **1890**

BULLETIN. (BE). **1600**

BULLETIN A B Q. (CN/0380-7150). **3197**

BULLETIN (ALABAMA MUSEUM OF NATURAL HISTORY). (US/0196-1039). **4163**

BULLETIN - AMERICAN ORCHID SOCIETY. (US). **2411**

BULLETIN - AMERICAN RAILWAY ENGINEERING ASSOCIATION. (US/0003-0694). **5430**

BULLETIN / AMERICAN SUNBATHING ASSOCIATION, THE. (US/0279-8158). **4849**

BULLETIN - AMIS DE GUSTAVE COURBET. (FR/0983-3943). **345**

BULLETIN AMQ. (CN/0316-8832). **3497**

BULLETIN ANALYTIQUE DE DOCUMENTATION POLITIQUE, ECONOMIQUE ET SOCIALE CONTEMPORAINE / FONDATION NATIONAL DES SCIENCES POLITIQUES. (FR/0007-4071). **5193**

BULLETIN & I.E. ET ANNALES DE LA SOCIETE ROYALE BELGE D'ENTOMOLOGIE. (BE/0374-6038). **5579**

BULLETIN ANTIEKE BESCHAVING : BABESCH. (NE/0165-9367). **2612**

BULLETIN - AQUACULTURE ASSOCIATION OF CANADA. (CN/0840-5417). **449**

BULLETIN ASPEA. (SZ). **1934**

BULLETIN - ASSOCIATION CANADIENNE POUR L'AVANCEMENT DES ETUDES NEERLANDAISES. (CN/0823-9487). **2680**

BULLETIN - ASSOCIATION DES MEDECINS DE LANGUE FRANCAISE DU CANADA (1977). (CN/0702-7656). **3559**

BULLETIN (ASSOCIATION FOR THE BIBLIOGRAPHY OF HISTORY (U.S.)). (US/0892-4600). **2635**

BULLETIN - ASSOCIATION QUEBECOISE POUR L'ETUDE DE L'IMPRIME. (CN/0838-5459). **431**

BULLETIN BAKHTINE, LE. (CN/0821-6886). **3338**

BULLETIN / BIBLIOGRAPHICAL SOCIETY OF AUSTRALIA AND NEW ZEALAND. (AT/0084-7852). **Adv Mgr:** Brian Hubber, **Tel** 61 3 6699032. **3198**

BULLETIN BIBLIOGRAPHIQUE AMERIQUE LATINE / RESEAU DOCUMENTAIRE AMERIQUE LATINE, GRECO 26, CNRS. (FR/0292-8515). **411**

BULLETIN BIBLIOGRAPHIQUE - INSTITUT NATIONALE DE LA STATISTIQUE ET DES ETUDES ECONOMIQUES. (FR/0020-2398). **1530**

BULLETIN / BRITISH SOCIETY FOR MUSIC THERAPY. (UK/0953-7511). **4105**

BULLETIN - CALIFORNIA WATER POLLUTION CONTROL ASSOCIATION. (US/0008-1620). **2225**

BULLETIN - CANADIAN BOTANICAL ASSOCIATION. (CN/0008-3046). **504**

BULLETIN / CANADIAN SOCIETY FOR MESOPOTAMIAN STUDIES. (CN/0844-3416). **Adv Mgr:** L. Wilding. **262**

BULLETIN - CANADIAN SOCIETY OF LABORATORY TECHNOLOGISTS. (CN/0381-5838). **5090**

BULLETIN - CANADIAN SOCIETY OF ZOOLOGISTS. (CN/0319-6674). **5579**

BULLETIN - CAVE EXPLORATION GROUP OF EAST AFRICA. (KE/1013-784X). **1403**

BULLETIN - CORPUS CHRISTI GEOLOGICAL SOCIETY. (US/0739-5620). **1368**

BULLETIN / COUNCIL OF SOCIETIES FOR THE STUDY OF RELIGION. (US/1060-1635). **4940**

BULLETIN CRITIQUE DU LIVRE FRANCAIS. (FR/0007-4209). **3338**

BULLETIN / CSD. (SA). **5193**

BULLETIN DE LA BANQUE NATIONALE DE BELGIQUE. (BE/0005-5611). **780**

BULLETIN DE LA SOCIETE BELGE DE GEOLOGIE. (BE/0379-1807). **Adv Mgr:** B DeBoose. **1368**

BULLETIN DE LA SOCIETE BOTANIQUE DE FRANCE. ACTUALITES BOTANIQUES. (FR/0181-1789). **504**

BULLETIN DE LA SOCIETE DES ETUDES OCEANIENNES (POLYNESIE ORIENTALE). (FP). **2669**

BULLETIN DE LA SOCIETE ENTOMOLOGIQUE DE FRANCE. (FR/0037-928X). **5606**

BULLETIN DE LA SOCIETE PAUL CLAUDEL. (FR/0037-9506). **3369**

BULLETIN DE L'ASSOCIATION DES PROFESSEURS DE MATHEMATIQUES ET L'ENSEIGNEMENT PUBLIC. (FR). **3498**

BULLETIN DE LIAISON DES LABORATOIRES DES PONTS ET CHAUSSEES. (FR/0458-5860). **1967**

BULLETIN DE LIAISON DU COMITE INTERAFRICAIN D'ETUDES HYDRAULIQUES. (UV/0379-3478). **2088**

BULLETIN DE L'INSTITUT DE GEOLOGIE DU BASSIN D'AQUITAINE. (FR/0524-0832). **1369**

BULLETIN DE L'INSTITUT DE READAPTATION DE MONTREAL, LE. (CN/0316-4454). **5275**

BULLETIN DE L'INSTITUT PASTEUR. (FR/0020-2452). **3667**

BULLETIN DE L'UNION DES PHYSICIENS. (FR/0366-3876). **Adv Mgr:** Mr. Neel, **Tel** 011 33 1 42203998. **4399**

BULLETIN DE L'UNION INTERNATIONALE CONTRE LA TUBERCULOSE ET LES MALADIES RESPIRATOIRES. (FR/1011-7903). **3949**

BULLETIN DE NOUVELLES - CORPORATION PROFESSIONNELLE DES TRAVAILLEURS SOCIAUX DU QUEBEC. (CN/0713-4290). **5275**

BULLETIN DE PSYCHOLOGIE SCOLAIRE ET D'ORIENTATION. (BE/0007-4411). **4578**

BULLETIN DES AGRICULTEURS. (CN/0007-4446). **69**

BULLETIN DES BIBLIOTHEQUES DE FRANCE. (FR/0006-2006). **3198**

BULLETIN DES DESSINS ET MODELES INTERNATIONAUX : PUBLICATION MENSUELLE DU BUREAU INTERNATIONAL DE L'ORGANISATION MONDIALE DE LA PROPRIETE INTELLECTUELLE. (SZ/0250-7730). **3476**

BULLETIN DES ETUDES AFRICAINES. (FR/0249-728X). **2498**

BULLETIN DES G.T.V. (FR/0399-2519). **Adv Mgr:** same as editor. **5506**

BULLETIN DES SCIENCES MATHEMATIQUES. (FR/0007-4497). **3498**

BULLETIN DES SEANCES - ACADEMIE ROYALE DES SCIENCES D'OUTRE-MER. (BE/0001-4176). **5091**

BULLETIN DES SOCIETES CHIMIQUES BELGES. (BE/0037-9646). **963**

BULLETIN D'INFORMATION DU BITS. (BE). **5465**

BULLETIN D'INFORMATIONS DE L'ASSOCIATION DES BIBLIOTHECAIRES FRANCAIS. (FR/0004-5365). **3198**

BULLETIN D'INFORMATIONS SCIENTIFIQUES - INSTITUT PASTEUR. (FR/1144-3464). **5091**

BULLETIN - DOLMETSCH FOUNDATION. (UK/0419-618X). **4106**

BULLETIN DU CENTRE GENEVOIS D'ANTHROPOLOGIE / MUSEE D'ETHNOGRAPHIE, DEPARTEMENT D'ANTHROPOLOGIE. (BE/0777-5466). **232**

BULLETIN DU CENTRE PROTESTANT D'ETUDES. (SZ). **5057**

BULLETIN DU GROUPEMENT D'INFORMATIONS MUTUELLES AMPERE. (SZ/0434-6971). **4399**

BULLETIN - ENTOMOLOGICAL SOCIETY OF CANADA. (CN/0071-0741). **5579**

BULLETIN - ENTOMOLOGICAL SOCIETY OF NEW ZEALAND. (NZ/0110-4527). **5579**

BULLETIN / FEDERATION INTERNATIONALE DE GYMNASTIQUE. (SZ/0428-1659). **4888**

BULLETIN FOR INTERNATIONAL FISCAL DOCUMENTATION. (NE/0007-4624). **4715**

BULLETIN / GENEALOGICAL FORUM OF OREGON, INC. (US). **2440**

BULLETIN - GENETICS SOCIETY OF CANADA. (CN/0316-4357). **543**

BULLETIN GEODESIQUE. (FR/0007-4632). **1403**

BULLETIN / GEOTHERMAL RESOURCES COUNCIL. (US/0160-7782). **Adv Mgr:** same as editor. **1934**

BULLETIN - GREATER ST. LOUIS DENTAL SOCIETY. (US/0360-2575). **1318**

BULLETIN - HUMAN FACTORS SOCIETY. (US/0438-1629). **Adv Mgr:** Lois Smith. **1250**

BULLETIN - ILLINOIS GEOGRAPHICAL SOCIETY. (US/0019-2031). **2557**

BULLETIN - INDIAN GEOLOGISTS' ASSOCIATION. (II/0379-5098). **1369**

BULLETIN / INSTITUTE FOR ANTIQUITY AND CHRISTIANITY. (US/0739-0459). **4941**

BULLETIN / INSTITUTE OF ADVANCED LEGAL STUDIES (UNIVERSITY OF LONDON). (UK/0963-9675). **Adv Mgr:** B. Crothers. **2944**

BULLETIN - INSTITUTE OF MATHEMATICAL STATISTICS. (US/0146-3942). **5324**

BULLETIN - INSTITUTE OF MATHEMATICS AND ITS APPLICATIONS. (UK/0950-5628). **3498**

BULLETIN (INTERNATIONAL ASSOCIATION OF LIGHTHOUSE AUTHORITIES). (FR/0379-2811). **4175**

BULLETIN - INTERNATIONAL ASSOCIATION OF ORIENTALIST LIBRARIANS. (US/0161-7397). **3198**

BULLETIN / INTERNATIONAL OLD LACERS. (US). **5348**

BULLETIN - JOURNAL OF THE TOKYO WOMEN'S MEDICAL COLLEGE. (JA/0495-7792). **3560**

BULLETIN - KING COUNTY MEDICAL SOCIETY, THE. (US/0023-1592). **3913**

BULLETIN - LUZERNE COUNTY MEDICAL SOCIETY, THE. (US/0098-5880). **3560**

BULLETIN / MAINE ARCHAEOLOGICAL SOCIETY. (US/0542-1292). **263**

BULLETIN / MANITOBA NATURALISTS SOCIETY. (CN/0823-2911). **4164**

BULLETIN - MICROSCOPICAL SOCIETY OF CANADA. (CN/0383-1825). **572**

BULLETIN - NEW JERSEY ACADEMY OF SCIENCE, THE. (US/0028-5455). **5091**

BULLETIN - NEW JERSEY MOTOR TRUCK ASSOCIATION. (US/0028-5838). **5378**

BULLETIN - NEW MEXICO BUREAU OF MINES & MINERAL RESOURCES. (US/0096-4581). **2135**

BULLETIN - NORTH AMERICAN GLADIOLUS COUNCIL. (US/0029-2370). **Adv Mgr:** Plummer, **Tel** (614)653-3517. **505**

BULLETIN - NORTH DAKOTA LEAGUE OF CITIES. (US/0279-800X). **4634**

BULLETIN OF BIBLIOGRAPHY (1979). (US/0190-745X). **412**

BULLETIN OF CONCERNED ASIAN SCHOLARS. (US/0007-4810). **2647**

BULLETIN OF DENTAL EDUCATION. (US/0007-4837). **Adv Mgr:** A. Siegel, **Tel** (202)667-9433. **1318**

BULLETIN OF EASTERN CARIBBEAN AFFAIRS. (BB). **2511**

BULLETIN OF ECONOMIC RESEARCH. (UK/0307-3378). **1590**

BULLETIN OF ENTOMOLOGICAL RESEARCH. (UK/0007-4853). **5606**

BULLETIN OF GRAIN TECHNOLOGY. (II/0007-4896). **200**

BULLETIN OF HISPANIC STUDIES. (UK/0007-490X). **3271**

BULLETIN OF INDONESIAN ECONOMIC STUDIES. (AT/0007-4918). **1466**

BULLETIN OF JUDAEO-GREEK STUDIES. (UK/0954-1179). **5046**

BULLETIN OF MEDIEVAL CANON LAW. (US/0146-2989). **2944**

BULLETIN OF NUMBER THEORY AND RELATED TOPICS. BOLETIN DE TEORIA DE NUMEROS Y TEMAS CONEXOS. (AG). **3498**

BULLETIN OF PEACE PROPOSALS. (NO/0007-5035). **4466**

BULLETIN OF PHYSICAL EDUCATION. (UK/0521-0011). **1855**

BULLETIN OF PURE & APPLIED SCIENCES. SEC. D, PHYSICS. (II). **4399**

BULLETIN OF PURE & APPLIED SCIENCES. SEC. E, MATHEMATICS. (II/0970-6577). **3498**

BULLETIN OF PURE & APPLIED SCIENCES. SECTION A, ANIMAL SCIENCE. (II/0970-0765). **5579**

BULLETIN OF PURE & APPLIED SCIENCES. SECTION B, PLANT SCIENCES. (II). **505**

BULLETIN OF TANZANIAN AFFAIRS. (UK/0952-2948). **2638**

BULLETIN OF THE AMATEUR ENTOMOLOGISTS' SOCIETY, THE. (UK/0266-836X). **Adv Mgr:** R. Dyke. **5606**

BULLETIN OF THE AMERICAN DAHLIA SOCIETY, INC. (US/0002-8150). **Adv Mgr:** Charles S. Conerty, Jr., **Tel** (201)694-4864. **2411**

BULLETIN OF THE AMERICAN IRIS SOCIETY. (US/0747-4172). **2411**

BULLETIN OF THE AMERICAN METEOROLOGICAL SOCIETY. (US/0003-0007). **1421**

BULLETIN OF THE AMERICAN PENSTEMON SOCIETY. (US/0065-9584). **2411**

BULLETIN OF THE AMERICAN ROCK GARDEN SOCIETY. (US/0003-0864). **Adv Mgr:** Al Deurbrouck. **2411**

BULLETIN OF THE AMERICAN SCHOOLS OF ORIENTAL RESEARCH. (US/0003-097X). **264**

BULLETIN OF THE AMERICAN SOCIETY FOR INFORMATION SCIENCE. (US/0095-4403). **3198**

BULLETIN OF THE ASSOCIATION FOR BUSINESS COMMUNICATION, THE. (US/8756-1972). **862**

BULLETIN OF THE ASSOCIATION OF BRITISH THEOLOGICAL AND PHILOSOPHICAL LIBRARIES. (UK/0305-781X). **3198**

BULLETIN OF THE ASSOCIATION OF COLLEGE UNIONS-INTERNATIONAL, THE. (US/0004-5659). **1861**

BULLETIN OF THE ASTRONOMICAL SOCIETY OF INDIA. (II/0304-9523). **394**

BULLETIN OF THE ATOMIC SCIENTISTS. (US/0096-3402). **5091**

BULLETIN OF THE AUSTRALIAN METEOROLOGICAL AND OCEANOGRAPHIC SOCIETY. (AT/1035-6576). **Adv Mgr:** Robert Wright, **Tel** 011 61 3 669 4000. **1421**

BULLETIN OF THE AUSTRALIAN PSYCHOLOGICAL SOCIETY. (AT). **4579**

BULLETIN OF THE CANADIAN BIOCHEMICAL SOCIETY. (CN/0008-302X). **484**

BULLETIN OF THE CHEMICAL SOCIETY OF JAPAN. (JA/0009-2673). **963**

BULLETIN OF THE ESSEX COUNTY MEDICAL SOCIETY, THE. (US/0014-0937). **3560**

BULLETIN OF THE EUROPEAN ASSOCIATION OF FISH PATHOLOGISTS. (NE/0108-0288). **2298**

BULLETIN OF THE GUILD OF CARILLONNEURS IN NORTH AMERICA. (US/0827-5955). **4106**

BULLETIN OF THE HEGEL SOCIETY OF GREAT BRITAIN, THE. (UK/0263-5232). **Adv Mgr:** Dr. Robert Stern. **4343**

BULLETIN OF THE HISTORY OF DENTISTRY. (US/0007-5132). **1318**

BULLETIN OF THE HISTORY OF MEDICINE. (US/0007-5140). **3560**

BULLETIN OF THE HOUSTON GEOLOGICAL SOCIETY, THE. (US/0018-6686). **Adv Mgr:** B. Falkenstein. **1370**

BULLETIN OF THE INDIAN SOCIETY OF EARTHQUAKE TECHNOLOGY. (II). **1403**

BULLETIN OF THE INSTITUTE FOR CONTINUING DENTAL EDUCATION OF THE QUEENS COUNTY DENTAL SOCIETY. (US/0739-1773). **1318**

BULLETIN OF THE INSTITUTE OF MARITIME AND TROPICAL MEDICINE IN GDYNIA. (PL/0324-8542). **3985**

BULLETIN OF THE INSTITUTE OF TRADITIONAL CULTURES. (II/0541-7562). **5194**

BULLETIN OF THE INSTITUTION OF ENGINEERS (INDIA). (II/0020-3343). **2037**

BULLETIN OF THE INTERNATIONAL ASSOCIATION OF ENGINEERING GEOLOGY. (GW/0074-1612). **2019**

BULLETIN OF THE INTERNATIONAL CENTRE FOR HEAT AND MASS TRANSFER. (US/0888-6911). **2111**

BULLETIN OF THE INTERNATIONAL PEAT SOCIETY. (FI/0355-1008). **1934**

BULLETIN OF THE INTERNATIONAL PEDIATRIC ASSOCIATION. (FR/0245-9337). **3901**

BULLETIN OF THE JEWISH HISTORICAL SOCIETY OF ENGLAND. (UK). **5046**

BULLETIN OF THE MARYLAND HERPETOLOGICAL SOCIETY. (US/0025-4231). **5579**

BULLETIN OF THE MASSACHUSETTS ARCHAEOLOGICAL SOCIETY. (US/0148-1886). **Adv Mgr:** Tom Lux. **264**

BULLETIN OF THE MEDICAL LIBRARY ASSOCIATION. (US/0025-7338). **3198**

BULLETIN OF THE MENNINGER CLINIC. (US/0025-9284). **3922**

BULLETIN OF THE MICHIGAN DENTAL HYGIENISTS' ASSOCIATION, THE. (US/0746-5564). **1318**

BULLETIN OF THE NATIONAL GUILD OF CATHOLIC PSYCHIATRISTS, INC, THE. (US/0547-7115). **3922**

BULLETIN OF THE NEEDLE AND BOBBIN CLUB, THE. (US/0273-0197). **5183**

BULLETIN OF THE OCMA, THE. (US/0199-7378). **3560**

BULLETIN OF THE OHIO BIOLOGICAL SURVEY. (US/0078-3994). **450**

BULLETIN OF THE PERMANENT INTERNATIONAL ASSOCIATION OF NAVIGATION CONGRESSES. (BE/0374-1001). **2088**

BULLETIN OF THE PHILADELPHIA HERPETOLOGICAL SOCIETY. (US/0553-9587). **5579**

BULLETIN — Advertising Accepted Index

BULLETIN OF THE SCHOOL OF ORIENTAL AND AFRICAN STUDIES. (UK/0041-977X). **3271**

BULLETIN OF THE SCIENCE FICTION WRITERS OF AMERICA. (US/0192-2424). **3370**

BULLETIN OF THE SOCIETY OF VECTOR ECOLOGISTS. (US/0146-6429). **Adv Mgr:** H. B. Munn, **Tel** (209)295-3540. **2212**

BULLETIN OF THE TORREY BOTANICAL CLUB, THE. (US/0040-9618). **505**

BULLETIN OF TOKYO MEDICAL AND DENTAL UNIVERSITY, THE. (JA/0040-8921). **3561**

BULLETIN OFFICIEL DE LA SOCIETE INTERNATIONALE DE PSYCHO-PROPHYLAXIE OBSTETRICALE. (FR/0037-9468). **3758**

BULLETIN - ORNITHOLOGICAL SOCIETY OF THE MIDDLE EAST. (UK). **5616**

BULLETIN - PENNSYLVANIA FLOWER GROWERS. (US/0031-448X). **2435**

BULLETIN / POLISH GENEALOGICAL SOCIETY, CALIFORNIA. (US/1056-568X). **2441**

BULLETIN - PORTLAND ART ASSOCIATION (OR.). (US/0887-4395). **345**

BULLETIN / PRINTING HISTORICAL SOCIETY. (UK/0144-7505). **4564**

BULLETIN - ROYAL SOCIETY OF NEW ZEALAND. (NZ/0370-6559). **5091**

BULLETIN - ROYAL TROPICAL INSTITUTE. (NE/0922-7911). **450**

BULLETIN - SEATTLE GENEALOGICAL SOCIETY. (US/0559-2526). **2441**

BULLETIN SIGNALETIQUE - DOC MNE. (FR/0989-1994). **208**

BULLETIN SKI NAUTIQUE. (CN/0824-0906). **4888**

BULLETIN - SOCIETE DES AMIS DU JARDIN VAN DEN HENDE INC. (CN/0711-6446). **2411**

BULLETIN (SOCIETE D'ETUDES HISTORIQUES DE LA NOUVELLE CALEDONIE). (NL). **2669**

BULLETIN - SOCIETE FRANCAISE DE PHOTOGRAMMETRIE ET DE TELEDETECTION. (FR/0244-6014). **4367**

BULLETIN - SOCIETY FOR SPANISH AND PORTUGUESE HISTORICAL STUDIES (U.S.). (US/0739-1824). **Adv Mgr:** Paul Freedman. **2681**

BULLETIN - SOCIETY OF WETLAND SCIENTISTS (U.S.). (US/0732-9393). **450**

BULLETIN - SPECIAL LIBRARIES ASSOCIATION. EDUCATION DIVISION. (US/1052-9454). **3198**

BULLETIN - SPECIAL LIBRARIES ASSOCIATION. GEOGRAPHY AND MAP DIVISION. (US/0036-1607). **2557**

BULLETIN - SPECIAL LIBRARIES ASSOCIATION, NORTH CAROLINA CHAPTER. (US/0195-9077). **3198**

BULLETIN - SPECIAL LIBRARIES ASSOCIATION. SAN FRANCISCO BAY REGION CHAPTER. (US/0277-2124). **3199**

BULLETIN TECHNIQUE DE L INSEMINATION ARTIFICIELLE. (FR/0153-6281). **5506**

BULLETIN, THE. (US). **1317**

BULLETIN - THE INSTITUTE OF MEAT. (UK). **2329**

BULLETIN (TOY TRAIN OPERATING SOCIETY : 1973). (US). **2772**

BULLETIN TRIMESTRIEL DE LA SOCIETE BELGE DE PHOTOGRAMMETRIE-TELEDETECTION ET CARTOGRAPHIE. (BE). **Adv Mgr:** J. Van Hemelrijck, **Tel** 011 32 2 2103598. **4367**

BULLETIN TRIMESTRIEL DI L'INSTITUT ARCHEOLOGIQUE DU LUXEMBOURG. (BE/0020-2177). **265**

BULLETIN - U.S. COAST GUARD ACADEMY ALUMNI ASSOCIATION. (US/0191-9814). **1101**

BULLETIN - UK CENTRE FOR ECONOMIC AND ENVIRONMENTAL DEVELOPMENT. (UK/0268-7402). **1466**

BULLETIN - UNITED BIBLE SOCIETIES. (UK/0041-719X). **5015**

BULLETIN - UNIVERSITY RELATIONS AND INFORMATION OFFICE, UNIVERSITY OF MANITOBA. (CN/0706-8549). **1813**

BULLETIN VOYAGES. (CN/0706-215X). **Adv Mgr:** Mrs. Honorat. **5465**

BULLETIN / WEST TEXAS GEOLOGICAL SOCIETY. (US/0739-5957). **1371**

BULLETIN - YAKIMA VALLEY GENEALOGICAL SOCIETY. (US/0513-6776). **2441**

BULLETIN / YORKSHIRE NATURALISTS' UNION. (UK/0265-6833). **4164**

BULLISIANA. (CN/0705-9108). **394**

BULL'S-EYE NEWS. (US/0885-0771). **Adv Mgr:** Jay Tomlinson. **4888**

BUNDES-TELEFONBUCH FUER DIE GEWERBLICHE WIRTSCHAFT DER BUNDESREPUBLIK DEUTSCHLAND MIT BERLIN (WEST). (GW). **1600**

BUNDESBAHN, DIE. (GW/0007-5876). **5430**

BUNDESBAUBLATT. (GW/0007-5884). **2816**

BUNDESGESUNDHEITSBLATT. (GW/0007-5914). **4770**

BUNSEKI. (JA). **1014**

BUNSEKI KAGAKU. (JA/0525-1931). **1014**

BUOYANT FLIGHT. (US/0361-5065). **15**

BUREAU NEWS / BUREAU OF WHOLESALE SALES REPRESENTATIVES. (US/0747-4598). **644**

BURGEN UND SCHLOSSER. (GW/0007-6201). **2682**

BURLESON COUNTY CITIZEN-TRIBUNE AND THE CALDWELL NEWS. (US). **Adv Mgr:** Charlotte Strong. **5747**

BURLINGTON MAGAZINE. (UK/0007-6287). **346**

BURLINGTON STANDARD-PRESS. (US/0749-7261). **Adv Mgr:** David Wright. **5765**

BURNS CHRONICLE. (UK). **431**

BURNSVILLE CURRENT, THE. (US/0193-3000). **Adv Mgr:** Paul Johnson, **Tel** (612)896-4700. **5694**

BURPEE GARDENS. (US/0749-4653). **2411**

BUS DATABASE. (US). **1172**

BUS RIDE. (US/0192-8902). **5378**

BUS RIDE: BUS INDUSTRY DIRECTORY. (US/0363-3764). **5378**

BUS VERKEHR. (GW). **5378**

BUS WORLD. (US/0162-9689). **5378**

BUSES SHEPPERTON. (UK/0007-6392). **5378**

BUSES YEARBOOK. (UK). **5378**

BUSH FIRE BULLETIN. (AT). **Adv Mgr:** John Jackson. **2288**

BUSHDRIVER. (AT/0155-0535). **5408**

BUSHWHACKER MUSINGS : VERNON COUNTY HISTORICAL SOCIETY NEWSLETTER. (US/1070-8243). **2725**

BUSINESS AND COMMERCIAL AVIATION. (US/0191-4642). **15**

BUSINESS AND FINANCE. (IE/0007-6473). **781**

BUSINESS AND FINANCE IN SCOTLAND. (UK). **Adv Mgr:** Helen Stuart, **Tel** same as publisher. **781**

BUSINESS AND HEALTH. (US/0739-9413). **645**

BUSINESS & INDUSTRY. (US/0021-0463). **Adv Mgr:** Robert Wagner. **645**

BUSINESS AND MANAGEMENT EDITIONS: BMB. (BE). **862**

BUSINESS & PROFESSIONAL WOMAN (OTTAWA). (CN/0045-3587). **AdvMgr Tel** (416)424-1393. **5552**

BUSINESS ARCHIVES. (UK/0007-6538). **Adv Mgr:** W. S. Quinn-Robinson. **3199**

BUSINESS AVIATION SAFETY. (US/0890-8664). **15**

BUSINESS COMPUTER NEWS. (CN/0838-438X). **646**

BUSINESS CONCEPTS. (US/1055-8217). **646**

BUSINESS CONTACT. (RU/0235-764X). **826**

BUSINESS CREDIT. (US/0897-0181). **Adv Mgr:** Diane Wade. **781**

BUSINESS CURRENTS. TECHNICAL REPORT. (US/0736-4415). **939**

BUSINESS DAY'S 1000 TOP CORPORATIONS IN THE PHILIPPINES. (PH). **647**

BUSINESS DIGEST. (US/1046-168X). **647**

BUSINESS DIGEST (DANBURY, CONN.). (US/8750-9520). **647**

BUSINESS DIRECTIONS. (AT/1031-2315). **Adv Mgr:** David Dell. **647**

BUSINESS ECONOMICS (CLEVELAND, OHIO). (US/0007-666X). **1466**

BUSINESS ECONOMICS. MEMBERSHIP DIRECTORY. (US). **1466**

BUSINESS EDUCATION FORUM. (US/0007-6678). **647**

BUSINESS EDUCATION TODAY. (UK). **1729**

BUSINESS EDUCATION TODAY. (UK/0951-1512). **647**

BUSINESS ETHICS (MADISON, WIS.). (US/0894-6582). **Adv Mgr:** M Kniaz. **2249**

BUSINESS FACILITIES. (US/0746-0023). **648**

BUSINESS FIRMS DIRECTORY OF THE DELAWARE VALLEY. (US/0091-2581). **648**

BUSINESS FIRST (BUFFALO, N.Y.). (US/0749-9418). **648**

BUSINESS FIRST (COLUMBUS, OHIO). (US/0748-6146). **648**

BUSINESS FIRST (LOUISVILLE, KY.). (US/0748-6138). **Adv Mgr:** Maureen O'Mearo. **648**

BUSINESS FOR CENTRAL NEW JERSEY. (US/1042-8704). **862**

BUSINESS FORUM (LOS ANGELES, CALIF.). (US/0733-2408). **648**

BUSINESS HISTORY. (UK/0007-6791). **Adv Mgr:** Anne Kidson. **648**

BUSINESS HISTORY REVIEW. (US/0007-6805). **Adv Mgr:** A. Chaney, **Tel** (617)495-6154. **648**

BUSINESS HISTORY REVIEW. (US/0007-6805). **648**

BUSINESS IN BROWARD. (US). **1466**

BUSINESS IN PALM BEACH COUNTY. (US). **649**

BUSINESS IN THAILAND. (TH/0125-0140). **649**

BUSINESS IN VANCOUVER. (CN/0849-5017). **Adv Mgr:** Sandi Gilmer, **Tel** same as publisher. **649**

BUSINESS INDIA. (II/0254-5268). **649**

BUSINESS INFORMATION ALERT. (US/1042-0746). **3199**

BUSINESS INSIGHT. (US/1056-6244). **649**

BUSINESS INSURANCE. (US/0007-6864). **2877**

BUSINESS INSURANCE. DIRECTORY OF CORPORATE BUYERS OF INSURANCE, BENEFIT PLANS AND RISK MANAGEMENT SERVICES. (US/0747-7937). **649**

BUSINESS JOURNAL (1988), THE. (US/1048-8812). **Adv Mgr:** Matt Toeldo. **649**

BUSINESS JOURNAL (MILWAUKEE, WIS.), THE. (US/0740-2899). **Adv Mgr:** Dan Meyer. **649**

BUSINESS JOURNAL (NEW YORK). (US). **Adv Mgr:** O. Sheahan. **649**

BUSINESS JOURNAL OF UPPER EAST TENNESSEE AND SOUTHWEST VIRGINIA. (US/1040-6360). **650**

BUSINESS JOURNAL (PHOENIX, ARIZ.), THE. (US/0895-1632). **650**

BUSINESS JOURNAL (PORTLAND, OR.), THE. (US/0742-6550). **650**

BUSINESS JOURNAL (SACRAMENTO, CALIF.). (US/8756-5897). **650**

BUSINESS JOURNAL / SONOMA & MARIN. (US). **Adv Mgr:** Ken Clark, **Tel** (707)579-2900. **650**

BUSINESS LAW REPORTS. (CN/0703-5551). **3096**

BUSINESS LAW REVIEW. (UK). **3096**

BUSINESS LAWYER, THE. (US/0007-6899). **3097**

BUSINESS (LUXEMBOURG). (LU). **650**

BUSINESS MARKETING. (US/0745-5933). **922**

BUSINESS MEXICO. (MX/0187-1455). **Adv Mgr:** Hector Abaroa, **Tel** 7243800. **650**

BUSINESS NEW HAMPSHIRE MAGAZINE. (US/1046-9575). **Adv Mgr:** David Kruger. **650**

BUSINESS/NEW YORK. (US/8750-927X). **651**

BUSINESS NEWS (EUGENE, OR.), THE. (US/1064-1661). **651**

BUSINESS, NORTH CAROLINA. (US/0279-4276). **Adv Mgr:** Glenn Benton. **651**

BUSINESS OF FILM, THE. (UK). **Adv Mgr:** E. Tavares, **Tel** 0101 310 657 2336. **4064**

BUSINESS OF FUR, THE. (US/0740-6258). **3183**

BUSINESS OPINION. (NZ). **651**

BUSINESS OPPORTUNITIES HANDBOOK. (US/1042-6175). **Adv Mgr:** Andrea Freedman, **Tel** (414)272-9977. **651**

BUSINESS OPPORTUNITIES JOURNAL. (US/0193-3221). **Adv Mgr:** Maria Nicolaidis, **Tel** (800)854-6570. **893**

BUSINESS PEOPLE MAGAZINE (WINNIPEG. 1990). (CN/0849-3901). **Adv Mgr:** (204)982-4000. **651**

BUSINESS PRESS (FORT WORTH, TEX.), THE. (US/1045-8697). **Adv Mgr:** Carolyn Ashford, **Tel** (817)336-8300. **651**

BUSINESS QUARTERLY, THE. (CN/0007-6996). **652**

BUSINESS QUEENSLAND. (AT/1038-1430). **Adv Mgr:** Mario Salvadori. **652**

BUSINESS RADIO. (US/0746-8911). **Adv Mgr:** Robin Little, **Tel** (703)739-0300. **1150**

BUSINESS RECORD (DES MOINES, IOWA). (US/0746-410X). **652**

BUSINESS REFERRAL DIRECTORY / GREATER SAN DIEGO CHAMBER OF COMMERCE. (US/1068-3038). **652**

BUSINESS REVIEW WEEKLY : BRW. (AT/0727-758X). **652**

BUSINESS SCOTLAND. (UK/0144-6096). **652**

BUSINESS STUDIES. (UK/0953-685X). **653**

BUSINESS TELECOMMUNICATIONS DIRECTORY. (US/1041-6137). **1150**

BUSINESS TIMES (EAST HARTFORD, CONN.), THE. (US/0744-172X). **653**

BUSINESS TODAY. (US/0007-7100). **Adv Mgr:** Elise Nicol, **Tel** (609)258-1111. **653**

BUSINESS TOKYO. (JA/0914-0026). **653**

BUSINESS TRAVEL MANAGEMENT. (US/1046-5057). **653**

BUSINESS TRAVEL NEWS. (US/8750-3670). **653**

BUSINESS UPDATE (SANTA ANA, CALIF.). (US/8750-7803). **818**

BUSINESS VENEZUELA. (VE/1013-2120). **653**

BUSINESS WEEK. (US/0007-7135). **653**

BUSINESS WHO'S WHO OF AUSTRALIA, THE. (AT/0068-4503). **Adv Mgr:** Max Cunningham. **727**

BUSINESS WHO'S WHO PRODUCTS AND TRADENAMES GUIDE. (AT/1031-1343). **Adv Mgr:** Max Cunningham. **727**

BUSINESS WORCESTER. (US/0738-8977). **654**

BUSINESSWEST (SPRINGFIELD, MASS.). (US/1049-9822). **654**

BUTCHER & PROCESSOR. (UK/0268-1781). **Adv Mgr:** Peter Fleming, **Tel** 0799 584 879. **2329**

BUTTERICK HOME CATALOG (1985). (US/0895-6871). **5183**

BUTTERWORTHS CURRENT LAW. (NZ/0110-070X). **3125**

BUTTERWORTHS JOURNAL OF INTERNATIONAL BANKING AND FINANCIAL LAW. (UK/0269-2694). **3086**

BUTTERWORTHS LAW DIGEST MALAYSIA, SINGAPORE AND BRUNEI. (SI/0951-5720). **2945**

BUTTERWORTHS LEGAL SERVICES DIRECTORY. (UK). **3159**

BUVAR. (HU/0007-7356). **450**

BUY BOOKS WHERE, SELL BOOKS WHERE. (US/0732-6599). **4812**

BUYERS' GUIDE. (UK/0306-204X). **2587**

BUYERS' GUIDE & DEALER DIRECTORY: NORTHEASTERN AREA. (US/0145-5915). **826**

BUYER'S GUIDE (HINSDALE, ILL.). (US/0078-2610). **2154**

BUYERS GUIDE - NATIONAL TOOLING & MACHINING ASSOCIATION. (US/0736-7112). **949**

BUYERS GUIDE TO OUTDOOR ADVERTISING, THE. (US/0095-5531). **756**

BUYER'S GUIDE TO REACTIVE CURE SYSTEMS, UV-IR-EB. (US). **1021**

BUYING FOR BABY. (AT). **Adv Mgr:** Matthew Chivers & David Knight. **2277**

BUYING FOR LIBRARIES. (UK). **3199**

BUZZ (LOS ANGELES, CALIF.). (US/1053-3605). **2529**

BUZZ (THUNDER BAY). (CN/0701-2837). **4941**

BUZZWORM (BOULDER, COLO.). (US/0898-2996). **2189**

BVDA JOURNAL : BRITISH VETERINARY DENTAL ASSOCIATION. (UK). **5507**

BWLETIN Y BWRDD GWYBODAU CELTAIDD. (UK/0142-3363). **3271**

BWR TWRH. (IS/0333-6298). **5046**

BYGG & TEKNIK. (SW/0281-658X). **606**

BYGGEKUNST. (NO/0007-7518). **294**

BYGGREFERAT. (SW/0345-1941). **294**

BYLAWS, RULES, AND SPECIFICATIONS - WOMEN'S INTERNATIONAL BOWLING CONGRESS. (US/0191-1902). **4888**

BYLINE (EVANSTON, ILL.). (US/0731-5449). **2917**

BYLINE (OKLAHOMA CITY, OKLA.). (US/0744-4249). **2918**

BYOIN YAKUGAKU. (JA/0389-9098). **4295**

BYPLAN. (DK/0007-7658). **2816**

BYRON JOURNAL. (UK/0301-7257). **3339**

BYTE. (US/0360-5280). **1273**

BYTE BUYER, THE. (US/0889-8200). **1172**

BYU JOURNAL OF PUBLIC LAW, THE. (US/0896-2383). **2945**

BYZANTINA VINDOBONENSIA. (AU/0525-3292). **2682**

BYZANTINE AND MODERN GREEK STUDIES. (UK/0307-0131). **2682**

BYZANTINE STUDIES. (US/0095-4608). **2682**

BZZLLETIN. (NE/0165-0858). **3461**

C.A.R.E. PACKAGE, THE. (US/1064-2609). **3370**

C & L APPLICATIONS. (UK/0957-4085). **3199**

C.C.A.I. MONTHLY NEWSLETTER. (II/0376-7787). **1294**

C C C N (CALIFORNIA COMMUNITY CARE NEWS). (US). **2529**

C.F.O. JOURNAL. (US/0362-9902). **5616**

C.F.P. CHAUD FROID PLOMBERIE. (FR/0750-1552). **2604**

C. H. A. C. REVIEW. (CN/0226-5923). **Adv Mgr:** Martine Leroux. **3777**

C I E N, CANADIAN INDUSTRIAL EQUIPMENT NEWS. (CN/0319-5902). **3476**

C I M REPORTER. (CN/0701-0710). **2136**

C.J. THE AMERICAS. (US/0896-9922). **3159**

C-MAGAZIN. (GW/0935-0373). **4941**

C MAGAZINE (1992). (CN/1193-8625). **Adv Mgr:** Carol Peaker. **317**

C O R S BULLETIN. (CN/0315-1417). **1236**

C P H A HEALTH DIGEST. (CN/0703-5624). **4770**

C R S PERSPECTIVES. (CN/0228-1821). **2136**

C (TORONTO. 1987). (CN/0838-0392). **Adv Mgr:** Ben Smith and Carol Peaker, **Tel** 416-539-9495. **346**

C USERS JOURNAL, THE. (US/0898-9788). **Adv Mgr:** Jeff Dickey-Chasins. **1278**

C1 MOLECULE CHEMISTRY. (SZ/0275-7567). **1035**

CA CRAFT CONNECTION, THE. (US/1042-6280). **370**

CA MAGAZINE. (CN/0317-6878). **740**

CA SELECTS: HEAT-RESISTANT & ABLATIVE POLYMERS. (US/0162-7821). **1003**

CA SELECTS: ORGANIC REACTION MECHANISMS. (US/0162-7848). **1006**

CA SELECTS: ORGANOPHOSPHORUS CHEMISTRY. (US/0162-783X). **1006**

CA SELECTS: THERMOCHEMISTRY. (US/0162-7864). **1010**

CABELL RECORD. (US/1041-2255). **5763**

CABINETMAKER (CHICAGO, ILL.). (US/1048-0196). **633**

CABLE COMMUNICATIONS MAGAZINE. (CN/0318-0069). **1128**

CABLE GUIDE. (US/0191-4871). **1129**

CABLE GUIDE (WYOMING, MI). (US). **1129**

CABLE TV INVESTOR. (US/0731-0250). **1129**

CABLE TV TECHNOLOGY. (US/0276-5713). **1129**

CABLE WEEK. ORANGE-SEMINOLE-OSEOLA ED. (US/0744-2327). **1129**

CABLE WORLD. (US/1042-7228). **1150**

CABLESPORTS NEWSLETTER. (US). **Adv Mgr:** Barry Gould, **Tel** (207)363-6222. **1129**

CAC NEWS - CHICAGO ARTISTS' COALITION. (US/0890-5908). **346**

CACD JOURNAL. (US/1052-3103). **5276**

CACHE REGISTER, THE. (US/0731-079X). **1236**

CACTUS AND SUCCULENT JOURNAL (SANTA BARBARA). (US/0007-9367). **Adv Mgr:** Mindy Fusaro, **Tel** (515)285-7760. **2411**

CACTUS AND SUCCULENT JOURNAL WOOLLAHRA. (AT/0526-7196). **2411**

CAD CAM. (UK). **1231**

CAD/CAM DIGEST. (UK/0263-6190). **1231**

CAD CAM REPORT. (GW). **1227**

CAD USER. (UK/0959-6259). **Adv Mgr:** Adam Ramzi, **Tel** 081 663 3818. **1222**

CADENCE. (US/0162-6973). **Adv Mgr:** Susan. **4106**

CADENCE (AUSTIN, TEX.). (US/0887-9141). **1173**

CADENZA (LOLO, MONT.). (US/0007-9405). **4106**

CADIZ RECORD, THE. (US). **Adv Mgr:** Jan Witty. **5679**

CADMOS. (SW). **2682**

CADRES CFDT. (FR/0398-3145). **Adv Mgr:** Pierre Vial. **1657**

CADSCAN. (UK). **3999**

CADUCEUS (SPRINGFIELD, ILL.). (US/0882-6447). **3561**

CAFE, CACAO, THE. (FR/0007-9510). **165**

CAFETAL: REVISTA BIMESTRAL DE ANACAFE. (GT). **2365**

CAHIERS AFRICAINS D'ADMINISTRATION PUBLIQUE. (MR/0007-9588). **4635**

CAHIERS BERNARD LAZARE. (FR). **5046**

CAHIERS BIBLIOGRAPHIQUES DE CHIMIE ORGANOMETALLIQUE. (FR). **966**

CAHIERS D'ANTHROPOLOGIE ET BIOMETRIE HUMAINE. (FR/0758-2714). **233**

CAHIERS DE CIVILISATION MEDIEVALE. (FR/0007-9731). **2682**

CAHIERS DE DEFENSE SOCIALE. (FR). **3159**

CAHIERS DE GEOGRAPHIE DU QUEBEC. (CN/0007-9766). **2557**

CAHIERS DE LA CINEMATHEQUE, LES. (FR/0764-8499). **4064**

CAHIERS DE LA DOCUMENTATION. (BE/0007-9804). **3199**

CAHIERS DE LA FONDATION, LES. (FR/0983-1851). **654**

CAHIERS DE LA NOUVELLE, LES. (FR/0294-0442). **3371**

CAHIERS DE LA SEIGNEURIE DE CHAMBLY. (CN/0228-0930). **2725**

CAHIERS DE L'ANALYSE DES DONNEES, LES. (FR/0339-3097). **5324**

CAHIERS DE LEXICOLOGIE. (FR/0007-9871). **3271**

CAHIERS DE LINGUISTIQUE. ASIE ORIENTALE. (FR/0153-3320). **3271**

CAHIERS DE MEDECINE DU TRAVAIL. (BE/0376-7639). **3561**

CAHIERS DE NUTRITION ET DE DIETETIQUE. (FR/0007-9960). **4188**

CAHIERS DE PSYCHOLOGIE COGNITIVE. (FR/0249-9185). **4579**

CAHIERS DE SOCIOLOGIE ECONOMIQUE ET CULTURELLE, ETHNOPSYCHOLOGIE. (FR/0761-9871). **5241**

CAHIERS DEBUSSY. (FR/0395-1200). **4106**

CAHIERS DES AMERIQUES LATINES (PARIS, FRANCE : 1985). (FR). **2725**

CAHIERS DES COMITES DE PREVENTION DU BATIMENT ET DES TRAVAUX PUBLICS. (FR/0010-244X). **2860**

CAHIERS DES RELIGIONS AFRICAINES. (CG/0008-0047). **4942**

CAHIERS D'HISTOIRE DE DEUX-MONTAGNES. (CN/0226-7063). **2725**

CAHIERS D'HISTOIRE DE L'INSTITUT DE RECHERCHES MARXISTES. (FR/0221-5047). **2682**

CAHIERS D'HISTOIRE ET DE PHILOSOPHIE DES SCIENCES. (FR/0221-3664). **5092**

CAHIERS D'HISTOIRE (MONTREAL). (CN/0712-2330). **2613**

CAHIERS D'OUTRE-MER. (FR/0373-5834). **2557**

CAHIERS DU CENTRE D'ETUDES DE L'ASIE DE L'EST. (CN/0839-4555). **2844**

CAHIERS DU CENTRE SCIENTIFIQUE ET TECHNIQUE DU BATIMENT. (FR/0008-9850). **5092**

CAHIERS DU CINEMA. (FR/0008-011X). **4064**

CAHIERS DU CREDIT MUTUEL. (FR/0395-8175). **781**

CAHIERS DU LACITO PARIS. (FR/0994-7736). **3272**

CAHIERS DU MONDE RUSSE ET SOVIETIQUE. (FR/0008-0160). **2682**

CAHIERS

Advertising Accepted Index

CAHIERS ECONOMIQUES DE BRUXELLES. (BE/0008-0195). **1467**

CAHIERS ECONOMIQUES ET MONETAIRES. (FR/0396-4701). **781**

CAHIERS ECONOMIQUES ET SOCIAUX (KINSHASA). (CG/0008-0209). **1550**

CAHIERS ELISABETHAINES. (FR/0184-7678). **3339**

CAHIERS FRANCO-CANADIENS DE LOUEST. (CN/0843-9559). **Adv Mgr:** Raymond Theberge, **Tel** (204)233-0210. **3272**

CAHIERS IVOIRIENS DE RECHERCHE LINGUISTIQUE / INSTITUT DE LINGUISTIQUE APPLIQUU.N.A.C.I-ABIDJAN. (IV/0252-9386). **3272**

CAHIERS NATURALISTES, LES. (FR/0008-0365). **3371**

CAHIERS PAUL-LOUIS COURIER. (FR/0084-8239). **3371**

CAHIERS RATIONALISTES, LES. (FR). **5092**

CAHIERS SAINT DOMINIQUE. (FR). **5025**

CAIRO PAPERS IN SOCIAL SCIENCE. (UA). **5194**

CALAO. (FR/0335-6469). **1060**

CALCUTTA LAW JOURNAL. (II). **2946**

CALDWELL MESSENGER (CALDWELL, KAN. 1942), THE. (US/0897-4551). **5674**

CALDWELL PROGRESS (1942). (US). **Adv Mgr:** Roger White. **5709**

CALEDONIAN-RECORD (SAINT JOHNSBURY, VT.). (US/1054-3716). **Adv Mgr:** George Wollpath. **5757**

CALENDAR FOR NEW MUSIC, THE. (US/0886-4594). **4106**

CALGARY COMMERCE. (CN/0707-8064). **826**

CALGARY SUN. (CN). **Adv Mgr:** G. Norrie. **5781**

CALHOUN NEWS, THE. (US). **Adv Mgr:** Mary Buchanan, **Tel** (618)576-2244. **5658**

CALICO JOURNAL. (US/0742-7778). **Adv Mgr:** E. Johnson. **1222**

CALIFORNIA AGRICULTURAL EXPORTER. (US). **71**

CALIFORNIA AND WESTERN STATES GRAPE GROWER. (US/0092-2145). **166**

CALIFORNIA ANGLER. (US/8750-8907). **2298**

CALIFORNIA APPAREL NEWS. (US/0008-0896). **1082**

CALIFORNIA-ARIZONA COTTON. (US/0008-090X). **166**

CALIFORNIA ARTS ADVOCATE. (US). **317**

CALIFORNIA BANKRUPTCY JOURNAL. (US/1047-0743). **782**

CALIFORNIA BLUE BOOK. (US). **1082**

CALIFORNIA BOWLING NEWS. (US/0008-0918). **4889**

CALIFORNIA BUILDER. (US/0527-2009). **606**

CALIFORNIA BUSINESS. (US/0008-0926). **654**

CALIFORNIA CATTLEMAN. (US/0008-0942). **Adv Mgr:** J. Danekas, **Tel** (916)965-6122. **208**

CALIFORNIA CONNECTIONS PUBLICATIONS. (US/0893-0694). **1658**

CALIFORNIA CORRECTIONAL NEWS. (US/0194-1682). **3159**

CALIFORNIA DEMOCRAT. (US). **5702**

CALIFORNIA ENGINEER. (US/0008-1027). **Adv Mgr:** Ivan Choi, **Tel** (510)642-8679. **1967**

CALIFORNIA EXPLORER. (US/0164-8748). **5465**

CALIFORNIA FARMER. (US/0008-1051). **71**

CALIFORNIA GARDEN. (US/0008-1116). **Adv Mgr:** Maianne Truby, **Tel** (619)232-5762. **2411**

CALIFORNIA GEOGRAPHER, THE. (US/0575-5700). **2557**

CALIFORNIA GROWER (VISTA, CALIF.). (US/0888-1715). **Adv Mgr:** R. Belieff, **Tel** (805)684-0916. **71**

CALIFORNIA HEALTH LAW REPORT. (US). **2946**

CALIFORNIA HIGHWAY PATROLMAN, THE. (US/0008-1140). **3159**

CALIFORNIA HISTORIAN. (US/0575-5751). **Adv Mgr:** A. Almeida, **Tel** (619)833-2872. **2725**

CALIFORNIA HISTORY ACTION. (US/0882-357X). **2725**

CALIFORNIA HORSE REVIEW. (US/0091-441X). **2797**

CALIFORNIA HORSEMAN'S NEWS. (US/0273-8287). **2797**

CALIFORNIA HOSPITALS. (US/0896-2766). **3777**

CALIFORNIA INNTOUCH. (US/0274-6093). **2804**

CALIFORNIA INTERNATIONAL TRADE REGISTER. (US/0270-4862). **1467**

CALIFORNIA JAZZ NOW. (US/1067-5213). **Adv Mgr:** A. Repke. **4106**

CALIFORNIA JOB JOURNAL. (US/0892-6395). **Adv Mgr:** Roz Hudnell. **1658**

CALIFORNIA JOURNAL. (US/0008-1205). **4466**

CALIFORNIA LAWYER. (US/0279-4063). **Adv Mgr:** Steven Phillips, **Tel** (415)252-0500. **2946**

CALIFORNIA LIBRARIES. (US/1056-1528). **Adv Mgr:** Christie Braziel. **3199**

CALIFORNIA MANAGEMENT REVIEW. (US/0008-1256). **862**

CALIFORNIA MANUFACTURERS REGISTER. (US/0068-5739). **Adv Mgr:** D Pearce. **3476**

CALIFORNIA MINING JOURNAL. (US/0008-1299). **Adv Mgr:** D.Craig. **2136**

CALIFORNIA MONTHLY. (US/0008-1302). **Adv Mgr:** Lora Dinga, **Tel** (510)526-4766. **1090**

CALIFORNIA NURSE. (US/0008-1310). **3852**

CALIFORNIA OPTOMETRY. (US/0273-804X). **4215**

CALIFORNIA PARALEGAL MAGAZINE. (US/1040-2640). **2946**

CALIFORNIA PARKS & RECREATION. (US/0733-5326). **4706**

CALIFORNIA PEACE OFFICER, THE. (US/0199-7025). **3159**

CALIFORNIA PEDIATRICIAN. (US/0882-3421). **3901**

CALIFORNIA PHARMACIST. (US/0739-0483). **Adv Mgr:** Lisa Clode, **Tel** (916)444-7811 ext.335. **4295**

CALIFORNIA PHYSICIAN. (US/8750-1813). **Adv Mgr:** Robert Shapiro. **3561**

CALIFORNIA POLITICAL WEEK. (US/0195-6175). **4636**

CALIFORNIA PRISONER, THE. (US/0884-0075). **3159**

CALIFORNIA PRIVATE SCHOOL DIRECTORY. (US/0098-5147). **1730**

CALIFORNIA PSYCHOLOGIST, THE. (US/0890-0302). **4579**

CALIFORNIA PUBLISHER. (US/0008-1434). **4813**

CALIFORNIA QUARTERLY. (US/0045-3978). **3371**

CALIFORNIA REAL ESTATE (1975). (US/0008-1450). **Adv Mgr:** Cindi Richardson, **Tel** (212)739-8321. **4835**

CALIFORNIA SCHOOL EMPLOYEE, THE. (US/0008-1515). **1861**

CALIFORNIA SENIOR CITIZEN. (US/0748-5727). **Adv Mgr:** Carol Osmon. **5633**

CALIFORNIA SERVICES REGISTER. (US/0271-6615). **Adv Mgr:** D Pearce. **654**

CALIFORNIA SOCIOLOGIST. (US/0162-8712). **5241**

CALIFORNIA SOUTHERN BAPTIST, THE. (US/0008-1558). **5057**

CALIFORNIA STAATS-ZEITUNG. (US/0890-1473). **5633**

CALIFORNIA TAX LAWYER. (US). **4716**

CALIFORNIA TECH, THE. (US/0008-1582). **1090**

CALIFORNIA TOMATO GROWER, THE. (US/0527-3277). **166**

CALIFORNIA TRUCKER. (US/1049-1023). **5378**

CALIFORNIA UNION LIST OF PERIODICALS. (US/0095-8034). **412**

CALIFORNIA VETERINARIAN, THE. (US/0008-1612). **5507**

CALIFORNIA WESTERN INTERNATIONAL LAW JOURNAL. (US/0886-3210). **3125**

CALIFORNIA WESTERN LAW REVIEW. (US/0008-1639). **2947**

CALIFORNIA WOMAN, THE. (US/0008-1663). **5552**

CALIFORNIAI MAGYARSAG. (US/0744-8600). **2257**

CALIFORNIAN (CUPERTINO, CALIF.), THE. (US/0742-5465). **2726**

CALIFORNIAN (TEMECULA, CALIF.), THE. (US/1045-5868). **Adv Mgr:** Paula Patton, **Tel** (909)676-4315. **5633**

CALIFORNIANS (SAN FRANCISCO, CALIF.), THE. (US/0745-5895). **Adv Mgr:** Robin Pendergraft, **Tel** (707)557-5552. **2726**

CALIOPE Y POLIMNIA : REVISTA DE POESIA Y CUENTOS. (SP). **3461**

CALIPER (TORONTO). (CN/0045-4001). **4385**

CALL-A.P.P.L.E. (US/8755-4909). **1265**

CALL BOARD (SAN FRANCISCO, CALIF.). (US/1064-0703). **5362**

CALL-NEWS DISPATCH, THE. (US). **5625**

CALLAHAN COUNTY STAR. (US). **Adv Mgr:** Carol Smith. **5747**

CALLALOO. (US/0161-2492). **3371**

CALLBOARD. (CN). **5362**

CALLIGRAPHY REVIEW (NORMAN, OKLA.). (US/0895-7819). **377**

CALS JOURNAL. (US/1061-2572). **Adv Mgr:** Bill Sleight. **1173**

CALUMET PRESS, THE. (US). **Adv Mgr:** Bill Palmateer, **Tel** (219)838-0717. **5663**

CALVACADE OF ACTS & ATTRACTIONS. (US). **384**

CALVERT CO. MARYLAND GENEALOGY NEWSLETTER. (US/0895-8939). **2441**

CALVINIST CONTACT. (CN/0410-3882). **5057**

CALYX (CORVALLIS). (US/0147-1627). **Adv Mgr:** Amy Agnello. **3371**

CAM MAGAZINE. (US/0883-7880). **606**

CAMAGUEYANO, EL. (US). **2726**

CAMARA DE COMERCIO DE GUATEMALA. (GT). **826**

CAMBRIA. (UK/0306-9796). **2557**

CAMBRIA COUNTY LEGAL JOURNAL. (US). **2947**

CAMBRIAN LAW REVIEW, THE. (UK/0084-8328). **2947**

CAMBRIAN MEDIEVAL CELTIC STUDIES. (UK). **3272**

CAMBRIDGE ANTHROPOLOGY. (UK). **233**

CAMBRIDGE CHRONICLE. (US). **Adv Mgr:** Edwin Vargas. **5688**

CAMBRIDGE MEDIEVAL CELTIC STUDIES. (UK/0260-5600). **3272**

CAMBRIDGE QUARTERLY. (UK/0008-199X). **3339**

CAMBRIDGE REVIEW OF INTERNATIONAL AFFAIRS. (UK/0955-7571). **4467**

CAMBRIDGE REVIEW, THE. (UK/0008-2007). **1090**

CAMBRIDGE UNIVERSITY GUIDE TO COURSES. (UK). **Adv Mgr:** Nick Kelley, **Tel** 0223 325757. **1090**

CAMDEN COUNTY TRIBUNE. (US/1055-6559). **Adv Mgr:** Tina Thompson. **5652**

CAMDEN NEWS, THE. (US). **Adv Mgr:** Sue Parnell. **5631**

CAMELLIA JOURNAL, THE. (US/0008-204X). **2411**

CAMERA AUSTRIA INTERNATIONAL. (AU). **4368**

CAMERA CANADA. (CN/0008-2090). **4368**

CAMERA OBSCURA (BERKELEY). (US/0270-5346). **4065**

CAMERART. (JA/0008-2082). **4368**

CAMERART PHOTO TRADE DIRECTORY. (JA). **4368**

CAMERAWORK. (US). **4368**

CAMERON HERALD (CAMERON, TEX.). (US). **5747**

CAMILLA ENTERPRISE, THE. (US). **Adv Mgr:** Sherie Kegrns. **5652**

CAMPAIGN AUSTRALIA. (AT). **Adv Mgr:** Dario Burgel, **Tel** (02)332 3666. **2793**

CAMPAIGN (LONDON. 1968). (UK/0008-2309). **757**

CAMPBELL LAW REVIEW. (US/0198-8174). **Adv Mgr:** Don Hegley, **Tel** (919)893-4111. **2947**

CAMPBELL RIVER UPPER ISLANDER, THE. (CN/0318-9538). **5781**

CAMPESINO, EL. (CL). **71**

CAMPING AND RV MAGAZINE. (US/0896-5706). **4849**

CAMPING CANADA. (CN/0384-9856). **4870**

CAMPING-FUHRER. BAND 1: SUDEUROPA. (GW). **4870**

CAMPING FUHRER BAND II : DEUTSCHLAND, MITTEL- UND NORD-EUROPA. (GW). **4870**

CAMPING MAGAZINE, THE. (US/0740-4131). **4870**

CAMPUS ACTIVITIES PROGRAMMING. (US/0746-2328). **1813**

CAMPUS CANADA (TORONTO, ONT.). (CN/0829-3309). **Adv Mgr:** H.Wolfe. **1090**

CAMPUS LAW ENFORCEMENT JOURNAL. (US/0739-0394). **3159**

CAMPUS LIFE (WHEATON, ILL.). (US/0008-2538). **1061**

CAMPUS OUTREACH. (US/1046-6975). **1813**

CAMPUS SAFETY REPORT NEWSLETTER. (US/0885-3398). **4770**

CANADA & THE WORLD. (CN/0043-8170). **5194**

CANADA CHINCHILLA. (CN/0823-2504). **5507**

CANADA JOURNAL (DEUTSCHE AUSG.). (CN/0829-0814). **Adv Mgr:** E. Tolles. **654**

CANADA LEGAL DIRECTORY. (CN/0315-8322). **3139**

CANADA LUTHERAN (NATIONAL ED.). (CN/0832-0179). **Adv Mgr:** Liz Olson. **5057**

CANADA NEWS (AUBURNDALE, FLA.). (US/0889-0412). **Adv Mgr:** Andy Steinbergs. **5649**

CANADA OFFSHORE BUYERS GUIDE. (CN/0822-8698). **4252**

CANADA POULTRYMAN. (CN/0008-2732). **Adv Mgr:** C. Greaves, **Tel** (604)585-3131. **208**

CANADA QUILTS. (CN/0381-7369). **5183**

CANADA-UNITED STATES LAW JOURNAL. (US/0163-6391). **3125**

CANADA YEARBOOK. (CN/0068-8142). **1923**

CANADAN UUTISET. (CN/0008-2775). **Adv Mgr:** Helena Itkonen, Tel 344-1611. **5781**

CANADA'S WHO'S WHO OF THE POULTRY INDUSTRY. (CN/0068-8134). **431**

CANADIAN ACOUSTICS. (CN/0711-6659). **2162**

CANADIAN ADVENTIST MESSENGER. (CN/0702-5084). **5057**

CANADIAN AIRCRAFT OPERATOR, THE. (CN/0008-2848). **15**

CANADIAN AMATEUR (1987). (CN/0834-3977). **2037**

CANADIAN-AMERICAN SLAVIC STUDIES. (US/0090-8290). **2683**

CANADIAN APPRAISER, THE. (CN/0827-2697). **4835**

CANADIAN ART SALES INDEX ..., THE. (CN/0229-8961). **346**

CANADIAN ART (TORONTO, 1984). (CN/0825-3854). **346**

CANADIAN ASSOCIATION OF RADIOLOGISTS JOURNAL. (CN/0846-5371). **3939**

CANADIAN AUCTIONEER, THE. (CN/0823-6429). **862**

CANADIAN AUTHOR (1992). (CN/1193-9974). **3372**

CANADIAN AUTHOR & BOOKMAN. (CN/0008-2937). **3372**

CANADIAN AUTOWORLD. (CN/1192-2745). **5408**

CANADIAN AVIATION NEWS (1984). (CN/0829-2132). **15**

CANADIAN AYRSHIRE REVIEW. (CN/0008-2961). **72**

CANADIAN BANKER (1983). (CN/0822-6830). **Adv Mgr:** Sally Longfiled. **782**

CANADIAN BANKRUPTCY REPORTS. (CN/0068-8347). **3086**

CANADIAN BAPTIST, THE. (CN/0008-2988). **Adv Mgr:** Don Besler. **4942**

CANADIAN BAR REVIEW. REVUE DU BARREAU CANADIEN, THE. (CN/0008-3003). **2947**

CANADIAN BAR REVIEW, THE. (CN/0008-3003). **3125**

CANADIAN BEEKEEPING. (CN/0576-4688). **Adv Mgr:** WJR Arnott. **72**

CANADIAN BIKER MAGAZINE, THE. (CN/0820-8344). **4080**

CANADIAN BIOTECH NEWS. (CN/1188-455X). **Adv Mgr:** Carole Cheetham. **3690**

CANADIAN BOOKSELLER (TORONTO). (CN/0225-2392). **4827**

CANADIAN BUSINESS (1977). (CN/0008-3100). **654**

CANADIAN C.S. LEWIS JOURNAL, THE. (CN/0711-2173). **3372**

CANADIAN CAMPER, THE. (CN/0316-280X). **4870**

CANADIAN CASES ON EMPLOYMENT LAW. (CN/0824-2607). **3145**

CANADIAN CASES ON THE LAW OF INSURANCE. (CN/0824-2585). **2947**

CANADIAN CASES ON THE LAW OF TORTS. (CN/0701-1733). **3089**

CANADIAN CAVER, THE. (CN/0833-0948). **4870**

CANADIAN CD-ROM NEWS. (CN/0848-8649). **1173**

CANADIAN CERAMICS QUARTERLY. (CN/0831-2974). **Adv Mgr:** B.Howell. **2587**

CANADIAN CHILDREN'S LITERATURE. (CN/0319-0080). **3372**

CANADIAN CIVIL ENGINEER. (CN/0825-7515). **2020**

CANADIAN CLEANER & LAUNDERER. (CN/0008-3224). **1600**

CANADIAN COIN BOX MAGAZINE. (CN/0045-4575). **Adv Mgr:** Peter Wilkinson, **Tel** (416)271-1366. **655**

CANADIAN COIN NEWS. (CN/0702-3162). **2780**

CANADIAN CONSTRUCTION CATALOGUE FILE. (CN/0082-0431). **606**

CANADIAN CONTROLS AND INSTRUMENTATION. BUYERS' GUIDE. (CN). **3476**

CANADIAN CRIMINAL CASES (BOUND CUMULATION). (CN/0008-3348). **3105**

CANADIAN CRITICAL CARE NURSING JOURNAL. (CN/0826-6778). **3852**

CANADIAN CURLING NEWS. (CN/0045-4648). **4889**

CANADIAN DANCERS NEWS (1988). (CN/0843-218X). **1311**

CANADIAN DEFENCE QUARTERLY (TORONTO). (CN/0315-3495). **4038**

CANADIAN DENTAL ASSISTANTS' ASSOCIATION : JOURNAL. (CN/0833-8264). **1318**

CANADIAN DIMENSION. (CN/0008-3402). **4467**

CANADIAN EMERGENCY NEWS. (CN/0847-947X). **AdvMgr Tel** (800)567-0911. **4770**

CANADIAN ENTOMOLOGIST, THE. (CN/0008-347X). **5606**

CANADIAN ENVIRONMENTAL PROTECTION. (CN). **Adv Mgr:** Ian Stuart, **Tel** (604)291-9900. **2162**

CANADIAN ETHNIC STUDIES. (CN/0008-3496). **AdvMgr Tel** (403)220-7257. **2257**

CANADIAN FACILITY MANAGEMENT & DESIGN. (CN/1193-7505). **863**

CANADIAN FAMILY PHYSICIAN. (CN/0008-350X). **3737**

CANADIAN FAR EASTERN NEWSLETTER, THE. (CN/0045-4737). **4517**

CANADIAN FICTION MAGAZINE. (CN/0045-477X). **Adv Mgr:** Bob. **3372**

CANADIAN FIREFIGHTER, THE. (CN/0704-6391). **2288**

CANADIAN FLIGHT. (CN/0008-3577). **16**

CANADIAN FLORIST, GREENHOUSE AND NURSERY. (CN/0008-3585). **2435**

CANADIAN FOLK MUSIC BULLETIN. (CN/0829-5344). **4107**

CANADIAN FOOTWEAR JOURNAL. (CN/0705-1433). **Adv Mgr:** Brian Murphy. **1082**

CANADIAN FORUM. (CN/0008-3631). **Adv Mgr:** M. Wile. **3339**

CANADIAN FRUITGROWER. (CN/0045-4885). **Adv Mgr:** Jim Countryman. **2412**

CANADIAN FUNERAL DIRECTOR. (CN/0319-3225). **2406**

CANADIAN FUNERAL NEWS. (CN/0382-5876). **2406**

CANADIAN FURNITURE AND FURNISHINGS DIRECTORY. (CN/0826-6204). **2904**

CANADIAN GEMMOLOGIST. (CN/0226-7446). **2913**

CANADIAN GENERAL AVIATION NEWS. (CN/0226-5648). **16**

CANADIAN GEOGRAPHER. (CN/0008-3658). **2558**

CANADIAN GEOGRAPHIC. (CN/0706-2168). **2558**

CANADIAN GEOTECHNICAL JOURNAL. (CN/0008-3674). **1352**

CANADIAN GUERNSEY JOURNAL. (CN/0831-3008). **192**

CANADIAN GUIDE. (CN/0008-3712). **2530**

CANADIAN GUIDER. (CN/0300-435X). **Adv Mgr:** Barbara Crocker, **Tel** (416)487-5281 ext. 264. **1730**

CANADIAN GUNNER (SHILO. 1965). (CN/0068-8843). **4038**

CANADIAN HAIRDRESSER. (CN/0008-3720). **402**

CANADIAN HEAVY EQUIPMENT GUIDE. (CN/0832-6533). **Adv Mgr:** John. **606**

CANADIAN HEREFORD DIGEST. (CN/0008-3739). **Adv Mgr:** Janice McCurdie. **208**

CANADIAN HIGHWAY CARRIERS GUIDE. (CN/0702-8733). **5378**

CANADIAN HISTORICAL REVIEW. (CN/0008-3755). **2726**

CANADIAN HOME ECONOMICS JOURNAL. (CN/0008-3763). **Adv Mgr:** M Martin, **Tel** (613)238-8817. **2789**

CANADIAN HORSEMAN (GUELPH). (CN/0840-6200). **Adv Mgr:** V. Evans. **2797**

CANADIAN HOSPITAL DIRECTORY. (CN/0068-8932). **3777**

CANADIAN HOUSE AND HOME. (CN/0826-7642). **Adv Mgr:** Kathryn O'Hara, **Tel** (416)593-0666. **2904**

CANADIAN HOUSING. (CN/0826-7278). **2817**

CANADIAN HR REPORTER. (CN/0838-228X). **939**

CANADIAN INDEPENDENT ADJUSTER, THE. (CN/0008-3828). **2877**

CANADIAN INDIA STAR, THE. (CN/0319-8715). **2648**

CANADIAN INFORMATION PROCESSING. (CN/1182-3097). **1173**

CANADIAN INSURANCE. (CN/0008-3879). **2877**

CANADIAN INSURANCE CLAIMS DIRECTORY. (CN/0318-0352). **Adv Mgr:** J. Young. **2877**

CANADIAN INSURANCE LAW REVIEW. (CN/0836-0456). **2948**

CANADIAN INTELLECTUAL PROPERTY REPORTS. (CN/0824-2623). **1302**

CANADIAN INVESTMENT REVIEW. (CN/0840-6863). **894**

CANADIAN JERSEY BREEDER. (CN/0008-3909). **208**

CANADIAN JEWELLER. (CN/0008-3917). **Adv Mgr:** A. Thomas, **Tel** (416)755-5799. **2913**

CANADIAN JEWISH NEWS MONTREAL ED. (CN). **Adv Mgr:** V. Gillman, **Tel** 422-2331. **5046**

CANADIAN JOURNAL OF ADMINISTRATIVE LAW & PRACTICE. (CN/0835-6742). **3092**

CANADIAN JOURNAL OF AFRICAN STUDIES. (CN/0008-3968). **Adv Mgr:** same as editor. **2638**

CANADIAN JOURNAL OF ANAESTHESIA. (CN/0832-610X). **3682**

CANADIAN JOURNAL OF ANIMAL SCIENCE. (CN/0008-3984). **208**

CANADIAN JOURNAL OF APPLIED SPECTROSCOPY. (CN/1183-7306). **4434**

CANADIAN JOURNAL OF BEHAVIOURAL SCIENCE. (CN/0008-400X). **4579**

CANADIAN JOURNAL OF BOTANY. (CN/0008-4026). **505**

CANADIAN JOURNAL OF CARDIOLOGY. (CN/0828-282X). **3700**

CANADIAN JOURNAL OF CARDIOVASCULAR NURSING. (CN/0843-6096). **Adv Mgr:** Barb Fenwick. **3700**

CANADIAN JOURNAL OF CHEMISTRY. (CN/0008-4042). **966**

CANADIAN JOURNAL OF CIVIL ENGINEERING. (CN/0315-1468). **2020**

CANADIAN JOURNAL OF COMMUNICATION. (CN/0705-3657). **1105**

CANADIAN JOURNAL OF COMMUNITY MENTAL HEALTH. (CN/0713-3936). **5276**

CANADIAN JOURNAL OF CRIMINOLOGY. (CN/0704-9722). **3159**

CANADIAN JOURNAL OF EARTH SCIENCES. (CN/0008-4077). **1353**

CANADIAN JOURNAL OF ECONOMICS, THE. (CN/0008-4085). **1468**

CANADIAN JOURNAL OF EDUCATION. (CN/0380-2361). **1730**

CANADIAN JOURNAL OF ELECTRICAL AND COMPUTER ENGINEERING. (CN/0840-8688). **AdvMgr Tel** (604)721-8617. **1227**

CANADIAN JOURNAL OF EXPERIMENTAL PSYCHOLOGY. (CN/1196-1961). **4579**

CANADIAN JOURNAL OF FOREST RESEARCH. (CN/0045-5067). **2377**

CANADIAN JOURNAL OF GASTROENTEROLOGY, THE. (CN/0835-7900). **3743**

CANADIAN JOURNAL OF HERBALISM. (CN/0848-9629). **2412**

CANADIAN JOURNAL OF HISTORY. (CN/0008-4107). **Adv Mgr:** J. Fraser, **Tel** (306)966-5794. **2613**

CANADIAN JOURNAL OF INFECTIOUS DISEASES, THE. (CN/1180-2332). **3712**

CANADIAN — Advertising Accepted Index

CANADIAN JOURNAL OF INFORMATION AND LIBRARY SCIENCE, THE. (CN/1195-096X). **3199**

CANADIAN JOURNAL OF INFORMATION SCIENCE. (CN/0380-9218). **3199**

CANADIAN JOURNAL OF IRISH STUDIES, THE. (CN/0703-1459). **Adv Mgr:** Ron Marken, **Tel** (306)966-5500. **3372**

CANADIAN JOURNAL OF ITALIAN STUDIES. (CN/0705-3002). **3372**

CANADIAN JOURNAL OF LAW AND JURISPRUDENCE, THE. (CN/0841-8209). **Adv Mgr:** Nanette Love. **2948**

CANADIAN JOURNAL OF LAW AND SOCIETY. (CN/0829-3201). **2948**

CANADIAN JOURNAL OF LINGUISTICS. (CN/0008-4131). **3272**

CANADIAN JOURNAL OF MEDICAL RADIATION TECHNOLOGY. (CN/0820-5930). **Adv Mgr:** S. Besner. **3939**

CANADIAN JOURNAL OF MEDICAL TECHNOLOGY. (CN/0008-4158). **3562**

CANADIAN JOURNAL OF MICROBIOLOGY. (CN/0008-4166). **560**

CANADIAN JOURNAL OF NATIVE EDUCATION. (CN/0710-1481). **1730**

CANADIAN JOURNAL OF NETHERLANDIC STUDIES. (CN/0225-0500). **2683**

CANADIAN JOURNAL OF NEUROLOGICAL SCIENCES. (CN/0317-1671). **3829**

CANADIAN JOURNAL OF NURSING ADMINISTRATION. (CN/0838-2948). **3852**

CANADIAN JOURNAL OF NURSING RESEARCH, THE. (CN/0844-5621). **3852**

CANADIAN JOURNAL OF OCCUPATIONAL THERAPY (1939). (CN/0008-4174). **3922**

CANADIAN JOURNAL OF OPHTHALMOLOGY. (CN/0008-4182). **3873**

CANADIAN JOURNAL OF OPTOMETRY. (CN/0045-5075). **4215**

CANADIAN JOURNAL OF PHILOSOPHY. (CN/0045-5091). **4343**

CANADIAN JOURNAL OF PHYSICS. (CN/0008-4204). **4399**

CANADIAN JOURNAL OF PHYSIOLOGY AND PHARMACOLOGY. (CN/0008-4212). **579**

CANADIAN JOURNAL OF PLANT SCIENCE. (CN/0008-4220). **505**

CANADIAN JOURNAL OF POLITICAL SCIENCE. (CN/0008-4239). **4467**

CANADIAN JOURNAL OF PROGRAM EVALUATION, THE. (CN/0834-1516). **Adv Mgr:** Kathy Jones, **Tel** (613)230-1007. **4636**

CANADIAN JOURNAL OF PSYCHIATRY. (CN/0706-7437). **3923**

CANADIAN JOURNAL OF PSYCHOLOGY. (CN/0008-4255). **4579**

CANADIAN JOURNAL OF PUBLIC HEALTH. (CN/0008-4263). **4770**

CANADIAN JOURNAL OF REGIONAL SCIENCE, THE. (CN/0705-4580). **2817**

CANADIAN JOURNAL OF REHABILITATION. (CN/0828-0827). **4379**

CANADIAN JOURNAL OF RESEARCH IN EARLY CHILDHOOD EDUCATION, THE. (CN/0827-0899). **1803**

CANADIAN JOURNAL OF SCHOOL PSYCHOLOGY. (CN/0829-5735). **1730**

CANADIAN JOURNAL OF SOCIOLOGY. (CN/0318-6431). **5241**

CANADIAN JOURNAL OF SOIL SCIENCE. (CN/0008-4271). **166**

CANADIAN JOURNAL OF SPORT SCIENCES. (US/0833-1235). **3953**

CANADIAN JOURNAL OF STATISTICS, THE. (CN/0319-5724). **5325**

CANADIAN JOURNAL OF SURGERY. (CN/0008-428X). **3961**

CANADIAN JOURNAL OF URBAN RESEARCH. (CN/1188-3774). **2817**

CANADIAN JOURNAL OF VETERINARY RESEARCH. (CN/0830-9000). **5507**

CANADIAN JOURNAL OF WOMEN AND THE LAW. (CN/0832-8781). **2948**

CANADIAN JOURNAL OF ZOOLOGY. (CN/0008-4301). **5580**

CANADIAN JOURNAL ON AGING. (CN/0714-9808). **Adv Mgr:** same as editor. **3750**

CANADIAN LACEMAKER GAZETTE. (CN/0824-1856). **5183**

CANADIAN LAW LIBRARIES. (CN/1180-176X). **2948**

CANADIAN LAWYER. (CN/0703-2129). **Adv Mgr:** Jayne Townsend. **2948**

CANADIAN LIBRARY JOURNAL. (CN/0008-4352). **3200**

CANADIAN LITERATURE. (CN/0008-4360). **3372**

CANADIAN LIVING. (CN/0382-4624). **5552**

CANADIAN MACHINERY AND METALWORKING. (CN/0008-4379). **2111**

CANADIAN MANAGER. (CN/0045-5156). **863**

CANADIAN METALLURGICAL QUARTERLY. (CN/0008-4433). **3999**

CANADIAN MINES HANDBOOK. (CN/0068-9289). **2136**

CANADIAN MINING JOURNAL. (CN/0008-4492). **2136**

CANADIAN MODERN LANGUAGE REVIEW, THE. (CN/0008-4506). **3272**

CANADIAN MUSIC EDUCATOR, THE. (CN/0008-4549). **4107**

CANADIAN MUSICIAN. (CN/0708-9635). **Adv Mgr:** Jan Smith, **Tel** (905)641-1512. **4107**

CANADIAN MUSLIM, THE. (CN/0707-2945). **5042**

CANADIAN NEWS INDEX (TORONTO). (CN/0225-7459). **5781**

CANADIAN NUMISMATIC JOURNAL, THE. (CN/0008-4573). **2780**

CANADIAN NURSE (1924). (CN/0008-4581). **3852**

CANADIAN OCCUPATIONAL SAFETY. (CN/0008-4611). **Adv Mgr:** Ralph Elliot. **2860**

CANADIAN OIL & GAS HANDBOOK. (CN/0710-622X). **4253**

CANADIAN OIL REGISTER. (CN/0068-9394). **4253**

CANADIAN ONCOLOGY NURSING JOURNAL. (CN/1181-912X). **Adv Mgr:** Pappin, **Tel** (613)735-0952. **3853**

CANADIAN ONCOLOGY NURSING JOURNAL. (CN/1181-912X). **Adv Mgr:** Pappin, **Tel** (613)735-0952. **3853**

CANADIAN OPERATING ROOM NURSING JOURNAL. (CN/0712-6778). **3853**

CANADIAN ORCHESTRAS AND YOUTH ORCHESTRAS DIRECTORY. (CN/1189-9956). **4107**

CANADIAN ORCHID JOURNAL, THE. (CN/0824-1554). **2412**

CANADIAN PATENT REPORTER. (CN/0008-4689). **1302**

CANADIAN PHILATELIST. (CN/0045-5253). **2784**

CANADIAN PHILOSOPHICAL REVIEWS. (CN/0228-491X). **4343**

CANADIAN PLASTICS. (CN/0008-4778). **4454**

CANADIAN PLASTICS DIRECTORY & BUYER'S GUIDE. (CN/0068-9459). **4454**

CANADIAN POETRY (LONDON, ONT.). (CN/0704-5646). **3461**

CANADIAN POLICE CHIEF NEWSLETTER. (CN/0713-4517). **3159**

CANADIAN PSYCHOLOGY. (CN/0708-5591). **4579**

CANADIAN PUBLIC ADMINISTRATION. (CN/0008-4840). **4636**

CANADIAN PUBLIC POLICY. (CN/0317-0861). **Adv Mgr:** J.R. Vanderkamp. **1468**

CANADIAN RAILWAY CLUB NEWS. (CN/0226-157X). **5430**

CANADIAN RAILWAY MODELLER. (CN/0849-2964). **5430**

CANADIAN RECORD, THE. (US). **Adv Mgr:** Tina Stock. **5747**

CANADIAN RENTAL SERVICE. (CN/0383-7920). **1600**

CANADIAN REVIEW OF SOCIAL POLICY (1987). (CN/0836-303X). **Adv Mgr:** Gerald de Montigny, **Tel** (613)788-2600 Ext. 5601. **5276**

CANADIAN REVIEW OF SOCIOLOGY AND ANTHROPOLOGY, THE. (CN/0008-4948). **233**

CANADIAN REVIEW OF STUDIES IN NATIONALISM. (CN/0317-7904). **2635**

CANADIAN SAILINGS. (CN/0821-5944). **5448**

CANADIAN SCHOOL EXECUTIVE (1982). (CN/0228-0914). **1861**

CANADIAN SCIENCE (DOWNSVIEW, ONT.). (CN/0712-4848). **5092**

CANADIAN SECURITY. (CN/0709-3403). **Adv Mgr:** Jack Percival. **5176**

CANADIAN SHAREOWNER. (CN/0836-0960). **Adv Mgr:** Dawn Paupst, **Tel** (519)252-9965. **894**

CANADIAN SLAVONIC PAPERS. (CN/0008-5006). **3272**

CANADIAN SOCIAL WORK REVIEW. (CN/0820-909X). **5276**

CANADIAN SOCIETY OF FORENSIC SCIENCE JOURNAL. (CN/0008-5030). **3740**

CANADIAN SPORTSMAN, THE. (CN/0008-5073). **2798**

CANADIAN STAMP NEWS. (CN/0702-3154). **2784**

CANADIAN THEATRE REVIEW. (CN/0315-0836). **5362**

CANADIAN TOBACCO GROWER, THE. (CN/0008-5189). **Adv Mgr:** Bill Arts. **5372**

CANADIAN TRAVEL COURIER. (CN/0008-5219). **5465**

CANADIAN TRAVEL PRESS WEEKLY. (CN/0831-9138). **5465**

CANADIAN TREASURER. (CN/0845-7328). **655**

CANADIAN ULTRALIGHT NEWS. (CN/0821-6673). **16**

CANADIAN VENDING MAGAZINE (L989). (CN/0848-8975). **Adv Mgr:** Pete Wilkinson, **Tel** (416)271-1366. **1600**

CANADIAN (VERNON, B.C.). (CN/0836-3196). **655**

CANADIAN VET SUPPLIES. (CN/0825-754X). **5507**

CANADIAN VOCATIONAL JOURNAL. (CN/0045-5520). **1911**

CANADIAN WATER RESOURCES JOURNAL. (CN/0701-1784). **5531**

CANADIAN WATER WELL. (CN/1180-050X). **5532**

CANADIAN WEST (1985). (CN/0829-5026). **2726**

CANADIAN WOMEN'S STUDIES. (CN/0713-3235). **5553**

CANADIAN WOOD PRODUCTS (1992). (CN/1183-9139). **1600**

CANADIAN WORKSHOP. (CN/0704-0717). **633**

CANADIAN WRESTLER (1985). (CN/0831-229X). **4889**

CANADIAN WRITER'S JOURNAL. (CN/0827-293X). **3372**

CANADIAN YACHTING. (CN/0384-0999). **592**

CANADO-AMERICAIN, LE. (US/0576-6478). **2530**

CANAL & RIVERBOAT. (UK/0141-2302). **4870**

CANAL TIMES : NEW YORK STATE CANAL SYSTEM NEWS. (US). **5448**

CANARSIE COURIER. (US). **Adv Mgr:** R.Sito. **5714**

CANBERRA ANTHROPOLOGY. (AT/0314-9099). **233**

CANBY NEWS. (US/0745-7251). **5695**

CANCER. (US/0008-543X). **3810**

CANCER BIOCHEMISTRY BIOPHYSICS. (US/0305-7232). **3810**

CANCER CAUSES & CONTROL : CCC. (UK/0957-5243). **3810**

CANCER DATA. (NZ/0548-9415). **3811**

CANCER EPIDEMIOLOGY, BIOMARKERS & PREVENTION. (US/1055-9965). **3811**

CANCER GENETICS AND CYTOGENETICS. (US/0165-4608). **3811**

CANCER INVESTIGATION. (US/0735-7907). **3811**

CANCER JOURNAL (VILLEJUIF), THE. (FR/0765-7846). **3811**

CANCER RESEARCH (BALTIMORE). (US/0008-5472). **3812**

CANCER SURVEYS. (US/0261-2429). **3812**

CANCER VICTORS JOURNAL. (US/0891-0766). **Adv Mgr:** Suzanne Landon. **3813**

CANDY BUYERS' DIRECTORY; A CLASSIFIED DIRECTORY OF CANDY MANUFACTURERS SELLING NATIONALLY OR SECTIONALLY, THE. (US). **2330**

CANDY WHOLESALER. (US/0162-5136). **Adv Mgr:** Mary Ann Paniccia, **Tel** (800)482-2962 or (202)463-2124. **2330**

CANELOBRE. (SP). **317**

CANMORE LEADER. (CN/0824-3646). **5781**

CANNON FALLS BEACON. (US). **Adv Mgr:** Dave Templin. **5695**

CANOE AND KAYAK RACING NEWS. (US). **592**

CANOE (CAMDEN, ME.). (US/0360-7496). **592**

CANPARA (1976). (CN/0227-5880). **Adv Mgr:** same as editor. **4889**

CANPLAY. (CN/0829-3627). **5362**

CANTERAS Y EXPLOTACIONES. (SP/0008-5677). **Adv Mgr:** Magdaleno Romo. **2111**

CANTIGUEIROS (LEXINGTON, KY.). (US/0898-8463). **3372**

CANTON EAGLE, THE. (US/0192-6446). **5691**

CANTON INDEPENDENT-SENTINEL, THE. (US). **Adv Mgr:** Janie Riggs. **5735**

CANYON COURIER WEEKENDER, THE. (US/0192-0197). **5642**

CANYON ECHO. (US/0164-7024). **Adv Mgr:** Richard L Isetts, **Tel** (602)945-5586. **2530**

CANYON NEWS (CANYON, TEX. : 1926). (US). **5748**

CAO TIMES. (US/0146-3365). **390**

CAP TODAY. (US/0891-1525). **3893**

CAPACITOR INDUSTRY NEWSLETTER : BIMONTHLY NEWS FOR THE FILM CAPACITOR TRADE AND ALLIED DIELECTRIC MARKETS. (US/1056-6813). **1600**

CAPE BRETON'S MAGAZINE. (CN/0319-4639). **2726**

CAPE COD LIFE. (US/0199-7238). **Adv Mgr:** Robin Mayer, **Tel** (508)564-4466. **2530**

CAPILANO REVIEW, THE. (CN/0315-3754). **3372**

CAPITAL. (FR). **1468**

CAPITAL & CLASS. (UK/0309-8168). **1590**

CAPITAL BAPTIST. (US/0528-0559). **5057**

CAPITAL CHEMIST, THE. (US/0411-0080). **966**

CAPITAL DISTRICT BUSINESS REVIEW. (US/0747-3699). **655**

CAPITAL ENERGY LETTER. (US/0195-5292). **1935**

CAPITAL JOURNAL (PIERRE, S.D.). (US/0893-5564). **Adv Mgr:** Terry Hipple. **5743**

CAPITAL NEWS. (AT/0812-1494). **Adv Mgr:** Terry Hill, **Tel** 067-650300. **4107**

CAPITAL NURSING. (US). **3853**

CAPITAL PRESS. (US/0740-3704). **Adv Mgr:** Mr. Schultz, **Tel** (503)364-4798. **5733**

CAPITAL (RHINEBECK, N.Y.), THE. (US/0885-4718). **2441**

CAPITAL SPORTS FOCUS. (US/1041-5742). **4889**

CAPITAL SPOTLIGHT, THE. (US/0411-0137). **5647**

CAPITAL TIMES, THE. (US/0749-4068). **5766**

CAPITALISM, NATURE, SOCIALISM. (US/1045-5752). **2212**

CAPITOL REVIEW, THE. (US/0746-3294). **5748**

CAPPER'S. (US/0892-1148). **5674**

CAPTAIN AMERICA. (US/0274-5267). **1061**

CAR AND DRIVER. (US/0008-6002). **5408**

CAR AND DRIVER ROAD TEST ANNUAL. (US/8755-626X). **5409**

CAR AND LOCOMOTIVE CYCLOPEDIA OF AMERICAN PRACTICE. (US). **5430**

CAR CARE MALL NEWS. (US). **5409**

CAR COLLECTOR & CAR CLASSICS MAGAZINE. (US/1057-4441). **5409**

CAR CORRAL. (US/1045-7216). **5409**

CAR-DEL SCRIBE. (US/0008-6029). **2441**

CAR MODELER. (US/1048-6194). **Adv Mgr:** Brain Taylor. **2772**

CAR PRICES. (US/0739-1722). **5409**

CARABELA. (SP/0213-9715). **3272**

CARAVAN BUSINESS. (UK/0268-5558). **5466**

CARBOHYDRATE POLYMERS. (UK/0144-8617). **1040**

CARBOHYDRATE RESEARCH. (NE/0008-6215). **1040**

CARBON COUNTY LAW JOURNAL, THE. (US/0090-8789). **2948**

CARBONATES AND EVAPORITES. (US/0891-2556). **1371**

CARCINOGENESIS (NEW YORK). (US/0143-3334). **3814**

CARDINAL NEWS, THE. (US). **5580**

CARDIO-VASCULAR NURSING. (US/0008-6355). **3853**

CARDIOLOGIA PER IMMAGINI. (IT/1120-3730). **3700**

CARDIOLOGY. (SZ/0008-6312). **3700**

CARDIOLOGY BOARD REVIEW. (US/0888-8418). **3700**

CARDIOLOGY IN PRACTICE. (UK/0262-5547). **3701**

CARDIOLOGY IN THE YOUNG. (US/1047-9511). **3701**

CARDIOLOGY MANAGEMENT. (US/0892-9327). **3701**

CARDIOMYOLOGY. (IT/0394-073X). **450**

CARDIOPULMONARY PHYSICAL THERAPY JOURNAL. (US). **4379**

CARDIOVASCULAR DRUGS AND THERAPY. (US/0920-3206). **3701**

CARDIOVASCULAR PHARMACOLOGY. (UK/0263-7243). **3701**

CARDIOVASCULAR PHYSIOLOGY. (UK/0142-8012). **579**

CARDIOVASCULAR REVIEWS & REPORTS. (US/0197-3118). **3702**

CARDOZO ARTS & ENTERTAINMENT LAW JOURNAL. (US/0736-7694). **2948**

CARDOZO LAW REVIEW. (US/0270-5192). **2948**

CARDOZO STUDIES IN LAW AND LITERATURE. (US/1043-1500). **Adv Mgr:** Averlyn Archer, **Tel** (212)790-0370. **2948**

CARE CONNECTION, THE. (CN/0843-9966). **3853**

CAREER DEVELOPMENT FOR EXCEPTIONAL INDIVIDUALS. (US/0885-7288). **1911**

CAREER DEVELOPMENT QUARTERLY, THE. (US/0889-4019). **4201**

CAREER EDUCATION AND GUIDANCE. (UK/0954-3732). **Adv Mgr:** Janice Cook, **Tel** 0291 672985. **1730**

CAREER FOCUS FOR TODAY'S RISING BLACK PROFESSIONAL. (US/1049-9954). **4202**

CAREER FOCUS FOR TODAY'S RISING HISPANIC PROFESSIONAL. (US/1049-9946). **4202**

CAREER FUTURES. (US/1045-4314). **Adv Mgr:** Glenn Mairano, **Tel** (203)227-1775. **4202**

CAREERS & COLLEGES. (US/1065-9935). **Adv Mgr:** Colleen Smith. **4202**

CAREERS & THE DISABLED. (US/1056-277X). **4202**

CAREERS FOR GRADUATES. (CN/0318-6229). **4202**

CAREERS GUIDANCE TODAY. (UK/0969-6431). **Adv Mgr:** Annie Van Heerden, **Tel** 0223 276737. **4202**

CAREFREE ENTERPRISE. (US/0738-9604). **Adv Mgr:** Lynn Grant. **2530**

CARETAKER GAZETTE, THE. (US/1074-3642). **Adv Mgr:** Gary C. Dunn, **Tel** same as publisher. **4203**

CARGO CLAIMS ANALYSIS. (UK/0265-427X). **3180**

CARGO FACTS. (US/0278-0801). **Adv Mgr:** John Riley, **Tel** (206)587-6538. **5379**

CARGO SYSTEMS INTERNATIONAL. (UK/0306-0985). **5379**

CARGONEWS ASIA. (HK/0252-9610). **Adv Mgr:** Chris Michaelides. **5379**

CARGOWARE INTERNATIONAL. (UK). **4218**

CARGOWORLD. (GW/0172-9314). **Adv Mgr:** Peter Wauker, **Tel** 040 23714165. **5448**

CARGUIDE. (CN/0384-9309). **Adv Mgr:** Grant Wells or Al Henderson. **5409**

CARIBBEAN AFFAIRS. (TR/1011-5765). **Adv Mgr:** Anna Aleong. **2511**

CARIBBEAN/AMERICAN DIRECTORY. (US/0275-2883). **655**

CARIBBEAN BUSINESS. (US/0194-8326). **655**

CARIBBEAN BUSINESS DIRECTORY. (CJ). **655**

CARIBBEAN CHALLENGE. (JM/0008-6436). **5015**

CARIBBEAN CONTACT. (TR). **4942**

CARIBBEAN DATELINE. (US). **894**

CARIBBEAN FLITE GUIDE. (US). **16**

CARIBBEAN HANDBOOK, THE. (AQ). **5466**

CARIBBEAN INSIGHT. (UK/0142-4742). **Adv Mgr:** Jeff, **Tel** 976-1493. **2726**

CARIBBEAN ISLANDS HANDBOOK. (UK). **5466**

CARIBBEAN JOURNAL OF EDUCATION. (JM/0376-7701). **1730**

CARIBBEAN LAW AND BUSINESS. (BB/1013-9230). **3097**

CARIBBEAN PORTS HANDBOOK. (JM). **5448**

CARIBBEAN QUARTERLY. (JM/0254-8038). **2486**

CARIBBEAN REVIEW. (US/0008-6525). **4467**

CARIBBEAN SHIPPING : THE JOURNAL OF THE CARIBBEAN SHIPPING ASSOCIATION. (JM). **5448**

CARIBBEAN TOURISM STATISTICAL REPORT. (BB). **5500**

CARIBBEAN TRAVEL AND LIFE. (US/1052-1011). **Adv Mgr:** Joe DiMarino. **5466**

CARIBBEAN WEEK. (BB/1019-5076). **Adv Mgr:** P Starr. **5778**

CARIBBEAN WRITER, THE. (VI/0893-1550). **Adv Mgr:** Carlyna Allard. **3373**

CARIBOO CALLING. (CN/0319-7360). **2558**

CARIBOU COUNTY SUN. (US). **5656**

CARICOM BULLETIN. (GY). **1550**

CARIES RESEARCH. (SZ/0008-6568). **1318**

CARITAS (FREIBURG IM BREISGAU). (GW/0008-6614). **4334**

CARLETON UNIVERSITY STUDENT JOURNAL OF PHILOSOPHY, THE. (CN/0317-073X). **4343**

CARLINVILLE DEMOCRAT, THE. (US). **Adv Mgr:** Laurie Flori. **5658**

CARLSONREPORT. (US/0889-2288). **952**

CARLYLE STUDIES ANNUAL. (US/1074-2670). **3373**

CARMEL PINE CONE AND CARMEL VALLEY OUTLOOK, THE. (US). **Adv Mgr:** Karen Carlson. **5633**

CARMELUS. (IT/0008-6673). **5025**

CARNIVOROUS PLANT NEWSLETTER. (US/0190-9215). **506**

CARO BULLETIN. (CN/0827-357X). **347**

CAROLINA AGENT, THE. (US/1065-1292). **2877**

CAROLINA CHRISTIAN. (US/0008-672X). **AdvMgr Tel** (704)465-6739. **4942**

CAROLINA COUNTRY. (US/0008-6746). **1541**

CAROLINA GARDENER. (US/1063-7451). **2412**

CAROLINA INDIAN VOICE, THE. (US/0739-1730). **Adv Mgr:** Helen Locklear. **2258**

CAROLINA JOURNAL OF PHARMACY, THE. (US/0528-1725). **4295**

CAROLINA PEACEMAKER. (US). **Adv Mgr:** Tom Price, Jr. **2258**

CAROLINA QUARTERLY. (US/0008-6797). **3373**

CAROLINIAN (RALEIGH), THE. (US/0045-5873). **Adv Mgr:** P.J. Monroe. **5722**

CAROUSEL NEWS & TRADER, THE. (US/0892-9769). **250**

CARP. CANADIAN ASSOCIATION OF RETIRED PERSONS. (CN/1193-8544). **Adv Mgr:** Keith Gardner, **Tel** (416)363-5562 ext.301. **5178**

CARPENTER. (US/0008-6843). **Adv Mgr:** David Peterson, **Tel** (202)546-6206. **633**

CARPET & RUG INDUSTRY. (US/0192-4486). **2899**

CARPET SPECIFIER'S HANDBOOK, THE. (US/0095-6457). **5348**

CARREFOUR. (CN/0706-1250). **Adv Mgr:** C. Campeau. **4343**

CARRIAGE JOURNAL, THE. (US/0008-6916). **Adv Mgr:** Diane Garrison. **2772**

CARRIAGE TRADE (SARNIA, ONT.). (CN/0831-2907). **5348**

CARRIER REPORT. (US). **5379**

CARROLL CABLES. (US/0892-2152). **2442**

CARROLL COUNTY HISTORY JOURNAL. (US). **2727**

CARROLL COUNTY TIMES. (US/0746-7494). **5685**

CARROLL GARDENS COBBLE HILL NEWSPAPER, THE. (US). **Adv Mgr:** Celia Weintraub. **5714**

CARROLL TODAY NEWS. (US). **5669**

CARROSSIER. (SZ). **1967**

CARROUSEL ART. (US/0740-0780). **250**

CARS & PARTS. (US/0008-6975). **5409**

CARSON PRESS, THE. (US/0899-7624). **Adv Mgr:** Duane Schatz, **Tel** (701)584-2900. **5725**

CARSON VALLEY CHRONICLE. (US). **Adv Mgr:** Loren Abbott, **Tel** (702)882-2111 ext.269. **5707**

CARSWELL'S PRACTICE CASES. (CN/0706-5388). **3089**

CARTA DE CLACSO. (AG). **Adv Mgr:** Jorge Fraga. **5194**

CARTACTUAL. (HU/0008-7009). **2558**

CARTE ITALIANE. (US/0737-9412). **3373**

CARTELLINA, LA. (IT/1120-4621). **Adv Mgr:** Paola Mazzini, **Tel** same as publisher. **4108**

CARTHAGE

CARTHAGE REPUBLICAN TRIBUNE. (US/0889-8715). **Adv Mgr:** Charles Howlett, **Tel** (315)788-3638. **5714**

CARTOGRAPHIC JOURNAL, THE. (UK/0008-7041). **2581**

CARTOGRAPHY. (AT/0069-0805). **2581**

CARTOGRAPHY AND GEOGRAPHIC INFORMATION SYSTEMS. (US/1050-9844). **2581**

CARTOMANIA. (US/0894-2595). **2558**

CARTONNAGES EMBALLAGES MODERNES. (FR). **4218**

CARTOUCHE ENGLISH EDITION (CALGARY). (CN/1183-2045). **2581**

CARTOUCHE FRENCH EDITION (CALGARY). (CN/1183-2045). **2581**

CARVER REPORTER. (US). **Adv Mgr:** Gary Higgins. **5688**

CAS. CURRENT AWARENESS SERVICE - BRITISH INSTITUTE OF MENTAL HANDICAP. (UK/0143-0289). **1793**

CAS JOURNAL. (US/1053-7694). **4108**

CASA DEL TIEMPO. (MX/0185-4275). **2511**

CASA STILE. (IT/0390-1513). **2583**

CASA TESSIL REPORTER. (IT/0394-882X). **Adv Mgr:** Za AL Tessile, **Tel** 02 38200080 1. **5348**

CASA VOGUE. (IT/0008-7173). **2899**

CASCADE CAVER, THE. (US/0008-7211). **1403**

CASCADE COURIER, THE. (US). **Adv Mgr:** Ellen & Pat Travis. **5705**

CASCADES EAST. (US/0194-8954). **4870**

CASE DIGEST (SACRAMENTO, CALIF.). (US/0890-8400). **3105**

CASE INDUSTRY DIRECTORY. (US/0898-5022). **1173**

CASE MANAGER. (US/1061-9259). **Adv Mgr:** Pam Adelstein, **Tel** (501)227-5553. **2877**

CASE RESEARCH JOURNAL. (US/0894-6043). **863**

CASE TRENDS. (US/1046-5944). **1227**

CASE UPDATE. (US/0749-7709). **2949**

CASE WESTERN RESERVE LAW REVIEW. (US/0008-7262). **Adv Mgr:** Carolyn Speaker. **2949**

CASH BOX, THE. (US/0008-7289). **5316**

CASHTON RECORD. (US). **5766**

CASINO CHRONICLE. (US/0889-9797). **2804**

CASINO EXPLORER. (US). **4858**

CASINOS : THE INTERNATIONAL CASINO GUIDE. (US/1040-9920). **4858**

CASS COUNTY REPORTER. (US). **Adv Mgr:** Peggy Hanson. **5725**

CASS COUNTY SUN (1897). (US). **Adv Mgr:** Betty Rhyne. **5748**

CASSVILLE DEMOCRAT (CASSVILLE, MO. : 1871). (US). **Adv Mgr:** Darlene Wierman. **5703**

CAST METALS. (UK/0953-4962). **3999**

CASTANEA. (US/0008-7475). **Adv Mgr:** Cynthia Aulbach-Smith, **Tel** (803)359-5027. **506**

CASTINE PATRIOT. (US). **Adv Mgr:** W. Sewall, **Tel** (207)367-2200. **5685**

CASTING WORLD. (US/0887-9060). **3999**

CASTINGS. (AT/0008-7521). **3999**

CASTLEGAR SUN, THE. (CN/1185-1899). **5781**

CASTME JOURNAL. (UK/0264-3138). **1890**

CASTRO, EL. (SP). **3461**

CASTRUM PEREGRINI. (NE/0008-7556). **3373**

CASUAL LIVING. (US/0740-8285). **2904**

CAT FANCIERS' NEWS. (US/0069-1003). **4286**

CAT FANCY (SAN JUAN CAPISTRANO, CALIF.). (US/0892-6514). **4286**

CATALOG AGE. (US/0740-3119). **757**

CATALOG HANDBOOK. (US/1042-6167). **Adv Mgr:** Andrea Freedman, **Tel** (414)272-9977. **656**

CATALOG PRODUCT NEWS. (US/1048-0633). **949**

CATALOGING & CLASSIFICATION QUARTERLY. (US/0163-9374). **3200**

CATALOGING SERVICE BULLETIN. (US/0160-8029). **3200**

CATALOGUE DE LIVRES AU FORMAT DE POCHE. (FR/0769-1696). **412**

CATALOGUE - FUNNEL. (CN/0826-2861). **4065**

CATALOGUE OF CONODONTS. (GW). **4226**

CATALOGUE OF GOVERNMENT PUBLICATIONS. (KE). **412**

CATALYSIS REVIEWS : SCIENCE AND ENGINEERING. (US/0161-4940). **2009**

CATALYSIS TODAY. (NE/0920-5861). **966**

CATALYST (ATLANTA, GA.). (US/0896-7423). **3373**

CATALYST (DES MOINES, IOWA : 1971), THE. (US/0730-711X). **3201**

CATALYST (GOROKA, PAPUA NEW GUINEA). (PP/0253-2921). **2669**

CATALYST (MONTPELIER, VT.). (US/0742-6534). **1468**

CATALYST (PHILADELPHIA), THE. (US/0008-767X). **967**

CATALYSTS IN CHEMISTRY. (UK/0309-5770). **967**

CATASTROPHISM AND ANCIENT HISTORY. (US/0733-8058). **2613**

CATECHIST. (US/0008-7726). **5025**

CATENA (GIESSEN). (GW/0341-8162). **166**

CATERING & HEALTH. (UK/0267-3851). **2330**

CATHAIR NO MART. (IE/0332-4117). **2683**

CATHEDRAL CITY POST. (US/0884-6189). **5633**

CATHETERIZATION AND CARDIOVASCULAR DIAGNOSIS. (US/0098-6569). **3702**

CATHOLIC ACCENT, THE. (US/0745-399X). **5025**

CATHOLIC ADVANCE, THE. (US/0008-7904). **5025**

CATHOLIC BULLETIN, THE. (US). **Adv Mgr:** Terri Broderick, **Tel** (612)290-1630. **5025**

CATHOLIC CHRONICLE, THE. (US/0008-7971). **5025**

CATHOLIC COURIER (1989). (US/1054-2728). **5025**

CATHOLIC DIGEST (SAINT PAUL, MINN.). (US/0008-7998). **5025**

CATHOLIC EXPONENT, THE. (US/0162-7031). **5025**

CATHOLIC FREE PRESS, THE. (US/0008-8056). **Adv Mgr:** R.C. Ballantine. **5026**

CATHOLIC GAZETTE. (UK/0008-8064). **5026**

CATHOLIC HEALTH WORLD. (US/8756-4068). **3778**

CATHOLIC HERALD. (UK/0008-8072). **5026**

CATHOLIC HERALD (SACRAMENTO, CALIF.). (US/0746-4185). **5026**

CATHOLIC HISTORICAL REVIEW, THE. (US/0008-8080). **5026**

CATHOLIC JOURNALIST. (US/0008-8129). **2918**

CATHOLIC LIBRARY WORLD, THE. (US/0008-820X). **3201**

CATHOLIC LIGHT, THE. (US/0164-9418). **5735**

CATHOLIC MEDICAL QUARTERLY : JOURNAL OF THE GUILD OF CATHOLIC DOCTORS. (UK/0008-8226). **3562**

CATHOLIC MESSENGER. (US/0008-8234). **Adv Mgr:** Kathy. **5026**

CATHOLIC NEW TIMES. (CN/0701-0788). **Adv Mgr:** Noreen Zarand. **5026**

CATHOLIC PRESS DIRECTORY. (US/0008-8307). **5012**

CATHOLIC REGISTER, THE. (CN/0383-1620). **Adv Mgr:** S. Tyson, **Tel** same as publisher. **5026**

CATHOLIC REVIEW (BALTIMORE, MD.), THE. (US/0008-8315). **Adv Mgr:** John McNulty, **Tel** (410)547-5562. **5026**

CATHOLIC SENTINEL - CATHOLIC CHURCH. DIOCESE OF BAKER (OR.). (US/0162-0363). **5026**

CATHOLIC SINGLES. (US/0886-8190). **5242**

CATHOLIC STANDARD (WASHINGTON, D.C.). (US/0411-2741). **5026**

CATHOLIC SUN (SYRACUSE, N.Y.), THE. (US/0744-267X). **5026**

CATHOLIC TELEGRAPH. (US). **5727**

CATHOLIC TIMES (COLUMBUS, OHIO), THE. (US/0745-6050). **Adv Mgr:** Jim Fath, **Tel** (614)224-5115. **5026**

CATHOLIC TIMES (MONTREAL). (CN/0703-1521). **5026**

CATHOLIC TRANSCRIPT, THE. (US). **Adv Mgr:** Roy J. Rowland. **5645**

CATHOLIC TWIN CIRCLE. (US/0273-6136). **Adv Mgr:** Frank Wright. **5026**

CATHOLIC UNIVERSE-BULLETIN, THE. (US/0162-7023). **Adv Mgr:** David Sarosy. **5027**

CATHOLIC VOICE (OAKLAND, CALIF.), THE. (US/0279-0645). **Adv Mgr:** Tim Holden. **5027**

CATHOLIC WORLD REPORT, THE. (US/1058-8159). **Adv Mgr:** Mary Jennett. **5027**

CATHOLICA (MUNSTER). (GW/0008-8501). **5027**

CATONSVILLE TIMES. (US/0748-5263). **5686**

CAT'S EAR. (US/1062-6379). **3461**

CATS MAGAZINE. (US/0008-8544). **4286**

CATSKILL MOUNTAIN NEWS. (US). **5714**

CATTLE GUARD. (US/0411-289X). **208**

CATTLEMAN. (US/0008-8552). **209**

CATTLEMEN. (CN/0008-3143). **209**

CAUCHO. (AG/0528-3280). **5075**

CAUT BULLETIN. (CN/0834-9614). **1814**

CAVE SCIENCE (1982). (UK/0263-760X). **1404**

CAVES & CAVING. (UK/0142-1832). **1371**

CAYMAN ISLANDS CONSOLIDATED INDEX OF STATUTES AND SUBSIDIARY LEGISLATION TO ... . (BB). **3126**

CAZENOVIA REPUBLICAN. (US). **Adv Mgr:** Barbara Dukette, **Tel** (315)655-3415. **5714**

CB VOICE. (US/0145-6806). **1151**

CBA RECORD. (US/0892-1822). **2949**

CBE VIEWS. (US/0164-5609). **451**

CBIA NEWS. (US/0199-686X). **656**

CBT DIRECTIONS. (US/0898-8498). **AdvMgr Tel** (716)542-0146. **1173**

CC AI. (BE/0773-4182). **Adv Mgr:** Yves Devlieher, **Tel** 32 9 264 39 52. **1212**

CCI. CLIMA COMMERCE INTERNATIONAL. (GW/0009-8914). **Adv Mgr:** Mrs. Finne. **2604**

CCLM NEWSLETTER. (US/0273-3315). **3373**

CD PLUS COMPACT DISC CATALOGUE. (US/0843-9532). **Adv Mgr:** Mary Thomson with Sheperd Media, **Tel** (416)485-2098. **4108**

CD REVIEW DIGEST. CLASSICAL. (US/1045-0114). **4108**

CD REVIEW DIGEST. JAZZ, POPULAR, ETC. (US/1045-0122). **4108**

CD-ROM DIRECTORY, THE. (UK). **1174**

CD-ROM ENDUSER. (US/1042-8623). **1174**

CD ROM INTERNATIONAL. (FR). **1276**

CD-ROM LIBRARIAN. (US/0893-9934). **1174**

CD-ROM MARKET PLACE. (US/1047-966X). **1174**

CD-ROM PROFESSIONAL. (US/1049-0833). **Adv Mgr:** John Bryans. **1276**

CD-ROMS IN PRINT. (US/0891-8198). **1276**

CDR IN. (DK). **1468**

CDS REVIEW. (US/0091-1666). **1318**

CEA ADVISOR. (US/0007-8050). **1731**

CEA FORUM. (US/0007-8034). **3273**

CEDAR CREEK PILOT. (US/1046-8633). **Adv Mgr:** Kathi Nailling. **5748**

CEDAR TREE, THE. (US/0738-1905). **2442**

CEDARTOWN STANDARD (1950). (US/1056-8271). **Adv Mgr:** Wilson Adam. **5652**

CEE NEWS. (US/1045-2710). **2038**

CEI. (UK). **1151**

CELL AND CHROMOSOME RESEARCH. (II/0254-2935). **533**

CELL AND TISSUE RESEARCH. (GW/0302-766X). **533**

CELL BIOCHEMISTRY AND FUNCTION. (UK/0263-6484). **484**

CELL BIOLOGY AND TOXICOLOGY (PRINCETON SCIENTIFIC PUBLISHERS). (NE/0742-2091). **Adv Mgr:** M A Mehlman. **533**

CELL BIOPHYSICS. (US/0163-4992). **495**

CELL CALCIUM (EDINBURGH). (UK/0143-4160). **533**

CELL (CAMBRIDGE). (US/0092-8674). **533**

CELL CONTACT PHENOMENA. (UK/0142-8039). **533**

CELL CYCLE. (UK/0263-7251). **533**

CELL DIFFERENTIATION SHEFFIELD. (UK/0263-726X). **533**

CELL GROWTH & DIFFERENTIATION. (US/1044-9523). **533**

CELL MEMBRANES. (UK/0142-8047). **533**

CELL STRUCTURE AND FUNCTION. (JA/0386-7196). **534**

CELLE NEWSLETTER. (US/0743-4979). **2442**

CELLULAR BUSINESS. (US/0741-6520). **1151**

CELLULAR PHYSIOLOGY AND BIOCHEMISTRY. (SZ/1015-8987). **534**

CELLULAR POLYMERS. (UK/0262-4893). **4454**

CELSIUS. (AT). **2604**

CELULOZA SI HIRTIE (BUCHAREST, ROMANIA : 1986). (RM). **4233**

CENCRASTUS. (UK). **317**

CENIMM; CENTRO NACIONAL DE INVESTIGACIONES METALURGICAS. (SP). **4000**

CENSO DO CALCADO RS / ASSOCIACAO COMERCIAL E INDUSTRIAL DE NOVO HAMBURGO. (BL). **1082**

CENSUS OF BUILDING AND CONSTRUCTION (FIJI). (FJ). **607**

CENTENNIAL REVIEW, THE. (US/0162-0177). **Adv Mgr:** C. Finney. **2844**

CENTER PAPER (PRINCETON, N.J.) (US/0513-1529). **4551**

CENTER QUARTERLY. (US/0890-4634). **Adv Mgr:** Larry Lewis. **4368**

CENTER STAGE (NEW YORK). (US). **5362**

CENTERS; UPSCALE SPECIALTY, URBAN MIXED-USE AND FESTIVAL. (US). **4835**

CENTRAL AFRICAN CHAMBER OF COMMERCE AND INDUSTRY DIRECTORY. (CM). **818**

CENTRAL AFRICAN JOURNAL OF MEDICINE. (RH/0008-9176). **3562**

CENTRAL ALABAMA INDEPENDENT ADVERTISER AND THE UNION-BANNER, THE. (US). **5625**

CENTRAL AMERICA UPDATE. (CN/0823-7689). **4467**

CENTRAL & INNER ASIAN STUDIES. (US/0893-2301). **2648**

CENTRAL ASIATIC JOURNAL. (GW/0008-9192). **2648**

CENTRAL BANKING. (UK/0960-6319). **782**

CENTRAL DISTRICT ALMANAC. (US). **2949**

CENTRAL EUROPEAN. (UK/0962-2543). **Adv Mgr:** Susan Christopherson. **1633**

CENTRAL EUROPEAN HISTORY. (US/0008-9389). **Adv Mgr:** J. Carnlin, **Tel** (908)872-1441. **2683**

CENTRAL FLORIDA MAGAZINE. (US/8750-2852). **2530**

CENTRAL IDAHO STAR-NEWS, THE. (US/0747-248X). **Adv Mgr:** Tom Grote. **5656**

CENTRAL IDAHO STAR-NEWS, THE. (US). **5656**

CENTRAL KENTUCKY NEWS-JOURNAL. (US). **Adv Mgr:** Cheryl Caulk. **5680**

CENTRAL MONTANA WAGON TRAILS. (US/0883-9603). **2442**

CENTRAL NEW YORK ENVIRONMENT. (US/0275-827X). **Adv Mgr:** Walt Aikman. **2162**

CENTRAL NORTH CAROLINA JOURNAL. (US/1050-1339). **2530**

CENTRAL RAILWAY CHRONICLE. (US/0008-9532). **5430**

CENTRAL RECORD (MEDFORD, N.J.). (US/0745-7030). **Adv Mgr:** Elain Kern. **5709**

CENTRAL THEMES. (CN/0821-4107). **4943**

CENTRALLY PLANNED ECONOMIES OUTLOOK. (US/0749-6508). **1469**

CENTRE DAILY TIMES. (US/0745-483X). **Adv Mgr:** Gene Kneller, **Tel** (814)231-4650. **5735**

CENTRE LETTER (BANFF). (CN/0705-6842). **317**

CENTREVILLE PRESS, THE. (US). **5625**

CENTZONTLE : REVISTA DE LA SOCIEDAD MEXICANA DE ORNITOLOGIA. (MX). **5580**

CEPA NEWSLETTER. (US/8756-0550). **1231**

CEPHALALGIA. (NO/0333-1024). **3829**

CERAMIC ARTS & CRAFTS. (US/0009-0190). **2587**

CERAMIC INDUSTRY. (US/0009-0220). **2587**

CERAMIC REVIEW. (UK/0144-1825). **2587**

CERAMIC SCOPE. (US/0009-0247). **2587**

CERAMIC SOURCE. (US/8756-8187). **2587**

CERAMIC STUDY GROUP NEWSLETTER. (AT). **2772**

CERAMICA ACTA. (IT/1121-6093). **2587**

CERAMICA INFORMAZIONE. (IT/0009-0271). **2587**

CERAMICA MADRID. (SP/0210-010X). **2587**

CERAMICA PER L'EDILIZIA INTERNATIONAL. (IT). **2587**

CERAMICA (SAO PAULO). (BL/0366-6913). **2587**

CERAMICA Y CRISTAL. (AG/0325-0229). **2588**

CERAMICS INTERNATIONAL. (IT/0272-8842). **2588**

CERAMICS MONTHLY. (US/0009-0328). **2588**

CERAMICS PADDINGTON. (AT/1035-1841). **2588**

CERAMIQUE MODERNE, LA. (FR/0009-0336). **2588**

CERAMURGIA. (IT/0045-6152). **Adv Mgr:** G. Bertoni, **Tel** 0546 22661. **2588**

CEREAL FOODS WORLD. (US/0146-6283). **2331**

CEREAL RESEARCH COMMUNICATIONS. (HU/0133-3720). **200**

CEREBRAL CORTEX (NEW YORK, N.Y. 1991). (US/1047-3211). **3829**

CEREBROVASCULAR DISEASES. (SZ/1015-9770). **3829**

CERN COURIER. (SZ/0304-288X). **Adv Mgr:** Micheline Falciola. **4446**

CERTIFIED ACCOUNTANT. (IE/0306-2406). **AdvMgr Tel** 44-420-477381. **740**

CERTIFIED ENGINEERING TECHNICIAN. (US/0746-6641). **Adv Mgr:** Kurt Schuler. **1968**

CERVANTES : REVISTA DE POESIA E INFORMACION CULTURAL. (SP). **3461**

CESKOSLOVENSKA FARMACIE. (XR/0009-0530). **4296**

CESKOSLOVENSKA FYSIOLOGIE. (XR/0009-0557). **579**

CESKOSLOVENSKA PSYCHOLOGIE. (XR/0009-062X). **4580**

CESKOSLOVENSKY ARCHITEKT. (XR/0009-0697). **295**

CESSNA OWNER MAGAZINE, THE. (US/0745-3523). **16**

CEW, CHEMICAL ENGINEERING WORLD. (II/0009-2517). **Adv Mgr:** Uday Rastogi, **Tel** 2042044. **2009**

CEYLON MEDICAL JOURNAL. (CE/0009-0875). **3562**

CEYLON VETERINARY JOURNAL. (CE/0009-0891). **5507**

CFE BATIMENT. (FR). **2038**

CFE INDUSTRIE. (FR/1146-1497). **2038**

CFI, CERAMIC FORUM INTERNATIONAL. (GW/0173-9913). **2588**

CGA MAGAZINE. (CN/0318-742X). **740**

CHAC INFO. (CN/0822-8426). **4771**

CHAIN DRUG REVIEW. (US/0164-9914). **656**

CHAIN MERCHANDISER. (US/0009-0921). **952**

CHAIN-REACTION (CARLTON, VIC.). (AT/0312-1372). **2189**

CHAKRA. (US). **3373**

CHALLENGE (BLOOMINGTON, ILL.). (US/0894-5535). **4858**

CHALLENGE (WHITE PLAINS). (US/0577-5132). **1469**

CHALLENGER (BUFFALO, N.Y.), THE. (US/1040-8886). **5714**

CHALLIS MESSENGER, THE. (US). **Adv Mgr:** Peggy Parks. **5669**

CHAMBER MUSIC (NEW YORK, N.Y.). (US/1071-1791). **4108**

CHAMBER OF MINES JOURNAL. (RH/0009-1162). **2136**

CHAMBEREXECUTIVE. (US/0884-8114). **819**

CHAMBRE BLANCHE. (CN/0820-781X). **347**

CHAMPAGNE ECONOMIQUE. (FR). **1469**

CHAMPAGNE VITICOLE, LA. (FR). **Adv Mgr:** Blaques Jawes. **2366**

CHAMPIGNONCULTUUR, DE. (NE/0009-1316). **166**

CHANGE (NEW ROCHELLE, N.Y.). (US/0009-1383). **1814**

CHANGING MEN (MADISON, WIS.). (US/0889-7174). **Adv Mgr:** Peter Bresnick. **3994**

CHANGING SCHOOLS (MUNCIE, IND. (US/0738-9418). **1731**

CHANGING WORK (NEW HAVEN, CONN.). (US/0883-1416). **1659**

CHANNEL GUIDE. (US/0744-6462). **1130**

CHANSONS D'AUJOURD'HUI. (CN/0227-5023). **4108**

CHANTIERS DE FRANCE. (FR/0397-4650). **607**

CHANUTE TRIBUNE (CHANUTE, KAN. : 1946). (US). **Adv Mgr:** Jo Anne Johnson. **5674**

CHAPEL HILL NEWSPAPER, THE. (US). **5723**

CHAPLAINCY TODAY. (US/0895-7916). **4943**

CHAPLEAU SENTINEL. (CN/0832-2414). **Adv Mgr:** Michelle, **Tel** (705)864-0640. **5781**

CHAPTER NEWSLETTER - BIG BAND SOCIETY. ED WALKER CHAPTER. (US/0731-4051). **4109**

CHAPTER ONE. (US/0895-3384). **1814**

CHARCUTERIE ET GASTRONOMIE PARIS. (FR/0222-0377). **2331**

CHARIHO TIMES (1993), THE. (US/1069-9473). **Adv Mgr:** Laurie Ramaker. **5741**

CHARIOTEER, THE. (US/0577-5574). **3374**

CHARISMA AND CHRISTIAN LIFE. (US/0895-156X). **Adv Mgr:** Bob Minotti, **Tel** (407)333-0600. **4943**

CHARITIES USA. (US/0364-0760). **Adv Mgr:** C. Anderson, **Tel** (703)549-1390. **5277**

CHARITON HERALD-PATRIOT, THE. (US). **Adv Mgr:** Norral Lowe, **Tel** (515)774-2137. **5669**

CHARITON LEADER (CHARITON, IOWA : 1904). (US). **Adv Mgr:** Norral Lowe, **Tel** (515)774-2137. **5669**

CHARITON REVIEW, THE. (US/0098-9452). **3374**

CHARITY LONDON. 1983. (UK/0265-5209). **4335**

CHARLES BELL JOURNAL, THE. (UK). **3778**

CHARLES CITY PRESS (1951). (US/1049-7242). **5669**

CHARLESTON DAILY MAIL (CHARLESTON, W.VA. : 1920). (US). **5763**

CHARLESTON MAGAZINE. (US/0162-2722). **Adv Mgr:** S. Faulkenberry, **Tel** (803)722-8018. **2486**

CHARLESTON MAGAZINE, THE. (UK/0963-4770). **Adv Mgr:** Jane Grylls, **Tel** 011 44 71 278 1927. **3374**

CHARLOTTESVILLE ALBEMARLE OBSERVER. (US/0882-9322). **5758**

CHARLTON COUNTY HERALD. (US). **5652**

CHARME MODA. (IT). **Adv Mgr:** Paola Riboldi. **5553**

CHAROLAIS BANNER. (CN/0824-1767). **Adv Mgr:** Rob Pek. **209**

CHAROLAIS CONNECTION. (CN/0828-7600). **Adv Mgr:** Rob Pek. **209**

CHAROLAIS JOURNAL. (US/0191-5444). **209**

CHART AND QUILL. (US/0737-2655). **2442**

CHART (CHICAGO. 1956). (US/0069-2778). **3853**

CHART MAGAZINE. (CN). **4109**

CHARTAC ACCOUNTANCY NEWS. (AT/1037-6267). **740**

CHARTER (SYDNEY, AUSTRALIA). (AT). **Adv Mgr:** Chris St. John, **Tel** (02)290-1344. **740**

CHARTERED ACCOUNTANT, THE. (II/0009-188X). **740**

CHARTERED BUILDER. (AT/0311-1903). **Adv Mgr:** Road Harrington, **Tel** 011 61 03 32995844. **607**

CHARTERED BUILDER (ASCOT, 1989). (UK/0957-8773). **Adv Mgr:** Pauline Sargent. **607**

CHARTERED QUANTITY SURVEYOR. (UK/0142-5196). **2020**

CHARTERED SECRETARY (NEW DELHI). (II/0376-7868). **863**

CHARTERED SURVEYOR : BUILDING AND QUANTITY SURVEYING QUARTERLY. (UK). **607**

CHARTERED SURVEYOR WEEKLY. (UK/0264-049X). **4835**

CHASQUI (WILLIAMSBURG, VA.). (US/0145-8973). **3374**

CHATELAINE (EDITION FRANCAISE). (CN/0317-2635). **5553**

CHATELAINE — Advertising Accepted Index

CHATELAINE (TORONTO, ONT.: 1928). (CN/0009-1995). **5553**

CHATHAM COURIER, THE ROUGH NOTES, THE. (US/1064-4644). **Adv Mgr:** James Fleming, **Tel** (518)392-5151. **5714**

CHATHAM HOUSE PAPERS. (UK/0143-5795). **4517**

CHATSWORTH TIMES. (US). **5652**

CHATTAHOOCHEE REVIEW, THE. (US/0741-9155). **3339**

CHATTANOOGA FREE PRESS. (US). **Adv Mgr:** Dan Mausley, **Tel** (615)757-6370. **5744**

CHATTOOGA PRESS, THE. (US). **5652**

CHAUSSER 1968. (FR/0151-4040). **Adv Mgr:** Chantelat. **1082**

CHAUTAUQUAN DAILY, THE. (US/0746-0414). **Adv Mgr:** Barney Shilling. **5714**

CHE-CHIANG HSUEH KAN. ZHEJIANGXUEKAN CHE-CHIANG SHENG SHE HUI KO HSUEH YEN CHIU SO. (CC). **5195**

CHE-CHIANG TA HSUEH HSUEH PAO. (CC). **5093**

CHEBOYGAN DAILY TRIBUNE. (US/0746-665X). **Adv Mgr:** Roy Trahan. **5691**

CHEEKTOWAGA TIMES. (US). **5714**

CHEER NEWS TODAY. (US/0893-8091). **4889**

CHEESE REPORTER. (US/0009-2142). **Adv Mgr:** Kevin Thome. **192**

CHELYS (VIOLA DA GAMBA SOCIETY). (UK/0952-8407). **4109**

CHEM 13 NEWS. CHEM 12 NEWS. (CN/0703-1157). **967**

CHEMICA. (FI). **1050**

CHEMICAL AGE OF INDIA. (II/0009-2320). **968**

CHEMICAL & ENGINEERING NEWS. (US/0009-2347). **1022**

CHEMICAL BUSINESS. (II/0970-3136). **2009**

CHEMICAL BUSINESS. (US/0731-8774). **968**

CHEMICAL CORRESPONDENCE. (JA). **968**

CHEMICAL DESIGN AUTOMATION NEWS. (US/0886-6716). **968**

CHEMICAL ENGINEER (LONDON). (UK/0302-0797). **2009**

CHEMICAL ENGINEERING AND PROCESSING. (SZ/0255-2701). **Adv Mgr:** Ms. W van Cattenburch (Amsterdam). **2009**

CHEMICAL ENGINEERING EDUCATION. (US/0009-2479). **2009**

CHEMICAL ENGINEERING EQUIPMENT BUYERS' GUIDE. (US/0272-4057). **2009**

CHEMICAL ENGINEERING JOURNAL AND THE BIOCHEMICAL ENGINEERING JOURNAL, THE. (SZ/0923-0467). **Adv Mgr:** Ms. W van Cattenburch (Amsterdam). **2010**

CHEMICAL ENGINEERING (NEW YORK). (US/0009-2460). **1034**

CHEMICAL ENGINEERING PROGRESS. (US/0360-7275). **2010**

CHEMICAL HAZARDS IN INDUSTRY. (UK/0265-5721). **2872**

CHEMICAL INDUSTRY. (JA). **1022**

CHEMICAL INFORMATION BULLETIN. (US/0364-1910). **968**

CHEMICAL MARKETING REPORTER. (US/0090-0907). **968**

CHEMICAL PACKAGING REVIEW, THE. (US/1054-5131). **2162**

CHEMICAL RESEARCH IN TOXICOLOGY. (US/0893-228X). **Adv Mgr:** Centcom, **Tel** (203)256-8211. **3979**

CHEMICAL REVIEWS. (US/0009-2665). **969**

CHEMICAL SENSES. (UK/0379-864X). **485**

CHEMICAL SPECIATION AND BIOAVAILABILITY. (UK/0954-2299). **2162**

CHEMICAL TIMES & TRENDS. (US/0149-2381). **969**

CHEMICAL WEEKLY. (II/0045-6500). **969**

CHEMICKE LISTY. (XR/0009-2770). **969**

CHEMIE DER ERDE. (GW/0009-2819). **1438**

CHEMIE MAGAZINE : MAANDBLAD VAN DE VLAAMSE CHEMISCHE VERENIGING. (BE). **969**

CHEMIE, MIKROBIOLOGIE, TECHNOLOGIE DER LEBENSMITTEL. (GW/0366-7154). **2331**

CHEMIE-TECHNIK. (GW/0340-9961). **2010**

CHEMINS DE FER : BULLETIN OFFICIEL. (FR/0009-2924). **5430**

CHEMISCH JAARBOEK. (NE). **969**

CHEMISCHE INDUSTRIE (DUSSELDORF). (GW/0009-2959). **970**

CHEMISCHE INDUSTRIE INTERNATIONAL. (GW/0009-2967). **1022**

CHEMIST & DRUGGIST. (UK/0009-3033). **4296**

CHEMIST & DRUGGIST DIRECTORY. (UK/0262-5881). **4296**

CHEMIST & DRUGGIST DIRECTORY AND TABLET & CAPSULE IDENTIFICATION GUIDE. (UK). **4296**

CHEMIST (NEW YORK), THE. (US/0009-3025). **970**

CHEMISTRY AND INDUSTRY (LONDON). (UK/0009-3068). **970**

CHEMISTRY IN AUSTRALIA. (AT/0314-4240). **970**

CHEMISTRY IN NEW ZEALAND. (NZ/0110-5566). **971**

CHEMISTRY INTERNATIONAL. (UK/0193-6484). **971**

CHEMISTRY OF MATERIALS. (US/0897-4756). **Adv Mgr:** Centcom, **Tel** (203)256-8211. **971**

CHEMOMETRICS AND INTELLIGENT LABORATORY SYSTEMS : LABORATORY INFORMATION MANAGEMENT. (NE/0925-5281). **1014**

CHEMOSPHERE (OXFORD). (UK/0045-6535). **2226**

CHEMOTHERAPY (BASEL). (SZ/0009-3157). **3814**

CHEMTECH. (US/0009-2703). **AdvMgr Tel** (203)256-8211. **1022**

CHEMUNG VALLEY REPORTER. (US/1064-4091). **Adv Mgr:** Marian Grushetsky. **5714**

CHENEY SENTINEL, THE. (US). **Adv Mgr:** Arla Tanner. **5674**

CHERAW CHRONICLE. (US/0889-0617). **Adv Mgr:** Sandy Garris. **5741**

CHEROKEE COUNTY HERALD, THE. (US). **5625**

CHEROKEE FAMILY HISTORY. (US). **2442**

CHEROKEE FAMILY RESEARCHER. (US). **2443**

CHEROKEE ONE FEATHER, THE. (US/0890-4448). **2258**

CHESAPEAKE BAY MAGAZINE. (US/0045-656X). **593**

CHESHIRE HERALD. (US). **Adv Mgr:** Joseph Jakubisyn. **5645**

CHESOPIEAN, THE. (US/0009-3300). **265**

CHESS. (UK/0009-3319). **4858**

CHESS COLLECTOR. (UK). **Adv Mgr:** Gareth Williams, **Tel** 071 262 6410. **4858**

CHESS CORRESPONDENT, THE. (US/0009-3327). **4858**

CHESS HORIZONS. (US/0147-2569). **Adv Mgr:** same as editor. **4858**

CHESS IN INDIANA. (US/1044-8888). **4858**

CHESS LIFE (1980). (US/0197-260X). **4858**

CHEST. (US/0012-3692). **3702**

CHEST DISEASES, THORACIC SURGERY AND TUBERCULOSIS. (NE/0014-4193). **3949**

CHESTER COUNTY PRESS. (US). **Adv Mgr:** Alan Turns. **5735**

CHESTERTON REVIEW, THE. (CN/0317-0500). **3374**

CHESTERTON TRIBUNE, THE. (US). **Adv Mgr:** Bill Mathe. **5663**

CHESTNUT HILL LOCAL, THE. (US/0009-3394). **Adv Mgr:** Frank Moeschlin, **Tel** (215)248-8815. **5735**

CHEVAL MAGAZINE. (FR). **2798**

CHEVAUX DE PENNY. (FR). **1061**

CHEVRON WORLD. (US/0148-3102). **4253**

CHICAGO & COOK COUNTY MARKETING DIRECTORY. (US/0896-4017). **Adv Mgr:** Charles Scherer. **922**

CHICAGO APPAREL NEWS. (US/0195-0819). **1082**

CHICAGO BOWLER, INC, THE. (US/1056-3547). **Adv Mgr:** Mariann Weglarz. **4890**

CHICAGO CRUSADER, THE. (US). **5658**

CHICAGO DEFENDER (1973). (US/0745-7014). **Adv Mgr:** Joseph Gilmore. **5659**

CHICAGO GALLERY NEWS. (US/1046-6185). **4086**

CHICAGO JEWISH STAR. (US/1054-1365). **5659**

CHICAGO LAWYER. (US/0199-8374). **2950**

CHICAGO MEDICINE. (US/0009-3637). **Adv Mgr:** Kristi Zernia, **Tel** (312)670-2550 ext. 228. **3563**

CHICAGO POST, THE. (US). **Adv Mgr:** James Boratyn. **5659**

CHICAGO PRODUCTION BIBLE. (US). **Adv Mgr:** Maureen Cany, **Tel** (312)664-5236. **4065**

CHICAGO PURCHASOR, THE. (US/0009-367X). **Adv Mgr:** Jackie Stinson, **Tel** (312)782-1940. **949**

CHICAGO REVIEW. (US/0009-3696). **3374**

CHICAGO SHORELAND NEWS, THE. (US). **5659**

CHICAGO SOURCEBOOK. (US/1078-5949). **757**

CHICAGO SUN-TIMES. (US). **5659**

CHICAGO TALENT SOURCEBOOK. (US/0734-6662). **757**

CHICAGO TIMES MAGAZINE. (US/0894-5640). **2530**

CHICAGO TRIBUNE (CHICAGO, ILL. : 1963). (US). **5659**

CHICO ENTERPRISE-RECORD. (US/0746-5548). **5633**

CHICO TEXAN, THE. (US). **Adv Mgr:** Keith Bridwell. **5748**

CHIEF EXECUTIVE (NEW YORK, N.Y. 1977). (US/0160-4724). **863**

CHIEF INFORMATION OFFICER JOURNAL. (US/0899-0182). **1174**

CHIEFTAIN (IROQUOIS). (CN/0821-7696). **Adv Mgr:** Sharron Bolte. **5782**

CHIEN CHU SHIH (TAIPEI, TAIWAN). (CH). **Adv Mgr:** Chou Yu Ying. **295**

CHIH WU SHENG LI HSUEH TUNG HSUN. (CC/0412-0914). **506**

CHIHUA XUEBAO. (CC/0253-9837). **1050**

CHIKASUI GAKKAI SHI. (JA/0913-4182). **1413**

CHIKUSAN NO KENKYU. ANIMAL HUSBANDRY. (JA). **5507**

CHILD & FAMILY BEHAVIOR THERAPY. (US/0731-7107). **4580**

CHILD AND MAN. (UK/0009-3890). **Adv Mgr:** Peter Ramm. **1731**

CHILD & YOUTH SERVICES. (US/0145-935X). **5278**

CHILD CARE. (CN/0838-9683). **Adv Mgr:** Carric Kelly. **3901**

CHILD CARE, HEALTH AND DEVELOPMENT. (UK/0305-1862). **3901**

CHILD CARE INFORMATION EXCHANGE. (US/0164-8527). **5278**

CHILD CARE WORKER, THE. (SA/0258-8927). **5242**

CHILD DEVELOPMENT. (US/0009-3920). **4580**

CHILD EDUCATION. (UK/0009-3947). **1890**

CHILD LIFE (INDIANAPOLIS, IND. 1922). (US/0009-3971). **1061**

CHILD NEPHROLOGY AND UROLOGY. (SZ/1012-6694). **3989**

CHILD (NEW YORK, N.Y.). (US/0894-7988). **2277**

CHILD PSYCHIATRY AND HUMAN DEVELOPMENT. (US/0009-398X). **3923**

CHILD PSYCHIATRY QUARTERLY. (II/0009-3998). **3901**

CHILD WELFARE. (US/0009-4021). **5278**

CHILDHOOD EDUCATION. (US/0009-4056). **1803**

CHILDREN & TEENS TODAY. (US/0882-942X). **5278**

CHILDREN AND WAR. (UK/0956-3113). **5195**

CHILDREN LOOKED AFTER BY LOCAL AUTHORITIES IN WALES / WELSH OFFICE / PLANT Y GOFELIR AM DANYNT GAN AWDURDODAU LLEOL CYMRU / Y SWYDDFA GYMREIG. (UK/0968-4050). **5278**

CHILDREN'S ADVOCATE, THE. (US/0739-425X). **Adv Mgr:** A. Gennino. **5279**

CHILDREN'S ALBUM, THE. (US/0749-8659). **1061**

CHILDREN'S BOOKS IN PRINT (LONDON, ENGLAND). (UK/0577-781X). **4827**

CHILDREN'S FOCUS. (US/0893-486X). **1061**

CHILDREN'S HEALTH CARE. (US/0273-9615). **3901**

CHILDREN'S LEGAL RIGHTS JOURNAL. (US/0278-7210). **3120**

CHILDREN'S LITERATURE ASSOCIATION QUARTERLY. (US/0885-0429). **3340**

CHILDREN'S MINISTRY. (US/1054-1144). **Adv Mgr:** Larry Boryour, **Tel** (303)669-3836. **4943**

CHILDREN'S PLAYMATE MAGAZINE. (US/0009-4161). **1062**

CHILDREN'S WELFARE ASSOCIATION OF VICTORIA NEWSLETTER. (AT). **5279**

CHILDREN'S WORLD (BOSTON, MASS.). (US/0895-2221). **1877**

CHILD'S PLAY (CHICAGO, ILL.). (US/0749-8632). **1803**

CHILE FORESTAL. (CL/0716-1190). **2377**

CHILEAN FORESTRY NEWS. (CL). **2377**

CHILTON COUNTY NEWS (CLANTON, ALA. : 1986). (US/0888-451X). **5625**

CHILTON TIMES-JOURNAL. (US). **5766**

CHILTON'S AUTOMOTIVE INDUSTRIES (1976). (US/0273-656X). **5410**

CHILTON'S AUTOMOTIVE MARKETING. (US/0193-3264). **5410**

CHILTON'S ELECTRONIC COMPONENT NEWS. (US/0193-614X). **2038**

CHILTON'S FOOD ENGINEERING. (US/0193-323X). **2331**

CHILTON'S FOOD ENGINEERING INTERNATIONAL. (US/0148-4478). **2331**

CHILTON'S IAN (1977). (US/0193-6174). **1968**

CHILTON'S I&CS. (US/0746-2395). **1968**

CHILTON'S IMPO. (US/8755-2523). **3476**

CHILTON'S INDUSTRIAL SAFETY & HYGIENE NEWS. (US/8755-2566). **2860**

CHILTON'S MOTOR/AGE (1970). (US/0193-7022). **5411**

CHILTON'S OWNER OPERATOR. (US). **5379**

CHILTON'S REVIEW OF OPTOMETRY. (US/0147-7633). **4215**

CHILTON'S TRUCK & OFF-HIGHWAY INDUSTRIES. (US/0194-1410). **5379**

CHIMICA E L'INDUSTRIA, LA. (IT/0009-4315). **971**

CHIMIE MAGAZINE. (FR/0245-940X). **972**

CHIMIE NOUVELLE. (BE/0771-730X). **972**

CHINA AKTUELL / INSTITUT FUER ASIENKUNDE. (GW/0341-6631). **4468**

CHINA & THE WORLD. (CC). **4517**

CHINA-BRITAIN TRADE REVIEW. (UK/0952-9756). **Adv Mgr:** Ms. Starbuck. **827**

CHINA BUSINESS & TRADE. (US/0731-7700). **Adv Mgr:** Justin Ford. **827**

CHINA BUSINESS REVIEW, THE. (US/0163-7169). **Adv Mgr:** Pat Jordan. **657**

CHINA COAL INDUSTRY YEARBOOK. (HK/0258-3062). **2136**

CHINA DAILY (INTERNATIONAL EDITION). (CC/0253-9543). **5798**

CHINA EARTH SCIENCES. (NE/0923-6805). **1353**

CHINA ECONOMIC REVIEW. (UK). **Adv Mgr:** Cordelia Boyd and Rachel Groves. **1551**

CHINA FAX AND TELEX DIRECTORY. (HK). **827**

CHINA GLASS & TABLEWARE. (US/0009-4382). **2588**

CHINA INFORMATION. (NE/0920-203X). **4468**

CHINA MARKET. (HK). **1633**

CHINA NOW. (UK/0045-6764). **Adv Mgr:** Ms. Ryder. **2502**

CHINA PHONE BOOK & BUSINESS DIRECTORY, THE. (HK). **827**

CHINA PLASTIC & RUBBER JOURNAL. (HK). **4454**

CHINA QUARTERLY (LONDON). (UK/0305-7410). **2648**

CHINA REPORT (NEW DELHI). (II/0009-4455). **5242**

CHINA TELECOMMUNICATIONS CONSTRUCTION. (HK/1017-5199). **Adv Mgr:** Alan Law. **1130**

CHINA TELECOMMUNICATIONS CONSTRUCTION. (HK/1017-5199). **Adv Mgr:** K.M. Han. **1151**

CHINA TEXTILE. (HK). **5349**

CHINAMAC JOURNAL. (HK). **3476**

CHINATOWN NEWS. (CN/0009-4501). **2486**

CHINESE AMERICA, HISTORY AND PERSPECTIVES. (US/1051-7642). **2258**

CHINESE AMERICAN FORUM. (US/0895-4690). **1731**

CHINESE ANNALS OF MATHEMATICS. SER. B. (CC/0252-9599). **3500**

CHINESE BUSINESS HISTORY. (US). **Adv Mgr:** A. McElderry, **Tel** same as publisher. **657**

CHINESE CULTURE. (CH/0009-4544). **3374**

CHINESE ECONOMIC STUDIES. (US/0009-4552). **1469**

CHINESE EDUCATION. (US/0009-4560). **1731**

CHINESE HISTORIANS. (US/1043-643X). **2649**

CHINESE JOURNAL OF ACOUSTICS. (CC). **4452**

CHINESE LAW AND GOVERNMENT. (US/0009-4609). **2950**

CHINESE LITERATURE (MADISON). (US/0161-9705). **3375**

CHINESE MUSIC. (US/0192-3749). **4109**

CHINESE PHYSICS LETTERS. (US/0256-307X). **4400**

CHINESE SCIENCE ABSTRACTS. PART A. (CC/0254-5179). **5093**

CHINESE SCIENCE ABSTRACTS. PART B. (CC/0254-4903). **5093**

CHINESE STUDIES IN HISTORY. (US/0009-4633). **2649**

CHINESE STUDIES IN PHILOSOPHY. (US/0023-8627). **4343**

CHING FENG (ENGLISH EDITION). (HK/0009-4668). **4943**

CHIP MADRID. (SP/0211-2841). **1174**

CHIRIHAK. (KO). **2558**

CHIRON. (GW/0069-3715). **1075**

CHIROPODY REVIEW. (UK/0009-4714). **Adv Mgr:** A.D. Nines. **3917**

CHIROPRACTIC JOURNAL OF AUSTRALIA. (AT/1036-0913). **4379**

CHIROPRACTIC PRODUCTS. (US/1041-2360). **3563**

CHIRURGIA. (IT/0394-9508). **3961**

CHIRURGIA DEGLI ORGANI DI MOVIMENTO. (IT/0009-4749). **3961**

CHIRURGIA GASTROENTEROLOGICA. (IT/0009-4765). **3743**

CHIRURGIA TRIVENETA. (IT/0009-4811). **3962**

CHIRURGICA (OULU). (FI/0358-4917). **3962**

CHIRURGIEN - DENTISTE DE FRANCE, LE. (FR/0009-4838). **1319**

CHISAGO COUNTY PRESS. (US). **Adv Mgr:** Ellen Glemna. **5695**

CHISHOLM TRAIL, THE. (US). **2443**

CHITARRE. (IT). **4109**

CHITTENANGO, BRIDGEPORT TIMES. (US). **Adv Mgr:** Diane Connors. **5715**

CHO TO GA. TYO TO GA. (JA). **5606**

CHOCOLATE NEWS. (UK). **2331**

CHOCOLATE SINGLES. (US/0882-4460). **2258**

CHOCOLATIER. (US/0887-591X). **2331**

CHOCTAW ADVOCATE, THE. (US). **Adv Mgr:** Lee Mosley. **5625**

CHOICE. (US/0009-4978). **3201**

CHOICE INDIA. (II). **5195**

CHOICES (AMES, IOWA). (US/0886-5558). **73**

CHOIRS ONTARIO. (CN/0822-4749). **Adv Mgr:** Bev Jahnke. **4109**

CHOLESTEROL AND LIPOPROTEINS. (UK/0964-7597). **485**

CHORAL JOURNAL, THE. (US/0009-5028). **4109**

CHORISTERS GUILD LETTERS. (US/0412-2801). **Adv Mgr:** B. Merry. **4109**

CHORUS! (DULUTH, GA.). (US/1044-7857). **4109**

CHORUS (HALIFAX). (CN/0821-1108). **4109**

CHOSON ILBO (MIJU PAN). (US/0743-7056). **Adv Mgr:** Elaine Kim, **Tel** (718)463-4443. **5715**

CHRISTIAN ACTIVITIES CALENDAR (MIDDLE ATLANTIC ED.). (US/0883-4210). **4944**

CHRISTIAN CENTURY (1902), THE. (US/0009-5281). **4944**

CHRISTIAN CHALLENGE, THE. (US/0890-6793). **5058**

CHRISTIAN COMMUNITY (COLUMBUS), THE. (US/0145-3297). **4944**

CHRISTIAN COUNSELING TODAY. (US/1076-9668). **Adv Mgr:** Dawn Emeigh, **Tel** (804)384-0564. **4944**

CHRISTIAN COURIER. (CN/1192-3415). **Adv Mgr:** Stan De Jong. **5058**

CHRISTIAN EDUCATORS JOURNAL. (US). **Adv Mgr:** P. Boogaart. **4944**

CHRISTIAN HERALD. (US/0009-5354). **431**

CHRISTIAN HERALD WORTHING. (UK/0953-4385). **Adv Mgr:** Ann Terry. **5058**

CHRISTIAN HOME AND SCHOOL. (US). **2278**

CHRISTIAN INDEX, THE. (US). **Adv Mgr:** Norma B. King, **Tel** (404)936-5312. **5058**

CHRISTIAN INFO DIRECTORY. (CN). **4945**

CHRISTIAN JOURNAL (FORT WORTH, TEX.). (US/1056-3644). **4945**

CHRISTIAN LEADER (HILLSBORO). (US/0009-5419). **5058**

CHRISTIAN LIBRARIAN (CEDARVILLE, OHIO), THE. (US/0412-3131). **3202**

CHRISTIAN MEDICAL & DENTAL SOCIETY JOURNAL. (US). **3563**

CHRISTIAN MESSENGER. (GH/0009-5478). **4945**

CHRISTIAN MINISTRY, THE. (US/0033-4138). **4945**

CHRISTIAN MUSIC. (UK). **4109**

CHRISTIAN MUSIC DIRECTORIES. PRINTED MUSIC, THE. (US). **4109**

CHRISTIAN NEW AGE QUARTERLY. (US/0899-7292). **4945**

CHRISTIAN OBSERVER (MANASSAS, VA.). (US/0899-2584). **4945**

CHRISTIAN PSYCHOLOGY FOR TODAY. (US/0892-4686). **4580**

CHRISTIAN RENEWAL. (CN/0820-7593). **AdvMgr Tel** (905)562-5719. **4945**

CHRISTIAN RESEARCH JOURNAL. (US). **Adv Mgr:** Melanie Cogdill, **Tel** (714)899-4428. **4945**

CHRISTIAN RETAILING. (US/0892-0281). **Adv Mgr:** Bob Minotti, **Tel** (407)333-0600. **952**

CHRISTIAN SCHOLAR'S REVIEW. (US/0017-2251). **4946**

CHRISTIAN SCIENCE MONITOR (1983), THE. (US/0882-7729). **Adv Mgr:** Nick Drinker, **Tel** (617)450-2652. **5688**

CHRISTIAN SOCIAL ACTION (WASHINGTON, D.C.). (US/0897-0459). **4946**

CHRISTIAN STATESMAN. (US/0009-5664). **4946**

CHRISTIAN VISION. (CN/0843-7602). **3375**

CHRISTIAN WEEK. (CN/0835-412X). **Adv Mgr:** Bryan Rempel. **4946**

CHRISTIAN WORLD REPORT, THE. (CN/0846-4243). **Adv Mgr:** T. Gray. **4946**

CHRISTIANISME AU VINGTIEME SIECLE, LE. (FR/0009-5729). **4946**

CHRISTIANITY AND CRISIS. (US/0009-5745). **4946**

CHRISTIANITY & LITERATURE. (US/0148-3331). **3375**

CHRISTIANITY TODAY (WASHINGTON). (US/0009-5753). **4946**

CHRISTIANS WRITING. (AT/0729-4042). **3375**

CHRISTMAS TREES. (US/0199-0217). **Adv Mgr:** Alice Wright. **2377**

CHRISTOPHER STREET. (US/0146-7921). **2793**

CHRISTOPHORUS STUTTGART. (GW/0412-3417). **5411**

CHRISTUS. (FR/0009-5834). **5027**

CHRONICA HORTICULTURAE. (NE/0578-039X). **2412**

CHRONICLE. (US). **Adv Mgr:** Paul Johnson, **Tel** (612)896-4700. **5695**

CHRONICLE (BARTON, VT.). (US/0746-438X). **Adv Mgr:** Ned Andrews. **5757**

CHRONICLE CAREER INDEX. (US/0276-0355). **4203**

CHRONICLE (CHARLESTON, S.C.), THE. (US/0746-1429). **Adv Mgr:** Nanette Smalls. **5742**

CHRONICLE (CRESWELL, OR.). (US/0739-9758). **Adv Mgr:** Gerri O'Rourke, **Tel** $503)895-2197. **5733**

CHRONICLE-EXPRESS. (US). **Adv Mgr:** Ken Miller. **5715**

CHRONICLE (MILFORD, DEL.). (US). **Adv Mgr:** Jerry Miller. **5648**

CHRONICLE-NEWS, THE. (US). **Adv Mgr:** Annette Girom. **5642**

CHRONICLE — Advertising Accepted Index

CHRONICLE OF HIGHER EDUCATION, THE. (US/0009-5982). **1815**

CHRONICLE OF PHILANTHROPY, THE. (US/1040-676X). **4335**

CHRONICLE OF THE HORSE, THE. (US/0009-5990). **2798**

CHRONICLE OF THE U.S. CLASSIC POSTAL ISSUES, THE. (US/0009-6008). **2784**

CHRONICLE (OMAHA, NEB.), THE. (US/0030-2201). **4188**

CHRONICLE SUMMARY REPORT. (US/0193-1601). **1815**

CHRONICLE-TELEGRAM, THE. (US). **5727**

CHRONICLE, THE. (US). **Adv Mgr:** Ralph Mann. **5230**

CHRONICLE TWO-YEAR COLLEGE DATABOOK. (US/0191-3662). **1815**

CHRONICLE VOCATIONAL SCHOOL MANUAL. (US/0276-0371). **1912**

CHRONICLES (PHILADELPHIA, PA.). (US/0893-2921). **2443**

CHRONICLES (ROCKFORD, ILL.). (US/0887-5731). **2844**

CHRONIQUE DE LA RECHERCHE MINIERE. (FR/0182-564X). **1371**

CHRONIQUE D'EGYPTE. (BE/0009-6067). **265**

CHRONIQUE INTERNATIONALE PARIS. (FR/1145-1408). **1470**

CHRONIQUE JUDICIAIRE D'HAITI, LA. (HT). **3126**

CHRONIQUES ITALIENNES. (FR/0766-4257). **3273**

CHRONOSTRATIGRAPHIE UND NEOSTRATOTYPEN. (GW/0578-0578). **1353**

CHRYSALIS (NEW YORK, N.Y.). (US/0888-9384). **Adv Mgr:** Susanna Lawson, **Tel** (804)983-3021. **4343**

CHRYSANTHEMUM. (US/0090-5771). **2412**

CHUAN PO KUNG CHENG. (CH). **4175**

CHULPAN MUNHWA. (KO/0009-6245). **4828**

CHUNG-HUA CH'I KUAN I CHIH TSA CHIH. (CC/0254-1785). **3564**

CHUNG-HUA MIN KUO CHI CHI SHE PEI HSUAN LU. (CH). **2111**

CHUNG-HUA PI FU KO TSA CHIH. (CC/0412-4030). **3718**

CHUNG-KUO CHIEN CHU FA CHAN. (HK). **607**

CHUNG-KUO FU NU / ZHONGGUO FUNU. (CC/0529-603X). **5553**

CHUNG-KUO HAI YUN. (HK). **5448**

CHUNG-KUO HSIN WEN NIEN CHIEN. (CC). **2918**

CHUNG-KUO SHENG WU I HSUEH KUNG CHENG HSUEH PAO. (CH/0258-8021). **3564**

CHUNG-KUO TA LU YEN CHIU (KUO LI CHENG CHIH TA HSUEH. KUO CHI KUAN HSI YEN CHIU CHUNG HSIN). (CH). **4518**

CHUNG-KUO TIEN YING NIEN CHIEN / CHUNG-KUO TIEN YING CHIA HSIEH HUI PIEN TSUAN. (CC). **4065**

CHUNG-KUO TUI WAI CHING CHI MAO I NIEN CHIEN. (HK). **AdvMgr Tel** 0852-5938831. **1551**

CHUNG-KUO TUI WAI MAO I. (CC/0009-4498). **827**

CHUNG WAI WEN HSUEH. (CH). **Adv Mgr:** Chun-yen Chen, **Tel** 886-2-363-9395. **3375**

CHURCH AND CLERGY FINANCE. (US/0045-6861). **783**

CHURCH & SYNAGOGUE LIBRARIES. (US/0009-6342). **Adv Mgr:** Judith Janzen. **3202**

CHURCH BYTES. (US/0884-7193). **4947**

CHURCH HERALD, THE. (US/0009-6393). **Adv Mgr:** S.Smith. **4947**

CHURCH HISTORY. (US/0009-6407). **4947**

CHURCH MANAGEMENT. (US/0009-6431). **4947**

CHURCH MUSIC QUARTERLY. (UK/0307-6334). **4109**

CHURCH MUSIC REPORT : TCMR, THE. (US/1071-9903). **Adv Mgr:** D. Yarlott, **Tel** (800)969-2670. **4109**

CHURCH MUSICIAN, THE. (US/0009-6466). **4109**

CHURCH (NEW YORK, N.Y.). (US/0883-5667). **4947**

CHURCH OBSERVER. (UK/0009-6482). **4947**

CHURCH OF ENGLAND NEWSPAPER : CEN. (UK/0964-816X). **Adv Mgr:** Chris Turner. **2514**

CHURCH OF ENGLAND YEAR BOOK, THE. (UK/0069-3987). **4947**

CHURCH RECREATION MAGAZINE. (US/0162-4652). **4849**

CHURCH RESOURCE DIRECTORY. (US). **4947**

CHURCH TIMES, THE. (US). **4948**

CHURCH WORLD. (US/0009-6601). **5027**

CHURCHMAN (LONDON. 1879). (UK/0009-661X). **Adv Mgr:** M J W Barker. **4948**

CIBOLA COUNTY BEACON. (US/1071-3506). **Adv Mgr:** Ken Wingat. **5712**

CICERO LIFE. (US). **Adv Mgr:** Pete Manning. **5659**

CIEL ET TERRE. (BE/0009-6709). **394**

CIEL VARIABLE :LE MANIFESTE DU TEMPS. (CN/0831-3091). **347**

CIENCIA DEL SUELO. (AG/0326-3169). **1353**

CIENCIA E INVESTIGACION AGRARIA. (CL/0304-5609). **74**

CIENCIA FORESTAL. (MX/0185-2418). **2377**

CIENCIA HOJE : REVISAT DE DIVULGACAO CIENTIFICA DA SOCIEDADE BRASILEIRA PARA O PROGRESSO DA CIENCIA. (BL/0101-8515). **5094**

CIENCIA (MEXICO CITY, MEXICO). (MX/0185-075X). **5094**

CIENCIA PEDIATRIKA (MADRID, SPAIN : 1986). (SP). **Adv Mgr:** McCarmen Alvarez, **Tel** 733-88-92. **3902**

CIENCIA PHARMACEUTICA. (SP). **4296**

CIENCIA Y DESARROLLO. (MX/0185-0008). **5094**

CIENCIAS MARINAS. (MX/0185-3880). **553**

CIENTIFICA (JABOTICABAL). (BL/0100-0039). **5507**

CIERVO, EL. (SP/0045-6896). **4948**

CIGAR AFICIONADO. (US/1063-7885). **Adv Mgr:** James Archambault, **Tel** (212)684-4224. **5372**

CIM BULLETIN. (CN/0317-0926). **2136**

CIM-MANAGEMENT. (GW/0179-2679). **1174**

CIMAISE. (FR/0009-6830). **347**

CIMENTS, BETONS, PLATRES, CHAUX. (FR/0397-006X). **607**

CINCINNATI. (US/0009-689X). **2530**

CINCINNATI ENQUIRER (CINCINNATI, OHIO : 1872). (US). **5727**

CINCINNATI MEDICINE. (US/0163-0075). **3564**

CINE & MEDIA. (BE/1016-9660). **1106**

CINE BULLES. (CN/0820-8921). **Adv Mgr:** Martine Mauroy. **4065**

CINE CUBANO. (CU/0009-6946). **4065**

CINE-FICHES DE GRAND ANGLE, LES. (BE/0773-2279). **4065**

CINEASTE (NEW YORK, N.Y.). (US/0009-7004). **4066**

CINEFANTASTIQUE. (US/0145-6032). **4066**

CINEFEX. (US/0198-1056). **4066**

CINEFORUM. (IT/0009-7039). **4066**

CINEMA D'OGGI. (IT/0392-9981). **4066**

CINEMA E CINEMA. (IT). **4066**

CINEMA IN INDIA. (II). **4066**

CINEMA JOURNAL. (US/0009-7101). **4066**

CINEMA NUOVO. (IT/0009-711X). **Adv Mgr:** R. Coga. **4066**

CINEMA PAPERS. (AT/0311-3639). **4066**

CINEMA (PORTO, PORTUGAL). (PO). **4066**

CINEMA TECHNOLOGY. (UK). **Adv Mgr:** Jackson Rudd, **Tel** 071-613-0717. **4066**

CINEMA (ZURICH, SWITZERLAND). (SZ/1010-3627). **4066**

CINEMACABRE. (US/0198-1064). **4066**

CINEMACTION. (FR/0243-4504). **4066**

CINEMAGIC (NEW YORK, N.Y.). (US/0009-3000). **4067**

CINEMAS (MONTREAL). (CN/1181-6945). **4067**

CINEMATOGRAPH. (US/0886-6570). **317**

CINEVUE. (US/0895-805X). **4368**

CIOMS CALENDAR. (SZ/0379-8100). **3564**

CIRCA (BELFAST, NORTHERN IRELAND). (UK/0263-9475). **347**

CIRCA. CONFLITS INTERNATIONAUX, LES REGIONS ET LE CANADA. (CN/0822-8418). **4518**

CIRCUIT CELLAR INK. (US/0896-8985). **Adv Mgr:** Sue Hodge. **1227**

CIRCUIT (MONTREAL). (CN/0821-1876). **Adv Mgr:** Malboeuf, **Tel** (514)334-6742. **3273**

CIRCUIT NEWS. (US/1058-9317). **Adv Mgr:** Irene Blanset. **2038**

CIRCUIT WORLD. (UK/0305-6120). **2038**

CIRCUITREE MAGAZINE. (US). **2038**

CIRCULAIRE D'INFORMATION. (CG). **819**

CIRCULAR / NATIONAL AUDUBON SOCIETY. (US). **AdvMgr Tel** (212)546-9127. **5617**

CIRCULATION MANAGEMENT (SPRINGFIELD, OR.). (US/0888-8191). **Adv Mgr:** G. Bartmen, **Tel** (212)979-0730. **2918**

CIRCULATION (NEW YORK, N.Y.). (US/0009-7322). **3702**

CIRCULATION RESEARCH. (US/0009-7330). **3702**

CIRCULATION (WILMETTE, ILL.). (US/0569-6704). **922**

CIRCUS (NEW YORK, N.Y. 1979). (US/0009-7365). **4110**

CIRCUS REPORT, THE. (US/0889-5996). **4849**

CIRP ANNALS. (SZ/0007-8506). **2111**

CIRUGIA DE URGENCIA. (SP/0213-5353). **3723**

CIRUGIA DEL URUGUAY. (UY/0009-7381). **3962**

CIRUGIA PLASTICA IBERO-LATINOAMERICANA. (SP/0376-7892). **3962**

CIRUGIA Y CIRUJANOS. (MX/0009-7411). **Adv Mgr:** Bruno Vanneuville, **Tel** 011 52 5 2600048. **3962**

CISCO PRESS, THE. (US). **Adv Mgr:** Bill Sanders, **Tel** (817)629-1707. **5748**

CISSNA PARK NEWS, THE. (US). **5659**

CITATION (CHICAGO, ILL.). (US/0009-7446). **2950**

CITE (HOUSTON, TEX.). (US/8755-0415). **Adv Mgr:** Lynn Kewt, **Tel** (713)526-4370. **295**

CITES NOUVELLES. (CN/0319-5198). **Adv Mgr:** Marc Forge, **Tel** (514)6200781. **5782**

CITHARA. (US/0009-7527). **4948**

CITIES & VILLAGES. (US/0009-7535). **4638**

CITIES (LONDON, ENGLAND). (UK/0264-2751). **2817**

CITIZEN (AMERICAN FORK, UTAH). (US/8750-4677). **Adv Mgr:** Brett Brezzant. **5756**

CITIZEN (AUBURN, N.Y.), THE. (US/0738-7520). **Adv Mgr:** Charles Kolsky. **5715**

CITIZEN (DENVER), THE. (US/0009-7543). **4702**

CITIZEN (HAMTRAMCK, MICH.), THE. (US/1042-6906). **Adv Mgr:** Chris Stamatel. **5691**

CITIZEN OF MORRIS COUNTY, THE. (US). **5709**

CITIZEN-STATESMAN. (US/0746-7745). **Adv Mgr:** Michelle Denton. **5744**

CITIZEN-TIMES, THE. (US). **Adv Mgr:** Quinn Wood. **5680**

CITRUS AND SUB-TROPICAL FRUIT JOURNAL, THE. (SA/0257-2095). **167**

CITRUS DEED REPORT. (US). **4835**

CITRUS INDUSTRY (BARTOW, FLA. : 1982), THE. (US). **Adv Mgr:** Jane Kutler. **2331**

CITY & COUNTRY CLUB LIFE. (US/0897-4926). **2530**

CITY & SOCIETY. (US/0893-0465). **2818**

CITY & TOWN (NORTH LITTLE ROCK, ARK.). (US/0193-8371). **Adv Mgr:** J. Woodruff. **4638**

CITY GUIDE (NEW YORK, N.Y.). (US/1043-3937). **5466**

CITY JOURNAL (NEW YORK, N.Y.), THE. (US/1060-8540). **Adv Mgr:** Margaret Laws. **4468**

CITY LIMITS. (US/0199-0330). **Adv Mgr:** Faith Wiggins, **Tel** (917)253-3887. **2818**

CITY OF CHICAGO BUILDING CODE. (US). **Adv Mgr:** Tom Youpel, **Tel** (312)644-7800. **2950**

CITY OF LONDON LAW REVIEW. (UK/0306-9788). **2950**

CITY OF LOS ANGELES PLANNING AND ZONING CODE : CHAPTER 1 OF THE LOS ANGELES MUNICIPAL CODE. (US). **2818**

CITY PAPER. (US/0195-0843). **5686**

CITY RECORD. (US). **4638**

CITY SUN, THE. (US/8750-2720). **Adv Mgr:** Barbara Sealy Rhoden. **5715**

CIUDAD DE DIOS, LA. (SP/0009-7756). **Adv Mgr:** Saturnino Alvarez. **4948**

CIVIC AFFAIRS. (II/0009-7772). **4638**

CIVIC CENTER NEWSOURCE. (US/1067-4357). **5634**

CIVIC PUBLIC WORKS. (CN/0829-772X). **4760**

CIVIL AIR PATROL NEWS. (US/0009-7810). **16**

CIVIL AVIATION TRAINING : CAT. (UK/0960-9024). **16**

CIVIL ENGINEER IN SOUTH AFRICA, THE. (SA/0009-7845). **Adv Mgr:** Mrs. Smith. **2020**

CIVIL ENGINEERING NEWS (MARIETTA, GA.). (US/1051-9629). **2021**

CIVIL ENGINEERING PRACTICE. (US/0886-9685). **2021**

CIVIL ENGINEERING SURVEYOR. (UK/0266-139X). **2021**

CIVIL ENGINEERING SYSTEMS. (UK/0263-0257). **2021**

CIVIL JUSTICE QUARTERLY. (UK/0261-9261). **3089**

CIVIL RIGHTS & CIVIL LIBERTIES LITIGATION : A GUIDE TO [SECTION SYMBOL] 1983 / SHELDON H. NAHMOD. (US). **4506**

CIVIL WAR COLLECTORS' DEALER DIRECTORY, THE. (US/0094-1182). **250**

CIVIL WAR HISTORY. (US/0009-8078). **2728**

CIVIL WAR NEWS, THE. (US/1053-1181). **2728**

CIVIL WAR REGIMENTS. (US/1055-3266). **AdvMgr Tel** (408)879-9073. **2728**

CIVIL WAR TOKEN JOURNAL, THE. (US). **2780**

CIVILIAN-BASED DEFENSE. (US/0886-6015). **4039**

CIVILISATIONS. (BE/0009-8140). **5242**

CIVILTA CATTOLICA, LA. (IT/0009-8167). **5027**

CIVIS MUNDI. (NE/0030-3283). **4540**

CIVITAN MAGAZINE, THE. (US/0194-5785). **5230**

CIVITAS. (IT/0009-8191). **4468**

CJ INTERNATIONAL. (US/0882-0244). **3160**

CLA HANDBOOK AND MEMBERSHIP DIRECTORY / CATHOLIC LIBRARY ASSOCIATION. (US). **3202**

CLA JOURNAL. (US/0007-8549). **3273**

CLADISTICS. (US/0748-3007). **451**

CLAIMS (SEATTLE, WASH.). (US/0895-7991). **2878**

CLAIRLIEU : TIJDSCHRIFT GEWIJD ANN DE GESCHIEDENIS DER KRUISHEREN. (BE). **2683**

CLAO JOURNAL, THE. (US/0733-8902). **3873**

CLAREMORE DAILY PROGRESS. (US). **Adv Mgr:** Dave Kucifer, **Tel** (918)341-1195. **5731**

CLARENCE COURIER (CLARENCE, MO. : 1946. (US). **Adv Mgr:** Dennis Williams, **Tel** (816)699-2344. **5703**

CLARENDON NEWS (1990), THE. (US/1048-8170). **5748**

CLARIN : REVISTA DE CULTURA. (SP). **3461**

CLARINET (POCATELLO, IDAHO), THE. (US/0361-5553). **4110**

CLARION-LEDGER, THE. (US/0744-9526). **5700**

CLARION (NEW YORK. 1972). (US/0191-8079). **1815**

CLARION TECH JOURNAL, THE. (US/1044-4750). **AdvMgr Tel** (507)452-2824. **5095**

CLARISWORKS JOURNAL. (US/1059-6542). **1174**

CLARK'S DIRECTORY OF SOUTHERN HOSPITALS. (US/0069-4428). **3778**

CLARKSVILLE TIMES, THE. (US/1040-2489). **Adv Mgr:** Barbara Mitchell. **5748**

CLASS ACT. (US). **1732**

CLASS ACTION REPORTS. (US/0746-7168). **2951**

CLASS (NEW YORK, N.Y.). (US/0747-3826). **2486**

CLASSIC AND SPORTSCAR. (UK). **Adv Mgr:** Matthew Newell, **Tel** (908)665-7811. **5411**

CLASSIC BIKE. (UK/0142-890X). **1294**

CLASSIC IMAGES. (US/0275-8423). **4067**

CLASSIC TOY TRAINS. (US/0895-0997). **2772**

CLASSICAL AND MODERN LITERATURE. (US/0197-2227). **1075**

CLASSICAL ANTIQUITY. (US/0278-6656). **1075**

CLASSICAL BULLETIN (ST. LOUIS, MO.), THE. (US/0009-8337). **Adv Mgr:** L. Bolchazy. **1075**

CLASSICAL JOURNAL (CLASSICAL ASSOCIATION OF THE MIDDLE WEST AND SOUTH), THE. (US/0009-8353). **1075**

CLASSICAL MUSIC. (UK) **4110**

CLASSICAL OUTLOOK, THE. (US/0009-8361). **1075**

CLASSICAL QUARTERLY. (UK/0009-8388). **1075**

CLASSICAL REVIEW. (UK/0009-840X). **1076**

CLASSICAL WORLD, THE. (US/0009-8418). **Adv Mgr:** Lawrence Gaichas. **1076**

CLASSIFIED BUSINESS DIRECTORY OF THE STATE OF CONNECTICUT. (US/0069-4517). **657**

CLAVIER. (US/0009-854X). **4110**

CLAVIER'S PIANO EXPLORER. (US/0279-0858). **4110**

CLAY COUNTY FREE PRESS. (US). **5763**

CLAY MINERALS. (UK/0009-8558). **1438**

CLAY SCIENCE. (JA/0009-8574). **1353**

CLAY TIMES-JOURNAL, THE. (US/1053-9123). **Adv Mgr:** David Proctor & Linda McDonald. **5625**

CLAYTON COUNTY REGISTER, THE. (US). **5669**

CLAYTON NEWS. (US). **5723**

CLAYTON SUN. (US/0199-7270). **Adv Mgr:** J. Hewitt. **5652**

CLE JOURNAL AND REGISTER, THE. (US). **Adv Mgr:** Kathy Lawner, **Tel** (215)243-1659. **2951**

CLEAN AIR. (UK/0300-5143). **2226**

CLEANFAX (COLUMBUS, OHIO). (US/1042-6442). **Adv Mgr:** Bill Yeadon, **Tel** (800)669-0803. **5349**

CLEANING AND RESTORATION. (US/0886-9901). **Adv Mgr:** Collen Carpenter, **Tel** (410)235-6500. **5349**

CLEANING MANAGEMENT MAGAZINE. (US/1051-5720). **863**

CLEANROOMS (FLEMINGTON, N.J.). (US/1043-8017). **2860**

CLEARING HOUSE (MENASHA, WIS.). (US/0009-8655). **1732**

CLEARINGHOUSE REVIEW. (US/0009-868X). **3179**

CLEARWATER TRIBUNE. (US). **Adv Mgr:** Marty Donner, **Tel** (208)476-4571. **5656**

CLEARY NEWS. (US/0883-7716). **2443**

CLEBURNE NEWS (HEFLIN, ALA.). (US). **5626**

CLEF, LA. (CN). **2951**

CLEM LABINE'S TRADITIONAL BUILDING. (US/0898-0284). **295**

CLERMONT SUN (BATAVIA, OHIO : 1854). (US). **5727**

CLEVELAND ADVOCATE (CLEVELAND, TEX.), THE. (US/0746-7125). **5748**

CLEVELAND BAR JOURNAL (1968). (US/0160-1598). **Adv Mgr:** John Moore, **Tel** (216)721-2455. **2951**

CLEVELAND CLINIC JOURNAL OF MEDICINE. (US/0891-1150). **3564**

CLEVELAND ENGINEERING. (US/0009-8809). **1968**

CLEVELAND ENTERPRISE (CLEVELAND, OHIO. 1991). (US/1059-3055). **Adv Mgr:** Lee Kuegsegger. **1601**

CLEVELAND MAGAZINE. (US/0160-8533). **Adv Mgr:** Lute Harmon. **2486**

CLEVELAND PHYSICIAN. (US). **3564**

CLEVELAND STATE LAW REVIEW. (US/0009-8876). **Adv Mgr:** John Dyer, **Tel** (216)687-2336. **2951**

CLIC QUARTERLY. (US/0736-0045). **3202**

CLIENT COUNSELING UPDATE : CCU. (US/0276-752X). **2951**

CLIFTON RECORD, THE. (US). **Adv Mgr:** James W. Smith. **5748**

CLIMATE RESEARCH. (GW/0936-577X). **1422**

CLIMATIC CHANGE. (NE/0165-0009). **1422**

CLIMBING (ASPEN, COLO.). (US/0045-7159). **4871**

CLINCH VALLEY NEWS, THE. (US/8750-1171). **Adv Mgr:** Audria Liffel. **5758**

CLINCH VALLEY TIMES. (US). **Adv Mgr:** Allen Gregory. **5758**

CLINICA. (UK/0144-7777). **3564**

CLINICA CHIMICA ACTA. (NE/0009-8981). **972**

CLINICA DIETOLOGICA, LA. (IT/0392-7318). **4188**

CLINICA E INVESTIGACION EN GINECOLOGIA Y OBSTETRICIA. (SP/0210-573X). **3758**

CLINICA E LABORATORIO (ROMA). (IT/0391-2035). **Adv Mgr:** Dott Dalla, **Tel** 06-86207165. **3565**

CLINICA EUROPEA. (IT/0009-9007). **3565**

CLINICAL ABSTRACTS/CURRENT THERAPEUTIC FINDINGS. (US/1043-3031). **4296**

CLINICAL AND EXPERIMENTAL DERMATOLOGY. (UK/0307-6938). **3718**

CLINICAL AND EXPERIMENTAL HYPERTENSION. PART A, THEORY AND PRACTICE. (US/0730-0077). **3703**

CLINICAL AND EXPERIMENTAL HYPERTENSION. PART B, HYPERTENSION IN PREGNANCY. (US/0730-0085). **3758**

CLINICAL AND EXPERIMENTAL IMMUNOLOGY. (UK/0009-9104). **3667**

CLINICAL & EXPERIMENTAL METASTASIS. (UK/0262-0898). **3815**

CLINICAL AND EXPERIMENTAL OBSTETRICS & GYNECOLOGY. (IT/0390-6663). **3758**

CLINICAL AND EXPERIMENTAL OPTOMETRY. (AT/0816-4622). **Adv Mgr:** Sandra Shaw, **Tel** 03 663 6833. **4215**

CLINICAL AND EXPERIMENTAL PHARMACOLOGY & PHYSIOLOGY. (AT/0305-1870). **4296**

CLINICAL AND EXPERIMENTAL RHEUMATOLOGY. (IT/0392-856X). **3565**

CLINICAL AND INVESTIGATIVE MEDICINE. (UK/0147-958X). **3565**

CLINICAL AND LABORATORY HAEMATOLOGY. (UK/0141-9854). **3771**

CLINICAL AUTONOMIC RESEARCH : OFFICIAL JOURNAL OF THE CLINICAL AUTONOMIC RESEARCH SOCIETY. (UK/0959-9851). **3565**

CLINICAL BIOCHEMIST REVIEWS. (AT/0159-8090). **485**

CLINICAL BIOFEEDBACK AND HEALTH. (CN/0827-1038). **4581**

CLINICAL BIOMECHANICS (BRISTOL). (UK/0268-0033). **3565**

CLINICAL CARDIOLOGY (MAHWAH, N.J.). (US/0160-9289). **3703**

CLINICAL CHEMICA (OULU). (FI/0358-4879). **3565**

CLINICAL CHEMISTRY (REFERENCE EDITION). (US/0009-9147). **972**

CLINICAL CYTOGENETICS. (UK/0260-5872). **535**

CLINICAL ECOLOGY. (US/0735-9306). **3565**

CLINICAL EEG ELECTROENCEPHALOGRAPHY. (US/0009-9155). **3830**

CLINICAL ENDOCRINOLOGY (OXFORD). (UK/0300-0664). **3727**

CLINICAL EYE AND VISION CARE. (US/0953-4431). **3873**

CLINICAL GENETICS. (DK/0009-9163). **543**

CLINICAL GERONTOLOGIST. (US/0731-7115). **3750**

CLINICAL HEMORHEOLOGY. (US/0271-5198). **3771**

CLINICAL HEMOSTASIS REVIEW. (US/0894-1025). **Adv Mgr:** G. Ens, **Tel** (803)399-3336. **3565**

CLINICAL INFECTIOUS DISEASES. (US/1058-4838). **3712**

CLINICAL INTENSIVE CARE : INTERNATIONAL JOURNAL OF CRITICAL & CORONARY CARE MEDICINE. (UK/0956-3075). **Adv Mgr:** Wendy Reinders. **3703**

CLINICAL LAB PRODUCTS. (US/0192-1282). **3565**

CLINICAL LABORATORY MANAGEMENT REVIEW. (US/0888-7950). **4771**

CLINICAL LABORATORY REFERENCE. (US/0093-8076). **3566**

CLINICAL LABORATORY SCIENCE. (US/0894-959X). **3566**

CLINICAL MANAGEMENT : THE MAGAZINE OF THE AMERICAN PHYSICAL THERAPY ASSOCIATION. (US). **4380**

CLINICAL MICROBIOLOGY REVIEWS. (US/0893-8512). **561**

CLINICAL NEPHROLOGY. (GW/0301-0430). **3989**

CLINICAL NEUROLOGY AND NEUROSURGERY. (NE/0303-8467). **3830**

CLINICAL

Advertising Accepted Index

CLINICAL NEUROPATHOLOGY. (GW/0722-5091). **3894**

CLINICAL NUCLEAR MEDICINE. (US/0363-9762). **3847**

CLINICAL NURSING RESEARCH. (US/1054-7738). **3853**

CLINICAL NUTRITION. (UK/0261-5614). **4188**

CLINICAL OTOLARYNGOLOGY AND ALLIED SCIENCES. (UK/0307-7772). **3887**

CLINICAL PEDIATRICS. (US/0009-9228). **3902**

CLINICAL PHARMACOKINETICS. (US/0312-5963). **4296**

CLINICAL PHARMACOLOGY AND THERAPEUTICS. (US/0009-9236). **4297**

CLINICAL PHARMACY. (US/0278-2677). **4297**

CLINICAL PHYSIOLOGY (OXFORD). (UK/0144-5979). **579**

CLINICAL PSYCHIATRY NEWS. (US/0270-6644). **3923**

CLINICAL PSYCHOLOGY REVIEW. (US/0272-7358). **4581**

CLINICAL RADIOLOGY. (UK/0009-9260). **3940**

CLINICAL REVIEWS IN ALLERGY. (US/0731-8235). **3668**

CLINICAL SCIENCE (1979). (UK/0143-5221). **485**

CLINICAL SPORTS MEDICINE. (UK/0953-9875). **3953**

CLINICAL SUPERVISOR, THE. (US/0732-5223). **4581**

CLINICAL TRANSPLANTATION. (DK/0902-0063). **3566**

CLINIQUE OPHTALMOLOGIQUE PARIS, LA. (FR/0009-9368). **3873**

CLINTON CHRONICLE (CLINTON, S.C.), THE. (US/0893-035X). **Adv Mgr:** Larry Franklin. **5742**

CLINTON COUNTY NEWS. (US). **Adv Mgr:** Jeff Forsythe. **5659**

CLINTON COUNTY NEWS. (US). **Adv Mgr:** Preston Odette. **5691**

CLINTON DAILY ITEM. (US). **Adv Mgr:** Joan Marino. **5688**

CLINTON DAILY JOURNAL. (US). **Adv Mgr:** Terrie Baker. **5659**

CLINTON DAILY NEWS. (US). **Adv Mgr:** Carla Miller. **5731**

CLINTON MONTHLY, THE. (US/1075-1130). **4468**

CLINTON RECORDER. (US). **5645**

CLIO (FORT WAYNE, IND.). (US/0884-2043). **3376**

CLIO MEDICA. (NE/0366-676X). **3567**

CLIO (SANTO DOMINGO). (DR/0009-9376). **2844**

CLIPPING SERVICE. (CN/1182-6665). **5279**

CLIS OBSERVER. (II/0970-0943). **3202**

CLOCKMAKER (HINCKLEY). (UK/0961-5032). **Adv Mgr:** Susi Bolzicco, **Tel** same as publisher. **2772**

CLOCKWATCH REVIEW. (US/0740-9311). **317**

CLOSED-END FUND DIGEST. (US). **895**

CLOSING THE GAP. (US/0886-1935). **Adv Mgr:** Mary Ann Harty. **1877**

CLOSING THE GAP RESOURCE DIRECTORY. (US). **1877**

CLOTH DIRECTORY. (UK). **1083**

CLOTH DOLL, THE. (US/8755-2655). **371**

CLOVER HERALD. (US). **Adv Mgr:** Angie Ferguson. **5742**

CLOVERDALE WEEKLY REVEILLE. (US). **5634**

CLOVIS INDEPENDENT (CLOVIS, CALIF. 1946), THE. (US/1068-5944). **Adv Mgr:** Deborah Brown. **5634**

CLOVIS NEWS-JOURNAL. (US). **Adv Mgr:** Mikie Bohannan. **5712**

CLS MARKET PLACE. (US/1061-6020). **657**

CLUB INDUSTRY. (US/0747-8283). **2596**

CLUB INTERNATIONAL (NEWTOWN, CONN.). (US/0747-0819). **3994**

CLUB LIVING. (US/0160-6166). **4890**

CLUB MANAGEMENT IN AUSTRALIA. (AT/0045-7205). **5230**

CLUES (BOWLING GREEN, OHIO). (US/0742-4248). **5074**

CLUMBER SPANIEL CORRESPONDENCE. (AT). **4286**

CLYDE REPUBLICAN (CLYDE, KAN. : 1986). (US). **Adv Mgr:** Ann Carlson. **5675**

CMAJ. CANADIAN MEDICAL ASSOCIATION JOURNAL. (CN/0820-3946). **3567**

CMBH CRIMINAL BEHAVIOUR AND MENTAL HEALTH. (UK/0957-9664). **3160**

CMEA NEWS. (US/0007-8638). **4110**

CMJ NEW MUSIC REPORT. (US/0890-0795). **4110**

CMLEA JOURNAL. (US/0196-3309). **3202**

CMM, CONFECTIONERY MANUFACTURE AND MARKETING. (UK/0007-8654). **3477**

CNC WEST. (US/0747-3362). **3477**

CO-EXISTENCE (DORDRECHT). (NE/0587-5994). **4518**

CO-OPERATEUR AGRICOLE, LE. (CN/0315-1204). **Adv Mgr:** Andre Leger. **75**

COACHING VOLLEYBALL. (US/0894-4237). **Adv Mgr:** Kevin Kaneshiro. **4890**

COACHING WOMEN'S BASKETBALL. (US/0894-4245). **4890**

COAL ABSTRACTS. (UK/0309-4979). **1961**

COAL CALENDAR. (UK/0143-6287). **1935**

COAL (CHICAGO, ILL. : 1988). (US/1040-7820). **2137**

COAL FOCUS / THE COAL ASSOCIATION OF CANADA. (CN/0821-7068). **2137**

COAL PEOPLE. (US/0748-6073). **2728**

COAL PREPARATION (NEW YORK, N.Y.). (US/0734-9343). **2137**

COAL VALLEY NEWS. (US/0745-7111). **5763**

COALFIELD PROGRESS, THE. (US/0889-3330). **5758**

COALINGA RECORD. (US). **Adv Mgr:** Jeff Rice. **5634**

COALTRANS INTERNATIONAL. (UK). **2137**

COALTRANS WORCESTER PARK. (UK/0269-381X). **1935**

COAST MARINE & TRANSPORTATION DIRECTORY. (US). **5379**

COASTAL COURIER (HINESVILLE, GA.), THE. (US/1047-6636). **Adv Mgr:** Matt Newton. **5653**

COASTAL CRUISING. (US/0897-750X). **Adv Mgr:** R. White, **Tel** (919)728-4661. **4890**

COASTAL MANAGEMENT. (US/0892-0753). **2190**

COASTAL OBSERVER (PAWLEYS ISLAND, S.C.). (US/8750-3425). **Adv Mgr:** Squeaky Swenson. **5742**

COASTAL PLAINS FARMER. ALABAMA, FLORIDA ED. (US/0737-1756). **75**

COASTGUARD. (UK). **4175**

COAT OF ARMS, THE. (UK/0010-003X). **2443**

COATING. (SZ/0590-8450). **2011**

COATINGS. (CN/0225-6363). **Adv Mgr:** L. Bonilowsky, **Tel** (416)844-9773. **4223**

COATNEY/COURTNEY EXCHANGE. (US). **2443**

COCHRANE TIMES. (CN/0319-745X). **5782**

COCKRELL CONNECTION, THE. (US/0891-5296). **2443**

COCONUT BULLETIN (LUNUWILA, SRI LANKA). (CE/0255-4119). **167**

COCONUT STATISTICS / COMPILED AND EXPANDED BY UCAP RESEARCH DEPARTMENT. (PH). **152**

COCONUT TELEGRAPH. (HO). **2511**

CODA MAGAZINE. (CN/0820-926X). **4110**

CODESRIA BULLETIN. (SG/0850-8712). **5195**

CODY ENTERPRISE, THE. (US/0747-2498). **Adv Mgr:** John T. Malmberg. **5772**

COFFEE & COCOA INTERNATIONAL. (UK/0262-5938). **2366**

COFFEY COUNTY TODAY. (US/0745-838X). **Adv Mgr:** B. J. Peterson. **5675**

COGENERATION & RESOURCE RECOVERY. (US). **1935**

COGNITION & EMOTION. (UK/0269-9931). **4581**

COGNITION AND INSTRUCTION. (US/0737-0008). **1891**

COGNITION (SCARBOROUGH). (CN/0227-0781). **167**

COGNITIVE DEVELOPMENT. (US/0885-2014). **4581**

COGNITIVE SCIENCE. (US/0364-0213). **1212**

COI. COUNTERTRADE AND OFFSET INTELLIGENCE. (UK/0950-916X). **Adv Mgr:** J Wain, **Tel** 071 584 1333. **827**

COIFFURE DE PARIS, LA. (FR). **402**

COIN MAGAZINE. (US). **2780**

COIN NEWS (HINDHEAD, ENGLAND). (UK/0955-4386). **Adv Mgr:** C. Hartman. **2780**

COIN SLOT (LUZERNE, PA.), THE. (US/0745-8533). **250**

COIN WORLD. (US/0010-0447). **2780**

COIN YEARBOOK. (UK/0307-6571). **2780**

COINAGE. (US/0010-0455). **2780**

COINS (IOLA, WIS.). (US/0010-0471). **2780**

COINS MARKET VALUES. (UK). **2780**

COKEMAKING INTERNATIONAL. (GW/0937-9258). **2137**

COLADA. (SP/0010-0544). **4000**

COLCHESTER COUNTY, NOVA SCOTIA, TRAVEL GUIDE. (CN/0828-7651). **5466**

COLD REGIONS SCIENCE AND TECHNOLOGY. (NE/0165-232X). **1968**

COLECCION ESTUDIOS CIEPLAN. (CL/0716-0631). **1552**

COLECCION JUVENIL MC. (SP). **2278**

COLEMAN COUNTY CHRONICLE. (US). **Adv Mgr:** Stan Brudney. **5748**

COLLAGE (CAMP HILL, PA.). (US/0883-2781). **4760**

COLLECTIBLE AUTOMOBILE. (US/0742-812X). **5411**

COLLECTIBLE NEWSPAPERS. (US/1076-4356). **2772**

COLLECTIBLES CANADA. (CN). **Adv Mgr:** C. Head, **Tel** (905)646-7744. **250**

COLLECTION BUILDING. (US/0160-4953). **3202**

COLLECTION FORUM (OTTAWA). (CN/0831-4985). **4165**

COLLECTION MANAGEMENT. (US/0146-2679). **3202**

COLLECTION PALEO-QUEBEC. (CN/0821-3801). **266**

COLLECTIONS (COLUMBIA, S.C.). (US/1046-2252). **4087**

COLLECTIONS FOR A HISTORY OF STAFFORDSHIRE. (UK). **2684**

COLLECTOR CAR NEWS. (US/0888-1944). **2772**

COLLECTORS BULLETIN (CANTON, ILL.). (US/1048-0951). **Adv Mgr:** T. Behymer, **Tel** (309)668-2211. **2780**

COLLECTORS JOURNAL (VINTON). (US/0164-6915). **Adv Mgr:** Leann Jones, **Tel** (319)472-4763. **5669**

COLLECTORS' SHOWCASE (SAN DIEGO, CALIF.). (US/0744-5989). **250**

COLLEGE AND JUNIOR TENNIS. (US/0279-1153). **4890**

COLLEGE & RESEARCH LIBRARIES. (US/0010-0870). **3203**

COLLEGE BOUND (EVANSTON, ILL.). (US/1068-7912). **1816**

COLLEGE BROADCASTER. (US/1055-0461). **Adv Mgr:** Gordon Kent, **Tel** (401)863-2225. **1130**

COLLEGE COMPOSITION AND COMMUNICATION. (US/0010-096X). **1816**

COLLEGE ENGLISH. (US/0010-0994). **3274**

COLLEGE HOCKEY. (US/1061-6357). **4890**

COLLEGE LITERATURE. (US/0093-3139). **3376**

COLLEGE MATHEMATICS JOURNAL, THE. (US/0746-8342). **3500**

COLLEGE MEDIA DIRECTORY, THE. (US/1046-4255). **1816**

COLLEGE MUSIC SYMPOSIUM. (US/0069-5696). **4110**

COLLEGE PLANNING QUARTERLY. (US/1071-3751). **1732**

COLLEGE STORE EXECUTIVE. (US/0010-1141). **922**

COLLEGE STORE JOURNAL, THE. (US/0010-115X). **1817**

COLLEGE TEACHING. (US/8756-7555). **1817**

COLLEGE UNION & ON-CAMPUS HOSPITALITY. (US/0887-431X). **1090**

COLLEGIATE BASEBALL. (US/0530-9751). **Adv Mgr:** Diane Pavlovich. **4890**

COLLEGIATE MICROCOMPUTER. (US/0731-4213). **1266**

COLLETTIVITA CONVIVENZE. (IT/1120-639X). **4771**

COLLIE REVIEW. (US/0744-0731). **4286**

COLLIERVILLE HERALD, THE. (US). **5744**

COLLIERY GUARDIAN. (UK/0010-1281). **2137**

Advertising Accepted Index — COMMUNICATIONS

COLLIN CHRONICLES. (US/1060-0949). **2443**

COLLINSVILLE HERALD (COLLINSVILLE, ILL.), THE. (US/0883-6574). **Adv Mgr:** Doug Cooper. **5659**

COLLISION. (US/0739-7437). **5411**

COLLOID AND POLYMER SCIENCE. (GW/0303-402X). **1050**

COLLOQUIUM. (AT/0588-3237). **4948**

COLOMBIA MEDICA : CM. (CK/0120-8322). **3567**

COLONIAL ECHO. (US). **1090**

COLONIAL LATIN AMERICAN HISTORICAL REVIEW. (US/1063-5769). **Adv Mgr:** Denise Padilla, **Tel** (505)277-1370. **2728**

COLONIAL WATERBIRDS. (US/0738-6028). **5617**

COLOQUIO/CIENCIAS. (PO/0870-7650). **5095**

COLOR PUBLISHING. (US/1055-9701). **Adv Mgr:** Robert Holton, **Tel** (508)692-2157. **4813**

COLOR RESEARCH AND APPLICATION. (US/0361-2317). **5095**

COLORADO BANKRUPTCY COURT REPORTER, THE. (US/1048-3683). **2952**

COLORADO BUSINESS MAGAZINE : CBM. (US/0898-6363). **658**

COLORADO COUNTRY LIFE. (US). **4760**

COLORADO EDUCATION DIRECTORY. (US/0588-4349). **1732**

COLORADO ENGINEER, THE. (US/0010-1583). **1968**

COLORADO ENVIRONMENTAL REPORT, THE. (US/0891-3463). **2190**

COLORADO GENEALOGIST, THE. (US/0010-1613). **Adv Mgr:** Barbara Henritze, **Tel** (303)499-3750. **2443**

COLORADO GREEN. (US/0195-0045). **2412**

COLORADO HOMES & LIFESTYLES. (US/0272-6904). **2904**

COLORADO LABOR ADVOCATE. (US/0190-8235). **5642**

COLORADO LAWYER. (US/0363-7867). **Adv Mgr:** Suellen Palcanis, **Tel** (303)377-1673. **2952**

COLORADO LIBRARIES. (US/0147-9733). **3203**

COLORADO MEDICINE (1980). (US/0199-7343). **3567**

COLORADO MUNICIPALITIES. (US/0010-1664). **4639**

COLORADO-NORTH REVIEW. (US/0194-0589). **3377**

COLORADO NURSE (1985). (US/8750-846X). **3854**

COLORADO PROSPECTOR. (US/0010-1702). **2729**

COLORADO REVIEW (1985). (US/1046-3348). **3340**

COLORADO SPRINGS GAZETTE-TELEGRAPH. (US). **Adv Mgr:** Doug Barnett, **Tel** (719)636-0113. **5642**

COLORADO WHEAT GROWER. (US/1078-5612). **167**

COLORADO WOMAN. (US/1042-9549). **Adv Mgr:** Sharon Silvas. **5553**

COLORBAT LAB PRO. (US/1055-0704). **347**

COLOURAGE. (II/0010-1826). **5349**

COLTON CLARION. (US/0896-9590). **2443**

COLUMBIA, A MAGAZINE OF POETRY AND PROSE. (US/0161-486X). **3377**

COLUMBIA COUNTY INDEPENDENT, THE. (US). **Adv Mgr:** Charles Schram. **5715**

COLUMBIA DAILY SPECTATOR. (US). **1090**

COLUMBIA DAILY TRIBUNE. (US). **5703**

COLUMBIA FLIER. (US/0192-7841). **5686**

COLUMBIA GORGE VISITOR & RECREATION GUIDE (1992). (US/1063-763X). **Adv Mgr:** Marie Cordell. **4849**

COLUMBIA HUMAN RIGHTS LAW REVIEW. (US/0090-7944). **4506**

COLUMBIA JESTER, THE. (US). **1090**

COLUMBIA JOURNAL OF ENVIRONMENTAL LAW. (US/0098-4582). **3110**

COLUMBIA JOURNAL OF TRANSNATIONAL LAW. (US/0010-1931). **3126**

COLUMBIA JOURNAL OF WORLD BUSINESS, THE. (US/0022-5428). **658**

COLUMBIA LAW REVIEW. (US/0010-1958). **2953**

COLUMBIA MAGAZINE (COLUMBIA, MD.). (US/0889-2342). **Adv Mgr:** Susan Econ. **2531**

COLUMBIA MISSOURIAN. (US/0747-1874). **Adv Mgr:** Jack Swartz. **5703**

COLUMBIA (NEW YORK, N.Y. 1978). (US/0162-3893). **1090**

COLUMBIA NEWS-TIMES, THE. (US/1053-7511). **Adv Mgr:** Gainette Haywood. **5653**

COLUMBIA (RHINEBECK, N.Y.), THE. (US/8755-2914). **2443**

COLUMBIA SPECTATOR. (US). **5715**

COLUMBIAN (VANCOUVER, WASH.). (US/1043-4151). **Adv Mgr:** Susan Hirtzel. **5760**

COLUMBIANA. (US/0893-276X). **2531**

COLUMBUS GAZETTE (COLUMBUS JUNCTION, IOWA), THE. (US/0747-2889). **Adv Mgr:** Tammy Virzi. **5669**

COLUMBUS JOURNAL-REPUBLICAN (COLUMBUS, WIS. : 1971). (US). **5766**

COLUMBUS TIMES, THE. (US). **5653**

COLUSA COUNTY SUN HERALD. (US/0897-8743). **5634**

COMBAT NATURE PERIGUEUX. (FR/0184-7473). **Adv Mgr:** same as editor. **2163**

COMBINED INDEX FOR THE JOURNALS SULPHUR, NITROGEN AND PHOSPHORUS & POTASSIUM. (UK). **1023**

COMBROAD. (UK/0951-0826). **1130**

COMBUSTION SCIENCE AND TECHNOLOGY. (US/0010-2202). **1051**

COME-ALL-YE (HATBORO, PA.). (US/0736-6132). **2319**

COMERCIO E INDUSTRIA DE LA MADERA. (SP/1131-8694). **633**

COMERCIO E INDUSTRIA (SAN SALVADOR, EL SALVADOR). (ES). **828**

COMIC PRESS NEWS. (US). **4859**

COMIC TALE EASY READER. (US/0748-2264). **1062**

COMICS JOURNAL, THE. (US/0194-7869). **377**

COMITE INTERNATIONAL DES POIDS ET MESURES, COMITE CONSULTATIF D'ELECTRICITE. RAPPORT. (FR). **4030**

COMLA NEWSLETTER. (JM/0378-1070). **3203**

COMMACK NEWS. (US/0746-7508). **Adv Mgr:** Jen Paley. **5715**

COMMAND (DENVER, COLO.). (US/0010-2474). **Adv Mgr:** Ted Shadid. **4039**

COMMAND MAGAZINE (SAN LUIS OBISPO, CALIF.). (US/1059-5651). **Adv Mgr:** Chris. **4039**

COMMENTAIRE (JULLIARD). (FR/0180-8214). **3377**

COMMENTARY (NEW YORK). (US/0010-2601). **5047**

COMMENTARY (SINGAPORE). (SI/0084-8956). **2503**

COMMENTS ON ARGENTINE TRADE (BUENOS AIRES, ARGENTINA : 1985). (AG). **828**

COMMENTS ON ASTROPHYSICS. (US/0146-2970). **394**

COMMENTS ON ATOMIC AND MOLECULAR PHYSICS. (UK/0010-2687). **4446**

COMMENTS ON MODERN CHEMISTRY. PART A, COMMENTS ON INORGANIC CHEMISTRY. (UK/0260-3594). **1036**

COMMENTS ON PLASMA PHYSICS AND CONTROLLED FUSION. (US/0374-2806). **4400**

COMMERCE (HACKENSACK, N.Y.). (US/0745-077X). **658**

COMMERCE INTERNATIONAL. (UK/0010-2733). **828**

COMMERCE NEWS. (CN/0704-8017). **819**

COMMERCE NEWS, THE. (US). **Adv Mgr:** Scott Buffington. **5653**

COMMERCIAL AGRICULTURE IN ZIMBABWE. (RH). **75**

COMMERCIAL AND FINANCIAL CHRONICLE (1978), THE. (US/0163-2876). **895**

COMMERCIAL AND INDUSTRIAL FLOORSPACE STATISTICS, WALES. (UK/0262-5334). **5325**

COMMERCIAL AND INDUSTRIAL REGISTER OF SOUTHERN AFRICA, THE. (SA). **Adv Mgr:** Alleen du Preez, **Tel** (031) 701 7026. **1602**

COMMERCIAL APPEAL, THE. (US/0745-4856). **5744**

COMMERCIAL FISHERIES NEWS. (US/0273-6713). **2299**

COMMERCIAL FISHING. (UK/0143-652X). **2299**

COMMERCIAL FISHING. (NZ/0110-1730). **2299**

COMMERCIAL LAW JOURNAL. (US/0010-3055). **3098**

COMMERCIAL LAWS OF EUROPE. (UK/0141-7258). **3098**

COMMERCIAL RECORD (SOUTH WINDSOR, CT.), THE. (US/0010-3098). **4836**

COMMERCIAL RENOVATION. (US/0747-0134). **608**

COMMERCIAL-REVIEW (PORTLAND, IND. : DAILY : 1922). (US). **Adv Mgr:** Don Gillespie, **Tel** (219)726-8141. **5663**

COMMERCIAL REVIEW (PORTLAND, OR.). (US/0010-3101). **75**

COMMITTEE BULLETIN. (AT). **4639**

COMMITTEE ON EAST ASIAN LIBRARIES BULLETIN. (US/0148-6225). **3203**

COMMLAW CONSPECTUS. (US/1068-5871). **2953**

COMMON BOUNDARY, THE. (US/0885-8500). **4582**

COMMON GROUND. (UK/0010-325X). **4949**

COMMON GROUND (CHARLOTTETOWN). (CN/0715-478X). **5553**

COMMON GROUND (VANCOUVER). (CN/0824-0698). **3774**

COMMON LIVES, LESBIAN LIVES. (US/0891-6969). **2794**

COMMON MARKET LAW REPORTS. (UK/0588-7445). **2953**

COMMON MARKET LAW REVIEW. (NE/0165-0750). **2953**

COMMON SENSE ECONOMICS. (CN/0319-7549). **1470**

COMMON SENSE PEST CONTROL QUARTERLY. (US/8756-7881). **4244**

COMMONWEAL. (US/0010-3330). **2531**

COMMONWEALTH. (FR/0395-6989). **3377**

COMMONWEALTH ESSAYS & STUDIES. (FR). **3377**

COMMONWEALTH FORESTRY HANDBOOK, THE. (UK). **2377**

COMMONWEALTH FORESTRY REVIEW, THE. (UK/0010-3381). **2399**

COMMONWEALTH-JOURNAL (SOMERSET, KY.), THE. (US/0899-1839). **Adv Mgr:** David Trimble, **Tel** (606)678-8191. **5680**

COMMONWEALTH LAW BULLETIN. (UK/0305-0718). **2953**

COMMONWEALTH OF DOMINICA CONSOLIDATED INDEX OF STATUTES AND SUBSIDIARY LEGISLATION TO ... . (BB). **3126**

COMMONWEALTH, THE. (US). **5703**

COMMUNICATE (HIGH WYCOMBE). (UK/0264-4509). **Adv Mgr:** Stuart Giddings, **Tel** 071 403 8989. **1151**

COMMUNICATIE. (BE/0771-7342). **1106**

COMMUNICATING TOGETHER. (CN/0822-0638). **1106**

COMMUNICATIO SOCIALIS YEARBOOK. (II/0970-0382). **4949**

COMMUNICATION ARTS. (US/0010-3519). **377**

COMMUNICATION - CANADIAN CO-ORDINATING COUNCIL ON DEAFNESS. (CN/0228-5401). **4385**

COMMUNICATION EDUCATION. (US/0363-4523). **1106**

COMMUNICATION ET INFORMATION. (CN/0382-7798). **1106**

COMMUNICATION MONOGRAPHS. (US/0363-7751). **1107**

COMMUNICATION OUTLOOK. (US/0161-4126). **1107**

COMMUNICATION QUARTERLY. (US/0146-3373). **1107**

COMMUNICATION RESEARCH REPORTS. (US/0882-4096). **1107**

COMMUNICATION THEORY. (US/1050-3293). **1107**

COMMUNICATION WORLD (SAN FRANCISCO, CALIF.). (US/0744-7612). **Adv Mgr:** T. Gradie. **1107**

COMMUNICATIONS & COGNITION. (BE/0378-0880). **1108**

COMMUNICATIONS AND THE LAW. (US/0162-9093). **2954**

COMMUNICATIONS FROM THE INTERNATIONAL BRECHT SOCIETY. (US/0740-8943). **3377**

COMMUNICATIONS IN ALGEBRA. (US/0092-7872). **3500**

COMMUNICATIONS IN APPLIED NUMERICAL METHODS. (UK/0748-8025). **3500**

COMMUNICATIONS IN LABORATORY MEDICINE. (UK/0267-3320). **3567**

COMMUNICATIONS — Advertising Accepted Index

COMMUNICATIONS IN PARTIAL DIFFERENTIAL EQUATIONS. (US/0360-5302). **3501**

COMMUNICATIONS IN SOIL SCIENCE AND PLANT ANALYSIS. (US/0010-3624). **167**

COMMUNICATIONS IN STATISTICS : SIMULATION AND COMPUTATION. (US/0361-0918). **1282**

COMMUNICATIONS IN STATISTICS : STOCHASTIC MODELS. (US/0882-0287). **5325**

COMMUNICATIONS IN STATISTICS : THEORY AND METHODS. (US/0361-0926). **3501**

COMMUNICATIONS OF THE ACM. (US/0001-0782). **1175**

COMMUNICATIONS OF THE DUBLIN INSTITUTE FOR ADVANCED STUDIES. SERIES D. GEOPHYSICAL BULLETIN. (IE/0070-7422). **1404**

COMMUNICATIONS ON PURE AND APPLIED MATHEMATICS. (US/0010-3640). **3501**

COMMUNICATIONS REPORT. SYDNEY. (AT/1035-6959). **1152**

COMMUNICATOR OF PHI DELTA CHI FRATERNITY, THE. (US/0746-3979). **5230**

COMMUNIO (SPOKANE, WASH.). (US/0094-2065). **Adv Mgr:** David Spesia. **4949**

COMMUNIQUE (COLUMBUS, OHIO). (US/1043-0695). **4949**

COMMUNIQUE HEBROMADAIRE (INSTITUT NATIONAL DE STATISTIQUE (BELGIUM) : 1982). (BE/0771-0410). **5325**

COMMUNIQUE / HUMAN FACTORS ASSOCIATION OF CANADA. (CN/0712-936X). **2860**

COMMUNIQUE (KENT). (US/0164-775X). **4582**

COMMUNIQUE - LEARNING DISABILITIES ASSOCIATION OF ONTARIO. (CN/0843-2236). **Adv Mgr:** K. Quinn. **1877**

COMMUNIQUE NATIONAL DE LA SCRP. (CN/0710-071X). **757**

COMMUNIQUE (RICHMOND, VA). (US). **1319**

COMMUNIQUE - SYNCHRO SWIM CANADA. (CN/0226-8701). **4891**

COMMUNIQUER. (FR). **1108**

COMMUNITIES (LOUISA). (US/0199-9346). **2818**

COMMUNITY ALTERNATIVES. (US/1052-7656). **5279**

COMMUNITY & JUNIOR COLLEGE LIBRARIES. (US/0276-3915). **3203**

COMMUNITY ANIMAL CONTROL. (US/0278-2863). **226**

COMMUNITY ASSOCIATION LAW REPORTER. (US/0190-1192). **Adv Mgr:** Jeff Sanderson. **2954**

COMMUNITY COLLEGE JOURNALIST : OFFICIAL PUBLICATION OF THE COMMUNITY COLLEGE JOURNALISM ASSOCIATION. (US). **2918**

COMMUNITY COLLEGE WEEK. (US/1041-5726). **1817**

COMMUNITY CRIER, THE. (US/0193-077X). **Adv Mgr:** Jack Armstrong. **5691**

COMMUNITY DENTISTRY AND ORAL EPIDEMIOLOGY. (DK/0301-5661). **1319**

COMMUNITY DEVELOPMENT JOURNAL. (UK/0010-3802). **5242**

COMMUNITY EDUCATION JOURNAL. (US/0045-7736). **Adv Mgr:** Ursula Ellis. **1733**

COMMUNITY HERALD (MONONA, WIS.), THE. (US/0745-6646). **5766**

COMMUNITY JOBS. (US/0195-1157). **Adv Mgr:** Jim Clark, **Tel** (212)475-1001. **1660**

COMMUNITY/JUNIOR COLLEGE. (US/0277-6774). **1817**

COMMUNITY LIVING OF FLORIDA. (US). **Adv Mgr:** Jeff Sanderson. **4639**

COMMUNITY NEWS (BROWNS MILLS, N.J.), THE. (US/0745-8150). **5709**

COMMUNITY PRESS (MILLBROOK, ALA.). (US/0739-9219). **5626**

COMMUNITY PUBLICATION RATES AND DATA. (US/0162-8887). **757**

COMMUNITY QUARTERLY. (AT/0814-401X). **2818**

COMMUNITY RADIO NEWS. (US). **1130**

COMMUNITY REVIEW (NEW BRUNSWICK). (US/0163-8475). **1818**

COMMUNITY SERVICE BUSINESS. (US/0747-6086). **5196**

COMMUNITY, TECHNICAL, AND JUNIOR COLLEGE JOURNAL. (US/0884-7169). **1818**

COMMUNITY TRANSPORTATION REPORTER : CTR. (US/0895-4437). **Adv Mgr:** Bill Shoemaker, **Tel** (302)436-4375. **5380**

COMMUTATION & TRANSMISSION. (FR/0242-1283). **Adv Mgr:** same as editor. **1152**

COMMUTER (COLLEGE PARK, MD.), THE. (US/0734-3817). **5380**

COMMUTER / REGIONAL AIRLINE NEWS. (US/1040-5402). **5380**

COMMUTER WORLD. (UK/0265-4504). **16**

COMPACT CAMBRIDGE MEDLINE [COMPUTER FILE]. (US). **3567**

COMPANIES HOLDING BOILER AND PRESSURE VESSEL CERTIFICATES OF AUTHORIZATION FOR USE OF CODE SYMBOL STAMPS. (US/0148-6594). **2112**

COMPANIES HOLDING NUCLEAR CERTIFICATES OF AUTHORIZATION. (US/0272-6777). **2154**

COMPANION (TORONTO). (CN/0010-3985). **5028**

COMPANY LAW DIGEST (NEW DELHI, INDIA). (II). **3098**

COMPANY LAW JOURNAL (NEW DELHI, INDIA). (II). **3098**

COMPANY RECOGNITION STUDY. RETAILER EDITION. (US/0275-7486). **1969**

COMPANY SECRETARY'S REVIEW. (UK/0309-703X). **3098**

COMPARABLE WORTH PROJECT NEWSLETTER. (US/0278-4122). **658**

COMPARATIVE AND INTERNATIONAL LAW JOURNAL OF SOUTHERN AFRICA, THE. (SA/0010-4051). **3126**

COMPARATIVE BIOCHEMISTRY AND PHYSIOLOGY. A, COMPARATIVE PHYSIOLOGY. (UK/0300-9629). **579**

COMPARATIVE BIOCHEMISTRY AND PHYSIOLOGY. B, COMPARATIVE BIOCHEMISTRY. (UK/0305-0491). **486**

COMPARATIVE ECONOMIC STUDIES. (US/0888-7233). **Adv Mgr:** Michael R. Dohan, Ph.D., **Tel** (718)997-5461. **1470**

COMPARATIVE EDUCATION. (UK/0305-0068). **1733**

COMPARATIVE LITERATURE IN CANADA. (CN/0045-7795). **3377**

COMPARATIVE LITERATURE STUDIES (URBANA). (US/0010-4132). **3377**

COMPARATIVE PHYSIOLOGY AND ECOLOGY. (II/0379-0436). **579**

COMPARATIVE STATE POLITICS. (US/1047-1006). **Adv Mgr:** Jackie Wright, **Tel** (218)786-6574. **4469**

COMPARATIVE STRATEGY. (US/0149-5933). **4518**

COMPARE. (UK/0305-7925). **1891**

COMPEL. (IE/0332-1649). **2039**

COMPENDIUM NEWSLETTER, THE. (US/0198-9103). **2190**

COMPENDIUM (NEWTOWN, PA.). (US/0894-1009). **Adv Mgr:** Dan Perkins. **1319**

COMPENDIUM ON CONTINUING EDUCATION FOR THE PRACTICING VETERINARIAN, THE. (US/0193-1903). **5508**

COMPETITION ANGLER. (US/1047-1669). **4871**

COMPETITIONS (LOUISVILLE, KY.). (US/1058-6539). **295**

COMPETITIVE ADVANCES. MATERIALS AND PROCESSES. (US). **5095**

COMPETITIVE GRADE FINDER FOR THE PAPER AND GRAPHIC ARTS INDUSTRIES, THE. (US). **Adv Mgr:** Mark Subers. **4233**

COMPETITIVE INTELLIGENCE REVIEW. (US/1058-0247). **659**

COMPILER, THE. (US/0742-2784). **1175**

COMPLEAT GOLFER. (SA/1015-8014). **Adv Mgr:** Dale Hayes, **Tel** 011 8837820. **4891**

COMPLEAT MOTHER, THE. (CN/0829-8564). **3759**

COMPLEMENTARY MEDICINE INDEX : CURRENT AWARENESS TOPICS SERVICES. (UK/0950-6667). **3567**

COMPLETE GUIDE TO AMERICAN POCKET WATCHES, THE. (US/0730-2924). **2916**

COMPLEX VARIABLES THEORY AND APPLICATION. (US/0278-1077). **3501**

COMPLIANCE ENGINEERING. (US/0898-3577). **Adv Mgr:** Michael Costa and Michael Mintzer, **Tel** same as publisher. **1152**

COMPOLUX. (IT). **2039**

COMPOSER NEWS. (US/0894-5950). **4111**

COMPOSER/USA. (US). **4111**

COMPOSITE POLYMERS. (UK/0952-6919). **4454**

COMPOSITE STRUCTURES. (UK/0263-8223). **2101**

COMPOSITES. (UK/0010-4361). **2101**

COMPOSITES & ADHESIVES NEWSLETTER, THE. (US/0888-1227). **1023**

COMPOSITES SCIENCE AND TECHNOLOGY. (UK/0266-3538). **2101**

COMPOSITIO MATHEMATICA. (NE/0010-437X). **3501**

COMPOSITION STUDIES : FRESHMAN ENGLISH NEWS. (US). **3274**

COMPOUNDINGS. (US/1042-508X). **4253**

COMPREHENSIVE DISSERTATION INDEX. (US). **3567**

COMPRESSED AIR (1965). (US/0010-4426). **1602**

COMPTES RENDUS DE THERAPEUTIQUE ET DE PHARMACOLOGIE CLINIQUE. (FR/0293-9908). **Adv Mgr:** Delorme. **4297**

COMPTES RENDUS DES TRAVAUX DES COLLOQUES. (FR/0223-6355). **4400**

COMPU-MART (RICHARDSON, TEX.). (US/1072-3544). **Adv Mgr:** Jim Reilly. **1236**

COMPU-MGR TELE-MGR. (US). **Adv Mgr:** Jim Reilly. **1175**

COMPUTATIONAL COMPLEXITY. (SZ/1016-3328). **Adv Mgr:** Bavdo Perry. **3501**

COMPUTATIONAL INTELLIGENCE. (CN/0824-7935). **1212**

COMPUTATIONAL LINGUISTICS (ASSOCIATION FOR COMPUTATIONAL LINGUISTICS). (US/0891-2017). **1175**

COMPUTE (GREENSBORO). (US/0194-357X). **1266**

COMPUTER AIDED DESIGN. (UK/0010-4485). **1231**

COMPUTER-AIDED ENGINEERING. (US/0733-3536). **1228**

COMPUTER-AIDED PROCESS CONTROL ABSTRACTS. (UK/0955-4319). **1232**

COMPUTER & ELECTRONICS GRADUATE, THE. (US/0882-200X). **4203**

COMPUTER & VIDEOGIOCHI. (IT). **4859**

COMPUTER APPLICATIONS IN THE BIOSCIENCES. (UK/0266-7061). **1176**

COMPUTER BUYER'S GUIDE AND HANDBOOK. (US/0738-9213). **Adv Mgr:** Mary Wohlberg. **1266**

COMPUTER COMMUNICATIONS. (UK/0140-3664). **1240**

COMPUTER DIRECTORY AND BUYERS' GUIDE, THE. (US/0734-0583). **1244**

COMPUTER DISPLAY REVIEW, THE. (US/0010-4582). **1264**

COMPUTER EDUCATION. (UK/0010-4590). **Adv Mgr:** Dr. HLW Jackson. **1222**

COMPUTER GAMES STRATEGY PLUS. (US). **1230**

COMPUTER GAMING WORLD. (US/0744-6667). **1230**

COMPUTER GRAPHICS FORUM : A JOURNAL OF THE EUROPEAN ASSOCIATION FOR COMPUTER GRAPHICS. (NE/0167-7055). **Adv Mgr:** Paula Stewart, **Tel** 0865 791100. **1232**

COMPUTER GRAPHICS WORLD. (US/0271-4159). **1232**

COMPUTER GRAPHICS WORLD BUYERS GUIDE. (US/0895-2760). **1232**

COMPUTER HOT LINE. (US/0192-6349). **1176**

COMPUTER INDUSTRY LITIGATION REPORTER. (US/0740-1469). **1303**

COMPUTER-INTEGRATED MANUFACTURING SYSTEMS. (UK/0951-5240). **1228**

COMPUTER JOURNAL (KALISPELL, MONT.). (US/0748-9331). **1177**

COMPUTER LANGUAGE. (US/0749-2839). **1218**

COMPUTER LIVING, NEW YORK. (US/8750-4375). **1177**

COMPUTER (LONG BEACH, CALIF.). (US/0018-9162). **1266**

COMPUTER MUSIC JOURNAL. (US/0148-9267). **1240**

COMPUTER NETWORKS AND ISDN SYSTEMS. (NE/0169-7552). **Adv Mgr:** W Van Cattenburch. **1240**

COMPUTER PAPER (BRITISH COLUMBIA ED.). (CN/0840-3929). **Adv Mgr:** Hari Singh. **1177**

COMPUTER PERIPHERALS REVIEW. (US/0149-5054). **1264**

COMPUTER POST. (CN/1194-305X). **Adv Mgr:** Brent Aubertin, **Tel** (204)947-9766. **1177**

COMPUTER PROCESSING OF CHINESE & ORIENTAL LANGUAGES. (US/0715-9048). **3274**

COMPUTER PRODUCT NEWS. (BE). **Adv Mgr:** Leo Por, **Tel** 02/242 2992. **1244**

COMPUTER REPORT & THE PC STREET PRICE INDEX. (US/1063-8369). **Adv Mgr:** Gian Ofria, **Tel** (609)784-8866. **1246**

COMPUTER RESELLER NEWS. (US/0893-8377). **1244**

COMPUTER REVIEW. (US/0093-416X). **1264**

COMPUTER SCIENCE EDUCATION. (US/0899-3408). **1177**

COMPUTER SCIENCE IN ECONOMICS AND MANAGEMENT. (NE/0921-2736). **1177**

COMPUTER SCIENCE SYLLABUS. (US/1065-2078). **1177**

COMPUTER SECURITY, AUDITING AND CONTROLS. (US/0738-4262). **1226**

COMPUTER SWEDEN. (SW/0280-9982). **1178**

COMPUTER SYSTEMS SCIENCE AND ENGINEERING. (UK/0267-6192). **1228**

COMPUTER TECHNOLOGY REVIEW. (US/0278-9647). **Adv Mgr:** Carol Stagg, **Tel** (310)208-1335. **1246**

COMPUTER TRADE WEEKLY. (UK). **Adv Mgr:** Russell Beadle, **Tel** 011 44 462 4424741. **1178**

COMPUTER USERS' YEAR BOOK. (UK/0268-6821). **1245**

COMPUTERS AND LAW SYDNEY. (AT/0811-7225). **1178**

COMPUTERS & MATHEMATICS WITH APPLICATIONS (1987). (UK/0898-1221). **1179**

COMPUTERS & MEDICINE. (US/0163-0547). **Adv Mgr:** Sam Limeton. **1179**

COMPUTERS & MINING. (US/1068-4425). **2138**

COMPUTERS & SECURITY. (UK/0167-4048). **1226**

COMPUTERS & STRUCTURES. (UK/0045-7949). **Adv Mgr:** R Fazzolari, **Tel** 914-333-2555. **1228**

COMPUTERS IN EDUCATION (TORONTO, ONT.). (CN/0823-9940). **1222**

COMPUTERS IN GENEALOGY. (UK/0263-3248). **Adv Mgr:** Mary Gandy, **Tel** 071-251-8799. **1266**

COMPUTERS IN HUMAN SERVICES. (US/0740-445X). **1179**

COMPUTERS IN LIBRARIES. (US/1041-7915). **3203**

COMPUTERS IN NURSING. (US/0736-8593). **Adv Mgr:** Susan Edison, **Tel** (215)238-4492. **3854**

COMPUTERS IN SCHOOL LIBRARIES. (CN/1188-6331). **3203**

COMPUTERS IN THE SCHOOLS. (US/0738-0569). **1222**

COMPUTERTALK FOR THE PHARMACIST. (US/0736-3893). **Adv Mgr:** W.A. Lockwood Jr., **Tel** (215)825-7686. **4297**

COMPUTERWORLD. (US/0010-4841). **Adv Mgr:** Kevin McPherson. **1236**

COMPUTERWORLD ITALIA. (IT/0392-8845). **1180**

COMPUTERWORLD SINGAPORE. (SI/0217-8362). **Adv Mgr:** Vera Chan. **1180**

COMPUTHINK WINDOWS WATCHER, THE. (US/1054-0784). **1180**

COMPUTING CANADA. (CN/0319-0161). **Adv Mgr:** Carmen Girard, **Tel** (416)497-9562. **1257**

COMPUTING NOW!. (CN/0823-6437). **Adv Mgr:** David Stone, **Tel** (416)696-5488. **1273**

COMPUTING RESEARCH NEWS. (US/1069-384X). **Adv Mgr:** Joan Bass, **Tel** (202)234-2111. **1180**

COMPUTING TEACHER, THE. (US/0278-9175). **1222**

COMPUTING TODAY (LONDON). (UK/0142-7210). **1266**

COMSTOCK'S. (US). **659**

COMUNI D'ITALIA. (IT/0394-8277). **4640**

COMUNICACION. (VE). **5242**

COMUNICACIONES (CORAL GABLES, FLA.). (US/0748-3104). **1152**

COMUNIMEF. (MX). **784**

CON TEXT MAGAZINE. (BE). **Adv Mgr:** Frans Van der Werff. **1083**

CONA JOURNAL. (CN/0708-6474). **3854**

CONAN THE BARBARIAN. (US/0273-0782). **4859**

CONAN THE KING. (US/0746-8237). **4859**

CONCEPT NEWS. (II/0970-6437). **5196**

CONCEPTS IN MAGNETIC RESONANCE. (US/1043-7347). **Adv Mgr:** L O'Neill. **4443**

CONCERN (REGINA). (CN/0836-7310). **Adv Mgr:** Judi Horning, **Tel** (306)565-3808. **3854**

CONCERTINA & SQUEEZEBOX. (US). **4111**

CONCERTINO MILANO. (IT/1121-6875). **2845**

CONCH REVIEW OF BOOKS, THE. (US/0092-7708). **3340**

CONCHO RIVER REVIEW. (US/1048-9568). **3377**

CONCORD BUSINESS. (US). **659**

CONCORD MONITOR (CONCORD, N.H. : 1970). (US). **5708**

CONCORDIA HISTORICAL INSTITUTE QUARTERLY. (US/0010-5260). **Adv Mgr:** Aug. R. Suelflow. **5058**

CONCORDIA THEOLOGICAL QUARTERLY. (US/0038-8610). **4949**

CONCORDIAN, THE. (US). **1091**

CONCOURS MEDICAL. (FR/0010-5309). **3568**

CONCRETE INTERNATIONAL. (US/0162-4075). **608**

CONCRETE (LONDON). (UK/0010-5317). **2021**

CONCRETE PLANT AND PRODUCTION. (UK/0264-0236). **608**

CONCRETE YEAR BOOK, THE. (UK/0069-8288). **608**

CONDITION MONITORING AND DIAGNOSTIC TECHNOLOGY. (UK). **1969**

CONDIZIONAMENTO DELL'ARIA, RISCALDAMENTO, REFRIGERAZIONE. (IT/0373-7772). **2604**

CONDO SALES REPORT. (US/8750-1236). **4836**

CONDOR (LOS ANGELES, CALIF.), THE. (US/0010-5422). **5617**

CONFECTIONER (1989), THE. (US/1047-8345). **2332**

CONFECTIONERY PRODUCTION. (UK/0010-5473). **2332**

CONFEDERACION DE CAMARAS INDUSTRIALES. (MX). **1552**

CONFEDERATE CHRONICLES OF TENNESSEE. (US/0895-9455). **2729**

CONFEDERATE VETERAN (MURFREESBORO, TENN.). (US/0890-2216). **Adv Mgr:** same as publisher. **2729**

CONFERENCE GREEN BOOK. (UK). **Adv Mgr:** Julia Allen. **2804**

CONFERENCE RECORD OF THE ... ANNUAL ACM SYMPOSIUM ON PRINCIPLES OF PROGRAMMING LANGUAGES. (US/0730-8566). **1279**

CONFETTI (ELK GROVE VILLAGE, ILL.). (US/0897-5973). **1109**

CONFIDENCIAL ECONOMICO NORDESTE. (BL). **1470**

CONFIDENTIAL REPORT FOR ATTORNEYS. (US/0890-3034). **2955**

CONFLICT INTERNATIONAL. (UK/0963-1674). **4518**

CONFLICT QUARTERLY. (CN/0227-1311). **4518**

CONFLICT STUDIES. (UK/0069-8792). **4518**

CONFRONTATION/CHANGE LITERARY REVIEW. (US/0363-9460). **5196**

CONFRONTI. (IT). **4950**

CONGENITAL ANOMALIES. (JA/0914-3505). **543**

CONGREGATIONALIST (BELOIT), THE. (US/0010-5856). **4950**

CONGRES ARCHEOLOGIQUE DE FRANCE. (FR/0069-8881). **266**

CONGRESS & THE PRESIDENCY. (US/0734-3469). **4469**

CONGRESS MONTHLY (1985). (US/0887-0764). **2258**

CONJUNCTIONS (NEW YORK, N.Y.). (US/0278-2324). **3340**

CONNAISSANCE DES ARTS, PLAISIR DE FRANCE. (FR/0395-5907). **348**

CONNAISSANCE DES TEMPS. (FR/0181-3048). **4175**

CONNAISSANCEG DES PERES DE L'EGGLISE. (FR). **4950**

CONNECT (ANN ARBOR, MICH.). (US/1070-0994). **Adv Mgr:** Mary, **Tel** (310)572-7272. **1180**

CONNECT. BRUNSWICK. (AT/0158-4995). **1733**

CONNECTICUT ANTIQUARIAN, THE. (US/0010-6054). **2729**

CONNECTICUT BAR JOURNAL. (US/0010-6070). **2955**

CONNECTICUT BEVERAGE JOURNAL. (US/0744-1843). **2366**

CONNECTICUT ENGLISH JOURNAL. (US/0893-0376). **1891**

CONNECTICUT HISTORICAL SOCIETY BULLETIN, THE. (US/0885-4831). **2729**

CONNECTICUT JOURNAL OF INTERNATIONAL LAW. (US/0897-1218). **3126**

CONNECTICUT LAW REVIEW. (US/0010-6151). **2955**

CONNECTICUT LAW TRIBUNE, THE. (US/0198-0289). **2955**

CONNECTICUT LIBRARIES (1954-). (US/0010-616X). **3204**

CONNECTICUT MAGAZINE (FAIRFIELD, CONN.). (US/0889-7670). **2531**

CONNECTICUT MARKET BULLETIN. (US/0161-5858). **76**

CONNECTICUT MEDICINE. (US/0010-6178). **3568**

CONNECTICUT NURSING NEWS (1980). (US/0278-4092). **3854**

CONNECTICUT NUTMEGGER, THE. (US/0045-8120). **2444**

CONNECTICUT POST (BRIDGEPORT, CONN.). (US/1070-874X). **Adv Mgr:** Paul Ward. **5645**

CONNECTICUT, RHODE ISLAND DIRECTORY OF MANUFACTURERS. (US/0193-5909). **3477**

CONNECTICUT TECHNOLOGY DIRECTORY. (US/1046-9672). **5096**

CONNECTICUT WEEKLY AGRICULTURAL REPORT. (US/1059-8723). **76**

CONNECTICUT WOODLANDS. (US/0010-6259). **2163**

CONNECTION (BOSTON, MASS.). (US/0895-6405). **Adv Mgr:** Sarah Laubner. **1818**

CONNECTION TECHNOLOGY. (US/8756-4076). **5096**

CONNECTION, THE. (US/1045-7445). **Adv Mgr:** Gina Cope, **Tel** (216)494-1996. **1279**

CONNECTIONS (POINTE CLAIRE). (CN/0707-7130). **2444**

CONNECTIONS (TORONTO). (CN/0226-1766). **5242**

CONNECTIVE ISSUES. (US/8756-9086). **3568**

CONNERSVILLE NEWS-EXAMINER. (US). **Adv Mgr:** Diane Howell, **Tel** (317)825-0581. **5663**

CONNEXIONS (OAKLAND, CALIF.). (US/0886-7062). **5553**

CONRADIAN : THE JOURNAL OF THE JOSEPH CONRAD SOCIETY (U.K.), THE. (UK). **3378**

CONRADIANA. (US/0010-6356). **431**

CONROE DAILY COURIER. (US). **Adv Mgr:** Brenda Roy. **5748**

CONSCIENCE CANADA NEWSLETTER. (CN/0823-8669). **4718**

CONSER TABLES. (US/0190-3608). **3204**

CONSERVATION ADMINISTRATION NEWS. (US/0192-2912). **3204**

CONSERVATION BIOLOGY. (US/0888-8892). **2190**

CONSERVATION DIRECTORY. (US/0069-911X). **2190**

CONSERVATIONIST, THE. (US/0010-650X). **2190**

CONSERVATIVE JUDAISM. (US/0010-6542). **5047**

CONSERVATIVE NEWSLINE. (UK). **4469**

CONSERVATIVE REVIEW (WASHINGTON, D.C.). (US/1047-5990). **1471**

CONSORT (DOLMETSCH FOUNDATION), THE. (UK/0268-9111). **Adv Mgr:** Jeremy Stewart. **4111**

CONSORT (HALIFAX). (CN/0823-8278). **4111**

CONSORTIUM DIRECTORY. (US/0091-701X). **1818**

CONSORTIUM NEWS / HEALTH SCIENCES CONSORTIUM. (US). **Adv Mgr:** Bret Kuner. **3913**

CONSTITUTIONAL FORUM. (CN/0847-3889). **Adv Mgr:** Christine Urouhart. **3092**

CONSTITUTIONAL POLITICAL ECONOMY. (US/1043-4062). **Adv Mgr:** V Vauberg. **3092**

CONSTRUCT IN STEEL. (AT/1030-2581). **Adv Mgr:** Micheal Carlton, **Tel** (02) 929-6666. **608**

CONSTRUCTION ALBERTA NEWS. (CN/0700-9178). **608**

CONSTRUCTION AND ENGINEERING, ZIMBABWE. (RH). **1969**

CONSTRUCTION

Advertising Accepted Index

CONSTRUCTION (ARLINGTON). (US/0010-6704). **608**

CONSTRUCTION BRIEFINGS COLLECTION, THE. (US/0747-5233). **609**

CONSTRUCTION BULLETIN. (US/0010-6720). **Adv Mgr:** John Saunders, **Tel** (612)537-7730. **609**

CONSTRUCTION CANADA. (CN/0228-8788). **609**

CONSTRUCTION COMPUTING. (UK/0264-6854). **1180**

CONSTRUCTION DIMENSIONS. (US/0194-8903). **609**

CONSTRUCTION EQUIPMENT (1970). (US/0192-3978). **609**

CONSTRUCTION EQUIPMENT, OPERATION AND MAINTENANCE. (US/0010-6771). **609**

CONSTRUCTION LABOR NEWS. (US/0161-990X). **1661**

CONSTRUCTION LAW REPORTS. (CN/0824-2593). **2956**

CONSTRUCTION (LONDON, 1977). (UK/0142-0410). **609**

CONSTRUCTION MANAGEMENT AND ECONOMICS. (UK/0144-6193). **610**

CONSTRUCTION NEWS (LITTLE ROCK). (US/0160-5607). **610**

CONSTRUCTION NOTEBOOK NEWS. (US). **Adv Mgr:** Paula. **610**

CONSTRUCTION SIGHTLINES. (CN/0708-1073). **610**

CONSTRUCTION SPECIFIER, THE. (US/0010-6925). **610**

CONSTRUCTIONAL REVIEW. (AT/0010-695X). **611**

CONSTRUCTIS. (UK). **611**

CONSTRUCTOR (WASHINGTON). (US/0162-6191). **611**

CONSTRUIRE (QUEBEC). (CN/0833-0239). **Adv Mgr:** Pierre Leduc, **Tel** (514)739-2381. **611**

CONSULENTE IMMOBILIARE. (IT/0010-7050). **AdvMgr Tel** 3022.1. **2819**

CONSULTANT - ASSOCIATION OF CONSULTING FORESTERS OF AMERICA, THE. (US/0010-7085). **2378**

CONSULTANT PHARMACIST, THE. (US/0888-5109). **Adv Mgr:** Mark Piluigi, **Tel** (215)348-4351. **4298**

CONSULTANT, THE. (US). **2378**

CONSULTING OPPORTUNITIES JOURNAL. (US/0273-4613). **659**

CONSULTING-SPECIFYING ENGINEER. (US/0892-5046). **2097**

CONSUMER FINANCE LAW QUARTERLY REPORT. (US/0883-4555). **3086**

CONSUMER HEALTH & NUTRITION INDEX. (US/0883-1963). **4200**

CONSUMER MAGAZINE AND AGRI-MEDIA RATES AND DATA / SRDS. (US/0746-2522). **758**

CONSUMER PHARMACIST, THE. (US/0738-0615). **4298**

CONSUMER PRICE INDICES (KINGSTON, JAMAICA). (JM). **1471**

CONSUMERS DIGEST (CHICAGO, ILL.). (US/0010-7182). **1296**

CONSUMERS INDEX TO PRODUCT EVALUATIONS AND INFORMATION SOURCES. (US/0094-0534). **1300**

CONSUMERS' RESEARCH MAGAZINE. (US/0095-2222). **1296**

CONTACT. (UK/0589-5014). **Adv Mgr:** M. Thompson. **939**

CONTACT. (UK). **4386**

CONTACT. (UK/0573-777X). **4950**

CONTACT - ASSOCIATION CANADIENNE DES PROFESSIONNELS DE LA VENTE. (CN/1193-7521). **Adv Mgr:** same as editor. **659**

CONTACT - ASSOCIATION DE SPINA-BIFIDA ET D'HYDROCEPHALIE DU QUEBEC. (CN/1195-6925). **Adv Mgr:** S. Beliale, **Tel** (514)340-9019. **4335**

CONTACT - CANADIAN ELECTROACOUSTIC COMMUNITY. (CN/0838-3340). **2039**

CONTACT - CANADIAN PROFESSIONAL SALES ASSOCIATION. (CN/1193-7513). **Adv Mgr:** same as editor. **659**

CONTACT DERMATITIS. (DK/0105-1873). **3718**

CONTACT (DON MILLS). (CN/0703-119X). **Adv Mgr:** Christine Paetkau. **4836**

CONTACT II. (US/0197-6796). **3461**

CONTACT LENS FORUM. (US/0363-1621). **4215**

CONTACT LENS JOURNAL. (US/0096-2716). **3873**

CONTACT LENS JOURNAL (THORNTON HEATH, SURREY), THE. (UK/0306-9575). **4215**

CONTACT LENS SPECTRUM. (US/0885-9175). **4215**

CONTACT-LINSE, DIE. (GW). **4215**

CONTACT QUARTERLY. (US/0198-9634). **1311**

CONTACT (TORONTO. 1972). (CN/0319-7379). **4386**

CONTACT - UNIVERSITE SIMON FRASER. FACULTE D'EDUCATION. (CN/0714-3192). **3275**

CONTACTS IN AGRICULTURE. (NZ). **76**

CONTADURIA UNIVERSIDAD DE ANTIOQUIA. (CK/0120-4203). **741**

CONTAINERISATION INTERNATIONAL. (UK/0010-7379). **864**

CONTAINERISATION INTERNATIONAL WORLD DIRECTORY OF LINER SHIPPING AGENTS. (UK/0951-5879). **Adv Mgr:** P. G. Owen, **Tel** 71 404 2763 Ext.2161. **829**

CONTAMINACION AMBIENTAL. (CK). **2226**

CONTAMINATION CONTROL ABSTRACTS. (UK/0952-1542). **2183**

CONTEMPORARY ACCOUNTING RESEARCH. (CN/0823-9150). **742**

CONTEMPORARY CHRISTIAN MUSIC (1986). (US/1049-3379). **4111**

CONTEMPORARY DIAGNOSTIC RADIOLOGY. (US/0149-9009). **3940**

CONTEMPORARY DRUG PROBLEMS. (US/0091-4509). **1342**

CONTEMPORARY FRENCH CIVILIZATION. (US/0147-9156). **2684**

CONTEMPORARY HYPNOSIS : THE JOURNAL OF THE BRITISH SOCIETY OF EXPERIMENTAL AND CLINICAL HYPNOSIS. (UK/0960-5290). **2857**

CONTEMPORARY INTERNAL MEDICINE. (US/1042-9646). **Adv Mgr:** Mark Branca. **3796**

CONTEMPORARY ISSUES IN CLINICAL NUTRITION. (US/0736-4369). **4189**

CONTEMPORARY JEWRY. (US/0147-1694). **2259**

CONTEMPORARY LONGTERM CARE. (US/8750-9652). **5280**

CONTEMPORARY MUSIC REVIEW. (UK/0749-4467). **4111**

CONTEMPORARY NEUROSURGERY. (US/0163-2108). **3963**

CONTEMPORARY NURSE : A JOURNAL FOR THE AUSTRALIAN NURSING PROFESSION. (AT/1037-6178). **Adv Mgr:** J. Chandler. **3854**

CONTEMPORARY OB/GYN. (US/0090-3159). **3759**

CONTEMPORARY PACIFIC, THE. (US/1043-898X). **2510**

CONTEMPORARY POLICY ISSUES. (US/0735-0007). **1471**

CONTEMPORARY PSYCHOLOGY. (US/0010-7549). **4582**

CONTEMPORARY RECORD : THE JOURNAL OF THE INSTITUTE OF CONTEMPORARY BRITISH HISTORY. (UK/0950-9224). **Adv Mgr:** Anne Kidson. **2684**

CONTEMPORARY REVIEW (LONDON, ENGLAND). (UK/0010-7565). **2486**

CONTEMPORARY SECURITY POLICY. (UK). **4519**

CONTEMPORARY SOCIOLOGY (WASHINGTON). (US/0094-3061). **5243**

CONTEMPORARY SSOCIAL PSYCHOLOGY. (US/1041-3030). **Adv Mgr:** Editor. **4582**

CONTEMPORARY TIMES. (US/1071-2917). **Adv Mgr:** Janice Alvey. **864**

CONTEMPORARY TOPICS IN LABORATORY ANIMAL SCIENCE. (US/1060-0558). **5508**

CONTEMPORARY WALES : AN ANNUAL REVIEW OF ECONOMIC AND SOCIAL RESEARCH. (UK/0951-4937). **1471**

CONTINENTAL MODELLER. (UK/0955-1298). **2773**

CONTINGENCIES (WASHINGTON, D.C.). (US/1048-9851). **Adv Mgr:** J. Solomon. **2878**

CONTINGENCY PLANNING & RECOVERY JOURNAL : CPR-J. (US/0899-4595). **1226**

CONTINUING CARE RESOURCES. (CN/0824-1384). **3778**

CONTINUING EDUCATION LECTURES. (US/0148-1010). **3568**

CONTINUING HIGHER EDUCATION REVIEW. (US/0893-0384). **1818**

CONTINUITE. (CN/0714-9476). **348**

CONTINUITY. (US/0277-1446). **2614**

CONTINUO. (CN/0705-6656). **4111**

CONTINUO (BRISBANE, QLD.). (AT/0310-6802). **4112**

CONTINUOUS JOURNEY. (US/1065-3406). **864**

CONTINUUM (MONTREAL). (CN/0226-6385). **5782**

CONTRA COSTA COUNTY POPULAR STREET ATLAS (CENSUS TRACT ED.). (US/0733-6845). **2559**

CONTRA MUNDUM. (US/1070-9495). **4950**

CONTRABAND. (US/0888-7586). **Adv Mgr:** Richard Allen. **5683**

CONTRACEPTION (STONEHAM). (US/0010-7824). **588**

CONTRACT EMPLOYMENT WEEKLY. (US/1063-9268). **4203**

CONTRACT MANAGEMENT. (US/0190-3063). **Adv Mgr:** Lee Tapp, **Tel** (703)448-9231. **2956**

CONTRACTORS GUIDE (LOMBARD, ILL.). (US/0273-5954). **611**

CONTREE / RAAD VIR GEESTESWETENSKAPLIKE NAVORSING, INSTITUUT VIR GESKIEDNISNAVORSING, AFDELING STREEKGESKIEDENIS. (SA/0379-9867). **2638**

CONTRETEMPS (MONTREAL). (CN/0829-240X). **Adv Mgr:** S. McKay. **2212**

CONTRIBUTIONS IN BLACK STUDIES. (US/0196-9099). **2845**

CONTRIBUTIONS IN ETHNIC STUDIES. (US/0196-7088). **2259**

CONTRIBUTIONS IN MILITARY STUDIES. (US/0883-6884). **4040**

CONTRIBUTIONS OF THE UNIVERSITY OF CALIFORNIA ARCHAEOLOGICAL RESEARCH FACILITY. (US/0068-5933). **266**

CONTRIBUTIONS TO ATMOSPHERIC PHYSICS. (GW/0303-4186). **1424**

CONTRIBUTIONS TO LIBRARY SCIENCE. BIBLIOTEEKKUNDIGE HYDRAES. (SA). **3204**

CONTRIBUTIONS TO THE STUDY OF CHILDHOOD AND YOUTH. (US/0273-124X). **4583**

CONTRIBUTIONS TO THE STUDY OF MASS MEDIA AND COMMUNICATIONS. (US/0732-4456). **1109**

CONTRIBUTIONS TO THE STUDY OF RELIGION. (US/0196-7053). **4950**

CONTROL AND COMPUTERS. (US/0730-9538). **1219**

CONTROL & INSTRUMENTATION. (UK/0010-8022). **1219**

CONTROL ENGINEERING. (US/0010-8049). **1219**

CONTROL SYSTEMS TONBRIDGE. (UK/0266-2493). **Adv Mgr:** Paul Johnson. **1180**

CONTROLLED CLINICAL TRIALS. (US/0197-2456). **3568**

CONTROLLER. (SZ/0010-8073). **17**

CONTROLLERS MAGAZINE. (NE). **660**

CONTROSPAZIO. (IT). **296**

CONVENIENCE STORE NEWS. (US/0194-8733). **660**

CONVENIENT AUTOMOTIVE SERVICES RETAILER. (US/0895-1047). **5412**

CONVERTING MAGAZINE. (US/0746-7141). **1602**

CONVEYANCER AND PROPERTY LAWYER, THE. (UK/0010-8200). **2956**

CONVEYING MATERIAL CATALOGUE. (SZ). **414**

COOKBOOK DIGEST. (US/0010-826X). **2789**

COOKING FOR PROFIT. (US/0091-861X). **2332**

COOKING LIGHT (SOUTHERN LIVING, INC.). (US/0886-4446). **4189**

COOPER REVIEW. (US). **5748**

COOPERATION AND CONFLICT. (NO/0010-8367). **4470**

COOPERATION (JEFFERSON CITY). (US/0192-4842). **3569**

COOPERATIVE ADVERTISING PLANS FOR YELLOW PAGES. (US/0883-4857). **758**

COOPERATIVE HOUSING JOURNAL. (US/0589-6355). **2819**

COOPERAZIONE EDUCATIVA. (IT). **1733**

COOPERAZIONE ITALIANA, LA. (IT). **AdvMgr Tel** (061) 8844942. **1542**

COOS COUNTY DEMOCRAT, THE. (US). **Adv Mgr:** Sue Hikel. **5708**

COOS GENEALOGICAL BULLETIN. (US/0591-2083). **2444**

COPENHAGEN PAPERS IN EAST AND SOUTHEAST ASIAN STUDIES. (DK/0903-2703). **5243**

COPIA. (IT). **4211**

COPIAH COUNTY COURIER. (US). **Adv Mgr:** Cardyn Runnells. **5700**

COPIERS OF THE WORLD. (GW). **4211**

COPPER STATE BULLETIN. (US/0098-4841). **Adv Mgr:** Jo Clark, **Tel** (602)885-2179. **2444**

COPYRIGHT (GENEVA). (SZ/0010-8626). **1303**

CORAL REEF NEWSLETTER. (US/0278-324X). **1448**

CORDAGE NEWS. (US/1063-746X). **5349**

CORDELE DISPATCH AND THE WILCOX COUNTY CHRONICLE, THE. (US). **5653**

CORDIALITY. (US). **2486**

CORDOVA TIMES, THE. (US/1048-8766). **Adv Mgr:** Joy Landaluce, **Tel** (907)424-7181. **5629**

CORE JOURNALS EN ENFERMEDADES PULMONARES. (SP/1130-0965). **3949**

CORINTHIAN HORSE SPORT. (CN/0829-2930). **Adv Mgr:** V. Mosher, **Tel** 727-0107. **2798**

CORMORANT NEWS BULLETIN, THE. (US/0045-8554). **5412**

CORNELL ALUMNI NEWS. (US/1058-3467). **1101**

CORNELL AND LAKE HOLCOMBE COURIER, THE. (US/0885-078X). **5766**

CORNELL DAILY SUN. (US). **5715**

CORNELL ENGINEER, THE. (US/0010-8790). **1969**

CORNELL VETERINARIAN. SUPPLEMENT. (US/0589-7432). **5508**

CORNELL VETERINARIAN, THE. (US/0010-8901). **5508**

CORNER BROOK WESTERN STAR. (CN). **Adv Mgr:** Dan Johnson, **Tel** (709)634-4348. **5782**

CORNERSTONE (CHICAGO, ILL.). (US/0275-2743). **4950**

CORNSTALK GAZETTE. (AT/0818-7339). **384**

CORONA (BOZEMAN). (US/0270-6687). **3378**

CORONARY ARTERY DISEASE. (US/0954-6928). **3703**

CORONICA, LA. (US/0193-3892). **3275**

CORPORATE CONDUCT QUARTERLY. (US/1061-8775). **2957**

CORPORATE CONSUMER FORUM TRENDLETTER. (US). **2789**

CORPORATE CONTROLLER. (US/0899-0174). **661**

CORPORATE FINANCE BLUEBOOK, THE. (US/0740-2546). **784**

CORPORATE FINANCE SOURCEBOOK, THE. (US/0163-3031). **785**

CORPORATE GIVING WATCH. (US/0747-8003). **5280**

CORPORATE GROWTH REPORT, THE. (US/1050-320X). **661**

CORPORATE LEGAL TIMES. (US). **3099**

CORPORATE MEETINGS AND INCENTIVES. (US/0745-1636). **Adv Mgr:** B Ventro. **5467**

CORPORATE MONEY. (UK/0951-3639). **Adv Mgr:** Phil Dwyer. **785**

CORPORATE PROFILES / BUSINESS DAY. (PH). **662**

CORPORATE REPORT MINNESOTA. (US/0279-5299). **662**

CORPORATE REPORT WISCONSIN. (US/0890-4278). **Adv Mgr:** Christine Schramek, **Tel** (414)255-9077. **662**

CORPORATE RISK MANAGEMENT. (US/1046-5626). **662**

CORPORATE SHOWCASE. (US/0742-9975). **377**

CORPORATE TAXATION. (US/0898-798X). **785**

CORPORATE TECHNOLOGY DIRECTORY. (US/0887-1930). **3477**

CORPUS CHRISTI CALLER-TIMES. (US/0894-5365). **Adv Mgr:** Barry Box. **5748**

CORPUS OF EARLY KEYBOARD MUSIC. (GW/0070-0371). **4112**

CORRECTIONS TODAY. (US/0190-2563). **Adv Mgr:** Jennifer Butz. **3161**

CORRESPONDENCE CHESS. (UK). **4859**

CORRIDOR REAL ESTATE JOURNAL, THE. (US/1048-7948). **4836**

CORRIERE TERMO IDRO SANITARIO, IL. (IT/0393-9723). **2604**

CORROSION & COATINGS SOUTH AFRICA. (SA/0377-8711). **2011**

CORROSION AUSTRALASIA. (AT/0155-6002). **2011**

CORROSION (HOUSTON, TEX.). (US/0010-9312). **2011**

CORROSION PREVENTION AND CONTROL. (UK/0010-9371). **2011**

CORROSION Y PROTECCION. (SP/0045-8678). **2012**

CORRY JOURNAL. (US). **5735**

CORSETERIA Y LENCERIA. (SP). **1083**

CORTEZ SENTINEL, THE. (US). **Adv Mgr:** Jeanne Scrivner. **5642**

CORVALLIS GAZETTE-TIMES. (US/0746-3995). **5733**

CORVETTE FEVER MAGAZINE. (US/0195-1661). **Adv Mgr:** Curt Patterson. **5412**

COSAS. (CL). **4640**

COSMETIC NEWS : CN. (IT). **Adv Mgr:** Franco Mattei. **403**

COSMETIC WORLD. (US/0589-8447). **403**

COSMETIC WORLD NEWS. (UK/0305-0319). **403**

COSMETICA DISTRIBUTION LEVALLOIS-PERRET. (FR/1150-1677). **403**

COSMETICS AND TOILETRIES. (US/0361-4387). **403**

COSMETICS & TOILETRIES. (IT). **403**

COSMETICS (DON MILLS). (CN/0315-1301). **403**

COSMETICS INTERNATIONAL. (UK). **403**

COSMOPOLITAN (1952). (US/0010-9541). **5554**

COSMOPOLITAN CONTACT. (US/0010-955X). **4541**

COSSMHO REPORTER, THE. (US). **2259**

COST ENGINEER. (UK/0010-9606). **864**

COST ENGINEERING (MORGANTOWN. 1980). (US/0274-9696). **1969**

COSTOS Y GESTION. (AG/0327-5345). **662**

COSTRUIRE IN LATERIZIO. (IT/0394-1590). **296**

COTON ET FIBRES TROPICALES. (FR/0010-9711). **2413**

COTTAGE CONNECTION, THE. (US). **662**

COTTAGE LIFE. (CN/0838-2395). **Adv Mgr:** Patricia Moylan. **4849**

COTTON DIGEST INTERNATIONAL, THE. (US/0090-2462). **Adv Mgr:** Anderson. **5349**

COTTON GIN AND OIL MILL PRESS, THE. (US/0010-9800). **5349**

COTTONWOOD CHRONICLE. (US). **Adv Mgr:** Pat Wherry. **5656**

COULICOU. (CN/0822-7098). **1062**

COUNSEL : THE JOURNAL OF THE BAR OF ENGLAND & WALES. (UK/0268-3784). **2957**

COUNSELING AND HUMAN DEVELOPMENT. (US/0193-7375). **5281**

COUNSELING AND VALUES. (US/0160-7960). **4583**

COUNSELING INTERVIEWER, THE. (US/0160-6794). **4583**

COUNSELOR (ARLINGTON, VA.), THE. (US/1047-7314). **1342**

COUNSELOR EDUCATION AND SUPERVISION. (US/0011-0035). **1877**

COUNTDOWN (ATHENS, OHIO). (US/0746-8830). **17**

COUNTDOWN / JUVENILE DIABETES FOUNDATION INTERNATIONAL. (US/1070-9282). **Adv Mgr:** Sandy Dylak. **3727**

COUNTED THREAD. (US/0164-3460). **5183**

COUNTERPOINT. (AT). **Adv Mgr:** Hugh Salmon, **Tel** 61-2-372-5222. **2810**

COUNTERPOINT (WASHINGTON, D.C.). (US/1053-1386). **Adv Mgr:** Mary Varillo, **Tel** (215)784-0860. **1877**

COUNTERTERRORISM & SECURITY REPORT. (US/1064-9093). **4519**

COUNTRY ALMANAC, THE. (US/0192-0111). **Adv Mgr:** Jennifer Brown. **5634**

COUNTRY COURIER (HINCKLEY, ILL.). (US/1061-3218). **Adv Mgr:** Dolores Bastian. **5659**

COUNTRY DECORATING IDEAS. (US/0731-2164). **2899**

COUNTRY GUIDE. (CN/0011-0140). **77**

COUNTRY HERITAGE. (US/0733-8759). **Adv Mgr:** Beverly King. **4112**

COUNTRY HOME. (US/0737-3740). **2899**

COUNTRY LIFE IN BRITISH COLUMBIA. (CN/0011-0183). **77**

COUNTRY LIVING (NEW YORK, N.Y.). (US/0732-2569). **2789**

COUNTRY MUSIC. (US/0090-4007). **4112**

COUNTRY MUSIC NEWS (OTTAWA). (CN/0714-8356). **4112**

COUNTRY MUSIC PEOPLE. (UK/0591-2237). **4112**

COUNTRY MUSIC ROUND UP. (UK/0140-5721). **Adv Mgr:** Doreen Holder. **4112**

COUNTRY SAMPLER. (US/1047-3955). **2899**

COUNTRY SAMPLER'S WEST. (US/1066-7245). **2899**

COUNTRY SHOPPER, THE. (US/0192-1126). **Adv Mgr:** Charles Seaman. **5715**

COUNTRY-SIDE. (UK/0011-023X). **2213**

COUNTRY SONG ROUNDUP. (US/0011-0248). **4112**

COUNTRY TODAY, THE. (US/0192-9658). **Adv Mgr:** Mike Straud. **5766**

COUNTRY (TORONTO). (CN/1180-8047). **4112**

COUNTRYMAN, THE. (UK/0011-0272). **2514**

COUNTRYSIDE AND SMALL STOCK JOURNAL (1985). (US/8750-7595). **209**

COUNTRYSIDE (NEW YORK, N.Y. 1990). (US/1061-6349). **2486**

COUNTY COMMENT. (US/1049-7838). **4641**

COUNTY LINE (PANAMA CITY, FLA.), THE. (US/0888-2851). **2444**

COUNTY MAGAZINE (BLOOMFIELD. 1983). (CN/0826-3035). **Adv Mgr:** Kim Klaver. **2729**

COUNTY PROGRESS. (US/0011-0353). **Adv Mgr:** Pat Coursey. **4641**

COUNTYLINE, THE. (US). **Adv Mgr:** Lee Bryce. **5727**

COUP D'OEIL GRANDVILLIERS. (FR/0987-0113). **3874**

COUP D'OEIL SUR L'HALTEROPHILIE. (CN/0227-6909). **4891**

COURANT (MONTREAL). (CN/0712-4570). **4871**

COURANTS PARIS. 1990. (FR/1146-5786). **5532**

COURIER (BROCKTON, MASS.), THE. (US/1062-8371). **Adv Mgr:** Tom Desmond. **4859**

COURIER (CANADA. CANADIAN FORCES BASE (COLD LAKE, ALTA.)). (CN/0045-8872). **5782**

COURIER HERALD, THE. (US). **5653**

COURIER JOURNAL. (US). **Adv Mgr:** Mary Sue Roberts. **5703**

COURIER (MIDDLETOWN, N.J.), THE. (US/0891-7272). **5709**

COURIER NEWS. (US/0746-9527). **Adv Mgr:** Christine Moore. **5631**

COURIER (PLANT CITY, FL). (US). **Adv Mgr:** Sherry Wheeler. **5649**

COURIER, THE. (US). **Adv Mgr:** Pam Carpenter. **5629**

COURIER, THE. (US). **Adv Mgr:** Eugene Weber. **5727**

COURIER, THE. (US). **Adv Mgr:** Georgia Golden. **5708**

COURIER-TIMES, THE. (US). **5723**

COURIER-TRIBUNE (SENECA, KAN.). (US). **Adv Mgr:** Janet Diehl, **Tel** (913)336-2175. **5675**

COURIER-WEDGE, THE. (US). **5766**

COURIER WEEKEND. (CN/0707-4905). **5782**

COURRIER AUSTRALIEN. (AT/0011-0442). **2486**

COURRIER CERN. (SZ). **4446**

COURRIER DE GAND, LE. (BE/0770-9021). **5778**

COURRIER DE LA NATURE, LE. (FR). **2191**

COURRIER DE LA SCLEROSE EN PLAQUES, LE. (FR/0290-5736). **3569**

COURRIER DES PAYS DE L'EST. (FR/0590-0239). **1478**

COURRIER DU BOIS, LE. (BE/0770-111X). **633**

COURRIER FRONTENAC. (CN/0704-0474). **5782**

COURRIER INTERNATIONAL PARIS. (FR/1154-516X). **2486**

COURRIER LAURENTIDES (EDITION EST). (CN/0829-2442). **5782**

COURRIER - O.C.C, LE. (FR/0249-9975). **Adv Mgr:** Philippe Brame, **Tel** 78.91.39.32. **5467**

COURRIER ROUMAIN (MONTREAL). (CN/0827-4045). **5196**

COURSE TRENDS. (US). **1734**

COURSES

Advertising Accepted Index

COURSES ET ELEVAGE. (FR). **4891**

COURT MANAGER, THE. (US/1046-249X). **3140**

COURT REVIEW. (US/0011-0647). **Adv Mgr:** Anne Kelly, **Tel** (801)259-1841. **3140**

COUSINS ET COUSINES. (US/0740-3046). **2444**

COVENANT COMPANION. (US/0011-0671). **5058**

COVENANT DISCIPLESHIP QUARTERLY. (US/1052-3790). **4951**

COVENANT QUARTERLY, THE. (US/0361-0934). **4951**

COVENANTER WITNESS. (US/0749-4319). **Adv Mgr Tel** (412)241-0436. **4951**

COVERED BRIDGE TOPICS. (US). **2022**

COVINGTON LEADER, THE. (US). **Adv Mgr:** Larry Whitley. **5745**

COVINGTON NEWS (COVINGTON, GA.), THE. (US/1049-4936). **5653**

COW COUNTRY. (US/0279-8204). **209**

COWLEY COUNTY REPORTER, THE. (US). **Adv Mgr:** Ann Alexander. **5675**

COYUNTURA ANDINA. (CK). **1554**

COYUNTURA ECONOMICA. (CK/0120-3576). **1554**

CPA COMPUTER REPORT. (US/0745-1342). **742**

CPA FREEWHEELER. (CN/0824-7226). **4386**

CPA JOURNAL (1975), THE. (US/0732-8435). **Adv Mgr:** David Boniface, **Tel** (212)719-8313. **742**

CPA SOFTWARE NEWS, THE. (US/1068-8285). **Adv Mgr:** L. Duncan, **Tel** (405)275-3100. **662**

CPCU JOURNAL. (US/0162-2706). **2878**

CPI (BALTIMORE, MD.). (US/0897-8751). **5412**

CPJ : CANADIAN PHARMACEUTICAL JOURNAL. (CN/0828-6914). **4298**

CPRS NATIONAL NEWSLETTER. (CN/0710-0701). **758**

CPU NEWS : JOURNAL OF THE COMMONWEALTH PRESS UNION. (UK). **Adv Mgr:** Ms. Wade. **2918**

CPU : QUARTERLY OF THE COMMONWEALTH PRESS UNION. (UK). **2918**

CQ-DL. (GW). **1109**

CRAB, THE. (US/0300-7561). **3204**

CRAFT & NEEDLEWORK AGE. (US/0887-9818). **5183**

CRAFT CONNECTION. (US/1067-8328). **Adv Mgr:** Jim Schiller. **371**

CRAFT CONTACTS (1983). (CN/0823-2148). **371**

CRAFT DIGEST. (US). **Adv Mgr:** Harry Langenheim, **Tel** (203)489-4723. **2773**

CRAFT FACTOR. (CN/0228-7498). **371**

CRAFT RANGE. (US/0199-5200). **371**

CRAFT SHOW DIGEST. (US/0882-7486). **371**

CRAFT SUPPLY DIRECTORY. (US). **2584**

CRAFTNEWS (TORONTO). (CN/0319-7832). **Adv Mgr:** Susan Browne, **Tel** (416)886-6640. **371**

CRAFTS (CRAFTS ADVISORY COMMITTEE). (UK/0306-610X). **371**

CRAFTS 'N THINGS. (US/0146-6607). **371**

CRAFTS (PEORIA, ILL.). (US/0148-9127). **371**

CRAFTS REPORT, THE. (US/0160-7650). **Adv Mgr:** Maryann Parker. **372**

CRAG AND CANYON. (CN/0701-3558). **4871**

CRAIN'S CLEVELAND BUSINESS. (US/0197-2375). **663**

CRANBERRIES (PORTLAND). (US/0011-0787). **168**

CRANE NEWS (CRANE, TEX. : 1945)-. (US). **Adv Mgr:** Skip Nichols. **5748**

CRANFORD CHRONICLE (1979). (US). **5709**

CRANIO. (US/0886-9634). **3569**

CRANK (PHILADELPHIA, PA.). (US/1076-9102). **Adv Mgr:** Jeff Koyen. **4113**

CRANSTON HERALD. (US). **Adv Mgr:** Alice Stanelun. **5741**

CRAZYHORSE (LITTLE ROCK, ARK.). (US/0011-0841). **3462**

CREATING EXCELLENCE. (US/1045-7011). **663**

CREATION MAGAZINE. (FR/0765-9911). **758**

CREATION SPIRITUALITY. (US/1053-9891). **4951**

CREATIVE. (US/0737-5883). **758**

CREATIVE CAMERA. (UK/0011-0876). **4368**

CREATIVE CHILD AND ADULT QUARTERLY, THE. (US/0884-4291). **1877**

CREATIVE FORECASTING. (US/1052-2573). **5281**

CREATIVE FORUM. (II). **3378**

CREATIVE HANDBOOK, THE. (UK). **377**

CREATIVE KIDS. (US/0892-9599). **1062**

CREATIVE LOAFING (1978). (US/0889-8685). **Adv Mgr:** Howard Landsman. **5653**

CREATIVE NURSING. (US). **Adv Mgr:** Eric Haukkala. **3854**

CREATIVE OHIO. (US/0741-6504). **372**

CREATIVE REAL ESTATE MAGAZINE. (US/0194-7222). **4836**

CREATIVE SOURCE AUSTRALIA. (AT/0726-3589). **4368**

CREATIVE WOMAN (PARK FOREST SOUTH, ILL.), THE. (US/0736-4733). **Adv Mgr:** Kristine Rynne, **Tel** (708)355-7693. **5554**

CREATIVITY AND INNOVATION MANAGEMENT. (UK/0963-1690). **Adv Mgr:** Paula Stewart, **Tel** 0865 791100. **864**

CREATIVITY RESEARCH JOURNAL. (US/1040-0419). **5196**

CREATOR (WICHITA, KAN.). (US/1045-0815). **Adv Mgr:** M. Sanders. **4113**

CREDIT & FINANCE. (US/1055-8225). **785**

CREDIT CARD MANAGEMENT. (US/0896-9329). **785**

CREDIT CONTROL. (UK/0143-5329). **785**

CREDIT MANAGEMENT. (UK/0265-2099). **785**

CREDIT UNION EXECUTIVE (MADISON, WIS. 1989). (US/1053-6744). **Adv Mgr:** Phyllis Peterson, **Tel** (608)231-4077. **786**

CREDIT UNION MAGAZINE. (US/0011-1066). **Adv Mgr:** Phyllis Peterson, **Tel** (608)231-4077. **786**

CREDIT UNION MANAGEMENT. (US/0273-9267). **786**

CREDIT UNION NEWS. (US/0199-9311). **Adv Mgr:** Brian K. Burkart. **1542**

CREDIT UNION REPORT. (US/0894-752X). **786**

CREDIT UNION TIMES. (US/1058-7764). **Adv Mgr:** Tim O'Hara. **786**

CREDIT UNION WAY. (CN/0829-2175). **Adv Mgr:** Diana Sneesby, **Tel** (306)566-1260. **786**

CREDIT (WASHINGTON). (US/0097-8345). **786**

CREDIT WORLD, THE. (US/0011-1074). **Adv Mgr:** Bill Murray. **786**

CREDO. (NO). **4951**

CREIGHTON LAW REVIEW. (US/0011-1155). **Adv Mgr:** Ron Dowse, **Tel** (402)280-2988. **2957**

CRESCENDO & JAZZ MUSIC. (UK/0962-7472). **Adv Mgr:** 1071 405 8911. **4113**

CRESCENT INTERNATIONAL. (CN/0705-3754). **4470**

CRESCENT-NEWS. (US). **Adv Mgr:** Jim Eitniear. **5727**

CRESTLINE ADVOCATE (CRESTLINE, OHIO : 1869). (US). **5727**

CRESTON NEWS ADVERTISER (CRESTON, IOWA : 1928 : DAILY). (US). **Adv Mgr:** Roger Lanning. **5669**

CREWE, BURKEVILLE JOURNAL, THE. (US/8755-9463). **5758**

CRIME AND DELINQUENCY. (US/0011-1287). **3161**

CRIMINAL APPEAL REPORTS (SENTENCING), THE. (UK/0144-3321). **3105**

CRIMINAL JUSTICE ABSTRACTS. (US/0146-9177). **3080**

CRIMINAL JUSTICE JOURNAL (SAN DIEGO, CALIF.). (US/0145-4226). **3162**

CRIMINAL JUSTICE REVIEW (ATLANTA, GA.). (US/0734-0168). **3162**

CRIMINAL LAW FORUM. (US/1046-8374). **3106**

CRIMINAL LAW JOURNAL. (AT/0314-1160). **3106**

CRIMINAL LAW REVIEW (LONDON, ENGLAND). (UK/0011-135X). **3106**

CRIMINAL REPORTS. (CN/0383-9494). **3106**

CRIMINOLOGIE (MONTREAL). (CN/0316-0041). **3162**

CRIMINOLOGIE (MONTREAL). (CN/0316-0041). **3163**

CRIMINOLOGIST (COLUMBUS), THE. (US/0164-0240). **3163**

CRIMINOLOGIST, THE. (US/0011-1376). **3163**

CRIMINOLOGY (BEVERLY HILLS). (US/0011-1384). **3163**

CRISIS (NEW YORK, N.Y.), THE. (US/0011-1422). **2259**

CRISIS (NOTRE DAME, IND.). (US). **5028**

CRISIS (TORONTO). (CN/0227-5910). **4583**

CRISTIANESIMO NELLA STORIA. (IT/0393-3598). **4951**

CRISWELL THEOLOGICAL REVIEW. (US/0892-5712). **Adv Mgr:** Klein, **Tel** (214)821-5433. **4951**

CRITERIO. (AG/0011-1473). **5028**

CRITICA HISPANICA. (US/0278-7261). **3275**

CRITICA (LA JOLLA, CALIF.). (US/8755-3325). **5243**

CRITICA MARXISTA. (IT/0011-152X). **4541**

CRITICA; REVISTA HISPANOAMERICANA DE FILOSOFIA. (MX/0011-1503). **Adv Mgr:** F Maxinoz, **Tel** 52 5 6227434. **4344**

CRITICAL ARTS. (SA/0256-0046). **1109**

CRITICAL CARE MEDICINE. (US/0090-3493). **3723**

CRITICAL CARE NURSE. (US/0279-5442). **3854**

CRITICAL INQUIRY. (US/0093-1896). **318**

CRITICAL ISCHAEMIA. (UK/0956-2257). **3569**

CRITICAL MATRIX. (US/1066-288X). **5554**

CRITICAL QUARTERLY, THE. (UK/0011-1562). **3379**

CRITICAL REVIEW (NEW YORK, N.Y.). (US/0891-3811). **Adv Mgr:** Dawn Herron, **Tel** (415)495-2157. **4470**

CRITICAL REVIEWS IN ORAL BIOLOGY AND MEDICINE. (US/1045-4411). **1319**

CRITICAL SOCIOLOGY. (US/0896-9205). **5243**

CRITICAL STUDIES IN MASS COMMUNICATION. (US/0739-3180). **1109**

CRITICAL TEXTS. (US/0730-2304). **3341**

CRITICISM (DETROIT). (US/0011-1589). **2845**

CRITIQUE. (FR/0011-1600). **3341**

CRITIQUE - BOLINGBROKE SOCIETY. (US/0011-1619). **3341**

CRITIQUE OF ANTHROPOLOGY. (UK/0308-275X). **234**

CRITTENDEN PRESS, THE. (US). **5680**

CROC. (CN/0226-6083). **3379**

CROCHET WORLD. (US/0164-7962). **5183**

CROISSANCE. (FR). **4519**

CRONACHE FARMACEUTICHE. (IT/0011-1783). **4298**

CROP PHYSIOLOGY ABSTRACTS. (UK/0306-7556). **152**

CROP PROTECTION (GUILDFORD, SURREY). (UK/0261-2194). **169**

CROP REPORT / ALBERTA WHEAT POOL. (CN). **169**

CROP SCIENCE. (US/0011-183X). **169**

CROSBY COUNTY NEWS AND THE CROSBYTON REVIEW. (US). **5748**

CROSBYTON REVIEW, THE. (US). **Adv Mgr:** Donna Gillespie. **5748**

CROSS COUNTRY SKIER. (US/0278-9213). **4892**

CROSS CURRENT. (UK/0260-6313). **1734**

CROSS CURRENTS. (US/0011-1953). **Adv Mgr:** Ronnie Carpini. **4951**

CROSS POINT. (US/1064-4490). **Adv Mgr:** Paraclete Press, **Tel** (508)255-4685. **4951**

CROSS STITCH AUSTRALIA. (AT). **5183**

CROSS STITCHER, THE. (US/1055-2871). **5183**

CROSSFACE, THE. (US/0273-9135). **4892**

CROSSROADS (DE KALB, ILL.). (US/0741-2037). **2503**

CROSSROADS (SHOAL LAKE, MAN.). (CN). **5783**

CROSSROADS (SPRINGDALE, ARK.). (US/1044-5544). **5281**

CROSSSTITCH SAMPLER. (US/1054-1551). **5183**

Advertising Accepted Index

CYCLODEXTRIN

CROSSTALK AND ANGLICAN JOURNAL EPISCOPAL. (CN/0845-4795). **5058**

CROSSTIES. (US/0097-4536). **2378**

CROSSVILLE CHRONICLE. (US). **Adv Mgr:** Becky Gilley. **5745**

CROSSWORD TREAT. (US/0194-3154). **4859**

CROSSWORD VARIETIES. (US/0194-3162). **4859**

CROTON REVIEW. (US/0741-6210). **3379**

CROWLEY POST-SIGNAL, THE. (US). **Adv Mgr:** Glenn Boudreux. **5683**

CROWLEY REVIEW. (US/1041-3081). **Adv Mgr:** Cathy Smith, **Tel** (817)295-0486. **2332**

CROWN JEWELS OF THE WIRE. (US/0884-7983). **1153**

CROW'S BUYER'S & SELLER'S GUIDE TO THE FOREST PRODUCTS INDUSTRIES. (US). **2400**

CRS PUBLICATIONS' CAREER OPPORTUNITY INDEX (EAST-SOUTH-CENTRAL). (US/0897-909X). **4203**

CRS PUBLICATIONS' CAREER OPPORTUNITY INDEX (WESTERN). (US/0898-218X). **4203**

CRUCIBLE. (UK/0011-2100). **4951**

CRUCIBLE (TORONTO). (CN/0381-8047). **5097**

CRUISE DIGEST. (US/0886-5604). **Adv Mgr:** D Ward. **5467**

CRUISE INDUSTRY NEWS (ANNUAL). (US/1047-3378). **5467**

CRUISE INDUSTRY NEWS QUARTERLY, THE. (US/0893-1240). **Adv Mgr:** Angel A. Mathison. **5467**

CRUISE TRAVEL MAGAZINE. (US/0199-5111). **5467**

CRUISING AROUND THE WORLD. (US/0744-6004). **5467**

CRUISING HELMSMAN. (AT/0812-4086). **593**

CRUISING WORLD. (US/0098-3519). **593**

CRUSADER (CENTERVILLE, IND.). (US). **Adv Mgr:** Peggy Patterson. **5663**

CRUX OF THE NEWS. (US/0591-2296). **4952**

CRUX (PRETORIA). (SA/0250-0035). **3275**

CRYO LETTERS. (UK/0143-2044). **452**

CRYOGAS INTERNATIONAL. (US/1052-0139). **Adv Mgr:** Lori Frieling. **2112**

CRYOGENICS (GUILFORD). (UK/0011-2275). **4401**

CRYPTOGAMIC BOTANY. (GW/0935-2147). **507**

CRYPTOGRAPHY MAGAZINE. (US/0732-5495). **2773**

CRYPTOLOGIA. (US/0161-1194). **1226**

CRYPTOZOOLOGY. (US/0736-7023). **5581**

CSAS NEWSLETTER. (CN/0714-8240). **209**

CSCC NEWS. (CN/0826-1024). **973**

CSD BULLETIN. (SA). **5197**

CSELT TECHNICAL REPORTS. (IT/0393-2648). **1153**

CSG BACKGROUNDER / COUNCIL OF STATE GOVERNMENTS. (US). **4641**

CSP. CRITICAL SOCIAL POLICY. (UK/0261-0183). **4541**

CSSE CONTACT. (CN/0713-3421). **2861**

CSSR BULLETIN. (US). **4952**

CSSR DIRECTORY OF DEPARTMENTS OF RELIGIOUS STUDIES IN NORTH AMERICA. (US). **4952**

CTA ACTION (1986). (US/0896-7326). **1862**

CTDNEWS (PHILADELPHIA, PA.). (US/1062-6743). **Adv Mgr:** Brad Aronson. **3569**

CTI JOURNAL. (US). **2112**

CTISS FILE. (UK/0959-3004). **1222**

CTOSIAN. (US). **Adv Mgr:** Teresa Davis, **Tel** (804) 547-8382. **1245**

CTVD, CINEMA, TV DIGEST. (US/0007-9219). **1109**

CUADERNOS AMERICANOS. (MX/0011-2356). **2730**

CUADERNOS DE ACTUALIDAD INTERNACIONAL. (VE/0798-0841). **5197**

CUADERNOS DE ECONOMIA (SANTIAGO). (CL/0716-0046). **1478**

CUADERNOS DE EDUCACION. (VE). **1734**

CUADERNOS DE INVESTIGACION FILOLOGICA. (SP/0211-0547). **3276**

CUADERNOS DE MARCHA. (UY). **2551**

CUADERNOS DEL CENDES. (VE). **1478**

CUADERNOS DEL CLAEH. (UY). **5197**

CUADERNOS DEL TERCER MUNDO. (UY). **1554**

CUADERNOS POLITICOS. (MX). **5197**

CUB CLUES. (US/0889-437X). **17**

CUBA FOREIGN TRADE. (CU). **Adv Mgr:** P. Medero, **Tel** 30-9643. **663**

CUBA UPDATE. (US/0196-0830). **4541**

CUBAN JOURNAL OF AGRICULTURAL SCIENCE. (CU/0253-5815). **77**

CUE MAGAZINE. (US/1064-2579). **4850**

CUISINE AUCKLAND. (NZ/0113-1206). **Adv Mgr:** M. Thomson, **Tel** 307 0702. **2789**

CULLMAN TRIBUNE, THE. (US/0739-523X). **Adv Mgr:** Barbara Blalock. **5626**

CULTIVADOR MODERNO, EL. (SP). **77**

CULTIVAR. (FR/0045-9216). **170**

CULTURA E FE. (BL). **4952**

CULTURA E NATURA. (IT). **5243**

CULTURA, LA. (IT). **2845**

CULTURA NEL MONDO, LA. (IT/0011-2798). **2486**

CULTURAL ANTHROPOLOGY. (US/0886-7356). **234**

CULTURAL CRITIQUE. (US/0882-4371). **5197**

CULTURAL FUTURES RESEARCH. (US/0748-772X). **234**

CULTURAL SURVIVAL QUARTERLY. (US/0740-3291). **4507**

CULTURAL VISTAS. (US/1048-8650). **2845**

CULTURE, MEDICINE AND PSYCHIATRY. (NE/0165-005X). **3924**

CULTURED DAIRY PRODUCTS JOURNAL OF THE AMERICAN CULTURED DAIRY PRODUCTS INSTITUTE. (US/0045-9259). **192**

CUMBERLAND ADVOCATE. (US/0748-965X). **5766**

CUMBERLAND COUNTY NEWS, THE. (US). **Adv Mgr:** Bruce Henson, **Tel** (502)864-3891. **5680**

CUMBERLAND FLAG, THE. (US/0011-2968). **4952**

CUMBERLAND PRESBYTERIAN, THE. (US/0011-2976). **5058**

CUMHURIYET. (TU). **5811**

CUMULATIVE INDEX TO NURSING & ALLIED HEALTH LITERATURE. (US/0146-5554). **3656**

CUNICULTURAL. (SP/0210-1912). **210**

CUOIO, PELLI, MATERIE CONCIANTI. (IT/0011-3034). **Adv Mgr:** A. M. Scandurra. **3183**

CUPA JOURNAL (WASHINGTON, D.C.: 1987). (US/1046-9508). **Adv Mgr:** Robert Kruhm. **939**

CUPA NEWS (WASHINGTON D.C.: 1987). (US/0892-7855). **1819**

CURARE. (GW/0344-8622). **3924**

CURRENT ADVANCES IN CLINICAL CHEMISTRY. (UK/0885-1980). **1011**

CURRENT AFFAIRS BULLETIN. (AT/0011-3182). **4470**

CURRENT ARCHAEOLOGY. (UK/0011-3212). **266**

CURRENT BIOLOGY. (UK/0960-9822). **452**

CURRENT BIOTECHNOLOGY. (UK/0960-5037). **3656**

CURRENT BOOKS MAGAZINE. (US/1063-9012). **Adv Mgr:** Natalie op de Beeck. **3341**

CURRENT BRITISH JOURNALS. (UK). **3258**

CURRENT CENTRAL LEGISLATION. (II). **2957**

CURRENT COINS OF THE WORLD. (US/0070-1882). **2781**

CURRENT CONTENTS. LIFE SCIENCES. (US/0011-3409). **5174**

CURRENT EMPLOYMENT. (US/1055-8292). **4203**

CURRENT EYE RESEARCH. (UK/0271-3683). **3874**

CURRENT GENETICS. (GW/0172-8083). **544**

CURRENT GEOGRAPHICAL PUBLICATIONS. (US/0011-3514). **2580**

CURRENT INDEX TO JOURNALS IN EDUCATION. (US/0011-3565). **1794**

CURRENT INDEX TO JOURNALS IN EDUCATION. SEMIANNUAL CUMULATION. (US). **1734**

CURRENT ISSUES IN MIDDLE LEVEL EDUCATION. (US/1059-7107). **1734**

CURRENT MUSICOLOGY. (US/0011-3735). **4113**

CURRENT (NEW YORK). (US/0011-3131). **2487**

CURRENT NOTES. (US/8750-1937). **1181**

CURRENT OPINION IN GENETICS AND DEVELOPMENT. (UK/0959-437X). **544**

CURRENT OPINION IN IMMUNOLOGY. (US/0952-7915). **3668**

CURRENT OPINION IN NEUROBIOLOGY. (UK/0959-4388). **453**

CURRENT OPINION IN ORTHOPAEDICS. (US/1041-9918). **3881**

CURRENT OPINION IN STRUCTURAL BIOLOGY. (UK/0959-440X). **453**

CURRENT OPINION IN THERAPEUTIC PATENTS. (UK). **1303**

CURRENT PRIMATE REFERENCES. (US/0590-4102). **5174**

CURRENT PROBLEMS IN DERMATOLOGY (CHICAGO, ILL.). (US/1040-0486). **3719**

CURRENT PROBLEMS IN PEDIATRICS (ENGLISH ED.). (US/0045-9380). **3903**

CURRENT RESEARCH IN LIBRARY & INFORMATION SCIENCE. (UK/0263-9254). **3205**

CURRENT SERIALS RECEIVED. (UK/0959-4914). **3205**

CURRENT SOCIOLOGY (PARIS, FRANCE). (UK/0011-3921). **5244**

CURRENT SURGERY. (US/0149-7944). **3963**

CURRENT THERAPEUTICS. (AT/0311-905X). **4298**

CURRENT TITLES IN ELECTROCHEMISTRY. (II/0300-4376). **1011**

CURRENT TOPICS IN HUMAN INTELLIGENCE. (US/8755-0040). **4584**

CURRENT TOPICS IN RESEARCH ON SYNAPSES. (US/0747-5454). **580**

CURRENTLY (TORONTO). (CN/0384-9627). **4087**

CURRENTS (CHAPEL HILL, N.C.). (US/0882-7915). **4189**

CURRENTS IN THEOLOGY AND MISSION. (US/0098-2113). **4952**

CURRENTS (WASHINGTON, D.C. 1983). (US/0748-478X). **1819**

CURRICULUM AND TEACHING. (AT/0726-416X). **Adv Mgr:** D. Murphy, **Tel** 696-5545. **1734**

CURRICULUM INQUIRY. (US/0362-6784). **1892**

CURRICULUM PERSPECTIVES. (AT/0159-7868). **1892**

CURRICULUM PRODUCT NEWS : CPN. (US/1063-3375). **Adv Mgr:** J.Horton. **1892**

CURRICULUM REVIEW. (US/0147-2453). **1892**

CUSHING CITIZEN, THE. (US). **Adv Mgr:** Brian Hammock. **5731**

CUSSCO NEWSLETTER. (CN/0823-3918). **4773**

CUSTOM BUILDER. (US/0895-2493). **612**

CUSTOM TAILOR, THE. (US/1071-1147). **1479**

CUSTOS. (SA). **4706**

CUTBANK. (US/0734-9963). **3379**

CUTTING TOOL ENGINEERING. (US/0011-4189). **4000**

CUTTINGTON RESEARCH JOURNAL. (LB). **3341**

CYBEREDGE JOURNAL. (US/1061-3099). **1181**

CYBERNETICS ABSTRACTS / SCIENTIFIC INFORMATION CONSULTANTS LIMITED, LONDON, ENGLAND. (UK/0011-4243). **1250**

CYBERNETICS AND SYSTEMS. (US/0196-9722). **1250**

CYBIUM. (FR/0399-0974). **2299**

CYCLE CANADA. (CN/0319-2822). **4081**

CYCLE NEWS EAST. (US/0274-7502). **428**

CYCLE TOURING & CAMPAIGNING. (UK). **Adv Mgr:** L. Warburton. **428**

CYCLIC AMP (SHEFFIELD, ENGLAND). (UK/0142-8055). **486**

CYCLING SCIENCE. (US/1049-8990). **Adv Mgr:** M. Katz, **Tel** (609)443-9202. **428**

CYCLING U.S.A. (US/0274-4813). **Adv Mgr:** Mary Ellen Davis. **428**

CYCLING WORLD. (UK/0143-0238). **Adv Mgr Tel** 011 41 332 874731. **4892**

CYCLODEXTRIN NEWS. (HU/0951-256X). **Adv Mgr:** G. Szejtli, **Tel** (361)1-115-1669. **1041**

CYCLOTOURISME — Advertising Accepted Index

CYCLOTOURISME ORGANE OFFICIEL DE LA FEDERATION FRANCAISE DE CYCLOTOURISME. (FR). **429**

CYPRUS JOURNAL OF ECONOMICS, THE. (CY/1013-3224). **1479**

CYPRUS REVIEW, THE. (CY/1015-2881). **4471**

CYPRUS REVIEW, THE. (CY). **5197**

CYTOGENETICS AND CELL GENETICS. (SZ/0301-0171). **544**

CYTOPATHOLOGY (OXFORD). (UK/0956-5507). **535**

CZECHOSLOVAK ECONOMIC PAPERS. (CS/0590-5001). **1479**

CZECHOSLOVAK LIFE. (CS/0011-4634). **Adv Mgr:** Mikatova. **2514**

CZECHOSLOVAK MARKET. (XR). **664**

D.A.C. NEWS. (US/0011-4707). **4892**

D & B REPORTS. (US/0746-6110). **664**

D (DALLAS. 1978). (US/0164-8292). **2532**

D.H. LAWRENCE REVIEW, THE. (US/0011-4936). **3341**

D.O., DIARIO OFICIAL, ESTADO DO RIO DE JANEIRO. PARTE III. (BL). **2958**

D.O.T.C. NEWS (1983). (CN/0822-6261). **5783**

D'A PALMA DE MALLORCA. (SP/1130-3794). **Adv Mgr:** Angel Hevia. **296**

DACHAUER HEFTE. (GW/0257-9472). **2685**

DACHAUER HEFTER. (GW/0934-361X). **2685**

DACHDECKER-HANDWERK, DAS. (GW/0012-124X). **612**

DADA SURREALISM. (US/0084-9537). **318**

DAFFODIL JOURNAL, THE. (US/0011-5290). **Adv Mgr:** L. Kitchens, **Tel** (609)829-6557. **2413**

DAGENS INDUSTRI. (SW/0346-640X). **664**

DAI DAMU / LARGE DAMS. (JA/0011-5347). **2088**

DAIDALOS. (GW/0721-4235). **296**

DAIHAN GUMSOG HAGHOI JI. (KO/0253-3847). **4000**

DAILY ASTORIAN, THE. (US/0739-5078). **Adv Mgr:** Charles Swift. **5733**

DAILY CALIFORNIAN. (US/1050-2300). **5634**

DAILY CHALLENGE. (US/0746-8865). **Adv Mgr:** Jean Wells. **5715**

DAILY CHIEF-UNION, THE. (US). **Adv Mgr:** Tom Martin, **Tel** (419)294-2332. **5727**

DAILY CITIZEN, THE. (US). **Adv Mgr:** Phil Weaver. **5631**

DAILY CLAY COUNTY ADVOCATE-PRESS, THE. (US). **5659**

DAILY CLINTONIAN, THE. (US). **Adv Mgr:** B. Bartlett, **Tel** (317)832-2443. **5663**

DAILY COMET, THE. (US). **Adv Mgr:** Alan Rini. **5683**

DAILY COMMERCE. (US/0279-4195). **830**

DAILY COMMERCIAL NEWS AND CONSTRUCTION RECORD. (CN/0317-3178). **612**

DAILY COMMERCIAL RECORDER, THE. (US/8750-734X). **5748**

DAILY CONSTRUCTION SERVICE. (US/0011-5401). **612**

DAILY COURT REVIEW. (US/0740-1949). **2958**

DAILY DEMOCRAT. DAVIS EDITION. (US). **5634**

DAILY DEMOCRAT (WOODLAND, CALIF.). (US/0747-1890). **5634**

DAILY DUNKLIN DEMOCRAT, THE. (US/1047-7160). **Adv Mgr:** Terri Coleman. **5703**

DAILY EASTERN NEWS, THE. (US/0894-1599). **1091**

DAILY FACTS, THE. (US). **Adv Mgr:** David Berkowitz. **5634**

DAILY FAVORITE, THE. (US). **Adv Mgr:** Elaine Ashlock. **5749**

DAILY GLOBE (WORTHINGTON, MINN.). (US/1045-487X). **Adv Mgr:** Denise McMillen, **Tel** (507)376-9711. **5695**

DAILY GRAPHIC (PORTAGE LA PRAIRIE. 1954). (CN/0832-4298). **Adv Mgr:** Barry Clayton. **5783**

DAILY HAMPSHIRE GAZETTE. (US/0739-3504). **Adv Mgr:** Bill Knittle. **5688**

DAILY HERALD (PROVO, UTAH. 1939), THE. (US/0891-2777). **Adv Mgr:** Mike Stausfield. **5756**

DAILY HERALD, THE. (US). **Adv Mgr:** Jane Ricker. **5728**

DAILY HOME. (US/1059-6461). **Adv Mgr:** Sandy Carden. **5626**

DAILY JOURNAL, THE. (US). **Adv Mgr:** Harry Swendsen, **Tel** (218)285-7411. **5695**

DAILY MAIL BOOK OF HOME PLANS. (UK). **296**

DAILY MESSENGER (UNION CITY, TENN.). (US/0745-5534). **5745**

DAILY MINER & NEWS. (CN). **5783**

DAILY MOUNTAIN EAGLE. (US/0893-0759). **5626**

DAILY NEWS. (US). **5683**

DAILY NEWS HALIFAX-DARTMOUTH EDITION. (CN/0715-4321). **5783**

DAILY NEWS (HAVRE, MONT.), THE. (US/1046-1590). **Adv Mgr:** Paula Carmean. **5705**

DAILY NEWS LEADER, THE. (US/0747-2501). **5758**

DAILY NEWS (LONGVIEW, WASH.), THE. (US/0889-0005). **5760**

DAILY OF THE UNIVERSITY OF WASHINGTON, THE. (US). **Adv Mgr:** Stephanie Pure. **5760**

DAILY PALM BEACH NEWS, THE. (US). **Adv Mgr:** Donna Moore, **Tel** (407)820-3820. **5649**

DAILY PRESS (1988). (US/1042-8496). **Adv Mgr:** Dean Strella, **Tel** (619)951-6260. **5634**

DAILY PRESS (ASHLAND, WIS.), THE. (US/1050-4095). **Adv Mgr:** J. Swiston, **Tel** (715)682-2313. **5766**

DAILY PRESS (ESCANABA, MICH.). (US). **5691**

DAILY PRESS (NEWPORT NEWS, VA.). (US). **Adv Mgr:** G. McDaniel, **Tel** (804)247-4665. **5758**

DAILY RECORD & THE KANSAS CITY DAILY NEWS PRESS. (US). **Adv Mgr:** Pam Weaver. **5703**

DAILY RECORD (PARSIPPANY, N.J.). (US). **5710**

DAILY RECORD (WOOSTER, OHIO), THE. (US/0892-8215). **Adv Mgr:** Bob Anderson, **Tel** (216)264-1125 ext.327. **5728**

DAILY RECORDER, THE. (US/0197-8055). **Adv Mgr:** Laura Enright, **Tel** (916)444-2355. **2958**

DAILY REGISTER (OELWEIN, IOWA). (US/1074-4487). **Adv Mgr:** Jeff Swor, **Tel** (218)624-3665. **5669**

DAILY REGISTER (PORTAGE, WIS.). (US/0747-2927). **Adv Mgr:** David Holgate. **5766**

DAILY REPORT (BAKERSFIELD, CALIF.), THE. (US/0276-5926). **2958**

DAILY REPORTER (COLUMBUS, OHIO). (US/0011-5487). **Adv Mgr:** Dan Shillinburg. **5728**

DAILY REPORTER (SIOUX CITY), THE. (US/0360-9510). **2958**

DAILY REPORTER, THE. (US). **Adv Mgr:** Faye Osenbaugh. **5675**

DAILY REVIEW, THE. (US). **Adv Mgr:** Andy Shirley. **5683**

DAILY REVIEW, THE. (US). **Adv Mgr:** H.R. Autz, **Tel** (510)293-2302. **5634**

DAILY SENTINEL (ROME, N.Y.). (US). **Adv Mgr:** Ronald D. O'Neil, **Tel** (315)337-1438. **5715**

DAILY SIFTINGS HERALD, THE. (US). **Adv Mgr:** Tim Hart. **5631**

DAILY SOUTHERNER. (US). **Adv Mgr:** Ellis W. Hooks. **5723**

DAILY STAR (ONEONTA, NEW YORK). (US). **5715**

DAILY SUN-NEWS. (US/1046-1612). **Adv Mgr:** Jim Applegate. **5760**

DAILY TELEGRAM, THE. (US). **Adv Mgr:** Betty Porter. **5766**

DAILY TERRITORIAL, THE. (US/0743-8397). **Adv Mgr:** David Stoler. **5630**

DAILY TEXAN, THE. (US). **Adv Mgr:** Jim Barger, **Tel** (512)471-1951. **5749**

DAILY TIMES. (NR). **5807**

DAILY TIMES. (US). **Adv Mgr:** Bill Standley. **5712**

DAILY TIMES-CALL. (US). **Adv Mgr:** Mike Gugliotto. **5642**

DAILY TIMES-NEWS, THE. (US). **Adv Mgr:** Trip Hatley, **Tel** (910)227-0131. **5723**

DAILY TIMES (PRIMOS, PA.). (US). **Adv Mgr:** Elaine Lyon. **5736**

DAILY TIMES (SALISBURY, MD.). (US). **Adv Mgr:** Clyde Pinson. **5686**

DAILY TIMES, THE. (US). **Adv Mgr:** Joan Heyers, **Tel** (815)433-2000. **5659**

DAILY TIMES, THE. (US). **Adv Mgr:** Ed Walker. **5772**

DAILY TRIBUNE (BAY CITY, TEX.). (US). **Adv Mgr:** Buzz Crainer. **5749**

DAILY TRIBUNE NEWS (CARTERSVILLE, GA.), THE. (US/1049-6750). **Adv Mgr:** Barbara Dolken. **5653**

DAILY WORLD (HELENA, ARK.), THE. (US/8750-5274). **Adv Mgr:** Ann Puckett. **5631**

DAIRY CONTACT. (CN/0383-6207). **193**

DAIRY EXPORTER. (NZ/0111-915X). **Adv Mgr:** C. Cook, **Tel** 09 358 8124. **193**

DAIRY FOODS. (US/0888-0050). **193**

DAIRY GOAT JOURNAL. (US/0011-5592). **193**

DAIRY INDIA. (II). **152**

DAIRY INDUSTRIES INTERNATIONAL. (UK/0308-8197). **193**

DAIRY (SAINT PAUL, MINN.). (US/0883-007X). **194**

DAIRY SCIENCE ABSTRACTS. (UK/0011-5681). **153**

DAIRY WORLD (MILLBURY, MASS.). (US/0736-4962). **194**

DAIRYMAN (ARMADALE), THE. (AT). **194**

DAIRYMAN (CORONA), THE. (US/0011-572X). **194**

DAIRYMEN'S DIGEST (MORNING GLORY FARMS ED.). (US/0894-1653). **194**

DAIRYMEN'S DIGEST. NORTH CENTRAL REGION EDITION. (US/0745-9033). **194**

DAIRYNEWS (PEARL RIVER, N.Y.). (US/0011-5738). **Adv Mgr:** Monica Coleman. **194**

DAKOTA COUNTRY. (US/0194-5769). **Adv Mgr:** Sylvia Shockman. **4871**

DAKOTA COUNTY TRIBUNE. (US/8750-2895). **5695**

DAKOTA FAMILY. (US/0199-7122). **78**

DAKOTA OUTDOORS. (US/1041-1968). **Adv Mgr:** Terry Hipple. **4871**

DALE NEWS, THE. (US). **Adv Mgr:** Kathy Treffer, **Tel** (812)367-2041. **5663**

DALHOUSIE DENTAL JOURNAL. (CN/0418-3010). **1320**

DALHOUSIE FRENCH STUDIES. (CN/0711-8813). **3379**

DALHOUSIE GAZETTE, THE. (CN/0011-5819). **1091**

DALHOUSIE JOURNAL OF LEGAL STUDIES. (CN/1188-4258). **2959**

DALHOUSIE REVIEW, THE. (CN/0011-5827). **3380**

DALLAS APPAREL NEWS. (US/0279-4888). **1083**

DALLAS BUSINESS JOURNAL. (US/0899-4129). **664**

DALLAS COWBOYS OFFICIAL WEEKLY. (US/0745-0370). **4892**

DALLAS MEDICAL JOURNAL. (US/0011-586X). **3570**

DALLAS NEW ERA, THE. (US/8750-1376). **Adv Mgr:** Annette Manning. **5653**

DALLAS OBSERVER. (US/0732-0299). **384**

DALLAS POST, THE. (US). **Adv Mgr:** Ron Bartizek. **5736**

DALLAS POST TRIBUNE, THE. (US/0746-7303). **5749**

DALLAS WEEKLY, THE. (US/0885-1271). **Adv Mgr:** Andrea Allen. **5749**

DALLES CHRONICLE, THE. (US/0747-3443). **Adv Mgr:** Skop Tschanz. **5733**

DAN CHUA. (US/0747-2315). **Adv Mgr:** Ann Mary. **5028**

DAN SHA. (CN/0833-3831). **5783**

DANCE AND DANCERS. (UK/0011-5983). **1311**

DANCE AUSTRALIA. (AT). **1311**

DANCE CONNECTION. (CN/0838-1313). **1311**

DANCE IN CANADA. (CN/0317-9737). **1312**

DANCE MAGAZINE. (US/0011-6009). **1312**

DANCE MATTERS. (UK). **1312**

DANCE MUSIC REPORT. (US/0883-1122). **Adv Mgr Tel** (212)677-6770. **4113**

DANCE NOW. (UK/0966-6346). **Adv Mgr:** S. Philo, **Tel** 0367 820367. **1312**

DANCE RESEARCH. (UK/0264-2875). **1312**

DANCE RESEARCH JOURNAL. (US/0149-7677). **1312**

DANCE TEACHER NOW. (US/0199-1795). **1312**

DANCE THEATRE JOURNAL. (UK/0264-9160). **Adv Mgr:** D Bromaue. **1312**

DANCEBAG (NORMAN, OKLA.). (US/1041-5564). **1312**

DANCING TIMES. (UK/0011-605X). **1312**

DANCING USA. (US/1053-5454). **Adv Mgr:** LeAnn Bamford. **1313**

DANCSCENE. (US/0745-3949). **1313**

DANDELION. (CN/0383-9575). **3380**

DANGEROUS GOODS : NEWSLETTER. (CN/0710-0914). **5380**

DANGEROUS PROPERTIES OF INDUSTRIAL MATERIALS REPORT. (US/0270-3777). **2861**

DANISH MEDICAL BULLETIN. (DK/0011-6092). **3570**

DANSER. (FR/0755-7639). **1313**

DANSK AUDIOLOGOPDI. (DK/0105-7200). **3887**

DANSK KEMI. (DK/0011-6335). **974**

DANSK UDSYN. (DK/0106-4622). **2685**

DANTE STUDIES, WITH THE ANNUAL REPORT OF THE DANTE SOCIETY. (US/0070-2862). **3380**

DANVILLE NEWS (DANVILLE, PA.). (US). **Adv Mgr:** Donna Keefer. **5736**

DANVILLE REGISTER, THE. (US/0744-3242). **Adv Mgr:** George Robinette, **Tel** (804)793-2311 ext. 3032. **5758**

DAPHNIS. (SZ/0300-693X). **3380**

DAQI KEXUE. (CC/0254-0002). **1424**

DAR ES SALAAM UNIVERSITY LAW JOURNAL. (TZ). **2959**

DAREDEVIL. (US/0279-8271). **4859**

DARIEN NEWS-REVIEW. (US/0744-3862). **5645**

DARIEN NEWS, THE. (US). **5653**

DARK SHADOWS ANNOUNCEMENT, THE. (US). **1131**

DARKNERVE. (US). **4241**

D'ARS. (IT). **348**

DARSHANA INTERNATIONAL. (II/0011-6734). **4344**

DARTMOUTH ALUMNI MAGAZINE. (US). **1101**

DARTMOUTH BUSINESS DIRECTORY. (CN/0827-2786). **664**

DARTMOUTH BUSINESS NEWS. (CN/0824-2682). **664**

DARTMOUTH REVIEW, THE. (US). **1091**

DARTS WORLD. (UK/0140-6000). **4892**

DASEIN. (US/0011-6807). **318**

DATA ARCHIVE BULLETIN / SSRC. (UK/0307-1391). **2481**

DATA BASED ADVISOR. (US/0740-5200). **1253**

DATA COMMUNICATIONS INTERNATIONAL. (US). **1241**

DATA ENTRY SERVICES DIRECTORY. (US/0899-4579). **1257**

DATA EXTRACT. (AT). **2510**

DATA JURIDICA. (NE). **2959**

DATA PAPERS ON PAPUA NEW GUINEA LANGUAGES. (PP). **3276**

DATA PROCESSING. (UK/0011-684X). **1257**

DATA PROCESSING & COMMUNICATIONS SECURITY. (US/0749-1484). **1257**

DATA PRODUCT NEWS (TORONTO). (CN/0226-6091). **1245**

DATA RESOURCE MANAGEMENT. (US/1053-5594). **Adv Mgr:** Phil Brady, **Tel** (212)971-5120. **865**

DATA TRAINING. (US/0884-2604). **Adv Mgr:** Steve. **1257**

DATABASE CANADA. (CN/0840-7797). **1253**

DATABASE PROGRAMMING & DESIGN. (US/0895-4518). **1253**

DATABASE SEARCHER. (US/0891-6713). **1253**

DATABASE (WESTON). (US/0162-4105). **Adv Mgr:** Corky Murray, **Tel** (203)761-1466. **1253**

DATAMATION. (US/0011-6963). **1258**

DATAPRO MANAGEMENT OF MICROCOMPUTER SYSTEMS. (US/8750-6858). **1274**

DATAPRO REPORTS ON OFFICE AUTOMATION. (US). **1258**

DATELINE HYPERTENSION. (US/0747-6124). **3704**

DATENSCHUTZ UND DATENSICHERUNG. (GW). **2959**

DATI E TARIFFE PUBBLICITARIE. (IT). **758**

DATZ : AQUARIEN TERRARIEN. (GW/0941-8393). **2773**

DAUGHTERS OF SARAH. (US/0739-1749). **4952**

DAUGHTERS OF THE AMERICAN REVOLUTION MAGAZINE. (US/0011-7013). **Adv Mgr:** Bob Fones, **Tel** (202)879-3286. **2730**

DAVE CAMPBELL'S TEXAS FOOTBALL. (US/0147-1287). **4892**

DAVID Y GOLIATH : BOLETIN CLACSO. (AG/0325-0431). **2551**

DAVIE COUNTY ENTERPRISE-RECORD. (US). **5723**

DAVIS ENTERPRISE. (US). **Adv Mgr:** Allison Perkes Felch. **5634**

DAVISON'S "SALESMAN'S BOOK.". (US/0363-5252). **5350**

DAVISON'S TEXTILE "BLUE BOOK". (US/0070-2951). **Adv Mgr:** Carol Nealy. **5350**

DAVISON'S TEXTILE BLUE BOOK : UNITED STATES AND CANADA. (US). **5350**

DAWN. (PK). **2503**

DAWSON SPRINGS PROGRESS, THE. (US). **Adv Mgr:** Faye Winfrey. **5680**

DAY (NEW LONDON, CONN.), THE. (US/0744-0499). **5645**

DAYLILY JOURNAL, THE. (US/0744-0219). **2413**

DAYTON BUSINESS REPORTER. (US/1063-3413). **664**

DAYTON DAILY NEWS (DAYTON, OHIO : 1987). (US/0897-0920). **5728**

DAYTON REVIEW (DAYTON, IOWA). (US). **Adv Mgr:** James A. Diehl. **5669**

DAZE INC, THE. (US/0895-3961). **2588**

DB; DEINE BAHN. (GW). **5431**

DB. DEUTSCHE BAUZEITUNG (1981). (GW/0721-1902). **296**

DBMS (REDWOOD CITY, CALIF.). (US/1041-5173). **1254**

DBZ. DEUTSCHE BRIEFMARKEN-ZEITUNG. (GW/0931-4393). **2773**

DDZ. DER DEUTSCHE ZOLLBEAMTE. (GW). **4719**

DE LLOYD / LE LLOYD. (BE). **Adv Mgr:** Koen Heinen. **5381**

DE PERE JOURNAL. (US/0748-6219). **Adv Mgr:** P. J. Creviere, Jr. **5766**

DE QUEEN BEE. (US). **5631**

DE SMET NEWS, THE. (US). **5743**

DEACON DIGEST. (US/8750-7749). **4952**

DEAF CANADA. (CN/1195-3349). **4386**

DEAF CANADIAN ADVOCATE. (CN/0841-9116). **4386**

DEAF LIFE. (US/0898-719X). **4386**

DEAF SPORTS REVIEW. (US/1059-3063). **4892**

DEAF USA. (US/0898-5480). **4386**

DEALERSCOPE MERCHANDISING. (US/0888-4501). **953**

DEALMAKERS (BELLE MEAD, N.J.), THE. (US/1055-0771). **4836**

DEARBORN TIMES-HERALD. (US/0193-0230). **5691**

DEATH STUDIES. (US/0748-1187). **4584**

DEATH VALLEY GATEWAY GAZETTE. (US/0746-7419). **5707**

DEBATE (LIMA, PERU). (PE). **4471**

DEBATES AND PROCEEDINGS - LEGISLATIVE ASSEMBLY OF MANITOBA. (CN/0542-5492). **4641**

DEBATES EN SOCIOLOGIA. (PE). **5244**

DEBRETT'S PEOPLE OF TODAY. (UK). **432**

DEC PROFESSIONAL, THE. (US/0744-9216). **1246**

DECANTER (LONDON. 1985). (UK/0954-4240). **Adv Mgr:** John Cullimore. **2366**

DECATUR-DEKALB NEWS/ERA. (US). **Adv Mgr:** J. Crane. **5653**

DECCAN GEOGRAPHER. (II/0011-7269). **Adv Mgr:** S.A. Todkar. **2559**

DECEMBER ROSE. (US/0748-1195). **5178**

DECIDUOUS FRUIT GROWER, THE. (SA/0302-7074). **2413**

DECISION (CANADIAN ED.). (CN/0820-9057). **4952**

DECISION LINE. (US/0732-6823). **664**

DECISION SCIENCES. (US/0011-7315). **664**

DECISIONS MEDIAS. (FR/1165-8606). **1109**

DECKS AWASH. (CN/0317-7076). **Adv Mgr:** Jeff, **Tel** (709)368-7670. **2487**

DECORAH JOURNAL. (US). **Adv Mgr:** Ken Eicle. **5669**

DECORAH PUBLIC OPINION (DECORAH, IOWA : 1954). (US). **Adv Mgr:** Ken Eicle. **5669**

DECORATION CHEZ-SOI. (CN/0705-1093). **2899**

DECORATIVE ARTS DIGEST. (US/0888-076X). **372**

DECORATIVE RUG, THE. (US/1045-8816). **Adv Mgr:** Peter Woodman, **Tel** (603)744-9191. **2904**

DECOY MAGAZINE. (US/1055-0364). **2773**

DEEP SKY. (US/0735-3073). **395**

DEER AND DEER HUNTING. (US/0164-7318). **4871**

DEER FARMER, THE. (NZ/0110-7992). **210**

DEER PARK BROADCASTER. (US). **Adv Mgr:** Randy Wilson, **Tel** (713)479-2760. **5749**

DEFAULTED BONDS NEWSLETTER. (US/1057-7521). **896**

DEFENCE (ETON). (UK/0142-6184). **4040**

DEFENCE HELICOPTER WORLD. (UK/0263-5062). **17**

DEFENCE INDUSTRY AND AEROSPACE REPORT. (AT/1033-2898). **4040**

DEFENCE JOURNAL. (PK). **4040**

DEFENCE SYSTEMS MODERNISATION. (UK/0953-4970). **Adv Mgr:** David Holmes, **Tel** 44 703 220189. **4040**

DEFENDER NORTH MELBOURNE. (AT/0811-6407). **Adv Mgr:** M. J. O'Connor, **Tel** 03 8426203. **3179**

DEFENDERS. (US/0162-6337). **2191**

DEFENSA MADRID. (SP/0211-3732). **17**

DEFENSE & FOREIGN AFFAIRS HANDBOOK. (US/0160-5836). **4041**

DEFENSE & FOREIGN AFFAIRS WEEKLY. (US/0884-4054). **4041**

DEFENSE & TECHNOLOGIE INTERNATIONAL PARIS. (FR/1155-3480). **4041**

DEFENSE CONTRACTING AGENCY AUDIT MANUAL. (US). **4642**

DEFENSE CONTRACTING AGENCY AUDIT MANUAL / DISKETTE. (US). **4041**

DEFENSE ELECTRONICS. (US/0278-3479). **2040**

DEFENSE LATIN AMERICA. (UK/0261-233X). **4041**

DEFENSE MANUAL. (US/0191-877X). **3089**

DEFENSE NATIONALE. (FR/0336-1489). **4041**

DEFENSE NEWS (SPRINGFIELD, VA.). (US/0884-139X). **4041**

DEFENSE TRANSPORTATION JOURNAL. (US/0011-7625). **Adv Mgr:** Ms. Scofield, **Tel** (804) 979-4913. **4042**

DEFENSOR CHIEFTAIN. (US/0011-7633). **Adv Mgr Tel** (505)835-0520. **5712**

DEFI-A.C.L. (CN/0835-0337). **318**

DEFI-SANTE. (CN/0848-9068). **2596**

DEFORMACION METALICA. (SP/0210-685X). **4000**

DEGRE SECOND. (US/0148-561X). **3341**

DEGRES. (BE/0376-8163). **3276**

DEI DELITTI E DELLE PENE. (IT). **Adv Mgr:** Lulena Ortauda, **Tel** 011 814 2748. **3163**

DELANO RECORD. (US/1074-410X). **Adv Mgr:** L. Lemons. **5634**

DELAVAN ENTERPRISE (1992), THE. (US/1064-4539). **5767**

DELAVAN TIMES, THE. (US). **5659**

DELAWARE BUSINESS REVIEW. (US/1061-4605). **Adv Mgr:** Nancy Carney. **665**

DELAWARE COAST PRESS. (US/0740-2023). **Adv Mgr:** Jane Meleady. **5647**

DELAWARE COUNTY TIMES. (US/0745-0206). **5715**

DELAWARE DIRECTORY OF COMMERCE AND INDUSTRY. (US/0272-8117). **1603**

DELAWARE GAZETTE (DELAWARE, OHIO 1932), THE. (US/1064-2013). **Adv Mgr:** Deirdre Warden. **5728**

DELAWARE JOURNAL OF CORPORATE LAW, THE. (US/0364-9490). **Adv Mgr:** B Glassman. **3099**

DELAWARE LAW MONTHLY, THE. (US/0193-4007). **2959**

DELAWARE LAWYER. (US/0735-6595). **2959**

DELAWARE MEDICAL JOURNAL. (US/0011-7781). **3571**

DELAWARE — Advertising Accepted Index

DELAWARE TODAY (WILMINGTON, DEL. : 1983). (US). **2532**

DELAWARE VALLEY RAIL PASSENGER, THE. (US). **Adv Mgr:** same as editor. **5431**

DELHI LAW REVIEW. (II). **2959**

DELI NEWS. (US/0011-7862). **2333**

DELICIOUS MAGAZINE. (US). **Adv Mgr:** Rick Prill. **2333**

DELIUS SOCIETY JOURNAL, THE. (UK/0306-0373). **4113**

DELL CROSSWORD PUZZLES. (US/0274-6301). **4859**

DELPHIN. (GW). **318**

DELTA COUNTY INDEPENDENT. (US/0891-9704). **Adv Mgr:** Linda Storm. **5642**

DELTA DEMOCRAT-TIMES, THE. (US). **5700**

DELTA OPTIMIST, THE. (CN/0710-1422). **5783**

DELTA (PALMERSTON NORTH). (NZ/0419-9855). **1735**

DELTA PI EPSILON JOURNAL. (US/0011-8052). **665**

DELTION AUTOKINETISTIKES NOMOTHESIAS KAI NOMOLOGIAS. (GR). **2959**

DEMAND SIDE MONTHLY. (US). **4760**

DEMENTIA (BASEL, SWITZERLAND). (SZ/1013-7424). **3831**

DEMING HEADLIGHT (1956). (US/0738-8349). **Adv Mgr:** Rachel Baldwin. **5712**

DEMOCRAT AND CHRONICLE. (US). **5715**

DEMOCRAT-LEADER (FAYETTE, MO.). (US/0746-9934). **5703**

DEMOCRAT-NEWS (FREDERICKTOWN, MO.). (US). **Adv Mgr:** Laura Yount. **5703**

DEMOCRAT-REPORTER, THE. (US). **Adv Mgr:** Linda Williams. **5626**

DEMOCRAT-TRIBUNE (MINERAL POINT, WIS.). (US). **Adv Mgr:** Sherry Byous, **Tel** (608)987-2141. **5767**

DEMOCRATIC LEFT. (US/0164-3207). **4471**

DEMOCRATIZATION. (UK). **Adv Mgr:** Anne Kidson. **4471**

DEMOLITION AGE. (US/0362-7772). **612**

DEMOPOLIS TIMES, THE. (US). **5626**

DENEUVE (SAN FRANCISCO, CALIF.). (US/1062-6247). **Adv Mgr:** Lisa Tripp, **Tel** (202)833-4749. **2794**

DENISON REVIEW, THE. (US). **5669**

DENMARK REVIEW. (DK/0418-6745). **665**

DENNI HLASATEL. (US/0744-6586). **5659**

DENNING LAW JOURNAL, THE. (UK/0269-1922). **2959**

DENPUN KAGAKU. (JA/0021-5406). **2333**

DENTAL COMPUTER NEWSLETTER. (US/0738-9744). **1320**

DENTAL DIMENSIONS. (US/0191-2542). **1320**

DENTAL-ECHO. (GW/0011-8575). **1320**

DENTAL ECONOMICS (PITTSBURGH. 1968). (US/0011-8583). **1320**

DENTAL GUIDE. (CN/0070-3656). **1320**

DENTAL HYGIENE NEWS (ROCHESTER, N.Y.). (US/0882-9543). **1321**

DENTAL LAB PRODUCTS. (US/0146-9738). **1321**

DENTAL-LABOR. LABORATOIRE DENTAIRE. DENTAL LABORATORY, DAS. (GW). **1321**

DENTAL MATERIALS. (DK/0109-5641). **1321**

DENTAL PRACTICE (EWELL). (UK/0011-8710). **1321**

DENTAL PRACTICE MANAGEMENT (DON MILLS, ONT.). (CN/0827-1305). **1321**

DENTAL PRODUCTS REPORT. (US/0011-8737). **1321**

DENTAL SUMMARIES. (SA). **1321**

DENTAL TECHNICIAN. (UK/0011-8796). **1321**

DENTAL UPDATE. (UK/0305-5000). **1321**

DENTEKSA. (SA/0259-563X). **1322**

DENTIST (WACO, TEX.). (US/0887-5669). **1322**

DENTISTRY (CHICAGO, ILL.). (US/0277-3635). **Adv Mgr:** Debbie Lorimor. **1322**

DENTISTRY TODAY. (US/8750-2186). **1322**

DENTO MAXILLO FACIAL RADIOLOGY. (UK/0250-832X). **1322**

DENTON RECORD-CHRONICLE. (US). **Adv Mgr:** Ron Ray, **Tel** (817)381-9515. **5749**

DENVER BUSINESS. (US/0746-2964). **665**

DENVER BUSINESS JOURNAL, THE. (US/0893-7745). **Adv Mgr:** Jill Hess. **665**

DENVER HERALD DISPATCH. (US/0898-1701). **5642**

DENVER MAGAZINE, THE. (US/0161-4886). **2532**

DENVER QUARTERLY. (US/0011-8869). **Adv Mgr:** J. Ward. **3380**

DENVER UNIVERSITY LAW REVIEW. (US/0883-9409). **2959**

DEO. (UK). **Adv Mgr:** Sue Mills. **4114**

DEPARTMENT CHAIR, THE. (US/1049-3255). **1862**

DEPARTMENT OF DEFENSE SUPPLEMENT / DISKETTE. (US). **4042**

DEPARTMENT OF THE NAVY SUPPLEMENT / DISKETTE. (US). **4176**

DEPAUL BUSINESS LAW JOURNAL. (US/1049-6122). **3099**

DEQUINCY NEWS, THE. (US). **Adv Mgr:** Jeffra DeViney. **5683**

DERBY (NORMAN, OKLA.). (US/0199-5928). **2798**

DERMATOLOGISCHE MONATSSCHRIFT. (GW/0011-9083). **3719**

DERMATOLOGY IN PRACTICE (LONDON). (UK/0262-5504). **3719**

DERMATOSEN IN BERUF UND UMWELT. (GW/0343-2432). **3720**

DERMO TIME. (IT). **3720**

DERRY NEWS, THE. (US). **Adv Mgr:** Ellen Wolslegel, **Tel** (603)437-7000. **5708**

DES LIVRES ET DES JEUNES. (CN/0706-795X). **3380**

DES MOINES BUSINESS RECORD. (US/1068-6681). **Adv Mgr:** Mary Day. **665**

DES PLAINES EDITION OF THE TIMES. (US/0895-0148). **Adv Mgr:** Bill Tapper. **5659**

DESALINATION. (NE/0011-9164). **5532**

DESARROLLO ECONOMICO (BUENOS AIRES). (AG/0046-001X). **Adv Mgr:** Getulio E. Steinbach. **5198**

DESARROLLO INDOAMERICANO. (CK/0418-7547). **Adv Mgr:** Ana de Consuegra. **2730**

DESARROLLO NACIONAL. (US/0279-2958). **5099**

DESARROLLO Y SOCIEDAD. (CK/0120-3584). **1555**

DESCANT (TORONTO). (CN/0382-909X). **Adv Mgr:** Elizabeth Mitchell, **Tel** (416)603-0223. **3380**

DESCENDER, THE. (US/0420-0063). **2445**

DESCENT (SYDNEY). (AT/0084-9731). **2445**

DESCENT WELLS. (UK/0046-0036). **1373**

DESERET NEWS (SALT LAKE CITY, UTAH : 1964). (US/0745-4724). **Adv Mgr:** Ed McCaffrey, **Tel** (801)237-2712. **5756**

DESERT LIFE. (US). **4871**

DESIGN. (II/0011-9261). **296**

DESIGN BOOK REVIEW. (US/0737-5344). **296**

DESIGN COST AND DATA. (US/1054-3163). **Adv Mgr:** Rob Rizzi. **297**

DESIGN ENGINEERING (LONDON, ENGLAND). (UK/0308-8448). **1970**

DESIGN FOR ARTS IN EDUCATION. (US/0732-0973). **318**

DESIGN FROM SCANDINAVIA. (DK/0108-0695). **372**

DESIGN IN FINLAND. (FI/0418-7717). **2899**

DESIGN ISSUES. (US/0747-9360). **297**

DESIGN (LONDON). (UK/0011-9245). **2097**

DESIGN MANAGEMENT JOURNAL. (US/1045-7194). **Adv Mgr:** Melissa Blanchette, **Tel** (617)338-6380. **1970**

DESIGN NEWS. (JA/0385-3462). **2097**

DESIGN PRODUCTS & APPLICATIONS. (UK). **Adv Mgr:** Andrew Quenault. **2097**

DESIGN SOLUTIONS. (US/0277-3538). **297**

DESIGN STUDIES. (UK/0142-694X). **2097**

DESIGN SYSTEMS STRATEGIES. (US/0895-6790). **1233**

DESIGN TECHNOLOGY TEACHING. (UK). **Adv Mgr Tel** 0222 360839. **372**

DESIGN TIMES. (US/1041-0422). **2899**

DESIGN (WASHINGTON, D.C., 1980). (US/1050-9224). **Adv Mgr:** Ray Chattman, **Tel** (703)620-1083. **2918**

DESIGN WITH FLOWERS. (US/1043-9145). **372**

DESIGN WORLD. (AT/0810-6029). **297**

DESIGNERS DIGEST MAGAZINE. (GW). **378**

DESIGNERS' JOURNAL. (UK/0264-8148). **297**

DESIGNERS WEST. (US/0192-1487). **2900**

DESIGNERS WEST RESOURCE DIRECTORY. (US). **2900**

DESIGNFAX. (US/0163-6669). **2097**

DESIGNINK. (AU/1035-0500). **Adv Mgr:** P Bernadou, **Tel** 61 3 8169895. **297**

DESKTOP COMMUNICATIONS. (US/1050-1800). **1182**

DESKTOP MAGAZINE. (AT/1037-7603). **Adv Mgr Tel** 03 525 5566. **1233**

DESKTOP PUBLISHER. (US). **1263**

DESOTO COUNTY TRIBUNE, THE. (US). **Adv Mgr:** Tam Ratcliff. **5700**

DESOTO TIMES (1981). (US/1064-4784). **Adv Mgr:** Tawanda Tanxersley. **5700**

DESPATCH. (UK/0046-0079). **4042**

DET BASTA UR READER'S DIGEST. (SW/0005-3856). **2515**

DETAIL (MUNCHEN). (GW/0011-9571). **297**

DETAILS (NEW YORK, N.Y.). (US/0740-4921). **3995**

DETROIT COLLEGE OF LAW ALUMNI NEWS. (US). **1101**

DETROIT COLLEGE OF LAW REVIEW. (US/0099-135X). **2960**

DETROIT DENTAL BULLETIN. (US/0011-9601). **1322**

DETROIT FREE PRESS (DETROIT, MICH., 1858). (US/1055-2758). **Adv Mgr:** Richard McClennen. **5691**

DETROIT LABOR NEWS. (US/1072-1525). **1662**

DETROIT LAWYER, THE. (US/0011-9652). **2960**

DETROIT LEGAL NEWS (DAILY ED.). (US/0739-9480). **2960**

DETROIT MEDICAL NEWS. (US/0098-471X). **3571**

DETROIT NEWS (DETROIT, MICH.), THE. (US/1055-2715). **5691**

DETROITER, THE. (US/0011-9709). **Adv Mgr:** Barbara Gatton, **Tel** (313)596-0366. **819**

DEUTSCH-AMERIKANISCHE GESCHAFTSBEZIEHUNGEN. (GW/0932-2973). **665**

DEUTSCH - BRASILIANISCHE HEFTE. CADERNOS GERMANO - BRASILEIROS. (GW). **2551**

DEUTSCHAMERIKANER (CHICAGO), DER. (US/0273-5261). **2532**

DEUTSCHE BUHNE, DIE. (GW). **5363**

DEUTSCHE HEBE- UND FORDERTECHNIK. (GW/0012-0278). **5099**

DEUTSCHE JUGEND. (GW/0012-0332). **5282**

DEUTSCHE KRANKENPFLEGEZEITSCHRIFT. (GW/0012-074X). **3855**

DEUTSCHE LEBENSMITTEL-RUNDSCHAU. (GW/0012-0413). **2333**

DEUTSCHE MILCHWIRTSCHAFT (HILDESHEIM). (GW/0012-0480). **194**

DEUTSCHE OPTIKERZEITUNG. (GW/0344-7103). **3874**

DEUTSCHE RICHTERZEITUNG. (GW). **2960**

DEUTSCHE SCHRIFT, DIE. (GW). **3276**

DEUTSCHE SCHWARZBUNTE. (GW/0343-3145). **210**

DEUTSCHE SPRACHE. (GW/0340-9341). **3276**

DEUTSCHE STOMATOLOGIE. (GW/0863-4904). **1322**

DEUTSCHE STUDIEN (SCHLOSS BLECKEDE). (GW/0012-0812). **2515**

DEUTSCHE UNIVERSITATSZEITUNG. (GW). **1820**

DEUTSCHE WEINBAU, DER. (GW). **2366**

DEUTSCHE ZAHNAERZTLICHE ZEITSCHRIFT. (GW/0012-1029). **1322**

DEUTSCHE ZEITSCHRIFT FUER MUND-, KIEFER- UND GESICHTS- CHIRURGIE. (GW/0343-3137). **3963**

DEUTSCHE ZEITSCHRIFT FUER ONKOLOGIE. (GW/0931-0037). **3816**

DEUTSCHE ZEITSCHRIFT FUER SPORTMEDIZIN. (GW/0344-5925). **3954**

DEUTSCHER GARTENBAU. (GW). **2413**

DEUTSCHES ALLGEMEINES SONNTAGSBLATT. (GW). **5801**

DEUTSCHES ARZTEBLATT. (GW/0012-1207). **3571**

DEUTSCHES TIERARZTEBLATT. (GW/0340-1898). **5508**

DEUTSCHES VERWALTUNGSBLATT. (GW/0012-1363). **2960**

DEUTSCHLAND ARCHIV. (GW/0012-1428). **4471**

DEVELOPMENT AND PSYCHOPATHOLOGY. (US/0954-5794). **4584**

DEVELOPMENT (CAMBRIDGE). (UK/0950-1991). **541**

DEVELOPMENT COOPERATION. (FR). **2909**

DEVELOPMENT DOSSIER / ACFOA. (AT). **2909**

DEVELOPMENT FORUM - UNITED NATIONS. (US/0251-6632). **1479**

DEVELOPMENT IN PRACTICE. (UK/0961-4524). **Adv Mgr:** T. Milner, **Tel** (0805)313196. **2909**

DEVELOPMENT JOURNAL (LONDON). (UK/0957-4115). **4642**

DEVELOPMENT POLICY AND ADMINISTRATION REVIEW. (II). **4642**

DEVELOPMENT POLICY REVIEW. (UK/0950-6764). **2909**

DEVELOPMENT SOUTHERN AFRICA (SANDTON, SOUTH AFRICA). (SA). **2909**

DEVELOPMENT. SUPPLEMENT. (UK). **Adv Mgr:** R Skaer, **Tel** 44 223 420482. **541**

DEVELOPMENTAL DISABILITIES BULLETIN. (CN/1184-0412). **Adv Mgr:** H. Groot, **Tel** (403)492-4505. **4386**

DEVELOPMENTAL MEDICINE & CHILD NEUROLOGY. (UK/0012-1622). **3657**

DEVELOPMENTAL NEUROPSYCHOLOGY. (US/8756-5641). **3571**

DEVELOPMENTAL NEUROSCIENCE. (SZ/0378-5866). **3831**

DEVELOPMENTAL PHARMACOLOGY AND THERAPEUTICS. (SZ/0379-8305). **4299**

DEVELOPMENTAL PSYCHOBIOLOGY. (US/0012-1630). **453**

DEVELOPMENTAL PSYCHOLOGY. (US/0012-1649). **4584**

DEVELOPPEMENT PERSONNEL. (FR/0985-3766). **1110**

DEVELOPPEURS LEVALLOIS-PERRET. (FR/1145-2099). **4836**

DEVENIR. (SZ). **3571**

DEVIANCE ET SOCIETE. (SZ/0378-7931). **4584**

DEVIANT BEHAVIOR. (US/0163-9625). **4584**

DEVON & CORNWALL NOTES & QUERIES. (UK/0012-1681). **2685**

DEVON DISPATCH, THE. (CN/0710-5495). **5783**

DEWAN MASYARAKAT. (MY). **5198**

DEXTER LEADER, THE. (US). **5691**

DGA NEWS. (US/1075-6116). **Adv Mgr:** Scott Burnell. **4067**

DHZ MARKT. (NE). **2811**

DIABETE ET NUTRITION. (FR/0012-1789). **3727**

DIABETES CARE. (US/0149-5992). **3727**

DIABETES DIALOGUE. (CN/0703-5764). **3727**

DIABETES EDUCATOR, THE. (US/0145-7217). **3727**

DIABETES FORECAST. (US/0095-8301). **3727**

DIABETES IN THE NEWS (1987). (US/0893-5939). **Adv Mgr:** Beth Kuzma. **3728**

DIABETES SELF-MANAGEMENT. (US/0741-6253). **3728**

DIABETES SPECTRUM. (US/1040-9165). **3728**

DIABETIC MEDICINE. (UK/0742-3071). **3728**

DIABETIC TRAVEL ER, THE. (US/0899-2398). **5468**

DIABLO BUSINESS. (US/1055-7431). **665**

DIACHRONICA. (GW/0176-4225). **3277**

DIACRITICS. (US/0300-7162). **3341**

DIAGNOSIS (ORADELL, N.J.). (US/0163-3228). **3571**

DIAGNOSTIC ENGINEERING : NEWSLETTER OF THE INSTITUTION OF DIAGNOSTIC ENGINEERS. (UK/0269-0225). **1970**

DIAGNOSTIC IMAGING (SAN FRANCISCO, CALIF.). (US/0194-2514). **3940**

DIAGNOSTIC MICROBIOLOGY AND INFECTIOUS DISEASE. (US/0732-8893). **562**

DIAGNOSTIC ONCOLOGY. (SZ/1013-8129). **3816**

DIAGNOSTICA PER IMMAGINI. (IT). **3941**

DIAKONIA (MAINZ, GERMANY : 1972). (GW/0341-9592). **4953**

DIAL ELECTRICAL ELECTRONICS SALES CONTACTS. (UK). **2041**

DIAL ENGINEERING SALES CONTACTS. (UK). **2112**

DIALECTICA. (SZ/0012-2017). **4345**

DIALECTICAL ANTHROPOLOGY. (NE/0304-4092). **235**

DIALOG (EDMONTON). (CN/0842-8336). **Adv Mgr:** Kim Harrold. **4386**

DIALOG (ST. PAUL). (US/0012-2033). **Adv Mgr:** Ruth Taylor, **Tel** (207)799-4387. **4953**

DIALOGHI DI ARCHEOLOGIA. (IT/0392-8535). **266**

DIALOGO ECUMENICO. (SP/0210-2870). **4953**

DIALOGO FILOSOFICO. (SP/0213-1196). **4345**

DIALOGOS. (UK). **Adv Mgr:** Anne Kidson. **3277**

DIALOGOS. (PR/0012-2122). **4345**

DIALOGUE & ALLIANCE. (US/0891-5881). **4953**

DIALOGUE - ANGLICAN CHURCH OF CANADA. DIOCESE OF ONTARIO. (CN/1184-6283). **Adv Mgr Tel** (613)544-4774. **4953**

DIALOGUE - CANADIAN PHILOSOPHICAL ASSOCIATION. (CN/0012-2173). **4345**

DIALOGUE IN INSTRUMENTAL MUSIC EDUCATION. (US/0147-7544). **4114**

DIALOGUE : JOURNAL OF ADDIS ABABA UNIVERSITY MAIN CAMPUS TEACHERS ASSOCIATION. (US). **Adv Mgr:** George Jones, **Tel** (607)256-4215. **1820**

DIALOGUE (MILWAUKEE, WIS.). (US/0012-2246). **4345**

DIALOGUE (MUNROE FALLS, OHIO). (US/0279-568X). **Adv Mgr:** Tiffany Komasara. **319**

DIALOGUES ET CULTURES. (CN/0226-6881). **3277**

DIALYSIS & TRANSPLANTATION. (US/0090-2934). **3571**

DIAMOND DEPOSITIONS, SCIENCE AND TECHNOLOGY. (US/1051-9084). **1023**

DIAMOND INTERNATIONAL. (UK/0957-0446). **Adv Mgr:** Diane Taylor. **2914**

DIAMOND NEWS & S.A. JEWELLER. (SA). **2914**

DIAMOND REGISTRY BULLETIN, THE. (US/0199-9753). **2914**

DIAMOND TRAIL NEWS. (US). **5669**

DIAMOND WORLD. (II). **Adv Mgr:** Alok Kala. **2914**

DIAMOND WORLD REVIEW. (IS). **2914**

DIAMONDBACK, THE. (US). **Adv Mgr:** Chris Stelzig. **5686**

DIAMOND'S JAPAN BUSINESS DIRECTORY. (JA). **665**

DIANDU YU HUANBAO. (CC/1000-4742). **2041**

DIANOIA (CAMROSE). (CN/1192-1854). **Adv Mgr:** C. Jensen McClog, **Tel** (403)679-1502. **1820**

DIAPASON (CHICAGO), THE. (US/0012-2378). **4114**

DIARIO DE HOY. REPERTORIO, EL. (ES). **Adv Mgr:** Fabricio Altamirano, **Tel** 503 2710122. **5800**

DIARIO LAS AMERICAS. (US/0744-3234). **5649**

DIARIST'S JOURNAL. (US). **3381**

DIASTEMA. (SA/0419-0955). **1322**

DICKENS QUARTERLY. (US/0742-5473). **3381**

DICKENSIAN, THE. (UK/0012-2440). **Adv Mgr:** Edward Preston. **3381**

DICKENSON STAR, THE. (US/0746-584X). **5758**

DICKEY COUNTY LEADER. (US). **Adv Mgr:** Doug Robb. **5725**

DICKINSON LAW REVIEW. (US/0012-2459). **2960**

DICKINSON PRESS (DICKINSON, N.D. 1942), THE. (US/1049-6718). **5725**

DICKINSON STUDIES. (US/0164-1492). **3462**

DICTA / NEWSLETTER FOR ATTORNEYS OF SAN DIEGO COUNTY. (US/0417-4569). **Adv Mgr:** Jana Davis. **2960**

DICTIONNAIRE DE L'INDUSTRIE FRANCAISE. (FR). **Adv Mgr:** Mr. Chombart. **665**

DIDAKTIEF. (NE). **1735**

DIDASCALIA (ROSARIO, SANTA FE, ARGENTINA). (AG). **Adv Mgr:** Nestor A. Nortega. **5028**

DIDSBURY BOOSTER AND MOUNTAIN VIEW COUNTY NEWS. (CN/0316-683X). **Adv Mgr:** Alison Wright. **5783**

DIE CASTING MANAGEMENT. (US/0745-449X). **3477**

DIEHARD (BOSTON, MASS.). (US/0896-7970). **Adv Mgr:** Jan Cheves. **2773**

DIELECTRICS & EI NEWS BULLETIN. (SW). **2041**

DIEN AN TH O. (US/0885-1255). **5758**

DIENSTLEISTUNGS UND BEHORDEN-COMPASS. (AU). **665**

DIESEL & GAS TURBINE WORLDWIDE. (US/0278-5994). **2112**

DIESEL CAR. (UK/0956-3806). **Adv Mgr:** Helen Kirkhope. **5412**

DIET AND HEALTH MAGAZINE. (US/1048-8391). **4189**

DIETETIQUE (MONTREAL). (CN/0701-1350). **4190**

DIETSCHE WARANDE EN BELFORT. (BE/0012-2645). **3381**

DIFESA PENALE, LA. (IT). **3106**

DIFFUSION DES PROGRAMMES AUDIOVISUELS, LA. (BE). **4368**

DIGEST BUSINESS & LAW JOURNAL. (CN/0315-811X). **3099**

DIGEST FOR HOME FURNISHERS. (US/1053-4571). **2905**

DIGEST OF CHIROPRACTIC ECONOMICS, THE. (US/0415-8407). **3572**

DIGEST OF INFORMATION AND PATENT REVIEW. (UK). **Adv Mgr:** T. Green. **2588**

DIGEST OF REPORT - TRANSPORT AND ROAD RESEARCH LABORATORY. (UK/0269-8196). **5440**

DIGEST OF SOFTWARE REVIEWS : EDUCATION, THE. (US/0749-9302). **1285**

DIGESTION. (SZ/0012-2823). **3744**

DIGESTIVE DISEASES (BASEL). (SZ/0257-2753). **3744**

DIGESTIVE ENDOSCOPY : OFFICIAL JOURNAL OF THE JAPAN GASTROENTEROLOGICAL ENDOSCOPY SOCIETY. (JA/0915-5635). **Adv Mgr:** Y. Matsumoto. **3744**

DIGHTON HERALD (DIGHTON, KAN. : 1916). (US). **5675**

DIKAIO KAI POLITIKE (THESSALONIKE, GREECE : 1982). (GR). **3127**

DILIMAN REVIEW, THE. (PH/0012-2858). **5198**

DILLON HERALD, THE. (US). **Adv Mgr:** Johnnie Daniels. **5742**

DIME NOVEL ROUND-UP (1953). (US/0012-2874). **3381**

DIMENSIONAL STONE. (US/0883-0258). **613**

DIMENSIONS (LITTLE ROCK, ARK. 1973). (US/0160-6425). **1892**

DIMENSIONS (NEW YORK, N.Y.). (US/0882-1240). **Adv Mgr:** C. Perkins, **Tel** (212)255-7951. **2685**

DIMENSIONS OF CRITICAL CARE NURSING. (US/0730-4625). **3855**

DIMENSIONS (WINONA, MINN.). (US/1057-4506). **Adv Mgr:** Gloria, **Tel** (507)452-0023. **1182**

DIMS. DRUG INDEX FOR MALAYSIA & SINGAPORE. (HK). **4299**

DINUBA SENTINEL. (US/0745-6654). **Adv Mgr:** Bob Raison. **5634**

DIOGENES (ENGLISH ED.). (IT/0392-1921). **4345**

DIONISO. (IT). **5363**

DIONYSOS (SUPERIOR, WISC.). (US/1044-4149). **1342**

DIOTIMA. (GR/1010-7363). **4345**

DIPLOMACY AND STATECRAFT. (UK/0959-2296). **Adv Mgr:** Anne Kidson. **4520**

DIPLOMAT (LONDON, ENGLAND), THE. (UK). **4520**

DIPLOMATIC HISTORY. (US/0145-2096). **Adv Mgr:** John Paschetto. **2731**

DIPLOMATIC WORLD BULLETIN AND DELEGATES WORLD BULLETIN, THE. (US/0363-8200). **4520**

DIPLOMES

DIPLOMES - UNIVERSITE DE MONTREAL. (CN/0228-9636). **1820**

DIQIU HUAXUE. (CC/0379-1726). **1373**

DIRECT MAGAZINE. (US). **923**

DIRECT MARKETING MARKET PLACE, THE. (US/0192-3137). **728**

DIRECT MARKETING NEWS (MARKHAM). (CN/1187-7111). **Adv Mgr:** George Gadjovich. **923**

DIRECTION. (US/0092-7449). **5381**

DIRECTION ET GESTION DES ENTREPRISES. (FR/0012-320X). **665**

DIRECTIONS (AUSTIN, TEX.). (US/0742-678X). **1237**

DIRECTIONS IN GOVERNMENT. (AT/1030-391X). **4472**

DIRECTIONS (NEW YORK, N.Y. 1975). (US/0360-473X). **3206**

DIRECTIONS (NEW YORK, N.Y. : 1985). (US/0883-9727). **923**

DIRECTOR (LONDON. 1935). (UK/0012-3242). **666**

DIRECTOR (MADISON, WIS.), THE. (US/0199-3186). **Adv Mgr:** kellie Schilling. **2407**

DIRECTOR, THE. (II/0012-3250). **665**

DIRECTORIO COMERCIAL E INDUSTRIAL DE EL SALVADOR. EL SALVADOR'S COMMERCIAL AND INDUSTRIAL DIRECTORY. (ES). **1604**

DIRECTORIO DE SOCIOS / CAMARA DE COMERCIO AMERICANA EN ESPANA. (SP). **819**

DIRECTORIO MPM : MEDIOS AUDIO/VISUALES; INFORMACION Y TARIFAS. (MX). **758**

DIRECTORIO POSTAL DE PANAMA. (PN). **1144**

DIRECTORS & BOARDS. (US/0364-9156). **865**

DIRECTORY. (US/0543-2774). **3206**

DIRECTORY - AMERICAN ACADEMY OF DERMATOLOGY. (US/0278-9000). **3720**

DIRECTORY / AMERICAN CHAMBER OF COMMERCE IN ITALY. (IT). **819**

DIRECTORY - AMERICAN GROUP PRACTICE ASSOCIATION. (US/0098-2377). **Adv Mgr:** Fred Haag. **3779**

DIRECTORY AND REGISTER / ROLLS-ROYCE OWNERS' CLUB. (US/0485-3695). **5413**

DIRECTORY AND YEAR BOOK OF AMERICAN BUSINESS IN IRELAND. (IE). **666**

DIRECTORY AND YEARBOOK - HUMAN FACTORS SOCIETY. (US/0270-5311). **1970**

DIRECTORY - BELGIAN AMERICAN CHAMBER OF COMMERCE IN THE UNITED STATES, INC, THE. (US/0196-7622). **819**

DIRECTORY - BRITISH COLUMBIA MOTOR TRANSPORT ASSOCIATION. (CN/0714-8658). **5381**

DIRECTORY - CANADIAN STAMP DEALERS' ASSOCIATION. (CN/0827-2034). **2785**

DIRECTORY / COMPOSERS' FORUM, INC, THE. (US). **4114**

DIRECTORY / ENGINEERING EMPLOYERS' FEDERATION. (UK/0141-7592). **1970**

DIRECTORY FOR EXCEPTIONAL CHILDREN, THE. (US/0070-5012). **1877**

DIRECTORY FOR ZAMBIA, MALAW, BOTSWANA AND ADJACENT TERRITORIES, THE. (ZA). **2639**

DIRECTORY - HOME ECONOMISTS IN BUSINESS, SECTION OF THE AMERICAN HOME ECONOMICS ASSOCIATION. (US/0569-5058). **2789**

DIRECTORY : JUVENILE AND ADULT CORRECTIONAL DEPARTMENTS, INSTITUTIONS, AGENCIES AND PAROLING AUTHORITIES, UNITED STATES AND CANADA. (US). **3163**

DIRECTORY OF ADMINISTRATORS OF COMMUNITY, TECHNICAL, AND JUNIOR COLLEGES. (US/8756-4254). **1820**

DIRECTORY OF AGRICULTURAL CO-OPERATIVES IN THE UNITED KINGDOM. (UK). **79**

DIRECTORY OF AMERICAN BUSINESS IN AUSTRIA. (AU). **666**

DIRECTORY OF ASSOCIATIONS IN CANADA. (CN/0316-0734). **5230**

DIRECTORY OF ATA MEMBERS. (US). **2785**

DIRECTORY OF AUSTRALIAN ACADEMIC AND RESEARCH LIBRARIES. (AT). **3206**

DIRECTORY OF BOOK, CATALOG, AND MAGAZINE PRINTERS. (US/0895-139X). **4564**

DIRECTORY OF BUILDERS AND CONTRACTORS. (II). **613**

DIRECTORY OF CANADIAN ARCHIVES. (CN/0711-0413). **2481**

DIRECTORY OF CANADIAN ORCHESTRAS AND YOUTH ORCHESTRAS / ANNUAIRE CANADIEN DES ORCHESTRES ET ORCHESTRES DES JEUNES. (CN/0705-6249). **4114**

DIRECTORY OF COLORADO LIBRARIES ... & LIBRARY STATISTICS / COLORADO DEPARTMENT OF EDUCATION. (US). **3206**

DIRECTORY OF COMMUNITY SERVICES IN METROPOLITAN TORONTO. (CN/0315-0631). **5282**

DIRECTORY OF CONTRACT SERVICE FIRMS. (US/0148-1819). **1970**

DIRECTORY OF DELAWARE LIBRARIES, A. (US/0730-5222). **3207**

DIRECTORY OF ENVIRONMENTAL ORGANIZATIONS (LOS ANGELES). (US/0270-1111). **2213**

DIRECTORY OF EUROPEAN RETAILERS. (UK). **953**

DIRECTORY OF FACILITIES AND SERVICES FOR LEARNING DISABLED. (US). **1877**

DIRECTORY OF FLORIDA INDUSTRIES. (US). **923**

DIRECTORY OF FOREST INDUSTRIES IN MALAYSIA. (MY). **2400**

DIRECTORY OF FURTHER EDUCATION. (UK). **1800**

DIRECTORY OF GEOSCIENCE DEPARTMENTS, NORTH AMERICA. (US). **Adv Mgr:** Jeannie Gay, **Tel** (703)379-2480. **1373**

DIRECTORY OF HIGHER EDUCATION COURSES. (AT). **Adv Mgr:** Colin Ritchie. **1821**

DIRECTORY OF HONG KONG INDUSTRIES. (HK). **1604**

DIRECTORY OF HOTEL & MOTEL SYSTEMS. (US). **2805**

DIRECTORY OF INDIAN ECONOMIC JOURNALS. (II). **1479**

DIRECTORY OF IOWA MUNICIPALITIES. (US/0363-1842). **4643**

DIRECTORY OF KANSAS PUBLIC OFFICIALS. (US/0196-7681). **4643**

DIRECTORY OF LIBRARIES AND INFORMATION SOURCES IN THE PHILADELPHIA AREA. (US/0278-5684). **3207**

DIRECTORY OF LIBRARIES IN NEWFOUNDLAND AND LABRADOR. (CN/0317-2465). **3207**

DIRECTORY OF LONG TERM CARE CENTRES IN CANADA. (CN/0226-5419). **3779**

DIRECTORY OF MAILING LIST COMPANIES. (US). **666**

DIRECTORY OF MAJOR MALLS. (US/0732-5983). **954**

DIRECTORY OF MEDICAL COMPUTER SYSTEMS. (US). **1182**

DIRECTORY OF MEMBER AGENCIES IN THE UNITED STATES AND CANADA. (US/1045-1684). **5283**

DIRECTORY OF MEMBERS / AMERICAN ASSOCIATION OF HOMES FOR THE AGING. (US). **5283**

DIRECTORY OF MEMBERS - AUSTRALIAN BOOK PUBLISHERS ASSOCIATION. (AT). **4828**

DIRECTORY OF MEMBERS - DIRECTORS GUILD OF AMERICA. (US/0419-2052). **Adv Mgr:** Adele Field. **4068**

DIRECTORY OF MEMBERS - FEDERATION OF INDIAN PUBLISHERS. (II). **4814**

DIRECTORY OF MEMBERS / LOS ANGELES COUNTY MEDICAL ASSOCIATION. (US). **3913**

DIRECTORY OF MEMBERS - PERIODICAL WRITERS ASSOCIATION OF CANADA. (CN/0833-9821). **2919**

DIRECTORY OF MEMBERS - PUNJAB HARYANA & DELHI CHAMBER OF COMMERCE AND INDUSTRY. (II/0376-8511). **819**

DIRECTORY OF MICHIGAN MUNICIPAL OFFICIALS. (US/0148-7442). **4643**

DIRECTORY OF MINING PROGRAMS. (US/0884-917X). **2138**

DIRECTORY OF MINNESOTA CITY OFFICIALS. (US/0890-1651). **4643**

DIRECTORY OF MULTIMEDIA EQUIPMENT, SOFTWARE, AND SERVICES / ICIA. (US). **Adv Mgr:** Kim Williams, **Tel** (703)273-7200. **1153**

DIRECTORY OF NORTH AMERICAN FAIRS AND EXPOSITIONS. (US). **4860**

DIRECTORY OF OBSOLETE SECURITIES. (US/0085-0551). **896**

DIRECTORY OF OKLAHOMA. (US/0095-0920). **4644**

DIRECTORY OF OKLAHOMA'S CITY AND TOWN OFFICIALS. (US/0099-197X). **4644**

DIRECTORY OF POETRY PUBLISHERS. (US). **3462**

DIRECTORY OF PROFESSIONAL GENEALOGISTS. (US/1055-6710). **Adv Mgr:** Suzanne McVetty, **Tel** (516)997-8393. **2445**

DIRECTORY OF PROFESSIONAL GENEALOGISTS AND RELATED SERVICES. (US/0272-3387). **2445**

DIRECTORY OF PROFESSIONAL RELOCATION AND REAL ESTATE SERVICES. (US). **4836**

DIRECTORY OF RELIGION BROADCASTING (1982/83), THE. (US/0731-0331). **Adv Mgr:** Dick Reynolds, **Tel** (704)393-0602. **4953**

DIRECTORY OF SAN FRANCISCO ATTORNEYS. (US/0092-9174). **2962**

DIRECTORY OF SMALL PRESS & MAGAZINE EDITORS & PUBLISHERS, THE. (US/0277-1519). **4814**

DIRECTORY OF SOURCES FOR EDITORS, REPORTERS & RESEARCHERS, THE. (CN/1197-5148). **2919**

DIRECTORY OF SOUTHEAST ASIAN ACADEMIC & SPECIAL LIBRARIES. (TH). **3208**

DIRECTORY OF TENNESSEE MANUFACTURERS. (US/0070-6450). **3478**

DIRECTORY OF TERTIARY EXTERNAL COURSES IN AUSTRALIA. (AT/0818-0687). **1736**

DIRECTORY OF THE AMERICAN PSYCHOLOGICAL ASSOCIATION (1978). (US/0196-6545). **1925**

DIRECTORY OF THE FOREST PRODUCTS INDUSTRY. (US/0070-6477). **2400**

DIRECTORY OF THE NATIONAL ASSOCIATION OF ADVISORS FOR THE HEALTH PROFESSIONS. (US/1043-6669). **3913**

DIRECTORY OF THE NEW MEXICO BENCH AND BAR. (US/8756-1611). **2962**

DIRECTORY OF THE PUBLIC AQUARIA OF THE WORLD. (US/0085-0039). **5581**

DIRECTORY OF UNDERGRADUATE POLITICAL SCIENCE FACULTY. (US/0884-5859). **4472**

DIRECTORY OF WIRE COMPANIES OF NORTH AMERICA. (US/1048-373X). **Adv Mgr:** Cliff Crawford, **Tel** (203)684-5877. **2113**

DIRECTORY OF WOMEN IN BUSINESS PROFESSIONS & MANAGEMENT. (AT). **5554**

DIRECTORY / ONTARIO AMATEUR FOOTBALL ASSOCIATION. (CN/0713-6781). **4892**

DIRECTORY - PARENT COOPERATIVE PRESCHOOLS INTERNATIONAL. (CN). **1803**

DIRECTORY - PERSEKUTUAN PEKILAND-PEKILANG MALAYSIA. (MY/0126-9801). **3478**

DIRECTORY. POSTAL CODE. (CN/0835-4693). **1144**

DIRECTORY / SPECTROSCOPY SOCIETY OF CANADA. (CN/0709-8448). **4401**

DIRECTORY - SPORTS FEDERATION OF CANADA. (CN/0229-3161). **4893**

DIRECTORY - STATE BAR OF GEORGIA. (US/1067-4861). **2962**

DIRECTORY - TEXAS OSTEOPATHIC MEDICAL ASSOCIATION. (US/0196-6340). **3572**

DIRECTORY / THE AMERICAN CHAMBER OF COMMERCE IN FRANCE. (FR). **Adv Mgr:** A. Salvan, **Tel** 33 1 47 23 70 28. **819**

DIRECTORY / THE ASSOCIATED CHURCH PRESS. (US/0066-8710). **4953**

DIRECTORY / TOY TRAIN OPERATING SOCIETY. (US/0732-9873). **2584**

DIRECTORY - U. S. COAST GUARD ACADEMY ALUMNI ASSOCIATION. (US). **1101**

DIRECTORY (UNITARIAN UNIVERSALIST ASSOCIATION : 1965). (US/0503-2636). **5059**

DIRECTORY / VIRGINIA HIGH SCHOOL LEAGUE, INC. (US). **1736**

DIRES. (CN/0820-0890). **5198**

DIREZIONE DEL PERSONALE. (IT). **Adv Mgr:** Brevi Melania, **Tel** 02 6709558. **940**

DIRIGENTE RURAL, O. (BL/0012-3374). **79**

DIRITTO AEREO. (IT/0012-3390). **2962**

DIRITTO DELLE RADIODIFFUSIONI E DELLE TELECOMUNICAZIONI, IL. (IT). **2962**

DIRITTO DELL'ECONOMIA, IL. (IT). **2962**

DIRITTO DI AUTORE, IL. (IT/0012-3420). **1304**

DIRITTO DI FAMIGLIA E DELLE PERSONE. (IT). **3120**

DIRITTO E PRATICA NELL ASSICURAZIONE. (IT). **2963**

DIRITTO ECCLESIASTICO E RASSEGNA DI DIRITTO MATRIMONIALE, IL. (IT/0012-3455). **2963**

DIRT BIKE. (US/0364-1546). **4081**

DIRT (NEW YORK, N.Y.). (US/1061-8481). **Adv Mgr:** Andrew Crossfield, **Tel** (212)551-9333. **3995**

DIRT RIDER. (US/0735-4355). **4081**

DIRT WHEELS MAGAZINE. (US/0745-0192). **4893**

DIRTY LINEN. (US/1047-4315). **Adv Mgr:** Linda Cohn, **Tel** (410)768-9261. **4115**

DIS COLLECTOR (CHESWOLD, DEL. : 1981). (US/0731-843X). **4115**

DISABILITY ISSUES. (US/1063-9373). **4387**

DISABILITY RAG, THE. (US/0749-8586). **Adv Mgr:** Sharon Kute Mellem, **Tel** (502)459-5343. **4387**

DISABILITY TODAY (ST. CATHARINES). (CN/1186-9666). **4387**

DISABLED OUTDOORS. (US). **4387**

DISABLED OUTDOORS MAGAZINE. (US/1067-098X). **4387**

DISASTER RECOVERY JOURNAL. (US). **Adv Mgr:** Patti Fitzgerald, **Tel** same as publisher. **5284**

DISASTERS. (UK/0361-3666). **5284**

DISC. (US/1052-4053). **1183**

DISC SPORTS. (US/0747-9956). **4893**

DISCIPLE (ST. LOUIS, MO.). (US/0092-8372). **5059**

DISCIPLESHIP JOURNAL. (US/0273-5865). **Adv Mgr:** Dave Wilson, **Tel** (719)531-3579. **4954**

DISCIPLIANA (1960). (US/0732-9881). **Adv Mgr:** J.Seale. **4954**

DISCLOSURE RECORD. (US/0094-2561). **788**

DISCOUNT MERCHANDISER, THE. (US/0012-3579). **954**

DISCOURSE. (UK/0159-6306). **1736**

DISCOURSE PROCESSES. (US/0163-853X). **3277**

DISCOVER COSTA RICA. (US). **5468**

DISCOVER GUATEMALA. (US). **5468**

DISCOVER INDIA. (HK). **Adv Mgr:** Xavier Collaco. **5468**

DISCOVER SOUTHWEST WISCONSIN'S HIDDEN VALLEYS. (US/0738-8071). **5468**

DISCOVERING ETHIOPIA. (ET). **5468**

DISCOVERY AND INNOVATION. (KE/1015-079X). **5101**

DISCOVERY (SKOKIE, ILL.). (US/0012-3641). **5468**

DISCOVERY (VANCOUVER. 1972). (CN/0319-8480). **2191**

DISCOVERY YMCA. (US). **4850**

DISCRETE MATHEMATICS. (NE/0012-365X). **3504**

DISCURSO LITERARIO. (PY/0737-8742). **3382**

DISEASE INFORMATION. (FR/1012-5329). **5509**

DISEASES OF THE COLON & RECTUM. (US/0012-3706). **3744**

DISEGNO MAGAZINE. (IT). **1233**

DISKUSSION DEUTSCH. (GW/0342-1589). **3277**

DISNEY ADVENTURES. (US/1050-2491). **1062**

DISNEY CHANNEL MAGAZINE, THE. (US/0747-4644). **Adv Mgr:** Myles Grossman, **Tel** (212)687-4442. **1131**

DISNEY MAGAZINE. (US/0362-1960). **Adv Mgr:** V. Barne. **1063**

DISNEY NEWS. (US/0095-7178). **Adv Mgr:** K. Helgason. **4850**

DISPATCH-NEWS, THE. (US). **5742**

DISPATCH (ROCKVILLE, MD.). (US/0743-7269). **5381**

DISPENSING OPTICS. (UK/0954-3201). **Adv Mgr:** I. McGhie, **Tel** 0303 262272. **4215**

DISPLAY & DESIGN IDEAS. (US/1049-9172). **759**

DISPLAYS. (UK/0141-9382). **1228**

DISPOSABLES AND NONWOVENS. (UK/0012-3811). **5350**

DISPOSITIO. (US/0734-0591). **Adv Mgr:** Kathe Johnson. **3382**

DISSENT (NEW YORK). (US/0012-3846). **4541**

DISTINGUISHED HOME PLANS. HOMES FOR SLOPING SITES. (US/0897-6236). **298**

DISTRIBUTION D'AUJOURD'HUI. (BE/0012-3935). **3478**

DISTRIBUTION MAPS OF PESTS. SERIES A (AGRICULTURAL). (UK/0588-778X). **79**

DISTRIBUTION MAPS OF PLANT DISEASES. (UK/0012-396X). **508**

DISTRIBUTORS LINK. (US). **923**

DISTRICT COUNCIL JOURNAL. (US/0748-1179). **4645**

DISTRICT HEATING AND COOLING. (US/0885-6621). **Adv Mgr:** Tammie Jackson. **2604**

DIVER. (UK). **4893**

DIVER MAGAZINE. (CN/0706-5132). **Adv Mgr:** Peter Vassilopoulos, **Tel** (604)273-4333. **4893**

DIVER (PORTLAND CONN.), THE. (US/0273-8589). **4893**

DIVERSION (TITUSVILLE). (US/0363-4825). **4850**

DIVERSITY & DIVISION. (US/1064-7430). **Adv Mgr:** Jeff Muir, **Tel** (202)833-1801. **5244**

DIVING WORLD (VAN NUYS, CALIF.). (US/1042-1343). **4893**

DIWEN WULI XUEBAO. (CC/1000-3258). **4402**

DIXIE CONTRACTOR, THE. (US/0012-4281). **Adv Mgr:** F J Aaron. **2022**

DIXIE GUN WORKS BLACKPOWDER ANNUAL. (US/0737-0105). **3478**

DIXIE LOGGER AND LUMBERMAN MAGAZINE. (US/0046-0435). **2400**

DIZHEN DIZHI. (CC/0253-4967). **1404**

DJ TIMES. (US/1045-9693). **1131**

DM NEWS. (US/0194-3588). **923**

DMA DANCE MUSIC AUTHORITY. (US). **4115**

DMT. DANSK MUSIK TIDSSKRIFT. (DK/0106-5629). **4115**

DNA PROBES. (UK/0266-6308). **453**

DNA REPORTER. (US). **Adv Mgr:** Delaware Nurses Assoc., **Tel** (302)368-2333. **3855**

DOAR, HA-. (US/0017-6524). **5047**

DOC ITALIA / ISTITUTO NAZIONALE DELL'INFORMAZIONE. (IT). **5230**

DOCENT EDUCATOR. (US). **1893**

DOCK AND HARBOUR AUTHORITY. (UK/0012-4419). **5449**

DOCKLANDS NEWS. (UK/0264-9691). **667**

DOCTOR GUILDFORD. (UK/0046-0451). **3737**

DOCTOR'S REVIEW. (CN/0821-5758). **4850**

DOCTRINE AND LIFE. (IE/0012-446X). **4954**

DOCUMENTA OPHTHALMOLOGICA. (NE/0012-4486). **3874**

DOCUMENTAIRE EN EUROPE, LE. (BE). **4068**

DOCUMENTALISTE (PARIS). (FR/0012-4508). **3208**

DOCUMENTATION CATHOLIQUE, LA. (FR/0012-4613). **5028**

DOCUMENTATION ET BIBLIOTHEQUES. (CN/0315-2340). **3208**

DOCUMENTATION IN PUBLIC ADMINISTRATION. (II/0377-7081). **4645**

DOCUMENTS D'ANALISI GEOGRAFICA / [PUBLICACIONS DEL DEPARTAMENT DE GEOGRAFIA, UNIVERSITAT AUTONOMA DE BARCELONA]. (SP/0212-1573). **2560**

DOCUMENTS D'ARCHEOLOGIE MERIDIONALE. (FR/0184-1068). **266**

DOCUMENTS TO THE PEOPLE. (US/0270-5095). **Adv Mgr:** Jill Mortearty. **3208**

DODGE COUNTY INDEPENDENT. (US). **Adv Mgr:** Marcia Seland, **Tel** (507)634-7503. **5695**

DOE HET VEILIG. (BE/0773-6231). **2861**

DOG FANCY (LOS ANGELES, CALIF.). (US/0892-6522). **4286**

DOG WATCH, THE. (AT). **4176**

DOG WORLD. (US/0012-4893). **4286**

DOGS IN CANADA. (CN/0012-4915). **4286**

DOHNER FAMILY NEWSLETTER. (US/0736-2412). **2445**

DOLL CASTLE NEWS. (US/0363-7972). **372**

DOLL DESIGNS. (US/1050-4796). **Adv Mgr:** Everett Knapp, **Tel** (800)226-0148. **372**

DOLL READER. (US/0744-0901). **2584**

DOLL TIMES. (US). **2584**

DOLLARS & SENSE (SOMERVILLE, MASS.). (US/0012-5245). **Adv Mgr:** Debbie Dover, **Tel** (617)628-8411. **1480**

DOLLS. (US/0733-2238). **372**

DOLOR. (SP/0214-0659). **3573**

DOLORES STAR. (US/0889-5155). **Adv Mgr:** Sam Green. **5642**

DOLPHIN DIGEST. (US/0744-3226). **Adv Mgr:** K. Keidel, **Tel** (305)594-0508. **4893**

DOMES (MILWAUKEE, WIS.). (US/1060-4367). **2768**

DOMESTIC ANIMAL ENDOCRINOLOGY. (US/0739-7240). **3728**

DOMINION LAW REPORTS. (CN/0012-5350). **3089**

DOMINION POST. (US). **Adv Mgr:** Titus Workman. **5763**

DOMODOMO : FIJI MUSEUM QUARTERLY. (FJ). **4087**

DOMUS. (IT/0012-5377). **2900**

DONEGAL ANNUAL. (IE/0416-2773). **2685**

DONGWUXUE JIKAN. (CC/1000-1786). **5581**

DONKEY DIGEST. (AT/1031-6280). **5582**

DONT ACTE. (CN/0381-1875). **669**

DOON PRESS. (US). **5670**

DOOR COUNTY ADVOCATE. (US/0749-7180). **Adv Mgr:** James Petersen. **5767**

DOORS AND HARDWARE. (US/0361-5294). **Adv Mgr:** R. Silverstein. **613**

DORCHESTER COUNTY GENEALOGICAL MAGAZINE, THE. (US/8755-2353). **2445**

DORCHESTER EAGLE-RECORD. (US). **5742**

DORM. (US/0743-2860). **1091**

DOS INTERNATIONAL. (GW/0933-1557). **1183**

DOSSIER. L'UFFICIO TECNICO. (IT/0394-8315). **298**

DOSSIERS DU MARKETING DIRECT, LES. (FR/0769-5918). **923**

DOSTOEVSKY STUDIES : JOURNAL OF THE INTERNATIONAL DOSTOEVSKY SOCIETY. (AU/1013-2309). **3382**

DOUBLE FEATURE (LETHBRIDGE). (CN/0824-278X). **2278**

DOUBLE-GUN JOURNAL, THE. (US/1050-2262). **4893**

DOUBLE LIAISON. (FR/0012-5709). **4223**

DOUBLE LIAISON-CHIMIE DES PEINTURES. (FR/0012-5709). **4223**

DOUBLE REED, THE. (US/0741-7659). **4115**

DOUGLAS COUNTY POST-GAZETTE. (US/0746-1437). **5706**

DOUGLAS DAILY DISPATCH. (US). **5630**

DOUGLAS ENTERPRISE, THE. (US). **Adv Mgr:** Jim Merritt. **5653**

DOWN BEAT. (US/0012-5768). **4115**

DOWN EAST. (US/0012-5776). **5468**

DOWN SYNDROME TODAY. (US). **4387**

DOWN THE ROAD. (US/1072-4656). **4203**

DOWN UNDER QUILTS. (AT/1033-4513). **5183**

DOWNEAST ANCESTRY. (US/0891-0960). **2446**

DOWNRIVER NEWS-HERALD, THE. (US/0194-7303). **Adv Mgr:** Bill Dillingham. **5691**

DOWNSIDE REVIEW, THE. (UK/0012-5806). **3382**

DOWNTOWN NEWS. (US). **Adv Mgr:** Maria Flannigan. **5634**

DOWNTOWN PROMOTION REPORTER. (US/0363-2830). **759**

DP, DANSK PRESSE. (DK). **2515**

DPN: DESIGN PRODUCT NEWS. (CN/0319-8413). **1971**

DR. ATKINS' HEALTH REVELATIONS. (US/1073-8169). **3573**

DR. FOX'S NEW HEALTH JOURNAL. (US/1043-8165). **4774**

DR : THE FASHION BUSINESS. (UK). **1083**

DRAFT HORSE JOURNAL, THE. (US/0012-5865). **2798**

DRAG RULES. (US/0277-4771). **4893**

DRAGON (LAKE GENEVA, WIS.). (US/0279-6848). **4860**

DRAHT. (GW/0012-5911). **4001**

DRAIN ENTERPRISE. (US). **5733**

DRAINAGE CONTRACTOR. (CN). **80**

DRAKE LAW REVIEW. (US/0012-5938). **2964**

DRAMA. (UK/0012-5946). **5363**

DRAMA BROADSHEET. (UK/0261-1651). **5363**

DRAMA-LOGUE. (US/0272-2720). **5364**

DRAMA/THEATRE TEACHER, THE. (US/1046-5022). **5364**

DRAMATHERAPY (NEWSLETTER). (UK). **5364**

DRAMATHERAPY : THE JOURNAL OF THE BRITISH ASSOCIATION OF DRAMATHERAPY. (UK). **5364**

DRAUDZES VESTIS. (CN/0701-0214). **4954**

DRAUGAS. (US). **Adv Mgr:** Nijole. **5659**

DRAUGHTING & DESIGN. (UK/0951-5704). **1183**

DRAWING (NEW YORK, N.Y. 1979). (US/0191-6963). **Adv Mgr:** Dianne Turner. **349**

DRESDEN ENTERPRISE AND SHARON TRIBUNE. (US). **5745**

DRESSAGE & CT. (US/0147-796X). **2798**

DREW GATEWAY, THE. (US/0012-6152). **4954**

DRILLING CONTRACTOR. (US/0046-0702). **4254**

DRINKING WATER & BACKFLOW PREVENTION. (US/1055-2782). **5533**

DRIPPING SPRINGS DISPATCH, THE. (US/0746-603X). **Adv Mgr:** Dale Roberson. **5749**

DRIVER/EDUCATION (TORONTO). (CN/1183-7314). **5413**

DRIVER (MIAMI, FLA.). (US/1062-9394). **Adv Mgr:** Mary Rizzotti, **Tel** (304)599-3482. **4893**

DRIVERS AND CONTROLS. (UK/0950-5490). **1971**

DROIT ET AFFAIRES INTERNATIONAL. (FR/0184-5926). **2964**

DROIT SOCIAL. (FR/0012-6438). **Adv Mgr:** Epstrin. **3146**

DRUCK PRINT. (GW/0012-6462). **4564**

DRUCKINDUSTRIE (ST. GALLEN). (SZ/0046-0737). **4564**

DRUCKWELT. (GW/0012-6519). **4564**

DRUG ABUSE UPDATE. (US/0739-6562). **1343**

DRUG AND CHEMICAL TOXICOLOGY (NEW YORK, N.Y. 1978). (US/0148-0545). **3980**

DRUG AND THERAPEUTICS BULLETIN. (ITALIAN EDITION). (UK). **4299**

DRUG DEVELOPMENT AND INDUSTRIAL PHARMACY. (US/0363-9045). **4300**

DRUG INFORMATION JOURNAL. (US/0092-8615). **4300**

DRUG METABOLISM AND DISPOSITION. (US/0090-9556). **4300**

DRUG NEWS & PERSPECTIVES. (SP/0214-0934). **4301**

DRUG STORE NEWS. (US/0191-7587). **4301**

DRUG STORE NEWS, INSIDE PHARMACY. (US/0891-9828). **4301**

DRUG TARGETING. (UK/0952-0317). **4301**

DRUG THERAPY (NEW YORK, N.Y.). (US/0001-7094). **3573**

DRUG THERAPY TOPICS. (US/0882-6684). **4301**

DRUG TOPICS. (US/0012-6616). **4301**

DRUG TOPICS REDBOOK UPDATE. (US/0731-8596). **4301**

DRUGLINK INFORMATION LETTER. (UK/0305-4349). **1343**

DRUGS & SOCIETY (NEW YORK, N.Y.). (US/8756-8233). **1344**

DRUGS IN PEDIATRICS. (CN/0824-703X). **3903**

DRUGS IN PSYCHIATRY (POINTE-CLAIRE). (CN/0824-7102). **4302**

DRUGS MADE IN GERMANY. (GW/0012-6683). **4302**

DRUGS OF THE FUTURE. (SP/0377-8282). **4302**

DRUM CORPS WORLD (MADISON). (US/0164-3223). **Adv Mgr:** Jeff Collins, **Tel** (916)392-6994. **4115**

DRUM. EAST AFRICAN EDITION. (KE/0419-7690). **2278**

DRUMMER (SAN FRANCISCO, CALIF.). (US/1055-7415). **2794**

DRVNA INDUSTRIJA. (CI/0012-6772). **2400**

DRYCLEANER NEWS. (US/0012-6802). **5350**

DTW. DEUTSCHE TIERAERZTLICHE WOCHENSCHRIFT. (GW/0341-6593). **5509**

DU. (SZ/0012-6837). **2515**

DUAL SPORTER. (US). **Adv Mgr:** Jean P. Offers. **4081**

DUBUQUE LEADER, THE. (US/0012-6918). **5670**

DUCKS UNLIMITED. (US/0012-6950). **2191**

DUKE JOURNAL OF COMPARATIVE & INTERNATIONAL LAW. (US/1053-6736). **3127**

DUKE LAW JOURNAL. (US/0012-7086). **2964**

DUKE MATHEMATICAL JOURNAL. (US/0012-7094). **3504**

DULCIMER PLAYER NEWS, THE. (US/0098-3527). **4115**

DULUTH BUDGETEER, THE. (US). **Adv Mgr:** Jeff Swor. **5695**

DUMAS CLARION, THE. (US). **Adv Mgr:** Glenda Ward. **5631**

DUNCANVILLE SUBURBAN. (US/0888-1960). **Adv Mgr:** Leslie Nasche. **5749**

DUNDALK EAGLE, THE. (US). **Adv Mgr:** Kim Boone. **5686**

DUNE BUGGIES AND HOT VWS. (US/0012-7132). **5413**

DUNGEON MASTER. (US). **2794**

DUNLAP REPORTER (DUNLAP, IOWA : 1913). (US). **Adv Mgr:** Agnes Morris. **5670**

DUNN COUNTY NEWS, THE. (US). **Adv Mgr:** Denny Bodoh. **5767**

DUODECIM. (FI/0012-7183). **3573**

DUQUESNE LAW REVIEW. (US/0093-3058). **2964**

DURANGO HERALD, THE. (US). **Adv Mgr:** Sharon Hermes. **5642**

DURHAM UNIVERSITY JOURNAL, THE. (UK/0012-7280). **1822**

DUTCH HARBOR FISHERMAN. (US). **Adv Mgr:** Deidre Fellner, **Tel** (907)581-2092. **5629**

DUTCHESS, THE. (US/0735-6242). **2446**

DVADTSAT DVA. (IS). **Adv Mgr:** M. Baz-Oz, **Tel** 972-3-394525. **3382**

DVZ DEUTSCHE VERKEHRS-ZEITUNG. (GW/0342-166X). **5381**

DW DOKUMENTATION WASSER. (GW/0012-5156). **5533**

DWB. (BE/0012-2645). **3383**

DWF. (IT). **5554**

DWJ, DEUTSCHES WAFFEN-JOURNAL. (GW). **Adv Mgr:** Norbert Rieger. **4893**

DX MAGAZINE, THE. (US/1043-4208). **1154**

DYES AND PIGMENTS. (UK/0143-7208). **4223**

DYNAMIC BUSINESS : A PUBLICATION OF THE SMALLER MANUFACTURER'S COUNCIL. (US/0279-4039). **670**

DYNAMIC (NEW YORK, N.Y.). (US/0741-0263). **4472**

DYNAMIC SYSTEMS AND APPLICATIONS. (US/1056-2176). **3504**

DYNAMICS. (BE). **Adv Mgr:** J. Laffineur. **670**

DYNAMICS AND STABILITY OF SYSTEMS. (UK/0268-1110). **1246**

DYNAMISCHE PSYCHIATRIE. (GW/0012-740X). **3924**

DZIENNIK ZWIAZKOWY. (US/0742-6615). **Adv Mgr:** Wanda Such. **5660**

E & MJ INTERNATIONAL DIRECTORY OF MINING. (US). **2138**

E I C, ELECTRONIQUE, INDUSTRIELLE & COMMERCIALE. (CN/0226-7748). **2056**

E.I.T.D. ELECTRONIC INDUSTRY TELEPHONE DIRECTORY. (US/0422-9053). **1605**

E (NORWALK, CONN.). (US/1046-8021). **Adv Mgr:** Alyssa Burger. **2164**

EAA EXPERIMENTER. (US/0894-1289). **18**

EAGLE (CAMBRIDGE, N.Y.), THE. (US/0745-9831). **Adv Mgr:** Richard Farrell, **Tel** (518)677-5158. **5716**

EAGLE, THE. (US). **3163**

EAP DIGEST. (US/0273-8910). **1344**

EAR AND HEARING. (US/0196-0202). **3887**

EAR (NEW YORK, N.Y.). (US/0893-9500). **4115**

EARLY AMERICAN LIFE. (US/0012-8155). **2731**

EARLY AMERICAN LITERATURE. (US/0012-8163). **3341**

EARLY CHILD DEVELOPMENT AND CARE. (UK/0300-4430). **2278**

EARLY CHILDHOOD NEWS. (US). **1803**

EARLY CHILDHOOD RESEARCH QUARTERLY. (US/0885-2006). **1803**

EARLY CHINA. (US/0362-5028). **2650**

EARLY EDUCATION AND DEVELOPMENT. (US/1040-9289). **1737**

EARLY KEYBOARD JOURNAL. (US/0899-8132). **Adv Mgr:** K. Jacob, **Tel** (704)334-3468. **4116**

EARLY KEYBOARD STUDIES NEWSLETTER. (US/0882-0201). **4116**

EARLY MUSIC. (UK/0306-1078). **4116**

EARLY MUSIC NEWS. (UK). **4116**

EARNINGS FORECASTER. (US/1073-631X). **Adv Mgr:** Eden Leviinson. **897**

EARNSHAW'S INFANTS-GIRLS-BOYS WEAR REVIEW. (US/0161-2786). **1083**

EARTH FIRST! (1991). (US/1055-8411). **2164**

EARTH GARDEN. (AT/0310-222x). **Adv Mgr:** Judith Gray, **Tel** (054)241399. **5244**

EARTH ISLAND JOURNAL. (US/1041-0406). **Adv Mgr:** Justin Lowe. **2164**

EARTH, MOON, AND PLANETS. (NE/0167-9295). **395**

EARTH SCIENCE BULLETIN. (US/0012-8236). **1354**

EARTH SCIENCE OPPORTUNITIES. (US/1058-0425). **1354**

EARTH SURFACE PROCESSES AND LANDFORMS. (UK/0197-9337). **1374**

EARTH (WAUKESHA, WIS.). (US/1056-148X). **Adv Mgr:** Kristi Rummel, **Tel** 800 558-1544. **1355**

EARTH WORK. (US/1060-5053). **Adv Mgr:** Devi Cannon, **Tel** (703)524-2441. **2192**

EARTHCARE NORTHWEST. (US/0732-684X). **2192**

EARTHKEEPER MAGAZINE. (CN/1181-7828). **Adv Mgr:** M. Johnson. **2164**

EARTHWORD. (US). **2164**

EAST AFRICAN AGRICULTURAL AND FORESTRY JOURNAL. (KE/0012-8325). **80**

EAST AFRICAN CERTIFICATE OF EDUCATION : REGULATIONS AND SYLLABUSES. (UG/0376-9151). **1862**

EAST AFRICAN MEDICAL JOURNAL, THE. (KE/0012-835X). **3573**

EAST ASIA QUARTERLY. (CH). **4541**

EAST ASIA SERIES. (US/0066-0957). **2503**

EAST ASIAN EXECUTIVE REPORTS. (US/0272-1589). **3099**

EAST ASIAN HISTORY. (AT/1036-6008). **2650**

EAST CAROLINA UNIVERSITY PUBLICATIONS IN HISTORY. (US/0070-8089). **2615**

EAST CENTRAL EUROPE. (US/0094-3037). **2846**

EAST COAST ANGLER. (US/0899-0506). **2300**

EAST COAST ROCKER. (US). **Adv Mgr:** D. Hein. **4116**

EAST COUNTY CHRONICLE. (US). **5656**

EAST EUROPEAN INVESTMENT MAGAZINE. (US/1063-4029). **Adv Mgr:** Mr. Drecun, **Tel** (212)388-1500. **897**

EAST EUROPEAN QUARTERLY. (US/0012-8449). **2686**

EAST HAMPTON STAR, THE. (US). **Adv Mgr:** Greg Robinson. **5716**

EAST LAUDERDALE NEWS. (US). **5626**

EAST LONDON RECORD. (UK/0141-6286). **2686**

EAST MIDLAND ARCHAEOLOGICAL BULLETIN. (UK). **267**

EAST MIDLAND GEOGRAPHER. (UK/0012-8481). **2560**

EAST ORANGE RECORD. (US). **Adv Mgr:** Erik Kent, **Tel** (908)686-7700. **5710**

EAST OREGONIAN. (US). **Adv Mgr:** Al Donnelly. **5733**

EAST ROCKAWAY LYNNBROOK OBSERVER. (US/0746-2093). **5716**

EAST TENNESSEE ROOTS. (US/0885-4025). **2446**

EAST TEXAS BANNER. (US). **Adv Mgr:** Lacole Mitchell. **5749**

EAST TEXAS HISTORICAL JOURNAL. (US/0424-1444). **2732**

EAST TEXAS MEDICINE. (US/1050-6675). **3573**

EAST (TOKYO, JAPAN). (JA/0012-8295). **Adv Mgr:** Y. Masaki, **Tel** 03 3446-7721. **2650**

EAST TROY NEWS, THE. (US/0749-5943). **Adv Mgr:** David Wright, **Tel** (414)763-3511. **5767**

EAST/WEST BUSINESS & TRADE. (US/1065-6790). **Adv Mgr:** Justin Ford. **832**

EAST/WEST EDUCATION. (US/0899-0247). **1737**

EASTERN ANTHROPOLOGIST, THE. (II/0012-8686). **235**

EASTERN BASKETBALL. (US/0195-0223). **4893**

EASTERN BLOC CHEMICALS. (UK). **974**

EASTERN BLOC ENERGY. (UK/0954-2981). **Adv Mgr:** n. **1937**

EASTERN DAILY PRESS. (UK/0307-0956). **Adv Mgr:** Marie Barnes, **Tel** same as publisher. **5812**

EASTERN ECONOMIC JOURNAL. (US/0094-5056). **1480**

EASTERN EUROPEAN & SOVIET TELECOM REPORT. (US/1054-6499). **1154**

EASTERN EUROPEAN ECONOMICS. (US/0012-8775). **1481**

EASTERN GAZETTE (1985), THE. (US/8750-961X). **5685**

EASTERN GREAT LAKES SALES GUIDE TO HIGH-TECH COMPANIES. (US/1040-0559). **5102**

EASTERN ITASCAN, THE. (US). **Adv Mgr:** Leanne Stanley, **Tel** (218)885-2100. **5695**

EASTERN PHARMACIST. (II/0012-8872). **4302**

EASTERN TRAVEL SALES GUIDE. (US/0739-4780). **5468**

EASTERN/WESTERN QUARTER HORSE JOURNAL. (US/0191-7714). **2798**

EASTLAND TELEGRAM (EASTLAND, TEX. : 1953). (US). **5749**

EASTSIDE MESSENGER. (US/0891-2300). **Adv Mgr:** Bruce Russel. **5728**

EASTSIDE PARENT. (US/1065-2655). **Adv Mgr:** Alayne Sulkin. **2278**

EASTSIDE SUN. (US). **Adv Mgr:** Jonathan Sanchez. **5634**

EASY LIVING GUIDE : THE ORIGINAL GUIDE FOR THE COMMUNITIES OF NEW WESTMINSTER, COQUITLAM, PORT MOODY, BURNABY. (CN/0821-7394). **2487**

EASY READER. (US/0194-6412). **5634**

EATERN AIZONA COURIER. (US). **5630**

EAU, L'INDUSTRIE, LES NUISANCES, L'. (FR/0755-5016). **2227**

EAU VIVE, L'. (CN/0046-1016). **5783**

EAWARUDO. (JA). **18**

EBA NEWSLETTER. (FR/0987-2507). **788**

EBONY. (US/0012-9011). **2259**

EBONY MAN. (US/0884-4879). **3995**

EBSCO BULLETIN OF SERIALS CHANGES. (US/0360-0637). **415**

ECCLESIA MADRID. (SP/0012-9038). **5029**

ECCTIS 2000 : THE UK COURSES INFORMATION SERVICE ON CD-ROM. (UK). **Adv Mgr:** Nicola Colley. **1822**

ECHEC +. (FR/0825-0049). **Adv Mgr:** Robert Finta, **Tel** same as publisher. **4860**

ECHO. (SZ/0012-9143). **1893**

ECHO DE LA PRESSE (PARIS, FRANCE). (FR). **2919**

ECHO DES BOIS, L'. (BE). **2400**

ECHO : QUOTIDIEN DE L'ECONOMIE ET DE LA BOURSE, L'. (BE). **Adv Mgr:** Francine Mirmovitch, **Tel** 011 32 2 526 5566. **1481**

ECHO-X. (CN/0820-6295). **3941**

ECHOCARDIOGRAPHY (MOUNT KISCO, N.Y.). (US/0742-2822). **3704**

ECHOES (BLAINE, ME.). (US/1043-3341). **Adv Mgr:** Gordon Hammond. **2732**

ECHOS DU CENTRE INTERNATIONAL D'ETUDES PEDAGOGIQUES DE SEVRES. (FR/0154-5280). **2686**

ECHOS DU MONDE CLASSIQUE. (CN/0012-9356). **267**

ECLIPSE-NEWS-REVIEW, THE. (US). **5670**

ECM POST-REVIEW, THE. (US/0891-0731). **5695**

ECN. EUROPEAN CHEMICAL NEWS. (UK/0014-2875). **974**

ECO E NOTIZIARIO DELL ECOLOGIA. (IT). **2213**

ECODECISION (MONTREAL). (CN/1183-2355). **2192**

ECOLE. (IT). **2213**

ECOLE DES PARENTS, L'. (FR/0424-2238). **2278**

ECOLOGICAL APPLICATIONS. (US/1051-0761). **2213**

ECOLOGICAL ENTOMOLOGY. (UK/0307-6946). **5607**

ECOLOGICAL ILLNESS LAW REPORT. (US/8755-9013). **3110**

ECOLOGICAL MONOGRAPHS. (US/0012-9615). **2214**

ECOLOGICAL SOCIETY OF AUSTRALIA BULLETIN. (AT). **2214**

ECOLOGIST (1979). (UK/0261-3131). **2214**

ECOLOGY AND FARMING : INTERNATIONAL IFOAM MAGAZINE. (GW). **81**

ECOLOGY LAW QUARTERLY. (US/0046-1121). **3110**

ECOLOGY OF FOOD AND NUTRITION. (US/0367-0244). **4190**

ECOLOGY (TEMPE). (US/0012-9658). **2214**

ECONEWS (ARCATA, CALIF.). (US/0885-7237). **Adv Mgr:** Joanie Weiser, **Tel** (707)822-6918. **2192**

ECONOMETRIC REVIEWS. (US/0747-4938). **1481**

ECONOMETRICA. (US/0012-9682). **1481**

ECONOMIA & LAVORO (1967). (IT/0012-978X). **1481**

ECONOMIA AZIENDALE : FOUR MONTHLY REVIEW OF THE ACCADEMIA ITALIANA DI ECONOMIA AZIENDALE. (IT). **1591**

ECONOMIA BRASILEIRA E SUAS PERSPECTIVAS, A. (BL/0424-2386). **1481**

ECONOMIA DELLE FONTI DI ENERGIA. (IT). **1937**

ECONOMIA E BANCA. (IT/0393-9243). **Adv Mgr:** Dr. Sergio Costa. **1481**

ECONOMIA INFORMA. (MX/0185-0849). **Adv Mgr:** Ernesto Bartolucci. **1481**

ECONOMIA (LISBOA). (PO/0870-3531). **1481**

ECONOMIA MONTANA. (IT). **1481**

ECONOMIA MONTANA ROMA. (IT/0012-9836). **Adv Mgr:** Flaminio Laureri, **Tel** 06 54 03 224. **2214**

ECONOMIC AFFAIRS (CALCUTTA). (II/0424-2513). **1482**

ECONOMIC AFFAIRS (LONDON, ENGLAND). (UK/0265-0665). **1482**

ECONOMIC ANALYSIS AND POLICY. (AT/0313-5926). **1591**

ECONOMIC AND FINANCIAL COMPUTING. (UK/0962-2780). **1482**

ECONOMIC AND INDUSTRIAL DEMOCRACY. (UK/0143-831X). **1664**

ECONOMIC AND LABOUR RELATIONS REVIEW : ELRR, THE. (AT/1035-3046). **2861**

ECONOMIC AWARENESS. (UK/0953-4997). **1482**

ECONOMIC BOOKS : CURRENT SELECTIONS. (US/0093-2485). **1482**

ECONOMIC BOTANY. (US/0013-0001). **508**

ECONOMIC BULLETIN - SINGAPORE INTERNATIONAL CHAMBER OF COMMERCE. (SI/0037-5659). **819**

ECONOMIC DEVELOPMENT QUARTERLY. (US/0891-2424). **1483**

ECONOMIC DEVELOPMENT REVIEW (SCHILLER PARK, ILL.). (US/0742-3713). **Adv Mgr:** Marion Morgan. **1483**

ECONOMIC FORUM MINORITY BUSINESS REVIEW. (US). **671**

ECONOMIC GEOLOGY (MONTPELIER, VT.). (US/0531-8262). **1374**

ECONOMIC HISTORY REVIEW, THE. (UK/0013-0117). **1557**

ECONOMIC HOME OWNER, THE. (US/1055-8284). **2821**

ECONOMIC INQUIRY. (US/0095-2583). **1483**

ECONOMIC MODELLING. (UK/0264-9993). **1591**

ECONOMIC PAPERS / THE ECONOMIC SOCIETY OF AUSTRALIA. (AT). **Adv Mgr:** C. Orchard. **1484**

ECONOMIC QUALITY CONTROL. (GW/0940-5151). **1484**

ECONOMIC RECORD, THE. (AT/0013-0249). **1484**

ECONOMIC REVIEW AND OUTLOOK. (SQ). **1484**

ECONOMIC REVIEW (COLOMBO). (CE/0259-9775). **1484**

ECONOMIC SYSTEMS RESEARCH. (UK/0953-5314). **Adv Mgr:** Linda Salter. **1485**

ECONOMIC THEORY. (GW/0938-2259). **1591**

ECONOMIC TIMES. (UK). **671**

ECONOMIC TRENDS (NEW DELHI). (II/0014-9470). **1591**

ECONOMIC WORLD DIRECTORY OF JAPANESE COMPANIES IN USA. (US/0163-4682). **832**

ECONOMIC WORLD (LOS ANGELES). (US/0164-3525). **Adv Mgr:** Herb Pressman, **Tel** (212)986-1588. **1486**

ECONOMICA. (IO). **1486**

ECONOMICA (LONDON). (UK/0013-0427). **1486**

ECONOMICS & POLITICS (OXFORD, ENGLAND). (UK/0954-1985). **1486**

ECONOMICS CLASSICS - OLD AND RARE BOOKS ON ECONOMICS. (US). **1486**

ECONOMICS ILLUSTRATED. (US). **Adv Mgr:** J. Simone, **Tel** (213)229-1961. **1486**

ECONOMICS (LONDON). (UK/0300-4287). **1486**

ECONOMICS OF EDUCATION REVIEW. (US/0272-7757). **1737**

ECONOMICS OF PLANNING. (NE/0013-0451). **1558**

ECONOMIE ET GESTION AGRO-ALIMENTAIRE. (FR/0981-8715). **81**

ECONOMIE ET HUMANISME. (FR/0245-9132). **1634**

ECONOMIE ET STATISTIQUE. (FR/0336-1454). **1532**

ECONOMIE FAMILIALE HOME ECONOMICS, L'. (FR/0397-8389). **2789**

ECONOMIE, L'. (FR/0013-0478). **1558**

ECONOMIE PROSPECTIVE INTERNATIONALE. (FR/0242-7818). **1634**

ECONOMIES ET SOCIETES. (FR/0013-0567). **1487**

ECONOMISCH EN SOCIAAL TIJDSCHRIFT. (BE/0013-0575). **Adv Mgr:** same as editor. **671**

ECONOMIST (LONDON). (UK/0013-0613). **1559**

ECONOMISTAS (MADRID, SPAIN). (SP/0212-4386). **1487**

ECONOMY AND SOCIETY. (UK/0308-5147). **5199**

ECONOMY BULLETINS. (UK). **1487**

ECOS. (AT/0311-4546). **2227**

ECOS. (UK/0143-9073). **Adv Mgr:** Rick Minter, **Tel** 0242 579059. **2192**

ECOSSISTEMA / FACULDADE DE AGRONOMIA E ZOOTECNIA "MANOEL CARLOS GONCALVES.". (BL/0100-4107). **81**

ECRITS SUR LE CINEMA (SUPPLEMENT). (CN/0822-6350). **4068**

ECRITURE FRANCAISE DANS LE MONDE. (CN/0228-7951). **3383**

ECUMENE. (UK/0967-4608). **Adv Mgr:** Mary Attree, **Tel** 071 873 6336. **2560**

ECUMENICAL REVIEW, THE. (SZ/0013-0796). **4955**

EDAD DE ORO (MADRID, SPAIN). (SP). **3383**

EDAV. EDUCAZIONE AUDIOVISIVA. (IT/0393-098X). **1737**

EDDA. (NO/0013-0818). **3341**

EDESIPAR. (HU/0013-0842). **2334**

EDGEBROOK EDITION OF THE TIMES REVIEW. (US/0895-0105). **Adv Mgr:** Bill Tapper. **5660**

EDGELEY MAIL, THE. (US). **Adv Mgr:** Robert L. Ketchum, **Tel** (701)493-2261. **5725**

EDGERTON ENTERPRISE. (US). **5695**

EDGERTON REPORTER, THE. (US). **Adv Mgr:** David Fitzgerald, **Tel** (608)884-3367. **5767**

EDGEWATER TRIBUNE. (US/0745-774X). **5642**

EDI (DALLAS, TEX.). (US/1045-5698). **1258**

EDI FORUM. (US/1048-3047). **Adv Mgr:** Trinda Gray O'Connor, **Tel** (708)848-0135. **671**

EDI MONTHLY REPORT. (US/1062-645X). **4645**

EDI WORLD. (US/1055-0399). **Adv Mgr:** R. Sessa. **2042**

EDI YELLOW PAGES INTERNATIONAL. (US). **1183**

EDINBURGH BIBLIOGRAPHICAL SOCIETY TRANSACTIONS. (UK/0140-7082). **415**

EDIOS. (CN/0707-2287). **4345**

EDISON-NORWOOD EDITION OF THE TIMES REVIEW. (US/0895-0091). **Adv Mgr:** Bill Tapper. **5660**

EDITING HISTORY. (US/0883-3532). **4814**

EDITIO. (GW/0931-3079). **3341**

EDITION ANNUELLE : AVIS AUX NAVIGATEURS. (CN). **4176**

EDITOR & PUBLISHER. (US/0013-094X). **4814**

EDITOR & PUBLISHER. (US). **924**

EDITOR & PUBLISHER. SYNDICATE DIRECTORY. (US). **2919**

EDITOR, EL. (US). **5749**

EDITOR'S DIGEST. (US). **4814**

EDITORS' NOTES. (US/0888-3173). **2919**

EDIZIONI PER LA CONSERVAZIONE. (IT/1120-1819). **4828**

EDMOND EVENING SUN, THE. (US). **Adv Mgr:** Jack Hovorka, **Tel** (405)341-2121 ext. 130. **5731**

EDMORE HERALD. (US/8750-5444). **5725**

EDMS JOURNAL. (US/1058-0379). **Adv Mgr:** Debra Fitzgibbons, **Tel** 617-247-1511. **1183**

EDON COMMERCIAL. (US). **Adv Mgr:** Mary Howard, **Tel** (419)298-2369. **5728**

EDP AUDITOR JOURNAL, THE. (US/0885-0445). **Adv Mgr:** M. Faddock. **1258**

EDUCA. (UK/0141-8459). **1912**

EDUCADORES; REVISTA LATINOAMERICANA DE EDUCACION. (AG/0422-6399). **1794**

EDUCATED TRAVELER, THE. (US/1052-0597). **5469**

EDUCATING ABLE LEARNERS, DISCOVERING & NURTURING TALENT. (US/0896-9574). **1878**

EDUCATION 3-13. (UK/0300-4279). **1804**

EDUCATION ALTERNATIVES. (AT/1037-5104). **1738**

EDUCATION AND HEALTH : JOURNAL OF THE HEA SCHOOLS HEALTH EDUCATION UNIT, UNIVERSITY OF EXETER. (UK/0265-1602). **Adv Mgr:** S. Forster. **1855**

EDUCATION AND SOCIETY (MELBOURNE). (AT/0726-2655). **1738**

EDUCATION & TREATMENT OF CHILDREN. (US/0748-8491). **Adv Mgr:** A. Reitz. **1893**

EDUCATION AUTHORITIES DIRECTORY AND ANNUAL, THE. (UK/0070-9131). **1862**

EDUCATION DIGEST, THE. (US/0013-127X). **1739**

EDUCATION (EDINBURGH). (UK/0013-1164). **1863**

EDUCATION ENFANTINE, L'. (FR/0013-1288). **1739**

EDUCATION FOR LIBRARY AND INFORMATION SERVICES, AUSTRALIA. (AT). **3209**

EDUCATION FORUM (TORONTO. 1988). (CN/0840-9269). **Adv Mgr:** R. Brandon. **1893**

EDUCATION IN SCIENCE. (UK/0013-1377). **5102**

EDUCATION LAW JOURNAL. (CN/0838-2875). **2965**

EDUCATION LIBRARIES. (US/0148-1061). **3209**

EDUCATION LIBRARIES JOURNAL. (UK/0957-9575). **3209**

EDUCATION MUSICALE, L'. (FR/0013-1415). **4116**

EDUCATION QUARTERLY, THE. (II/0013-1482). **1740**

EDUCATION, RESEARCH AND PERSPECTIVES. (AT/0311-2543). **1822**

EDUCATION STATISTICS - (SWAZILAND). (SQ). **1794**

EDUCATION TODAY (TORONTO). (CN/0843-5081). **Adv Mgr:** Wendy Agostino, **Tel** (905)841-3118. **1740**

EDUCATION WEEK. (US/0277-4232). **1741**

EDUCATION WITH PRODUCTION. (BS). **1741**

EDUCATION YEAR BOOK. (UK/0143-5469). **1741**

EDUCATIONAL ADMINISTRATION AND POLICY REVIEW. (AT). **1863**

EDUCATIONAL ADMINISTRATION QUARTERLY. (US/0013-161X). **1863**

EDUCATIONAL & TRAINING TECHNOLOGY INTERNATIONAL : ETTI. (UK/0954-7304). **1741**

EDUCATIONAL ASSESSMENT. (US/1062-7197). **1741**

EDUCATIONAL CHANGE. (US/0748-0806). **1741**

EDUCATIONAL COMPUTING AND TECHNOLOGY. (UK). **Adv Mgr:** Tina Kirkby. **1223**

EDUCATIONAL FACILITY PLANNER. (US/1059-7417). **1863**

EDUCATIONAL FOUNDATIONS (ANN ARBOR, MICH.). (US/1047-8248). **1741**

EDUCATIONAL GERONTOLOGY. (US/0360-1277). **1800**

EDUCATIONAL HORIZONS. (US/0013-175X). **1741**

EDUCATIONAL MANAGEMENT & ADMINISTRATION : JOURNAL OF THE BRITISH EDUCATIONAL MANAGEMENT AND ADMINISTRATION SOCIETY. (UK/0263-211X). **1863**

EDUCATIONAL MEASUREMENT, ISSUES AND PRACTICE. (US/0731-1745). **1893**

EDUCATIONAL PLANNING. (US/0315-9388). **1742**

EDUCATIONAL POLICY (LOS ALTOS, CALIF.). (US/0895-9048). **1742**

EDUCATIONAL PSYCHOLOGIST. (US/0046-1520). **4586**

EDUCATIONAL PSYCHOLOGY IN PRACTICE. (UK/0266-7363). **4586**

EDUCATIONAL RECORD, THE. (US/0013-1873). **1822**

EDUCATIONAL RESEARCH QUARTERLY. (US/0196-5042). **1742**

EDUCATIONAL RESEARCH (WINDSOR). (UK/0013-1881). **1742**

EDUCATIONAL RESEARCHER (WASHINGTON, D.C. : 1972). (US/0013-189X). **1742**

EDUCATIONAL REVIEW (BIRMINGHAM). (UK/0013-1911). **1742**

EDUCATIONAL STUDIES. (UK/0305-5698). **1743**

EDUCATIONAL STUDIES IN MATHEMATICS. (NE/0013-1954). **1743**

EDUCATIONAL TECHNOLOGY. (US/0013-1962). **1893**

EDUCATIONAL THEORY. (US/0013-2004). **Adv Mgr:** D. Becket. **1743**

EDUCATORE. (IT). **Adv Mgr:** Alessandra Piazzoni. **1743**

EDUCATORS GUIDE TO FREE HEALTH, PHYSICAL EDUCATION AND RECREATION MATERIALS. (US). **1855**

EDUCATOR'S INTERNATIONAL GUIDE TO FREE & LOW COST HEALTH AUDIO-VISUAL TEACHING AIDS. (US). **4774**

EDUCAZIONE SANITARIA E PROMOZIONE DELLA SALUTE. (IT). **Adv Mgr:** Dott Dalla, **Tel** 06-86207165. **4774**

EDUCOM REVIEW. (US/1045-9146). **1822**

EEO REVIEW, THE. (US/0148-6934). **1664**

EESTI HAAL. (UK). **5812**

EFFECTIVE SCHOOL PRACTICES. (US/1068-7378). **Adv Mgr Tel** (503)485-1293. **1894**

EFRYDIAU ATHRONYDDOL. (UK). **4345**

EFTHINI. (GR). **2515**

EGALITE (MONCTON). (CN/0226-6873). **Adv Mgr:** Jean-Claude Bellefeuille, **Tel** (506)383-5653. **4472**

EGESZSEGNEVELES. EDUCATIO SANITARIA. (HU). **4774**

EGLISE CANADIENNE, L'. (CN/0013-2322). **4955**

EGO KIDS MAGAZINE. (CN). **1083**

EGON RONAY'S GUIDE TO HOTELS, RESTAURANTS, PUBS, INNS IN GREAT BRITAIN AND IRELAND AND LONDON PENSIONS. (UK). **2805**

EGREGIOUS STEAMBOAT JOURNAL, THE. (US/1058-3556). **Adv Mgr:** Sandra Custer. **4176**

EGYPT INVESTMENT & BUSINESS DIRECTORY. (UA). **897**

EGYPTIAN HOTEL GUIDE. (UA). **2805**

EGYPTIAN JOURNAL OF DAIRY SCIENCE. (UA/0378-2700). **2334**

EGYPTIAN ORTHOPEDIC JOURNAL. (UA/0013-242X). **Adv Mgr Tel** (03)422 5626. **3881**

EGYPTIAN POPULATION AND FAMILY PLANNING REVIEW, THE. (UA). **4552**

EIA GUIDE. (US). **949**

EIGHTEENTH-CENTURY FICTION (DOWNSVIEW, ONT.). (CN/0840-6286). **3383**

EIGHTEENTH CENTURY (LUBBOCK), THE. (US/0193-5380). **2686**

EIGHTEENTH-CENTURY STUDIES. (US/0013-2586). **319**

EIGSE CHEOL TIRE. (IE/0332-298X). **4160**

EINKAUFS-1X1 DER DEUTSCHEN INDUSTRIE. (GW/0343-5881). **Adv Mgr:** Mr. Rinas. **832**

EINTRACHT HARMONY. (US). **2515**

EIRE-IRELAND (ST. PAUL). (US/0013-2683). **3341**

EISEI DOBUTSU. (JA/0424-7086). **5607**

EISENBAHN INGENIEUR KALENDER. (GW/0071-0075). **5431**

EISENBAHNINGENIEUR, DER. (GW/0013-2810). **5431**

EISMA 'S VAKPERS. (NE/0920-2099). **4223**

EISZEITALTER UND GEGENWART. (GW/0424-7116). **1374**

EJHP, EUROPEAN JOURNAL OF HOSPITAL PHARMACY. (GW/0992-4663). **Adv Mgr Tel** 0711-2582-245. **4302**

EKATA. (CN/0715-3902). **2532**

EKKLESIA KAI THEOLOGIA : EKKLESIASTIKE KAI THEOLOGIKE EPETERIS TES HIERAS ARCHIEPISKOPES THYATEIRON KAI MEGALES VRETANNIAS. (GR). **5039**

EKLITRA / ASSOCIATION CULTURELLE PICARDE. (FR/0424-7175). **2515**

EKONOMICKY CASOPIS. (XO/0013-3035). **1488**

EKONOMSKA POLITIKA. (YU/0013-3248). **Adv Mgr Tel** 381 11 334464. **671**

EKSPOR (INDONESIA. BIRO PUSAT STATISTIK). (IO). **832**

EKSPORT AKTUELT / FRA NORGES EKSPORTRAD. (NO/0800-6733). **833**

EKSPORT KOEBENHAVN. (DK/0900-3177). **833**

EL CHICANO (COLTON, CALIF.). (US/0893-3502). **Adv Mgr:** Christine Donelan. **5634**

EL DORADO GAZETTE, GEORGETOWN GAZETTE & TOWN CRIER. (US/8750-6289). **Adv Mgr:** Megan Costa. **5634**

EL DORADO NEWS-TIMES. (US). **Adv Mgr:** Betty Pattings. **5631**

EL PASO ARCHAEOLOGY. (US/0013-4023). **267**

EL SOL (SALINAS, CALIF.). (US/1064-1998). **5635**

ELAEIS. (MY/0128-1828). **5102**

ELASTOMERS. (US). **4455**

ELBA CLIPPER, THE. (US). **Adv Mgr:** Ferrin Cox, **Tel** (205)897-2823. **5626**

ELBERT ROGERS' WASHINGTON STATE SCORE. (US/0736-881X). **2532**

ELBERTON STAR, THE. (US). **Adv Mgr:** Amanda Slaughterback. **5653**

ELDERS WEEKLY. (AT). **Adv Mgr:** Pete Maye & Margaret Green, **Tel** 356-0320. **210**

ELECTORAL STUDIES. (UK/0261-3794). **4645**

ELECTRE BIBLIO FRENCH BOOKS IN PRINT. CD-ROM. (FR). **415**

ELECTRIC CONSUMER. (US/0745-4651). **1937**

ELECTRIC LINES. (US/0895-2116). **2043**

ELECTRIC MACHINES AND POWER SYSTEMS. (US/0731-356X). **2043**

ELECTRIC POWER SYSTEMS RESEARCH. (SZ/0378-7796). **Adv Mgr:** Ms. W van Cattenburch (Amsterdam). **2044**

ELECTRIC VEHICLE DEVELOPMENTS. (UK/0141-9811). **5381**

ELECTRICAL ADVERTISER. (US). **2044**

ELECTRICAL APPARATUS. (US/0190-1370). **2044**

ELECTRICAL BLUE BOOK, THE. (CN/0149-6174). **2044**

ELECTRICAL COMPONENT LOCATOR. DOMESTIC CARS, LIGHT TRUCKS & VANS, IMPORTED CARS & TRUCKS. (US/0743-6076). **5414**

ELECTRICAL DESIGN & MFG. (US/1065-7436). **Adv Mgr:** Jackie Fanella. **2044**

ELECTRICAL EQUIPMENT LONDON. (UK/0013-4317). **2045**

ELECTRICAL INDIA. (II/0013-435X). **2045**

ELECTRICAL MANUFACTURING (LIBERTYVILLE, ILL.). (US/0895-3716). **3478**

ELECTRICAL MARKETING. (US/0149-5771). **2045**

ELECTRICAL PRODUCTS TUNBRIDGE WELLS, KENT. (UK/0260-1656). **Adv Mgr:** Stuart Wetherall. **2045**

ELECTRICAL WHOLESALING. (US/0013-4430). **2045**

ELECTRICAL WORLD. (US/0013-4457). **2045**

ELECTRICIDADE. (PO/0870-5364). **2045**

ELECTRICITY TODAY (PICKERING). (CN/0843-7343). **Adv Mgr:** Michele LeGresley. **2046**

ELECTRICITY WEEK. (AT/1032-5565). **2046**

ELECTROMAGNETIC NEWS REPORT. (US/0270-4935). **2046**

ELECTROMAGNETICS. (US/0272-6343). **2046**

ELECTROMYOGRAPHY AND CLINICAL NEUROPHYSIOLOGY. (BE/0301-150X). **3796**

ELECTRON SPIN RESONANCE. (UK/0305-9758). **1015**

ELECTRON (WILLOUGHBY, OHIO), THE. (US/0740-1922). **Adv Mgr:** Denise M. Zakrajsek. **5728**

ELECTRONIC ATLAS NEWSLETTER, THE. (US/1053-0924). **1183**

ELECTRONIC BUSINESS. (US/0163-6197). **2046**

ELECTRONIC BUSINESS ASIA. (HK). **2046**

ELECTRONIC BUYERS' NEWS. (US/0164-6362). **2046**

ELECTRONIC DESIGN'S GOLD BOOK. (US/0738-0399). **2047**

ELECTRONIC ENGINEERING. (UK/0013-4902). **2047**

ELECTRONIC FUEL INJECTION, DIAGNOSIS & TESTING. (US/0741-6334). **5414**

ELECTRONIC GREEN JOURNAL. (US/1076-7975). **Adv Mgr:** Katie Manjotich, **Tel** (510)841-9975. **2165**

ELECTRONIC HOUSE / INTELLIGENCE REPORT. (US). **Adv Mgr:** Steve Gragert. **1212**

ELECTRONIC MEDIA. (US/0745-0311). **1131**

ELECTRONIC MODELING. (US/0275-9136). **2047**

ELECTRONIC MUSICIAN. (US/0884-4720). **Adv Mgr:** Robin Boyce. **4116**

ELECTRONIC PRODUCT DESIGN. (UK/0263-1474). **Adv Mgr:** Patrick Flynn. **2048**

ELECTRONIC PRODUCTS (1981). (US/0013-4953). **2048**

ELECTRONIC PRODUCTS AND TECHNOLOGY. (CN/0708-4366). **Adv Mgr:** R Luton, **Tel** (416)624-8100. **2048**

ELECTRONIC SERVICING & TECHNOLOGY. (US/0278-9922). **2048**

ELECTRONIC SOURCE BOOK FOR SOUTHERN CALIFORNIA, THE. (US/8755-1527). **2048**

ELECTRONIC TECHNOLOGY (LONDON). (UK/0141-061X). **2048**

ELECTRONIC TRADER. (UK). **Adv Mgr:** Kate Lauton. **2048**

ELECTRONICA & COMUNICACIONES MAGAZINE. (SP/1130-6971). **Adv Mgr:** Corenzo Aulesa. **1110**

ELECTRONICS (1985). (US/0883-4989). **2048**

ELECTRONICS INFORMATION & PLANNING. (II/0304-9876). **2049**

ELECTRONICS KOREA. (KO). **2049**

ELECTRONICS LETTERS. (UK/0013-5194). **2049**

ELECTRONICS MANUFACTURE & TEST. (UK/0265-301X). **Adv Mgr:** Simon Eliis. **2049**

ELECTRONICS RETAILING. (US/0149-9203). **954**

ELECTRONICS SOURCE BOOK FOR SOUTH ATLANTIC, THE. (US). **2050**

ELECTRONICS TIMES. (UK). **2050**

ELECTRONICS TODAY INTERNATIONAL. (UK/0811-0727). **2050**

ELECTRONIQUE EUROPE 2000 PARIS. (FR/0994-1894). **2050**

ELECTROSOURCE : PRODUCT REFERENCE GUIDE AND TELEPHONE DIRECTORY. (CN/0826-192X). **2050**

ELEGANT BRIDE. (US). **Adv Mgr:** T.Reeves, **Tel** (919)378-6065. **2278**

ELEKTOR AACHEN. (GW/0932-5468). **Adv Mgr Tel** 749-241-8890911. **2051**

ELEKTOR ELECTRONICS. (UK/0268-4519). **2051**

ELEKTRICESTVO. (RU/0013-5380). **2051**

ELEKTRICHESKIE STANTSII. (RU/0201-4564). **2051**

ELEKTRIE. (GW/0013-5399). **2051**

ELEKTRISCHE BAHNEN. (GW/0013-5437). **5431**

ELEKTRISCHE ENERGIE-TECHNIK. (GW/0170-2033). **1937**

ELEKTROMEISTER + DEUTSCHES ELEKTROHANDWERK. (GW/0012-1258). **2051**

ELEKTRONIK VARLDEN. (SW/0033-7749). **2052**

ELEKTRONIKAI ES HRADASTECHNIKAI SZAKIRODALMI TAJEKOZTATO. (HU/0231-066X). **2052**

ELEKTROTEHNIKA (ZAGREB). (CI/0013-5844). **2052**

ELEKTROWARME INTERNATIONAL. EDITION A : ELEKTOWARME IM TECHNISCHEN AUSBAU. (GW/0174-6189). **2604**

ELEKTROWARME INTERNATIONAL. EDITION B : INDUSTRIELLE ELEKTROWARME. (GW/0340-3521). **2605**

ELEKTUUR. (NE/0013-5895). **2052**

ELEMENTARY SCHOOL GUIDANCE AND COUNSELING. (US/0013-5976). **1878**

ELEMENTARY SCHOOL JOURNAL. MICROFORM, THE. (US/0013-5984). **1743**

ELENCHUS OF BIBLICA. (IT). **4955**

ELETTRIFICAZIONE. (IT/0013-6093). **2052**

ELETTRONICA E TELECOMUNICAZIONI. (IT/0013-6123). **2052**

ELEVATOR WORLD. (US/0013-6158). **Adv Mgr:** Patricia Cartee, **Tel** (205)479-4514. **2113**

ELEVATORI MODERNI : SOLLEVAMENTO E TRASPORTO A FUNE. (IT/1121-7995). **Adv Mgr:** Arch. Colonna, **Tel** 11 39 2 27203245. **5381**

ELEX. (NE). **Adv Mgr:** U Van Noordenne. **2053**

ELF (TONAWANDA, N.Y.). (US/1054-3376). **Adv Mgr Tel** (716)695-2669. **3341**

ELGAR SOCIETY JOURNAL, THE. (UK). **5230**

ELH. (US/0013-8304). **3342**

ELIZABETHAN REVIEW, THE. (US/1066-7059). **3384**

ELIZABETHTOWN CHRONICLE (ELIZABETHTOWN, PA. : 1989). (US). **Adv Mgr:** Dave Wagner. **5736**

ELK CITY DAILY NEWS, THE. (US). **Adv Mgr:** Sharon Penny. **5732**

ELK POINT LAKELAND REVIEW. (CN/0828-7759). **5784**

ELKHART TRUTH, THE. (US/0746-7516). **5663**

ELKHORN INDEPENDENT (ELKHORN, WIS. : 1892). (US). **Adv Mgr:** R. Johnson. **5767**

ELKO DAILY FREE PRESS. (US). **Adv Mgr:** Glenas Bir. **5707**

ELKO INDEPENDENT (1915). (US). **Adv Mgr:** Sean Thompson. **5707**

ELKS MAGAZINE, THE. (US/0013-6263). **5231**

ELKTON RECORD, THE. (US/0899-966X). **5743**

ELLE. (NE). **5554**

ELLE (NEW YORK, N.Y.). (US/0888-0808). **5555**

ELLE (SPANISH EDITION). (SP). **5555**

ELLENIKA NEA (LONDON, ONT.). (CN/0821-7270). **5784**

ELLENIKE KTENIATRIKE. (GR/0018-0068). **5509**

ELLENOKANADIKA CHRONIKA. (CN/0820-7801). **5784**

ELLIS COUNTY STAR, THE. (US). **Adv Mgr:** Pat Taylor. **5675**

ELLIS REVIEW (ELLIS, KAN. : 1930). (US). **5675**

ELLSWORTH AMERICAN. (US). **Adv Mgr:** Terry L. Young. **5685**

ELLSWORTH REPORTER. (US). **Adv Mgr:** Karl Gaston. **5675**

ELMIRA INDEPENDENT. (CN/1194-1030). **Adv Mgr:** Kathy Beisel. **5784**

ELMONT HERALD. (US/1070-7328). **Adv Mgr:** Rita Mezzapelle. **5716**

ELMWOOD ARGUS, THE. (US) **5767**

ELT JOURNAL. (UK/0951-0893). **3278**

ELTEKNIK MED AKTUELL ELEKTRONIK. (SW/0346-6310). **2053**

ELVIS COSTELLO INFORMATION SERVICE. (NE). **4116**

ELVIS MONTHLY. (UK/0013-6484). **4116**

ELY ECHO. (US/0746-7087). **5695**

EMA, ELEKTRISCHE MASCHINEN. (GW). **2053**

EMAJL-KERAMIKA-STAKLO. (CI/0350-3607). **2588**

EMBEDDED SYSTEMS PROGRAMMING. (US/1040-3272). **1228**

EMBROIDERY. (UK/0013-6611). **5184**

EMBRYO TRANSFER NEWSLETTER. (US). **3760**

EMC. EDUCATIONAL MEDIA SPECIAL INTEREST COUNCIL. (CN/0824-782X). **3209**

EMC TECHNOLOGY. (US/1055-6230). **Adv Mgr:** Walter Loop, **Tel** (703)347-0030. **2053**

EMC TECHNOLOGY ... ANTHOLOGY. (US/0748-108X). **2053**

EMERALD CITY COMIX AND STORIES. (US/1042-9166). **3384**

EMERGE (NEW YORK, N.Y.). (US/0899-1154). **2533**

EMERGENCIAS. (SP). **3724**

EMERGENCY. (US/0162-5942). **4774**

EMERGENCY LIBRARIAN. (US/0315-8888). **3209**

EMERGENCY MEDICAL UPDATE. (US/1064-5934). **Adv Mgr:** Karen Douglas. **3724**

EMERGENCY MEDICINE. (US/0013-6654). **3724**

EMERGENCY PREHOSPITAL MEDICINE. (CN/0836-7272). **Adv Mgr:** John Moir, **Tel** (416)722-9839. **3724**

EMERY ENTERPRISE. (US). **5743**

EMI. EDUCATIONAL MEDIA INTERNATIONAL. (UK/0952-3987). **1894**

EMIE BULLETIN. (US/0737-9021). **3209**

EMIGRE (BERKELEY, CALIF.). (US/1045-3717). **378**

EMMA. (GW). **5555**

EMMANATIONS. (US/0734-6158). **1744**

EMMANUEL (NEW YORK, N.Y.). (US/0013-6719). **4955**

EMMY. (US/0164-3495). **Adv Mgr:** John Mccarthy. **1131**

EMOTIONAL FIRST AID. (US/0739-828X). **4586**

EMPIRE STATE MASON. (US/0013-6794). **5231**

EMPIRE STATE REPORT (1982). (US/0747-0711). **4645**

EMPIRE STATE SURVEYOR. (US). **2023**

EMPIRICAL ECONOMICS. (AU/0377-7332). **1488**

EMPIRISCHE PADAGOGIK. (GW/0931-5020). **Adv Mgr:** R.S. Jaeger. **1744**

EMPLOYEE ASSISTANCE PROGRAM MANAGEMENT LETTER. (US/0896-0941). **866**

EMPLOYEE ASSISTANCE QUARTERLY. (US/0749-0003). **2861**

EMPLOYEE BENEFIT NEWS. (US/1044-6265). **1665**

EMPLOYEE BENEFIT PLAN REVIEW. (US/0013-6808). **2879**

EMPLOYEE BENEFITS. (US/0194-3499). **1665**

EMPLOYEE RELATIONS LAW JOURNAL. (US/0098-8898). **3146**

EMPLOYEE SERVICES MANAGEMENT. (US/0744-3676). **940**

EMPLOYMENT AND WAGES. (SQ). **1666**

EMPLOYMENT INFORMATION IN THE MATHEMATICAL SCIENCES. (US/0163-3287). **1666**

EMPLOYMENT RELATIONS TODAY. (US/0745-7790). **1667**

EMPRESS CHINCHILLA BREEDER (1974). (US/0094-3282). **3183**

EMTP NEWS. (BE). **2053**

EMU TODAY & TOMORROW. (US/1062-6034). **Adv Mgr:** Denise Whitehead. **5582**

ENBI TO PORIMA. (JA/0367-021X). **4455**

ENCEPHALE. (FR/0013-7006). **3832**

ENCHANTMENT. (US/0046-1946). **2533**

ENCLITIC. (US/0193-5798). **3342**

ENCOMIA. (US/0363-4841). **3342**

ENCORE. (US/0071-0164). **5364**

ENCOUNTERS (ST. PAUL, MINN.). (US/0273-5717). **5102**

END PAPERS. (UK/0262-7922). **4473**

ENDLESS VACATION - RESORT CONDOMINIUMS INTERNATIONAL, THE. (US/0279-4853). **5469**

ENDOCRINE RESEARCH. (US/0743-5800). **3729**

ENDOCRINE REVIEWS. (US/0163-769X). **3729**

ENDOCRINE SOCIETY - ANNUAL MEETING, PROGRAM AND ABSTRACTS, THE. (US). **3729**

ENDOCRINOLOGY (PHILADELPHIA). (US/0013-7227). **3730**

ENDOCURIETHERAPY — Advertising Accepted Index

ENDOCURIETHERAPY / HYPERTHERMIA ONCOLOGY. (US/8756-1689). **Adv Mgr:** Khalid Sheikh, PhD. **3816**

ENDODONTICS & DENTAL TRAUMATOLOGY. (DK/0109-2502). **1323**

ENDOSCOPY REVIEW. (US/8756-968X). **3744**

ENDOTHELIUM. (UK/0957-3518). **454**

ENDS REPORT. (UK). **Adv Mgr:** Gail Davis. **2228**

ENERGIA E MATERIE PRIME. (IT). **1938**

ENERGIA ELETTRICA. (IT/0013-7308). **2053**

ENERGIA NUCLEAR E AGRICULTURA. (BL/0100-3593). **2154**

ENERGIE ALTERNATIVE HTE. (IT/0391-5360). **5103**

ENERGIE DIALOG. (GW). **1938**

ENERGIE PLUS. (FR/0292-1731). **1938**

ENERGY AND BUILDINGS. (SZ/0378-7788). **Adv Mgr:** Ms. W van Cattenburch (Amsterdam). **614**

ENERGY & FUELS. (US/0887-0624). **1939**

ENERGY CONSERVATION NEWS. (US/0161-6595). **1939**

ENERGY DAILY, THE. (US/0364-5274). **1939**

ENERGY DEVELOPMENTS. (GW/0342-5665). **1940**

ENERGY DIGEST. (UK/0367-1119). **1940**

ENERGY ECONOMICS. (UK/0140-9883). **1940**

ENERGY EXPLORATION & EXPLOITATION. (UK/0144-5987). **1940**

ENERGY JOURNAL (CAMBRIDGE, MASS.). (US/0195-6574). **1940**

ENERGY LAW JOURNAL. (US/0270-9163). **Adv Mgr:** William Miller, **Tel** (202)986-8000. **2966**

ENERGY MANAGEMENT TECHNOLOGY. (US/0745-984X). **5103**

ENERGY POLICY. (UK/0301-4215). **1941**

ENERGY PROCESSING CANADA. (CN/0319-5759). **Adv Mgr:** Jim Graham. **1941**

ENERGY SOURCES. (US/0090-8312). **1942**

ENERGY (STAMFORD, CONN. 1975). (US/0149-9386). **1942**

ENERGY STUDIES REVIEW. (CN/0843-4379). **1942**

ENERGY UNLIMITED. (US/0279-621X). **1942**

ENERGY USER NEWS. (US/0162-9131). **1942**

ENERGY WORLD. (UK/0307-7942). **Adv Mgr:** H. Howland. **1943**

ENFANCE MAJUSCULE PARIS. (FR/1164-8589). **3164**

ENFANT D'ABORD, L'. (FR/0399-4988). **3903**

ENFERMERA AL DIA. (MX/0185-0970). **3855**

ENFIELD PRESS (1984), THE. (US/8750-3123). **Adv Mgr Tel** (413)562-4181. **5645**

ENFO. (US/0276-9956). **2165**

ENFOQUES EN ATENCION PRIMARIA. (CL/0716-2774). **Adv Mgr:** Suzamme Aurelius, **Tel** 6394560. **3574**

ENGINEER OF CALIFORNIA. (US/0277-1233). **Adv Mgr:** A. Schilling, **Tel** 799-1246. **1972**

ENGINEERED SYSTEMS. (US/0891-9976). **2113**

ENGINEERING ANALYSIS WITH BOUNDARY ELEMENTS. (UK/0955-7997). **1972**

ENGINEERING AND MINING JOURNAL (1926). (US/0095-8948). **2138**

ENGINEERING & SCIENCE. (US/0013-7812). **1972**

ENGINEERING AND TECHNOLOGY DEGREES. (US/0071-0393). **1972**

ENGINEERING DESIGN GRAPHICS JOURNAL. (US/0046-2012). **Adv Mgr:** Craig Miller. **1972**

ENGINEERING DESIGNER. (UK/0013-7898). **2098**

ENGINEERING DIGEST (TORONTO). (CN/0013-7901). **Adv Mgr:** Fran Hetherington. **1972**

ENGINEERING DIMENSIONS. (CN/0820-8190). **Adv Mgr:** Susan Browne, **Tel** (416)886-6640. **1972**

ENGINEERING HORIZONS (VAN NUYS, CALIF.). (US/1040-1679). **1973**

ENGINEERING IN MINIATURE. (UK/0955-7644). **Adv Mgr:** Susi Bolzicco, **Tel** same as publisher. **2773**

ENGINEERING MANPOWER BULLETIN. (US/0013-8037). **1973**

ENGINEERING OPTIMIZATION. (UK/0305-215X). **1973**

ENGINEERING PLASTICS. (UK/0952-6900). **4455**

ENGINEERING STRUCTURES. (UK/0141-0296). **2023**

ENGINEERING TIMES (WASHINGTON, D.C.). (US/0195-6876). **Adv Mgr Tel** (410)882-0050. **1974**

ENGINEERING WORLD (LONDON, ENGLAND). (UK). **1974**

ENGINEERS AND ENGINES MAGAZINE. (US/0013-8142). **158**

ENGINEERS AUSTRALIA. (AT/1032-1195). **1974**

ENGLISCH AMERIKANISCHE STUDIEN. (GW/0172-1992). **3384**

ENGLISH AND AMERICAN STUDIES IN GERMAN; SUMMARIES OF THESES AND MONOGRAPHS. (GW). **3278**

ENGLISH DANCE AND SONG. (UK/0013-8231). **384**

ENGLISH FOR SPECIFIC PURPOSES (NEW YORK, N.Y.). (US/0889-4906). **3278**

ENGLISH HISTORICAL REVIEW, THE. (UK/0013-8266). **2615**

ENGLISH IN AUSTRALIA. (AT/0155-2147). **3279**

ENGLISH IN EDUCATION. (UK/0425-0494). **3279**

ENGLISH JOURNAL. (US/0013-8274). **1894**

ENGLISH LANGUAGE NOTES. (US/0013-8282). **3342**

ENGLISH LITERARY RENAISSANCE. (US/0013-8312). **3342**

ENGLISH LITERATURE IN TRANSITION, 1880-1920. (US/0013-8339). **3342**

ENGLISH (LONDON). (UK/0013-8215). **3384**

ENGLISH RECORD, THE. (US/0013-8363). **1744**

ENGLISH STUDIES. (NE/0013-838X). **3384**

ENGLISH STUDIES IN AFRICA. (SA/0013-8398). **3384**

ENGLISH TRANSLATIONS OF GERMAN STANDARDS CATALOGUE / ISSUED BY DIN DEUTSCHES INSTITUT FUER NORMUNG E.V. (GW/0936-0530). **4030**

ENGLISH WESTERNERS' TALLY SHEET. (UK/0013-841X). **2732**

ENGLISH WORLD-WIDE. (NE/0172-8865). **3279**

ENGRAVERS JOURNAL, THE. (US/0099-0043). **4564**

ENLIGHTENMENT AND DISSENT. (UK/0262-7612). **4473**

ENNIS DAILY NEWS, THE. (US/8756-9056). **5749**

ENQUETE SOCIO-ECONOMIQUE. (BE). **4562**

ENR. (US/0891-9526). **1975**

ENR DIRECTORY OF DESIGN FIRMS. (US/0098-6305). **1975**

ENRICH!. (US). **671**

ENROUTE. (CN/0703-0312). **2533**

ENSAYOS ECONOMICOS. (AG/0325-3937). **1591**

ENSEIGNANTS (MONTREAL). (CN/0046-2101). **1744**

ENSEIGNEMENT DU RUSSE, L'. (FR/0300-2608). **3279**

ENSEIGNEMENT MATHEMATIQUE. (FR/0013-8584). **3505**

ENSEIGNEMENT PHILOSOPHIQUE, L'. (FR/0986-1653). **4365**

ENSEMBLE. (CN/0842-8409). **4956**

ENSEMBLE. (US). **384**

ENSIGN (SAN MATEO, CALIF.), THE. (US/0744-3129). **593**

ENTENDRE. (CN/0318-9139). **4387**

ENTERPRISE. (SA). **671**

ENTERPRISE-COURIER. (US). **5703**

ENTERPRISE LEDGER (ENTERPRISE, ALA. : 1977). (US). **Adv Mgr:** Kelly Speigner. **5626**

ENTERPRISE (PONCHATOULA, LA.). (US/0889-0684). **Adv Mgr:** Sharyn Brecheen. **5683**

ENTERPRISE SYSTEMS JOURNAL. (US/1053-6566). **1184**

ENTERPRISE, THE. (US). **Adv Mgr:** Dave Palmer. **5686**

ENTERPRISE (VANCOUVER). (CN/0319-8626). **1542**

ENTERTAINMENT LAW REPORTER. (US/0270-3831). **2966**

ENTERTAINMENT MAGAZINE, THE. (US/0883-1890). **4850**

ENTERTAINMENT WEEKLY. (US/1049-0434). **Adv Mgr:** Michael J. Kelly. **385**

ENTOMOLOGIA EXPERIMENTALIS ET APPLICATA. (NE/0013-8703). **5607**

ENTOMOLOGICA SCANDINAVICA. (DK/0013-8711). **5607**

ENTOMOLOGICAL NEWS. (US/0013-872X). **5607**

ENTOMOLOGICAL RESEARCH BULLETIN. (KO). **5607**

ENTOMOLOGICAL REVIEW. (US/0013-8738). **5607**

ENTOMOLOGIST'S GAZETTE. (UK/0013-8894). **Adv Mgr:** G. Morton, **Tel** 44-491-33882. **5608**

ENTOMOLOGIST'S MONTHLY MAGAZINE, THE. (UK/0013-8908). **Adv Mgr:** G. Morton, **Tel** 011 44 1491-33882. **5608**

ENTOMOLOGIST'S RECORD AND JOURNAL OF VARIATION, THE. (UK/0013-8916). **5582**

ENTOURAGE (DOWNSVIEW, ONT.). (CN/0829-8815). **5284**

ENTRAINEMENTS & SYSTEMES. (FR/0765-006X). **2113**

ENTRE-NOUS - SOCIETE DES ELEVEURS DE BOVINS CANADIENS. (CN/0709-8510). **210**

ENTREMETTEUR. (CN/0225-3569). **5784**

ENTREPRENEUR (SANTA MONICA, CALIF.). (US/0163-3341). **672**

ENTREPRENEURIAL MANAGER'S NEWSLETTER. (US/0272-0396). **672**

ENTREPRENEURIAL WOMAN. (US/1051-2624). **5555**

ENTREPRENEURSHIP AND REGIONAL DEVELOPMENT. (UK/0898-5626). **672**

ENTREPRISE 1951, L'. (BE/0777-6357). **2605**

ENTREPRISE ET L'HOMME. (BE). **2249**

ENTROPIE. (FR/0013-9084). **1975**

ENTRY (ANN ARBOR, MICH.). (US/0886-845X). **4369**

ENVIRONMENT & PLANNING A. (UK/0308-518X). **2821**

ENVIRONMENT AND PLANNING. B, PLANNING & DESIGN. (UK/0265-8135). **2821**

ENVIRONMENT AND PLANNING. C, GOVERNMENT & POLICY. (UK/0263-774X). **4646**

ENVIRONMENT AND PLANNING. D, SOCIETY & SPACE. (UK/0263-7758). **5199**

ENVIRONMENT BUSINESS. (UK/0959-7042). **Adv Mgr:** Steven Voss, **Tel** (081)877-9130. **2165**

ENVIRONMENT BUSINESS MAGAZINE. (UK/1352-8882). **Adv Mgr:** Steven Voss. **2228**

ENVIRONMENT INSTITUTE OF AUSTRALIA NEWSLETTER. (AT/1030-1429). **2165**

ENVIRONMENT INTERNATIONAL. (UK/0160-4120). **2165**

ENVIRONMENT PROTECTION ENGINEERING. (PL/0324-8828). **2166**

ENVIRONMENT TODAY. (US/1054-7517). **2166**

ENVIRONMENTAL ACTION (WASHINGTON, D.C.). (US/0013-922X). **Adv Mgr:** Jim Pierce, **Tel** (301)891-1100. **2166**

ENVIRONMENTAL AND PLANNING LAW JOURNAL. (AT/0813-300X). **3111**

ENVIRONMENTAL BIOLOGY OF FISHES. (NE/0378-1909). **2300**

ENVIRONMENTAL CARCINOGENESIS REVIEWS. (US/0882-8164). **3816**

ENVIRONMENTAL CONTROL NEWS FOR SOUTHERN INDUSTRY. (US/0013-9238). **2167**

ENVIRONMENTAL EDUCATION AND INFORMATION. (UK/0144-9281). **2167**

ENVIRONMENTAL ENGINEERING (BURY SAINT EDMUNDS, ENG. : 1988). (UK/0954-5824). **1975**

ENVIRONMENTAL ENTOMOLOGY. (US/0046-225X). **5608**

ENVIRONMENTAL ETHICS. (US/0163-4275). **Adv Mgr:** Jan Dickson. **2167**

ENVIRONMENTAL GEOCHEMISTRY AND HEALTH. (UK/0269-4042). **2167**

ENVIRONMENTAL GEOLOGY AND WATER SCIENCES. (US/0177-5146). **1375**

ENVIRONMENTAL HEALTH (LONDON). (UK/0013-9270). **2822**

ENVIRONMENTAL HEALTH REVIEW. (CN/0319-6771). **4774**

ENVIRONMENTAL HEALTH REVIEW, AUSTRALIA : THE OFFICIAL JOURNAL OF THE AUSTRALIAN INSTITUTE OF ENVIRONMENTAL HEALTH. (AT/0818-5670). **Adv Mgr:** Neil Wilson, **Tel** 02 319 3933. **2167**

ENVIRONMENTAL HISTORY REVIEW : EHR. (US/1053-4180). **2228**

ENVIRONMENTAL IMPACT. (UK). **2167**

ENVIRONMENTAL LAB. (US/1042-5209). **5103**

ENVIRONMENTAL LAW (PORTLAND, ORE.). (US/0046-2276). **3111**

ENVIRONMENTAL LAW SECTION JOURNAL. (US/8756-9280). **Adv Mgr:** Mary Beth Martin. **3111**

ENVIRONMENTAL LIABILITY REPORT, THE. (US/1043-2698). **2168**

ENVIRONMENTAL MANAGER. (US/1043-786X). **2228**

ENVIRONMENTAL MONITORING AND ASSESSMENT. (NE/0167-6369). **2168**

ENVIRONMENTAL POLITICS. (UK/0964-4016). **Adv Mgr:** Anne Kidson. **2168**

ENVIRONMENTAL POLLUTION (1987). (UK/0269-7491). **2229**

ENVIRONMENTAL PROFESSIONAL, THE. (US/0191-5398). **2169**

ENVIRONMENTAL PROGRESS. (US/0278-4491). **2229**

ENVIRONMENTAL REVIEWS. (CN/1181-8700). **Adv Mgr:** Bob Barrette, **Tel** (613)993-9085. **2215**

ENVIRONMENTAL SCIENCE & ENGINEERING (AURORA). (CN/0835-605X). **1975**

ENVIRONMENTAL SCIENCE & TECHNOLOGY. (US/0013-936X). **Adv Mgr Tel** (203)256-8211. **2169**

ENVIRONMENTAL SOFTWARE. (UK/0266-9838). **2170**

ENVIRONMENTAL SOFTWARE DIRECTORY. (US/1043-9056). **Adv Mgr:** Veronica Deschambault, **Tel** (703)659-1954. **2170**

ENVIRONMENTAL SOFTWARE REPORT. (US/1043-2884). **2170**

ENVIRONMENTAL TECHNOLOGY. (UK/0959-3330). **2170**

ENVIRONMENTAL TESTING & ANALYSIS. (US/1068-7432). **2170**

ENVIRONMENTAL WASTE MANAGEMENT. (US/1049-4715). **Adv Mgr:** Katie Keegan, **Tel** (215)683-5098. **2229**

ENVIRONMENTALIST, THE. (UK/0251-1088). **2193**

ENVIRONNEMENT. (BE). **2171**

ENVIROSOUTH. (US/0272-1120). **2171**

ENVOI. (UK/0013-9394). **3462**

ENVOI (MONTREAL). (CN/0823-1834). **4894**

ENZYME. (SZ/0013-9432). **486**

EOS (WASHINGTON, D.C.). (US/0096-3941). **1404**

EPE. (UK/0963-5920). **2053**

EPHRATA REVIEW, THE. (US). **Adv Mgr:** Doug Dussinger. **5736**

EPI. EQUIPOS PRODUCTOS INDUSTRIALES. (SP/1130-9571). **1606**

EPICIER (MONTREAL). (CN/0013-9521). **2334**

EPIDEMIOLOGIA E PSICHIATRIA SOCIALE. (IT/1121-189X). **Adv Mgr:** Dott Dalla, **Tel** 06-86207165. **3734**

EPIDEMIOLOGIC REVIEWS. (US/0193-936X). **3734**

EPIDEMIOLOGY MONITOR, THE. (US/0744-0898). **4775**

EPIEGRAM (1988). (US/1046-1493). **Adv Mgr:** Earl Fultz, **Tel** (516)765-2378. **1241**

EPILOGE. (GR). **1560**

EPIPHANY. (US). **4956**

EPISCOPAL CHURCH ANNUAL, THE. (US/0071-1012). **5059**

EPISCOPAL LIFE. (US/1050-0057). **Adv Mgr:** D. Kelso, **Tel** (215)564-2010. **5059**

EPISCOPAL NEWS, THE. (US/0195-0681). **4956**

EPISODES. (US). **2533**

EPISTEME NS : REVISTA DEL INSTITUTE DE FILOSOFIA. (VE). **4345**

EPISTEMOLOGIA. (IT). **5103**

EPOCH (ITHACA). (US/0145-1391). **3384**

EPOPTEIA. (GR). **4345**

EPWORTH REVIEW. (UK/0308-0382). **5059**

EQUAL MEANS. (US/1059-164X). **5555**

EQUAL OPPORTUNITY. (US/0071-1039). **1822**

EQUAL TIME (MENTOR, OHIO). (US/1063-0589). **Adv Mgr Tel** 473-1020. **5555**

EQUESTRIAN TRAILS. (US/0013-9831). **2798**

EQUINE PRACTICE. (US/0162-8941). **2798**

EQUINE VETERINARY JOURNAL. (UK/0425-1644). **5509**

EQUINEWS. (US/0828-864X). **2799**

EQUINOX (CAMDEN EAST). (CN/0710-9911). **2560**

EQUIPMENT JOURNAL. (CN/0710-2720). **Adv Mgr:** Jon Baker, **Tel** (416)274-4883. **2114**

EQUIPMENT MANAGEMENT. (US/0733-3056). **1975**

EQUIPMENT TODAY. (US/0891-141X). **614**

EQUIPOS PRODUCTOS ELECTRONICOS. (SP). **2053**

EQUITIES (NEW YORK, N.Y.). (US/1053-2544). **Adv Mgr:** Jean Flaherty, **Tel** (212)685-6244. **897**

EQUITY AND CHOICE. (US/0882-3863). **1744**

EQUUS. (US/0149-0672). **2799**

ERA, ELEKTRICITETENS RATIONELLA ANVANDNING. (SW). **2054**

ERANOS. (SW/0013-9947). **1076**

ERASMUS IN ENGLISH. (CN/0071-1063). **4346**

ERBA D'ARNO. (IT). **319**

ERBA D'ARNO. (IT/0394-5618). **2615**

ERBE UND AUFTRAG (BEURON). (GW/0013-9963). **5029**

ERDE. (GW/0013-9998). **2560**

ERDKUNDE. (GW/0014-0015). **1375**

ERDOGAZDASAG ES FAIPAR. (HU/0014-0066). **2400**

ERDOL, ERDGAS, KOHLE. (GW/0179-3187). **4255**

ERDOL-INFORMATIONSDIENST. (GW/0343-6705). **672**

ERES MAGAZINE. (US). **Adv Mgr:** A. Schoutton, **Tel** (619)276-8709. **5555**

ERETZ MAGAZINE. (IS). **267**

ERFAHRUNGSHEILKUNDE. (GW/0014-0082). **3575**

ERFRISCHUNGSGETRANK, DAS. (GW/0342-2232). **2367**

ERGANZUNGSHEFT ZU PETERMANNS GEOGRAPHSCHISCHEN MITTEILUNGEN. (GW). **2560**

ERGEBNISSE DER AEROLOGISCHEN UND BODENNAHEN OZONMESSUNGEN. (GW). **1425**

ERGO-MED. (GW/0170-2327). **3575**

ERGONOMICS IN DESIGN. (US/1064-8046). **Adv Mgr:** Lois Smith. **1975**

ERIA, EL. (SP). **3385**

ERIE DAILY TIMES, THE. (US). **Adv Mgr:** Al Haskins, **Tel** (814)870-1657. **5736**

ERIE RECORD (ERIE, KAN. : 1904). (US). **5675**

ERIGENIA. (US/8755-2000). **509**

ERKENNTNIS. (NE/0165-0106). **4346**

ERNAHRUNG (VIENNA, AUSTRIA). (AU/0250-1554). **Adv Mgr:** Ms. Allacher. **4190**

ERNAHRUNGSWIRTSCHAFT. (GW). **2334**

ERROR TRENDS. (US). **2781**

ERSKINE ECHO, THE. (US). **Adv Mgr:** Robert M. Hole. **5695**

ERWERBSOBSTBAU. (GW/0014-0309). **170**

ERYTHROCYTES. (UK/0268-808X). **536**

ERZIEHUNG UND WISSENSCHAFT. (GW/0342-0671). **1745**

ESA BULLETIN. (FR/0376-4265). **18**

ESA JOURNAL. (FR/0379-2285). **18**

ESCALE (QUEBEC). (CN/0822-4056). **4176**

ESCAPE TO THE MINNESOTA GOOD TIMES. (US/0740-9648). **2533**

ESCRITOS DEL VEDAT. (SP/0210-3133). **4956**

ESCRITURA (CARACAS). (VE/1011-7989). **3342**

ESPACE GEOGRAPHIQUE. (FR/0046-2497). **2560**

ESPACE (MONTREAL). (CN/0821-9222). **Adv Mgr:** Y. O'Reilly. **349**

ESPACES ET SOCIETES. (FR/0014-0481). **298**

ESPANOL EN AUSTRALIA. (AT). **3279**

ESPERANTO. (NE/0014-0635). **Adv Mgr:** O. Buller. **3279**

ESPIAL CANADIAN DATA BASE DIRECTORY, THE. (CN/0834-3888). **Adv Mgr:** H. Cambell, **Tel** (416)485-8063. **1259**

ESPIONAGE MAGAZINE. (US/8756-8535). **5074**

ESPRIT CREATEUR, L'. (US/0014-0767). **3342**

ESPRIT DE CORPS, CANADIAN MILITARY THEN & NOW. (CN/1194-2266). **Adv Mgr:** S.R. Taylor. **4043**

ESQ. (US/0093-8297). **3385**

ESQUIRE (1979). (US/0194-9535). **2533**

ESSAYS IN ARTS AND SCIENCES. (US/0361-5634). **2846**

ESSAYS IN CRITICISM. (UK/0014-0856). **3385**

ESSAYS IN POETICS. (UK/0308-888X). **3385**

ESSAYS IN THEATRE. (CN/0821-4425). **5364**

ESSAYS ON CANADIAN WRITING. (CN/0316-0300). **3385**

ESSE. (CN/0831-859X). **349**

ESSECOME. (IT/0394-8625). **Adv Mgr:** Fabrina Montanari. **3164**

ESSENTIAL GUIDE TO PRESCRIPTION DRUGS, THE. (US/0894-7058). **Adv Mgr:** Kathy Lynch, **Tel** (212)207-7000. **4303**

ESSEX FAMILY HISTORIAN, THE. (UK/0140-7503). **2446**

ESSEX INDEPENDENT, THE. (US). **Adv Mgr:** Bob Jackson, **Tel** (712)379-3313. **5670**

ESSEX INSTITUTE HISTORICAL COLLECTIONS. (US). **2732**

ESSEX SUCCULENT REVIEW. (UK). **2414**

EST MEDECINE. (FR/0248-9643). **Adv Mgr:** A. Trebucq. **3575**

EST-OVEST. (IT/0046-256X). **4473**

ESTADISTICA. (US/0014-1135). **5327**

ESTADO DA PARAIBA, ANUARIO ESTATISTICO. (BL). **5327**

ESTATES & TRUSTS REPORTS. (CN/0706-5655). **3118**

ESTES PARK TRAIL-GAZETTE, THE. (US). **5642**

ESTES TRAILS. (US/0737-481X). **2446**

ESTEVAN MERCURY. (CN). **5784**

ESTIMATES OF LABOUR INCOME (OTTAWA). (CN/0318-9007). **1532**

ESTRATEGIA ECONOMICA Y FINANCIERA. (CK/0121-4802). **Adv Mgr:** Graciela Gonzalez Sanguino, **Tel** 243 7911 1213. **1489**

ESTRENO. (US/0097-8663). **5364**

ESTUAIRE. (CN/0700-365X). **3462**

ESTUDIOS DE ECONOMIA. (CL). **1591**

ESTUDIOS DEL DESARROLLO. (INT/1013-4069). **5199**

ESTUDIOS ECLESIASTICOS. (SP/0210-1610). **5029**

ESTUDIOS FILOLOGICOS. (CL/0071-1713). **3280**

ESTUDIOS FILOSOFICOS. (VE). **4346**

ESTUDIOS - INSTITUTO DE ESTUDIO ECONOMICOS SOBRE LA REALIDAD ARGENTINA Y LATINOAMERICANA. (AG/0325-6928). **1489**

ESTUDIOS MADRID. (SP/0210-0525). **3385**

ESTUDIOS PARAGUAYOS. (PY/0251-2483). **2732**

ESTUDIOS SOCIALES (SANTIAGO, CHILE). (CL/0716-0321). **5199**

ESTUDIOS SOCIALES (SANTO DOMINGO). (DR/1017-0596). **Adv Mgr:** Manuel Maza. **5199**

ETC. (US/0014-164X). **3280**

ETC (MONTREAL). (CN/0835-7641). **Adv Mgr:** Annie Molin Vasseur, **Tel** (514)842-4319. **350**

ETCETERA. (US). **250**

ETHICS & INTERNATIONAL AFFAIRS. (US/0892-6794). **Adv Mgr:** C. Wakeman. **4520**

ETHICS, EASIER SAID THAN DONE. (US/0897-0106). **2250**

ETHICS IN-SERVICE. (CN/0824-5622). **2250**

ETHIOPIAN MEDICAL JOURNAL. (ET/0014-1755). **3575**

ETHIOPIAN PUBLICATIONS. (ET/0071-1772). **416**

ETHIOPIAN REVIEW. (US/1056-2354). **Adv Mgr:** Hailu. **2639**

ETHIOPIAN TRADE JOURNAL. (ET/0014-1763). **833**

ETHNIC AND RACIAL STUDIES. (UK/0141-9870). **2260**

ETHNIC FORUM. (US/0278-9078). **Adv Mgr Tel** (216)672-2782. **2260**

ETHNIC GROUPS. (US/0308-6860). **2260**

ETHNIC REPORTER (CLAREMONT, CALIF.), THE. (US/0893-7362). **2260**

ETHNIC SCHOOLS IN FOCUS. (AT/1035-3682). **Adv Mgr:** Inta Rumpe. **1745**

ETHNICITY & DISEASE. (US/1049-510X). **3735**

ETHNIKOS KERUX. (US). **Adv Mgr:** Victoria Diamatard, **Tel** (718)784-5255. **5716**

ETHNOARTS INDEX. (US/0893-0120). **334**

ETHNOHISTORY. (US/0014-1801). **2261**

ETHNOLOGIA EUROPAEA. (DK/0425-4597). **235**

ETHNOMUSICOLOGY. (US/0014-1836). **4117**

ETHOLOGY. (GW/0179-1613). **5583**

ETHOS. (US/0091-2131). **4586**

ETNOS (LUBLIN, POLAND). (PL). **4956**

ETR. (GW/0013-2845). **5431**

ETTELAAT. (IR). **5803**

ETUDES ANGLAISES. (FR/0014-195X). **3342**

ETUDES CANADIENNES. (FR/0153-1700). **Adv Mgr:** Lacroix. **2732**

ETUDES CLASSIQUES (NAMUR, BELGIUM). (BE/0014-200X). **1076**

ETUDES DE LINGUISTIQUE APPLIQUEE. (FR/0071-190X). **3280**

ETUDES ET STATISTIQUES - BANQUE DES ETATS DE L'AFRIQUE CENTRALE. (CM/0014-2069). **728**

ETUDES FRANCAISES (MONTREAL). (CN/0014-2085). **3385**

ETUDES GERMANIQUES. (FR/0014-2115). **3280**

ETUDES INTERNATIONALES (QUEBEC). (CN/0014-2123). **4521**

ETUDES INTERNATIONALES (QUEBEC). (CN/0014-2123). **4473**

ETUDES INUIT. (CN/0701-1008). **236**

ETUDES IRLANDAISES. (FR/0183-973X). **2687**

ETUDES LITTERAIRES (UNIVERSITE LAVAL). (CN/0014-214X). **3386**

ETUDES STATISTIQUES (BRUSSELS, BELGIUM). (BE/0522-7585). **5327**

ETUDES THEOLOGIQUES ET RELIGIEUSES. (FR/0014-2239). **4956**

ETV NEWSLETTER. (US/0012-8023). **1745**

EUDISED R & D BULLETIN. (FR). **1745**

EUDORA WELTY NEWSLETTER. (US/0146-7220). **3386**

EUFAULA TRIBUNE, THE. (US). **Adv Mgr:** Jack Jackson. **5626**

EUGENE O'NEILL REVIEW, THE. (US/1040-9483). **3386**

EULAR BULLETIN. MONOGRAPH SERIES. (SZ/0253-0333). **3804**

EUNTES DOCETE. (IT). **4956**

EUPHORION (HEIDELBERG, GERMANY). (GW/0014-2328). **3386**

EUPHYTICA. (NE/0014-2336). **509**

EURASIAN LANGUAGE ARCHIVES. (US/0898-0454). **3280**

EUREKA (BECKENHAM). (UK/0261-2097). **2098**

EUREKA HERALD, THE. (US). **5675**

EUREKA SENTINEL (EUREKA, NEV. : 1902). (US). **5707**

EUREKA : THE ARCHIMEDEANS' JOURNAL. (UK/0071-2248). **3505**

EURO FILE MUSIC INDUSTRY DIRECTORY. (NE). **Adv Mgr:** Ron Betist. **4117**

EURO-FOCUS RATINGEN. (GW/0936-1928). **4215**

EURO P.V. (FR/0245-8438). **833**

EURO PRINTER. (GW/0938-1236). **4564**

EURODIENCE. (FR). **Adv Mgr:** Joelle Chausiemier, **Tel** 011 33 1 49 83 24 87. **385**

EUROFACH ELECTRONICA. (SP/0211-2973). **Adv Mgr:** Carlos Gomez Yepes. **2054**

EUROFILE RADIO INDUSTRY DIRECTORY. (NE). **Adv Mgr:** Ron Betist. **1132**

EUROFRUIT. (UK). **Adv Mgr:** Erica Nicholson. **2414**

EUROIL. (NO/0802-9474). **4255**

EUROMARKETING : THE WEEKLY EUROPEAN NEWS BULLETIN FROM ADVERTISING AGE. (UK/0952-3820). **Adv Mgr:** J. Palley. **759**

EUROP. (FR). **Adv Mgr:** same as editor. **1489**

EUROPA-ARCHIV. (GW/0014-2476). **4521**

EUROPA CHEMIE. (GW/0014-2484). **2012**

EUROPA DELLA CEE. (IT). **Adv Mgr Tel** 3022.1. **1634**

EUROPA DOMANI. (IT/0390-2102). **Adv Mgr:** Diana Giani, **Tel** 70635333. **833**

EUROPA E LA CEE, L'. (IT). **Adv Mgr:** V Systeece. **4521**

EUROPA ETHNICA. (AU/0014-2492). **2261**

EUROPA STAR. (SZ/0014-2603). **2916**

EUROPAEISCHE GRUNDRECHTE - ZEITSCHRIFT. (GW/0341-9800). **4507**

EUROPAEISCHE RUNDSCHAU. (AU/0304-2782). **4521**

EUROPAISCHE INTEGRATION AUSWAHLBIBLIOGRAPHIE. (GW). **4473**

EUROPAISCHE ZEITUNG. (GW). **4473**

EUROPAMARKT : MILCH. (GW). **194**

EUROPE. (FR/0014-2751). **3342**

EUROPE EN FORMATION, L'. (FR/0014-2808). **4521**

EUROPE PLURILINGUE. (FR/1161-8884). **Adv Mgr:** N. Dormoy. **2487**

EUROPE (WASHINGTON, D.C.). (US/0191-4545). **833**

EUROPEAN ACCESS. (UK/0264-7362). **4473**

EUROPEAN ACCOUNTING REVIEW. (UK/0963-8180). **Adv Mgr:** David Polley. **743**

EUROPEAN ADHESIVES AND SEALANTS. (UK/0264-9047). **4223**

EUROPEAN APPLIED RESEARCH REPORTS. ENVIRONMENT AND NATURAL RESOURCES SECTION. (UK/0272-4626). **2171**

EUROPEAN APPLIED RESEARCH REPORTS. NUCLEAR SCIENCE AND TECHNOLOGY SECTION. (SZ/0379-4229). **2155**

EUROPEAN BUSINESS JOURNAL. (UK/0955-808X). **673**

EUROPEAN BUSINESS REVIEW. (UK/0955-534X). **673**

EUROPEAN COMMERCIAL CASES. (UK/0141-7266). **3100**

EUROPEAN COMMUNICATIONS. (UK/0955-4041). **1111**

EUROPEAN COMPANION, THE. (UK). **4521**

EUROPEAN CONSORTIUM FOR POLITICAL RESEARCH NEWS. (UK). **4473**

EUROPEAN COSMETIC MARKETS. (UK). **404**

EUROPEAN DESIGN DIRECTORY. (UK). **2114**

EUROPEAN ENVIRONMENTAL YEARBOOK. (UK). **2171**

EUROPEAN FILMFILE. (UK). **Adv Mgr:** L Martin. **4068**

EUROPEAN GOURMET: THE GRAND DINING TOUR OF EUROPE, THE. (US). **2334**

EUROPEAN HANDBOOK. (UK/0966-4858). **Adv Mgr:** Kevin Brady. **673**

EUROPEAN HUMAN RIGHTS REPORTS. (UK/0260-4868). **4508**

EUROPEAN INFORMATION SERVICE. (UK/0261-2747). **2516**

EUROPEAN INTELLECTUAL PROPERTY REVIEW. (UK/0142-0461). **1304**

EUROPEAN JOURNAL OF CANCER PREVENTION. (UK/0959-8278). **3817**

EUROPEAN JOURNAL OF CELL BIOLOGY. (GW/0171-9335). **536**

EUROPEAN JOURNAL OF CHIROPRACTIC. (UK/0263-9114). **3575**

EUROPEAN JOURNAL OF CLINICAL INVESTIGATION. (GW/0014-2972). **3575**

EUROPEAN JOURNAL OF CLINICAL MICROBIOLOGY & INFECTIOUS DISEASES. (GW/0934-9723). **562**

EUROPEAN JOURNAL OF CLINICAL NUTRITION. (UK/0954-3007). **4190**

EUROPEAN JOURNAL OF COGNITIVE PSYCHOLOGY, THE. (UK/0954-1446). **4586**

EUROPEAN JOURNAL OF COMMUNICATION (LONDON). (UK/0267-3231). **1111**

EUROPEAN JOURNAL OF DEVELOPMENT RESEARCH, THE. (UK/0957-8811). **Adv Mgr:** Anne Kidson. **2909**

EUROPEAN JOURNAL OF DISORDERS OF COMMUNICATION. (UK/0963-7273). **Adv Mgr:** Sarah Vicary, **Tel** 071 359 0579. **1111**

EUROPEAN JOURNAL OF EDUCATION. (UK/0141-8211). **1745**

EUROPEAN JOURNAL OF ENGINEERING EDUCATION. (UK/0304-3797). **1975**

EUROPEAN JOURNAL OF EPIDEMIOLOGY. (IT/0393-2990). **3735**

EUROPEAN JOURNAL OF FOREST PATHOLOGY. (GW/0300-1237). **2379**

EUROPEAN JOURNAL OF GASTROENTEROLOGY & HEPATOLOGY. (UK/0954-691X). **3744**

EUROPEAN JOURNAL OF GYNAECOLOGICAL ONCOLOGY. (IT/0392-2936). **3817**

EUROPEAN JOURNAL OF HAEMATOLOGY. (DK/0902-4441). **3771**

EUROPEAN JOURNAL OF IMPLANT AND REFRACTIVE SURGERY, THE. (FR/0955-3681). **3874**

EUROPEAN JOURNAL OF INFORMATION SYSTEMS. (UK/0960-085X). **1184**

EUROPEAN JOURNAL OF INTERCULTURAL STUDIES. (UK/0952-391X). **2261**

EUROPEAN JOURNAL OF INTERNATIONAL AFFAIRS, THE. (IT/0394-6444). **4473**

EUROPEAN JOURNAL OF MECHANICAL ENGINEERING. (BE/0777-2734). **2114**

EUROPEAN JOURNAL OF MEDICINAL CHEMISTRY. (FR/0223-5234). **3575**

EUROPEAN JOURNAL OF MEDICINE. (FR/1165-0478). **Adv Mgr:** Mme Laska, **Tel** 33 1 45 502308. **3575**

EUROPEAN JOURNAL OF MINERALOGY (STUTTGART). (GW/0935-1221). **1439**

EUROPEAN JOURNAL OF NON-DESTRUCTIVE TESTING, THE. (UK/0957-767X). **5104**

EUROPEAN JOURNAL OF ORIENTAL MEDICINE. (UK). **Adv Mgr:** Carol Daglish, **Tel** 081 883 8431. **3575**

EUROPEAN JOURNAL OF ORTHODONTICS. (UK/0141-5387). **1323**

EUROPEAN JOURNAL OF PERSONALITY. (UK/0890-2070). **4587**

EUROPEAN JOURNAL OF POLITICAL RESEARCH. (NE/0304-4130). **4473**

EUROPEAN JOURNAL OF PROTISTOLOGY. (GW/0932-4739). **562**

EUROPEAN JOURNAL OF PSYCHIATRY, THE. (SP/0213-6163). **3925**

EUROPEAN JOURNAL OF SERIALS LIBRARIANSHIP. (US/1048-5287). **3209**

EUROPEAN JOURNAL OF ULTRASOUND. (IE/0929-8266). **3941**

EUROPEAN JUDAISM. (UK/0014-3006). **5047**

EUROPEAN MAC PROFESSIONAL. (SP). **1237**

EUROPEAN MANAGEMENT JOURNAL. (UK/0263-2373). **867**

EUROPEAN MICROSCOPY AND ANALYSIS. (UK/0958-1952). **Adv Mgr:** Mrs. Gordon. **572**

EUROPEAN MICROSCOPY & ANALYSIS. (UK). **Adv Mgr:** Mrs Gordon. **572**

EUROPEAN NEUROLOGY. (SZ/0014-3022). **3832**

EUROPEAN PACKAGING MAGAZINE (HEUSENSTAMM, GERMANY). (GW). **Adv Mgr:** G. Bitterlich. **4219**

EUROPEAN PATENT OFFICE REPORTS. (UK/0269-0802). **1304**

EUROPEAN PETROLEUM DIRECTORY. (US/0275-3871). **4256**

EUROPEAN POWER NEWS. (UK/0261-8214). **1944**

EUROPEAN RESPIRATORY REVIEW : AN OFFICIAL JOURNAL OF THE EUROPEAN RESPIRATORY SOCIETY. (DK/0905-9180). **3949**

EUROPEAN REVIEW OF AGRICULTURAL ECONOMICS. (NE/0165-1587). **82**

EUROPEAN REVIEW OF NATIVE AMERICAN STUDIES. (GW/0238-1486). **2261**

EUROPEAN ROMANTIC REVIEW. (US/1050-9585). **3386**

EUROPEAN RUBBER DIRECTORY. (UK/0306-414X). **5075**

EUROPEAN RUBBER JOURNAL (LONDON, ENGLAND : 1982). (UK/0266-4151). **5075**

EUROPEAN SCIENCE EDITING : BULLETIN OF THE EUROPEAN ASSOCIATION OF SCIENCE EDITORS. (UK/0309-4715). **4815**

EUROPEAN SECURITY. (UK/0966-2839). **4521**

EUROPEAN SECURITY STUDIES. (UK). **Adv Mgr Tel** same as editor. **4043**

EUROPEAN SEMICONDUCTOR. (UK/0957-5685). **2054**

EUROPEAN SOCIOLOGICAL REVIEW. (UK/0266-7215). **5245**

EUROPEAN STEEL REVIEW. (UK). **4001**

EUROPEAN STUDIES NEWSLETTER. (US/0046-2802). **2687**

EUROPEAN SURGICAL RESEARCH. (SZ/0014-312X). **3964**

EUROPEAN TABLEWARE BUYERS GUIDE. (UK/0264-5041). **2589**

EUROPEAN TAXATION. (NE/0014-3138). **4722**

EUROPEAN TAXATION. SUPPLEMENTARY SERVICE. (NE/0531-4577). **4722**

EUROPEAN UROLOGY. (SZ/0302-2838). **3999**

EUROPEAN WATER POLLUTION CONTROL : OFFICIAL PUBLICATION OF THE EUROPEAN WATER POLLUTION CONTROL ASSOCIATION (EWPCA). (NE/0925-5060). **5533**

EUROPE'S 15,000 LARGEST COMPANIES DIE 15,000 GROSSTEN UNTERNEHMEN EUROPAS LES 15,000 PLUS GRANDES SOCIETES DE L'EUROPE. (UK/0800-0638). **673**

EUROPHYSICS NEWS. (SZ/0531-7479). **4402**

EUROPROPERTY LONDON. (UK/0961-9712). **Adv Mgr:** John Taylor. **897**

EUROSLOT OLDHAM. (UK/0966-0259). **Adv Mgr:** J. Lancaster. **4860**

EUSKAL HERRIKO POETAK. (SP). **3386**

EVALUATION & RESEARCH IN EDUCATION. (UK/0950-0790). **1745**

EVALUATION ENGINEERING. (US/0149-0370). **2054**

EVANGELICAL BAPTIST. (CN/0014-3324). **5059**

EVANGELICAL BEACON, THE. (US/0014-3332). **4957**

EVANGELICAL FRIEND. (US/0014-3340). **4957**

EVANGELICAL MISSIONS QUARTERLY. (US/0014-3359). **Adv Mgr:** Jan Warren. **4957**

EVANGELICAL QUARTERLY. (UK/0014-3367). **4957**

EVANGELICAL REVIEW OF THEOLOGY. (II/0144-8153). **4957**

EVANGELICAL STUDIES BULLETIN. (US/0890-703X). **4957**

EVANGELICAL TIMES. (UK). **5060**

EVANGELISCHE ERZIEHER, DER. (GW/0014-3413). **4957**

EVANGELISCHE KOMMENTARE. (GW/0300-4236). **4957**

EVANGELISCHE THEOLOGIE. (GW/0014-3502). **4957**

EVANGELISM (MEQUON, WIS.). (US/0890-667X). **4957**

EVANGELIST (ALBANY, N.Y.), THE. (US/0738-8489). **5029**

EVANGELIUM / GOSPEL / EUAGGELION. (GW). **4957**

EVANGELIZING TODAY'S CHILD. (US/0891-3846). **Adv Mgr:** AA Baker, **Tel** (803)370-3717. **4958**

EVANSVILLE PRESS. (US/0896-6249). **5664**

EVELYN WAUGH NEWSLETTER AND STUDIES. (US/1058-8272). **432**

EVENING CHRONICLE (OLDHAM). (UK/0968-3623). **Adv Mgr:** Jim Whittingham, **Tel** same as publisher. **5812**

EVENING JOURNAL (LUBBOCK, TEX.). (US/0745-547X). **5749**

EVENING JOURNAL, THE. (US). **Adv Mgr:** James Connors. **5763**

EVENING NEWS (HARRISBURG, PA.), THE. (US/0887-7939). **5736**

EVENING NEWS (JEFFERSONVILLE, IND. : 1924). (US). **Adv Mgr:** Donna Barrett. **5664**

EVENING NEWS (NORWICH. 1991). (UK/0964-4946). **5812**

EVENING OBSERVER, THE. (US). **Adv Mgr:** Karl Davis, **Tel** (716)366-3000. **5716**

EVENING REVIEW, THE. (US). **Adv Mgr:** Lisa Lynn. **5728**

EVENING SUN (NORWICH, N.Y.). (US/0747-0355). **Adv Mgr:** Russell Foote, **Tel** (607)334-3276. **5716**

EVENING TELEGRAM (HERKIMER, N.Y.). (US). **Adv Mgr:** Wesley Williams, **Tel** (315)866-2220. **5716**

EVENING TELEGRAM (SUPERIOR, WIS. : 1922). (US). **Adv Mgr:** Betty Porter. **5767**

EVENING TIMES. (US). **Adv Mgr:** Bob Bruce. **5631**

EVENING TIMES (LITTLE FALLS, N.Y.), THE. (US). **Adv Mgr:** Peggy Vespi and Elaine McEvoy. **5716**

EVENING TIMES (SAYRE, PA.). (US/0746-4843). **5736**

EVENT (NEW WESTMINSTER). (CN/0315-3770). **3386**

EVEREST WORLD, THE. (US). **Adv Mgr:** Becky Williams. **5675**

EVERGREEN CHRONICLES, THE. (US/1043-3333). **2794**

EVERGREEN COURANT, THE. (US). **5626**

EVERGREEN STATE FILM & VIDEO INDEX, THE. (US/0737-0113). **1132**

EVERMAN TIMES. (US). **Adv Mgr:** Jedd Blessing. **5749**

EVERYDAY ELECTRONICS. (UK/0262-3617). **2054**

EVERYDAY WITH PRACTICAL ELECTRONICS. (UK). **Adv Mgr:** P. Mew, **Tel** 0255 850596. **2054**

EVERYONE'S BACKYARD. (US/0749-3940). **2171**

EVERYTHING NATURAL. (US/0889-8421). **2790**

EVOLUTION. (US/0014-3820). **544**

EVOLUTION PSYCHIATRIQUE, L'. (FR/0014-3855). **3925**

EVOLUTIONARY ECOLOGY. (UK/0269-7653). **2216**

EVOLUTIONARY TRENDS IN PLANTS. (UK/1011-3258). **509**

EVOLUZIONE DEI SETTORI INDUSTRIALI NEL ... / CONFINDUSTRIA, CENTRO STUDI. (IT). **1606**

EWGS BULLETIN. (US/0738-5234). **2446**

EWING EXCHANGE. (US/0892-2144). **2446**

EWOKS. (US/0888-0743). **4860**

EX AUDITU. (US/0883-0053). **4958**

EX AUDITU : AN INTERNATIONAL JOURNAL OF THEOLOGICAL INTERPRETATION OF SCRIPTURE. (US). **4958**

EX LIBRIS (PORTSMOUTH, N.H.). (US/1042-6647). **3386**

EX TEMPORE. (CN/0276-6795). **4117**

EXAMINER (BARRIE). (CN/0839-4164). **Adv Mgr:** Chuck McCaren, **Tel** (705)726-6539. **5784**

EXCALIBUR (DOWNSVIEW, ONT.). (CN/0823-1915). **5784**

EXCAVATING CONTRACTOR. (US/0014-3995). **614**

EXCEL (SAN FRANCISCO, CALIF.). (US/0893-5017). **5200**

EXCELLENCE (ROSS, CALIF.). (US/0896-0798). **5414**

EXCEPTIONAL CHILDREN. (US/0014-4029). **1878**

EXCEPTIONAL PARENT, THE. (US/0046-9157). **2278**

EXCERPTA INDONESICA. (NE/0046-0885). **5227**

EXCERPTA INFORMATICA. (NE/0169-5509). **1219**

EXCERPTA MEDICA. SECTION 1. ANATOMY, ANTHROPOLOGY, EMBRYOLOGY AND HISTOLOGY. (NE/0014-4053). **3657**

EXCERPTA MEDICA. SECTION 6. INTERNAL MEDICINE. (NE/0014-410X). **3657**

EXCERPTA MEDICA. SECTION 7. PEDIATRICS AND PEDIATRIC SURGERY. (NE/0373-6512). **3657**

EXCERPTA MEDICA. SECTION 9. SURGERY. (NE/0014-4134). **3657**

EXCERPTA MEDICA. SECTION 13. DERMATOLOGY AND VENEREOLOGY. (NE/0014-4177). **3658**

EXCERPTA MEDICA. SECTION 18. CARDIOVASCULAR DISEASES AND CARDIOVASCULAR SURGERY. (NE/0014-4223). **3658**

EXCERPTA MEDICA. SECTION 19. REHABILITATION AND PHYSICAL MEDICINE. (NE/0014-4231). **3658**

EXCERPTA MEDICA. SECTION 22. HUMAN GENETICS. (NE/0014-4266). **3658**

EXCERPTA MEDICA. SECTION 23. NUCLEAR MEDICINE. (NE/0014-4274). **3658**

EXCERPTA MEDICA. SECTION 24. ANESTHESIOLOGY. (NE/0014-4282). **3658**

EXCERPTA MEDICA. SECTION 25. HEMATOLOGY. (NE/0014-4290). **3658**

EXCERPTA MEDICA. SECTION 27. BIOPHYSICS, BIOENGINEERING AND MEDICAL INSTRUMENTATION. (NE/0014-4312). **3658**

EXCERPTA MEDICA. SECTION 28. UROLOGY AND NEPHROLOGY. (NE/0014-4320). **3658**

EXCHANGE. (NE/0166-2740). **4958**

EXCHANGE & COMMISSARY NEWS. (US/0014-4452). **4044**

EXCHANGE (KITCHENER). (CN/0824-457X). **833**

EXCHANGE (PROVO). (US/0146-4000). **1091**

EXE. (UK/0268-6872). **Adv Mgr:** Sandra Inniss-Palmer, **Tel** 81-994-6477. **1184**

EXECUTIVE : AN ACADEMY OF MANAGEMENT PUBLICATION, THE. (US). **867**

EXECUTIVE DEVELOPMENT. (UK). **867**

EXECUTIVE EDUCATOR, THE. (US/0161-9500). **1863**

EXECUTIVE (HONG KONG EDITION). (HK). **Adv Mgr:** Lesley Kelly. **674**

EXECUTIVE HOUSEKEEPING TODAY. (US/0738-6583). **Adv Mgr:** Dan Cufford. **2790**

EXECUTIVE INTELLIGENCE REVIEW. (US/0273-6314). **Adv Mgr:** Stanley Ezrol, **Tel** (703)777-9451. **1490**

EXECUTIVE REPORT ON MANAGED CARE, THE. (US/0898-9753). **940**

EXECUTIVE REPORT (PITTSBURGH, PA.). (US/0279-1382). **Adv Mgr:** Karen Schade. **674**

EXERCISE EXCHANGE. (US/0531-531X). **1894**

EXERCISE STANDARDS & MALPRACTICE REPORTER, THE. (US/0891-0278). **Adv Mgr:** Molly Romig. **2968**

EXETER NEWS-LETTER (1867), THE. (US/0886-3962). **5708**

EXETER TIMES-ADVOCATE. (CN). **5784**

EXHAUST NEWS. (US/0192-7469). **5104**

EXHIBIT BUILDER. (US/0887-6878). **Adv Mgr:** Jill Brookman, **Tel** (818)225-0100. **1606**

EXHIBIT BUILDER SOURCE BOOK DIRECTORY. (US). **674**

EXHIBIT REVIEW, THE. (US/1046-2872). **Adv Mgr:** Cameron Perry, **Tel** (503)643-2783. **759**

EXHIBITION BULLETIN. (UK/0014-4649). **Adv Mgr:** L. Colls. **759**

EXHIBITIONS 'ROUND THE WORLD. (CH). **759**

EXHIBITS DIRECTORY - ASSOCIATION OF AMERICAN PUBLISHERS. (US/0147-0310). **4815**

EXILFORSCHUNG. (GW). **5245**

EXPANSION. (MX). **Adv Mgr:** Elena Bayardo. **4647**

EXPANSION MANAGEMENT. (US/1073-8355). **674**

EXPANSION MANAGEMENT REVIEW, L'. (FR). **Adv Mgr:** Philippe Guillanton, **Tel** 011 33 1 40604060. **867**

EXPERIENTIAL EDUCATION. (US/0739-2338). **1746**

EXPERIMENT. (US/0014-4770). **3463**

EXPERIMENTAL AGING RESEARCH. (US/0361-073X). **3750**

EXPERIMENTAL AND CLINICAL IMMUNOGENETICS. (SZ/0254-9670). **3669**

EXPERIMENTAL ASTRONOMY. (NE/0922-6435). **395**

EXPERIMENTAL DERMATOLOGY. (DK/0906-6705). **3720**

EXPERIMENTAL HEAT TRANSFER. (UK/0891-6152). **4430**

EXPERIMENTAL LUNG RESEARCH. (US/0190-2148). **3949**

EXPERIMENTAL PATHOLOGY (1981). (GW/0232-1513). **3894**

EXPERIMENTAL ROCKET FLYER. (US/1062-8576). **18**

EXPERIMENTAL TECHNIQUES (WESTPORT, CONN.). (US/0732-8818). **2114**

EXPERIMENTAL THERMAL AND FLUID SCIENCE. (US/0894-1777). **4427**

EXPERT AND THE LAW, THE. (US/0737-8726). **2968**

EXPERT SYSTEMS FOR INFORMATION MANAGEMENT. (UK/0953-5551). **1212**

EXPERT WITNESS JOURNAL. (US/0277-0555). **2968**

EXPLICATOR — Advertising Accepted Index

EXPLICATOR, THE. (US/0014-4940). **3386**

EXPLORATION GEOPHYSICS. (US/0071-3473). **1405**

EXPLORATION GEOPHYSICS (MELBOURNE). (AT/0812-3985). **Adv Mgr:** G. Dickson, **Tel** 011 61 3 8892522. **4402**

EXPLORATION INTERNATIONAL NEWS. (UK/0960-9989). **4256**

EXPLORATIONS (DAYTON, OHIO). (US/0889-8693). **4958**

EXPLORATIONS IN ETHNIC STUDIES. (US/0730-904X). **2261**

EXPLORATIONS IN KNOWLEDGE. (UK/0261-1376). **Adv Mgr:** same as editor. **4346**

EXPLORATIONS IN RENAISSANCE CULTURE. (US/0098-2474). **2846**

EXPLORE (CALGARY). (CN/0714-816X). **4871**

EXPLORERS JOURNAL. (US/0014-5025). **5104**

EXPLORING B. (US/0162-4431). **5060**

EXPLOSIVES AND PYROTECHNICS. (US/0014-505X). **2012**

EXPO NEWS. (FR/0757-4223). **834**

EXPO (WAUCONDA, ILL.). (US/1046-3925). **867**

EXPORT CONTROL NEWS. (US/0896-0682). **834**

EXPORT DIRECTORY CHILE. (CL). **834**

EXPORT DIRECTORY OF BRAZIL. (BL). **834**

EXPORT DIRECTORY OF CHILE. GUIA CHILENA DE LA EXPORTACION. (CL). **Adv Mgr:** ITV, **Tel** 232-4316. **834**

EXPORT GAZETTE. (II). **834**

EXPORT GRAFICAS USA. (US/0741-7160). **378**

EXPORT HANDBOOK SYDNEY. (AT/0312-3774). **Adv Mgr:** Andrew Pomeroy. **674**

EXPORT LEADS. (US/1064-1513). **Adv Mgr:** Barbara MacIntyre, **Tel** (206)779-1511. **834**

EXPORT (NEW YORK, N.Y.). (US/0014-519X). **2811**

EXPORT POLYGRAPH INTERNATIONAL. (GW/0344-2039). **378**

EXPORT TIMES (NEW DELHI), THE. (II/0257-8018). **834**

EXPORT TODAY. (US/0882-4711). **Adv Mgr:** Pat Steele. **834**

EXPORT TRADE TODAY (ENGINEERING EDITION). (GW). **3478**

EXPORTADOR, EL. (US/0279-456X). **835**

EXPOSITIONES MATHEMATICAE. (GW/0723-0869). **3505**

EXPOSITORY TIMES, THE. (UK/0014-5246). **5016**

EXPRESS (DRUMMONDVILLE). (CN/0713-5483). **5784**

EXTRACELLULAR MATRIX. (UK/0268-1617). **536**

EXTRACTA ORTHOPAEDICA. (GW/0344-5046). **3881**

EXTRACTA UROLOGICA. (GW/0344-5038). **3990**

EXTRAPOLATION. (US/0014-5483). **3342**

EXTRUSION COMMUNIQUE. (UK/0958-0549). **Adv Mgr:** Ms. Taylor, **Tel** 011 44 242 676645. **2334**

EYE : THE INTERNATIONAL REVIEW OF GRAPHIC DESIGN. (UK/0960-779X). **378**

EYECARE BUSINESS. (US/0885-9167). **4215**

EYELINE. (AT). **373**

EYEPIECE. (UK/0950-737X). **Adv Mgr:** Ron Bowyer, **Tel** 081 464 6738. **4369**

F.A.R.O.G. FORUM JOURNAL BILINGUE. (US/0741-577X). **5200**

F.I.B.A. RULES CASEBOOK. (CN/0712-5585). **4894**

F.I.D. NEWS BULLETIN. (NE/0014-5874). **3210**

F.O.C. REVIEW. (US/1041-8164). **3387**

FABIAN REVIEW. (UK). **Adv Mgr:** T. Upton. **4541**

FABIAN TRACT. (UK/0307-7535). **Adv Mgr:** T. Upton. **4474**

FABIS. (SY/0255-6448). **171**

FABRICATOR (ROCKFORD, ILL.). (US/0888-0301). **Adv Mgr:** Mike Lacny. **3478**

FABRICS & ARCHITECTURE. (US/1045-0483). **298**

FABRIMETAL. (BE/0377-9084). **3478**

FABULA. (GW/0014-6242). **2319**

FACE A LA JUSTICE. (CN/0710-1090). **3164**

FACE (MALIBU, CALIF.). (US/1064-7953). **2533**

FACEPLATE. (US/1040-807X). **4176**

FACES ROCKS. (US/0882-2921). **4117**

FACET TALK. (AT/1035-0977). **2773**

FACETS FEATURES. (US/0736-3745). **Adv Mgr:** M. Reyes. **4068**

FACHBERICHTE HUTTENPRAXIS METALLWEITERVERARBEITUNG. (GW/0340-8043). **4001**

FACHSPRACHE. (AU/0251-1207). **3281**

FACHVORTRAGE DES WVAO-JAHRESKONGRESSES, DIE. (GW). **4215**

FACIAL PLASTIC SURGERY. (US/0736-6825). **3964**

FACILITIES DESIGN & MANAGEMENT. (US/0279-4438). **2900**

FACILITIES MANAGER : THE OFFICIAL PUBLICATION OF THE ASSOCIATION OF PHYSICAL PLANT ADMINISTRATORS OF UNIVERSITIES AND COLLEGES. (US/0882-7249). **867**

FACILITIES PLANNING NEWS. (US/1045-7089). **Adv Mgr:** Todd Stone, **Tel** (510)254-1744. **298**

FACILITY MANAGEMENT JOURNAL : A PUBLICATION OF THE INTERNATIONAL FACILITY MANAGEMENT ASSOCIATION. (US/1059-3667). **867**

FACILITY MANAGER. (US/0888-0085). **Adv Mgr:** Carole Snyder, **Tel** (616)345-3230. **868**

FACS OF THE WEEK. (US/1056-2540). **898**

FACTS ABOUT COAL. (US). **2139**

FACTS FOR YOU. (II). **1561**

FACTS ON FILE NEWS DIGEST CD-ROM. (US/1062-9572). **2487**

FACTS (SEATTLE, WASH. : 1962). (US/0427-8879). **5760**

FACTSHEET FIVE. (US/0890-6823). **385**

FACTUM. (SZ). **5060**

FACTUM : BOLETIN OFICIAL DEL COLEGIO DE ABOGADOS DE PUERTO RICO. (PR). **2968**

FACULTY DIALOGUE. (US/8756-2146). **4958**

FAG TIDSSKRIFTET SYKEPLEIEN. (NO/0802-9768). **3856**

FAIR SCOPE. (CN). **674**

FAIR TIMES. (US/0889-0714). **Adv Mgr:** Jack McAndrew, **Tel** (215)887-5700. **4860**

FAIRBANKS DAILY NEWS-MINER. (US/8750-5495). **Adv Mgr:** Marilyn Romano, **Tel** (907)456-6661 ext. 257. **5629**

FAIRCHILD'S TRAVEL INDUSTRY PERSONNEL DIRECTORY. (US). **5469**

FAIRFAX JOURNAL (SPRINGFIELD. 1980). THE. (US/0273-6403). **Adv Mgr:** Bob Saupp, **Tel** (703)846-8380. **5758**

FAIRMONT SENTINEL. (US). **Adv Mgr:** Gary Audersen, **Tel** (507)235-3303. **5695**

FAIRPLAY WORLD PORTS DIRECTORY. (UK/0261-2356). **5449**

FAIRPRESS. (US/0192-3110). **5645**

FAIRVIEW REPUBLICAN. (US). **5732**

FAITH & FORM. (US/0014-7001). **298**

FAITH AND FREEDOM OXFORD. (UK/0014-701X). **4958**

FAITH AND PHILOSOPHY : JOURNAL OF THE SOCIETY OF CHRISTIAN PHILOSOPHERS. (US/0739-7046). **4346**

FAITH TODAY (TORONTO). (CN/0706-7003). **4958**

FAITH TODAY (WILLOWDALE). (CN/0832-1191). **4958**

FAITS & CHIFFRES. (FR/0290-0378). **1532**

FAIZULISLAM. (PK). **5285**

FAJR (JERUSALEM). (IS). **2503**

FALFURRIAS FACTS. (US). **Adv Mgr:** San Juanita Olivarez. **5749**

FALMOUTH OUTLOOK, THE. (US/0891-8694). **5680**

FAMILIA. (SA/0014-7117). **2447**

FAMILIA CRISTIANA. (MX). **5029**

FAMILIES IN SOCIETY. (US/1044-3894). **5285**

FAMILJA KANA. (MM). **Adv Mgr:** Crest Publicity, **Tel** 224876, 238467. **2279**

FAMILLE ET DEVELOPPEMENT. (TG). **Adv Mgr:** K. Attigno. **4775**

FAMILLE MAGAZINE. (FR). **2279**

FAMILLE QUEBEC. (CN/0318-0581). **2279**

FAMILY ADVOCATE. (US/0163-710X). **3120**

FAMILY AFFAIRS. (US). **2279**

FAMILY AND CONCILIATION COURTS REVIEW. (US/1047-5699). **3120**

FAMILY ASSOCIATION NEWSLETTER, DRODDY, DRODY, DRAWDY & VARIANTS, THE. (US/0749-4505). **2447**

FAMILY CIRCLE. (US/0014-7206). **2790**

FAMILY CONNECTIONS. (CN/1195-9428). **2279**

FAMILY COURT REPORTER. (UK/0952-8199). **3120**

FAMILY HANDYMAN, THE. (US/0014-7230). **2790**

FAMILY HISTORY. (UK/0014-7265). **2447**

FAMILY LAW (CHICHESTER). (UK/0014-7281). **3120**

FAMILY LIFE. (UK). **2279**

FAMILY LIFE (NEW YORK, N.Y.). (US/1072-0332). **2279**

FAMILY MATTERS (MELBOURNE, VIC.). (AT/1030-2646). **Adv Mgr:** Liz Sharmon. **2279**

FAMILY MEDICINE. (US/0742-3225). **3737**

FAMILY MOTOR COACHING. (US/0360-3024). **5382**

FAMILY PHYSICIAN (KUALA LUMPUR, MALAYSIA). (MY). **3737**

FAMILY PLANNING PERSPECTIVES. (US/0014-7354). **588**

FAMILY PRACTICE. (UK/0263-2136). **3737**

FAMILY PRACTICE RECERTIFICATION. (US/0163-6642). **3737**

FAMILY PROCESS. (US/0014-7370). **2279**

FAMILY RECORDS TODAY. (US/0736-1858). **2447**

FAMILY RELATIONS. (US/0197-6664). **2279**

FAMILY ROOTS : JOURNAL OF THE FAMILY ROOTS FAMILY HISTORY SOCIETY. EASTBOURNE AND DISTRICT. (UK). **2447**

FAMILY SYSTEMS MEDICINE. (US/0736-1718). **3737**

FAMILY TIES (HOLLAND GENEALOGICAL SOCIETY). (US/0736-9883). **2447**

FAMILY TREE MAGAZINE. (UK/0267-1131). **Adv Mgr:** J. Boon. **2447**

FAMILY TREE TALK. (US/0747-9441). **2447**

FAMILYFUN (NEW YORK, N.Y.). (US/1056-6333). **2280**

FAMUAN (TALLAHASSEE, FLA.), THE. (US/1063-9942). **5649**

FAN CLUB DIRECTORY, THE. (US). **5231**

FANFARE (TENAFLY, N.J.). (US/0148-9364). **4117**

FANGORIA. (US/0164-2111). **4068**

FANTASTIC FOUR. (US/0274-5291). **4861**

FANTASY & SCIENCE FICTION. (US/0024-984X). **3387**

FANTASY BOOK. (US/0277-0717). **3387**

FAR EASTERN ECONOMIC REVIEW. (HK/0014-7591). **1561**

FAR EASTERN TECHNICAL REVIEW. (UK/0144-8218). **835**

FARBE. (GW/0014-7680). **1024**

FARBE + I.E. UND LACK ADRESSBUCH MIT BEZUGSQUELLENNACHWEIS. (GW). **4223**

FARBE + LACK. (GW/0014-7699). **4223**

FARE ELETTRONICA. (IT). **2054**

FARM AND COUNTRY (TORONTO). (CN/0046-3299). **84**

FARM AND DAIRY (SALEM, OHIO : 1914). (US/0014-7826). **Adv Mgr:** Scot Darling. **5728**

FARM & POWER EQUIPMENT DEALER. (US/0892-6085). **158**

FARM BUILDING PROGRESS. (UK/0309-4111). **Adv Mgr:** same as editor. **158**

FARM BUILDINGS AND ENGINEERING : JOURNAL OF THE FARM BUILDINGS INFORMATION CENTRE AND THE FARM BUILDINGS ASSOCIATION. (UK/0265-5373). **614**

FARM BUREAU JOURNAL. (US). **84**

FARM EQUIPMENT. (US/0014-7958). **159**

FARM GATE, THE. (CN/0705-8748). **84**

FARM INDUSTRY NEWS (1984). (US/0892-8312). **159**

FARM JOURNAL (PHILADELPHIA. 1956). (US/0014-8008). **85**

FARM NEWS OF ERIE AND WYOMING COUNTIES. (US). **85**

FARM REVIEW (JOLIET, ILL.). (US). **85**

FARMACEUTICO HOSPITALES, EL. (SP/0214-4697). **4304**

FARMACEUTSKI GLASNIK. (CI/0014-8202). **4304**

FARMACEVTISK REVY. (SW/0014-8210). **4304**

FARMACI. (IT). **4304**

FARMACOTERAPIA MADRID. (SP/0214-8935). **4305**

FARMER STOCKMAN OF THE MIDWEST. (US/0739-9235). **Adv Mgr:** Robert Deterding. **85**

FARMERS' ADVANCE, THE. (US/0745-211X). **5692**

FARMER'S DIGEST. (US/0046-3337). **85**

FARMERS EXCHANGE. (US). **85**

FARMER'S EXCHANGE, THE. (US). **85**

FARMERS HOT LINE. (US/0192-6322). **86**

FARMERS' NEWSLETTER, LARGE AREA. (AT/0467-5282). **86**

FARMERSVILLE HERALD (FARMERSVILLE, CALIF.). (US/1072-1827). **Adv Mgr:** V. Spencer, **Tel** (209)592-3171. **5635**

FARMFUTURES. (US/0091-1305). **86**

FARMING JAPAN. (JA). **86**

FARMING NEWS. (UK). **86**

FARMING TODAY (NAIROBI, KENYA). (KE). **86**

FARMINGTON NEWS, THE. (US). **Adv Mgr:** Frank Chilinski. **5645**

FARMINGTON OBSERVER. (US/0888-6199). **Adv Mgr:** Mark Lewis, **Tel** (313)591-2300. **5692**

FARMVILLE HERALD. (US). **5758**

FARMWEEK (EASTERN ED.). (US/0164-8640). **86**

FARO DEL POETA : REVISTA TRIMESTRAL DE POESIA. (SP). **3463**

FARO DEL SILENCIO. (SP). **4388**

FARR FOOTNOTES. (US/0897-778X). **2448**

FASEB JOURNAL, THE. (US/0892-6638). **455**

FASHION ACCESSORIES. (HK/0255-7290). **1084**

FASHION FORECAST. (UK). **1084**

FASHION GALLERIA, THE. (US/0274-5100). **1084**

FASHION GUIDE DUSSELDORF. (GW/0942-8151). **1084**

FAST AND HEALTHY MAGAZINE. (US/1078-0203). **2597**

FAST FERRY INTERNATIONAL. (UK/0954-3988). **Adv Mgr:** D. Woodgate, **Tel** 81-549-1077. **593**

FAST FOLK MUSICAL MAGAZINE. (US/8755-9137). **4117**

FASTENER TECHNOLOGY INTERNATIONAL. (US/0746-2441). **2114**

FATE (MARION). (US/0014-8776). **4241**

FATIGUE & FRACTURE OF ENGINEERING MATERIALS & STRUCTURES. (UK/8756-758X). **2102**

FAULKNER & GRAY'S BANKRUPTCY LAW REVIEW. (US/1043-0547). **2968**

FAULKNER JOURNAL, THE. (US/0884-2949). **Adv Mgr:** Dawn Trouard. **3387**

FAULKNER NEWSLETTER AND YOKNAPATAWPHA REVIEW, THE. (US/0733-6357). **Adv Mgr:** D. Wells. **432**

FAUNA D'ITALIA. (IT/0430-1226). **5583**

FAUNA OF NEW ZEALAND. (NZ/0111-5383). **5608**

FAUNA (OSLO). (NO/0014-8881). **5583**

FAUQUIER TIMES-DEMOCRAT. (US/1050-7655). **Adv Mgr:** John T. Toler. **5758**

FAXON PLANNING REPORT, THE. (US/1043-1187). **3210**

FAYETTE ADVERTISER, THE. (US/0746-9942). **5703**

FAYETTE CONNECTION, THE. (US/0739-8093). **2448**

FAYETTE FALCON, THE. (US). **5745**

FAYETTE REVIEW, THE. (US/1065-0083). **5728**

FCM FORUM (ENGLISH ED.). (CN/0381-1352). **4647**

FCX CAROLINA COOPERATOR. (US/0195-3346). **86**

FDGB REVIEW. (GW/0323-7028). **1669**

FDM, FURNITURE DESIGN & MANUFACTURING. (US/0192-8058). **634**

FEATURED FILL-IT-INS. (US/0194-3170). **4861**

FEDERAL AQUISITION REGULATIONS / DISKETTE. (US). **4647**

FEDERAL BAR NEWS & JOURNAL. (US/0279-4691). **Adv Mgr:** Beth Kemper. **2969**

FEDERAL COMMUNICATIONS LAW JOURNAL. (US/0163-7606). **2969**

FEDERAL COMPUTER WEEK. (US/0893-052X). **Adv Mgr:** Julie Savage. **1247**

FEDERAL FACILITIES ENVIRONMENTAL JOURNAL. (US/1048-4078). **3112**

FEDERAL JOBS DIGEST. (US/0739-1684). **4204**

FEDERAL LABOR RELATIONS REPORTER. (US/0199-4883). **1669**

FEDERAL MANAGERS QUARTERLY. (US/0893-8415). **868**

FEDERAL MERIT SYSTEMS REPORTER. (US/0746-035X). **4702**

FEDERAL PERSONNEL GUIDE. (US/0163-7665). **4702**

FEDERAL PROPERTY MANAGEMENT REGULATIONS / DISKETTE. (US). **4648**

FEDERAL-STATE-LOCAL GOVERNMENT DIRECTORY, THE. (US/1041-6722). **4648**

FEDERAL TIMES. (US/0014-9233). **4703**

FEDERAL VETERINARIAN, THE. (US/0164-6257). **5510**

FEDERAL WAY NEWS. (US). **Adv Mgr:** Pam Schairbaum. **5760**

FEDERALIST (WASHINGTON, D.C. : 1980), THE. (US/0736-8151). **2733**

FEDNEWS, THE. (US/0430-2761). **1669**

FEED & FARM SUPPLY DEALER. (CN/0046-3604). **200**

FEED & GRAIN. (US/1055-3223). **200**

FEED COMPOUNDER. (UK/0950-771X). **Adv Mgr:** Simon Mounsey. **200**

FEED INTERNATIONAL. (US/0274-5771). **201**

FEED MANAGEMENT. (US/0014-956X). **201**

FEEDS & FEEDING. (US/0961-978X). **201**

FELD WALD WASSER. SCHWEIZERISCHE JAGDZEITUNG. (SZ/0014-9756). **4871**

FELIX. (US). **320**

FELLOWSHIP (NEW YORK). (US/0014-9810). **4521**

FELL'S INTERNATIONAL COIN BOOK. (US/0430-2958). **2781**

FELL'S UNITED STATES COIN BOOK. (US/1041-6951). **Adv Mgr:** Don Lessane. **2781**

FEM. (MX/0185-4666). **Adv Mgr:** Patricia Gonzalez, **Tel** 011 52 5 536 9261. **5555**

FEMALE BODYBUILDING AND WEIGHT TRAINING. (US/0888-4102). **2597**

FEMINIE. (CN). **Adv Mgr:** Sharon Barlow, **Tel** (416)921-3682. **5555**

FEMINISM & PSYCHOLOGY. (UK/0959-3535). **5555**

FEMINIST BOOKSTORE NEWS. (US/0741-6555). **Adv Mgr:** Sandy. **5556**

FEMINIST, DER. (GW/0179-8367). **5556**

FEMINIST ISSUES. (US/0270-6679). **5556**

FEMINIST REVIEW. (UK/0141-7789). **5556**

FEMINIST STUDIES. (US/0046-3663). **5556**

FEMINIST TEACHER. (US/0882-4843). **1894**

FEMMES D'ACTION. (CN/0226-9902). **5556**

FEMS MICROBIOLOGY. (NE/0921-8254). **562**

FEN. FINITE ELEMENT NEWS. (UK/0309-6688). **5105**

FENESTRATION (RIVERTON, N.J.). (US/0895-450X). **614**

FENXI HUAXUE. (CC/0253-3820). **Adv Mgr:** Shi Youlin. **1015**

FERDINAND NEWS, THE. (US). **Adv Mgr:** Kathy Tretter. **5664**

FERGUSON FILES. (US/1040-2276). **2448**

FERGUSON'S SRI LANKA DIRECTORY. (CE). **2503**

FERMENT (LONDON). (UK/0957-7041). **Adv Mgr:** F. Bolton. **2367**

FERN GAZETTE, THE. (UK/0308-0838). **510**

FERNANDINA BEACH NEWS-LEADER. (US). **Adv Mgr:** Mike H., **Tel** (904)261-3696. **5649**

FERNSEH- UND KINOTECHNIK. (GW/0015-0142). **4068**

FERRARI WORLD. (UK/0958-7462). **5415**

FERRO-ALLOY DIRECTORY & DATABOOK. (UK/0266-3198). **4002**

FERROELECTRICS. (US/0015-0193). **4402**

FERROELECTRICS. LETTERS SECTION. (US/0731-5171). **2054**

FERTIGUNGSTECHNIK UND BETRIEB. (GW/0015-024X). **2114**

FERTILISER MARKETING NEWS. (II). **87**

FERTILISER NEWS. (II/0015-0266). **87**

FERTILITY AND STERILITY. (US/0015-0282). **3576**

FERTILIZER INTERNATIONAL. (UK/0015-0304). **87**

FERTILIZER RESEARCH. (NE/0167-1731). **171**

FERTILIZER TECHNOLOGY. (US/0378-0430). **171**

FESTIVAL QUARTERLY. (US/8750-3530). **4959**

FETUS (NASHVILLE, TENN.), THE. (US/1057-137X). **3761**

FEUILLETS DE BIOLOGIE. (FR/0428-2779). **455**

F+I-BAU. (GW/0340-2967). **615**

F+I-BAU BAUEN MIT SYSTEMEN. (GW). **Adv Mgr:** Brigitte Zugel. **615**

FIA JOURNAL. (AT/1322-4409). **2597**

FIBER AND INTEGRATED OPTICS. (US/0146-8030). **4434**

FIBEROPTIC PRODUCT NEWS. (US/0890-653X). **1155**

FIBERSCOPE. (US/0198-8387). **5351**

FIBERWORKS QUARTERLY. (US/8756-7121). **5351**

FIBRE BOX HANDBOOK. (US/0196-7215). **4219**

FIBRE MARKET NEWS. (US/0046-3728). **Adv Mgr:** M Gladstone. **5351**

FIBRINOLYSIS. (UK/0268-9499). **455**

FICHERO BIBLIOGRAFICO HISPANOAMERICANO. (PR/0015-0592). **416**

FICTION INTERNATIONAL. (US/0092-1912). **Adv Mgr:** S. Dollente, **Tel** (619)357-5536. **3387**

FIDDLEHEAD, THE. (CN/0015-0630). **3387**

FIELD CROP ABSTRACTS. (UK/0015-069X). **153**

FIELD HOCKEY RULES. NATIONAL FEDERATION ED. (US/0275-5394). **4894**

FIELD (OBERLIN, OHIO). (US/0015-0657). **3463**

FIELD TRIP GUIDEBOOK (COLUMBIA). (US/0197-0976). **1375**

FIELDIANA. BOTANY. (US/0015-0746). **510**

FIELDIANA : GEOLOGY. (US/0096-2651). **1375**

FIELDIANA : ZOOLOGY. (US/0015-0754). **5583**

FIFTY-FIVE PLUS (BATTERSEA). (CN/0840-4496). **Adv Mgr:** J. Walsh. **5179**

FIFTY SOMETHING. (AT). **Adv Mgr:** K. Osgood. **5179**

FIGA. (US/0196-187X). **4117**

FIGHT DIRECTOR, THE. (UK). **5364**

FIGHTING WOMAN NEWS. (US/0146-8812). **2597**

FIJI LIBRARY ASSOCIATION NEWSLETTER. (FJ). **3210**

FIJI TIMES, THE. (FJ). **5800**

FIKR O NAZAR. (PK/0430-4055). **5042**

FILIPINAS (SAN FRANCISCO, CALIF.). (US/1063-4630). **Adv Mgr:** B.Bitagon. **2261**

FILIPINO CATHOLIC. (US/0273-7280). **5029**

FILLES D'AUJOURD'HUI. (CN/0227-0315). **1063**

FILM & HISTORY (NEWARK, N.J.). (US/0360-3695). **4069**

FILM AND TELEVISION TECHNICIAN. (UK). **4069**

FILM & VIDEO (LOS ANGELES, CALIF.). (US/1041-1933). **4069**

FILM AND VIDEO MAKERS DIRECTORY, THE. (US/0270-3289). **4069**

FILM COMMENT. (US/0015-119X). **4069**

FILM

Advertising Accepted Index

FILM CULTURE. (US/0015-1211). **4069**

FILM DIRECTIONS. (IE). **4069**

FILM DOPE. (UK/0305-1706). **4069**

FILM EN TELEVISIE EN VIDEO. (BE). **Adv Mgr:** Ronnie Pede. **4069**

FILM INDEX. (AT). **4070**

FILM JOURNAL (HOLLINS), THE. (US/0046-3787). **4070**

FILM (LONDON, ENGLAND : 1954). (UK/0015-1025). **4070**

FILM QUARTERLY. (US/0015-1386). **4070**

FILM REVIEW (ENGLAND). (UK). **Adv Mgr Tel** 081-878-5486. **4070**

FILM : TUTTI I FILM DELLA STAGIONE. (IT). **4070**

FILM UND FARBE. (GW/0934-0378). **4070**

FILMFAUST. (GW). **4070**

FILMFAX. (US/0895-0393). **4070**

FILMKUNST. (AU/0015-1599). **4071**

FILMS IN REVIEW. (US/0015-1688). **4071**

FILMS ON OFFER ... / COMPILED BY NIGEL ALGAR AND STEPHEN JENKINS. (UK). **4071**

FILOLOGIA POLSKA. (PL). **3388**

FILOSOFIA E SOCIETA. (IT). **5200**

FILOZOFIA (BRATISLAVA). (XO/0046-385X). **4347**

FILSON CLUB HISTORY QUARTERLY, THE. (US/0015-1874). **2733**

FILTER (BRANTFORD). (CN/0833-8493). **3941**

FILTRATION & SEPARATION. (UK/0015-1882). **2012**

FINAL FRONTIER. (US/0899-4161). **20**

FINANCE AND COMMERCE (REGULAR DAILY ED.). (US/8750-6149). **2970**

FINANCIAL ACCOUNTABILITY & MANAGEMENT IN GOVERNMENTS, PUBLIC SERVICES, AND CHARITIES. (UK/0267-4424). **4649**

FINANCIAL ANALYSTS JOURNAL, THE. (US/0015-198X). **898**

FINANCIAL COUNSELING AND PLANNING. (US/1052-3073). **Adv Mgr:** Tahara. **898**

FINANCIAL DAILY CARD SERVICE, CUMULATIVE. (US/0093-4070). **898**

FINANCIAL EXECUTIVE (1987). (US/0895-4186). **675**

FINANCIAL FUTURES. (US/0890-1309). **1490**

FINANCIAL MANAGERS' STATEMENT. (US/0887-4808). **868**

FINANCIAL PLANNING NEWS. (US/0893-7060). **898**

FINANCIAL PLANNING ON WALL STREET. (US). **898**

FINANCIAL PLANNING SERIES. MONEYLINES MAGAZINE. (US). **675**

FINANCIAL TIMES (LONDON ED.). (UK/0307-1766). **5812**

FINANCIAL TIMES NORTH SEA LETTER AND EUROPEAN OFFSHORE NEWS. (UK/0950-1037). **1944**

FINANCIAL TIMES WHO'S WHO IN WORLD OIL AND GAS. (UK/0141-3236). **1607**

FINANCIAL TIMES WORLD HOTEL DIRECTORY, THE. (UK/0308-8464). **2805**

FINANCIAL TIMES WORLD INSURANCE YEARBOOK, THE. (UK). **2897**

FINANCIAL WOMAN TODAY. (US/1059-3950). **5556**

FINANCIAL WORLD. (US/0015-2064). **898**

FINANCIEEL OVERHEIDSMANAGEMENT. (NE/0922-1026). **4649**

FINANZ-RUNDSCHAU. (GW/0340-9007). **4726**

FINANZARCHIV. (GW/0015-2218). **4726**

FINCASTLE HERALD, THE. (US/8750-7323). **Adv Mgr:** Joan Bowles. **5758**

FINDING. (US/0892-7367). **3210**

FINE ART & AUCTION REVIEW. (CN/0833-0891). **350**

FINE GARDENING. (US/0896-6281). **2414**

FINE HOMEBUILDING. (US/0273-1398). **615**

FINE LINE. (AT/0818-3473). **3388**

FINE PRINT (SAN FRANCISCO). (US/0361-3801). **4565**

FINE TOOL JOURNAL, THE. (US/0745-6824). **Adv Mgr:** S. Ward. **250**

FINE WOODWORKING. (US/0361-3453). **634**

FINESCALE MODELER. (US/0277-979X). **2773**

FINEST HOUR. (US/0882-3715). **2688**

FINGER LAKES TRAVEL GUIDE, THE. (US). **2773**

FINGERPRINT WHORLD. (UK/0951-1288). **Adv Mgr:** M. Crockett, **Tel** 0926-415833. **3164**

FINISHERS' MANAGEMENT. (US/0015-2358). **868**

FINISHING. (UK/0264-2506). **4224**

FINNISH MUSIC QUARTERLY. (FI/0782-1069). **4117**

FINNISH TRADE REVIEW. (FI/0015-2463). **835**

FIRA BULLETIN. (UK/0014-5904). **2905**

FIRE & MOVEMENT. (US/0147-0051). **Adv Mgr:** James Cason. **4861**

FIRE & SECURITY PROTECTION. (UK). **5177**

FIRE APPARATUS JOURNAL. (US/0885-8837). **2289**

FIRE CHIEF. (US/0015-2552). **2289**

FIRE ENGINEERING. (US/0015-2587). **2289**

FIRE ENGINEERS JOURNAL. (UK/0143-5337). **2289**

FIRE FIGHTING IN CANADA. (CN/0015-2595). **Adv Mgr:** Dave Douglas, **Tel** (519)582-2513. **2289**

FIRE INTERNATIONAL. (UK/0015-2609). **2289**

FIRE PREVENTION (LONDON, 1971). (UK/0309-6866). **2289**

FIRE PROTECTION CONTRACTOR, THE. (US/1043-2485). **2289**

FIRE SERVICE INFORMATION. (US/0015-2668). **2290**

FIRE SURVEYOR. (UK/0262-7981). **2290**

FIRE (TUNBRIDGE WELLS). (UK/0142-2510). **2290**

FIREFIGHTER'S NEWS. (USUS/1061-4818). **Adv Mgr:** Al Frazier. **2290**

FIREHEART (MAYNARD, MASS.). (US/1046-6029). **4185**

FIREHOUSE. (US/0145-4064). **2290**

FIREMAN MELBOURNE, THE. (AT/0812-0056). **2290**

FIREPOINT ROSEVILLE. (AT/1035-2287). **2290**

FIRESIDE CHATS. (US/0015-2714). **2785**

FIREWATCH / NAFED. (US). **2290**

FIREWEED. (CN/0706-3857). **Adv Mgr:** Z. Dhanam. **5556**

FIREWORKS BUSINESS. (US/8755-4372). **675**

FIRM FOUNDATION. (US/8750-9377). **5060**

FIRST BREAK. (UK/0263-5046). **1405**

FIRST CHOICE CANADA. (CN/0820-8859). **5382**

FIRST CLASS ALFELD. (GW/0939-8414). **Adv Mgr:** Uwe Krist. **2805**

FIRST DAYS. (US/0428-4836). **2785**

FIRST DROP / COASTER NEWS. (UK). **Adv Mgr:** A. Hine. **4861**

FIRST FOR WOMEN. (US/1040-9467). **5557**

FIRST HAND. (US/0744-6349). **2794**

FIRST LANGUAGE. (UK/0142-7237). **3281**

FIRST PERSPECTIVE. (CN). **2261**

FIRST STEPS ON THE LADDER OF LEARNING. (AT). **Adv Mgr:** Margaret Sasse, Suzie Rosenstraus. **1804**

FIRST STRIKE. (US/0896-4432). **2781**

FIRST TEACHER. (US/0744-7434). **1895**

FIRST THINGS (NEW YORK, N.Y.). (US/1047-5141). **Adv Mgr:** Richard Vaughan, **Tel** (815)398-8569. **4959**

FIRSTS (LOS ANGELES, CALIF.). (US/1066-5471). **4821**

FISCAL STUDIES. (UK/0143-5671). **4726**

FISCH UND FANG. (GW/0015-2838). **4894**

FISCHWAID (1982). (GW/0722-706X). **2301**

FISH CULTURIST, THE. (US/0015-2919). **2301**

FISH FARM NEWS, THE. (CN/1180-5633). **Adv Mgr:** Catherine Egan. **2301**

FISH FARMING INTERNATIONAL. (UK/0262-0820). **2301**

FISH INTERNATIONAL. (GW/0930-6552). **Adv Mgr:** Eckhard Preuss. **2301**

FISH PHYSIOLOGY AND BIOCHEMISTRY. (NE/0920-1742). **2301**

FISH SNIFFER (NORTHERN CALIFORNIA-NEVADA ED.), THE. (US/0747-3397). **5635**

FISH SUPPLIES INTERNATIONAL : PROCESSING & MARKETING NEWS. (CN/0229-1924). **2301**

FISHERIES (BETHESDA). (US/0363-2415). **2302**

FISHERIES PRODUCT NEWS. (US/1047-2525). **2302**

FISHERMAN (GRAND HAVEN, MICH.), THE. (US/8755-4216). **2302**

FISHERMAN (NEW ENGLAND ED.), THE. (US/1040-0125). **Adv Mgr Tel** (203)572-0564. **2302**

FISHERMAN (NEW JERSEY, DELAWARE BAY ED.), THE. (US/1040-0117). **Adv Mgr:** Cullen Monahan. **4894**

FISHERMAN, THE. (CN/0015-2986). **2302**

FISHERMEN'S NEWS, THE. (US/0015-2994). **2303**

FISHING & HUNTING NEWS (WESTERN WASHINGTON ED.). (US/0015-301X). **4872**

FISHING BOAT WORLD. (HK/1033-1247). **2303**

FISHING FACTS (NORTHERN ED.). (US/0899-9597). **2303**

FISHING FACTS (SOUTHERN ED.). (US/0899-9589). **2303**

FISHING IN MARYLAND. (US/0164-0941). **2303**

FISHING (NEW YORK, N.Y.). (US/0742-0587). **2303**

FISHING NEWS INTERNATIONAL. (UK/0015-3044). **2303**

FISHING SECRETS. (US/0742-0595). **2303**

FISHING TACKLE RETAILER (1984). (US/8750-1287). **675**

FISHING TACKLE TRADE NEWS. (US/0015-3060). **2303**

FISHING WORLD. (US/0015-3079). **2303**

FISICA E TECNOLOGIA. (IT/0391-9757). **5105**

FISK(E) FAMILY ASSOCIATION : NEWSLETTER. (US). **2448**

FITECH. (UK/0307-2118). **2290**

FITECH INTERNATIONAL. (UK). **2290**

FITNESS MANAGEMENT (SOLANA BEACH, CALIF.). (US/0882-0481). **2597**

FITNESS PLUS. (US/1054-674X). **2597**

FITOPATOLOGIA. (PE/0430-6155). **Adv Mgr:** Hebert Torres, **Tel** 51 14 366920 - 2048. **510**

FITOPATOLOGIA BRASILEIRA. (BL/0100-4158). **172**

FIVE OWLS, THE. (US/0892-6735). **1063**

FLAG BULLETIN, THE. (US/0015-3370). **2616**

FLAGSCAN. (CN/0833-1510). **2448**

FLAMBOROUGH NEWS. (CN/0710-5339). **5784**

FLAMING CRESCENT, THE. (US). **4474**

FLANNERY O'CONNOR BULLETIN. (US/0091-4924). **Adv Mgr:** same as editor. **432**

FLARE (TORONTO). (CN/0708-4927). **5557**

FLASH ART (INTERNATIONAL EDITION). (IT/0394-1493). **350**

FLAT EARTH NEWS. (US/8756-0313). **1405**

FLATBUSH GUIDE, THE. (US). **5470**

FLAVOUR AND FRAGRANCE JOURNAL. (UK/0882-5734). **2335**

FLEET EQUIPMENT. (US/0747-2544). **Adv Mgr:** Bill White. **5382**

FLEET MANAGEMENT NEWS (PORT READING, N.J.). (US/1042-1769). **Adv Mgr:** J. Dickenson. **5382**

FLEISCH. (GW/0015-3575). **2335**

FLEISCHEREI. (GW/0015-3613). **2335**

FLETCHER FORUM OF WORLD AFFAIRS, THE. (US/1046-1868). **4521**

FLEXPACK MATERIALS & MARKETS BULLETIN. (UK). **4219**

FLIGHT INTERNATIONAL DIRECTORY. PART 1, UNITED KINGDOM. (UK). **Adv Mgr:** Rowena Shelley, **Tel** 44 473 696661. **21**

FLIGHT INTERNATIONAL DIRECTORY. PART II, MAINLAND EUROPE AND IRELAND. (UK). **21**

FLINDERS JOURNAL OF HISTORY AND POLITICS. (AT/0726-7215). **4474**

FLINT JOURNAL (1935). (US). **Adv Mgr:** R. Samuel. **5692**

FLOATING. (US). **4850**

FLOODTIDE. (US). **4959**

FLOOR COVERING PLUS. (CN/1193-8781). **Adv Mgr:** A. Thomas. **615**

FLOOR COVERING WEEKLY. (US/0015-3761). **2905**

FLOOR FOCUS. (US/1064-7627). **615**

FLORA-LINE, THE. (US/1062-855X). **Adv Mgr:** Dody Lyness, **Tel** (310)377-7040. **2435**

FLORA (LONDON). (UK/0306-882X). **2435**

FLORA. MORPHOLOGIE, GEOBOTANIK, OKOLOGIE. (GW/0367-2530). **2216**

FLORA NEOTROPICA. (US/0071-5794). **510**

FLORACULTURE INTERNATIONAL. (US/1051-9076). **2414**

FLORAL & NURSERY TIMES. (US/1042-2145). **511**

FLORALA NEWS, THE. (US). **5626**

FLORENCE CITIZEN, THE. (US). **5642**

FLORENCE MORNING NEWS. (US). **5742**

FLORESVILLE CHRONICLE-JOURNAL. (US). **Adv Mgr:** James J. Fietsam. **5750**

FLORIDA ADMINISTRATIVE WEEKLY. (US/0098-874X). **2970**

FLORIDA ANTHROPOLOGIST, THE. (US/0015-3893). **236**

FLORIDA ARCHITECT. (US/0015-3907). **298**

FLORIDA ARCHITECTURE (1966). (US/1040-0893). **298**

FLORIDA BAPTIST WITNESS / ORGAN OF THE FLORIDA BAPTIST STATE CONVENTION. (US). **5060**

FLORIDA BAR JOURNAL, THE. (US/0015-3915). **2970**

FLORIDA BAR NEWS. (US/0360-0114). **2970**

FLORIDA BLUE SHEET. (US). **4071**

FLORIDA BUILDER. (US). **Adv Mgr:** D. Williams. **615**

FLORIDA BUSINESS GUIDE, THE. (US/0733-964X). **676**

FLORIDA BUSINESS PUBLICATIONS INDEX. (US/0191-183X). **676**

FLORIDA BUSINESS SOUTHWEST. (US/1047-6105). **676**

FLORIDA CATHOLIC, THE. (US/0746-4584). **5029**

FLORIDA CATTLEMAN AND LIVESTOCK JOURNAL, THE. (US/0015-3958). **211**

FLORIDA CONTRACTOR. (US/0046-4112). **2605**

FLORIDA CPA TODAY : A PUBLICATION OF THE FLORIDA INSTITUTE OF CERTIFIED PUBLIC ACCOUNTANTS. (US). **744**

FLORIDA ENVIRONMENTS. (US/0894-9743). **Adv Mgr:** M Hutchens. **2172**

FLORIDA FAMILY PHYSICIAN. (US/0015-4067). **3737**

FLORIDA FIELD NATURALIST. (US/0738-999X). **5584**

FLORIDA FIREMAN. (US/0274-8797). **2290**

FLORIDA FLAMBEAU, THE. (US). **Adv Mgr:** Rose Rodriguez, **Tel** (904)681-6692 ext. 29. **5649**

FLORIDA FOLIAGE. (US). **2414**

FLORIDA FOLIAGE. (US/0741-1448). **Adv Mgr:** Elaine Hudson, **Tel** (407)886-1036. **511**

FLORIDA FORUM. (US/0191-4618). **615**

FLORIDA FUNERAL DIRECTOR, THE. (US/0273-9747). **2407**

FLORIDA GARDENER, THE. (US/0426-5750). **2414**

FLORIDA GEOGRAPHER, THE. (US/0739-0041). **2560**

FLORIDA GROCER. (US/0191-586X). **2335**

FLORIDA GROWER & RANCHER. (US/0015-4091). **Adv Mgr:** Sondra Abrahamson. **87**

FLORIDA HOTEL & MOTEL JOURNAL. (US/8750-6807). **Adv Mgr:** Helen Sanders. **2805**

FLORIDA INDUSTRIES GUIDE, THE. (US). **1561**

FLORIDA JOURNAL OF ENVIRONMENTAL HEALTH. (US/0897-4624). **2172**

FLORIDA LAND OWNER MAGAZINE. (US/1047-1413). **4837**

FLORIDA LAW REVIEW. (US/1045-4241). **2971**

FLORIDA LIVING. (US/0888-9600). **Adv Mgr:** Jill Teter. **2533**

FLORIDA MANUFACTURERS REGISTER. (US/0882-9438). **3479**

FLORIDA MEDICAL DIRECTORY. (US). **3576**

FLORIDA NATURALIST, THE. (US/0015-4172). **Adv Mgr:** Mike Nelson. **226**

FLORIDA NURSE, THE. (US/0015-4199). **3856**

FLORIDA NURSERYMAN. (US). **2414**

FLORIDA ORCHIDIST, THE. (US/0430-778X). **Adv Mgr:** S. Taylor. **2414**

FLORIDA PAINTBALL PRESS. (US). **4895**

FLORIDA READING QUARTERLY, THE. (US/0015-4261). **1747**

FLORIDA REALTOR. (US/0199-5839). **Adv Mgr:** Tracy Lawton, **Tel** (407)438-1400 Ext. 2322. **4838**

FLORIDA RESTAURATEUR. (US/0192-348X). **5071**

FLORIDA RESTAURATEUR & PURVEYOR NEWS. (US/0046-418X). **5071**

FLORIDA RETIREMENT LIVING. (US/0160-5739). **Adv Mgr:** R. Dummer. **5179**

FLORIDA SHIPPER, THE. (US/0884-8548). **Adv Mgr:** Brian Neuhart. **5449**

FLORIDA SPORTSMAN (MIAMI). (US/0015-3885). **4895**

FLORIDA STAR (JACKSONVILLE, FLA. : 1951), THE. (US/0740-798X). **Adv Mgr:** T. J. Stafford, **Tel** (904)765-7940. **2616**

FLORIDA STATE UNIVERSITY LAW REVIEW. (US/0096-3070). **2971**

FLORIDA TIMES-UNION (JACKSONVILLE, FLA. : 1910). (US/0740-2325). **5649**

FLORIDA TRUCK NEWS. (US/0015-4334). **5382**

FLORIDA VOCATIONAL JOURNAL. (US/0145-9376). **1913**

FLORIDA WATER RESOURCES JOURNAL. (US/0896-1794). **5533**

FLORIDAGRICULTURE (GAINESVILLE, FLA.). (US/0015-3869). **87**

FLORISSANT VALLEY REPORTER, THE. (US). **5703**

FLORIST (GUNZBURG, GERMANY). (GW/0015-4393). **Adv Mgr:** D. Winkler. **2435**

FLORIST (SOUTHFIELD, MICH.). (US/0015-4385). **Adv Mgr:** Denise Mazzetti, **Tel** (810)355-6264. **2435**

FLORIST TRADE MAGAZINE. (UK/0015-4415). **2435**

FLORISTS' REVIEW. (US/0015-4423). **2435**

FLORTECNICA. (IT). **2414**

FLOTATION SLEEP INDUSTRY. (US/0164-5749). **2905**

FLOWER AND GARDEN (KANSAS CITY, MO. : 1982). (US/0891-9534). **2414**

FLOWER NEWS : THE FLORAL INDUSTRY'S NATIONAL WEEKLY. (US/0015-4490). **2414**

FLOWER OF THE FOREST BLACK GENEALOGICAL JOURNAL. (US/0738-159X). **2448**

FLOWERS&. (US/0199-4751). **Adv Mgr:** Peter Nicolaysen, **Tel** (310)826-5253. **2435**

FLUE CURED TOBACCO FARMER, THE. (US/0015-4512). **5373**

FLUG REVUE. (GW/0015-4547). **21**

FLUID MECHANICS : SOVIET RESEARCH. (US/0096-0764). **2089**

FLUID PHASE EQUILIBRIA. (NE/0378-3812). **1052**

FLUID POWER ABSTRACTS. (UK/0015-4644). **2089**

FLUSHING TIMES. (US). **Adv Mgr:** Howard Swengler. **5716**

FLUSSIGES OBST. (GW/0015-4539). **2335**

FLUTE TALK. (US/0744-6918). **4118**

FLUTIST QUARTERLY, THE. (US/8756-8667). **4118**

FLY FISHERMAN. (US/0015-4741). **2304**

FLY ROD & REEL. (US/1045-0149). **Adv Mgr:** Bill Anderson, **Tel** (207)594-9544. **2304**

FLY-TACKLE DEALER. (US). **2304**

FLYFISHING. (US/0744-7191). **Adv Mgr:** Joyce Sherman, **Tel** (503)653-8108. **2304**

FLYING BUYERS' GUIDE. (US/0738-3800). **21**

FLYING MODELS. (US/0015-4849). **2773**

FLYING NEEDLE, THE. (US/0270-2959). **5184**

FLYING REVIEW. (US/0274-5798). **21**

FLYPAPER (CALGARY). (CN/0317-2481). **4895**

FMR (ENGLISH ED.). (US/0747-6388). **350**

FOCUS (AUSTIN, TEX. 1985). (US/0883-8194). **1247**

FOCUS (AUSTIN, TEX. 1989). (US/1041-2549). **1185**

FOCUS (BURBANK, CALIF.). (US/1054-4208). **4241**

FOCUS : CHICAGO. (US/0362-0905). **4071**

FOCUS (CHICAGO. 1977). (US/0148-026X). **2971**

FOCUS, FIBRE OPTIC COMMUNICATION & USER SYSTEMS. (UK/0959-0188). **Adv Mgr:** Alex Henner (UK); Willy R. Mattes (CN). **1155**

FOCUS (MATHEMATICAL ASSOCIATION OF AMERICA). (US/0731-2040). **3505**

FOCUS (NEW YORK, N.Y. 1950). (US/0015-5004). **2561**

FOCUS ON AFRICA : BBC MAGAZINE. (UK/0959-9576). **2499**

FOCUS ON COMMERICAL AVIATION SAFETY. (UK). **21**

FOCUS ON CRITICAL CARE. (US/0736-3605). **3856**

FOCUS ON EXCEPTIONAL CHILDREN. (US/0015-511X). **1879**

FOCUS ON FARMING. (US/0745-8355). **88**

FOCUS ON INDIANA LIBRARIES. (US/0015-5152). **Adv Mgr:** Editor, **Tel** (317)257-2040. **3211**

FOCUS ON INTERNATIONAL & COMPARATIVE LIBRARIANSHIP. (UK/0305-8468). **3211**

FOCUS ON LEARNING PROBLEMS IN MATHEMATICS. (US/0272-8893). **1879**

FOCUS ON SECURITY. (US/1071-9997). **Adv Mgr:** Jon Gustafson. **3211**

FOERDERN UND HEBEN. (GW/0373-6482). **2114**

FOGLI DI COLLEGAMENTO DELLA L O C. (IT). **Adv Mgr:** Annalisa Marini. **4521**

FOKUS PA FAMILIEN. (NO/0332-5415). **2280**

FOLDRAJZI KOZLEMENYEK. (HU/0015-5411). **2561**

FOLIA HEREDITARIA ET PATHOLOGICA. (IT/0015-5578). **545**

FOLIA PHONIATRICA. (SZ/0015-5705). **3888**

FOLIA PRIMATOLOGICA. (SZ/0015-5713). **5584**

FOLIO (BROCKPORT, N.Y.). (US/0882-3030). **3388**

FOLIO : THE MAGAZINE FOR MAGAZINE MANAGEMENT. (US/0046-4333). **4815**

FOLIO'S PUBLISHING NEWS. (US/1053-4563). **Adv Mgr:** Shirley Sax, **Tel** (203)358-9900. **4815**

FOLK ART FINDER. (US/0738-8357). **350**

FOLK DANCE SCENE. (US). **1313**

FOLK DIRECTORY, THE. (UK/0430-876X). **5231**

FOLK HARP JOURNAL. (US/0094-8934). **4118**

FOLK LIFE. (UK/0430-8778). **2319**

FOLK MUSIC JOURNAL. (UK/0531-9684). **4118**

FOLK ROOTS. (UK/0951-1326). **Adv Mgr:** Gina Jennings. **4118**

FOLKLOR ARCHIVUM. (HU). **2319**

FOLKLORE (CALCUTTA). (II/0015-5896). **2320**

FOLKLORE DE FRANCE. (FR/0015-5918). **Adv Mgr:** Feybesse JC. **2320**

FOLKLORE (LONDON). (UK/0015-587X). **2320**

FOLKLORE (MOOSE JAW). (CN/0824-3085). **2320**

FOLKLORE SUISSE. (SZ/0015-5969). **2320**

FOLLETOS MUNDO CRISTIANO. (SP). **2280**

FOLLIA DI NEW YORK. (US/0015-6000). **2846**

FONDERIE, FONDEUR D'AUJOURD'HUI. (FR/0249-3136). **4002**

FONTES ARTIS MUSICAE. (SZ/0015-6191). **4118**

FONTI ORALI-STUDI E RICERCHE. (IT). **2688**

FOOD AND CHEMICAL TOXICOLOGY. (UK/0278-6915). **3980**

FOOD

Advertising Accepted Index

FOOD AND DRUG PACKAGING. (US/0015-6272). **4219**

FOOD & SERVICE / TEXAS RESTAURANT ASSOCIATION. (US/0891-0154). **2336**

FOOD AUSTRALIA : OFFICIAL JOURNAL OF CAFTA AND AIFST. (AT/1032-5298). **2336**

FOOD BROKER QUARTERLY. (US/0884-7185). **2336**

FOOD CHEMISTRY. (UK/0308-8146). **1024**

FOOD CONTROL. (UK). **2336**

FOOD DISTRIBUTION MAGAZINE : FDM. (US/1048-8197). **Adv Mgr:** Ray Rehn. **2337**

FOOD EUROPE ENGLISH ED. (UK/0956-6783). **Adv Mgr:** Frank Blackwell. **2337**

FOOD FIRST DEVELOPMENT REPORT. (US/0895-3090). **5285**

FOOD INDUSTRIES OF SOUTH AFRICA. (SA/0015-6450). **2337**

FOOD INDUSTRY NEWS AUCKLAND. (NZ/0113-8901). **Adv Mgr:** Heather Braae. **2337**

FOOD MANAGEMENT. (US/0091-018X). **2338**

FOOD MANAGEMENT AMERSFOORT. (NE/0168-325X). **2338**

FOOD MANUFACTURE INGREDIENT & MACHINERY SURVEY. (UK). **2338**

FOOD MARKETING & TECHNOLOGY. (GW/0932-2744). **2338**

FOOD MERCHANTS ADVOCATE. (US/0015-6493). **2338**

FOOD PEOPLE AND THEIR COMPANIES. (US/0279-9839). **Adv Mgr:** Laura Mikszan, **Tel** (404)974-1077 or (800)647-3724. **2338**

FOOD PERSONALITY. (NE/0925-8051). **2339**

FOOD PLANT EQUIPMENT. (US/0887-3895). **2339**

FOOD POLICY. (UK/0306-9192). **2339**

FOOD PROCESSING (BROMLEY, LONDON, ENGLAND). (UK/0264-9462). **Adv Mgr:** Frank Blackwell. **2339**

FOOD PROCESSOR. (AT). **Adv Mgr:** Ros Richards. **2339**

FOOD PRODUCTION MANAGEMENT. (US/0191-6181). **Adv Mgr:** R.Gerstmyer. **2339**

FOOD REVIEW. (SA/0257-8867). **Adv Mgr:** G Wells. **2339**

FOOD SCIENCE AND TECHNOLOGY ABSTRACTS. (UK/0015-6574). **2362**

FOOD SCIENCE & TECHNOLOGY TODAY. (UK/0950-9623). **Adv Mgr:** Mr. B. Broome, **Tel** 0732-866360. **2340**

FOOD-SERVICE EAST. (US/0885-6877). **Adv Mgr:** Richard E. Dolby, **Tel** (800)852-5212. **2340**

FOOD TECHNOLOGY (CHICAGO). (US/0015-6639). **2340**

FOOD TECHNOLOGY IN NEW ZEALAND. (NZ/0015-6655). **2340**

FOOD TRADE NEWS. (US/0015-6663). **2340**

FOOD TRADE REVIEW. (UK/0015-6671). **Adv Mgr:** Adrain Rinsted. **2340**

FOOD TRENDS NEWSLETTER. (US). **2340**

FOOD WORLD (COLUMBIA). (US/0191-619X). **Adv Mgr:** Nina Weiland. **2340**

FOODLINES. (US/0736-0010). **5286**

FOODSERVICE & HOSPITALITY. (CN/0007-8972). **5071**

FOODSERVICE DISTRIBUTOR, THE. (US/0896-4505). **2341**

FOODSERVICE EQUIPMENT SPECIALIST. BUYERS GUIDE AND PRODUCT DIRECTORY. (US). **2341**

FOODSERVICE OPERATORS GUIDE. (US/1040-4546). **2341**

FOOKIEN TIMES PHILIPPINES YEARBOOK, THE. (PH). **Adv Mgr:** William Velasco. **2651**

FOOT & ANKLE. (US/0198-0211). **3881**

FOOT & ANKLE INTERNATIONAL. (US/1071-1007). **3918**

FOOT WORSHIP NEWS. (US). **5268**

FOOTBALL, BASKETBALL & HOCKEY COLLECTOR. (US/1051-1997). **2773**

FOOTBALL DIGEST. (US/0015-6760). **4895**

FOOTBALL NEWS (DETROIT). (US/0161-9020). **Adv Mgr:** K Ballew, **Tel** (313)881-9554. **4895**

FOOTHILLS SENTINEL. (US/8750-3026). **5630**

FOOTHILLS TRADER. (US/0191-7463). **5645**

FOOTLOOSE LIBRARIAN, THE. (US/0733-3196). **5474**

FOOTNOTES. (US). **1313**

FOOTNOTES (RESTON, VA.). (US/8755-9048). **4895**

FOOTNOTES (WASHINGTON, D.C.). (US/0749-6931). **5245**

FOOTPRINTS. (UK). **2448**

FOOTPRINTS (FORT WORTH). (US/0426-8261). **2448**

FOOTWEAR FORUM. (CN/0706-7534). **Adv Mgr:** S. Boake, **Tel** (416)755-5799. **1084**

FOOTWEAR NEWS AUSTRALIA. (AT/0725-3362). **1084**

FOOTWEAR NEWS FACT BOOK. (US/0429-0208). **1084**

FOOTWORK. (US/0743-2259). **2846**

FOR FORMULATION CHEMISTS ONLY. (US/0887-736X). **975**

FOR THE LOVE OF CROSS STITCH. (US/1040-3965). **5184**

FOR THE RECORD (PORTLAND, OR.). (US). **2971**

FOR YOUR INFORMATION (NEW YORK, N.Y.). (US/0890-2992). **Adv MgrAdv Mgr Tel** (212)366-6900 ext.212. **320**

FORBES. (US/0015-6914). **676**

FORCE (ROME, ITALY). (IT/0394-5243). **3164**

FORDHAM INTERNATIONAL LAW JOURNAL. (US/0747-9395). **3128**

FORDHAM LAW REVIEW. (US/0015-704X). **2971**

FORD'S DECK PLAN GUIDE. (US/0096-1353). **5474**

FORD'S INTERNATIONAL CRUISE GUIDE. (US/0015-7066). **5449**

FORDYCE LETTER, THE. (US/0733-0324). **1675**

FORDYCE NEWS-ADVOCATE. (US/8750-4995). **Adv Mgr:** Ann Mathews. **5631**

FOREIGN LANGUAGE ANNALS. (US/0015-718X). **3282**

FOREIGN POLICY. (US/0015-7228). **4522**

FOREIGN SERVICE JOURNAL. (US/0146-3543). **Adv Mgr Tel** (202)338-4045. **4522**

FOREIGN TRADE BULLETIN. (II/0015-7317). **836**

FORENSIC REPORTS. (US/0888-692X). **3740**

FORENSIC SERVICES DIRECTORY. (US/0192-3145). **2972**

FORESIGHT (EDMONTON). (CN/0711-3927). **Adv Mgr:** Eric, **Tel** (604)275-7971. **5179**

FORESKRIFTER OM STATLIG TJANSTEPENSIONERING / STATENS ARBETSGIVARVERK. (SW/0348-1115). **1675**

FOREST AND BIRD. (NZ). **4165**

FOREST & CONSERVATION HISTORY. (US/1046-7009). **2379**

FOREST CITY SUMMIT (FOREST CITY, IOWA : 1947). (US). **5670**

FOREST FARMER. (US/0015-7406). **Adv Mgr:** Joye Moore. **2379**

FOREST INDUSTRIES DIRECTORY, BUYERS' AND SELLERS' GUIDE. (AT). **2380**

FOREST NOTES. (US/0015-7457). **2380**

FOREST PLANNING-CANADA. (CN/0832-1655). **2380**

FOREST PRESS (TIONESTA, PA. : 1953). (US). **Adv Mgr:** Leslie Holt, **Tel** 755-4900. **5736**

FOREST PRODUCTS ABSTRACTS. (UK/0140-4784). **2399**

FOREST SCIENCE. (US/0015-749X). **2381**

FOREST SCIENCE. MONOGRAPH. (US/0071-7568). **2381**

FORESTRY ABSTRACTS. (UK/0015-7538). **2399**

FORESTRY AND BRITISH TIMBER. (UK). **2400**

FORESTRY CHRONICLE, THE. (CN/0015-7546). **2381**

FORESTRY (LONDON). (UK/0015-752X). **2382**

FORESTRY ON THE HILL. (CN/1185-9598). **2382**

FORESTS AND PEOPLE. (US/0015-7589). **2382**

FORET CONSERVATION. (CN/0380-321X). **Adv Mgr:** Christine Cote. **2382**

FORET PRIVEE (1977), LA. (FR/0153-0216). **Adv Mgr:** C. Chavet. **2382**

FORET WALLONE. (BE). **2382**

FORM. (SW/0015-766X). **2900**

FORM (ALEXANDRIA). (US/0532-1700). **Adv Mgr:** Katie Davis. **4565**

FORM FUNCTION FINLAND. (FI/0358-8904). **2098**

FORM (SEEHEIM-JUGENHEIM, WEST GERMANY). (GW/0015-7678). **2098**

FORMAT (MINNETONKA, MINN.). (US/0279-6058). **Adv Mgr:** M.Johnson. **759**

FORMAT (ST. CHARLES). (US/0190-678X). **350**

FORMAZIONE PSICHIATRICA : PERIODICO TRIMESTRALE A CURA DELLA CLINICA PSICHIATRICA DELL'UNIVERSITA DI CATANIA. (IT). **3925**

FORME E LA STORIA, LE. (IT). **3388**

FORMS AND DIRECT MAIL MANUFACTURERS MARKET PLACE. (US). **Adv Mgr Tel** (800)327-7652. **676**

FORMSMFG. (US/1042-3028). **676**

FORNEY MESSENGER. (US). **Adv Mgr:** Judy P. Griffin. **5750**

FORO AMMINISTRATIVO (ANNUAL). (IT). **3093**

FORO INTERNACIONAL. (MX/0185-013X). **4474**

FORSCHUNGEN ZUR RELIGION UND LITERATUR DES ALTEN UND NEUEN TESTAMENTS. (GW). **5016**

FORSCHUNGEN ZUR SYSTEMATISCHEN UND OEKUMENISCHEN THEOLOGIE. (GW/0429-162X). **4959**

FORSCHUNGS- UND SITZUNGSBERICHTE. (GW/0515-9083). **2823**

FORSCHUNGSFORDERUNGEN UND FORSCHUNGSAUFTRAGE. (AU). **5106**

FORSTLICHE UMSCHAU. (GW/0015-7988). **2383**

FORSTWISSENSCHAFTLICHES CENTRALBLATT. (GW/0015-8003). **2383**

FORT BRAGG ADVOCATE-NEWS. (US/0886-8840). **Adv Mgr:** Bill Bodany, **Tel** (707)964-5642. **5635**

FORT COLLINS COLORADOAN. (US). **Adv Mgr:** Bob Williams, **Tel** (303)224-7702. **5642**

FORT FRANCES TIMES. (CN). **Adv Mgr:** Debbie Logan. **5784**

FORT MCMURRAY TODAY. (CN/0316-7542). **5784**

FORT MILL TIMES. (US). **Adv Mgr:** Carol Rose Mantle. **5742**

FORT MORGAN TIMES, THE. (US). **Adv Mgr:** Harold Bohm. **5643**

FORT MYERS BEACH OBSERVER. (US/0199-2945). **5649**

FORT RILEY POST, THE. (US). **Adv Mgr:** Doris Peterson, **Tel** (913)762-5000. **5675**

FORT WORTH. (US/0015-8089). **2533**

FORT WORTH COMMERCIAL RECORDER. (US/0015-8097). **2972**

FORT WORTH STAR-TELEGRAM. (US/0889-0013). **Adv Mgr:** Mac Tully, **Tel** (817)390-7802. **5750**

FORTNIGHT (BELFAST). (IE/0046-4694). **3343**

FORTRAN JOURNAL. (US/1060-0221). **1185**

FORTSCHRITTE DER KIEFERORTHOPAEDIE. (GW/0015-816X). **1323**

FORTSCHRITTE DER MEDIZIN. (GW/0015-8178). **3577**

FORTSCHRITTLICHE LANDWIRT, DER. (AU). **88**

FORTUNE. (US/0015-8259). **676**

FORUM BARCELONA. (SP/0212-9965). **3577**

FORUM (BONNER, MONT.). (US/0883-4970). **5016**

FORUM / CONFERENCE OF DEFENCE ASSOCIATIONS. (CN/0848-8886). **Adv Mgr:** P.Fogg, **Tel** (416)472-2801. **4044**

FORUM DER LETTEREN. (NE/0015-8496). **3388**

FORUM DES AUDIOPHILES PARIS. (FR/0760-7245). **4118**

FORUM (DON MILLS). (CN/0380-3147). **2881**

FORUM (FARGO, N.D.), THE. (US/0895-1292). **Adv Mgr:** Robert Hiemenz. **5725**

FORUM FOR COMMERCE AND INDUSTRY. (UK). **836**

FORUM FOR EKONOMI OCH TEKNIK. (FI/0533-070X). **5106**

FORUM FOR MODERN LANGUAGE STUDIES. (UK/0015-8518). **3282**

FORUM FOR PROMOTING 3-19 COMPREHENSIVE EDUCATION. (UK/0963-8253). **1747**

FORUM HOMOSEXUALITAT UND LITERATUR. (GW/0931-4091). **Adv Mgr:** Wolfgang Popp. **3388**

FORUM ITALICUM. (US/0014-5858). **3388**

FORUM LINGUISTICUM. (US/0163-0768). **3282**

FORUM (NORTH HOLLYWOOD). (US/0164-6931). **Adv Mgr:** Mary Warner. **3107**

FORUM OF PHI SIGMA IOTA, THE. (US/0883-5640). **3282**

FORUM (REGINA, SASK.). (CN/0831-3016). **3211**

FORUM, STADTE, HYGIENE. (GW/0342-202X). **2194**

FORUM WARE. (GW/0340-7705). **Adv Mgr:** I. Wagner. **2194**

FOTO MAGAZIN. (GW/0340-6660). **4369**

FOTOGESCHICHTE. (GW/0720-5260). **4369**

FOTOHANDEL. (NE). **4369**

FOUNDATION DRILLING. (US/0274-5186). **Adv Mgr:** Ted Ledgar, **Tel** (214)343-2091. **615**

FOUNDATION NEWS. (US/0015-8976). **4336**

FOUNDRYMAN, THE. (UK/0007-0718). **Adv Mgr:** Les Rivers, **Tel** 0432 350448. **4002**

FOUNTAIN COUNTY NEIGHBOR. (US/1060-5495). **Adv Mgr:** Judy Buchley, **Tel** (317)762-2411. **5664**

FOUR DIRECTIONS (TELLICO PLAINS, TENN.), THE. (US/1070-7549). **Adv Mgr:** William Meyer. **3388**

FOUR QUARTERS. (US/0015-9107). **Adv Mgr:** J. Cawley. **3388**

FOUR-TOWN JOURNAL. (CN/0712-6387). **5784**

FOUR WHEELER. (US/0015-9123). **5382**

FOURNEE, LA. (CN/0015-9158). **2341**

FOX FAMILY FACTS. (US/1044-9809). **2449**

FOX (NEW YORK, N.Y. 1984). (US/1041-9470). **3995**

FRA FYSIKKENS VERDEN. (NO/0015-9247). **4403**

FRACASTORO, IL. (IT/0015-9271). **3577**

FRAME/WORK (LOS ANGELES, CALIF.). (US/0895-6030). **4369**

FRAMERS FORUM. (US). **1185**

FRANCE AMERIQUE (NEW YORK, N.Y.). (US/0747-2757). **5716**

FRANCE COMPOSITES. (FR/0985-0503). **2102**

FRANCE ITALIE. (FR/1146-0024). **4474**

FRANCE... SPECIALIZED CATALOGUE OF ARTIST PROOFS, DE LUXE SHEETS, IMPERFORATES, COLOR ESSAYS, FIRST DAY COVERS, COLLECTIVE PROOFS, PRINTERS INSPECTION PROOFS, ILLUSTRATIONS. (US/0197-7202). **2785**

FRANCE TODAY (SAN FRANCISCO, CALIF. 1987). (US/0895-3651). **2688**

FRANCEXPORT. (FR/0244-710X). **837**

FRANCHISE ANNUAL HANDBOOK AND DIRECTORY. (US). **Adv Mgr:** Denise Muir. **954**

FRANCHISE ANNUAL (LEWISTON), THE. (CN/0318-8752). **Adv Mgr:** D. Muir. **677**

FRANCHISE HANDBOOK, THE. (US/0882-5505). **Adv Mgr:** Barbara Monfeli, **Tel** (414)272-9977. **1297**

FRANCHISE LEGAL DIGEST. (US/0739-8239). **3100**

FRANCHISE MAGAZINE. (UK/0268-8395). **Adv Mgr:** Wendy Sanders. **677**

FRANCHISING WORLD. (US/1041-7311). **677**

FRANCISCAN, THE. (UK). **5029**

FRANCISCANA. (BE/0015-9840). **5029**

FRANCISCANUM. (CK/0120-1468). **4347**

FRANCOFONIA. (IT). **3389**

FRANCOPHONIE RUGBY. (UK/0957-1744). **3282**

FRANK. (FR/0738-9299). **3343**

FRANKFURTER ALLGEMEINE. (GW/0174-4909). **5801**

FRANKFURTER FORSCHUNGEN ZUR ARCHITEKTURGESCHICHTE. (GW/0429-5714). **299**

FRANKLIN ADVOCATE, THE. (US). **5700**

FRANKLIN CHALLENGER. (US/8750-7390). **5664**

FRANKLIN COUNTY GRAPHIC. (US). **Adv Mgr:** Debbie Rochester. **5761**

FRANKLIN COUNTY TRIBUNE. (US). **Adv Mgr:** Jeannie York, **Tel** (314)583-2545. **5703**

FRANKLIN JOURNAL AND FARMINGTON CHRONICLE, THE. (US). **Adv Mgr:** Carol A. Lanier, **Tel** (207)778-2075. **5685**

FRANKLIN SUN (WINNSBORO, LA.). (US). **Adv Mgr:** Monica Huff. **5684**

FRASER'S CANADIAN TRADE DIRECTORY. (CN/0071-9277). **729**

FRASER'S POTATO NEWSLETTER. (CN/0384-7322). **172**

FRATERNITY NEWS - FRATERNITY FOR CANADIAN ASTROLOGERS. (CN/0710-510X). **390**

FRAUEN UND FILM. (GW). **4071**

FRAZEE FORUM. (US). **5696**

FREDDO. (IT/0016-0296). **2605**

FREDERICK FINDINGS. (US/0899-4188). **2449**

FREE ASSOCIATIONS. (UK/0267-0887). **3925**

FREE CHINA JOURNAL, THE. (CH). **5798**

FREE CHURCH CHRONICLE. (UK/0016-0326). **4960**

FREE FLIGHT (OTTAWA ONT.). (CN/0827-2557). **4895**

FREE INQUIRY IN CREATIVE SOCIOLOGY. (US/0736-9182). **5246**

FREE LANCE STAR, THE. (US). **Adv Mgr:** C. Murphy Street, **Tel** (703)374-5470. **5758**

FREE LUNCH. (US/1041-0945). **3463**

FREE MATERIALS FOR SCHOOLS AND LIBRARIES. (US/0836-0073). **Adv Mgr:** Ms. S. Lim, **Tel** (604)689-1568. **1895**

FREE PRESS. (US). **5696**

FREE PRESS (SPARWOOD). (CN/0715-5131). **5784**

FREE PRESS STANDARD, THE. (US). **5728**

FREE RADICAL RESEARCH COMMUNICATIONS. (SZ/8755-0199). **1052**

FREE SPIRIT (MIAMI, FLA.). (US/1062-8134). **Adv Mgr:** Dee Johns. **4388**

FREE SPIRIT (MINNEAPOLIS, MINN.). (US/0895-2256). **1063**

FREE TIME. (US/1064-2757). **2533**

FREE VENICE BEACHHEAD. (US/0884-9641). **5635**

FREEBIES (SANTA MONICA). (US/0148-2092). **1297**

FREEDOM SPEECH. (US/1057-3682). **Adv Mgr:** Jean Bolrmon, **Tel** (408)626-6600. **5635**

FREEDOM WRITER (GREAT BARRINGTON, MASS.). (US/1059-6372). **Adv Mgr:** 6. **4960**

FREELANCE (REGINA). (CN/0705-1379). **3389**

FREELANCE WRITER'S REPORT. (US/0731-549X). **2920**

FREER PRESS, THE. (US). **5750**

FREESAIL. (AT/0727-615X). **Adv Mgr:** Stephen Kay. **4895**

FREESTONE FRONTIERS. (US/0735-3278). **2449**

FREETHOUGHT HISTORY. (US/1071-7269). **4347**

FREETHOUGHT TODAY. (US/0882-8512). **4960**

FREIBURGER ZEITSCHRIFT FUER PHILOSOPHIE UND THEOLOGIE. (SZ/0016-0725). **4347**

FREIGHT MANAGEMENT. (UK/0016-0873). **5383**

FREIGHT MANAGEMENT INTERNATIONAL. (UK/0965-4704). **5383**

FREIGHT NEWS EXPRESS. (UK). **5383**

FREIGHTER, THE. (CN/0820-5280). **Adv Mgr:** Lou Thibault. **5784**

FREIGHTER TRAVEL NEWS. (US/0016-089X). **837**

FREMONT COUNTY NOSTALGIA NEWS. (US/8756-8446). **2449**

FREMONTIA (SACRAMENTO, CALIF.). (US/0092-1793). **Adv Mgr:** Dalheite, **Tel** (415)939-4911. **511**

FRENCH FORUM. (US/0098-9355). **3343**

FRENCH LITERATURE SERIES. (US/0271-6607). **3343**

FRENCH PERIODICAL INDEX. (US/0362-5044). **416**

FRENCH POLITICS AND SOCIETY. (US/0882-1267). **4474**

FRENCH REVIEW, THE. (US/0016-111X). **3283**

FRENCH STUDIES. (UK/0016-1128). **3343**

FRENCH STUDIES IN SOUTHERN AFRICA. (SA/0259-0247). **3389**

FRESHWATER BIOLOGY. (UK/0046-5070). **456**

FRESHWATER FISHING AUSTRALIA. (AT/1032-125X). **Adv Mgr:** Pamela Gibson. **2304**

FRESNO BEE, THE. (US/0889-6070). **5635**

FRIDAY WEEKLY. (SI). **Adv Mgr:** Lawrence Loh, **Tel** 740-2038. **1063**

FRIEDENSWARTE, DIE. (SZ/0340-0255). **3128**

FRIENDLY EXCHANGE. (US/0279-6856). **5474**

FRIENDLY LETTER, A. (US/0739-5418). **5060**

FRIENDS JOURNAL. (US/0016-1322). **Adv Mgr:** Caitlyn Frost, **Tel** (215)241-7277. **4960**

FRIENDS OF FINANCIAL HISTORY. (US/0278-8861). **Adv Mgr:** D. Moore, **Tel** (212)908-4519. **899**

FRIENDS OF FLORIDA FOLK. (US/0892-2500). **2320**

FRIGHTEN THE HORSES. (US/1072-5644). **Adv Mgr:** Nishauga Bliss, **Tel** (510)704-9736. **5187**

FRIO, CALOR, AIRE ACONDICIONADO. (SP/0210-0665). **Adv Mgr:** Senor de la Pezuela. **2605**

FRIONA STAR. (US). **5750**

FRISKO. (US). **2533**

FRONIMO; RIVISTA TRIMESTRALE DI CHITARRA E LIUTO, IL. (IT). **4118**

FRONTIER CHRONICLES. (US/1050-3560). **Adv Mgr:** Paul Taylor. **2616**

FRONTIERS (BOULDER). (US/0160-9009). **5557**

FRONTIERS OF MEDICAL AND BIOLOGICAL ENGINEERING. (NE/0921-3775). **3692**

FRONTLINE DUNEDIN. (NZ/0113-1990). **3724**

FROSTPROOF NEWS, THE. (US). **Adv Mgr:** Amy Stealy. **5649**

FROZEN FOOD DIGEST. (US/0889-5902). **2341**

FROZEN FOOD EXECUTIVE, THE. (US/0279-1498). **Adv Mgr:** JoAnne Meyers. **2341**

FROZEN FOOD REPORT. (US/0192-0367). **2342**

FRUCHTHANDEL DUSSELDORF. (GW/0429-7830). **Adv Mgr:** M Tedet, **Tel** 49 211 9910420. **172**

FRUIT BELGE, LE. (BE/0016-2248). **2415**

FRUIT COUNTRY. (US). **89**

FRUIT GARDENER, THE. (US/1049-4545). **2415**

FRUIT GROWER MAIDSTONE. (UK/0953-2188). **172**

FRUIT SOUTH. (US/0192-0847). **172**

FRUIT VARIETIES JOURNAL. (US/0091-3642). **2415**

FRUITS. (FR/0016-2299). **2415**

FRUITS & LEGUMES. (FR/0754-0698). **2342**

FU INFO / [HERAUSGEGEBEN VON DER PRESSE- UND INFORMATIONSSTELLE DER FREIEN UNIVERSITAT BERLIN (FU)]. (GW). **1825**

FU-NACHRICHTEN. (GW). **Adv Mgr:** Gabriela Gast-Anhzith, **Tel** 49 30 838 73 185. **1825**

FUEL CONSUMPTION GUIDE. (CN/0225-9214). **5415**

FUEL (GUILFORD). (UK/0016-2361). **4256**

FUEL OIL NEWS. (US/0016-2396). **4256**

FUEL PROCESSING TECHNOLOGY. (NE/0378-3820). **1025**

FUERZA AEREA (SANTIAGO, CHILE). (CL). **4044**

FUJIAN NONGYE KEJI. (CC/0253-2301). **89**

FULDAER HOCHSCHULSCHRIFTEN / HERAUSGEGEBEN VON DER THEOLOGISCHEN FAKULTAT FULDA. (GW). **4960**

FULL-COURT PRESS, THE. (US/0892-5364). **5696**

FULL CRY (SEDALIA). (US/0016-2620). **4872**

FULTON COUNTY NEWS (MCCONNELLSBURG, PA.). (US). **5736**

FULTON SUN, THE. (US/8750-6696). **5703**

FUNCTIONAL ORTHODONTIST, THE. (US/8756-3150). **1324**

FUNCTIONS. (CN/0821-2708). **3506**

FUND RAISING MANAGEMENT. (US/0016-268X). **868**

FUNDAMENTA PSYCHIATRICA. (GW/0931-0428). **3925**

FUNDAMENTAL & CLINICAL PHARMACOLOGY. (FR/0767-3981). **4305**

FUNDAMENTALS OF COSMIC PHYSICS. (US/0094-5846). **395**

FUNDBERICHTE AUS BADEN-WURTTEMBERG. (GW). **268**

FUNDS, AGENTS, CUSTODIANS, SUPPLIERS. (US/0887-8161). **899**

FUNGICIDE AND NEMATICIDE TESTS. (US/0148-9038). **172**

FUNK-TECHNIK. AUSGABE ZV (MUNCHEN). (GW/0342-0426). **1156**

FUNKSCHAU. (GW/0016-2841). **2055**

FUNKTIONSKRANKHEITEN DES BEWEGUNGSAPPARATES. (GW/0258-2015). **3804**

FUNPARKS DIRECTORY. (US/0147-5606). **4861**

FUNWORLD. (US/0892-3752). **4861**

FUR AGE WEEKLY. (US/0016-2884). **3184**

FUR-FISH-GAME. (US/0016-2922). **4872**

FURIOUS FICTIONS. (US/1065-7983). **3389**

FURMAN STUDIES. (US/0190-4701). **2846**

FURNISHING FLOORS. DOMESTIC AND CONTRACT. (AT/0816-5947). **Adv Mgr:** Joanne Royal. **2905**

FURNITURE/TODAY. (US/0194-360X). **2905**

FURNITURE WORLD (NEW YORK, N.Y.). (US/0738-890X). **2906**

FURROW, THE. (IE/0016-3120). **5029**

FUSE MAGAZINE. (CN/0838-603X). **Adv Mgr:** K. Mootoo. **320**

FUSION ASIA. (II/0970-0080). **2504**

FUSION FACTS (SALT LAKE CITY, UTAH). (US/1051-8738). **1945**

FUSION MAGAZINE. (CN/0832-9656). **2589**

FUSION WILMINGTON, DEL. (US/0016-3155). **2589**

FUTURA. (IE/0016-3252). **1084**

FUTURE (NEW DELHI, INDIA). (II/0252-1873). **2280**

FUTURES AND OPTIONS WORLD. (UK/0953-6620). **924**

FUTURES (LONDON). (UK/0016-3287). **1492**

FUTURIBLES (PARIS). (FR/0337-307X). **5246**

FUTURICS. (US/0164-1220). **5107**

FUTURIST, THE. (US/0016-3317). **5107**

FV. FOTO-VIDEO ACTUALIDAD. (SP/0214-2244). **4369**

FWP JOURNAL. (SA/0015-9026). **4027**

G.A.S. LITES. (US/0882-8377). **2449**

G. GESCHICHTE MIT PFIFF. (GW/0173-539X). **2616**

G.I. JOE. (US/0746-7397). **4861**

GABONAIPAR. (HU/0133-0918). **201**

GACETA ARQUEOLOGICA ANDINA. (PE/0254-8240). **268**

GACETA POETICA : REVISTA TRIMESTRAL DE POESIA. (SP). **3463**

GADSDEN COUNTY TIMES. (US). **Adv Mgr:** Bev Kirk. **5649**

GADSDEN TIMES (GADSDEN, ALA. : 1925). (US). **5626**

GAELIC GLEANINGS. (US/0882-2166). **2449**

GAFFNEY LEDGER, THE. (US/0748-934X). **Adv Mgr:** Robert Martin. **5742**

GAIRM. (UK/0016-3929). **3343**

GAITHERSBURG GAZETTE, THE. (US/0195-2447). **5686**

GAKKAI SENTA NEWS. (JA). **5107**

GALAKSIJA. (YU/0350-123X). **5107**

GALESVILLE REPUBLICAN. (US). **5767**

GALLERIES. (UK/0265-7511). **4088**

GALLERIES (WASHINGTON, D.C.). (US/0739-0475). **4088**

GALLERY (NEW YORK, N.Y.). (US/0195-072X). **Adv Mgr:** T. Martoran. **3995**

GALLERY OF FINE HOME PLANS. (US/0899-4404). **299**

GALPAGUCCHA. (II). **3283**

GALVA NEWS, THE. (US/0747-282X). **5660**

GALVANOTECNICA & NUOVE FINITURE. (IT/1120-6454). **487**

GALVESTON DAILY NEWS (HOUSTON, TEX. : 1865). (US/0738-8047). **5750**

GAM ON YACHTING. (CN/0016-4259). **Adv Mgr:** Craig Green. **593**

GAMA NEWS JOURNAL. (US/1058-0808). **2881**

GAMBIT (NEW ORLEANS, LA.). (US/0279-6589). **Adv Mgr:** Susan Crichton. **5684**

GAMC NEWS. (US/0743-7307). **868**

GAME BIRD BULLETIN. (US). **2194**

GAME JOURNAL : THE BEST OF HUNTING AND FISHING. (US). **4872**

GAMECOCK, THE. (US/0016-4313). **211**

GAMEPRO (BELMONT, CALIF.). (US/1042-8658). **4861**

GAMEROOM (NEW ALBANY, IND.). (US/1049-3948). **4861**

GAMES JUNIOR. (US/0897-196X). **4861**

GAMUT (TORONTO). (CN/0713-3545). **321**

GANG JOURNAL, THE. (US/1061-5326). **Adv Mgr:** John Fitzholm, **Tel** (616)695-3442. **3165**

GAONENG WULI YU HE WULI. (CC/0254-3052). **4447**

GARBAGE (BROOKLYN, NEW YORK, N.Y.). (US/1044-3061). **2194**

GARBO. (SP). **2517**

GARDEN CENTER BULLETIN, THE. (US/0892-564X). **2415**

GARDEN CITY OBSERVER. (US). **Adv Mgr:** Mark Lewis, **Tel** (313)591-2300. **5692**

GARDEN CITY TELEGRAM (GARDEN CITY, KAN. : 1953). (US). **Adv Mgr:** Kent O'Toole. **5675**

GARDEN CLIPPINGS. (CN/0318-7705). **2415**

GARDEN DESIGN. (US/0733-4923). **2415**

GARDEN RAILWAYS. (US/0747-0622). **5431**

GARDEN STATE REPORT. (US/8756-6605). **4650**

GARDENING IN ALBERTA. (CN/1188-2972). **Adv Mgr:** C. Dack. **2416**

GARDENING NEWS. (AT). **2416**

GARDENS' BULLETIN, SINGAPORE, THE. (SI/0374-7859). **89**

GARDENS WEST. (CN/0836-4974). **Adv Mgr:** T.Wilson, **Tel** (604)879-4991. **2416**

GARFIELD COUNTY NEWS (TROPIC, UTAH). (US/1064-7309). **5756**

GARFIELD-MAPLE HEIGHTS SUN. (US/0746-2611). **5728**

GARMENT MANUFACTURERS INDEX. (US/1065-1330). **Adv Mgr:** Edward Klevens. **1084**

GARTENPRAXIS. (GW/0341-2105). **Adv Mgr:** Mr. Kretschmer, **Tel** 49 711 4507-126. **2416**

GARTNERBORSE. (GW/0945-9111). **2416**

GARY CRUSADER. (US). **5664**

GAS. (NE/0016-4828). **4257**

GAS (BARCELONA, SPAIN). (SP). **4257**

GAS CHROMATOGRAPHY LITERATURE, ABSTRACTS AND INDEX. (US/0016-4895). **1015**

GAS DIRECTORY AND WHO'S WHO. (UK/0307-3084). **4257**

GAS ENGINE MAGAZINE. (US/0435-1304). **250**

GAS INDUSTRIES (1978). (US/0194-2468). **Adv Mgr:** Bill Dannhausen. **4257**

GAS (MUNCHEN). (GW/0343-2092). **4257**

GAS SEPARATION & PURIFICATION. (UK/0950-4214). **4258**

GAS TURBINE WORLD (1984). (US/0747-7988). **2114**

GAS TURBINE WORLD HANDBOOK. (US/0883-458X). **2114**

GAS WARME INTERNATIONAL. (GW/0020-9384). **4258**

GAS WORLD (LONDON, ENGLAND : 1974). (UK/0308-7654). **4258**

GASKELL SOCIETY JOURNAL, THE. (UK/0951-7200). **3389**

GASKIYA TA FI KWABO. (NR). **5807**

GASLIGHT (CLEVELAND, MINN.). (US/1062-015X). **Adv Mgr:** Melissa Gish. **3389**

GASPESIE (GASPE. 1979). (CN/0227-1370). **2734**

GASTECH : PREPRINTS OF CONFERENCE PAPERS / THE ... INTERNATIONAL LNG/LPG CONFERENCE & EXHIBITION ; ORGANISED BY GASTECH LTD. (UK). **4258**

GASTRIC SECRETION. (UK/0142-8098). **3744**

GASTROENTEROLOGIA CLINICA. (IT/1120-3757). **Adv Mgr:** Dott Dalla, **Tel** 06-86207165. **3745**

GASTROENTEROLOGIA JAPONICA. (JA/0435-1339). **3745**

GASTROENTEROLOGY & ENDOSCOPY NEWS. (US/0883-8348). **3745**

GASTROENTEROLOGY (NEW YORK, N.Y. 1943). (US/0016-5085). **3745**

GASTROINTESTINAL ENDOSCOPY. (US/0016-5107). **3746**

GASTROPODIA. (US/0435-1363). **5584**

GASTRUM. (SP/0211-058X). **3746**

GATELODGE : THE PRISON OFFICERS' MAGAZINE. (UK). **3165**

GATEWAY: THE JOURNAL OF THE BELL COUNTY HISTORICAL SOCIETY. (US). **2734**

GATHERING GIBSONS. (US/0893-3162). **2449**

GATHERING OF THE TRIBES, A. (US/1058-9112). **Adv Mgr:** Christian Howe. **3390**

GATO TUERTO, EL. (US/8755-3651). **3390**

GATOR BAIT. (US/0744-0995). **Adv Mgr:** Dwight Johnson, **Tel** (813)351-5469. **4896**

GAUGE RAIL-ROADING, O. (US/1062-1482). **2773**

GAUHATI LAW REPORTS. (II). **2973**

GAVEA-BROWN. (US/0276-7910). **3390**

GAY AIRLINE & TRAVEL CLUB NEWSLETTER, THE. (US). **2794**

GAYELLOW PAGES. NORTHEAST ED. (US). **2794**

GAZ D'AUJOURD'HUI. (FR/0016-5328). **4259**

GAZDASAG. (HU/0016-5360). **1492**

GAZETA MERCANTIL. (BL). **Adv Mgr:** M. Fares. **1562**

GAZETA OBSERWATORA. (PL). **1425**

GAZETTE - CANADIAN FORCES BASE GAGETOWN (1981). (CN/0713-391X). **4044**

GAZETTE (CEDAR RAPIDS, IOWA), THE. (US/1066-0291). **Adv Mgr:** David Storey, **Tel** (319)398-8208. **5670**

GAZETTE DE L'HOTEL DROUOT, LA. (FR). **321**

GAZETTE DES ARCHIVES, LA. (FR/0016-5522). **2481**

GAZETTE LEADER. (US). **5710**

GAZETTE (NEOLA, IOWA). (US). **5670**

GAZETTE, THE. (US). **5728**

GB+GW; GARTNERBORSE UND GARTENWELT. (GW/0342-4731). **2416**

GC/MS UPDATE. PART A ENVIRONMENTAL. (UK/0962-9327). **2172**

GEAR TECHNOLOGY. (US/0743-6858). **2114**

GEFAEHRLICHE LADUNG. (GW/0016-5808). **5383**

GEGENWART. (SZ/0016-5867). **4960**

GEGENWARTSKUNDE. (GW/0016-5875). **5200**

GEIJUTSU SHINCHO. (JA). **351**

GEIST GAZETTE. (US). **Adv Mgr:** John McNatt. **5664**

GEIST UND LEBEN (WURZBURG). (GW/0016-5921). **3390**

GEIST (VANCOUVER). (CN/1181-6554). **Adv Mgr:** Kevin Barefoot. **3390**

GEITEHOUDER, DE. (NE). **211**

GEKA TO TAISHA, EIYO. (JA/0389-5564). **3965**

GEKKAN HAIKIBUTSU. (JA/0285-6220). **2230**

GEMATOLOGIYA I TRANSFUZIOLOGIYA. (RU). **3771**

GEMMA : REVISTA INTERNACIONAL DE LITERATURA. (SP). **3390**

GEMSTONE REGISTRY BULLETIN, THE. (US/0882-6269). **2914**

GEN, GASTROENTEROLOGIA, ENDOCRINOLOGIA I NUTRICION. (VE/0016-3503). **3746**

GENDAI KAGAKU. CHEMISTRY TODAY. (JA). **976**

GENDAI KORIA. (JA). **2651**

GENDER & HISTORY. (UK/0953-5233). **5557**

GENDER & SOCIETY. (US/0891-2432). **5200**

GENDERS (AUSTIN, TEX.). (US/0894-9832). **2846**

GENE. (NE/0378-1119). **545**

GENE EXPRESSION. (US/1052-2166). **Adv Mgr:** Carole Timkovich, **Tel** (708)578-3259. **545**

GENE EXPRESSION. (UK/0957-3526). **545**

GENEAGRAM. (US/8756-7989). **2449**

GENEALOGICAL & LOCAL HISTORY BOOKS IN PRINT. (US/0146-616X). **4828**

GENEALOGICAL CLEARINGHOUSE QUARTERLY, THE. (US/0882-0422). **2449**

GENEALOGICAL COMPUTER PIONEER. (US/0735-0287). **2449**

GENEALOGICAL COMPUTING. (US/0277-5913). **Adv Mgr:** Gary Sagers, **Tel** (801)531-1490. **2450**

GENEALOGICAL GOLDMINE. (US/0738-3770). **2450**

GENEALOGICAL RECORD (HOUSTON, TEX.), THE. (US/0433-3209). **2450**

GENEALOGIST (MANCHESTER, N.H.), THE. (US/0196-4259). **2450**

GENEALOGIST MELBOURNE. (AT). **2450**

GENEALOGIST (NEW YORK), THE. (US/0197-1468). **2450**

GENEALOGISTS' MAGAZINE : OFFICIAL ORGAN OF THE SOCIETY OF GENEALOGISTS, THE. (UK/0016-6391). **Adv Mgr:** M. Gandy. **2450**

GENEESKUNDE EN SPORT. (NE/0016-6448). **3954**

GENEESKUNDIG ADRESBOEK VOOR NEDERLAND. (NE). **3914**

GENERAL AVIATION NEWS. (US/0191-927X). **22**

GENERAL AVIATION NEWS AND FLYER. (US/1052-9136). **Adv Mgr:** Larry Price. **22**

GENERAL DENTISTRY. (US/0363-6771). **1324**

GENERAL HOSPITAL PSYCHIATRY. (US/0163-8343). **3925**

GENERAL INSURANCE REGISTER. (CN/0380-223X). **2881**

GENERAL PRACTITIONER. (UK/0046-5607). **3737**

GENERATIONS (FREDERICTON). (CN/0821-5359). **2450**

GENERATIONS (SAN FRANCISCO, CALIF.). (US/0738-7806). **5179**

GENERATIONS (WINNIPEG). (CN/0226-6105). **2451**

GENES & DEVELOPMENT. (US/0890-9369). **545**

GENESIS 2. (US/0016-6669). **5047**

GENESIS (WASHINGTON, D.C.). (US/0744-0596). **3761**

GENETIC ENGINEER & BIOTECHNOLOGIST, THE. (UK/0959-020X). **3692**

GENETIC ENGINEERING LETTER. (US/0276-1882). **545**

GENETIC ENGINEERING NEWS. (US/0270-6377). **545**

GENETIC EPISTEMOLOGIST, THE. (GW/0740-9583). **546**

GENETIC, SOCIAL, AND GENERAL PSYCHOLOGY MONOGRAPHS. (US/8756-7547). **4587**

GENETICA. (NE/0016-6707). **546**

GENETIKA I SELEKTSIYA. (BU/0016-6766). **2416**

GENEVE-AFRIQUE. (SZ/0016-6774). **5246**

GENIE BUG. (US/0739-6090). **2451**

GENIE LOGICIEL & SYSTEMES EXPERTS. (FR/1166-4738). **1286**

GENIE, THE. (US/0534-0020). **2451**

GENII. (US/0016-6855). **4862**

GENITOURINARY MEDICINE. (UK/0266-4348). **4776**

GENOME. (CN/0831-2796). **546**

GENRE (NORMAN, OKLA.). (US/0016-6928). **3343**

GENTE. (MX). **Adv Mgr:** Juan Azcarraga. **2488**

GEO. (GW/0342-8311). **4165**

GEO-KATALOG. (GW). **5478**

GEO PLEIN-AIR. (CN/1194-5303). **Adv Mgr:** Dalpe, **Tel** (514)228-7559. **4896**

GEOARCHAEOLOGY. (US/0883-6353). **269**

GEOBOTANISCHE KOLLOQUIEN. (GW/0940-6581). **Adv Mgr:** Dr. Ballach, **Tel** 69 798 4757. **2216**

GEOBOTANISCHE KOLLOQUIEN. (GW/0940-6581). **Adv Mgr:** Dr. Ballach, **Tel** 69 798 4757. **2216**

GEOBYTE. (US/0885-6362). **2139**

GEOCARTO INTERNATIONAL. (HK/1010-6049). **2561**

GEOCHEMISTRY INTERNATIONAL. (US/0016-7029). **1376**

GEOCHRONIQUE. (FR/0292-8477). **1376**

GEODESIA. (NE). **2561**

GEODEZIA ES KARTOGRAFIA. (HU/0016-7118). **2581**

GEODRILLING. (UK/0268-0165). **1405**

GEODYNAMICS SERIES. (US/0277-6669). **1376**

GEOFIZICHESKII ZHURNAL. (UN/0203-3100). **1405**

GEOGRAFIA. (BL). **2561**

GEOGRAFICKY CASOPIS. GEOGRAFICHESKII ZHURNAL. GEOGRAPHICAL REVIEW. GEOGRAPHISCHE ZEITSCHRIFT. REVUE DE GEOGRAPHIE. (XO/0016-7193). **2562**

GEOGRAFISKA ANNALER. SERIES A, PHYSICAL GEOGRAPHY. (SW/0435-3676). **2562**

GEOGRAFISKA ANNALER. SERIES B, HUMAN GEOGRAPHY. (NO/0435-3684). **2823**

GEOGRAPHIA. (PL). **2562**

GEOGRAPHIA MEDICA (BUDAPEST). (HU/0300-807X). **3735**

GEOGRAPHICA. (FI). **2562**

GEOGRAPHICA (KUALA LUMPUR). (MY/0126-6101). **2562**

GEOGRAPHICAL ABSTRACTS. HUMAN GEOGRAPHY. (UK/0953-9611). **2580**

GEOGRAPHICAL ABSTRACTS : PHYSICAL GEOGRAPHY. (UK/0954-0504). **2580**

GEOGRAPHICAL ANALYSIS. (US/0016-7363). **2562**

GEOGRAPHICAL JOURNAL, THE. (UK/0016-7398). **2563**

GEOGRAPHICAL PAPERS. DEPARTMENT OF GEOGRAPHY, UNIVERSITY OF READING. (UK/0305-5914). **2563**

GEOGRAPHICAL PERSPECTIVES. (US/0199-994X). **2563**

GEOGRAPHICAL REVIEW. (US/0016-7428). **2563**

GEOGRAPHICAL REVIEW OF INDIA. (II). **2563**

GEOGRAPHICAL : THE MONTHLY MAGAZINE OF THE ROYAL GEOGRAPHICAL SOCIETY. (UK). **2563**

GEOGRAPHIE PHYSIQUE ET QUATERNAIRE. (CN/0705-7199). **2563**

GEOGRAPHISCHE RUNDSCHAU. (GW/0016-7460). **2564**

GEOGRAPHY. (UK/0016-7487). **2564**

GEOGRAPHY BULLETIN. (AT). **2564**

GEOGRAPHY RESEARCH FORUM. (US/0333-5275). **2564**

GEOGRAPHY REVIEW. (UK). **2564**

GEOJOURNAL. (GE/0343-2521). **2564**

GEOLIT. (GW). **2564**

GEOLOGICAL ABSTRACTS. (UK/0954-0512). **1362**

GEOLOGICAL CONTRIBUTIONS / ABILENE GEOLOGICAL SOCIETY. (US). **1377**

GEOLOGICAL MILESTONES. (US/0196-3090). **1378**

GEOLOGICAL SOCIETY OF AMERICA BULLETIN. (US/0016-7606). **1378**

GEOLOGIE EN MIJNBOUW. (NE/0016-7746). **1379**

GEOLOGIJA RUDNYH MESTOROZDENIJ. (RU/0016-7770). **2139**

GEOLOGISCHES JAHRBUCH, REIHE F : BODENKUNDE. (GW/0341-6445). **1379**

GEOLOGUES. (FR/0016-7916). **1380**

GEOLOGY (BOULDER). (US/0091-7613). **1380**

GEOMAGNETISM AND AERONOMY. (US/0016-7932). **22**

GEOMETRIAE DEDICATA. (NE/0046-5755). **3507**

GEOMETRIC AND FUNCTIONAL ANALYSIS : GAFA. (SZ/1016-443X). **3507**

GEOMICROBIOLOGY JOURNAL. (US/0149-0451). **563**

GEOMIMET. (MX/0185-1314). **2139**

GEOMUNDO. (PN/0256-7253). **2564**

GEOPHYSICAL AND ASTROPHYSICAL FLUID DYNAMICS. (US/0309-1929). **1405**

GEOPHYSICAL DIRECTORY, THE. (US). **1405**

GEOPHYSICAL JOURNAL. (US/0275-9128). **1405**

GEOPHYSICAL MONOGRAPH. (US/0065-8448). **1406**

GEOPHYSICAL PROSPECTING. (NE/0016-8025). **1406**

GEOPHYSICS. (US/0016-8033). **1406**

GEOPHYSICS, THE LEADING EDGE OF EXPLORATION. (US/0732-989X). **1406**

GEOPOLITIQUE. (FR/0752-1693). **4522**

GEORGE D. HALL'S DIRECTORY OF MASSACHUSETTS MANUFACTURERS. (US/0149-6913). **3479**

GEORGE D. HALL'S MASSACHUSETTS SERVICE DIRECTORY. (US/0196-7185). **1607**

GEORGE D. HALL'S NEW JERSEY MANUFACTURERS DIRECTORY. (US/0278-9124). **3479**

GEORGE D. HALL'S NEW YORK MANUFACTURERS DIRECTORY. (US/0272-1074). **3479**

GEORGE HERBERT JOURNAL. (US/0161-7435). **Adv Mgr:** same as editor. **3390**

GEORGE MASON UNIVERSITY LAW REVIEW. (US/0741-8736). **2973**

GEORGE SAND STUDIES. (US/0897-0483). **3343**

GEORGE WASHINGTON JOURNAL OF INTERNATIONAL LAW AND ECONOMICS, THE. (US/0748-4305). **3128**

GEORGE WASHINGTON LAW REVIEW, THE. (US/0016-8076). **2973**

GEORGETOWN CURRENT. (US). **Adv Mgr:** Simone Diggs. **5647**

GEORGETOWN INDEPENDENT. (CN/0834-6518). **Adv Mgr:** S Dorsey. **5785**

GEORGETOWN INTERNATIONAL REVIEW. (US/0360-6082). **3128**

GEORGETOWN LAW JOURNAL, THE. (US/0016-8092). **2974**

GEORGETOWNER, THE. (US/0730-9082). **2534**

GEORGIA ADVANCE SHEETS. (US/8750-0515). **2974**

GEORGIA ALERT; A LOOK AT EDUCATION'S ROLE TODAY. (US). **1748**

GEORGIA ALUMNI RECORD. (US/0016-8130). **1102**

GEORGIA ANCHORAGE. (US/0016-8149). **5449**

GEORGIA BULLETIN. (US). **Adv Mgr:** Leonard Markum. **5030**

GEORGIA COUNTY GOVERNMENT. (US/1066-0119). **Adv Mgr:** John McCurley, **Tel** (404)256-1116. **4650**

GEORGIA JOURNAL (ATHENS, GA.). (US/0746-5963). **Adv Mgr:** Ann Shepherd. **2534**

GEORGIA JOURNAL OF INTERNATIONAL AND COMPARATIVE LAW, THE. (US/0046-578X). **3128**

GEORGIA LIBRARIAN, THE. (US/0016-8319). **Adv Mgr:** Dale Luchsinger. **3212**

GEORGIA LIVING. (US/1049-6432). **2488**

GEORGIA MUSIC NEWS. (US/0046-5798). **4119**

GEORGIA NURSING. (US/0016-8335). **3856**

GEORGIA REVIEW, THE. (US/0016-8386). **3390**

GEORGIA STATE BAR JOURNAL. (US/0016-8416). **Adv Mgr Tel** (404)527-8791. **2974**

GEORGIA STATE BAR NEWS. (US). **2974**

GEORGIA VETERINARIAN, THE. (US/0886-5760). **5510**

GEOSCIENCE CANADA. (CN/0315-0941). **1380**

GEOSCIENCE CONTENTS. (US/0883-895X). **1380**

GEOSCIENTIST. (UK/0961-5628). **1380**

GEOSCOPE (OTTAWA). (CN/0046-581X). **2564**

GEOSUR / [ASOCIACION SUDAMERICANA DE ESTUDIOS GEOPOLITICOS E INTERNACIONALES]. (UY). **4522**

GEOTECHNICAL ENGINEERING. (TH/0046-5828). **2023**

GEOTECHNICAL FABRICS REPORT. (US/0882-4983). **5351**

GEOTECHNICAL NEWS. (CN/0823-650X). **Adv Mgr:** Lynn Pugh. **1381**

GEOTECHNIK. (GW/0172-6145). **2023**

GEOTECHNIQUE. (UK/0016-8505). **2023**

GEOTIMES. (US/0016-8556). **1381**

GERALDTON-LONGLAC TIMES STAR. (CN/0834-6275). **Adv Mgr:** Donna, **Tel** (807)854-1919. **5785**

GERANIUMS — Advertising Accepted Index

GERANIUMS AROUND THE WORLD. (US/0016-8599). **2416**

GERIATRIC NURSING (NEW YORK). (US/0197-4572). **3856**

GERIATRICS. (US/0016-867X). **3751**

GERIATRICS ED. ITALIANA. (IT/0392-9663). **Adv Mgr:** Uff. Marketing. **3751**

GERMAN GENEALOGICAL DIGEST. (US). **2451**

GERMAN HISTORY : THE JOURNAL OF THE GERMAN HISTORY SOCIETY. (UK/0266-3554). **2689**

GERMAN JOURNAL OF PSYCHOLOGY, THE. (GW/0705-5870). **4587**

GERMAN POLITICS. (UK/0964-4008). **Adv Mgr:** Anne Kidson. **4474**

GERMAN POLITICS AND SOCIETY. (US/1045-0300). **5200**

GERMAN QUARTERLY, THE. (US/0016-8831). **3390**

GERMAN STUDIES REVIEW. (US/0149-7952). **2689**

GERMAN TEACHING. (UK/0953-4822). **3283**

GERMAN TRIBUNE, THE. (GW/0016-8858). **2517**

GERMANIC NOTES AND REVIEWS. (US). **2846**

GERMANIC REVIEW, THE. (US/0016-8890). **3343**

GERMANISCHE DENKMALER DER VOLKERWANDERUNGSZEIT. SERIES B. DIE FRANKISCHEN ALTERTUMER DES RHEINLANDES. (GW/0418-9779). **269**

GERMANISTIK (BERLIN). (GW/0524-8414). **3284**

GERMANISTIK (TUEBINGEN). (GW/0016-8912). **3336**

GERMANISTISCHE ABHANDLUNGEN (STUTTGART). (GW/0435-5903). **3284**

GERMANISTISCHE LINGUISTIK. (GW/0072-1492). **3284**

GERMANISTISCHE MITTEILUNGEN. (BE/0771-3703). **3284**

GERMANO-SLAVICA. (CN/0317-4956). **3391**

GERMANTOWN CRIER. (US/0742-6631). **2734**

GERMANTOWN PAPER, THE. (US). **Adv Mgr:** James Mitchell, **Tel** (215)885-4111. **5736**

GERMINATION. (CN/0704-6286). **3463**

GERODONTOLOGY. (US/0734-0664). **3751**

GERONTOLOGIST, THE. (US/0016-9013). **3751**

GERONTOLOGY & GERIATRICS EDUCATION. (US/0270-1960). **3752**

GERONTOLOGY (BASEL). (SZ/0304-324X). **3752**

GESAMTSCHUL-INFORMATIONEN. (GW/0340-7268). **1748**

GESCHICHTE. (SZ). **2616**

GESCHMACKSMUSTERBLATT. (GW/0934-7062). **2974**

GESELLSCHAFT UND POLITIK. (AU/0016-9099). **5201**

GESHER (WORLD JEWISH CONGRESS. ISRAEL EXECUTIVE). (IS/0435-8406). **5047**

GESTION 2000. (BE/0773-0543). **868**

GESTION (LAVAL). (CN/0701-0028). **868**

GESTIONESCUOLA. (IT/0393-5523). **Adv Mgr:** Gabriella Crusco. **869**

GESTIONS HOSPITALIERES. (FR/0016-9218). **Adv Mgr:** J. Ganavat. **3780**

GESTOS (IRVINE, CALIF.). (US/1040-483X). **5364**

GESUNDE PFLANZEN. (GW/0367-4223). **2230**

GET READY SHEET, THE. (US/0148-7566). **3212**

GET RICH NEWS. (US). **677**

GETAWAY. (SA). **4872**

GETTING ABOUT BRITAIN. (UK/0954-0369). **5478**

GETTING MARRIED. (US/0891-1657). **2280**

GETTYSBURG REVIEW (1988). (US/0898-4557). **Adv Mgr:** E. Clarke, **Tel** (717)337-6771. **3391**

GEWERKSCHAFTLICHE RUNDSCHAU. (SZ). **1676**

GFWC CLUBWOMAN. (US/0745-2209). **5557**

GHANA REVIEW. (GH). **2499**

GIA QUARTERLY. (US/1070-7794). **Adv Mgr:** Alec Harris, **Tel** (708)496-3800. **4119**

GIAIDS. GIORNALE ITALIANO DELL' AIDS. (IT/1120-7892). **3669**

GIANTS NEWSWEEKLY, THE. (US/0279-0238). **Adv Mgr:** Dave Klein. **4896**

GIATROS DERMATOLOGIE. (GW/0932-8661). **3720**

GIATROS HNO. (GW/0930-8318). **3888**

GIATROSERTHOPAEDIE. (GW/0930-8326). **3881**

GIATROSGYNAKOLOGIE. (GW/0177-9109). **3761**

GIATROSPAEDIATRIE. (GW/0177-9095). **3903**

GIATROSUROLOGIE. (GW/0178-7527). **3990**

GIBBONS STAMP MONTHLY. (UK). **Adv Mgr:** Carol Flynn. **2785**

GIDS (AMSTERDAM, NETHERLANDS). (NE). **4475**

GIESSEREI. (GW/0016-9765). **4003**

GIESSEREIFORSCHUNG. (GW/0046-5933). **4003**

GIFTED CHILD TODAY, THE. (US/0892-9580). **1063**

GIFTED CHILDREN MONTHLY. (US/8750-684X). **1879**

GIFTED EDUCATION INTERNATIONAL. (UK/0261-4294). **1879**

GIFTED EDUCATION REVIEW. (US/1060-3166). **1879**

GIFTS TODAY. (UK). **Adv Mgr:** J. Baulch. **2584**

GIGUERERIE (EDITION FRANCAISE). (CN/0713-3162). **2451**

GILBERT & SULLIVAN NEWS. (UK/0263-7995). **385**

GILGAMESH. (IQ). **321**

GILMORE SUGAR MANUAL, THE. (US/0748-6782). **173**

GIMTOJI KALBA. (LI). **1112**

GINECOLOGIA DELL'INFANZIA E DELL'ADOLESCENZA. (IT/0393-5337). **3761**

GINECOLOGIA Y OBSTETRICIA DE MEXICO. (MX/0300-9041). **3761**

GIORNALE DEGLI ECONOMISTI E ANNALI DI ECONOMIA. (IT/0017-0097). **1492**

GIORNALE DELL' INSTALLATORE ELETTRICO, IL. (IT/0392-3630). **2056**

GIORNALE DELL' OFFICINA. (IT/0017-0240). **2115**

GIORNALE DELLA LIBRERIA. (IT). **4815**

GIORNALE DELLA SUBFORNITURA, IL. (IT/0392-3622). **1607**

GIORNALE DELL'ARTE (TURIN, ITALY). (IT/0394-0543). **Adv Mgr:** Patrizia Sbodio. **321**

GIORNALE DELL'INGEGNERE, IL. (IT). **1976**

GIORNALE DELL'INSTALLATORE TELEFONICO, IL. (IT/1120-219X). **1976**

GIORNALE DI ANESTESIA STOMATOLOGICA. (IT/0391-5670). **1324**

GIORNALE DI EMODINAMICA. (IT/0392-7679). **3704**

GIORNALE DI GEOLOGIA. (IT/0017-0291). **1381**

GIORNALE DI MALATTIE INFETTIVE E PARASSITARIE. (IT/0017-0321). **4777**

GIORNALE DI MEDICINA MILITARE. (IT/0017-0364). **3578**

GIORNALE DI METAFISICA. (IT). **4347**

GIORNALE ITALIANO DELLE MALATTIE DEL TORACE. (IT/0017-0437). **3949**

GIORNALE ITALIANO DI ANGIOLOGIA. (IT/0392-1387). **3705**

GIORNALE ITALIANO DI CARDIOLOGIA. (IT/0046-5968). **3705**

GIORNALE ITALIANO DI CHEMIOTERAPIA. (IT/0017-0445). **3578**

GIORNALE ITALIANO DI CHIMICA CLINICA. (IT/0392-2227). **976**

GIORNALE ITALIANO DI DERMATOLOGIA E VENEREOLOGIA. (IT/0392-0488). **3720**

GIORNALE ITALIANO DI ENTOMOLOGIA. (IT/0392-7296). **5609**

GIORNALE ITALIANO DI ONCOLOGIA. (IT/0392-128X). **3817**

GIORNALE ITALIANO DI OSTETRICIA E GINECOLOGIA. (IT/0391-9013). **3761**

GIORNALE STORICO DI PSICOLOGIA DINAMICA. (IT/0391-2515). **4588**

GIORNI CANTATI (ROME, ITALY). (IT). **351**

GIRARD GAZETTE, THE. (US). **Adv Mgr:** Nathan Jones. **5660**

GIRARD PRESS, THE. (US). **Adv Mgr:** Tammy Merrett. **5675**

GIRL GROUPS GAZETTE, THE. (US). **4119**

GIRONALE DEI GIOCATTOLI. (IT). **2584**

GIS WORLD. (US/0897-5507). **2565**

GISTER EN VANDAG. (SA). **1895**

GIURISPRUDENZA COMMERCIALE. (IT). **3100**

GIURISPRUDENZA COSTITUZIONALE. (IT/0436-0222). **3093**

GIURISPRUDENZA DI MERITO. (IT). **2974**

GIVEAWAY, THE. (US). **Adv Mgr:** John C. Roberts, **Tel** (812)967-3176. **5664**

GLADIATOR SPORTS MAGAZINE. (US). **4896**

GLADWIN COUNTY RECORD AND BEAVERTON CLARION, THE. (US/1071-0019). **Adv Mgr:** Dick Malosh. **5692**

GLAMOUR. (US/0017-0747). **5557**

GLAS. (RU). **Adv Mgr:** Arch Tait. **3391**

GLAS OCH PORSLIN. (SW/0017-078X). **2589**

GLAS UND RAHMEN. (GW/0036-3065). **2589**

GLASCO SUN (GLASCO, KAN. : 1937). (US). **5675**

GLASFORUM. (GW/0017-0852). **2589**

GLASGOW NATURALIST. (UK/0373-241X). **4165**

GLASGOW REPUBLICAN, THE. (US). **5680**

GLASNIK SLOVENSKEGA ETNOLOSKEGA DRUSTVA. (XV/0351-2908). **237**

GLASS ART (BROOMFIELD, COLO.). (US/1068-2147). **Adv Mgr:** Kevin, **Tel** (303)791-8998. **2589**

GLASS ART MAGAZINE (BROOMFIELD, COLO.). (US/0886-8131). **2589**

GLASS ART SOCIETY PHOTOGRAPHIC DIRECTORY. (US/0740-8889). **2589**

GLASS COLLECTOR'S DIGEST. (US/0893-8660). **2589**

GLASS DIGEST. (US/0017-1018). **2589**

GLASS FACTORY DIRECTORY. (US). **2590**

GLASS INDUSTRY, THE. (US/0017-1026). **2590**

GLASS INTERNATIONAL. (UK/0143-7836). **2590**

GLASS MAGAZINE. (US/0747-4261). **2590**

GLASS NEWS. (US/0890-3743). **2590**

GLASS ON METAL. THE ENAMELISTS' NEWSLETTER. (US). **2590**

GLASS (REDHILL). (UK/0017-0984). **2590**

GLASS TECHNOLOGY. (UK/0017-1050). **2590**

GLASTECHNISCHE BERICHTE. (GW/0017-1085). **2590**

GLASTEKNISK TIDSKRIFT. (SW/0017-1093). **2590**

GLASTONBURY CITIZEN, THE. (US). **Adv Mgr:** Carol Saucier. **5645**

GLAUCOMA (MIAMI). (US/0164-4645). **3875**

GLEANER INDEX / NATIONAL LIBRARY OF JAMAICA, THE. (JM/0259-0336). **5805**

GLEANINGS IN BEE CULTURE. (US/0017-114X). **5585**

GLEN RIDGE PAPER. (US). **5710**

GLENBOW (EXHIBITIONS AND EVENTS). (CN/0710-3697). **4088**

GLENDIVE RANGER-REVIEW. (US). **Adv Mgr:** Pat Boese. **5705**

GLENWOOD POST. (US). **Adv Mgr:** Bob Zanella. **5643**

GLIDER RIDER'S ULTRALIGHT FLYING. (US/0883-7937). **Adv Mgr:** David Prestridge, **Tel** (615)629-5375. **22**

GLIM NEWSLETTER, THE. (UK). **5328**

GLOBAL AFFAIRS. (US/0886-6198). **4522**

GLOBAL CHURCH GROWTH. (US/0731-1125). **Adv Mgr:** Shelly Hinkley. **4960**

GLOBAL COMMUNICATIONS. (US/0195-2250). **1112**

GLOBAL CUSTODIAN. (US/1047-8736). **Adv Mgr:** Ana Pacheco. **899**

GLOBAL INVESTMENT TECHNOLOGY. (US/1058-3920). **Adv Mgr:** M. Horton. **899**

GLOBAL JOURNAL ON CRIME AND CRIMINAL LAW. (NE/0928-9313). **3165**

GLOBAL JUSTICE. (US/1060-0884). **Adv Mgr Tel** (303)871-2523. **4523**

GLOBAL RISK ASSESSMENTS: ISSUES, CONCEPTS, AND APPLICATIONS. (US/0739-4640). **900**

GLOBAL TAPESTRY. (UK). **3463**

GLOBE AND LAUREL. (UK/0017-1204). **4044**

GLOBEHOPPER. (CN/0711-7108). **5478**

GLOBOSPORTS. (US). **Adv Mgr:** Barry Gould, **Tel** (207)363-6222. **1132**

GLORY OF INDIA. (II). **2504**

GLOUCESTERSHIRE FAMILY HISTORY SOCIETY JOURNAL. (UK/0143-0513). **2451**

GLOXINIAN, THE. (US/0017-1352). **512**

GLYCOBIOLOGY (OXFORD). (UK/0959-6658). **487**

GMDA BULLETIN. (US/0884-6898). **1324**

GNOSIS (MONTREAL). (CN/0316-618X). **4347**

GNOSIS (SAN FRANCISCO, CALIF.). (US/0894-6159). **Adv Mgr:** Jeff Chiutouras, **Tel** (415)255-0400. **4960**

GNOSTICA. (US/0145-885X). **4241**

GOAL (NEW YORK, N.Y.). (US/0273-5601). **Adv Mgr:** Neil Butwin, **Tel** (212)308-6666. **4896**

GOAT VETERINARY SOCIETY JOURNAL. (UK). **Adv Mgr:** J. Matthews. **5510**

GOBBLES. (US/0017-1506). **211**

GOD'S SPECIAL PEOPLE. (US/0896-2413). **4960**

GOING DOWN SWINGING. (AT/0157-3950). **3391**

GOLD BOOK OF NAVAL AVIATION, THE. (US/0884-1128). **22**

GOLD COAST GAZETTE (SEA CLIFF, N.Y.). (US/1065-1748). **Adv Mgr:** Kevin Horton and John O'Connell. **5716**

GOLD + SILBER, UHREN + SCHMUCK. (GW/0017-1573). **2914**

GOLDBELT GAZETTE. (CN/0849-8288). **5785**

GOLDEN GATE UNIVERSITY LAW REVIEW. (US/0363-0307). **2975**

GOLDEN PRAIRIE NEWS. (US). **Adv Mgr:** Angela Pamery. **5660**

GOLDEN ROOTS OF THE MOTHER LODE. NEWSLETTER. (US/8755-5697). **2451**

GOLDEN TRANSCRIPT, THE. (US/0746-6382). **Adv Mgr:** John Tracy. **5643**

GOLDEN VALLEY NEWS. (US). **Adv Mgr:** Sandy Culleim. **5725**

GOLDEN YEARS MAGAZINE. (US). **5179**

GOLDFINCH, THE. (US/0278-0208). **Adv Mgr:** Deborah G. Ohrn, **Tel** (319)335-3916. **1063**

GOLEM NEWSLETTER. (IT). **5108**

GOLF COURSE MANAGEMENT. (US/0192-3048). **Adv Mgr:** Mick Urban, **Tel** 800 422 6383. **4896**

GOLF DIGEST. (US/0017-176X). **Adv Mgr:** Peter Gross, **Tel** (212)789-3030. **4896**

GOLF FOR WOMEN : GFW. (US/0898-4719). **Adv Mgr:** Vicki Richards, **Tel** (212)551-7177. **4896**

GOLF ILLUSTRATED (COVINA, CALIF.). (US/0160-6808). **4896**

GOLF NEWS MAGAZINE. (US). **4896**

GOLF PRO. (US/1072-1274). **4897**

GOLF PROPERTY. (US). **4838**

GOLF REPORTER, THE. (US/0745-7502). **4897**

GOLF TRAVELER, THE. (US/0191-717X). **4897**

GOLF WORLD. (UK/0017-1883). **4897**

GOLF WORLD. (US/0017-1891). **Adv Mgr:** Robert Carney, **Tel** (212)789-3009. **4897**

GOLFSHOP OPERATIONS. (US/0017-1824). **924**

GOLFWEEK. (US/0890-3514). **4897**

GONGYE WEISHENGWU. (CC/1001-6678). **563**

GONZAGA LAW REVIEW. (US/0046-6115). **2975**

GOOD FOOD MAGAZINE. (US/0885-0690). **2342**

GOOD FRUIT & VEGETABLES. (AT). **2417**

GOOD HEALTH (DON MILLS). (CN/0229-5903). **1297**

GOOD HOUSEKEEPING (U.S. ED.). (US/0017-209X). **2790**

GOOD NEWS. (US). **5767**

GOOD NEWS (WILMORE). (US/0436-1563). **5060**

GOOD OLD DAYS. (US/0046-6158). **3391**

GOOD OLD DAYS. SPECIAL ISSUES. (US/0160-7510). **2735**

GOOD PACKAGING MAGAZINE. (US/1049-3158). **Adv Mgr:** K. Dean. **4219**

GOOD TIMES (GREENVILLE, NY.). (US/0191-4995). **2534**

GOODFRUIT GROWER, THE. (US/0046-6174). **2417**

GOODING COUNTY LEADER. (US). **5656**

GOOSE CREEK GAZETTE. (US). **5742**

GORDIAN (1948). (GW/0017-2243). **2342**

GORDON JOURNAL. (US). **Adv Mgr:** Neal Ziller, **Tel** (308)282-0118. **5706**

GORDON'S PRINT PRICE ANNUAL. (US/0160-6298). **378**

GORGET ET SASH : JOURNAL OF THE EARLY MODERN WARFARE SOCIETY. (US/0892-466X). **4044**

GOSPEL HERALD BEAMSVILLE. (CN/0829-4666). **Adv Mgr:** E.C. Perry. **4961**

GOSPEL STANDARD, OR, FEEBLE CHRISTIAN'S SUPPORT, THE. (UK). **Adv Mgr:** C. Pearce. **4961**

GOSPEL TIDINGS (OMAHA, NEB.). (US/0745-7618). **5060**

GOSPEL VOICE. (US). **Adv Mgr:** Rick Francis. **4119**

GOUE VAG. (SA). **211**

GOURMET. (US/0017-2553). **2790**

GOUT DE VIVRE, LE. (CN/0383-6738). **5246**

GOVERNANCE (OXFORD). (UK/0952-1895). **4651**

GOVERNING (WASHINGTON, D.C.). (US/0894-3842). **4475**

GOVERNMENT AND OPPOSITION (LONDON). (UK/0017-257X). **4475**

GOVERNMENT BUSINESS WORLD REPORT. (US/0017-2588). **678**

GOVERNMENT EXECUTIVE. (US/0017-2626). **4651**

GOVERNMENT FINANCE REVIEW. (US/0883-7856). **4728**

GOVERNMENT IMAGING. (US). **4651**

GOVERNMENT MICROCOMPUTER LETTER. (US/0882-6587). **1267**

GOVERNMENT PRODUCT NEWS. (US/0017-2642). **950**

GOVERNMENT PROGRAMS. (US/1055-825X) **4652**

GOVERNMENT PUBLICATIONS REVIEW (1982). (US/0277-9390). **3212**

GOVERNMENT PURCHASING GUIDE (TORONTO). (CN/0046-6220). **950**

GOVERNMENT REFERENCE BOOKS. (US/0072-5188). **4652**

GOVERNMENTS OF ALABAMA. (US/0883-3753). **4728**

GOVERNMENTS OF ARKANSAS. (US/0883-3761). **4728**

GOVERNMENTS OF CALIFORNIA. (US/0883-377X). **4728**

GOVERNMENTS OF COLORADO. (US/0883-3788). **4728**

GOVERNMENTS OF CONNECTICUT. (US/0883-3796). **4728**

GOVERNMENTS OF FLORIDA. (US/0883-380X). **4728**

GOVERNMENTS OF GEORGIA. (US/0883-3818). **4728**

GOVERNMENTS OF ILLINOIS. (US/0883-3826). **4728**

GOVERNMENTS OF INDIANA. (US/0883-3834). **4728**

GOVERNMENTS OF IOWA. (US/0883-3842). **4728**

GOVERNMENTS OF KANSAS. (US/0883-3850). **4728**

GOVERNMENTS OF KENTUCKY. (US/0883-3869). **4728**

GOVERNMENTS OF LOUISIANA. (US/0883-3877). **4728**

GOVERNMENTS OF MAINE. (US/0883-3885). **4728**

GOVERNMENTS OF MASSACHUSETTS. (US/0883-3893). **4728**

GOVERNMENTS OF MICHIGAN. (US/0883-3907). **4728**

GOVERNMENTS OF MINNESOTA. (US/0883-3915). **4728**

GOVERNMENTS OF MISSISSIPPI. (US/0883-3923). **4728**

GOVERNMENTS OF MISSOURI. (US/0883-3931). **4728**

GOVERNMENTS OF NEBRASKA. (US/0883-394X). **1493**

GOVERNMENTS OF NEW JERSEY. (US/0883-3958). **4729**

GOVERNMENTS OF NEW YORK. (US/0883-3966). **4729**

GOVERNMENTS OF NORTH DAKOTA. (US/0883-3974). **4729**

GOVERNMENTS OF OHIO. (US/0883-3982). **4729**

GOVERNMENTS OF OKLAHOMA. (US/0883-3990). **4729**

GOVERNMENTS OF PENNSYLVANIA. (US/0883-4008). **4729**

GOVERNMENTS OF SOUTH DAKOTA. (US/0883-4016). **4729**

GOVERNMENTS OF TENNESSEE. (US/0883-4024). **4729**

GOVERNMENTS OF TEXAS. (US/0883-4032). **4729**

GOVERNMENTS OF THE CAROLINAS. (US/0883-4091). **4729**

GOVERNMENTS OF THE NORTHEAST. (US/0883-4121). **4729**

GOVERNMENTS OF THE NORTHWEST. (US/0883-4105). **4729**

GOVERNMENTS OF THE WEST. (US/0883-4113). **4729**

GOVERNMENTS OF VERMONT. (US/0883-4040). **4729**

GOVERNMENTS OF VIRGINIA. (US/0883-4059). **4729**

GOVERNMENTS OF WASHINGTON. (US/0883-4067). **4729**

GOVERNMENTS OF WEST VIRGINIA. (US/0883-4075). **4729**

GOVERNMENTS OF WISCONSIN. (US/0883-4083). **4729**

GOYA. (SP/0017-2715). **351**

GQ. (US/0016-6979). **3995**

GQ (UK EDITION). (UK/0954-8750). **Adv Mgr:** Tony Long, **Tel** 011 44 71 499 9080. **3995**

GR. GROCERS REPORT. (US/0160-8894). **2342**

GRADHIVA. (FR/0764-8928). **237**

GRADIVA. (US/0363-8057). **3343**

GRADUATE FACULTY PHILOSOPHY JOURNAL. (US/0093-4240). **4347**

GRADUATE OUTLOOK. (AT/0314-0679). **Adv Mgr:** Colin Ritchie. **1826**

GRADUATE STUDIES (LONDON, ENGLAND). (UK/0072-5269). **1826**

GRADUATING ENGINEER. (US/0193-2276). **1976**

GRAFISCH NIEUWS. (BE/0773-591X). **Adv Mgr:** Kris Mortier. **4815**

GRAFISKT FORUM. (SW). **378**

GRAIN & FEED MERCHANT, THE. (US/0199-2287). **201**

GRAIN JOURNAL (DECATUR, ILL.). (US/0274-7138). **Adv Mgr:** Mark Avery. **201**

GRAINEWS. (CN/0229-8090). **173**

GRAINGER SOCIETY JOURNAL, THE. (UK/0141-5085). **4119**

GRAMOPHONE INCLUDING COMPACT DISC NEWS AND REVIEWS. (UK/0017-310X). **5316**

GRAMOPHONE. SPOKEN WORD AND MISCELLANEOUS CATALOGUE. (UK). **5317**

GRAMPIAN BUSINESS DIRECTORY. (UK). **3480**

GRAMPIAN DIRECTORY. (UK/0261-572X). **1926**

GRAND FALLS ADVERTISER. (CN/0833-1014). **Adv Mgr:** B. Andrews. **5785**

GRAND FORKS GAZETTE. (CN). **Adv Mgr:** Sandra Huffner. **5785**

GRAND RIVER VALLEY REVIEW, THE. (US/0739-084X). **2735**

GRAND SLAM (OTTAWA). (CN/0701-0745). **4897**

GRAND STREET. (US/0734-5496). **3391**

GRAND TIMES. (US/1068-1345). **5179**

GRAND VALLEY STAR AND VIDETTE. (CN/0834-616X). **Adv Mgr:** Shirley Gade, **Tel** (519)941-2230. **5785**

GRANGE NEWS, THE. (US/0043-0587). **90**

GRANMA (DAILY EDITION, SPANISH). (CU/0017-3223). **Adv Mgr:** Jose Polo, **Tel** 707290. **5799**

GRANMA INTERNATIONAL. (CU/0864-4624). **5799**

GRANT COUNTY HERALD INDEPENDENT. (US). **Adv Mgr:** Kevin Kelly. **5767**

GRANT COUNTY JOURNAL. (US). **5761**

GRANT COUNTY NEWS, THE. (US). **Adv Mgr:** Duane Schatz, **Tel** (701)584-2900. **5725**

GRANT COUNTY PRESS. (US). **Adv Mgr:** Jodi Fouch. **5763**

GRANT COUNTY REVIEW (MILBANK, S.D.). (US). **Adv Mgr:** Holli Seehafer. 5743

GRANTA. (UK/0017-3231). 3343

GRANT'S INTEREST RATE OBSERVER. (US/0748-8424). 1493

GRANTSVILLE GAZETTE. (US/8750-7684). 5756

GRANVILLE SENTINEL (GRANVILLE, N.Y. : 1885). (US). **Adv Mgr:** John Manchester, **Tel** (518)642-1234. 5716

GRAPELAND MESSENGER, THE. (US). 5750

GRAPHIC ARTS BLUE BOOK (METROPOLITAN NEW YORK-NEW JERSEY ED.). (US/1044-8527). 4565

GRAPHIC ARTS BLUE BOOK (MIDWESTERN ED.). (US/1044-8535). 378

GRAPHIC ARTS PRODUCT NEWS (CHICAGO). (US/0274-5976). 379

GRAPHIC DESIGN, USA. (US). 379

GRAPHIC MONTHLY, THE. (CN/0227-2806). 4565

GRAPHICUS. (IT/0017-3436). 2488

GRAPHIS. (SZ/0017-3452). 379

GRAPHOSCOPE, THE. (CN/0046-631X). 900

GRASAS Y ACEITES (SEVILLA). (SP/0017-3495). 488

GRASS AND FORAGE SCIENCE. (UK/0142-5242). 90

GRASS ROOTS SHEPPARTON. (AT/0310-2890). **Adv Mgr:** C. Ballard, **Tel** 057-947-256. 90

GRASSLANDS AND FORAGE ABSTRACTS. (UK/1350-9837). 153

GRASSROOTS CATALOG. (US). 2452

GRASSROOTS ECONOMIC ORGANIZING NEWSLETTER. (US/1071-0590). 1592

GRASSROOTS FUNDRAISING JOURNAL. (US/0740-4832). 4337

GRAVURE (NEW YORK, N.Y. 1987). (US/0894-4946). 4565

GRAY AREAS. (US/1062-5712). 2534

GRAY PANTHER NETWORK. (US/0739-2001). 5286

GRAY'S SPORTING JOURNAL. (US/0273-6691). **Adv Mgr:** Lea Cockerherm, **Tel** (800)458-4010. 4873

GREAT BARRINGTON HISTORICAL SOCIETY NEWSLETTER. (US/0895-7851). 2617

GREAT BEND TRIBUNE (1972). (US/0891-7078). **Adv Mgr:** Debbie Piland. 5676

GREAT EXPEDITIONS. (US/0706-7682). 5478

GREAT FALLS TRIBUNE (GREAT FALLS, MONT. : 1921). (US). 5705

GREAT LAKES ENTOMOLOGIST, THE. (US/0090-0222). 5609

GREAT LAKES FISHERMAN. (CN/0847-0685). 2304

GREAT LAKES FISHERMAN (COLUMBUS, OHIO). (US/0194-5564). 2304

GREAT LAKES NAVIGATION. (CN/0824-8583). 5449

GREAT LAKES SAILOR (AKRON, OHIO). (US/0892-5410). 593

GREAT LAKES TRAVEL & LIVING. (US/0887-6223). 5478

GREAT LAKES VEGETABLE GROWERS NEWS, THE. (US/1049-8494). **Adv Mgr:** Dee Rau. 173

GREAT METROPOLIS, OR NEW-YORK ALMANAC, THE. (US). 2534

GREAT OUTDOORS. (SA). 2194

GREAT PLAINS QUARTERLY. (US/0275-7664). **Adv Mgr:** Linda Ratcliffe, **Tel** (407)472-3082. 2735

GREAT PLAINS RESEARCH. (US/1052-5165). 4166

GREAT PLAINS SOCIOLOGIST, THE. (US/0896-0054). 5246

GREATER AVOYELLES JOURNAL, THE. (US). 5684

GREATER GREENWOOD BUSINESS JOURNAL, THE. (US). **Adv Mgr:** Brian Kelly. 678

GREATER LANSING BUSINESS MONTHLY. (US). **Adv Mgr:** Denise Parks. 678

GREATER LLANO ESTACADO SOUTHEAST HERITAGE, THE. (US/0145-8825). 2735

GREATER LONDON LOCAL HISTORY DIRECTORY AND BIBLIOGRAPHY. (UK). 2689

GREATER LOS ANGELES PUBLIC SERVICE GUIDE. (US). 4653

GREATER PHOENIX JEWISH NEWS. (US/0747-444X). 5047

GREATER WASHINGTON BOARD OF TRADE NEWS, THE. (US/0274-5496). **Adv Mgr:** Suzanne Trump-Warring, **Tel** (202)857-5944. 1564

GREATER WINNIPEG BUSINESS. (CN/0830-8535). 678

GREECE & ROME. (UK/0017-3835). 1077

GREECE POST, THE. (US). **Adv Mgr:** Catharene Gardner. 5716

GREEK ACCENT. (US/0279-1234). 2689

GREEK HERALD. (AT). 5777

GREEKAMERICAN, THE. (US/0890-0035). 2262

GREEN. (CN/0823-6380). 4897

GREEN BAY NEWS-CHRONICLE, THE. (US). **Adv Mgr:** Al Rasmussen. 5767

GREEN BOOK BUYERS' GUIDE FOR GARDEN MERCHANDISE. (US/0147-3891). 2417

GREEN BOOK (LONDON). (UK/0017-3932). 159

GREEN BOOK REPORT, THE. (US/1062-4589). **Adv Mgr:** Chris McIntosh, **Tel** (617)935-4800. 2172

GREEN EGG. (US/1066-7385). **Adv Mgr:** Ron Johnson. 4241

GREEN LAKE COUNTY REPORTER (GREEN LAKE, WIS. : 1983). (US/8755-3988). **Adv Mgr:** Betty Van Sistine. 5767

GREEN LIBRARY JOURNAL (BERKELEY, CALIF. 1992). (US/1059-0838). **Adv Mgr:** Katie Manjotich, **Tel** (510)841-9975. 2173

GREEN SCENE, THE. (US/0190-9789). **Adv Mgr:** Joe Robinson, **Tel** (215)625-8280. 2417

GREEN TEACHER (TORONTO). (CN/1192-1285). 2173

GREENBELT NEWS REVIEW. (US). 5686

GREENBOOK (NEW YORK, N.Y.). (US/8756-534X). 925

GREENE COUNTY DEMOCRAT (EUTAW, ALA.), THE. (US/0889-518X). **Adv Mgr:** Laddi Jones & Ed Jordan. 5626

GREENE COUNTY INDEPENDENT. (US). **Adv Mgr:** Betty Banks. 5626

GREENE COUNTY NEWS. (US). **Adv Mgr:** Barb Cragie, **Tel** (518)943-2100. 5716

GREENER MANAGEMENT INTERNATIONAL. (UK). 2173

GREENFIELD QUARTERLY. (US/0883-170X). 2452

GREENHOUSE CANADA. (CN/0712-4996). **Adv Mgr:** Mark Crandon, **Tel** (519)582-2513. 2417

GREENHOUSE MANAGER. (US/0744-8988). 2417

GREENHOUSE PRODUCT NEWS. (US/1053-7104). 2417

GREENMASTER. (CN/0380-3333). 4897

GREENPOINT GAZETTE. (US). 5717

GREEN'S MAGAZINE. (CN/0824-2992). 3392

GREENSBORO WATCHMAN. (US). **Adv Mgr:** Ed Lowry. 5626

GREENSBURG DAILY NEWS. (US). **Adv Mgr:** Pamela Jackson Abel. 5664

GREENSWARD. (UK/0017-4092). 90

GREENVILLE ADVOCATE. (US). 5626

GREENVILLE ADVOCATE (GREENVILLE, ILL.). (US). 5660

GREENVILLE PIEDMONT, THE. (US). **Adv Mgr:** Mark Johnston. 5742

GREENWICH (GREENWICH, CONN.). (US/1072-2432). **Adv Mgr:** M. McDonnel. 2488

GREENWICH MAGAZINE. (US/1051-0745). 2488

GREENWOOD AND SOUTHSIDE CHALLENGER, THE. (US/1068-6673). 5664

GREENWOOD COMMONWEALTH (GREENWOOD, MISS. : 1976). (US). **Adv Mgr:** Larry Alderman. 5700

GREENWOOD ENCYCLOPEDIA OF BLACK MUSIC, THE. (US/0272-0264). 4119

GREENWOOD GAZETTE, THE. (US). **Adv Mgr:** Brian Kelly. 5664

GREENWOOD LAKE AND WEST MILFORD NEWS. (US/1065-1144). **Adv Mgr:** Ann Chaimowitz. 5717

GREENWOOD'S GUIDE TO GREAT LAKES SHIPPING. (US/0072-7490). 5449

GREER CITIZEN, THE. (US). 5742

GREETINGS AND GIFT STATIONER. (UK). 2584

GREETINGS AND GIFTS. (AT/1036-5915). **Adv Mgr:** M. Merrick, **Tel** 02 9070366. 2584

GREGORIUSBLAD. (NE). 4119

GRENADA CONSOLIDATED INDEX OF STATUTES AND SUBSIDIARY LEGISLATION TO .... (US). 3081

GRIDIRON COACH. (US/1071-1902). 4897

GRIDLEY HERALD, THE. (US). **Adv Mgr:** John Skaggs. 5635

GRIFFIN REPORT OF FOOD MARKETING, THE. (US/0192-4400). **Adv Mgr:** Kevin Griffin. 2342

GRIFFIN REPORT, THE. (US). 2342

GRIMSBY INDEPENDENT. (CN/0834-6623). **Adv Mgr:** Robert Van Wyngaarden, **Tel** (905)563-5393. 5785

GRIO' (BLACK HISTORY ED.). (US/0886-1668). **Adv Mgr:** Al Thomas. 2735

GRIOT (HOUSTON, TEX.), THE. (US/0737-0873). 2735

GRIPE/ GROUP FOR RESEARCH IN PATHOLOGY EDUCATION. (US). **Adv Mgr:** M. Libman, **Tel** (213)342-1283. 3894

GRIT AND STEEL. (US/0017-4297). 4873

GRIT (NATIONAL ED.). (US/0017-4289). 5676

GRNLAND (1953). (DK/0017-4556). 4553

GROCER FOOD & DRINK DIRECTORY, THE. (UK/0967-5892). 2342

GROCER TODAY. (CN/1196-0817). **Adv Mgr:** Pat Sasso. 838

GROCERS JOURNAL OF CALIFORNIA. (US/0745-4104). 2342

GROCERS' REVIEW. (NZ/0113-1850). 2342

GROCERY DISTRIBUTION. (US/0361-4034). 2342

GROCERY INDUSTRY ANNUAL REPORT, THE. (US). 2342

GROCERY MARKETING. (US/0888-0360). 2343

GROENTEN EN FRUIT : G & F. (NE/0017-4491). 2417

GROESBECK JOURNAL. (US). 5750

GRONDBOOR EN HAMER. (NE/0017-4505). 1381

GROOM & BOARD. (US/0199-8366). 4286

GROSS DOMESTIC PRODUCT AND EXPENDITURE. (PP). 5328

GROSSE POINTER, THE. (US/0017-4629). 5478

GROSSEN 500, DIE. (GW). 678

GROTIANA (1980). (NE). 3128

GROUND ENGINEERING. (UK/0017-4653). 2024

GROUND ENGINEERING YEARBOOK. (UK/0959-9959). 2024

GROUND WATER. (US/0017-467X). 1413

GROUND WATER AGE. (US/0046-645X). 5533

GROUND WATER MONITORING REVIEW. (US/0277-1926). 1413

GROUNDS MAINTENANCE. (US/0017-4688). 2417

GROUNDSMAN. (UK/0017-4696). **Adv Mgr:** Anthony Harvey, **Tel** (077)837-9363. 2418

GROUP ANALYSIS. (UK/0533-3164). 3926

GROUP (LOVELAND, COLO.). (US/0163-8971). **Adv Mgr:** Larry Boryour, **Tel** (303)669-3836. 1064

GROUP (NEW YORK. 1977). (US/0362-4021). 4588

GROUP PRACTICE JOURNAL. (US/0199-5103). **Adv Mgr:** Fred Haag. 3780

GROUP PRACTICE (NEWSLETTER). (US/0190-440X). 3780

GROUP'S JR. HIGH MINISTRY. (US/0884-0504). 1064

GROVE CITY SOUTHWEST MESSENGER. (US/0891-2270). **Adv Mgr:** Bruce Russel, **Tel** (614272-5422. 5728

GROVE EXAMINER, THE. (CN/0318-1650). 5785

GROWER. (UK/0017-4785). 2418

GROWER (SHAWNEE MISSION, KAN.), THE. (US/0745-1784). 173

GROWER TALKS. (US/0276-9433). 2418

GROWER (TORONTO). (CN/0017-4777). **Adv Mgr:** James Shaw, **Tel** (416)463-0007. 2418

GROWING EDGE (CORVALLIS, OR.), THE. (US/1043-2906). 2418

GROWING WITHOUT SCHOOLING. (US/0745-5305). **Adv Mgr:** Patrick Farenga, **Tel** (617)864-3100. 1895

GROWTH AND CHANGE. (US/0017-4815). 2823

Advertising Accepted Index — HANDBOOK

GROWTH INDEX, THE. (US/0744-7205). **820**

GROWTH (PRETORIA, SOUTH AFRICA). (SA). **1564**

GRUNDLAGEN DER GERMANISTIK. (GW/0533-3350). **3284**

GRUVER STATESMAN. (US). **5750**

GSA TODAY. (US/1052-5173). **1381**

GUAM BUSINESS NEWS. (GU/1045-053X). **Adv Mgr:** Vicki Anderson. **678**

GUARDIAN (LONDON). (UK/0261-3077). **5812**

GUARDIAN (NEW YORK, N.Y.), THE. (US/0017-5021). **2920**

GUARDIAN OF TRUTH. (US/0273-5504). **4961**

GUARDIAN - WRIGHT STATE'S STUDENT NEWSPAPER. (US). **Adv Mgr:** Elizabeth Green. **5728**

GUARDMOUNT. (US/0883-0843). **3182**

GUERNSEY BREEDERS' JOURNAL. (US/0017-5110). **211**

GUERNSEY BREEDERS' JOURNAL. (UK). **211**

GUERNSEY EVENING PRESS AND STAR. (UK). **5812**

GUERNSEY GAZETTE, THE. (US/1061-1789). **Adv Mgr:** Cheri Fegler. **5772**

GUIA DE CONCURSOS : REVISTA DE INFORMACION CULTURAL Y LITERARIA. (SP). **3392**

GUIA DE EXPORTADORES E IMPORTADORES ARGENTINOS. (AG). **Adv Mgr:** Telmo Mirat, **Tel** 011 54 1 771 7940. **838**

GUIA DE LA INDUSTRIA ALIMENTARIA. (MX). **2343**

GUIA, EL. (SP). **321**

GUIDANCE & COUNSELLING. (CN/0831-5493). **Adv Mgr:** Denise Hughes. **1748**

GUIDE D'ACHAT DE LA VOITURE USAGEE. (CN/0820-8964). **5415**

GUIDE DE LA MUSIQUE, LE. (BE). **4119**

GUIDE DE LA ROUTE, FLORIDE. (CN/0838-0015). **5478**

GUIDE DE LA ROUTE, PROVINCES DE L'ATLANTIQUE ET DU QUEBEC. (CN/0225-2600). **5478**

GUIDE DE L'AUDIOVISUEL EUROPEEN, LE. (FR). **4071**

GUIDE DE L'EQUIPEMENT ET DE L'OUTILLAG. (FR). **5415**

GUIDE DU CADEAU ET DES ARTS DE LA TABLE. (FR/0997-2676). **351**

GUIDE DU PRODUCTEUR DE DISQUES, LE. (BE). **5317**

GUIDE DU TRANSPORT PAR CAMION INC. (CN/0706-9995). **Adv Mgr:** Raymond Patry. **5383**

GUIDE ECONOMIQUE DE LA TUNISIE. (TI). **1565**

GUIDE TO ACCREDITED CAMPS. (US/1046-5774). **1064**

GUIDE TO ELECTRONICS INDUSTRY IN INDIA. (II/0376-5229). **2056**

GUIDE TO FLORIDA RETIREMENT LIVING. (US/0889-051X). **5179**

GUIDE TO GEORGIA. (US/0434-8877). **Adv Mgr:** Jim Crawford. **5479**

GUIDE TO INDIAN PERIODICAL LITERATURE. (II/0017-5285). **416**

GUIDE TO JEWISH EUROPE. (US). **5479**

GUIDE TO MICROFORMS IN PRINT. AUTHOR, TITLE. (GW/0164-0747). **416**

GUIDE TO MICROFORMS IN PRINT. SUPPLEMENT. (US/0164-0739). **416**

GUIDE TO MICROGRAPHIC EQUIPMENT. (US/0360-8654). **4370**

GUIDE TO NEW INDUSTRIAL POLICY OF GOVERNMENT OF INDIA. (II). **1608**

GUIDE TO SPRINGFIELD. (US). **2534**

GUIDE TO SUMMER CAMPS AND SUMMER SCHOOLS, THE. (US/0072-8705). **4850**

GUIDE TO THE ANTIQUE SHOPS OF BRITAIN. (UK). **Adv Mgr:** Jean Johnson. **250**

GUIDE TO THE CANADIAN FINANCIAL SERVICES INDUSTRY. (CN/0827-0864). **789**

GUIDE TO THE COALFIELDS. (UK/0072-8713). **2140**

GUIDE TO THE HOUSE OF COMMONS. (UK). **4475**

GUIDE TO THE MOTOR INDUSTRY OF JAPAN. (JA). **5415**

GUIDE (TORONTO). (CN/0533-5051). **1676**

GUIDEBOOK - NEW MEXICO GEOLOGICAL SOCIETY. (US/0077-8567). **1382**

GUIDEBOOK - WYOMING GEOLOGICAL ASSOCIATION. (US/0160-2829). **1382**

GUIDELINES (SASKATOON). (CN/0048-9190). **1749**

GUIDEPOST (WASHINGTON, D.C.). (US/0017-5323). **4588**

GUIDING IN AUSTRALIA. (AT/0159-0340). **1064**

GUILD (NEW YORK, N.Y.). (US/0885-3975). **373**

GUILD OF BOOK WORKERS JOURNAL. (US/0434-9245). **4828**

GUION. (CK). **2488**

GUITAR FOR THE PRACTICING MUSICIAN. (US). **Adv Mgr:** Barbara Seerman, **Tel** (914)935-5243. **4120**

GUITAR INTERNATIONAL. (UK). **4120**

GUITAR REVIEW, THE. (US/0017-5471). **4120**

GUJARAT AGRICULTURAL UNIVERSITY RESEARCH JOURNAL. (II/0250-5193). **91**

GUJARATA SAMSODHANA MANDALANUM TRAIMASIKA. (II). **2504**

GULF COAST CATTLEMAN. (US/0017-5552). **211**

GULF COAST HISTORICAL REVIEW. (US/0892-9025). **2735**

GULF COAST OIL DIRECTORY. (US/0739-3547). **4259**

GULF COUNTY BREEZE. (US). **5649**

GULF NEWS. (CN/0833-1065). **5785**

GULFSHORE LIFE. (US/0745-0079). **2534**

GULLET. (UK/0952-0643). **3579**

GULLIVER (BARI, ITALY). (IT). **1112**

GUMMI BEREIFUNG. (GW). **5075**

GUMMI, FASERN, KUNSTSTOFFE. (GW/0176-1625). **5076**

GUN DOG. (US/0279-5086). **Adv Mgr:** Mary Stearns, **Tel** same as publisher. **4873**

GUN REPORT. (US/0017-5617). **250**

GUN WORLD. (US/0017-5641). **4897**

GUNNER. (UK). **4045**

GUNRUNNER. (CN). **4897**

GUNS & WEAPONS FOR LAW ENFORCEMENT. (US/1058-2975). **Adv Mgr:** Parker Gentry. **3165**

GUNS REVIEW. (UK). **4897**

GUNZO. (JA). **3392**

GUOJI RIBAO. (US/0741-126X). **Adv Mgr:** Fred King. **5635**

GURNEE PRESS. (US/0745-810X). **Adv Mgr:** Jill DePasquale. **5660**

GURU NANAK JOURNAL OF SOCIOLOGY. (II/0970-0242). **5246**

GUTENBERG-JAHRBUCH. (GW/0072-9094). **4565**

GUTHRIE CENTER TIMES (GUTHRIE CENTER, IOWA : 1952). (US). **5670**

GUYANA CONSOLIDATED INDEX TO STATUTES AND SUBSIDIARY LEGISLATION TO 1ST JAN. .... (US). **3081**

GUYANA LIBRARY ASSOCIATION BULLETIN. (GY). **3212**

GWIAZDA POLARNA. (US/0740-5944). **Adv Mgr:** Barbara Bublitz. **5767**

GYERMEKGYOGYASZAT. (HU/0017-5900). **3903**

GYMNASIUM (HEIDELBERG). (GW/0342-5231). **1077**

GYNECOLOGIC AND OBSTETRIC INVESTIGATION. (SZ/0378-7346). **3761**

GYNECOLOGICAL ENDOCRINOLOGY. (UK/0951-3590). **3730**

GYPSY BLOOD REVIEW. (US/1071-5126). **Adv Mgr:** Stan Faulkner. **3392**

GZ : GOLDSCHMIEDE UND UHRMACHER ZEITUNG. (GW). **2914**

H.A.C. JOURNAL. (AT). **1092**

H.A.N.D.S. ON GUIDE. (US/0897-5345). **373**

H. G. WELLS NEWSLETTER, THE. (UK/0306-5480). **3392**

H + G ZEITSCHRIFT FUER HAUTKRANKHEITEN. (GW/0301-0481). **3720**

H2O TIJDSCHRIFT VOOR DRINKWATERVOORZIENING EN AFVALWATERBEHANDELING. (NE). **5534**

HA-SHILTH-SA. (CN/0715-4143). **5785**

HA'ARETZ. (IS). **5804**

HABILITATIVE MENTAL HEALTHCARE NEWSLETTER, THE. (US/1057-3291). **3926**

HABITAT (FALMOUTH, ME.). (US/0739-2052). **2194**

HABITAT (LONDON). (UK/0028-9043). **2194**

HABITAT (MELBOURNE). (AT/0310-2939). **2194**

HAC. THE HEATING AND AIR CONDITIONING JOURNAL. (UK/0307-7950). **2605**

HACK'D (WOODBRIDGE, VA.). (US/1055-033X). **4081**

HACTION. (CN/0714-7066). **5287**

HADASSAH MAGAZINE. (US/0017-6516). **5048**

HAEGI. (KO). **4176**

HAEMATOLOGIA. (HU/0017-6559). **3797**

HAEMATOLOGICA (ROMA). (IT/0390-6078). **Adv Mgr:** Dott Dalla, **Tel** 06-86207165. **3772**

HAEMOSTASEOLOGIE. (GW/0720-9355). **3580**

HAEMOSTASIS. (SZ/0301-0147). **3580**

HAEUSER. (GW/0724-6528). **299**

HAFTEN FOR KRITISKA STUDIER. (SW/0345-4789). **4475**

HAIR DESIGN. (US). **404**

HAIR INTERNATIONAL NEWS. (US/0887-803X). **404**

HAIYANG YUYE. (CC/1004-2490). **2305**

HALASZAT. (HU). **2305**

HALF MOON BAY REVIEW AND PESCADERO PEBBLE. (US). **5635**

HALI. (UK/0142-0798). **5351**

HALIFAX METROPOLITAN AREA BUSINESS DIRECTORY. (CN/0834-0676). **678**

HALLE YEARBOOK. (UK). **4120**

HALSBURY'S STATUTES OF ENGLAND AND WALES. (UK). **2976**

HALSTAD VALLEY JOURNAL. (US). **5696**

HALTON BUSINESS JOURNAL (1986). (CN/0833-384X). **Adv Mgr:** V. McKee. **678**

HAMBRO COMPANY GUIDE, THE. (UK/0144-2015). **678**

HAMBURGER BEITRAEGE ZUR FRIEDENSFORSCHUNG UND SICHERHEITSPOLITIK. (GW/0936-0018). **4523**

HAMDARD ISLAMICUS. (PK/0250-7196). **5042**

HAMERSKY & ALLIED FAMILIES NEWSLETTER. (US/0882-4150). **2452**

HAMILTON COUNTY NEWS, THE. (US). **5717**

HAMILTON LAWYER. (CN/1188-4827). **Adv Mgr:** D. Sexton. **2976**

HAMILTON REPORT. (CN/0834-0536). **Adv Mgr:** Heather Rose. **678**

HAMILTON THIS MONTH. (CN/0829-1373). **Adv Mgr:** Heather Rose. **678**

HAMLET STUDIES. (II/0256-2480). **3392**

HAMLINE LAW REVIEW. (US/0198-7364). **2976**

HAMMER & DOLLY. (US/1064-4822). **Adv Mgr:** Scott DeSimone. **5416**

HAMMOND VINDICATOR, THE. (US). **5684**

HAMPTON COUNTY GUARDIAN. (US). **5742**

HAN HSUEH YEN CHIU TUNG HSUN. (CH). **2504**

HANCEVILLE HERALD, THE. (US). **5626**

HANCOCK CLARION, THE. (US). **Adv Mgr:** Kathy Sabelhaus. **5680**

HANCOCK COUNTY COURIER (NEW CUMBERLAND, W. VA. : 1943). (US). **Adv Mgr:** Hugh Taylor. **5764**

HANCOCK HERALD, THE. (US). **Adv Mgr:** Millie Triff, **Tel** (607)637-3591. **5717**

HAND PAPERMAKING. (US/0887-1418). **4234**

HANDBOOK - COMMONWEALTH BROADCASTING ASSOCIATION. (UK). **Adv Mgr:** Derek Inall, **Tel** 011 44 462 684231. **1132**

HANDBOOK OF CERTIFICATION/LICENSURE REQUIREMENTS FOR SCHOOL PSYCHOLOGISTS, THE. (US). **4588**

HANDBOOK OF PRIVATE SCHOOLS, THE. (US/0072-9884). **1749**

HANDBOOK OF THE BRITISH ASTRONOMICAL ASSOCIATION, THE. (UK/0068-130X). **395**

HANDBOOK - OKLAHOMA BAR ASSOCIATION. (US/0271-2571). **2976**

HANDBOOK TO THE SEASON / CINCINNATI SYMPHONY ORCHESTRA. (US/0732-2321). **4120**

HANDBUCH

Advertising Accepted Index

HANDBUCH DER DATENBANKEN FUER NATURWISSENSCHAFT, TECHNIK, PATENTE. (GW/0936-1375). **1185**

HANDBUCH DER GROSSUNTERNEHMEN. (GW/0073-0068). **1493**

HANDBUCH DER PFLANZENANATOMIE. (GW). **512**

HANDBUCH DER WIRTSCHAFTSDATENBANKEN. (GW/0931-2234). **679**

HANDCHIRURGIE, MIKROCHIRURGIE, PLASTISCHE CHIRURGIE. (GW/0722-1819). **3965**

HANDGUNNER. (UK/0260-8693). **Adv Mgr:** Tony Smith. **4898**

HANDLING EQUIPMENT DIRECTORY. (UK). **2115**

HANDLOADER. (US/0017-7393). **4898**

HANDMADE (ASHEVILLE, N.C.). (US/0275-9640). **5184**

HANDWOVEN. (US/0198-8212). **5351**

HANFORD SENTINEL, THE. (US). **Adv Mgr:** Bob Randall. **5635**

HANG GLIDING. (US/0895-433X). **Adv Mgr:** Jeff Elgart, **Tel** (719)632-8300. **4898**

HANG KUNG CHIH SHIH. (CC/1000-0119). **22**

HAN'GUK CHUKSAN HAKHOE CHI. (KO/0367-5807). **5510**

HANGUK ILBO, SAEN PURANSISUKO. (US/0747-8356). **Adv Mgr:** Michael Kang. **5635**

HANGUK KIDIKKYO CHANGNOHOE HOEBO. (KO). **5061**

HANGUK KISUL YONGUSO CHONGNAM. (KO). **5109**

HAN'GUK NONGHWA HAKHOE CHI. (KO/0368-2897). **91**

HANGZHOU DAXUE XUEBAO. ZIRAN KEXUE BAN. (CC/0253-3618). **5109**

HANJIE XUEBAO. (CC/0253-360X). **4027**

HANOVER POST POSTSCRIPTS, THE. (CN/0847-8988). **Adv Mgr:** Marie David. **5786**

HANSA. (GW/0017-7504). **4177**

HANSFORD PLAINSMAN, THE. (US). **5750**

HANZAIGAKU ZASSHI. (JA/0302-0029). **3740**

HAPPY WANDERER, THE. (US/0195-2080). **5479**

HARALSON GATEWAY-BEACON, THE. (US/0746-4169). **Adv Mgr:** Glenn Smith. **5653**

HARAMBEE. (US). **Adv Mgr:** C. Diggs. **2262**

HARBOR SOUND, THE. (US). **Adv Mgr:** Jim Dryden. **5653**

HARBOUR & SHIPPING. (CN/0017-7636). **5450**

HARDIN COUNTY HISTORICAL QUARTERLY. (US/8755-6073). **2735**

HARDWARE MERCHANDISER (CHICAGO). (US/0017-7709). **2811**

HARDWARE MERCHANDISING, BUILDING SUPPLY DEALER. (CN/0831-0807). **2811**

HARDWICK GAZETTE, THE. (US/0744-5512). **Adv Mgr:** Susan Javzyna. **5757**

HARDWOOD FLOORS. (US/0897-022X). **2401**

HARLEY WOMEN. (US/0893-6447). **Adv Mgr:** Bonnie, **Tel** (602)451-9655. **4851**

HARMONIE-QUEBEC : BULLETIN OFFICIEL, FEDERATION DES HARMONIES DU QUEBEC. (CN/0713-8059). **4120**

HARMONIZER (KENOSHA, WIS.), THE. (US/0017-7849). **4120**

HARPER'S BAZAAR. (US/0017-7873). **1085**

HARPER'S BAZAAR ITALIA. (IT/1121-7375). **1085**

HARPER'S (NEW YORK, N.Y.). (US/0017-789X). **3343**

HARPIES & QUINES. (UK/0966-2995). **Adv Mgr:** Helen Chambers. **5558**

HARRIS COUNTY REAL ESTATE REPORT. (US). **4838**

HARRIS INDIANA INDUSTRIAL DIRECTORY. (US/0888-8175). **1608**

HARRIS MICHIGAN INDUSTRIAL DIRECTORY (TWINSBURG, OHIO: 1984). (US/0888-8167). **1608**

HARRISON INDEPENDENT. (US/0892-4163). **Adv Mgr:** Ray Martin. **5717**

HARRISONBURG DAILY NEWS RECORD. (US). **Adv Mgr:** Linda Wsecker. **5758**

HARRISTON REVIEW, THE. (CN/0381-0283). **Adv Mgr:** B. Newman. **5786**

HARROWSMITH (CANADIAN ED.). (CN/0381-6885). **2534**

HARROWSMITH COUNTRY LIFE. (US/1049-4618). **2534**

HART BEAT, THE. (US/0892-239X). **5750**

HART COUNTY NEWS-HERALD. (US/1075-4628). **5680**

HARTFORD CITY NEWS-TIMES. (US). **Adv Mgr:** Connie Murray. **5664**

HARTLEPOOL MAIL. (UK). **5812**

HARTSVILLE MESSENGER, THE. (US/8750-3972). **5742**

HARTSVILLE VIDETTE, THE. (US/0891-169X). **Adv Mgr:** Rosemary Denham. **5745**

HARTVILLE NEWS, THE. (US/0746-8016). **Adv Mgr:** Rosalee Haines. **5728**

HARVARD ADVOCATE (CAMBRIDGE, MASS.), THE. (US/0017-8004). **Adv Mgr:** Thomas Cheung. **3393**

HARVARD BUSINESS SCHOOL BULLETIN. (US/0017-8020). **679**

HARVARD CRIMSON, THE. (US). **5688**

HARVARD DIVINITY BULLETIN. (US/0017-8047). **4962**

HARVARD EDUCATIONAL REVIEW. (US/0017-8055). **1749**

HARVARD INDEPENDENT, THE. (US). **1092**

HARVARD INTERNATIONAL REVIEW. (US/0739-1854). **Adv Mgr:** Matt Price, **Tel** (617)495-9607. **4523**

HARVARD JOURNAL OF LAW & PUBLIC POLICY. (US/0193-4872). **2976**

HARVARD JOURNAL ON LEGISLATION. (US/0017-808X). **2977**

HARVARD LAW RECORD. (US/0017-8101). **2977**

HARVARD LAW REVIEW. (US/0017-811X). **2977**

HARVARD, L'EXPANSION. (FR/0397-5495). **Adv Mgr:** Philippe Guillanton, **Tel** 33 1 40604060. **869**

HARVARD MAGAZINE. (US/0095-2427). **1092**

HARVARD MEDICAL ALUMNI BULLETIN. (US/0191-7757). **1102**

HARVARD POLITICAL REVIEW. (US/0090-1032). **4475**

HARVARD REVIEW. (US). **Adv Mgr:** Joyce Wilson. **3393**

HARVARD SEMITIC MONOGRAPHS. (US/0073-0637). **5016**

HARVARD THEOLOGICAL REVIEW, THE. (US/0017-8160). **4962**

HARVEST (PORT MORESBY). (PP/0378-8865). **91**

HARVESTER, THE. (UK/0017-8217). **5017**

HASKELL COUNTY MONITOR-CHIEF, THE. (US). **Adv Mgr:** Doris Birney. **5676**

HASSADEH. (IS/0017-8314). **91**

HASTINGS COMMUNICATIONS AND ENTERTAINMENT LAW JOURNAL (COMM/ENT). (US/1061-6578). **Adv Mgr:** A. Kaba, **Tel** (415)565-4738. **2977**

HASTINGS CONSTITUTIONAL LAW QUARTERLY. (US/0094-5617). **Adv Mgr:** A Kaba, **Tel** (415)565-4738. **3093**

HASTINGS INTERNATIONAL AND COMPARATIVE LAW REVIEW. (US/0149-9246). **Adv Mgr:** A Kava, **Tel** (415)565-4738. **3129**

HASTINGS LAW JOURNAL. (US/0017-8322). **Adv Mgr:** A Kaba, **Tel** (415)565-4738. **2977**

HASTINGS WOMEN'S LAW JOURNAL. (US/1061-0901). **Adv Mgr:** A Kaba, **Tel** (415)565-4738. **2977**

HATTIESBURG AMERICAN. (US). **5700**

HAUSFRAU, MONATSSCHRIFT FUR DIE FRAUENWELT AMERIKAS, DIE. (US/0017-842X). **2517**

HAUSTECHNISCHE RUNDSCHAU. (GW/0017-8438). **616**

HAVANA HERALD. (US). **5649**

HAWAII ARCHITECT. (US/0191-8311). **299**

HAWAII BAR JOURNAL (1992). (US/1063-1585). **Adv Mgr:** Brett Pruitt, **Tel** (808)521-1929. **2977**

HAWAII BAR JOURNAL MICROFORM. (US). **2977**

HAWAII BEVERAGE GUIDE. (US/0017-8543). **2367**

HAWAII BUSINESS. (US/0440-5056). **679**

HAWAII BUSINESS DIRECTORY. (US). **679**

HAWAII DENTAL JOURNAL. (US/0891-9933). **1324**

HAWAII HERALD (1969). (US/8750-913X). **2262**

HAWAII INVESTOR. (US/0745-7073). **Adv Mgr:** Mary Winpenny, **Tel** (808)524-7400. **4838**

HAWAII MEDICAL JOURNAL (1962). (US/0017-8594). **3581**

HAWAII REVIEW. (US/0093-9625). **3393**

HAWAII, THE BIG ISLAND UPDATE. (US/1042-8046). **5479**

HAWAII TV DIGEST. (US/0745-6565). **1132**

HAWAIIAN ARCHAEOLOGY. (US/0890-1678). **269**

HAWAIIAN JOURNAL OF HISTORY, THE. (US/0440-5145). **2669**

HAWAIIAN SHELL NEWS. (US/0017-8624). **1449**

HAWK EYE, THE. (US). **Adv Mgr:** Nelson H. Showalter. **5670**

HAWK : THE INDEPENDENT JOURNAL OF THE ROYAL AIR STAFF COLLEGE. (UK). **22**

HAWKEYE HERITAGE. (US/0440-5234). **2452**

HAWKEYE OSTEOPATHIC JOURNAL. (US). **3581**

HAWLEY HERALD, THE. (US). **5696**

HAXTUN HERALD, THE. (US). **Adv Mgr:** Holly Barnett. **5643**

HAYDEN VALLEY PRESS, THE. (US). **5643**

HAYES DRUGGIST DIRECTORY. (US). **4306**

HAYS DAILY NEWS, THE. (US). **Adv Mgr:** Mike Haas, **Tel** (913)628-1081. **5676**

HAZ-MAT TECHNOLOGY. (US/0888-6849). **4777**

HAZ PACKS. (US/1042-6574). **2230**

HAZARD HERALD-VOICE. (US). **Adv Mgr:** Wilma Thomas. **5681**

HAZARD MONTHLY. (US/0742-6410). **2230**

HAZARD PREVENTION. (US/0743-8826). **2862**

HAZARD TIMES, THE. (US/0883-752X). **5681**

HAZARDOUS CARGO BULLETIN. (UK/0143-6864). **5450**

HAZARDOUS MATERIALS INTELLIGENCE REPORT. (US/0272-9628). **2231**

HAZARDOUS MATERIALS MANAGEMENT. (CN/1193-2074). **Adv Mgr:** Arnie Gess. **2231**

HAZARDOUS MATERIALS NEWSLETTER (BARRE, VT.). (US/0889-3454). **2231**

HAZCHEM ALERT. (US/0891-3072). **4777**

HAZELL'S GUIDE AND THE BAR LIST. (UK/0266-3597). **2977**

HAZELL'S GUIDE TO THE JUDICIARY AND THE COURTS. (UK/0266-3597). **3141**

HAZMAT WORLD. (US/0898-5685). **2232**

HB. HOOSIER BANKER. (US/0018-473X). **790**

HE HUAXUE YU FANGSHE HUAXUE. (CC/0253-9950). **976**

HEAD INJURY UPDATE. (US/0887-1779). **3965**

HEAD OFFICE AT HOME. (CN/1183-6709). **679**

HEADACHE. (US/0017-8748). **3833**

HEADLAND OBSERVER, THE. (US). **Adv Mgr:** Betty Rowland. **5626**

HEADLINES. (UK/0957-8714). **1864**

HEADQUARTERS HELIOGRAM (COUNCIL ON AMERICA'S MILITARY PAST). (US). **4045**

HEALDSBURG TRIBUNE-ENTERPRISE AND SCIMITAR. (US/0017-8810). **5635**

HEALING (SACRAMENTO, CALIF.). (US/1064-4237). **4777**

HEALTH & FITNESS MAGAZINE FOR HEALTHY, SOUND LIVING : HF. (US/1048-8405). **4777**

HEALTH AND HYGIENE (LONDON). (UK/0140-2986). **Adv Mgr Tel** (071)580 2731. **4777**

HEALTH & NUTRITION UPDATE. (CN/0831-8530). **4191**

HEALTH & SAFETY AT WORK (CROYDON). (UK/0141-8246). **2862**

HEALTH & SAFETY SPECIFIER. (UK). **Adv Mgr:** Debbie Preece, **Tel** 011 44 242 581480. **4778**

HEALTH & SOCIAL WORK. (US/0360-7283). **5287**

HEALTH CARE FOR WOMEN INTERNATIONAL. (US/0739-9332). **3762**

HEALTH CARE LABOR MANUAL. (US/0095-3792). **1676**

HEALTH CARE MANAGEMENT. (UK/0269-2104). **3781**

HEALTH CARE STRATEGIC MANAGEMENT. (US/0742-1478). **3781**

HEALTH CITY SUN. (US). **Adv Mgr:** A. D. Collado. **5712**

HEALTH CONSCIOUSNESS (OVIEDO, FLA.). (US/0895-9986). **Adv Mgr:** John Zielinski. **4779**

HEALTH DIET & NUTRITION. (US/1055-8241). **4191**

HEALTH EDUCATION INDEX AND GUIDE TO VOLUNTARY SOCIAL WELFARE ORGANISATIONS. (UK). **2598**

HEALTH EDUCATION JOURNAL, THE. (UK/0017-8969). **2598**

HEALTH EDUCATION QUARTERLY. (US/0195-8402). **4779**

HEALTH EDUCATION RESEARCH. (UK/0268-1153). **4779**

HEALTH ESTATE JOURNAL : JOURNAL OF THE INSTITUTE OF HOSPITAL ENGINEERING. (UK/0957-7742). **3781**

HEALTH FACILITIES ENERGY REPORT. (US/0272-8443). **1946**

HEALTH FACILITIES MANAGEMENT. (US/0899-6210). **4779**

HEALTH FACT NEWS. (US/0279-5639). **2598**

HEALTH FOODS BUSINESS. (US/0149-9602). **2343**

HEALTH FORUM. (AT/1030-6072). **4779**

HEALTH FUNDS DEVELOPMENT LETTER. (US/0193-7928). **3581**

HEALTH INDUSTRY BUYERS GUIDE : HIBG. (US/0892-7731). **3581**

HEALTH INDUSTRY TODAY. (US/0745-4678). **3581**

HEALTH INFORMATION AND LIBRARIES. (HU/0864-991X). **3213**

HEALTH MARKETING QUARTERLY. (US/0735-9683). **3582**

HEALTH MATRIX. (US/0748-383X). **Adv Mgr:** Carolyn Speaker, **Tel** (216)368-3304. **3740**

HEALTH NEWS & REVIEW. (US/1056-1900). **4191**

HEALTH/PAC BULLETIN. (US/0017-9051). **4780**

HEALTH POLICY AND PLANNING. (UK/0268-1080). **4780**

HEALTH PROGRESS (SAINT LOUIS, MO.). (US/0882-1577). **3781**

HEALTH PROMOTION INTERNATIONAL. (UK/0957-4824). **4781**

HEALTH PSYCHOLOGY. (US/0278-6133). **4588**

HEALTH SCIENCE (1985). (US/0883-8216). **4781**

HEALTH SERVICE JOURNAL, THE. (UK/0952-2271). **4781**

HEALTH SERVICES INTERNATIONAL. (UK/1011-5153). **4781**

HEALTH SERVICES MANAGEMENT. (UK/0953-8534). **3781**

HEALTH SERVICES MANAGEMENT RESEARCH : AN OFFICIAL JOURNAL OF THE ASSOCIATION OF UNIVERSITY PROGRAMS IN HEALTH ADMINISTRATION. (UK/0951-4848). **3781**

HEALTH VALUES. (US/0147-0353). **Adv Mgr:** P Glover. **4782**

HEALTH VISITOR : THE JOURNAL OF THE HEALTH VISITORS' ASSOCIATION. (UK/0017-9140). **3856**

HEALTH WATCH (LOUISVILLE, KY.). (US/1051-9726). **4782**

HEALTH WORLD. (US/0888-7330). **4782**

HEALTHCARE ADVERTISING REVIEW. (US/8756-4513). **760**

HEALTHCARE ADVOCATE (EDMONTON). (CN/1197-4710). **Adv Mgr:** Jan Henry, **Tel** (403)484-3895. **3782**

HEALTHCARE COMMUNITY RELATIONS & MARKETING LETTER. (US/0894-9980). **3583**

HEALTHCARE EXECUTIVE. (US/0883-5381). **3782**

HEALTHCARE FINANCIAL MANAGEMENT. (US/0735-0732). **3782**

HEALTHCARE FORUM JOURNAL, THE. (US/0899-9287). **Adv Mgr:** Gayle Samuelson. **3583**

HEALTHCARE INFORMATICS. (US/1050-9135). **3782**

HEALTHCARE MARKETING REPORT. (US/0741-9368). **3782**

HEALTHSHARING. (CN/0226-1510). **Adv Mgr:** Lisa Huncar, **Tel** (416)532-0812. **4782**

HEALTHTEXAS (AUSTIN, TEX.). (US/1048-4167). **Adv Mgr:** Martin Bevins. **3782**

HEARING HEALTH. (US/0888-2517). **Adv Mgr:** Dave Bakker. **1297**

HEARING INSTRUMENTS. (US/0092-4466). **3888**

HEARING JOURNAL, THE. (US/0745-7472). **3888**

HEARING REHABILITATION QUARTERLY. (US/0360-9278). **4388**

HEARSAY. (US). **4388**

HEART & LUNG. (US/0147-9563). **3856**

HEART DISEASE AND STROKE. (US/1058-2819). **Adv Mgr:** Krista Curnutt, **Tel** (214)706-1426. **3705**

HEARTH AND HOME (GILFORD, N.H. : 1989). (US/0273-5695). **Adv Mgr:** Jackie Avignone, **Tel** (800)258-3772. **1946**

HEARTLAND BOATING. (US/1042-1009). **Adv Mgr:** Kelly Smith. **593**

HEARTLAND JOURNAL. (US/0887-2597). **3393**

HEAT SHOCK PROTEINS. (UK/0950-0510). **488**

HEAT TRANSFER ENGINEERING. (US/0145-7632). **2012**

HEAT TRANSFER. JAPANESE RESEARCH. (US/0096-0802). **4431**

HEAT TREATMENT OF METALS. (UK/0305-4829). **4003**

HEATHER SOCIETY BULLETIN, THE. (UK). **5231**

HEATING & VENTILATING REVIEW. (UK/0017-9396). **2605**

HEAVY HORSE WORLD. (UK/0951-2640). **2799**

HEAVY METAL. (US/0885-7822). **3393**

HEBDO DE LAVAL, L'. (CN/0822-7535). **5786**

HEBREW STUDIES. (US/0146-4094). **5048**

HECATE. (AT/0311-4198). **5558**

HEENSCHUT. (NE/0017-9515). **Adv Mgr:** A Moolenaak, **Tel** 31 21 5482211. **299**

HEILIGER DIENST. (AU/0017-9620). **Adv Mgr:** P. Winfried. **4962**

HEILPADAGOGISCHE FORSCHUNG. (GW). **1750**

HEIMEN. (NO/0017-9841). **2690**

HEISEY NEWS. (US/0731-8014). **2590**

HEJNA. (US/0748-7568). **2262**

HELICOPTER ANNUAL. (US/0739-5728). **Adv Mgr:** M. Beames. **22**

HELICOPTER WORLD (LONDON. 1982). (UK/0262-0448). **23**

HELICOPTERS. (CN/0227-3160). **23**

HELICTITE. (AT/0017-9973). **5109**

HELIOS (LUBBOCK). (US/0160-0923). **1077**

HELLAS. (US/1044-5331). **3393**

HELLO. (UK). **Adv Mgr:** Sarah Pearson. **2517**

HELPER (AMERICAN SOCIAL HEALTH ASSOCIATION). (US). **4782**

HELSINGIN SANOMAT. (FI/0355-2047). **5800**

HELVETICA CHIMICA ACTA. (SZ/0018-019X). **976**

HELVETICA CHIRURGICA ACTA. (SZ/0018-0181). **3903**

HELVETICA PAEDIATRICA ACTA. (SZ/0018-022X). **3903**

HEM O FRITID. (SW). **2517**

HEMATOLOGICAL ONCOLOGY. (UK/0278-0232). **3772**

HEMEL HEMPSTEAD & DISTRICT BUSINESS DIRECTORY. (UK/0957-1043). **679**

HEMET NEWS, THE. (US). **Adv Mgr Tel** (909)487-2211. **5635**

HEMISPHERE (MIAMI, FLA.). (US/0898-3038). **Adv Mgr:** R. Jurado. **4475**

HEMMINGS MOTOR NEWS. (US). **5416**

HEMOGLOBIN. (US/0363-0269). **3797**

HENDERSON HOME NEWS. (US). **5707**

HENDERSONVILLE STAR NEWS. (US/0193-5143). **Adv Mgr:** Judi McMinn. **5745**

HENNEPIN LAWYER, THE. (US). **2978**

HENRY HERALD, THE. (US/1045-6678). **5653**

HENRY JAMES REVIEW, THE. (US/0273-0340). **3344**

HENSTON VETERINARY VADE MECUM. LARGE ANIMALS, THE. (UK/0268-4276). **5511**

HENSTON VETERINARY VADE MECUM. SMALL ANIMALS, THE. (UK/0268-4268). **Adv Mgr:** John O'Hara. **5511**

HEPATOLOGY (BALTIMORE, MD.). (US/0270-9139). **3797**

HER WORLD ANNUAL. (SI). **5558**

HERALD AND TRIBUNE (JONESBORO, TENN. : 1869). (US). **Adv Mgr:** Lois D. Hicks. **5745**

HERALD-CHRONICLE (WINCHESTER, TENN.), THE. (US/0893-3707). **Adv Mgr:** Rebekah Moorehead. **5745**

HERALD-CITIZEN (COOKEVILLE, TENN.). (US/8750-5541). **Adv Mgr:** Allen Profant. **5745**

HERALD-COASTER, THE. (US). **Adv Mgr:** Debra Anthony. **5750**

HERALD-DISPATCH (LOS ANGELES, CALIF. : 1981). (US/8750-2038). **Adv Mgr:** L. Holoman. **5635**

HERALD (EVERETT, WASH.), THE. (US). **Adv Mgr:** John Hill, **Tel** (206)339-3026. **5761**

HERALD-LEADER, THE. (US). **Adv Mgr:** Becky Anderson. **5653**

HERALD-NEWS (EDMONTON, KY.), THE. (US/0889-9711). **Adv Mgr:** Kandis Shive. **5681**

HERALD OF LIBRARY SCIENCE. (II/0018-0521). **3213**

HERALD-PRESS (HUNTINGTON, IND.). (US). **Adv Mgr:** Claude Good. **5664**

HERALD RECORD (WEST UNION, W. VA.). (US). **Adv Mgr:** Virginia Nicholson. **5764**

HERALD (RINCON, GA.), THE. (US/0899-627X). **5654**

HERALD-STANDARD (UNIONTOWN, PA. : 1980). (US). **Adv Mgr:** Maureen Lorichak, **Tel** (412)439-7582. **5736**

HERALD-STAR, THE. (US/0890-8656). **5728**

HERALD, THE. (PK). **2504**

HERALD, THE. (US). **5712**

HERALD, THE. (US). **5645**

HERALD, THE. (US). **Adv Mgr:** Jeff Forsythe. **5660**

HERALDRY IN CANADA. (CN/0441-6619). **2453**

HERANCA JUDAICA. (BL). **Adv Mgr:** Ernesto Strauss, **Tel** 282-5844. **5048**

HERB QUARTERLY, THE. (US/0163-9900). **Adv Mgr:** J. Keough, **Tel** (415)455-9540. **2418**

HERBAGE ABSTRACTS. (UK/0018-0602). **154**

HERBALGRAM (AUSTIN, TEX.). (US/0899-5648). **Adv Mgr:** M. Wright. **512**

HERBARIST, THE. (US/0740-5979). **Adv Mgr:** Linda Wells. **2418**

HERD BOOK - BRITISH GOAT SOCIETY. (UK). **195**

HEREDITY. (UK/0018-067X). **547**

HERINGTON TIMES (HERINGTON, KAN. : 1973). (US). **5676**

HERITAGE (AUSTIN, TEX.). (US/1047-5613). **2736**

HERITAGE (CARSON, CALIF.). (US/0895-0792). **2262**

HERITAGE COUNTRY. (US/1055-9515). **2736**

HERITAGE HEARTH. (CN/0841-923X). **4088**

HERITAGE OF VERMILION COUNTY, THE. (US/0018-0718). **2617**

HERITAGE OUTLOOK. (UK/0261-1988). **300**

HERITAGE SCOTLAND : THE MAGAZINE OF THE NATIONAL TRUST FOR SCOTLAND. (UK/0264-9144). **2690**

HERIZONS. (CN/0711-7485). **5558**

HERMATHENA. (IE/0018-0750). **4348**

HERMES (1936). (GW). **1077**

HERMES AMERICANUS. (US/0741-1286). **3285**

HERMISTON HERALD AND BUYER'S BONUS, THE. (US/8750-4782). **Adv Mgr:** Dan Zimmerman. **5733**

HERPETOFAUNA NEWS. (UK/0269-8498). **5585**

HERPETOLOGICAL JOURNAL, THE. (UK/0268-0130). **5585**

HERPETOLOGICAL REVIEW. (US/0018-084X). **5585**

HERVORMDE TEOLOGIESE STUDIES. (SA). **4962**

HERVORMER, DIE. (SA). **4962**

HESPERUS REVIEW. (II). **3393**

HESSTON RECORD, THE. (US). **5676**

HETEROCYCLES. (JA/0385-5414). **1041**

HETEROFONIA. (MX/0018-1137). **4121**

HETI VILAGGAZDASAG : HVG. (HU/0139-1682). **1635**

HEURISTICS — Advertising Accepted Index

HEURISTICS (ROCKVILLE, MD.). (US/1040-6433). **Adv Mgr:** V. Sullivan, **Tel** (301)948-4890. **1229**

HEYTHROP JOURNAL. (UK/0018-1196). **5030**

HFD. (US/0746-7885). **2906**

HI-RISE. (CN/0715-5948). **2534**

HIBALLER FOREST MAGAZINE. (CN/0708-2169). **2384**

HIBBING TRIBUNE. (US). **5696**

HIBOU (ST-LAMBERT). (CN/0709-9177). **1064**

HIDUP. (IO/0377-9610). **5030**

HIFU. SKIN RESEARCH. (JA/0018-1390). **3720**

HIGH BLOOD PRESSURE AND CARDIOVASCULAR PREVENTION. (US/1120-9879). **3705**

HIGH COLOR. (US/1060-5282). **1233**

HIGH COUNTRY INDEPENDENT PRESS. (US/0746-3359). **5705**

HIGH COUNTRY NEWS. (US/0191-5657). **2195**

HIGH ENERGY PHYSICS INDEX / HOCHENERGIEPHYSIK-INDEX. (GW/0018-1447). **4404**

HIGH INTEGRITY SYSTEMS. (UK/0967-2648). **Adv Mgr:** Peter Carpenter, **Tel** 081 786 7376. **1247**

HIGH PERFORMANCE (LOS ANGELES). (US/0160-9769). **385**

HIGH-PERFORMANCE PONTIAC. (US/0745-5941). **5416**

HIGH PERFORMANCE REVIEW. (US/0277-1357). **5317**

HIGH PLAINS APPLIED ANTHROPOLOGIST. (US/0882-4894). **237**

HIGH PLAINS JOURNAL, THE. (US/0018-1471). **Adv Mgr:** Tom Taylor. **5676**

HIGH PLAINS LITERARY REVIEW. (US/0888-4153). **3344**

HIGH ROLLER. (US/0197-6044). **3213**

HIGH SCHOOL WRITER, THE. (US/1048-3373). **2920**

HIGH SOLIDS COATINGS. (US/0146-4752). **977**

HIGH SPRINGS HERALD. (US/0746-1046). **Adv Mgr:** Carol Chidlow. **5649**

HIGH TEMPERATURE SCIENCE. (US/0018-1536). **1052**

HIGH TEMPERATURES - HIGH PRESSURES. (UK/0018-1544). **4431**

HIGH TIMBER TIMES. (US). **Adv Mgr:** John Ellis. **5643**

HIGH VOLUME PRINTING. (US/0737-1020). **4565**

HIGHER EDUCATION. (NE/0018-1560). **1828**

HIGHER EDUCATION ABSTRACTS. (US/0748-4364). **1795**

HIGHER EDUCATION DIRECTORY. (US/0740-9230). **1828**

HIGHER EDUCATION IN EUROPE. (RM/0379-7724). **1828**

HIGHER EDUCATION POLICY. (UK/0952-8733). **1828**

HIGHER EDUCATION QUARTERLY / SOCIETY FOR RESEARCH INTO HIGHER EDUCATION. (UK/0951-5224). **1828**

HIGHER EDUCATION REVIEW. (UK/0018-1609). **1828**

HIGHLAND HERITAGE. (CN/0707-2554). **2453**

HIGHLAND NEWS LEADER. (US/8750-0957). **Adv Mgr:** Gay Bentlage. **5660**

HIGHLANDER (BARRINGTON), THE. (US/0161-5378). **2262**

HIGHLANDER, THE. (US). **5649**

HIGHLANDER, THE. (US). **5750**

HIGHLANDS PRESS. (US). **Adv Mgr:** Barbara Wagoner. **5650**

HIGHLIGHT QUEBEC. (CN/0825-4850). **Adv Mgr:** Carole Tapin. **4963**

HIGHLIGHTS : BUDGET SPEECH AND ESTIMATES. (CN). **1493**

HIGHLINE TIMES. (US). **Adv Mgr:** Carla Royter. **5761**

HIGHWAY 12 WEEKENDER. (CN/0821-4824). **5786**

HIGHWAY BUILDER. (US). **Adv Mgr:** Naylor Publications, **Tel** (800)879-1107. **2024**

HIKAKU BUNKA ZASSHI. (JA). **2617**

HIKAKU KAGAKU. (JA/0018-1811). **3184**

HILLSBORO ARGUS (HILLSBORO, OR.). (US/8750-5479). **Adv Mgr:** Kent Johnson, **Tel** (503)648-1131. **5733**

HILLSBORO SENTRY-ENTERPRISE. (US/0749-7016). **Adv Mgr:** Scott Hughes. **5768**

HIMALAYAN JOURNAL, THE. (II). **4873**

HIMALAYAN PLANT JOURNAL. (II). **2418**

HIMALAYAN RESEARCH BULLETIN. (US/0891-4834). **2652**

HINDU (MADRAS, INDIA : DAILY). (II). **5803**

HINDUSTAN ANTIBIOTICS BULLETIN. (II/0018-1935). **4306**

HINDUSTAN YEAR-BOOK AND WHO'S WHO. (II/0970-1168). **5012**

HINE'S DIRECTORY OF INSURANCE ADJUSTERS. (US). **2882**

HINE'S INSURANCE COUNSEL. (US). **2978**

HIPPO MAGAZINE. (US/1050-6802). **3393**

HIRATRA / SAMPANA TENY SY LAHABOLANA ARY RIBA MALAGASY. (MG). **3393**

HIROSHIMA DAIGAKU SEIBUTSU GAKKAI SHI. (JA/0367-5912). **457**

HISLA. (PE). **1565**

HISPALIS MEDICA. (SP/0018-2125). **3584**

HISPAMERICA (COLLEGE PARK). (US/0363-0471). **3394**

HISPANIA. (US/0018-2133). **3285**

HISPANIC AMERICAN HISTORICAL REVIEW, THE. (US/0018-2168). **2262**

HISPANIC BOOKS BULLETIN. (US/0894-2358). **4828**

HISPANIC BUSINESS. (US/0199-0349). **679**

HISPANIC FOCUS. (US/0737-7029). **2276**

HISPANIC HOTLINE. (US/1064-0916). **4204**

HISPANIC JOURNAL OF BEHAVIORAL SCIENCES. (US/0739-9863). **2262**

HISPANIC LINGUISTICS. (US/0742-5287). **3285**

HISPANIC LINK. (US). **2262**

HISPANIC LINK WEEKLY REPORT. (US). **Adv Mgr:** Carlos, **Tel** (210)239-0280. **2262**

HISPANIC OUTLOOK IN HIGHER EDUCATION, THE. (US/1054-2337). **1829**

HISPANIC REVIEW. (US/0018-2176). **3285**

HISPANIC TIMES MAGAZINE. (US/0892-1369). **Adv Mgr:** D. Lopez. **4204**

HISPANIC (WASHINGTON, D.C.). (US/0898-3097). **2262**

HISPANO NEWS, EL. (US). **Adv Mgr:** A. B. Collado. **2263**

HISPANO (SACRAMENTO, CALIF.). (US). **5635**

HISTOCHEMICAL JOURNAL. (UK/0018-2214). **536**

HISTOIRE DE L'ART (PARIS, 1988). (FR/0992-2059). **Adv Mgr:** Loire Natalie. **321**

HISTOIRE DE L'EDUCATION. (FR/0221-6280). **1750**

HISTOIRE, L'. (FR/0182-2411). **2617**

HISTOIRE SOCIALE. (CN/0018-2257). **5201**

HISTOLOGY AND HISTOPATHOLOGY. (SP/0213-3911). **537**

HISTOPATHOLOGY. (UK/0309-0167). **3894**

HISTORIA CRITICA (BOGOTA, COLOMBIA). (CK). **Adv Mgr:** Hugo Fazio, **Tel** 572-2819260. **2736**

HISTORIA MEDICINAE VETERINARIAE. (DK/0105-1423). **5511**

HISTORIA MEXICANA. (MX/0185-0172). **2736**

HISTORIA, QUESTOES & DEBATES. (BL/0100-6932). **2736**

HISTORIA (SANTIAGO). (CL/0073-2435). **2736**

HISTORIA (THREE RIVERS). (SA/0018-229X). **Adv Mgr:** J. Grobler. **2640**

HISTORIA (WIESBADEN). (GW/0018-2311). **2617**

HISTORIA Y CULTURA (LIMA). (PE/0073-2486). **2617**

HISTORIAN (KINGSTON), THE. (US/0018-2370). **2618**

HISTORIANS OF EARLY MODERN EUROPE. (US/0883-3559). **2691**

HISTORIANS OF NETHERLANDISH ART NEWSLETTER. (US/1067-4284). **352**

HISTORIC BRASS SOCIETY JOURNAL. (US/1045-4616). **Adv Mgr:** Jeff Nussbaum, **Tel** (212)627-3820. **4121**

HISTORIC BRASS SOCIETY NEWSLETTER. (US/1045-4594). **Adv Mgr:** Jeff Nussbaun. **4121**

HISTORIC HOUSES, CASTLES, AND GARDENS IN GREAT BRITAIN AND IRELAND. (UK/0073-2567). **2691**

HISTORICA (LIMA). (PE/0252-8894). **2737**

HISTORICAL ARCHAEOLOGY. (US/0440-9213). **269**

HISTORICAL FOOTNOTES (STONINGTON, CONN.). (US/0886-5272). **2737**

HISTORICAL GEOGRAPHY. (US). **2565**

HISTORICAL JOURNAL OF FILM, RADIO, AND TELEVISION. (UK/0143-9685). **4071**

HISTORICAL JOURNAL OF MASSACHUSETTS. (US/0276-8313). **2737**

HISTORICAL METALLURGY. (UK/0142-3304). **4003**

HISTORICAL METHODS. (US/0161-5440). **5201**

HISTORICAL NEWS. (NZ/0439-2345). **2618**

HISTORICAL PERFORMANCE. (US/0898-8587). **4121**

HISTORICAL REFLECTIONS. (CN/0315-7997). **2618**

HISTORICAL RESEARCH : THE BULLETIN OF THE INSTITUTE OF HISTORICAL RESEARCH. (UK/0950-3471). **2618**

HISTORICAL REVIEW OF BERKS COUNTY. (US/0018-2524). **2737**

HISTORICAL STUDIES IN THE PHYSICAL AND BIOLOGICAL SCIENCES. (US/0890-9997). **4404**

HISTORIE; JYSKE SAMLINGER. (DK). **2691**

HISTORISCH GEOGRAFISCH TIJDSCHRIFT. (NE/0167-9775). **2565**

HISTORISCH-POLITISCHE BUCH, DAS. (GW/0018-2605). **2618**

HISTORISCHE ZEITSCHRIFT. (GW/0018-2613). **2619**

HISTORISK TIDSKRIFT FOR FINLAND. (FI/0046-7596). **2691**

HISTORY AND ANTHROPOLOGY. (SZ/0275-7206). **237**

HISTORY & COMPUTING. (UK/0957-0144). **Adv Mgr:** Kathryn MacLean. **1186**

HISTORY AND TECHNOLOGY. (SZ/0734-1512). **5110**

HISTORY AND THEORY. (US/0018-2656). **2635**

HISTORY IN AFRICA. (US/0361-5413). **2640**

HISTORY (LONDON). (UK/0018-2648). **2619**

HISTORY OF ECONOMIC THOUGHT NEWSLETTER. (UK/0440-9884). **1592**

HISTORY OF EDUCATION QUARTERLY. (US/0018-2680). **1750**

HISTORY OF PHOTOGRAPHY. (UK/0308-7298). **4370**

HISTORY OF POLITICAL ECONOMY. (US/0018-2702). **1565**

HISTORY OF POLITICAL THOUGHT. (UK/0143-781X). **4476**

HISTORY OF RELIGIONS. (US/0018-2710). **4963**

HISTORY OF SCIENCE. (UK/0073-2753). **5110**

HISTORY TEACHER BRISBANE. (AT/0729-154X). **Adv Mgr:** Gail Fellows, **Tel** 07 864 3075. **1896**

HISTORY TEACHER (LONG BEACH, CALIF.), THE. (US/0018-2745). **1896**

HISTORY TODAY. (UK/0018-2753). **2619**

HISTORY (WASHINGTON). (US/0361-2759). **2619**

HISTORY WORKSHOP. (UK/0309-2984). **2619**

HITCHCOCK ANNUAL. (US/1062-5518). **4072**

HITOTSUBASHI RONSO. (JA/0018-2818). **5201**

HLABC FORUM. (CN/0826-0125). **3213**

HLASATEL. (US). **Adv Mgr:** Josef Kucera and Martha Jerabek. **5660**

HLH. (GW/0017-9906). **2605**

HMO PRACTICE. (US/0891-6624). **Adv Mgr:** Hank Townsend, PMI, **Tel** (212)685-5010. **5287**

HOARD'S DAIRYMAN. (US/0018-2885). **195**

HOBBES STUDIES. (NE/0921-5891). **4348**

HOBBY GREENHOUSE. (US/1040-6212). **2418**

Advertising Accepted Index   HOSPITAL

HOBBY MERCHANDISER (NEW YORK, N.Y.). (US/0744-1738). **2774**

HOBIE HOT LINE. (US/0745-1628). **593**

HOCKEY CIRCLE. (AT). **4898**

HOCKEY DIGEST (EVANSTON, ILL.). (US/0046-7693). **4899**

HOCKEY DIGEST (HARROW). (UK/0950-9550). **4899**

HOCKEY NEWS, THE. (CN/0018-3016). **4899**

HOFSTRA ENVIRONMENTAL LAW DIGEST. (US/0882-6765). **3113**

HOFSTRA LAW REVIEW. (US/0091-4029). **2978**

HOG MARKET PLACE QUARTERLY. (CN/0380-3651). **212**

HOGAKU. (US/0886-1862). **4121**

HOHLE, DIE. (AU/0018-3091). **1356**

HOISINGTON DISPATCH, THE. (US). **5676**

HOKHMAH. (SZ/0379-7465). **5061**

HOKUBEI HOCHI. (US/8756-6451). **Adv Mgr:** Reiko Henry. **5761**

HOLBROOK TRIBUNE-NEWS AND SNOWFLAKE HERALD. (US/8750-5363). **Adv Mgr:** Matthew Barger. **5630**

HOLDSWORTH LAW REVIEW / UNIVERSITY OF BIRMINGHAM. (UK). **2979**

HOLISTIC EDUCATION REVIEW. (US/0898-0926). **1751**

HOLISTIC MASSAGE. (US/0748-6855). **2598**

HOLISTIC MEDICINE (SEATTLE, WASH.). (US/0898-6029). **Adv Mgr:** R. Dowtin. **3584**

HOLISTIC RESOURCE MANAGEMENT NEWSLETTER. (US/1048-8472). **93**

HOLLAND HERALD. (NE). **2517**

HOLLAND SENTINEL (1977), THE. (US/1050-4044). **Adv Mgr:** Margaret Van Sant. **5692**

HOLLANDSE KRANT. (CN/0837-1342). **2263**

HOLLINS CRITIC, THE. (US/0018-3644). **3344**

HOLLIS EUROPE. (UK/0962-3590). **Adv Mgr:** Richard Bagnall. **760**

HOLLIS PRESS & PUBLIC RELATIONS ANNUAL. (UK/0073-3059). **760**

HOLLY SOCIETY JOURNAL. (US/0738-2421). **5231**

HOLLYWOOD MAGAZINE. (US/1045-361X). **2488**

HOLOCAUST STUDIES ANNUAL. (US/0738-0739). **2691**

HOLOCENE (SEVENOAKS). (UK/0959-6836). **1382**

HOLOGRAPHICS INTERNATIONAL. (UK/0951-3914). **4434**

HOLSTEIN JOURNAL. (CN/0710-1309). **Adv Mgr:** Peter English. **195**

HOLY LAND. (US). **4963**

HOLZ IM HANDWERK. (AU/0018-3776). **2906**

HOLZ-KUNSTSTOFF. (GW). **2401**

HOLZ-ZENTRALBLATT. (GW/0018-3792). **2384**

HOLZFORSCHUNG. (GW/0018-3830). **2401**

HOLZFORSCHUNG UND HOLZVERWERTUNG. (AU/0018-3849). **2401**

HOME. (IT). **Adv Mgr:** Ernesto Cipriani. **5351**

HOME & AWAY. (US/8750-5649). **5479**

HOME & AWAY (OMAHA, NEB.). (US/0199-7009). **5479**

HOME AND CONDO. (US). **2418**

HOME-BASED & SMALL BUSINESS NETWORK. (US/1067-7739). **680**

HOME BUILDER MAGAZINE. (CN/0840-4348). **616**

HOME BUSINESS ADVOCATE, THE. (CN/0832-8595). **680**

HOME CARE REPORT. (US/1072-3617). **3584**

HOME ECONOMICS. (UK). **2791**

HOME ECONOMIST, THE. (UK). **2791**

HOME EDUCATION MAGAZINE. (US/0888-4633). **Adv Mgr:** Mark Hegener. **1751**

HOME ENERGY (BERKELEY, CALIF.). (US/0896-9442). **Adv Mgr:** Emily Polsby, **Tel** (510)524-5405. **1946**

HOME FURNISHINGS EXECUTIVE (GREENSBORO, N.C.). (US/1073-5585). **2906**

HOME FURNISHINGS REPRESENTATIVES CONTACT. (US/8750-4979). **2906**

HOME HEALTH CARE SERVICES QUARTERLY. (US/0162-1424). **5288**

HOME HEALTH JOURNAL. (US/0734-7588). **3584**

HOME HEALTHCARE NURSE. (US/0884-741X). **3856**

HOME LIFE (NASHVILLE). (US/0018-4071). **5061**

HOME LIGHTING & ACCESSORIES. (US/0162-9077). **2906**

HOME NEWS (BATH, PA.). (US). **Adv Mgr:** Kevin Halbfoerster. **5736**

HOME (ORADELL, N.J.). (US/0278-2839). **2900**

HOME PLANET NEWS. (US/0273-303X). **3394**

HOME PLANNER. (US/1040-547X). **616**

HOME PLANS GUIDE. (US/0899-4374). **300**

HOME PLANS TO BUILD. (US/0899-4366). **300**

HOME POWER. (US/1050-2416). **Adv Mgr:** K. Perez. **1946**

HOME SCHOOL RESEARCHER. (US/1054-8033). **1751**

HOME SHOP MACHINIST, THE. (US/0744-6640). **2115**

HOME TEXTILES TODAY. (US/0195-3184). **5351**

HOMECARE (LOS ANGELES, CALIF.). (US/0882-2700). **5288**

... HOMECARE MARKET REPORT, THE. (US/0882-9152). **3584**

HOMEHEALTH MAGAZINE. (US/0883-0835). **4783**

HOMEMAKER OF THE NATIONAL EXTENSION HOMEMAKERS COUNCIL, THE. (US/0146-9487). **2791**

HOMEMAKER'S MAGAZINE. (CN/0318-7802). **5558**

HOMEOWNER, THE. (US/0747-3176). **616**

HOMER NEWS. (US). **Adv Mgr:** Jane Alberts. **5629**

HOMESCHOOLING TODAY. (US). **Adv Mgr:** Allan Ward. **1751**

HOMESTEAD (KENTVILLE). (CN/0712-6476). **5786**

HOMETOWN PRESS. (US/1064-1742). **Adv Mgr:** Dana Jenson. **2534**

HOMEWORLD BUSINESS. (US/1048-0641). **Adv Mgr:** M. Colangelo. **1608**

HOMILETIC. (US/0738-0534). **4963**

HOMILETIC & PASTORAL REVIEW. (US/0018-4268). **5030**

HOMILY HINTS. (CN/1184-2652). **4963**

HOMINES. (PR/0252-8908). **5201**

HOMME. (FR/0439-4216). **237**

HOMO. (GW/0018-442X). **237**

HONDO ANVIL HERALD, THE. (US). **5751**

HONDURAS ROTARIA. (HO). **680**

HONEY HOLE. (US/0895-4046). **Adv Mgr:** Roger Romines, **Tel** (817)738-5596. **4899**

HONG KONG BUILDER DIRECTORY. (HK). **616**

HONG KONG ELECTRONICS. (HK). **2056**

HONG KONG GIFTS & PREMIUMS. (HK). **2584**

HONG KONG GOVERNMENT GAZETTE, THE. (HK). **4654**

HONG KONG LIBRARY ASSOCIATION JOURNAL. (HK). **3213**

HONG KONG MANAGER. K'O HSUEH KUAN LI. (HK). **869**

HONG KONG MONTHLY DIGEST OF STATISTICS. (HK/0300-418X). **4698**

HONG KONG WATCHES & CLOCKS. (HK). **2916**

HONOLULU. (US/0441-2044). **Adv Mgr:** Mary Meese. **2534**

HONOLULU STAR-BULLETIN. (US). **Adv Mgr:** Howard Mullenary, **Tel** (808)525-7658. **5656**

HONOLULU WEEKLY. (US/1057-414X). **Adv Mgr:** Laurie Carlson. **5656**

HOOF BEATS (COLUMBUS, OHIO). (US/0018-4683). **2799**

HOOFBEATS. (AT/0811-8698). **Adv Mgr:** same as editor. **2799**

HOOK (BONITA, CALIF.), THE. (US/0736-9220). **4177**

HOOKUP. (US). **2305**

HOOSIER CONSERVATION. (US/0199-6894). **2216**

HOOSIER JOURNAL OF ANCESTRY, THE. (US/0147-1228). **2454**

HOOSIER OUTDOORS. (US/0018-4780). **4873**

HOPKINS QUARTERLY. (CN/0094-9086). **3344**

HOPSCOTCH (SARATOGA SPRINGS, N.Y.). (US/1044-0488). **1064**

HORA DE POESIA. (SP/0212-9442). **3464**

HORECO. (SP). **5071**

HOREN : JUNGER LITERATURKREIS, DIE. (GW/0018-4942). **3394**

HORGESCHADIGTEN PADAGOGIK. (GW/0342-4898). **4388**

HORIZONS (GAMBRILLS, MD.). (US/1064-6434). **4388**

HORIZONS (SAINT JOHN. 1982). (CN/0823-2393). **4088**

HORIZONS SF. (CN/0229-1215). **3394**

HORIZONS (VILLANOVA). (US/0360-9669). **4963**

HORIZONTE EMPRESARIAL. (SP/0212-0607). **Adv Mgr:** Rosa Guillen, **Tel** 484-12-00. **1566**

HORMONE RESEARCH. (SZ/0301-0163). **3730**

HORN BOOK GUIDE TO CHILDREN'S AND YOUNG ADULT BOOKS, THE. (US/1044-405X). **1064**

HORN BOOK MAGAZINE (1945), THE. (US/0018-5078). **1064**

HORN CALL, THE. (US/0046-7928). **4121**

HORN OF AFRICA. (US/0161-4703). **2640**

HORNBILL. (II). **457**

HORNERO, EL. (AG/0073-3407). **5586**

HOROLOGICAL JOURNAL. (UK/0018-5108). **Adv Mgr:** Helen Bartlett. **2916**

HOROLOGICAL TIMES. (US/0145-9546). **2916**

HORROR SHOW, THE. (US/0748-2914). **3394**

HORRY INDEPENDENT, THE. (US). **5742**

HORS CADRE. (FR/0755-0863). **4072**

HORS LIGNE. (SZ). **680**

HORSE AND HORSEMAN. (US/0094-3355). **2799**

HORSE & RIDER. (US/0018-5159). **2799**

HORSE AND RIDER (LONDON, ENGLAND). (UK). **2799**

HORSE MAGAZINE. (AT/0817-7686). **2799**

HORSE PLAY. (US/0092-6353). **2799**

HORSE TIMES. (US/0744-4257). **2799**

HORSE WORLD. (US/0018-5191). **2800**

HORSEMEN'S JOURNAL, THE. (US/0018-5256). **2800**

HORSEMEN'S YANKEE PEDLAR. (US/0199-6436). **Adv Mgr:** Kelley Small. **2800**

HORSEPOWER (AURORA). (CN/0840-6715). **Adv Mgr:** V. Mosher. **2800**

HORSES ALL. (CN/0225-4913). **2800**

HORSES (CARLSBAD, CALIF.). (US/0046-7936). **2800**

HORSESHOE PITCHER'S NEWS DIGEST, THE. (US). **4899**

HORSETRADER, THE. (US/0742-7999). **2800**

HORTICULTURAL ABSTRACTS. (UK/0018-5280). **2434**

HORTICULTURAL NEWS (NEW BRUNSWICK, N.J.). (US/0886-5779). **2419**

HORTICULTURE. (US/0018-5329). **2419**

HORTICULTURE IN NEW ZEALAND : JOURNAL OF THE ROYAL NEW ZEALAND INSTITUTE OF HORTICULTURE. (NZ/1170-1803). **2419**

HORTICULTURE REVIEW. (CN/0823-8472). **2419**

HORTICULTURIST/ INSTITUTE OF HORTICULTURE, THE. (UK/0964-8992). **2419**

HORTON HEADLIGHT (HORTON, KAN. : 1933). (US). **Adv Mgr:** Renee Wilburn, **Tel** 486-2512. **5676**

HORTSCIENCE. (US/0018-5345). **2419**

HORTTECHNOLOGY (ALEXANDRIA, VA.). (US/1063-0198). **2419**

HORTUS (FARNHAM). (UK/0950-1657). **2419**

HOSE & NOZZLE (SHREVEPORT). (US/0191-6653). **4260**

HOSPICE JOURNAL, THE. (US/0742-969X). **5288**

HOSPICE LETTER. (US/0193-6816). **3783**

HOSPITAL 2000. (SP/0214-2422). **300**

HOSPITAL & COMMUNITY PSYCHIATRY. (US/0022-1597). **3926**

HOSPITAL — Advertising Accepted Index

HOSPITAL & HEALTHCARE AUSTRALIA. (AT/0813-7471). **3783**

HOSPITAL AND SELECTED MORBIDITY DATA. (NZ/0548-9938). **4810**

HOSPITAL CONTRACTS MANUAL. (US/0734-0028). **2979**

HOSPITAL DOCTOR. (UK/0262-3145). **3584**

HOSPITAL, EL. (US/0018-5485). **3783**

HOSPITAL FUND RAISING NEWSLETTER. (US/0193-9939). **3784**

HOSPITAL GIFT SHOP MANAGEMENT. (US/0738-7946). **869**

HOSPITAL MANAGEMENT INTERNATIONAL / INTERNATIONAL HOSPITAL FEDERATION. (UK/0953-9743). **3784**

HOSPITAL MATERIALS MANAGEMENT. (US/0888-3068). **3784**

HOSPITAL MATERIEL MANAGEMENT QUARTERLY. (US/0192-2262). **3784**

HOSPITAL MEDICINE (NEW YORK, N.Y.). (US/0441-2745). **3584**

HOSPITAL MORBIDITY - CANADIAN CENTRE FOR HEALTH INFORMATION. (CN/1195-4000). **3659**

HOSPITAL NEWS (PITTSBURGH, PA. 1986). (US/1071-0582). **Adv Mgr:** Bob Milie, **Tel** (412)341-1775. **3784**

HOSPITAL PHARMACY (PHILADELPHIA). (US/0018-5787). **4306**

HOSPITAL PHYSICIAN (SURGERY/EMERGENCY/SPECIALTIES ED.). (US/0888-2428). **3584**

HOSPITAL PRACTICE (OFFICE EDITION). (US/8750-2836). **3584**

HOSPITAL PRODUCTS AND TECHNOLOGY. (CN/0823-6798). **3584**

HOSPITAL PURCHASING NEWS. (US/0279-4799). **3785**

HOSPITAL TOPICS. (US/0018-5868). **3785**

HOSPITAL TRUSTEE. (CN/0704-0407). **3785**

HOSPITALITE (TORONTO). (CN/0704-6359). **5071**

HOSPITALITY & TOURISM EDUCATOR. (US). **2806**

HOSPITALS & HEALTH SERVICES YEAR BOOK AND DIRECTORY OF HOSPITAL SUPPLIERS, THE. (UK/0300-5968). **Adv Mgr:** M. Nasser. **3785**

HOSPITALS & HEALTH SERVICES YEARBOOK AUSTRALIA. (AT). **3786**

HOT BOAT. (US/0892-8320). **593**

HOT HOUSE. (US). **4121**

HOT LINE CONSTRUCTION EQUIPMENT MONTHLY UPDATE. (US/1047-4382). **616**

HOT LINE FARM EQUIPMENT GUIDE'S QUICK REFERENCE GUIDE FOR FARM TRACTORS AND COMBINES. (US/0743-7730). **159**

HOT ROD. (US/0018-6031). **5416**

HOT ROD ... ANNUAL. (US/0735-083X). **5416**

HOT ROD MAGAZINE CHEVROLET. (US/0271-0919). **5416**

HOT ROD MAGAZINE ENGINES. (US/0730-4811). **5416**

HOT ROD MAGAZINE KIT CAR. (US/0731-3314). **5416**

HOT SHOE INTERNATIONAL. (UK/0959-6933). **4370**

HOT WIRE. (US/0747-8887). **5558**

HOTEL & CATERING REVIEW (BLACKROCK, DUBLIN). (US/0332-4400). **2806**

HOTEL & MOTEL MANAGEMENT. (US/0018-6082). **2806**

HOTEL & RESORT INDUSTRY. (US/0149-3639). **2806**

HOTEL BUSINESS. (US). **2806**

HOTEL RESTAURANT. (GW). **5071**

HOTEL- UND GASTGEWERBE RUNDSCHAU. (SZ). **2806**

HOTELDOMANI. (IT). **2806**

HOTELS (NEWTON, MASS.). (US/1047-2975). **2807**

HOUALLET. (CN/0714-8275). **2454**

HOUILLE BLANCHE, LA. (FR/0018-6368). **2090**

HOUNDS AND HUNTING. (US/0018-6384). **4286**

HOUR (MONTREAL). (CN/1192-6708). **Adv Mgr:** Claudia Pharand. **2535**

HOUSE & GARDEN (NEW YORK). (US/0018-6406). **2901**

HOUSE BEAUTIFUL. (US/0018-6422). **300**

HOUSE BEAUTIFUL'S HOME BUILDING. (US). **616**

HOUSE BEAUTIFUL'S HOME REMODELING AND DECORATING. (US). **2901**

HOUSE BEAUTIFUL'S HOUSES AND PLANS. (US). **300**

HOUSE BEAUTIFUL'S KITCHENS, BATHS. (US). **2901**

HOUSE BUILDER. (UK). **2824**

HOUSE MAGAZINE. (UK/0309-0426). **4476**

HOUSE PRICES. (UK/0263-3639). **4838**

HOUSE (WESTHAMPTON BEACH, N.Y.). (US/1074-4274). **Adv Mgr Tel** (516)288-5400. **2901**

HOUSEHOLD & PERSONAL PRODUCTS INDUSTRY : HAPPI. (US/0090-8878). **977**

HOUSEPLANT MAGAZINE. (US/1061-4079). **Adv Mgr:** Mark Branciaroli, **Tel** (304)636-1212. **2420**

HOUSING & PLANNING REVIEW. (UK/0018-6589). **2824**

HOUSING (LONDON. 1978). (UK/0261-0280). **Adv Mgr:** H Cox, **Tel** 44 71 8374280. **2824**

HOUSING REVIEW (LONDON). (UK/0018-6651). **2825**

HOUSING STUDIES. (UK/0267-3037). **2825**

HOUSMAN SOCIETY JOURNAL. (UK/0305-926X). **3394**

HOUSTON BUSINESS JOURNAL. (US/0277-4976). **Adv Mgr:** Linda Harris. **680**

HOUSTON INTERNATIONAL BUSINESS DIRECTORY. (US/0197-3630). **680**

HOUSTON LAW REVIEW. (US/0018-6694). **2979**

HOUSTON LAWYER. (US/0439-660X). **Adv Mgr:** Lisa Kennedy, **Tel** (713)236-1048. **2979**

HOUSTON MONTHLY. (US/0272-8060). **2535**

HOUSTON OIL DIRECTORY. (US/0739-3555). **4260**

HOUSTON SUN, THE. (US/1071-2941). **Adv Mgr:** Lonal Robinson. **5751**

HOUSTON TIMES-JOURNAL. (US/1075-1874). **5654**

HOUSTONIAN (HUNTSVILLE, TEX.). (US). **Adv Mgr:** Keri Toma. **5751**

HOWARD COUNTY TIMES (COLUMBIA, MD.). (US/0748-5298). **5686**

HOWARD JOURNAL OF COMMUNICATIONS, THE. (US/1064-6175). **1112**

HOWARD LAW JOURNAL. (US/0018-6813). **2979**

HOWE ENTERPRISE, THE. (US). **Adv Mgr:** Lana Rideout. **5751**

HP PALMTOP PAPER, THE. (US/1065-6189). **1186**

HP PROFESSIONAL. (US/0896-145X). **1186**

HPV NEWS (INDIANAPOLIS, IND.). (US/0898-6894). **1977**

HR/PC. (US/0884-9129). **941**

HSI TUNG KO HSUEH YU SHU HSUEH. (CC/1000-0577). **3508**

HSIEN TAI TUNG HSIN. (CC). **1156**

HSIEN TAI WU LI CHIH SHIH / MODERN PHYSICS. (CC/1001-0610). **4404**

HSUEH PAO (SHAN-TUNG CHUNG I HSUEH YUAN). (CH). **3585**

HUAGONG JIXIE. (CC/0254-6094). **Adv Mgr:** Z. Laimeng. **2013**

HUANJING HUAXUE. (CC/0254-6108). **2173**

HUAXUE SHIJI. (CH/0258-3283). **5365**

HUDSON REGISTER STAR. (US). **Adv Mgr:** Steven Mortefolio. **5717**

HUDSON REVIEW, THE. (US/0018-702X). **322**

HUDSON VALLEY. (US/0191-9288). **2535**

HUDSON VALLEY BUSINESS JOURNAL (ORANGE COUNTY ED.). (US/1050-1096). **680**

HUDSON VALLEY GREEN TIMES. (US/0888-661X). **2173**

HUDSON'S STATE CAPITALS NEWS MEDIA CONTACTS DIRECTORY. (US/0885-1328). **1133**

HUDSON'S SUBSCRIPTION NEWSLETTER DIRECTORY. (US/1046-8110). **2488**

HUDSON'S WASHINGTON NEWS MEDIA CONTACTS DIRECTORY. (US/0441-389X). **2920**

HUGO DAILY NEWS, THE. (US). **Adv Mgr:** Linda Packard. **5732**

HUISARTS NU : MAANDBLAD VAN DE WETENSCHAPPELIJKE VERENIGING DER VLAAMSE HUISARTSEN : HANU. (BE/0775-0501). **Adv Mgr:** Ludo Truyons, **Tel** (03)287-1616. **3738**

HUMAN ANTIBODIES AND HYBRIDOMAS. (US/0956-960X). **Adv Mgr:** M. Rawlins. **457**

HUMAN CAPITAL. (US/1043-8998). **869**

HUMAN DEVELOPMENT. (SZ/0018-716X). **4588**

HUMAN ECOLOGIST, THE. (US/8755-7878). **Adv Mgr:** L. Jones. **5202**

HUMAN EVENTS (WASHINGTON). (US/0018-7194). **4476**

HUMAN EVOLUTION. (IT/0393-9375). **237**

HUMAN GENE THERAPY. (US/1043-0342). **547**

HUMAN HEREDITY. (SZ/0001-5652). **547**

HUMAN IMMUNOLOGY. (US/0198-8859). **3670**

HUMAN ORGANIZATION. (US/0018-7259). **237**

HUMAN PATHOLOGY. (US/0046-8177). **3895**

HUMAN POWER. (US/0898-6908). **1977**

HUMAN REPRODUCTION (OXFORD). (UK/0268-1161). **541**

HUMAN RESOURCE EXECUTIVE. (US/1040-0443). **941**

HUMAN RESOURCE MANAGEMENT. (SA/1010-8092). **Adv Mgr:** same as editor. **941**

HUMAN RESOURCE MANAGEMENT YEARBOOK, THE. (UK). **942**

HUMAN RESOURCES PROFESSIONAL. (CN/0847-9453). **Adv Mgr:** Marta Pawych. **942**

HUMAN RESOURCES PROFESSIONAL (NEW YORK, N.Y.), THE. (US/1040-5232). **942**

HUMAN RIGHTS (CHICAGO, ILL.). (US/0046-8185). **2979**

HUMAN RIGHTS LAW JOURNAL : HRLJ. (GW/0174-4704). **3129**

HUMAN RIGHTS QUARTERLY. (US/0275-0392). **4509**

HUMAN SERVICES IN THE RURAL ENVIRONMENT. (US/0193-9009). **5288**

HUMAN SYSTEMS MANAGEMENT. (NE/0167-2533). **5111**

HUMANE MEDICINE. (CN/0828-7090). **3585**

HUMANIST (BUFFALO, N.Y.), THE. (US/0018-7399). **4348**

HUMANIST IN CANADA. (CN). **Adv Mgr:** Dan Morrison, **Tel** (613)225-7216. **4348**

HUMANISTIC PSYCHOLOGIST, THE. (US/0887-3267). **4589**

HUMANITAS (BRESCIA, ITALY). (IT). **4348**

HUMANITIES EDUCATION. (US/0882-5475). **2847**

HUMBOLDT BEACON AND FORTUNA ADVANCE, THE. (US/0746-777X). **5635**

HUMBOLDT SUN. (US). **5707**

HUME PAPERS ON PUBLIC POLICY. (UK). **Adv Mgr:** Kathryn MacLean. **4655**

HUME STUDIES. (US/0319-7336). **Adv Mgr Tel** (801)261-8971. **4348**

HUMPTY DUMPTY'S MAGAZINE. (US/0273-7590). **1064**

HUNGARIAN CINEMA. (HU). **4072**

HUNGARIAN ECONOMIC REVIEW : HER. (HU/1215-2439). **839**

HUNGARIAN HERITAGE REVIEW. (US/0889-2695). **2263**

HUNGARIAN JOURNAL OF INDUSTRIAL CHEMISTRY. (HU/0133-0276). **977**

HUNGARIAN LIBRARY AND INFORMATION SCIENCE ABSTRACTS. (HU/0046-8304). **3258**

HUNGARIAN STUDIES NEWSLETTER. (US/0194-164X). **2692**

HUNGER NOTES. (US/0740-1116). **2910**

HUNGRY MIND REVIEW. (US/0887-5499). **Adv Mgr:** Philip Patrick. **4829**

HUNT. (US). **4873**

HUNTERDON COUNTY DEMOCRAT. (US/0018-7844). **Adv Mgr:** A. Angreli, **Tel** (908)782-4747 Ext 631. **5710**

HUNTER'S HORN, THE. (US/0018-7860). **4899**

HUNTING HORIZONS. (US/1059-3837). **Adv Mgr:** Jana Kosco. **4873**

HUNTING (NEW YORK, N.Y.). (US/0276-8895). **4899**

HUNTSVILLE TIMES, THE. (US). **Adv Mgr:** J. Michael Venable, **Tel** (205)532-4450. **5627**

HURON SOIL AND CROP NEWS (1964). (CN/0319-6038). **173**

HURRICANE ALICE. (US/0882-7907). **Adv Mgr:** Jayne Paynek. **5558**

Advertising Accepted Index ILLINOIS

HUSSERL STUDIES. (NE/0167-9848). **4348**

HUSTLER (COLUMBUS). (US/0149-4635). **3995**

HUSTLER, THE. (US/1074-0236). **760**

HUTCHINSON LEADER. (US). **5696**

HUTCHINSON NEWS (HUTCHINSON, KAN. : 1957). (US). **Adv Mgr:** Debbie Lemen. **5676**

HUTOIPAR. (HU/0018-8085). **2343**

HUTTON CONSTRUCTION CATALOG : MECHANICAL PRODUCTS. (US/0737-6316). **2115**

HYBRID CIRCUIT TECHNOLOGY. (US/0747-1599). **5111**

HYBRID CIRCUITS : JOURNAL OF THE INTERNATIONAL SOCIETY FOR HYBRID MICROELECTRONICS-UK / INTERNATIONAL SOCIETY FOR HYBRID ELECTRONICS, UNITED KINGDOM. (UK/0265-3028). **2056**

HYBRIDOMA. (US/0272-457X). **3670**

HYDATA NEWS AND VIEWS. (US). **5534**

HYDE PARK TRIBUNE, THE MATTAPAN TRIBUNE. (US/0745-9262). **Adv Mgr:** K. Willette. **5689**

HYDROBIOLOGIA. (NE/0018-8158). **457**

HYDROBIOLOGICAL BULLETIN. (NE/0165-1404). **457**

HYDROBIOLOGICAL JOURNAL. (US/0018-8166). **457**

HYDROBIOLOGICAL STUDIES. (XR/0577-3644). **1414**

HYDROCARBON PROCESSING (U.S. ED.). (US/0887-0284). **4260**

HYDROGRAPHIC JOURNAL. (UK/0309-7846). **1414**

HYDROLOGICAL PROCESSES. (UK/0885-6087). **1414**

HYDROLOGICAL SCIENCES JOURNAL. (UK/0262-6667). **1415**

HYDROMETALLURGY. (NE/0304-386X). **4003**

HYGIE. (FR/0751-7149). **4783**

HYGIENE + MEDIZIN. (GW/0172-3790). **3585**

HYMN, THE. (US/0018-8271). **4121**

HYPATIA (EDWARDSVILLE, ILL.). (US/0887-5367). **5558**

HYPERLINK MAGAZINE. (US/1045-4624). **1186**

HYPERTENSION (DALLAS, TEX. 1979). (US/0194-911X). **3705**

HYPERTENSION RESEARCH, CLINICAL AND EXPERIMENTAL. (JA/0916-9636). **3706**

HYSTERIA (KITCHENER). (CN/0229-5385). **5558**

I A S M H F NEWSLETTER. (US). **4089**

I & P. (FR). **4523**

I.C.I.D. BULLETIN. (II/0300-2810). **2090**

I C O M NEWS. (FR/0018-8999). **4089**

I.D.E.A.S. INTERIORS, DESIGN, ENVIRONMENT, ARTS, STRUCTURES. (US/0161-1895). **Adv Mgr:** R. Rachlin. **2901**

I-D MAGAZINE. (UK). **Adv Mgr:** Jo Peters. **1064**

I/O NEWS. (US/0274-9998). **1267**

I YUAN TO YING. (CC). **322**

IA. INGEGNERIA AMBIENTALE. (IT/0394-5871). **2232**

IA, THE JOURNAL OF THE SOCIETY FOR INDUSTRIAL ARCHEOLOGY. (US/0160-1040). **269**

IACD QUARTERLY. (US/8756-2189). **4589**

IACEE NEWSLETTER. (FI/0786-9916). **1977**

IAEI NEWS. (US/0020-5974). **2290**

IAHPER JOURNAL, THE. (US). **1855**

IAHR BULLETIN. (NE). **2090**

IAJRC JOURNAL. (US/0098-9487). **4122**

IALL JOURNAL OF LANGUAGE LEARNING TECHNOLOGIES, THE. (US/1050-0049). **3286**

IAPA NEWS. (US/0018-8409). **2920**

IAS NEWSLETTER (INTERNATIONAL ASSOCIATION OF SEDIMENTOLOGISTS). (DK). **1382**

IASLIC BULLETIN. (II/0018-8441). **3214**

IBERO-AMERIKANISCHES ARCHIV. (GW/0340-3068). **2738**

IBEROAMERICANA. (GW/0342-1864). **2738**

IBI DIENST. (GW/0946-4441). **2920**

IBIS LINKS. (AT/0811-5559). **2454**

IBIS (LONDON, ENGLAND). (UK/0019-1019). **5617**

IBIS REVIEW. (US). **2882**

IBRO NEWS. (US/0361-0713). **3834**

IC MASTER. (US/0894-6809). **2057**

ICARBS. (US/0360-8409). **3214**

ICB. INTERNATIONAL CARPET BULLETIN. (UK/0268-2966). **Adv Mgr:** Julie Smith, **Tel** same as publisher. **5351**

ICC BUSINESS WORLD : MAGAZINE OF THE INTERNATIONAL CHAMBER OF COMMERCE. (FR). **820**

ICE. (UK/0019-1043). **1415**

ICE CREAM AND FROZEN CONFECTIONERY. (UK). **2343**

ICE RIVER. (US/1043-7010). **3395**

ICELAND REVIEW (REYKJAVIK, ICELAND : 1984). (IC/0019-1094). **2692**

ICELANDIC CANADIAN. (CN/0046-8452). **Adv Mgr:** Rosemary Isford, **Tel** (204)284-2169. **2263**

ICES JOURNAL. (US/0882-2115). **2024**

ICIDH AND ENVIRONMENTAL FACTORS INTERNATIONAL NETWORK. (CN/1198-3795). **Adv Mgr Tel** (418)529-9141 ext. 6274. **5289**

ICIDH INTERNATIONAL NETWORK. (CN/1182-5049). **5289**

ICL TECHNICAL JOURNAL. (UK/0142-1557). **1187**

ICLAS NEWS. (FI/1018-4635). **5111**

ICLAS NEWS. (FI/1018-4635). **5511**

ICO. INTELLIGENCE ARTIFICIELLE ET SCIENCES COGNITIVES AU QUEBEC. (CN/1189-6078). **5111**

ICP INFORMATION NEWSLETTER. (US/0161-6951). **1015**

ICPS NEWLETTER / INSTITUTE FOR CULTURAL POLICY STUDIES. (AT). **Adv Mgr:** Sharon Clifford. **5268**

ICSID REVIEW. (US/0258-3690). **3129**

ICSSR JOURNAL OF ABSTRACTS AND REVIEWS : ECONOMICS. (II). **1533**

ICSSR JOURNAL OF ABSTRACTS AND REVIEWS: GEOGRAPHY. (II). **2565**

ICSSR JOURNAL OF ABSTRACTS AND REVIEWS : POLITICAL SCIENCE. (II/0250-9660). **4476**

ICSSR JOURNAL OF ABSTRACTS AND REVIEWS. SOCIOLOGY AND SOCIAL ANTHROPOLOGY / INDIAN COUNCIL OF SOCIAL SCIENCE RESEARCH. (II). **5202**

ICSSR RESEARCH ABSTRACTS QUARTERLY. (II). **5202**

ID SYSTEM BUYER'S GUIDE. (US/1043-8319). **1494**

ID SYSTEMS. (US/0892-676X). **5111**

IDA COUNTY PIONEER RECORD. (US). **5670**

IDAHO BUSINESS REVIEW, THE. (US/8750-4022). **Adv Mgr:** Kitty Fleischman. **681**

IDAHO CITIES. (US). **4655**

IDAHO ENTERPRISE, THE. (US). **5656**

IDAHO FARMER-STOCKMAN. (US/1041-1682). **212**

IDAHO FRUIT TREE CENSUS / U.S. DEPARTMENT OF AGRICULTURE, ECONOMICS AND STATISTICS SERVICE AND IDAHO DEPARTMENT OF AGRICULTURE. (US). **2420**

IDAHO GENEALOGICAL SOCIETY QUARTERLY. (US/0445-2127). **2454**

IDAHO LAW REVIEW. (US/0019-1205). **2979**

IDAHO LIBRARIAN, THE. (US/0019-1213). **Adv Mgr:** Diane Prorak, **Tel** (208)885-6235. **3214**

IDAHO MOUNTAIN EXPRESS. (US/0279-8964). **5656**

IDAHO PRESS-TRIBUNE. (US). **Adv Mgr:** John Rybarczyk. **5657**

IDAHO STATE JOURNAL. (US). **5657**

IDAHO STATESMAN, THE. (US). **Adv Mgr:** Debbie Pantenburg, **Tel** (208)377-6358. **5657**

IDAHO WOOL GROWER'S BULLETIN. (US). **212**

IDEA. (JA/0019-1299). **380**

IDEA INK. (US/8755-6871). **5030**

IDEA (ROME). (IT/0019-1280). **2620**

IDEA SPEKTRUM. (GW). **4964**

IDEA TODAY. (US/1040-8126). **1313**

IDEAL TRAVELER. (US/1055-8314). **5480**

IDEAS '92: A PUBLICATION OF THE 1992 INSTITUTE. (US). **2620**

IDEAS AND DEBATES : A JOURNAL OF ART WRITING. (CN). **352**

IDEAS EN ARTE Y TECNOLOGIA / UNIVERSIDAD DE BELGRANO. (AG/0326-3878). **300**

IDEAS EN CIENCIAS SOCIALES / UNIVERSIDAD DE BELGRANO. (AG/0326-386X). **5202**

IDENTIFICATION JOURNAL. (US/0747-962X). **870**

IDENTITY (CINCINNATI, OHIO). (US/0899-3483). **380**

IDF BULLETIN. (US/0306-4980). **3731**

IDIOM 23. (AT/1032-1640). **3395**

IDISHER KEMFER. (US/1050-5296). **2504**

IDLER (TORONTO). (CN/0828-1289). **2535**

IDOJARAS (BUDAPEST 1897). (HU/0367-7443). **1426**

IDR. INDUSTRIAL DIAMOND REVIEW. (UK/0019-8145). **2115**

IDS BULLETIN (UNIVERSITY OF SUSSEX. INSTITUTE OF DEVELOPMENT STUDIES : 1985). (UK). **1494**

IDYLLWILD TOWN CRIER. (US). **Adv Mgr:** Lisa Swett. **5635**

IE, INVESTMENT EXECUTIVE. (CN/0840-9137). **Adv Mgr:** B. Hyland. **900**

IEE NEWS. (UK/0308-0684). **2057**

IEE PROCEEDINGS. PART H, MICROWAVES, ANTENNAS, AND PROPAGATION. (UK/0950-107X). **2058**

IEE PRODUCTRONIC. (GW). **2058**

IEEE BULLETIN. (US/0162-3842). **2059**

IEEE COMPUTER GRAPHICS AND APPLICATIONS. (US/0272-1716). **1233**

IEEE DESIGN & TEST OF COMPUTERS. (US/0740-7475). **1229**

IEEE EXPERT. (US/0885-9000). **1229**

IEEE MICRO. (US/0272-1732). **1267**

IEEE SOFTWARE. (US/0740-7459). **1286**

IFCO NEWS. (US/1065-1675). **4964**

IFDA DOSSIER / INTERNATIONAL FOUNDATION FOR DEVELOPMENT ALTERNATIVES. (SZ). **4523**

IFLA JOURNAL. (GW/0340-0352). **3214**

IFO SCHNELLDIENST. (GW/0018-974X). **681**

IFW. INTERNATIONAL FREIGHTING WEEKLY. (UK/0032-5007). **5383**

IGIENE E SANITA PUBBLICA. (IT/0019-1639). **4783**

IGIENE MODERNA. (IT/0019-1655). **4783**

IIC DOCUMENT SERVICE. (US/0738-7938). **1113**

IIC; INTERNATIONAL REVIEW OF INDUSTRIAL AND COPYRIGHT LAW. (GW/0018-9855). **1304**

IIMS, INDONESIA INDEX OF MEDICAL SPECIALITIES. (SI/0300-4147). **4307**

IIPA NEWSLETTER. (II/0536-1761). **4655**

IKUSHUGAKU ZASSHI. (JA/0536-3683). **94**

ILCA RESEARCH REPORT / INTERNATIONAL LIVESTOCK CENTRE FOR AFRICA. (ET). **212**

ILE CAMERA. (US). **Adv Mgr:** L. Atkinson. **5692**

ILGA PINK BOOK. (NE). **2794**

ILLINOIAN-STAR DAILY. (US). **Adv Mgr:** Lillian Mitchell. **5660**

ILLINOIS AGRI-NEWS. (US/0194-7443). **94**

ILLINOIS ARCHITECTURE REFERENCE DIRECTORY, THE. (US/0747-6345). **300**

ILLINOIS AUDUBON. (US/1061-9801). **4166**

ILLINOIS AVIATION (SPRINGFIELD, ILL. : 1979). (US/0276-640X). **23**

ILLINOIS BANKER. (US/0019-185X). **Adv Mgr:** Ms. Richle. **790**

ILLINOIS BAR JOURNAL. (US/0019-1876). **2980**

ILLINOIS BEVERAGE JOURNAL. (US/0019-1892). **2367**

ILLINOIS CONSTRUCTION LAW. (US/8755-691X). **2980**

ILLINOIS COUNTY AND TOWNSHIP OFFICIAL. (US/0019-1949). **Adv Mgr:** Bryan E. Smith. **4655**

ILLINOIS DENTAL JOURNAL. (US/0019-1973). **1324**

ILLINOIS ENGINEER. (US/0019-2015). **1977**

ILLINOIS ISSUES. (US/0738-9663). **4476**

ILLINOIS JOURNAL OF HEALTH, PHYSICAL EDUCATION, RECREATION, AND DANCE. (US/1062-2764). **Adv Mgr:** Bonnie, **Tel** (309)274-2049. **1751**

ILLINOIS MAGAZINE. (US/0747-9794). **2738**

ILLINOIS — Advertising Accepted Index

ILLINOIS MANUFACTURERS DIRECTORY. (US/0160-3302). **3480**

ILLINOIS MASTER PLUMBER. (US/0019-2112). **2606**

ILLINOIS MEDICINE. (US/1044-6400). **Adv Mgr:** Carla Nolen. **3585**

ILLINOIS MUSIC EDUCATOR, THE. (US/0019-2147). **4122**

ILLINOIS PARKS & RECREATION. (US/0019-2155). **4706**

ILLINOIS PHARMACIST (1979). (US/0195-2099). **4307**

ILLINOIS PRINCIPAL. (US/0019-218X). **1864**

ILLINOIS PSYCHOLOGIST : NEWSLETTER OF THE ILLINOIS PSYCHOLOGICAL ASSOCIATION. (US/0019-2198). **4589**

ILLINOIS REVIEW, THE. (US/1067-4128). **3344**

ILLINOIS SCHOOL BOARD JOURNAL. (US/0019-221X). **Adv Mgr:** Ruth Ann Ferris. **1864**

ILLINOIS SCHOOL RESEARCH AND DEVELOPMENT. (US/0163-822X). **1751**

ILLINOIS SERVICES DIRECTORY. (US/0092-3818). **1609**

ILLINOIS TIMES. (US/0199-7823). **Adv Mgr:** Simon Mulverhill. **5660**

ILLINOIS WILDLIFE. (US/0019-2317). **2195**

ILLINOIS WRITERS REVIEW. (US/0733-9526). **3344**

ILLNESS CRISIS & LOSS. (US/1054-1373). **Adv Mgr:** C. Drivas, **Tel** (215)925-3995. **2251**

ILLUSTRATED DIRECTORY OF HANDICAPPED PRODUCTS, THE. (US/1053-6035). **4389**

ILLUSTRATED LONDON NEWS, THE. (UK/0019-2422). **2517**

ILLUSTRATOR, THE. (US/0019-2465). **380**

ILMU MASYARAKAT : TERBITAN PERSATUAN SAINS SOSIAL MALAYSIA. (MY). **5203**

ILP MAGAZINE. (UK/0951-2187). **1677**

ILVS REVIEW. (US/1043-3023). **Adv Mgr:** P. Hinske, **Tel** (414)238-1916. **4089**

IMA JOURNAL OF APPLIED MATHEMATICS. (UK/0272-4960). **3508**

IMA JOURNAL OF MATHEMATICAL CONTROL AND INFORMATION. (UK/0265-0754). **3508**

IMA JOURNAL OF MATHEMATICS APPLIED IN MEDICINE AND BIOLOGY. (UK/0265-0746). **3508**

IMA JOURNAL OF NUMERICAL ANALYSIS. (UK/0272-4979). **3508**

IMAGE AND VISION COMPUTING. (UK/0262-8856). **1233**

IMAGE DE LA MAURICIE. (CN/0704-7428). **5480**

IMAGE TECHNOLOGY (LONDON). (UK/0950-2114). **4072**

IMAGE--THE JOURNAL OF NURSING SCHOLARSHIP. (US/0743-5150). **3857**

IMAGE (VANCOUVER). (CN/0383-9710). **3586**

IMAGEN (SAN JUAN, P.R.). (PR/0890-6548). **Adv Mgr:** Arnaldo Jimenez. **2488**

IMAGES (NELSON). (CN/0384-5990). **5558**

IMAGES (RESTON, VA.). (US/1055-1476). **Adv Mgr Tel** (708)571-9072. **3941**

IMAGINE (MONTREAL). (CN/0709-8855). **3395**

IMAGING SERVICE BUREAU NEWS. (US/1055-8098). **1609**

IMAGING UPDATE. (US/0889-9142). **4565**

IMAGINGWORLD (CAMDEN, ME.). (US/1060-894X). **Adv Mgr Tel** (207)236-8524. **4212**

IMAGO MUNDI (LYMPNE). (UK/0308-5694). **2582**

IMBALLAGGIO : ORGANO UFFICIALE DELL'ISTITUTO ITALIANO IMBALLAGGIO. (IT/0019-2708). **5112**

IMC JOURNAL. (US/0019-0012). **Adv Mgr:** Chris Lacy. **4212**

IMFAMA. (SA/0019-2724). **Adv Mgr:** same as editor. **4389**

IMM ABSTRACTS. (UK/0019-0020). **4003**

IMMAGINE RIFLESSA, L'. (IT). **3395**

IMMIGRANTS & MINORITIES. (UK/0261-9288). **Adv Mgr:** Anne Kidson. **1919**

IMMIGRATION LAW REPORTER (DON MILLS). (CN/0835-3808). **2980**

IMMUNOBIOLOGY (1979). (GW/0171-2985). **3670**

IMMUNOCLONES. (FR/0994-9895). **458**

IMMUNOHEMATOLOGY. (US/0894-203X). **3772**

IMMUNOLOGICAL REVIEWS. (DK/0105-2896). **3671**

IMMUNOLOGY. (UK/0019-2805). **3671**

IMMUNOLOGY & ALLERGY PRACTICE. (US/0194-7508). **3671**

IMMUNOLOGY AND INFECTIOUS DISEASES. (UK/0959-4957). **3671**

IMMUNOLOGY TODAY (AMSTERDAM. REGULAR ED.). (UK/0167-5699). **3671**

IMMUNOPHARMACOLOGY. (US/0162-3109). **3672**

IMP, INDUSTRIAL MODELS & PATTERNS. (US/0146-0161). **3481**

IMPACT / ACADEMY OF GENERAL DENTISTRY. (US). **Adv Mgr:** Todd Goldman, **Tel** (813)264-2772. **1324**

IMPACT INTERNATIONAL. (UK/0046-8703). **4523**

IMPACT (MANILA). (PH/0300-4155). **5203**

IMPACT PUMP NEWS & PATENTS. (US/1056-1536). **2115**

IMPACT SINGAPORE. (SI/0129-2862). **4964**

IMPACT VALVE NEWS & PATENTS. (US/1056-1544). **2115**

IMPACT YEARBOOK. (US/0749-7946). **2367**

IMPART. (AT/0813-6939). **3214**

IMPERIAL QUARTERLY MAGAZINE. (CN/1188-0066). **2517**

IMPERIAL VALLEY PRESS. (US). **Adv Mgr:** John Yanni. **5635**

IMPIANTISTICA ITALIANA. (IT/0394-1582). **617**

IMPLEMENT & TRACTOR. (US/0019-2953). **159**

IMPOR MENURUT JENIS BARANG DAN NEGERI ASAL. (IO). **839**

IMPORT AUTOMOTIVE PARTS & ACCESSORIES. (US/0199-4468). **Adv Mgr:** Lana Meyers, **Tel** (818)761-4272. **5416**

IMPORTED CARS & TRUCKS, ELECTRICAL SERVICE & REPAIR. (US). **5416**

IMPORTED CARS & TRUCKS, TRANSMISSION SERVICE & REPAIR. (US/0741-0158). **5416**

IMPORTWEEK. (CN/0702-8385). **839**

IMPRESA. (IT/0035-6816). **1609**

IMPRINT (NEW YORK, NEW YORK). (US/0019-3062). **3857**

IMPRINT (WATERLOO). (CN/0706-7380). **1829**

IMPRINTING BUSINESS. (US/1066-7083). **1085**

IMPROVISOR. (US/0892-1911). **Adv Mgr:** LaDonna Smith, **Tel** (205)930-0914. **4122**

IMSA JOURNAL. (US/1064-2560). **Adv Mgr:** Sharon Earl. **5441**

IN BUSINESS. (US/0190-2458). **2232**

IN DANCE. (US/0883-9956). **1313**

IN DEPTH (WASHINGTON, D.C.). (US/1055-9809). **Adv Mgr:** Larry Orman, **Tel** (202)293-7443. **4476**

IN FACT (MILWAUKEE, WIS.). (US). **2980**

IN-FISHERMAN, THE. (US/0276-9905). **Adv Mgr:** Jim Bessenfelder. **2305**

IN JOPLIN METROPOLITAN. (US/0743-1503). **5480**

IN OTHER WORDS NUNAWADING. (AT/1036-1421). **Adv Mgr:** same as editor. **3286**

IN-PLANT PRINTER & ELECTRONIC PUBLISHER. (US/0891-8996). **4565**

IN PRACTICE (LONDON 1979). (UK/0263-841X). **5511**

IN SITU. (US/0146-2520). **1440**

IN THE MARKETPLACE. (US/1064-0649). **Adv Mgr:** Roy Taylor. **4964**

IN THEORY ONLY. (US/0360-4365). **4122**

IN THESE TIMES. (US/0160-5992). **Adv Mgr:** Bruce Embry. **5203**

IN TRANSIT (WASHINGTON). (US/0019-3291). **5384**

IN VIVO (ATHENS). (GR/0258-851X). **458**

IN VIVO (NEW YORK, N.Y.). (US/0733-1398). **681**

INA NEWSLETTER. (UK/0255-013X). **4227**

INA NEWSLETTER / INTERNATIONAL NANNOPLANKTON ASSOCIATION. (NE). **4231**

INCAST (DALLAS, TEX.). (US/1045-5779). **4003**

INCENTIVE MARKETING AND SALES PROMOTION: ANNUAL REVIEW AND BUYERS' GUIDE. (UK). **760**

INCHIESTA. (IT). **Adv Mgr:** R. Coga. **5247**

INCIDENTS OF THE WAR. (US). **4370**

INCIPIT. (AG/0326-0941). **3395**

INCITE (SYDNEY). (AT/0158-0876). **3214**

INCL JOURNAL. (US/0270-2061). **2980**

INCREDIBLE HULK, THE. (US/0274-5275). **4862**

INCREMENTAL MOTION CONTROL SYSTEMS AND DEVICES NEWSLETTER. (US/0362-3858). **2064**

INDAGINI E QUADERNI. (IT). **3344**

INDEPENDENCE. (AT). **Adv Mgr:** Janine Watson Chevron, **Tel** 011 03 3295844. **1751**

INDEPENDENT ADJUSTER, THE. (US). **Adv Mgr:** Duane Brady, **Tel** (206)624-6965. **2882**

INDEPENDENT BANKER. (US/0019-3674). **Adv Mgr:** F Moeckel, **Tel** (301)469-0800. **790**

INDEPENDENT BAPTIST VOICE, THE. (US/8756-1816). **5061**

INDEPENDENT DEMOCRAT (WAVERLY). (US). **Adv Mgr:** Jayne Thomas Hall. **5670**

INDEPENDENT ENERGY. (US/1043-7320). **Adv Mgr:** Rick Huntzicker, **Tel** (612)983-6892. **1946**

INDEPENDENT LIVING. (AT/0815-2276). **Adv Mgr:** Maria Hermanson, **Tel** (07)341-0461. **4389**

INDEPENDENT (LONDON, ENGLAND). (UK). **5812**

INDEPENDENT MONTHLY, THE. (AT/1033-9957). **Adv Mgr:** Steve Congerton. **4476**

INDEPENDENT (NEW YORK, N.Y. : 1978). (US/0731-5198). **Adv Mgr:** Laura Davis, **Tel** (212)473-3400. **4072**

INDEPENDENT NEWSPAPER FROM RUSSIA. (US/1064-4431). **Adv Mgr:** Cynthia Neu, **Tel** (703)827-0414. **5759**

INDEPENDENT-OBSERVER (CONRAD, MONT.). (US). **Adv Mgr:** Pat Loran. **5705**

INDEPENDENT-OBSERVER (SCOTTDALE, PA.). (US). **Adv Mgr:** Bob Cummingham or Peggy Milliron, **Tel** (412)887-6102. **5736**

INDEPENDENT PRESS (BLOOMFIELD, N.J.). (US/0747-4075). **Adv Mgr:** Peter Worrall, **Tel** (908)686-7700. **5710**

INDEPENDENT REPUBLICAN. (US/8750-2364). **4476**

INDEPENDENT REPUBLICAN, 1812. (US). **Adv Mgr:** E. Wright, **Tel** (914)294-6111 ext.3. **2488**

INDEPENDENT (ROBERTSDALE, ALA.). (US). **Adv Mgr:** Jeniece Hooper, **Tel** (205)947-7712. **5627**

INDEPENDENT SCHOLAR, THE. (US/1066-5633). **1829**

INDEPENDENT SCHOOL (BOSTON, MASS.). (US/0145-9635). **Adv Mgr:** Rob Whitmore. **1751**

INDEPENDENT SENIOR, THE. (CN/0847-5288). **Adv Mgr:** Phil Vachon. **5179**

INDEPENDENT SHAVIAN, THE. (US/0019-3763). **3396**

INDEPENDENT TEACHER FORTITUDE VALLEY. (AT/1033-2464). **Adv Mgr:** Terry Burke. **1896**

INDEX COMMERCIAL DE MONTREAL. (CN/0821-7254). **839**

INDEX INDIA. (II/0019-3844). **417**

INDEX INDO-ASIATICUS. (II/0019-3852). **2653**

INDEX INTERNATIONALIS INDICUS. (II). **5021**

INDEX-JOURNAL, THE. (US/0747-0231). **Adv Mgr:** Harry L. Garrett. **5742**

INDEX OF CONFERENCE PROCEEDINGS. ANNUAL CUMULATION. (UK/0959-4906). **3214**

INDEX OF CONFERENCE PROCEEDINGS RECEIVED. (UK). **3214**

INDEX OF CURRENT RESEARCH ON PIGS / AGRICULTURAL RESEARCH COUNCIL. (UK/0568-2800). **94**

INDEX OF ISLAMIC LITERATURE. (UK). **3458**

INDEX OF STATISTICS PUBLISHED BY THE DEPARTMENT OF HEALTH / NATIONAL HEALTH STATISTICS CENTRE, DEPARTMENT OF HEALTH (NEW ZEALAND). (NZ). **4810**

INDEX OF VETERINARY SPECIALITIES. (UK/0019-3941). **5511**

INDEX ON CENSORSHIP. (UK/0306-4220). **3344**

INDEX TO BOOK REVIEWS IN RELIGION. (US/0887-1574). **5012**

INDEX TO FREE PERIODICALS. (US/0147-5630). **2496**

INDEX TO INDIAN ECONOMIC JOURNALS. (II/0019-4026). **1494**

INDEX TO INDIAN LEGAL PERIODICALS. (II/0019-4034). **2981**

INDEX TO PERIODICAL ARTICLES RELATED TO LAW. (US/0019-4093). **3081**

INDEX TO REPRODUCTIONS IN ART PERIODICALS : IRAP. (US/0893-0139). **352**

INDEX VETERINARIUS. (UK/0019-4123). **5528**

INDEXER. (UK/0019-4131). **3215**

INDIA, A REFERENCE ANNUAL. (II/0073-6090). **2653**

INDIA ABROAD. (US/0046-8932). **2263**

INDIA CALLING. (II). **1133**

INDIA CURRENTS. (US/0896-095X). **2488**

INDIA INTERNATIONAL CENTRE QUARTERLY. (II/0376-9771). **2653**

INDIA LEATHER & LEATHER PRODUCTS DIRECTORY. (II/0376-978X). **3184**

INDIA MAGAZINE OF HER PEOPLE AND CULTURE, THE. (II). **2263**

INDIA TODAY. (II). **2504**

INDIA TODAY (INTERNATIONAL ED). (II). **2488**

INDIA-WEST. (US/0883-721X). **Adv Mgr:** Prem Dutt, **Tel** (510)652-9064. **5636**

INDIA WHO'S WHO. (II/0073-6244). **433**

INDIAN ANTHROPOLOGIST. (II). **238**

INDIAN-ARTIFACT MAGAZINE. (US/0736-265X). **Adv Mgr:** JoAnne Fogelman. **270**

INDIAN BEE JOURNAL. (II/0019-4425). **94**

INDIAN BOOK INDUSTRY. (II/0019-4433). **4829**

INDIAN BOOK REVIEW. (II). **4829**

INDIAN CASHEW JOURNAL. (II/0019-4484). **2344**

INDIAN CERAMICS. (II/0019-4492). **Adv Mgr:** Ms. Suchhandadas. **2591**

INDIAN CHEMICAL ENGINEER. (II/0019-4506). **2013**

INDIAN CHURCH HISTORY REVIEW. (II/0019-4530). **4964**

INDIAN COFFEE. (II/0019-4549). **174**

INDIAN CONCRETE JOURNAL, THE. (II/0019-4565). **617**

INDIAN COUNTRY TODAY. (US/1066-5501). **Adv Mgr:** John Painter. **5743**

INDIAN DAIRYMAN. (II/0019-4603). **195**

INDIAN DISSERTATION ABSTRACTS. (II). **5203**

INDIAN ECONOMIC AND SOCIAL HISTORY REVIEW, THE. (II/0019-4646). **1566**

INDIAN ENERGY AND POWER UPDATE. (II). **1946**

INDIAN EXPORT TRADE JOURNAL, THE. (II/0019-4735). **4523**

INDIAN EXPORT YEAR-BOOK. (II). **840**

INDIAN FARMING. (II/0019-4786). **94**

INDIAN FOOD INDUSTRY. (II/0253-5025). **2344**

INDIAN FOOD PACKER. (II/0019-4808). **2344**

INDIAN FORESTER, THE. (II/0019-4816). **2384**

INDIAN GEOGRAPHICAL JOURNAL, THE. (II/0019-4824). **2566**

INDIAN HIGHWAYS. (II/0376-7256). **5441**

INDIAN HISTORICAL REVIEW, THE. (II/0376-9836). **2653**

INDIAN HISTORY AND GENEALOGY. (US). **2454**

INDIAN HORTICULTURE. (II/0019-4875). **2420**

INDIAN JOURNAL OF ADULT EDUCATION. (US/0019-5006). **1801**

INDIAN JOURNAL OF AGRICULTURAL ECONOMICS, THE. (II/0019-5014). **94**

INDIAN JOURNAL OF AGRICULTURAL RESEARCH. (II/0367-8245). **95**

INDIAN JOURNAL OF AGRICULTURAL SCIENCES, THE. (II/0019-5022). **95**

INDIAN JOURNAL OF AGRONOMY. (II/0537-197X). **95**

INDIAN JOURNAL OF AMERICAN STUDIES. (II/0019-5030). **2738**

INDIAN JOURNAL OF ANIMAL HEALTH. (II/0019-5057). **5511**

INDIAN JOURNAL OF APPLIED LINGUISTICS. (II/0379-0037). **3286**

INDIAN JOURNAL OF BEHAVIOUR. (II/0970-0897). **4589**

INDIAN JOURNAL OF BOTANY. (II/0250-829X). **513**

INDIAN JOURNAL OF CANCER. (II/0019-509X). **3818**

INDIAN JOURNAL OF CHEST DISEASES & ALLIED SCIENCES, THE. (II/0377-9343). **3706**

INDIAN JOURNAL OF CLINICAL PSYCHOLOGY. (II/0303-2582). **4589**

INDIAN JOURNAL OF CRYOGENICS. (II/0379-0479). **4405**

INDIAN JOURNAL OF DAIRY SCIENCE. (II/0019-5146). **195**

INDIAN JOURNAL OF DERMATOLOGY. (II/0019-5154). **3720**

INDIAN JOURNAL OF DERMATOLOGY, VENEREOLOGY AND LEPROLOGY. (II/0378-6323). **3720**

INDIAN JOURNAL OF ECONOMICS. (II/0019-5170). **1494**

INDIAN JOURNAL OF ENVIRONMENTAL HEALTH. (II/0367-827X). **2174**

INDIAN JOURNAL OF ENVIRONMENTAL PROTECTION. (II/0253-7141). **2174**

INDIAN JOURNAL OF EXPERIMENTAL BIOLOGY. (II/0019-5189). **458**

INDIAN JOURNAL OF GASTROENTEROLOGY. (II/0254-8860). **3746**

INDIAN JOURNAL OF HEREDITY. (II/0374-826X). **548**

INDIAN JOURNAL OF HOSPITAL PHARMACY. (II/0019-526X). **4307**

INDIAN JOURNAL OF INDUSTRIAL RELATIONS. (II/0019-5286). **681**

INDIAN JOURNAL OF LEPROSY. (II/0254-9395). **4784**

INDIAN JOURNAL OF MARINE SCIENCES. (II/0379-5136). **1450**

INDIAN JOURNAL OF MATHEMATICS. (II/0019-5324). **3508**

INDIAN JOURNAL OF MEDICAL RESEARCH. SECTION A, INFECTIOUS DISEASES. (II/0970-955X). **3586**

INDIAN JOURNAL OF MEDICAL RESEARCH. SECTION B, BIOMEDICAL RESEARCH OTHER THAN INFECTIOUS DISEASES. (II/0970-9568). **3586**

INDIAN JOURNAL OF MEDICAL SCIENCES. (II/0019-5359). **3586**

INDIAN JOURNAL OF MICROBIOLOGY. (II/0046-8991). **563**

INDIAN JOURNAL OF NUTRITION AND DIETETICS, THE. (II/0022-3174). **4192**

INDIAN JOURNAL OF OPHTHALMOLOGY. (II/0301-4738). **3875**

INDIAN JOURNAL OF OTOLARYNGOLOGY. (II/0019-5421). **3888**

INDIAN JOURNAL OF PATHOLOGY & MICROBIOLOGY. (II/0377-4929). **3895**

INDIAN JOURNAL OF PEDIATRICS. (II/0019-5456). **3904**

INDIAN JOURNAL OF PHARMACEUTICAL SCIENCES. (II/0250-474X). **4307**

INDIAN JOURNAL OF PHARMACOLOGY. (II/0253-7613). **4307**

INDIAN JOURNAL OF PHYSICAL ANTHROPOLOGY AND HUMAN GENETICS. (II/0378-8156). **548**

INDIAN JOURNAL OF PHYSICS AND PROCEEDINGS OF THE INDIAN ASSOCIATION FOR THE CULTIVATION OF SCIENCE. (II/0019-5480). **5112**

INDIAN JOURNAL OF PHYSIOLOGY AND PHARMACOLOGY. (II/0019-5499). **581**

INDIAN JOURNAL OF PLANT PHYSIOLOGY. (II/0019-5502). **513**

INDIAN JOURNAL OF PLANT PROTECTION. (II/0253-4355). **513**

INDIAN JOURNAL OF POWER AND RIVER VALLEY DEVELOPMENT. (II/0019-5537). **5534**

INDIAN JOURNAL OF PSYCHIATRIC SOCIAL WORK. (II/0302-1610). **5289**

INDIAN JOURNAL OF PUBLIC ADMINISTRATION, THE. (II/0019-5561). **4656**

INDIAN JOURNAL OF PUBLIC HEALTH. (II/0019-557X). **4784**

INDIAN JOURNAL OF PURE & APPLIED PHYSICS. (II/0019-5596). **4405**

INDIAN JOURNAL OF REGIONAL SCIENCE. (II/0046-9017). **2825**

INDIAN JOURNAL OF SOCIAL RESEARCH. (II/0019-5626). **Adv Mgr:** Vivek Pori, **Tel** 11 91 11 2420827. **5203**

INDIAN JOURNAL OF SOCIAL WORK, THE. (II/0019-5634). **5289**

INDIAN JOURNAL OF TECHNOLOGY. (II/0019-5669). **5112**

INDIAN JOURNAL OF VETERINARY MEDICINE. (II/0970-051X). **5512**

INDIAN JUDGMENT REPORTER : IJR. (II). **2981**

INDIAN MANAGEMENT ABSTRACTS. (II). **870**

INDIAN MARKET. (US/0892-6409). **Adv Mgr:** J. Young. **2264**

INDIAN MINING & ENGINEERING JOURNAL, THE. (II/0019-5944). **2140**

INDIAN PEDIATRICS. (II/0019-6061). **3904**

INDIAN PERFUMER. (II/0019-607X). **404**

INDIAN PHILOSOPHICAL QUARTERLY. (II/0376-415X). **4349**

INDIAN PRACTITIONER. (II/0019-6169). **3587**

INDIAN PSYCHOLOGICAL ABSTRACTS. (II). **4589**

INDIAN PSYCHOLOGICAL REVIEW. (II/0019-6215). **4589**

INDIAN REVIEW OF LIFE SCIENCES. (II/0253-4436). **458**

INDIAN SCHOLAR. (II). **3344**

INDIAN SCIENCE INDEX. (II). **5112**

INDIAN SHIPPING. (II/0970-4299). **5450**

INDIAN SPICES. (II/0019-6401). **840**

INDIAN SUGAR. (II/0019-6428). **2344**

INDIAN TEXTILE JOURNAL, THE. (II/0019-6436). **5351**

INDIAN THEOLOGICAL STUDIES. (II/0253-620X). **4964**

INDIAN TRADER, THE. (US/0046-9076). **2738**

INDIAN VETERINARY JOURNAL, THE. (II/0019-6479). **5512**

INDIANA BEVERAGE JOURNAL. (US/0274-547X). **2367**

INDIANA BUSINESS MAGAZINE. (US/1060-4154). **Adv Mgr:** Amy Krieg. **682**

INDIANA CRIMINAL LAW REVIEW. (US). **3107**

INDIANA FREEMASON, THE. (US/0019-6622). **5232**

INDIANA GRAPPLER. (US). **Adv Mgr:** Dianne Chitwood. **4900**

INDIANA JOURNAL OF POLITICAL SCIENCE. (US/0737-7355). **4477**

INDIANA LAW REVIEW. (US/0090-4198). **2982**

INDIANA LIBRARIES. (US/0275-777X). **Adv Mgr Tel** (317)257-2040. **3215**

INDIANA MANUFACTURERS DIRECTORY. (US/0735-2417). **3481**

INDIANA MEDIA JOURNAL. (US/0164-7660). **Adv Mgr:** Callison, **Tel** (812)855-2018. **3215**

INDIANA MEDICINE. (US/0746-8288). **Adv Mgr:** same as editor. **3587**

INDIANA MUSICATOR. (US/0273-9933). **4122**

INDIANA NEWSPAPER DIRECTORY AND RATE BOOK. (US). **5664**

INDIANA PHARMACIST. (US). **4307**

INDIANA PRESERVATIONIST, THE. (US/0737-8602). **Adv Mgr:** Stacey Gray. **5480**

INDIANA PUBLISHER, THE. (US/0019-6711). **4815**

INDIANA READING QUARTERLY. (US/0019-672X). **Adv Mgr:** Loren Braught, **Tel** (812)237-2836. **1896**

INDIANA REVIEW. (US/0738-386X). **Adv Mgr:** Mikki Smith. **3344**

INDIANA STATE BOARD OF HEALTH BULLETIN, THE. (US/0019-6754). **4784**

INDIANA THEORY REVIEW. (US/0271-8022). **4122**

INDIANAPOLIS 500 YEARBOOK, THE. (US/1055-3355). **5417**

INDIANAPOLIS BUSINESS JOURNAL. (US/0274-4929). **Adv Mgr:** Greg Morris. **682**

INDIANAPOLIS MONTHLY. (US/0899-0328). **2535**

INDIANAPOLIS RECORDER, THE. (US). **5664**

INDICADORES DE COYUNTURA. (AG/0537-3468). **1534**

INDICATEUR SUISSE. (SZ). **2916**

INDICATOR (NANAIMO). (CN/0381-0917). **4848**

INDICATOR, THE. (US/0019-6924). **Adv Mgr:** Herman Burwasser, **Tel** (201)335-0912. **978**

INDICE COLOMBIANO DE ECONOMIA Y NEGOCIOS. (CK/0121-2613). **682**

INDICE DE PROFESIONALES DEL URUGUAY. (UY). **4205**

INDICE GENERAL DE PUBLICACIONES PERIODICAS CUBANAS. (CU). **5203**

INDICE — Advertising Accepted Index

INDICE HISPANOAMERICANO DE CIENCIAS SOCIALES. (CK/0120-6478). **5203**

INDICE INDUSTRIAL. (UY/0376-9941). **1609**

INDICI MENSILI PIROLA. (IT). **Adv Mgr Tel** 3022.1. **1495**

INDIKATOR EKONOMI. (IO). **1567**

INDIKATOR KESEJAHTERAAN RAKYAT / WELFARE INDICATORS. (IO). **5289**

INDIKATOR PEMBANGUNAN INDUSTRI PERTANIAN. (IO). **95**

INDIVIDUAL PSYCHOLOGY. (US/0277-7010). **4590**

INDO-CANADIAN TIMES. (CN/0708-949X). **5786**

INDO-IRANIAN JOURNAL. (NE/0019-7246). **4349**

INDONESIA CIRCLE : [JOURNAL]. (UK/0306-2848). **2505**

INDOOR AIR. (DK/0905-6947). **2232**

INDOOR GARDEN, THE. (US/8750-4081). **2420**

INDRAMA. (II). **2505**

INDUSTRIA. (BL). **1567**

INDUSTRIA AVICOLA. (US/0019-7467). **213**

INDUSTRIA AZUCARERA, LA. (AG/0325-0326). **95**

INDUSTRIA CARNICA LATINOAMERICANA, LA. (AG/0325-3414). **Adv Mgr:** Nestor Galibert. **213**

INDUSTRIA CONSERVE. (IT/0019-7483). **2344**

INDUSTRIA COTONIERA. (IT/0019-7491). **5352**

INDUSTRIA DEL LEGNO & DEL MOBILE, L'. (IT/0392-9086). **Adv Mgr:** Paola Govoni, **Tel** 76 02 16 48. **634**

INDUSTRIA DEL MOBILE, L'. (IT). **634**

INDUSTRIA DELLA CARTA. (IT/0019-7548). **4234**

INDUSTRIA DELLA GOMMA, L'. (IT/0019-7556). **5076**

INDUSTRIA INTERNACIONAL. (SP). **1610**

INDUSTRIA LEMNULUI (BUCHAREST, ROMANIA : 1986). (RM). **2384**

INDUSTRIA PORCINA. (US/0279-7771). **Adv Mgr:** Clay Schreiber. **213**

INDUSTRIA SACCARIFERA ITALIANA. (IT/0019-7734). **2344**

INDUSTRIA Y QUIMICA. (AG). **978**

INDUSTRIAL AND CORPORATE CHANGE. (UK/0960-6491). **1610**

INDUSTRIAL & ENGINEERING CHEMISTRY RESEARCH. (US/0888-5885). **2013**

INDUSTRIAL AND TRADE DIRECTORY. (KE). **840**

INDUSTRIAL AND TRADE DIRECTORY OF MALAWI. (MW/0377-0028). **840**

INDUSTRIAL ARCHAEOLOGY REVIEW. (UK/0309-0728). **270**

INDUSTRIAL ARCHAEOLOGY (TAVISTOCK). (UK/0019-7971). **270**

INDUSTRIAL CASES REPORTS. (UK/0306-2163). **3149**

INDUSTRIAL CERAMICS. (IT). **Adv Mgr:** G. Bertoni, **Tel** 0546 22661. **2591**

INDUSTRIAL COMPUTING PLUS PROGRAMMABLE CONTROLS. (US/1045-0203). **1238**

INDUSTRIAL CORROSION. (UK/0265-0584). **Adv Mgr:** Paul Green. **2102**

INDUSTRIAL CRISIS QUARTERLY. (NE/0921-8106). **682**

INDUSTRIAL EDUCATION. (US/0091-8601). **1913**

INDUSTRIAL EQUIPMENT NEWS (NEW YORK). (US/0019-8285). **2098**

INDUSTRIAL FABRIC PRODUCTS REVIEW. (US/0019-8307). **5352**

INDUSTRIAL FINISHING. BUYERS' GUIDE. (US). **4224**

INDUSTRIAL FINISHING (WHEATON). (US/0019-8323). **4224**

INDUSTRIAL FIRE JOURNAL. (UK/0964-9719). **2291**

INDUSTRIAL FIRE WORLD. (US/0749-890X). **2291**

INDUSTRIAL HEATING. (US/0019-8374). **4431**

INDUSTRIAL HYGIENE NEWS (PITTSBURGH). (US/0147-5401). **2863**

INDUSTRIAL LAUNDERER. (US/0046-9211). **Adv Mgr:** Mittie Spruill. **5352**

INDUSTRIAL LAW JOURNAL, INCLUDING THE INDUSTRIAL LAW REPORTS. (SA). **2982**

INDUSTRIAL LAW REPORTS (KUALA LUMPUR, MALAYSIA). (MY/0127-3051). **3149**

INDUSTRIAL MARKET PLACE. (US). **Adv Mgr:** Adrienne Gallender. **1610**

INDUSTRIAL MARKETING MANAGEMENT. (US/0019-8501). **926**

INDUSTRIAL MATHEMATICS. (US/0019-8528). **3509**

INDUSTRIAL METROLOGY. (NE/0921-5956). **4030**

INDUSTRIAL MINERALS. (UK/0019-8544). **1440**

INDUSTRIAL NEWS (IAEGER, W.VA.). (US). **Adv Mgr:** Ruby McCoy. **5764**

INDUSTRIAL ORGANIZATIONAL PSYCHOLOGIST, THE. (US/0739-1110). **Adv Mgr:** Jennifer Rinas, **Tel** (708)640-0068. **4590**

INDUSTRIAL PRODUCT BULLETIN. (US/0199-2074). **3481**

INDUSTRIAL PROPERTY. (SZ/0019-8625). **1304**

INDUSTRIAL PSYCHOLOGY. (SA/0258-5200). **Adv Mgr:** F. Crous. **4590**

INDUSTRIAL PURCHASING AGENT. (US/0019-8641). **950**

INDUSTRIAL REHABILITATION QUARTERLY. (US). **1611**

INDUSTRIAL RELATIONS (BERKELEY). (US/0019-8676). **1678**

INDUSTRIAL RELATIONS JOURNAL (KARACHI, PAKISTAN). (PK). **1678**

INDUSTRIAL RELATIONS JOURNAL (LONDON, ENGLAND). (UK/0019-8692). **1678**

INDUSTRIAL RELATIONS LAW JOURNAL. (US/0145-188X). **3149**

INDUSTRIAL RELATIONS RESEARCH ASSOCIATION SERIES NEWSLETTER. (US/0749-2162). **1678**

INDUSTRIAL RESEARCHER. (II). **901**

INDUSTRIAL WASTEWATER. (US/1067-5337). **Adv Mgr:** Tom Wolfe. **5534**

INDUSTRIE ALIMENTARI (PINEROLO). (IT/0019-901X). **2344**

INDUSTRIE-ANZEIGER. (GW/0019-9036). **617**

INDUSTRIE CERAMIQUE, L'. (FR/0019-9044). **2591**

INDUSTRIE DELLE BEVANDE. (IT/0390-0541). **2367**

INDUSTRIE DU CUIR (PARIS, FRANCE : 1987). (FR/0980-1367). **Adv Mgr:** J. Verry. **3184**

INDUSTRIE LACKIER BETRIEB. (GW/0019-9109). **4224**

INDUSTRIE SERVICE. (GW). **3481**

INDUSTRIE TEXTILE (PARIS). (FR/0019-9176). **5352**

INDUSTRIEBAU HANNOVER. (GW/0935-2023). **617**

INDUSTRIEL SUR BOIS. (SZ). **2401**

INDUSTRIELLE OBST- UND GEMUESEVERWERTUNG, DIE. (GW/0367-939X). **2344**

INDUSTRIES AGRO-ALIMENTAIRES. (FR/0245-985X). **2344**

INDUSTRIES DES CEREALES. (FR/0245-4505). **202**

INDUSTRISTATISTIK. (DK/0070-3532). **1534**

INDUSTRY & HIGHER EDUCATION. (UK/0950-4222). **1611**

INDUSTRY INTERNATIONAL. (US/0276-7317). **682**

INDUSTRY NEWS (RICHMOND, VA.). (US/8750-5525). **5071**

INDUSTRY PERFORMANCE IN ... AND PROSPECTS FOR ... . (PH). **682**

INDUSTRYGUIDE. (US). **1612**

INDY CAR RACING MAGAZINE. (US/1071-1759). **Adv Mgr:** Kevin Kelly. **4900**

INF INN : INFORMAZIONE INNOVATIVA. (IT). **5113**

INFANCIA Y APRENDIZAJE. (SP/0210-3702). **4590**

INFANT BEHAVIOR & DEVELOPMENT. (US/0163-6383). **4590**

INFANT MENTAL HEALTH JOURNAL. (US/0163-9641). **4590**

INFECTION. (GW/0300-8126). **Adv Mgr:** E. Caesar, **Tel** 089-43189-642. **3714**

INFECTION AND IMMUNITY. (US/0019-9567). **563**

INFECTIOUS AND MEDICAL DISEASE LETTERS FOR OBSTETRICS AND GYNECOLOGY, THE. (US). **3762**

INFECTIOUS DISEASE ALERT. (US/0739-7348). **3672**

INFECTOLOGIA. (MX/0185-0628). **Adv Mgr:** Oscar Baqnarelli. **3714**

INFERTILITY. (US/0160-7626). **3762**

INFINITY LIMITED. (US/1050-7280). **3396**

INFO COMMERCE. (CN/0823-5414). **840**

INFO DGA. (FR). **682**

INFO-INFOGETTABLE. (GW). **1064**

INFO MEP. (CN/0822-0409). **1752**

INFO-QUEBEC. (CN/0226-6598). **1259**

INFO SECURITY NEWS. (US/1066-7822). **1226**

INFO-SOUTH ABSTRACTS. (US/1059-5910). **1534**

INFOAAU. (US/0279-9863). **2598**

INFOCUS NEWS MAGAZINE. (AT/0815-6905). **2264**

INFOCUS (PORTLAND, OR.). (US/1040-2179). **870**

INFOFISH INTERNATIONAL. (MY/0127-2012). **Adv Mgr:** Paul H S Tan. **2305**

INFOR MARECHALERIE. (BE/0774-4323). **Adv Mgr:** F. Dominique. **3396**

INFORM (SILVER SPRING, MD.). (US/0892-3876). **4370**

INFORMACION SISTEMATICA. (MX/0185-2973). **5806**

INFORMACIONES Y MEMORIAS DE LA SOCIEDAD DE INGENIEROS DEL PERU. (PE). **1978**

INFORMATEUR CATHOLIQUE (1985). (CN/0833-9228). **4964**

INFORMATIC USERS. (BE). **1188**

INFORMATIK - FORSCHUNG UND ENTWICKLUNG. (GW/0178-3564). **1188**

INFORMATION AGE. (UK/0261-4103). **1226**

INFORMATION & MANAGEMENT. (NE/0378-7206). **1254**

INFORMATION AND REFERRAL. (US/0278-2383). **5289**

INFORMATION AND SOCIETY. (AT/1033-6273). **5247**

INFORMATION AND SOFTWARE TECHNOLOGY. (UK/0950-5849). **1260**

INFORMATION BULLETIN - AMERICAN BAR ASSOCIATION. STANDING COMMITTEE ON SPECIALIZATION. (US/0736-2765). **2982**

INFORMATION BULLETIN / WESTERN ASSOCIATION OF MAP LIBRARIES. (US/0049-7282). **3215**

INFORMATION - CANADIAN ASSOCIATION OF SOCIAL WORKERS. (CN/0315-3150). **5289**

INFORMATION CARDIOLOGIQUE, L'. (FR/0220-2476). **3706**

INFORMATION CHICAGO. (US/0196-3643). **2535**

INFORMATION DEVELOPMENT. (UK/0266-6669). **3215**

INFORMATION ECONOMICS AND POLICY. (NE/0167-6245). **1157**

INFORMATION INTELLIGENCE, ONLINE LIBRARIES, AND MICROCOMPUTERS. (US/0737-7770). **3216**

INFORMATION INTELLIGENCE ONLINE NEWSLETTER. (US/0194-0694). **1274**

INFORMATION - L'ASSOCIATION QUEBECOISE DU TRANSPORT ET DES ROUTES. (CN/0319-1818). **5384**

INFORMATION MANAGEMENT & TECHNOLOGY. (UK). **Adv Mgr:** Cathy Godfrey, **Tel** 11 44 707 284692. **3258**

INFORMATION MANAGEMENT BULLETIN. (US/1046-9303). **1188**

INFORMATION MANAGEMENT SOURCEBOOK. (US/0897-3199). **3216**

INFORMATION RESEARCH NEWS. (UK/0959-8928). **3216**

INFORMATION RESOURCES MANAGEMENT JOURNAL. (US/1040-1628). **3216**

INFORMATION SCIENCES. (US/0020-0255). **3216**

INFORMATION SEARCHER. (US/1055-3916). **Adv Mgr:** Bill Berger, **Tel** (914)723-3156. **1752**

INFORMATION SOCIETY, THE. (US/0197-2243). **3216**

INFORMATION STRATEGY. (US/0743-8613). **Adv Mgr Tel** (212)971-5000. **870**

INFORMATION SYSTEMS MANAGEMENT. (US/1058-0530). **Adv Mgr Tel** (212)971-5000. **870**

INFORMATION SYSTEMS RESEARCH. (US/1047-7047). **Adv Mgr:** Pamela Battis. **1188**

INFORMATION SYSTEMS SECURITY. (US/1065-898X). **1226**

INFORMATION TECHNOLOGY & LEARNING. (UK/0952-7923). **1286**

INFORMATION TECHNOLOGY & PUBLIC POLICY. (UK/0266-8513). **1188**

INFORMATION TECHNOLOGY MANAGEMENT. (AT/1322-3526). **5113**

INFORMATION TECHNOLOGY NEWSLETTER (HARRISBURG, PA.). (US/1057-7939). **3217**

INFORMATION TODAY. (US/8755-6286). **Adv Mgr:** Michael V. Zarrello. **3217**

INFORMATION UPDATE / LEAGUE OF OREGON CITIES. (US/0731-1443). **Adv Mgr:** Kim Bentley. **2535**

INFORMATIONS CANADIENNES 1969. (FR/0768-9098). **820**

INFORMATIONS MONDIALES - UNDA. (BE/0258-9494). **1133**

INFORMATIONS TECHNIQUES DE SERVICES VETERINAIRES. (FR). **5512**

INFORMATIONSDIENST SUDLICHES AFRIKA. (GW/0721-5088). **4477**

INFORMATIONWEEK (MANHASSET, N.Y.). (US/8750-6874). **1260**

INFORMATIQUE ET BUREAUTIQUE : L'HEBDO ROMAND DE L'INFORMATIQUE. (SZ). **1229**

INFORMATIQUE QUEBEC. (CN/0706-1773). **1260**

INFORMATORE AGRARIO, L'. (IT). **96**

INFORMATORE PIROLA. (IT). **Adv Mgr** Tel 02 3022.1. **2982**

INFORMATORE SCOLASTICO. (IT). **1092**

INFORMAZIONE CARDIOLOGICA. (IT). **Adv Mgr:** Sig. Boscarello Walter, Tel 011 39 2 29572541. **3706**

INFORME AGROPECUARIO (BELO HORIZONTE). (BL/0100-3364). **96**

INFORME SOBRE CHILE. (CK). **5329**

INFORMER. (IT). **2517**

INFORMER (RALEIGH), THE. (US/0195-4318). **3217**

INFOWORLD. (US/0199-6649). **1268**

INGAA RATE AND POLICY ANALYSIS DEPARTMENTS REPORTS. (US). **4260**

INGEGNERIA ALIMENTARE. LE CONSERVE ANIMALI. (IT/0394-588X). **Adv Mgr:** Wanda Moroni. **2344**

INGEGNERIA ELETTRONICA. (IT). **2065**

INGEGNERIA SISMICA. (IT/0393-1420). **2024**

INGENIERIA HIDRAULICA (LA HABANA). (CU/0253-0678). **2091**

INGENIEUR (DEN HAAG). (NE/0020-1146). **1978**

INGENUITY. (UK/1354-9952). **1189**

INGLESIDE INDEX, THE. (US). **Adv Mgr:** Patsy Dicken, Tel (512)758-5391. **5751**

INHALO-SCOPE. (CN/0824-8281). **4308**

INITIATIVE EUROPE MONITOR. (UK/0955-1697). **682**

INITIATIVES IN POPULATION. (PH/0115-2181). **4553**

INJURY. (UK/0020-1383). **3587**

INJURY PREVENTION NETWORK NEWSLETTER. (US). **4784**

INK & GALL. (US/0894-0479). **353**

INLAND ARCHITECT. (US/0020-1472). **Adv Mgr:** T.W.Hill. **301**

INLAND EMPIRE MAGAZINE. (US/0199-5073). **Adv Mgr:** Brenda Lorenzi. **682**

INLAND RIVER GUIDE. (US/0198-859X). **5450**

INLAND SEAS. (US/0020-1537). **2739**

INN BUSINESS (ESSEX, ONT.). (CN/0821-7610). **2807**

INNER HORIZONS. (US/0897-229X). **Adv Mgr:** Sister Mary Paula Kolar. **5030**

INNER WOMAN. (US/1049-9709). **5559**

INNISFIL SCOPE, THE. (CN/0225-1604). **Adv Mgr:** John, **Tel** (416)729-2287. **5786**

INNOVATION (MCLEAN, VA.). (US/0731-2334). **2099**

INNOVATIONS & IDEAS. (US/1059-2091). **5114**

INNOVATIONS & RESEARCH IN CLINICAL SERVICES, COMMUNITY SUPPORT, AND REHABILITATION. (US/1062-7553). **Adv Mgr:** LeRoy Spaniol, Tel (617)353-3549. **3926**

INNOVATIVE PACKAGING PARIS. (FR/0988-6249). **4219**

INNSIDE ISSUES. (US). **4839**

INORGANIC CHEMISTRY. (US/0020-1669). **1036**

INQUINAMENTO. (IT/0001-4982). **2233**

INQUIRER, THE. (UK/0020-1723). **4965**

INQUIRY (KINGSTON). (CN/0714-7198). **682**

INQUIRY (OSLO). (NO/0020-174X). **4349**

INSATSU ZASSHI. (JA). **4566**

INSCAPE LONDON. (UK/0264-7141). **353**

INSECTA MUNDI. (US/0749-6737). **5609**

INSERVICE (SYRACUSE, N.Y.). (US/0732-3808). **1864**

INSIDE (ALBANY, N.Y.). (US/0736-0150). **3100**

INSIDE ARTS. (US/1069-2029). **Adv Mgr:** Kim Kerker, **Tel** (202)833-2787. **385**

INSIDE BLUEGRASS. (US/0891-0537). **4122**

INSIDE CHICAGO. (US). **5480**

INSIDE COLLECTOR, THE. (US/1052-861X). **Adv Mgr:** Keith Kaonis. **251**

INSIDE DPMA. (US/0898-171X). **Adv Mgr:** Mike Wright, **Tel** (301)577-4030. **683**

INSIDE INFORMATION WHITCHURCH. (UK/0958-1790). **1189**

INSIDE IRELAND. (IE/0332-2483). **2518**

INSIDE ISHM MAGAZINE. (US). **Adv Mgr:** Bob Stegle. **2065**

INSIDE MEDIA (STAMFORD, CONN.). (US/1046-5316). **760**

INSIDE MS. (US/0739-9774). **3834**

INSIDE/OUT (NEW YORK, N.Y. : 1980). (US/0275-021X). **3396**

INSIDE RADIO. (US/0731-9312). **1133**

INSIDE SPORTS. (US/0195-3478). **4900**

INSIDE TEXAS RUNNING. (US/1042-3664). **4900**

INSIDE THE AUBURN TIGERS (AUBURN, ALA.). (US/0279-2273). **4900**

INSIDE THE LEADING MAIL ORDER HOUSES. (US/0743-2895). **760**

INSIDE TRACK (HAMMONTON, N.J.). (US/1052-1607). **Adv Mgr:** Gary Slade, **Tel** (817)640-8316. **4851**

INSIDE WELFARE BULLETIN. (AT/0313-8496). **1496**

INSIDE WOMEN'S TENNIS. (US/0738-7040). **4900**

INSIDE WORCESTER. (US). **2535**

INSIDE WRESTLING. (US/1047-9562). **4900**

INSIDER, THE. (BU/0861-3117). **Adv Mgr:** Rossitsa Tsoleva. **2518**

INSIEME. (IT/0020-1871). **683**

INSIGHT LAGOS. 1987. (NR/0794-7968). **4965**

INSIGHT (NORTHAMPTON). (UK/1354-2575). **2102**

INSIGHT ON COLLECTABLES (1987). (CN/0836-5873). **251**

INSIGHT ON THE NEWS (WASHINGTON, D.C.). (US/1051-4880). **Adv Mgr:** Desiree DeLoatch, **Tel** (202) 636-8888. **4477**

INSIGHT (SAN FRANSISCO, CALIF.). (US/1060-135X). **Adv Mgr:** Robin Brandes, **Tel** (213)624-0900. **3857**

INSIGHTS INTO CHRISTIAN EDUCATION. (US/8756-3347). **4965**

INSIGHTS INTO OPEN EDUCATION/ UNIVERSITY OF NORTH DAKOTA. (US/0740-5596). **1896**

INSIGHTS (WASHINGTON, D.C.). (US/0747-007X). **4900**

INSOLVENCY INTELLIGENCE. (UK/0950-2645). **2983**

INSPIRATION. (SZ/0020-2061). **926**

INSPIRED. (US). **301**

INSTALACIONES DEPORTIVAS XXI. (SP/0212-8519). **617**

INSTALACIONES Y TECNICAS DEL CONFORT. (SP/0214-4034). **Adv Mgr:** Victorio Redondo Polo. **2606**

INSTALADOR, EL. (SP). **Adv Mgr:** Jose Moreno, **Tel** 302 5240. **2065**

INSTALLATION & CLEANING SPECIALIST. (US/0192-1657). **Adv Mgr:** Phil Johnson. **2901**

INSTALLATORE ITALIANO. (IT/0020-2118). **2606**

INSTITUTE OF CRIMINOLOGY & FORENSIC SCIENCES BULLETIN. (US/0739-8514). **3166**

INSTITUTE TODAY. (US/0897-4527). **791**

INSTITUTIONAL DISTRIBUTION. (US/0020-3572). **2344**

INSTITUTIONAL REAL ESTATE LETTER, THE. (US/1044-1662). **Adv Mgr:** Mike Mollo, **Tel** (510)933-4040. **4839**

INSTRUCTION DELIVERY SYSTEMS. (US/0892-4872). **1189**

INSTRUCTIONAL DEVELOPMENT AT WATERLOO. (CN/0228-2313). **1896**

INSTRUCTOR (1990). (US/1049-5851). **1896**

INSTRUMENTALIST, THE. (US/0020-4331). **4122**

INSTRUMENTENBAU ZEITSCHRIFT, MUSIK INTERNATIONAL : IZ. (GW/0934-3962). **Adv Mgr:** T Leugendorf, Tel 224 64039. **4122**

INSULATION GUIDE. (US/0737-2817). **1947**

INSULIN AND GLUCAGON. (UK/0142-8144). **3731**

INSURANCE ADVOCATE. (US/0020-4587). **2882**

INSURANCE ALMANAC (ENGLEWOOD. 1933), THE. (US/0074-0675). **2882**

INSURANCE BROKERS' MONTHLY AND INSURANCE ADVISER. (UK/0260-2385). **Adv Mgr:** Jane Sones, **Tel** 0689 785156. **2883**

INSURANCE CONFERENCE PLANNER. (US/0193-0516). **Adv Mgr:** B Ventre. **2883**

INSURANCE JOURNAL. (US/0020-4714). **Adv Mgr:** Dena Kaplan. **2883**

INSURANCE MARKETING INSIDER. (US/1040-6867). **2884**

INSURANCE RECORD (DALLAS, TEX.), THE. (US/0020-4803). **Adv Mgr:** C. J. Hargis. **2884**

INSURANCE RECORD OF AUSTRALIA & NEW ZEALAND, THE. (AT). **2884**

INSURANCE TIMES (NEWTON, MASS.). (US/1042-7333). **2884**

INSURANCEWEEK. (US/0020-4846). **2884**

INTEGRAL YOGA. (US/0161-1380). **4965**

INTEGRATED MANUFACTURING SYSTEMS. (UK/0957-6061). **2116**

INTEGRATION (AMSTERDAM). (NE/0167-9260). **2066**

INTEGRATIVE PSYCHIATRY. (US/0735-3847). **3926**

INTELLECTUAL PROPERTY JOURNAL. (CN/0824-7064). **1305**

INTELLECTUAL PROPERTY LAW (CHUR, SWITZERLAND). (UK/0892-2365). **1305**

INTELLIGENCE AND NATIONAL SECURITY. (UK/0268-4527). **Adv Mgr:** Anne Kidson. **4524**

INTELLIGENCE (NEW YORK, N.Y. 1984). (US/1042-4296). **1189**

INTELLIGENCE (NORWOOD). (US/0160-2896). **4590**

INTELLIGENCER JOURNAL. (US/0889-4140). **5737**

INTELLIGENCER (WHEELING, W.VA.) (US). **Adv Mgr:** Robert Diehl. **5764**

INTELLIGENT INSTRUMENTS & COMPUTERS. (US/0889-8308). **1220**

INTENSIVBEHANDLUNG. (GW/0341-3063). **3588**

INTENSIVE CARE WORLD (BALDOCK). (UK/0266-7037). **3588**

INTENSIVE THERAPY AND CLINICAL MONITORING. (UK). **3588**

INTER ALIA (RENO). (US/0092-6086). **Adv Mgr:** C. Cendagorta, **Tel** (702)329-4100. **2983**

INTER-AMERICAN ARBITRATION. (CN/0715-4771). **2983**

INTER CDI ETAMPES. (FR/0242-2999). **Adv Mgr:** same as editor. **683**

INTER-CITY EXPRESS (OAKLAND, CALIF.). (US/0274-7464). **5636**

INTER DEPENDENT, THE. (US/0094-5072). **Adv Mgr:** Susan Woolfson. **4524**

INTER ECONOMICS. (GW/0020-5346). **1636**

INTER (HAUTE-VILLE, QUEBEC). (CN/0825-8708). **Adv Mgr:** Sylvie Martel, **Tel** (418)5299600. **385**

INTER-MECANIQUE DU BATIMENT. (CN/0831-411X). **617**

INTERACTING WITH COMPUTERS. (UK/0953-5438). **1189**

INTERACTION - CANADIAN CHILD DAY CARE FEDERATION. (CN/0835-5819). **Adv Mgr:** T. Wittur. **5290**

INTERACTION (CANBERRA, A.C.T.). (AT/0818-6286). **1880**

INTERACTIONS (TILLSONBURG). (CN/1188-3146). **2174**

INTERACTIVE LEARNING INTERNATIONAL. (UK/0748-5743). **1223**

INTERAVIA (ENGLISH ED.). (UK/0020-5168). **24**

INTERBEHAVIORIST, THE. (US/8755-612X). **4590**

INTERCAMBIO. (MX). **840**

INTERCERAM. (GW/0020-5214). **2591**

INTERCHAMBER. (ET). **841**

INTERCHANGE   Advertising Accepted Index

INTERCHANGE SYDNEY. (AT/0814-4834). **1801**

INTERCHANGE (TORONTO. 1984). (CN/0826-4805). **1753**

INTERCOLLEGIATE REVIEW, THE. (US/0020-5249). **1831**

INTERCOM (LETCHWORTH DEVELOPMENTAL SERVICES). (US). **1753**

INTERDISCIPLINARY SCIENCE REVIEWS : ISR. (UK/0308-0188). **5114**

INTERFACE. (US/0163-6626). **Adv Mgr:** Judith Hug, **Tel** (408)724-0915. **1223**

INTERFACE (AMSTERDAM). (NE/0303-3902). **4123**

INTERFACE (CHICAGO). (US/0270-6717). **3217**

INTERFACE (MONTREAL. 1984). (CN/0826-4864). **Adv Mgr:** Pierette LeFrancois, **Tel** (514)466-3095. **5114**

INTERFERENCE TECHNOLOGY ENGINEER'S MASTER. (US/0190-0943). **Adv Mgr Tel** (610)825-1960 ext. 223. **2066**

INTERGEO BULLETIN. (FR/0396-5880). **2582**

INTERIOR CONSTRUCTION. (US/0888-0387). **Adv Mgr:** Sharon Mathison. **617**

INTERIOR DECORATORS' HANDBOOK. (US/0733-8511). **2901**

INTERIOR JOURNAL (1984). (US/8750-7609). **Adv Mgr:** Sharmon P. Moore. **5681**

INTERIOR LANDSCAPE INDUSTRY. (US/0742-1648). **2420**

INTERIORS & SOURCES. (US/1059-5287). **Adv Mgr Tel** (708)498-9880. **2901**

INTERIORSCAPE. (US/0744-8635). **2420**

INTERLAKEN REVIEW, THE. (US). **Adv Mgr:** Del Hall, Jim Graney. **5717**

INTERMEDIAIR BELGIE. (BE). **1567**

INTERMODAL ASIA. (HK). **5450**

INTERMODAL REPORTER. (US/0882-8059). **5384**

INTERMOUNTAIN CATHOLIC. (US/0273-6187). **4965**

INTERMOUNTAIN CONTRACTOR. (US/0020-5656). **617**

INTERMOUNTAIN JEWISH NEWS. (US/0047-0511). **5643**

INTERMOUNTAIN LOGGING NEWS. (US/0300-7405). **2401**

INTERNAL AUDITOR, THE. (US/0020-5745). **745**

INTERNAL MEDICINE NEWS & CARDIOLOGY NEWS. (US/0274-5542). **3746**

INTERNAMERICA (NEEDHAM, MASS.). (US/1061-7337). **Adv Mgr:** Ellen Miller. **1680**

INTERNASJONAL POLITIKK (OSLO, NORWAY). (NO/0020-577X). **4524**

INTERNATIONAL AEROSPACE DIRECTORY. (US/0882-6730). **24**

INTERNATIONAL AFFAIRS BULLETIN. (SA/0258-7270). **4524**

INTERNATIONAL AFFAIRS (LONDON). (UK/0020-5850). **4524**

INTERNATIONAL AFFAIRS STUDIES. (PL/0867-4493). **4524**

INTERNATIONAL AGRICULTURAL DEVELOPMENT (CROWBOROUGH, EAST SUSSEX). (UK/0261-4413). **96**

INTERNATIONAL AND COMPARATIVE LAW QUARTERLY, THE. (UK/0020-5893). **3129**

INTERNATIONAL ASSOCIATION OF PANORAMIC PHOTOGRAPHERS :. (US/1063-7478). **4370**

INTERNATIONAL ATOMIC ENERGY AGENCY BULLETIN. (AU/0020-6067). **1947**

INTERNATIONAL AUCTION RECORDS. (US/0074-1922). **353**

INTERNATIONAL AVIATION MECHANICS JOURNAL. (US/0045-1193). **24**

INTERNATIONAL BAR NEWS (LONDON, ENGLAND). (UK/0143-7453). **3129**

INTERNATIONAL BIBLIOGRAPHY OF STUDIES ON ALCOHOL. (US). **1350**

INTERNATIONAL BLOOD/PLASMA NEWS. (US/0742-7719). **3772**

INTERNATIONAL BONSAI. (US/0198-9561). **2420**

INTERNATIONAL BOOKS IN PRINT. (GW/0170-9348). **4821**

INTERNATIONAL BOTTLER AND PACKER, THE. (UK/0020-6199). **4219**

INTERNATIONAL BROADCAST ENGINEER : IBE. (UK/0020-6229). **1133**

INTERNATIONAL BROADCASTING. (UK/0957-4425). **1133**

INTERNATIONAL BUILDING SCIENCE & CONSTRUCTION ABSTRACTS. (IE/0790-5769). **2024**

INTERNATIONAL BULK JOURNAL : IBJ. (UK/0260-1087). **5384**

INTERNATIONAL BULLETIN OF MISSIONARY RESEARCH. (US/0272-6122). **4965**

INTERNATIONAL BUSINESS LAWYER. (UK/0309-7676). **3129**

INTERNATIONAL CALIFORNIA MINING JOURNAL. (US). **Adv Mgr:** D.Craig. **2140**

INTERNATIONAL CD-ROM REPORT, THE. (CN/0847-0456). **1189**

INTERNATIONAL CEMENT REVIEW. (UK/0959-6038). **Adv Mgr:** Paul Brown. **617**

INTERNATIONAL CHEMICAL ENGINEERING. (US/0020-6318). **2013**

INTERNATIONAL CHILDREN'S RIGHTS MONITOR. (SZ/0259-3696). **Adv Mgr:** same as editor. **4477**

INTERNATIONAL CHORAL BULLETIN. (US/0896-0968). **4123**

INTERNATIONAL CIVIL ENGINEERING ABSTRACTS. (IE/0332-4095). **2005**

INTERNATIONAL CLASSIFICATION. (GW/0340-0050). **3218**

INTERNATIONAL CLINICAL PSYCHOPHARMACOLOGY. (UK/0268-1315). **4308**

INTERNATIONAL COMET QUARTERLY, THE. (US/0736-6922). **395**

INTERNATIONAL CONGRESS OF THE INTERNATIONAL COUNCIL ON HEALTH, PHYSICAL EDUCATION, AND RECREATION. (US/0074-4417). **1856**

INTERNATIONAL COUNTERMEASURES HANDBOOK, THE. (US/0145-2584). **4046**

INTERNATIONAL DEFENCE EQUIPMENT CATALOG : IDEC. (GW). **4046**

INTERNATIONAL DEFENCE ET TECHNOLOGY. (FR). **5114**

INTERNATIONAL DEFENSE REVIEW. (SZ/0020-6512). **4046**

INTERNATIONAL DENTAL JOURNAL. (UK/0020-6539). **1325**

INTERNATIONAL DEVELOPMENT ABSTRACTS. (UK/0262-0855). **2913**

INTERNATIONAL DIRECTORY OF BOOK COLLECTORS. (UK). **4829**

INTERNATIONAL DIRECTORY OF COMPUTER ANIMATION PRODUCERS. (CN/0840-5905). **1234**

INTERNATIONAL DIRECTORY OF LITTLE MAGAZINES & SMALL PRESSES. (US/0092-3974). **1926**

INTERNATIONAL DIRECTORY OF MARKETING RESEARCH HOUSES AND SERVICE; GREEN BOOK. (US/0074-459X). **926**

INTERNATIONAL DIRECTORY OF RESOURCES FOR ARTISANS, THE. (US/0898-1094). **373**

INTERNATIONAL DOCUMENTARY. (US/0742-5333). **Adv Mgr Tel** (213)962-1396. **4072**

INTERNATIONAL DOCUMENTS REVIEW. (US/1054-4933). **Adv Mgr:** Lauren Carner, **Tel** (212)355-5510. **4524**

INTERNATIONAL DOMOTIQUE NEWS PARIS. (FR/1148-3555). **5115**

INTERNATIONAL DREDGING REVIEW. (US/0737-8181). **1979**

INTERNATIONAL DRUG THERAPY NEWSLETTER. (US/0020-6571). **4308**

INTERNATIONAL ECONOMIC REVIEW (PHILADELPHIA). (US/0020-6598). **1496**

INTERNATIONAL ECONOMY, THE. (US/0898-4336). **1636**

INTERNATIONAL EDUCATION FORUM (PULLMAN, WASHINGTON). (US/1053-1750). **1831**

INTERNATIONAL EDUCATOR (WASHINGTON, D.C.). (US/1059-4221). **Adv Mgr:** Jennifer Kemp. **1753**

INTERNATIONAL EMPLOYMENT GAZETTE. (US/1058-0506). **Adv Mgr:** Del McCaleb. **4205**

INTERNATIONAL ENDODONTIC JOURNAL. (UK/0143-2885). **1325**

INTERNATIONAL ENERGY STATISTICS SOURCEBOOK. (US/1058-2487). **Adv Mgr:** Jay Kilburn, **Tel** (918)831-9416. **1963**

INTERNATIONAL ENGINEERING DIRECTORY. (US/0074-5774). **1979**

INTERNATIONAL ENVIRONMENT & SAFETY. (UK/0141-4836). **2174**

INTERNATIONAL EXAMINER (SEATTLE, WASH. 1973). (US/1065-1500). **Adv Mgr:** Ron Bruan, **Tel** (206)624-3925. **2654**

INTERNATIONAL EXECUTIVE. (US/0020-6652). **4502**

INTERNATIONAL EXPLORATION NEWSLETTER. (US/1064-9042). **4261**

INTERNATIONAL FIBER JOURNAL. (US/1049-801X). **5352**

INTERNATIONAL FINANCIAL LAW REVIEW. (UK/0262-6969). **3100**

INTERNATIONAL FIRE AND SECURITY PRODUCT NEWS. (UK/0961-3730). **2291**

INTERNATIONAL FIRE PHOTOGRAPHERS ASSOCIATION : NEWSLETTER : IFPA. (US). **4371**

INTERNATIONAL FLYING FARMER. (US/0020-675X). **96**

INTERNATIONAL FOOD INGREDIENT. (NE/0924-5863). **2345**

INTERNATIONAL FORUM FOR LOGOTHERAPY, THE. (US/0191-3379). **4349**

INTERNATIONAL FORUM ON INFORMATION AND DOCUMENTATION. (NE/0304-9701). **3218**

INTERNATIONAL FREE TRADE ZONE. (UK). **5384**

INTERNATIONAL FREEDOM FOUNDATION. (SA/0897-5086). **Adv Mgr:** J. Duncan Berry. **1636**

INTERNATIONAL FRUIT WORLD. (SZ/0250-944X). **2345**

INTERNATIONAL FUR FASHION REVIEW. (CN/0823-6976). **3184**

INTERNATIONAL GLASS/METAL CATALOG. (US/0147-300X). **2591**

INTERNATIONAL GYMNAST (1986). (US/0891-6616). **Adv Mgr:** Peter Koch, **Tel** (310)836-2642. **4900**

INTERNATIONAL HAIR ROUTE. (CN/0820-6880). **3720**

INTERNATIONAL HEPATOLOGY COMMUNICATIONS. (NE/0928-4346). **3797**

INTERNATIONAL HISTORY REVIEW, THE. (CN/0707-5332). **2620**

INTERNATIONAL HYDROGRAPHIC REVIEW, THE. (MC/0020-6946). **1415**

INTERNATIONAL INFORMATION, COMMUNICATION & EDUCATION. (II/0970-1850). **Adv Mgr Tel** 381497. **3218**

INTERNATIONAL INSIDER. (UK/0953-2714). **Adv Mgr:** Mary Adams, **Tel** 071 353 7311. **1496**

INTERNATIONAL INSURANCE MONITOR. (US/0020-6997). **2884**

INTERNATIONAL INTERACTIONS. (UK/0305-0629). **4524**

INTERNATIONAL INVENTION REGISTER. (US/8755-9609). **1305**

INTERNATIONAL INVESTOR'S DIRECTORY. (US/1040-6921). **Adv Mgr:** Dan Dent. **902**

INTERNATIONAL JOURNAL. (CN/0020-7020). **2692**

INTERNATIONAL JOURNAL FOR HOUSING SCIENCE AND ITS APPLICATIONS. (US/0146-6518). **2825**

INTERNATIONAL JOURNAL FOR NUMERICAL METHODS IN FLUIDS. (UK/0271-2091). **2091**

INTERNATIONAL JOURNAL FOR VITAMIN AND NUTRITION RESEARCH (SUPPLEMENT). (SZ/0300-9831). **4192**

INTERNATIONAL JOURNAL OF ACAROLOGY. (US/0164-7954). **5586**

INTERNATIONAL JOURNAL OF ADHESION AND ADHESIVES. (UK/0143-7496). **1053**

INTERNATIONAL JOURNAL OF ADOLESCENCE AND YOUTH. (UK/0267-3843). **2281**

INTERNATIONAL JOURNAL OF ADULT ORTHODONTICS AND ORTHOGNATHIC SURGERY, THE. (US/0742-1931). **1325**

INTERNATIONAL JOURNAL OF ADVERTISING. (UK/0265-0487). **760**

INTERNATIONAL JOURNAL OF AFRICAN HISTORICAL STUDIES, THE. (US/0361-7882). **Adv Mgr:** Laura Scott, **Tel** (617)353-7306. **2640**

INTERNATIONAL JOURNAL OF ANDROLOGY. (UK/0105-6263). **3588**

INTERNATIONAL JOURNAL OF ANGIOLOGY, THE. (US/1061-1711). **3706**

INTERNATIONAL JOURNAL OF APPLIED ELECTROMAGNETICS IN MATERIALS. (NE/0925-2096). **4444**

INTERNATIONAL JOURNAL OF APPLIED LINGUISTICS. (NO/0802-6106). **3287**

INTERNATIONAL JOURNAL OF APPLIED PHILOSOPHY, THE. (US/0739-098X). **2251**

INTERNATIONAL JOURNAL OF APPROXIMATE REASONING. (US/0888-613X). **1213**

INTERNATIONAL JOURNAL OF ARTIFICIAL ORGANS, THE. (IT/0391-3988). **3798**

INTERNATIONAL

INTERNATIONAL JOURNAL OF BANK MARKETING. (UK/0265-2323). **792**

INTERNATIONAL JOURNAL OF BIOCHEMISTRY, THE. (UK/0020-711X). **488**

INTERNATIONAL JOURNAL OF BIOLOGICAL MACROMOLECULES. (UK/0141-8130). **581**

INTERNATIONAL JOURNAL OF BIOLOGICAL MARKERS, THE. (IT/0393-6155). **3818**

INTERNATIONAL JOURNAL OF BIOMETEOROLOGY. (NE/0020-7128). **1426**

INTERNATIONAL JOURNAL OF CANADIAN STUDIES. (CN/1180-3991). **Adv Mgr:** Guy Leclair. **2739**

INTERNATIONAL JOURNAL OF CANCER. (US/0020-7136). **3818**

INTERNATIONAL JOURNAL OF CARDIAC IMAGING. (US/0167-9899). **3706**

INTERNATIONAL JOURNAL OF CAREER MANAGEMENT, THE. (HK/0955-6214). **4205**

INTERNATIONAL JOURNAL OF CELL CLONING. (US/0737-1454). **537**

INTERNATIONAL JOURNAL OF CHILDBIRTH EDUCATION, THE. (US/0887-8625). **3762**

INTERNATIONAL JOURNAL OF CLINICAL AND EXPERIMENTAL HYPNOSIS, THE. (US/0020-7144). **2858**

INTERNATIONAL JOURNAL OF CLINICAL MONITORING AND COMPUTING. (NE/0167-9945). **1190**

INTERNATIONAL JOURNAL OF CLINICAL NEUROPSYCHOLOGY, THE. (US/0749-8470). **4591**

INTERNATIONAL JOURNAL OF COGNITIVE EDUCATION & MEDIATED LEARNING. (UK/0957-4964). **1753**

INTERNATIONAL JOURNAL OF COMPARATIVE AND APPLIED CRIMINAL JUSTICE. (US/0192-4036). **3166**

INTERNATIONAL JOURNAL OF COMPUTER AIDED VLSI DESIGN. (US/1042-7988). **2066**

INTERNATIONAL JOURNAL OF COMPUTER APPLICATIONS IN TECHNOLOGY. (SZ/0952-8091). **1190**

INTERNATIONAL JOURNAL OF COMPUTER MATHEMATICS. (UK/0020-7160). **Adv Mgr:** Kathy Langdale. **3509**

INTERNATIONAL JOURNAL OF COMPUTER SYSTEMS SCIENCE & ENGINEERING. (UK). **1190**

INTERNATIONAL JOURNAL OF COMPUTER VISION. (US/0920-5691). **1190**

INTERNATIONAL JOURNAL OF CONSTRUCTION MAINTENANCE & REPAIR, THE. (UK/0959-5090). **618**

INTERNATIONAL JOURNAL OF CONTEMPORARY HOSPITALITY MANAGEMENT. (HK/0959-6119). **2807**

INTERNATIONAL JOURNAL OF CONTINUING ENGINEERING EDUCATION. (SZ/0957-4344). **1979**

INTERNATIONAL JOURNAL OF COSMETIC SCIENCE. (UK/0142-5463). **404**

INTERNATIONAL JOURNAL OF DERMATOLOGY. (US/0011-9059). **3721**

INTERNATIONAL JOURNAL OF DEVELOPMENT BANKING : IJDB. (II). **792**

INTERNATIONAL JOURNAL OF DEVELOPMENTAL BIOLOGY, THE. (SP/0214-6282). **541**

INTERNATIONAL JOURNAL OF EARLY CHILDHOOD. (CN/0020-7187). **Adv Mgr:** M. C. Hewitt. **1753**

INTERNATIONAL JOURNAL OF EATING DISORDERS, THE. (US/0276-3478). **3798**

INTERNATIONAL JOURNAL OF ECOLOGY AND ENVIRONMENTAL SCIENCES. (II/0377-015X). **2217**

INTERNATIONAL JOURNAL OF EDUCATIONAL MANAGEMENT. (UK). **871**

INTERNATIONAL JOURNAL OF ELECTRICAL ENGINEERING EDUCATION. (UK/0020-7209). **2066**

INTERNATIONAL JOURNAL OF ELECTRICAL POWER & ENERGY SYSTEMS. (UK/0142-0615). **2066**

INTERNATIONAL JOURNAL OF ENERGY SYSTEMS. (US/0226-1472). **1947**

INTERNATIONAL JOURNAL OF ENGINEERING EDUCATION, THE. (GW). **1980**

INTERNATIONAL JOURNAL OF ENVIRONMENTAL ANALYTICAL CHEMISTRY. (US/0306-7319). **1015**

INTERNATIONAL JOURNAL OF EPIDEMIOLOGY. (UK/0300-5771). **3735**

INTERNATIONAL JOURNAL OF EXPERT SYSTEMS. (US/0894-9077). **1213**

INTERNATIONAL JOURNAL OF FATIGUE. (UK/0142-1123). **2102**

INTERNATIONAL JOURNAL OF FERTILITY. (US/0020-725X). **581**

INTERNATIONAL JOURNAL OF FETO-MATERNAL MEDICINE. (GW/0933-0445). **3762**

INTERNATIONAL JOURNAL OF FLEXIBLE MANUFACTURING SYSTEMS. (US/0920-6299). **3481**

INTERNATIONAL JOURNAL OF FOOD SCIENCE AND TECHNOLOGY. (UK/0950-5423). **2345**

INTERNATIONAL JOURNAL OF FRACTURE. (NE/0376-9429). **2102**

INTERNATIONAL JOURNAL OF FRONTIER MISSIONS. (US/0743-2429). **4965**

INTERNATIONAL JOURNAL OF GENERAL SYSTEMS. (US/0308-1079). **1247**

INTERNATIONAL JOURNAL OF GOVERNMENT AUDITING. (CN/0047-0724). **4732**

INTERNATIONAL JOURNAL OF GROUP PSYCHOTHERAPY, THE. (US/0020-7284). **3927**

INTERNATIONAL JOURNAL OF GYNAECOLOGY AND OBSTETRICS. (IE/0020-7292). **3762**

INTERNATIONAL JOURNAL OF HEALTH CARE QUALITY ASSURANCE. (UK/0952-6862). **4785**

INTERNATIONAL JOURNAL OF HEALTH PLANNING & MANAGEMENT, THE. (UK/0749-6753). **4785**

INTERNATIONAL JOURNAL OF HEALTH SCIENCES. (NE/0924-2287). **4785**

INTERNATIONAL JOURNAL OF HEAT AND FLUID FLOW, THE. (US/0142-727X). **2116**

INTERNATIONAL JOURNAL OF HUMAN-COMPUTER INTERACTION. (US/1044-7318). **1220**

INTERNATIONAL JOURNAL OF IMMUNOPATHOLOGY AND PHARMACOLOGY. (IT/0394-6320). **3672**

INTERNATIONAL JOURNAL OF INFORMATION MANAGEMENT. (UK/0268-4012). **3218**

INTERNATIONAL JOURNAL OF INTELLIGENT SYSTEMS. (US/0884-8173). **1213**

INTERNATIONAL JOURNAL OF ISLAMIC AND ARABIC STUDIES. (US/0740-5375). **2768**

INTERNATIONAL JOURNAL OF LAW AND THE FAMILY. (UK/0950-4109). **3121**

INTERNATIONAL JOURNAL OF LEGAL INFORMATION. (US/0731-1265). **3218**

INTERNATIONAL JOURNAL OF LEXICOGRAPHY. (UK/0950-3846). **3287**

INTERNATIONAL JOURNAL OF MARITIME HISTORY. (CN/0843-8714). **4177**

INTERNATIONAL JOURNAL OF MATERIALS & PRODUCT TECHNOLOGY. (SZ/0268-1900). **1980**

INTERNATIONAL JOURNAL OF MECHANICAL ENGINEERING EDUCATION, THE. (UK/0306-4190). **2116**

INTERNATIONAL JOURNAL OF MEDICAL MICROBIOLOGY AND HYGIENE ABSTRACTS OF MICROBIOLOGY, VIROLOGY, PARASITOLOGY, PREVENTIVE MEDICINE AND ENVIRONMENTAL HYGIENE. (GW/0937-1591). **564**

INTERNATIONAL JOURNAL OF MENTAL HEALTH. (US/0020-7411). **3927**

INTERNATIONAL JOURNAL OF MICROCIRCULATION: CLINICAL AND EXPERIMENTAL. (NE/0167-6865). **3798**

INTERNATIONAL JOURNAL OF MINI & MICROCOMPUTERS. (US/0702-0481). **1274**

INTERNATIONAL JOURNAL OF MINING AND GEOLOGICAL ENGINEERING. (UK/0269-0136). **2141**

INTERNATIONAL JOURNAL OF MODELLING & SIMULATION. (US/0228-6203). **1282**

INTERNATIONAL JOURNAL OF MORAL AND SOCIAL STUDIES. (UK/0267-9655). **2251**

INTERNATIONAL JOURNAL OF MUSIC EDUCATION / INTERNATIONAL SOCIETY FOR MUSIC EDUCATION. (UK). **Adv Mgr:** Elizabeth Smith. **4123**

INTERNATIONAL JOURNAL OF NETWORK MANAGEMENT. (UK/1055-7148). **1113**

INTERNATIONAL JOURNAL OF NUMERICAL METHODS FOR HEAT & FLUID FLOW. (UK/0961-5539). **1980**

INTERNATIONAL JOURNAL OF OBSTETRIC ANESTHESIA. (UK/0959-289X). **3763**

INTERNATIONAL JOURNAL OF OFFSHORE AND POLAR ENGINEERING. (US/1053-5381). **1980**

INTERNATIONAL JOURNAL OF ONCOLOGY. (GR/1019-6439). **3818**

INTERNATIONAL JOURNAL OF OPTOELECTRONICS. (UK/0952-5432). **4435**

INTERNATIONAL JOURNAL OF ORAL AND MAXILLOFACIAL IMPLANTS, THE. (US/0882-2786). **1325**

INTERNATIONAL JOURNAL OF ORAL AND MAXILLOFACIAL SURGERY. (DK/0901-5027). **3966**

INTERNATIONAL JOURNAL OF ORTHODONTICS. (US/0020-7500). **1325**

INTERNATIONAL JOURNAL OF ORTHOPAEDIC TRAUMA. (UK/0960-2941). **Adv Mgr:** Wendy Reinders. **3882**

INTERNATIONAL JOURNAL OF PATTERN RECOGNITION AND ARTIFICIAL INTELLIGENCE. (SI/0218-0014). **Adv Mgr:** Gilbert Low. **1213**

INTERNATIONAL JOURNAL OF PEPTIDE AND PROTEIN RESEARCH. (DK/0367-8377). **1042**

INTERNATIONAL JOURNAL OF PERIODONTICS & RESTORATIVE DENTISTRY, THE. (US/0198-7569). **1325**

INTERNATIONAL JOURNAL OF PHARMACEUTICAL TECHNOLOGY & PRODUCT MANUFACTURE. (UK/0260-6267). **4308**

INTERNATIONAL JOURNAL OF PHARMACY PRACTICE. (UK/0961-7671). **4309**

INTERNATIONAL JOURNAL OF PHYSICAL DISTRIBUTION & LOGISTICS MANAGEMENT. (UK/0960-0035). **871**

INTERNATIONAL JOURNAL OF POLITICAL ECONOMY. (US/0891-1916). **4477**

INTERNATIONAL JOURNAL OF POLITICS, CULTURE, AND SOCIETY. (US/0891-4486). **5248**

INTERNATIONAL JOURNAL OF POLYMERIC MATERIALS. (US/0091-4037). **978**

INTERNATIONAL JOURNAL OF POWDER METALLURGY (PRINCETON, N.J.). (US/0888-7462). **4004**

INTERNATIONAL JOURNAL OF PRESSURE VESSELS AND PIPING, THE. (UK/0308-0161). **2116**

INTERNATIONAL JOURNAL OF PROJECT MANAGEMENT. (UK/0263-7863). **1980**

INTERNATIONAL JOURNAL OF PSYCHO-ANALYSIS, THE. (UK/0020-7578). **4591**

INTERNATIONAL JOURNAL OF PSYCHOSOMATICS. (US/0884-8297). **3589**

INTERNATIONAL JOURNAL OF PUBLIC ADMINISTRATION. (US/0190-0692). **4657**

INTERNATIONAL JOURNAL OF PUBLIC SECTOR MANAGEMENT, THE. (UK/0951-3558). **4657**

INTERNATIONAL JOURNAL OF QUALITY & RELIABILITY MANAGEMENT, THE. (UK/0265-671X). **871**

INTERNATIONAL JOURNAL OF RADIATION APPLICATIONS AND INSTRUMENTATION. PART E, NUCLEAR GEOPHYSICS, THE. (UK/0886-0130). **1407**

INTERNATIONAL JOURNAL OF REFRACTORY METALS & HARD MATERIALS. (UK/0263-4368). **4004**

INTERNATIONAL JOURNAL OF REFRIGERATION. (UK/0140-7007). **2606**

INTERNATIONAL JOURNAL OF REHABILITATION RESEARCH. (GW/0342-5282). **4389**

INTERNATIONAL JOURNAL OF REMOTE SENSING. (UK/0143-1161). **1980**

INTERNATIONAL JOURNAL OF ROBOTICS & AUTOMATION. (US/0826-8185). **1213**

INTERNATIONAL JOURNAL OF ROBOTICS RESEARCH, THE. (US/0278-3649). **1220**

INTERNATIONAL JOURNAL OF SATELLITE COMMUNICATIONS. (UK/0737-2884). **1158**

INTERNATIONAL JOURNAL OF SCIENCE AND TECHNOLOGY. (US/0891-5083). **Adv Mgr:** Dina Soliman, **Tel** (317)839-8157. **5115**

INTERNATIONAL — Advertising Accepted Index

INTERNATIONAL JOURNAL OF SEDIMENT RESEARCH. (CC/1013-7866). **1383**

INTERNATIONAL JOURNAL OF SOCIAL EDUCATION, THE. (US/0889-0293). **5204**

INTERNATIONAL JOURNAL OF SOCIOLOGY. (US/0020-7659). **5248**

INTERNATIONAL JOURNAL OF SOLAR ENERGY. (SZ/0142-5919). **1948**

INTERNATIONAL JOURNAL OF SPORT BIOMECHANICS. (US/0740-2082). **495**

INTERNATIONAL JOURNAL OF SPORT PSYCHOLOGY. (IT/0047-0767). **4900**

INTERNATIONAL JOURNAL OF SUPERCOMPUTER APPLICATIONS, THE. (US/0890-2720). **1287**

INTERNATIONAL JOURNAL OF SYSTEMATIC BACTERIOLOGY. (US/0020-7713). **564**

INTERNATIONAL JOURNAL OF TECHNOLOGY MANAGEMENT. (SZ/0267-5730). **5115**

INTERNATIONAL JOURNAL OF THE ADDICTIONS. (US/0020-773X). **1345**

INTERNATIONAL JOURNAL OF THE HISTORY OF SPORT, THE. (UK/0952-3367). **Adv Mgr:** Anne Kidson. **4901**

INTERNATIONAL JOURNAL OF THE SOCIOLOGY OF LANGUAGE. (NE/0165-2516). **3287**

INTERNATIONAL JOURNAL OF THE STRUCTURAL DESIGN OF TALL BUILDINGS, THE. (UK/1062-8002). **Adv Mgr:** Michael Levermore, **Tel** 0243 770351. **2025**

INTERNATIONAL JOURNAL OF THERAPEUTIC COMMUNITIES. (UK/0196-1365). **3589**

INTERNATIONAL JOURNAL OF TRANSLATION. (II). **3288**

INTERNATIONAL JOURNAL OF TROPICAL PLANT DISEASES. (II/0254-0126). **Adv Mgr:** S Jain. **514**

INTERNATIONAL JOURNAL OF TURBO & JET-ENGINES. (IS/0334-0082). **24**

INTERNATIONAL JOURNAL OF TURKISH STUDIES. (US/0272-7919). **2692**

INTERNATIONAL JOURNAL OF UNIVERSITY ADULT EDUCATION. (CN/0074-3992). **1801**

INTERNATIONAL JOURNAL OF VEHICLE DESIGN. (SZ/0143-3369). **5417**

INTERNATIONAL JOURNAL OF WATER RESOURCES DEVELOPMENT. (UK/0790-0627). **5534**

INTERNATIONAL JOURNAL OF WILDLAND FIRE, THE. (US/1049-8001). **Adv Mgr:** Lane Shaw, **Tel** (509)283-2397. **2291**

INTERNATIONAL JOURNAL OF WINE MARKETING. (HK/0954-7541). **2368**

INTERNATIONAL JOURNAL ON DRUG POLICY, THE. (UK/0955-3959). **1345**

INTERNATIONAL JOURNAL ON POLICY AND INFORMATION. (US/0251-1266). **5204**

INTERNATIONAL JOURNAL ON THE UNITY OF THE SCIENCES. (US/0896-2294). **5115**

INTERNATIONAL LABMATE. (UK/0143-5140). **1015**

INTERNATIONAL LABOR AND WORKING CLASS HISTORY. (US/0147-5479). **1680**

INTERNATIONAL LABORATORY. EUROPEAN ED. (US/0010-2164). **1016**

INTERNATIONAL LAW PRACTICUM. (US/1041-3405). **3130**

INTERNATIONAL LAWYER, THE. (US/0020-7810). **3130**

INTERNATIONAL LEGAL MATERIALS. (US/0020-7829). **3130**

INTERNATIONAL LEGAL PRACTITIONER. (UK/0309-7684). **3130**

INTERNATIONAL LIAISON GROUP ON GOLD MINERALIZATION NEWSLETTER. (UK). **1383**

INTERNATIONAL LIBRARY MOVEMENT. (II/0970-0048). **3218**

INTERNATIONAL LICENSING DIRECTORY, THE. (UK). **Adv Mgr:** Jerry Wooldridge. **1305**

INTERNATIONAL LICHENOLOGICAL NEWSLETTER. (GW/0731-2830). **514**

INTERNATIONAL LIVING (WASHINGTON, D.C.). (US/0277-2442). **5481**

INTERNATIONAL MANAGEMENT. (UK). **684**

INTERNATIONAL MARINE BUSINESS. (UK/0965-0644). **Adv Mgr:** Madeline Lowe. **684**

INTERNATIONAL MARINE BUSINESS JOURNAL. (US). **593**

INTERNATIONAL MARKETING REVIEW. (UK/0265-1335). **926**

INTERNATIONAL MARXIST REVIEW : IMR / ORGAN OF THE REVOLUTIONARY MARXIST TENDENCY OF THE FOURTH INTERNATIONAL. (UK). **4477**

INTERNATIONAL MAURITIUS DIRECTORY. (MF). **2499**

INTERNATIONAL MEDIA GUIDE. EDITION, BUSINESS/PROFESSIONAL PUBLICATIONS, EUROPE. (US/0730-5273). **761**

INTERNATIONAL MEDIA GUIDE. EDITION, BUSINESS/PROFESSIONAL PUBLICATIONS, MIDDLE EAST/AFRICA. (US). **761**

INTERNATIONAL MEDIEVAL BIBLIOGRAPHY. (UK/0020-7950). **3458**

INTERNATIONAL MIGRATION (GENEVA, SWITZERLAND). (SZ/0020-7985). **1919**

INTERNATIONAL MIGRATION REVIEW : IMR. (US/0197-9183). **1919**

INTERNATIONAL MONEY MARKETING. (UK/0958-3785). **Adv Mgr:** Tony Hay, **Tel** 011 44 71 287 1536. **902**

INTERNATIONAL MOTION PICTURE ALMANAC (1956). (US/0074-7084). **4073**

INTERNATIONAL NETWORKS. (US/0739-9898). **1158**

INTERNATIONAL NEWS ON FATS, OILS AND RELATED MATERIALS. (US/0897-8026). **1025**

INTERNATIONAL NURSING INDEX. (US/0020-8124). **3660**

INTERNATIONAL NURSING REVIEW (LONDON, ENGLAND). (SZ/0020-8132). **3857**

INTERNATIONAL OLD LACERS INC., BULLETIN. (US/0740-6746). **5352**

INTERNATIONAL OLYMPIC LIFTER. (US/0739-5396). **Adv Mgr:** Sandra Hise. **4901**

INTERNATIONAL OPHTHALMOLOGY. (NE/0165-5701). **3875**

INTERNATIONAL ORGANIZATION. (US/0020-8183). **4525**

INTERNATIONAL PAF USERS GROUP SOFTWARE. (US). **1190**

INTERNATIONAL PEACEKEEPING. (UK/1353-3312). **4525**

INTERNATIONAL PEDIATRICS. (US/0885-6265). **3904**

INTERNATIONAL PERMACULTURE SPECIES YEARBOOK, THE. (US/0896-5781). **2217**

INTERNATIONAL PERSPECTIVES IN PUBLIC HEALTH. (US/8755-5328). **4785**

INTERNATIONAL PEST CONTROL. (UK/0020-8256). **4245**

INTERNATIONAL PETROLEUM ENCYCLOPEDIA. (US/0148-0375). **4261**

INTERNATIONAL PHARMACEUTICAL ABSTRACTS. (US/0020-8264). **4334**

INTERNATIONAL PHILOSOPHICAL QUARTERLY. (US/0019-0365). **Adv Mgr:** Sara Penella. **4349**

INTERNATIONAL PHOTOGRAPHER. (US/0020-8299). **4371**

INTERNATIONAL POLITICAL SCIENCE ABSTRACTS. (FR/0020-8345). **4502**

INTERNATIONAL POLITICAL SCIENCE REVIEW. (UK/0192-5121). **4477**

INTERNATIONAL POLYMER PROCESSING. (GW/0930-777X). **4455**

INTERNATIONAL POPULAR BRIDGE MONTHLY. (UK/0951-1555). **4851**

INTERNATIONAL PROBLEMS. (IS/0020-840X). **4525**

INTERNATIONAL PSYCHOLOGIST. (US/0047-116X). **4591**

INTERNATIONAL PUBLIC RELATIONS REVIEW. (UK/0269-0357). **Adv Mgr:** V.Glenn. **761**

INTERNATIONAL PULP & PAPER DIRECTORY. (US/0097-2509). **4234**

INTERNATIONAL QUARTERLY OF ENTOMOLOGY. (TU/0256-6672). **5610**

INTERNATIONAL QUARTERLY (TALLAHASS., FLA.). (US/1060-6084). **Adv Mgr:** Van K. Brock. **3396**

INTERNATIONAL RAILWAY JOURNAL AND RAPID TRANSIT REVIEW. (UK/0744-5326). **5432**

INTERNATIONAL RAILWAY TRAVELER, THE. (US/0891-7655). **5432**

INTERNATIONAL REAL ESTATE JOURNAL. (US/8755-6138). **Adv Mgr:** Troy E. Johnson. **4839**

INTERNATIONAL RELATIONS (LONDON). (UK/0047-1178). **4525**

INTERNATIONAL REPORT (IRVINE, CALIF.). (US/0740-669X). **4477**

INTERNATIONAL REVIEW FOR THE SOCIOLOGY OF SPORT. (GW/0074-7769). **4901**

INTERNATIONAL REVIEW OF ADMINISTRATIVE SCIENCES. (BE/0020-8523). **4657**

INTERNATIONAL REVIEW OF AFRICAN AMERICAN ART, THE. (US/1045-0920). **353**

INTERNATIONAL REVIEW OF LAW AND ECONOMICS. (US/0144-8188). **1636**

INTERNATIONAL REVIEW OF NEUROBIOLOGY. (US/0074-7742). **459**

INTERNATIONAL REVIEW OF SOCIAL HISTORY. (NE/0020-8590). **5248**

INTERNATIONAL REVIEW OF SOCIOLOGY OF EDUCATION. (AT/0726-4178). **5248**

INTERNATIONAL ROUND TABLE, THE. (US). **841**

INTERNATIONAL SATELLITE DIRECTORY. (US/1041-4541). **1113**

INTERNATIONAL SAUDI-REPORT. (UK/0265-5799). **2505**

INTERNATIONAL SCHOOLS JOURNAL, THE. (UK). **1754**

INTERNATIONAL SECURITY. (US/0162-2889). **4525**

INTERNATIONAL SECURITY DIRECTORY. (UK/0074-7890). **3166**

INTERNATIONAL SEMIOTIC SPECTRUM. (CN/0825-0456). **2848**

INTERNATIONAL SMALL BUSINESS JOURNAL. (UK/0266-2426). **684**

INTERNATIONAL SOCIAL SCIENCE JOURNAL. (FR/0020-8701). **5204**

INTERNATIONAL SOCIAL WORK. (UK/0020-8728). **5290**

INTERNATIONAL SOCIETY OF BASSISTS. (US/0892-0532). **4123**

INTERNATIONAL SPECTRUM. (US/1050-9070). **Adv Mgr:** Jill Dennis. **1190**

INTERNATIONAL SPORTS MAGAZINE. (HU). **4901**

INTERNATIONAL STATISTICAL REVIEW. (NE/0306-7734). **5329**

INTERNATIONAL STUDIES NOTES. (US/0094-7768). **4525**

INTERNATIONAL STUDIES OF MANAGEMENT & ORGANIZATION. (US/0020-8825). **872**

INTERNATIONAL STUDIES QUARTERLY. (US/0020-8833). **4525**

INTERNATIONAL STUDIES (SAHIBABAD). (II/0020-8817). **3131**

INTERNATIONAL SUGAR JOURNAL. (UK/0020-8841). **2345**

INTERNATIONAL SURGERY. (IT/0020-8868). **3966**

INTERNATIONAL TAX FREE TRADER. (UK). **Adv Mgr:** Stuart Velden, **Tel** 011 44 737 768611 ext. 3519. **1636**

INTERNATIONAL TELEVISION & VIDEO ALMANAC. (US/0895-2213). **1133**

INTERNATIONAL TELEX-DIRECTORY ITD. (GW). **1158**

INTERNATIONAL TENNIS. (US/1063-0333). **Adv Mgr:** Erika Green. **4901**

INTERNATIONAL TENNIS WEEKLY. (US/0199-0853). **4901**

INTERNATIONAL TEXTILE BULLETIN. DYEING/PRINTING/FINISHING. (SZ/1012-8417). **5352**

INTERNATIONAL TEXTILE BULLETIN. FABRIC FORMING. (SZ/1012-8425). **5352**

INTERNATIONAL TEXTILES. (NE/0020-8914). **5352**

INTERNATIONAL, THE. (UK). **Adv Mgr:** R. Symondon. **792**

INTERNATIONAL THIRD WORLD STUDIES JOURNAL & REVIEW. (US/1041-3944). **4526**

INTERNATIONAL TRADE JOURNAL, THE. (US/0885-3908). **841**

INTERNATIONAL TRAVEL NEWS (SACRAMENTO, CALIF.). (US/0191-8761). **5481**

INTERNATIONAL TREE CROPS JOURNAL, THE. (UK/0143-5698). **2385**

INTERNATIONAL TROMBONE ASSOCIATION SERIES. (US/0363-5708). **4123**

INTERNATIONAL TV & VIDEO GUIDE. (UK). **1133**

INTERNATIONAL UNDERWATER SYSTEMS DESIGN. (UK/0267-1085). **Adv Mgr:** T. Barrett, **Tel** 0926 641640. **2091**

INTERNATIONAL UROLOGY AND NEPHROLOGY. (HU/0301-1623). **3990**

INTERNATIONAL WATER & IRRIGATION REVIEW. (IS). **Adv Mgr:** Amir Cohen. **175**

INTERNATIONAL YOUTH HOSTELS HANDBOOK. (UK). **5481**

INTERNATIONAL ZOO-NEWS. (UK/0020-9155). **5586**

INTERNATIONALE BIBLIOGRAPHIE DER REZENSIONEN WISSENSCHAFTLICHER LITERATUR. (GW/0020-918X). **3357**

INTERNATIONALE BIBLIOGRAPHIE DER ZEITSCHRIFTENLITERATUR AUS ALLEN GEBIETEN DES WISSENS. (GW). **3357**

INTERNATIONALE JAHRESBIBLIOGRAPHIE DER FESTSCHRIFTEN : IJBF. (GW). **417**

INTERNATIONALE JAHRESBIBLIOGRAPHIE DER KONGRESSBERICHTE. (GW/0933-1905). **417**

INTERNATIONALE KATHOLISCHE ZEITSCHRIFT. (GW/0341-8693). **5030**

INTERNATIONALE MATHEMATISCHE NACHRICHTEN. (AU). **3510**

INTERNATIONALE ZEITSCHRIFT FUER PHILOSOPHIE. (GW/0942-3028). **4349**

INTERNATIONALE ZEITSCHRIFTENSCHAU FUER BIBELWISSENSCHAFT UND GRENZGEBIETE. (GW/0074-9745). **5013**

INTERNATIONALER HOLZMARKT. (AU/0020-9422). **2402**

INTERNATIONALES ARCHIV FUER SOZIALGESCHICHTE DER DEUTSCHEN LITERATUR. (GW/0340-4528). **3397**

INTERNATIONALES SAUNA-ARCHIV. (GW/0178-7764). **2599**

INTERNATIONALES VERKEHRSWESEN. (GW/0020-9511). **5384**

INTERNISTISCHE WELT. (GW/0344-4201). **3798**

INTERNSHIPS. (US/0272-5460). **4205**

INTERPLASTICS (MILANO). (IT/0392-3800). **4455**

INTERPRES. (IT). **3397**

INTERPRETATION (RICHMOND). (US/0020-9643). **4966**

INTERPRETE, L'. (SZ/0047-1291). **3288**

INTERPRETER (EVANSTON, ILL.), THE. (US/0020-9678). **Adv Mgr:** Laura O'Kumu, **Tel** (615)742-5104. **5061**

INTERRACE (SCHENECTADY, N.Y.). (US/1047-5370). **Adv Mgr:** Gabe Grosz. **2264**

INTERSCAMBIO. (IT/0394-087X). **1497**

INTERSCHOLASTIC ATHLETIC ADMINISTRATION. (US/0097-871X). **Adv Mgr:** Brad Rumble, **Tel** (816)464-5400. **4901**

INTERSTATE ACCOMODATION DIRECTORY. (AT). **Adv Mgr:** Karen Shields. **2807**

INTERTAX. (NE/0165-2826). **4733**

INTERVAL (SAN DIEGO, CALIF.). (US/0276-3052). **4123**

INTERVALLE. (GW). **4123**

INTERVENTION IN SCHOOL AND CLINIC. (US/1053-4512). **1880**

INTERVENTION (QUEBEC). (CN/0705-1972). **2535**

INTERVENTIONS ECONOMIQUES POUR UNE ALTERNATIVE SOCIALE. (CN/0715-3570). **1497**

INTERVENTIONS SONORES. (CN/1181-7739). **4124**

INTERVIEW (NEW YORK, N.Y. 1977). (US/0149-8932). **2535**

INTERVIROLOGY. (SZ/0300-5526). **564**

INTI (PROVIDENCE, R.I.). (US/0732-6750). **3397**

INTIMATE FASHION NEWS. (US/1061-5792). **Adv Mgr:** E.A. Greenberg, **Tel** (212)679-6677. **1085**

INTIMO PIU MARE. (IT). **1085**

INTOWNER, THE. (US/0887-9400). **Adv Mgr:** Mr. Wolfe. **5647**

INUIT ART QUARTERLY. (CN/0831-6708). **Adv Mgr:** S. Green. **353**

INVASION & METASTASIS. (SW/0251-1789). **537**

INVENTAIRE DES MOYENS DE FORMATION DEPENDANT DES MINISTERES TECHNIQUES. (IV). **1913**

INVENTORS' DIGEST (COLORADO SPRINGS, COLO.). (US/0883-9859). **5116**

INVENTORS' VOICE. (US/0748-7851). **5116**

INVERT MAGAZINE. (UK/0957-3828). **429**

INVERTEBRATE REPRODUCTION & DEVELOPMENT. (IS/0792-4259). **5586**

INVERTEBRATE TAXONOMY. (AT/0818-0164). **5587**

INVEST IN HUNGARY. (HU/0239-1929). **902**

INVEST YOURSELF. (US/0148-6802). **5290**

INVESTAMERICA (SAN FRANCISCO, CALIF.). (US/1040-2934). **902**

INVESTIGACION MEDICA INTERNACIONAL. (MX/0377-0206). **Adv Mgr:** Oscar Bagnarelli. **3590**

INVESTIGACION Y TECNICA DEL PAPEL. (SP/0368-0789). **4234**

INVESTIGATING. (AT/0815-9602). **Adv Mgr:** Ian Pattie, **Tel** (003)314048. **5116**

INVESTMENT ADVISOR (SHREWSBURY, N.J.). (US/1069-1731). **Adv Mgr:** David Smith, **Tel** (908)389-8700 Ext. 111. **902**

INVESTMENT DEALERS' DIGEST, THE. (US/0021-0080). **793**

INVESTOR'S DAILY. (US). **903**

INVIVO. (CN/0836-3838). **459**

INVOLVEMENT & PARTICIPATION / IPA. (UK). **872**

INVOLVEMENT : THE JOURNAL OF THE INVOLVEMENT & PARTICIPATION ASSOCIATION. (UK). **872**

IO, MANAGEMENT-ZEITSCHRIFT INDUSTRIELLE ORGANISATION. (SZ/0019-9281). **872**

IOLA HERALD, THE. (US/0886-8360). **Adv Mgr:** Trey Foerster. **5768**

IOLA REGISTER (IOLA, KAN. : 1939). (US). **Adv Mgr:** Jack Hastings. **5676**

IOWA ARCHITECT. (US/0021-0439). **Adv Mgr:** Kelly Roberson. **301**

IOWA CITY MAGAZINE. (US). **2536**

IOWA DENTAL JOURNAL, THE. (US/0021-0498). **1325**

IOWA INTERLINK. (US/1050-2270). **4657**

IOWA JOURNAL OF COMMUNICATION. (US). **1114**

IOWA LAW REVIEW. (US/0021-0552). **2984**

IOWA MANUFACTURERS REGISTER. (US/0737-7940). **3481**

IOWA MEDICINE. (US/0746-8709). **Adv Mgr:** Jane Nieland. **3590**

IOWA MUNICIPALITIES. (US/0021-0595). **4657**

IOWA REVIEW, THE. (US/0021-065X). **3397**

IOWA SCHOOL BOARD DIALOGUE, THE. (US/0021-0668). **1865**

IOWA SCIENCE TEACHERS' JOURNAL. (US/0021-0676). **5116**

IOWA STATE DAILY. (US). **Adv Mgr:** Kathy Davis, **Tel** (515)294-4121. **5670**

IOWA STATE UNIVERSITY VETERINARIAN. (US/0099-5851). **5512**

IOWA WOMAN. (US/0271-8227). **5559**

IOWAN, THE. (US/0021-0722). **2536**

IP MARK. (SP). **684**

IPA REVIEW (1986). (AT/1030-4177). **4733**

IPADE ALAGBARA. (US/0883-6620). **5268**

IPEF, INSTITUTO DE PESQUISAS E ESTUDOS FORESTAIS. (BL/0100-4557). **2385**

IPM, INTERPRESS MAGAZIN. (HU). **2518**

IPM PRACTITIONER, THE. (US/0738-968X). **4245**

IPPOGRIFO (BOLOGNA, ITALY). (IT). **3344**

IPSWICH & SUFFOLK DIRECTORY OF INDUSTRY & COMMERCE, THE. (UK/0269-2716). **684**

IPTC NEWS. (UK/1012-8719). **1158**

IQBAL REVIEW. (PK/0021-0773). **3397**

IR. INVESTOR RELATIONS. (UK/0958-6679). **903**

IRAL, INTERNATIONAL REVIEW OF APPLIED LINGUISTICS IN LANGUAGE TEACHING. (GW/0019-042X). **3288**

IRAN NAMEH. BUNYAD-I MUTALAAT-I IRAN. (US/0892-4147). **2654**

IRAN TIMES, THE. (US). **5647**

IRAN-UNITED STATES CLAIMS TRIBUNAL REPORTS. (UK). **3131**

IRANIAN STUDIES. (US/0021-0862). **2768**

IRANIAN WOMEN QUARTERLY. (CN). **5559**

IRANIYAN (TORONTO). (CN/0832-2007). **5786**

IRANSHINASI (BETHESDA, MD.). (US/1051-5364). **3397**

IRCIHE BULLETIN / INTERNATIONAL REFERRAL CENTRE FOR INFORMATION HANDLING EQUIPMENT. (CI/0351-0123). **3218**

IRELAND : A PARLIAMENTARY DIRECTORY. (IE). **4658**

IRELAND OF THE WELCOMES. (IE/0021-0943). **2518**

IRIS (CHARLOTTESVILLE, VA.). (US/0896-1301). **5204**

IRIS YEAR BOOK / BRITISH IRIS SOCIETY, THE. (UK/0075-0700). **2420**

IRISH AMERICA. (US/0884-4240). **Adv Mgr:** Eilleen McMahon. **2739**

IRISH ASTRONOMICAL JOURNAL, THE. (UK/0021-1052). **396**

IRISH BIBLICAL STUDIES. (IE/0268-6112). **5017**

IRISH BIOTECH NEWS. (IE/0790-1747). **459**

IRISH BIRDS. (IE/0332-0111). **Adv Mgr:** O. O'sullivan. **5617**

IRISH ECHO. (US/0192-1215). **2264**

IRISH ECONOMIC AND SOCIAL HISTORY. (IE/0332-4893). **2692**

IRISH EDITION. (US/1063-7532). **Adv Mgr:** Mary Kay Cavanaugh. **2264**

IRISH EDUCATIONAL STUDIES. (IE/0332-3315). **1755**

IRISH FARMER'S JOURNAL. (IE). **97**

IRISH FORESTRY. (IE/0021-1192). **2385**

IRISH HERITAGE LINKS. (UK/0957-0837). **2454**

IRISH HISTORICAL STUDIES. (IE/0021-1214). **2692**

IRISH JOURNAL OF EDUCATION, THE. (IE/0021-1257). **1755**

IRISH JOURNAL OF MEDICAL SCIENCE. (IE/0021-1265). **Adv Mgr:** D. Korcel. **3590**

IRISH JOURNAL OF PSYCHOLOGICAL MEDICINE. (IE/0790-9667). **Adv Mgr:** Ray Hurrell. **3927**

IRISH JOURNAL OF PSYCHOLOGY, THE. (IE/0303-3910). **4592**

IRISH JURIST, THE. (IE/0021-1273). **2985**

IRISH LITERARY SUPPLEMENT. (US/0733-3390). **3397**

IRISH MEDICAL JOURNAL. (IE/0332-3102). **3590**

IRISH NATURALISTS' JOURNAL, THE. (UK/0021-1311). **Adv Mgr:** Catherine Tyrie. **4166**

IRISH NEWS AND BELFAST MORNING NEWS, THE. (IE). **5803**

IRISH QUERIES. (US/1044-6923). **2454**

IRISH REVIEW (CORK, IRELAND). (IE/0790-7850). **2518**

IRISH SLAVONIC STUDIES. (UK/0260-2067). **Adv Mgr:** same as editor. **2692**

IRISH TRAVEL TRADE NEWS. (IE/0021-1419). **5481**

IRISH UNIVERSITY REVIEW. (IE/0021-1427). **3344**

IRISH VETERINARY JOURNAL. (IE/0368-0762). **5512**

IRISH VETERINARY NEWS. (IE). **5512**

IRISH VOICE (NEW YORK, N.Y.). (US/0895-4534). **Adv Mgr:** Paddy McCarthy. **5717**

IRON. (UK). **3397**

IRON AND STEEL ENGINEER. (US/0021-1559). **Adv Mgr:** S. Seem. **4004**

IRON AND STEEL INDUSTRY. ANNUAL STATISTICS FOR THE UNITED KINGDOM. (UK/0572-709X). **1612**

IRON AND STEEL WORKS OF THE WORLD. (UK). **4005**

IRON & STEELMAKER. (US/0275-8687). **4005**

IRON MAN. (US/0047-1496). **2599**

IRON-MEN ALBUM MAGAZNE. (US). **2117**

IRON ORE MANUAL. (JA). **4005**

IRONMAKING & STEELMAKING. (UK/0301-9233). **4005**

IRPI. INTERNATIONAL REINFORCED PLASTICS INDUSTRY. (UK/0261-5487). **4455**

IRRIGATION AND DRAINAGE ABSTRACTS / COMMONWEALTH AGRICULTURAL BUREAUX. (UK/0306-7327). **2005**

IRRIGATION AND POWER. (II/0367-9993). **2091**

IRRIGATION FARMER, THE. (AT). **175**

IRRIGATION JOURNAL. (US/0047-1518). **159**

IS AUDIT & CONTROL JOURNAL. (US/1076-4100). **Adv Mgr:** M. Faddock. **1260**

IS. INTER SERVICE. (US/0273-7485). **955**

ISA DIRECTORY OF INSTRUMENTATION (TRADE EDITION). (US/0272-8141). **3481**

ISA TRANSACTIONS. (US/0019-0578). **5116**

ISAAS — Advertising Accepted Index

ISAAS NEWSLETTER / INDIAN SOCIETY FOR AFRO-ASIAN STUDIES. (II). **4526**

ISANTI COUNTY NEWS. (US/8750-2267). **5696**

ISEA COMMUNIQUE. (US/0019-0624). **1865**

ISIS. (US/0021-1753). **5116**

ISIS GUIDE TO THE HISTORY OF SCIENCE. (US). **5116**

ISIS MAGAZINE : MAGAZINE OF THE INDEPENDENT SCHOOLS INFORMATION SERVICE, THE. (UK). **Adv Mgr:** R. Lambert, **Tel** 071 630 8795. **1755**

ISKCON WORLD REVIEW, THE. (US/0748-2280). **4966**

ISLAH (DUBAYY, UNITED ARAB EMIRATES). (TS). **4526**

ISLAMIC AFFAIRS. (US/0748-0482). **5043**

ISLAMIC STUDIES. (PK/0578-8072). **5043**

ISLAMOCHRISTIANA. ISLAMIYAT MASIHIYAT. (IT). **4966**

ISLAND. (AT/1035-3127). **3397**

ISLAND DISPATCH. (US/0892-2497). **5717**

ISLAND GROWER, THE. (CN/0827-2824). **2420**

ISLAND (OAKLAND, CALIF.). (US/0894-3494). **2693**

ISLAND PACKET, THE. (US/0746-4886). **Adv Mgr:** Phil Porter. **5742**

ISLAND PARENT MAGAZINE. (CN/0838-5505). **2281**

ISLAND, SANDY BAY. (AT/1035-3127). **Adv Mgr:** Lynne Hardwick. **3397**

ISLANDER, THE. (US). **5654**

ISLANDS (SANTA BARBARA, CALIF.). (US/0745-7847). **5481**

ISLANDWIDE RUNNER. (US/0740-6266). **4901**

ISLE OF MAN OFFICIAL YEAR BOOK. (UK). **2693**

ISOKINETICS AND EXERCISE SCIENCE. (US). **2599**

ISOZYMES. (US/0160-3787). **488**

ISPT JOURNAL OF RESEARCH. (II). **4592**

ISR, INTERNATIONLE BERG- UND SEILBAHNRUNDSCHAU. INTERNATIONAL AERIAL TRAMWAY REVIEW. (AU). **2117**

ISRAEL AFFAIRS. (UK). **2768**

ISRAEL BOOK TRADE DIRECTORY. (IS). **4829**

ISRAEL HORIZONS. (US/0021-2083). **5048**

ISRAEL JOURNAL OF BOTANY. (IS/0021-213X). **514**

ISRAEL JOURNAL OF CHEMISTRY. (IS/0021-2148). **978**

ISRAEL JOURNAL OF MEDICAL SCIENCES. (IS/0021-2180). **Adv Mgr:** S. Noy, **Tel** (2) 972-817727. **3590**

ISRAEL JOURNAL OF PLANT SCIENCES. (IS/0792-9978). **514**

ISRAEL JOURNAL OF PSYCHIATRY AND RELATED SCIENCES, THE. (IS/0333-7308). **3927**

ISRAEL JOURNAL OF VETERINARY MEDICINE. (IS/0334-9152). **5512**

ISRAEL JOURNAL OF ZOOLOGY. (IS/0021-2210). **5587**

ISRAEL LAW REVIEW. (IS/0021-2237). **2985**

ISRAEL YEARBOOK AND ALMANAC. (IS). **1927**

ISRAEL YEARBOOK OF HUMAN RIGHTS. (NE/0333-5925). **4510**

ISRAELI JOURNAL OF AQUACULTURE, BAMIDGEH. (IS/0792-156X). **2306**

ISS DIRECTORY OF OVERSEAS SCHOOLS. (US/0732-7862). **1755**

ISSAQUAH PRESS, THE. **Adv Mgr:** Brian Bretland. **5761**

ISSLEDOVANIE ZEMLI IZ KOSMOSA. (SZ/0275-911X). **1981**

ISSO NEWSLETTER, THE. (US/1064-4393). **Adv Mgr:** Melanie Horn. **25**

ISSUE (WALTHAM, MASS.). (US/0047-1607). **2499**

ISSUES, EVENTS & IDEAS. (CN/0704-6936). **1804**

ISSUES IN COMPREHENSIVE PEDIATRIC NURSING. (US/0146-0862). **3857**

ISSUES IN INTEGRATIVE STUDIES. (US). **Adv Mgr:** Sechelow. **1755**

ISSUES IN MENTAL HEALTH NURSING. (US/0161-2840). **3858**

ISSUES IN REPRODUCTIVE AND GENETIC ENGINEERING : JOURNAL OF INTERNATIONAL FEMINIST ANALYSIS. (US/0958-6415). **3693**

ISSUES IN SCIENCE AND TECHNOLOGY. (US/0748-5492). **5116**

ISSUES IN SOCIAL WORK EDUCATION / ASSOCIATION OF TEACHERS IN SOCIAL WORK EDUCATION. (UK/0261-4154). **5291**

ISSUES IN WRITING. (US/0897-0696). **2921**

ISSX PROCEEDINGS. (US/1061-3439). **4309**

ISTF NEWS. (US/0276-2056). **2385**

ISTF NOTICIAS. (US/0743-5991). **Adv Mgr:** Rodney Young. **2385**

ISTINA. (FR/0021-2423). **4966**

ISTMO. (MX/0021-261X). **5249**

ISTORICHESKI PREGLED. (BU/0021-2636). **2693**

IT LINK. (UK/0954-2612). **3219**

IT TRAINING. (UK/0954-7940). **Adv Mgr:** Sam Stevens. **1223**

ITALIA GRAFICA, L'. (IT/0021-2784). **4566**

ITALIAN-AMERICAN BUSINESS. (IT). **1636**

ITALIAN AMERICANA. (US/0096-8846). **2264**

ITALIAN CARS. (UK/0960-3204). **5417**

ITALIAN GENERAL REVIEW OF DERMATOLOGY. (IT/0021-292X). **3721**

ITALIAN GREYHOUND, THE. (US/0735-8504). **4286**

ITALIAN JOURNAL OF BIOCHEMISTRY. (IT/0021-2938). **488**

ITALIAN JOURNAL OF GASTROENTEROLOGY, THE. (IT/0392-0623). **3746**

ITALIAN JOURNAL OF SPORTS TRAUMATOLOGY. (IT/0391-4089). **3954**

ITALIAN JOURNAL OF SURGICAL SCIENCES, THE. (US/0392-3525). **3966**

ITALIAN LIGHTING. (IT). **Adv Mgr:** Renato Pisaniello. **2067**

ITALIAN QUARTERLY. (US/0021-2954). **2693**

ITALIAN TRIBUNE NEWS. (US). **Adv Mgr:** David Aaron. **5710**

ITALIANA VITA. (CN/0700-3234). **2693**

ITALIANIST. (UK/0261-4340). **3397**

ITALIENISCH. (GW/0171-4996). **3288**

ITALIQUES / UNIVERSITE DE LA SORBONNE NOUVELLE (PARIS III), U.E.R. D'ITALIEN ET ROUMAIN, CENTRE DE RECHERCHES SUR L'ITALIE MODERNE ET CONTEMPORAINE. (FR/0751-2163). **3397**

ITAWAMBA COUNTY TIMES. (US). **Adv Mgr:** Terry Miller. **5700**

ITC JOURNAL, THE. (NE/0303-2434). **1356**

ITE JOURNAL. (US/0162-8178). **5384**

ITEM. (SP/0214-0349). **3219**

ITEM OF MILLBURN AND SHORT HILLS, THE. (US). **Adv Mgr:** Tracy Dupuis. **5710**

ITEM, THE. (US). **Adv Mgr:** C. F Olavania. **5742**

ITG JOURNAL. (US/0363-2849). **4124**

ITHACA JOURNAL (ITHACA, N.Y. : 1934). (US). **5717**

ITHACA TIMES. (US/0277-1187). **5717**

ITI. INTERNATIONAL TELECOMMUNICATIONS INTELLIGENCE. (UK/0268-9960). **1158**

ITPI JOURNAL. (II). **2825**

IUS CANONICUM. (SP/0021-325X). **2985**

IUS COMMUNE. (GW). **2985**

IUSTITIA (BLOOMINGTON). (IT/0092-3524). **2985**

IVS ANNUAL CROWS NEST. (AT/1033-2863). **Adv Mgr:** G Hand. **5512**

IVS. INDEX OF VETERINARY SPECIALITIES. (SA/0019-0918). **5512**

IVY JOURNAL. (US/0882-4142). **514**

IVY LEAF (CHICAGO). (US/0021-3276). **1102**

IWGIA DOCUMENTS. (DK/0105-4503). **238**

IWK INTERNATIONALE WISSENSCHAFTLICHE KORRESPONDENZ ZUR GESCHICHTE DER DEUTSCHEN ARBEITERBEWEGUNG. (GW/0046-8428). **Adv Mgr:** same as editor. **1681**

IWSA YEAR BOOK : AN OFFICIAL PUBLICATION OF THE INTERNATIONAL WATER SUPPLY ASSOCIATION. (UK). **5535**

IYO DENSHI TO SEITAI KOGAKU. (JA/0021-3292). **3693**

IZVESTIYA, ACADEMY OF SCIENCES, USSR. PHYSICS OF THE SOLID EARTH. (US/0001-4354). **1407**

J P 4. (IT/0394-3437). **25**

J.P. WEEKLY LAW DIGEST, THE. (UK/0264-3723). **2986**

J U C O REVIEW. (US/0047-2956). **4901**

JA QUARTERLY. (JA). **301**

JAARBOEK VAN DE HAVEN VAN ANTWERPEN. ANNUAIRE DU PORT D'ANVERS. ANTWERP PORT ANNUAL. (BE). **Adv Mgr:** Koen Heinen. **5450**

JAARBOEK (VLAAMS INSTITUUT VOOR AMERIKAANSE KULTUREN). (BE). **270**

JAB MAGAZINE. (US). **2536**

JACK-PINE WARBLER. (US). **5617**

JACKSON ADVOCATE. (US/0047-1704). **Adv Mgr:** O.J.Daniels. **5700**

JACKSON COUNTY FLORIDAN. (US). **5650**

JACKSON COUNTY PILOT. (US). **Adv Mgr:** Dallas Luhmann. **5696**

JACKSON HERALD. (US). **Adv Mgr:** Scott Buffington. **5654**

JACKSON HOLE GUIDE, THE. (US). **Adv Mgr:** Monty Nethercott. **5772**

JACKSONIANA. (US/0738-6648). **2455**

JACKSONVILLE BUSINESS JOURNAL. (US/0885-453X). **Adv Mgr:** L Chasteen. **685**

JACKSONVILLE (JACKSONVILLE, FLA.). (US/1070-5163). **Adv Mgr:** Bruce Beresford. **2536**

JACKSONVILLE NEWS (JACKSONVILLE, ALA.). (US). **Adv Mgr:** Roy Roberts. **5627**

JACKSONVILLE PATRIOT. (US/1064-7260). **Adv Mgr:** Susie Magie. **5631**

JACKSONVILLE TODAY. (US/0885-4769). **Adv Mgr:** Mischelle Grant, **Tel** (904)396-8666. **2536**

JACT REVIEW. (UK/0268-0181). **1077**

JAEGER'S INTERTRAVEL. (GW). **5481**

JAHRBUCH DER GRAPHISCHEN UNTERNEHMUNGEN OSTERREICHS. (AU/0075-2266). **4566**

JAHRBUCH DER PSYCHOANALYSE. (GW/0075-2363). **3927**

JAHRBUCH DER TURNKUNST. (GW). **4901**

JAHRBUCH DES EISENBAHNWESENS. (GW/0075-2479). **5432**

JAHRBUCH DES FREIEN DEUTSCHEN HOCHSTIFTS. (GW/0071-9463). **3398**

JAHRBUCH DES VEREINS FUER GESCHICHTE DER STADT WIEN. (AU/1011-4726). **2694**

JAHRBUCH DES VEREINS ZUM SCHUTZ DER BERGWELT. (GW/0171-4694). **2196**

JAHRBUCH DES WIENER GOETHE-VEREINS. (AU). **3398**

JAHRBUCH FUER FINNISCH-DEUTSCHE LITERATURBEZIEHUNGEN. (FI/0781-3619). **3398**

JAHRBUCH FUER INTERNATIONALE GERMANISTIK. (GW/0449-5233). **3289**

JAHRBUCH FUER VOLKSLIEDFORSCHUNG. (GW/0075-2789). **4124**

JAHRBUCH - MAX-PLANCK-GESELLSCHAFT. (GW/0341-0218). **5117**

JAHRBUCH SCHWEISSTECHNIK / HERAUSGEBER, DEUTSCHER VERBAND FUER SCHWEISSTECHNIK E.V. (DVS). (GW). **5117**

JAHRBUCHER DER ZENTRALANSTALT FUER METEOROLOGIE UND GEODYNAMIK. (AU). **1426**

JAHRBUCHER FUER GESCHICHTE OSTEUROPAS. (PL/0021-4019). **2694**

JAHRESBERICHT (AKADEMIE FUR RAUMFORSCHUNG UND LANDESPLANUNG (GERMANY)). (GW/0515-9091). **2825**

JAHRESBERICHT DER DEUTSCHEN MATHEMATIKER-VEREINIGUNG. (GW/0012-0456). **3511**

JAHRESBERICHT - DEUTSCHE GESELLSCHAFT FUER AUSWAERTIGE POLITIK. (GW). **4526**

JAHRESBERICHTE UND MITTEILUNGEN DES OBERRHEINISCHEN GEOLOGISCHEN VEREINES. (GW/0078-2947). **1384**

JAHRESFACHKATALOG: RECHT, WIRTSCHAFT, STEUERN. (GW/0075-2886). **2986**

JAHRESSCHAU DER DEUTSCHEN INDUSTRIE. DIE ELEKTRO-INDUSTRIE, ELEKTRONIK UND IHRE HELFER. (GW). **2067**

JAHRESSCHRIFT FUER MITTELDEUTSCHE VORGESCHICHTE. (GW/0075-2932). **271**

JAHRESSTATISTIK DES AUSSENHANDELS DER SCHWEIZ. STATISTIQUE ANNUELLE DU COMMERCE EXTERIEUR DE LA SUISSE. (SZ). **730**

JAMA : THE JOURNAL OF THE AMERICAN MEDICAL ASSOCIATION. (US/0098-7484). **3591**

JAMAICA CONSOLIDATED INDEX OF STATUTES AND SUBSIDIARY LEGISLATION TO .... (BB). **3131**

JAMAICA JOURNAL. (JM/0021-4124). **2536**

JAMAICA PLAIN CITIZEN ROXBURY CITIZEN. (US/0745-9254). **Adv Mgr**: K. Willette. **5689**

JAMAICAN HISTORICAL REVIEW, THE. (JM/1010-6367). **Adv Mgr**: Anthont Gambrill, **Tel** (509)965-7280. **2740**

JAMES DICKEY NEWSLETTER. (US/0749-0291). **3464**

JAMES JOYCE LITERARY SUPPLEMENT. (US/0899-3114). **3345**

JAMES JOYCE QUARTERLY. (US/0021-4183). **3345**

JAMES MADISON JOURNAL, THE. (US/0147-2046). **745**

JAMES WHITE REVIEW, THE. (US/0891-5393). **3345**

JAMESTOWN SUN, THE. (US). **Adv Mgr**: Gene Keller. **5725**

JANASAMKHYA. (II). **4554**

JANE'S A F V SYSTEMS. (UK). **4046**

JANE'S AIRPORT EQUIPMENT. (UK). **25**

JANE'S ALL THE WORLD'S AIRCRAFT (LONDON, ENGLAND). (UK/0075-3017). **4046**

JANE'S ARMOUR AND ARTILLERY. (UK/0143-9952). **4046**

JANE'S ARMOURED FIGHTING VEHICLE RETROFIT SYSTEMS. (UK). **4046**

JANE'S AVIONICS. (UK). **4047**

JANE'S DEFENCE WEEKLY. (UK/0265-3818). **4047**

JANE'S FIGHTING SHIPS. (UK/0075-3025). **4177**

JANE'S INFANTRY WEAPONS. (UK). **4047**

JANE'S LAND-BASED AIR DEFENCE. (UK). **4047**

JANE'S MERCHANT SHIPS. (UK). **4177**

JANE'S MILITARY COMMUNICATIONS. (UK/0144-0004). **4047**

JANE'S MILITARY TRAINING SYSTEMS. (UK). **4047**

JANE'S NBC PROTECTION EQUIPMENT. (UK). **4047**

JANE'S RADAR AND ELECTRONIC WARFARE SYSTEMS. (US). **4047**

JANE'S URBAN TRANSPORT SYSTEMS. (UK). **5385**

JANE'S WORLD RAILWAYS. (UK/0075-3084). **5432**

JANESVILLE ARGUS. (US). **5696**

JANG. (II). **5803**

JAPAN AVIATION DIRECTORY. (JA/0286-0635). **25**

JAPAN CHEMICAL ANNUAL. (JA). **1026**

JAPAN CHEMICAL WEEK. (JA/0047-1755). **1026**

JAPAN COMPANY HANDBOOK. SECOND SECTION. (JA). **Adv Mgr**: Ms. W. Ito, **Tel** (81) 3 3246 5655. **685**

JAPAN DIRECTORY. (JA). **842**

JAPAN ECONOMIC DAILY. (US/0734-0575). **1498**

JAPAN GRAPHIC ARTS. (JA). **4566**

JAPAN HARVEST. (JA/0021-440X). **4967**

JAPAN INSURANCE NEWS. (JA/0910-4534). **2885**

JAPAN M&A REPORTER. (US/1049-4383). **Adv Mgr**: Dan Schwartz. **793**

JAPAN MISSIONARY BULLETIN, THE. (JA/0021-4531). **4967**

JAPAN PICTORIAL (NORTH AMERICAN EDITION). (JA/0388-6115). **2536**

JAPAN PLASTICS AGE. (JA/0021-4582). **4455**

JAPAN PLASTICS INDUSTRY ANNUAL. (JA/0448-8679). **4455**

JAPANESE ANAESTHESIA JOURNALS' REVIEW. (NE/0169-1066). **3683**

JAPANESE CIRCULATION JOURNAL. (JA/0047-1828). **3706**

JAPANESE ECONOMIC STUDIES. (US/0021-4841). **1569**

JAPANESE JOURNAL OF ANTIBIOTICS, THE. (JA/0368-2781). **4309**

JAPANESE JOURNAL OF THORACIC SURGERY. (JA). **3949**

JAPANESE PHILATELY. (US/0146-0994). **2785**

JAPANESE PRESS, THE. (JA). **5805**

JAPANESE RELIGIONS. (JA/0448-8954). **4967**

JAPANINFO. (GW/0931-3230). **685**

JAPAN'S IRON & STEEL INDUSTRY. (JA/0075-3475). **Adv Mgr**: Vehara. **1613**

JAPOS BULLETIN. (US/0278-436X). **2785**

JARN : JAPAN AIR CONDITIONING, HEATING & REFRIGERATION NEWS. (JA). **2606**

JASNA NEWS. (US/0892-8665). **3398**

JASO : JOURNAL OF THE ANTHROPOLOGICAL SOCIETY OF OXFORD. (UK/0044-8370). **238**

JASPER JOURNAL, THE. (US/0744-3110). **Adv Mgr**: Delores Quissel. **5696**

JASPER JOURNAL, THE. (US). **Adv Mgr**: Sue Lond. **5745**

JAVELIER (LA POCATI'ERE). (CN/0841-9787). **Adv Mgr**: Michael D., **Tel** (418)856-2104. **2740**

JAX FAX TRAVEL MARKETING MAGAZINE. (US/0279-7984). **5481**

JAZYKOVEDNY CASOPIS. (XO/0021-5597). **3289**

JAZZ EDUCATORS JOURNAL. (US/0730-9791). **Adv Mgr Tel** (913)776-8744. **4124**

JAZZ FORUM. (US/0021-5635). **4124**

JAZZ JOURNAL INTERNATIONAL. (UK/0140-2285). **4125**

JAZZ-PODIUM. (GW/0021-5686). **4125**

JAZZ REPORT (TORONTO). (CN/0843-3151). **Adv Mgr**: Bill King, **Tel** (416)656-7366. **4125**

JAZZ SCENE, LA. (US). **4125**

JAZZ TIMES (WASHINGTON). (US/0272-572X). **Adv Mgr**: Lee Mergner. **4125**

JAZZFREUND (MENDEN), DER. (GW/0021-5724). **4125**

JAZZIZ (GAINESVILLE, FLA.). (US/0741-5885). **4125**

JBI JOURNAL, THE. (JM). **1613**

JBSP. JOURNAL OF THE BRITISH SOCIETY FOR PHENOMENOLOGY. (UK/0007-1773). **4350**

JCT, JOURNAL OF COATINGS TECHNOLOGY. (US/0361-8773). **4224**

JCU : JOURNAL OF CLINICAL ULTRASOUND. (US/0091-2751). **3591**

JE ME PETITDERBROUILLE. (CN/0714-4067). **5117**

JE ME SOUVIENS. (US/0195-7384). **2455**

JEANNETTE SPIRIT, THE. (US/0746-5971). **5737**

JEC BATTERY NEWSLETTER. (US). **Adv Mgr**: Robert Morey, **Tel** same as publisher. **979**

JEEVADHARA (ENGLISH ED.). (II/0970-1125). **4967**

JEFF DAVIS LEDGER. (US). **Adv Mgr**: Kay Purser. **5654**

JEFFERSON. (SW/0345-5653). **4125**

JEFFERSON COUNTY LEGAL JOURNAL. (US). **2986**

JEFFERSON JIMPLECUTE. (US/1060-3476). **5751**

JEFFERSON REPORTER, THE. (US/8755-9501). **Adv Mgr**: Joyce Drinkwater. **5654**

JEFFERSONIAN, THE. (US). **5686**

JEI. JOURNAL OF ECONOMIC ISSUES. (US/0021-3624). **1592**

JEI, JOURNAL OF THE ELECTRONICS INDUSTRY. (JA/0385-4515). **2068**

JEMS. (US/0197-2510). **3724**

JEN MIN JIH PAO SO YIN. (CC). **5798**

JEN WEN TSA CHIH RENWEN ZAZHI. (CC). **2505**

JERSEY JOURNAL. (US/0021-5953). **Adv Mgr**: Kim Billman, **Tel** (614)861-3636. **213**

JERSEY WOMAN. (US/0197-4610). **5559**

JERUSALEM JOURNAL OF INTERNATIONAL RELATIONS, THE. (US/0363-2865). **4526**

JESUP CITIZEN HERALD. (US). **5671**

JESUS PARIS. 1973. (FR/1154-7138). **Adv Mgr**: M. Ponchon. **4967**

JET. (US/0021-5996). **2265**

JET CARGO NEWS. (US/0021-6003). **5385**

JET. JOURNAL OF EDUCATION FOR TEACHING. (UK/0260-7476). **1897**

JEU. (CN/0382-0335). **5365**

JEUNE CINEMA. (FR). **4073**

JEWELLERY INTERNATIONAL. (UK/0961-4559). **Adv Mgr**: Diane Taylor. **2914**

JEWELLERY NEWS ASIA. (HK). **Adv Mgr**: Karen Chow. **2914**

JEWELLERY REVIEW. (HK). **2914**

JEWELLERY WORLD. (CN/0383-9818). **Adv Mgr**: G Staines. **2914**

JEWISH ADVOCATE, THE. (US). **Adv Mgr**: Eleanor Grosser, **Tel** (617)367-9100 ext. 36. **2265**

JEWISH AFFAIRS. (SA). **5048**

JEWISH BIBLE QUARTERLY, THE. (IS/0792-3910). **5017**

JEWISH CHRONICLE (LONDON, ENGLAND : 1845). (UK/0021-633X). **5048**

JEWISH CURRENTS. (US/0021-6399). **5048**

JEWISH EDUCATION. (US/0021-6429). **5049**

JEWISH EDUCATION NEWS. (US). **1755**

JEWISH FOLKLORE AND ETHNOLOGY REVIEW. (US/0890-9113). **Adv Mgr**: A. Fromm. **2321**

JEWISH FRONTIER. (US/0021-6453). **2265**

JEWISH HISTORICAL STUDIES : TRANSACTIONS OF THE JEWISH HISTORICAL SOCIETY OF ENGLAND. (UK). **5049**

JEWISH JOURNAL OF GREATER LOS ANGELES, THE. (US/0888-0468). **Adv Mgr**: Toni Van Ness. **5049**

JEWISH JOURNAL OF SOCIOLOGY, THE. (UK/0021-6534). **5249**

JEWISH NEWS OF GREATER PHOENIX. (US/1070-5848). **5630**

JEWISH NEWS (RICHMOND, VA.), THE. (US/0744-6632). **5049**

JEWISH OBSERVER, THE. (US/0021-6615). **5049**

JEWISH PRESS (BROOKLYN), THE. (US/0021-6674). **2265**

JEWISH QUARTERLY REVIEW (PHILADELPHIA, PA.). (US/0021-6682). **5049**

JEWISH QUARTERLY, THE. (UK/0449-010X). **5049**

JEWISH SOCIAL WORK FORUM, THE. (US/0021-6712). **5291**

JEWISH STANDARD (TORONTO). (CN/0021-6739). **5049**

JEWISH STAR (CALGARY). (CN/0228-2283). **5787**

JEWISH STAR (EDMONTON EDITION). (CN/0228-6017). **5787**

JEWISH TIMES. (US). **Adv Mgr**: Larry Salomon. **5737**

JEWISH TRANSCRIPT, THE. (US/0021-678X). **Adv Mgr**: Karen Chachkes, **Tel** (206)441-4553. **2265**

JEWISH TRAVEL GUIDE, THE. (UK/0075-3750). **5481**

JEWISH VETERAN, THE. (US/0047-2018). **Adv Mgr**: Howard Metzger. **2265**

JEWISH VOICE, THE. (US/0021-6828). **5049**

JEWISH WEEKLY NEWS. (US/0021-6860). **2265**

JEWISH WESTERN BULLETIN. (CN/0021-6879). **Adv Mgr**: R Freedman. **5787**

JEWISH WORLD (ALBANY), THE. (US/0199-4441). **Adv Mgr**: Lisa Shaw. **2265**

JIB GEMS. (CN/0839-105X). **4089**

JICARILLA CHIEFTAIN. (US/0021-695X). **2265**

JIHAD (TEHRAN, IRAN). (IR). **2505**

JIJNASA (CALCUTTA, INDIA). (II). **2654**

JIKKEN DOBUTSU. (JA/0007-5124). **3592**

JIKKEN SHAKAI SHINRIGAKU KENKYU. (JA/0387-7973). **4592**

JIM RENNIE'S SPORTS LETTER. (CN/0712-2632). **4901**

JIM TAYLOR'S CURRENTS. (CN/0828-9662). **4967**

JINSHAN SHIBAO. (US/0746-5432). **5636**

JISUANJI YU YINGYONG HUAXUE. (CC/1001-4160). **1191**

JMR, JOURNAL OF MARKETING RESEARCH. (US/0022-2437). **927**

JMR. JOURNAL OF MOLECULAR RECOGNITION. (UK/0952-3499). **460**

JNMM : JOURNAL OF THE INSTITUTE OF NUCLEAR MATERIALS MANAGEMENT. (US/0893-6188). **2156**

JOB HUNTER, THE. (US/0889-9908). **Adv Mgr:** Barb Thornton. **4205**

JOB INFORMATION LETTER. (US/8756-1670). **4205**

JOB MARKET. (US). **685**

JOB TRAINING AND PLACEMENT REPORT. (US/1041-1488). **872**

JOBBER NEWS (TORONTO). (CN/0021-7050). **5417**

JOBBER TOPICS. (US/0021-7069). **5417**

JOBS AVAILABLE (WESTERN ED.). (US/1065-6944). **4205**

JOBS MAGAZINE. (US). **1681**

JOBSON'S MINING YEAR BOOK. (AT/0075-3777). **Adv Mgr:** Chris Peuegrinetti, Tel 001 02 368 2299. **2141**

JOBSON'S QUARTERLY. (AT/0813-7455). **Adv Mgr:** Max Cunningham. **685**

JOE WEIDER'S MUSCLE & FITNESS. (US/0744-5105). **2599**

JOERNAAL VIR EIETYDSE : GESKIEDENIS EN INTERNASIONALE VERHOUDINGE. (SA). **2620**

JOGU. (GW). **1832**

JOHN DONNE JOURNAL. (US/0738-9655). **3345**

JOHN MARSHALL LAW REVIEW, THE. (US/0270-854X). **2986**

JOHN TWIGG'S REPORT ON B.C. (CN/0838-1542). **1498**

JOHNS HOPKINS MAGAZINE. (US/0021-7255). **Adv Mgr:** Susan Smart, Tel (410)532-2136. **1102**

JOHNSON COUNTY GENEALOGIST, THE. (US/0749-6850). **2455**

JOHNSON JOURNAL. (US/8755-1721). **2455**

JOJOBA HAPPENINGS. (US/0746-3766). **98**

JONATHAN (MONTREAL). (CN/0711-026X). **5049**

JONESREPORT. (US/0889-485X). **Adv Mgr:** Marsha Davis. **927**

JONG HOLLAND. (NE/0168-9193). **354**

JONQUIL. (US/0744-3943). **5232**

JOPLIN GLOBE. (US). **5703**

JORDANS REGIONAL DIRECTORIES OF KEY BUSINESS PROSPECTS. VARIOUS AREAS IN UK. (UK). **685**

JORDEMODERN. (SW/0021-7468). **3763**

JORNAL BRASILEIRO DE PSIQUIATRIA. (BL/0047-2085). **3928**

JORNAL BRASILEIRO DE UROLOGIA. (BL/0100-0519). **3990**

JORNAL DA LIGA BRASILEIRA DE EPILEPSIA. (BL). **Adv Mgr:** Magda Nunes. **3834**

JORNAL DO BRASIL. (BL). **5779**

JORNAL PORTUGUES (SAN PABLO, CALIF.). (US/8756-2200). **Adv Mgr:** Magda Bettencourt. **5636**

JOSEPH CONRAD TODAY. (US/0162-413X). **433**

JOSLIN'S JAZZ JOURNAL. (US/0735-1585). **4125**

JOUETS ET JEUX. (FR/0075-4056). **2584**

JOURNAL - ADDICTION RESEARCH FOUNDATION, THE. (CN/0044-6203). **4786**

JOURNAL-ADVOCATE. (US). **Adv Mgr:** Myron House. **5643**

JOURNAL (AMERICAN ACADEMY OF GNATHOLOGIC ORTHOPEDICS). (US/0886-1064). **1325**

JOURNAL / AMERICAN RHODODENDRON SOCIETY. (US/0745-7839). **2421**

JOURNAL / AMERICAN WATER WORKS ASSOCIATION. (US/0003-150X). **5535**

JOURNAL - AMERICAN WINE SOCIETY. (US/0364-698X). **2368**

JOURNAL AND REPORT OF PROCEEDINGS - PERMANENT WAY INSTITUTION. (UK/0031-5524). **2025**

JOURNAL AND REPUBLICAN, THE. (US). **Adv Mgr:** Bonnie Franklin. **5717**

JOURNAL AND THE NOBLE COUNTY LEADER, THE. (US). **Adv Mgr:** Fred Powell, Tel (614)732-2341. **5729**

JOURNAL BELGE DE RADIOLOGIE (1924). (BE/0021-7646). **3942**

JOURNAL / CALIFORNIA RARE FRUIT GROWERS. (US/0894-8445). **98**

JOURNAL / CALIFORNIA TRADITIONAL MUSIC SOCIETY. (US/1053-3664). **2321**

JOURNAL - CAMBORNE SCHOOL OF MINES. (UK/0308-3845). **2141**

JOURNAL (CAMP VERDE, ARIZ.), THE. (US/0744-3285). **5630**

JOURNAL - CANADIAN DENTAL ASSOCIATION. (CN/0709-8936). **Adv Mgr:** Trish Sullivan. **1325**

JOURNAL - CANADIAN OLDTIMERS' HOCKEY ASSOCIATION. (CN/0826-5887). **4901**

JOURNAL / CHARTERED INSURANCE INSTITUTE, THE. (UK). **Adv Mgr:** David Hughes, Tel 011 44 071 5833030. **2885**

JOURNAL - COLORADO DENTAL ASSOCIATION. (US/0010-1559). **1326**

JOURNAL / COLORADO EDUCATION ASSOCIATION. (US/0279-3326). **1755**

JOURNAL - CONNECTICUT STATE DENTAL ASSOCIATION, THE. (US/0010-6232). **Adv Mgr:** Sarah Van Dyke, Tel (203)278-5550. **1326**

JOURNAL / CORNWALL FAMILY HISTORY SOCIETY. (UK/0141-7614). **2455**

JOURNAL COTE-DES-NEIGES. (CN/0822-0794). **5787**

JOURNAL (CROSBY, N.D.), THE. (US/0886-6007). **5725**

JOURNAL D' ANALYSE MATHEMATIQUE (JERUSALEM). (IS/0021-7670). **3511**

JOURNAL DE CORNWALL, LE. (CN/0704-0660). **5787**

JOURNAL DE DROIT FISCAL. (BE). **2986**

JOURNAL DE LA SOCIETE DES AMERICANISTES. (FR/0037-9174). **271**

JOURNAL DE L'IMMERSION, LE. (CN/0833-1812). **3289**

JOURNAL DE MATHEMATIQUES PURES ET APPLIQUEES. (FR/0021-7824). **3511**

JOURNAL DE MEDECINE DE LYON. (FR/0021-7883). **Adv Mgr:** F. Balula. **3592**

JOURNAL DE MUSIQUE ANCIENNE. (CN/0838-9349). **4125**

JOURNAL DE PHARMACIE CLINIQUE. (FR/0291-1981). **4310**

JOURNAL DE RECHERCHE OCEANOGRAPHIQUE. (FR/0397-5347). **1450**

JOURNAL DENTAIRE DU QUEBEC. (CN). **1326**

JOURNAL DENTAIRE DU QUEBEC. (CN). **1326**

JOURNAL DES DEBATS (QUEBEC). (CN/0709-3632). **4478**

JOURNAL DES INGENIEURS (BRUSSELS, BELGIUM : 1984). (BE/0021-8065). **Adv Mgr:** Publicarto. **1981**

JOURNAL D'OUTREMONT, LE. (CN/0824-1317). **2536**

JOURNAL (ELLETTSVILLE, IND.). (US). **Adv Mgr:** Jane Fiscus. **5665**

JOURNAL-ENTERPRISE, THE. (US). **5681**

JOURNAL-EXPRESS. (US). **Adv Mgr:** Don Abens, Tel (515)842-2155. **5671**

JOURNAL / FLORIDA ENGINEERING SOCIETY. (US/0015-4032). **Adv Mgr:** Nancy Taylor. **1981**

JOURNAL - FLORIDA GENEALOGICAL SOCIETY (1978). (US/0735-6420). **2455**

JOURNAL FOR ANTHROPOSOPHY. (US/0021-8235). **4967**

JOURNAL FOR CONTEMPORARY HISTORY / JOERNAAL VIR EIETYDSE GESKIEDENIS. (SA). **4526**

JOURNAL FOR PEACE & JUSTICE STUDIES. (US). **4526**

JOURNAL FOR QUALITY AND PARTICIPATION, THE. (US/1040-9602). **1681**

JOURNAL FOR RESEARCH IN MATHEMATICS EDUCATION. (US/0021-8251). **3511**

JOURNAL FOR SPECIALISTS IN GROUP WORK, THE. (US/0193-3922). **4592**

JOURNAL FOR THE CALLIGRAPHIC ARTS. (US). **Adv Mgr:** James Michae. **380**

JOURNAL FOR THE EDUCATION OF THE GIFTED. (US/0162-3532). **1880**

JOURNAL FOR THE HISTORY OF ARABIC SCIENCE. (SY/0379-2927). **5118**

JOURNAL FOR THE HISTORY OF ASTRONOMY. (UK/0021-8286). **396**

JOURNAL FOR THE SCIENTIFIC STUDY OF RELIGION. (US/0021-8294). **Adv Mgr:** Harve Horowitz, Tel (410)997-0763. **4967**

JOURNAL FOR THE STUDY OF RELIGION. (SA/1011-7601). **4967**

JOURNAL FOR THE STUDY OF THE NEW TESTAMENT. (UK/0142-064X). **5017**

JOURNAL FOR THE STUDY OF THE OLD TESTAMENT. (UK/0309-0892). **5017**

JOURNAL FOR THE THEORY OF SOCIAL BEHAVIOUR. (UK/0021-8308). **4593**

JOURNAL FOR VOCATIONAL SPECIAL NEEDS EDUCATION, THE. (US/0195-7597). **1880**

JOURNAL - FORENSIC SCIENCE SOCIETY. (UK/0015-7368). **3741**

JOURNAL FRANCAIS D'AMERIQUE. (US/0195-2889). **Adv Mgr:** A. Kautmann. **5636**

JOURNAL FRANCAIS D'OTO-RHINO-LARYNGOLOGIE. (FR/0398-9771). **3889**

JOURNAL FUER DIE FRAU. (GW/0178-7284). **Adv Mgr:** D. Koring. **5559**

JOURNAL FUER DIE REINE UND ANGEWANDTE MATHEMATIK. (GW/0075-4102). **3511**

JOURNAL FUER ORNITHOLOGIE. (GW/0021-8375). **5618**

JOURNAL - GALPIN SOCIETY. (UK/0072-0127). **4125**

JOURNAL-GAZETTE (FORT WAYNE, IND.), THE. (US/0734-3701). **Adv Mgr:** Tom Eason, Tel (219)461-8232. **5665**

JOURNAL - GEOLOGICAL SOCIETY OF JAMAICA. (JM). **1384**

JOURNAL / GLASS ART SOCIETY. (US/0278-9426). **2591**

JOURNAL-HERALD (WHITE HAVEN, PA.). (US). **Adv Mgr:** Seth Isenberg, Tel (717)443-9131. **5737**

JOURNAL - HISTORICAL FIREARMS SOCIETY OF SOUTH AFRICA. (SA). **251**

JOURNAL / INSTITUTE OF MUSLIM MINORITY AFFAIRS. (UK/0266-6952). **2265**

JOURNAL - INTERNATIONAL CHINESE SNUFF BOTTLE SOCIETY. (US/0734-5534). **251**

JOURNAL INTERNATIONAL DES SCIENCES DE LA VIGNE ET DU VIN. (FR/1151-0985). **175**

JOURNAL - JAPANESE ASSOCIATION OF GROUNDWATER HYDROLOGY. (JA). **1415**

JOURNAL - MAINE WATER UTILITIES ASSOCIATION. (US/0025-0805). **4761**

JOURNAL MICHIGAN PHARMACIST. (US/1045-6481). **Adv Mgr:** Bryan Deutsch. **4310**

JOURNAL - MINING AND METALLURGICAL INSTITUTE OF JAPAN. (JA). **4006**

JOURNAL - NATIONAL ASSOCIATION OF CAREERS AND GUIDANCE TEACHERS. (UK/0954-3732). **Adv Mgr:** Janice Cook. **1756**

JOURNAL (NEW ULM, MINN.). (US/1059-1338). **5696**

JOURNAL - NEW ZEALAND DIETETIC ASSOCIATION. (NZ/0110-635X). **4192**

JOURNAL (ODON, IND.). (US). **5665**

JOURNAL OF ABNORMAL PSYCHOLOGY (1965). (US/0021-843X). **4593**

JOURNAL OF ABSTRACTS (AND ARTICLES) IN INTERNATIONAL EDUCATION. (US/1064-0746). **1795**

JOURNAL OF ACADEMIC LIBRARIANSHIP. (US/0099-1333). **3219**

JOURNAL OF ACCESS STUDIES / FORUM FOR ACCESS STUDIES. (UK/0269-2562). **1801**

JOURNAL OF ACCOUNTANCY. (US/0021-8448). **746**

JOURNAL OF ACCOUNTING & ECONOMICS. (NE/0165-4101). **746**

JOURNAL OF ACCOUNTING AND PUBLIC POLICY. (US/0278-4254). **746**

JOURNAL OF ACCOUNTING EDUCATION. (US/0748-5751). **746**

JOURNAL OF ADHESION SCIENCE AND TECHNOLOGY. (NE/0169-4243). **1053**

JOURNAL OF ADHESION, THE. (UK/0021-8464). **1053**

JOURNAL OF ADOLESCENT CHEMICAL DEPENDENCY. (US/0896-7768). **1345**

JOURNAL OF ADOLESCENT RESEARCH. (US/0743-5584). **4593**

JOURNAL OF ADVANCED COMPOSITION. (US/0731-6755). **3289**

JOURNAL OF ADVANCED NURSING. (UK/0309-2402). **3858**

JOURNAL OF ADVANCED ZOOLOGY. (II/0253-7214). **5587**

JOURNAL OF ADVANCES IN HEALTH AND NURSING CARE. (UK/0960-9857). **3858**

JOURNAL OF ADVENTIST EDUCATION, THE. (US/0021-8480). **1897**

JOURNAL OF ADVERTISING. (US/0091-3367). **761**

JOURNAL OF ADVERTISING RESEARCH. (US/0021-8499). **761**

JOURNAL OF AESTHETIC EDUCATION, THE. (US/0021-8510). **2848**

JOURNAL OF AESTHETICS AND ART CRITICISM, THE. (US/0021-8529). **354**

JOURNAL OF AFRICAN AMERICAN MALE STUDIES. (US/1063-4460). **2265**

JOURNAL OF AFRICAN EARTH SCIENCES (AND THE MIDDLE EAST). (UK/0899-5362). **1384**

JOURNAL OF AFRICAN ECONOMIES. (UK/0963-8024). **1637**

JOURNAL OF AFRICAN LANGUAGES AND LINGUISTICS. (NE/0167-6164). **3289**

JOURNAL OF AFRICAN LAW. (UK/0021-8553). **2986**

JOURNAL OF AFRICAN ZOOLOGY. (BE/0776-7943). **5587**

JOURNAL OF AGING AND HEALTH. (US/0898-2643). **3752**

JOURNAL OF AGING & SOCIAL POLICY. (US/0895-9420). **5179**

JOURNAL OF AGRICULTURAL & ENVIRONMENTAL ETHICS. (CN/1187-7863). **2251**

JOURNAL OF AGRICULTURAL AND FOOD CHEMISTRY. (US/0021-8561). **99**

JOURNAL OF AGRICULTURAL & FOOD INFORMATION. (US/1049-6505). **99**

JOURNAL OF AGRICULTURAL ECONOMICS. (UK/0021-857X). **99**

JOURNAL OF AGRICULTURAL ENTOMOLOGY. (US/0735-939X). **Adv Mgr:** Howard W. Fescemyer, **Tel** (803)656-5050. **5610**

JOURNAL OF AGRICULTURAL LENDING / AMERICAN BANKERS ASSOCIATION. (US). **Adv Mgr:** K Gotsick, **Tel** (202)663-5111. **793**

JOURNAL OF AIR TRAFFIC CONTROL, THE. (US/0021-8650). **Adv Mgr:** Aida Gregory. **25**

JOURNAL OF ALLERGY AND CLINICAL IMMUNOLOGY. (US/0091-6749). **3673**

JOURNAL OF ALLOYS AND COMPOUNDS. (SZ/0925-8388). **Adv Mgr:** Ms. W van Cattenburch (Amsterdam). **4006**

JOURNAL OF ALTERNATIVE AND COMPLEMENTARY MEDICINE. (UK/0959-9886). **Adv Mgr:** Elaine Curtis, **Tel** 0932 874333. **3593**

JOURNAL OF AMBULATORY CARE MANAGEMENT, THE. (US/0148-9917). **3786**

JOURNAL OF AMBULATORY CARE MARKETING. (US/0886-9723). **3725**

JOURNAL OF AMERICAN COLLEGE HEALTH. (US/0744-8481). **3593**

JOURNAL OF AMERICAN CULTURE. (US/0191-1813). **2740**

JOURNAL OF AMERICAN ETHNIC HISTORY. (US/0278-5927). **2265**

JOURNAL OF AMERICAN FOLKLORE. (US/0021-8715). **2321**

JOURNAL OF AMERICAN HISTORY, THE. (US/0021-8723). **2740**

JOURNAL OF AMERICAN INDIAN FAMILY RESEARCH, THE. (US/0730-6148). **2455**

JOURNAL OF AMERICAN ORGANBUILDING. (US/1048-2482). **Adv Mgr:** Howard Maple, **Tel** (713)529-2212. **4125**

JOURNAL OF ANALYTICAL AND APPLIED PYROLYSIS. (NE/0165-2370). **1016**

JOURNAL OF ANALYTICAL TOXICOLOGY. (US/0146-4760). **3981**

JOURNAL OF ANDROLOGY. (US/0196-3635). **581**

JOURNAL OF ANIMAL ECOLOGY, THE. (UK/0021-8790). **5587**

JOURNAL OF ANIMAL MORPHOLOGY AND PHYSIOLOGY, THE. (II/0021-8804). **5587**

JOURNAL OF ANTHROPOSOPHIC MEDICINE. (US/1067-4640). **3593**

JOURNAL OF ANTIBIOTICS (NIHON KOSEIBUSSHITSU GAKUJUTSU KYOGIKAI : 1968). (JA/0021-8820). **4310**

JOURNAL OF ANXIETY DISORDERS. (US/0887-6185). **4593**

JOURNAL OF APHIDOLOGY. (II/0970-3810). **5610**

JOURNAL OF APICULTURAL RESEARCH. (UK/0021-8839). **5587**

JOURNAL OF APPLIED AQUACULTURE. (US/1045-4438). **2306**

JOURNAL OF APPLIED BEHAVIOR ANALYSIS. (US/0021-8855). **4593**

JOURNAL OF APPLIED BEHAVIORAL SCIENCE, THE. (US/0021-8863). **5205**

JOURNAL OF APPLIED BUSINESS RESEARCH. (US/0892-7626). **Adv Mgr:** Ron Clute, **Tel** (303)972-6604. **685**

JOURNAL OF APPLIED COMMUNICATION RESEARCH : JACR. (US/0090-9882). **1114**

JOURNAL OF APPLIED COSMETOLOGY. (IT/0392-8543). **Adv Mgr:** P. Morganti. **3721**

JOURNAL OF APPLIED CRYSTALLOGRAPHY. (DK/0021-8898). **1032**

JOURNAL OF APPLIED DEVELOPMENTAL PSYCHOLOGY. (US/0193-3973). **4593**

JOURNAL OF APPLIED ECOLOGY, THE. (UK/0021-8901). **2217**

JOURNAL OF APPLIED ELECTROCHEMISTRY. (UK/0021-891X). **1034**

JOURNAL OF APPLIED GERONTOLOGY. (US/0733-4648). **3753**

JOURNAL OF APPLIED ICHTHYOLOGY. (GW/0175-8659). **2306**

JOURNAL OF APPLIED MANUFACTURING SYSTEMS, THE. (US/0899-0956). **1613**

JOURNAL OF APPLIED MATHEMATICS AND STOCHASTIC ANALYSIS. (US/1048-9533). **1282**

JOURNAL OF APPLIED MEDICINE. (II/0377-0400). **3593**

JOURNAL OF APPLIED NUTRITION, THE. (US/0021-8960). **4192**

JOURNAL OF APPLIED PHYSIOLOGY (1985). (US/8750-7587). **581**

JOURNAL OF APPLIED POLYMER SCIENCE. (US/0021-8995). **2013**

JOURNAL OF APPLIED PROBABILITY. (UK/0021-9002). **3511**

JOURNAL OF APPLIED PSYCHOLOGY. (US/0021-9010). **4593**

JOURNAL OF APPLIED RABBIT RESEARCH, THE. (US/0738-9760). **460**

JOURNAL OF APPLIED REHABILITATION COUNSELING. (US/0047-2220). **1880**

JOURNAL OF APPLIED SEED PRODUCTION. (US/8755-8750). **Adv Mgr:** Editor. **175**

JOURNAL OF APPLIED SOCIAL SCIENCES, THE. (US/0146-4310). **5291**

JOURNAL OF APPLIED SOCIOLOGY - SOCIETY FOR APPLIED SOCIOLOGY (U.S.). (US/0749-0232). **5249**

JOURNAL OF APPLIED SPORT SCIENCE RESEARCH, THE. (US). **1856**

JOURNAL OF AQUACULTURE & AQUATIC SCIENCES. (US/0733-2076). **460**

JOURNAL OF AQUATIC FOOD PRODUCTS TECHNOLOGY. (US/1049-8850). **2306**

JOURNAL OF ARAB AFFAIRS. (US/0275-3588). **4527**

JOURNAL OF ARACHNOLOGY, THE. (US/0161-8202). **5587**

JOURNAL OF ARBORICULTURE. (US/0278-5226). **2421**

JOURNAL OF ARTS & IDEAS. (II/0970-5309). **323**

JOURNAL OF ARTS MANAGEMENT AND LAW, THE. (US/0733-5113). **386**

JOURNAL OF ASIAN CULTURE. (US/0162-6795). **2505**

JOURNAL OF ASIAN HISTORY. (GW/0021-910X). **2655**

JOURNAL OF ASIAN MARTIAL ARTS. (US/1057-8358). **2599**

JOURNAL OF ASIAN STUDIES, THE. (US/0021-9118). **2655**

JOURNAL OF ASSOCIATION OF EXPLORATION GEOPHYSICISTS. (II/0257-1412). **1407**

JOURNAL OF ASTHMA, THE. (US/0277-0903). **3950**

JOURNAL OF ATMOSPHERIC CHEMISTRY. (NE/0167-7764). **1426**

JOURNAL OF AUDIOLOGICAL MEDICINE. (UK/0963-7133). **3889**

JOURNAL OF AUDIOVISUAL MEDIA IN MEDICINE, THE. (UK/0140-511X). **3593**

JOURNAL OF AUSTRALIAN POLITICAL ECONOMY, THE. (AT/0156-5826). **1498**

JOURNAL OF AUTOMATED REASONING. (NE/0168-7433). **1220**

JOURNAL OF AUTONOMIC PHARMACOLOGY. (UK/0144-1795). **4310**

JOURNAL OF AVIAN BIOLOGY. (DK/0908-8857). **5618**

JOURNAL OF BACTERIOLOGY. (US/0021-9193). **564**

JOURNAL OF BALLISTICS. (US/0146-4140). **2014**

JOURNAL OF BALTIC STUDIES. (US/0162-9778). **2694**

JOURNAL OF BANK ACCOUNTING & AUDITING, THE. (US/0895-853X). **793**

JOURNAL OF BANK TAXATION, THE. (US/0895-4720). **793**

JOURNAL OF BANKING & FINANCE. (NE/0378-4266). **793**

JOURNAL OF BASIC WRITING. (US/0147-1635). **3289**

JOURNAL OF BASQUE STUDIES. (US/0747-6256). **2694**

JOURNAL OF BECKETT STUDIES. (US). **3399**

JOURNAL OF BEHAVIORAL OPTOMETRY. (US/1045-8395). **4216**

JOURNAL OF BIOCHEMICAL AND BIOPHYSICAL METHODS. (NE/0165-022X). **489**

JOURNAL OF BIOGEOGRAPHY. (UK/0305-0270). **2567**

JOURNAL OF BIOLOGICAL CHEMISTRY, THE. (US/0021-9258). **Adv Mgr:** Linda Acuff, **Tel** (301)530-7107. **489**

JOURNAL OF BIOLOGICAL CURATION. (UK/0958-7608). **4090**

JOURNAL OF BIOLOGICAL EDUCATION. (UK/0021-9266). **460**

JOURNAL OF BIOLOGICAL PHYSICS. (NE/0092-0606). **495**

JOURNAL OF BIOLOGICAL REGULATORS AND HOMEOSTATIC AGENTS. (IT/0393-974X). **460**

JOURNAL OF BIOMECHANICAL ENGINEERING. (US/0148-0731). **3694**

JOURNAL OF BIOMEDICAL ENGINEERING. (UK/0141-5425). **3694**

JOURNAL OF BIOMEDICAL MATERIALS RESEARCH. (US/0021-9304). **3593**

JOURNAL OF BIOMOLECULAR NMR. (NE/0925-2738). **461**

JOURNAL OF BIOMOLECULAR STRUCTURE & DYNAMICS. (US/0739-1102). **461**

JOURNAL OF BIOSOCIAL SCIENCE. (UK/0021-9320). **5205**

JOURNAL OF BLACK PSYCHOLOGY, THE. (US/0095-7984). **4594**

JOURNAL OF BONE AND JOINT SURGERY. AMERICAN VOLUME (PRINT ED.). (US/0021-9355). **3882**

JOURNAL OF BORDERLANDS STUDIES. (US/0886-5655). **2740**

JOURNAL OF BRITISH MUSIC THERAPY. (UK/0951-5038). **4125**

JOURNAL OF BRYOLOGY. (UK/0373-6687). **515**

JOURNAL OF BURN CARE & REHABILITATION, THE. (US/0273-8481). **3594**

JOURNAL OF BUSINESS. (US). **Adv Mgr:** Scott Crytser. **686**

JOURNAL OF BUSINESS ADMINISTRATION (VANCOUVER). (CN/0021-941X). **686**

JOURNAL OF BUSINESS & FINANCE LIBRARIANSHIP. (US/0896-3568). **3219**

JOURNAL OF BUSINESS & INDUSTRIAL MARKETING, THE. (US/0885-8624). **927**

JOURNAL OF BUSINESS AND SOCIAL STUDIES, THE. (NR/0021-9428). **686**

JOURNAL OF BUSINESS COMMUNICATION (1973). (US/0021-9436). **1114**

JOURNAL OF BUSINESS ETHICS. (NE/0167-4544). **2251**

JOURNAL OF BUSINESS FINANCE & ACCOUNTING. (UK/0306-686X). **746**

JOURNAL OF BUSINESS LAW, THE. (UK/0021-9460). **3101**

JOURNAL OF BUSINESS RESEARCH. (US/0148-2963). **686**

JOURNAL OF BUSINESS (SINGAPORE). (SI/0377-0419). **686**

JOURNAL OF BUSINESS STRATEGIES. (US/0887-2058). **686**

JOURNAL OF BUSINESS VENTURING. (US/0883-9026). **686**

JOURNAL OF CALIFORNIA AND GREAT BASIN ANTHROPOLOGY. (US/0191-3557). **238**

JOURNAL OF CALIFORNIA TAXATION, THE. (US/1046-400X). **2987**

JOURNAL OF CANADIAN PETROLEUM TECHNOLOGY, THE. (CN/0021-9487). **4262**

JOURNAL OF CANADIAN POETRY. (CN/0705-1328). **Adv Mgr:** Glenn Clever, **Tel** (613)224-6837. **3464**

JOURNAL OF CANADIAN STUDIES. (CN/0021-9495). **Adv Mgr:** J. Manson, **Tel** (709)748-1279. **2740**

JOURNAL OF CANCER EDUCATION, THE. (US/0885-8195). **3819**

JOURNAL OF CARBOHYDRATE CHEMISTRY. (US/0732-8303). **1042**

JOURNAL — Advertising Accepted Index

JOURNAL OF CARDIAC SURGERY. (US/0886-0440). **3966**

JOURNAL OF CARDIOPULMONARY REHABILITATION. (US/0883-9212). **3706**

JOURNAL OF CARDIOVASCULAR ELECTROPHYSIOLOGY. (US/1045-3873). **3707**

JOURNAL OF CAREER PLANNING & EMPLOYMENT. (US/0884-5352). **4206**

JOURNAL OF CARIBBEAN HISTORY, THE. (BB/0047-2263). **2741**

JOURNAL OF CASE MANAGEMENT. (US/1061-3706). **Adv Mgr:** Linda Mappleback. **3787**

JOURNAL OF CELL SCIENCE. (UK/0021-9533). **537**

JOURNAL OF CELLULAR PLASTICS. (US/0021-955X). **4455**

JOURNAL OF CEPHALOPOD BIOLOGY. (US/0843-6150). **461**

JOURNAL OF CHEMICAL AND ENGINEERING DATA. (US/0021-9568). **2014**

JOURNAL OF CHEMICAL DEPENDENCY TREATMENT. (US/0885-4734). **1345**

JOURNAL OF CHEMICAL EDUCATION. (US/0021-9584). **980**

JOURNAL OF CHEMICAL INFORMATION AND COMPUTER SCIENCES. (US/0095-2338). **980**

JOURNAL OF CHEMICAL NEUROANATOMY. (UK/0891-0618). **3834**

JOURNAL OF CHEMICAL RESEARCH. MINIPRINT. (UK/0308-2350). **980**

JOURNAL OF CHEMICAL RESEARCH. SYNOPSES. (UK/0308-2342). **980**

JOURNAL OF CHILD AND ADOLESCENT PSYCHIATRIC AND MENTAL HEALTH NURSING. (US/0897-9685). **Adv Mgr:** Joseph Braden, **Tel** (215)545-7222. **3928**

JOURNAL OF CHILD AND YOUTH CARE. (CN/0840-982X). **5291**

JOURNAL OF CHILD NEUROLOGY. (US/0883-0738). **3904**

JOURNAL OF CHILD PSYCHOTHERAPY. (UK/0075-417X). **3928**

JOURNAL OF CHILD SEXUAL ABUSE. (US/1053-8712). **5291**

JOURNAL OF CHILDHOOD COMMUNICATION DISORDERS. (US/0735-3170). **1880**

JOURNAL OF CHINESE LINGUISTICS. (US/0091-3723). **3289**

JOURNAL OF CHINESE MEDICINE, THE. (UK/0143-8042). **3594**

JOURNAL OF CHINESE PHILOSOPHY. (US/0301-8121). **4350**

JOURNAL OF CHINESE STUDIES (ALBUQUERQUE, N.M.). (US/0742-5929). **2505**

JOURNAL OF CHIROPRACTIC. (US/0744-9984). **3594**

JOURNAL OF CHRISTIAN HEALING, THE. (US/0738-2944). **4968**

JOURNAL OF CHRISTIAN JURISPRUDENCE. (US/0741-6075). **2987**

JOURNAL OF CHRISTIAN NURSING. (US/0743-2550). **3858**

JOURNAL OF CHRISTIAN RECONSTRUCTION, THE. (US/0360-1420). **4968**

JOURNAL OF CHROMATOGRAPHIC SCIENCE. (US/0021-9665). **1016**

JOURNAL OF CHURCH AND STATE. (US/0021-969X). **Adv Mgr Tel** (817)755-1510. **4478**

JOURNAL OF CIVIL DEFENSE. (US/0740-5537). **1073**

JOURNAL OF CLASSIFICATION. (US/0176-4268). **3512**

JOURNAL OF CLASSROOM INTERACTION, THE. (US/0749-4025). **1756**

JOURNAL OF CLEAN TECHNOLOGY AND ENVIRONMENTAL SCIENCES. (US/1052-1062). **Adv Mgr:** MA Mehlman. **2175**

JOURNAL OF CLINICAL AND EXPERIMENTAL GERONTOLOGY. (US/0192-1193). **3753**

JOURNAL OF CLINICAL AND EXPERIMENTAL NEUROPSYCHOLOGY. (NE/0168-8634). **3834**

JOURNAL OF CLINICAL & LABORATORY IMMUNOLOGY. (UK/0141-2760). **3673**

JOURNAL OF CLINICAL ANESTHESIA. (US/0952-8180). **3683**

JOURNAL OF CLINICAL CHILD PSYCHOLOGY. (US/0047-228X). **4594**

JOURNAL OF CLINICAL COMPUTING. (US/0090-1091). **3787**

JOURNAL OF CLINICAL ENDOCRINOLOGY AND METABOLISM, THE. (US/0021-972X). **3731**

JOURNAL OF CLINICAL ENGINEERING. (US/0363-8855). **3694**

JOURNAL OF CLINICAL IMMUNOASSAY. (US/0736-4393). **3673**

JOURNAL OF CLINICAL INVESTIGATION, THE. (US/0021-9738). **3594**

JOURNAL OF CLINICAL MICROBIOLOGY. (US/0095-1137). **565**

JOURNAL OF CLINICAL ORTHODONTICS. (US/0022-3875). **1326**

JOURNAL OF CLINICAL PERIODONTOLOGY. (DK/0303-6979). **1326**

JOURNAL OF CLINICAL PHARMACY AND THERAPEUTICS. (UK/0269-4727). **4310**

JOURNAL OF CLINICAL PSYCHIATRY, THE. (US/0160-6689). **3928**

JOURNAL OF CLINICAL PSYCHOANALYSIS. (US). **Adv Mgr:** David Loiterstein, **Tel** (203)245-0775. **3928**

JOURNAL OF CLINICAL PSYCHOLOGY. (US/0021-9762). **4595**

JOURNAL OF CLINICAL PSYCHOPHARMACOLOGY. (US/0271-0749). **4310**

JOURNAL OF COAL QUALITY, THE. (US/0732-8087). **1948**

JOURNAL OF COASTAL RESEARCH. (US/0749-0208). **1357**

JOURNAL OF COFFEE RESEARCH. (II/0374-8537). **176**

JOURNAL OF COGNITIVE NEUROSCIENCE, THE. (US/0898-929X). **3835**

JOURNAL OF COGNITIVE PSYCHOTHERAPY, THE. (US/0889-8391). **Adv Mgr:** Beth Albert. **4595**

JOURNAL OF COLLEGE & UNIVERSITY FOODSERVICE. (US/1053-8739). **2345**

JOURNAL OF COLLEGE AND UNIVERSITY LAW, THE. (US/0093-8688). **2987**

JOURNAL OF COLLEGE AND UNIVERSITY STUDENT HOUSING, THE. (US/0161-827X). **Adv Mgr:** D. Lehner. **1832**

JOURNAL OF COLLEGE MANAGEMENT. (UK). **1832**

JOURNAL OF COLLEGE READING AND LEARNING. (US). **1832**

JOURNAL OF COLLEGE SCIENCE TEACHING. (US/0047-231X). **5118**

JOURNAL OF COLLEGE STUDENT PSYCHOTHERAPY. (US/8756-8225). **4595**

JOURNAL OF COMMERCE (VANCOUVER). (CN/0709-1230). **842**

JOURNAL OF COMMON MARKET STUDIES. (UK/0021-9886). **1569**

JOURNAL OF COMMONWEALTH & COMPARATIVE POLITICS, THE. (UK/0306-3631). **Adv Mgr:** Anne Kidson. **4478**

JOURNAL OF COMMONWEALTH LITERATURE. (UK/0021-9894). **3399**

JOURNAL OF COMMUNICATION. (US/0021-9916). **1114**

JOURNAL OF COMMUNICATION DISORDERS. (US/0021-9924). **3835**

JOURNAL OF COMMUNICATION INQUIRY, THE. (US/0196-8599). **1114**

JOURNAL OF COMMUNICATION THERAPY. (US/0734-4368). **4595**

JOURNAL OF COMMUNITY HEALTH NURSING. (US/0737-0016). **3858**

JOURNAL OF COMMUNITY PSYCHOLOGY. (US/0090-4392). **4595**

JOURNAL OF COMPARATIVE FAMILY STUDIES. (CN/0047-2328). **2281**

JOURNAL OF COMPARATIVE LITERATURE & AESTHETICS. (II/0252-8169). **354**

JOURNAL OF COMPARATIVE PSYCHOLOGY (1983). (US/0735-7036). **4595**

JOURNAL OF COMPREHENSIVE HEALTH IN SOUTH AFRICA. (SA). **4786**

JOURNAL OF COMPUTATIONAL CHEMISTRY. (US/0192-8651). **981**

JOURNAL OF COMPUTER-AIDED MOLECULAR DESIGN. (NE/0920-654X). **1229**

JOURNAL OF COMPUTER-ASSISTED MICROSCOPY. (US/1040-7286). **1223**

JOURNAL OF COMPUTER INFORMATION SYSTEMS, THE. (US/0887-4417). **1260**

JOURNAL OF COMPUTING & SOCIETY. (US/1044-0755). **5205**

JOURNAL OF CONCHOLOGY. (UK/0022-0019). **5587**

JOURNAL OF CONSTRUCTION ACCOUNTING & TAXATION. (US/1054-3007). **Adv Mgr:** Phil Brady, **Tel** (212)971-5120. **618**

JOURNAL OF CONSTRUCTIONAL STEEL RESEARCH. (UK/0143-974X). **618**

JOURNAL OF CONSULTING AND CLINICAL PSYCHOLOGY. (US/0022-006X). **4595**

JOURNAL OF CONSUMER AFFAIRS, THE. (US/0022-0078). **1297**

JOURNAL OF CONSUMER POLICY. (NE/0168-7034). **1297**

JOURNAL OF CONSUMER RESEARCH, THE. (US/0093-5301). **927**

JOURNAL OF CONSUMER STUDIES AND HOME ECONOMICS. (UK/0309-3891). **1298**

JOURNAL OF CONTEMPORARY AFRICAN STUDIES : JCAS. (SA/0258-9001). **2848**

JOURNAL OF CONTEMPORARY ART. (US/0897-2400). **354**

JOURNAL OF CONTEMPORARY ASIA. (UK/0047-2336). **2655**

JOURNAL OF CONTEMPORARY HEALTH LAW AND POLICY, THE. (US/0882-1046). **2987**

JOURNAL OF CONTEMPORARY HISTORY. (UK/0022-0094). **2621**

JOURNAL OF CONTEMPORARY LAW. (US/0097-9937). **2987**

JOURNAL OF CONTEMPORARY LEGAL ISSUES. (US/0896-5595). **2987**

JOURNAL OF CONTINUING SOCIAL WORK EDUCATION. (US/0276-0878). **1756**

JOURNAL OF CORPORATE ACCOUNTING AND FINANCE. (US/1044-8136). **746**

JOURNAL OF CORPORATE FINANCE. (NE/0929-1199). **793**

JOURNAL OF CORPORATE MANAGEMENT, THE. (AT/1038-2410). **Adv Mgr Tel** (02)223-5744. **3101**

JOURNAL OF CORPORATION LAW, THE. (US/0360-795X). **3101**

JOURNAL OF COST MANAGEMENT FOR THE MANUFACTURING INDUSTRY. (US/0899-5141). **873**

JOURNAL OF COUNSELING AND DEVELOPMENT. (US/0748-9633). **1913**

JOURNAL OF COUNSELING PSYCHOLOGY. (US/0022-0167). **4595**

JOURNAL OF COUPLES THERAPY. (US/0897-4446). **2281**

JOURNAL OF CRIMINAL JUSTICE EDUCATION. (US/1051-1253). **3167**

JOURNAL OF CRIMINAL LAW & CRIMINOLOGY. (US/0091-4169). **3107**

JOURNAL OF CRIMINAL LAW (HERTFORD). (UK/0022-0183). **3107**

JOURNAL OF CRITICAL ANALYSIS, THE. (US/0022-0213). **1756**

JOURNAL OF CRITICAL ILLNESS, THE. (US/1040-0257). **3595**

JOURNAL OF CROSS-CULTURAL GERONTOLOGY. (NE/0169-3816). **3753**

JOURNAL OF CRYPTOLOGY. (US/0933-2790). **3512**

JOURNAL OF CULINARY PRACTICE. (US/1052-9241). **2346**

JOURNAL OF CULTURAL DIVERSITY. (US/1071-5568). **Adv Mgr:** Monique, **Tel** (708)969-3809. **5206**

JOURNAL OF CULTURAL GEOGRAPHY. (US/0887-3631). **2567**

JOURNAL OF CURRENT LASER ABSTRACTS. (CN/0022-0264). **4426**

JOURNAL OF CUTANEOUS PATHOLOGY. (DK/0303-6987). **3721**

JOURNAL OF DAIRY SCIENCE. (US/0022-0302). **195**

JOURNAL OF DANISH ARCHAEOLOGY. (DK/0108-464X). **271**

JOURNAL OF DATA & COMPUTER COMMUNICATIONS. (US/1054-089X). **1260**

JOURNAL OF DATABASE MANAGEMENT. (US/1063-8016). **1254**

JOURNAL OF DEMOCRACY. (US/1045-5736). **4478**

JOURNAL OF DENTAL EDUCATION. (US/0022-0337). **Adv Mgr:** A. Siegel, **Tel** (202)667-9433. **1326**

JOURNAL OF DENTAL HYGIENE. (US/1043-254X). **1326**

JOURNAL OF DENTAL RESEARCH. (US/0022-0345). **1326**

JOURNAL OF DENTISTRY. (UK/0300-5712). **1326**

JOURNAL OF DENTISTRY FOR CHILDREN. (US/0022-0353). **1326**

JOURNAL OF DEPRESSION & STRESS. (US). **Adv Mgr:** David Loitorston. **3928**

JOURNAL OF DERMATOLOGIC SURGERY AND ONCOLOGY, THE. (US/0148-0812). **3967**

JOURNAL OF DERMATOLOGICAL SCIENCE. (NE/0923-1811). **3721**

JOURNAL OF DERMATOLOGICAL TREATMENT, THE. (UK/0954-6634). **3721**

JOURNAL OF DESIGN HISTORY. (UK/0952-4649). **2099**

JOURNAL OF DEVELOPING AREAS, THE. (US/0022-037X). **Adv Mgr:** Joan Pano. **2910**

JOURNAL OF DEVELOPMENT AND ADMINISTRATIVE STUDIES, THE. (NP). **1613**

JOURNAL OF DEVELOPMENT COMMUNICATION, THE. (MY/0128-3863). **1114**

JOURNAL OF DEVELOPMENT ECONOMICS. (NE/0304-3878). **1569**

JOURNAL OF DEVELOPMENT STUDIES, THE. (UK/0022-0388). **Adv Mgr:** Anne Kidson. **1569**

JOURNAL OF DEVELOPMENTAL AND BEHAVIORAL PEDIATRICS. (US/0196-206X). **3904**

JOURNAL OF DEVELOPMENTAL EDUCATION. (US/0894-3907). **1756**

JOURNAL OF DEVELOPMENTAL PHYSIOLOGY. (UK/0141-9846). **3763**

JOURNAL OF DIETETIC SOFTWARE. (US/0742-826X). **4193**

JOURNAL OF DISABILITY POLICY STUDIES, THE. (US/1044-2073). **4389**

JOURNAL OF DISPERSION SCIENCE AND TECHNOLOGY. (US/0193-2691). **4428**

JOURNAL OF DISTANCE EDUCATION / REVUE DE L'ENSEIGNEMENT A DISTANCE. (CN/0830-0445). **1756**

JOURNAL OF DIVORCE & REMARRIAGE. (US/1050-2556). **2281**

JOURNAL OF DOCUMENT AND TEXT MANAGEMENT. (UK). **1192**

JOURNAL OF DOCUMENTATION. (UK/0022-0418). **3219**

JOURNAL OF DRUG DEVELOPMENT. (UK/0952-9500). **Adv Mgr:** Kathryn Wilkinson, **Tel** 44 625 618507. **4311**

JOURNAL OF DRUG ISSUES. (US/0022-0426). **1346**

JOURNAL OF DYNAMIC SYSTEMS, MEASUREMENT, AND CONTROL. (US/0022-0434). **1982**

JOURNAL OF EARLY ADOLESCENCE, THE. (US/0272-4316). **4596**

JOURNAL OF EAST-WEST BUSINESS. (US/1066-9868). **686**

JOURNAL OF EASTERN AFRICAN RESEARCH & DEVELOPMENT. (KE/0251-0405). **2640**

JOURNAL OF ECOLOGY, THE. (UK/0022-0477). **515**

JOURNAL OF ECONOMIC AND SOCIAL INTELLIGENCE. (UK). **5206**

JOURNAL OF ECONOMIC AND TAXONOMIC BOTANY. (II/0250-9768). **515**

JOURNAL OF ECONOMIC BEHAVIOR & ORGANIZATION. (NE/0167-2681). **1498**

JOURNAL OF ECONOMIC COOPERATION AMONG ISLAMIC COUNTRIES. (TU). **1498**

JOURNAL OF ECONOMIC DYNAMICS & CONTROL. (NE/0165-1889). **1499**

JOURNAL OF ECONOMIC EDUCATION, THE. (US/0022-0485). **1499**

JOURNAL OF ECONOMIC ENTOMOLOGY. (US/0022-0493). **5610**

JOURNAL OF ECONOMIC HISTORY, THE. (US/0022-0507). **1569**

JOURNAL OF ECONOMIC LITERATURE. (US/0022-0515). **1535**

JOURNAL OF ECONOMIC PSYCHOLOGY. (NE/0167-4870). **1593**

JOURNAL OF ECONOMIC SURVEYS. (UK/0950-0804). **1570**

JOURNAL OF ECONOMICS AND BUSINESS. (US/0148-6195). **1499**

JOURNAL OF ECONOMICS AND INTERNATIONAL RELATIONS. (HK/1013-1809). **1570**

JOURNAL OF ECUMENICAL STUDIES. (US/0022-0558). **Adv Mgr:** Nancy Krody. **4968**

JOURNAL OF EDUCATION & PSYCHOLOGY. (II/0022-0590). **4596**

JOURNAL OF EDUCATION (BOSTON, MASS.). (US/0022-0574). **1756**

JOURNAL OF EDUCATION FINANCE. (US/0098-9495). **1865**

JOURNAL OF EDUCATION FOR BUSINESS. (US/0883-2323). **687**

JOURNAL OF EDUCATIONAL MEASUREMENT. (US/0022-0655). **1757**

JOURNAL OF EDUCATIONAL RESEARCH (WASHINGTON, D.C.), THE. (US/0022-0671). **1757**

JOURNAL OF EDUCATIONAL STATISTICS. (US/0362-9791). **1795**

JOURNAL OF EDUCATIONAL TELEVISION. (UK/0260-7417). **1757**

JOURNAL OF EDUCATIONAL THOUGHT. (CN/0022-0701). **1757**

JOURNAL OF ELASTICITY. (NE/0374-3535). **4428**

JOURNAL OF ELDER ABUSE & NEGLECT. (US/0894-6566). **5291**

JOURNAL OF ELECTRICAL AND ELECTRONICS ENGINEERING, AUSTRALIA. (AT/0725-2986). **2068**

JOURNAL OF ELECTROCARDIOLOGY. (US/0022-0736). **3707**

JOURNAL OF ELECTRON MICROSCOPY. (JA/0022-0744). **572**

JOURNAL OF ELECTRONIC DEFENSE. (US/0192-429X). **4048**

JOURNAL OF ELECTRONIC ENGINEERING : JEE. (JA/0385-4507). **2068**

JOURNAL OF ELECTRONIC IMAGING. (US/1017-9909). **2068**

JOURNAL OF ELECTRONIC MATERIALS. (US/0361-5235). **2068**

JOURNAL OF ELECTRONIC PACKAGING. (US/1043-7398). **2069**

JOURNAL OF ELECTROPHYSIOLOGICAL TECHNOLOGY. (UK/0307-5095). **Adv Mgr:** B. Bragg. **3595**

JOURNAL OF ELECTROPHYSIOLOGY. (US/0892-1059). **2069**

JOURNAL OF ELECTROSTATICS. (NE/0304-3886). **2069**

JOURNAL OF EMERGENCY NURSING. (US/0099-1767). **3858**

JOURNAL OF EMOTIONAL AND BEHAVIORAL PROBLEMS. (US/1064-7023). **Adv Mgr:** Nancy Shin, **Tel** (812)336-7700. **4596**

JOURNAL OF EMPLOYMENT COUNSELING. (US/0022-0787). **4206**

JOURNAL OF END USER COMPUTING. (US/1063-2239). **1192**

JOURNAL OF ENDOCRINOLOGICAL INVESTIGATION. (IT/0391-4097). **3731**

JOURNAL OF ENDOCRINOLOGY, THE. (UK/0022-0795). **3731**

JOURNAL OF ENDODONTICS. (US/0099-2399). **1327**

JOURNAL OF ENERGY AND DEVELOPMENT, THE. (US/0361-4476). **1948**

JOURNAL OF ENERGY ENGINEERING. (US/0733-9402). **2118**

JOURNAL OF ENERGY, NATURAL RESOURCES & ENVIRONMENTAL LAW. (US/1053-377X). **3113**

JOURNAL OF ENGINEERING DESIGN. (UK/0954-4828). **2099**

JOURNAL OF ENGINEERING FOR INDUSTRY. (US/0022-0817). **1982**

JOURNAL OF ENGINEERING MATERIALS AND TECHNOLOGY. (US/0094-4289). **2118**

JOURNAL OF ENGINEERING MATHEMATICS. (NE/0022-0833). **1982**

JOURNAL OF ENGINEERING TECHNOLOGY. (US/0747-9964). **Adv Mgr:** Richard Moore, **Tel** (503)725-3066. **1982**

JOURNAL OF ENGLISH AND GERMANIC PHILOLOGY, THE. (US/0363-6941). **3290**

JOURNAL OF ENGLISH LINGUISTICS. (US/0075-4242). **3290**

JOURNAL OF ENTOMOLOGICAL RESEARCH. (II/0378-9519). **5587**

JOURNAL OF ENVIRONMENT & DEVELOPMENT, THE. (US/1070-4965). **1499**

JOURNAL OF ENVIRONMENTAL BIOLOGY. (II/0254-8704). **2233**

JOURNAL OF ENVIRONMENTAL ENGINEERING (NEW YORK N.Y.). (US/0733-9372). **2233**

JOURNAL OF ENVIRONMENTAL HEALTH. (US/0022-0892). **Adv Mgr:** Scott Houston, **Tel** (303)756-9090. **2175**

JOURNAL OF ENVIRONMENTAL LAW. (UK/0952-8873). **3113**

JOURNAL OF ENVIRONMENTAL LAW AND LITIGATION. (US/1049-0280). **Adv Mgr:** Derek Snelling. **3113**

JOURNAL OF ENVIRONMENTAL PATHOLOGY, TOXICOLOGY AND ONCOLOGY. (US/0731-8898). **3819**

JOURNAL OF ENVIRONMENTAL SCIENCE AND HEALTH. PART A, ENVIRONMENTAL SCIENCE AND ENGINEERING. (US/0360-1226). **1982**

JOURNAL OF ENVIRONMENTAL SCIENCE AND HEALTH. PART B, PESTICIDES, FOOD CONTAMINANTS, AND AGRICULTURAL WASTES. (US/0360-1234). **2176**

JOURNAL OF ENZYME INHIBITION. (SZ/8755-5093). **461**

JOURNAL OF EPILEPSY. (US/0896-6974). **3835**

JOURNAL OF EQUINE VETERINARY SCIENCE. (US/0737-0806). **2800**

JOURNAL OF ESSENTIAL OIL RESEARCH, THE. (US/1041-2905). **1026**

JOURNAL OF ETHIOPIAN STUDIES. (ET/0304-2243). **2640**

JOURNAL OF ETHNIC STUDIES, THE. (US/0091-3219). **2266**

JOURNAL OF ETHNOBIOLOGY. (US/0278-0771). **238**

JOURNAL OF ETHNOPHARMACOLOGY. (SZ/0378-8741). **4311**

JOURNAL OF EURO MARKETING. (US/1049-6483). **927**

JOURNAL OF EUROPEAN BUSINESS, THE. (US/1044-002X). **1613**

JOURNAL OF EUROPEAN STUDIES. (UK/0047-2441). **2694**

JOURNAL OF EVOLUTIONARY BIOLOGY. (SZ/1010-061X). **548**

JOURNAL OF EVOLUTIONARY ECONOMICS. (GW/0936-9937). **1593**

JOURNAL OF EXPERIMENTAL & CLINICAL CANCER RESEARCH : CR. (IT/0392-9078). **3819**

JOURNAL OF EXPERIMENTAL & THEORETICAL ARTIFICIAL INTELLIGENCE. (UK/0952-813X). **1214**

JOURNAL OF EXPERIMENTAL BIOLOGY. (UK/0022-0949). **582**

JOURNAL OF EXPERIMENTAL BOTANY. (UK/0022-0957). **515**

JOURNAL OF EXPERIMENTAL EDUCATION, THE. (US/0022-0973). **1898**

JOURNAL OF EXPERIMENTAL PSYCHOLOGY : ANIMAL BEHAVIOR PROCESSES. (US/0097-7403). **4596**

JOURNAL OF EXPERIMENTAL PSYCHOLOGY : GENERAL. (US/0096-3445). **4596**

JOURNAL OF EXPERIMENTAL PSYCHOLOGY. LEARNING, MEMORY, AND COGNITION. (US/0278-7393). **4597**

JOURNAL OF EXPLOSIVES ENGINEERING, THE. (US/0889-0668). **1982**

JOURNAL OF EXPOSURE ANALYSIS AND ENVIRONMENTAL EPIDEMIOLOGY. (US/1053-4245). **Adv Mgr:** M A Mehlman. **2176**

JOURNAL OF FAMILY PRACTICE, THE. (US/0094-3509). **3738**

JOURNAL OF FAMILY PSYCHOLOGY. (US/0893-3200). **4597**

JOURNAL OF FAMILY PSYCHOTHERAPY. (US/0897-5353). **2282**

JOURNAL OF FAMILY WELFARE, THE. (II/0022-1074). **589**

JOURNAL OF FEMINIST FAMILY THERAPY. (US/0895-2833). **2282**

JOURNAL OF FEMINIST STUDIES IN RELIGION. (US/8755-4178). **4969**

JOURNAL OF FERROCEMENT. (TH/0125-1759). **Adv Mgr Tel** 66-2-524-5864. **632**

JOURNAL OF FIELD ARCHAEOLOGY. (US/0093-4690). **271**

JOURNAL OF FIELD ORNITHOLOGY. (US/0273-8570). **5618**

JOURNAL OF FILM AND VIDEO. (US/0742-4671). **4073**

JOURNAL OF FINANCIAL ABSTRACTS. (US). **794**

JOURNAL OF FINANCIAL AND QUANTITATIVE ANALYSIS. (US/0022-1090). **794**

JOURNAL OF FINANCIAL ENGINEERING, THE. (US/1062-8924). **1982**

JOURNAL OF FINANCIAL INTERMEDIATION. (US/1042-9573). **904**

JOURNAL OF FINANCIAL MANAGEMENT AND ANALYSIS. (II/0970-4205). **794**

JOURNAL OF FINANCIAL PLANNING (DENVER, COLO.). (US/1040-3981). **Adv Mgr:** Farley Associates, Greenwich, CT, **Tel** (203)629-3400. **794**

JOURNAL OF FINANCIAL RESEARCH, THE. (US/0270-2592). **794**

JOURNAL OF FISH DISEASES. (UK/0140-7775). **2306**

JOURNAL OF FLUENCY DISORDERS. (US/0094-730X). **3595**

JOURNAL OF FLUID CONTROL, THE. (US/8755-8564). **2091**

JOURNAL — Advertising Accepted Index

JOURNAL OF FLUIDS ENGINEERING. (US/0098-2202). **2092**

JOURNAL OF FLUORINE CHEMISTRY. (SZ/0022-1139). **Adv Mgr:** Ms. W van Cattenburch (Amsterdam). **981**

JOURNAL OF FOETAL MEDICINE. (IT/0392-9507). **3763**

JOURNAL OF FOLKLORE RESEARCH. (US/0737-7037). **2321**

JOURNAL OF FOOD BIOCHEMISTRY. (US/0145-8884). **2346**

JOURNAL OF FOOD ENGINEERING. (UK/0260-8774). **2346**

JOURNAL OF FOOD PROCESS ENGINEERING. (US/0145-8876). **2346**

JOURNAL OF FOOD PROCESSING AND PRESERVATION. (US/0145-8892). **2346**

JOURNAL OF FOOD PRODUCTS MARKETING. (US/1045-4446). **2346**

JOURNAL OF FOOD PROTECTION. (US/0362-028X). **2346**

JOURNAL OF FOOD QUALITY. (US/0146-9428). **2346**

JOURNAL OF FOOD SAFETY. (US/0149-6085). **2346**

JOURNAL OF FOODSERVICE SYSTEMS. (US/0196-4283). **2347**

JOURNAL OF FOOT SURGERY, THE. (US/0449-2544). **3918**

JOURNAL OF FORAMINIFERAL RESEARCH. (US/0096-1191). **5588**

JOURNAL OF FOREIGN EXCHANGE AND INTERNATIONAL FINANCE. (II). **794**

JOURNAL OF FORENSIC ECONOMICS. (US/0898-5510). **1499**

JOURNAL OF FORESTRY. (US/0022-1201). **2385**

JOURNAL OF FUNCTIONAL PROGRAMMING. (UK/0956-7968). **1279**

JOURNAL OF FURTHER AND HIGHER EDUCATION. (UK/0309-877X). **1832**

JOURNAL OF FUTURES MARKETS, THE. (US/0270-7314). **Adv Mgr:** Roberta Frederick. **904**

JOURNAL OF GAY & LESBIAN PSYCHOTHERAPY. (US/0891-7140). **2794**

JOURNAL OF GAY & LESBIAN SOCIAL SERVICES. (US/1053-8720). **2794**

JOURNAL OF GEM INDUSTRY. (II/0022-1244). **2915**

JOURNAL OF GEMMOLOGY AND PROCEEDINGS OF THE GEMMOLOGICAL ASSOCIATION OF GREAT BRITAIN. (UK/0022-1252). **1440**

JOURNAL OF GENERAL EDUCATION (UNIVERSITY PARK, PA.), THE. (US/0021-3667). **1757**

JOURNAL OF GENERAL INTERNAL MEDICINE. (US/0884-8734). **3798**

JOURNAL OF GENERAL MICROBIOLOGY, THE. (UK/0022-1287). **565**

JOURNAL OF GENERAL ORTHODONTICS. (US/1048-1990). **1327**

JOURNAL OF GENERAL PSYCHOLOGY, THE. (US/0022-1309). **4597**

JOURNAL OF GENERAL VIROLOGY, THE. (UK/0022-1317). **565**

JOURNAL OF GENETIC PSYCHOLOGY, THE. (US/0022-1325). **4597**

JOURNAL OF GENETICS & BREEDING. (IT/0394-9257). **548**

JOURNAL OF GEOGRAPHY (HOUSTON). (US/0022-1341). **2567**

JOURNAL OF GEOGRAPHY IN HIGHER EDUCATION. (UK/0309-8265). **2567**

JOURNAL OF GEOLOGICAL EDUCATION. (US/0022-1368). **1384**

JOURNAL OF GEOMAGNETISM AND GEOELECTRICITY. (JA/0022-1392). **1407**

JOURNAL OF GERIATRIC DRUG THERAPY. (US/8756-4629). **3753**

JOURNAL OF GERIATRIC PSYCHIATRY. (US/0022-1414). **3928**

JOURNAL OF GERIATRIC PSYCHIATRY AND NEUROLOGY. (US/0891-9887). **3753**

JOURNAL OF GERONTOLOGICAL NURSING. (US/0098-9134). **3858**

JOURNAL OF GERONTOLOGICAL SOCIAL WORK. (US/0163-4372). **5292**

JOURNAL OF GERONTOLOGY (KIRKWOOD). (US/0022-1422). **3753**

JOURNAL OF GLOBAL BUSINESS (HARRISONBURG, VA.). (US/1053-7287). **687**

JOURNAL OF GLOBAL INFORMATION MANAGEMENT. (US/1062-7375). **3220**

JOURNAL OF GLOBAL MARKETING. (US/0891-1762). **927**

JOURNAL OF GRAPH THEORY. (US/0364-9024). **3513**

JOURNAL OF GREAT LAKES RESEARCH. (US/0380-1330). **1416**

JOURNAL OF GROUP PSYCHOTHERAPY, PSYCHODRAMA AND SOCIOMETRY. (US/0731-1273). **3929**

JOURNAL OF HAND SURGERY (ST. LOUIS, MO.), THE. (US/0363-5023). **3967**

JOURNAL OF HAND THERAPY. (US/0894-1130). **4380**

JOURNAL OF HARD MATERIALS. (UK/0954-027X). **Adv Mgr:** Sarah Alder, **Tel** 0272 297481. **5118**

JOURNAL OF HAZARDOUS MATERIALS. (NE/0304-3894). **2234**

JOURNAL OF HEAD & NECK PATHOLOGY. (BE/0770-9471). **3595**

JOURNAL OF HEALTH AND SOCIAL BEHAVIOR. (US/0022-1465). **4786**

JOURNAL OF HEALTH & SOCIAL POLICY. (US/0897-7186). **5292**

JOURNAL OF HEALTH CARE CHAPLAINCY. (US/0885-4726). **4969**

JOURNAL OF HEALTH CARE MARKETING. (US/0737-3252). **927**

JOURNAL OF HEALTH ECONOMICS. (NE/0167-6296). **1499**

JOURNAL OF HEALTH EDUCATION. ASSOCIATION FOR THE ADVANCEMENT OF HEALTH EDUCATION. (US/1055-6699). **4786**

JOURNAL OF HEALTH POLITICS, POLICY AND LAW. (US/0361-6878). **2987**

JOURNAL OF HEALTHCARE MATERIAL MANAGEMENT. (US/0889-2482). **3787**

JOURNAL OF HELLENIC STUDIES. (UK/0075-4269). **1078**

JOURNAL OF HELMINTHOLOGY. (UK/0022-149X). **5588**

JOURNAL OF HERBS, SPICES & MEDICINAL PLANTS. (US/1049-6475). **2421**

JOURNAL OF HEREDITY, THE. (US/0022-1503). **548**

JOURNAL OF HIGH RESOLUTION CHROMATOGRAPHY : HRC. (GW/0935-6304). **1017**

JOURNAL OF HIGHER EDUCATION. (AT/1034-3350). **1832**

JOURNAL OF HIMALAYAN STUDIES & REGIONAL DEVELOPMENT. (II). **2218**

JOURNAL OF HISPANIC PHILOLOGY. (US/0147-5460). **3290**

JOURNAL OF HISTOCHEMISTRY AND CYTOCHEMISTRY, THE. (US/0022-1554). **537**

JOURNAL OF HISTORICAL SOCIOLOGY. (UK/0952-1909). **5249**

JOURNAL OF HISTOTECHNOLOGY. (US/0147-8885). **538**

JOURNAL OF HOME ECONOMICS (WASHINGTON). (US/0022-1570). **2791**

JOURNAL OF HOMOSEXUALITY. (US/0091-8369). **2795**

JOURNAL OF HOSPITAL MARKETING. (US/0883-7570). **3787**

JOURNAL OF HOSPITALITY & LEISURE MARKETING. (US/1050-7051). **4851**

JOURNAL OF HOUSING (1979). (US/0272-7374). **2826**

JOURNAL OF HOUSING FOR THE ELDERLY. (US/0276-3893). **2826**

JOURNAL OF HUMAN HYPERTENSION. (UK/0950-9240). **3707**

JOURNAL OF HUMAN JUSTICE, THE. (CN/0847-2971). **2987**

JOURNAL OF HUMAN LACTATION. (US/0890-3344). **3763**

JOURNAL OF HUMAN MOVEMENT STUDIES. (UK/0306-7297). **583**

JOURNAL OF HUMAN NUTRITION AND DIETETICS. (UK/0952-3871). **4193**

JOURNAL OF HUMAN RESOURCES, THE. (US/0022-166X). **1914**

JOURNAL OF HUMANISTIC EDUCATION. (US/0890-0493). **1898**

JOURNAL OF HUMANITIES (ZOMBA, MALAWI). (MW). **2848**

JOURNAL OF HYDRAULIC RESEARCH. (NE/0022-1686). **2092**

JOURNAL OF HYDROLOGY, NEW ZEALAND. (NZ/0022-1708). **1416**

JOURNAL OF HYPERBARIC MEDICINE. (US/0884-1225). **3595**

JOURNAL OF HYPERTENSION. (US/0263-6352). **3707**

JOURNAL OF ICHTHYOLOGY. (US/0032-9452). **2307**

JOURNAL OF IMA, THE. (US/0899-8299). **3595**

JOURNAL OF IMAGING SCIENCE AND TECHNOLOGY, THE. (US/1062-3701). **5118**

JOURNAL OF IMMUNOASSAY. (US/0197-1522). **3673**

JOURNAL OF IMPERIAL AND COMMONWEALTH HISTORY, THE. (UK/0308-6534). **Adv Mgr:** Anne Kidson. **2695**

JOURNAL OF INDIAN COUNCIL OF PHILOSOPHICAL RESEARCH. (II). **4350**

JOURNAL OF INDIAN PHILOSOPHY. (NE/0022-1791). **4350**

JOURNAL OF INDIAN WRITING IN ENGLISH, THE. (II/0302-1319). **3400**

JOURNAL OF INDO-EUROPEAN STUDIES, THE. (US/0092-2323). **3290**

JOURNAL OF INDUSTRIAL ECONOMICS, THE. (UK/0022-1821). **1614**

JOURNAL OF INDUSTRIAL IRRADIATION TECHNOLOGY. (US/0735-7923). **981**

JOURNAL OF INDUSTRIAL TECHNOLOGY / THE NATIONAL ASSOCIATION OF INDUSTRIAL TECHNOLOGY. (US/0882-6404). **5118**

JOURNAL OF INFECTIOUS DISEASES, THE. (US/0022-1899). **3714**

JOURNAL OF INFERENTIAL AND DEDUCTIVE BIOLOGY. (US/0883-1378). **461**

JOURNAL OF INFORMATION ETHICS. (US/1061-9321). **Adv Mgr:** Steve Wilson. **2251**

JOURNAL OF INFORMATION NETWORKING. (UK/0966-9248). **1242**

JOURNAL OF INFORMATION TECHNOLOGY MANAGEMENT. (US/1042-1319). **873**

JOURNAL OF INFUSIONAL CHEMOTHERAPY, THE. (US/1060-0051). **Adv Mgr:** Charles Healy, **Tel** (619)320-0118. **3819**

JOURNAL OF INHERITED METABOLIC DISEASE. (UK/0141-8955). **3798**

JOURNAL OF INORGANIC BIOCHEMISTRY. (US/0162-0134). **489**

JOURNAL OF INSTITUTE OF ECONOMIC RESEARCH. (II/0020-2851). **1570**

JOURNAL OF INSTITUTIONAL AND THEORETICAL ECONOMICS : JITE. (GW/0932-4569). **5206**

JOURNAL OF INSURANCE MEDICINE (NEW YORK, N.Y.). (US/0743-6661). **2885**

JOURNAL OF INTELLIGENT SYSTEMS. (UK/0334-1860). **1214**

JOURNAL OF INTENSIVE ENGLISH STUDIES. (US/0899-885X). **3290**

JOURNAL OF INTERAMERICAN STUDIES AND WORLD AFFAIRS. (US/0022-1937). **Adv Mgr Tel** (908)932-2280. **4527**

JOURNAL OF INTERCULTURAL STUDIES. (AT/0725-6868). **1919**

JOURNAL OF INTERDISCIPLINARY CYCLE RESEARCH. (NE/0022-1945). **461**

JOURNAL OF INTERDISCIPLINARY HISTORY, THE. (US/0022-1953). **2621**

JOURNAL OF INTERDISCIPLINARY STUDIES. (US/0890-0132). **4969**

JOURNAL OF INTERFERON RESEARCH. (US/0197-8357). **565**

JOURNAL OF INTERGROUP RELATIONS. (US/0047-2492). **5250**

JOURNAL OF INTERLIBRARY LOAN & INFORMATION SUPPLY. (US/1042-4458). **3220**

JOURNAL OF INTERNATIONAL AND COMPARATIVE SOCIAL WELFARE. (US/0898-5847). **5292**

JOURNAL OF INTERNATIONAL BANKING LAW. (UK/0267-937X). **3087**

JOURNAL OF INTERNATIONAL BUSINESS STUDIES. (CN/0047-2506). **687**

JOURNAL OF INTERNATIONAL CONSUMER MARKETING. (US/0896-1530). **928**

JOURNAL OF INTERNATIONAL FINANCIAL MARKETS, INSTITUTIONS & MONEY. (US/1042-4431). **1637**

JOURNAL OF INTERNATIONAL FOOD & AGRIBUSINESS MARKETING. (US/0897-4438). **2347**

JOURNAL OF INTERNATIONAL MARKETING AND MARKETING RESEARCH. (UK). **Adv Mgr:** T. A. Voss. **928**

JOURNAL OF INTERNATIONAL MEDICAL RESEARCH, THE. (UK/0300-0605). **3595**

JOURNAL OF INTERNATIONAL TRADE AND ECONOMIC DEVELOPMENT. (UK/0963-8199). **Adv Mgr:** David Polley. **1637**

JOURNAL OF INTERPERSONAL VIOLENCE. (US/0886-2605). **5292**

Advertising Accepted Index — JOURNAL

JOURNAL OF INTERVENTIONAL CARDIOLOGY. (US/0896-4327). **3707**

JOURNAL OF INTRAVENOUS NURSING. (US/0896-5846). **3858**

JOURNAL OF INTRAVENOUS THERAPY (LOS ANGELES). (US/0194-1658). **3595**

JOURNAL OF INVASIVE CARDIOLOGY, THE. (US/1042-3931). **3707**

JOURNAL OF INVESTIGATIVE SURGERY. (US/0894-1939). **3967**

JOURNAL OF IRREPRODUCIBLE RESULTS, THE. (US/0022-2038). **5118**

JOURNAL OF ISLAMIC BANKING & FINANCE : QUARTERLY PUBLICATION OF THE INTERNATIONAL ASSOCIATION OF ISLAMIC BANKS, KARACHI (ASIAN REGION). (PK). **795**

JOURNAL OF ITALIAN FOOD & WINE. (US/1073-3124). **Adv Mgr:** Andrew Pappas. **2347**

JOURNAL OF JAPANESE LINGUISTICS. (JA). **3290**

JOURNAL OF JAPANESE STUDIES, THE. (US/0095-6848). **2655**

JOURNAL OF JAPANESE TRADE & INDUSTRY. (JA/0285-9556). **687**

JOURNAL OF JEWISH COMMUNAL SERVICE. (US/0022-2089). **2266**

JOURNAL OF JEWISH EDUCATION. (US). **5050**

JOURNAL OF JEWISH STUDIES, THE. (UK/0022-2097). **5050**

JOURNAL OF JUVENILE LAW. (US/0160-2098). **3121**

JOURNAL OF KANSAS PHARMACY, THE. (US/0194-5106). **4311**

JOURNAL OF KEW GUILD. (UK). **Adv Mgr:** Mr. Gaggini, **Tel** 0604 811839. **2421**

JOURNAL OF KOREAN STUDIES (SEATTLE, WASH. : 1979), THE. (US/0731-1613). **2655**

JOURNAL OF LABOR RESEARCH. (US/0195-3613). **1682**

JOURNAL OF LABORATORY AND CLINICAL MEDICINE, THE. (US/0022-2143). **3595**

JOURNAL OF LAND USE & ENVIRONMENTAL LAW. (US/0892-4880). **3113**

JOURNAL OF LANGUAGE AND SOCIAL PSYCHOLOGY. (US/0261-927X). **3290**

JOURNAL OF LANGUAGE FOR INTERNATIONAL BUSINESS, THE. (US/8755-0504). **3290**

JOURNAL OF LAPAROENDOSCOPIC SURGERY. (US/1052-3901). **3967**

JOURNAL OF LARYNGOLOGY AND OTOLOGY. (UK/0022-2151). **3889**

JOURNAL OF LATIN AMERICAN LORE. (US/0360-1927). **2321**

JOURNAL OF LAW AND COMMERCE, THE. (US/0733-2491). **2988**

JOURNAL OF LAW & EDUCATION. (US/0275-6072). **1865**

JOURNAL OF LAW AND ETHICS IN DENTISTRY. (US/0894-8879). **1327**

JOURNAL OF LAW AND INFORMATION SCIENCE. (AT/0729-1485). **Adv Mgr:** David McGuire. **2988**

JOURNAL OF LAW & POLITICS. (US/0749-2227). **2988**

JOURNAL OF LAW AND RELIGION, THE. (US/0748-0814). **Adv Mgr:** J Matson, **Tel** (612)641-2082. **2988**

JOURNAL OF LAW AND SOCIETY. (UK/0263-323X). **2988**

JOURNAL OF LEARNING DISABILITIES. (US/0022-2194). **1880**

JOURNAL OF LEARNING SKILLS, THE. (US/0740-5715). **1757**

JOURNAL OF LEGAL ASPECTS OF SPORT. (US/1072-0316). **2988**

JOURNAL OF LEGAL ECONOMICS. (US/1054-3023). **1500**

JOURNAL OF LEGAL HISTORY, THE. (UK/0144-0365). **Adv Mgr:** Anne Kidson. **2988**

JOURNAL OF LEGAL MEDICINE (CHICAGO. 1979), THE. (US/0194-7648). **3741**

JOURNAL OF LEGAL STUDIES, THE. (US/0047-2530). **2988**

JOURNAL OF LEGISLATION. (US/0146-9584). **2989**

JOURNAL OF LIBERTARIAN STUDIES, THE. (US/0363-2873). **5206**

JOURNAL OF LIBRARY ADMINISTRATION. (US/0193-0826). **3220**

JOURNAL OF LIBRARY AND INFORMATION SCIENCE (DELHI). (II/0970-714X). **3220**

JOURNAL OF LIGHT CONSTRUCTION (NEW ENGLAND ED), THE. (US/1050-2610). **Adv Mgr:** Nellie Callahan, **Tel** (802)434-4747. **618**

JOURNAL OF LITERARY SEMANTICS. (NE/0341-7638). **Adv Mgr:** R. Wiendl. **3290**

JOURNAL OF LITERARY STUDIES (PRETORIA, SOUTH AFRICA). (SA/0256-4718). **3345**

JOURNAL OF LOGIC PROGRAMMING, THE. (US/0743-1066). **1280**

JOURNAL OF LONG TERM CARE ADMINISTRATION, THE. (US/0093-4445). **Adv Mgr:** Jan Lamoglia, **Tel** (703)739-7913. **3787**

JOURNAL OF LOSS PREVENTION IN THE PROCESS INDUSTRIES. (UK/0950-4230). **2099**

JOURNAL OF MACROECONOMICS. (US/0164-0704). **1500**

JOURNAL OF MACROMARKETING. (US/0276-1467). **928**

JOURNAL OF MACROMOLECULAR SCIENCE. PHYSICS. (US/0022-2348). **4409**

JOURNAL OF MACROMOLECULAR SCIENCE. REVIEWS IN MACROMOLECULAR CHEMISTRY. (US/0022-2356). **1042**

JOURNAL OF MAGNETIC RESONANCE IMAGING. (US/1053-1807). **Adv Mgr:** Tom Shimala, **Tel** (708) 571-7819. **3942**

JOURNAL OF MAMMALOGY. (US/0022-2372). **5588**

JOURNAL OF MANAGEMENT. (US/0149-2063). **873**

JOURNAL OF MANAGEMENT CONSULTING (AMSTERDAM). (US/0168-7778). **Adv Mgr:** Michael Shays. **873**

JOURNAL OF MANAGEMENT STUDIES, THE. (UK/0022-2380). **874**

JOURNAL OF MANAGEMENT SYSTEMS, THE. (US/1041-2808). **943**

JOURNAL OF MANAGERIAL ISSUES. (US/1045-3695). **874**

JOURNAL OF MANAGERIAL PSYCHOLOGY. (UK/0268-3946). **4598**

JOURNAL OF MANIPULATIVE AND PHYSIOLOGICAL THERAPEUTICS. (US/0161-4754). **4380**

JOURNAL OF MANUAL & MANIPULATIVE THERAPY, THE. (US/1066-9817). **Adv Mgr:** M. Holton, **Tel** (407)677-5194. **3882**

JOURNAL OF MARITAL AND FAMILY THERAPY. (US/0194-472X). **2282**

JOURNAL OF MARKETING. (US/0022-2429). **928**

JOURNAL OF MARKETING CHANNELS. (US/1046-669X). **928**

JOURNAL OF MARKETING EDUCATION. (US/0273-4753). **928**

JOURNAL OF MARKETING FOR HIGHER EDUCATION. (US/0884-1241). **1833**

JOURNAL OF MARKETING FOR MENTAL HEALTH. (US/0883-7589). **4787**

JOURNAL OF MARKETING MANAGEMENT. (UK/0267-257X). **928**

JOURNAL OF MARRIAGE AND THE FAMILY. (US/0022-2445). **2282**

JOURNAL OF MATERIALS RESEARCH. (US/0884-2914). **2103**

JOURNAL OF MATERIALS SCIENCE. (UK/0022-2461). **4006**

JOURNAL OF MATERIALS SCIENCE LETTERS. (UK/0261-8028). **2103**

JOURNAL OF MATERIALS SCIENCE. MATERIALS IN ELECTRONICS. (UK/0957-4522). **2069**

JOURNAL OF MATHEMATICAL BEHAVIOR, THE. (US/0732-3123). **3513**

JOURNAL OF MATHEMATICAL SOCIOLOGY, THE. (US/0022-250X). **5250**

JOURNAL OF MAYAN LINGUISTICS. (US/0195-475X). **3291**

JOURNAL OF MEDIA ECONOMICS. (US/0899-7764). **1115**

JOURNAL OF MEDICAL COLLEGES OF PLA. (CC/1000-9094). **3596**

JOURNAL OF MEDICAL ENTOMOLOGY. (US/0022-2585). **5611**

JOURNAL OF MEDICAL PRACTICE MANAGEMENT, THE. (US/8755-0229). **3914**

JOURNAL OF MEDICINAL CHEMISTRY. (US/0022-2623). **490**

JOURNAL OF MEDICINE AND PHILOSOPHY, THE. (NE/0360-5310). **3596**

JOURNAL OF MEDICINE (WESTBURY). (US/0025-7850). **3596**

JOURNAL OF MEDIEVAL AND RENAISSANCE STUDIES, THE. (US/0047-2573). **2695**

JOURNAL OF MEDITERRANEAN STUDIES. (MM/1016-3476). **Adv Mgr:** Tita Bonnica, **Tel** 356 343572. **2848**

JOURNAL OF MEMBRANE SCIENCE. (NE/0376-7388). **5119**

JOURNAL OF MENNONITE STUDIES. (CN/0824-5053). **4969**

JOURNAL OF MEN'S STUDIES, THE. (US/1060-8265). **3995**

JOURNAL OF MENTAL HEALTH ADMINISTRATION. (US/0092-8623). **5292**

JOURNAL OF MENTAL HEALTH COUNSELING. (US/1040-2861). **5292**

JOURNAL OF METAMORPHIC GEOLOGY. (UK/0263-4929). **1458**

JOURNAL OF METEOROLOGY. (UK/0307-5966). **1426**

JOURNAL OF MICROCOLUMN SEPARATIONS, THE. (US/1040-7685). **981**

JOURNAL OF MICROCOMPUTER SYSTEMS MANAGEMENT. (US/1043-6464). **1192**

JOURNAL OF MICROPALEONTOLOGY. (UK/0262-821X). **4227**

JOURNAL OF MICROSCOPY (OXFORD). (UK/0022-2720). **572**

JOURNAL OF MILITARY HISTORY, THE. (US/0899-3718). **Adv Mgr:** F. Richards. **4048**

JOURNAL OF MIND AND BEHAVIOR, THE. (US/0271-0137). **4598**

JOURNAL OF MINES, METALS & FUELS. (II/0022-2755). **2141**

JOURNAL OF MINISTRY IN ADDICTION & RECOVERY. (US/1053-8755). **1346**

JOURNAL OF MINORITY AGING, THE. (US/0742-6291). **5180**

JOURNAL OF MISSISSIPPI HISTORY, THE. (US/0022-2771). **Adv Mgr:** Chrissy Wilson, **Tel** (601)359-6850. **2741**

JOURNAL OF MODERN AFRICAN STUDIES, THE. (UK/0022-278X). **2640**

JOURNAL OF MODERN GREEK STUDIES. (US/0738-1727). **2695**

JOURNAL OF MODERN KOREAN STUDIES, THE. (US/8756-2235). **2655**

JOURNAL OF MODERN LITERATURE. (US/0022-281X). **3345**

JOURNAL OF MOLECULAR GRAPHICS. (UK/0263-7855). **1234**

JOURNAL OF MOLECULAR STRUCTURE. (NE/0022-2860). **1054**

JOURNAL OF MOLLUSCAN STUDIES. (UK/0260-1230). **5588**

JOURNAL OF MONETARY ECONOMICS. (NE/0304-3932). **1500**

JOURNAL OF MONEY, CREDIT, AND BANKING. (US/0022-2879). **795**

JOURNAL OF MORAL EDUCATION. (UK/0305-7240). **1758**

JOURNAL OF MOTOR BEHAVIOR. (US/0022-2895). **583**

JOURNAL OF MOTOR VEHICLE LAW. (CN/0840-7754). **2989**

JOURNAL OF MULTI-CULTURAL AND CROSS-CULTURAL RESEARCH IN ART EDUCATION. (US/0740-1833). **354**

JOURNAL OF MULTICULTURAL SOCIAL WORK. (US/1042-8224). **5292**

JOURNAL OF MULTILINGUAL AND MULTICULTURAL DEVELOPMENT. (UK/0143-4632). **3291**

JOURNAL OF MULTINATIONAL FINANCIAL MANAGEMENT. (US/1042-444X). **1637**

JOURNAL OF MUSCLE RESEARCH AND CELL MOTILITY. (UK/0142-4319). **538**

JOURNAL OF MUSIC THEORY PEDAGOGY, THE. (US/0891-7639). **Adv Mgr:** A. Lanning, **Tel** (405)364-7328. **4126**

JOURNAL OF MUSICOLOGICAL RESEARCH, THE. (US/0141-1896). **4126**

JOURNAL OF MUSICOLOGY (ST. JOSEPH, MICH.), THE. (US/0277-9269). **4126**

JOURNAL OF MUTUAL FUND SERVICES, THE. (US/1071-846X). **904**

JOURNAL OF NATUROPATHIC MEDICINE, THE. (US/1047-7837). **3596**

JOURNAL OF NAVIGATION, THE. (UK/0373-4633). **4177**

JOURNAL OF NEAR INFRARED SPECTROSCOPY. (UK). **Adv Mgr:** Ian Michael. **4436**

JOURNAL OF NEGRO EDUCATION, THE. (US/0022-2984). **1758**

JOURNAL OF NERVOUS AND MENTAL DISEASE, THE. (US/0022-3018). **3835**

JOURNAL OF NEUROBIOLOGY. (US/0022-3034). **3835**

JOURNAL OF NEUROCYTOLOGY. (UK/0300-4864). **538**

JOURNAL OF NEUROIMMUNOLOGY. (NE/0165-5728). **3836**

JOURNAL OF NEUROLOGIC REHABILITATION. (US/0888-4390). **3836**

JOURNAL — Advertising Accepted Index

JOURNAL OF NEUROLOGICAL & ORTHOPAEDIC MEDICINE & SURGERY, THE. (US/0890-6599). **3967**

JOURNAL OF NEUROPATHOLOGY AND EXPERIMENTAL NEUROLOGY. (US/0022-3069). **3836**

JOURNAL OF NEUROPHYSIOLOGY. (US/0022-3077). **3836**

JOURNAL OF NEUROPSYCHIATRY AND CLINICAL NEUROSCIENCES, THE. (US/0895-0172). **3929**

JOURNAL OF NEUROSCIENCE METHODS. (NE/0165-0270). **3837**

JOURNAL OF NEUROSCIENCE NURSING, THE. (US/0888-0395). **3859**

JOURNAL OF NEUROSCIENCE, THE. (US/0270-6474). **3836**

JOURNAL OF NEUROSURGICAL SCIENCES. (IT/0390-5616). **3968**

JOURNAL OF NEW GENERATION COMPUTER SYSTEMS. (GW/0863-0445). **1192**

JOURNAL OF NEW ZEALAND LITERATURE : JNZL. (NZ/0112-1227). **3400**

JOURNAL OF NEWSPAPER AND PERIODICAL HISTORY. (UK/0265-5942). **2921**

JOURNAL OF NIH RESEARCH, THE. (US/1043-609X). **461**

JOURNAL OF NON-EQUILIBRIUM THERMODYNAMICS. (GW/0340-0204). **4431**

JOURNAL OF NONPROFIT & PUBLIC SECTOR MARKETING. (US/1049-5142). **928**

JOURNAL OF NORTHEAST ASIAN STUDIES. (US/0738-7997). **4479**

JOURNAL OF NUCLEAR AGRICULTURE AND BIOLOGY. (II/0379-5489). **100**

JOURNAL OF NUCLEAR MEDICINE (1978), THE. (US/0161-5505). **3848**

JOURNAL OF NUCLEAR MEDICINE. SUPPLEMENT. (US/0075-4315). **3848**

JOURNAL OF NUCLEAR MEDICINE TECHNOLOGY. (US/0091-4916). **3848**

JOURNAL OF NURSE-MIDWIFERY. (US/0091-2182). **3859**

JOURNAL OF NURSING. (CH/0047-262X). **3859**

JOURNAL OF NURSING ADMINISTRATION, THE. (US/0002-0443). **3859**

JOURNAL OF NURSING EDUCATION, THE. (US/0148-4834). **3859**

JOURNAL OF NUTRITION EDUCATION. (US/0022-3182). **4193**

JOURNAL OF NUTRITION FOR THE ELDERLY. (US/0163-9366). **4193**

JOURNAL OF NUTRITION IN RECIPE & MENU DEVELOPMENT. (US/1055-1379). **4193**

JOURNAL OF NUTRITION, THE. (US/0022-3166). **Adv Mgr Tel** (301)530-7103. **4193**

JOURNAL OF NUTRITIONAL IMMUNOLOGY. (US/1049-5150). **4193**

JOURNAL OF OBJECTIVE STUDIES. (II). **5043**

JOURNAL OF OBSTETRICS AND GYNAECOLOGY. (UK/0144-3615). **3763**

JOURNAL OF OCCUPATIONAL AND ORGANIZATIONAL PSYCHOLOGY. (UK/0963-1798). **Adv Mgr:** H Dauker, **Tel** 44 81 444 1040. **4598**

JOURNAL OF OCCUPATIONAL MEDICINE AND TOXICOLOGY. (US/1054-044X). **Adv Mgr:** M A Mehlman. **3981**

JOURNAL OF OCULAR PHARMACOLOGY. (US/8756-3320). **3876**

JOURNAL OF OFFENDER MONITORING. (US/1043-500X) **3167**

JOURNAL OF OFFENDER REHABILITATION. (US/1050-9674). **3167**

JOURNAL OF OMAN STUDIES, THE. (MK/0378-8180). **2655**

JOURNAL OF ONE-DAY SURGERY. (UK/0963-5386). **3968**

JOURNAL OF OPHTHALMIC NURSING & TECHNOLOGY. (US/0744-7132). **3859**

JOURNAL OF OPHTHALMIC PHOTOGRAPHY, THE. (US/0198-6155). **3876**

JOURNAL OF OPTOMETRIC EDUCATION. (US/0098-6917). **4216**

JOURNAL OF OPTOMETRIC VISION DEVELOPMENT (1976). (US/0149-886X). **4216**

JOURNAL OF ORAL AND MAXILLOFACIAL SURGERY. (US/0278-2391). **3968**

JOURNAL OF ORAL IMPLANTOLOGY, THE. (US/0160-6972). **1327**

JOURNAL OF ORGANIC CHEMISTRY. (US/0022-3263). **1043**

JOURNAL OF ORGANIZATIONAL BEHAVIOR MANAGEMENT. (US/0160-8061). **4599**

JOURNAL OF ORGANIZATIONAL CHANGE MANAGEMENT. (UK/0953-4814). **874**

JOURNAL OF ORGANOMETALLIC CHEMISTRY. (SZ/0022-328X). **Adv Mgr:** Ms. W van Cattenburch (Amsterdam). **1043**

JOURNAL OF ORIENTAL STUDIES (HONG KONG). (HK/0022-331X). **2655**

JOURNAL OF ORTHOMOLECULAR MEDICINE. (CN/0834-4825). **3929**

JOURNAL OF ORTHOPAEDIC AND SPORTS PHYSICAL THERAPY, THE. (US/0190-6011). **3882**

JOURNAL OF ORTHOPAEDIC RHEUMATOLOGY. (UK/0951-9580). **3882**

JOURNAL OF ORTHOPAEDIC SURGICAL TECHNIQUES, THE. (UK/0334-0236). **3882**

JOURNAL OF OTOLARYNGOLOGY. SUPPLEMENT, THE. (CN/0707-7270). **3889**

JOURNAL OF OTOLARYNGOLOGY, THE. (CN/0381-6605). **3889**

JOURNAL OF PACIFIC HISTORY, THE. (AT/0022-3344). **2669**

JOURNAL OF PACKAGING TECHNOLOGY. (US/0892-029X). **4219**

JOURNAL OF PAIN AND SYMPTOM MANAGEMENT. (US/0885-3924). **3596**

JOURNAL OF PALEOLIMNOLOGY. (NE/0921-2728). **461**

JOURNAL OF PALESTINE STUDIES. (US/0377-919X). **2655**

JOURNAL OF PAN AFRICAN STUDIES, THE. (US/0888-6601). **5206**

JOURNAL OF PARAMETRICS. (US/1015-7891). **Adv Mgr:** Amy Johnson. **747**

JOURNAL OF PARAPSYCHOLOGY, THE. (US/0022-3387). **4241**

JOURNAL OF PARENTERAL SCIENCE AND TECHNOLOGY. (US/0279-7976). **4311**

JOURNAL OF PASTORAL CARE, THE. (US/0022-3409). **4969**

JOURNAL OF PASTORAL COUNSELING, THE. (US/0449-508X). **4969**

JOURNAL OF PASTORAL PSYCHOTHERAPY. (US/0886-5477). **4599**

JOURNAL OF PASTORAL THEOLOGY. (US/1064-9867). **Adv Mgr:** Glenn Asquith, **Tel** (215)861-1521. **4969**

JOURNAL OF PATHOLOGY. (UK/0022-3417). **3895**

JOURNAL OF PEACE RESEARCH. (NO/0022-3433). **4527**

JOURNAL OF PEASANT STUDIES, THE. (UK/0306-6150). **Adv Mgr:** Anne Kidson. **5250**

JOURNAL OF PEDIATRIC & PERINATAL NUTRITION. (US/8756-6206). **3905**

JOURNAL OF PEDIATRIC ENDOCRINOLOGY, THE. (UK/0334-018X). **3905**

JOURNAL OF PEDIATRIC HEALTH CARE. (US/0891-5245). **3905**

JOURNAL OF PEDIATRIC OPHTHALMOLOGY AND STRABISMUS. (US/0191-3913). **3905**

JOURNAL OF PEDIATRICS, THE. (US/0022-3476). **3905**

JOURNAL OF PENSION PLANNING AND COMPLIANCE. (US/0148-2181). **904**

JOURNAL OF PENTECOSTAL THEOLOGY. (UK/0966-7369). **Adv Mgr:** Anne Dolling, **Tel** 670043. **5062**

JOURNAL OF PEPTIDE SCIENCE. (UK/1075-2617). **Adv Mgr:** Michael J. Levermore. **1043**

JOURNAL OF PERINATAL & NEONATAL NURSING, THE. (US/0893-2190). **3859**

JOURNAL OF PERINATAL EDUCATION, THE. (US/1058-1243). **Adv Mgr:** Megan Thompson, **Tel** (202)857-1128. **3764**

JOURNAL OF PERINATAL MEDICINE. (GW/0300-5577). **3764**

JOURNAL OF PERIODONTAL RESEARCH. (DK/0022-3484). **1327**

JOURNAL OF PERIODONTOLOGY (1970). (US/0022-3492). **1327**

JOURNAL OF PERSONAL SELLING & SALES MANAGEMENT, THE. (US/0885-3134). **928**

JOURNAL OF PERSONALITY. (US/0022-3506). **4599**

JOURNAL OF PERSONALITY AND SOCIAL PSYCHOLOGY. (US/0022-3514). **4599**

JOURNAL OF PERSONALITY ASSESSMENT. (US/0022-3891). **4599**

JOURNAL OF PERSONALITY DISORDERS. (US/0885-579X). **4599**

JOURNAL OF PETROLEUM GEOLOGY. (UK/0141-6421). **4262**

JOURNAL OF PETROLEUM SCIENCE & ENGINEERING. (NE/0920-4105). **4262**

JOURNAL OF PETROLEUM TECHNOLOGY. (US/0149-2136). **4262**

JOURNAL OF PETROLOGY. (UK/0022-3530). **1458**

JOURNAL OF PHARMACEUTICAL CARE IN PAIN & SYMPTOM CONTROL. (US/1056-4950). **4311**

JOURNAL OF PHARMACEUTICAL MARKETING & MANAGEMENT. (US/0883-7597). **4311**

JOURNAL OF PHARMACEUTICAL SCIENCES. (US/0022-3549). **4312**

JOURNAL OF PHARMACOEPIDEMIOLOGY. (US/0896-6966). **3596**

JOURNAL OF PHARMACOLOGY AND EXPERIMENTAL THERAPEUTICS, THE. (US/0022-3565). **4312**

JOURNAL OF PHARMACY AND PHARMACOLOGY. (UK/0022-3573). **4312**

JOURNAL OF PHARMACY TEACHING. (US/1044-0054). **4312**

JOURNAL OF PHARMACY TECHNOLOGY, THE. (US/8755-1225). **4313**

JOURNAL OF PHENOMENOLOGICAL PSYCHOLOGY. (US/0047-2662). **Adv Mgr:** J. Camlin, **Tel** (308)872-1441. **4599**

JOURNAL OF PHILIPPINE LIBRARIANSHIP. (PH/0022-359X). **3220**

JOURNAL OF PHILOSOPHICAL LOGIC. (NE/0022-3611). **3291**

JOURNAL OF PHILOSOPHY OF EDUCATION. (UK/0309-8249). **1898**

JOURNAL OF PHILOSOPHY, THE. (US/0022-362X). **4350**

JOURNAL OF PHOTOCHEMISTRY AND PHOTOBIOLOGY. A, CHEMISTRY. (SZ/1010-6030). **Adv Mgr:** Ms. W van Cattenburch (Amsterdam). **1054**

JOURNAL OF PHOTOCHEMISTRY AND PHOTOBIOLOGY. B, BIOLOGY. (SZ/1011-1344). **Adv Mgr:** Ms. W van Cattenburch (Amsterdam). **1054**

JOURNAL OF PHOTOGRAPHIC SCIENCE, THE. (UK/0022-3638). **4371**

JOURNAL OF PHYCOLOGY. (US/0022-3646). **515**

JOURNAL OF PHYSICAL CHEMISTRY (1952). (US/0022-3654). **Adv Mgr Tel** (203)256-8211. **1054**

JOURNAL OF PHYSICAL EDUCATION, RECREATION & DANCE. (US/0730-3084). **1856**

JOURNAL OF PLANKTON RESEARCH. (US/0142-7873). **5588**

JOURNAL OF PLANNING EDUCATION AND RESEARCH. (US/0739-456X). **Adv Mgr:** C. Kyser. **2826**

JOURNAL OF PLANT ANATOMY AND MORPHOLOGY. (II/0256-436X). **515**

JOURNAL OF PLANT BIOLOGY. (KO). **515**

JOURNAL OF PLANT NUTRITION. (US/0190-4167). **515**

JOURNAL OF PLANT PHYSIOLOGY. (GW/0176-1617). **516**

JOURNAL OF PLANTATION CROPS. (II/0304-5242). **176**

JOURNAL OF POLICE AND CRIMINAL PSYCHOLOGY. (US/0882-0783). **Adv Mgr:** same as editor. **3167**

JOURNAL OF POLICY MODELING. (US/0161-8938). **5206**

JOURNAL OF POLITICS, THE. (US/0022-3816). **4479**

JOURNAL OF POLYMER ENGINEERING. (IS/0334-6447). **2104**

JOURNAL OF POLYMORPHOUS PERVERSITY. (US/0737-1195). **4599**

JOURNAL OF POPULAR CULTURE. (US/0022-3840). **2741**

JOURNAL OF POPULAR FILM AND TELEVISION, THE. (US/0195-6051). **4073**

JOURNAL OF POPULAR LITERATURE. (US/0897-3075). **3400**

JOURNAL OF POPULATION ECONOMICS. (GW/0933-1433). **4554**

JOURNAL OF POST KEYNESIAN ECONOMICS. (US/0160-3477). **1593**

JOURNAL OF POSTGRADUATE MEDICINE (BOMBAY). (II/0022-3859). **3597**

JOURNAL OF POWDER & BULK SOLIDS TECHNOLOGY. (UK/0147-698X). **2014**

JOURNAL OF PRACTICAL HYGIENE, THE. (US/1072-7965). **Adv Mgr:** L. W. Scott Clements, **Tel** (201)236-0700 ext. 117. **1327**

JOURNAL OF PRACTICAL NURSING, THE. (US/0022-3867). **3860**

JOURNAL OF PREHISTORIC RELIGION. (SW/0283-8486). **4969**

JOURNAL OF PRESSURE VESSEL TECHNOLOGY. (US/0094-9930). **2118**

JOURNAL OF PROBATION AND PAROLE : THE JOURNAL OF THE NEW YORK STATE PROBATION OFFICERS ASSOCIATION. (US/0278-1042). **3167**

JOURNAL OF PROCESS CONTROL. (UK/0959-1524). **3482**

JOURNAL OF PRODUCT INNOVATION MANAGEMENT, THE. (US/0737-6782). **687**

JOURNAL OF PRODUCTIVITY ANALYSIS. (US/0895-562X). **1614**

JOURNAL OF PROFESSIONAL NURSING. (US/8755-7223). **3860**

JOURNAL OF PROFESSIONAL SERVICES MARKETING. (US/0748-4623). **929**

JOURNAL OF PROGRESSIVE HUMAN SERVICES. (US/1042-8232). **5292**

JOURNAL OF PROMOTION MANAGEMENT. (US/1049-6491). **874**

JOURNAL OF PROPERTY RESEARCH. (UK/0959-9916). **4839**

JOURNAL OF PROSTHETIC DENTISTRY, THE. (US/0022-3913). **1327**

JOURNAL OF PROSTHETICS AND ORTHOTICS. (US/1040-8800). **Adv Mgr:** Amy Coniglio, **Tel** (703)836-7118. **3597**

JOURNAL OF PROTECTIVE COATINGS & LININGS. (US/8755-1985). **5119**

JOURNAL OF PROTOZOOLOGY, THE. (US/0022-3921). **5588**

JOURNAL OF PSYCHIATRY & LAW, THE. (US/0093-1853). **2989**

JOURNAL OF PSYCHIATRY & NEUROSCIENCE. (CN/1180-4882). **Adv Mgr:** M. Watkins. **3929**

JOURNAL OF PSYCHOACTIVE DRUGS. (US/0279-1072). **1346**

JOURNAL OF PSYCHOHISTORY, THE. (US/0145-3378). **4599**

JOURNAL OF PSYCHOLOGICAL RESEARCHES. (II/0022-3972). **4600**

JOURNAL OF PSYCHOLOGICAL TYPE. (US/0895-8750). **4600**

JOURNAL OF PSYCHOLOGY AND CHRISTIANITY. (US/0733-4273). **4969**

JOURNAL OF PSYCHOLOGY & HUMAN SEXUALITY. (US/0890-7064). **4600**

JOURNAL OF PSYCHOLOGY AND JUDAISM. (US/0700-9801). **4600**

JOURNAL OF PSYCHOLOGY, THE. (US/0022-3980). **4600**

JOURNAL OF PSYCHOPHARMACOLOGY (OXFORD, ENGLAND). (UK/0269-8811). **4313**

JOURNAL OF PSYCHOPHYSIOLOGY. (UK/0269-8803). **4600**

JOURNAL OF PSYCHOSOCIAL NURSING AND MENTAL HEALTH SERVICES. (US/0279-3695). **3860**

JOURNAL OF PSYCHOSOCIAL ONCOLOGY. (US/0734-7332). **3819**

JOURNAL OF PSYCHOTHERAPY PRACTICE AND RESEARCH, THE. (US/1055-050X). **3929**

JOURNAL OF PUBLIC ADMINISTRATION RESEARCH AND THEORY. (US/1053-1858). **4659**

JOURNAL OF PUBLIC HEALTH DENTISTRY. (US/0022-4006). **Adv Mgr:** Dr. Gary Rozier, **Tel** (919)966-7388. **1328**

JOURNAL OF PUBLIC HEALTH POLICY. (US/0197-5897). **4787**

JOURNAL OF PURE AND APPLIED ALGEBRA. (NE/0022-4049). **3514**

JOURNAL OF QUANTITATIVE ANTHROPOLOGY. (NE/0922-2995). **239**

JOURNAL OF RANGE MANAGEMENT. (US/0022-409X). **100**

JOURNAL OF READING. (US/0022-4103). **Adv Mgr Tel** (302)731-1600, ext. 261. **1898**

JOURNAL OF REAL ESTATE FINANCE AND ECONOMICS, THE. (US/0895-5638). **4839**

JOURNAL OF RECEPTOR RESEARCH. (US/0197-5110). **538**

JOURNAL OF RECONSTRUCTIVE MICROSURGERY. (US/0743-684X). **3968**

JOURNAL OF REFUGEE STUDIES. (UK/0951-6328). **1919**

JOURNAL OF REGULATION AND SOCIAL COSTS. (US/1054-8939). **Adv Mgr:** T.Armstrong. **1500**

JOURNAL OF REGULATORY ECONOMICS. (US/0922-680X). **843**

JOURNAL OF REHABILITATION. (US/0022-4154). **5292**

JOURNAL OF REHABILITATION ADMINISTRATION. (US/0148-3846). **4390**

JOURNAL OF REHABILITATION IN ASIA, THE. (II/0022-4162). **4380**

JOURNAL OF RELIGION IN AFRICA. (NE/0022-4200). **4970**

JOURNAL OF RELIGION IN PSYCHOTHERAPY. (US/1045-5876). **3929**

JOURNAL OF RELIGIOUS & THEOLOGICAL INFORMATION. (US/1047-7845). **3220**

JOURNAL OF RELIGIOUS ETHICS, THE. (US/0384-9694). **2251**

JOURNAL OF RELIGIOUS GERONTOLOGY. (US/1050-2289). **5180**

JOURNAL OF RELIGIOUS HISTORY, THE. (AT/0022-4227). **4970**

JOURNAL OF RELIGIOUS THOUGHT, THE. (US/0022-4235). **4970**

JOURNAL OF REPRODUCTION & FERTILITY. (UK/0022-4251). **3597**

JOURNAL OF REPRODUCTIVE AND INFANT PSYCHOLOGY. (UK/0264-6838). **Adv Mgr Tel** 011 44 532 335734. **3764**

JOURNAL OF REPRODUCTIVE MEDICINE. (US/0024-7758). **3764**

JOURNAL OF RESEARCH IN CHILDHOOD EDUCATION. (US/0256-8543). **1758**

JOURNAL OF RESEARCH IN PHARMACEUTICAL ECONOMICS. (US/0896-6621). **4313**

JOURNAL OF RESEARCH IN SCIENCE TEACHING. (US/0022-4308). **5119**

JOURNAL OF RESEARCH ON CHRISTIAN EDUCATION. (US/1065-6219). **Adv Mgr:** Debi Robertson, **Tel** (616)471-6080. **4970**

JOURNAL OF RESEARCH ON COMPUTING IN EDUCATION. (US/0888-6504). **1224**

JOURNAL OF RETAIL BANKING. (US/0195-2064). **795**

JOURNAL OF RETAILING. (US/0022-4359). **955**

JOURNAL OF RHEOLOGY (NEW YORK, N.Y.). (US/0148-6055). **4428**

JOURNAL OF RHEUMATOLOGY, THE. (CN/0315-162X). **3805**

JOURNAL OF RISK AND INSURANCE, THE. (US/0022-4367). **2885**

JOURNAL OF RISK AND UNCERTAINTY. (US/0895-5646). **1500**

JOURNAL OF RITUAL STUDIES. (US/0890-1112). **4970**

JOURNAL OF ROBOTIC SYSTEMS. (US/0741-2223). **1214**

JOURNAL OF ROMAN STUDIES, THE. (UK/0075-4358). **Adv Mgr Tel** 071-387-8157. **1078**

JOURNAL OF RURAL AND SMALL SCHOOLS. (US/0890-9520). **1758**

JOURNAL OF RURAL COMMUNITY PSYCHOLOGY. (US/0276-2285). **Adv Mgr:** Smith. **4601**

JOURNAL OF RURAL HEALTH, THE. (US/0890-765X). **Adv Mgr:** Steve Levine, **Tel** (816)649-1681. **4787**

JOURNAL OF SCHOOL HEALTH, THE. (US/0022-4391). **4787**

JOURNAL OF SCHOOL PSYCHOLOGY. (US/0022-4405). **4601**

JOURNAL OF SCIENCE AND MATHEMATICS EDUCATION IN SOUTHEAST ASIA. (MY/0126-7663). **1758**

JOURNAL OF SCIENTIFIC AND APPLIED PHOTOGRAPHY AND CINEMATOGRAPHY. (US). **4371**

JOURNAL OF SCOUTING HISTORY. (US). **5232**

JOURNAL OF SECURITY ADMINISTRATION. (US/0195-9425). **3168**

JOURNAL OF SEDIMENTARY PETROLOGY. (US/0022-4472). **1458**

JOURNAL OF SEMANTICS (NIJMEGEN). (NE/0167-5133). **3291**

JOURNAL OF SEMI-CUSTOM ICS. (UK/0264-3375). **2069**

JOURNAL OF SEMITIC STUDIES. (UK/0022-4480). **2266**

JOURNAL OF SERVICES MARKETING, THE. (US/0887-6045). **929**

JOURNAL OF SEX & MARITAL THERAPY. (US/0092-623X). **5187**

JOURNAL OF SEX EDUCATION AND THERAPY. (US/0161-4576). **5187**

JOURNAL OF SEX RESEARCH, THE. (US/0022-4499). **5187**

JOURNAL OF SEXUAL HEALTH. (UK/0963-6757). **Adv Mgr:** P. Bradbury. **5187**

JOURNAL OF SHOULDER AND ELBOW SURGERY. (US/1058-2746). **3968**

JOURNAL OF SIKH STUDIES. (II/0379-8194). **4970**

JOURNAL OF SLAVIC LINGUISTICS. (US/1068-2090). **3292**

JOURNAL OF SLAVIC MILITARY STUDIES, THE. (UK). **Adv Mgr:** Anne Kidson. **4048**

JOURNAL OF SMALL ANIMAL PRACTICE, THE. (UK/0022-4510). **5513**

JOURNAL OF SMALL BUSINESS MANAGEMENT. (US/0047-2778). **874**

JOURNAL OF SMOKING-RELATED DISORDERS, THE. (UK/0959-2431). **Adv Mgr:** Kathryn Wilkinson, **Tel** 44 625 618507. **3981**

JOURNAL OF SOCIAL AND CLINICAL PSYCHOLOGY. (US/0736-7236). **4601**

JOURNAL OF SOCIAL AND PERSONAL RELATIONSHIPS. (UK/0265-4075). **4601**

JOURNAL OF SOCIAL BEHAVIOR AND PERSONALITY. (US/0886-1641). **4601**

JOURNAL OF SOCIAL DEVELOPMENT IN AFRICA. (RH). **5206**

JOURNAL OF SOCIAL PHILOSOPHY. (US/0047-2786). **Adv Mgr:** K.Eicher. **5206**

JOURNAL OF SOCIAL POLICY. (UK/0047-2794). **5293**

JOURNAL OF SOCIAL PSYCHOLOGY, THE. (US/0022-4545). **4601**

JOURNAL OF SOCIAL SCIENCE. (MW). **5207**

JOURNAL OF SOCIAL SERVICE RESEARCH. (US/0148-8376). **5293**

JOURNAL OF SOCIAL STUDIES, THE. (BG). **5207**

JOURNAL OF SOCIAL WORK & HUMAN SEXUALITY. (US/0276-3850). **5293**

JOURNAL OF SOCIAL WORK EDUCATION. (US/1043-7797). **5293**

JOURNAL OF SOCIAL WORK PRACTICE. (UK/0265-0533). **5293**

JOURNAL OF SOCIOLOGICAL STUDIES, THE. (II). **5250**

JOURNAL OF SOCIOLOGY AND SOCIAL WELFARE. (US/0191-5096). **Adv Mgr:** Barbara Dennison, **Tel** (717) 867-6336. **5293**

JOURNAL OF SOIL AND WATER CONSERVATION. (US/0022-4561). **2196**

JOURNAL OF SOIL SCIENCE, THE. (UK/0022-4588). **176**

JOURNAL OF SOLAR ENERGY ENGINEERING. (US/0199-6231). **1949**

JOURNAL OF SOUTH ASIAN AND MIDDLE EASTERN STUDIES. (US/0149-1784). **Adv Mgr:** Havsman, **Tel** 215-645-4738. **2769**

JOURNAL OF SOUTH ASIAN LITERATURE. (US/0091-5637). **3400**

JOURNAL OF SOUTHEAST ASIAN STUDIES (SINGAPORE). (SI/0022-4634). **Adv Mgr:** same as editor. **2655**

JOURNAL OF SOUTHERN AFRICAN STUDIES. (UK/0305-7070). **2641**

JOURNAL OF SOUTHERN HISTORY, THE. (US/0022-4642). **2742**

JOURNAL OF SOUTHWEST GEORGIA HISTORY, THE. (US/0739-1943). **2742**

JOURNAL OF SOVIET MILITARY STUDIES, THE. (UK/0954-254X). **4048**

JOURNAL OF SPACE LAW. (US/0095-7577). **2989**

JOURNAL OF SPECIAL EDUCATION, THE. (US/0022-4669). **1881**

JOURNAL OF SPECULATIVE PHILOSOPHY, THE. (US/0891-625X). **4351**

JOURNAL OF SPEECH AND HEARING RESEARCH. (US/0022-4685). **4390**

JOURNAL OF SPEECH-LANGUAGE PATHOLOGY AND AUDIOLOGY. (CN/0848-1970). **Adv Mgr:** C. Saindon. **4390**

JOURNAL OF SPELEAN HISTORY, THE. (US/0022-4693). **1357**

JOURNAL OF SPINE RESEARCH. (US/1058-1588). **3597**

JOURNAL OF SPORT AND SOCIAL ISSUES. (US/0193-7235). **5250**

JOURNAL OF SPORT HISTORY. (US/0094-1700). **4902**

JOURNAL OF SPORT MANAGEMENT. (US/0888-4773). **4902**

JOURNAL OF SPORTS MEDICINE AND PHYSICAL FITNESS. (IT/0022-4707). **3954**

JOURNAL — Advertising Accepted Index

JOURNAL OF SPORTS PHILATELY. (US/0447-953X). **2785**

JOURNAL OF SPORTS SCIENCES. (UK/0264-0414). **4902**

JOURNAL OF STAFF DEVELOPMENT, THE. (US/0276-928X). **1801**

JOURNAL OF STAFF, PROGRAM & ORGANIZATION DEVELOPMENT, THE. (US/0736-7627). **1898**

JOURNAL OF STAINED GLASS : THE JOURNAL OF THE BRITISH SOCIETY OF MASTER GLASS PAINTERS, THE. (UK). **2591**

JOURNAL OF STATE GOVERNMENT, THE. (US/1043-2248). **4479**

JOURNAL OF STATISTICAL COMPUTATION AND SIMULATION. (US/0094-9655). **1282**

JOURNAL OF STRAIN ANALYSIS FOR ENGINEERING DESIGN, THE. (UK/0309-3247). **2118**

JOURNAL OF STRATEGIC AND SYSTEMIC THERAPIES, THE. (CN/0711-5075). **3929**

JOURNAL OF STRATEGIC STUDIES, THE. (UK/0140-2390). **Adv Mgr:** Anne Kidson. **4048**

JOURNAL OF STROKE AND CEREBROVASCULAR DISEASES. (US/1052-3057). **3837**

JOURNAL OF STRUCTURAL LEARNING. (US/0022-4774). **1758**

JOURNAL OF STUDIES ON ALCOHOL. (US/0096-882X). **1346**

JOURNAL OF SUBSTANCE ABUSE. (US/0899-3289). **1346**

JOURNAL OF SUNG-YUAN STUDIES. (US/1059-3152). **2505**

JOURNAL OF SURGICAL ONCOLOGY. (US/0022-4790). **3820**

JOURNAL OF SURVEYING ENGINEERING. (US/0733-9453). **2026**

JOURNAL OF SUSTAINABLE AGRICULTURE. (US/1044-0046). **100**

JOURNAL OF SWIMMING RESEARCH, THE. (US/0747-5993). **4902**

JOURNAL OF SYSTEMS MANAGEMENT. (US/0022-4839). **687**

JOURNAL OF TAXATION OF ESTATES & TRUSTS, THE. (US/1044-9418). **3118**

JOURNAL OF TAXATION OF EXEMPT ORGANIZATIONS, THE. (US/1043-0539). **4735**

JOURNAL OF TAXATION OF S CORPORATIONS, THE. (US/1040-502X). **795**

JOURNAL OF TEACHER EDUCATION. (US/0022-4871). **1865**

JOURNAL OF TEACHING IN INTERNATIONAL BUSINESS. (US/0897-5930). **688**

JOURNAL OF TEACHING IN PHYSICAL EDUCATION. (US/0273-5024). **1856**

JOURNAL OF TEACHING IN SOCIAL WORK. (US/0884-1233). **5293**

JOURNAL OF TEXAS CATHOLIC HISTORY AND CULTURE / TEXAS CATHOLIC HISTORICAL SOCIETY, THE. (US/1048-2431). **5031**

JOURNAL OF TEXTURE STUDIES. (US/0022-4901). **2347**

JOURNAL OF THE ABRAHAM LINCOLN ASSOCIATION. (US/0898-4212). **2742**

JOURNAL OF THE ACADEMY OF FLORIDA TRIAL LAWYERS. (US/0515-2046). **Adv Mgr:** L. Garcia, **Tel** (904)224-9403. **2989**

JOURNAL OF THE ACADEMY OF MARKETING SCIENCE. (US/0092-0703). **929**

JOURNAL OF THE AERONAUTICAL SOCIETY OF INDIA, THE. (II/0001-9267). **26**

JOURNAL OF THE ALABAMA DENTAL ASSOCIATION, THE. (US/0002-4198). **1328**

JOURNAL OF THE AMERICAN ACADEMY OF CHILD AND ADOLESCENT PSYCHIATRY. (US/0890-8567). **3929**

JOURNAL OF THE AMERICAN ACADEMY OF DERMATOLOGY. (US/0190-9622). **3721**

JOURNAL OF THE AMERICAN ACADEMY OF PHYSICIAN ASSISTANTS. (US/0893-7400). **3597**

JOURNAL OF THE AMERICAN ACADEMY OF PSYCHOANALYSIS, THE. (US/0090-3604). **3930**

JOURNAL OF THE AMERICAN ACADEMY OF RELIGION. (US/0002-7189). **4970**

JOURNAL OF THE AMERICAN ANALGESIA SOCIETY. (US/0002-7243). **3597**

JOURNAL OF THE AMERICAN ANIMAL HOSPITAL ASSOCIATION, THE. (US/0587-2871). **5513**

JOURNAL OF THE AMERICAN BOARD OF FAMILY PRACTICE, THE. (US/0893-8652). **3738**

JOURNAL OF THE AMERICAN CHAMBER OF COMMERCE IN JAPAN / ACCJ, THE. (JA/0002-7847). **820**

JOURNAL OF THE AMERICAN CHEMICAL SOCIETY. (US/0002-7863). **982**

JOURNAL OF THE AMERICAN COLLEGE OF CARDIOLOGY. (US/0735-1097). **3707**

JOURNAL OF THE AMERICAN COLLEGE OF DENTISTS, THE. (US/0002-7979). **1328**

JOURNAL OF THE AMERICAN COLLEGE OF TOXICOLOGY. (US/0730-0913). **3982**

JOURNAL OF THE AMERICAN DIETETIC ASSOCIATION. (US/0002-8223). **4194**

JOURNAL OF THE AMERICAN GERIATRICS SOCIETY. (US/0002-8614). **3753**

JOURNAL OF THE AMERICAN HELICOPTER SOCIETY. (US/0002-8711). **26**

JOURNAL OF THE AMERICAN INSTITUTE FOR CONSERVATION. (US/0197-1360). **323**

JOURNAL OF THE AMERICAN INSTITUTE OF HOMEOPATHY. (US/0002-8967). **3775**

JOURNAL OF THE AMERICAN LEATHER CHEMISTS ASSOCIATION, THE. (US/0002-9726). **Adv Mgr:** Velma Becker, **Tel** (513)556-1197. **3184**

JOURNAL OF THE AMERICAN LISZT SOCIETY. (US/0147-4413). **4126**

JOURNAL OF THE AMERICAN MEDICAL WOMEN'S ASSOCIATION (1972). (US/0098-8421). **3597**

JOURNAL OF THE AMERICAN MOSQUITO CONTROL ASSOCIATION. (US/8756-971X). **4245**

JOURNAL OF THE AMERICAN MUSICAL INSTRUMENT SOCIETY. (US/0362-3300). **4126**

JOURNAL OF THE AMERICAN MUSICOLOGICAL SOCIETY. (US/0003-0139). **4126**

JOURNAL OF THE AMERICAN OPTOMETRIC ASSOCIATION. (US/0003-0244). **Adv Mgr Tel** (314)991-4100. **4216**

JOURNAL OF THE AMERICAN ORIENTAL SOCIETY. (US/0003-0279). **3292**

JOURNAL OF THE AMERICAN OSTEOPATHIC ASSOCIATION, THE. (US/0098-6151). **3598**

JOURNAL OF THE AMERICAN PLANNING ASSOCIATION. (US/0194-4363). **2826**

JOURNAL OF THE AMERICAN PODIATRIC MEDICAL ASSOCIATION. (US/8750-7315). **3918**

JOURNAL OF THE AMERICAN PSYCHOANALYTIC ASSOCIATION. (US/0003-0651). **4601**

JOURNAL OF THE AMERICAN SHETLAND PONY CLUB. (US). **2800**

JOURNAL OF THE AMERICAN SOCIETY FOR INFORMATION SCIENCE. (US/0002-8231). **3220**

JOURNAL OF THE AMERICAN SOCIETY FOR MASS SPECTROMETRY. (US/1044-0305). **1017**

JOURNAL OF THE AMERICAN SOCIETY OF BREWING CHEMISTS. (US/0361-0470). **982**

JOURNAL OF THE AMERICAN SOCIETY OF CLU & CHFC. (US/1052-2875). **2886**

JOURNAL OF THE AMERICAN SOCIETY OF OCULARISTS, THE. (US/1055-5161). **Adv Mgr:** Ted Johnson. **3876**

JOURNAL OF THE AMERICAN STATISTICAL ASSOCIATION. (US/0162-1459). **5329**

JOURNAL OF THE AMERICAN STUDIES ASSOCIATION OF TEXAS. (US/0587-5064). **Adv Mgr:** Lois E. Myers, **Tel** (817)755-3437. **2742**

JOURNAL OF THE AMERICAN TAXATION ASSOCIATION, THE. (US/0198-9073). **4735**

JOURNAL OF THE AMERICAN VETERINARY MEDICAL ASSOCIATION. (US/0003-1488). **5513**

JOURNAL OF THE ANATOMICAL SOCIETY OF INDIA. (II/0003-2778). **3679**

JOURNAL OF THE ARKANSAS MEDICAL SOCIETY, THE. (US/0004-1858). **Adv Mgr:** Editor. **3598**

JOURNAL OF THE ARNOLD SCHOENBERG INSTITUTE. (US/0146-5856). **4126**

JOURNAL OF THE ASSOCIATION FOR PERSONS WITH SEVERE HANDICAPS, THE. (US/0749-1425). **1881**

JOURNAL OF THE ASSOCIATION OF AVIAN VETERINARIANS. (US/1044-8314). **5513**

JOURNAL OF THE ASSOCIATION OF CHILDREN'S PROSTHETIC-ORTHOTIC CLINICS. (US/0884-8424). **3883**

JOURNAL OF THE ASSOCIATION OF NURSES IN AIDS CARE, THE. (US/1055-3290). **Adv Mgr:** Joseph Braden, **Tel** (215)545-7222. **3860**

JOURNAL OF THE ASSOCIATION OF PHYSICIANS OF INDIA. (II). **Adv Mgr Tel** 2611719. **3799**

JOURNAL OF THE ASSOCIATION OF SURVEYORS OF PAPUA NEW GUINEA, THE. (PP). **2026**

JOURNAL OF THE ATMOSPHERIC SCIENCES. (US/0022-4928). **1427**

JOURNAL OF THE AUSTRALIAN CATHOLIC HISTORICAL SOCIETY. (AT/0084-7259). **5031**

JOURNAL OF THE AUSTRALIAN NAVAL INSTITUTE. (AT/0312-5807). **4178**

JOURNAL OF THE AUSTRALIAN WAR MEMORIAL. (AT/0729-6274). **4048**

JOURNAL OF THE BRISTOL AND AVON FAMILY HISTORY SOCIETY. (UK/0308-4183). **2455**

JOURNAL OF THE BRITISH ASSOCIATION FOR IMMEDIATE CARE, THE. (UK). **3725**

JOURNAL OF THE BRITISH ASSOCIATION OF TEACHERS OF THE DEAF, THE. (UK/0266-4062). **1881**

JOURNAL OF THE BRITISH ASTRONOMICAL ASSOCIATION. (UK/0007-0297). **396**

JOURNAL OF THE BRITISH CONTACT LENS ASSOCIATION. (UK/0141-7037). **3876**

JOURNAL OF THE BROMELIAD SOCIETY. (US/0090-8738). **516**

JOURNAL OF THE CALIFORNIA DENTAL ASSOCIATION. (US/1043-2256). **Adv Mgr:** Sue Hummel, **Tel** (916)443-3382. **1328**

JOURNAL OF THE CAMBRIDGESHIRE FAMILY HISTORY SOCIETY. (UK/0309-5800). **Adv Mgr:** Mrs. J. Hurst, **Tel** 0734-420194. **2455**

JOURNAL OF THE CANADIAN ATHLETIC THERAPISTS ASSOCIATION, THE. (CN/0225-9877). **3954**

JOURNAL OF THE CANADIAN CHIROPRACTIC ASSOCIATION, THE. (CN/0008-3194). **3805**

JOURNAL OF THE CHINESE LANGUAGE TEACHERS ASSOCIATION. (US/0009-4595). **3292**

JOURNAL OF THE CHINESE LANGUAGE TEACHERS ASSOCIATION / CHUNG WEN CHIAO SHIH HSUEH HUI HSUEH PAO. (US). **Adv Mgr:** Nikki Bado, **Tel** (614)292-5816. **3292**

JOURNAL OF THE CLAN CAMPBELL SOCIETY (UNITED STATES OF AMERICA). (US/0731-955X). **2455**

JOURNAL OF THE COIN LAUNDRY AND DRYCLEANING INDUSTRY, THE. (US/1062-8088). **Adv Mgr:** Brian Wallace. **1026**

JOURNAL OF THE COMMUNITY DEVELOPMENT SOCIETY. (US/0010-3829). **5250**

JOURNAL OF THE CONDUCTORS' GUILD. (US/0734-1032). **Adv Mgr:** Judy Voois. **4127**

JOURNAL OF THE CORK HISTORICAL AND ARCHAEOLOGICAL SOCIETY. (IE/0010-8731). **2695**

JOURNAL OF THE DAGUERREIAN SOCIETY. (US). **Adv Mgr:** John Grat, **Tel** (414)339-9389. **4371**

JOURNAL OF THE DECORATIVE ARTS SOCIETY 1890-1940. (UK/0260-9568). **373**

JOURNAL OF THE EARLY REPUBLIC. (US/0275-1275). **2742**

JOURNAL OF THE ELECTROCHEMICAL SOCIETY. (US/0013-4651). **1034**

JOURNAL OF THE ELECTROCHEMICAL SOCIETY OF INDIA. (II/0013-466X). **1026**

JOURNAL OF THE EUROPEAN ASSOCIATION OF MARINE SCIENCES AND TECHNIQUES. (NE/0924-7963). **1450**

JOURNAL OF THE EXPERIMENTAL ANALYSIS OF BEHAVIOR. (US/0022-5002). **4601**

JOURNAL OF THE FLORIDA MEDICAL ASSOCIATION (1974). (US/0015-4148). **Adv Mgr:** Joy Freiha. **3598**

JOURNAL OF THE FLORIDA MOSQUITO CONTROL ASSOCIATION. (US/1055-355X). **4787**

JOURNAL OF THE ... GENERAL SYNOD / ANGLICAN CHURCH OF CANADA. (CN/0826-3205). **5062**

JOURNAL OF THE GEOGRAPHICAL ASSOCIATION OF TANZANIA. (TZ/0016-738X). **2567**

JOURNAL OF THE GEOLOGICAL SOCIETY. (UK/0016-7649). **1385**

JOURNAL OF THE GEOLOGICAL SOCIETY OF IRAQ. (IQ/0533-8301). **1385**

JOURNAL OF THE GREATER HOUSTON DENTAL SOCIETY, THE. (US/1062-0265). **Adv Mgr:** Becky Ricks. **1328**

JOURNAL OF THE GYPSY LORE SOCIETY. (US/0017-6087). **2321**

JOURNAL OF THE HELLENIC DIASPORA. (US/0364-2976). **2695**

JOURNAL OF THE HISTORICAL SOCIETY OF SOUTH AUSTRALIA. (AT/0312-9640). **Adv Mgr:** Marcia Dunshore. **2669**

JOURNAL OF THE HISTORY OF BIOLOGY. (NE/0022-5010). **462**

JOURNAL OF THE HISTORY OF IDEAS. (US/0022-5037). **4351**

JOURNAL OF THE HISTORY OF MEDICINE AND ALLIED SCIENCES. (US/0022-5045). **3598**

JOURNAL OF THE HISTORY OF PHILOSOPHY. (US/0022-5053). **4351**

JOURNAL OF THE HISTORY OF SEXUALITY. (US/1043-4070). **5187**

JOURNAL OF THE HISTORY OF THE BEHAVIORAL SCIENCES. (US/0022-5061). **4601**

JOURNAL OF THE HISTORY OF THE NEUROSCIENCES. (UK/0964-704X). **Adv Mgr:** Clare Parker. **490**

JOURNAL OF THE IES. (US/1052-2883). **2176**

JOURNAL OF THE ILLINOIS OPTOMETRIC ASSOCIATION. (US/0279-6422). **4216**

JOURNAL OF THE INDIAN ACADEMY OF FORENSIC SCIENCES. (II/0579-4749). **3741**

JOURNAL OF THE INDIAN ACADEMY OF MATHEMATICS, THE. (II/0970-5120). **3515**

JOURNAL OF THE INDIAN ACADEMY OF PHILOSOPHY, THE. (II/0019-4271). **4351**

JOURNAL OF THE INDIAN CHEMICAL SOCIETY. (II/0019-4522). **982**

JOURNAL OF THE INDIAN DENTAL ASSOCIATION. (II/0019-4611). **1328**

JOURNAL OF THE INDIAN INSTITUTE OF ARCHITECTS. (II/0019-4913). **302**

JOURNAL OF THE INDIAN INSTITUTE OF SCIENCE. (II/0019-4964). **5120**

JOURNAL OF THE INDIAN MUSICOLOGICAL SOCIETY. (II/0251-012X). **4127**

JOURNAL OF THE INDIAN SOCIETY OF SOIL SCIENCE. (II/0019-638X). **177**

JOURNAL OF THE INDIAN STATISTICAL ASSOCIATION. (II/0537-2585). **5330**

JOURNAL OF THE INDIANA DENTAL ASSOCIATION. (US/0019-6568). **Adv Mgr:** Jody Eagan. **1328**

JOURNAL OF THE INSTITUTE OF BREWING. (UK/0046-9750). **Adv Mgr:** F. Bolton, **Tel** (071)499-8144. **2368**

JOURNAL OF THE INSTITUTE OF HEALTH EDUCATION. (UK/0307-3289). **Adv Mgr:** P. Davies. **4787**

JOURNAL OF THE INSTITUTE OF MINE SURVEYORS OF SOUTH AFRICA. (SA/0020-2983). **2142**

JOURNAL OF THE INSTITUTE OF WOOD SCIENCE. (UK/0020-3203). **2402**

JOURNAL OF THE INSTITUTION OF CHEMISTS, CALCUTTA. (II/0020-3254). **983**

JOURNAL OF THE INSTITUTION OF ENGINEERS (INDIA). (II/0020-3386). **2070**

JOURNAL OF THE INSTITUTION OF ENGINEERS (INDIA). CIVIL ENGINEERING DIVISION. (II/0373-1995). **2026**

JOURNAL OF THE INSTITUTION OF ENGINEERS (INDIA). ELECTRONICS & TELECOMMUNICATION ENGINEERING DIVISION. (II/0251-1096). **2070**

JOURNAL OF THE INSTITUTION OF ENGINEERS (INDIA). MECHANICAL ENGINEERING DIVISION. (II/0020-3408). **2118**

JOURNAL OF THE INSTITUTION OF ENGINEERS (INDIA). PART EN CALCUTTA, ENVIRONMENTAL ENGINEERING DIVISION, THE. (II/0251-110X). **2176**

JOURNAL OF THE INTERNATIONAL ASSOCIATION OF BUDDHIST STUDIES, THE. (US/0193-600X). **5021**

JOURNAL OF THE INTERNATIONAL PHONETIC ASSOCIATION. (UK/0025-1003). **3292**

JOURNAL OF THE IOWA ACADEMY OF SCIENCE, THE. (US/0896-8381). **5121**

JOURNAL OF THE IRISH COLLEGES OF PHYSICIANS AND SURGEONS. (IE/0374-8405). **3598**

JOURNAL OF THE IRISH DENTAL ASSOCIATION, THE. (IE/0021-1133). **1328**

JOURNAL OF THE IRISH SOCIETY FOR LABOUR LAW. (IE/0790-0473). **3150**

JOURNAL OF THE KAFKA SOCIETY OF AMERICA. (US/0894-6388). **3345**

JOURNAL OF THE KANSAS BAR ASSOCIATION, THE. (US/0022-8486). **2989**

JOURNAL OF THE KENTUCKY MEDICAL ASSOCIATION, THE. (US/0023-0294). **Adv Mgr:** Sue Tharp, **Tel** (502)426-6200. **3598**

JOURNAL OF THE KOREAN INSTITUTE OF SURFACE ENGINEERING. (KO). **1983**

JOURNAL OF THE KUWAIT MEDICAL ASSOCIATION, THE. (KU/0023-5776). **3598**

JOURNAL OF THE LANCASTER COUNTY HISTORICAL SOCIETY. (US/0023-7477). **Adv Mgr:** Denise Baer, **Tel** (717)393-8880. **2742**

JOURNAL OF THE LAW SOCIETY OF SCOTLAND, THE. (UK/0458-8711). **Adv Mgr:** N Kelly, **Tel** 44 31 2282792. **2989**

JOURNAL OF THE LEPIDOPTERISTS' SOCIETY. (US/0024-0966). **5589**

JOURNAL OF THE LINCOLN ASSASSINATION. (US). **2742**

JOURNAL OF THE LINGUISTIC ASSOCIATION OF NIGERIA : JOLAN. (NR/0189-5680). **3292**

JOURNAL OF THE LOUISIANA STATE MEDICAL SOCIETY, THE. (US/0024-6921). **Adv Mgr:** Ann Goocer. **3599**

JOURNAL OF THE LYCOMING COUNTY HISTORICAL SOCIETY, THE. (US/0887-543X). **2742**

JOURNAL OF THE MALACOLOGICAL SOCIETY OF AUSTRALIA. (AT/0085-2988). **5589**

JOURNAL OF THE MARKET RESEARCH SOCIETY. (UK/0025-3618). **929**

JOURNAL OF THE MASSACHUSETTS DENTAL SOCIETY. (US/0025-4800). **Adv Mgr:** C. Peterson. **1328**

JOURNAL OF THE MEDICAL ASSOCIATION OF GEORGIA. (US/0025-7028). **3599**

JOURNAL OF THE MICHIGAN DENTAL ASSOCIATION, THE. (US/0026-2102). **1328**

JOURNAL OF THE MIDWEST FINANCE ASSOCIATION. (US/0272-6637). **905**

JOURNAL OF THE MIDWEST MODERN LANGUAGE ASSOCIATION, THE. (US/0742-5562). **3292**

JOURNAL OF THE MINE VENTILATION SOCIETY OF SOUTH AFRICA. (SA/0368-3206). **2142**

JOURNAL OF THE MISSISSIPPI ACADEMY OF SCIENCES. (US/0076-9436). **5121**

JOURNAL OF THE MISSISSIPPI STATE MEDICAL ASSOCIATION. (US/0026-6396). **3599**

JOURNAL OF THE MISSOURI BAR. (US/0026-6485). **2989**

JOURNAL OF THE MISSOURI WATER AND SEWERAGE CONFERENCE. (US/0096-4255). **2234**

JOURNAL OF THE MUHYIDDIN IBN ARABI SOCIETY. (UK/0266-2183). **5043**

JOURNAL OF THE N.J. ASSOCIATION OF OSTEOPATHIC PHYSICIANS AND SURGEONS, THE. (US/0892-0249). **3599**

JOURNAL OF THE NATIONAL AGRICULTURAL SOCIETY OF CEYLON. (CE/0547-3616). **101**

JOURNAL OF THE NATIONAL ASSOCIATION OF ADMINISTRATIVE LAW JUDGES. (US/0735-0821). **Adv Mgr:** S. Cyean. **3093**

JOURNAL OF THE NATIONAL ASSOCIATION OF DOCUMENT EXAMINERS. (US/8755-1020). **3168**

JOURNAL OF THE NATIONAL BUILDINGS ORGANISATION. (II/0027-8815). **618**

JOURNAL OF THE NATIONAL MEDICAL ASSOCIATION. (US/0027-9684). **3599**

JOURNAL OF THE NEW ENGLAND LUTHERAN HISTORICAL SOCIETY. (US/1051-0605). **Adv Mgr:** Reverend Kim Williams. **4971**

JOURNAL OF THE NEW ENGLAND WATER POLLUTION CONTROL ASSOCIATION. (US/0548-4502). **2234**

JOURNAL OF THE NEW ENGLAND WATER WORKS ASSOCIATION. (US/0028-4939). **4761**

JOURNAL OF THE NEW JERSEY DENTAL ASSOCIATION. (US/0093-7347). **1328**

JOURNAL OF THE NEW YORK STATE NURSES ASSOCIATION, THE. (US/0028-7644). **3860**

JOURNAL OF THE NEW ZEALAND SOCIETY OF PERIODONTOLOGY. (NZ/0111-1485). **1328**

JOURNAL OF THE NORTH-EAST INDIA COUNCIL FOR SOCIAL SCIENCE RESEARCH, THE. (II). **5207**

JOURNAL OF THE NORTH MIDDLESEX FAMILY HISTORY SOCIETY. (UK/0141-9544). **2456**

JOURNAL OF THE OPERATIONAL RESEARCH SOCIETY, THE. (UK/0160-5682). **3515**

JOURNAL OF THE ORDERS AND MEDALS SOCIETY OF AMERICA, THE. (US). **2781**

JOURNAL OF THE OREGON DENTAL ASSOCIATION, THE. (US/0030-4670). **1329**

JOURNAL OF THE ORIENTAL INSTITUTE, M.S. UNIVERSITY OF BARODA. (II/0030-5324). **2505**

JOURNAL OF THE ORIENTAL SOCIETY OF AUSTRALIA, THE. (AT/0030-5340). **2656**

JOURNAL OF THE PAKISTAN HISTORICAL SOCIETY. (PK/0030-9796). **2656**

JOURNAL OF THE PAKISTAN MEDICAL ASSOCIATION. (PK/0030-9982). **3599**

JOURNAL OF THE PATENT AND TRADEMARK OFFICE SOCIETY. (US/0882-9098). **1305**

JOURNAL OF THE PENNSYLVANIA ACADEMY OF SCIENCE. (US/1044-6753). **5121**

JOURNAL OF THE PENNSYLVANIA OSTEOPATHIC MEDICAL ASSOCIATION, THE. (US/0479-9534). **3599**

JOURNAL OF THE PLAYING-CARD SOCIETY. (UK/0305-2133). **4862**

JOURNAL OF THE POLYNESIAN SOCIETY. (NZ/0032-4000). **3292**

JOURNAL OF THE PRINT WORLD. (US/0737-7436). **Adv Mgr:** Sophia Lane, **Tel** (603)279-6479. **4566**

JOURNAL OF THE RESEARCH SOCIETY OF PAKISTAN. (PK/0034-5431). **5207**

JOURNAL OF THE RIO GRANDE VALLEY HORTICULTURAL SOCIETY. (US/0485-2044). **2421**

JOURNAL OF THE ROCKY MOUNTAIN MEDIEVAL AND RENAISSANCE ASSOCIATION. (US/0195-8453). **2621**

JOURNAL OF THE ROYAL AGRICULTURAL SOCIETY OF ENGLAND. (UK/0080-4134). **101**

JOURNAL OF THE ROYAL ARMY MEDICAL CORPS. (UK/0035-8665). **3599**

JOURNAL OF THE ROYAL ARTILLERY, THE. (UK). **4048**

JOURNAL OF THE ROYAL ASIATIC SOCIETY OF GREAT BRITAIN & IRELAND. (UK/0035-869X). **2769**

JOURNAL OF THE ROYAL AUSTRALIAN HISTORICAL SOCIETY. (AT/0035-8762). **2670**

JOURNAL OF THE ROYAL COLLEGE OF PHYSICIANS OF LONDON. (UK/0035-8819). **Adv Mgr:** PRC Assoc., **Tel** 081-786-7376. **3599**

JOURNAL OF THE ROYAL COLLEGE OF SURGEONS OF EDINBURGH. (UK/0035-8835). **3968**

JOURNAL OF THE ROYAL MUSICAL ASSOCIATION. (UK/0269-0403). **4127**

JOURNAL OF THE ROYAL NAVAL MEDICAL SERVICE. (UK/0035-9033). **3599**

JOURNAL OF THE ROYAL SOCIETY OF HEALTH. (UK/0264-0325). **4787**

JOURNAL OF THE ROYAL SOCIETY OF MEDICINE. (UK/0141-0768). **3599**

JOURNAL OF THE ROYAL SOCIETY OF NEW ZEALAND. (NZ/0303-6758). **5121**

JOURNAL OF THE ROYAL STATISTICAL SOCIETY. SERIES A (GENERAL). (UK/0035-9238). **5330**

JOURNAL OF THE ROYAL STATISTICAL SOCIETY. SERIES A: (STATISTICS IN SOCIETY). (UK). **5330**

JOURNAL OF THE ROYAL STATISTICAL SOCIETY. SERIES B (METHODOLOGICAL). (UK/0035-9246). **5330**

JOURNAL OF THE ROYAL UNITED SERVICES INSTITUTE OF AUSTRALIA. (AT/0728-1188). **Adv Mgr:** N. Wainwright, **Tel** (6)248-6866. **4048**

JOURNAL OF THE SAN JUAN ISLANDS. (US/0734-3809). **5761**

JOURNAL OF THE SOCIETY FOR ARMENIAN STUDIES. (US/0747-9301). **2656**

JOURNAL OF THE SOCIETY FOR ARMY HISTORICAL RESEARCH. (UK/0037-9700). **4048**

JOURNAL OF THE SOCIETY FOR GYNECOLOGIC INVESTIGATION. (US/1071-5576). **Adv Mgr:** Andrea Cernichiari, **Tel** (212)633-3813. **3764**

JOURNAL Advertising Accepted Index

JOURNAL OF THE SOCIETY FOR ITALIC HANDWRITING, THE. (UK/0037-9743). **380**

JOURNAL OF THE SOCIETY FOR UNDERWATER TECHNOLOGY. (UK/0141-0814). **1450**

JOURNAL OF THE SOCIETY OF ARCHITECTURAL HISTORIANS. (US/0037-9808). **302**

JOURNAL OF THE SOCIETY OF COSMETIC CHEMISTS. (US/0037-9832). **1026**

JOURNAL OF THE SOCIETY OF DAIRY TECHNOLOGY. (UK/0037-9840). **196**

JOURNAL OF THE SOCIETY OF DYERS AND COLOURISTS. (UK/0037-9859). **1026**

JOURNAL OF THE SOCIETY OF LEATHER TECHNOLOGISTS AND CHEMISTS. (UK/0144-0322). **Adv Mgr:** Robert Blakey, **Tel** 11 44 0532 621005. **3184**

JOURNAL OF THE SOUTH AFRICAN INSTITUTE OF MINING & METALLURGY. (SA/0038-223X). **2142**

JOURNAL OF THE SOUTH AFRICAN VETERINARY ASSOCIATION. (SA/0301-0732). **5513**

JOURNAL OF THE SOUTH CAROLINA BAPTIST HISTORICAL SOCIETY. (US/0146-0196). **5062**

JOURNAL OF THE SOUTH CAROLINA MEDICAL ASSOCIATION (1975). (US/0038-3139). **3599**

JOURNAL OF THE SOUTHERN CALIFORNIA DENTAL HYGIENISTS' ASSOCIATION. (US/0038-3899). **1329**

JOURNAL OF THE SOUTHERN ORTHOPAEDIC ASSOCIATION. (US/1059-1052). **Adv Mgr:** Wendy Reid. **3883**

JOURNAL OF THE SOUTHWEST. (US/0894-8410). **2742**

JOURNAL OF THE TENNESSEE DENTAL ASSOCIATION, THE. (US/0040-3385). **Adv Mgr:** Sharon Melvin, **Tel** same as publisher. **1329**

JOURNAL OF THE TENNESSEE MEDICAL ASSOCIATION. (US/0040-3318). **3600**

JOURNAL OF THE UNITED SERVICE INSTITUTION OF INDIA, THE. (II/0041-770X). **4048**

JOURNAL OF THE VIOLIN SOCIETY OF AMERICA. (US/0148-6845). **Adv Mgr:** Rachel Goodkind. **4127**

JOURNAL OF THE WALTER ROTH MUSEUM OF ARCHAEOLOGY AND ANTHROPOLOGY. (GY). **239**

JOURNAL OF THE WEST. (US/0022-5169). **Adv Mgr:** Carol Williams. **2742**

JOURNAL OF THE WESTERN PACIFIC ORTHOPAEDIC ASSOCIATION, THE. (HK/0043-4019). **3883**

JOURNAL OF THE WESTERN SOCIETY OF PERIODONTOLOGY / PERIODONTAL ABSTRACTS, THE. (US/0148-4893). **1329**

JOURNAL OF THE WILLIAM MORRIS SOCIETY, THE. (UK/0084-0254). **373**

JOURNAL OF THE WRITERS GUILD OF AMERICA. WEST. (US/1055-1948). **Adv Mgr:** Dianna Hightower, **Tel** (310)455-4210. **3400**

JOURNAL OF THE YUGOSLAV FOREIGN TRADE. (YU/0022-5452). **4527**

JOURNAL OF THE ZOOLOGICAL SOCIETY OF INDIA. (II/0049-8769). **5589**

JOURNAL OF THEOLOGICAL STUDIES. (UK/0022-5185). **4971**

JOURNAL OF THEOLOGY FOR SOUTHERN AFRICA. (SA/0047-2867). **4971**

JOURNAL OF THERMAL BIOLOGY. (UK/0306-4565). **462**

JOURNAL OF THERMAL STRESSES. (UK/0149-5739). **2119**

JOURNAL OF THIRD WORLD SPECTRUM. (US/1072-5040). **4527**

JOURNAL OF THIRD WORLD STUDIES. (US/8755-3449). **1637**

JOURNAL OF THORACIC AND CARDIOVASCULAR SURGERY. (US/0022-5223). **3968**

JOURNAL OF THORACIC IMAGING. (US/0883-5993). **3600**

JOURNAL OF THOUGHT. (US/0022-5231). **1759**

JOURNAL OF TIME SERIES ANALYSIS. (UK/0143-9782). **3516**

JOURNAL OF TISSUE CULTURE METHODS. (NE/0271-8057). **538**

JOURNAL OF TISSUE VIABILITY. (UK/0965-206X). **Adv Mgr:** J. G. Gisby. **538**

JOURNAL OF TOURISM STUDIES, THE. (AT/1035-4662). **5481**

JOURNAL OF TOXICOLOGY AND ENVIRONMENTAL HEALTH. (US/0098-4108). **3982**

JOURNAL OF TOXICOLOGY. CLINICAL TOXICOLOGY. (US/0731-3810). **3982**

JOURNAL OF TOXICOLOGY. CUTANEOUS AND OCULAR TOXICOLOGY. (US). **3982**

JOURNAL OF TOXICOLOGY. TOXIN REVIEWS. (US/0731-3837). **3982**

JOURNAL OF TRACE AND MICROPROBE TECHNIQUES. (US/0733-4680). **1017**

JOURNAL OF TRACE ELEMENTS AND ELECTROLYTES IN HEALTH AND DISEASE. (GW/0931-2838). **3600**

JOURNAL OF TRADITIONAL CHINESE MEDICINE. (CC/0254-6272). **3600**

JOURNAL OF TRAFFIC SAFETY EDUCATION. (US/0164-1344). **5441**

JOURNAL OF TRANSCULTURAL NURSING. (US/1043-6596). **3860**

JOURNAL OF TRANSNATIONAL LAW & POLICY. (US/1067-8182). **3131**

JOURNAL OF TRANSPLANT COORDINATION : OFFICIAL PUBLICATION OF THE NORTH AMERICAN TRANSPLANT COORDINATORS ORGANIZATION (NATCO). (DK/0905-9199). **3799**

JOURNAL OF TRANSPORT ECONOMICS AND POLICY. (UK/0022-5258). **5385**

JOURNAL OF TRANSPORT HISTORY, THE. (UK/0022-5266). **5385**

JOURNAL OF TRANSPORTATION ENGINEERING. (US/0733-947X). **2026**

JOURNAL OF TRAUMA, THE. (US/0022-5282). **3969**

JOURNAL OF TRAVEL AND TOURISM MARKETING. (US/1054-8408). **5482**

JOURNAL OF TRAVEL RESEARCH. (US/0047-2875). **5482**

JOURNAL OF TREE FRUIT PRODUCTION. (US/1055-1387). **177**

JOURNAL OF TROPICAL MEDICINE AND HYGIENE. (UK/0022-5304). **3986**

JOURNAL OF TROPICAL PEDIATRICS (1980). (UK/0142-6338). **3905**

JOURNAL OF TURFGRASS MANAGEMENT. (US/1070-437X). **2422**

JOURNAL OF UFO STUDIES, THE. (US/0730-5478). **26**

JOURNAL OF UGANDAN LIBRARIES. (UG). **3221**

JOURNAL OF UKRAINIAN GRADUATE STUDIES. (CN/0701-1792). **2695**

JOURNAL OF ULTRASOUND IN MEDICINE. (US/0278-4297). **3943**

JOURNAL OF UNCONVENTIONAL HISTORY. (US). **2621**

JOURNAL OF URBAN AFFAIRS. (US/0735-2166). **2826**

JOURNAL OF URBAN AND CULTURAL STUDIES. (US/1054-1802). **1759**

JOURNAL OF URBAN PLANNING AND DEVELOPMENT. (US/0733-9488). **2026**

JOURNAL OF UROLOGICAL NURSING. (US/0738-7350). **3991**

JOURNAL OF UROLOGY, THE. (US/0022-5347). **3991**

JOURNAL OF VAISNAVA STUDIES, THE. (US/1062-1237). **Adv Mgr:** Barbara Berasl, **Tel** (718)522-2335. **4971**

JOURNAL OF VASCULAR AND INTERVENTIONAL RADIOLOGY. (US/1051-0443). **3943**

JOURNAL OF VASCULAR SURGERY. (US/0741-5214). **3969**

JOURNAL OF VASCULAR TECHNOLOGY, THE. (US/1044-4122). **3708**

JOURNAL OF VEGETABLE CROP PRODUCTION. (US/1049-6467). **177**

JOURNAL OF VETERINARY EMERGENCY AND CRITICAL CARE (SANTA BARBARA, CALIF.). (US/1056-6392). **5514**

JOURNAL OF VIETNAMESE STUDIES. (AT/1030-6390). **Adv Mgr Tel** 03 353 9294. **2656**

JOURNAL OF VIROLOGY. (US/0022-538X). **566**

JOURNAL OF VISION REHABILITATION (LINCOLN, NEB.). (US/1041-0384). **3876**

JOURNAL OF VISUAL IMPAIRMENT & BLINDNESS. (US/0145-482X). **4390**

JOURNAL OF VOLUNTEER ADMINISTRATION, THE. (US/0733-6535). **Adv Mgr:** M. Martin. **5293**

JOURNAL OF WATER BORNE COATINGS. (US/0163-4526). **4224**

JOURNAL OF WATER RESOURCES. (IQ/0255-0148). **5535**

JOURNAL OF WATER RESOURCES PLANNING AND MANAGEMENT. (US/0733-9496). **5535**

JOURNAL OF WATERWAY, PORT, COASTAL, AND OCEAN ENGINEERING. (US/0733-950X). **2092**

JOURNAL OF WEATHER MODIFICATION, THE. (US/0739-1781). **1427**

JOURNAL OF WEST AFRICAN LANGUAGES, THE. (UK/0022-5401). **3292**

JOURNAL OF WEST INDIAN LITERATURE. (BB/0258-8501). **3400**

JOURNAL OF WILDLIFE REHABILITATION. (US/1071-2232). **2196**

JOURNAL OF WIND ENGINEERING AND INDUSTRIAL AERODYNAMICS. (NE/0167-6105). **1983**

JOURNAL OF WOMEN & AGING. (US/0895-2841). **5559**

JOURNAL OF WOMEN'S HEALTH. (US/1059-7115). **3600**

JOURNAL OF WOMEN'S HISTORY. (US/1042-7961). **5559**

JOURNAL OF WOOD CHEMISTRY AND TECHNOLOGY. (US/0277-3813). **1055**

JOURNAL OF WORKERS COMPENSATION, THE. (US/1059-4167). **2886**

JOURNAL OF WORLD FOREST RESOURCE MANAGEMENT. (UK/0261-4286). **2386**

JOURNAL OF WORLD HISTORY. (US/1045-6007). **2621**

JOURNAL OF XIAN MEDICAL UNIVERSITY. (CC/0258-0659). **Adv Mgr:** Yue Mangsheng, **Tel** 029 5261609-2266. **3600**

JOURNAL OF ZOO AND WILDLIFE MEDICINE : OFFICIAL PUBLICATION OF THE AMERICAN ASSOCIATION OF ZOO VETERINARIANS. (US/1042-7260). **Adv Mgr Tel** (215)387-9094. **5514**

JOURNAL OF ZOOLOGY (1987). (UK/0952-8369). **5589**

JOURNAL (OGDENSBURG, N.Y.), THE. (US/0893-5149). **Adv Mgr:** Mary McGreg. **5717**

JOURNAL / OHIO SCHOOL BOARDS ASSOCIATION. (US/0893-5289). **Adv Mgr:** Rick Lewis. **1865**

JOURNAL - OKLAHOMA STATE MEDICAL ASSOCIATION. (US/0030-1876). **3601**

JOURNAL ON EXCELLENCE IN COLLEGE TEACHING. (US/1052-4800). **Adv Mgr:** Dr. Richlin, **Tel** (412)624-6593. **1833**

JOURNAL - ONTARIO ASSOCIATION OF CHILDREN'S AID SOCIETIES. (CN/0030-283X). **Adv Mgr:** S. Devine. **5293**

JOURNAL - ONTARIO OCCUPATIONAL HEALTH NURSES ASSOCIATION. (CN/0828-542X). **3860**

JOURNAL-OPINION. (US/0746-1674). **Adv Mgr:** James Jung. **5757**

JOURNAL : PAPER OF THE NATIONAL UNION OF CIVIL AND PUBLIC SERVANTS. (UK/0957-8978). **Adv Mgr:** G. Ellis, **Tel** 071 928 9671. **4704**

JOURNAL-PATRIOT, THE. (US). **Adv Mgr:** Carolyn Sipes, **Tel** (910)838-4117. **5723**

JOURNAL RECORD (HAMILTON, AL.). (US). **5627**

JOURNAL RECORD (OKLAHOMA CITY, OKLA.), THE. (US/0737-5468). **Adv Mgr:** M. Dunbar, **Tel** (405)278-6077. **688**

JOURNAL / RHODE ISLAND BAR ASSOCIATION. (US/1073-8800). **Adv Mgr:** Beth Bailey. **2990**

JOURNAL - SEATTLE-KING COUNTY DENTAL SOCIETY. (US). **1329**

JOURNAL - SINGAPORE COMPUTER SOCIETY. (SI). **1261**

JOURNAL STAR, THE. (US). **5660**

JOURNAL - TEXAS SOCIETY FOR ELECTRON MICROSCOPY. (US/0196-5662). **572**

JOURNAL, THE. (US). **Adv Mgr:** David C. Meade. **5742**

JOURNAL : THE LITERARY MAGAZINE OF THE OHIO STATE UNIVERSITY, THE. (US/1045-084X). **3400**

JOURNAL - THE LOS ANGELES INSTITUTE OF CONTEMPORARY ART. (US/0094-8985). **354**

JOURNAL : THE MAGAZINE OF THE INDIANA SCHOOL BOARDS ASSOCIATION, THE. (US). **1865**

JOURNAL - TIMBER DEVELOPMENT ASSOCIATION OF INDIA. (II/0377-936X). **2402**

JOURNAL - WORLD PHEASANT ASSOCIATION. (UK). **2196**

JOURNALEN SYKEPLEIEN. (NO). **3860**

JOURNALISM HISTORY. (US/0094-7679). **2921**

JOURNALISMUS. (GW). **2921**

JOURNALIST. (UK/0022-5541). **2921**

JOURNALIST (EDMONTON). (CN/0823-1672). **1092**

JOURNEY (LYNCHBURG, VA.). (US/0887-8854). **4971**

JOURNEYMEN (CANDIA, N.H.). (US/1061-8538). **3995**

JOY OF HERBS, THE. (US/1040-8134). **2422**

JOYAS & JOYEROS. (SP/0213-120X). **2915**

JOYFUL WOMAN MAGAZINE, THE. (US/0885-8004). **5559**

JP AIRLINE-FLEETS INTERNATIONAL. (SZ). **26**

JPC. JOURNAL OF PLANAR CHROMATOGRAPHY, MODERN TLC. (GW/0933-4173). **983**

JPEN, JOURNAL OF PARENTERAL AND ENTERAL NUTRITION. (US/0148-6071). **4194**

JPMS; JOURNAL OF POLITICAL & MILITARY SOCIOLOGY. (US/0047-2697). **5250**

JR. HIGH MINISTRY. (US/1055-1409). **Adv Mgr:** Larry Boryour, **Tel** (303)669-3836. **4971**

JSAE REVIEW. (JA/0389-4304). **5418**

JSE HANDBOOK / JOHANNESBURG STOCK EXCHANGE, THE. (SA). **Adv Mgr:** D. Wood. **905**

JSN INTERNATIONAL. (JA). **5353**

JU BU SAENG HWAL. (KO). **Adv Mgr:** Doug Park, **Tel** (213)487-4702. **5559**

JUDAICA. (SZ/0022-572X). **5050**

JUDAICA BOOK NEWS. (US/0022-5754). **5013**

JUDAISM. (US/0022-5762). **5050**

JUDGE, THE. (US). **3141**

JUDICATURE. (US/0022-5800). **Adv Mgr:** David Richart, **Tel** (312)558-6900. **2990**

JUDO. (UK/0022-5819). **2599**

JUGENDWOHL. (GW/0022-5975). **1065**

JUGHEAD (MAMARONECK, ILL.). (US/0022-5991). **4862**

JUGHEAD WITH ARCHIE. (US/8750-0639). **4862**

JUGUETES Y JUEGOS DE ESPANA. (SP/0022-6157). **2584**

JUILLIARD JOURNAL, THE. (US/1064-1580). **386**

JUKE BLUES. (UK). **4127**

JUKEBOX COLLECTOR. (US/1053-6884). **Adv Mgr:** Rick Botts. **4127**

JULESBURG ADVOCATE. (US). **5643**

JULIET ART MAGAZINE. (IT). **355**

JUMELLO, LE. (CN/0823-776X). **2282**

JUMP CUT. (US/0146-5546). **1115**

JUNCTION EAGLE, THE. (US). **5751**

JUNEAU EMPIRE. (US). **Adv Mgr:** Robin Paul, **Tel** (907)586-3740. **5629**

JUNGE KIRCHE; EINE ZEITSCHRIFT EUROPAISCHER CHRISTEN. (GW/0022-6319). **4971**

JUNIATA NEWS. (US). **Adv Mgr:** Thomas Lineman. **5737**

JUNIOR BOOKSHELF. (UK/0022-6505). **1072**

JUNIOR SCHOLASTIC. (US/0022-6688). **1065**

JUNIOR TENNIS. (US/1074-0554). **4902**

JURIS. (US/0022-6807). **2990**

JURISPRUDENCE EXPRESS. (CN/0705-3061). **2991**

JURISPRUDENTIE VOOR GEMEENTEN. (NE/0924-4824). **4659**

JURISTENZEITUNG. (GW/0022-6882). **2991**

JURUPA THIS WEEK. (US). **Adv Mgr:** Bob Umphress. **5636**

JUS GENTIUM. (IT/0022-6963). **3131**

JUSER (LOS ANGELES, CALIF.). (US/0888-9007). **Adv Mgr:** Robert Bond. **2769**

JUSSENS VENNER. (NO/0022-6971). **2991**

JUST BETWEEN FRIENDS. (CN/0849-5718). **2489**

JUST B'TWX US. (US/0075-4587). **3221**

JUST CROSSSTITCH. (US/0883-0797). **Adv Mgr:** Mike Nish, **Tel** (309)682-6626. **5184**

JUSTICE OF THE PEACE (CHICHESTER). (UK/0141-5859). **2991**

JUSTICE OF THE PEACE REPORTS (CHICHESTER, WEST SUSSEX). (UK/0264-3731). **2991**

JUSTICE PROFESSIONAL, THE. (US/0888-4315). **2991**

JUSTICE QUARTERLY. (US/0741-8825). **Adv Mgr:** Pat Delancey. **3168**

JUSTICE TRENDS. (AT/0157-6011). **4510**

JUVENILE AND FAMILY COURT NEWSLETTER. (US/0162-9859). **3121**

JUVENILE LAW REPORTS. (US/0276-9603). **3121**

K & I.E. EN C. KUNST EN CULTUUR. (BE/0022-7277). **323**

K & K. (DK). **3401**

K : INTERNATIONAL CERAMICS MAGAZINE. (IT/1120-2343). **2592**

K-THEORY. (NE/0920-3036). **3516**

K.V.P. MANITOBA NEWS. (CN/0828-5942). **3896**

KADAMBINI. (II). **3401**

KAEHYOK SINANG. (KO). **4971**

KAGAN CABLE TV FINANCIAL DATABOOK, THE. (US). **1134**

KAHPER JOURNAL (RICHMOND, KY.). (US/0022-7269). **1856**

KAHPERD JOURNAL (PITTSBURG, KAN.). (US/0893-3316). **Adv Mgr:** C. Daniel, **Tel** (502)745-6042. **1857**

KAHTOU. (CN/0827-2077). **Adv Mgr:** Garth. **2536**

KAIIN JITTAI CHOSA. (JA). **3860**

KAILASH. (NP/0377-7499). **239**

KAIROS (OAKLAND, CALIF.). (US/0277-710X). **3345**

KAIROS; ZEITSCHRIFT FUER RELIGIONSWISSENSCHAFT UND THEOLOGIE. (AU/0022-7757). **4971**

KAJIAN MALAYSIA : JOURNAL OF MALAYSIAN STUDIES. (MY/0127-4082). **2656**

KAKAO + ZUCKER. (GW/0022-7838). **2347**

KALAVRITT / KALAVRTTA. (II). **Adv Mgr:** Virendra Patni, **Tel** 316628. **355**

KALENDAR HOLOSU SPASYTELJA. (CN/0381-5110). **5039**

KALENDARZ DZIENNIKA POLSKIEGO. (UK). **196**

KALENDER FUER DEN BIOGARTEN. (GW/0931-380X). **462**

KALISPELL'S WEEKLY NEWS. (US). **5705**

KALONA NEWS, THE. (US). **5671**

KALORI; JOURNAL OF THE MUSEUMS ASSOCIATION OF AUSTRALIA. (AT/0047-312X). **4090**

KALTE UND KLIMATECHNIK. (GW/0343-2246). **2606**

KAMERA UND SCHULE. (GW/0022-8109). **4371**

KAMI PA GIKYOSHI. (JA/0022-815X). **4234**

KANADA KURIER (ALBERTA AUSG.). (CN/0712-8878). **5787**

KANADA KURIER (AUSGABE FUER BRITISH COLUMBIA). (CN/0712-8886). **5787**

KANADA KURIER (MANITOBA AUSG.). (CN/0712-8894). **5787**

KANADA KURIER (MONTREAL AUSG.). (CN/0712-8908). **5787**

KANADA KURIER (ONTARIO AUSGABE). (CN/0712-8916). **5787**

KANADA KURIER (OTTAWA AUSG.). (CN/0712-8924). **5787**

KANADA KURIER (SASKATCHEWAN AUSG.). (CN/0712-8932). **5787**

KANADA KURIER (TORONTO AUSGABE). (CN/0712-8940). **5788**

KANADSKE LISTY (TORONTO. 1973). (CN/0449-7368). **5788**

KANAWA MAGAZINE FOR RECREATIONAL PADDLING IN CANADA. (CN/1189-5152). **4874**

KANG SHENG SU. (CC/0254-6116). **4313**

KANHISTIQUE. (US/0738-9736). **2743**

KANSANTALOUDELLINEN AIKAKAUSKIRJA. (FI/0022-8427). **1501**

KANSAS BANKER, THE. (US/0022-8478). **795**

KANSAS BUSINESS NEWS. (US/0199-3607). **688**

KANSAS BUSINESS TEACHER / KANSAS BUSINESS TEACHERS ASSOCIATION, THE. (US). **688**

KANSAS CITY BUSINESS JOURNAL. (US/0734-2748). **688**

KANSAS CITY GENEALOGIST, THE. (US/0451-3991). **2456**

KANSAS CITY GRAIN MARKET REVIEW. (US/0738-7296). **1501**

KANSAS CITY KANSAN, THE. (US). **Adv Mgr:** Joie Millenbruch. **5676**

KANSAS CITY SMALL BUSINESS MONTHLY. (US/1068-2422). **Adv Mgr:** John Holson. **688**

KANSAS ENGLISH. (US/0739-0157). **1899**

KANSAS GEOGRAPHER, THE. (US). **2567**

KANSAS GOVERNMENT JOURNAL. (US/0022-8613). **4659**

KANSAS INSURANCE AGENT & BROKER. (US/1069-1847). **2886**

KANSAS LEGAL DIRECTORY, THE. (US). **2992**

KANSAS MEDICINE. (US/8755-0059). **Adv Mgr:** Susan Ward. **3601**

KANSAS MUSIC REVIEW. (US/0022-8702). **4127**

KANSAS NURSE, THE. (US/0022-8710). **3860**

KANSAS QUARTERLY. (US/0022-8745). **2536**

KANSAS RESTAURANT. (US/0022-8753). **5071**

KANSAS STOCKMAN, THE. (US/0022-8826). **Adv Mgr:** Tammy Jauker. **213**

KANSAS WORKS. (US). **Adv Mgr:** Karl Gaston. **5676**

KANT-STUDIEN. (GW/0022-8877). **4351**

KANTOOR EN EFFICIENCY. (NE). **4212**

KANZUME JIHO. (JA). **2347**

KAPPA ALPHA JOURNAL, THE. (US/0888-8868). **5232**

KARADA NO KAGAKU. (JA). **3601**

KARATE AND ORIENTAL ARTS. (UK). **4902**

KARATE, KUNG-FU ILLUSTRATED. (US/0888-031X). **4902**

KARIKAZO. (US/0164-2537). **2321**

KARTER NEWS. (US/0096-3216). **4903**

KARTHAGO. (FR/0453-3429). **272**

KARTING. (UK/0022-913X). **4903**

KASARINLAN. (PH/0116-0923). **Adv Mgr:** Carlites Escueta, **Tel** 995071 loc. 6783. **2656**

KASHRUS MAGAZINE. (US/1074-3502). **2347**

KASHU MAINICHI. (US/0893-8962). **5636**

KATAHDIN TIMES. (US/1064-0657). **Adv Mgr:** Robin Stevens. **5685**

KATES KIN. (US/0741-2045). **2456**

KATHMANDU REVIEW. (NP). **1501**

KATHOLIEKE VERENIGING GEHANDICAPTEN. (BE). **4390**

KATY KEENE. (US/0886-4748). **4862**

KAUAI UPDATE, THE. (US/0898-1418). **5482**

KAUFMAN KOUNTY KONNECTIONS. (US/0884-7525). **2456**

KAUKAUNA TIMES. (US). **Adv Mgr:** George Kailhofer. **5768**

KAVAKA. (II/0379-5179). **575**

KAWASAKI MEDICAL JOURNAL. (JA/0385-0234). **3601**

KAYHAN. (UK). **4480**

KAYHAN-I VARZISHI. (IR). **4903**

KEADAAN ANGKATEN KERJA DI INDONESIA : ANGKA SEMENTARA. (IO). **1682**

KEATS-SHELLEY REVIEW. (UK). **3401**

KEENELAND. (US). **2800**

KEEPER'S LOG. (US/0883-0061). **2026**

KEEPER'S VOICE. (US/0274-4872). **3168**

KEHRWIEDER. (GW/0176-473X). **5451**

KEIKINZOKU KOGYO TOKEI NEMPO. (JA). **4025**

KEKKAKU. (JA/0022-9776). **3950**

KELLY'S BUSINESS DIRECTORY. (UK/0269-9265). **843**

KELLY'S POST OFFICE LONDON BUSINESS DIRECTORY. (UK/0266-3791). **688**

KELLY'S U.K. EXPORTS. (UK/0268-3105). **843**

KELTICA. (US/0192-1207). **2696**

KEMIA. (FI/0355-1628). **1027**

KEMIAI KOEZLEMENYEK. (HU/0022-9814). **983**

KEMIJA U INDUSTRIJI. (CI/0022-9830). **983**

KEMIVARLDEN. (SW/1102-6650). **Adv Mgr:** Ellinor Jenneholt. **1055**

KEMMERER GAZETTE, THE. (US). **5772**

KEMPER COUNTY MESSENGER. (US). **Adv Mgr:** Jayne Jowers, **Tel** (601)743-5760. **5701**

KEMPE'S Advertising Accepted Index

KEMPE'S ENGINEER'S YEAR-BOOK. (UK/0075-5400). **1984**

KENDRICK GAZETTE, THE. (US) **5657**

KENNEBEC JOURNAL (AUGUSTA, ME. : 1975). (US/0745-2039). **Adv Mgr:** Molly Evans. **5685**

KENNEL REVIEW. (US/0164-4289). **4287**

KENNIS EN METHODE. (NE/0165-1773). **4351**

KENT COUNTY NEWS. (US). **Adv Mgr:** Mary Burton. **5686**

KENT FAMILY HISTORY SOCIETY JOURNAL. (UK/0305-9359). **2456**

KENTUCKY BENCH & BAR. (US/0164-9345). **2992**

KENTUCKY CITY (1968), THE. (US/0453-5677). **4660**

KENTUCKY CLUBWOMAN, THE. (US/0740-6185). **5232**

KENTUCKY COLLEGES AND UNIVERSITIES : DEGREES CONFERRED. (US/0145-9120). **1833**

KENTUCKY DENTAL JOURNAL. (US/0744-396X). **1329**

KENTUCKY EXPLORER, THE. (US/0890-8362). **2743**

KENTUCKY FARM BUREAU NEWS. (US/0023-0200). **102**

KENTUCKY FARMER, THE. (US/0023-0219). **102**

KENTUCKY JOURNAL (LEXINGTON, KY.). (US/1063-9357). **2536**

KENTUCKY JOURNAL OF COMMERCE AND INDUSTRY, THE. (US/0279-5388). **843**

KENTUCKY LIBRARIES. (US/0732-5452). **3221**

KENTUCKY LIVING. (US/1043-853X). **2536**

KENTUCKY MANUFACTURERS REGISTER. (US/0741-9031). **3482**

KENTUCKY MARQUEE. (US/0892-4899). **5365**

KENTUCKY NEW ERA (HOPKINSVILLE, KY. : DAILY). (US). **5681**

KENTUCKY NURSE. (US/0742-8367). **Adv Mgr:** Spectrum Publications, **Tel** (800)728-4101. **3860**

KENTUCKY PHARMACIST, THE. (US/0194-567X). **4313**

KENTUCKY POETRY REVIEW. (US/0889-647X). **3345**

KENTUCKY REVIEW (LEXINGTON. 1979), THE. (US/0191-1031). **2849**

KENTUCKY'S GROWING GOLD. (US). **2386**

KENYA NATIONAL BIBLIOGRAPHY. (KE). **418**

KENYA PAST AND PRESENT. (KE/0257-8301). **2641**

KENYAN PERIODICALS DIRECTORY. (KE). **418**

KENYON REVIEW, THE. (US/0163-075X). **3345**

KEP ES HANGTECHNIKA. (HU/0023-0480). **4437**

KEPADATAN PERUSAHAAN INDUSTRI DAN TENAGA KERJA DI SEKTOR INDUSTRI TERHADAP JUMLAH PENDUDUK DI TIAP-TIAP PROPINSI, KABUPATEN, KOTA MADYA. (IO). **1682**

KERALA SOCIOLOGIST. (II). **5250**

KERAMISCHE ZEITSCHRIFT. (GW/0023-0561). **2592**

KERK EN THEOLOGIE. (NE/0450-1489). **4972**

KERNTECHNIK (1987). (GW/0932-3902). **2156**

KERRANG!. (UK/0262-6624). **1298**

KERSHNER KINFOLK. (US/0736-0886). **2456**

KERYGMA (OTTAWA). (CN/0023-0693). **4972**

KEY BRITISH ENTERPRISES : KBE / COMPILED AND PUBLISHED BY PUBLICATIONS DIVISION, DUN & BRADSTREET LIMITED. (UK/0142-5048). **688**

KEY BUSINESS DIRECTORY OF AUSTRALIA : KBD. (AT/0726-0288). **688**

KEY INTERVENTIONAL RADIOLOGY. (US/1040-8479). **3943**

KEY NOTES MUSICAL LIFE IN THE NETHERLANDS. (NE). **4127**

KEY VIVE. (AT/0310-8260). **4127**

KEY WEST CITIZEN, THE. (US). **Adv Mgr:** Randy Erikson. **5650**

KEYBOARD ARTS. (US/0090-3361). **4127**

KEYBOARD COMPANION. (US). **Adv Mgr:** Elizabeth Van Ness. **4127**

KEYBOARD (CUPERTINO, CALIF.). (US/0730-0158). **4128**

KEYSTONE COAL INDUSTRY MANUAL. (US). **2142**

KEYSTONE FOLKLORE. (US/0149-8444). **2321**

KEYSTONE WATER QUALITY MANAGER. (US/1069-0212). **5535**

KHIMICHESKAIA FIZIKA. (US/0733-2831). **1055**

KHIPU. (GW/0170-0391). **323**

KIBBUTZ TRENDS. (IS/5792-7290). **4542**

KID PROOF. (CN/0843-0284). **1065**

KIDRON NEWS THE DALTON GAZETTE, THE. (US). **5729**

KIDS FASHIONS MAGAZINE. (US/0362-6660). **1085**

KIDS, KIDS, KIDZ MAGAZINE. (US). **2282**

KIDS TORONTO. (CN/0826-9696). **4851**

KIDSPORTS (ARLINGTON, VA.). (US/1054-7002). **1065**

KIEL TRI COUNTY RECORD. (US). **Adv Mgr:** Joe Mathes. **5768**

KIJK OP HET NOORDEN. (NE/0023-1363). **1501**

KIKAI TO KOGU. (JA/0387-1053). **2119**

KIKAIKA NOGYO. (JA). **159**

KIKAN ANIMA. (JA). **4167**

KIKAN NIHON SHISO SHI. (JA). **2656**

KILLEEN DAILY HERALD. (US). **Adv Mgr:** Thad Byars. **5751**

KILLSHOT. (CN/0711-7094). **4862**

KILLSHOT (PADUCAH, KY.). (US/1069-2614). **Adv Mgr Tel** same as publisher. **4903**

KINAADMAN. WISDOM. (PH). **2656**

KINATUINAMOT ILLENGAJUK / LABRADOR INUIT ASSOCIATION. (CN/0715-4437). **2536**

KINCARDINE INDEPENDENT, THE. (CN/0834-6674). **5788**

KINDER. (GW). **1804**

KINDEX. (US/0733-8937). **3081**

KINESIOLOGY AND MEDICINE FOR DANCE. (US/1058-7438). **1313**

KINESIS (CARBONDALE, ILL.). (US/0023-1568). **4351**

KINESIS (VANCOUVER). (CN/0317-9095). **5560**

KINETOSCOPIO, EL. (CK/0121-3776). **Adv Mgr:** Ana Ramos. **4073**

KINGFISHER (BERKELEY, CALIF.). (US). **3402**

KINGFISHER FREE PRESS, THE. (US). **Adv Mgr:** Barry Reid. **5732**

KINGSTON THIS WEEK. (CN/0712-9068). **5788**

KINISTINO POST [MICROFORM], THE. (CN). **5788**

KINSHIP KRONICLE. (US/0882-9802). **2457**

KIPLING JOURNAL. (UK/0023-1738). **Adv Mgr:** Dr. Karim. **3402**

KIPU. (EC). **5250**

KIRCHE IM OSTEN. (GW/0453-9273). **5039**

KIRCHE UND KONFESSION. (GW/0453-929x). **4972**

KIRCHENMUSIKER, DER. (GW/0023-1819). **4128**

KIRCHLICHES MONATSBLATT FUER DAS EVANGELISCH-LUTHERISCH HAUS. (US). **5062**

KIRKE OG KULTUR. (NO/0023-186X). **4972**

KIRSCHNER'S INSURANCE DIRECTORIES. NORTHERN CALIFORNIA. (US/1071-8230). **2886**

KIRSCHNER'S INSURANCE DIRECTORY. SOUTHERN CALIFORNIA. (US/1071-8249). **2886**

KITABAT. (BA). **3402**

KITELINES. (US/0192-3439). **4851**

KITPLANES. (US/0891-1851). **27**

KITTSON COUNTY ENTERPRISE. (US). **Adv Mgr:** Gail Norland. **5696**

KIVA (TUSCON, ARIZ.), THE. (US/0023-1940). **Adv Mgr Tel** (602)621-4794. **272**

KJEMI. (NO/0023-1983). **1027**

KLANSMAN, THE. (US/0749-0763). **2266**

KLERONOMIA : PERIODIKON DEMODIEUMA TOU PATRIARCHIKOU HIDRYMATOS PATERIKON MELETON. (GR). **4972**

KLINISCHES LABOR. (GW/0941-2131). **Adv Mgr:** E. Buck. **5123**

KNIFE WORLD. (US/0276-9042). **2774**

KNIT & CHAT. (CN/0711-639X). **5184**

KNITTERS. (US/0747-9026). **Adv Mgr:** Karen Bright. **5184**

KNITTING INTERNATIONAL. (UK/0266-8394). **5353**

KNITTING TIMES. (US/0023-2300). **5184**

KNITTING WORLD (SEABROOK, N.H.). (US/0194-8083). **5184**

KNJIZNICA. (XV/0023-2424). **3221**

KNOWLEDGE-BASED SYSTEMS (GUILDFORD, SURREY). (UK/0950-7051). **1193**

KNOWLEDGE MATTERS. (US/0886-4063). **4351**

KNOX COUNTY DAILY NEWS (BICKNELL, IND. : 1991). (US/1060-6173). **5665**

KODALY ENVOY. (US). **Adv Mgr:** Jim Lovell. **1899**

KODIAK DAILY MIRROR, THE. (US/0740-2112). **Adv Mgr:** Amy Willis. **5629**

KODIKAS. (GW/0171-0834). **3293**

KOERS. (SA/0023-270X). **4351**

KOGAI. (JA/0454-9015). **2235**

KOGNITIONSWISSENSCHAFT. (GW/0938-7986). **4602**

KOI USA. (US/0748-7320). **Adv Mgr:** T. Graham, **Tel** (619)673-0955. **2422**

KOINONIA (PRINCETON, N.J.). (US/1047-1057). **4972**

KOKALOS : STUDI PUBBLICATI DALL'ISTITUTO DI STORIA ANTICA DELL'UNIVERSITA DI PALERMO. (IT/0454-1596). **1078**

KOKUBUNGAKU KENKYU SHIRYOKAN KIYO. (JA). **3402**

KOLNER MUSEUMS-BULLETIN. (GW/0933-257X). **4090**

KOLNER ZEITSCHRIFT FUER SOZIOLOGIE UND SOZIALPSYCHOLOGIE. (GW/0023-2653). **5251**

KOMBA. (KE). **5590**

KOMMUNIKATION. (SZ). **1159**

KOMPASS; AUSTRALIA. (AT). **731**

KOMPASS-SVERIGE. (SW). **1615**

KONOMISK REVY. (NO). **1571**

KONSTRUKTIVER IGENIEURBAU. (GW/0023-3633). **619**

KONTINENT (BERLIN, GERMANY). (GW/0176-4179). **4480**

KONYVTARI FIGYELO. (HU/0023-3773). **3222**

KOOKS MAGAZINE. (US/1045-103X). **4242**

KOREA BUSINESS WORLD. (KO). **689**

KOREA ECONOMIC REPORT. (KO). **Adv Mgr:** M.H. Jeon, **Tel** (02)783-5283. **1571**

KOREA HERALD, THE. (KO). **5805**

KOREA JOURNAL. (KO/0023-3900). **2657**

KOREA NEWSREVIEW. (US/0146-9657). **2506**

KOREA OBSERVER. (KO). **Adv Mgr:** B.Y. Kim. **2849**

KOREAN BUSINESS REVIEW. (KO). **689**

KOREAN JOURNAL OF INTERNATIONAL STUDIES, THE. (KO/0377-0451). **4528**

KOREAN JOURNAL OF OPHTHALMOLOGY : KJO. (KO). **3876**

KOREAN SOCIAL SCIENCE JOURNAL. (KO). **5207**

KOREAN STUDIES. (US/0145-840X). **2657**

KOREAN TRADE DIRECTORY. (KO). **843**

KOREANA. (KO). **355**

KORNYEZETVEDELMI SZAKIRODALMI TAJEKOZTATO. (HU/0231-0716). **2218**

KORT SAGT !. (DK/0902-7270). **3222**

KORTARS. (HU/0023-415X). **3402**

KOSHER GOURMET MAGAZINE, THE. (US/0888-4811). **2791**

KOSMETIK INTERNATIONAL. (GW). **404**

KOSMORAMA. (DK/0023-4222). **4073**

KOSMOS + OEKUMENE. (NE). **4972**

KOSMOS (STUTTGART). (GW/0023-4230). **5124**

KOTAI BUTSURI. A SHIRIZU. (JA). **4411**

KOUNTRY KORRAL MAGAZINE. (SW). **4128**

KOVOVE MATERIALY. (XO/0023-432X). **4007**

KOZGAZDASAGI SZEMLE. (HU/0023-4346). **689**

KOZUTI KOZLEKEDESI SZAKIRODALMI TAJEKOZTATO. (HU/0231-0724). **5441**

KRAFTFUTTER. (GW/0023-4427). **202**

KRANKENDIENST. (GW/0023-4486). **3602**

KRANKENHAUS-HYGIENE + INFEKTIONSVERHUTUNG. (GW/0720-3373). **4788**

KRANKENHAUSPHARMAZIE. (GW/0173-7597). **4313**

KRANKENHAUSTECHNIK. (GW/0720-3977). **3787**

KRANKENHAUSUMSCHAU. (GW/0023-4508). **Adv Mgr:** Mr. Geist, **Tel** 011 49 9221 949234. **3787**

KRANKENPFLEGE. (SZ/0253-0465). **3861**

KRANKENVERSICHERUNG (BERLIN), DIE. (GW/0301-4835). **2886**

KREFELD IMMIGRANTS AND THEIR DESCENDANTS. (US/0883-7961). **2457**

KRIMINALISTIK. (GW/0023-4699). **3168**

KRISIS (INTERNATIONAL CIRCLE FOR RESEARCH IN PHILOSOPHY). (US/0894-5233). **4351**

KRITIKON LITTERARUM. (GW). **3293**

KRITISCHE STUDIEN ZUR GESCHICHTSWISSENSCHAFT. (GW). **2622**

KRMIVA. (CI/0023-4850). **103**

KRONIKA; CASOPIS ZA SLOVENSKO KRAJENO ZGODOVINO. (XV/0023-4923). **2696**

KRONIKA (TORONTO). (CN/0704-4380). **2536**

KRONOS. (US/0361-6584). **2622**

KRYTYKA. (PL/0867-5244). **2696**

KUANGCHUANG DIZHI. (CC/0258-7106). **1441**

KUANGYE GONGCHENG. (CC/0253-6099). **2143**

KUCHE. (GW/0344-4376). **2348**

KUEI SUAN YEN HSUEH PAO. (CC/0454-5648). **Adv Mgr:** Shi Keshun. **1037**

KUKCHE MUNJE. (KO). **4528**

KULTURA (PARIS). (FR/0023-5148). **3403**

KULTURA SLOVA. (XO/0023-5202). **3293**

KULTUURLEVEN. (BE/0023-5288). **Adv Mgr:** M. Verminh. **5251**

K'UN CH'UNG HSUEH PAO. (CC/0454-6296). **5611**

KUNA-MELBA NEWS. (US). **5657**

KUNAPIPI. (DK/0106-5734). **3403**

KUNG CHENG CHI HSIEH. (CH). **619**

KUNG FU MASTERS. (US/1068-7645). **4903**

KUNST & ANTIQUITATEN. (GW/0341-4159). **355**

KUNST & MUSEUMJOURNAAL (DUTCH EDITION). (NE/0924-5251). **355**

KUNST & MUSEUMJOURNAAL (ENGLISH EDITION). (NE/0924-526X). **356**

KUNST IN HESSEN UND AM MITTELRHEIN. (GW/0452-8514). **356**

KUNST OG KULTUR. (NO/0023-5415). **373**

KUNST UND KIRCHE. (AU/0023-5431). **356**

KUNSTHANDEL, DER. (GW/0023-5504). **356**

KUNSTPREISJAHRBUCH. (GW/0174-3511). **356**

KUNSTSTOFF-JOURNAL. (GW/0047-3766). **4456**

KUNSTSTOFFE. (GW/0023-5563). **4456**

KUO CHI HANG KUNG / GUOJI HANGKONG. (CC). **27**

KUO CHI HUO I. (CC/1002-5030). **843**

KUPRIAKAI SPOUDAI. (CY/0081-1580). **2696**

KURIER (ORANGE, VA), DER. (US/1059-9762). **2457**

KW MAGAZINE. (CN/0822-8140). **2536**

KWARTALNIK HISTORII I TEORII RUCHU ZAWODOWEGO. (PL/0860-9357). **1683**

KYKLOS. (SZ/0023-5962). **5208**

KYOKA PURASUCHIKKUSU. (JA/0452-9685). **4456**

KYONGYONG NONJIP (SOUL TAEHAKKYO. KYONGYONG YONGUSO). (KO/0023-369X). **1615**

KYRIAKATIKA NEA. (US/0746-4479). **5689**

KYRKOHISTORISK AARSSKRIFT. (SW/0085-2619). **4972**

KYUSHU SHINKEI SEISHIN IGAKU. (JA/0023-6144). **3930**

L.A. 411. (US/1062-6603). **Adv Mgr:** C VanDecaslede. **4073**

L. A. ARCHITECT. (US/0885-7377). **302**

L.A.S.I.E. (AT/0047-3774). **3222**

L.A. WEEKLY. (US/0192-1940). **Adv Mgr Tel** (213)465-9909. **5636**

L.C. CLASSIFICATION: ADDITIONS AND CHANGES. (US/0041-7912). **3222**

L UNION VICTORIAVILLE CANADA. (CN). **5788**

LA CROSSE TRIBUNE. (US/0745-9793). **5768**

LA FERIA NEWS, THE. (US). **5751**

LA PORTE HERALD-ARGUS, THE. (US). **Adv Mgr:** Thomas Avery. **5665**

LA RECORD. (UK). **Adv Mgr:** Andrew Nelson-Cole, **Tel** 071 636 7543, ext 245; FAX 071 323 6675. **3222**

LA YOUTH. (US). **1066**

LAB 2000. (SP/0213-7275). **5125**

LAB PRODUCTS INTERNATIONAL. BRUSSELS. (BE/0775-602X). **463**

LABOR ARBITRATION IN GOVERNMENT. (US/0047-3839). **3150**

LABOR HISTORY. (US/0023-656X). **1683**

LABOR HOSPITALARIA. (SP/0211-8262). **3787**

LABOR PAGE, THE. (US/8755-1284). **1685**

LABOR RESEARCH REVIEW. (US/0885-4238). **1685**

LABOR STUDIES JOURNAL. (US/0160-449X). **1685**

LABOR WORLD, THE. (US/0023-6667). **1685**

LABORATORIO 2000. (IT/1120-8376). **Adv Mgr:** Marcnesu Nibuca, **Tel** 02 69001267. **984**

LABORATORIUM PRAKTIJK. (NE). **463**

LABORATORIUMSMEDIZIN. (GW/0342-3026). **3603**

LABORATORY AND RESEARCH METHODS IN BIOLOGY AND MEDICINE. (US/0160-8584). **463**

LABORATORY ANIMALS (LONDON). (UK/0023-6772). **5515**

LABORATORY BUYERS GUIDE. (CN/0381-6729). **5125**

LABORATORY EQUIPMENT DIGEST. (UK/0023-6829). **5125**

LABORATORY EQUIPMENT DIRECTORY. (UK/0141-8963). **5125**

LABORATORY HAZARDS BULLETIN. (UK/0261-2917). **2872**

LABORATORY INVESTIGATION. (US/0023-6837). **3896**

LABORATORY MEDICINE. (US/0007-5027). **3603**

LABORATORY MICROCOMPUTER. (UK/0262-2955). **1268**

LABORATORY NEWS. (UK/0266-7169). **Adv Mgr:** Ian Sprange, **Tel** 011 44 81 688 7788. **463**

LABORATORY NEWS. (AT). **Adv Mgr:** David Strong. **463**

LABORATORY PRODUCT NEWS. (CN/0047-3855). **5125**

LABORATORY ROBOTICS AND AUTOMATION. (US/0895-7533). **1214**

LABORPRAXIS. (GW/0344-1733). **3603**

LABORSCOPE. (SZ). **1985**

LABOUR ARBITRATION CASES. (CN/0023-690X). **3151**

LABOUR FORCE / DEPARTMENT OF STATISTICS, THE. (JM). **1686**

LABOUR (HALIFAX). (CN/0700-3862). **Adv Mgr:** Irene Whitfield, **Tel** (709)737-2144. **1686**

LABOUR (HALIFAX). (CN/0700-3862). **1686**

LABOUR HISTORY (CANBERRA). (AT/0023-6942). **1686**

LABOUR NETWORK. (AT). **1686**

LABOUR RESEARCH (LONDON). (UK/0023-7000). **1686**

LABRADOR QUARTERLY : LQ, THE. (US/8750-3557). **Adv Mgr:** Cindy Kerstiens. **4287**

LABYRINTHOS. (IT/0393-0807). **356**

LACERTA. (NE/0023-7051). **5590**

LACIO DROM : RIVISTA BIMESTRALE DI STUDI ZINGARI. (IT/0394-2791). **2321**

LACKAWANNA JURIST. (US/0023-7078). **2993**

LACMA PHYSICIAN. (US/0162-7163). **3914**

LACON HOME JOURNAL (LACON, ILL. : 1866 : WEEKLY). (US). **5660**

LACROSSE (BALTIMORE, MD.). (US/0194-7893). **Adv Mgr:** Network Publications, **Tel** (410)235-0500. **4903**

LACTATION REVIEW, THE. (US/0362-3173). **3764**

LADENBAU. (SZ/0458-6123). **302**

LADIES' HOME JOURNAL. (US/0023-7124). **5560**

LADY. (UK/0023-7167). **2518**

LADY'S CIRCLE. (US/0023-7191). **5560**

LADY'S CIRCLE PATCHWORK QUILTS. (US/0731-9916). **5184**

LAE NEWS. (US/0162-3052). **1760**

LAFAYETTE BUSINESS DIGEST. (US/1048-2822). **689**

LAFAYETTE LEADER (LAFAYETTE, IND. : 1952). (US). **Adv Mgr:** Kim Critchlow. **5665**

LAG & [I.E. OCH] AVTAL. (SW). **3151**

LAGRANGE STANDARD. (US). **5665**

LAI NOTES / THE UNIVERSITY OF NEW MEXICO LATIN AMERICAN INSTITUTE. (US). **1833**

LAIFS. (US/0146-910X). **2422**

LAIT ET NOUS, LE. (BE/0770-2515). **196**

LAKARTIDNINGEN. (SW/0023-7205). **3603**

LAKE ALFRED PRESS. (US). **Adv Mgr:** Barbara Wagoner. **5650**

LAKE CHARLES AMERICAN-PRESS. (US/0739-1196). **5684**

LAKE CITIES SUN, THE. (US). **5751**

LAKE CITY SILVER WORLD. (US). **5643**

LAKE COUNTRY REPORTER. (US). **Adv Mgr:** Gary Jasiek. **5768**

LAKE COUNTY RECORD-BEE. (US/0746-4304). **Adv Mgr:** Roy Dufrain and Ursula Gallas. **5636**

LAKE ELSINORE VALLEY SUN-TRIBUNE. (US/0745-1350). **5636**

LAKE MARTIN LIVING MAGAZINE. (US/1070-8103). **Adv Mgr:** Debbie Bain. **4851**

LAKE NEWS, THE. (US/8750-3689). **5681**

LAKE PARK JOURNAL. (US). **5696**

LAKE PLACID NEWS. (US). **Adv Mgr:** Sue Harrington, **Tel** (518)891-2600. **5717**

LAKE STEVENS JOURNAL. (US). **Adv Mgr:** D. Cahoon. **5761**

LAKE SUPERIOR MAGAZINE. (US/0890-3050). **2537**

LAKE VIEW RESORT (LAKE VIEW, IOWA : 1910). (US). **Adv Mgr:** Deb Druivenga, **Tel** (712)657-8588 or (712)664-2830. **5671**

LAKELAND BOATING (1982). (US/0744-9194). **594**

LAKELAND TIMES. (US/0746-4274). **Adv Mgr:** John Benton. **5768**

LAKES DISTRICT NEWS. (CN). **5788**

LAKESHORE CHRONICLE. (US). **5768**

LAKESIDE LEADER. (CN/0821-3372). **5788**

LAKEVILLE JOURNAL, THE. (US). **Adv Mgr:** Anna Mae Kupferer. **5645**

LAKEWOOD JEFFERSON SENTINEL (1991), THE. (US/1060-5215). **5643**

LAKOTA TIMES, THE. (US/0744-2238). **5744**

LAM-MISPAHA. (US/0894-9816). **5050**

LAMAR DAILY NEWS AND HOLLY CHIEFTAIN, THE. (US). **Adv Mgr:** Sandee Leighty. **5643**

LAMAR DEMOCRAT. (US/0745-9300). **Adv Mgr:** Stephanie Morgan. **5703**

LAMAR DEMOCRAT AND THE SULLIGENT NEWS. (VERNON, AL.), THE. (US). **Adv Mgr:** Tammy Bardon. **5627**

LAMBDA BOOK REPORT. (US/1048-9487). **Adv Mgr:** L. Smith. **2795**

LAMBERTON NEWS. (US). **5696**

LAMB'S PASTURES. (US/0883-7708). **2457**

LAMESA PRESS-REPORTER. (US). **Adv Mgr:** Dee Ann McCormick. **5751**

LAMIERA. (IT/0391-5891). **4007**

LAMOURE CHRONICLE. (US). **5725**

LAMP, THE. (AT/0047-3936). **3861**

LAMPAS. (NE/0165-8204). **3294**

LAMPASAS DISPATCH RECORD. (US/8750-1759). **5751**

LAN-CHOU HSUEH KAN LAN ZHOU XUE KAN. (CC). **5233**

LAN MAGAZINE. (NE). **1242**

LANCASHIRE LIFE. (UK). **2518**

LANCASTER COUNTY CONNECTIONS. (US/0748-1071). **2457**

LANCASTER — Advertising Accepted Index

LANCASTER FARMING. (US/0023-7485). **103**

LANCASTER LIVESTOCK REPORTER. (US/0738-730X). **214**

LANCASTER NEW ERA. (US). **5737**

LANCE K. LERAY'S BAKERY WORLD OF CANADA. (CN/0710-569X). **Adv Mgr:** Frank Grennan. **2348**

LANCET (NORTH AMERICAN EDITION), THE. (US/0099-5355). **3603**

LAND AND MINERALS SURVEYING. (UK/0265-4210). **2027**

LAND AND WATER (FORT DODGE). (US/0192-9453). **Adv Mgr:** Amy Dencklau. **2197**

LAND COMPENSATION REPORTS. (CN/0380-4208). **2993**

LAND JUGEND. (AU). **103**

LAND (MANKATO, MINN.), THE. (US/0279-1633). **103**

LAND- UND FORSTWIRTSCHAFLICHE BETRIEB, DER. (AU). **2386**

LAND USE POLICY. (UK/0264-8377). **1502**

LAND + WATER / MILIEUTECHNIEK. (NE). **2027**

LANDBOTE, DER. (GW). **104**

LANDBOUWLEVEN. (BE/0772-7240). **Adv Mgr:** Eyben Sylvie, **Tel** 02 730 3316. **104**

LANDBOUWMECHANISATIE. (NE/0023-7795). **159**

LANDEIGENAAR. (NE/0166-5839). **4840**

LANDFALL. (NZ/0023-7930). **3403**

LANDINSPEKTREN; TIDSSKRIFT FOR OPMALINGSOG MATRIKELVAESEN. (DK/0105-4570). **2027**

LANDMAN (FT. WORTH). (US/0457-088X). **Adv Mgr:** L. Wiert, **Tel** (817)847-7700. **4263**

LANDMARK (CALGARY). (CN/0843-459X). **Adv Mgr:** W. Whalen, **Tel** (613)930-9020. **2422**

LANDMARK (PLATTE CITY, MO.). (US). **Adv Mgr Tel** Ivan Foley. **5703**

LANDMARK, THE. (US). **Adv Mgr:** Kathleen Puffer. **5689**

LANDMARKS OBSERVER. (US/0272-1384). **2743**

LANDMARKS (SEATTLE, WASH.). (US/0734-4007). **2743**

LANDSCAPE & IRRIGATION. (US/0745-3795). **2422**

LANDSCAPE ARCHITECT & SPECIFIER NEWS. (US/1060-9962). **Adv Mgr:** Bob Erber, **Tel** (714)979-5276. **2422**

LANDSCAPE ARCHITECTURAL REVIEW. (CN/0228-6963). **2422**

LANDSCAPE AUSTRALIA. (AT/0310-9011). **2423**

LANDSCAPE CONTRACTOR, THE. (US/0194-7257). **Adv Mgr:** Esther Baricza, **Tel** (708)932-8443. **2423**

LANDSCAPE DESIGN. (UK/0020-2908). **2423**

LANDSCAPE ECOLOGY. (NE/0921-2973). **2218**

LANDSCAPE JOURNAL. (US/0277-2426). **2423**

LANDSCAPE RESEARCH. (UK/0142-6397). **2423**

LANDSCAPE, THE. (NZ/0110-1439). **2422**

LANDSCAPE TRADES. (CN/0225-6398). **2423**

LANDSCAPER. (AT). **2423**

LANDSCHAFTSARCHITEKTUR. (GW/0323-3162). **2423**

LANDSCOPE. (AT/0815-4465). **2197**

LANDSTINGENS PLANER. (SW) **5294**

LANDTECHNIK, DIE. (GW/0023-8082). **159**

LANDWIRTSCHAFTLICHES WOCHENBLATT FUR WESTFALEN UND LIPPE. (GW). **104**

LANE REPORT, THE. (US/1063-925X). **Adv Mgr:** Joe Oliver. **689**

LANG VAN. (CN/0832-1922). **2489**

LANGAGE ET SOCIETE. (FR/0181-4095). **3294**

LANGENSCHEIDT'S SPRACH-ILLUSTRIERTE. (GW/0023-8252). **3294**

LANGMUIR. (US/0743-7463). **1055**

LANGSTON HUGHES REVIEW, THE. (US/0737-0555). **3345**

LANGUAGE AND COMPUTERS. (NE/0921-5034). **3294**

LANGUAGE AND EDUCATION. (UK/0950-0782). **3294**

LANGUAGE AND LEARNING. (UK). **1899**

LANGUAGE AND LITERATURE (SAN ANTONIO, TEX.). (US/1057-6037). **3294**

LANGUAGE AND SPEECH. (UK/0023-8309). **3295**

LANGUAGE AND STYLE. (US/0023-8317). **3295**

LANGUAGE ARTS. (US/0360-9170). **1804**

LANGUAGE ASSOCIATION BULLETIN. (US/0889-6917). **1899**

LANGUAGE (BALTIMORE). (US/0097-8507). **3295**

LANGUAGE, CULTURE, AND CURRICULUM. (UK/0790-8318). **3295**

LANGUAGE INTERNATIONAL. (NE/0923-182X). **3295**

LANGUAGE LEARNING JOURNAL : THE JOURNAL OF THE ASSOCIATION OF LANGUAGE LEARNING. (UK/0957-1736). **3295**

LANGUAGE PROBLEMS & LANGUAGE PLANNING. (US/0272-2690). **3295**

LANGUAGE, SPEECH & HEARING SERVICES IN SCHOOLS. (US/0161-1461). **1881**

LANGUAGE TEACHER / JAPAN ASSOCIATION OF LANGUAGE TEACHERS, THE. (JA/0289-7938). **3296**

LANGUAGE TRAINING. (UK). **689**

LANGUAGES IN EUROPE. (UK/0965-240X). **Adv Mgr:** S. Downing. **1761**

LANGUAGES OF DESIGN. (NE/0927-3034). **3296**

LANGUES ET LINGUISTIQUE. (CN/0226-7144). **3296**

LANGUES MODERNES, LES. (FR/0023-8376). **3296**

LANIGAN ADVISOR. (CN). **Adv Mgr:** Karen. **5788**

LANSING METROPOLITAN QUARTERLY. (US). **Adv Mgr:** Jeanne Castro, **Tel** (517)372-8433. **2622**

LANSING STATE JOURNAL. (US/0274-9742). **Adv Mgr:** Stan Howard. **5692**

LANTERN. (SA/0023-8422). **2499**

LANTMANNEN. (SW). **104**

LANTZVILLE LOG, THE. (CN/0710-5487). **5788**

LAOGRAPHIA. (GR/1010-7266). **2321**

LAPIDARY JOURNAL, THE. (US/0023-8457). **2915**

LAPIS (MUNCHEN). (GW/0342-2933). **1357**

LAPIZ : REVISTA MENSUAL DE ARTE. (SP/0212-1700). **356**

LAPORAN TAHUNAN PUSAT DOKUMENTASI ILMIAH NASIONAL. (IO). **396**

LARAMIE DAILY BOOMERANG (LARAMIE, WYO. : 1957). (US). **Adv Mgr:** Sheryn Pulse, **Tel** (307)742-2176. **5772**

LARGE ANIMAL VETERINARIAN COVERING HEALTH & NUTRITION. (US/1043-7533). **Adv Mgr:** Clay Schreiber. **5515**

LARGE ANIMAL VETERINARY REPORT. (US/1069-1774). **5515**

LARGO CONSUMO. (IT). **929**

LARIMORE PIONEER, THE. (US). **Adv Mgr:** Arlo Sbedberg. **5725**

LARUE COUNTY HERALD NEWS, THE. (US). **5681**

LARYNGOSCOPE. SUPPLEMENT, THE. (US). **3889**

LARYNGOSCOPE, THE. (US/0023-852X). **3889**

LAS CRUCES BULLETIN. (US/0885-8527). **5814**

LAS VEGAS OPTIC. (US). **Adv Mgr:** Anna Huie. **5712**

LAS VEGAS REVIEW-JOURNAL. (US). **Adv Mgr:** Jack Harpster, **Tel** (702)383-0388. **5707**

LASA FORUM / LATIN AMERICAN STUDIES ASSOCIATION. (US/0890-7218). **2743**

LASER AND PARTICLE BEAMS. (UK/0263-0346). **4437**

LASER CHEMISTRY. (SZ/0278-6273). **984**

LASER FOCUS WORLD BUYERS' GUIDE. (US). **4437**

LASER UND OPTOELEKTRONIK. (GW/0722-9003). **4411**

LASERS AND LIGHT IN OPHTHALMOLOGY. (NE/0922-5307). **3876**

LASERS & OPTRONICS. (US/0892-9947). **4438**

LAST OG BUSS. (NO/0802-7870). **5418**

LATE IMPERIAL CHINA. (US/0884-3236). **2658**

LATEINAMERIKA-KURIER. (SZ). **689**

LATIN AMERICA AND CARIBBEAN CONTEMPORARY RECORD. (US/0736-9700). **2743**

LATIN AMERICAN ANTIQUITY. (US/1045-6635). **273**

LATIN AMERICAN INDEX. (US/0090-9416). **Adv Mgr:** Justin Ford. **4480**

LATIN AMERICAN INDIAN LITERATURES JOURNAL. (US/0888-5613). **3403**

LATIN AMERICAN JEWISH STUDIES NEWSLETTER (1983). (US/0738-1379). **5050**

LATIN AMERICAN LITERARY REVIEW. (US/0047-4134). **3345**

LATIN AMERICAN MINING LETTER. (UK/0267-5099). **2143**

LATIN AMERICAN PERSPECTIVES. (US/0094-582X). **4542**

LATIN AMERICAN RESEARCH REVIEW. (US/0023-8791). **2743**

LATIN AMERICAN TRAVEL & PAN AMERICAN HIGHWAY GUIDE. (US/0075-8159). **5482**

LATINITAS. (VC/0023-883X). **3296**

LATVIAN DIMENSIONS. (US/1062-9505). **2267**

LAUGH COMICS DIGEST MAGAZINE. (US/8750-0612). **4862**

LAUGHING BEAR NEWSLETTER. (US/1056-0327). **4816**

LAUREL LEADER. (US/0748-528X). **5686**

LAUREL OUTLOOK. (US). **Adv Mgr:** Milton E. Wester. **5705**

LAUREL REVIEW / WEST VIRGINIA WESLEYAN COLLEGE, THE. (US/0023-9003). **Adv Mgr:** Loren Gruber, **Tel** (816)562-1265. **3404**

LAURENTIANUM. (IT/0023-902X). **5031**

LAURIER CAMPUS. (CN/0700-5105). **1834**

LAURISTON S. TAYLOR LECTURES IN RADIATION PROTECTION AND MEASUREMENTS. (US/0277-9196). **4788**

LAVAL THEOLOGIQUE ET PHILOSOPHIQUE. (CN/0023-9054). **4973**

LAVORO E PREVIDENZA OGGI. (IT/0390-251X). **3151**

LAVOURA ARROZEIRA. (BL/0023-9143). **104**

LAW AND CONTEMPORARY PROBLEMS. (US/0023-9186). **2994**

LAW & INEQUALITY. (US/0737-089X). **2994**

LAW AND ORDER. (US/0023-9194). **3168**

LAW AND PHILOSOPHY. (NE/0167-5249). **2994**

LAW & POLICY. (UK/0265-8240). **2994**

LAW & SOCIAL INQUIRY. (US/0897-6546). **2994**

LAW & SOCIETY REVIEW. (US/0023-9216). **2994**

LAW CALENDAR. (AT). **2995**

LAW ENFORCEMENT LEGAL REVIEW. (US/1070-9967). **3107**

LAW ENFORCEMENT NEWS. (US/0364-1724). **3169**

LAW ENFORCEMENT TECHNOLOGY. (US/0747-3680). **3169**

LAW FIRM PROFIT REPORT. (US/0895-9412). **Adv Mgr:** L Thinnes. **2995**

LAW IN CONTEXT (BUNDOORA, VIC.). (AT/0811-5796). **2995**

LAW INSTITUTE JOURNAL. (AT/0023-9267). **Adv Mgr:** B. Holt, **Tel** (03)6079345. **2995**

LAW LIBRARIAN (LONDON). (UK/0023-9275). **3222**

LAW LIBRARY JOURNAL. (US/0023-9283). **3222**

LAW LIBRARY LIGHTS. (US/0457-2483). **3222**

LAW, MEDICINE & HEALTH CARE. (US/0277-8459). **2995**

LAW NOW. (CN/0841-2626). **2995**

LAW OFFICE MANAGEMENT JOURNAL. (CN/0843-7076). **2996**

LAW REPORTS. CHANCERY DIVISION, FAMILY DIVISION. (UK/0265-1211). **3121**

LAW REVIEW JOURNAL. (US/0734-1938). **2996**

LAW SCHOOL ADMINISTRATOR'S JOURNAL. (US/0741-1170). **2996**

LAW SOCIETY JOURNAL (SYDNEY, N.S.W. : 1982). (AT). **Adv Mgr:** John Tottrup. **2997**

LAW SOCIETY'S GAZETTE. (UK/0262-1495). **Adv Mgr:** M. Manning, **Tel** 071 320 5852. **2997**

LAW TALK (WELLINGTON, N.Z.). (NZ). **2997**

LAW TEACHER'S JOURNAL. (US/0741-1197). **2997**

LAW TIMES, THE. (SI). **2997**

LAWASIA HUMAN RIGHTS BULLETIN. (AT). **4510**

LAWN & GARDEN TRADE. (CN/0705-212X). **2423**

LAWN & LANDSCAPE MAINTENANCE. (US/1046-154X). **Adv Mgr:** M Mertz. **2423**

LAWRENCE COUNTY ADVOCATE. (US/0883-6531). **Adv Mgr:** Kathy Burroughs. **5745**

LAWRENCE DAILY JOURNAL-WORLD. (US). **5677**

LAWRENCE EAGLE-TRIBUNE. (US). **Adv Mgr:** Vincent Cottone. **5689**

LAWYER'S ALERT. (US/0278-9817). **2998**

LAWYERS DIARY AND MANUAL INCLUDING BAR DIRECTORY OF NEW JERSEY. (US). **2998**

LAWYERS IN EUROPE. (UK/0959-0889). **Adv Mgr:** M R Cane. **3132**

LAWYER'S PC, THE. (US/0740-0942). **2998**

LAWYER'S REGISTER INTERNATIONAL BY SPECIALTIES AND FIELDS OF LAW INCLUDING A DIRECTORY OF CORPORATE COUNSEL. (US/1061-7272). **3101**

LAWYERS WEEKLY (SCARBOROUGH). (CN/0830-0151). **2998**

LC & YOU. (US/8755-4313). **404**

LC GC. (US/0888-9090). **984**

LC GC INTERNATIONAL. (US/0895-5441). **984**

LC-MS UPDATE. (UK/0964-1645). **5125**

LCOMM NEWS / LIBRARY COUNCIL OF METROPOLITAN MILWAUKEE. (US). **3222**

LDA JOURNAL. (US/0092-4458). **1329**

LEABHARLANN, AN. (IE/0023-9542). **3223**

LEADER COURIER, THE. (US). **Adv Mgr:** Sarah Solomon. **5677**

LEADER (LANSING, KAN.), THE. (US/1050-5806). **5677**

LEADER (MORRISBURG). (CN/0834-6666). **5788**

LEADER-NEWS (WASHBURN, N.D.), THE. (US/0888-0220). **Adv Mgr:** Dave Freuer, **Tel** (701)463-2201. **5725**

LEADER (OTTAWA. 1976). (CN/0711-5377). **4851**

LEADER (POINT PLEASANT BEACH, N.J.). (US/0745-6816). **Adv Mgr:** Tom Bateman. **5710**

LEADER (RESEARCH TRIANGLE PARK, N.C.), THE. (US/0195-0622). **5723**

LEADER-TELEGRAM. (US/0891-0227). **Adv Mgr:** Lori Peterson, **Tel** (715)833-9238. **5768**

LEADER-TRIBUNE (FORT VALLEY, GA.), THE. (US/8750-250X). **Adv Mgr:** Maria Kitchens. **5654**

LEADER-VINDICATOR, THE. (US). **Adv Mgr:** Jas R. Shaffer, **Tel** (814)275-3131. **5737**

LEADERS MAGAZINE (LEXINGTON). (US/0023-9631). **2886**

LEADERSHIP (CAROL STREAM). (US/0199-7661). **4973**

LEADERSHIP IN HEALTH SERVICES. (CN/1188-3669). **Adv Mgr:** Michelle Garneau. **3787**

LEADERSHIP (WASHINGTON). (US/0195-9204). **875**

LEADING EDGE (PROVO, UTAH), THE. (US/1049-5983). **Adv Mgr:** Lee Ann Setzer. **3404**

LEADVILLE HERALD DEMOCRAT. (US). **5643**

LEAFLET, THE. (US/0023-964X). **1761**

LEAGUE BULLETIN. (US). **2744**

LEARNING AND INDIVIDUAL DIFFERENCES. (US/1041-6080). **1761**

LEARNING AND MEMORY / ISSUED BY UNIVERSITY OF SHEFFIELD BIOMEDICAL INFORMATION SERVICE. (UK/0143-7534). **3930**

LEARNING DISABILITY QUARTERLY. (US/0731-9487). **1881**

LEARNING ENGLISH IN BRITAIN. (UK). **3297**

LEARNING (PALO ALTO, CALIF.). (US/0090-3167). **1900**

LEASING AND FINANCIAL SERVICES MONITOR, THE. (US/0888-8981). **Adv Mgr:** S. Angelucci. **690**

LEATHER AND FOOTWEAR IN ASIA. (UK). **Adv Mgr:** Graham Bond. **3185**

LEATHER MANUFACTURER, THE. (US/0023-9763). **3185**

LEATHER SCIENCE (MADRAS). (II/0023-9771). **3185**

LEATHERNECK. (US/0023-981X). **4049**

LEAVEN (FRANKLIN PARK, ILL.). (US/8750-2011). **2282**

LEAVENWORTH TIMES LEAVENWORTH, KAN. : 1878). (US). **5677**

LEBANON LIGHT. (US/1075-8852). **Adv Mgr:** Kyle Good. **1093**

LEBANON TIMES, THE. (US). **5677**

LEBENDE SPRACHEN. (GW/0023-9909). **3297**

LEBENDIGE SEELSORGE. (GW). **4973**

LEBENSMITTEL TECHNOLOGIE. (SZ). **Adv Mgr:** W. Frieden. **2348**

LEBENSMITTEL- UND BIOTECHNOLOGIE. (AU/0254-9298). **2348**

LEBENSMITTEL-WISSENSCHAFT + I.E. UND TECHNOLOGIE. (UK/0023-6438). **2348**

LEBENSMITTELTECHNIK. (GW/0047-4290). **2348**

LEBER, MAGEN, DARM. (GW/0300-8622). **3747**

L'ECOUTE, A. (CN/0700-3900). **4128**

LECTINS SHEFFIELD. (UK/0143-4217). **490**

LECTOR (BERKELEY, CALIF.). (US/0732-8001). **3346**

LECTURAS DE HISTORIA DEL ARTE. (SP). **357**

LEDER. (GW/0024-0176). **3185**

LEDGE, THE. (US/1046-2724). **3465**

LEDGER (RIDGEFIELD, CONN.), THE. (US/0888-3017). **Adv Mgr:** Jim DeFillipo. **5645**

LEDGER, THE. (US). **5677**

LEE COUNTY OBSERVER. (US). **5742**

LEEDS NEWS, THE. (US). **Adv Mgr:** Stephen A. Adams. **5627**

LEETOWN NEWS. (US). **Adv Mgr:** Dennis Cook. **5671**

LEFT BANK. (US/1056-7429). **3404**

LEFT CURVE. (US/0160-1857). **Adv Mgr:** same as editor. **4480**

LEGACY (AMHERST, MASS.). (US/0748-4321). **3404**

LEGACY (FORT COLLINS, COLO.). (US/1052-3774). **Adv Mgr:** Ted Wood, **Tel** (406)442-6597. **4706**

LEGAL ACTION. (UK/0266-3953). **2999**

LEGAL ALERT. (CN/0712-841X). **3101**

LEGAL ASPECTS OF MEDICAL PRACTICE. (US/0190-2350). **2999**

LEGAL BIBLIOGRAPHY JOURNAL. (US/0741-1189). **3081**

LEGAL BUSINESS. (UK/0958-4609). **2999**

LEGAL EDGE, THE. (US/1063-9888). **2999**

LEGAL EXECUTIVE, THE. (UK/0024-0362). **2999**

LEGAL HISTORY. (II/0377-0907). **2999**

LEGAL INFORMATION ALERT. (US/0883-1297). **3081**

LEGAL INTELLIGENCER, THE. (US/0277-495X). **2999**

LEGAL INVESTIGATOR, THE. (US/0741-417X). **3000**

LEGAL LOOSELEAFS IN PRINT. (US/0275-4088). **3082**

LEGAL NEWSLETTERS IN PRINT. (US/8755-416X). **3082**

LEGAL REFERENCE SERVICES QUARTERLY. (US/0270-319X). **3000**

LEGAL REGISTER, METROPOLITAN WASHINGTON, THE. (US/8756-2006). **3000**

LEGAL TIMES. (US/0732-7536). **3001**

LEGGERE. (IT). **3404**

LEGGERE DONNA. (IT). **5560**

LEGGI NUOVE. (IT). **Adv Mgr Tel** 02 3022.1. **3001**

LEGION. (CN/0024-0435). **4049**

LEGISLATIVE MANUAL - GENERAL ASSEMBLY OF SOUTH CAROLINA. (US/0362-272X). **4661**

LEGISLATIVE NETWORK FOR NURSES. (US/8756-0054). **3002**

LEGISLATIVE REPORTING SERVICE / COMMERCE CLEARING HOUSE. (US). **4661**

LEGISLAZIONE VALUTARIA ITALIANA. (IT). **690**

LEGNO, IL. (IT). **844**

LEGON OBSERVER, THE. (GH/0024-0540). **2641**

LEHREN UND LERNEN. (GW/0341-8294). **1761**

LEICA-FOTOGRAFIE. (GW/0024-0621). **4371**

LEICA FOTOGRAFIE INTERNATIONAL. (GW/0937-3977). **4371**

LEIDSE GERMANISTISCHE EN ANGLISTISCHE REEKS. (NE/0458-9971). **3404**

LEIDSE ROMANTISCHE REEKS. (NE/0075-8647). **3404**

LEISURE INDUSTRY REPORT. (US). **4851**

LEISURE LINES (SACRAMENTO, CALIF.). (US/0733-5377). **4706**

LEISURE PAINTER AND CRAFTSMAN. (UK). **Adv Mgr:** P. Hunter. **4224**

LEISURE, RECREATION, AND TOURISM ABSTRACTS. (UK/0261-1392). **4856**

LEISURE SCIENCES. (US/0149-0400). **5208**

LEISURE STUDIES. (UK/0261-4367). **4852**

LEISURE TIME ELECTRONICS. (US/0273-6586). **2070**

LEISURE WHEELS. (CN/0709-7093). **5385**

LEISURE WORLD. (CN/1184-146X). **5482**

LEISUREWAYS. (US/0712-5747). **Adv Mgr:** J. Tarbat. **4852**

LEMEL. (AT/0729-5898). **Adv Mgr:** Felicity Peters. **2915**

LEMONT METROPOLITAN. (US/8750-6998). **5661**

LEMOUZI. (FR/0024-0761). **2321**

LENTIL ABSTRACTS. (UK/0260-8464). **105**

LEONARDO (KISSING). (GW/0935-1108). **302**

LEPROSY REVIEW. (UK/0305-7518). **Adv Mgr:** Jennet Batten, **Tel** 11 44 0865 873899. **3604**

LESBIAN AND GAY STUDIES NEWSLETTER : LGSN. (CN/1064-5950). **2795**

LESBIAN NEWS (CANOGA PARK, CALIF.), THE. (US/0739-1803). **2795**

LESOTHO STATISTICAL YEARBOOK / COMPILED AND ISSUED BY BUREAU OF STATISTICS. (LO). **5332**

LETHBRIDGE MAGAZINE. (CN/0821-5278). **2537**

LETRAS DE BUENOS AIRES. (AG/0326-2928). **3404**

LETRAS FEMENINAS. (US/0277-4356). **3404**

LETRAS PENINSULARES. (US/0897-7542). **3404**

LET'S CHEER. (US/0733-9674). **4903**

LET'S DANCE. (US/0024-1253). **1313**

LET'S LIVE. (US/0024-1288). **4194**

LET'S PLAY HOCKEY. (US/0889-4795). **Adv Mgr:** Doug Johnson. **4903**

LETTER EXCHANGE, THE. (US/0882-3804). **3404**

LETTERS IN MATHEMATICAL PHYSICS. (NE/0377-9017). **4411**

LETTERS OF CREDIT REPORT. (US/0886-0459). **796**

LETTORE DI PROVINCIA, IL. (IT/0024-1350). **3405**

LETTRE ADA, LA. (FR). **1280**

LETTRE AFRIQUE EXPANSION, LA. (FR/0996-9888). **4480**

LETTRE DE LA SURETE DE FONCTIONNEMENT, LA. (FR). **1616**

LETTRE DE L'EDI PARIS, LA. (FR/1145-9646). **1115**

LETTRE DES MUSEES ET DES EXPOSITIONS. (FR/0993-9067). **4090**

LETTRE. FRENCH TV MARKET NEWSLETTER, LA. (FR/0996-7826). **1159**

LETTRE MENSUELLE DE FRANCE PHARMACIE LABORATOIRES, LA. (FR/1145-4881). **4314**

LETTRE TOURISTIQUE PARIS, LA. (FR/1146-1918). **Adv Mgr:** Maria Porcher, **Tel** 42610916. **5483**

LETTRES QUEBECOISES. (CN/0382-084X). **Adv Mgr:** Benoit Marion. **3405**

LETTURE. (IT/0024-144X). **5365**

LEUCOCYTES. (UK/0142-8160). **3674**

LEUKEMIA. (UK/0887-6924). **3820**

LEVANT (MONTPELLIER, FRANCE). (FR/0992-0757). **2658**

LEVELLAND AND HOCKLEY COUNTY NEWS-PRESS. (US). **5751**

LEVENDE TALEN. (NE/0024-1539). **3297**

LEVIATAN — Advertising Accepted Index

LEVIATAN (MADRID, SPAIN). (SP/0210-6337). **Adv Mgr:** Mercedes Garcia Lenberg. **4528**

LEVIATHAN (DUSSELDORF). (GW/0340-0425). **5208**

LEWISTON MORNING TRIBUNE. (US/0892-2586). **Adv Mgr:** Rob Minervini. **5657**

LEWISTON - PORTER SENTINEL. (US). **5718**

LEWISVILLE DAILY LEADER. (US/0745-6174). **5751**

LEXIS. (PE/0254-9239). **3297**

LHAT BULLETIN. (US). **302**

LIAISON ENERGIE FRANCOPHONIE. (CN/0840-7827). **1949**

LIAISON - INTERGOVERNMENTAL COMMITTEE ON URBAN AND REGIONAL RESEARCH. (CN/0843-5278). **2827**

LIAISON (THEATRE-ACTION). (CN/0227-227X). **5365**

LIAISONS (MONTREAL). (CN/0707-7726). **3297**

LIAN HE RI BAO. (US/0891-1436). **5718**

LIANHE WANBAO. (SI). **Adv Mgr:** Lawrence Loh, **Tel** 740-2038. **5810**

LIANHE ZAO BOA. (SI). **Adv Mgr:** Lawrence Loh, **Tel** 740-2038. **5810**

LIBER ANNUUS - STUDIUM BIBLICUM FRANCISCANUM. (IS). **5017**

LIBERAL OPINION WEEK. (US/1051-6433). **Adv Mgr:** Tim Stephany, **Tel** (515)282-8220. **5671**

LIBERATION (MILTON. 1984). (CN/0829-0954). **4973**

LIBERATOR (1988), THE. (US/1040-3760). **5251**

LIBERTARIAN DIGEST, THE. (US/0272-5959). **4480**

LIBERTAS. (GW/0341-9762). **Adv Mgr:** Ute Hirschburger, **Tel** 07031 81 1855. **4480**

LIBERTY GAZETTE (LIBERTY, TEX.). (US). **Adv Mgr:** Lawrence Kuslich. **5752**

LIBERTY (PORT TOWNSEND, WASH.). (US/0894-1408). **4481**

LIBRARIANS' HANDBOOK (BIRMINGHAM). (US/0093-1888). **3223**

LIBRARIAN'S WORLD. (US/0739-0297). **3223**

LIBRARIES & CULTURE. (US/0894-8631). **4829**

LIBRARIES DIRECTORY. (UK/0961-4575). **Adv Mgr:** Lucy Simcox, **Tel** 0223-350865. **3223**

LIBRARIUM. (SZ/0024-2152). **4830**

LIBRARY. (UK/0024-2160). **Adv Mgr:** O. Donoglue, **Tel** 0732 453503. **418**

LIBRARY ADMINISTRATION & MANAGEMENT. (US/0888-4463). **3224**

LIBRARY & ARCHIVAL SECURITY. (US/0196-0075). **3224**

LIBRARY AND INFORMATION NEWS. (UK/0269-8161). **3224**

LIBRARY AND INFORMATION RESEARCH NEWS. (UK/0141-6561). **3224**

LIBRARY & INFORMATION SCIENCE RESEARCH. (US/0740-8188). **3224**

LIBRARY AND INFORMATION SERVICE. (CC/0252-3116). **3224**

LIBRARY ASSOCIATION OF ALBERTA OCCASIONAL PAPER, THE. (CN/0075-904X). **3224**

LIBRARY BOOKSELLER, THE. (US/0024-2217). **Adv Mgr:** S. Snifes, **Tel** (510)540-6951. **3224**

LIBRARY BULLETIN (INSTITUTE OF SOUTHEAST ASIAN STUDIES). (SI/0073-9723). **3225**

LIBRARY CHRONICLE OF THE UNIVERSITY OF TEXAS AT AUSTIN, THE. (US/0024-2241). **2849**

LIBRARY HI TECH. (US/0737-8831). **Adv Mgr:** Annette Wall, **Tel** 313-434-5530. **3225**

LIBRARY HI TECH NEWS. (US/0741-9058). **3225**

LIBRARY HISTORY. (UK/0024-2306). **3225**

LIBRARY HOTLINE. (US/0740-736X). **3225**

LIBRARY JOURNAL (1976). (US/0363-0277). **3225**

LIBRARY LIFE : NEW ZEALAND LIBRARY ASSOCIATION NEWSLETTER. (NZ/0110-4373). **3226**

LIBRARY MANAGEMENT QUARTERLY. (US). **3226**

LIBRARY OUTREACH REPORTER. (US/0895-1179). **3226**

LIBRARY PR NEWS. (US/0164-9566). **3226**

LIBRARY PROGRESS (INTERNATIONAL). (II/0970-1052). **3226**

LIBRARY QUARTERLY (CHICAGO), THE. (US/0024-2519). **3226**

LIBRARY SOFTWARE REVIEW. (US/0742-5759). **1288**

LIBRARY TALK. (US/1043-237X). **3227**

LIBRARY TECHNOLOGY NEWS LTN. (UK/0964-7627). **Adv Mgr:** Lynda Agili, **Tel** 44 71 8157870. **3227**

LIBRARY WORK. (UK/0953-9638). **3228**

LIBRI (KBENHAVN). (DK/0024-2667). **3228**

LIBRO EN AMERICA LATINA Y EL CARIBE, EL. (CK/0121-1242). **4830**

LIBROS EN VENTA EN HISPANOAMERICA Y ESPANA. (PR/0075-918X). **419**

LIBYA ANTIQUA / KINGDOM OF LIBYA, MINISTRY OF NATIONAL ECONOMY. (LY/0459-2980). **273**

LICENSED BEVERAGE JOURNAL. (US/0024-2764). **2369**

LICENSING BOOK, THE. (US/0741-0107). **4830**

LICENSING BUSINESS REVIEW. (UK/1073-8983). **1306**

LICENSING JOURNAL, THE. (US/1040-4023). **1616**

LICENSING REPORTER EUROPE. (UK/1073-8991). **Adv Mgr:** Jerry Wooldridge, **Tel** 384-4400591. **1306**

LICHT (MUNCHEN). (GW/0171-5496). **2070**

LICKING LANTERN, THE. (US/0748-1012). **2458**

LIDOVE NOVINY. (XR/0862-5921). **Adv Mgr:** Iva Sladka. **5799**

LIEN HORTICOLE. (FR/0293-6852). **2424**

LIETUVIU DIENOS. (US/0024-2950). **2267**

LIFE & PEACE REVIEW. (SW/0284-0200). **4973**

LIFE AND WORK. (UK/0024-306X). **5062**

LIFE ASSOCIATION NEWS. (US/0024-3078). **2886**

LIFE CHEMISTRY REPORTS. (US/0278-6281). **490**

LIFE (CHICAGO). (US/0024-3019). **2489**

LIFE FORUM. (PH). **5031**

LIFE INSURANCE SELLING. (US/0024-3140). **2887**

LIFE LINES (LINCOLN, NEB.). (US/0744-0677). **5180**

LIFE SCIENCE LAB PRODUCTS. (US/1056-0866). **463**

LIFE SUPPORT SYSTEMS. (UK/0261-989X). **3604**

LIFE WITH ARCHIE. (US/0024-3248). **4863**

LIFELINER. (US/0047-4630). **2458**

LIFTOFF (GRAND RAPIDS, MICH.). (US/1060-7692). **27**

LIGAND QUARTERLY NOTIZIE TECHNICHE. (IT). **Adv Mgr:** Dott Roseua Rebuglio. **3604**

LIGEIA. (FR/0989-6023). **324**

LIGHT AND LIFE (WINONA LAKE). (US/0024-3299). **5062**

LIGHT AVIATION. (UK). **27**

LIGHT (CHICAGO, ILL.). (US/1064-8186). **Adv Mgr:** John Mella, **Tel** (708)853-1028. **3405**

LIGHT METAL AGE. (US/0024-3345). **4007**

LIGHT OF CONSCIOUSNESS. (US/1040-7448). **4973**

LIGHT OF LIFE. (II/0970-2571). **4974**

LIGHTBEARER. (UK). **5062**

LIGHTHOUSE (BURLINGTON). (CN/0711-5628). **Adv Mgr:** Keith Weaver. **1357**

LIGHTHOUSE (UNIVERSITY PARK, PA.), THE. (US/1070-6690). **4128**

LIGHTING DESIGN & APPLICATION. (US/0360-6325). **Adv Mgr:** Beth Bay. **2070**

LIGHTING DIMENSIONS. (US/0191-541X). **4074**

LIGHTING IN AUSTRALIA. (AT/0728-5639). **2071**

LIGHTING JOURNAL (RUGBY, WARWICKSHIRE). (UK). **2071**

LIGHTING + SOUND INTERNATIONAL. (UK/0268-7429). **5126**

LIGHTWAVE. (US/0741-5834). **4438**

LIHC MONTHLY REPORT. (US). **2827**

LIJECNICKI VJESNIK. (CI/0024-3477). **3604**

LILITH (NEW YORK). (US/0146-2334). **5050**

LILLE MEDICAL (1987). (FR/0981-1095). **3604**

LILY YEARBOOK OF THE NORTH AMERICAN LILY SOCIETY, INC, THE. (US/0741-9910). **2424**

LIMA NEWS, THE. (US). **Adv Mgr:** Ken Carpenter. **5729**

LIMA TIMES. (PE). **2552**

LIMELIGHT. (US). **324**

LIMESFORSCHUNGEN. (GW/0459-4371). **273**

LIMITED MOBILITY & IMMOBILIZED PATIENT PRODUCTS. (US). **3605**

LIMOUSIN LEADER, THE. (CN/0381-5552). **214**

LINCOLN COUNTY JOURNAL. (US). **5657**

LINCOLN COUNTY RECORD (PIOCHE, NEV. : 1968). (US/8755-3260). **5707**

LINCOLN HERALD. (US/0024-3671). **2744**

LINCOLN JOURNAL (LINCOLN, NEB.). (US/1054-7983). **5706**

LINCOLN LAW REVIEW (SAN FRANCISCO, CALIF.). (US/0024-368X). **3003**

LINCOLN REVIEW. (US/0192-5083). **Adv Mgr:** Lori Saxon. **2744**

LINDEN LANE MAGAZINE. (US/0736-1084). **Adv Mgr:** C. Brunet. **324**

LINEA D'OMBRA. (IT). **Adv Mgr:** Miriam Corradi. **3405**

LINEA EDP. (IT). **Adv Mgr:** Giacomo Bernini. **1193**

LINEA INTIMA ITALIA. (IT). **1085**

LINEAGE (COMMACK, N.Y.). (US/0899-1871). **2458**

LINEAGRAFICA. (IT/0024-3744). **Adv Mgr:** Brivio Givsi. **380**

LINEAPELLE. (IT). **Adv Mgr:** F. Bacchi, **Tel** 02-801020. **3185**

LINEAR ALGEBRA AND ITS APPLICATIONS. (US/0024-3795). **3517**

LINEAR AND MULTILINEAR ALGEBRA. (US/0308-1087). **3517**

LINGUA FRANCA : THE REVIEW OF ACADEMIC LIFE. (US/1051-3310). **Adv Mgr:** B Kimmel, **Tel** (914)698-9427. **1834**

LINGUE DEL MONDO. (IT). **3298**

LINGUIST (LONDON, ENGLAND : 1986). (UK/0268-5965). **3298**

LINGUISTIC INQUIRY. (US/0024-3892). **3298**

LINGUISTIC REVIEW, THE. (NE/0167-6318). **3298**

LINGUISTICS. (NE/0024-3949). **3299**

LINGUISTICS AND EDUCATION. (US/0898-5898). **3299**

LINGUISTICS AND LANGUAGE BEHAVIOR ABSTRACTS. (US/0888-8027). **3336**

LINGUISTICS AND PHILOSOPHY. (NE/0165-0157). **3299**

LINGUISTISCHE BERICHTE. (GW/0024-3930). **3299**

LININGTON LINEUP. (US/8756-5609). **3405**

LINK. (IS/0792-9765). **690**

LINK. (II/0459-469X). **2506**

LINK (TROY, MICH.). (US/1045-9723). **761**

LINK-UP (MINNEAPOLIS, MINN. 1983). (US/0739-988X). **Adv Mgr:** Michael V. Zarrello. **1242**

LINK (WINNIPEG. 1974). (CN/0380-299X). **Adv Mgr:** R. Gupta. **2658**

LINKS (SACRAMENTO). (US/0163-2205). **5295**

LINKS : SOZIALISTISCHE ZEITUNG. (GW/0024-404X). **Adv Mgr:** Sigrid Schoenecker. **4543**

LINN'S STAMP NEWS. (US/0161-6234). **2785**

LINSCOTT'S DIRECTORY OF IMMUNOLOGICAL AND BIOLOGICAL REAGENTS. (US/0740-7394). **3674**

LINTUMIES / SUOMEN LINTUTIETEELLINEN YHDISTYS. (FI/0357-3524). **5618**

LION AND THE UNICORN (BROOKLYN), THE. (US/0147-2593). **3346**

LION (UNITED STATES ED.), THE. (US/0024-4163). **Adv Mgr:** Mary Kay Rietz, **Tel** (708)571-5466. **5233**

LIP (LANCASTER, PA.). (US/0744-3722). **3346**

LIP SERVICE. (US/0893-620X). **4129**

LIPOSOMES. (UK/0264-9659). **490**

LIPS (MONTCLAIR, N.J.). (US/0278-0933). **3465**

LIQUID CHROMATOGRAPHY LITERATURE, ABSTRACTS AND INDEX. (US/0147-328X). **1017**

LIQUIDS HANDLING. (UK/0268-9219). **Adv Mgr:** Phil Norgal. **4263**

LIQUOR STORE MONTHLY. (SA) **2369**

LISAN AL-ARAB. (CN/0833-3858) **5788**

LISTE D'ABREVIATIONS DE MOTS DES TITRES DE PUBLICATIONS EN SERIE. (FR/0259-000X). **3228**

LISTE DES DIPLOMES INSTITUES SUR LE PLAN NATIONAL ET SANCTIONNANT UNE FORMATION PROFESSIONNELLE. (FR). **1834**

LISTE OFFICIELLE DES NAVIRES DE MER BELGES ET DE LA FLOTTE DE LA FORCE NAVALE. (BE). **5451**

LISTEN (FRANKFURT AM MAIN, GERMANY). (GW/0179-7417). **3346**

LISTEN (FRENCH EDITION, OTTAWA). (CN/1183-1820). **Adv Mgr:** Ian Fraser. **4390**

LISTENING (RIVER FOREST). (US/0024-4414). **4974**

LISTENING (WASHINGTON). (US/0196-7258). **4390**

LISTINO DEI PREZZI ALL'INGROSSO SULLA PIAZZA DI MILANO. (IT). **1616**

LISZT SOCIETY JOURNAL, THE. (UK). **4129**

LITCHFIELD COUNTY TIMES, THE. (US/0744-6705). **Adv Mgr:** Marty Sweeney, **Tel** (203)355-4141. **5645**

LITCHVILLE BULLETIN. (US). **5725**

LITERARY AND LINGUISTIC COMPUTING. (UK/0268-1145). **1193**

LITERARY CRITERION, THE. (II/0024-452X). **3406**

LITERARY CRITICISM REGISTER. (US/0733-2165). **Adv Mgr:** same as editor. **3357**

LITERARY ENDEAVOUR, THE. (II/0255-2779). **3406**

LITERARY HALF-YEARLY, THE. (II/0024-4554). **3406**

LITERARY ONOMASTICS STUDIES. (US/0160-8703). **3406**

LITERARY RESEARCH. (US/0891-6365). **3406**

LITERARY REVIEW (EDINBURGH). (UK/0144-4360). **3346**

LITERARY REVIEW OF CANADA, THE. (CN/1188-7494). **3406**

LITERARY SKETCHES. (US/0024-4597). **3406**

LITERAT, DER. (GW/0024-4627). **3406**

LITERATUR FUER LESER. (GW/0343-1657). **3406**

LITERATUR IN WISSENSCHAFT UND UNTERRICHT : LWU. (GW/0024-4643). **3406**

LITERATURA (BUDAPEST). (HU/0133-2368). **3406**

LITERATURE & HISTORY. (UK/0306-1973). **3407**

LITERATURE AND MEDICINE. (US/0278-9671). **3605**

LITERATURE AND PSYCHOLOGY. (US/0024-4759). **3407**

LITERATURE & THEOLOGY. (UK/0269-1205). **3407**

LITERATURE FILM QUARTERLY. (US/0090-4260). **4074**

LITERATURE SCAN. ANESTHESIOLOGY. (US/0892-2438). **3683**

LITERATURE SCAN. TRANSPLANTATION. (US/0883-8410). **3969**

LITHIUM (EDINBURGH). (UK/0954-1381). **4314**

LITIGATION (CHICHESTER, ENGLAND). (UK/0263-2160). **3003**

LITORAL. (SP). **3407**

LITTLE CANADA PRESS. (US). **Adv Mgr:** Michelle Larson. **5696**

LITTLE NECK LEDGER. (US). **Adv Mgr:** Howard Sweugle. **5718**

LITURGISCHES JAHRBUCH. (GW/0024-5100). **4974**

LIVE ANIMAL TRADE & TRANSPORT MAGAZINE. (US/1043-1039). **226**

LIVE (LAVAL). (CN/0713-4991). **4129**

LIVE LINES. (NZ). **2071**

LIVE OAK (OAKLAND, CALIF. 1982), THE. (US/0897-9839). **2458**

LIVE/PRO LIGHT & SOUND. (UK). **Adv Mgr:** Jay Green, **Tel** 0 727 821861. **386**

LIVER (COPENHAGEN). (DK/0106-9543). **3799**

LIVERPOOL FAMILY HISTORIAN. (UK/0260-759X). **2458**

LIVERPOOL LAW REVIEW, THE. (UK/0144-932X). **3003**

LIVESTOCK MARKET DIGEST. (US/0024-5208). **214**

LIVESTOCK WEEKLY (SAN ANGELO). (US/0162-5601). **215**

LIVING ARCHITECTURE. (DK/0108-4135). **302**

LIVING BLUES. (US/0024-5232). **Adv Mgr:** Brett Bonner. **4129**

LIVING CHURCH (1942), THE. (US/0024-5240). **4974**

LIVING EARTH (BRISTOL). (UK/0954-1098). **105**

LIVING (HOUSTON, ED.). (US/0741-5486). **4840**

LIVING IN SOUTH CAROLINA. (US/0047-486X). **1298**

LIVING IN VENEZUELA. (VE). **2552**

LIVING LIGHT, THE. (US/0024-5275). **Adv Mgr:** Chuck Bugge. **5031**

LIVING MARXISM. (UK/0955-2448). **4543**

LIVING MUSIC. (US/8755-092X) **Adv Mgr:** same as editor. **4129**

LIVING SAFETY. (CN/1200-2275) **4789**

LIVING SAFETY FOR THE CANADIAN FAMILY. (CN/0714-5896). **4789**

LIVING WITH TEENAGERS. (US/0162-4261). **2283**

LIVING WORLD (LOS ANGELES, CALIF.). (US/0896-2154). **Adv Mgr:** Ruth Phillips. **2252**

LIVINGSTON ENTERPRISE. (US). **5745**

LIVRE DES FEUX, DES BOUEES ET DES SIGNAUX DE BRUME. EAUX INTERIEURES. (CN/0381-3398). **4178**

LIVRE ET L'ESTAMPE, LE. (BE/0024-533X). **4830**

LIVRES JEUNES AUJOURD'HUI. (FR/0223-4289). **Adv Mgr:** M. J. Cartalel. **3408**

LIXUE YU SHIJIAN. (CC/1000-0879). **4428**

LJUSKULTUR. (SW). **2235**

LLA BULLETIN. (US/0196-3023). **3228**

LLAMA BANNER. (US/0899-6202). **105**

LLEN CYMRU. (UK/0076-0188). **3346**

LLETRA DE CANVI. (SP). **3408**

LLEWELLYN'S ... DAILY PLANETARY GUIDE. (US/0743-6408). **390**

LLEWELLYN'S MOON SIGN BOOK AND DAILY PLANETARY GUIDE. (US). **390**

LLEWELLYN'S NEW WORLDS OF MIND AND SPIRIT. (US). **Adv Mgr:** Nancy Trudelle. **4242**

LLOYD'S CANADIAN CHEMICAL, PHARMACEUTICAL, AND PRODUCT DIRECTORY. (CN/0068-8452). **4314**

LLOYD'S CANADIAN ENGINEERING & INDUSTRIAL YEAR BOOK. (CN/0068-8665). **2099**

LLOYD'S CANADIAN FOOTWEAR AND LEATHER DIRECTORY. (CN/0068-8762). **3185**

LLOYD'S CANADIAN HARDWARE, ELECTRICAL AND BUILDING SUPPLY DIRECTORY. (CN/0456-3867). **Adv Mgr:** P.Young. **619**

LLOYD'S CANADIAN JEWELLERY AND GIFTWARE DIRECTORY. (CN/0068-9041). **2915**

LLOYD'S CANADIAN MUSIC DIRECTORY. (CN/0381-5730). **4129**

LLOYD'S CANADIAN TEXTILE DIRECTORY. (CN/0068-9858). **5354**

LLOYD'S CANADIAN VARIETY MERCHANDISE DIRECTORY. (CN/0068-9955). **2584**

LLOYD'S INTERNATIONAL MARINE EQUIPMENT GUIDE. (UK). **4178**

LLOYD'S LAW REPORTS. (UK/0024-5488). **3181**

LLOYD'S LIST. (UK). **5451**

LLOYD'S LIST MARITIME ASIA. (HK/1015-227X). **Adv Mgr:** Jonathon Hughes, **Tel** 011 44 71 250 1500. **5451**

LLOYD'S LOADING LIST. (UK). **5386**

LLOYD'S MARITIME ASIA. (HK/0217-1120). **5451**

LLOYD'S MARITIME DIRECTORY. (UK/0268-327X). **5451**

LLOYD'S NAUTICAL YEAR BOOK. (UK). **4178**

LLOYD'S PROFESSIONAL LIABILITY TODAY. (UK/0268-9669). **3004**

LLOYD'S SHIPPING ECONOMIST. (UK/0144-6673). **5452**

LLOYD'S SHIPPING INDEX. (UK/0144-4549). **5452**

LLOYD'S VOYAGE RECORD. (UK/0144-4557). **5452**

LLOYD'S WEEKLY CASUALTY REPORTS. (UK). **5452**

LMT (NORWALK, CONN.). (US/1058-7845). **Adv Mgr:** Jim Pouilliard. **1329**

LOBBY DIGEST & PUBLIC AFFAIRS MONTHLY, THE. (CN/1193-4034). **4662**

LOCAL COUNCIL REVIEW. (UK/0308-3594). **4662**

LOCAL ECONOMY. (UK/0269-0942). **1573**

LOCAL GOVERNMENT FOCUS. (AT/0819-470X). **Adv Mgr:** Marie. **4662**

LOCAL GOVERNMENT IN SOUTHERN AFRICA. (SA/1015-0048). **4662**

LOCAL GOVERNMENT POLICY MAKING. (UK/0264-2050). **4663**

LOCAL GOVERNMENT REVIEW. (UK). **4663**

LOCAL GOVERNMENT STUDIES. (UK/0300-3930). **Adv Mgr:** Anne Kidson. **876**

LOCAL HISTORIAN (LONDON. 1968). (UK/0024-5585). **2697**

LOCAL HISTORY. (UK/0266-2698). **2697**

LOCAL POPULATION STUDIES. (UK/0143-2974). **4554**

LOCAL TRANSPORT TODAY. (UK/0962-6220). **5386**

LOCATION UPDATE. (US/1058-3238). **Adv Mgr:** L. Burns. **4074**

LOCATOR. (US). **2120**

LOCATOR OF USED MACHINERY & EQUIPMENT. (US/0740-3712). **Adv Mgr:** Bill Wood. **2120**

LOCKE NEWSLETTER, THE. (UK/0307-2606). **4352**

LOCUS (CAMBRIDGE, MASS.). (US/0047-4959). **3408**

LOCUS (DENTON, TEX.). (US/0898-8056). **Adv Mgr:** Jane Tanner, **Tel** (817)565-2124. **2744**

LODGING MAGAZINE. (US/1078-6503). **Adv Mgr:** Janet Dodson, **Tel** (202)289-3160. **2807**

LOFTY TIMES. (US). **3465**

LOG ANALYST, THE. (US/0024-581X). **1949**

LOG (ANNAPOLIS), THE. (US/0024-5801). **4863**

LOG (HAYES), THE. (UK/0024-5798). **28**

LOG HOME LIVING. (US/1041-830X). **302**

LOG TRAIN, THE. (US/0743-281X). **5432**

LOGBUCH, DAS. (GW/0175-7601). **2774**

LOGGER (VANCOUVER). (CN/1193-5855). **2402**

LOGIA (FORT WAYNE, INDIANA). (US/1064-0398). **Adv Mgr:** Rodney E Zwonitzer. **4974**

LOGISTICA MANAGEMENT. (IT/1120-3587). **876**

LOGISTICS SPECTRUM. (US/0024-5852). **5126**

LOGOPEDIE EN FONIATRIE. (NE/0166-252X). **4391**

LOGOS (SANTA CLARA, CALIF.). (US/0276-5667). **4352**

LOHN + GEHALT. (GW/0172-9047). **690**

L'OISEAU MAGAZINE : REVUE DE LA LIGUE FRANCAISE POUR LA PROTECTION DES OISEAUX. (FR/0297-5785). **5618**

LOK-MAGAZIN. (GW). **5432**

LONDON ARCHAEOLOGIST, THE. (UK/0024-5984). **273**

LONDON CORN CIRCULAR, THE. (UK). **202**

LONDON MAGAZINE. (UK/0024-6085). **3408**

LONDON MAGAZINE (LONDON, ONT.). (CN/0711-6233). **2537**

LONDON MATHEMATICAL SOCIETY NEWSLETTER, THE. (UK). **3517**

LONDON PHILATELIST, THE. (UK). **2785**

LONDON REVIEW OF BOOKS, THE. (UK/0260-9592). **3346**

LONDON THEATRE GUIDE. (UK). **Adv Mgr:** David Burns. **5365**

LONDON THEATRE NEWS. (US/1064-0312). **Adv Mgr:** Ellen Wilk-Harris. **5365**

LONE STAR HORSE REPORT. (US/0892-6271). **2800**

LONE STAR SIERRAN. (US/0195-1955). **2177**

LONG BEACH COMMUNITY NEWS. (US). **5636**

LONG ISLAND ASSOCIATION DIRECTORY OF DIVERSIFIED SERVICES. (US/0882-3626). **690**

LONG ISLAND BUSINESS DIRECTORY & BUYERS GUIDE, THE. (US/1052-8431). **690**

LONG ISLAND BUSINESS NEWS. (US/0894-4806). **Adv Mgr:** T. Masterson. **690**

LONG ISLAND FORUM. (US/0024-628X). **2744**

LONG ISLAND HISTORICAL JOURNAL, THE. (US/0898-7084). **2744**

LONG ISLAND JEWISH WEEK, THE. (US/0745-5607). **5051**

LONG ISLAND JEWISH WORLD. (US/0199-2899). **Adv Mgr:** Harriet Lippman. **2267**

LONG ISLAND POETRY COLLECTIVE NEWSLETTER, THE. (US). **3465**

LONG ISLAND TRAVELER, MATTITUCK WATCHMAN, THE. (US). **5718**

LONG ISLAND'S NIGHTLIFE MAGAZINE. (US/0744-7590). **4852**

LONG POND REVIEW. (US/8756-5099). **3408**

LONG-TERM CARE ADMINISTRATOR. (US/0146-275X). **Adv Mgr:** J. Lamoglia. **3788**

LOOK AT FINLAND. (FI/0024-6379). **2519**

LOOK BACK AT BOB DYLAN. (US/1049-4340). **4129**

LOOK JAPAN. (JA/0456-5339). **2506**

LOOKINGFIT. (US/0890-4189). **2599**

LOOKOUT, THE. (SP). **2519**

LOOKS LONDON. (UK/0268-4969). **2489**

LOONFEATHER. (US/0734-0699). **3346**

LOOSE CHANGE. (US/0278-4114). **Adv Mgr:** Nora Mead. **2774**

LORE AND LANGUAGE. (UK/0307-7144). **2322**

LORIS. (CE/0024-6514). **2197**

LOS ALTOS TOWN CRIER. (US/8750-4588). **Adv Mgr:** Susan Glaze. **5636**

LOS ANGELES. (US/0024-6522). **2537**

LOS ANGELES BUSINESS JOURNAL. (US/0194-2603). **690**

LOS ANGELES COUNTY ALMANAC. (US/0092-1882). **4663**

LOS ANGELES COUNTY POPULAR STREET ATLAS (CENSUS TRACT ED.). (US/0733-6918). **2568**

LOS ANGELES DAILY JOURNAL, THE. (US/0362-5575). **Adv Mgr:** Nell Fields. **3004**

LOS ANGELES LAWYER. (US/0162-2900). **3004**

LOS ANGELES NEWS CONSERVANCY. (US). **2537**

LOS ANGELES OBSERVER. (US/0890-0949). **2537**

LOS ANGELES TIMES, THE. (US/0458-3035). **5636**

LOS BANOS ENTERPRISE, THE. (US). **5636**

LOSS, GRIEF & CARE. (US/8756-4610). **4603**

LOST AND FOUND TIMES. (US). **3408**

LOST CREEK LETTERS. (US/1048-2172). **Adv Mgr:** same as Editor. **3408**

LOST GENERATION JOURNAL. (US/0091-2948). **3408**

LOST IN CANADA?. (US/0362-4293). **2458**

LOST TREASURE. (US/0195-2692). **Adv Mgr Tel** (918)786-2182. **5074**

LOT OF BUNKUM. YEARBOOK, A. (US/0882-2425). **2458**

LOT'S WIFE (MICROFICHE). (AT). **5777**

LOTTA CONTRO LA TUBERCOLOSI E LE MALATTIE POLMONARI SOCIALI. (IT/0368-7546). **3950**

LOTTERY PLAYER'S MAGAZINE. (US/0277-5565). **4863**

LOTUS (CAMBRIDGE, MASS.). (US/8756-7334). **1288**

LOTUS (MUSKOGEE, ILL.). (US/1056-3954). **Adv Mgr:** J Tramel, **Tel** (918)683-4560. **4603**

LOUISBURG HERALD, THE. (US/8750-6378). **Adv Mgr:** Larry Roth. **5677**

LOUISIANA CONTRACTOR. (US/0195-7074). **619**

LOUISIANA HISTORY. (US/0024-6816). **Adv Mgr:** G. R. Conrad, **Tel** (318)231-6871. **2745**

LOUISIANA INTERNATIONAL TRADE DIRECTORY. (US/0147-4464). **844**

LOUISIANA LAW REVIEW. (US/0024-6859). **Adv Mgr:** M. Pourcian. **3004**

LOUISIANA OUT-OF-DOORS. (US/0738-8098). **4874**

LOUISIANA PHARMACIST, THE. (US/0192-3838). **4314**

LOUISIANA SPORTSMAN. (US/8750-9016). **Adv Mgr:** L. Behan. **4903**

LOUISIANA WEEKLY, THE. (US). **Adv Mgr:** Bertel Dejoie. **5684**

LOUISVILLE. (US/0024-6948). **2537**

LOUISVILLE DEFENDER, THE. (US). **Adv Mgr:** V. Woodson. **5681**

LOUISVILLE LAW EXAMINER. (US/0890-8605). **3004**

LOUISVILLE TIMES. (US). **Adv Mgr:** Doug Conarroe. **5643**

LOUVAIN BREWING LETTERS. (BE/0777-8805). **2369**

LOV OG RETT. (NO/0024-6980). **3004**

LOVELAND DAILY REPORTER-HERALD. (US). **Adv Mgr:** Sally Lee. **5643**

LOVELOCK REVIEW-MINER. (US). **5707**

LOW INTENSITY CONFLICT AND LAW ENFORCEMENT. (UK/0966-2847). **Adv Mgr:** Anne Kidson. **3169**

LOW RIDER. (US/0199-9362). **5418**

LOW TEMPERATURE DIRECTORY : THE NEWSLETTER OF THE BRITISH CRYOGENICS COUNCIL. (UK). **4411**

LOWDOWN 1982. (AT/0158-099X). **Adv Mgr:** Polly O'Neil, **Tel** 08 2675111. **386**

LOWNDES SIGNAL, THE. (US). **Adv Mgr:** Trey Cross. **5627**

LOWRY AIRMAN. (US). **Adv Mgr:** Jim Gourley. **5643**

LOYALIST GAZETTE, THE. (CN/0047-5149). **2745**

LOYOLA LAW REVIEW. (US/0192-9720). **3004**

LOYOLA OF LOS ANGELES INTERNATIONAL AND COMPARATIVE LAW JOURNAL. (US/0277-5417). **3132**

LOYOLA OF LOS ANGELES LAW REVIEW. (US/0147-9857). **3004**

LOYOLA UNIVERSITY OF CHICAGO LAW JOURNAL. (US/0024-7081). **3005**

LOZANIA. (CK/0085-2899). **5590**

LP GAS REVIEW. (UK). **4263**

LRA'S ECONOMIC NOTES. (US/0895-5220). **1688**

LUA NOVA. (BL). **4352**

LUAS & INTENSITAS SERANGAN HAMA & PENYAKIT DI INDONESIA. (IO). **2424**

LUBRICATION ENGINEERING. (US/0024-7154). **2120**

LUCAS. (AT/1030-4428). **4975**

LUCAS-SYLVAN NEWS. (US). **Adv Mgr:** Carolyn Schultz, **Tel** (913)525-6355. **5677**

LUCHA STRUGGLE. (US/0885-4378). **5208**

LUCKNOW LAW TIMES. (II). **3005**

LUCRARI STIINTIFICE, INSTITUL AGRONOMIC "N. BALCESCU," BUCURESTI, SERIA D, ZOOTEHNIE. (RM/0374-8898). **5590**

LUCRURI NOI SI VECHI. (US/8756-8012). **4975**

LUDOWICI NEWS, THE. (US). **5654**

LUFT- UND RAUMFAHRT. (GW/0173-6264). **28**

LUFTFAHRT-NORMEN-VERZEICHNIS. (GW). **28**

LUFTWAFFEN-FORUM. (GW). **28**

LUMBER CO-OPERATOR, THE. (US/0024-7294). **Adv Mgr:** Christine S. Mattke. **2402**

LUMEN VITAE. (BE/0024-7324). **4975**

LUMIERE ET VIE. (FR/0024-7359). **4975**

LUNDIAN : AN INTERNATIONAL MAGAZINE, THE. (SW). **2519**

LURELU. (CN/0705-6567). **1066**

LURZER'S INT'L ARCHIVE. (US/0893-0260). **762**

LUSAKA PROVINCE ANNUAL REPORT FOR THE YEAR ... / REPUBLIC OF ZAMBIA, OFFICE OF THE PRIME MINISTER. (ZA). **4663**

LUSCOMBE ASSOCIATION NEWS. (US/0889-4361). **28**

LUSK'S PRINCE WILLIAM COUNTY REAL ESTATE DIRECTORY SERVICE. (US/0094-8713). **4840**

LUSO-BRAZILIAN REVIEW. (US/0024-7413). **1078**

LUSOAMERICANO (NEWARK, N.J.). (US/0898-9052). **Adv Mgr:** David Matinho. **5710**

LUSTRUM. (GW/0024-7421). **1078**

LUTHERAN DIGEST, THE. (US/0458-497X). **5063**

LUTHERAN EDUCATION. (US/0024-7448). **5063**

LUTHERAN JOURNAL, THE. (US/0360-6945). **5063**

LUTHERAN PARTNERS. (US/0885-9922). **5063**

LUTHERAN, THE. (AT). **5062**

LUTHERAN WITNESS REPORTER. (US/0024-7588). **5063**

LUTHERAN WITNESS (ST. LOUIS), THE. (US/0024-757X). **Adv Mgr:** Roberta Hipenbecker, **Tel** (314)268-1129. **5063**

LUTHERJAHRBUCH. (GW/0342-0914). **4975**

LUTRA. (NE/0024-7634). **5590**

LUVERNE JOURNAL (AND NEWS), THE. (US). **Adv Mgr:** James Morgan. **5627**

LUX; LA REVUE DE L'ECLAIRAGE. (FR/0024-7669). **2071**

LVNW NIEUWS. (NE). **5295**

LYCHNOS: LARDOMSHISTORISKA SAMFUNDETS ARSBOK. (SW/0076-1648). **5126**

LYMPHOCYTES SHEFFIELD. (UK/0142-8179). **490**

LYNDEN TRIBUNE, THE. (US). **5761**

LYON COUNTY NEWS (GEORGE, IOWA). (US). **5671**

LYONS DAILY NEWS (1929). (US/1040-1504). **Adv Mgr:** Paul Jonet, **Tel** (316)257-2368. **5677**

M + A MESSEPLANER. (GW). **762**

M + A MESSEPLANER FUR MESSEN UND AUSSTELLUNGEN INTERNATIONAL. (GW). **929**

M & A EUROPE. (SZ). **691**

M & A JAPAN. (UK). **797**

M/C HEALTH AND FITNESS NEWSLETTER. (AT). **4789**

M.D. COMPUTING. (US/0724-6811). **1268**

M.D.P. MONOGRAFIAS DE PEDIATRIA. (SP). **3906**

M D T, MOTORCYCLE DEALER & TRADE. (CN/0705-2030). **4081**

M. MACINTOSH MAGAZINE. (IT/1120-8465). **1264**

M.O.C.A. BULLETIN. (AT/0819-9000). **Adv Mgr:** E. Camp. **357**

M P & P, METAL-WORKING PRODUCTION & PURCHASING. (CN/0383-090X). **4007**

MAARIV. (IS). **Adv Mgr:** Tali Sever, **Tel** (212)687-1632. **5684**

MAAS JOURNAL OF ISLAMIC SCIENCE. (II/0970-1672). **5043**

MAB 'S-GRAVENHAGE. (NE/0924-6304). **747**

MABUE HA-NAHAL. (IS). **5051**

MAC/CHICAGO (CHICAGO, ILL.). (US/1045-5825). **Adv Mgr:** same as editor. **1193**

MAC HOME JOURNAL. (US). **1268**

MACCHINE. (IT/0024-8959). **2120**

MACEDONIAN REVIEW. (XN/0350-3089). **2849**

MACH. (US). **2795**

MACHINE AND TOOL DIRECTORY. (US). **2120**

MACHINE DESIGN. (US/0024-9114). **2120**

MACHINE KNITTING MONTHLY. (UK/0269-9761). **5184**

MACHINE-MEDIATED LEARNING. (US/0732-6718). **1224**

MACHINE OUTIL. (FR/0024-9149). **2120**

MACHINE VISION AND APPLICATIONS. (US/0932-8092). **1252**

MACHINERY AND PRODUCTION ENGINEERING. (UK/0024-919X). **2120**

MACHINERY BUYERS GUIDE. (UK). **950**

MACHINES PRODUCTION PARIS. (FR/0047-536X). **2121**

MACHINISME AGRICOLE TROPICAL. (FR/0242-2565). **159**

MACINTOSH BUSINESS REVIEW. (US/0899-725X). **691**

MACINTOUCH. (US/0887-9648). **1194**

MACKINAC, THE. (US/0744-5288). **2177**

MACKLIN MIRROR. (CN/0706-7240). **5789**

MACKNIT. (US/0886-1188). **5184**

MACLEAN'S. (CN/0024-9262). **2489**

MACON COUNTY TIMES. (US/0745-5976). **Adv Mgr:** Linda McDonald. **5745**

MACON MAGAZINE. (US). **Adv Mgr:** Judy Sherling. **2537**

MACON TELEGRAPH. (US/1054-2485). **Adv Mgr:** Alton Brown, **Tel** (912)-477-8434. **5654**

MACOUPIN COUNTY ENQUIRER. (US). **Adv Mgr:** Mary Schmitt. **5661**

MACPLAS. (IT/0394-3453). **4456**

MACROMOLECULES. (US/0024-9297). **1044**

MACTUTOR. (US/8756-8810). **Adv Mgr:** Barbara McPike. **1280**

MACTUTOR COMPANION SOURCE CODE DISKS. (US). **Adv Mgr:** Barbara McRice. **1280**

MACUSER LONDON. (UK/0269-3275). **Adv Mgr:** Caroline Evans. **1268**

MACWEEK. (US/0892-8118). **Adv Mgr:** Peter J Longo. **1238**

MACWORLD (LONDON). (UK/0957-2341). **1194**

MADAME AU FOYER. (CN/0541-6620). **5560**

MADAMINA. (US/0740-5812). **4129**

MADDEN FAMILY NEWSLETTER. (US/0883-556X). **2459**

MADDUX REPORT, THE. (US/0889-0838). **Adv Mgr:** Marcia Turner. **691**

MADEMOISELLE (NEW YORK, N.Y. 1935). (US/0024-9394). **5560**

MADERPRESS BARCELONA. (SP/1131-897X). **634**

MADILL RECORD, THE. (US). **Adv Mgr:** Sam McKenzie. **5732**

MADISON AVENUE HANDBOOK, THE. (US/0076-2148). **762**

MADISON COUNTY CARRIER. (US). **5650**

MADISON COUNTY RECORD. (US/0889-4205). **5627**

MADISON COURIER (MADISON, IND : 1892 : DAILY). (US). **Adv Mgr:** Edward Eggers, **Tel** (812)265-3641. **5665**

MADISON MAGAZINE. (US/0192-7442). **2537**

MADISON MESSENGER. (US/0891-2262). **Adv Mgr:** Jim Durban. **5729**

MADISON NEWS (MADISON, KAN. : 1915). (US). **5677**

MADISON REVIEW, THE. (US). **3409**

MADISONIAN, THE. (US). **Adv Mgr:** Sara Speer. **5654**

MADISON'S CANADIAN LUMBER DIRECTORY. (CN/0316-6414). **Adv Mgr:** same as editor. **2402**

MADRAS AGRICULTURAL JOURNAL, THE. (II/0024-9602). **106**

MADRAS PIONEER, THE. (US). **Adv Mgr:** Shannon Ahern. **5733**

MAGAZIN FUER AMERIKANISTIK. (GW/0170-2513). **2745**

MAGAZIN'ART (WESTMOUNT). (CN/0844-1707). **324**

MAGAZINE & BOOKSELLER. (US/0744-3102). **4816**

MAGAZINE - CANADIAN ORNAMENTAL PHEASANT AND GAME BIRD ASSOCIATION. (CN/0225-0721). **2774**

MAGAZINE CARGUIDE. (CN/1187-9475). **Adv Mgr:** Grant Wells or Al Henderson. **5418**

MAGAZINE DESIGN & PRODUCTION. (US/0882-049X). **2922**

MAGAZINE ISSUES. (US/0899-7039). **4816**

MAGAZINE LITTERAIRE. (FR/0024-9807). **3409**

MAGAZINE OF AMERICA'S BEST RECIPES, THE. (US/1048-8383). **4194**

MAGAZINE OF HISTORY. (US/0882-228X). **Adv Mgr:** Debby J. Davis, **Tel** (812)855-9854. **2622**

MAGAZINE OF SPECULATIVE POETRY, THE. (US/8755-8785). **3465**

MAGAZINE PROVIGO (ED. FRANCAISE). (CN/1192-6929). **2538**

MAGAZINE PROVIGO (ENGLISH EDITION). (CN/1192-6937). **2538**

MAGAZINEWEEK (FRAMINGHAM, MASS.). (US/0895-2124). **4816**

MAGHREB REPORT. (US/1071-7579). **Adv Mgr Tel** (609)258-3392. **2499**

MAGHREB REVIEW, THE. (UK/0309-457X). **2641**

MAGIC MAGAZINE (ORLANDO, FLA.). (US/1054-6723). **4904**

MAGICAL BLEND (1989). (US/1073-5879). **4242**

MAGICAL BLEND MAGAZINE. (US/1040-4287). **Adv Mgr:** Neal Powers, **Tel** (916)893-9037. **4242**

MAGICK CIRCLE DIRECTORY OF OCCULT GOODS AND SERVICES, THE. (US/0742-8898). **4242**

MAGILL. (IE/0332-1754). **2519**

MAGISTRA. (CN). **5031**

MAGISTRATE, THE. (UK). **3169**

MAGNESIUM RESEARCH : OFFICIAL ORGAN OF THE INTERNATIONAL SOCIETY FOR THE DEVELOPMENT OF RESEARCH ON MAGNESIUM. (UK/0953-1424). **3605**

MAGNETIC RESONANCE IN CHEMISTRY : MRC. (UK/0749-1581). **1044**

MAGNETIC RESONANCE REVIEW. (US/0097-7330). **4444**

MAGNETIC SEPARATION NEWS. (US/0731-3632). **4444**

MAGNETOHYDRODYNAMICS (NEW YORK, N.Y. 1989). (US/0891-9801). **2071**

MAGNETS IN YOUR FUTURE. (US/0887-5707). **3943**

MAGNOLIA (HAMMOND, LA.). (US/0738-3053). **5233**

MAGYAR ALLATORVOSOK LAPJA. (HU/0025-004X). **5516**

MAGYAR ALUMINUM. (HU/0025-0058). **4008**

MAGYAR ELET. (CN/0833-0883). **5789**

MAGYAR GEOFIZIKA. (HU/0025-0120). **1408**

MAGYAR GRAFIKA. (HU/0479-480X). **380**

MAGYAR KONYVTARI SZAKIRODALOM BIBLIOGRAFIAJA, A. (HU/0133-736X). **3259**

MAGYAR NAPTAR (NEW YORK). (US/0094-1484). **2489**

MAGYAR PEDAGOGIA. (HU/0025-0260). **1762**

MAGYAR TEXTILTECHNIKA. (HU/0025-0309). **5354**

MAGYAR TUDOMANY. (HU/0025-0325). **5126**

MAHA BODHI, THE. (II/0025-0406). **5021**

MAHARASHTRA TAIMSA VARSHIKA. (II). **2506**

MAHASAGAR. (II/0542-0938). **1451**

MAHD BULLETIN. (US/1064-5608). **3229**

MAIL ORDER PRODUCT GUIDE. (US/1040-1296). **691**

MAILING LIST COMPANIES AND CATAGORIES ... DIRECTORY. (US/1043-4372). **1145**

MAILING LIST TIDBITS. (US). **Adv Mgr:** Wayne Stoler, **Tel** (410)358-8973. **929**

MAIN GROUP METAL CHEMISTRY. (UK/0334-7575). **4008**

MAIN SHEET. (US/0025-0600). **594**

MAINE ANTIQUE DIGEST. (US/0147-0639). **Adv Mgr:** Alice Greene, **Tel** (207)832-4888. **251**

MAINE FISH AND WILDLIFE. (US/0360-005X). **2308**

MAINE LEGIONNAIRE, THE. (US/0161-584X). **5233**

MAINE NATURALIST (STEUBEN, ME.). (US/1063-3626). **4167**

MAINE NURSE, THE. (US/0025-0767). **3861**

MAINE ORGANIC FARMER & GARDENER, THE. (US/0891-9194). **Adv Mgr:** Janice Clark. **106**

MAINE (ORONO, ME.). (US). **1102**

MAINE REGISTER, STATE YEAR-BOOK AND LEGISLATIVE MANUAL. (US/0145-9597). **4663**

MAINE SNOWMOBILER. (US/0195-2870). **4904**

MAINE SPORTSMAN, THE. (US/0199-0365). **4904**

MAINE TIMES. (US/0025-0783). **5685**

MAINE TOWNSMAN, THE. (US/0025-0791). **4664**

MAINE, VERMONT, NEW HAMPSHIRE DIRECTORY OF MANUFACTURERS. (US/0197-1220). **3483**

MAINLINE MODELER. (US/0199-5421). **5432**

MAINLINES (INDIANAPOLIS, IND.). (US/0278-9450). **Adv Mgr:** J Spain, **Tel** (317)541-3600. **3861**

MAINSTREAM (SAN DIEGO, CALIF.). (US/0278-8225). **Adv Mgr Tel** (617)444-0600. **4391**

MAINTENANCE FARNHAM. (UK/0953-2110). **1985**

MAINTENANCE SUPPLIES. (US/0025-0929). **2236**

MAINTENANCE TECHNOLOGY. (US/0899-5729). **619**

MAIRENA (RIO PIEDRAS, SAN JUAN, P.R.). (PR/1050-835X). **3465**

MAITRE ELECTRICIEN, LE. (CN/0025-0988). **2071**

MAITRE IMPRIMEUR, LE. (CN/0025-0996). **Adv Mgr:** J. Cote, **Tel** (514)227-7300. **4566**

MAJALAH DEMOGRAFI INDONESIA. (IO/0126-0251). **4554**

MAJALAH FAKULTAS HUKUM UNIVERSITAS AIRLANGGA. (IO). **3005**

MAJALAH PEMBINAAN BAHASA INDONESIA. (IO/0126-4737). **3300**

MAJALLA (LONDON), AL. (UK/0261-0876). **Adv Mgr:** Lisa Cheng. **2489**

MAJALLAT AL-BUHUTH ABTARIKHIYAH. (LY). **2641**

MAJALLAT AL-TAWTHIQ AL-TARBAWI. (SU). **1762**

MAJALLAT DIRASAT AL-KHALIJ WA-AL-JAZIRAH AL-ARABIYAH. (KU). **2769**

MAJALLAT GHURFAT TIJARAT WA-SINAAT ABU ZABY. (TS). **844**

MAJOR COMPANIES OF NIGERIA. (UK). **844**

MAJOR COMPANIES OF THE ARAB WORLD. (UK/0144-0594). **691**

MAKEDONSKA TRIBUNA. (US/0024-9009). **5665**

MAKING WAVES (PORT ALBERNI). (CN/1192-2427). **1504**

MAKROMOLEKULARE CHEMIE (BASEL, SWITZERLAND : 1981). (SZ/0025-116X). **1044**

MAKROMOLEKULARE CHEMIE. RAPID COMMUNICATIONS, DIE. (SZ/0173-2803). **1044**

MAKTABA. (KE/0253-5971). **3229**

MAL SORI. (KO). **3301**

MALACOLOGY DATA NET. (US/0892-6506). **5590**

MALAHAT REVIEW, THE. (CN/0025-1216). **3409**

MALAWIAN GEOGRAPHER, THE. (MW/1010-5549). **2568**

MALAWIAN WRITERS SERIES. (MW). **3409**

MALAYALAM LITERARY SURVEY. (II). **3465**

MALAYAN LAW JOURNAL (BILINGUAL ED.). (SI/0025-1283). **3005**

MALAYAN NATURE JOURNAL, THE. (MY/0025-1291). **4167**

MALAYSIA AGRICULTURAL DIRECTORY & INDEX. (MY). **106**

MALAYSIAN APPLIED BIOLOGY. (MY/0126-8643). **463**

MALAYSIAN BUSINESS. (MY). **691**

MALAYSIAN JOURNAL OF PATHOLOGY, THE. (MY/0126-8635). **Adv Mgr:** Dr. PL Chzah, **Tel** 603 7502481. **3896**

MALAYSIAN MANAGEMENT REVIEW. (MY/0025-1348). **691**

MALCOLM LOWRY REVIEW, THE. (CN/0828-5020). **3347**

MALIBU SURFSIDE NEWS, THE. (US/0191-7307). **Adv Mgr:** C. Stoddard. **5636**

MALIBU TIMES. (US/1050-4931). **Adv Mgr:** Gloria Neiman and Mary Abbott. **5637**

MALL OG MINNE. (NO/0024-855X). **3301**

MALLAS JA OLUT. (FI/0356-3014). **2369**

MALLET, THE. (US/0162-8879). **634**

MALLORN. (UK/0308-6674). **3409**

MALPRACTICE REPORTER. ANESTHESIOLOGY, THE. (US/0738-1018). **3005**

MALPRACTICE REPORTER. HOSPITALS, THE. (US/0738-1956). **3005**

MALT NEWSLETTER. (CN/0710-3417). **3229**

MALVERN DAILY RECORD. (US). **Adv Mgr:** Richard Folds. **5631**

MALVERN LEADER (MALVERN, IOWA : 1883). (US). **5671**

MAMMAL REVIEW. (UK/0305-1838). **5590**

MAMMARY GLAND. (UK/0964-7600). **464**

MAN AT ARMS. (US/0191-3522). **4049**

MAN! (AUSTIN, TEX.). (US/1056-5175). **Adv Mgr:** Judi Roberts, **Tel** (512)474-6401. **3995**

MAN (CHICAGO, ILL.). (US/1062-2543). **2267**

MAN-ENVIRONMENT SYSTEMS. (US/0025-1550). **303**

MAN IN THE NORTHEAST. (US/0191-4138). **240**

MAN — Advertising Accepted Index

MAN (LONDON). (UK/0025-1496). **240**

MAN-MADE TEXTILES IN INDIA. (II/0377-7537). **5354**

MAN UNDERWATER. (CN/0383-7777). **4904**

MANA MEMBERS DIRECTORY OF MANUFACTURERS' SALES AGENCIES. (US/0890-7641). **3483**

MANAB MON. (II/0025-1615). **4603**

MANAGE. (US/0025-1623). **876**

MANAGED CARE (LANGHORNE, PA.). (US/1062-3388). **Adv Mgr:** Timothy Search. **3788**

MANAGEMENT ACCOUNTANT, THE. (II/0025-1674). **747**

MANAGEMENT ACCOUNTING (LONDON). (UK/0025-1682). **747**

MANAGEMENT ACCOUNTING (NEW YORK, N.Y.). (US/0025-1690). **747**

MANAGEMENT COMMUNICATION QUARTERLY. (US/0893-3189). **1115**

MANAGEMENT DAN USAHAWAN INDONESIA. (IO/0302-9859). **876**

MANAGEMENT (DUBLIN). (IE/0025-164X). **Adv Mgr:** Roger Cole. **877**

MANAGEMENT INFORMATION SYSTEMS QUARTERLY. (US/0276-7783). **Adv Mgr:** Editor. **1194**

MANAGEMENT INTERNATIONAL REVIEW. (GW/0025-181X). **877**

MANAGEMENT JAPAN. (JA/0025-1828). **877**

MANAGEMENT NEWS : THE NEWSPAPER OF THE BRITISH INSTITUTE OF MANAGEMENT. (UK/0025-1844). **877**

MANAGEMENT REPORT (NEW YORK, N.Y.). (US/0745-4880). **944**

MANAGEMENT REVIEW. (US). **878**

MANAGEMENT S.A. (AT). **Adv Mgr:** Pauline Fowles. **878**

MANAGEMENT SCIENCE. (US/0025-1909). **878**

MANAGEMENT SERVICES (ENFIELD). (UK/0307-6768). **878**

MANAGEMENT TODAY. (UK/0025-1925). **878**

MANAGERIAL AUDITING JOURNAL. (UK/0268-6902). **748**

MANAGING TECHNOLOGY TODAY. (US/1062-3310). **878**

MANASABHARATI : SRI RAMACARITAMANASA CATUSSATABDI SAMAROHA SAMITI, MADHYAPRADESA, BHOPALA KI MASIKA MUKHAPATRIKA. (II). **3409**

MANCHESTER STAR-MERCURY. (US). **Adv Mgr:** Mike Hale, **Tel** (706)846-3188. **5654**

MANCUNION : THE OFFICIAL NEWSPAPER OF MANCHESTER UNIVERSITY STUDENTS UNION. (UK). **1093**

MANDATE (TORONTO. 1979). (CN/0225-7068). **4975**

M&R. MARINE AND RECREATION NEWS. (US/0025-312X). **594**

MANEDSSTATISTIKK OVER UTENRIKSHANDELEN. (NO/0332-6403). **1536**

MANGAJIN (ATLANTA, GA.). (US/1051-8177). **Adv Mgr:** Greg Tenhover, **Tel** (404)590-0270. **380**

MANHATTAN MEDICINE. (US/0744-4966). **3606**

MANHATTAN OFFICE BUILDINGS. DOWNTOWN. (US/0886-2737). **4840**

MANHATTAN OFFICE BUILDINGS. MIDTOWN. (US/0886-3725). **4840**

MANHATTAN REVIEW (NEW YORK, N.Y. : 1980), THE. (US/0275-6889). **3465**

MANIPULATOR, THE. (GW/0178-3556). **5801**

MANITOBA BUSINESS. (CN/0709-2423). **Adv Mgr:** Louise Ayre, **Tel** (204)477-4620. **691**

MANITOBA CO-OPERATOR. (CN/0025-2239). **Adv Mgr:** Champ Rossenholt, **Tel** (204)934-0416. **5789**

MANITOBA CONSTRUCTION & RESOURCE INDUSTRIES. (CN/0712-2594). **619**

MANITOBA DAIRYMAN. (CN). **196**

MANITOBA LAW JOURNAL (1966). (CN/0076-3861). **Adv Mgr:** J. Epp. **3006**

MANITOBA PSYCHOLOGIST. (CN/0711-1533). **4603**

MANITOBA TEACHER. (CN/0025-228X). **1762**

MANITOBA TRADE DIRECTORY. (CN/0076-390X). **845**

MANITOBA WINNIPEG BUILDING AND CONSTRUCTION TRADES COUNCIL YEARBOOK. (CN/0714-3222). **1689**

MANITOBAN. (CN). **5789**

MANITOULIN EXPOSITOR. (CN/0834-6682). **Adv Mgr:** Ruth Mohammed. **5789**

MANKIND QUARTERLY. (US/0025-2344). **240**

MANLEY FAMILY NEWSLETTER. (US/0883-7805). **2459**

MANNHEIMER SOZIALWISSENSCHAFTLICHE STUDIEN. (GW). **5251**

MANNING TIMES, THE. (US). **Adv Mgr:** Sheila Touchberry. **5742**

MANOA. (US/1045-7909). **3347**

MANORAMA YEAR BOOK. (II/0542-5778). **1927**

MANSFIELD NEWS-MIRROR. (US/0746-3847). **5752**

MANTHANA. (II). **2506**

MANTI MESSENGER (MANTI, UTAH : 1981). (US). **5756**

MANUAL. NEW YORK BUILDING LAWS. (US). **3006**

MANUFACTURED HOME MERCHANDISER. (US/1047-2967). **2827**

MANUFACTURER NZ. (NZ). **Adv Mgr:** Jill Wood. **3483**

MANUFACTURERS DIRECTORY, WINDSOR-ESSEX COUNTY, ONTARIO, CANADA. (CN/0826-7413). **3483**

MANUFACTURING AUTOMATION. (US/1060-2712). **Adv Mgr:** Sarah Collings. **3483**

MANUFACTURING CHEMIST (LONDON: 1981). (UK/0262-4230). **985**

MANUFACTURING CLOTHIER (LONDON). (UK/0025-2565). **1085**

MANUFACTURING CONFECTIONER, THE. (US/0163-4364). **3483**

MANUFACTURING SYSTEMS. (US/0748-948X). **1617**

MANUFACTURING TODAY. (US/0164-968X). **3484**

MANUSCRIPT SOCIETY NEWS, THE. (US/0195-7813). **2774**

MANUSCRIPTS FOR TUBA SERIES. (US/0363-6585). **4130**

MANUSCRIPTS (NEW YORK, N.Y.). (US/0025-262X). **2774**

MANUSCRITO. (BL/0100-6045). **Adv Mgr:** Marcos Munhoz. **4352**

MANUSCRITOS POETICOS. (SP). **3465**

MANUSKRIPTE. (AU/0025-2638). **3410**

MANUTENCION Y ALMACENAJE. (SP/0025-2646). **5127**

MANUTENZIONE : TECNICA E MANAGEMENT. (IT). **5127**

MANY CORNERS. (US). **3347**

MAP COLLECTOR, THE. (UK/0140-427X). **Adv Mgr:** Ben Lane. **2582**

MAPICS THE MAGAZINE. (US/0891-7973). **Adv Mgr:** same as Managing Editor. **879**

MAPLE SHADE PROGRESS. (US). **Adv Mgr:** Barbara Bethard. **5710**

MAPLEWOOD REVIEW. (US). **Adv Mgr:** Paula Greene. **5697**

MAPPE, DIE. (GW/0025-2697). **2902**

MAPPING AWARENESS. (UK/0954-7126). **1194**

MAPPING AWARENESS & GIS EUROPE. (UK/0954-712636). **1242**

MAQUILA (EL PASO, TEX.). (US/1050-6497). **1617**

MAR Y PESCA. (CU/0025-2735). **2308**

MARATHI PRAKASANA VARSHIKA ANI PRAKASANA DAYARI. (II). **4830**

MARCHE MONDIAL DE L'AUDIOVISUEL, LE. (BE). **4371**

MARCHES AGRICOLES, ALIMENTAIRES ET FONCIERS. (FR). **107**

MARCHES TROPICAUX ET MEDITERRANEENS. (FR/0025-2859). **845**

MARCONI'S INTERNATIONAL REGISTER. (US/0076-4418). **1116**

MARCONI'S INTERNATIONAL REGISTER. (US/0076-4418). **Adv Mgr:** L.G.Smith. **1159**

MARFA INDEPENDENT AND THE BIG BEND SENTINEL, THE. (US/0747-119X). **Adv Mgr:** Rosario Halpern. **5752**

MARG. (II/0025-2913). **357**

MARIN COUNTY COURT REPORTER. (US/0745-8959). **3006**

MARIN INDEPENDENT JOURNAL. (US/0891-5164). **5637**

MARINE AND PETROLEUM GEOLOGY. (UK/0264-8172). **1386**

MARINE BEHAVIOUR AND PHYSIOLOGY. (US/0091-181X). **583**

MARINE CORPS GAZETTE. (US/0025-3170). **4049**

MARINE DIGEST AND TRANSPORTATION NEWS. (US/1059-2970). **Adv Mgr:** Jim Lengell. **845**

MARINE DOCK AGE. (US). **594**

MARINE ECOLOGY (BERLIN, WEST). (GW/0173-9565). **2218**

MARINE ECOLOGY. PROGRESS SERIES (HALSTENBEK). (GW/0171-8630). **2218**

MARINE ENGINEERING DIGEST. (CN/0824-734X). **1986**

MARINE ENVIRONMENTAL RESEARCH. (UK/0141-1136). **2177**

MARINE EQUIPMENT DIRECTORY. (CN/0824-8729). **4179**

MARINE FISH MONTHLY. (US/1045-3555). **Adv Mgr Tel** (615)992-3892. **2308**

MARINE GEODESY. (US/0149-0419). **1358**

MARINE GEOPHYSICAL RESEARCHES. (NE/0025-3235). **1451**

MARINE GEOTECHNOLOGY. (US/0360-8867). **1451**

MARINE INDUSTRY FAX DIRECTORY. (US). **1159**

MARINE MAMMAL SCIENCE. (US/0824-0469). **1452**

MARINE NEWS. (UK). **5452**

MARINE ORNITHOLOGY. (SA). **5618**

MARINE POLICY. (UK/0308-597X). **1452**

MARINE POLLUTION RESEARCH TITLES. (UK). **2236**

MARINE RESOURCE ECONOMICS. (US/0738-1360). **2308**

MARINE STORES INTERNATIONAL. (UK). **1617**

MARINE STRUCTURES. (UK/0951-8339). **4179**

MARINE TECHNOLOGY AND SNAME NEWS. (US). **1452**

MARINE TECHNOLOGY SOCIETY JOURNAL. (US/0025-3324). **1452**

MARINE TEXTILES. (US/0885-9949). **Adv Mgr:** Jim Penningroth, **Tel** (612)473-5088. **5354**

MARINE TRADES (1978). (CN/0705-8993). **845**

MARINEBLAD. (NE/0025-3340). **4179**

MARINER (VANCOUVER, B.C.). (CN/0829-545X). **5452**

MARINER'S MIRROR. (UK/0025-3359). **4179**

MARINETTE EAGLE-STAR, THE. (US). **5768**

MARION ZIMMER BRADLEY'S FANTASY MAGAZINE. (US/0897-9286). **Adv Mgr:** Rachel Holman, **Tel** (510)644-9222. **3410**

MARIPOSA FOLK FESTIVAL. (CN/0712-6263). **4130**

MARIPOSA WEEKLY GAZETTE AND MINER. (US). **5637**

MARITIME ANTHROPOLOGICAL STUDIES : MAST. (NE/0922-1476). **241**

MARITIME DEFENCE. (UK/0950-558X). **4179**

MARITIME PATROL AVIATION. (CN). **28**

MARITIME WORKER. (AT). **1690**

MARJORIE KINNAN RAWLINGS JOURNAL OF FLORIDA LITERATURE, THE. (US/1060-3409). **3410**

MARK. (FI). **930**

MARKEE (SANFORD, FLA.). (US/1073-8924). **4074**

MARKET LETTER. (UK/0951-3175). **Adv Mgr:** Joan Kairis, **Tel** (071)828-7272. **4314**

MARKET REPORT & NEWSLETTER. (US/0747-4121). **215**

MARKET WATCH (NEW YORK, N.Y.). (US/0277-9277). **2369**

MARKETING BULLETIN - DEPARTMENT OF MARKETING, MASSEY UNIVERSITY. (NZ/0113-6895). **930**

MARKETING BULLETIN (SYRACUSE). (US/0093-2736). **930**

MARKETING EDUCATORS' JOURNAL. (US). **930**

MARKETING INTELLIGENCE & PLANNING. (UK/0263-4503). **931**

MARKETING MIX (JOHANNESBURG, SOUTH AFRICA). (SA). **931**

MARKETING NEWS. (US/0025-3790). **931**

MARKETING OPTIONS. (CN/0822-3998). **931**

MARKETING RESEARCH (CHICAGO, ILL.). (US/1040-8460). **932**

MARKETING REVIEW. (US). **932**

MARKETING SCIENCE (PROVIDENCE, R.I.). (US/0732-2399). **932**

MARKETING (TORONTO). (CN/0025-3642). **932**

MARKETPLACE MAGAZINE. (US/1054-2264). **692**

MARKING INDUSTRY MAGAZINE. (US/0164-4939). **933**

MARKT, DER. (AU). **933**

MARKWICK MIDDEN. (CN/0821-3275). **2459**

MARLBORO HERALD-ADVOCATE. (US). **Adv Mgr:** Linda Wilson. **5743**

MARLIN. (US/0749-2006). **2308**

MARMAC GUIDE TO PHILADELPHIA, A. (US/0736-8127). **5483**

MARQUEE (TORONTO). (CN/0700-5008). **4074**

MARQUEE (WASHINGTON, D.C.). (US). **5365**

MARQUETTE COUNTY TRIBUNE, THE. (US). **5768**

MARQUETTE LAW REVIEW. (US/0025-3987). **3006**

MARQUETTE TRIBUNE (MILWAUKEE), THE. (US/0025-3995). **Adv Mgr:** A. Scott DeVouton, **Tel** (414)288-1739. **5768**

MARRIAGE & FAMILY REVIEW. (US/0149-4929). **2283**

MARRIAGE PARTNERSHIP. (US/0897-5469). **4975**

MARS DAILY SENTINEL, LE. (US). **5671**

MARSHALL ISLANDS JOURNAL (1980). (XE/0892-2098). **5806**

MARSHFIELD MAIL, THE. (US) **Adv Mgr:** Rita Ritterhouse, **Tel** (417)859-2014. **5704**

MART (MONTREAL). (CN/0319-2709). **2121**

MARTHA'S KIDLIT NEWSLETTER. (US/1045-4292). **1066**

MARTHA'S VINEYARD. (US/1052-5785). **107**

MARTHA'S VINEYARD TIMES, THE. (US/8750-1449). **Adv Mgr:** Don Lyons and Nelson Sigelman. **5689**

MARVEL AGE. (US/8750-4367). **4863**

MARVEL FANFARE (NEW YORK, N.Y.). (US/0746-7664). **4863**

MARXISM TODAY. (UK/0025-4118). **2519**

MARXIST REVIEW. LONDON. (UK/0965-9749). **4543**

MARXISTISCHE BLATTER. (GW/0542-7770). **4543**

MARYLAND AND DELAWARE GENEALOGIST, THE. (US/0025-4150). **2459**

MARYLAND BAR JOURNAL, THE. (US/0025-4177). **3006**

MARYLAND FARMER (BALTIMORE, MD. : 1979). (US/0279-7895). **107**

MARYLAND GRAPEVINE, THE. (US/1052-6161). **Adv Mgr:** Myra Novak. **178**

MARYLAND HISTORIAN, THE. (US/0025-424X). **2622**

MARYLAND HISTORICAL MAGAZINE. (US/0025-4258). **2745**

MARYLAND LAW REVIEW (1936). (US/0025-4282). **3006**

MARYLAND LAWYERS' MANUAL. (US). **3007**

MARYLAND MAGAZINE (1988). (US/1040-7936). **2745**

MARYLAND MEDICAL JOURNAL (1985). (US/0886-0572). **3606**

MARYLAND MUSIC EDUCATOR. (US). **4130**

MARYLAND NURSE, THE. (US/0047-6080). **3861**

MARYLAND PROSECUTOR, THE. (US/0748-2957). **3108**

MARYLAND REGISTER. (US/0360-2834). **3007**

MARYLAND TIMES-PRESS. (US). **Adv Mgr:** Sue Lathbery. **5686**

MARYSVILLE ADVOCATE, THE. (US). **Adv Mgr:** Randy Meerian. **5677**

MARYSVILLE JOURNAL-TRIBUNE. (US/1069-2207). **Adv Mgr:** Peyton Rardin. **5729**

MAS (NEW YORK, N.Y.). (US/1046-5634). **2267**

MASABEY 'ENWS. (IS/0792-0970). **1690**

MASCHINE, DIE. (GW/0340-5737). **2121**

MASCHINENBAU. (SZ). **2121**

MASON COUNTY NEWS. (US). **5752**

MASS COMM REVIEW. (US/0193-7707). **1116**

MASS HIGH TECH. (US/8750-2100). **5127**

MASS MEDIA : RIVISTA BIMESTRALE DELLA COMUNICAZIONE. (IT). **1116**

MASS SPECTROMETRY BULLETIN. (UK/0025-4738). **1011**

MASS SPECTROMETRY REVIEWS. (US/0277-7037). **1017**

MASS TRANSIT (WASHINGTON, D.C.). (US/0364-3484). **5386**

MASSACHUSETTS CPA REVIEW. (US/0025-4770). **748**

MASSACHUSETTS DAILY COLLEGIAN, THE. (US/0890-0434). **Adv Mgr:** Danielle Yaniro, **Tel** (413)545-3500. **5689**

MASSACHUSETTS DIRECTORY OF MANUFACTURERS. (US/0195-5810). **3484**

MASSACHUSETTS LAW REVIEW. (US/0163-1411). **3007**

MASSACHUSETTS LAWYERS DIARY AND MANUAL : INCLUDING BAR DIRECTORY. (US/0738-369X). **Adv Mgr:** N. Bergamo. **3007**

MASSACHUSETTS LAWYERS WEEKLY. (US/0196-7509). **3007**

MASSACHUSETTS MUSIC NEWS. (US/0147-2550). **4130**

MASSACHUSETTS NURSE, THE. (US/0163-0784). **3861**

MASSACHUSETTS POLITICAL ALMANAC, THE. (US/0277-1314). **4664**

MASSACHUSETTS REVIEW, THE. (US/0025-4878). **2850**

MASSACHUSETTS VOTER / LEAGUE OF WOMEN VOTERS OF MASSACHUSETTS, THE. (US). **4481**

MASSAGE (DAVIS, CALIF.). (US/1057-378X). **Adv Mgr:** C Gerhard. **2599**

MASSIMARIO DI GIURISPRUDENZA DEL LAVORO. (IT). **3151**

MASSOG. (US/0738-1549). **2459**

MAST (MADISON, WIS.). (US/1051-824X). **Adv Mgr:** same as editor. **1145**

MAST. MANITOBA ASSOCIATION OF SCHOOL TRUSTEES. (CN/0381-9531). **4664**

MASTER CARD. (US). **2490**

MASTER DRAWINGS. (US/0025-5025). **380**

MASTER SERMON SERIES. (US/0362-0808). **4976**

MASTERING FOOD ALLERGIES. (US). **2349**

MASTHEAD (MISSISSAUGA). (CN/0832-512X). **4816**

MATATU. (NE/0932-9714). **3410**

MATEKON. (US/0025-1127). **1504**

MATEMAATTISTEN AINEIDEN AIKAKAUSKIRJA. (FI/0025-5149). **3517**

MATERIA MEDICA POLONA (ENGLISH EDITION). (PL/0025-5246). **4314**

MATERIAL CULTURE. (US/0883-3680). **241**

MATERIAL UND ORGANISMEN; BEIHEFT. (GW/0025-5270). **1017**

MATERIALI E STRUTTURE. (IT). **303**

MATERIALIEN / LANDESUMWELTAMT. (GW). **2177**

MATERIALIEN ZUR POLITISCHEN BILDUNG. (GW/0340-0476). **4481**

MATERIALPRUFUNG. (GW/0025-5300). **2104**

MATERIALS AUSTRALIA. (AT/1037-7107). **4008**

MATERIALS EDGE. (UK/0952-5211). **4008**

MATERIALS ENGINEERING. (US/0025-5319). **2105**

MATERIALS EVALUATION. (US/0025-5327). **2105**

MATERIALS FORUM. (AT/0883-2900). **1986**

MATERIALS MANAGEMENT AND DISTRIBUTION. (CN/0025-5343). **1618**

MATERIALS PERFORMANCE. (US/0094-1492). **2105**

MATERIALS SCIENCE & ENGINEERING. A, STRUCTURAL MATERIALS : PROPERTIES, MICROSTRUCTURE AND PROCESSING. (SZ/0921-5093). **Adv Mgr:** Ms. W van Cattenburch (Amsterdam). **2105**

MATERIALY BADAWCZE - INSTYTUT METEOROLOGII I GOSPODARKI WODNEJ. SERIA, HYDROLOGIA I OCEANOLOGIA. (PL/0239-6297). **1416**

MATERIALY BADAWCZE. SERIA: GOSPODARKA WODNA I OCHRONA WOD. (PL). **5536**

MATERIAUX ET TECHNIQUES. (FR/0032-6895). **2106**

MATERIAY BADAWCZE. SERIA: INZYNIERIA WODNA. (PL). **2093**

MATERNAL & CHILD HEALTH (RICHMOND, SURREY). (UK/0262-0200). **3738**

MATH NOTEBOOK. (US/0272-8885). **1882**

MATHEMATICA IN EDUCATION. (US/1065-2965). **1763**

MATHEMATICAL BIOSCIENCES. (US/0025-5564). **464**

MATHEMATICAL GAZETTE. (UK/0025-5572). **3519**

MATHEMATICAL METHODS IN THE APPLIED SCIENCES. (GW/0170-4214). **3519**

MATHEMATICAL REPORTS (CHUR, SWITZERLAND). (SZ/0275-7214). **3520**

MATHEMATICAL REVIEWS. (US/0025-5629). **3542**

MATHEMATICAL SPECTRUM. (UK/0025-5653). **3520**

MATHEMATICAL SYSTEMS IN ECONOMICS. (GW/0344-3302). **3520**

MATHEMATICS AND COMPUTER EDUCATION. (US/0730-8639). **3520**

MATHEMATICS AND COMPUTERS IN SIMULATION. (NE/0378-4754). **1282**

MATHEMATICS IN SCHOOL. (UK/0305-7259). **3520**

MATHEMATICS MAGAZINE. (US/0025-570X). **3521**

MATHEMATICS OF COMPUTATION. (US/0025-5718). **3521**

MATHEMATICS STUDENT (AHMEDABAD), THE. (II/0025-5742). **3521**

MATHEMATICS TEACHER, THE. (US/0025-5769). **3521**

MATHEMATICS TEACHING. (UK/0025-5785). **3521**

MATHS & STATS. (UK/0959-3950). **3522**

MATRIART (TORONTO). (CN/1182-6169). **358**

MATRIMONIAL STRATEGIST, THE. (US/0736-4881). **Adv Mgr:** Nancy Gedder, **Tel** (212)741-8300. **3121**

MATRIX (LENNOXVILLE). (CN/0318-3610). **Adv Mgr:** Beryl Parker or Linda Leith. **3410**

MATSYA. (II/0253-9314). **2308**

MATURE HEALTH. (US/0891-9232). **4789**

MATURE LIVING (NASHVILLE). (US/0162-427X). **5180**

MATURE OUTLOOK. (US/0742-0935). **5180**

MATURE OUTLOOK NEWSLETTER. (US/0748-4003). **5180**

MATURE TRAVELER. (US/1043-2280). **5484**

MAUI UPDATE, THE. (US/0895-9390). **5484**

MAURITIUS POLICE MAGAZINE, THE. (MF). **3169**

MAXIMUM ROCKNROLL. (US/0743-3530). **4130**

MAY DAY PICTORIAL NEWS. (US/0025-6129). **5452**

MAYBERRY GAZETTE, THE. (US/1043-2639). **1134**

MAYGAMV. (II). **3301**

MAYO CLINIC PROCEEDINGS. (US/0025-6196). **3799**

MAYVILLE MONITOR. (US). **5692**

MAZAL U'BRACHA. (IS/0334-6838). **Adv Mgr:** Erez Yemini. **1618**

MBB : BELASTINGBESCHOUWINGEN. (NE/0005-8335). **4737**

MBEA TODAY. (US/0892-9831). **1763**

MBI. MEDICO-BIOLOGIC INFORMATION. (BU/0324-119X). **3606**

MBI MUSIC BUSINESS INFORMATIONS. (UK/0768-8172). **4130**

MC : THE MODERN CHURCHMAN. (UK/0025-7597). **4976**

MCALESTER NEWS-CAPITAL, THE. (US). **Adv Mgr:** Kay Coffee. **5732**

MCCALL'S. (US/0024-8908). **5561**

MCCOOK DAILY GAZETTE. (US). **5706**

MCCORMICK MESSENGER. (US). **5743**

MCCURTAIN GAZETTE. (US). **Adv Mgr:** Margie Jones. **5732**

MCCUTCHEON'S DETERGENTS & EMULSIFIERS. NORTH AMERICAN EDITION. (US/0145-7055). **1044**

MCCUTCHEON'S EMULSIFIERS & DETERGENTS (INTERNATIONAL EDITION). (US/0734-0567). **1027**

MCCUTCHEON'S FUNCTIONAL MATERIALS. NORTH AMERICAN EDITION. (US/0734-0559). **1027**

MCDUFFIE PROGRESS, THE. (US). 5654

MCFARLAND COMMUNITY LIFE. (US/0883-6566). 5769

MCGILL LAW JOURNAL. (CN/0024-9041). 3132

MCGILL NEWS, THE. (CN/0024-9068). 1093

MCGREGOR'S WHO OWNS WHOM. (SA). 692

MCINTOSH TIMES, THE. (US). 5697

MCKEAN COUNTY MINER (SMETHPORT, PA. : 1974). (US). Adv Mgr: G. Nichols, Tel (814)362-6563. 5737

MCKINNEY MAZE, THE. (US/0736-2420). 2460

MCKNIGHT'S LONG-TERM CARE NEWS. (US/1048-3314). 5295

MCLEAN PROVIDENCE JOURNAL AND FAIRFAX HERALD, THE. (US). Adv Mgr: Chris Brockway, Tel (703)356-3181. 5759

MCM. (IT/0393-8190). 324

MCN, THE AMERICAN JOURNAL OF MATERNAL CHILD NURSING. (US/0361-929X). 3861

MCVILLE MESSENGER. (US/8750-5436). 5725

MDE. MANAGERIAL AND DECISION ECONOMICS. (UK/0143-6570). 1504

MDI MANAGEMENT JOURNAL. (II/0970-6623). 692

ME NAISET. (FI/0025-6277). 5561

MEADVILLE TRIBUNE (1955). (US/0747-2412). 5737

MEANING OF LIFE, THE. (US/1071-328X). 4352

MEANJIN (PARKVILLE, VIC.). (AT/0815-953X). 3410

MEANS CONCRETE COST DATA. (US/1075-0533). 620

MEANS CONSTRUCTION COST INDEXES. (US/0361-9591). 620

MEANS ELECTRICAL COST DATA. (US/0748-7002). 620

MEANS HISTORICAL COST INDEXES. (US/0277-8610). 620

MEANS SQUARE FOOT COSTS : RESIDENTIAL, COMMERCIAL, INDUSTRIAL, INSTITUTIONAL. (US/0732-815X). 621

MEASUREMENT AND EVALUATION IN COUNSELING AND DEVELOPMENT. (US/0748-1756). 1763

MEASUREMENTS & CONTROL. (US/0148-0057). 5127

MEAT & POULTRY. (US/0892-6077). 2349

MEAT INDUSTRY DIGEST. (AT). Adv Mgr: D. Curtis. 2349

MEAT SCIENCE. (UK/0309-1740). 215

MECANIQUE, MATERIAUX, ELECTRICITE. (FR/0025-6439). 2121

MECCANICA (MILAN). (NE/0025-6455). 4428

MECHANICAL ENGINEERING (NEW YORK, N.Y. 1919). (US/0025-6501). 2122

MECHANICAL ENGINEERING NEWS (FAYETTEVILLE, ARK.). (US/0025-651X). 2122

MECHANICAL INCORPORATED ENGINEER. (UK/0954-6529). Adv Mgr: Sydney Jary Ltd., Tel 44 272 741640. 2122

MECHANICAL MUSIC. (US/1045-795X). 4130

MECHANICAL PARTS/LABOR ESTIMATING GUIDE. DOMESTIC GLASS. (US/0884-0156). 5418

MECHANISMS OF AGEING AND DEVELOPMENT. (SZ/0047-6374). 584

MECHANO BUYERS DIRECTORY. NORTHERN CALIFORNIA. (US). 3484

MECHATRONICS (OXFORD). (UK/0957-4158). 1195

MECHELECIV. (US/0047-6382). 5127

MECKLENBURG GAZETTE, THE. (US). Adv Mgr: Lou Sullivan. 5723

MECKLENBURG TIMES. (US). Adv Mgr: Norris Rumfelt. 5723

MED TEC INTERNATIONAL. (NZ). 3607

MEDAL LONDON. (UK/0263-7707). 2781

MEDAL NEWS HINDHEAD. 1989. (UK/0958-4986). Adv Mgr: Mrs. C. Hartman. 2781

MEDALS YEARBOOK. (US/0737-6529). 4049

MEDDELANDEN FRAN INSTITUTIONEN FOR NORDISKA SPRAK VID STOCKHOLMS UNIVERSITET: MINS. (SW/0348-3568). 3301

MEDDELELSER OM GRNLAND. BIOSCIENCE. (DK/0106-1054). 464

MEDDELELSER OM GRNLAND. GEOSCIENCE. (DK/0106-1046). 1358

MEDDELELSER OM GRNLAND. MAN & SOCIETY. (DK/0106-1062). 2519

MEDECIN BIOPATHOLOGISTE PARIS, LE. (FR/0999-6338). Adv Mgr: Dr. Laget, Tel 33 1 40476060. 3607

MEDECIN DU QUEBEC. (CN/0025-6692). 3607

MEDECINE DU SPORT. (FR/0025-6722). 3955

MEDECINE ET ARMEES. (FR/0300-4937). 4049

MEDECINE FOETALE ET ECHOGRAPHIE EN GYNECOLOGIE. (FR/1150-5966). Adv Mgr: Dr. Niddam. 3607

MEDECINE TROPICALE. (FR/0025-682X). 3986

MEDEDELINGEN VAN DE WERKGROEP VOOR TERTIAIRE EN KWARTAIRE GEOLOGIE. (NE/0165-280X). 1387

MEDEX. (BE). 3607

MEDIA AND METHODS. (US/0025-6897). 1900

MEDIA BOX. (BE). 4852

MEDIA, CULTURE & SOCIETY. (UK/0163-4437). 5251

MEDIA FORUM. (IT/0394-9575). Adv Mgr: Piero Silvesvri. 762

MEDIA GUIDE INTERNATIONAL. EDITION : BUSINESS/PROFESSIONAL PUBLICATIONS. (US/0164-1743). 762

MEDIA HISTORY DIGEST. (US/0195-6779). 2922

MEDIA INFORMATION AUSTRALIA. (AT/0312-9616). 1116

MEDIA MARKET GUIDE (NEW YORK, N.Y.). (US). 762

MEDIA MARKET GUIDE. TOP 100 MARKETING AREAS. (US/0149-7626). 762

MEDIA MARKETING NEWS. (BE). 933

MEDIA SCANDINAVIA. (DK/0076-5821). 4816

MEDIA SELECTION. (GW/0934-4217). 692

MEDIA SPECTRUM. (US/0731-3675). Adv Mgr: B.H Brooks, Tel (517)699-1717. 3230

MEDIAEVAL SCANDINAVIA SUPPLEMENTS. (DK/0106-102X). 2697

MEDIAEVALIA (BINGHAMTON). (US/0361-946X). 2697

MEDIAFILE. (US/0885-4610). 2922

MEDIAPLUSNEWS. (IT/1120-1932). 692

MEDIASPOUVOIRS. (FR/0762-5642). 1117

MEDIATORS OF INFLAMMATION. (UK/0962-9351). 3607

MEDIAWATCH (ALEXANDRIA, VA.). (US/1053-8321). 1117

MEDIC. METODOLOGIA E DIDATTICA CLINICA. (US). 3607

MEDICAL ABBREVIATIONS - 8600 CONVENIENCES AT THE EXPENSE OF COMMUNICATIONS AND SAFETY. (US). 3607

MEDICAL ADVERTISING NEWS. (US/0745-0907). Adv Mgr: Maureen Williams, Tel (609)530-0044. 762

MEDICAL & BIOLOGICAL ENGINEERING & COMPUTING. (UK/0140-0118). 3695

MEDICAL ANTHROPOLOGY. (US/0145-9740). 241

MEDICAL ANTHROPOLOGY QUARTERLY. (US/0745-5194). 241

MEDICAL ASPECTS OF HUMAN SEXUALITY. (US/0025-7001). 5188

MEDICAL AUDIT NEWS. (UK/0959-2903). 748

MEDICAL CARE. (US/0025-7079). 3608

MEDICAL DECISION MAKING. (US/0272-989X). Adv Mgr: Diane Sherel, Tel 215-546-0313 or FAX: 215-790-9330. 1215

MEDICAL DEVICES, DIAGNOSTICS & INSTRUMENTATION REPORTS. (US/0163-2426). 3608

MEDICAL DEVISE REGISTER. (US/0278-808X). 3788

MEDICAL DIGEST, THE. (SA). 3608

MEDICAL DIRECTORY. (UK/0305-3342). 3915

MEDICAL DIRECTORY OF NEW YORK STATE. (US/0273-0561). 3608

MEDICAL EDUCATION. (UK/0308-0110). 3609

MEDICAL ELECTRONICS (PITTSBURGH, PA.). (US/0149-9734). 3609

MEDICAL FOCUS (WURZBURG, GERMANY). (GW/0724-8172). 3609

MEDICAL GROUP MANAGEMENT JOURNAL. (US/0899-8949). 3609

MEDICAL GROUP NEWS. (US/0025-7265). 3609

MEDICAL HISTORY. (UK/0025-7273). 3609

MEDICAL HUMANITIES REVIEW. (US/0892-2772). Adv Mgr: Diane Pfeil. 3609

MEDICAL HYPNOANALYSIS JOURNAL. (US/0894-5098). Adv Mgr: Rhonda Shipley, Tel (216)867-6677. 4603

MEDICAL IMAGING AND MONITORING. (AT). Adv Mgr: David Strong. 3609

MEDICAL INDUSTRY EXECUTIVE. (US/1060-5193). Adv Mgr: Larry Jacobs, Tel (603)772-0730. 3609

MEDICAL INTERFACE. (US/0896-4831). Adv Mgr: Jane Armstrong. 3609

MEDICAL JOURNAL OF AUSTRALIA. (AT/0025-729X). 3610

MEDICAL JOURNAL - UNIVERSITY OF TORONTO. (CN/0833-2207). Adv Mgr: Kenmars Inc., Tel (416)864-9132. 3610

MEDICAL LABORATORY SCIENCES. (UK/0308-3616). 3610

MEDICAL LABORATORY WORLD. (UK/0140-3028). 3610

MEDICAL LAW REPORTS. (UK/0957-9346). Adv Mgr: J. Arcker, Tel 011 44 494 79262. 3008

MEDICAL MALPRACTICE DEFENSE REPORTER, THE. (US/0893-8229). 3008

MEDICAL MALPRACTICE PREVENTION. (US/0885-744X). 3008

MEDICAL MARKETING & MEDIA. (US/0025-7354). 933

MEDICAL MEETINGS. (US/0093-1314). Adv Mgr: B Ventre. 3610

MEDICAL MEETINGS ANNUAL DIRECTORY. (US). Adv Mgr: B. Ventre. 3610

MEDICAL PRINCIPLES AND PRACTICE. (SZ/1011-7571). 3611

MEDICAL PROBLEMS OF PERFORMING ARTISTS. (US/0885-1158). 3611

MEDICAL PRODUCT MANUFACTURING NEWS. (US/0893-6250). 3611

MEDICAL PRODUCTS MARKETERS DIRECTORY. (US/0275-4940). 3695

MEDICAL PRODUCTS SALES. (US/0279-4802). 3611

MEDICAL PROGRESS THROUGH TECHNOLOGY. (NE/0047-6552). 3695

MEDICAL REFERENCE SERVICES QUARTERLY. (US/0276-3869). 3230

MEDICAL RESEARCH FUNDING BULLETIN. (US). 3611

MEDICAL TEACHER. (UK/0142-159X). 3611

MEDICAL TECHNOLOGIST AND SCIENTIST, THE. (UK/0309-2666). 3612

MEDICAL TRIBUNE (1980). (US/0279-9340). 3612

MEDICAL WORLD NEWS. (US/0025-763X). 3612

MEDICAMENTOS DE ACTUALIDAD. (SP/0025-7656). 4315

MEDICARE-MEMORANDUM (OUTPATIENT CLINIC ED.). (US/0896-4815). 5296

MEDICINA (BUENOS AIRES). (AG/0025-7680). Adv Mgr: Delisio Horacio J. 3613

MEDICINA CLINICA. (SP/0025-7753). 3613

MEDICINA DE REHABILITACION. (SP/0214-8714). 4381

MEDICINA DEL LAVORO. (IT/0025-7818). 3613

MEDICINA DELLO SPORT. (IT). 3955

MEDICINA E INFORMATICA. (IT/1120-3773). Adv Mgr: Dott Dalla, Tel 06-86207165. 3613

MEDICINAL & AROMATIC PLANTS ABSTRACTS. (II/0250-4367). 517

MEDICINAL RESEARCH REVIEWS. (US/0198-6325). 4315

MEDICINE AND LAW. (GW/0723-1393). 3742

MEDICINE AND SCIENCE IN SPORTS AND EXERCISE. (US/0195-9131). 3955

MEDICINE AND WAR. (UK/0748-8009). Adv Mgr: Anne Kidson. 3613

MEDICINE (BALTIMORE). (US/0025-7974). 3613

MEDICINE DIGEST. (UK). 3613

MEDICINE DIGEST. ASIA. (HK). Adv Mgr: Mary, Tel 519 9303. 3613

MEDICINE INTERNATIONAL. THE MONTHLY ADD-ON JOURNAL. UK EDITION. (UK/0144-0403). 3613

Advertising Accepted Index

MEDICINE NORTH AMERICA. (CN/0225-3895). **Adv Mgr:** C.Bourke. **3614**

MEDICINE, SCIENCE, AND THE LAW. (UK/0025-8024). **Adv Mgr:** Alex Reeve. **3742**

MEDICINSKI PREGLED. (YU/0025-8105). **3614**

MEDICINSKI RAZGLEDI. (XV/0025-8121). **3614**

MEDICOM. (NR/0253-0961). **3614**

MEDIEN + ERZIEHUNG. (GW/0341-6860). **1117**

MEDIEN KONKRET. (GW/0931-9808). **1117**

MEDIEVAL CERAMICS. (UK). **2592**

MEDIEVAL PROSOPOGRAPHY. (US/0198-9405). **2698**

MEDIFACTS [SOUND RECORDING]. (CN/0317-7017). **3738**

MEDIFAX ROMA. (IT/1121-2810). **3614**

MEDIOS AUDIO-VISUALES. (SP). **4074**

MEDISCH CONTACT. (NE). **3614**

MEDISTAT / WORLD MEDICAL MARKET ANALYSIS. (UK). **3614**

MEDITERRANEAN HISTORICAL REVIEW. (UK). **Adv Mgr:** Anne Kidson. **2698**

MEDITERRANEAN LANGUAGE REVIEW. (GW/0724-7567). **3301**

MEDITERRANEE MEDICALE. (FR/0302-9263). **Adv Mgr:** A. Trebucq. **3614**

MEDIUM AEVUM. (UK/0025-8385). **3301**

MEDIUM (BOTHELL, WASH.). (US/0889-0773). **Adv Mgr:** Marilyn Camp, **Tel** (509)534-8776. **3230**

MEDIUM (FRANKFURT). (GW/0025-8350). **1117**

MEDIZIN AKTUELL. (GW/0323-5386). **3615**

MEDIZIN, GESELLSCHAFT, UND GESCHICHTE : JAHRBUCH DES INSTITUTS FUER GESCHICHTE DER MEDIZIN DER ROBERT BOSCH STIFTUNG. (GW/0939-351X). **Adv Mgr:** MS. Szoradi. **3615**

MEDIZIN IN WEST-BERLIN, DIE. (GW). **3915**

MEDIZIN UND GESELLSCHAFT. (GW/0323-6153). **3615**

MEDIZINISCHE MONATSSCHRIFT FUER PHARMAZEUTEN. (GW/0342-9601). **4315**

MEDIZINISCHE MONATSSCHRIFT (STUTTGART). (GW/0025-8474). **3615**

MEDIZINTECHNIK (STUTTGART). (GW/0344-9416). **3615**

MEDWAY VALLEY NEWS (1978). (CN/0711-1754). **2198**

MEED. (UK/0047-7230). **1574**

MEEKER HERALD, THE. (US). **Adv Mgr:** Lisa Cook. **5643**

MEER & YACHTEN. (FR). **594**

MEERESFORSCHUNG. (GW/0341-6836). **1452**

MEERESTECHNIK. (GW/0025-8644). **2093**

MEETING MANAGER, THE. (US/8750-7218). **Adv Mgr:** B. McGlynn, **Tel** (214)712-7733. **692**

MEETING REPORTS, CARDIOVASCULAR. (US/1063-2468). **3708**

MEETINGS MONTHLY, NEWS BULLETIN. (CN/0841-9663). **5484**

MEETINGS (NEW YORK, N.Y. 1980). (US/8755-1810). **3230**

MEGAFON. (AG). **3410**

MEGAMOT / MOSAD SOLD LEMAAN HA-YELED VEHA-NOAR. (IS/0025-8679). **5209**

MEIE ELU OUR LIFE. (CN/0047-665X). **Adv Mgr:** Astrid Vaikla, **Tel** (416)466-0951. **5789**

MEIERIPOSTEN. (NO/0025-8776). **196**

MEITAN KEXUE JISHU. (CC/0253-2336). **2143**

MEJ : MEDIA EDUCATION JOURNAL. (UK). **Adv Mgr:** M. Hubbard. **1763**

MEKEEL'S WEEKLY STAMP NEWS. (US). **2785**

MELA NOTES. (US/0364-2410). **3230**

MELANESIAN JOURNAL OF THEOLOGY : JOURNAL OF THE MELANESIAN ASSOCIATION OF THEOLOGICAL SCHOOLS. (PP). **4976**

MELANGES DE SCIENCE RELIGIEUSE. (FR/0025-8911). **4976**

MELANOMA RESEARCH. (UK/0960-8931). **3821**

MELBOURNE JOURNAL OF POLITICS. (AT/0085-3224). **4481**

MELBURNER BLETER. (AT). **3410**

MELITA THEOLOGICA. (MM/1012-9588). **4976**

MELUS. (US/0163-755X). **3410**

MELVILLE ADVANCE. (CN). **Adv Mgr:** Mark Orosz. **5789**

MELYEPITESI ES VIZEPITESI SZAKIRODALMI TAJEKOZTATO. (HU/0231-0732). **2027**

MEMBERS' DIRECTORY / FEDERATION OF HONG KONG INDUSTRIES. (HK). **1618**

MEMBERS DIRECTORY / THE INSTITUTION OF ENVIRONMENTAL HEALTH OFFICERS. (UK/0264-5947). **4790**

MEMBERSHIP DIRECTORY / AMERICAN ASSOCIATION OF EXPORTERS AND IMPORTERS. (US). **845**

MEMBERSHIP DIRECTORY - AMERICAN CHAMBER OF COMMERCE IN EGYPT. (UA). **820**

MEMBERSHIP DIRECTORY AND BUYERS' GUIDE - AMERICAN FROZEN FOOD INSTITUTE. (US/0361-0888). **2350**

MEMBERSHIP DIRECTORY - GYPSY LORE SOCIETY, NORTH AMERICAN CHAPTER. (US/0193-1598). **2322**

MEMBERSHIP DIRECTORY / MARYLAND GENEALOGICAL SOCIETY. (US/1056-0394). **2460**

MEMBERSHIP DIRECTORY / NATIONAL ASSOCIATION FOR MUSIC THERAPY. (US/8755-2892). **4130**

MEMBERSHIP DIRECTORY / NATIONAL ASSOCIATION OF BUSINESS ECONOMISTS. (US). **Adv Mgr:** David Williams. **1504**

MEMBERSHIP DIRECTORY - NATIONAL SOCIETY FOR PERFORMANCE AND INSTRUCTION. (US/0730-7675). **1224**

MEMBERSHIP DIRECTORY OF THE AMERICAN PSYCHOLOGICAL SOCIETY. (US/1051-1830). **4603**

MEMBERSHIP DIRECTORY - PHILATELIC TRADERS' SOCIETY. (UK/0305-3245). **2785**

MEMBERSHIP DIRECTORY - SUBURBAN NEWSPAPERS OF AMERICA. (US/0270-4641). **5661**

MEMBERSHIP LIST - AMERICAN MENSA LIMITED. (US/0363-3616). **Adv Mgr:** Shoshana Shafran. **5233**

MEMBERSHIP LIST - CANADIAN ASSOCIATION OF MUSIC LIBRARIES (1984). (CN/0828-7007). **3231**

MEMBERSHIP LIST - THE GALPIN SOCIETY. (UK). **Adv Mgr:** T.K. Diblet, **Tel** 0304 374772. **4130**

MEMBRANE BIOCHEMISTRY. (US/0149-046X). **490**

MEMBRANE LIPIDS. (UK/0952-0422). **490**

MEMBRANE PROTEINS. (UK/0143-4233). **490**

MEMBRANE QUARTERLY. (US/1052-0953). **Adv Mgr:** V. Totten, **Tel** (512)471-4033. **1027**

MEMO. (LE). **1505**

MEMO (QUEBEC). (CN/0848-0877). **Adv Mgr:** Maire-Claire Dupre. **693**

MEMOIR - NEW MEXICO BUREAU OF MINES & MINERAL RESOURCES. (US/0548-5975). **2143**

MEMOIRES DE BIOSPEOLOGIE. (FR/0184-0266). **464**

MEMOIRES DE LA SOCIETE GENEALOGIQUE CANADIENNE-FRANCAISE. (CN/0037-9387). **2460**

MEMOIRES VIVES MONTREAL. (CN/1188-8296). **303**

MEMOIRES VIVES (MONTREAL). (CN/1188-8296). **274**

MEMOIRS OF THE CONNECTICUT ACADEMY OF ARTS AND SCIENCES. (US/0069-8970). **2850**

MEMORANDUM - AMERICAN NEWSPAPER PUBLISHERS ASSOCIATION. (US/0270-9864). **4816**

MEMORIA DEL CONGRESO INTERNACIONAL DE LITERATURA IBEROAMERICANA. (PE). **3347**

MEMORIA (TURIN, ITALY). (IT/0392-4564). **2623**

MEMORIE DELLA SOCIETA ENTOMOLOGICA ITALIANA. (IT/0037-8747). **5612**

MEMORIES PLUS. (US/1062-9556). **5180**

MEMORY LANE (LEIGH-ON-SEA, ESSEX). (UK/0266-8033). **4130**

MEMPHIS. (US/0162-282X). **Adv Mgr:** Jeffrey Goldberg. **2538**

MEMPHIS BUSINESS JOURNAL. (US/0747-167X). **693**

MEMPHIS FLYER, THE. (US). **2490**

MEMPHIS STATE UNIVERSITY LAW REVIEW. (US/0047-6714). **3009**

MENARD NEWS AND MESSENGER, THE. (US). **5752**

MENDOCINO BEACON, THE. (US). **5637**

MENDY AND THE GOLEM. (US/0278-4432). **5018**

MENNESKER OG RETTIGHETER. (NO/0800-0735). **4510**

MENNONITE (1936), THE. (US/0025-9330). **Adv Mgr:** Larry Penner. **5063**

MENNONITE BRETHREN HERALD. (CN/0025-9349). **Adv Mgr:** S. Brandt. **5063**

MENNONITE FAMILY HISTORY. (US/0730-5214). **2460**

MENNONITE HISTORIAN. (CN/0700-8066). **5064**

MENNONITE REPORTER. (CN/0380-0121). **5789**

MENNONITE WEEKLY REVIEW. (US/0889-2156). **5677**

MENNONITISCHE POST. (CN/0705-4041). **5064**

MENOMINEE TRIBAL NEWS. (US). **Adv Mgr Tel** (715)799-5167. **2267**

MENS & MELODIE. (NE/0025-9462). **4131**

MEN'S EXERCISE. (US/1059-9169). **Adv Mgr:** Bruce Soffer. **2599**

MEN'S WEAR OF CANADA. (CN/0025-9535). **1086**

MENSA BULLETIN. (US/0025-9543). **5233**

MENSAJE (SANTIAGO, CHILE). (CL/0025-956X). **4976**

MENSAJERO (SAN FRANCISCO, CALIF.), EL. (US/1040-5712). **2746**

MENSALOHA. (US/8750-4529). **4603**

MENSCH & BUERO. (GW/0933-8241). **4212**

MENSCH + RECHT : QUARTALSZEITSCHRIFT DER SCHWEIZERISCHEN GESELLSCHAFT FUR DIE EUROPAISCHE MENSCHENRECHTSKONVENTION (SGEMKO) / HERAUSGEBERIN SGEMKO. (SZ). **4510**

MENSCH UND BUERO. (GW/0933-8241). **4212**

MENTAL HANDICAP : JOURNAL OF THE BRITISH INSTITUTE OF MENTAL HANDICAP. (UK/0261-9997). **5296**

MENTAL HEALTH-HUMAN RESOURCES CONFERENCE GUIDE. (US/1064-685X). **Adv Mgr:** Jody Bowland. **3616**

MENTAL HEALTH NURSING. (UK). **Adv Mgr:** Graham Watt, **Tel** 011 44 532 730973. **3861**

MENTAL RETARDATION (WASHINGTON). (US/0047-6765). **1882**

MENTALITIES. (NZ/0111-8854). **4604**

MENTOR (SINGAPORE). (SI). **1763**

MENTORING INTERNATIONAL. (CN/0843-5405). **4604**

MER & BATEAUX PARIS. (FR/0999-7148). **594**

MER. MARINE ENGINEERS REVIEW. (UK/0047-5955). **1987**

MER (TOKYO, JAPAN). (JA/0503-1540). **1452**

MERCADO. (AG/0325-0687). **1574**

MERCANTILE AGENT. (AT). **846**

MERCATO METALSIDERURGICO. (IT). **4008**

MERCED SUN-STAR. (US). **5637**

MERCER BUSINESS : A PUBLICATION OF MERCER COUNTY CHAMBER. (US/0194-9101). **Adv Mgr:** Donna Hill. **693**

MERCER ISLAND REPORTER. (US). **5761**

MERCER LAW REVIEW. (US/0025-987X). **Adv Mgr:** Jonathan Martin, **Tel** (912)752-2624. **3009**

MERCHANT MAGAZINE, THE. (US/0739-9723). **2402**

MERCURY (POTTSTOWN, PA.). (US). **Adv Mgr:** 52. **5737**

MERCURY-REGISTER. (US). **Adv Mgr:** Lonnie Steedman. **5637**

MERCURY (SAN FRANCISCO). (US/0047-6773). **397**

MEREDITH NEWS, THE. (US). **Adv Mgr:** David French. **5708**

MERGER AND ACQUISITION SOURCEBOOK. (US/0742-602X). **693**

MERGERS & ACQUISITIONS. (US/0026-0010). **798**

MERIDIAN (BUNDOORA, VIC.). (AT/0728-5914). **3347**

MERIDIAN - MAP & GEOGRAPHY ROUND TABLE (AMERICAN LIBRARY ASSOCIATION). (US/1040-7421). **Adv Mgr:** David Cobb, **Tel** (617) 495-2417. **2582**

MERI'S MONTHLY CIRCULAR. (JA/0026-6809). **1574**

MERKBLATTER — Advertising Accepted Index

MERKBLATTER / LANDESUMWELTAMT. (GW). **2236**

MERLYN'S PEN. (US/0882-2050). **1066**

MERRILL LYNCH EUROMONEY DIRECTORY, THE. (UK). **798**

MERRILL-PALMER QUARTERLY (1960). (US/0272-930X). **4604**

MERRILL'S ILLINOIS LEGAL TIMES. (US/1063-3014). **Adv Mgr:** Chuck Carman. **3009**

MESPA PRINCIPAL. (US). **1866**

MESQUITE MESSENGER. (US). **2402**

MESSAGE (1993). (US/1071-5215). **Adv Mgr:** Tariq Kahn. **5043**

MESSENGER (FORT DODGE, IOWA), THE. (US/0740-6991). **5671**

MESSENGER (MADISON, N.C.). (US/0892-1814). **5723**

MESSENGER-PRESS. (US). **5710**

MESSENGER (SCARBOROUGH). (CN/0228-2828). **5789**

MESSING ABOUT IN BOATS. (US). **4904**

MESTER (LOS ANGELES). (US/0160-2764). **Adv Mgr Tel** (310)825-6014. **3411**

META (MONTREAL). (CN/0026-0452). **3302**

METABOLIC, PEDIATRIC AND SYSTEMIC OPHTHALMOLOGY (1985). (US/0882-889X). **3876**

METAL ARCHITECTURE. (US/0885-5781). **Adv Mgr:** J.Riester, **Tel** (708)674-2200. **303**

METAL BULLETIN MONTHLY. (UK/0373-4064). **4009**

METAL BULLETIN, THE. (UK/0026-0533). **4009**

METAL CD. (UK/0967-442X). **Adv Mgr:** Elspeth Thomson. **4131**

METAL CONSTRUCTION NEWS. (US/8756-2014). **Adv Mgr:** J.Garvey, **Tel** (708)674-2200. **621**

METAL FABRICATING NEWS. (US/0026-055X). **3484**

METAL FINISHING. (US/0026-0576). **4009**

METAL POWDER REPORT. (UK/0026-0657). **4009**

METAL STAMPING. (US/1040-967X). **Adv Mgr:** Kathy Delollis. **4027**

METALL (BERLIN). (GW/0026-0746). **4009**

METALLBEWERKING. (NE). **4009**

METALLI. (IT). **4009**

METALLOBERFLACHE. (GW/0026-0797). **4009**

METALLOFIZIKA (KIEV). (UN/0204-3580). **4009**

METALLURGICAL PLANT AND TECHNOLOGY : MPT. (GW/0171-4511). **4010**

METALLURGICAL TRANSACTIONS. A. PHYSICAL METALLURGY AND MATERIALS SCIENCE. (US/0360-2133). **4010**

METALLURGICAL TRANSACTIONS. B, PROCESS METALLURGY. (US/0360-2141). **4010**

METALSMITH. (US/0270-1146). **374**

METALURGIA (SAO PAULO). (BL/0026-0983). **4011**

METALURGIA Y ELECTRICIDAD. (SP/0026-0991). **Adv Mgr:** Antonio Recio Cuevas. **4011**

METAPHILOSOPHY. (UK/0026-1068). **4352**

METAPHYSICAL REVIEW, THE. (AT/0814-8805). **3411**

METASCIENCE. (AT/0815-0796). **5128**

METEOR NEWS. (US/0146-9959). **397**

METHOD (LOS ANGELES, CALIF.). (US/0736-7392). **4353**

METHODIST HISTORY. (US/0026-1238). **5064**

METHODIST RECORDER. (UK). **Adv Mgr:** R. Blanchard. **5064**

METHODOLOGY AND SCIENCE. (NE/0543-6095). **5209**

METHODS AND FINDINGS IN EXPERIMENTAL AND CLINICAL PHARMACOLOGY. (SP/0379-0355). **4315**

METHODS IN ORGANIC SYNTHESIS. (UK/0265-4245). **1012**

METHODS OF INFORMATION IN MEDICINE. (GW/0026-1270). **3616**

METLFAX. (US/0026-1297). **4012**

METRIC TODAY. (US/1050-5628). **Adv Mgr:** V. Antoine, **Tel** (818)363-5606. **4031**

METRIKA. (GW/0026-1335). **3523**

METRO HANDBOOK AND DIRECTORY OF MEMBERS. (US/0887-1973). **3231**

METRO NEW YORK DIRECTORY OF MANUFACTURERS. (US/0731-7417). **3484**

METRO PRESS. (US). **Adv Mgr:** Patty Toneff, **Tel** (418)836-2221. **5729**

METRO (SAN JOSE, CALIF.). (US/0882-4290). **2538**

METRO SPORTS MAGAZINE. (US). **4904**

METRO TELECASTER (1977). (CN/0708-2568). **1134**

METRO TIMES (DETROIT, MICH.), THE. (US/0746-4045). **Adv Mgr:** Rick Ficorelli. **5692**

METROPOLIS (PARIS). (FR/0223-5633). **2828**

METROPOLITAN ALMANAC (1989). (US/1045-5108). **2538**

METROPOLITAN HOME. (US/0273-2858). **2902**

METROPOLITAN NEWS-ENTERPRISE. (US/0897-2281). **5637**

METROPOLITAN REVIEW (CHICAGO, ILL.). (US/0893-8490). **2828**

METROPOLITAN TORONTO ... ANNUAL VISITORS GUIDE. (CN/0836-4443). **5484**

METU KALENDORIUS - PRISIKELIMO PARAPIJA, EKONOMINE SEKCIJA. (CN/0380-1373). **2490**

METUCHEN, EDISON REVIEW. (US/0747-2390). **5710**

MEUBELECHO. (BE/0772-6287). **2906**

MEXICAN STUDIES. (US/0742-9797). **1505**

MEXICO & CENTRAL AMERICAN HANDBOOK. (UK). **5484**

MEXICO DESCONOCIDO. (MX). **Adv Mgr:** Alejandro Guerrero Molina. **5484**

MEXICON. (GW/0720-5988). **2746**

MEYER'S DIRECTORY OF GENEALOGICAL SOCIETIES IN THE U.S.A. AND CANADA. (US/0732-3395). **2460**

MEZOGAZDASAGI ELELMISZERIPARI STATISZTIKAI ZSEBKONYU / LOZPONTI STATISZTIKAI HIVATAL. (HU/0238-7891). **5333**

MIAMI CHIEF (CANADIAN, TEX.). (US/0746-0082). **5752**

MIAMI MEDICAL LETTER. (US/1047-2509). **3616**

MIAMI MEDICAL LETTER EN ESPANOL. (US/1047-2495). **3616**

MIAMI MEDICINE : THE OFFICIAL PUBLICATION OF THE DADE COUNTY MEDICAL ASSOCIATION. (US). **Adv Mgr:** Karn Cochrane. **3616**

MIAMI MENSUAL. (US/0273-9372). **Adv Mgr:** Ana Soler. **2538**

MIAMI REPUBLICAN, THE. (US). **Adv Mgr:** Lori, **Tel** (913)294-2311. **5677**

MIAMI TODAY. (US/0889-2296). **Adv Mgr:** Alicia Coya. **5650**

MICHIANA SEARCHER. (US/0736-5004). **2460**

MICHIGAN AFL-CIO NEWS. (US/0026-1998). **1690**

MICHIGAN ALUMNUS. (US/0746-2565). **1102**

MICHIGAN BAR JOURNAL, THE. (US/0164-3576). **Adv Mgr:** Mary Stowell, **Tel** (517)372-9030 ext. 3035. **3009**

MICHIGAN BEVERAGE NEWS. (US/0026-2021). **2369**

MICHIGAN CHRISTIAN ADVOCATE. (US/0026-2072). **4977**

MICHIGAN CHRONICLE, THE. (US). **Adv Mgr:** Sherry Hatcher, **Tel** (313)963-5522 ext. 246. **5692**

MICHIGAN CITIZEN. (US/1072-2041). **Adv Mgr:** Mark Hicks. **5693**

MICHIGAN COUNTIES. (US/0896-646X). **4665**

MICHIGAN CPA, THE. (US/0026-2064). **Adv Mgr:** Sara Bocketti. **748**

MICHIGAN DAILY, THE. (US/0745-967X). **Adv Mgr:** Harris Winters, **Tel** (313)764-0554. **5693**

MICHIGAN DISTRIBUTORS DIRECTORY. (US/0890-4049). **694**

MICHIGAN FIRE SERVICE NEWS. (US). **2291**

MICHIGAN FLORIST, THE. (US/0026-217X). **Adv Mgr:** Barbara Doyle. **2435**

MICHIGAN GERMANIC STUDIES. (US/0098-8030). **Adv Mgr:** Harold Scholler. **3302**

MICHIGAN GOLFER. (US). **Adv Mgr Tel** (312)227-4200. **4904**

MICHIGAN GOLFER. (US/1071-2313). **4904**

MICHIGAN HISTORICAL REVIEW, THE. (US/0890-1686). **Adv Mgr:** Carol Riddle. **2746**

MICHIGAN HOSPITALS. (US/0026-220X). **3789**

MICHIGAN JOURNAL OF POLITICAL SCIENCE. (US/0733-4486). **4481**

MICHIGAN LAW REVIEW. (US/0026-2234). **3009**

MICHIGAN LIVING. (US/0735-1798). **Adv Mgr:** Kerry Rende. **5484**

MICHIGAN MANUFACTURERS DIRECTORY. (US/0736-2889). **3484**

MICHIGAN MEDICINE. (US/0026-2293). **3616**

MICHIGAN MIDDLE SCHOOL JOURNAL. (US/0270-6571). **1764**

MICHIGAN MUNICIPAL REVIEW. (US/0026-2331). **Adv Mgr:** Judi Campbell. **4665**

MICHIGAN NURSE. (US/0026-2366). **Adv Mgr Tel** (517)349-5640. **3861**

MICHIGAN OPTOMETRIST, THE. (US/1071-1627). **Adv Mgr:** Amy Holmes. **4216**

MICHIGAN OUT-OF-DOORS. (US/0026-2382). **Adv Mgr:** Bill Donahue. **2198**

MICHIGAN PROFESSIONAL ENGINEER (1990). (US/1054-5840). **Adv Mgr:** Jim Hagerty, **Tel** (414)466-0610. **1987**

MICHIGAN QUARTERLY REVIEW. (US/0026-2420). **Adv Mgr:** Doris Knight. **3347**

MICHIGAN RETAILER, THE. (US/0889-0439). **Adv Mgr:** Wright, **Tel** (800)366-3699. **879**

MICHIGAN ROMANCE STUDIES. (US/0270-3629). **3302**

MICHIGAN RUNNER, THE. (US/0279-1773). **4904**

MICHIGAN SLAVIC MATERIALS. (US/0543-9930). **3302**

MICHIGAN SNOWMOBILER. (US/0746-2298). **5386**

MICHIGAN SPEECH-LANGUAGE-HEARING ASSOCIATION JOURNAL / MSHA. (US/0742-3284). **4391**

MICHIGAN SPORTSMAN (OSHKOSH WIS.). (US/0539-8908). **4874**

MICHIGAN TOWNSHIP NEWS. (US). **Adv Mgr:** Daynell McCall, **Tel** (517)321-6467. **4665**

MICHIGANA. (US/0462-372X). **2460**

MICHIGAN'S OIL & GAS NEWS (1983). (US/0746-5769). **Adv Mgr:** Emily, **Tel** (517)772-5181. **4264**

MICKLE STREET REVIEW, THE. (US/0194-1313). **3411**

MICKY MAUS. (GW). **1066**

MICRO ECONOMICS / THE BOSTON COMPUTER SOCIETY. (US/0883-4296). **694**

MICRO MONEY. (US/0742-9398). **1269**

MICRO SOFTWARE REPORT. (US/8755-5786). **3231**

MICROBIAL ECOLOGY IN HEALTH AND DISEASE. (UK/0891-060X). **3616**

MICROBIOLOGICA. (IT/0391-5352). **567**

MICROBIOLOGICAL REVIEWS. (US/0146-0749). **567**

MICROCIRCULATION, ENDOTHELIUM, AND LYMPHATICS. (US/0740-9451). **3616**

MICROCOMPUTER APPLICATIONS (ANAHEIM). (US/0820-0750). **1269**

MICROCOMPUTER REVIEW. (US/8755-7525). **1269**

MICROCOMPUTERS FOR INFORMATION MANAGEMENT. (US/0742-2342). **1269**

MICROELECTRONICS AND RELIABILITY. (UK/0026-2714). **2072**

MICROFORM MARKET PLACE. (US/0362-0999). **4822**

MICROFORM REVIEW. (US/0002-6530). **3231**

MICROGRAPHICS NEWSLETTER. (US/0883-9808). **1195**

MICROGRAVITY SCIENCE AND TECHNOLOGY. (GW/0938-0108). **4412**

MICROMATH : A JOURNAL OF THE ASSOCIATION OF TEACHERS OF MATHEMATICS. (UK/0267-5501). **3523**

MICRON AND MICROSCOPICA ACTA. (UK/0739-6260). **573**

MICROPOROUS MATERIALS. (NE/0927-6513). **986**

MICROPROCESSING AND MICROPROGRAMMING. (NE/0165-6074). **Adv Mgr:** W Van Cattenburch. **1269**

MICROPROCESSORS AND MICROSYSTEMS. (UK/0141-9331). **1230**

MICROPSYCH NETWORK. (US/0748-2051). **4604**

MICROSCOPE (LONDON). (US/0026-282X). **573**

MICROSCOPIA ELECTRONICA Y BIOLOGIA CELULAR : ORGANO OFICIAL DE LAS SOCIEDADES LATINOAMERICANA DE MICROSCOPIA ELECTRONICA E IBEROAMERICANA DE BIOLOGIA CELULAR. (AG/0326-3142). **573**

MICROSCOPY. (UK/0026-2838). **573**

MICROSCOPY SOCIETY OF AMERICA BULLETIN. (US/1062-9785). **573**

MICROSTATION MANAGER. (US/1057-9567). **Adv Mgr Tel** (505)471-8822. **1195**

MICROTECNIC. (SZ/0026-2854). **4031**

MICROTIMES (PLEASANT HILL, CALIF.). (US/1065-0148). **1270**

MICROWAVE JOURNAL (EURO-GLOBAL ED.). (US/0192-6217). **2072**

MID-AMERICA COMMERCE & INDUSTRY. (US/0193-2047). **950**

MID AMERICA FARMER GROWER, THE. (US/1040-1423). **Adv Mgr:** Lisa LaRose, **Tel** (314)547-2244. **108**

MID-AMERICA FOLKLORE. (US/0275-6013). **2322**

MID AMERICA INSURANCE. (US/0026-2935). **2888**

MID-AMERICA THEOLOGICAL JOURNAL. (US/0734-9882). **4977**

MID-AMERICAN REVIEW. (US/0747-8895). **Adv Mgr:** Wayne Barham. **3411**

MID-AMERICAN REVIEW OF SOCIOLOGY. (US/0732-913X). **5252**

MID-ATLANTIC COUNTRY. (US/0888-1022). **2538**

MID-ATLANTIC FOODSERVICE NEWS. (US/0888-5311). **2350**

MID-ATLANTIC JOURNAL OF BUSINESS, THE. (US/0732-9334). **694**

MID-ATLANTIC SALES GUIDE TO HIGH-TECH COMPANIES. (US/1040-0575). **5128**

MID-ATLANTIC THOROUGHBRED. (US/1056-3245). **Adv Mgr:** Kristen Mowery. **2800**

MID-CONTINENT BOTTLER. (US/0026-2978). **2369**

MID-NORTH MONITOR, THE. (CN/0227-3853). **5789**

MID-SOUTH HUNTING & FISHING NEWS. (US/0894-7767). **4874**

MID-WEST CONTRACTOR. (US/0026-3044). **621**

MID-YORK WEEKLY, THE. (US). **Adv Mgr:** Charles Mahaffy, **Tel** (315)853-6103. **5718**

MIDCONTINENTAL JOURNAL OF ARCHAEOLOGY, MCJA. (US/0146-1109). **274**

MIDDLE EAST, ABSTRACTS AND INDEX. (US/0162-766X). **2635**

MIDDLE EAST AND WORLD CONSTRUCTION DIRECTORY. (LE). **621**

MIDDLE EAST AND WORLD FOOD DIRECTORY. (LE). **2350**

MIDDLE EAST CIVIL AVIATION. (US/1054-9838). **28**

MIDDLE EAST EXECUTIVE REPORTS. (US/0271-0498). **3132**

MIDDLE EAST FOOD TRADE & CATERING EQUIPMENT. (UK/0265-6469). **2350**

MIDDLE EAST INDUSTRY & TRANSPORT. (UK/0261-1473). **5387**

MIDDLE EAST INSIGHT. (US/0731-9371). **4482**

MIDDLE EAST JOURNAL OF ANESTHESIOLOGY. (LE/0544-0440). **3683**

MIDDLE EAST JOURNAL, THE. (US/0026-3141). **2635**

MIDDLE EAST (LONDON, ENGLAND : 1985). (UK/0305-0734). **Adv Mgr:** Chris Irwin. **1505**

MIDDLE EAST MONITOR. (US/0026-315X). **4482**

MIDDLE EAST POLICY. (US/1061-1924). **4528**

MIDDLE EAST QUARTERLY. (US). **2526**

MIDDLE EAST REPORT (NEW YORK, N.Y. : 1988). (US/0899-2851). **Adv Mgr:** M. Zanger. **2526**

MIDDLE EAST REVIEW (SAFFRON WALDEN, ESSEX). (UK). **1638**

MIDDLE EAST STUDIES ASSOCIATION BULLETIN. (US/0026-3184). **2769**

MIDDLE EASTERN STUDIES. (UK/0026-3206). **Adv Mgr:** Anne Kidson. **2769**

MIDDLE SCHOOL JOURNAL. (US/0094-0771). **1764**

MIDDLEBURY INDEPENDENT (MIDDLEBURY, IND. : 1974). (US). **5665**

MIDDLETOWN NEWS (MIDDLETOWN, IND. : 1913). (US). **Adv Mgr:** Jack White. **5665**

MIDDLETOWN PRESS, THE. (US). **Adv Mgr:** Tom Howard. **5645**

MIDGETS & MINI-SPRINTS RACING NEWS. (US/0889-5279). **4904**

MIDI MEDIA. (FR/0295-3943). **Adv Mgr:** Rebecca Arditti. **1117**

MIDLAND HISTORY. (UK/0047-729X). **2698**

MIDLANDS BUSINESS JOURNAL. (US/0194-4525). **694**

MIDLOTHIAN MIRROR, THE. (US). **Adv Mgr:** Debbie Garvin. **5752**

MIDSTREAM (NEW YORK). (US/0026-332X). **5051**

MIDWEEK EAGLE. (US). **5725**

MIDWEST ALLIANCE IN NURSING JOURNAL / MAIN. (US/1048-499X). **Adv Mgr:** J. Spain, **Tel** (317)541-3600. **3861**

MIDWEST ENGINEER. (US/0026-3370). **1987**

MIDWEST FLYER MAGAZINE. (US/0273-7515). **28**

MIDWEST HISTORICAL AND GENEALOGICAL REGISTER. (US/0271-8685). **2460**

MIDWEST MOTORIST, THE. (US/0026-3435). **Adv Mgr:** Deborah Klein. **5484**

MIDWEST RACING NEWS. (US/0047-732X). **4904**

MIDWEST REVIEW (WAYNE, NEB. : 1975). (US/0740-3208). **2746**

MIDWESTERN DENTIST. (US/0026-3478). **1330**

MIDWIFERY TODAY. (US/0891-7701). **3765**

MIDWIFERY TODAY AND CHILDBIRTH EDUCATION. (US). **Adv Mgr:** Nicole Van DeVeere. **3765**

MIDWIVES CHRONICLE AND NURSING NOTES. (UK/0026-3524). **3765**

MIFFLINBURG TELEGRAPH. (US). **Adv Mgr:** John Stamm. **5737**

MIGRATION (BERLIN, WEST). (GW/0721-2887). **1920**

MIGRATION NEWS. (SZ/0026-3583). **1920**

MIJU HAN'GUK ILBO. (US/1041-7281). **Adv Mgr:** Yang Ho Lee, **Tel** (202)723-3060. **5647**

MIKE SHAYNE MYSTERY MAGAZINE. (US/0026-3621). **5074**

MIKROELEKTRONIK. (GW). **2072**

MIKROKOSMOS (STUTTGART). (GW/0026-3680). **573**

MILANO FINANZA : MF. (IT). **798**

MILCH PRAXIX UND RINDERMAST, DIE. (GW/0343-0200). **215**

MILCHWIRTSCHAFTLICHE BERICHTE AUS DEN BUNDESANSTALTEN WOLFPASSING UND ROTHOLZ. (AU/0544-1706). **196**

MILCHWISSENSCHAFT. (GW/0026-3788). **196**

MILFORD CABINET AND WILTON JOURNAL, THE. (US). **Adv Mgr:** K. Johnson. **5708**

MILIEU MAGAZINE ALPHEN AAN DEN RIJN. (NE/0924-6282). **2177**

MILITAIRE SPECTATOR, DE. (NE). **4050**

MILITARY & POLICE UNIFORM ASSOCIATION NEWSLETTER, THE. (US/1072-8112). **2795**

MILITARY BUSINESS REVIEW. (US/0883-3427). **950**

MILITARY CHAPLAIN, THE. (US/0026-3958). **4050**

MILITARY CLUB & HOSPITALITY. (US/0886-8832). **2350**

MILITARY CLUBS & RECREATION. (US/0192-2718). **4050**

MILITARY ENGINEER, THE. (US/0026-3982). **1987**

MILITARY HISTORY JOURNAL. (SA/0026-4016). **4050**

MILITARY HISTORY OF THE SOUTHWEST. (US/0898-8064). **Adv Mgr:** Jane Tanner, **Tel** (817)565-2124. **4050**

MILITARY HISTORY OF THE WEST. (US/1071-2011). **Adv Mgr:** Jane Tanner. **4050**

MILITARY LIFESTYLE (UNITED STATES EDITION). (US/0885-8403). **Adv Mgr:** Mike Jennings, **Tel** (914)997-6440. **4051**

MILITARY LIVING. (US/0740-5065). **4051**

MILITARY LIVING'S R & R REPORT. (US/0740-5073). **4051**

MILITARY MARKET. (US/0026-4067). **4051**

MILITARY MEDICINE. (US/0026-4075). **3617**

MILITARY MODELLING. (UK/0026-4083). **2774**

MILITARY (SACRAMENTO, CALIF.). (US/1046-2511). **Adv Mgr:** Rosalie Hernandez, **Tel** (800)4-info-ad. **4051**

MILITARY VEHICLES. (US/0893-3863). **4051**

MILITARY YEAR-BOOK. (II/0076-8782). **4051**

MILK AND LIQUID FOOD TRANSPORTER. (US/0199-2317). **5387**

MILK INDUSTRY. (UK/0026-4172). **196**

MILK PRODUCER. (UK/0026-4180). **197**

MILKWEED CHRONICLE. (US/0275-8113). **325**

MILLARD COUNTY CHRONICLE PROGRESS. (US/8750-3093). **5757**

MILLARD COUNTY GAZETTE, THE. (US). **5757**

MILLE LACS MESSENGER, THE. (US). **Adv Mgr:** Kevin Anderson, Patrice O'Leary. **5697**

MILLENNIUM. (UK/0305-8298). **4529**

MILLENNIUM FILM JOURNAL. (US/1064-5586). **4074**

MILLIMETER. (US/0164-9655). **4074**

MILLIMETRO, IL. (IT/0392-5498). **2922**

MILLING AND BAKING NEWS. (US/0091-4843). **202**

MILNE'S POULTRY DIGEST. (AT/1032-3767). **Adv Mgr:** Tracie Murray. **215**

MILPITAS POST. (US/0745-6212). **Adv Mgr:** Linda Schmitz. **5637**

MILTON COURIER, THE. (US). **5769**

MILTON QUARTERLY. (US/0026-4326). **Adv Mgr:** Jason Holtman, **Tel** (614)593-2831. **3347**

MILTONVALE RECORD, THE. (US). **Adv Mgr:** Richard Phelps. **5677**

MILWAUKEE COURIER. (US/0026-4350). **Adv Mgr:** Faithe Colas, **Tel** (414)449-4863. **5769**

MILWAUKEE JOURNAL, THE. (US/1052-4452). **5769**

MILWAUKEE LABOR PRESS. (US/0279-3741). **1690**

MILWAUKEE LAWYER, THE. (US/0148-3242). **3010**

MILWAUKEE MAGAZINE. (US/0741-1243). **Adv Mgr:** Pat Replia. **2538**

MILWAUKEE PROFESSIONAL NURSE. (US/0026-4369). **3861**

MILWAUKEE SENTINEL (1883), THE. (US/1052-4479). **5769**

MIMS. (UK/0027-0431). **4315**

MIMS AFRICA. (UK/0140-4415). **4315**

MIMS ANNUAL, AUSTRALIAN EDITION. (AT/0725-4709). **4315**

MIMS CARIBBEAN. (UK). **4315**

MIMS CROWS NEST. (AT/1035-5723). **4315**

MIMS DESK REFERENCE. (SA/0076-8847). **4316**

MIMS DISEASE INDEX. (AT/1035-5693). **Adv Mgr:** M McCathey. **3715**

MIMS HOSPITAL EQUIPMENT AND SUPPLIES. (AT/0159-9100). **Adv Mgr:** G. Hard, **Tel** 02 438-3558. **3789**

MIMS INDIA. (II/0970-1036). **Adv Mgr:** Pooja Sharma. **4316**

MIMS MEDICAL SPECIALTIES. (SA/0027-0431). **4316**

MIMS MIDDLE EAST. (UK/0302-4172). **3617**

MIMS UK. (UK). **Adv Mgr:** Kate Locks. **4316**

MIND. (UK/0026-4423). **4353**

MIND & LANGUAGE. (UK/0268-1064). **3302**

MIND BODY HEALTH DIGEST. (US/0898-3127). **3799**

MINE AND QUARRY. (UK/0369-1632). **Adv Mgr:** Graeme Ringsell. **2144**

MINE AND QUARRY MECHANISATION. (AT/0085-3453). **2144**

MINERACAO METALURGIA (1968). (BL/0100-6908). **4012**

MINERAL AND ELECTROLYTE METABOLISM. (SZ/0378-0392). **3799**

MINERAL PLANNING. (UK/0267-1409). **1441**

MINERAL PROCESSING AND EXTRACTIVE METALLURGY REVIEW. (UK/0882-7508). **2144**

MINERALOGICAL MAGAZINE. (UK/0026-461X). **1441**

MINERALOGICAL RECORD, THE. (US/0026-4628). **1441**

MINERALOGICAL SOCIETY BULLETIN. (UK/0263-9513). **1441**

MINERALOLTECHNIK — Advertising Accepted Index

MINERALOLTECHNIK. (GW/0341-1893). **1442**

MINERALS & METALLURGICAL PROCESSING. (US/0747-9182). **4012**

MINERALS ENGINEERING. (UK/0892-6875). **2144**

MINERAUX ET FOSSILES, LE GUIDE DU COLLECTIONNEUR. (FR/0335-6566). **Adv Mgr:** same as editor. **1358**

MINER'S NEWS. (US/0890-6157). **Adv Mgr:** Arnie Weber. **2145**

MINERVA ANESTESIOLOGICA. (IT/0375-9393). **3683**

MINERVA CARDIOANGIOLOGICA. (IT/0026-4725). **3708**

MINERVA CHIRURGICA. (IT/0026-4733). **3970**

MINERVA GINECOLOGICA. (IT/0026-4784). **3765**

MINERVA (LONDON). (UK/0026-4695). **Adv Mgr:** G. Anderson, **Tel** (081)682-1782. **5129**

MINERVA MEDICA. (IT/0026-4806). **3799**

MINERVA MEDICOLEGALE : ORGANO UFFICIALE DELLA SOCIETA ITALIANA DI MMEDICINA LEGALE E DELLE ASSICURAZIONI. (IT/0026-4849). **3742**

MINERVA OFTALMOLOGICA. (IT/0026-4903). **3876**

MINERVA ORTOPEDICA E TRAUMATOLOGICA. (IT). **3883**

MINERVA PEDIATRICA. (IT/0026-4946). **3906**

MINERVA PSICHIATRICA. (IT/0391-1772). **3931**

MINERVA STOMATOLOGICA. (IT/0026-4970). **1330**

MINERVA UROLOGICA E NEFROLOGICA. (IT/0393-2249). **3991**

MINERVA'S BULLETIN BOARD. (US/0897-6104). **4051**

MINES DIRECTORY. (US/0197-9965). **2145**

MINES MAGAZINE. (US/0096-4859). **1442**

MINI JOURNAL, LE. (CN/0225-5529). **1804**

MINI STORAGE MESSENGER, THE. (US/0273-5822). **695**

MINIATURE QUILTS. (US/1065-0245). **Adv Mgr:** Carol Newman. **5185**

MINIATURE WARGAMES. (UK). **2774**

MINIATURES DEALER (CLIFTON, VA. : 1985). (US/0882-9187). **2774**

MINIATURES SHOWCASE. (US/0896-7288). **2775**

MINING ANNUAL REVIEW. (UK/0076-8995). **2145**

MINING DEPARTMENT MAGAZINE. (UK/0307-9066). **2145**

MINING ENGINEER (LONDON). (UK/0026-5179). **2145**

MINING ENGINEERING. (US/0026-5187). **2145**

MINING EXPLORATION AND DEVELOPMENT REVIEW, BRITISH COLUMBIA AND YUKON TERRITORY. (CN/0318-1766). **2145**

MINING JOURNAL (1954). (US/0898-4964). **Adv Mgr:** Gail England. **5693**

MINING JOURNAL (LONDON. 1908). (UK/0026-5225). **2146**

MINING MAGAZINE (LONDON). (UK/0308-6631). **2146**

MINING MIRROR. (US). **2146**

MINING RECORD (1968), THE. (US/0026-5241). **2146**

MINING REVIEW (NORTH VANCOUVER). (CN/0711-3277). **2146**

MINING TECHNOLOGY (MANCHESTER). (UK/0026-5276). **2146**

MINING WORLD NEWS. (US/1047-7551). **2146**

MINISTRIES TODAY. (US/0891-5725). **Adv Mgr:** Bob Minotti, **Tel** (407)333-0600. **4977**

MINISTRY (WASHINGTON, D.C.). (US/0026-5314). **4977**

MINNEAPOLIS LABOR REVIEW, THE. (US/0274-9017). **1690**

MINNEAPOLIS/ST. PAUL CITYBUSINESS. (US/0883-3044). **Adv Mgr Tel** 591-2659. **695**

MINNEOLA RECORD (MINNEOLA, KAN. : 1976). (US). **Adv Mgr:** Jane Unruh. **5677**

MINNESOTA BUSINESS JOURNAL. (US/0192-5504). **695**

MINNESOTA CALLS. (US). **2539**

MINNESOTA CITIES. (US/0148-8546). **4665**

MINNESOTA DAILY, THE. (US). **Adv Mgr:** Michael Armel. **5697**

MINNESOTA FIRE CHIEF. (US/0026-5470). **Adv Mgr:** James Heim. **2291**

MINNESOTA FLYER. (US/0889-4809). **Adv Mgr:** Mary Ellen. **28**

MINNESOTA GENEALOGIST. (US/0581-0086). **2460**

MINNESOTA GROCER. (US). **2350**

MINNESOTA HORTICULTURIST, THE. (US/0026-5500). **2424**

MINNESOTA INSURANCE. (US/0740-8366). **2888**

MINNESOTA LITERATURE NEWSLETTER. (US/0890-0566). **Adv Mgr:** same as publisher. **3412**

MINNESOTA MANUFACTURERS REGISTER. (US/0738-1514). **3484**

MINNESOTA MEDICINE. (US/0026-556X). **3617**

MINNESOTA MONTHLY (COLLEGEVILLE, MINN.). (US/0739-8700). **Adv Mgr:** Steve Fox, **Tel** (612)371-5808. **2539**

MINNESOTA OUT-OF-DOORS. (US/0026-5608). **Adv Mgr:** Dan Hinton. **4874**

MINNESOTA POLICE JOURNAL. (US/0026-5624). **3169**

MINNESOTA REAL ESTATE JOURNAL. (US/0893-2255). **4841**

MINNESOTA REVIEW (NEW YORK, N.Y.). (US/0026-5667). **3347**

MINNESOTA SPORTSMAN. (US/0274-8622). **4874**

MINNESOTA UNITED METHODIST REPORTER. (US/0893-4142). **5697**

MINORITIES & WOMEN IN BUSINESS. (US/1053-2749). **Adv Mgr:** John Enoch. **5561**

MINORITY BUSINESS ENTREPRENEUR. (US/1048-0919). **Adv Mgr:** Barbara Daley. **695**

MINORITY BUSINESS NEWS U.S.A. (US). **Adv Mgr:** Sharon Davis, **Tel** (214)221-5501. **695**

MINORITY ENGINEER : ME, THE. (US/0884-1829). **1988**

MINORITY ENTRPRENEUR. A CLEARINGHOUSE FOR BUSINESS DEVELOPMENT. (US). **Adv Mgr:** Francois Leach, **Tel** (312)939-7222. **695**

MINORITY MBA. (US/1040-1547). **695**

MINORITY NURSE NEWSLETTER. (US/1071-9946). **3861**

MINOSEG ES MEGBIZHATOSAG. (HU/0580-4485). **4220**

MINOT DAILY NEWS, THE. (US/0885-3053). **Adv Mgr:** S. Baker, **Tel** (701)857-1927. **5726**

MINUTES / OCIC. (BE/0771-0461). **Adv Mgr:** Guido Convents. **4074**

MINWA NO TECHO. (JA). **2322**

MIO CONNECTION. (US). **2460**

MIRROR (DAWSON CREEK). (CN/0712-1105). **5790**

MIRROR-EXAMINER. (CN/1196-071X). **5790**

MIRROR MONTREAL. 1990. (CN/1182-5812). **Adv Mgr:** Paul Cassar. **2539**

MIRROR NEWS. (US/0191-4677). **3484**

MIRRORS : INTERNATIONAL HAIKU FORUM. (US). **3466**

MISCELLANEA MUSICOLOGICA (ADELAIDE). (AT/0076-9355). **4131**

MISCELLANIA ZOOLOGICA. (SP/0211-6529). **5591**

MISE A JOUR DE LA LISTE DES MEMBRES DU CIEE AU ... . (CN/0820-6309). **2699**

MISHPACHA (VIENNA, VA.). (US/1050-9348). **Adv Mgr:** Susan Wynne, **Tel** (301)657-3389. **5051**

MISINFORMATION. (US). **1195**

MISION (BUENOS AIRES, ARGENTINA). (AG). **4977**

MISSIOLOGY. (US/0091-8296). **Adv Mgr:** Steve Shenk, **Tel** (703)433-7477. **4977**

MISSION: JOURNAL OF MISSION STUDIES. (CN/1198-0400). **4978**

MISSIONALIA. (SA/0256-9507). **5013**

MISSIONARY HERALD (LONDON, ENGLAND : 1921). (UK). **5064**

MISSIONARY MONTHLY. (US/0161-7133). **4978**

MISSIONARY SEER. (US). **Adv Mgr:** Seth Moulton. **4978**

MISSISSAUGA BUSINESS REPORT. (CN). **Adv Mgr:** Bob Leuschner, **Tel** (416)273-8241. **695**

MISSISSAUGA NEWS. (CN). **5790**

MISSISSIPPI BANKER, THE. (US/0026-6159). **799**

MISSISSIPPI BUSINESS EDUCATION ASSOCIATION JOURNAL. (US). **695**

MISSISSIPPI BUSINESS JOURNAL, THE. (US/0195-0002). **695**

MISSISSIPPI COAST. (US/1045-1021). **Adv Mgr:** Jeff Bell. **2539**

MISSISSIPPI COLLEGE LAW REVIEW. (US/0277-1152). **3010**

MISSISSIPPI DENTAL ASSOCIATION JOURNAL. (US/0098-4329). **1330**

MISSISSIPPI EDUCATOR, THE. (US/0164-8683). **1764**

MISSISSIPPI FARM BUREAU NEWS. (US/0026-6205). **109**

MISSISSIPPI FOLKLORE REGISTER. (US/0026-6248). **2322**

MISSISSIPPI GENEALOGICAL EXCHANGE. (US/0540-3995). **2461**

MISSISSIPPI (JACKSON, MISS. 1982). (US/0747-1602). **2539**

MISSISSIPPI LAW JOURNAL. (US/0026-6280). **3011**

MISSISSIPPI LAW JOURNAL. CUMULATIVE TEN-YEAR INDEX FOR VOLUMES 41-50. (US). **3011**

MISSISSIPPI LEGION'AIRE. (US/0026-6299). **5233**

MISSISSIPPI LIBRARIES. (US/0194-388X). **3231**

MISSISSIPPI MAGAZINE (JACKSON). (US/0199-5677). **Adv Mgr:** Richard Roper, **Tel** (601)982-8418. **2539**

MISSISSIPPI MUD, THE. (US/0739-0424). **325**

MISSISSIPPI MUNICIPALITIES. (US/0026-6337). **4666**

MISSISSIPPI QUARTERLY, THE. (US/0026-637X). **2850**

MISSISSIPPI RAG, THE. (US/0742-4612). **4131**

MISSISSIPPI REVIEW. (US/0047-7559). **3412**

MISSISSIPPI RN, THE. (US/0026-6388). **3861**

MISSISSIPPI STATE MEDICAL ASSOCIATION DIRECTORY. (US). **3617**

MISSISSIPPI SUPERVISOR AND CHANCERY CLERK, CIRCUIT CLERK, TAX ASSESSOR & COLLECTOR. (US/0738-727X). **4666**

MISSISSIPPI WILDLIFE. (US/1044-0062). **4874**

MISSOULIAN (MISSOULA, MONT. 1961). (US/0746-4495). **5693**

MISSOURI ALUMNUS. (US/0745-0583). **1102**

MISSOURI DENTAL JOURNAL (JEFFERSON CITY, MO.). (US/0887-4646). **Adv Mgr:** Tammy Miller. **1330**

MISSOURI FB NEWS. (US/0026-6574). **109**

MISSOURI JOURNAL OF MATHEMATICAL SCIENCES. (US/0899-6180). **3523**

MISSOURI LAW REVIEW. (US/0026-6604). **3011**

MISSOURI MEDICINE. (US/0026-6620). **3617**

MISSOURI MUNICIPAL REVIEW. (US/0026-6647). **4666**

MISSOURI NURSE, THE. (US/0026-6655). **3861**

MISSOURI PRESS NEWS. (US/0026-6671). **4817**

MISSOURI REVIEW, THE. (US/0191-1961). **3412**

MISSOURI VALLEY TIMES-NEWS. (US). **Adv Mgr:** Charles Hickman, **Tel** (712)642-2791. **5671**

MISSOURI WILDLIFE. (US). **2218**

MITCHELL TECH SERVICE BULLETIN. (US/8755-4453). **5419**

MITTEILUNGEN AUS DER ARBEITSMARKT- UND BERUFSFORSCHUNG. (GW/0340-3254). **1691**

MITTEILUNGEN DER KARL-MAY-GESELLSCHAFT. (GW/0941-7842). **3412**

MITTEILUNGEN DER MATHEMATISCHEN GESELLSCHAFT IN HAMBURG. (GW/0340-4358). **3523**

MITTEILUNGEN DER OSTERREICHISCHEN GEOGRAPHISCHEN GESELLSCHAFT. (AU). **2569**

MITTEILUNGEN DER OSTERREICHISCHEN GEOLOGISCHEN GESELLSCHAFT. (AU/0378-8199). **1388**

MITTEILUNGEN DES DEUTSCHEN GERMANISTENVERBANDES. (GW/0418-9426). **1764**

MITTEILUNGEN DES VEREINS DEUTSCHER EMAILFACHLEUTE E.V. UND DES DEUTSCHEN EMAIL ZENTRUSM E.V. (GW/0723-886X). **2592**

Advertising Accepted Index — MONGOLIA

MITTEILUNGEN - DEUTSCHE GESELLSCHAFT FUR PHARMAKOLOGIE UND TOXIKOLOGIE. (GW/0934-4640). **4316**

MITTEILUNGEN FUER DIE VIEH- UND FLEISCHWIRTSCHAFT. (GW). **Adv Mgr:** Christel Adam. **216**

MITTEILUNGEN KLOSTERNEUBURG : REBE UND WEIN, OBSTBAU UND FRUCHTEVERWERTUNG. (AU/0007-5922). **2369**

MITTEILUNGEN - PTB. (GW/0030-834X). **5129**

MITTEILUNGSBLATT DER ARBEITSGEMEINSCHAFT KATHOLISCH-THEOLOGISCHER BIBLIOTHEKEN, AKTHB. (GW/0177-8358). **3231**

MITTEILUNGSBLATT - VERBAND DER BIBLIOTHEKEN DES LANDES NORDRHEIN WESTFALEN. (GW/0042-3629). **3232**

MITTELLATEINISCHES JAHRBUCH. (GW/0076-9762). **3302**

MIX (BERKELEY, CALIF.), THE. (US/0164-9957). **Adv Mgr:** Robin Boyce. **5317**

MK. MOBEL-KULTUR. (GW/0047-7796). **2906**

ML NEWSLETTER. (AT). **3303**

MLA JOB INFORMATION LIST. ENGLISH ED. (US). **4206**

MLA NEWS LETTER - MINNESOTA LIBRARY ASSOCIATION. (US/0748-9285). **3232**

MLA NEWSLETTER (NEW YORK). (US/0160-5720). **3303**

MLJEKARSTVO. (CI/0026-704X). **197**

MLO, MEDICAL LABORATORY OBSERVER. (US/0580-7247). **3617**

MM. (DK/0105-6972). **4131**

MM NEWS. (US). **3617**

MMR, MINERALS & METALS REVIEW. (II/0378-6366). **4012**

MMW. MUNCHENER MEDIZINISCHE WOCHENSCHRIFT. (GW/0341-3098). **Adv Mgr:** W. Beuse, **Tel** 089-43189-642-676. **3617**

MNA ACCENT. (US/0026-5586). **3862**

MO INFO. (US/0884-2205). **3232**

MOBILE & CELLULAR. (UK). **1160**

MOBILE & HOLIDAY HOMES. (UK). **2828**

MOBILE BEACON & ALABAMA CITIZEN, THE. (US). **Adv Mgr:** Cleretta Blackmon. **5627**

MOBILE BEAT INTERNATIONAL. (US/1058-0212). **Adv Mgr:** Bob Lindquist. **4131**

MOBILE EUROPE. (UK/1350-7362). **1160**

MOBILE HOME LIVING. (US/8750-0655). **2828**

MOBILE OFFICE. (US/1047-1952). **695**

MOBILE PRODUCT NEWS. (US/1044-1190). **1160**

MOBILE TELECOMMUNICATIONS NEWS. (UK/0267-1255). **1160**

MOBILIA (AMSTERDAM). (NE/0165-5302). **Adv Mgr:** Paul Pekelharing. **2906**

MOBILITY (WASHINGTON). (US/0195-8194). **Adv Mgr:** Richard McGuire. **695**

MOCI; MONITEUR DU COMMERCE INTERNATIONAL, LE. (FR/0026-9719). **3011**

MOD CONTRACTS BULLETIN. (UK/0269-0365). **695**

MODA. (IT). **1086**

MODA E BIJOUX. (IT). **2915**

MODASPORT VACANZE. (IT). **1086**

MODEL AUTO REVIEW. (UK/0267-2715). **2775**

MODEL AVIATION. (US/0744-5059). **2775**

MODEL AVIATION CANADA. (CN/0317-7831). **28**

MODEL BOATS. (UK/0144-2910). **594**

MODEL BUILDER (1981). (US/0731-4795). **2775**

MODEL RAILROADER. (US/0026-7341). **2775**

MODEL RAILROADING. (US/0199-1914). **Adv Mgr:** Chris Lane. **2775**

MODEL RETAILER (CLIFTON, VA.). (US/0191-6904). **2775**

MODEL SHIP BUILDER. (US/0199-7068). **4179**

MODEL SHIPWRIGHT. (UK). **Adv Mgr:** J. Mannering, **Tel** 071 583 2412. **2775**

MODELING OF GEO-BIOSPHERE PROCESSES. (GW/0938-9563). **1358**

MODELTEC. (US/0742-7107). **5129**

MODEM & TELECOMUNICAZIONI. (IT). **1160**

MODERN AFRICA. (UK/0264-8067). **Adv Mgr:** C. Herriman. **696**

MODERN AGE (CHICAGO). (US/0026-7457). **2539**

MODERN AGING RESEARCH. (US/0275-360X). **3754**

MODERN APPLICATIONS NEWS. (US/0277-9951). **4012**

MODERN ATHLETE AND COACH. (AT). **Adv Mgr:** same as editor. **4905**

MODERN AUSTRIAN LITERATURE. (US/0026-7503). **3412**

MODERN BREWERY AGE. (US/0026-7538). **2369**

MODERN BREWERY AGE BLUE BOOK. (US). **2369**

MODERN BRIDE. (US/0026-7546). **2283**

MODERN CASTING. (US/0026-7562). **4012**

MODERN DAIRY. (CN/0026-7651). **197**

MODERN DRAMA. (CN/0026-7694). **5366**

MODERN DRUMMER. (US/0194-4533). **Adv Mgr:** Robert Berenson. **4131**

MODERN FINISHING METHODS. (CN/0380-2299). **4012**

MODERN FOOD SERVICE NEWS. (US/0888-7645). **5072**

MODERN GROCER. (US/0026-7805). **Adv Mgr:** K. Gallagher. **2350**

MODERN HEALTHCARE (1977). (US/0160-7480). **3789**

MODERN INTERNATIONAL DRAMA. (US/0026-7856). **3412**

MODERN JEWISH STUDIES ANNUAL. (US/0270-9406). **3412**

MODERN JUDAISM. (US/0276-1114). **5051**

MODERN LANGUAGE JOURNAL (BOULDER, COLO.), THE. (US/0026-7902). **3303**

MODERN LANGUAGE STUDIES. (US/0047-7729). **3303**

MODERN LAW REVIEW. (UK/0026-7961). **3011**

MODERN LITURGY. (US/0363-504X). **4978**

MODERN LOGIC. (US/1047-5982). **3523**

MODERN MACHINE SHOP. (US/0026-8003). **2122**

MODERN MATURITY (NRTA ED.). (US/0747-6302). **5180**

MODERN MEDICINE (MINNEAPOLIS). (US/0026-8070). **3661**

MODERN MEDICINE (NEDERLANDSE ED.). (NE/0929-0141). **3617**

MODERN OFFICE TECHNOLOGY. (US/0746-3839). **4212**

MODERN PAINTERS (LONDON, ENGLAND). (UK/0953-6698). **358**

MODERN PLASTICS. (US/0026-8275). **4456**

MODERN POWER SYSTEMS. (UK/0260-7840). **1950**

MODERN RAILWAYS. (UK/0026-8356). **5433**

MODERN RECORDING & MUSIC. (US/0273-8511). **5317**

MODERN SCHOOLMAN, THE. (US/0026-8402). **4353**

MODERN SHORT STORIES. (US/1040-9068). **3412**

MODERNA SPRAK. (SW/0026-8577). **3303**

MODERNE MATHEMATIK IN ELEMENTARER DARSTELLUNG. (GW). **3523**

MODESTO BEE, THE. (US). **Adv Mgr:** Gary Moore, **Tel** (209)578-2080. **5637**

MODO DESIGN MAGAZINE. (IT/0391-3635). **2902**

MODOC COUNTY RECORD, THE. (US). **Adv Mgr:** Karen Badmark. **5637**

MODULAR HI-FI COMPONENTS SERVICE DATA. (US/0730-1197). **2073**

MOEBIUS. (CN/0225-1582). **3412**

MOHAIR AUSTRALIA. (AT). **5354**

MOHAVE COUNTY MINER (KINGMAN, ARIZ. : 1931). (US). **Adv Mgr:** Kathi Wright. **5630**

MOHAWK, THE. (US/0740-9699). **2461**

MOL. (JA/0386-5495). **2015**

MOLE. (CN/0827-2387). **4131**

MOLECULAR AND CELLULAR BIOLOGY. (US/0270-7306). **568**

MOLECULAR AND CELLULAR ENDOCRINOLOGY. (IE/0303-7207). **3732**

MOLECULAR AND CELLULAR NEUROSCIENCES. (US/1044-7431). **3838**

MOLECULAR AND CHEMICAL NEUROPATHOLOGY. (US/1044-7393). **3838**

MOLECULAR BIOLOGY OF THE CELL. (US/1059-1524). **Adv Mgr:** Edward Newman. **539**

MOLECULAR BIOLOGY REPORTS. (NE/0301-4851). **465**

MOLECULAR BIOTHERAPY. (US/0952-8172). **465**

MOLECULAR BRAIN RESEARCH. (NE/0169-328X). **3838**

MOLECULAR DYNAMICS NEWS. (US/1046-5219). **986**

MOLECULAR ENDOCRINOLOGY (BALTIMORE, MD.). (US/0888-8809). **3732**

MOLECULAR MEMBRANE BIOLOGY. (US/0968-7688). **491**

MOLECULAR PHARMACOLOGY. (US/0026-895X). **4316**

MOLEKULIARNAIA SPEKTROSKOPIIA. (RU). **4438**

MOLINI D'ITALIA. (IT/0026-9018). **202**

MOLODA UKRAINA. (CN/0026-9042). **2519**

MOLTEN SALTS BULLETIN. (FR). **1442**

MOM ... GUESS WHAT ... !. (US). **2795**

MOMENT (NEW YORK). (US/0099-0280). **5051**

MOMENTUM (WASHINGTON). (US/0026-914X). **4978**

MONAHANS NEWS (MONAHANS, TEX. : 1931). (US). **Adv Mgr:** David McCaffity, **Tel** (915)943-4313. **5752**

MONARCHY CANADA. (CN/0319-4019). **Adv Mgr:** same as editor. **4482**

MONASH UNIVERSITY LAW REVIEW. (AT/0311-3140). **3011**

MONASTIC STUDIES. (CN/0026-9190). **5032**

MONATSBERICHTE - OESTERREICHISCHES INSTITUT FUER WIRTSCHAFTSFORSCHUNG. (AU/0029-9898). **Adv Mgr:** Mrs. Shulz. **1505**

MONATSHEFTE FUER VETERINAERMEDIZIN. (GW/0026-9263). **5516**

MONATSSCHRIFT FUER DEUTSCHES RECHT. (GW/0340-1812). **3011**

MONATSSCHRIFT FUER KRIMINOLOGIE UND STRAFRECHTSREFORM. (GW/0026-9301). **3169**

MONDAY DEVELOPMENTS. (US/1043-8157). **5296**

MONDAY MAGAZINE (1983). (CN/0832-4719). **Adv Mgr:** Craig Maxwell, **Tel** (604)382-6188. **696**

MONDAY MORNING (INDIANAPOLIS, IND.). (US/0360-6171). **5065**

MONDE A BICYCLETTE, LE. (CN/0823-5570). **429**

MONDE DE LA BIBLE, LE. (FR/0154-9049). **5018**

MONDE DU ROCK. (CN/0823-0498). **4132**

MONDE ET LES MINERAUX, LE. (FR/0153-9167). **1442**

MONDE INFORMATIQUE, LE. (FR/0242-5769). **1195**

MONDE JUIF, LE. (FR/0026-9425). **2699**

MONDE JURIDIQUE, LE. (CN/0828-4989). **3011**

MONDES EN DEVELOPPEMENT. (FR/0302-3052). **Adv Mgr:** M. Scohy, **Tel** same as publisher. **1505**

MONDO APERTO. (IT/0026-9492). **1638**

MONDO BANCARIO. (IT/0026-9506). **799**

MONDO CINESE. (IT/0390-2811). **2507**

MONDO DEL LATTE, IL. (IT/0368-9123). **Adv Mgr:** Sede di Roma, **Tel** 06 4885648. **197**

MONDO E MISSIONE. (IT/0026-6094). **Adv Mgr:** Ferrari Andrea. **5032**

MONDO GIUDIZIARIO, IL. (IT). **3011**

MONETARIA. (MX/0185-1136). **Adv Mgr:** Claudio Antonovich. **799**

MONEY AFFAIRS / CEMLA, CENTRE FOR LATIN AMERICAN MONETARY STUDIES. (MX). **1506**

MONEY (CHICAGO, ILL.). (US/0149-4953). **906**

MONEY LAUNDERING ALERT. (US/1046-3070). **3087**

MONEY MANAGEMENT FOR PHYSICIANS. (US/0162-6507). **799**

MONGOLIA SOCIETY NEWSLETTER (1985), THE. (US/0894-6523). **2659**

MONGOLIA

Advertising Accepted Index

MONGOLIA SOCIETY OCCASIONAL PAPERS, THE. (US/0077-0396). **2659**

MONGOLIA SOCIETY SPECIAL PAPERS, THE. (US/0896-0925). **2659**

MONGOLIAN STUDIES. (US/0190-3667). **Adv Mgr:** Susie Drost. **2659**

MONIST, THE. (US/0026-9662). **4353**

MONITEUR ARCHITECTURE AMC, LE. (FR/0998-4194). **303**

MONITEUR BELGE. BELGISCH STAATSBLAD. (US). **3011**

MONITEUR DES TRAVAUX PUBLICS ET DU BATIMENT, LE. (FR/0026-9700). **Adv Mgr:** Dominique Laneyrie, **Tel** 011 33 1 40133319. **621**

MONITOR. (AT). **2073**

MONITOR (CLEARWATER, FLA.). (US/0895-8777). **933**

MONITOR DE LA FARMACIA Y DE LA TERAPEUTICA, EL. (SP). **4316**

MONITOR (TRENTON, N.J.), THE. (US/0746-8350). **Adv Mgr:** James Cassidy. **5710**

MONITORING TIMES. (US/0889-5341). **1135**

MONK (SAN FRANCISCO, CALIF.). (US/0899-6059). **Adv Mgr:** Jim Crotty. **4604**

MONOCLONAL ANTIBODIES. (UK/0261-4960). **3675**

MONOGRAPH AND RESEARCH SERIES (UNIVERSITY OF CALIFORNIA, LOS ANGELES. INSTITUTE OF INDUSTRIAL RELATIONS). (US/0739-439X). **5209**

MONOGRAPH / ONTARIO ASSOCIATION GEOGRAPHIC ENVIRONMENTAL EDUCATION, THE. (CN/0048-1793). **2569**

MONOGRAPH SERIES - FACULTY OF COMMERCE AND BUSINESS ADMINISTRATION, UNIVERSITY OF BRITISH COLUMBIA. (CN/0572-6972). **696**

MONOGRAPH SERIES IN WORLD AFFAIRS. (US/0077-0582). **4529**

MONOGRAPH SERIES ON MINERAL DEPOSITS. (GW/0341-6356). **1442**

MONOGRAPHIC REVIEW. (US/0885-7512). **3413**

MONOGRAPHIEN ZUR GESCHICHTE DES MITTELALTERS. (GW/0026-9832). **2699**

MONOGRAPHIEN ZUR PHILOSOPHISCHEN FORSCHUNG. (GW). **4353**

MONOGRAPHS OF THE HEBREW UNION COLLEGE. (US/0190-5627). **5051**

MONROE COUNTY GENEALOGICAL SOCIETY NEWS. (US/0893-5718). **Adv Mgr:** V. Shelquist. **2461**

MONROE COURIER. (US). **Adv Mgr:** Robin Glowa. **5645**

MONROE EVENING TIMES (MONROE, WIS. 1898). (US/1068-5820). **Adv Mgr:** Gary Guralski, **Tel** (608)328-4202. **5769**

MONROE JOURNAL, THE. (US/0884-8750). **5627**

MONROE LEGACY, THE. (US). **Adv Mgr:** Kathleen Burman. **5671**

MONROE MONITOR/VALLEY NEWS. (US/0890-2879). **5761**

MONTAGNE ET ALPINISME, LA. (FR/0047-7923). **4875**

MONTAGUE'S MODERN BOTTLE IDENTIFICATION AND PRICE GUIDE. (US/0192-3900). **2592**

MONTANA. (US/0026-9891). **2747**

MONTANA FARMER-STOCKMAN. (US/1041-1674). **216**

MONTANA FOOD DISTRIBUTOR. (US/0047-7931). **2350**

MONTANA GRAIN NEWS. (US/1046-6088). **Adv Mgr:** Nancy Anderson. **203**

MONTANA LAW REVIEW. (US/0026-9972). **3012**

MONTANA NEWSPAPER RATES AND DATA. (US). **Adv Mgr:** Linda Fromm. **5705**

MONTANA OIL JOURNAL (1953). (US/0047-794X). **4264**

MONTANA WOOLGROWER. (US/0027-0024). **216**

MONTCLAIR TIMES, THE. (US). **Adv Mgr:** Sara Singleton, **Tel** (201)746-1100. **5710**

MONTEREY LIFE. (US/0274-8770). **2539**

MONTESSORI OBSERVER / IMS, THE. (US/0889-5643). **1765**

MONTEZUMA VALLEY JOURNAL. (US). **Adv Mgr:** Jeanne Scrivner. **5643**

MONTGOMERY ADVERTISER (1987), THE. (US/0892-4457). **5627**

MONTGOMERY BUSINESS. (US/0889-4442). **696**

MONTGOMERY HERALD, THE. (US). **Adv Mgr:** Nancy Shelton, **Tel** (304)469-3373. **5764**

MONTGOMERY INDEPENDENT, THE. (US). **Adv Mgr:** Alan Cutler. **5627**

MONTH (LONDON. 1882), THE. (UK/0027-0172). **4979**

MONTHLY COMMENTARY ON INDIAN ECONOMIC CONDITIONS. (II/0027-030X). **Adv Mgr:** Inderjit Rai. **1574**

MONTHLY DIRECTORY OF S. ASIAN ASSOCIATIONS & BUSINESSES, THE. (CN/0700-3471). **696**

MONTHLY INDICATORS OF CURRENT ECONOMIC SITUATION OF BANGLADESH. (BG). **1575**

MONTHLY NEWSLETTER - INDIAN INVESTMENT CENTRE. (II/0019-4999). **907**

MONTHLY NOTES OF THE ASTRONOMICAL SOCIETY OF SOUTHERN AFRICA. (SA/0024-8266). **397**

MONTHLY PRESCRIBING REFERENCE. (US/0883-0266). **3618**

MONTHLY PUBLIC OPINION SURVEYS. (II). **4482**

MONTHLY REVIEW (NEW YORK. 1949). (US/0027-0520). **4543**

MONTHLY WEATHER REVIEW. NORTHERN TERRITORY / COMMONWEALTH OF AUSTRALIA, BUREAU OF METEOROLOGY, DEPARTMENT OF THE INTERIOR. (AT). **1432**

MONTREAL CE MOIS-CI. (CN/0316-8530). **4852**

MONTREAL CUISINE. (CN/0823-2857). **5072**

MONTREAL MAGAZINE. (CN/0831-5213). **4863**

MONTROSE DAILY PRESS. (US). **5643**

MONTSERRAT CONSOLIDATED INDEX OF STATUTES AND SUBSIDIARY LEGISLATION TO 1ST JANUARY .... (BB). **3132**

MONUMENTA ARCHAEOLOGICA (LOS ANGELES). (US/0363-7565). **275**

MONUMENTA NIPPONICA. (JA/0027-0741). **2659**

MONUMENTA NIPPONICA MONOGRAPHS. (JA). **2507**

MONUMENTA SERICA. (GW/0254-9948). **2623**

MONUMENTS HISTORIQUES (1980). (FR/0242-830X). **304**

MOODY COUNTY ENTERPRISE (FLANDREAU, S.D. : 1938). (US). **5744**

MOODY COURIER, THE. (US). **5752**

MOODY STREET IRREGULARS. (US/0196-2604). **3413**

MOP : GEBAEUDEUNTERHALT & REINIGUNG. (SZ). **621**

MORAL EDUCATION FORUM. (US/0163-6480). **1765**

MORALITY IN MEDIA INC. NEWSLETTER. (US/0027-1004). **3170**

MORAVIA REPUBLICAN REGISTER. (US). **5718**

MORAVIAN (1989), THE. (US/1041-0961). **4979**

MORE FROM THE SHORE. (US/1067-7402). **2461**

MOREANA. (FR/0047-8105). **Adv Mgr:** Marc Hadour. **3413**

MORGAN HORSE, THE. (US/0027-1098). **2801**

MORGAN MESSENGER, THE. (US). **Adv Mgr:** Arlene Olson. **5697**

MORGAN REPORT ON DIRECTORY PUBLISHING. (US/0890-9512). **Adv Mgr:** Mr. Wolden, **Tel** (609)259-1695. **4817**

MORICHES BAY TIDE. (US). **5718**

MORNING HERALD, THE. (US). **Adv Mgr:** Terry McDaniel. **5686**

MORNING NEWS (BLACKFOOT, IDAHO), THE. (US/0893-3812). **Adv Mgr:** Leslie Bare. **5657**

MORNING NEWS (ERIE, PA.). (US). **Adv Mgr:** John Anderson, **Tel** (814)870-1655. **5737**

MORNING NEWS TRIBUNE. (US/1042-3621). **5761**

MORNING STAR, THE. (UK). **5812**

MORNING SUN, THE. (US). **5677**

MOROCCO COURIER, THE. (US/1060-5231). **Adv Mgr:** Sally Snow. **5665**

MORPHE / UNIVERSIDAD AUTONOMA DE PUEBLA, MAESTRIA EN CIENCIAS DEL LENGUAJE. (MX). **3304**

MORRELL, MORRILL FAMILIES ASSOCIATION NEWSLETTER. (US/0889-7247). **2461**

MORRIS SUN-TRIBUNE. (US). **Adv Mgr:** Anne Erichson. **5697**

MORSKOI GIDROFIZICHESKII ZHURNAL. (NE/0920-5047). **1453**

MORTGAGE BANKING. (US/0730-0212). **800**

MORTGAGE MARKETPLACE, THE. (US/0744-3927). **800**

MORTON JOURNAL (MORTON, WASH. : 1988). (US). **5761**

MORTON TRIBUNE. (US). **5752**

MORTUARY MANAGEMENT. (US/0027-1268). **2407**

MOSAIC (WINNIPEG). (CN/0027-1276). **Adv Mgr:** M. McLean. **3413**

MOSCOW NEWS. (RU/0027-1306). **5809**

MOSELLE FRUIT. (FR). **2350**

MOSQUITO SYSTEMATICS. (US/0091-3669). **2177**

MOSSBAUER EFFECT REFERENCE AND DATA JOURNAL. (US/0163-9587). **Adv Mgr:** Christine R. Boss, **Tel** (704)251-6617. **4426**

MOSSBAUER HANDBOOK. (US/0272-2755). **1012**

MOSSE SWISS ADRESS. (SZ). **696**

MOT : DIE AUTOZEITSCHRIFT. (GW). **5419**

MOTHER & CHILD (LAHORE). (PK/0379-2617). **2283**

MOTHERING. (US/0733-3013). **2283**

MOTHEROOT JOURNAL. (US/0739-5272). **4830**

MOTO JOURNAL. (CN/0319-2865). **4081**

MOTOCROSS ACTION MAGAZINE. (US/0146-3292). **4082**

MOTONEIGE QUEBEC. (CN/0836-7264). **4905**

MOTOR. (NE). **4082**

MOTOR 16. (SP/0212-9000). **5419**

MOTOR BOATING & SAILING. (US/0027-1799). **594**

MOTOR IN CANADA. (CN/0027-190X). **5420**

MOTOR INDUSTRY JOURNAL. (AT/0729-0799). **Adv Mgr:** Betty Billett. **5420**

MOTOR INDUSTRY YEAR BOOK. (NZ). **5420**

MOTOR ITALIA. (IT). **5420**

MOTOR REISEN REVUE. (GW). **5420**

MOTOR SERVICE (CHICAGO, ILL. : 1951). (US/0027-1977). **5420**

MOTOR SPECIFICATIONS AND PRICES. (UK). **5387**

MOTOR TRADE JOURNAL. (AT). **5420**

MOTOR TREND. (US/0027-2094). **5420**

MOTOR VEHICLE REPORTS. (CN/0709-5341). **3012**

MOTOR WORLD (LOS ANGELES, CALIF.). (US/1055-8233). **5420**

MOTORCYCLE DRAG RACING. (US/0883-7228). **4082**

MOTORCYCLE INDUSTRY MAGAZINE : MI. (US/0884-626X). **4082**

MOTORCYCLE PRODUCT NEWS. (US/0164-8349). **4082**

MOTORCYCLE ROAD RACER ILLUSTRATED. (US/1056-1455). **4082**

MOTORCYCLIST'S POST, THE. (US/0164-9256). **5387**

MOTORI. (IT). **5420**

MOTORIK. (GW/0170-5792). **4792**

MOTORING NEWS LONDON. (UK/0027-2264). **4905**

MOTORISTS GUIDE TO NEW & USED CAR PRICES. (UK/0027-2302). **Adv Mgr:** Adam. **5421**

MOTORSPORTS MARKETING NEWS. (US). **Adv Mgr:** Ernie Saxton. **762**

MOTRIX. (US/0027-2396). **5421**

MOTS. (FR/0243-6450). **4482**

MOTS A TROUVER RG. (CN/0823-7123). **4863**

MOTS CACHES J'AIME, LES. (CN/0826-4740). **4863**

MOTS CACHES SUPERMAGAZINE. (CN/0822-4145). **4863**

MOULTON ADVERTISER (1933), THE. (US/1071-0337). **Adv Mgr:** Amy Thrasher. **5627**

MOULTRIE OBSERVER, THE. (US). **Adv Mgr:** Velda Duke. **5654**

MOUNDSVILLE DAILY ECHO, THE. (US). **5764**

MOUNT AYR RECORD-NEWS. (US). **Adv Mgr:** Helen Terry, **Tel** (515)464-2440. **5671**

MOUNT PLEASANT NEWS, THE. (US). **Adv Mgr:** Doug Kofoed. **5671**

MOUNT PROSPECT TIMES. (US/0747-2595). **Adv Mgr:** Bill Tapper. **5661**

MOUNT SHASTA HERALD. (US/1064-6477). **Adv Mgr:** Genny Axtman. **5637**

MOUNTAIN ADVOCATE (BARBOURVILLE, KY.). (US). **Adv Mgr:** Carolyn Kennedy. **5681**

MOUNTAIN CITIZEN. (US). **2490**

MOUNTAIN EMPIRE GENEALOGICAL QUARTERLY, THE. (US/0882-4266). **2461**

MOUNTAIN HOME NEWS. (US). **5657**

MOUNTAIN MAIL. (US). **Adv Mgr:** Vicki Sue Vigil. **5643**

MOUNTAIN RECORD. (US/0896-8942). **5021**

MOUNTAINEER-HERALD, THE. (US). **Adv Mgr:** David Thompson, **Tel** (814)472-8240. **5737**

MOUNTAINEER (SEATTLE, WASH.). (US/0027-2620). **4875**

MOUNTRAIL COUNTY RECORD. (US). **Adv Mgr:** Dave Freuer, **Tel** (701)463-2201. **5726**

MOUSE GENOME. (UK/0959-0587). **466**

MOUVEMENT SOCIAL, LE. (FR/0027-2671). **2623**

MOUVEMENTS. (CN/0823-5651). **1691**

MOVEMENT AND DANCE : MAGAZINE OF THE LABAN GUILD. (UK). **1314**

MOVEMENT THEATRE QUARTERLY. (US/1065-1519). **5366**

MOVIE COLLECTOR'S WORLD. (US/8750-5401). **2775**

MOVIE/TV MARKETING. (JA). **933**

MOVIELINE (LOS ANGELES, CALIF.). (US/1055-0917). **4075**

MOVIES USA. (US/1044-1336). **4075**

MOVIMENTO. (IT). **4604**

MOVING FORWARD : THE NATIONAL NEWSPAPER FOR PEOPLE WITH DISABILITIES. (US/1056-7240). **Adv Mgr:** WG Holdsworth, **Tel** (714)544-2555 (West), (708)934-0084 (Midwest). **4391**

MOVING OUT. (US). **3413**

MOVING TO & AROUND ALBERTA. (CN/0713-8369). **4841**

MOVING TO & AROUND SASKATCHEWAN. (CN/0713-8385). **4841**

MOVING TO & AROUND TORONTO & AREA. (CN/0713-8377). **4841**

MOVING TO & AROUND VANCOUVER & B.C. (CN/0713-8407). **4841**

MOVING TO & AROUND WINNIPEG & MANITOBA. (CN/0715-7053). **4841**

MOVING TO OTTAWA/HULL (1978). (CN/0226-7837). **4841**

MOZAMBIQUEFILE : A MOZAMBIQUE NEWS AGENCY MONTHLY / AIM. (MZ). **4482**

MOZNAYIM. (IS/0027-2892). **3413**

MPLA NEWSLETTER (1975). (US/0145-6180). **3232**

MRAX INFORMATION. (BE/0024-8320). **Adv Mgr:** Myriam Mottard. **5209**

MRS BULLETIN. (US/0883-7694). **2107**

MS. (US/0047-8318). **5561**

MS. TREE. (US/0826-2586). **5074**

MSBA IN BRIEF. (US/0884-1667). **3012**

MSOS JOURNAL. (CN/0831-3040). **Adv Mgr:** Ray Gislason. **5180**

MT. STERLING ADVOCATE, THE. (US). **Adv Mgr:** Doug Taylor. **5681**

MT. VERNON OPTIC-HERALD. (US). **5752**

MTA. PEDIATRIA. (SP/0210-8135). **3906**

MTL. MONTREAL. (CN/0833-0026). **Adv Mgr:** Sharon Dawe. **2539**

MU KARA SANI NOUVELLE FORMULE : BULLETIN D'INFORMATION ET DE LIAISON DE L'INSTITUT DE RECHERCHES EN SCIENCES HUMAINES L'UNIVERSITE DE NIAMEY. (NG). **5210**

MUCCHIO SELVAGGIO, IL. (IT). **4132**

MUEHLE + MISCHFUTTERTECHNIK, DIE. (GW/0027-2949). **203**

MUEMLEKVEDELEM. (HU/0541-2439). **275**

MUIR'S ORIGINAL LOG HOME GUIDE FOR BUILDERS AND BUYERS. (US/0844-3459). **621**

MUKWONAGO CHIEF, THE. (US). **Adv Mgr:** Terri Blazek. **5769**

MULBERRY PRESS. (US). **Adv Mgr:** Barbara Wagoner. **5650**

MULIKA. (TZ). **3413**

MULLENS ADVOCATE, THE. (US/1064-6132). **Adv Mgr:** Eva Smith. **5764**

MULLMAGAZIN. (GW/0934-3482). **Adv Mgr:** Anne Wispler, **Tel** 030 2628027. **2236**

MULTI-MEDIA COMPUTING. (NE/0923-8182). **1196**

MULTICHANNEL NEWS. (US/0276-8593). **1135**

MULTICULTURAL EDUCATION ABSTRACTS. (UK/0260-9770). **1795**

MULTICULTURAL EDUCATION REVIEW. (AT/1033-6281). **1765**

MULTICULTURAL EDUCATION (SAN FRANCISCO, CALIF.). (US/1068-3844). **1765**

MULTICULTURAL REVIEW. (US/1058-9236). **Adv Mgr:** Garance Inc, **Tel** (914)834-7070. **2268**

MULTIHULL INTERNATIONAL. (UK). **1988**

MULTIHULLS. (US/0749-4122). **4905**

MULTINATIONAL EXECUTIVE TRAVEL COMPANION. (US/0093-7487). **5485**

MULTIVARIATE BEHAVIORAL RESEARCH. (US/0027-3171). **4605**

MUNDAY COURIER, THE. (US/8750-6750). **5752**

MUNDELEIN NEWS. (US/0746-8938). **Adv Mgr:** Jill DePasquale. **5661**

MUNDO CRISTIANO. (SP/0027-3252). **5032**

MUNDO EJECUTIVO. (MX). **800**

MUNDO ELETRICO. (BL). **2073**

MUNDO FINANCIERO. (SP/0300-3884). **1506**

MUNDO GANADERO. (SP). **216**

MUNDO HISPANICO (ATLANTA, GA.). (US/1051-4147). **Adv Mgr:** Tabiola Dorrh. **5654**

MUNDO MECANICO. (BL). **2123**

MUNICIPAL AND PLANNING LAW REPORTS. (CN/0702-7206). **3012**

MUNICIPAL CODE OF CHICAGO. (US). **3012**

MUNICIPAL DIRECTORY (AUGUSTA). (US/0272-4596). **4667**

MUNICIPAL FINANCE JOURNAL. (US/0199-6134). **4738**

MUNICIPAL REVIEW & AMA NEWS. (UK/0027-3562). **4667**

MUNICIPAL WORLD. (CN/0027-3589). **879**

MUNICIPALITY (1916), THE. (US/0027-3597). **Adv Mgr:** John O. Kirkpatrick. **4667**

MUNSTER (MUNCHEN), DAS. (GW/0027-299X). **359**

MUNSTERS & THE ADDAMS FAMILY REUNION, THE. (US). **1135**

MUNZEN REVUE. (SZ). **2782**

MUPPET MAGAZINE. (US/0737-6855). **1066**

MURRAY LEDGER & TIMES, THE. (US). **5681**

MUSCLE & NERVE. (US/0148-639X). **3838**

MUSCLE CARS OF THE ... . (US/0898-5820). **5421**

MUSCLE MAG INTERNATIONAL. (CN/0317-087X). **Adv Mgr:** Gina Logan, **Tel** (416)678-7312. **2600**

MUSCOGIANA (COLUMBUS, GA.). (US/1042-3419). **2461**

MUSCULAR DEVELOPMENT. (US/0047-8415). **Adv Mgr:** Ann Fortz, **Tel** (516)467-3140 Ext. 161. **2600**

MUSE. ARTS AND ENTERTAINMENT IN CANBERRA. (AT/0158-9571). **359**

MUSE (OTTAWA). (CN/0820-0165). **4091**

MUSEES. (CN/0706-098X). **4091**

MUSEES ET COLLETIONS PUBLIQUES DE FRANCE. (FR/0027-383X). **Adv Mgr:** M A Sonrier. **4091**

MUSEOGRAMME. (CN/0380-4623). **4091**

MUSEOLOGIA. (IT/0392-5528). **4091**

MUSE'S MILL. (US). **3414**

MUSEUM (BRAUNSCHWEIG). (GW/0341-8634). **4092**

MUSEUM CRITICUM. (IT). **4092**

MUSEUM HELVETICUM. (SZ/0027-4054). **275**

MUSEUM NEWS (WASHINGTON). (US/0027-4089). **4092**

MUSEUM ROUND-UP. (CN/0045-3005). **4092**

MUSEUM STORE. (US/1040-6999). **4092**

MUSEUMS AND ART GALLERIES IN GREAT BRITAIN AND IRELAND. (UK/0141-6723). **4093**

MUSEUMS JOURNAL. (UK/0027-416X). **4093**

MUSEUMS YEARBOOK. (UK/0307-7675). **4093**

MUSEUMSKUNDE. (GW/0027-4178). **4093**

MUSHING (ESTER, ALASKA). (US/0895-9668). **Adv Mgr:** Roy Earnest. **4905**

MUSHROOM JOURNAL. (UK/0144-0551). **2424**

MUSHROOM (MOSCOW, IDAHO). (US/0740-8161). **575**

MUSHROOM NEWS. (US/0541-3869). **Adv Mgr:** Tim King, **Tel** (215)296-9611. **179**

MUSIC ANALYSIS. (UK). **4132**

MUSIC & AUTOMATA. (UK/0262-8260). **4132**

MUSIC & LETTERS. (UK/0027-4224). **4132**

MUSIC AND LITURGY. (UK/0305-4438). **4133**

MUSIC & SOUND RETAILER, THE. (US/0894-1238). **4133**

MUSIC AND THE TEACHER. (AT/0047-8431). **Adv Mgr:** J. Thomas, **Tel** 03 853-7861. **4133**

MUSIC BOX, THE. (UK). **4133**

MUSIC BUSINESS INTERNATIONAL. (FR). **Adv Mgr:** Rudi Blackett, **Tel** 011 44 71 921 5981. **4133**

MUSIC CITY NEWS. (US/0027-4291). **4133**

MUSIC CLUBS MAGAZINE (1963). (US/0161-2654). **4133**

MUSIC DIRECTORY CANADA. (CN/0820-0416). **4133**

MUSIC EDUCATORS JOURNAL. (US/0027-4321). **4133**

MUSIC FOR THE LOVE OF IT. (US/0898-8757). **4133**

MUSIC-IN-PRINT SERIES. (US/0146-7883). **4133**

MUSIC LEADER, THE. (US/0027-4372). **4134**

MUSIC LIBRARIAN. (US/1065-1179). **4134**

MUSIC OF THE SPHERES. (US/0892-2721). **4186**

MUSIC PERCEPTION. (US/0730-7829). **4134**

MUSIC PERFORMANCE RESOURCES. (US/0896-1352). **4134**

MUSIC REFERENCE SERVICES QUARTERLY. (US/1058-8167). **4134**

MUSIC REVIEW, THE. (UK/0027-4445). **4134**

MUSIC ROW. (US/0745-5054). **4135**

MUSIC SCENE (DIETIKON, SWITZERLAND). (SZ). **4135**

MUSIC TEACHER. (UK/0027-4461). **4135**

MUSIC TECHNOLOGY (ELY). (UK/0957-6606). **4135**

MUSIC THEORY SPECTRUM. (US/0195-6167). **Adv Mgr:** James Baker, **Tel** (401)863-3234. **4135**

MUSIC THERAPY PERSPECTIVES. (US/0734-6875). **4135**

MUSIC WEEK DIRECTORY. (UK/0267-3290). **4135**

MUSICA. (GW/0027-4518). **4135**

MUSICA. (IT). **4135**

MUSICA DISCIPLINA. (IT/0077-2461). **4135**

MUSICA DOMANI : ORGANO DELLA SOCIETA ITALIANA PER L'EDUCAZIONE MUSICALE. (IT/0391-4380). **4135**

MUSICAL AMERICA (1987). (US/1042-3443). **4136**

MUSICAL AMERICA. INTERNATIONAL DIRECTORY OF THE PERFORMING ARTS. (US/0735-7788). **386**

MUSICAL DENMARK. (US/0027-4585). **4160**

MUSICAL MERCHANDISE REVIEW. (US/0027-4615). **4136**

MUSICAL NEWS (SAN FRANCISCO, CALIF.). (US/0748-9293). **4136**

MUSICAL OPINION. (UK/0027-4623). **Adv Mgr:** Liz Biddle, **Tel** 44 81 6690011. **4136**

MUSICAL QUARTERLY, THE. (US/0027-4631). **4136**

MUSICAL TIMES (LONDON, ENGLAND : 1957). (UK/0027-4666). **4136**

MUSICK. (CN/0226-8620). **4137**

MUSICOLOGICAL STUDIES & DOCUMENTS. (GW/0077-2496). **4137**

MUSICOLOGY AUSTRALIA. (AT/0814-5857). **4137**

MUSICUS. (SA). **4137**

MUSICWORKS. (CN/0225-686X). **4137**

MUSIK-ALMANACH — Advertising Accepted Index

MUSIK-ALMANACH (KASSEL, GERMANY). (GW/0930-8954). **4137**

MUSIK IN BAYERN : HALBJAHRESSCHRIFT DER GESELLSCHAFT FUER BAYERISCHE MUSIKGESCHICHTE E.V. (GW). **4137**

MUSIK UND BILDUNG. (GW/0027-4747). **4138**

MUSIK UND GOTTESDIENST. (SZ/1015-6798). **4138**

MUSIK UND KIRCHE. (GW/0027-4771). **4138**

MUSIKBRANCHENS ARBOG. (DK). **4138**

MUSIKFORSCHUNG. (GW/0027-4801). **4138**

MUSIKHANDEL. (GW). **4138**

MUSIKINSTRUMENT, DAS. (GW/0027-4828). **4138**

MUSIKREVY. (SW/0027-4844). **4138**

MUSIKTHEORIE. (GW/0177-4182). **4138**

MUSIKWISSENSCHAFTLICHE STUDIENBIBLIOTHEK. (GW). **4138**

MUSKEGON CHRONICLE, THE. (US). **Adv Mgr:** Kevin Newton. **5693**

MUSKOGEE DAILY PHOENIX AND TIMES-DEMOCRAT. (US). **Adv Mgr:** DeAnn Anderson, **Tel** (918)684-2804. **5732**

MUSKY HUNTER MAGAZINE. (US/1041-6366). **Adv Mgr:** B. Krammer, **Tel** (800)23-Musky. **4875**

MUSLIM EDUCATION QUARTERLY. (UK/0267-615X). **1765**

MUSLIM JOURNAL. (US/0883-816X). **5044**

MUSLIM SCIENTIST. (US/0148-0995). **5210**

MUSLIM WORLD BOOK REVIEW, THE. (UK/0260-3063). **5044**

MUSLIM WORLD (HARTFORD), THE. (US/0027-4909). **5044**

MUSLIM WORLD LEAGUE JOURNAL, THE. (SU). **5044**

MUSTANG!. (US/1043-2590). **2801**

MUSTANG MONTHLY MAGAZINE. (US/0274-8460). **Adv Mgr:** Curt Patterson, **Tel** (813)644-7610. **5421**

MUSTANG TIMES. (US/0744-2572). **5421**

MUSU ZINIOS. (US). **4979**

MUSZAKI INFORMACIO. KORSZERU MUNKAFELTETELEK, MUNKAVEDELEM. (HU/0230-2896). **2865**

MUTANTIA : ZONA DE LUCIDEZ IMPLACABLE. (AG). **5252**

MUTISIA. (CK/0027-5123). **518**

MUTTERSPRACHE (WIESBADEN). (GW/0027-514X). **3304**

MUTUAL AID. (US/0734-9998). **4792**

MUTUAL FUND SOURCEBOOK. (US/8755-4151). **908**

MUTUAL FUNDS MAGAZINE. (US). **909**

MUTUAL MAGAZINE (PHILADELPHIA, PA. : 1980), THE. (US/0740-672X). **5433**

MUZIEK & DANS. (NE/0166-0535). **4139**

MUZSIKA. (HU/0027-5336). **4139**

MUZZLELOADER, THE. (US/0274-5720). **Adv Mgr Tel** (903)832-4347. **4205**

MYCOLOGIA. (US/0027-5514). **575**

MYCOLOGIST, THE. (UK/0269-915X). **576**

MYCOTOXIN RESEARCH. (GW/0178-7888). **Adv Mgr:** Editor. **519**

MYOTIS. (GW/0580-3896). **5592**

MYRTLE BEACH JOURNAL, THE. (US/0745-8584). **5637**

MYSTERY READERS JOURNAL. (US/1043-3473). **3414**

MYSTERY REVIEW, THE. (CN/1192-8700). **Adv Mgr:** Chris von Hessert. **3414**

MYSTICS QUARTERLY (IOWA CITY, IOWA). (US/0742-5503). **3414**

MYSTIQUE (TORONTO). (CN/0710-1988). **5188**

N.A.C.W.P.I JOURNAL. (US/0027-576X). **4139**

N.A.R.D. JOURNAL. (US/0162-1602). **4316**

N & M. NATUR OG MILJ. (NO/0802-4618). **2198**

N. B. NATURALIST. (CN/0047-9551). **4168**

N.C. ... ANNUAL REPORT OF HAZARDOUS WASTE GENERATED, STORED, TREATED OR DISPOSED. (US). **2237**

N.R.S., LA NOUVELLE REVUE SOCIALISTE. (FR). **4543**

N.S.W. MASTER PLUMBER. (AT/0819-1824). **Adv Mgr:** R. Rolls. **2607**

N-SCALE (EDMONDS, WASH.). (US/1045-5140). **5433**

N.Y. HABITAT. (US/0745-0893). **4841**

NAACOG NEWSLETTER. (US/0889-0579). **3862**

NAAMAT. (IS). **5562**

NAATI NEWS. (AT/1031-5411). **3304**

NABE NEWS (CLEVELAND, OHIO). (US/0745-3205). **1506**

NACA NEWS. (US). **226**

NACADA JOURNAL / NATIONAL ACADEMIC ADVISING ASSOCIATION. (US/0271-9517). **1836**

NACE CORROSION ENGINEERING BUYER'S GUIDE : OFFICIAL PUBLICATION OF NACE. (US). **2015**

NACHRICHTEN DER AKADEMIE DER WISSENSCHAFTEN IN GOTTINGEN. PHILOLOGISCH-HISTORISCHE KLASSE. (GW/0065-5287). **3304**

NACHRICHTEN FUER DOKUMENTATION. (GW/0027-7436). **3232**

NACHRICHTENDIENST. (GW/0012-1185). **Adv Mgr:** Ralt Mulot. **5297**

NACION, LA. (AG). **5777**

NACOI FORUM. (CN/0708-5249). **2268**

NACTA JOURNAL. (US/0149-4910). **110**

NAFSA DIRECTORY OF INSTITUTIONS AND INDIVIDUALS IN INTERNATIONAL EDUCATIONAL EXCHANGE. (US/0736-4660). **1836**

NAFTILIAKI. (GR). **Adv Mgr:** Natassa Vassilaki. **5453**

NAGA, THE ICLARM QUARTERLY. (PH/0116-290X). **2308**

NAHNU AL-ARAB. (UA). **2507**

NAHRO ROSTER. (US/0363-6453). **2829**

NAIA NEWS. (US/0740-5995). **Adv Mgr:** Nancy Rhees. **4905**

NAIKA. (JA/0547-1729). **3800**

NAMIBIA ABSTRACTS. (ZA). **4482**

NAMIBIANA. (SX/0259-2010). **2642**

NANJING HANGKONG XUEYUAN XUEBAO. (CC/1000-1956). **29**

NANNY TIMES. (US). **2283**

NANTUCKET JOURNAL (NANTUCKET, MASS. 1987). (US/1056-2265). **2747**

NAPA COUNTY RECORD AND NAPA VALLEY NEWS. (US/0744-6942). **Adv Mgr:** David Barker. **5637**

NAPA VALLEY REGISTER, THE. (US). **Adv Mgr:** Micheal Stansfield. **5637**

NAPOLEON HOMESTEAD. (US). **Adv Mgr:** Terry Schwartzemberger. **5726**

NAPSAC DIRECTORY OF ALTERNATIVE BIRTH SERVICES AND CONSUMER GUIDE. (US/0273-3730). **3765**

NAPSAC NEWS. (US/0192-1223). **589**

NARC OFFICER, THE. (US/0889-7794). **3170**

NARODNO ZEMEDELSKO ZNAME. (US/8755-9706). **4482**

NARROW GAUGE AND SHORT LINE GAZETTE. (US/0148-2122). **5433**

NASA TECH BRIEFS (WASHINGTON, D.C. 1976). (US/0145-319X). **5130**

NASE DEJINY. (US/0745-239X). **2461**

NASE RODINA (SAINT PAUL, MINN.). (US/1045-8190). **2461**

NASHR-I DANISH. (IR/0259-9090). **5044**

NASHRAT MAHAD SHUUN AL-AQALLIYAT AL-MUSLIMAH, JAMIAT AL-MALIK ABD AL-AZIZ BI-JIDDAH. (SU). **5044**

NASHUA REPORTER AND WEEKLY NASHUA POST, THE. (US). **Adv Mgr:** Wanda Orric, **Tel** (515)435-4151. **5672**

NASHVILLE BUSINESS JOURNAL. (US/0889-2873). **696**

NASHVILLE RECORD, THE. (US). **Adv Mgr:** H. Hayward. **696**

NASSAU LITERARY REVIEW, THE. (US/0883-2374). **1093**

NASSAUISCHE ANNALEN. (GW/0077-2887). **2700**

NASW NEWS. (US/0027-6022). **5297**

NATA DIRECTORY SYDNEY. (AT/0311-8185). **2123**

NATA NEWS SYDNEY. (AT/0311-662X). **2123**

NATATION (PARIS). (FR/1169-8152). **Adv Mgr:** B. Rayaune, **Tel** same as editor. **4852**

NATAT'S REPORTER. (US/0735-9691). **4668**

NATCHEZ DEMOCRAT (1916), THE. (US/0888-8744). **5701**

NATCHEZ TRACE NEWSLETTER. (US/0739-1412). **2461**

NATION (NEW YORK, N.Y.), THE. (US/0027-8378). **3348**

NATIONAL ALLIANCE. (US/0027-8513). **1692**

NATIONAL AQUATICS JOURNAL. (US). **4906**

NATIONAL ASSOCIATION FOR OLMSTED PARKS. (US/0895-819X). **4707**

NATIONAL AUCTIONS & SALES. (US/1055-8268). **1298**

NATIONAL BANKRUPTCY REPORTER. (US/0275-0252). **3087**

NATIONAL BAR ASSOCIATION MAGAZINE. (US/0741-0115). **Adv Mgr:** H. Carter. **3013**

NATIONAL BAR BULLETIN, THE. (US). **3013**

NATIONAL BLACK LAW JOURNAL. (US/0896-0194). **3013**

NATIONAL BUILDER (LONDON). (UK/0027-8807). **621**

NATIONAL BUS TRADER. (US/0194-939X). **Adv Mgr:** J. Plachno. **5388**

NATIONAL BUSINESS REVIEW. (NZ/0110-6813). **697**

NATIONAL BUSINESS REVIEW. (NZ). **Adv Mgr:** Amanda Harrison-Kyle. **697**

NATIONAL BUSINESS WOMAN. (US/0027-8831). **5562**

NATIONAL BUTTON BULLETIN, THE. (US/0027-884X). **2775**

NATIONAL CAPITAL PHARMACIST, THE. (US/0027-8890). **4317**

NATIONAL CATHOLIC REGISTER. (US/0027-8920). **Adv Mgr:** Frank Wright, **Tel** same as publisher. **5032**

NATIONAL CATHOLIC REPORTER. (US/0027-8939). **5033**

NATIONAL CATTLEMEN. (US/0885-7679). **216**

NATIONAL CHRISTIAN REPORTER, THE. (US/0279-8913). **4980**

NATIONAL CIVIC REVIEW. (US/0027-9013). **4668**

NATIONAL CLOTHESLINE (MIDWEST ED.), THE. (US/0744-6306). **5354**

NATIONAL COAL LEADER. (US). **2865**

NATIONAL CULINARY REVIEW, THE. (US/0747-7716). **2350**

NATIONAL DEFENSE (WASHINGTON). (US/0092-1491). **4052**

NATIONAL DENTAL ASSOCIATION JOURNAL. (US/1050-530X). **1330**

NATIONAL DEVELOPMENT. MIDDLE EAST/AFRICA. (US/0738-1670). **622**

NATIONAL DIRECTORY / CANADIAN INSTITUTE OF FOOD SCIENCE AND TECHNOLOGY. (CN/0823-2717). **2350**

NATIONAL DIRECTORY OF ADDRESSES AND TELEPHONE NUMBERS (NEW YORK, N.Y.), THE. (US/0740-7203). **697**

NATIONAL DIRECTORY OF AIDS CARE. (US). **4792**

NATIONAL DIRECTORY OF BULLETIN BOARD SYSTEMS. (US/0884-9536). **1196**

NATIONAL DIRECTORY OF COLLEGE ATHLETICS (WOMEN'S EDITION), THE. (US/0739-1226). **4906**

NATIONAL DIRECTORY OF COMMUNITY NEWSPAPERS (1992). (US/1066-0887). **Adv Mgr:** Gwen Smith. **5697**

NATIONAL DIRECTORY OF HEAD INJURY REHABILITATION SERVICES. (US/0892-6972). **Adv Mgr:** Kim Arline, **Tel** (202)296-6443. **3618**

NATIONAL DIRECTORY OF HIGH SCHOOL COACHES, THE. (US). **4906**

NATIONAL DIRECTORY OF LAW ENFORCEMENT ADMINISTRATORS, CORRECTIONAL INSTITUTIONS, AND RELATED GOVERNMENTAL AGENCIES. (US/1066-5595). **Adv Mgr:** Jennifer Bailey, **Tel** (715)345-2772. **3170**

NATIONAL DIRECTORY OF LOCAL RESEARCHERS. (US/0742-9045). **2462**

NATIONAL DIRECTORY OF MAGAZINES, THE. (US/0895-4321). **2539**

NATIONAL DIRECTORY OF OCCUPATIONAL HEALTH PROVIDERS. (US). **3789**

NATIONAL DIRECTORY OF WOMEN-OWNED BUSINESS FIRMS. (US/0886-389X). **697**

NATIONAL DRAGSTER. (US/0466-2199). **4906**

NATIONAL DRILLERS BUYERS GUIDE. (US/0279-7739). **5536**

NATIONAL EDUCATOR, THE. (US/0739-1617). **Adv Mgr:** Max Goldberg. **5637**

NATIONAL EMPLOYMENT LISTING SERVICE FOR HUMAN SERVICES. (US/0194-0775). **1692**

NATIONAL EMPLOYMENT OPPORTUNITIES NEWSLETTER. COMPUTER/ELECTRONIC FIELD ENGINEERING. (US/0895-5778). **1692**

NATIONAL ENGINEER, THE. (US/0027-9218). **1988**

NATIONAL ENVIRONMENTAL ENFORCEMENT JOURNAL. (US). **3114**

NATIONAL ENVIRONMENTAL JOURNAL, THE. (US/1067-2583). **Adv Mgr:** C.B. Campbell. **2178**

NATIONAL ESTIMATOR. (US/1040-2926). **2889**

NATIONAL FIRE & ARSON REPORT, THE. (US/1064-4814). **3170**

NATIONAL FISHERMAN. (US/0027-9250). **2309**

NATIONAL FORENSIC JOURNAL. (US/0749-1042). **3742**

NATIONAL FORUM OF APPLIED EDUCATIONAL RESEARCH JOURNAL. (US/0895-3880). **1867**

NATIONAL FORUM OF EDUCATIONAL ADMINISTRATION AND SUPERVISION JOURNAL. (US/0888-8132). **1766**

NATIONAL FORUM OF SPECIAL EDUCATION JOURNAL. (US/1043-2167). **Adv Mgr Tel** (318)477-0008. **1882**

NATIONAL GARDENER, THE. (US/0027-9331). **2424**

NATIONAL GARDENING. (US/1052-4096). **Adv Mgr:** Bob Bennett. **2425**

NATIONAL GENEALOGICAL SOCIETY QUARTERLY. (US/0027-934X). **2462**

NATIONAL GEOGRAPHER. (II/0470-0929). **2570**

NATIONAL GEOGRAPHIC. (US/0027-9358). **2570**

NATIONAL GREENHOUSE GARDENER. (US/0883-8313). **2425**

NATIONAL GUARD ALMANAC. (US/0363-8618). **4052**

NATIONAL GUARD (WASHINGTON. 1978). (US/0163-3945). **4052**

NATIONAL HIGHWAY AND AIRWAY CARRIERS AND ROUTES. (US/0275-3286). **5401**

NATIONAL HISPANIC JOURNAL. (US/0734-9920). **2268**

NATIONAL HIV/AIDS LEGAL LINK NEWSLETTER. (AT/1037-6615). **3013**

NATIONAL HOG FARMER. (US/0027-9447). **216**

NATIONAL HOME CENTER NEWS. (US/0192-6772). **2792**

NATIONAL HOOKUP. (US/0194-4754). **4391**

NATIONAL INSTITUTE OF ARTS AND LETTERS, AMERICAN ACADEMY OF ARTS AND LETTERS. (US). **325**

NATIONAL INTEREST, THE. (US/0884-9382). **4529**

NATIONAL JAIL AND ADULT DETENTION DIRECTORY. (US/0192-8228). **3170**

NATIONAL JEWISH POST & OPINION (INDIANAPOLIS, INC. : 1984). (US/0888-0379). **Adv Mgr:** Sam Schulman, **Tel** (317)927-7800. **5665**

NATIONAL JOB MARKET. (US/0747-4296). **4206**

NATIONAL JOURNAL (1975). (US/0360-4217). **4483**

NATIONAL JOURNAL OF SOCIOLOGY. (US/0892-4287). **5252**

NATIONAL KNIFE MAGAZINE, THE. (US/1051-4600). **2775**

NATIONAL LAMPOON. (US/0027-9587). **2539**

NATIONAL LEGAL EAGLE. (AT/0813-9741). **3013**

NATIONAL LIBRARIAN : THE NLA NEWSLETTER. (US/0191-359X). **3233**

NATIONAL MARKET PLACE NEWS. (AT/1030-8784). **Adv Mgr:** Brian Garrett. **2350**

NATIONAL MILK RECORDS. ANNUAL REPORT, ENGLAND & WALES. (UK). **197**

NATIONAL MINORITY POLITICS. (US/1057-1655). **Adv Mgr:** Willie Richardson. **2268**

NATIONAL MORTGAGE NEWS. (US/1050-3331). **Adv Mgr:** Jim Hollander, **Tel** (212)563-4008. **801**

NATIONAL MOTORIST. (US/0279-3083). **5485**

NATIONAL NEWS - AMERICAN LEGION AUXILIARY. (US/1062-4244). **5234**

NATIONAL NEWS - NATIONAL PENSIONERS AND SENIOR CITIZENS FEDERATION. (CN/0849-2115). **5180**

NATIONAL NOTARY, THE. (US/0894-7872). **4668**

NATIONAL NOW TIMES. (US/0149-4740). **5562**

NATIONAL OIL & LUBE NEWS, THE. (US/1071-1260). **Adv Mgr:** B. Tinsley. **4265**

NATIONAL OTC STOCK JOURNAL, THE. (US/0745-7049). **909**

NATIONAL (OTTAWA. 1978). (CN/0709-1370). **Adv Mgr:** J. Voyer, **Tel** (613)238-5721. **1882**

NATIONAL PACKING NEWS. (US/1073-6948). **2351**

NATIONAL PARALEGAL REPORTER. (US/1058-482X). **3014**

NATIONAL PARK GUIDE (NEW YORK, N.Y.). (US/0734-7960). **4707**

NATIONAL PARKS JOURNAL. (AT/0047-9012). **2198**

NATIONAL PARKS (WASHINGTON, D.C.). (US/0276-8186). **4707**

NATIONAL PASTIME, THE. (US/0734-6905). **4906**

NATIONAL PETROLEUM NEWS. (US/0149-5267). **4265**

NATIONAL PRODUCTIVITY REVIEW. (US/0277-8556). **880**

NATIONAL PROVISIONER, THE. (US/0027-996X). **2351**

NATIONAL PUBLIC ACCOUNTANT (1957), THE. (US/0027-9978). **748**

NATIONAL RADIO GUIDE. (CN/0849-3952). **Adv Mgr:** Jane McIvor. **1135**

NATIONAL RADIO PUBLICITY DIRECTORY. (US/0276-4520). **1135**

NATIONAL RAILWAYS OF ZIMBABWE. (RH). **5433**

NATIONAL REAL ESTATE INDEX. MARKET MONITOR. (US). **Adv Mgr:** Ami Loventhal. **4842**

NATIONAL REAL ESTATE INVESTOR. DIRECTORY ISSUE. (US/0731-8693). **4842**

NATIONAL REFERRAL ROSTER. (US/1075-1084). **Adv Mgr:** Mark Neujahr, **Tel** same as publisher. **4842**

NATIONAL REGISTER OF NON-GOVERNMENT SECONDARY SCHOOLS OF AUSTRALIA. (AT). **Adv Mgr:** Noel Crow. **1766**

NATIONAL RELOCATION AND REAL ESTATE MAGAZINE. (US). **4842**

NATIONAL REVIEW (NEW YORK). (US/0028-0038). **4483**

NATIONAL REVIEW OF CORPORATE ACQUISITIONS, THE. (US/0097-6202). **Adv Mgr:** Tish Stanny. **697**

NATIONAL ROSTER OF REALTORS. (US/0090-1741). **4842**

NATIONAL RUGBY POST. (CN). **Adv Mgr:** D. Graham. **4906**

NATIONAL SACRED HARP NEWSLETTER. (US). **4139**

NATIONAL SPEED SPORT NEWS. (US/0028-0208). **4906**

NATIONAL SQUARE DANCE DIRECTORY. (US/0196-0040). **1314**

NATIONAL STAMPAGRAPHIC. (US/0747-5527). **381**

NATIONAL STOCK DOG MAGAZINE. (US/0028-0267). **4287**

NATIONAL STONE ASSOCIATION BUYER'S GUIDE. (US). **2147**

NATIONAL STRENGTH & CONDITIONING ASSOCIATION JOURNAL. (US/0744-0049). **1857**

NATIONAL TANK TRUCK CARRIER DIRECTORY. (US/0077-586X). **5388**

NATIONAL TELEPHONE DIRECTORY FOR BROKERS, DEALERS, BANKS, MUTUAL FUNDS. (US/0730-3823). **801**

NATIONAL TOMBSTONE EPITAPH, THE. (US/0890-068X). **2747**

NATIONAL TRADE INDEX OF SOUTH AFRICA AND RHODESIA. (SA). **2499**

NATIONAL TRIAL LAWYER (FLORIDA ED.). (US/1066-7733). **Adv Mgr:** Par Haffert. **3014**

NATIONAL TRIAL LAWYER (NATIONAL ED.). (US/1049-684X). **3014**

NATIONAL TRIAL LAWYER (NEW YORK ED.). (US/1060-9210). **Adv Mgr:** Pat Haffert, **Tel** (800)331-9000. **3014**

NATIONAL UTILITY CONTRACTOR, THE. (US/0192-0359). **622**

NATIONAL VOTER, THE. (US/0028-0372). **4483**

NATIONAL WEATHER DIGEST. (US/0271-1052). **1432**

NATIONAL WOODLANDS. (US/0279-9812). **2388**

NATIONAL WOOL GROWER. (US/0028-0410). **110**

NATIONALITIES PAPERS. (US/0090-5992). **2268**

NATIONALKONOMISK TIDSSKRIFT. (DK/0028-0453). **1507**

NATION'S BUILDING NEWS. (US/8750-6580). **622**

NATION'S BUSINESS. (US/0028-047X). **697**

NATION'S CITIES WEEKLY. (US/0164-5935). **Adv Mgr:** J. Rowley, **Tel** (215)675-9133. **4668**

NATION'S HEALTH (1971), THE. (US/0028-0496). **4792**

NATIONWIDE DIRECTORY. MAJOR MASS MARKET MERCHANDISERS. (US/0737-061X). **1086**

NATIVE NEVADAN, THE. (US/0028-0534). **2539**

NATIVE PEOPLES. (US/0895-7606). **Adv Mgr:** J. Sixkiller. **2747**

NATIVE VOICE. (CN/0028-0542). **Adv Mgr:** Robert MacDonald. **2539**

NATO-WARSAW AND STRATEGIES. (NP/0749-0674). **4483**

NATO'S FIFTEEN NATIONS. (GW/0027-6065). **4529**

NATO'S SIXTEEN NATIONS. (NE/0169-1821). **4052**

NATS JOURNAL / NATIONAL ASSOCIATION OF TEACHERS OF SINGING JOURNAL, THE. (US/0884-8106). **4139**

NATSO TRUCKERS NEWS. (US/1040-2284). **5388**

NATUR + I.E. UND RECHT. (GW). **3114**

NATUR-UND GANZHEITSMEDIZIN : NGM. (GW/0934-7909). **3619**

NATUR UND LAND. (AU/0028-0607). **2178**

NATUR UND MUSEUM (FRANKFURT AM MAIN : 1962). (GW/0028-1301). **4168**

NATURA. (NE/0028-0631). **4168**

NATURA & MED. (GW/0931-1513). **3775**

NATURAL BODYBUILDING AND FITNESS. (US/1071-555X). **Adv Mgr Tel** (212)947-4322. **4906**

NATURAL FOODS MERCHANDISER. (US/0164-338X). **Adv Mgr:** Cassandra, **Tel** (303)939-8440. **2351**

NATURAL GAS (NEW YORK, N.Y.). (US/0743-5665). **4265**

NATURAL HISTORY. (US/0028-0712). **4168**

NATURAL HISTORY BOOK REVIEWS. (UK). **4174**

NATURAL LANGUAGE AND LINGUISTIC THEORY. (NE/0167-806X). **3305**

NATURAL LIFE MAGAZINE. (CN/0830-0887). **4194**

NATURAL LIFE (UNIONVILLE. 1991). (CN/0701-8002). **2600**

NATURAL PHYSIQUE. (US/1044-6583). **Adv Mgr:** Bruce Soffer, **Tel** (212)947-4322. **4906**

NATURAL RESOURCES COMPUTER NEWSLETTER. (US/0890-5673). **2199**

NATURAL RESOURCES FORUM. (NE/0165-0203). **2199**

NATURAL RESOURCES FORUM LIBRARY. (NE/0167-4110). **2199**

NATURAL RESOURCES JOURNAL. (US/0028-0739). **3115**

NATURAL STONE DIRECTORY : DIMENSION STONE SOURCES FOR BRITAIN AND IRELAND. (UK). **622**

NATURALIST (LEEDS). (UK/0028-0771). **4168**

NATURALIST REVIEW. (US/0888-6547). **2199**

NATURALIST (TRINIDAD AND TOBAGO). (TR). **4168**

NATURE CANADA. (CN/0374-9894). **2199**

NATURE GENETICS. (US/1061-4036). **550**

NATURE (LONDON). (UK/0028-0836). **5131**

NATURE NORTHWEST. (CN/0836-4702). **4169**

NATURE NOTEBOOK. (US). **466**

NATURE, SOCIETY, AND THOUGHT. (US/0890-6130). **5210**

NATUREN. (NO/0028-0887). **5131**

NATUREN. (NO). **5131**

NATUROPATHIC PHYSICIAN / THE AMERICAN ASSOCIATION OF NATUROPATHIC PHYSICIANS, THE. (US). **3619**

NATUUR EN TECHNIEK. (NE/0028-1093). **5131**

NATUURHISTORISCH — Advertising Accepted Index

NATUURHISTORISCH MAANBLAD : ORGAAN VAN HET NATUURHISTORISCH GENOOTSCHAP IN LIMBURG. (NE). **4169**

NAUGATUCK DAILY NEWS. (US). **5646**

NAUTICA. (IT/0392-369X). **4179**

NAUTICAL BRASS, ETC. (US). **4179**

NAUTICAL MAGAZINE. (UK/0028-1336). **Adv Mgr:** D. Provan. **4179**

NAUTICAL RESEARCH JOURNAL. (US/0738-7245). **4179**

NAVAJO NATION MESSENGER, THE. (US). **Adv Mgr:** Bob Zollinger. **5712**

NAVAJO TIMES (WINDOW ROCK, ARIZ. : 1987). (US). **Adv Mgr:** Gene Tapahe, **Tel** (602)871-7358. **5630**

NAVAL AFFAIRS. (US/0028-1409). **4179**

NAVAL ARCHITECT, THE. (UK/0306-0209). **5453**

NAVAL FORCES. (UK/0722-8880). **4180**

NAVAL HISTORY. (US/1042-1920). **4180**

NAVAL REVIEW. (UK). **Adv Mgr:** A. Gorst-Williams, **Tel** 089283-2232. **4180**

NAVAL STORES REVIEW (1979). (US/0164-4580). **2403**

NAVALAKATHA. (II/0028-1492). **3414**

NAVIGATION. (AT/0077-6262). **4180**

NAVIGATION (PARIS). (FR/0028-1530). **4180**

NAVIGATION (WASHINGTON). (US/0028-1522). **4180**

NAVIRES, PORTS & CHANTIERS. (FR/0028-159X). **4180**

NAVY INTERNATIONAL. (UK/0144-3194). **4180**

NAVY NEWS. (US/0028-1670). **5759**

NAVY TIMES. (US/0028-1697). **4180**

NAZARETH (COMBERMERE). (CN/1183-1863). **Adv Mgr:** J. Nordholt. **5033**

NC HOME. (US/1059-3500). **Adv Mgr:** Glenn Benton. **2902**

NCA/TCS NEWSLETTER. (US/0163-772X). **Adv Mgr:** Marietta W Ellis, **Tel** (410)992-0946. **539**

NCAA BASKETBALL. (US/0276-1017). **4906**

NCAA FOOTBALL RULES AND INTERPRETATIONS. (US/0736-5160). **4906**

NCAA MEN'S AND WOMEN'S BASKETBALL RULES AND INTERPRETATIONS. (US/1042-3877). **4907**

NCAA MEN'S WATER POLO RULES. (US/0734-0508). **4907**

NCAA NEWS, THE. (US/0027-6170). **4907**

NCBA COOPERATIVE BUSINESS JOURNAL. (US/1065-7207). **697**

NCCA ILLUSTRATED MEN'S AND WOMEN'S BASKETBALL RULES. (US/1042-3869). **4907**

NCEOA JOURNAL. (US/0889-8405). **1766**

NCGR JOURNAL. (US). **390**

NCJW JOURNAL. (US/0161-2115). **2268**

NCOA JOURNAL (SAN ANTONIO, TEX.). (US/0747-0150). **4052**

NCOA NETWORKS. (US/1045-9073). **5180**

NCPHS NEWSLETTER. (US/1054-9188). **1146**

NCVO NEWS. (UK/0955-2170). **Adv Mgr:** Anne Hodgson. **5297**

NEA TOY HAMILTON. (CN/0715-4410). **5790**

NEAR EAST ARCHAEOLOGICAL SOCIETY BULLETIN. (US/0739-0068). **Adv Mgr:** same as editor. **275**

NEAR EAST REPORT. (US/0028-176X). **4529**

NEAR NORTH NEWS. (US/0028-1778). **5661**

NEARA JOURNAL. (US/0149-2551). **Adv Mgr:** Suzanne, **Tel** (508)752-3490. **2748**

NEBRASKA ANCESTREE. (US/0270-4463). **2462**

NEBRASKA CATTLEMAN. (US/1062-8274). **216**

NEBRASKA DAILY NEWS-PRESS. (US). **Adv Mgr:** Greg Dillon. **5706**

NEBRASKA FARMER, THE. (US/1049-1880). **111**

NEBRASKA LAW REVIEW. (US/0047-9209). **Adv Mgr:** Jane Kemper. **3014**

NEBRASKA LIBRARY ASSOCIATION QUARTERLY. (US/0028-1883). **3233**

NEBRASKA MEDICAL JOURNAL, THE. (US/0091-6730). **3619**

NEBRASKA MUNICIPAL REVIEW. (US/0028-1905). **4668**

NEBRASKA MUSIC EDUCATOR, THE. (US/0732-1503). **4139**

NEBRASKA NEWSPAPER. (US/0028-1913). **Adv Mgr:** Mary Burt, **Tel** (402)476-2851. **5706**

NEBRASKA NURSE. (US/0028-1921). **Adv Mgr:** Arthur Davis Company, **Tel** (319)277-2414. **3862**

NEBRASKA REVIEW (OMAHA, NEB.), THE. (US/8755-514X). **2851**

NEBRASKA SPEECH AND HEARING JOURNAL. (US/0470-570X). **4391**

NEBRASKALAND. (US/0028-1964). **4852**

NEDERLANDS BOSBOUW TIJDSCHRIFT. (NE/0369-3651). **2389**

NEDERLANDS THEOLOGISCH TIJDSCHRIFT. (NE/0028-212X). **4980**

NEDERLANDS TIJDSCHRIFT VOOR FOTONICA. (NE/0925-5338). **4413**

NEDERLANDS TIJDSCHRIFT VOOR NATUURKUNDE (AMSTERDAM. 1991). (NE/0926-4264). **Adv Mgr:** M Bruning, **Tel** FAX - 0175-41847. **5132**

NEDERLANDS TIJDSCHRIFT VOOR TANDHEELKUNDE. (NE/0028-2200). **1330**

NEDERLANDS VAN NU. (BE/0771-5080). **3305**

NEDERLANDSCHE LEEUW; MAANDBLAD VAN HET KONINKLIJK NEDERLANDSCH GENOOTSCHAP VOOR GESLACHT- EN WAPENKUNDE, DE. (NE). **2462**

NEDERLANDSE BOEK. (NE/0166-0586). **3348**

NEDERLANDSE CHEMISCHE INDUSTRIE. (NE/0470-6021). **987**

NEDERLANDSE COURANT (WILLOWDALE). (CN/0316-9782). **2268**

NEEDLE ARTS. (US). **5185**

NEEDLEPOINT PLUS. (US/1040-5518). **5185**

NEGATIVE CAPABILITY. (US/0277-5166). **3414**

NEGOCIO A NEGOCIO. (SP). **1619**

NEGOCIOS Y BANCOS : REVISTA PARA EL EJECUTIVO. (MX/0028-2456). **801**

NEGRO HISTORY BULLETIN. (US/0028-2529). **Adv Mgr:** Dr. J. Harris, **Tel** (202)667-2822. **2748**

NEHGS NEXUS. (US/0747-9891). **2462**

NEIGHBORHOOD WORKS, THE. (US/0193-791X). **2829**

NEIL SPERRY'S GARDENS. (US/1061-3994). **2425**

NELSON COUNTY ARENA (MICHIGAN, N.D. : 1919). (US/0895-5344). **5726**

NELSON'S DIRECTORY OF INSTITUTIONAL REAL ESTATE. (US/1060-5789). **Adv Mgr:** Peter McCuen, **Tel** (914)937-8400. **4842**

NELSON'S DIRECTORY OF INVESTMENT MANAGERS. (US/0896-0143). **909**

NELSON'S DIRECTORY OF INVESTMENT RESEARCH. (US/0896-0135). **909**

NEMA NEWS. (US). **4093**

NEMATROPICA. (US/0099-5444). **5592**

NENKAN NIHON NO IRASUTORESHON. (JA). **381**

NEODESHA SUN-REGISTER, THE. (US). **Adv Mgr:** Dorothy Campbell. **5677**

NEONATAL NETWORK. (US/0730-0832). **3906**

NEONATOLOGY LETTER. (US/0747-6132). **3765**

NEPAL TRADE DIRECTORY. (II). **847**

NEPHROLOGY NEWS & ISSUES. (US/0896-1263). **Adv Mgr:** Lawrence Coutts. **3992**

NEPTUNUS. (BE). **4181**

NERVE CELL BIOLOGY / UNIVERSITY OF SHEFFIELD BIOMEDICAL INFORMATION SERVICE. (UK/0142-8225). **466**

NERVENHEILKUNDE. (GW/0722-1541). **3839**

NERVLINE. A MICROCOMPUTER INFORMATION RETRIEVAL SYSTEM IN THE CLINICAL NEUROSCIENCES. (US). **Adv Mgr Tel** debra A. Finelli. **3839**

NERVURE PARIS. (FR/0988-4068). **3931**

NESHOBA DEMOCRAT, THE. (US). **Adv Mgr:** Charlie Howell. **5701**

NESS COUNTY NEWS. (US). **5677**

NESTOR. (US/0028-2812). **286**

NET RESULTS. (US/0270-4900) **Adv Mgr:** J. Latimer. **4980**

NETBALL MAGAZINE. (UK/0959-1117). **4907**

NETHERLANDS-BRITISH TRADE DIRECTORY. (UK). **847**

NETHERLANDS INTERNATIONAL LAW REVIEW. (NE/0165-070X). **3133**

NETHERLANDS JOURNAL OF AGRICULTURAL SCIENCE. (NE/0028-2928). **111**

NETHERLANDS JOURNAL OF ZOOLOGY. (NE/0028-2960). **5592**

NETSUSOKUTEI. (JA/0386-2615). **987**

NETWORK ADMINISTRATOR. (US/1073-1164). **Adv Mgr:** Donna Ward, **Tel** (913)841-0239. **1243**

NETWORK COMPUTING. (US/1046-4468). **1243**

NETWORK COMPUTING. (UK/0966-7873). **Adv Mgr:** Stuart Leigh. **1243**

NETWORK (MELBOURNE (VIC.). (AT/0159-7302). **Adv Mgr:** M. Reeves, **Tel** same as publisher. **5433**

NETWORK OF SASKATCHEWAN WOMEN (1983). (CN/0826-4929). **5562**

NETWORK (SALT LAKE CITY, UTAH). (US/0890-3530). **Adv Mgr:** Kate Olson, **Tel** (801)262-8091. **5562**

NETWORK (TORONTO. 1987). (CN/0836-0197). **Adv Mgr:** H.Wolfe. **386**

NETWORKER (ASHEVILLE, N.C.), THE. (US/1070-762X). **Adv Mgr:** Ken Burke. **4186**

NETWORKING MANAGEMENT. (US/1052-049X). **1243**

NEU. (IT). **3839**

NEUE CHINA, DAS. (GW). **2660**

NEUE ENTOMOLOGISCHE NACHRICHTEN. (GW/0722-3773). **5592**

NEUE FREIE ZEITUNG. (AU). **2520**

NEUE HEIMAT UND WELT. (AT/0817-6922). **5777**

NEUE HOCHSCHULE, DIE. (GW). **1914**

NEUE KERAMIK. (GW/0933-2367). **3466**

NEUE ORDNUNG, DIE. (GW). **4980**

NEUE POLITISCHE LITERATUR. (GW/0028-3320). **5210**

NEUE TECHNIK. (SZ/0028-3398). **5132**

NEUE ZEITSCHRIFT FUER MISSIONSWISSENSCHAFT. NOUVELLE REVUE DE SCIENCE MISSIONAIRE. (SZ/0028-3495). **4980**

NEUEREN SPRACHEN, DIE. (GW/0342-3816). **3305**

NEUES GLAS. (GW/0723-2454). **2592**

NEUES JAHRBUCH FUER GEOLOGIE UND PALAONTOLOGIE. ABHANDLUNGEN. (GW/0077-7749). **1389**

NEUES JAHRBUCH FUER GEOLOGIE UND PALAONTOLOGIE. MONATSHEFTE. (GW/0028-3630). **1389**

NEUES JAHRBUCH FUER MINERALOGIE. ABHANDLUNGEN. (GW/0077-7757). **1443**

NEUES JAHRBUCH FUER MINERALOGIE. MONATSHEFTE. (GW/0028-3649). **1443**

NEUF; ARCHITECTURES NOUVELLES, MATERIAUX NOUVEAUX. (BE). **304**

NEURAL COMPUTATION. (US/0899-7667). **1215**

NEURAL, PARALLEL AND SCIENTIFIC COMPUTATIONS. (US/1061-5369). **Adv Mgr:** S. Revathi. **1197**

NEURO-CHIRURGIE. (FR/0028-3770). **3839**

NEURO-OPHTHALMOLOGY (AMSTERDAM : AEOLUS PRESS. 1980). (NE/0165-8107). **3876**

NEUROBIOLOGIA (RECIFE). (BL/0028-3800). **3839**

NEUROBIOLOGY OF AGING. (US/0197-4580). **3839**

NEUROCHEMISTRY SHEFFIELD. (UK/0142-8403). **491**

NEUROCOMPUTING (AMSTERDAM). (NE/0925-2312). **1215**

NEUROENDOCRINOLOGY. (SZ/0028-3835). **3840**

NEUROEPIDEMIOLOGY. (SZ/0251-5350). **3840**

NEUROHYPOPHYSIAL HORMONES. (UK/0143-4276). **3732**

NEUROLOGIA CROATICA : GLASILO UDRUZENJA NEUROLOGA JUGOSLAVIJE, OFFICIAL JOURNAL OF YUGOSLAV NEUROLOGICAL ASSOCIATION. (CI/0353-8842). **3840**

NEUROLOGIA PSICHIATRIA SCIENZE UMANE. (IT). **3931**

NEUROLOGICAL RESEARCH (NEW YORK). (UK/0161-6412). **3840**

NEUROLOGY AND NEUROBIOLOGY. (US/0736-4563). **3841**

NEUROLOGY, INDIA. (II/0028-3886). **3841**

NEUROMUSCULAR DISEASES. (UK/0261-8412). **3841**

NEUROPATHOLOGY AND APPLIED NEUROBIOLOGY. (UK/0305-1846). **3896**

NEUROPEPTIDES (EDINBURGH). (UK/0143-4179). **3841**

NEUROPEPTIDES (SHEFFIELD). (UK/0142-8233). **3841**

NEUROPHYSIOLOGIE CLINIQUE. (NE/0987-7053). **3841**

NEUROPSYCHOBIOLOGY. (SZ/0302-282X). **3842**

NEUROREPORT. (UK/0959-4965). **3842**

NEUROSCIENCE AND BIOBEHAVIORAL REVIEWS. (US/0149-7634). **3842**

NEUROSCIENCE LETTERS. (NE/0304-3940). **3842**

NEUROSCIENCE RESEARCH. (IE/0168-0102). **3842**

NEUROSURGERY. (US/0148-396X). **3970**

NEUROSURGICAL REVIEW. (GW/0344-5607). **3970**

NEUROTOXICOLOGY (PARK FOREST SOUTH). (US/0161-813X). **3843**

NEUSPRACHLICHE MITTEILUNGEN AUS WISSENSCHAFT UND PRAXIS : NM. (GW/0028-3983). **1767**

NEVADA APPEAL (CARSON CITY, NEV. : 1968). (US). **Adv Mgr:** Loren Abbott, **Tel** (702)882-2111 ext. 269. **5708**

NEVADA BAPTIST, THE. (US/0279-4535). **4980**

NEVADA BUSINESS JOURNAL. (US). **698**

NEVADA (CARSON CITY, NEV.). (US/0199-1248). **2540**

NEVADA HISTORICAL SOCIETY QUARTERLY (1961). (US/0047-9462). **2748**

NEVADA JOURNAL (NEVADA, IOWA). (US/0747-430X). **Adv Mgr:** Annette Forbes. **5672**

NEVADA LAWYER. (US/1068-882X). **Adv Mgr:** C. Cendagonla, **Tel** (702)329-4100. **3015**

NEVADA LEGAL NEWS. (US/0744-8902). **3015**

NEVADA RNFORMATION. (US/0273-4117). **3862**

NEVADA STATISTICAL ABSTRACT. (US). **5334**

NEVADA WAGE SURVEY. (US). **1693**

NEVIPENS ROMANI : NOTICIAS GITANAS. (SP). **Adv Mgr:** Olga Sanchez. **2269**

NEW ACCOUNTANT. (US/0882-8067). **749**

NEW ADVOCATE (BOSTON, MASS.), THE. (US/0895-1381). **3415**

NEW AFRICAN (LONDON. 1978). (UK/0142-9345). **2499**

NEW AFRICAN YEARBOOK (LONDON, ENGLAND : 1987). (UK). **2499**

NEW AGE JOURNAL (1983). (US/0746-3618). **4186**

NEW AGE RETAILER. (US/1042-6566). **4186**

NEW AGE WEEKLY. (II/0047-9500). **4483**

NEW AMBEROLA GRAPHIC, THE. (US/0028-4181). **5318**

NEW AMERICAN (BELMONT, MASS.), THE. (US/0885-6540). **4483**

NEW AMERICAN (NEW YORK, N.Y.). (US). **2269**

NEW AMERICAN PRESS, THE. (US/1045-8093). **Adv Mgr:** Al LeRoy, **Tel** (904)434-3973. **5650**

NEW AMERICAN, THE. (US). **Adv Mgr:** Jean Wells. **5718**

NEW AMERICAN WRITING. (US/0893-7842). **3415**

NEW ART EXAMINER. (US/0886-8115). **Adv Mgr:** Art Stone. **359**

NEW BLACKFRIARS. (UK/0028-4289). **4980**

NEW BODY. (US/0732-4782). **2600**

NEW BOOKBINDER, THE. (UK/0261-5363). **4830**

NEW BREED MICROFORM, THE. (US). **2269**

NEW BREEZE. (JA/0915-3160). **Adv Mgr:** A. Manabe. **1118**

NEW BREWER, THE. (US/0741-0506). **2369**

NEW BUSINESS OPPORTUNITIES (IRVINE, CALIF.). (US/1041-3707). **698**

NEW CANAAN ADVERTISER. (US). **5646**

NEW CANADIAN REVIEW. (CN/0832-932X). **3415**

NEW CATALYST. (CN/0834-969X). **2540**

NEW CATHOLIC EXPLORER. (US/1044-8322). **5033**

NEW CHARLOTTE, THE. (US). **2540**

NEW CHEROKEE ADVOCATE, THE. (US). **5732**

NEW CHOICES FOR THE BEST YEARS. (US/1041-6277). **5180**

NEW CIVIL ENGINEER. (UK/0307-7863). **2027**

NEW COMMUNITY. (UK/0047-9586). **2269**

NEW CONTRAST. (SA/1017-5415). **3415**

NEW COVENANT (ANN ARBOR, MICH.). (US/0744-8589). **5033**

NEW CRITERION (NEW YORK, N.Y.), THE. (US/0734-0222). **326**

NEW DANCE REVIEW, THE. (US/1040-8908). **1314**

NEW DAY (PHILADELPHIA). (US/0028-453X). **4980**

NEW DELTA REVIEW. (US/1050-415X). **3415**

NEW DEPARTURES. (UK/0028-4580). **326**

NEW DIMENSIONS. (US). **1298**

NEW DIRECTIONS. (US). **4391**

NEW DIRECTIONS FOR WOMEN. (US/0160-1075). **Adv Mgr:** Susan Valentine. **5562**

NEW DIRECTIONS (VANCOUVER. 1985). (CN/0827-6153). **4483**

NEW DOCTOR. (AT/0313-2153). **Adv Mgr:** C. Zarresh. **3916**

NEW DRIVER (HIGHLAND PARK, ILL.). (US/0279-6384). **5421**

NEW DRUGS SURVEY. (JA). **Adv Mgr:** Kiyonori Shiina. **4317**

NEW EDUCATION (MELBOURNE, VIC.). (AT). **1767**

NEW ELECTRIC RAILWAY JOURNAL, THE. (US/1048-3845). **5433**

NEW ELECTRONIC ENCYCLOPEDIA. [COMPUTER FILE], THE. (US). **Adv Mgr:** Maryanne Piazza, **Tel** (203)797-3365. **1927**

NEW ELECTRONICS. (NZ). **Adv Mgr:** John Emmanuet. **2073**

NEW ENERGY NEWS. (US/1075-0045). **Adv Mgr Tel** (801)583-6232. **1951**

NEW ENGLAND ANTIQUES JOURNAL. (US/0897-5795). **251**

NEW ENGLAND BUSINESS. (US/0164-3533). **698**

NEW ENGLAND DIRECTORY FOR COMPUTER PROFESSIONALS. (US/0739-6120). **1238**

NEW ENGLAND ELECTRICAL BLUE BOOK. (US). **2073**

NEW ENGLAND ENTERTAINMENT DIGEST. (US/0896-1506). **5366**

NEW ENGLAND ENTERTAINMENT DIGEST [MICROFORM]. (US). **5366**

NEW ENGLAND FARM BULLETIN & GARDEN GAZETTE. (US). **2425**

NEW ENGLAND FARMER (ST. JOHNSBURY). (US/0193-0923). **111**

NEW ENGLAND FRUIT MEETINGS. (US/0099-426X). **111**

NEW ENGLAND HISTORICAL AND GENEALOGICAL REGISTER, THE. (US/0028-4785). **2462**

NEW ENGLAND JOURNAL OF BLACK STUDIES. (US/0747-4970). **2269**

NEW ENGLAND JOURNAL OF HUMAN SERVICES. (US/0277-996X). **5298**

NEW ENGLAND JOURNAL OF MEDICINE, THE. (US/0028-4793). **Adv Mgr Tel** (617)893-6742. **3620**

NEW ENGLAND JOURNAL OF OPTOMETRY. (US/0028-4807). **Adv Mgr:** Jon C. Lundell. **4216**

NEW ENGLAND JOURNAL OF PUBLIC POLICY. (US/0749-016X). **4668**

NEW ENGLAND MINORITY NEWS. (US). **2269**

NEW ENGLAND PRINTER & PUBLISHER. (US/0162-8771). **4567**

NEW ENGLAND PROGRESS MAGAZINE. (US). **2607**

NEW ENGLAND PURCHASER. (US/0028-4858). **950**

NEW ENGLAND QUARTERLY, THE. (US/0028-4866). **2748**

NEW ENGLAND READING ASSOCIATION JOURNAL. (US/0028-4882). **1901**

NEW ENGLAND REAL ESTATE JOURNAL. (US/0028-4890). **Adv Mgr Tel** (617)878-4540. **4842**

NEW ENGLAND RUNNER. (US/1041-4800). **4907**

NEW ENGLAND SALES GUIDE TO HIGH-TECH COMPANIES. (US/1040-0591). **5132**

NEW ENGLAND SENIOR CITIZEN. (US/0163-2248). **5180**

NEW ENGLAND THEATRE JOURNAL. (US/1050-9720). **Adv Mgr:** Corey. **5366**

NEW EQUIPMENT DIGEST. (US/0028-4963). **2123**

NEW EQUIPMENT NEWS. (CN/0028-4971). **3485**

NEW ERA (LANARK). (CN/0227-8030). **5790**

NEW ERA LAUNDRY & CLEANING LINES. (US/0028-5056). **698**

NEW ETHICALS CATALOGUE. (NZ/0110-9510). **4334**

NEW FARMER AND GROWER. (UK/0952-1402). **111**

NEW FEDERALIST. (US/1043-2264). **Adv Mgr:** Stanley Ezrol. **4484**

NEW FOOD & DRUG PACKAGING, THE. (US/1075-3028). **Adv Mgr:** Sharon Needham. **4220**

NEW FORMATIONS. (UK/0950-2378). **Adv Mgr:** R. Borthwick. **3348**

NEW FRONTIERS IN EDUCATION. (II/0047-9705). **1837**

NEW GERMAN CRITIQUE. (US/0094-033X). **3415**

NEW GERMAN STUDIES. (UK/0307-2770). **3305**

NEW GLASS REVIEW (PRAHA). (XR/1210-2741). **2592**

NEW GROUND. (SA/1016-9075). **Adv Mgr:** L. De Bruyn. **2178**

NEW GUARD. (US/0028-5137). **4484**

NEW GUN WEEK, THE. (US/0195-1599). **Adv Mgr:** Peggy Tartaro, **Tel** (716)885-6408. **4907**

NEW HAMPSHIRE BAR JOURNAL. (US/0548-4928). **3015**

NEW HAMPSHIRE BUSINESS REVIEW. (US/0164-8152). **698**

NEW HAMPSHIRE GENEALOGICAL RECORD, THE. (US/1055-0763). **2462**

NEW HAMPSHIRE MAGAZINE (DURHAM). (US/0199-0306). **1093**

NEW HAMPSHIRE PREMIER. (US/1050-5512). **2540**

NEW HAMPSHIRE REGISTER, STATE YEAR-BOOK AND LEGISLATIVE MANUAL. (US/0545-1671). **4669**

NEW HAMPSHIRE TOWN & CITY. (US/0545-171X). **4669**

NEW HAVEN REGISTER, THE. (US). **5646**

NEW HEAVEN, NEW EARTH. (US/0896-3150). **5665**

NEW HI-FI SOUND. (UK). **5318**

NEW HOLSTEIN REPORTER. (US/0749-6982). **Adv Mgr:** Joe Mathes. **5769**

NEW HOMES. (US/0890-4723). **Adv Mgr:** Dan Ciavri. **4842**

NEW HORIZON (LONDON, ENGLAND). (UK/0955-095X). **5044**

NEW HUMANIST (LONDON, ENGLAND). (UK/0306-512x). **4353**

NEW IN CHESS YEARBOOK. (NE/0168-7697). **4864**

NEW INTERNATIONALIST. (UK/0305-9529). **4529**

NEW JERSEY 50 PLUS. (US). **Adv Mgr:** Patricia Jasin, **Tel** (908)240-3000. **5711**

NEW JERSEY BEVERAGE JOURNAL. (US/0028-5552). **2369**

NEW JERSEY BRIDE. (US). **2283**

NEW JERSEY BUSINESS. (US/0028-5560). **698**

NEW JERSEY DIRECTORY OF MANUFACTURERS. (US/0195-9352). **3485**

NEW JERSEY LAKE SURVEY FISHING MAPS GUIDE. (US/1054-4623). **Adv Mgr:** Steve Perrone. **2309**

NEW JERSEY LAW JOURNAL, THE. (US/0028-5803). **3015**

NEW JERSEY LAWYER (MAGAZINE). (US/0195-0983). **3015**

NEW JERSEY LAWYERS DIARY AND MANUAL. (US/1053-1955). **3015**

NEW JERSEY LIBRARIES. (US/0028-5811). **3234**

NEW JERSEY MEDICINE. (US/0885-842X). **3620**

NEW JERSEY MONTHLY. (US/0273-270X). **2540**

NEW JERSEY NURSE (1978). (US/0196-4895). **3862**

NEW JERSEY PARENT-TEACHER. (US/0028-5897). **1867**

NEW — Advertising Accepted Index

NEW JERSEY REALTOR. (US/0028-5919). **4842**

NEW JERSEY RESTAURANT GUIDE. (US). **5072**

NEW JERSEY REVIEW OF LITERATURE, THE. (US/1073-8576). **3415**

NEW JERSEY TRACK. (US). **2600**

NEW JERSEY TRIAL LAWYER, THE. (US/1051-8746). **Adv Mgr:** Pat Haffert. **3015**

NEW JERSEY WOMAN MAGAZINE. (US). **Adv Mgr:** Leslie Malon. **5562**

NEW JOURNAL (NEW HAVEN, CONN.), THE. (US/0028-6001). **1093**

NEW KOREA (LOS ANGELES, CALIF.). (US/1054-5891). **5637**

NEW LAW FOR SURVEYORS. (UK/0264-8121). **4842**

NEW LEADER (NEW YORK, N.Y.), THE. (US/0028-6044). **4543**

NEW LETTERS. (US/0146-4930). **3416**

NEW LIBRARY SCENE, THE. (US/0735-8571). **3234**

NEW LIFE. (AT). **Adv Mgr:** W. Zegelis. **5777**

NEW LITERARY HISTORY. (US/0028-6087). **3348**

NEW LITERATURE REVIEW. (AT/0314-7495). **Adv Mgr:** K. Brooks. **3348**

NEW MAP OF THE EUROPEAN PULP & PAPER INDUSTRY. (BE). **4235**

NEW MARITIMES. (CN/0713-4789). **5790**

NEW MENORAH. (US/0883-0215). **Adv Mgr:** M Katz, **Tel** (215)247-9700. **4981**

NEW METHODS (SAN FRANCISCO, CALIF.). (US/0277-3015). **5517**

NEW MEXICO ARCHITECTURE. (US/0545-3151). **304**

NEW MEXICO BUSINESS JOURNAL. (US/0164-6796). **Adv Mgr Tel** (505)889-2911. **698**

NEW MEXICO DENTAL JOURNAL. (US/0028-6176). **Adv Mgr:** M.E. Nelson. **1330**

NEW MEXICO FARM AND RANCH. (US/0028-6192). **Adv Mgr:** Erik Ness, **Tel** (505)526-5521. **112**

NEW MEXICO GENEALOGIST. (US). **2462**

NEW MEXICO HISTORICAL REVIEW. (US/0028-6206). **Adv Mgr:** Bill Broughton, **Tel** (505)277-0991. **2748**

NEW MEXICO HUMANITIES REVIEW. (US/0738-9671). **2851**

NEW MEXICO LAW REVIEW. (US/0028-6214). **3015**

NEW MEXICO MAGAZINE (SANTA FE, N.M. : 1974). (US/0028-6249). **2540**

NEW MEXICO MUSICIAN, THE. (US/0742-8278). **4140**

NEW MEXICO NURSE. (US/0028-6273). **3862**

NEW MILFORD TIMES, THE. (US) **Adv Mgr:** Bernie Schraer. **5646**

NEW MYTHS. (US/1055-9868). **3416**

NEW OBSERVATIONS. (US/0737-5387). **3416**

NEW ON THE CHARTS. (US/0276-7031). **4140**

NEW ORLEANS MAGAZINE (1988). (US/0897-8174). **Adv Mgr:** Amy Taylor, **Tel** (504)834-9292. **2540**

NEW ORLEANS MUSIC. (UK/0308-1990). **4140**

NEW ORLEANS OIL DIRECTORY. (US). **Adv Mgr:** Fran Hart. **4266**

NEW OUTLOOK (TEL AVIV). (IS/0028-6427). **4529**

NEW OXFORD REVIEW. (US/0149-4244). **4981**

NEW PACIFIC (SEATTLE, WASH.), THE. (US/1050-3080). **Adv Mgr:** Bev Scorey. **2540**

NEW PAGES. (US/0271-8197). **4817**

NEW PALTZ NEWS COMBINED WITH THE WALLKILL VALLEY WORLD, THE. (US). **Adv Mgr:** Barbara Walters. **5718**

NEW PERSPECTIVE (HAMILTON). (CN/0715-4445). **2269**

NEW PERSPECTIVES ON TURKEY. (TU/0896-6346). **5210**

NEW PERSPECTIVES QUARTERLY. (US/0893-7850). **4484**

NEW PHYSICIAN. (US/0028-6451). **3620**

NEW PITTSBURGH COURIER (CITY ED.). (US/1047-8051). **Adv Mgr:** Donna Walker, **Tel** (412)481-8302. **5738**

NEW PITTSBURGH COURIER (NATIONAL ED.). (US/1047-806X). **Adv Mgr:** D. Walker. **5738**

NEW POLITICAL SCIENCE. (US/0739-3148). **Adv Mgr:** John C. Berg. **4484**

NEW POLYMERIC MATERIALS. (NE). **987**

NEW PRESS (QUEENS, N.Y.), THE. (US/0894-6078). **3416**

NEW PRODUCTS REVIEW. (UK). **405**

NEW REPUBLIC (NEW YORK, N.Y.). (US/0028-6583). **2851**

NEW SCHOLAR, THE. (US/0028-6613). **5210**

NEW SETTLER'S GUIDE FOR WASHINGTON, D.C. AND COMMUNITIES IN NEARBY MARYLAND AND VIRGINIA, THE. (US/0097-8213). **2829**

NEW SOLIDARITY. (US/0028-6737). **2540**

NEW TECHNOLOGY IN THE HUMAN SERVICES. (UK). **5252**

NEW TECHNOLOGY, WORK, AND EMPLOYMENT. (UK/0268-1072). **1694**

NEW TESTAMENT ABSTRACTS. (US/0028-6877). **5013**

NEW THOUGHT (SCOTTSDALE, ARIZ.). (US/0146-7832). **4981**

NEW TIMES (MOBILE, ALA.), THE. (US/0885-1662). **5627**

NEW TIMES (PHOENIX, ARIZ.) (US/0279-3962). **5630**

NEW TIMES (SEATTLE, WASH.). (US/1044-2782). **4186**

NEW TIMES : THE JOURNAL OF DEMOCRATIC LEFT. (UK/0960-748X). **5210**

NEW TRAIL (1982). (CN/0824-8125). **1102**

NEW TREND (BALTIMORE, MD.). (US/0732-1848). **4530**

NEW TRENDS IN CLINICAL NEUROPHARMACOLOGY : OFFICIAL JOURNAL OF THE EUROPEAN ASSOCIATION FOR CLINICAL NEUROPHARMACOLOGY. (IT/0393-5345). **3843**

NEW VICO STUDIES. (US/0733-9542). **Adv Mgr:** G. Tagliacozzo, **Tel** (212)989-2909. **4353**

NEW VIEWS (FORREST CITY, ARK.). (US/1062-9378). **Adv Mgr:** H Hunter, **Tel** (501)633-7547. **2540**

NEW VOICES (DIEGO MARTIN, TRINIDAD AND TOBAGO). (TR/0387-4185). **3416**

NEW WASHINGTON HERALD. (US). **5729**

NEW WAYS (EVANSTON, ILL.). (US). **3931**

NEW WELSH REVIEW, THE. (UK/0954-2116). **3416**

NEW WOLCOTT ENTERPRISE, THE. (US). **5666**

NEW WOMAN. (US/0028-6974). **5562**

NEW WORDS DIGEST. (US/1044-8578). **1882**

NEW WORLD (1989), THE. (US/1043-3538). **Adv Mgr:** Joyce Peterson. **5033**

NEW WORLD OUTLOOK. (US/0043-8812). **Adv Mgr:** Ruth Kurtz. **5065**

NEW YORK (1968). (US/0028-7369). **2540**

NEW YORK AMSTERDAM NEWS (1962). (US/1059-1818). **5718**

NEW YORK APPAREL NEWS. (US/0279-7844). **1086**

NEW YORK AUTO REPAIR NEWS. (US/0191-4979). **5421**

NEW YORK BAPTIST, THE. (US/0893-9063). **4981**

NEW YORK BEACON. (US). **Adv Mgr:** Daye, **Tel** (212)213-8585. **5718**

NEW YORK CONSTRUCTION NEWS. (US/0028-7164). **Adv Mgr:** Mr. Kelly, **Tel** (212)512-4775. **622**

NEW YORK FOLKLORE. (US/0361-204X). **2323**

NEW YORK GENEALOGICAL AND BIOGRAPHICAL RECORD, THE. (US/0028-7237). **Adv Mgr:** H. Macy. **2462**

NEW YORK GUARDIAN, THE. (US/1060-0167). **5711**

NEW YORK HERALD TIMES CROSSWORD PUZZLES ONLY. (US/0886-9936). **4864**

NEW YORK HERALD TRIBUNE LARGE PRINT CROSSWORDS. (US/0892-0168). **4864**

NEW YORK HOLSTEIN NEWS. (US/0279-8611). **216**

NEW YORK INTERNATIONAL LAW REVIEW. (US/1050-9453). **3133**

NEW YORK JEWISH WEEK, THE. (US/0745-5356). **Adv Mgr:** Richard Waloff. **2269**

NEW YORK JURY VERDICT REPORTER (METROPOLITAN ED.), THE. (US/0738-1697). **Adv Mgr:** Karen Hertz. **3016**

NEW YORK LAW JOURNAL. (US/0028-7326). **3016**

NEW YORK LITERARY FORUM. (US/0149-1040). **3416**

NEW YORK METRO SALES GUIDE TO HIGH-TECH COMPANIES. (US/1040-0583). **5133**

NEW YORK METS INSIDE PITCH. (US/0887-5863). **Adv Mgr:** Jan Cheves. **4907**

NEW YORK NATIVE. (US/0744-060X). **2795**

NEW YORK OPERA NEWSLETTER, THE. (US/1043-2361). **Adv Mgr:** Jeanne Whiting, **Tel** (201)762-9561. **386**

NEW YORK PEDIATRICIAN. (US/0737-4216). **3906**

NEW YORK QUARTERLY : NYQ, THE. (US/0028-7482). **3467**

NEW YORK REAL ESTATE JOURNAL. (US/1057-2104). **4842**

NEW YORK REVIEW OF SCIENCE FICTION, THE. (US/1052-9438). **3416**

NEW YORK RUNNING NEWS. (US/0161-7338). **4907**

NEW YORK SPORTS. (US/0740-2384). **4907**

NEW YORK STATE BAR JOURNAL. (US/0028-7547). **3016**

NEW YORK STATE CONSERVATION COUNCIL COMMENTS. (US/0745-8835). **2200**

NEW YORK STATE DENTAL JOURNAL. (US/0028-7571). **Adv Mgr:** Patricia Zahner. **1330**

NEW YORK STATE GFOA NEWSLETTER. (US/1064-0762). **801**

NEW YORK STATE JOURNAL OF MEDICINE. (US/0028-7628). **3621**

NEW YORK STATE JOURNAL OF PHARMACY, THE. (US/0279-8778). **4318**

NEW YORK STATE MUNICIPAL BULLETIN. (US). **4669**

NEW YORK STYLE & DESIGN. (US). **2540**

NEW YORK TIMES BOOK REVIEW, THE. (US/0028-7806). **3349**

NEW YORK TIMES, THE. (US/0362-4331). **Adv Mgr:** Janet L. Robinson. **5719**

NEW YORK UNIVERSITY LAW REVIEW (1950). (US/0028-7881). **3016**

NEW YORKER (NEW YORK, N.Y. : 1925). (US/0028-792X). **2490**

NEW YORKIN UUTISET. (US/0895-5549). **Adv Mgr:** Eija Hendel, **Tel** (718)435-0800. **5719**

NEW YOUTH CONNECTIONS. (US/0737-285X). **1067**

NEW ZEALAND AGRICHEMICAL AND PLANT PROTECTION MANUAL. (NZ/0114-4022). **112**

NEW ZEALAND ANTARCTIC RECORD. (NZ/0110-5124). **2570**

NEW ZEALAND BEEKEEPER, THE. (NZ). **112**

NEW ZEALAND BOOKS. (NZ/1170-9103). **Adv Mgr:** Jane Gayers. **4831**

NEW ZEALAND BOOKS IN PRINT / NEW ZEALAND BOOK PUBLISHERS ASSOCIATION. (AT/0157-7662). **4822**

NEW ZEALAND BUSINESS WHO'S WHO, THE. (NZ/0071-9571). **699**

NEW ZEALAND COMMERCIAL GROWER : OFFICIAL JOURNAL OF THE NEW ZEALAND VEGETABLE AND PRODUCE GROWERS' FEDERATION. (NZ). **2425**

NEW ZEALAND DENTAL JOURNAL. (NZ/0028-8047). **Adv Mgr:** Ms. McCort, **Tel** 011 64 634 5567. **1330**

NEW ZEALAND DISABLED. (NZ). **Adv Mgr:** Patricia Zimmerman, **Tel** (04)818-9329. **4391**

NEW ZEALAND ENGINEERING. (NZ/0028-808X). **Adv Mgr:** Jackie Enright, **Tel** 011 64 4952399. **1988**

NEW ZEALAND ENTOMOLOGIST, THE. (NZ/0077-9962). **Adv Mgr:** same as editor. **5592**

NEW ZEALAND FAMILY PHYSICIAN, THE. (NZ/0110-022X). **3738**

NEW ZEALAND FARMER, THE. (NZ). **112**

NEW ZEALAND FISHERMAN. (NZ/0113-9606). **4908**

NEW ZEALAND FORESTRY. (NZ/0112-9597). **2389**

NEW ZEALAND GEOLOGICAL SURVEY PALEONTOLOGICAL BULLETIN. (NZ). **1389**

NEW ZEALAND HISTORIC PLACES. (NZ). **Adv Mgr:** T. Reeves. **2670**

NEW ZEALAND HOME AND BUILDING. (NZ/0110-098X). **Adv Mgr:** Gaye Billings. **2902**

Advertising Accepted Index   NEWSLETTER

NEW ZEALAND INTERNATIONAL BUSINESS. (NZ/0113-8138). **Adv Mgr:** Linda Brickland. **699**

NEW ZEALAND INTERNATIONAL REVIEW. (NZ/0110-0262). **4530**

NEW ZEALAND JOURNAL OF AGRICULTURAL RESEARCH. (NZ/0028-8233). **112**

NEW ZEALAND JOURNAL OF BOTANY. (NZ/0028-825X). **519**

NEW ZEALAND JOURNAL OF CROP AND HORTICULTURAL SCIENCE. (NZ/0114-0671). **2425**

NEW ZEALAND JOURNAL OF ENVIRONMENTAL HEALTH. (NZ/0112-0212). **4793**

NEW ZEALAND JOURNAL OF GEOGRAPHY. (NZ/0028-8292). **2570**

NEW ZEALAND JOURNAL OF GEOLOGY AND GEOPHYSICS. (NZ/0028-8306). **1389**

NEW ZEALAND JOURNAL OF HISTORY, THE. (NZ/0028-8322). **2670**

NEW ZEALAND JOURNAL OF INDUSTRIAL RELATIONS. (NZ/0110-0637). **1694**

NEW ZEALAND JOURNAL OF MARINE AND FRESHWATER RESEARCH. (NZ/0028-8330). **556**

NEW ZEALAND JOURNAL OF MEDICAL LABORATORY SCIENCE. (NZ/1171-0195). **3621**

NEW ZEALAND JOURNAL OF OCCUPATIONAL THERAPY. (NZ/1171-0462). **2865**

NEW ZEALAND JOURNAL OF PHYSIOTHERAPY. (NZ/0303-7193). **4381**

NEW ZEALAND JOURNAL OF SPORTS MEDICINE, THE. (NZ/0110-6384). **3955**

NEW ZEALAND JOURNAL OF ZOOLOGY. (NZ/0301-4223). **5592**

NEW ZEALAND LAW SOCIETY'S NEWS SHEET, THE. (NZ). **3016**

NEW ZEALAND LIBRARIES. (NZ/0028-8381). **3234**

NEW ZEALAND LISTENER. (NZ). **1135**

NEW ZEALAND LOCAL GOVERNMENT. (NZ). **4669**

NEW ZEALAND MARINE SCIENCES NEWSLETTER. (NZ). **1453**

NEW ZEALAND MATHEMATICS MAGAZINE, THE. (NZ/0549-0510). **3524**

NEW ZEALAND MEDICAL JOURNAL. (NZ/0028-8446). **3621**

NEW ZEALAND MONTHLY REVIEW 1986. (NZ/0112-9120). **2510**

NEW ZEALAND NEWS UK. (UK/0028-8500). **Adv Mgr:** Ana Hensley, **Tel** 11 44 71 9306451. **5812**

NEW ZEALAND NURSING FORUM. (NZ/0110-7968). **3862**

NEW ZEALAND NURSING JOURNAL, THE. (NZ/0028-8535). **3862**

NEW ZEALAND OUTLOOK. (NZ/0113-1982). **2510**

NEW ZEALAND PHARMACY. (NZ/0111-431X). **Adv Mgr:** Kerry McKenzie, **Tel** 09 523 1754. **4318**

NEW ZEALAND PRINTER MAGAZINE. (NZ/1171-0829). **Adv Mgr:** P. Callahan, **Tel** 922-6133. **4567**

NEW ZEALAND RAILWAY OBSERVER. (NZ/0028-8624). **5433**

NEW ZEALAND RECENT LAW REVIEW. (NZ/0114-0655). **3016**

NEW ZEALAND SCIENCE REVIEW. (NZ/0028-8667). **5133**

NEW ZEALAND SHIPPING GAZETTE CHRISTCHURCH. (NZ/0027-724X). **Adv Mgr:** H. Driver, **Tel** (09)3094892. **5453**

NEW ZEALAND SPEECH-LANGUAGE THERAPISTS' JOURNAL, THE. (NZ/0110-571X). **3889**

NEW ZEALAND STOCK EXCHANGE WEEKLY DIARY. (NZ). **909**

NEW ZEALAND VISITOR STATISTICS. ASIA. (NZ). **5334**

NEW ZEALAND VISITOR STATISTICS. AUSTRALIA AND PACIFIC. (NZ). **5334**

NEW ZEALAND VISITOR STATISTICS. EUROPE. (NZ). **5334**

NEW ZEALAND VISITOR STATISTICS. TOTAL VISITORS. (NZ). **5334**

NEW ZEALAND WILDLIFE. (NZ/0028-8802). **4875**

NEW ZEALAND WINGS. (NZ/0110-1471). **30**

NEW ZEALAND WOOL MARKET REVIEW. (NZ/0113-2792). **5354**

NEWARK POST, THE. (US). **Adv Mgr:** Tina Winibell. **5647**

NEWBERG ON CLASS ACTIONS. (US). **3017**

NEWCOMERSTOWN NEWS (1953). (US). **Adv Mgr:** Laura Bridges. **5729**

NEWEST REVIEW, THE. (CN). **3349**

NEWFOUNDLAND ANCESTOR. (CN/0838-049X). **Adv Mgr:** R. Fitzpatrick. **2462**

NEWFOUNDLAND & LABRADOR BUSINESS JOURNAL. (CN). **699**

NEWFOUNDLAND HERALD, THE. (CN/0824-3581). **Adv Mgr:** G. Greene. **2490**

NEWFOUNDLAND LIFESTYLE. (CN/0827-3960). **Adv Mgr:** Hubert Hutton. **2748**

NEWFOUNDLAND SOCIAL AND ECONOMIC PAPERS. (CN/0078-0332). **5211**

NEWINGTON TOWN CRIER. (US/0745-0796). **5646**

NEWNAN TIMES-HERALD, THE. (US/0883-2536). **Adv Mgr:** Lamar Truitt. **5654**

NEWPORT HISTORY. (US/0028-8918). **2749**

NEWPORT MINER, THE. (US/0892-6239). **5761**

NEWPORT NAVALOG. (US). **Adv Mgr:** Mary Jane Mann. **5741**

NEWPORT THIS WEEK. (US). **Adv Mgr:** James Marazitti. **5741**

NEWS 3X/400. (US/1040-6093). **1238**

NEWS ADVERTISER (AJAX CANADA). (CN). **Adv Mgr:** Bruce Dunford, **Tel** same as publisher. **5790**

NEWS & CITIZEN. (US). **5757**

NEWS AND NOTES FROM ALL OVER, NEWSLETTER OF THE SOCIETY FOR THE ERADICATION OF TELEVISION. (US). **2490**

NEWS & OBSERVER (RALEIGH, N.C. : 1894). (US). **5724**

NEWS & RECORD. (US/0747-2862). **Adv Mgr:** Tucker McLaughlin Jr., **Tel** (804)572-2928. **5759**

NEWS AND REPORTER. (US). **5743**

NEWS - ASSOCIATION OF COLLEGIATE SCHOOLS OF ARCHITECTURE. (US/0149-2446). **Adv Mgr:** John Edwards, **Tel** (202)785-2324. **304**

NEWS / BRITISH COLUMBIA MEDICAL ASSOCIATION. (CN/0715-5379). **3621**

NEWS BULLETIN / MICHIGAN BUSINESS EDUCATION ASSOCIATION. (US/0026-2048). **Adv Mgr Tel** (616)531-0608. **699**

NEWS BULLETIN OF THE AUSTRALIAN DENTAL ASSOCIATION. (AT/0810-7440). **1331**

NEWS (CALIFORNIA ASSOCIATION OF COMMUNITY COLLEGES). (US). **1837**

NEWS-CHRONICLE (SHIPPENSBURG, PA.). (US). **Adv Mgr:** Steve Helm, **Tel** (717)532-4101. **5738**

NEWS CIRCLE, THE. (US/0193-1814). **2269**

NEWS (CLAY CITY, IND.). (US). **Adv Mgr:** Rhonda Riggle, **Tel** (812)939-2163. **5666**

NEWS-COMMERCIAL, THE. (US). **5701**

NEWS-DIGEST (AMITE, LA.). (US). **5684**

NEWS DIGEST INTERNATIONAL. (AT). **2670**

NEWS-EXAMINER, THE. (US). **5657**

NEWS FOR SENIORS. (CN/0710-958X). **5180**

NEWS FROM DBDH. (DK/0904-9681). **2607**

NEWS FROM ICELAND. (IC). **2520**

NEWS FROM NATIVE CALIFORNIA. (US/1040-5437). **Adv Mgr:** Yolanda Montijo. **2749**

NEWS FROM WITHIN. (IS). **Adv Mgr:** Ingrid. **2770**

NEWS-GAZETTE (CHAMPAIGN, ILL.). (US/1042-3354). **Adv Mgr:** Sue Trippiedi, **Tel** (217)351-5282. **5661**

NEWS-GAZETTE (SAINT CLOUD, FLA.). (US/8750-5029). **Adv Mgr:** Paula Stark. **5650**

NEWS-HERALD (MORGANTON, N.C.), THE. (US/8750-3980). **Adv Mgr:** Randy Hart. **5724**

NEWS - INTERNATIONAL ASSOCIATION OF PERSONNEL IN EMPLOYMENT SECURITY. (US/0020-6008). **1694**

NEWS JOURNAL (MANSFIELD, OHIO). (US). **Adv Mgr:** Ann Danuloff, **Tel** (419)522-3311. **5729**

NEWS JOURNAL - SOCIETY FOR COMMERCIAL ARCHAEOLOGY (U.S.). (US/0735-1399). **304**

NEWS JOURNAL (WILMINGTON, DEL.), THE. (US/1042-4121). **Adv Mgr:** Kitty Burns Esenberg, **Tel** (302)324-2617. **5647**

NEWS LEADER. (US). **Adv Mgr:** Diana. **5764**

NEWS LEADER, THE. (US). **Adv Mgr:** Don Bailey. **5654**

NEWS LETTER - BAR ASSOCIATION OF SRI LANKA. (CE). **3017**

NEWS LETTER / MATHEMATICAL ASSOCIATION. (UK/0465-3696). **3524**

NEWS LETTER / MONTANA GEOLOGICAL SOCIETY. (US). **1389**

NEWS LIBRARY NEWS. (US/1047-417X). **Adv Mgr:** Gay Nemeti, **Tel** (305)376-3403. **3234**

NEWS OF NEW YORK. (US/0028-9264). **Adv Mgr:** Colleen Caplan. **3621**

NEWS OF ORANGE COUNTY, THE. (US/1071-1716). **Adv Mgr:** David Jones, **Tel** (919)732-2171. **5724**

NEWS - ONTARIO PUBLIC SCHOOL TEACHERS' FEDERATION (1989). (CN/0846-4715). **Adv Mgr:** Charlotte Morgan. **1768**

NEWS PHOTOGRAPHER. (US/0199-2422). **4372**

NEWS-RECORD (GILLETTE, WYO.), THE. (US/0739-4926). **Adv Mgr:** Paul Treide, Jr. **5772**

NEWS-RECORD OF MAPLEWOOD AND SOUTH ORANGE. (US). **Adv Mgr:** Steve Ward. **5711**

NEWS REGISTER. (US). **Adv Mgr:** Rick McDonald. **5733**

NEWS-REPORTER. (US). **Adv Mgr:** Bonnie Miller. **5644**

NEWS REPORTER, THE. (US). **5724**

NEWS-REVIEW (INYOKERN, CALIF.), THE. (US/0893-9004). **Adv Mgr:** Pat Farris. **5637**

NEWS, THE. (US). **5627**

NEWS TIMES (NEWPORT, OR.). (US/0888-2010). **Adv Mgr:** Rhonda Persyn. **5733**

NEWSBOY. (US/0028-9396). **3416**

NEWSLETTER. (CN/0705-0216). **2200**

NEWSLETTER - AFRICAN-AMERICAN FAMILY HISTORY ASSOCIATION. (US/0893-4290). **2463**

NEWSLETTER - AMERICAN ASSOCIATION FOR THE ADVANCEMENT OF SLAVIC STUDIES. (US/0883-9549). **2700**

NEWSLETTER / AMERICAN ASSOCIATION OF PASTORAL COUNSELORS. (US/1065-383X). **4981**

NEWSLETTER / AMERICAN FEDERATION FOR CLINICAL RESEARCH. (US/1052-7982). **3621**

NEWSLETTER - AMERICAN MUSICAL INSTRUMENT SOCIETY. (US/0160-2365). **4140**

NEWSLETTER - AMERICAN SHORE AND BEACH PRESERVATION ASSOCIATION. (US/0517-4856). **2200**

NEWSLETTER - AMERICAN SOCIETY OF BREWING CHEMISTS. (US/0149-7308). **987**

NEWSLETTER / AMERICAN SOCIETY OF INDEXERS. (US/0733-3048). **3234**

NEWSLETTER / APPLIED SCIENCE TECHNOLOGISTS AND TECHNICIANS OF BRITISH COLUMBIA. (CN/0834-1788). **Adv Mgr:** Ted Noowell. **5133**

NEWSLETTER - ASSOCIATION FOR NATIVE DEVELOPMENT IN THE PERFORMING AND VISUAL ARTS. (CN/0316-8409). **326**

NEWSLETTER - ASSOCIATION FOR WOMEN IN MATHEMATICS. (US). **5562**

NEWSLETTER - ASSOCIATION OF SYSTEMATICS COLLECTIONS. (US/0147-7889). **4094**

NEWSLETTER / ATLANTIC CANADA INSTITUTE. (CN/0713-4479). **2541**

NEWSLETTER - AUSTRALIAN AND NEW ZEALAND SOCIETY OF NUCLEAR MEDICINE. (AT/0159-8376). **Adv Mgr:** S. Bass. **3848**

NEWSLETTER / AUSTRALIAN LAW LIBRARIANS' GROUP. (AT/0311-5984). **3235**

NEWSLETTER - BEATRIX POTTER SOCIETY. (UK/0260-3780). **3416**

NEWSLETTER - BRITISH COLUMBIA COUNCIL FOR THE FAMILY. (CN/0706-9022). **2284**

NEWSLETTER - BRITISH SCIENCE FICTION ASSOCIATION. (UK/0307-3335). **3417**

NEWSLETTER / CALIFORNIA NATIVE PLANT SOCIETY, BRISTLECONE CHAPTER. (US). **519**

NEWSLETTER / CANADIAN ASSOCIATION OF MUSIC LIBRARIES. (CN/0383-1299). **3235**

NEWSLETTER - CANADIAN ASSOCIATION OF SLAVISTS. (CN/0381-6133). **2520**

NEWSLETTER - CANADIAN ASSOCIATION ON GERONTOLOGY. (CN/0712-676X). **5180**

NEWSLETTER - CANADIAN ATHLETIC THERAPISTS ASSOCIATION. (CN/0822-7578). **3955**

NEWSLETTER

Advertising Accepted Index

NEWSLETTER (CANADIAN BOOKBINDERS AND BOOK ARTISTS GUILD). (CN/0822-9538). **4831**

NEWSLETTER - CANADIAN INSTITUTE OF UKRAINIAN STUDIES. (CN/0702-8474). **2700**

NEWSLETTER - CANADIAN PHYSIOTHERAPY ASSOCIATION. SPORTS PHYSIOTHERAPY DIVISION. (CN/0824-2917). **3955**

NEWSLETTER - CANADIAN RESEARCH INSTITUTE FOR THE ADVANCEMENT OF WOMEN. (CN/0229-7256). **5562**

NEWSLETTER - CANADIAN SOCIETY OF ENVIRONMENTAL BIOLOGISTS. (CN/0318-5133). **2200**

NEWSLETTER - CENTER FOR HOLOCAUST STUDIES (BROOKLYN, NEW YORK, N.Y.). (US/0737-8092). **2700**

NEWSLETTER - CENTER FOR MIGRATION STUDIES (U.S.). (US/8756-4467). **1920**

NEWSLETTER (CHINESE AMERICAN LIBRARIANS ASSOCIATION). (US/0736-8887). **3235**

NEWSLETTER / CLERMONT COUNTY GENEALOGICAL SOCIETY. (US/0749-0631). **2463**

NEWSLETTER / CONFERENCE GROUP ON ITALIAN POLITICS & SOCIETY. (US/0896-9825). **4530**

NEWSLETTER / COUNCIL OF NOVA SCOTIA ARCHIVES. (CN/0829-7142). **2482**

NEWSLETTER (CRIMINAL LAWYERS' ASSOCIATION (TORONTO, ONT.)). (CN/0715-5980). **3108**

NEWSLETTER - DANISH CENTRE FOR TECHNICAL AIDS FOR REHABILITATION AND EDUCATION. (DK). **1882**

NEWSLETTER, EAST ASIAN ART & ARCHAEOLOGY. (US/8755-4593). **360**

NEWSLETTER - EUBIOS ETHICS INSTITUTE. (NZ/1170-5485). **2252**

NEWSLETTER - EXECUTIVE COMMITTEE, LEAGUE OF CANADIAN POETS. (CN/0319-6658). **3467**

NEWSLETTER FOR RSEEA. (US/8756-8942). **112**

NEWSLETTER FROM THE COMMISSION FOR SCIENTIFIC RESEARCH IN GREENLAND. (DK/0106-1372). **5133**

NEWSLETTER - GLASGOW & WEST OF SCOTLAND FAMILY HISTORY SOCIETY. (UK/0141-8009). **2463**

NEWSLETTER - GUIDANCE AND COUNSELLING ASSOCIATION. (CN/0315-2995). **1882**

NEWSLETTER / INDIANA COVERED BRIDGE SOCIETY. (US). **2749**

NEWSLETTER - INSTITUTE FOR STUDIES IN AMERICAN MUSIC. (US/0145-8396). **4141**

NEWSLETTER - LEAGUE OF OREGON CITIES (1980). (US/0731-1435). **4669**

NEWSLETTER - LONG POINT BIRD OBSERVATORY. (CN/0317-9575). **5618**

NEWSLETTER / MAINE HISTORICAL SOCIETY. (US/0882-4223). **2749**

NEWSLETTER - MANITOBA UNDERWATER COUNCIL. (CN/0383-7742). **4908**

NEWSLETTER (MATHEMATICAL ASSOCIATION). (UK). **3524**

NEWSLETTER / MUSICOLOGICAL SOCIETY OF AUSTRALIA. (AT/0155-0543). **4141**

NEWSLETTER - NAFSA: ASSOCIATION OF INTERNATIONAL EDUCATORS (WASHINGTON, D.C.). (US/1067-4780). **Adv Mgr:** Bill Vual. **1768**

NEWSLETTER / NATIONAL ALOPECIA AREATA FOUNDATION, NAAF. (US/0894-1769). **Adv Mgr:** Carol ,Mayer. **3715**

NEWSLETTER - NATIONAL ASSOCIATION FOR THE VISUAL ARTS. (AT/1032-9617). **326**

NEWSLETTER - NATIONAL ASSOCIATION OF SOCIAL WORKERS. WASHINGTON STATE CHAPTER. (US/0745-3531). **5299**

NEWSLETTER - NATIONAL COUNCIL FOR THERAPY AND REHABILITATION THROUGH HORTICULTURE (U.S.). (US/0739-1609). **2425**

NEWSLETTER / NEW HAMPSHIRE SOCIETY OF GENEALOGISTS. (US/8755-173X). **2463**

NEWSLETTER - NEW MEXICO LIBRARY ASSOCIATION. (US/0893-2956). **Adv Mgr:** Carol Myers. **3235**

NEWSLETTER - NEW ZEALAND. NATURE CONSERVATION COUNCIL. (NZ/0111-686X). **2200**

NEWSLETTER OF THE AMERICAN ASSOCIATION OF AUSTRALIAN LITERARY STUDIES. (US/0894-7945). **3349**

NEWSLETTER OF THE AMERICAN COMMITTEE TO ADVANCE THE STUDY OF PETROGLYPHS AND PICTOGRAPHS. (US/0278-2871). **242**

NEWSLETTER OF THE AMERICAN DIALECT SOCIETY. (US/0002-8193). **3306**

NEWSLETTER OF THE AMERICAN HANDEL SOCIETY. (US/0888-8701). **4141**

NEWSLETTER OF THE AUSTRALIAN ROBOT ASSOCIATION. (AT/0726-3716). **1220**

NEWSLETTER OF THE NEW YORK STATE COUNCIL FOR THE SOCIAL STUDIES, THE. (US). **5211**

NEWSLETTER ON NEWSLETTERS, THE. (US/0028-9507). **2922**

NEWSLETTER / ONTARIO FORESTRY ASSOCIATION. (CN/0834-2008). **Adv Mgr:** J.D.C., **Tel** (416)493-4565. **2389**

NEWSLETTER - PENNSYLVANIA ACADEMY OF SCIENCE. (US/0160-4228). **5133**

NEWSLETTER - PLANETARY ASSOCIATION FOR CLEAN ENERGY. (CN/0708-918X). **1951**

NEWSLETTER/ REMOTE SENSING SOCIETY. (UK). **1358**

NEWSLETTER / SOCIETY FOR ARMENIAN STUDIES. (US/0740-5510). **2660**

NEWSLETTER - SOCIETY FOR HISTORIANS OF AMERICAN FOREIGN RELATIONS. (US/0740-6169). **4530**

NEWSLETTER / SOCIETY OF THE SEVEN SAGES. (CN/0701-9890). **3417**

NEWSLETTER / THE CROW WING COUNTY HISTORICAL SOCIETY. (US/0895-0822). **2750**

NEWSLETTER - THE SOCIETY OF ARCHITECTURAL HISTORIANS. (US/0049-1195). **304**

NEWSLETTER TRENDS. (CN/1185-5088). **Adv Mgr:** same as editor. **4817**

NEWSLETTER / W.H. AUDEN SOCIETY. (UK). **3467**

NEWSLETTER / WEST COAST ENVIRONMENTAL LAW RESEARCH FOUNDATION. (CN/0715-4275). **3115**

NEWSLETTER-WRITERS GUILD OF AMERICA, WEST. (US/0043-9533). **Adv Mgr:** Dianna Hightower, **Tel** (310)455-4210. **3417**

NEWSLETTERS ON STRATIGRAPHY. (NE/0078-0421). **1389**

NEWSLINE / AMERICAN ASSEMBLY OF COLLEGIATE SCHOOLS OF BUSINESS. (US/0360-697X). **699**

NEWSLINE - MANITOBA LIBRARY ASSOCIATION. (CN/0227-6569). **3236**

NEWSLINK. (US). **4606**

NEWSPAPER FINANCIAL EXECUTIVE JOURNAL. (US/0889-4590). **2922**

NEWSPAPER RATES AND DATA. (US/0038-9544). **763**

NEWSPAPER TECHNIQUES (DARMSTADT, GERMANY). (GW). **4817**

NEWSPAPERS & TECHNOLOGY. (US/1052-5572). **Adv Mgr:** Mary Van Meter. **5644**

NEWSPEACE. (UK/0048-0304). **Adv Mgr:** Ben Rees, **Tel** 051 724 1989. **4982**

NEWSTIME (LONDON, ENGLAND). (UK). **4817**

NEWSWATCH (LAGOS). (NR/0189-8892). **2499**

NEWSWEEK (U.S. ED.). (US/0028-9604). **2490**

NEWTON COUNTY ENTERPRISE. (US). **Adv Mgr:** Eric Drain. **5666**

NEWTON GRAPHIC, THE. (US/0739-3849). **Adv Mgr:** Susan Robinson, **Tel** (617)487-7255. **5689**

NEWTON KANSAN (NEWTON, KAN. : 1952). (US). **5677**

NEWTON RECORD, THE. (US). **5701**

NEXUS (HAMILTON, ONT.). (CN/0711-5342). **242**

NFAIS NEWSLETTER. (US/0090-0893). **3236**

NFM-THEMAREEKS AMSTERDAM. (NE/0926-3411). **4075**

NG. NIEUWSBLAD GEZONDHEIDSZORG. (NE/0922-744X). **3621**

NGOUI VIET DAILY NEWS. ENGLISH SECTION. (US/1056-5124). **5637**

NHAC VIET. (US/1063-1909). **Adv Mgr:** Tonnu, **Tel** (216)677-9703. **4141**

NHAN BAN. (FR/0153-3762). **5801**

NIAGARA BRUCE TRAIL CLUB. (CN/0706-7429). **4876**

NIAGARA FALLS REVIEW. (CN/0839-1572). **Adv Mgr:** Tony Bove, **Tel** (416)358-5711 Ext.181. **5790**

NIAGARA - WHEATFIELD TRIBUNE. (US). **5719**

NIBBLE. (US/0734-3795). **1280**

NICHE (BALTIMORE, MD.). (US/1064-0347). **955**

NICHI-BEI JOSEI JANARU. (US/0898-8900). **5563**

NICHI BEI TIMES. (US/0739-2443). **Adv Mgr:** Mr. Tsutomu Umezu, **Tel** (415)921-6820. **5637**

NICOLA VALLEY HISTORICAL QUARTERLY. (CN/0708-8132). **2750**

NIEDEROSTERREICHISCHE SOZIALHILFE UND JUGENDWOHLFAHRTSPFLEGE. (AU). **5299**

NIEDERSAECHSISCHE WIRTSCHAFT. (GW). **1575**

NIEN GIAM VIET-NAM, MONTREAL. (CN/0712-5054). **2750**

NIEREN- UND HOCKDRUCKKRANKHEITEN. (GW/0300-5224). **3622**

NIEUW NEUF. (BE). **305**

NIEUW WERELDTIJDSCHRIFT : NWT. (BE/0773-3577). **2520**

NIEUWE WEST-INDISCHE GIDS. (NE/0028-9930). **5211**

NIGERIAN CHRISTIAN, THE. (NR/0029-005X). **4982**

NIGERIAN CURRENT LAW REVIEW : THE JOURNAL OF THE NIGERIAN INSTITUTE OF ADVANCED LEGAL STUDIES. (NR/0189-207X). **3017**

NIGERIAN FIELD. (UK/0029-0076). **4169**

NIGERIAN JOURNAL OF ECONOMIC AND SOCIAL STUDIES, THE. (NR/0029-0092). **1508**

NIGERIAN JOURNAL OF FORESTRY. (NR/0374-9584). **2389**

NIGERIAN JOURNAL OF NUTRITIONAL SCIENCES. (NR/0189-0913). **4195**

NIGERIAN JOURNAL OF PUBLIC AFFAIRS, THE. (NR). **4669**

NIGERIAN LIBRARY AND INFORMATION SCIENCE REVIEW. (NR/0189-4412). **3236**

NIGERIAN PETROLEUM NEWS. (NR/0189-7233). **4266**

NIGERIAN YELLOW PAGES : AN A TO Z TRADE DIRECTORY. (NR/0331-0973). **847**

NIGHTINGALE REPORT. (CN). **4075**

NIHON BUNGAKU. (JA). **3417**

NIHON HAKUYO KIKAN GAKKAI SHI. JOURNAL OF THE MARINE ENGINEERING SOCIETY IN JAPAN. (JA). **1989**

NIHON KAGAKU RYOHO GAKKAI SOKAI SHOROKUSHU. (JA). **3622**

NIHON KANGO KYOKAI CHOSA KENKYU HOKOKU. (JA/0911-0844). **3862**

NIHON KAZE KOGAKKAI SHI. (JA). **1989**

NIHON OYO DOBUTSU KONCHU GAKKAISHI. (JA/0021-4914). **5612**

NIHON PURANKUTON GAKKAI HO. (JA). **556**

NIHON SEMPAKU MUSEN DENSHINKYOKU KYOKUMEIROKU. (JA). **1135**

NIHON SHOKUHIN KOGYO GAKKAI SHI. (JA/0029-0394). **2351**

NIHON SUISAN GAKKAI SHI. (JA/0021-5392). **2309**

NIKKAN KOKUBO KEIZAI TSUSHIN. THE KOKUBO KEIZAI TSUSHIN. (JA). **4052**

NIKKEI PASOKON. (JA). **1238**

NIKKEI SANGYO SHIMBUN. (JA). **5805**

NIKKEI WEEKLY. (JA). **1638**

NIMHANS JOURNAL. (II). **3931**

NIMROD (TULSA). (US/0029-053X). **Adv Mgr:** Elizabeth Thompson, **Tel** (918)584-3333. **3417**

NINETEENTH CENTURY CONTEXTS. (US/0890-5495). **3417**

NINETEENTH-CENTURY FRENCH STUDIES. (US/0146-7891). **3349**

NINETEENTH-CENTURY LITERATURE. (US/0891-9356). **3417**

NINETEENTH-CENTURY STUDIES (CHARLESTON, S.C.). (US/0893-7931). **3417**

NINETEENTH CENTURY : THE MAGAZINE OF THE VICTORIAN SOCIETY IN AMERICA. (US). **360**

NINETEENTH CENTURY THEATRE. (US/0893-3766). **5367**

NINNAU : THE NORTH AMERICAN WELSH NEWSLETTER. (US/0890-0485). **2270**

NIP (CINCINNATI, OHIO. 1993). (US/1074-0791). **Adv Mgr:** H. Bond, **Tel** (513)281-5416. **2491**

NIR NEWS. (UK/0960-3360). **4413**

NIRSA JOURNAL. (US). **4908**

NISQUALLY VALLEY NEWS, THE. (US). **5761**

NITROGEN. (UK/0029-0777). **987**

NITTANY GROTTO NEWS. (US/0732-5398). **1358**

NIYOJANA. (NP). **590**

NJ AUDUBON. (US/0886-6619). **2200**

NJEA REVIEW. (US/0027-6758). **1769**

NLGI SPOKESMAN. (US/0027-6782). **2123**

NMR IN BIOMEDICINE. (UK/0952-3480). **3622**

NO-DIG INTERNATIONAL. (UK/0960-4405). **Adv Mgr:** Mike Bellenger. **2027**

NO-TILL FARMER. (US/0091-9993). **179**

NO TO SHINKEI. (JA/0006-8969). **3844**

NOBLES COUNTY REVIEW. (US). **Adv Mgr:** Patricia Jansen. **5697**

NOGYO KISHO. (JA/0021-8588). **1432**

NOISE CONTROL ENGINEERING JOURNAL. (US/0736-2501). **2178**

NOISE POLLUTION PUBLICATIONS ABSTRACTS. (US/0733-172X). **2179**

NOK LAPJA. (HU). **5563**

NOMA. (NR/0331-6742). **114**

NOME NUGGET (NOME, ALASKA : 1938). (US/0745-9106). **5629**

NOMINA. (UK/0141-6340). **3306**

NOMOS (FORTALEZA, BRAZIL). (BL). **3018**

NON-DESTRUCTIVE TESTING - AUSTRALIA. (AT/0157-6461). **1989**

NON-FERROUS METAL WORKS OF THE WORLD. (UK/0078-0987). **4013**

NONPROFIT TIMES, THE. (US/0896-5048). **Adv Mgr:** Kevin Landers. **880**

NONPROFIT WORLD. (US). **Adv Mgr:** Dave Hilsenhoff, **Tel** (608)274-9777. **5299**

NONRENEWABLE RESOURCES. (US/0961-1444). **2201**

NONVIOLENT ACTIVIST, THE. (US/8755-7428). **Adv Mgr:** Andy Mager, **Tel** (607)842-6858. **3133**

NONWOVENS INDUSTRY. (US/0163-4429). **1620**

NOR KIANK. (US/0194-0074). **5637**

NOR OR. (US). **5637**

NORD E SUD. (IT/0029-1188). **2700**

NORD (HEARST). (CN/0382-8883). **5790**

NORDEN (NEW YORK, N.Y.). (US/0895-2612). **5719**

NORDEN; NORD-NORGES LANDBRUKSTIDSSKRIFT. (NO). **114**

NORDIC JOURNAL OF BOTANY. (DK/0107-055X). **520**

NORDIC JOURNAL OF LINGUISTICS. (NO/0332-5865). **3306**

NORDIC JOURNAL OF SOVIET AND EAST EUROPEAN STUDIES. (SW/0281-8353). **2700**

NORDIC WEST. (US/0749-601X). **4908**

NORDISK ADMINISTRATIVT TIDSSKRIFT. (DK/0029-1285). **4669**

NORDISK ALKOHOL TIDSKRIFT. (FI/0782-9671). **1347**

NORDISK DOMSSAMLING. (NO/0029-1315). **3018**

NORDISK JARNBANETIDSKRIFT. (SW). **5433**

NORDISK PEDAGOGIK. (DK/0901-8050). **1769**

NORDISK PSYKOLOGI. (DK/0029-1463). **4606**

NORDISK ST-FORUM. (NO/0801-7220). **5211**

NORDISK TIDSKRIFT FOR DOVUNDERVISNINGEN. (SW/0029-1471). **1883**

NORDISK TIDSSKRIFT FOR INTERNATIONAL RET. PUBLIKATIONSSERIE. (DK). **3133**

NORDISK TIDSSKRIFT FOR SPECIALPAEDAGOGIK. (NO/0048-0509). **1883**

NORDSTJERNAN (1991). (US/1059-7670). **Adv Mgr:** Mette Barlsund. **5719**

NORFOLK ANCESTOR : JOURNAL OF THE NORFOLK & NORWICH GENEALOGICAL SOCIETY, THE. (UK/0140-5403). **2464**

NORGES KOMMUNEKALENDER. (NO). **1576**

NORIN SUISANSHO TOKEIHYO. (JA). **114**

NORMALISATIE-NIEUWS (DELFT). (NE/0929-2985). **4032**

NORMAS LEGALES. (PE). **3018**

NORMAT. (NO/0801-3500). **3524**

NORMATIVA TECNICA. (IT). **5134**

NOROIL. (NO/0332-544X). **4266**

NORRIDGE HARWOOD HEIGHTS NEWS. (US/1054-7932). **Adv Mgr:** Julie Ross. **5661**

NORSEMAN. (NO/0029-1846). **2520**

NORSK ANTHROPOLOGISK TIDSSKRIFT. (NO/0802-7285). **242**

NORSK ARTILLERI TIDSSKRIFT. (NO). **4053**

NORSK FARMACEUTISK TIDSSKRIFT. (DK/0029-1935). **4318**

NORSK FILOSOFISK TIDSSKRIFT. (NO/0029-1943). **4353**

NORSK GEOGRAFISK TIDSSKRIFT. (NO/0029-1951). **2571**

NORSK GEOLOGISK TIDSSKRIFT. (NO/0029-196X). **1390**

NORSK HAGETIDEND. (NO/0029-1986). **2426**

NORSK IDRETT. (NO/0029-1994). **4908**

NORSK LANDBRUK. (NO). **114**

NORSK LINGVISTISK TIDSSKRIFT : NLT. (NO/0800-3076). **3306**

NORSK MILITRT TIDSSKRIFT. (NO/0029-2028). **4053**

NORSK MUSIKERBLAD. (NO/0029-2044). **4142**

NORSK MUSIKKTIDSSKRIFT. (NO/0332-5482). **4142**

NORSK OLJEREVY. (NO/0332-5490). **4266**

NORSK PEDAGOGISK TIDSKRIFT. (NO). **1769**

NORSK SKOGBRUK. (NO/0029-2087). **2389**

NORSK SLEKTSHISTORISK TIDSSKRIFT. (NO/0029-2141). **2464**

NORSK STATSVITENSKAPELIG TIDSSKRIFT. (NO/0801-1745). **4484**

NORSK TEOLOGISK TIDSSKRIFT. (NO/0029-2176). **4982**

NORSK TIDSSKRIFT FOR MISJON. (NO/0029-2214). **4982**

NORSK VETERINARTIDSSKRIFT. (NO). **5517**

NORTH AMERICAN DIRECTORY & REFERENCE GUIDE OF ASIAN INDIAN BUSINESSES AND INDEPENDENT PROFESSIONAL PRACTITIONERS ALONG WITH COMMUNITY REFERENCE GUIDE & TRAVEL INFORMATION. (US/0883-3583). **699**

NORTH AMERICAN DIRECTORY OF CONTRACT MANUFACTURERS IN ELECTRONICS. (US/1052-0716). **2074**

NORTH AMERICAN FARM EQUIPMENT JOURNAL. (US). **160**

NORTH AMERICAN FISHERMAN. (US/1043-2450). **Adv Mgr:** Mike Edison. **2309**

NORTH AMERICAN HUNTER. (US/0194-4320). **4876**

NORTH AMERICAN LICENSING TRIBUNE. (UK). **1306**

NORTH BATTLEFORD NEWS OPTIMIST. (CN). **5790**

NORTH CAROLINA. (US). **Adv Mgr:** C. Couch, P. deLuca. **699**

NORTH CAROLINA ARCHITECTURE. (US/1045-3253). **305**

NORTH CAROLINA BEACON. (US/1064-4830). **Adv Mgr:** Jim Tucker. **5724**

NORTH CAROLINA CHRISTIAN ADVOCATE. (US/0029-2435). **5724**

NORTH CAROLINA COUNCIL OF WOMEN'S ORGANIZATIONS ANNUAL DIRECTORY. (US). **5234**

NORTH CAROLINA DENTAL GAZETTE. (US/0091-164X). **1331**

NORTH CAROLINA ENGLISH TEACHER. (US/0887-5596). **1901**

NORTH CAROLINA FARM BUREAU NEWS. (US/0744-9593). **115**

NORTH CAROLINA INDEPENDENT, THE. (US/0737-8254). **Adv Mgr:** B. Thorp. **5724**

NORTH CAROLINA JOURNAL OF INTERNATIONAL LAW AND COMMERCIAL REGULATION. (US/0743-1759). **3133**

NORTH CAROLINA LAW REVIEW. (US/0029-2524). **3018**

NORTH CAROLINA LAWYERS WEEKLY. (US/1041-1747). **Adv Mgr:** Laura Price. **3018**

NORTH CAROLINA LIBRARIES. (US/0029-2540). **Adv Mgr:** Judy Stoddard, **Tel** (910)592-4153. **3237**

NORTH CAROLINA LITERARY REVIEW. (US/1063-0724). **3418**

NORTH CAROLINA MEDICAL JOURNAL (WINSTON-SALEM). (US/0029-2559). **Adv Mgr:** Don French, **Tel** (919)467-8515. **3916**

NORTH CAROLINA PLUMBING-HEATING-COOLING FORUM. (US/0739-3830). **Adv Mgr:** Annette Forsythe, **Tel** (919)833-0372. **2607**

NORTH CAROLINA RECREATIONAL AND PARK REVIEW. (US/0164-4254). **Adv Mgr:** Mike Waters, **Tel** (919)832-5868. **4853**

NORTH CAROLINA STATE BAR QUARTERLY. (US/0164-6850). **3018**

NORTH CENTRAL SALES GUIDE TO HIGH-TECH COMPANIES. (US/1040-0540). **5134**

NORTH CHESHIRE FAMILY HISTORIAN 1975. (UK/0306-9206). **2464**

NORTH COUNTRY ANVIL. (US). **2541**

NORTH DAKOTA MUSIC EDUCATOR. (US/0029-2753). **4142**

NORTH DAKOTA R E C MAGAZINE. (US). **1542**

NORTH EAST OUT DOORS. (US/0199-8463). **4876**

NORTH FRONTENAC NEWS. (CN/0700-950X). **5790**

NORTH GEORGIA JOURNAL. (US/8756-9256). **Adv Mgr:** Carole Webster, **Tel** (404)642-5569. **2750**

NORTH IRISH ROOTS. (UK/0264-9217). **2464**

NORTH JACKSON PROGRESS. (US/0164-9108). **5627**

NORTH JEFFERSON NEWS, THE. (US). **Adv Mgr:** Mona Richards. **5627**

NORTH JERSEY PROSPECTOR, THE. (US/0745-8908). **5711**

NORTH KAWARTHA TIMES. (CN/0823-7387). **5791**

NORTH LAKE TAHOE BONANZA. (US/0192-3129). **Adv Mgr:** Lucy Karnes, **Tel** (702)831-4666. **5708**

NORTH LOUISIANA GENEALOGICAL SOCIETY JOURNAL. (US). **2464**

NORTH SAN ANTONIO TIMES, THE. (US). **Adv Mgr:** Jim Kennedy. **5753**

NORTH SCOTT PRESS, THE. (US). **Adv Mgr:** Jayne Carstersen. **5672**

NORTH SEA OIL & GAS DIRECTORY. (UK). **4266**

NORTH SHORE. (US/0164-5366). **2541**

NORTH SHORE SENTINEL. (CN/0715-5786). **5791**

NORTH / SOUTH ISSUES : BIBLIOGRAPHY OF THEORETICAL AND CURRENT EVENT ANALYSIS. (FR). **421**

NORTH SUBURBAN PRESS. (US/0892-1792). **5697**

NORTH TEXAS TRAIL TRACERS. (US/0893-2948). **2464**

NORTH VERNON PLAIN DEALER, THE. (US). **Adv Mgr:** Paula Lamb. **5666**

NORTH VERNON SUN. (US). **Adv Mgr:** Paula Lamb. **5666**

NORTH-WESTERN EUROPEAN LANGUAGE EVOLUTION. (DK/0108-8416). **3306**

NORTH WOODS CALL, THE. (US/0029-2958). **4876**

NORTHAMPTONSHIRE PAST & PRESENT. (UK). **2700**

NORTHEAST EQUINE JOURNAL. (US). **2801**

NORTHEAST IMPROVER, THE. (US/0145-9112). **197**

NORTHEAST JOURNAL OF BUSINESS & ECONOMICS, THE. (US/8755-5123). **1508**

NORTHEAST MISSISSIPPI DAILY JOURNAL. (US/0744-5431). **5701**

NORTHEAST SUN. (US/0738-971X). **1951**

NORTHEAST TIMES (PHILADELPHIA, PA. : 1971). (US). **Adv Mgr:** Timothy Smylie, **Tel** (215)355-9009 ext. 121. **5738**

NORTHEASTER. (US). **5697**

NORTHEASTERN GEOLOGY. (US/0194-1453). **1390**

NORTHERN CALIFORNIA HOME & GARDEN. (US/0898-1191). **2902**

NORTHERN CALIFORNIA MEDICINE. (US). **Adv Mgr:** Kate Lynn, **Tel** (510)832-3364. **3623**

NORTHERN CALIFORNIA SUN. (US/8755-8866). **1951**

NORTHERN ILLINOIS UNIVERSITY LAW REVIEW. (US/0734-1490). **3018**

NORTHERN IRELAND LAW REPORTS, THE. (IE). **3018**

NORTHERN IRELAND LEGAL QUARTERLY, THE. (IE/0029-3105). **Adv Mgr:** Patricia McCann. **3018**

NORTHERN — Advertising Accepted Index

NORTHERN JOURNAL OF APPLIED FORESTRY. (US/0742-6348). **2389**

NORTHERN LIFE (SUDBURY). (CN/0700-527X). **Adv Mgr:** K. Johansson. **5791**

NORTHERN LIGHTS. (US). **2541**

NORTHERN LOGGER AND TIMBER PROCESSOR, THE. (US/0029-3156). **Adv Mgr:** Pamela Leach, **Tel** (315)369-3078. **2403**

NORTHERN MINER, THE. (CN/0029-3164). **2147**

NORTHERN MOSAIC (THUNDER BAY). (CN/0384-0840). **5791**

NORTHERN MOSIAC (LLOYDMINSTER). (CN/0824-3484). **326**

NORTHERN NECK OF VIRGINIA HISTORICAL MAGAZINE. (US/0549-9186). **2751**

NORTHERN NEW ENGLAND REVIEW. (US/0190-3012). **3418**

NORTHERN OHIO LIVE. (US/0271-5147). **Adv Mgr:** Gail Kerzner. **2541**

NORTHERN ONTARIO BUSINESS. (CN/0710-2755). **700**

NORTHERN PEN. (CN/0229-0391). **Adv Mgr:** Sharon Warren. **5791**

NORTHERN REVIEW, THE. (US/0894-3362). **326**

NORTHERN REVIEW (WHITEHORSE) (CN). **Adv Mgr:** A. Graham. **326**

NORTHERN TIMES (WHITEHORSE). (CN/0227-2512). **5791**

NORTHERN VIRGINIA SUN. (US/1065-1632). **Adv Mgr:** David Blakeslee. **5759**

NORTHERN VIRGINIAN. (US/0164-6710). **2541**

NORTHERN WOMAN JOURNAL. (CN/0824-4081). **5563**

NORTHGLENN-THORNTON SENTINEL. (US). **Adv Mgr:** Scott Bumgardner. **5644**

NORTHLAND QUARTERLY, THE. (US/0899-708X). **3418**

NORTHPOINT. (CN/0380-0881). **5134**

NORTHROP UNIV. LAW J. AEROSP., BUS. TAX. (US/0887-4301). **3019**

NORTHSHORE CITIZEN (1990). (US/1057-3771). **Adv Mgr:** Kim VanderKooy. **5761**

NORTHUMBERLAND NEWS. (CN/0228-0531). **5791**

NORTHUMBRIANA. (UK). **2520**

NORTHWARD JOURNAL. (CN/0706-0955). **360**

NORTHWEST ARKANSAS TIMES (FAYETTEVILLE, AR.). (US/1066-3355). **Adv Mgr:** Carmen Collen, **Tel** (501)447-1735. **5632**

NORTHWEST BOAT TRAVEL. (US/0192-1169). **594**

NORTHWEST CHESS. (US/0146-6941). **4864**

NORTHWEST DENTISTRY. (US/0029-2915). **Adv Mgr:** Patty Lein. **1331**

NORTHWEST ENVIRONMENTAL JOURNAL, THE. (US/0749-7962). **Adv Mgr:** Ellen Chu, **Tel** (206)543-1812. **2179**

NORTHWEST ETHNIC NEWS. (US/0894-3109). **2270**

NORTHWEST EXPLORER (YELLOWKNIFE). (CN/0820-6724). **2541**

NORTHWEST FARM EQUIPMENT JOURNAL. (US/0029-3350). **160**

NORTHWEST LABOR PRESS. (US/0894-444X). **5733**

NORTHWEST PALATE, THE. (US/0892-8363). **2351**

NORTHWEST PUBLIC POWER BULLETIN. (US/1055-6761). **1951**

NORTHWEST REVIEW (EUGENE, OR.). (US/0029-3423). **3349**

NORTHWEST RUNNER. (US/0883-7945). **4908**

NORTHWEST SAILBOARD. (US). **Adv Mgr:** Marie Cordell, **Tel** (503)386-7440. **594**

NORTHWEST SAILBOARD. (US/1063-8164). **Adv Mgr:** Marie Cordell. **4908**

NORTHWEST SALES GUIDE TO HIGH-TECH COMPANIES. (US/1040-0516). **5134**

NORTHWEST SCIENCE. (US/0029-344X). **5134**

NORTHWEST TERRITORIES REPORTS. (CN/0824-3433). **3019**

NORTHWEST TRAVEL. (US/1059-9681). **5486**

NORTHWESTERN DENTAL RESEARCH. (US/1062-0311). **Adv Mgr Tel** (312)503-6869. **1331**

NORTHWESTERN JEWELER, THE. (US/0029-3490). **2915**

NORTHWESTERN JOURNAL OF INTERNATIONAL LAW & BUSINESS. (US/0196-3228). **3102**

NORTHWESTERN NATURALIST : A JOURNAL OF VERTEBRATE BIOLOGY. (US/1051-1733). **4169**

NORTHWESTERNER (LARKSPUR, CALIF.). (US/0894-0800). **5433**

NORTON NOTES. (US/1049-1821). **2284**

NORVEG. (NO/0029-3601). **242**

NORWALK REFLECTOR (NORWALK, OHIO : DAILY). (US/0745-4023). **Adv Mgr:** John Ringenbeng. **5729**

NORWAY CURRENT, THE. (US/1071-2607). **Adv Mgr:** L. A. Underhill. **5693**

NORWAY TIMES. (US/0891-6322). **Adv Mgr:** Judith Anderson. **5719**

NORWEGIAN ARCHAEOLOGICAL REVIEW. (NO/0029-3652). **276**

NOR'WESTING. (US/0739-747X). **594**

NOS SOURCES. (CN/0227-0404). **2464**

NOSA TERRA, A. (SP/0213-3105). **Adv Mgr:** Cesar Pazos, **Tel** 43-86-433830. **5269**

NOSTOC MAGAZINE. (US). **3467**

NOTE TRIMESTRIELLE DE CONJONCTURE / STATEC, LUXEMBOURG. (LU). **1508**

NOTES AND QUERIES. (UK/0029-3970). **3306**

NOTES & QUERIES FOR SOMERSET AND DORSET. (UK/0029-3989). **2700**

NOTES BIBLIOGRAPHIQUES. (FR/0468-8678). **Adv Mgr:** J. Cartalas. **3418**

NOTES DE RECHERCHES - GEOGRAPHIE. UNIVERSITE D'OTTAWA. (CN/0824-295X). **2571**

NOTES ET DOCUMENTS (INSTITUT INTERNATIONAL JACQUES MARITAIN). (IT). **4354**

NOTES FROM UNDERGROUND. (US/0550-0974). **5388**

NOTES ON CONTEMPORARY LITERATURE. (US/0029-4047). **3349**

NOTES ON LITERACY. (US/0737-6707). **3307**

NOTES ON MODERN IRISH LITERATURE. (US/1045-6619). **3418**

NOTES ON SCRIPTURE IN USE. (US/0737-2876). **5018**

NOTFALL-MEDIZIN (ERLANGEN). (GW/0341-2903). **3725**

NOTICES OF THE AMERICAN MATHEMATICAL SOCIETY. (US/0002-9920). **3525**

NOTICIARIO DE HISTORIA AGRARIA. (SP/1132-1261). **115**

NOTICIAS DEL MUNDO. (US/0888-143X). **Adv Mgr:** David Rosa. **5719**

NOTICIERO DE LA AMBAC. (MX). **Adv Mgr:** Lec. Jose Antonio Yanez, **Tel** 011 52 5 2279012. **3237**

NOTIZIARIO ASSICURATIVO. (IT). **2889**

NOTIZIARIO CHIMICO E FARMACEUTICO. (IT/0550-1156). **988**

NOTIZIARIO SULLE MALATTIE DELLE PIANTE. (IT/0468-9291). **520**

NOTIZIARIO TESSILE ABBIGLIAMENTO. (IT). **5354**

NOTIZIE AIRI. (IT). **5134**

NOTIZIE DELLA SCUOLA. (IT). **Adv Mgr:** Gabriella Crusco. **1867**

NOTRE DAME JOURNAL OF FORMAL LOGIC. (US/0029-4527). **4354**

NOTRE DAME JOURNAL OF LAW, ETHICS & PUBLIC POLICY. (US/0883-3648). **3019**

NOTRE DAME LAW REVIEW, THE. (US/0745-3515). **3019**

NOTRE HOPITAL. (CN/0704-8815). **3790**

NOUS. (FR). **Adv Mgr:** Rene Boue. **5253**

NOUS (BLOOMINGTON). (US/0029-4624). **4354**

NOUS VOULONS LIRE PESSAC. (FR/0153-9027). **3349**

NOUVEAU BIOLOGISTE, LE. (FR/0181-3684). **467**

NOUVEAU RECUEIL COMPLET DES FABLIAUX. (NE). **3418**

NOUVEAUX CAHIERS D'ALLEMAND. (FR/0758-170X). **3418**

NOUVEAUX CAHIERS, LES. (FR/0550-1350). **5051**

NOUVEL AFRIQUE ASIE, LE. (FR/1141-9946). **4484**

NOUVEL ECONOMISTE, LE. (FR). **1576**

NOUVEL OFFICIEL DE L'AMEUBLEMENT. (FR). **2906**

NOUVELLE (BEAUMONT). (CN/0827-2085). **5791**

NOUVELLE REVUE DU SON PARIS, LA. (FR/0397-3190). **2491**

NOUVELLE REVUE PEDAGOGIQUE. (FR/0029-4837). **1769**

NOUVELLE REVUE THEOLOGIQUE. (BE/0029-4845). **4982**

NOUVELLE TOUR DE FEU, LA. (FR/0294-4030). **5791**

NOUVELLES ARCHIVES HOSPITALIERES. (FR/0029-4853). **3790**

NOUVELLES (CENTRALE DE L'ENSEIGNEMENT DU QUEBEC). (CN/0710-5568). **1695**

NOUVELLES DE L'A.Q.T. (CN/0826-2799). **4413**

NOUVELLES DE LA REPUBLIQUE DES LETTRES (NAPLES, ITALY). (IT/0392-2332). **3307**

NOUVELLES DE LA SCIENCE ET DES TECHNOLOGIES. (BE/0771-7369). **5135**

NOUVELLES DE L'ACADEMIE / ACADEMIE DES SCIENCES, LES. (FR/0246-1226). **5135**

NOUVELLES DE L'ESTAMPE. (FR/0029-4888). **4567**

NOUVELLES DERMATOLOGIQUES, LES. (FR/0752-5370). **Adv Mgr:** Frederique Nartz. **3722**

NOUVELLES ESTHETIQUES (FRENCH ED.), LES. (FR). **405**

NOUVELLES FISCALES (PARIS), LES. (FR/0399-1636). **Adv Mgr:** JB Monier, **Tel** 1 48 05 91 05. **801**

NOUVELLES GRAPHIQUES. (BE/0029-4926). **381**

NOUVELLES / LA FEDERATION DES SOCIETES D'HISTOIRE DU QUEBEC. (CN/0829-2612). **2751**

NOUVELLES QUESTIONS FEMINISTES. (FR/0248-4951). **5563**

NOVA ET VETERA (FRIBOURG). (SZ/0029-5027). **4982**

NOVA HRVATSKA. (UK/0143-3563). **2660**

NOVA LAW REVIEW. (US/1049-0248). **3019**

NOVA MATICA. (YU/0353-8052). **Adv Mgr:** Babic, **Tel** (41)539 212. **3349**

NOVA SCOTIA BUSINESS JOURNAL. (CN/0820-2737). **700**

NOVA SCOTIA CHRISTMAS TREE JOURNAL. (CN/0832-8293). **2390**

NOVA SCOTIA HISTORICAL REVIEW. (CN/0227-4752). **2751**

NOVA SCOTIA LAW NEWS. (CN/0316-6325). **3019**

NOVA SCOTIA MEDICAL JOURNAL, THE. (CN/0838-2638). **3623**

NOVARA. (IT). **1508**

NOVASCOPE. (US/0892-5003). **2491**

NOVEL. (US/0029-5132). **3349**

NOVENYTERMELES. (HU/0546-8191). **179**

NOVI DNI. (CN/0048-1017). **2270**

NOVIJ SLAH. (CN/0029-5310). **5791**

NOVOE RUSSKOE SLOVO. (US/0730-8949). **5719**

NOVUM GEBRAUCHSGRAPHIK. (GW/0302-9794). **381**

NOW AND THEN (MUNCY). (US/0029-5361). **Adv Mgr:** Bill Ritter, **Tel** (717)546-2211. **2751**

NOW DIG THIS. (UK). **Adv Mgr Tel** (091) 2624006. **4142**

NOW L.A. / OFFICIAL PUBLICATION OF THE LOS ANGELES CHAPTER, NATIONAL ORGANIZATION FOR WOMEN (NOW). (US/0741-9627). **5563**

NOW (TORONTO. 1981). (CN/0712-1326). **Adv Mgr:** Bill Malcolm, **Tel** (416)461-0871. **4853**

NPTA MANAGEMENT NEWS. (US/0739-2214). **Adv Mgr:** Carl Dunby, **Tel** (516)829-3070 ext. 19. **4235**

NRC HANDELSBLAD. (NE). **5806**

NRMA AD/PRO. (US/0748-8327). **763**

NSCA MEMBERS' HANDBOOK. (UK/0140-6787). **2179**

NSCLC WASHINGTON WEEKLY. (US/0277-7460). **3020**

NSPA WASHINGTON REPORTER, THE. (US/0469-3922). **749**

NSS NEWS. (US/0027-7010). **Adv Mgr:** Brandon Fee, **Tel** (205)854-7487. **1359**

NSUKKA LIBRARY NOTES. (NR/0331-1481). **3237**

NSW DAIRYMEN'S DIGEST. (AT). **197**

NT, TECNICA & TECNOLOGIA / AMMA. (IT). **2123**

NTDRA DEALER NEWS. (US/0027-7045). **Adv Mgr:** Joan Senn. **5076**

NTZ : NACHRICTENTECHNISCHE ZEITSCHRIFT. (GW/0027-707X). **1161**

NUCLEAR CANADA YEARBOOK. (CN/0383-8536). **1951**

NUCLEAR ENERGY (1978). (UK/0140-4067). **1951**

NUCLEAR ENGINEER, THE. (UK/0262-5091). **2156**

NUCLEAR EUROPE WORLDSCAN. (SZ/1016-5975). **Adv Mgr:** A. Hunter. **2157**

NUCLEAR MEDICINE COMMUNICATIONS. (UK/0143-3636). **3848**

NUCLEAR NEWS (HINSDALE). (US/0029-5574). **2157**

NUCLEAR PLANT JOURNAL. (US/0892-2055). **1952**

NUCLEAR SCIENCE APPLICATIONS. (SZ/0191-1686). **4449**

NUCLEAR SCIENCE APPLICATIONS. (SZ/0191-1686). **4449**

NUCLEAR TIMES (NEW YORK, N.Y.). (US/0734-5836). **4485**

NUCLEIC ACIDS RESEARCH. (UK/0305-1048). **491**

NUCLEOSIDES & NUCLEOTIDES. (US/0732-8311). **491**

NUDE & NATURAL. (US/1070-9835). **2491**

NUESTRAS RAICES (QUARTERLY). (US/1045-2427). **2465**

NUESTRO. (US/0147-3247). **2270**

NUEVA LUZ. (US/0887-5855). **Adv Mgr:** M. Romais. **4372**

NUEVA REVISTA DE FILOLOGIA HISPANICA. (MX/0185-0121). **3307**

NUEVAMERICA. (AG/0325-6960). **Adv Mgr:** Gema Romero. **1769**

NUEZ (NEW YORK, N.Y.), LA. (US/0898-1140). **3419**

NUMEN (INTERNATIONAL ASSOCIATION FOR THE HISTORY OF RELIGIONS). (NE/0029-5973). **4982**

NUMERICAL FUNCTIONAL ANALYSIS AND OPTIMIZATION. (US/0163-0563). **3525**

NUMERICAL HEAT TRANSFER. PART A, APPLICATIONS. (US/1040-7782). **4432**

NUMERICAL HEAT TRANSFER. PART B, FUNDAMENTALS. (US/1040-7790). **4432**

NUMERICAL METHODS FOR PARTIAL DIFFERENTIAL EQUATIONS. (US/0749-159X). **3525**

NUMISMATIC NEWS (KRAUSE PUBLICATIONS : 1977). (US/0029-604X). **2782**

NUMISMATICA, LA. (IT). **2782**

NUMISMATIST, THE. (US/0029-6090). **2782**

NUNATSIAQ NEWS. (CN/0702-7915). **5791**

NUOVA ANTOLOGIA. (IT/0029-6147). **2491**

NUOVA CORRENTE. (IT/0029-6155). **4354**

NUOVA ELETTRONICA. (IT). **2074**

NUOVA EUROPA, LA. (IT). **4983**

NUOVA FINESTRA. (IT). **634**

NUOVA RIVISTA DI NEUROLOGIA. (IT). **Adv Mgr:** Dott Dalla, **Tel** 06-49914675. **3844**

NUOVA RIVISTA MUSICALE ITALIANA. (IT/0029-6228). **4142**

NUOVA RIVISTA STORICA. (IT/0029-6236). **2624**

NUOVO MEZZOGIORNO. (IT/0029-6376). **1509**

NUOVO OSSERVATORE, IL. (IT). **Adv Mgr:** Antonella Massaroni. **1509**

NUOVO PAESE. (AT/0311-6166). **2701**

NURADEEN. (US/8756-4637). **5044**

NURSCENE. (CN/0382-8476). **3862**

NURSE ANESTHESIA. (US/0897-7437). **3683**

NURSE EDUCATOR. (US/0363-3624). **3863**

NURSE PRACTITIONER, THE. (US/0361-1817). **3863**

NURSE, THE PATIENT & THE LAW, THE. (US/0196-6790). **Adv Mgr:** S Berntson. **3020**

NURSERY MANAGER. (US). **2426**

NURSING. (US/0360-4039). **3863**

NURSING ADMINISTRATION QUARTERLY. (US/0363-9568). **Adv Mgr:** Frances S. Ray, **Tel** (301)417-7584. **3863**

NURSING & ALLIED HEALTH CINAHL CAMBRIDGE. CD-ROM. (US). **3661**

NURSING & ALLIED HEALTH (CINAHL) ... SUBJECT HEADING LIST. (US/0888-0530). **3863**

NURSING & HEALTH CARE. (US/0276-5284). **3863**

NURSING AND HEALTH SCIENCE EDUCATION REVIEW. (AT/1033-6273). **3863**

NURSING BC. (CN/1185-3638). **Adv Mgr:** Doug Davison, **Tel** (604)688-6819. **3863**

NURSING ECONOMIC$. (US/0746-1739). **3864**

NURSING FORUM (HILLSDALE). (US/0029-6473). **Adv Mgr:** Joseph M Braden. **3864**

NURSING JOURNAL OF INDIA. (II/0029-6503). **3864**

NURSING MATTERS. (US/0272-9512). **Adv Mgr:** Kaye Lillesand. **3864**

NURSING NEW ZEALAND. (NZ/1172-1979). **3864**

NURSING OUTLOOK. (US/0029-6554). **3865**

NURSING (OXFORD). (UK/0142-0372). **3865**

NURSING QUEBEC. (CN/0381-6419). **3865**

NURSING RESEARCH ABSTRACTS. (UK/0141-3899). **3865**

NURSING RESEARCH (NEW YORK). (US/0029-6562). **3865**

NURSING RSA. (SA/0258-1647). **3865**

NURSINGCONNECTIONS (WASHINGTON, D.C.). (US/0895-2809). **3866**

NURSINGWORLD JOURNAL. (US/0745-8630). **Adv Mgr:** Richard DeVito. **3866**

NUT EDUCATION REVIEW. (UK/0951-7855). **Adv Mgr:** T. Kresky. **1769**

NUT GROWER. (US/0745-3469). **180**

NUT KERNEL, THE. (US/0738-596X). **2426**

NUTRICION HOSPITALARIA. (SP/0212-1611). **4195**

NUTRITION ABSTRACTS AND REVIEWS. SERIES A: HUMAN & EXPERIMENTAL. (UK/0309-1295). **4201**

NUTRITION ABSTRACTS AND REVIEWS. SERIES B. LIVESTOCK FEEDS AND FEEDING. (UK/0309-135X). **155**

NUTRITION AND CANCER. (US/0163-5581). **4195**

NUTRITION & DIETARY CONSULTANT, THE. (US/8750-8370). **4195**

NUTRITION AND HEALTH (BERKHAMSTED). (UK/0260-1060). **4195**

NUTRITION (BURBANK, LOS ANGELES COUNTY, CALIF.). (US/0899-9007). **4196**

NUTRITION RESEARCH (NEW YORK, N.Y.). (US/0271-5317). **4196**

NUTRITION TODAY (ANNAPOLIS). (US/0029-666X). **4197**

NUTRITIONAL PERSPECTIVES. (US/0160-3922). **4197**

NUTSHELL NEWS. (US/0164-3290). **374**

NUTZFAHRZEUG, DAS. (GW). **5388**

NUUSBRIEF. (SA/0039-4807). **5234**

NV; NEUE VERPACKUNG. (GW/0341-0390). **4220**

NVB. NOISE & VIBRATION BULLETIN. (UK/0144-7785). **2179**

NVS NIEUWS. (NE). **4794**

NYA ANTIK & AUKTION. (SW/0346-9212). **251**

NYAC NEWS. (US/0275-5114). **4670**

NYALA / NATIONAL FAUNA PRESERVATION SOCIETY OF MALAWI. (MW). **2201**

NYLA BULLETIN. (US/0027-7134). **Adv Mgr:** C. Raphael, **Tel** (518)432-6952. **3238**

NYLON HIGHWAY. (US/1071-2615). **1409**

NYT FRA ISLAND. (DK). **2701**

NYTT NORSK TIDSSKRIFT. (NO/0800-336X). **4485**

NZ BUSINESS. (NZ/0113-4957). **700**

O A C E T T NEWSLETTER. (CN/0318-5338). **1989**

O.S.B.E.R. OIL SPILL BULLETIN AND ENVIRONMENTAL REVIEW. (UK/0959-9134). **Adv Mgr:** Frances Johnson, **Tel** 0224 878188 x 32. **2238**

O SOLO. (BL/0584-0821). **180**

OAG AIR CARGO GUIDE. (US/0191-152X). **5388**

OAG TRAVEL PLANNER (EUROPEAN ED.). (US/1075-1548). **2808**

OAG WORLDWIDE CRUISE & SHIPLINE GUIDE. (US/0097-8779). **5487**

OAH NEWSLETTER. (US/1059-1125). **2751**

OAHA NEWS BULETIN. (CN). **Adv Mgr:** B. Sherrer, **Tel** (416)884-3710. **3623**

OAHU UPDATE, THE. (US/1042-8038). **5487**

OAK LEAVES. (US). **5661**

OAK LEAVES (BAY CITY, TEX.). (US/0740-8013). **2465**

OAKDALE LEADER. (US). **Adv Mgr:** John Burden. **5638**

OAKES ACORNS. (US/0897-7771). **2465**

OAKLAND BUSINESS MONTHLY. (US/8750-0981). **700**

OAKLAND POST. (US). **5638**

OAPSE/AFSCME ADVOCATE. (US/0893-5106). **1868**

OAZ, OSTERREICHISCHE APOTHEKER-ZEITUNG. (AU/0253-5238). **4318**

OB. GYN. NEWS. (US/0029-7437). **3766**

OBERFLACHE - SURFACE. (SZ/0048-1270). **4014**

OBERLIN HERALD (OBERLIN, KAN. : 1951). (US). **Adv Mgr:** Stan Chupin. **5678**

OBESITY & HEALTH. (US/1044-1522). **4197**

OBESITY RESEARCH. (US/1071-7323). **3623**

OBESITY SURGERY. (UK/0960-8923). **3970**

OBG MANAGEMENT. (US/1044-307X). **3766**

OBITER DICTA (1963). (CN/0029-7585). **3020**

OBJECTIF EUROPE STRASBOURG. (FR/0221-0703). **2520**

OBJECTIF PREVENTION (MONTREAL). (CN/0705-0577). **Adv Mgr:** Claude Gallant. **4794**

OBJEKTIV HELLERUP. (DK/0107-6329). **4372**

OBSERVADOR ECONOMICO, EL. (UY). **1509**

OBSERVATORY, THE. (UK/0029-7704). **397**

OBSERVER (DE WITT, IOWA. NATIONAL ED.). (US/0886-8808). **Adv Mgr:** Jean Bormann. **5672**

OBSERVER ECCENTRIC. (US). **Adv Mgr:** Mark Lewis, **Tel** (313)591-2300. **5693**

OBSERVER (LONDON). (UK/0029-7712). **5813**

OBSERVER-PATRIOT, THE. (US). **5646**

OBSERVER (RIO RANCHO, N.M.), THE. (US/1049-7374). **Adv Mgr:** Marisa Gilles. **5712**

OBSERVER (ROCKFORD), THE. (US/0029-7739). **Adv Mgr Tel** (815)963-3471. **5033**

OBSERVER, THE. (US). **Adv Mgr:** Anthony J. Urillo, **Tel** (203)628-9645. **5646**

OBSIDIAN II. (US/0888-4412). **3419**

OBST UND GARTEN. (GW/0029-7798). **2426**

OBSTETRICA ET GYNECOLOGICA (OULU). (FI/0358-4844). **3766**

OBSTETRICAL & GYNECOLOGICAL SURVEY. (US/0029-7828). **3766**

OBSTETRICIA Y GINECOLOGIA LATINO-AMERICANAS. (AG/0029-7836). **3766**

OBSTETRICS AND GYNECOLOGY (NEW YORK. 1953). (US/0029-7844). **3766**

OBZORNIK ZA MATEMATIKO IN FIZIKO. (XV/0473-7466). **3525**

OCCASIONAL PAPERS ON RELIGION IN EASTERN EUROPE. (US/0731-5465). **4983**

OCCASIONAL PAPERS. SOUTH ASIA SERIES. (US/0076-812X). **2661**

OCCASIONAL PUBLICATION - BOREAL INSTITUTE FOR NORTHERN STUDIES. (CN/0068-0303). **2751**

OCCASIONAL PUBLICATIONS IN NORTHEASTERN ANTHROPOLOGY. (US/0276-8607). **242**

OCCUPATIONAL BRIEFS / CGP. (US/1064-7333). **4207**

OCCUPATIONAL HAZARDS. (US/0029-7909). **2866**

OCCUPATIONAL HEALTH. (UK/0029-7917). **Adv Mgr:** Peter Collis. **2866**

OCCUPATIONAL SAFETY & HEALTH (BIRMINGHAM). (UK/0143-5353). **2867**

OCCUPATIONAL

Advertising Accepted Index

OCCUPATIONAL THERAPY IN HEALTH CARE. (US/0738-0577). **1883**

OCCUPATIONAL THERAPY IN MENTAL HEALTH. (US/0164-212X). **2867**

OCCUPATIONAL THERAPY INDEX : CURRENT AWARENESS TOPICS SERVICE. (UK/0950-6675). **1883**

OCCUPATIONAL THERAPY INTERNATIONAL. (UK/0966-7903). **4381**

OCEAN AIR INTERACTIONS. (US/0743-0876). **1359**

OCEAN CHALLENGE. (UK). **1453**

OCEAN DEVELOPMENT AND INTERNATIONAL LAW. (US/0090-8320). **3182**

OCEAN INDUSTRY. (US/0029-8026). **4267**

OCEAN NAVIGATOR. (US/0886-0149). **1453**

OCEAN REALM. (US/0738-9833). **Adv Mgr:** Lori Cutler, **Tel** (305)470-2458. **1453**

OCEAN SPORTS INTERNATIONAL. (US/0899-2622). **4908**

OCEAN SPRINGS RECORD. (US). **Adv Mgr:** Peter Logan, **Tel** (601)875-2791. **5701**

OCEAN VOICE. (UK/0261-6777). **4181**

OCEANIA. (AT/0029-8077). **Adv Mgr:** D. Koller, **Tel** (02)692-2666. **2670**

OCEANIC LINGUISTICS. (US/0029-8115). **3307**

OCEANOLOGICA ACTA. (FR/0399-1784). **1454**

OCEANS. (FR). **4908**

OCEANUS (WOODS HOLE). (US/0029-8182). **1454**

OCLC MICRO. (US/8756-5196). **3238**

OCONOMOWOC ENTERPRISE, THE. (US). **Adv Mgr:** Jan Gust. **5769**

OCTANE. (CN/0835-1740). **4267**

OCTOBER (CAMBRIDGE, MASS.). (US/0162-2870). **327**

OCULAR SURGERY NEWS. (US/8750-3085). **3971**

ODENSE UNIVERSITY STUDIES IN ENGLISH. (DK/0078-3293). **3308**

ODESSA RECORD, THE. (US/1062-2934). **5761**

ODONTO-STOMATOLOGIE TROPICALE. (FR/0251-172X). **1331**

O'DWYER'S DIRECTORY OF CORPORATE COMMUNICATIONS. (US/0149-1091). **763**

O'DWYER'S DIRECTORY OF PUBLIC RELATIONS EXECUTIVES. (US/0191-0051). **763**

O'DWYER'S DIRECTORY OF PUBLIC RELATIONS FIRMS. (US/0078-3374). **763**

O'DWYER'S PR SERVICES REPORT. (US/1043-2957). **763**

ODYSSEUS (FLUSHING, N.Y.). (US/0883-3664). **5487**

ODYSSEY (PETERBOROUGH, N.H.). (US/0163-0946). **398**

OEA FOCUS. (US/0743-7986). **1770**

OECOLOGIA AQUATICA. (SP/0210-9352). **2219**

OEM INDUSTRY. (US/1072-2580). **3485**

OEM OFF-HIGHWAY. (US/1048-3039). **3485**

OEP : OFFICE EQUIPMENT & PRODUCTS. (JA/0387-5245). **4213**

OESTERREICHISCHE BIBLIOGRAPHIE. REIHE A. (AU). **Adv Mgr:** W. Lang. **421**

OESTERREICHISCHE BIBLIOGRAPHIE. REIHE B, VERZEICHNIS DER OSTERREICHISCHEN HOCHSCHULSCHRIFTEN. (AU). **1796**

OESTERREICHISCHE GLASER-ZEITUNG. (AU/0029-9162). **2592**

OESTERREICHISCHE ZEITSCHRIFT FUER VOLKSKUNDE. (AU/0029-9669). **2323**

OEUVRES ET CRITIQUES. (FR/0338-1900). **3349**

OF A LIKE MIND. (US/0892-5984). **4186**

OF COUNSEL (NEW YORK, N.Y.). (US/0730-3815). **3021**

OFF-LEAD. (US/0094-0186 #y 0094-0816). **4287**

OFF OUR BACKS. (US/0030-0071). **5563**

OFF-ROAD (LOS ANGELES). (US/0363-1745). **5422**

OFF ROAD MUNCHEN. (GW/0172-4185). **Adv Mgr:** R. Muhlberger. **5388**

OFF THE SHELF (HUMBLE, TEX.). (US/1059-3993). **3420**

OFFENTLICHE DIENST, DER. (AU). **1699**

OFFICE AUTOMATION. (US/0472-6049). **4213**

OFFICE BUYER. (UK). **4207**

OFFICE DEALER. (UK). **4207**

OFFICE GUIDE TO ORLANDO. (US/0733-1266). **4213**

OFFICE-MANAGEMENT (BADEN-BADEN). (GW/0722-2572). **880**

OFFICE NURSE, THE. (US/0893-6595). **Adv Mgr:** Tom Jones, **Tel** (201)391-6306. **3866**

OFFICE SECRETARY. (UK/0951-6824). **4207**

OFFICE (STAMFORD. 1936), THE. (US/0030-0128). **4213**

OFFICE SYSTEMS (GEORGETOWN, CONN.). (US/8750-3441). **4213**

OFFICE SYSTEMS RESEARCH JOURNAL. (US/0737-8998). **700**

OFFICER REVIEW. (US/0736-7317). **4053**

OFFICER, THE. (US/0030-0268). **4053**

OFFICERSFORBUNDSBLADET. (SW). **Adv Mgr:** Monica Wistedt. **4053**

OFFICIAL BOARD MARKETS. (US/0030-0284). **4235**

OFFICIAL CALIFORNIA APARTMENT JOURNAL. (US/0191-6335). **2829**

OFFICIAL CITY GUIDE. (US/1055-1778). **Adv Mgr:** Paul Insalaco, **Tel** (212)315-0800. **5487**

OFFICIAL DETECTIVE. (US/0894-1211). **Adv Mgr:** J. Burriesci, **Tel** (212)947-6500. **5074**

OFFICIAL DIRECTORY OF CANADIAN MUSEUMS AND RELATED INSTITUTIONS, THE. (CN/0829-0474). **4094**

OFFICIAL DIRECTORY OF INDUSTRIAL AND COMMERCIAL TRAFFIC EXECUTIVES, THE. (US/0192-2629). **5388**

OFFICIAL DIRECTORY OF NEW JERSEY LIBRARIES AND MEDIA CENTERS. (US/0748-2469). **3238**

OFFICIAL GUIDE - TIME FINANCE ADJUSTERS (FIRM). (US/0732-2798). **802**

OFFICIAL GUIDE, TRACTORS AND FARM EQUIPMENT. (US/0162-6809). **160**

OFFICIAL HANDBOOK OF THE AAU CODE. (US/0091-3405). **4909**

OFFICIAL HELICOPTER BLUE BOOK, THE. (US/0890-7498). **30**

OFFICIAL HIGH SCHOOL BOYS GYMNASTICS RULES. (US/0740-9532). **4909**

OFFICIAL HOTEL AND RESORT GUIDE. (US). **2808**

OFFICIAL INTERMODAL EQUIPMENT REGISTER, THE. (US/0190-6690). **5388**

OFFICIAL IOWA MANUFACTURERS DIRECTORY. (US/1056-6872). **Adv Mgr:** Charles Scherer. **3485**

OFFICIAL JOURNAL - ILLINOIS POLICE ASSOCIATION. (US/0019-2171). **3171**

OFFICIAL JOURNAL (PATENTS). (UK/0030-0330). **1307**

OFFICIAL (LOS ANGELES). (US/0192-5784). **2607**

OFFICIAL MANITOBA SHIP-BY-TRUCK DIRECTORY (1983). (CN/0713-8776). **5388**

OFFICIAL MOTOR CARRIER DIRECTORY. (US/0472-6243). **5388**

OFFICIAL MUSEUM PRODUCTS AND SERVICES DIRECTORY, THE. (US/0276-637X). **4094**

OFFICIAL NASCAR YEARBOOK AND PRESS GUIDE, THE. (US/0891-4648). **4909**

OFFICIAL RULES FOR COMPETITIVE SWIMMING. (US/0091-3413). **4910**

OFFICIAL RULES / RINGETTE CANADA. (CN/0711-0537). **4910**

OFFICIAL SOUVENIR PROGRAM OF SPOLETO FESTIVAL U.S.A, THE. (US/0147-5991). **386**

OFFICIAL STEAMSHIP GUIDE INTERNATIONAL. (US/0030-0381). **5487**

OFFICIAL UNITED STATES TENNIS ASSOCIATION YEARBOOK AND TENNIS GUIDE WITH THE OFFICIAL RULES, THE. (US/0196-5425). **4910**

OFFICIAL WATER POLO RULES. (US). **4910**

OFFSHORE (CONROE, TEX.). (US/0030-0608). **4267**

OFFSHORE ENGINEER. (UK/0305-876X). **2094**

OFFSHORE RIG LOCATION REPORT, THE. (US/0733-0928). **4267**

OFFSHORE TAX PLANNING REVIEW. (UK). **4739**

OFFSHORE (WEST NEWTON). (US/0274-9394). **594**

OGEMAW COUNTY HERALD. (US). **Adv Mgr:** R. Eaton. **5693**

OGGI. (IT/0030-0705). **2491**

OGGI 7. (US/1059-4760). **5711**

OH CALCUTTA. (II/0377-7596). **2507**

OH! IDAHO. (US/1051-2373). **2541**

OH&S CANADA. (CN/0827-4576). **2867**

OHIO. (US/0279-3504). **2541**

OHIO BANKER, THE. (US/0030-0802). **Adv Mgr Tel** (614)222-0106. **802**

OHIO BEVERAGE JOURNAL. (US/0740-1361). **2370**

OHIO CIVIL LIBERTIES. (US/0274-5615). **4511**

OHIO CPA JOURNAL, THE. (US/0749-8284). **749**

OHIO DENTAL JOURNAL, THE. (US/0030-087X). **1331**

OHIO ENGINEER, THE. (US/0194-9276). **1989**

OHIO HOLSTEIN NEWS. (US/0199-7580). **197**

OHIO JOURNAL OF SCIENCE, THE. (US/0030-0950). **Adv Mgr:** L. Elfner. **5136**

OHIO LAWYER (COLUMBUS, OHIO : 1987). (US). **3021**

OHIO LIBRARIES (COLUMBUS, OHIO. 1988). (US/1046-4336). **3239**

OHIO MANUFACTURERS DIRECTORY. (US/0737-7495). **3485**

OHIO MEDIA SPECTRUM. (US/0192-6942). **3239**

OHIO MEDICINE. (US/0892-2454). **Adv Mgr:** G. Auigley, **Tel** (513)779-7177. **3624**

OHIO MONTHLY RECORD. (US/0163-0008). **3021**

OHIO MOTOR VEHICLE LAWS. (US). **3021**

OHIO NEWS (WOOSTER, OHIO). (US/0899-4862). **197**

OHIO NORTHERN UNIVERSITY LAW REVIEW. (US/0094-534X). **3021**

OHIO READING TEACHER. (US/0030-1035). **3308**

OHIO REGISTER OF MANUFACTURERS. (US/0884-173X). **3485**

OHIO REVIEW (ATHENS), THE. (US/0360-1013). **3420**

OHIO RUNNER, THE. (US/0279-9634). **Adv Mgr:** same as editor. **4910**

OHIO SCHOOLS - OHIO EDUCATION ASSOCIATION. (US/0030-1086). **Adv Mgr:** Maxine Flynn, **Tel** (614)227-3050. **1868**

OHIO SPEECH JOURNAL, THE. (US/0078-4052). **1119**

OHIO STATE BAR ASSOCIATION REPORT (1981). (US/0744-8376). **3022**

OHIO STATE JOURNAL ON DISPUTE RESOLUTION. (US/1046-4344). **3022**

OHIO STATE LAW JOURNAL. (US/0048-1572). **3022**

OHIO TAVERN NEWS. (US/0030-1183). **Adv Mgr:** Tom Weeks, **Tel** (614)224-4835. **5072**

OHIO THOROUGHBRED, THE. (US). **2801**

OHIO WOODLANDS. (US). **Adv Mgr:** AgComm Advertising Agency, **Tel** (614)889-6604. **2390**

OHIO WRITER. (US/0896-5730). **2923**

OHS BULLETIN. (CN/0714-6736). **2541**

OIKOS. (DK/0030-1299). **2220**

OIL & GAS DIRECTORY (HOUSTON, TEX. 1970). (US). **4268**

OIL & GAS FINANCE & ACCOUNTANCY. (UK/0902-3752). **749**

OIL & GAS FINANCE AND ACCOUNTING. (UK/0962-3752). **749**

OIL & GAS INVESTOR. (US/0744-5881). **4268**

OIL & GAS JOURNAL. (US/0030-1388). **4268**

OIL & GAS (OXFORD, OXFORDSHIRE). (UK/0263-5070). **3022**

OIL & GAS PRODUCING INDUSTRY IN YOUR STATE, THE. (US). **4268**

OIL & GAS RUSSIA & POST SOVIET REPUBLICS. HYDROCARBONS BRIEF. (UK/0967-537X). **4269**

OIL DAILY, THE. (US/0030-1434). **4269**

OIL GAS. (GW/0342-5622). **4269**

OIL, GAS & PETROCHEM EQUIPMENT. (US/0030-1353). **4269**

OIL MILL GAZETTEER. (US/0030-1442). **2015**

Advertising Accepted Index — OPEN

OIL PACKER INTERNATIONAL. (UK/0957-655X). **4220**

OIL PRODUCING INDUSTRY IN YOUR STATE, THE. (US/0191-0396). **4270**

OILGAS. (SP). **4270**

OILS AND OILSEEDS JOURNAL. (II/0369-769X). **1044**

OILWEEK. (CN/0030-1515). **4270**

OJANCANO (CHAPEL HILL, N.C.). (US/0899-983X). **3420**

OJC THE OHIO JEWISH CHRONICLE, THE. (US). **Adv Mgr:** Stephen Pinsky. **5729**

OKANAGAN LIFE (KELOWNA. 1988). (CN/0840-5492). **Adv Mgr:** Gerry Lee, **Tel** (604)861-5399. **2541**

OKIKA O HAWAII, NA. (US/0099-8745). **2426**

OKIKE. (NR/0331-0566). **3420**

OKLAHOMA ALMANAC. (US). **Adv Mgr:** P. Lester. **1927**

OKLAHOMA BANKER. (US/0030-1647). **Adv Mgr:** Beth Payne. **802**

OKLAHOMA BAR JOURNAL, THE. (US/0030-1655). **3022**

OKLAHOMA BUSINESS. (US/0192-9593). **701**

OKLAHOMA CITY UNIVERSITY LAW REVIEW. (US/0364-9458). **3022**

OKLAHOMA CONSTITUTION, THE. (US/0890-1007). **4671**

OKLAHOMA COWMAN. (US/0030-1698). **217**

OKLAHOMA DAILY, THE. (US/0030-171X). **Adv Mgr:** Susan Sasso, **Tel** (405)325-2521. **5732**

OKLAHOMA DENTAL ASSOCIATION JOURNAL. (US/0164-9442). **1331**

OKLAHOMA EAGLE, THE. (US/0745-385X). **Adv Mgr:** Jerry Goodwin. **5732**

OKLAHOMA FARMER-STOCKMAN, THE. (US/0145-9392). **117**

OKLAHOMA HOME & LIFE STYLE. (US/0895-1586). **2542**

OKLAHOMA LAW REVIEW. (US/0030-1752). **Adv Mgr:** Michael Waters. **3022**

OKLAHOMA LIBRARIAN. (US/0030-1760). **3239**

OKLAHOMA NURSE, THE. (US/0030-1787). **3866**

OKLAHOMA OBSERVER, THE. (US/0030-1795). **Adv Mgr:** Helen Troy. **4485**

OKLAHOMA READER, THE. (US/0030-1833). **3308**

OKLAHOMA REALTOR. (US/0745-5046). **4842**

OKLAHOMA RETAILER. (US/0030-1841). **956**

OKLAHOMA RURAL NEWS. (US/0048-1610). **117**

OKLAHOMA TODAY. (US/0030-1892). **2752**

OKLAHOMA WOMEN'S FRONT PAGE NEWS. (US/1071-1643). **5563**

OKONOMI OG POLITIK. (DK/0030-1906). **1577**

OKUMENISCHE RUNDSCHAU. (GW/0029-8654). **4983**

OLD BOTTLE MAGAZINE. (US/0030-1965). **252**

OLD CAR VALUE GUIDE. (US/0475-1876). **5422**

OLD CARS. (US/0048-1637). **5422**

OLD CARS PRICE GUIDE. (US/0194-6404). **5422**

OLD COLONY MEMORIAL. (US). **Adv Mgr:** Gary Higgins. **5689**

OLD DOMINION GARDENER. (US/0274-6956). **2426**

OLD FARMER'S ALMANAC. SPECIAL CANADIAN EDITION, THE. (US/0276-3060). **1927**

OLD-HOUSE JOURNAL CATALOG, THE. (US/0271-7220). **623**

OLD-HOUSE JOURNAL, THE. (US/0094-0178). **623**

OLD LYONS RECORDER, THE. (US). **5644**

OLD MILL NEWS. (US/0276-3338). **Adv Mgr:** Tom Freestone. **305**

OLD TESTAMENT ABSTRACTS. (US/0364-8591). **5013**

OLD TIME COUNTRY. (US/1044-1042). **4143**

OLD-TIME HERALD. (US/1040-3582). **Adv Mgr:** L. Copulsky. **4143**

OLD TOY SOLDIER. (US/1064-4164). **2585**

OLD WEST. (US/0030-2058). **2752**

OLD WORLD ARCHAEOLOGY NEWSLETTER. (US/0732-1635). **Adv Mgr:** D. Sierpinsk, **Tel** (203)347-9411 ext. 2804. **277**

OLDE MACHINERY MART. (AT/1031-4555). **2123**

OLDE TIMES. (US/0883-6442). **2752**

OLDIE (LONDON). (UK/0965-2507). **Adv Mgr:** Hamish Miller. **2520**

OLEAGINEUX. (FR/0030-2082). **117**

OLIVIA TIMES-JOURNAL. (US). **Adv Mgr:** Rose He Hig. **5697**

OLJYPOSTI. (FI). **4270**

OLMSTE(A)D'S GENEALOGY RECORDED. (US/0162-0800). **2465**

OLNEY ENTERPRISE, THE. (US). **Adv Mgr:** David Penn, **Tel** (817)564-5558. **5753**

OLNEY TIMES. (US). **Adv Mgr:** Melissa Reilly. **5738**

O'LOCHLAINNS PERSONAL JOURNAL OF IRISH FAMILIES. (US/1056-0378). **2465**

OLS NEWS : THE INDEPENDENT VOICE OF OPEN LEARNING. (UK/0169-9729). **1770**

OLSEN'S FISHERMAN'S NAUTICAL ALMANACK, CONTAINING TIDE TABLES AND DIRECTORY OF BRITISH FISHING VESSELS. (UK). **Adv Mgr:** B. Rumford. **5453**

OLTON ENTERPRISE (OLTON, TEX. : 1926). (US). **5753**

OLYMPIAN (NEW YORK, N.Y.), THE. (US/0094-9787). **4910**

OLYMPIC REVIEW. (SZ/0377-192X). **4910**

OMAHA STAR, THE. (US). **Adv Mgr:** Preston Love Sr. **5707**

OMAHA WORLD-HERALD (OMAHA, NB : 1954 : SUNRISE ED.). (US). **5707**

OMAK-OKANOGAN COUNTY CHRONICLE, THE. (US/1064-2617). **Adv Mgr:** Marilyn Ries. **5761**

OMEGA (FARMINGDALE). (US/0030-2228). **4606**

OMH. OFFICES MUNICIPAUX D'HABITATION. (FR/0228-8494). **2830**

OMNI (NEW YORK, N.Y.). (US/0149-8711). **2542**

OMRO HERALD, THE. (US/8755-3961). **Adv Mgr:** Betty Van Sistine. **5769**

ON DISENO. (SP). **2902**

ON GUARD (CLEVELAND, TENN.). (US/0738-758X). **4983**

ON-LINE REVIEW. (UK/0309-314X). **1275**

ON LOCATION. (US/0149-7014). **4075**

ON ONE WHEEL. (US/0893-4606). **429**

ON OUR BACKS. (US/0890-2224). **Adv Mgr:** Marnie De Bois. **2795**

ON PRODUCTION AND POST-PRODUCTION. (US/1067-6120). **4075**

ON-SHORE WEEKLY. (UK). **2147**

ON-STAGE STUDIES. (US/0749-1549). **Adv Mgr:** same as editor. **5367**

ON THE ISSUES. (US/0895-6014). **5563**

ON THE LEVEL ASHFIELD. (AT/1036-8124). **2600**

ON THE RISK. (US/0885-4416). **2889**

ON TRACK (SANTA ANA, CALIF.). (US/0279-2737). **Adv Mgr:** David Amette, **Tel** same as publisher. **4911**

ONALASKA COMMUNITY LIFE. (US/1053-6906). **5769**

ONCE UPON A TIME (ST. PAUL, MINN.). (US/1071-2526). **1067**

ONCOGENE. (UK/0950-9232). **3821**

ONCOGENES. (UK/0950-0561). **550**

ONCOLOGY. (SZ/0030-2414). **3821**

ONCOLOGY ISSUES. (US/1046-3356). **3822**

ONCOLOGY NURSING FORUM. (US/0190-535X). **3866**

ONDE ELECTRIQUE. (FR/0030-2430). **2074**

ONDERNEMEN. (BE/0772-3326). **5065**

ONDERNEMING, DE. (BE/0777-6349). **2607**

ONE ON ONE (ALBANY, N.Y.). (US/0733-639X). **3022**

ONE PEACEFUL WORLD. (US). **2220**

ONE SKY REPORT. (CN/0713-7753). **1638**

ONE TO ONE. (US/0739-5442). **1135**

ONE WORLD (GENEVA). (SZ/0303-125X). **4983**

ONION WORLD. (US/0892-578X). **Adv Mgr:** Mike Stoken. **2426**

ONKOLOGIE. (SZ/0378-584X). **3822**

ONLINE ACCESS. (US/0898-2015). **Adv Mgr:** Robert Jordan, **Tel** (312)573-1700. **1248**

ONLINE & CDROM REVIEW : THE INTERNATIONAL JOURNAL OF ONLINE & OPTICAL INFORMATION SYSTEMS. (UK). **Adv Mgr:** Michael Hislop (Europe) and Michael V. Zarrello (US), **Tel** 011 44 865 730275 ext. 226 (Europe) or (609)654-4888 (US). **1275**

ONLINE (COLOGNE, GERMANY : 1982). (GW). **1197**

ONLINE HELIDATA. (UK/0951-9904). **31**

ONLINE HOTLINE NEWS SERVICE. (US/1040-6646). **1197**

ONLINE TODAY. (US/0891-4672). **3239**

ONLINE (WESTON, CONN.). (US/0146-5422). **Adv Mgr:** Corky Murray, **Tel** (203)761-1466. **1275**

ONOMASTICKY ZPRAVODAJ CSAV. (XR). **3308**

ONS AMSTERDAM. (NE/0166-1809). **2701**

ONS ERFDEEL. (BE/0030-2651). **327**

ONT. SHEEP NEWS. (CN/0844-5303). **217**

ONTARIO AMATEUR WRESTLING ASSOCIATION RESULTS BOOK. (CN/0822-6806). **4911**

ONTARIO ANNUAL PRACTICE (1973). (CN/0318-3556). **3142**

ONTARIO BRANCH NEWS. (CN/0710-345X). **4795**

ONTARIO BUSINESS. (CN/0227-1397). **701**

ONTARIO CORN PRODUCER. (CN/0008-7297). **117**

ONTARIO CRAFT. (CN/0229-1320). **Adv Mgr:** Susan Browne, **Tel** (416)886-6640. **374**

ONTARIO CRICKET "PITCH". (CN/1183-4072). **4911**

ONTARIO DEMOCRAT, THE. (CN/0827-2247). **4485**

ONTARIO DENTIST. (CN/0300-5275). **Adv Mgr Tel** (416)691-5155. **1332**

ONTARIO FISHERMAN. (CN/0822-8736). **2309**

ONTARIO FOLKDANCER. (CN/0384-5052). **1314**

ONTARIO HISTORY. (CN/0030-2953). **2752**

ONTARIO LAND SURVEYOR, THE. (CN/0316-2001). **2028**

ONTARIO LAWYER'S PHONE BOOK, THE. (CN/0845-4825). **3023**

ONTARIO MEDICAL REVIEW. (CN/0030-302X). **3624**

ONTARIO MEDICAL TECHNOLOGIST / ONTARIO SOCIETY OF MEDICAL TECHNOLOGISTS. (CN/0228-877X). **3624**

ONTARIO MILK PRODUCER. (CN/0030-3038). **197**

ONTARIO MUNICIPAL BOARD REPORTS. (CN/0318-7527). **3023**

ONTARIO NURSING HOME JOURNAL. (CN/0829-6340). **3790**

ONTARIO OUT OF DOORS. (CN/0707-3178). **4876**

ONTARIO PSYCHOLOGIST, THE. (CN/0030-3054). **Adv Mgr:** S. Traub. **4606**

ONTARIO PUBLIC SECTOR. (CN/0841-0798). **Adv Mgr:** James McGillis, **Tel** (604)482-3104. **4671**

ONTARIO RECYCLING UPDATE. (CN/0823-6143). **2238**

ONTARIO REVIEW (WINDSOR, ONT.). (CN/0316-4055). **3420**

ONTARIO SNOWMOBILER. (CN/0383-7009). **Adv Mgr:** John Hildebrandt, **Tel** (705)484-1511. **4911**

ONTARIO TECHNOLOGIST, THE. (CN/0380-1969). **5136**

ONTARIO WATER SKIER, THE. (CN/0226-5702). **4911**

ONTHEBUS (LOS ANGELES, CALIF.). (US/1043-884X). **3420**

ONTONAGON HERALD. (US). **5693**

ONZE VOGELS. (NE). **5619**

OP CIT. (IT/0030-3305). **Adv Mgr:** Renato De Fusco. **361**

OPADY ATMOSFERYCZNE. (PL). **1433**

OPASQUIA TIMES. (CN/0707-5448). **5791**

OPEC BULLETIN. (AU/0474-6279). **4270**

OPEC REVIEW. (US/0277-0180). **4270**

OPELIKA AUBURN NEWS. (US/1044-7539). **Adv Mgr:** Jack Nolan. **5627**

OPEN EARTH. (UK/0141-3619). **1359**

OPEN HANDS. (US/0888-8833). **2795**

OPEN LEARNING. (UK/0268-0513). **1801**

OPEN SPACE (OPEN SPACES SOCIETY, GREAT BRITAIN). (UK) **Adv Mgr:** Nicole Bentham. **2201**

OPEN SQUARES, THE. (US/0891-3447). **1314**

OPEN WHEEL. (US/0279-0254). **4911**

OPENBAAR KUNSTBEZIT IN VLAANDEREN. (BE). **327**

OPER UND KONZERT (MUNCHEN). (GW/0030-3518). **4143**

OPERA AUSTRALIA. (AT). **4143**

OPERA CANADA. (CN/0030-3577). **Adv Mgr:** Robert de Vrij, **Tel** 538-0395. **4143**

OPERA FANATIC. (US/0891-3757). **4143**

OPERA JOURNAL, THE. (US/0030-3585). **4143**

OPERA (LONDON). (UK/0030-3526). **4143**

OPERA MILANO. 1987, L'. (IT/1121-4112). **Adv Mgr:** Sabino Lenoci. **4143**

OPERA MONTHLY. (US/0897-6554). **4143**

OPERA NEWS. (US/0030-3607). **4143**

OPERA QUARTERLY, THE. (US/0736-0053). **4144**

OPERATIONAL GEOGRAPHER, THE. (CN/0822-4838). **2571**

OPERATIONS FORESTIERES ET DE SCIERIE. (CN/0030-3631). **2390**

OPERATIONS MANAGEMENT REVIEW. (US/0734-1458). **881**

OPERATIONS OF BANK PEMBANGUNAN INDONESIA. (IO). **802**

OPERATIONS RESEARCH. (US/0030-364X). **3525**

OPERATIVE ORTHOPADIE UND TRAUMATOLOGIE. (GW/0934-6694). **3883**

OPERATORE SANITARIO, L'. (IT/0392-5153). **3624**

OPHEA JOURNAL. (CN/0840-822X). **1857**

OPHELIA. (DK/0078-5326). **556**

OPHTHALMIC & PHYSIOLOGICAL OPTICS. (UK/0275-5408). **4216**

OPHTHALMIC LITERATURE. (UK/0030-3720). **3877**

OPHTHALMIC PAEDIATRICS AND GENETICS. (NE/0167-6784). **550**

OPHTHALMIC PRACTICE. (CN/0832-9869). **Adv Mgr:** Sara Wilkins. **3877**

OPHTHALMIC SURGERY. (US/0022-023X). **3971**

OPHTHALMOLOGICA (BASEL). (SZ/0030-3755). **3877**

OPHTHALMOLOGICA ET OTO-RHINO-LARYNGOLOGICA (OULU). (FI/0358-4852). **3877**

OPHTHALMOLOGY MANAGEMENT. (US/0746-1070). **3878**

OPHTHALMOLOGY (ROCHESTER, MINN.). (US/0161-6420). **3878**

OPHTHALMOLOGY TIMES. (US/0193-032X). **3878**

OPINION. (US). **3023**

OPINION DE BAGDAD, L'. (IQ). **4485**

OPINION (LOS ANGELES, CALIF.), LA. (US/0276-590X). **5638**

OPP NEWS, THE. (US) **Adv Mgr:** Jennifer Cosby. **5627**

OPPORTUNITIES FOR MATRICULANTS AND SCHOOL LEAVERS. (SA). **4208**

OPPORTUNITIES IN AGRICULTURE, DEVELOPMENT & BIOLOGICALLY RELATED ARTS & SCIENCES. (UK). **117**

OPPORTUNITY (CHICAGO, ILL. : 1983). (US/0741-3750). **701**

OPPORTUNITY VALLEY NEWS. (US). **Adv Mgr:** Jan Bromley, **Tel** (409)883-3571. **5753**

OPSEARCH. (II/0030-3887). **881**

OPTICAL AND QUANTUM ELECTRONICS. (UK/0306-8919). **4439**

OPTICAL COMPUTING & PROCESSING. (UK/0954-2264). **1277**

OPTICAL ENGINEERING. (US/0091-3286). **4439**

OPTICAL INDUSTRY & SYSTEMS ENCYCLOPEDIA & DICTIONARY, THE. (US/0191-0639). **4439**

OPTICAL PRISM. (CN/0824-3441). **4216**

OPTICS AND LASER TECHNOLOGY. (UK/0030-3992). **4439**

OPTIK; ZEITSCHRIFT FUER LICHT- UND ELEKTRONENOPTIK. (GW). **4440**

OPTIMIST (ABILENE), THE. (US/0030-4069). **1094**

OPTIMIST MAGAZINE, THE. (US/0744-4672). **5234**

OPTIMST, THE. (CN/0384-5230). **5563**

OPTION/BIO PARIS. (FR/0992-5945). **467**

OPTION FINANCE ED. FRANCAISE. (FR/0989-1900). **Adv Mgr:** F Fahys. **802**

OPTION (LOS ANGELES, CALIF.). (US/0882-178X). **Adv Mgr:** Scott Becker. **4144**

OPTION PAIX. (CN/0823-9703). **4530**

OPTO MAGAZINE. (BE). **Adv Mgr:** B. Denis. **3878**

OPTOLASER MILANO. (IT/1120-8724). **2074**

OPTOMETRIC ECONOMICS. (US/1052-7346). **Adv Mgr:** Raeber, **Tel** (314)991-4100. **4216**

OPTOMETRIC MANAGEMENT. (US/0030-4085). **4216**

OPTOMETRIE. (GW/0030-4123). **Adv Mgr:** Ball. **4216**

OPTOMETRISTE. (CN/0708-3173). **Adv Mgr:** Mrs. Lucie English. **4216**

OPTOMETRY TODAY. (II). **Adv Mgr:** same as editor. **4217**

OPTOMETRY TODAY (LONDON). (UK/0268-5485). **Adv Mgr:** MA Callender. **4217**

OPUS INTERNATIONAL. (FR/0048-2056). **327**

OPUSCULA ZOOLOGICA - INSTITUTUM ZOOSYSTEMATICUM UNIVERSITATIS BUDAPESTINENSIS. (HU/0473-1034). **5593**

OR MANAGER. (US/8756-8047). **Adv Mgr:** John Schmes, **Tel** (609)589-2319. **3866**

OR/MS TODAY. (US). **5136**

ORACION DE LAS HORAS. (SP). **4984**

ORACLE MAGAZINE. (US/1065-3171). **Adv Mgr:** Kevin Canady, **Tel** (415)506-3430. **1198**

ORACLE, THE. (US). **1094**

ORAFO ITALIANO. (IT/0471-7376). **2915**

ORAL HEALTH. (CN/0030-4204). **1332**

ORAL HISTORY ASSOCIATION OF AUSTRALIA JOURNAL. (AT/0158-7366). **2670**

ORAL HISTORY (COLCHESTER). (UK/0143-0955). **2625**

ORAL HISTORY REVIEW, THE. (US/0094-0798). **2625**

ORAL RADIOLOGY. (JA/0911-6028). **1332**

ORAL SURGERY, ORAL MEDICINE, ORAL PATHOLOGY. (US/0030-4220). **1332**

ORANA. (AT/0045-6705). **3239**

ORANGE COAST. (US/0279-0483). **Adv Mgr:** Linda Goldstein. **2542**

ORANGE COUNTY APARTMENT NEWS. (US/0747-3435). **2830**

ORANGE COUNTY BUSINESS JOURNAL (NEWPORT BEACH, CALIF.). (US/1051-7480). **Adv Mgr:** Roger Kranz. **701**

ORANGE COUNTY BUSINESS TO BUSINESS. (US/0733-9534). **701**

ORANGE COUNTY GENEALOGICAL SOCIETY. (US/0736-0185). **2465**

ORANGE COUNTY LAWYER. (US/0897-5698). **Adv Mgr:** Susan Serpa, **Tel** (714)222-4782. **3023**

ORANGE COUNTY POST. (US). **Adv Mgr:** Pam Lewis. **5720**

ORANGE LEADER (ORANGE, TEX.). (US/0885-8047). **Adv Mgr:** Jan Bromley. **5753**

ORANGEVILLE CITIZEN, THE. (CN/0319-180X). **5792**

ORATORI DEL GIORNO, GLI. (IT/0393-4012). **3023**

ORBIS BIBLICUS ET ORIENTALIS. (SZ). **4984**

ORBIS GEOGRAPHICUS. ADRESSAR GEOGRAPHIQUE DU MONDE. WORLD DIRECTORY OF GEOGRAPHY. GEOGRAPHISCHES WELTADRESSBUCH. (GW/0030-4395). **2571**

ORBIS LITTERARUM. (DK/0105-7510). **3420**

ORBIS (PHILADELPHIA). (US/0030-4387). **4485**

ORBIS (YOULGREAVE, DERBYSHIRE). (UK/0030-4425). **3467**

ORBIT (AMSTERDAM). (NE/0167-6830). **3878**

ORBIT (TORONTO). (CN/0030-4433). **1902**

ORBIT VIDEO. (US/1042-1149). **4075**

ORBUS. (US/0890-6432). **701**

ORC REPORT. (CN/0826-3019). **4876**

ORCHARDIST OF NEW ZEALAND, THE. (NZ/0110-6260). **180**

ORCHESTER, DAS. (GW/0030-4468). **4144**

ORCHESTRA CANADA. (CN/0380-1799). **4144**

ORCHID ADVOCATE, THE. (US/0097-9546). **2426**

ORCHID DIGEST, THE. (US/0199-9559). **2426**

ORCHID REVIEW. (UK/0030-4476). **2436**

ORCHIDEE, DIE. (GW/0473-1425). **Adv Mgr:** E. Wermuth, **Tel** (08466)8228. **2426**

ORDER (DORDRECHT). (NE/0167-8094). **3526**

OREGON BUSINESS. (US/0279-8190). **701**

OREGON COAST. (US/0744-8317). **5487**

OREGON LAW REVIEW. (US/0196-2043). **Adv Mgr:** Julie Martil, **Tel** (503)346-1551. **3023**

OREGON NURSE. (US/0030-4751). **Adv Mgr:** Cathi, **Tel** (503)293-0011. **3866**

OREGON OPTOMETRY. (US/0274-6549). **4217**

OREGON STATE BAR BULLETIN, THE. (US/0030-4816). **Adv Mgr:** Art Greisser. **3023**

OREGONIAN (PORTLAND, OR. 1937), THE. (US/8750-1317). **Adv Mgr:** Denny Atkin, **Tel** (503)221-8279. **5734**

ORFF ECHO, THE. (US/0095-2613). **4144**

ORGAN (BOURNEMOUTH). (UK/0030-4883). **4144**

ORGAN YEARBOOK, THE. (NE/0920-3192). **4144**

ORGANI DI TRASMISSIONE. (IT). **2123**

ORGANIC FARMER (MONTPELIER, VT.). (US/1063-6803). **117**

ORGANIC MASS SPECTROMETRY. (UK/0030-493X). **1018**

ORGANIC PREPARATIONS AND PROCEDURES INTERNATIONAL. (US/0030-4948). **1045**

ORGANIST'S COMPANION, THE. (US/0749-3533). **Adv Mgr:** J. Atwood. **4144**

ORGANISTS' REVIEW. (UK/0048-2161). **Adv Mgr:** Marcus Knight. **4144**

ORGANIZACIJA IN KADRI. (YU/0350-1531). **881**

ORGANIZATION DEVELOPMENT JOURNAL. (US/0889-6402). **Adv Mgr Tel** (216)461-4333. **881**

ORGANIZATION STUDIES. (GW/0170-8406). **5211**

ORGANIZZAZIONE SANITARIA. (IT/0394-283X). **3790**

ORGANO, L'. (IT). **4144**

ORGANO OFICIAL DE LA JUNTA CIVICO-MILITAR CUBANA. (US/0272-4650). **2752**

ORGANOMETALLIC COMPOUNDS. (UK/0030-5138). **1045**

ORGANOMETALLICS. (US/0276-7333). **1045**

ORGEL (AMERSFOORT, NETHERLANDS). (NE). **4144**

ORGUE (PARIS), L'. (FR/0030-5170). **4145**

ORIENT (DEUTSCHES ORIENT-INSTITUT). (GW/0030-5227). **2661**

ORIENTAL ART. (UK/0030-5278). **Adv Mgr:** P. Law, **Tel** (071)586 4109. **361**

ORIENTAL INSECTS. (US/0030-5316). **5612**

ORIENTATIONS (HONG KONG). (HK/0030-5448). **2661**

ORIENTEERING NORTH AMERICA. (US/0886-1080). **4911**

ORIENTEERING WORLD. (SW/1015-4965). **4911**

ORIENTO. (JA). **2661**

ORIGINAL NEW ENGLAND GUIDE, THE. (US/0734-4066). **5487**

ORIGINAL WNC BUSINESS JOURNAL, THE. (US/1065-027X). **Adv Mgr:** Michelle Ramsey, **Tel** (704)258-1341. **701**

ORION. (IT). **Adv Mgr:** M. Murelli, **Tel** same as publisher. **4486**

ORION. (SZ/0030-557X). **398**

ORITA. (NR/0030-5596). **4984**

ORKESTER JOURNALEN. (SW/0030-5642). **4145**

ORL-HEAD AND NECK NURSING. (US/1064-3842). **Adv Mgr:** Sandra Schwartz. **3890**

ORL; JOURNAL FOR OTO-RHINO-LARYNGOLOGY AND ITS BORDERLANDS. (SZ/0301-1569). **3890**

ORLANDO BUSINESS JOURNAL. (US/8750-8656). **Adv Mgr:** Joan Watts. **702**

ORLANDO MAGAZINE. (US/0279-1323). **Adv Mgr:** Karen Poulsen, **Tel** (407)539-3939. **2542**

ORLANDO SPECTATOR, THE. (US/1070-860X). **5650**

ORNAMENT COLLECTOR, THE. (US/0895-9730). **2776**

ORNAMENT (LOS ANGELES, CALIF.). (US/0148-3897). **2915**

ORNAMENTAL/MISCELLANEOUS METAL FABRICATOR. (US/0191-5940). **4014**

ORNIS FENNICA. (FI/0030-5685). **5619**

ORNIS SCANDINAVICA. (NO/0030-5693). **5619**

ORNITHOLOGISCHE BEOBACHTER. (SZ/0030-5707). **5619**

ORODHA MAALUM YA BEI / JAMHURI YA MUUNGANO WA TANZANIA, TUME YA BEI YA TAIFA. (TZ). **1594**

OROMOCTO POST, THE. (CN/0710-5460). **5792**

ORQUIDEA (MEXICO. 1971). (MX/0300-3701). **520**

ORTE. (SZ). **3421**

ORTHODONTIC DIRECTORY OF THE WORLD. (US). **1332**

ORTHODOX CATHOLIC VOICE, THE. (US). **5039**

ORTHODOX OBSERVER. (US/0731-2547). **4984**

ORTHOPAEDIC PRODUCT NEWS. (UK/0954-4755). **3883**

ORTHOPAEDIC REVIEW. (US/0094-6591). **3883**

ORTHOPEDIC NURSING / NATIONAL ASSOCIATION OF ORTHOPEDIC NURSES. (US/0744-6020). **3884**

ORTHOPEDIC SURGERY. (NE/0014-4371). **3661**

ORTHOPEDICS (THOROFARE). (US/0147-7447). **3884**

ORYX. (UK/0030-6053). **2201**

OS2 PROFESSIONAL. (US/1069-6814). **Adv Mgr:** Richard Dubin, **Tel** (518)489-4034. **1289**

OSAGE COUNTY CHRONICLE (BURLINGAME, KAN. : 1983). (US/1040-6077). **Adv Mgr:** Kurt Kessinger, **Tel** (913)654-3621. **5678**

OSAWATOMIE GRAPHIC-NEWS, THE. (US). **5678**

OSCAR ISRAELOWITZ'S GUIDE TO JEWISH NEW YORK CITY. (US). **5269**

OSGOOD JOURNAL, THE. (US). **Adv Mgr:** Linda Chandler, **Tel** (812)689-6364. **5666**

OSGOODE HALL LAW JOURNAL. (CN). **3023**

OSHKOSH ADVANCE-TITAN. (US/0300-676X). **Adv Mgr:** Barb Lvedtke, **Tel** (414)424-3049. **5769**

OSIRIS (SCHENECTADY, N.Y.). (US/0095-019X). **3467**

OSMOSE (MONTREAL). (CN/0829-5131). **3866**

OSNABRUCKER LAND HEIMAT-JAHRBUCH. (GW). **2701**

OSPEDALE. (IT/0030-6231). **3790**

OSPEDALI D'ITALIA-CHIRURGIA. (IT/0030-6266). **3971**

OSSERVATORE ROMANO, L'. (VC/0030-6312). **5813**

OSSERVATORIO SUL MERCATO IMMOBILIARE. (IT). **4842**

OSSIAN BEE, THE. (US). **Adv Mgr:** Dirk Amundsen, **Tel** (319)532-9113. **5672**

OSSIAN JOURNAL, THE. (US). **Adv Mgr:** Nila Dafforn. **5666**

OSTEOPATHIE : THERAPIES MANUELLES. (FR/0753-6019). **4795**

OSTERREICHISCHE AMTSVORMUND, DER. (AU). **3122**

OSTERREICHISCHE BEITRAGE ZU METEOROLOGIE UND GEOPHYSIK. (AU/1016-6254). **1433**

OSTERREICHISCHE BIBLIOGRAPHIE. REIHE C, NEUERE AUSLANDISCHE AUSTRIACA. AUSWAHLBIBLIOGRAPHIE / BEARBEITET UND HERAUSGEGEBEN VON DER OSTERREICHISCHEN NATIONALBIBLIOTHEK. (AU). **Adv Mgr:** W. Lang. **421**

OSTERREICHISCHE FORSTZEITUNG (1987). (AU). **2390**

OSTERREICHISCHE JURISTEN-ZEITUNG. (AU/0029-9251). **3024**

OSTERREICHISCHE ZEITSCHRIFT FUER POLITIKWISSENSCHAFT. (AU/0378-5149). **4486**

OSTERREICHISCHER FRISEUR. (AU). **405**

OSTERREICHISCHES RECHT DER WIRTSCHAFT. (AU). **3024**

OSTERREICHS FISCHEREI. (AU/0029-9987). **2310**

OSTEUROPA (STUTTGART). (GW/0030-6428). **4486**

OSTEUROPA WIRTSCHAFT. (GW/0030-6460). **1511**

OSTOMY QUARTERLY. (US/0030-6517). **3971**

OTAR. (NE). **2028**

OTC NEWS & MARKET REPORT. (UK/0956-2559). **4318**

OTHER ISRAEL : NEWSLETTER OF THE ISRAELI COUNCIL FOR ISRAELI-PALESTINIAN PEACE, THE. (IS/0792-4615). **2270**

OTHER SIDE (SAVANNAH), THE. (US/0145-7675). **4984**

OTHER VOICES (HIGHLAND PARK, ILL.). (US/8756-4696). **3421**

OTIS RUSH. (AT/0819-7288). **327**

OTOLARYNGOLOGY AND HEAD AND NECK SURGERY. (US/0194-5998). **3971**

OTORINOLARINGOLOGIA. (IT/0392-6621). **3890**

OTTAR. (NO/0030-6703). **4170**

OTTAWA BANDING GROUP. (CN/0827-2298). **5619**

OTTAWA BRANCH NEWS - ONTARIO GENEALOGICAL SOCIETY. (CN/0708-5583). **2466**

OTTAWA JEWISH BULLETIN (1993). (CN/1196-1929). **Adv Mgr:** A. Baker. **2270**

OTTAWA LAW REVIEW. (CN/0048-2331). **Adv Mgr:** Donald Legal, **Tel** (613)564-2919. **3024**

OTTAWA SUN, THE. (CN/0843-2570). **Adv Mgr:** L. Desgrosilliers. **5792**

OUA/DATA'S ... GUIDE TO CORPORATE GIVING IN MAINE. (US/0883-2730). **4338**

OUDTESTAMENTISCHE STUDIEN. (NE/0169-7226). **5018**

OUR FAMILY (BATTLEFORD). (CN/0030-6843). **4984**

OUR GENERATION (MONTREAL). (CN/0030-686X). **4544**

OUR OWN. (US). **Adv Mgr:** Michelle Romano. **2795**

OUR SUNDAY VISITOR. (US/0030-6967). **5034**

OUR TIMES (TORONTO). (CN/0822-6377). **1700**

OUR WORLD (DAYTONA BEACH, FLA.). (US/1044-6699). **5487**

OURAY COUNTY PLAINDEALER. (US). **5644**

OURS (MINNEAPOLIS, MINN.). (US/0899-9333). **Adv Mgr:** Sue Slominski. **5300**

OUSLEY NEWSLETTER. (US/0733-6381). **2466**

OUT AUCKLAND. (NZ/0110-4454). **2795**

OUT/LOOK (SAN FRANCISCO, CALIF.). (US/0896-7733). **2795**

OUT (NEW YORK, N.Y.). (US/1062-7928). **Adv Mgr:** Harry Taylor, **Tel** (212)334-9119. **2795**

OUTCROP (DENVER, COLO.). (US/0888-5184). **1390**

OUTDOOR AMERICA (1971). (US/0021-3314). **4170**

OUTDOOR CANADA. (CN/0315-0542). **4876**

OUTDOOR CREST (1975). (CN/0700-9909). **4876**

OUTDOOR JOURNAL. (US/0890-7196). **4877**

OUTDOOR LIFE (NEW YORK, N.Y.). (US/0030-7076). **4877**

OUTDOOR NETWORK NEWSLETTER, THE. (US/1050-7485). **1771**

OUTDOOR NEWS (OKLAHOMA CITY, OKLA.). (US/0279-9065). **Adv Mgr:** Randy Goodman, **Tel** (405)733-3050. **2201**

OUTDOOR OKLAHOMA. (US/0030-7106). **4877**

OUTDOOR SPORTS & RECREATION. (US/0892-8355). **4877**

OUTDOORS ILLUSTRATED. (UK/0962-1016). **4877**

OUTLOOK. (US). **1094**

OUTLOOK (OTHELLO, WASH.), THE. (US/1056-8328). **Adv Mgr:** Dick Rex, **Tel** (509)488-3342. **5761**

OUTLOOK (PALO ALTO). (US/0273-835X). **749**

OUTLOOK (SANTA MONICA, CALIF.), THE. (US/0898-5375). **Adv Mgr:** Paul Wrosch. **5638**

OUTLOOK (WASHINGTON, D.C. : 1988). (US/0898-5766). **623**

OUTLOOK (WASHINGTON, D.C. 1989). (US/1044-5706). **5564**

OUTPOST EXCHANGE. (US/0748-8394). **1298**

OUTPUT. (SZ/0303-8351). **1261**

OUTPUT OESTERREICH. (AU). **702**

OUTPUT (RICHMOND HILL). (CN/1184-9770). **1224**

OUTREMER (PARIS, FRANCE : 1982). (FR/0014-2816). **2500**

OUTSIDE (1980). (US/0278-1433). **4877**

OUTSIDE PLANT. (US/0747-8763). **1119**

OUTSTATE BUSINESS. (US/1064-3621). **702**

OVERHEIDSMANAGEMENT : VAKBLAD VOOR FINANCIEN AUTOMATISERING EN PERSONEEL 7 ORGANISATIE. (NE/0928-8503). **4672**

OVERLAND. (AT/0030-7416). **2511**

OVERLAND JOURNAL. (US/0738-1093). **Adv Mgr Tel** (816)252-2276. **2752**

OVERSEAS JOBS EXPRESS. (UK/0966-7660). **4208**

OVERSEAS LIVING. (US/0882-8938). **2542**

OVERSEAS TRADING. (AT). **Adv Mgr:** E. Livingstone. **848**

OVERTURE (LOS ANGELES). (US/0030-7556). **4145**

OWEN SOUND SUN TIMES. (CN). **Adv Mgr:** Warren Elder. **5792**

OWINGS MILLS TIMES. (US/1041-0880). **Adv Mgr:** Tim Biringer, **Tel** (410)337-2455. **5686**

OWL OF MINERVA, THE. (US/0030-7580). **4354**

OWNER BUILDER MAGAZINE. (AT/0728-7275). **623**

OWNER BUILT HOME PLANS. (US). **305**

OWOSSO ARGUS-PRESS, THE. (US). **Adv Mgr:** Thomas E. Campbell. **5693**

OXBRIDGE DIRECTORY OF NEWSLETTERS. (US/0163-7010). **2923**

OXFORD ART JOURNAL. (UK/0142-6540). **361**

OXFORD BULLETIN OF ECONOMICS AND STATISTICS. (UK/0305-9049). **1577**

OXFORD ECONOMIC PAPERS. (UK/0030-7653). **1594**

OXFORD GERMAN STUDIES. (UK/0078-7191). **3421**

OXFORD JOURNAL OF LEGAL STUDIES. (UK/0143-6503). **3024**

OXFORD LITERARY REVIEW, THE. (UK/0305-1498). **3349**

OXFORD POETRY (OXFORD, OXFORDSHIRE). (UK). **Adv Mgr:** Kate Reeves. **3467**

OXFORD REVIEW OF ECONOMIC POLICY. (UK/0266-903X). **1511**

OXFORD REVIEW OF EDUCATION. (UK/0305-4985). **1771**

OXFORD SLAVONIC PAPERS. (UK/0078-7256). **3336**

OXFORD STUDIES IN COMPARATIVE EDUCATION. (UK/0961-2149). **1771**

OXIDATION COMMUNICATIONS. (BU/0209-4541). **Adv Mgr:** M. Boneva. **1045**

OXYGEN RADICALS. (UK/0950-057X). **491**

OYO YAKURI. (JA/0300-8533). **4319**

OZ ARTS MAGAZINE. (AT/1037-1311). **327**

OZ (MANHATTAN, KAN.). (US/0888-7802). **305**

OZARKS MOUNTAINEER, THE. (US/0030-7769). **2753**

OZAUKEE COUNTY NEWS GRAPHIC. (US/1056-9006). **Adv Mgr:** Monika Hughes. **5770**

OZONE NEWS. (US/1065-5905). **Adv Mgr:** same as editor. **5212**

P C DISC. (SP). **1198**

P-D NEWS. (US/0478-9997). **944**

P FORM. (US/1067-2222). **Adv Mgr:** Ken. **361**

P.H.M. - REVUE HORTICOLE. (FR). **2427**

P I B C NEWS. (CN/0048-4326). **2830**

P I Q PRODUITS POUR L'INDUSTRIE QUEBECOISE. (CN/0701-1687). **3486**

P.J.R. PRAXIS JURIDIQUE ET RELIGION. (FR/0758-802X). **4984**

P-O-P TIMES. (US/1040-8169). **763**

PA. TOWNSHIP NEWS. (US/0162-5160). **4672**

PAAC NOTES (CHICAGO, ILL.). (US/1059-7913). **Adv Mgr:** Gordon Nary. **3715**

PACE LAW REVIEW. (US/0272-2410). **3024**

PACIFIC AFFAIRS. (CN/0030-851X). **4486**

PACIFIC BOATING ALMANAC. NORTHERN CALIFORNIA & NEVADA. (US/0193-3515). **595**

PACIFIC BOATING ALMANAC. SOUTHERN CALIFORNIA, ARIZONA & BAJA. (US/0193-3507). **595**

PACIFIC BUILDER & ENGINEER. (US/0030-8544). **2028**

PACIFIC CITIZEN, THE. (US/0030-8579). **5638**

PACIFIC COAST NURSERYMAN & GARDEN SUPPLY DEALER. (US/0192-7159). **2427**

PACIFIC COAST OIL DIRECTORY. (US). **4271**

PACIFIC COAST PHILOLOGY. (US/0078-7469). **3421**

PACIFIC COAST STUDIO DIRECTORY. (US/0731-2059). **4075**

PACIFIC CONSERVATION BIOLOGY. (AT/1038-2097). **2201**

PACIFIC DISCOVERY. (US/0030-8641). **Adv Mgr:** Doug Corwin, **Tel** (415)750-7116. **5137**

PACIFIC FISHING. (US/0195-6515). **2310**

PACIFIC FRUIT NEWS. (US/0030-8668). **2352**

PACIFIC GILLNETTER. (CN/1195-3365). **2310**

PACIFIC ISLANDS MONTHLY. (AT/0030-8722). **2670**

PACIFIC ISLANDS YEAR BOOK. (FJ). **2511**

PACIFIC MAGAZINE (HONOLULU, HAWAII). (US/0744-1754). **2511**

PACIFIC MARITIME MAGAZINE. (US/0741-7586). **5453**

PACIFIC NORTHWEST. (US/0199-6363). **2542**

PACIFIC NORTHWEST INSECT CONTROL HANDBOOK. (US). **4246**

PACIFIC NORTHWEST PLANT DISEASE CONTROL HANDBOOK. (US). **2427**

PACIFIC NORTHWEST TRADE DIRECTORY. (US). **848**

PACIFIC OIL WORLD. (US/0008-1329). **4271**

PACIFIC PERSPECTIVE. (FJ/0377-2543). **2670**

PACIFIC PHILOSOPHICAL QUARTERLY. (UK/0279-0750). **4354**

PACIFIC RAIL NEWS. (US/8750-8486). **5433**

PACIFIC REPORT (RED HILL). (AT/1031-6981). **702**

PACIFIC REVIEW (OXFORD, ENGLAND). (UK/0951-2748). **4486**

PACIFIC SCIENCE. (US/0030-8870). **5137**

PACIFIC SHIPPER. (US/0030-8900). **5453**

PACIFIC STUDIES. (US/0275-3596). **2670**

PACIFIC SUN. (US/0048-2641). **5638**

PACIFIC TELECOMMUNICATIONS REVIEW. (US/1066-3894). **Adv Mgr:** J. Savage. **1119**

PACIFIC THEOLOGICAL REVIEW. (US/0360-1897). **4984**

PACIFIC TRAFFIC. (US/0030-8943). **5442**

PACIFIC TRIBUNE (VANCOUVER, B.C.). (CN). **5792**

PACIFIC VIEWPOINT. (NZ/0030-8978). **1577**

PACIFIC YACHTING. (CN/0030-8986). **595**

PACIFICA : AUSTRALIAN THEOLOGICAL STUDIES. (AT). **4984**

PACING AND CLINICAL ELECTROPHYSIOLOGY. (US/0147-8389). **3708**

PACK & PADDLE. (US/1059-4493). **4911**

PACK-O-FUN. (US/0030-901X). **1067**

PACKAGING. (AT). **Adv Mgr:** Ms Ros Richards, **Tel** 372-5222. **4220**

PACKAGING JAPAN. (JA/0288-3864). **4220**

PACKAGING NEWS (LONDON). (UK/0030-9133). **4220**

PACKAGING SCIENCE AND TECHNOLOGY ABSTRACTS. (GW/0722-3218). **Adv Mgr:** J. Elze. **5175**

PACKAGING TODAY LONDON. (UK/0268-0920). **4221**

PACKAGING TRENDS : JAPAN. (JA). **4221**

PACKER, THE. (US/0030-9168). **2352**

PADAGOGIK (WEINHEIM AN DER BERGSTRASSE, GERMANY). (GW/0043-3446). **1771**

PADDLE POWER. (AT/0818-0210). **4877**

PADDLER. (CN/0835-0310). **595**

PADUCAH SUN (1978), THE. (US/1050-0030). **Adv Mgr:** Jana Thomasson. **5682**

PAEDAGOGICA HISTORICA. (BE/0030-9230). **1771**

PAEDAGOGISCHE STUDIEN. (NE/0165-0645). **1771**

PAEDIATRIC ANAESTHESIA. (FR/1155-5645). **3907**

PAEDIATRIC NURSING. (UK). **3866**

PAEDIATRICA INDONESIANA. (IO/0030-9311). **3907**

PAGAN MUSE & WORLD REPORT. (US/1068-2473). **4186**

PAGE PEDIGREE. (US/0897-7763). **2466**

PAGEANTRY (ALTAMONTE SPRINGS, FLA.). (US/1075-3133). **Adv Mgr:** C. Dunn. **2542**

PAGELAND PROGRESSIVE JOURNAL, THE. (US/1063-8415). **Adv Mgr:** Jane Hough. **5743**

PAGES (NORTHEAST ED.). (US/0742-4981). **5488**

PAGINAS (CENTRO DE ESTUDIOS Y PUBLICACIONES). (PE). **Adv Mgr:** Eduardo Urdanivia. **4985**

PAIDEUMA (ORONO). (US/0090-5674). **Adv Mgr Tel** (207)581-3814. **434**

PAIDEUMA (WIESBADEN). (GW/0078-7809). **243**

PAINT & COATINGS INDUSTRY. (US/0884-3848). **4224**

PAINT & INK INTERNATIONAL. (UK/0953-9891). **4224**

PAINT & RESIN. (UK/0261-5746). **4224**

PAINT CHECK. (US/1059-6313). **4853**

PAINT HORSE JOURNAL (1979). (US/0164-5706). **Adv Mgr:** Jackie McGinnis, **Tel** (817)439-3400 ext. 219. **2801**

PAINTBRUSH (LARAMIE). (US/0094-1964). **3467**

PAINTED BRIDE QUARTERLY, THE. (US/0362-7969). **Adv Mgr:** Jerry Haging. **3467**

PAINTINDIA. ANNUAL. (II/0030-9540). **4224**

PAINTING & WALLCOVERING CONTRACTOR. (US/0735-9713). **4224**

PAIS (MADRID, SPAIN : EDICION INTERNACIONAL). (SP). **5810**

PAKISTAN ACCOUNTANT, THE. (PK). **749**

PAKISTAN & GULF ECONOMIST. (PK). **702**

PAKISTAN EXPORTS. (PK/0030-977X). **848**

PAKISTAN EXPORTS (KARACHI, PAKISTAN : 1982). (PK). **848**

PAKISTAN HOTEL & RESTAURANT GUIDE. (PK/0250-4359). **2808**

PAKISTAN HOTEL AND TRAVEL REVIEW. (PK). **2808**

PAKISTAN HOTEL GUIDE. (PK/0552-8968). **2808**

PAKISTAN JOURNAL OF AGRICULTURE, AGRICULTURAL ENGINEERING & VETERINARY SCIENCES. (PK/1015-3055). **118**

PAKISTAN JOURNAL OF APPLIED ECONOMICS. (PK/0254-9204). **1511**

PAKISTAN JOURNAL OF BOTANY. (PK/0556-3321). **520**

PAKISTAN JOURNAL OF FORESTRY, THE. (PK/0030-9818). **2390**

PAKISTAN JOURNAL OF OTOLARYNGOLOGY. (PK/0257-4985). **Adv Mgr:** Asif Afzal. **3890**

PAKISTAN JOURNAL OF PSYCHOLOGY. (PK/0030-9869). **4606**

PAKISTAN JOURNAL OF SCIENCE. (PK/0030-9877). **5137**

PAKISTAN JOURNAL OF SCIENTIFIC AND INDUSTRIAL RESEARCH. (PK/0030-9885). **Adv Mgr:** Dr. J. N. Usmani, **Tel** 7725943. **5137**

PAKISTAN JOURNAL OF SCIENTIFIC RESEARCH. (PK/0552-9050). **5137**

PAKISTAN JOURNAL OF ZOOLOGY. (PK/0030-9923). **5593**

PAKISTAN LAW JOURNAL. (PK). **3024**

PAKISTAN LIBRARY BULLETIN. (PK/0030-9966). **3240**

PAKISTAN MANAGEMENT REVIEW. (PK). **881**

PAKISTAN PEDIATRIC JOURNAL. (PK). **3907**

PAKISTAN SEAFOOD DIGEST. (PK/1010-3562). **2352**

PAKISTAN SYSTEMATICS. (PK). **520**

PAKISTAN VETERINARY JOURNAL. (PK/0253-8318). **5518**

PAKIZAH INTIRNASHINAL. (CN/0711-4222). **5564**

PALABRA. (SP). **4985**

PALABRA Y EL HOMBRE, LA. (MX/0185-5727). **2851**

PALAEONTOGRAPHICA. ABTEILUNG B : PALAOPHYTOLOGIE. (GW/0375-0299). **4229**

PALAEONTOLOGY. (UK/0031-0239). **4229**

PALAEONTOLOGY NEWSLETTER. (UK/0954-9900). **4229**

PALAESTRA (MACOMB, ILL.). (US/8756-5811). **4392**

PALEOBIOLOGY. (US/0094-8373). **4229**

PALEONTOLOGICAL JOURNAL. (US/0031-0301). **4229**

PALESTINE EXPLORATION QUARTERLY. (UK/0031-0328). **278**

PALESTINE PERSPECTIVES. (US/0163-3716). **4531**

PALETTEN. (SW/0031-0352). **361**

PALIMPSEST (IOWA CITY), THE. (US/0031-0360). **Adv Mgr:** Debi Meyers, **Tel** (815)242-4861. **2753**

PALISADE TRIBUNE & VALLEY REPORT, THE. (US). **Adv Mgr:** Cindy O'Keeffe. **5644**

PALLADIUM-TIMES, THE. (US). **Adv Mgr:** Craig Nessck. **5720**

PALLET ENTERPRISE. (US/1065-3651). **Adv Mgr:** E. Scott Brindley. **2403**

PALLIATIVE CARE INDEX. (UK/0961-4591). **3625**

PALM BEACH LIFE. (US/0031-0417). **2542**

PALM SPRINGS LIFE. (US/0031-0425). **Adv Mgr:** F. Jones, **Tel** (619)325-2333. **2542**

PALMETTO BANKER. (US/0164-5773). **Adv Mgr:** Linda Vazquez, **Tel** same as publisher. **802**

PALMETTO (ORLANDO, FLA.), THE. (US/0276-4164). **2427**

PALO ALTO WEEKLY. (US/0199-1159). **5638**

PALOMINO HORSES. (US/0031-045X). **2801**

PALOS VERDES REVIEW. (US/0745-2462). **2542**

PAMATKY ARCHEOLOGICKE. (XR/0031-0506). **278**

PAN. (MX). **Adv Mgr:** Dulce Ma.Perarta. **2352**

PAN-AFRICAN SOCIAL SCIENCE REVIEW. (NR/8755-7436). **5212**

PAN PIPES. (US/0889-7581). **Adv Mgr:** M. Maxwell. **4145**

PANADERIA NOTICIAS. (SP). **2352**

PANCREATIC AND SALIVARY SECRETION. (UK/0142-825X). **3732**

PANDORA (DENVER, COLO.). (US/0275-519X). **3422**

PANEL RESOURCE PAPER. (US/0739-2346). **1902**

PANHANDLE HERALD, THE. (US/8756-2464). **5753**

PANIM LE-KHAN ULE-KHAN. (IS). **4486**

PANOLA WATCHMAN (CARTHAGE, TEX. : 1873). (US). **Adv Mgr:** Bill Holder. **5753**

PANOPTICON. (BE). **3171**

PANORAMA. (UK). **Adv Mgr:** M. Hart, **Tel** 0664 500055. **4221**

PANORAMA CONTITERO. (SP). **Adv Mgr:** Marisa Hernandez, **Tel** 011 34 1 5219228. **2352**

PANORAMA (LEVALLOIS). (FR/0299-4690). **956**

PANORAMA MODA & ABBIGLIAMENTO. (IT). **2491**

PANORAMA PANADERO. (SP/0212-6524). **Adv Mgr:** Marisa Hernandez, **Tel** 91-5215194. **2352**

PANTOGRAPH OF POSTAL STATIONERY, THE. (US/0893-9055). **2786**

PAPEL, O. (BL/0031-1057). **4235**

PAPER AGE. (US/0031-1081). **4235**

PAPER BUYERS' ENCYCLOPEDIA : FINE PAPER DIRECTORY AND SAMPLE BOOK, THE. (US). **Adv Mgr:** Mark Subers. **4235**

PAPER CONSERVATION NEWS (LONDON). (UK/0140-1033). **4235**

PAPER CONSERVATOR. (UK/0309-4227). **4235**

PAPER EUROPE. (UK/0955-7806). **Adv Mgr:** Jaret Smith. **4236**

PAPER, FILM AND FOIL CONVERTER. (US/0031-1138). **4236**

PAPER (LONDON). (UK/0306-8234). **4236**

PAPER MONEY. (US/0031-1162). **2783**

PAPER (NEW YORK, N.Y.). (US/0892-3809). **327**

PAPER PILE QUARTERLY. (US/1049-6572). **4236**

PAPER. SOUTHERN AFRICA. (SA/0254-3494). **4236**

PAPER SUMMARIES - AMERICAN SOCIETY FOR NONDESTRUCTIVE TESTING. (US/0272-4723). **1990**

PAPERBOARD PACKAGING'S OFFICIAL CONTAINER DIRECTORY. (US/0198-8867). **4221**

PAPERI JA PUU. (FI/0031-1243). **4236**

PAPERS. (AT). **3422**

PAPERS AND DISCUSSIONS - ASSOCIATION OF MINE MANAGERS OF SOUTH AFRICA. (SA). **2147**

PAPERS AND STUDIES IN CONTRASTIVE LINGUISTICS. (PL/0137-2459). **3309**

PAPERS ON FRENCH SEVENTEENTH CENTURY LITERATURE. (GW/0343-0758). **Adv Mgr:** Editor. **3422**

PAPERS ON LANGUAGE & LITERATURE. (US/0031-1294). **3422**

PAPERS PRESENTED AT THE SHORT COURSE IN PAINT TECHNOLOGY. (US). **2015**

PAPETIER DE FRANCE, LE. (FR). **4236**

PAPIER AUS OSETERREICH. (AU/1011-0186). **4236**

PAPIER, CARTON ET CELLULOSE. (FR/0031-1367). **Adv Mgr:** F. Henin, **Tel** 42 3695 59. **4236**

PAPIER, DAS. (GW/0031-1340). **4236**

PAPIER- UND ZELLSTOFF-DIENST. (GW/0171-1458). **4237**

PAPIERE ZUR LINGUISTIK. (GW). **3309**

PAPRIPARI ES NYOMDAIPARI SZAKIRODALMI TAJEKOZTATO. (HU/0231-0740). **4237**

PAPUA NEW GUINEA MEDICAL JOURNAL. (PP/0031-1480). **3626**

PAPYRUS BODMER. (SZ). **3422**

PAR EXCELLANCE MAGAZINE. (US/0886-4527). **4911**

PAR. PUBLIC ADMINISTRATION REVIEW POPULATION. (US/0033-3352). **4672**

PARA-LEGAL UPDATE. (US/0146-2954). **3025**

PARABOLA. (AT). **Adv Mgr:** D. Tait. **3526**

PARABOLA (MT. KISCO). (AT/0362-1596). **2323**

PARACHUTE. (CN/0318-7020). **361**

PARACHUTIST (WASHINGTON). (US/0031-1588). **4911**

PARACLETE (SPRINGFIELD, MO.). (US/0190-4639). **5065**

PARADES AND PAGEANTRY. (CN). **4145**

PARADOX INFORMANT. (US/1058-7071). **Adv Mgr:** Mitchell Koulouris. **1280**

PARAGLIDE. (US/0745-9688). **4053**

PARAGLIDE (FORT BRAGG, N.C.). (US/0891-7965). **5724**

PARAGRAPH (MODERN CRITICAL THEORY GROUP). (UK/0264-8334). **3309**

PARAGRAPH POOLE. (UK/0953-8577). **Adv Mgr:** Kathryn MacLean. **2851**

PARAGRAPH (STRATFORD). (CN/1182-543X). **Adv Mgr:** B. Barber. **3422**

PARALEGAL, THE. (US/0739-3601). **3025**

PARALLELOGRAMME (VANCOUVER). (CN/0703-8712). **Adv Mgr:** AnneMarie Beneteau, **Tel** (416)869-3854. **361**

PARAMETRO; MENSILE INTERNATIONALE DI ARCHITETTURA & URBANISTICA. (IT). **305**

PARAPLEGIA NEWS. (US/0031-1766). **4392**

PARASITE IMMUNOLOGY. (UK/0141-9838). **3675**

PARASITICA. (BE/0031-1812). **521**

PARASITOLOGY. (UK/0031-1820). **492**

PARATUS. (SA). **4053**

PARCHEMIN, LE. (BE). **2466**

PARENT & CHILD. (US/1041-178X). **Adv Mgr:** Fran Gianaris. **2284**

PARENTGUIDE NEWS. (US/0896-1468). **2284**

PARENTS AND CHILDREN TOGETHER. (US/1050-7108). **2284**

PARENTS & TEENAGERS. (US/0897-8697). **Adv Mgr:** Debbie Mitchell, **Tel** (503)549-8261. **2284**

PARENTS' CHOICE. (US/0161-8164). **Adv Mgr:** A. Braithwaite. **2284**

PARENTS' PRESS. (US/0889-8863). **2285**

PARENT'S SAY. (AT/0818-8114). **1772**

PARENTS SHOPPING GUIDE. (AT/1030-1968). **2285**

PARENTWISE. (UK). **4985**

PARFUMERIE UND KOSMETIK. (GW/0031-1952). **405**

PARIS NEWS, THE. (US/8756-2081). **Adv Mgr:** Larry Reynolds. **5753**

PARIS PASSION : THE MAGAZINE OF THE FRENCH CAPITAL. (FR). **2521**

PARIS POST-INTELLIGENCER, THE. (US/0893-3669). **Adv Mgr:** Brenda Stubblefield. **5746**

PARIS REVIEW, THE. (US/0031-2037). **3422**

PARK & GROUNDS MANAGEMENT. (US/1057-204X). **Adv Mgr:** Hooper Jones, **Tel** (708)486-1021. **4707**

PARK CITIES NEWS, THE. (US). **5753**

PARK RECORD (1964), THE. (US/0745-9483). **Adv Mgr:** Pamela Hamsworth, **Tel** (801)649-9014. **5757**

PARK RIDGE EDITION OF THE TIMES HERALD. (US/0895-013X). **Adv Mgr:** Bill Tapper. **5661**

PARK WORLD. (UK). **Adv Mgr:** John Slattery, **Tel** same as publisher. **3486**

PARKE COUNTY SENTINEL. (US/1044-7822). **Adv Mgr:** Jane Moss. **5666**

PARKER DIRECTORY OF CALIFORNIA ATTORNEYS. (US/0196-6138). **3025**

PARKING (WASHINGTON, D.C.). (US/0031-2193). **Adv Mgr:** Dawn Newman. **5423**

PARKINSON NETWORK. (CN/0824-7315). **3626**

PARKS AND GROUNDS. (SA). **2427**

PARKS & SPORTS GROUNDS. (UK/0031-224X). **Adv Mgr:** Jennifer Archer. **5488**

PARKWATCH. (AT). **2202**

PARLEMENTS ET FRANCOPHONIE. (FR/0258-4751). **Adv Mgr:** Frank Borotra. **4486**

PARLIAMENTARIAN. (UK/0031-2282). **4672**

PARLIAMENTARY HISTORY : A YEARBOOK. (UK/0264-2824). **Adv Mgr:** Kathryn MacLean. **4672**

PARLIAMENTARY WEEKLY QUARTERLY REPORT, THE. (CN/1188-2387). **Adv Mgr:** Robert Renaud. **4487**

PARLIAMENTS, ESTATES & REPRESENTATION. (UK/0260-6755). **4487**

PARNASSUS : POETRY IN REVIEW. (US/0048-3028). **3467**

PAROLA DEL PASSATO, LA. (IT/0031-2355). **1079**

PARSONS ADVOCATE. (US/0747-3303). **Adv Mgr:** Gail Jones. **5764**

PARSONS NEWS, THE. (US). **Adv Mgr:** Silva Staten. **5678**

PARSONS SUN (PARSONS, KAN. : 1929). (US). **5678**

PARTICLE ACCELERATORS. (US/0031-2460). **4413**

PARTICULATE SCIENCE AND TECHNOLOGY. (US/0272-6351). **2015**

PARTISAN REVIEW (1936). (US/0031-2525). **4544**

PASADENA HERITAGE. (US/0889-5864). **Adv Mgr:** H. Tobin, **Tel** (818)793-0617. **2753**

PASADENA JOURNAL OF BUSINESS. (US/0743-6610). **702**

PASADENA STAR-NEWS. (US/1069-2827). **5638**

PASCAL. F 10, MECANIQUE, ACOUSTIQUE ET TRANSFERT DE CHALEUR. (FR/1146-5107). **Adv Mgr:** Ms. Guinuarc. **4453**

PASO ROBLES COUNTRY NEWS, THE. (US/0195-0134). **Adv Mgr:** Mary Baldwin, **Tel** (805)237-6060. **5638**

PASOS SAN JOSE. (CR/1016-9857). **4985**

PASS PROMOTER, THE. (CN/0380-4135). **5792**

PASSAGES NORTH. (US/0278-0828). **3422**

PASSAIC REVIEW. (US/0731-4663). **3349**

PASSANT, EN. (CN/0822-5672). **4864**

PASSATO E PRESENTE. (IT). **4544**

PASSATO E PRESENTE (FLORENCE, ITALY). (IT/0392-4815). **2625**

PASSENGER PIGEON, THE. (US/0031-2703). **5619**

PASSENGER TRAIN JOURNAL. (US/0160-6913). **5433**

PASSENGER TRANSPORT. (US/0364-345X). **Adv Mgr:** Cecilia Barber, **Tel** (202)898-4122. **5389**

PASSPORT TO WORLD BAND RADIO. (US/0897-0157). **1136**

PAST & PRESENT. (UK/0031-2746). **2625**

PAST, PRESENT & FUTURE. (US/0895-0857). **2543**

PASTA JOURNAL. (US/8750-9393). **2352**

PASTICCERIA INTERNAZIONALE. (IT/0392-4718). **2352**

PASTORAL CARE IN EDUCATION. (UK/0264-3944). **1772**

PASTORAL LIFE. (US/0031-2762). **Adv Mgr:** D' Ann J. Montpet, **Tel** (216)799-1306. **4985**

PASTORAL MUSIC. (US/0363-6569). **4145**

PASTORAL SCIENCES. (CN/0713-3383). **Adv Mgr:** Jacques Gauthier. **4985**

PASTRYCOOKS AND BAKERS NEWS MONTHLY. (AT/0818-6561). **Adv Mgr:** R. J. Corner. **2353**

PATENTNI GLASNIK. (YU/0031-2908). **1308**

PATHOLOGY. (AT/0031-3025). **3897**

PATHOS. MONOGRAFIAS DE PATOLOGIA MEDICA. (SP). **3709**

PATHWAY TO GOD. (II). **4985**

PATHWAYS (HAMILTON). (CN/0840-8114). **2179**

PATIENT CARE. (US/0031-305X). **3738**

PATIENT EDUCATION NEWSLETTER. (US/0278-8209). **4795**

PATIENT MANAGEMENT (SEAFORTH). (NZ/0314-660X). **3626**

PATIENT UPDATE. (CN/0847-8090). **Adv Mgr:** K. Secord. **3790**

PATIO. (FR). **4607**

PATRE. (FR). **217**

PATRICIAN, THE. (CN/0316-4942). **4053**

PATRIDES (TORONTO). (CN/0824-359X). **2270**

PATRIOT (HARRISBURG, PA. : DAILY). (US/1041-4029). **5738**

PATRIOT LEDGER (CITY EDITION), THE. (US). **Adv Mgr:** George White, **Tel** (617)786-7175. **5689**

PATRIOT LEDGER (SOUTH EDITION), THE. (US). **Adv Mgr:** George White, **Tel** (617)786-7175. **5689**

PATRIOT LEDGER (SUBURBAN EDITION), THE. (US). **Adv Mgr:** George White, **Tel** (617)786-7175. **5689**

PATRISTIC AND BYZANTINE REVIEW, THE. (US/0737-738X). **4985**

PAULDING COUNTY PROGRESS. (US). **Adv Mgr:** Teri Daniels. **5729**

PAULLINA TIMES-SUTHERLAND COURIER (PAULLINA ED.). (US). **5672**

PAVING FORUM. (US). **2028**

PAY TV NEWSLETTER, THE. (US/0146-0072). **1136**

PAYROLL EXCHANGE. (US/0194-6196). **1701**

PAYS D'EUROPE OCCIDENTALE EN ..., LES. (FR). **2702**

PAYTECH (NEW YORK, N.Y.). (US/1063-9047). **749**

PAZIFISCHE RUNDSCHAU. (CN/0048-3095). **5792**

PC ACTIVE. (NE/0925-5745). **Adv Mgr:** R Lie, **Tel** 020-6249969. **1270**

PC AI. (US/0894-0711). **Adv Mgr:** Robin Okun, **Tel** (602)971-1869. **1215**

PC GRAPHICS & VIDEO. (US/1077-5862). **1234**

PC GUIDE USA. CD-ROM. (US). **1198**

PC MAGAZINE. (UK/0953-7708). **Adv Mgr:** Tim Munson. **1271**

PC NOVICE. (US/1052-1186). **1271**

PC-PRAXIS 1989. (GW/0940-6743). **Adv Mgr:** Peter Staesche, **Tel** 211 31081 50. **1199**

PC PUBLISHING. (US/0896-8209). **4818**

PC REPORT. (US). **1271**

PC-SIG — Advertising Accepted Index

PC-SIG MAGAZINE. (US/1042-0681). **Adv Mgr:** Jerry Pearson, **Tel** (408)730-9291. **1289**

PC TECHNIQUES. (US/1053-6205). **Adv Mgr:** T.Mayer. **1289**

PC TODAY. (US/1040-6484). **1271**

PC USER (LONDON, ENGLAND). (UK/0263-5720). **1271**

PC WEEK (U.S. ED.). (US/0740-1604). **1271**

PCA MESSENGER, THE. (US/0191-4162). **Adv Mgr:** Bill Savage. **4986**

PCGAMES. (US/0897-893X). **1230**

PCIM EUROPE. (GW). **1990**

PCM. (US/0747-0460). **Adv Mgr:** Carol Fenwick, **Tel** (502)228-4492. **1271**

PCR METHODS AND APPLICATIONS. (US/1054-9803). **1045**

PCR / PRODUCTION AND CASTING REPORT. (UK/0142-632X). **1621**

PCSO BULLETIN. (US/0191-7951). **1332**

PCTE NEWSLETTER. (FR). **1199**

PCWORLD. (HK). **Adv Mgr:** Vera Chan. **1271**

PEACE AND CHANGE. (US/0149-0508). **4531**

PEACE & DEMOCRACY NEWS. (US/0749-5900). **4531**

PEACE AND TRUTH. (UK). **4986**

PEACE MAGAZINE. (CN/0826-9521). **Adv Mgr:** Jean Smith. **4531**

PEACE NEWSLETTER (SYRACUSE, N.Y.). (US/0735-4134). **4531**

PEACE RESEARCH. (CN/0008-4697). **Adv Mgr:** Mrs. T. Sowia, **Tel** (204)729-9010. **4531**

PEACE REVIEW (PALO ALTO, CALIF.). (US/1040-2659). **4531**

PEACEKEEPING & INTERNATIONAL RELATIONS. (CN/1187-3485). **Adv Mgr:** Fred Russell. **4531**

PEACEMAKER, THE. (US/0031-3602). **4487**

PEACH TIMES. (US/0031-3610). **2427**

PEAK RUNNING PERFORMANCE. (US). **4911**

PEAKE STUDIES. (SZ/1013-1191). **3422**

PEANUT FARMER, THE. (US/0031-3653). **180**

PEANUT GROWER, THE. (US/1042-9379). **180**

PEANUT INDUSTRY GUIDE. (US/0740-2562). **119**

PEASANT STUDIES. (US/0149-1547). **5212**

PEAT NEWS. (CN/0706-1307). **119**

PECOS FREE PRESS AND ENTERPRISE. (US). **Adv Mgr:** Cristina Bitolas. **5753**

PECUNIA. BRUXELLES, DE. (BE/1015-6283). **881**

PEDAGOGIA MEDICA. (IT/1120-8627). **3626**

PEDAGOGIKA. (XR/0031-3815). **1772**

PEDIATRE, LE. (FR/0397-9180). **Adv Mgr:** same as editor. **3907**

PEDIATRIA MEDICA E CHIRURGICA, LA. (IT/0391-5387). **3907**

PEDIATRIA MODERNA. (BL/0031-3920). **3907**

PEDIATRIC ALLERGY AND IMMUNOLOGY : OFFICIAL PUBLICATION OF THE EUROPEAN SOCIETY OF PEDIATRIC ALLERGY AND IMMUNOLOGY. (DK/0905-6157). **3675**

PEDIATRIC ANNALS. (US/0090-4481). **3908**

PEDIATRIC DERMATOLOGY. (US/0736-8046). **3908**

PEDIATRIC EMERGENCY CARE. (US/0749-5161). **3725**

PEDIATRIC EXERCISE SCIENCE. (US/0899-8493). **3908**

PEDIATRIC HEMATOLOGY AND ONCOLOGY. (US/0888-0018). **3773**

PEDIATRIC NEUROLOGY. (US/0887-8994). **Adv Mgr:** Richard Geyer. **3909**

PEDIATRIC NEUROSURGERY. (SZ/1016-2291). **3909**

PEDIATRIC NURSING. (US/0097-9805). **3866**

PEDIATRIC PATHOLOGY. (US/0277-0938). **3897**

PEDIATRIC RESEARCH. (US/0031-3998). **3909**

PEDIATRIC REVIEWS AND COMMUNICATION. (SZ/0882-9225). **3909**

PEDIATRICS (EVANSTON). (US/0031-4005). **Adv Mgr Tel** (708)981-7902. **3910**

PEDIATRIE. (FR/0031-4021). **3910**

PEDMED. (SA/1017-1711). **3626**

PEDOBIOLOGIA. (GW/0031-4056). **181**

PEDRALBES. (SP). **2702**

PEEK (65). (US/0739-0653). **1264**

PEEKE REPORT / METRO WASHINGTON DC EDITION / (MONDAY ONLY, BY MAIL). (US). **5686**

PEGASUS. (UK/0031-4080). **4053**

PEGBAR. (CN/0828-9247). **381**

PEGBOARD (MENLO PARK, CALIF.). (US/0892-5763). **1230**

PEGG. ASSOCIATION OF PROFESSIONAL ENGINEERS, GEOLOGISTS AND GEOPHYSICISTS OF ALBERTA (MONTHLY ED.). (CN/0823-1745). **1990**

PEGG, THE. (CN/0030-7912). **1990**

PELANCAR. (MY). **1543**

PELIZZA'S POSITIVE PRINCIPLES FOR BETTER LIVING. (US/1070-6674). **Adv Mgr:** John Pelizza. **4607**

PELUQUERIAS. (SP). **405**

PEM : PLANT ENGINEERING AND MAINTENANCE. (CN/0710-362X). **Adv Mgr:** Julie Clifford. **2124**

PEMBIMBING PEMBACA. (IO). **3240**

PEMBROKE MAGAZINE, THE. (US/0097-496X). **3423**

PEMBROKE REPORTER. (US/0746-6056). **Adv Mgr:** Gary Higgins. **5689**

PEN WORLD. (US/1045-1188). **2776**

PENDER POST. (US). **5724**

PENINSULA GATEWAY, THE. (US/1066-2065). **Adv Mgr:** Tom Taylor, **Tel** (206)851-9921. **5761**

PENINSULA HERITAGE. (US/0895-8165). **5034**

PENINSULA (REDWOOD CITY, CALIF.). (US/0888-4846). **2543**

PENINSULA (SAN MATEO), LA. (US/0197-2197). **2754**

PENN DENTAL JOURNAL, THE. (US/0031-4331). **1332**

PENN JERSEY BAPTIST. (US/0195-1815). **5065**

PENN SOUNDS. (US/1046-0292). **4145**

PENNSBORO NEWS, THE. (US). **Adv Mgr:** Randa Gregg. **5764**

PENNSYLVANIA ARCHITECT. (US/1062-8649). **305**

PENNSYLVANIA BAR ASSOCIATION LAWYERS DIRECTORY. (US/8755-0342). **Adv Mgr:** Leonard and Associates, **Tel** (215)675-9133. **3025**

PENNSYLVANIA CHIEFS OF POLICE ASSOCIATION BULLETIN. (US/0031-4404). **3171**

PENNSYLVANIA CPA JOURNAL. (US/0746-1062). **749**

PENNSYLVANIA DAIRY FARMSHINE. (US/0195-1971). **197**

PENNSYLVANIA DENTAL JOURNAL. (US/0031-4439). **Adv Mgr:** Stephanie Kalina, **Tel** (717)234-5941. **1332**

PENNSYLVANIA DIRECTORY OF MANUFACTURERS (HOHOKUS, N.J.). (US/0733-5237). **3486**

PENNSYLVANIA FORESTS. (US/0031-4501). **2390**

PENNSYLVANIA FRUIT NEWS. (US). **181**

PENNSYLVANIA GENEALOGICAL MAGAZINE, THE. (US/0882-3685). **2467**

PENNSYLVANIA HISTORY. (US/0031-4528). **2754**

PENNSYLVANIA JOURNAL OF HEALTH, PHYSICAL EDUCATION, RECREATION, DANCE. (US/0279-0033). **1902**

PENNSYLVANIA LAW JOURNAL-REPORTER. (US/0279-8166). **3025**

PENNSYLVANIA LAWYER, THE. (US/0193-4821). **Adv Mgr:** Leonard and Associates, **Tel** (215)675-9133. **3025**

PENNSYLVANIA MAGAZINE (CAMP HILL, PA.). (US/0744-4230). **Adv Mgr:** Susan Getter. **5488**

PENNSYLVANIA MAGAZINE OF HISTORY AND BIOGRAPHY, THE. (US/0031-4587). **2754**

PENNSYLVANIA MEDICINE. (US/0031-4595). **3626**

PENNSYLVANIA NURSE, THE. (US/0031-4617). **3866**

PENNSYLVANIA PHARMACIST. (US/0031-4633). **4319**

PENNSYLVANIA RECREATION & PARKS. (US/0742-793X). **Adv Mgr:** Marcie Lynch. **4707**

PENNSYLVANIA REVIEW (PITTSBURGH, PA.), THE. (US/8756-5668). **3423**

PENNSYLVANIA SPEECH COMMUNICATION ANNUAL, THE. (US/0889-5570). **1119**

PENNSYLVANIAN. (US/0031-4714). **4673**

PENORRA : REVISTA TRIMESTRAL DE POESIA, LA. (SP). **3468**

PENSACOLA NEWS JOURNAL. (US). **Adv Mgr:** Kit Carson, **Tel** (904)435-8667. **5650**

PENSAMIENTO IBEROAMERICANO. (SP/0212-0208). **1512**

PENSAMIENTO PROPIO : BOLETIN DE INFORMACION Y ANALISIS. (NQ). **Adv Mgr:** Walter Hernandez. **1512**

PENSE PROGRESS. (CN/0715-5735). **5792**

PENSIERO MAZZINIANO, IL. (IT). **Adv Mgr:** Gian Franco Fontana, **Tel** 054220908. **4487**

PENSION FUNDS AND THEIR ADVISERS. (UK/0140-6647). **911**

PENSION WORLD. (US/0098-1753). **1701**

PENSIONS & INVESTMENT AGE. EDITORIAL INDEX. (US/0275-0333). **911**

PENTECOSTAL EVANGEL. (US/0031-4897). **5066**

PENTECOSTAL MESSENGER, THE. (US/0031-4919). **Adv Mgr:** P. Allen. **5066**

PENTECOSTAL TESTIMONY, THE. (CN/0031-4927). **Adv Mgr:** D. Niles. **4986**

PEOPLE & THE PLANET / IPPF, UNFPA, IUCN. (UK/0968-1655). **4556**

PEOPLE (CHICAGO. 1974). (US/0093-7673). **2543**

PEOPLE DYNAMICS. (SA/1019-6196). **Adv Mgr:** Barbara Spence, **Tel** 011 886-5954. **944**

PEOPLE (ENGLISH ED.). (UK/0301-5645). **590**

PEOPLE'S FOLK DANCE DIRECTORY. (US/0160-5550). **1314**

PEOPLE'S KOREA, THE. (JA/0031-5036). **5805**

PEOPLE'S WEEKLY WORLD [MICROFORM]. (US). **Adv Mgr:** Audrey West. **5720**

PEOPLE'S WORLD (BERKELEY). (US/0031-5044). **5638**

PEP (MAMARONECK, N.Y.). (US/0031-5060). **4864**

PEPTIDE HORMONE RECEPTORS. (UK/0268-1552). **492**

PEPTIDE RESEARCH. (US/1040-5704). **1046**

PEPTIDES (NEW YORK, N.Y, : 1980). (US/0196-9781). **492**

PER LA FILOSOFIA. (IT). **Adv Mgr:** Cesare Crespi, **Tel** 5521-1220. **4354**

PERCEPTION & PSYCHOPHYSICS. (US/0031-5117). **4607**

PERCEPTION (LONDON). (UK/0301-0066). **4607**

PERCEPTION (OTTAWA). (CN/0704-5263). **5301**

PERCUSSIONER INTERNATIONAL AUDIO MAGAZINE. (US/0743-8621). **5318**

PERCUSSIVE NOTES. (US/0553-6502). **4145**

PERDESI PANJAB. (CN/0708-9503). **5792**

PERFECT VISION, THE. (US/0895-4143). **1136**

PERFORMANCE & INSTRUCTION (1985). (US/0884-1985). **1773**

PERFORMANCE EVALUATION. (NE/0166-5316). **Adv Mgr:** W Van Cattenburch, **Tel** 31 20 515 3220. **1261**

PERFORMANCE (FORT WORTH, TEX.). (US/0882-9314). **Adv Mgr:** Diana McClure. **387**

PERFORMANCE MANAGEMENT MAGAZINE. (US/0734-029X). **Adv Mgr:** Tracy Keever. **882**

PERFORMANCE PRACTICE REVIEW. (US/1044-1638). **4145**

PERFORMANCE RANKING GUIDE. (UK). **Adv Mgr:** Andy Parson. **802**

PERFORMANCE (VANIER). (CN/0832-8196). **4912**

PERFORMANCES MARSEILLE. (FR/0996-5882). **1773**

PERFORMING ARTS & ENTERTAINMENT IN CANADA. (CN/1185-3433). **Adv Mgr:** Peter Steen, **Tel** (416)785-4300. **387**

PERFORMING ARTS FORUM. (US/0739-1161). **387**

PERFORMING ARTS (HOUSTON). (US/0192-4192). **387**

PERFORMING ARTS JOURNAL. (US/0735-8393). **387**

PERFORMING ARTS (LOS ANGELES EDITION). (US/0031-5222). **387**

PERFUMER & FLAVORIST. (US/0272-2666). **1028**

PERFUSION LIFE. (US/0747-3079). **3773**

PERIOD HOME RENOVATOR BUYER'S GUIDE. (AT/1036-3181). **Adv Mgr:** Liz Webster, **Tel** 6466788. **2907**

PERIODICA ISLAMICA : AN INTERNATIONAL CONTENTS JOURNAL. (MY/0128-3715). **5044**

PERIODICA MATHEMATICA HUNGARICA. (HU/0031-5303). **3526**

PERIODICA POLYTECHNICA. CIVIL ENGINEERING. (HU/0553-6626). **2028**

PERIODICAL (COUNCIL ON AMERICA'S MILITARY PAST). (US). **4053**

PERIODICOS Y REVISTAS ESPANOLAS E HISPANOAMERICANAS. (SP). **4818**

PERIODICUM BIOLOGORUM. (CI/0031-5362). **468**

PERIODONTOLOGY. (AT). **1333**

PERIODONTOLOGY 2000. (DK/0906-6713). **1333**

PERIPHERY LISMORE. (AT/1034-0580). **374**

PERITONEAL DIALYSIS INTERNATIONAL. (US/0896-8608). **3800**

PERMACULTURE INTERNATIONAL JOURNAL. (AT/1037-8480). **Adv Mgr:** Andrew. **119**

PERRIS PROGRESS, THE. (US). **5638**

PERRY COUNTY TIMES, THE. (US). **Adv Mgr:** Rick White, **Tel** (717)582-4305. **5738**

PERRY HERALD (1912). (US/1065-1128). **Adv Mgr:** Lois Taylor. **5720**

PERRYSBURG MESSENGER-JOURNAL. (US/1064-2021). **Adv Mgr:** Matt Welch, **Tel** (419)874-4491. **5730**

PERSISTENCE OF VISION. (US). **4076**

PERSON-CENTERED REVIEW. (US/0883-2293). **4607**

PERSONAL ENGINEERING & INSTRUMENTATION NEWS. (US/0748-0016). **Adv Mgr:** Al Shackil, **Tel** (201)808-0165. **1230**

PERSONAL SELLING POWER. (US/0738-8594). **934**

PERSONNEL GUIDE TO CANADA'S TRAVEL INDUSTRY. (CN/0048-3451). **Adv Mgr:** Celyne Benitah & Robin Catto. **5488**

PERSONNEL JOURNAL. (US/0031-5745). **945**

PERSONNEL MANAGEMENT ABSTRACTS. (US/0031-577X). **732**

PERSONNEL MANAGEMENT (LONDON. 1969). (UK/0031-5761). **945**

PERSONNEL NEWS. (US). **Adv Mgr:** Ken Whelan, **Tel** (408)988-8991. **4704**

PERSONNEL PSYCHOLOGY. (US/0031-5826). **4607**

PERSONNES C.L.E.F. (CN/0824-1902). **3028**

PERSOON EN GEMEENSCHAP. (BE/0031-5842). **1773**

PERSPECTIVA (SOUTH HADLEY, MASS.). (US/1059-0536). **Adv Mgr:** Sarah Clay. **3310**

PERSPECTIVE (ALBANY, N.Y. 1983). (US/0743-6475). **3029**

PERSPECTIVE ON AGING. (US/0096-2740). **3754**

PERSPECTIVES : A JOURNAL OF REFORMED THOUGHT. (US). **4986**

PERSPECTIVES AGRICOLES. (FR/0399-8533). **119**

PERSPECTIVES - GERONTOLOGICAL NURSING ASSOCIATION. (CN/0831-7445). **Adv Mgr:** HLR & Associates, **Tel** (613)623-6975. **3866**

PERSPECTIVES IN BIOLOGY AND MEDICINE. (US/0031-5982). **468**

PERSPECTIVES IN EDUCATION AND DEAFNESS. (US/1051-6204). **4392**

PERSPECTIVES IN ENGINEERING. (US). **1990**

PERSPECTIVES IN PLASTIC SURGERY. (US/0892-3957). **3972**

PERSPECTIVES IN PSYCHIATRIC CARE. (US/0031-5990). **Adv Mgr:** Joseph M Braden. **3866**

PERSPECTIVES IN RELIGIOUS STUDIES. (US/0093-531X). **4986**

PERSPECTIVES OF NEW MUSIC. (US/0031-6016). **1240**

PERSPECTIVES ON ADDICTIONS NURSING. (US/1057-1639). **Adv Mgr:** Kathy Checea, **Tel** (708)966-5010. **3867**

PERSPECTIVES ON SCIENCE. (US/1063-6145). **5137**

PERSPECTIVES ON SCIENCE AND CHRISTIAN FAITH. (US/0892-2675). **4986**

PERSPECTIVES ON THE MEDICAL TRANSCRIPTION PROFESSION. (US/1066-3533). **3626**

PERSPECTIVES (SASKATOON). (CN/0316-3334). **5212**

PERSPECTIVES (TOLEDO, OHIO). (US/0883-6086). **3350**

PERSPEKTIEF. (NE/0167-9104). **4372**

PERSPEKTIVEN (VIENNA, AUSTRIA). (AU). **623**

PERTANIKA. (MY/0126-6128). **119**

PESQUISA VETERINARIA BRASILEIRA. (BL/0100-736X). **Adv Mgr:** Luis Carlos de Oliveira, **Tel** (021)263-7561. **5518**

PEST CONTROL TECHNOLOGY. (US/0730-7608). **Adv Mgr:** D Foster. **4246**

PEST MANAGEMENT. (US/0744-6357). **4246**

PESTALK. (AT). **4246**

PET AGE. (US/0098-5406). **4287**

PET BUSINESS. (US/0191-4766). **4287**

PET DEALER. (US/0553-8572). **4287**

PET DEALER ANNUAL GUIDE. (US/0553-8572). **Adv Mgr:** Arline Wasserman. **4287**

PETA NEWS. (US/0899-9708). **226**

PETERBOROUGH EXAMINER. (CN). **Adv Mgr:** B. Barthorpe, **Tel** 745-4641. **5792**

PETERBOROUGH EXAMINER (DAILY ED.). (CN/0839-0878). **Adv Mgr:** B. Barthorpe, **Tel** 745-4644. **5792**

PETERBOROUGH TRANSCRIPT, THE. (US). **Adv Mgr:** Cher Powers, **Tel** (603)924-3333. **5708**

PETERSEN'S 4 WHEEL & OFF-ROAD. (US/0162-3214). **4912**

PETERSEN'S FISHING. (US/1041-4703). **4912**

PETERSEN'S HUNTING. (US/0146-4671). **4912**

PETERSEN'S PHOTOGRAPHIC. (US/0199-4913). **4372**

PETFOOD INDUSTRY. (US/0031-6245). **4287**

PETIT JOURNAL DU BRASSEUR. (BE/0031-6253). **2370**

PETITE NATION, LA. (CN/0228-9954). **5792**

PETOSKEY NEWS REVIEW. (US). **Adv Mgr:** Tari Calouette. **5693**

PETROCHEMICALS & REFINING. (SI). **4271**

PETROLEUM. (VE). **Adv Mgr:** Aristides Villalobos. **4272**

PETROLEUM ECONOMIST (ENGLISH EDITION). (UK/0306-395X). **4272**

PETROLEUM ENGINEER INTERNATIONAL. (US/0164-8322). **4272**

PETROLEUM EXPLORATION IN NEW ZEALAND NEWS. (NZ/0113-0501). **Adv Mgr:** R. Gregg, **Tel** (04)4720 030. **4272**

PETROLEUM INDEPENDENT. (US/0747-2528). **Adv Mgr:** Rick Carbo, **Tel** (202)857-4775. **4272**

PETROLEUM MANAGEMENT (HOUSTON, TEX.). (US/0884-4550). **4273**

PETROLEUM MARKETER (NEW HAVEN). (US/0362-7799). **4273**

PETROLEUM REVIEW (LONDON. 1978). (UK/0020-3076). **4273**

PETROLEUM SOFTWARE DIRECTORY. (US). **4273**

PETROLEUM TERMINAL ENCYCLOPEDIA. (US/0897-2001). **4274**

PETS MAGAZINE (1985). (CN/0831-2621). **4287**

PEUPLE BRETON, LE. (FR/0245-9507). **2271**

PEUPLE-TRIBUNE. (CN/0383-7572). **5792**

PEUPLES DU MONDE. (FR/0555-9952). **4986**

PEUPLES MEDITERRANEENS. (FR/0399-1253). **2702**

PFLANZENARZT, DER. (AU/0031-6733). **521**

PHALGU : PHALGU SAHITYA SAMSADARA MUKHAPATRA. (II). **3423**

PHARMA INTERNATIONAL (TRI-LINGUAL EDITION). (SZ/0301-1348). **4319**

PHARMA-MARKETING-JOURNAL. (GW/0721-5665). **1512**

PHARMACEUTICA ACTA HELVETIAE. (SZ/0031-6865). **4319**

PHARMACEUTICAL & COSMETIC REVIEW. (SA/1015-4760). **Adv Mgr:** G Wells. **4320**

PHARMACEUTICAL ENGINEERING. (US/0273-8139). **Adv Mgr:** David Hall. **4320**

PHARMACEUTICAL EXECUTIVE. (US/0279-6570). **4320**

PHARMACEUTICAL JOURNAL OF KENYA. (KE/0378-228X). **4320**

PHARMACEUTICAL MARKETING. (UK). **Adv Mgr:** Ben Brazelle. **4320**

PHARMACEUTICAL MEDICINE (BASINGSTOKE). (UK/0265-0673). **4320**

PHARMACEUTICAL TECHNOLOGY. (US/0147-8087). **4321**

PHARMACEUTICAL TECHNOLOGY INTERNATIONAL. (US/0164-6826). **4321**

PHARMACEUTICAL TIMES. (UK). **Adv Mgr:** Angela Fernandez. **4321**

PHARMACEUTIQUES PARIS. (FR/1240-0866). **4321**

PHARMACOLOGIA ET PHYSIOLOGICA (OULU). (FI/0358-4828). **4322**

PHARMACOLOGICAL REVIEWS. (US/0031-6997). **4322**

PHARMACOLOGY. (SZ/0031-7012). **4322**

PHARMACOLOGY & TOXICOLOGY. (DK/0901-9928). **4322**

PHARMACOLOGY, BIOCHEMISTRY AND BEHAVIOR. (US/0091-3057). **4322**

PHARMACOPSYCHIATRY. (GW/0176-3679). **4323**

PHARMACOTHERAPY. (US/0277-0008). **4323**

PHARMACTUEL. (CN/0834-065X). **4323**

PHARMACY TIMES. (US/0003-0627). **4323**

PHARMACY WEST. (US/0191-6394). **4323**

PHARMAZEUTISCHE INDUSTRIE, DIE. (GW/0031-711X). **4324**

PHARMAZEUTISCHE ZEITUNG. (GW/0031-7136). **4324**

PHARMINDEX. (US/0031-7152). **4324**

PHASE. (SP). **5034**

PHASE TRANSITIONS. (US/0141-1594). **4414**

PHAT : PRESENTATION HOUSE ARTS TABLOID. (CN/0711-7515). **381**

PHELON'S WOMEN'S APPAREL SHOPS. (US/0737-3430). **1086**

PHELPS COUNTY GENEALOGICAL SOCIETY QUARTERLY. (US/0884-2140). **2467**

PHENIX. (FR/0300-3639). **4864**

PHENIX CITIZEN (1973). (US). **5627**

PHI DELTA KAPPAN. (US/0031-7217). **1773**

PHILADELPHIA ARCHITECT. (US/1071-1651). **306**

PHILADELPHIA CITY PAPER. (US/0733-6349). **5738**

PHILADELPHIA FOLKSONG SOCIETY NEWSLETTER. (US). **4146**

PHILADELPHIA GAY NEWS. (US). **Adv Mgr:** Tony Lombardo. **5738**

PHILADELPHIA MAGAZINE (1967). (US/0031-7233). **2543**

PHILADELPHIA MEDICINE. (US/0031-7306). **3627**

PHILADELPHIA NEW OBSERVER, THE. (US/0890-8435). **Adv Mgr:** Frank Green. **5738**

PHILADELPHIA TRIBUNE (1884). (US/0746-956X). **5738**

PHILANTHROPY MONTHLY, THE. (US/1071-6661). **4338**

PHILANTHROPY. THE QUARTERLY NEWSLETTER OF THE AUSTRALIAN ASSOCIATION OF PHILANTHROPY. (AT). **4338**

PHILATELIC EXPORTER, THE. (UK/0031-7381). **1146**

PHILATELIC JOURNALIST, THE. (US/0048-3710). **2786**

PHILATELIC LITERATURE REVIEW. (US/0270-1707). **2786**

PHILATELIE AU QUEBEC. (CN/0381-7547). **Adv Mgr:** Ivan Latulippe. **2786**

PHILATELIST AND PJGB, THE. (UK/0260-6739). **2786**

PHILIPPINE CONSTRUCTION DIRECTORY. (PH). **623**

PHILIPPINE ECONOMIC JOURNAL, THE. (PH/0031-7500). **1512**

PHILIPPINE ENTOMOLOGIST. (PH/0369-9536). **5594**

PHILIPPINE GEOGRAPHICAL JOURNAL. (PH/0031-7551). **2572**

PHILIPPINE JOURNAL OF CROP SCIENCE, THE. (PH/0115-2025). **181**

PHILIPPINE JOURNAL OF EDUCATION, THE. (PH/0031-7624). **1773**

PHILIPPINE JOURNAL OF LINGUISTICS. (PH/0048-3796). **3310**

PHILIPPINE JOURNAL OF OPHTHALMOLOGY. (PH/0031-7659). **3878**

PHILIPPINE JOURNAL OF VETERINARY MEDICINE. (PH/0031-7705). **5518**

PHILIPPINE JOURNAL OF WEED SCIENCE. (PH). **181**

PHILIPPINE LAW GAZETTE. (PH/0115-2483). **Adv Mgr:** Arlene Dabu-Foz. **3142**

PHILIPPINE LAW JOURNAL. (PH/0031-7721). **3029**

PHILIPPINE LUMBERMAN, THE. (PH/0024-7316). **2403**

PHILIPPINE PHYTOPATHOLOGY. (PH/0115-0804). **521**

PHILIPPINE QUARTERLY OF CULTURE AND SOCIETY. (PH/0115-0243). **5253**

PHILIPPINE SOCIOLOGICAL REVIEW. (PH/0031-7810). **5253**

PHILIPPINE STATISTICIAN, THE. (PH/0031-7829). **5336**

PHILIPPINE TECHNOLOGY JOURNAL. (PH/0116-7294). **5138**

PHILIPPINES BUSINESS DIRECTORY. (PH). **703**

PHILOLOGICAL QUARTERLY. (US/0031-7977). **3310**

PHILOLOGOS. (GR). **1079**

PHILOMEL (PHILADELPHIA, PA.). (US/1052-4878). **3423**

PHILOSOPHER (MONTREAL, QUEBEC). (CN/0827-1887). **4355**

PHILOSOPHER, THE. (UK). **4355**

PHILOSOPHER'S INDEX. (US/0031-7993). **4365**

PHILOSOPHIA MATHEMATICA. (US/0031-8019). **3526**

PHILOSOPHIA NATURALIS. (GW/0031-8027). **4355**

PHILOSOPHIA (RAMAT GAN). (IS/0048-3893). **4355**

PHILOSOPHIA REFORMATA. (NE/0031-8035). **4355**

PHILOSOPHICA. (BE/0379-8402). **4355**

PHILOSOPHICAL BOOKS. (UK/0031-8051). **4355**

PHILOSOPHICAL FORUM, THE. (US/0031-806X). **4355**

PHILOSOPHICAL PAPERS (GRAHAMSTOWN). (SA/0556-8641). **4356**

PHILOSOPHICAL QUARTERLY, THE. (UK/0031-8094). **4356**

PHILOSOPHICAL REVIEW, THE. (US/0031-8108). **4356**

PHILOSOPHICAL STUDIES. (NE/0031-8116). **4356**

PHILOSOPHICAL TOPICS. (US/0276-2080). **4356**

PHILOSOPHISCHE RUNDSCHAU. (GW/0031-8159). **4356**

PHILOSOPHISCHE RUNDSCHAU. BEIHEFT. (GW/0554-0828). **4356**

PHILOSOPHISCHER LITERATURANZEIGER. (GW/0031-8175). **4356**

PHILOSOPHY AND LITERATURE. (US/0190-0013). **4356**

PHILOSOPHY AND PHENOMENOLOGICAL RESEARCH. (US/0031-8205). **Adv Mgr:** S. Berwnad, **Tel** (401)863-3215. **4356**

PHILOSOPHY & PUBLIC AFFAIRS. (US/0048-3915). **5212**

PHILOSOPHY AND SOCIAL ACTION. (II/0377-2772). **5253**

PHILOSOPHY & SOCIAL CRITICISM. (US/0191-4537). **4357**

PHILOSOPHY EAST & WEST. (US/0031-8221). **4357**

PHILOSOPHY IN CONTEXT. (US/0742-2733). **4357**

PHILOSOPHY (LONDON). (UK/0031-8191). **4357**

PHILOSOPHY OF SCIENCE (EAST LANSING). (US/0031-8248). **5138**

PHILOSOPHY OF THE SOCIAL SCIENCES. (US/0048-3931). **5212**

PHILOSOPHY TODAY (CELINA). (US/0031-8256). **4357**

PHLEBOLOGIE UND PROKTOLOGIE. (GW/0340-305X). **3800**

PHLS MICROBIOLOGY DIGEST. (UK/0265-3400). **568**

PHOEBE (ONEONTA, N.Y.). (US/1045-0904). **Adv Mgr:** D. Simons. **5564**

PHOENICS JOURNAL OF COMPUTATIONAL FLUID DYNAMICS & ITS APPLICATIONS, THE. (UK). **Adv Mgr:** Miss S.J. Barnes. **1289**

PHOENIX (1989). (US/1045-1773). **2543**

PHOENIX AND VICINITY POPULAR STREET ATLAS, INCLUDING MARICOPA COUNTY (CENSUS TRACT EDITION). (US/0733-7574). **2572**

PHOENIX HOME/GARDEN. (US/0270-9341). **2902**

PHOENIX (MINNEAPOLIS, MINN.), THE. (US/0893-4509). **4608**

PHOENIX RISING (TORONTO, ONT.). (CN/0710-1457). **3932**

PHOENIX (TORONTO). (CN/0031-8299). **1079**

PHOLEOS. (US/0733-8864). **1409**

PHONETICA. (SZ/0031-8388). **3310**

PHOSPHOLIPIDS. (UK/0264-9624). **492**

PHOSPHORUS AND POTASSIUM. (UK/0031-8426). **988**

PHOTO COMMUNIQUE. (CN/0708-5435). **4373**

PHOTO ELECTRONIC IMAGING. (US/1060-4936). **Adv Mgr:** Donna McMahan. **4373**

PHOTO - FORUM. (AT). **4373**

PHOTO INFORMATION ALMANAC. (US/0093-1365). **4373**

PHOTO-LAB-INDEX. (US/0884-9528). **4373**

PHOTO LAB MANAGEMENT. (US/0164-4769). **4373**

PHOTO LIFE. (CN/0700-3021). **4373**

PHOTO MARKETING. (US/0031-8531). **Adv Mgr:** Terri Cameron. **4373**

PHOTO OPPORTUNITY. (US/0899-4587). **882**

PHOTOCHEMISTRY AND PHOTOBIOLOGY. (UK/0031-8655). **1056**

PHOTOGRAMMETRIC ENGINEERING AND REMOTE SENSING. (US/0099-1112). **1990**

PHOTOGRAMMETRIC RECORD, THE. (UK/0031-868X). **2572**

PHOTOGRAPH COLLECTOR, THE. (US/0271-0838). **4374**

PHOTOGRAPH COLLECTORS' RESOURCE DIRECTORY / THE PHOTOGRAPHIC ARTS CENTER, THE. (US). **4374**

PHOTOGRAPHER, THE. (UK/0031-8698). **4374**

PHOTOGRAPHER'S FORUM. (US/0194-5467). **4374**

PHOTOGRAPHIC ART MARKET. (US/1053-7031). **4374**

PHOTOGRAPHIC JOURNAL (1956). (UK/0031-8736). **4374**

PHOTOGRAPHICA. (US). **4374**

PHOTOGRAPHIE. (SZ). **4374**

PHOTOGRAPHIES MAGAZINE. (FR/0988-7679). **Adv Mgr:** P. Hevllant. **4374**

PHOTOGRAPHY IN NEW YORK. (US/1040-0346). **4374**

PHOTONICS SPECTRA (PITTSFIELD, MASS. 1982). (US/0731-1230). **4440**

PHOTOSCOOP / PICTORIAL MAGAZINE. (BE). **4375**

PHOTOSYNTHESIS RESEARCH. (NE/0166-8595). **521**

PHRONESIS. (NE/0031-8868). **4357**

PHRONESIS (HEIDELBERG, GERMANY). (NE/0031-8868). **4357**

PHU NU DIEN DAN. (VM). **5564**

PHYCOLOGIA (OXFORD). (UK/0031-8884). **521**

PHYLON (1960). (US/0031-8906). **5213**

PHYSICAL & OCCUPATIONAL THERAPY IN GERIATRICS. (US/0270-3181). **4381**

PHYSICAL & OCCUPATIONAL THERAPY IN PEDIATRICS. (US/0194-2638). **4381**

PHYSICAL EDUCATION GOLD BOOK. (US/0733-7272). **1857**

PHYSICAL EDUCATION REVIEW. (UK/0140-7708). **1857**

PHYSICAL THERAPY. (US/0031-9023). **4381**

PHYSICIAN AND SPORTSMEDICINE, THE. (US/0091-3847). **3955**

PHYSICIAN ASSISTANT (1983). (US/8750-7544). **3627**

PHYSICIAN ASSISTANT NEWSLETTER OF ETHICS. (US). **Adv Mgr:** Bernard Stuetz, **Tel** (215)884-7972. **2252**

PHYSICIAN EXECUTIVE. (US/0898-2759). **3916**

PHYSICIAN REFERRAL UPDATE. (US). **3627**

PHYSICIANS & COMPUTERS. (US/0891-8163). **1261**

PHYSICIANS' DESK REFERENCE (PRINT ED.). (US/0093-4461). **4325**

PHYSICIAN'S MANAGEMENT. (US/0031-9066). **3627**

PHYSICIAN'S MANAGEMENT MANUALS. (CN/0705-6311). **3916**

PHYSICS AND CHEMISTRY OF LIQUIDS. (US/0031-9104). **1056**

PHYSICS ESSAYS. (CN/0836-1398). **Adv Mgr:** Ken Charbobbeau, **Tel** (819)777-0548. **4415**

PHYSICS IN CANADA. (CN/0031-9147). **Adv Mgr:** F Brule. **4415**

PHYSICS OF METALS. (US/0275-9144). **4014**

PHYSICS TEACHER, THE. (US/0031-921X). **1902**

PHYSIK DATEN. (GW/0344-8401). **4416**

PHYSIK UND DIDAKTIK. (GW/0340-8515). **1902**

PHYSIOLOGIA PLANTARUM. (DK/0031-9317). **521**

PHYSIOLOGICAL CHEMISTRY AND PHYSICS AND MEDICAL NMR. (US/0748-6642). **469**

PHYSIOLOGICAL ENTOMOLOGY. (UK/0307-6962). **5612**

PHYSIOLOGICAL REVIEWS. (US/0031-9333). **585**

PHYSIOLOGIST, THE. (US/0031-9376). **585**

PHYSIOTHERAPY. (UK/0031-9406). **4382**

PHYSIOTHERAPY CANADA. (CN/0300-0508). **3627**

PHYSIOTHERAPY IN SPORT. (UK/0954-0741). **Adv Mgr:** Joanne Mansfield. **3955**

PHYTOMORPHOLOGY. (II/0031-9449). **522**

PHYTON (BUENOS AIRES). (AG/0031-9457). **522**

PHYTOPATHOLOGIA MEDITERRANEA. (IT/0031-9465). **522**

PHYTOPHTHORA NEWSLETTER. (UK/0748-6693). **523**

PI QUALITY. (US). **1199**

PIANO GUILD NOTES. (US/0031-9546). **4146**

PIANO JOURNAL / EUROPEAN PIANO TEACHERS ASSOCIATION. (UK/0267-7253). **4146**

PIANO QUARTERLY, THE. (US/0031-9554). **4146**

PIANO TECHNICIAN'S JOURNAL. (US/0031-9562). **4146**

PICKENS COUNTY HERALD. (US/0893-0767). **Adv Mgr:** Brian Hood. **5627**

PICKWORLD IRVINE, CALIF. (US/1066-2154). **1199**

PICTON, LE. (FR/0151-6086). **2702**

PICTORIAL NEW VAUTIER MAGAZINE. (BE). **4375**

PICTURE PERFECT. (US/1045-0629). **4375**

PIEDMONT JOURNAL-INDEPENDENT, THE. (US/0890-6017). **Adv Mgr:** Carol Weatherbee. **5627**

PIEDMONT LITERARY REVIEW. (US/0275-357X). **3423**

PIERCE COUNTY POPULAR STREET ATLAS (CENSUS TRACT ED.). (US/0733-7663). **2572**

PIERCE COUNTY TRIBUNE, THE. (US). **Adv Mgr:** Kim Brown, **Tel** (701)776-5252. **5726**

PIERCE PIANO ATLAS. (US/0733-429X). **4146**

PIERRE-FORT - PIERRE GENEALOGICAL SOCIETY, THE. (US/0737-7975). **2467**

PIG FARMER, THE. (AT/0031-9740). **217**

PIG FARMING. (UK/0031-9759). **217**

PIG INTERNATIONAL (EUROPE, ASIA, AFRICA, LATIN AMERICA AND OCEANIA EDITION. (US/0191-8834). **217**

PIG NEWS AND INFORMATION. (UK/0143-9014). **155**

PIG VETERINARY JOURNAL. (UK/0956-0939). **Adv Mgr:** J. Heard. **5518**

PIGMENT & RESIN TECHNOLOGY. (UK/0369-9420). **4225**

PIGS. (NE/0168-9533). **217**

PIK. PRAXIS DER INFORMATIONSVERARBEITUNG UND KOMMUNIKATION. (GW/0930-5157). **Adv Mgr:** Elisabeth Grubev, **Tel** 089-76902235. **1199**

PIKES PEAK JOURNAL, THE. (US). **5644**

PILLSBURY FAST AND HEALTHY MAGAZINE. (US/1059-8073). **4197**

PILOT (BOSTON, MASS.), THE. (US/0744-933X). **Adv Mgr:** Joan McAllister, **Tel** (617)482-4316. **31**

PILOT (MONTREAL). (CN/0380-6618). **31**

PILOT UND FLUGZEUG. (GW). **31**

PIMA CATALOG. (US/0739-2133). **4237**

PIMA MAGAZINE. (US/1046-4352). **4237**

PIMIENTA. (US/0146-2075). **3996**

PINE CITY PIONEER. (US/0892-2012). **5698**

PINE COUNTY COURIER. (US). **Adv Mgr:** Patty McQuiston. **5698**

PINE LOG, THE. (US). **Adv Mgr:** Emmeline Aguirre. **5753**

PINE RIVER JOURNAL. (US). **Adv Mgr:** Debbie Hughes, **Tel** (218)587-2360. **5698**

PINELLAS COUNTY REVIEW. (US/0746-746X). **803**

PING PANG SHIH CHIEH. (CC). **Adv Mgr:** Mr. Su Pixian, **Tel** 7031505. **4912**

PINHOLE JOURNAL. (US/0885-1476). **4375**

PINTURAS Y ACABADOS INDUSTRIALES. (SP/0031-9953). **4225**

PIONEER (BEMIDJI, MINN.), THE. (US/0899-1812). **Adv Mgr:** Jeff Haverson. **5698**

PIONEER (BIG RAPIDS, MICH.), THE. (US/8750-5533). **Adv Mgr Tel** (616)796-4831. **5693**

PIONEER (CHETWYND). (CN/0228-0523). **5793**

PIONEER PATHFINDER. (US/0736-8208). **Adv Mgr:** Dee Krohse, **Tel** 9605)338-3441. **2467**

PIONEER, THE. (US). **Adv Mgr:** Irv Smith. **5638**

PIP COLLEGE "HELPS" NEWSLETTER. (US/0732-5258). **Adv Mgr:** Hazel Morse. **1883**

PIPE BAND. (UK). **4146**

PIPE LINE INDUSTRY (HOUSTON, TEX.). (US/0032-0145). **2124**

PIPELINE & GAS JOURNAL. (US/0032-0188). **4274**

PIPELINE DIGEST. (US/0197-1506). **4274**

PIPELINE INTELLIGENCE REPORT. (US). **Adv Mgr:** Margie Moses. **4274**

PIPES & PIPELINES INTERNATIONAL (1965). (UK/0032-020X). **4274**

PIPESTONE COUNTY STAR. (US). **Adv Mgr:** Ray Fuder, **Tel** (507)825-3333. **5698**

PIQUALITY. (US/1058-8787). **Adv Mgr:** Jim Losm, **Tel** (708)462-2316. **1199**

PISCINAS. (SP/0210-6868). **623**

PITCH PIPE, THE. (US/0882-214X). **4146**

PITT MAGAZINE. (US). **1102**

PITTSBURGH BUSINESS TIMES-JOURNAL. (US/0883-7910). **Adv Mgr:** Rick Linder, **Tel** (412)481-6397. **703**

PITTSBURGH HISTORY. (US/1069-4706). **2754**

PITTSBURGH LEGAL JOURNAL. (US/0032-0331). **3029**

PIZZA TODAY. (US/0743-3115). **Adv Mgr:** Kaye Durnell. **2353**

PJG (MIAMI, FLA.). (US/1043-0083). **2427**

PLA BULLETIN. (US/0197-9299). **3241**

PLACES (CAMBRIDGE, MASS.). (US/0731-0455). **306**

PLAIN RAPPER, THE. (US/0032-0412). **5301**

PLAINDEALER (WICHITA, KAN. 1919), THE. (US/0898-4360). **Adv Mgr:** Linda Powell. **5678**

PLAN AND PRINT. (US/0032-0595). **1234**

PLAN CANADA. (CN/0032-0544). **2830**

PLAN (MONTREAL). (CN/0032-0536). **Adv Mgr:** France Cadieux. **1990**

PLAN OG ARBEID. (NO/0032-0609). **1702**

PLAN SPONSOR. (US). **Adv Mgr:** Dan Dent. **911**

PLANET TODAY. (CN/1183-6040). **2179**

PLANETARIAN, THE. (US/0090-3213). **398**

PLANNER (LONDON). (UK/0309-1384). **2830**

PLANNING. (UK). **Adv Mgr:** Prue Warne, **Tel** 011 44 384 373421. **4673**

PLANNING & ZONING NEWS. (US/0738-114X). **2831**

PLANNING (CHICAGO, ILL. 1969). (US/0001-2610). **2831**

PLANNING FOR HIGHER EDUCATION. (US/0736-0983). **1841**

PLANNING HISTORY. (UK/0959-5805). **2702**

PLANNING HISTORY PRESENT. (US/1071-1953). **2831**

PLANNING NEWS (ALBANY, N.Y.). (US/0885-6737). **2831**

PLANNING NEWS SOUTH MELBOURNE. (AT/0313-3796). **Adv Mgr:** J. Jenkins, **Tel** 05 819 0930. **2831**

PLANNING PERSPECTIVES : PP. (UK/0266-5433). **2831**

PLANNING PRACTICE + RESEARCH. (UK/0269-7459). **2831**

PLANNING QUARTERLY (NEW ZEALAND PLANNING INSTITUTE). (NZ). **Adv Mgr:** Chris Joel. **2831**

PLANNING REVIEW. (US/0094-064X). **882**

PLANO STAR COURIER (1986). (US/0895-4305). **5753**

PLANT AND CELL PHYSIOLOGY. (JA/0032-0781). **523**

PLANT & GARDEN. (CN). **Adv Mgr:** Barbara Paul. **2427**

PLANT AND SOIL. (NE/0032-079X). **181**

PLANT & WORKS ENGINEERING. (UK). **Adv Mgr:** Steve Aslett. **1990**

PLANT BIOTECHNOLOGY. (UK/0260-5902). **523**

PLANT BREEDING. (GW/0179-9541). **523**

PLANT BREEDING ABSTRACTS. (UK/0032-0803). **155**

PLANT, CELL AND ENVIRONMENT. (UK/0140-7791). **523**

PLANT CELL, THE. (US/1040-4651). **539**

PLANT CELL, TISSUE AND ORGAN CULTURE. (NE/0167-6857). **523**

PLANT DISEASE. (US/0191-2917). **181**

PLANT ENGINEERING. (US/0032-082X). **1990**

PLANT FOODS FOR HUMAN NUTRITION (DORDRECHT). (NE/0921-9668). **4197**

PLANT GROWTH REGULATION. (NE/0167-6903). **523**

PLANT GROWTH REGULATOR ABSTRACTS. (UK/0305-9154). **155**

PLANT JOURNAL : FOR CELL AND MOLECULAR BIOLOGY, THE. (UK/0960-7412). **523**

PLANT MOLECULAR BIOLOGY. (NE/0167-4412). **550**

PLANT/OPERATIONS PROGRESS. (US/0278-4513). **2015**

PLANT PATHOLOGY. (UK/0032-0862). **524**

PLANT PROTECTION QUARTERLY. (AT/0815-2195). **120**

PLANT SCIENCE (LIMERICK). (IE/0168-9452). **524**

PLANT VARIETIES JOURNAL. (AT/1030-9748). **2428**

PLANTA MEDICA. (GW/0032-0943). **4325**

PLANTER, THE. (MY/0126-575X). **120**

PLANTLINE. (AT/0726-4623). **Adv Mgr:** Peter Symonds, **Tel** 372-5222. **3486**

PLANTS, SITES & PARKS. (US/0191-2933). **703**

PLANTSMAN, THE. (UK/0143-0106). **2428**

PLASMAPHERESIS. (US/0894-6779). **3627**

PLASTFORUM SCANDINAVIA. (SW/0347-8262). **4457**

PLASTIC AND RECONSTRUCTIVE SURGERY (1963). (US/0032-1052). **3972**

PLASTIC FIGURE AND PLAYSET COLLECTOR. (US). **2585**

PLASTIC NEWS INTERNATIONAL. (AT). **2107**

PLASTIC SURGERY. (NE/0014-438X). **3972**

PLASTICOS UNIVERSALES. (SP/0303-4011). **4457**

PLASTICS AND RUBBER INTERNATIONAL. (UK/0309-4561). **4457**

PLASTICS BULLETIN. (BE). **Adv Mgr:** Robert De Craene. **4457**

PLASTICS DESIGN FORUM. (US/0362-9376). **4458**

PLASTICS ENGINEERING. (US/0091-9578). **4458**

PLASTICS INDUSTRY DIRECTORY, THE. (UK). **4458**

PLASTICS NEWS (AKRON, OHIO). (US/1042-802X). **4458**

PLASTICS SOUTHERN AFRICA. (SA/0032-2660). **2107**

PLASTICS TECHNOLOGY. (US/0032-1257). **4458**

PLASTICS WORLD. (US/0032-1273). **4458**

PLASTICULTURE. (FR). **4459**

PLASTIZINE. (CN/0715-5719). **381**

PLASTVERARBEITER, DER. (GW/0032-1338). **4459**

PLATE WORLD. (US/0195-5780). **2593**

PLATEAUX. (FR). **387**

PLATELETS SHEFFIELD. (UK/0142-8268). **3773**

PLATING AND SURFACE FINISHING. (US/0360-3164). **4225**

PLATTE COUNTY GAZETTE (1988), THE. (US/0899-5737). **Adv Mgr:** Carol Allen, **Tel** (816)781-1044. **5704**

PLAY & CULTURE. (US/0894-4253). **5213**

PLAY AND PARENTING CONNECTIONS. (CN/0835-4014). **3241**

PLAY METER MAGAZINE. (US/1048-8243). **4864**

PLAYBACK AND FAST FORWARD. (II). **703**

PLAYBACK (TORONTO). (CN/0836-2114). **1136**

PLAYBILL. (US/0551-0678). **Adv Mgr:** B Charles. **5367**

PLAYBOARD. (CN/0048-4415). **387**

PLAYERS. (US/0149-466X). **3996**

PLAYGIRL. (US/0032-1494). **5564**

PLAYING-CARD WORLD. (UK/0966-4033). **4865**

PLAYS & PLAYWRIGHTS. (US). **3424**

PLAYS (BOSTON). (US/0032-1540). **5367**

PLAYWRIGHT'S COMPANION, THE. (US/0887-1507). **5367**

PLAZA MAYOR. (PE). **2831**

PLC INSIDER'S NEWSLETTER, THE. (US/1040-9718). **1265**

PLEASANT GROVE REVIEW. (US/8755-9072). **Adv Mgr:** Brett Brezzant. **5757**

PLEASANTS COUNTY LEADER. (US). **Adv Mgr:** Vermice Simonton. **5764**

PLEASURE BOATING. (US/0191-7366). **595**

PLEIN SOLEIL (MONTREAL). (CN/0384-7810). **Adv Mgr:** L. Bouchard, **Tel** (514)259-3422 Ext. 24. **3732**

PLEINE MARGE. (FR/0295-1630). **362**

PLENTYWOOD HERALD. (US). **Adv Mgr:** Tim Polk. **5706**

PLERUS. (PR/0048-4466). **1512**

PLEXUS (OAKLAND, CALIF.). (US/0274-5526). **5564**

PLONGEE. (CN/0228-3530). **4912**

PLOUGHSHARES. (US/0048-4474). **3424**

PLOWMAN (BROOKLIN). (CN/0840-707X). **3468**

PLUIMVEEHOUDERIJ, DE. (NE). **217**

PLUM CREEK ALMANAC. (US/0898-5197). **2468**

PLUMBING. (UK/0032-1656). **Adv Mgr:** Marilyn Sansom. **2607**

PLUMBING BUSINESS. (US). **2607**

PLURAL. (MX/0185-4925). **328**

PLURAL SOCIETIES. (NE/0048-4482). **5213**

PLUS (BAIERSBRONN). (GW). **1086**

PLYMOUTH BULLETIN. (US/0032-1737). **5423**

PM NET WORK, THE. (US/1040-8754). **882**

PM PLUS. (UK). **946**

PM. PRAXIS DER MATHEMATIK. (GW/0032-7042). **3527**

PMC. PRACTICE OF MINISTRY IN CANADA. (CN/0825-0391). **4986**

PMD, PHARMACEUTICAL MARKETERS DIRECTORY. (US/0149-0885). **4325**

PME (LAVAL). (CN/0828-8089). **703**

PMEA NEWS. (US/0030-8102). **4146**

PMI. POWDER METALLURGY INTERNATIONAL. (GW/0048-5012). **4015**

PN REVIEW (MANCHESTER, GREATER MANCHESTER : 1979). (UK/0144-7076). **3350**

PNCC STUDIES. (US/0734-4570). **4987**

PNLA QUARTERLY. (US/0030-8188). **3241**

PNPA PRESS. (US/0030-8196). **4818**

POA (1985). (US/0882-9624). **2801**

POCAHONTAS STAR HERALD. (US). **Adv Mgr:** Becky Blisener, **Tel** (501)892-4451. **5632**

PODIATRIC PRODUCTS. (US/0890-3972). **3918**

PODIATRY MANAGEMENT. (US/0744-3528). **3918**

POE STUDIES. (US/0090-5224). **434**

POEM. (US/0032-1885). **3468**

POET LORE. (US/0032-1966). **3468**

POET (SHREVEPORT, LA.), THE. (US/0748-4062). **Adv Mgr:** P. Cooper. **3468**

POETICA (MUNCHEN). (NE/0303-4178). **3424**

POETICS. (US/1043-0814). **3468**

POETICS TODAY. (US/0333-5372). **3424**

POETRY & AUDIENCE. (UK/0032-2040). **3469**

POETRY CANADA REVIEW. (CN/0709-3373). **Adv Mgr:** Melanie. **3350**

POETRY (CHICAGO). (US/0032-2032). **3469**

POETRY DURHAM. (UK). **3469**

POETRY EAST. (US/0197-4009). **3469**

POETRY FLASH. (US/0737-4747). **3469**

POETRY IRELAND REVIEW, THE. (IE/0332-2998). **Adv Mgr:** Niamh Morris, **Tel** (353)1-610320. **3469**

POETRY NIPPON. (JA/0032-2105). **3469**

POETRY PILOT. (US/0554-3983). **3469**

POETRY REVIEW (LONDON). (UK/0032-2156). **3350**

POETRY TORONTO. (CN/0381-6591). **3469**

POETS & WRITERS. (US/0891-6136). **3470**

POETS AT WORK. (US). **3470**

POINT OF BEGINNING- POB. (US/0739-3865). **Adv Mgr:** Ed Miller. **2028**

POINT SERIES. (PP/0253-2913). **4987**

POINT THEOLOGIQUE, LE. (FR). **4987**

POINT VETERINAIRE, LE. (FR/0335-4997). **5518**

POINTER, THE. (US/0554-4246). **1883**

POLAR AND GLACIOLOGICAL ABSTRACTS. (UK/0957-5073). **2572**

POLAR RECORD, THE. (UK/0032-2474). **5138**

POLAR TIMES, THE. (US/0032-2482). **Adv Mgr Tel** (503)759-3589. **2572**

POLEMIC. (AT). **3029**

POLICE AND SECURITY NEWS. (US/1070-8111). **Adv Mgr:** Al Menear, **Tel** (215)538-1240. **3171**

POLICE CAREER DIGEST. (US/8756-355X). **3171**

POLICE CHIEF, THE. (US/0032-2571). **3171**

POLICE COLLECTORS NEWS. (US/1071-1724). **3172**

POLICE COMPUTER REVIEW. (US/1061-1509). **Adv Mgr:** Kappeler. **1289**

POLICE JOURNAL (CHICHESTER). (UK/0032-258X). **Adv Mgr:** Dora Curtis. **3172**

POLICE MARKSMAN, THE. (US/0164-8365). **3172**

POLICE REVIEW (LONDON). (UK/0309-1414). **3172**

POLICE STUDIES. (US/0141-2949). **3172**

POLICY ANALYSIS. (PH/0115-1746). **703**

POLICY ANALYSIS (CATO INSTITUTE). (US/1069-8124). **4487**

POLICY AND POLITICS. (UK/0305-5736). **4487**

POLICY REVIEW (WASHINGTON). (US/0146-5945). **5213**

POLICY STUDIES JOURNAL. (US/0190-292X). **4488**

POLICY STUDIES REVIEW. (US/0278-4416). **4488**

POLIMERI (ZAGREB). (CI/0351-1871). **4459**

POLIN. (UK/0268-1056). **5052**

POLIO NETWORK NEWS. (US). **3628**

POLISH AMERICAN JOURNAL (1985 : NATIONAL ED.). (US). **Adv Mgr:** Kathy Sobocinski. **5720**

POLISH AMERICAN STUDIES (CHICAGO, ILL.). (US/0032-2806). **2754**

POLISH AMERICAN WORLD. (US). **Adv Mgr:** Tom Poster. **5720**

POLISH DIGEST & EASTERN EUROPEAN AFFAIRS. (US). **2271**

POLISH GENEALOGICAL SOCIETY NEWSLETTER. (US/0735-9349). **2468**

POLISH HERITAGE. (US/0735-9209). **Adv Mgr:** W. West. **2754**

POLISH JOURNAL OF OCCUPATIONAL MEDICINE AND ENVIRONMENTAL HEALTH. (PL/0867-8383). **3628**

POLISH POLAR RESEARCH. (PL/0138-0338). **5138**

POLISH REVIEW (NEW YORK. 1956), THE. (US/0032-2970). **Adv Mgr:** Jane Kedron. **5213**

POLITICA. (DK/0105-0710). **4488**

POLITICA EXTERIOR. (SP/0213-6856). **Adv Mgr:** Jaime Garcia de Vinuesa. **4532**

POLITICAL AFFAIRS. (US/0032-3128). **4488**

POLITICAL RESEARCH QUARTERLY. (US/1065-9129). **4489**

POLITICAL RESOURCE DIRECTORY (NATIONAL ED.). (US/0898-4271). **4489**

POLITICAL SCIENCE. (NZ/0032-3187). **4490**

POLITICAL SCIENCE QUARTERLY. (US/0032-3195). **4490**

POLITICAL SCIENCE REVIEWER, THE. (US/0091-3715). **4490**

POLITICAL STUDIES. (UK/0032-3217). **4490**

POLITICAL THEORY. (US/0090-5917). **4490**

POLITICS & SOCIETY. (US/0032-3292). **5213**

POLITICS AND THE INDIVIDUAL. (GW/0939-6071). **4490**

POLITICS AND THE LIFE SCIENCES. (US/0730-9384). **4490**

POLITIE-ALMANAK. (NE). **3172**

POLITIK UND KULTUR. (GW). **4491**

POLITIQUE INTERNATIONALE. (FR/0221-2781). **4532**

POLITIQUES ET MANAGEMENT PUBLIC. (FR/0758-1726). **4491**

POLITY. (US/0032-3497). **4491**

POLIZEI, VERKEHR + TECHNIK. (GW). **3172**

POLKA NEWS, THE. (US/0273-6454). **1314**

POLK'S MINNEAPOLIS SUBURBAN CITY DIRECTORY. (US). **2572**

POLLED HEREFORD WORLD (1965). (US/0162-7953). **217**

POLLUTION ENGINEERING. (US/0032-3640). **2238**

POLLUTION EQUIPMENT NEWS. (US/0032-3659). **2239**

POLLUTION PREVENTION. (UK). **2239**

POLO (GAITHERSBURG, MD.). (US/0146-4574). **4912**

POLYGRAPH, DER. (GW/0032-3845). **4567**

POLYGRAPH (LINTHICUM HEIGHTS). (US/0197-7024). **3172**

POLYHEDRON. (UK/0277-5387). **1037**

POLYMER BULLETIN (BERLIN, WEST). (GW/0170-0839). **1056**

POLYMER COMPOSITES. (US/0272-8397). **4459**

POLYMER CONTENTS. (UK/0883-153X). **4461**

POLYMER DEGRADATION AND STABILITY. (UK/0141-3910). **988**

POLYMER (GUILFORD). (UK/0032-3861). **1046**

POLYMER JOURNAL. (JA/0032-3896). **1046**

POLYMER NETWORKS & BLENDS. (CN/1181-9510). **1046**

POLYMER-PLASTICS TECHNOLOGY AND ENGINEERING (SOFTCOVER ED.). (US/0360-2559). **2015**

POLYMER PREPRINTS, AMERICAN CHEMICAL SOCIETY, DIVISION OF POLYMER CHEMISTRY. (US/0032-3934). **989**

POLYMER TESTING. (UK/0142-9418). **4459**

POLYMERS & RUBBER ASIA. (UK/0268-9812). **4459**

POLYMERS PAINT COLOUR YEAR BOOK. (UK/0078-7817). **4225**

POLYSCOPE, COMPUTER, ELECTRONICS, COMMUNICATION. (SZ). **2075**

POLYSCOPE (MONTREAL). (CN/0710-3522). **1094**

POMONA : NORTH AMERICAN FRUIT EXPLORERS' QUARTERLY. (US/0748-6510). **2428**

POMPANO LEDGER. (US). **Adv Mgr:** Karen Foley. **5650**

POMPEIIANA NEWSLETTER. (US/0892-5941). **3311**

PONCA CITY NEWS, THE. (US). **Adv Mgr:** Elec Rains. **5732**

PONCHATOULA TIMES, THE. (US). **5684**

PONTIAC-OAKLAND COUNTY LEGAL NEWS. (US/0739-0203). **3029**

PONY JOURNAL, THE. (US/0199-5537). **2801**

POODLE REVIEW, THE. (US/0477-5449). **4287**

POODLE VARIETY. (US/0882-2816). **4287**

POOL & BILLIARD MAGAZINE. (US/1049-2852). **Adv Mgr:** Mark Haddad. **4912**

POOL & SPA MARKETING. (CN/0711-2998). **934**

POOL & SPA NEWS. (US/0194-5351). **703**

POOL & SPA NEWS DIRECTORY ISSUE. (US). **4853**

POOP SHEET, THE. (US/0195-0037). **4912**

POPOLI. (IT/0394-4247). **2521**

POPULAR ARCHAEOLOGY. (US/0300-774X). **278**

POPULAR ARCHAEOLOGY. TECHNICAL PUBLICATION. (US). **278**

POPULAR CERAMICS. (US/0032-4477). **2593**

POPULAR COMMUNICATIONS. (US/0733-3315). **1119**

POPULAR CULTURE IN LIBRARIES. (US/1053-8747). **3241**

POPULAR HOT RODDING. (US/0032-4523). **5423**

POPULAR MECHANICS (NEW YORK. 1959). (US/0032-4558). **5139**

POPULAR MINING. (US/8756-6257). **2148**

POPULAR MUSIC AND SOCIETY. (US/0300-7766). **4147**

POPULAR MUSIC PERIODICALS INDEX (LONDON, ENGLAND). (UK). **4147**

POPULAR PHOTOGRAPHY (1955). (US/0032-4582). **4375**

POPULAR PLASTICS & PACKAGING. (II). **4459**

POPULAR SCIENCE (NEW YORK, N.Y.). (US/0161-7370). **5139**

POPULAR WOODWORKING. (US/0884-8823). **2403**

POPULATION ET SOCIETES. (FR/0184-7783). **4557**

POPULATION INDEX. (US/0032-4701). **Adv Mgr:** G Hancock. **4562**

POPULATION REVIEW. (US/0032-471X). **4558**

POPULATION STUDIES. (UK/0032-4728). **4558**

POPULATION STUDIES. (II). **4558**

POPULATION TIMES, THE. (BG). **590**

PORCELAIN ARTIST. (US/0888-0336). **2593**

PORK CITY PRESS. (US). **Adv Mgr:** Barbara Wagoner. **5650**

PORK JOURNAL. (AT/1032-3759). **Adv Mgr:** Tracie Murray. **218**

PORT CONSTRUCTION AND OCEAN TECHNOLOGY. (UK/0264-8733). **624**

PORT DOVER MAPLE LEAF. (CN/0834-7166). **5793**

PORT GIBSON REVEILLE (PORT GIBSON, MISS.: 1890). (US). **Adv Mgr:** Janice G. Bufkin. **5701**

PORT ISABEL SOUTH PADRE ISLAND PRESS. (US). **5753**

PORT OF DETROIT WORLD HANDBOOK. (US/0160-5526). **5454**

PORT OF LONDON. (UK/0030-8064). **5454**

PORT OF NEW ORLEANS ANNUAL DIRECTORY. (US/0085-5030). **5454**

PORT OF NEW ORLEANS RECORD. (US/1046-9265). **849**

PORT ORCHARD INDEPENDENT. (US). **Adv Mgr:** Doug Weese. **5762**

PORT TOWNSEND JEFFERSON COUNTY LEADER, THE. (US/1050-1460). **Adv Mgr:** Dan Huntingford. **5762**

PORTABLE 100 (1986). (US/0888-0131). **Adv Mgr:** Bob Liddil. **1199**

PORTABLE COMPANION, THE. (US/0732-7501). **1272**

PORTABLE PAPER, THE. (US/0886-9138). **1199**

PORTAGE LAKES HERALD, THE. (US/0746-6021). **5730**

PORTE & CANCELLI. (IT/1120-2637). **1621**

PORTHOLE (DEERFIELD BEACH, FLA.). (US/1070-9479). **Adv Mgr:** Bill Panoff, **Tel** (305)426-0046. **5489**

PORTLAND MONTHLY. (US/0887-5340). **2573**

PORTLAND OBSERVER. (US). **Adv Mgr:** Chuck Washington, **Tel** (503)288-1897. **5734**

PORTLAND PRESS HERALD, THE. (US). **5685**

PORTLAND REV. (1981). (US/0885-7121). **3424**

PORTSMOUTH HERALD, THE. (US/0746-6218). **5709**

PORTUGUESE TIMES (NEW BEDFORD, MASS.). (US/0746-3928). **5689**

PORZELLAN + GLAS : P + G / ORGAN DES BUNDESVERBANDES DES GLAS-, PORZELLAN- UND KERAMIK-EINZELHANDELS. (GW). **2593**

POSEBNA IZDANJA INSTITUTA ZA ZASTITU BILJA. (YU/0408-9952). **525**

POSEV. (GW/0032-5201). **4491**

POSEY COUNTY NEWS & THE TIMES. (US). **Adv Mgr:** Jim Kohlmeyer. **5666**

POSITIF. (FR/0048-4911). **4076**

POSITIVE APPROACH, A. (US/0891-8791). **Adv Mgr:** Pat Swart, **Tel** (609)451-4777 ext. 3. **4392**

POSITIVE ATTITUDE POSTERS. (US). **946**

POSITIVE HEALTH. (UK/0958-5737). **4795**

POSITIVE INK. (US/1040-0494). **1774**

POSITIVE (LONDON, ONT.). (CN/0229-9712). **3241**

POSSIBLES. (CN/0703-7139). **5213**

POST (CARLE PLACE, N.Y.). (US/0891-5628). **1162**

POST DISPATCH, THE. (US). **Adv Mgr:** Lillie Hart. **5753**

POST-GAZETTE (BOSTON, MASS.). (US/0888-0107). **5689**

POST, KENYA. (KE/0253-5963). **5139**

POST-SEARCH LIGHT, THE. (US). **5654**

POST-STAR (GLENS FALLS, N.Y. : 1974). (US/0897-0505). **5720**

POST-TELEGRAPH (PRINCETON, MO.). (US). **Adv Mgr:** Carrie Haouck. **5704**

POST-TRIBUNE (GARY, IND.). (US/8750-3492). **Adv Mgr:** Todd Brownrout, **Tel** (219)881-3166. **5666**

POSTA (LAKE OSWEGO, OR.), LA. (US/0885-7385). **2786**

POSTAL HISTORY JOURNAL. (US/0032-5341). **1146**

POSTAL STATIONERY. (US/0554-8373). **2786**

POSTCARD CLASSICS. (US/0897-4020). **375**

POSTCARD COLLECTOR. (US/0746-6102). **2777**

POSTGESCHICHTE. (SZ). **2786**

POSTGRADUATE DOCTOR. AFRICA. (UK/0142-7946). **3628**

POSTGRADUATE DOCTOR. MIDDLE EAST EDITION. (UK/0140-7724). **3628**

POSTGRADUATE MEDICAL JOURNAL. (UK/0032-5473). **3628**

POSTGRADUATE MEDICINE. (US/0032-5481). **3628**

POSTGRADUATE RADIOLOGY. (US/0273-0278). **3944**

POSTHARVEST NEWS AND INFORMATION. (UK/0957-7505). **155**

POSTPRAXIS, DIE. (GW/0554-842X). **1147**

POTASH REVIEW. (SZ/0032-5546). **182**

POTATO ABSTRACTS. (UK/0308-7344). **156**

POTATO BUSINESS WORLD. (UK/0968-7661). **Adv Mgr:** David Brenchley. **2353**

POTATO COUNTRY. (US/0886-4780). **Adv Mgr:** Mike Stoken, **Tel** (509)248-2452. **182**

POTATO GROWER. (AT/0815-6514). **182**

POTATO GROWER OF IDAHO. (US/0146-499X). **182**

POTATO GROWER : POTATO GROWER OF IDAHO MAGAZINE. (US). **182**

POTATO REVIEW. (UK/0961-7655). **Adv Mgr:** G. Davidon, **Tel** 011 44 494 86412. **182**

POTATO STATISTICAL YEARBOOK. (US/0739-0238). **156**

POTENTIALS IN MARKETING. (US/0032-5619). **935**

POTOMAC ALMANAC. (US/0194-2182). **5687**

POTTER LEADER-ENTERPRISE. (US/0895-6839). **5738**

POTTERSFIELD PORTFOLIO, THE. (CN/0226-0840). **3424**

POTTERY IN AUSTRALIA. (AT/0048-4954). **Adv Mgr:** Trish Wilkinds. **2593**

POTTSBORO PRESS. (US/0747-4253). **5753**

POULTRY AND EGG MARKETING. (US/0032-5716). **218**

POULTRY INTERNATIONAL. (US/0032-5767). **218**

POULTRY PRESS. (US/0032-5783). **218**

POULTRY TIMES (NATIONAL ED.). (US/0885-3371). **218**

POUR LA SCIENCE. (FR/0153-4092). **5139**

POVERKHNOST. (US/0734-1520). **4417**

POVERTY. (UK/0032-5856). **5301**

POWDER/BULK SOLIDS. (US/8750-6653). **4221**

POWDER COATINGS. (US/0163-4542). **4225**

POWDER DIFFRACTION. (US/0885-7156). **4015**

POWDER HANDLING & PROCESSING. (GW/0934-7348). **2148**

POWDER TECHNOLOGY. (SZ/0032-5910). **Adv Mgr:** Ms. W van Cattenburch (Amsterdam). **2016**

POWELL TRIBUNE, THE. (US/0740-1078). **Adv Mgr:** Diane E. Bonner, **Tel** (307)754-2221. **5772**

POWER. (US/0032-5929). **1953**

POWER BOATING CANADA. (CN/0838-0872). **595**

POWER COUNTY PRESS, THE. (US). **Adv Mgr:** Leslie Lusk. **5657**

POWER ENGINEERING (BARRINGTON, ILL.). (US/0032-5961). **2124**

POWER EQUIPMENT AUSTRALASIA. (AT/0817-6043). **2124**

POWER FARMING MAGAZINE. (AT/0311-1911). **160**

POWER INTERNATIONAL. (UK/0950-1487). **2124**

POWER LINE (WASHINGTON, D.C.), THE. (US/0738-5676). **1953**

POWER TRANSMISSION DESIGN. (US/0032-6070). **2124**

POWERBOAT (VAN NUYS, CALIF.). (US/0032-6089). **595**

POWERLIFTING USA. (US/0199-8536). **4913**

POWERTECHNICS MAGAZINE. (US/0882-7419). **4417**

POWYS NOTES. (US/1058-7691). **3350**

POWYS REVIEW, THE. (UK/0309-1619). **3350**

PR & V : PR EN VOORLICHTING. (NE). **763**

PRABUDDHA BHARATA. (II/0032-6178). **5041**

PRACE VYZKUMNEHO USTAVU GEOLOGICKEHO INZENYRSTVI. (XR/0139-763X). **4275**

PRACI BHASA-VIJNAN (CALCUTTA). (II/0970-9940). **3311**

PRACTICAL ACCOUNTANT, THE. (US/0032-6321). **749**

PRACTICAL ALLERGY & IMMUNOLOGY. (CN/0831-0998). **3675**

PRACTICAL AQUACULTURE & LAKE MANAGEMENT. (US/1057-218X). **Adv Mgr:** Jean Roberts, **Tel** (919)772-8548. **2310**

PRACTICAL CARDIOLOGY. (US/0361-3372). **3709**

PRACTICAL DIABETES. (UK/0266-447X). **3732**

PRACTICAL DIABETOLOGY. (US/0730-3491). **3732**

PRACTICAL ENGLISH TEACHING. (UK/0260-4752). **1902**

PRACTICAL GASTROENTEROLOGY. (US/0277-4208). **3747**

PRACTICAL HOMEOWNER. (US/1042-4601). **624**

PRACTICAL HORSEMAN. (US/0090-8762). **2801**

PRACTICAL LAW FOR COMPANIES. (UK). **3030**

PRACTICAL LAWYER, THE. (US/0032-6429). **Adv Mgr:** K. Lawner, **Tel** (215)243-1659. **3030**

PRACTICAL LITIGATOR, THE. (US/1047-6261). **Adv Mgr:** Kathy Lawner, **Tel** (215)243-1659. **3030**

PRACTICAL PERIODONTICS AND AESTHETIC DENTISTRY. (US/1042-2722). **Adv Mgr:** L. W. Scott Clements, **Tel** (201)236-0700 ext. 117. **1333**

PRACTICAL REAL ESTATE LAWYER, THE. (US/8756-0372). **Adv Mgr:** K. Lawner, **Tel** (215)243-1659. **3030**

PRACTICAL TAX LAWYER, THE. (US/0890-4898). **Adv Mgr:** K. Lawner, **Tel** (215)243-1659. **3030**

PRACTICAL WINERY/VINEYARD. (US/1057-2694). **2370**

PRACTICE (NEW YORK, N.Y.). (US/0742-9940). **Adv Mgr:** C Helm, **Tel** (212)941-8844. **4545**

PRACTICE NURSE. (UK/0953-6612). **3867**

PRACTICING ANTHROPOLOGY. (US/0888-4552). **243**

PRACTICING ARCHITECT. (US/0888-3424). **306**

PRACTISING MANAGER. (AT/0159-1193). **882**

PRACTITIONER, THE. (UK/0032-6518). **3738**

PRAGMATICS : QUARTERLY PUBLICATION OF THE INTERNATIONAL PRAGMATICS ASSOCIATION. (BE/1018-2101). **3311**

PRAIRIE FIRE (WINNIPEG). (CN/0821-1124). **3424**

PRAIRIE JOURNAL OF CANADIAN LITERATURE, THE. (CN/0827-2921). **3424**

PRAIRIE MESSENGER. (CN/0032-664X). **Adv Mgr:** Rose Marie Strueby. **5793**

PRAIRIE ROSE, THE. (US/0032-6666). **Adv Mgr Tel** (319)277-2414. **3867**

PRAIRIE SCHOONER. (US/0032-6682). **3424**

PRAIRIELAND PIONEER. (US/0892-6131). **2468**

PRAJNAN. (II/0032-6690). **803**

PRAKTIJKBLAD VOOR MEDEZEGGENSCHAP. (NE/0921-2442). **946**

PRAKTISCHE SCHADLINGSBEKAMPFER, DER. (GW/0032-6801). **182**

PRAKTISCHE THEOLOGIE. (NE). **4987**

PRAKTISCHE TIERARZT. (GW/0032-681X). **5518**

PRAPARATOR. (GW/0032-6542). **4170**

PRASADA (CALCUTTA, INDIA). (II). **3425**

PRASARA. (II). **1802**

PRATIBHA INDIA. (II). **1842**

PRATICA AZIENDALE. (IT). **Adv Mgr Tel** 02 3022.1. **704**

PRATICA SOCIALE. (IT). **4608**

PRATIQUE DU SOUDAGE, LA. (BE). **4027**

PRATIQUE LONDON. (UK/0269-1396). **3715**

PRATIQUES. (FR/0338-2389). **3311**

PRATT TRIBUNE (PRATT, KAN. : 1964). (US/1048-3675). **5678**

PRAVNIK (PRAGUE, CZECHOSLOVAKIA). (XR). **3030**

PRAXIS DER KLINISCHEN VERHALTENSMEDIZIN UND REHABILITATION. (GW/0933-842X). **3932**

PRAXIS DER PSYCHOMOTORIK. (GW/0170-060X). **1884**

PRAXIS GRUNDSCHULE. (GW/0170-3722). **1094**

PRAXIS: JOURNAL OF POLITICAL SCIENCE. (PH/0116-709X). **4492**

PRAXIS MEDIZINISCHER DOKUMENTATION / DEUTSCHER VERBAND MEDIZINISCHER DOKUMENTARE E.V. (GW/0722-477X). **Adv Mgr:** Doris Tegethoff, **Tel** (0891)5919 64 ext. 165. **3629**

PRC NEWSLETTER. (US/8755-3902). **4375**

PRC OFFICIAL ACTIVITIES AND MONTHLY BIBLIOGRAPHY / INSTITUTE OF ASIAN AFFAIRS. (GW). **4502**

PRE-LAW JOURNAL. (US/0741-1162). **3030**

PRE- (PRAIRIE VILLAGE, KAN.). (US/1042-0304). **4818**

PRE/TEXT. (US/0731-0714). **3311**

PREACHING (JACKSONVILLE, FLA.). (US/0882-7036). **4987**

PRECIOS DE PRODUCTOS E INSUMOS AGROPECUARIOS. (UY). **121**

PRECIOUS

Advertising Accepted Index

PRECIOUS FIBERS. (US/0886-4268). **5355**

PRECISION ENGINEERING. (US/0141-6359). **2125**

PRECISION SHOOTING. (US/0048-5144). **4877**

PREDICAMENT, THE. (US/0199-0705). **4913**

PREFERRED SHARES & WARRANTS. (CN/0829-383X). **911**

PREGONERO (WASHINGTON, D.C.), EL. (US/8750-9326). **5647**

PREMIERE (NEW YORK, N.Y. 1987). (US/0894-9263). **4076**

PREMISES & FACILITIES MANAGEMENT. (UK/0965-4739). **Adv Mgr:** Mark Wiles. **4214**

PREMIUM CHANNELS TV BLUEPRINT. (US/1040-5534). **Adv Mgr:** Steve Goldmintz, **Tel** (516)234-5200. **1136**

PREMONITIONS ARRETON. (UK/0968-6185). **3425**

PRENATAL DIAGNOSIS. (UK/0197-3851). **3767**

PRENSA MEDICA ARGENTINA. (AG/0032-745X). **3629**

PRENSA (ORLANDO, FLA.), LA. (US/0888-756X). **Adv Mgr:** Sandra Gonzalez. **5650**

PRENSA SAN DIEGO, LA. (US/0738-9183). **2271**

PREP POWER POLL. (US). **4913**

PREPARATIVE BIOCHEMISTRY. (US/0032-7484). **492**

PREPODAVANIE ISTORII V SHKOLE. (RU/0132-0696). **2626**

PREPRESS BULLETIN, THE. (US/8750-2224). **Adv Mgr:** H. Yocherer, **Tel** (708)369-7442. **5034**

PREPRINTS OF PAPERS PRESENTED - AMERICAN CHEMICAL SOCIETY. DIVISION OF FUEL CHEMISTRY. (US/0569-3772). **989**

PREPRINTS OF PAPERS PRESENTED AT THE AES CONVENTIONS. (US). **5318**

PREREFUNDED BOND SERVICE. (US/0737-9595). **803**

PRESBYTERIAN RECORD (MONTREAL). (CN/0032-7573). **5066**

PRESBYTERIAN SURVEY. (US/0032-759X). **Adv Mgr Tel** (502)569-5634. **5066**

PRESCOTT JOURNAL (PRESCOTT, WIS. : 1930). (US). **5770**

PRESCOTT'S WEEKLY. (US/0194-9748). **5630**

PRESCRIBER. (UK/0959-6682). **Adv Mgr:** Peter Saver. **3629**

PRESCRIPTION PRODUCTS GUIDE. (AT/0818-4445). **4325**

PRESENCE (MONTREAL. 1992). (CN/1188-5580). **4987**

PRESENTATION PRODUCTS MAGAZINE. (US/1041-9780). **Adv Mgr:** Bill Slapin, **Tel** (310)456-2283. **704**

PRESENTING THE SEASON. (US). **5235**

PRESERVATION PROGRESS (CHARLESTON). (US/0478-1392). **306**

PRESIDENTIAL STUDIES QUARTERLY. (US/0360-4918). **4674**

PRESIDENTS & PRIME MINISTERS. (US/1060-5088). **Adv Mgr:** Anu Agnihotci, **Tel** (208)858-6161. **4492**

PRESQUE ISLE COUNTY ADVANCE. (US). **5693**

PRESS AND ADVERTISERS YEAR BOOK. (II). **764**

PRESS & SUN-BULLETIN. (US/0886-8816). **Adv Mgr:** Scott Putnicki. **5720**

PRESS ARGUS-COURIER. (US/0885-9086). **5632**

PRESS DEMOCRAT (SANTA ROSA, CALIF.). (US/0747-220X). **Adv Mgr:** Ken Svanum, **Tel** (707)526-8577. **5638**

PRESS-DISPATCH, THE. (US). **Adv Mgr:** John Heuring. **5666**

PRESS-ENTERPRISE (BLOOMSBURG, PA.). (US/0746-0724). **Adv Mgr:** Sandy Bower, **Tel** (717)387-1234 ext. 1216. **5739**

PRESS-ENTERPRISE (RIVERSIDE, CALIF.). (US/0746-4258). **Adv Mgr:** David Cornwall, **Tel** (909)782-7670. **5638**

PRESS FOR CONVERSION. (CN/1183-8892). **Adv Mgr:** Sylvis, **Tel** (613)749-3147. **4054**

PRESS INDEPENDENT. (CN/1182-9931). **Adv Mgr:** Teresa Sanderson. **2543**

PRESS, RADIO AND TV GUIDE : AUSTRALIA, NEW ZEALAND AND THE PACIFIC ISLANDS. (AT). **1125**

PRESS REVIEW (TORONTO). (CN/0706-9286). **2923**

PRESS-SENTINEL, THE. (US). **5654**

PRESS WOMAN, THE. (US/0032-7824). **2923**

PRESSE HANDBUCH / VERBAND OSTERREICHISCHER ZEITUNGSHERAUSGEBER UND ZEITUNGSVERLEGER. (AU). **4567**

PRESSE MEDICALE (1983), LA. (FR/0755-4982). **3629**

PRESSE (MONTREAL). (CN). **5793**

PRESSE UND SPRACHE. (GW/0935-8064). **2923**

PRESSTIME. (US/0194-3243). **4818**

PRESSURE (BETHESDA, MD.). (US/0889-0242). **3629**

PRESTEL DIRECTORY, THE. (UK/0266-0288). **1162**

PRETRE ET PASTEUR. (CN/0383-8307). **4987**

PREVENTION (EMMAUS). (US/0032-8006). **4796**

PREVENTION IN HUMAN SERVICES. (US/0270-3114). **4810**

PREVIDENCIA, A. (BL). **2890**

PREVIEW. (US/0899-9821). **3241**

PREVIEW (RICHARDSON, TEX.). (US/0892-6468). **387**

PREVIEWS GUIDE TO THE WORLD'S FINE REAL ESTATE. (US). **4843**

PREVUE (READING, PA.). (US/1045-1234). **1119**

PREZZI INFORMATIVI DELL EDILIZIA MATERIALI ED OPERE COMPIUTE : IMPIANTI TECNICI. (IT). **624**

PREZZI INFORMATIVI DELL EDILIZIA MATERIALI ED OPERE COMPIUTE : NUOVE COSTRUZIONI. (IT). **624**

PRI REVIEW. INTERNATIONAL ROAD SAFETY. (LU). **4796**

PRIEST RIVER TIMES. (US/0740-3348). **Adv Mgr:** Jeanine Hinchleff. **5657**

PRIEST, THE. (US/0032-8200). **5034**

PRIESTS & PEOPLE. (UK/0952-6390). **5034**

PRIKLADNYE PROBLEMY PROCHNOSTI I PLASTICHNOSTI. (RU). **2107**

PRIMA COMUNICAZIONE. (IT/0390-3311). **Adv Mgr:** Sig. Buonacasa. **1119**

PRIMARILY NURSING. (US/0739-4446). **Adv Mgr:** Eric Haukkala, **Tel** (612)339-7766. **3867**

PRIMARY CARE & CANCER. (US/0743-8176). **3822**

PRIMARY CARE NEWSLETTER. (US/1071-2496). **5301**

PRIMARY CARE UPDATE FOR OB/GYNS. (US/1068-607X). **3767**

PRIMARY EDUCATION AUSTRALIA. (AT/0048-5284). **Adv Mgr Tel** 011 61 3 8958131. **1805**

PRIMARY GEOGRAPHER. (UK/0956-277X). **2573**

PRIMARY SOURCES AND ORIGINAL WORKS. (US/1042-8216). **3241**

PRIMARY TEACHING STUDIES. (UK/0268-2176). **Adv Mgr:** Susan Powell. **1902**

PRIMATE EYE. (UK/0305-8417). **5594**

PRIME NUMBER. (AT/0816-9349). **3527**

PRIME REAL ESTATE. (US). **4843**

PRIME TIME (NEW YORK). (US/0194-2611). **5181**

PRIME TIMES (MADISON). (US/0195-5934). **5181**

PRIMROSES. (US/0162-6671). **2428**

PRINCE RUPERT DAILY NEWS. (CN). **5793**

PRINCETON ALUMNI WEEKLY. (US/0149-9270). **Adv Mgr:** L. O'Brien, **Tel** (609)258-4886. **1102**

PRINCETON LEADER, THE. (US). **5682**

PRINCETON RECOLLECTOR. (US/0196-1136). **2755**

PRINCETON TIMES-REPUBLIC. (US/8755-397X). **Adv Mgr:** Betty Van Sistine. **5770**

PRINCIPAL (ARLINGTON, VA.). (US/0271-6062). **1868**

PRINCIPAL (EAST LANSING). (US/0199-6371). **1805**

PRINCIPAL MATTERS. (AT). **Adv Mgr:** John Gilmore. **1868**

PRINSBURG NEWS. (US/8750-0698). **5698**

PRINT ACTION. (CN/0380-2752). **4567**

PRINT BUYING. (UK). **4568**

PRINT COLLECTOR'S NEWSLETTER, THE. (US/0032-8537). **381**

PRINT-EQUIP NEWS. (US/0048-5314). **Adv Mgr:** Jeff Jotras, **Tel** (818)954-9495. **381**

PRINT MEDIA PRODUCTION DATA. (US/0555-1633). **764**

PRINT (NEW YORK). (US/0032-8510). **381**

PRINT PRODUCTION DIRECTORY. (AT/1033-6885). **4568**

PRINT QUARTERLY. (UK/0265-8305). **4568**

PRINTED CIRCUIT FABRICATION. (US/0274-8096). **2075**

PRINTERS BUYER'S GUIDE AND HANDBOOK. (US/0890-7234). **Adv Mgr:** Mary Wohlberg. **1265**

PRINTERS HOT LINE. (US/0192-6314). **4568**

PRINTER'S NEWS (WELLINGTON). (NZ/0048-5330). **4568**

PRINTERS YEARBOOK : THE COMPREHENSIVE GUIDE TO THE PRINTING INDUSTRY. (UK). **4568**

PRINTING AND GRAPHIC ARTS BUYERS : PGAB. (US/0741-1979). **4568**

PRINTING HISTORY. (US/0192-9275). **4568**

PRINTING IMPRESSIONS. (US/0032-860X). **4568**

PRINTING INDUSTRIES. (UK/0307-7195). **4568**

PRINTING JOURNAL. (US/0191-8273). **4568**

PRINTING TRADES DIRECTORY. (UK). **4568**

PRINTING WORLD. (UK/0032-8715). **4568**

PRINTINGNEWS. MIDWEST. (US/1048-6860). **Adv Mgr:** Steve Lovie. **4568**

PRINTWEAR MAGAZINE. (US/0898-3313). **5355**

PRINTWORLD DIRECTORY OF CONTEMPORARY PRINTS AND PRICES. (US/0734-2721). **381**

PRIORITIES. (US). **2601**

PRIORITIES (VANCOUVER). (CN/0700-6543). **5564**

PRISM INTERNATIONAL. (CN/0032-8790). **3425**

PRISMA. (IO). **1513**

PRISMA LATINOAMERICANO. (CU). **4532**

PRISMET. (NO/0032-8447). **4988**

PRITEL LIDU : CASOPIS SLEZSKE CIRKVE EVANGELICKE. (XR). **4988**

PRIVACY EN REGISTRATIE. (NE). **4512**

PRIVATE CARRIER. (US/0032-8871). **5389**

PRIVATE EQUITY ANALYST, THE. (US/1057-526X). **Adv Mgr:** Leanne Cowley. **911**

PRIVATE EYE WEEKLY. (US). **Adv Mgr:** Kim Gregory, **Tel** (801)575-7003. **2543**

PRIVATE LABEL PRODUCT NEWS. (US/0892-6727). **3486**

PRIVATE LIBRARY. (UK/0032-8898). **3241**

PRIVATE PRACTICE. (US/0032-891X). **Adv Mgr:** Debra Griffith. **3629**

PRIVATE PRESS BOOKS. (UK). **4831**

PRIVATE VARNISH. (US/1047-9473). **5434**

PRIVATISATION INTERNATIONAL. (UK/0961-4206). **1639**

PRO/E, THE MAGAZINE. (US/1069-6113). **1200**

PRO ECCLESIA (NORTHFIELD, MINN.). (US/1063-8512). **4988**

PRO FOOTBALL WEEKLY. (US/0032-9053). **Adv Mgr:** Bob Sherman. **4913**

PRO (FORT ATKINSON, WIS.). (US/1041-5610). **2428**

PRO-LIFE NEWS. (CN/0715-4356). **3767**

PRO-NAT. (SA). **2500**

PRO SOUND NEWS (U.S. ED.). (US/0164-6338). **5318**

PRO WRESTLING ILLUSTRATED. (US/1043-7576). **4913**

PROA. (CK/0032-9150). **306**

PROBABILISTIC ENGINEERING MECHANICS. (UK/0266-8920). **2125**

PROBABILITY AND MATHEMATICAL STATISTICS. (PL/0208-4147). **3542**

PROBATE AND PROPERTY (CHICAGO, ILL. : 1987). (US/0164-0372). **3118**

PROBATE LAW JOURNAL. (US/0737-3112). **3031**

PROBATION AND PAROLE DIRECTORY (COLLEGE PARK, MD.). (US/0732-0965). **3173**

PROBATION AND PAROLE LAW REPORTS. (US/0276-6965). **3173**

PROBATION JOURNAL. (UK). **3173**

PROBE (LONDON. 1954). (UK/0032-9185). **1333**

PROBIN HITAISHI. (BG/1012-9197). **3754**

PROBLEMI DELLA PEDAGOGIA, I. (IT). **1774**

PROBLEMI DI GESTIONE. (IT). **704**

PROBLEMS OF COMMUNISM. (UK). **4545**

PROBLEMS OF ECONOMICS. (US/0032-9436). **1513**

PROBUS. (NE/0921-4771). **3312**

PROCEEDINGS - ABRASIVE ENGINEERING SOCIETY (U.S). CONFERENCE/EXHIBITION. (US/0734-9629). **4016**

PROCEEDINGS - AMERICAN SOCIETY FOR THE ADVANCEMENT ANESTHESIA IN DENTISTRY. (US/0164-1700). **3684**

PROCEEDINGS AND ADDRESSES OF THE AMERICAN PHILOSOPHICAL ASSOCIATION. (US/0065-972X). **Adv Mgr:** Donna Benedetti, **Tel** (302)831-2012. **4357**

PROCEEDINGS AND PAPERS OF THE ANNUAL CONFERENCE OF THE CALIFORNIA MOSQUITO AND VECTOR CONTROL ASSOCIATION. (US/0160-6751). **2239**

PROCEEDINGS AND REPORTS - FLORIDA STATE UNIVERSITY, CENTER FOR YUGOSLAV-AMERICAN STUDIES, RESEARCH AND EXCHANGES. (US/0196-9730). **2703**

PROCEEDINGS; ANNUAL AAZPA CONFERENCE. (US/0090-4473). **5595**

PROCEEDINGS ... ANNUAL CONFERENCE / AGRONOMY SOCIETY OF NEW ZEALAND. (NZ/0110-6589). **121**

PROCEEDINGS ... ANNUAL CONFERENCE OF THE AMERICAN COUNCIL ON CONSUMER INTERESTS. (US/0275-1356). **1299**

PROCEEDINGS, ANNUAL MEETING OF THE AMERICAN WOOD-PRESERVERS' ASSOCIATION. (US/0066-1198). **2403**

PROCEEDINGS, ANNUAL MEETING - WASHINGTON STATE HORTICULTURAL ASSOCIATION. (US/0149-6905). **2428**

PROCEEDINGS. ANNUAL SYMPOSIUM. INCREMENTAL MOTION CONTROL SYSTEMS AND DEVICES. (US/0092-1661). **2076**

PROCEEDINGS / ... ANNUAL THIRD WORLD CONFERENCE. (US/0885-2316). **1639**

PROCEEDINGS - INTERNATIONAL COMPUTER SOFTWARE & APPLICATIONS CONFERENCE. (US/0730-3157). **1289**

PROCEEDINGS OF AMERICAN PEANUT RESEARCH AND EDUCATION SOCIETY, INC. (US/0197-8748). **183**

PROCEEDINGS OF INNOVATION CANADA INC. (CN/0711-0235). **704**

PROCEEDINGS OF ... PAKISTAN CONGRESS OF ZOOLOGY. (PK). **5595**

PROCEEDINGS OF THE ACADEMY OF POLITICAL SCIENCE. (US). **4492**

PROCEEDINGS OF THE AMERICAN ANTIQUARIAN SOCIETY. (US/0044-751X). **2755**

PROCEEDINGS OF THE AMERICAN ETHNOLOGICAL SOCIETY. (US/0731-4108). **243**

PROCEEDINGS OF THE ANNUAL CONFERENCE. (UK/0582-303X). **3242**

PROCEEDINGS OF THE ANNUAL CONFERENCE - CANADIAN COUNCIL ON INTERNATIONAL LAW. (CN/0317-9087). **3134**

PROCEEDINGS OF THE ANNUAL CONFERENCE OF THE FORESTRY ASSOCIATION OF NIGERIA. (NR). **2391**

PROCEEDINGS OF THE ... ANNUAL CONFERENCE ON TAXATION HELD UNDER THE AUSPICES OF THE NATIONAL TAX ASSOCIATION-TAX INSTITUTE OF AMERICA. (US/1066-8608). **4742**

PROCEEDINGS OF THE ANNUAL CONGRESS OF THE SOUTH AFRICAN SUGAR TECHNOLOGISTS' ASSOCIATION. (SA/0373-045X). **2353**

PROCEEDINGS OF THE ANNUAL CONVENTION - AMERICAN ASSOCIATION OF BOVINE PRACTITIONERS. CONVENTION. (US/0743-0450). **5519**

PROCEEDINGS OF THE ANNUAL MEETING - AMERICAN SOCIETY OF INTERNATIONAL LAW. (US/0272-5037). **3134**

PROCEEDINGS OF THE ANNUAL MEETING / ARKANSAS STATE HORTICULTURAL SOCIETY. (US/0749-4327). **2429**

PROCEEDINGS OF THE ANNUAL MEETING OF THE ENTOMOLOGICAL SOCIETY OF ALBERTA. (CN/0071-0709). **5612**

PROCEEDINGS OF THE ARISTOTELIAN SOCIETY. (UK/0066-7374). **4358**

PROCEEDINGS OF THE AUSTRALIAN PHYSIOLOGICAL AND PHARMACOLOGICAL SOCIETY. (AT/0067-2084). **585**

PROCEEDINGS OF THE BRITISH SOCIETY FOR THE STUDY OF PROSTHETIC DENTISTRY. (UK). **1333**

PROCEEDINGS OF THE ... CONFERENCE OF THE AUSTRALIAN SOCIETY OF SUGAR CANE TECHNOLOGISTS. (AT/0726-0822). **183**

PROCEEDINGS OF THE ENTOMOLOGICAL SOCIETY OF MANITOBA. (CN/0315-2146). **5613**

PROCEEDINGS OF THE FIRST BIANNUAL INTERNATIONAL CONFERENCE ON ADVANCES IN MANAGEMENT. (US/1059-356X). **883**

PROCEEDINGS OF THE GEOLOGISTS' ASSOCIATION. (UK/0016-7878). **1391**

PROCEEDINGS OF THE INSTITUTION OF ELECTRICAL ENGINEERS. (UK/0020-3270). **2077**

PROCEEDINGS OF THE IRISH BIBLICAL ASSOCIATION. (IE/0332-4427). **5019**

PROCEEDINGS OF THE LONDON MATHEMATICAL SOCIETY. (UK/0024-6115). **3528**

PROCEEDINGS OF THE MICROSCOPICAL SOCIETY OF CANADA. (CN/0381-1751). **573**

PROCEEDINGS OF THE MUSKEG RESEARCH CONFERENCE. (CN/0541-4393). **2573**

PROCEEDINGS OF THE NEW ZEALAND GEOGRAPHY CONFERENCE. (NZ/1170-5698). **2573**

PROCEEDINGS OF THE NEW ZEALAND GRASSLAND ASSOCIATION. (NZ/0369-3902). **122**

PROCEEDINGS OF THE NEW ZEALAND SOCIETY OF ANIMAL PRODUCTION. (NZ/0370-2731). **219**

PROCEEDINGS OF THE ROYAL SOCIETY OF NEW ZEALAND. (NZ/0557-4161). **5141**

PROCEEDINGS OF THE ... SEMINAR OF CATASTROPHISM AND ANCIENT HISTORY. (US/0890-5592). **2626**

PROCEEDINGS OF THE SOUTH CAROLINA HISTORICAL ASSOCIATION, THE. (US/0361-6207). **Adv Mgr:** W. S. Brockington, **Tel** (803)648-6851. **2755**

PROCEEDINGS OF THE SOUTH DAKOTA ACADEMY OF SCIENCE. (US/0096-378X). **5142**

PROCEEDINGS OF THE SPECIAL CONVENTION OF THE NATIONAL COLLEGIATE ATHLETIC ASSOCIATION. (US/0094-4459). **4913**

PROCEEDINGS OF THE UNITARIAN UNIVERSALIST HISTORICAL SOCIETY, THE. (US/0731-4078). **5066**

PROCEEDINGS OF THE WESTERN PHARMACOLOGY SOCIETY. (US/0083-8969). **Adv Mgr:** same as Editor. **4326**

PROCEEDINGS OF THE ZOOLOGICAL SOCIETY. (II/0373-5893). **5595**

PROCEEDINGS - ROYAL MICROSCOPICAL SOCIETY. (UK/0035-9017). **573**

PROCEEDINGS - THE RADIO CLUB OF AMERICA, INC. (US/0033-779X). **1120**

PROCEEDINGS - UNITED STATES NAVAL INSTITUTE. (US/0041-798X). **4182**

PROCESS AND CHEMICAL ENGINEERING. (UK/0960-5045). **2006**

PROCESS, ARCHITECTURE. (JA/0386-037X). **306**

PROCESS CONTROL & QUALITY. (US/0924-3089). **2016**

PROCESS ENGINEERING. (UK/0370-1859). **2016**

PROCESS ENGINEERING INDEX. (UK/0264-7176). **2016**

PROCESS INDUSTRIES CANADA. (CN/0826-7243). **2016**

PROCESS MAGAZINE : LE MENSUEL DES TECHNIQUES LAITIERES ET ALIMENTAIRES. (FR). **2354**

PROCESS STUDIES. (US/0360-6503). **4358**

PROCESSING. (UK/0305-439X). **Adv Mgr:** David Lewis. **2016**

PROCLAIM (NASHVILLE). (US/0162-4326). **4988**

PROCOMM ENTERPRISES MAGAZINE. (US/0896-7229). **1162**

PROCTOR. (AT). **3032**

PROCUREMENT. (UK). **951**

PRODEI. (SP/0079-5836). **3486**

PRODUCE BUSINESS. (US/0886-5663). **Adv Mgr:** Whit Acre, **Tel** (407)241-4333. **2354**

PRODUCE NEWS. (US/0032-969X). **2354**

PRODUCER (PORT WASHINGTON, N.Y.). (US/1067-439X). **1162**

PRODUCER'S MASTERGUIDE, THE. (US/0732-6653). **1136**

PRODUCT DATA INTERNATIONAL. (US/1050-7043). **5142**

PRODUCT LIABILITY INTERNATIONAL. (UK). **3032**

PRODUCT SAFETY NEWS. (US). **2868**

PRODUCTEUR DE PORC QUEBECOIS. (CN/0229-7876). **219**

PRODUCTEUR PLUS, LE. (CN/1183-9929). **122**

PRODUCTION. (US/0032-9819). **2126**

PRODUCTION JOURNAL. (UK/0032-9878). **Adv Mgr:** Terry Gunter, **Tel** 071 404 1501. **4818**

PRODUCTION OF MILK AND MILK PRODUCTS. (IE/0791-3036). **198**

PRODUCTION PLANNING & CONTROL. (UK/0953-7287). **1622**

PRODUCTS FINISHING. (US/0032-9940). **3486**

PRODUCTS FINISHING DIRECTORY. (US/0478-4251). **4016**

PRODUKSI PERIKANAN LAUT YANG DIJUAL DI PELELANGAN/TEMPAT PENDARATAN IKAN DI JAWA-MADURA. (IO). **2311**

PROEDUCATION. (US/8756-5188). **1774**

PROFESSION COMPTABLE, LA. (FR/0766-9208). **Adv Mgr:** Pascale Borjolami. **750**

PROFESSIONAL AGENT, THE. (US/0148-8899). **2890**

PROFESSIONAL CALENDAR. (UK/0953-7279). **3242**

PROFESSIONAL CARWASHING. (US/0191-6823). **935**

PROFESSIONAL CARWASHING & DETAILING. (US). **5423**

PROFESSIONAL COMMUNICATOR, THE. (US/0891-1207). **1120**

PROFESSIONAL DIRECTORY / THE AMERICAN INSTITUTE OF CHEMISTS. (US/0084-6376). **990**

PROFESSIONAL DOCUMENT RETRIEVAL. (US/8755-0253). **3242**

PROFESSIONAL ELECTRONICS / THE OFFICIAL JOURNAL OF NESDA AND ISCET. (US). **2077**

PROFESSIONAL ENGINEERING. (UK/0953-6639). **2127**

PROFESSIONAL GEOGRAPHER, THE. (US/0033-0124). **2573**

PROFESSIONAL HOTEL & RESTAURANT INTERIORS. (UK/0959-2687). **2902**

PROFESSIONAL LANDSCAPER. (UK). **2429**

PROFESSIONAL MEDICAL ASSISTANT, THE. (US/0033-0140). **3630**

PROFESSIONAL MEETING MANAGEMENT. (US). **764**

PROFESSIONAL MONITOR / MICHIGAN ASSOCIATION OF THE PROFESSIONS, THE. (US/0744-7817). **3032**

PROFESSIONAL NEGLIGENCE LAW REPORTER. (US/1051-3744). **3032**

PROFESSIONAL PHOTOGRAPHER. (UK/0019-784X). **4375**

PROFESSIONAL PHOTOGRAPHER (1964), THE. (US/0033-0167). **Adv Mgr:** Donna McMahon, **Tel** (708)299-8161. **4375**

PROFESSIONAL PILOT. (US/0191-6238). **Adv Mgr:** Earlene Chandler, **Tel** (703)370-0606. **32**

PROFESSIONAL PRINTER. (UK/0308-4205). **4569**

PROFESSIONAL PSYCHOLOGY, RESEARCH AND PRACTICE. (US/0735-7028). **4609**

PROFESSIONAL PULIZIE. (IT/1120-8368). **2127**

PROFESSIONAL QUILTER MAGAZINE, THE. (US/0891-5237). **5185**

PROFESSIONAL READING GUIDE FOR EDUCATIONAL ADMINISTRATORS. (AT). **1869**

PROFESSIONAL RENOVATION. (CN/1182-0470). **2903**

PROFESSIONAL ROOFING. (US/0896-5552). **Adv Mgr:** Mary Carravallah, **Tel** (708)299-9070. **624**

PROFESSIONAL SAFETY. (US/0099-0027). **2868**

PROFESSIONAL SKATER, THE. (US/8750-9369). **4913**

PROFESSIONAL — Advertising Accepted Index

PROFESSIONAL STAINED GLASS. (US/0885-1808). **2593**

PROFESSIONAL SURVEYOR. (US/0278-1425). **2029**

PROFESSIONAL TRANSLATOR & INTERPRETER. (UK/0995-616X). **3312**

PROFESSIONAL UPHOLSTERER, THE. (US/0882-1518). **2903**

PROFESSIONALS. (US/0744-3471). **Adv Mgr:** R. Seliger, **Tel** (414)895-6098. **3725**

PROFESSIONI INFERMIERISTICHE. (IT/0033-0205). **3867**

PROFIL : SOZIALDEMOKRATISCHE ZEITSCHRIFT FUR POLITIK, WIRTSCHAFT UND KULTUR. (SZ/0555-3482). **4545**

PROFIL (VIENNA, AUSTRIA : 1979). (AU). **2521**

PROFILE (OMAHA). (US/0162-5241). **705**

PROFILE (SOUTH PORTLAND, ME.). (US/1071-3808). **705**

PROFILES (SOLANA BEACH, CALIF.). (US/8755-464X). **1272**

PROFIT (ARMONK, N.Y.). (US/1061-9194). **Adv Mgr:** M. Feinberg. **705**

PROFIT (TORONTO). (CN/1183-1324). **705**

PROFITRAVEL. (GW). **705**

PROGENITOR. (AT/0725-914X). **2468**

PROGNOSIS. (XR). **Adv Mgr:** Anne Harvey, **Tel** 011 42 2 6631 2620. **5799**

PROGRAM AND ABSTRACTS OF PAPERS - INTERNATIONAL ASSOCIATION FOR DENTAL RESEARCH. (US/0534-669X). **1333**

PROGRAM (ASLIB). (UK/0033-0337). **3242**

PROGRAM LONDON. 1987. (UK/0952-8865). **1248**

PROGRAMME SOUVENIR. FESTIVAL DU VOYAGEUR, ST. BONIFACE, MANITOBA. (CN/0229-2572). **4853**

PROGRAMMER'S PROVANTAGE COMPUTER PRODUCTS BUYER'S GUIDE. (US/1076-9714). **Adv Mgr:** Gina Cope, **Tel** (216)494-1996. **1281**

PROGRES AGRICOLE ET VITICOLE, LE. (FR/0369-8173). **122**

PROGRES TECHNIQUE, LE. (FR/0397-8060). **Adv Mgr:** M. Pagezy. **5142**

PROGRESOS DE OBSTETRICIA Y GINECOLOGIA. (SP/0304-5013). **3767**

PROGRESOS EN DIAGNOSTICO PRENATAL. (SP/1130-0523). **3767**

PROGRESS (CAVE CITY, KY. 1988), THE. (US/1055-9531). **Adv Mgr:** A. C. Wilson Jr., **Tel** $502)773-3401. **5682**

PROGRESS IN BATTERIES & SOLAR CELLS. (US/0198-7259). **2077**

PROGRESS IN NUCLEAR ENERGY (NEW SERIES). (UK/0149-1970). **2158**

PROGRESS IN ORGANIC COATINGS. (SZ/0300-9440). **Adv Mgr:** Ms. W van Cattenburch (Amsterdam). **4225**

PROGRESS IN PAPER RECYCLING. (US/1061-1452). **Adv Mgr:** J. Schiel. **4237**

PROGRESS IN RUBBER AND PLASTICS TECHNOLOGY. (UK/0266-7320). **5077**

PROGRESS OF EDUCATION, THE. (II/0033-0663). **1775**

PROGRESS REPORT - AMERICAN PHYSICAL THERAPY ASSOCIATION. (US/0162-3907). **4382**

PROGRESS (SEATTLE, WASH.), THE. (US/0739-6023). **5034**

PROGRESS TIMES. (US/0890-2666). **Adv Mgr:** Anna Carrillo. **5753**

PROGRESSI IN PATOLOGIA CARDIOVASCOLARE. (IT/0033-0701). **Adv Mgr:** Dott Dalla. **3709**

PROGRESSIONS : A TECHNICAL JOURNAL FOR DEVELOPERS IN PROGRESS. (US). **1201**

PROGRESSIVE ARCHITECTURE. (US/0033-0752). **306**

PROGRESSIVE FARMER. (US/0033-0760). **123**

PROGRESSIVE FISH-CULTURIST, THE. (US/0033-0779). **2311**

PROGRESSIVE GROCER, THE. (US/0033-0787). **2354**

PROGRESSIVE LIBRARIAN. (US/1052-5726). **3242**

PROGRESSIVE (MADISON), THE. (US/0033-0736). **4532**

PROGRESSIVE PERIODICALS DIRECTORY. (US/1054-1985). **4822**

PROGRESSIVE RAILROADING. (US/0033-0817). **5434**

PROGRESSIVE RENTALS. (US/8750-6106). **705**

PROGRESSO MEDICO (ROMA). (IT/0370-1514). **3972**

PROJECT INFORMATION REPORT. (KE). **2832**

PROJECT MANAGEMENT JOURNAL. (US/8756-9728). **883**

PROJET. (FR/0033-0884). **Adv Mgr:** Monique Bellas, **Tel** 44 39 48 48. **1639**

PROLACTIN SHEFFIELD. (UK/0142-8276). **3732**

PROMETEO (MILAN, ITALY). (IT). **5214**

PROMETHEUS. (AT/0810-9028). **3242**

PROMISE (REGINA). (CN/0826-533X). **5066**

PROMOBIL SPEZIAL. (GW). **5489**

PROMOTION AND EDUCATION. (FR/0751-7149). **4797**

PROMOTIONS & INCENTIVES. (UK/0266-7991). **883**

PROOFS (TULSA). (US/0033-1236). **1333**

PROOFTEXTS. (US/0272-9601). **3425**

PROP. 65 NEWS. (US/0895-5042). **3115**

PROPAGANDA (NEW HYDE PARK, N.Y.). (US/0737-0776). **4147**

PROPANE CANADA. (CN/0033-1260). **Adv Mgr:** Jim Graham. **4275**

PROPELLER (EAST DETROIT). (US/0194-6218). **4913**

PROPERTY DISPOSITION HANDBOOK. (US). **2832**

PROPERTY FINANCE. (UK/0955-8658). **804**

PROPERTY LAW BULLETIN. (UK). **3032**

PROPERTY MANAGEMENT. (LONDON). (UK/0263-7472). **4843**

PROPERTY TAX JOURNAL. (US/0731-0285). **4742**

PROPOS DE CUISINE. (CN/0821-1264). **624**

PRORODEO SPORTS NEWS. (US/0161-5815). **4913**

PROSE STUDIES. (UK/0144-0357). **Adv Mgr:** Anne Kidson. **3425**

PROSPECTING IN AREAS OF GLACIATED TERRAIN. (UK/0141-3376). **2148**

PROSPECTIVE ET SANTE. (FR/0152-2108). **3543**

PROSPECTIVE (MONTREAL. 1984). (CN/0823-8138). **2891**

PROSPECTOR : EXPLORATION AND INVESTMENT BULLETIN, THE. (CN/1181-6414). **Adv Mgr:** Barry McNeil, **Tel** (604)688-2271. **2149**

PROSPETTIVE PSICOANALITICHE NEL LAVORO ISTITUZIONALE. (IT). **Adv Mgr:** Dott Dalla. **4609**

PROSPICE. (UK/0308-2776). **3426**

PROSTAGLANDINS. (US/0090-6980). **585**

PROSTHETICS AND ORTHOTICS INTERNATIONAL. (DK/0309-3646). **4392**

PROSVETA ENLIGHTENMENT. (US). **Adv Mgr:** Jean. **2891**

PROTEIN ABNORMALITIES. (US/0736-4547). **586**

PROTEIN SCIENCE : A PUBLICATION OF THE PROTEIN SOCIETY. (US/0961-8368). **Adv Mgr:** James Alexander. **493**

PROTESTANTESIMO. (IT/0033-1767). **5066**

PROTOCOL DIGEST. (US/1071-2194). **4054**

PROTOTYPE MODELER. (US/0734-1482). **2777**

PROTOZOOLOGICAL ABSTRACTS. (UK/0309-1287). **5604**

PROVERBIUM (COLUMBUS, OHIO). (US/0743-782X). **2323**

PROVIDENCE BUSINESS NEWS. (US/0887-8226). **Adv Mgr:** John Lamp. **5741**

PROVIDENCE VISITOR (1984), THE. (US/8750-5452). **5741**

PROVIDER (WASHINGTON, D.C.). (US/0888-0352). **5302**

PROVINCIA CREMONA. (IT). **5804**

PROZAH. (IS). **3426**

PRUDENTIA. (NZ). **3426**

PRZEGLAD INFORMACYJNO-DOKUMENTACYJNY. SERIA: HYDROLOGIA I OCEANOLOGIA. (PL). **1417**

PRZEGLAD SPAWALNICTWA. (PL/0033-2364). **5142**

PRZEWALSKI HORSE. (NE/0167-7926). **2801**

PSA JOURNAL. (US/0030-8277). **Adv Mgr:** T Dresser, **Tel** (405)843-1437. **4376**

PSBA BULLETIN. (US/0162-3559). **1869**

PSI RESEARCH. (US/0749-2898). **4242**

PSICHIATRIA E PSICOTERAPIA ANALITICA. (IT/0393-9774). **3932**

PSICHIATRIA GENERALE E DELL'ETA EVOLUTIVA. (IT/0555-5299). **Adv Mgr:** A. Pagamento. **3932**

PSICOANALISI CONTRO. (IT/0393-6902). **Adv Mgr:** Pietro de Santis. **3932**

PSICOLOGIA, PSICOPATOLOGIA & PSICOSOMATICA DELLA DONNA. (US). **4609**

PSIQUIS. (SP/0210-8348). **Adv Mgr:** Carmen Acuadez. **3933**

PSSC SOCIAL SCIENCE INFORMATION. (PH). **5214**

PSYCHIATRIC ANNALS. (US/0048-5713). **3933**

PSYCHIATRIC GENETICS. (UK/0955-8829). **551**

PSYCHIATRIC HOSPITAL, THE. (US/0885-7717). **3791**

PSYCHIATRIC LENGTH OF STAY BY DIAGNOSIS, UNITED STATES. (US/0898-0543). **3791**

PSYCHIATRIC LENGTH OF STAY BY DIAGNOSIS, UNITED STATES, NORTHEASTERN REGION. (US/0898-0527). **3791**

PSYCHIATRIC LENGTH OF STAY BY DIAGNOSIS, UNITED STATES, SOUTHERN REGION. (US/0898-0519). **3791**

PSYCHIATRIC LENGTH OF STAY BY DIAGNOSIS. UNITED STATES, WESTERN REGION. (US/0898-0535). **3791**

PSYCHIATRIC NEWS. (US/0033-2704). **3933**

PSYCHIATRIC TIMES, THE. (US/0893-2905). **3933**

PSYCHIATRIE, RECHERCHE ET INTERVENTION EN SANTE MENTALE DE L'ENFANT : P.R.I.S.M.E. (CN/1180-5501). **3934**

PSYCHIATRY IN PRACTICE. (UK/0262-5377). **3934**

PSYCHIATRY (WASHINGTON, D.C.). (US/0033-2747). **3934**

PSYCHIC OBSERVER. (US/0048-573X). **4242**

PSYCHOANALYSIS AND CONTEMPORARY THOUGHT. (US/0161-5289). **4610**

PSYCHOANALYTIC PSYCHOLOGY. (US/0736-9735). **4610**

PSYCHOBIOLOGY (AUSTIN, TEX.). (US/0889-6313). **4610**

PSYCHOHISTORY REVIEW, THE. (US/0363-891X). **2626**

PSYCHOLOGIA. (JA/0033-2852). **4610**

PSYCHOLOGIA UNIVERSALIS. (GW/0555-5582). **4610**

PSYCHOLOGICAL ASSESSMENT. (US/1040-3590). **4610**

PSYCHOLOGICAL BULLETIN. (US/0033-2909). **4610**

PSYCHOLOGICAL MEDICINE. MONOGRAPH SUPPLEMENT. (UK/0264-1801). **4611**

PSYCHOLOGICAL PERSPECTIVES. (US/0033-2925). **4611**

PSYCHOLOGICAL RECORD, THE. (US/0033-2933). **4611**

PSYCHOLOGICAL SCIENCE. (US/0956-7976). **4611**

PSYCHOLOGICAL STUDIES. (II/0033-2968). **4611**

PSYCHOLOGIE & EDUCATION. (FR). **Adv Mgr:** Herve Jo. **4611**

PSYCHOLOGIE IN ERZIEHUNG UND UNTERRICHT. (GW/0342-183X). **1903**

PSYCHOLOGIE PREVENTIVE. (CN/0714-3494). **4612**

PSYCHOLOGIES. (FR). **4612**

PSYCHOLOGISCHE BEITRAEGE. (GW/0033-3018). **4612**

PSYCHOLOGISCHE RUNDSCHAU. (GW/0033-3042). **4612**

PSYCHOLOGY AND AGING. (US/0882-7974). **4612**

PSYCHOLOGY AND DEVELOPING SOCIETIES. (II/0971-3336). **4612**

PSYCHOLOGY IN THE SCHOOLS. (US/0033-3085). **4612**

PSYCHOLOGY (SAVANNAH). (US/0033-3077). **4613**

PSYCHOLOGY TODAY. (US/0033-3107). **4613**

PSYCHOLOOG. (NE/0033-3115). **4613**

PSYCHOPATHOLOGY. (SZ/0254-4962). **3934**

PSYCHOPHYSIOLOGY. (US/0048-5772). **586**

PSYCHOSOCIAL REHABILITATION JOURNAL. (US/0147-5622). **Adv Mgr:** LeRoy Spaniol, **Tel** (617)353-3549. **3934**

PSYCHOSOMATICS (WASHINGTON, D.C.). (US/0033-3182). **3631**

PSYCHOTHERAPY AND PSYCHOSOMATICS. (SZ/0033-3190). **3935**

PSYCHOTHERAPY IN PRIVATE PRACTICE. (US/0731-7158). **4614**

PSYCHOTHERAPY PATIENT, THE. (US/0738-6176). **3935**

PSYCHOTHERAPY RESEARCH. (US/1050-3307). **4614**

PSYCHOTROPES (MONTREAL). (CN/0715-9684). **1348**

PSYCSCAN. APPLIED PSYCHOLOGY. (US/0271-7506). **4623**

PSYCSCAN. CLINICAL PSYCHOLOGY. (US/0197-1484). **4623**

PSYCSCAN. DEVELOPMENTAL PSYCHOLOGY. (US/0197-1492). **4623**

PSYCSCAN. LD/MR. (US/0730-1928). **4623**

PTERIDINES. (GW/0933-4807). **5143**

PTI JOURNAL. (US). **5390**

PTIT FOCUS. (TH/0857-7749). **4276**

PTR. PHYTOTHERAPY RESEARCH. (UK/0951-418X). **525**

PUB NEWSLETTER. (BE). **4818**

PUBBLICITA IN ITALIA. (US). **764**

PUBBLICITA ITALIA. (IT). **Adv Mgr:** Danieue Monai. **764**

PUBLI 10. (FR/0751-5464). **764**

PUBLIC ADMINISTRATION (LONDON). (UK/0033-3298). **4704**

PUBLIC ADMINISTRATION TIMES. (US/0149-8797). **4676**

PUBLIC ART REVIEW. (US/1040-211X). **362**

PUBLIC AUTHORITIES DIRECTORY. (UK). **4676**

PUBLIC BUDGETING & FINANCE. (US/0275-1100). **4743**

PUBLIC CITIZEN. (US/0738-5927). **1299**

PUBLIC COMMUNICATIONS MAGAZINE. (US/1041-6943). **Adv Mgr:** Denise Fisher, **Tel** (804)320-4675. **1120**

PUBLIC CONTRACT LAW JOURNAL. (US/0033-3441). **3033**

PUBLIC FINANCE. (NE/0033-3476). **4743**

PUBLIC FUND DIGEST. (US/0736-7848). **4743**

PUBLIC GARDEN, THE. (US/0885-3894). **2429**

PUBLIC HEALTH (LONDON). (UK/0033-3506). **4797**

PUBLIC HEALTH NURSING (BOSTON, MASS.). (US/0737-1209). **3867**

PUBLIC HEALTH REVIEWS. (IS/0301-0422). **4797**

PUBLIC HISTORIAN, THE. (US/0272-3433). **2626**

PUBLIC LEDGER, THE. (UK). **5813**

PUBLIC LIBRARIES. (US/0163-5506). **3243**

PUBLIC LIBRARY JOURNAL. (UK/0268-893X). **3243**

PUBLIC LIBRARY QUARTERLY (NEW YORK, N.Y.). (US/0161-6846). **3243**

PUBLIC MANAGER (POTOMAC, MD.), THE. (US/1061-7639). **4676**

PUBLIC MONEY & MANAGEMENT. (UK/0954-0962). **4743**

PUBLIC PERSONNEL MANAGEMENT. (US/0091-0260). **946**

PUBLIC POWER. (US/0033-3654). **4762**

PUBLIC RELATIONS. (UK). **764**

PUBLIC RELATIONS CAREER DIRECTORY. (US/0882-8288). **764**

PUBLIC RELATIONS JOURNAL. PRSA REGISTER ISSUE. (US). **765**

PUBLIC RELATIONS JOURNAL, THE. (US/0033-3670). **764**

PUBLIC RELATIONS QUARTERLY. (US/0033-3700). **765**

PUBLIC RELATIONS REVIEW (RIVERDALE, N.Y.). (US/0363-8111). **765**

PUBLIC RISK. (US/0891-7183). **1514**

PUBLIC SECTOR JOB BULLETIN. (US/1072-3773). **4209**

PUBLIC SECTOR QUALITY REPORT. (US/1067-4489). **732**

PUBLIC SERVANT. DIE STAATSAMPTENAAR, THE. (SA/0033-376X). **Adv Mgr:** S. Frisby. **4677**

PUBLIC (TORONTO). (CN/0845-4450). **328**

PUBLIC TRANSPORT INTERNATIONAL. (BE/1016-796X). **5390**

PUBLIC UTILITIES FORTNIGHTLY. (US/0033-3808). **4762**

PUBLIC WELFARE (WASHINGTON). (US/0033-3816). **5303**

PUBLIC WORKS. (US/0033-3840). **1992**

PUBLIC WORKS FINANCING. (US). **4743**

PUBLICACIONES ESPECIALES - INSTITUTO ESPANOL DE OCEANOGRAFIA. (SP/0214-7378). **1455**

PUBLICACIONES - INSTITUTO DE FISIOGRAFIA Y GEOLOGIA. (AG/0041-8684). **1392**

PUBLICATION / ALASKA GEOLOGICAL SOCIETY. (US/0749-9671). **1392**

PUBLICATION B / CENTRE INTERNATIONAL DE RECERCHES SUR LE BILINGUISME. (CN/0704-7037). **3312**

PUBLICATIONES MATHEMATICAL (DEBRECEN). (HU/0033-3883). **3529**

PUBLICATIONS. (US). **4148**

PUBLICATIONS INDEX / NATIONAL HEALTH STATISTICS CENTRE. (NZ). **4811**

PUBLICATIONS OF THE INTERNATIONAL BUREAU OF FISCAL DOCUMENTATION. (NE/0074-2112). **750**

PUBLICATIONS OF THE MODERN LANGUAGE ASSOCIATION OF AMERICA. (US/0030-8129). **Adv Mgr:** Cynthia Port. **3313**

PUBLICATIONS (TOPOR & ASSOCIATES). (US/1063-1771). **Adv Mgr:** R. Topor, **Tel** (415)962-1105. **1843**

PUBLISH! (SAN FRANCISCO, CALIF.). (US/0897-6007). **1263**

PUBLISHED. (US/0882-7400). **3426**

PUBLISHER (OTTAWA). (CN/0380-8025). **4818**

PUBLISHERS' AUXILIARY. (US/0048-5942). **4818**

PUBLISHER'S MONTHLY. (II). **4818**

PUBLISHERS REPORTS. (UK/0953-7899). **4819**

PUBLISHERS' TRADE LIST ANNUAL, THE. (US/0079-7855). **4822**

PUBLISHERS WEEKLY. (US/0000-0019). **4831**

PUBLISHING HISTORY. (UK/0309-2445). **4819**

PUBLIUS. (US/0048-5950). **4492**

PUBLIZISTIK. (GW/0033-4006). **2923**

PUCE A L'ORIELLE (MONTREAL). (CN/0824-068X). **1776**

PUCKERBRUSH REVIEW. (US/0890-3433). **3350**

PUEBLO CHIEFTAIN. (US). **Adv Mgr:** Jack Wyss. **5644**

PUERTO DEL SOL. (US/0738-517X). **3426**

PUERTO RICO HEALTH SCIENCES JOURNAL. (PR/0738-0658). **3631**

PUERTO RICO LIVING. (US/0033-4049). **2544**

PUGET SOUND BUSINESS JOURNAL. (US/8750-7757). **705**

PUGET SOUND COMPUTER USER. (US/0886-8174). **Adv Mgr:** Ray Kehl, **Tel** (206)547-4950. **1201**

PULASKI CITIZEN (PULASKI, TENN. : 1866). (US). **Adv Mgr:** Juanita Hoover, **Tel** (615)363-3544. **5746**

PULASKI COUNTY JOURNAL. (US). **5666**

PULASKI NEWS. (US). **Adv Mgr:** Mary Lepak. **5770**

PULCE. (IT). **1514**

PULIZIA INDUSTRIALE E SANIFICAZIONE. (IT). **Adv Mgr:** Dr Pellizzari. **2868**

PULLER, THE. (US/8750-4219). **160**

PULMONARY PHARMACOLOGY (EDINBURGH). (UK/0952-0600). **3951**

PULP & PAPER CANADA ANNUAL AND DIRECTORY. (CN/0709-2563). **4238**

PULP & PAPER INTERNATIONAL. (US/0033-409X). **4238**

PULPIT DIGEST (1978). (US/0160-838X). **4988**

PULSE BUYERS GUIDE. (SA). **2078**

PULSE (KLOOF). (SA/0256-6028). **2078**

PULSE (PICO RIVERA). (US/0555-6953). **5519**

PULSO DEL PERIODISMO. (US/1051-8126). **Adv Mgr:** Mary Van Meter, **Tel** (303)964-8400. **2923**

PUNCH (LONDON). (UK/0033-4278). **3426**

PUNCTURE (SAN FRANCISCO, CALIF.). (US/1047-4528). **Adv Mgr:** Steve Connell. **4148**

PUNTO. (VE). **307**

PUNTO CRITICO. (MX). **1514**

PUNTO DE VISTA. (AG/0326-3061). **2552**

PUPIL TRANSPORTATION NEWS. (US/0730-5443). **Adv Mgr:** J. Dickinson, **Tel** (908)937-0058. **5390**

PUPPETRY JOURNAL, THE. (US/0033-443X). **5367**

PURCELL REGISTER, THE. (US). **Adv Mgr:** Vickie Foreaker, **Tel** (405)527-2126. **5732**

PURCHASING & SUPPLY MANAGEMENT / INSTITUTE OF PURCHASING AND SUPPLY. (UK/0309-7242). **951**

PURCHASING MANAGEMENT. (CN/0841-615X). **951**

PURDUE ALUMNUS, THE. (US/0033-4502). **1102**

PURDUE EXPONENT, THE. (US). **5666**

PURE AND APPLIED CHEMISTRY. (UK/0033-4545). **990**

PURE AND APPLIED MATHEMATIKA SCIENCES. (II). **3529**

PURE-BRED DOGS, AMERICAN KENNEL GAZETTE. (US/0033-4561). **Adv Mgr Tel** (212)696-8261. **4287**

PUREBRED PICTURE, THE. (US/8750-1880). **219**

PUSH! (NEW YORK, N.Y.). (US/1054-3686). **382**

PUTNAM COUNTY COURIER (CARMEL, N.Y. : 1852). (US/0890-1147). **5646**

PUTNAM COURIER-TRADER, THE. (US). **5646**

PUTNAM DEMOCRAT (WINFIELD, W. VA.). (US). **Adv Mgr:** Fritzi Whitney. **5764**

PUXICO PRESS. (US). **5704**

PW PERSONEELSMANAGEMENT. (NE). **705**

PWACONTACT. (CN/0822-4706). **Adv Mgr:** Paulette Pelletier-Kelly. **1928**

PYNCHON NOTES. (US/0278-1891). **3426**

PYRAMID (MOUNT PLEASANT, UTAH). (US). **5757**

PYROTECHNICA. (US/0272-6521). **1028**

PYTTERSEN'S NEDERLANDSE ALMANAK. (NE). **2521**

QINGBAO KEXUE. (CC/1000-8489). **3243**

QJM : MONTHLY JOURNAL OF THE ASSOCIATION OF PHYSICIANS. (UK). **3631**

QST. (US/0033-4812). **1136**

QST CANADA. (CN/0840-6170). **1992**

QTGO. QUADERNI DI TECNICA E GESTIONE OSPEDALIERA. (IT/1120-7906). **Adv Mgr:** Dott Dalla, **Tel** 06-86207165. **3791**

QUAD-CITY HERALD. (US). **5762**

QUAD COMMUNITY PRESS. (US/0892-1806). **Adv Mgr:** Michelle Larson. **5698**

QUADERNI DI ARCHEOLOGIA DELLA LIBIA. (IT/0079-8258). **279**

QUADERNI DI STORIA. (IT). **Adv Mgr:** R. Coga. **2626**

QUADERNI DI TERZO MONDO. (IT/0391-7312). **4492**

QUADERNI D'ITALIANISTICA. (CN/0226-8043). **3426**

QUADERNI FIORENTINI PER LA STORIA DEL PENSIERO GIURIDICO MODERNO. (IT). **3033**

QUADERNI IBERO-AMERICANI. (IT/0033-4960). **3350**

QUADERNI MARCHIGIANI DI MEDICINA. (IT/0392-9620). **3632**

QUADERNI MEDIEVALI. (IT). **Adv Mgr:** R. Coga. **2704**

QUADERNO MONTESSORI. (IT). **1884**

QUADERNS D'ARQUITECTURA I URBANISME. (SP/0211-9595). **Adv Mgr:** Ignasi Perez Arnal, **Tel** 301-50-00 Ext. 296. **307**

QUADERNS D'ARQUITECTURA I URBANISME. (SP). **307**

QUADRANT. (AT/0033-5002). **2511**

QUADRANT (NEW YORK). (US/0033-5010). **4614**

QUAERENDO. (NE/0014-9527). **4831**

QUAIL UNLIMITED MAGAZINE. (US/0746-2638). **5619**

QUAKER LIFE. (US/0033-5061). **Adv Mgr:** Carol Beals. **4989**

QUALITE — Advertising Accepted Index

QUALITE (DOLLARD-DES-ORMEAUX). (CN/0226-3432). **883**

QUALITE TOTALE. (CN). **Adv Mgr:** S. King. **883**

QUALITY AND PRODUCTIVITY MANAGEMENT. (US/0895-2272). **Adv Mgr:** K. Denson. **883**

QUALITY AND RELIABILITY ENGINEERING INTERNATIONAL. (UK/0748-8017). **1992**

QUALITY AUSTRALIA. (AT/0813-0272). **Adv Mgr:** Geoff Govllet. **883**

QUALITY CITIES. (US/0892-4171). **Adv Mgr:** Priscilla Dawson, **Tel** (904)222-9684. **4677**

QUALITY DIGEST. (US/1049-8699). **1705**

QUALITY OBSERVER, THE. (US/1057-9583). **Adv Mgr:** M. Jones, **Tel** same as publisher. **884**

QUALITY OF LIFE RESEARCH. (UK/0962-9343). **4392**

QUALITY PROGRESS. (US/0033-524X). **1993**

QUALITY (WHEATON). (US/0360-9936). **884**

QUANAH TRIBUNE-CHIEF. (US). **Adv Mgr:** Judy Nelson. **5753**

QUARRY (KINGSTON). (CN/0033-5266). **3427**

QUARRY WEST. (US/0736-4628). **3427**

QUART DE ROND. (CN/0709-0692). **625**

QUARTER CIRCLE. (CN/0228-0612). **2801**

QUARTER HORSE JOURNAL (1953), THE. (US/0164-6656). **Adv Mgr:** Doug Hayes, **Tel** (806)372-1163. **2801**

QUARTER RACING RECORD, THE. (US/0091-7516). **2802**

QUARTERLY - ASSOCIATION OF PROFESSIONAL GENEALOGISTS (U.S.). (US/1056-6732). **Adv Mgr:** S. McVetty, **Tel** (516)997-4757. **2468**

QUARTERLY BULLETIN OF THE ALPINE GARDEN SOCIETY. (UK/0002-6476). **2429**

QUARTERLY BULLETIN OF THE NORTH AMERICAN LILY SOCIETY, INC. (US). **2429**

QUARTERLY BULLETIN OF THE SOUTH AFRICAN LIBRARY. (SA/0038-2418). **3243**

QUARTERLY - CANADIAN CAT ASSOCIATION. (CN/0828-4865). **4287**

QUARTERLY DEC JOURNAL. (US/1063-1216). **Adv Mgr:** Kate Davis. **706**

QUARTERLY ECONOMIC REVIEW / UGANDA COMMERCIAL BANK. (UG). **1580**

QUARTERLY JOURNAL - FLORIDA AGRICULTURAL AND MECHANICAL UNIVERSITY, TALLAHASSEE, THE. (US). **1843**

QUARTERLY JOURNAL OF ADMINISTRATION, THE. (NR/0001-8333). **1869**

QUARTERLY JOURNAL OF ENGINEERING GEOLOGY, THE. (UK/0481-2085). **2029**

QUARTERLY JOURNAL OF FORESTRY. (UK/0033-5568). **2391**

QUARTERLY JOURNAL OF IDEOLOGY. (US/0738-9752). **5254**

QUARTERLY JOURNAL OF MATHEMATICS. (UK/0033-5606). **3530**

QUARTERLY JOURNAL OF MECHANICS AND APPLIED MATHEMATICS, THE. (UK/0033-5614). **2127**

QUARTERLY JOURNAL OF MEDICINE, THE. (UK/0033-5622). **3632**

QUARTERLY JOURNAL OF THE ROYAL ASTRONOMICAL SOCIETY, THE. (UK/0035-8738). **399**

QUARTERLY JOURNAL OF THE ROYAL METEOROLOGICAL SOCIETY. (UK/0035-9009). **1434**

QUARTERLY NEWS-LETTER - BOOK CLUB OF CALIFORNIA. (US/0006-7202). **Adv Mgr Tel** (415)781-7532. **4831**

QUARTERLY OF THE NATIONAL ASSOCIATION FOR OUTLAW AND LAWMAN HISTORY, INC. (US/1071-4189). **2756**

QUARTERLY - ORANGE COUNTY CALIFORNIA GENEALOGICAL SOCIETY. (US/0030-4263). **Adv Mgr:** same as editor. **2469**

QUARTERLY / OREGON GENEALOGICAL SOCIETY. (US/0738-1891). **2469**

QUARTERLY - PHI LAMBDA KAPPA MEDICAL FRATERNITY. (US/0739-2079). **3917**

QUARTERLY REVIEW - CIPEC. (FR/1015-0064). **1623**

QUARTERLY REVIEW OF BIOLOGY, THE. (US/0033-5770). **471**

QUARTERLY REVIEW OF HISTORICAL STUDIES, THE. (II/0033-5800). **2627**

QUARTERLY REVIEW OF WINES. (US/0740-1248). **Adv Mgr:** Jack Lynch, **Tel** same as editor. **2370**

QUARTERLY REVIEW - UNITED METHODIST BOARD OF HIGHER EDUCATION AND MINISTRY (U.S.). (US/0270-9287). **5066**

QUARTERLY REVIEWS OF BIOPHYSICS. (UK/0033-5835). **496**

QUARTERLY - ST. LAWRENCE COUNTY HISTORICAL ASSOCIATION, THE. (US/0558-1931). **2756**

QUARTERLY WEST. (US/0194-4231). **Adv Mgr:** Maggie Welsh. **3427**

QUARTZ DEVICES DIRECTORY. (US). **Adv Mgr:** L. Aiken. **3487**

QUATRE SAISONS DU JARDINAGE, LES. (FR/0242-4959). **2429**

QUATRE-TEMPS. (CN/0820-5515). **525**

QUATRE-TEMPS (MONTREAL). (CN/0820-5515). **Adv Mgr:** P. Feugere, **Tel** (514)872-0650. **526**

QUE PASA SAN ANTONIO. (US). **5489**

QUE PASA (TEANECK, N.J.). (US/0899-2576). **2491**

QUEBEC CHRONICLE-TELEGRAPH. (CN). **5793**

QUEBEC FRANCAIS. (CN/0316-2052). **3427**

QUEBEC PHARMACIE (MONTREAL, 1981). (CN/0826-9874). **Adv Mgr:** Y. LaCroix, **Tel** (514)626-0024. **4327**

QUEBEC SCIENCE. (CN/0021-6127). **5143**

QUEBEC STUDIES. (US/0737-3759). **2756**

QUEBEC VERT. (CN/0705-6923). **2202**

QUEBEC YACHTIING, VOILE & MOTEUR. (CN/0833-918X). **595**

QUEBECOISEAUX (MONTREAL). (CN/0843-9656). **5619**

QUEEN CHARLOTTE ISLANDS OBSERVER. (CN). **5793**

QUEEN'S LAW JOURNAL. (CN/0316-778X). **3033**

QUEEN'S QUARTERLY. (CN/0033-6041). **5214**

QUEENSLAND ACCOMMODATION AND CARAVANNING DIRECTORY. (AT). **Adv Mgr:** Kayleen Dunsford. **5489**

QUEENSLAND COUNTRY LIFE. (AT/0033-6084). **124**

QUEENSLAND DAIRY FARMER. (AU). **Adv Mgr:** Morris Lake. **198**

QUEENSLAND FAMILY HISTORIAN : JOURNAL OF THE QUEENSLAND FAMILY HISTORY SOCIETY, INC. (AT/0811-3394). **2469**

QUEENSLAND FRUIT AND VEGETABLE NEWS. (AT/0033-6122). **2429**

QUEENSLAND GEOGRAPHICAL JOURNAL. NEW SERIES. (AT/0155-400X). **2574**

QUEENSLAND GOVERNMENT MINING JOURNAL. (AT/0033-6149). **2149**

QUEENSLAND GRAINGROWER, THE. (AT). **203**

QUEENSLAND LAW SOCIETY JOURNAL, THE. (AT/0313-4253). **Adv Mgr:** Gail Baker, **Tel** same as publisher. **3034**

QUEENSLAND LAWYER, THE. (AT/0312-1658). **3034**

QUEENSLAND MASTER BUILDER. (AT/0048-6361). **Adv Mgr:** Denis Manahan. **625**

QUEENSLAND PROPERTY REPORT. (AT). **Adv Mgr:** R. Weiler. **4843**

QUEENSLAND TEACHERS PROFESSIONAL MAGAZINE. (AT/0813-8206). **Adv Mgr:** Margaret Hinchliffe. **1903**

QUEENSLAND YEAR BOOK. (AT/0085-5359). **1928**

QUEL CORPS?. (FR/0337-6338). **Adv Mgr:** JM Brohm. **1776**

QUELLEN UND FORSCHUNGEN AUS ITALIENISCHEN ARCHIVEN UND BIBLIOTHEKEN. (GW/0079-9068). **2627**

QUERY. (US). **1249**

QUESNEL CARIBOO OBSERVER. (CN/1195-5023). **Adv Mgr:** Dave Sales. **5793**

QUEST : FOR A POSITIVE LIFESTYLE. (US/1064-4059). **2796**

QUEST (LUSAKA, ZAMBIA). (ZA/1011-226X). **4358**

QUEST: MANHATTAN PROPERTIES & COUNTRY ESTATES. (UK). **4843**

QUEST (WHEATON, ILL.), THE. (US/1040-533X). **Adv Mgr:** Ray. **4358**

QUESTIONS (BIRMINGHAM). (UK/0954-920X). **1903**

QUI PARLE. (US/1041-8385). **2852**

QUICK FROZEN FOODS ANNUAL PROCESSORS' DIRECTORY AND BUYERS' GUIDE. (US/0890-5517). **2355**

QUICK FROZEN FOODS INTERNATIONAL. (US/0033-6416). **2355**

QUICK 'N EASY COOKIN'. (US/0893-2247). **2792**

QUICK PRINTING. (US/0191-4588). **4569**

QUILL AND SCROLL (IOWA CITY). (US/0033-6505). **2923**

QUILL (CHICAGO), THE. (US/0033-6475). **Adv Mgr:** Gregory Christopher. **2923**

QUILL, QUEENSLAND INTER-LIBRARY LIAISON. (AT). **3243**

QUILT WORLD. (US/0149-8045). **5185**

QUILTER'S NEWSLETTER MAGAZINE. (US/0274-712X). **5185**

QUIMERA (BARCELONA, SPAIN). (SP/0211-3325). **3351**

QUINCY COLLEGE BULLETIN. (US/0033-6556). **1094**

QUINCY SUN, THE. (US). **Adv Mgr:** Mark Crosby. **5690**

QUINCY VALLEY POST-REGISTER, THE. (US). **5762**

QUINTESSENCE INTERNATIONAL (BERLIN : 1985). (GW). **1334**

QUINTO LINGO. (US/0033-6602). **3313**

QUINZAINE LITTERAIRE, LA. (FR/0048-6493). **3427**

QUIPU. (MX/0185-5093). **5144**

QUIRK'S MARKETING RESEARCH REVIEW. (US/0893-7451). **Adv Mgr:** E. Tweed, **Tel** same as publisher. **765**

QUMRAN CHRONICLE. (PL/0867-8715). **5019**

QUONDAM ET FUTURUS (BIRMINGHAM, ALA.). (US/8755-3627). **3351**

QUOTIDIEN DE PARIS. (FR). **5801**

QUOTIDIEN DU PHARMACIEN, LE. (FR/0764-5104). **4327**

R A C V S OUT AND ABOUT. (AT). **5489**

R A C V'S ATTRACTIONS AUSTRALIA. (AT). **5489**

R & D MANAGEMENT. (UK/0033-6807). **5144**

R & R (LOS ANGELES, CALIF.). (US/1076-6502). **1137**

R.C.M. MAGAZINE. (UK/0033-684X). **4148**

R. E. TODAY. (UK). **Adv Mgr:** Mr. Cyril Lowden, **Tel** 0628 890700. **4989**

R.F. DESIGN. (US/0163-321X). **1993**

R.I.A. (PARIS, 1977). (FR/0035-4244). **2355**

R P M WEEKLY. (CN/0033-7064). **4148**

RABBINICS TODAY. (US/1066-0585). **5052**

RABELS ZEITSCHRIFT FUER AUSLAENDISCHES UND INTERNATIONALES PRIVATRECHT. (GW/0033-7250). **3134**

RAC CAMPING & CARAVANNING GUIDE - EUROPE. (UK). **5489**

RAC, REFRIGERATION AND AIR CONDITIONING. (UK). **2607**

RACCOON. (US/0148-0162). **3470**

RACE & CLASS. (UK/0306-3968). **2271**

RACECAR ENGINEERING. (UK/0961-1096). **5423**

RACER (TORONTO). (CN/0380-7762). **Adv Mgr:** Brenda Gallagher, **Tel** (613)748-5669. **4914**

RACER (TUSTIN, CALIF.). (US/1066-6060). **Adv Mgr:** Donna Chamberlain. **4914**

RACINE LABOR. (US). **Adv Mgr:** Sherry Horton, **Tel** (414)634-7186. **1705**

RACING FOR KIDS. (US/1056-7623). **Adv Mgr:** Zeta Smith, **Tel** (704)786-7131. **1068**

RACING GREYHOUNDS. (US/1042-9174). **4865**

RACING PIGEON BULLETIN. (US/0146-8383). **4914**

RACING PIGEON PICTORIAL. (UK/0033-7404). **4914**

RACING PIGEON, THE. (UK/0033-7390). **4914**

RACING STAR WEEKLY. (US/0033-7439). **2802**

RACKHAM JOURNAL OF THE ARTS AND HUMANITIES, THE. (US/0731-4817). **2852**

RAD HARLOW. (UK/0264-6412). **Adv Mgr:** D. Roberts. **3944**

RAD! : REVIEW AND DISCUSSION OF ROCK & ROLL CULTURE. (US). **4148**

RADDLE MOON. (CN/0826-5909). **3427**

RADIANCE (OAKLAND, CALIF.). (US/0889-9495). **405**

RADIATION CURING BUYER'S GUIDE. (US/0197-8039). **3944**

RADIATION MEDICINE. (JA/0288-2043). **3944**

RADIATION PROTECTION DOSIMETRY. (UK/0144-8420). **4440**

RADIATION PROTECTION IN AUSTRALIA. (AT/0729-7963). **4798**

RADIATION PROTECTION MANAGEMENT. (US/0740-0640). **2868**

RADICAL AMERICA. (US/0033-7617). **4493**

RADICAL HISTORY REVIEW. (US/0163-6545). **4545**

RADICAL PHILOSOPHY. (UK/0300-211X). **4358**

RADICAL TEACHER (CAMBRIDGE). (US/0191-4847). **1776**

RADIO AGE (AUGUSTA, GA.). (US/0892-6360). **1137**

RADIO & RECORDS. (US/0277-4860). **1137**

RADIO ATIVITE INC. (CN/0822-7926). **4148**

RADIO-CHICAGO. (US/1044-9647). **1137**

RADIO COMMUNICATION. (UK/0033-7803). **2078**

RADIO CONTROL BUYERS GUIDE. (US/0098-9215). **2777**

RADIO CONTROL CAR ACTION. (US/0886-1609). **2777**

RADIO CONTROL MODELS & ELECTRONICS. (UK/0033-7838). **2777**

RADIO IN THE UNITED STATES. (US/0740-2341). **1137**

RADIO MODELLER. (UK/0144-0713). **2777**

RADIO WORLD (FALLS CHURCH, VA.). (US/0274-8541). **1138**

RADIO Y TELEVISION. (US/0033-8133). **1138**

RADIOACTIVE WASTE MANAGEMENT AND THE NUCLEAR FUEL CYCLE. (SZ/0739-5876). **2240**

RADIOACTIVE WASTE MANAGEMENT (CHUR, SWITZERLAND : 1981). (SZ/0275-7273). **2240**

RADIOACTIVITY & RADIOCHEMISTRY. (US/1045-845X). **Adv Mgr:** Laura Roop, **Tel** (404)352-4620. **1029**

RADIOCHIMICA ACTA. (US/0033-8230). **1057**

RADIOCOMM MAGAZINE. (CN/1196-0809). **1138**

RADIOGRAPHER. (AT/0033-8273). **3632**

RADIOGRAPHICS. (US/0271-5333). **3945**

RADIOISOTOPES. (JA/0033-8303). **5144**

RADIOLOGIA MEDICA. (IT/0033-8362). **3945**

RADIOLOGIC TECHNOLOGY. (US/0033-8397). **3945**

RADIOLOGICA (OULU). (FI/0358-4887). **3945**

RADIOLOGY. (US/0033-8419). **3945**

RADIOLOGY MANAGEMENT. (US/0198-7097). **Adv Mgr:** Teresa Cryan. **3946**

RADIOSCAN MAGAZINE (SPANISH ED.). (US/1050-3641). **1120**

RADIOTEHNIKA (MOSKVA). (RU/0033-8486). **1138**

RADIOTEKHNIKA I ELEKTRONIKA. (RU/0033-8494). **2078**

RADIOTHERAPY AND ONCOLOGY. (NE/0167-8140). **3823**

RADIUS (MENDOCINO, CALIF.). (US/0886-7771). **328**

RADIUS (STUTTGART, GERMANY). (GW/0033-8532). **4989**

RADIX (BERKELEY, CALIF.). (US/0275-0147). **4989**

RADON NEWS DIGEST. (US/0896-7180). **2241**

RAFT (CLEVELAND, OHIO). (US/0891-0545). **3314**

RAFU SHIMPO. (US). **Adv Mgr:** Mr. Ubukata. **5638**

RAG MAG (GOODHUE, MINN.). (US/0742-2768). **3427**

RAG TIMES. (US/0090-4570). **4148**

RAGGUAGLIO LIBRARIO, IL. (IT/0033-8648). **423**

RAGIUSAN. RASSEGNA GIURIDICA DELLA SANITA. (IT/1120-1762). **3034**

RAICES (MADRID, SPAIN). (SP/0212-6753). **2271**

RAIL CLASSICS & RAILWAY QUARTERLY. (US/0743-9075). **5434**

RAIL ENGINEERING INTERNATIONAL (1981). (UK/0141-4615). **5434**

RAIL INTERNATIONAL. (BE/0020-8442). **5434**

RAIL MART, THE. (US/1070-7751). **5434**

RAIL PARIS, LE. (FR/0989-8220). **5435**

RAILFAN & RAILROAD. (US/0163-7266). **5435**

RAILPACE NEWSMAGAZINE. (US/0745-5267). **5435**

RAILROAD MODEL CRAFTSMAN. (US/0033-877X). **2777**

RAILROAD REVENUES, EXPENSES, AND INCOME: CLASS I RAILROADS IN THE UNITED STATES. (US). **5435**

RAILROADER. (RH). **5435**

RAILS (WELLINGTON). (NZ/0110-6155). **5435**

RAILWATCH. (UK/0267-5943). **5435**

RAILWAY WORLD ANNUAL. (UK/0082-5891). **5436**

RAILWAYS. (SA/0254-2218). **5436**

RAINBOW (PROSPECT, KY.). (US/0746-4797). **1272**

RAINS COUNTY LEADER. (US). **5753**

RAJASTHAN BOARD JOURNAL OF EDUCATION. RAJASTHANA BORDA SIKSHANA PATRIKA, THE. (II/0033-9083). **1776**

RAJASTHAN LAW WEEKLY, THE. (II/0377-7723). **3034**

RAKENNUSTUOTANTO. (FI). **625**

RAKENTAJAIN KALENTERI / SUOMEN RAKENNUSMESTARILIITTO. (FI/0355-550X). **625**

RAM DIGEST, THE. (US/0147-9059). **2832**

RAMBLING ON. (AT). **4914**

RAM'S HORN (HANOVER, N.H.), THE. (US/0272-2747). **3314**

RAMUS. (AT/0048-671X). **1079**

RANCH MAGAZINE, THE. (US/0145-8515). **220**

RAND MCNALLY CAMPGROUND & TRAILER PARK GUIDE, EASTERN. (US/0733-8309). **4708**

RANDALLSTOWN NEWS. (US/0883-7104). **5687**

RANDAX EDUCATION GUIDE TO COLLEGES SEEKING STUDENTS. (US). **1843**

RANDOL MINING DIRECTORY. (US/1054-027X). **Adv Mgr Tel** (303)278-9199. **2149**

RANDOM LENGTHS BUYERS' & SELLERS' GUIDE. (US/0891-7833). **2404**

RANDOM LENGTHS (SAN PEDRO, CALIF.). (US/0891-8627). **Adv Mgr:** Tom Davidson. **5638**

RANGE HISTORY. (US). **2627**

RANGEFINDER (SANTA MONICA), THE. (US/0033-9202). **Adv Mgr:** Jerry Goldstein, **Tel** (310)451-8506. **4376**

RANGER. (US). **4708**

RANKIN COUNTY NEWS. (US). **5701**

RAPID CITY JOURNAL, THE. (US). **Adv Mgr:** Brad Slater. **5744**

RAPPORT ANNUEL DE LA BANQUE DE LA REPUBLIQUE DU BURUNDI. (BD). **806**

RAPPORT BIPM. (FR/0026-1394). **1434**

RAPPORT DE RECHERCHE LPC. (FR/0222-8394). **2030**

RAPPORT - GRONLANDS GEOLOGISKE UNDERSOGELSE. (DK/0418-6559). **1393**

RAPPORT (LOS ANGELES, CALIF.). (US/1061-6861). **Adv Mgr:** Glen Kenyon. **388**

RAPPORTO CSC / CONFINDUSTRIA, CENTRO STUDI. (IT). **1623**

RAPPORTS HET FRANSE BOEK. (NE). **3427**

RARE BOOKS AND MANUSCRIPTS LIBRARIANSHIP. (US/0884-450X). **3244**

RARE BOOKS NEWSLETTER. (UK). **4832**

RARE FRUIT COUNCIL OF AUSTRALIA INC. NEWSLETTER. (AT/0726-1470). **2430**

RARITAN. (US/0275-1607). **3351**

RASAYANA SAMIKSHA. (II/0379-7635). **990**

RASSEGNA (BOLOGNA). (IT/0393-0203). **307**

RASSEGNA CHIMICA. (IT/0033-9334). **990**

RASSEGNA CONGIUNTURALE / CONFINDUSTRIA, CENTRO STUDI. (IT). **1537**

RASSEGNA DEI BENI CULTURALI. (IT). **252**

RASSEGNA DELL IMBALLAGGIO E CONFEZIONAMENTO. (IT). **4221**

RASSEGNA DI STATISTICHE DEL LAVORO. (IT/0033-961X). **1537**

RASSEGNA GRAFICA. (IT). **4569**

RASSEGNA IBERISTICA. (IT/0392-4777). **3428**

RASSEGNA PARLAMENTARE. (IT/0486-0373). **3093**

RASSEGNA SINDACALE. (IT/0033-9849). **1705**

RASSEGNA TAR. (IT). **4678**

RAT NEWS LETTER. (US/0309-1848). **5519**

RATEL. (UK/0305-1218). **5596**

RATING AND VALUATION REPORTER. (UK). **3034**

RATING APPEALS. (UK). **3034**

RATIO JURIS. (UK/0952-1917). **3034**

RATIO (OXFORD). (UK/0034-0006). **4358**

RATIONALITY AND SOCIETY. (US/1043-4631). **5214**

RATON RANGE (1985). (US/0896-1093). **Adv Mgr:** Paula Pachoruk. **5713**

RAUMFORSCHUNG UND RAUMORDNUNG. (GW/0034-0111). **33**

RAVALLI REPUBLIC. (US). **Adv Mgr:** Cindi. **5706**

RAVEN (TRENTON, N.J.). (US/1071-0043). **Adv Mgr:** Jon T. Radel, **Tel** (703)960-5128. **5214**

RAW MATERIALS REPORT. (SW/0349-6287). **2203**

RAW VISION. (UK/0955-1182). **363**

RAWLINSON'S AUSTRALIAN CONSTRUCTION HANDBOOK. (AT/0810-8064). **Adv Mgr:** Ron Murphy, **Tel** 02 360 4922. **625**

RAWLINSONS NEW ZEALAND CONSTRUCTION HANDBOOK. (NZ). **625**

RAYNE ACADIAN TRIBUNE. (US). **5684**

RAYON JEUNESSE. (CN/0841-758X). **1068**

RAYS. (IT/0390-7740). **Adv Mgr:** Dott Dalla, **Tel** 06-86207165. **3946**

RAZA, LA. (US/0034-0219). **2271**

RAZON Y FE. (SP/0034-0235). **2853**

RC MODELER (1969). (US/0033-6866). **2777**

RCD. ROCK COMPACT DISC MAGAZINE. (UK/0965-190X). **Adv Mgr:** Elspeth Thomson. **4148**

RCDA. RELIGION IN COMMUNIST DOMINATED AREAS. (US/0034-3978). **4546**

RDH. (US/0279-7720). **1334**

RE-NEW (PORT HOPE). (CN/0845-5341). **Adv Mgr:** Vicki Mosher. **2832**

RE. REVISTA DE EDIFICACION. (SP/0213-8948). **307**

RE-VIEW (NEW YORK). (US/0161-5114). **363**

REACTIONS. (AT/0157-7271). **3632**

READ, AMERICA!. (US/0891-4214). **1776**

READER (HOUGHTON, MICH.). (US/0742-9681). **Adv Mgr:** F. Peschlu. **1777**

READER (SAN DIEGO, CALIF.). (US). **5638**

READER'S DIGEST BASIA ED. (HK/0034-0383). **2271**

READING & WRITING. (NE/0922-4777). **3314**

READING IN A FOREIGN LANGUAGE. (UK/0264-2425). **3314**

READING INSTRUCTION JOURNAL, THE. (US/0275-441X). **Adv Mgr Tel** 444-6740. **1843**

READING MEDIEVAL STUDIES : ANNUAL PROCEEDINGS OF THE GRADUATE CENTRE FOR MEDIEVAL STUDIES IN THE UNIVERSITY OF READING. (UK). **2704**

READING PSYCHOLOGY. (UK/0270-2711). **4615**

READING RESEARCH AND INSTRUCTION. (US/0886-0246). **3314**

READING (SUNDERLAND). (UK/0034-0472). **1903**

READING TEACHER, THE. (US/0034-0561). **3314**

READING TODAY : A BIMONTHLY NEWSPAPER OF THE INTERNATIONAL READING ASSOCIATION. (US). **1777**

READINGS

Advertising Accepted Index

READINGS - AMERICAN ORTHOPSYCHIATRIC ASSOCIATION. (US/0886-3784). **3935**

REAL ESTATE CAPITAL MARKETS REPORT. (US/1064-1491). **1515**

REAL ESTATE DIGEST, THE. (US/0882-8733). **4844**

REAL ESTATE FINANCE. (US/0748-318X). **Adv Mgr:** Frank Eaton, **Tel** (617)457-0600. **4844**

REAL ESTATE FORUM. (US/0034-0707). **Adv Mgr:** J. Schein, **Tel** same as publisher. **4844**

REAL ESTATE ISSUES. (US/0146-0595). **4844**

REAL ESTATE RECORD AND BUILDER'S GUIDE (1941). (US/0034-0774). **4845**

REAL ESTATE TODAY. (US/0034-0804). **4845**

REAL PEOPLE. (US/1040-9335). **2544**

REAL POTTERY. (UK). **2593**

REAL PROPERTY LAW SECTION NEWSLETTER. (US/0147-135X). **4845**

REAL PROPERTY REPORTS. (CN/0703-4687). **3035**

REAL TIME MAGAZINE. (BE/1018-0303). **Adv Mgr:** Rene Giden. **1221**

REAL WEST. (US/0034-0898). **2756**

REALITES INDUSTRIELLES. (FR). **2149**

REALITES THERAPEUTIQUES EN DERMATO-VENEROLOGIE. (FR/1155-2492). **Adv Mgr:** G. Koster. **3722**

REALTOR NEWS. (US/0279-6309). **4846**

REALTY. (IT). **4846**

REALTY. (US/0481-9004). **4846**

REALTY AND BUILDING. (US/0034-1045). **4846**

REALTY STOCK REVIEW. (US). **Adv Mgr:** A. Goldfinger, **Tel** (908)389-8700 Ext.122. **4846**

REAPER; NEW ZEALAND'S EVANGELICAL MONTHLY. (NZ/0034-107X). **4989**

REASON. (US/0048-6906). **Adv Mgr:** Mike Griffin. **5214**

REBUS, DE. (SA/0250-0329). **3035**

REC NEWSLETTER, THE. (US/0899-014X). **3530**

RECAREERING NEWSLETTER. (US/1068-199X). **4209**

RECENTI PROGRESSI IN MEDICINA. (IT/0034-1193). **Adv Mgr:** Dott Dalla, **Tel** 06-86207165. **3801**

RECEPTOR (CLIFTON, N.J. JOURNAL). (US/1052-8040). **493**

RECHERCHE EN DANSE, LA. (FR/0752-5729). **1314**

RECHERCHE ET INDUSTRIE. (FR/0767-0273). **5145**

RECHERCHE (PARIS. 1970). (FR/0029-5671). **5145**

RECHERCHES ANGLAISES ET NORD-AMERICAINES : RANAM. (FR). **3428**

RECHERCHES DE SCIENCE RELIGIEUSE. (FR/0034-1258). **4989**

RECHERCHES GERMANIQUES. (FR/0399-1989). **2853**

RECHT DER DATENVERARBEITUNG : RDV. (GW/0178-8930). **1227**

RECHT DER JUGEND UND DES BILDUNGSWESEN. (GW/0034-1312). **3035**

RECHT DER WIRTSCHAFT, DAS. (GW). **3102**

RECHT IN OST UND WEST. (GW/0486-1485). **3036**

RECHT UND POLITIK. (GW/0344-7871). **3036**

RECHT UND SCHADEN. (GW/0343-9771). **3036**

RECHTSKUNDIG WEEKBLAD. (BE). **3036**

RECHTSMEDIZIN BERLIN. (GW/0937-9819). **3742**

RECHTSRHEINISCHES KOLN. (GW/0179-2938). **2704**

RECHTSTHEORIE. (GW/0034-1398). **3036**

RECOMBINANT DNA. (UK/0261-4979). **551**

RECOMMEND FLORIDA. (US/0034-1452). **5490**

RECOMMENDED REFERENCE BOOKS FOR SMALL AND MEDIUM-SIZED LIBRARIES AND MEDIA CENTERS. (US/0277-5948). **1928**

RECONCILIATION QUARTERLY (NEW MALDEN, SURREY). (UK/0034-1479). **Adv Mgr:** Ben Rees, **Tel** 051 724 1989. **4990**

RECONSTRUCTIONIST. (US/0034-1495). **5052**

RECORD COLLECTOR, THE. (UK/0034-155X). **4149**

RECORD COLLECTOR'S MONTHLY. (US/8755-6154). **2777**

RECORD-COURIER (GARDNERVILLE, NEV.). (US/8755-4631). **Adv Mgr:** Toni. **5708**

RECORD ENTERPRISE (PLYMOUTH, N.H.), THE. (US/1070-745X). **Adv Mgr:** Georgia Golden. **5709**

RECORD-HERALD AND INDIANOLA TRIBUNE, THE. (US/0895-3287). **Adv Mgr:** Brian Weber, **Tel** (515)961-2511. **5672**

RECORD-JOURNAL. (US). **5646**

RECORD (LOUISVILLE, KY.), THE. (US/0746-8474). **5682**

RECORD OF THE ASSOCIATION OF THE BAR OF THE CITY OF NEW YORK, THE. (US/0004-5837). **3036**

RECORD-OUTLOOK, THE. (US/0747-2161). **Adv Mgr:** Carolyn Windows. **5739**

RECORD ROUNDUP (NORTH CAMBRIDGE, MASS.). (US/1071-4170). **Adv Mgr:** Leland Stern. **4149**

RECORD SEARCHLIGHT. (US). **Adv Mgr:** Bill Dawson. **5638**

RECORD STOCKMAN, THE. (US/0034-1614). **220**

RECORD (TORONTO). (CN/0712-8290). **Adv Mgr:** Kathleen Miller. **4149**

RECORD (TROY, N.Y.). (US/1053-8976). **Adv Mgr:** Regina Burkhart, **Tel** (518)270-1241. **5720**

RECORDER. (AT/0155-8722). **1705**

RECORDER (GREENFIELD, MASS.). (US). **Adv Mgr:** Rich Foley. **5690**

RECORDER HERALD. (US). **Adv Mgr:** Sheila Hodges. **5657**

RECORDER MAGAZINE, THE. (UK/0306-4409). **4149**

RECORDER, THE. (US/0362-6121). **3036**

RECORDER, THE. (UK). **Adv Mgr:** J. Burbidge. **4149**

RECORDER (TORONTO). (CN/0704-7231). **4149**

RECORDS OF EARLY ENGLISH DRAMA. (CN/0700-9283). **5367**

RECORDS OF NEW JERSEY BIRDS. (US). **5620**

RECORDS OF THE AMERICAN CATHOLIC HISTORICAL SOCIETY OF PHILADELPHIA. (US/0002-7790). **Adv Mgr:** Dr Greene, **Tel** (215)645-4677. **5035**

RECOUP. (CN/0709-6402). **2241**

RECOUP'S MATERIALS RECYCLING MARKETS. (CN/0884-4526). **2241**

RECOVERING (SAN FRANCISCO, CALIF.). (US/0896-2391). **Adv Mgr:** Corin Hylton. **1348**

RECREATION BRITISH COLUMBIA (1985). (CN/0830-1913). **4853**

RECREATION CANADA. (CN/0031-2231). **4853**

RECREATION CANADA (FRENCH EDITION). (CN/0031-2231). **4853**

RECREATION EXCHANGE. (AT). **4853**

RECREATION EXECUTIVE REPORT. (US/0890-2194). **4853**

RECREATION RESOURCES. (US/1046-316X). **4854**

RECREATIONAL SPORTS DIRECTORY. (US). **4914**

RECRUITING & SUPERVISION TODAY. (CN/1187-9378). **946**

RECUEIL DE MEDECINE VETERINAIRE. (FR/0034-1843). **5520**

RECUEIL DES FILMS (MONTREAL). (CN/0085-543X). **4076**

RECUEIL DES TRAVAUX CHIMIQUES DES PAYS-BAS (1920). (NE/0165-0513). **991**

RECUPERARE. EDILIZIA DESIGN IMPIANTI. (IT/0392-4599). **307**

RECURRING BIBLIOGRAPHY OF HYPERTENSION. (US/0090-1326). **3710**

RECYCLAGE RECUPERATION PARIS. (FR/1156-962X). **2220**

RECYCLING TODAY (MUNICIPAL (POST-CONSUMER) MARKET ED.). (US/1051-0109). **Adv Mgr:** S France. **2241**

RECYCLING TODAY (SCRAP PROCESSING MARKET ED.). (US/1051-1091). **Adv Mgr:** S France. **2241**

RED APPLE BULLETIN. (US). **5657**

RED BASS. (US/0883-0126). **329**

RED BAY NEWS (RED BAY, ALA. : 1963). (US). **Adv Mgr:** LaVale Mills. **5628**

RED BLUFF TEHAMA COUNTY DAILY NEWS. (US). **5639**

RED BOOK OF OPHTHALMOLOGY, THE. (US/0146-4582). **3878**

RED CEDAR REVIEW. (US/0034-1967). **3428**

RED WING REPUBLICAN EAGLE. (US). **Adv Mgr:** Mary Foley. **5698**

REDBOOK. (US/0034-2106). **5565**

REDDING PILOT, THE. (US). **Adv Mgr:** J. DeFillipo. **5646**

REDEMPTION DIGEST AND CORPORATE ACTIONS. (US/1056-506X). **Adv Mgr:** Rafi Reguer, **Tel** (212)966-9031. **807**

REDNECK REVIEW OF LITERATURE, THE. (US/0887-5715). **3428**

REDS REPORT. (US/1057-9540). **Adv Mgr:** Jan Cheves. **4914**

REDWOOD CITY ALMANAC. (US/0195-0533). **5639**

REED'S COMMERCIAL SALVAGE PRACTICE. (UK). **5455**

REEDUCATION POSTURALE GLOBALE. (FR/0294-0922). **3806**

REEL DIRECTORY, THE. (US/8755-786X). **4077**

REEL WEST DIGEST. (CN/0821-7947). **4077**

REESE RIVER REVEILLE (AUSTIN, NEV. : 1950). (US). **5708**

REEVES JOURNAL. (US/0048-7066). **2608**

REFER. (UK/0144-2384). **3244**

REFERATIVNYI ZHURNAL: ELEKTRONIKA. (RU). **2078**

REFERATIVNYI ZHURNAL FARMAKOLOGIYA OBSHCHAYA FARMAKOLOGIYA NERVNOI SISTEMY. (RU/0134-580X). **471**

REFEREE (FRANKSVILLE, WIS.). (US/0733-1436). **4914**

REFERENCE AND RESEARCH BOOK NEWS. (US/0887-3763). **3244**

REFERENCE LIBRARIAN, THE. (US/0276-3877). **3244**

REFERENCE REVIEWS. (UK/0950-4125). **1928**

REFERENCE SERVICES REVIEW. (US/0090-7324). **Adv Mgr:** Annette Ferguson and Ken Wachsberger. **1928**

REFERENCES DE LA POSTE PARIS. (FR/0983-1924). **1147**

REFERENCES DESIGN MALAKOFF. (FR/0996-5912). **375**

REFLECTIONS (TAZEWELL, TENN.). (US/1071-0515). **2756**

REFLECTOR (1983), THE. (US/0893-3286). **Adv Mgr:** Pratap Velagapudi, **Tel** (601)325-7907. **5701**

REFLETS ET PERSPECTIVES DE LA VIE ECONOMIQUE. (BE/0034-2971). **1639**

REFLEX (SEATTLE, WASH.). (US/1054-3465). **Adv Mgr:** Judy Kitzman, **Tel** (206)522-6865. **329**

REFLEXIONES (SANTA FE, N.M.). (US/1040-0265). **5490**

REFORM. (UK/0306-7262). **5067**

REFORM JUDAISM. (US/0482-0819). **5052**

REFORMA NEWSLETTER. (US/0891-8880). **3244**

REFORMATUSOK LAPJA. (HU). **5067**

REFORMED PERSPECTIVE. (CN/0714-8208). **4990**

REFORMED REVIEW (HOLLAND, MICH.). (US/0034-3064). **Adv Mgr:** Norman Donkersloot. **4990**

REFRACTORY GIRL. (AT/0310-4168). **5565**

REFRIGERATED TRANSPORTER. (US/0034-3129). **5391**

REFRIGERATION. (US). **2608**

REFUGEE ABSTRACTS : A PUBLICATION OF THE INTERNATIONAL REFUGEE INTEGRATION RESOURCE CENTRE. (SZ/0253-1445). **1921**

REFUNDLE BUNDLE. (US/0194-0139). **1299**

REFUSE NEWS. (US). **Adv Mgr:** Kurt Bullen. **2241**

REGATTA. (UK). **Adv Mgr:** A. Todd. **4914**

REGGAE REPORT. (US/1065-3023). **4149**

REGINA. (CN/0315-212X). **2544**

REGIONAL ANESTHESIA. (US/0146-521X). **3684**

REGIONAL CANCER TREATMENT. (GW/0935-0411). **3823**

REGIONAL DEVELOPMENT DIALOGUE. (JA/0250-6505). **2833**

REGIONAL DIRECTORY OF MINORITY & WOMEN-OWNED BUSINESS FIRMS (CENTRAL ED.). (US/1047-7799). **706**

REGIONAL DIRECTORY OF MINORITY AND WOMEN-OWNED BUSINESS FIRMS (EASTERN ED.). (US/1047-7802). **706**

REGIONAL DIRECTORY OF MINORITY & WOMEN-OWNED BUSINESS FIRMS. (WESTERN EDITION). (US/0886-3946). **706**

REGIONAL JOURNAL OF SOCIAL ISSUES. (AT/0158-7102). **5255**

REGIONAL POLITICS & POLICY. (UK). **Adv Mgr:** Anne Kidson. **4493**

REGIONAL SCIENCE AND URBAN ECONOMICS. (NE/0166-0462). **2833**

REGIONAL THEATRE DIRECTORY. (US/1041-9411). **5367**

REGISTER (KANSAS CITY, MO.), THE. (US/0899-3572). **220**

REGISTER (MONTREAL, 1980). (CN/0226-7586). **2627**

REGISTER OF AUSTRALIAN MINING. (AT). **2149**

REGISTER OF GRADUATES AND FORMER CADETS OF THE UNITED STATES MILITARY ACADEMY. (US/0090-2357). **4055**

REGISTER OF THE SPENCER MUSEUM OF ART, THE. (US/0733-866X). **4095**

REGISTERED NURSE (TORONTO). (CN/0840-8831). **Adv Mgr:** Ellen Kral. **3868**

REGISTRY OF MEMBERS - CLINICAL SOCIOLOGY ASSOCIATION. (US/0733-0251). **5255**

REGLEMENTATION POUR LE TRANSPORT DES MARCHANDISES DANGEREUSES. (CN/0256-3231). **2180**

REGULAE BENEDICTI STUDIA. (GW). **4990**

REGULATED RIVERS. (UK/0886-9375). **1359**

REGULATORY AFFAIRS JOURNAL. (UK/0960-7889). **3633**

REHAB & COMMUNITY CARE MANAGEMENT. (CN/1192-2508). **3633**

REHAB MANAGEMENT. (US/0899-6237). **4382**

REHABILITATION COUNSELING BULLETIN. (US/0034-3552). **1884**

REHABILITATION DIGEST. (CN/0048-7139). **4393**

REHABILITATION GAZETTE. (US/0361-4166). **4393**

REHABILITATION NURSING. (US/0278-4807). **3868**

REHABILITATION PSYCHOLOGY. (US/0090-5550). **4615**

REIDSVILLE REVIEW, THE. (US). **Adv Mgr:** T. Talley. **5724**

REIGOS Y DRENAJES XXI. (SP/0213-3660). **2095**

REINBECK COURIER. (US). **Adv Mgr:** Gregg Moser, **Tel** (319)345-2031. **5672**

REINFORCED PLASTICS (LONDON). (UK/0034-3617). **4460**

REINIGER + WASCHER. (GW/0034-3625). **5355**

REINRAUMTECHNIK. (GW/0931-9190). **5145**

REINSURANCE LAW REPORTS. (UK/0961-7264). **Adv Mgr:** J. Arcker, **Tel** 011 44 494 79262. **3037**

REITEN UND FAHREN. (GW/0720-5104). **4914**

REJOICE! (UNIVERSITY, MISS.). (US/1044-1034). **Adv Mgr:** Brett Bonner. **4149**

REKAMAN PERISTIWA .... (IO). **5255**

REKINDLE. (US/0193-7359). **2292**

RELACION DE LOS INGENIEROS DE CAMINOS, CANALES Y PUERTOS. (SP). **Adv Mgr:** Tonice Baeze. **2030**

RELACIONES DE LA SOCIEDAD ARGENTINA DE ANTROPOLOGIA. (AG). **244**

RELACIONES INTERNACIONALES. (MX/0185-0814). **4533**

RELACIONES MEXICO-ESTADOS UNIDOS, BIBLIOGRAFIA ANUAL. (MX). **4502**

RELATIONAL DATABASE JOURNAL. (US/1074-6404). **1255**

RELATORIO DE ATIVIDADES - FUNDACAO PARA O LIVRO DO CEGO NO BRASIL. (BL). **5304**

RELAZIONE DEL CONSIGLIO DIRETTIVO ALLA ASSEMBLEA GENERALE DEI SOCI. (IT). **1624**

RELAZIONI INTERNAZIONALI. (IT/0034-3846). **4533**

RELC JOURNAL. (SI/0033-6882). **3315**

RELEASE. (AT/0157-3470). **3174**

RELEASE PRINT. (US/0890-5231). **4077**

RELEASE (VANCOUVER). (CN/1182-3976). **Adv Mgr:** Frank Chimento, **Tel** (615)872-8080 ext. 2159. **4149**

RELEASING HORMONES. (UK/0142-8314). **3733**

RELEVE, LA. (RW). **2642**

RELIABILITY REVIEW (MILWAUKEE, WIS.). (US/0277-9633). **1993**

RELIGION & LITERATURE. (US/0888-3769). **4990**

RELIGION & PUBLIC EDUCATION. (US/1056-7224). **1777**

RELIGION INDEX ONE. PERIODICALS. (US/0149-8428). **5013**

RELIGION INDEX TWO : MULTI-AUTHOR WORKS. (US/0149-8436). **4991**

RELIGION TEACHER'S JOURNAL. (US/0034-401X). **4991**

RELIGIONEN DER MENSCHHEIT, DIE. (GW/0486-3585). **4991**

RELIGIONSGESCHICHTLICHE VERSUCHE UND VORARBEITEN. (GW). **4991**

RELIGIONSVIDENSKABELIGT TIDSSKRIFT. (DK/0108-1993). **4991**

RELIGIOUS BROADCASTING. (US/0034-4079). **Adv Mgr:** Dick Reynolds, **Tel** (704)393-0602. **1138**

RELIGIOUS EDUCATION. (US/0034-4087). **4991**

RELIGIOUS HERALD, THE. (US/0738-7318). **4992**

RELIGIOUS LIFE (CHICAGO, ILL.). (US/0279-0459). **4992**

RELIGIOUS STUDIES AND THEOLOGY. (CN/0829-2922). **4992**

RELIGIOUS STUDIES REVIEW. (US/0319-485X). **4992**

RELIGIOUS TRADITIONS. (AT/0156-1650). **4992**

RELIX. (US/0146-3489). **4149**

RELOCATION COMPASS. (US/1069-5923). **884**

RELOCATION / REALTY UPDATE. (US). **946**

REMAINS TO BE FOUND. (US/0738-5889). **2469**

REMEDIAL AND SPECIAL EDUCATION. (US/0741-9325). **1884**

REMEMBER THAT SONG. (US/0889-8790). **4149**

REMINDER. ZONE ONE. BRANDON, GROVELAND, ATLAS AND HADLEY TOWNSHIPS, THE. (US/0194-245X). **5693**

REMINERALIZE THE EARTH. (US/1066-4106). **184**

REMITTANCE AND DOCUMENT PROCESSING TODAY. (US/1050-9186). **5145**

REMODELING (WASHINGTON, D.C.). (US/0885-8039). **626**

REMONSTRANTS WEEKBLAD : RW. (NE). **4992**

REMOTE SENSING REVIEWS. (SZ/0275-7257). **1993**

REMSEN BELL-ENTERPRISE. (US). **5672**

RENAISSANCE (ARDMORE, PA.). (US/1072-3625). **Adv Mgr:** W. Nasir. **2271**

RENAISSANCE STUDIES. (UK/0269-1213). **2705**

RENAISSANCE UNIVERSAL JOURNAL. (US/0712-4767). **4533**

RENAL EDUCATOR. (AT/0816-990X). **3992**

RENAL FAILURE. (US/0886-022X). **3992**

RENAL PHYSIOLOGY AND BIOCHEMISTRY. (SZ/1011-6524). **3993**

RENAL TRANSPLANTATION AND DIALYSIS. (UK/0142-8357). **3633**

RENDER. (US/0090-8932). **2355**

RENDICONTI DEL SEMINARIO MATEMATICO. (IT). **3531**

RENDITIONS. (HK/0377-3515). **Adv Mgr:** Janice K. Wickeri, **Tel** 11 852 0 6097407. **3429**

RENEGADE (BLOOMFIELD HILLS). (US). **3429**

RENEWAL MAGAZINE. (UK). **Adv Mgr:** P. Thomas. **4992**

RENIN, ANGIOTENSIN & KININS. (UK/0143-4284). **471**

RENLEIXUE XUEBAO. (CC/1000-3193). **244**

RENNINGER'S ANTIQUE GUIDE. (US). **252**

RENO GAZETTE-JOURNAL. (US/0745-1415). **Adv Mgr:** John Zidich, **Tel** (702)788-6236. **5708**

RENOVATEC BARCELONA. (SP/0214-3127). **626**

RENOVATION BRICOLAGE. (CN/0381-0992). **626**

RENSSELAER ENGINEER. (US/0034-4508). **1993**

RENTAL EQUIPMENT REGISTER. (US/0034-4524). **935**

RENTAL PRODUCT NEWS (1992). (US/1067-0904). **707**

RENVILLE COUNTY FARMER. (US). **Adv Mgr:** Gloria Abrahamson, **Tel** (701)756-6363. **5726**

RENVILLE COUNTY STAR FARMER NEWS. (US). **Adv Mgr:** Rich McCube. **5698**

REPERTOIRE DE LA VIE FRANCAISE EN AMERIQUE. (CN/0708-1510). **2544**

REPERTOIRE DES ASSOCIATIONS. (CN/0318-4595). **707**

REPERTOIRE DES GEOGRAPHES FRANCAIS PARIS. (FR/1147-9558). **Adv Mgr:** Gerard Jolly. **2574**

REPERTOIRE DES LABORATOIRES D'ESSAIS ET D'ANALYSES DU QUEBEC .... (CN/0229-9534). **1993**

REPERTOIRE DES MEMBRES / ORDRE DES AGRONOMES DU QUEBEC. (CN/0822-9430). **125**

REPERTOIRE MENSUEL DU MINISTERE DE L'INTERIEUR. (FR/0240-4729). **4680**

REPERTORIEN ZUR DEUTSCHEN LITERATURGESCHICHTE. (GW/0486-4166). **3429**

REPERTORIO CHIMICO ITALIANO. (IT). **991**

REPLICA (MIAMI, FLA. 1970). (US/0146-2008). **2492**

REPORT & REVIEW / WORLD FEDERATION OF ADVERTISERS, WFA. (BE). **765**

REPORT - AUDUBON SOCIETY OF RHODE ISLAND. (US/0274-502X). **2203**

REPORT - CENTRAL SOYA, INC., FORT WAYNE IND. (US/0411-4094). **2627**

REPORT - FEDERAL BAR ASSOCIATION. SECTION OF TAXATION. (US/0742-5317). **3037**

REPORT FROM THE INSTITUTE FOR PHILOSOPHY & PUBLIC POLICY. (US/1051-6972). **5215**

REPORT / NATIONAL COUNCIL ON FAMILY RELATIONS. (US/0278-6168). **2285**

REPORT OF INVESTIGATIONS / NEW WORLD RESEARCH. (US). **280**

REPORT OF RESEARCH - DIVISION OF FOOD RESEARCH. (AT). **2355**

REPORT OF THE COMMITTEE ON FOREIGN AFFAIRS FOR THE ... SESSION OF THE ... NATIONAL ASSEMBLY APPOINTED ON ... / REPUBLIC OF ZAMBIA. (ZA). **4533**

REPORT OF THE COMMITTEE ON INFECTIOUS DISEASES. (US). **Adv Mgr Tel** (708)981-7902. **3715**

REPORT ON BUSINESS, CANADA COMPANY HANDBOOK. (CN/0847-2831). **707**

REPORT ON PUBLICATIONS OF THE SCHOOL OF INTERNATIONAL AFFAIRS AND THE REGIONAL INSTITUTES. (US/0084-8921). **4533**

REPORT ON THE BACKGROUND, CURRENT PROGRAMMES AND PLANNED DEVELOPMENT OF THE BANGLADESH INSTITUTE OF DEVELOPMENT STUDIES, A. (BG). **5215**

REPORT ON THE ... PDCP SURVEY OF BUSINESS PERFORMANCE FOR MANILA, A. (PH). **707**

REPORT ON THE SWAZILAND POPULATION CENSUS. (SQ). **4562**

REPORT - ROYAL GREENWICH OBSERVATORY. (UK/0308-3322). **399**

REPORT / THE OHIO GENEALOGICAL SOCIETY. (US). **2470**

REPORTER. (US). **Adv Mgr:** Leslie Knight. **5698**

REPORTER ARGUS. (US). **5739**

REPORTER (FOND DU LAC, WIS.), THE. (US/0749-7172). **5770**

REPORTER - NEW JERSEY ASSOCIATION FOR HEALTH, PHYSICAL EDUCATION AND RECREATION, THE. (US/0034-477X). **4799**

REPORTER - ONTARIO ENGLISH CATHOLIC TEACHERS' ASSOCIATION. (CN/0384-5648). **Adv Mgr:** Barbara Nair. **1903**

REPORTER. ROCKLEDGE EDITION, THE. (US/0740-4166). **5651**

REPORTER, THE. (US). **5753**

REPORTS OF FAMILY LAW. (CN/0317-4859). **3122**

REPORTS ON MATHEMATICAL PHYSICS. (PL/0034-4877). **4419**

REPOSITORY (CANTON, OHIO), THE. (US/0745-7545). **Adv Mgr:** Michael Miller. **5730**

REPRESENTATIONS

Advertising Accepted Index

REPRESENTATIONS (BERKELEY, CALIF.). (US/0734-6018). **2853**

REPRESENTATIVE, FOX LAKE, WISCONSIN, THE. (US/8755-4011). **Adv Mgr:** Betty Van Sistine. **5770**

REPRESENTATIVE RESEARCH IN SOCIAL PSYCHOLOGY. (US/0034-4907). **4615**

REPRODUCER, THE. (US/0742-9088). **2777**

REPRODUCTION. (UK/0034-4958). **4569**

REPRODUCTION, FERTILITY, AND DEVELOPMENT. (AT/1031-3613). **586**

REPROGRAF, DER. (GW). **4376**

REPTILE & AMPHIBIAN MAGAZINE. (US/1059-0668). **5596**

REPUBLICAN (DANVILLE, IND.). (US). **5667**

REPUBLICAN JOURNAL (BELFAST, ME.). (US/0034-5075). **5685**

REPULESI SZAKIRODALMI TAJEKOZTATO. (HU/0231-3928). **33**

RERIC HOLDINGS LIST : / AN OCCASIONAL PUBLICATION OF RERIC. (TH). **1955**

RES PUBLICA. (PL/0860-4592). **2492**

RES PUBLICA (CLAREMONT). (US/0092-671X). **4683**

RESCUE-EMS MAGAZINE. (US/1073-9998). **Adv Mgr:** Al Frazier. **4799**

RESCUE NEWS. (UK/0950-5830). **280**

RESEARCH & DEVELOPMENT. TELEPHONE DIRECTORY. (US). **1929**

RESEARCH EVALUATION. (UK/0958-2029). **5146**

RESEARCH FOR DEVELOPMENT : THE JOURNAL OF THE NIGERIAN INSTITUTE OF SOCIAL & ECONOMIC RESEARCH. (NR/0189-0085). **1517**

RESEARCH (GOTTINGEN, GERMANY). (GW/0722-6349). **244**

RESEARCH IN AFRICAN LITERATURES. (US/0034-5210). **3429**

RESEARCH IN EDUCATION (MANCHESTER). (UK/0034-5237). **1779**

RESEARCH IN NONDESTRUCTIVE EVALUATION. (US/0934-9847). **1994**

RESEARCH IN NURSING & HEALTH. (US/0160-6891). **3868**

RESEARCH IN PHENOMENOLOGY. (US/0085-5553). **Adv Mgr:** J. Camlin, **Tel** (908)872-1441. **4358**

RESEARCH IN SCIENCE EDUCATION. (AT/0157-244X). **1779**

RESEARCH IN THE TEACHING OF ENGLISH. (US/0034-527X). **1903**

RESEARCH IN VETERINARY SCIENCE. (UK/0034-5288). **5520**

RESEARCH INTO HIGHER EDUCATION ABSTRACTS. (UK/0034-5326). **1797**

RESEARCH INTO PRACTICE DIGEST, THE. (US/0885-2324). **1904**

RESEARCH NEWS - FAMILY HISTORY WORLD. (US/0884-3716). **2470**

RESEARCH NOTES (LIVINGSTONE MUSEUM). (ZA). **4095**

RESEARCH ON LANGUAGE AND SOCIAL INTERACTION. (CN/0835-1813). **3315**

RESEARCH PAPER - CENTRE FOR URBAN AND COMMUNITY STUDIES. UNIVERSITY OF TORONTO. (CN/0316-0068). **2833**

RESEARCH PAPER (UNIVERSITY OF WISCONSIN--MADISON. TENURE CENTER). (US/0090-7170). **1517**

RESEARCH PAPERS (CENTRE FOR THE STUDY OF ISLAM AND CHRISTIAN-MUSLIM RELATIONS (BIRMINGHAM, WEST MIDLANDS, ENGLAND)). (UK/0260-3772). **5044**

RESEARCH, POLICY AND PLANNING : THE JOURNAL OF THE SOCIAL SERVICES RESEARCH GROUP. (UK/0264-519X). **5215**

RESEARCH REPORT SERIES - BROCK UNIVERSITY. DEPARTMENT OF GEOLOGICAL SCIENCES. STUDIES IN PALEOZOIC STRATIGRAPHIC INVESTIGATIONS. (CN/0824-3247). **1395**

RESEARCH REPORTS / DEPARTMENT OF ANTHROPOLOGY, UNIVERSITY OF MASSACHUSETTS, AMHERST. (US). **244**

RESEARCH REVIEW - INSTITUTE OF AFRICAN STUDIES. (GH/0020-2703). **2643**

RESEARCH STRATEGIES. (US/0734-3310). **3245**

RESEAU - ASSOCIATION DES ENSEIGNANTES ET DES ENSEIGNANTS FRANCO-ONTARIENS. (CN/1192-2796). **1779**

RESERVE FORCES ALMANAC. (US/0363-860X). **4055**

RESIDENT AND STAFF PHYSICIAN. (US/0034-5555). **3634**

RESIDENTIAL TREATMENT FOR CHILDREN & YOUTH. (US/0886-571X). **5306**

RESOLUTION. (US/1050-3978). **1201**

RESOLUTION TRUST REPORTER. (US/1045-0130). **Adv Mgr:** Jim Hollander. **809**

RESORT DEVELOPMENT & OPERATION. (US/8750-1252). **2809**

RESORTS & GREAT HOTELS. (US/0897-5833). **Adv Mgr:** Don Fritzen, **Tel** (805)687-1422. **2809**

RESOURCE. (CN/0832-9354). **4992**

RESOURCE (ATLANTA, GA.). (US/0887-1752). **2892**

RESOURCE DIRECTORY (TORONTO). (CN/0822-2479). **2903**

RESOURCE (DON MILLS, ONT.). (CN/0828-9522). **4846**

RESOURCE MANAGEMENT AND OPTIMIZATION. (UK/0142-2391). **2204**

RESOURCE RECYCLING / NORTH AMERICA'S RECYCLING JOURNAL. (US/0744-4710). **Adv Mgr:** Rick Downing, **Tel** (216)255-1454. **2242**

RESOURCE RECYCLING'S PLASTICS RECYCLING UPDATE. (US/1052-4908). **Adv Mgr:** R. Downing, **Tel** (216)255-1454. **4460**

RESOURCE REVIEW (ANCHORAGE, ALASKA). (US/8755-1918). **2204**

RESOURCE RICHMOND. (AT/1031-3796). **5777**

RESOURCE SHARING & INFORMATION NETWORKS. (US/0737-7797). **3245**

RESOURCES AND ENERGY. (NE/0165-0572). **1517**

RESOURCES FOR AMERICAN LITERARY STUDY. (US/0048-7384). **3351**

RESOURCES FOR FEMINIST RESEARCH : RFR. (CN/0707-8412). **5565**

RESOURCES IN AGING. (US/0892-0818). **5306**

RESOURCES IN EDUCATION. ANNUAL CUMULATION. (US/0197-9973). **1797**

RESOURCES POLICY. (UK/0301-4207). **2204**

RESPIRATION. (SZ/0025-7931). **3951**

RESPIRATORY CARE. (US/0020-1324). **3951**

RESPIRATORY DISEASES RESEARCH CENTER. (KE). **3951**

RESPIRATORY SYSTEM. (UK/0142-8780). **3951**

RESPONSA MERIDIANA. (SA/0486-5588). **3039**

RESPONSABILITA CIVILE E PREVIDENZA. (IT). **3039**

RESPONSE (NEW YORK. 1967). (US/0034-5709). **5052**

RESPONSE (SOLANA BEACH, CALIF.). (US/0732-2933). **4799**

RESPONSIVE COMMUNITY, THE. (US/1053-0754). **Adv Mgr:** Jun Lee, **Tel** (202)994-7907. **5256**

RESPONSIVE PHILANTHROPY. (US/1065-0008). **Adv Mgr:** Beth Daley. **4339**

RESTAURANT BUSINESS. (US/0097-8043). **5072**

RESTAURANT HOSPITALITY. (US/0147-9989). **5072**

RESTAURANTS & INSTITUTIONS (CHICAGO, ILL.). (US/0273-5520). **5073**

RESTAURATOR. (DK/0034-5806). **2483**

RESTAURO & CITTA. (IT). **308**

RESTO DEL CARLINO. (IT). **5805**

RESTORATION & MANAGEMENT NOTES. (US/0733-0707). **2204**

RESTORATION (KNOXVILLE). (US/0162-9905). **3429**

RESTORATION QUARTERLY. (US/0486-5642). **4993**

RESTORATION (TUCSON, ARIZ.). (US/0736-5934). **252**

RESTORATION WITNESS. (US/0191-0167). **Adv Mgr:** G. Booz, **Tel** (816)252-5010. **4993**

RESTORICA. (SA). **626**

RESUMENES ANALITICOS EN EDUCACION. (CL/0716-0151). **1797**

RESUMES DE JURISPRUDENCE PENALE DU QUEBEC. (CN/0822-7616). **3083**

RESURGENCE. (UK/0034-5970). **4494**

RESUSCITATION. (IE/0300-9572). **3951**

RETAIL DIRECTORY. (UK). **956**

RETAIL NEWS WEST. (US/8750-4286). **957**

RETAIL TENANT DIRECTORY. (US/0887-0470). **957**

RETAIL WORLD. (AT). **957**

RETAILER AND MARKETING NEWS. (US/0192-9151). **936**

RETHINKING MARXISM. (US/0893-5696). **1594**

RETINA (PHILADELPHIA, PA.). (US/0275-004X). **3878**

RETIRED MILITARY ALMANAC. (US/0149-7197). **4055**

RETIRED OFFICER (ALEXANDRIA, VA.), THE. (US/0034-6160). **4055**

RETIRED OFFICER MAGAZINE (ALEXANDRIA, VA.), THE. (US/1061-3102). **Adv Mgr:** Hacker. **4055**

RETIREMENT INDUSTRY JOURNAL, THE. (AT). **5181**

RETIREMENT LIFESTYLE. (CN/0844-5982). **Adv Mgr:** Eric, **Tel** (604)275-7971. **5181**

RETREADER'S JOURNAL. (US/0482-430X). **707**

RETURN TO THE SOURCE. (US/0743-1244). **4993**

REUMATOLOGO : PUBBLICA IL BOLLETTINO DELLA SOCIETA ITALIANA DI REUMATOLOGIA, IL. (IT/0391-8963). **3806**

REUNIONS (MILWAUKEE, WIS.). (US/1046-5235). **Adv Mgr:** Lynn Ryan, **Tel** same as publisher. **2470**

REVELSTOKE TIMES. (CN). **5794**

REVIEW AND EXPOSITOR (BERNE). (US/0034-6373). **Adv Mgr:** Joel Drinkard Jr. **5067**

REVIEW (CHARLOTTESVILLE). (US/0190-3233). **3351**

REVIEW : LATIN AMERICAN LITERATURE AND ARTS. (US). **Adv Mgr:** Editor, **Tel** (212)249-8950. **329**

REVIEW OF AFRICAN POLITICAL ECONOMY. (UK/0305-6244). **1581**

REVIEW OF BLACK POLITICAL ECONOMY, THE. (US/0034-6446). **1517**

REVIEW OF BOOKS ON THE BOOK OF MORMON. (US/1050-7930). **4993**

REVIEW OF CONTEMPORARY FICTION. (US/0276-0045). **3351**

REVIEW OF ECONOMIC STUDIES, THE. (UK/0034-6527). **1517**

REVIEW OF EDUCATION, THE. (US/0098-5597). **1779**

REVIEW OF ENGLISH STUDIES. (UK/0034-6551). **3429**

REVIEW OF EXISTENTIAL PSYCHOLOGY AND PSYCHIATRY (1972). (US/0361-1531). **Adv Mgr:** J. Camlin, **Tel** (908)872-1441. **4615**

REVIEW OF INTERNATIONAL BROADCASTING. (US/0149-9971). **1138**

REVIEW OF INTERNATIONAL STUDIES. (UK/0260-2105). **4534**

REVIEW OF LITIGATION, THE. (US/0734-4015). **3040**

REVIEW OF METAPHYSICS, THE. (US/0034-6632). **4359**

REVIEW OF NATIONAL LITERATURES. (US/0034-6640). **3351**

REVIEW OF POLITICS, THE. (US/0034-6705). **4494**

REVIEW OF PROGRESS IN COLORATION AND RELATED TOPICS. (UK/0557-9325). **1029**

REVIEW OF PUBLIC PERSONNEL ADMINISTRATION. (US/0734-371X). **Adv Mgr:** P Whitheld, **Tel** (803)777-8157. **4705**

REVIEW OF RADICAL POLITICAL ECONOMICS, THE. (US/0486-6134). **1594**

REVIEW OF RELIGIOUS RESEARCH. (US/0034-673X). **4993**

REVIEW OF THE RIVER PLATE, THE. (AG/0325-7487). **1581**

REVIEW (SHIDLER, OKLA.), THE. (US/8750-8508). **Adv Mgr:** Brenda Lawless, **Tel** (918)793-3841. **5732**

REVIEW, THE. (UK/0034-6349). **2892**

REVIEW (WINSLOW, WASH.), THE. (US/1053-2889). **Adv Mgr:** Chris Allen. **5762**

REVIEWS IN AMERICAN HISTORY. (US/0048-7511). **2757**

REVIEWS IN ANTHROPOLOGY. (US/0093-8157). **244**

REVIEWS IN CHEMICAL ENGINEERING. (UK/0264-8431). **2017**

REVIEWS IN CLINICAL GERONTOLOGY. (UK/0959-2598). **3754**

REVIEWS IN INORGANIC CHEMISTRY (LONDON, ENGLAND). (UK/0193-4929). **1037**

REVIEWS JOURNAL. (AT/0157-3705). **3351**

Advertising Accepted Index — REVISTA

REVISION (CAMBRIDGE, MASS.). (US/0275-6935). **3429**

REVISTA AEREA. (US/0279-4519). **Adv Mgr:** M.Z. Dicker. **33**

REVISTA AMRIGS. (BL/0102-2105). **3634**

REVISTA ANDINA. (PE). **Adv Mgr:** same as editor. **5216**

REVISTA ANTIOGUENA DE ECONOMIA Y DESARROLLO. (CK/0121-0017). **1518**

REVISTA ARGENTINA DE CIRUGIA. (AG). **3973**

REVISTA ARGENTINA DE LINGUISTICA. (AG/0326-6400). **3315**

REVISTA ARGENTINA DE MICROBIOLOGIA. (AG/0325-7541). **569**

REVISTA ARGENTINA NUCLEAR. (AG/0326-7873). **2158**

REVISTA ASTRONOMICA. (AG/0374-4272). **399**

REVISTA AVICULTURA. (CU/0257-9162). **220**

REVISTA BIBLICA. (AG/0034-7078). **5019**

REVISTA BRASILEIRA DE ANESTESIOLOGIA. (BL/0034-7094). **3684**

REVISTA BRASILEIRA DE ENTOMOLOGIA. (BL/0085-5626). **5613**

REVISTA BRASILEIRA DE ESTUDOS POLITICOS. (BL/0034-7191). **4494**

REVISTA BRASILEIRA DE FARMACIA. (BL/0370-372X). **4328**

REVISTA BRASILEIRA DE FISICA. (BL/0374-4922). **4420**

REVISTA BRASILEIRA DE GENETICA. (BL/0100-8455). **551**

REVISTA BRASILEIRA DE MEDICINA. (BL/0034-7264). **3634**

REVISTA BRASILEIRA DE PATOLOGIA CLINICA. (BL/0034-7302). **Adv Mgr:** Cristina Maria Regis Morgado. **3897**

REVISTA CHILENA DE ENTOMOLOGIA. (CL/0034-740X). **5613**

REVISTA CHILENA DE PEDIATRIA. (CL/0370-4106). **3911**

REVISTA COLOMBIANA DE EDUCACION (BOGOTA, COLOMBIA : 1978). (CK). **1780**

REVISTA COLOMBIANA DE OBSTETRICIA Y GINECOLOGIA. (CK/0034-7434). **3768**

REVISTA COSTARRICENSE DE CIENCIAS MEDICAS. (CR/0253-2948). **3635**

REVISTA CRITICA DE CIENCIAS SOCIAIS. (PO). **5216**

REVISTA CUBANA DE HIGIENE Y EPIDEMIOLOGIA. (CU/0253-1151). **3736**

REVISTA DA ACADEMIA SOBRALENSE DE ESTUDOS E LETRAS. (BL). **2757**

REVISTA DA BIBLIOTECA NACIONAL (LISBOA). (PO/0251-1711). **3260**

REVISTA DA SOCIEDADE BRASILEIRA DE MEDICINA TROPICAL. (BL/0037-8682). **3986**

REVISTA DE ADMINISTRACAO DE EMPRESAS. (BL/0034-7590). **885**

REVISTA DE ADMINISTRACAO MUNICIPAL. (BL). **4683**

REVISTA DE ADMINISTRACION PUBLICA. (MX/0482-5209). **4683**

REVISTA DE ARQUEOLOGIA (RIO DE JANEIRO, BRAZIL). (BL). **280**

REVISTA DE ASCOLBI / ASOCIATION COLOMBIANA DE BIBLIOTECOLOGOS Y DOCUMENTALISTAS, ASCOLBI. (CK/0121-0203). **3246**

REVISTA DE BIOLOGIA MARINA. (CL/0080-2115). **557**

REVISTA DE CHIRURGIE ONCOLOGIE, RADIOLOGIE, O.R.L., OFTALMOLOGIE, STOMATOLOGIE. ONCOLOGIA. (RM/0377-4724). **3823**

REVISTA DE CHIRURGIE, ONCOLOGIE, RADIOLOGIE, O.R.L. OFTALMOLOGIE, STOMATOLOGIE. SERIA : STOMATOLOGIE. (RM/0377-7871). **3635**

REVISTA DE CIENCIA POLITICA (SANTIAGO). (CL/0716-1417). **Adv Mgr Tel** 011 56 2 2224516 Ext. 2581. **4494**

REVISTA DE CIENCIAS SOCIALES (SAN JOSE). (CR/0482-5276). **5216**

REVISTA DE CRITICA LITERARIA LATINOAMERICANA. (PE/0252-8843). **3351**

REVISTA DE DIAGNOSTICO BIOLOGICO. (SP/0034-7973). **Adv Mgr:** Juan Jose Serrano Cadamia. **471**

REVISTA DE DIREITO CIVIL. (BL). **3091**

REVISTA DE DIREITO DO TRABALHO (SAO PAULO). (BL/0102-8774). **3153**

REVISTA DE DIVULGACAO CULTURAL / FURB. (BL). **2757**

REVISTA DE EDUCACION. (CL). **1780**

REVISTA DE ESTUDIOS HISPANICOS (RIO PIEDRAS, P.R.). (PR/0378-7974). **3315**

REVISTA DE ESTUDIOS HISPANICOS (UNIVERSITY, AL.). (US/0034-818X). **3315**

REVISTA DE ESTUDIOS REGIONALES. (SP/0213-7585). **5216**

REVISTA DE FARMACOLOGIA CLINICA Y EXPERIMENTAL. (SP). **4328**

REVISTA DE FILOSOFIA. (MX/0185-3481). **4359**

REVISTA DE FOMENTO SOCIAL. (SP/0015-6043). **5216**

REVISTA DE HISTORIA DE ROSARIO. (AG/0556-5995). **2758**

REVISTA DE INTERPRETACION BIBLICA LATINOAMERICANA : RIBLA. (CR/1018-5763). **5019**

REVISTA DE INVESTIGACION CLINICA. (MX/0034-8376). **3801**

REVISTA DE INVESTIGACIONES MARINAS. (CU/0252-1962). **557**

REVISTA DE LA ASOCIACION CASTELLANA DE APARATO DIGESTIVO. (SP/0213-1463). **3801**

REVISTA DE LA ASOCIACION ESPANOLA DE NEUROPSIQUIATRIA. (SP/0211-5735). **3935**

REVISTA DE LA ASOCIACION ODONTOLOGICA ARGENTINA. (AG/0004-4881). **1334**

REVISTA DE LA EDUCACION SUPERIOR. (MX). **1846**

REVISTA DE LA FACULTAD DE DERECHO DE MEXICO. (MX/0185-1810). **3041**

REVISTA DE LA FEDERACION MEXICANA DE QUIMICOS Y TECNICOS DEL CUERO. (MX). **3185**

REVISTA DE LA IMAGEN Y EL SONIDO: EIKONOS. (SP). **4376**

REVISTA DE LA MEDICINA TRADICIONAL CHINA. (SP/1130-4405). **3635**

REVISTA DE LA SANIDAD DE LAS FUERZAS POLICIALES. (PE/0254-3435). **3635**

REVISTA DE LA SOCIEDAD ESPANOLA DE QUIMICA CLINICA. (SP/0213-8514). **1018**

REVISTA DE LLENGUA I DRET. (SP/0212-5056). **1079**

REVISTA DE MEDICINA DE LA UNIVERSIDAD DE NAVARRA. (SP/0556-6177). **3973**

REVISTA DE MEDICINA VETERINARIA. (AG/0325-6391). **5520**

REVISTA DE METALURGIA (MADRID). (SP/0034-8570). **4018**

REVISTA DE MICROBIOLOGIA. (BL/0001-3714). **569**

REVISTA DE MUSICA LATINOAMERICANA. (US/0163-0350). **4149**

REVISTA DE NEFROLOGIA, DIALISIS Y TRANSPLANTE : PUBLICACION CONJUNTA DE LA ASOCIACION REGIONAL DE DIALISIS Y TRASPLANTES RENALES DE CAPITAL FEDERAL Y PROVINCIA DE BUENOS AIRES Y LA SOCIEDAD ARGENTINA DE NEFROLOGIA. (AG/0326-3428). **Adv Mgr:** Nelida Pecoraro, **Tel** 01 825 0023. **3635**

REVISTA DE NEURO-PSIQUIATRIA. (PE/0034-8597). **Adv Mgr:** Jose C. Mariategui, **Tel** 51 14 907207. **3845**

REVISTA DE OBRAS PUBLICAS. (SP/0034-8619). **Adv Mgr:** Monica Baeza. **2030**

REVISTA DE PEDIATRIA PREVENTIVA E SOCIALE. NIPIOLOGIA. (IT/0392-4416). **3911**

REVISTA DE PROCESSO. (BL). **3091**

REVISTA DE PSICOLOGIA GENERAL Y APLICADA. (SP/0373-2002). **Adv Mgr:** Palonea Rivero. **4616**

REVISTA DE SOLDADURA. (SP/0048-7759). **4027**

REVISTA DEL ARCHIVO HISTORICO DEL GUAYAS. (EC). **2483**

REVISTA DEL INSTITUTO DE ESTUDIOS HISTORICO-MARITIMOS DEL PERU. (PE). **2758**

REVISTA DEL PENSAMIENTO CENTROAMERICANO. (NQ/0378-3340). **2512**

REVISTA DO COLEGIO BRASILEIRO DE CIRURGIOES. (BL/0100-6991). **3973**

REVISTA DO HOSPITAL DAS CLINICAS. (BL/0041-8781). **Adv Mgr Tel** 282-2811 R.4235. **3635**

REVISTA DO INSTITUTO DE MEDICINA TROPICAL DE SAO PAULO. (BL/0036-4665). **3986**

REVISTA DO IRB / INSTITUTO DE RESSEGUROS DO BRASIL. (BL/0019-0446). **2892**

REVISTA ESPANOLA DE ALERGOLOGIA E INMUNOLOGIA CLINICA : ORGANO OFICIAL DE LA SOCIEDAD ESPANOLA DE ALERGOLOGIA E INMUNOLOGIA CLINICA. (SP/0214-1477). **3676**

REVISTA ESPANOLA DE ANESTESIOLOGIA Y REANIMACION. (SP/0034-9356). **3684**

REVISTA ESPANOLA DE CARDIOLOGIA. (SP/0300-8932). **3710**

REVISTA ESPANOLA DE CIENCIA Y TECNOLOGIA DE ALIMENTOS / EDITADA POR EL CONSEJO SUPERIOR DE INVESTIGACIONES CIENTIFICAS. (SP/1131-799X). **2356**

REVISTA ESPANOLA DE ENFERMEDADES DIGESTIVAS. (SP/1130-0108). **3747**

REVISTA ESPANOLA DE GERIATRIA Y GERONTOLOGIA. (SP/0211-139X). **3755**

REVISTA ESPANOLA DE LECHERIA. (SP/0300-5550). **Adv Mgr:** Luis Rincon, **Tel** 011 34 1 759 57 15. **198**

REVISTA ESPANOLA DE MICROPALEONTOLOGIA. (SP/0556-655X). **4230**

REVISTA EUROPEA DE ESTUDIOS LATINOAMERICANOS Y DEL CARIBE. EUROPEAN REVIEW OF LATIN AMERICAN AND CARIBBEAN STUDIES. (NE/0924-0608). **5216**

REVISTA FARMACEUTICA (SAN JUAN, P.R.). (PR/1070-5015). **Adv Mgr:** Janet James, **Tel** (809)759-9794. **4328**

REVISTA IBEROAMERICANA. (US/0034-9631). **3430**

REVISTA IBEROAMERICANA DE FERTILIDAD Y REPRODUCCION HUMANA. (SP). **3636**

REVISTA INTERAMERICANA DE BIBLIOTECOLOGIA / UNIVERSIDAD DE ANTIOQUIA, ESCUELA INTERAMERICANA DE BIBLIOTECOLOGIA. (CK/0120-0976). **3246**

REVISTA INTERAMERICANA DE PLANIFICACION. (US/0185-1861). **2834**

REVISTA INTERAMERICANA DE PSICOLOGIA. (US/0034-9690). **4616**

REVISTA INTERNACIONAL DE METODOS NUMERICOS PARA CALCULO Y DISEfNO EN INGENIERIA. (SP/0213-1315). **1994**

REVISTA JAVERIANA (BOGOTA). (CK/0120-3088). **Adv Mgr:** Estela de Alaran. **2552**

REVISTA JURIDICA DE LA UNIVERSIDAD DE PUERTO RICO. (PR/0886-2516). **Adv Mgr:** same as editor. **3042**

REVISTA JURIDICA DEL PERU. (PE). **3042**

REVISTA LATINOAMERICANA DE ESTUDIOS EDUCATIVOS. (MX/0185-1284). **1780**

REVISTA LATINOAMERICANA DE ESTUDIOS ETNOLINGUISTICOS. (PE). **3316**

REVISTA LATINOAMERICANA DE MICROBIOLOGIA (1970). (MX/0187-4640). **569**

REVISTA LATINOAMERICANA DE PATOLOGIA. (VE/0300-9068). **3897**

REVISTA LATINOAMERICANA DE PSICOLOGIA. (CK/0120-0534). **4616**

REVISTA LATINOAMERICANA DE QUIMICA. (MX/0370-5943). **1047**

REVISTA MARITIMA BRASILEIRA. (BL/0034-9860). **4182**

REVISTA MEDICA DE CHILE. (CL/0034-9887). **3801**

REVISTA MEDICA DE COSTA RICA. (CR/0034-9909). **3636**

REVISTA MEDICA DE PANAMA. (PN/0379-1629). **3636**

REVISTA MEXICANA DE ANALISIS DE LA CONDUCTA. (MX). **4616**

REVISTA MEXICANA DE ANESTESIOLOGIA Y REANIMACION. (MX/0185-1012). **Adv Mgr:** Yolanda Celis. **3684**

REVISTA MEXICANA DE MICOLOGIA. (MX/0187-3180). **576**

REVISTA MEXICANA DE PEDIATRIA. (MX/0035-0052). **3911**

REVISTA MEXICANA DE POLITICA EXTERIOR. (MX/0185-6022). **2758**

REVISTA MUSICAL CHILENA. (CL/0716-2790). **Adv Mgr Tel** 11 56 2 6713326. **4150**

REVISTA ODONTOLOGICA ECUATORIANA. (EC/0484-8020). **1334**

REVISTA ORL. (AG/0326-7067). **3891**

REVISTA PAULISTA DE HOSPITAIS. (BL/0048-7864). **3636**

REVISTA PERUANA DE DERECHO DE LA EMPRESA. (PE). **3042**

REVISTA PORTUGUESA DE CIENCIAS VETERINARIAS. (PO/0035-0389). **5520**

REVISTA — Advertising Accepted Index

REVISTA PORTUGUESA DE ESTOMATOLOGIA E CIRURGIA MAXILO-FACIAL. (PO/0035-0397). **1334**

REVISTA PORTUGUESA DE FILOSOFIA. (PO/0870-5283). **4359**

REVISTA PORTUGUESA DE QUIMICA. (PO/0035-0419). **991**

REVISTA/REVIEW INTERAMERICANA. (PR/0360-7917). **5216**

REVISTA ROL DE ENFERMERIA. (SP/0210-5020). **Adv Mgr:** Tomas Lavandeira, **Tel** (93)200.80.33. **3868**

REVISTA TELEGRAFICA ELECTRONICA. (AG/0035-0516). **2079**

REVISTA TEOLOGICA LIMENSE. (PE). **5035**

REVISTA UNIVERSIDAD EAFIT. (CK/0120-033X). **4683**

REVISTA URUGUAYA DE ESTUDIOS INTERNACIONALES. (UY). **4534**

REVISTI DI ARCHEOLOGIA CRISTIANA. (VC/0035-6042). **281**

REVMEDIA LONDON. (UK/0955-8500). **Adv Mgr:** C A McKenney. **1183**

REVOLUCIONES POR MINUTO : RPM. (SP). **4150**

REVOLUTION (STATEN ISLAND, N.Y.). (US/1059-0927). **Adv Mgr:** Roe, **Tel** (800)331-6534. **3868**

REVOLUTIONARY RUSSIA. (UK/0954-6545). **Adv Mgr:** Anne Kidson. **2706**

REVTECH. (US). **Adv Mgr:** Betty. **1202**

REVUE A. C. C. S. (CN/0226-5931). **Adv Mgr:** Martine Leroux. **3792**

REVUE ACEDA. (CN/0382-7976). **1884**

REVUE ADMINISTRATIVE, LA. (FR/0035-0672). **4683**

REVUE ARBIDO. (SZ/0258-0772). **3246**

REVUE BELGE DE DROIT INTERNATIONAL. (BE/0035-0788). **3135**

REVUE BELGE DE MEDECINE DENTAIRE 1984. (BE/0775-0293). **1334**

REVUE BELGE DE PHILOLOGIE ET D'HISTOIRE. (BE/0035-0818). **3316**

REVUE BELGE D'HISTOIRE CONTEMPORAINE. (BE). **2706**

REVUE BELGE DU FEU. (BE/0771-4033). **2292**

REVUE COMMERCE (MONTREAL. 1975). (CN/0380-9811). **850**

REVUE D'ALLEMAGNE. (FR/0035-0974). **2706**

REVUE DE DROIT CANONIQUE. (FR/0556-7378). **4993**

REVUE DE DROIT COMMERCIAL BELGE. (BE). **3102**

REVUE DE DROIT INTERNATIONAL ET DE DROIT COMPARE. (BE/0775-4663). **3135**

REVUE DE DROIT (SHERBROOKE). (CN/0317-9656). **3043**

REVUE DE GEOGRAPHIE ALPINE. (FR/0035-1121). **2575**

REVUE DE GEOMORPHOLOGIE DYNAMIQUE. (FR/0556-7432). **2575**

REVUE DE LA BANQUE, LA. (BE). **810**

REVUE DE LA CERAMIQUE ET DU VERRE, LA. (FR/0294-202X). **Adv Mgr:** same as editor. **2593**

REVUE DE LA CERAMIQUE, LA. (FR). **2593**

REVUE DE LA CINEMATHEQUE, LA. (CN/0843-6827). **4077**

REVUE DE LA SOCIETE HISTORIQUE DU MADAWASKA (1982). (CN/0820-0793). **2758**

REVUE DE LA SOUDURE (BRUXELLES). (BE/0035-127X). **4027**

REVUE DE L'ACLA. (CN/1193-1493). **3316**

REVUE DE L'ALIMENTATION ANIMALE. (FR/0242-6595). **220**

REVUE DE L'ART. (FR/0035-1326). **363**

REVUE DE LARYNGOLOGIE, D'OTOLOGIE ET DE RHINOLOGIE. (FR/0035-1334). **Adv Mgr:** V. Lombard. **3891**

REVUE DE L'ATEQ, LA. (CN/0835-0868). **1870**

REVUE DE L'EDUCATION PHYSIQUE. (BE). **1858**

REVUE DE L'ENERGIE. (FR/0303-240X). **Adv Mgr:** Epstein. **1956**

REVUE DE L'INSTITUT DE SOCIOLOGIE. (BE/0771-6796). **5217**

REVUE DE L'IRES, LA. (FR/1145-1378). **1518**

REVUE DE LITTERATURE COMPAREE. (FR/0035-1466). **3430**

REVUE DE L'OCEAN INDIEN, ECONOMIE. (MG). **1518**

REVUE DE MATHEMATIQUES SPECIALES. (FR/0035-1504). **3531**

REVUE DE MEDECINE INTERNE, LA. (FR/0248-8663). **3801**

REVUE DE MEDECINE VETERINAIRE. (FR/0035-1555). **5520**

REVUE DE METALLURGIE (PARIS). (FR/0035-1563). **4018**

REVUE DE NEUROPSYCHOLOGIE / SOCIETE DE NEUROPSYCHOLOGIE DE LANGUE FRANCAISE. (FR/1155-4452). **3845**

REVUE DE PALEOBIOLOGIE. (SZ). **4230**

REVUE DE THEOLOGIE ET DE PHILOSOPHIE. (SZ/0035-1784). **4359**

REVUE DE TOURISME. (SZ/0251-3102). **Adv Mgr:** Evelyn Moeckli. **5490**

REVUE DES DEUX MONDES (1982). (FR/0750-9278). **3430**

REVUE DES ECHANGES DE L'ASSOCIATION FRANCOPHONE INTERNATIONALE DES DIRECTEURS D'ETABLISSEMENTS SCOLAIRES, LA. (CN/0822-8329). **1780**

REVUE DES ETUDES ARMENIENNES (PARIS). (FR/0080-2549). **2663**

REVUE DES ETUDES AUGUSTINIENNES. (FR/0035-2012). **4993**

REVUE DES ETUDES BYZANTINES. (FR/0373-5729). **2706**

REVUE DES ETUDES GEORGIENNES ET CAUCASIENNES. (FR/0373-1537). **3316**

REVUE DES ETUDES JUIVES. (FR/0484-8616). **5052**

REVUE DES LABORATOIRES D'ESSAIS, LA. (FR/0296-5321). **Adv Mgr:** Johane Cagna, **Tel** 33 1 45085009. **5148**

REVUE DES LANGUES ROMANES. (FR/0223-3711). **3316**

REVUE DES LIVRES POUR ENFANTS, LA. (FR). **3351**

REVUE DES QUESTIONS SCIENTIFIQUES. (BE/0035-2160). **5148**

REVUE DES REVUES, LA. (FR/0980-2797). **424**

REVUE DES SCIENCES RELIGIEUSES. (FR/0035-2217). **4993**

REVUE DES SCIENCES SOCIALES DE LA FRANCE DE L'EST. (FR/0336-1578). **5217**

REVUE D'ETUDES PALESTINIENNES. (LE/0252-8290). **4534**

REVUE D'HISTOIRE DE LA COTE-NORD. (CN/0828-9468). **2758**

REVUE D'HISTOIRE DE L'AMERIQUE FRANCAISE. (CN/0035-2357). **2758**

REVUE D'HISTOIRE DIPLOMATIQUE. (FR/0035-2365). **4534**

REVUE D'HISTOIRE DU BAS ST-LAURENT. (CN/0381-8454). **2758**

REVUE D'HISTOIRE DU THEATRE. (FR/0035-2373). **5368**

REVUE D'HISTOIRE ECCLESIASTIQUE. (BE/0035-2381). **5013**

REVUE D'HISTOIRE MAGHREBINE. (TI). **2643**

REVUE D'INTEGRATION EUROPEENNE. (CN/0703-6337). **4494**

REVUE DIPLOMATIQUE DE L'OCEAN INDIEN. (MG). **4534**

REVUE D'ODONTO-STOMATOLOGIE DU MIDI DE LA FRANCE. (FR/0035-2470). **1334**

REVUE DU BARREAU, LA. (CN/0383-669X). **3043**

REVUE DU BOIS ET DE SES APPLICATIONS. (FR/0373-5133). **2404**

REVUE DU JOUET, LA. (FR/0035-2594). **2585**

REVUE DU MARCHE COMMUN ET DE L'UNION EUROPEENNE. (FR). **Adv Mgr:** Epstein. **1582**

REVUE DU NORD. (FR/0035-2624). **2706**

REVUE DU NOTARIAT, LA. (CN/0035-2632). **3043**

REVUE DU PALAIS DE LA DECOUVERTE. (FR/0339-7521). **Adv Mgr:** same as editor. **5148**

REVUE DU PRACTICIEN, LA. (FR/0035-2640). **3636**

REVUE DU RHUMATISME ET DES MALADIES OSTEO-ARTICULAIRES. (FR/0035-2659). **3806**

REVUE DU TRAVAIL. (BE). **5217**

REVUE ECONOMIQUE. (FR/0035-2764). **1595**

REVUE ECONOMIQUE - CHAMBRE DE COMMERCE DE LAVAL. (CN/0825-0707). **1518**

REVUE ECONOMIQUE ET SOCIALE (LAUSANNE). (SZ/0035-2772). **1595**

REVUE FIDUCIAIRE. INFORMATION HEBDOMADAIRES. (FR). **3043**

REVUE FRANCAISE DE GEOTECHNIQUE. (FR/0181-0529). **1395**

REVUE FRANCAISE DE GYNECOLOGIE ET D'OBSTETRIQUE. (FR/0035-290X). **3768**

REVUE FRANCAISE DE SCIENCE POLITIQUE. (FR/0035-2950). **4495**

REVUE FRANCAISE DE SERVICE SOCIAL, LA. (FR). **5306**

REVUE FRANCAISE D'ETUDES AMERICAINES. (FR/0397-7870). **2759**

REVUE FRANCAISE D'OENOLOGIE. (FR/0395-899X). **2370**

REVUE FRANCAISE DU MARKETING. (FR/0035-3051). **936**

REVUE FRANCOPHONE DE LA DEFICIENCE INTELLECTUELLE. (CN/0847-5733). **Adv Mgr:** H. Gascon, **Tel** (418)228-2051. **3845**

REVUE FRONTENAC. (CN/0715-9994). **3431**

REVUE GENERAL NUCLEAIRE. (FR/0335-5004). **1956**

REVUE GENERALE DE L'ELECTRICITE. (FR/0035-3116). **2079**

REVUE GENERALE DU FROID, LA. (FR/0035-3205). **2608**

REVUE GEOGRAPHIQUE DE L'EST. (FR/0035-3213). **2575**

REVUE HISTORIQUE DES ARMEES. (FR/0035-3299). **4056**

REVUE INTERNATIONALE DE CRIMINOLOGIE ET DE POLICE TECHNIQUE. (FR/0035-3329). **3175**

REVUE INTERNATIONALE DE DROIT COMPARE. (FR/0035-3337). **3135**

REVUE INTERNATIONALE DE PARODONTIE & DENTISTERIE RESTAURATRICE. (FR/0721-0078). **1335**

REVUE INTERNATIONALE DE PHILOSOPHIE. (BE/0048-8143). **4359**

REVUE INTERNATIONALE DES SERVICES DE SANTE DES FORCES ARMEES : ORGANE DU COMITE INTERNATIONAL DE MEDECINE ETUDE PHARMACIE MILITAIRES. (BE/0259-8582). **3636**

REVUE INTERNATIONALE P M E. (BE). **708**

REVUE INTERNATIONALE POUR L'ENSEIGNEMENT COMMERCIAL. INTERNATIONAL REVIEW FOR BUSINESS EDUCATION. INTERNATIONAL ZEITSCHRIFT FUR KAUFMANNISCHES BILDUNGSWESEN. RIVISTA INTERNAZIONALE PER LA CULTURA COMMERCIALE. REVISTA INTERNACIONAL PARA LA ENSENANZA COMMERCIAL. (SZ/0035-354X). **708**

REVUE JURIDIQUE DU RWANDA. IGAZETI ISOBANURA AMATEGEKO MU RWANDA. (NR). **3043**

REVUE JURIDIQUE DU ZAIRE; DROIT ECRIT ET DROIT COUTUMIER. (CG). **3043**

REVUE JURIDIQUE THEMIS (1970). (CN/0556-7963). **Adv Mgr:** M. Joubert. **3044**

REVUE JURIDIQUE THEMIS (1970). (CN/0556-7963). **Adv Mgr:** M. Joubert. **3044**

REVUE LAITIERE FRANCAISE. (FR/0035-3590). **220**

REVUE MARITIME 1990, LA. (FR/1146-2132). **4182**

REVUE MEDICALE DE BRUXELLES. (BE/0035-3639). **3636**

REVUE MEDICALE DE LA SUISSE ROMANDE. (SZ/0035-3655). **3637**

REVUE MUNICIPALE (MONTREAL). (CN/0035-3728). **4684**

REVUE MUSICALE DE SUISSE ROMANDE. (SZ). **4150**

REVUE NOIRE. (FR/1157-4127). **330**

REVUE NOUVELLE, LA. (BE/0035-3809). **2522**

REVUE OFFICIELLE DE LA SOCIETE FRANCAISE D'ORL ET DE PATHOLOGIE CERVICO-FACIALE. (FR/1155-1087). **3891**

REVUE PHILOSOPHIQUE DE LOUVAIN. (BE/0035-3841). **4360**

REVUE POLYTECHNIQUE. (SZ/0374-4256). **5148**

REVUE PRATIQUE DU FROID ET DU CONDITIONNEMENT DE L'AIR. (FR/0370-6699). **2608**

REVUE QUEBECOISE DE DROIT INTERNATIONAL. (CN/0828-9999). **3135**

REVUE QUEBECOISE DE LINGUISTIQUE THEORIQUE ET APPLIQUEE. (CN/0835-3581). **3317**

REVUE ROUMAINE DE MATHEMATIQUES PURES ET APPLIQUEES. (RM/0035-3965). **3531**

REVUE SCHWEIZ. (SZ). **708**

REVUE SUISSE D'AGRICULTURE. (SZ/0375-1325). **130**

REVUE SUISSE DE VITICULTURE, ARBORICULTURE, HORTICULTURE. (SZ/0375-1430). **2430**

REVUE SYNDICALE SUISSE. (SZ/0035-421X). **1708**

REVUE TECHNIQUE MACHINISME AGRICOLE. (FR/0223-0135). **5424**

REVUE THOMISTE. (FR/0035-4295). **4994**

REVUE VERVIETOISE D'HISTOIRE NATURELLE. (BE/0375-1465). **4171**

REVUE VOILE QUEBEC, LA. (CN/0820-4969). **595**

REVUE VOYAGEUR, LA. (CN/0824-1309). **5490**

REXBURG STANDARD/JOURNAL, THE. (US). **Adv Mgr:** Garph Lords. **5657**

REYNOLDS COUNTY COURIER (ELLINGTON, MO.). (US). **5704**

RFD (WOLF CREEK). (US/0149-709X). **2796**

RFE. REVISTA FORESTAL ESPANOLA. (SP/1130-958X). **Adv Mgr:** Angel Garcia-Rodrigo, **Tel** 532-3875. **2394**

RG. (CN/0831-375X). **2796**

RHETORIC REVIEW. (US/0735-0198). **Adv Mgr:** Ed. **3317**

RHETORIC SOCIETY QUARTERLY. (US/0277-3945). **Adv Mgr:** same as editor. **3317**

RHETORICA. (US/0734-8584). **3317**

RHETORIK. (GW/0720-5775). **3317**

RHEUMA (MADRID). (SP/0211-7274). **3637**

RHINOLOGY. (NE/0300-0729). **3891**

RHODE ISLAND BAR JOURNAL. (US/0556-8595). **Adv Mgr:** Beth Bailey. **3044**

RHODE ISLAND HISTORY. (US/0035-4619). **2759**

RHODE ISLAND MEDICINE. (US/1061-222X). **Adv Mgr:** James P.Wilson. **3637**

RHODE ISLAND MONTHLY. (US/1041-1380). **Adv Mgr:** K. Schultz, **Tel** (401)421-2552. **5490**

RHODE ISLAND RESOURCES. (US/0035-4635). **130**

RHODESIANS WORLDWIDE. (UK). **Adv Mgr:** Mrs. J. Hagelthorn. **2500**

RHODODENDRON, THE. (AT/0485-0637). **2430**

RHONDA WHITE-WARNER'S TIDBITS. (US/1041-9799). **2492**

RIA INTERNATIONAL, REVUE DES INDUSTRIES D'ART EXPORT. (FR). **363**

RIABILITAZIONE E APPRENDIMENTO. (IT/0393-7518). **4382**

RIBOSOMES & TRANSLATION. (UK/0952-0414). **551**

RICARDA HUCH, STUDIEN ZU IHREM LEBEN UND WERK. (GW). **3431**

RICARDIAN. (UK/0048-8267). **5236**

RICE ABSTRACTS. (UK/0141-0164). **1012**

RICE WORLD. (US). **Adv Mgr:** same as editor. **185**

RICE WORLD & SOYBEAN NEWS, THE. (US/0738-5943). **Adv Mgr:** John Hart, **Tel** (318)497-0007. **185**

RICERCA E INNOVAZIONE. (IT). **5148**

RICERCHE PEDAGOGICHE. (IT). **1781**

RICHARDSON FAMILY RESEARCHER AND HISTORICAL NEWS. (US/0147-2488). **2470**

RICHFIELD REAPER, THE. (US/0746-6730). **Adv Mgr Tel** same as publisher. **5757**

RICHMOND POST. (US). **5639**

RICHMOND SURROUNDINGS. (US/1064-1785). **Adv Mgr:** R. Malkman. **4854**

RICHTON DISPATCH, THE. (US). **5701**

RIDER. (US/0095-1625). **4082**

RIDGEFIELD PRESS. (US). **Adv Mgr:** Jim DeFillipo. **5646**

RIFLE. (US/0162-3583). **4915**

RIFLEMAN. (UK). **4915**

RIFORMA MEDICA. (IT/0035-5259). **3637**

RIGHT HERE. (US/0895-3139). **2492**

RIGHT OF WAY. (US/0035-5275). **4846**

RIGHTING WORDS. (US/0892-581X). **2924**

RIGHTS (NEW YORK, N.Y. 1953). (US/0035-5283). **Adv Mgr:** Barbara Kross, **Tel** (212)673-2040. **4512**

RILA BULLETIN. (US/0146-8685). **3247**

RILEVAZIONE DEI PREZZI ALL INGROSSO : ASSOMET. (IT). **4018**

RIMBEY RECORD. (CN). **5794**

RINSHO KENSA. (JA/0485-1420). **3637**

RINSHO SHINKEIGAKU. (JA/0009-918X). **3845**

RIPLEY BEE (RIPLEY, OHIO : 1887). (US). **5730**

RIPON FORUM. (US/0035-5526). **4495**

RIRON TO HOHO. (JA/0913-1442). **Adv Mgr:** Fumiaki Ojima. **5256**

RISALAT AL-MAKTABAH. (JO). **3247**

RISALAT MAHAD AL-TURATH AL-ILMI AL-ARABI. (SY). **5148**

RISC USER. (UK/0966-1913). **1202**

RISING STAR (RISING STAR, TEX. : 1965). (US). **5754**

RISK & BENEFITS MANAGEMENT. (US/0893-2654). **2892**

RISK (LONDON. 1987). (UK/0952-8776). **810**

RISK MANAGEMENT. (US/0035-5593). **2892**

RISTORAZIONE COLLETTIVA. (IT/1120-6039). **2356**

RITCHIE GAZETTE AND THE CAIRO STANDARD. (US). **Adv Mgr:** Judy Newbrough, **Tel** (304)643-2221. **5765**

RITMO (MEXICO CITY, MEXICO). (MX). **4150**

RIVER CITIES. (US/0744-7418). **1299**

RIVER CITY (MEMPHIS, TENN.). (US/1048-129X). **3431**

RIVER CITY REVIEW (LOUISVILLE, KY.). (US/0734-497X). **3431**

RIVER FALLS JOURNAL (RIVER FALLS, WIS. : 1872). (US). **Adv Mgr:** Paul Charbonneau. **5770**

RIVER REPORTER, THE. (US). **Adv Mgr:** Laurie Stuart. **5720**

RIVER RUNNER MAGAZINE. (US). **595**

RIVER STYX. (US/0149-8851). **3431**

RIVERDALE PRESS, THE. (US). **Adv Mgr:** Phyllis Steele. **5720**

RIVERINE GRAZIER, THE. (AT). **5777**

RIVERLANDER. (AT). **5539**

RIVERTON RANGER, THE. (US). **Adv Mgr:** Anita Ellis. **5772**

RIVISTA AERONAUTICA. (IT). **33**

RIVISTA BIBLICA. (IT/0035-5798). **5019**

RIVISTA DEI COMBUSTIBILI. (IT/0370-5463). **4277**

RIVISTA DELLA GUARDIA DI FINANZA. (IT/0035-595X). **4056**

RIVISTA DELLA SOCIETA ITALIANA DI SCIENZA DELL'ALIMENTAZIONE, LA. (IT/0391-4887). **2356**

RIVISTA DELLA STAZIONE SPERIMENTALE DEL VETRO. (IT). **5148**

RIVISTA DELLE SOCIETA. (IT/0035-6018). **3103**

RIVISTA DELLE TECNOLOGIE TESSILI. (IT/0394-5413). **5355**

RIVISTA DELL'INFERMIERE. (IT). **Adv Mgr:** Dott Dalla, **Tel** 06-86207165. **3792**

RIVISTA D'EUROPA. (IT). **2707**

RIVISTA DI ARCHEOLOGIA. (IT/0392-0895). **281**

RIVISTA DI BIOLOGIA. (IT/0035-6050). **472**

RIVISTA DI DIRITTO INDUSTRIALE. (IT/0035-614X). **1308**

RIVISTA DI DIRITTO INTERNAZIONALE. (IT/0035-6158). **3135**

RIVISTA DI ESTETICA. (IT/0035-6212). **4360**

RIVISTA DI GRAMMATICA GENERATIVA. (IT). **3317**

RIVISTA DI INFORMATICA. (IT/0390-668X). **1202**

RIVISTA DI MATEMATICA PER LE SCIENZE ECONOMICHE E SOCIALI / ASSOCIAZIONE PER LA MATEMATICA APPLICATA ALLE SCIENZE ECONOMICHE E SOCIALI. (IT). **3532**

RIVISTA DI MATEMATICA PURA ED APPLICATA. (IT). **3532**

RIVISTA DI MECCANICA. (IT/0035-6301). **2128**

RIVISTA DI NEUROBIOLOGIA. (IT/0035-6336). **3845**

RIVISTA DI NEURORADIOLOGIA. (IT). **Adv Mgr:** M. Leonardi. **3845**

RIVISTA DI OSTETRICIA GINECOLOGIA PRATICA E MEDICINA PERINATALE. (IT/0391-0970). **3768**

RIVISTA DI PARASSITOLOGIA. (IT/0035-6387). **569**

RIVISTA DI PATOLOGIA NERVOSA E MENTALE. (IT/0035-6433). **3936**

RIVISTA DI PATOLOGIA VEGETALE. (IT/0035-6441). **526**

RIVISTA DI POLITICA ECONOMICA. (IT/0391-6170). **1595**

RIVISTA DI PSICHIATRIA. (IT/0035-6484). **Adv Mgr:** Dott Dalla, **Tel** 06-86207165. **3936**

RIVISTA DI PSICOLOGIA DELL'ARTE. (IT). **330**

RIVISTA DI STORIA DELLA STORIOGRAFIA MODERNA. (IT). **2628**

RIVISTA DI STUDI ITALIANI. (CN/0821-3216). **3431**

RIVISTA DI TEOLOGIA MORALE. (IT). **4994**

RIVISTA INTERNAZIONALE DI FILOSOFIA DEL DIRITTO. (IT/0035-6727). **3044**

RIVISTA ITALIANA DEGLI ODONTOTECNICI. (IT/0391-5611). **1335**

RIVISTA ITALIANA DELLA SALDATURA. (IT/0035-6794). **4027**

RIVISTA ITALIANA DELLE SOSTANZE GRASSE. (IT/0035-6808). **Adv Mgr:** L. Cariboni. **1029**

RIVISTA ITALIANA DI CHIRURGIA MAXILLO-FACCIALE. (IT/1120-7558). **Adv Mgr:** Uff. Starpa Calderini, **Tel** 051 492211. **3974**

RIVISTA ITALIANA DI CHIRURGIA PLASTICA. (IT/0391-2221). **3974**

RIVISTA ITALIANA DI DIRITTO DEL LAVORO. (IT/0393-2494). **3154**

RIVISTA ITALIANA DI DIRITTO E PROCEDURA PENALE. (IT). **3109**

RIVISTA ITALIANA DI GEOTECNICA. (IT/0557-1405). **1395**

RIVISTA ITALIANA DI OTORINOLARINGOLOGIA, AUDIOLOGIA E FONIATRIA. (IT/0392-1360). **3891**

RIVISTA MILITARE. (IT/0035-6980). **4056**

RIVISTA SPERIMENTALE DI FRENIATRIA E MEDICINA LEGALE DELLE ALIENAZIONI MENTALI. (IT/0370-7261). **3936**

RIVISTA STORICA ITALIANA. (IT/0035-7073). **2707**

RIVISTA SVIZZERA SICUREZZA LAVORO. (SZ). **2869**

RIVISTA TRIMESTRALE DI DIRITTO E PROCEDURA CIVILE. (IT). **3045**

RIVISTA TRIMESTRALE DI DIRITTO PUBBLICO. (IT/0557-1464). **3094**

RIV'ON LE-MEHKAR HEVRATI. (IS/0334-4762). **5217**

RLA, REVISTA DE LINGUISTICA TEORICA Y APLICADA. (CL/0033-698X). **3317**

RMCLAS REVIEW. (US/0749-9728). **2552**

RN. (US/0033-7021). **3868**

RN IDAHO. (US/0192-298X). **3868**

RNT. (BL). **1163**

ROAD AND TRACK. (US/0035-7189). **5424**

ROAD LAW AND ROAD LAW REPORTS. (UK/1352-0717). **Adv Mgr:** Mrs. Curtis. **5443**

ROAD TRAFFIC LAW BULLETIN. (UK/0265-7937). **5443**

ROAD WAY, THE. (UK). **5391**

ROADRUNNER REFUNDER. (US/0196-383X). **1299**

ROADS & BRIDGES (DES PLAINS, ILL.). (US/8750-9229). **2030**

ROANOKE BEACON, THE. (US). **Adv Mgr:** Sherrie Phelps. **5724**

ROANOKE TIMES & WORLD-NEWS. (US). **5759**

ROANOKER, THE. (US/0274-9734). **2544**

ROBB REPORT, THE. (US/0279-1447). **2492**

ROBERT FROST REVIEW, THE. (US/1062-6999). **Adv Mgr:** Jeff Glassen, **Tel** (803)323-4566. **3431**

ROBERTS REGISTOR. (US/8756-7741). **2470**

ROBESON COUNTY REGISTER, THE. (US/0888-3807). **2470**

ROBOT. (SA). **5444**

ROBOT (TOKYO, 1971). (JA/0387-1940). **Adv Mgr:** Keiichi Takai. **1216**

ROBOTICA. (UK/0263-5747). **1216**

ROBOTICS WORLD DIRECTORY. (US). **1216**

ROCAS Y MINERALES. (SP/0378-3316). **2150**

ROCHAS DE QUALIDADE. (BL). **2150**

ROCHESTER — Advertising Accepted Index

ROCHESTER BUSINESS JOURNAL (ROCHESTER, N.Y. : 1987). (US/0896-3274). **708**

ROCHESTER GOLF WEEK & SPORTS LEDGER. (US). **4915**

ROCHESTER SENTINEL (ROCHESTER, IND. : DAILY : 1961). (US). **Adv Mgr:** Arthur Hoffman. **5667**

ROCK & GEM. (US/0048-8453). **1444**

ROCK & ICE. (US/0885-5722). **Adv Mgr:** Wendy Levison. **4878**

ROCK CREEK CURRENT, THE. (US/1062-2721). **Adv Mgr:** Simone Diggs. **5647**

ROCK MECHANICS. SUPPLEMENT. (AU/0080-3375). **1994**

ROCKCASTLE REMINISCENCE. (US). **2628**

ROCKDALE CITIZEN, THE. (US/1050-1401). **Adv Mgr:** Jane Patterson. **5654**

ROCKET (SEATTLE, WA). (US). **Adv Mgr:** Courtney Miller, **Tel** (206)728-7625. **4151**

ROCKFORD LABOR NEWS (MICROFICHE). (US). **1708**

ROCKFORD MAGAZINE. (US/0899-9414). **Adv Mgr:** G. Kazuk. **1299**

ROCKIN' 50'S. (US/0738-7717). **4151**

ROCKLAND COUNTY TIMES, THE. (US). **5720**

ROCKS AND MINERALS. (US/0035-7529). **1444**

ROCKY FORD DAILY GAZETTE, THE. (US). **5644**

ROCKY HILL POST, THE. (US). **5646**

ROCKY MOUNTAIN BAPTIST. (US/0485-294X). **5067**

ROCKY MOUNTAIN CAVING. (US/8756-033X). **Adv Mgr:** Robert Phillips, **Tel** (303)798-0663. **1410**

ROCKY MOUNTAIN GARDENER. (US/1054-9552). **2430**

ROCKY MOUNTAIN HIGH TECHNOLOGY DIRECTORY. (US/0883-8046). **5148**

ROCKY MOUNTAIN LIVESTOCK JOURNAL. (US/1072-5636). **220**

ROCKY MOUNTAIN PAY DIRT. (US/0886-0912). **2150**

ROCKY MOUNTAIN PETROLEUM DIRECTORY. (US/0278-9299). **4277**

ROCKY MOUNTAIN REVIEW OF LANGUAGE AND LITERATURE. (US/0361-1299). **3431**

ROCZNIK HYDROLOGICZNY WOD PODZIEMNYCH. (PL). **1417**

ROCZNIK HYDROLOGICZNY WOD POWIERZCHNIOWYCH. DORECZE ORDY I RZEKI PRZYMORA MIEDZY ODRA I WISLA. (PL). **1417**

ROCZNIK HYDROLOGICZNY WOD POWIERZCHNIOWYCH. DORZECZE WISLY I RZEKI PRZYMORZA NA WSCHOD OD WISLY. (PL). **1417**

ROCZNIK METEOROLOGICZNY. (PL). **1434**

ROCZNIK METEOROLOGICZNY STACJI ARCTOWSKIEGO. (PL). **1434**

ROCZNIK METEOROLOGICZNY STACJI HORNSUNDU. (PL). **1434**

ROCZNIKI AKADEMII MEDYCZNEJ W BIAYMSTOKU. (PL/0067-6489). **3637**

ROCZNIKI AKADEMII ROLNICZEJ W POZNANIU - WYDZIA ZOOTECHNICZNY. (PL). **220**

ROD SERLING'S THE TWILIGHT ZONE MAGAZINE. (US/0279-6090). **3431**

RODDY REPORT. BOULDER COUNTY. (US). **Adv Mgr:** G Roddy. **4847**

RODDY REPORT. DALLAS COUNTY, THE. (US/0889-1842). **Adv Mgr:** G Roddy. **4847**

RODDY REPORT. TARRANT COUNTY, THE. (US). **Adv Mgr:** G Roddy. **4847**

RODEO NEWS. (US/0149-6425). **Adv Mgr:** Tom Vietzke. **4915**

RODEO TIMES /NATIONAL HIGH SCHOOL RODEO ASSOCIATION. (US). **4915**

RODNA GRUDA SLOVENIJA. (XV/0557-2282). **2272**

RODO KAGAKU. (JA/0035-7774). **1708**

ROELAND PARK SUN, THE. (US). **Adv Mgr:** Peggy Flora. **5678**

ROEPER REVIEW. (US/0278-3193). **Adv Mgr:** Vicki Rossbach. **1885**

ROGUE DIGGER. (US/0048-8534). **2470**

ROHSTOFFPREISINDEX. (GW). **Adv Mgr:** G. Mantwill. **1519**

ROLL CALL (WASHINGTON, D.C.). (US/0035-788X). **4495**

ROLLER SKATING BUSINESS. (US/0191-7617). **4854**

ROLLERCOASTER! MAGAZINE. (US/0896-7261). **4865**

ROLLING STONE. (US/0035-791X). **4151**

ROMA. (II). **2628**

ROMANCE PHILOLOGY. (US/0035-8002). **3318**

ROMANCE QUARTERLY. (US/0883-1157). **3318**

ROMANCE STUDIES : A JOURNAL OF THE UNIVERSITY OF WALES. (UK/0263-9904). **1846**

ROMANIAN ECONOMIC NEWS. (RM). **1582**

ROMANIAN FOREIGN TRADE. (RM). **1519**

ROMANIC REVIEW. (US/0035-8118). **3431**

ROMANISTISCHE ZEITSCHRIFT FUER LITERATURGESCHICHTE. (GW/0343-379X). **3318**

ROMANTIC TIMES. (US/0747-3370). **5074**

ROMANTIST, THE. (US/0161-682X). **3432**

RONTGENPRAXIS (STUTTGART). (GW/0035-7820). **3946**

ROOF. (US). **2834**

ROOFER MAGAZINE, THE. (US/0279-4616). **Adv Mgr:** G. Abrell. **3487**

ROOFING, CLADDING & INSULATION. (UK). **626**

ROOM OF ONE'S OWN. (CN/0316-1609). **3432**

ROOT CELLAR PRESERVES. (US/0748-6251). **2470**

ROOTS DIGEST. (US/8755-8343). **2471**

ROSEBUD COUNTY PRESS. (US/8750-2097). **Adv Mgr:** Pearl Ryckman, **Tel** (406)356-2149. **5706**

ROSEVILLE PRESS-TRIBUNE. (US). **5639**

ROSSFORD RECORD JOURNAL. (US). **Adv Mgr:** Matt Welch, **Tel** (419)874-4491. **5730**

ROSTER ISSUE OF THE NORTH CAROLINA MEDICAL JOURNAL. (US). **Adv Mgr:** Don French, **Tel** (919)467-8515. **3637**

ROSTRUM, THE. (US). **1121**

ROSWELL DAILY RECORD, THE. (US). **Adv Mgr:** J Pettit, **Tel** (505)622-7710. **5713**

ROTA-GENE. (US/0730-5168). **2471**

ROTARIAN, THE. (US/0035-838X). **Adv Mgr Tel** (708)866-3195. **5236**

ROTKIN REVIEW, THE. (US/0883-735X). **4376**

ROTOR (ALEXANDRIA, VA.). (US/0897-831X). **Adv Mgr:** M. Beames. **34**

ROTOR & WING INTERNATIONAL. (US/0191-6408). **34**

ROTOR ROSTER. (US). **34**

ROTORCRAFT (CLINTON, LA.). (US/1041-2735). **34**

ROTUNDA (TORONTO). (CN/0035-8495). **Adv Mgr:** John Jory, **Tel** (416)447-7999. **4096**

ROUGH NOTES (INDIANAPOLIS). (US/0035-8525). **2893**

ROUGHNECK, THE. (CN/0048-864X). **Adv Mgr:** J. Graham. **4277**

ROUND BOBBIN. (US/1076-058X). **5185**

ROUND ROCK LEADER. (US/0164-9124). **Adv Mgr:** Bobby Seijerman, **Tel** (512)255-5827. **5754**

ROUND TABLE, THE. (UK/0035-8533). **4534**

ROUND UP (UNIVERSITY PARK, N.M.). (US/0744-5555). **5713**

ROUNDUP (MINNEAPOLIS, MINN.), THE. (US/0485-5140). **1314**

ROUNDUP RECORD-TRIBUNE & WINNETT TIMES. (US/0890-9660). **Adv Mgr Tel** (406)323-1105. **5706**

ROUTES ET TRANSPORTS. (CN/0319-3780). **5392**

ROW (PETALUMA, CALIF.). (US/1043-2345). **4915**

ROYAL AIR FORCE COLLEGE JOURNAL, THE. (UK/0035-8606). **Adv Mgr:** same as editor. **1094**

ROYAL AIR FORCE YEARBOOK. (UK/0954-092X). **34**

ROYAL ASTRONOMICAL SOCIETY OF NEW ZEALAND VARIABLE STAR MONTHLY CIRCULARS M. (NZ). **Adv Mgr:** Audrey Walsh. **399**

ROYAL COLLEGE OF MUSIC MAGAZINE. (UK). **4151**

ROYAL ENGINEERS JOURNAL, THE. (UK/0035-8878). **1995**

ROYAL LIFE SAVING SOCIETY LIFESAVER UK, THE. (UK). **4800**

ROYAL MILITARY POLICE JOURNAL. (UK). **3183**

ROYALTY DIGEST. (UK/0967-5744). **2522**

RPCV WRITERS & READERS. (US/1062-4694). **3432**

RRT. (CN/0831-2478). **3952**

RS. RIFIUTI SOLIDI. (IT/0394-5391). **2242**

RSA CALLING. (SA). **2643**

RSA JOURNAL. (UK). **5149**

RSG. RICHTING SPORT-GERICHT. (NE/0926-7638). **1904**

RSGB AMATEUR RADIO CALL BOOK. (UK). **Adv Mgr:** Victor Brand, **Tel** 0953 898422. **1138**

RTTY JOURNAL. (US/0033-7161). **1163**

RTW REVIEW. (US/0887-3003). **Adv Mgr:** Jim Windler. **1087**

RUBBER & PLASTICS NEWS. (US/0300-6123). **5077**

RUBBER BOARD BULLETIN. (II/0537-0507). **5077**

RUBBER CHEMISTRY AND TECHNOLOGY. (US/0035-9475). **5077**

RUBBER INDIA. (II/0035-9491). **5077**

RUBBER NEWS. (II/0035-9513). **Adv Mgr:** Lalitha Eswaran. **5077**

RUBBERSTAMPMADNESS. (US/0746-7672). **Adv Mgr:** Susan Shumway. **2777**

RUG HOOKING. (US/1045-4373). **Adv Mgr:** Diana Marcum, **Tel** (717)238-6401. **375**

RUG NEWS. (US/0278-9795). **5355**

RUGBY (NEW YORK). (US/0162-1297). **4915**

RUIMTE VOOR CULTUUR. (BE). **2853**

RULES FOR INBOARD, INBOARD ENDURANCE, UNLIMITED RACING. (US/0272-3468). **595**

RULES FOR STOCK OUTBOARD, PRO OUTBOARD, MODIFIED OUTBOARD. (US/0272-3476). **595**

RUMANIAN REVIEW. (RM/0035-8088). **3352**

RUN. (US/0741-4285). **1272**

RUNDFUNK UND FERNSEHEN. (GW/0035-9874). **1138**

RUNDFUNKTECHNISCHE MITTEILUNGEN. (GW/0035-9890). **1138**

RUNDSCHAU FUER FLEISCHUNTERSUCHUNG UND LEBENSMITTELUBERWACHUNG. (GW/0341-0668). **2356**

RUNGH (VANCOUVER). (CN/1188-9950). **330**

RUNNER'S GAZETTE. (US/0199-6983). **4916**

RUNNING. (UK). **4916**

RUNNING JOURNAL. (US/0892-5038). **Adv Mgr:** M.L. Day, **Tel** same as publisher. **4916**

RUNNING TIMES. (US/0147-2968). **4916**

RUNZHEIMER REPORTS ON TRANSPORTATION. (US/0730-8655). **5392**

RURAL AFRICANA. (US/0085-5839). **1582**

RURAL BUILDER. (US/0888-3025). **627**

RURAL BUSINESS MAGAZINE. (AT/1031-3079). **131**

RURAL COUNCILLOR, THE. (CN/0036-0007). **131**

RURAL DELIVERY. (CN/0703-7724). **2544**

RURAL DEVELOPMENT ABSTRACTS / [PREPARED BY THE COMMONWEALTH BUREAU OF AGRICULTURAL ECONOMICS]. (UK/0140-4768). **2840**

RURAL EDUCATOR (FORT COLLINS), THE. (US/0273-446X). **1781**

RURAL ELECTRIFICATION MAGAZINE (1987). (US/1054-0474). **Adv Mgr:** Andrea Smith, **Tel** (202)857-9581. **1543**

RURAL HERITAGE. (US/0889-2970). **252**

RURAL HISTORY. (UK/0956-7933). **5256**

RURAL LIVING (A&N ELECTRIC COOPERATIVE ED.). (US/1054-4801). **Adv Mgr:** Kathy Lake. **131**

RURAL MONTANA. (US/0199-6401). **131**

RURAL NEW ENGLAND MAGAZINE. (US). **Adv Mgr:** same as editor. **131**

RURAL TELECOMMUNICATIONS. (US/0744-2548). **Adv Mgr:** Dave Bolton, **Tel** (202)298-2331. **1163**

RURAL VOICE (BLYTH). (CN/0700-5385). **Adv Mgr:** Gerry Fortune. **131**

Advertising Accepted Index — SAN

RUSH COUNTY NEWS (LA CROSSE, KAN.). (US). **Adv Mgr:** Duane Engel, **Tel** (913)222-2555. **5678**

RUSI JOURNAL / ROYAL UNITED SERVICES INSTITUTE FOR DEFENCE STUDIES, THE. (UK). **4056**

RUSISTIKA : THE RUSSIAN JOURNAL OF THE ASSOCIATION FOR LANGUAGE LEARNING. (UK/0957-1760). **Adv Mgr:** Glenda Simmonds, **Tel** 0788 546443. **3318**

RUSSELL'S OFFICIAL NATIONAL MOTOR COACH GUIDE. (US/0036-0171). **5392**

RUSSIA AND HER NEIGHBORS. (US/1066-0127). **5217**

RUSSIAN ECONOMIC TRENDS. (UK/0967-0793). **1583**

RUSSIAN FAR EAST UPDATE. (US/1061-5679). **1519**

RUSSIAN HISTORY (PITTSBURGH). (US/0094-288X). **2707**

RUSSIAN LINGUISTICS. (NE/0304-3487). **3318**

RUSSIAN ORTHODOX JOURNAL, THE. (US/0036-0317). **5040**

RUSSIAN PETROLEUM INVESTOR. (US/1072-155X). **Adv Mgr:** Moira Brennan. **4277**

RUSSIAN REVIEW (STANFORD), THE. (US/0036-0341). **2708**

RUSSISTIK. (GW/0935-8072). **3318**

RUSSKAIA ZHIZN. (US). **Adv Mgr:** Anna Zeltzer. **5639**

RUSSKII GOLOS (NEW YORK, N.Y.). (US/0036-0406). **2272**

RUTGERS ART REVIEW, THE. (US/0194-049X). **363**

RUTGERS COMPUTER & TECHNOLOGY LAW JOURNAL. (US/0735-8938). **1202**

RUTGERS LAW JOURNAL. (US/0277-318X). **3045**

RUTGERS LAW REVIEW. (US/0036-0465). **Adv Mgr:** Brenda McDonough. **3045**

RUTLAND DAILY HERALD (RUTLAND, VT. : 1885). (US). **5757**

RUTLAND RECORD. (UK/0260-3322). **2708**

RV TRADE DIGEST (CHICAGO, ILL. 1981). (US/0745-0389). **5392**

RX ET CETERA. (US/0744-7736). **4328**

S.A.A.D. DIGEST. (UK/0049-1160). **1335**

S.A. ARGIEFBLAD. (SA/1012-2796). **2483**

S.A.M. ADVANCED MANAGEMENT JOURNAL (1984). (US/0749-7075). **885**

S & B REPORT. (US). **2903**

S D; SPACE DESIGN. (JA/0563-0991). **308**

S. KLEIN DIRECTORY OF COMPUTER GRAPHICS SUPPLIERS, THE. (US/0732-9199). **1235**

S.S.A. NEWSLETTER : A PUBLICATION OF THE SUDAN STUDIES ASSOCIATION. (US/0899-3785). **2500**

SA JOURNAL OF FOOD SCIENCE AND NUTRITION, THE. (SA/1013-3666). **Adv Mgr:** J. Sharland, **Tel** same as publisher. **4199**

SA POLICE. (AT). **3176**

SAA NEWSLETTER. (US/0091-5971). **2483**

SAAGVERKEN. (SW). **2404**

SAARLANDISCHE KREBSDOKUMENTATION. (GW). **3823**

SABINE INDEX (MANY, LA. : 1879). (US/0739-0017). **5684**

SABORD, LE. (CN/0822-2908). **Adv Mgr:** L.A. Gervais. **330**

SABRETACHE. (AT/0486-8013). **4056**

SAC NEWS MONTHLY. (US). **Adv Mgr Tel** (800)825-3722. **5684**

SACRAMENTAL LIFE. (US/0899-2061). **Adv Mgr:** T. Crouch, **Tel** (216)535-8656. **4995**

SACRAMENTO BEE, THE. (US/0890-5738). **Adv Mgr:** Lisa Leonard, **Tel** (916)321-1476. **5639**

SACRAMENTO (JONSSON COMMUNICATIONS CORPORATION). (US/0747-8712). **2544**

SACRAMENTO MEDICINE. (US/0886-2826). **Adv Mgr:** Chris Albeson, **Tel** (916)452-2671. **3638**

SACRAMENTO NEWS & REVIEW. (US/1065-3287). **Adv Mgr:** D. Gillen, **Tel** (916)737-1234. **2544**

SACRAMENTO OBSERVER, THE. (US/0036-2212). **Adv Mgr:** Joe Stinson. **5639**

SACRED ART JOURNAL. (US/0741-9163). **364**

SACRED MUSIC. (US/0036-2255). **5035**

SADA AL-USBU. (BA). **2508**

SADCC DIRECTORY AND TRADERS GUIDE. (RH). **708**

SADDLE AND BRIDLE. (US/0036-2271). **Adv Mgr:** Chris Thompson. **2802**

SADDLE HORSE REPORT. (US/0161-7842). **2802**

SAFARI (TUCSON, ARIZ.). (US/0199-5316). **Adv Mgr:** Eric Hubbell, **Tel** (602)620-1220. **4916**

SAFE JOURNAL. (US/0191-6319). **34**

SAFETY & HEALTH. (US/0891-1797). **2869**

SAFETY AND HEALTH AT WORK : ILO-CIS BULLETIN. (SZ/1010-7053). **2872**

SAFETY & HEALTH PRACTITIONER. (UK/0958-479X). **4800**

SAFETY MANAGEMENT. (SA/0377-8592). **2869**

SAFETY MANAGEMENT LONDON. (UK). **Adv Mgr:** Bill Bateman, **Tel** 0676-23435. **4801**

SAG HARBOR EXPRESS. (US). **5720**

SAGETRIEB. (US/0735-4665). **3470**

SAGGI NEUROPSICOLOGIA INFANTILE PSICOPEDAGOGIA RIABILITAZIONE. (IT/0390-5179). **4617**

SAGINAW NEWS (1929). (US). **Adv Mgr:** Charles Kretschmer. **5693**

SAHIFAT AL-MAKTABAH. (UA). **3247**

SAHITYA SANKETA. (II). **3433**

SAHOVSKI GLASNIK. (CI). **4865**

SAIKO TO HOAN. (JA/0370-8217). **2870**

SAIL. (US/0036-2700). **595**

SAILBOARD EXTRA. (AT/0817-2773). **4916**

SAILBOARD RETAILER. (US/1063-8180). **Adv Mgr:** Marie Cordell. **4916**

SAILING. (US/0036-2719). **596**

SAILING CANADA. (CN/0709-4744). **596**

SAILING QUARTERLY. (US/1071-1392). **Adv Mgr:** Bob Timm. **596**

SAILING WORLD. (US/0889-4094). **Adv Mgr:** Mark Herlyn. **596**

SAINNYAG HAGHOI JI (SENUR). (KO/0253-3073). **4329**

SAINT BARTHOLOMEW'S HOSPITAL JOURNAL. (UK/0036-2778). **3638**

SAINT CHRISTOPHER AND NEVIS CONSOLIDATED INDEX OF STATUTES AND SUBSIDIARY LEGISLATION TO ... . (BB). **3135**

SAINT JO TRIBUNE, THE. (US). **Adv Mgr:** Rebecca Smith. **5754**

SAINT LOUIS UNIVERSITY LAW JOURNAL. (US/0036-3030). **Adv Mgr:** Mark Boatman. **3045**

SAINT LOUIS UNIVERSITY PUBLIC LAW REVIEW. (US/0898-8404). **3045**

SAINT LUCIA CONSOLIDATED INDEX OF STATUTES AND SUBSIDIARY LEGISLATION TO ... . (BB). **3135**

SAINT PAUL LEGAL LEDGER. (US). **5698**

SAINT VINCENT AND THE GRENADINES CONSOLIDATED INDEX OF STATUTES AND SUBSIDIARY LEGISLATION TO ... . (BB). **3135**

SAINTPAULIA INTERNATIONAL NEWS. (US). **2430**

SAINTS HERALD. (US/0036-3251). **Adv Mgr:** G Booz, **Tel** (816)252-5010. **5067**

SAIPA. (SA/0036-0767). **4684**

SAIS REVIEW (JOHNS HOPKINS UNIVERSITY. SCHOOL OF ADVANCED INTERNATIONAL STUDIES: 1981). (US/0036-0775). **Adv Mgr:** Sheila Ward, **Tel** same as publisher. **4534**

SAISONS D'ALSACE STRASBOURG. (FR/0048-9018). **2522**

SAKSHARATA SANDESA. (II). **5257**

SAL TERRAE. (SP). **4995**

SALALM NEWSLETTER. (US/0098-6275). **3247**

SALAR. (CN/0827-3472). **2312**

SALEM OBSERVER. (US). **Adv Mgr:** Armend Beliyeau. **5709**

SALES & MARKETING MANAGEMENT. (US/0163-7517). **936**

SALES MOTIVATION (SANTA MONICA, CALIF.). (US/0892-8193). **709**

SALESMAN'S GUIDE NATIONWIDE DIRECTORY: MAJOR MASS MARKET MERCHANDISERS (EXCLUSIVE OF NEW YORK METROPOLITAN AREA), THE. (US). **709**

SALING AKTIENFUHRER. (GW). **Adv Mgr:** Susanne Kinhn, **Tel** 6151 380 260. **596**

SALISBURY POST, THE. (US/0747-0738). **Adv Mgr:** Steve Johnson. **5724**

SALLY ANN. (CN/0838-7397). **4995**

SALMAGUNDI (SARATOGA SPRINGS). (US/0036-3529). **2853**

SALMON AND TROUT MAGAZINE, THE. (UK/0036-3545). **2312**

SALMON FARMING. (UK/0951-9882). **2312**

SALMON TROUT STEELHEADER. (US/0029-3431). **Adv Mgr:** Sherry Gullings, **Tel** (503)653-8108. **4854**

SALMONID (HARPERS FERRY, W.VA.). (US/1071-1635). **2312**

SALOME (CHICAGO, ILL.). (US/0749-6435). **1314**

SALON MAGAZINE. (CN/1197-1495). **405**

SALT (CHICAGO, ILL.). (US/0883-2587). **4995**

SALT (KENNEBUNK). (US/0160-7537). **1094**

SALT LAKE TRIBUNE (SALT LAKE CITY, UTAH : 1890). (US/0746-3502). **5757**

SALT WATER SPORTSMAN. (US/0036-3618). **4916**

SALUD RURAL. T.S.R. (SP). **3638**

SALUDOS HISPANOS. (US/0898-4875). **2492**

SALZBURGER JAHRBUCH FUER PHILOSOPHIE. (AU/0080-5696). **4360**

SAMAB. (SA/0370-8314). **4096**

SAMFERDSEL (1979). (NO/0332-8988). **5392**

SAMISDAT. (US/0226-840X). **3352**

SAMMAMISH VALLEY NEWS. (US). **5762**

SAMMLUNG GEOGRAPHISCHER FUHRER. (GW/0344-6565). **2575**

SAMMLUNG METZLER. (GW/0558-3667). **3433**

SAMPE JOURNAL. (US/0091-1062). **1995**

SAMPSON INDEPENDENT, THE. (US). **Adv Mgr:** Gary Pate. **5724**

SAMS AUTO RADIO SERVICE DATA. (US/0163-3627). **2080**

SAMS TRANSISTOR RADIO. (US). **5149**

SAMTIDEN. (NO/0036-3928). **2522**

SAN ANGELO STANDARD-TIMES. (US). **5754**

SAN ANTONIO BUSINESS JOURNAL. (US/0895-1551). **Adv Mgr:** Mary Jonas. **709**

SAN ANTONIO EXPRESS-NEWS. (US/1065-7908). **Adv Mgr:** Bruce Ford, **Tel** (210)351-7413. **5754**

SAN BERNARDINO COUNTY SUN, THE. (US). **Adv Mgr:** John Bennett. **5639**

SAN BERNARDINO, RIVERSIDE COUNTIES STREET ATLAS AND DIRECTORY (ZIP CODE ED.). (US/0883-0118). **2575**

SAN BERNARDINO STREET ATLAS. ZIP CODE EDITION. (US/0733-2297). **1147**

SAN DIEGO BUSINESS JOURNAL. (US/8750-6890). **709**

SAN DIEGO COUNTY BUSINESS DIRECTORY. (US/1047-9619). **709**

SAN DIEGO EXECUTIVE. (US/1067-6384). **709**

SAN DIEGO HOME / GARDEN. (US). **2792**

SAN DIEGO HOME/GARDEN LIFESTYLES. (US/1073-6891). **2792**

SAN DIEGO LAW REVIEW, THE. (US/0036-4037). **3046**

SAN DIEGO MAGAZINE (1949). (US/0036-4045). **2544**

SAN DIEGO PHYSICIAN. (US). **Adv Mgr:** E. Persian. **3638**

SAN DIEGO UNION (SAN DIEGO, CALIF. : 1930). (US). **5639**

SAN DIEGO WRITERS MONTHLY. (US/1054-6774). **2924**

SAN FRANCISCO BAY GUARDIAN, THE. (US/0036-4096). **Adv Mgr:** K. Close, **Tel** (415)255-4600. **2545**

SAN FRANCISCO BAY TIMES. (US). **Adv Mgr:** Bob Gordon. **5639**

SAN FRANCISCO BUSINESS. (US/0036-410X). **Adv Mgr:** Carol Haynosch and Joann Serafini, **Tel** (415)392-4511 ext. 806 or ext. 831. **709**

SAN FRANCISCO CHRONICLE. (US). **5639**

SAN FRANCISCO DAILY JOURNAL (1990). (US/1059-2636). **Adv Mgr:** Linda Hubbell, **Tel** (415)252-0500. **3046**

SAN FRANCISCO JOURNAL. CHINESE EDITION, THE. (US/0199-462X). **5639**

SAN FRANCISCO JUNG INSTITUTE LIBRARY JOURNAL, THE. (US/0270-6210). **Adv Mgr Tel** (415)221-2266. **4617**

SAN FRANCISCO MEDICINE. (US/0361-705X). **3638**

SAN FRANCISCO POST. (US). **5639**

SAN FRANCISCO PROGRESS, THE. (US/0191-8192). **5639**

SAN FRANCISCO REVIEW OF BOOKS. (US/0194-0724). **Adv Mgr:** Donald Paul. **330**

SAN JOSE POST-RECORD, THE. (US/0036-4185). **5640**

SAN JUAN RECORD (1953), THE. (US/0894-3273). **Adv Mgr:** Bill Boyle. **5757**

SAN JUAN STAR, THE. (PR/8750-6122). **5808**

SAN LUIS OBISPO COUNTY TELEGRAM-TRIBUNE. (US). **Adv Mgr:** Devon Goetz, **Tel** (805)781-7849. **5640**

SAN MARCOS COURIER. (US/0273-9259). **5640**

SAN MARCOS NEWS REPORTER. (US). **Adv Mgr:** M. Ferdo. **5640**

SANCTUARY ASIA. (II). **2204**

SAND MOUNTAIN REPORTER. (US/0890-1724). **Adv Mgr:** Debra Hedgepath. **5628**

SANDERS COUNTY LEDGER (THOMPSON FALLS, MONT. : 1959). (US). **Adv Mgr:** Sherry Hagerman-Benton, **Tel** (406)827-4375. **5706**

SANDERSVILLE PROGRESS, THE. (US/0747-3710). **Adv Mgr:** Melissa Brown. **5655**

SANDLAPPER (1990). (US/1046-3267). **2628**

SANDPOINT DAILY BEE. (US). **Adv Mgr:** Herb, **Tel** 263-9534. **5657**

SANDRA : TOLLE STRICKMODE. (GW). **5185**

SANDY PARKER'S FUR WORLD. (US/0747-3753). **3185**

SANFORD EVANS GOLD BOOK OF USED CAR PRICES. (CN/0381-8179). **5425**

SANGER HERALD. (US). **Adv Mgr:** Cheri Chastain. **5640**

SANGYO SHARYO. (JA). **5392**

SANITAR UND HEIZUNGTECHNIK. (GW/0036-4401). **2608**

SANITARY MAINTENANCE. (US/0036-4436). **2242**

SANSEVIERIA JOURNAL, THE. (US/1062-8908). **2430**

SANTA BARBARA NEWS-PRESS (1932). (US). **Adv Mgr:** John Leonard, **Tel** (805)564-5248. **5640**

SANTA BARBARA SENIOR WORLD, THE. (US/0276-0800). **5181**

SANTA CLARA COUNTY CONNECTIONS. (US/0895-6103). **2471**

SANTA CLARA COUNTY POPULAR STREET ATLAS (ZIP CODE ED.). (US/0733-740X). **2575**

SANTA FE NEW MEXICAN, THE. (US). **Adv Mgr:** Virginia Sohn-Shihi, **Tel** (505)986-3006. **5713**

SANTA FE REPORTER, THE. (US/0744-477X). **Adv Mgr:** Andrew Strong Jordan. **5713**

SANTA FEAN MAGAZINE (SANTA FE, N.M.). (US/1046-2708). **2545**

SANTA GERTRUDIS JOURNAL, THE. (US/0036-455X). **221**

SANTA GERTRUDIS TRIBUNE. (US/8750-3743). **221**

SANTA MARIA TIMES. (US/0745-6166). **5640**

SANTA MONICA REVIEW : SMR. (US/0899-9848). **3433**

SANTA ROSA NEWS (1987). (US/0894-783X). **Adv Mgr:** Virginia Freeman. **5713**

SANTIAGO. (CU/0048-9115). **3433**

SAO PAULO YEAR BOOK. (BL). **850**

SAP, SPECTRA OF ANTHROPOLOGICAL PROGRESS. (II). **245**

SAPERE. (IT/0036-4681). **Adv Mgr:** R. Coga. **5149**

SAPIENTIA. (AG/0036-4703). **4360**

SAR MAGAZINE, THE. (US/0161-0511). **5236**

SARASOTA MAGAZINE. (US/1048-2245). **2545**

SARATOGA NEWS. (US/0745-6255). **5640**

SARATOGA (RHINEBECK, N.Y.), THE. (US/0740-9702). **2471**

SARATOGIAN (SARATOGA SPRINGS, N.Y., 1910), THE. (US/1071-4448). **5720**

SARCOIDOSIS. (IT/0393-1447). **3638**

SARMATIAN REVIEW, THE. (US/1059-5872). **Adv Mgr:** C. Allen. **2708**

SAS BULLETIN. (US/0899-8922). **282**

SAS COMMUNICATIONS. (US/0270-9422). **1121**

SASK. REPORT. (CN/0820-5043). **Adv Mgr:** Bill Clewes. **2545**

SASKATCHEWAN ASSOCIATION OF SOCIAL WORKERS NEWSLETTER. (CN). **Adv Mgr:** M. Hicks, **Tel** same as publisher. **5306**

SASKATCHEWAN BULLETIN, THE. (CN/0036-4886). **1781**

SASKATCHEWAN BUSINESS. (CN/0709-0854). **Adv Mgr:** Mark Reis. **709**

SASKATCHEWAN MULTICULTURAL MAGAZINE. (CN/0714-9050). **Adv Mgr:** Elaine Lee. **2272**

SASKATCHEWAN TRADE DIRECTORY (1986). (CN/0831-9057). **3487**

SASSY (NEW YORK, N.Y. 1988). (US/0899-9953). **1068**

SATELLITE BUSINESS NEWS. (US/1043-0865). **Adv Mgr:** Collette Loescher, **Tel** same as publisher. **1121**

SATELLITE COMMUNICATIONS. (US/0147-7439). **1163**

SATELLITE LEARNING. (US/1054-9935). **1846**

SATELLITE NEWS. (UK). **34**

SATELLITE RETAILER. (US/0890-1252). **Adv Mgr Tel** (704)482-9673. **957**

SATELLITE TV WEEK. NORTH AMERICAN EDITION. (US/0744-7841). **Adv Mgr:** Dan Eliason, **Tel** (207)725-6951. **1163**

SATMER ED. FRANCAISE. (FR/0294-1910). **1434**

SATURDAY EVENING POST (1839), THE. (US/0048-9239). **2492**

SATURDAY NIGHT. (CN/0036-4975). **2545**

SAUDI BULLETIN OF OPHTHALMOLOGY : OFFICIAL JOURNAL OF THE SAUDI OPHTHALMOLOGICAL SOCIETY. (SU). **3879**

SAUDI ECONOMIC SURVEY. (SU). **1583**

SAUDI MEDICAL JOURNAL. (SU/0379-5284). **Adv Mgr:** Peter Carpenter. **3638**

SAUGETIERKUNDLICHE MITTEILUNGEN. (GW/0036-2344). **472**

SAUL BELLOW JOURNAL. (US/0735-1550). **434**

SAUSSUREA. (SZ/0373-2525). **527**

SAUVEGARDE DES CHANTIERS. (FR/0036-505X). **Adv Mgr:** M. Francais, **Tel** 33 1 46092651. **627**

SAVACOU. (JM/0036-5068). **364**

SAVANNAH EVENING PRESS. (US/8750-4685). **5655**

SAVING AND PRESERVING ARTS AND CULTURAL ENVIRONMENTS. (US/0748-8378). **330**

SAVINGS AND DEVELOPMENT. (IT). **1519**

SAVINGS BANKS INTERNATIONAL. (SZ/1010-4038). **810**

SAVINGS INSTITUTIONS. (US/0746-1321). **810**

SAVVY SHOPPER, THE. (US/1057-3275). **5490**

SAWADDI. (TH/0581-8893). **2663**

SAXOPHONE JOURNAL. (US/0276-4768). **4152**

SAYYIDATI. (UK/0265-5780). **2601**

SBANE ENTERPRISE. (US/8750-3158). **709**

SBORNIK K DEJINAM 19. A 20. STOLETI. (XR). **2628**

SBORNIK VYSOKE SKOLY CHEMICKO-TECHNOLOGICKE V PRAZE. POLYMERY-CHEMIE, VLASTNOSTI A ZPRACOVANI. (XR/0139-908X). **1047**

SCALA. (GW/0303-4232). **2522**

SCALA INTERNATIONAL. (GW/0581-9385). **2522**

SCALE AIRCRAFT MODELLING. (UK). **Adv Mgr:** Andy Hale. **2777**

SCALE AUTO ENTHUSIAST. (US). **Adv Mgr:** Brian Taylor, **Tel** (414)783-7740. **2777**

SCALE CABINETMAKER, THE. (US/0145-8213). **2777**

SCAN (NORTH SYDNEY). (AT/0726-4127). **1904**

SCANDINAVIAN ACTUARIAL JOURNAL. (SW/0346-1238). **2893**

SCANDINAVIAN DAIRY INFORMATION. (SW/1101-2706). **198**

SCANDINAVIAN DAIRY INFORMATION - SDI. (SW/1101-2706). **198**

SCANDINAVIAN ECONOMIC HISTORY REVIEW, THE. (SW/0358-5522). **1583**

SCANDINAVIAN JOURNAL OF CLINICAL & LABORATORY INVESTIGATION. (UK/0036-5513). **586**

SCANDINAVIAN JOURNAL OF DENTAL RESEARCH. (DK/0029-845X). **1335**

SCANDINAVIAN JOURNAL OF DEVELOPMENT ALTERNATIVES. (SW/0280-2791). **4535**

SCANDINAVIAN JOURNAL OF ECONOMICS, THE. (UK/0347-0520). **1520**

SCANDINAVIAN JOURNAL OF EDUCATIONAL RESEARCH. (UK/0031-3831). **1781**

SCANDINAVIAN JOURNAL OF GASTROENTEROLOGY. (NO/0036-5521). **3747**

SCANDINAVIAN JOURNAL OF IMMUNOLOGY. (UK/0300-9475). **3676**

SCANDINAVIAN JOURNAL OF METALLURGY. (SW/0371-0459). **4018**

SCANDINAVIAN JOURNAL OF PSYCHOLOGY. (SW/0036-5564). **4617**

SCANDINAVIAN JOURNAL OF RHEUMATOLOGY. (SW/0300-9742). **3807**

SCANDINAVIAN JOURNAL OF SOCIAL WELFARE. (DK/0907-2055). **5307**

SCANDINAVIAN JOURNAL OF STATISTICS. (SW/0303-6898). **5338**

SCANDINAVIAN JOURNAL OF UROLOGY AND NEPHROLOGY. (SW/0036-5599). **3993**

SCANDINAVIAN PSYCHOANALYTIC REVIEW, THE. (NO/0106-2301). **4617**

SCANDINAVIAN REVIEW [MICROFORM]. (US). **2272**

SCANDINAVIAN STUDIES: PUBLICATION OF THE SOCIETY FOR THE ADVANCEMENT OF SCANDINAVIAN STUDY. (US/0036-5637). **Adv Mgr:** W.Reading. **3433**

SCANDINAVICA. (UK/0036-5653). **3433**

SCANFAX. (US/0018-9227). **2080**

SCANNING. (US/0161-0457). **574**

SCAPE (LOS ANGELES, CALIF.). (US/1049-7455). **2492**

SCARLET & GOLD. (CN/0316-4209). **3176**

SCARSDALE INQUIRER, THE. (US). **Adv Mgr:** D White. **5721**

SCEA EMPHASIS. (US/0273-7906). **1870**

SCENE ENTERTAINMENT WEEKLY. (US/1064-6116). **330**

SCENIC TRIPS TO THE GEOLOGIC PAST. (US/0548-5983). **1396**

SCHATZKAMMER DER DEUTSCHEN SPRACHE, DICHTUNG UND GESCHICHTE. (US/0740-1965). **3433**

SCHAULADE, DIE. (GW). **2593**

SCHAUSPIELFUHRER, DER. (GW). **5372**

SCHIFF & HAFEN/SEEWIRTSCHAFT. (GW/0938-1643). **Adv Mgr:** Helmut Moller. **5455**

SCHIFF REPORT, THE. (US/1055-8969). **4801**

SCHNAUZER SHORTS. (US/0276-1521). **Adv Mgr:** Dan Kiedrowski. **4288**

SCHOLARLY PUBLISHING. (CN/0036-634X). **4819**

SCHOLARS OF EARLY MODERN STUDIES. (US/1059-9185). **2708**

SCHOLASTIC CHOICES. (US/0883-475X). **2792**

SCHOLASTIC COACH. (US/0036-6382). **4917**

SCHOLASTIC COACH AND ATHLETIC DIRECTOR. (US/1077-5625). **4917**

SCHOLASTIC UPDATE (TEACHERS' ED.). (US/0886-4551). **2545**

SCHOLASTIC VOICE. (US/0032-6380). **3319**

SCHOOL AND COMMUNITY (COLUMBIA). (US/0036-6447). **Adv Mgr:** N. Bailey, **Tel** (314)442-3127. **1782**

SCHOOL ARTS. (US/0036-6463). **364**

SCHOOL BUSINESS AFFAIRS. (US/0036-651X). **1871**

SCHOOL COUNSELOR, THE. (US/0036-6536). **1885**

SCHOOL EN COMPUTER. (BE). **1224**

SCHOOL EN WET. (NE). **1782**

SCHOOL FOOD SERVICE JOURNAL. (US/0160-6271). **Adv Mgr:** Tina Farah, **Tel** (703)739-3900. **2356**

SCHOOL FOODSERVICE & NUTRITION. (US/1075-3885). **Adv Mgr:** Tina Farah, **Tel** (703)739-3900. **2356**

SCHOOL LEADER. (US). **Adv Mgr:** Chris Gadekar. **1871**

SCHOOL LIBRARIAN, THE. (UK/0036-6595). **3247**

SCHOOL LIBRARIES IN CANADA. (CN/0227-3780). **3248**

SCHOOL LIBRARY JOURNAL (NEW YORK, N.Y.). (US/0362-8930). **3248**

SCHOOL LIBRARY MEDIA ANNUAL. (US/0739-7712). **3248**

SCHOOL LIBRARY MEDIA QUARTERLY. (US/0278-4823). **3248**

SCHOOL MUSIC NEWS, THE. (US/0036-6668). **4152**

SCHOOL ORGANISATION & MANAGEMENT ABSTRACTS. (UK/0261-2755). **1797**

SCHOOL PSYCHOLOGY REVIEW. (US/0279-6015). **4618**

SCHOOL SCIENCE AND MATHEMATICS. (US/0036-6803). **5149**

SCHOOL SCIENCE REVIEW. (UK/0036-6811). **5149**

SCHOOL SOCIAL WORK JOURNAL. (US/0161-5653). **Adv Mgr:** Joan Fedota. **1871**

SCHOOL TRANSPORTATION NEWS. (US/1070-3586). **5392**

SCHOOL TRUSTEE (REGINA). (CN/0036-6854). **1872**

SCHOOLS ABROAD OF INTEREST TO AMERICANS. (US/0899-2002). **1782**

SCHOOLS (OLYMPIA, WASH.). (US). **1847**

SCHUHTECHNIK 1987. (GW/0933-808X). **1087**

SCHUMPERT MEDICAL QUARTERLY. (US/0731-5406). **3639**

SCHWEISSEN UND SCHNEIDEN. (GW/0036-7184). **4027**

SCHWEIZER ALUMINIUM RUNDSCHAU. (SZ/0036-7257). **4018**

SCHWEIZER INGENIEUR UND ARCHITEKT. (SZ/0251-0960). **1995**

SCHWEIZER LOGISTIK-KATALOG / SWISS LOGISITICS CATALOGUE. (SZ). **Adv Mgr:** W. Meier. **1929**

SCHWEIZER MONATSSCHRIFT FUER ZAHNMEDIZIN. (SZ/1011-4203). **1335**

SCHWEIZER OPTIKER. L'OPTICIEN SUISSE. L'OTTICO SVIZZERO, DER. (SZ). **4217**

SCHWEIZER SPITAL. (SZ/0304-4432). **3792**

SCHWEIZER VERPACKUNGSKATALOG. (SZ). **4222**

SCHWEIZER WAFFEN-MAGAZIN. (SZ/0253-4878). **4056**

SCHWEIZERISCHE APOTHEKER-ZEITUNG. GIORNALE SVIZZERO DI FARMACIA. (SZ/0036-7508). **4329**

SCHWEIZERISCHE BLASMUSIKZEITUNG. (SZ). **4152**

SCHWEIZERISCHE MEDIZINISCHE WOCHENSCHRIFT. (SZ/0036-7672). **3639**

SCHWEIZERISCHE RUNDSCHAU FUER MEDIZIN PRAXIS. (SZ/1013-2058). **3801**

SCHWEIZERISCHE ZEITSCHRIFT FUER GESCHICHTE. (SZ/0036-7834). **2708**

SCHWEIZERISCHE ZEITSCHRIFT FUER SPORTMEDIZIN. (SZ/0036-7885). **3955**

SCHWEIZERISCHE ZEITSCHRIFT FUER VOLKSWIRTSCHAFT UND STATISTIK. (SZ/0303-9692). **1538**

SCHWEIZERISCHES IDIOTIKON. WORTERBUCH DER SCHWEIZERDEUTSCHEN SPRACHE. (SZ). **3319**

SCHWENDEMAN'S DIRECTORY OF COLLEGE GEOGRAPHY OF THE UNITED STATES. (US/0734-8185). **2576**

SCI-TECH NEWS. (US/0036-8059). **Adv Mgr:** Mary Lee Kennedy, **Tel** (403)992-5066. **3248**

SCIENCE ACTIVITIES. (US/0036-8121). **5150**

SCIENCE AND CHILDREN. (US/0036-8148). **1904**

SCIENCE & CULTURE. (II/0036-8156). **5150**

SCIENCE AND INDUSTRY. (NE/0925-5842). **5150**

SCIENCE & PUBLIC POLICY. (UK/0302-3427). **4685**

SCIENCE & RELIGION NEWS. (US/1048-8642). **4995**

SCIENCE AND SOCIETY (NEW YORK. 1936). (US/0036-8237). **5218**

SCIENCE & TECHNOLOGY IN JAPAN (TOKYO. 1982). (JA/0286-0406). **5150**

SCIENCE & TECHNOLOGY LIBRARIES (NEW YORK, N.Y.). (US/0194-262X). **3248**

SCIENCE AS CULTURE. (UK/0950-5431). **5151**

SCIENCE BOOKS & FILMS. (US/0098-342X). **5151**

SCIENCE BUDGET. (IE/0332-1126). **5151**

SCIENCE EDUCATION (SALEM, MASS.). (US/0036-8326). **5151**

SCIENCE ET COMPORTEMENT. (CN/0841-7741). **4618**

SCIENCE ET VIE. (FR/0036-8369). **5151**

SCIENCE FICTION. (AT/0314-6677). **Adv Mgr:** same as editor. **3434**

SCIENCE FICTION AGE (HERNDON, VA.). (US/1065-1829). **3434**

SCIENCE FICTION CHRONICLE. (US/0195-5365). **Adv Mgr:** A. Porter. **3434**

SCIENCE-FICTION STUDIES. (CN/0091-7729). **3434**

SCIENCE FOR PEOPLE (LONDON). (UK/0144-8447). **5151**

SCIENCE IN NEW GUINEA. (PP/0310-4303). **5152**

SCIENCE IN PARLIAMENT. (UK/0263-6271). **5152**

SCIENCE LINK. (CN/0821-7246). **2924**

SCIENCE NEWS (WASHINGTON). (US/0036-8423). **5152**

SCIENCE OF COMPUTER PROGRAMMING. (NE/0167-6423). **1281**

SCIENCE OF MIND. (US/0036-8458). **4360**

SCIENCE OF THE TOTAL ENVIRONMENT, THE. (NE/0048-9697). **2181**

SCIENCE PROGRESS (1916). (UK/0036-8504). **5152**

SCIENCE REPORTER. (II/0036-8512). **5153**

SCIENCE SCOPE (WASHINGTON, D.C.). (US/0887-2376). **5153**

SCIENCE TEACHER (WASHINGTON, D.C.), THE. (US/0036-8555). **5153**

SCIENCE, TECHNOLOGY & DEVELOPMENT. (UK/0950-0707). **Adv Mgr:** Anne Kidson. **5153**

SCIENCE, TECHNOLOGY & HUMAN VALUES. (US/0162-2439). **5153**

SCIENCE TODAY. (UK). **5153**

SCIENCE (WASHINGTON, D.C.). (US/0036-8075). **5154**

SCIENCES ET TECHNIQUES DE L'EAU. (CN). **1418**

SCIENCES ET TECHNIQUES EN PERSPECTIVE. (FR/0294-0264). **5154**

SCIENCES GEOLOGIQUES. BULLETIN. (FR/0302-2692). **1396**

SCIENCES (NEW YORK), THE. (US/0036-861X). **5154**

SCIENTIA CANADENSIS. (CN/0829-2507). **5154**

SCIENTIA PHARMACEUTICA. (AU/0036-8709). **4329**

SCIENTIFIC AMERICAN MEDICINE. (US/0194-9063). **3639**

SCIENTIFIC AMERICAN. SPECIAL ISSUE. (US/1048-0943). **5155**

SCIENTIFIC DRILLING. (GW/0934-4365). **1410**

SCIENTIFIC PRESENTATIONS OF THE ANNUAL MEETING - AMERICAN ANIMAL HOSPITAL ASSOCIATION. (US/0164-1999). **5521**

SCIENTIFIC PUBLICATION - FRESHWATER BIOLOGICAL ASSOCIATION. (UK/0367-1887). **472**

SCIENTIFIC REVIEWS ON ARID ZONE RESEARCH. (II/0254-0568). **2220**

SCIENTIFIC SLEUTHING REVIEW. (US/1043-4224). **5155**

SCIENTIFIC WORLD. (UK/0036-8857). **5156**

SCIENTIFUR. (DK/0105-2403). **3186**

SCIENTIST (PHILADELPHIA, PA.), THE. (US/0890-3670). **Adv Mgr:** Pat LaValley, **Tel** (215)386-0100, Ext. 1544. **5156**

SCIENTOMETRICS. (NE/0138-9130). **5156**

SCIFANT. (US/0882-1348). **5074**

SCIMA. (II). **1252**

SCIMP SELECTIVE CO-OPERATIVE INDEX OF MANAGEMENT PERIODICALS. (FI/0782-2979). **733**

SCINTILLA (TORONTO). (CN/0824-6009). **3434**

SCITECH BOOK NEWS. (US/0196-6006). **5156**

SCLC (ATLANTA, GA.). (US/0735-7443). **4995**

SCOOP. (CN). **2835**

SCORE (NASHVILLE, TENN.). (US/1074-5769). **Adv Mgr:** Mr. Nowlin, **Tel** same as publisher. **4152**

SCORE (TORONTO). (CN/0711-3226). **Adv Mgr:** Peter Simpson. **4917**

SCOT LIT. (UK). **3434**

SCOTLANDS. (UK/1350-7508). **Adv Mgr:** Kathryn MacLean. **2854**

SCOTLANDS REGIONS. (UK/0305-6562). **4685**

SCOTS LAW TIMES; THE LANDS TRIBUNAL FOR SCOTLAND REPORTS, THE. (UK/0036-908X). **3047**

SCOTS MAGAZINE, THE. (UK). **2522**

SCOTT KING'S DIABETES INTERVIEW. (US/1058-6598). **3676**

SCOTTISH ARCHITECTS DIRECTORY, THE. (UK). **308**

SCOTTISH BANNER, THE. (CN/0707-073X). **2272**

SCOTTISH BAPTIST MAGAZINE. (UK/0036-9136). **5067**

SCOTTISH BEEKEEPER. (UK/0370-8918). **132**

SCOTTISH BIRDS. (UK/0036-9144). **5620**

SCOTTISH BOOK COLLECTOR. (UK/0954-8769). **4819**

SCOTTISH BUILDING AND CIVIL ENGINEERING YEAR BOOK. (UK/0085-6002). **627**

SCOTTISH BUSINESS INSIDER. (UK/0952-1488). **Adv Mgr:** Grant Johnstone, **Tel** 011 44 31 459 5500. **709**

SCOTTISH EDUCATIONAL REVIEW. (UK/0141-9072). **1783**

SCOTTISH FORESTRY. (UK/0036-9217). **2395**

SCOTTISH GENEALOGIST, THE. (UK/0300-337X). **2472**

SCOTTISH GEOGRAPHICAL MAGAZINE. (UK/0036-9225). **2576**

SCOTTISH HISTORICAL REVIEW, THE. (UK/0036-9241). **Adv Mgr:** Kathryn MacLean. **2709**

SCOTTISH JOURNAL OF GEOLOGY. (UK/0036-9276). **1396**

SCOTTISH JOURNAL OF PHYSICAL EDUCATION. (UK/0140-2315). **1858**

SCOTTISH JOURNAL OF POLITICAL ECONOMY. (UK/0036-9292). **1595**

SCOTTISH JOURNAL OF RELIGIOUS STUDIES, THE. (UK/0143-8301). **4995**

SCOTTISH JOURNAL OF THEOLOGY. (UK/0036-9306). **4995**

SCOTTISH LANGUAGE. (UK/0264-0198). **3319**

SCOTTISH LAW DIRECTORY FOR ..., THE. (UK/0080-8083). **Adv Mgr:** Raylene Davidson, **Tel** 011 44 31 225 4703. **3047**

SCOTTISH LAW GAZETTE, THE. (UK/0036-9314). **Adv Mgr:** Derek Flyn. **3047**

SCOTTISH LIBRARIES (1987). (UK/0950-0189). **3248**

SCOTTISH LITERARY JOURNAL. (UK/0305-0785). **3434**

SCOTTISH LITERARY JOURNAL. THE YEAR'S WORK IN SCOTTISH LITERARY AND LINGUISTIC STUDIES. (UK). **3319**

SCOTTISH PHOTOGRAPHY BULLETIN. (UK/0269-1787). **4376**

SCOTTISH PLANNING LAW & PRACTICE. (UK/0144-8196). **3047**

SCOTTISH RITE JOURNAL. (US/0279-7011). **5739**

SCOTTISH SLAVONIC REVIEW. (UK/0265-3273). **3319**

SCOTT'S DIRECTORIES, WESTERN MANUFACTURERS. (CN/0829-2248). **3487**

SCOTTSDALE MAGAZINE. (US). **2545**

SCOUT MID-RANGE SOFTWARE DIRECTORY. (US/1047-1812). **Adv Mgr:** Dusty Johnson. **1202**

SCRANTON TIMES (SCRANTON, PA. : 1891 : DAILY). (US). **5739**

SCRAP PROCESSING AND RECYCLING. (US/0898-0756). **4018**

SCRAP TIRE NEWS. (US). **Adv Mgr:** Mike Sikora. **2181**

SCRAP TIRE USERS DIRECTORY. (US). **Adv Mgr:** Mike Sikora, **Tel** (703)280-9112. **2181**

SCRATCHING RIVER POST, THE. (CN/0707-2333). **5794**

SCREAMING EAGLE, THE. (US). **4056**

SCREEN. (UK/0036-9543). **4077**

SCREEN (CHICAGO, ILL.). (US/1070-7573). **4077**

SCREEN PRINTING. (US). **4569**

SCREEN PRINTING TECHNIQUES. (US/0362-160X). **4569**

SCRIBLERIAN AND THE KIT-CATS, THE. (US/0190-731X). **2854**

SCRIP — Advertising Accepted Index

SCRIP (RICHMOND). (UK/0143-7690). **4329**

SCRIPT (PARIS, 1988). (FR/0993-2097). **Adv Mgr:** Rene Thevenet, **Tel** 16 1 47 23 70 30. **4077**

SCRIPTA THEOLOGICA. (SP/0036-9764). **4996**

SCRIPTURE BULLETIN. (UK/0036-9780). **5019**

SCRIPTWRITERS MARKET. (US/0748-6456). **4077**

SCRIVENER. (CN/0227-5090). **3435**

SCROGGINS NATIONAL LAW ENFORCEMENT DIRECTORY. (US/0882-1909). **3176**

SCROLL (MALVERNE, N.Y.). (US/0890-524X). **1292**

SCULPTURE REVIEW. (US/0747-5284). **364**

SCULPTURE (WASHINGTON, D.C.). (US/0889-728X). **Adv Mgr:** H. Singer, **Tel** (212)343-0202. **364**

SCUOLA CATTOLICA, LA. (IT/0036-9810). **5036**

SCUOLAOFFICINA. (IT). **5156**

SEA BREEZE (BOSTON, MASS.). (US). **5455**

SEA BREEZES. (UK/0036-9977). **Adv Mgr:** M. Shacklady. **5455**

SEA FRONTIERS (1988). (US/0897-2249). **1456**

SEA HERITAGE NEWS. (US/0270-5524). **2545**

SEA (LOS ANGELES, CALIF.). (US/0746-8601). **596**

SEA POWER (1971). (US/0199-1337). **4183**

SEA SWALLOW, THE. (UK). **Adv Mgr:** same as editor. **5620**

SEA TECHNOLOGY. (US/0093-3651). **1456**

SEA TECHNOLOGY. BUYERS GUIDE, DIRECTORY. (US). **1456**

SEACOAST LIFE. (US/0885-6435). **2545**

SEAFARER (LONDON). (UK/0037-007X). **4183**

SEAFOOD AUSTRALIA. (AT/1320-9663). **2357**

SEAFOOD BUSINESS (CAMDEN, ME.). (US/0889-3217). **2357**

SEAFOOD INTERNATIONAL. (UK/0268-1293). **2313**

SEAFOOD LEADER. (US/0744-4664). **2313**

SEAFOOD PRICE - CURRENT. (US/0270-417X). **2357**

SEAISI DIRECTORY. (MY). **4019**

SEAISI QUARTERLY. (SI/0129-5721). **4019**

SEALY NEWS (SEALY, TEX. : 1915). (US). **Adv Mgr:** Jim Grimes. **5754**

SEAMAN, THE. (UK/0037-0142). **1710**

SEAPORT. (US/0743-6246). **Adv Mgr:** Ann Wells, **Tel** (203)855-9750. **2760**

SEAPORTS AND THE SHIPPING WORLD. (CN/0037-0150). **5455**

SEAPORTS AND THE SHIPPING WORLD. SPRING ISSUE. (CN). **5455**

SEAPOSTER. (US). **2787**

SEARCH AND RESCUE MAGAZINE. (US/0092-5136). **4802**

SEARCH MAGAZINE (AMHERST). (US/0037-0290). **35**

SEARCH (MIAMI), THE. (US/0272-5827). **2664**

SEARCH (NASHVILLE). (US/0048-9913). **5067**

SEARCH (SYDNEY). (AT/0004-9549). **5156**

SEARCHER (MEDFORD, N.J.). (US/1070-4795). **Adv Mgr:** Michael V. Zarrello. **1202**

SEARCHING TOGETHER. (US/0739-2281). **5067**

SEARCHLIGHT (CULBERTSON, MONT.). (US). **5706**

SEARCHLIGHT (LONDON). (UK/0262-4591). **Adv Mgr:** S. Gable, **Tel** 011 49 71 284-4040. **5257**

SEARMG NEWSLETTER. (AT/0158-1953). **2854**

SEASONS. (CN/0227-793X). **Adv Mgr:** C Davidson, **Tel** (416)477-4297. **4171**

SEATRADE REVIEW. (UK/0964-8895). **5455**

SEATTLE HOME AND GARDEN. (US). **2431**

SEATTLE REVIEW, THE. (US/0147-6629). **Adv Mgr:** J Smith. **3435**

SEATTLE TIMES, THE. (US/0745-9696). **5762**

SEATTLE'S CHILD. (US/1064-4512). **Adv Mgr:** Alayne Sulkin. **2286**

SEAWAY MARITIME DIRECTORY. (US/0582-3668). **5456**

SEAWAY REVIEW. (US/0037-0487). **5456**

SEAWAYS (1980). (UK/0144-1019). **Adv Mgr:** Tina Scott. **4183**

SEBREE BANNER, THE. (US). **Adv Mgr:** Betty P. Catlett, **Tel** (502)835-7521. **5682**

SEC REPORT. (US/0885-9078). **4917**

SECHERESSE MONTROUGE. (FR/1147-7806). **1360**

SECHZIG - NA UND ?. (GW). **5181**

SECOND BOAT, THE. (US/0274-6441). **2472**

SECOND CENTURY (ABILENE, TEX.), THE. (US/0276-7899). **4996**

SECOND LANGUAGE RESEARCH. (UK/0267-6583). **3320**

SECOND STONE, THE. (US/1047-3971). **Adv Mgr:** J. Bailey, **Tel** (504)891-7555. **2796**

SECONDS (NEW YORK, N.Y.). (US/1052-5025). **Adv Mgr:** Ken Senudato. **4152**

SECRET PARIS. (FR/1163-2747). **Adv Mgr:** Besse V. **710**

SECRETARY, THE. (US/0037-0622). **710**

SECTION A - REVUE D'ARCHITECTURE. (CN/0715-9781). **308**

SECURED LENDER, THE. (US/0888-255X). **811**

SECURITE, ENVIRONEMENT. (SZ/1015-6356). **2870**

SECURITE ET MEDECINE DU TRAVAIL. (FR/0755-2386). **2870**

SECURITIES JOURNAL. (HK). **Adv Mgr:** Ricky Ma, **Tel** 011 852 896 8333. **811**

SECURITY AFFAIRS. (US/0889-4876). **4535**

SECURITY MANAGEMENT (ARLINGTON, VA.). (US/0145-9406). **Adv Mgr:** S. Wade, **Tel** (703)312-6353. **885**

SECURITY SPECIFIER. (UK). **Adv Mgr:** Chris Musk, **Tel** 0242 236336. **5177**

SECURITY STUDIES. (UK/0963-6412). **Adv Mgr:** Ann Kidson. **4535**

SECURITY TRADERS HANDBOOK. (US/0885-2693). **1520**

SEDIMENTOLOGY. (UK/0037-0746). **1410**

SEDONA RED ROCK NEWS. (US/1044-7555). **5630**

SEE THE MUSIC. (CN/0826-5216). **4152**

SEED ABSTRACTS. (UK/0141-0180). **156**

SEED TRADE NEWS. (US/0037-0789). **Adv Mgr:** James R. Laird. **133**

SEED WORLD. (US/0037-0797). **186**

SEEDS (DECATUR, GA.). (US/0194-4495). **Adv Mgr:** Susan Hansen, **Tel** (817)755-7745. **2912**

SEGNO PESCARA. (IT/0391-3910). **330**

SEIDENKI GAKKAI KOEN RONBUNSHU : SEIDENKI GAKKAI ZENKOKU TAIKAI. (JA). **4445**

SEIDENKI GAKKAI SHI. (JA/0386-2550). **4445**

SEIJI HANDOBUKKU. (JA). **4495**

SEIRBHIS PHOIBLI : JOURNAL OF THE DEPARTMENT OF THE PUBLIC SERVICE. (IE/0332-2688). **4705**

SEISMOLOGICAL RESEARCH LETTERS. (US/0895-0695). **1397**

SEITAI NO KAGAKU. (JA/0370-9531). **473**

SEL & POIVRE. (CN/0714-6116). **5073**

SELECCIONES AVICOLAS. (SP/0582-4818). **221**

SELECCIONES DEL READER'S DIGEST (UNITED STATES ED.). (US/0885-0496). **2492**

SELECTED EDUCATIONAL STATISTICS. (II). **1797**

SELECTED MONOGRAPHS ON TAXATION. (NE). **4747**

SELECTION DU READER'S DIGEST (EDITION CANADIENNE). (CN/0037-1378). **2492**

SELECTWARE SYSTEM. CD-ROM. (US). **1239**

SELEZIONE DAL READER'S DIGEST. (IT/0037-1483). **2522**

SELEZIONE VETERINARIA. (IT/0037-1521). **5521**

SELF ADHESIVE MATERIALS & MARKETS BULLETIN. (UK). **4222**

SELF (NEW YORK). (US/0149-0699). **5566**

SELF PUBLISHING UPDATE. (US/0736-1882). **710**

SELMA ENTERPRISE, THE. (US). **Adv Mgr:** Gerald Latham. **5640**

SEM DNEI. (US). **2492**

SEMAINE VETERINAIRE, LA. (FR/0396-5015). **5521**

SEMANA. (IS). **2508**

SEMANA ECONOMICA. (PE). **Adv Mgr:** Roberto. **1520**

SEMANA MEDICA (BUENOS AIRES, ARGENTINA : 1894). (AG). **3640**

SEMANTIKOS. (FR/0395-3556). **3320**

SEMENCE, LA. (CN/0228-670X). **5019**

SEMENCES ET PROGRES. (FR/0395-8930). **5156**

SEMICONDUCTOR INTERNATIONAL. (US/0163-3767). **2080**

SEMICONDUCTOR WORLD. (JA). **2108**

SEMICONDUCTORS AND INSULATORS. (US/0309-5991). **4421**

SEMINARS IN COLON & RECTAL SURGERY. (US/1043-1489). **3974**

SEMINARS IN HEARING. (US/0734-0451). **3891**

SEMINARS IN INTERVENTIONAL RADIOLOGY. (US/0739-9529). **3946**

SEMINARS IN LIVER DISEASE. (US/0272-8087). **3801**

SEMINARS IN NEUROLOGY. (US/0271-8235). **3846**

SEMINARS IN REPRODUCTIVE ENDOCRINOLOGY. (US/0734-8630). **3733**

SEMINARS IN RESPIRATORY MEDICINE. (US/0192-9755). **3952**

SEMINARS IN SPEECH AND LANGUAGE. (US/0734-0478). **3320**

SEMINARS IN SURGICAL ONCOLOGY. (US/8756-0437). **3824**

SEMINARS IN THROMBOSIS AND HEMOSTASIS. (US/0094-6176). **3774**

SEMINOLE OUTLOOK. (US/8750-2070). **5651**

SEMINOLE TRIBUNE, THE. (US/0891-8252). **5651**

SEMIOSIS. (GW/0170-219X). **3320**

SEMIOTEXTE (NEW YORK). (US/0093-9579). **5257**

SEMIOTIC REVIEW OF BOOKS. (CN/0847-1622). **1121**

SEMIOTICA. (NE/0037-1998). **3320**

SENECA REVIEW, THE. (US/0037-2145). **3435**

SENIOR CITIZENS' CONSULTANTS OF ST. CATHARINES INC. (CN/0714-5756). **5181**

SENIOR CITIZENS TODAY. (US/0049-0199). **5181**

SENIOR DIGEST. (US). **Adv Mgr:** Carolyn Giordana. **5181**

SENIOR NEWS. (SA/0037-2234). **5181**

SENIOR SCENE. (AT). **5182**

SENIOR SPECTRUM. (US). **Adv Mgr:** J.Walacek. **5182**

SENIOR WORLD NEWSMAGAZINE. (US). **5182**

SENIOR WORLD QUARTERLY. (CN/0714-8798). **5182**

SENIORS TODAY. (CN/0715-4046). **5182**

SENSIBLE SOUND, THE. (US/0199-4654). **5318**

SENSOR BUSINESS DIGEST. (US/1060-1902). **Adv Mgr:** Sarah Collings. **3487**

SENSORS AND ACTUATORS. A, PHYSICAL. (SZ/0924-4247). **Adv Mgr:** Ms. W van Cattenburch (Amsterdam). **2080**

SENSORS AND ACTUATORS. B, CHEMICAL. (SZ/0925-4005). **Adv Mgr:** Ms. W van Cattenburch (Amsterdam). **2081**

SENSORS BUYER'S GUIDE. (US/1042-2757). **3488**

SENSORS (PETERSBOROUGH, N.H.). (US/0746-9462). **1996**

SENSORY PERCEPTION AND INFORMATION PROCESSING. (UK/0143-7526). **4618**

SENTIER CHASSE-PECHE. (CN/0711-7957). **4878**

SENTINEL (CARLISLE, PA.), THE. (US/0887-0802). **Adv Mgr:** Steve Crowley, **Tel** (717)243-2611 ext. 244. **5739**

SENTINEL (CHICAGO, ILL.). (US/0037-2331). **5662**

SENTINEL (RADCLIFF, KY.). (US). **Adv Mgr:** Sandy Bowen. **5682**

SENTINEL-RECORD, THE. (US). **Adv Mgr:** Floyd Emerson. **5632**

SENTINEL (TORONTO. 1957). (CN/0049-0202). **5067**

SEOUL JOURNAL OF ECONOMICS. (KO). **1520**

SEPARATION AND PURIFICATION METHODS (SOFTCOVER ED.). (US/0360-2540). **1029**

SEPARATION SCIENCE AND TECHNOLOGY. (US/0149-6395). **1029**

SEPARATIONS TECHNOLOGY. (US/0956-9618). **1996**

SEPTS (SAINT PAUL, MINN.), THE. (US/1049-1783). **2472**

SEQUENCES. (FR/0559-4871). **3471**

SEQUENCES (MONTREAL). (CN/0037-2412). **4077**

SEQUENTIAL ANALYSIS. (US/0747-4946). **3533**

SEQUOIA (SAN FRANCISCO). (US/0199-8153). **Adv Mgr:** Robert Forsberg. **4996**

SERB WORLD U.S.A. (US/8756-5579). **2760**

SERGIO ARAGONES GROO THE WANDERER (NEW YORK, N.Y.). (US/0887-5952). **4866**

SERIAL NUMBER GUIDE. (US/8756-2987). **627**

SERIALS LIBRARIAN, THE. (US/0361-526X). **3249**

SERIALS REVIEW. (US/0098-7913). **3249**

SERICHAI. (US/0888-238X). **Adv Mgr:** Siriwan Plsuttipong. **5640**

SERIDIM. (IS). **5052**

SERIES IN PSYCHOSOCIAL EPIDEMIOLOGY. (US/1044-5633). **3936**

SERIES ON ROCK AND SOIL MECHANICS. (US/0080-9004). **1397**

SERIGRAFIA (MILANO, ITALY). (IT). **4569**

SERRA D'OR. (SP/0037-2501). **3352**

SERVAMUS. (SA). **3176**

SERVICE BUSINESS. (US/0736-5764). **710**

SERVICE INDUSTRIES JOURNAL, THE. (UK/0264-2069). **Adv Mgr:** Ann Kidson. **1626**

SERVICE NEWS PARIS. (FR/1144-2433). **886**

SERVICE REPORTER. (US/0193-2128). **2608**

SERVICE STATION. (AT). **Adv Mgr:** M. Malone. **5392**

SERVICE STATION MANAGEMENT. (US/0488-3896). **5425**

SERVICES MARKETING NEWSLETTER. (US/0891-0952). **886**

SERVICES (VIENNA, VA.). (US/0279-0548). **4214**

SESAME STREET MAGAZINE. (US/0049-0253). **1069**

SESSION / COMITE INTERNATIONAL DES POIDS ET MESURES, COMITE CONSULTATIF DE THERMOMETRIE. (FR). **4032**

SESSIONAL YEARBOOK ... AND DIRECTORY OF MEMBERS. (UK/0073-9847). **Adv Mgr Tel** same as publisher. **2030**

SETON HALL LAW REVIEW. (US/0586-5964). **3048**

SETON HALL LEGISLATIVE JOURNAL. (US/0361-8951). **3048**

SETTLER (TOWANDA, PA. 1952), THE. (US/0488-4965). **2760**

SEVENTEEN. (US/0037-301X). **1069**

SEVENTEENTH-CENTURY FRENCH STUDIES. (UK/0265-1068). **3435**

SEVENTEENTH CENTURY NEWS. (US/0037-3028). **3435**

SEVENTEENTH CENTURY, THE. (UK/0268-117X). **2709**

SEW. (NE). **3136**

SEW BEAUTIFUL. (US/1063-9160). **Adv Mgr:** Kathy McMakin, **Tel** same as publisher. **5185**

SEW IT SEAMS. (US/0888-577X). **5186**

SEWANEE REVIEW, THE. (US/0037-3052). **3352**

SEWARD PHOENIX LOG. (US). **Adv Mgr:** Claire Rodgers, **Tel** (907)224-8070. **5629**

SEWICKLEY HERALD (1968), THE. (US/1047-0697). **5739**

SEWTRADE C F I YEARBOOK AND DIRECTORY. (AT/1035-1272). **1087**

SEX EDUCATION COALITION NEWS. (US/0741-9686). **1783**

SEXTANT (WASHINGTON, D.C.). (US/0731-2180). **1272**

SEXUAL COERCION & ASSAULT. (US/0884-4372). **5257**

SEXUALLY TRANSMITTED DISEASES. (US/0148-5717). **4802**

SEYMOUR HERALD, THE. (US). **5672**

SEZ. (US/0190-3640). **3435**

SF WEEKLY (SAN FRANCISCO, CALIF.). (US/1060-2526). **5640**

SFINX. (DK/0105-7618). **2629**

SHADES. (CN/0228-3115). **4152**

SHADOWS CHRIST CHURCH. (NZ/1170-9758). **3947**

SHAHID (TEHRAN, IRAN : 1983). (IR). **2493**

SHAIR INTERNATIONAL FORUM. (CN/1185-3158). **2545**

SHAKER MESSENGER, THE. (US/0270-9368). **Adv Mgr Tel** (616)396-4588. **2760**

SHAKESPEARE BULLETIN. (US/0748-2558). **5368**

SHAKESPEARE IN SOUTHERN AFRICA : JOURNAL OF THE SHAKESPEARE SOCIETY OF SOUTHERN AFRICA. (SA/1011-582X). **5368**

SHAKESPEARE ON FILM NEWSLETTER. (US/0739-6570). **3435**

SHAKESPEARE QUARTERLY. (US/0037-3222). **3435**

SHAKESPEARE SURVEY (CAMBRIDGE). (UK/0080-9152). **434**

SHAKHTNYI I KARERNYI TRANSPORT. (RU). **2151**

SHALE SHAKER. (US/0037-3257). **1397**

SHAMAN'S DRUM. (US/0887-8897). **4997**

SHAMROCK TEXAN, THE. (US). **5754**

SHAN CHA. (CC). **3435**

SHAN-HSI SHIH TA HSUEH PAO. CHE HSUEH SHE HUI KO HSUEH PAN. (CC). **5218**

SHANG-HAI CHEN CHIU TSA CHIH. (CC). **3640**

SHANG-HAI WEN HSUEH. (CC). **3436**

SHANGHAI NONGXUEYUAN XUEBAO. (CC/1000-193X). **134**

SHANNON COUNTY CURRENT WAVE. (US). **Adv Mgr:** Rita Johnson. **5704**

SHANTIH. (US/0037-329X). **3436**

SHAONIEN ZHONGGUO (SAN FRANCISCO, CALIF.). (US/0749-7679). **5640**

SHAPE (WOODLAND HILLS, CALIF.). (US/0744-5121). **2601**

SHARE (TORONTO). (CN/0709-4647). **5794**

SHAREWARE MAGAZINE. (US/1042-0681). **1202**

SHARING IDEAS. (US/0886-1501). **2545**

SHARING THE PRACTICE. (US/0193-8274). **4997**

SHARING THE VICTORY. (US/0745-1245). **Adv Mgr:** John Dodderidge, **Tel** (816)921-0909. **4917**

SHARON REPORTER, THE. (US). **Adv Mgr:** Mabel Jackson. **5770**

SHAW'S DIRECTORY OF COURTS IN ENGLAND AND WALES. (UK/0307-3343). **3048**

SHAW'S DIRECTORY OF COURTS IN THE UNITED KINGDOM. (UK). **Adv Mgr:** Crispin Williams. **3048**

SHEEP BREEDER AND SHEEPMAN MAGAZINE. (US/0037-3400). **221**

SHEEP CANADA MAGAZINE. (CN/0702-8881). **221**

SHEEP MAGAZINE. (US/0279-9200). **221**

SHEET METAL INDUSTRIES. (UK/0037-3435). **4019**

SHEET MUSIC EXCHANGE, THE. (US/0741-7780). **4152**

SHEET MUSIC MAGAZINE. STANDARD PIANO/GUITAR. (US/0273-6462). **Adv Mgr:** Josephine Sblendorio, **Tel** (914)232-8108. **4153**

SHEFFIELD AND SOUTH YORKSHIRE CHAMBERS OF COMMERCE DIRECTORY. (UK/0950-8945). **851**

SHELBY COUNTY REPORTER (1955). (US/1063-9489). **Adv Mgr:** Terri Quarles. **5628**

SHELBY EXCHANGE. (US). **2472**

SHELBY PROMOTER, THE. (US). **Adv Mgr:** Cindy Combs, **Tel** (406)434-5171. **5706**

SHELBY REPORT OF THE SOUTHEAST, THE. (US/0194-1968). **Adv Mgr:** D. Heller. **2357**

SHELBY REPORT OF THE SOUTHWEST. (US/0192-916X). **Adv Mgr:** D. Heller, **Tel** (404)534-8380. **2357**

SHELDON'S RETAIL DIRECTORY OF THE UNITED STATES AND CANADA. (US). **1087**

SHELLS AND SEA LIFE. (US/0747-6078). **5597**

SHELTER ISLAND REPORTER. (US/0746-066X). **Adv Mgr:** Patricia Binder, **Tel** (516)749-1000. **5721**

SHELTERFORCE. (US/0885-9612). **Adv Mgr:** Dale Coleman & Bernice Henry, **Tel** (201)678-3110. **2835**

SHELTIE INTERNATIONAL. (US/0745-2012). **4288**

SHELTIE PACESETTER. (US/0744-6608). **4288**

SHELTON-MASON COUNTY JOURNAL, THE. (US). **Adv Mgr:** Michael Politz. **5762**

SHEM TOV. (CN/0843-6924). **2472**

SHENANDOAH. (US/0037-3583). **3436**

SHENANDOAH HERALD, SHENANDOAH VALLEY, THE. (US/0746-6846). **Adv Mgr:** Carol Holmes. **5759**

SHENG LI KO HSUEH CHIN CHAN. (CC/0559-7765). **587**

SHENGWU GONGCHENG XUEBAO. (CC/1000-3061). **3696**

SHENGWU HUAXUE YU SHENGWU WULI JINZHAN. (CH/0253-9918). **473**

SHENGWU HUAXUE ZAZHI. (CC/1000-8543). **3696**

SHEPARD'S MANUAL OF FEDERAL PRACTICE / EDITORIAL STAFF, EDITOR IN CHIEF, RUDOLPH W. FISCHER ... [ET AL.]. (US). **3051**

SHEPHERD EXPRESS. (US/1071-5185). **Adv Mgr:** Mary Henschel. **5770**

SHEPHERD (NEW WASHINGTON, OHIO), THE. (US/8750-7897). **Adv Mgr:** Ken Kark, **Tel** (419)492-2364. **221**

SHEPPARD'S BOOK DEALERS IN EUROPE. (UK/0963-0171). **4832**

SHEPPARD'S BOOK DEALERS IN NORTH AMERICA. (UK/0269-1469). **4832**

SHEPPARD'S BOOK DEALERS IN THE BRITISH ISLES. (UK/0950-0715). **4832**

SHERIDAN HEADLIGHT, THE. (US). **5632**

SHERIDAN PRESS (SHERIDAN, WYO.), THE. (US/1074-682X). **5772**

SHERIFF (ALEXANDRIA, VA.). (US/1070-8170). **Adv Mgr:** D. Strigel, **Tel** (703)838-5330. **3176**

SHERMAN SENTINEL, THE. (US/1071-4480). **Adv Mgr:** David and Janet Hopkins. **2493**

SHHH. (US/0883-1688). **4393**

SHHH NEWS. (AT/1033-792X). **4393**

SHIBAO ZHOU KAN (MEIZHOU-BAN). (US/0883-6655). **Adv Mgr:** Hai-Hwa Yuan, **Tel** (718)937-6110. **5721**

SHIH CHIEH CHIH SHIH / SHIJIE ZHISHI. (CC). **4535**

SHIH CHIEH CHING CHI (CHUNG-KUO SHIH CHIEH CHING CHI HSUEH HUI). (CC). **1583**

SHIH TZU REPORTER, THE. (US/1040-5801). **4288**

SHIJIE RIBAO (SAN FRANCISCO, CALIF.). (US/0747-5071). **Adv Mgr:** Shirley Chan. **5640**

SHINGLE, THE. (US/0037-377X). **Adv Mgr Tel** (215)238-6342. **3055**

SHINING STAR (CARTHAGE, ILL.). (US/0884-5514). **1905**

SHIP & BOAT INTERNATIONAL. (UK/0037-3834). **5456**

SHIP & BOAT INTERNATIONAL. ANNUAL GUIDE. (UK). **4183**

SHIP-BY-TRUCK OFFICIAL ONTARIO DIRECTORY AND BUYER'S GUIDE. (CN/0711-303X). **5392**

SHIPBROKER, THE. (UK/0142-6680). **5456**

SHIPCARE & MARITIME MANAGEMENT. (UK/0263-7944). **5456**

SHIPMATE (ANNAPOLIS, MD.). (US/0488-6720). **4183**

SHIPPERS' TIMES. (SI/0217-1139). **5456**

SHIPPING & MARINE INDUSTRIES JOURNAL. (II/0970-0285). **5456**

SHIPS ATLAS, THE. (UK). **5456**

SHIPS MONTHLY. (UK/0037-394X). **4183**

SHIYOU KANTAN KAIFA. (CC/1000-0747). **4278**

SHO-BAN NEWS, THE. (US/0197-7954). **5657**

SHOAL LAKE STAR. (CN). **Adv Mgr Tel** same as publisher. **5794**

SHOE FACTORY BUYERS' GUIDE. (US). **1087**

SHOFAR (MELVILLE, N.Y.). (US/0748-9706). **1069**

SHONI GEKA. (JA/0385-6313). **3911**

SHOOTING INDUSTRY, THE. (US/0037-4148). **4917**

SHOOTING — Advertising Accepted Index

SHOOTING SPORTS RETAILER. (US/0887-9397). **957**

SHOOTING SPORTSMAN (WILLIAMSPORT, PA.). (US/1050-5717). **Adv Mgr:** Bill Anderson. **4878**

SHOOTING STAR REVIEW. (US/0892-1407). **3436**

SHOOTING TIMES. (US/0038-8084). **Adv Mgr:** Ken Ramage. **4917**

SHOP (DON MILLS). (CN/0381-8667). **Adv Mgr:** M. C. Figurel, **Tel** 274-4883. **2128**

SHOPPER & OBSERVER NEWS, THE. (US). **1299**

SHOPPING CENTER DIGEST. (US/0885-209X). **957**

SHOPPING CENTER WORLD PRODUCT AND SERVICE DIRECTORY. (US/0049-0393=). **957**

SHOPPING CENTERS TODAY. (US/0885-9841). **957**

SHOPPING CENTRE NEWS. (AT). **1299**

SHORE AND BEACH. (US/0037-4237). **2205**

SHOREVIEW PRESS. (US). **Adv Mgr:** Michelle Larson. **5698**

SHORT FICTION BY WOMEN. (US). **3436**

SHORTHORN COUNTRY. (US/0149-9319). **Adv Mgr:** A. K. Sears, **Tel** (402)393-7051. **221**

SHORTHORN NEWS. (CN/0037-427X). **221**

SHORTHORN, THE. (US/0892-6603). **Adv Mgr:** Arnie Phillips. **1095**

SHOSHI SAKUIN TEMBO. (JA). **3249**

SHOSHONE NEWS-PRESS. (US/1044-9353). **Adv Mgr:** Judy Binkley, **Tel** (208)783-1107. **5657**

SHOTS (DANVILLE, KY.). (US/1048-793X). **4376**

SHOW HORSE (BANGOR, ME.). (US/8755-3929). **2802**

SHOW-ME UNDERWRITER, THE. (US/0883-6825). **2893**

SHOW MUSIC. (US/8755-9560). **4153**

SHOW STEER, THE. (US/0195-2463). **221**

SHOWCASE (MINNEAPOLIS). (US/0196-1586). **4153**

SHOWCASE (NEW YORK). (US/0361-3232). **3186**

SHOWCAST. (AT). **388**

SHROPSHIRE FAMILY HISTORY JOURNAL. (UK/0261-135X). **2472**

SHUKAN ASAHI. (JA). **2508**

SHUPIHUI. (PE/0254-2021). **2273**

SHUTTERBUG. (US/0895-321X). **4376**

SHUTTLE, SPINDLE & DYEPOT. (US/0049-0423). **375**

SI YU YAN. (CH/0258-8412). **2854**

SIAJ - JOURNAL OF THE SINGAPORE INSTITUTE OF ARCHITECTS. (SI/0049-0520). **308**

SIAM JOURNAL ON APPLIED MATHEMATICS. (US/0036-1399). **3534**

SIAM JOURNAL ON COMPUTING. (US/0097-5397). **1262**

SIAM JOURNAL ON CONTROL AND OPTIMIZATION. (US/0363-0129). **3534**

SIAM JOURNAL ON MATHEMATICAL ANALYSIS. (US/0036-1410). **3534**

SIAM JOURNAL ON NUMERICAL ANALYSIS. (US/0036-1429). **3535**

SIAM NEWS : A PUBLICATION OF SOCIETY FOR INDUSTRIAL AND APPLIED MATHEMATICS. (US). **3535**

SIAM REVIEW. (US/0036-1445). **3535**

SIBBALD GUIDE TO THE TEXAS TOP TWO-FIFTY, THE. (US/0278-3266). **710**

SIBERIAN QUARTERLY, THE. (US/0274-7286). **Adv Mgr:** Cindy Kerstiens. **4288**

SIC. (VE/0049-0431). **4496**

SICANGU SUN TIMES. (US/1070-7786). **2273**

SICHERHEITSBEAUFTRAGTER. (GW/0300-3337). **3176**

SICHERHEITSINGENIEUR. (GW/0300-3329). **2870**

SICILIA PARRA. (US/8755-6987). **2273**

SIDA RAPPORT. (SW/0282-6011). **2912**

SIDDHA VANI. (II). **5041**

SIDE-SADDLE NEWS. (US/0744-3056). **2802**

SIDE STREETS OF THE WORLD. (US/0741-7624). **5491**

SIDELINES. (US). **4918**

SIDNEY ARGUS-HERALD, THE. **Adv Mgr:** Ellen Longman, **Tel** (712)374-2251. **5672**

SIDNEY TELEGRAPH (SIDNEY, NEB. : 1951). (US). **Adv Mgr:** Sue Kilgore, **Tel** (308)254-5555. **5707**

SIECUS REPORT. (US/0091-3995). **5188**

SIEMENS REVIEW. (GW/0302-2528). **2081**

SIERRA. (US/0161-7362). **2205**

SIERRA COUNTY SENTINEL. (US). **5713**

SIERRA HERITAGE. (US/0886-6503). **Adv Mgr:** Donna Lewis, **Tel** (916)823-3986. **5491**

SIGHT AND SOUND (LONDON). (UK/0037-4806). **Adv Mgr:** Hucksters, **Tel** 11 44 89 2784804. **4078**

SIGHTHOUND REVIEW. (US/8750-1953). **4288**

SIGHTLINES (NEW YORK, N.Y.). (US/0037-4830). **4078**

SIGN BUSINESS. (US/0893-9888). **Adv Mgr:** Ken Higgins. **710**

SIGN LANGUAGE STUDIES. (US/0302-1475). **3321**

SIGN WORLD. (UK/0049-0466). **766**

SIGNAL. (US). **3436**

SIGNAL (1950). (US/0037-4938). **Adv Mgr Tel** (703)631-6187. **1121**

SIGNAL (LISBON, OHIO). (US/0893-4592). **Adv Mgr:** Tammy Thacker. **5730**

SIGNAL PROCESSING. (NE/0165-1684). **2081**

SIGNAL PROCESSING. IMAGE COMMUNICATION. (NE/0923-5965). **2081**

SIGNAL (RYCROFT). (CN/0712-1296). **5794**

SIGNAL TRANSDUCTION & CYCLIC NUCLEOTIDES. (UK/0964-7589). **493**

SIGNAL UND DRAHT. (GW/0037-4997). **5436**

SIGNALMAN'S JOURNAL, THE. (US/0037-5020). **5436**

SIGNALNAYA INFORMATSIYA KATALIZ I KATALIZATORY. (RU/0234-9736). **1058**

SIGNALNAYA INFORMATSIYA KHIMIYA VYSOKIKH ENERGII. (RU/0234-968X). **992**

SIGNALNAYA INFORMATSIYA NAPOLNENNYE I ARMIROVANNYE PLASTIKI. (RU/0234-971X). **992**

SIGNALNAYA INFORMATSIYA OCHISTKA I UTILIZATSIYA OTKHODOV KHIMICHESKIK PROIZVODSTV. (RU/0234-9701). **992**

SIGNALNAYA INFORMATSIYA SORBENTY POVERKHNOSTNO-AKTIVNYE VESHCHESTVA. (RU/0234-9698). **992**

SIGNATURE (PRAIRIE VILLAGE, KAN.). (US/1068-1957). **4569**

SIGNCRAFT. (US/0270-4757). **382**

SIGNPOST. (UK). **2809**

SIGNS (CHICAGO, ILL.). (US/0097-9740). **5566**

SIGNUM. (FI/0355-0036). **3249**

SIIRTOLAISUUS / SIIRTOLAISUUSINSTITUUTTI. (FI/0355-3779). **1921**

SIKH COURIER, THE. (UK). **Adv Mgr:** B. S. Grewal, **Tel** same as publisher. **4997**

SIKH REVIEW, THE. (II/0037-5128). **4997**

SIKSI : THE NORDIC ART REVIEW. (FI/0782-7423). **330**

SILENCIUM. (GW). **2809**

SILENT NEWS. (US/0049-0490). **Adv Mgr Tel** (716)272-4900. **5721**

SILICATES INDUSTRIELS. (BE/0037-5225). **2594**

SILSBEE BEE, THE. (US). **5754**

SILVAE GENETICA. (GW/0037-5349). **528**

SILVER (WHITTIER, CALIF.). (US/0899-6105). **4019**

SILVERFISH REVIEW. (US/0164-1085). **Adv Mgr:** R. Moody, **Tel** (503)344-5060. **3437**

SILVERTON STANDARD AND THE MINER, THE. (US). **Adv Mgr:** Sharon Denious. **5644**

SIMAN KERIAH. (IS). **3352**

SIMANTIKA. (US/8755-7517). **3437**

SIMG : MEDICINA GENERALE. (IT/1120-673X). **3641**

SIMIOLUS. (NE/0037-5411). **364**

SIMMENTAL SHIELD. (US/0192-3072). **221**

SIMON'S TAXES. (UK). **3055**

SIMPSON COUNTY NEWS. (US). **Adv Mgr:** Jean Butler, **Tel** (601)849-3434. **5701**

SIMSBURY NEWS, THE. (US/0891-9542). **Adv Mgr:** Frank Chilinski. **5646**

SIMULATION & GAMING. (US/1046-8781). **1283**

SIMULATION/GAMES FOR LEARNING. (UK/0142-9361). **1905**

SIMULATION PRACTICE AND THEORY. (NE/0928-4869). **Adv Mgr:** W Van Cattenburch. **1244**

SIMULATION (SAN DIEGO, CALIF.). (US/0037-5497). **1283**

SINFONIAN (1980), THE. (US/8750-5347). **4153**

SING OUT. (US/0037-5624). **4153**

SING OUT EAST DONCASTER. (AT/0818-0555). **Adv Mgr Tel** 03 568-7374. **4153**

SINGAPORE BUSINESS. (SI/0129-2951). **851**

SINGAPORE JOURNAL OF EDUCATION. (SI/0129-4776). **1784**

SINGAPORE JOURNAL OF OBSTETRICS & GYNAECOLOGY. (SI/0129-3273). **3768**

SINGAPORE JOURNAL OF PRIMARY INDUSTRIES. (SI/0129-6485). **134**

SINGAPORE LAW REVIEW. (SI/0080-9705). **3055**

SINGAPORE MANAGEMENT REVIEW. (SI). **886**

SINGENDE KIRCHE. (AU/0037-5721). **4153**

SINGING NEWS MAGAZINE, THE. (US/1060-3956). **Adv Mgr:** Rick Templeton, **Tel** same as publisher. **4153**

SINGLE ADULT MINISTRY INFORMATION. (US/0887-1167). **4997**

SINGLE GENTLEMEN & WOMEN. (US). **3996**

SINGLE LIVING MAGAZINE : AN IOWA PERSPECTIVE. (US). **2493**

SINGLE PARENT, THE. (US/0037-5748). **Adv Mgr Tel** (301)588-9354. **2286**

SINGLELIFE (MILWAUKEE, WIS.). (US/8756-0380). **Adv Mgr:** David Rose. **2493**

SINGMUL CHOJIK PAEYANG HAKHOE CHI. (KO). **528**

SINGMUL HAKHOE CHI. (KO/0583-421X). **Adv Mgr:** Young Myung Kwon. **528**

SINISTER WISDOM. (US/0196-1853). **Adv Mgr:** Jamie Lee Evans. **2796**

SINN UND FORM. (GW/0037-5756). **2522**

SINO-AMERICAN RELATIONS. (CH). **4535**

SINO-JAPANESE STUDIES. (US). **2664**

SINOPSE ESTATISTICA DA REGIAO NORTE / SECRETARIA DE PLANEJAMENTO DA PRESIDENCIA DA REPUBLICA, FUNDACAO INSTITUTO BRASILEIRO DE GEOGRAFIA E ESTATISTICA, IBGE. (BL). **5338**

SINTESE. (BL/0103-4332). **5219**

SINTEZA. (XV/0049-0601). **364**

SIOUX COUNTY CAPITAL-DEMOCRAT, THE. (US). **Adv Mgr:** Dennis Hartog. **5673**

SISKIYOU PIONEER IN FOLKLORE, FACT AND FICTION, THE. (US/0196-0725). **2324**

SISMODINAMICA (DURHAM, N.H.). (US/1051-6441). **2031**

SISTEMA (MADRID). (SP/0210-0223). **5219**

SISTEMI INTELLIGENTI. (IT). **1217**

SISTEMNOE OPISANIE LEKSIKI GERMANSKIKH IAZYKOV. (RU). **3321**

SISTERS TODAY. (US/0037-590X). **5036**

SITE REPORT, THE. (US/0275-1488). **3488**

SITE SELECTION & INDUSTRIAL DEVELOPMENT. (US/1041-3073). **4847**

SITES ET MONUMENTS. (FR/0489-0280). **2709**

SITES (NEW YORK, N.Y.). (US/0747-9409). **330**

SITREP. (CN/0316-5620). **4057**

SITUATIONS DIGEST. (US/1059-1958). **2545**

SIXTEENTH CENTURY JOURNAL, THE. (US/0361-0160). **2629**

SIYYON. (IS/0044-4758). **5052**

SIZZLE SHEET, THE. (US/0738-6516). **936**

SKAGIT VALLEY HERALD. (US/1071-197X). **Adv Mgr:** Paul Wood. **5762**

SKANNER, THE. (US). **Adv Mgr:** Ted Banks, **Tel** (503)287-3562 ext. 507. **5734**

SKATING. (US/0037-6132). **Adv Mgr:** Luann Duda, **Tel** (719)635-5200. **4918**

SKATTERETT. (NO/0333-2810). **3055**

SKEET SHOOTING REVIEW. (US/0037-6140). **Adv Mgr:** Susie Fluckiger, **Tel** (800)US-SKEET. **4918**

SKEPTIC (ALTADENA, CALIF.). (US/1063-9330). **5158**

SKEPTIKER. (GW/0936-9244). **4243**

SKI AREA MANAGEMENT. (US/0037-6175). **4918**

SKI BUSINESS. (US/0037-6191). **4918**

SKI CANADA. (CN/0702-701X). **4918**

SKI NAUTIQUE NEWS. (CN/0714-8267). **4918**

SKI (NEW YORK, N.Y.). (US/0037-6159). **4918**

SKI RACING. (US/0037-6213). **Adv Mgr:** Phil Knaub. **4918**

SKIING (NEW YORK, N.Y.). (US/0037-6264). **4918**

SKILLINGS' MINING REVIEW. (US/0037-6329). **2151**

SKIN & ALLERGY NEWS. (US/0037-6337). **3722**

SKIN DIVER. (US/0037-6345). **4918**

SKIN PHARMACOLOGY. (SZ/1011-0283). **3723**

SKINNED KNUCKLES. (US/0164-3509). **5425**

SKOG & FORSKNING. (SW/1101-9506). **2395**

SKOG INDUSTRI. (NO/0800-8582). **4239**

SKY AND TELESCOPE. (US/0037-6604). **399**

SKY CALENDAR. (US/0733-6314). **399**

SKY-HI NEWS. (US). **5644**

SKYDIVING. (US/0192-7361). **4918**

SKYWAYS. (II). **35**

SKYWAYS (POUGHKEEPSIE, N.Y.). (US/1051-6956). **35**

SKYWAYS: THE JOURNAL OF THE AIRPLANE 1920-1940. (US). **35**

SL RIVISTA DI ORGANIZZAZIONE. (IT). **1520**

SLAGER. (NE). **2357**

SLAVE RIVER JOURNAL. (CN/0707-4964). **Adv Mgr:** Tony Dowler, **Tel** (403)872-2764. **5794**

SLAVERY & ABOLITION. (UK/0144-039X). **Adv Mgr:** Ann Kidson. **4513**

SLAVIC AND EAST EUROPEAN JOURNAL. (US/0037-6752). **3321**

SLAVIC REVIEW. (US/0037-6779). **2854**

SLAVIC SYNTAX NEWSLETTER, THE. (US/1070-5775). **3321**

SLAVICA SLOVACA. (XO/0037-6787). **3321**

SLEEP (NEW YORK, N.Y.). (US/0161-8105). **3641**

SLEEP WATCHERS. (US/0748-5352). **3641**

SLEEPY EYE HERALD-DISPATCH. (US). **5698**

SLOAN MANAGEMENT REVIEW. (US/0019-848X). **886**

SLOVAK MUSIC. (XO/0862-0407). **4153**

SLOVAK V AMERIKE. (US/0199-6819). **5739**

SLOVENIJA (SLOVENSKA IZSELJENSKA MATICA). (XV). **2273**

SLOVENSKA ARCHEOLOGIA. (XO/0037-6949). **282**

SLOVENSKA DRZAVA. (CN/0037-6957). **4496**

SLOVENSKA LITERATURA. (XO/0037-6973). **3437**

SLOVENSKA REC. (XO/0037-6981). **3322**

SLOVENSKE DIVADLO. (XO/0037-699X). **5368**

SLOVENSKY NARODOPIS. (XO/0037-7023). **245**

SMALL BUSINESS CHRONICLE. (US). **711**

SMALL BUSINESS ECONOMICS. (NE/0921-898X). **1520**

SMALL BUSINESS EXCHANGE. (US/0892-5992). **Adv Mgr:** Robert Kratz. **711**

SMALL BUSINESS REPORT (MONTEREY, CALIF.). (US/0164-5382). **711**

SMALL BUSINESS TODAY. (US). **Adv Mgr:** Lena, **Tel** (216)331-6397. **711**

SMALL COMPANY INVESTOR. (UK). **914**

SMALL COMPUTERS IN THE ARTS NEWS. (US/0748-2043). **330**

SMALL ENTERPRISE DEVELOPMENT. (UK/0957-1329). **711**

SMALL FARMER'S JOURNAL. (US/0743-9989). **135**

SMALL POND MAGAZINE OF LITERATURE, THE. (US/0737-1535). **3437**

SMALL PRESS. (US/0000-0485). **Adv Mgr:** Lisa Phelps. **4569**

SMALL PRESS BOOK REVIEW, THE. (US/8756-7202). **4832**

SMALL PRESS RECORD OF BOOKS IN PRINT. (US/0148-9720). **4832**

SMALL PRESS REVIEW. (US/0037-7228). **3353**

SMALL SIBLINGS. (US/0897-7860). **2472**

SMALL TOWN OBSERVER, THE. (US/1061-9933). **Adv Mgr:** Thom Evons, **Tel** (503)383-3746. **2835**

SMALL WARS AND INSURGENCIES. (UK/0959-2318). **Adv Mgr:** Anne Kidson. **4057**

SMALL WORLD (GUILFORD). (US/0037-7260). **2907**

SMARANDACHE FUNCTION JOURNAL. (US/1053-4792). **Adv Mgr:** L. Jones. **3536**

SMART (NEW YORK, N.Y.). (US/0899-2347). **2546**

SMASH HITS. (UK/0260-3004). **1300**

SMITH COUNTY REFORMER, THE. (US). **Adv Mgr:** Brenda Ingram, **Tel** (601)785-6525. **5701**

SMITH PAPERS. (US/0278-3134). **2472**

SMITHSONIAN. (US/0037-7333). **4172**

SMOKESHOP. (US/0146-9266). **712**

SMOOTH MUSCLE. (UK/0261-4928). **3807**

SMPTE JOURNAL (1976). (US/0036-1682). **4078**

SMT TRENDS. (US/0890-7900). **2081**

SMYTH COUNTY NEWS. (US/0744-0766). **5759**

SNACK WORLD. (US/0896-1670). **2358**

SNACKS MAGAZINE, THE. (UK). **Adv Mgr:** Dawn Dubsky, **Tel** 44 33 46090756. **2358**

SNAKE. (JA/0386-3425). **5597**

SNIPS. (US/0037-7457). **2608**

SNOHOMISH COUNTY TRIBUNE. (US). **Adv Mgr:** Becky Reed. **5762**

SNOW COUNTRY. (US/0896-758X). **Adv Mgr:** Tom Brown, **Tel** (212)789-3090. **4919**

SNOWMOBILE ANNUAL. (CN/0700-3315). **4919**

SNYDER DAILY NEWS, THE. (US). **Adv Mgr:** Wayne Burney. **5754**

SOAP, COSMETICS, CHEMICAL SPECIALTIES. (US/0091-1372). **1030**

SOAP OPERA UPDATE. (US/0898-1485). **2546**

SOAP OPERA WORD-FIND HIDDEN WORD PUZZLES. (US/0194-3197). **4866**

SOARING. (US/0037-7503). **35**

SOBORNOST. (UK/0144-8722). **5040**

SOBRE LOS DERIVADOS DE LA CANA DE AZUCAR (HAVANA, CUBA : 1983). (CU). **2358**

SOBREVIVENCIA. (BL). **2205**

SOCCER AMERICA. (US/0163-4070). **4919**

SOCCER DIGEST (EVANSTON). (US/0149-2365). **4919**

SOCCER INTERNATIONAL. (US/1053-4199). **Adv Mgr:** P. Herbison. **4919**

SOCCER JOURNAL. (US/0560-3617). **Adv Mgr:** Lee & Associates, **Tel** (800)364-0426. **4919**

SOCCER JR. (US/1060-9911). **Adv Mgr:** M. Haisch, **Tel** (203)259-5766. **1069**

SOCCER MAGAZINE (TITUSVILLE, FLA.). (US/1070-9754). **4919**

SOCCER MATCH. (US/0744-964X). **4919**

SOCIAAL BESTEK. (NE). **5258**

SOCIAL ACTION & THE LAW. (US/0272-765X). **3056**

SOCIAL ACTION (NEW DELHI). (II/0037-7627). **5258**

SOCIAL ALTERNATIVES. (AT/0155-0306). **5258**

SOCIAL ANALYSIS (ADELAIDE, S. AUST.). (AT/0155-977X). **5219**

SOCIAL ANARCHISM. (US/0196-4801). **4546**

SOCIAL AND ECONOMIC STUDIES. (JM/0037-7651). **Adv Mgr:** Ms. A Paul, **Tel** (809)927-1020. **5219**

SOCIAL AND LABOUR BULLETIN. (US/0377-5380). **1710**

SOCIAL BEHAVIOR AND PERSONALITY. (NZ/0301-2212). **5258**

SOCIAL BIOLOGY. (US/0037-766X). **551**

SOCIAL CHANGE. (II/0049-0857). **Adv Mgr:** R.S. Somi. **5308**

SOCIAL CHANGE AND DEVELOPMENT. (RH). **4546**

SOCIAL CHOICE AND WELFARE. (GW/0176-1714). **5308**

SOCIAL COGNITION. (US/0278-016X). **5258**

SOCIAL CONCEPT. (US/0737-7762). **5219**

SOCIAL DEVELOPMENT ISSUES. (US/0147-1473). **5308**

SOCIAL DYNAMICS. (SA/0253-3952). **5258**

SOCIAL EDUCATION. (US/0037-7724). **5219**

SOCIAL FORCES. (US/0037-7732). **5258**

SOCIAL HISTORY (LONDON). (UK/0307-1022). **2630**

SOCIAL HISTORY OF MEDICINE : THE JOURNAL OF THE SOCIETY FOR THE SOCIAL HISTORY OF MEDICINE. (UK/0951-631X). **3641**

SOCIAL HOUSING. (UK/1351-4288). **5308**

SOCIAL INDICATORS FOR FIJI. (FJ). **5259**

SOCIAL INDICATORS NETWORK NEWS. (US/0885-6729). **5219**

SOCIAL INDICATORS RESEARCH. (NE/0303-8300). **5219**

SOCIAL JUSTICE (SAN FRANCISCO, CALIF.). (US/1043-1578). **3177**

SOCIAL LIST OF WASHINGTON, D.C. AND SOCIAL PRECEDENCE IN WASHINGTON, THE. (US/1063-7516). **Adv Mgr:** P. Murray, **Tel** (301)949-4445. **4686**

SOCIAL ONCOLOGY NETWORK ... NEWSLETTER. (US/0882-4398). **5259**

SOCIAL PLANNING, POLICY & DEVELOPMENT ABSTRACTS. (US/1042-8380). **5266**

SOCIAL POLICY. (US/0037-7783). **5259**

SOCIAL PROBLEMS. (US/0037-7791). **5220**

SOCIAL PROCESS IN HAWAII (1979). (US/0737-6871). **5220**

SOCIAL PSYCHOLOGY QUARTERLY. (US/0190-2725). **5259**

SOCIAL SCIENCE & MEDICINE (1982). (US/0277-9536). **5220**

SOCIAL SCIENCE COMPUTER REVIEW. (US/0894-4393). **1272**

SOCIAL SCIENCE HISTORY. (US/0145-5532). **5220**

SOCIAL SCIENCE JOURNAL (FORT COLLINS), THE. (US/0362-3319). **5220**

SOCIAL SCIENCE RECORD. (US/0037-7872). **5221**

SOCIAL SCIENTIST (NEW DELHI). (II/0970-0293). **5221**

SOCIAL SERVICE JOBS. (US). **5308**

SOCIAL SERVICES EMPLOYMENT BULLETIN. (US/1054-3384). **5309**

SOCIAL SERVICES RESEARCH JOURNAL. (UK/0265-6957). **Adv Mgr:** Helen Harris. **5309**

SOCIAL STUDIES OF SCIENCE. (UK/0306-3127). **5221**

SOCIAL STUDIES (PHILADELPHIA, PA. : 1953). (US/0037-7996). **5222**

SOCIAL STUDIES REVIEW (MILLBRAE, CALIF.). (US/1056-6325). **Adv Mgr:** Mezzetta, Sabato. **5222**

SOCIAL TEXT. (US/0164-2472). **5259**

SOCIAL THEORY AND PRACTICE. (US/0037-802X). **5222**

SOCIAL THOUGHT (WASHINGTON, D.C.). (US/0099-183X). **4997**

SOCIAL WELFARE. (II/0037-8038). **5309**

SOCIAL WORK AND CHRISTIANITY. (US/0737-5778). **5309**

SOCIAL WORK EDUCATION REPORTER. (US/0037-8062). **5309**

SOCIAL WORK IN HEALTH CARE. (US/0098-1389). **5309**

SOCIAL WORK (MANILA). (PH/0583-7057). **5309**

SOCIAL WORK (NEW YORK). (US/0037-8046). **5309**

SOCIAL WORK RESEARCH & ABSTRACTS. (US/0148-0847). **5267**

SOCIAL WORK REVIEW (NEWTON, AUCKLAND, N.Z.). (NZ/0111-7351). **5310**

SOCIAL WORK STELLENBOSCH. (SA/0037-8054). **5310**

SOCIAL — Advertising Accepted Index

SOCIAL WORK TODAY. (UK/0037-8070). **5310**

SOCIAL WORK WITH GROUPS (NEW YORK. 1978). (US/0160-9513). **5310**

SOCIAL WORKER. TRAVAILLEUR SOCIAL. (CN/0037-8089). **Adv Mgr:** same as editor. **5310**

SOCIALISM AND DEMOCRACY. (US/0885-4300). **4546**

SOCIALISMO Y PARTICIPACION. (PE). **4546**

SOCIALIST PERSPECTIVE. (II). **Adv Mgr Tel** 525196. **4547**

SOCIALIST REVIEW (SAN FRANCISCO). (US/0161-1801). **4547**

SOCIALISTA (P.S.O.E. (POLITICAL PARTY) : WEEKLY). (SP). **4547**

SOCIETA E STORIA. (IT). **2630**

SOCIETY AND NATURE. (US/1062-9599). **Adv Mgr:** Pavlos, **Tel** (303)730-6232. **2182**

SOCIETY FOR GERMAN-AMERICAN STUDIES NEWSLETTER. (US/0741-5753). **2273**

SOCIETY FOR ORGANIC PETROLOGY NEWSLETTER, THE. (US/0743-3816). **1459**

SOCIETY (MONTREAL). (CN/0381-1794). **5260**

SOCIETY (NEW BRUNSWICK). (US/0147-2011). **5222**

SOCIETY NEWS (BROOMALL, PA.). (US/8756-8861). **4153**

SOCIO-ECONOMIC PLANNING SCIENCES. (US/0038-0121). **1521**

SOCIOCRITICISM. (US/1041-9861). **5260**

SOCIOLINGUISTICA. (GW/0933-1883). **3322**

SOCIOLOGIA. (XO/0049-1225). **5260**

SOCIOLOGIA DEL LAVORO. (IT/0392-5048). **5260**

SOCIOLOGIA INTERNATIONALIS. (GW/0038-0164). **5260**

SOCIOLOGIA RURALIS. (NE/0038-0199). **5260**

SOCIOLOGICAL ABSTRACTS. (US/0038-0202). **5267**

SOCIOLOGICAL ANALYSIS. (US/0038-0210). **4998**

SOCIOLOGICAL BULLETIN. (II/0038-0229). **5260**

SOCIOLOGICAL FOCUS (KENT, OHIO). (US/0038-0237). **5260**

SOCIOLOGICAL IMAGINATION. (US/1077-5048). **5260**

SOCIOLOGICAL INQUIRY. (US/0038-0245). **5260**

SOCIOLOGICAL METHODOLOGY. (US/0081-1750). **5260**

SOCIOLOGICAL QUARTERLY. (US/0038-0253). **5261**

SOCIOLOGICAL REVIEW MONOGRAPH, THE. (UK/0081-1769). **5261**

SOCIOLOGICAL REVIEW, THE. (UK/0038-0261). **5261**

SOCIOLOGICAL SPECTRUM. (US/0273-2173). **5261**

SOCIOLOGICAL THEORY. (UK/0735-2751). **5261**

SOCIOLOGIE DU TRAVAIL (PARIS). (FR/0038-0296). **1711**

SOCIOLOGIE ET SOCIETES. (CN/0038-030X). **5262**

SOCIOLOGISCHE GIDS. (BE/0038-0334). **5262**

SOCIOLOGISK FORSKNING. (SW/0038-0342). **5262**

SOCIOLOGUS; ZEITSCHRIFT FUER EMPIRISCHE ETHNOSOZIOLOGIE UND ETHNOPSYCHOLOGIE. JOURNAL FOR EMPIRICAL ETHNO-SOCIOLOGY AND ETHNO-PSYCHOLOGY. (GW/0038-0377). **5262**

SOCIOLOGY OF EDUCATION. (US/0038-0407). **1784**

SOCIOLOGY OF EDUCATION ABSTRACTS. (UK/0038-0415). **1797**

SOCIOLOGY OF HEALTH & ILLNESS. (UK/0141-9889). **5262**

SOCIOLOGY OF SPORT JOURNAL. (US/0741-1235). **4919**

SOCIOLOGY (OXFORD). (UK/0038-0385). **Adv Mgr:** J. Ward, **Tel** 0564 772402. **5262**

SODA TO ENSO. (JA/0371-3768). **2371**

SOEDRA SKOG. (SW). **2395**

SOFT DRINKS MANAGEMENT INTERNATIONAL. (UK/0953-4776). **Adv Mgr:** Keith Bailey. **2371**

SOFT TECHNOLOGY. (AT/0810-1434). **Adv Mgr:** Jo Wick, **Tel** (03)853 8055. **1957**

SOFTWARE ABSTRACTS FOR ENGINEERS : SAFE. (IE/0790-150X). **Adv Mgr:** Ken Kelly, **Tel** 353 1 2886227. **1210**

SOFTWARE DEVELOPER'S MONTHLY. (US). **1290**

SOFTWARE FOR ENGINEERING AND WORKSTATIONS. (UK/0952-8768). **1203**

SOFTWARE-KURIER FUER MEDIZINER UND PSYCHOLOGEN. (GW/0934-5841). **1203**

SOFTWARE MAGAZINE (WESTBOROUGH, MASS.). (US/0897-8085). **1290**

SOFTWARE MAINTENANCE NEWS. (US/0741-4501). **Adv Mgr:** Judith Marx Golub. **1291**

SOFTWARE MANUFACTURING NEWS. (US/1064-878X). **1203**

SOFTWARE : PRACTICE & EXPERIENCE. (UK/0038-0644). **1291**

SOFTWARE TESTING, VERIFICATION & RELIABILITY. (UK/0960-0833). **1291**

SOIL & TILLAGE RESEARCH. (NE/0167-1987). **186**

SOIL DYNAMICS AND EARTHQUAKE ENGINEERING (1984). (UK/0267-7261). **1996**

SOIL SCIENCE. (US/0038-075X). **187**

SOIL SCIENCE SOCIETY OF AMERICA JOURNAL. (US/0361-5995). **187**

SOIL TECHNOLOGY. (GW/0933-3630). **187**

SOIL USE AND MANAGEMENT. (UK/0266-0032). **187**

SOILS AND FERTILIZERS. (UK/0038-0792). **156**

SOINS PARIS. (FR/0038-0814). **3869**

SOINS. PSYCHIATRIE. (FR/0241-6972). **3937**

SOJOURNER (CAMBRIDGE). (US/0191-8699). **5566**

SOL DE TEXAS, EL. (US). **Adv Mgr:** Jaime Montano. **5754**

SOL (PHOENIX, ARIZ. : 1939). (US). **5630**

SOL (WINNIPEG). (CN/0709-504X). **1957**

SOLANUS. (UK/0038-0903). **3250**

SOLAR LAW : CUMULATIVE SUPPLEMENT / PRESENT AND FUTURE : WITH PROPOSED FORMS. SANDY F. KRAEMER. (US). **3056**

SOLAR PHYSICS. (NE/0038-0938). **400**

SOLAR PROGRESS. (AT/0729-6436). **Adv Mgr:** T. Lee. **1957**

SOLAR TODAY. (US/1042-0630). **Adv Mgr:** McFadden, **Tel** (303)443-4308. **1957**

SOLARIS. (CN/0709-8863). **3437**

SOLDADURA Y TECNOLOGIAS DE UNION. (SP/1130-0280). **4019**

SOLDAT UND TECHNIK. (GW/0038-0989). **4057**

SOLDERING & SURFACE MOUNT TECHNOLOGY : JOURNAL OF THE SMART (SURFACE MOUNT & RELATED TECHNOLOGIES) GROUP. (UK/0954-0911). **4019**

SOLDIER. (UK). **4057**

SOLDIER OF FORTUNE. (US/0145-6784). **Adv Mgr:** Facets Advertising, **Tel** (303)494-1177. **4057**

SOLDIERS TODAY. (US/1059-194X). **4057**

SOLETTER. (US/0747-623X). **1997**

SOLICITORS' JOURNAL (LONDON, ENGLAND : 1928). (UK/0038-1047). **3056**

SOLID FUEL. (UK). **1030**

SOLID STATE COMMUNICATIONS. (US/0038-1098). **4421**

SOLID STATE TECHNOLOGY. (US/0038-111X). **2081**

SOLIDARIDAD SAN JUAN, METRO MANILA. (PH/0117-3138). **4496**

SOLOINTIMO SOLOMARE. (IT). **1087**

SOLON TIMES, THE. (US/0194-3677). **Adv Mgr:** Carole Vigliotti. **5730**

SOLPLAN REVIEW. (CN/0828-6574). **2835**

SOMA (SAN FRANCISCO, CALIF.). (US/0896-5005). **Adv Mgr Tel** same as publisher. **2546**

SOMATICS. (US/0147-5231). **4361**

SOMATOSENSORY & MOTOR RESEARCH. (US/0899-0220). **5597**

SOMATOTHERAPIES ET SOMATOLOGIE. (FR). **3642**

SOME DATA ABOUT SWEDEN. (SW). **2523**

SOMERSET HERALD (PRINCESS ANNE, MD. : 1985). (US/8756-6397). **Adv Mgr:** Tom Sexton. **5687**

SOMERSET LEGAL JOURNAL. (US). **3056**

SOMETHING SPECIAL PATTERN CLUB. (US/0883-3710). **5186**

SOMOS (BUENOS AIRES, ARGENTINA. (AG). **2552**

SON, VIDEO MAGAZINE. (FR/0765-3530). **5319**

SONANCES. (CN/0712-2438). **4153**

SONDERHEFT - DEUTSCHE KERAMISCHE GESELLSCHAFT. (GW/0417-2256). **2594**

SONDERPADAGOGIK. (GW). **1885**

SONG NEWS. (CN/0704-5859). **187**

SONG (TORONTO). (CN/0822-4226). **3471**

SONNECK SOCIETY BULLETIN, THE. (US). **4153**

SONORA REVIEW. (US/0275-5203). **Adv Mgr:** J Barnet, **Tel** (602)791-2257. **3353**

SONOVISION PARIS. (FR/0768-956X). **1121**

SONS OF NORWAY VIKING, THE. (US/0038-1462). **2273**

SOO, THE. (US/0733-5296). **5436**

SOONER, THE. (US/0038-1497). **1095**

SOPERTON NEWS, THE. (US). **5655**

SOPHIA. (AT/0038-1527). **4998**

SORGHUM AND MILLETS ABSTRACTS. (UK/03082970). **156**

SORKIN'S DIRECTORY OF BUSINESS & GOVERNMENT (KANSAS CITY ED.). (US/0894-1033). **712**

SORKINS' DIRECTORY OF BUSINESS & GOVERNMENT (ST. LOUIS ED.). (US/0748-0458). **712**

SOROUSH / SURUSH. (IR). **2508**

SORTIE (MONTREAL). (CN/0714-7376). **2796**

SOSIALKONOMEN. (NO). **1595**

SOTSIALNOE OBESPECHENIE. (RU). **2894**

SOUDAGE ET TECHNIQUES CONNEXES. (FR/0038-173X). **4027**

SOUDERTON INDEPENDENT. (US). **Adv Mgr:** John Derr, **Tel** (215)723-4801. **5739**

SOUND & COMMUNICATIONS. (US/0038-1845). **1122**

SOUND & IMAGE. (US/1050-2777). **4154**

SOUND & VIDEO CONTRACTOR. (US/0741-1715). **5319**

SOUND & VISION (TORONTO). (CN/0829-3678). **Adv Mgr:** M Briant. **1627**

SOUND OF VIENNA, THE. (US/0192-5180). **Adv Mgr Tel** (703)281-0474. **2546**

SOUND POST (GRANITE FALLS, MINN.). (US/0749-0755). **4154**

SOUND WAVES : MONTHLY NEWSLETTER. (US). **252**

SOUNDBOARD. (US/0145-6237). **Adv Mgr:** Gunnar Eisel. **4154**

SOUNDINGS (ESSEX, CONN.). (US). **596**

SOUNDINGS (KNOXVILLE, TENN.). (US/0038-1861). **4998**

SOUNDINGS. TRADE ONLY. (US/0194-8369). **596**

SOUNDS AUSTRALIAN : AUSTRALIAN MUSIC CENTRE JOURNAL. (AT/0811-3149). **Adv Mgr:** F. Harvey. **4154**

SOUNDS OF GOSPEL RECORDINGS. (US). **4998**

SOUNDTRACK. (BE/0771-6303). **5319**

SOUNDTRACK!. (BE). **4078**

SOUNDTRACK (RINGWOOD, N.J.). (US/1042-0649). **5319**

SOURCE (WINTER PARK, FLA.). (US/0898-8811). **Adv Mgr:** Janie Graziani. **712**

SOURCES CHRETIENNES. (FR/0750-1978). **5040**

SOURCES OF ORIENTAL LANGUAGES AND LITERATURES / DOGU DILLERI VE EDEBIYATLARNN KAYNAKLAR. (US). **2664**

SOURCES OF SUPPLY : BUYERS GUIDE. (US/0190-8200). **4239**

SOURCES (TORONTO). (CN/0700-480X). **2924**

SOURCEWORLD. (US/0270-496X). **1276**

SOURDS DU CANADA. (CN/1195-3349). **4393**

SOUS-TERRE. (CN/0827-9772). **1411**

SOUTH AFRICA INTERNATIONAL. (SA/0015-5055). **2500**

SOUTH AFRICAN ARCHAEOLOGICAL BULLETIN, THE. (SA/0038-1969). **Adv Mgr:** C. Borr, **Tel** (021)243330 ext. 2086. **282**

SOUTH AFRICAN BUILDER, THE. (SA). **Adv Mgr:** J. Emery. **627**

SOUTH AFRICAN CLEANING REVIEW. (SA). **1711**

SOUTH AFRICAN CULTURAL HISTORY MUSEUM ANNALS. (SA). **2643**

SOUTH AFRICAN EXPORTERS. (SA). **851**

SOUTH AFRICAN FORESTRY JOURNAL. (SA/0038-2167). **2395**

SOUTH AFRICAN HAIRDRESSING AND BEAUTY CULTURE. (SA/0036-0759). **405**

SOUTH AFRICAN HISTORICAL JOURNAL. (SA). **Adv Mgr:** K. Harris. **2643**

SOUTH AFRICAN JOURNAL FOR ENOLOGY AND VITICULTURE. (SA/0253-939X). **2371**

SOUTH AFRICAN JOURNAL OF ANIMAL SCIENCE. (SA/0375-1589). **222**

SOUTH AFRICAN JOURNAL OF COMMUNICATION DISORDERS. (SA/0379-8046). **3846**

SOUTH AFRICAN JOURNAL OF ECONOMICS, THE. (SA/0038-2280). **1521**

SOUTH AFRICAN JOURNAL OF PHYSICS. (SA/0379-4377). **4421**

SOUTH AFRICAN JOURNAL OF PHYSIOTHERAPY. (SA/0379-6175). **3642**

SOUTH AFRICAN JOURNAL OF SCIENCE. (SA/0038-2353). **5158**

SOUTH AFRICAN JOURNAL OF SURGERY. (SA/0038-2361). **3975**

SOUTH AFRICAN JOURNAL ON HUMAN RIGHTS. (SA/0258-7203). **4513**

SOUTH AFRICAN LABOUR BULLETIN. (SA/0377-5429). **1711**

SOUTH AFRICAN MACHINE TOOL REVIEW. (SA/0036-0848). **2129**

SOUTH AFRICAN MEDICAL JOURNAL. (SA/0038-2469). **3642**

SOUTH AFRICAN MUSIC TEACHER. (SA/0038-2493). **4154**

SOUTH AFRICAN OPTOMETRIST, SUID-AFRIKAANSE OOGKUNDIGE, THE. (SA/0378-9411). **4217**

SOUTH AFRICAN ORCHID JOURNAL. SUID-AFRIKAANSE ORGIDEEJOERNAAL. (SA). **Adv Mgr:** L. Davies. **2431**

SOUTH AFRICAN SHIPPING NEWS AND FISHING INDUSTRY REVIEW, THE. (SA/0038-2671). **5457**

SOUTH AFRICAN SUGAR JOURNAL, THE. (SA/0038-2728). **187**

SOUTH AFRICAN SUGAR YEAR BOOK, THE. (SA). **136**

SOUTH AFRICAN THEATRE JOURNAL : SATJ. (SA). **Adv Mgr Tel** 021 808 3216. **5368**

SOUTH AFRICAN TREASURER, THE. (SA/0038-2779). **4748**

SOUTH ALABAMIAN (JACKSON, ALA.), THE. (US/0890-8168). **Adv Mgr:** Cammie Breedlove. **5628**

SOUTH AMBOY CITIZEN (SOUTH AMBOY, N.J. 1884), THE. (US/1041-2514). **Adv Mgr:** Jim Gotti. **5711**

SOUTH AMERICAN EXPLORER. (US/0889-7891). **4878**

SOUTH ASIA. (AT/0085-6401). **2664**

SOUTH ASIA BULLETIN. (US/0732-3867). **2665**

SOUTH ASIA IN REVIEW. (US/0889-8650). **2665**

SOUTH ASIA JOURNAL : QUARTERLY JOURNAL OF INDIAN COUNCIL FOR SOUTH ASIAN COOPERATION. (II). **5222**

SOUTH ASIA LIBRARY NOTES & QUERIES. (US/0197-5366). **3250**

SOUTH ASIA RESEARCH. (UK/0262-7280). **2854**

SOUTH ASIAN ANTHROPOLOGIST. (II/0257-7348). **245**

SOUTH ATLANTIC QUARTERLY, THE. (US/0038-2876). **2854**

SOUTH ATLANTIC REVIEW. (US/0277-335X). **Adv Mgr:** Christel Bell. **3322**

SOUTH AUSTRALIAN ANGLER. (AT). **Adv Mgr:** S. Mensforth. **4919**

SOUTH AUSTRALIAN DAIRY FARMER'S JOURNAL, THE. (AT/0049-1446). **199**

SOUTH AUSTRALIAN GENEALOGIST. (AT/0311-2756). **2473**

SOUTH AUSTRALIAN GEOGRAPHICAL JOURNAL. (AT/1030-0481). **2576**

SOUTH AUSTRALIAN MASTER BUILDER. (AT). **Adv Mgr:** O Harrarine. **1627**

SOUTH AUSTRALIAN SCHOOL POST. (AT). **1784**

SOUTH AUSTRALIAN SCIENCE TEACHERS JOURNAL. (AT). **Adv Mgr:** J. Morton. **1905**

SOUTH BEND TRIBUNE IRISH SPORTS REPORTS. (US). **Adv Mgr:** Smith, **Tel** (219)235-6161. **5667**

SOUTH BEND TRIBUNE, THE. (US). **5667**

SOUTH CAROLINA BUSINESS. (US/1050-7698). **712**

SOUTH CAROLINA BUSINESS JOURNAL. (US/0745-4473). **712**

SOUTH CAROLINA HISTORICAL MAGAZINE. (US/0038-3082). **2761**

SOUTH CAROLINA LAW REVIEW. (US/0038-3104). **3057**

SOUTH CAROLINA LAWYER. (US/1044-4238). **3057**

SOUTH CAROLINA NURSE, THE. (US/1046-7394). **Adv Mgr:** Art Davis, **Tel** (319)277-2414. **3869**

SOUTH CAROLINA OUT-OF-DOORS. (US/0887-9249). **2205**

SOUTH CAROLINA REVIEW, THE. (US/0038-3163). **3353**

SOUTH CAROLINA VOTER. (US). **Adv Mgr:** Laurel Suggs, **Tel** (803)782-9147. **2493**

SOUTH CENTRAL REVIEW. (US/0743-6831). **Adv Mgr:** Jo Hebert. **3322**

SOUTH CENTRAL SALES GUIDE TO HIGH-TECH COMPANIES. (US/1040-0532). **5159**

SOUTH COAST POETRY JOURNAL. (US/0887-2074). **Adv Mgr:** Jennifer Boyle, **Tel** (909)985-2959. **3471**

SOUTH COAST SPORTFISHING. (US/0279-2249). **4854**

SOUTH COAST WEEK. (US/0744-785X). **Adv Mgr:** Juan Mejia. **5734**

SOUTH DADE NEWS LEADER. (US/1048-5406). **Adv Mgr:** M. Davis. **5651**

SOUTH DAKOTA HIGH LINER MAGAZINE. (US/1067-4977). **Adv Mgr:** Bernie Ripperger, **Tel** (605)224-8823. **2493**

SOUTH DAKOTA JOURNAL OF MEDICINE. (US/0038-3317). **Adv Mgr:** J. Spars, **Tel** (605)336-1965. **3642**

SOUTH DAKOTA LAW REVIEW. (US/0038-3325). **3057**

SOUTH DAKOTA MAGAZINE (YANKTON, S.D.). (US/0886-2680). **2546**

SOUTH DAKOTA MUNICIPALITIES. (US/0300-6182). **Adv Mgr:** M. Gienger. **4686**

SOUTH DAKOTA REVIEW. (US/0038-3368). **3438**

SOUTH EAST ASIAN PRINTER MAGAZINE. (SI/0129-1262). **Adv Mgr:** C. Chong, **Tel** 299-8577. **4569**

SOUTH EAST ASIAN REVIEW, THE. (II). **2665**

SOUTH EASTERN LATIN AMERICANIST. (US/0049-1527). **2761**

SOUTH FLORIDA. (US/0895-5352). **Adv Mgr:** Muriel Sommers. **2546**

SOUTH FLORIDA BUSINESS JOURNAL. (US/0746-2271). **Adv Mgr:** Karen Van Der Eems. **712**

SOUTH FLORIDA PIONEERS. (US/8756-2766). **2473**

SOUTH GEORGIA BUSINESS JOURNAL. (US). **712**

SOUTH GIBSON STAR-TIMES. (US). **Adv Mgr:** John Heuring. **5667**

SOUTH HAMILTON RECORD/NEWS (JEWELL, IOWA : 1978). (US). **5673**

SOUTH HAVEN DAILY TRIBUNE. (US). **Adv Mgr:** Michael Eastman. **5694**

SOUTH JERSEY MAGAZINE. (US/0275-4428). **Adv Mgr:** Ella Batcheler, **Tel** (609)455-3286. **2761**

SOUTH PIERCE COUNTY DISPATCH, THE. (US). **5762**

SOUTH PITTSBURG HUSTLER. (US). **Adv Mgr:** Jim Shanks. **5746**

SOUTH PITTSBURGH REPORTER. (US). **Adv Mgr:** W. T. Smith, **Tel** (412)481-0266. **5739**

SOUTH-REPORTER. (US). **Adv Mgr:** Betty Webb. **5701**

SOUTH SHORE NEWS (WEST HANOVER, MASS.). (US/0192-4869). **Adv Mgr:** Paul A. Mark. **5690**

SOUTH SHORE RECORD. (US/0038-352X). **2546**

SOUTH SLAV JOURNAL, THE. (UK). **2710**

SOUTH VANCOUVER REVUE. (CN/0821-0187). **Adv Mgr:** R. Raglin. **5795**

SOUTH WHIDBEY RECORD. (US/1064-0622). **Adv Mgr:** Kayla Conner. **5762**

SOUTHAMPTON MEDICAL JOURNAL. (UK/0266-0342). **3642**

SOUTHEAST ASIAN BULLETIN OF MATHEMATICS. (HK/0129-2021). **3536**

SOUTHEAST ASIAN JOURNAL OF SOCIAL SCIENCE. (SI). **5222**

SOUTHEAST ASIAN JOURNAL OF TROPICAL MEDICINE AND PUBLIC HEALTH, THE. (TH/0038-3619). **4803**

SOUTHEAST DRAGSTER : AN NHRA PUBLICATION. (US). **Adv Mgr:** Scott Lowden. **4919**

SOUTHEAST FOOD SERVICE NEWS. (US/0199-2805). **2358**

SOUTHEAST MESSENGER. (US/0891-2289). **Adv Mgr:** Bruce Russel, **Tel** (614)272-5422. **5730**

SOUTHEAST MISSOURIAN. (US/0746-4452). **5704**

SOUTHEAST SALES GUIDE TO HIGH-TECH COMPANIES. (US/1040-0567). **5159**

SOUTHEASTERN ARCHAEOLOGY. (US/0734-578X). **282**

SOUTHEASTERN EUROPE (PITTSBURGH). (US/0094-4467). **2523**

SOUTHEASTERN FRONT. (US). **3438**

SOUTHEASTERN GEOGRAPHER. (US/0038-366X). **2576**

SOUTHEASTERN LIBRARIAN, THE. (US/0038-3686). **3250**

SOUTHEASTERN PEANUT FARMER. (US/0038-3694). **188**

SOUTHEASTERN POLITICAL REVIEW. (US/0730-2177). **Adv Mgr Tel** (912)681-5698. **4496**

SOUTHERN ACCENTS. (US/0149-516X). **2903**

SOUTHERN AFRICA RECORD. (SA). **4535**

SOUTHERN AFRICAN ECONOMIST. (RH). **1521**

SOUTHERN AFRICAN JOURNAL OF EPIDEMIOLOGY & INFECTION : OFFICIAL JOURNAL OF THE SEXUALLY TRANSMITTED DISEASES, INFECTIOUS DISEASES, AND EPIDEMIOLOGICAL SOCIETIES OF SOUTHERN AFRICA, THE. (SA). **3716**

SOUTHERN BANKER, THE. (US/0038-383X). **812**

SOUTHERN BANKERS DIRECTORY. (US/0734-7812). **812**

SOUTHERN BEVERAGE JOURNAL. (US/0193-0613). **2371**

SOUTHERN BOATING. (US/0192-3579). **Adv Mgr:** Steve Beck. **596**

SOUTHERN BUILDING. (US/0038-3864). **628**

SOUTHERN BUSINESS & ECONOMIC JOURNAL, THE. (US/0743-779X). **712**

SOUTHERN CALIFORNIA ANTHOLOGY, THE. (US/0743-1406). **3438**

SOUTHERN CALIFORNIA BEVERAGE BULLETIN. (US/0192-1835). **2371**

SOUTHERN CALIFORNIA BUSINESS. (US/0038-3880). **821**

SOUTHERN CALIFORNIA BUSINESS DIRECTORY AND BUYERS GUIDE. (US/0093-3090). **Adv Mgr:** D. Pearce. **712**

SOUTHERN CALIFORNIA LAW REVIEW. (US/0038-3910). **3057**

SOUTHERN CALIFORNIA SENIOR LIFE. (US). **5182**

SOUTHERN CALIFORNIA WOODWORKER, THE. (US/0898-3550). **635**

SOUTHERN CHANGES. (US/0193-2446). **4513**

SOUTHERN CITY. (US/0361-7130). **4686**

SOUTHERN COMMUNICATION JOURNAL, THE. (US/1041-794X). **Adv Mgr:** Jef Dolan. **1122**

SOUTHERN COUNTY NEWS, THE. (US). **Adv Mgr:** Wm. F. Scharader. **5673**

SOUTHERN CROSS (SAN DIEGO, CALIF.). (US/0745-0257). **5036**

SOUTHERN DUTCHESS NEWS. (US/0192-9631). **Adv Mgr:** Audrey Morgenstern. **5721**

SOUTHERN ECONOMIC JOURNAL. (US/0038-4038). **1521**

SOUTHERN ECONOMIST. (II/0038-4046). **1521**

SOUTHERN EXPOSURE (DURHAM, N.C.). (US/0146-809X). **2761**

SOUTHERN FOLKLORE. (US/0899-594X). **Adv Mgr:** K. Shaw. **2324**

SOUTHERN FUNERAL DIRECTOR. (US/0038-4135). **2407**

SOUTHERN GENEALOGICAL INDEX. (US/8755-1748). **2473**

SOUTHERN GENEALOGIST'S EXCHANGE QUARTERLY, THE. (US/0584-4487). **2473**

SOUTHERN — Advertising Accepted Index

SOUTHERN GRAPHICS. (US/0274-774X). **382**

SOUTHERN HERALD (LIBERTY, MISS.), THE. (US/0893-3790). **5701**

SOUTHERN HISTORIAN, THE. (US/0738-5102). **2761**

SOUTHERN HOSPITALS. (US/0038-4178). **3792**

SOUTHERN HUMANITIES REVIEW. (US/0038-4186). **2854**

SOUTHERN ILLINOIS UNIVERSITY LAW JOURNAL. (US/0145-3432). **3057**

SOUTHERN INSURANCE. (US/0038-4216). **2894**

SOUTHERN JOURNAL OF APPLIED FORESTRY. (US/0148-4419). **2395**

SOUTHERN JOURNAL OF PHILOSOPHY, THE. (US/0038-4283). **Adv Mgr:** Leigh Tanner. **4361**

SOUTHERN LAWNMOWERS DEALERS NEWSLETTER. (US). **2431**

SOUTHERN LINKS (HILTON HEAD ISLAND, S.C.). (US/1043-6375). **Adv Mgr Tel** (203)977-8600. **4919**

SOUTHERN LIVING. (US/0038-4305). **2546**

SOUTHERN LOGGIN' TIMES. (US/0744-2106). **2404**

SOUTHERN LUMBERMAN. (US/0038-4313). **Adv Mgr:** Lori Fisher, **Tel** (615)790-0790. **2404**

SOUTHERN MEDICAL JOURNAL (BIRMINGHAM). (US/0038-4348). **3975**

SOUTHERN MOTOR CARGO. (US/0038-4372). **5425**

SOUTHERN MOTORACING. (US/0049-1616). **5425**

SOUTHERN OUTDOORS (MONTGOMERY). (US/0199-3372). **4878**

SOUTHERN PARTISAN, THE. (US/0739-1714). **Adv Mgr:** Alicia LeJeune. **4496**

SOUTHERN PLUMBING, HEATING, COOLING. (US/0038-4461). **2608**

SOUTHERN QUARTERLY, THE. (US/0038-4496). **331**

SOUTHERN QUERIES : THE CONTACT MAGAZINE FOR PEOPLE SEARCHING FOR THEIR SOUTHERN ANCESTORS. (US/1048-8057). **Adv Mgr:** Frank Monachelli, **Tel** (205)322-7700. **2473**

SOUTHERN READER. (US/1042-6604). **3438**

SOUTHERN REVIEW (ADELAIDE). (AT/0038-4526). **3353**

SOUTHERN REVIEW (BATON ROUGE), THE. (US/0038-4534). **Adv Mgr:** Joanne Mcmullen, **Tel** (504)388-5108. **3438**

SOUTHERN SHIPPER. (US/1054-7150). **Adv Mgr:** Bill Barrs, **Tel** (904)355-26013. **5457**

SOUTHERN SOCIAL STUDIES JOURNAL. (US/1047-7942). **5222**

SOUTHERN STAR. (US). **Adv Mgr:** Charlie Dawkins. **5628**

SOUTHERN STARS. (NZ/0049-1640). **400**

SOUTHERN STUDIES. (US/0735-8342). **2761**

SOUTHERN TEXTILE NEWS. (US/0038-4607). **Adv Mgr:** David O'Neal. **5356**

SOUTHERN THEATRE. (US/0584-4738). **5368**

SOUTHERN UNIVERSITY LAW REVIEW. (US/0099-1465). **3057**

SOUTHERN UTAH NEWS. (US/0049-1659). **5757**

SOUTHERN UTE DRUM, THE. (US/0587-0674). **2273**

SOUTHERN WASTE INFORMATION EXCHANGE CATALOG, THE. (US/0892-5739). **Adv Mgr:** Gene Jones, **Tel** (800)441-7949. **2243**

SOUTHFIELD ECCENTRIC. (US). **Adv Mgr:** Mark Lewis, **Tel** (313)591-2300. **5694**

SOUTHLAND TIMES. (NZ/0112-9910). **Adv Mgr:** A. R. Wills, **Tel** (03)218 1909. **5807**

SOUTHSIDE CHALLENGER, THE. (US). **Adv Mgr:** Don Guerreta. **5667**

SOUTHSIDE VIRGINIAN, THE. (US/0736-5683). **2473**

SOUTHWEST & TEXAS WATER WORKS JOURNAL. (US/0196-0717). **5539**

SOUTHWEST CONTRACTOR (PHOENIX, ARIZ.). (US/1064-6914). **Adv Mgr:** Bill Davis, **Tel** same as publisher. **628**

SOUTHWEST DAILY TIMES, THE. (US/0745-8916). **Adv Mgr:** Jodie Harless. **5678**

SOUTHWEST DIGEST. (US). **5754**

SOUTHWEST JOURNAL OF LINGUISTICS. (US/0737-4143). **Adv Mgr:** E. Hernandez, **Tel** (505)277-3347. **3322**

SOUTHWEST MUSEUM PAPERS. (US/0076-0994). **4096**

SOUTHWEST OIL WORLD. (US/0884-6219). **4278**

SOUTHWEST PHILOSOPHY REVIEW. (US/0897-2346). **4361**

SOUTHWEST PROFILE. (US/0895-6049). **2546**

SOUTHWEST REFERENCE .... (US). **222**

SOUTHWEST REVIEW. (US/0038-4712). **Adv Mgr:** same as editor. **3353**

SOUTHWEST SALES GUIDE TO HIGH-TECH COMPANIES. (US/1040-0524). **5159**

SOUTHWEST SAMPLER. (US/1047-4242). **2903**

SOUTHWEST TIMES RECORD. (US). **Adv Mgr:** Mr. Beasley, **Tel** (501)785-7726. **5632**

SOUTHWEST VIRGINIA ENTERPRISE. (US). **Adv Mgr:** Suelyn Arnold, **Tel** (703)228-6611. **5759**

SOUTHWEST WAVE. (US). **5640**

SOUTHWESTERN AMERICAN LITERATURE. (US/0049-1675). **3438**

SOUTHWESTERN ARCHIVIST. (US/1056-1021). **Adv Mgr:** Ed, **Tel** (504)865-5685. **3250**

SOUTHWESTERN HISTORICAL QUARTERLY. (US/0038-478X). **2761**

SOUTHWESTERN JOURNAL OF ECONOMIC ABSTRACTS. (US/8756-2278). **1522**

SOUTHWESTERN JOURNAL OF THEOLOGY. (US/0038-4828). **5067**

SOUTHWESTERN MASS COMMUNICATION JOURNAL. (US/0891-9186). **Adv Mgr:** Gil Fowlee, **Tel** (501)972-3075. **1122**

SOUTHWESTERN MUSICIAN COMBINED WITH THE TEXAS MUSIC EDUCATOR, THE. (US). **4154**

SOUTHWESTERN PAY DIRT. (US/0886-0920). **2151**

SOUVENIR NAPOLEONIEN, LE. (FR/0246-1919). **2630**

SOUVENIRS & NOVELTIES. (US/0038-4968). **2585**

SOU'WESTER (EDWARDSVILLE), THE. (US/0038-4976). **3438**

SOVIET AND EASTERN EUROPEAN FOREIGN TRADE. (US/0038-5263). **1640**

SOVIET ANTHROPOLOGY AND ARCHAEOLOGY. (US/0038-528X). **245**

SOVIET BIOGRAPHICAL SERVICE. (US). **435**

SOVIET BUSINESS & TRADE (1982). (US/0731-7727). **851**

SOVIET LAW AND GOVERNMENT. (US/0038-5530). **3057**

SOVIET MATERIALS SCIENCE REVIEWS. (US/0888-689X). **2129**

SOVIET NEUROLOGY & PSYCHIATRY. (US/0038-559X). **3846**

SOVIET REVIEW. (AT/1033-6257). **1522**

SOVIET REVIEW (WHITE PLAINS), THE. (US/0038-5794). **2523**

SOVIET STUDIES. (UK/0038-5859). **4547**

SOVIET STUDIES IN HISTORY. (US/0038-5867). **2710**

SOVIET STUDIES IN PHILOSOPHY. (US/0038-5883). **4361**

SOVIET WEEKLY. (UK). **2523**

SOYA BLUEBOOK. (US/0275-4509). **Adv Mgr:** Sharyn Kingma. **188**

SOYABEAN ABSTRACTS. (UK/0141-0172). **156**

SOYBEAN DIGEST. (US/0038-6014). **188**

SOZIAL- UND PRAEVENTIVMEDIZIN. (SZ/0303-8408). **4803**

SOZIALE BEWEGUNGEN : ANALYSE UND DOKUMENTATION DES IMSF. (GW). **1711**

SOZIALE SICHERHEIT (WIEN). (AU/0038-6065). **5310**

SOZIALE WELT. (GW/0038-6073). **5223**

SOZIOLOGISCHE REVUE. (GW/0343-4109). **5263**

SPA AND SAUNA TRADE JOURNAL. BUYERS GUIDE. (US). **713**

SPACE AGE TIMES. (US/0738-0968). **35**

SPACE AND SECURITY NEWS. (US/1071-2569). **35**

SPACE (BEACONSFIELD). (UK/0267-954X). **35**

SPACE CALENDAR. (US/0741-1731). **35**

SPACE NEWS (SPRINGFIELD, VA.). (US/1046-6940). **36**

SPACE POLICY. (UK/0265-9646). **36**

SPACE POWER. (US/0883-6272). **1958**

SPACE R & D ALERT. (US/0743-8982). **36**

SPACE RESEARCH IN BULGARIA. (BU/0204-9104). **400**

SPACE SCIENCE REVIEWS. (NE/0038-6308). **400**

SPACE TODAY. (US/0889-6054). **400**

SPANISH STUDIES. (UK). **2710**

SPANISH TODAY. (US/0049-1802). **3439**

SPARE RIB. (UK/0306-7971). **5566**

SPE DRILLING ENGINEERING. (US/0885-9744). **4278**

SPE FORMATION EVALUATION. (US/0885-923X). **4279**

SPE PRODUCTION ENGINEERING. (US/0885-9221). **4279**

SPE RESERVOIR ENGINEERING. (US/0885-9248). **4279**

SPEAK UP. (CN/0383-9370). **2762**

SPEAKER BUILDER. (US/0199-7920). **5319**

SPEAKIN' OUT NEWS. (US). **Adv Mgr Tel** (205)852-9449. **2273**

SPEAQ-OUT. (CN/0229-6535). **3323**

SPEAR (TORONTO). (CN/0315-0208). **2273**

SPEARHEAD. (UK). **4535**

SPEARMAN REPORTER, THE. (US). **5754**

SPEC-COM. (US/0883-2560). **1139**

SPEC (NEW CARLISLE). (CN/0226-9120). **5795**

SPECCHIO ECONOMICO. (IT). **Adv Mgr:** Paola Nardella. **1522**

SPECIAL CARE IN DENTISTRY. (US/0275-1879). **1335**

SPECIAL CHILDREN (BIRMINGHAM). (UK/0951-6875). **1885**

SPECIAL-INTEREST AUTOS. (US/0049-1845). **5425**

SPECIAL PUBLICATION - CUSHMAN FOUNDATION FOR FORAMINIFERAL RESEARCH. (US/0070-2242). **5597**

SPECIAL PUBLICATIONS. (US/0067-6179). **4096**

SPECIAL RECREATION DIGEST. (US/0747-0185). **4854**

SPECIAL REPORT - WHITTLE COMMUNICATIONS. (US/1059-5201). **Adv Mgr:** Mike Huddleston, **Tel** (615) 595-5304. **2546**

SPECIALIST (NEW YORK, N.Y.). (US/0273-9399). **3251**

SPECIALITY PAPER & BOARD MATERIALS & MARKETS BULLETIN. (UK). **4222**

SPECIALTY ADVERTISING BUSINESS. (US/0195-0495). **766**

SPECIALTY & CUSTOM DEALER. (US/0193-7278). **5425**

SPECIALTY BOOKSELLERS DIRECTORY. (US/0895-254X). **4820**

SPECIALTY CHEMICALS (REDHILL). (UK/0262-2262). **993**

SPECIALTY COOKING. (US/1048-8413). **4199**

SPECIALTY TRAVEL INDEX: THE DIRECTORY TO SPECIAL INTEREST TRAVEL. (US/0889-7085). **5491**

SPECIFICATION. (UK). **628**

SPECTACLE DU MONDE, LE. (FR/0038-6944). **3353**

SPECTACLE DU MONDE / PERSPECTIVES / REALITIES, LE. (FR). **3353**

SPECTATOR (LONDON. 1828). (UK/0038-6952). **2523**

SPECTROSCOPY INTERNATIONAL. (US/1040-7669). **993**

SPECTROSCOPY LETTERS. (US/0038-7010). **4442**

SPECTROSCOPY (OTTAWA, ONT.). (CN/0712-4813). **993**

SPECTRUM. (US/0892-9459). **1122**

SPECTRUM (CHATSWORTH, CALIF.). (US/1047-2371). **4154**

SPECTRUM (SANTA BARBARA, CALIF.). (US/0038-7061). **1095**

SPECTRUM (TAKOMA PARK, MD.). (US/0890-0264). **Adv Mgr:** Chip Cassano. **4999**

SPECTRUM (TEL AVIV, ISRAEL). (IS/0334-1046). **1711**

SPECULATIONS IN SCIENCE AND TECHNOLOGY. (UK/0155-7785). **5159**

SPECULUM. (US/0038-7134). **2710**

SPECULUM (COLUMBUS, OHIO), THE. (US/0739-3806). **5522**

SPEECH AND DRAMA. (UK/0038-7142). **5368**

SPEECH COMMUNICATION. (NE/0167-6393). **1122**

SPEECH COMMUNICATION DIRECTORY. (US/0190-2075). **1122**

SPEECH TECHNOLOGY. (US/0744-1355). **1122**

SPEEDHORSE (MONTHLY), THE. (US/0364-9237). **2802**

SPEEDNEWS. (US/0271-2598). **Adv Mgr:** Scott Daniels. **36**

SPEEDWAY SCENE. (US/0747-5403). **4920**

SPEEDY BEE. (US/0190-6798). **5598**

SPEKTROSKOPIJA GAZORAZRJADNOJ PLAZMY. (RU/0134-9007). **4445**

SPELD. (AT). **1885**

SPETTACOLO, LO. (IT/0038-738X). **331**

SPICE NEWSLETTER. (II). **2358**

SPIDR NEWS. (US/0888-9325). **1711**

SPIEGEL (HAMBURG), DER. (GW/0038-7452). **2523**

SPIEGEL HISTORIAEL. (NE/0038-7487). **2630**

SPIELRAUM. (GW/0934-4853). **2601**

SPILL SCIENCE AND TECHNOLOGY BULLETIN. (UK/1353-2561). **2243**

SPIN-OFF (LOVELAND, COLO.). (US/0198-8239). **5356**

SPINAL COLUMNS. (CN/1195-5767). **4394**

SPINE (PHILADELPHIA, PA. 1976). (US/0362-2436). **3642**

SPINE REHABILITATION. (US/1058-1421). **3642**

SPINNER (NEW BEDFORD, MASS.). (US/0730-2657). **2762**

SPIRIT OF DEMOCRACY (WOODSFIELD, OHIO : 1844). (US). **5730**

SPIRIT OF JEFFERSON FARMERS ADVOCATE. (US). **Adv Mgr:** Meade Dorsey. **5765**

SPIRIT (SISTERS, OR.). (US/0885-0291). **4999**

SPIRIT (SOUTH ORANGE). (US/0038-7584). **3471**

SPIRITUALITY TODAY. (US/0162-6760). **5036**

SPITBALL. (US/8755-741X). **3439**

SPOKEN ENGLISH. (UK/0038-772X). **3323**

SPOKESMAN (EDMONTON). (CN/0700-5229). **4394**

SPOKESMAN-REVIEW (1894), THE. (US/1064-7317). **5762**

SPOON RIVER POETRY REVIEW. (US). **Adv Mgr:** Jean Lee, **Tel** (309)438-3024. **3471**

SPORT & MEDICINA. (IT/0392-9647). **3956**

SPORT AVIATION. (US/0038-7835). **4920**

SPORT CONSTRUCTION BUYERS GUIDE. (US). **2031**

SPORT FLYER. (US/8750-8117). **4920**

SPORT MARKETING QUARTERLY. (US/1061-6934). **Adv Mgr:** Eric Noble. **4920**

SPORT MEDIA BUYERS GUIDE. (US). **4920**

SPORT MEDICINE DIRECTORY. (CN/0229-1541). **3956**

SPORT (NEW YORK). (US/0038-7797). **4920**

SPORT PSYCHOLOGIST, THE. (US/0888-4781). **4619**

SPORT REPORT. (AT). **4921**

SPORT ROCKETRY. (US/1076-2701). **2778**

SPORT SCENE. (US/0270-1812). **4921**

SPORT TRUCK. (US/1044-7903). **5425**

SPORTCARE & FITNESS. (US/0899-3815). **4921**

SPORTING CLASSICS. (US). **4921**

SPORTING CLAYS. (US/1061-2424). **4879**

SPORTING GOODS BUYERS. NATIONAL DIRECTORY. (US). **951**

SPORTING NEWS ... BASEBALL YEARBOOK, THE. (US/0275-0732). **4921**

SPORTING NEWS, THE. (US/0038-805X). **4921**

SPORTS. (SI). **Adv Mgr:** Sharon Lau, **Tel** 011 65 3409663. **4922**

SPORTS AFIELD DEER. (US/0160-1830). **4879**

SPORTS BUSINESS. (CN/0830-1921). **958**

SPORTS CAR INTERNATIONAL. (US/1042-9662). **Adv Mgr:** Stan. **5425**

SPORTS ILLUSTRATED. (US/0038-822X). **4922**

SPORTS ILLUSTRATED FOR KIDS. (US/1042-394X). **1069**

SPORTS MEDICINE NEWS. (US). **3956**

SPORTS MEDICINE STANDARDS AND MALPRACTICE REPORTER, THE. (US/1041-696X). **3956**

SPORTS 'N SPOKES. (US/0161-6706). **Adv Mgr Tel** (602)246-9426. **4923**

SPORTS, PARKS & RECREATION LAW REPORTER, THE. (US/0893-8210). **Adv Mgr:** Molly Romig. **3058**

SPORTS PROFILES. (US). **4923**

SPORTS REVIEW WRESTLING (AMBLER, PA.). (US/1073-1326). **4923**

SPORTSEARCH. (US/0882-553X). **4856**

SPORTSWEAR INTERNATIONAL'S KIDS. (US). **Adv Mgr:** Constantine Floris. **1087**

SPORTUNTERRICHT. (GW/0342-2402). **1858**

SPORTWISSENSCHAFT. (GW). **4923**

SPOT (HOUSTON, TEX.). (US/1049-0450). **4377**

SPOT RADIO RATES AND DATA. (US/0038-9560). **766**

SPOT TELEVISION RATES AND DATA. (US/0038-9552). **766**

SPOTLIGHT. ACTORS. (UK/0309-0183). **388**

SPOTLIGHT. ACTRESSES. (UK/0308-9827). **388**

SPOTLIGHT (BROOKLYN, N.Y.). (US/1044-1247). **2512**

"SPOTLIGHT" CASTING DIRECTORY, THE. (UK). **4078**

SPOTLIGHT CONTACTS. (UK/0010-7344). **388**

SPOTLIGHT (INDIANAPOLIS, IND.). (US). **Adv Mgr:** Ron Douglas. **5667**

SPOTLIGHT (WASHINGTON), THE. (US/0191-6270). **5648**

SPRACHDIENST, DER. (GW/0038-8459). **3323**

SPRACHE. (AU/0376-401X). **Adv Mgr:** A. Weddigen. **3323**

SPRACHE IM TECHNISCHEN ZEITALTER. (GW/0038-8475). **3353**

SPRACHE UND DATENVERARBEITUNG. (GW/0343-5202). **3323**

SPRACHE UND LITERATUR IN WISSENSCHAFT UND UNTERRICHT. (GW/0724-9713). **3323**

SPRACHKUNST. (AU/0038-8483). **3323**

SPRACHWISSENSCHAFT. (GW/0344-8169). **3323**

SPRAKVARD. (SW/0038-8440). **3323**

SPRECHSAAL. (GW/0341-0439). **2594**

SPRING. (US/0362-0522). **Adv Mgr:** Jay Livernois, **Tel** (203)974-3229. **4619**

SPRING (NEW YORK, N.Y. : 1982). (US/0735-6889). **3472**

SPRING VALLEY SUN (SPRING VALLEY, WIS. : 1952). (US). **5771**

SPRINGFIELD ADVANCE-PRESS. (US). **Adv Mgr:** Peter Hedstrom. **5698**

SPRINGFIELD MAGAZINE. (US/0164-6745). **2546**

SPRINGFIELD MAGAZINE (SPRINGFIELD, MO.). (US/0195-0894). **Adv Mgr:** R. C. Glazier, **Tel** (417)831-1640. **2546**

SPRINGFIELD NEWS-SUN. (US/0744-6101). **5730**

SPRINGHOUSE, THE. (US/0888-3319). **2324**

SPRINGS MAGAZINE (COLORADO SPRINGS, COLO.). (US/0748-6405). **Adv Mgr:** Sharon Friedman. **2546**

SPRINGS VALLEY HERALD. (US). **5667**

SPRINGVILLE HERALD (SPRINGVILLE, UTAH). (US). **Adv Mgr:** Martin Conover. **5757**

SPUDMAN. (US/0038-8661). **137**

SPUMS JOURNAL. (AT/0813-1988). **3642**

SPUR (DELAPLANE). (US/0098-5422). **2802**

SPURS & FEATHERS. (US/0745-4368). **4923**

SPUTNIK (ANGL. JAZ.). (RU/0131-8721). **2523**

SQL FORUM. (US/1068-0950). **Adv Mgr:** Marya C Fischer. **1204**

SQUASH NEWS (HOPE VALLEY, R.I.). (US/0164-7148). **Adv Mgr:** Tom Jones. **4924**

SR. TEXAS. (US). **Adv Mgr:** S. Schwaller, **Tel** (214)341-9429. **5182**

SRASHTA. (II). **3439**

SRDS SPOT RADIO SMALL MARKETS EDITION. (US). **766**

SRI LANKA VETERINARY JOURNAL : THE OFFICIAL JOURNAL OF THE SRI LANKA VETERINARY ASSOCIATION, THE. (CE). **5522**

SRINAGAR LAW JOURNAL. (II). **3058**

SRPSKA BORBA. (US/0279-1293). **2273**

ST. CLAIR NEWS-AEGIS. (US/1044-1964). **5628**

ST. CLOUD STATE UNIVERSITY CHRONICLE. (US/0747-1025). **1095**

ST COMPUTER. (GW). **1204**

ST. CROIX VALLEY PRESS. (US/0892-1784). **Adv Mgr:** Michelle Larson. **5698**

ST. GEORGE MAGAZINE. (US/0882-8741). **5491**

ST. IGNACE NEWS. (US). **Adv Mgr:** Richard Hayden. **5694**

ST. LOUIS. (US/0272-1279). **2546**

ST. LOUIS BUSINESS JOURNAL. (US/0271-6453). **713**

ST. LOUIS COMMERCE. (US/0036-293X). **851**

ST. LOUIS COUNTIAN, THE. (US/0036-2948). **5704**

ST. LOUIS DAILY RECORD. (US). **Adv Mgr Tel** (314)421-1880. **3058**

ST. LOUIS JOURNALISM REVIEW, THE. (US/0036-2972). **2924**

ST. LOUIS METROPOLITAN MEDICINE. (US/0892-1334). **3642**

ST. LOUIS POST-DISPATCH. (US). **Adv Mgr:** Tom Rees, **Tel** (314)340-8577. **5704**

ST. LOUIS REVIEW. (US/0036-3022). **5036**

ST. LOUIS SENTINEL. (US). **Adv Mgr:** O. Smith. **5704**

ST. MARK'S REVIEW. (AT/0036-3103). **4999**

ST. MARY'S LAW JOURNAL. (US/0581-3441). **3058**

ST. MARYS STAR (ST. MARYS, KAN. : 1978). (US). **Adv Mgr:** Carla Opliger. **5678**

ST. PAUL RECORDER. (US). **5698**

ST. PAUL'S FAMILY MAGAZINE. (US/0896-8276). **Adv Mgr:** Sandra Leek. **365**

ST. PETERSBURG TIMES. (US). **5651**

ST. TAMMANY FARMER. (US). **Adv Mgr:** Vera Hardman. **5684**

ST. THOMAS'S HOSPITAL GAZETTE (1981). (UK/0263-3507). **3792**

ST. VLADIMIR'S THEOLOGICAL QUARTERLY. (US/0036-3227). **5040**

STA PHANTOM, THE. (US/0890-3603). **1627**

STAATSCOURANT. (NE/0169-5037). **4687**

STADEN-JAHRBUCH. (BL/0582-1150). **2762**

STADION (COLOGNE, GERMANY). (GW/0172-4029). **4924**

STAFDA ... DIRECTORY. (US/1051-2136). **1627**

STAGE AND TELEVISION TODAY, THE. (UK/0038-9099). **Adv Mgr:** C. Finnlpy, **Tel** 071-11031818. **5368**

STAGE DIRECTIONS (WEST SACRAMENTO, CALIF.). (US/1047-1901). **Adv Mgr:** Lori Viffa. **5368**

STAHL UND EISEN. (GW/0340-4803). **4020**

STAHLBAU RUNDSCHAU. (AU/0561-7855). **2031**

STAINLESS STEEL DATABOOK. (UK). **4020**

STAINLESS STEEL EUROPE. (NE). **Adv Mgr:** Gert-Jan Kloos. **1030**

STAINLESS STEEL INDUSTRY. (UK/0306-2988). **1627**

STAL. (RU/0038-920X). **4020**

STALLION REGISTER FOR ... . (US). **2802**

STALSBY/ WILSON'S WHO'S WHO IN NATURAL GAS SUPPLY. (US/0897-2028). **4279**

STAMFORD AMERICAN (STAMFORD, TEX. : 1965). (US). **Adv Mgr:** Chandra Mathis. **5754**

STAMM LEITFADEN DURCH PRESSE UND WERBUNG. (GW/0341-7093). **5802**

STAMP COLLECTOR. (US/0277-3899). **2787**

STAMP — Advertising Accepted Index

STAMP DEALER FORUM. (US/8755-3139). **2787**

STAMP LOVER, THE. (UK/0038-9277). **2787**

STAMP WHOLESALER, THE. (US/0038-9315). **2787**

STAMPA MEDICA. (IT/0038-9323). **3642**

STAMPING QUARTERLY. (US/1043-5093). **Adv Mgr:** Penni Korte. **4020**

STAMPS (NEW YORK, N.Y. 1932). (US/0038-9358). **2787**

STANDARD AND TIMES LAUDERDALE COUNTY NEWS, THE. (US). **Adv Mgr:** Estelle W., **Tel** (250)383-8471. **5628**

STANDARD (BOSTON), THE. (US/0038-9390). **Adv Mgr:** Barbara Crockett. **2894**

STANDARD (ELLIOT LAKE). (CN/0827-6609). **Adv Mgr:** Sandra Dudeck. **5795**

STANDARD (EVANSTON, ILL.), THE. (US/0038-9382). **Adv Mgr:** Pam Nelsen. **5068**

STANDARD-EXAMINER, THE. (US). **Adv Mgr:** Brad Roghaar, **Tel** (801)625-4310. **5757**

STANDARD GUIDEBOOK TO THE ISLES OF SCILLY, THE. (UK). **5491**

STANDARD METHODS FOR ANALYSIS AND TESTING OF PETROLEUM AND RELATED PRODUCTS. (UK). **4279**

STANDARD PERIODICAL DIRECTORY, THE. (US/0085-6630). **3251**

STANDARD-TIMES (WAKEFIELD, R.I), THE. (US/1040-3337). **5741**

STANDARD TRADE & INDUSTRY DIRECTORY OF INDONESIA. (IO). **852**

STANDARD TRADE DIRECTORY OF INDONESIA. (IO). **852**

STANDARDBRED, THE. (CN/0705-2553). **2802**

STANDARDS ENGINEERING. (US/0038-9668). **4032**

STANDARDS MONITOR. (US/0739-0564). **3642**

STANDORTWAHL DER BETRIEBE IN DER BUNDESREPUBLIK DEUTSCHLAND UND BERLIN (WEST) / BUNDESMINISTER FUR ARBEIT UND SOZIALORDNUNG, DIE. (GW). **1585**

STANFORD FRENCH AND ITALIAN STUDIES. (US/0886-0750). **3439**

STANFORD FRENCH REVIEW. (US/0163-657X). **3353**

STANFORD HUMANITIES REVIEW. (US/1048-3721). **2855**

STANFORD ITALIAN REVIEW. (US/0730-6857). **3353**

STANFORD JOURNAL OF INTERNATIONAL LAW. (US/0731-5082). **3136**

STANFORD LAW & POLICY REVIEW. (US/1044-4386). **3058**

STANFORD LAWYER. (US/0585-0576). **3058**

STANFORD LITERATURE REVIEW. (US/0886-666X). **3353**

STANFORD MAGAZINE, THE. (US/0745-3981). **1095**

STANGER REPORT, THE. (US/0195-6620). **Adv Mgr:** Kathy Phillips. **916**

STANGER'S INVESTMENT ADVISOR. (US/1052-5912). **916**

STANISLAUS FARM NEWS. (US/8750-4960). **137**

STAPLES WORLD. (US). **Adv Mgr:** Gary Mueller. **5698**

STAR AND LAMP OF PI KAPPA PHI, THE. (US/0038-9854). **1095**

STAR (CHICAGO HEIGHTS AREA ED.]), THE. (US/0746-5181). **Adv Mgr:** Jay Frederickson. **5662**

STAR-COURIER, THE. (US). **5754**

STAR-DEMOCRAT (EASTON, MD.), THE. (US/1065-2345). **Adv Mgr:** David Fike. **5687**

STAR (FRANKFORT, ILL.), THE. (US/0746-5742). **5662**

STAR-LEDGER (NEWARK, N.J. : 1964). (US). **Adv Mgr:** Fred Marks. **5711**

STAR PROGRESS, THE. (US) **Adv Mgr:** Judith Hurler. **5632**

STARS AND STRIPES, THE NATIONAL TRIBUNE, THE. (US/0894-8542). **4057**

STARS MARIEMBOURG. (BE/0776-0698). **425**

START (SAN FRANCISCO, CALIF.). (US/0889-6216). **1204**

STARTEXT INK. (US/0890-6688). **Adv Mgr:** Gerry Barker. **1122**

STAT. (US/0038-9986). **3869**

STAT (VANCOUVER). (CN/0844-3955). **852**

STATE (CHARLOTTE, N.C.), THE. (US/0038-9994). **Adv Mgr:** S. Rogers, **Tel** (704)371-3269. **2762**

STATE (COLUMBIA, S.C. : 1891 : DAILY). (US). **5743**

STATE GOVERNMENT NEWS. (US/0039-0119). **4687**

STATE HOUSE WATCH. (US/1070-7719). **4687**

STATE JOURNAL, THE. (US). **Adv Mgr:** LoreNelle White. **713**

STATE JOURNAL, THE. (US). **5682**

STATE LIBRARIAN. (UK/0305-9189). **3251**

STATE NEWS. (US). **Adv Mgr:** D. Decoste, **Tel** (517)353-6400. **5694**

STATE OF HAWAII DATA BOOK. (US/0073-1080). **5339**

STATE PORT PILOT, THE. (US). **Adv Mgr:** Kim Adams, **Tel** (910)457-4568. **5724**

STATE REVENUE NEWSLETTER, THE. (US/0883-6760). **2787**

STATEMENT (FORT COLLINS, CO.). (US). **3324**

STATEMENTS (CHICAGO, ILL. 1985). (US/1054-7746). **Adv Mgr Tel** (312)787-2018. **309**

STATEN ISLAND HISTORIAN, THE. (US/0039-0232). **2762**

STATEN ISLAND REGISTER. (US/0890-9881). **5721**

STATESMAN JOURNAL. (US/0739-5507). **Adv Mgr:** Lorna Danielson, **Tel** (503)399-6645. **5734**

STATESMAN (STONY BROOK, N.Y.). (US). **1848**

STATESMAN, THE. (PK/0039-0313). **3353**

STATION RELAY, THE. (US). **5223**

STATIONERY NEWS. (AT/1033-758X). **Adv Mgr:** M. Merrick, **Tel** 02 9070366. **713**

STATIONERY TRADE NEWS. (UK/0951-7820). **Adv Mgr:** Paula Sandmann. **713**

STATISTICAL PROFILE OF IOWA. (US). **1538**

STATISTICAL RECORD, THE. (UK). **2803**

STATISTICAL REVIEW - AUSTRALIAN TOURIST COMMISSION. (AT). **5491**

STATISTICAL SCIENCE. (US/0883-4237). **5340**

STATISTICAL THEORY AND METHOD ABSTRACTS. (UK/0039-0518). **5340**

STATISTICAL YEARBOOK OF THE SOCIALIST REPUBLIC OF ROMANIA. (RM/0377-5739). **5341**

STATISTICIAN, THE. (UK/0039-0526). **5341**

STATISTICS AND COMPUTING. (UK/0960-3174). **Adv Mgr:** Rachel Kelly, **Tel** 44-71-865-0066. **1210**

STATISTICS & DECISIONS. (GW/0721-2631). **5342**

STATISTICS (BERLIN, DDR). (GW/0233-1888). **3543**

STATISTICS OF PAPER, PAPERBOARD AND WOOD PULP. (US/0731-8863). **4240**

STATISTIK ENERGI. (IO). **1963**

STATISTIK IN DER RENTENVERSICHERUNG. (GW). **5311**

STATISTIK INDONESIA. STATISTICAL YEARBOOK OF INDONESIA. (IO/0126-2912). **5342**

STATISTIK INDUSTRI KECIL. (IO). **1539**

STATISTIK PENDIDIKAN DILUAR LINGKUNGAN DEPARTEMEN P & K. (IO). **1798**

STATISTIK PENDIDIKAN DILUAR LINGKUNGAN DEPARTEMEN P & K DI-SUMATERA UTARA. (IO). **1798**

STATISTIK PERHUBUNGAN - BIRO PUSAT STATISTIK (LALU LINTAS ANGKUTAN BARANG ANTAR PULAU MENURUT JENIS PELAYARAN). (IO/0216-6909). **5457**

STATISTIK PERKEBUNAN BESAR. (IO). **138**

STATISTIQUE CRIMINELLE DE LA BELGIQUE. (BE). **3083**

STATISTIQUE DU TRAFIC INTERNATIONAL DES PORTS, U.E.B.L. / ROYAUME DE BELGIQUE, MINISTERE DES AFFAIRES ECONOMIQUES, INSTITUT NATIONAL DE BELGIQUE. (BE). **5402**

STATISTIQUES DE LA CONSTRUCTION ET DU LOGEMENT. (BE/0772-7712). **633**

STATISTIQUES DEMOGRAPHIQUES. (BE/0067-5490). **4563**

STATISTIQUES DIVERSES. (FR). **3083**

STATISTIQUES DU COMMERCE EXTERIEUR DE L'UNION ECONOMIQUE BELGO-LUXEMBURGEOISE. (BE/0772-6694). **734**

STATISTIQUES DU COMMERCE INTERIEUR ET DES TRANSPORTS / ROYAUME DE BELGIQUE, MINISTERE DES AFFAIRES ECONOMIQUES, INSTITUT NATIONAL DE STATISTIQUE. (BE). **734**

STATISTIQUES FINANCIERES. (BE). **734**

STATISTIQUES INDUSTRIELLES. (BE/0772-7704). **1539**

STATISTIQUES JUDICIAIRES. (BE/0775-311X). **3083**

STATISTISCHE BEIHEFTE ZU DEN MONATSBERICHTEN DER DEUTSCHEN BUNDESBANK. REIHE 4 : SAISONBEREINIGTE WIRTSCHAFTSZAHLEN. (GW/0418-8330). **1539**

STATISTISCHES JAHRBUCH BERLIN. (GW). **5343**

STATISTISK ARBOG. (DK). **5343**

STATISZTIKAI HAVI KOZLEMENYEK. (HU/0018-781X). **5344**

STATISZTIKAI SZEMLE. (HU/0039-0690). **1540**

STATSVETENSKAPLIG TIDSKRIFT. (SW/0039-0747). **4497**

STATUTE LAW REVIEW. (UK/0144-3593). **3059**

STAUB, REINHALTUNG DER LUFT. (GW/0039-0771). **2244**

STAVIVO. (XR/0039-0801). **628**

STAYNER SUN [MICROFORM], THE. (CN/0834-7425). **Adv Mgr:** Sue Nicholson. **5795**

STEAM PASSENGER SERVICE DIRECTORY. (US/0081-542X). **5437**

STEAMBOAT BILL (1958). (US/0039-0844). **2762**

STEAMBOAT PILOT, THE. (US). **5644**

STEEL GUITAR INTERNATIONAL NEWSLETTER. (US). **4154**

STEEL RESEARCH. (GW/0177-4832). **4020**

STEELVILLE STAR-CRAWFORD MIRROR. (US). **Adv Mgr:** Delma Pascoe. **5704**

STEERING WHEEL (AUSTIN). (US/0039-1298). **5393**

STEINBECK QUARTERLY. (US/0039-100X). **435**

STEM CELLS (DAYTON, OHIO). (US/1066-5099). **540**

STEP-BY-STEP GRAPHICS. (US/0886-7682). **382**

STEPPING BACK IN TIME. (US/0894-8313). **Adv Mgr:** E.B. Sherrill, **Tel** same as publisher. **2473**

STEPPING OUT ARTS MAGAZINE. (US). **Adv Mgr:** J. R. Reimann. **331**

STEPPKE. (GW/0938-0914). **1069**

STEREO-ATLAS OF OSTRACOD SHELLS; EDITED BY P.C. SYLVESTER-BRADLEY AND DAVID J. SIVETER. (UK). **557**

STEREO FM RADIO. (AT/0313-0797). **Adv Mgr:** M. Pena, **Tel** 439-4777. **1139**

STEREO REVIEW'S STEREO ... BUYERS GUIDE. (US/0736-6515). **5319**

STEREO REVIEWS TAPE RECORDING BUYERS' GUIDE. (US). **5319**

STEREOPHILE. (US/0585-2544). **5319**

STERNE UND WELTRAUM. (GW/0039-1263). **400**

STERN'S PERFORMING ARTS DIRECTORY. (US). **1314**

STEROID RECEPTORS. (UK/0142-8330). **540**

STEROIDS. (US/0039-128X). **473**

STERRENGIDS. (NE). **400**

STETSON LAW REVIEW. (US/0739-9731). **Adv Mgr Tel** (813)343-1344. **3059**

STEUBEN NEWS. (US). **4513**

STEUBENVILLE REGISTER, THE. (US/0744-771X). **Adv Mgr:** Janice Ward, **Tel** (614)282-6831. **5730**

STEUER UND WIRTSCHAFT. (GW). **4750**

STEWARTVILLE STAR. (US). **5699**

STILL HERE : JOB/SCHOLARSHIP REFERRAL NEWSLETTER / SCHOOL OF COMMUNICATIONS, HOWARD UNIVERSITY. (US). **1122**

STIMULOGRAPHY. (FR/0989-2192). **3710**

STIRPES. (US/0039-1522). **2473**

STITCH 'N SEW QUILTS. (US/0744-1649). **5186**

STITCHES : THE JOURNAL OF MEDICAL HUMOUR. (CN). **3643**

STOCK CAR RACING. (US/0734-7340). **4924**

STOCK MARKET MAGAZINE, THE. (US/0039-1638). **916**

STOCK SHOW, THE. (US/0273-5776). **222**

STOCKS, BONDS, BILLS, AND INFLATION YEARBOOK. (US/1047-2436). **916**

STOCKTON RECORD (STOCKTON, CALIF.). (US). **Adv Mgr:** Dave Winegarden, **Tel** (209)546-8238. **5640**

STOFF MISBRUK : INFORMASJON FRA SENTRALRADET FOR NARKOTIKAPROBLEMER. (NO). **1349**

STOMATOLOGIJA. (RU/0039-1735). **1336**

STOMATOLOSKI GLASNIK SRBIJE. (YU/0039-1743). **1336**

STONE COUNTRY. (US/0146-1397). **3472**

STONE COUNTY ENTERPRISE. (US). **Adv Mgr:** Christy Groves. **5702**

STONE COUNTY LEADER (1956). (US/1066-3983). **5632**

STONE IN AMERICA. (US/0160-7243). **365**

STONE INDUSTRIES. (UK/0039-1778). **Adv Mgr:** Les Hawkins. **1445**

STONE LION REVIEW. (US/0747-6744). **3440**

STONE REVIEW. (US/8750-9210). **2151**

STONE SOUP (SANTA CRUZ, CALIF.). (US/0094-579X). **1069**

STONEHAM CATALOGUE OF BRITISH STAMPS, THE. (UK/0142-615X). **2787**

STONEHAM INDEPENDENT, THE. (US). **Adv Mgr:** Jon Haggesty, **Tel** (617)438-1660. **5690**

STOP (BRATISLAVA). (XO/0139-6501). **5426**

STOP (MONTREAL). (CN/0831-0319). **Adv Mgr:** Andre Lenelin. **3440**

STORES. (US/0039-1867). **958**

STORES OF THE YEAR. (US/0192-8732). **2903**

STORIA ARCHITETTURA. (IT/0390-4253). **309**

STORIA DEL PENSIERO ECONOMICO. BOLLETTINO DI INFORMAZIONE. (IT). **1585**

STORIA DELLA STORIOGRAFIA. (IT). **2630**

STORIES (BOSTON, MASS.). (US/0742-2113). **3440**

STORY CITY HERALD (STORY CITY, IOWA : 1892). (US). **Adv Mgr:** Tricia Sawyer. **5673**

STORYQUARTERLY (NORTHBROOK, ILL.). (US/1041-0708). **3440**

STORYTELLING MAGAZINE. (US/1048-1354). **2324**

STORYVILLE (CHIGWELL). (UK/0039-2030). **4154**

STOUGHTON COURIER HUB (STOUGHTON, WIS. : 1981). (US/1049-0655). **5771**

STOUTONIA, THE. (US). **1095**

STRAD, THE. (UK/0039-2049). **4154**

STRAFFORD FESTIVAL. (CN/0085-6770). **388**

STRAIN. (UK/0039-2103). **2129**

STRAITS TIMES, THE. (SI). **5810**

STRANGE MAGAZINE. (US/0894-8968). **2493**

STRANI JEZICI. (CI/0351-0840). **3440**

STRASSE UND AUTOBAHN. (GW/0039-2162). **2031**

STRATEGIC PLANNING FOR ENERGY AND THE ENVIRONMENT. (US/1048-5236). **1958**

STRATEGIC REVIEW FOR SOUTHERN AFRICA. (SA). **5223**

STRATEGIES & SOLUTIONS. (US/1067-9537). **Adv Mgr:** Kim Branko, **Tel** (612)881-1082. **4804**

STRATEGIES (BIRMINGHAM). (UK/0959-8936). **1905**

STRATEGIES (LOS ANGELES, CALIF.). (US/1040-2136). **4497**

STRATEGY & TACTICS (CAMBRIA, CALIF.). (US/1040-886X). **4058**

STRATEGY (TORONTO. 1991). (CN/1187-4309). **937**

STRATFORD JOURNAL (STRATFORD, WIS.). (US). **5771**

STRATTON MAGAZINE. (US/1064-1629). **Adv Mgr:** Lee Romand. **4924**

STREET BEAT (PITTSBURGH, PA.). (US/1069-5478). **3440**

STREET MACHINE (LONDON, ENGLAND). (UK/0143-5949). **5426**

STREET NEWS. (US). **2547**

STREET RODDING ILLUSTRATED. (US/8750-3298). **5426**

STRELEC (JERSEY CITY, N.J.). (US/0747-7287). **3440**

STRENGTH AND HEALTH. (US/0039-2308). **2601**

STRINGS (SAN ANSELMO, CALIF.). (US/0888-3106). **4155**

STRIPER. (US/0199-5634). **2314**

STROEZ I FUNKCII NA MOZKA. (BU/0204-4560). **3846**

STROITELNYE MATERIALY I KONSTRUKTSII. (RU/0136-7773). **629**

STROJNISKI VESTNIK. (XV/0039-2480). **5160**

STROKE (1970). (US/0039-2499). **3710**

STROKE CONNECTION. (US/1047-014X). **5312**

STROLLING ASTRONOMER, THE. (US/0039-2502). **400**

STROM + SEE. (SZ/0039-2510). **5393**

STROMATA. (AG/0049-2353). **4999**

STRUCTURAL ENGINEERING AND MECHANICS. (KO/1225-4568). **Adv Mgr:** N.H. Lee, **Tel** same as publisher. **1997**

STRUCTURAL ENGINEERING INTERNATIONAL : JOURNAL OF THE INTERNATIONAL ASSOCIATION FOR BRIDGE AND STRUCTURAL ENGINEERING (IABSE). (SZ/1016-8664). **5393**

STRUCTURAL ENGINEERING REVIEW. (UK/0952-5807). **2031**

STRUCTURAL SURVEY. (US). **629**

STRUCTURED PROGRAMMING. (US/0935-1183). **1204**

STRUGGLE : MATHEMATICS FOR LOW ATTAINERS. (UK). **1885**

STRUKTURNAIA I PRIKLADNAIA LINGVISTIKA. (RU). **3324**

STRUMENTI MUSICALI. (IT/0392-890X). **4155**

STUART HERALD, THE. (US). **Adv Mgr:** Norma Thurman. **5673**

STUART NEWS, THE. (US). **5651**

STUDENT ASSISTANCE JOURNAL. (US/1042-6388). **1349**

STUDENT CONTRIBUTION SERIES. (US). **3251**

STUDENT GUIDE TO: GRADUATE LAW STUDY PROGRAMS. (US/0196-9773). **3060**

STUDENT GUIDE TO: SUMMER LAW STUDY PROGRAMS. (US/0197-6656). **3060**

STUDENT GUIDE TO THE SAT. (US/1043-8378). **1848**

STUDENT HANDBOOK OF INFORMATION ON UNIVERSITY POLICIES AND PRACTICES. (NR). **1848**

STUDENT LAWYER (CHICAGO. 1972). (US/0039-274X). **3060**

STUDENT PUBLICATION OF THE SCHOOL OF DESIGN. (US/0078-1444). **309**

STUDENT SUCCESS TUTOR DIRECTORY. SARASOTA COUNTY. (US/0899-2355). **1786**

STUDENT TIMES (MONTREAL). (CN/0712-7944). **5795**

STUDENT TRAVELS MAGAZINE. (US). **5491**

STUDENT VOICE. (US/0039-2804). **1095**

STUDI CATTOLICI. (IT/0039-2901). **5036**

STUDI DI LETTERATURA ISPANO-AMERICANA. (IT/0585-4776). **3440**

STUDI DI TEOLOGIA DOGMATICA. (IT). **Adv Mgr:** F. Zucchelli Giuseppe. **4999**

STUDI ECONOMICI E SOCIALI. (IT/0391-8750). **1628**

STUDI ETNO-ANTROPOLOGICI E SOCIOLOGICI / PUBBLICATA SOTTO GLI AUSPICI DEL CONSIGLIO NAZIONALE DELLE RICHERCHE. (IT). **246**

STUDI FRANCESI. (IT/0039-2944). **3440**

STUDI ITALIANI DI FILOLOGIA CLASSICA. (IT/0039-2987). **1080**

STUDI PIEMONTESI. (IT). **Adv Mgr:** Albina Malerba. **2711**

STUDI STORICI. (IT/0039-3037). **2711**

STUDIA CELTICA. (UK/0081-6353). **3324**

STUDIA DIPLOMATICA. (BE/0770-2965). **4497**

STUDIA IRANICA. (NE/0772-7852). **2665**

STUDIA LEIBNITIANA. (GW/0039-3185). **4361**

STUDIA LOGICA. (PL/0039-3215). **4362**

STUDIA MUSICOLOGICA NORVEGICA. (NO/0332-5024). **4155**

STUDIA MYSTICA. (US/0161-7222). **3441**

STUDIA NEOPHILOLOGICA. (SW/0039-3274). **3325**

STUDIA PHONETICA POSNANIENSIA. (PL/0861-2085). **3325**

STUDIA PSYCHOLOGICA. (XO) **4619**

STUDIA ROSENTHALIANA. (NE/0039-3347). **2273**

STUDIA SLAVICA ACADEMIAE SCIENTIARUM HUNGARICAE. (HU/0039-3363). **3325**

STUDIA SPINOZANA. (GW). **4362**

STUDIA THEOLOGICA. (NO/0039-338X). **5000**

STUDIEN UND MITTEILUNGEN ZUR GESCHICHTE DES BENEDIKTINER-ORDENS UND SEINER ZWEIGE. (GW). **5037**

STUDIEN ZUM WANDEL VON GESELLSCHAFT UND BILDUNG IM NEUNZEHNTEN JAHRHUNDERT. (GW). **2631**

STUDIEN ZUR MEDIZINGESCHICHTE DES NEUNZEHNTEN JAHRHUNDERTS. (GW/0081-7333). **3643**

STUDIEN ZUR UMWELT DES NEUEN TESTAMENTS. (GW/0585-6272). **5000**

STUDIENFUHRER. (GW). **1849**

STUDIES. (IE/0039-3495). **2523**

STUDIES IN 20TH CENTURY LITERATURE. (US/0145-7888). **3354**

STUDIES IN AFRICAN LINGUISTICS. (US/0039-3533). **3325**

STUDIES IN AMERICAN DRAMA, 1945-PRESENT. (US/0886-7097). **5369**

STUDIES IN AMERICAN FICTION. (US/0091-8083). **3354**

STUDIES IN AMERICAN INDIAN LITERATURE. (US). **Adv Mgr:** R.M. Nelson, **Tel** (809)289-8311. **3441**

STUDIES IN AMERICAN JEWISH LITERATURE (ALBANY, N.Y.). (US/0271-9274). **3441**

STUDIES IN APPLIED MATHEMATICS (CAMBRIDGE). (US/0022-2526). **3537**

STUDIES IN CANADIAN LITERATURE (FREDERICTON, N.B.). (CN/0380-6995). **Adv Mgr:** S. Campbell. **3441**

STUDIES IN CENTRAL AND EAST ASIAN RELIGIONS : JOURNAL OF THE SEMINAR FOR BUDDHIST STUDIES, COPENHAGEN & AARHUS. (DK/0904-2431). **5022**

STUDIES IN CHRISTIAN ETHICS. (UK). **5000**

STUDIES IN COMPARATIVE COMMUNISM. (UK/0039-3592). **4548**

STUDIES IN COMPARATIVE INTERNATIONAL DEVELOPMENT. (US/0039-3606). **5223**

STUDIES IN COMPARATIVE RELIGION. (UK/0039-3622). **5000**

STUDIES IN CONSERVATION. (UK/0039-3630). **366**

STUDIES IN CONTEMPORARY SATIRE. (US/0163-4143). **3441**

STUDIES IN EDUCATIONAL ADMINISTRATION. (AT). **Adv Mgr:** Bernadette Taylor. **1872**

STUDIES IN EIGHTEENTH-CENTURY CULTURE. (US/0360-2370). **2631**

STUDIES IN ENGLISH LITERATURE, 1500-1900. (US/0039-3657). **3442**

STUDIES IN HISTORY (SAHIBABAD). (US/0258-1698). **2665**

STUDIES IN HUMAN RIGHTS. (US/0146-3586). **4513**

STUDIES IN LATIN AMERICAN POPULAR CULTURE. (US/0730-9139). **Adv Mgr:** same as editor. **331**

STUDIES IN MUSIC. (AT/0081-8267). **4155**

STUDIES IN PHILOLOGY. (US/0039-3738). **3326**

STUDIES IN PHILOSOPHY AND EDUCATION. (US/0039-3746). **4362**

STUDIES IN RELIGION. (CN/0008-4298). **5001**

STUDIES IN ROMANTICISM. (US/0039-3762). **3442**

STUDIES IN SCIENCE EDUCATION. (UK/0305-7267). **5160**

STUDIES IN SECOND LANGUAGE ACQUISITION. (US/0272-2631). **3326**

STUDIES IN SOVIET THOUGHT. (NE/0039-3797). **4362**

STUDIES IN THE AMERICAN RENAISSANCE. (US/0149-015X). **3354**

STUDIES IN THE HUMANITIES. (US). **2855**

STUDIES — Advertising Accepted Index

STUDIES IN THE NOVEL. (US/0039-3827). **3354**

STUDIES IN ZIONISM. (IS/0334-1771). **Adv Mgr:** Anne Kidson. **5053**

STUDIES ON NEOTROPICAL FAUNA AND ENVIRONMENT. (NE/0165-0521). **5598**

STUDIES ON WOMEN ABSTRACTS. (UK/0262-5644). **5572**

STUDII SI MATERIALE DE ISTORIE MEDIE. (RM/0567-6312). **2712**

STUDII SI MATERIALE DE ISTORIE MODERNA. (RM/0567-6320). **2712**

STUDIUM (MADRID). (SP/0585-766X). **3443**

STUTTGART DAILY LEADER, THE. (US). **Adv Mgr:** Gene Austin. **5632**

STUTTGARTER BEITRAEGE ZUR NATURKUNDE. SERIES C. ALLGEMEINVERSTAENDLICHE AUFSAETZE. (GW/0341-0161). **4172**

STYLE (FAYETTEVILLE). (US/0039-4238). **3443**

STYLE (TORONTO). (CN/0039-4246). **Adv Mgr:** S. Swan, **Tel** (416)755-5799. **1087**

SUB-STANCE. (US/0049-2426). **3443**

SUBCONTRACTOR, THE. (US/0195-1459). **629**

SUBSEA ENGINEERING NEWS. (UK/0266-2205). **2095**

SUBURBAN. COTE DES NEIGES EDITION. (CN/0229-2998). **5795**

SUBURBAN (COTE-SAINT-LUC ED.). (CN/0226-9686). **5795**

SUBURBAN. DOLLARD DES ORMEAUX EDITION. (CN/0229-298X). **5795**

SUBURBAN GAZETTE. (US). **Adv Mgr:** James Dinaudo. **5739**

SUBURBAN (LAVAL EDITION). (CN/0229-3048). **2547**

SUBURBAN. NEW BORDEAUX, CARTIERVILLE EDITION. (CN/0229-3013). **5795**

SUBURBAN NEWS (READING), THE. (US/0194-276X). **Adv Mgr:** Paul Mack. **5690**

SUBURBAN. NOTRE DAME DE GRACE EDITION. (CN/0229-2971). **5795**

SUBURBAN. ST. LAURENT EDITION. (CN/0229-303X). **5795**

SUBURBAN (WESTMOUNT EDITION). (CN/0229-3005). **5795**

SUCCESSFUL CALIFORNIA ACCOUNTANT, THE. (US). **Adv Mgr:** Diana Granger, **Tel** (916)427-0227. **752**

SUCCESSFUL FARMING. (US/0039-4432). **138**

SUCCESSFUL HOTEL MARKETER, THE. (US/1040-600X). **2809**

SUCCESSFUL SELLING & MANAGING. (AT/1036-1693). **937**

SUCCESSO. (IT). **813**

SUCCULENTA. (NE/0039-4467). **528**

SUCHASNIST. (US/0585-8364). **3443**

SUD; INFORMATION ECONOMIQUE : PROVENCE ALPES COTE D'AZUR. (FR). **1585**

SUDAN NOTES AND RECORDS. (SJ/0375-2984). **2855**

SUDOST EUROPA : [MONATSSCHRIFT DER ABTEILUNG GEGENWARTSFORSCHUNG DES SUDOST-INSTITUTS]. (GW/0722-480X). **5224**

SUFFOLK BANNER, THE. (US/0194-7230). **222**

SUFFOLK COUNTY AGRICULTURAL NEWS. (US/0039-467X). **Adv Mgr:** Caryn Popowitch. **138**

SUFFOLK COUNTY AGRICULTURAL NEWS. (US). **138**

SUFFOLK TIMES, THE. (US). **Adv Mgr:** Janice Robinson. **5721**

SUFISM (SAN RAFAEL, CALIF.). (US/0898-3380). **Adv Mgr:** Blake Ross, **Tel** (415)472-6959. **5001**

SUGAR BULLETIN, THE. (US/0039-4726). **2358**

SUGAR CANE (1983). (UK/0265-7406). **188**

SUGAR JOURNAL. (US/0039-4734). **188**

SUGAR PRODUCER, THE. (US/0199-8498). **2359**

SUGAR Y AZUCAR. (US/0039-4742). **Adv Mgr:** Alan Berg. **138**

SUGAR Y AZUCAR. YEARBOOK. (US/0081-9212). **Adv Mgr:** A. Berg. **2359**

SUGARBEET GROWER, THE. (US/0039-4750). **188**

SUGARLAND. (PH/0039-4777). **188**

SUICIDE & LIFE-THREATENING BEHAVIOR. (US/0363-0234). **4619**

SUID-AFRIKAAN, DIE. (SA/1011-7547). **1523**

SUID-AFRIKAANSE GEOGRAAF. (SA). **2577**

SUID-AFRIKAANSE TEATERSUSTER. (US). **Adv Mgr:** G. Espost. **3870**

SUID-AFRIKAANSE TYDSKRIF VIR APTEEKWESE. (SA/0038-2558). **Adv Mgr:** Felicity Wilson. **4330**

SUID-AFRIKAANSE TYDSKRIF VIR NATUURWETENSKAP EN TEGNOLOGIE. (SA/0254-3486). **5160**

SUISAN KAIYO KENKYU. (JA/0916-1562). **2314**

SULFUR LETTERS. (UK/0278-6117). **1038**

SULFUR (PASADENA, CALIF.). (US/0730-305X). **Adv Mgr:** Caryl Eshleman, **Tel** same as publisher. **3443**

SULFUR REPORTS. (SZ/0196-1772). **1038**

SULLIVAN COUNTY DEMOCRAT. (US). **Adv Mgr:** J Price. **4497**

SULPHUR. (UK/0039-4890). **1030**

SULPHUR SPRINGS NEWS-TELEGRAM. (US/0745-6425). **5755**

SUMMA. (AG/0325-4615). **309**

SUMMA+. (AG/0327-9022). **309**

SUMMA MUSICAE MEDII AEVI. (GW/0585-9158). **4155**

SUMMARIOS. (AG/0325-6448). **309**

SUMMER THEATRE DIRECTORY (DORSET, VT.). (US/0884-5840). **Adv Mgr:** Gene Siratof. **5369**

SUMMERVILLE NEWS, THE. (US). **5655**

SUMMIT (BIG BEAR LAKE). (US/0039-5056). **4879**

SUMTER COUNTY JOURNAL. (US). **Adv Mgr:** Judi Johnston. **5628**

SUMTER JOURNAL, THE. (US/0747-0304). **5651**

SUN (1993). (US/1072-8619). **Adv Mgr:** Bob Alexsander. **5721**

SUN-ADVOCATE, THE. (US). **Adv Mgr:** Bonnie Johnson. **5757**

SUN AT WORK IN EUROPE. (UK/0269-1159). **1958**

SUN BELT FLOOR COVERING. (US/0895-934X). **2907**

SUN (BREMERTON, WASH.), THE. (US/1050-3692). **Adv Mgr:** Steve Howes. **5762**

SUN/COAST ARCHITECT/BUILDER. (US/0744-8872). **629**

SUN-DIAMOND GROWER. (US/0899-8809). **2432**

SUN (GRAND CENTRE). (CN/0710-0019). **5795**

SUN HERALD (BILOXI, MISS.). (US). **Adv Mgr:** Stone Ellis. **5702**

SUN (HUMMELSTOWN, PA.). (US). **Adv Mgr:** Rosemary Jackson. **5739**

SUN-NEWS (LOWDEN, IOWA). (US). **Adv Mgr:** Pat Kroemer. **5673**

SUN-REPORTER, THE. (US/0890-0930). **Adv Mgr:** J Castle. **5640**

SUN-TIMES (HEBER SPRINGS, ARK.). (US/1050-5105). **Adv Mgr:** John Jennings. **5632**

SUN TRIBUNE. (US). **Adv Mgr:** Tolley Evans. **5734**

SUNBELT FOODSERVICE. (US/1069-3475). **Adv Mgr:** D. Heller. **2359**

SUNBURST (ROSEVILLE). (US/0274-9181). **5224**

SUNBURY NEWS, THE. (US). **Adv Mgr:** Mary Ann Pemberton. **5730**

SUNDAY NEWS (LANCASTER, PA.). (US). **5740**

SUNDAY TELEGRAM, THE. (US). **5685**

SUNDAY TIMES (LONDON, ENGLAND : 1931). (UK). **5813**

SUNFLOWER (FARGO), THE. (US/0192-8988). **188**

SUNSET (MENLO PARK, CALIF.). (US/0039-5404). **2547**

SUNSHINE ARTISTS, U.S.A. (US/0199-9370). **375**

SUNSTONE. (US/0363-1370). **Adv Mgr:** K. Kolan, **Tel** (801)355-5926. **5001**

SUNWORLD. (AT/0149-1938). **Adv Mgr:** P. Riches. **1958**

SUOMEN HAMMASLAAKARISEURAN TOIMITUKSIA. (FI/0039-551X). **1336**

SUOMEN MATKAILU. (FI/0359-0607). **2523**

SUOMEN SHAKKI. (FI). **4924**

SUPER AUTOMOTIVE SERVICE. (US/0896-0437). **5426**

SUPER GROUP MAGAZINE. (US/1043-2418). **1204**

SUPER STOCK & DRAG ILLUSTRATED. (US/0039-5692). **4924**

SUPERB FILL-IT-INS. (US/0194-3227). **4866**

SUPERB WORD-FIND PUZZLES. (US/0194-3235). **4866**

SUPERB WORD-TWISTS. (US/0199-218X). **4866**

SUPERCOMPUTER. (NE/0168-7875). **1204**

SUPERCOMPUTING REVIEW. (US/1048-6836). **1204**

SUPERCONDUCTOR INDUSTRY. (US/1042-4105). **5161**

SUPERMAGAZINE D'ARTISANAT LES MOUSTARTS. (CN/0824-6254). **376**

SUPERMARKET SCOOP. (US/1065-3260). **2359**

SUPERPREP. AMERICA'S RECRUITING MAGAZINE. (US). **4924**

SUPERSTAR WRESTLER. (US/0887-1035). **4866**

SUPERTRAX. (CN). **Adv Mgr:** T. Kehoe. **4855**

SUPERVISOR (ENGLEWOOD, N.J.), EL. (US/1043-2191). **2871**

SUPLEMENTO ANTROPOLOGICO - UNIVERSIDAD CATOLICA. (PY/0378-9896). **246**

SUPPLEMENTARY VOLUME - ARISTOTELIAN SOCIETY. (UK/0309-7013). **4363**

SUPPLEMENTS TO NOVUM TESTAMENTUM. (NE/0167-9732). **5001**

SUPPLEMENTS TO VETUS TESTAMENTUM. (NE/0083-5889). **5001**

SUPPLY LINE. (US/8750-0124). **Adv Mgr:** Kay, **Tel** (816)737-5111. **4058**

SUPPORT FOR LEARNING. (UK/0268-2141). **1786**

SUPREME COURT BULLETIN (MANCHESTER, N.H.). (US/0199-5030). **3061**

SUPREME COURT CASES, THE. (II). **3061**

SUPREME COURT RECORD. (US/0892-810X). **3061**

SUREPAY UPDATE. (US/0195-5225). **813**

SURFACE & COATINGS TECHNOLOGY. (SZ/0257-8972). **Adv Mgr:** Ms. W van Cattenburch (Amsterdam). **2108**

SURFACE AND INTERFACE ANALYSIS : SIA. (UK/0142-2421). **1019**

SURFACE COATING & RAW MATERIAL DIRECTORY. (UK/0268-9766). **Adv Mgr:** John Lane, **Tel** 011 44 061 442 5828. **4225**

SURFACE COATINGS AUSTRALIA. (AT/0815-709X). **Adv Mgr:** G. Goullet. **1030**

SURFACE DESIGN JOURNAL. (US/0197-4483). **Adv Mgr:** Joy Stocksdale, **Tel** (510)841-2008. **5356**

SURFACE ENGINEERING. (UK/0267-0844). **1997**

SURFACE MOUNT TECHNOLOGY. (US/0893-3588). **Adv Mgr:** Paula Solomini. **2083**

SURFACE TREATMENT TECHNOLOGY ABSTRACTS. (UK). **4026**

SURFACES. (FR/0585-9840). **4021**

SURFER. (US/0039-6036). **4924**

SURFER'S JOURNAL, THE. (US/1062-3892). **4924**

SURGERY. (US/0039-6060). **3975**

SURGERY ALERT. (US/0748-1942). **3975**

SURGERY, GYNECOLOGY & OBSTETRICS. (US/0039-6087). **3975**

SURGERY (OXFORD). (UK/0263-9319). **3975**

SURGICAL NEUROLOGY. (US/0090-3019). **3976**

SURGICAL PRODUCT NEWS. (US/0279-4829). **3684**

SURGICAL TECHNOLOGIST, THE. (US/0164-4238). **3644**

SURNAME AND PUBLICATION INDEX. (US/0270-9856). **2474**

SURPLUS RECORD, THE. (US/0039-615X). **Adv Mgr Tel** (312)372-9077. **2129**

SURPRISES. (US/0890-3573). **1070**

SURVEILLANT (WASHINGTON, D.C.). (US/1051-0923). **Adv Mgr:** Bagley Fordyce, **Tel** (202)797-1234. **4058**

SURVEY OF ANESTHESIOLOGY. (US/0039-6206). **3684**

SURVEY OF CHAINS AND GROUPS. (CN). **2359**

SURVEY OF DISTRIBUTIVE TRADE. (FJ). **958**

SURVEY OF OPHTHALMOLOGY. (US/0039-6257). **3879**

SURVEYING AND LAND INFORMATION SYSTEMS. (US/1052-2905). **2583**

SURVEYING TECHNICIAN. (UK/0952-5793). **2032**

SURVEYS IN GEOPHYSICS. (NE/0169-3298). **1411**

SURVEYS IN HIGH ENERGY PHYSICS. (SZ/0142-2413). **4451**

SURVEYS ON MATHEMATICS FOR INDUSTRY. (AU/0938-1953). **1997**

SURVIVAL (LONDON). (UK/0039-6338). **4058**

SURVIVING TOGETHER. (US/0895-6286). **Adv Mgr:** T. Speiser. **4536**

SURYA INDIA. (II). **2508**

SUSPECT CHEMICALS SOURCEBOOK. UPDATE SERVICE. (US/0893-7044). **Adv Mgr:** Karen Winstedt. **1030**

SUSSEX-SURRY DISPATCH. (US/0745-9467). **5759**

SUSTAINABLE FARMING. (CN/1180-1506). **Adv Mgr:** R. Samson. **138**

SV. SOUND AND VIBRATION. (US/0038-1810). **Adv Mgr:** Lisa King. **4453**

SVA BULLETIN : OFFIZIELLES ORGAN DER SVA UND DESOAF. (SZ/0036-777X). **4451**

SVENSK FARMACEUTISK TIDSKRIFT. (SW/0039-6524). **4330**

SVENSK INDUSTRIKALENDER. (SW). **1628**

SVENSK MISSIONSTIDSKRIFT. (SW/0346-217X). **5001**

SVENSK PAPPERSTIDNING. (SW/0039-6680). **4239**

SVENSK TIDSKRIFT. (SW/0039-677X). **3354**

SVENSK TRAVARU- OCH PAPPERSMASSETIDNING. (SW/0039-6796). **2405**

SVENSK VETERINARTIDNING. (SW/0346-2250). **5522**

SVERIGES FRIMARKEN OCH HELSAKER / SVERIGES FILATELIST-FORBUND. (SW/0347-1152). **2787**

SVETSEN. (SW/0039-7091). **4028**

SVOBODA (JERSEY CITY). (US/0274-6964). **Adv Mgr:** Maria Szeparowycz, **Tel** (201)434-0237. **5711**

SVOBODNYJ MIR. (US/0892-6379). **426**

SWARA / EAST AFRICAN WILD LIFE SOCIETY. (KE). **5598**

SWEDEN INTERNATIONAL. (SW/1101-4989). **Adv Mgr:** Robin Courtenay. **714**

SWEDISH AMERICAN GENEALOGIST. (US/0275-9314). **Adv Mgr:** same as editor. **2474**

SWEDISH-AMERICAN HISTORICAL QUARTERLY. (US/0730-028X). **2762**

SWEDISH DENTAL JOURNAL. (SW/0347-9994). **1336**

SWEDISH TOWN AND COUNTRY PLANNING REVIEW, THE. (SW/0032-0560). **2836**

SWEET POTATO. (US/0147-5282). **4155**

SWEET'S CATALOG FILE. PRODUCTS FOR HOME BUILDING AND REMODELING. (US/0743-5789). **629**

SWIFT COUNTY MONITOR-NEWS. (US/0747-1653). **5699**

SWIM (ARLINGTON, VA.). (US/8755-2027). **4924**

SWIMMING TEACHER. (UK/0306-0403). **4925**

SWIMMING TECHNIQUE. (US/0039-7415). **4925**

SWIMMING TIMES. (UK). **4925**

SWIMMING WORLD AND JUNIOR SWIMMER (1965). (US/0039-7431). **4925**

SWISS AMERICAN REVIEW. (US). **Adv Mgr:** Nadja C. Leonard, **Tel** (202)408-1200. **5721**

SWISS BUSINESS. (SZ). **714**

SWISS MATERIALS. (SZ/1013-4476). **1997**

SWISS PACKAGING CATALOGUE. (SZ). **4222**

SWORD OF THE LORD, THE. (US/0039-7547). **5001**

SYDNEY REVIEW 1988. (AT/1032-2892). **331**

SYDNEY'S CHILD. (AT/1034-6384). **Adv Mgr:** Joanna, **Tel** 02 484-5334. **2286**

SYGEPLEJERSKEN. (DK/0106-8350). **3870**

SYLLABUS. (US). **1225**

SYLLECTA CLASSICA. (US/1040-3612). **1080**

SYMBOLS. (US/0889-7425). **246**

SYMBOLS OF AMERICAN LIBRARIES. (US/0095-0874). **3252**

SYMPOSIUM (SYRACUSE). (US/0039-7709). **3327**

SYN OG SEGN. (NO/0039-7717). **2523**

SYNAPSE. (FR/0762-7475). **3846**

SYNOPSES OF THE BRITISH FAUNA. (UK/0082-1101). **5598**

SYNTHESIS AND REACTIVITY IN INORGANIC AND METAL-ORGANIC CHEMISTRY. (US/0094-5714). **994**

SYNTHETIC COMMUNICATIONS. (US/0039-7911). **1048**

SYNTHETIC FIBRES / ASSOCIATION OF SYNTHETIC FIBRE INDUSTRY. (II). **5356**

SYNTHETIC METALS. (SZ/0379-6779). **Adv Mgr:** Ms. W van Cattenburch (Amsterdam). **4021**

SYRACUSE JOURNAL OF INTERNATIONAL LAW AND COMMERCE. (US/0093-0709). **3136**

SYRACUSE LAW REVIEW. (US/0039-7938). **3062**

SYRACUSE NEW TIMES. (US/0893-844X). **Adv Mgr:** Karen Belgrader. **2493**

SYSDATA. (SZ). **Adv Mgr:** B U Schonenberger. **1262**

SYSTEM (LINKOPING). (UK/0346-251X). **3327**

SYSTEMATIC ENTOMOLOGY. (UK/0307-6970). **5613**

SYSTEMATIC PARASITOLOGY. (NE/0165-5752). **5598**

SYSTEMES SOLAIRES. (FR/0295-5873). **Adv Mgr:** Liebard. **1959**

SYSTEMS RESEARCH AND INFORMATION SCIENCE. (US/0882-3014). **3252**

SYSTEMS SCIENCE. (PL/0137-1223). **1249**

SYSTEMS USER. (US/0199-8951). **1262**

SZACHY. (PL). **4866**

T & D. (AT/1037-9687). **887**

T & G RECORD. (UK). **Adv Mgr:** Steve McGowan, **Tel** 071 831 8864. **1713**

T.E.L. THE ELECTRIC LETTER. (US/0093-5379). **2083**

T.U.B.A. JOURNAL. (US/0363-4787). **Adv Mgr:** Jim Shearer, **Tel** (505)646-2601. **4156**

T.U.B.A. MEMBERSHIP ROSTER. (US/0163-5360). **4156**

TA NEA. (GR). **5802**

TAA REPORT. (US/1041-1453). **4832**

TAAMULI. (TZ). **4497**

TABLET (LONDON), THE. (UK/0039-8837). **5002**

TABLET, THE. (US/0039-8845). **5037**

TACD JOURNAL. (US/1046-171X). **4620**

TACT : THE AIR CARGO TARIFF. (NE). **5394**

TAE KWON DO TIMES. (US/0741-028X). **Adv Mgr:** C Hart. **4925**

TAEKWONDO WORLD. (US/1043-1047). **Adv Mgr:** Carla Dailey. **2601**

TAFRIJA (TUCKER, GA.). (US/1070-7522). **389**

TAGLICHE PRAXIS. (GW/0494-464X). **3644**

TAGLINE (OLNEY). (UK/0968-0349). **Adv Mgr:** Leigh Foster, **Tel** 01234 241454. **4820**

TAHOE DAILY TRIBUNE AND THE LAKE TAHOE NEWS. (US/8750-3948). **Adv Mgr:** Marianne Archibald. **5640**

TAHQIQAT-I ISLAMI. (II). **5045**

T'AI CHI. (US/0730-1049). **2601**

TAI-WAN SHUI LI. (CH). **2244**

TAIDE. (FI/0039-8977). **366**

TAIKABUTSU. (JA/0039-8993). **4021**

TAIKABUTSU OVERSEAS. (JA/0285-0028). **5161**

TAITEEN KESKUSTOIMIKUNNAN TIEDOTUSLEHTI. (FI). **331**

TAITO. (FI/0355-7421). **376**

TAIWAN BUSINESS DIRECTORY. (CH). **714**

TAIWAN BUYERS' GUIDE. (US/0082-1470). **3488**

TAIWAN ENTERPRISE. (CH). **1628**

TAIWAN EXPORTERS GUIDE. (CH). **853**

TAIWAN GONGLUNBAO. (US/0743-5355). **5640**

TAIWAN STATISTICAL DATA BOOK. (CH). **5344**

TAIYO CHIKYU KEIHO EISEI CHOSA HOKOKU. (JA). **37**

TAIYO (HEIBONSHA). (JA). **2509**

TAKAHE CHRISTCHURCH. (NZ/0114-4138). **3444**

TAKE FIVE (SASKATOON, SASK.). (CN/0821-0160). **2547**

TAKING CARE. (US). **4804**

TALEN GRONINGEN. (NE/0922-1166). **3327**

TALISMAN (HOBOKEN, N.J.). (US/0898-8684). **Adv Mgr Tel** same as publisher. **3472**

TALK (LONDON, ENGLAND). (UK). **Adv Mgr:** Emma Kelly. **1122**

TALKIN' UNION (TAKOMA PARK MD.). (US/0738-7911). **1713**

TALKING LEAF (LOS ANGELES, CALIF. : 1972). (US/0300-6247). **2274**

TALKS OF POPE JOHN PAUL II. (US). **5037**

TALLAHASSEE DEMOCRAT. (US/0738-5153). **5651**

TALLASSEE TRIBUNE, THE. (US). **5628**

TALON (WASHINGTON, D.C.). (US). **1849**

TAMA NEWS-HERALD, THE. (US). **Adv Mgr:** Maraly Hotchkiss. **5673**

TAMARIND PAPERS, THE. (US/0276-3397). **382**

TAMIL EELAM DOCUMENTATION BULLETIN. (CN/0822-2762). **4513**

TAMKANG REVIEW. (CH/0049-2949). **3354**

TAMPA BAY BUSINESS JOURNAL. (US/0896-467X). **714**

TAMPA BAY LIFE (TAMPA, FLA.). (US/1048-0056). **2547**

TAMS JOURNAL. (US/0039-8233). **2783**

TAN MAGAZINE. (US/1042-3036). **405**

TANDLAKARTIDNINGEN. (SW/0039-6982). **1336**

TANK. (UK/0039-9418). **Adv Mgr:** J. Cutler. **4058**

TANTRA (TORREON, N.M.). (US/1064-0584). **4363**

TANZANIAN MATHEMATICAL BULLETIN / THE MATHEMATICAL ASSOCIATION OF TANZANIA, THE. (TZ). **3538**

TANZANIAN VETERINARY BULLETIN : THE TROPICAL VETERINARIAN / TANZANIA VETERINARY ASSOCIATION. (TZ). **5522**

TAPER & SHAVE. (US/1059-6364). **4925**

TAPPI JOURNAL. (US/0734-1415). **4239**

TAPROOT. (US/0887-9257). **3444**

TAR HEEL NURSE. (US/0039-9620). **3870**

TARA. (SZ). **Adv Mgr:** R. Schmuki. **4222**

TARGET GUN. (UK/0143-8751). **4925**

TARGET MARKETING. (US/0889-5333). **937**

TARHEEL BANKER, THE. (US/0039-9663). **Adv Mgr:** Editor. **813**

TARIF DES SPECIALITES PHARMACEUTIQUES. (BE/0770-1772). **4330**

TARIFAS Y DATOS: MEDIOS IMPRESOS. (MX). **767**

TARIQ AL-SALAMAH / AL-JAMIYAH AL-URDUNIYAH LIL-WIQAYAH MIN HAWADITH AL-TURUQ. (JO). **5394**

TARKIO AVALANCHE, THE. (US). **Adv Mgr:** Will Johnson, **Tel** 736-4411. **5704**

TAS TOTS. (AT). **1070**

TASCHENBUCH INFORMATION & DOKUMENTATION. (GW/0723-4074). **3252**

TASCHENBUCH-KATALOG. (GW). **4833**

TASMANIAN ANCESTRY. (AT/0159-0677). **2474**

TASMANIAN BUILDING JOURNAL. (AT). **630**

TASMANIAN COUNTRY. (AT). **Adv Mgr:** Ann Brown. **2511**

TASPO MAGAZIN. (GW/0177-5014). **2432**

TASTE FULL. (US). **2359**

TATE'S EXPORT. (UK). **853**

TATTOO ADVOCATE. (US/0896-8063). **5269**

TATTVALOKAH / TATTVALOKA. (II). **5041**

TAVERN SPORTS INTERNATIONAL. (US). **4866**

TAVERNA

Advertising Accepted Index

TAVERNA DE AUERBACH, LA. (IT/0394-3518). **3472**

TAX ADVISER, THE. (US/0039-9957). **4751**

TAX EXECUTIVE, THE. (US/0040-0025). **4752**

TAX, FINANCIAL AND ESTATE PLANNING FOR THE OWNER OF A CLOSELY-HELD CORPORATION. (US/0194-8822). **3119**

TAX LAWYER : BULLETIN OF THE SECTION OF TAXATION, AMERICAN BAR ASSOCIATION, THE. (US/0040-005X). **3062**

TAX MAGAZINE. (US). **4753**

TAX NEWS SERVICE. (NE/0040-0076). **3062**

TAX NOTES (ARLINGTON). (US/0270-5494). **4753**

TAXATION. (UK/0040-0149). **4754**

TAXATION OF PATENT ROYALTIES, DIVIDENDS, INTEREST IN EUROPE. (NE). **4755**

TAXATION OF PRIVATE INVESTMENT INCOME. (NE). **4755**

TAXIDERMY TODAY. (US/0279-9731). **2778**

TAXON. (GW/0040-0262). **529**

TC. TWIN CITIES. (US/0274-5151). **2547**

TE & MS TELECOM ASIA. (HK). **1164**

TE AVEIA. (FP/0293-2547). **1586**

TE REO. (NZ/0494-8440). **3327**

TEA & COFFEE TRADE JOURNAL, THE. (US/0040-0343). **2371**

TEACHER EDUCATION. (II/0312-4886). **1905**

TEACHER EDUCATION AND SPECIAL EDUCATION. (US/0888-4064). **1886**

TEACHER EDUCATION QUARTERLY (CLAREMONT, CALIF.). (US/0737-5328). **1906**

TEACHER EDUCATOR, THE. (US/0887-8730). **1906**

TEACHER (HALIFAX). (CN/0382-408X). **1906**

TEACHER MAGAZINE. (US/1046-6193). **1906**

TEACHER (VANCOUVER). (CN/0841-9574). **Adv Mgr:** K. Kolisnik, **Tel** (604)871-1876. **1787**

TEACHERS COLLEGE RECORD (1970). (US/0161-4681). **1849**

TEACHERS OF THE WORLD. (GW/0492-4134). **1906**

TEACHING EARTH SCIENCES. (UK/0957-8005). **1360**

TEACHING EDUCATION (COLUMBIA, S.C.). (US/1047-6210). **1906**

TEACHING ELEMENTARY PHYSICAL EDUCATION. (US/1045-4853). **1805**

TEACHING ENGLISH IN THE TWO-YEAR COLLEGE. (US/0098-6291). **1850**

TEACHING ENGLISH TO DEAF AND SECOND-LANGUAGE STUDENTS. (US). **1886**

TEACHING EXCEPTIONAL CHILDREN. (US/0040-0599). **1886**

TEACHING GEOGRAPHY. (UK). **1907**

TEACHING HISTORY (EMPORIA, KAN.). (US/0730-1383). **2631**

TEACHING HISTORY (LONDON). (UK/0040-0610). **1907**

TEACHING HOME, THE. (US). **Adv Mgr:** Kevin Bradley. **1787**

TEACHING MATHEMATICS. (AT/0313-7767). **3538**

TEACHING MATHEMATICS AND ITS APPLICATIONS. (UK/0268-3679). **3538**

TEACHING OF PSYCHOLOGY. (US/0098-6283). **4620**

TEACHING OPPORTUNITIES (NORTH BRUNSWICK, N.J.). (US/1060-8958). **Adv Mgr:** C. Shomers. **1907**

TEACHING PHILOSOPHY. (US/0145-5788). **4363**

TEACHING POLITICS. (II). **4498**

TEACHING PRE-K-8. (US/0891-4508). **1805**

TEACHING PUBLIC ADMINISTRATION : TPA. (UK/0144-7394). **4690**

TEACHING SCIENCE. (UK/0028-0763). **5161**

TEACHING SOCIOLOGY. (US/0092-055X). **5264**

TEACHING STATISTICS. (UK/0141-982X). **1798**

TEACHING TODAY (EDMONTON). (CN/0827-3049). **Adv Mgr:** Dian Gonn, **Tel** (403)435-0835. **1907**

TEAM AND TRAIL. (US). **4925**

TEAM LICENSING BUSINESS. (US/1065-738X). **1628**

TEAM MARKETING REPORT. (US). **4925**

TECH-EUROPE. (BE). **Adv Mgr:** Lucyna Grauer. **3252**

TECH, THE. (US/0148-9607). **5690**

TECHN. BIOL. - 1985. (FR/0766-5725). **3644**

TECHNI-PORC. (FR/0181-6764). **222**

TECHNICA (BASEL). (BE/0040-0866). **2915**

TECHNICAL AID TO THE DISABLED JOURNAL. (AT/0725-2919). **4394**

TECHNICAL ANALYSIS OF STOCKS AND COMMODITIES (JOURNAL). (US/0738-3355). **917**

TECHNICAL COMMUNICATION QUARTERLY. (US/1057-2252). **Adv Mgr:** Dr. B. Wahlstrom, **Tel** (612)624-7750. **1122**

TECHNICAL CONFERENCE PROCEEDINGS / IRRIGATION ASSOCIATION. (US/0160-7499). **Adv Mgr:** Ryan Eliades. **2095**

TECHNICAL DIAGNOSTICS AND NONDESTRUCTIVE TESTING. (UK/0955-3835). **1998**

TECHNICAL MONOGRAPH - GREAT BRITAIN. SOIL SURVEY. (UK/0072-7210). **189**

TECHNICAL REPORT SERIES OF THE LABORATORY FOR RESEARCH IN STATISTICS AND PROBABILITY. (CN/0823-1664). **3538**

TECHNICAL REVIEW MIDDLE EAST. (UK/0267-5307). **Adv Mgr:** Patricia Fairfield. **5162**

TECHNICAL SERVICES LAW LIBRARIAN. (US/0195-4857). **3252**

TECHNICAL SERVICES QUARTERLY. (US/0731-7131). **3252**

TECHNICAL TEXTILES INTERNATIONAL. (UK/0964-5993). **5356**

TECHNICALITIES. (US/0272-0884). **3252**

TECHNICIAN ASSOCIATION NEWS. (US). **2083**

TECHNICIEN DU FILM ET DE LA VIDEO, LA TECHNIQUE, L'EXPLOITATION CINEMAGRAPHIQUE, LE. (FR). **4078**

TECHNIK UND GESELLSCHAFT (FRANKFURT AM MAIN, GERMANY). (GW/0723-0664). **5162**

TECHNIQUE LAITIERE. (FR/0040-1242). **199**

TECHNIQUE MODERNE, LA. (FR/0040-1250). **5162**

TECHNIQUES DE PECHE. (CN/0225-199X). **2314**

TECHNIQUES IN ORTHOPAEDICS (ROCKVILLE, MD.). (US/0885-9698). **3885**

TECHNIQUES, SCIENCES, METHODES : TSM. (FR/0299-7258). **2244**

TECHNISCH-OEKONOMISCHE INFORMATION DER ZIVILEN LUFTFAHRT. (GW). **37**

TECHNISCHE MITTEILUNGEN DER SCHWEIZERISCHEN TELEGRAPHEN- UND TELEPHON-VERWALTUNG. (SZ/0040-1471). **5162**

TECHNISCHE MITTEILUNGEN FUER SAPPEURE, PONTONIERE, UND MINEURE. (SZ). **2032**

TECHNISCHES MESSE : TM. (GW/0171-8096). **4033**

TECHNOLOGIES BANCAIRES. (FR/0765-3069). **813**

TECHNOLOGUE. (CN/0825-5172). **5163**

TECHNOLOGY & CONSERVATION. (US/0146-1214). **366**

TECHNOLOGY IRELAND. (IE/0040-1676). **Adv Mgr:** D. Black. **5164**

TECHNOLOGY REVIEW. (US/0040-1692). **5164**

TECHNOLOGY TEACHER, THE. (US/0746-3537). **5164**

TECHNOLOGY UPDATE (PALO ALTO, CALIF.). (US/0896-8586). **4394**

TECHNOLOGY WATCH FOR THE GRAPHIC ARTS AND INFORMATION INDUSTRIES. (CN/0738-9507). **382**

TECHNOVA. (HK). **1998**

TECHTRENDS. (US/8756-3894). **Adv Mgr:** LMB Marketing, **Tel** 312-554-0931. **1225**

TECNICA DELLA SCUOLA, LA. (IT). **1873**

TECNICA E INDUSTRIA. (AG). **3488**

TECNICA ITALIANA. (IT/0040-1846). **2032**

TECNICA MOLITORIA. (IT/0040-1862). **204**

TECNICA PESQUERA. (MX). **2314**

TECNICA TEXTIL INTERNACIONAL. (SP/0040-1900). **5356**

TECNOLOGIA DEL AGUA. (SP/0211-8173). **5541**

TECNOLOGIA ELETTRICHE. INDUSTRIA ITALIANA ELETTROTECNICA ED ELETTRONICA. (IT/0390-6698). **2083**

TECNOLOGIA MILITAR. (GW/0722-2904). **4059**

TECNOLOGIE DEI SERVIZI PUBBLICI. (IT). **4690**

TECNOLOGIE MECCANICHE. (IT/0391-1683). **2130**

TECOLOTE, EL. (US/0741-0034). **2493**

TECTONICS (WASHINGTON, D.C.). (US/0278-7407). **1411**

TEDDY BEAR AND FRIENDS, THE. (US/0745-7189). **2778**

TEDDY BEAR REVIEW. (US/0890-4162). **376**

TEELINE : THE SHORTHAND AND BUSINESS STUDIES MAGAZINE. (UK). **1850**

'TEEN. (US/0040-2001). **1070**

TEEN SET. (US/1058-9856). **1070**

TEENQUEST. (US/0890-4006). **Adv Mgr:** Mike Stephens, **Tel** (214)570-7597. **1070**

TEHACHAPI NEWS, THE. (US). **Adv Mgr:** Al Crisaui. **5640**

TEHNICESKAJA ELEKTRODINAMIKA. (UN/0204-3599). **2084**

TEHNOLOGIJA MESA. (YU/0494-9846). **3488**

TEHO / TYOTEHOSEURA. (FI/0355-0567). **Adv Mgr:** Atte Kaksonen. **140**

TEIKOKU GINKO KAISHA NENKAN. HIGASHI NIHON. (JA). **1629**

TEILHARD REVIEW, THE. (UK/0040-2184). **Adv Mgr:** T. Baxter. **246**

TEJAS JOURNAL OF AUDIOLOGY AND SPEECH PATHOLOGY. (US/0738-8837). **3891**

TEKAWENNAKE. (CN/0300-3159). **2547**

TEKNOS. (IT). **5165**

TEL AVIV UNIVERSITY STUDIES IN LAW. (IS). **3063**

TELE-C.L.E.F. (CN/0822-451X). **3063**

TELECOM. (FR). **Adv Mgr:** S. Mariani, **Tel** 011 33 1 45818048. **1164**

TELECOM ADVISOR, THE. (CN/1195-5759). **1164**

TELECOM OUTLOOK : THE TELECOMMUNICATIONS & DATA COMMUNICATIONS NEWSLETTER. (US/1045-6562). **1164**

TELECOM WORLD. (UK/0963-0597). **1165**

TELECOMMUNICATION JOURNAL (ENGLISH EDITION). (SZ/0497-137X). **1165**

TELECOMMUNICATION JOURNAL OF AUSTRALIA, THE. (AT/0040-2486). **1165**

TELECOMMUNICATIONS AND RADIO ENGINEERING. (US/0040-2508). **1165**

TELECOMMUNICATIONS (NORTH AMERICAN EDITION). (US/0278-4831). **1166**

TELECOMMUNICATIONS POLICY. (UK/0308-5961). **1166**

TELECOMMUNICATIONS STRATEGIES REPORT. (AT/1322-3518). **1166**

TELECONNECT. (US/0740-9354). **Adv Mgr:** Gerry Friesen, **Tel** (215)355-2886. **1166**

TELEGRAM & GAZETTE. (US/1050-4184). **5690**

TELEGRAPH HERALD (1935). (US/1041-293X). **Adv Mgr:** Jim Hart. **5673**

TELEMARKETING. (US/0730-6156). **1167**

TELEPHONE ENGINEER & MANAGEMENT DIRECTORY. (US). **1167**

TELESPECTATEUR, LE. (CN/0712-6891). **1140**

TELEVISION & CABLE FACTBOOK. (US/0732-8648). **1140**

TELEVISION BROADCAST. (US/0898-767X). **1140**

TELEVISION (LONDON). (UK/0308-454X). **1141**

TELEVISION QUARTERLY (BEVERLY HILL). (US/0040-2796). **1141**

TELEXPORT : LES EXPORTATEURS ET IMPORTATEURS FRANCAIS. (FR). **Adv Mgr:** Philippe Do. **853**

TELL. (AT/1030-8768). **5002**

TELLURIDE TIMES-JOURNAL, THE. (US). **Adv Mgr:** Bruce Kinsey. **5644**

TELLUS. SERIES A, DYNAMIC METEOROLOGY AND OCEANOGRAPHY. (SW/0280-6495). **1436**

TELOCATOR. (US/0193-1458). **1168**

TELOS (ST. LOUIS). (US/0090-6514). **5224**

TEMA CELESTE. (IT). **Adv Mgr Tel** 011 39 2 4813734. **366**

TEMAS (NEW YORK, N.Y.). (US/0040-2869). **2493**

TEMISCAMIEN (1976). (CN/0382-0653). **5796**

TEMPDIGEST (HOUSTON, TEX.). (US/0897-5574). **4209**

TEMPLE LAW REVIEW. (US/0899-8086). **3063**

TEMPLE POLITICAL & CIVIL RIGHTS LAW REVIEW. (US/1062-5887). **4513**

TEMPO. (MZ). **2500**

TEMPO MEDICO. (IT). **Adv Mgr:** Cozzi Elisabetta, **Tel** 011 39 2 422 1240. **3645**

TEMPO PRESENTE. (IT). **4498**

TEMPS DE VIVRE (MONTREAL). (CN/0708-7632). **5182**

TEMPS LIBRE (MONTREAL). (CN/0823-5708). **5492**

TEMPS STRATEGIQUE, LA. (SZ). **2493**

TEN.8. (UK/0142-9663). **4377**

TENANTS BULLETIN. (CN/1195-423X). **2836**

TENDERS AUSTRALIA. (AT). **715**

TENDRIL. (US/0197-890X). **3444**

TENKI. (JA/0546-0921). **1436**

TENNESSEE ATTORNEYS DIRECTORY. (US/0742-4329). **3063**

TENNESSEE BANKER, THE. (US/0040-3199). **Adv Mgr:** D. Martin, **Tel** same as publisher. **813**

TENNESSEE BAR JOURNAL. (US/0497-2325). **3063**

TENNESSEE FARMER (NASHVILLE, TENN.). (US/0040-3245). **140**

TENNESSEE JOURNAL OF HEALTH, PHYSICAL EDUCATION, RECREATION, AND DANCE / TENNESSEE ASSOCIATION OF HEALTH, PHYSICAL EDUCATION, RECREATION, AND DANCE. (US/0890-1597). **1859**

TENNESSEE JUDICIAL NEWSLETTER. (US). **3063**

TENNESSEE LAW REVIEW. (US/0040-3288). **3063**

TENNESSEE LIBRARIAN. (US/0162-1564). **Adv Mgr:** B.P. Ponnappa, **Tel** (615)974-4240. **3252**

TENNESSEE NURSE. (US/1055-3134). **3870**

TENNESSEE PUBLIC WORKS. (US/0892-5380). **4690**

TENNESSEE REGISTER, THE. (US/1041-1569). **Adv Mgr:** Marilyn Rubin. **5746**

TENNESSEE RESTAURANTEUR. (US). **5073**

TENNESSEE SCHOOL BOARDS JOURNAL. (US/0747-6159). **1873**

TENNESSEE TEACHER. (US/0040-3407). **1907**

TENNESSEE TOWN & CITY. (US/0040-3415). **4690**

TENNESSEE TRUCKER, THE. (US/0887-3526). **5394**

TENNESSEE VOLUNTEERS MAGAZINE. (US). **1095**

TENNIS INDUSTRY. (US/0191-5851). **4925**

TENNIS LONDON. 1981. (UK/0262-9224). **4925**

TENNIS MAGAZINE. AUSTRALIA. (AT). **Adv Mgr:** Cameron. **4926**

TENNIS (NORWALK, CONN.). (US/0040-3423). **4926**

TENNIS WEEK. (US/0194-9098). **Adv Mgr:** Roberta Faig. **4926**

TENNIS WORLD. (UK/0040-3474). **4926**

TENNISPRO. (US). **4926**

TENOLAI. (II). **5176**

TENOR. (II). **3445**

TEOLOGIA (BRESCIA, ITALY). (IT). **Adv Mgr:** Lovati Claudio. **5037**

TEOLOGIA Y VIDA. (CL/0049-3449). **Adv Mgr:** Marciano Barrios V., **Tel** 274.40.41. ax.2075. **5002**

TEOLOGINEN AIKAKAUSKIRJA. TEOLOGISK TIDSKRIFT. (FI/0040-3555). **5002**

TEOLOGISK FORUM. (NO). **5002**

TEORIIA MASHIN METALLURGICHESKOGO I GORNOGO OBORUDOVANIIA. (RU). **2130**

TER HERKENNING. (NE). **5002**

TERATOLOGY (PHILADELPHIA). (US/0040-3709). **474**

TERMNET NEWS : JOURNAL OF THE INTERNATIONAL NETWORK FOR TERMINOLOGY (TERMNET). (AU/0251-5253). **3328**

TERRA GRISCHUNA. (SZ). **2712**

TERRA (LOS ANGELES, CALIF.). (US/0040-3733). **4173**

TERRAZZO. (IT). **309**

TERRE DE CHEZ NOUS. DOSSIER D'INFORMATION TECHNIQUE ET PROFESSIONNELLE, LA. (CN/0823-2784). **141**

TERRE DE CHEZ NOUS (MONTREAL). (CN/0040-3830). **141**

TERRITOIRES. (FR). **4498**

TERRITORIAL, THE. (US/0890-4235). **2547**

TERROR AUSTRALIS: THE AUSTRALIAN HORROR & FANTASY MAGAZINE. (AT/1031-3001). **3445**

TERRORISM AND POLITICAL VIOLENCE. (UK/0954-6553). **Adv Mgr:** Anne Kidson. **4536**

TERZIARIA. (IT). **1524**

TERZO MONDO. (IT/0040-392X). **5264**

TERZOOCCHIO. (IT). **366**

TESL CANADA JOURNAL. (CN/0826-435X). **3328**

TESOL MATTERS. (US/1051-8886). **Adv Mgr:** Maria Minor, **Tel** (703)836-0774. **1907**

TESOL MEMBERSHIP DIRECTORY. (US/0730-9325). **3328**

TESOL QUARTERLY. (US/0039-8322). **3328**

TESSERA (BURNABY). (CN/0840-4631). **Adv Mgr:** Jennifer Henderson. **3445**

TEST & MEASUREMENT WORLD. (US/0744-1657). **2084**

TEST (OAKHURST, N.J.). (US/0193-4120). **2130**

TESTO UNICO IMPOSTE DIRETTE. (IT). **3063**

TETE, EN. (CN/0822-8531). **1850**

TETON. (US/0049-3481). **4879**

TETON VALLEY NEWS. (US/0889-9851). **Adv Mgr:** Eileen Foster. **5657**

TEX HOME. (IT). **Adv Mgr:** Aldo Gerbert. **5357**

TEX-RAYS : OFFICIAL JOURNAL TEXAS SOCIETY OF RADIOLOGIC TECHNOLOGISTS, INC. (US). **3947**

TEXARKANA GAZETTE. (US). **Adv Mgr:** Rick Meredith. **5632**

TEXAS AIRPORT DIRECTORY. (US). **37**

TEXAS ALCALDE. (US/1061-561X). **Adv Mgr:** Amy Katz, **Tel** (512)471-8086. **1103**

TEXAS ALMANAC AND STATE INDUSTRIAL GUIDE (1967). (US/0363-4248). **2547**

TEXAS ARCHITECT. (US/0040-4179). **Adv Mgr:** Ray Don Tilley. **310**

TEXAS BANKING. (US/0885-6907). **Adv Mgr:** L. Cafferty. **813**

TEXAS BANKING REDBOOK. (US). **Adv Mgr:** Beth Wilson. **813**

TEXAS BAR JOURNAL. (US/0040-4187). **3063**

TEXAS BASKETBALL MAGAZINE. (US). **4926**

TEXAS BICYCLIST. (US). **429**

TEXAS BLUE BOOK OF LIFE INSURANCE STATISTICS (1982), THE. (US/0739-4691). **Adv Mgr:** C. J. Hargis. **2898**

TEXAS BOOKS IN REVIEW. (US/0739-3202). **4833**

TEXAS CITY SUN. (US). **Adv Mgr:** Larry Cooke. **5755**

TEXAS COACH. (US/0040-4241). **Adv Mgr:** E Wolski, **Tel** (512)454-6709. **4926**

TEXAS DENTAL JOURNAL. (US/0040-4284). **1336**

TEXAS DO. (US/0275-1453). **3645**

TEXAS FACT BOOK. (US/0163-4666). **1586**

TEXAS FARMER STOCKMAN. (US/0279-165X). **141**

TEXAS FIREMEN. (US/0278-9930). **Adv Mgr:** same as editor. **2293**

TEXAS FOOD MERCHANT. (US/0040-4322). **2359**

TEXAS GARDENER (WACO, TX.). (US/0744-0987). **2432**

TEXAS GULF HISTORICAL AND BIOGRAPHICAL RECORD, THE. (US). **2763**

TEXAS HEREFORD. (US/0744-4761). **Adv Mgr:** same as editor. **222**

TEXAS HISTORIAN, THE. (US/0022-6602). **2763**

TEXAS HORTICULTURIST, THE. (US). **2432**

TEXAS HOTEL REVIEW (SAN ANTONIO, TEX. : 1988). (US). **2809**

TEXAS INTERNATIONAL LAW JOURNAL. (US/0163-7479). **3136**

TEXAS JEWISH POST, THE. (US/0040-439X). **5755**

TEXAS JOURNAL OF IDEAS, HISTORY, AND CULTURE. (US/0894-3354). **Adv Mgr:** Judith H. Diaz. **2855**

TEXAS JOURNAL OF POLITICAL STUDIES. (US/0191-0930). **Adv Mgr Tel** (409)294-1457. **4498**

TEXAS LAWMAN, THE. (US/0040-442X). **3178**

TEXAS LAWYER, THE. (US/0267-8306). **3064**

TEXAS LIBRARY JOURNAL. (US/0040-4446). **3253**

TEXAS LIVESTOCK MARKET NEWS. (US/0199-7041). **222**

TEXAS LONE STAR. (US/0749-9310). **1873**

TEXAS MANUFACTURERS REGISTER. (US/0743-1163). **3488**

TEXAS MATHEMATICS TEACHER. (US/0277-030X). **3538**

TEXAS MEDICINE. (US/0040-4470). **3645**

TEXAS MONTHLY (AUSTIN). (US/0148-7736). **2547**

TEXAS NURSING. (US/0095-036X). **3870**

TEXAS OBSERVER, THE. (US). **5755**

TEXAS OUTLOOK, THE. (US/0040-4551). **1787**

TEXAS PARKS & WILDLIFE. (US/0040-4586). **4708**

TEXAS PHARMACY. (US/0362-7926). **Adv Mgr:** Lori Alcala. **4330**

TEXAS PRINTER. (US/1043-2302). **4570**

TEXAS PROFESSIONAL ENGINEER (1981). (US/0747-1262). **1998**

TEXAS PROFESSIONAL PHOTOGRAPHER. (US). **Adv Mgr:** same as editor. **4377**

TEXAS PUBLIC EMPLOYEE. (US/0040-4640). **1714**

TEXAS REVIEW (HUNTSVILLE, TEX.), THE. (US/0885-2685). **3354**

TEXAS SAVINGS & LOAN DIRECTORY. (US). **813**

TEXAS SCHOOL BUSINESS. (US/0563-2978). **Adv Mgr:** J. Garrett. **1787**

TEXAS STATE DIRECTORY. (US/0363-7530). **4690**

TEXAS STUDIES IN LITERATURE AND LANGUAGE. (US/0040-4691). **3445**

TEXAS TECH LAW REVIEW. (US/0564-6197). **3064**

TEXAS TELLER QUARTERLY NEWSLETTER. (US/0892-5186). **3445**

TEXAS THOROUGHBRED (WICHITA FALLS, KAN.). (US/0164-6168). **2802**

TEXAS VETERINARIAN. (US/1071-0566). **Adv Mgr:** Ellen Smith. **5522**

TEXAS VETERINARY MEDICAL JOURNAL. (US/0040-4756). **5522**

TEXAS WOMAN (FORT WORTH, TEX.). (US/0279-2443). **5567**

TEXINCON AHMEDABAD. (II/0970-5686). **5357**

TEXT AND PRESENTATION. (US/1054-724X). **Adv Mgr:** J. Grady, **Tel** (800)524-0634. **5369**

TEXT + KRITIK. (GW/0040-5329). **3445**

TEXT TECHNOLOGY. (US/1053-900X). **1205**

TEXTES - SOCIETE HISTORIQUE DE QUEBEC. (CN/0081-1130). **Adv Mgr:** Gilles Mathieu. **2763**

TEXTIL- ES TEXTILRUHAZATI IPARI SZAKIRODALMI TAJEKOZTATO. (HU/0209-9578). **5357**

TEXTIL PRAXIS INTERNATIONAL. (GW/0040-4853). **5357**

TEXTILE ASIA. (HK/0049-3554). **5357**

TEXTILE ASIA INDEX. (HK). **5357**

TEXTILE CHEMIST AND COLORIST. (US/0040-490X). **5357**

TEXTILE DYER & PRINTER. (II/0040-4926). **5357**

TEXTILE FLAMMABILITY DIGEST. (US/0738-9620). **5357**

TEXTILE INDUSTRIES DYEGEST OF SOUTHERN AFRICA. (SA/0254-0533). **5358**

TEXTILE INDUSTRY & TRADE JOURNAL. (II/0040-4993). **5358**

TEXTILE MAGAZINE, THE. (II/0040-5078). **5358**

TEXTILE MANUFACTURING. (US/1065-1713). **5358**

TEXTILE — Advertising Accepted Index

TEXTILE TECHNOLOGY DIGEST. (US/0040-5191). **5360**

TEXTILE TRENDS. (II/0040-5205). **5358**

TEXTILE VIEW MAGAZINE. (NE). **5358**

TEXTILE WORLD. (US/0040-5213). **5358**

TEXTILES. (UK/0306-0748). **5359**

TEXTILES PANAMERICANOS. (US/0049-3570). **5359**

TEXTILES SUISSES. (SZ/0040-5248). **5359**

TEXTILFORUM. (GW). **5359**

TEXTILVEREDLUNG. (SZ/0040-5310). **5359**

TEXTUAL STUDIES IN CANADA. (CN). **Adv Mgr:** Ron Smith. **3355**

TEXTURES AND MICROSTRUCTURES. (US/0730-3300). **1033**

THAI BUILDER DIRECTORY. (TH). **630**

THAI INDUSTRIAL DIRECTORY. (TH). **1629**

THAI JOURNAL OF AGRICULTURAL SCIENCE. (TH/0049-3589). **141**

THAI JOURNAL OF SURGERY. (TH/0125-6068). **3976**

THALIA (OTTAWA). (CN/0706-5604). **3445**

THANATOLOGY ABSTRACTS. (US/0196-0121). **4620**

(THE) BRAVE NEW TICK. (US/1070-0161). **2796**

THE UNCANNY X-MEN. (US/0274-5372). **4867**

THEATER. (GW). **Adv Mgr:** Marion Schaduthe. **5369**

THEATER IN OSTERREICH / WIENER GESELLSCHAFT FUER THEATERFORSCHUNG, INSTITUT FUER THEATERWISSENSCHAFT AN DER UNIVERSITAT WIEN. (AU). **5370**

THEATER (NEW HAVEN, CONN.). (US/0161-0775). **Adv Mgr Tel** (203)432-9664. **5370**

THEATER RUNDSCHAU. (GW). **5370**

THEATER WEEK. (US/0896-1956). **Adv Mgr:** Wendy Daigneault. **5370**

THEATERZEITSCHRIFT. (GW/0723-1172). **Adv Mgr:** Bernward Debus. **389**

THEATRE & THERAPY. (UK). **5370**

THEATRE CRAFTS. (US/0040-5469). **5370**

THEATRE CRAFTS DIRECTORY. (US). **5370**

THEATRE CRAFTS INTERNATIONAL. (US/1060-3042). **5370**

THEATRE DIRECTORY OF THE SAN FRANCISCO BAY AREA. (US/0737-0172). **5370**

THEATRE HISTORY STUDIES. (US/0733-2033). **5370**

THEATRE INSIGHT. (US). **5370**

THEATRE IRELAND. (IE/0263-6344). **5370**

THEATRE JOBLIST. (US/0892-0796). **389**

THEATRE JOURNAL (WASHINGTON, D.C.). (US/0192-2882). **5371**

THEATRE NOTEBOOK. (UK/0040-5523). **5371**

THEATRE ORGAN (1970). (US/0040-5531). **Adv Mgr Tel** (503)233-7276. **4156**

THEATRE/PUBLIC. (FR/0335-2927). **Adv Mgr:** A. Girault. **5371**

THEATRE RECORD. (UK/0962-1792). **5371**

THEATRE RESEARCH INTERNATIONAL. (UK/0307-8833). **5371**

THEATRE SOUTHWEST. (US/0743-5452). **5371**

THEATRE SURVEY. (US/0040-5574). **5371**

THEATRE TIMES. (US/0732-300X). **5371**

THEATRE TOPICS. (US/1054-8378). **5371**

THEATREPHILE. (UK/0265-2609). **5371**

THEMA UMWELT (OSNABRUCK). (GW/0939-8767). **426**

THEMATA CHOROU + TECHNON. (GR/0074-1191). **Adv Mgr:** Orestis Doumanis. **310**

THEMEN DER PRAKTISCHEN THEOLOGIE, THEOLOGIA PRACTICA. (GW/0720-9525). **5003**

THEODORE ROOSEVELT ASSOCIATION JOURNAL. (US/0161-8423). **435**

THEOLOGIAI SZEMLE. (HU/0133-7599). **5003**

THEOLOGICA XAVERIANA. (CK). **5037**

THEOLOGICAL DIGEST & OUTLOOK. (CN/1184-8901). **5003**

THEOLOGICAL EDUCATOR, THE. (US/0198-6856). **5003**

THEOLOGIE DER GEGENWART. (GW). **5003**

THEOLOGIE UND GLAUBE. (GW/0049-366X). **5003**

THEOLOGISCH-PRAKTISCHE QUARTALSCHRIFT. (AU/0040-5663). **5037**

THEOLOGISCHE BEITRAEGE. (GW/0342-2372). **5003**

THEOLOGISCHE QUARTALSCHRIFT (MUNCHEN). (GW/0342-1430). **5004**

THEOLOGISCHE REVUE. (GW/0040-568X). **5004**

THEOLOGISCHE RUNDSCHAU. (GW/0040-5698). **5004**

THEOLOGISCHE ZEITSCHRIFT. (SZ/0040-5701). **5004**

THEOLOGY DIGEST. (US/0040-5728). **5004**

THEOLOGY TODAY (EPHRATA, PA.). (US/0040-5736). **5004**

THEORETICAL CHEMICAL ENGINEERING. (UK/0960-5053). **2007**

THEORETICAL COMPUTER SCIENCE. (NE/0304-3975). **1205**

THEORETICAL LINGUISTICS. (GW/0301-4428). **3328**

THEORETICAL MEDICINE. (NE/0167-9902). **3645**

THEORIA. (SW/0040-5825). **4363**

THEORIA (DENTON, TEX.). (US). **4156**

THEORIA/PRAXIS: A GRADUATE JOURNAL OF THEORY AND CRITICISM. (CN). **5224**

THEORY AND DECISION. (NE/0040-5833). **4363**

THEORY & PSYCHOLOGY. (UK/0959-3543). **4620**

THEORY AND RESEARCH IN SOCIAL EDUCATION. (US/0093-3104). **5224**

THERAPEUTISCHE UMSCHAU. (SZ/0040-5930). **3976**

THERAPIE. (FR/0040-5957). **4330**

THERAPIE DER GEGENWART. (GW/0040-5965). **3645**

THERE IS. (CN/0823-3276). **3472**

THERIOGENOLOGY. (US/0093-691X). **5522**

THERIOS : REVISTA DE MEDICINA VETERINARIA Y PRODUCCION ANIMAL. (AG). **Adv Mgr:** Juan Jose Ruiz. **5523**

THERMOLOGY. (US/0882-3758). **3645**

THERMOPOLIS INDEPENDENT RECORD. (US). **Adv Mgr:** Patrick Schmidt. **5773**

THESAURUS - INSTITUTO CARO Y CUERVO. (CK/0040-604X). **Adv Mgr:** Ignacio Chaves Cevas. **3328**

THESAURUS LINGUAE LATINAE. (GW). **1929**

THESIS ELEVEN. (US/0725-5136). **5264**

THIEF RIVER FALLS TIMES. (US/8750-3883). **Adv Mgr:** Ken Kohler. **5699**

THIN SOLID FILMS. (SZ/0040-6090). **Adv Mgr:** Ms. W van Cattenburch (Amsterdam). **2084**

THIN-WALLED STRUCTURES. (UK/0263-8231). **2032**

THIRD OPINION. (AT/1030-5467). **2511**

THIRD RAIL (LOS ANGELES, CALIF.). (US/0741-5958). **3446**

THIRD WAY. (UK/0309-3492). **5004**

THIRD WORLD PLANNING REVIEW. (UK/0142-7849). **2836**

THIRD WORLD QUARTERLY. (UK/0143-6597). **1587**

THIRD WORLD REPORTS. (UK). **2912**

THIRD WORLD RESOURCES. (US/8755-8831). **2912**

THIRTEEN TOWNS, THE. (US). **Adv Mgr:** Peter Carr. **5699**

THIS IS WEST TEXAS. (US/0040-6201). **2547**

THIS MAGAZINE. (CN/0381-3746). **2493**

THIS MONTH ON LONG ISLAND. (US/0896-4599). **5492**

THIS PEOPLE. (US/0273-6527). **5004**

THIS WEEK MAGAZINE (PORTLAND, ORE.). (US/0746-1100). **Adv Mgr:** Ken Raddle. **5734**

THISTLE, THE. (CN). **2493**

THOMAS COOK EUROPEAN TIMETABLE. (UK/0952-620X). **5437**

THOMAS COOK OVERSEAS TIMETABLE. (UK/0144-7475). **5492**

THOMAS COOK RAILPASS GUIDE. (UK). **5492**

THOMAS HARDY YEAR BOOK. (UK/0082-416X). **3446**

THOMAS REGISTER'S MID-YEAR GUIDE TO FACTORY AUTOMATION PRODUCTS, SYSTEMS, SERVICES. (US/0894-4288). **1235**

THOMAS WOLFE REVIEW, THE. (US/0276-5683). **3446**

THOMASTON TIMES AND THE FREE PRESS, THE. (US). **5655**

THOMIST, THE. (US/0040-6325). **4363**

THORAX. (UK/0040-6376). **3952**

THOROUGHBRED OF CALIFORNIA, THE. (US/0049-3821). **2803**

THOROUGHBRED RECORD. FOREIGN STATISTICAL REVIEW, THE. (US). **2803**

THOROUGHBRED TIMES. (US/0887-2244). **2803**

THOUGHT & ACTION (WASHINGTON, D.C.). (US/0748-8475). **1850**

THOUGHT (NEW YORK). (US/0040-6457). **5005**

THOUGHTS FOR ALL SEASONS. (US/0886-6481). **3446**

THOUGHTS ON ECONOMICS. (BG). **1587**

THREADS MAGAZINE. (US/0882-7370). **5359**

THREE VILLAGE HERALD. (US/1053-2684). **Adv Mgr:** Barbara Farley. **5721**

THREE WIRE WINTER. (US). **2763**

THREEPENNY REVIEW, THE. (US/0275-1410). **3446**

THRESHOLDS IN EDUCATION. (US/0196-9641). **1787**

THRIFTY NICKEL WEEKLY NEWSPAPER. BIRMINGHAM. (US). **Adv Mgr:** Elizabeth Laird. **5628**

THROMBOSIS AND HAEMOSTASIS. (GW/0340-6245). **3801**

THROMBOSIS RESEARCH. (US/0049-3848). **3710**

THRUST. (US/0190-3381). **1714**

THUNDER BAY MAGAZINE. (CN/0823-6542). **2547**

THUNDERCATS MAGAZINE. (US/0890-0256). **1070**

THURGOOD MARSHALL LAW REVIEW. (US/0749-1646). **3064**

THURIES MAGAZINE. (FR/0989-6333). **Adv Mgr Tel** 011 33 1 63561601. **2793**

THYMUS. (NE/0165-6090). **3677**

TIANJIN YIYAO. (CC/0253-9896). **3645**

TIBET JOURNAL, THE. (II). **2666**

TIBETAN REVIEW. (II/0040-6708). **2577**

TIBIA. (GW). **4156**

TIDE, DISTANCE AND SPEED TABLES. (UK). **Adv Mgr:** D. Provan. **4184**

TIDE : TERI INFORMATION DIGEST ON ENERGY. (II/0971-085X). **Adv Mgr Tel** same as publisher. **1959**

TIDINGS INTERNATIONAL BUSINESS DIRECTORY. (II). **1587**

TIDINGS (LOS ANGELES). (US/0040-6791). **5037**

TIDSKRIFT FOR MEDICINSK OCH TEKNISK FOTOGRAFI. (SW/1100-6323). **4377**

TIDSKRIFT FOR RATTSSOCIOLOGI. (SW). **3064**

TIDSKRIFT I FORTIFIKATION. (SW/0040-6937). **4059**

TIDSSKRIFT FOR DEN NORSKE LAEGEFORENING; TIDSSKRIFT FOR PRAKTISK MEDISIN. THE JOURNAL OF THE NORWEGIAN MEDICAL ASSOCIATION. (NO/0029-2281). **3645**

TIDSSKRIFT FOR RETTSVIDENSKAP. (NO/0040-7143). **3064**

TIDSSKRIFT FOR SAMFUNNSFORSKNING. (NO/0040-716X). **5224**

TIDSSKRIFT FOR TEOLOGI OG KIRKE. (NO/0040-7194). **5005**

TIE JA LIIKENNE. (FI). **2032**

TIE REPORT. (NE/0196-254X). **1714**

TIEMPO LIBRE / PUBLICACION SEMANAL DE UNO MAS UNO. (MX). **Adv Mgr:** Javier Flores. **4855**

TIEMPOS MEDICOS DE ESPANA. (SP/0210-9999). **1788**

TIEN HSIA TSA CHIH. (CH). **715**

TIERARZTLICHE PRAXIS. (GW/0303-6286). **5523**

TIERARZTLICHE UMSCHAU. (GW/0049-3864). **5523**

TIETOPALVELU. (FI/0782-825X). **3253**

TIFTON GAZETTE (DAILY), THE. (US/1065-2884). **Adv Mgr:** Randy Blalock. **5655**

TIGER BEAT. (US/0040-7380). **1070**

TIGER RAG. (US/0744-7604). **4926**

TIJDSCHRIFT RECHTSDOCUMENTATIE. (BE/0771-0704). **3064**

TIJDSCHRIFT VAN DE VERENIGING VOOR NEDERLANDSE MUZIEKGESCHIEDENIS. (NE/0042-3874). **4156**

TIJDSCHRIFT VOOR ALCOHOL, DRUGS EN ANDERE PSYCHOTROPE STOFFEN. (NE/0378-2778). **1349**

TIJDSCHRIFT VOOR ANTILLIAANS RECHT, JUSTICIA / UITGEVER STICHTING TIJDSCHRIFT VOOR ANTILLIAANS RECHT, JUSTICIA. (NA). **3064**

TIJDSCHRIFT VOOR ARBITRAGE. (NE/0167-1359). **3064**

TIJDSCHRIFT VOOR BELGISCH BURGERLIJK RECHT : TBBR. (BE/0775-2814). **3091**

TIJDSCHRIFT VOOR BESTUURSWETENCHAPPEN EN PUBLEKRECHT. (BE/0040-7437). **Adv Mgr:** P. Berckx, **Tel** 011 32 2 2694109. **3064**

TIJDSCHRIFT VOOR BESTUURSWETENSCHAPPEN EN PUBLEKRECHT. (BE). **4690**

TIJDSCHRIFT VOOR CRIMINOLOGIE. (NE/0165-182X). **3178**

TIJDSCHRIFT VOOR DIERGENEESKUNDE. (NE/0040-7453). **5523**

TIJDSCHRIFT VOOR ECONOMIE EN MANAGEMENT. (BE/0772-7674). **1524**

TIJDSCHRIFT VOOR ECONOMISCHE EN SOCIALE GEOGRAFIE : TESG. (NE/0040-747X). **1524**

TIJDSCHRIFT VOOR FAMILIE- EN JEUGDRECHT. (NE). **3122**

TIJDSCHRIFT VOOR GENEESKUNDE. (BE/0371-683X). **3802**

TIJDSCHRIFT VOOR GESCHIEDENIS (1920). (NE/0040-7518). **2631**

TIJDSCHRIFT VOOR MARKETING. (NE). **937**

TIJDSCHRIFT VOOR ONDERWIJSRESEARCH. (NE/0166-591X). **5165**

TIJDSCHRIFT VOOR PARAPSYCHOLOGIE. (NE). **4243**

TIJDSCHRIFT VOOR PSYCHIATRIE. (NE/0303-7339). **3937**

TIJDSCHRIFT VOOR SEKSUOLOGIE. (NE/0167-5915). **5188**

TIJDSCHRIFT VOOR SOCIAAL WETENSCHAPPELIJK ONDERZOEK VAN DE LANDBOUW. (NE/0921-481X). **Adv Mgr:** J.H.M. Wijnands. **141**

TIJDSCHRIFT VOOR THEOLOGIE. (NE/0168-9959). **5005**

TIJDSCHRIFT VOOR VERVOERSWETENSCHAP. (NE/0040-7623). **5394**

TIJDSCHRIFT VOOR WELZIJNSWERK. (BE). **5312**

TIKHOOKEANSKAIA GEOLOGIIA. ENGLISH. (SZ/8755-755X). **1399**

TILBURG FOREIGN LAW REVIEW. (NE/0926-874X). **3064**

TILBURY TIMES. (CN). **Adv Mgr:** Victoria Charron. **5796**

TILBURY TIMES. (CN/0834-7344). **5796**

TILE & DECORATIVE SURFACES. (US/0192-9550). **2907**

TILLER AND TOILER (1986), THE. (US/0888-1189). **Adv Mgr:** Dennis Martin. **5678**

TIMBER GROWER. (UK/0040-7763). **2396**

TIMBER HARVESTING. (US/0160-6433). **2405**

TIMBER PROCESSING. (US/0885-906X). **2405**

TIMBER TRADE REVIEW. (MY). **1629**

TIMBER/WEST. (US/0192-0642). **2405**

TIMBERTALK. (US/0744-8511). **2405**

TIMBERTRADER NEWS (1990). (AT/1035-4298). **Adv Mgr:** Mr. King, **Tel** 011 61 3 8821972. **2405**

TIME & TIDE. (II/0040-7836). **4078**

TIME AUSTRALIA. (AT/0818-0628). **2511**

TIME (CHICAGO, ILL.). (US/0040-781X). **2493**

TIME OUT (KANNAPOLIS, N.C.). (US/8756-8497). **4926**

TIMEPIECE. (UK). **2916**

TIMES 1000, THE. (UK). **715**

TIMES-ARGUS (CENTRAL CITY, KY). (US). **5682**

TIMES-BULLETIN, THE. (US/8750-1503). **5730**

TIMES (CANAL WINCHESTER, OHIO). (US/0884-4135). **Adv Mgr:** Carol Zimmer. **5730**

TIMES-CHRONICLE. (US/0746-4606). **Adv Mgr:** Leslie Hamada, **Tel** (215)885-1345. **5740**

TIMES CLARION (HARLOWTON, MONT.), THE. (US/0889-5627). **Adv Mgr:** Julie Killorn. **5706**

TIMES-COURIER. (US). **Adv Mgr:** Bob Yamamoto. **5662**

TIMES EDUCATIONAL SUPPLEMENT, THE. (UK/0040-7887). **1788**

TIMES-GEORGIAN (CARROLLTON, GA.). (US/1049-9458). **Adv Mgr:** Bill Chaple. **5655**

TIMES-HERALD (FORREST CITY, ARK.). (US). **Adv Mgr:** Truman Beasley. **5632**

TIMES HERALD (NORRISTOWN, PA.). (US). **5740**

TIMES HERALD RECORD, THE. (US). **Adv Mgr:** Dan Stewart. **5721**

TIMES INTERNATIONAL (LAGOS, NIGERIA : 1979). (NR). **2644**

TIMES JOURNAL (RUSSELL SPRINGS, KY.). (US). **Adv Mgr:** Kathy Haynes-Ellis. **5682**

TIMES-LEADER, THE. (US). **Adv Mgr:** Kathy Metcalf. **5662**

TIMES-LEADER, THE. (US). **Adv Mgr:** Chip Hutcheson. **5682**

TIMES LEADER (WILKES-BARRE, PA.). (US/0896-4084). **Adv Mgr:** Dennis Shealey, **Tel** (717)829-7122. **5740**

TIMES (MOORESVILLE, IND.). (US). **Adv Mgr:** Sharon Clipp, **Tel** (317)831-0280. **5667**

TIMES-NEWS (LEHIGHTON, PA.). (US). **Adv Mgr:** Don Reese, **Tel** (610)377-2051. **5740**

TIMES OF OMAN. (MK). **5807**

TIMES OF THE AMERICAS, THE. (US/0040-7917). **2552**

TIMES OF TI. (US/0746-0392). **5721**

TIMES-PICAYUNE (NEW ORLEANS, LA. 1986), THE. (US/1055-3053). **5684**

TIMES-PLAIN DEALER, THE. (US). **Adv Mgr:** H.D. Moore. **5673**

TIMES-POST. (US/0746-3901). **5702**

TIMES PRESS HARTFORD PUBLICATIONS. (US). **Adv Mgr:** Jackie Michalowski. **5771**

TIMES PRESS (SEYMOUR, WIS. : 1978). (US). **Adv Mgr:** Ken Hodgden. **5771**

TIMES RECORD (BRUNSWICK, ME), THE. (US/0747-1300). **Adv Mgr:** John Bamford. **5685**

TIMES RECORD NEWS. (US/0895-6138). **5755**

TIMES-RECORD, THE. (US). **5628**

TIMES RECORDER (ZANESVILLE, OHIO : 1965). (US). **Adv Mgr:** Mike Kimmons, **Tel** (614)452-4561. **5730**

TIMES (SMITHFIELD, VA). (US). **Adv Mgr:** Lona Ellis. **5760**

TIMES STANDARD, THE. (US). **Adv Mgr:** Gary Siegal. **5640**

TIMES, THE. (US). **Adv Mgr:** Roxanne Muehlberg. **5699**

TIMES, THE. (US). **Adv Mgr:** Rebecca Ladewig. **5655**

TIMES (TRENTON, N.J. PRINCETON METRO ED.), THE. (US/8750-9083). **5711**

TIMES TRIBUNE (CORBIN, KY.). (US). **Adv Mgr:** Rochelle Stadlin. **5682**

TIMES (WALWORTH, WIS.). (US). **Adv Mgr:** Marge Moore. **5771**

TIMES (WEBSTER, MASS.), THE. (US/0747-2900). **Adv Mgr:** Ernest Mayotte. **5690**

TIMIX BUYERS' GUIDE. (US). **1245**

TIMMINS TIMES, THE. (CN/1191-0771). **Adv Mgr:** J.Lapraik, **Tel** (705)268-6252. **5796**

TIN INTERNATIONAL. (UK/0040-795X). **2152**

TIN NEWS. (US/0040-7968). **4022**

TINCTORIA. (IT/0040-7984). **5359**

TINKLE. (II). **1070**

TINTA (SANTA BARBARA, CALIF.). (US/0739-7003). **3446**

TIPTON CONSERVATIVE AND ADVERTISER, THE. (US). **Adv Mgr:** Sally Taylor. **5673**

TIRE REVIEW (1966). (US/0040-8085). **5078**

TIRRA LIRRA. (AT/1038-8400). **3446**

TISSUE & CELL. (UK/0040-8166). **540**

TISSUE ANTIGENS. (DK/0001-2815). **3802**

TITLE INDEX OF CURRENT REVIEWS. (US/0739-4616). **426**

TITLE MASTER. (US/0747-6418). **426**

TITLE NEWS. (US/0040-8190). **2894**

TITLES MAGAZINE. (US/1049-2704). **2925**

TITRA. (FR). **Adv Mgr:** Ryng, **Tel** 67753229. **3446**

TITUSVILLE HERALD, THE. (US). **Adv Mgr:** Michael Sample. **5740**

TIZ. (GW/0722-9488). **2152**

TJFR BUSINESS NEWS REPORTER. (US). **2925**

TJFR HEALTH NEWS REPORTER. (US). **3646**

TJI : TOBACCO JOURNAL INTERNATIONAL. (GW/0721-5185). **5373**

TJURUNGA; AN AUSTRALASIAN BENEDICTINE REVIEW. (AT). **5037**

TJUSTBYGDEN. (SW). **2712**

TLC -- FOR PLANTS. (US/0835-3271). **Adv Mgr:** Josee Brault, **Tel** same as publisher. **2432**

TLC MONTHLY. (US). **2494**

TLTA NEWS. (US). **2894**

TMSA AEROSPACE MARKET OUTLOOK. (US/0271-7417). **37**

TO VIMA. (GR). **5802**

TOASTMASTER, THE. (US/0040-8263). **1123**

TOBACCO NEWS / TOBACCO BOARD INDIA. (II). **5374**

TOBACCO, WORLD MARKETS & TRADE / UNITED STATES DEPARTMENT OF AGRICULTURE, FOREIGN AGRICULTURAL SERVICE. (US). **5374**

TOCHER; TALES, SONGS, TRADITION. (UK/0049-397X). **4156**

TOCQUEVILLE REVIEW, THE. (US/0730-479X). **5224**

TODAY CEDAR HILL. (US/1065-2876). **Adv Mgr:** Leslie Nasche. **5755**

TODAY IN MISSISSIPPI. (US/1052-2433). **2084**

TODAY LANCASTER. (US/1065-0644). **Adv Mgr:** Leslie Nasche. **5755**

TODAY'S BRIDE (DON MILLS). (CN/0226-1758). **2286**

TODAY'S CATHOLIC (SAN ANTONIO, TEX.). (US/0745-3612). **5037**

TODAY'S CATHOLIC TEACHER. (US/0040-8441). **1873**

TODAY'S CHEMIST AT WORK. (US/1062-094X). **Adv Mgr:** Dean Baldwin, **Tel** (908)738-8200. **994**

TODAY'S CHICAGO WOMAN. (US/1071-3786). **Adv Mgr:** Karen Iglar. **5567**

TODAY'S CHIROPRACTIC. (US/0091-2360). **Adv Mgr:** Cheryl DiDuro. **3646**

TODAY'S CHRISTIAN WOMAN. (US/0163-1799). **5005**

TODAY'S CPA. (US/0889-4337). **Adv Mgr:** J. Ouerton, **Tel** (214)689-6036. **752**

TODAY'S DAILY NEWS. (LAKE HAVASU CITY). (US/1068-1876). **Adv Mgr:** John Schneider. **5630**

TODAY'S DISTRIBUTOR. (US/0898-5561). **1629**

TODAY'S FACILITY MANAGER. (US/1059-0307). **2903**

TODAY'S FEED LOTTING. (AT/1034-6147). **223**

TODAY'S HEALTH (TORONTO). (CN/0821-6819). **4805**

TODAY'S IMAGE. (US/0898-1434). **715**

TODAY'S LIFE SCIENCE. (AT/1033-6893). **5166**

TODAY'S MOTOR. (AT/1033-1069). **2130**

TODAY'S OR NURSE. (US/0194-5181). **3870**

TODAY'S PARENT. (CN/0823-9258). **2286**

TODAY'S PARISH. (US/0040-8549). **5005**

TODAY'S REFINERY. (US/1048-0935). **4280**

TODAY'S SENIORS. (CN/0827-6854). **5182**

TODAY'S SPIRIT. (US/8755-9315). **Adv Mgr:** Herbert Hoover, **Tel** (215)675-3430. **5740**

TODAY'S TRANSPORT INTERNATIONAL. (US/0040-859X). **853**

TODAY'S TRUCKING. (CN/0837-1512). **5394**

TODD COUNTY TRIBUNE. (US). **Adv Mgr:** Ervin Figert, **Tel** (605)856-4469. **5744**

TOK BLONG PASIFIK. (CN). **2671**

TOKUSHU KYOKUGAKU KENKYU. (JA/0387-3374). **1886**

TOLDOT HA-DOAR SHEL ERETS YISRAEL. (IS). **2787**

TOLE WORLD. (US/0199-4514). **332**

TOLEDO SPORTSMAN, THE. (US/8750-6726). **4926**

TOLERIE PONTAULT-COMBAULT. (FR/0985-5637). **4022**

TOLLEY'S COMPUTER LAW AND PRACTICE. (UK/0266-4801). **Adv Mgr:** David Nossitar. **1227**

TOMBALL SUN, THE. (US/8750-619X). **Adv Mgr:** Lindsay Lewis. **5755**

TOMBSTONE, THE. (US/0893-7664). **2475**

TOMORROW'S NATION. (US/1068-1817). **5699**

TONGA YONGU. (KO). **2666**

TONIC (ROBERT SIMPSON SOCIETY). (UK/0260-7425). **4156**

TONKAWA NEWS, THE. (US). **Adv Mgr:** Lyle Becker, **Tel** $405)628-2532. **5732**

TONOPAH TIMES-BONANZA AND GOLDFIELD NEWS. (US). **5708**

TOOELE TRANSCRIPT-BULLETIN. (US). **Adv Mgr:** Clayton Dunn, **Tel** (801)882-0050. **5757**

TOOL & ALLOY STEELS. (II/0377-9408). **2130**

TOP 10'S AND TRIVIA OF ROCK & ROLL AND RHYTHM & BLUES. (US). **4156**

TOP AGRAR : DAS MAGAZIN FUR MODERNE LANDWIRTSCHAFT. (GW). **141**

TOP LINE. (US/0738-6699). **888**

TOP SHELF. (US/1040-0885). **5073**

TOPEKA GENEALOGICAL SOCIETY QUARTERLY, THE. (US/0734-8495). **2475**

TOPICAL STUDIES. (US). **2763**

TOPICAL TIME. (US/0040-9332). **Adv Mgr:** Don Smith, **Tel** (814)539-6301. **2788**

TOPICS IN CLINICAL NUTRITION. (US/0883-5691). **4199**

TOPICS IN EARLY CHILDHOOD SPECIAL EDUCATION. (US/0271-1214). **1886**

TOPICS IN GERIATRIC REHABILITATION. (US/0882-7524). **3755**

TOPICS IN HEALTH CARE FINANCING. (US/0095-3814). **814**

TOPICS IN MAGNETIC RESONANCE IMAGING. (US/0899-3459). **3947**

TOPOI. (NE/0167-7411). **4364**

TORONTO & AREA AIRPORT BUSINESS DIRECTORY. (CN/0822-7748). **37**

TORONTO CONSTRUCTION NEWS. (CN/0712-5895). **630**

TORONTO HERALD, THE. (US/0899-9635). **5744**

TORONTO IRISH NEWS. (CN/0821-2740). **2763**

TORONTO LIFE. (CN/0049-4194). **2548**

TORONTO REVIEW OF CONTEMPORARY WRITING ABROAD, THE. (CN). **Adv Mgr:** N. Aziz, **Tel** (416)483-7191. **3447**

TORONTO ROYALIST. (CN). **2494**

TORONTO SOUTH ASIAN REVIEW, THE. (CN/0714-3508). **3447**

TORONTO'S WEDDING BELLS. (CN/0831-2184). **Adv Mgr:** Alethea Wakefield. **2286**

TORRE (RIO PIEDRAS (SAN JUAN), P.R.), LA. (PR/0040-9588). **3447**

TORRINGTON TELEGRAM. (US). **Adv Mgr:** Bill Hanson. **5773**

TOSCANA QUI. (IT). **332**

TOSHO SHINYOROKU. KANTO-BAN. (JA). **814**

TOT TALK. (CN/0824-507X). **4805**

TOTAH TRACINGS. (US). **2475**

TOTAL HEALTH. (US/0274-6743). **4805**

TOULADI. (CN/0712-3299). **5796**

TOUNG PAO. (NE/0082-5433). **2666**

TOUR DE SUTTON, LE. (CN/0826-5224). **4855**

TOURBILLON DE LA SQTRP, LE. (CN/0836-7655). **3646**

TOURISM MANAGEMENT (1982). (UK/0261-5177). **888**

TOURISME+, LE JOURNAL DES VOYAGES. (CN/0836-205X). **5493**

TOURIST ATTRACTIONS & PARKS. (US/0194-4894). **4855**

TOURIST GUIDE BOOK OF ONTARIO. (CN/0319-0439). **5494**

TOURNAMENT CHESS. (UK/0276-7090). **4867**

TOURNAMENTS ILLUMINATED. (US/0732-6645). **2713**

TOURO JOURNAL OF TRANSNATIONAL LAW. (US/1046-3445). **Adv Mgr:** Sean Conway, **Tel** (516)421-2244 Ext. 508. **3136**

TOURS & RESORTS. (US/0890-2852). **5494**

TOURS ON MOTORCOACH. (CN/0847-9348). **5494**

TOWARD AN ELECTRONIC PATIENT RECORD. (US/1063-973X). **Adv Mgr:** S. Dreskin, **Tel** (617)964-3923. **1205**

TOWARD FREEDOM (1990). (US/1063-4134). **Adv Mgr:** Pamela Polston. **4536**

TOWARD FREEDOM EUROFILE. (US). **4536**

TOWERS CLUB USA NEWSLETTER. (US/0193-4953). **2925**

TOWN AND COUNTRY FARMER. (AT/0814-4540). **142**

TOWN & COUNTRY PLANNING. (UK/0040-9960). **4691**

TOWN & VILLAGE. (US/0040-9979). **5721**

TOWN MEETING. (US). **Adv Mgr:** Lynn Genow. **5694**

TOWN PLANNING REVIEW. (UK/0041-0020). **2837**

TOWNSEND STAR. (US). **5706**

TOWNSHIPS SUN, THE. (CN/0316-022X). **Adv Mgr:** Patricia Ball, **Tel** (819_566-7424. **5796**

TOWSON STATE JOURNAL OF INTERNATIONAL AFFAIRS. (US/0041-0063). **4536**

TOXIC SUBSTANCES JOURNAL. (US/0199-3178). **2871**

TOXICOLOGIC PATHOLOGY. (US/0192-6233). **3898**

TOXICOLOGICAL AND ENVIRONMENTAL CHEMISTRY. (UK/0277-2248). **3984**

TOXICOLOGY AND INDUSTRIAL HEALTH. (US/0748-2337). **Adv Mgr:** M A Mehlman. **3984**

TOXICOLOGY IN VITRO. (UK/0887-2333). **3984**

TOY BOOK, THE. (US/0885-3991). **2585**

TOY FARMER, THE. (US/0894-5055). **Adv Mgr:** Gwen Chappell. **2778**

TOY SHOP. (US/0898-5650). **2585**

TOYS AND PLAYTHINGS. (UK/0041-0187). **Adv Mgr:** John Baulch. **4867**

TPA MESSENGER. (US/0194-9802). **Adv Mgr:** Ed Sterling. **4820**

TPUG MAGAZINE. (CN/0825-0367). **1205**

TR NEWS. (US/0738-6826). **5394**

TRABAJADORES. (CU). **5799**

TRAC, TRENDS IN ANALYTICAL CHEMISTRY (PERSONAL EDITION). (NE/0165-9936). **1019**

TRACE (MEXICO CITY, MEXICO). (MX/0185-6286). **5224**

TRACES (MONTREAL). (CN/0841-6397). **Adv Mgr:** Lina Forest, **Tel** (514)374-2621. **1908**

TRACK & FIELD NEWS. (US/0041-0284). **4926**

TRACK & FIELD QUARTERLY REVIEW. (US/0041-0292). **Adv Mgr:** George Dales, **Tel** same as publisher. **4926**

TRACKER, THE. (US/0041-0330). **4157**

TRACKS. (AT). **Adv Mgr:** Stephen Kay. **4927**

TRACTEURS & MACHINES AGRICOLES PARIS. (FR/0754-121X). **161**

TRACTRIX. (NE/0924-0829). **5166**

TRADE AND COMMERCE (WINNIPEG). (CN/0049-4321). **853**

TRADE CONNECTIONS. (CN/0713-634X). **854**

TRADE DIRECTORY. (MM). **854**

TRADE NEWS SERVICE, THE. (US/1071-0604). **1630**

TRADE REPORT - SEYCHELLES. (SE). **854**

TRADESHOW & EXHIBIT MANAGER. (US/0893-2662). **767**

TRADESHOW WEEK. (US/0733-0170). **767**

TRADESHOW WEEK'S MAJOR EXHIBIT HALL DIRECTORY. (US). **767**

TRADESHOW WEEK'S ... TRADESHOW SERVICES DIRECTORY. (US). **767**

TRADING LAW. (UK/0262-9240). **3136**

TRADING LAW AND TRADING LAW REPORTS. (UK/1352-061X). **Adv Mgr:** Mrs. Curtis. **3104**

TRADISJON. (NO/0332-5997). **2325**

TRADITION MAGAZINE. (FR/0980-8493). **Adv Mgr:** Sbraire, **Tel** 33 1 40211829. **4157**

TRADITION (WALNUT, IOWA). (US/1071-1864). **4157**

TRADITIONAL MEDICAL SYSTEMS. (II/0025-7109). **3647**

TRADITIONAL MUSICLINE, THE. (US/1059-5953). **4157**

TRADITIONAL QUILTWORKS. (US/1050-4435). **Adv Mgr:** Carol Newman. **5186**

TRADITIONAL TAEKWON-DO. (US/0745-2365). **4927**

TRADO, ASIAN AFRICAN DIRECTORY OF EXPORTERS-IMPORTERS & MANUFACTURERS. (II). **854**

TRADUIRE / SOCIETE FRANCAISE DES TRADUCTEURS. (FR/0395-773X). **3329**

TRAFFIC ENGINEERING & CONTROL. (UK/0041-0683). **5394**

TRAFFIC MANAGEMENT. (US/0041-0691). **5394**

TRAFFIC WORLD, THE. (US/0041-073X). **5394**

TRAFIK-SKADOR. (SW/0347-6359). **5446**

TRAI TIM DU'C ME. (US/0744-6128). **5005**

TRAIL AND TIMBERLINE. (US/0041-0756). **Adv Mgr Tel** (303)279-3080. **4879**

TRAIL BLAZER (PASO ROBLES). (US/0274-8274). **2803**

TRAIL RIDER MAGAZINE. (US/0892-3922). **4855**

TRAIL SEEKERS. (US/0739-6643). **2475**

TRAILER BOATS. (US/0300-6557). **596**

TRAILER/BODY BUILD. (US/0041-0772). **5394**

TRAILER LIFE. (US/0041-0780). **4855**

TRAILHEAD. (US). **2397**

TRAINING AND DEVELOPMENT IN AUSTRALIA. (AT/0310-4664). **Adv Mgr:** C. Felle, **Tel** 03 465 1107. **716**

TRAINING DIRECTORY, THE. (UK). **4209**

TRAINING (MINNEAPOLIS). (US/0095-5892). **948**

TRAINING OFFICER, THE. (UK/0041-090X). **948**

TRAINING TOMORROW. (UK/0957-0004). **4691**

TRAINS. (US/0041-0934). **5437**

TRAIT D'UNION - FEDERATION DES CAISSES POPULAIRES ACADIENNES. (CN/0822-3521). **1543**

TRAMES (MONTREAL). (CN/0847-9119). **Adv Mgr:** C Nadeau. **2837**

TRANS F M. (CN/0704-478X). **1141**

TRANSACTIONAL ANALYSIS JOURNAL. (US/0362-1537). **4620**

TRANSACTIONS - AMERICAN CRYSTALLOGRAPHIC ASSOCIATION. (US/0065-8006). **1033**

TRANSACTIONS / GULF COAST ASSOCIATION OF GEOLOGICAL SOCIETIES. (US/0533-6562). **1400**

TRANSACTIONS OF SHASE JAPAN. (JA/0081-1610). **2608**

TRANSACTIONS OF THE AMERICAN CRYSTALLOGRAPHIC ASSOCIATION. (US/0065-8006). **Adv Mgr:** American Crystallographic Association, **Tel** (716)856-9600. **1033**

TRANSACTIONS OF THE AMERICAN FISHERIES SOCIETY (1900). (US/0002-8487). **2315**

TRANSACTIONS OF THE AMERICAN SOCIETY FOR NEUROCHEMISTRY. (US/0066-0132). **3847**

TRANSACTIONS OF THE ANNUAL MEETING OF THE ORTHOPAEDIC RESEARCH SOCIETY. (US/0149-6433). **Adv Mgr:** Amber Howard, **Tel** (617)449-9745. **3885**

TRANSACTIONS OF THE CHARLES S. PIERCE SOCIETY. (US/0009-1774). **4364**

TRANSACTIONS OF THE DELAWARE ACADEMY OF SCIENCE. (US/0093-6456). **5166**

TRANSACTIONS OF THE ILLINOIS STATE ACADEMY OF SCIENCE. (US/0019-2252). **5166**

TRANSACTIONS OF THE INDIAN CERAMIC SOCIETY. (II/0371-750X). **2594**

TRANSACTIONS OF THE PHILOLOGICAL SOCIETY. (UK/0079-1636). **3329**

TRANSACTIONS OF THE ROYAL SOCIETY OF TROPICAL MEDICINE AND HYGIENE. (UK/0035-9203). **3987**

TRANSACTIONS OF THE SAEST. (II/0036-0678). **1035**

TRANSACTIONS OF THE UNITARIAN HISTORICAL SOCIETY. (UK/0082-7800). **5068**

TRANSACTIONS. SECTION A, MINING INDUSTRY / INSTITUTION OF MINING & METALLURGY. (UK/0371-7844). **2152**

TRANSACTIONS - THE SOCIETY OF NAVAL ARCHITECTS AND MARINE ENGINEERS. (US/0081-1661). **4184**

TRANSACTOR, THE. (CN/0827-2530). **1273**

TRANSAFRICA FORUM. (US/0730-8876). **4536**

TRANSCEND. (US). **1070**

TRANSCRIPT, THE. (US). **1123**

TRANSCRIPTASE : REVUE CRITIQUE DE L'ACTUALIT,E SCIENTIFIQUE INTERNATIONALE SUR LE SIDA. (FR/1166-5300). **Adv Mgr:** Mayle Didier. **3677**

TRANSFIL EUROPE PARIS. (FR/1143-3760). **1168**

TRANSFORMATION (EXETER). (UK/0265-3788). **5005**

TRANSFUSION MEDICINE REVIEWS. (US/0887-7963). **3647**

TRANSFUSION (PHILADELPHIA). (US/0041-1132). **3774**

TRANSILVANIA. (RM). **2713**

TRANSITION. (AT/0157-7344). **Adv Mgr:** Callum Fraser, **Tel** 011 61 3 660 2968. **310**

TRANSITION (LONDON, ENGLAND). (UK/0267-8950). **1917**

TRANSITION METAL CHEMISTRY. (UK/0340-4285). **4022**

TRANSITIONS ABROAD. (US/1061-2343). **Adv Mgr:** M. Slaff, **Tel** (413)247-3300. **1788**

TRANSLATION AND LITERATURE. (UK/0968-1361). **Adv Mgr:** Kathryn Maclean. **3447**

TRANSLATION (NEW YORK). (US/0093-9307). **Adv Mgr:** Timothy Sultan, **Tel** (212)854-2305. **3447**

TRANSLATION REVIEW. (US/0737-4836). **3329**

TRANSLATION SERVICES DIRECTORY. (US/0738-4750). **3329**

TRANSMISSION & DISTRIBUTION. (US/0041-1280). **2085**

TRANSMISSION DIGEST. (US/0277-8300). **Adv Mgr:** Robert Mace. **5426**

TRANSNATIONAL DATA AND COMMUNICATIONS REPORT. (US/0892-399X). **1168**

TRANSNATIONAL LAW & CONTEMPORARY PROBLEMS : A JOURNAL OF THE UNIVERSITY OF IOWA COLLEGE OF LAW. (US/1058-1006). **3136**

TRANSPACIFIC (VENICE, CALIF.). (US/1047-7977). **2274**

TRANSPLANTATION. (US/0041-1337). **3647**

TRANSPLANTATION AND IMMUNOLOGY LETTER. (US/0748-1861). **3976**

TRANSPLANTATION PROCEEDINGS. (US/0041-1345). **3977**

TRANSPORT-DIENST + WIRTSCHAFTS-CORRESPONDENT. (GW). **5395**

TRANSPORT ECHO ED. BILINGUE. (BE/0009-6083). **5395**

TRANSPORT ENGINEER, THE. (UK/0020-3122). **1999**

TRANSPORT HISTORY. (UK/0041-1469). **5395**

TRANSPORT (LONDON. 1980). (UK/0144-3453). **5395**

TRANSPORT MANAGEMENT; THE BRITISH JOURNAL OF TRADE AND TRANSPORT. (UK/0041-1515). **Adv Mgr:** MMA Associates, **Tel** 0580 753221. **5395**

TRANSPORT REVIEW. (UK). **5396**

TRANSPORT ROUTIER DU QUEBEC. (CN/0049-447X). **5396**

TRANSPORT THEORY AND STATISTICAL PHYSICS. (US/0041-1450). **4430**

TRANSPORT TOPICS. (US/0041-1558). **5396**

TRANSPORTATION BUILDER. (US/1043-4054). **5396**

TRANSPORTATION (DORDRECHT). (NE/0049-4488). **5396**

TRANSPORTATION LAW JOURNAL, THE. (US/0049-450X). **3065**

TRANSPORTATION PLANNING AND TECHNOLOGY. (US/0308-1060). **5396**

TRANSPORTATION PLANNING SYSTEMS. (UK/0962-7146). **5396**

TRANSPORTATION PRACTITIONERS JOURNAL. (US/8756-9302). **5396**

TRANSPORTATION QUARTERLY. (US/0278-9434). **5397**

TRANSPORTATION SCIENCE. (US/0041-1655). **5397**

TRANSPORTATION TELEPHONE TICKLER. (US). **5397**

TRANSPORTATION WORLDWIDE. (US/8750-8397). **854**

TRANSPORTS. (FR/0564-1373). **Adv Mgr:** Epstein. **5397**

TRANSYLVANIA TIMES, THE. (US). **5724**

TRAP & FIELD. (US/0041-1760). **4927**

TRAPPER AND PREDATOR CALLER, THE. (US/8750-233X). **3186**

TRAPPER (NORTH BATTLEFORD. 1990). (CN/1184-7417). **4879**

TRASFUSIONE DEL SANGUE. (IT/0041-1787). **3802**

TRASGRESSIONI. (IT). **4498**

TRATTAMENTI E FINITURA. (IT/0041-1833). **4022**

TRAVAIL ET MAITRISE. (FR/0750-8964). **948**

TRAVAIL ET METHODES. (FR/0041-185X). **888**

TRAVAIL ET SANTE. (CN/0829-0369). **2871**

TRAVAIL SOCIAL ACTUALITES PARIS. (FR/0753-9711). **Adv Mgr:** M Villeneuve. **5313**

TRAVAUX. (FR/0041-1906). **1999**

TRAVEL 50 & BEYOND. (US/1049-6211). **5494**

TRAVEL A LA CARTE. (CN/0836-7353). **5494**

TRAVEL AGENCY. (UK/0041-1981). **5494**

TRAVEL AND DESCRIPTION SERIES. (US). **2763**

TRAVEL & LEISURE. (US/0041-2007). **5495**

TRAVEL & TOURISM EXECUTIVE REPORT. (US/1070-8855). **5495**

TRAVEL AUSTRALIA SYDNEY. (AT/0817-2935). **Adv Mgr:** I. Burgess. **5495**

TRAVEL BUSINESS ANALYST ASIA ED. (HK/1011-7768). **5495**

TRAVEL BUSINESS ANALYST EUROPE ED. (HK/0256-419X). **5495**

TRAVEL COURIER (TORONTO). (CN/1182-9699). **Adv Mgr:** Celyne Benitah / Robin Catto. **5495**

TRAVEL HOLIDAY. (US/0199-025X). **5495**

TRAVEL INDUSTRY PERSONNEL DIRECTORY. (US/0082-6146). **5496**

TRAVEL NEWS ASIA. (HK). **Adv Mgr:** Sue Dyer. **5496**

TRAVEL PREVIEW. (US/0898-0055). **5496**

TRAVEL TIDINGS. (US/0895-4135). **5496**

TRAVEL TO THE USSR. (RU/0320-0167). **5496**

TRAVEL TRADE DIRECTORY. (UK). **5497**

TRAVEL TRENDS IN THE UNITED STATES AND CANADA. (US). **5497**

TRAVELAGE WEST. (US/0041-1973). **5497**

TRAVELLER'S GUIDE TO THE MIDDLE EAST. (UK). **5497**

TRAVELWARE. (US/0747-475X). **1630**

TRAVELWEEK BULLETIN. (CN/0225-6207). **Adv Mgr:** Tina Cancilla. **5497**

TRAVERSE (TRAVERSE CITY, MICH.). (US/1071-3719). **2494**

TRAVLTIPS. (US/0162-9816). **5497**

TREASURE CHEST (NEW YORK, N.Y.). (US/0897-814X). **252**

TREASURY MANAGEMENT INTERNATIONAL. (UK/0967-523X). **Adv Mgr:** Geert Reinders. **814**

TREATING ABUSE TODAY. (US/1052-3995). **Adv Mgr:** Anna Machan, **Tel** (206)466-5654. **5313**

TREBEDE : REVISTA DE POESIA. (SP). **3472**

TREE PHYSIOLOGY. (CN/0829-318X). **2397**

TREES AND NATURAL RESOURCES. (AT/0814-4680). **2207**

TREESPEAK ADELAIDE. (AT/1032-6111). **2207**

TREFILE, LE. (GW/0374-2261). **4022**

TRELLIS. (CN/0380-1470). **2432**

TREMBLAIE. (CN/0713-4282). **2476**

TREND. (II). **2667**

TRENDS & TECHNIQUES IN THE CONTEMPORARY DENTAL LABORATORY. (US/0746-8962). **1337**

TRENDS & WORDS. (IT). **937**

TRENDS IN BIOCHEMICAL SCIENCES (AMSTERDAM. REGULAR ED.). (UK/0167-7640). **493**

TRENDS IN BIOTECHNOLOGY (PERSONAL EDITION). (NE/0167-7799). **3697**

TRENDS IN HEALTH CARE, LAW & ETHICS. (US/1062-5364). **Adv Mgr:** same as editor. **2253**

TRENDS IN HOUSING. (US/0300-6026). **2837**

TRENDS (SCOTTSDALE, ARIZ.). (US/0742-034X). **332**

TRENTONIAN (TRENTON, N.J.), THE. (US/1064-3567). **Adv Mgr:** M Gebhart, **Tel** (609)989-7800, ext. 218. **5711**

TRI-CITY COMPUTING MAGAZINE. (US). **Adv Mgr:** Josie Soto. **1205**

TRI-CITY GENEALOGICAL SOCIETY BULLETIN, THE. (US/0496-1803). **Adv Mgr:** same as editor. **2476**

TRI-CITY REPORTER, THE. (US). **5746**

TRI-CITY TRIBUNE. (US). **Adv Mgr:** Judy Chase. **5632**

TRI-COUNTY NEWS (OSSEO, WIS.), THE. (US/0749-7040). **5771**

TRI-COUNTY SEARCHER, THE. (US/0742-5015). **2476**

TRI-COUNTY SUN (FORDVILLE, N.D.). (US). **5726**

TRI-COUNTY TIMES, THE. (US). **Adv Mgr:** Sharon Rood, **Tel** (515)685-3416. **5673**

TRI-STATE FOOD NEWS. (US/0041-249X). **2360**

TRI STATE LIVESTOCK NEWS. (US). **223**

TRIAD BUSINESS. (US/0897-0408). **716**

TRIAD (FARMINGTON, MICH.). (US/1046-4948). **Adv Mgr:** Mark Scheible, **Tel** (313)476-2800. **3647**

TRIAD (OHIO MUSIC EDUCATION ASSOCIATION). (US/0041-2511). **4157**

TRIAL. (US/0041-2538). **3066**

TRIAL DIPLOMACY JOURNAL. (US/0160-7308). **3066**

TRIAL TALK. (US/0747-1378). **3066**

TRIATHLON SPORTS. (AT). **Adv Mgr:** A. Mitchell. **4927**

TRIBAL TRIBUNE. (US). **5733**

TRIBOLOGIE UND SCHMIERUNGSTECHNIK. (GW/0724-3472). **1048**

TRIBOLOGY INTERNATIONAL. (UK/0301-679X). **2108**

TRIBOMATERIALS NEWS. (US/1063-9195). **Adv Mgr Tel** (615)574-5377. **4424**

TRIBORO BANNER. (US/1055-9590). **Adv Mgr:** Carol Carey. **5740**

TRIBUNA DE NEW YORK & NEW JERSEY, LA. (US). **Adv Mgr:** Soraya Molenaar. **5712**

TRIBUNAUX CORRECTIONNELS, COURS D'APPEL, CONSEILS DE GUERRE ET COUR MILITAIRE. (BE). **3083**

TRIBUNE. (UK/0041-2821). **5813**

TRIBUNE BUSINESS WEEKLY. (US/1051-7367). **Adv Mgr:** Smith, **Tel** (219)235-6161. **716**

TRIBUNE (COSHOCTON, OHIO). (US). **Adv Mgr:** David Rich. **5731**

TRIBUNE-COURIER (1989). (US/1046-302X). **Adv Mgr:** Terri Dunnigan, **Tel** (501)527-4565. **5683**

TRIBUNE DE L'ORGUE, LA. (SZ/1013-6835). **4157**

TRIBUNE-PHONOGRAPH. (US). **Adv Mgr:** Carol O'Leary. **5771**

TRIBUNE PRESS REPORTER. (US). **Adv Mgr:** Shawn DeWitt. **5771**

TRIBUNE RECORD-GLEANER, THE. (US). **Adv Mgr:** Nancy Meyer. **5771**

TRIBUNE-STAR, THE. (US/0745-9599). **5667**

TRIBUNE, THE. (US). **5644**

TRIBUNE-TIMES. (US/0747-1165). **Adv Mgr:** Marsha Justice. **5743**

TRICYCLE (NEW YORK, N.Y.). (US/1055-484X). **5022**

TRIDENT (WASHINGTON, D.C.). (US/0882-1674). **2788**

TRIERER THEOLOGISCHE ZEITSCHRIFT. (GW/0041-2945). **5006**

TRIMESTRE ECONOMICO, EL. (MX/0041-3011). **Adv Mgr:** Guillermo Escalante. **1640**

TRINITY DIGEST. (US). **2925**

TRINITY WEEKLY JOURNAL. (US). **Adv Mgr:** Fran Wittmann. **5641**

TRIPLE I. (SI). **716**

TRIQUARTERLY / NORTHWESTERN UNIVERSITY. (US/0041-3097). **3447**

TRIVIA. (US/0736-928X). **3355**

TRO OCH LIV. (SW/0346-2803). **Adv Mgr:** Stefan Claesson, **Tel** 011 46 8 7433172. **5006**

TROPICAL AGRICULTURE. (UK/0041-3216). **142**

TROPICAL AND GEOGRAPHICAL MEDICINE. (NE/0041-3232). **3987**

TROPICAL ANIMAL HEALTH AND PRODUCTION. (UK/0049-4747). **Adv Mgr:** Kathryn MacLean. **5523**

TROPICAL DISEASES BULLETIN. (UK/0041-3240). **3662**

TROPICAL ECOLOGY. (II/0564-3295). **2222**

TROPICAL FISH HOBBYIST. (US/0041-3259). **Adv Mgr:** Amy Manning. **2315**

TROPICAL LEPIDOPTERA. (US/1048-8138). **5614**

TROPICAL SCIENCE. (UK/0041-3291). **142**

TROPICAL VETERINARIAN. (NR/0253-4851). **Adv Mgr:** Dr S A Agbede, **Tel** 022 400550 Ext 1538. **3987**

TROUBADOUR (FREDERICTON). (CN/0713-8113). **4157**

TROUBLE AND STRIFE. (UK). **5567**

TROUT AND SALMON. (UK/0041-3372). **2315**

TRUBUS. (IO/0126-0057). **142**

TRUCK CANADA. (CN/0315-5501). **5398**

TRUCKERS/USA (TUSCALOOSA, ALA.). (US/0897-9219). **5398**

TRUCKSTOP WORLD. (US/0894-962X). **5398**

TRUE DETECTIVE. (US/0041-350X). **Adv Mgr:** J Burriesci. **5075**

TRUE EXPERIENCE (NEW YORK). (US/0199-0012). **2494**

TRUE WEST. (US/0041-3615). **2764**

TRUMANN DEMOCRAT, THE. (US). **Adv Mgr:** John Hampton. **5632**

TRUMANSBURG FREE PRESS. (US). **Adv Mgr:** Del Hall, Jim Graney. **5721**

TRUMPETER (LONDON). (CN/0148-673X). **2788**

TRUPPENPRAXIS. (GW). **4059**

TRUST NEWS. (AT). **2207**

TRUSTEE (EDMONTON, ALTA.). (CN/0229-4141). **1873**

TRUXBOOK. (CN/0820-5655). **855**

TRY US. (US/0191-6106). **2274**

TRYON DAILY BULLETIN, THE. (US). **5724**

TSO WU PIN CHUNG TZU YUAN. (CC/1000-6435). **189**

TSUKUBA DAIGAKU TAIIKU KAGAKUKEI KIYO. (JA/0386-7129). **1859**

TTS BLUE BOOK OF TRUCKING COMPANIES. (US/1056-0440). **Adv Mgr:** Thomas R. Fugee. **5398**

TTS NATIONAL MOTOR CARRIER DIRECTORY. (US/1061-477X). **Adv Mgr:** Thomas R. Fugee. **5398**

TTT, INTERDISCIPLINAIR TIJDSCHRIFT VOOR TAAL- & TEKSTWETENSCHAP. (NE/0167-4773). **3330**

TU CHE WEN CHAI. (HK/0041-3836). **2509**

TUBE & PIPE QUARTERLY, THE. (US/1051-4120). **Adv Mgr:** Mike Lacny. **4023**

TUBE & PIPE TECHNOLOGY. (UK/0953-2366). **Adv Mgr:** Caroline Page. **4023**

TUBE SUBSTITUTION HANDBOOK. (US). **2085**

TUCKERTON BEACON (TUCKERTON, N.J. : 1985). (US/0882-9616). **Adv Mgr:** Tim Wallace, **Tel** (609)597-3211. **5712**

TUCSON CITIZEN (1977). (US/0888-5478). **Adv Mgr:** Sam Adkins, **Tel** (602)573-4398. **5630**

TUCSON GUIDE QUARTERLY. (US). **Adv Mgr:** Mike Levy. **2548**

TUDOMANYOS KOZLEMENYEK. (HU). **Adv Mgr:** Pal Nagy, **Tel** 036 1 1564 444 234. **1859**

TUESDAY LETTER. (US/0047-8733). **2207**

TUG LINES. (US/0892-4961). **Adv Mgr:** C D Taylor. **1281**

TUIN EN LANDSCHAP. (NE). **2432**

TUINBOUW VISIE. (BE/0776-4472). **2432**

TULANE LAW REVIEW. (US/0041-3992). **3066**

TULANE LAWYER. (US). **3066**

TULANE STUDIES IN ROMANCE LANGUAGES AND LITERATURE. (US/0564-4380). **3448**

TULIAO GONGYE. (CH/0253-4312). **4225**

TULSA ANNALS. (US/0564-4437). **Adv Mgr:** same as editor. **2476**

TULSA BUSINESS CHRONICLE. (US/0745-5747). **5733**

TULSA LAW JOURNAL. (US/0041-4050). **3067**

TULSA STUDIES IN WOMEN'S LITERATURE. (US/0732-7730). **3448**

TUMOUR BIOLOGY. (SZ/0289-5447). **475**

TUMOUR MARKER UPDATE. (UK/0955-5102). **3825**

TUNDRA DRUMS, THE. (US). **Adv Mgr:** Natalia Akerlund, **Tel** (907)543-3500. **5629**

TUNDRA TIMES. (US/0049-4801). **Adv Mgr:** Debi Smith. **5629**

TUNICA TIMES-DEMOCRAT, THE. (US). **Adv Mgr:** Anita Reed, **Tel** (601)363-2503. **5702**

TUNNELLING AND UNDERGROUND SPACE TECHNOLOGY. (UK/0886-7798). **2033**

TUNNELS & TUNNELLING. (UK/0041-414X). **2033**

TUNNELS ET OUVRAGES SOUTERRAINS VILLEURBANNE. (FR/0399-0834). **2033**

TUPPER LAKE FREE PRESS AND TUPPER LAKE HERALD. (US). **Adv Mgr:** Betty Bell. **5721**

TURBOMACHINERY INTERNATIONAL. (US/0149-4147). **2131**

TURBOMACHINERY INTERNATIONAL HANDBOOK. (US/0748-0903). **2131**

TURCICA (PARIS). (BE/0082-6847). **3330**

TURF & RECREATION. (CN/1186-0170). **2433**

TURF AND SPORT DIGEST. (US/0041-4158). **4927**

TURISMO D'ITALIA. (IT). **2809**

TURKEY WORLD (1968). (US/0041-4271). **223**

TURKEYS. (US/0041-428X). **223**

TURKISH JOURNAL OF NUCLEAR SCIENCES. (TU/0254-5446). **4451**

TURKISH SHIPPING. (UK/0266-7193). **5458**

TURKISH STUDIES ASSOCIATION BULLETIN. (US/0275-6048). **3355**

TURLOCK JOURNAL. (US). **Adv Mgr:** Ted Emory. **5641**

TURNOUT, THE. (CN/0227-244X). **5437**

TURNSTILE (NEW YORK, N.Y.). (US/0896-5951). **3448**

TURTLE MAGAZINE FOR PRESCHOOL KIDS. (US/0191-3654). **1071**

TURTLE QUARTERLY. (US/0896-2022). **2274**

TUSCALOOSA NEWS, THE. (US). **5628**

TUTTITALIA. (UK). **Adv Mgr:** Glenda Simmonds, **Tel** 0788 546443. **3330**

TUTTO SCUOLA. (IT). **1788**

TV CROSSWORDS. (US/0734-5585). **4867**

TV ENTERTAINMENT. (US/1049-1163). **1141**

TV ETC. (US/1054-2329). **1141**

TV EXECUTIVE, THE. (US/0736-2986). **1141**

TV GUIDE. (US/0039-8543). **1141**

TV TECHNOLOGY. (US/0887-1701). **1168**

TV WORLD. (UK/0142-7466). **1142**

TVZ : VAKBLAD VOOR DE VERPLEGKUNDIGEN. (NE/0303-6456). **3870**

TWI JOURNAL. (UK/0963-6927). **4028**

TWIN CITIES CHRISTIAN, THE. (US/0745-8606). **5006**

TWIN CITIES READER. (US/0193-2802). **2548**

TWIN CITY NEWS (CHATTAHOOCHEE, FLA.). (US/0889-2245). **5651**

TWIN FALLS TIMES-NEWS. (US). **5657**

TWIN PLANT NEWS. (US/1046-9427). **Adv Mgr:** W. Davis, **Tel** (915)532-1567. **855**

TWINS. (US/0890-3077). **Adv Mgr:** Brenda Schifman, **Tel** (913)722-1090. **2286**

TWO THIRDS. (CN/0705-3452). **2912**

TWR'S INSIDER REPORT. (US). **5567**

TYDSKRIF VAN DIE TANDHEELKUNDIGE VERENIGING VAN SUID AFRIKA. (SA/0011-8516). **1337**

TYDSKRIF VIR LETTERKUNDE. (SA/0041-476X). **2315**

TYDSKRIF VIR REGSWETENSKAP. (SA/0258-252X). **3067**

TYDSKRIF VIR VOLKSKUNDE EN VOLKSTAAL. (SA/0049-4933). **2325**

TYLER TODAY. (US). **Adv Mgr:** Pene Bridges. **2548**

TYO TERVEYS TURVALLISUUS. (FI/0041-4816). **Adv Mgr:** Mr. Ingmar Quist, **Tel** 358 0 213246. **2871**

TYPOGRAFISCHE MONATSBLATTER. (SZ). **4570**

TYPOGRAPHIC : THE JOURNAL OF THE SOCIETY OF TYPOGRAPHIC DESIGNERS. (UK). **4570**

TZ FUER METALLBEARBEITUNG. (GW/0170-9577). **4023**

U.C. DAVIS LAW REVIEW. (US/0197-4564). **Adv Mgr:** A. Trujillo. **3067**

U-CHOOSE. (CN/0706-4713). **Adv Mgr:** Anita Wood, **Tel** (416)441-1168. **1095**

U.I.T. JOURNAL. (GW). **4927**

U.K. MAGAZINE. (US/8750-1082). **2524**

U.S.A. OIL INDUSTRY DIRECTORY. (US/0082-8599). **4281**

U.S.A. OILFIELD SERVICE, SUPPLY, AND MANUFACTURERS DIRECTORY. (US). **4281**

U S AIRBOAT. (US). **596**

U.S. CATHOLIC. (US/0041-7548). **5037**

U.S. CONGRESS HANDBOOK, THE. (US/0196-7614). **4691**

U.S. FIRMS IN TAIWAN : DIRECTORY. (CH). **716**

U.S. FOAMED PLASTICS MARKETS & DIRECTORY. (US/0083-0968). **4460**

U.S. GLASS, METAL & GLAZING. (US/0041-7661). **2595**

U.S. IMMIGRATION. (US/1055-8276). **1921**

U.S. INDUSTRIAL DIRECTORY. (US/0095-7046). **1630**

U.S.-JAPAN WOMEN'S JOURNAL. ENGLISH SUPPLEMENT. (US/1059-9770). **5567**

U.S. JOURNAL OF DRUG AND ALCOHOL DEPENDENCE, THE. (US/0148-8619). **1350**

U.S. KIDS. (US/0895-9471). **1071**

U.S. MEDICINE. (US/0191-6246). **3917**

U.S. NEWS & WORLD REPORT. (US/0041-5537). **2494**

U.S. PHARMACIST. (US/0148-4818). **4331**

U.S. RAIL NEWS. (US/0743-7994). **5437**

U.S. REAL ESTATE REGISTER. (US/8755-1608). **4848**

U.S. WATER NEWS. (US/0749-1980). **Adv Mgr:** Phil Friedman, **Tel** (201)461-5422. **5541**

U.S. WOMAN ENGINEER. (US/0272-7838). **2000**

U : THE NATIONAL COLLEGE NEWSPAPER. (US). **Adv Mgr:** Greg Dickson. **5641**

U&C UNIFICAZIONE & CERTIFICAZIONE. (IT/0394-9605). **630**

UBD CONFERENCE DIRECTORY. (AT). **717**

UBERSEE RUNDSCHAU. (GW/0041-5707). **856**

UCLA HISTORICAL JOURNAL. (US/0276-864X). **2632**

UCLA LAW REVIEW. (US/0041-5650). **Adv Mgr:** Brian Hofstra. **3067**

UCLA MAGAZINE (1989). (US/1075-2749). **1103**

UCLA PACIFIC BASIN LAW JOURNAL. (US/0884-0768). **3067**

UFAHAMU. (US/0041-5715). **2500**

UFFICIOSTILE. (IT). **310**

UFO TIMES. (UK/0958-4846). **38**

UFONTAS, AS. (BL). **38**

UGOL. (RU/0041-5790). **2152**

UHF. ULTRA HIGH FIDELITY. (CN/0847-1851). **Adv Mgr:** R. Lessard, **Tel** (514)651-5720. **5319**

UHREN, JUWELEN, SCHMUCK. (GW). **2916**

UJ TUKOR. (HU). **2524**

UKIAH DAILY JOURNAL. (US). **5641**

UKRAINIAN QUARTERLY, THE. (US/0041-6010). **4498**

UKRAINIAN REPORTER. (UN/0964-4326). **4537**

UKRAINIAN REVIEW (LONDON, ENGLAND). (UK/0041-6029). **4499**

UKRAINIAN WEEKLY, THE. (US/0273-9348). **Adv Mgr:** Maria Szeparowycz, **Tel** (201)434-0237. **2274**

UKRAINSKA RSR. (UN). **5398**

UKRAINSKI VISTI (EDMONTON). (CN/0041-6002). **Adv Mgr:** Richard Sheps. **5796**

UKRAINSKYI FILATELIST / SOIUZ UKRAINSKYKH FILATELISTIV I NUMIZMATYKIV. (US/0198-6252). **2788**

UKRAINSKYI ISTORYK. (US/0041-6061). **2714**

ULEN UNION, THE. (US). **Adv Mgr:** David Evans. **5699**

ULSTER JOURNAL OF ARCHAEOLOGY. (UK/0082-7355). **285**

ULSTER MEDICAL JOURNAL. (UK/0041-6193). **3648**

ULTIMISSIME PELLICCERIA. (IT). **3186**

ULTRA (HOUSTON, TEX.). (US/0279-4322). **2548**

ULTRAFIT AUSTRALIA. (AT). **Adv Mgr:** Karen Fode, **Tel** 03 4392828. **2601**

ULTRAPURE WATER. (US/0747-8291). **5541**

ULTRASONICS. (UK/0041-624X). **4424**

ULTRASOUND IN MEDICINE & BIOLOGY. (US/0301-5629). **3648**

ULTRASTRUCTURAL PATHOLOGY. (US/0191-3123). **3898**

ULYSSES NEWS, THE. (US). **5678**

UMAP JOURNAL, THE. (US/0197-3622). **3540**

UMBEN. (PP). **5264**

UMBRELLA (GLENDALE). (US/0160-0699). **367**

UMI'S SOUTHEASTERN BASKETBALL HANDBOOK. (US). **4927**

UMPQUA FREE PRESS. (US/0745-7588). **5734**

UMSATZSTEUER-RUNDSCHAU (COLOGNE, GERMANY : 1986). (GW/0341-8669). **3067**

UMWELT (DUSSELDORF). (GW/0041-6355). **2245**

UNA SANCTA (METTINGEN). (GW/0342-1465). **5006**

UNABASHED LIBRARIAN, THE. (US/0049-514X). **3254**

UNB LAW JOURNAL. (CN/0836-6632). **3067**

UNCAPTIVE MINDS. (US/0897-9669). **Adv Mgr:** Eric Chenoweth. **2714**

UNCLASSIFIED (WASHINGTON, D.C.). (US/1062-3450). **5177**

UNDER WESTERN SKIES. (US/0279-6244). **4079**

UNDERCAR DIGEST. (US/0893-6943). **Adv Mgr:** Larry Dixon. **5427**

UNDERGROUND WINE JOURNAL, THE. (US/1047-6865). **2371**

UNDERLINE. (US/0276-0398). **310**

UNDERSEA BIOMEDICAL RESEARCH. (US/0093-5387). **3697**

UNDERSTANDING JAPAN. (JA/0041-6576). **2509**

UNDERWATER MEDICINE AND RELATED SCIENCES. (US/0191-2534). **3648**

UNDERWATER NEWS & TECHNOLOGY. (US/1069-6547). **1458**

UNDERWATER USA. (US/0749-1794). **4927**

UNDERWOOD NEWS, THE. (US/8750-7285). **Adv Mgr:** Dave Freuer, **Tel** (701)463-2201. **5726**

UNDERWRITERS' REPORT. (US/0041-6622). **2895**

UNDISCOVERED COUNTRIES JOURNAL. (US/1068-3267). **Adv Mgr:** Gary Breckenridge. **3449**

UNDRO NEWS. (SZ/0250-9377). **2912**

UNDZER VEG (TORONTO). (CN/0382-0610). **2274**

UNESCO KOERIER. (BE/0304-3169). **332**

UNICORN (CARLTON, TAS.). (AT/0311-4775). **1788**

UNIDOS : JOURNAL OF OPPORTUNITY. (US). **Adv Mgr:** Irma Rey. **717**

UNIE GOODWOOD, DIE. (SA/0259-5591). **Adv Mgr:** N. Kotze. **1908**

UNIFICATION NEWS. (US/1061-0871). **5006**

UNIFORM BUILDING CODE. (US). **630**

UNIFORMED SERVICES ALMANAC. (US/0503-1982). **4059**

UNIGEO - SBORNIK PRACI. (XR). **5167**

UNIGRAM. X. (UK/0952-3359). **Adv Mgr:** S Thompson. **1249**

UNIMETRO : ORGANO DE INFORMACION E INVESTIGACION. (CK/0120-7504). **3648**

UNION (1987), THE. (US/1050-7906). **5641**

UNION ADVOCATE. (US/8750-1562). **5699**

UNION BANNER. (US). **Adv Mgr:** Mike Langham. **5662**

UNION COUNTY LEADER, THE. (US). **5713**

UNION DEMOCRAT, THE. (US). **Adv Mgr:** Bud Vogel. **5641**

UNION EXPRESS, L'. (CN/0715-6359). **1716**

UNION LABOR NEWS (MADISON, WIS.). (US/0041-6924). **1716**

UNION LEADER. (US/0161-9292). **2548**

UNION LIST OF SERIALS IN MONTREAL HOSPITAL LIBRARIES. (CN/0316-5043). **426**

UNION MEDICALE DU CANADA. (CN/0041-6959). **3648**

UNION POSTALE. (SZ). **1147**

UNION RECORDER. (US). **Adv Mgr:** Percy Canon. **5655**

UNION SPRINGS HERALD. (US). **5628**

UNION, THE. (US). **Adv Mgr:** Richard Larimer. **5641**

UNION WRITES NEWSLETTER. (US/0748-6839). **1716**

UNISPHERE. (US/0279-1579). **1249**

UNITARIAN QUEST. (AT). **1071**

UNITARIAN UNIVERSALIST CHRISTIAN, THE. (US/0362-0492). **5068**

UNITAS FRATRUM. (GW/0344-9254). **5068**

UNITED CHURCH NEWS (NATIONAL EDITION). (US/0882-7214). **5731**

UNITED CHURCH OBSERVER, THE. (CN/0041-7238). **5006**

UNITED DAILY NEWS. (CH). **5799**

UNITED DAUGHTERS OF THE CONFEDERACY MAGAZINE. (US). **2764**

UNITED EVANGELICAL. (US/0041-7262). **5040**

UNITED EVANGELICAL ACTION. (US/0041-7270). **5006**

UNITED FLY TYERS' ROUNDTABLE. (US/0747-9832). **2315**

UNITED METHODIST CHRISTIAN ADVOCATE, THE. (US/8750-7668). **5068**

UNITED METHODIST REPORTER (DALLAS, TEX.), THE. (US/0737-5581). **5068**

UNITED STATES AIR FORCE YEARBOOK. (UK/0956-2828). **4059**

UNITED STATES BANKER (COS COB). (US/0148-8848). **815**

UNITED STATES-GERMAN ECONOMIC YEARBOOK. (US/1044-4351). **717**

UNITED STATES SPACE FOUNDATION PROCEEDINGS. (US). **38**

UNITED STATES SPECIALIST, THE. (US/0164-923X). **1147**

UNITED STATES SWIMMING RULES AND REGULATIONS. (US/0742-7808). **4927**

UNITED STATES TRADE FAIR. (US/0742-3675). **952**

UNITED SYNAGOGUE REVIEW. (US/0041-8153). **5053**

UNIVERSAL MESSAGE, THE. (PK). **5045**

UNIVERSAL MILITARY ABSTRACTS. (II). **Adv Mgr:** R. K. Arora. **4059**

UNIVERSALIST FRIENDS. (US). **5068**

UNIVERSALIST - QUAKER UNIVERSALIST GROUP. (UK/0267-6648). **5068**

UNIVERSE MANCHESTER. (UK/0041-8226). **5813**

UNIVERSITAS. ENGLISH LANGUAGE EDITION (STUTTGART). (GW/0341-0129). **2856**

UNIVERSITES (MONTREAL). (CN/0226-7454). **1852**

UNIVERSITY ADMINISTRATION. OSMANIA UNIVERSITY. HYDERABAD. (II/0970-9584). **1852**

UNIVERSITY AFFAIRS / AFFAIRES UNIVERSITAIRES. (CN/0041-9257). **Adv Mgr:** D. Sheehan. **1852**

UNIVERSITY CALENDAR SIMON FRASER. UNIVERSITY OF BC. (CN). **1096**

UNIVERSITY CITY LIGHT. (US/0889-8154). **Adv Mgr:** Leah Hansen. **5641**

UNIVERSITY COMPUTING : THE BULLETIN OF THE IUCC. (UK/0265-4385). **1852**

UNIVERSITY DAILY KANSAN. (US/0746-4967). **Adv Mgr:** (913)864-7661. **5679**

UNIVERSITY DAILY, THE. (US). **Adv Mgr:** Susan Peterson. **5755**

UNIVERSITY OF ARKANSAS AT LITTLE ROCK LAW JOURNAL. (US/0162-8372). **3068**

UNIVERSITY OF BALTIMORE LAW REVIEW. (US/0091-5440). **3068**

UNIVERSITY OF CHICAGO LAW REVIEW, THE. (US/0041-9494). **3068**

UNIVERSITY OF CINCINNATI LAW REVIEW. (US/0009-6881). **3068**

UNIVERSITY OF COLORADO LAW REVIEW. (US/0041-9516). **3068**

UNIVERSITY OF DAYTON LAW REVIEW. (US/0162-9174). **3068**

UNIVERSITY OF EDINBURGH JOURNAL. (UK/0041-9567). **1852**

UNIVERSITY OF FLORIDA JOURNAL OF LAW AND PUBLIC POLICY. (US/1047-8035). **Adv Mgr:** Keith Riffardi, **Tel** (904)373-7139. **3068**

UNIVERSITY OF GHANA LAW JOURNAL. (GH/0041-9605). **3068**

UNIVERSITY OF HAWAII LAW REVIEW. (US/0271-9835). **3068**

UNIVERSITY OF ILLINOIS LAW REVIEW. (US/0276-9948). **3068**

UNIVERSITY OF MIAMI ENTERTAINMENT & SPORTS LAW REVIEW. (US/1051-2225). **3069**

UNIVERSITY OF MIAMI INTER-AMERICAN LAW REVIEW, THE. (US/0884-1756). **3137**

UNIVERSITY OF MIAMI LAW REVIEW. (US/0041-9818). **3069**

UNIVERSITY OF MICHIGAN JOURNAL OF LAW REFORM. (US/0363-602X). **3069**

UNIVERSITY OF NEW SOUTH WALES LAW JOURNAL, THE. (AT/0313-0096). **Adv Mgr:** Rhoda Yung, **Tel** 011 61 2 6972237. **3069**

UNIVERSITY OF PENNSYLVANIA LAW REVIEW. (US/0041-9907). **3069**

UNIVERSITY OF PITTSBURGH LAW REVIEW. (US/0041-9915). **3069**

UNIVERSITY OF RICHMOND LAW REVIEW. (US/0566-2389). **3069**

UNIVERSITY OF TASMANIA LAW REVIEW. (AT/0082-2108). **3069**

UNIVERSITY OF TORONTO LAW JOURNAL, THE. (CN/0042-0220). **3069**

UNIVERSITY OF TORONTO QUARTERLY. (CN/0042-0247). **2856**

UNIVERSITY PRESS BOOK NEWS. (US/1040-8991). **427**

UNIVERSITY PUBLISHING. (US/0191-4146). **4833**

UNIVERSO. (IT/0042-0409). **2578**

UNIX/BUSINESS. (UK/0958-6253). **1239**

UNIX NEWS LONDON. (UK/0956-2753). **Adv Mgr:** Oren Wolfe, **Tel** 44 071 528 7083. **1249**

UNIX PRODUCTS DIRECTORY. (US/0886-2575). **1206**

UNIX/WORLD. (US/0739-5922). **1265**

UNLISTED DRUGS. (US/0042-0441). **4331**

UNMUZZLED OX. (US/0049-5557). **3472**

UNSER WALD : ZEITSCHRIFT DER SCHUTZGEMEINSCHAFT DEUTSCHER WALD. (GW). **Adv Mgr:** Ulrike Migende. **2397**

UNSERE JUGEND. (GW/0342-5258). **1789**

UNSERE STIMME. (GW). **3355**

UNTERNEHMUNG. (SZ/0042-059X). **889**

UNTERRICHTSPRAXIS, DIE. (US/0042-062X). **3331**

UNTERRICHTSWISSENSCHAFT. (GW/0340-4099). **1789**

UNVEILING. (US/0747-931X). **3449**

UOMO HARPER'S BAZAAR. (IT/1121-5496). **1088**

UP-DATE - B.C. NUTRITION COUNCIL. (CN/0823-8332). **4199**

UP HERE : LIFE IN CANADA'S NORTH. (CN). **2548**

UP INFORMATION. (BE). **4499**

UPDATE & DIALOG. (DK/0906-7272). **5007**

UPDATE (ARLINGTON). (US/0162-945X). **1917**

UPDATE CAPE TOWN. (SA/0258-929X). **3649**

UPDATE - GEORGIA ASSOCIATION OF EDUCATORS. (US/8750-2283). **1789**

UPDATE / INTERPRETATION CANADA. (CN/0715-3392). **1789**

UPDATE ON LAW-RELATED EDUCATION. (US/0147-8648). **3070**

UPDATE - ONTARIO TRUCKING ASSOCIATION. (CN/0841-2472). **5399**

UPDATE - UNIVERSITY OF SOUTH CAROLINA. DEPT. OF MUSIC. (US/8755-1233). **4157**

UPHOLSTERY DESIGN & MANUFACTURING. (US/1056-2052). **3489**

UPPER — Advertising Accepted Index

UPPER ARLINGTON NEWS, THE. (US/0194-2131). **Adv Mgr Tel** Carol Zimmer. **5731**

UPPER CANADIAN, THE. (CN/0711-0081). **Adv Mgr:** same as editor. **252**

UPPER COUNTY NEWS-REPORTER, THE. (US). **5657**

UPSIDE (U.S. ED.). (US/1052-0341). **1239**

UPSTATE NEW YORK DIRECTORY OF MANUFACTURERS. (US/0732-2860). **3489**

UPTOWN SAN DIEGO EXAMINER. (US/0898-4581). **5641**

UQAR-INFORMATION. (CN/0711-2254). **1853**

URAL-ALTAISCHE JAHRBUCHER. (GW/0042-0786). **3331**

URAL-ALTAISCHE JAHRBUCHER (WIESBADEN, GERMANY : 1981). (GW/0042-0786). **3331**

URBA. (CN/0709-9444). **Adv Mgr:** Pierre Christiane. **4692**

URBAN ABSTRACTS. (UK/0305-103X). **2837**

URBAN ACADEMIC LIBRARIAN. (US/0276-9298). **3255**

URBAN ANTHROPOLOGY AND STUDIES OF CULTURAL SYSTEMS AND WORLD ECONOMIC DEVELOPMENT. (US/0894-6019). **247**

URBAN DESIGN UPDATE: NEWSLETTER OF THE INSTITUTE FOR URBAN DESIGN. (US/0895-8076). **2837**

URBAN LEAGUE REVIEW, THE. (US/0147-1740). **2274**

URBAN TRANSPORTATION MONITOR, THE. (US/1040-4880). **Adv Mgr:** C. Reeves. **5399**

URBANISTICA INFORMAZIONI. (IT/0392-5005). **2838**

URETHANES TECHNOLOGY. (UK/0265-637X). **4460**

URJA. (II/0378-9535). **1960**

URNER BARRY'S MEAT & POULTRY DIRECTORY. (US/0738-6745). **223**

URNER BARRY'S PRICE-CURRENT. WEST COAST EDITION. (US/0273-5016). **143**

UROLOGIA. (IT/0391-5603). **3993**

UROLOGIA INTERNATIONALIS. (SZ/0042-1138). **3993**

UROLOGIC NURSING. (US/1053-816X). **3870**

UROLOGY (RIDGEWOOD, N.J.). (US/0090-4295). **3994**

URPE. (US/0743-1694). **Adv Mgr:** D. Olsen. **1525**

US ARCHER, THE. (US/0738-9949). **4927**

US-CHINA REVIEW. (US/0164-3886). **4537**

US (NEW YORK, N.Y. 1985). (US/0147-510X). **2548**

USA GYMNASTICS. (US/0748-6006). **4928**

USA OUTDOORS. (US/0883-6841). **4880**

USA TODAY (ARLINGTON, VA.). (US/0734-7456). **5687**

USA TODAY (INTERNATIONAL ED.). (US/1051-7405). **Adv Mgr:** Alex Clemente. **5722**

USA TODAY (NEW YORK, N.Y.). (US/0161-7389). **2548**

USAE. (US/0894-8194). **Adv Mgr:** Ross Heller. **5687**

USCTA NEWS. (US/0744-0103). **2803**

USDF CALENDAR OF COMPETITIONS. (US/0882-5009). **2803**

USE OF ENGLISH, THE. (UK/0042-1243). **1789**

USQR, UNION SEMINARY QUARTERLY REVIEW. (US/0362-1545). **5007**

USSR AND THIRD WORLD. (UK/0041-5545). **4537**

USYSA NETWORK. (US). **4928**

UTAH BUSINESS MAGAZINE. (US). **Adv Mgr:** Karen. **717**

UTAH DIRECTORY OF BUSINESS AND INDUSTRY. (US/8755-2841). **1630**

UTAH FISHING. (US/0897-7283). **Adv Mgr:** James Archie, **Tel** (801)521-8223. **4880**

UTAH LAW REVIEW. (US/0042-1448). **3070**

UTAH LIBRARIES/NEWS. (US). **3255**

UTAH MUSIC EDUCATOR. (US/0502-871X). **4157**

UTAH SYMPHONY. (US/0191-1635). **4157**

UTBLICK LANDSKAP. (SW). **310**

UTENSIL. (IT/0392-6567). **2131**

UTILITIES INDUSTRY LITIGATION REPORTER. (US/1053-0258). **3070**

UTILITY COMMUNICATOR'S EXCHANGE. (US/0889-4248). **Adv Mgr:** Kathy Staskal, **Tel** (319)438-6101. **4762**

UTILITY PURCHASING AND STORES. (US/0042-1588). **952**

UTNE READER, THE. (US/8750-0256). **2549**

UV/EB NEWS. (US/0275-3901). **4442**

UWI STUDENT'S LAW REVIEW. (BB). **3070**

UXBRIDGE TIMES-JOURNAL. (CN/0834-7336). **5796**

VACANCES POUR TOUS. (CN/0831-3067). **Adv Mgr:** Eric Chasse, **Tel** (418)682-5464. **5498**

VACATION STUDY ABROAD (NEW YORK, N.Y.). (US/1046-2104). **5498**

VACATIONS (HOUSTON, TEX.). (US/0894-9093). **5498**

VACCINE. (UK/0264-410X). **3649**

VACHER'S EUROPEAN COMPANION & CONSULTANTS' REGISTER. (UK/0958-0336). **4693**

VACUUM CIRCUITS. (US/0747-5063). **5399**

VADNAIS HEIGHTS PRESS. (US). **Adv Mgr:** Michelle Larson. **5699**

VADO E TORNO. (IT/0042-2096). **5399**

VAIL TRAIL, THE. (US). **5644**

VAJRADHATU SUN, THE. (US/0882-0813). **5022**

VALDERS JOURNAL, THE. (US). **5771**

VALDEZ VANGUARD. (US). **Adv Mgr:** Linda Wakefield, **Tel** (907)835-2211. **5629**

VALDOSTA DAILY TIMES, THE. (US). **Adv Mgr:** Bill Wallace. **5655**

VALENCIA FRUITS. (SP). **143**

VALFARDS BULLETINEN / SCB. (SW/0280-1418). **5313**

VALLEJO TIMES-HERALD. (US). **5641**

VALLEY CATHOLIC, THE. (US/8750-6238). **Adv Mgr:** M. Hawkins. **5038**

VALLEY COURIER (ALAMOSA, COLO.). (US/1047-1170). **Adv Mgr:** Keith Cerny. **5644**

VALLEY-FOOTHILLS NEWS, THE. (US/0745-5321). **5630**

VALLEY FORGE JOURNAL, THE. (US/0734-5712). **2764**

VALLEY GAZETTE, THE. (US/1056-4853). **Adv Mgr:** Ed Gildea. **5740**

VALLEY JOURNAL, THE. (US). **5644**

VALLEY MAGAZINE (GRANADA HILLS, CALIF.). (US/8750-1430). **Adv Mgr:** Fred Braden. **1300**

VALLEY MAGAZINE (SELINSGROVE, PA.). (US/1046-0454). **5498**

VALLEY NEWS. (US). **Adv Mgr:** Terri Dudley. **5709**

VALLEY NEWS. (US). **5657**

VALLEY NEWS (FULTON, N.Y.), THE. (US/1067-7755). **5722**

VALLEY POTATO GROWER. (US/0889-4787). **143**

VALLEY SENTINEL (VALEMOUNT). (CN/0845-4183). **5797**

VALLEY TRIBUNE, THE. (US). **Adv Mgr:** Eunice McFull, **Tel** (806)455-1101. **5755**

VALUE ENGINEERING & MANAGEMENT DIGEST. (US/0275-4371). **2000**

VALUE RETAIL NEWS : THE JOURNAL OF VALUE-ORIENTED RETAILING & DEVELOPMENT. (US). **Adv Mgr:** Fran Tolson. **1300**

VALUE WORLD. (US). **1525**

VAN BUREN COUNTY DEMOCRAT. (US). **5632**

VAN BUREN ECHOES. (US/0897-9413). **2476**

VAN HORN ADVOCATE. (US). **5755**

VAN WERT AND SURROUNDING COUNTIES, OHIO. (US/0898-641X). **2549**

VANCOUVER & AREA AIRPORT BUSINESS DIRECTORY. (CN/0828-4504). **39**

VANCOUVER (VANCOUVER, 1975). (CN/0380-9552). **Adv Mgr:** Janet MacDonald. **5498**

VANDANCE (VANCOUVER). (CN/0705-8063). **1314**

VANDERBILT JOURNAL OF TRANSNATIONAL LAW. (US/0090-2594). **3137**

VANDERBILT LAW REVIEW. (US/0042-2533). **3070**

VANDERBILT STREET REVIEW. (US/0275-7672). **3450**

VANGUARD. (US/0892-6433). **2838**

VANGUARD (VANCOUVER). (CN/0315-5226). **367**

VANIEROIS, LE. (CN/0823-0153). **1525**

VAR FAGELVARLD. (SW/0042-2649). **5620**

VARBUSINESS. (US/0894-5802). **1239**

VARIETY. (US/0042-2738). **4079**

VARIETY CROSSPATCHES. (US/0194-3278). **4867**

VARIETY WORD-FIND PUZZLES. (US/0194-3286). **4867**

VARLIK. (TU). **3450**

VARSITY OUTDOOR CLUB JOURNAL, THE. (CN/0524-5613). **4880**

VARSITY (TORONTO). (CN/0042-2789). **1096**

VART FORSVAR, TIDSKRIFT UTG. AF ALLMANNA FORSVARSFORENINGEN OCH FORENINGEN FOR NORRLANDS FASTA FORSVAR. (SW/0042-2800). **4060**

VASA. (SZ/0301-1526). **3802**

VASA STAR, THE. (US/0746-0627). **2274**

VASCULAR REPORTS. (US/0748-8971). **3977**

VASCULAR SURGERY. (US/0042-2835). **3977**

VASLA. (US/0042-1723). **3255**

VASUTI KOZLEKEDESI SZAKIRODALMI TAJEKOZTATO. (HU/0231-0767). **5437**

VATTEN. (SW/0042-2886). **5541**

VAX PROFESSIONAL, THE. (US/8750-9628). **1206**

VDI-Z. (GW/0042-1766). **2131**

VDT NEWS. (US/0742-938X). **Adv Mgr:** Barbara Gerson. **4806**

VE VENEZUELA. (VE/0042-2932). **5498**

VEA (HATO REY, P.R.). (PR/0738-7628). **2494**

VEALER, THE. (US/0749-6664). **2360**

VECTOR KLOOF. (SA/0256-7008). **2796**

VECTOR LONDON. (UK/0955-1433). **1206**

VECTOR (READING). (UK/0505-0448). **3450**

VEDANTA KESARI, THE. (II/0042-2983). **4364**

VEDERE CONTACT INTERNATIONAL. (IT/0392-0453). **4217**

VEDERE INTERNATIONAL. (IT/0302-6256). **4217**

VEDIC LIGHT. (II). **5041**

VEGETARIAN (ALTRINCHAM, CHESHIRE : 1980). (UK/0260-3233). **Adv Mgr:** Sue Stobart. **4200**

VEGETARIAN TIMES. (US/0164-8497). **4200**

VEGETARIAN VOICE. (US/0271-1591). **4806**

VEGETATIO. (NE/0042-3106). **529**

VEGYIPARI SZAKIRODALMI TAJEKOZTATO MUANYAG- ES GUMIIPARI KULONLENYOMATA. (HU/0231-0775). **995**

VEHICLE AND TRAFFIC LAW. (US). **3070**

VEHICLE LEASING TODAY. (US). **Adv Mgr:** Deborah Dember. **5399**

VEHICLE SYSTEM DYNAMICS. (NE/0042-3114). **2131**

VEHICULES A MOTEUR NEUFS MIS EN CIRCULATION. (BE). **5427**

VEJVISER I STATISTIKKEN. (DK/0109-8314). **5345**

VELD & FLORA. (SA/0042-3203). **530**

VELDWERK AMSTERDAM. (NE/0922-2782). **2912**

VELO-NEWS. (US/0161-1798). **429**

VELTRO, IL. (IT/0042-3254). **2524**

VELVET LIGHT TRAP, THE. (US/0149-1830). **4079**

VENDING INTERNATIONAL. (UK/0954-6235). **Adv Mgr:** Conrad Chant. **937**

VENDING TIMES. (US/0042-3327). **4214**

VENEREOLOGY : OFFICIAL PUBLICATION OF THE NATIONAL VENEREOLOGY COUNCIL OF AUSTRALIA. (AT). **Adv Mgr:** Heather McDuff, **Tel** 03 347 0309. **3716**

VENTES AUX ENCHERES PUBLIQUES. (CN/0849-0465). **367**

VENTURA COUNTY STAR-FREE PRESS. (US). **Adv Mgr:** Harvey Hopkins, **Tel** (805)655-1780. **5641**

VENTURE ROAD. (US/0883-7821). **5498**

VERA LEX. (US/0893-4851). **2253**

VERANDA (ATLANTA, GA.). (US/1040-8150). **2903**

VERBATIM. (US/0162-0932). **3331**

VERBINDING ROTTERDAM. (NE/0922-6540). **1168**

VERBONDSNIEUWS VOOR DE BELGISCHE SIERTEELT. (BE). **2436**

VERBUM (SAN DIEGO, CALIF.). (US/0889-4507). **382**

VERDAD (CORPUS CHRISTI, TEX. : 1942). (US). **2275**

VERDE AMBIENTE. (IT). **2222**

VERDE INDEPENDENT, THE. (US). **Adv Mgr:** Kathy Bartlett. **5630**

VERDI NEWSLETTER. (US/0160-2667). **4158**

VEREINTE NATIONEN. (GW/0042-384X). **4537**

VERFASSUNG UND RECHT IN UBERSEE. (GW/0506-7286). **3094**

VERGILIUS (1959). (US/0506-7294). **1080**

VERHANDLUNGEN DER DEUTSCHEN GESELLSCHAFT FUER HERZ- UND KREISLAUFFORSCHUNG. (GW/0174-2817). **3711**

VERHANDLUNGEN DER ORNITHOLOGISCHE GESELLSCHAFT IN BAYERN. (GW). **5620**

VERHANDLUNGEN - INTERNATIONALE VEREINIGUNG FUER THEORETISCHE UND ANGEWANDTE LIMNOLOGIE. (GW/0368-0770). **1418**

VERKOPEN! VAKMAGAZINE VOOR COMMERCIELE AKTIE. (NE). **952**

VERKSTADERNA. (SW/0042-4056). **2131**

VERKUNDIGUNG UND FORSCHUNG. (GW/0342-2410). **5007**

VERMESSUNG, PHOTOGRAMMETRIE, KULTURTECHNIK. (SZ/0252-9424). **Adv Mgr:** Mr Signer. **2000**

VERMONT BAR JOURNAL & LAW DIGEST, THE. (US/0748-4925). **3071**

VERMONT LIFE. (US/0042-417X). **Adv Mgr:** Gerianne Smart, **Tel** (802)425-2283. **2549**

VERMONT NATURAL HISTORY. (US/0270-5982). **4173**

VERMONT REGISTERED NURSE. (US/0191-1880). **3870**

VERMONT YEAR BOOK. (US/0083-5781). **718**

VERNON COUNTY BROADCASTER. (US). **Adv Mgr:** Peter Hollister. **5771**

VEROFFENTLICHUNGEN. (GW/0568-4358). **1080**

VEROFFENTLICHUNGEN DES MUSEUMS FUER UR- UND FRUHGESCHICHTE POTSDAM. (GE/0079-4376). **285**

VEROFFENTLICHUNGEN - MAX-PLANCK-INSTITUT FUER GESCHICHTE. (GW/0436-1180). **2632**

VERONA PRESS, THE. (US). **Adv Mgr:** Terry Leonard, **Tel** (608)845-9559. **5771**

VERPACKUNG. (GW/0042-4269). **4222**

VERPLEEGKUNDIGEN EN GEMEENSCHAPSZORG. (BE). **Adv Mgr:** Michel Foulon. **3870**

VERRE (PARIS, FRANCE). (FR/0984-7979). **2595**

VERSAILLES POLICY, THE. (US). **Adv Mgr:** Lynn Langston, **Tel** (513)526-9131. **5731**

VERSAILLES REPUBLICAN (VERSAILLES, IND. : 1893). (US). **Adv Mgr:** Linda Chandler. **5668**

VERSION (SIDNEY, N.S.W.). (AT). **Adv Mgr:** P. Jeavons, **Tel** 02 630 5982. **2511**

VERTIFLITE. (US/0042-4455). **39**

VERWALTUNG UND FORTBILDUNG. (GW). **4693**

VERWALTUNGSARCHIV. (GW/0042-4501). **3071**

VERWARMING EN VENTILATIE. (NE/0042-451X). **2608**

VESTIRAMA. (SP). **1088**

VESTNIK CESKOSLOVENSKYCH SPOLKU V MONTREALE. (CN/0700-8171). **2764**

VESTNIK, LE MESSAGER. (FR/0767-7294). **2524**

VESTNIK (OWINGS MILLS, MD.). (US/1055-2278). **Adv Mgr:** Gennady Krochik. **2275**

VETERA CHRISTIANORUM. (IT/0506-8126). **Adv Mgr:** Ceglie. **5020**

VETERINARIA ARGENTINA. (AG/0326-4629). **Adv Mgr:** Sr Speroni. **5523**

VETERINARIA (MEXICO). (MX/0301-5092). **Adv Mgr:** Renate Thumule. **5523**

VETERINARIAN MAGAZINE. (CN/0849-5009). **Adv Mgr:** L. Hewitt. **5524**

VETERINARY AND COMPARATIVE ORTHOPAEDICS AND TRAUMATOLOGY. (GW/0932-0814). **5524**

VETERINARY AND HUMAN TOXICOLOGY. (US/0145-6296). **5524**

VETERINARY BULLETIN (LONDON). (UK/0042-4854). **5528**

VETERINARY CLINICAL PATHOLOGY. (US/0275-6382). **5525**

VETERINARY ECONOMICS. (US/0042-4862). **5525**

VETERINARY HISTORY. (UK/0301-6943). **5525**

VETERINARY MEDICINE (1985). (US/8750-7943). **5526**

VETERINARY PATHOLOGY. (US/0300-9858). **5526**

VETERINARY PRACTICE. (UK/0042-4897). **5526**

VETERINARY QUARTERLY, THE. (NE/0165-2176). **5526**

VETERINARY RADIOLOGY & ULTRASOUND. (US/1058-8183). **Adv Mgr:** L. Ayres. **5526**

VETERINARY RECORD. (UK/0042-4900). **5526**

VETERINARY SURGERY. (US/0161-3499). **5527**

VETERINARY TECHNICIAN. (US/8750-8990). **5527**

VETERINARY TIMES. (UK/1352-9374). **Adv Mgr:** Trisha Anderson, **Tel** same as publisher. **5527**

VETSKAP. (SW/0283-8708). **1096**

VETTE. (US/0199-7890). **5427**

VETTE VUES MAGAZINE. (US/0279-8476). **5427**

VETUS TESTAMENTUM. (NE/0042-4935). **5020**

VFW, VETERANS OF FOREIGN WARS MAGAZINE. (US/0161-8598). **4060**

VGB-KRAFTWERKSTECHNIK. (GW/0372-5715). **2000**

VI. (SW/0346-4180). **2524**

VIATOR (BERKELEY). (US/0083-5897). **1080**

VIBE (NEW YORK, N.Y.). (US/1070-4701). **Adv Mgr:** Susan Coppa, **Tel** (212)522-7082. **2494**

VIBRATIONS (TORONTO). (CN/0227-6755). **Adv Mgr:** Bob Hickey. **4394**

VICA JOURNAL. (US/1044-0151). **4209**

VICE VERSA (MONTREAL, QUEBEC). (CN/0829-2299). **Adv Mgr:** Josee Bellemare. **2549**

VICKSBURG EVENING POST. (US/0884-8912). **Adv Mgr:** David Gillis. **5702**

VICTOR VALLEY MAGAZINE. (US/0738-8586). **2549**

VICTORIA ADVOCATE (VICTORIA, TEX. : DAILY). (US) **5755**

VICTORIA COUNTY RECORD. (CN/0703-8747). **5797**

VICTORIA INSIDER. (CN/0843-4395). **2765**

VICTORIA NATURALIST, THE. (CN/0049-612X). **4173**

VICTORIAN BRANCH NEWS. (AT/0813-6394). **3650**

VICTORIAN HOMES. (US/0744-415X). **310**

VICTORIAN NATURALIST. (AT/0042-5184). **4173**

VICTORIAN NETBALLER. (AT). **Adv Mgr:** same as editor. **4928**

VICTORIAN ORGAN JOURNAL. (AT/0310-4834). **4158**

VICTORIAN PERIODICALS REVIEW. (US/0709-4698). **3355**

VICTORIAN POETRY. (US/0042-5206). **Adv Mgr:** Dr. H. Ward. **3450**

VICTORIAN REAL ESTATE JOURNAL. (AT/0815-3132). **Adv Mgr:** G. Kyrros. **4848**

VICTORIAN REVIEW. (CN/0848-1512). **3450**

VICTORIAN SAMPLER. (US/1047-3947). **2903**

VICTORIAN STUDIES. (US/0042-5222). **3450**

VICTORIAN TRADES HALL COUNCIL OFFICIAL TRADE UNION DIRECTORY & DIGEST. (AT). **Adv Mgr:** Phil Wicks. **1716**

VICTORIAN VEGETABLE GROWER, THE. (AT). **190**

VICTORIAN YEAR-BOOK. (AT/0067-1223). **4701**

VICTORIANS INSTITUTE JOURNAL. (US/0886-3865). **5237**

VICTORY LANE. (US/0887-1426). **Adv Mgr:** R. Lichty, **Tel** (415)321-4605. **4928**

VIDA HISPANICA (1972). (UK/0308-4957). **3332**

VIDA Y PENSAMIENTO. (CR). **5007**

VIDE, LES COUCHES MINCES, LE. (FR/0223-4335). **4424**

VIDEO AGE INTERNATIONAL. (US/0278-5013). **1142**

VIDEO & AUDIO REPORT. (NE). **1123**

VIDEO CHOICE. (US/0896-2871). **4079**

VIDEO COMPUTING. (US/8756-5250). **1142**

VIDEO GUIDE (VANCOUVER). (CN/0228-6726). **1142**

VIDEO JOURNAL OF COLOR FLOW IMAGING. (US/1052-2182). **3947**

VIDEO JOURNAL OF ECHOCARDIOGRAPHY. (US/1052-2174). **Adv Mgr:** M. Linzer. **3711**

VIDEO NETWORKS. (US/0738-7563). **1142**

VIDEO-PRESSE. (CN/0315-3975). **1071**

VIDEO RATING GUIDE FOR LIBRARIES. (US/1045-3393). **3255**

VIDEO : REVISTA DE CIRURGIA. (SP). **3977**

VIDEO SOURCE BOOK, THE. (US/0748-0881). **4377**

VIDEO STORE. (US/0195-1750). **1142**

VIDEO SYSTEMS. (US/0361-0942). **1142**

VIDEO TIMES (SKOKIE, ILL.). (US/0742-8111). **4378**

VIDEODISC COMPENDIUM FOR EDUCATION AND TRAINING, THE. (US/1047-921X). **Adv Mgr:** Rubyanna Pollak. **1790**

VIDEOGRAPHY. (US/0363-1001). **1143**

VIDEOLOG. (US/0746-7699). **4079**

VIDEOMAKER. (US/0889-4973). **1168**

VIDEOMANIA. (CN/0711-7914). **4867**

VIDEOTEL INTERNATIONAL REVIEW. (IT). **1143**

VIDEOVISIE. (NE). **1143**

VIDURA. (II). **1123**

VIDYAJYOTI (DELHI). (II/0970-1222). **5038**

VIE DES ARTS. (CN/0042-5435). **332**

VIE E TRASPORTI. (IT). **5399**

VIE FRANCAISE (QUEBEC). (CN/0382-0262). **2549**

VIE OUVRIERE (MONTREAL, QUEBEC). (CN/0229-3803). **1716**

VIE SOCIALE. (FR/0042-5605). **5225**

VIE WALLONNE. (BE/0042-5648). **2715**

VIER BULLETIN. (AT). **1790**

VIERTELJAHRESBERICHTE PROBLEMS OF INTERNATIONAL COOPERATION. (GW/0936-451X). **Adv Mgr:** Margret Reichert. **4537**

VIERTELJAHRESSCHRIFT FUER HEILPADAGOGIK UND IHRE NACHBARGEBIETE. (SZ/0017-9655). **1790**

VIERTELJAHRSHEFTE FUER ZEITGESCHICHTE. (GW/0042-5702). **2632**

VIETNAM GENERATION. (US/1042-7597). **2765**

VIETNAM TODAY. (AT/1030-9985). **4537**

VIETNAM UPDATE. (US/0899-6601). **2632**

VIETNAM WAR NEWSLETTER. (US/0743-2496). **4060**

VIETNAMESE STUDIES. HANOI, VIETNAM (1966). (VM/0085-7823). **2667**

VIEWCAMERA (SACRAMENTO, CALIF.). (US/1066-6958). **4378**

VIEWS (BOSTON, MASS.). (US/0743-8044). **Adv Mgr:** Darsie Alexander. **4378**

VIGENCIA. (AG). **2856**

VIGIL. (UK/0954-0881). **3451**

VIGILANCE. (FR/0398-9399). **1790**

VIGILIAE CHRISTIANAE. (NE/0042-6032). **3451**

VIKALPA. (II/0256-0909). **889**

VIKING TOURIST GUIDE. (CN/0828-4849). **5498**

VILAG ES NYELV. (HU). **3332**

VILAS COUNTY NEWS-REVIEW. (US). **Adv Mgr:** Byron McNutt. **5771**

VILLAGE CRIER (TOMS RIVER, N.J.), THE. (US/1066-1204). **Adv Mgr:** Patricia Jasin, **Tel** (908)240-3000. **5712**

VILLAGE TIMES, THE. (US/0889-8677). **Adv Mgr:** Kathryn Mandracchia. **5722**

VILLAGE

Advertising Accepted Index

VILLAGE VOICE (NEW YORK), THE. (US/0042-6180). **2549**

VILLAGER (MISSISSAUGA). (CN/0226-5907). **5797**

VILLAGER, THE. (US). **Adv Mgr:** Gerri Sweeney. **5644**

VILLAGER, THE. (US). **Adv Mgr:** T. Wyatt. **2275**

VILLAMOSSAG. (HU/0042-6210). **2085**

VILLANOVA LAW REVIEW. (US/0042-6229). **3071**

VILLE (MONTREAL), EN. (CN/0826-7731). **5498**

VILLE PLATTE GAZETTE, THE. (US/8750-6785). **Adv Mgr:** Jerry Matt. **5684**

VIM & VIGOR. (US/0886-6554). **2601**

VINCENNES SUN-COMMERCIAL, THE. (US). **Adv Mgr:** V. Kopp. **5668**

VINCULUM. (AT/0157-759X). **3540**

VINDICATOR (LIBERTY, TEX.). (US/0746-6838). **5755**

VINEYARD & WINERY MANAGEMENT. (US/1047-4951). **Adv Mgr:** Hope Merletti, **Tel** (800)535-5670. **2371**

VINEYARD GAZETTE, THE. (US). **Adv Mgr:** Eileen Holley. **5690**

VINIFERA WINE GROWERS JOURNAL, THE. (US/0095-3563). **190**

VINTAGE AIRPLANE, THE. (US/0091-6943). **39**

VINTAGE FORD, THE. (US/0042-6350). **5427**

VINTAGE JAZZ MART. (UK/0042-6369). **4158**

VINTAGE (NEW YORK, N.Y. 1971). (US/0049-6456). **2360**

VINTON COUNTY COURIER, THE. (US). **Adv Mgr:** Ardena Kessler. **5731**

VINUM. (SZ/0177-2570). **2372**

VIOLEXCHANGE, THE. (US/0892-5437). **4158**

VIP. VAKBLAD VOOR IMAGE PROCESSING. (NE/0926-3241). **Adv Mgr:** Dennis Landman. **1221**

VIRGINIA BUSINESS. (US/0888-1340). **718**

VIRGINIA COUNTRY. (US/0734-6603). **2549**

VIRGINIA DENTAL JOURNAL. (US/0049-6472). **1337**

VIRGINIA ENGINEER (1974), THE. (US/0504-4251). **2000**

VIRGINIA ENGLISH BULLETIN. (US/0504-426X). **3332**

VIRGINIA FARMER (BALTIMORE, MD.). (US/0746-1186). **144**

VIRGINIA FORESTS (1974). (US/0740-011X). **2398**

VIRGINIA FRUIT. (US/0097-1782). **2433**

VIRGINIA GAZETTE (1930). (US/0049-6480). **5760**

VIRGINIA GEOGRAPHER, THE. (US/0042-6512). **2579**

VIRGINIA JOURNAL OF EDUCATION (1980). (US/0270-837X). **Adv Mgr:** Yolanda Morris. **1908**

VIRGINIA JOURNAL OF INTERNATIONAL LAW. (US/0042-6571). **3137**

VIRGINIA JOURNAL, THE. (US/0739-4586). **1859**

VIRGINIA LAND USE DIGEST. (US). **4848**

VIRGINIA LAW REVIEW. (US/0042-6601). **3071**

VIRGINIA LAW WEEKLY. (US/0042-661X). **3072**

VIRGINIA MAGAZINE OF HISTORY AND BIOGRAPHY, THE. (US/0042-6636). **2765**

VIRGINIA MARITIMER. (US). **5458**

VIRGINIA MEDICAL QUARTERLY : VMQ. (US/1052-4231). **Adv Mgr:** Anne Hill, **Tel** (804)353-2721. **3650**

VIRGINIA NUMISMATIST, THE. (US). **2783**

VIRGINIA NURSE. (US/0270-7780). **Adv Mgr:** Pat Taylor. **3870**

VIRGINIA PHARMACIST, THE. (US/0042-6717). **4332**

VIRGINIA POULTRYMAN, THE. (US/0042-6733). **223**

VIRGINIA QUARTERLY REVIEW, THE. (US/0042-675X). **3355**

VIRGINIA REVIEW. (US/0732-9156). **Adv Mgr:** Roger Habeck. **4693**

VIRGINIA SOCIAL SCIENCE JOURNAL. (US/0507-1305). **5225**

VIRGINIA TAX REVIEW. (US/0735-9004). **3072**

VIRGINIA TOWN & CITY. (US/0042-6784). **4693**

VIRGINIA UNITED METHODIST ADVOCATE. (US/0891-5598). **5069**

VIRGINIAN (STAUNTON, VA.), THE. (US/0743-4243). **2549**

VIRTUAL REALITY REPORT. (US/1052-6242). **1283**

VIRTUE. (US/0164-7288). **5007**

VIRUS BULLETIN. (UK/0956-9979). **1227**

VIRUS GENES. (US/0920-8569). **571**

VISALIA TIMES-DELTA. (US). **5641**

VISAO. (BL/0042-6873). **2553**

VISIBILITIES. (US/0892-7375). **2796**

VISIBLE LANGUAGE. (US/0022-2224). **Adv Mgr:** Carrie Harris, **Tel** (401)454-6171. **4570**

VISION. (US). **5008**

VISION. (UK). **Adv Mgr:** Michele Pollock. **5568**

VISION LETTER, THE. (US/0042-6962). **4499**

VISION (PASADENA, CALIF.). (US/0882-6609). **5008**

VISIONMONDAY (NEW YORK, N.Y.). (US/1054-7665). **Adv Mgr:** Frank Giammanco, **Tel** (212)24-7070. **4217**

VISIONS. (US/1043-4194). **2601**

VISIONS MAGAZINE (BOSTON, MASS.). (US/1064-8658). **4378**

VISITANTE DOMINICAL, EL. (US/0194-9160). **5038**

VISITANTE, EL. (PR). **Adv Mgr:** Carola Llompart. **5008**

VISITOR (KITCHENER, ONT.). (CN/0839-1335). **5499**

VISTA DE MEXICO, LA. (US/0895-6464). **5499**

VISTA PRESS, THE. (US/0893-3464). **Adv Mgr:** Helen Woods. **5641**

VISTA/U.S.A. (US/0507-1577). **5499**

VISTAZO. (EC). **Adv Mgr:** Roberto Comacho. **5800**

VISUAL ARTS NEWS. (CN/0704-0512). **368**

VISUAL MERCHANDISING & STORE DESIGN. (US/0745-4295). **958**

VISUAL RESOURCES. (US/0197-3762). **368**

VISUAL RESOURCES ASSOCIATION BULLETIN. (US/1046-9001). **368**

VISUM NIEUWS. (NE/0925-8275). **1853**

VISVA HINDI DARSANA. (II). **3332**

VITA E PENSIERO. (IT/0042-725X). **4364**

VITA E SALUTE. (IT/0042-7268). **Adv Mgr:** Franco Evangelist. **2495**

VITA SOCIALE. (IT/0042-7365). **5038**

VITAE SCHOLASTICAE. (US/0735-1909). **1790**

VITAL CHRISTIANITY (1994). (US/1077-6982). **Adv Mgr:** George Nalywaiko. **5008**

VITAL SIGNS (STORRS, CONN.). (US/0749-856X). **4621**

VITAL STATISTICS IN CORRECTIONS. (US). **3084**

VITALITY. (CN/0829-6014). **2602**

VITAMIN CONNECTION. (UK/0957-6436). **4200**

VITICULTURA ENOLOGIA PROFESIONAL. (SP). **145**

VITREOUS ENAMELLER. (UK/0042-7519). **2017**

VITRIINI. (FI/0357-749X). **2810**

VIVA. (KE). **5568**

VIVA (NEW YORK). (NE/0149-4473). **2549**

VIVANT UNIVERS. (BE/0042-7527). **2579**

VIVARIUM. (NE/0042-7543). **4364**

VIVARIUM (LAKESIDE, CALIF.), THE. (US/1047-2665). **Adv Mgr Tel** (619)747-4948. **5599**

VIVRE LE PRIMAIRE. (CN/0835-5169). **1806**

VLA NEWSLETTER. (US/0896-0720). **3255**

VLAAMS DIERGENEESKUNDIG TIJDSCHRIFT. (BE/0303-9021). **5527**

VLAAMSE GIDS, DE. (BE). **2856**

VLAANDEREN. (BE/0042-7683). **332**

VMEBUS SYSTEMS. (US/0884-1357). **1273**

VOCATIONAL EDUCATION JOURNAL. (US/0884-8009). **1917**

VOCATIONAL EVALUATION AND WORK ADJUSTMENT BULLETIN. (US/0160-8312). **4395**

VOEDING. (NE/0042-7926). **4200**

VOGELWELT, DIE. (GW/0042-7993). **5620**

VOGUE KNITTING INTERNATIONAL. (US/0890-9237). **5186**

VOGUE MUNCHEN. (GW/0176-6104). **Adv Mgr:** Dagmar Huber. **5568**

VOGUE (NEW YORK). (US/0042-8000). **5568**

VOGUE PATTERNS (BRITISH EDITION). (UK/0142-338X). **5186**

VOICE (EAST LANSING, MICH.). (US/0883-573X). **Adv Mgr:** Gertie Buren. **1790**

VOICE (FRANKLIN, WIS.), THE. (US/0889-3543). **3793**

VOICE LONDON. 1992. (UK/0966-789X). **3891**

VOICE M.A.N, THE. (US/0505-8708). **Adv Mgr:** (same as editor). **2433**

VOICE OF THE DIABETIC. (US/1041-8490). **3733**

VOICE OF THE PEDESTRIAN, THE. (NE). **2839**

VOICE OF THE TENNESSEE WALKING HORSE. (US/0505-8813). **Adv Mgr:** David Kranich, **Tel** (615)359-1567. **2803**

VOICE OF THE TRAPPER. (US/0194-6927). **4880**

VOICE OF THE TURTLE (SAN DIEGO, CALIF.). (US/0739-9324). **5237**

VOICE OF THE WORKING WOMAN, THE. (II). **1717**

VOICE OF UNITED SENIOR CITIENS OF ONTARIO, INC. (CN/0382-0068). **5182**

VOICE OF WASHINGTON MUSIC EDUCATORS. (US/0147-4367). **4158**

VOICE OF YOUTH ADVOCATES. (US/0160-4201). **3451**

VOICE. OFFICIAL PUBLICATION OF MICHIGAN ASSOCIATION OF NURSEYMEN. (US). **Adv Mgr:** K. Ebert. **2433**

VOICE PROCESSING MAGAZINE. (US/1042-0460). **Adv Mgr:** Webster. **1206**

VOICE, THE. (US/1040-1121). **2293**

VOICE, THE. (US). **2433**

VOICE (WESTCHESTER). (US/0049-6669). **5008**

VOICES (AMERICAN ACADEMY OF PSYCHOTHERAPISTS). (US/0042-8272). **3937**

VOICES IN ITALIAN AMERICANA. (US/1048-292X). **Adv Mgr:** A J Tamburri, **Tel** (317)494-3839. **3451**

VOICES ISRAEL. (IS). **3473**

VOICES OF MEXICO. (MX/0186-9418). **2512**

VOICES OF THE AFRICAN DIASPORA. (US/1054-4283). **2275**

VOICES (SOUTHBURY). (US/0193-1474). **5646**

VOIE LACTEE. (CN/0710-5479). **3769**

VOIES FERREES. (FR/0249-4914). **857**

VOIR DIRE (MONTREAL). (CN/0826-4503). **4395**

VOIX DU SANCTUAIRE. (CN/0700-9313). **5008**

VOIX SEFARAD. (CN/0704-5352). **Adv Mgr:** Jean Claude Leon. **2275**

VOLGA TRIBUNE, THE. (US/0163-6154). **5744**

VOLLEYBALL RULE BOOK. (US/0882-1372). **4928**

VOLTA REVIEW, THE. (US/0042-8639). **4395**

VOLUNTAS : INTERNATIONAL JOURNAL OF VOLUNTARY AND NON-PROFIT ORGANISATIONS. (UK/0957-8765). **4339**

VOPROSY TEORII SISTEM AVTOMATICESKOGO UPRAVLENIJA. (RU/0130-0415). **2131**

VORGANGE. (GW/0507-4150). **2524**

VORWARTS (NEW YORK, N.Y.). (US/0746-7869). **Adv Mgr Tel** (212)889-8200 ext. 406. **5722**

VOTRE SUCCES. (CN/0843-6665). **718**

VOX BENEDICTINA. (CN/0715-8726). **5038**

VOX LATINA. (GW/0172-5300). **3332**

VOX MAGAZINE (NEW YORK, N.Y. 1990). (US/1052-8814). **3451**

VOX PATRUM. (PL). **5008**

VOX REFORMATA. (AT/0728-0912). **5008**

VOX SANGUINIS. (SZ/0042-9007). **3774**

VOYAGE EN GROUPE. (CN/0711-6136). **5499**

VOYAGER. (US). **5651**

VOYAGER INTERNATIONAL. (US/1040-8541). **2579**

VOYAGEUR (GREEN BAY, WIS.). (US/1062-7634). **Adv Mgr:** P. Viets, **Tel** (414)465-2446. **2633**

VOZ DE HOUSTON, LA. (US). **Adv Mgr:** Jorge Duarte, **Tel** (713)644-7449. **5755**

VOZ DE LA CULTURA, LA. (SP). **332**

VOZ DE LA VALDERIA, LA. (SP). **2524**

VOZ, LA. (US). **2495**

VOZ (SEATTLE, WASH.). (US). **2495**

VOZAC I SAOBRACAJ. (CI). **5427**

VR. VERMESSUNGSWESEN UND RAUMORDNUNG. (GW/0340-5141). **2579**

VR VIDEOREGISTRARE. (IT/0394-2384). **4079**

VRIJ NEDERLAND : VN. (NE). **2524**

VS NEWS. (US/0748-7886). **Adv Mgr:** Joan Berkley. **1273**

V+T. VERKEHR UND TECHNIK. (GW/0340-4536). **5399**

VUELTA. (MX/0185-1586). **Adv Mgr:** Patricia Rodriguez. **2512**

VULKANOLOGIIA I SEISMOLOGIA. (US/0742-0463). **1412**

VVS BULLETIN. (NE). **5346**

VXI JOURNAL. (US/1072-9933). **Adv Mgr:** M. Hopper, **Tel** (810)774-8180. **1206**

W. (US/0162-9115). **1088**

W.W. 1 AERO. (US/0736-198X). **39**

WACO CITIZEN, THE. (US). **Adv Mgr:** Sharon Witcowski. **5755**

WACO FARM AND LABOR JOURNAL (1986). (US/0889-3233). **145**

WACO TRIBUNE-HERALD. (US). **Adv Mgr:** Bob Nay. **5755**

WACONDA ROOTS AND BRANCHES. (US/8755-2167). **2477**

WADENA NEWS [MICROFORM], THE. (CN). **Adv Mgr:** Headington. **5797**

WAGNER. (UK). **4158**

WAGNER NEWS (LONDON, ENGLAND). (UK/0261-3468). **389**

WAGONER (JOURNAL). (US). **2477**

WAHKIAKUM COUNTY EAGLE. (US). **Adv Mgr Tel** 795-3391. **5763**

WAITOMO NEWS. (NZ). **Adv Mgr:** F. Rawling, **Tel** (07)878 8005 Ext. 13. **5807**

WAKARUSA TRIBUNE, THE. (US). **Adv Mgr:** Ginger Rodgers. **5668**

WAKE FOREST LAW REVIEW. (US/0043-003X). **3072**

WALDEN'S ABC GUIDE AND PAPER PRODUCTION YEARBOOK. (US/0731-2571). **4239**

WALDEN'S PAPER CATALOG. (US). **4239**

WALKING HORSE REPORT. (US/0093-6928). **2803**

WALKING MAGAZINE, THE. (US/1042-2102). **2602**

WALL PAPER (NEW YORK, N.Y.), THE. (US/0273-6837). **2903**

WALL STREET JOURNAL (EUROPE). (BE/0921-9986). **5778**

WALLACE ENTERPRISE. (US). **Adv Mgr:** Mary Oswald. **5724**

WALLACE MINER, THE. (US/0883-671X). **Adv Mgr:** Judi Binkley, **Tel** (208)783-1107. **5658**

WALLACE STEVENS JOURNAL, THE. (US/0148-7132). **3473**

WALLACEANA. (MY). **2222**

WALLCOVERINGS, WINDOWS & INTERIOR FASHION. (US/1055-4394). **2903**

WALLEYE. (US/0744-1266). **4880**

WALLEYE IN-SIDER. (US/1068-2112). **Adv Mgr:** Jim Besenfelder. **2315**

WALLS & CEILINGS. (US/0043-0161). **Adv Mgr:** Paula Graham, **Tel** (800)533-5653. **631**

WALNUT COUNCIL BULLETIN. (US/1041-5769). **2398**

WALSH COUNTY RECORD (1992), THE. (US/1067-5922). **Adv Mgr:** Don Tuff. **5726**

WALT WHITMAN QUARTERLY REVIEW. (US/0737-0679). **3452**

WALTON TRIBUNE, THE. (US/0893-410X). **5655**

WANT ADVERTISER. (US). **Adv Mgr:** Mrs. Halter, **Tel** (508)443-4100. **2779**

WANTOK. (PP). **2511**

WAR & SOCIETY. (AT/0729-2473). **2633**

WAR, LITERATURE, AND THE ARTS. (US/1046-6967). **Adv Mgr:** Donald Anderson. **3452**

WAR RESEARCH INFO SERVICE. (US/1058-823X). **4060**

WARBIRDS. (US/0744-6624). **39**

WARD'S AUTO WORLD. (US/0043-0315). **5428**

WARP AND WEFT (MCMINNVILLE, OR.). (US/0732-6890). **5359**

WARREN-NEWPORT PRESS. (US/0745-8118). **Adv Mgr:** Jill DePasquale. **5662**

WARREN SHEAF. (US). **5699**

WARREN'S MOVIE POSTER PRICE GUIDE. (US/0884-3791). **4079**

WARRIOR (SHEARWATER. 1978). (CN/0707-8056). **4060**

WARROAD PIONEER. (US). **Adv Mgr:** Pam Pederson. **5699**

WARSAW VOICE, THE. (PL/0860-7591). **5808**

WARTA GEOLOGI. (MY/0126-5539). **1401**

WARUNKI SRODOWISKOWE POLSKIEJ STREFY POLUDNIOWEGO BALTYKU-MATERIALY ODDZIALU MORSKIEGO. (PL). **1458**

WARWICK BEACON. (US). **Adv Mgr:** Alice Stanelun. **5741**

WAS TUN. (GW/0043-0404). **4499**

WASAFIRI. (UK/0269-0055). **3452**

WASECA COUNTY NEWS. (US/0745-8177). **Adv Mgr:** Cheryl Neid. **5699**

WASHBURN COUNTY REGISTER (SHELL LAKE, WIS. : 1928). (US/8755-0520). **5771**

WASHINGTON AFRO-AMERICAN AND THE WASHINGTON TRIBUNE. (US). **5687**

WASHINGTON AND LEE LAW REVIEW. (US/0043-0463). **3072**

WASHINGTON APPLE PI. (US/1056-7682). **Adv Mgr:** Beth Medlin, **Tel** (301)654-8060. **1207**

WASHINGTON BUSINESS JOURNAL. (US/0737-3147). **Adv Mgr:** Lisa Bormaster, **Tel** (703)816-0307. **719**

WASHINGTON CEO. (US/1048-4981). **Adv Mgr:** June Ford. **719**

WASHINGTON COUNSELETTER. (US/0740-8501). **1790**

WASHINGTON COUNTY NEWS. (US). **Adv Mgr:** Pauline Jackson. **5628**

WASHINGTON FOOD DEALER MAGAZINE, THE. (US/0043-0560). **2361**

WASHINGTON INFORMER, THE. (US/0741-9414). **2275**

WASHINGTON INQUIRER. (US/0749-1050). **4538**

WASHINGTON ISLAND OBSERVER. (US). **Adv Mgr:** G. L. Toerpe, **Tel** (414)847-2661. **5771**

WASHINGTON JEWISH WEEK. (US/0746-9373). **5053**

WASHINGTON JOB SOURCE, THE. (US/1067-0769). **4209**

WASHINGTON JOURNALISM REVIEW (1983). (US/0741-8876). **2925**

WASHINGTON LAW REVIEW (1967). (US/0043-0617). **3072**

WASHINGTON LAWYER, THE. (US/0890-8761). **Adv Mgr:** Maureen Muller, **Tel** ext. 205. **3072**

WASHINGTON MANUFACTURERS REGISTER. (US/0148-5687). **3489**

WASHINGTON MONTHLY, THE. (US/0043-0633). **4499**

WASHINGTON NURSE, THE. (US/0734-5666). **3871**

WASHINGTON PARK ARBORETUM BULLETIN. (US/1046-8749). **2433**

WASHINGTON POST BOOK WORLD, THE. (US). **4833**

WASHINGTON POST (WASHINGTON, D.C. : 1974). (US/0190-8286). **5648**

WASHINGTON QUARTERLY, THE. (US/0163-660X). **4538**

WASHINGTON REPORT ON AFRICA. (US/0733-8104). **Adv Mgr:** Justin Ford. **4499**

WASHINGTON REPORT ON MIDDLE EAST AFFAIRS, THE. (US/8755-4917). **Adv Mgr:** Greg Noakes, **Tel** 800-368-5788. **2526**

WASHINGTON REVIEW. (US/0163-903X). **333**

WASHINGTON STATE BAR NEWS. (US/0886-5213). **3073**

WASHINGTON TIMES-HERALD (WASHINGTON, IND.). (US). **Adv Mgr:** Don Brown. **5668**

WASHINGTON UNIVERSITY JOURNAL OF URBAN AND CONTEMPORARY LAW. (US/8756-0801). **3073**

WASHINGTON UNIVERSITY LAW QUARTERLY. (US/0043-0862). **3073**

WASHINGTON VIEW. (US/1042-4229). **2549**

WASHINGTONIAN (WASHINGTON, D.C.), THE. (US/0043-0897). **2549**

WASSER-KALENDER (BERLIN). (GW/0511-3520). **5541**

WASSER UND BODEN. (GW/0043-0951). **145**

WASSERWIRTSCHAFT. (GW/0043-0978). **5541**

WASTE AGE. (US/0043-1001). **2245**

WASTE AGE'S RECYCLING TIMES. (US/1042-0614). **2246**

WASTE BUSINESS WEST. (CN/1185-4731). **2246**

WASTE MANAGEMENT & ENVIRONMENT. (AT). **Adv Mgr:** D. Williams, **Tel** 02 555 1944. **2246**

WASTE PLANNING. (UK/0965-3147). **Adv Mgr:** Liz Harrison, **Tel** 0609-748709. **2246**

WASTES MANAGEMENT. (UK). **Adv Mgr:** Jennie Harris. **2246**

WATAUGA DEMOCRAT. (US/0745-1903). **5724**

WATCH & CLOCK REVIEW. (US/0279-6198). **2916**

WATCH REVIEW. (HK). **2916**

WATER, AIR, AND SOIL POLLUTION. (NE/0049-6979). **2247**

WATER AND ENVIRONMENTAL MANAGEMENT : JOURNAL OF THE INSTITUTION OF WATER AND ENVIRONMENTAL MANAGEMENT. (UK/0951-7359). **2247**

WATER AND WASTES DIGEST. (US/0043-1141). **5542**

WATER & WASTEWATER DIGEST. (US/0748-2612). **2247**

WATER & WASTEWATER INTERNATIONAL. (US/0891-5385). **5542**

WATER CONDITIONING & PURIFICATION. (US/0746-4029). **5542**

WATER ENGINEERING & MANAGEMENT. (US/0273-2238). **2096**

WATER ENVIRONMENT & TECHNOLOGY. (US/1044-9493). **2247**

WATER EQUIPMENT NEWS. (US/0194-1194). **5542**

WATER LAW. (UK/0959-9754). **5543**

WATER NEWS (CAMBRIDGE). (CN/0821-0233). **5543**

WATER POLLUTION CONTROL ASSOCIATION OF PENNSYLVANIA MAGAZINE. (US/0890-4553). **2247**

WATER RESOURCES BULLETIN (URBANA). (US/0043-1370). **5544**

WATER RESOURCES DATA FOR MINNESOTA. (US/0364-4383). **5544**

WATER RESOURCES MANAGEMENT (DORDRECHT, NETHERLANDS). (NE/0920-4741). **5547**

WATER RESOURCES MONOGRAPH. (US/0270-9600). **5547**

WATER RESOURCES RESEARCH. (US/0043-1397). **5547**

WATER S. A. (SA/0378-4738). **5547**

WATER SCOOTER. (US/0899-9775). **596**

WATER SERVICES. (UK/0301-7028). **2248**

WATER SKIER (WINTER HAVEN), THE. (US/0049-7002). **4928**

WATER SUPPLY. (UK/0735-1917). **5548**

WATER TECHNOLOGY. (US/0192-3633). **5548**

WATER TREATMENT. (CC/0921-2639). **5548**

WATER WELL JOURNAL. (US/0043-1443). **5548**

WATERBULLETIN. (UK/0262-9909). **5548**

WATERBURY REPUBLICAN-AMERICAN. (US). **4500**

WATERFRONT NEWS. (US/8756-0038). **596**

WATERFRONT WORLD. (US/0733-0677). **2839**

WATERLINES. (UK/0262-8104). **5548**

WATERLOO CHRONICLE. (CN). **Adv Mgr:** Bill Karges. **5797**

WATERSCHAPSBELANGEN. (NE/0043-1486). **5548**

WATERSKI (WINTER PARK, FLA.). (US/0883-7813). **4929**

WATERTOWN PUBLIC OPINION. (US). **Adv Mgr:** Almon W. Johnson, **Tel** (605)886-6901. **5744**

WATERWAY GUIDE. NORTHERN EDITION. (US/0090-712X). **597**

WATERWAYS JOURNAL, THE. (US/0043-1524). **5399**

WATERWORLD NEWS. (US/0747-9735). **2248**

WATFORD BUSINESS DIRECTORY. (UK/0957-1124). **719**

WATHENA — Advertising Accepted Index

WATHENA TIMES, THE FRIDAY TROY REPUBLICAN, THE. (US). **5679**

WATKINS REVIEW & EXPRESS, THE. (US/1041-6250). **Adv Mgr:** Joe Fazzary. **5722**

WATSONVILLE REGISTER-PAJARONIAN. (US). **5641**

WAUPACA COUNTY POST. (US). **Adv Mgr:** Tim Williams. **5771**

WAUSAU DAILY HERALD. (US/0887-4271). **Adv Mgr:** Vic Brakinder, **Tel** (715)845-0622. **5771**

WAVE. (US). **Adv Mgr:** Susan Lyons. **5647**

WAVE (ROCKAWAY BEACH, N.Y.), THE. (US/0882-7028). **Adv Mgr:** Sanford Benstein. **5722**

WAVELENGTH (NEW ORLEANS, LA.). (US/0741-2460). **4158**

WAVERLY GAZETTE (WAVERLY, KAN. : 1898). (US). **Adv Mgr:** B. J. Peterson, **Tel** (316-264-5325. **5679**

WAVES (SPRING VALLEY, CALIF.). (US/1055-0348). **2096**

WAWATAY NEWS. (CN/0703-9387). **2275**

WAY, THE. (UK/0043-1575). **5008**

WAYCROSS JOURNAL-HERALD. (US). **Adv Mgr:** David Tanner. **5655**

WAYNE COUNTY MAIL. (US/0745-7685). **Adv Mgr:** Donna Herzog, **Tel** (716)671-3554. **5722**

WAYNE LAW REVIEW. (US/0043-1621). **3073**

WBAI FOLIO. (US). **1143**

WCA NATIONAL UPDATE. (US). **333**

WDA JOURNAL. (US/1046-9338). **1337**

WEAR. (SZ/0043-1648). **Adv Mgr:** Ms. W van Cattenburch (Amsterdam). **2132**

WEATHER. (UK/0043-1656). **1436**

WEATHER VANE (CHARLESTON, W. VA.), THE. (US/0043-1664). **3871**

WEATHERWISE. (US/0043-1672). **1436**

WEAVER'S (SIOUX FALLS, S.D.). (US/1042-7643). **Adv Mgr:** Karen Bright. **5359**

WEB ABBOTSFORD. (AT/1036-3912). **1908**

WEB OF SPIDER-MAN. (US/0887-9702). **4867**

WEBER STUDIES. (US/0891-8899). **2856**

WEBSTER HERALD, THE. (US/0745-1377). **Adv Mgr:** Greg Rickard. **5722**

WEBSTER PROGRESS-TIMES, THE. (US). **Adv Mgr:** Tim James. **5702**

WEED ABSTRACTS. (UK/0043-1729). **157**

WEED PRESS. (US/1064-6469). **Adv Mgr:** Genny Axtman. **5641**

WEED RESEARCH. (UK/0043-1737). **530**

WEEKENDS. (US). **5499**

WEEKLY BULLETIN - WEEKLY BULLETIN LEATHER SHOE NEWS CO. (US). **3186**

WEEKLY COLLEGIAN. (US). **5740**

WEEKLY INDIA TRIBUNE. (US/0744-4524). **5662**

WEEKLY INSIDERS TURKEY LETTER. (US/0160-4910). **157**

WEEKLY LAW REPORTS. (UK). **3073**

WEEKLY LIVESTOCK REPORTER, THE. (US/0043-1842). **223**

WEEKLY MARKET BULLETIN (CONCORD). (US/0043-1850). **145**

WEEKLY NEWS (MIAMI, FLA.), THE. (US/0199-4395). **2796**

WEEKLY RECORDER, THE. (US). **Adv Mgr:** Susan Burd. **5740**

WEEKLY REGISTER-CALL (CENTRAL CITY, COLO. : 1861). (US). **Adv Mgr:** Debra Soucy, **Tel** (303)582-5395. **5644**

WEEKLY REVIEW, THE. (KE). **4538**

WEEKLY WEATHER AND CROP BULLETIN. (US/0043-1974). **1437**

WEEKLY WESTPORT REPORTER, THE. (US/0738-8055). **5704**

WEEKLY WORLD NEWS. (US/0199-574X). **5651**

WEGEN. (NE/0043-2067). **2033**

WEHRAUSBILDUNG. (GW/0178-3084). **4061**

WEHRMEDIZIN UND WEHRPHARMAZIE. (GW). **4332**

WEHRMEDIZINISCHE MONATSSCHRIFT. (GW/0043-2156). **3650**

WEHRTECHNIK. (GW/0043-2172). **4061**

WEIGHING & MEASUREMENT. (US/0095-537X). **4033**

WEIGHT ENGINEERING. (US). **2001**

WEIGHT WATCHERS. (US/0043-2180). **2602**

WEIGHTWATCHERS. (UK). **4200**

WEIMARER BEITRAEGE. (GW/0323-4223). **Adv Mgr:** Mr. Winkler. **3452**

WEIRD TALES. (US/0898-5073). **Adv Mgr:** Carol Adams. **3452**

WEISER SIGNAL-AMERICAN, THE. (US). **Adv Mgr:** James R. Simpson. **5658**

WEISHENGWUXUE TONGBAO. (CC/0253-2654). **571**

WELDING ABSTRACTS / WELDING INSTITUTE. (UK/0952-0287). **4028**

WELDING AND METAL FABRICATION. (UK/0043-2245). **4028**

WELDING DATA BOOK. (US/0511-4365). **4028**

WELDING DESIGN & FABRICATION. (US/0043-2253). **4028**

WELDING DISTRIBUTOR (1966). (US/0192-7671). **938**

WELDING INTERNATIONAL. (UK/0950-7116). **4028**

WELDING JOURNAL. (US/0043-2296). **4028**

WELEETKAN, THE. (US/0746-4339). **Adv Mgr:** Polly Everett or Ronda Clinesmith. **5733**

WELFARE IN AUSTRALIA. (AT/0310-4869). **5314**

WELFARE MANCHESTER. (UK/0269-879X). **5314**

WELFARE TO WORK. (US/1060-5622). **5314**

WELL SERVICING. (US/0043-2393). **Adv Mgr:** Katherine Leidy, **Tel** (214)692-0771. **4282**

WELLNESS PERSPECTIVES. (US/0748-1764). **4807**

WELLSIAN (EDWALTON, NOTTINGHAMSHIRE : 1976). (UK/0263-1776). **3452**

WELSH JOURNAL OF EDUCATION, THE. (UK/0957-297X). **1791**

WELT DES ISLAMS, DIE. (NE/0043-2539). **5045**

WELTKUNST, DIE. (GW/0043-261X). **368**

WELTMISSION, DIE. (GW/0723-6204). **Adv Mgr:** Eike Rahn. **5008**

WELTMISSION (EVANGELISCHES MISSIONSWERK IN DER BUNDESREPUBLIK DEUTSCHLAND UND BERLIN WEST). (GW/0341-082X). **5008**

WELTWOCHE, DIE. (SZ). **2525**

WELZYNSWEEKBLAD 1981. (NE/0169-0639). **5314**

WEN HSUEH YUEH PAO (CHANG-SHA SHIH, CHINA). (CC). **3452**

WEN HUA YU SHENG HUO. (CC). **2668**

WEN HUI YUEH KAN / WEN HUI YUEH KAN PIEN CHI PU. (CC). **333**

WERELDWIJD. (BE). **Adv Mgr:** Anckaert Goedele. **5009**

WERKBLAD NEDERLANDSE DIDACTIEK. (BE). **1791**

WERKSTOFFE, BETRIEBSLEITUNG + TECHNIK. (GW). **2033**

WESLEYAN ADVOCATE, THE. (US/0043-289X). **5069**

WESLEYAN CHRISTIAN ADVOCATE. (US/0190-6097). **5069**

WESLEYAN THEOLOGICAL JOURNAL. (US/0092-4245). **5009**

WEST AFRICA (LONDON). (UK/0043-2962). **2500**

WEST AFRICAN JOURNAL OF ARCHAEOLOGY. (NR/0083-8160). **285**

WEST AFRICAN JOURNAL OF BIOLOGICAL AND APPLIED CHEMISTRY. (NR/0043-2989). **995**

WEST AFRICAN JOURNAL OF MEDICINE. (NR/0189-160X). **3650**

WEST AFRICAN JOURNAL OF SURGERY. (NR/0331-054X). **3977**

WEST ALLIS STAR. (US). **5772**

WEST BRANCH TIMES (WEST BRANCH, IOWA : 1889). (US). **5673**

WEST ENDER. (CN/0229-6012). **Adv Mgr:** Heidi Franke. **5797**

WEST ESSEX TRIBUNE. (US). **Adv Mgr:** Judith Dressel. **5712**

WEST EUROPEAN POLITICS. (UK/0140-2382). **Adv Mgr:** Anne Kidson. **4500**

WEST HARTFORD NEWS. (US/1057-1272). **Adv Mgr:** Frank Chilinski. **5646**

WEST HAVEN NEWS. (US). **Adv Mgr:** Bill Flaucher. **5646**

WEST HAWAII TODAY. (US/0744-4591). **5656**

WEST INDIAN LAW JOURNAL. (JM/0253-7370). **3073**

WEST INDIAN MEDICAL JOURNAL, THE. (JM/0043-3144). **3650**

WEST KENTUCKY NEWS. (US). **Adv Mgr:** Greg LeNeave. **5683**

WEST OF ENGLAND MEDICAL JOURNAL. (UK). **3650**

WEST ORANGE TIMES. (US). **Adv Mgr:** Andrew Bailey. **5651**

WEST OST JOURNAL. (AU). **4500**

WEST TEXAS HISTORICAL ASSOCIATION YEAR BOOK, THE. (US/0886-6155). **2765**

WEST TOLEDO HERALD. (US/8750-1872). **Adv Mgr:** Thomas Nishwitz. **5731**

WEST VIRGINIA ADVOCATE, THE. (US/0891-9240). **5765**

WEST VIRGINIA BUSINESS INDEX. (US/0195-4644). **719**

WEST VIRGINIA COAL BELL. (US). **2153**

WEST VIRGINIA HILLBILLY (RICHWOOD, W.VA. : 1986). (US/0888-0409). **5765**

WEST VIRGINIA HILLS & STREAMS. (US/0279-0580). **2208**

WEST VIRGINIA LAW REVIEW. (US/0043-3268). **3073**

WEST VIRGINIA LIBRARIES. (US/0043-3276). **Adv Mgr:** Judy Duncan, **Tel** (304)722-4244. **3256**

WEST VIRGINIA MANUFACTURERS REGISTER. (US/0893-2824). **3489**

WEST VIRGINIA MEDICAL JOURNAL. (US/0043-3284). **Adv Mgr:** Michelle Young. **3650**

WEST VIRGINIA SCHOOL JOURNAL (1990). (US/1056-733X). **1791**

WESTAF'S NATIONAL ARTS JOB BANK. (US/1046-7718). **333**

WESTBOROUGH NEWS, THE. (US/0893-3782). **5690**

WESTBRIDGE ART MARKET REPORT. (CN/1191-3371). **368**

WESTCHESTER BAR JOURNAL. (US/0746-1844). **3073**

WESTCHESTER FAMILY. (US/1043-6774). **1071**

WESTCHESTER HISTORIAN, THE. (US/0049-7266). **2765**

WESTCHESTER LAW JOURNAL. (US/0049-7274). **3073**

WESTERLY. (AT/0043-342X). **3452**

WESTERLY SUN, THE. (US/1065-1209). **5741**

WESTERN AMERICAN LITERATURE. (US/0043-3462). **3453**

WESTERN & EASTERN TREASURES. (US/0890-0876). **Adv Mgr:** S. Anderson, **Tel** (206)230-9224. **4880**

WESTERN ANGLER. (AT/1035-493X). **Adv Mgr Tel** 09 227 7266. **2316**

WESTERN AUSTRALIA IN BRIEF. (AT/0727-2022). **Adv Mgr:** Tony Stevens. **3073**

WESTERN BIRDS. (US/0160-1121). **Adv Mgr:** Dorothy S. Myers. **5620**

WESTERN CANADA OUTDOORS (ALBERTA EDITION). (CN/0836-446X). **2208**

WESTERN CANADA OUTDOORS (SASKATCHEWAN EDITION). (CN/0836-4451). **2208**

WESTERN CATHOLIC REPORTER. (CN/0512-5235). **5038**

WESTERN CITY (SACRAMENTO, CALIF. : 1976). (US/0279-5337). **Adv Mgr:** J. Flagg. **4694**

WESTERN CLEANER & LAUNDERER. (US/0049-741X). **1031**

WESTERN COLLEGE READING & LEARNING ASSOCIATION NEWSLETTER. (US/0746-1305). **1853**

WESTERN COMMERCE & INDUSTRY MAGAZINE. (CN). **2361**

WESTERN EXPRESS. (US/0510-2332). **2788**

WESTERN FARMER AND GRAZIER. WESTERN FARM WEEKLY. (AT). **145**

WESTERN FLOORS. (US/0049-7398). **Adv Mgr:** Phil Johnson. **2904**

WESTERN FOLKLORE. (US/0043-373X). **2325**

WESTERN GROCER MAGAZINE (1977). (CN/0705-906X). **2361**

WESTERN GROWER & SHIPPER. (US/0043-3799). **Adv Mgr Tel** (510)653-2122. **190**

WESTERN HISTORICAL QUARTERLY. (US/0043-3810). **Adv Mgr:** Barbara Stewart, **Tel** (801)750-1301. **2636**

WESTERN HOG JOURNAL. (CN/0225-3488). **Adv Mgr:** W Toma. **223**

WESTERN HORSEMAN, THE. (US/0043-3837). **2803**

WESTERN HUMANITIES REVIEW. (US/0043-3845). **3453**

WESTERN HVACR NEWS. (US/0273-5687). **Adv Mgr Tel** (213)225-8034. **2608**

WESTERN JOURNAL OF APPLIED FORESTRY. (US/0885-6095). **2398**

WESTERN JOURNAL OF BLACK STUDIES, THE. (US/0197-4327). **2275**

WESTERN JOURNAL OF MEDICINE, THE. (US/0093-0415). **Adv Mgr:** John Cook, **Tel** (415)882-5178. **3650**

WESTERN JOURNAL OF NURSING RESEARCH. (US/0193-9459). **3871**

WESTERN KANSAS WORLD. (US). **Adv Mgr:** Jerry Millard. **5679**

WESTERN LIVING (VANCOUVER ED.). (CN/0824-0604). **Adv Mgr:** Janet McDonald. **2904**

WESTERN METALWORKING DIRECTORY. (US). **4023**

WESTERN MINING DIRECTORY. (US/0162-9026). **2153**

WESTERN MINING NEWS. (US/0300-662X). **919**

WESTERN NEW YORK. (US/0149-5070). **719**

WESTERN NEW YORK FAMILY MAGAZINE. (US). **Adv Mgr:** Doug Carpenter. **2286**

WESTERN NEWS (LIBBY, MONT.), THE. (US/0745-0362). **5706**

WESTERN NEWS (LONDON). (CN/0316-8654). **Adv Mgr:** Chris Amyot. **1853**

WESTERN OIL WORLD. (US/0884-7592). **4282**

WESTERN OUTDOOR NEWS. (US/0049-7479). **4880**

WESTERN OUTDOORS. (US/0043-4000). **4880**

WESTERN PETROLEUM REGISTER. (US/0273-1762). **4282**

WESTERN PLANNER, THE. (US/0279-0602). **4695**

WESTERN POLITICAL QUARTERLY, THE. (US/0043-4078). **4500**

WESTERN PRODUCER. (CN/0043-4094). **146**

WESTERN QUEENS GAZETTE, THE. (US). **Adv Mgr:** Tony Brasamian. **5722**

WESTERN RACING NEWS. (US/0510-2626). **5428**

WESTERN RECORDER (MIDDLETOWN). (US/0043-4132). **Adv Mgr Tel** (502)244-6473. **5009**

WESTERN RIDER (1987). (CN/0820-571X). **2803**

WESTERN ROOFING INSULATION AND SIDING. (US/0164-5803). **631**

WESTERN SKIER. (CN/1184-2679). **4929**

WESTERN SPORTSMAN. (CN/0709-1532). **4929**

WESTERN STAR (BESSEMER, ALA.), THE. (US/0889-0080). **Adv Mgr:** Cathy Calure. **5628**

WESTERN STATE UNIVERSITY LAW REVIEW. (US/0362-8892). **Adv Mgr:** Debora Paul. **3073**

WESTERN TIMES (SHARON SPRINGS, KAN. : 1934). (US). **Adv Mgr:** Jackie Walker or Julie Samuelson. **5679**

WESTERN VIKING. (US). **2275**

WESTERN WEEKLY REPORTS. (CN/0049-7525). **3074**

WESTERN WHEEL. (CN/0701-1571). **2550**

WESTFALEN (MUNSTER). (GW/0043-4337). **2715**

WESTFIELD LEADER, THE. (US). **5712**

WESTINDIAN DIGEST. (UK/0143-6619). **2525**

WESTINE REPORT. (US/0749-6990). **Adv Mgr:** David Wright, **Tel** (414)763-3511. **5772**

WESTLAKER TIMES, THE. (US/0746-9802). **Adv Mgr:** Eleaner J. Gottschaek. **5731**

WESTMINISTER WINDOW. (US). **Adv Mgr:** Scott Bumgardner. **5644**

WESTMINSTER STUDIES IN EDUCATION. (UK/0140-6728). **1791**

WESTON DEMOCRAT, THE. (US). **Adv Mgr:** Julia Spelsberg. **5765**

WESTON FORUM, THE. (US). **Adv Mgr:** Jim DeFillipo. **5646**

WESTOSHA REPORT. (US/0192-9356). **Adv Mgr:** David Wright. **5772**

WESTPREUSSEN-JAHRBUCH. (GW/0511-8484). **2715**

WESTSIDE GAZETTE. THURSDAY. (US). **Adv Mgr:** Sonia Henry, **Tel** (305)523-5115. **5651**

WESTSIDE MESSENGER. (US/0891-2297). **Adv Mgr:** Bruce Russel. **5731**

WESTVILLE INDICATOR. (US). **5668**

WESTWARD INTO NEBRASKA. (US/0738-0380). **2477**

WESTWAYS. (US/0043-4434). **Adv Mgr:** S. Kilets, **Tel** (213)741-4765. **5428**

WESTWIND (LOS ANGELES, CALIF.). (US/0508-6191). **333**

WESTWORD. (US/0194-7710). **Adv Mgr:** Amy Cobb. **5644**

WESTWORD (EDMONTON). (CN/1184-678X). **Adv Mgr:** Darlene Diver. **2925**

WESTWORLD MAGAZINE (BRITISH COLUMBIA ED.). (CN/0843-3356). **2495**

WETENSCHAP EN SAMENLEVING. (NE/0043-4442). **146**

WETENSCHAPPELIJKE TIJDINGEN. (BE). **2715**

WETHERSFIELD POST. (US). **Adv Mgr:** Frank Chilinski. **5646**

WETTBEWERB IN RECHT UND PRAXIS : WRP. (GW/0172-049X). **3104**

WETTER UND LEBEN. (AU/0043-4450). **1437**

WETUMPKA HERALD, THE. (US). **Adv Mgr:** JoAnn Lambert, **Tel** (205)567-2266. **5628**

WFCD COMMUNICATOR. (CN/0822-8183). **146**

WFS QUARTERLY. (US/1071-1767). **2293**

WHALEWATCHER. (US/0273-4419). **5600**

WHARTON JOURNAL-SPECTATOR, THE. (US/1076-7266). **Adv Mgr:** Missy Justice. **5756**

WHAT CAR?. (UK). **5428**

WHAT THEY SAID. (US/0512-5804). **2633**

WHAT'S BREWING. (CN/0714-2056). **2372**

WHAT'S BREWING?. (US/0279-9707). **4929**

WHAT'S NEW IN COMPUTING. (SI). **1245**

WHAT'S NEW IN FARMING. (UK). **146**

WHAT'S NEW IN HOME ECONOMICS. (US/0043-4590). **2793**

WHAT'S ON VIDEO AND CINEMA. (AT). **4378**

WHEAT, BARLEY AND TRITICALE ABSTRACTS. (UK/0265-7880). **157**

WHEAT GROWER (WASHINGTON, D.C.), THE. (US/0882-9691). **146**

WHEAT LIFE. (US/0043-4701). **146**

WHEAT RIDGE JEFFERSON SENTINEL, THE. (US/1060-5223). **5644**

WHEEL-O-RAMA. (US/0882-6676). **5428**

WHEELERS RV RESORT & CAMPGROUND GUIDE. (US/0194-0384). **Adv Mgr:** Kevin Dempsey. **4880**

WHEELING NEWS-REGISTER. (US). **Adv Mgr:** Robert Diehl. **5765**

WHEELS OF TIME. (US/0738-565X). **5399**

WHERE CALGARY. (CN/1182-1981). **4867**

WHERE TO GO IN MINNEAPOLIS & ST. PAUL. (US/0739-9693). **5499**

WHERE TO LEARN ENGLISH IN GREAT BRITAIN. (UK/0143-2214). **3333**

WHERE TO STAY IN SCOTLAND, BED AND BREAKFAST. (UK). **2810**

WHICH COMPUTER?. (UK/0140-3435). **1207**

WHIDBEY NEWS-TIMES. (US/1060-7161). **Adv Mgr:** M. Smith. **5763**

WHISKEY, WOMEN, AND ... . (US/0091-7664). **4159**

WHISPERING WIND. (US/0300-6565). **2275**

WHISTLE PUNK. (CN/0825-477X). **2398**

WHISTLER QUESTION. (CN/0383-820X). **5797**

WHITBY FREE PRESS. (CN/0844-398X). **5797**

WHITBY FREE PRESS. (CN/0844-398X). **5797**

WHITE BEAR PRESS, THE. (US/0892-1326). **Adv Mgr:** Michelle Larson. **5699**

WHITE COUNTY RECORD (JUDSONIA, ARK.). (US/8750-5177). **5632**

WHITE HOUSE NEWS PHOTOGRAPHERS ANNUAL AWARDS. (US/0163-3430). **4378**

WHITE LEADER, THE. (US/0899-9805). **5744**

WHITE LIGHT, THE. (US/0742-8820). **4243**

WHITE RIVER JOURNAL. (US). **Adv Mgr:** Dean Walls. **5632**

WHITE ROCKER (1990), THE. (US/1049-3387). **Adv Mgr:** Frances, **Tel** (214)327-9336. **5756**

WHITE TOPS, THE. (US/0043-499X). **4867**

WHITE WOLF MAGAZINE. (US/0897-9391). **4867**

WHITECOURT STAR. (CN/0847-8597). **5798**

WHITESBORO NEWS-RECORD. (US). **5756**

WHITEWALLS (CHICAGO, ILL.). (US/0190-9835). **368**

WHITEWRIGHT SUN, THE. (US). **Adv Mgr:** Clara Combs, **Tel** (903)364-2276. **5756**

WHITTIER LAW REVIEW. (US/0195-7643). **Adv Mgr:** T. Jeha. **3075**

WHO MAKES MACHINERY IN GERMANY. (GW). **Adv Mgr:** Thomas Wengenroth. **2132**

WHO OWNS WHAT IN WORLD BANKING. (UK). **816**

WHOLE AGAIN RESOURCE GUIDE, THE. (US/0734-9033). **5265**

WHOLE FOODS. (US/0193-1504). **2361**

WHOLE LIFE. (US/0888-2061). **4807**

WHOLE LIFE TIMES. (US/0279-5604). **4200**

WHOLESALE DRUGS MAGAZINE. (US/0743-3778). **4332**

WHOLESALER (ELMHURST), THE. (US/0032-1680). **2609**

WHO'S MAILING WHAT!. (US/8755-2671). **767**

WHO'S WHO, CHICANO OFFICEHOLDERS. (US/0738-4637). **436**

WHO'S WHO - COMMONWEALTH BROADCASTING ASSOCIATION. (UK). **Adv Mgr:** Derek Inall, **Tel** 011 44 462 684231. **1143**

WHO'S WHO IN DENTAL TECHNOLOGY. (US). **1337**

WHO'S WHO IN FRANCE. (FR/0083-9531). **437**

WHO'S WHO IN INDIAN SCIENCE. (II). **437**

WHO'S WHO IN LANDSCAPE CONTRACTING (1979). (US/0730-7225). **2433**

WHO'S WHO IN LIVE ANIMAL TRADE & TRANSPORT. (US/1042-2633). **224**

WHO'S WHO IN P/M. (US/0361-6304). **437**

WHO'S WHO IN SPECIAL LIBRARIES. (US/0278-842X). **437**

WHO'S WHO IN THE DENTAL LABORATORY INDUSTRY. (US/0195-6221). **1337**

WHO'S WHO IN THE EMERGENCY & RESCUE SERVICES. (UK). **4807**

WHO'S WHO IN THE FISH INDUSTRY. (US/0270-160X). **2316**

WHO'S WHO IN THE FISH INDUSTRY, CANADA. (US/1040-7804). **2316**

WHO'S WHO IN THE MOTION PICTURE INDUSTRY. (US/0278-6516). **438**

WHO'S WHO IN THE PICTURE FRAMING INDUSTRY. (US/0147-2119). **438**

WHO'S WHO IN TRAINING AND DEVELOPMENT. (US/0092-4598). **438**

WHO'S WHO (LONDON. 1849). (UK/0083-937X). **438**

WIADOMOSCI INSTYTUTU METEOROLOGII I GOSPODARKI WODNEJ. (PL/0208-6263). **1437**

WIADOMOSCI STATYSTYCZNE (WARSAW, POLAND : 1956). (PL). **5346**

WIBAUX PIONEER-GAZETTE, THE. (US). **Adv Mgr:** F. Datta, **Tel** (406)795-2218. **5706**

WICAZO SA REVIEW. (US/0749-6427). **2766**

WICHITA BUSINESS JOURNAL. (US/0894-4032). **720**

WICHITA COMMERCE. (US/1048-8782). **857**

WICHITA JOURNAL. (US/1048-3365). **Adv Mgr:** Faye Osenbaugh. **5679**

WIDE ANGLE. (US/0160-6840). **4080**

WIDE SMILES. (US/1056-7402). **5314**

WIEL. (SA/0257-5426). **5428**

WIENER BEITRAEGE ZUR ENGLISCHEN PHILOLOGIE. (AU/0083-9914). **3333**

WIENER GESCHICHTSBLATTER. (AU/0043-5317). **2716**

WIENER HUMANISTISCHE BLATTER. (AU/0083-9965). **1081**

WIENER JAHRBUCH FUR PHILOSOPHIE. (AU/0083-999X). **4365**

WIENER — Advertising Accepted Index

WIENER MEDIZINISCHE WOCHENSCHRIFT. (AU/0043-5341). **3651**

WIENER STUDIEN. (AU/0084-005X). **3333**

WIENER STUDIEN. (AU). **2716**

WIENER TIERARZTLICHE MONATSSCHRIFT. (AU/0043-535X). **5527**

WIENER VOLKERKUNDLICHE MITTEILUNGEN. (AU/0084-0068). **247**

WIENER ZEITSCHRIFT FUER DIE KUNDE DES MORGENLANDES. (AU/0084-0076). **2633**

WILBUR REGISTER, THE. (US). **Adv Mgr:** Karen Tilson. **5763**

WILCOX PROGRESSIVE ERA. (US). **Adv Mgr:** Melissa Dove. **5628**

WILD EARTH. (US/1055-1166). **Adv Mgr:** Tom Butler. **2183**

WILDERNESS. (AT). **2208**

WILDERNESS ALBERTA. (CN/0830-8284). **2209**

WILDERNESS MEDICINE LETTER : THE OFFICIAL NEWSLETTER OF THE WILDERNESS MEDICAL SOCIETY. (US). **3651**

WILDERNESS RECORD. (US/0194-3030). **2209**

WILDERNESS (WASHINGTON, D.C.). (US/0736-6477). **2209**

WILDFLOWER. (CN/0842-5132). **2209**

WILDFLOWER (AUSTIN, TEX. 1984). (US/0898-8803). **Adv Mgr:** Tela Mange. **530**

WILDFOWL (ADEL, IOWA). (US/0886-0637). **Adv Mgr:** Mary Stearns, **Tel** same as publisher. **4880**

WILDFOWL CARVING AND COLLECTING. (US/0886-3407). **Adv Mgr:** Diana Marcum. **376**

WILDLIFE ART NEWS. (US/0746-9640). **368**

WILDLIFE AUSTRALIA. (AT/0043-5481). **2209**

WILDLIFE COLLECTABLES JOURNAL, THE. (CN/0827-2409). **2209**

WILDLIFE HARVEST. (US/0886-3458). **4880**

WILDLIFE JOURNAL. (US/0893-6560). **2209**

WILDLIFE REHABILITATION TODAY. (US/1044-2618). **227**

WILDLIFE RESEARCH. (AT/1035-3712). **5600**

WILKAMITE RECORD, THE. (US). **5702**

WILLAMETTE LAW REVIEW. (US/0191-9822). **Adv Mgr Tel** (503)370-6300 Ext. 4343. **3075**

WILLAMETTE WEEK. (US). **Adv Mgr:** Meeker, **Tel** (503)243-2122. **5734**

WILLAPA HARBOR HERALD, THE. (US/1065-3805). **5763**

WILLIAM AND MARY LAW REVIEW. (US/0043-5589). **3075**

WILLIAM AND MARY QUARTERLY, THE. (US/0043-5597). **2766**

WILLIAM CARLOS WILLIAMS REVIEW. (US/0196-6286). **3356**

WILLIAM MITCHELL LAW REVIEW. (US/0270-272X). **3075**

WILLIAMS NEWS. (US). **Adv Mgr:** Joyce McNelly. **5630**

WILLIAMSON COUNTY SUN, THE. (US). **Adv Mgr:** Mike Winton. **5756**

WILLIAMSPORT SUN-GAZETTE. (US/1056-3083). **Adv Mgr:** John Yahner. **5740**

WILLOW TRANSFER QUARTERLY. (CN/0826-2098). **2595**

WILLOWS JOURNAL. (US). **Adv Mgr:** Patricia Begrin, **Tel** (916)934-6804. **5641**

WILMINGTON JOURNAL (WILMINGTON, N.C.), THE. (US/0049-7649). **Adv Mgr:** Gwendolyn Hamilton. **5724**

WILMOT ENTERPRISE, THE. (US). **5744**

WILSHIRE CENTER'S LARCHMONT CHRONICLE. (US/0192-1932). **Adv Mgr:** Dawne P. Goodwin. **5641**

WILSON LIBRARY BULLETIN. (US/0043-5651). **Adv Mgr:** Raissa Fomerand (Advertising sales director), **Tel** (914)834-2400 or FAX (914)834-2562. **3256**

WILSON QUARTERLY (WASHINGTON), THE. (US/0363-3276). **2495**

WILTON BULLETIN. (US). **Adv Mgr:** Jim DeFillipo. **5646**

WIN NEWS. (US/0145-7985). **5568**

WINCHESTER STAR (WINCHESTER, VA.). (US/1064-0665). **Adv Mgr:** Jerry Howard, **Tel** (800)296-8639. **5760**

WINCHESTER SUN (WINCHESTER, KY. : 1912). (US). **Adv Mgr:** Ann Laurence. **5683**

WIND ENERGY ABSTRACTS. (US/0277-2140). **1960**

WIND ENERGY NEWS. (US/0886-2818). **1960**

WIND ENERGY REPORT. (US/0162-8623). **1960**

WIND ENGINEERING. (UK/0309-524X). **1437**

WINDER NEWS, THE. (US). **Adv Mgr:** Debbie Burgamy. **5655**

WINDIRECTIONS. (UK/0950-0642). **1960**

WINDMILL HERALD. (CN/0712-6417). **5798**

WINDOW FASHIONS. (US/0886-9669). **Adv Mgr:** Dori Michard. **2904**

WINDOWS KONKRET. (GW). **1207**

WINDOWS MAGAZINE. (FR). **2904**

WINDOWS SHOPPER'S GUIDE, THE. (US/1049-071X). **Adv Mgr:** Jolene Andoniodis, **Tel** (503)629-5612. **1207**

WINDOWS USER. (US/1065-3481). **1207**

WINDPOWER MONTHLY. (DK/0109-7318). **1960**

WINDRIDER. (US/0279-4659). **4929**

WINDS OF CHANGE (BOULDER, COLO.). (US/0888-8612). **Adv Mgr:** B. Wakshul, **Tel** (303)443-2270. **5169**

WINDSCRIPT. (CN/0822-2363). **3453**

WINDSOR JOURNAL, THE. (US). **Adv Mgr:** Frank Chilinski. **5646**

WINDSOR LOCKS JOURNAL, THE. (US). **Adv Mgr:** Frank Chilinski. **5647**

WINDSOR THIS MONTH. (CN/0318-2460). **2550**

WINDSPEAKER. (CN/0834-177X). **Adv Mgr:** Cliff. **5798**

WINDSPORT. (CN/0826-5003). **4929**

WINDSURF MAGAZINE. (UK). **Adv Mgr:** Jim Peskett. **597**

WINDSURFING CALIFORNIA. (US/1063-8172). **Adv Mgr:** Marie Cordell. **4929**

WINE & SPIRITS (BERKELEY, CALIF.). (US/0890-0299). **Adv Mgr:** Michael Kinney, **Tel** (415)255-9659. **2372**

WINE EAST. (US/0892-662X). **2372**

WINE INVESTOR. EXECUTIVE EDITION, THE. (US/0889-4256). **2372**

WINE NEWS (CORAL GABLES, FLA.), THE. (US/1065-4895). **2372**

WINE NEWS, THE. (US). **Adv Mgr:** Elizabeth Kuehner, **Tel** (303)444-6110. **2372**

WINE PRODUCTION, AUSTRALIA AND STATES / AUSTRALIAN BUREAU OF STATISTICS. (AT). **2362**

WINE SPECTATOR, THE. (US/0193-497X). **2372**

WINE TIDINGS. (CN/0228-6157). **2372**

WINE WORLD. (US/0199-7483). **2373**

WINES AND VINES. (US/0043-583X). **2373**

WINES & VINES. BUYER'S GUIDE ISSUE. (US/0043-583X). **2373**

WINESBURG EAGLE, THE. (US/0147-3166). **439**

WINESTATE. (AT/0156-6490). **Adv Mgr:** P. Simic. **2373**

WING & SHOT. (US/0892-1849). **Adv Mgr:** Mary Stearns, **Tel** same as publisher. **4880**

WING WORLD. (US/0745-273X). **4083**

WINGING IT. (US/1042-511X). **Adv Mgr:** Susanna Lawson, **Tel** (804)983-3021. **5600**

WINGS (CALGARY). (CN/0701-1369). **39**

WINGS OF ALOHA. (US). **39**

WINGS OF GOLD (PENSACOLA, FLA.). (US/0274-7405). **Adv Mgr:** Nancy Fullen. **39**

WINGTIPS (LANSING, N.Y.). (US/8756-4505). **5600**

WINNING (TULSA, OKLA.). (US/0744-2467). **4867**

WINNIPEG FREE PRESS. (CN/0828-1785). **5798**

WINNIPEG MAGAZINE. (CN/0707-6185). **2550**

WINNIPEG SUN (1980). (CN/0711-3773). **5798**

WINSTON CUP ILLUSTRATED. (US/1048-6119). **Adv Mgr:** Zeta Smith, **Tel** (704)786-7131. **4930**

WINSTON CUP SCENE. (US/1053-461X). **Adv Mgr:** Zeta Smith, **Tel** (704)786-7131. **4930**

WINSTON-SALEM CHRONICLE. (US). **Adv Mgr:** Mike Pitt. **5724**

WINSTON-SALEM JOURNAL. (US). **5724**

WINSTON-SALEM MAGAZINE. (US/8755-9587). **Adv Mgr:** Jennifer Valentine, **Tel** (910)722-8706. **2550**

WINTER HAVEN DAILY NEWS-CHIEF. (US). **Adv Mgr:** Rick Etzkorn. **5651**

WINTER PARK-MAITLAND OBSERVER. (US/1064-3613). **Adv Mgr:** G. Munster. **5651**

WINTER PARK OUTLOOK. (US/0745-9203). **5651**

WIRE INDUSTRY. (UK/0043-6011). **2086**

WIRE JOURNAL INTERNATIONAL. (US/0277-4275). **4023**

WIRE (LONDON, ENGLAND). (UK/0952-0686). **4159**

WIRE ROPE NEWS & SLING TECHNOLOGY. (US/0740-1809). **Adv Mgr:** Ed Bluvias. **3489**

WIRE TECHNOLOGY INTERNATIONAL. (US/0898-9850). **4023**

WIRE WORLD INTERNATIONAL. (GW/0043-6046). **2086**

WIRED (SAN FRANCISCO, CALIF.). (US/1059-1028). **Adv Mgr:** Kathleen Lyman. **1207**

WIRELESS FOR THE CORPORATE USER. (US). **1169**

WIREWORLD. (GW/0934-5906). **2001**

WIRTSCHAFT UND GESELLSCHAFT. (AU/0378-5130). **1588**

WIRTSCHAFT UND WETTBEWERB. (GW/0043-6151). **857**

WIRTSCHAFTSDIENST (HAMBURG). (GW/0043-6275). **1526**

WIRTSCHAFTSINFORMATIK. (GW/0937-6429). **1263**

WIRTSCHAFTSPRUFUNG, DIE. (GW/0043-6313). **753**

WIRTSCHAFTSRECHT. (GW/0512-6320). **Adv Mgr:** Mr. Kassner, **Tel** (030)4287323. **3104**

WIRTSCHAFTSSCHUTZ + SICHERHEITSTECHNIK. (GW/0173-3303). **3179**

WISCONSERVATION. (US/0164-3649). **2210**

WISCONSIN AGRICULTURIST. (US/0043-6356). **146**

WISCONSIN ARBORIST, THE. (US/0887-8927). **Adv Mgr:** David Eastman, **Tel** 471-8420. **2183**

WISCONSIN ARCHITECT. (US). **310**

WISCONSIN CHINA SERIES. (US/0084-053X). **3453**

WISCONSIN COUNTIES. (US/0749-6818). **4695**

WISCONSIN ENGINEER. (US/0043-6453). **2001**

WISCONSIN GOLF. (US/1042-6620). **4930**

WISCONSIN HOLSTEIN NEWS. (US/0194-4401). **199**

WISCONSIN HOME GALLERY MAGAZINE. (US/0888-6822). **Adv Mgr:** Dick Strauss. **2904**

WISCONSIN JEWISH CHRONICLE, THE. (US/0043-6488). **Adv Mgr:** Joni Oxmoor. **5053**

WISCONSIN LAW REVIEW. (US/0043-650X). **3075**

WISCONSIN LAWYER. (US/1043-0490). **4695**

WISCONSIN MANUFACTURERS REGISTER. (US/0738-0070). **3489**

WISCONSIN MASTER PLUMBER. (US/0199-1639). **2609**

WISCONSIN MEDICAL JOURNAL. (US/0043-6542). **Adv Mgr:** Lynne Bjorgo. **3651**

WISCONSIN NEWMONTH. (US/1059-0935). **2550**

WISCONSIN PHARMACIST, THE. (US/0043-6585). **4332**

WISCONSIN REALTOR, THE. (US/0279-2583). **4848**

WISCONSIN REC NEWS. (US). **1543**

WISCONSIN RESTAURATEUR, THE. (US/0274-7472). **Adv Mgr:** Kerry Koppen. **5073**

WISCONSIN SCHOOL MUSICIAN, THE. (US/0043-6658). **Adv Mgr:** Ms. Pharo. **4159**

WISCONSIN SCHOOL NEWS. (US). **1874**

WISCONSIN SILENT SPORTS. (US/0882-9640). **4930**

WISCONSIN SMALL BUSINESS COUNSELOR. (US/0897-5116). **889**

WISCONSIN SOCIOLOGIST, THE. (US/0043-6666). **5265**

WISCONSIN SPORTSMAN. (US/0361-9451). **4880**

WISCONSIN TRAILS. (US/0095-4314). **2550**

WISCONSIN WOOD MARKETING BULLETIN. (US). **2405**

WISCONSIN WOODS & WATER. (US/1041-1291). **4881**

WISDEN'S CRICKETERS ALMANAC. (UK). **Adv Mgr:** Colin Ackehurst. **4930**

WISE WOMAN, THE. (US/0883-119X). **5568**

WISENET. (AT/0815-0753). **5568**

WISSENSCHAFT UND WEISHEIT. (GW/0043-678X). **5009**

WISSENSCHAFTLICHE ZEITSCHRIFT DER UNIVERSITAT ROSTOCK. NATURWISSENSCHAFTLICHE REIHE. (GW/0863-1204). **5170**

WISTRA. (GW/0721-6890). **3109**

WITHOUT PREJUDICE. (US/0892-9408). **4514**

WITHOUT PREJUDICE (EDMONTON). (CN/0706-5574). **2896**

WITNESS (FARMINGTON HILLS, MICH.). (US/0891-1371). **3453**

WITTYWORLD. (US/0892-9807). **Adv Mgr:** same as editor. **376**

WIZARD: THE GUIDE TO COMICS. (US). **Adv Mgr:** Colin Campbell, **Tel** (212)265-0986. **2779**

WLW JOURNAL. (US/0272-1996). **3256**

WNC BUSINESS JOURNAL. (US/1049-7145). **723**

WOCHE IN AUSTRALIEN, DIE. (AT). **5777**

WOCHENBLATT FUER PAPIERFABRIKATION. (GW/0043-7131). **4240**

WOHNBAUFORSCHUNG IN OSTERREICH. (AU). **2839**

WOLFENBUTTELER NOTIZEN ZUR BUCHGESCHICHTE. (GW/0341-2253). **4833**

WOLFENBUTTELER RENAISSANCE MITTEILUNGEN. (GW/0342-4340). **2716**

WOLGAN KONSOL. (KO). **311**

WOLGAN KWAHAK. (CH). **Adv Mgr:** Mr. Lee Wen Lung. **5170**

WOLSLEY BULLETIN, THE. (CN/0842-084X). **Adv Mgr:** E. Dahlman. **5798**

WOLVES AND RELATED CANIDS. (US/0899-9317). **5600**

WOMAN ACTIVIST, THE. (US/0049-7770). **4500**

WOMAN ALIVE. (UK/0962-2152). **Adv Mgr:** Steven Bayes. **5009**

WOMAN BOWLER, THE. (US/0043-7255). **Adv Mgr:** Leslie Smith, **Tel** (414)421-9000. **4930**

WOMAN ENGINEER. (GREENLAWN, N.Y.), THE. (US/0887-2120). **2001**

WOMAN ENGINEER, THE. (UK). **2001**

WOMAN LOCALLY. (US/0163-3244). **5569**

WOMAN OF POWER. (US/0743-2356). **5569**

WOMANIST (OTTAWA). (CN/0849-4975). **5569**

WOMAN'S ART JOURNAL. (US/0270-7993). **368**

WOMAN'S DAY. (US/0043-7336). **5569**

WOMAN'S ENTERPRI$E. (US/0898-6126). **5569**

WOMAN'S WORLD (ENGLEWOOD, N.J.). (US/0272-961X). **5569**

WOMANSPEAK. (AT/0311-8479). **5569**

WOMBAT. (US). **1071**

WOMEN. (UK/0957-4042). **5569**

WOMEN & CRIMINAL JUSTICE. (US/0897-4454). **3179**

WOMEN AND ENVIRONMENTS. (CN/0229-480X). **Adv Mgr:** Kim Pearson. **5569**

WOMEN & GUNS. (US/1045-7704). **5569**

WOMEN & HEALTH. (US/0363-0242). **3769**

WOMEN & PERFORMANCE. (US/0740-770X). **5372**

WOMEN & POLITICS. (US/0195-7732). **4500**

WOMEN & THERAPY. (US/0270-3149). **5569**

WOMEN ARTISTS NEWS. (US/0149-7081). **333**

WOMEN IN BUSINESS (KANSAS CITY, MO.). (US/0043-7441). **Adv Mgr:** Lynn Weddle-Judkins. **723**

WOMEN IN MANAGEMENT. (CN/1185-4863). **889**

WOMEN IN NATURAL RESOURCES. (US). **5570**

WOMEN IN THE ARTS BULLETIN. (US). **369**

WOMEN LAWYERS' JOURNAL. (US/0043-7468). **3076**

WOMEN LIKE ME. (CN/0821-4794). **723**

WOMEN POLICE MAGAZINE. (US). **3179**

WOMEN UNLIMITED. (US). **5570**

WOMEN WITH WHEELS. (US/1043-979X). **5428**

WOMEN'S & CHILDREN'S WEAR AND FASHION ACCESSORIES BUYERS. (US/0741-0735). **1088**

WOMEN'S ART MAGAZINE. (UK). **369**

WOMENS ART REGISTER BULLETIN. (AT). **333**

WOMEN'S CIRCLE. (US/0509-089X). **5186**

WOMENS CIRCLE CROCHET. (US/0279-1978). **5186**

WOMEN'S FASTPITCH WORLD. (US/0899-5508). **4930**

WOMEN'S HOUSEHOLD. (US/0510-7385). **5571**

WOMEN'S HOUSEHOLD CROCHET. (US/0745-0575). **5186**

WOMEN'S LARGE & HALF SIZE SPECIALTY STORES. (US/0743-3972). **1088**

WOMEN'S LEAGUE OUTLOOK. (US/0043-7557). **5053**

WOMEN'S QUARTERLY REVIEW. (US/0882-1135). **5571**

WOMEN'S RECORD, THE. (US/0888-4609). **5571**

WOMEN'S REVIEW OF BOOKS, THE. (US/0738-1433). **3356**

WOMEN'S RIGHTS LAW REPORTER. (US/0085-8269). **3076**

WOMEN'S SPORTS AND FITNESS. (US/8750-653X). **4930**

WOMEN'S STUDIES. (US/0049-7878). **5571**

WOMEN'S STUDIES INTERNATIONAL FORUM. (UK/0277-5395). **5571**

WOMEN'S STUDIES JOURNAL. (NZ). **5571**

WOMEN'S STUDIES QUARTERLY. (US/0732-1562). **Adv Mgr:** S. Cozzi, **Tel** (212) 360-5790. **5571**

WOMEN'S TRAVELLER. (US). **5499**

WOMENWISE. (US/0890-9695). **4808**

WOOD DESIGN FOCUS. (US). **Adv Mgr:** Jennifer McBlaine, **Tel** (503)228-0819. **311**

WOOD RIVER JOURNAL. (US). **5658**

WOODALL'S CAMPGROUND DIRECTORY. EASTERN EDITION. (US/0162-7406). **4881**

WOODALL'S CAMPGROUND DIRECTORY. NORTH AMERICAN EDITION. (US/0146-1362). **4881**

WOODALL'S FLORIDA (GERMAN ED.). (US/0198-1110). **5499**

WOODALL'S MISSOURI/ARKANSAS CAMPGROUND DIRECTORY. (US/0163-5328). **4881**

WOODALL'S ... RETIREMENT DIRECTORY. (US/0731-6526). **5182**

WOODENBOAT, THE. (US/0095-067X). **597**

WOODFORD SUN. (US). **Adv Mgr:** Robert H. Atres. **5683**

WOODLAKE ECHO AND THE THREE RIVERS CURRENT. (US/1072-1819). **Adv Mgr:** V. Spencer, **Tel** (209)592-3171. **5641**

WOODMEN OF THE WORLD MAGAZINE. (US/0043-7751). **2896**

WOODS 'N' WATER. (US/0194-8253). **4881**

WOODSHOP NEWS. NORTHEAST. (US/0894-5403). **2406**

WOODSTOCK TIMES. (US). **5722**

WOODVILLE LEADER AND DUNN COUNTY PICTORIAL MESSENGER, THE. (US/0748-6812). **Adv Mgr:** Sue Heim, **Tel** (715)698-2401. **5772**

WOODVILLE REPUBLICAN (WOODVILLE, MISS. : 1861). (US). **Adv Mgr:** Lili Lewis, **Tel** (601)888-4293. **5702**

WOODWORK (ROSS, CALIF.). (US/1045-3040). **635**

WOODWORKER (HEMEL HEMPSTEAD. (1910)). (UK/0043-776X). **635**

WOODWORKER'S JOURNAL (NEW MILFORD), THE. (US/0199-1892). **635**

WOODWORKING INTERNATIONAL. (UK). **635**

WOODWORKING INTERNATIONAL NURNBERG. (GW/0177-7114). **635**

WOODWORKING (MARKHAM). (CN/0838-4185). **2406**

WOOL & WOOLLENS OF INDIA. (II/0043-7808). **Adv Mgr:** same as editor. **5359**

WOOL (PALMERSTON NORTH). (NZ/0110-6015). **5360**

WOOL RECORD WEEKLY MARKET REPORT. (UK). **Adv Mgr:** Wynn Home, **Tel** 0274 726357. **5360**

WOOL REPORT NEW ZEALAND. (NZ/0112-6059). **5360**

WOOL SACK, THE. (US/0043-7840). **224**

WOOL TECHNOLOGY AND SHEEP BREEDING. (AT/0043-7875). **224**

WOORD EN DAAD WORD AND ACTION. (SA/0257-8921). **Adv Mgr:** E. M. Strydom. **5009**

WORCESTER BUSINESS JOURNAL. (US/1063-6595). **Adv Mgr:** Donna Rickoff. **723**

WORCESTER MAGAZINE (WORCESTER). (US/0191-4960). **4855**

WORD & WORLD. (US/0275-5270). **Adv Mgr:** Ruth Taylor, **Tel** (207)799-4387. **5009**

WORD OF LIFE LIFE LINES. (US/0194-6684). **Adv Mgr:** Beverly Schmaker, **Tel** (518)532-7111. **5009**

WORD OF MOUTH (SAN ANTONIO, TEX.). (US/1048-3950). **1886**

WORD WAYS. (US/0043-7980). **Adv Mgr Tel** (201)538-4584. **3333**

WORDPERFECT FOR WINDOWS MAGAZINE. (US/1058-9783). **Adv Mgr:** Maurice Beaujeu. **1292**

WORDPERFECT (OREM, UTAH). (US/1042-5152). **Adv Mgr:** Mo Beaujeu. **1292**

WORDS & PHRASES LEGALLY DEFINED. (UK). **3076**

WORDS (WILLOW GROVE). (US/0164-4742). **4214**

WORDSWORTH CIRCLE. (US/0043-8006). **3356**

WORK BOAT, THE. (US/0043-8014). **597**

WORK, EMPLOYMENT AND SOCIETY. (UK/0950-0170). **1718**

WORK INJURY MANAGEMENT. (US). **2896**

WORKAMERICA. (US/0740-4077). **1718**

WORKAMPER NEW$. (US/0895-3678). **1718**

WORKBASKET AND HOME ARTS MAGAZINE, THE. (US/0162-9123). **376**

WORKBENCH. (US/0043-8057). **635**

WORKBOAT INTERNATIONAL. (UK). **Adv Mgr:** Marilyn Stansell. **597**

WORKBOOK, THE. (US/0195-4636). **1300**

WORKER CO-OPS (TORONTO. 1980). (CN/0829-576X). **1543**

WORKERS EDUCATION. (II). **1719**

WORKERS VOICE, THE. (BM). **1719**

WORKFORCE (WASHINGTON, D.C.). (US/1063-4363). **1719**

WORKING CLASS, THE. (II). **1719**

WORKING MOTHER (NEW YORK, N.Y. 1981). (US/0278-193X). **2287**

WORKING PAPER SERIES - UNIVERSITY OF ARIZONA. MEXICAN AMERICAN STUDIES AND RESEARCH CENTER. (US/0732-7749). **5226**

WORKING PAPERS IN LINGUISTICS (SEATTLE, WASH.). (US/0892-8886). **3333**

WORKING PAPERS ON LANGUAGE, GENDER & SEXISM. (AT/1036-4099). **3333**

WORKING TOGETHER (SEATTLE, WASH.). (US/1064-8585). **5314**

WORKING WOMAN. (US/0145-5761). **5572**

WORKS AND DAYS. (US/0886-2060). **333**

WORLD ACROBATICS. (AT/1038-6963). **389**

WORLD AFFAIRS (WASHINGTON). (US/0043-8200). **4538**

WORLD AGRICULTURAL ECONOMICS AND RURAL SOCIOLOGY ABSTRACTS. (UK/0043-8219). **157**

WORLD AIRNEWS. (SA). **40**

WORLD AIRNEWS. (SA/0261-2399). **40**

WORLD AIRSHOW NEWS. (US/0888-5265). **40**

WORLD ALUMINIUM DATABOOK. (UK/0951-2233). **4023**

WORLD & I, THE. (US/0887-9346). **2495**

WORLD AND PRESS. (GW/0509-1632). **3334**

WORLD & SCIENCE, THE. (US/1059-1931). **5170**

WORLD AND UNITED STATES AVIATION AND SPACE RECORDS AS OF ... . (US/0890-510X). **40**

WORLD AQUACULTURE. (US/1041-5602). **2316**

WORLD — Advertising Accepted Index

WORLD ARCHAEOLOGY. (UK/0043-8243). **285**

WORLD AROUND YOU, THE. (US/0199-8293). **4395**

WORLD (ASHEVILLE, N.C.). (US/0888-157X). **Adv Mgr:** Roger Schoffer. **2550**

WORLD BIRDWATCH : THE NEWSLETTER OF THE INTERNATIONAL COUNCIL FOR BIRD PRESERVATION. (UK). **Adv Mgr:** Leslie Stanton, **Tel** same as publisher. **2210**

WORLD BUSINESS (OTTAWA). (CN/1182-0993). **Adv Mgr:** Tom Eyres. **723**

WORLD CEMENT. (UK/0263-6050). **631**

WORLD CEMENT DIRECTORY. (FR). **1031**

WORLD CHRISTIAN : TODAY'S MISSION MAGAZINE. (US/0743-2399). **5010**

WORLD COFFEE & TEA. (US/0043-8340). **2373**

WORLD COGENERATION. (US/1053-5802). **2132**

WORLD COIN NEWS. (US/0145-9090). **2783**

WORLD COLLECTORS ANNUARY. (NE/0084-1498). **369**

WORLD (COOS BAY, OR.), THE. (US/1062-8495). **Adv Mgr:** Juna Mejia, **Tel** (503)269-1222. **5734**

WORLD COPPER DATABOOK. (UK/0950-2262). **4024**

WORLD DIRECTORY OF FERTILIZER PRODUCTS. (UK). **147**

WORLD ECONOMY, THE. (UK/0378-5920). **1641**

WORLD FAITHS ENCOUNTER. (UK). **5010**

WORLD FISHING. (UK/0043-8480). **2316**

WORLD FOOTWEAR. (US/0894-3079). **1088**

WORLD FUTURES. (US/0260-4027). **4365**

WORLD HOCKEY. (UK/0964-0681). **4930**

WORLD HOSPITALS. (UK/0512-3135). **3793**

WORLD JOURNAL OF MICROBIOLOGY & BIOTECHNOLOGY. (UK/0959-3993). **571**

WORLD JOURNAL OF PSYCHOSYNTHESIS. (US/0043-860X). **3937**

WORLD JOURNAL OF UROLOGY. (GW/0724-4983). **3994**

WORLD LEATHER. (US/0894-3087). **3186**

WORLD LEISURE & RECREATION. (US). **4855**

WORLD LITERATURE TODAY. (US/0196-3570). **Adv Mgr:** David D. Clark. **3454**

WORLD LITERATURE WRITTEN IN ENGLISH. (CN/0093-1705). **3356**

WORLD MARKET PERSPECTIVE. (US/0229-4044). **817**

WORLD MONITOR. (US/0897-9472). **2495**

WORLD MUSIC CONNECTIONS. (US/1049-0140). **4159**

WORLD NEUROLOGY. (UK/0899-9465). **Adv Mgr:** Clare Parker. **3847**

WORLD (NEW YORK, N.Y. : 1967), THE. (US/0043-8154). **3473**

WORLD NEWS. (UK). **Adv Mgr:** M. Mathews. **1527**

WORLD OF BANKING, THE. (US/0730-8736). **817**

WORLD OF BEER, THE. (IT/1121-158X). **Adv Mgr:** Edwin Janus, **Tel** 02 6682834. **2373**

WORLD OF GYMNASTICS. (SZ). **4930**

WORLD OF LUBAVITCH. (CN/0824-7420). **5053**

WORLD OF MUSIC (WILHELMSHAVEN). (SZ/0043-8774). **4159**

WORLD OF PERSONNEL. (US/0892-6247). **1720**

WORLD OIL (HOUSTON, TEX.). (US/0043-8790). **4282**

WORLD OPERA SCHEDULE. (US/1042-931X). **Adv Mgr:** L. Morton, **Tel** (505)983-8786. **4159**

WORLD PATENT INFORMATION. (UK/0172-2190). **1309**

WORLD PLASTICS & RUBBER TECHNOLOGY. (UK). **4461**

WORLD POLICY JOURNAL. (US/0740-2775). **4538**

WORLD POLITICS. (US/0043-8871). **4538**

WORLD PRESS REVIEW. (US/0195-8895). **4539**

WORLD PUMPS. (UK/0262-1762). **2132**

WORLD RADIO TV HANDBOOK. (UK/0144-7750). **1143**

WORLD RECORD GAME FISHES. (US/0194-3340). **2316**

WORLD RESOURCE REVIEW. (US/1042-8011). **2210**

WORLD REVIEW. (AT/0043-8960). **4501**

WORLD SOCCER. (UK). **4930**

WORLD STUDENT NEWS. (XR/0014-2255). **1792**

WORLD SUGAR JOURNAL. (UK). **147**

WORLD TELEMEDIA. (UK/0961-6284). **1169**

WORLD TEXTILE ABSTRACTS. (UK/0043-9118). **5361**

WORLD TOBACCO. (UK/0043-9126). **5374**

WORLD TOBACCO SITUATION / UNITED STATES DEPARTMENT OF AGRICULTURE, FOREIGN AGRICULTURAL SERVICE. (US). **5374**

WORLD TODAY, THE. (UK/0043-9134). **4539**

WORLD TRADE INDEX. (UK). **858**

WORLD TRADE NEWSPAPER. (CN/0843-4174). **858**

WORLD TRANSLATIONS INDEX : A JOINT PUBLICATION OF INTERNATIONAL TRANSLATIONS CENTRE [AND] CENTRE NATIONAL DE LA RECHERCHE SCIENTIFIQUE IN CO-OPERATION WITH THE NATIONAL TRANSLATIONS CENTER AT THE JOHN CRERAR LIBRARY OF THE UNIVERSITY OF CHICAGO. (NE/0259-8264). **5171**

WORLD TRAVELING. (US/0163-1780). **5500**

WORLD WAR II INVESTIGATOR. (UK/0953-4857). **2633**

WORLD WEIGHTLIFTING. (HU/0230-3035). **2602**

WORLD-WIDE PRINTER. (GW/0147-4804). **4570**

WORLDRADIO, INC. (US). **1169**

WORLD'S FAIR (CORTE MADERA, CALIF.). (US/0273-480X). **5226**

WORLD'S FAIR, THE. (UK). **Adv Mgr:** B. Gunn. **4868**

WORLD'S POULTRY SCIENCE JOURNAL. (UK/0043-9339). **224**

WORLDWIDE BROCHURES (PRINT ED.). (US/1053-9158). **5500**

WORLDWIDE OFFSHORE CONTRACTORS & EQUIPMENT DIRECTORY. (US/1058-9686). **4285**

WORLDWIDE PETROCHEMICAL DIRECTORY. (US/0084-2583). **4282**

WORLDWIDE PROJECTS. (US/0192-5512). **2001**

WORLDWIDE REFINING AND GAS PROCESSING DIRECTORY (1978). (US/0277-0962). **4283**

WORLDWIDE TRAVEL PLANNER. (US/0890-4766). **5500**

WORLDWISE (HANOVER, N.H.). (US/1053-1572). **Adv Mgr:** Grace Kelly, **Tel** same as publisher. **5709**

WORSHIP. (US/0043-941X). **5010**

WORSHIP AND ARTS. (US/0890-5754). **5010**

WORSHIP AND PREACHING. (UK/0032-7407). **5010**

WORSHIP WORKS. (US/1051-9653). **5010**

WOUND REPAIR AND REGENERATION. (US/1067-1927). **3651**

WPA, WRITING PROGRAM ADMINISTRATION. (US/0196-4682). **3454**

WPNR, WEEKBLAD VOOR PRIVAATRECHT, NOTARIAAT EN REGISTRATIE. (NE). **3076**

WRANGELL SENTINEL. (US). **Adv Mgr:** Sara Bird. **5629**

WRAP. (US/0896-1697). **1124**

WRAP. (UK). **4808**

WRAP UP (NORWOOD, N.J.). (US/0741-8523). **3652**

WRAY GAZETTE, THE. (US). **Adv Mgr:** Jeanette B. Rieb. **5644**

WRECKING AND SALVAGE JOURNAL. (US/0043-9460). **Adv Mgr:** Karen Duane, **Tel** (617)848-6160. **631**

WREE-VIEW OF WOMEN FOR RACIAL AND ECONOMIC EQUALITY, THE. (US/0892-3116). **4514**

WRESTLER (ROCKVILLE CENTRE, N.Y.), THE. (US/1052-0899). **Adv Mgr Tel** (800)678-9321. **4930**

WRESTLING SUPERSTARS. (US/1042-5284). **4931**

WRESTLING USA (LAHABRA). (US/0199-6258). **4931**

WRESTLING'S MAIN EVENT. (US/0278-9612). **4931**

WRIGHTSVILLE HEADLIGHT, THE. (US/0747-3737). **Adv Mgr:** Sherry Lanier. **5655**

WRIT (TORONTO). (CN/0316-3768). **3454**

WRITE NOW!. (US). **3454**

WRITER (BOSTON). (US/0043-9517). **Adv Mgr:** Ann-Margaret Hemings Caljouw. **3454**

WRITER'S DIGEST, THE. (US/0043-9525). **3454**

WRITER'S GUIDELINES (PITTSBURG, MO.). (US/1053-1793). **2925**

WRITERS' JOURNAL (SAINT PAUL, MINN.). (US/0891-8759). **3454**

WRITER'S LIFELINE. (CN/0225-610X). **2926**

WRITER'S NORTHWEST HANDBOOK. (US/0896-7946). **4820**

WRITING CENTER JOURNAL, THE. (US). **1854**

WRITING INSTRUCTOR, THE. (US/0277-7789). **3334**

WRITING ON THE EDGE. (US/1064-6051). **Adv Mgr:** Margaret Eldred. **3455**

WRITING TEACHER (SAN ANTONIO, TEX.). (US/0894-5837). **1908**

WURTTEMBERGISCHES WOCHENBLATT FUR LANDWIRTSCHAFT. (GW). **147**

WURZBURGER JAHRBUCHER FUR DIE ALTERTUMSWISSENSCHAFT. (GW/0342-5932). **1081**

WWD. (US/0149-5380). **1088**

WWF MAGAZINE. (US/8756-7792). **Adv Mgr Tel** (212)593-2228. **4931**

WWS, WORLD WIDE SHIPPING GUIDE. (US/0162-0088). **5458**

WXXI PROGRAM GUIDE (1985). (US/0883-1106). **1143**

WXXI (ROCHESTER, N.Y.). (US/1055-2960). **Adv Mgr:** Judith Lemoncelli, **Tel** (716)325-7500. **1143**

WYANDOTTE WEST. (US). **Adv Mgr:** Carol A. Bland, **Tel** (915)788-5565. **5679**

WYNIKI POMIAROW PIONOWEGO ROZKLADU OZONU W ATMOSFERZE. (PL). **1437**

WYNNE PROGRESS, THE. (US). **Adv Mgr:** Brandon Boger. **5632**

WYOMING CATHOLIC REGISTER, THE. (US/0746-5580). **5038**

WYOMING NURSE. (US). **Adv Mgr:** Mark Miller, **Tel** (319)277-2414. **3871**

WYOMING STOCKMAN FARMER. (US/0043-9800). **147**

WYOMING WOOL GROWER. (US/0043-9827). **224**

X-RAY SPECTROMETRY. (UK/0049-8246). **1020**

XANADU (WANTAGH). (US/0146-0463). **3473**

XAVIER REVIEW. (US/0887-6681). **3356**

XIBEI SHI-DI. (CH/1000-4076). **2668**

XIYOU JINSHU. (CC/0258-7076). **4024**

Y.E.S. QUARTERLY. (US/0884-6677). **5600**

Y WEEKLY, THE. (US/0883-3133). **5756**

YA HOTLINE. (CN/0701-8894). **1071**

YACHT PREMIERE ENGLISH ED. (IT/1120-2424). **Adv Mgr:** Paola Pellegrino, **Tel** 39 2 48012417. **4856**

YACHTING (NEW YORK, N.Y.). (US/0043-9940). **Adv Mgr:** Rick Becker, **Tel** (212)779-5086. **597**

YAKIMA HERALD-REPUBLIC. (US). **Adv Mgr:** Brian Vaillancourt, **Tel** (509)577-7732. **5763**

YALE ALUMNI MAGAZINE (1984). (US/8750-409X). **Adv Mgr:** Barbara Durland. **1103**

YALE DAILY NEWS. (US/0890-2240). **Adv Mgr:** Anastasia Katsetos, **Tel** (203)432-2401. **5647**

YALE JOURNAL OF BIOLOGY AND MEDICINE, THE. (US/0044-0086). **3652**

YALE JOURNAL OF INTERNATIONAL LAW, THE. (US/0889-7743). **Adv Mgr:** Aaron Fellmeth. **3138**

YALE JOURNAL OF LAW AND FEMINISM. (US/1043-9366). **3076**

YALE JOURNAL ON REGULATION. (US/0741-9457). **3076**

YALE LAW & POLICY REVIEW. (US/0740-8048). **3077**

YALE LAW JOURNAL, THE. (US/0044-0094). **3077**

YALE REVIEW, THE. (US/0044-0124). **5226**

YALE SCIENTIFIC. (US/0091-0287). **5171**

YANKEE (DUBLIN, N.H.). (US/0044-0191). **2550**

YANKEE FOOD SERVICE. (US/0195-2552). **Adv Mgr:** Kevin Griffin. **2361**

YANKEE HOMES. (US/8756-0259). **4848**

YANKEE HORSETRADER. (US/0192-5210). **2803**

YANKEE OILMAN. (US/0044-0205). **4283**

YANKTON DAILY PRESS & DAKOTAN. (US). **5744**

YAO HSUEH HSUEH PAO. (CC/0513-4870). **4333**

YAOWU FENXI ZAZHI. (CC/0254-1793). **4333**

YARD & GARDEN. (US/0896-6834). **2434**

YATES CENTER NEWS (YATES CENTER, KAN. : 1948). (US). **5679**

YEAR BOOK. (UK/0305-0998). **821**

YEAR BOOK, AUSTRALIA. (AT/0810-8633). **5346**

YEAR BOOK - BRITISH FEDERATION OF MUSIC FESTIVALS. (UK/0309-8044). **389**

YEAR BOOK - CANADIAN RACING PIGEON UNION. (CN/0316-2559). **4931**

YEAR BOOK / DUTCHESS COUNTY HISTORICAL SOCIETY. (US/0739-8565). **2766**

YEAR BOOK - FLORIDA GENEALOGICAL SOCIETY, TAMPA, FLA. (US/0428-7282). **2478**

YEAR BOOK - NATIONAL AURICULA & PRIMULA SOCIETY (NORTHERN SECTION). (UK). **148**

YEAR BOOK OF ADULT EDUCATION. (UK/0084-3601). **1802**

YEAR BOOK - ROYAL SOCIETY OF TROPICAL MEDICINE AND HYGIENE. (UK/0080-4711). **3987**

YEAR BOOK - UNITED REFORMED CHURCH. (UK). **Adv Mgr:** Everest Media, **Tel** 01628 897000. **5069**

YEAR BOOK - VENEZUELAN-AMERICAN CHAMBER OF COMMERCE & INDUSTRY. (VE). **821**

YEAR BOOK ... (... YEAR OF ISSUE) / THE CHURCH OF SCOTLAND. (UK/0069-3995). **5010**

YEARBOOK - AMERICAN SOCIETY OF SANITARY ENGINEERING. (US/0066-068X). **2248**

YEARBOOK AND CHURCH DIRECTORY OF THE ORTHODOX CHURCH IN AMERICA. (US/0145-7950). **5040**

YEARBOOK AND DIRECTORY OF OSTEOPATHIC PHYSICIANS. (US/0084-358X). **3652**

YEARBOOK AND PHILATELIC SOCIETIES' DIRECTORY. (UK/0260-1265). **2788**

YEARBOOK & REGISTER OF MEMBERS / INCORPORATED SOCIETY OF MUSICIANS. (UK). **4159**

YEARBOOK - CALIFORNIA MACADAMIA SOCIETY. (US/0068-5720). **2434**

YEARBOOK : COMMERCIAL ARBITRATION. (NE). **3104**

YEARBOOK - CREDIT UNION NATIONAL ASSOCIATION. (US). **817**

YEARBOOK / LUTHERAN CHURCH IN AMERICA. (US). **5069**

YEARBOOK - NEW YORK COUNTY LAWYERS' ASSOCIATION. (US/0548-8729). **3077**

YEARBOOK OF COMPARATIVE AND GENERAL LITERATURE. (US/0084-3695). **3356**

YEARBOOK OF CONSTRUCTION ARTICLES. (US/0747-8399). **631**

YEARBOOK OF EXPERTS, AUTHORITIES & SPOKESPERSONS. AN ENCYCLOPEDIA OF SOURCES. (US/1051-4058). **1930**

YEARBOOK OF GERMAN-AMERICAN STUDIES. (US/0741-2827). **2766**

YEARBOOK OF LANGLAND STUDIES, THE. (US/0890-2917). **3473**

YEARBOOK OF THE CALIFORNIA AVOCADO SOCIETY. (US/0096-5960). **2434**

YEARBOOK OF THE HEATHER SOCIETY. (UK/0440-5757). **Adv Mgr:** Arnold Stow, **Tel** (0494)449397. **5237**

YELLOW SILK. (US/0736-9212). **Adv Mgr:** Shelly Hebert. **3455**

YELLOW SPRINGS NEWS. (US). **Adv Mgr:** Karen Hernandez, **Tel** (513)767-7373. **5731**

YELLOWBACK LIBRARY. (US). **3455**

YESTERYEAR (PRINCETON). (US/0194-9349). **252**

YESTERYEARS. (US/0044-037X). **2478**

YHA ACCOMODATION GUIDE. ENGLAND & WALES / YHA. (UK). **Adv Mgr:** Vicki King. **5314**

YICHUAN. (CC/0253-9772). **552**

YICHUAN XUEBAO. (CC/0379-4172). **552**

YIDDISH. (US/0364-4308). **3455**

YIDDISHKEIT. (IS/0792-044X). **5054**

YIDISHE SHPRAKH. (US/0044-0442). **3334**

YIHUA BAO. (US/0745-2322). **Adv Mgr:** Mark Shriner. **5763**

YINGYONG SHUXUE XUEBAO. (CC). **3541**

YM. (US/0888-5842). **1071**

YO YO TIMES. (US/0897-7704). **1071**

YOGA AND HEALTH. (UK/0953-2161). **4365**

YOGA INTERNATIONAL. (US/1055-7911). **4186**

YOGA JOURNAL. (US/0191-0965). **2602**

YONHAP (TAEGU, KOREA). (KO). **2495**

YORK COUNTY COAST STAR. (US). **5685**

YORK DAILY RECORD (YORK, PA. : 1973). (US/1043-4313). **5741**

YORK DISPATCH, THE. (US/1050-267X). **5741**

YORKSHIRE JOURNAL. (US/0044-0612). **5527**

YORKVILLE ENQUIRER. (US). **Adv Mgr:** Angie Hoccomb. **5743**

YOSUI TO HAISUI. (JA/0513-5907). **2248**

YOU! (AGOURA HILLS, CALIF.). (US/1064-8682). **Adv Mgr:** Anita Birsa. **5038**

YOU TORONTO. 1990. (CN/1189-4695). **Adv Mgr:** Faye Gruenspan. **1088**

YOUNG. (CN/0702-1755). **1096**

YOUNG EAST. (JA/0513-5974). **5022**

YOUNG FASHIONS MAGAZINE. (US/0884-7630). **1088**

YOUNG GENERATION. (SI). **1071**

YOUNG PEOPLE NOW. (UK). **5314**

YOUNG SOCIALIST (NEW YORK. 1972). (US/0360-0157). **3356**

YOUNG VOICES (OLYMPIA, WASH.). (US/1046-8404). **1072**

YOUR CHURCH. (US/0049-8394). **5010**

YOUR CLASSIC. (UK/0957-6525). **5429**

YOUR COMPUTER CAREER. (US/0884-4615). **4210**

YOUR HEALTH & FITNESS. (US/0279-9324). **4808**

YOUR MORTGAGE MAGAZINE. (AT/1039-0081). **Adv Mgr:** Bruce Ewan. **817**

YOUR SCHOOL & THE LAW. (US/0094-0399). **3077**

YOUTH AND POLICY. (UK/0262-9798). **1072**

YOUTH IN SOCIETY. (UK/0307-1790). **5314**

YOUTH LEADER (SPRINGFIELD, MO.), THE. (US/0190-4566). **Adv Mgr:** Chuck Goldberg. **5011**

YOUTH MARKETING REPORT. (US). **938**

YOUTH POLICY. (US). **5314**

YOUTH THEATRE JOURNAL. (US/0892-9092). **5372**

YOUTHWORKER JOURNAL. (US/0747-3486). **Adv Mgr:** J. Hatcherian, **Tel** (813)822-0109. **5011**

YU WEN HSUEH HSI (JEN MIN CHIAO YU CHU PAN SHE). (CH). **3334**

YU YEN CHIAO HSUEH YU YEN CHIU. (CC). **3334**

YUANZIHE WULI. (CC/0253-3790). **4451**

YUANZINING NONGYE YINGYONG. (CC/0253-3596). **1961**

YUGNTRUF. (US/0098-3640). **3456**

YUGOSLAV REVIEW [A MONTHLY MAGAZINE OF THE SERBS, CROATS AND SLOVENES], THE. (YU/0512-9907). **2525**

YUGOSLAV SURVEY. (YU/0044-1341). **Adv Mgr:** Gordana Maljkovic. **2716**

YUKON NEWS (1972). (CN/0318-1952). **5798**

YUMA PIONEER, THE. (US). **Adv Mgr:** Mary Lynne Groshans. **5644**

Z MAGAZINE. (ZA). **2644**

ZABS REVIEW : A PUBLICATION OF THE ZAMBIA BUREAU OF STANDARDS. (ZA). **4033**

ZAC, ZEITSCHRIFT FUER ANTIMIKROBIELLE, ANTINEOPLASTISCHE CHEMOTHERAPIE. (GW/0724-9004). **3652**

ZAHNAERZTLICHE MITTEILUNGEN. (GW/0044-1643). **1337**

ZAHNARZTEBLATT BADEN-WURTTEMBERG. (GW/0340-3017). **1337**

ZAIRE-AFRIQUE. (CG/0251-298X). **2644**

ZAMBEZIA. (RH/0379-0622). **5226**

ZAMBIA INDUSTRIAL CASES REPORTS / REPUBLIC OF ZAMBIA, MINISTRY OF LABOUR AND SOCIAL SERVICES, INDUSTRIAL RELATIONS COURT, THE. (ZA). **3155**

ZAMBIA NURSE (KITWE, ZAMBIA : 1978). (ZA/0044-1740). **3871**

ZAMBIAN GEOGRAPHICAL JOURNAL. (ZA). **2579**

ZAPAD. (CN/0226-3068). **2275**

ZAPAD TODAY. (CN). **2275**

ZAVALA COUNTY SENTINEL (LA PRYOR, TEX. : 1913). (US). **5756**

ZAVODSKAJA LABORATORIJA. (RU/0321-4265). **1020**

ZEITGEMASSE SCHAFHALTUNG : MIT EINEM KAPITEL UBER MILCHSCHAFHALTUNG. (AU). **Adv Mgr:** J. Tritscher. **199**

ZEITSCHRIFT DER DEUTSCHEN GEMMOLOGISCHEN GESELLSCHAFT. (GW). **2915**

ZEITSCHRIFT DER SAVIGNY-STIFTUNG FUER RECHTSGESCHICHTE. KANONISTISCHE ABTEILUNG. (GW/0323-4142). **3077**

ZEITSCHRIFT DER SAVIGNY-STIFTUNG FUER RECHTSGESCHICHTE. ROMANISTISCHE ABTEILUNG. (AU). **3077**

ZEITSCHRIFT FUER ACKER- UND PFLANZENBAU. (GW/0931-2250). **148**

ZEITSCHRIFT FUER ALTHEBRAISTIK. (GW/0932-4461). **3335**

ZEITSCHRIFT FUER ANALYSIS UND IHRE ANWENDUNGEN. (GW/0232-2064). **3541**

ZEITSCHRIFT FUER ANGEWANDTE ENTOMOLOGIE. (GW/0044-2240). **5614**

ZEITSCHRIFT FUER ARBEITSRECHT UND SOZIALRECHT. (AU/0044-2321). **3155**

ZEITSCHRIFT FUER ARBEITSWISSENSCHAFT. (GW/0340-2444). **1720**

ZEITSCHRIFT FUER ARZTLICHE FORTBILDUNG. (GW/0044-2178). **3739**

ZEITSCHRIFT FUER AUSLAENDISCHES OEFFENTLICHES RECHT UND VOELKERRECHT. (GW/0044-2348). **3138**

ZEITSCHRIFT FUER AUSLANDISCHE LANDWIRTSCHAFT. (GW/0049-8599). **148**

ZEITSCHRIFT FUER BALKANOLOGIE. (GW/0044-2356). **2717**

ZEITSCHRIFT FUER BERUFS- UND WIRTSCHAFTSPADAGOGIK 1980. (GW/0172-2875). **1918**

ZEITSCHRIFT FUER BEWASSERUNGSWIRTSCHAFT. (GW/0049-8602). **148**

ZEITSCHRIFT FUER CELTISCHE PHILOLOGIE. (GW/0084-5302). **3335**

ZEITSCHRIFT FUER DEUTSCHE PHILOLOGIE. (GW/0044-2496). **3335**

ZEITSCHRIFT FUER DEUTSCHE PHILOLOGIE. BEIHEFT. (GW). **3335**

ZEITSCHRIFT FUER DEUTSCHES ALTERTUM UND DEUTSCHE LITERATUR. (GW/0044-2518). **3335**

ZEITSCHRIFT FUER DIALEKTOLOGIE UND LINGUISTIK. (GW/0044-1449). **3335**

ZEITSCHRIFT FUER DIE ALTTESTAMENTLICHE WISSENSCHAFT. (GW/0044-2526). **5020**

ZEITSCHRIFT FUER DIE ALTTESTAMENTLICHE WISSENSCHAFT. BEIHEFTE. (GW). **5020**

ZEITSCHRIFT FUER EISENBAHNWESEN UND VERKEHRSTECHNIK. (GW/0373-322X). **5438**

ZEITSCHRIFT FUER ENERGIEWIRTSCHAFT. (GW/0343-5377). **1961**

ZEITSCHRIFT FUER ENTWICKLUNGSPSYCHOLOGIE UND PADAGOGISCHE PSYCHOLOGIE. (GW/0049-8637). **1792**

ZEITSCHRIFT FUER ERKRANKUNGEN DER ATMUNGSORGANE. (GW/0303-657X). **3952**

ZEITSCHRIFT FUER ETHNOLOGIE. (GW/0044-2666). **248**

ZEITSCHRIFT — Advertising Accepted Index

ZEITSCHRIFT FUER EVANGELISCHES KIRCHENRECHT. (GW/0044-2690). **5070**

ZEITSCHRIFT FUER EXPERIMENTELLE UND ANGEWANDTE PSYCHOLOGIE. (GW/0044-2712). **4622**

ZEITSCHRIFT FUER FLUGWISSENSCHAFTEN UND WELTRAUMFORSCHUNG. (GW/0342-068X). **40**

ZEITSCHRIFT FUER FRANZOSISCHE SPRACHE UND LITERATUR. (GW/0044-2747). **3335**

ZEITSCHRIFT FUER GASTROENTEROLOGIE. (GW/0044-2771). **3748**

ZEITSCHRIFT FUER GEMEINWIRTSCHAFT. (AU). **1589**

ZEITSCHRIFT FUER GEOMORPHOLOGIE. (GW/0372-8854). **1401**

ZEITSCHRIFT FUER GERONTOLOGIE. (GW/0044-281X). **3755**

ZEITSCHRIFT FUER GESCHICHTSWISSENSCHAFT. (GW/0044-2828). **2634**

ZEITSCHRIFT FUER HERZ THORAX UND GEFAESSCHIRURGIE. (GW/0930-9225). **3978**

ZEITSCHRIFT FUER INTERNATIONALE ERZIEHUNGS- UND SOZIALWISSENSCHAFTLICHE FORSCHUNG. (GW/0930-9381). **Adv Mgr:** Stephanie Jancke. **1792**

ZEITSCHRIFT FUER JAGDWISSENSCHAFT. (GW/0044-2887). **4931**

ZEITSCHRIFT FUER KIRCHENGESCHICHTE. (GW/0044-2925). **5011**

ZEITSCHRIFT FUER KLINISCHE PSYCHOLOGIE. (GW/0084-5345). **4622**

ZEITSCHRIFT FUER KLINISCHE PSYCHOLOGIE, PSYCHOPATHOLOGIE UND PSYCHOTHERAPIE. (GW/0723-6557). **4622**

ZEITSCHRIFT FUER KRISTALLOGRAPHIE. (GW). **1033**

ZEITSCHRIFT FUER KULTURTECHNIK UND LANDENWICKLUNG. (GW/0934-666X). **148**

ZEITSCHRIFT FUER LUFT- UND WELTRAUMRECHT. (GW/0340-8329). **3078**

ZEITSCHRIFT FUER LYMPHOLOGIE. (GW/0343-8554). **3653**

ZEITSCHRIFT FUER MISSION. (GW). **5011**

ZEITSCHRIFT FUER MORPHOLOGIE UND ANTHROPOLOGIE. (GW/0044-314X). **248**

ZEITSCHRIFT FUER MYKOLOGIE. (GW/0170-110X). **576**

ZEITSCHRIFT FUER NATURFORSCHUNG. (GW/0932-0784). **4425**

ZEITSCHRIFT FUER PAEDAGOGIK. (GW/0044-3247). **1792**

ZEITSCHRIFT FUER PAEDAGOGISCHE PSYCHOLOGIE. (SZ/1010-0652). **Adv Mgr Tel** 0041 31 24 25 33. **4622**

ZEITSCHRIFT FUER PARAPSYCHOLOGIE UND GRENZGEBIETE DER PSYCHOLOGIE. (GW/0028-3479). **4243**

ZEITSCHRIFT FUER PARLAMENTSFRAGEN. (GW/0340-1758). **4695**

ZEITSCHRIFT FUER PHILOSOPHISCHE FORSCHUNG. (GW/0044-3301). **4365**

ZEITSCHRIFT FUER PHYSIKALISCHE CHEMIE (NEUE FOLGE). (GW/0044-3336). **1059**

ZEITSCHRIFT FUER PLANUNG : ZP. (GW/0936-8787). **890**

ZEITSCHRIFT FUER POLITIK. (GW/0044-3360). **4501**

ZEITSCHRIFT FUER RELIGIONS- UND GEISTESGESCHICHTE. (GW/0044-3441). **5011**

ZEITSCHRIFT FUER SAUGETIERKUNDE. (GW/0044-3468). **476**

ZEITSCHRIFT FUER SCHWEIZERISCHE ARCHAEOLOGIE UND KUNSTGESCHICHTE. (SZ/0044-3476). **286**

ZEITSCHRIFT FUER SEMIOTIK. (GW/0170-6241). **5172**

ZEITSCHRIFT FUER SLAVISCHE PHILOLOGIE. (GW/0044-3492). **3335**

ZEITSCHRIFT FUER THEOLOGIE UND KIRCHE. (GW/0044-3549). **5011**

ZEITSCHRIFT FUER TIERPHYSIOLOGIE, TIERERNAHRUNG UND FUTTERMITTELKUNDE. (GW/0044-3565). **5600**

ZEITSCHRIFT FUER TRANSPLANTATIONSMEDIZIN. (GW). **3653**

ZEITSCHRIFT FUER UNFALLCHIRURGIE UND VERSICHERUNGSMEDIZIN. (SZ/1017-1584). **3653**

ZEITSCHRIFT FUER UNTERNEHMENSGESCHICHTE. (GW/0342-2852). **725**

ZEITSCHRIFT FUER VERMESSUNGSWESEN. ZFV. (GW/0340-4560). **2034**

ZEITSCHRIFT FUER VERWALTUNG. (AU). **3094**

ZEITSCHRIFT FUER WIRTSCHAFTS- UND SOZIALWISSENSCHAFTEN. (GW/0342-1783). **1528**

ZEITSCHRIFT FUER WIRTSCHAFTSGEOGRAPHIE. (GW/0044-3751). **2580**

ZEITSCHRIFT FUER ZIVILPROZESS. (GW/0342-3468). **3078**

ZEITSCHRIFT FUER ZOOLOGISCHE SYSTEMATIK UND EVOLUTIONSFORSCHUNG. (GW/0044-3808). **5600**

ZEITSCHRIFT FUHRUNG + ORGANISATION : ZFO. (GW/0722-7485). **725**

ZEITSCHRIFT FUR GANZHEITSFORSCHUNG. (AU). **Adv Mgr:** M. Stueckler. **4365**

ZEITSCHRIFT FUR KULTUR, POLITIK, KIRCHE. (SW). **5070**

ZEITSCHRIFT FUR NATURFORSCHUNG. (GW/0939-5075). **476**

ZEITSCHRIFT FUR NATURFORSCHUNG. (GW/0932-0776). **996**

ZEITSCHRIFT FUR SCHWEIZERISCHE KIRCHENGESCHICHTE. REVUE D'HISTOIRE ECCLESIASTIQUE SUISSE. (SZ/0044-3484). **5011**

ZEITSCHRIFT FUR TIERZUCHTUNG UND ZUCHTUNGSBIOLOGIE (HAMBURG, GERMANY : 1939). (GW/0044-3581). **224**

ZEITSCHRIFT FUR VERKEHRSRECHT. (AU). **5400**

ZEITSCHRIFT INTERNE REVISION. (GW/0044-3816). **725**

ZEITSCRHIFT FUR KLINISCHE MEDIZIN (BERLIN, DDR). (GW/0233-1608). **3653**

ZEITUNG FUER KOMMUNALE WIRTSCHAFT. (GW). **Adv Mgr Tel** 49 89 4376045. **4695**

ZEITWENDE. (GW/0341-7166). **3356**

ZEMLEDELIE. (RU/0044-3913). **148**

ZENAIR NEWS. (US/0889-4353). **40**

ZENTRALASIATISCHE STUDIEN DES SEMINARS FUER SPRACH- UND KULTURWISSENSCHAFT ZENTRALASIENS DER UNIVERSITAT BONN. (GW/0514-857X). **2668**

ZENTRALBLATT FUER CHIRURGIE. (GW/0044-409X). **3978**

ZENTRALBLATT FUER CHIRURGIE. SONDERBAND. (GW/0044-409X). **3978**

ZENTRALBLATT FUER MIKROBIOLOGIE. (GW/0232-4393). **571**

ZENTRALBLATT FUER NEUROCHIRURGIE. (GW/0044-4251). **3978**

ZENTRALBLATT FUER VETERINARMEDIZIN. REIHE A. (GW/0514-7158). **5528**

ZEOLITES. (US/0144-2449). **1038**

ZESZYTY LITERACKIE : ZL. (FR). **3456**

ZEV, DET, GLASERS ANNALEN, DIE EISENBAHNTECHNIK. (GW/0941-0589). **5438**

ZFA, ZEITSCHRIFT FUER ARBEITSRECHT. (GW). **3156**

ZFBR, ZEITSCHRIFT FUER DEUTSCHES UND INTERNATIONALES BAURECHT. (GW). **3078**

ZHEJIANG YIKE DAXUE XUEBAO. (CC/1000-1743). **Adv Mgr:** Z. Lianrong. **3653**

ZHONGGUO CHUBAN NIANJIAN / CHINA PUBLISHING YEARBOOK. (CC/1001-8859). **4820**

ZHONGGUO KANGSHENGSU ZAZHI. (CC/1001-8689). **4333**

ZHONGGUO YIXUE WENZHAI. ZHONGYI. (CC/0254-9042). **3653**

ZHONGGUO ZAOZHI. (CC/0254-508X). **Adv Mgr:** Ms. Li Ping. **4240**

ZHONGGUO ZHI CHUN. (US/0735-8237). **2668**

ZHONGHUA GUKE ZAZHI. (CC/0253-2352). **3885**

ZHONGHUA LILIAO ZAZHI. (CC/0254-1408). **4382**

ZHONGHUA NEIFENMI DAIXIE ZAZHI. (CC/1000-6699). **3733**

ZHONGHUA WULIYIXUE ZAZHI. (CC/0254-1424). **3654**

ZHONGHUA XUEYEXUE ZAZHI. (CC/0253-2727). **3774**

ZHONGNAN KUANGYE XUEYUAN XUEBAO. (CH/0253-4347). **2153**

ZHURNAL NAUCHNOI I PRIKLADNOI FOTOGRAFII I KINEMATOGRAFII. (US/0734-1504). **4378**

ZI INTERNATIONAL. (GW/0341-0552). **631**

ZIEKENHUIS, HET. (NE/0044-4715). **3794**

ZIELSPRACHE DEUTSCH. (GW/0341-5864). **3336**

ZIELSPRACHE ENGLISCH. (GW/0342-6173). **Adv Mgr:** A. Ruhland. **3336**

ZIMBABWE AGRICULTURAL JOURNAL. (RH/1017-5156). **149**

ZIMBABWE AT WORK. (RH). **Adv Mgr:** R. Mahleka. **1632**

ZIMBABWE JOURNAL OF AGRICULTURAL RESEARCH, THE. (RH/0251-1045). **149**

ZIMBABWE LIBRARIAN, THE. (RH/1015-6828). **3257**

ZIMBABWE VETERINARY JOURNAL. (RH/1016-1511). **5528**

ZINCSCAN. (UK/0950-1592). **4025**

ZINOTAJS. (CN/0227-2423). **2717**

ZION'S HERALD (1975). (US/0098-9282). **5070**

ZIRAN KEXUESHI YANJIU. (CC/1000-0224). **1361**

ZLODZENIE POLSKIEJ STREFY PRZYBRZEZNEJ-MATERIALY ODDZIALU MORSKIEGO. (PL). **1458**

ZLR, ZEITSCHRIFT FUER DAS GESAMTE LEBENSMITTELRECHT. (GW/0342-3476). **3078**

ZNAMJA (MOSKVA). (RU/0130-1616). **3356**

ZONA ABIERTA. (SP/0210-2692). **Adv Mgr:** Mercedes Garcia Lenberg. **5226**

ZOO ANVERS. (BE/0044-5029). **5601**

ZOO GOER, THE. (US/0163-416X). **5601**

ZOOLOGICA SCRIPTA. (UK/0300-3256). **5601**

ZOOLOGICAL PARKS AND AQUARIUMS IN THE AMERICAS. (US/0740-7610). **5601**

ZOOLOGICAL SCIENCE. (JA/0289-0003). **5602**

ZOOLOGISCHE GARTEN; ZEITSCHRIFT FUER DIE GESAMTE TIERGARTNEREI. (GW/0044-5169). **5603**

ZOOLOGISCHE JAHRBUCHER. ABTEILUNG FUER ALLGEMEINE ZOOLOGIE UND PHYSIOLOGIE DER TIERE. (GW/0044-5185). **5603**

ZOOLOGISCHE JAHRBUCHER. ABTEILUNG FUER ANATOMIE UND ONTOGENIE DER TIERE. (GW/0044-5177). **5603**

ZOOLOGISCHE JAHRBUCHER. ABTEILUNG FUER SYSTEMATIK, OKOLOGIE UND GEOGRAPHIE DER TIERE. (GW/0044-5193). **5603**

ZOOLOGISCHER ANZEIGER. (GW/0044-5231). **5603**

ZOON. (SA/0044-5274). **5603**

ZOR. ZEITSCHRIFT FUER OPERATIONS-RESEARCH. (GW/0340-9422). **5173**

ZPA. ZEITSCHRIFT FUER PRAKTISCHE AUGENHEILKUNDE. (GW/0173-2595). **3880**

ZUCKER- UND SUSSWAREN WIRTSCHAFT. (GW/0373-0204). **2362**

ZUCKERINDUSTRIE. (GW/0344-8657). **1031**

ZUPNI VJESNIK NASE GOSPE KRALJICE HRVATA, TORONTO, HRVATSKIH MUCENIKA, MISSISSAUGA. (CN/0820-6449). **5038**

ZVAIGZNOTA DEBESS. (LV/0135-129X). **401**

ZWF CIM. (GW/0932-0482). **2132**

ZWIAZKOWIEC. (CN). **5798**

ZWIERZETA LABORATORYJNE. (PL/0084-5825). **5604**

ZWR. (GW/0044-166X). **1337**

ZYGON. (UK/0591-2385). **5012**

ZYMURGY. (US/0196-5921). **2373**

ZYZZYVA. (US/8756-5633). **3457**

ZZAP! 64. (UK/0954-867X). **1245**

Serials with Controlled Circulation

The following index lists all serials in the Directory with controlled circulation. The country code, ISSN, and circulation figures [printing within brackets] are provided when available. The page number in bold refers you to the complete serial listing in Volume I, II or III of the Directory.

3 R'S (FREDERICTON, N.B.) (CN/0710-7722). **1720**

4-H SOUNDER (US/0740-848X). [2,300] **1059**

9-1-1 MAGAZINE (US/1040-7316). [20,000] **1103**

13TH STREET JOURNAL, THE (US/1041-3111). **311**

16MM FILM ADDENDUM - MIDWESTERN REGIONAL LIBRARY SYSTEM (CN/0821-1116). **4062**

19TH CENTURY MUSIC (US/0148-2076). [1,350] **4098**

20/20 (US/0192-1304). [34,000] **4214**

33 METAL PRODUCING (US/0149-1210). **3996**

50 PLUS (DURHAM, ONT.) (CN/0840-5395). [35,000 monthly] **5177**

68 MICRO JOURNAL (US/0194-5025). [10,000] **1265**

100 A1 (UK/0266-8971). [30,000] **5447**

1000 UND 1 BUCH (AU). **1059**

1199 NEWS (US/0012-6535). [100,000] **1642**

A & V, MONOGRAFIAS DE ARQUITECTURA Y VIVIENDA (SP/0213-487X). [5,000] **286**

A C P NOTEBOOK (CN/0705-6621). **4811**

A.D.P.H.S.O (FR/0339-8854). [800] **3775**

A-E BUSINESS REVIEW (US). [3,000] **286**

A.E. LEGAL NEWSLETTER (US/0090-2411). [800] **286**

A.F.P. SCIENCES (FR/0397-829X). **5079**

A.G.T. DOKUMENTATION (GW). [10,000] **2034**

A.I.D. ECONOMIC DATA BOOK, LATIN AMERICA (US). **1459**

A.I.D. ECONOMIC DATA BOOK, NEAR EAST AND SOUTH ASIA (US/0503-4922). [18,500] **2913**

A.I.D. RESEARCH AND DEVELOPMENT ABSTRACTS (US/0096-1507). [4,000] **2913**

A I M L S SELF ASSESSMENT PROGRAMMES SERIES (AT). [2,400] **3891**

A.I.P.P.I. : JOURNAL OF THE JAPANESE GROUP OF AIPPI (JA). **1300**

A L'AUTRE, UNE (CN/0824-8230). [2,000] **3755**

A. MAGAZINE (US/1070-9401). [100,000] **2253**

A P C O PUBLIC SAFETY COMMUNICATIONS (US). [6,000] **4763**

A RAYONS OUVERTS (CN/0835-8672). [1,000] **3186**

A.S.A. ARTISAN (US/0892-3582). **335**

A + T (AT). [3,500] **335**

A.T.A. JOURNAL (HK/1015-8138). [12,300] **5347**

A TO Z OF WHO IS WHO IN AUSTRALIA'S HISTORY, THE (AT). **2668**

A.U.M.L.A (AT/0001-2793). [1,300] **3260**

A.W.R. BULLETIN (AU/0001-2947). [1,000] **5269**

A-Z OF UK MARKETING DATA, THE (UK). [250] **920**

AA FILES (UK/0261-6823). [2,500] **287**

AAA, ARBEITEN AUS ANGLISTIK UND AMERIKANISTIK (AU/0171-5410). [750] **3260**

AADE EDITORS' JOURNAL (US/0160-6999). [325] **4811**

AAHS JOURNAL (US/0882-9365). [3,000] **3**

AAMI NEWS (US/0739-0270). [5,000] **3543**

AAMVA BULLETIN / AMERICAN ASSOCIATION OF MOTOR VEHICLE ADMINISTRATORS (US/0001-0154). [1,500] **5399**

AANA JOURNAL (US/0094-6354). [24,000] **3849**

AANA NEWSBULLETIN (US/0199-2554). [24,000] **3849**

AAOHN NEWS / AMERICAN ASSOCIATION OF OCCUPATIONAL HEALTH NURSES, INC (US/0746-620X). [13,000] **3850**

AAPG BULLETIN (US/0149-1423). [37,000] **4248**

AAPG EXPLORER (US/0195-2986). [45,000] **1364**

AAR STUDIES IN RELIGION (US/0145-2789). **4931**

AARBGER FOR NORDISK OLDKYNDIGHED OG HISTORIE / UDGIVNE AF DET KONGELIGE NORDISKE OLDSKRIFT-SELSKAB (DK). **2671**

AARDRIJKSKUNDE, DE (BE). [1,300] **2553**

AATF NATIONAL BULLETIN (US/0883-6795). [12,000] **3260**

AATSEEL'S NEWSLETTER / AMERICAN ASSOCIATION OF TEACHERS OF SLAVIC AND EAST EUROPEAN LANGUAGES (US). [1,400] **1720**

AAVSO CIRCULAR (US/0197-2979). [300] **391**

AAVSO MONOGRAPH (US/0892-4244). [500] **391**

ABA/BNA LAWYERS' MANUAL ON PROFESSIONAL CONDUCT. CURRENT REPORTS (US/0740-4050). [2,000] **2926**

ABA JOURNAL (US/0747-0088). [370,000] **2926**

ABACUS (SYDNEY) (AT/0001-3072). [1,000] **735**

ABBEY (US). [200] **3357**

ABC AND D. ARCHITECT BUILDER CONTRACTOR AND DEVELOPER (UK/0966-9647). [24,350] **287**

ABC DER DEUTSCHEN WIRTSCHAFT. CD-ROM (GW). [30,000] **1596**

ABD (US/0001-0502). [16,000] **3**

ABEGWEIT REVIEW (CN/0382-4632). [500] **2253**

ABEILLE (CN/0821-5111). **5572**

ABERDEEN AMERICAN-NEWS (US/1074-7117). [20,000] **5743**

ABERDEEN PETROLEUM REPORT (UK/0263-5054). **4249**

ABERDEEN UNIVERSITY REVIEW (UK/0001-320X). [1,650] **1088**

ABHANDLUNGEN - BAYERISCHE AKADEMIE DER WISSENSCHAFTEN, PHILOSOPHISCH-HISTORISCHE KLASSE (GW). **1073**

ABHANDLUNGEN DER AKADEMIE DER WISSENSCHAFTEN IN GOTTINGEN. PHILOLOGISCH-HISTORISCHE KLASSE (GW/0930-4304). **1073**

ABHANDLUNGEN DER GEOLOGISCHEN BUNDESANSTALT (AU/0378-0864). **1364**

ABHANDLUNGEN DER HEIDELBERGER AKADEMIE DER WISSENSCHAFTEN, PHILOSOPHISCH-HISTORISCHE KLASSE (GW/0017-9574). [1,000] **4339**

ABHANDLUNGEN DER SENCKENBERGISCHEN NATURFORSCHENDEN GESELLSCHAFT (GW/0365-7000). **4161**

ABHANDLUNGEN UND MATERIALIEN ZUR PUBLIZISTIK (GW/0065-0323). [1,000] **2609**

ABHATH (MR). [6,500] **5189**

ABHINAYA (II). [5,200] **3357**

ABILENE REFLECTOR-CHRONICLE (US/0890-345X). [4,823] **5668**

ABIRA DIGEST (US/0196-0652). [1,550] **429**

ABITARE CON ARTE (IT/1120-6772). **2898**

ABLATIVE (AT/0814-5180). [400] **636**

ABMS DIRECTORY OF CERTIFIED COLON AND RECTAL SURGEONS (US/0884-1470). [250] **3957**

ABMS DIRECTORY OF CERTIFIED DERMATOLOGISTS (US/0884-1489). [600] **3717**

ABMS DIRECTORY OF CERTIFIED OBSTETRICIANS AND GYNECOLOGISTS (US/0884-1535). **3755**

ABMS DIRECTORY OF CERTIFIED PLASTIC SURGEONS (US/0749-839X). [600] **3957**

ABMS DIRECTORY OF CERTIFIED UROLOGISTS (US/0742-0374). [1,250] **3987**

ABN NEWS / NATIONAL LIBRARY OF AUSTRALIA, AUSTRALIAN BIBLIOGRAPHIC NETWORK (AT/0726-0644). [2,500] **3186**

ABORIGINAL CHILD AT SCHOOL, THE (AT). [2,000] **1874**

ABORIGINAL

ABORIGINAL LAW BULLETIN (AT). [2,600] **2926**

ABOUT THE HOUSE (UK/0001-3242). [21,000] **4098**

ABOVE & BEYOND (CN/0843-7815). [30,000] **2553**

ABRIDGED CATHOLIC PERIODICAL AND LITERATURE INDEX, THE (US/0737-3457). [350] **5012**

ABSTRACT REVIEW IN SCIENCE EXTENSION (HU/0238-6178). [1,000] **5079**

ABSTRACTS (CN). [1,000] **1412**

ABSTRACTS, ANNUAL MEETING - ASSOCIATION OF AMERICAN GEOGRAPHERS (US/0197-1700). [2,500] **2553**

ABSTRACTS IN BIOCOMMERCE (UK/0263-6778). [500] **3654**

ABSTRACTS IN MARYLAND ARCHEOLOGY (US/0743-4251). [100] **253**

ABSTRACTS OF AIT REPORTS AND PUBLICATIONS ON ENERGY (TH/0857-6181). [500] **1961**

ABSTRACTS OF BULGARIAN SCIENTIFIC MEDICAL LITERATURE (BU/0001-3536). [515] **3543**

ABSTRACTS OF PAPERS PRESENTED AT THE ... ANNUAL MEETING ... / THE AMERICAN INSTITUTE FOR CONSERVATION OF HISTORIC AND ARTISTIC WORKS (US). **335**

ABSTRACTS OF PAPERS PRESENTED AT THE ... TOBACCO ROOT GEOLOGICAL SOCIETY CONFERENCE (US/8755-1942). [150] **1364**

ABSTRACTS OF RESEARCH IN PASTORAL CARE AND COUNSELING (US/0733-2599). [250] **5012**

ABSTRACTS OF SOVIET AND EAST EUROPEAN EMIGRE PERIODICAL LITERATURE (US/0738-2707). [600] **2513**

ABSTRACTS ON RURAL DEVELOPMENT IN THE TROPICS (NE/0169-605X). [500] **5189**

ABSTRACTS ON TROPICAL AGRICULTURE (NE/0304-5951). [1,000] **149**

AC. THE ADCRAFTER (US/0001-8066). [4,000] **753**

AC/UNU NEWSLETTER / THE AMERICAN COUNCIL FOR THE UNITED NATIONS UNIVERSITY (US). [5,200] **1806**

ACA BULLETIN - ASSOCIATION FOR COMMUNICATION ADMINISTRATION (US/0360-0939). [400] **1103**

ACA NEWS (EDMONTON) (CN/0826-497X). [6,000] **5177**

ACAATO HANDBOOK (CN/0822-5710). **1806**

ACADEMIC LIBRARY BOOK REVIEW (US/0894-993X). [2,400] **4822**

ACADEMY ACCENTS (US/1071-376X). [1,200] **4931**

ACADEMY BOOKMAN, THE (US/0001-4249). [400] **3654**

ACADEMY FORUM (NEW YORK), THE (US/0192-1088). [4,000] **3918**

ACADEMY NEWSLETTER, THE (US/0897-5523). [25,000] **5079**

ACADEMY OF MANAGEMENT JOURNAL (US/0001-4273). [10,350] **858**

ACADIAN GENEALOGY EXCHANGE (US/0199-9591). [750] **2436**

ACADIANA PROFILE (US/0001-4397). [10,000] **2254**

ACADIENSIS (FREDERICTON) (CN/0044-5851). [900] **2717**

ACAFO (AG). [10,000] **4366**

ACCC COMMUNITY (CN/0839-0088). [16,000] **1807**

ACCENT (US/0192-7507). **2913**

ACCENT (US/0162-1955). [106,000] **4931**

ACCENT ON ARTS (CN/0821-0209). **5054**

ACCENT ON WORSHIP (US/0276-2358). [4,500] **4931**

ACCESS REPORTS REFERENCE FILE (US/0191-6696). [200] **2926**

ACCESS (SYRACUSE) (US/0095-5698). **2496**

ACCESS USA NEWS (US/1069-6784). [30,000] **4383**

ACCESS (VICTORIA, AUSTRALIA) (AT/1030-0155). **1802**

ACCESSIONS LIST, BRAZIL. CUMULATIVE LIST OF SERIALS / LIBRARY OF CONGRESS (BL/0731-4515). [500] **406**

ACCESSIONS LIST, EASTERN AFRICA (KE/0090-371X). [1,150] **406**

ACCESSIONS LIST, EASTERN AFRICA. ANNUAL SERIAL SUPPLEMENT (KE/0192-7388). [800] **406**

ACCESSIONS LIST, SOUTHEAST ASIA. CUMULATIVE LIST OF INDONESIAN SERIALS (IO/0163-4054). [1,050] **406**

ACCESSIONS LIST, SOUTHEAST ASIA. CUMULATIVE LIST OF MALAYSIA, SINGAPORE AND BRUNEI SERIALS (IO/0163-4046). [1,050] **406**

ACCESSIONS LIST, SOUTHEAST ASIA. CUMULATIVE LIST OF SERIALS, BURMA, THAILAND AND LAOS (IO/0732-7374). [1,050] **406**

ACCESSIONSKATALOG FOR DRAMATISK BIBLIOTEK (DK). [400] **3187**

ACCIAIO INOSSIDABILE, L' (IT/0515-2291). [2,000] **3996**

ACCIDENT PREVENTION (CN/0044-5878). [18,000] **2858**

ACCIDENT PREVENTION MAGAZINE (CN). [37,000] **2858**

ACCION (PY). [1,000] **5189**

ACCORD (CALGARY) (CN/0226-7845). [1,000] **2254**

ACCOUNTANCY SA (SA/0258-7254). [18,000] **735**

ACCOUNTANT (NAIROBI), THE (KE/1010-4135). [14,000] **735**

ACCOUNTANTS' JOURNAL (PH/0001-4753). **735**

ACCOUNTANT'S MAGAZINE, THE (UK/0001-4761). [13,500] **736**

ACCOUNTING AND FINANCE PARKVILLE (AT/0810-5391). [1,300] **736**

ACCOUNTING EDUCATORS' JOURNAL, THE (US/1041-0392). [450] **736**

ACCOUNTING HISTORIANS JOURNAL, THE (US/0148-4184). [850] **737**

ACCOUNTING HISTORIANS NOTEBOOK, THE (US/1075-1416). [1,000] **737**

ACCREDITATION (US/0099-0256). [6,000] **1807**

ACER NEWSLETTER (AT). [20,000] **1722**

ACHIEVEMENT (LONDON. 1969) (UK/0001-4907). [10,760] **1596**

ACHIEVEMENTS (WASHINGTON) (US/0270-7578). [5,000] **4701**

ACHTZEHNTE JAHRHUNDERT, DAS (GW). [800] **2672**

ACIS : JOURNAL OF THE ASSOCIATION FOR CONTEMPORARY IBERIAN STUDIES (UK/0955-4270). [300] **3260**

Controlled Circulation Index

ACJ (PLATTE CITY, MO.) (US/1068-8021). [2,000] **204**

ACORN JOURNAL : OFFICIAL JOURNAL OF THE AUSTRALIAN CONFEDERATION OF OPERATING ROOM NURSES (AT/0156-3491). [3,500] **3850**

ACORN (PLATTEVILLE), THE (US/0274-8762). [2,000] **1887**

ACQUISITION, BIBLIOGRAPHY, CATALOGUING NEWS / NATIONAL LIBRARY OF AUSTRALIA (AT/0725-0037). [60] **3187**

ACQUISIZIONI FUSIONI CONCORRENZA (IT). [400] **1596**

ACS NEWSLETTER / ASSOCIATION FOR CANADIAN STUDIES (CN/0714-2579). [1,000] **2526**

AC'S TECH FOR THE COMMODORE AMIGA (US/1053-7929). **1170**

ACSI-ON (CN/0821-5049). **3187**

ACSUS. CANADIAN STUDIES UPDATE (US/0734-4546). **2717**

ACSUS MEMBERSHIP DIRECTORY (US/0892-7111). [1,300] **2717**

ACT. ADVERTISING/COMMUNICATIONS TIMES (US/0193-4457). [40,000] **753**

ACT NEWSLETTER (SIMSBURY, CONN.) (US/0742-7751). [250] **1887**

ACTA AD ARCHAEOLOGIAM ET ARTIUM HISTORIAM PERTINENTIA (IT/0065-0900). [300] **335**

ACTA ADRIATICA (CI/0001-5113). **552**

ACTA AMAZONICA (BL/0044-5967). [1,500] **439**

ACTA ANAESTHESIOLOGICA ITALICA (IT/0374-4965). [1700] **3680**

ACTA ARCHAEOLOGICA (DK/0065-101X). [500] **253**

ACTA BIO-MEDICA DE L'ATENEO PARMENSE (IT/0392-4203). [500] **3544**

ACTA BIOLOGICA LEOPOLDENSIA (BL/0101-5354). [600] **531**

ACTA BIOQUIMICA CLINICA LATINOAMERICANA (AG/0325-2957). [2,200] **479**

ACTA BIOTECHNOLOGICA (GW/0138-4988). [450] **3685**

ACTA BOTANICA INDICA (II/0379-508X). [600] **497**

ACTA BOTANICA MALACITANA (SP/0210-9506). [500] **497**

ACTA - BRATISLAVA. UNIVERZITA. FAKULTA TELESNEJ VYCHOVY A SPORTU (XO). **4881**

ACTA CARDIOLOGICA (BE/0001-5385). [1,000] **3697**

ACTA CARDIOLOGICA MEDITERRANEA (IT/0392-9698). **3697**

ACTA CHIRURGICA BELGICA (BE/0001-5458). [1,050] **3957**

ACTA CHIRURGICA ITALICA (IT/0001-5466). [1500] **3957**

ACTA CIENTIFICA VENEZOLANA (VE/0001-5504). [21,000] **5080**

ACTA CYTOLOGICA (US/0001-5547). [6,500] **531**

ACTA DIRECTORY (CN/0848-2497). [9,500] **5460**

ACTA ENDOCRINOLOGICA (COPENHAGEN) (DK/0001-5598). [2,000] **3726**

ACTA FARMACEUTICA BONAERENSE (AG/0326-2383). [1,000] **4288**

ACTA GASTROENTEROLOGICA LATINOAMERICANA (AG/0300-9033). [2,500] **3794**

ACTA GENETICAE MEDICAE ET GEMELLOLOGIAE (IT/0001-5660). **541**

ACTA GEOGRAPHICA LOVANIENSIA (BE/0065-1257). [300] **2553**

ACTA GEOLOGICA LEOPOLDENSIA (BL/0102-1249). [200] **1364**

ACTA HISTOCHEMICA ET CYTOCHEMICA (JA/0044-5991). **531**

ACTA HORTICULTURAE (NE/0567-7572). [300] **2407**

ACTA JURIDICA (CAPE TOWN) (SA/0065-1346). [378] **2927**

ACTA LITERARIA (CL/0716-0909). [600] **3337**

ACTA MATHEMATICA HUNGARICA (HU/0236-5294). [1,000] **3490**

ACTA MEDICA AUXOLOGICA (IT/0001-6004). [1,200] **3544**

ACTA MEDICA (MEXICO) (MX/0001-5997). [1,200] **3544**

ACTA MEDICA PHILIPPINA (PH/0001-6071). **3544**

ACTA MOZARTIANA (GW/0001-6233). **4098**

ACTA MUSICOLOGICA (GW/0001-6241). [7,600] **4098**

ACTA NATURALIA DE L'ATENEO PARMENSE (IT/0392-419X). [350] **5080**

ACTA NEUROLOGICA SCANDINAVICA (DK/0001-6314). [1,350] **3825**

ACTA OBSTETRICIA ET GYNECOLOGICA SCANDINAVICA (SW/0001-6349). [2,200] **3756**

ACTA ONCOLOGICA (STOCKHOLM, SWEDEN) (SW/0284-186X). [2,500] **3808**

ACTA OPHTHALMOLOGICA (DK/0001-639X). [2,000] **3545**

ACTA ORIENTALIA (KBENHAVN) (DK/0001-6438). [500] **3261**

ACTA PEDIATRICA ESPANOLA (SP). [8,000] **3899**

ACTA PHARMACEUTICA FENNICA (FI/0356-3456). [1,000] **4288**

ACTA PHARMACEUTICA TURCICA (TU/1010-0849). **4289**

ACTA PHONIATRICA LATINA (IT/0392-3088). [1000] **3885**

ACTA PSYCHIATRICA SCANDINAVICA (DK/0001-690X). [1,400] **3919**

ACTA RADIOLOGICA (STOCKHOLM, SWEDEN : 1987) (SW/0284-1851). [6,000] **3938**

ACTA SLAVICA IAPONICA (JA/0288-3503). [500] **2672**

ACTA SOCIETATIS BOTANICORUM POLONIAE (PL/0001-6977). [1,200] **497**

ACTA STEREOLOGICA (XV/0351-580X). [500] **3491**

ACTA ZOOLOGICA ET PATHOLOGICA ANTVERPIENSIA (BE/0001-7280). [1,200] **5573**

ACTES. / ASSOCIATION CANADIENNE DE LINGUISTIQUE APPLIQUEE (CN). [600] **3261**

ACTES DE LECTURE, LES (FR/0758-1475). [2,500] **1722**

ACTION (UK). [2,000] **4932**

ACTION FOR CANADA'S CHILDREN (CN/0229-2653). [1,000] **1059**

ACTION FRANCAISE HEBDO, L' (FR/1166-3286). [10,000] **4461**

ACTION (GREENWOOD, IND.) (US/0744-0375). **4623**

ACTION IN TEACHER EDUCATION (US/0162-6620). [3,500] **1887**

ACTION INFORMATION (US). [7,000] **4932**

ACTION JURIDIQUE CFDT (FR). [5,600] **2927**

ACTION MISSIONNAIRE PARIS (FR/0184-6345). [5,000] **4932**

ACTION (TORONTO. 1970) (CN/0315-6036). [30,000] **4932**

ACTION (WINNIPEG) (CN/0701-1547). [500] **5550**

ACTIVE AND PASSIVE ELECTRONIC COMPONENTS (US/0882-7516). **2034**

ACTIVE (BELCONNEN) (AT/1031-282X). [25,000] **4881**

ACTIVIDAD MINERA (AG/0326-6672). [1,500] **2132**

ACTIVITE DES COURS ET TRIBUNAUX. STATISTIQUES DIVERSES (BE). [350] **3078**

ACTIVITIES / CHEMICAL INDUSTRY INSTITUTE OF TOXICOLOGY (US/8755-4259). [5,000] **3978**

ACTON FREE PRESS (CN). [4,650] **5779**

ACTS AND FACTS (US). **4932**

ACTS AND PROCEEDINGS OF THE GENERAL ASSEMBLY OF THE PRESBYTERIAN CHURCH IN CANADA (CN/0079-4996). [5,000] **5054**

ACTUALITE CHIMIQUE, L' (FR/0151-9093). [3,636] **959**

ACTUALITE DIOCESAINE (CN/0823-552X). [8,000] **4932**

ACTUALITE ECONOMIQUE (CN/0001-771X). [1,200] **1589**

ACTUALITE IMMOBILIERE (CN/0701-0516). [4,000] **4833**

ACTUALITE RELIGIEUSE DANS LE MONDE (1983) (FR/0757-3529). [20,000] **4932**

ACTUALITES ODONTO-STOMATOLOGIQUES (FR/0001-7817). **1315**

ACTUALITES (PARIS) (FR/0183-5017). [3,000] **821**

ACTUALITES PREVENTION (CN/0711-169X). **4763**

ACTUALITES SDM (CN/0842-1854). **1103**

ACTUARIAL RESEARCH CLEARING HOUSE (US/0732-5428). [320] **2872**

ACTUARY (US/0001-7825). [13,000] **2872**

ACTUEL CIDJ (FR/0337-9566). [5,500] **2484**

ACUCAA BULLETIN (US). [1,700] **383**

ACUTE CARE THERAPEUTICS (US/0898-2783). **3546**

AD 2000 (AT/1031-8453). [8,000] **4932**

AD ASTRA (WASHINGTON, D.C.) (US/1041-102X). [30,000] **3**

ADA STRATEGIES (US/0893-0570). [200] **1255**

ADB QUARTERLY REVIEW (PH/0115-074X). [10,000] **768**

ADB REVIEW / ASIAN DEVELOPMENT BANK (PH). [10,000] **768**

ADC TIMES (US/0749-2642). [15,000] **2254**

ADCA, AMERICAN DIRECTORY OF COLLECTION AGENCIES AND ATTORNEYS (US/0148-5350). **768**

ADDVANTAGE (US/0149-4082). [5,000] **4881**

ADELAIDE LAW REVIEW, THE (AT/0065-1915). [700] **2927**

ADELAIDE REVIEW (AT/0815-5992). [40,000] **312**

ADELPHI PAPERS (UK/0567-932X). [7,500] **4514**

ADEPT REPORT, THE (US/1053-2668). **1315**

ADHAESION (GW/0001-8198). [3,608] **1049**

ADHESIVES AGE (US/0001-821X). [23,000] **2007**

ADISTA : AGENZIA D'INFORMAZIONE STAMPA (IT). [12,000] **4461**

ADLER MUSEUM BULLETIN (SA). [1,500] **4083**

ADMINISTRATION & MANAGEMENT SPECIAL INTEREST SECTION NEWSLETTER (US/8756-629X). [3,500] **859**

ADMINISTRATION ET GESTION (CN/0704-9765). [1,000] **4624**

ADMINISTRATION OF JUSTICE MEMORANDA (US/0147-3603). [1,000] **2927**

ADMINISTRATIVE LAW REVIEW (US/0001-8368). **3092**

ADMINISTRATIVE REGISTER OF KENTUCKY (US/0096-1493). [800] **2928**

ADMINISTRATOR'S NOTEBOOK (US/0001-8430). [700] **1859**

ADMISSIONS DECISIONS STUDY - FLORIDA. UNIVERSITY, GAINESVILLE. GRADUATE SCHOOL (US/0148-9097). [1,000] **1792**

ADNEWS (OCT. 13, 1981) (CN/0712-9041). [6,500] **754**

ADOPTED CHILD (US/0745-3167). [3,000] **2276**

ADRICHALUT YISRAELIT (IS). [10,000] **287**

ADTALK (CN/0225-6991). **754**

ADULT AND CONTINUING EDUCATION TODAY (US/0001-8473). [1,900] **1799**

ADULT FAITH RESOURCES NETWORKER (US/0898-9729). [800] **4932**

ADULT VIDEO NEWS (US/0883-7090). [27,000] **4366**

ADVANCE DATA SERVICE / INTERNATIONAL LEAD AND ZINC STUDY GROUP (UK). **3997**

ADVANCE (DES MOINES, IOWA) (US/0889-8170). [70,000] **1125**

ADVANCE (SPRINGFIELD) (US/0001-8589). **5054**

ADVANCE (ZURICH) (CN/0824-6610). [3,124] **5779**

ADVANCED IMAGING (WOODBURY, N.Y.) (US/1042-0711). [35,000] **1276**

ADVANCED MATERIALS TECHNOLOGY (UK/0957-4778). [15,000] **5080**

ADVANCED PACKAGING (US/1065-0555). **2034**

ADVANCES (US/0741-9783). [5,000] **3546**

ADVANCES IN DENTAL RESEARCH (US/0895-9374). [3,000] **1315**

ADVANCES IN NEUROIMMUNOLOGY (UK/0960-5428). [500] **3826**

ADVANCES IN PHYSIOLOGY EDUCATION (US/1043-4046). [2,500 to 6,500] **577**

ADVANCES IN THERAPY (US/0741-238X). [5,000] **3546**

ADVANCES IN VLSI AND COMPUTER SYSTEM SERIES (US/0888-224X). **1246**

ADVENTURING IN CONSERVATION (CN/0225-6533). [1,000] **2185**

ADVERTISING EXPENDITURE IN MAIN MEDIA (AT/0313-2382). **1103**

ADVOCATE (DENVER, COLO.) (US/1040-2225). [28,500] **4285**

ADVOCATE (EDMONTON) (CN/0847-2890). [1,500] **5270**

ADVOCATE (LOS ANGELES, CALIF.), THE (US/0001-8996). [350,000] **2793**

ADVOCATE (MUNCIE, IND.), THE (US/0279-7097). **5228**

AEA ADVOCATE (US/0194-8849). [23,000] **1860**

AED (LONDON, ENGLAND) (UK/0144-8234). [6,000] **1544**

AEGEAN REVIEW (US/0891-7213). **3358**

AEGIS (WASHINGTON, D.C.) (US/0883-0029). [1,500] **4503**

AEJMC NEWS (US/0747-8909). [5,000] **2917**

AERIAL APPLICATOR, FARM, FOREST AND FIRE (US). [8,214] **158**

AERO REVUE (SZ/0001-9186). [24,000] **4**

AEROCOMERCIAL (AG/0326-1360). [11,500] **4**

AEROESPACIO (BUENOS AIRES, ARGENTINA) (AG). [27,000] **4**

AEROKURIER (GW/0341-1281). [48,000] **4**

AERONAUTICAL INFORMATION SERVICES PROVIDED BY STATES / SERVICES D'INFORMATION AERONAUTIQUE ASSURES PAR LES ETATS / SERVICIOS DE INFORMACION AERONAUTICA SUMINISTRADOS POR LOS ESTADOS (CN). [2,300] **4**

AERONAUTICAL JOURNAL, THE (UK/0001-9240). [2,000] **4**

AERONOMICA ACTA. A (BE/0572-3159). **5**

AEROSPACE ENGINEERING (WARRENDALE, PA.) (US/0736-2536). [45,000] **5**

AESIS QUARTERLY (AT/0313-704x). [400] **1361**

AETEI JOURNAL (II). [2,000] **4932**

AETS YEARBOOK (US). [1,000] **5081**

AFA WATCHBIRD, THE (US/0199-543X). [10,100] **4285**

AFFAIRES (MONTREAL. 1981) (CN/0229-3404). [94,000] **636**

AFFARSVARLDEN (1974) (SW/0345-3766). [25,000] **1544**

AFFIRMATIONS (US/0162-8038). **4932**

AFFIRMATIVE ACTION REGISTER (US/0146-2113). [52,000] **938**

AFGHANISTAN STUDIES JOURNAL (US/1046-9834). [500] **2501**

AFP ANNUAL REPORT (PH). **4033**

AFRICA DEVELOPMENT (SG/0378-3006). [1,000] **1544**

AFRICA ENTERPRISE UPDATE (SA). [40,000] **2254**

AFRICA FORUM (UK/0961-1142). **2501**

AFRICA HEALTH (UK/0141-9536). [5,000] **3547**

AFRICA INSIGHT (SA/0256-2804). [4,000] **5189**

AFRICA QUARTERLY (II/0001-9828). [650] **2636**

AFRICA TODAY (US/0001-9887). [2,300] **4462**

AFRICA (WASHINGTON, D.C.) (US/0084-2281). **2636**

AFRICAN-AMERICAN TRAVELER, THE (US/0895-6235). [1,000] **2553**

AFRICAN ECONOMIC HISTORY (US/0145-2258). [350] **1544**

AFRICAN FARMING AND FOOD PROCESSING (UK). [8,000] **45**

AFRICAN HERALD, THE (US/1069-8205). **5746**

AFRICAN RECORDER (II/0002-0125). [1,000] **2497**

AFRICAN REVIEW (DAR ES SALAAM, TANZANIA) (TZ/0002-0117). [500] **5189**

AFRICAN STATISTICAL YEARBOOK. ANNUAIRE STATISTIQUE POUR L'AFRIQUE (ET). [1,500] **5320**

AFRICAN STUDIES BY SOVIET SCHOLARS (RU). [3,000] **4539**

AFRICAN STUDIES REVIEW (US/0002-0206). **2498**

AFRICAN STUDY MONOGRAPHS (JA/0285-1601). [1,000] **2498**

AFRICAN STUDY MONOGRAPHS. SUPPLEMENTARY ISSUE (JA/0286-9667). [1,000] **2498**

AFRICAN VIOLET MAGAZINE (US/0002-0265). [12,000] **2408**

AFRICAN WOMAN (UK/0953-9816). [5,000] **5550**

AFRICANA NOTES AND NEWS (SA/0002-032X). [450] **2498**

AFRIKA JAHRBUCH (GW). **4462**

AFRIKA-POST (GW/0002-0389). [3,000] **4515**

AFRIKASPECTRUM (GW/0002-0397). [500] **5189**

AFRIQUE ET L'ASIE MODERNES, L' (FR/0399-0370). [3,000] **2637**

AFRIQUE HISTOIRE U.S (US/0741-2592). [2,500] **2637**

AFRO-AMERICANS IN NEW YORK LIFE AND HISTORY (US/0364-2437). [800] **2254**

AFRO SCHOLAR NEWSLETTER (US/0894-0762). [5,000] **5189**

AFSM INTERNATIONAL (US/1049-2135). [6,000] **1235**

AFTERMATH (US/0737-1381). [10,000] **4856**

AFVA BULLETIN / AMERICAN FILM AND VIDEO ASSOCIATION (US). [900] **4062**

AFVA EVALUATIONS (US/1051-5925). [1,000] **4062**

AG ALERT (US/0161-5408). [51,316] **45**

AG-ALERT (LONDON, ONT.) (CN). [500] **45**

AG IMPACT (US/0196-0857). **45**

AG. REVIEW (PUTNAM, CONN.) (US/0194-6625). [45,000] **45**

AGADA (US/0740-2392). [1,000] **5045**

AGARD HIGHLIGHTS (FR/0302-5020). **6**

AGATE. ALBERTA GIFTED AND TALENTED EDUCATION (CN/0833-0603). [250] **1874**

AGE & NUTRITION (FR). **4186**

AGE REFDEX (TH). **5081**

AGEING INTERNATIONAL (US/0163-5158). [2,000] **5270**

AGENCY SALES (US/0749-2332). [20,000] **921**

AGENDA, L' (IT). [8,000] **3547**

AGENDA OF REGULATIONS (US/1044-9876). **2153**

AGENDEN / AKTIVITATEN 90/91 (AU). [4,500] **4625**

AGENOR (BE/0002-080X). **4515**

AGENT & MANAGER (US/1065-5921). [22,000] **859**

AGENTS AND ACTIONS (SZ/0065-4299). [900] **4289**

AGID NEWS (TH). [2,500] **1351**

AGIS : ATTORNEY-GENERAL'S INFORMATION SERVICE (AT/0312-4592). **2928**

AGLOW NEWSLETTER (MELVILLE) (CN/0823-0315). **5054**

AGO NEWS (CN/0829-4437). [23,000] 335

AGORA, PAPELES DE FILOSOFIA (SP). [600] 4339

AGORA PARIS. 1986 (FR/0984-4783). 2249

AGRARISCH RECHT (NE/0167-4242). [1,600] 2928

AGRARTECHNIK INTERNATIONAL (GW). [15,450] 158

AGRI-BOOK MAGAZINE (CN/0705-3878). 47

AGRI-BOOK MAGAZINE. TOP CROP MANAGER (CN). [23,000] 47

AGRI FINANCE (US/0002-1164). [22,000] 768

AGRI MARKETING (US/0002-1180). [10,000] 47

AGRI NEWS (US/0745-3450). [21,800] 5694

AGRI-PLASTICS REPORT, THE (US/1073-1776). [300] 47

AGRIBUSINESS DECISION (AT/0311-0370). [500] 48

AGRIBUSINESS NEWS FOR KENTUCKY (US/0899-1294). [3,500] 48

AGRIBUSINESS WORLDWIDE (US). [25,000] 48

AGRICULTURA DE LAS AMERICAS (OVERLAND PARK, KANS.) (US/0002-1350). [40,000] 48

AGRICULTURA EM SAO PAULO (BL/0044-6793). [2,000] 48

AGRICULTURA (MADRID, SPAIN) (SP/0002-1334). [8,000] 49

AGRICULTURAL AVIATION (WASHINGTON, D.C.) (US/0745-4864). [8,500] 6

AGRICULTURAL CREDIT CONDITIONS SURVEY (US/0737-948X). [4,000] 49

AGRICULTURAL EDUCATION MAGAZINE, THE (US/0732-4677). [5,500] 50

AGRICULTURAL ENGINEER, THE (UK/0308-5732). [4,000] 50

AGRICULTURAL FINANCE REVIEW (US/0002-1466). [1,800] 769

AGRICULTURAL HISTORY (US/0002-1482). [1,250] 50

AGRICULTURAL HISTORY REVIEW, THE (UK/0002-1490). [1,000] 50

AGRICULTURAL NEWSLETTER (SUDBURY) (CN/0228-2038). 50

AGRICULTURAL RESEARCH IN KANSAS (US/0749-2197). [3,000] 51

AGRICULTURAL SCIENCE IN FINLAND (FI/0789-600X). [1,500] 52

AGRICULTURAL SITUATION IN INDIA (II/0002-1679). [1,100] 52

AGRICULTURE & RESOURCES QUARTERLY (AT/1032-9722). 53

AGRICULTURE (MONTREAL) (CN/0002-1687). [4,000] 54

AGRICULTURE TEACHERS DIRECTORY (US). [12,993] 54

AGRIPROMO ABIDJAN (IV/1018-8568). [8,000] 2813

AGRISEARCH (CARBONDALE, ILL.) (US). [7,000] 54

AGRITROP [ENGLSIH ED.] (FR). [450] 54

AGRO SUR (CL/0304-8802). [500] 55

AGRONOMIA COSTARRICENSE (CR/0377-9424). [1,400] 56

AGROPECUARIA : PRECOS, MEDIOS E INDICES DE ARRENDAMENTOS, VENDAS DE TERRAS, SALARIOS, SERVICOS (BL). [2,800] 56

AGROTECHNOLOGY TRANSFER (US/0883-8631). [3,000] 57

AGROTECNIA DE CUBA (CU/0568-3114). [400,000] 57

AGROTIKE (ATHENS, GREECE, : 1983) (GR). [30,000] 57

AGSCENE (US/0279-666X). [9,000] 57

AHA NEWS (CHICAGO, ILL.) (US/0891-6608). [40,000] 3775

AHMADIYYA GAZETTE (CN/0229-5644). 5041

AI APPLICATIONS (US/1051-8266). 1210

AI DIRECTORY (US/1050-7965). [12,000] 1210

AI MAGAZINE (US/0738-4602). [12,000] 1211

AI TODAY (US/0893-6552). [10,000] 1211

AIBC BULLETIN (US/1040-6018). [75] 1419

AICHE JOURNAL (US/0001-1541). [4,300] 2007

AIDA PARKER NEWSLETTER (SA). 4515

AIDS & SOCIETY (US/1055-0380). [2,000] 3663

AIDS BULLETIN TYGERBERG (SA/1019-8334). [2,000] 3711

AIDS CASES, STATE OF NEW JERSEY, AS OF ... (US). 3663

AIDS TREATMENT NEWS (US/1052-4207). [5,000] 3664

AIGA JOURNAL OF GRAPHIC DESIGN (US/0736-5322). [9,000] 376

AIMER ET SERVIR (FR). 3547

AIPE FACILITIES (US/1054-7541). [10,000] 1964

AIPE NEWSLINE (US/8750-2046). [9,200] 1964

AIR CARGO WORLD (US/0745-5100). [22,000] 5375

AIR FAN (FR/0223-0038). [16,000] 4033

AIR NAVIGATION PLAN, CARRIBBEAN AND SOUTH AMERICAN REGIONS / PLAN DE NAVIGATION AERIENNE, REGIONS CARAIBES ET AMERIQUE DU SUD. PLAN DE NAVEGACION AEREA, REGIONES DEL CARIBE Y DE SUDAMERICA (CN). 7

AIR PROFESSIONAL FILE, THE (US/8756-6168). 1807

AIR PROGRESS (US/0002-2500). 8

AIR TRANSPORT STATISTICS. FLIGHT CREW LICENCES (AT/0727-2774). [285] 41

AIR UNIVERSITY LIBRARY INDEX TO MILITARY PERIODICALS (US/0002-2586). [1,600] 4061

AIRCRAFT MAINTENANCE INTERNATIONAL (UK/0955-8063). [10,000] 9

AIRCRAFT TECHNOLOGY ENGINEERING & MAINTENANCE (UK/0967-439X). 1964

AIRFAIR (US/0044-7005). [55,000] 5460

AIRFINANCE ANNUAL (UK/0266-2132). [5,000] 9

AIRFINANCE JOURNAL (UK/0143-2257). [8,000] 9

AIRPORT FORUM (GW/0002-2802). [9,335] 10

AIRPORT POCKET GUIDE (DOMESTIC ED.) (US/0894-1513). [1,200] 5460

AIRPORT SUPPORT (UK). 10

AIRPORTS INTERNATIONAL (UK/0002-2853). [12,000] 11

AIRPOWER JOURNAL (US/0897-0823). [20,000] 4034

AISPICH CHAKWAN (CN/0824-4715). [2,000] 5271

AIT. ARCHITEKTUR, INNENARCHITEKTUR, TECHNISCHER AUSBAU (GW/0173-8046). [10,000] 287

AITIM : BOLETIN DE INFORMACION TECNICA / ASOCIACION DE INVESTIGACION TECHNICA DE LAS INDUSTRIAS DE LA MADERNA Y CORCHO (PO). 2374

AJS REVIEW (US/0364-0094). [1,000] 5045

AKIKI, THE (US/0091-1607). [150] 2436

AKRON BUGLE (US). [1,650] 5713

AKRON BUSINESS AND ECONOMIC REVIEW (US/0044-7048). [2,500] 637

AKTUELL (UK/0959-5740). 3262

AL-AALAM (UK). 2501

AL-DARAH (SU). [13,000] 2645

AL-FIHRIST (LE). [500] 407

AL-GEZIRA (SP/0213-2966). [1,000] 2609

AL-JAWHARAH (QA). [16,000] 5550

AL-MAGALLA AL-TIBBIYYA AL-URDUNIYYA (JO/0446-9283). 3547

AL-MAWQIF AL-ADABI (SY). 3358

AL-MUJTAMA AL-MADANI WA-AL-TAHAWWUL AL-DIMUQRATI FI AL-WATAN AL-ARABI (UA). 4625

AL-MUSAFIR AL-ARABI (UK/0267-0194). [23,000] 5460

AL-RIYADAH WA-AL-SHABAB (TS). [40,000] 4882

AL-TAMWIL WA-AL-TANMIYAH (US/0250-7455). [8,500] 4708

AL-TAWTHIQ AL-ILAMI / TASDURU AN MARKAZ AL-TAWTHIQ AL-ILAMI LI-DUWAL AL-KHALIJ AL-ARABI (IQ). [2,500] 3188

AL-THAQAFAH AL-AJNABIYAH (IQ). 3359

AL-TIJARAH (TS). [7,000] 1545

AL-ZIMAM WA-AL-MISAHAT AL-MUNZARIAH FI JUMHURIYAT MISR AL-ARABIYAH / AL-JIHAZ AL-MARKAZI LIL-TABIAH AL-AMMAH WA-AL-IHSA (UA). 1461

ALA BULLETIN : A PUBLICATION OF THE AFRICAN LITERATURE ASSOCIATION (CN/0146-4965). [1,000] 3359

ALA WASHINGTON NEWSLETTER (US/0001-1746). [1,900] 3188

ALA WHERE TO STAY BOOK, EAST (US/0731-3152). 2803

ALA WHERE TO STAY BOOK, WEST (US/8755-9242). 2803

ALABAMA ARCHITECTURE (US). [1,800] 287

ALABAMA CATTLEMAN (US/0516-3889). [16,000] 204

ALABAMA DEVELOPMENT NEWS (US/0889-7468). [15,000] 1545

ALABAMA ECONOMIC OUTLOOK / DEVELOPED BY CENTER FOR BUSINESS AND ECONOMIC RESEARCH, UNIVERSITY OF ALABAMA (US). [600] 1545

ALABAMA FARMER (US). [12,134] 57

ALABAMA FORESTS (US/0275-6625). [3,500] 2374

ALABAMA INDUSTRIAL DIRECTORY (US/1061-9585). [5,000] 2133

ALABAMA JOURNAL, THE (US/0745-323X). [20,686] 5625

ALABAMA LAWYER, THE (US/0002-4287). [9,000] 2929

ALABAMA LIBRARIAN, THE (US/0002-4295). [975] 3188

ALABAMA PEACE OFFICERS' JOURNAL (US/0279-5175). [4,000] 3156

ALABAMA PURCHASOR (US/0002-4325). [5,300] 948

ALABAMA SCHOOL JOURNAL (US/0002-435X). [64,000] 1860

ALABAMA WILDLIFE (US/0894-8356). [6,000] 4868

ALABAMA'S HEALTH (US/0145-6857). [1,200] 4764

ALALUZ (US/0044-7064). [1,000] 3359

ALAM AL-ISTITHMAR AL-ARABI. ARAB BUSINESS REPORT (NE). [25,000] 1545

ALAM TUB AL-ASSNAN (GW). [8,000] 1315

ALAMANCE GENEALOGIST (US). [150] 2436

ALAMBRE (GW/0002-4406). [3,370] 3475

ALASKA AIRLINES MAGAZINE (US). [35,000] 2527

ALASKA BAPTIST MESSENGER (US/0194-7834). [2,500] 5054

ALASKA BUSINESS MONTHLY (US/8756-4092). [10,000] 637

ALASKA ECONOMIC REPORT, THE (US). [650] 1461

ALASKA ECONOMIC TRENDS (US/0160-3345). [3,000] 1461

ALASKA EDUCATION NEWS (US/0516-4842). [1,500] 1723

ALASKA FISHERMAN'S JOURNAL (US/0164-8330). [12,000] 2293

ALASKA GEOGRAPHIC (US/0361-1353). [7,000] 2553

ALASKA MARINE RADIO DIRECTORY (US/8755-3422). [11,000] 1148

ALASKA MEDICINE (US/0002-4538). [1,300] 3547

ALASKA NURSE, THE (US/0002-4546). [500] 3850

ALASKA STATE DRUG ABUSE PLAN. REVISED UPDATE (US). 1339

ALASKA STATISTICAL QUARTERLY (US/0401-1961). [800] 1528

ALASKA'S WILDLIFE (US/1052-2727). [10,000] 4868

ALBANIA REPORT (US/0002-4651). [3,000] 4462

ALBANIAN CATHOLIC BULLETIN (US/0272-7250). [1,500] 5022

ALBANY LAW JOURNAL OF SCIENCE & TECHNOLOGY (US/1059-4280). [750] 2929

ALBANY LAW REVIEW (US/0002-4678). [800] 2929

ALBANY NEWS (ALBANY, TEX.) (US). [2,100] 5746

ALBANY STATE COLLEGE JOURNAL OF ARTS AND SCIENCES (US/0199-9826). [500] 1808

ALBEMARLE MAGAZINE, THE (US/0273-7841). [10,000] 2527

ALBERTA BUSINESS (CALGARY) (CN/0827-2603). [10,000] 637

ALBERTA CATHOLIC DIRECTORY (CN/0316-473X). [1,500] 5022

ALBERTA CATTLEMAN, THE (CN/0226-6075). 205

ALBERTA COUNSELLETTER (CN/0381-5951). 1723

ALBERTA CRAFT MAGAZINE (CN/0834-910X). [1,200] 369

ALBERTA DOCTORS' DIGEST, THE (CN/0833-8477). [4,400] 3547

ALBERTA ENGLISH (CN/0382-5191). 3262

ALBERTA FACT SHEET (CN/0704-4488). [3,000] **5178**

ALBERTA FAMILY HISTORIES SOCIETY QUARTERLY (CN/0228-9288). [180] **2436**

ALBERTA GREENHOUSE NOTES (CN). [700] **2408**

ALBERTA LIBRARY BOARD REPORT (CN/0715-1640). [500] **3189**

ALBERTA MODERN LANGUAGE JOURNAL (CN/0318-5176). [420] **3263**

ALBERTA PERSPECTIVE (CN/0713-8067). [1,200] **5271**

ALBERTA SCIENCE EDUCATION JOURNAL (CN/0701-1024). [800] **5082**

ALBERTA SCIENCE TEACHER, THE (CN/0229-3099). [820] **5082**

ALBERTA WILD ROSE QUARTER HORSE JOURNAL (CN/0227-0579). [10,000] **2796**

ALBERTOA (BL). [1,000] **498**

ALBION (UK). [450] **4563**

ALBION (BOONE) (US/0095-1390). [1,400] **2672**

ALBUM (SP). [25,000] **2841**

ALBUM (MADRID, SPAIN) (SP). [25,000] **335**

ALBUM NETWORK, THE (US/0739-1641). [5,000] **4099**

ALCHEMIST (LASALLE) (CN/0384-8523). [500] **3359**

ALCOHOL (FAYETTEVILLE, N.Y.) (US/0741-8329). **1339**

ALCOHOL HEALTH AND RESEARCH WORLD (US/0090-838X). [8,000] **1339**

ALCOOL OU SANTE PARIS (FR/0002-5054). [10,000] **1340**

ALDERSGATE NEWS (CN/0711-2769). [4,000] **4933**

ALDRICHIMICA ACTA (US/0002-5100). [250,000] **960**

ALDUS MAGAZINE (US/1046-0616). [230,000] **1284**

ALERGIA (MEXICO) (MX/0002-5151). [3,000] **3665**

ALERT (US). **637**

ALERT (SACRAMENTO, CALIF.) (US/0882-0929). [9,500] **817**

ALEXANDRIA DAILY TOWN TALK, THE (US). [39,773 daily 41,270 Sunday] **5683**

ALEXANOR (FR/0002-5208). [1,250] **5574**

ALFA (BL/0002-5216). [1,000] **3359**

ALFRED DEAKIN LECTURE, THE (AT). [1000] **4625**

ALGEMEEN NEDERLANDS TIJDSCHRIFT VOOR WIJSBEGEERTE (NE/0002-5275). [800] **4340**

ALGONQUIAN AND IROQUOIAN LINGUISTICS (CN/0711-382X). [200] **3263**

ALGONQUIN IMPACT (CN/0704-707X). **5780**

ALI-ABA CLE REVIEW (US/0044-7560). [89,000] **1808**

ALI ANTICHE (IT/0394-6185). [1,000] **11**

ALI REPORTER, THE (US/0164-5757). [2,750] **2931**

ALIGARH JOURNAL OF ENGLISH STUDIES, THE (II/0258-0365). [300] **3359**

ALIMENTALEX (MADRID) (SP/0214-803X). [1,000] **2326**

ALIMENTARIA (SP/0300-5755). [5,000] **4764**

ALIMENTOLOGUE (CN/0823-9355). **2326**

ALIMENTOS PROCESADOS (US/0744-625X). [21,000] **2326**

ALISO (US/0065-6275). [500] **498**

ALIVE (VANCOUVER) (CN/0228-586X). [20,000] **4187**

ALKI (US/8756-4173). [1,300] **3189**

ALKOHOL- OG NARKOTIKAMISBRUGET KBENHAVN. 1988 (DK/0904-4450). [25,000] **1340**

ALL ABOUT BLOWOUT (NO). [10,000] **4249**

ALLEGRO (NEW YORK, N.Y.) (US/0002-5704). [20,000] **4099**

ALLERGIE UND IMMUNOLOGIE (GW/0323-4398). **3665**

ALLERGOLOGIE (GW/0344-5062). **3665**

ALLERGY ALERT (CN/0824-1333). [650] **3665**

ALLERGY PROCEEDINGS (US/1046-9354). [3,000] **3666**

ALLERTONIA (US/0735-8032). [200] **498**

ALLES UBER WEIN (GW/0175-8314). **2363**

ALLESTIRE (IT). [8,000] **287**

ALLGEMEINE SCHWEIZERISCHE MILITARZEITSCHRIFT (SZ). [31,539] **4034**

ALLGEMEINE ZEITSCHRIFT FUER PHILOSOPHIE (GW). [1,200] **4340**

ALLIANCE (IE). **5803**

ALLIANCE LIFE (US/1040-6794). [55,000] **4933**

ALLIANCE (OTTAWA. ENGLISH ED.) (CN/0838-7990). [180,000 (Canada)] **1643**

ALLIANZ REPORT (GW/0943-4569). [6,000] **2109**

ALLIED HEALTH EDUCATION NEWSLETTER (US). [1,500] **3548**

ALLIED INDUSTRIAL WORKER (US/0002-6107). [72,000] **1643**

ALLMAN MANADSSTATISTIK (SW/0039-7253). [3,000] **5320**

ALLPRISER (CN). [8,000] **2603**

ALLUMINIO E LEGHE (IT). [5,500] **3997**

ALMANAC OF THE 50 STATES (US/0887-0519). **1923**

ALMANACH MODERNE (CN/0315-2898). [150,000] **2484**

AL'MANAKH VYDAVNYTSTVA "TRYZUB" (CN/0824-5908). [4,100] **4812**

ALMANAQUE PUERTORRIQUENO (PR). [15,000] **2527**

ALMOND FACTS (US/0886-4365). [9,000] **2408**

ALMOST FREE RECIPES AND COOKBOOKS UPDATES (US/0736-170X). [1,200] **2788**

ALOE (SA). [1,300] **498**

ALPES, LES (SZ). [70,000] **5461**

ALPHA ACTION REPORTER (CN/0227-0897). [100] **4383**

ALPHA DELTA KAPPAN (US/0002-6387). [58,000] **5228**

ALPHA DELTA PHI LITERARY JOURNAL, THE (CN/0712-4589). **1089**

ALPHA OMEGAN (US/0002-6417). [9000] **1315**

ALPHABET : THE JOURNAL OF THE FRIENDS OF CALLIGRAPHY (US). [700] **369**

ALPHABETICAL DIRECTORY OF ATTORNEYS IN NEW YORK STATE (US/0738-8152). [1,000] **2932**

ALPHABETICAL INDEX OF CONSTITUENT PARTICULARS OF TRADE MARKS (AT/0312-3278). [60] **1301**

ALSHP NEWSLETTER (US). [750] **4290**

ALTA DIRECCION (SP/0002-6549). [15,000] **1596**

ALTADENA REVIEW, THE (US/0162-8208). [200] **3337**

ALTERNATE ROUTES (CN/0702-8865). [350] **5238**

ALTERNATIVE ENERGY RETAILER (US/0273-8163). [16,000] **1931**

ALTERNATIVE PRESS INDEX (US/0002-662X). [1,000] **4186**

ALTERNATIVES ECONOMIQUES DIJON (FR/0247-3739). [46,000] **1589**

ALTERNATIVES (INGRAM, TEX.) (US/0893-5025). [100,000] **2595**

ALTERNATIVES TO THE HIGH COST OF LITIGATION (US/0736-3613). [4,000] **3095**

ALTERNATIVES (WASHINGTON, D.C.) (US/1070-3047). [3,000] **4625**

ALUMI-NEWS (CN/0705-4157). [19,000] **598**

ALUMINIUM INDUSTRY (UK/0268-5280). [5,000] **3997**

ALUMNAE DIRECTORY OF SWEET BRIAR COLLEGE (US). [12,000] **1096**

ALUMNAE MAGAZINE - SWEET BRIAR COLLEGE (US/0039-7342). [12,000] **1808**

ALUMNI DIRECTORY - BOSTON UNIVERSITY. SCHOOL OF MEDICINE. ALUMNI ASSOCIATION (US/0743-5533). [4,200] **3548**

ALUMNI DIRECTORY - CHRISTIAN BROTHERS COLLEGE (MEMPHIS, TENN.) (US/0740-1779). [300] **1098**

ALUMNI DIRECTORY - THE UNIVERSITY OF CHICAGO LAW SCHOOL (US/0162-0371). **1099**

ALUMNI DIRECTORY - UNIVERSITY OF VIRGINIA. ALUMNI ASSOCIATION (US/0738-3762). [50,000] **1100**

ALUMNI MAGAZINE (MORGANTOWN, W. VA.) (US). [100,000] **1100**

ALUMNI UPDATE : PHILADELPHIA COLLEGE OF TEXTILES AND SCIENCE (US). [9,000] **1101**

ALUMNINEWS - CARLETON UNIVERSITY (CN/0226-5389). [40,000] **1101**

ALVARADO POST (US). [2,600] **5746**

ALWAYS JUKIN' (US/0896-9345). [3,000] **4099**

AMANECER (ENGLISH ED.) (US/1055-7008). [3,000] **4933**

AMATEUR ENTOMOLOGIST : THE JOURNAL OF THE AMATEUR ENTOMOLOGISTS' SOCIETY, THE (UK). [2,000] **5605**

AMATEUR WRESTLING NEWS (US/0569-1796). [9,000] **4882**

AMBC NEWS (US/1064-1599). [4,500] **205**

AMBIENTE (IT). [15,000] **2211**

AMBIENTE CUCINA, L' (IT/0392-5730). [22,100] **2898**

AMBIENTE MEDICO : REVISTA DEL HOSPITAL J.A. FERNANDEZ (AG/0326-0674). [500] **3775**

AMBIENTE SALUTE TERRITORIO (IT). [4,000] **2211**

AMBIX (UK/0002-6980). [550] **960**

AMBULATORY RECORD MONITOR (US/1057-753X). [500] **3776**

AMC. ACTA MEDICA COLOMBIANA (CK/0120-2448). [3,000] **3794**

AMC NEWSLETTER (US). [1,800] **4099**

AME JOURNAL (US). **11**

AMEGHINIANA (AG/0002-7014). [800] **4226**

AMENAGEMENT ET NATURE (FR/0044-7463). [4,000] **2186**

AMERICA OGGI (US/1042-6965). [60,000 (daily, morning)] **5709**

AMERICAN AERONAUT (US/0279-7968). [15,000] **1643**

AMERICAN AGENT & BROKER (US/0002-7200). [39,000] **2873**

AMERICAN AMATEUR JOURNALIST, THE (US/1046-0470). [350] **2770**

AMERICAN ANTHROPOLOGIST (US/0002-7294). [12,000] **227**

AMERICAN ANTIQUITY; A QUARTERLY REVIEW OF AMERICAN ARCHAEOLOGY (US/0002-7316). [6,000] **253**

AMERICAN-ARAB AFFAIRS (US/0731-6763). [18,500] **4515**

AMERICAN ARCHIVIST, THE (US/0360-9081). [4,600] **2478**

AMERICAN ART JOURNAL, THE (US/0002-7359). [1,400] **336**

AMERICAN ART THERAPY ASSOCIATION NEWSLETTER (US/1066-4076). [4,100] **4572**

AMERICAN ASIAN REVIEW, THE (US/0737-6650). [400] **2645**

AMERICAN ATHEIST, THE (US/0516-9623). [30,000] **4933**

AMERICAN BABY (US/0044-7544). [1,000,000] **2276**

AMERICAN BABY'S CHILDBIRTH EDUCATOR (US/0279-490X). [22,000] **3756**

AMERICAN BAPTIST WOMAN, THE (US/0191-0183). **5055**

AMERICAN BAR, THE CANADIAN BAR, THE INTERNATIONAL BAR, THE (US). [33,000] **3123**

AMERICAN BENEDICTINE REVIEW, THE (US/0002-7650). [1,000] **5023**

AMERICAN BIBLE SOCIETY RECORD (US/0006-0801). [350,000] **5014**

AMERICAN BICYCLIST AND MOTORCYCLIST (US/0002-7677). [11,025] **427**

AMERICAN BIOLOGY TEACHER, THE (US/0002-7685). [10,000] **441**

AMERICAN BOOKSELLER (NEW YORK. 1977) (US/0148-5903). [9,500] **4823**

AMERICAN BUSINESS LAW JOURNAL (US/0002-7766). [2,300] **3095**

AMERICAN CAMELLIA YEARBOOK, THE (US/0065-762X). [4,000] **2408**

AMERICAN CERAMIC CIRCLE JOURNAL (US/0899-806X). [400] **2586**

AMERICAN CERAMIC SOCIETY BULLETIN (US/0002-7812). [13,000] **2586**

AMERICAN CHIANINA JOURNAL (US/0198-8816). [4,000] **205**

AMERICAN CHIROPRACTOR, THE (US/0194-6536). [32,000] **4379**

AMERICAN CHRISTMAS TREE JOURNAL (US/0569-3845). [2,000] **58**

AMERICAN CLINICAL LABORATORY (US/1041-3235). [72,000] **3548**

AMERICAN COLLECTOR'S JOURNAL, THE (US/0164-7008). [51,000] **248**

AMERICAN COMPUTER LAW DIGEST (US/8755-1675). [2,000] **2932**

AMERICAN CURRENTS (US/1070-7352). [350] **2294**

AMERICAN DELI-BAKERY NEWS (US/0891-3331). **2326**

AMERICAN — Controlled Circulation Index

AMERICAN DEMOGRAPHICS (US/0163-4089). [34,000] **4549**

AMERICAN DOCTORAL DISSERTATIONS (US/0065-809X). [700] **1808**

AMERICAN DRUGGIST (1974) (US/0190-5279). [92,000] **4290**

AMERICAN DYESTUFF REPORTER (US/0002-8266). [11,500] **5347**

AMERICAN ECONOMIST (NEW YORK, N.Y. 1960), THE (US/0569-4345). [6,000] **1461**

AMERICAN EDUCATOR (US/0148-432X). **1723**

AMERICAN ELM, THE (US/0736-9794). [225] **2436**

AMERICAN ENTERPRISE (WASHINGTON, D.C.), THE (US/1047-3572). [15,000] **638**

AMERICAN ETHNOLOGIST (US/0094-0496). [3,500] **228**

AMERICAN EXPORT REGISTER (US/0272-1163). [22,000] **822**

AMERICAN EXPRESS SKY GUIDE (US/0744-091X). **11**

AMERICAN FAMILY PHYSICIAN (1970) (US/0002-838X). [140,000] **3736**

AMERICAN FARM & HOME ALMANAC, THE (US/0065-8278). [650,000] **2527**

AMERICAN FARRIERS' JOURNAL (US/0274-6565). [4,000] **2796**

AMERICAN FASTENER JOURNAL (US/1064-3834). **1596**

AMERICAN FENCING (US/0002-8436). [8,000] **4882**

AMERICAN FERN JOURNAL (US/0002-8444). [1,300] **498**

AMERICAN FITNESS (US/0893-5238). [30,000] **2595**

AMERICAN FOLKLORE SOCIETY NEWSLETTER, THE (US/0745-5178). [2,216] **2318**

AMERICAN FOOD AND AG EXPORTER (US/1065-3775). [12,500] **2326**

AMERICAN FUCHSIA SOCIETY BULLETIN (US/0194-3456). [1,400] **2408**

AMERICAN GENEALOGICAL-BIOGRAPHICAL INDEX (US). **2478**

AMERICAN GLASS REVIEW (US/0002-8649). [1,400] **2586**

AMERICAN GO JOURNAL, THE (US/0148-0243). [1,200] **4856**

AMERICAN HARP JOURNAL, THE (US/0002-869X). [3,400] **4099**

AMERICAN HOCKEY MAGAZINE (US/8756-3789). [30,000] **4882**

AMERICAN ILLUSTRATION SHOWCASE (US/0278-8128). [34,550] **376**

AMERICAN IMAGO (US/0065-860X). [1,000] **4572**

AMERICAN INDIAN CULTURE AND RESEARCH JOURNAL (US/0161-6463). [1,000] **2254**

AMERICAN INDIAN LAW NEWSLETTER (US/0002-8886). [700] **2932**

AMERICAN INDIAN LAW REVIEW (US/0094-002X). [850] **2932**

AMERICAN INDIAN REPORT (US/0894-4040). [550] **2719**

AMERICAN INDUSTRY (US/0002-8908). [25,000] **859**

AMERICAN INVENTOR (BLOOMINGTON, IND.) (US/1042-1890). [5,000] **5082**

AMERICAN JEWISH ARCHIVES (US/0002-905X). [5,000] **2255**

AMERICAN JEWISH HISTORY (US/0164-0178). [3,300] **2255**

AMERICAN JOURNAL OF ARCHAEOLOGY (US/0002-9114). [3,400] **254**

AMERICAN JOURNAL OF BOTANY (US/0002-9122). [5,000] **498**

AMERICAN JOURNAL OF CHINESE MEDICINE, THE (US/0192-415X). **3548**

AMERICAN JOURNAL OF COSMETIC SURGERY, THE (US/0748-8068). [5,000] **3958**

AMERICAN JOURNAL OF CRIMINAL LAW (US/0092-2315). [750] **3105**

AMERICAN JOURNAL OF EEG TECHNOLOGY, THE (US/0002-9238). [3,200] **3827**

AMERICAN JOURNAL OF ENOLOGY AND VITICULTURE (US/0002-9254). [3,400] **2363**

AMERICAN JOURNAL OF FAMILY THERAPY, THE (US/0192-6187). [2,800] **4573**

AMERICAN JOURNAL OF GERMANIC LINGUISTICS AND LITERATURES (US/1040-8207). [200] **3263**

AMERICAN JOURNAL OF HEALTH PROMOTION (US/0890-1171). [6,000] **4764**

AMERICAN JOURNAL OF OCCUPATIONAL THERAPY, THE (US/0272-9490). [43,000] **1874**

AMERICAN JOURNAL OF OPHTHALMOLOGY (US/0002-9394). [18,000] **3871**

AMERICAN JOURNAL OF OTOLOGY (NEW YORK, N.Y.), THE (US/0192-9763). [1,500] **3886**

AMERICAN JOURNAL OF PERINATOLOGY (US/0735-1631). [1,500] **3756**

AMERICAN JOURNAL OF PHARMACEUTICAL EDUCATION (US/0002-9459). [2,200] **4290**

AMERICAN JOURNAL OF PHYSICS (US/0002-9505). [7,700] **4396**

AMERICAN JOURNAL OF PHYSIOLOGY (US/0002-9513). [2,800] **577**

AMERICAN JOURNAL OF PHYSIOLOGY : CELL PHYSIOLOGY (US/0363-6143). [390] **577**

AMERICAN JOURNAL OF PHYSIOLOGY : ENDOCRINOLOGY AND METABOLISM (US/0193-1849). [358] **577**

AMERICAN JOURNAL OF PHYSIOLOGY : GASTROINTESTINAL AND LIVER PHYSIOLOGY (US/0193-1857). [400] **578**

AMERICAN JOURNAL OF PHYSIOLOGY : HEART AND CIRCULATORY PHYSIOLOGY (US/0363-6135). [660] **578**

AMERICAN JOURNAL OF PHYSIOLOGY. LUNG CELLULAR AND MOLECULAR PHYSIOLOGY (US/1040-0605). [500] **3948**

AMERICAN JOURNAL OF PHYSIOLOGY : REGULATORY, INTEGRATIVE AND COMPARATIVE PHYSIOLOGY (US/0363-6119). [250] **578**

AMERICAN JOURNAL OF PHYSIOLOGY RENAL, FLUID AND ELECTROLYTE PHYSIOLOGY (US/0363-6127). [600] **578**

AMERICAN JOURNAL OF POLITICAL SCIENCE (US/0092-5853). [2,800] **4463**

AMERICAN JOURNAL OF RHINOLOGY (US/1050-6586). [3,000] **3886**

AMERICAN JOURNAL OF SEMIOTICS (US/0277-7126). [750] **3263**

AMERICAN JOURNAL OF THEOLOGY & PHILOSOPHY (US/0194-3448). [550] **4340**

AMERICAN JOURNAL OF TROPICAL MEDICINE AND HYGIENE, THE (US/0002-9637). [3,800] **3985**

AMERICAN LABORATORY (FAIRFIELD) (US/0044-7749). [130,000] **960**

AMERICAN LEGION, THE (US/0886-1234). [2,600,000] **4034**

AMERICAN LIBRARIES (CHICAGO, ILL.) (US/0002-9769). [45,000] **3189**

AMERICAN LITERATURE (US/0002-9831). [4,500] **3360**

AMERICAN LUTHERIE (US/1041-7176). [2,000] **4099**

AMERICAN MAGAZINE AND HISTORICAL CHRONICLE, THE (US/0882-5351). [1,000] **2719**

AMERICAN MARKETING ASSOCIATION INTERNATIONAL MEMBERSHIP DIRECTORY AND MARKETING SERVICES GUIDE (US). [32,000] **921**

AMERICAN MENSA REGISTER (US/0738-5218). [55,000] **5228**

AMERICAN MIDDLE SCHOOL EDUCATION (US/0889-552X). **1860**

AMERICAN MIDLAND NATURALIST, THE (US/0003-0031). [1,500] **4161**

AMERICAN MINERALOGIST, THE (US/0003-004X). [4,500] **1437**

AMERICAN MOTOR CARRIER (US/0003-0066). [28,000] **5375**

AMERICAN MOTORCYCLIST (US/0277-9358). [143,740] **4080**

AMERICAN MUSEUM NOVITATES (US/0003-0082). [1,500] **5574**

AMERICAN MUSIC TEACHER, THE (US/0003-0112). [25,000] **4099**

AMERICAN OIL & GAS REPORTER, THE (US/0145-9198). [11,500] **4249**

AMERICAN OPTOMETRIC ASSOCIATION NEWS (US/0094-9620). [30,390] **4215**

AMERICAN ORCHID SOCIETY BULLETIN (US/0003-0252). [27,000] **2408**

AMERICAN ORGANIST (1979), THE (US/0164-3150). [25,000] **4099**

AMERICAN OXONIAN, THE (US/0003-0295). [2,300] **1808**

AMERICAN PAINT & COATINGS JOURNAL (US/0098-5430). [7,000] **4222**

AMERICAN PAINT & COATINGS JOURNAL. CONVENTION DAILY (US/0097-4749). [40,000] **4222**

AMERICAN PAINTING CONTRACTOR (US/0003-0325). [25,000] **4222**

AMERICAN PAPERMAKER (1991) (US/1056-4772). [32,000] **4232**

AMERICAN PHILATELIST, THE (US/0003-0473). [50,000] **2784**

AMERICAN PHOTOGRAPHY SHOWCASE (US/0278-8314). [33,600] **4366**

AMERICAN POSTAL WORKER, THE (US/0044-7811). [290,000] **1643**

AMERICAN POTATO JOURNAL (US/0003-0589). [1,500] **162**

AMERICAN PRACTICE ADVISOR (US). [2,300] **2596**

AMERICAN PREMIERE (US/0279-0041). [17,500] **4063**

AMERICAN PRESBYTERIANS (US/0886-5159). **5055**

AMERICAN PRINTER (1982) (US/0744-6616). [93,664] **4563**

AMERICAN PROFESSIONAL CONSTRUCTOR, THE (US/0146-7557). [1,700] **2018**

AMERICAN PURPOSE (US/0891-446X). [2,500] **4515**

AMERICAN QUILTER (US/8756-6591). [75,000] **5182**

AMERICAN RABBI (CANOGA PARK, LOS ANGELES, CALIF.), THE (US/0164-3916). [900] **5045**

AMERICAN RED ANGUS (US/0886-4357). **205**

AMERICAN REGISTER OF PRINTING AND GRAPHIC ARTS SERVICES, THE (US/0276-5519). [55,000] **4563**

AMERICAN REVIEW OF CANADIAN STUDIES, THE (US/0272-2011). [2,500] **2719**

AMERICAN REVIEW OF RESPIRATORY DISEASE, THE (US/0003-0805). [15,500] **3948**

AMERICAN ROWING (US/0888-1154). [26,000] **4883**

AMERICAN SAILOR (US/0279-9553). [30,000] **591**

AMERICAN SALESMAN, THE (US/0003-0902). [1,625] **859**

AMERICAN SALON: OFFICIAL PUBLICATION OF THE NHCA (US/0741-5737). [122,053] **402**

AMERICAN SCHLESWIG-HOLSTEIN HERITAGE SOCIETY NEWSLETTER (US/1045-9960). [600] **2437**

AMERICAN SCHOOL & UNIVERSITY (US/0003-0945). [44,000] **1860**

AMERICAN SHIPPER (1991) (US/1074-8350). **822**

AMERICAN SHOWCASE. ILLUSTRATION (US). [34,550] **376**

AMERICAN SHOWCASE OF ILLUSTRATION AND PHOTOGRAPHY (US/0278-8683). [35,000] **4366**

AMERICAN SQUARE DANCE (US/0091-3383). [24,000] **1310**

AMERICAN STRING TEACHER (US/0003-1313). [10,000] **4100**

AMERICAN STUDIES (LAWRENCE) (US/0026-3079). [1,600] **2719**

AMERICAN SUZUKI JOURNAL (US/0193-5372). [6,200] **4100**

AMERICAN TAXIDERMIST MAGAZINE (US). [2,700] **2771**

AMERICAN TEACHER (US/0003-1380). [600,000] **1888**

AMERICAN TRAIL SERIES (US/0066-0884). [1,000] **2719**

AMERICAN TRAPPER (US/1050-4036). [17,000] **2186**

AMERICAN TURF MONTHLY (US/0003-1445). **2796**

AMERICAN VOICE (LOUISVILLE, KY.), THE (US/0884-4356). [2,000] **3360**

AMERICAN WAY (DALLAS, TEX.) (US/0003-1518). [270,000] **11**

AMERICAN WEATHER OBSERVER (US/8755-9552). [2,100] **1419**

AMERICAN WORKER, THE (US/1047-7136). [60,000] **1643**

AMERICAN ZOOLOGIST (US/0003-1569). [6,300] **5574**

AMERICANA (US/0090-9114). [330,000] **2527**

AMERICAS REVIEW (HOUSTON, TEX.) (US/1042-6213). [1,000] **3360**

AMERICA'S TEXTILES INTERNATIONAL (US/0890-9970). [35,250] **5347**

AMERIKA WOCHE (US/0745-6557). [25,000] **5658**

AMERIKAI MAGYAR SZO (US/0194-7990). **5713**

AMERIKANSKI SLOVENEC (CHICAGO, ILL.) (US/0745-5453). [12,000] **5658**

AMERINDIA (FR/0221-8852). [200] **3263**

AMERRIKUA! (SCHUYLER FALLS, N.Y.) (US/1043-7029). [500] **2255**

ANNALS

AMI (MISSISSAUGA, ONT.) (CN/0830-8586). [2,500] **383**

AMICA NEWS BULLETIN, THE (US/1043-5379). **4100**

AMIS DE JESUS, LES (CN/0823-6178). **4934**

AMIS DE LA BANQUE D'YEUX DU QUEBEC (CN/0710-1368). **3872**

AMNESTY ACTION / AI, USA (US). [300,000] **4503**

AMNESTY INTERNATIONAL NEWSLETTER (UK/0308-6887). [60,000] **4503**

AMOEBA AMSTERDAM. 1976 (NE/0926-3543). [1,500] **4161**

AMON HEN (UK). [600] **3360**

AMONG THE COLES (US/0743-2801). [250] **2437**

AMPHIBIA-REPTILIA (GW/0173-5373). **5575**

AMPLEFORTH JOURNAL, THE (UK/0003-2018). [3,000] **5023**

AMRO (UK). [1,000] **3549**

AN COSANTOIR (IE). [5,000] **4040**

AN-HUI SHIH TA HSUEH PAO (CC). **2841**

ANACRUSIS (CN/0826-7464). [600] **4100**

ANAESTHESIOLOGICA (OULU) (FI/0358-4836). [450] **3680**

ANAIS BRASILEIROS DE DERMATOLOGIA (BL/0365-0596). [3,000] **3717**

ANAIS DA CONFERENCIA NACIONAL DE SAUDE (BL). [5,000] **4765**

ANAIS DO INSTITUTO DE HIGIENE E MEDICINA TROPICAL (PO/0303-7762). [1,000] **3549**

ANAIS HIDROGRAFICOS (BL). [1,300] **5529**

ANALECTA CALASANCTIANA (SP/0569-9789). [400] **5023**

ANALECTA PRAEMONSTRATENSIA (BE). **2610**

ANALELE UNIVERSITATI DIN GALATI. FASCICULA II - MATEMATICA, FIZICA, MECANICA TEORETICA (RM). [250] **3492**

ANALELE UNIVERSITATII DIN GALATI. FASCICULA I, STIINTE SOCIALE SI UMANISTE (RM/1015-9606). [250] **5190**

ANALELE UNIVERSITATII DIN GALATI.FASCICULA VII, TEHNICA PISCICOLA (RM). [250] **2294**

ANALES DE CIENCIAS - UNIVERSIDAD DE MURCIA (SP/0213-5469). [300] **960**

ANALES DE LA ESCUELA NACIONAL DE CIENCIAS BIOLOGICAS (MEXICO) (MX/0365-1932). [1,000] **441**

ANALES DE LA ESTACION EXPERIMENTAL DE AULA DEI (SP/0365-1800). [1,000] **58**

ANALES DE LA FACULTAD DE VETERINARIA DE LEON (SP/0373-1170). [800] **5502**

ANALES DE LA FUNDACION JUAN MARCH (SP/0532-8500). **4334**

ANALES DE LA REAL ACADEMIA NACIONAL DE MEDICINA, MADRID (SP/0034-0634). [2,200] **3549**

ANALES DE LITERATURA HISPANOAMERICANA (SP). **3361**

ANALES DE VETERINARIA DE MURCIA (SP/0213-5434). **5502**

ANALES DEL INSTITUTO DE BIOLOGIA, UNIVERSIDAD NACIONAL AUTONOMA DE MEXICO. SERIE BOTANICA (MX/0374-5511). [600] **498**

ANALES DEL INSTITUTO DE BIOLOGIA, UNIVERSIDAD NACIONAL AUTONOMA DE MEXICO. SERIE ZOOLOGIA (MX/0368-8720). [600] **5575**

ANALES DEL INSTITUTO DE ESTUDIOS MADRILENOS (SP/0584-6374). **2673**

ANALES DEL INSTITUTO DE INVESTIGACIONES ESTETICAS (MX/0185-1276). [2,000] **336**

ANALES DEL INSTITUTO DE LA PATAGONIA. SERIE CIENCIAS NATURALES (CL/0716-6486). [1,000] **4161**

ANALES DEL INSTITUTO DE LA PATAGONIA. SERIE CIENCIAS SOCIALES (CL/0716-6478). [1,000] **5190**

ANALES DEL INSTITUTO DE MATEMATICAS (MX/0185-0644). [500] **3492**

ANALES DEL MUSEO DE HISTORIA NATURAL DE VALPARAISO (CL). [350] **4161**

ANALES ESPANOLES DE PEDIATRIA (SP/0302-4342). **3900**

ANALES GALDOSIANOS (US/0569-9924). [1,000] **3337**

ANALES OTORRINOLARINGOLOGICOS IBERO-AMERICANOS (SP/0303-8874). [1,000] **3886**

ANALISIS ESTADISTICO, URUGUAY: IMPORTACION - EXPORTACION (UY). [2,000] **822**

ANALISIS FILOSOFICO (AG/0326-1301). [500] **4340**

ANALISIS FINANCIERO (SP). [2,000] **770**

ANALUSIS (FR/0365-4877). [3,000] **1012**

ANALYSE (NE/0166-7688). [4,000] **3549**

ANALYSES DE LA S.E.D.E.I.S (FR/0399-1245). **1461**

ANALYSIS (NEW YORK (N.Y.) (US/0003-2638). [600] **4340**

ANALYSIS OF WORKMEN'S COMPENSATION LAWS (US/0191-118X). **3144**

ANALYTIC TEACHING (US/0890-5118). [300] **4340**

ANALYTICAL ABSTRACTS (UK/0003-2689). [3,800] **996**

ANALYTICAL AND QUANTITATIVE CYTOLOGY AND HISTOLOGY (US/0884-6812). [2,500] **531**

ANALYTICAL CHEMISTRY (WASHINGTON) (US/0003-2700). [27,500] **1013**

ANALYTISCHE PSYCHOLOGIE (SZ/0301-3006). [5,500] **4573**

ANARCHY (UK/0003-2751). [2,000] **4539**

ANATOLIAN STUDIES (UK/0066-1546). [850] **254**

ANATOLICA (NE/0066-1554). [300] **3264**

ANATOMICA, PATHOLOGICA, MICROBIOLOGICA (FI/0358-4895). [450] **3678**

ANCESTOR (AT/0044-8222). [6,500] **2437**

ANCESTOR HUNT (US/0736-9115). [325] **2437**

ANCESTOR UPDATE (US/1064-0738). [330] **2437**

ANCESTORS WEST (US/0734-4988). [450] **2437**

ANCESTRY NEWSLETTER (US/0749-5927). [7,000] **2437**

ANCETRE (QUEBEC) (CN/0316-0513). [1,250] **2437**

ANCHORAGE TIMES (US). [35,524 daily, 45,267 Sunday] **5628**

ANCIENT CITY GENEALOGIST, THE (US/1072-8953). [150] **2437**

ANCIENT TL (UK/0735-1348). [150] **254**

ANCIENT WORLD, THE (US/0160-9645). [1,000] **254**

ANDALUCIA ECONOMICA (SP/1130-4413). [15,000] **1462**

ANDERSON REPORT, THE (US/0197-7040). **1231**

ANDERSON'S CAMPGROUND DIRECTORY (US/0163-268X). [18,000] **4869**

ANDHRA AGRICULTURAL JOURNAL, THE (II/0003-2956). [1,200] **58**

ANDRADE : REVISTA TRIMESTRAL DE POESIA (SP). **3361**

ANELLO CHE NON TIENE, L' (US/0899-5273). [300] **3361**

ANESTESIA E RIANIMAZIONE (IT/0570-0760). [4,000] **3681**

ANESTHESIA PROGRESS (US/0003-3006). [3,500] **1316**

ANESTHESIOLOGY (GLENDALE, CALIF.) (US/0271-1265). **3681**

ANG NEWS / AUSTRALIAN NATIONAL GALLERY (AT). [12,000] **4083**

ANGLICAN, THE (CN/0517-7731). [44,000] **5055**

ANGLO-SOVIET JOURNAL, THE (UK/0044-8265). [1,000] **2673**

ANGORABOT & SYBOTHAAR -BLAD (SA/0003-3464). [3,000] **205**

ANGUS TIMES (CN/0849-6188). [3500] **205**

ANGUS TOPICS (US/0402-4265). [8,000] **205**

ANIMAL KEEPERS' FORUM (US/0164-9531). [2,650] **5575**

ANIMAL LIBERATION ACTION (AT/0816-486X). [500] **225**

ANIMAL NUTRITION RESEARCH HIGHLIGHTS (US). [6,000] **58**

ANIMAL PRODUCTION (UK/0003-3561). **205**

ANIMAL WELFARE INSTITUTE QUARTERLY, THE (US/0743-0841). [25,000] **225**

ANIMATION MAGAZINE (US/1041-617X). [25,000] **4063**

ANLA BULLETIN / ASSOCIATION OF NEWFOUNDLAND AND LABRADOR ARCHIVISTS (CN/0821-7157). **2479**

ANN ARBOR OBSERVER (US/0192-5717). [56,000] **2484**

ANNALEN DER METEOROLOGIE (GW/0072-4122). **1419**

ANNALES (TI). **59**

ANNALES ACADEMIAE SCIENTIARUM FENNICAE. DISSERTATIONES HUMANARUM LITTERARUM (FI/0355-113X). [500-800] **2841**

ANNALES CHIRURGIAE ET GYNAECOLOGIAE (FI/0355-9521). [2,000] **3756**

ANNALES DE BIOCHIMIE CLINIQUE DU QUEBEC (CN/0709-8502). [900] **480**

ANNALES DE BOURGOGNE (FR/0003-3901). [550] **2674**

ANNALES DE L'A C F A S (CN/0066-8842). [6,000] **5083**

ANNALES DE L'EST (FR/0365-2017). [800] **2674**

ANNALES DE L'INSTITUT PHYTOPATHOLOGIQUE BENAKI (GR/0365-5814). [1,000] **499**

ANNALES DES MINES DE BELGIQUE (BE/0003-4290). [500] **2133**

ANNALES DES TELECOMMUNICATIONS (FR/0003-4347). [1,300] **1148**

ANNALES HISTORICO-NATURALES MUSEI NATIONALIS HUNGARICI (BUDAPEST, HUNGARY : 1965) (HU). [700] **4161**

ANNALES HYDROGRAPHIQUES (FR/0373-3629). **1412**

ANNALES MEDICALES DE NANCY ET DE L'EST (FR/0221-3796). [3,000] **3550**

ANNALES MUSEI GOULANDRIS (GR/0302-1033). [800] **4161**

ANNALES POLONICI MATHEMATICI (PL/0066-2216). [1,500] **3493**

ANNALES THEOLOGICI (IT/0394-8226). [650] **4934**

ANNALES UNIVERSITATIS MARIAE CURIE-SKODOWSKA. SECTIO C. BIOLOGIA (PL/0066-2232). [950] **442**

ANNALES UNIVERSITATIS SCIENTIARUM BUDAPENTINENSIS DE ROLANDO EOTVOS NOMINATAE. SECTIO PHILOLOGICA MODERNA (HU). [500] **3264**

ANNALES UNIVERSITATIS SCIENTIARUM BUDAPESTINENSIS DE ROLANDO EOTVOS NOMINATAE. SECTIO GEOGRAPHICA (HU/0524-8965). **2554**

ANNALES UNIVERSITATIS SCIENTIARUM BUDAPESTINENSIS DE ROLANDO EOTVOS NOMINATAE. SECTIO HISTORICA (HU/0524-8981). **2841**

ANNALES UNIVERSITATIS SCIENTIARUM BUDAPESTINENSIS DE ROLANDO EOTVOS NOMINATAE. SECTIO PHILOSOPHICA ET SOCIOLOGICA (HU/0524-9023). [550] **4341**

ANNALI ITALIANI DI CHIRURGIA (IT/0003-469X). [2,000] **3959**

ANNALI SCLAVO (IT/0003-472X). [5,000] **558**

ANNALS - JAPAN ASSOCIATION FOR PHILOSOPHY OF SCIENCE (JA). [600] **5083**

ANNALS OF AIR AND SPACE LAW (CN/0701-158X). [1,000] **3123**

ANNALS OF APPLIED BIOLOGY (UK/0003-4746). [1,500] **442**

ANNALS OF BEHAVIORAL MEDICINE (US/0883-6612). [3,000] **3654**

ANNALS OF CLINICAL AND LABORATORY SCIENCE (US/0091-7370). [2,000] **3893**

ANNALS OF EMERGENCY MEDICINE (US/0196-0644). [18,500] **3723**

ANNALS OF GLACIOLOGY (UK/0260-3055). [800] **1412**

ANNALS OF IOWA (US/0003-4827). [1,000] **2720**

ANNALS OF OPHTHALMOLOGY (BIRMINGHAM) (US/0003-4886). **3872**

ANNALS OF OTOLOGY, RHINOLOGY & LARYNGOLOGY, THE (US/0003-4894). [6,002] **3886**

ANNALS OF REGIONAL SCIENCE, THE (GW/0570-1864). [1,100] **2814**

ANNALS OF SAUDI MEDICINE (SU/0256-4947). [14,000] **3550**

ANNALS OF THE ACADEMY OF MEDICINE, SINGAPORE (SI/0304-4602). [1,500] **3550**

ANNALS OF THE ENTOMOLOGICAL SOCIETY OF AMERICA (US/0013-8746). [2,000] **5605**

ANNALS OF THE NATAL MUSEUM, PIETERMARITZBURG (SA/0304-0798). [350] **4162**

ANNALS OF THE ROYAL COLLEGE OF PHYSICIANS AND SURGEONS OF CANADA (CN/0035-8800). [28,000] **3913**

ANNALS

Controlled Circulation Index

ANNALS OF THE SCHOOL OF BUSINESS ADMINISTRATION, KOBE UNIVERSITY, THE (JA/0085-2570). [600] **638**

ANNALS OF THE TRANSVAAL MUSEUM (SA/0041-1752). [400] **4162**

ANNALS OF WARSAW AGRICULTURAL UNIVERSITY - SGGW-AR. FORESTRY AND WOOD TECHNOLOGY (PL/0208-5704). **2374**

ANNALS (SOCIETY OF LOGISTICS ENGINEERS) (US/0885-3916). [2,000] **1964**

ANNEE SOCIALE / INSTITUT DE SOCIOLOGIE, UNIVERSITE LIBRE DE BRUXELLES, L' (BE/0066-2380). [1,000] **5191**

ANNOTATED GUIDE TO WOMEN'S PERIODICALS IN THE U.S. & CANADA, THE (US/0741-9899). [200] **5550**

ANNOTATION (US/0160-8460). [3,000] **2720**

ANNUAIRE (FR). **4445**

ANNUAIRE - ASSOCIATION DES INSTITUTIONS D'ENSEIGNEMENT SECONDAIRE (CN/0066-8990). [6,000] **1724**

ANNUAIRE - ASSOCIATION DES ROUTES ET TRANSPORTS DU CANADA (CN/0701-1636). [550] **5376**

ANNUAIRE DE L'ADMINISTRATION DES DIRECTIONS REGIONALES DE L'INDUSTRIE ET DE LA RECHERCHE (FR/1140-7123). [10,000] **2133**

ANNUAIRE DE L'EGLISE CATHOLIQUE AU CANADA (CN/0821-9885). [5,000] **5023**

ANNUAIRE DE L'EGLISE CATHOLIQUE AU CANADA (CN/0821-9885). [5,000] **5023**

ANNUAIRE DENTAIRE (FR). [10,000] **1316**

ANNUAIRE DENTAIRE / ORDRE DES DENTISTES DU QUEBEC (CN/0826-2233). **1316**

ANNUAIRE DES COLLECTIVITES LOCALES / C.N.R.S., G.R.A.L (FR/0248-0573). **4626**

ANNUAIRE DES COMMUNAUTES EUROPEENNES ET DES AUTRES ORGANISATIONS EUROPEENNES (BE/0771-7962). [8,000] **4515**

ANNUAIRE DES MEMBRES DE L'ASSOCIATION DES BIBLIOTHECAIRES FRANCAIS (FR). [2,500] **3190**

ANNUAIRE DU MARKETING (FR). [2,000] **921**

ANNUAIRE DU PAPIER, L' (FR/0337-4971). [2,500] **4232**

ANNUAIRE EGYPTIEN DES ENTREPRISES, DES SERVICES, DE L'INDUSTRIE ET DU COMMERCE EXTERIEUR (UA). [5,000] **822**

ANNUAIRE : L'EGLISE DE MONTREAL (CN/0826-0338). **5023**

ANNUAIRE STATISTIQUE DE LA BELGIQUE (BE/0066-3646). [1,350] **5321**

ANNUAIRE STATISTIQUE DE POCHE - INSTITUT NATIONAL DE STATISTIQUE (BE/0067-5431). [1,200] **5321**

ANNUAIRE STATISTIQUE DU MAROC (RABAT, MOROCCO : 1982) (MR). **5321**

ANNUAL AREA LABOR REVIEW (US/0149-3779). [1,000] **1644**

ANNUAL BENZENE & DERIVATIVES (US/1042-8364). **4249**

ANNUAL CBAC SURVEY OF PERFORMING ARTS ORGANIZATIONS (CN/0229-3153). **383**

ANNUAL CONFERENCE OF THE ATLANTIC CANADA ECONOMICS ASSOCIATION (CN/0319-003X). [200] **1462**

ANNUAL CONFERENCE / THE ONTARIO PETROLEUM INSTITUTE (CN/0078-5040). **4249**

ANNUAL DESCRIPTIVE REPORT OF PROGRAM ACTIVITIES FOR VOCATIONAL EDUCATION (US/0091-5882). **1910**

ANNUAL ECONOMIC REPORT / STATISTICAL, ECONOMIC AND SOCIAL RESEARCH AND TRAINING CENTRE FOR ISLAMIC COUNTRIES, ORGANIZATION OF THE ISLAMIC CONFERENCE (TU). **1545**

ANNUAL ECONOMIC SURVEY (PORT OF SPAIN, TRINIDAD AND TOBAGO) (TR/1011-6311). [1,200] **1545**

ANNUAL EDITION: NOTICES TO MARINERS (CN). [15,000] **4174**

ANNUAL EXHIBITION OF THE CANADIAN SOCIETY OF PAINTERS IN WATER COLOUR (CN/0318-4978). [350] **336**

ANNUAL FINANCIAL REPORT AND REPORT OF OPERATIONS / PUBLIC EMPLOYEES' RETIREMENT SYSTEM, STATE OF CALIFORNIA (US/0732-4618). **4626**

ANNUAL HOUSE MARKET REPORT : THE STATE OF THE HOUSING MARKET (US). **2814**

ANNUAL INDEX OF FOUNDATION REPORTS / OFFICES OF THE ATTORNEY GENERAL (US). **4334**

ANNUAL - KAJAKS TRACK AND FIELD CLUB (CN/0229-0618). **4883**

ANNUAL MEETING - AMERICAN INSTITUTE OF ORAL BIOLOGY (US/0098-6119). [250] **1316**

ANNUAL MEETING & INTERNATIONAL CONFERENCE ON NUCLEAR ENERGY (US). [250] **1932**

ANNUAL OF ARMENIAN LINGUISTICS (US/0271-9800). [200] **3265**

ANNUAL OF CARDIAC SURGERY (UK/0952-0562). [3,000] **3959**

ANNUAL PLAN ... OF THE ILLINOIS DEPARTMENT OF MENTAL HEALTH AND DEVELOPMENTAL DISABILITIES (US/0276-6922). [2,000] **4765**

ANNUAL PLANNING INFORMATION. CHARLESTON, WEST VIRGINIA STANDARD METROPOLITAN STATISTICAL AREA (US). [250] **5321**

ANNUAL PLANNING INFORMATION REPORT. PITTSBURGH PRIMARY METROPOLITAN STATISTICAL AREA, LABOR MARKET AREA NO. 6280 (US). [700] **1529**

ANNUAL PROGRAM; LIBRARY SERVICES AND CONSTRUCTION ACT - SOUTH CAROLINA. STATE LIBRARY, COLUMBIA (US/0364-7803). **3190**

ANNUAL PROGRAM PLAN / WASHINGTON STATE, COMMISSION FOR VOCATIONAL EDUCATION (US). [600] **1910**

ANNUAL REPORT (AT). [7,000] **4626**

ANNUAL REPORT (AT). [6,000] **3475**

ANNUAL REPORT (AT). [15,000] **2186**

ANNUAL REPORT / ADMINISTRATIVE CONFERENCE OF THE UNITED STATES (US/0898-3100). **4626**

ANNUAL REPORT - ALABAMA. DEPT. OF INDUSTRIAL RELATIONS. DIVISION OF SAFETY AND INSPECTION (US). [1,500] **2859**

ANNUAL REPORT / ALBERTA CULTURE AND MULTICULTURALISM (CN/0848-2128). **2528**

ANNUAL REPORT / ALBERTA LAW REFORM INSTITUTE (CN). [2,000] **2934**

ANNUAL REPORT / AMHC, ALBERTA MORTGAGE AND HOUSING CORPORATION (CN/0837-6816). **2814**

ANNUAL REPORT AND ACCOUNTS - BHARAT PUMPS & COMPRESSORS LIMITED (II). [2,000] **2109**

ANNUAL REPORT AND ACCOUNTS - BRITISH TRUST FOR ORNITHOLOGY (UK). [10,000] **5614**

ANNUAL REPORT AND AUDITED FINANCIAL STATEMENTS AS OF ... (US). [13,000] **4709**

ANNUAL REPORT AND BALANCE SHEET AND REVENUE AND EXPENDITURE ACCOUNT (RH). [600] **312**

ANNUAL REPORT AND FINANCIAL STATEMENTS FOR THE YEAR ENDED ... (TS). [1,500] **770**

ANNUAL REPORT AND STATEMENT OF ACCOUNTS - CENTRAL BANK OF MALTA (MM). [1,600] **770**

ANNUAL REPORT AND STATEMENT OF ACCOUNTS FOR THE YEAR ENDED ... / ELECTRICITY SUPPLY COMMISSION OF MALAWI (MW). [2,000] **2035**

ANNUAL REPORT ... ANNUAL MEETING / OREGON HORTICULTURAL SOCIETY (US/0885-7849). [700] **2409**

ANNUAL REPORT ... / ARIZONA COUNCIL FOR THE DEAF (US). [500] **4383**

ANNUAL REPORT / ARKANSAS FORESTRY COMMISSION (US/8756-8292). **2374**

ANNUAL REPORT - ASIAN DEVELOPMENT BANK (PH/0066-8370). [15,000] **770**

ANNUAL REPORT - ASIAN PRODUCTIVITY ORGANIZATION (JA/0066-846X). **1597**

ANNUAL REPORT - AUSTRALIA COUNCIL (AT). [3,000] **312**

ANNUAL REPORT - AUSTRALIAN ACADEMY OF TECHNOLOGICAL SCIENCES (AT/0313-6736). **5083**

ANNUAL REPORT / AUSTRALIAN NATIONAL RAILWAYS COMMISSION (AT). [3,000] **5429**

ANNUAL REPORT / BATTELLE MEMORIAL INSTITUTE (US/0736-6159). [23,000] **5084**

ANNUAL REPORT - BRITISH LIBRARY (UK/0305-7887). [4,000] **3190**

ANNUAL REPORT - BUCKNELL UNIVERSITY (US/0099-1198). [3,000] **1809**

ANNUAL REPORT / CANADIAN NATIONAL (CN/0824-8265). [40,000] **5376**

ANNUAL REPORT / CAPE BRETON DEVELOPMENT CORPORATION (CN/0228-4723). [2,000] **4627**

ANNUAL REPORT ... / CEDEFOP (GW). [1,000] **1910**

ANNUAL REPORT - CENTRAL BANK OF BARBADOS (BB/0304-6796). [2,400] **1546**

ANNUAL REPORT - CENTRAL INSTITUTE OF FISHERIES NAUTICAL & ENGINEERING TRAINING (INDIA) (II). [500] **2294**

ANNUAL REPORT - CENTRE FOR POLICY ON AGING (LONDON, ENGLAND) (UK). [3,000] **5178**

ANNUAL REPORT - CITIZENS ADVISORY COUNCIL (HARRISBURG) (US/0092-7937). [500] **2160**

ANNUAL REPORT / COLD SPRING HARBOR LABORATORY (US). **442**

ANNUAL REPORT - COMMISSIONER OF OFFICIAL LANGUAGES (CN/0382-1161). [12,000] **3265**

ANNUAL REPORT / COUNCIL FOR MINERAL TECHNOLOGY (SA). [1,700] **2133**

ANNUAL REPORT - COUNCIL OF MARITIME PREMIERS (CN/0380-0768). [2,100] **4515**

ANNUAL REPORT - CSIRO. COAL AND ENERGY TECHNOLOGY (AT/1036-1367). [800] **1932**

ANNUAL REPORT / CURTIN UNIVERSITY OF TECHNOLOGY (AT/1031-1378). [2000] **5084**

ANNUAL REPORT - CYPRUS ORNITHOLOGICAL SOCIETY (CY/0590-4935). [500] **5614**

ANNUAL REPORT - CYPRUS PORTS AUTHORITY (CY). [1,000] **5447**

ANNUAL REPORT / DELAWARE RIVER BASIN COMMISSION (US/0418-5455). [800] **5529**

ANNUAL REPORT - DENNISON MANUFACTURING COMPANY (US). [35,000] **3475**

ANNUAL REPORT - DEPARTMENT OF EDUCATION (US). **1725**

ANNUAL REPORT - DEPARTMENT OF OCEANOGRAPHY. UNIVERSITY OF BRITISH COLUMBIA (CN/0828-1939). **1446**

ANNUAL REPORT - DEPARTMENT OF PRIMARY INDUSTRIES, QUEENSLAND (AT/0480-9696). [2,400] **60**

ANNUAL REPORT - DEPARTMENT OF SAFETY (US/0095-1994). **5438**

ANNUAL REPORT - DEPARTMENT OF TOURISM (CN/0837-4171). **5461**

ANNUAL REPORT - DEPARTMENT OF TRANSPORT AND COMMUNICATIONS (AT/1032-1896). [1,500] **5376**

ANNUAL REPORT / DET NORSKE VERITAS (NO). [20,000] **5447**

ANNUAL REPORT / DEVELOPMENT BANK OF SEYCHELLES (SE). [100] **771**

ANNUAL REPORT / ETHNOGRAPHICAL MUSEUM (HU). **228**

ANNUAL REPORT / EUROPEAN SCIENCE FOUNDATION (FR). [1,500] **5084**

ANNUAL REPORT FOR ... / NEW YORK POWER AUTHORITY (US). [20,000] **4759**

ANNUAL REPORT FOR ... / THE AUSTRALIAN NATIONAL UNIVERSITY, DEPARTMENT OF ECONOMICS, RESEARCH SCHOOL OF PACIFIC STUDIES (AT). [300] **1462**

ANNUAL REPORT FOR THE YEAR ENDED 30TH JUNE ... / ABORIGINAL AFFAIRS PLANNING AUTHORITY (AT). [1,000] **4627**

ANNUAL REPORT FOR THE YEAR ENDED ... / DAIRY CONTROL BOARD (SOUTH AFRICA) (SA). [1,000] **191**

ANNUAL REPORT FOR THE YEAR ENDED ... / EMPLOYMENT APPEALS TRIBUNAL (IE). [1,000] **3144**

ANNUAL REPORT FOR YEAR ENDING 30 JUNE ... CONSERVATION COMMISSION OF THE NORTHERN TERRITORY (AT). [250] **2186**

ANNUAL REPORT - GREAT LAKES FISHERY COMMISSION (US/0072-7296). [500] **2294**

ANNUAL REPORT, HIGHWAY SAFETY IMPROVEMENT PROGRAMS IN VIRGINIA / PREPARED BY THE DIVISION OF TRAFFIC AND SAFETY FOR THE VIRGINIA DEPARTMENT OF HIGHWAYS AND TRANSPORTATION (US). **4766**

ANNUAL REPORT - HUNTINGTON LIBRARY, ART GALLERY, BOTANICAL GARDENS (US/0363-3306). [5,000] **3190**

ANNUAL REPORT - INDONESIAN NATIONAL SCIENTIFIC DOCUMENTATION CENTER (IO). [500] **5084**

ANNUAL REPORT, INFORMATION COMMISSIONER (CN/0826-9904). [7,000] **4627**

ANNUAL REPORT / INSTITUTE OF OCCUPATIONAL HEALTH (FI). [4,000] **2859**

ANNUAL REPORT - INTERNATIONAL CENTRE FOR THEORETICAL PHYSICS (IT/0304-7091). [2,000] **4397**

ANNUAL REPORT / INTERNATIONAL FERTILIZER DEVELOPMENT CENTER (US/0748-5875). [4,000] **163**

ANNUAL REPORT - INTERNATIONAL PLANNED PARENTHOOD FEDERATION (UK/0307-6857). [20,000] **2276**

ANNUAL REPORT / INTERNATIONAL PLANNED PARENTHOOD FEDERATION (US). [10,000] **4549**

ANNUAL REPORT / KENYA TUBERCULOSIS AND RESPIRATORY DISEASES RESEARCH CENTRE (KE/1015-0072). [200] **3948**

ANNUAL REPORT - LAND RESOURCE SCIENCE. UNIVERSITY OF GUELPH (CN/0820-3997). **163**

ANNUAL REPORT / MACAULAY LAND USE RESEARCH INSTITUTE (UK/0954-7010). [850] **163**

ANNUAL REPORT / MISSISSIPPI, STATE DEPARTMENT OF HEALTH (US). [3,000] **4766**

ANNUAL REPORT / MISSOURI HIGHWAY & TRANSPORTATION COMMISSION (US). **5438**

ANNUAL REPORT / NATIONAL BANK OF HUNGARY (HU). **771**

ANNUAL REPORT - NATIONAL FOUNDATION FOR ADVANCEMENT IN THE ARTS (U.S.) (US/0882-245X). [2,000] **313**

ANNUAL REPORT - NATIONAL GALLERY OF ART (U.S.) (US/0091-7222). [3,500-5,000] **336**

ANNUAL REPORT - NATIONAL HYDATIDS COUNCIL (NZ/0110-9901). [5,000] **5503**

ANNUAL REPORT / NATIONAL INSTITUTE FOR COAL RESEARCH (SA/0250-2348). [1,000] **2133**

ANNUAL REPORT / NATIONAL INSTITUTE OF RURAL DEVELOPMENT (II). [1,000] **2814**

ANNUAL REPORT - NATIONAL MULTIPLE SCLEROSIS SOCIETY (US). [400,000] **3827**

ANNUAL REPORT - NATIONAL TRUST OF AUSTRALIA, W.A (AT). [2,200] **4628**

ANNUAL REPORT / NEW MEXICO STATE LAND OFFICE (US). [500] **4628**

ANNUAL REPORT ... NEW YORK, NEW JERSEY / PALISADES INTERSTATE PARK COMMISSION (US). **4628**

ANNUAL REPORT / NEW YORK STATE, OFFICE OF ADVOCATE FOR THE DISABLED (US). [12,000] **4628**

ANNUAL REPORT - NEW ZEALAND COUNCIL FOR EDUCATIONAL RESEARCH (NZ/0545-7564). [1,500] **1725**

ANNUAL REPORT - NORTHERN TERRITORY. DEPARTMENT OF PRIMARY INDUSTRY AND FISHERIES (AT/1034-7356). [1,000] **2294**

ANNUAL REPORT / OAK RIDGE ASSOCIATED UNIVERSITIES (US/0078-2904). [2,000] **4446**

ANNUAL REPORT OF MUNICIPAL STATISTICS (CN). [800] **4696**

ANNUAL REPORT OF OHIONET (US/0270-0107). [250] **3190**

ANNUAL REPORT OF THE ACTIVITIES OF THE ALABAMA DEPT. OF PUBLIC HEALTH (US). [1,000] **4766**

ANNUAL REPORT OF THE AMERICAN BIBLE SOCIETY (US/0740-6401). [2,000] **5014**

ANNUAL REPORT OF THE CHIEF ELECTORAL OFFICER ADMINISTERING THE ELECTION FINANCES AND CONTRIBUTIONS DISCLOSURE ACT (CN/0227-8073). [1,000] **4628**

ANNUAL REPORT OF THE COLORADO JUDICIARY (US/0731-3195). **3139**

ANNUAL REPORT OF THE COUNCIL AND INSTITUTE ACCOUNTS (UK). [16,500] **2018**

ANNUAL REPORT OF THE DELAWARE RACING COMMISSION TO THE GOVERNOR OF THE STATE OF DELAWARE (US). **2797**

ANNUAL REPORT OF THE DEPARTMENT OF ANTIQUITIES FOR THE YEAR ... / REPUBLIC OF CYPRUS, MINISTRY OF COMMUNICATIONS WORKS (CY). [1,000] **255**

ANNUAL REPORT OF THE DIRECTOR TO THE BOARD OF GOVERNORS (UK). [1,500] **4628**

ANNUAL REPORT OF THE EUROPEAN FREE TRADE ASSOCIATION (SZ/0531-4127). [7,000] **823**

ANNUAL REPORT OF THE NEW MEXICO STATE PERMANENT FUND AND SEVERENCE TAX PERMANENT FUND (US). [250] **891**

ANNUAL REPORT OF THE SECRETARY OF THE STATE HORTICULTURAL SOCIETY OF MICHIGAN (US/0096-7688). [2,200] **2409**

ANNUAL REPORT ON THE KENYA METEOROLOGICAL DEPARTMENT FOR THE PERIOD 1ST JULY ... TO 30TH JUNE ... (KE). [800] **1420**

ANNUAL REPORT ON THE RESULTS OF TREATMENT IN GYNECOLOGICAL CANCER (SW/0348-8799). [2,000] **3809**

ANNUAL REPORT--ONTARIO HERITAGE FOUNDATION (CN/0706-0106). [1,000] **2721**

ANNUAL REPORT / POSTS AND TELECOMMUNICATIONS CORPORATION (RH). [1,500] **1149**

ANNUAL REPORT / PRINCE EDWARD ISLAND HOUSING CORPORATION (CN). [250] **2815**

ANNUAL REPORT - PUBLIC SAFETY SERVICES (ALBERTA) (CN/0833-7659). [400] **4766**

ANNUAL REPORT / PUERTO RICO INDUSTRIAL DEVELOPMENT COMPANY (PR/0748-5530). [20,000] **891**

ANNUAL REPORT - RAILROAD RETIREMENT BOARD (US/0891-8066). [1,850] **1650**

ANNUAL REPORT - ROYAL ONTARIO MUSEUM (CN/0082-5115). **4084**

ANNUAL REPORT - SOIL SURVEY. ENGLAND AND WALES (UK/0141-1675). [200] **163**

ANNUAL REPORT - SOUTHEASTERN LIBRARY NETWORK (US/0099-085X). [800] **3191**

ANNUAL REPORT - TECHNISCH-PHYSISCHE DIENST TNO-TH (NE/0304-8292). [2,500] **4397**

ANNUAL REPORT / THE ATLANTIC SALMON FEDERATION (CN/0837-1059). [7,500] **2295**

ANNUAL REPORT / THE HAKLUYT SOCIETY (UK). [2,300] **5461**

ANNUAL REPORT - THE MANITOBA HYDRO-ELECTRIC BOARD (CN/0460-9581). **4759**

ANNUAL REPORT / THE ROWETT RESEARCH INSTITUTE (UK/0952-7222). [1,500] **5503**

ANNUAL REPORT / THE SOUTH AFRICAN TRANSPORT SERVICES (SA). **5376**

ANNUAL REPORT - THE SOUTHWESTERN LEGAL FOUNDATION (US/0561-1784). [2,000] **2935**

ANNUAL REPORT TO THE GOVERNOR AND LEGISLATURE - STATE BOARD OF INDIGENTS' DEFENSE SERVICES (KANSAS) (US). **4035**

ANNUAL REPORT - TOWN AND COUNTRY PLANNING ASSOCIATION (UK/0308-082X). [1,300] **2815**

ANNUAL REPORT - UNITED PLANTING ASSOCIATION OF MALAYSIA (MY/0304-8349). **61**

ANNUAL REPORT / UNIVERSITY OF LONDON, INSTITUTE OF ADVANCED LEGAL STUDIES (UK). [400] **2935**

ANNUAL REPORT - UTAH. DEPT. OF NATURAL RESOURCES (US/0882-7583). [1,800] **4630**

ANNUAL REPORT - VICTORIA, AUSTRALIA. ENVIRONMENT PROTECTION AUTHORITY (AT). **3109**

ANNUAL REPORT / VICTORIAN ETHNIC AFFAIRS COMMISSION (AT/0812-566X). [500] **4630**

ANNUAL REPORT / VICTORIAN MINISTRY OF IMMIGRATION & ETHNIC AFFAIRS (AT). **1918**

ANNUAL REPORT - VIRGINIA ENVIRONMENTAL ENDOWMENT (US/0191-4049). [5,000] **2161**

ANNUAL REPORT / WATER AUTHORITY OF WESTERN AUSTRALIA (AT/1031-5225). [1,500] **5530**

ANNUAL REPORT / WORKERS' COMPENSATION BOARD, NEWFOUNDLAND AND LABRADOR (CN/0225-3291). [7,500] **1650**

ANNUAL REPORT - WYOMING STATE BOARD OF NURSING (US/0098-2679). **3851**

ANNUAL REPORTS FOR ... / UNIVERSITY OF OXFORD, INSTITUTE OF ECONOMICS AND STATISTICS (UK). [300] **1590**

ANNUAL REPORTS OF THE NATIONAL COLLEGIATE ATHLETIC ASSOCIATION (US/0077-3794). **4883**

ANNUAL REVIEW / CHIEF, NATIONAL GUARD BUREAU (US/0192-4559). [3,000] **4035**

ANNUAL REVIEW OF ANTHROPOLOGY (US/0084-6570). **228**

ANNUAL REVIEW OF ASTRONOMY AND ASTROPHYSICS (US/0066-4146). **391**

ANNUAL REVIEW OF BIOCHEMISTRY (US/0066-4154). **480**

ANNUAL REVIEW OF CALIFORNIA OIL AND GAS PRODUCTION (US/0197-5641). [800] **4250**

ANNUAL REVIEW OF CELL BIOLOGY (US/0743-4634). **532**

ANNUAL REVIEW OF EARTH AND PLANETARY SCIENCES (US/0084-6597). **1351**

ANNUAL REVIEW OF ECOLOGY AND SYSTEMATICS (US/0066-4162). **2211**

ANNUAL REVIEW OF ENTOMOLOGY (US/0066-4170). **5605**

ANNUAL REVIEW OF FLUID MECHANICS (US/0066-4189). **2087**

ANNUAL REVIEW OF GENETICS (US/0066-4197). **542**

ANNUAL REVIEW OF IMMUNOLOGY (US/0732-0582). **3666**

ANNUAL REVIEW OF MATERIALS SCIENCE (US/0084-6600). **2100**

ANNUAL REVIEW OF MEDICINE (US/0066-4219). **3551**

ANNUAL REVIEW OF NEUROSCIENCE (US/0147-006X). **3827**

ANNUAL REVIEW OF NUCLEAR AND PARTICLE SCIENCE (US/0163-8998). **4446**

ANNUAL REVIEW OF NUTRITION (US/0199-9885). **4187**

ANNUAL REVIEW OF PHARMACOLOGY AND TOXICOLOGY (US/0362-1642). **4291**

ANNUAL REVIEW OF PHYSICAL CHEMISTRY (US/0066-426X). **1050**

ANNUAL REVIEW OF PHYSIOLOGY (US/0066-4278). **578**

ANNUAL REVIEW OF PHYTOPATHOLOGY (US/0066-4286). **500**

ANNUAL REVIEW OF PLANT PHYSIOLOGY AND PLANT MOLECULAR BIOLOGY (US/1040-2519). **500**

ANNUAL REVIEW OF POPULATION LAW (US/0364-3417). **2935**

ANNUAL REVIEW OF PSYCHOLOGY (US/0066-4308). **4574**

ANNUAL REVIEW OF PUBLIC HEALTH (US/0163-7525). **4767**

ANNUAL REVIEW OF SOCIOLOGY (US/0360-0572). **5239**

ANNUAL REVIEW OF THE ROYAL INSCRIPTIONS OF MESOPOTAMIA PROJECT (CN/0822-2525). [500] **3265**

ANNUAL REVIEW - THE JUNIOR CHAMBER OF COMMERCE FOR LONDON (UK/0306-8501). [2,000] **818**

ANNUAL STATISTICAL REPORT - SOUTH DAKOTA DEPARTMENT OF SOCIAL SERVICES (US/0147-6467). [315] **5266**

ANNUAL STATUS REPORT ON FEMALE AND MALE STUDENTS AND EMPLOYEES IN VOCATIONAL EDUCATION (OKLAHOMA) (US). [200] **1910**

ANNUAL SUMMARY OF VITAL STATISTICS, KANSAS (1969) (US/0364-2372). [750] **5321**

ANNUAL SUPPLEMENT TO HONG KONG TRADE STATISTICS, COUNTRY BY COMMODITY IMPORTS (HK/0304-8489). [900] **726**

ANNUAL SURVEY OF COMMUNITY PHARMACY OPERATIONS (CN/0829-2078). [1,000] **4291**

ANNUAL SURVEY OF INDIAN LAW (II/0570-2666). [1,000] **2935**

ANNUAL SYMPOSIUM ON FOUNDATIONS OF COMPUTER SCIENCE (US). **1250**

ANNUAL TECHNICAL REPORT / UNITED STATES DEPARTMENT OF AGRICULTURE, SOIL CONSERVATION SERVICE, BISMARCK PLANT MATERIALS CENTER (US). **5084**

ANNUAL U.S. ECONOMIC DATA (US/0891-8414). [8,954] **1463**

ANNUAL VOLUME / THE OLD WATER-COLOUR SOCIETY'S CLUB (UK/0958-8825). [1,000] **337**

ANNUARIO DEL GRUPPO IRI (IT). [24,000] **1463**

ANNUARIO FILOSOFICO (IT/0394-1809). **4341**

ANNUARIO SEAT. VOL. A, SIDERURGIA E MECCANICA (IT). [28,300] **3998**

ANNUARIO SEAT. VOL. B, ELETTROTECNICA, TERMOTECNICA E ATTREZZATURE INDUSTRIALI (IT). [30,100] **5084**

ANNUARIO SEAT. VOL. C, CHIMICA, MATERIE PLASTICHE, MEDICINA (IT). [23,600] **961**

ANNUARIO SEAT. VOL. I, TRASPORTI, CARTOTECNICA ED EDITORIA (IT). [30,200] **1598**

ANNUARIO SEAT. VOL. L, CREDITO, ASSICURAZIONI E SERVIZI PER LE AZIENDE (IT). [31,600] **772**

ANNUELLES ET LEGUMES. RESULTATS DES CULTURES D'ESSAI (CN/0319-3098). [500] **2409**

ANNUITIES FROM THE BUYER'S POINT OF VIEW (US). [1,000,000] **2874**

ANO PEDAGOGICO (SP/0577-8484). [500] **1725**

ANPHI PAPERS, THE (PH/0065-0676). **3851**

ANSEARCHIN' NEWS (US/0003-5246). [2,100] **2437**

ANTARTIDA (BUENOS AIRES) (AG/0302-5691). [350] **2554**

ANTELOPE VALLEY PRESS (US/0744-5830). [58,150] **5633**

ANTENNA (UK/0140-1890). [2,250] **5576**

ANTENNE (MONTREAL) (CN/0701-1865). [2,000] **3265**

ANTHOLOGY OF MAGAZINE VERSE AND YEARBOOK OF AMERICAN POETRY (1980) (US/0196-2221). **3460**

ANTHROPOLOGICAL PAPERS OF THE AMERICAN MUSEUM OF NATURAL HISTORY (US/0065-9452). [1,500] **4162**

ANTHROPOLOGIE (PARIS) (FR/0003-5521). [30] **229**

ANTHROPOLOGY & EDUCATION QUARTERLY (US/0161-7761). [1,400] **230**

ANTHROPOLOGY NEWSLETTER (US/0098-1605). [10,000] **230**

ANTHROPOS (BARCELONA, SPAIN) (SP/0211-5611). [10,000] **2842**

ANTHROPOS. SUPLEMENTOS (SP/1130-2089). [5,000] **2842**

ANTHROPOZOOLOGICA PARIS (FR/0761-3032). [350] **5576**

ANTHROQUEST (US/0749-1751). [5,000] **230**

ANTI (GR). [18,000] **4515**

ANTICHITA VIVA (IT/0003-5645). [1,500] **337**

ANTIGONISH REVIEW, THE (CN/0003-5661). [800] **3337**

ANTIKE KUNST (SZ/0003-5688). [1,100] **255**

ANTIMICROBIAL AGENTS AND CHEMOTHERAPY (US/0066-4804). [7,127] **559**

ANTIMICROBIAL NEWSLETTER (NZ/1170-8875). [140] **559**

ANTIPODES (BROOKLYN, NEW YORK, N.Y.) (US/0893-5580). [600] **3362**

ANTIQUARIAN BOOK MONTHLY (UK). [3,000] **4823**

ANTIQUARIAN HOROLOGY AND THE PROCEEDINGS OF THE ANTIQUARIAN HOROLOGICAL SOCIETY (UK/0003-5785). [3,000] **2916**

ANTIQUE AUTOMOBILE, THE (US/0003-5831). [40,000] **5404**

ANTIQUE BOTTLE & GLASS COLLECTOR (US/8750-1481). [4,200] **248**

ANTIQUE CAR TIMES (US/0164-7237). [800] **248**

ANTIQUE GAZETTE (US). [10,000] **249**

ANTIQUE POWER MAGAZINE (US/1042-7392). **249**

ANTIQUE REVIEW (US/0883-833X). [9,500] **249**

ANTIQUES & COLLECTIBLES (GREENVALE, N.Y.) (US/0274-6085). [10,000] **249**

ANTIQUES & COLLECTING HOBBIES (US/0884-6294). [25,000] **249**

ANTIQUES & FINE ART (US/0886-7208). [40,000] **249**

ANTIQUITE CLASSIQUE, L' (BE/0770-2817). **1074**

ANTISEPTIC, THE (II/0003-5998). **3551**

ANTONIANUM (IT/0003-6064). [1,000] **4935**

ANUARIO ANTROPOLOGICO (BL). [2,000] **231**

ANUARIO DE DERECHO INTERNACIONAL (SP/0212-0747). [100] **3124**

ANUARIO DE HISTORIA DEL DERECHO ESPANOL (SP/0304-4319). [500] **2935**

ANUARIO DE LA NIEVE (SP). [24,000] **4883**

ANUARIO DE PSICOLOGIA (SP). [1,500] **4574**

ANUARIO ESTADISTICO DE ANTIOQUIA (CK/0120-3495). [1,500] **5322**

ANUARIO ESTADISTICO (INSTITUTO NACIONAL DE ESTADISTICA Y CENSOS (ARGENTINA)) (AG). **5322**

ANUARIO ESTADISTICO DAS FERROVIAS DO BRASIL (BL). [1,200] **5400**

ANUARIO ESTADISTICO DO BRASIL / MINISTERIO DA AGRICULTURA, INDUSTRIA E COMMERCIO, DIRECTORIA GERAL DE ESTATISTICA (BL/0100-1299). [7,000] **5322**

ANUARIO IEHS (AG/0326-9671). [1,000] **2721**

ANUARIO JURIDICO (MX/0185-3295). [1,000] **2935**

ANUARIO MINERAL BRASILEIRO (BL/0100-9303). **1361**

ANUARUL INSTUTUTULUI DE GEOLOGIE SI GEOFIZICA (RM/0250-2933). [700] **1365**

ANZEIGER DER ORNITHOLOGISCHE GESELLSCHAFT IN BAYERN (GW/0030-5715). [1,200] **5614**

AOHA PROGRESS : A PUBLICATION OF THE AMERICAN OSTEOPATHIC HOSPITAL ASSOCIATION (US). [1,200] **3777**

AONTAS NEWSLETTER (IE/1805-1157). [750] **1799**

AOPA PILOT, THE (US/0001-2084). [265,000] **12**

AORN JOURNAL (US/0001-2092). [39,659] **3851**

AOYAMA SHAKAI KAGAKU KIYO (JA). [1,100] **5191**

APA NEWSLETTERS ON THE BLACK EXPERIENCE, COMPUTER USE, FEMINISM, LAW, MEDICINE, TEACHING (US/1067-9464). **4341**

APAGAY (MONTREAL) (CN/0382-9251). [1,200] **5780**

APARTMENT AGE (US/0192-0030). [38,300] **2815**

APCA DIRECTORY AND RESOURCE BOOK (US/0094-9191). [9,000] **2224**

APCO BULLETIN, THE (US/0001-2165). [9,750] **4767**

APEC JOURNAL (US/0893-0457). [1,500] **1965**

APERCU ECONOMIQUE TRIMESTRIEL (BE/0773-9664). [1,500 French1,000 Dutch] **1546**

APF REPORTER (US/0193-4562). [4,000] **2917**

APHA NEWSLETTER : A PUBLICATION OF THE AMERICAN PRINTING HISTORY ASSOCIATION, THE (US). [900] **4563**

API ACCOUNT, THE (US/0883-2102). [2,500] **738**

APIACTA (RM/0003-6455). [6,000] **62**

APICULTURAL ABSTRACTS (UK/0003-648X). [1,000] **5604**

APIS, THE (US/0887-7386). [750] **226**

APLASTIC ANEMIA FOUNDATION OF AMERICAN NEWSLETTER (US). [4,500] **4767**

APLIC BULLETIN (CN/0825-186X). [125] **3191**

APLUS (BE). [10,000] **288**

APOLLO (LONDON. 1925) (UK/0003-6536). [10,000] **337**

APOTHECARY (BOSTON), THE (US/0003-6560). [67,400] **4292**

APOTHEKENHELFERIN, DIE (GW). [22,000] **4292**

APOTHEKER-JAHRBUCH (GW/0066-5347). [4,000] **4292**

APOTHEKER-ZEITUNG STUTTGART (GW/0178-4862). [30,000] **4292**

APPALACHIA (BOSTON) (US/0003-6587). [10,000] **4869**

APPALACHIA (WASHINGTON) (US/0003-6595). [22,500] **1463**

APPALACHIAN FAMILIES (US/1041-8466). [500] **2437**

APPALACHIAN READER, THE (US/1043-2809). [500] **5273**

APPALACHIAN ROOTS (US/0888-6814). [450] **2437**

APPALACHIAN TRAILWAY NEWS (US/0003-6641). [24,500] **4869**

APPAREL (NZ). [3,200] **1081**

APPAREL INDUSTRY MAGAZINE (US/0192-1878). [18,600] **1081**

APPAREL INTERNATIONAL (UK/0263-1008). [6,000] **1081**

APPAREL NEWS SOUTH (US/0744-6403). [13,000] **1081**

APPAREL STRATEGIST (US). **1081**

APPEL, DE (NE). [750] **755**

APPLAUSE THEATRE BOOK REVIEW & CATALOG, THE (US). [50,000] **383**

APPLESEED QUARTERLY (CN/1183-3785). [500] **3363**

APPLEWOOD TRANSCRIPT (US). [8,000] **5641**

APPLIANCE (US/0003-6781). [29,000] **2810**

APPLIANCE MANUFACTURER (US/0003-679X). [35,000] **2810**

APPLIANCE SERVICE NEWS (US/0003-6803). [52,000] **2810**

APPLICATIONS OF COMPUTER SCIENCE SERIES (US/0888-2231). **1171**

APPLIED CYTOGENETICS (US/1056-5191). [2,000] **542**

APPLIED HEALTH PHYSICS ABSTRACTS AND NOTES (UK/0305-7615). [1,000] **4433**

APPLIED PLANT SCIENCE (SA/0259-5605). [800] **163**

APPLIED PSYCHOLOGICAL MEASUREMENT (US/0146-6216). [975] **4574**

APPLIED RADIOLOGY (1976) (US/0160-9963). [27,000] **3939**

APPLIED SPECTROSCOPY REVIEWS (SOFTCOVER ED.) (US/0570-4928). **1013**

APPLIED STATISTICS (UK/0035-9254). [5,500] **5322**

APPRAISAL JOURNAL, THE (US/0003-7087). [38,000] **4834**

APPRAISAL REVIEW & MORTGAGE UNDERWRITING JOURNAL (US/1041-1593). **4834**

APPRAISERS' INFORMATION EXCHANGE, THE (US/8755-4348). [2,500] **4834**

APPRENTICE (OTTAWA) (CN/0706-7399). [1,000] **4857**

APS OBSERVER (US/1050-4672). [15,000] **4575**

APSA DIRECTORY OF DEPARTMENT CHAIRPERSONS (US/0196-5255). [1,000] **4464**

APT. REVIEW. EGLINTON EDITION (CN/0226-6040). **383**

APUA NEWSLETTER (UK). [625] **62**

APUA NEWSLETTER / ALLIANCE FOR THE PRUDENT USE OF ANTIBIOTICS (US). [1,000] **4292**

APUNTS. MEDICINA DE L'ESPORT (SP/0213-3717). [2,000] **3953**

AQUA FENNICA (FI/0356-7133). **1412**

AQUACULTURAL ENGINEERING (UK/0144-8609). **2295**

AQUACULTURE IRELAND (IE/0790-0929). [800] **2295**

AQUACULTURE MAGAZINE (US/0199-1388). [7,360] **2295**

AQUACULTURE MAGAZINE. BUYER'S GUIDE ... AND INDUSTRY DIRECTORY (US/0898-9540). [7,200] **2296**

AQUACULTURE NEWS (US). [6,000] **2296**

AQUALINE ABSTRACTS (UK/0263-5534). [3,600] **2002**

AQUAPHYTE (US/0893-7702). [5,000] **500**

AQUARAMA (FR/0151-6981). [10,000] **4285**

AQUARIUM (US). **553**

AQUATIC MICROBIOLOGY NEWSLETTER (US/0570-5118). **559**

AQUATICS INTERNATIONAL (US/1058-7039). [30,000] **4883**

AQUEDUCT (LOS ANGELES) (US/0092-0622). [40,000] **5530**

AQUI MAGAZINE (US). [15,000] **2484**

AQUILON (YELLOWKNIFE) (CN/0834-1443). [1,000] **3266**

AQUITANIA (FR/0758-9670). [800] **2675**

AR FALZ (FR/0755-883X). **3363**

ARAB GULF JOURNAL OF SCIENTIFIC RESEARCH (SU/1015-4442). **5085**

ARAB OIL & GAS DIRECTORY (FR/0304-8551). [4,560] **4250**

ARAB STUDIES QUARTERLY (US/0271-3519). [2,000] **2645**

ARABESQUE (NEW YORK, N.Y.) (US/0148-5865). [6,000] **4100**

ARABIAN COMPUTER NEWS (UK/0950-5075). **1235**

ARABIAN HORSE EXPRESS (US/0194-6803). [10,500] **2797**

ARABIAN HORSE TIMES, THE (US/0279-8425). [25,000] **2797**

ARABIAN SYSTEMS GUIDE (UK). [12,000] **1171**

ARABICA (NE/0570-5398). [575] **2767**

ARABIDOPSIS INFORMATION SERVICE (GW/0066-5657). [500] **500**

ARABLE FARMING (UK/0269-6797). [32,000] **62**

ARAMCO WORLD (1987) (US/1044-1891). [180,000] **2768**

ARANCEL ADUANERO DE CHILE (CL). [1,500] **823**

ARANCEL DE ADUANAS (TARIC) UPDATES (SP). [2,500] **823**

ARARAT (NEW YORK) (US/0003-7583). [2,200] **3363**

ARBA SICULA (US/0271-0730). [1,500] **3363**

ARBEIDERVERN (NO/0332-7124). [41,000] **2859**

ARBEIDSMARKED OG ARBEIDSMARKEDSPOLITIKK I NORDEN. TYOMARKKINAT JA TYOMARKKINAPOLITIIKKA (DK). [400] **1651**

ARBEITEN ZUR ANGEWANDTEN STATISTIK (GW/0066-5673). [300] **3495**

ARBEITSBERICHT DES INSTITUTS FUR MITTELSTANDSFORSCHUNG (GW). **639**

ARBEITSBLATTER FUER RESTAURATOREN (GW/0066-5738). [2,400] **256**

ARBEITSMARKT IN BADEN-WURTTEMBERG; JAHRESBERICHT, DER (GW). [900] **1529**

ARBEITSSCHUTZ, ARBEITSHYGIENE (GW/0138-1555). [8,000] **2859**

ARBITRATION IN THE SCHOOLS (US/0003-7885). [3,500] **1726**

ARBITRATION JOURNAL, THE (US/0003-7893). [8,500] **2936**

ARBITRATION TIMES (US/8756-5455). [70,000] **2936**

ARBITRIUM : ZEITSCHRIFT FUER REZENSIONEN ZUR GERMANISTISCHEN LITERATURWISSENSCHAFT (GW). [500] **3337**

ARBOR AGE (US/0279-0106). [15,000] **2375**

ARBORESCENCES (PARIS) (FR/0767-337X). **2375**

ARBORICULTURE FRUITIERE, L' (FR/0003-794X). [5,000] **163**

ARC-EN-CIEL (ROUYN) (CN/0712-3310). [750] **313**

ARC (MONTREAL) (CN/0229-2807). [600-700] **5055**

ARC TODAY, THE (US). **5273**

ARCADE HERALD (US/0746-102X). [4,900] **5713**

ARCADE (SEATTLE, WASH.) (US). [1,400] **288**

ARCHAEOLOGIA CANTIANA (UK/0066-5894). [1,500] **256**

ARCHAEOLOGIA ZAMBIANA (ZA). [500] **256**

ARCHAEOLOGICA PRAGENSIA : ARCHEOLOGICKY SBORNIK MUZEA HLAVNIHO MESTA PRAHY (XR). [500] **256**

ARCHAEOLOGICAL JOURNAL, THE (UK/0066-5983). [2,000] **256**

ARCHAEOLOGICAL SERIES (TUCSON) (US/0196-5409). [150] **257**

ARCHAIOLOGIKON DELTION (GR). [1,200] **258**

ARCHAOLOGIE DER SCHWEIZ (SZ). [3,500] **258**

ARCHEOLOGICKE ROZHLEDY (XR/0044-8605). [1,400] **259**

ARCHERY ACTION WITH OUTDOOR CONNECTIONS (AT/1037-6720). [11,000] **4884**

ARCHI FUER MITTELRHEINISCHE KIRCHENGESCHICHTE (GW/0066-6432). [1,900] **4935**

ARCHIE AT RIVERDALE HIGH (US/0746-8660). **4857**

ARCHIE (NEW YORK, N.Y.) (US/0735-6455). **4857**

ARCHIE'S PALS 'N GALS (US/0745-7774). **4857**

ARCHIFACTS (NZ/0303-7940). [600] **2479**

ARCHIPELAG : A (GW). [10,000] **4540**

ARCHITECT & SURVEYOR (UK/0308-8596). [5,000] **288**

ARCHITECT, W.A. : THE OFFICIAL JOURNAL OF THE ROYAL AUSTRALIAN INSTITUTE OF ARCHITECTS, W.A. CHAPTER, THE (AT/0003-8393). [1,200] **288**

ARCHITECTS' EMPLOYMENT CLEARINGHOUSE (US). [7,000] **288**

ARCHITECTURAL DESIGN (UK/0003-8504). [12,000] **288**

ARCHITECTURAL LIGHTING (US/0894-0436). [57,000] **289**

ARCHITECTURE CALIFORNIA (US/0738-1131). [10,000] **290**

ARCHITECTURE CONCEPT (CN/0003-8687). [4,052] **290**

ARCHITECTURE D'AUJOURD'HUI, L' (BE/0003-8695). [25,791] **290**

ARCHITECTURE MINNESOTA (US/0149-9106). [7,000] **290**

ARCHITECTURE NEW ZEALAND (NZ/0113-4566). [8,500] **290**

ARCHITECTURE SA (SA/0250-054X). [4,100] **290**

ARCHITECTURE TODAY (UK/0958-6407). [22,000] **290**

ARCHITEKT (STUTTGART), DER (GW/0003-875X). [8,000] **290**

ARCHITEKTUR AKTUELL FACH-JOURNAL (AU/0570-6602). **290**

ARCHITEKTUR WETTBEWERBE (GW/0341-2784). [4,000] **291**

ARCHITEKTURA A URBANIZMUS (XO/0044-8680). [1,150] **291**

ARCHITETTURA, STORIA E DOCUMENTI : RIVISTA SEMESTRALE DI STORIA DELL'ARCHITETTURA DEL CENTRO DI STUDI STORICO-ARCHIVISTICI PER LA STORIA DELL'ARTE E DELL'ARCHITETTURA MEDIOEVALE E MODERNA (IT). [900] **291**

ARCHIV FUER KOMMUNALWISSENSCHAFTEN (GW/0003-9209). **4630**

ARCHIV FUER MOLLUSKENKUNDE DER SENCKENBERGISCHE NATURFORSCHENDE GESELLSCHAFT (GW/0003-9284). [750] **5576**

ARCHIV FUR SIPPENFORSCHUNG UND ALLE VERWANDTEN GEBIETE (GW/0003-9403). **2437**

ARCHIVE OF AUSTRALIAN JUDAICA HOLDINGS TO ... (AT). [200] **2479**

ARCHIVE (TUCSON, ARIZ.), THE (US/0735-5572). [2,000] **4366**

ARCHIVES AND MANUSCRIPTS (AT/0157-6895). [800] **2479**

ARCHIVES BELGES DE MEDECINE SOCIALE HYGIENE, MEDECINE DU TRAVAIL ET MEDECINE LEGALE (BE/0003-9578). [1,000] **3552**

ARCHIVES DE L'ART FRANCAIS (FR). **337**

ARCHIVES DE L'INSTITUT PASTEUR DE MADAGASCAR (MG/0020-2495). [900] **3666**

ARCHIVES DE PHILOSOPHIE (FR/0003-9632). [1,200] **4341**

ARCHIVES ET BIBLIOTHEQUES DE BELGIQUE (BE/0003-9748). [400] **2479**

ARCHIVES FRANCAISES DE PEDIATRIE (FR/0003-9764). [3,100] **3900**

ARCHIVES INFORMATION CIRCULAR (US/0093-9056). **2479**

ARCHIVES JUIVES (FR). [600] **2676**

ARCHIVES OF COMPLEX ENVIRONMENTAL STUDIES : ACES (FI/0787-0396). **2161**

ARCHIVES OF NATURAL HISTORY (UK/0260-9541). [800] **4162**

ARCHIVES OF PHYSICAL MEDICINE AND REHABILITATION (US/0003-9993). [8,300] **4379**

ARCHIVI (IT). [4,500] **337**

ARCHIVI & COMPUTER (IT/1121-2462). [1,300] **1171**

ARCHIVIO DI ORTOPEDIA E REUMATOLOGIA (IT/0390-7368). [3,000] **3803**

ARCHIVIO EDILE (IT). [6,000] **599**

ARCHIVIO ITALIANO DI ANATOMIA E DI EMBRIOLOGIA (IT/0004-0223). [500] **3678**

ARCHIVIO PER L'ANTROPOLOGIA E LA ETNOLOGIA (IT/0373-3009). **231**

ARCHIVIO PUTTI DI CHIRURGIA DEGLI ORGANI DI MOVIMENTO (IT/0066-670X). [3,000] **3960**

ARCHIVIO SICILIANO DI MEDICINA E CHIRURGIA. 1, ACTA CHIRURGICA MEDITERRANEA (IT). [4,000] **3960**

ARCHIVOS DE BRONCONEUMOLOGIA (SP/0300-2896). [5,000] **3948**

ARCHIVOS DE CRIMINOLOGIA, NEUROPSIQUIATRIA Y DISCIPLINAS CONEXAS (EC). [1,000] **3158**

ARCHIVOS DE MEDICINA VETERINARIA (CL/0301-732X). [1,000] **5504**

ARCHIVOS DE OFTALMOLOGIA DE BUENOS AIRES (AG/0066-6777). [2,000] **3872**

ARCHIVOS DEL INSTITUTO DE CARDIOLOGIA DE MEXICO (MX/0020-3785). [2,500] **3699**

ARCHIVOS ESPANOLES DE UROLOGIA (SP/0004-0614). [2,500] **3988**

ARCHIVOS LATINOAMERICANOS DE NUTRICION (VE/0004-0622). [500] **4187**

ARCHIVUM FRANCISCANUM HISTORICUM (IT/0004-0665). [550] **5024**

ARCHIVUM MATHEMATICUM (XR/0044-8753). [500] **3496**

ARCHOLOGIAI ERTESITO (HU/0003-8032). [900] **259**

ARCTIC (CN/0004-0843). [2,300] **2555**

ARCTIC AND ALPINE RESEARCH (US/0004-0851). [950] **2555**

ARCTIC MEDICAL RESEARCH (FI/0782-226X). [2,200] **3552**

ARCTIC NEWS (CN/0518-3839). [4,000] **4936**

AREA (MILAN, ITALY) (IT/0394-0055). **291**

AREEA REPORT, THE (US/1064-1092). **4834**

ARENA (AT/0004-0932). [3,000] **4464**

ARENA JOURNAL (AT). [1,000] **4540**

ARENA MAGAZINE (AT/1039-1010). [2,000] **4540**

ARETE (US/0885-9787). [1,000] **5273**

ARFFAS VIEWPOINT (AT). [5,000] **4035**

ARGOMENTI DI CARDIOLOGIA (IT/1120-8635). [15,000] **3699**

ARGUMENTATION AND ADVOCACY (US/1051-1431). [1,000] **1104**

ARGUS (MONTREAL) (CN/0315-9930). [1,200] **3191**

ARGUS (SAN FRANCISCO) (US/0194-8172). [14,000] **3872**

ARHIV ZA HIGIJENU RADA I TOKSIKOLOGIJU (CR/0004-1254). [1,000] **2859**

ARIEL (ENGLISH EDITION) (IS/0004-1343). [20,000] **3363**

ARION / BOSTON UNIVERSITY (US). [750 controlled 2500 printed] **3363**

ARISTOS (US/0737-0407). **313**

ARITHMETIC TEACHER, THE (US/0004-136X). [44,000] **3496**

ARIZONA ATTORNEY (US/1040-4090). [11,200] **2936**

ARIZONA BEVERAGE ANALYST (US/0164-6281). [5,000] **2363**

ARIZONA GROCER (US/0004-1505). [2,600] **2327**

ARIZONA HUNTER & ANGLER (US/0888-840X). **4884**

ARIZONA LABOR MARKET NEWSLETTER (US/0743-5657). [5,500] **1653**

ARIZONA MUSIC NEWS (US/0518-6129). [1,000] **4101**

ARIZONA NURSE (US/0004-1599). [1.300] **3851**

ARIZONA ONLINE USER GROUP (US/0894-9948). [90] **1274**

ARIZONA PHARMACIST, THE (US/0004-1602). [1,400] **4292**

ARIZONA PORTFOLIO, THE (US/0882-4932). **337**

ARIZONA REALTOR DIGEST (US/0199-9206). [21,000] **4834**

ARIZONA REVIEW (US/0004-1629). [3,000] **639**

ARIZONA SENIOR WORLD, THE (US/0270-0425). [200,000] **5629**

ARIZONA STATE LAW JOURNAL (US/0164-4297). [770] **2937**

ARIZONA THOROUGHBRED, THE (US/0091-4401). [4,000] **2797**

ARIZONA TREND AZ (US/1046-476X). [60,000] **2528**

ARIZONA WILDLIFE VIEWS (US/0882-5572). [20,000] **2187**

ARIZONA'S ECONOMY (US). [3,600] **1463**

ARKANSAS AMATEUR, THE (US/0518-6617). [450] **259**

ARKANSAS ARCHEOLOGICAL SURVEY RESEARCH SERIES (US/0882-5491). [500] **259**

ARKANSAS ARCHEOLOGICAL SURVEY TECHNICAL PAPER (US/0882-5483). [100] **259**

ARKANSAS BUSINESS (US/1053-6582). [8,000] **639**

ARKANSAS CATTLE BUSINESS (US/0004-1750). [7,200] **206**

ARKANSAS CITY TRAVELER (ARKANSAS CITY, KAN. : 1970) (US/0888-8485). [7,000] **5674**

ARKANSAS DAILY LEGISLATIVE DIGEST (US). [400] **4630**

ARKANSAS DENTISTRY (US/1056-4764). [1200] **1316**

ARKANSAS EDUCATOR (US/0161-7753). [18,000] **1888**

ARKANSAS EPISCOPALIAN, THE (US/0890-5258). [8,200] **5055**

ARKANSAS FAMILY HISTORIAN, THE (US/0571-0472). [1,200] **2438**

ARKANSAS GAZETTE INDEX (US/0273-4001). [50] **2528**

ARKANSAS LIBRARIES (US/0004-184X). [800] **3191**

ARKANSAS NURSING NEWS (US). [1,000] **3851**

ARKANSAS REGISTER, THE (US). [300] **4630**

ARKANSAS STATE DIRECTORY (US). [3,500] **4630**

ARKANSAS VALLEY JOURNAL (US/0004-1890). [5,893] **63**

ARKITEKTEN (DK/0004-198X). [7,100] **291**

ARKITEKTUR

ARKITEKTUR DK (DK/0004-2013). [4,300] **292**

ARKKITEHTI (FI/0004-2129). [5,000] **292**

ARLINGTON CATHOLIC HERALD (US/0361-3712). [30,000] **5024**

ARLIS/ANZ NEWS (AT/0157-4043). [130] **408**

ARLIS/NA UPDATE (US/0743-040X). [1,300] **3192**

ARMADA INTERNATIONAL (SZ/0252-9793). [30,000] **4035**

ARMEES D'AUJOURD'HUI (FR). [150,000] **4036**

ARMENIAN CAUSE, THE (CN/0826-2667). [2,500] **2645**

ARMENIAN MIRROR-SPECTATOR, THE (US/0004-234X). [3,300] **5687**

ARMENIAN WEEKLY, THE (US/0004-2374). [2,500] **5687**

ARMOUR CHRONICLE, THE (US/8750-2488). [670] **5743**

ARMS COLLECTING (CN/0380-982X). [1,500] **2771**

ARMS CONTROL (LONDON, ENGLAND) (UK/0144-0381). **4036**

ARMS CONTROL REPORTER, THE (US/0886-3490). **4516**

ARMS REGISTER (US). [350] **755**

ARMSTRONG CHRONICLES (US/0898-1329). [200] **2438**

ARMY COMMUNICATOR, THE (US/0362-5745). [12,000] **4036**

ARMY HISTORY (US). [6,000] **4036**

ARMY LOGISTICIAN (US/0004-2528). [438,348] **4036**

ARMY QUARTERLY AND DEFENCE JOURNAL, THE (UK/0004-2552). [20,000] **4036**

ARNOLDIA (JAMAICA PLAIN) (US/0004-2633). [4,000] **2409**

AROIDEANA (US/0197-4033). [450] **2409**

ARQ : ARCHITECTURE/QUEBEC (CN/0710-1163). [5,000] **292**

ARQUITECTURA CUBA (CU/1010-3821). [20,000] **292**

ARQUITECTURA VIVA (SP/0214-1256). [8,000] **292**

ARQUIVOS DE BIOLOGIA E TECNOLOGIA (BL/0365-0979). [500] **443**

ARQUIVOS DE NEURO-PSIQUIATRIA (BL/0004-282X). [1,500] **3827**

ARQUIVOS DE ZOOLOGIA (BL/0066-7870). [684] **5576**

ARQUIVOS DO MUSEU NACIONAL (BL/0365-4508). **4084**

ARS CERAMICA (US/1043-3317). [500-600] **2586**

ARS MEDICI, MONATSSCHRIFT FUER ALLGEMEINMEDIZIN (SZ/0004-2897). [4,500] **3552**

ARS NOVA (SA). [500] **4101**

ARS ORIENTALIS (US/0571-1371). **337**

ARSBERETNING / DANTEST (DK). **4029**

ARSBERETNING - GRONLANDS GEOLOGISKE UNDERSOGELSE (DK). [100] **860**

ARSBERETNING - JUSTERVSENET (DK). [1,000] **4029**

ARSBOK FOR SVERIGES KOMMUNER (SW/0065-020X). [2,500] **4696**

ARSRAPPORT (NO/0800-4072). [4,000] **12**

ARSREDOVISNING / NOBELSTIFTELSEN (SW). [9,500] **3144**

ARSSKRIFT - DANSK GEOLOGISK FORENING (DK). [800] **1366**

ARSSKRIFT - LOKALHISTORISK FORENING FOR SONDERHALD KOMMUNE (DK). **2676**

ART AND ARCHAEOLOGY TECHNICAL ABSTRACTS (US/0004-2994). [4,500] **333**

ART & AUCTION (NEW YORK, N.Y.) (US/0197-1093). [22,000] **250**

ART & CRAFTS CATALYST (US). **370**

ART & DESIGN NEWS (US/1055-2286). [47,000] **376**

ART AND POETRY TODAY (II). [1,100] **338**

ART BUSINESS NEWS (US/0273-5652). [27,989] **338**

ART BUYER'S HANDBOOK (GW/0932-3333). [10,000] **338**

ART EDUCATION (RESTON) (US/0004-3125). [15,902] **338**

ART EDUCATION (SASKATOON) (CN/0708-5354). [200] **338**

ART HERITAGE : CATALOG (II). [1,000] **339**

ART INDEX (US/0004-3222). **334**

ART INDEX. CD-ROM (US/0004-3222). **334**

ART ISSUES (US/1046-8471). [9,000] **339**

ART LINE (CN/0711-1312). **370**

ART LOVERS' ART & CRAFT FAIR BULLETIN (US/0892-1202). **370**

ART MUSCLE (US). [17,000] **313**

ART NEW ENGLAND (US/0274-7073). [28,000] **339**

ART POST, THE (CN/0829-0784). [8,000] **340**

ART PRESS (PARIS, FRANCE : 1981) (FR/0245-5676). **313**

ART-TALK (US/0741-496X). [38,000] **340**

ART THERAPY : JOURNAL OF THE AMERICAN ART THERAPY ASSOCIATION (US/0742-1656). [4,200] **4575**

ART TO SCIENCE IN TISSUE CULTURE (US). [30,000] **443**

ART TO ZOO (US/0882-6838). [75,000] **1888**

ART TRIBAL (SZ). **340**

ARTE CRISTIANA (IT/0004-3400). [1000] **340**

ARTE, DE (SA). [800] **340**

ARTE IN (IT). [20,000] **341**

ARTE MEDIEVALE (IT/0393-7267). [500] **341**

ARTEFACT, THE (AT/0044-9075). [400] **260**

ARTES CONSTRUCTIONUM (FI/0355-3213). [450] **2018**

ARTHRITIS FOUNDATION ANNUAL REPORT (US/0191-2836). [15,000] **3803**

ARTHRITIS TODAY (US/0890-1120). [600,000] **3803**

ARTIFACT, THE (US/0004-3680). [215] **260**

ARTIFICIAL INTELLIGENCE ABSTRACTS (US/0882-1410). **1208**

ARTINF (AG). [2,000] **341**

ARTIST (CALCUTTA) (II/0304-8640). [5,000] **314**

ARTLINK (AT/0727-1239). [3,000] **342**

ARTPAPER (US/0739-8646). [3,000] **342**

ARTPARK (US/0164-1298). **342**

ARTS AND ACTIVITIES (US/0004-3931). [24,114] **314**

ARTS & METIERS (FR/0004-4008). [19,000] **5086**

ARTS & SCIENCES JOURNAL (PH). [500] **314**

ARTS BULLETIN OF THE CANADIAN CONFERENCE OF THE ARTS (CN/0707-9532). [2,500] **314**

ARTS D'AFRIQUE NOIRE (FR/0337-1603). **314**

ARTS EDUCATION : THE MAGAZINE OF THE NATIONAL FOUNDATION FOR ARTS EDUCATION (UK). [1,500] **315**

ARTS IN PSYCHOTHERAPY, THE (US/0197-4556). **3921**

ARTS IN VIRGINIA (US/0004-4032). [16,000] **315**

ARTS MANAGEMENT (US/0004-4067). **315**

ARTS QUARTERLY (NEW ORLEANS, LA. 1978) (US/0740-9214). [20,000] **342**

ARTSAMERICA FINE ART FILM & VIDEO SOURCE BOOK (US). **4063**

ARTSOURCE (RENAISSANCE, CALIF.) (US/1064-6620). [3,000] **315**

ARTWORLD HOTLINE (US/1057-5413). [100] **315**

ARUKORU KENKYU TO YAKUBUTSU IZON (JA/0389-4118). **1341**

ARUP JOURNAL (UK/0951-0850). [5,000] **292**

ARVADA JEFFERSON SENTINEL, THE (US/1060-5207). [19,000] **5641**

ARZNEIMITTEL FORSCHUNG (GW/0004-4172). [5,100] **4292**

ARZNEIMITTELBRIEF (GW). [2,500] **3553**

ASA NEWS (LOS ANGELES, CALIF.) (US/0278-2219). [2,000] **2498**

ASA NEWSLETTER - APPLIED SCIENCE AND ANALYSIS, INC, THE (US/1057-9419). [1,000] **4037**

ASBESTOS LITIGATION REPORTER (US/0273-3048). **2937**

ASBESTOS MANAGEMENT SOURCEBOOK (US/1046-0438). [35,000] **599**

ASBSD BULLETIN (US/0001-2408). [2,700] **1860**

ASBURY PARK PRESS (US). [140,000 daily 210,000 Sunday] **5709**

ASCA NEWSLETTER (FORT LAUDERDALE, FLA.) (US/0747-6000). [3,000] **4884**

ASCENT (CN/0707-5588). [15,000] **1933**

ASCENT (KOOTENAY BAY) (CN/0315-8179). [1,500] **4936**

ASCENT (URBANA, ILL.) (US/0098-9363). **3364**

ASDA NEWS (1981) (US/0277-3627). [15,000] **1317**

ASEA TIDNING (SW/0346-6582). [90,000] **2036**

ASEAN BRIEFING (US). **1547**

ASEAN FOOD JOURNAL (MY/0127-7324). [2,000] **2327**

ASHA MONOGRAPHS (US/0066-071X). [5,000] **4384**

ASHCROFT CACHE CREEK JOURNAL (CN). [1,700] **5780**

ASHMOLEAN, THE (UK). [2,000] **4084**

ASHRAE HANDBOOK. REFRIGERATION SYSTEMS AND APPLICATIONS (US). [50,000] **2603**

ASHRAE JOURNAL (US/0001-2491). [50,000] **2603**

ASHTREE ECHO (US/0004-4377). [300] **2438**

ASIA COMPUTER WEEKLY (SI/0129-5896). [20,000] **1235**

ASIA FOUNDATION QUARTERLY, THE (US). **2842**

ASIA INSURANCE REVIEW (SI/0218-2696). [5,000] **2874**

ASIA LETTER, THE (US/0004-4466). **1463**

ASIA-OCEANIA JOURNAL OF OBSTETRICS AND GYNAECOLOGY (JA/0389-2328). [4,000] **3757**

ASIA PACIFIC JOURNAL OF HUMAN RESOURCES (AT/1038-4111). [12,500] **938**

ASIA-PACIFIC JOURNAL OF PUBLIC HEALTH : ASIA-PACIFIC ACADEMIC CONSORTIUM FOR PUBLIC HEALTH (TH/1010-5395). [2,000] **4767**

ASIA PACIFIC PAPERMAKER (AT/1320-9787). [6,000] **4232**

ASIA-PACIFIC POPULATION & POLICY (US/0891-6683). [3,500] **4549**

ASIA PACIFIC TRAVEL (US/1045-3881). [125,000] **5461**

ASIA PULP & PAPER, TECHNOLOGY MARKETS (JA). [7,500] **4232**

ASIA THEOLOGICAL NEWS (CH). [2,000] **4936**

ASIA TRAVEL TRADE (HK). [20,000] **5462**

ASIAMAC JOURNAL (HK/1015-5023). [15,000] **2110**

ASIAN AFFAIRS (LONDON) (UK/0306-8374). [1,900] **2646**

ASIAN ALMANAC (SI/0004-4520). **2646**

ASIAN AMERICAN NEWS (HOUSTON, TEX.) (US/1070-3969). [2,000] **2255**

ASIAN AND AFRICAN STUDIES (JERUSALEM) (IS/0066-8281). [800] **2638**

ASIAN AND PACIFIC POPULATION FORUM (US/0891-2823). [2,000] **4549**

ASIAN AQUACULTURE (PH/0115-4974). **2296**

ASIAN ARCHITECT AND CONTRACTOR (HK). [17,600] **292**

ASIAN-AUSTRALASIAN JOURNAL OF ANIMAL SCIENCES (KO/1011-2367). [600] **5504**

ASIAN AVIATION (SI). [12,000] **12**

ASIAN BUSINESS (HK/0254-3729). [87,500] **640**

ASIAN COMMUNICATIONS (UK/0952-7516). [8,500] **1149**

ASIAN CULTURE QUARTERLY (CH/0378-8911). [1,000] **2646**

ASIAN DEFENCE JOURNAL (MY/0126-6403). [11,500] **4037**

ASIAN DEVELOPMENT REVIEW (PH/0116-1105). [6,000] **1547**

ASIAN ECONOMIC AND SOCIAL REVIEW, THE (II/0970-6305). [3,000] **1547**

ASIAN ENVIRONMENT (PH/0116-2993). **2161**

ASIAN HOSPITAL (HK/1011-596X). [5,000] **3777**

ASIAN HOTEL AND CATERING TIMES (HK). **2804**

ASIAN LIVESTOCK : MONTHLY PUBLICATION OF THE ANIMAL PRODUCTION AND HEALTH COMMISSION FOR ASIA, THE FAR EAST AND THE SOUTH-WEST PACIFIC (TH). [3,500] **206**

ASIAN PACIFIC JOURNAL OF ALLERGY AND IMMUNOLOGY (TH/0125-877X). [1,000] **3666**

ASIAN PERSPECTIVE (KO). [1,500] **4516**

ASIAN RECORDER (II/0004-4644). [2,000] **2646**

ASIAN SOURCES COMPUTER PRODUCTS (HK/0254-5586). **1235**

ASIAN SOURCES ELECTRONICS (HK/0254-1114). **2036**

ASIAN SOURCES HARDWARES FOR WORLD MARKETS (HK). [21,200] **1598**

ASIAN SOURCES TIMEPIECES (HK/0254-1173). [19,500] **2916**

ASIAN STUDIES (PH/0004-4679). [1,000] **2501**

ASIAN STUDIES (CALCUTTA, INDIA) (II). [500] **2501**

ASIAN TIMES (UK/0264-8490). [20,000] **2485**

ASIATHEQUE (CN/0228-4138). **2646**

ASIFA. ASSOCIATION INTERNATIONALE DU FILM D'ANIMATION, CANADA (CN/0828-7511). [300] **4063**

ASKOV AMERICAN (US). [1,800] **5694**

ASMAT SKETCH BOOK, AN (US). **231**

ASME NEWS (1981) (US/0279-9316). [120,000] **2110**

ASPAREZ (US/0004-4229). [10,000] **5633**

ASPECTS DE LA FRANCE (FR). [30,000] **4464**

ASPIRE (NASHVILLE, TENN.) (US/1076-5778). [50,000] **2596**

ASRT SCANNER (US/0161-3863). **3939**

ASSEMBLIES OF GOD EDUCATOR (US/0196-9560). [1,100] **1726**

ASSEMBLY (US). [1,500] **5024**

ASSERTIVE UTILIZATION MANAGEMENT REPORT, THE (US/1064-4962). **3553**

ASSESSMENT AND VALUATION LEGAL REPORTER (US/0090-6352). [700] **4711**

ASSESSMENT DIGEST (US/0731-0277). [8,500] **4711**

ASSET FINANCE & LEASING DIGEST (UK). [8,000] **773**

ASSET (ST. LOUIS, MO.), THE (US/0883-7384). [7,300] **738**

ASSISTANT LIBRARIAN (UK/0004-5152). [1,300] **3192**

ASSOCIATION & SOCIETY MANAGER (US/0004-5292). [18,000] **860**

ASSOCIATION MEETINGS (US/1042-3141). [21,000] **756**

ASSOCIATION NEWS - INDUSTRIAL FIRST AID ATTENDANTS ASSOCIATION OF BRITISH COLUMBIA (CN/0844-0506). [500] **3795**

ASSOCIATION OF HISTORIANS OF AMERICAN ART NEWSLETTER (GW). [500] **343**

ASSOCIATIONS OF DELAWARE VALLEY (US/0161-0023). **5228**

ASSUMPTION PIONEER, THE (US). [2,600] **5683**

ASSYRIOLOGICAL STUDIES (US/0066-9903). [750] **3267**

ASTHMA WELFARER (AT). [5,500] **3948**

ASTM GEOTECHNICAL TESTING JOURNAL (US/0149-6115). [1,200] **1965**

ASTR, AMERICAN SOCIETY FOR THEATRE RESEARCH NEWSLETTER (US/0044-7927). [700] **5361**

ASTRO-NEWS (BATON ROUGE, LA.) (US/0743-4227). [300] **390**

ASTROGRAPH (ARLINGTON, THE (US/0094-1417). [1,000] **391**

ASTROLOGICAL MAGAZINE, THE (II/0004-6140). [25,000] **390**

ASTROLOGICAL REVIEW, THE (US/0044-9784). **390**

ASTRUIM (NE). **393**

ASTUTE INVESTOR (KINGSTON, TENN.), THE (US/0736-7643). [1,000] **891**

ASWEA: JOURNAL FOR SOCIAL WORK EDUCATION IN AFRICA (ET). [200] **5274**

AT A GLANCE (CN/0708-0263). **3192**

AT HOME IN CANADA'S CAPITAL (CN/0225-9761). **4834**

AT RANDOM (US/1062-0036). [100,000] **4812**

AT WORK (SAN FRANCISCO, CALIF.) (US/1061-9925). [1,500] **4201**

ATA JOURNAL. ASIA THEOLOGICAL ASSOCIATION. INDIA (II). [700] **4936**

ATA NEWS (II). [700] **4936**

ATAC, ASOCIACION DE TECNICOS AZUCAREROS DE CUBA (CU/0366-242X). [10,000] **2328**

ATACC NEWSLETTER (CN/0828-6949). **1222**

ATALANTA (MUNCHEN) (GW/0171-0079). [1,200] **5605**

AT&T DATALINE (US/1041-2530). **1149**

AT&T TECHNICAL JOURNAL (US/8756-2324). [35,000] **1149**

ATCC QUARTERLY NEWSLETTER (US/0894-9026). [25,000] **443**

ATCP (MX). [2,250] **4232**

ATE NEWS LETTER (US/0001-2718). [3,500] **1888**

ATEMWEGS- UND LUNGENKRANKHEITEN (GW/0341-3055). **3948**

ATENCION MEDICA (MX/0185-6235). [16,500] **3553**

ATENEA (CONCEPCION, CHILE: 1972) (CL/0004-6507). [2,500] **2611**

ATHANOR (TALLAHASSEE, FLA.) (US/0732-1619). [300] **343**

ATHAREP (FR/0985-0120). [150] **5274**

ATHELINGS (US/0149-0125). **2528**

ATHENAEUM (PAVIA, ITALY) (IT/0004-6574). [800] **1074**

ATHENS OBSERVER, THE (US/0744-4001). [6,000] **5652**

ATHLETE, THE (US/0892-6166). [3,700] **4884**

ATHLETIC ADMINISTRATION (US/0044-9873). [5,000] **1855**

ATHLETIC BUSINESS (US/0747-315X). [40,000] **640**

ATHLETIC MANAGEMENT (US). **4884**

ATIKOKAN PROGRESS (CN). [1,800] **5780**

ATJ NEWSLETTER (US/0894-6728). [600] **3267**

ATLANTA BUSINESS CHRONICLE (US/0164-8071). [30,000] **640**

ATLANTA BUSINESS MAKERS & SHAKERS SERIES (US/1054-5182). [800] **640**

ATLANTA JEWISH TIMES, THE (US/0892-3345). [10,000] **5652**

ATLANTA SMALL BUSINESS MONTHLY, THE (US). [28,000] **640**

ATLANTA VOICE, THE (US). [103,000] **5652**

ATLANTIC (UK). [4,200] **823**

ATLANTIC (BOSTON, MASS. : 1981), THE (US/0276-9077). [450,000] **2528**

ATLANTIC BUSINESS REPORT (CN/1192-0203). [16,000] **641**

ATLANTIC CANADA RESEARCH LETTER (CN/0823-6933). [400] **2722**

ATLANTIC CHARISMATIC (CN/0821-6479). [4,500] **5024**

ATLANTIC CITY MAGAZINE (US/0194-9993). [40,000] **2485**

ATLANTIC CO-OPERATOR, THE (CN/0703-5357). [65,000] **1541**

ATLANTIC CONSTRUCTION JOURNAL (CN/0842-9588). **599**

ATLANTIC CONTROL STATES BEVERAGE JOURNAL (US/0044-9881). [7,450] **5070**

ATLANTIC FIREFIGHTER (CN/0838-679X). **2288**

ATLANTIC FORESTRY JOURNAL (CN/0832-5502). **2375**

ATLANTIC LIFESTYLE BUSINESS (CN/1184-051X). [25,000] **641**

ATLANTIC MATHEMATICS BULLETIN (CN/0705-9078). **3496**

ATLANTIC MINING JOURNAL (CN/0840-6693). **2134**

ATLANTIC MONTHLY (1993), THE (US/1072-7825). **2485**

ATLANTIC PROVINCES BOOK REVIEW, THE (CN/0316-5981). [55,000] **3337**

ATLANTIC REPORT (HALIFAX, N.S.) (CN/0004-6841). [1,200] **1547**

ATLANTIC SALMON JOURNAL, THE (CN/0044-992X). **2296**

ATLANTIS (WOLFVILLE) (CN/0702-7818). [800] **5551**

ATLETICA LEGGERA (IT/0392-2251). [7,000] **2596**

ATLETICA : RIVISTA MENSILE DELLA FIDAL (IT). [30,000] **4884**

ATOMWIRTSCHAFT, ATOMTECHNIK (GW/0365-8414). **2154**

ATOSSEMENT VOTRE (CN/0826-5321). [500] **2296**

ATR; AUSTRALIAN TELECOMMUNICATION RESEARCH (AT/0001-2777). **1149**

ATRI TURF NOTES (AT/0729-9397). **2797**

ATS FOCUS (AT/0727-3096). [1,000] **5086**

ATTAKAPAS GAZETTE (US/0571-8236). [625] **2722**

ATTI DELLA FONDAZIONE GIORGIO RONCHI (1976) (IT/0391-2051). [500] **4433**

ATTI E MEMORIE DELLA SOCIETA ISTRIANA DI ARCHEOLOGIA E STORIA PATRIA (IT). [500] **260**

ATTI E MEMORIE - DEPUTAZIONE DI STORIA PATRIA PER LE ANTICHE PROVINCIE MODENESI (IT/0418-7296). [400] **2677**

ATTORNEY-CPA, THE (US/0571-8279). [2,000] **2938**

ATTORNEY FEE AWARDS REPORTER (US/0732-7552). [500] **2938**

ATTORNEYS PERSONNEL REPORT (US/8750-2763). **2938**

ATTUALITA CINEMATOGRAFICHE (IT). [1,500] **4064**

ATULU, L' (CN/0226-3688). **3192**

ATV NEWS (US/0744-7809). [50,000] **4080**

ATZ. AUTOMOBILTECHNISCHE ZEITSCHRIFT (GW/0001-2785). [3,900] **5404**

AU COEUR DE L'AFRIQUE (BD). [1,000] **4937**

AU-COURANT (HYDRO-QUEBEC. BIBLIOTHEQUE) (CN/0229-8937). **408**

AU FIL DES COLLECTIONS (CN/0711-7086). **4084**

AU FIL DU BOIS (CN/0383-0047). [5,000] **2399**

AU POINT (CN/0824-3069). [1,500] **1810**

AUBURN PLAINSMAN, THE (US/1071-1279). [19.500] **5625**

AUDECIBEL (US/0004-7473). [21,000] **4384**

AUDIBLE (TORONTO) (CN/0710-2038). [2,000] **4884**

AUDIO-DIGEST. OBSTETRICS AND GYNECOLOGY (US/0571-8635). **3757**

AUDIO VISUAL (UK/0305-2249). [20,000] **1104**

AUDIO-VISUAL PRESENTATIONS / CANADIAN JEWISH CONGRESS, AUDIO-VISUAL DEPARTMENT (CN/0821-5529). **5315**

AUDIOFILE (PORTLAND, ME.) (US/1063-0244). [1,000 per month] **1104**

AUDIOTEX NEWS (US/1063-1348). [500] **1149**

AUDIVIDEO INTERNATIONAL (US/0362-1162). [42,000] **5315**

AUDUBON NATURALIST NEWS : A PUBLICATION OF THE AUDUBON NATURALIST SOCIETY OF THE CENTRAL ATLANTIC STATES (US/0888-6555). [7,400] **4162**

AUERBACH DATA WORLD (US/0190-6585). **1256**

AUFTRAG (BASEL. 1967) (SZ/0004-7880). [47,000] **4937**

AUGENOPTIKER, DER (GW/0004-7929). [12,466] **3872**

AUGUSTA AREA TIMES (US/0749-7083). **5765**

AUGUSTA EAGLE, THE (US). [1,600] **5658**

AUGUSTA HISTORICAL BULLETIN (US/0571-8899). [500] **2722**

AUGUSTINUS (SP/0004-802X). [700] **4937**

AUJOURD'HUI CREDO (CN/0383-2554). [1,000] **4937**

AULA ORIENTALIS (SP/0212-5730). [150] **2646**

AUNT EDNA'S READING LIST (US). [300] **5551**

AURA (BIRMINGHAM, ALA.) (US/0889-7433). [250] **3364**

AURA (FORT WORTH, TEX.) (US/1054-5441). [20,000] **2528**

AURISA NEWS (AT/0811-3130). [900] **2815**

AUSGRABUNGEN UND FUNDE IN WESTFALEN-LIPPE / IM AUFTRAG DES LANDSCHAFTSVERBANDES WESTFALEN-LIPPE HERAUSGEGEBEN VON WESTFALISCHES MUSEUM FUER ARCHAOLOGIE, AMT FUER BODENDENKMALPFLEGE (GW/0175-6133). [500] **2677**

AUSLANDISCHE MESSEN, AUSSTELLUNGEN, KONGRESSE (AU). [10,000] **1598**

AUSSENDIENST-INFORMATIONEN. TRAININGSKURS FUR SYSTEMATISCHES VERKAUFEN (GW/0933-8357). [18,000] **2874**

AUSSENWIRTSCHAFT: ZEITSCHRIFT FUER INTERNATIONALE WIRTSCHAFTSBEZIEHUNGEN (SZ/0004-8216). [1,600] **4516**

AUSTRALASIAN ANGORA MOHAIR JOURNAL (AT). **3183**

AUSTRALASIAN BUS AND COACH (AT). [3,500] **5377**

AUSTRALASIAN JOURNAL OF AMERICAN STUDIES : AJAS (AT/0705-7113). [170] **2722**

AUSTRALASIAN — Controlled Circulation Index

AUSTRALASIAN JOURNAL OF DERMATOLOGY, THE (AT/0004-8380). **3718**

AUSTRALASIAN JOURNAL OF PHILOSOPHY (AT/0004-8402). [1,200] **4342**

AUSTRALASIAN JOURNAL OF SPECIAL EDUCATION (AT/1030-0112). [1,800] **1875**

AUSTRALASIAN RADIOLOGY (AT/0004-8461). [1,950] **3939**

AUSTRALASIAN RELIGION INDEX (AT/1033-2626). **4937**

AUSTRALASIAN SHIPPING RECORD (AT). **5447**

AUSTRALASIAN SHIPS & PORTS (AT/1032-3449). [4,600] **5447**

AUSTRALASIAN TEXTILES (AT/0725-086X). [2,350] **5348**

AUSTRALIA AND NEW ZEALAND JOURNAL OF DEVELOPMENTAL DISABILITIES (AT/0726-3864). [1,500] **4384**

AUSTRALIAN & NEW ZEALAND JOURNAL OF CRIMINOLOGY, THE (AT/0004-8658). [1,167] **3158**

AUSTRALIAN AND NEW ZEALAND JOURNAL OF MEDICINE (AT/0004-8291). [6,000] **3795**

AUSTRALIAN AND NEW ZEALAND JOURNAL OF OBSTETRICS AND GYNAECOLOGY (AT/0004-8666). [3,000] **3757**

AUSTRALIAN AND NEW ZEALAND JOURNAL OF PSYCHIATRY (AT/0004-8674). [2,500] **3921**

AUSTRALIAN AND NEW ZEALAND JOURNAL OF SOCIOLOGY, THE (AT/0004-8690). [1,100] **5240**

AUSTRALIAN & NEW ZEALAND PHYSICIST : A PUBLICATION OF THE AUSTRALIAN INSTITUTE OF PHYSICS & THE NEW ZEALAND INSTITUTE OF PHYSICS, THE (AT/1036-3831). [2,900] **4398**

AUSTRALIAN & NEW ZEALAND THEATRE RECORD : ANZTR (AT). [275] **5361**

AUSTRALIAN ANTIQUE BOTTLE COLLECTOR (AT). [2,000] **250**

AUSTRALIAN ARCHAEOLOGY (AT/0312-2417). [400] **260**

AUSTRALIAN AUTHOR, THE (AT/0045-026X). [2,750] **3364**

AUSTRALIAN BANKER (AT/0814-2912). [21,000] **773**

AUSTRALIAN BEAUTY COUNTER (AT/0726-2566). [8,500] **402**

AUSTRALIAN BEE JOURNAL (AT/0045-0294). [1,000] **63**

AUSTRALIAN BOOK COLLECTOR (AT/1034-0785). [500] **4823**

AUSTRALIAN BOOKSELLER & PUBLISHER (AT). [9,000] **4823**

AUSTRALIAN BUILDING, CONSTRUCTION AND HOUSING (AT/1032-240X). [6,150] **599**

AUSTRALIAN CANEGROWER (AT/0157-3039). [7,924] **63**

AUSTRALIAN CITRUS NEWS (AT/0004-8283). [3,000] **2328**

AUSTRALIAN COMMUNICATION REVIEW (AT/0726-3252). [250] **1104**

AUSTRALIAN COMPUTER JOURNAL, THE (AT/0004-8917). [12,500] **1256**

AUSTRALIAN CONCRETE CONSTRUCTION (AT/1031-3249). [11,500] **599**

AUSTRALIAN CONSULTING ENGINEER / JOURNAL FO THE ASSOCIATION OF CONSULTING ENGINEERS (AT). [4,000] **1966**

AUSTRALIAN CYCLIST (AT). [20,000] **428**

AUSTRALIAN DAIRY FOODS (AT). **192**

AUSTRALIAN DEER (AT). [5,500] **2187**

AUSTRALIAN DENTAL JOURNAL (AT/0045-0421). [7,000] **1317**

AUSTRALIAN DRILLING (AT/1037-3535). [5,000] **1966**

AUSTRALIAN EDUCATION INDEX (AT/0004-9026). [300] **1793**

AUSTRALIAN EDUCATION REVIEW / AUSTRALIAN COUNCIL FOR EDUCATIONAL RESEARCH (AT). [1,500] **1726**

AUSTRALIAN ENTOMOLOGICAL MAGAZINE (AT/0311-1881). [420] **5605**

AUSTRALIAN EQUINE VETERINARIAN (AT/1032-6626). [1,000] **2797**

AUSTRALIAN FAMILY MELBOURNE (AT/0811-3661). [2,500] **2276**

AUSTRALIAN FARMERS' AND DEALERS' JOURNAL (AT/1036-4242). [17,500] **158**

AUSTRALIAN FISHERIES (AT/0004-9115). [11,000] **2297**

AUSTRALIAN FORESTRY (AT/0004-9158). [2,000] **2375**

AUSTRALIAN GAS INDUSTRY DIRECTORY, THE (AT/0727-3525). **4251**

AUSTRALIAN GEMMOLOGIST (AT/0004-9174). [2,500] **2913**

AUSTRALIAN GOAT WORLD, THE (AT). [800] **206**

AUSTRALIAN GRAPEGROWER AND WINEMAKER (AT/0727-3606). [4,300] **2363**

AUSTRALIAN HAND WEAVER AND SPINNER / HAND WEAVERS AND SPINNERS GUILD OF NEW SOUTH WALES, THE (AT). [600] **5183**

AUSTRALIAN HEALTH REVIEW (AT/0156-5788). [1,000] **3777**

AUSTRALIAN HISTORY TEACHER (AT/0312-2530). [2,000] **1888**

AUSTRALIAN JOURNAL OF AGRICULTURAL RESEARCH (AT/0004-9409). [1,000] **64**

AUSTRALIAN JOURNAL OF ANTHROPOLOGY, THE (AT/1035-8811). [700] **231**

AUSTRALIAN JOURNAL OF ART (AT/0314-6464). [300] **343**

AUSTRALIAN JOURNAL OF CLINICAL AND EXPERIMENTAL HYPNOSIS (AT/0156-0417). [1,400] **2857**

AUSTRALIAN JOURNAL OF EDUCATION, THE (AT/0004-9441). [1,200] **1726**

AUSTRALIAN JOURNAL OF FORENSIC SCIENCES, THE (AT/0045-0618). [500] **3740**

AUSTRALIAN JOURNAL OF HISTORICAL ARCHAEOLOGY, THE (AT/0810-1868). [430] **260**

AUSTRALIAN JOURNAL OF HOSPITAL PHARMACY (AT/0310-6810). [2,100] **4293**

AUSTRALIAN JOURNAL OF HUMAN COMMUNICATION DISORDERS (AT/0310-6853). [2,500] **4384**

AUSTRALIAN JOURNAL OF INSTRUMENTATION AND CONTROL (AT). [1,000] **1966**

AUSTRALIAN JOURNAL OF INTERNATIONAL AFFAIRS (AT/1035-7718). [3,000] **4516**

AUSTRALIAN JOURNAL OF MARINE AND FRESHWATER RESEARCH (AT/0067-1940). [1,100] **1446**

AUSTRALIAN JOURNAL OF MEDICAL SCIENCE (AT/1038-1643). [2,500] **3554**

AUSTRALIAN JOURNAL OF MUSIC THERAPY, THE (AT/1036-9457). [1400] **3554**

AUSTRALIAN JOURNAL OF PHARMACY (AT/0311-8002). [8,500] **4293**

AUSTRALIAN JOURNAL OF PHYSIOTHERAPY, THE (AT/0004-9514). [6,995] **4379**

AUSTRALIAN JOURNAL OF PLANT PHYSIOLOGY (AT/0310-7841). [1,000] **501**

AUSTRALIAN JOURNAL OF PSYCHOLOGY (AT/0004-9530). [5,600] **4575**

AUSTRALIAN JOURNAL OF PSYCHOTHERAPY (AT/0728-6155). [1,000] **4575**

AUSTRALIAN JOURNAL OF SCIENCE AND MEDICINE IN SPORT (AT). [2,800] **3953**

AUSTRALIAN JOURNAL OF SOCIAL ISSUES, THE (AT/0157-6321). [1,000] **5274**

AUSTRALIAN JOURNAL OF SOIL AND WATER CONSERVATION (AT/1032-2426). [3,000] **5530**

AUSTRALIAN JOURNAL OF STATISTICS (AT/0004-9581). [1,600] **5322**

AUSTRALIAN JOURNAL OF ZOOLOGY (AT/0004-959X). [1,400] **5577**

AUSTRALIAN KEY BUSINESS DIRECTORY, THE (AT). [5,000] **641**

AUSTRALIAN LAW JOURNAL, THE (AT/0004-9611). **2938**

AUSTRALIAN LAW NEWS (AT). [28,000] **2939**

AUSTRALIAN LEGAL DIRECTORY (AT). [2,000] **2939**

AUSTRALIAN LEGAL MONTHLY DIGEST (AT/0004-9646). [3,500] **3078**

AUSTRALIAN LIBRARY REVIEW (AT/1034-8042). **3193**

AUSTRALIAN LITHOGRAPHER, PRINTER AND PACKAGER, THE (AT). [8,960] **4563**

AUSTRALIAN MACHINERY AND PRODUCTION ENGINEERING (AT/0004-9719). [5,030] **2110**

AUSTRALIAN MEAT INDUSTRY BULLETIN, THE (AT/0156-2681). [8,000] **206**

AUSTRALIAN MINING (AT/0004-976X). [7,040] **2134**

AUSTRALIAN NUGGET JOURNAL (AT/1030-7915). [4,000] **3998**

AUSTRALIAN NURSES' JOURNAL (AT/0045-0758). [42,000] **3852**

AUSTRALIAN NUTGROWER (AT/0819-7849). [500] **164**

AUSTRALIAN OCCUPATIONAL THERAPY JOURNAL (AT/0045-0766). [3,200] **1875**

AUSTRALIAN OFFICIAL JOURNAL OF PATENTS (CANBERRA, A.C.T. : 1987) (AT). [255] **1301**

AUSTRALIAN OLYMPIAN (AT). [5,000] **4885**

AUSTRALIAN ORCHID REVIEW (AT/0045-0782). [10,000] **2409**

AUSTRALIAN PACKAGING (AT/0004-9921). [5,096] **4218**

AUSTRALIAN PARKS AND RECREATION (AT/0311-8223). [1,800] **4706**

AUSTRALIAN PHARMACIST / PHARMACEUTICAL SOCIETY OF AUSTRALIA (AT/0728-4632). [9,500] **4293**

AUSTRALIAN PLANTS (AT/0005-0008). [9,500] **2410**

AUSTRALIAN POLICE JOURNAL (AT/0005-0024). [23,000] **3158**

AUSTRALIAN POLL DORSET JOURNAL (AT). [1,900] **206**

AUSTRALIAN PRESBYTERIAN LIFE (AT). [5,500] **5055**

AUSTRALIAN PRESCRIBER (AT/0312-8008). [60,000] **3554**

AUSTRALIAN PRINTER MAGAZINE (AT). [9,814] **4563**

AUSTRALIAN PRIVATE DOCTOR : THE JOURNAL OF PRIVATE DOCTORS OF AUSTRALIA (AT). [2,000] **3554**

AUSTRALIAN PROFILE (AT). **1464**

AUSTRALIAN PROJECT MANAGER (AT). [3,000] **861**

AUSTRALIAN PROPERTY MARKET INVESTMENT STRATEGY REPORT (AT/1035-364X). **891**

AUSTRALIAN PROSTHODONTIC JOURNAL (AT/0819-0887). [1,000] **1317**

AUSTRALIAN PSYCHOLOGIST (AT/0005-0067). [5,800] **4575**

AUSTRALIAN PURCHASING AND SUPPLY (WATERLOO) (AT/1035-0357). [3,500] **949**

AUSTRALIAN RECORD AND MUSIC REVIEW (AT/1033-1352). [120] **4101**

AUSTRALIAN REFRIGERATION, AIR CONDITIONING AND HEATING (AT). [2,900] **2603**

AUSTRALIAN ROAD AND TRACK (AT/1036-3254). [20,000] **5404**

AUSTRALIAN SCIENCE TEACHERS' JOURNAL, THE (AT/0045-0855). [5,200] **5087**

AUSTRALIAN SOCIETY OF INDEXERS NEWSLETTER (AT/0314-3767). [250] **3193**

AUSTRALIAN STOCK HORSE JOURNAL (AT/0817-8550). [6,250] **2797**

AUSTRALIAN STRING TEACHER (AT/0312-9950). [1,200] **4101**

AUSTRALIAN TABLE TENNIS (AT/0814-3668). [3,000] **4885**

AUSTRALIAN TEACHER OF THE DEAF (AT/0005-0334). [400] **1875**

AUSTRALIAN TEACHER, THE (AT). [150,000] **1888**

AUSTRALIAN VETERINARY JOURNAL (AT/0005-0423). [4,000] **5505**

AUSTRALIAN WELDING JOURNAL (AT/0005-0431). [20,000] **4026**

AUSTRALIAN WOMEN'S BOOK REVIEW (AT/1033-9434). [1,200] **5551**

AUSTRALIAN WORKER : OFFICIAL JOURNAL OF THE AUSTRALIAN WORKERS' UNION, THE (AT). [95,000] **1654**

AUSTRALIAN YEAR BOOK OF INTERNATIONAL LAW, THE (AT/0084-7658). [800] **3124**

AUSTRALIAN ZOOLOGIST, THE (AT/0067-2238). [1,500] **5577**

AUSTRALIANA (AT). [350] **2510**

AUSTRALIA'S MINING MONTHLY (AT). [7,480] **2134**

AUSTRIA TODAY (AU/0304-8713). [16,000] **2513**

AUSTRIACA (FR/0396-4590). **2677**

AUTHENTIK AUTHENTIK IN ENGLISH (IE/0791-0797). [40,000] **3267**

AUTHOR SERIES (US/0567-1744). [1,500] **2722**

AUTHORWARE MAGAZINE (US). [5,000] **1171**

AUTO ADVERTISING REPORT (US/0885-8292). [1,000] **756**

AUTO INDEX, THE (US/0145-6776). **5404**

AUTO-JOURNAL (PARIS), L' (FR/0005-0768). **5404**

AUTO LAUNDRY NEWS (US/0005-0776). [15,000] **5404**

AUTO MARKET REPORT (AT/1035-1051). **5405**

AUTO MERCHANDISING NEWS (US/0192-186X). [26,000] **641**

AUTOCAD USER (CN). [17,000] **1171**

AUTOGRAPH COLLECTOR (US/1071-3425). [20,000] **2438**

AUTOMATED BUILDER (US/0899-5540). [26,000] **2815**

AUTOMATIC MACHINING (US/0005-1071). [16,000] **2110**

AUTOMATICA E INSTRUMENTACION (SP/0213-3113). **1217**

AUTOMATION AND CONTROL (NZ/0110-6295). [7,000] **1217**

AUTOMATION NEWS (NEW YORK, N.Y.) (US/0736-3737). [40,000] **1218**

AUTOMOBIL-INDUSTRIE (GW/0005-1306). [4,000] **5405**

AUTOMOBILE (DON MILLS) (CN/0005-1330). [12,000] **5405**

AUTOMOBILE INTERNATIONAL (US/0099-2615). [28,046] **5405**

AUTOMOTIVE ENGINEERING (US/0098-2571). [67,000] **2110**

AUTOMOTIVE LITIGATION REPORTER (US/0278-4726). **2939**

AUTOMOTIVE MARKET REPORT (US/0733-2084). [10,000] **921**

AUTOMOTIVE PRODUCTS REPORT (US/8750-4103). [35,000] **5407**

AUTOMOTIVE REBUILDER (US/0567-2317). [24,000] **5407**

AUTONEWS (UK). [15,000] **5407**

AUTRES TEMPS (FR). [700] **4937**

AV KOMMUNIKACIO (HU/0237-9740). [830] **1104**

AVALOKA (US/0890-5541). [500] **4937**

AVANCES EN CIENCIAS VETERINARIAS (CL/0716-260X). [300] **5505**

AVE MARIA (LEMONT, ILL.) (US/0746-3499). [1,560] **5024**

AVENIR MONTREAL. 1991 (CN/1187-6611). **1464**

AVENUE (NEW YORK, N.Y.) (US/0279-1226). [81,000] **2528**

AVES (BE/0005-1993). [1,000] **5615**

AVIAN PATHOLOGY (UK/0307-9457). [700] **5505**

AVIATION BUSINESS REPORT (CN/0711-8163). **13**

AVIATION DESIGN THIAIS (FR/0997-3753). [35,000] **13**

AVIATION DIGEST (US/0884-4755). [25,000] **13**

AVIATION EQUIPMENT MAINTENANCE (US/0745-0214). [30,000] **13**

AVIATION LITIGATION REPORTER (US/0737-7746). **2939**

AVIATION QUARTERLY (US/0360-8670). **13**

AVIATORS HOT LINE (US/0195-0347). **14**

AVIAZIONE (IT/0391-7738). [15,000] **14**

AVICULTURAL JOURNAL, THE (CN/0317-5650). [310] **5615**

AVICULTURAL MAGAZINE, THE (UK/0005-2256). [800] **5615**

AVIDEO (US/0747-1335). [60,000] **1104**

AVIONICS (POTOMAC, MD.) (US/0273-7639). [17,500] **14**

AVIRON (ED QUEBECOISE) (CN/0821-1477). [14,535] **5780**

AVIS MUNICIPAL - VILLE DE CHARNY (CN/0820-6503). [5,000] **4631**

AVISTA FORUM (US/1041-6994). [200] **316**

AVKO NEWSLETTER (US). [200] **1875**

AVOTAYNU (US/0882-6501). [2,000] **2438**

AVTOMATIKA (KIEV) (UN/0572-2691). [2,290] **1218**

AWARE (US/0162-6833). [39,000] **4937**

AWIS MAGAZINE (US/1057-5839). [4,000] **5087**

AWP NEWSLETTER (NORFOLK) (US/0194-6498). [10,000] **3365**

AXONE (DARTMOUTH) (CN/0834-7824). [500] **3852**

AYRSHIRE DIGEST (US/0005-2450). [3,000] **192**

AZURE (TORONTO) (CN/0829-982X). [12,000] **2898**

B. C. AREA ANNUAL DOCKET (CN/0227-2962). **5055**

B. C. CATHOLIC, THE (CN/0007-0483). [17,000] **5024**

B.C. NATURALIST (CN/0228-8842). [8,000] **2187**

B.C. PROFESSIONAL ENGINEER. ANNUAL DIRECTORY NUMBER, THE (CN). [16,000] **1966**

B.T.I. NEWSLETTER (US/0145-7934). **4937**

B.T.O. NEWS (UK/0005-3392). [8,000] **5615**

B70 (DK/0905-4650). [6,000] **3193**

BABEL (AT/0005-3503). [2,000] **3267**

BABRAHAM (UK). **5505**

BABY CONNECTION, THE (US/0894-3990). [20,000] **1727**

BABY TALK (1977) (US/0749-971X). [1,050,000 (monthly)] **3900**

BACA (IO/0125-9008). [1,000] **3193**

BACK FORTY (ALEXANDRIA, VA.), THE (US/1049-3972). [500] **2188**

BACK HOME IN KENTUCKY (US/0199-6290). [20,000] **2722**

BACK STAGE (US/0005-3635). **4064**

BACK STAGE. TV FILM & TAPE PRODUCTION DIRECTORY (US/0734-9777). [10,000] **1126**

BACKER UND KONDITOR (GW/0005-383X). **2328**

BAD FAITH LAW REPORT, THE (US/8756-5374). [850] **2939**

BADGER BAPTIST (US). [1,600] **4937**

BADGER HERALD (US/0045-1304). [20,000] **1089**

BADMINTON MAGAZINE, THE (US/0747-9069). [2,500] **4886**

BADMINTON NEW-NOUVEAU BRUNSWICK : NEWSLETTER (CN/0229-3862). **4886**

BADMINTON NOW (UK). [5,500] **4886**

BADMINTON U S A (US/0045-1312). **4886**

BAGNO OGGI E DOMANI, IL (IT). [31,700] **2898**

BAHAI NEWS (WILMETTE) (US/0195-9212). [5,000] **5042**

BAHAMIAN REVIEW (BF/0005-397X). [25,000] **2528**

BAHASA DAN SASTRA (IO). [500] **3267**

BAIQUIEN YIKE DAXUE XUEBAO (CC/0253-3707). [2.500 (paid)1,000 other] **2937**

BAKER & TAYLOR'S SCHOOL SELECTION GUIDE (US/0732-8052). [100,000] **1727**

BAKERS JOURNAL (CN/0005-4097). [6,400] **2328**

BAKERY PRODUCTION AND MARKETING (US/0005-4127). [40,000] **2328**

BAKING & SNACK SYSTEMS (US/1040-9254). [9,400] **2328**

BAKO MAGAZINE (GW). **3475**

BALANCE LONDON (UK/0005-4216). [137,500] **3555**

BALANCING THE SCALES (US/0734-1822). [3,000] **3179**

BALKAN STUDIES (GR/0005-4313). **2677**

BALKANMEDIA (BU/0861-5047). [3,000] **1104**

BALL AND ROLLER BEARING ENGINEERING (GW/0522-0629). [90,000] **2111**

BALLET-HOO (CN/0045-1347). [55,000] **1310**

BALLOONS TODAY (US/1049-9970). [15,000] **2528**

BALLS AND BURLAPS (US/0404-6927). [1,600] **2410**

BALNEOLOGIA BOHEMICA (XR/0302-8070). [1,500] **4379**

BALSHANUT 'IVRIT (IS). **3268**

BALTIMORE/ANNAPOLIS (US/1052-0996). [2,000] **641**

BALTIMORE JEWISH TIMES (US/0005-450X). [20,000] **5046**

BAM (US/0194-5793). [130,000] **4102**

'BAMA (US/0195-0975). [15,000] **4886**

BAMBOO RIDGE (US/0733-0308). [350] **3365**

BANAR (CN/0225-6193). **2528**

BANCA Y FINANZAS (CK/0120-7040). [1,000] **773**

BANCNI VESTNIK (XV/0005-4631). [2,700] **774**

BAND & FESTIVAL GUIDE (US/0735-4711). [5,000] **4102**

BAND INTERNATIONAL : THE JOURNAL OF THE INTERNATIONAL MILITARY MUSIC SOCIETY (UK). [1,100] **4102**

BAND NEWS (AT). [500] **4102**

BANDER BLECHE ROHRE (GW/0005-3848). [5,000] **3475**

BANDON HISTORICAL JOURNAL (IE/0790-4304). [1,000] **2611**

BANDWAGON (COLUMBUS, OHIO : 1957) (US/0005-4968). [1,500] **4857**

BANGKO SENTRAL REVIEW : A MONTHLY PUBLICATION OF THE BANGKO SENTRAL NG PILIPINAS (PH). [4,500] **774**

BANGKOK POST, THE (TH). **5811**

BANGLADESH EXPORT STATISTICS (BG). [4,000] **726**

BANGLADESH EXPORTERS' DIRECTORY (BG). [4,000] **824**

BANGLADESH JOURNAL OF BOTANY (BG/0253-5416). [500] **501**

BANGLADESH MEDICAL RESEARCH COUNCIL BULLETIN (BG/0377-9238). [1,000] **3555**

BANGOR DAILY NEWS (US/0892-8738). [83,276] **5687**

BANK CREDIT ANALYST. INVESTMENT AND BUSINESS FORECAST, THE (CN/0822-5788). **892**

BANK EXPANSION QUARTERLY (US/0160-130X). [500] **774**

BANK NOTE REPORTER (US/0164-0828). [4,361] **2780**

BANK OF CANADA REVIEW (CN/0045-1460). **775**

BANK OPERATIONS BULLETIN (US). [3,000] **775**

BANK PERSONNEL NEWS (US/0272-3271). [2,600] **775**

BANK PROTECTION BULLETIN (US/0091-0392). [14,000] **775**

BANKERS' ALMANAC AND YEAR BOOK, THE (UK). [20,000] **776**

BANKERS MONTHLY (US/0005-5476). [25,000] **776**

BANKING & FINANCIAL TRAINING (UK/0265-7988). [4,000] **777**

BANKING LAW REVIEW (US/0898-7998). [1,000] **3085**

BANNER OF TRUTH, THE (US/0408-4748). [5,000] **4937**

BANQUIER (MONTREAL) (CN/0822-6849). [7,700] **778**

BAPTIST BIBLICAL HERITAGE (US). [1,000] **4938**

BAPTIST CHALLENGE, THE (US/8756-9612). [5,300] **5056**

BAPTIST HISTORY AND HERITAGE (US/0005-5719). [2,500] **5056**

BAPTIST MESSENGER (OKLAHOMA CITY, OKLA.) (US/0744-9518). [115,000] **5056**

BAPTIST PROGRESS (US/0005-5751). [15,500] **5056**

BAPTIST QUARTERLY (LONDON) (UK/0005-576X). [650] **5056**

BAPTIST TIMES (UK/0005-5786). **5056**

BAPTIST TRUMPET (LITTLE ROCK, ARK.) (US/0888-9074). [13,110] **5056**

BAPTIST WORLD (WASHINGTON, D.C.) (US/0005-5808). [10,000] **5056**

BAR: BEVERAGE ALCOHOL REPORTER (CN/0006-0348). [16,000] **2364**

BAR BRIEF (BEVERLY HILLS, CALIF.) (US/0749-0615). [2,600] **2939**

BAR EXAMINER, THE (US/0005-5824). [2,500] **2940**

BARATAINKNAK A MAGYAR JEZSUITAK (CN/0228-9873). **4938**

BARBOUR COMPENDIUM. BUILDING PRODUCTS (UK/0260-9169). [21,000] **599**

BARCELONA QUIRURGICA (SP/0304-4475). [3,500] **3960**

BARCLAYS INSURANCE LAW REPORT (CALIFORNIA EDITION) (US). [275] **2940**

BARNESVILLE RECORD-REVIEW, THE (US). [2,000] **5694**

BARNSTORMER (FORT WAYNE, IND.), THE (US/1062-7413). [15,000] **14**

BARRE GAZETTE (BARRE, MASS. : 1839) (US). [1,850] **5687**

BARRISTER (CHICAGO) (US/0094-5277). [150,000] **2940**

BARRON FAMILY NEWSLETTER, THE (US/0882-8202). [50] **2438**

BARTENDER (US/0199-8404). **2364**

BARTLETTIA : NOTES FROM THE MATTHAEI BOTANICAL GARDENS OF THE UNIVERSITY OF MICHIGAN (US). **501**

BARTONIA (US/0198-7356). [350] **501**

BASE (BERKELEY, CALIF.) (US/0732-7706). **5087**

BASEBALL BULLETIN (US/0199-0128). [20,000] **4886**

BASEBALL CARDS (US/8750-5851). [184,860] **2771**

BASEBALL HOBBY NEWS (US/0199-946X). [16,500] **2771**

BASEBALL RESEARCH JOURNAL (US/0734-6891). [8,000] **4886**

BASELINE

Controlled Circulation Index

BASELINE DATA REPORT (US/0739-6279). [500] **4632**

BASIC PETROLEUM DATA BOOK (WASHINGTON, D.C. : 1981) (US/0730-5621). **4252**

BASIS (IO/0005-6138). [2,000] **2647**

BASKET BITS (US). **370**

BASKETBALL WEEKLY (US/0005-6170). [60,000] **4887**

BASS MASTER MAGAZINE (US/0199-3291). [550,000] **2297**

BAT RESEARCH NEWS (US/0005-6227). **5577**

BATH & KITCHEN MARKETER (CN/0225-9206). **2898**

BATHROOMS (UK/0950-0197). [15,000] **600**

BATTALION (COLLEGE STATION, TEX. 1893), THE (US/1055-4726). [22,000] **1089**

BATTELLE TODAY (US/0145-8477). [35,000] **5087**

BATTERIES INTERNATIONAL (UK/0957-9249). [6,000] **2036**

BATTERY MAN (US/0005-6359). [5,500] **1933**

BAUDETTE REGION, THE (US). [2,385] **5694**

BAUEN MIT HOLZ (GW/0005-6545). [6,200] **600**

BAUEN + [I.E. UND] FERTIGHAUS (GW). **600**

BAUMEISTER (GW/0005-674X). [13,723] **293**

BAUVERWALTUNG (GW/0005-6847). [2,010] **4632**

BAUVORAUSSCHAETZUNG (GW). [200] **600**

BAUWIRTSCHAFT (HAUPTVERBAND DER DEUTSCHEN BAUINDUSTRIE) (GW/0341-3810). [6,000] **600**

BAUWIRTSCHAFTLICHE INFORMATIONEN / BETRIEBSWIRTSCHAFTLICHES INSTITUT DER WESTDEUTSCHEN BAUINDUSTRIE (GW/0721-6173). [2,000] **600**

BAY STATE LIBRARIAN (US/0005-6944). [1,100] **3193**

BAYERISCHES LANDWIRTSCHAFTLICHES JAHRBUCH (GW/0375-8621). [1,700] **65**

BAYERNMETALL (GW). [5,000] **3998**

BAYLOR COUNTY BANNER, THE (US). [2,900] **5747**

BAYREUTH (GW). **2513**

BAYRUT TAYMZ (US/0888-6016). [15,000] **5633**

BBL. BIBLIOTEKSBLADET (SW/0006-1867). [5,400] **3193**

BBSRC BUSINESS (US). [5,000] **3686**

BC AGRICULTURE (CN/0847-1444). [9,000] **65**

BC STUDIES (CN/0005-2949). [800] **2722**

BCATML NEWSLETTER, THE (CN/0229-0235). **3268**

BCG NEWSLETTER BOLTON (UK/0144-588X). [300] **4084**

BEACH CONSERVATION (AT/0313-7872). [5000] **2188**

BEACON FREE PRESS (US). [8,300] **5714**

BEAGLE : OCCASIONAL PAPERS OF THE TERRITORY MUSEUM OF ARTS AND SCIENCES, THE (AT/0811-3653). [300] **2843**

BEALOIDEAS (IE/0332-270X). [1,000] **2318**

BEATRIX POTTER STUDIES (UK). **3365**

BEAUFORTIA (NE/0067-4745). [650] **5577**

BEAUTIFUL GLASS FOR HOME & OFFICE (US/1043-5468). [25,000] **2586**

BEAUTY AGE (US/0887-414X). [27,719] **402**

BEAUTY CLASSIC (US/0886-8751). [27,000] **402**

BEAUTY COUNTER LONDON (UK/0960-3751). [14,000] **402**

BEAUX ARTS MAGAZINE (FR/0757-2271). [72,000] **343**

BEAUX LIVRES DE L'ANNEE, LES (FR). **4824**

BEBIDAS (US/0005-7533). [8,800] **2364**

BECKETT CIRCLE, THE (US/0732-2224). **3365**

BECKMAN FOCUS (GW). [11,000] **4029**

BECKMAN REPORT (GW/0005-755X). [11,000] **4029**

BEDFORD SUN BANNER (US/0746-262X). [5,442] **5727**

BEDFORDSHIRE FAMILY HISTORY SOCIETY JOURNAL (UK). [700] **2438**

BEE CULTURE (US/1071-3190). [12,000] **65**

BEEF CATTLE RESEARCH IN TEXAS (US). [1,500] **207**

BEEF (ST. PAUL, MINN.) (US/0005-7738). [120,000] **207**

BEEFMASTER COWMAN, THE (US/0194-4282). [8,500] **207**

BEEHIVE HISTORY (US/0883-8380). [3,200] **2722**

BEELDENAAR, DE (NE). [4,000] **2780**

BE'EMET?! (IS/0334-973X). [1,000] **1060**

BEER PAPER, THE (US/0738-8799). [860] **2364**

BEER WHOLESALER (US/0005-7770). [3,800] **2364**

BEETHOVEN NEWSLETTER, THE (US/0898-6185). [1,000] **4102**

BEFFROI (CN/0832-9966). [800] **3365**

BEFORE AND AFTER (US/1049-0035). **4824**

BEGONIAN, THE (US/0096-8684). [2,000] **2410**

BEHAVIOR ANALYSIS DIGEST (US/1052-0082). [200] **4576**

BEHAVIOR ANALYST, THE (US/0738-6729). [2,500] **4576**

BEHAVIOR THERAPIST, THE (US/0278-8403). [3,800] **4576**

BEHAVIORAL DISORDERS (US/0198-7429). [550] **1875**

BEHEER EN ONDERHOUD (NE/0165-2540). **600**

BEIRUT REVIEW, THE (LE/1019-0732). [1,000] **4516**

BEITRAEGE ZUR ALGEBRA UND GEOMETRIE (GW). **3497**

BEITRAEGE ZUR GESCHICHTE DER ARBEITERBEWEGUNG (BERLIN, DDR) (GW/0005-8068). [7,000] **2678**

BEITRAEGE ZUR HOCHSCHULFORSCHUNG (GW/0171-645X). [750] **1811**

BEITRAEGE ZUR NAMENFORSCHUNG (GW/0005-8114). [550] **2438**

BEITRAEGE ZUR NATURKUNDE NIEDERSACHSENS (GW/0340-4277). **4162**

BEITRAEGE ZUR TABAKFORSCHUNG INTERNATIONAL (GW/0173-783X). [1,100] **5372**

BEITRAEGE ZUR UR- UND FRUEHGESCHICHTE DER BEZIRKE ROSTOCK, SCHWERIN UND NEUBRANDENBURG (GW). **261**

BEITRAGE ZUR GESCHICHTE DER FDJ (GW). [350] **5240**

BEITRAGE ZUR PALAONTOLOGIE VON OSTERREICH (AU/1017-5563). **4226**

BELEIDSINFORMATICA (BE). [600] **1218**

BELGIAN JOURNAL OF ZOOLOGY (BE/0777-6276). **5577**

BELGISCH TIJDSCHRIFT VOOR TANDHEELKUNDE (BE/0775-0285). [3,500] **1317**

BELGISCHE PROTESTANTSE (BE). **5056**

BELL TOWER, THE (US/0092-8666). [2,000] **4102**

BELLE FRANCE, LA (US/8750-9180). [10,000] **5462**

BELLEFONTAINE EXAMINER (US/0747-3273). [11,134] **5727**

BELLES LETTRES (ARLINGTON, VA.) (US/0884-2957). [5,000] **3366**

BELLINGHAM REVIEW, THE (US/0734-2934). [700] **3366**

BELL'ITALIA (IT). [115,000] **2513**

BELL'S ALASKA, YUKON & BRITISH COLUMBIA TRAVEL GUIDE (US/1054-5034). [60,000] **5462**

BELMONTIA (NE/0169-4375). [150] **501**

BELOIT DAILY CALL, THE (US/8750-1791). [3,000] **5674**

BELSER KUNSTQUARTAL (GW). [33,000] **4084**

BENBROOK NEWS, THE (US). [6,000] **5747**

BENCH AND BAR OF MINNESOTA, THE (US/0276-1505). [13,000] **2941**

BENCHMARK OBAN (UK/0951-6859). [4,000] **2111**

BEND OF THE RIVER (US/1063-9241). [3,600] **4162**

BENDEL LIBRARY JOURNAL (NR/0331-555X). **3194**

BENEDICTINA (IT/0392-0356). [1,000] **4938**

BENEDICTINES (US/0005-8726). [1,000] **5024**

BENEFITS CANADA (CN/0703-7732). [14,000] **938**

BENEFITS NEWS ANALYSIS (US/0199-3100). [10,000] **642**

BENEVOLE, LE (CN/0227-1567). **1341**

BENSON TRACE, THE (US/0734-0214). [300] **2439**

BENT COUNTY DEMOCRAT (US). **5642**

BENT OF TAU BETA PI, THE (US/0005-884X). [95,000] **1966**

BENTON COUNTY PIONEER, THE (US/0409-0829). [300] **2723**

BEPPU DAIGAKU KIYO (JA). [500] **2843**

BEREA ALUMNUS, THE (US/0005-8874). [30,000] **1101**

BEREAN AMBASSADOR, THE (CN/0227-5554). **5056**

BERETNING FOR ... / ROSKILDE UNIVERSITETSCENTER (DK). [1,150] **1811**

BERGBAU (HATTINGEN) (GW/0342-5681). [11,000] **2135**

BERGSMANNEN (SW/0284-0448). [4500] **2135**

BERICHT DER ROMISCH-GERMANISCHEN KOMMISSION (GW). **261**

BERICHT DES PRASIDENTEN, ZAHLENSPIEGEL (GW/0723-2659). [3,000] **1811**

BERICHTE DER BUNSENGESELLSCHAFT FUER PHYSIKALISCHE CHEMIE (GW/0005-9021). [3,000] **1050**

BERICHTE DES VEREINS NATUR UND HEIMAT UND DES NATURHISTORISCHEN MUSEUMS ZU LUBECK (GW/0505-2793). [500] **4163**

BERITA BIBLIOGRAFI (JAKARTA, INDONESIA : 1984) (IO/0216-1273). [500] **408**

BERKELEY MONTHLY, THE (US/0191-7080). [80,000] **3338**

BERKS COUNTY LAW JOURNAL (US/8750-3379). [715] **2941**

BERKSHIRE GENEALOGIST, THE (US/0887-0713). [700] **2439**

BERLINER ARZTEBLATT (GW/0172-8490). [18,500] **3555**

BERLINER THEOLOGISCHE ZEITSCHRIFT : THEOLOGIA VIATORUM NEUE FOLGE : HALBJAHRESSCHRIFT FUER THEOLOGIE IN DER KIRCHE (GW/0724-6137). [1,000] **4938**

BERLINGSKE TIDENDE (DK). [135,000] **5799**

BERNAN ASSOCIATES' GOVERNMENT PUBLICATIONS NEWS (US/0897-5728). [4,500] **4632**

BERYTUS; ARCHAEOLOGICAL STUDIES (LE/0067-6195). [500] **261**

BESCHAFTIGUNGSTHERAPIE UND REHABILITATION (GW/0340-529X). **1875**

BEST 'N' MOST IN DFS, THE (SW/1100-3006). [6,000] **824**

BESTE AUS READER'S DIGEST, DAS (GW/0005-9668). [1,450,000] **2485**

BET (UK). [10,000] **642**

BETTER BREEDING (UK). [95,000] **192**

BETTER CROPS WITH PLANT FOOD (US/0006-0089). [20,000] **164**

BETTER HOMES AND GARDENS DECORATING IDEAS (US). **2899**

BETTER RADIO AND TELEVISION (US). [2,500] **1127**

BETTER ROADS (US/0006-0208). [40,000] **5439**

BETTER SUPERVISION (US). [43,000] **939**

BETTY AND ME (US/0006-0267). **4857**

BETTY AND VERONICA COMICS DIGEST MAGAZINE (US/0886-134X). **4857**

BETWEEN THE LINES (WASHINGTON, D.C.) (US/1049-4421). [400] **4465**

BETWEEN US (CN/0714-4601). [500] **1811**

BEVERAGE WORLD (US/0098-2318). [34,000] **2364**

BEVERAGE WORLD INTERNATIONAL (US). [10,400] **2364**

BEVERLY HILLS BAR ASSOCIATION JOURNAL (US/1051-628X). [3,300] **2941**

BEVERLY HILLS COURIER, THE (US/0892-645X). [48,000] **5633**

BEVOLKINGSSTATISTIEKEN - NATIONAAL INSTITUUT VOOR DE STATISTIEK (BE/0304-8888). [525] **4561**

BEYOND APARTHEID (NE/0923-4284). **1464**

BEYOND SIGHT (CN/0712-2446). [2,000 English, 500 French] **4887**

BHASHA ANI JIVANA : MARATHI-ABHYASA-PARISHAD-PATRIKA (II). [250] **3268**

BI-STATE REPORTER (US/0745-4813). [8,521] **5658**

BIA BULLETIN (UK). [350] **443**

BIA REPORT (GW/0173-0487). [400-800] **2859**

BIANNUAL NEWSLETTER OF THE CONFERENCE GROUP ON ITALIAN POLITICS & SOCIETY, THE (US/1077-9043). **4516**

BIBBIA E ORIENTE (IT/0006-0585). **5014**

BIBEL UND KIRCHE (GW/0006-0623). [25,000] **5014**

BIBEL UND LITURGIE (AU/0006-064X). [1,200] **5014**

BIBLE ADVOCATE (BROOMFIELD, COLO.) (US/0746-0104). [12,000] **5014**

BIBLE AND SPADE (US). **4938**

BIBLE DISTRIBUTOR. ENGLISH (US/0256-9361). [8,000] **5014**

BIBLE JOURNEYS FOR CHRISTIANS (US/0747-3893). [varies] **5014**

BIBLE JOURNEYS FOR CHRISTIANS (US). [800] **4938**

BIBLE-SCIENCE NEWSLETTER (US/0164-5587). [12,000] **5014**

BIBLE TEACHING FOR CONFIDENT LIVING (US/0890-457X). [95,000] **5015**

BIBLE TODAY, THE (US/0006-0836). [12,000] **5015**

BIBLICAL EVANGELIST, THE (US/0740-7998). [27,300] **4938**

BIBLICAL ILLUSTRATOR (US/0195-1351). [82,000] **4938**

BIBLICAL MISSIONS (US/0006-0909). [2,500] **5057**

BIBLICAL RESEARCH (US/0067-6535). [700] **5015**

BIBLICAL THEOLOGY BULLETIN (US/0146-1079). [1,500] **5015**

BIBLIO SERVICE (CN/0710-6319). [600] **1727**

BIBLIOGRAFI OVER DANMARKS OFFENTLIGE PUBLIKATIONER (DK/0067-6543). [400] **4696**

BIBLIOGRAFIA AGROMETEOROLOGII (PL/0239-958X). [120] **1420**

BIBLIOGRAFIA GOSPODARKI I INZYNIERII WODNEJ (PL/0239-622X). [220] **5531**

BIBLIOGRAFIA HYDROLOGII I OCEANOLOGII (PL/0239-6246). [250] **1412**

BIBLIOGRAFIA METEOROLOGII: POLSKA (PL/0239-6270). [500] **1421**

BIBLIOGRAFIA MEXICANA (BIBLIOTECA NACIONAL DE MEXICO) (MX/0006-1069). [850] **409**

BIBLIOGRAFIE NEDERLANDSE SOCIOLOGIE (NE/0167-8272). [200] **5240**

BIBLIOGRAFIIA NA BULGARSKATA BIBLIOGRAFIIA (BU). [400] **409**

BIBLIOGRAPHICAL SERIES / SOUTH AFRICAN INSTITUTE OF INTERNATIONAL AFFAIRS / BIBLIOGRAFIESE REEKS / SUID-AFRIKAANSE INSTITUUT VAN INTERNASIONALE AANGELEENTHEDE (SA). [300] **4501**

BIBLIOGRAPHIE BILDENDE KUNST (GW). [280] **334**

BIBLIOGRAPHIE DE L'AFRIQUE SUD-SAHARIENNE, SCIENCES HUMAINES ET SOCIALES (BE). [500] **5192**

BIBLIOGRAPHIE DU QUEBEC (CN/0006-1441). [500] **410**

BIBLIOGRAPHIE INTERNATIONALE DE LA DEMOGRAPHIE HISTORIQUE (BE/0255-0849). [4,000] **4561**

BIBLIOGRAPHIE LATINOAMERICAINE D'ARTICLES / INSTITUT DES HAUTES ETUDES DE L'AMERIQUE LATINE, CENTRE DE DOCUMENTATION (FR/0752-4080). [250] **410**

BIBLIOGRAPHIE PADAGOGIK. REIHE A, ZEITSCHRIFTEN- AUFSATZE (GW). **1793**

BIBLIOGRAPHIE SOZIALISATION UND SOZIALPAEDAGOGIK (GW/0342-3964). [700] **5266**

BIBLIOGRAPHIEN ZUR DEUTSCHEN LITERATUR DES MITTELALTERS (GW/0523-2767). **3457**

BIBLIOGRAPHY AND INDEX OF MICROPALEONTOLOGY (US/0300-7227). [300] **4231**

BIBLIOGRAPHY - INTERNATIONAL INSTITUTE FOR LAND RECLAMATION AND IMPROVEMENT (NE/0074-6436). **151**

BIBLIOGRAPHY OF AGRICULTURE : ANNUAL CUMULATION (US/0364-829X). [550] **66**

BIBLIOGRAPHY OF AMERICAN PALEOBOTANY (US/0193-5720). [500] **502**

BIBLIOGRAPHY OF ASIAN STUDIES (US/0067-7159). [3,000] **2634**

BIBLIOGRAPHY OF BIOETHICS (US/0363-0161). [2,000] **3555**

BIBLIOGRAPHY OF FOSSIL VERTEBRATES (US/0272-8869). **4231**

BIBLIOGRAPHY OF MODERN HEBREW LITERATURE IN TRANSLATION / BY ISAAC GOLDBERG (IS/0334-309X). [300] **3366**

BIBLIOGRAPHY OF NOISE, A (US/0092-5756). [200] **2161**

BIBLIOGRAPHY OF REPRODUCTION (UK/0006-1565). [900] **477**

BIBLIOGRAPHY OF SEISMOLOGY (UK/0523-2988). [350] **1362**

BIBLIOGRAPHY ON CABLE TELEVISION : BCTV (US/0742-4914). [100,000] **1124**

BIBLIOTEKSVEJVISER (DK). [2,000] **3194**

BIBLIOTERM (AU/0255-2795). [300] **3269**

BIBLIOTHECA EPHEMERIDUM THEOLOGICARUM LOVANIENSIUM (BE). **4939**

BIBLIOTHECA FRANCISCANA SCHOLASTICA MEDII AEVI (IT). [900] **4939**

BIBLIOTHECA HUMANISTICA ET REFORMATORICA (NE). **1074**

BIBLIOTHECA MEDICA CANADIANA (CN/0707-3674). [600] **3195**

BIBLIOTHECA MYCOLOGIA (GW). **443**

BIBLIOTHECA ORIENTALIS (NE/0006-1913). [700] **2647**

BIBLIOTHECA SACRA (1864) (US/0006-1921). [10,000] **4939**

BIBLIOTHEEK EN SAMENLEVING (NE/0165-1048). [3,500] **3195**

BIBLIOTHEK (GW/0341-4183). [500] **3195**

BIBLIOTHEKSFORUM BAYERN (GW/0340-000X). **3195**

BIBLISCHE ZEITSCHRIFT (GW/0006-2014). [900] **5015**

BIC US. BUSINESS INDUSTRY COORDINATOR (US). **643**

BICYCLE USA (US/0747-0371). [23,000] **428**

BIENNIAL EVALUATION REPORT - MICHIGAN. STATE ADVISORY COUNCIL FOR VOCATIONAL EDUCATION (US). [2,000] **1911**

BIENNIAL REPORT (US). [1,500] **3158**

BIENNIAL REPORT / NORTH DAKOTA, DEPT. OF HUMAN SERVICES (US). [600] **5274**

BIENNIAL REPORT OF EMPLOYMENT BY GEOGRAPHIC AREA (US/8756-7156). **4701**

BIENNIAL REPORT OF EXAMINING AND LICENSING BOARDS / MINNESOTA BOARD OF PSYCHOLOGY (US). [20] **4577**

BIENNIAL REPORT OF THE TEXAS STATE LIBRARY AND ARCHIVES COMMISSION (US). [300] **3195**

BIENNIAL REPORT OF THE VERMONT DEPARTMENT OF LIBRARIES (US/0363-3500). [500] **3195**

BIENNIAL REPORT / TENNESSEE DEPARTMENT OF EMPLOYMENT SECURITY (US). **1655**

BIENNIAL REPORT TO THE LEGISLATURE / LEGISLATIVE COMMISSION ON MINNESOTA RESOURCES (US). **4632**

BIENNIAL REPORT - WISCONSIN ARTS BOARD (US). [2,000] **316**

BIFIDUS, FLORES ET FRUCTUS (JA/0285-7006). [500] **477**

BIG BEND REGISTER (US/0736-7074). [100] **2439**

BIG BYTE, THE (CN/0045-1991). [1,800] **1246**

BIJDRAGEN TIJDSCHRIFT VOOR FILOSOFIE EN THEOLOGIE (NE). [600] **4342**

BIJINESU REBYU. BUSINESS REVIEW (JA). [1,000] **643**

BIKORET U-FARSHANUT (IS). [500] **3338**

BILAKABIDE : REVISTA DE POESIA (SP). [3,000] **3460**

BILANZ (SZ). [50,100] **1464**

BILDGEBUNG (BASEL) (SZ/1012-5655). [5,000] **3939**

BILDUNG UND WISSENSCHAFT (GW/0177-4212). [10,000] **5088**

BILLIKEN (AG). [120,000] **1060**

BILLINGSLEY YESTERDAY & TODAY (US/0899-1707). **2439**

BILTEN ZA HEMATOLOGIJU I TRANSFUZIJU (YU/0350-2023). [2,000] **3770**

BIMCO BULLETIN (DK/0901-814X). [3,000] **5447**

BINDEREPORT (GW/0342-3573). **4824**

BIO-SCIENCE RESEARCH BULLETIN (II/0970-0889). [100] **444**

BIO/TECHNOLOGY (NEW YORK, N.Y. 1983) (US/0733-222X). [20,000] **5088**

BIOCHEMICAL JOURNAL (LONDON. 1984) (UK/0264-6021). [3,500] **481**

BIOCHEMICAL SOCIETY SYMPOSIA (UK/0067-8694). [2,000] **481**

BIOCHEMICAL SOCIETY TRANSACTIONS (UK/0300-5127). [2,500] **481**

BIOCHEMIST LONDON (UK/0954-982X). [8,337] **481**

BIOCHEMISTRY AND CELL BIOLOGY (CN/0829-8211). [2,200] **481**

BIOCHEMISTRY INTERNATIONAL (AT/0158-5231). **482**

BIOCHIMICA CLINICA (IT/0393-0564). [8,500] **482**

BIOCHIMICA ET BIOPHYSICA ACTA (NE/0006-3002). [3,000] **482**

BIOCHIMICA ET BIOPHYSICA ACTA. PROTEIN STRUCTURE AND MOLECULAR ENZYMOLOGY (NE/0167-4838). [1,920] **482**

BIOCHROMATOGRAPHY (US/0888-4404). [20,000] **483**

BIOGRAPHY INDEX (US/0006-3053). **439**

BIOGRAPHY INDEX (CD-ROM ED.) (US/1063-3286). **439**

BIOINFORMATION MANAGER (GW). [6,000] **444**

BIOLOGIA & CLINICA HEMATOLOGICA (SP/0210-895X). [1,500] **3770**

BIOLOGIA MORA (VLADIVOSTOK) (RU/0134-3475). [1,100] **553**

BIOLOGICA (FI). [500] **502**

BIOLOGICAL & AGRICULTURAL INDEX (US/0006-3177). **477**

BIOLOGICAL NOTES (COLUMBUS) (US/0078-3986). [1,200] **445**

BIOLOGICAL RESEARCH REPORTS FROM THE UNIVERSITY OF JYVASKYLA (FI). [400] **445**

BIOLOGICAL THERAPY (US/0733-2661). [2,000] **3774**

BIOLOGISCHE ABHANDLUNGEN (GW/0006-3282). **446**

BIOLOGIST (LONDON) (UK/0006-3347). [15,000] **446**

BIOLOGUE (WATERLOO) (CN/0840-8548). [500] **446**

BIOLOGY INTERNATIONAL (FR/0253-2069). [2,000] **447**

BIOLOGY INTERNATIONAL. SPECIAL ISSUES : THE NEWS MAGAZINE OF THE INTERNATIONAL UNION OF BIOLOGICAL SCIENCES (IUBS) (FR). [1,000-1,500] **447**

BIOLOGY OF THE CELL (FR/0248-4900). [2,000] **532**

BIOMEDICA BIOCHIMICA ACTA (GW/0232-766X). [1,000] **447**

BIOMEDICAL LETTERS (UK/0961-088X). **3556**

BIOMEDICAL NEWS SOURCE MIDWEST (US/1057-7424). **3557**

BIOMETRICS (US/0006-341X). [7,500] **5323**

BIOPEOPLE (SAN MATEO, CALIF.) (US/1065-612X). [4,000] **447**

BIOPHARM (EUGENE, OR.) (US/1040-8304). [20,000] **4293**

BIOPROBES (EUGENE, OR.) (US/1064-251X). [40,000] **5088**

BIOTEC WURZBURG (GW). [10,000] **448**

BIOTECH KNOWLEDGE SOURCES (UK/0953-2226). [200] **3688**

BIOTECHNIQUES (US/0736-6205). [50,000] **3557**

BIOTECHNOLOGY IN JAPAN NEWSSERVICE (US/0891-9283). **3689**

BIOTECHNOLOGY INFORMATION NEWS (UK/0952-147X). [1,300] **3689**

BIOTECHNOLOGY THERAPEUTICS (US/0898-2848). **3690**

BIOTECNOLOGIA APLICADA : REVISTA DE LA SOCIEDAD IBEROLATINOAMERICANA PARA INVESTIGACIONES SOBRE INTERFERON Y BIOTECNOLOGIA EN SALUD (CU/0864-4551). [3,000] **3690**

BIOVENTURE VIEW (US/0892-1903). [850] **448**

BIPAC ACTION REPORT (US/0272-1694). **4465**

BIPAC POLITICS (US/0032-3276). [30,000] **4465**

BIRD STUDY (UK/0006-3657). [3,000] **5615**

BIRD WORLD (NORTH HOLLYWOOD) (US/0199-5979). [15,000] **5615**

BIRDING (US/0161-1836). [13,000] **5578**

BIRDING IN SOUTHERN AFRICA (SA/0006-5838). [5,000] **5616**

BIRMINGHAM

Controlled Circulation Index

BIRMINGHAM AREA INDUSTRIAL DIRECTORY (US/0147-2097). [432] **1599**

BIRMINGHAM BUSINESS JOURNAL (US/0889-2237). [10,500] **643**

BIRTH-ORIGIN STUDY OF TEXAS NEWBORNS, A (US/0891-3641). [250] **4550**

BIRTH TRAUMA (US/0892-7227). [250] **2942**

BISMARCK TRIBUNE, THE (US). [32,500 (a.m. Mon.-Sat.)34,000 (a.m. Sunday)] **5725**

BIT (IT). [45,000] **1172**

BITAMIN (VITAMIN) (JA). **962**

BITAON LAMOREH LEARVIT (IS). [1,300] **1728**

BITS & BYTES REVIEW (US/0891-2955). **1172**

BITS AND PIECES (NEWCASTLE) (US/0006-3894). [300,000] **861**

BITZARON (US/0006-3932). **5046**

BIULETYN STATYSTYCZNY (PL/0006-4025). [2,250] **5323**

BIULETYN ZWIAAZKU NAUCZYCIELSTWA POLSKIEGO W KANADZIE (CN/0821-3917). [1,200] **3269**

BIULLETEN RADIOASTROFIZICHESKOI OBSERVATORII AKADEMII NAUK LATVIISKOI (LV). **393**

BLACK & WHITE (BIRMINGHAM, ALA.) (US/1064-0134). [100,000] **2485**

BLACK BEAR (US/8756-0666). [500] **3367**

BLACK COLLEGIAN (NEW ORLEANS), THE (US/0192-3757). [123,128] **1811**

BLACK EMPLOYMENT & EDUCATION (US/1053-704X). [153,287] **643**

BLACK FAMILY (US/0279-0718). [250,000] **2256**

BLACK HEALTH (US/1042-329X). [26,000] **4768**

BLACK MARIA (US/0045-222X). [1,000] **3367**

BLACK RESOURCE GUIDE, THE (US/0882-0643). [25,000] **2257**

BLACK SCHOLAR, THE (US/0006-4246). [9,000] **2257**

BLACK VOICE NEWS, THE (US). [7,500] **2257**

BLACK WARRIOR REVIEW, THE (US/0193-6301). [1,500] **3338**

BLACK'S OFFICE LEASING GUIDE. CONNECTICUT/NEW YORK SUBURBS (US). [7,500-10,000] **4210**

BLACK'S OFFICE LEASING GUIDE. HOUSTON OFFICE SPACE MARKET (US). [7,500-10,000] **4210**

BLACK'S OFFICE LEASING GUIDE. PHILADELPHIA & SUBURBS, SOUTHERN NEW JERSEY, DELAWARE (US). [7,500-10,000] **4210**

BLACK'S OFFICE LEASING GUIDE. WASHINGTON / BALTIMORE METRO AREA (US). [7,500-10,000] **4210**

BLAIN FAMILY NEWSLETTER, THE (CN/0712-127X). **2439**

BLATTER FUER DEUTSCHE LANDESGESCHICHTE (GW/0006-4408). [800] **2611**

BLAUE JUNGS (GW). [25,000] **4175**

BLE. BOLETIN DE LEGISLACION EXTRANJERA (SP/0212-5617). [1500] **3124**

BLIND (AMSTERDAM, NETHERLANDS) (NE). [1,500] **344**

BLM. BONNIERS LITTERARA MAGASIN (SW/0005-3198). **3367**

BLONDE COUNTRY / ANNUAL HEARD REFERENCE ED (CN/0711-1797). [800] **207**

BLOODROOT (US/0161-2506). [800] **3367**

BLOOMFIELD JOURNAL, THE (US/0746-9632). [2,400] **5645**

BLOOMSBURY REVIEW, THE (US/0276-1564). [50,000] **3338**

BLOUNT JOURNAL, THE (US/1056-6252). [350] **2439**

BLUE & GRAY MAGAZINE (US/0741-2207). [50,000] **2723**

BLUE BOOK OF MAJOR HOMEBUILDERS, THE (US/0195-8461). [500] **601**

BLUE BOOK OF PHOTOGRAPHY PRICES (US/0738-8322). [10,000] **4367**

BLUE BUFFALO (CN/0820-8352). [350-500] **3367**

BLUE GRASS ROOTS (US/0278-8071). [1,500] **2439**

BLUE JAY (CN/0006-5099). [2,000] **4163**

BLUE JAY NEWS (CN/0822-9988). [2,000] **4163**

BLUE MOUNTAIN HERITAGE (US/0743-183X). [100] **2439**

BLUE RIBBON HOME PLANS (US/0899-4382). **2899**

BLUE UNICORN (US/0197-7016). [500] **3460**

BLUEGRASS UNLIMITED (US/0006-5137). [23,500] **4104**

BLUEPRINT FOR SOCIAL JUSTICE (US/0895-5786). [3,000] **5193**

BLUEPRINTS - NATIONAL BUILDING MUSEUM (U.S.) (US/0742-0552). [10,000] **293**

BLUMEN EINZELHANDEL (GW). [4,200] **2434**

BLYTTIA (NO/0006-5269). [1,400] **502**

... BMUG NEWSLETTER, THE (US/0899-1014). [12,000] **1172**

BNAC COMMUNICATOR (US/1051-208X). **1105**

BNA'S PATENT, TRADEMARK & COPYRIGHT JOURNAL (US/0148-7965). [2,500] **1301**

BNB NBB COMPTES ANNUELS DES ENTERPRISES BELGES. CD-ROM (BE). [160] **739**

BNF NUTRITION BULLETIN (UK/0141-9684). [1,500] **4188**

BOARD CONVERTING NEWS ESPANOL (US). [2,850] **4218**

BOARD OF DIRECTORS, COMMITTEE CHAIRMEN - CANADIAN CHAMBER OF COMMERCE (CN/0709-0285). **818**

BOARD REPORT FOR GRAPHIC ARTISTS (US/1062-7774). **377**

BOAT AND MOTOR DEALER (US/0006-5366). [32,000] **591**

BOAT GUIDE (CN/0826-2802). [55,000] **592**

BOATING INDUSTRY, THE (US/0006-5404). [27,000] **592**

BOATING NEWS (VANCOUVER) (CN/0700-7388). [21,000] **592**

BOATING PRODUCT NEWS (US/0190-4507). [24,288] **592**

BODOBOKA (NO). **4085**

BOECKH BUILDING COST GUIDE. COMMERCIAL (CN/0225-9389). [500] **601**

BOECKH BUILDING COST GUIDE. INSTITUTIONAL (CN/0225-9397). [300] **601**

BOECKH BUILDING COST GUIDE. LIGHT INDUSTRIAL (CN/0225-9400). [400] **601**

BOECKH BUILDING COST GUIDE. RESIDENTIAL (CN/0225-9419). [800] **601**

BOER EN DE TUINDER, DE (BE). [40,000] **67**

BOGENS VERDEN (DK/0006-5692). [3,600] **3196**

BOGG (ARLINGTON, VA.) (US/0882-648X). [800] **3368**

BOHEMIA (CU/0523-8579). [200,000] **2485**

BOIS NATIONAL (EDITION VERTE), LE (FR). [23,000] **2376**

BOITE A OUTILS (CN/0229-9909). **1800**

BOKVAENNEN (SW/0006-5846). [1,400] **3368**

BOLETIM / CEHILA (BL). [1,500] **2723**

BOLETIM DA FILMOTECA ULTRAMARINA PORTUGUESA (PO/0430-4497). [1,000] **2611**

BOLETIM DA SOCIEDADE BROTERIANA (PO/0081-0657). [1,100] **502**

BOLETIM DE CIENCIAS SOCIAIS (BL). [500] **5193**

BOLETIM DE GEOGRAFIA TEORETICA (BL). [1,200] **2556**

BOLETIM DE ZOOLOGIA (BL/0101-3580). [500] **5578**

BOLETIM DO INSTITUTO DE ARQUEOLOGIA BRASILEIRA (BL). [500] **262**

BOLETIM DO INSTITUTO DE PESQUISAS VETERINARIAS DESIDERIO FINAMOR (BL). **5506**

BOLETIM DO MINISTERIO DA JUSTICA (PO). [5,000] **2942**

BOLETIM DO MUSEU NACIONAL. NOVA SERIE, ZOOLOGIA (BL/0080-312X). [1,000] **5578**

BOLETIM FBCN (BL). [3,500] **2188**

BOLETIM IG-USP. SERIE CIENTIFICA / UNIVERSIDADE DE SAO PAULO, INSTITUTO DE GEOCIENCIAS (BL). [1,000] **1367**

BOLETIM MENSUAL DE ESTATISTICA (MH). [400] **5323**

BOLETIM PAULISTA DE GEOGRAFIA (BL/0006-6079). [3,000] **2556**

BOLETIM TECNICO DO SENAC (BL). [1,650] **1728**

BOLETIM TRIMESTRAL DE ESTATISTICA (FUNCHAL) (PO/0303-1705). [500] **5323**

BOLETIN ANTARTICO CHILENO (CL/0716-0763). [1,000] **2551**

BOLETIN ANUARIO - BANCO CENTRAL DEL ECUADOR (EC). **5323**

BOLETIN ASTRONOMICO DEL OBSERVATORIO DE MADRID (SP/0373-7101). [400] **393**

BOLETIN CHILENO DE PARASITOLOGIA (CL/0365-9402). [1,000] **449**

BOLETIN / CIRCA, CENTRO DE INFORMACION Y REFERENCIA SOBRE CENTROAMERICA Y EL CARIBE (CR). [1500] **2511**

BOLETIN COMERCIAL / INSTITUTO NACIONAL DE PESCA (UY). [300] **1599**

BOLETIN - COMISION DE INTEGRACION ELECTRICA REGIONAL (UY). [1,400] **4633**

BOLETIN DE ANTROPOLOGIA (CK/0120-2510). [1,000] **232**

BOLETIN DE ESTADISTICA MINERA (CL/0577-7933). **2002**

BOLETIN DE ESTUDIOS ECONOMICOS (SP/0006-6249). [4,500] **1465**

BOLETIN DE ESTUDIOS MEDICOS Y BIOLOGICOS (MX/0067-9666). [1,000] **449**

BOLETIN DE LA ACADEMIA ARGENTINA DE LETRAS (AG/0001-3757). [1,000] **3368**

BOLETIN DE LA ACADEMIA COLOMBIANA (CK/0001-3773). **2513**

BOLETIN DE LA ACADEMIA PUERTORRIQUENA DE LA HISTORIA (PR/0567-6037). **2723**

BOLETIN DE LA CAMARA DE CUENTAS Y DEL TRIBUNAL SUPERIOR ADMINISTRATIVO (DR). [400] **4713**

BOLETIN DE LA ESCUELA DE CIENCIAS ANTROPOLOGICAS DE LA UNIVERSIDAD DE YUCATAN (MX). [1,000] **232**

BOLETIN DE LA INSTITUCION LIBRE DE ENSENANZA (SP). [1,000] **1728**

BOLETIN DE LA OFICINA SANITARIA PANAMERICANA (US/0030-0632). [16,000] **4769**

BOLETIN DE LA SOCIEDAD ESPANOLA DE ANTROPOLOGIA BIOLOGICA (SP). **232**

BOLETIN DE LA SOCIEDAD QUIMICA DEL PERU (PE/0037-8623). [1,000] **962**

BOLETIN DEL ARCHIVO HISTORICO DE MIRAFLORES (VE/0042-3386). [8,000] **2480**

BOLETIN DEL INSTITUTO ESPANOL DE OCEANOGRAFIA (1983) (SP/0074-0195). [1,000] **1447**

BOLETIN DEL INSTITUTO GEMOLOGICO ESPANOL (SP/0210-7228). [5,000] **2913**

BOLETIN DEL MUSEO DE CIENCIAS NATURALES Y ANTROPOLOGICAS JUAN CORNELIO MOYANO (AG/0326-1484). [800] **262**

BOLETIN INFORMATIVO TECHINT (AG/0497-0292). [4,000] **1599**

BOLETIN MEDICO DEL HOSPITAL INFANTIL DE MEXICO (SPANISH EDITION) (MX/0539-6115). [3,500] **3901**

BOLETIN MENSUAL - BANCO CENTRAL DE CHILE (CL/0716-2367). [1,300] **779**

BOLETIN MEXICANO DE DERECHO COMPARADO (MX/0041-8633). [1,000] **3124**

BOLETIN OFICIAL DEL MINISTERIO DE ECONOMIA Y HACIENDA (SP). [6,200] **4633**

BOLLETTINO (CIVICI MUSEI VENEZIANI D'ARTE E DI STORIA) (IT/0394-1027). **4085**

BOLLETTINO DEI CONTRATTI (IT). [317] **949**

BOLLETTINO DEL CENTRO CAMUNO DI STUDI PREISTORICI (IT/0577-2168). [4,300] **344**

BOLLETTINO DELLA DOMUS MAZZINIANA (IT/0012-5385). [500] **2679**

BOLLETTINO DELLA DOXA (IT). [2,000] **5240**

BOLLETTINO DELLA SOCIETA DI STUDI VALDESI (IT/0037-8739). [850] **4939**

BOLLETTINO DELLA SOCIETA ENTOMOLOGICA ITALIANA (IT/0373-3491). [1,500] **5606**

BOLLETTINO DELLA SOCIETA ITALIANA DI TOPOGRAFIA E FOTOGRAMMETRIA (IT/0392-4424). **2556**

BOLLETTINO DELL'ISTITUTO STORICO ARTISTICO ORVIETANO (IT/0391-8211). [1,000] **2612**

BOLLETTINO DI GEODESIA E SCIENZE AFFINI (IT/0006-6710). [500] **1352**

BOLLETTINO DI GEOFISICA TEORICA ED APPLICATA (IT/0006-6729). [500] **1403**

BOLLETTINO DI OCEANOLOGIA TEORICA ED APPLICATA (IT/0393-196X). [500] **1447**

BOLLETTINO DI OCULISTICA (IT/0006-677X). **3872**

BOLLETTINO DI PSICOLOGIA APPLICATA (IT/0006-6761). [1,000] **4577**

BOLLETTINO DI STORIA DELLE SCIENZE MATEMATICHE (IT/0392-4432). [1,000] **3497**

BOLLETTINO DI ZOOLOGIA (IT/0373-4137). [1,500] **5578**

BOLLETTINO DI ZOOLOGIA AGRARIA E DI BACHICOLTURA (IT/0366-2403). [250] **68**

BOLLETTINO ECONOMICO (IT). [1,000] **1465**

BOLLETTINO STORICO-BIBLIOGRAFICO SUBALPINO (IT/0391-6715). **2679**

BOLLETTINO TRIBUTARIO D'INFORMAZIONI (IT/0006-6893). [20,000] **2942**

BOLLETTINO UFFICIALE REGIONE : EMILIA ROMAGNA - PART III (IT). **4633**

BOLLETTINO UFFICIALE REGIONE : UMBRIA. PART 1 & 2 (IT). **4633**

BOLLETTINO UFFICIALE REGIONE : UMBRIA. PART 4 (IT). **4633**

BOMA EXPERIENCE EXCHANGE REPORT (US/0738-2170). [11,000] **4834**

BOND LAW REVIEW (AT/1033-4505). [1,000] **2943**

BOND MANAGEMENT REVIEW (AT/1036-1456). [200] **861**

BONDHOLDER / IFR, THE (UK/0961-8171). **779**

BONNER ZOOLOGISCHE BEITRAEGE (GW/0006-7172). [500] **5578**

BONSAI CLUBS INTERNATIONAL (US/0744-3277). [3,600] **2410**

BONSAI TODAY (US/1044-2529). [9,000] **2410**

BOOK - AMERICAN ANTIQUARIAN SOCIETY, THE (US/0740-8439). [2,100] **4824**

BOOK NEWSLETTER (MINNEAPOLIS, MINN.) (US/1043-352X). [37,000] **3338**

BOOK OF THE OLD EDINBURGH CLUB, THE (UK). [500] **5229**

BOOK PRODUCTION (BENN PUBLICATIONS LTD.) (UK). **4825**

BOOK REVIEW DIGEST (US/0006-7326). **3356**

BOOK REVIEW DIGEST. CD-ROM (US/0006-7326). **4821**

BOOK TALK (ALBUQUERQUE) (US/0145-627X). [500] **4825**

BOOKBIRD (DK/0006-7377). **3368**

BOOKMARK (MOSCOW, IDAHO), THE (US/0735-0295). [1,150] **3197**

BOOKMARK, THE (US/0006-7407). **3197**

BOOKPLATE JOURNAL, THE (UK/0264-3693). [300] **4825**

BOOKS AND ARTICLES ON ORIENTAL SUBJECTS PUBLISHED IN JAPAN. / TOHOGAKU KANKEI CHOSHO RONBUN MOKUROKU (JA/0524-0654). [1,100] **2634**

BOOKS AT BROWN (US/0147-0787). [800] **4821**

BOOKS AT IOWA (US/0006-7474). [500] **3197**

BOOKS FOR YOUR CHILDREN (UK/0006-7482). [12,000] **3338**

BOOKS FROM ISRAEL (IS/0578-932X). [2,500] **4825**

BOOKS IN ARABIC (1980) (CN/0713-4460). **4825**

BOOKS IN ARMENIAN (CN/0705-8209). [307] **4825**

BOOKS IN BENGALI (1980) (CN/0713-5335). **4825**

BOOKS IN CHINESE (1980) (CN/0713-4495). **4825**

BOOKS IN CROATIAN (CN/0713-4568). **4825**

BOOKS IN DUTCH (1980) (CN/0713-4533). [307] **4825**

BOOKS IN ESTONIAN (1980) (CN/0714-2129). **4825**

BOOKS IN FINNISH (1980) (CN/0714-2382). [307] **4825**

BOOKS IN FRISIAN (1980) (CN/0714-2420). **4826**

BOOKS IN GERMAN (1980) (CN/0714-2455). **4826**

BOOKS IN GREEK (1980) (CN/0714-2471). **4826**

BOOKS IN GUJARATI (CN/0714-2501). **4826**

BOOKS IN HINDI (1980) (CN/0714-2528). **4826**

BOOKS IN HUNGARIAN (1980) (CN/0714-2544). [307] **4826**

BOOKS IN ITALIAN (CN/0714-2609). **4826**

BOOKS IN LITHUANIAN (CN/0705-8225). [307] **4826**

BOOKS IN MARATHI (CN/0317-2406). [307] **4826**

BOOKS IN PANJABI (1980) (CN/0714-282X). **4826**

BOOKS IN PERSIAN (1980) (CN/0227-2741). [307] **4826**

BOOKS IN POLISH (1980) (CN/0714-2773). [307] **4826**

BOOKS IN POLISH OR RELATING TO POLAND (UK). [100] **2514**

BOOKS IN PORTUGUESE (1980) (CN/0714-279X). **4826**

BOOKS IN SPANISH (1980) (CN/0713-5998). **4826**

BOOKS IN TAGALOG (1980) (CN/0824-5592). **4826**

BOOKS IN UKRAINIAN (1980) (CN/0714-2927). **4826**

BOOKS IN URDU (1980) (CN/0714-296X). **4826**

BOOKS IN VIETNAMESE (1980) (CN/0227-2776). **4826**

BOOKS IN YIDDISH (CN/0705-8268). **4826**

BOOKS--NOTED FOR YOU (CN/0829-4976). **4821**

BOOKS NOW (CN/0707-6924). **3368**

BOOKS ON TRIAL (NEW YORK, N.Y.) (US/0749-5323). [5,000] **2943**

BOOKSTORE JOURNAL (US/0006-7563). [9,000] **4939**

BOOKWOMAN, THE (US/0163-1128). [1,000] **4827**

BOONE COUNTY RECORDER, THE (US). [7,000] **5679**

BOONVILLE HERALD AND ADIRONDACK TOURIST (US). [3,400] **5714**

BORDER/LINES (CN/0826-967X). **4185**

BOREAS (NO/0300-9483). [800] **1368**

BORTHWICK PAPERS / UNIVERSITY OF YORK, BORTHWICK INSTITUTE OF HISTORICAL RESEARCH (UK/0524-0913). [400] **2679**

BORTHWICK TEXTS AND CALENDARS : RECORDS OF THE NORTHERN PROVINCE (UK). [350] **2480**

BOSTON BAR JOURNAL (US/0524-1111). [8,000] **2943**

BOSTON COLLEGE LAW REVIEW (US/0161-6587). [1,000] **2943**

BOSTON PARENTS' PAPER, THE (US/1059-1710). [80,000] **2277**

BOSTON PHOENIX, THE (US/0163-3015). [128,000] **5688**

BOSTON REVIEW (CAMBRIDGE, MASS. : 1982) (US/0734-2306). [20,000] **3368**

BOTANICAL REVIEW, THE (US/0006-8101). [2,000] **503**

BOTSCHAFT, DIE (US). [7,000] **5735**

BOTTIN COMMUNES (FR). **4634**

BOTTIN MONDAIN; TOUT PARIS, TOUTE LA FRANCE (FR). **5465**

BOTTOM LINE (CHARLESTON, S.C.), THE (US/0279-1889). [3,600] **739**

BOUKWOSTEN (NE). **601**

BOUT DE PAPIER (CN/0833-9864). [2,800] **2485**

BOUT DE PAPIER (CN/0833-9864). [2,600] **4517**

BOUWWERELD (NE/0026-5942). **602**

BOVINE PRACTITIONER, THE (US/0524-1685). [6,000] **5506**

BOWNE DIGEST FOR CORPORATE & SECURITIES LAWYERS (US/0896-906X). **3079**

BOXBOARD CONTAINERS (US/0006-8497). [13,529] **4218**

BOYCOTT REPORT (US/0738-5161). [5,000] **2257**

BP STATISTICAL REVIEW OF WORLD ENERGY (UK/0263-9815). [40,000] **1961**

BP&R BRITISH PLASTICS AND RUBBER (UK/0307-6164). [14,380] **4454**

BRADFORD STUDIES ON SOUTH EASTERN EUROPE (UK/1354-7739). **2679**

BRAILLE BOOK REVIEW (US/0006-873X). [5,000] **4384**

BRAIN DYSFUNCTION (SZ/0259-1278). [1,200] **3828**

BRAIN RESEARCH BULLETIN (US/0361-9230). **3829**

BRAKE & FRONT END (US/0193-726X). [29,000] **5408**

BRANCH NOTES / WATERLOO-WELLINGTON BRANCH, ONTARIO GENEALOGICAL SOCIETY (CN/0383-7505). [500] **2439**

BRANDON NEWS (US). [37,350] **5649**

BRANDSTOFFEN BRUSSEL (BE/0778-5097). **1021**

BRANDWACHT (GW/0006-9116). **2288**

BRANGUS JOURNAL (US/0006-9132). [3,500] **207**

BRANSON'S COUNTRY REVIEW (US/1066-4033). [27,000] **4105**

BRANT NEWS (CN/0707-7998). [38,000] **5781**

BRASS BULLETIN (SZ/0303-3848). [7,000] **4105**

BRASS RESEARCH SERIES (US/0363-454X). [700] **4105**

BRAUINDUSTRIE (GW/0341-7115). [7,000] **2365**

BRAUWELT (1978) (GW/0724-696X). [6,375] **2329**

BRAXTON CITIZEN'S NEWS (US). [6,500] **5763**

BRAZILIAN BIBLE QUARTERLY (BL). [1,000] **4940**

BRAZILIAN JOURNAL OF MEDICAL AND BIOLOGICAL RESEARCH (BL/0100-879X). [2,100] **3558**

BRAZORIA COUNTY NEWS, THE (US). **5747**

BRAZOSPORT FACTS, THE (US/1065-7886). [21,000] **5747**

BRE NEWS OF CONSTRUCTION RESEARCH (UK/0265-9611). [20,000] **602**

BRE NEWS OF FIRE RESEARCH (UK/0265-962X). **2288**

BREAKTHROUGH (HAMMOND, LA.) (US/1056-0130). [8,500] **2771**

BRECHT YEARBOOK, THE (US/0734-8665). [1,100] **3369**

BREESE JOURNAL, THE (US). [5,600] **5658**

BREEZE (CN/0700-3641). [150] **3197**

BREF (OTTAWA), EN (CN/0714-5578). **1889**

BREMER COUNTY BROWSINGS (US/0896-7415). [60-80] **2440**

BREPOLS PUBLISHERS NEWSLETTER (BE). **4812**

BRETHREN LIFE AND THOUGHT (US/0006-9663). [850] **4940**

BRETHREN MISSIONARY HERALD (US/0161-5238). [2,600] **4940**

BREVIORA (US/0006-9698). [900] **5578**

BREWER (LONDON) (UK/0006-9736). [2,500] **2365**

BREWERS' GUARDIAN (UK/0006-9728). [3,000] **2365**

BREWING & DISTILLING INTERNATIONAL (UK/0308-1265). [4,000] **2365**

BRIAN COSTELLO ON MONEY MANAGEMENT (CN/0827-2794). **4713**

BRIAR PATCH (CN/0703-8968). [2,000] **5193**

BRICK (CN/0382-8565). [2,000] **3338**

BRICKMAN LETTER, THE (US/0748-1853). [100] **893**

BRIDAL APPAREL NEWS (US). [10,000] **1082**

BRIDGE RIVER LILLOOET NEWS (CN). [2,300] **5781**

BRIDGES (SEATTLE, WASH.) (US/1046-8358). [3,000] **5552**

BRIEF (CHICAGO. 1980), THE (US/0273-0995). [22,000] **2943**

BRIEF TO THE ONTARIO COUNCIL ON UNIVERSITY AFFAIRS (YORK UNIVERSITY) (CN/0706-6775). **1812**

BRIEFING (TU). [2,000] **4466**

BRIEFLY SPEAKING (CN/0715-3759). [15,000] **2943**

BRIEFS / AMERICAN INSTITUTE OF FISHERY RESEARCH BIOLOGISTS (US/8755-0075). [1,200] **2297**

BRIERCREST ECHO (CN/0821-5839). [24,000] **4940**

BRIGHAM YOUNG UNIVERSITY EDUCATION AND LAW JOURNAL (US). [200] **2943**

BRIGHAM YOUNG UNIVERSITY LAW REVIEW (US/0360-151X). [600] **2943**

BRIO (UNITED KINGDOM BRANCH, INTERNATIONAL ASSOCIATION OF MUSIC LIBRARIES) (UK/0007-0173). [400] **4105**

BRISTOL HERALD COURIER, BRISTOL VIRGINIA-TENNESSEAN (US/8750-6505). [45,000] **5758**

BRITISH-AMERICAN DEAL REVIEW, THE (US/1044-2944). [800] **1633**

BRITISH BULLETIN OF PUBLICATIONS ON LATIN AMERICA, THE CARIBBEAN, PORTUGAL AND SPAIN / CANNING HOUSE, HISPANIC AAN LUSO-BRAZILIAN COUNCIL (UK/0268-2400). [1,000] **4827**

BRITISH — Controlled Circulation Index

BRITISH CERAMIC REVIEW (UK/0306-7076). [7,000] **2586**

BRITISH COLUMBIA (CN/0704-6278). [2,000] **3476**

BRITISH COLUMBIA & ALBERTA HOME BUSINESS REPORT (CN/1191-8640). [25,000] **644**

... BRITISH COLUMBIA COLLECTIVE BARGAINING REVIEW AND OUTLOOK, THE (CN/0829-8319). **1656**

BRITISH COLUMBIA GENEALOGIST, THE (CN/0315-3835). [1,500] **2440**

BRITISH COLUMBIA MEDICAL JOURNAL (CN/0007-0556). [7,400] **3558**

BRITISH COLUMBIA'S WEDDING BELLS (CN/0840-464X). [100,000] **2277**

BRITISH DEAF NEWS (UK/0007-0602). [6,000] **4385**

BRITISH DENTAL SURGERY ASSISTANT (UK/0007-0629). [3,000] **1317**

BRITISH DIGEST ILLUSTRATED (US/0196-7517). **2514**

BRITISH EXPORTS TO NORTH AMERICA (UK). [20,000] **825**

BRITISH HOTELIER & RESTAURATEUR : OFFICIAL MAGAZINE OF THE BRITISH HOTELS, RESTAURANTS & CATERERS ASSOCIATION (UK). [10,500] **2804**

BRITISH JOURNAL OF ACUPUNCTURE (UK/0143-4977). [500] **3558**

BRITISH JOURNAL OF CANADIAN STUDIES (UK/0269-9222). [700] **2724**

BRITISH JOURNAL OF CLINICAL PHARMACOLOGY (UK/0306-5251). [2,000] **4294**

BRITISH JOURNAL OF EDUCATIONAL PSYCHOLOGY, THE (UK/0007-0998). **4578**

BRITISH JOURNAL OF HAEMATOLOGY (UK/0007-1048). [300] **3771**

BRITISH JOURNAL OF HEALTHCARE COMPUTING, THE (UK/0265-5217). [12,500] **1172**

BRITISH JOURNAL OF MENTAL SUBNORMALITY (UK/0374-633X). **1876**

BRITISH JOURNAL OF NON-DESTRUCTIVE TESTING (UK/0007-1137). [2,950] **2101**

BRITISH JOURNAL OF OBSTETRICS AND GYNAECOLOGY (UK/0306-5456). [4,700] **3758**

BRITISH JOURNAL OF ORTHODONTICS (UK/0301-228X). [1,500] **1317**

BRITISH JOURNAL OF PHYSICAL EDUCATION (UK/0144-3569). [6,000] **1855**

BRITISH JOURNAL OF PHYTOTHERAPY, THE (UK/0959-6879). **504**

BRITISH JOURNAL OF THEATRE NURSING : NATNEWS : THE OFFICIAL JOURNAL OF THE NATIONAL ASSOCIATION OF THEATRE NURSES, THE (UK). [7,000] **3852**

BRITISH JOURNAL OF VISUAL IMPAIRMENT, THE (UK/0264-6196). [2,500] **4385**

BRITISH MUSEUM MAGAZINE (UK/0965-8297). [10,000] **4085**

BRITISH MUSEUM MAGAZINE : JOURNAL OF THE BRITISH MUSEUM SOCIETY (UK). [10,000] **4085**

BRITISH ORTHOPTIC JOURNAL (UK/0068-2314). [1,600] **3873**

BRITISH PRINTER, THE (UK/0007-1684). [13,926] **4564**

BRITISH SUGAR BEET REVIEW (UK/0007-1854). [15,500] **165**

BRITISH TRAVEL LETTER (US/1041-4010). [5,000] **5465**

BRITISH WILDLIFE (UK). [4,750] **4869**

BRITTONIA (US/0007-196X). [800] **504**

BRMNA JOURNAL (CN/0229-0553). **5430**

BRNO STUDIES IN ENGLISH (XR/0524-6881). [500] **3270**

BROADCAST ENGINEERING NEWS (AT/0155-3720). [3850] **1127**

BROADCAST ENGINEERING (OVERLAND PARK) (US/0007-1994). [35,000] **1127**

BROADCAST FINANCIAL JOURNAL (US/0161-9063). [1,600] **1127**

BROADCAST HARDWARE INTERNATIONAL (UK/0269-493X). **1127**

BROADCAST SYSTEMS ENGINEERING (UK/0267-565X). [15,000] **1128**

BROADCASTER (TORONTO) (CN/0008-3038). [9,000] **1128**

BROADCASTING & CABLE INTERNATIONAL (US). [8,500] **1128**

BROADCASTING AND THE LAW (US/0161-5823). [1,500] **2943**

BROADCASTING (WASHINGTON, D.C. 1957) (US/0007-2028). [39,000] **1128**

BROADSIDE (NEW YORK, N.Y. : 1940) (US/0068-2748). [500] **5362**

BROADWATER MARKET LETTER (CN/0711-7590). **68**

BROILER INDUSTRY (US/0007-2176). [14,000] **207**

BROKEN SPOKE, THE (CN/0045-3226). [200] **5408**

BROMINE IN ... (US). [200] **1362**

BRONTE NEWSLETTER (US/0737-6340). [500] **3369**

BRONTE SOCIETY PUBLICATIONS. TRANSACTIONS (UK/0309-7765). [3,500] **3369**

BRONX TIMES REPORTER (US/8750-4499). [17,000] **5714**

BROOKFIELD ZOO BISON (US/8756-3479). [30,000] **5578**

BROOKGREEN JOURNAL (US/0884-8815). [2,500] **345**

BROOKLYN LAW REVIEW (US/0007-2362). [1,000] **2944**

BROOM, BRUSH & MOP (US/0890-2933). [1,200] **1600**

BROT & BACKWAREN (GW/0172-8180). [7,200] **2329**

BROTHERHOOD ACTION (AT/0300-4678). [7,000] **5229**

BROWN SWISS BULLETIN, THE (US/0007-2516). [2,800] **207**

BROWN'S NAUTICAL ALMANAC (UK/0068-290X). [12,000] **4175**

BROWNSTONER, THE (US/0883-962X). [1,000] **293**

BRUCE & GREY BRANCH OF O.G.S (CN/0849-0848). [700] **2440**

BRUEL & KJAER TECHNICAL REVIEW (DK/0007-2621). [14,000] **1967**

BRUG, DE (NE). [50] **5806**

BRUNDTLAND BULLETIN / THE CENTRE FOR OUR COMMON FUTURE (SZ). **2162**

BRUNSWICK BUSINESS JOURNAL, THE (CN/0829-5239). [16,000] **644**

BRYGMESTEREN (DK/0007-2737). [1,000] **2365**

BRYOLOGIST, THE (US/0007-2745). [1,000] **504**

BUC ... NEW BOAT PRICE GUIDE (US/0195-346X). **592**

BUC USED BOAT PRICE GUIDE (US/0735-973X). **592**

BUCH DER ZEIT (GW/0007-2761). [12,000] **4812**

BUCH UND BIBLIOTHEK (GW/0340-0301). [6,000] **3197**

BUCHEREI DES PADIATERS (GW/0373-3165). **3901**

BUCHREIHE DER SUDOSTDEUTSCHEN HISTORISCHEN KOMMISSION (GW/0562-5270). [1,000] **2680**

BUCKER NEWS LETTER, THE (US/0889-4388). [200] **15**

BUCKEYE OSTEOPATHIC PHYSICIAN (US/0898-3070). [2,700] **4294**

BUCKLEY-LITTLE CATALOGUE OF BOOKS AVAILABLE FROM AUTHORS, THE (US/0749-615X). [12,000] **411**

BUCKSKIN BULLETIN (US/0045-3307). [4,500] **2724**

BUDDHIST-CHRISTIAN STUDIES (US/0882-0945). [350] **5020**

BUDDY (DALLAS, TEX.) (US/0192-9097). [100] **4105**

BUDESHTE (FR). [6,550] **2514**

BUDGET MONITOR (AT). **4714**

BUDGETING FOR BASIC NEEDS AND BUDGETING FOR MINIMUM ADEQUATE STANDARD OF LIVING (CN/0822-7918). [300] **2789**

BUDZETY GOSPODARSTW DOMOWYCH (PL). [900] **1465**

BUFFALO BULLETIN, THE (US). [4,300] **5765**

BUFFALO CHIPS (US/0736-2463). [100] **2440**

BUFFALO (CUSTER) (US/0196-9137). [1,200] **208**

BUFFALO JOURNAL (TH/0857-1554). **5090**

BUFFALO LAW REVIEW (US/0023-9356). [600] **2944**

BUFFALO SPREE (US/0300-7499). [21,000] **2529**

BUGLE (US/0889-6445). [150,000] **2189**

BUILD; JOURNAL OF THE INDUSTRY (IE/0007-3229). [4,836] **602**

BUILDCORE INDEX (CN/0227-0595). [14,000] **602**

BUILDER & CONTRACTOR (US/0273-7965). [24,000] **602**

BUILDER/DEALER (US/0892-824X). [25,000] **602**

BUILDERS MERCHANTS JOURNAL (TONBRIDGE AND MALLING, KENT : 1985) (UK/0268-1323). [7,080] **602**

BUILDING AND CONSTRUCTION LAW (AT/0815-6050). **602**

BUILDING AUTOMATION (IT). [27,000] **603**

BUILDING COST FILE. WESTERN EDITION (US/0194-0295). [6,900] **603**

BUILDING COST GUIDE. AGRICULTURAL (CN/0821-7327). [1,400] **603**

BUILDING COST GUIDE. MOBILE HOME (CN/0821-7300). [500] **603**

BUILDING COST MANUAL (US/0732-5789). **603**

BUILDING ECONOMIC ALTERNATIVES (US/0885-9930). [50,000] **1465**

BUILDING ECONOMIST, THE (AT/0007-3431). [3,800] **603**

BUILDING ENGINEER (UK). [5,000] **603**

BUILDING OKLAHOMA (OKLAHOMA CITY, OKLA. 1989) (US/1071-2879). [3,200] **603**

BUILDING OPERATING MANAGEMENT (US/0007-3490). [65,000] **603**

BUILDING-PERMIT ACTIVITY IN FLORIDA (MONTHLY) (US/0007-3555). **603**

BUILDING PRODUCTS DIGEST (US/0742-5694). [12,750] **2399**

BUILDING RESEARCH ESTABLISHMENT UPDATE (UK). **604**

BUILDING SERVICES CONTRACTOR (US/0007-3644). [7,500] **604**

BUILDING SERVICES : THE CIBSE JOURNAL (UK). **604**

BUILDING SUPPLY & HOME CENTERS (US/0890-9008). [43,000] **604**

BUILDING SURVEYOR MELBOURNE (AT/0728-9820). [3,500] **605**

BUILDING SYSTEMS BUILDER (US/1064-5896). **605**

BUILDING TRADES INDEX, STATE OF WYOMING (US). [250] **1656**

BUILDINGS (CEDAR RAPIDS. 1947) (US/0007-3725). [42,000] **605**

BUILDINGS ENERGY TECHNOLOGY (US/0891-3730). **1934**

BUILT ENVIRONMENT (LONDON, 1978) (UK/0263-7960). [600] **2816**

BU$INESS OF HERBS, THE (US/0736-9050). [2,000 subscribers 10,000 readership] **2411**

BUKU MAKLUMAT PERANGKAAN GETAH BAGI MALAYSIA. RUBBER STATISTICS HANDBOOK OF MALAYSIA (MY). [180] **5078**

BUKU SAKU STATISTIK INDONESIA (IO). **5324**

BULETIN PENELITIAN INSTITUT PERTANIAN BOGOR (IO/0216-3500). [500] **68**

BULETINUL BIBLIOTECII ROMANE (GW). [300] **2680**

BULETINUL INSTITUTUL AGRONOMIC CLUJ-NAPOCA. SERIA ZOOTEHNIE SI MEDICINA VETERINARA (RM/0557-4668). [500] **208**

BULETINUL INSTITUTULUI AGRONOMIC CLUJ-NAPOCA. SERIA AGRICULTURA (RM/0557-465X). [500] **68**

BULETINUL INSTITUTULUI DE PETROL SI GAZE (RM/0376-4516). **4252**

BULGARIAN CO-OPERATIVE REVIEW (BU). [5,600] **1541**

BULGARSKI KNIGOPIS (BU). [700] **4821**

BULGARSKO MUZIKOZNANIE (SOFIA, BULGARIA : 1979) (BU/0204-823X). **4105**

BULLDOG (LOS ANGELES, CALIF.) (US/0744-1797). [880] **4201**

BULLETIN (CN). [500] **411**

BULLETIN (US). [4,250] **2411**

BULLETIN A B Q (CN/0380-7150). [200] **3197**

BULLETIN : A VDOT MONTHLY NEWSPAPER (US). [17,000] **5378**

BULLETIN (ALABAMA MUSEUM OF NATURAL HISTORY) (US/0196-1039). **4163**

BULLETIN / ALBERTA RESEARCH COUNCIL (CN/0383-5359). **5090**

BULLETIN (ALBERTA TEACHERS' ASSOCIATION. SCIENCE COUNCIL) (CN/0820-7941). [820] **5090**

BULLETIN - AMERICAN ACADEMY OF ARTS AND SCIENCES (US/0002-712X). [3,500] **316**

BULLETIN / AMERICAN ACADEMY OF ORTHOPAEDIC SURGEONS (US/1049-9741). [18,000] **3880**

BULLETIN / AMERICAN ASSOCIATION FOR THE HISTORY OF NURSING (US/0898-6622). [400] **3852**

Controlled Circulation Index — BULLETIN

BULLETIN - AMERICAN ASTRONOMICAL SOCIETY (US/0002-7537). [1,900] **402**

BULLETIN - AMERICAN FEDERATION OF ASTROLOGERS (US/0735-4797). [5,000] **390**

BULLETIN / AMERICAN SUNBATHING ASSOCIATION, THE (US/0279-8158). [30,000] **4849**

BULLETIN ANTIEKE BESCHAVING : BABESCH (NE/0165-9367). **2612**

BULLETIN (ARTICLE 19 ORGANIZATION) (UK/1011-3983). [8,500] **4504**

BULLETIN / ASSOCIATION CANADIENNE DE LINGUISTIQUE (CN/0825-2823). **3270**

BULLETIN - ASSOCIATION CANADIENNE POUR L'AVANCEMENT DES ETUDES NEERLANDAISES (CN/0823-9487). [300] **2680**

BULLETIN - ASSOCIATION DES MEDECINS DE LANGUE FRANCAISE DU CANADA (1977) (CN/0702-7656). [15,000] **3559**

BULLETIN - ASSOCIATION FOR PSYCHOANALYTIC MEDICINE (US/0004-542X). [2,000] **3922**

BULLETIN - ASSOCIATION QUEBECOISE POUR L'ETUDE DE L'IMPRIME (CN/0838-5459). [300] **431**

BULLETIN BAKHTINE, LE (CN/0821-6886). [200] **3338**

BULLETIN BIBLIOGRAPHIQUE DE DOCUMENTATION TECHNIQUE / GROUPEMENT DE DOCUMENTATION DES INDUSTRIES EXTRACTIVES (FR/0395-7322). [600] **411**

BULLETIN BIBLIOGRAPHIQUE DE LA SOCIETE INTERNATIONALE ARTHURIENNE (FR/0074-1388). [1,400] **3457**

BULLETIN / BRITISH SOCIETY FOR MUSIC THERAPY (UK/0953-7511). [400] **4105**

BULLETIN - C P A A C M P A (CN/0701-0575). **1144**

BULLETIN - CALCUTTA STATISTICAL ASSOCIATION (II/0008-0683). [355] **5324**

BULLETIN - CALIFORNIA WATER POLLUTION CONTROL ASSOCIATION (US/0008-1620). [6,000] **2225**

BULLETIN - CANADIAN ASSOCIATION FOR UNIVERSITY CONTINUING EDUCATION (CN/0823-1168). [500] **1812**

BULLETIN - CANADIAN ASSOCIATION OF COLLEGE AND UNIVERSITY STUDENT SERVICES (CN/0711-2416). **1812**

BULLETIN - CANADIAN COMMISSION FOR UNESCO (CN/0008-4557). [5,000] **5193**

BULLETIN / CANADIAN SOCIETY FOR MESOPOTAMIAN STUDIES (CN/0844-3416). [300] **262**

BULLETIN - CANADIAN SOCIETY OF LABORATORY TECHNOLOGISTS (CN/0381-5838). [22,500] **5090**

BULLETIN - CANADIAN SOCIETY OF ZOOLOGISTS (CN/0319-6674). [1,000] **5579**

BULLETIN / CANADIAN WATER AND WASTEWATER ASSOCIATION (CN/0836-0278). [8,000] **5531**

BULLETIN (CARDINAL OTUNGA HIGH SCHOOL HISTORICAL SOCIETY) (KE). [300] **2612**

BULLETIN - CENTRE INTERUNIVERSITAIRE D'ETUDES EUROPEENNES (CN/0319-1095). **2680**

BULLETIN - CHINESE HISTORICAL SOCIETY OF AMERICA (US/0577-9065). [500] **2724**

BULLETIN - CORPORATION PROFESSIONNELLE DES MEDECINS DU QUEBEC (CN/0315-2979). [20,000] **3559**

BULLETIN (CRANBROOK INSTITUTE OF SCIENCE) (US/0070-1416). **5090**

BULLETIN - DAYTON ART INSTITUTE (US). [3,500] **345**

BULLETIN DE DOCUMENTATION - BELGIQUE, MINISTERE DES FINANCES (BE). [1,000] **4715**

BULLETIN DE LA CLASSE DE BEAUX-ARTS ACADEMIE ROYALE DE BELGIQUE (BE/0378-0716). [500] **316**

BULLETIN DE LA CLASSE DES LETTRES ET DES SCIENCES MORALES ET POLITIQUES (BE). [500] **3339**

BULLETIN DE LA CLASSE DES SCIENCES. ACADEMIE ROYALE DE BELGIQUE (BE/0001-4141). [500] **5090**

BULLETIN DE LA DIRECTION DES ETUDES ET RECHERCHES. SERIE A. NUCLEAIRE, HYDRAULIQUE, THERMIQUE (FR/0013-449X). [1,600] **2087**

BULLETIN DE LA DIRECTION DES ETUDES ET RECHERCHES. SERIE B. RESEAUX ELECTRIQUES, MATERIELS ELECTRIQUES (FR/0013-4503). [1,600] **2037**

BULLETIN DE LA MAISON FRANCO-JAPONAISE (JA/0495-7725). [1,000] **2843**

BULLETIN DE LA SOCIETE ARCHEOLOGIQUE ET HISTORIQUE DU LIMOUSIN (FR/0184-7651). [1,000] **263**

BULLETIN DE LA SOCIETE BELGE DE GEOLOGIE (BE/0379-1807). [1,300] **1368**

BULLETIN DE LA SOCIETE BELGE D'ETUDES GEOGRAPHIQUES (BE/0037-8925). [600] **2556**

BULLETIN DE LA SOCIETE DE L'HISTOIRE DU PROTESTANTISME FRANCAIS (1981) (FR/0037-9050). **5057**

BULLETIN DE LA SOCIETE DES ETUDES OCEANIENNES (POLYNESIE ORIENTALE) (FP). [600] **2669**

BULLETIN DE LA SOCIETE FRANCAISE DE NUMISMATIQUE (FR/0037-9344). [800] **2780**

BULLETIN DE LA SOCIETE PAUL CLAUDEL (FR/0037-9506). [130] **3369**

BULLETIN DE LA SOCIETE ROYALE DES SCIENCES DE LIEGE (BE/0037-9565). [700] **5090**

BULLETIN DE L'ACADEMIE DES SCIENCES ET LETTRES DE MONTPELLIER (FR). **2843**

BULLETIN DE L'ACADEMIE NATIONALE DE CHIRURGIE DENTAIRE (FR/0339-9710). [300] **3961**

BULLETIN DE L'AGE D'OR, LE (CN/0229-866X). **5178**

BULLETIN DE L'ASSOCIATION DE GEOGRAPHES FRANCAIS (FR/0004-5322). [950] **2556**

BULLETIN DE L'ASSOCIATION DES PROFESSEURS DE MATHEMATIQUES ET L'ENSEIGNEMENT PUBLIC (FR). [7,500] **3498**

BULLETIN DE LIAISON - CENTRE DE LINGUISTIQUE THEORIQUE ET APPLIQUEE, UNIVERSITE NATIONALE DU ZAIRE (CG). **3270**

BULLETIN DE LIAISON DES LABORATOIRES DES PONTS ET CHAUSSEES (FR/0458-5860). [6,500] **1967**

BULLETIN DE LIAISON / FEDERATION DES ASSOCIATIONS DE FAMILLES MONOPARENTALES DU QUEBEC (CN/0822-6768). [700] **2277**

BULLETIN DE L'INSTITUT DE GEOLOGIE DU BASSIN D'AQUITAINE (FR/0524-0832). [500] **1369**

BULLETIN DE L'INSTITUT DE READAPTATION DE MONTREAL, LE (CN/0316-4454). [8,500] **5275**

BULLETIN DE L'INSTITUT D'HISTOIRE DE L'AMERIQUE FRANCAISE (CN/0712-2187). [1,400] **2724**

BULLETIN DE L'INSTITUT PASTEUR (FR/0020-2452). [1,000] **3667**

BULLETIN DE L'INSTITUT ROYAL DU PATRIMOINE ARTISTIQUE. MICROFORM (US). [1,000] **316**

BULLETIN DE L'OIV (FR/0029-7127). [1,200] **69**

BULLETIN DE L'UNION INTERNATIONALE CONTRE LA TUBERCULOSE ET LES MALADIES RESPIRATOIRES (FR/1011-7903). [5,000] **3949**

BULLETIN DE NOUVELLES - CORPORATION PROFESSIONNELLE DES TRAVAILLEURS SOCIAUX DU QUEBEC (CN/0713-4290). [2,500] **5275**

BULLETIN DE NOUVELLES - PRESSE ETUDIANTE DU QUEBEC (CN/0228-1252). [90] **1089**

BULLETIN DE NOUVELLES - SOCIETE CANADIENNE DE DROIT CANONIQUE (CN/0703-1963). [425] **5025**

BULLETIN DE PHILOSOPHIE MEDIEVALE (BE/0068-4023). [1,000] **4343**

BULLETIN DE PSYCHOLOGIE (FR/0007-4403). **4578**

BULLETIN DE PSYCHOLOGIE SCOLAIRE ET D'ORIENTATION (BE/0007-4411). [350] **4578**

BULLETIN DES AGRICULTEURS (CN/0007-4446). [35,000] **69**

BULLETIN DES ETUDES VALERYENNES (FR/0335-508X). [500] **3369**

BULLETIN DES G.T.V (FR/0399-2519). [2,800] **5506**

BULLETIN DES RECHERCHES AGRONOMIQUES DE GEMBLOUX (BE/0435-2033). [1,000] **69**

BULLETIN DES SOCIETES CHIMIQUES BELGES (BE/0037-9646). [1,500] **963**

BULLETIN D'INFORMATION - BUREAU GRAVIMETRIQUE INTERNATIONAL (FR/0373-9023). **4399**

BULLETIN D'INFORMATION - CONSEIL REGIONAL DE DEVELOPPEMENT DE L'OUTAOUAIS (07) (CN/0226-5540). **1466**

BULLETIN D'INFORMATION ET DE LIAISON - ASSOCIATION DES SERVICES GEOLOGIQUES AFRICAINS (FR/0396-8863). **1369**

BULLETIN D'INFORMATION UFOLOGIQUE (CN/0828-4938). [100] **15**

BULLETIN D'INFORMATIONS DE L'ASSOCIATION DES BIBLIOTHECAIRES FRANCAIS (FR/0004-5365). [2,200] **3198**

BULLETIN D'INFORMATIONS SCIENTIFIQUES - INSTITUT PASTEUR (FR/1144-3464). **5091**

BULLETIN - DIVISION OF GEOLOGY AND EARTH RESOURCES (OLYMPIA) (US). [2,500] **1369**

BULLETIN - DOLMETSCH FOUNDATION (UK/0419-618X). [750] **4106**

BULLETIN DU CENTRE PROTESTANT D'ETUDES (SZ). **5057**

BULLETIN DU GROUPEMENT D'INFORMATIONS MUTUELLES AMPERE (SZ/0434-6971). [300] **4399**

BULLETIN DU MUSEE HONGROIS DES BEAUX-ARTS (HU). [1,400] **4085**

BULLETIN / EASTERN FISHERMEN'S FEDERATION (CN/0821-6576). **2297**

BULLETIN - ENTOMOLOGICAL SOCIETY OF CANADA (CN/0071-0741). [1,800] **5579**

BULLETIN / FEDERATION INTERNATIONALE DE GYMNASTIQUE (SZ/0428-1659). **4888**

BULLETIN FOR INTERNATIONAL FISCAL DOCUMENTATION (NE/0007-4624). [2,500] **4715**

BULLETIN FRANCAIS DE LA PECHE ET DE LA PISCICULTURE (FR/0767-2861). [1,000] **2298**

BULLETIN - FRANCE. PARLEMENT (1946-). ASSEMBLEE NATIONALE (FR/0755-2793). [7,000] **4634**

BULLETIN / GDR COMMITTEE FOR HUMAN RIGHTS (GW). **4505**

BULLETIN - GENETICS SOCIETY OF CANADA (CN/0316-4357). [450] **543**

BULLETIN - GEOLOGICAL SURVEY OF IRELAND (IE/0085-0985). [800] **1369**

BULLETIN / GEOLOGICAL SURVEY OF SOUTH AUSTRALIA (AT/0016-7671). [300] **1352**

BULLETIN (GEOLOGICAL SURVEY OF WYOMING) (US/0096-6053). [1,000] **1369**

BULLETIN / GEOTHERMAL RESOURCES COUNCIL (US/0160-7782). [1,200] **1934**

BULLETIN - GREATER ST. LOUIS DENTAL SOCIETY (US/0360-2575). [1,400] **1318**

BULLETIN / HEALTH SCIENCES ASSOCIATION OF ALBERTA (CN/0712-4775). **1657**

BULLETIN - HYMN SOCIETY OF GREAT BRITAIN AND IRELAND (UK/0018-828X). [500] **4106**

BULLETIN - I C S S (CN/0700-8090). **4888**

BULLETIN - INDIAN MUSEUM (II/0019-5987). [500] **4085**

BULLETIN (INSTITUT ROYAL DU PATRIMOINE ARTISTIQUE (BRUXELLES)) (BE/0085-1892). [1,000] **345**

BULLETIN / INSTITUTE FOR ANTIQUITY AND CHRISTIANITY (US/0739-0459). [1,000] **4941**

BULLETIN - INSTITUTE OF CLASSICAL STUDIES (UK/0076-0730). [500] **1075**

BULLETIN - INSTITUTE OF MATHEMATICS AND ITS APPLICATIONS (UK/0950-5628). [7,000] **3498**

BULLETIN - INTERNATIONAL COUNCIL ON ARCHIVES (FR/0252-9785). [1,500] **2481**

BULLETIN (INTERNATIONAL DAIRY FEDERATION) (BE/0250-5118). [1,000] **192**

BULLETIN - INTERNATIONAL NORTH PACIFIC FISHERIES COMMISSION (CN/0074-7157). [1,000] **2298**

BULLETIN / INTERNATIONAL OLD LACERS (US). [2,100] **5348**

BULLETIN - JOURNAL OF THE TOKYO WOMEN'S MEDICAL COLLEGE (JA/0495-7792). [1,700] **3560**

BULLETIN - KANSAS AGRICULTURAL EXPERIMENT STATION (US/0097-0484). [3,000] **69**

BULLETIN - KANSAS ORNITHOLOGICAL SOCIETY (US/0022-8729). [400] **5616**

BULLETIN - KING COUNTY MEDICAL SOCIETY, THE (US/0023-1592). [4,000] **3913**

BULLETIN / MAINE ARCHAEOLOGICAL SOCIETY (US/0542-1292). [350] **263**

BULLETIN MATCH (CN/0229-5814). **5552**

BULLETIN — Controlled Circulation Index

BULLETIN - MICROSCOPICAL SOCIETY OF CANADA (CN/0383-1825). [700] **572**

BULLETIN - MOUNT DESERT ISLAND BIOLOGICAL LABORATORY (1934) (US/0097-0883). **450**

BULLETIN MUNICIPAL - CONSEIL MUNICIPAL DE SAINT-LOUIS-DE-TERREBONNE (CN/0711-7744). **4634**

BULLETIN, NATIONAL EMPLOYMENT LISTING SERVICE FOR THE CRIMINAL JUSTICE SYSTEM (US/0194-0767). [2,000] **4201**

BULLETIN - NATIONAL PSYCHOLOGICAL ASSOCIATION FOR PSYCHOANALYSIS (US/0077-5339). [5,000] **4579**

BULLETIN - NATIONAL SHEVCHENKO MUSICAL ENSEMBLE GUILD OF CANADA (CN/0703-9999). [4,000] **4106**

BULLETIN - NATIONAL TROPICAL BOTANICAL GARDEN (US/1057-3968). [5,000] **505**

BULLETIN - NEW JERSEY MOTOR TRUCK ASSOCIATION (US/0028-5838). [2,800] **5378**

BULLETIN - NEW MEXICO BUREAU OF MINES & MINERAL RESOURCES (US/0096-4581). **2135**

BULLETIN (NEW YORK STATE ARCHEOLOGICAL ASSOCIATION : 1987) (US/1046-2368). [750] **264**

BULLETIN (NEW YORK STATE SCHOOL OF INDUSTRIAL AND LABOR RELATIONS) (US/0070-0134). [10,000] **1657**

BULLETIN - NORTH AMERICAN GLADIOLUS COUNCIL (US/0029-2370). [1,500] **505**

BULLETIN - NORTH DAKOTA LEAGUE OF CITIES (US/0279-800X). [2,800] **4634**

BULLETIN OF ANIMAL HEALTH AND PRODUCTION IN AFRICA (KE/0378-9721). [1,000] **208**

BULLETIN OF CARNEGIE MUSEUM OF NATURAL HISTORY (US/0145-9058). [500] **4164**

BULLETIN OF CENTRE FOR INFORMATICS (JA/0911-3622). [1,000] **3198**

BULLETIN OF CONCERNED ASIAN SCHOLARS (US/0007-4810). [1,800] **2647**

BULLETIN OF EASTERN CARIBBEAN AFFAIRS (BB). **2511**

BULLETIN OF ELECTROCHEMISTRY (II/0256-1654). [800] **1034**

BULLETIN OF INDONESIAN ECONOMIC STUDIES (AT/0007-4918). [1,500] **1466**

BULLETIN OF LAW, SCIENCE & TECHNOLOGY (US/0362-3769). **2944**

BULLETIN OF MARINE SCIENCE (US/0007-4977). [900] **1447**

BULLETIN OF MEDIEVAL CANON LAW (US/0146-2989). [600] **2944**

BULLETIN OF PEACE PROPOSALS (NO/0007-5035). [800] **4466**

BULLETIN OF PROCEEDINGS - CANADA. SUPREME COURT (CN/1193-8536). [250] **2944**

BULLETIN OF PURE & APPLIED SCIENCES. SEC. E, MATHEMATICS (II/0970-6577). **3498**

BULLETIN OF PURE & APPLIED SCIENCES. SECTION A, ANIMAL SCIENCE (II/0970-0765). [50] **5579**

BULLETIN OF PURE & APPLIED SCIENCES. SECTION B, PLANT SCIENCES (II). [500] **505**

BULLETIN OF TAU BETA PI, THE (US/8755-5670). [12,000] **5229**

BULLETIN OF THE ABERDEEN UNIVERSITY AFRICAN STUDIES GROUP (UK/0001-3196). [350] **2638**

BULLETIN OF THE AMATEUR ENTOMOLOGISTS' SOCIETY, THE (UK/0266-836X). [2,000] **5606**

BULLETIN OF THE AMERICAN ACADEMY OF PSYCHIATRY AND THE LAW (US/0091-634X). [2,000] **3922**

BULLETIN OF THE AMERICAN DAHLIA SOCIETY, INC (US/0002-8150). [1,800] **2411**

BULLETIN OF THE AMERICAN IRIS SOCIETY (US/0747-4172). [6,000] **2411**

BULLETIN OF THE AMERICAN ROCK GARDEN SOCIETY (US/0003-0864). [4,500] **2411**

BULLETIN OF THE ARCHAEOLOGICAL SOCIETY OF CONNECTICUT (US/0739-5612). [500] **264**

BULLETIN OF THE ARCHAEOLOGICAL SOCIETY OF NEW JERSEY (US/0196-8319). [500] **264**

BULLETIN OF THE ASTRONOMICAL SOCIETY OF INDIA (II/0304-9523). [600] **394**

BULLETIN OF THE AUSTRALIAN PSYCHOLOGICAL SOCIETY (AT). [5,400] **4579**

BULLETIN OF THE BIOLOGICAL SOCIETY OF WASHINGTON (US/0097-0298). [1,000] **4164**

BULLETIN OF THE BRACKISHWATER AQUACULTURE DEVELOPMENT CENTRE (IO/0126-1924). [500] **2298**

BULLETIN OF THE CALIFORNIA INSECT SURVEY (US/0068-5631). [800] **5606**

BULLETIN OF THE CHEMICAL SOCIETY OF JAPAN (JA/0009-2673). [8,000] **963**

BULLETIN OF THE CLEVELAND MUSEUM OF ART, THE (US/0009-8841). [20,000] **345**

BULLETIN OF THE CONGREGATIONAL LIBRARY (US/0010-5821). [1,000] **3198**

BULLETIN OF THE DEPARTMENT OF GEOGRAPHY, UNIVERSITY OF TOKYO (JA/0082-478X). [800] **2557**

BULLETIN OF THE DEPARTMENT OF INTERNATIONAL AFFAIRS, AFL-CIO, THE (US/0890-6165). [8,500] **4517**

BULLETIN OF THE EARTHQUAKE RESEARCH INSTITUTE, UNIVERSITY OF TOKYO (JA). **1403**

BULLETIN OF THE EUROPEAN ASSOCIATION FOR JAPANESE STUDIES (UK). [300] **2502**

BULLETIN OF THE FACULTY OF SCIENCE, IBARAKI UNIVERSITY. SERIES A : MATHEMATICS (JA). [300] **3498**

BULLETIN OF THE FRIENDS OF JADE, THE (US/0261-7080). [200] **370**

BULLETIN OF THE GLOUCESTER COUNTY HISTORICAL SOCIETY (US/0887-5413). [1,900] **2725**

BULLETIN OF THE HISTORICAL SOCIETY OF MONTGOMERY COUNTY, PENNSYLVANIA (US/0362-8590). [1,250] **2725**

BULLETIN OF THE HISTORY OF DENTISTRY (US/0007-5132). [1,500] **1318**

BULLETIN OF THE INDIAN SOCIETY OF EARTHQUAKE TECHNOLOGY (II). [900] **1403**

BULLETIN OF THE INSTITUTE OF ARCHAEOLOGY / UNIVERSITY OF LONDON, INSTITUTE OF ARCHAEOLOGY (UK/0076-0722). [750] **264**

BULLETIN OF THE INSTITUTE OF CHEMISTRY. ACADEMIA SINICA (CH/0366-0370). [300] **963**

BULLETIN OF THE INSTITUTION OF ENGINEERS (INDIA) (II/0020-3343). [50,000] **2037**

BULLETIN OF THE INTERNATIONAL ASSOCIATION FOR SHELL AND SPATIAL STRUCTURES (SP/0304-3622). [1000] **605**

BULLETIN OF THE INTERNATIONAL ASSOCIATION OF ENGINEERING GEOLOGY (GW/0074-1612). [4,500] **2019**

BULLETIN OF THE INTERNATIONAL COUNCIL FOR BIRD PRESERVATION (UK). [4,000] **2189**

BULLETIN OF THE INTERNATIONAL ORGANIZATION FOR SEPTUAGINT AND COGNITE STUDIES (US/0145-3890). [500] **5046**

BULLETIN OF THE INTERNATIONAL PEAT SOCIETY (FI/0355-1008). [1,500] **1934**

BULLETIN OF THE INTERNATIONAL SEISMOLOGICAL CENTRE (UK/0020-8671). [350] **1403**

BULLETIN OF THE INTERNATIONAL STATISTICAL INSTITUTE (GW/0074-8609). [2,500] **5324**

BULLETIN OF THE JEWISH HISTORICAL SOCIETY OF ENGLAND (UK). [1,000] **5046**

BULLETIN OF THE JOHN RYLANDS UNIVERSITY LIBRARY OF MANCHESTER (UK/0301-102X). [1,000] **2843**

BULLETIN OF THE MALAYSIAN MATHEMATICAL SOCIETY (MY/0126-6705). [1,000] **3498**

BULLETIN OF THE MARX MEMORIAL LIBRARY - LONDON (UK). [2,000] **4540**

BULLETIN OF THE NATIONAL BRAILLE ASSOCIATION, INC (US/0550-5666). [2,000] **1876**

BULLETIN OF THE NATIONAL GUILD OF CATHOLIC PSYCHIATRISTS, INC, THE (US/0547-7115). [250] **3922**

BULLETIN OF THE NEW YORK ACADEMY OF MEDICINE (1925) (US/0028-7091). [4,000] **3560**

BULLETIN OF THE NEW ZEALAND NATIONAL SOCIETY FOR EARTHQUAKE ENGINEERING (NZ/0110-0718). [800] **2019**

BULLETIN OF THE OHIO BIOLOGICAL SURVEY (US/0078-3994). [1,200] **450**

BULLETIN OF THE PAN AMERICAN HEALTH ORGANIZATION (US/0301-5750). [6,000] **4769**

BULLETIN OF THE PERMANENT INTERNATIONAL ASSOCIATION OF NAVIGATION CONGRESSES (BE/0374-1001). **2088**

BULLETIN OF THE SEISMOGRAPHIC STATIONS (US/0041-9435). [450] **1403**

BULLETIN OF THE SEISMOLOGICAL SOCIETY OF AMERICA (US/0037-1106). [2,700] **1403**

BULLETIN OF THE SOUTHERN CALIFORNIA PALEONTOLOGICAL SOCIETY (US/0160-4937). [120] **4226**

BULLETIN OF THE TEXAS ORNITHOLOGICAL SOCIETY (US/0040-4543). [600] **5616**

BULLETIN OF THE UNESCO REGIONAL OFFICE OF SCIENCE AND TECHNOLOGY FOR AFRICA (KE/0304-9590). [English 1,000 French 650] **5091**

BULLETIN OF ZOOLOGICAL NOMENCLATURE, THE (UK/0007-5167). [380] **5580**

BULLETIN - OFFICE INTERNATIONAL DES EPIZOOTIES (PARIS) (FR/0300-9823). [600] **5506**

BULLETIN - ORNITHOLOGICAL SOCIETY OF THE MIDDLE EAST (UK). [850] **5616**

BULLETIN / OVERHOLSER FAMILY ASSOCIATION (US/0742-8472). [450] **2441**

BULLETIN OZANAM / SOCIETE DE SAINT-VINCENT DE PAUL, HULL ET GATINEAU (CN/0823-7883). **4941**

BULLETIN PERTAMINA (IO). [7,500] **4252**

BULLETIN / POLISH GENEALOGICAL SOCIETY, CALIFORNIA (US/1056-568X). [300] **2441**

BULLETIN - PORTLAND ART ASSOCIATION (OR.) (US/0887-4395). **345**

BULLETIN PROVINCIAL (CANADIAN CHILD AND YOUTH DRAMA ASSOCIATION. NEW BRUNSWICK) (CN/0228-8079). **5362**

BULLETIN / RESERVE BANK OF AUSTRALIA (AT/0725-0320). [4,500] **781**

BULLETIN ROUTIER; QUEBEC (CN/0226-1014). **4635**

BULLETIN - ROYAL SOCIETY OF NEW ZEALAND (NZ/0370-6559). [300] **5091**

BULLETIN / SASKATCHEWAN CHORAL FEDERATION (CN/0838-6730). [1,000] **4106**

BULLETIN - SASKATCHEWAN GENEALOGICAL SOCIETY (CN/0048-9182). [1,100] **2441**

BULLETIN SKI NAUTIQUE (CN/0824-0906). [2,000] **4888**

BULLETIN - SOCIETE CHATEAUBRIAND (FR/0081-0754). [600] **3370**

BULLETIN - SOCIETE DES AMIS DU JARDIN VAN DEN HENDE INC (CN/0711-6446). [850] **2411**

BULLETIN - SOCIETE FRANCAISE DE PHOTOGRAMMETRIE ET DE TELEDETECTION (FR/0244-6014). [650] **4367**

BULLETIN - SOCIETY FOR SPANISH AND PORTUGUESE HISTORICAL STUDIES (U.S.) (US/0739-1824). [500] **2681**

BULLETIN / SOUTH DAKOTA GEOLOGICAL SURVEY (US/0085-6479). [700] **1370**

BULLETIN / SOUTHERN CALIFORNIA ACADEMY OF SCIENCES (US/0038-3872). [600] **5092**

BULLETIN - SPECIAL LIBRARIES ASSOCIATION. GEOGRAPHY AND MAP DIVISION (US/0036-1607). [750] **2557**

BULLETIN SSQ SUR LES LOIS SOCIALES. FRANCAIS (CN/0713-8431). [85,000 French, 5,000 English] **5276**

BULLETIN TECHNIQUE DE L INSEMINATION ARTIFICIELLE (FR/0153-6281). [3,000] **5506**

BULLETIN - THE AMERICAN ASSOCIATION OF VARIABLE STAR OBSERVERS (US/0516-9518). [1,300] **394**

BULLETIN / THE DAYTON ART INSTITUTE (US/0883-9239). [4,000] **346**

BULLETIN - THE INSTITUTE OF MEAT (UK). **2329**

BULLETIN - THE MARIE SELBY BOTANICAL GARDENS (US/0197-6265). [3,300] **505**

BULLETIN - THE ST. LOUIS ART MUSEUM (US/0009-7691). [18,000] **4086**

BULLETIN (TOY TRAIN OPERATING SOCIETY : 1973) (US). **2772**

BULLETIN TRIMESTRIEL DE LA FONDATION AUSCHWITZ (BE/0772-6961). **2681**

BULLETIN - U.S. COAST GUARD ACADEMY ALUMNI ASSOCIATION (US/0191-9814). [6,400] **1101**

BULLETIN - UNDERHILL SOCIETY OF AMERICA (US/0501-0918). [1,000] **2725**

BULLETIN - UNITED BIBLE SOCIETIES (UK/0041-719X). [200] **5015**

BULLETIN (UNITED STATES. BUREAU OF JUSTICE STATISTICS) (US/0742-7271). **3079**

BULLETIN - UNIVERSITY RELATIONS AND INFORMATION OFFICE, UNIVERSITY OF MANITOBA (CN/0706-8549). [6,800] **1813**

BULLETIN - UTAH GEOLOGICAL AND MINERAL SURVEY (US/0098-4825). [1,000] **1370**

BULLETIN / VILLE DE MONT-LAURIER (CN/0710-3689). **4635**

BULLETIN - VIRGINIA MUSEUM OF FINE ARTS (US/0363-3519). [16,000] **4086**

BULLETIN VOYAGES (CN/0706-215X). [8,000] **5465**

BULLETIN / WEST TEXAS GEOLOGICAL SOCIETY (US/0739-5957). [1,800] **1371**

BULLETIN - WEST VIRGINIA SPELEOLOGICAL SURVEY (US/0161-0392). **1403**

BULLETIN / WESTERN SYDNEY CLEARINGHOUSE (AT). [350] **5227**

BULLETIN / YORKSHIRE NATURALISTS' UNION (UK/0265-6833). [500] **4164**

BULLETINS OF AMERICAN PALEONTOLOGY (US/0007-5779). [500] **4226**

BULLETTINO DELL'ISTITUTO STORICO ITALIANO PER IL MEDIO EVO E ARCHIVIO MURATORIANO (IT). **2681**

BULLISIANA (CN/0705-9108). **394**

BULWARK, THE (UK/0045-3536). [5,000] **5057**

BUNDES-TELEFONBUCH FUER DIE GEWERBLICHE WIRTSCHAFT DER BUNDESREPUBLIK DEUTSCHLAND MIT BERLIN (WEST) (GW). [8,000] **1600**

BUNDESBAHN, DIE (GW/0007-5876). [10,000] **5430**

BUNDESGESUNDHEITSBLATT (GW/0007-5914). [2,500] **4770**

BUNGEI KENKYU (JA). [750] **3370**

BUNKAGAKU NENPO (KOBE DAIGAKU. BUNKAGAKU KENKYUKA) (JA). [700] **2843**

BUNKER BANNER / BUNKER FAMILY ASSOCIATION OF AMERICA (US). [500] **2441**

BUNRIN (JA). [1,800] **3370**

BUNSEKI (JA). [9,100] **1014**

BUREAU NEWS / BUREAU OF WHOLESALE SALES REPRESENTATIVES (US/0747-4598). [14,000] **644**

BUREAU OF MINES INFORMATION CIRCULAR (US/1066-5544). [2,000] **2135**

BURGEN UND SCHLOSSER (GW/0007-6201). **2682**

BURIED HISTORY (AT/0007-6260). [500] **265**

BURIED TREASURES (US/0882-5653). [225] **2441**

BURNETT FAMILY NEWSLETTER (US/0730-4978). [100] **2441**

BURPEE GARDENS (US/0749-4653). **2411**

BUS RIDE (US/0192-8902). [12,700] **5378**

BUS RIDE: BUS INDUSTRY DIRECTORY (US/0363-3764). [2,000] **5378**

BUS VERKEHR (GW). [7,000] **5378**

BUS WORLD (US/0162-9689). [5,500] **5378**

BUSH FIRE BULLETIN (AT). [30,000] **2288**

BUSINESS ACCOUNTING FOR LAWYERS NEWSLETTER / PRACTISING LAW INSTITUTE (US/0885-1034). [3,500] **3096**

BUSINESS ADVISORY REVIEW (CN/0823-9665). **645**

BUSINESS AND COMMERCIAL AVIATION (US/0191-4642). [52,000] **15**

BUSINESS AND FINANCE IN SCOTLAND (UK). [14,500] **781**

BUSINESS & INDUSTRY (US/0021-0463). [12000] **645**

BUSINESS & MANAGEMENT EDUCATION FUNDING ALERT (US/1042-5217). [225] **1813**

BUSINESS AND SOCIETY (US/0007-6503). [2,500] **645**

BUSINESS & TELECOM (NEDERLANDSE ED.) (BE/0778-7588). [16000] **645**

BUSINESS AVIATION SAFETY (US/0890-8664). [20,000] **15**

BUSINESS BOOK REVIEW (US/0741-8132). [3,000] **646**

BUSINESS COMMUNICATIONS REVIEW (US/0162-3885). [6,000] **646**

BUSINESS COMPUTER NEWS (CN/0838-438X). [16,000] **646**

BUSINESS CREDIT (US/0897-0181). [35,000] **781**

BUSINESS DAY'S 1000 TOP CORPORATIONS IN THE PHILIPPINES (PH). [2,000] **647**

BUSINESS DIGEST (US/1046-168X). [24] **647**

BUSINESS DIGEST (DANBURY, CONN.) (US/8750-9520). [6,500] **647**

BUSINESS DIRECTIONS (AT/1031-2315). [10,000] **647**

BUSINESS DYNAMICS (100 MILE HOUSE) (CN/0831-7291). [1,000] **647**

BUSINESS ECONOMICS (CLEVELAND, OHIO) (US/0007-666X). [4,600] **1466**

BUSINESS ECONOMICS. MEMBERSHIP DIRECTORY (US). [4000] **1466**

BUSINESS EDUCATION FORUM (US/0007-6678). [17,000] **647**

BUSINESS EDUCATION INDEX (US/0068-4414). [10,000] **727**

BUSINESS EDUCATION NEWS (FREDERICTON) (CN/0710-7714). **647**

BUSINESS EDUCATION TODAY (UK). [7,000-8,000] **1729**

BUSINESS EDUCATION TODAY (UK/0951-1512). [6,000] **647**

BUSINESS ETHICS RESOURCE (US/1064-0223). [1,400] **648**

BUSINESS FACILITIES (US/0746-0023). [30000] **648**

BUSINESS FIRST (COLUMBUS, OHIO) (US/0748-6146). [13,500] **648**

BUSINESS FOR CENTRAL NEW JERSEY (US/1042-8704). [13,000] **862**

BUSINESS GUIDE, THE (CN/0847-3900). **648**

BUSINESS HISTORY REVIEW (US/0007-6805). [2,100] **648**

BUSINESS IDEAS NEWSLETTER (US/0738-7024). [4,000] **649**

BUSINESS IN BROWARD (US). [20,000] **1466**

BUSINESS IN PALM BEACH COUNTY (US). [15,000] **649**

BUSINESS IN THAILAND (TH/0125-0140). [16,000] **649**

BUSINESS INDIA (II/0254-5268). [90,000] **649**

BUSINESS INDICATORS (AT). [45,000] **649**

BUSINESS INFORMATION REVIEW (UK/0266-3821). [600] **3199**

BUSINESS INSIGHT (US/1056-6244). [9,000] **649**

BUSINESS JOURNAL (1988), THE (US/1048-8812). [15,000] **649**

BUSINESS JOURNAL (NEW YORK) (US). [9,500] **649**

BUSINESS JOURNAL OF UPPER EAST TENNESSEE AND SOUTHWEST VIRGINIA (US/1040-6360). **650**

BUSINESS JOURNAL / SONOMA & MARIN (US). [8,500] **650**

BUSINESS LAWYER, THE (US/0007-6899). [60,000] **3097**

BUSINESS LIBRARY NEWSLETTER (US/0191-4006). [400] **3199**

BUSINESS (LUXEMBOURG) (LU). [6,000] **650**

BUSINESS MARKETING (US/0745-5933). [46,000] **922**

BUSINESS MEXICO (MX/0187-1455). [10,000] **650**

BUSINESS NEW HAMPSHIRE MAGAZINE (US/1046-9575). [13,000] **650**

BUSINESS NEWS (EUGENE, OR.), THE (US/1064-1661). [35,000] **651**

BUSINESS, NORTH CAROLINA (US/0279-4276). [26,000] **651**

BUSINESS OF FUR, THE (US/0740-6258). [8,000] **3183**

BUSINESS OPINION (NZ). [1,000] **651**

BUSINESS OPPORTUNITIES JOURNAL (US/0193-3221). [102,000] **893**

BUSINESS OUTLOOK FOR WEST MICHIGAN (US). [600] **651**

BUSINESS PEOPLE MAGAZINE (WINNIPEG. 1990) (CN/0849-3901). [11,000] **651**

BUSINESS PERIODICALS INDEX (US/0007-6961). **727**

BUSINESS PERIODICALS INDEX. CD-ROM (US/0007-6961). **727**

BUSINESS PRESS (CN/0707-493X). **651**

BUSINESS QUEENSLAND (AT/1038-1430). [14,000] **652**

BUSINESS RADIO (US/0746-8911). [3,000] **1150**

BUSINESS REVIEW (MONTREAL) (CN/0005-531X). [12,000] **652**

BUSINESS REVIEW (PHILADELPHIA) (US/0007-7011). [20,000] **1467**

BUSINESS TIMES (EAST HARTFORD, CONN.), THE (US/0744-172X). [30,000] **653**

BUSINESS TODAY (US/0007-7100). [200,000] **653**

BUSINESS TOKYO (JA/0914-0026). **653**

BUSINESS TRAVEL MANAGEMENT (US/1046-5057). [40,000] **653**

BUSINESS TRAVEL NEWS (US/8750-3670). [52,462] **653**

BUSINESS UPDATE (SANTA ANA, CALIF.) (US/8750-7803). [15,600] **818**

BUSINESS WORCESTER (US/0738-8977). [16,000] **654**

BUSINESSGRAM (TAMPA, FLA.) (US/1064-2412). **654**

BUSINESSWEST (SPRINGFIELD, MASS.) (US/1049-9822). [12,000] **654**

BUSSEIKEN DAYORI (TOKYO) (JA/0385-9843). [630] **4427**

BUTCHER & PROCESSOR (UK/0268-1781). [10,000] **2329**

BUTTERICK HOME CATALOG (1985) (US/0895-6871). [200,000] **5183**

BUTTERWORTHS CURRENT LAW (NZ/0110-070X). **3125**

BUTTERWORTHS INDEX AND NOTER-UP TO THE SOUTH AFRICAN LAW REPORTS (SA). **2945**

BUTTERWORTHS LEGAL SERVICES DIRECTORY (UK). **3159**

BUYER (MONITOR PRESS) (UK). **949**

BUYERS' GUIDE & DEALER DIRECTORY: NORTHEASTERN AREA (US/0145-5915). [3,400] **826**

BUYERS GUIDE - NATIONAL TOOLING & MACHINING ASSOCIATION (US/0736-7112). [25,000] **949**

BUYING FOR LIBRARIES (UK). [15,000] **3199**

BVDA JOURNAL : BRITISH VETERINARY DENTAL ASSOCIATION (UK). [130] **5507**

BYGG & TEKNIK (SW/0281-658X). [6,500] **606**

BYGGEKUNST (NO/0007-7518). [5,440] **294**

BYLAWS, RULES, AND SPECIFICATIONS - WOMEN'S INTERNATIONAL BOWLING CONGRESS (US/0191-1902). **4888**

BYLINE (EVANSTON, ILL.) (US/0731-5449). [2,000] **2917**

BYOIN YAKUGAKU (JA/0389-9098). [5,000] **4295**

BYRON JOURNAL (UK/0301-7257). [3,000] **3339**

BYTE BUYER, THE (US/0889-8200). [50,000] **1172**

BYTOWN TIMES (CN/0712-2799). [500] **2916**

BYU JOURNAL OF PUBLIC LAW, THE (US/0896-2383). [250] **2945**

BYZANTINE STUDIES (US/0095-4608). **2682**

C A F C DIALOGUE (CN/0706-1382). **2288**

C A L ANTHOLOGY (US). [1,000] **3370**

C/A/S/E OUTLOOK (US/0895-2108). [1000] **1172**

C. B. REVIEW (PH/0115-1401). [4,500] **1467**

C.C.A.I. MONTHLY NEWSLETTER (II/0376-7787). [3,000] **1294**

C C C N (CALIFORNIA COMMUNITY CARE NEWS) (US). [15,000] **2529**

C C U M C LEADER (US). [300] **1813**

C.F.A. DIGEST, THE (US/0046-9777). [12,000] **781**

C. H. A. C. REVIEW (CN/0226-5923). [1,500] **3777**

C.H.W. LETTER (CN/0834-1508). **893**

C I E N, CANADIAN INDUSTRIAL EQUIPMENT NEWS (CN/0319-5902). [35,000] **3476**

C I M REPORTER (CN/0701-0710). [6,200] **2136**

C O R S BULLETIN (CN/0315-1417). [600] **1236**

C P H A HEALTH DIGEST (CN/0703-5624). [4,000] **4770**

C S S E NEWS (CN/0382-8018). [1,100] **1730**

CA SELECTS: CHEMISTRY OF IR, OS, RH, & RU (US/1040-7146). **999**

CA SELECTS: COMPOSITE MATERIALS (POLYMERIC) (US/1040-7154). **1000**

Controlled Circulation Index

CA SELECTS. FOOD, DRUGS, & COSMETICS (US/1051-3914). **1002**

CA SELECTS: HEAT-RESISTANT & ABLATIVE POLYMERS (US/0162-7821). **1003**

CA SELECTS: NITROGEN FIXATION (US/1047-8108). **1005**

CA SELECTS: OMEGA THREE FATTY ACIDS & FISH OIL (US/1052-1984). **1006**

CA SELECTS: ORGANIC REACTION MECHANISMS (US/0162-7848). **1006**

CA SELECTS: ORGANOPHOSPHORUS CHEMISTRY (US/0162-783X). **1006**

CA SELECTS: ORGANOSULFUR CHEMISTRY (JOURNALS) (US/1040-7189). **1006**

CA SELECTS: THERMOCHEMISTRY (US/0162-7864). **1010**

CAAS NEWS (US/8755-3732). [1,000] **4835**

CAB, CURRENT AWARENESS BULLETIN (US). [4,200] **3999**

CABINETMAKER (CHICAGO, ILL.) (US/1048-0196). [27,000] **633**

CABLE TV ADVERTISING (US/0270-885X). **756**

CABLE WEEK. ORANGE-SEMINOLE-OSEOLA ED (US/0744-2327). [12,000] **1129**

CABLE WORLD (US/1042-7228). [14,000] **1150**

CABLESPORTS NEWSLETTER (US). [150] **1129**

CAC NEWS - CHICAGO ARTISTS' COALITION (US/0890-5908). [3,000] **346**

CACD JOURNAL (US/1052-3103). [3,000] **5276**

CACHE REGISTER, THE (US/0731-079X). [250] **1236**

CACTUS AND SUCCULENT JOURNAL WOOLLAHRA (AT/0526-7196). [400] **2411**

CAD CAM (UK). [20,000] **1231**

CAD/CAM ABSTRACTS (US/0882-1437). **1231**

CAD CAM REPORT (GW). **1227**

CAD USER (UK/0959-6259). [21,407] **1222**

CADDET NEWSLETTER (NE). **1934**

CADENCE (US/0162-6973). **4106**

CADENZA (LOLO, MONT.) (US/0007-9405). [1,100] **4106**

CADERNOS FUNDAP (BL/0101-3211). [2,500] **4466**

CAFE SOLO (US/0007-9537). [500] **3461**

CAHIERS AFRICAINS D'ADMINISTRATION PUBLIQUE (MR/0007-9588). [750] **4635**

CAHIERS DE BIOLOGIE MARINE (FR/0007-9723). **553**

CAHIERS DE CIVILISATION MEDIEVALE (FR/0007-9731). **2682**

CAHIERS DE LA CINEMATHEQUE, LES (FR/0764-8499). **4064**

CAHIERS DE LA DOCUMENTATION (BE/0007-9804). [300] **3199**

CAHIERS DE LA FONDATION, LES (FR/0983-1851). **654**

CAHIERS DE LA NOUVELLE, LES (FR/0294-0442). [200] **3271**

CAHIERS DE LA SEIGNEURIE DE CHAMBLY (CN/0228-0930). [500] **2725**

CAHIERS DE L'ACADEMIE (MONTREAL) (CN/0824-6602). [200] **2784**

CAHIERS DE L'ARMUQ, LES (CN/0821-1817). **4106**

CAHIERS DE LEXICOLOGIE (FR/0007-9871). [2,000] **3271**

CAHIERS DE MEDECINE DU TRAVAIL (BE/0376-7639). **3561**

CAHIERS DE NUTRITION ET DE DIETETIQUE (FR/0007-9960). **4188**

CAHIERS DE SOCIOLOGIE ECONOMIQUE ET CULTURELLE, ETHNOPSYCHOLOGIE (FR/0761-9871). [50] **5241**

CAHIERS DE TOPOLOGIE ET GEOMETRIE DIFFERENTIELLE CATEGORIQUES (FR). [500] **3499**

CAHIERS DES AMERIQUES LATINES (PARIS, FRANCE : 1985) (FR). [600] **2725**

CAHIERS DES COMITES DE PREVENTION DU BATIMENT ET DES TRAVAUX PUBLICS (FR/0010-244X). [18,000] **2860**

CAHIERS DES RELIGIONS AFRICAINES (CG/0008-0047). [1,000] **4942**

CAHIERS D'HISTOIRE DE LA SOCIETE D'HISTOIRE DE BELOEIL-MONT-SAINT-HILAIRE, LES (CN/0225-5359). [400] **2612**

CAHIERS D'HISTOIRE (MONTREAL) (CN/0712-2330). [350] **2613**

CAHIERS D'OUTRE-MER (FR/0373-5834). [1,200] **2557**

CAHIERS DU CENTRE SCIENTIFIQUE ET TECHNIQUE DU BATIMENT (FR/0008-9850). [3,500] **5092**

CAHIERS DU CINEMA (FR/0008-011X). [40,000] **4064**

CAHIERS DU CREDIT MUTUEL (FR/0395-8175). [15,000] **781**

CAHIERS DU LABRAPS (CN/0824-0736). [200] **1813**

CAHIERS DU MONDE RUSSE ET SOVIETIQUE (FR/0008-0160). [550] **2682**

CAHIERS ECONOMIQUES (BE). **1530**

CAHIERS ECONOMIQUES ET MONETAIRES (FR/0396-4701). [2,500] **781**

CAHIERS ECONOMIQUES ET SOCIAUX (KINSHASA) (CG/0008-0209). **1550**

CAHIERS JEAN GIRAUDOUX (FR/0150-6943). [2,000] **3371**

CAHIERS PAUL-LOUIS COURIER (FR/0084-8239). [300] **3371**

CAHIERS PEDAGOGIQUES (FEDERATION DES CERCLES DE RECHERCHE ET D'ACTION PEDAGOGIQUES (FRANCE)) (FR). [8,000] **1730**

CAHIERS QUEBECOIS DE DEMOGRAPHIE (CN/0380-1721). [800] **4550**

CAHIERS SAINT DOMINIQUE (FR). [2,000] **5025**

CAHIERS SIMONE WEIL (FR/0181-1126). [600] **4343**

CAHIERS VERTS DE L'ECONOMIE PARIS, LES (FR/1167-5217). [400] **1467**

CAHS JOURNAL, THE (CN/0007-7771). [1,300] **15**

CAI NEWS / WASHINGTON METROPOLITAN CHAPTER (US/0277-2949). [3,000] **654**

CAIMAN BARBUDO (MICROFICHE) (CU). [20,000] **3339**

CAIRN, THE (CN/0701-0281). [3,000] **4086**

CAJANUS (JM/0376-7655). [2,500] **4188**

CAL-OSHA REPORTER (US/1054-1209). [1,080] **2860**

CALDWELL COUNTY GENEALOGICAL SOCIETY, INC (US/0747-4849). [225] **2441**

CALENDAR OF COLLECTIVE BARGAINING, NEW YORK STATE (US). [1,500] **1657**

CALENDAR OF EVENTS (VICTORIA. 1979) (CN/0709-2121). **2486**

CALENDAR YEAR REPORT / NATIONAL MANPOWER AND YOUTH COUNCIL (PH). [2,000] **1657**

CALGARY SUN (CN). [70,000 daily 96,000 Sunday] **5781**

CALICO JOURNAL (US/0742-7778). [6,000] **1222**

CALIFORNIA AGRICULTURAL DIRECTORY (BERKELEY, CALIF.) (US/0575-5298). [1,000] **71**

CALIFORNIA AGRICULTURAL EXPORTER (US). [12,000] **71**

CALIFORNIA APPAREL NEWS (US/0008-0896). [15,000] **1082**

CALIFORNIA BLUE BOOK (US). [10,000] **1082**

CALIFORNIA BOWLING NEWS (US/0008-0918). [15,000] **4889**

CALIFORNIA BUILDER (US/0527-2009). [10,000] **606**

CALIFORNIA BUSINESS (US/0008-0926). [70,000] **654**

CALIFORNIA CATTLEMAN (US/0008-0942). [4,300] **208**

CALIFORNIA, CITIES, TOWNS & COUNTIES (US/0891-2718). **4636**

CALIFORNIA CONNECTIONS PUBLICATIONS (US/0893-0694). **1658**

CALIFORNIA ECONOMIC INDICATORS (US/0364-2895). [500] **1550**

CALIFORNIA ENGINEER (US/0008-1027). [10,000] **1967**

CALIFORNIA EYE, THE (US/0279-0246). [250] **4466**

CALIFORNIA FISH AND GAME (US/0008-1078). [2,000] **2189**

CALIFORNIA FORESTRY NOTE (US/0889-0102). [750] **2377**

CALIFORNIA GEOGRAPHER, THE (US/0575-5700). [500] **2557**

CALIFORNIA GROWER (VISTA, CALIF.) (US/0888-1715). [5,000] **71**

CALIFORNIA HAZARDOUS MATERIALS PROGRAM COMMENTARY (CN). **2226**

CALIFORNIA HAZARDOUS MATERIALS PROGRAM MATRIX (CN). **2226**

CALIFORNIA HEALTH LAW REPORT (US). [350] **2946**

CALIFORNIA HIGH WATER (1979-80) (US). [600] **1413**

CALIFORNIA HIGHWAY PATROLMAN, THE (US/0008-1140). [20,000] **3159**

CALIFORNIA HISTORY ACTION (US/0882-357X). [200] **2725**

CALIFORNIA HOSPITALS (US/0896-2766). **3777**

CALIFORNIA INNTOUCH (US/0274-6093). [7,300] **2804**

CALIFORNIA INTERNATIONAL TRADE REGISTER (US/0270-4862). [1,000] **1467**

CALIFORNIA LAWYER (US/0279-4063). [140,000] **2946**

CALIFORNIA LIBRARIES (US/1056-1528). [2,500] **3199**

CALIFORNIA MANUFACTURERS REGISTER (US/0068-5739). [5,000] **3476**

CALIFORNIA MONTHLY (US/0008-1302). [90,000] **1090**

CALIFORNIA MUNICIPAL BOND ADVISOR (US/0749-2375). **893**

CALIFORNIA ORNAMENTAL CROPS REPORT (US/0744-2653). [200] **2435**

CALIFORNIA PARALEGAL MAGAZINE (US/1040-2640). [2,000] **2946**

CALIFORNIA PARKS & RECREATION (US/0733-5326). [4,000] **4706**

CALIFORNIA PEACE OFFICER, THE (US/0199-7025). [11,600] **3159**

CALIFORNIA PEDIATRICIAN (US/0882-3421). [5,000] **3901**

CALIFORNIA PHARMACIST (US/0739-0483). [6,300] **4295**

CALIFORNIA POLICY CHOICES (US/0742-0927). [1,500] **4636**

CALIFORNIA POLL, THE (US/0195-4520). [300] **4561**

CALIFORNIA PSYCHOLOGIST, THE (US/0890-0302). [3,200] **4579**

CALIFORNIA PUBLIC EMPLOYEE RELATIONS : CPER SERIES (US/0194-3073). [700] **1658**

CALIFORNIA REGULATORY LAW REPORTER, THE (US/0739-7860). [1,500] **2946**

CALIFORNIA REGULATORY NOTICE REGISTER (US/1041-2654). [950] **2946**

CALIFORNIA SCHOOL EMPLOYEE, THE (US/0008-1515). [92,000] **1861**

CALIFORNIA SENIOR CITIZEN (US/0748-5727). [69,000] **5633**

CALIFORNIA SERVICES REGISTER (US/0271-6615). [1,500] **654**

CALIFORNIA STAATS-ZEITUNG (US/0890-1473). **5633**

CALIFORNIA STRAWBERRY REPORT (US/0194-8504). [100] **2330**

CALIFORNIA VOTER (US). [15,000] **4466**

CALIFORNIA WATER PLAN OUTLOOK, THE (US/0147-9164). [1,000] **5531**

CALIFORNIA WESTERN INTERNATIONAL LAW JOURNAL (US/0886-3210). [600] **3125**

CALIFORNIA WESTERN LAW REVIEW (US/0008-1639). [1,400] **2947**

CALIFORNIA WOMAN, THE (US/0008-1663). [12,000] **5552**

CALIFORNIA WORKERS' COMPENSATION REPORTER (US/0363-129X). [1,350] **3145**

CALIOPE Y POLIMNIA : REVISTA DE POESIA Y CUENTOS (SP). [4,600] **3461**

CALIPER (TORONTO) (CN/0045-4001). [5,000] **4385**

CALL BOARD (SAN FRANCISCO, CALIF.) (US/1064-0703). **5362**

CALL-NEWS DISPATCH, THE (US). [3,300] **5625**

CALL OF THE PLATEAU (US/0575-6383). [100] **2726**

CALL SHEET / SCREEN ACTORS GUILD (US). [75,000] **4064**

CALLALOO (US/0161-2492). [1,000] **3371**

CALLBOARD (CN). [1,200] **5362**

CALLIOPE (BRISTOL, R.I.) (US/0889-7158). [550] **3371**

CALVACADE OF ACTS & ATTRACTIONS (US). [7,000] **384**

CALVINIST CONTACT (CN/0410-3882). [7,000] **5057**

CALZADO Y TENERIA (MX). [3,500] **1082**

CAM MAGAZINE (US/0883-7880). [4,000] **606**

CAMAGUEYANO, EL (US). [2,250] **2726**

CAMBRIA COUNTY LEGAL JOURNAL (US). **2947**

CAMBRIDGE FUTURES CHARTS (UK/0961-0480). **1467**

CAMBRIDGE REVIEW, THE (UK/0008-2007). [1,000,000] **1090**

CAMELLIA JOURNAL, THE (US/0008-204X). [4,000] **2411**

CAMERA AUSTRIA INTERNATIONAL (AU). [3,000] **4368**

CAMERA CANADA (CN/0008-2090). [2,500] **4368**

CAMERA OBSCURA (BERKELEY) (US/0270-5346). [3,000] **4065**

CAMERAWORK (US). **4368**

CAMERON HERALD (CAMERON, TEX.) (US). [7,000] **5747**

CAMERON'S READYART BULLETIN (US/0894-8186). **346**

CAMINUS QUARTERLY POOL PRICE REVIEW (UK). [50] **2037**

CAMLS NEWS (US/0730-093X). [900] **3199**

CAMP FIRE LEADERSHIP (US/0092-1289). [45,000] **5229**

CAMP RESORT LAW REPORT (US/0748-2396). [200] **2947**

CAMPAIGN AUSTRALIA (AT). [16,000] **2793**

CAMPBELL RIVER UPPER ISLANDER, THE (CN/0318-9538). [8,000] **5781**

CAMPBELL'S LIST (US/0742-8987). [6,500] **2947**

CAMPESINO, EL (CL). [10,000] **71**

CAMPING AND RV MAGAZINE (US/0896-5706). [13,500] **4849**

CAMPING CANADA (CN/0384-9856). [56,000] **4870**

CAMPING-FUHRER. BAND 1: SUDEUROPA (GW). [280,000] **4870**

CAMPING FUHRER BAND II : DEUTSCHLAND, MITTEL- UND NORD-EUROPA (GW). [90,226] **4870**

CAMPING TRAILER & TRAVEL TRAILER TRADE-IN-GUIDE (US/0736-1939). **5378**

CAMPUS ACTIVITIES PROGRAMMING (US/0746-2328). [6,500] **1813**

CAMPUS CANADA (TORONTO, ONT.) (CN/0829-3309). **1090**

CAMPUS OUTREACH (US/1046-6975). [2,000] **1813**

CAMPUS REPORT (STANFORD) (US/0049-2108). [16,000] **1090**

CAMPUS SAFETY REPORT NEWSLETTER (US/0885-3398). [200] **4770**

CANADA CHINCHILLA (CN/0823-2504). [400] **5507**

CANADA HEALTH ACT ANNUAL REPORT (CN/0842-3202). [1,200] **5276**

CANADA JOURNAL (DEUTSCHE AUSG.) (CN/0829-0814). [14,000] **654**

CANADA LEGAL DIRECTORY (CN/0315-8322). **3139**

CANADA OFFSHORE BUYERS GUIDE (CN/0822-8698). [6,000] **4252**

CANADA POULTRYMAN (CN/0008-2732). [9,000] **208**

CANADA QUILTS (CN/0381-7369). [3,500] **5183**

CANADA TODAY (WASHINGTON) (US/0045-4257). [80,000] **2529**

CANADA (WASHINGTON, D.C. 1985) (US/0883-8135). **2726**

CANADA YEARBOOK (CN/0068-8142). [10,000] **1923**

CANADA'S WHO'S WHO OF THE POULTRY INDUSTRY (CN/0068-8134). [7,000] **431**

CANADEAN WORLD NEW PRODUCTS (UK/0260-7352). **2330**

CANADIAN ADVENTIST MESSENGER (CN/0702-5084). [13,400] **5057**

CANADIAN AIRCRAFT OPERATOR, THE (CN/0008-2848). [8,200] **15**

CANADIAN ALPINE JOURNAL, THE (CN/0068-8207). [3,000] **4870**

CANADIAN AMATEUR (1987) (CN/0834-3977). [5,000] **2037**

CANADIAN-AMERICAN SLAVIC STUDIES (US/0090-8290). [700] **2683**

CANADIAN AMPUTEE SPORTS ASSOCIATION (CN/0823-6674). **4889**

CANADIAN APPRAISER, THE (CN/0827-2697). [6,600] **4835**

CANADIAN ARABIAN HORSE STUD BOOK (CN). [1,700] **2797**

CANADIAN AUCTIONEER, THE (CN/0823-6429). [800] **862**

CANADIAN AUTHOR & BOOKMAN (CN/0008-2937). [6,000] **3372**

CANADIAN AVIATION NEWS (1984) (CN/0829-2132). [10,000] **15**

CANADIAN AYRSHIRE REVIEW (CN/0008-2961). [1,800] **72**

CANADIAN BANKER (1983) (CN/0822-6830). [36,384] **782**

CANADIAN BANKING REVIEW / CANADIAN BOND RATING SERVICE (CN/0836-3021). [300] **727**

CANADIAN BAR REVIEW. REVUE DU BARREAU CANADIEN, THE (CN/0008-3003). [35,000] **2947**

CANADIAN BAR REVIEW, THE (CN/0008-3003). [34,000] **3125**

CANADIAN BIKER MAGAZINE, THE (CN/0820-8344). [20,000] **4080**

CANADIAN BOOK OF CHARITIES (CN/0226-0409). [13,000] **5276**

CANADIAN BOOKSELLER (TORONTO) (CN/0225-2392). [1,300] **4827**

CANADIAN BUSINESS REVIEW, THE (CN/0317-4026). [10,000] **1467**

CANADIAN CAVER, THE (CN/0833-0948). [200] **4870**

CANADIAN CERAMICS QUARTERLY (CN/0831-2974). [1,000] **2587**

CANADIAN CHILDREN'S LITERATURE (CN/0319-0080). [1,000] **3372**

CANADIAN CIVIL ENGINEER (CN/0825-7515). [7,500] **2020**

CANADIAN CONSTRUCTION CATALOGUE FILE (CN/0082-0431). [22,000] **606**

CANADIAN CONSUMER (1963) (CN/0008-3275). [150,000] **1294**

CANADIAN CONTROLS AND INSTRUMENTATION. BUYERS' GUIDE (CN). [40,000] **3476**

CANADIAN COPPER (CN/0008-3291). [15,000] **3999**

CANADIAN CREDIT REVIEW (CN/0827-4312). [700] **782**

CANADIAN CRITICAL CARE NURSING JOURNAL (CN/0826-6778). [4,500] **3852**

CANADIAN CURLING NEWS (CN/0045-4648). [10,000] **4889**

CANADIAN DANCERS NEWS (1988) (CN/0843-218X). [1,200] **1311**

CANADIAN DEFENCE QUARTERLY (TORONTO) (CN/0315-3495). [10,000] **4038**

CANADIAN DISCIPLE (CN/0008-3410). [600] **4942**

CANADIAN EDUCATION INDEX (CN/0008-3453). [400] **1793**

CANADIAN EMERGENCY NEWS (CN/0847-947X). [4,000] **4770**

CANADIAN ENVIRONMENTAL PROTECTION (CN). **2162**

CANADIAN FACILITY MANAGEMENT & DESIGN (CN/1193-7505). **863**

CANADIAN FAMILY LAW QUARTERLY (CN/0832-6983). **3119**

CANADIAN FAMILY PHYSICIAN (CN/0008-350X). [25,000] **3737**

CANADIAN FAR EASTERN NEWSLETTER, THE (CN/0045-4737). [1,500] **4517**

CANADIAN FICTION MAGAZINE (CN/0045-477X). [1,000] **3372**

CANADIAN FIREFIGHTER, THE (CN/0704-6391). [12,000] **2288**

CANADIAN FISHERIES. ANNUAL STATISTICAL REVIEW / ECONOMIC POLICY BRANCH, ECONOMIC DEVELOPMENT DIRECTORATE, FISHERIES AND OCEANS (CN). [1,000] **2317**

CANADIAN FLIGHT (CN/0008-3577). [20,000] **16**

CANADIAN FOLK MUSIC BULLETIN (CN/0829-5344). [1,000] **4107**

CANADIAN FOOTWEAR JOURNAL (CN/0705-1433). [9,000] **1082**

CANADIAN FRUITGROWER (CN/0045-4885). [4,000] **2412**

CANADIAN FUNERAL DIRECTOR (CN/0319-3225). [1,635] **2406**

CANADIAN FURNITURE AND FURNISHINGS DIRECTORY (CN/0826-6204). [7,412] **2904**

CANADIAN GAS FACTS (CN/0316-3547). [2,000] **4760**

CANADIAN GEMMOLOGIST (CN/0226-7446). [1,000] **2913**

CANADIAN GENERAL AVIATION NEWS (CN/0226-5648). [20,000] **16**

CANADIAN GEOGRAPHER (CN/0008-3658). [2,400] **2558**

CANADIAN GEOTECHNICAL JOURNAL (CN/0008-3674). [2,800] **1352**

CANADIAN GIDEON (CN/0316-2907). [4,200] **4942**

CANADIAN GUERNSEY JOURNAL (CN/0831-3008). [500] **192**

CANADIAN GUIDE (CN/0008-3712). [2,000] **2530**

CANADIAN GUIDER (CN/0300-435X). [55,000] **1730**

CANADIAN HEAVY EQUIPMENT GUIDE (CN/0832-6533). **606**

CANADIAN HEREFORD DIGEST (CN/0008-3739). [3,300] **208**

CANADIAN HISTORICAL REVIEW (CN/0008-3755). [3,000] **2726**

CANADIAN HOME ECONOMICS JOURNAL (CN/0008-3763). [3,300] **2789**

CANADIAN HOSPITAL DIRECTORY (CN/0068-8932). [4,500] **3777**

CANADIAN HOUSING (CN/0826-7278). [10,000] **2817**

CANADIAN HOUSING. MONTHLY ANALYSIS (CN/0823-020X). [300] **2817**

CANADIAN HUMAN RIGHT REPORTER (CN/0226-2177). [800] **4505**

CANADIAN INDEPENDENT ADJUSTER, THE (CN/0008-3828). [5,000] **2877**

CANADIAN INDIA STAR, THE (CN/0319-8715). [5,000] **2648**

CANADIAN INFORMATION INDUSTRY ASSOCIATION (CN/0227-8804). **3199**

CANADIAN INSURANCE (CN/0008-3879). [11,000] **2877**

CANADIAN INTELLIGENCE SERVICE (CN/0576-5501). [2,400] **4636**

CANADIAN INVESTMENT REVIEW (CN/0840-6863). [8,100] **894**

CANADIAN IRIS SOCIETY NEWSLETTER (CN/0715-3775). [470] **5229**

CANADIAN JERSEY BREEDER (CN/0008-3909). [1,800] **208**

CANADIAN JEWELLER (CN/0008-3917). [7,000] **2913**

CANADIAN JOURNAL OF ARCHAEOLOGY (CN/0705-2006). [600] **265**

CANADIAN JOURNAL OF BEHAVIOURAL SCIENCE (CN/0008-400X). [2,500] **4579**

CANADIAN JOURNAL OF BOTANY (CN/0008-4026). [2,000] **505**

CANADIAN JOURNAL OF CARDIOVASCULAR NURSING (CN/0843-6096). [700] **3700**

CANADIAN JOURNAL OF CHEMISTRY (CN/0008-4042). [2,300] **966**

CANADIAN JOURNAL OF CIVIL ENGINEERING (CN/0315-1468). [5,474] **2020**

CANADIAN JOURNAL OF COMMUNICATION (CN/0705-3657). [400] **1105**

CANADIAN JOURNAL OF COUNSELLING (CN/0828-3893). [1,300] **1876**

CANADIAN JOURNAL OF CRIMINOLOGY (CN/0704-9722). [1,200] **3159**

CANADIAN JOURNAL OF EDUCATION (CN/0380-2361). [1,200] **1730**

CANADIAN JOURNAL OF EXPERIMENTAL PSYCHOLOGY (CN/1196-1961). **4579**

CANADIAN JOURNAL OF GASTROENTEROLOGY, THE (CN/0835-7900). [18,500] **3743**

CANADIAN JOURNAL OF GERIATRICS, THE (CN/0845-2970). [24,000] **3750**

CANADIAN JOURNAL OF INFORMATION SCIENCE (CN/0380-9218). [400] **3199**

CANADIAN JOURNAL OF IRISH STUDIES, THE (CN/0703-1459). [800] **3372**

CANADIAN JOURNAL OF LAW AND SOCIETY (CN/0829-3201). [300] **2948**

CANADIAN JOURNAL OF MATHEMATICS (CN/0008-414X). [1,200] **3499**

CANADIAN JOURNAL OF MEDICAL TECHNOLOGY (CN/0008-4158). [22,500] **3562**

CANADIAN JOURNAL OF MICROBIOLOGY (CN/0008-4166). [2,300] **560**

CANADIAN JOURNAL OF NETHERLANDIC STUDIES (CN/0225-0500). [350] **2683**

CANADIAN JOURNAL OF OPTOMETRY (CN/0045-5075). [3,000] **4215**

CANADIAN JOURNAL OF PHILOSOPHY (CN/0045-5091). [1,000] **4343**

CANADIAN JOURNAL OF PSYCHIATRY (CN/0706-7437). [3,300] **3923**

CANADIAN JOURNAL OF PSYCHOLOGY (CN/0008-4255). [2,200] **4579**

CANADIAN JOURNAL OF PUBLIC HEALTH (CN/0008-4263). [4,000] **4770**

CANADIAN JOURNAL OF SPORT SCIENCES (US/0833-1235). [1,300] **3953**

CANADIAN JOURNAL OF VETERINARY RESEARCH (CN/0830-9000). **5507**

CANADIAN — Controlled Circulation Index

CANADIAN LAWYER (CN/0703-2129). [29,816] **2948**

CANADIAN LIBRARY JOURNAL (CN/0008-4352). [6,000] **3200**

CANADIAN MACHINERY AND METALWORKING (CN/0008-4379). [16,000] **2111**

CANADIAN MANAGER (CN/0045-5156). [5,200] **863**

CANADIAN MATHEMATICAL BULLETIN (CN/0008-4395). [1,000] **3499**

CANADIAN MINING JOURNAL (CN/0008-4492). [10,470] **2136**

CANADIAN MULTICULTURAL SCENE (CN/0707-7300). **2258**

CANADIAN MUSIC EDUCATOR, THE (CN/0008-4549). [2,600] **4107**

CANADIAN MUSLIM, THE (CN/0707-2945). **5042**

CANADIAN NATURAL GAS FOCUS (CN/0847-0316). [200] **4253**

CANADIAN NEWS INDEX (TORONTO) (CN/0225-7459). **5781**

CANADIAN NEWSLETTER FOR OPEN GOVERNMENT, THE (CN/0703-1378). **4636**

CANADIAN NUMISMATIC JOURNAL, THE (CN/0008-4573). [2,300] **2780**

CANADIAN OCCUPATIONAL SAFETY (CN/0008-4611). [10,500] **2860**

CANADIAN OIL REGISTER (CN/0068-9394). [4,500] **4253**

CANADIAN OPERATING ROOM NURSING JOURNAL (CN/0712-6778). [5,000] **3853**

CANADIAN PARLIAMENTARY GUIDE (CN/0315-6168). [3,800] **4636**

CANADIAN PHILATELIST (CN/0045-5253). [6,000] **2784**

CANADIAN PHILOSOPHICAL REVIEWS (CN/0228-491X). [350] **4343**

CANADIAN PLAINS BULLETIN (CN/0316-0343). [4,500] **2726**

CANADIAN PLASTICS (CN/0008-4778). [11,000] **4454**

CANADIAN PLASTICS DIRECTORY & BUYER'S GUIDE (CN/0068-9459). [11,500] **4454**

CANADIAN POLICE CHIEF NEWSLETTER (CN/0713-4517). [1,200] **3159**

CANADIAN PROCESS EQUIPMENT & CONTROL NEWS (CN/0318-0859). **2101**

CANADIAN PSYCHOLOGY (CN/0708-5591). [3,500] **4579**

CANADIAN RAILWAY CLUB NEWS (CN/0226-157X). [1,600] **5430**

CANADIAN RATIOS FOR PROFIT PLANNING (CN/0317-2074). [650] **1600**

CANADIAN RENTAL SERVICE (CN/0383-7920). [3,265] **1600**

CANADIAN REVIEW OF AMERICAN STUDIES (CN/0007-7720). [500] **2530**

CANADIAN REVIEW OF ART EDUCATION, RESEARCH AND ISSUES (CN/0706-8107). [600] **346**

CANADIAN REVIEW OF SOCIAL POLICY (1987) (CN/0836-303X). [500] **5276**

CANADIAN REVIEW OF STUDIES IN NATIONALISM (CN/0317-7904). [600] **2635**

CANADIAN ROSE ANNUAL (1983) (CN/0826-743X). [800] **2412**

CANADIAN SAILINGS (CN/0821-5944). [11,000] **5448**

CANADIAN SAILOR (CN/0008-4972). [1,000] **5448**

CANADIAN SCHOOL EXECUTIVE (1982) (CN/0228-0914). [5,000] **1861**

CANADIAN SCIENCE (DOWNSVIEW, ONT.) (CN/0712-4848). **5092**

CANADIAN SECURITY (CN/0709-3403). [11,182] **5176**

CANADIAN SLAVONIC PAPERS (CN/0008-5006). [1,000] **3272**

CANADIAN SOCIETY OF FORENSIC SCIENCE JOURNAL (CN/0008-5030). [1,000] **3740**

CANADIAN SPORTSMAN, THE (CN/0008-5073). [6,000] **2798**

CANADIAN STUDIES IN POPULATION (CN/0380-1489). **4550**

CANADIAN TAX PLANNER'S NEWSLETTER (CN/0227-8375). **740**

CANADIAN THEATRE REVIEW (CN/0315-0836). [1,500] **5362**

CANADIAN TOBACCO GROWER, THE (CN/0008-5189). [3,500] **5372**

CANADIAN TOKEN, THE (CN/0703-895X). [300] **2772**

CANADIAN TRAVEL COURIER (CN/0008-5219). [18,500] **5465**

CANADIAN TRAVEL PRESS WEEKLY (CN/0831-9138). [13,000] **5465**

CANADIAN ULTRALIGHT NEWS (CN/0821-6673). [20,000] **16**

CANADIAN (VERNON, B.C.) (CN/0836-3196). [115,000] **655**

CANADIAN VOCATIONAL JOURNAL (CN/0045-5520). [1,000] **1911**

CANADIAN WATER RESOURCES JOURNAL (CN/0701-1784). **5531**

CANADIAN WATER WELL (CN/1180-050X). **5532**

CANADIAN WOMEN'S STUDIES (CN/0713-3235). [5,000] **5553**

CANADIAN WOOD PRODUCTS (1992) (CN/1183-9139). [7,000] **1600**

CANADIAN WRITER'S JOURNAL (CN/0827-293X). [300] **3372**

CANADIAN YEARBOOK OF INTERNATIONAL LAW (CN/0069-0058). [1,000] **3125**

CANADIANA GERMANICA (CN/0703-1599). [400] **2683**

CANADO-AMERICAIN, LE (CN/0576-6478). [22,000] **2530**

CANBERRA HISTORICAL JOURNAL (AT/0313-5977). [600] **2669**

CANCER FORUM (AT/0311-306X). [4,000] **3811**

CANCER INVESTIGATION (US/0735-7907). **3811**

CANCER NEWS (NEW YORK, N.Y.) (US/0008-5464). [150,000] **3812**

CANCER VICTORS JOURNAL (US/0891-0766). [4,000] **3813**

CANDID FACTS (CN/0226-2347). **3795**

CANDLE COMPUTER REPORT (US/1071-2976). [70,000] **1173**

CANDY WHOLESALER (US/0162-5136). [11,597] **2330**

CANNATA REPORT (US). **4211**

CANPARA (1976) (CN/0227-5880). [5,000] **4889**

CANSPA COMMUNICATOR (CN/0823-0145). **4849**

CANTERBURY AND YORK SOCIETY (SERIES) (UK/0262-995X). [400] **5229**

CANTON EAGLE, THE (US/0192-6446). [4,143] **5691**

CANTRILL'S FILMNOTES (AT/0158-4154). [1,000] **4065**

CANYON COURIER WEEKENDER, THE (US/0192-0197). [8,600] **5642**

CANYON ECHO (US/0164-7024). [15,000] **2530**

CAO TIMES (US/0146-3365). [1,000] **390**

CAP TODAY (US/0891-1525). [40,000] **3893**

CAPACITY CHANGES IN LEAD AND ZINC IN THE 1980'S (UK). **3999**

CAPE BRETON'S MAGAZINE (CN/0319-4639). [6,000] **2726**

CAPE LIBRARIAN, THE (SA/0008-5790). [1,200] **3200**

CAPITAL ENERGY LETTER (US/0195-5292). **1935**

CAPITAL NURSING (US). **3853**

CAPITAL SPORTS FOCUS (US/1041-5742). [100,000] **4889**

CAR CARE MALL NEWS (US). [6,000] **5409**

CAR COLLECTOR & CAR CLASSICS MAGAZINE (US/1057-4441). [43,087] **5409**

CARABELA (SP/0213-9715). [4,000] **3272**

CARBONATES AND EVAPORITES (US/0891-2556). [300] **1371**

CARDIOLOGIC CONSULTATION (US/0741-7454). **3700**

CARDIOLOGY BOARD REVIEW (US/0888-8418). [67,000] **3700**

CARDIOLOGY IN THE YOUNG (US/1047-9511). [1,200] **3701**

CARDIOLOGY MANAGEMENT (US/0892-9327). [14,000] **3701**

CARDIOMYOLOGY (IT/0394-073X). **450**

CARDIOPULMONARY PHYSICAL THERAPY JOURNAL (US). [1,000] **4379**

CARDIOVASCULAR REVIEWS & REPORTS (US/0197-3118). [110,000] **3702**

CARDOZO ARTS & ENTERTAINMENT LAW JOURNAL (US/0736-7694). [300] **2948**

CARE CONNECTION, THE (CN/0843-9966). [5,000] **3853**

CAREER CENTER BULLETIN, THE (US). [2,000] **4201**

CAREER CHOICES NEWSLETTER, THE (US/0888-2770). [1,000] **4201**

CAREER DEVELOPMENT FOR EXCEPTIONAL INDIVIDUALS (US/0885-7288). [2,000] **1911**

CAREER FOCUS FOR TODAY'S RISING BLACK PROFESSIONAL (US/1049-9954). [750,000] **4202**

CAREER FOCUS FOR TODAY'S RISING HISPANIC PROFESSIONAL (US/1049-9946). [750,000] **4202**

CAREER FUTURES (US/1045-4314). [400,000] **4202**

CAREER INFO CUS (CN/1182-9192). [200] **1911**

CAREER PILOT JOB REPORT (US/0891-0855). [15,000] **16**

CAREERS & COLLEGES (US/1065-9935). [500,000] **4202**

CAREERS FOR GRADUATES (US/0318-6229). [13,000] **4202**

CAREERS GUIDANCE TODAY (UK/0969-6431). [3,300] **4202**

CAREFREE ENTERPRISE (US/0738-9604). [12,000-16,000] **2530**

CARETAKER GAZETTE, THE (US/1074-3642). [2,500] **4203**

CARGONEWS ASIA (HK/0252-9610). [13,000] **5379**

CARGOWARE INTERNATIONAL (UK). [8,000] **4218**

CARIB (JM). [500] **3372**

CARIBBEAN BUSINESS (US/0194-8326). [45,000] **655**

CARIBBEAN CONTACT (TR). **4942**

CARIBBEAN GEOGRAPHY (JM/0252-9939). [500] **2558**

CARIBBEAN HANDBOOK, THE (AQ). [12,000] **5466**

CARIBBEAN JOURNAL OF EDUCATION (JM/0376-7701). [400] **1730**

CARIBBEAN JOURNAL OF SCIENCE (PR/0008-6452). [1,000] **5092**

CARIBBEAN WEEK (BB/1019-5076). **5778**

CARIBOO CALLING (CN/0319-7360). [15,000] **2558**

CARICOM BULLETIN (GY). [525] **1550**

CARICOM PERSPECTIVE (GY). [6,000] **2551**

CARILLON NEWS (US/0730-5001). [500] **4107**

CARING FOR ANIMALS (OTTAWA, ONT.) (CN/0825-1711). [2,500] **226**

CARING : THE BENEVOLENCES STORY (US). [50,000] **4942**

CARLETON GERMANIC PAPERS (CN/0317-7254). [150] **3373**

CARLETON INTERNATIONAL (CN/0704-5174). [1,000] **1731**

CARMEL PINE CONE AND CARMEL VALLEY OUTLOOK, THE (US). **5633**

CARNATION (US). [59,000] **5229**

CARNIVOROUS PLANT NEWSLETTER (US/0190-9215). [850] **506**

CARO BULLETIN (CN/0827-357X). **347**

CAROLINA AGENT, THE (US/1065-1292). [800-1,000] **2877**

CAROLINA CHEMTIPS (US/0748-0466). **966**

CAROLINA COMMENTS (US/0576-808X). [1,800] **2481**

CAROLINA COUNTRY (US/0008-6746). [335,000] **1541**

CAROLINA PEACEMAKER (US). [6,500] **2258**

CAROLINA TIPS (US/0045-5865). [125,000] **5092**

CAROLINAS GENEALOGICAL SOCIETY BULLETIN, THE (US/0363-440X). [250] **2441**

CAROLINIAN (RALEIGH), THE (US/0045-5873). [14,000] **5722**

CARP. CANADIAN ASSOCIATION OF RETIRED PERSONS (CN/1193-8544). [90,000] **5178**

CARPATHO-RUSYN AMERICAN (US/0749-9213). [1,200] **2258**

CARPENTER (US/0008-6843). [650,000] **633**

CARPET & RUG INDUSTRY (US/0192-4486). [5,500] **2899**

CARPET MANAGEMENT : A QUARTERLY REVIEW OF THE INTERNATIONAL CARPET AND RUG INDUSTRY (US). [1,000] **5348**

CARREFOUR (CN/0706-1250). [560] **4343**

CARREFOUR SALESIEN (CN/0823-9428). [10,000] **1814**

CARRELL, THE (US/0008-6894). [500] **3373**

CARRIAGE TRADE (SARNIA, ONT.) (CN/0831-2907). [3,000] **5348**

CARRIER REPORT (US). **5379**

CARRIEROLOGIE (CN/0820-5000). [1,000] **1658**

CARROLL COUNTY GENEALOGICAL QUARTERLY (US/0734-5682). [225] **2442**

CARROLL COUNTY HISTORICAL SOCIETY QUARTERLY, THE (US/0191-6637). [780] **2727**

CARROLL COUNTY HISTORY JOURNAL (US). [1,200] **2727**

CARROUSEL ART (US/0740-0780). [1,200] **250**

CARRYING STREAM, THE (UK/0961-4532). [1,500] **2683**

CARTA DE CLACSO (AG). [2,000] **5194**

CARTA INFORMATIVA PARA LOS SOCIOS (ES). [1,500] **818**

CARTACTUAL (HU/0008-7009). [900] **2558**

CARTE ITALIANE (US/0737-9412). [2,000] **3373**

CARTELLINA, LA (IT/1120-4621). [3,000] **4108**

CARTELLO METEOROLOGICO (IT). [400] **1421**

CARTES SYNOPTIQUES DE LA CHROMOSPHERE SOLAIRE ET CATALOGUES DES FILAMENTS ET DES CENTRES D'ACTIVITE (FR). **394**

CARTHAGE REPUBLICAN TRIBUNE (US/0889-8715). **5714**

CARTOGRAPHIC ACTIVITIES IN THE UNITED KINGDOM, REPORT (UK). **2581**

CARTOGRAPHIC JOURNAL, THE (UK/0008-7041). [2,000] **2581**

CARTOGRAPHICA (1980) (CN/0317-7173). [1,200] **2581**

CARTOGRAPHY (AT/0069-0805). [2,200] **2581**

CARTOUCHE ENGLISH EDITION (CALGARY) (CN/1183-2045). [500] **2581**

CARTOUCHE FRENCH EDITION (CALGARY) (CN/1183-2045). [500] **2581**

CAS. CURRENT AWARENESS SERVICE - BRITISH INSTITUTE OF MENTAL HANDICAP (UK/0143-0289). **1793**

CAS JOURNAL (US/1053-7694). [800] **4108**

CASA DEL TIEMPO (MX/0185-4275). [1,500] **2511**

CASA VOGUE (IT/0008-7173). [50,000] **2899**

CASE COMMENTARIES AND BRIEFS (US/0736-8240). [7,000] **3105**

CASE INDUSTRY DIRECTORY (US/0898-5022). [1,000] **1173**

CASE REGISTER (US/0272-2119). [1,000] **949**

CASE UPDATE (US/0749-7709). [700] **2949**

CASHTON RECORD (US). [1,500] **5766**

CASINOS : THE INTERNATIONAL CASINO GUIDE (US/1040-9920). [50,000] **4858**

CASS COUNTY GENEALOGICAL SOCIETY QUARTERLY (US). **2442**

CASSAVA BIBLIOGRAPHIC BULLETIN (CK). [3,000] **72**

CASSAVA NEWSLETTER (CK/0120-1824). [2,200] **166**

CASSIOPEIA (VICTORIA) (CN/0715-4747). [400] **394**

CASTING WORLD (US/0887-9060). [70,000] **3999**

CASTME JOURNAL (UK/0264-3138). [500] **1890**

CASTRO, EL (SP). [6,000] **3461**

CASUAL BULLETIN / ARCHIVE OF AUSTRALIAN JUDAICA (AT). [500] **5046**

CASUAL LIVING (US/0740-8285). **2904**

CATALAN REVIEW (SP/0213-5949). [500] **2258**

CATALOG AGE (US/0740-3119). [13,500] **757**

CATALOG OF PROFESSIONAL DEVELOPMENT SEMINARS / INSTITUTE FOR ADVANCED TECHNOLOGY, CONTROL DATA CORPORATION (US). [500,000] **5092**

CATALOG OF STATE ASSISTANCE PROGRAMS (US/0097-9309). [300] **4637**

CATALOG PRODUCT NEWS (US/1048-0633). [23,000] **949**

CATALOGUE & INDEX (UK/0008-7629). [3,500] **3200**

CATALOGUE DE LIVRES AU FORMAT DE POCHE (FR/0769-1696). [40,000] **412**

CATALOGUE DES PUBLICATIONS UNESCO (FR). [30,000] **412**

CATALOGUE - FUNNEL (CN/0826-2861). [2,000] **4065**

CATALOGUE / JOHN F. KENNEDY SCHOOL OF GOVERNMENT, HARVARD UNIVERSITY (US). **1814**

CATALOGUE - LAURENCE WITTEN RARE BOOKS (US/8756-7083). **4827**

CATALOGUE - NATIONAL INDIAN LAW LIBRARY (US/0092-3419). [1,000] **3079**

CATALOGUE OF ACCESSIONED PUBLICATIONS. SUPPLEMENT (US/0162-0827). [600] **1447**

CATALOGUE OF FORAMINIFERA. SUPPL (US/0885-7083). [300] **4164**

CATALONIA CULTURE (SP). **2514**

CATALYST / CITIZENS FOR PUBLIC JUSTICE (CN/0824-2062). [3,500] **4467**

CATALYST (DES MOINES, IOWA : 1971), THE (US/0730-711X). [1,800] **3201**

CATALYST (GOROKA, PAPUA NEW GUINEA) (PP/0253-2921). [750] **2669**

CATALYST (PHILADELPHIA), THE (US/0008-767X). [5,200] **967**

CATHAIR NO MART (IE/0332-4117). [1,000] **2683**

CATHEDRAL AGE (US/0008-7874). [34,500] **294**

CATHOLIC ADVANCE, THE (US/0008-7904). [27,000] **5025**

CATHOLIC ANCESTOR (UK). [1,000] **2442**

CATHOLIC ARCHIVES : THE JOURNAL OF THE CATHOLIC ARCHIVES SOCIETY (UK/0261-4316). [500] **5025**

CATHOLIC BIBLICAL QUARTERLY. MONOGRAPH SERIES (US). [1,000] **5016**

CATHOLIC CHRONICLE, THE (US/0008-7971). [39,000] **5025**

CATHOLIC FREE PRESS, THE (US/0008-8056). [21,000] **5026**

CATHOLIC HERALD (SACRAMENTO, CALIF.) (US/0746-4185). [38,500] **5026**

CATHOLIC JOURNALIST (US/0008-8129). [2,600] **2918**

CATHOLIC PERIODICAL AND LITERATURE INDEX, THE (US/0008-8285). [1,400] **5012**

CATHOLIC PRESS DIRECTORY (US/0008-8307). [2,200] **5012**

CATHOLIC REGISTER, THE (CN/0383-1620). [45,000] **5026**

CATHOLIC SINGLES (US/0886-8190). [20,000] **5242**

CATHOLIC STANDARD (WASHINGTON, D.C.) (US/0411-2741). [47,000] **5026**

CATHOLIC TELEGRAPH (US). [24,000] **5727**

CATHOLIC TIMES (MONTREAL) (CN/0703-1521). [12,500] **5026**

CATHOLIC TWIN CIRCLE (US/0273-6136). [56,878] **5026**

CATHOLIC VOICE (OAKLAND, CALIF.), THE (US/0279-0645). [102,000] **5027**

CATHOLIC YOUTH MINISTRY (US/0277-8165). [1,300] **5027**

CATO POLICY REPORT (US/0743-605X). [10,000] **1468**

CATTLE GUARD (US/0411-289X). [3,500] **208**

CATTLEMAN (US/0008-8552). [19,169] **209**

CAUCHO (AG/0528-3280). [2,000] **5075**

CAUSE/EFFECT (US/0164-534X). [3000] **1814**

CAYMAN ISLANDS LAW REPORTS, THE (UK/0269-977X). [200] **2949**

CBA RECORD (US/0892-1822). [22,000] **2949**

CBASSE NEWSLETTER (US/0734-5119). [2,500] **5195**

CBC CLASSICAL CATALOGUE (CN/0713-1283). **4108**

CBC FEATURES (US). [40,000] **3373**

CBC JAZZ AND POPULAR RECORD CATALOGUE (CN/0713-1291). **4108**

CBE VIEWS (US/0164-5609). [1,200] **451**

CBMR MONOGRAPHS (US/1042-8836). [450] **4108**

CBN NEWSLETTER (CK/1022-1492). [900] **166**

CBT DIRECTIONS (US/0898-8498). [10,000] **1173**

CC AI (BE/0773-4182). [300] **1212**

CCI. CLIMA COMMERCE INTERNATIONAL (GW/0009-8914). [5,500] **2604**

CCI NOUVELLES (CN/0822-5192). [100] **1967**

CCLM NEWSLETTER (US/0273-3315). [1,500] **3373**

CCPE NEWS (CN/0712-5844). [1,000] **1967**

CD-ROM ENDUSER (US/1042-8623). [18,000] **1174**

CDB NEWS / CARIBBEAN DEVELOPMENT BANK (BB). [4,000] **782**

CDC HIV : AIDS PREVENTION NEWSLETTER (US). [16,500] **3712**

CDR IN (DK). [2,000] **1468**

CDR PROJECT PAPERS (DK/0106-0805). [400] **2908**

CDR RESEARCH REPORT (DK/0108-6596). [500] **5195**

CDROM DATABASES (US/0897-3296). **1174**

CDS REVIEW (US/0091-1666). [9,000] **1318**

CED DIRECTORY OF ENGINEERING AND ENGINEERING TECHNOLOGY CO-OP PROGRAMS (US). [300] **1968**

CEE NEWS (US/1045-2710). [109,000] **2038**

CELEBRATE (AT). [5,041] **4943**

CELESTINESCA (US/0147-3085). [370] **3373**

CELL AND CHROMOSOME RESEARCH (II/0254-2935). [200] **533**

CELL STRUCTURE AND FUNCTION (JA/0386-7196). [403] **534**

CELLE NEWSLETTER (US/0743-4979). [120] **2442**

CELLULAR BUSINESS (US/0741-6520). [12,000] **1151**

CELLULAR POLYMERS (UK/0262-4893). [200] **4454**

CENSORSHIP NEWS (US/0749-6001). [5,000] **1106**

CENSUS OF BUILDING AND CONSTRUCTION (FIJI) (FJ). [150] **607**

CENSUS OF MAINE MANUFACTURES (US/0090-7111). [650] **1601**

CENTER CITY REPORT (US/0891-1029). [1,000] **2817**

CENTER FOR LIFE CYCLE SCIENCES NEWSLETTER (US). [1,000] **863**

CENTER RESEARCH REPORTS AND RECORD OF ACTIVITIES (US/0737-7010). **347**

CENTER STAGE (NEW YORK) (US). [25,000] **5362**

CENTINELA (NAMPA, IDAHO), EL (US/8750-4308). [100,000] **5057**

CENTRAL ALABAMA GENEALOGICAL SOCIETY : NEWSLETTER (US). [350] **2442**

CENTRAL AMERICA UPDATE (CN/0823-7689). [1,200] **4467**

CENTRAL AMERICA UPDATE (ALBUQUERQUE, N.M.) (US). [2,500] **4467**

CENTRAL AMERICA UPDATE (ALBUQUERQUE, N.M.) (US/1054-8882). [2,500] **4467**

CENTRAL & INNER ASIAN STUDIES (US/0893-2301). [200] **2648**

CENTRAL ASIA (PK). [500] **2648**

CENTRAL BANKING (UK/0960-6319). [500] **782**

CENTRAL CONFERENCE OF AMERICAN RABBIS ANNUAL CONVENTION (US/0069-1607). [1,650] **5046**

CENTRAL FLORIDA MAGAZINE (US/8750-2852). [25,000] **2530**

CENTRAL ILLINOIS GENEALOGICAL QUARTERLY (US/0577-0807). [800] **2442**

CENTRAL KENTUCKY NEWS-JOURNAL (US). **5680**

CENTRAL MONTANA WAGON TRAILS (US/0883-9603). [125] **2442**

CENTRAL NORTH CAROLINA JOURNAL (US/1050-1339). [300] **2530**

CENTRAL RAILWAY CHRONICLE (US/0008-9532). [300] **5430**

CENTRAL STATE BUSINESS REVIEW (US/8756-4521). **656**

CENTRAL STATES ARCHAEOLOGICAL JOURNAL (US/0008-9559). [8,000] **265**

CENTRALLY PLANNED ECONOMIES OUTLOOK (US/0749-6508). **1469**

CENTRE LETTER (BANFF) (CN/0705-6842). [500] **317**

CENTRE THIRD (CN/0712-1334). **4889**

CENTRO PRO UNIONE : [BOLLETTINO] (IT). [1,000] **4467**

CEO UPDATE (US). **656**

CEP RESEARCH REPORT (US/0898-4328). [4,500] **1469**

CEPHALALGIA (NO/0333-1024). [800] **3829**

CERAMIC ABSTRACTS (US/0095-9960). [3,800] **2595**

CERAMIC ARTS & CRAFTS (US/0009-0190). [45,000] **2587**

CERAMIC INDUSTRY (US/0009-0220). [9,850] **2587**

CERAMIC REVIEW (UK/0144-1825). [9,000] **2587**

CERAMIC SCOPE (US/0009-0247). [14,000] **2587**

CERAMIC

CERAMIC STUDY GROUP NEWSLETTER (AT). [600] **2772**

CERAMICA ACTA (IT/1121-6093). **2587**

CERAMICA (SAO PAULO) (BL/0366-6913). [2,000] **2587**

CERAMICS MONTHLY (US/0009-0328). [34,000] **2588**

CERAMICS PADDINGTON (AT/1035-1841). [10,000] **2588**

CEREAL FOODS WORLD (US/0146-6283). [4,000] **2331**

CEREBUS (CN/0712-7774). **4858**

CERN COURIER (SZ/0304-288X). **4446**

CERTIFIED COPY, THE (US/0749-5684). [250] **2442**

CERTIFIED ENGINEERING TECHNICIAN (US/0746-6641). [2,500] **1968**

CERTIFIED PUBLIC HOSPITAL LIST (CN/0828-0967). [450] **3778**

CESKOSLOVENSKA FYSIOLOGIE (XR/0009-0557). [650] **579**

CESKOSLOVENSKA PSYCHOLOGIE (XR/0009-062X). [2,800] **4580**

CESKOSLOVENSKY ARCHITEKT (XR/0009-0697). [7,500] **295**

CESSNA OWNER MAGAZINE, THE (US/0745-3523). [6,000] **16**

C'EST POUR QUAND (CN/0705-3215). **3758**

CEYLON MEDICAL JOURNAL (CE/0009-0875). [1,000] **3562**

CFI, CERAMIC FORUM INTERNATIONAL (GW/0173-9913). [4,500] **2588**

CGA MAGAZINE (CN/0318-742X). [40,000] **740**

CHAIN DRUG REVIEW (US/0164-9914). [43,000] **656**

CHAIN MERCHANDISER (US/0009-0921). [14,000] **952**

CHAINON (OTTAWA. 1983) (CN/0823-6186). [900] **2727**

CHALLENGE (US). [145,000] **5553**

CHALLENGE (CARTHAGE, ILL.) (US/0745-6298). [9,000] **1877**

CHALLENGE IN EDUCATIONAL ADMINISTRATION (CN/0045-625X). **1861**

CHALLENGE OF CONSERVATIVE BAPTIST HOME MISSIONS, THE (US/0745-2918). [95,000] **5057**

CHALLENGE (WHITE PLAINS) (US/0577-5132). [4,500] **1469**

CHALLENGER (BUFFALO, N.Y.), THE (US/1040-8886). **5714**

CHALLENGES OF THE CHANGING ECONOMY OF NEW YORK CITY (US). [500] **1469**

CHAMBER OF MINES JOURNAL (RH/0009-1162). [1,200] **2136**

CHAMBEREXECUTIVE (US/0884-8114). [4,500] **819**

CHAMBERLAIN ASSOCIATION NEWS (US/0882-987X). [300] **2442**

CHAMBRE BLANCHE (CN/0820-781X). [350] **347**

CHAMPAIGN COUNTY GENEALOGICAL SOCIETY QUARTERLY (US/0277-2086). [320] **2442**

CHAMPIGNONCULTUUR, DE (NE/0009-1316). [1,725] **166**

CHAMPIONS OF FREEDOM (US/0741-3408). [1,000] **1590**

CHANGING WORK (NEW HAVEN, CONN.) (US/0883-1416). [3,000] **1659**

CHANNEL GUIDE (US/0744-6462). [52,000] **1130**

CHANNELS (NEWBURY PARK, CALIF.) (US/0744-4079). [60,000] **4943**

CHAOS NETWORK, THE (US/1070-8146). [600] **5242**

CHAPEAU (CN/0228-5045). **1541**

CHAPEL HILL NEWSPAPER, THE (US). [25,000] **5723**

CHAPLEAU SENTINEL (CN/0832-2414). [1,400] **5781**

CHAPTER NEWSLETTER - BIG BAND SOCIETY. ED WALKER CHAPTER (US/0731-4051). [750] **4109**

CHARACTERISTICS OF PERSONS ENTERING PAROLE (US/0749-3347). **3160**

CHARACTERISTICS OF WORK-RELATED INJURIES AND ILLNESSES IN MAINE (US/0733-8384). [1,000] **2860**

CHARITON COLLECTOR, THE (US/0742-129X). [1,250] **2727**

CHARITY LONDON. 1983 (UK/0265-5209). [2,500] **4335**

CHARLES LAMB BULLETIN, THE (UK/0308-0951). [350] **3339**

CHARLESTON MAGAZINE, THE (UK/0963-4770). [3,000] **3374**

CHAROLAIS BANNER (CN/0824-1767). **209**

CHAROLAIS CONNECTION (CN/0828-7600). **209**

CHAROLAIS JOURNAL (US/0191-5444). [5,000] **209**

CHART AND QUILL (US/0737-2655). [100] **2442**

CHARTER (SYDNEY, AUSTRALIA) (AT). [33,000] **740**

CHARTERED ACCOUNTANT, THE (II/0009-188X). [65,000] **740**

CHARTERED BUILDER (AT/0311-1903). [2,800] **607**

CHARTERED BUILDER (ASCOT, 1989) (UK/0957-8773). [25,000] **607**

CHARTERED QUANTITY SURVEYOR (UK/0142-5196). [32,219] **2020**

CHARTERED SURVEYOR : BUILDING AND QUANTITY SURVEYING QUARTERLY (UK). [30,000] **607**

CHARTERED SURVEYOR WEEKLY (UK/0264-049X). [48,104] **4835**

CHARTIST (US). [5,000] **894**

CHASSE MAREE (FR). [25,000] **233**

CHAUSSER 1968 (FR/0151-4040). [8,000] **1082**

CHECKLIST OF INDIANA STATE DOCUMENTS (US/0361-0284). [600] **413**

CHECKLIST OF OFFICIAL NORTH CAROLINA STATE PUBLICATIONS (US/0193-9432). [225] **413**

CHECKLIST OF OFFICIAL PUBLICATIONS OF THE STATE OF NEW YORK, A (US/0077-9296). **413**

CHECKLIST OF SOUTH CAROLINA STATE PUBLICATIONS (US). **413**

CHECKPOINT (AT). [7,500] **4943**

CHEER NEWS TODAY (US/0893-8091). [30,000] **4889**

CHEESE REPORTER (US/0009-2142). [2,400] **192**

CHELYS (VIOLA DA GAMBA SOCIETY) (UK/0952-8407). [600] **4109**

CHEM 13 NEWS. CHEM 12 NEWS (CN/0703-1157). [4,700] **967**

CHEM SOURCES INTERNATIONAL (US). [500] **1021**

CHEM SOURCES U.S.A. (US/0094-6567). [5,000] **967**

CHEMECOLOGY (US/0738-7776). [24,000] **2162**

CHEMICA (FI). [450] **1050**

CHEMICAL AGE OF INDIA (II/0009-2320). [6,500] **968**

CHEMICAL & ENGINEERING NEWS (US/0009-2347). [139,000] **1022**

CHEMICAL BUSINESS (US/0731-8774). [45,000] **968**

CHEMICAL COMMUNICATIONS / UNIVERSITY OF STOCKHOLM (SW/0366-5607). **968**

CHEMICAL CORRESPONDENCE (JA). [200] **968**

CHEMICAL ENGINEERING EDUCATION (US/0009-2479). [1,900] **2009**

CHEMICAL INDUSTRY (JA). [32,000] **1022**

CHEMICAL INSIGHT (UK/0045-6403). **1022**

CHEMICAL MATTERS (UK). **1022**

CHEMICAL PACKAGING REVIEW, THE (US/1054-5131). [7,800] **2162**

CHEMICAL REVIEWS (US/0009-2665). [5,054] **969**

CHEMICAL SPOTLIGHT (US/0411-8871). **969**

CHEMICAL WEEKLY (II/0045-6500). [35,000] **969**

CHEMICKE LISTY (XR/0009-2770). [1,900] **969**

CHEMIE MAGAZINE : MAANDBLAD VAN DE VLAAMSE CHEMISCHE VERENIGING (BE). [4,000] **969**

CHEMIE-TECHNIK (GW/0340-9961). [19,000] **2010**

CHEMINS DE FER : BULLETIN OFFICIEL (FR/0009-2924). [4,000] **5430**

CHEMISCH JAARBOEK (NE). **969**

CHEMISCHE INDUSTRIE (DUSSELDORF) (GW/0009-2959). [5,000] **970**

CHEMISTRY IN AUSTRALIA (AT/0314-4240). [8,000] **970**

CHEMUNG VALLEY REPORTER (US/1064-4091). [1,500] **5714**

CHENE (CN/0228-5037). **4637**

CHEROKEE FAMILY HISTORY (US). [100] **2442**

CHEROKEE ONE FEATHER, THE (US/0890-4448). [2,000] **2258**

CHESNAIE (CN/0822-6342). **4637**

CHEST (US/0012-3692). [19,500] **3702**

CHEVAL MAGAZINE (FR). [130,000] **2798**

CHEVAUX DE PENNY (FR). **1061**

CHEVRON WORLD (US/0148-3102). [300,000] **4253**

CHI CHE TIEN CHUAN TUNG (CC). [5,000] **5430**

CHICAGO APPAREL NEWS (US/0195-0819). [8,000] **1082**

CHICAGO BOWLER, INC, THE (US/1056-3547). [3000] **4890**

CHICAGO CRUSADER, THE (US). [50,000] **5658**

CHICAGO GENEALOGIST (US/0009-3556). [800] **2443**

CHICAGO HISTORY (US/0272-8540). [9,000] **2727**

CHICAGO LAWYER (US/0199-8374). [6,000] **2950**

CHICAGO PURCHASOR, THE (US/0009-367X). [6,000] **949**

CHICAGO SOURCEBOOK (US/1078-5949). [12,000] **757**

CHICAGO STUDIES (US/0009-3718). [10,000] **5027**

CHICAGO TALENT SOURCEBOOK (US/0734-6662). [12,000] **757**

CHICAGO TIMES MAGAZINE (US/0894-5640). [55,000] **2530**

CHICAGO TRIBUNE (CHICAGO, ILL. : 1963) (US). [744,969 daily1,112,200 Sun.] **5659**

CHICANO-LATINO LAW REVIEW (US/1061-8899). **2950**

CHICO ENTERPRISE-RECORD (US/0746-5548). [27,208] **5633**

CHIEF EXECUTIVE (NEW YORK, N.Y. 1977) (US/0160-4724). [35,000] **863**

CHIEF EXECUTIVE OPINION (US). **656**

CHIEF INFORMATION OFFICER JOURNAL (US/0899-0182). [2,000] **1174**

CHIEN CHU SHIH (TAIPEI, TAIWAN) (CH). [6,500] **295**

CHIIKIGAKU KENKYU (JA). [700] **2817**

CHILD ANALYSIS (US). **4580**

CHILD AND FAMILY (US/0009-3882). [1,500] **2277**

CHILD CARE, HEALTH AND DEVELOPMENT (UK/0305-1862). [740] **3901**

CHILD CARE WORKER, THE (SA/0258-8927). **5242**

CHILD NEPHROLOGY AND UROLOGY (SZ/1012-6694). [1,200] **3989**

CHILD PROTECTION REPORT (US/0147-1260). [1,000] **4771**

CHILD SAFETY REVIEW (UK/0957-4107). [500] **4771**

CHILD SUPPORT REPORT (US/0884-8076). [10,000] **3120**

CHILD WELFARE (US/0009-4021). [12,000] **5278**

CHILDREN & TEENS TODAY (US/0882-942X). [2,500] **5278**

CHILDREN IN THE TROPICS (FR/0379-2269). [15,000] **3985**

CHILDREN LOOKED AFTER BY LOCAL AUTHORITIES IN WALES / WELSH OFFICE / PLANT Y GOFELIR AM DANYNT GAN AWDURDODAU LLEOL CYMRU / Y SWYDDFA GYMREIG (UK/0968-4050). [450] **5278**

CHILDREN OF THE AMERICAN REVOLUTION MAGAZINE (US). [5,000] **2443**

CHILDREN'S BOOK REVIEW SERVICE (US/0090-7987). [350] **3339**

CHILDREN'S BOOKS. AWARDS & PRIZES (US/0069-3472). [2,500] **1061**

CHILDREN'S HEALTH CARE (US/0273-9615). [4,500] **3901**

CHILDREN'S LEGAL RIGHTS JOURNAL (US/0278-7210). [550] **3120**

CHILDREN'S LITERATURE ASSOCIATION QUARTERLY (US/0885-0429). [700] **3340**

CHILDREN'S SERMONS SERVICE PLUS (US/8750-1929). [4,000] **1062**

CHILDREN'S VIDEO REVIEW NEWSLETTER (US/0895-2094). **4065**

CHILDREN'S WELFARE ASSOCIATION OF VICTORIA NEWSLETTER (AT). [300] **5279**

CHILDREN'S WORLD (BOSTON, MASS.) (US/0895-2221). [48,470] **1877**

CHILDSCOPE (US/0882-6390). [250] **3902**

CHILE ECOMOMIC REPORT (US/0884-4488). [7,500] **1551**

CHILEANS, THE (UK). [600] **506**

CHILTON COUNTY NEWS (CLANTON, ALA. : 1986) (US/0888-451X). [2,000] **5625**

CHILTON'S AUTOMOTIVE INDUSTRIES (1976) (US/0273-656X). [89,000] **5410**

CHILTON'S AUTOMOTIVE MARKETING (US/0193-3264). [26,621] **5410**

CHILTON'S ELECTRONIC COMPONENT NEWS (US/0193-614X). [110,000] **2038**

CHILTON'S FOOD ENGINEERING (US/0193-323X). [60,130] **2331**

CHILTON'S FOOD ENGINEERING INTERNATIONAL (US/0148-4478). [14,000] **2331**

CHILTON'S IAN (1977) (US/0193-6174). [112,000] **1968**

CHILTON'S I&CS (US/0746-2395). **1968**

CHILTON'S IMPO (US/8755-2523). [120,000] **3476**

CHILTON'S INDUSTRIAL SAFETY & HYGIENE NEWS (US/8755-2566). [57,000] **2860**

CHILTON'S MOTOR/AGE (1970) (US/0193-7022). [136,000] **5411**

CHILTON'S OWNER OPERATOR (US). [90,515] **5379**

CHILTON'S TRUCK & OFF-HIGHWAY INDUSTRIES (US/0194-1410). [33,000] **5379**

CHIMIE MAGAZINE (FR/0245-940X). **972**

CHINA AND OURSELVES (CN/0828-1602). [250] **4943**

CHINA COAL INDUSTRY YEARBOOK (HK/0258-3062). [1,500] **2136**

CHINA FACTS & FIGURES ANNUAL (US/0190-602X). **2502**

CHINA GLASS & TABLEWARE (US/0009-4382). [3,300] **2588**

CHINA INFORMATION (NE/0920-203X). [350] **4468**

CHINA LAW REPORTER (US/0891-6829). **2950**

CHINA LETTER (US/0529-3189). **657**

CHINA MARKET (HK). [20,000] **1633**

CHINA PLASTIC & RUBBER JOURNAL (HK). [15,000] **4454**

CHINA REPORT (NEW DELHI) (II/0009-4455). **2648**

CHINA TELECOMMUNICATIONS CONSTRUCTION (HK/1017-5199). [8,300] **1130**

CHINA TELECOMMUNICATIONS CONSTRUCTION (HK/1017-5199). [20,000] **1151**

CHINA TEXTILE (HK). [35,000] **5349**

CHINAMAC JOURNAL (HK). [20,000] **3476**

CHINATOWN NEWS (CN/0009-4501). [24,000] **2486**

CHINESE AMERICA, HISTORY AND PERSPECTIVES (US/1051-7642). [1,000] **2258**

CHINESE ECONOMIC STUDIES (US/0009-4552). [400] **1469**

CHINESE EDUCATION (US/0009-4560). [300] **1731**

CHINESE JOURNAL OF PSYCHOLOGY (CC). [500] **4580**

CHINESE LAW AND GOVERNMENT (US/0009-4609). [300] **2950**

CHINESE LITERATURE (MADISON) (US/0161-9705). [325] **3375**

CHINESE STUDIES IN PHILOSOPHY (US/0023-8627). [200] **4343**

CHING FENG (ENGLISH EDITION) (HK/0009-4668). [1,000] **4943**

CHINOOK REGIONAL LIBRARY DIRECTORY (CN/0705-2480). [175] **3201**

CHIROPODY REVIEW (UK/0009-4714). [1,400] **3917**

CHIROPRACTIC JOURNAL OF AUSTRALIA (AT/1036-0913). **4379**

CHIROPRACTIC PRODUCTS (US/1041-2360). [35,000] **3563**

CHIROPRACTIC RESEARCH JOURNAL (US/0899-6938). [3,000] **3804**

CHIRURGIA (IT/0394-9508). [6,000] **3961**

CHIRURGIA DEGLI ORGANI DI MOVIMENTO (IT/0009-4749). [3,500] **3961**

CHIRURGIA TRIVENETA (IT/0009-4811). [900] **3962**

CHIRURGICA (OULU) (FI/0358-4917). [450] **3962**

CHIRURGIEN - DENTISTE DE FRANCE, LE (FR/0009-4838). **1319**

CHISAGO COUNTY PRESS (US). [4,000] **5695**

CHITARRE (IT). [20,000] **4109**

CHO TO GA. TYO TO GA (JA). [1,500] **5606**

CHOCOLATE SINGLES (US/0882-4460). [110,000] **2258**

CHOCTAW COMMUNITY NEWS (US). [5,400] **5700**

CHOICE (CHIPPENDALE, N.S.W.) (AT). [200,000] **1294**

CHOICES (EVANSTON, ILL.) (US/0735-6358). **1062**

CHOIRS ONTARIO (CN/0822-4749). [1,500] **4109**

CHOIX: DOCUMENTATION AUDIOVISUELLE (CN/0706-2257). [400] **1891**

CHOIX : DOCUMENTATION IMPRIMEE (CN/0706-2249). [800] **3201**

CHOIX JEUNESSE : DOCUMENTATION IMPRINEE (CN/0706-2265). **3201**

CHOLTO CHARYANG KISUL ROLLING STOCK ENGINEERING (KO). [1,000] **5430**

CHONGUK KAJOK POGON SILTAE CHOSA POGO (KO). [300] **588**

CHON'GUK TAEHAKSAENG HAKSUL YON'GU PALPYO NONMUNJIP : SAHOE KWAHAK PUNYA (KO). **5195**

CHORAL JOURNAL, THE (US/0009-5028). [16,000] **4109**

CHORISTERS GUILD LETTERS (US/0412-2801). [7,600] **4109**

CHORUS (HALIFAX) (CN/0821-1108). [350] **4109**

CHOSEN MINSHU SHUGI JINMIN KYOWAKOKU SOSHIKIBETSU JINMEIBO (JA). [800] **4637**

CHRISTIAN ACTIVITIES CALENDAR (MIDDLE ATLANTIC ED.) (US/0883-4210). [20,000] **4944**

CHRISTIAN COMMUNITY : THE MAGAZINE OF THE NATIONAL CENTRE FOR CHRISTIAN COMMUNITIES AND NETWORKS (UK). [700] **4944**

CHRISTIAN CONQUEST (US/0892-9300). **4944**

CHRISTIAN COURIER (CN/1192-3415). **5058**

CHRISTIAN ENDEAVOR WORLD, THE (US/0009-5338). **4945**

CHRISTIAN HISTORY (WORCESTER, PA.) (US/0891-9666). [8,000] **4945**

CHRISTIAN INDEX (MEMPHIS, TENN.), THE (US/0744-4060). [6,000] **5058**

CHRISTIAN INDEX, THE (US). [65,000] **5058**

CHRISTIAN IRELAND TODAY (US/1040-8622). [475] **4945**

CHRISTIAN JOURNAL (FORT WORTH, TEX.) (US/1056-3644). [9-10,000] **4945**

CHRISTIAN LEADER (HILLSBORO) (US/0009-5419). [9,500] **5058**

CHRISTIAN MISSION (US/8750-7765). [15,000] **4945**

CHRISTIAN MONTHLY (US/0009-5494). [2,000] **4945**

CHRISTIAN PARAPSYCHOLOGIST, THE (UK/0308-6194). [1,400] **4241**

CHRISTIAN PSYCHOLOGY FOR TODAY (US/0892-4686). [5,600] **4580**

CHRISTIAN RETAILING (US/0892-0281). [11,000] **952**

CHRISTIAN SOCIAL ACTION (WASHINGTON, D.C.) (US/0897-0459). [3,500] **4946**

CHRISTIAN STATESMAN (US/0009-5664). [2,000] **4946**

CHRISTIAN THEOLOGICAL SEMINARY BULLETIN (US/0529-472X). [16,000] **4946**

CHRISTIANISME AU VINGTIEME SIECLE, LE (FR/0009-5729). [5,000] **4946**

CHRISTIANITY & LITERATURE (US/0148-3331). [1,500] **3375**

CHRISTIANS WRITING (AT/0729-4042). [300] **3375**

CHRISTMAS TREES (US/0199-0217). [8,000] **2377**

CHROMIUM REVIEW (SA/0256-0038). [5,500] **4000**

CHRONIC DISEASES IN CANADA (CN/0228-8699). [4,000] **3563**

CHRONICA (DAVIS) (US/0009-5931). [425] **3375**

CHRONICA HORTICULTURAE (NE/0578-039X). [3,500] **2412**

CHRONICLE-EXPRESS (US). **5715**

CHRONICLE FOUR-YEAR COLLEGE DATABOOK (US/0191-3670). [10,000] **1815**

CHRONICLE OF HIGHER EDUCATION, THE (US/0009-5982). [84,300] **1815**

CHRONICLE OF LATIN AMERICAN ECONOMIC AFFAIRS (US/1054-8874). **1469**

CHRONICLE OF THE EARLY AMERICAN INDUSTRIES ASSOCIATION, INC, THE (US/0012-8147). [3,300] **5094**

CHRONICLE OF THE HORSE, THE (US/0009-5990). [20,959] **2798**

CHRONICLE-TELEGRAM, THE (US). **5727**

CHRONICLES OF OKLAHOMA (US/0009-6024). [6,000] **2728**

CHRONICLES (PHILADELPHIA, PA.) (US/0893-2921). **2443**

CHRONIQUE FEMINISTE (BE). [2,000] **5553**

CHRONIQUE / INSTITUT CATHOLIQUE DE TOULOUSE (FR/0495-9396). [1,300] **1732**

CHRONIQUE JUDICIAIRE D'HAITI, LA (HT). [10,000] **3126**

CHRONIQUES DU PROTECTEUR DU CITOYEN (CN/1188-0856). **4637**

CHRONIQUES ITALIENNES (FR/0766-4257). **3273**

CHRYSANTHEMUM (US/0090-5771). [1,800] **2412**

CHUCHOTERIES (CN/0825-8449). **1861**

CHUGOKU KENKYU GEPPO (JA/0910-4348). **5195**

CHULPAN MUNHWA (KO/0009-6245). [3,000] **4828**

CHUNG-HUA MIN KUO CHI CHI SHE PEI HSUAN LU (CH). [2,000] **2111**

CHUNG-KUO CHIEN CHU FA CHAN (HK). [20,000] **607**

CHUNG-KUO HAI YUN (HK). [6,000] **5448**

CHUNG-SO YONGU (KO). [1,600] **2649**

CHUNG WAI WEN HSUEH (CH). [3,000] **3375**

CHUNG YANG MIN TSU HSUEH YUAN HSUEH PAO / ZHONGYANG MINZU XUEYUAN XUEBAO (CC). [4,500] **2258**

CHUNG YANG YEN CHIU YUAN TUNG WU YEN CHUI SO CHI KAN (CH/0001-3943). **5580**

CHURCH & SYNAGOGUE LIBRARIES (US/0009-6342). [3,200] **3202**

CHURCH GROWTH (KO). [12,615] **4947**

CHURCH HERALD, THE (US/0009-6393). [108,000] **4947**

CHURCH MUSIC QUARTERLY (UK/0307-6334). [16,500] **4109**

CHURCH MUSIC REPORT : TCMR, THE (US/1071-9903). **4109**

CHURCH OBSERVER (UK/0009-6482). [5,500] **4947**

CHURCH OF ENGLAND NEWSPAPER : CEN (UK/0964-816X). [12,000] **2514**

CHURCH OF GOD MISSIONS (US/0009-6504). [8,500] **4947**

CHURCH RECREATION MAGAZINE (US/0162-4652). **4849**

CHURCH RESOURCE DIRECTORY (US). [150,000] **4947**

CHURCH TEACHERS (US/0164-6451). [10,000] **4948**

CHUTAEK KUMYUNG (KO). [3,000] **2817**

CHUTO KIHO (JA). [150] **2649**

CIAT INTERNATIONAL (CK). [8,000] **74**

CID : ELECTRONICA Y PROCESO DE DATOS EN CUBA (CU). [6,000] **1174**

CIEL ET TERRE (BE/0009-6709). [1,200] **394**

CIENCIA DA INFORMACAO (BL/0100-1965). [1,000] **3202**

CIENCIA DEL SUELO (AG/0326-3169). [400] **1353**

CIENCIA E INVESTIGACION AGRARIA (CL/0304-5609). [500] **74**

CIENCIA FORESTAL (MX/0185-2418). [2,000] **2377**

CIENCIA HOJE : REVISAT DE DIVULGACAO CIENTIFICA DA SOCIEDADE BRASILEIRA PARA O PROGRESSO DA CIENCIA (BL/0101-8515). [40,000] **5094**

CIENCIA (MEXICO CITY, MEXICO) (MX/0185-075X). [2,000] **5094**

CIENCIA PEDIATRIKA (MADRID, SPAIN : 1986) (SP). [6,500] **3902**

CIENCIA PHARMACEUTICA (SP). [6000] **4296**

CIENCIA Y DESARROLLO (MX/0185-0008). [50,000] **5094**

CIENCIAS MARINAS (MX/0185-3880). [1,000] **553**

CIENTIFICA (JABOTICABAL) (BL/0100-0039). [1,000] **5507**

CIERVO, EL (SP/0045-6896). [5,000] **4948**

CIFRAS (CK/0120-5331). [2,000] **5799**

CIM BULLETIN (CN/0317-0926). [11,000] **2136**

CIMAISE (FR/0009-6830). [15,000] **347**

CIMBEBASIA : JOURNAL OF THE STATE MUSEUM, WINDHOEK (SX/1012-4926). [350] **5095**

CIMENTS, BETONS, PLATRES, CHAUX (FR/0397-006X). [1500] **607**

CINCINNATI

CINCINNATI (US/0009-689X). [20,000] **2530**

CINCINNATI POETRY REVIEW (US). [1,100] **3461**

CINE BULLES (CN/0820-8921). [1,500] **4065**

CINEASTE (NEW YORK, N.Y.) (US/0009-7004). [6,000] **4066**

CINEFAN (US/0095-1447). [1,500] **4066**

CINEFEX (US/0198-1056). [15,000] **4066**

CINEMA IN INDIA (II). [5,000] **4066**

CINEMA NUOVO (IT/0009-711X). **4066**

CINEMA PAPERS (AT/0311-3639). [15,000] **4066**

CINEMA (PORTO, PORTUGAL) (PO). [1,500] **4066**

CINEMA TECHNOLOGY (UK). [4,500] **4066**

CINEMACABRE (US/0198-1064). [3,000] **4066**

CINEMATOGRAPH (US/0886-6570). [1,800] **317**

CIP CIRCULAR (ENGLISH ED.) (PE/0256-8632). **167**

CIRCA. CONFLITS INTERNATIONAUX, LES REGIONS ET LE CANADA (CN/0822-8418). [400] **4518**

CIRCUIT (MONTREAL) (CN/0821-1876). [2,500] **3273**

CIRCUIT RIDER (FRANKFORT, KY.), THE (US/0898-0330). [400] **2728**

CIRCUIT RIDER (NASHVILLE), THE (US/0146-9924). [46,000] **5058**

CIRCUIT RIDER (SPRINGFIELD, ILL.), THE (US/0741-8264). [450] **2443**

CIRCUIT (TORONTO. 1977) (CN/0711-1355). [10,000] **1541**

CIRCUIT WORLD (UK/0305-6120). **2038**

CIRCUITREE MAGAZINE (US). [8,000] **2038**

CIRCULAIRE AUX PRETRES ET AUTRES AGENTS DE PASTORALE (CN/0227-552X). [500 to 600] **5027**

CIRCULAIRE D'INFORMATION (CG). [2,300] **819**

CIRCULAR / SOUTH DAKOTA GEOLOGICAL SURVEY (US/0085-6487). [500] **1372**

CIRCULARS - SOUTH AFRICAN ASTRONOMICAL OBSERVATORY (SA/0376-7884). [500] **394**

CIRCULATION MANAGEMENT (SPRINGFIELD, OR.) (US/0888-8191). [10,000] **2918**

CIRCULATION (NEW YORK, N.Y.) (US/0009-7322). [23,000] **3702**

CIRCULATION RESEARCH (US/0009-7330). [4,000] **3702**

CIRCULO - CIRCULO DE CULTURA PANAMERICANO (US/0009-7349). [800] **3376**

CIRCUS REPORT, THE (US/0889-5996). [2,100] **4849**

CIRUGIA DEL URUGUAY (UY/0009-7381). [500] **3962**

CIRUGIA Y CIRUJANOS (MX/0009-7411). [3,000] **3962**

CISEM INFORMAZIONI (IT). **1732**

CITATION (CHICAGO, ILL.) (US/0009-7446). [2,400] **2950**

CITE (HOUSTON, TEX.) (US/8755-0415). [6,000] **295**

CITIZEN (AUBURN, N.Y.), THE (US/0738-7520). [15,787 daily 16,226 Sunday] **5715**

CITIZEN (DENVER), THE (US/0009-7543). [10,000] **4702**

CITIZEN PARTICIPATION (MEDFORD) (US/0198-8468). [5,000] **4468**

CITIZENS' GUIDE TO LOCAL GOVERNMENT (OLYMPIA, WASH.) (US). [5,000] **4638**

CITRUS AND SUB-TROPICAL FRUIT JOURNAL, THE (SA/0257-2095). [3,750] **167**

CITRUS DEED REPORT (US). **4835**

CITY & COUNTRY CLUB LIFE (US/0897-4926). [30,000] **2530**

CITY & SOCIETY (US/0893-0465). [500] **2818**

CITY GUIDE (NEW YORK, N.Y.) (US/1043-3937). **5466**

CITY OPERA SPOTLIGHT (US/0737-8009). [5,000] **4110**

CITY PAPER (US/0195-0843). [86,000] **5686**

CITY RECORD, THE (US). [3,000] **4638**

CITY SUN, THE (US/8750-2720). [56,863] **5715**

CIVIC AFFAIRS (II/0009-7772). [5,000] **4638**

CIVIC PUBLIC WORKS (CN/0829-772X). [13,500] **4760**

CIVIL AIR PATROL NEWS (US/0009-7810). [70,000] **16**

CIVIL AVIATION TRAINING : CAT (UK/0960-9024). [11,436] **16**

CIVIL ENGINEER IN SOUTH AFRICA, THE (SA/0009-7845). [7,200] **2020**

CIVIL ENGINEERING EDUCATION (US/0884-1926). [1,100] **2020**

CIVIL ENGINEERING SURVEYOR (UK/0266-139X). [3,100] **2021**

CIVIL LAW OPINIONS OF THE JUDGE ADVOCATE GENERAL, UNITED STATES AIR FORCE (US/0748-7657). **3089**

CIVIL PROTECTION (UK/0961-2564). [43,000] **1072**

CIVIL WAR REGIMENTS (US/1055-3266). [1,200] **2728**

CIVITAN MAGAZINE, THE (US/0194-5785). [38,000] **5230**

CLA HANDBOOK AND MEMBERSHIP DIRECTORY / CATHOLIC LIBRARY ASSOCIATION (US). [3,000] **3202**

CLAIRON (MONTREAL) (CN/0710-099X). [800] **5016**

CLAN DIGGER (US/8755-3635). [100] **2443**

CLANDIGGER (EDMONTON) (CN/0226-2436). [400] **2443**

CLARIN : REVISTA DE CULTURA (SP). [5,000] **3461**

CLARION (NEW YORK. 1972) (US/0191-8079). [15,000] **1815**

CLARK CLARION, THE (US/0883-2692). [100] **2443**

CLARK COUNTY HISTORY (US/0090-449X). [800] **2728**

CLASS ACTION REPORTS (US/0746-7168). **2951**

CLASS (NEW YORK, N.Y.) (US/0747-3826). [250,000] **2486**

CLASS RACEHORSES OF AUSTRALIA AND NEW ZEALAND (AT/0814-2513). **2798**

CLASSIC CAR (US/0009-8310). [5,000] **5411**

CLASSICAL ANTIQUITY (US/0278-6656). [650] **1075**

CLASSMATE (CN/0315-906X). [650] **1732**

CLAUDEL STUDIES (US/0090-1237). [400] **3376**

CLAVIER (US/0009-854X). [21,000] **4110**

CLAVIER'S PIANO EXPLORER (US/0279-0858). [85,000] **4110**

CLAY COUNTY FREE PRESS (US). [5,200] **5763**

CLAY SCIENCE (JA/0009-8574). [800] **1353**

CLAYS AND CLAY MINERALS (US/0009-8604). [1,550] **1438**

CLAYTON CONSUMER REPORT (CN/1183-7446). **1294**

CLEANING MANAGEMENT MAGAZINE (US/1051-5720). [34,000] **863**

CLEANROOMS (FLEMINGTON, N.J.) (US/1043-8017). [45,000] **2860**

CLEARWATER NAVIGATOR (US/0747-2218). [9,000] **2226**

CLEARY NEWS (US/0883-7716). [150] **2443**

CLEBURNE COUNTY HISTORICAL SOCIETY JOURNAL (US/0740-5987). [300] **2728**

CLEF, LA (CN). **2951**

CLEM LABINE'S TRADITIONAL BUILDING (US/0898-0284). [15,400] **295**

CLEVELAND ENGINEERING (US/0009-8809). [2,000] **1968**

CLEVELAND STATE LAW REVIEW (US/0009-8876). [900] **2951**

CLIENT COUNSELING UPDATE : CCU (US/0276-752X). **2951**

CLIFTON RECORD, THE (US). [3,300] **5748**

CLIMATE RESEARCH (GW/0936-577X). [300] **1422**

CLIN-ALERT (US/0069-4770). **3564**

CLINICA CHIMICA ACTA (NE/0009-8981). [1,780] **972**

CLINICA E INVESTIGACION EN GINECOLOGIA Y OBSTETRICIA (SP/0210-573X). [5,000] **3758**

CLINICA Y ANALISIS GRUPAL (SP/0210-0657). [1,000] **4581**

CLINICAL AND EXPERIMENTAL HYPERTENSION. PART B, HYPERTENSION IN PREGNANCY (US/0730-0085). **3758**

CLINICAL AND EXPERIMENTAL IMMUNOLOGY (UK/0009-9104). [1,740] **3667**

CLINICAL AND EXPERIMENTAL OBSTETRICS & GYNECOLOGY (IT/0390-6663). [500] **3758**

CLINICAL AND EXPERIMENTAL OPTOMETRY (AT/0816-4622). [2,500] **4215**

CLINICAL AND LABORATORY HAEMATOLOGY (UK/0141-9854). [700] **3771**

CLINICAL BIOCHEMIST REVIEWS (AT/0159-8090). [1,100] **485**

CLINICAL CARDIOLOGY (MAHWAH, N.J.) (US/0160-9289). [22,000] **3703**

CLINICAL CHEMICA (OULU) (FI/0358-4879). [500] **3565**

CLINICAL CONNECTION, THE (US/0890-409X). **4385**

CLINICAL ECOLOGY (US/0735-9306). [1,200] **3565**

CLINICAL GENETICS (DK/0009-9163). [1,000] **543**

CLINICAL HEMOSTASIS REVIEW (US/0894-1025). [5,000] **3565**

CLINICAL LAB PRODUCTS (US/0192-1282). [53,000] **3565**

CLINICAL LABORATORY SCIENCE (US/0894-959X). [20,000] **3566**

CLINICAL MANAGEMENT : THE MAGAZINE OF THE AMERICAN PHYSICAL THERAPY ASSOCIATION (US). [51,000] **4380**

CLINICAL MICROBIOLOGY REVIEWS (US/0893-8512). [7,400] **561**

CLINICAL NEPHROLOGY (GW/0301-0430). **3989**

CLINICAL NEUROLOGY AND NEUROSURGERY (NE/0303-8467). [1,250] **3830**

CLINICAL NEUROPATHOLOGY (GW/0722-5091). **3894**

CLINICAL OTOLARYNGOLOGY AND ALLIED SCIENCES (UK/0307-7772). [935] **3887**

CLINICAL PHARMACOKINETICS (US/0312-5963). [1,500] **4296**

CLINICAL PSYCHIATRY NEWS (US/0270-6644). [28,000] **3923**

CLINICAL RC MANAGER (US/0896-5765). [800] **3778**

CLINICAL SCIENCE (1979) (UK/0143-5221). [2,500] **485**

CLINICAL THERAPEUTICS (US/0149-2918). [2,000] **4297**

CLINICAL TRANSPLANTATION (DK/0902-0063). [1,000] **3566**

CLINIQUE OPHTALMOLOGIQUE PARIS, LA (FR/0009-9368). **3873**

CLIS OBSERVER (II/0970-0943). [1,000] **3202**

CLOTHING AND TEXTILES RESEARCH JOURNAL (US/0887-302X). [1,300] **5349**

CLUB DES AMIS DE GILLES VILLENEUVE INC (CN/0228-4839). **4890**

CLUB INDUSTRY (US/0747-8283). [30,000] **2596**

CLUB INTERNATIONAL (NEWTOWN, CONN.) (US/0747-0819). [295,000] **3994**

CLUB LIVING (US/0160-6166). [51,000] **4890**

CLUB MANAGEMENT IN AUSTRALIA (AT/0045-7205). **5230**

CM BULLETIN (US/0738-5099). [3,000] **4638**

CMEA NEWS (US/0007-8638). [2,700] **4110**

CMN OFFICE MACHINE NEWS (US/0889-5880). [1,750] **4211**

CMS NEWS-LETTER (UK). [5,000] **4948**

CN LINES (US/1061-9739). [350] **5430**

CNSW NEWSLETTER (US/0164-7032). [1,000] **3989**

COACHES REPORT (US). [5,000] **1855**

COAL (CHICAGO, ILL. : 1988) (US/1040-7820). [30,000] **2137**

COAL FOCUS / THE COAL ASSOCIATION OF CANADA (CN/0821-7068). [700] **2137**

COAL PEOPLE (US/0748-6073). [11,000] **2728**

COAL STATISTICS INTERNATIONAL (US/0276-1890). [500] **1438**

COAL TRANSPORTATION STATISTICS (US/1046-9486). **1439**

COALTRANS INTERNATIONAL (UK). [4,728] **2137**

COALTRANS WORCESTER PARK (UK/0269-381X). **1935**

COASTAL MANAGEMENT (US/0892-0753). [800] **2190**

COASTAL PLAINS FARMER. ALABAMA, FLORIDA ED (US/0737-1756). [100,000] **75**

COASTGUARD (UK). [17,000] **4175**

COATINGS (CN/0225-6363). [7,300] **4223**

COMMUNICATION

COCHRANE TIMES (CN/0319-745X). [2,300] **5782**

COCKTAIL MOLOTOV, LE (CN/0228-9067). **1090**

COCOMUNITY NEWSLETTER (IO/0215-1502). [200] **75**

COCONUT STATISTICS / COMPILED AND EXPANDED BY UCAP RESEARCH DEPARTMENT (PH). [500] **152**

CODE NEWS (CLEVELAND, OHIO) (US/0735-9330). **608**

CODE ONE (US/1071-3816). [28,000] **16**

CODESRIA BULLETIN (SG/0850-8712). **5195**

COFFEE & COCOA INTERNATIONAL (UK/0262-5938). [5,000] **2366**

COGNITION (SCARBOROUGH) (CN/0227-0781). [3,000] **167**

COI. COUNTERTRADE AND OFFSET INTELLIGENCE (UK/0950-916X). [1,000] **827**

COIFFURE DE PARIS, LA (FR). **402**

COIFFURE Q : INTERNATIONAL HAIR MAGAZINE (UK). [100,000] **403**

COIN MAGAZINE (US). **2780**

COLD-DRILL MAGAZINE (US/0890-0086). [500] **3376**

COLECCION ESTUDIOS CIEPLAN (CL/0716-0631). [2,500] **1552**

COLECCION JUVENIL MC (SP). [3,000] **2278**

COLLABORATION (HIGH FALLS) (US/0164-1522). [1,500] **4344**

COLLAGE (CAMP HILL, PA.) (US/0883-2781). [7,500] **4760**

COLLECTANEA MATHEMATICA (BARCELONA) (SP/0010-0757). **3500**

COLLECTED PAPERS FROM THE NATIONAL CANCER RESEARCH INSTITUTE (JA/0077-3662). [300] **3815**

COLLECTED REPRINTS (SOUTHWEST FISHERIES CENTER) (US). [125] **2299**

COLLECTED REPRINTS - UNIVERSITY OF GEORGIA MARINE INSTITUTE (US/0072-1328). [500] **553**

COLLECTED REPRINTS - WATER RESOURCES RESEARCH CENTER, UNIVERSITY OF HAWAII (US). [300] **5532**

COLLECTION FORUM (OTTAWA) (CN/0831-4985). [300] **4165**

COLLECTION MANAGEMENT (US/0146-2679). [529] **3202**

COLLECTION ORGANISATION PEDAGOGIQUE (CN/0820-7860). [300] **1861**

COLLECTION UPDATE (CN/0226-3300). [100] **3203**

COLLECTIONS (COLUMBIA, S.C.) (US/1046-2252). [3,500] **4087**

COLLECTIONS (NEWARK, DEL.) (US/8755-3473). [500] **3203**

COLLECTIONS (PHILADELPHIA, PA.) (US/0275-8091). [8,500] **3567**

COLLECTIVE BARGAINING HANDBOOK (CN/0710-5193). **939**

COLLECTORS' AUCTION (BALTIMORE) (US/0093-1047). [1,000] **4087**

COLLEGE AND JUNIOR TENNIS (US/0279-1153). [5,000] **4890**

COLLEGE AND UNIVERSITY (US/0010-0889). [9,200] **1816**

COLLEGE AND UNIVERSITY ADMISSIONS AND ENROLLMENT, NEW YORK STATE (US/0147-5894). **1816**

COLLEGE BOARD NEWS (US/0530-9581). [100,000] **1816**

COLLEGE BOARD REVIEW, THE (US/0010-0951). **1816**

COLLEGE COMMENT (THUNDER BAY) (CN/0700-3668). **1816**

COLLEGE COMPOSITION AND COMMUNICATION (US/0010-096X). [100,000] **1816**

COLLEGE ENGLISH (US/0010-0994). [16,000] **3274**

COLLEGE LITERATURE (US/0093-3139). [1,000] **3376**

COLLEGE REVIEW (DENVER, COLO.), THE (US/0742-8057). [765] **3567**

COLLEGE STORE EXECUTIVE (US/0010-1141). **922**

COLLEGE STORE JOURNAL, THE (US/0010-115X). [6,142] **1817**

COLLEGE STUDENT AFFAIRS JOURNAL, THE (US/0888-210X). [1,100] **1817**

COLLEGE STUDENT AND THE COURTS, THE (US/0145-1472). [2,800] **2952**

COLLEGE STUDENT JOURNAL (US/0146-3934). [1,000] **1817**

COLLEGE UNION & ON-CAMPUS HOSPITALITY (US/0887-431X). **1090**

COLLEGIATE SPORTS REPORT (US/0748-9668). **4890**

COLLEGIATE TRENDS (RIDGEWOOD, N.J.) (US/1065-0296). [3,000] **1817**

COLLOID AND POLYMER SCIENCE (GW/0303-402X). [3,000] **1050**

COLLOQUIUM MATHEMATICUM (PL/0010-1354). [2,000] **3500**

COLONIAL ECHO (US). [4,000] **1090**

COLOQUIO : LETRAS (PO/0010-1451). [4,000] **3376**

COLORADO BANKRUPTCY COURT REPORTER, THE (US/1048-3683). **2952**

COLORADO BUSINESS MAGAZINE : CBM (US/0898-6363). [22,000] **658**

COLORADO ENGINEER, THE (US/0010-1583). [3,000] **1968**

COLORADO GENEALOGIST, THE (US/0010-1613). [650] **2443**

COLORADO GREEN (US/0195-0045). [7,500] **2412**

COLORADO HERITAGE (US/0272-9377). [6,500] **2729**

COLORADO INSURANCE INDUSTRY STATISTICAL REPORT (US/0277-9595). [250] **2897**

COLORADO LAWYER (US/0363-7867). [13,000] **2952**

COLORADO LIBRARIES (US/0147-9733). [1,200] **3203**

COLORADO MUNICIPALITIES (US/0010-1664). [4,500] **4639**

COLORADO-NORTH REVIEW (US/0194-0589). [1,500] **3377**

COLORADO NURSE (1985) (US/8750-846X). [2,000] **3854**

COLORADO OUTDOORS (US/0010-1699). [48,000] **2190**

COLORADO SCHOOL OF MINES QUARTERLY (US/0163-9153). [950] **2137**

COLORADO STATE AND COUNTY RETAIL SALES BY STANDARD INDUSTRIAL CLASSIFICATION (ANNUAL) (US/0732-1015). [75] **953**

COLUMBAN MISSION (US/0095-4438). [150,000] **4948**

COLUMBIA, A MAGAZINE OF POETRY AND PROSE (US/0161-486X). [2,000] **3377**

COLUMBIA BUSINESS LAW REVIEW (US/0898-0721). **3097**

COLUMBIA DOCUMENTS OF ARCHITECTURE AND THEORY (US/1065-304X). [3,000] **295**

COLUMBIA FLIER (US/0192-7841). [34,000] **5686**

COLUMBIA HUMAN RIGHTS LAW REVIEW (US/0090-7944). [600] **4506**

COLUMBIA JOURNAL OF WORLD BUSINESS, THE (US/0022-5428). [5,000] **658**

COLUMBIA LAW REVIEW (US/0010-1958). [3,200] **2953**

COLUMBIA MISSOURIAN (US/0747-1874). [5,527] **5703**

COLUMBIA (NEW HAVEN) (US/0010-1869). [1,402,000] **5028**

COLUMBIA (NEW YORK, N.Y. 1978) (US/0162-3893). [66,000] **1090**

COLUMBIA SPECTATOR (US). [10,000] **5715**

COLUMBUS JOURNAL-REPUBLICAN (COLUMBUS, WIS. : 1971) (US). **5766**

COLUMNS (MADISON) (US/0196-1306). [5,500] **2729**

COLUSA COUNTY SUN HERALD (US/0897-8743). **5634**

COM-AND, COMPUTER AUDIT NEWS DEVELOPMENTS (US/0738-4270). **741**

COMBAT NATURE PERIGUEUX (FR/0184-7473). [12,000] **2163**

COMBINED CUMULATIVE INDEX TO OBSTETRICS AND GYNECOLOGY (US/0884-8092). **3655**

COMBINED CUMULATIVE INDEX TO PEDIATRICS (US/0190-4981). [2,000] **3655**

COMBINED INDEX FOR THE JOURNALS SULPHUR, NITROGEN AND PHOSPHORUS & POTASSIUM (UK). [1,000] **1023**

COMBINED PROCEEDINGS / INTERNATIONAL PLANT PROPAGATORS' SOCIETY (US/0538-9143). [3,500] **2412**

COMBONI MISSIONS (US/0279-3652). [22,000] **4949**

COME-ALL-YE (HATBORO, PA.) (US/0736-6132). [2,000] **2319**

COME AND SEE (CN/0316-3040). [7,000] **5016**

COME BACK SAFELY (US). [14,000] **5380**

COMEDIE FRANCAISE (FR). [3,000] **5363**

COMERCIO E INDUSTRIA (SAN SALVADOR, EL SALVADOR) (ES). [3,000] **828**

COMIC PRESS NEWS (US). [35,000] **4859**

COMIC TALE EASY READER (US/0748-2264). [3,000] **1062**

COMICS JOURNAL, THE (US/0194-7869). [12,000] **377**

COMITEXTIL. BULLETIN (BE). [400] **5349**

COMLA NEWSLETTER (JM/0378-1070). [500] **3203**

COMMENT (DON MILLS) (CN/0382-7038). [25,000] **2878**

COMMENTARY (NEW YORK) (US/0010-2601). [37,000] **5047**

COMMENTARY (SINGAPORE) (SI/0084-8956). [5,000] **2503**

COMMENTS FROM THE FRIENDS (US/1063-7575). [2,000] **4949**

COMMERCE (HACKENSACK, N.Y.) (US/0745-077X). [15,000] **658**

COMMERCE INTERNATIONAL (UK/0010-2733). [7,000] **828**

COMMERCE NEWS (CN/0704-8017). [6,500] **819**

COMMERCIAL AGRICULTURE IN ZIMBABWE (RH). [10,000] **75**

COMMERCIAL CARPET DIGEST (US/0890-0027). **5349**

COMMERCIAL FISHERIES NEWS (US/0273-6713). [8,500] **2299**

COMMERCIAL FISHING (UK/0143-652X). [2,000] **2299**

COMMERCIAL FISHING (NZ/0110-1730). [2,000] **2299**

COMMERCIAL LAWS OF THE WORLD. CLASS C (US). [500] **3126**

COMMERCIAL LENDING NEWSLETTER (US). [19,000] **783**

COMMERCIAL RECORD (SOUTH WINDSOR, CT.), THE (US/0010-3098). [4,000] **4836**

COMMERCIAL RENOVATION (US/0747-0134). [45,000] **608**

COMMERCIAL REVIEW (PORTLAND, OR.) (US/0010-3101). [1,000] **75**

COMMISSAIRE D'ECOLES (CN/0228-7684). **1861**

COMMITTEE BULLETIN (AT). [1,000] **4639**

COMMITTEE ON EAST ASIAN LIBRARIES BULLETIN (US/0148-6225). [350] **3203**

COMMLAW CONSPECTUS (US/1068-5871). **2953**

COMMODITIES LAW LETTER (US/0277-2930). [300] **2953**

COMMON FOCUS (US). [8,000] **4582**

COMMON GROUND (UK/0010-325X). [4,000] **4949**

COMMON GROUND. (OTTAWA) (CN/1189-6892). [300] **1732**

COMMON SENSE PEST CONTROL QUARTERLY (US/8756-7881). [1,000] **4244**

COMMONWEALTH CURRENTS (UK/0141-8513). [30,000] **2908**

COMMONWEALTH OF AUSTRALIA NATIONAL REPORT (AT). **2581**

COMMONWEALTH (SAN FRANCISCO), THE (US/0010-3349). [18,000] **2531**

COMMONWEALTH SCIENTIFIC & INDUSTRIAL RESEARCH ORGANISATION. DIVISION OF HORTICULTURE. REPORT (AT/0069-7435). [1000] **2412**

COMMONWEALTH, THE (US). **5703**

COMMUNAL SOCIETIES (US/0739-1250). [1,000] **5242**

COMMUNAUTE CHRETIENNE (CN/0010-3454). [1,300] **4949**

COMMUNICATE (HIGH WYCOMBE) (UK/0264-4509). [17,118] **1151**

COMMUNICATIE (BE/0771-7342). [1,000] **1106**

COMMUNICATION BOOKNOTES (US/0748-657X). [1,700] **1125**

COMMUNICATION EDUCATION (US/0363-4523). [5,000] **1106**

COMMUNICATION ET INFORMATION (CN/0382-7798). [500] **1106**

COMMUNICATION - INTERNATIONAL SKATING UNION (SZ). [1,700] **4891**

COMMUNICATION LONDON. 1967 (UK/0045-7663). **3923**

COMMUNICATION MONOGRAPHS (US/0363-7751). [4,500] **1107**

COMMUNICATION OUTLOOK (US/0161-4126). [2,649] **1107**

COMMUNICATION QUARTERLY (US/0146-3373). [3,000] **1107**

COMMUNICATION QUARTERLY (EAST LANSING) (US/0274-6530). [10,000] **1891**

COMMUNICATION

COMMUNICATION RESEARCH REPORTS (US/0882-4096). [500] **1107**

COMMUNICATION WORLD (SAN FRANCISCO, CALIF.) (US/0744-7612). [12,500] **1107**

COMMUNICATIONES ARCHEOLOGICAE HUNGARIAE (HU). [800] **266**

COMMUNICATIONS & STRATEGIES MONTPELLIER (FR/1157-8637). [1,000] **1175**

COMMUNICATIONS FROM THE INTERNATIONAL BRECHT SOCIETY (US/0740-8943). [250] **3377**

COMMUNICATIONS FROM THE KAMERLINGH ONNES LABORATORY OF THE UNIVERSITY OF LEIDEN (NE). **4400**

COMMUNICATIONS IN ALGEBRA (US/0092-7872). **3500**

COMMUNICATIONS IN PARTIAL DIFFERENTIAL EQUATIONS (US/0360-5302). **3501**

COMMUNICATIONS IN SOIL SCIENCE AND PLANT ANALYSIS (US/0010-3624). **167**

COMMUNICATIONS TECHNOLOGY (US/0884-2272). **1130**

COMMUNIO (SPOKANE, WASH.) (US/0094-2065). [2,700] **4949**

COMMUNION (FR/0042-370X). [400] **5028**

COMMUNIQUE / CANADIAN COMMUNICATION ASSOCIATION (CN/0821-4379). [350] **1108**

COMMUNIQUE - CDA (CN/0711-8112). **4189**

COMMUNIQUE - CHILDREN'S AID SOCIETY OF OTTAWA (CN/0319-7468). **5279**

COMMUNIQUE HEBROMADAIRE (INSTITUT NATIONAL DE STATISTIQUE (BELGIUM) : 1982) (BE/0771-0410). [500] **5325**

COMMUNIQUE / HUMAN FACTORS ASSOCIATION OF CANADA (CN/0712-936X). [400] **2860**

COMMUNIQUE (KENT) (US/0164-775X). [15,000] **4582**

COMMUNIQUE (LAW SOCIETY OF MANITOBA) (CN/0824-2186). [2,000] **2954**

COMMUNIQUE - LEARNING DISABILITIES ASSOCIATION OF ONTARIO (CN/0843-2236). [5,000] **1877**

COMMUNIQUE / NATIONAL ASSOCIATION FOR GIFTED CHILDREN (US/0884-3643). [6,700] **1877**

COMMUNIQUE (RICHMOND, VA) (US). [800] **1319**

COMMUNIQUE - SOCIETE D'ARTHRITE (CN/0824-4154). **3804**

COMMUNIQUE - SOCIETY FOR INTERCULTURAL EDUCATION, TRAINING AND RESEARCH (US/0276-1386). [1800-2000] **1733**

COMMUNIQUE - SYNCHRO SWIM CANADA (CN/0226-8701). [2,700] **4891**

COMMUNITY (ALEXANDRIA, VA. : 1982) (US/0736-2099). [6,400] **5279**

COMMUNITY ALTERNATIVES (US/1052-7656). **5279**

COMMUNITY ANIMAL CONTROL (US/0278-2863). [7,500] **226**

COMMUNITY BANK PRESIDENT, THE (US/0276-0908). **783**

COMMUNITY CHANGE (US/0896-9159). [3,000] **2818**

COMMUNITY COLLEGE JOURNALIST : OFFICIAL PUBLICATION OF THE COMMUNITY COLLEGE JOURNALISM ASSOCIATION (US). [400] **2918**

COMMUNITY DENTISTRY AND ORAL EPIDEMIOLOGY (DK/0301-5661). [800] **1319**

COMMUNITY DEVELOPMENT JOURNAL (UK/0010-3802). [1,500] **5242**

COMMUNITY DIGEST (VANCOUVER) (CN/0826-4260). **2531**

COMMUNITY EDUCATION JOURNAL (US/0045-7736). [1,400] **1733**

COMMUNITY JOBS (US/0195-1157). [15,000] **1660**

COMMUNITY LEADERS OF AMERICA (1981) (US/0741-4161). **431**

COMMUNITY MARKETS CANADA : THE COMPREHENSIVE GUIDE TO THE LATEST COMMUNITY NEWSPAPER MARKET DATA (CN/0229-1630). **757**

COMMUNITY NEWS (BROWNS MILLS, N.J.), THE (US/0745-8150). [2,500] **5709**

COMMUNITY PRESS (MILLBROOK, ALA.) (US/0739-9219). [1,850] **5626**

COMMUNITY PUBLICATION RATES AND DATA (US/0162-8887). [2,000] **757**

COMMUNITY RELATIONS REPORT (BARTLESVILLE, OKLA.), THE (US/0736-7147). [500] **757**

COMMUNITY SERVICE BUSINESS (US/0747-6086). [150] **5196**

COMMUNITY SERVICE NEWSLETTER (US/0277-6189). [400] **2818**

COMMUNITY, TECHNICAL, AND JUNIOR COLLEGE JOURNAL (US/0884-7169). [23,120] **1818**

COMMUTATION & TRANSMISSION (FR/0242-1283). [7500] **1152**

COMMUTER (COLLEGE PARK, MD.), THE (US/0734-3817). [500] **5380**

COMMUTER WORLD (UK/0265-4504). [13,000] **16**

COMPANY LAW DIGEST (NEW DELHI, INDIA) (II). [10,000] **3098**

COMPANY RECOGNITION STUDY. RETAILER EDITION (US/0275-7486). **1969**

COMPANY SECRETARY'S REVIEW (UK/0309-703X). [8,500] **3098**

COMPARATIVE AND INTERNATIONAL LAW JOURNAL OF SOUTHERN AFRICA, THE (SA/0010-4051). [500] **3126**

COMPARATIVE DRAMA (US/0010-4078). [1,000] **5363**

COMPARATIVE EDUCATION (UK/0305-0068). **1733**

COMPARATIVE LABOR LAW JOURNAL (US/1043-5255). [800] **3145**

COMPARATIVE LITERATURE (US/0010-4124). [2,500] **3377**

COMPARATIVE LITERATURE STUDIES (URBANA) (US/0010-4132). [1,000] **3377**

COMPASS (UK). [100] **4469**

COMPASS ROSE (US/0742-8928). **658**

COMPASS (TORONTO) (CN/0715-8777). **4949**

COMPENDIO DE ESTADISTICAS SOCIALES / ESTADO LIBRE ASOCIADO DE PUERTO RICO, OFICINA DEL GOBERNADOR, JUNTA DE PLANIFICACION (PR). **5325**

COMPENDIUM DE INVESTIGACIONES CLINICAS LATINOAMERICANAS (MX/0185-1934). [5,500] **3567**

COMPETITION ANGLER (US/1047-1669). [1,000] **4871**

COMPETITION LAW IN THE EUROPEAN COMMUNITIES (UK). **3098**

COMPETITIONS (LOUISVILLE, KY.) (US/1058-6539). [2,000] **295**

COMPETITIVE ADVANCES. MATERIALS AND PROCESSES (US). [16,000] **5095**

COMPETITIVE INTELLIGENCE REVIEW (US/1058-0247). [1,700] **659**

COMPLEAT GOLFER (SA/1015-8014). [30,000] **4891**

COMPLEAT MOTHER, THE (CN/0829-8564). [15,000] **3759**

COMPLETE GUIDE TO HAZARDOUS MATERIALS ENFORCEMENT AND LIABILITY (CN). **2226**

COMPLICATIONS IN ORTHOPEDICS (US/0887-1736). [18,000] **3881**

COMPOLUX (IT). **2039**

COMPOSER NEWS (US/0894-5950). [2,500] **4111**

COMPOSITE POLYMERS (UK/0952-6919). [200] **4454**

COMPOSITES & ADHESIVES NEWSLETTER, THE (US/0888-1227). [250] **1023**

COMPOSITIO MATHEMATICA (NE/0010-437X). [650] **3501**

COMPREHENSIVE ANNUAL FINANCIAL REPORT, STATE OF MISSOURI (US). [800] **4718**

COMPREHENSIVE DISSERTATION INDEX (US). [3,000] **3567**

COMPRENDRE (IT/0010-4418). [2,000] **5242**

COMPRESSED AIR (1965) (US/0010-4426). [143,000] **1602**

COMPTES RENDUS DE L'ACADEMIE D'AGRICULTURE DE FRANCE (FR/0989-6988). [1,400] **76**

COMPU-MART (RICHARDSON, TEX.) (US/1072-3544). [60,000] **1236**

COMPU-MGR TELE-MGR (US). [40,000] **1175**

COMPUT-A-CAL (US/0742-5686). **5174**

COMPUTATIONAL COMPLEXITY (SZ/1016-3328). [400] **3501**

COMPUTER AIDED DESIGN REPORT (US/0276-749X). [2,600] **1232**

COMPUTER-AIDED ENGINEERING (US/0733-3536). [40,000] **1228**

COMPUTER AIDED SELLING (US/8756-8780). [5,000] **659**

COMPUTER AND COMMUNICATIONS BUYER (US/0272-4553). **1244**

COMPUTER & ELECTRONICS GRADUATE, THE (US/0882-200X). [18,000] **4203**

COMPUTER & VIDEOGIOCHI (IT). [40,000] **4859**

COMPUTER DISPLAY REVIEW, THE (US/0010-4582). [250] **1264**

COMPUTER GAMING WORLD (US/0744-6667). [25,000] **1230**

COMPUTER GRAPHICS FORUM : A JOURNAL OF THE EUROPEAN ASSOCIATION FOR COMPUTER GRAPHICS (NE/0167-7055). [1430] **1232**

COMPUTER GRAPHICS WORLD (US/0271-4159). [50,000] **1232**

COMPUTER HOT LINE (US/0192-6349). **1176**

COMPUTER INDUSTRY REPORT (US/0889-082X). **1256**

COMPUTER-INTEGRATED MANUFACTURING SYSTEMS (UK/0951-5240). [1,200] **1228**

COMPUTER LAW MONITOR, THE (US/0741-8809). [250] **2954**

COMPUTER LAW REPORTER (US/0739-7771). [300] **2954**

COMPUTER LETTER (US). **5096**

COMPUTER LITERACY NEWSLETTER (US). [2,500] **1177**

COMPUTER MUSIC JOURNAL (US/0148-9267). [3,700] **1240**

COMPUTER PAPER (BRITISH COLUMBIA ED.) (CN/0840-3929). [350,000] **1177**

COMPUTER PERIPHERALS REVIEW (US/0149-5054). [750] **1264**

COMPUTER POST (CN/1194-305X). [11,000] **1177**

COMPUTER PRICE GUIDE (US/0045-7841). **1244**

COMPUTER PRICE WATCH (US/1052-3502). **1244**

COMPUTER PRODUCT NEWS (BE). [50,000] **1244**

COMPUTER PUBLICITY NEWS (US/0276-9972). [600] **758**

COMPUTER RESELLER NEWS (US/0893-8377). [64,000] **1244**

COMPUTER REVIEW (US/0093-416X). [1,000] **1264**

COMPUTER SECURITY, AUDITING AND CONTROLS (US/0738-4262). **1226**

COMPUTER SECURITY JOURNAL (US/0277-0865). [30,000] **1226**

COMPUTER SOFTWARE ENGINEERING SERIES (US/0888-2088). **1178**

COMPUTER SWEDEN (SW/0280-9982). [21000] **1178**

COMPUTER TECHNOLOGY REVIEW (US/0278-9647). [67,000] **1246**

COMPUTER TRADE WEEKLY (UK). **1178**

COMPUTER USERS' YEAR BOOK (UK/0268-6821). **1245**

COMPUTERIZED DRAFTING AND DESIGN NEWSLETTER (US/0748-660X). [1,867] **1232**

COMPUTERIZED INVESTING (US/0734-4597). [45,000] **895**

COMPUTERS AND LAW SYDNEY (AT/0811-7225). [1,000] **1178**

COMPUTERS AND MATH SERIES (US/0888-2193). **1179**

COMPUTERS IN CARDIOLOGY (US/0276-6574). **3703**

COMPUTERS IN EDUCATION JOURNAL (US/1069-3769). [1,500] **1179**

COMPUTERS IN EDUCATION SERIES (US/0888-2177). **1179**

COMPUTERTALK FOR THE PHARMACIST (US/0736-3893). [50,000] **4297**

COMPUTERWORLD ITALIA (IT/0392-8845). [25,000] **1180**

COMPUTHINK WINDOWS WATCHER, THE (US/1054-0784). **1180**

COMPUTING AND THE CLASSICS (US/8756-596X). [500] **1222**

COMPUTING CANADA (CN/0319-0161). [32,000] **1257**

COMPUTING IN MUSICOLOGY (US/1057-9478). [3500] **1240**

COMPUTING NEWS / YORK UNIVERSITY (CN/0226-9201). [1200] **1180**

COMPUTING RESEARCH NEWS (US/1069-384X). [5,000] **1180**

COMPUTING RESOURCES FOR THE PROFESSIONAL (US/0276-5756). [100] **659**

COMPUTING TEACHER, THE (US/0278-9175). [14,000] **1222**

COMSTOCK'S (US). [16,000] **659**

COMUNICACION (VE). **5242**

COMUNICACIONES (CU). [10,000] **1109**

COMUNICACIONES BIOLOGICAS (AG/0326-1956). [300] **452**

COMUNICACIONES (CORAL GABLES, FLA.) (US/0748-3104). [12,000] **1152**

COMUNICACOES DO INSTITUTO DE INVESTIGACAO CIENTIFICA TROPICAL, SERIE DE CIENCIAS AGRARIAS (PO). [1,000] **76**

COMUNICACOES DO INSTITUTO DE INVESTIGACAO CIENTIFICA TROPICAL, SERIE DE CIENCIAS BIOLOGICAS (PO/0871-1755). [1,000] **452**

COMUNICACOES DO INSTITUTO DE INVESTIGACAO CIENTIFICA TROPICAL, SERIE DE CIENCIAS ETNOLOGICAS E ETNOMUSEOLOGICAS (PO/0871-178X). [1,000] **2258**

COMUNICACOES DO INSTITUTO DE INVESTIGACAO CIENTIFICA TROPICAL, SERIE DE CIENCIAS HISTORICAS, ECONOMICAS E SOCIOLOGICAS (PO/0871-1771). [1,000] **1470**

COMUNICACOES - INSTITUTO DE INVESTIGACAO CIENTIFICA TROPICAL. SERIE DE CIENCIAS DA TERRA (PO/0871-1798). [1,000] **1354**

COMUNICACOES - INSTITUTO DE INVESTIGACAO CIENTIFICA TROPICAL. SERIE DE CIENCIAS DE ENGENHARIA GEOGRAFICA (PO/0871-1747). [1,000] **2559**

COMUNIMEF (MX). **784**

CON TEXT MAGAZINE (BE). [4,800] **1083**

CONA JOURNAL (CN/0708-6474). [400] **3854**

CONCERN (REGINA) (CN/0836-7310). [10,500] **3854**

CONCERTACTION (CN/0226-5729). **5280**

CONCERTINA & SQUEEZEBOX (US). [750] **4111**

CONCORD BUSINESS (US). [5,000] **659**

CONCORDIA THEOLOGICAL QUARTERLY (US/0038-8610). [9,000] **4949**

CONCORDIAN, THE (US). [3,500] **1091**

CONCOURS MEDICAL (FR/0010-5309). [55,000] **3568**

CONDENSER (TONGAAT, SOUTH AFRICA) (SA). [18,000] **659**

CONDITION MONITORING AND DIAGNOSTIC TECHNOLOGY (UK). [500] **1969**

CONDIZIONAMENTO DELL'ARIA, RISCALDAMENTO, REFRIGERAZIONE (IT/0373-7772). [5,300] **2604**

CONFECTIONER (1989), THE (US/1047-8345). [12,200] **2332**

CONFEDERATE CHRONICLES OF TENNESSEE (US/0895-9455). [1,000] **2729**

CONFEDERATE VETERAN (MURFREESBORO, TENN.) (US/0890-2216). [20,000] **2729**

CONFERENCE BOARD BRIEFING, THE (US/0899-6741). **864**

CONFERENCE GREEN BOOK (UK). [7,000] **2804**

CONFERENCE PROCEEDINGS - INTERNATIONAL SOCIETY FOR MUSIC EDUCATION (UK). [2,000] **4111**

CONFERENCE RECORD OF THE ... ANNUAL ACM SYMPOSIUM ON PRINCIPLES OF PROGRAMMING LANGUAGES (US/0730-8566). **1279**

CONFERENZE DEL SEMINARIO DI MATEMATICA DELL'UNIVERSITA DI BARI (IT/0374-2113). **3502**

CONGREGATIONALIST (BELOIT), THE (US/0010-5856). [5,000] **4950**

CONGRES ARCHEOLOGIQUE DE FRANCE (FR/0069-8881). **266**

CONGRESS & THE PRESIDENCY (US/0734-3469). **4469**

CONGRESS MONTHLY (1985) (US/0887-0764). [30,000] **2258**

CONGRESSIONAL INFORMATION BUREAU (US/1062-6506). [1,000] **4175**

CONJUNCTIONS (NEW YORK, N.Y.) (US/0278-2324). [8,000] **3340**

CONNAISSANCE DES ARTS, PLAISIR DE FRANCE (FR/0395-5907). [47,118] **348**

CONNECTICARD ANNUAL STATISTICAL REPORT (US). [250] **3258**

CONNECTICUT ANCESTRY (US/0197-2103). [400] **2444**

CONNECTICUT ANTIQUARIAN, THE (US/0010-6054). [1,000] **2729**

CONNECTICUT BAR JOURNAL (US/0010-6070). [11,300] **2955**

CONNECTICUT ENGLISH JOURNAL (US/0893-0376). [600] **1891**

CONNECTICUT GREENHOUSE NEWSLETTER (US). [900] **2412**

CONNECTICUT LIBRARIES (1954-) (US/0010-616X). [1,000] **3204**

CONNECTICUT MARKET DATA (US/0573-665X). [5,000] **1531**

CONNECTICUT MEDICINE (US/0010-6178). [6,500] **3568**

CONNECTICUT NURSING NEWS (1980) (US/0278-4092). [1,700] **3854**

CONNECTICUT NUTMEGGER, THE (US/0045-8120). [4,300] **2444**

CONNECTICUT WOODLANDS (US/0010-6259). [3,000] **2163**

CONNECTION (BOSTON, MASS.) (US/0895-6405). [15,000] **1818**

CONNECTION TECHNOLOGY (US/8756-4076). [35,000] **5096**

CONNECTION, THE (US/1045-7445). [195,000] **1279**

CONNECTIONS JOURNAL (CN/0714-8550). **2190**

CONNOISSEURS' GUIDE TO CALIFORNIA WINE (US/0161-6668). [10,000] **2366**

CONRAD GREBEL REVIEW, THE (CN/0829-044X). [600] **4950**

CONRADIAN : THE JOURNAL OF THE JOSEPH CONRAD SOCIETY (U.K.), THE (UK). [300] **3378**

CONRADIANA (US/0010-6356). [650] **431**

CONROE DAILY COURIER (US). [13,500] **5748**

CONSCIOUSNESS (AT). [350] **4241**

CONSECRATED LIFE (ENGLISH ED.) (US/0884-7010). [2,300] **4950**

CONSENSUS (OTTAWA) (CN/0380-1314). [16,000] **4030**

CONSERVATION BIOLOGY (US/0888-8892). [3,000] **2190**

CONSERVATION DIRECTORY (US/0069-911X). [8,000] **2190**

CONSERVATIONEWS (US). [150] **4828**

CONSERVATIONIST, THE (US/0010-650X). [175,000] **2190**

CONSERVATIVE JUDAISM (US/0010-6542). [2,000] **5047**

CONSORT (DOLMETSCH FOUNDATION), THE (UK/0268-9111). [600] **4111**

CONSORT (HALIFAX) (CN/0823-8278). [150] **4111**

CONSORTIUM NEWS / HEALTH SCIENCES CONSORTIUM (US). [3,000] **3913**

CONSTITUTIONAL AND PARLIAMENTARY INFORMATION (SZ/0010-6623). [1,500] **3092**

CONSTITUTIONAL REFORM : THE QUARTERLY REVIEW (UK/0269-2511). [2,000] **3092**

CONSTRUCTION ALBERTA NEWS (CN/0700-9178). [4,300] **608**

CONSTRUCTION AND ENGINEERING, ZIMBABWE (RH). [3,000] **1969**

CONSTRUCTION & SURETY LAW DIVISION NEWSLETTER (US/0148-933X). [500] **2956**

CONSTRUCTION (ARLINGTON) (US/0010-6704). [6,900] **608**

CONSTRUCTION CANADA (CN/0228-8788). [3,900] **609**

CONSTRUCTION COMPUTING (UK/0264-6854). [30,000] **1180**

CONSTRUCTION DIMENSIONS (US/0194-8903). [16,288] **609**

CONSTRUCTION EQUIPMENT (1970) (US/0192-3978). [80,195] **609**

CONSTRUCTION EQUIPMENT, OPERATION AND MAINTENANCE (US/0010-6771). [69,240] **609**

CONSTRUCTION LABOR NEWS (US/0161-990X). [17,000] **1661**

CONSTRUCTION LAWYER, THE (US/0272-0116). [7,000] **2956**

CONSTRUCTION (LONDON, 1977) (UK/0142-0410). [10,000] **609**

CONSTRUCTION MANITOBA (CN/0832-5804). [1,865] **610**

CONSTRUCTION NEWS (LITTLE ROCK) (US/0160-5607). [7,680] **610**

CONSTRUCTION SIGHTLINES (CN/0708-1073). [4,200] **610**

CONSTRUCTION SPECIFIER, THE (US/0010-6925). [19,500] **610**

CONSTRUCTIONAL REVIEW (AT/0010-695X). [3,000] **611**

CONSTRUIRE (QUEBEC) (CN/0833-0239). [14,000] **611**

CONSULTANT PHARMACIST, THE (US/0888-5109). [11,100] **4298**

CONSULTING-SPECIFYING ENGINEER (US/0892-5046). [50,000] **2097**

CONSUMER ALERT (US). **1294**

CONSUMER ALERT COMMENTS (US/0740-4964). **1294**

CONSUMER BUYING GUIDE (SKOKIE, ILL.) (US). **1294**

CONSUMER CURRENTS (MY/0128-1143). [350] **1294**

CONSUMER HEALTH (US/0736-010X). **4772**

CONSUMER HEALTH & NUTRITION INDEX (US/0883-1963). **4200**

CONSUMER PHARMACIST, THE (US/0738-0615). [6,000] **4298**

CONSUMER TRENDS (US). [1,150] **784**

CONSUMERS INDEX TO PRODUCT EVALUATIONS AND INFORMATION SOURCES (US/0094-0534). [2,000] **1300**

CONSUMING PASSIONS (US/0741-7748). [5,000] **4189**

CONTACT (CN). [15,000] **5096**

CONTACT (UK). **4386**

CONTACT - ASSOCIATION CANADIENNE DES PROFESSIONNELS DE LA VENTE (CN/1193-7521). [30,000] **659**

CONTACT - ASSOCIATION OF REGISTRARS OF THE UNIVERSITIES AND COLLEGES OF CANADA (CN/0822-7632). [550] **1818**

CONTACT - CANADIAN PROFESSIONAL SALES ASSOCIATION (CN/1193-7513). [30,000] **659**

CONTACT DERMATITIS (DK/0105-1873). [1,500] **3718**

CONTACT (DON MILLS) (CN/0703-119X). [5000] **4836**

CONTACT II (US/0197-6796). [2,500] **3461**

CONTACT LENS FORUM (US/0363-1621). [20,000] **4215**

CONTACT LENS SPECTRUM (US/0885-9175). [26,227] **4215**

CONTACT (MONTREAL. 1977) (CN/0703-5780). **1661**

CONTACT - NATIONAL ASSOCIATION OF FREE WILL BAPTISTS (US/0573-7796). [5,000] **5058**

CONTACT (SOCIETE DE RELATIONS D'AFFAIRES, ECOLE DES HAUTES ETUDES COMMERCIALES. 1981) (CN/0713-5009). **659**

CONTACT (TEMISCAMING) (CN/0821-2341). **2531**

CONTACT (TORONTO. 1972) (CN/0319-7379). [1,800] **4386**

CONTADURIA UNIVERSIDAD DE ANTIOQUIA (CK/0120-4203). [1,000] **741**

CONTAGIOUS MAGAZINE (AT). **1062**

CONTAMINACION AMBIENTAL (CK). [1,500] **2226**

CONTEMPO (BIRMINGHAM, ALA.) (US/0162-1971). [61,000] **4950**

CONTEMPORARY DIAGNOSTIC RADIOLOGY (US/0149-9009). [1,700] **3940**

CONTEMPORARY INTERNAL MEDICINE (US/1042-9646). [90,000] **3796**

CONTEMPORARY LONGTERM CARE (US/8750-9652). [33,000] **5280**

CONTEMPORARY OB/GYN (US/0090-3159). [31,000] **3759**

CONTEMPORARY PSYCHOANALYSIS (US/0010-7530). [1,650] **3923**

CONTEMPORARY TIMES (US/1071-2917). [5,500] **864**

CONTINENTAL COMMENTS (US/0573-8164). [4,000] **5412**

CONTINENTAL MODELLER (UK/0955-1298). **2773**

CONTINGENCIES (WASHINGTON, D.C.) (US/1048-9851). [20,000] **2878**

CONTINUING EDUCATION (TORONTO) (CN/0318-5141). [7,200] **4298**

CONTINUING HIGHER EDUCATION REVIEW (US/0893-0384). [2,000] **1818**

CONTINUO (BRISBANE, QLD.) (AT/0310-6802). [80] **4112**

CONTINUOUS IMPROVEMENT (US/1071-2240). [2,000] **3477**

CONTINUOUS JOURNEY (US/1065-3406). **864**

CONTINUOUS SAMPLE SURVEY OF POPULATION (TR/0564-2612). [400] **4551**

CONTINUUM (MONTREAL) (CN/0226-6385). [15,000] **5782**

CONTRACEPTION (STONEHAM) (US/0010-7824). [900] **588**

CONTRACT MANAGEMENT (US/0190-3063). **2956**

CONTRACTORS GUIDE (LOMBARD, ILL.) (US/0273-5954). [30,000] **611**

CONTRACTORS MANAGEMENT JOURNAL (US). [1,000] **295**

CONTRADDIZIONE, LA (IT). [650] **4470**

CONTREE — Controlled Circulation Index

CONTREE / RAAD VIR GEESTESWETENSKAPLIKE NAVORSING, INSTITUUT VIR GESKIEDENISNAVORSING, AFDELING STREEKGESKIEDENIS (SA/0379-9867). [1,500] **2638**

CONTRIBUCIONES CIENTIFICAS DEL INSTITUTO ANTARTICO ARGENTINO (AG). [350] **5097**

CONTRIBUTION - UNIVERSITY OF MARYLAND, NATURAL RESOURCES INSTITUTE (US/0097-0832). **2191**

CONTRIBUTIONS FROM THE BERMUDA BIOLOGICAL STATION FOR RESEARCH (BM). [150] **2226**

CONTRIBUTIONS FROM THE UNIVERSITY OF KANSAS HERBARIUM (US/0735-3669). **507**

CONTRIBUTIONS IN ANTHROPOLOGY (PORTALES, N.M.) (US/0070-8232). [300] **234**

CONTRIBUTIONS IN SCIENCE (LOS ANGELES, CALIF.) (US/0459-8113). [1,000] **4165**

CONTRIBUTIONS TO GEOLOGY (LARAMIE) (US/0010-7980). [750] **1372**

CONTROL & INSTRUMENTATION (UK/0010-8022). [18,000] **1219**

CONTROL CIBERNETICA Y AUTOMATIZACION (CU/1013-2287). [10,000] **1250**

CONTROL ENGINEERING (US/0010-8049). [95,000] **1219**

CONTROL THEORY AND ADVANCED TECHNOLOGY (JA/0911-0704). [400] **1180**

CONTROSPAZIO (IT). **296**

CONVENIENCE STORE NEWS (US/0194-8733). [118,000] **660**

CONVENIENT AUTOMOTIVE SERVICES RETAILER (US/0895-1047). [5,500] **5412**

CONVENTION REPORT - C U P E (CN/0380-7789). **1661**

CONVERGENCE (FRIBOURG) (SZ/0010-8154). [2,500] **5028**

CONVERTING MAGAZINE (US/0746-7141). [41,000] **1602**

CONVEYING MATERIAL CATALOGUE (SZ). **414**

COOPER REVIEW (US). [2,550] **5748**

COOPERATION AND CONFLICT (NO/0010-8367). [600] **4470**

COOPERATION (JEFFERSON CITY) (US/0192-4842). [1,800] **3569**

COOPERATIVE ACCOUNTANT, THE (US/0010-8391). [2,500] **742**

COOPERAZIONE EDUCATIVA (IT). [3,500] **1733**

COPEIA (US/0045-8511). [3,600] **5581**

CORAL REEF NEWSLETTER (US/0278-324X). [1,400] **1448**

CORD. COCONUT RESEARCH & DEVELOPMENT (IO/0215-1162). **168**

CORD (HAMILTON) (CN/0225-7033). **5280**

CORD NEWSLETTER (US/0734-4856). **1311**

CORD (ST. BONAVENTURE, N.Y.), THE (US/0010-8685). [1,500] **5028**

CORDAGE NEWS (US/1063-746X). [1,000] **5349**

CORE (NORTH YORK) (CN/1183-1944). [4,000] **1818**

CORE TEACHER (US/0045-8538). [250] **1891**

CORMORANT NEWS BULLETIN, THE (US/0045-8554). [3,100] **5412**

CORNELL ENGINEER, THE (US/0010-8790). [4,000] **1969**

CORNELL LAW FORUM (ITHACA, N.Y. : 1974) (US/0010-8839). [8,000] **2956**

CORNELL LAW REVIEW (US/0010-8847). [3,500] **2956**

CORNER BROOK WESTERN STAR (CN). **5782**

CORNERSTONE CLUES (US/0739-0904). [700] **2444**

CORNSTALK GAZETTE (AT/0818-7339). [480] **384**

CORONARY CLUB BULLETIN, THE (US/8755-5271). [8,000] **3703**

CORPORATE CONTROLLER (US/0899-0174). [2,500] **661**

CORPORATE EXAMINER, THE (US/0361-2309). [2000] **661**

CORPORATE FINANCE BLUEBOOK, THE (US/0740-2546). **784**

CORPORATE FINANCE SOURCEBOOK, THE (US/0163-3031). [5,000] **785**

CORPORATE LEGAL LETTER, THE (UK). **3099**

CORPORATE LEGAL TIMES (US). [40,000] **3099**

CORPORATE MEETINGS AND INCENTIVES (US/0745-1636). [48,000] **5467**

CORPORATE OFFICERS & DIRECTORS LIABILITY LITIGATION REPORTER (US/0887-7793). **3099**

CORPORATE PROFILES / BUSINESS DAY (PH). [2,000] **662**

CORPORATE PUBLIC ISSUES AND THEIR MANAGEMENT (US/0730-5192). [4,000] **662**

CORPORATE REPORT WISCONSIN (US/0890-4278). [28,000] **662**

CORPORATE SHOWCASE (US/0742-9975). [18,450] **377**

CORPUS CHRISTI CALLER-TIMES (US/0894-5365). [68,000 daily 94,000 sunday] **5748**

CORPUS PHILOSOPHORUM DANICORUM MEDII AEVI (DK/0589-8080). [600] **4344**

CORPUS SCRIPTORUM CHRISTIANORUM ORIENTALIUM (FR). **4951**

CORRELATION (UK/0260-8790). [500] **390**

CORRIDOR REAL ESTATE JOURNAL, THE (US/1048-7948). [9,000] **4836**

CORRIERE EUROPEO (IT). **1634**

CORROSION ABSTRACTS (US/0010-9339). [850] **2003**

CORROSION & COATINGS SOUTH AFRICA (SA/0377-8711). [2,500] **2011**

CORROSION AUSTRALASIA (AT/0155-6002). [1,200] **2011**

CORROSION (HOUSTON, TEX.) (US/0010-9312). [4,000] **2011**

CORROSION PREVENTION AND CONTROL (UK/0010-9371). **2011**

CORROSION Y PROTECCION (SP/0045-8678). [1,000] **2012**

CORSETERIA Y LENCERIA (SP). [5,000] **1083**

CORYELL NEWSLETTER (US/0883-7600). [200] **2444**

COSMETIC NEWS : CN (IT). [3,000] **403**

COSMETICS & TOILETRIES (IT). [18,000] **403**

COSMETICS (DON MILLS) (CN/0315-1301). **403**

COSMETICS INTERNATIONAL (UK). [10,000] **403**

COST ENGINEER (UK/0010-9606). [2,300] **864**

COST OF LIVING NEWS (US/0743-2569). **1552**

COSTRUIRE IN LATERIZIO (IT/0394-1590). [17,500] **296**

COSTRUZIONI (IT/0010-9665). [8,000] **611**

COSTUME (UK/0590-8876). [1,500] **1083**

COTTAGE CONNECTION, THE (US). [8,000] **662**

COTTON GIN AND OIL MILL PRESS, THE (US/0010-9800). [1,800] **5349**

COTTON : WORLD STATISTICS (US). **5360**

COULICOU (CN/0822-7098). [25,000] **1062**

COUNCIL COLUMNS / COUNCIL ON FOUNDATIONS (US). [8,000] **4335**

COUNCIL OF GENEALOGY COLUMNISTS NEWSLETTER (US/1046-641X). [80-90] **2444**

COUNCIL SPOTLIGHT BOOKNOTES (US/0740-1183). [10,000] **4502**

COUNSELOR EDUCATION AND SUPERVISION (US/0011-0035). [911] **1877**

COUNTED THREAD (US/0164-3460). [6,000] **5183**

COUNTERFEITS AND FORGERIES (NE). [16,500] **785**

COUNTERPOINT (AT). [5050] **2810**

COUNTRY ALMANAC, THE (US/0192-0111). [21,000] **5634**

COUNTRY AMERICA (US/1043-4488). [400,000] **4112**

COUNTRY HERITAGE (US/0733-8759). [300] **4112**

COUNTRY-SIDE (UK/0011-023X). [15,000] **2213**

COUNTRY TIMES (THORNHILL) (CN/0821-7971). [1,000] **4112**

COUNTRYSIDE (NEW YORK, N.Y. 1990) (US/1061-6349). [250,000] **2486**

COUNTY AGENT, THE (US/0164-3932). [7,500] **77**

COUNTY COMMENT (US/1049-7838). **4641**

COUNTY LINE, THE (US). [3,000] **3204**

COUNTY LINES (ALBERT LEA, MINN.) (US/8755-9099). [5,200] **1542**

COUP D'OEIL GRANDVILLIERS (FR/0987-0113). [1,000] **3874**

COUP D'OEIL (VICTORIAVILLE) (CN/0715-8238). **1818**

COURANT (MONTREAL) (CN/0712-4570). [2,000] **4871**

COURIER (CANADA. CANADIAN FORCES BASE (COLD LAKE, ALTA.)) (CN/0045-8872). [3,100] **5782**

COURIER (EDMONTON) (CN/0318-0220). **3275**

COURIER (MIDDLETOWN, N.J.), THE (US/0891-7272). [11,500] **5709**

COURIER OF HISTORICAL EVENTS (US). [300] **2614**

COURRIER AGRIROYAL (CN/0822-7144). [1,800] **77**

COURRIER CERN (SZ). [18,000] **4446**

COURRIER DE LA NATURE, LE (FR). [10,000] **2191**

COURRIER DE LOTBINIERE, LE (CN/0226-9139). **5782**

COURRIER DU CENTRE INTERNATIONAL D'ETUDES POETIQUES (BE/0577-1757). [1,000] **3461**

COURRIER FRONTENAC (CN/0704-0474). [18,746] **5782**

COURRIER INTERNATIONAL PARIS (FR/1154-516X). [100,000] **2486**

COURRIER P.R.H. MONTREAL (CN/0821-0101). [500] **4583**

COURRIER ROUMAIN (MONTREAL) (CN/0827-4045). [250] **5196**

COURT COMMENTARIES (US/0731-7972). [1,600] **3140**

COURT MANAGER, THE (US/1046-249X). [1,400] **3140**

COURT REVIEW (US/0011-0647). [3,600] **3140**

COUSINS ET COUSINES (US/0740-3046). [600] **2444**

COUTTS LIBRARY SERVICES. CURRENT CANADIAN BOOKS (CN/0316-9448). **414**

COVENANT DISCIPLESHIP QUARTERLY (US/1052-3790). [1,000] **4951**

COVENANT QUARTERLY, THE (US/0361-0934). [1,800] **4951**

COVENANTER WITNESS (US/0749-4319). [2,000] **4951**

COVERTACTION INFORMATION BULLETIN (US/0275-309X). [10,000] **4519**

COVINGTON LEADER, THE (US). [8,400] **5745**

COW COUNTRY (US/0279-8204). [1,650] **209**

COYUNTURA ECONOMICA (CK/0120-3576). [1,500] **1554**

CPA FREEWHEELER (CN/0824-7226). **4386**

CPA PROFIT REPORT (US/1047-5834). **742**

CPA SOFTWARE NEWS, THE (US/1068-8285). [50,000] **662**

CPA'S PC NETWORK ADVISOR (US/1059-4590). **1241**

CPCU JOURNAL (US/0162-2706). [20,000] **2878**

CPI NATIONAL REPORT (US/0740-7947). [5,000] **4583**

CPJ : CANADIAN PHARMACEUTICAL JOURNAL (CN/0828-6914). [12,200] **4298**

CPL BIBLIOGRAPHY (US/0743-1635). [300] **2840**

CPN. CRIME PREVENTION NEWS (UK/0961-0286). [115,000] **3161**

CPOA TRAINING BULLETIN (US). [180] **3161**

CPRS CROSS-REFERENCE LIST (CN/0229-3870). **758**

CPU NEWS : JOURNAL OF THE COMMONWEALTH PRESS UNION (UK). [2,000] **2918**

CPU : QUARTERLY OF THE COMMONWEALTH PRESS UNION (UK). **2918**

CQ-DL (GW). [60,000] **1109**

CRA REVIEW, THE (US/0889-7395). [15,000] **1590**

CRAB, THE (US/0300-7561). [1,100] **3204**

CRAFT & NEEDLEWORK AGE (US/0887-9818). [32,000] **5183**

CRAFT CONNECTION (US/1067-8328). [800] **371**

CRAFT CONTACTS (1983) (CN/0823-2148). **371**

CRAFT DIGEST (US). [3,500] **2773**

CRAFT RANGE (US/0199-5200). [10,000] **371**

CRAFT SHOW DIGEST (US/0882-7486). [12,000] **371**

CRAG AND CANYON (CN/0701-3558). [4,500] **4871**

CRAIN'S CLEVELAND BUSINESS (US/0197-2375). [25,000] **663**

CRANBERRIES (PORTLAND) (US/0011-0787). [800] **168**

CRANFORD CHRONICLE (1979) (US). **5709**

CRANK (PHILADELPHIA, PA.) (US/1076-9102). [1,000] **4113**

CRAWFORD COUNTY IOWA GENEALOGICAL SOCIETY (US/1059-0374). [55] **2444**

CRAZYHORSE (LITTLE ROCK, ARK.) (US/0011-0841). [1,000] **3462**

CREATING EXCELLENCE (US/1045-7011). [20,000] **663**

CREATION MAGAZINE (FR/0765-9911). [14,132] **758**

CREATIVE (US/0737-5883). [12,800] **758**

CREATIVE BLACK BOOK (PORTFOLIO ED.), THE (US/0740-283X). [10,000] **758**

CREATIVE BLACK BOOK (PRODUCER'S ED.), THE (US/0889-6372). [30,000] **758**

CREATIVE BLACK BOOK, THE (US/0738-9000). [30,000] **758**

CREATIVE FORECASTING (US/1052-2573). [5,000] **5281**

CREATIVE FORUM (II). [450] **3378**

CREATIVE HANDBOOK, THE (UK). [10,000] **377**

CREATIVE LOAFING (1978) (US/0889-8685). [120,000] **5653**

CREATIVE OHIO (US/0741-6504). **372**

CREATIVE WOMAN (PARK FOREST SOUTH, ILL.), THE (US/0736-4733). [500] **5554**

CREATIVITY AND INNOVATION MANAGEMENT (UK/0963-1690). [120] **864**

CREATOR (WICHITA, KAN.) (US/1045-0815). [6,500] **4113**

CREDIT CARD MANAGEMENT (US/0896-9329). [4,500] **785**

CREDIT UNION NEWSWATCH (US/0889-5597). [24,000] **786**

CREDIT UNION REPORT (US/0894-752X). [5,000] **786**

CREDIT UNION TIMES (US/1058-7764). [11,000] **786**

CREDIT UNION WAY (CN/0829-2175). [5,300] **786**

CREDIT WORLD, THE (US/0011-1074). [9,000] **786**

CREDO (NO). [4,000] **4951**

CREIGHTON LAW REVIEW (US/0011-1155). [900] **2957**

CRESCENT INTERNATIONAL (CN/0705-3754). [20,000] **4470**

CRESSET (VALPARAISO), THE (US/0011-1198). [4,700] **3340**

CRESTLINE ADVOCATE (CRESTLINE, OHIO : 1869) (US). [2,300] **5727**

CRIME LABORATORY DIGEST (US/0743-1872). [3,000] **3080**

CRIMINAL DEFENSE NEWSLETTER (US/0731-082X). [1,500] **3105**

CRIMINAL JUSTICE ABSTRACTS (US/0146-9177). [1,000] **3080**

CRIMINAL JUSTICE POLICY REVIEW (US/0887-4034). [600] **3162**

CRIMINAL JUSTICE REVIEW (ATLANTA, GA.) (US/0734-0168). [1,000] **3162**

CRIMINOLOGIE (MONTREAL) (CN/0316-0041). **3163**

CRIMINOLOGIST (COLUMBUS), THE (US/0164-0240). [2,000] **3163**

CRIMINOLOGY (BEVERLY HILLS) (US/0011-1384). [3,000] **3163**

CRISIS (NEW YORK, N.Y.), THE (US/0011-1422). [300,000] **2259**

CRISTIANESIMO NELLA STORIA (IT/0393-3598). [1,200] **4951**

CRISWELL THEOLOGICAL REVIEW (US/0892-5712). [1,250] **4951**

CRITICA HISPANICA (US/0278-7261). [812] **3275**

CRITICA MARXISTA (IT/0011-152X). [6,000] **4541**

CRITICA; REVISTA HISPANOAMERICANA DE FILOSOFIA (MX/0011-1503). [1,000] **4344**

CRITICA SOCIOLOGICA, LA (IT/0011-1546). [2,000] **5243**

CRITICAL CARE NURSE (US/0279-5442). [95,000] **3854**

CRITICAL MATRIX (US/1066-288X). [500] **5554**

CRITICAL REVIEWS IN ORAL BIOLOGY AND MEDICINE (US/1045-4411). **1319**

CRITICAL SOCIOLOGY (US/0896-9205). [800] **5243**

CRITICAL STUDIES IN MASS COMMUNICATION (US/0739-3180). [3,200] **1109**

CRITICAL TEXTS (US/0730-2304). [850] **3341**

CRITICISM (DETROIT) (US/0011-1589). [1,200] **2845**

CROC (CN/0226-6083). [76,168] **3379**

CROCKER COMMUNICATION RESOURCES NEWSLETTER (US/1042-217X). [500] **663**

CRONACHE ECONOMICHE (IT/0011-1775). [3,500] **1478**

CROP PROTECTION NEWSLETTER (CN/0225-5774). [350] **169**

CROP REPORT / ALBERTA WHEAT POOL (CN). [1,000] **169**

CROSS STITCH & COUNTRY CRAFTS (US/0886-6600). [1,800] **5183**

CROSS STITCH! MAGAZINE (US/1056-7542). [130,000] **372**

CROSSOSOMA (US/0891-9100). [400] **507**

CROSSROAD TRAILS (US/0735-6196). [250] **2444**

CROSSROADS (DE KALB, ILL.) (US/0741-2037). [150] **2503**

CROSSROADS (SHOAL LAKE, MAN.) (CN). [6,200] **5783**

CROSSTALK AND ANGLICAN JOURNAL EPISCOPAL (CN/0845-4795). [273,000] **5058**

CROSSTIES (US/0097-4536). [1,800] **2378**

CROSSWORLD (LONDON, ONT.) (CN/0225-3992). [2,500] **2908**

CRREL BENCHNOTES : U.S. ARMY CORPS OF ENGINEERS INFORMATION EXCHANGE BULLETIN (US). [500] **1970**

CRS PUBLICATIONS' CAREER OPPORTUNITY INDEX (EAST-SOUTH-CENTRAL) (US/0897-909X). [35,000] **4203**

CRS PUBLICATIONS' CAREER OPPORTUNITY INDEX (WESTERN) (US/0898-218X). [50,000] **4203**

CRSSS 09 (CN/0701-8967). **5281**

CRU METAL MONITOR (UK). **4000**

CRUCIBLE (UK/0011-2100). [2,000] **4951**

CRUCIBLE (TORONTO) (CN/0381-8047). [1,600] **5097**

CRUISING AROUND THE WORLD (US/0744-6004). [23,000] **5467**

CRYO LETTERS (UK/0143-2044). [250] **452**

CRYPTOGAMIE. ALGOLOGIE (FR/0181-1568). [400] **452**

CRYPTOGAMIE. BRYOLOGIE, LICHENOLOGIE (FR/0181-1576). [400] **507**

CRYPTOLOGIA (US/0161-1194). [1,000] **1226**

CRYPTOZOOLOGY (US/0736-7023). [900] **5581**

CSA JOURNAL, THE (US/0195-9050). **5230**

CSAS NEWSLETTER (CN/0714-8240). [500] **209**

CSCC NEWS (CN/0826-1024). [600] **973**

CSELT TECHNICAL REPORTS (IT/0393-2648). [1,200] **1153**

CSG BACKGROUNDER / COUNCIL OF STATE GOVERNMENTS (US). **4641**

CSSE CONTACT (CN/0713-3421). [2,000] **2861**

CSSR BULLETIN (US). [6,000] **4952**

CSSS DIGEST : CENTER FOR THE STUDY OF SPORT IN SOCIETY (US). **4892**

CTA ACTION (1986) (US/0896-7326). **1862**

CTC BULLETIN : OCCASIONAL BULLETIN OF THE COMMISSION ON THEOLOGICAL CONCERNS, CHRISTIAN CONFERENCE OF ASIA (SI). [700] **4952**

CTI JOURNAL (US). [6,000] **2112**

CUADERNOS AMERICANOS (MX/0011-2356). [2,500] **2730**

CUADERNOS DE ACTUALIDAD INTERNACIONAL (VE/0798-0841). [1,000] **5197**

CUADERNOS DE ECONOMIA SOCIAL (AG/0325-9757). [3,000] **1478**

CUADERNOS DE FILOSOFIA (CL). [500] **4344**

CUADERNOS DE INFORMACION ECONOMICA (SP). [2,000] **1554**

CUADERNOS DE MARCHA (UY). **2551**

CUADERNOS DE TRADUCCION E INTERPRETACION (SP/0212-0550). [1,500] **3276**

CUADERNOS DEL CENDES (VE). [2,000] **1478**

CUB CLUES (US/0889-437X). [2,500] **17**

CUBA, ECONOMIA PLANIFICADA (CU/0864-1420). [2,000] **1478**

CUBA FOREIGN TRADE (CU). [3,000] **663**

CUBA INTERNACIONAL (CU/0011-2593). [30,000] **2486**

CUBA UPDATE (US/0196-0830). **4541**

CUBAN JOURNAL OF AGRICULTURAL SCIENCE (CU/0253-5815). [400] **77**

CUBAN STUDIES (US/0361-4441). [600] **2730**

CUE MAGAZINE (US/1064-2579). **4850**

CUE SHEET, THE (US/0888-9015). **4113**

CUED SPEECH ANNUAL (US/1041-6226). **3276**

CUED SPEECH CENTER LINES (US/1041-6196). [1,000] **4386**

CULLMAN TRIBUNE, THE (US/0739-523X). [13,400] **5626**

CULPEPPER LETTER, THE (US/8750-3697). [1,000] **1285**

CULTIC STUDIES JOURNAL (US/0748-6499). [350] **5243**

CULTIVAR (FR/0045-9216). [66,000] **170**

CULTURA E FE (BL). [2,500] **4952**

CULTURA E NATURA (IT). [5,000] **5243**

CULTURA NEL MONDO, LA (IT/0011-2798). **2486**

CULTURAL ANTHROPOLOGY (US/0886-7356). [1,200] **234**

CULTURAL CRITIQUE (US/0882-4371). [2,000] **5197**

CULTURAL INFORMATION SERVICE (US/0097-952X). [4,000] **4952**

CULTURAL SURVIVAL QUARTERLY (US/0740-3291). [8,000] **4507**

CULTURE & HISTORY (US/0195-2714). [15,000] **2730**

CULTURE & TRADITION (CN/0701-0184). [250] **2319**

CUMBERLAND FLAG, THE (US/0011-2968). [750] **4952**

CUMBERLAND LAWYER, THE (US/0590-3378). [7,000] **2957**

CUMULATIVE BOOK INDEX. CD-ROM (US/0011-300X). **3458**

CUMULATIVE BOOK INDEX, THE (US/0011-300X). **3458**

CUOIO, PELLI, MATERIE CONCIANTI (IT/0011-3034). [18,000] **3183**

CUPA JOURNAL (WASHINGTON, D.C.: 1987) (US/1046-9508). **939**

CUPA NEWS (WASHINGTON D.C. : 1987) (US/0892-7855). [4,200] **1819**

CURACAO TRADE INFORMATION GUIDE (NE). [4,000] **830**

CURRENT AFFAIRS BULLETIN (AT/0011-3182). [4,500] **4470**

CURRENT ANTARCTIC LITERATURE (US/0096-879X). [800] **2559**

CURRENT ARCHAEOLOGY (UK/0011-3212). [6,000] **266**

CURRENT AWARENESS IN BIOTECHNOLOGY (US/0735-956X). **3691**

CURRENT BIOLOGY (UK/0960-9822). **452**

CURRENT BOOKS MAGAZINE (US/1063-9012). [29,000] **3341**

CURRENT CONTENTS OF PERIODICALS ON THE MIDDLE EAST (IS/0333-9858). [1,000] **2650**

CURRENT DIGEST OF THE POST-SOVIET PRESS, THE (US/1067-7542). [1,000] **4502**

CURRENT DIGEST OF THE SOVIET PRESS, THE (US/0011-3425). [1,200] **4470**

CURRENT ESTIMATES - CITY OF WINNIPEG (CN/0317-9664). **4719**

CURRENT EVENTS SWEEPSTAKES (US/0739-1145). **2730**

CURRENT INDEX TO JOURNALS IN EDUCATION (US/0011-3565). [1,600] **1794**

CURRENT INDEX TO JOURNALS IN EDUCATION. SEMIANNUAL CUMULATION (US). [1,700] **1734**

CURRENT INDEX TO STATISTICS (US/0364-1228). [2,000] **3542**

CURRENT ISSUES IN MUSIC EDUCATION (US). [300] **4113**

CURRENT LAW CASE CITATOR (UK). [6,000] **2958**

CURRENT MEDICAL LITERATURE-INFECTIOUS DISEASES (UK/0951-9602). **3980**

CURRENT MEDICAL LITERATURE / NEPHROLOGY AND UROLOGY (UK/0951-9629). **3989**

CURRENT MUSICOLOGY (US/0011-3735). [1,000] **4113**

CURRENT
Controlled Circulation Index

CURRENT NOTES (US/8750-1937). [3,000] **1181**

CURRENT OPINION IN GENETICS AND DEVELOPMENT (UK/0959-437X). [1,000] **544**

CURRENT OPINION IN NEUROBIOLOGY (UK/0959-4388). [1,000] **453**

CURRENT OPINION IN STRUCTURAL BIOLOGY (UK/0959-440X). **453**

CURRENT PRIMATE REFERENCES (US/0590-4102). [500] **5174**

CURRENT PROTOCOLS IN MOLECULAR BIOLOGY (US). **453**

CURRENT RESEARCH IN THE PLEISTOCENE (US/8755-898X). [600] **235**

CURRENT SOUTH AFRICAN PERIODICALS. HUIDIGE SUID-AFRIKAANSE TYDSKRIFTE (SA). [650] **414**

CURRENT TECHNOLOGY INDEX : CTI (UK/0260-6593). **5174**

CURRENT THERAPEUTICS (AT/0311-905X). [21,000] **4298**

CURRENT THERAPY NEWSLETTER (US/0893-763X). **3570**

CURRENT TITLES IN ELECTROCHEMISTRY (II/0300-4376). [850] **1011**

CURRENTS (CHAPEL HILL, N.C.) (US/0882-7915). [2,500] **4189**

CURRENTS (WASHINGTON, D.C. 1983) (US/0748-478X). [14,000] **1819**

CURRICULUM AND TEACHING (AT/0726-416X). **1734**

CURRICULUM EXCHANGE (AT/0727-6826). [1,000] **1892**

CURRICULUM PERSPECTIVES (AT/0159-7868). [1,500] **1892**

CURRICULUM PLANS (US/0160-0885). [400] **5059**

CURRICULUM PRODUCT NEWS : CPN (US/1063-3375). [50,000] **1892**

CURRICULUM REPORT (US/0547-4205). [43,000] **1892**

CURRY COUNTY ECHOES (US). [350] **2730**

CUSO FORUM (OTTAWA, ONT. : 1980) (CN/0823-5740). [16,000] **1634**

CUSTOM BUILDER (US/0895-2493). [30,000] **612**

CUSTOM TAILOR, THE (US/1071-1147). [1,000] **1479**

CUTTING TOOL ENGINEERING (US/0011-4189). [38,000] **4000**

CVRD REVISTA (BL/0102-9541). [3,500] **1970**

CWA NEWS (US/0007-9227). [650,000] **1662**

CYBERNETICA (BE/0011-4227). [1,000] **1250**

CYBERNETICS ABSTRACTS / SCIENTIFIC INFORMATION CONSULTANTS LIMITED, LONDON, ENGLAND (UK/0011-4243). **1250**

CYBIUM (FR/0399-0974). [500] **2299**

CYCLE TOURING & CAMPAIGNING (UK). [33,500] **428**

CYCLING WORLD (UK/0143-0238). **4892**

CYCLOTOURISME ORGANE OFFICIEL DE LA FEDERATION FRANCAISE DE CYCLOTOURISME (FR). [10,000] **429**

CYLA QUARTERLY (US/8750-944X). [38,000] **2958**

CYLCHGRAWN LLYFRGELL GENEDLAETHOL CYMRU (UK/0011-4421). [400] **3205**

CYTOLOGIA (JA/0011-4545). **535**

CZECHOSLOVAK AND CENTRAL EUROPEAN JOURNAL (US/1056-005X). [500] **2685**

CZECHOSLOVAK MARKET (XR). **664**

D.A.C. NEWS (US/0011-4707). [4,000] **4892**

D.O., DIARIO OFICIAL, ESTADO DO RIO DE JANEIRO. PARTE III (BL). [20,000] **2958**

D.O., DIARIO OFICIAL, ESTADO DO RIO DE JANEIRO. PARTE V (BL). [24,000] **2958**

D O R L S TECHNICAL SERVICES COMMITTEE'S INFORMATION EXCHANGE (CN/0703-1688). **3205**

D.O.T.C. NEWS (1983) (CN/0822-6261). [1,500] **5783**

D'A PALMA DE MALLORCA (SP/1130-3794). [2000] **296**

DAAT (IS/0334-2336). [600] **5047**

DACHAUER HEFTER (GW/0934-361X). [5,000] **2685**

DADSWELL FAMILY BULLETIN (CN/0824-7730). [125] **2444**

DAFFODIL JOURNAL, THE (US/0011-5290). [1,400] **2413**

DAFTAR TAMBAHAN KOLEKSI MIKROFIS (IO). [500] **2650**

DAI DAMU / LARGE DAMS (JA/0011-5347). [1,600] **2088**

DAIDALOS (GW/0721-4235). [2,653] **296**

DAIGAKU KENKYU NOTO (JA). [1,000] **1819**

DAIHAN GUMSOG HAGHOI JI (KO/0253-3847). [2,500] **4000**

DAILY BULLETIN / INSTITUTE OF GOVERNMENT, UNIVERSITY OF NORTH CAROLINA AT CHAPEL HILL (US). [2,200] **4641**

DAILY CALIFORNIAN (US/1050-2300). [25,000] **5634**

DAILY COMMERCIAL NEWS AND CONSTRUCTION RECORD (CN/0317-3178). [6,500] **612**

DAILY GRAPHIC (PORTAGE LA PRAIRIE. 1954) (CN/0832-4298). [5,000] **5783**

DAILY GRAPHS. STOCK OPTION GUIDE (US/0195-2021). [25,000] **896**

DAILY HAMPSHIRE GAZETTE (US/0739-3504). [22,491] **5688**

DAILY HERALD (PROVO, UTAH. 1939), THE (US/0891-2777). [32,395 paid evenings33,607 Sunday] **5756**

DAILY MESSENGER (UNION CITY, TENN.) (US/0745-5534). [9,000] **5745**

DAILY MOUNTAIN EAGLE (US/0893-0759). [12,553] **5626**

DAILY NEWS HALIFAX-DARTMOUTH EDITION (CN/0715-4321). [22,000] **5783**

DAILY NEWS (LONGVIEW, WASH.), THE (US/0889-0005). [25,000] **5760**

DAILY PRESS (ASHLAND, WIS.), THE (US/1050-4095). [8,500] **5766**

DAILY RECORD (PARSIPPANY, N.J.) (US). [63,000 daily74,000 Sunday] **5710**

DAILY RECORDER, THE (US/0197-8055). [2,100] **2958**

DAILY REPORTER (SIOUX CITY), THE (US/0360-9510). [500] **2958**

DAILY REVIEW, THE (US). [41,782] **5634**

DAILY SENTINEL (ROME, N.Y.) (US). [18,500 (daily)] **5715**

DAILY TERRITORIAL, THE (US/0743-8397). [1,492] **5630**

DAILY TIMES (NR). [250,000] **5807**

DAIRY CATTLE (CN/0821-7440). **210**

DAIRY COUNCIL DIGEST (US/0011-5568). [85,000] **193**

DAIRY FOODS (US/0888-0050). [20,000] **193**

DAIRY (SAINT PAUL, MINN.) (US/0883-007X). [90,000] **194**

DAIRY WORLD (MILLBURY, MASS.) (US/0736-4962). [38,406] **194**

DAIRYMAN (ARMADALE), THE (AT). [4,000] **194**

DAIRYMAN (CORONA), THE (US/0011-572X). [32,500] **194**

DAIRYMEN'S DIGEST (MORNING GLORY FARMS ED.) (US/0894-1653). [6,000] **194**

DAIRYMEN'S DIGEST. NORTH CENTRAL REGION EDITION (US/0745-9033). [13,000] **194**

DAKOTA COUNTRY (US/0194-5769). [10,000 paid] **4871**

DAKOTA COUNTY GENEALOGIST, THE (US/1044-6524). [300] **2444**

DAKOTA FAMILY (US/0199-7122). [25,500] **78**

DAKOTA OUTDOORS (US/1041-1968). [7,000] **4871**

DALGETY FARMERS' ANNUAL WOOL DIGEST (AT). [15,000] **5360**

DALHOUSIE DENTAL JOURNAL (CN/0418-3010). [2,000] **1320**

DALHOUSIE FRENCH STUDIES (CN/0711-8813). [200] **3379**

DALHOUSIE GAZETTE, THE (CN/0011-5819). [10,000] **1091**

DALHOUSIE REVIEW, THE (CN/0011-5827). [1,000] **3380**

DALIL AL-KUWAYT AL-YAWM / WIZARAT AL-TAKHTIT, MARKAZ AL-KUWAYT LIL-MALUMAT WA-AL-MIKROFILM (KU). [1,000] **2959**

DALLAS APPAREL NEWS (US/0279-4888). [17,000] **1083**

DALLAS COWBOYS OFFICIAL WEEKLY (US/0745-0370). [83,075] **4892**

DALLAS MEDICAL JOURNAL (US/0011-586X). [4,400] **3570**

DALLAS OBSERVER (US/0732-0299). [70,000] **384**

DALLAS POST TRIBUNE, THE (US/0746-7303). [30,000] **5749**

DALLAS WEEKLY, THE (US/0885-1271). [20,300] **5749**

DAN CHUA (US/0747-2315). [2,500] **5028**

DAN SHA (CN/0833-3831). **5783**

DANCE IN CANADA (CN/0317-9737). [3,000] **1312**

DANCE INK (US/1047-823X). [15,000] **1312**

DANCEBAG (NORMAN, OKLA.) (US/1041-5564). [15,000] **1312**

DANCEVIEW (US). [600] **1312**

DANDELION (CN/0383-9575). [700] **3380**

DANGEROUS GOODS : NEWSLETTER (CN/0710-0914). [18,000 (English)5,500 (French)] **5380**

DANIA POLYGLOTTA (DK/0070-2714). [400] **3458**

DANISH FILMS (DK). [4,000] **4067**

DANSALAN QUARTERLY (PH). [500] **2650**

DANSER (FR/0755-7639). **1313**

DANSK AUDIOLOGOPDI (DK/0105-7200). **3887**

DANSK ELFORSYNING (DK). [3,000] **2003**

DANSK ORNITHOLOGISK FORENINGS TIDSSKRIFT (DK/0011-6394). [8,500] **5617**

DANSK TEOLOGISK TIDSSKRIFT (DK/0105-3191). **4952**

DANSKE MALERMESTRE (DK/0905-6440). [3,000] **4223**

DAR ES SALAAM UNIVERSITY LAW JOURNAL (TZ). **2959**

DARI DE SEAMA ALE SEDINTELOR - INSTITUTUL DE GEOLOGIE SI GEOFIZICA. 4, STRATIGRAFIE (RM/0254-7309). **1373**

DARI DE SEAMA ALE SEDINTELOR - INSTITUTUL DE GEOLOGIE SI GEOFIZICA. 5. TECTONICA SI GEOLOGIE REGIONALA (RM/0253-1798). [700] **1373**

DARSHANA INTERNATIONAL (II/0011-6734). [1,000] **4344**

DARTMOUTH ALUMNI MAGAZINE (US). [43,000] **1101**

DARTMOUTH BUSINESS DIRECTORY (CN/0827-2786). **664**

DARTMOUTH BUSINESS NEWS (CN/0824-2682). **664**

DARTMOUTH REVIEW, THE (US). **1091**

DARWINIANA (AG/0011-6793). [800] **508**

DASEIN (US/0011-6807). [4,500] **318**

DATA BASE (US/0095-0033). **1257**

DATA/COMM INDUSTRY REPORT (US/0149-9556). **1257**

DATA COMMUNICATIONS (US/0363-6399). **1241**

DATA DIGEST ON IOWA POSTSECONDARY INSTITUTIONS (US). [600] **1819**

DATA FROM THE DRUG ABUSE WARNING NETWORK. SEMIANNUAL REPORT (US/0884-2132). [800] **1342**

DATA INDIA (II/0377-6832). **2650**

DATA JURIDICA (NE). [700] **2959**

DATA PRODUCT NEWS (TORONTO) (CN/0226-6091). [30,000] **1245**

DATA RESOURCES MODEL OF CANADIAN ENERGY MARKETS, THE (CN/0823-9584). **1936**

DATA SCOPE (OAKVILLE) (CN/0228-9512). **1603**

DATA TRAINING (US/0884-2604). [10,000] **1257**

DATABASE (WESTON) (US/0162-4105). [3,550] **1253**

DATAPRO MANAGEMENT OF MICROCOMPUTER SYSTEMS (US/8750-6858). **1274**

DATEK PRINTER DATABASE SERVICE (US/0739-4519). **1258**

DATELINE HYPERTENSION (US/0747-6124). [55,000] **3704**

DATEN DES GESUNDHEITSWESENS (GW/0172-3723). [3,000] **4809**

DATI E TARIFFE PUBBLICITARIE (IT). [10,700] **758**

DAVID DUNLAP DOINGS, THE (CN/0713-5904). [200] **395**

DAVID Y GOLIATH : BOLETIN CLACSO (AG/0325-0431). [1,500] **2551**

DAVISON'S "SALESMAN'S BOOK." (US/0363-5252). **5350**

DAWN : A HERALD OF CHRIST'S PRESENCE, THE (US). **5016**

DAWSON AND HIND (CN/0703-6507). [300] **4087**

DAY RESEARCHER (US/0743-216X). [70] **2445**

DAYTON BUSINESS REPORTER (US/1063-3413). **664**

DEUTSCHE

DAZE INC, THE (US/0895-3961). [20,000] **2588**

DB; DEINE BAHN (GW). **5431**

DB. DEUTSCHE BAUZEITUNG (1981) (GW/0721-1902). [35,000] **296**

DBS NEWS (US/0733-9739). **1153**

DBZ. DEUTSCHE BRIEFMARKEN-ZEITUNG (GW/0931-4393). [48,000] **2773**

DDZ. DER DEUTSCHE ZOLLBEAMTE (GW). [33,000] **4719**

DE HAEN NEW PRODUCT SURVEY (US). [300] **4299**

DE HAEN'S DRUG PRODUCT INDEX. INTERNATIONAL (US). [300] **4299**

DE PAUL LAW REVIEW (US/0011-7188). [800] **2959**

DEACON DIGEST (US/8750-7749). [4,000] **4952**

DEADLINE (US). [500] **1285**

DEAF LIFE (US/0898-719X). [35,000] **4386**

DEALERSCOPE MERCHANDISING (US/0888-4501). [61,500] **953**

DEARBORN TIMES-HERALD (US/0193-0230). [27,000] **5691**

DEATHS, TASMANIA (AT/0814-8155). **4561**

DEBATE (LIMA, PERU) (PE). [8,000] **4471**

DEBATES AND PROCEEDINGS - LEGISLATIVE ASSEMBLY OF MANITOBA (CN/0542-5492). [300] **4641**

DEBATES EN SOCIOLOGIA (PE). **5244**

DEBATES OF PARLIAMENT / REPUBLIC OF SOUTH AFRICA (SA). [5,000] **4641**

DEBRETT'S PEOPLE OF TODAY (UK). **432**

DEC PROFESSIONAL, THE (US/0744-9216). [95,510] **1246**

DECEMBER ROSE (US/0748-1195). [80,000] **5178**

DECISION (CANADIAN ED.) (CN/0820-9057). [2,000,000] **4952**

DECISION LINE (US/0732-6823). [5,000] **664**

DECISION (NORTH AMERICA ED.) (US/0011-7307). [2,000,000] **4952**

DECISION SCIENCES (US/0011-7315). [4,000] **664**

DECISIONES SEU SENTENTIAE (VC). **5028**

DECISIONS MEDIAS (FR/1165-8606). [10,000] **1109**

DECKS AWASH (CN/0317-7076). [1,600] **2487**

DECORATION CHEZ-SOI (CN/0705-1093). [100,000] **2899**

DECORATIVE ARTS SOCIETY NEWSLETTER, THE (US/0884-4011). [300] **372**

DECORMAG (CN/0315-047X). [75,000] **2899**

DEFAULTED BONDS NEWSLETTER (US/1057-7521). **896**

DEFENCE (ETON) (UK/0142-6184). [30,185] **4040**

DEFENCE HELICOPTER WORLD (UK/0263-5062). **17**

DEFENCE SYSTEMS MODERNISATION (UK/0953-4970). [5200] **4040**

DEFENSE CONTRACTING AGENCY AUDIT MANUAL (US). **4642**

DEFENSE CONTRACTING AGENCY AUDIT MANUAL / DISKETTE (US). **4041**

DEFENSE COUNSEL JOURNAL (US/0895-0016). [4,000] **3089**

DEFENSE ELECTRONICS (US/0278-3479). [48,000] **2040**

DEFENSE MONITOR, THE (US/0195-6450). [90,000] **4041**

DEFENSE NEWS (SPRINGFIELD, VA.) (US/0884-139X). [35,000] **4041**

DEFENSE TRANSPORTATION JOURNAL (US/0011-7625). [8,000] **4042**

DEFENSOR CHIEFTAIN (US/0011-7633). [2,850] **5712**

DEFI-SANTE (CN/0848-9068). [25,000] **2596**

DEGREES AND OTHER AWARDS CONFERRED IN VIRGINIA / STATE COUNCIL OF HIGHER EDUCATION FOR VIRGINIA (US). [75] **1819**

DEGRES (BE/0376-8163). **3276**

DEHAEN'S NEW PRODUCT SURVEY. MONTHLY SUPPLEMENT (US). [300] **4299**

DEKALB COUNTY HERITAGE (US/8755-8459). [300] **2614**

DELANO RECORD (US/1074-410X). [4,650] **5634**

DELAWARE BUSINESS REVIEW (US/1061-4605). [11,000] **665**

DELAWARE GAZETTE (DELAWARE, OHIO 1932), THE (US/1064-2013). [7,612] **5728**

DELAWARE GENEALOGICAL SOCIETY JOURNAL (US/0731-3896). [250] **2445**

DELAWARE HISTORY (GW/0011-7765). [1,200] **2730**

DELAWARE JOURNAL OF CORPORATE LAW, THE (US/0364-9490). [1,100] **3099**

DELECTUS SEMINUM ET SPORARUM QUAE HORTUS BOTANICUS MONTIS-REGII PRO MUTUA COMMUTATIONE OFFERT (CN/0318-059X). [800] **508**

DELFT INTEGRAAL (NE). [23,500] **5099**

DELI NEWS (US/0011-7862). [6,000] **2333**

DELIUS SOCIETY JOURNAL, THE (UK/0306-0373). [450] **4113**

DELTA EPSILON SIGMA JOURNAL (US/0745-0958). [12,000] **5230**

DELTA OPTIMIST, THE (CN/0710-1422). [13,000] **5783**

DELTA PI EPSILON JOURNAL (US/0011-8052). [10,000] **665**

DELTION AUTOKINETISTIKES NOMOTHESIAS KAI NOMOLOGIAS (GR). [2,000] **2959**

DELTION ELLENIKIS MATHEMATIKIS ETAIREIAS (GR). [1,000] **3503**

DEMOCRATE (PARTI NOUVEAU DEMOCRATIQUE DU QUEBEC) (CN/0228-488X). **4471**

DEMOCRATIC JOURNALIST, THE (XR/0011-8214). [8,000] **2918**

DEMOCRATIC LEFT (US/0164-3207). [9,000] **4471**

DEMOGRAFIE (XR/0011-8265). [1,800] **4551**

DENISON REVIEW, THE (US). [5,800] **5669**

DENKI-SEIKO (JA/0011-8389). **4001**

DENNING LAW JOURNAL, THE (UK/0269-1922). **2959**

DENPUN KAGAKU (JA/0021-5406). [1,200] **2333**

DENTAL ADMISSION TESTING PROGRAM REPORT (US/0161-7540). [200] **1320**

DENTAL ADVISOR (US/0748-4666). **1320**

DENTAL ASEPSIS REVIEW (US/0733-9836). [310] **1320**

DENTAL DIMENSIONS (US/0191-2542). [2,000] **1320**

DENTAL ECONOMICS (PITTSBURGH. 1968) (US/0011-8583). [110,000] **1320**

DENTAL GUIDE (CN/0070-3656). **1320**

DENTAL LAB PRODUCTS (US/0146-9738). [21,000] **1321**

DENTAL MATERIALS (DK/0109-5641). [800] **1321**

DENTAL OUTLOOK, THE (AT/0418-694X). [7,000] **1321**

DENTAL PRACTICE (EWELL) (UK/0011-8710). [23,300] **1321**

DENTAL PRACTICE MANAGEMENT (DON MILLS, ONT.) (CN/0827-1305). **1321**

DENTAL PRODUCTS REPORT (US/0011-8737). [140,000] **1321**

DENTAL SUMMARIES (SA). [1,300] **1321**

DENTAL UPDATE (UK/0305-5000). [10,000] **1321**

DENTALETTER, THE (CN/0822-1596). **1322**

DENTEKSA (SA/0259-563X). [750] **1322**

DENTIST (WACO, TEX.) (US/0887-5669). [139,000] **1322**

DENTISTRY TODAY (US/8750-2186). [132,418] **1322**

DENTO MAXILLO FACIAL RADIOLOGY (UK/0250-832X). [600] **1322**

DENVER BUSINESS (US/0746-2964). [17,700] **665**

DENVER QUARTERLY (US/0011-8869). [1,000] **3380**

DENVER UNIVERSITY LAW REVIEW (US/0883-9409). [900] **2959**

DENVER WESTERNERS ROUNDUP, THE (US/0278-7970). [250] **2730**

DEPARTMENT OF DEFENSE SUPPLEMENT / DISKETTE (US). **4042**

DEPARTMENT OF EDUCATION REPORTS / NATIONAL CENTER FOR EDUCATION INFORMATION (US). **1735**

DEPARTMENT OF THE NAVY SUPPLEMENT / DISKETTE (US). **4176**

DERBY (NORMAN, OKLA.) (US/0199-5928). [3,500] **2798**

DERECHO Y REFORMA AGRARIA; REVISTA (VE/0304-2820). [1,000] **2960**

DERMATOLOGIC CAPSULE & COMMENT (US/0741-7489). **3719**

DERMATOLOGISCHE MONATSSCHRIFT (GW/0011-9083). **3719**

DERMATOLOGY IN PRACTICE (LONDON) (UK/0262-5504). [20,700] **3719**

DERWENT BIOTECHNOLOGY ABSTRACTS (UK/0262-5318). **3691**

DES LITIGATION REPORTER (US/0276-5675). **2960**

DES MOINES BUSINESS RECORD (US/1068-6681). [9,300] **665**

DES MOINES COUNTY GENEALOGICAL SOCIETY (US/0736-3931). [175] **2445**

DESARROLLO ECONOMICO (BUENOS AIRES) (AG/0046-001X). [2,000] **5198**

DESARROLLO INDOAMERICANO (CK/0418-7547). **2730**

DESARROLLO NACIONAL (US/0279-2958). **5099**

DESCANT (FORT WORTH, TEX.) (US/0011-9210). [500] **1091**

DESCENDER, THE (US/0420-0063). [100] **2445**

DESCENT (SYDNEY) (AT/0084-9731). [6,500] **2445**

DESCENT WELLS (UK/0046-0036). [3,500] **1373**

DESERT LIFE (US). [19,300] **4871**

DESIGN (II/0011-9261). [2,000] **296**

DESIGN COST AND DATA (US/1054-3163). [12,500] **297**

DESIGN DK (DK). [6,000] **297**

DESIGN ENGINEERING (LONDON, ENGLAND) (UK/0308-8448). [26,231] **1970**

DESIGN PRODUCTS & APPLICATIONS (UK). [36,110] **2097**

DESIGN SOLUTIONS (US/0277-3538). [33,000] **297**

DESIGN TIMES (US/1041-0422). [15,000] **2899**

DESIGNERS' JOURNAL (UK/0264-8148). [15,000] **297**

DESIGNERS WEST (US/0192-1487). [34,000] **2900**

DESIGNFAX (US/0163-6669). [110,047] **2097**

DESKTOP COMMUNICATIONS (US/1050-1800). [80,000] **1182**

DESKTOP PUBLISHER (US). [2,000] **1263**

DESOTO TIMES (1981) (US/1064-4784). [6,000] **5700**

DESSAUER'S JOURNAL (US). [4,000] **4519**

DESTINATION (TORONTO, ONT.) (CN/0229-2130). **5468**

DET BASTA UR READER'S DIGEST (SW/0005-3856). [200,000] **2515**

DET FORSTLIGE FORSOEGSVAESEN I DANMARK : BERETNINGER UTGIVNE VED DEN FORSTLIGE FORSOEGSKOMMISSION (DK/0367-2174). [800] **2378**

DETAIL (MUNCHEN) (GW/0011-9571). [13,058] **297**

DETAILED MORTALITY STATISTICS, SOUTH CAROLINA (US/8755-2744). [200] **5326**

DETROIT COLLEGE OF LAW ALUMNI NEWS (US). [6,500] **1101**

DETROIT DENTAL BULLETIN (US/0011-9601). [1,400] **1322**

DETROIT LABOR NEWS (US/1072-1525). [4,500] **1662**

DETROIT LAWYER, THE (US/0011-9652). **2960**

DETROIT LEGAL NEWS (DAILY ED.) (US/0739-9480). [2,600] **2960**

DETROIT MARINE HISTORIAN (US). [1,200] **5448**

DETROITER, THE (US/0011-9709). [18,000] **819**

DEUTSCH - BRASILIANISCHE HEFTE. CADERNOS GERMANO - BRASILEIROS (GW). [10,000] **2551**

DEUTSCHE ARCHITEKTUR (GE/0011-9865). **311**

DEUTSCHE HEBE- UND FORDERTECHNIK (GW/0012-0278). [11,250] **5099**

DEUTSCHE KRANKENPFLEGEZEITSCHRIFT (GW/0012-074X). [20,000] **3855**

DEUTSCHE LEBENSMITTEL-RUNDSCHAU (GW/0012-0413). [1,700] **2333**

DEUTSCHE OPTIKERZEITUNG (GW/0344-7103). [9,500] **3874**

DEUTSCHE RICHTERZEITUNG (GW). [12,500] **2960**

DEUTSCHE SCHRIFT, DIE (GW). [1,100] **3276**

DEUTSCHE

Controlled Circulation Index

DEUTSCHE SCHWARZBUNTE (GW/0343-3145). [38,000] **210**

DEUTSCHE STOMATOLOGIE (GW/0863-4904). [5,800] **1322**

DEUTSCHE WEINBAU, DER (GW). [11,273] **2366**

DEUTSCHE ZAHNAERZTLICHE ZEITSCHRIFT (GW/0012-1029). [6,000] **1322**

DEUTSCHE ZEITSCHRIFT FUER MUND-, KIEFER- UND GESICHTS-CHIRURGIE (GW/0343-3137). [7,900] **3963**

DEUTSCHER GARTENBAU (GW). [7,000] **2413**

DEUTSCHES ALLGEMEINES SONNTAGSBLATT (GW). [125,000] **5801**

DEUTSCHES ARZTEBLATT (GW/0012-1207). [210,000] **3571**

DEUTSCHES TIERARZTEBLATT (GW/0340-1898). [17,700] **5508**

DEUTSCHES VERWALTUNGSBLATT (GW/0012-1363). [3,650] **2960**

DEUTSCHSPRACHIGE ZEITSCHRIFTEN (GW/0419-005X). **414**

DEVELOPING ECONOMIES, THE (JA/0012-1533). **5198**

DEVELOPMENT ADMINISTRATION JOURNAL (PH). [500] **4642**

DEVELOPMENT (CAMBRIDGE) (UK/0950-1991). [1,300] **541**

DEVELOPMENT COMMUNICATION REPORT (US/0192-1312). [6,500] **1110**

DEVELOPMENT FORUM - UNITED NATIONS (US/0251-6632). [70,000] **1479**

DEVELOPMENT JOURNAL (LONDON) (UK/0957-4115). [5,300] **4642**

DEVELOPMENT SOUTHERN AFRICA (SANDTON, SOUTH AFRICA) (SA). [1,800-2,000] **2909**

DEVELOPMENTAL DISABILITIES BULLETIN (CN/1184-0412). [350-400] **4386**

DEVELOPMENTS (EDMONTON) (CN/0714-1017). [10,000] **1342**

DEVELOPMENTS IN MENTAL HEALTH LAW (US/1063-9977). [3,200] **2960**

DEVELOPPEMENT SOCIAL EN PERSPECTIVES (CN/0822-7128). [3,000] **5282**

DEVIANCE ET SOCIETE (SZ/0378-7931). [750] **4584**

DEVON DISPATCH, THE (CN/0710-5495). [1,546] **5783**

DEWITT POLYMER SERVICE (US). **4454**

DHZ MARKT (NE). **2811**

DI. DECISIONS INFORMATION (CN/0318-6377). [700] **1662**

DIABETE ET NUTRITION (FR/0012-1789). [6,000] **3727**

DIABETES DATELINE : THE NDIC BULLETIN (US). [6,000] **3727**

DIABETES FORECAST (US/0095-8301). [215,455] **3727**

DIABETES IN THE NEWS (1987) (US/0893-5939). [110,000] **3728**

DIABLO BUSINESS (US/1055-7431). [15,000] **665**

DIAGNOSIS (ORADELL, N.J.) (US/0163-3228). [100,000] **3571**

DIAGNOSTIC IMAGING (SAN FRANCISCO, CALIF.) (US/0194-2514). [30,000] **3940**

DIAKONIA (MAINZ, GERMANY : 1972) (GW/0341-9592). [1,050] **4953**

DIALOGHI DI ARCHEOLOGIA (IT/0392-8535). **266**

DIALOGO FILOSOFICO (SP/0213-1196). [1,000] **4345**

DIALOGUE & ALLIANCE (US/0891-5881). [2000] **4953**

DIALOGUE - ANGLICAN CHURCH OF CANADA. DIOCESE OF ONTARIO (CN/1184-6283). [7,000] **4953**

DIALOGUE (BRAILLE ED.) (US/1069-6865). [10,000] **4386**

DIALOGUE (CASSETTE ED.) (US/1069-6873). [10,000] **4386**

DIALOGUE IMMERSION (CN/0824-4189). [350] **3277**

DIALOGUE IN INSTRUMENTAL MUSIC EDUCATION (US/0147-7544). [400] **4114**

DIALOGUE : JOURNAL OF ADDIS ABABA UNIVERSITY MAIN CAMPUS TEACHERS ASSOCIATION (US). [100] **1820**

DIALOGUE (MUNROE FALLS, OHIO) (US/0279-568X). [15,000] **319**

DIALOGUES ET CULTURES (CN/0226-6881). [1,500] **3277**

DIALYSIS & TRANSPLANTATION (US/0090-2934). [18,000] **3571**

DIAMANT-, GOUD- EN ZILVERVERWERKENDE INDUSTRIE, SIERADENINDUSTRIE (NE/0920-5578). **2914**

DIAMOND DEPOSITIONS, SCIENCE AND TECHNOLOGY (US/1051-9084). [1,000] **1023**

DIAMOND TRAIL NEWS (US). [1,800] **5669**

DIAMOND WORLD (II). [12,000] **2914**

DIAMOND WORLD REVIEW (IS). [5,000] **2914**

DIAMOND'S JAPAN BUSINESS DIRECTORY (JA). [50,000] **665**

DIAPASON (CHICAGO), THE (US/0012-2378). [6,000] **4114**

DIARI OFICIAL DE LA GENERALITAT DE CATALUNYA (SP). [8,200] **2960**

DIARIO LAS AMERICAS (US/0744-3234). [64,093] **5649**

DIASTEMA (SA/0419-0955). [2,000] **1322**

DICKENSON STAR, THE (US/0746-584X). [3,600] **5758**

DICKINSON LAW REVIEW (US/0012-2459). [1,800] **2960**

DICKINSON MAGAZINE (US/0271-9134). [22,500] **1091**

DICKINSON PRESS (DICKINSON, N.D. 1942), THE (US/1049-6718). [8,450] **5725**

DICKINSON STUDIES (US/0164-1492). [250] **3462**

DICTIONARY CATALOG OF OFFICIAL PUBLICATIONS OF THE STATE OF NEW YORK (US). **4697**

DIDASCALIA (ROSARIO, SANTA FE, ARGENTINA) (AG). [2,000] **5028**

DIDASKALIA (LISBOA) (PO/0253-1674). [1,000] **4953**

DIDASKALIA (OTTERBURNE) (CN/0847-1266). **4953**

DIDSBURY BOOSTER AND MOUNTAIN VIEW COUNTY NEWS (CN/0316-683X). [2,100] **5783**

DIE CASTING MANAGEMENT (US/0745-449X). [3,300] **3477**

DIECIOCHO (US/0163-0415). [160] **3381**

DIEHARD (BOSTON, MASS.) (US/0896-7970). [9,000] **2773**

DIESEL & GAS TURBINE WORLDWIDE (US/0278-5994). [20,000] **2112**

DIETSCHE WARANDE EN BELFORT (BE/0012-2645). [3,000] **3381**

DIEU EST AMOUR SAINT-CENERE (FR/0180-9288). **5028**

DIGEST BUSINESS & LAW JOURNAL (CN/0315-811X). [2,000] **3099**

DIGEST FOR HOME FURNISHERS (US/1053-4571). [3,000] **2905**

DIGEST OF ADVISORY OPINIONS (US). [600] **2249**

DIGEST OF CHIROPRACTIC ECONOMICS, THE (US/0415-8407). [41,200] **3572**

DIGEST OF COMMISSION POLICIES AND COURT DECISIONS. WATER AND SEWER (US). [50] **2961**

DIGEST OF DECISIONS (US). [200] **939**

DIGEST OF INFORMATION AND PATENT REVIEW (UK). [300] **2588**

DIGEST OF OFFICIAL OPINIONS - ATTORNEY GENERAL (TALLAHASSEE) (US/0092-0843). [1,200] **3140**

DIGEST OF SELECTED REPORTS - UNITED WAY OF AMERICA (US/0146-9088). [2,000] **5282**

DIGEST OF STATE LAND SALES REGULATIONS, THE (US/0739-6368). [400] **4836**

DIGESTIVE DISEASES (BASEL) (SZ/0257-2753). [600] **3744**

DIGHTON HERALD (DIGHTON, KAN. : 1916) (US). **5675**

DIGITAL SYSTEM DESIGN SERIES (US/0888-2118). **1182**

DIKAIO KAI POLITIKE (THESSALONIKE, GREECE : 1982) (GR). [3,000] **3127**

DILIMAN REVIEW, THE (PH/0012-2858). [4,000] **5198**

DIMENSION (US/0162-6825). [45,700] **4953**

DIMENSIONAL STONE (US/0883-0258). [15,289] **613**

DIMENSIONS ECONOMIQUES DE LA BOURGOGNE (FR). [1,500] **5227**

DIMENSIONS OF EARLY CHILDHOOD (US/0160-6425). [20,000] **1803**

DIMS. DRUG INDEX FOR MALAYSIA & SINGAPORE (HK). [7,200] **4299**

DINNY'S CALGARY DIGEST (CN/0046-029X). [11,000] **5581**

DIONISO (IT). **5363**

DIOTIMA (GR/1010-7363). [1,000] **4345**

DIPLOMAT (LONDON, ENGLAND), THE (UK). [2,197] **4520**

DIPLOMES - UNIVERSITE DE MONTREAL (CN/0228-9636). [80,000] **1820**

DIRECT ACCESS (CALGARY) (CN/0843-5979). [350] **4386**

DIRECT MAGAZINE (US). [27,000] **923**

DIRECT MARKETING MARKET PLACE, THE (US/0192-3137). [5,000] **728**

DIRECT MARKETING NEWS (MARKHAM) (CN/1187-7111). [5,600] **923**

DIRECTION ET GESTION DES ENTREPRISES (FR/0012-320X). [2,800] **665**

DIRECTION (WINNIPEG) (US/0384-8515). [500] **4953**

DIRECTIONS : A NEWSLETTER FROM EBSCO PUBLISHING (US/0897-9499). **3206**

DIRECTIONS AT RIDER COLLEGE (US/0279-408X). [35,000] **1101**

DIRECTIONS IN GOVERNMENT (AT/1030-391X). [8,430] **4472**

DIRECTIONS (NEW YORK, N.Y. 1975) (US/0360-473X). [7,800] **3206**

DIRECTIONS (NEW YORK, N.Y. : 1985) (US/0883-9727). [5,600] **923**

DIRECTIONS (TORONTO. 1981) (CN/0711-0561). **1820**

DIRECTOR (LONDON. 1935) (UK/0012-3242). [36,000] **666**

DIRECTORIES OF HAWAII (US/0094-209X). **2559**

DIRECTORIO COMERCIAL E INDUSTRIAL DE EL SALVADOR. EL SALVADOR'S COMMERCIAL AND INDUSTRIAL DIRECTORY (ES). [1,800] **1604**

DIRECTORIO DE SOCIOS / CAMARA DE COMERCIO AMERICANA EN ESPANA (SP). [2,600] **819**

DIRECTORIO POSTAL DE PANAMA (PN). [50,000] **1144**

DIRECTORIO PROFESIONAL HISPANO (US/0147-5657). [107] **1663**

DIRECTORIO TURISTICO / DEPARTAMENTO DE ASUNTOS ECONOMICOS, DIVISION DE COMERCIO INTERNACIONAL Y TURISMO (US). [1,000] **5468**

DIRECTORY (US/0543-2774). [5,500] **3206**

DIRECTORY - AGRICULTURAL COMMUNICATORS IN EDUCATION (U.S.) (US/8755-5972). **79**

DIRECTORY / AMATEUR ATHLETIC UNION OF THE UNITED STATES (US). **4892**

DIRECTORY - AMERICAN ACADEMY OF DERMATOLOGY (US/0278-9000). [7,600] **3720**

DIRECTORY / AMERICAN BAR ASSOCIATION (US/1046-0349). [12,000] **2961**

DIRECTORY / AMERICAN CHAMBER OF COMMERCE IN ITALY (IT). [5,000] **819**

DIRECTORY - AMERICAN GROUP PRACTICE ASSOCIATION (US/0098-2377). [26,000] **3779**

DIRECTORY / AMERICAN MUSICOLOGICAL SOCIETY (US). [4,500] **4114**

DIRECTORY - AMERICAN RECOVERY ASSOCIATION, INC (US/0149-5216). [50,000] **666**

DIRECTORY - AMERICAN WATER WORKS ASSOCIATION, ONTARIO SECTION (CN/0704-7878). **5532**

DIRECTORY & CALENDAR / IAAF (UK). **4892**

DIRECTORY & CONSUMER GUIDE - BETTER BUSINESS BUREAU GREATER TORONTO (CN/0225-2686). **1296**

DIRECTORY AND REGISTER / ROLLS-ROYCE OWNERS' CLUB (US/0485-3695). [6,500] **5413**

DIRECTORY AND STATISTICS OF OREGON LIBRARIES (US/0162-0290). [625] **3206**

DIRECTORY - ASSOCIATION OF ACADEMIC HEALTH CENTERS (U.S.) (US/0276-6590). **3779**

DIRECTORY - CANADIAN ASSOCIATION OF GEOGRAPHERS (CN/0707-3844). [1,500] **2559**

DIRECTORY / CANADIAN GAS ASSOCIATION (CN/0229-1142). **4760**

DIRECTORY - CANADIAN RELIGIOUS CONFERENCE (CN/0705-3118). **4953**

DIRECTORY / CANADIAN SOCIETY FOR RENAISSANCE STUDIES (CN/0822-6369). [2,000] **2685**

DIRECTORY, CERTIFIED APPLIANCES AND ACCESSORIES (US/0732-1252). [4,500] **2811**

DIRECTORY / COLLEGE OF VETERINARIANS OF ONTARIO. [DISKETTE] (CN/1193-7998). [2,700] **5509**

DIRECTORY / COMPOSERS' FORUM, INC, THE (US). [2,000] **4114**

DIRECTORY : FLORIDA PORTS AND WATERWAYS (US/0091-8458). [10,000] **5448**

DIRECTORY - HOME ECONOMISTS IN BUSINESS, SECTION OF THE AMERICAN HOME ECONOMICS ASSOCIATION (US/0569-5058). [2,200] **2789**

DIRECTORY / MANITOBA DENTAL ASSOCIATION (CN/0711-2238). **1322**

DIRECTORY / MENNONITE CONFERENCE OF EASTERN CANADA (CN/1182-1701). [300] **5059**

DIRECTORY - NATIONAL FLUID POWER ASSOCIATION (US/0145-3866). [2,000] **2113**

DIRECTORY, NON-OPERATING LIBRARY BOARDS / GEORGIAN BAY REGIONAL LIBRARY SYSTEMS (CN/0712-9777). **3206**

DIRECTORY OF ACCREDITED AND RECOGNIZED PRACTITIONERS OF INTERPRETING & TRANSLATING (AT). [200] **3277**

DIRECTORY OF ACCREDITED INSTITUTIONS, CANDIDATES FOR ACCREDITATION (US/0882-6870). **1820**

DIRECTORY OF ADMINISTRATORS OF COMMUNITY, TECHNICAL, AND JUNIOR COLLEGES (US/8756-4254). **1820**

DIRECTORY OF ALBERTA GOVERNMENT LIBRARIES (CN/0382-3482). [250] **3206**

DIRECTORY OF ANIMAL DISEASE DIAGNOSTIC LABORATORIES (US/0146-1621). [1,000] **5509**

DIRECTORY OF ASSOCIATIONS IN CANADA (CN/0316-0734). [2,000] **5230**

DIRECTORY OF ATA MEMBERS (US). **2785**

DIRECTORY OF BILINGUAL SPEECH-LANGUAGE PATHOLOGISTS AND AUDIOLOGISTS (US/0743-5096). **4386**

DIRECTORY OF CANADIAN ARCHIVES (CN/0711-0413). **2481**

DIRECTORY OF CANADIAN MAP COLLECTIONS (CN/0070-5217). [300] **2559**

DIRECTORY OF CANADIAN UNIVERSITIES (CN/0706-2338). [5,500] **1820**

DIRECTORY OF CERTIFICATES OF AUTHORIZATION HOLDERS AUTHORIZED TO PRACTISE PROFESSIONAL ENGINEERING IN THE PROVINCE OF ONTARIO (CN/0712-7499). **1970**

DIRECTORY OF CERTIFIED PUBLIC ACCOUNTANTS AND PUBLIC ACCOUNTANTS OF OKLAHOMA (US/0361-4115). [8,000] **743**

DIRECTORY OF CHEMICAL PRODUCERS : UNITED STATES OF AMERICA (US/0012-3277). **1023**

DIRECTORY OF CHEMICAL PRODUCERS, WESTERN EUROPE (US). [1,000] **1023**

DIRECTORY OF COLORADO LIBRARIES ... & LIBRARY STATISTICS / COLORADO DEPARTMENT OF EDUCATION (US). [2,000] **3206**

DIRECTORY OF CONTRACT SERVICE FIRMS (US/0148-1819). [18,000] **1970**

DIRECTORY OF DIPLOMATES (US). [3,000] **3881**

DIRECTORY OF EDUCATIONAL INSTITUTIONS ACCREDITED BY THE ACCREDITING COMMISSION OF THE ASSOCIATION OF INDEPENDENT COLLEGES AND SCHOOLS (US/0733-2858). [20,000] **1820**

DIRECTORY OF EDUCATIONAL INSTITUTIONS AND APPRENTICESHIP AND OTHER ON- THE-JOB TRAINING FACILITIES APPROVED BY THE WEST VIRGINIA DEPARTMENT OF EDUCATION FOR VETERANS EDUCATIONAL BENEFITS UNDER PUBLIC LAW 96-466 (US). [1,000] **1912**

DIRECTORY OF FLORIDA INDUSTRIES (US). [9,000] **923**

DIRECTORY OF FOOD SERVICE DISTRIBUTORS (BUSINESS GUIDES, INC.) (US/0271-7662). **2333**

DIRECTORY OF FURTHER EDUCATION (UK). [1,250] **1800**

DIRECTORY OF GEOSCIENCE DEPARTMENTS, NORTH AMERICA (US). [2000] **1373**

DIRECTORY OF HIGHER EDUCATION COURSES (AT). [8,000] **1821**

DIRECTORY OF HONG KONG INDUSTRIES (HK). **1604**

DIRECTORY OF HUMAN SERVICES IN THE KALAMAZOO AREA (US). [1,000] **5283**

DIRECTORY OF LABOR MARKET INFORMATION (US/0190-3217). [2,000] **1663**

DIRECTORY OF LABOR MARKET INFORMATION (COLUMBIA, S.C.) (US). **1663**

DIRECTORY OF LAW LIBRARIES (US). **3207**

DIRECTORY OF LIBRARIES AND ARCHIVAL INSTITUTIONS IN PRINCE EDWARD ISLAND (CN/0715-1624). **3207**

DIRECTORY OF LICENSES (US). **4380**

DIRECTORY OF LONG TERM CARE CENTRES IN CANADA (CN/0226-5419). [2,000] **3779**

DIRECTORY OF MEDICAL COMPUTER SYSTEMS (US). [185,000] **1182**

DIRECTORY OF MEDICAL INSTITUTIONS CONDUCTING RESEARCH AND SERVICES FOR PERSONS WITH THE MARFAN SYNDROME AND RELATED CONNECTIVE TISSUE DISORDERS (US). **3572**

DIRECTORY OF MEMBER AGENCIES IN THE UNITED STATES AND CANADA (US/1045-1684). **5283**

DIRECTORY OF MEMBERS / AMERICAN ASSOCIATION OF HOMES FOR THE AGING (US). [6,000] **5283**

DIRECTORY OF MEMBERS - FEDERATION OF INDIAN PUBLISHERS (II). [500] **4814**

DIRECTORY OF MEMBERS - FREELANCE EDITORS' ASSOCIATION OF CANADA (CN/0226-9031). [3,500] **4814**

DIRECTORY OF MEMBERS - INSTITUTE OF MANAGEMENT CONSULTANTS (US/0097-6547). [2,500] **865**

DIRECTORY OF MEMBERS - INTERNATIONAL BAR ASSOCIATION, SECTION ON BUSINESS LAW (UK). [8,500] **3099**

DIRECTORY OF MEMBERS / LOS ANGELES COUNTY MEDICAL ASSOCIATION (US). [13,000] **3913**

DIRECTORY OF MEMBERS, OFFICERS, COMMITTEES - AMERICAN VACUUM SOCIETY (US/0360-8794). **2113**

DIRECTORY OF MICHIGAN MUNICIPAL OFFICIALS (US/0148-7442). [10,000] **4643**

DIRECTORY OF MISSOURI LIBRARIES (US/0092-4067). [1,000] **3207**

DIRECTORY OF O.C.U.L. LIBRARIES (CN/0822-935X). **3207**

DIRECTORY OF OKLAHOMA AIRPORTS (US/0094-5390). [5,000] **18**

DIRECTORY OF OPERATING LIBRARIES / GEORGIAN BAY REGIONAL LIBRARY SYSTEM (CN/0712-9785). **3207**

DIRECTORY OF PATHOLOGY TRAINING PROGRAMS IN THE UNITED STATES AND CANADA (US). [2,400] **3894**

DIRECTORY OF PUBLIC LIBRARY SERVICES, WESTERN AUSTRALIA (AT). [600] **3208**

DIRECTORY OF PUBLISHED PROCEEDINGS. SERIES PCE : POLLUTION CONTROL/ECOLOGY (US/0093-5816). **2227**

DIRECTORY OF PUBLISHED PROCEEDINGS. SERIES - SCIENCE/ENGINEERING/MEDICINE/TECHNOLOGY (US). **5174**

DIRECTORY OF RETAIL CHAINS IN CANADA (CN/0225-9443). **954**

DIRECTORY OF RETAILER OWNED COOPERATIVES, WHOLESALER SPONSORED VOLUNTARIES, WHOLESALE GROCERS, SERVICES MERCHANDISERS (US/0277-1969). **1604**

DIRECTORY OF SOURCES FOR EDITORS, REPORTERS & RESEARCHERS, THE (CN/1197-5148). [15,000] **2919**

DIRECTORY OF SOUTHEAST ASIAN ACADEMIC & SPECIAL LIBRARIES (TH). **3208**

DIRECTORY OF STATE AND PUBLIC LIBRARY SERVICES IN QUEENSLAND (AT/0314-9307). **3208**

DIRECTORY OF SUPERMARKET, GROCERY, AND CONVENIENCE STORE CHAINS (US/0196-1845). **2333**

DIRECTORY OF TELEFACSIMILE SITES IN NORTH AMERICAN LIBRARIES (US/1049-7218). [2,000] **1153**

DIRECTORY OF TENNESSEE MANUFACTURERS (US/0070-6450). [6,500] **3478**

DIRECTORY OF THE AMERICAN BAPTIST CHURCHES IN THE U.S.A (US/0091-9381). [6,000] **5059**

DIRECTORY OF THE ARTS (OTTAWA) (CN/0832-865X). **319**

DIRECTORY OF THE NEW MEXICO BENCH AND BAR (US/8756-1611). [3,826] **2962**

DIRECTORY OF UNDERGRADUATE POLITICAL SCIENCE FACULTY (US/0884-5859). [2,500] **4472**

DIRECTORY / ONTARIO AMATEUR FOOTBALL ASSOCIATION (CN/0713-6781). **4892**

DIRECTORY - OUTDOOR WRITERS ASSOCIATION OF AMERICA (US/0195-6124). [2,500] **2919**

DIRECTORY - PERSEKUTUAN PEKILAND-PEKILANG MALAYSIA (MY/0126-9801). [2,000] **3478**

DIRECTORY PERUSAHAAN BIS (ANTAR PROPINSI) (IO/0126-4613). **5381**

DIRECTORY / SPECTROSCOPY SOCIETY OF CANADA (CN/0709-8448). [1,200] **4401**

DIRECTORY - STATE BAR OF GEORGIA (US/1067-4861). [20,500] **2962**

DIRECTORY - TEXAS OSTEOPATHIC MEDICAL ASSOCIATION (US/0196-6340). [3,500] **3572**

DIRECTORY / TOY TRAIN OPERATING SOCIETY (US/0732-9873). [5,000] **2584**

DIRECTORY - U. S. COAST GUARD ACADEMY ALUMNI ASSOCIATION (US). [5,800] **1101**

DIRECTORY (UNITARIAN UNIVERSALIST ASSOCIATION : 1965) (US/0503-2636). [2,000] **5059**

DIRECTORY / VIRGINIA HIGH SCHOOL LEAGUE, INC (US). **1736**

DIRES (CN/0820-0890). [500] **5198**

DIREZIONE DEL PERSONALE (IT). [2,500] **940**

DIRIGENTE RURAL, O (BL/0012-3374). [43,000] **79**

DIRITTO DELLE RADIODIFFUSIONI E DELLE TELECOMUNICAZIONI, IL (IT). [3,000] **2962**

DIRITTO FALLIMENTARE E DELLE SOCIETA COMMERCIALI (IT/0391-5239). [2,500] **2963**

DIS COLLECTOR (CHESWOLD, DEL. : 1981) (US/0731-843X). [950] **4115**

DISABLED OUTDOORS (US). **4387**

DISABLED OUTDOORS MAGAZINE (US/1067-098X). [6,000] **4387**

DISASTER PREPAREDNESS IN THE AMERICAS. AMERICAN SANITARY BUREAU (US/0251-4494). [18,000] **4773**

DISC (US/1052-4053). [5,000] **1183**

DISC SPORTS (US/0747-9956). [15,000] **4893**

DISCERNER (US/0416-0274). [4,000] **4954**

DISCERNING TRAVELER, THE (US/0898-6231). **5468**

DISCIPLES THEOLOGICAL DIGEST, THE (US/0888-1111). [700] **4954**

DISCIPULOS RESPONSABLES (US/1052-3804). [750] **4954**

DISCLOSURE RECORD (US/0094-2561). [10,000] **788**

DISCLOSURES (US). [5,200] **743**

DISCOUNT MERCHANDISER, THE (US/0012-3579). [50,000] **954**

DISCOVER COSTA RICA (US). [10,000] **5468**

DISCOVER GUATEMALA (US). [8,000] **5468**

DISCOVER SOUTHWEST WISCONSIN'S HIDDEN VALLEYS (US/0738-8071). **5468**

DISCOVER THE BIBLE (CN/0018-912X). [2,500] **5016**

DISCOVERY AND INNOVATION (KE/1015-079X). [500] **5101**

DISCOVERY (AUSTIN) (US/0197-4947). [10,000] **2532**

DISCOVERY (BIRMINGHAM, ALA.) (US/0162-198X). [209,000] **5059**

DISCOVERY (NEW HAVEN, CONN.) (US/0012-3625). [1,000] **4087**

DISCOVERY (SKOKIE, ILL.) (US/0012-3641). [1,600,000] **5468**

DISCOVERY YMCA (US). [75,000] **4850**

DISCRETE MATHEMATICS (NE/0012-365X). **3504**

DISCUSSION PAPER - CENTER FOR LATIN AMERICA IN THE UNIVERSITY OF WISCONSIN, MILWAUKEE (US/0146-258X). [75] **1821**

DISCUSSION PAPER - CENTER FOR RESEARCH ON ECONOMIC DEVELOPMENT, THE UNIVERSITY OF MICHIGAN (US/0580-6062). [200] **1480**

DISEASE INFORMATION (FR/1012-5329). [250] **5509**

DISEGNO MAGAZINE (IT). [30,000] **1233**

DISNEY CHANNEL MAGAZINE, THE (US/0747-4644). [4,250,000] **1131**

DISNEY NEWS (US/0095-7178). [300,000] **4850**

DISP (SZ). **2022**

DISPATCH (ROCKVILLE, MD.) (US/0743-7269). [600] **5381**

DISPATCHER Controlled Circulation Index

DISPATCHER, THE (US/0012-3765). [44,000] **1663**

DISPLAY & DESIGN IDEAS (US/1049-9172). [18,000] **759**

DISPOSITIO (US/0734-0591). [800] **3382**

DISSERTATION ABSTRACTS INTERNATIONAL. A, THE HUMANITIES AND SOCIAL SCIENCES. B, THE SCIENCES AND ENGINEERING. CUMULATED AUTHOR INDEX (MICROFORM) (US). **5227**

DISTANCE EDUCATION (AT/0158-7919). [300] **1736**

DISTRIBUTIVE WORKER, THE (US/0012-3986). [50,000] **1663**

DISTRIBUTORS LINK (US). **923**

DISTRICT COUNCIL JOURNAL (US/0748-1179). [400] **4645**

DISTRICT MEMOIR / GEOLOGICAL SURVEY OF WEST MALAYSIA (MY). **1373**

DISTRICT OF COLUMBIA REAL ESTATE REPORTER (US/0738-6931). [250] **4837**

DIVER (UK). [39,376] **4893**

DIVER DOWN (CN/0700-3994). **4893**

DIVER MAGAZINE (CN/0706-5132). [20,000] **4893**

DIVERSION (TITUSVILLE) (US/0363-4825). [160,085] **4850**

DIVIDEND RECORD (CN/0046-0419). **4720**

DIVING WORLD (VAN NUYS, CALIF.) (US/1042-1343). [11,000] **4893**

DIXIE CONTRACTOR, THE (US/0012-4281). [10,000] **2022**

DIXIE LOGGER AND LUMBERMAN MAGAZINE (US/0046-0435). [25,000] **2400**

DIY WEEK (UK). **2811**

DJ TIMES (US/1045-9693). **1131**

DJAWAL IDI (AT/0314-7797). [1,500] **1803**

DK NEWSLETTER (II). [3,100] **415**

DM NEWS (US/0194-3588). [34,000] **923**

DMT. DANSK MUSIK TIDSSKRIFT (DK/0106-5629). [1,100] **4115**

DNA REPORTER (US). [700] **3855**

DNZ INTERNATIONAL (GW/0011-507X). **5350**

DOBOKU GAKKAI RONBUN HOKOKUSHU (JA/0385-5392). **2022**

DOBUTSU IYAKUHIN KENSAJO NEMPO (JA/0388-7421). [630] **5509**

DOCKLANDS NEWS (UK/0264-9691). [140,000] **667**

DOCTOR GUILDFORD (UK/0046-0451). [40,000] **3737**

DOCTOR'S REVIEW (CN/0821-5758). [34,000] **4850**

DOCTRINA PENAL (AG). [2,000] **3107**

DOCUMENT DE TRAVAIL - UNIVERSITE D'OTTAWA. FACULTE D'ADMINISTRATION (CN/0824-4316). **667**

DOCUMENTATION BIBLIOTECOLOGICA (AG). [250] **3208**

DOCUMENTATION CATHOLIQUE, LA (FR/0012-4613). [23,000] **5028**

DOCUMENTATION DU MINISTERE DE L'ENERGIE ET DES RESSOURCES, REPERTOIRE (CN/0824-3689). **1555**

DOCUMENTATION ET BIBLIOTHEQUES (CN/0315-2340). **3208**

DOCUMENTATION IN PUBLIC ADMINISTRATION (II/0377-7081). **4645**

DOCUMENTI DI ARCHITETTURA ARMENA (IT/0420-0810). [3,000] **298**

DOCUMENTO DE TRABAJO / INSTITUTO TORCUATO DI TELLA, CENTRO DE INVESTIGACIONES SOCIALES (AG/0325-8483). [300] **1663**

DOCUMENTOS DE TRABAJO (UNIVERSIDAD DE COSTA RICA, INSTITUTO DE INVESTIGACIONES EN CIENCIAS ECONOMICAS) (CR). [300] **1664**

DOCUMENTS D'ARCHEOLOGIE MERIDIONALE (FR/0184-1068). **266**

DOCUMENTS JURIDIQUES INTERNATIONAUX (CN/0714-931X). **3127**

DOCUMENTS - VIRGINIA HISTORICAL SOCIETY (US/0083-6389). **2731**

DODO (TRINITY) (UK/0265-5640). [3,000] **5581**

DOD'S REPORT (UK/0956-0580). [1,000] **1605**

DOE HET VEILIG (BE/0773-6231). [2,000] **2861**

DOE THIS MONTH (US/1057-5782). [27,000] **1936**

DOG WATCH, THE (AT). [1,500] **4176**

DOHNER FAMILY NEWSLETTER (US/0736-2412). [100] **2445**

DOKUMENTATIONSDIENST AFRIKA. AUSGEWAEHLTE NEUERE LITERATUR (GW/0342-040X). [100] **2496**

DOKUMENTATIONSDIENST LATEINAMERIKA. AUSGEWAEHLTE NEUERE LITERATUR (GW/0342-037X). [500] **5198**

DOLL READER (US/0744-0901). [60,000] **2584**

DOLLAR$ENSE (LOS ANGELES) (US/0194-8490). [750,000] **1296**

DOLPHIN LOG (US/8756-6362). [100,000] **1448**

DOMES (MILWAUKEE, WIS.) (US/1060-4367). **2768**

DOMESTIC AND INTERNATIONAL COMMERCIAL LOAN CHARGE-OFFS (US/0192-7639). [4,000] **788**

DOMODOMO : FIJI MUSEUM QUARTERLY (FJ). [1,000] **4087**

DONEGAL ANNUAL (IE/0416-2773). [900] **2685**

DONKEY DIGEST (AT/1031-6280). [500] **5582**

DONNEES SUR LA POPULATION ACTIVE : QUEBEC, ONTARIO ET CANADA (CN/0715-1055). [125] **5326**

DONT ACTE (CN/0381-1875). **669**

DON'T MISS OUT (US/0277-6987). [100,000] **1822**

DORITSU MIGISHI KOTARO BIJUTSUKAN HO (JA). [1,600] **349**

DORM (US/0743-2860). [1,000,000] **1091**

DOS INTERNATIONAL (GW/0933-1557). [230,000] **1183**

DOSHISHA DAIGAKU DAIGAKUIN SHOGAKU RONSHU (JA). [400] **1556**

DOSHISHA DANSO (JA). [1,000] **1822**

DOSHISHA GAIKOKU BUNGAKU KENKYU (JA). [2,000] **3382**

DOSSIER. L'UFFICIO TECNICO (IT/0394-8315). [6,100] **298**

DOSSIERS CSN (1980 OCT.) (CN/0821-4433). **1664**

DOSSIERS DU CEPED, LES (FR/0993-6165). [100] **4552**

DOSTOEVSKY STUDIES : JOURNAL OF THE INTERNATIONAL DOSTOEVSKY SOCIETY (AU/1013-2309). **3382**

DOTOKU TO KYOIKU (JA). [5,000] **1737**

DOUBLE REED, THE (US/0741-7659). [2,900] **4115**

DOUGHTY TREE, THE (US/0897-3350). [250] **2446**

DOW THEORY FORECASTS (US/0300-7324). [24,500] **897**

DOWN BEAT (US/0012-5768). [91,000] **4115**

DOWN TO EARTH (US/0012-5792). [6,000] **80**

DOWN UNDER QUILTS (AT/1033-4513). [11,000] **5183**

DOWNS SYNDROME ASSOCIATION OF NEW SOUTH WALES NEWSLETTER (AT). [1,300] **4387**

DOWNTOWNER (TORONTO) (CN/0710-1619). **5783**

DP, DANSK PRESSE (DK). [1,983] **2515**

DP MARKET FACTS (CN/0711-7884). [150] **1258**

DPN: DESIGN PRODUCT NEWS (CN/0319-8413). [19,000] **1971**

DR. MCBIRNIE'S NEWSLETTER (US). [30,000] **4472**

DRAGON (LAKE GENEVA, WIS.) (US/0279-6848). [85,000] **4860**

DRAHT (GW/0012-5911). [4,855] **4001**

DRAINAGE CONTRACTOR (CN). [8,800] **80**

DRAKE UPDATE (US). [43,000] **1091**

DRAMA/THEATRE TEACHER, THE (US/1046-5022). [1,100] **5364**

DRAMATHERAPY : THE JOURNAL OF THE BRITISH ASSOCIATION OF DRAMATHERAPY (UK). [400] **5364**

DRAMATISTS GUILD QUARTERLY, THE (US/0012-6004). [7,000] **5364**

DRAUGHTING & DESIGN (UK/0951-5704). [18,000] **1183**

DRESS (US/0361-2112). [1,500] **1083**

DRESSAGE & CT (US/0147-796X). [10,000] **2798**

DREW GATEWAY, THE (US/0012-6152). [600] **4954**

DRILLING CONTRACTOR (US/0046-0702). [18,500] **4254**

DRILLING WEEKLY (UK). **4255**

DRINKING WATER & BACKFLOW PREVENTION (US/1055-2782). [3,000] **5533**

DRIVE SAFELY (US). **5440**

DRIVER/EDUCATION (TORONTO) (CN/1183-7314). [700-1,000] **5413**

DRIVERS AND CONTROLS (UK/0950-5490). [18,000] **1971**

DROCHAID (CN/0703-1491). **2259**

DROIT ET AFFAIRES INTERNATIONAL (FR/0184-5920). [400] **2964**

DRUCK PRINT (GW/0012-6462). [9,420] **4564**

DRUCKWELT (GW/0012-6519). **4564**

DRUG ABUSE & ALCOHOLISM NEWSLETTER (US/0160-0028). [12,000] **1343**

DRUG ABUSE UPDATE (US/0739-6562). [16,000] **1343**

DRUG AND CHEMICAL TOXICOLOGY (NEW YORK, N.Y. 1978) (US/0148-0545). **3980**

DRUG AND DEVICE RECALL BULLETIN (US/8756-5935). [5,000] **4299**

DRUG AND THERAPEUTICS BULLETIN (UK/0012-6543). [80,000] **4299**

DRUG DEVELOPMENT AND INDUSTRIAL PHARMACY (US/0363-9045). **4300**

DRUG INTERACTIONS NEWSLETTER (US/0271-8707). [10,000] **4300**

DRUG STORE NEWS, INSIDE PHARMACY (US/0891-9828). [56,537] **4301**

DRUG THERAPY (NEW YORK, N.Y.) (US/0001-7094). [110,000] **3573**

DRUG TOPICS (US/0012-6616). [85,000] **4301**

DRUG TOPICS REDBOOK UPDATE (US/0731-8596). [8,100] **4301**

DRUGLINK INFORMATION LETTER (UK/0305-4349). [1,300] **1343**

DRUGS AND THERAPEUTICS FOR MARITIME PRACTITIONERS (CN/0705-291X). [5,100] **4302**

DRUGS IN PEDIATRICS (CN/0824-703X). [1,500] **3903**

DRUGS IN PSYCHIATRY (POINTE-CLAIRE) (CN/0824-7102). [2,600] **4302**

DRUGS MADE IN GERMANY (GW/0012-6683). [5,500] **4302**

DRUMMER (SAN FRANCISCO, CALIF.) (US/1055-7415). [30,000] **2794**

DRVNA INDUSTRIJA (CI/0012-6772). [2,000] **2400**

DRYCLEANER NEWS (US/0012-6802). [9,000] **5350**

DSIR BULLETIN (NZ/0077-961X). **5102**

DU (SZ/0012-6837). [20,606] **2515**

DU PONT MAGAZINE (US/0095-8808). [200,000] **1024**

DUCKS OLD TIME JOURNAL (US). [200] **2615**

DUCKS UNLIMITED (US/0012-6950). [600,000] **2191**

DUCTILE IRON PIPE NEWS (US). **4001**

DUKE MATHEMATICAL JOURNAL (US/0012-7094). [1,200] **3504**

DULCIMER PLAYER NEWS, THE (US/0098-3527). [2,200] **4115**

DULUTH BUSINESS INDICATORS (US/0419-814X). [800] **669**

DUMBARTON OAKS PAPERS (US/0070-7546). [800] **2650**

DUNN REPORT, ELECTRONIC PUBLISHING & PREPRESS SYSTEMS NEWS & VIEWS (US/0741-6547). **4814**

DUODECIM (FI/0012-7183). [17,500] **3573**

DUQUESNE LAW REVIEW (US/0093-3058). [1,200] **2964**

DURBAN MUSEUM NOVITATES (SA/0012-723X). [400] **4165**

DUTCH & FLEMISH ETCHINGS, ENGRAVINGS AND WOODCUTS (NE). [600] **349**

DUTCHESS, THE (US/0735-6242). [250] **2446**

DVW HESSEN MITTEILUNGEN (GW/0173-6280). [1,100] **2022**

DVZ DEUTSCHE VERKEHRS-ZEITUNG (GW/0342-166X). [13,000] **5381**

DWF (IT). **5554**

DWJ, DEUTSCHES WAFFEN-JOURNAL (GW). [72,000] **4893**

DX NEWS (US/0737-1659). [750] **2773**

DYNAMIC BUSINESS : A PUBLICATION OF THE SMALLER MANUFACTURER'S COUNCIL (US/0279-4039). [5,300] **670**

DYNAMIC (NEW YORK, N.Y.) (US/0741-0263). [30,000] **4472**

DYNAMICA (SA). [5,300] **670**

DYNIX DATALINE (US/8756-2294). [3,500] **3208**

DZIENNIK ZWIAZKOWY (US/0742-6615). [22,000] **5660**

E & MJ INTERNATIONAL DIRECTORY OF MINING (US). [2,500] **2138**

E I C, ELECTRONIQUE, INDUSTRIELLE & COMMERCIALE (CN/0226-7748). [10,000] **2056**

E.P.A.'S IRIS CHEMICAL INFORMATION DATABASE [COMPUTER FILE] (US). **2164**

EAA EXPERIMENTER (US/0894-1289). [6,500] **18**

EAGLE, THE (US). [3,000] **3163**

EAGLEVIEW POST, THE (CN/0821-2171). **5783**

EANHS BULLETIN (KE/0374-7387). [1,000] **4165**

EAP DIGEST (US/0273-8910). [16,000] **1344**

EARLY AMERICAN LITERATURE (US/0012-8163). [700] **3341**

EARLY CHILDHOOD EDUCATION (CN/0012-8171). **1737**

EARLY CHILDHOOD NEWS (US). [36,000] **1803**

EARLY CHINA (US/0362-5028). [300] **2650**

EARLY DAYS (AT/0312-6145). [1,000] **2669**

EARLY DRAMA, ART, AND MUSIC MONOGRAPH SERIES (US). **319**

EARLY ENGLISH CHURCH MUSIC (UK/0424-0359). **4116**

EARLY GEORGIA (US/0422-0374). [175] **267**

EARLY INTERVENTION (US/1058-8396). [4,000] **5284**

EARLY MUSIC NEWS (UK). [1,000] **4116**

EARNSHAW'S INFANTS-GIRLS-BOYS WEAR REVIEW (US/0161-2786). [10,000] **1083**

EARTH AND MINERAL SCIENCES (US/0026-4539). [18,000] **1354**

EARTH GARDEN (AT/0310-222x). [18,000] **5244**

EARTH SCIENCES HISTORY (US/0736-623X). [700] **1355**

EARTHCARE NORTHWEST (US/0732-684X). [5,500] **2192**

EARTHWATCH OREGON (US/0890-1201). [1,600] **2164**

EAST AFRICAN AGRICULTURAL AND FORESTRY JOURNAL (KE/0012-8325). [3,000] **80**

EAST ASIA AND THE WESTERN PACIFIC (US/1043-2140). **2650**

EAST ASIA MILLIONS (ROBESONIA) (US/0012-8406). [28,000] **4954**

EAST ASIA SERIES (US/0066-0957). [200] **2503**

EAST ASIAN BUSINESS INTELLIGENCE (US/0888-580X). [150] **923**

EAST ASIAN EXECUTIVE REPORTS (US/0272-1589). [600] **3099**

EAST ASIAN PASTORAL REVIEW (PH/0116-0257). [1,200] **4954**

EAST CAROLINA MANUSCRIPT COLLECTION BULLETIN (US/0360-5191). [500] **415**

EAST CAROLINA UNIVERSITY PUBLICATIONS IN HISTORY (US/0070-8089). [500] **2615**

EAST CENTRAL EUROPE (US/0094-3037). [300] **2846**

EAST COAST ANGLER (US/0899-0506). **2300**

EAST COUNTY CHRONICLE (US). [5,000] **5656**

EAST EUROPEAN INVESTMENT MAGAZINE (US/1063-4029). [9,800] **897**

EAST EUROPEAN MARKETS (UK/0262-0456). **897**

EAST EUROPEAN QUARTERLY (US/0012-8449). [900] **2686**

EAST EUROPEAN STATISTICS SERVICE (BE). [500] **1531**

EAST KENTUCKIAN, THE (US/0424-107X). [780] **2446**

EAST LONDON RECORD (UK/0141-6286). [2,000] **2686**

EAST TEXAS HISTORICAL JOURNAL (US/0424-1444). [575] **2732**

EAST TEXAS MEDICINE (US/1050-6675). [2,500] **3573**

EAST WEST FORTNIGHTLY BULLETIN (BE/0012-8570). **1634**

EASTER SEALER (CN/0844-5559). [12,500] **5284**

EASTERN BASKETBALL (US/0195-0223). [10,000] **4893**

EASTERN BLOC ENERGY (UK/0954-2981). [500] **1937**

EASTERN CHALLENGE (US/0898-9346). [22,000] **4954**

EASTERN ECONOMIC JOURNAL (US/0094-5056). [1,000] **1480**

EASTERN EUROPEAN ECONOMICS (US/0012-8775). [450] **1481**

EASTERN JOURNAL OF PRACTICAL THEOLOGY (CN). [1,000] **5059**

EASTERN TRAVEL SALES GUIDE (US/0739-4780). [2,000] **5468**

EASTERN/WESTERN QUARTER HORSE JOURNAL (US/0191-7714). [9,000] **2798**

EASTERN WORKER (PK/0012-8953). [1,000] **1664**

EASTMAN NOTES (US/0147-345X). [8,000] **4116**

EASTSIDE SUN (US). [63,000] **5634**

EASY LIVING GUIDE : THE ORIGINAL GUIDE FOR THE COMMUNITIES OF NEW WESTMINSTER, COQUITLAM, PORT MOODY, BURNABY (CN/0821-7394). [355,000] **2487**

EASY READER (US/0194-6412). [60,000] **5634**

EATERN AIZONA COURIER (US). **5630**

EAU VIVE, L' (CN/0046-1016). [1,400] **5783**

EAWARUDO (JA). [55,000] **18**

EBARA JIHO (JA/0385-3004). [4,000] **1971**

EBONY (US/0012-9011). [1,850,000] **2259**

EBSCO BUGLE (US). [3,000] **670**

EC NEWSLETTER - DELEGATION OF THE COMMISSION OF THE EUROPEAN COMMUNITIES (CN/0835-8451). [1,500] **1634**

EC UPDATE (UK). **2515**

ECCLESIA ORANS (IT/1010-3872). [1,000] **4954**

ECHO DES RECHERCHES, L' (FR/0012-9283). [10,000] **1154**

ECHO MUNICIPAL (CN/0713-8024). [450] **4645**

ECHOES (BLAINE, ME.) (US/1043-3341). [6,200] **2732**

ECHOS DU MONDE CLASSIQUE (CN/0012-9356). [700] **267**

ECO ALERT / CONSERVATION COUNCIL (CN/0833-448X). [500] **2192**

ECO/LOG WEEK (CN/0315-0380). **2227**

ECOLOGICAL ILLNESS LAW REPORT (US/8755-9013). [1,200] **3110**

ECOLOGIST (1979) (UK/0261-3131). [5,000] **2214**

ECOLOGY LAW QUARTERLY (US/0046-1121). [1300] **3110**

ECONOMIA & LAVORO (1967) (IT/0012-978X). [4,000] **1481**

ECONOMIA BRASILEIRA E SUAS PERSPECTIVAS, A (BL/0424-2386). [2,000] **1481**

ECONOMIA DELLE FONTI DI ENERGIA (IT). [3,300] **1937**

ECONOMIA E BANCA (IT/0393-9243). **1481**

ECONOMIA INFORMA (MX/0185-0849). [2,000] **1481**

ECONOMIA (LISBOA) (PO/0870-3531). [3,000] **1481**

ECONOMIC ANALYSIS AND POLICY (AT/0313-5926). [400] **1591**

ECONOMIC ANALYSIS OF BRITISH COLUMBIA (CN/0824-3980). [100,000] **1482**

ECONOMIC AND FINANCIAL STATISTICS (BB/0378-178X). **1531**

ECONOMIC AND SOCIAL REVIEW, THE (IE/0012-9984). [450] **5199**

ECONOMIC BOTANY (US/0013-0001). [2,000] **508**

ECONOMIC BULLETIN - SINGAPORE INTERNATIONAL CHAMBER OF COMMERCE (SI/0037-5659). [2,500] **819**

ECONOMIC DEVELOPMENT REVIEW (SCHILLER PARK, ILL.) (US/0742-3713). [2,900] **1483**

ECONOMIC EYE (JA/0389-0503). [15,500] **1557**

ECONOMIC GEOLOGY REPORT (ALBERTA RESEARCH COUNCIL) (CN). **1374**

ECONOMIC GROWTH AND LEAD AND ZINC CONSUMPTION (UK). **4001**

ECONOMIC HISTORY REVIEW, THE (UK/0013-0117). [4,500] **1557**

ECONOMIC MODELLING (UK/0264-9993). [800] **1591**

ECONOMIC PAPERS / THE ECONOMIC SOCIETY OF AUSTRALIA (AT). [2,200] **1484**

ECONOMIC POLICY PAPERS (NEW YORK, N.Y.) (US). [2,285] **1484**

ECONOMIC QUALITY CONTROL (GW/0940-5151). [200] **1484**

ECONOMIC RECORD, THE (AT/0013-0249). [4,000] **1484**

ECONOMIC REPORT (ALBUQUERQUE, N.M.), THE (US/0738-7210). **1484**

ECONOMIC REPORT - TURKIYE IS BANKAS A.S (TU/0376-9275). [2,000] **1558**

ECONOMIC REVIEW (COLOMBO) (CE/0259-9775). [12,000] **1484**

ECONOMIC REVIEW (CYPRUS POPULAR BANK) (CY/0254-3214). [2,800] **1484**

ECONOMIC REVIEW (KANSAS CITY) (US/0161-2387). [30,000] **1485**

ECONOMIC REVIEW OF TRAVEL IN AMERICA, THE (US/0733-642X). [300] **5469**

ECONOMIC STUDIES (CALCUTTA, INDIA) (II/0013-0362). [22,000] **1558**

ECONOMIC SURVEY (UK). **4828**

ECONOMIC SYSTEMS RESEARCH (UK/0953-5314). [550] **1485**

ECONOMIC TIMES (UK). [120,000] **671**

ECONOMIC TRENDS (NEW DELHI) (II/0014-9470). [1,500] **1591**

ECONOMIC UPDATE - DOMINION SECURITIES AMES. ECONOMICS (CN/0824-3425). **1558**

ECONOMIC WORLD DIRECTORY OF JAPANESE COMPANIES IN USA (US/0163-4682). [5,000] **832**

ECONOMICA (IO). [2,500] **1486**

ECONOMICS (LONDON) (UK/0300-4287). [3,200] **1486**

ECONOMICS MONITOR (AT). **1486**

ECONOMICS OF PLANNING (NE/0013-0451). [750] **1558**

ECONOMICS (TUBINGEN) (GW/0341-616X). [3,000] **1487**

ECONOMIE AND GESTION AGRO-ALIMENTAIRE (FR/0981-8715). [700] **81**

ECONOMIE FAMILIALE HOME ECONOMICS, L' (FR/0397-8389). [5,000] **2789**

ECONOMY WIDE CENSUS : AGRICULTURAL SERVICES, FORESTRY AND FISHING (NZ). [250] **1605**

ECOSSISTEMA / FACULDADE DE AGRONOMIA E ZOOTECNIA "MANOEL CARLOS GONCALVES." (BL/0100-4107). [1,000] **81**

ECRITS SUR LE CINEMA (SUPPLEMENT) (CN/0822-6350). [1,000] **4068**

EDAD DE ORO (MADRID, SPAIN) (SP). **3383**

EDC TODAY (CN/0839-9549). [23,000] **832**

EDI (DALLAS, TEX.) (US/1045-5698). **1258**

EDI MONTHLY REPORT (US/1062-645X). [1,000] **4645**

EDI RESEARCH AUSTRALIA (AT/1034-8360). **1183**

EDI UPDATE LONDON (UK/0954-6154). [1,000] **4721**

EDI WORLD (US/1055-0399). [42,000] **2042**

EDI YELLOW PAGES INTERNATIONAL (US). [33,000] **1183**

EDINBURGH BIBLIOGRAPHICAL SOCIETY TRANSACTIONS (UK/0140-7082). [170] **415**

EDITING HISTORY (US/0883-3532). [200] **4814**

EDITOR & PUBLISHER (US/0013-094X). [30,000] **4814**

EDITOR & PUBLISHER (US). [4,500] **924**

EDITOR, EL (US). [15,000] **5749**

EDITORS' NOTES (US/0888-3173). [600] **2919**

EDITORS ONLY (US/0735-8490). [500] **2919**

EDMONTON AUTISM SOCIETY UPDATE (CN). [850] **3831**

EDMONTON REPORT ON ECONOMIC DEVELOPMENT, THE (CN/0824-409X). **1559**

EDMS JOURNAL (US/1058-0379). [2500] **1183**

EDO JIDAI BUNGAKUSHI / RYUMONSHA HEN (JA). **3383**

EDON COMMERCIAL (US). [1,000] **5728**

EDP AUDITOR JOURNAL, THE (US/0885-0445). [12,000] **1258**

EDUCACION MEDICA Y SALUD (US/0013-1091). [5,800] **3573**

EDUCAMUS (SA/0250-152X). [60,000] **1738**

EDUCARE (PRETORIA) (SA/0256-8829). [8,500] **1738**

EDUCATING ABLE LEARNERS, DISCOVERING & NURTURING TALENT (US/0896-9574). [1,000] **1878**

EDUCATING AT-RISK YOUTH (US/1040-0729). **5284**

EDUCATION

EDUCATION AND SOCIETY (MELBOURNE) (AT/0726-2655). **1738**

EDUCATION & TRAINING (BRADFORD) (UK/0040-0912). [3,000] **1912**

EDUCATION FOR LIBRARY AND INFORMATION SERVICES, AUSTRALIA (AT). [250] **3209**

EDUCATION FORUM (TORONTO. 1988) (CN/0840-9269). [49,000] **1893**

EDUCATION IN SCIENCE (UK/0013-1377). [23,000] **5102**

EDUCATION INDEX (US/0013-1385). **1794**

EDUCATION INDEX. CD-ROM (US/0013-1385). **1794**

EDUCATION LIBRARIES (US/0148-1061). [400] **3209**

EDUCATION LIBRARIES JOURNAL (UK/0957-9575). [500] **3209**

EDUCATION MILLE-ILES (CN/0712-9688). **1863**

EDUCATION MUSICALE, L' (FR/0013-1415). [7,000] **4116**

EDUCATION NEWSLETTER / EDUCATION FAITS NOUVEAUX (FR). [5,000] **1740**

EDUCATION, RESEARCH AND PERSPECTIVES (AT/0311-2543). [500] **1822**

EDUCATION SAN DIEGO COUNTY (US). [15,000] **1740**

EDUCATION STATISTICS BULLETIN (CN/0826-8258). [475] **1740**

EDUCATION TODAY (TORONTO) (CN/0843-5081). [3,800] **1740**

EDUCATION (TUBINGEN, GERMANY) (GW/0341-6178). [2,000] **1741**

EDUCATION UPDATE (CHICAGO, ILL.) (US/0731-941X). [2,000] **1323**

EDUCATIONAL DIRECTORY. STATE & DISTRICT OFFICES (HONOLULU) (US/0092-1777). [14,000] **1741**

EDUCATIONAL FACILITY PLANNER (US/1059-7417). [1,600] **1863**

EDUCATIONAL FORUM (WEST LAFAYETTE, IND.), THE (US/0013-1725). [46,000] **1741**

EDUCATIONAL FREEDOM (US/0013-1741). **2965**

EDUCATIONAL OASIS (US/0892-2853). [10,000] **1893**

EDUCATIONAL PERSPECTIVES (US/0013-1849). [1,000] **1742**

EDUCATIONAL PLANNING (US/0315-9388). [800] **1742**

EDUCATIONAL RESEARCH QUARTERLY (US/0196-5042). [2,000] **1742**

EDUCATIONAL SERIES - NORTH DAKOTA GEOLOGICAL SURVEY (US/0091-9004). [3,000] **1374**

EDUCATORS GRADE GUIDE TO FREE TEACHING AIDS (US/0070-9387). **1893**

EDUCATORS GUIDE TO FREE HOME ECONOMICS AND CONSUMER EDUCATION MATERIALS (US). **2789**

EDUCATOR'S INTERNATIONAL GUIDE TO FREE & LOW COST HEALTH AUDIO-VISUAL TEACHING AIDS (US). [250,000] **4774**

EDUCO (CN/0712-810X). **1863**

EDUCOM REVIEW (US/1045-9146). [9,000] **1822**

EESTI HAAL (UK). [650] **5812**

EFAC BULLETIN (UK/0951-1105). **4955**

EFFECTIFS HUMAINS - COMMISSION SCOLAIRE L'ISLET-SUD (CN/0226-9023). **1743**

EFFECTIVE SCHOOL PRACTICES (US/1068-7378). [3,000] **1894**

EFFECTIVE SPECIAL SERVICES MANAGEMENT (US/0890-4790). **866**

EFTERRETNINGER FOR SOFARENDE (DK). [1,300] **4176**

EGALITE (MONCTON) (CN/0226-6873). [300] **4472**

EGATIKA NEA (CN/0710-0272). **5784**

EGE COGRAFYA DERGISI / [EGE UNIVERSITESI, EDEBIYAT FAKULTESI, COGRAFYA BOLUMU] (TU). [1,000] **2560**

EGESZSEGNEVELES. EDUCATIO SANITARIA (HU). [4,300] **4774**

EGG PRODUCER, THE (CN/0821-4689). [3,500] **210**

EGLISE CANADIENNE, L' (CN/0013-2322). [6,500] **4955**

EGLISE ET THEOLOGIE (CN/0013-2349). [500] **4955**

EGO KIDS MAGAZINE (CN). [10,000] **1083**

EGYPT THEN AND NOW (US/0736-945X). [2,000] **2768**

EGYPTIAN HOTEL GUIDE (UA). [20,000] **2805**

EGYPTIAN JOURNAL OF PHYSICS (UA/0376-8724). [700] **4402**

EIA GUIDE (US). [16,000] **949**

EIGHTEENTH-CENTURY FICTION (DOWNSVIEW, ONT.) (CN/0840-6286). [500] **3383**

EIGHTEENTH CENTURY (LUBBOCK), THE (US/0193-5380). [750] **2686**

EIGHTEENTH-CENTURY STUDIES (US/0013-2586). [3,000] **319**

EINKAUFS-1X1 DER DEUTSCHEN INDUSTRIE (GW/0343-5881). [21,000] **832**

EISEI DOBUTSU (JA/0424-7086). [1,100] **5607**

EKKLESIA KAI THEOLOGIA : EKKLESIASTIKE KAI THEOLOGIKE EPETERIS TES HIERAS ARCHIEPISKOPES THYATEIRON KAI MEGALES VRETANNIAS (GR). [1,000] **5039**

EKONOMICKY CASOPIS (XO/0013-3035). [2,900] **1488**

EKONOMIKA PRACE (XO). [4,500] **1488**

EKSPOR (INDONESIA. BIRO PUSAT STATISTIK) (IO). **832**

EKSPORT AKTUELT / FRA NORGES EKSPORTRAD (NO/0800-6733). [3,000] **833**

ELAEIS (MY/0128-1828). [2,000] **5102**

ELASTOMERS (US). [100,000] **4455**

ELBERT ROGERS' WASHINGTON STATE SCORE (US/0736-881X). [63,000] **2532**

ELECTION FINANCING FACT BOOK (US). [1,000] **4645**

ELECTRE BIBLIO FRENCH BOOKS IN PRINT. CD-ROM (FR). **415**

ELECTRIC CONSUMER (US/0745-4651). [260,000] **1937**

ELECTRIC LINES (US/0895-2116). [5,000] **2043**

ELECTRICAL ADVERTISER (US). [60,000] **2044**

ELECTRICAL APPARATUS (US/0190-1370). [16,000] **2044**

ELECTRICAL BLUE BOOK, THE (CN/0149-6174). [24,000] **2044**

ELECTRICAL COMMUNICATION (US/0013-4252). [30,000] **1154**

ELECTRICAL COMPONENT LOCATOR. DOMESTIC CARS, LIGHT TRUCKS & VANS, IMPORTED CARS & TRUCKS (US/0743-6076). **5414**

ELECTRICAL DESIGN & MFG (US/1065-7436). **2044**

ELECTRICAL ENGINEERING COMMUNICATIONS AND SIGNAL PROCESSING (US/0888-2134). **2045**

ELECTRICAL EQUIPMENT LONDON (UK/0013-4317). [30,383] **2045**

ELECTRICAL INDIA (II/0013-435X). [6,000] **2045**

ELECTRICAL MANUFACTURING (LIBERTYVILLE, ILL.) (US/0895-3716). **3478**

ELECTRICIDADE (PO/0870-5364). [4000] **2045**

ELECTRICITY DAILY REPORT, THE (US/1070-8928). [200] **1488**

ELECTRICITY JOURNAL, THE (US/1040-6190). [1,700] **4761**

ELECTRICITY TODAY (PICKERING) (CN/0843-7343). [14,000] **2046**

ELECTROMAGNETIC NEWS REPORT (US/0270-4935). [1,200] **2046**

ELECTRON DISPLAY WORLD (US/0742-1532). **2046**

ELECTRONIC ATLAS NEWSLETTER, THE (US/1053-0924). [50-100] **1183**

ELECTRONIC BUSINESS ASIA (HK). [41,000] **2046**

ELECTRONIC BUYERS' NEWS (US/0164-6362). [61,000] **2046**

ELECTRONIC DESIGN'S GOLD BOOK (US/0738-0399). [120,000] **2047**

ELECTRONIC ENGINEERING (UK/0013-4902). **2047**

ELECTRONIC FUEL INJECTION, DIAGNOSIS & TESTING (US/0741-6334). **5414**

ELECTRONIC HOUSE / INTELLIGENCE REPORT (US). **1212**

ELECTRONIC MARKET TRENDS (US/0886-8506). **2047**

ELECTRONIC MEDIA (US/0745-0311). [28,000] **1131**

ELECTRONIC PRODUCT DESIGN (UK/0263-1474). **2048**

ELECTRONIC PRODUCTS (1981) (US/0013-4953). [126,000] **2048**

ELECTRONIC PRODUCTS AND TECHNOLOGY (CN/0708-4366). [22,000] **2048**

ELECTRONIC SOURCE BOOK FOR SOUTHERN CALIFORNIA, THE (US/8755-1527). [12,000] **2048**

ELECTRONIC TRADER (UK). [5000] **2048**

ELECTRONICS (1985) (US/0883-4989). [97,116] **2048**

ELECTRONICS INFORMATION & PLANNING (II/0304-9876). **2049**

ELECTRONICS INTERNATIONAL (US/0149-5542). **2049**

ELECTRONICS KOREA (KO). [5,000] **2049**

ELECTRONICS MANUFACTURE & TEST (UK/0265-301X). [12,000] **2049**

ELECTRONICS SOURCE BOOK FOR SOUTH ATLANTIC, THE (US). [12,000] **2050**

ELECTRONICS SOURCE BOOK. SOUTHWEST, THE (US). [12,000] **2050**

ELECTRONICS TIMES (UK). [42,000] **2050**

ELECTROSOURCE : PRODUCT REFERENCE GUIDE AND TELEPHONE DIRECTORY (CN/0826-192X). [22,000] **2050**

ELEKTRISCHE ENERGIE-TECHNIK (GW/0170-2033). [12,500] **1937**

ELEKTROMEISTER + DEUTSCHES ELEKTROHANDWERK (GW/0012-1258). **2051**

ELEKTRONIK VARLDEN (SW/0033-7749). [21,000] **2052**

ELEKTRONIKAI ES HRADASTECHNIKAI SZAKIRODALMI TAJEKOZTATO (HU/0231-066X). [135] **2052**

ELEKTROTECHNICKY CASOPIS (XO/0013-578X). **2052**

ELEKTROTEHNIKA (ZAGREB) (CI/0013-5844). [1,000] **2052**

ELENCHUS OF BIBLICA (IT). [1,000] **4955**

ELEPAIO (US/0013-6069). [2,400] **2192**

ELEPHANT (DETROIT, MICH.) (US/0737-108X). [500] **5582**

ELETTRONICA E TELECOMUNICAZIONI (IT/0013-6123). [12,000] **2052**

ELEVAGE INSEMINATION (FR/0422-9703). **210**

ELEVATORI MODERNI : SOLLEVAMENTO E TRASPORTO A FUNE (IT/1121-7995). [2,500] **5381**

ELGAR SOCIETY JOURNAL, THE (UK). [1,300] **5230**

ELK POINT LAKELAND REVIEW (CN/0828-7759). [2,500] **5784**

ELKHORN INDEPENDENT (ELKHORN, WIS. : 1892) (US). [33,500] **5767**

ELKS MAGAZINE, THE (US/0013-6263). [1,500,000] **5231**

ELKTON RECORD, THE (US/0899-966X). [900] **5743**

ELLENOKANADIKA CHRONIKA (CN/0820-7801). [6,000] **5784**

ELLIOTT WAVE COMMODITY LETTER, THE (US/0742-891X). [6,000] **897**

ELLIOTT WAVE THEORIST, THE (US/0742-5252). [15,000] **897**

ELLIPSE (CN/0046-1830). [750] **3384**

ELLSWORTH REPORTER (US). [2,900] **5675**

ELMIRA INDEPENDENT (CN/1194-1030). [6,800] **5784**

ELMWOOD ARGUS, THE (US). **5767**

ELT JOURNAL (UK/0951-0893). [5,000] **3278**

ELVIS COSTELLO INFORMATION SERVICE (NE). [700] **4116**

EMAJL-KERAMIKA-STAKLO (CI/0350-3607). [1,000] **2588**

EMBEDDED SYSTEMS PROGRAMMING (US/1040-3272). [26,000] **1228**

EMBOUTEILLEUR QUEBECOIS, L' (CN/0705-6761). **2366**

EMC. EDUCATIONAL MEDIA SPECIAL INTEREST COUNCIL (CN/0824-782X). [500] **3209**

EMC TECHNOLOGY (US/1055-6230). [28,000] **2053**

EMC TECHNOLOGY ... ANTHOLOGY (US/0748-108X). [35,000] **2053**

EMENTARIO DO TIT (BL). [12,000] **2965**

EMERGENCIAS (SP). [3,000] **3724**

EMERGENCY LIBRARIAN (US/0315-8888). [10,000] **3209**

EMERGENCY MEDICAL UPDATE (US/1064-5934). **3724**

EMERGENCY MEDICINE (US/0013-6654). [140,000] **3724**

EMERGENCY MEDICINE (GLENDALE, CALIF.) (US/0748-8947). **3574**

EMERGENCY PREPAREDNESS DIGEST (CN/0837-5771). [15,000] **1073**

EMIE BULLETIN (US/0737-9021). [800] **3209**

EMIGRE (BERKELEY, CALIF.) (US/1045-3717). [7000] **378**

EMMA (GW). [45,000] **5555**

EMMANATIONS (US/0734-6158). **1744**

EMPIRE STATE MASON (US/0013-6794). [150,000] **5231**

EMPIRE STATE REPORT (1982) (US/0747-0711). [10,500] **4645**

EMPIRE STATE SURVEYOR (US). [1,970] **2023**

EMPIRISCHE PADAGOGIK (GW/0931-5020). [170] **1744**

EMPLOI AU QUEBEC (CN/0837-2470). [600] **1664**

EMPLOYEE BENEFIT NEWS (US/1044-6265). **1665**

EMPLOYEE BENEFIT PLAN REVIEW (US/0013-6808). [15,200] **2879**

EMPLOYEE BENEFITS (US/0194-3499). [75,000] **1665**

EMPLOYEE COUNSELLING TODAY (UK/0933-8217). [400] **4586**

EMPLOYEE SERVICES MANAGEMENT (US/0744-3676). [5,500] **940**

EMPORIA STATE RESEARCH STUDIES, THE (US/0424-9399). **1744**

EMTP NEWS (BE). **2053**

EMULSION POLYMERISATION AND POLYMER EMULSIONS (UK/0955-2804). [65] **4223**

ENCEPHALARTOS (SA/1012-9987). [1,000] **2413**

ENCHANTMENT (US/0046-1946). [90,000] **2533**

ENCOUNTER (INDIANAPOLIS) (US/0013-7081). [600] **4956**

ENCOUNTERS (ST. PAUL, MINN.) (US/0273-5717). [24,000] **5102**

ENCUENTRO (NQ). [6,000] **2732**

ENCUESTA NACIONAL DEL EMPLEO, GRAN SANTIAGO (SP). [350] **1667**

ENCYCLIA (US/0196-9110). [1,000] **5102**

ENDOCRINE SOCIETY - ANNUAL MEETING, PROGRAM AND ABSTRACTS, THE (US). [8,500] **3729**

ENDODONTIC REPORT, THE (US/0899-8973). [8,000] **1323**

ENDODONTICS & DENTAL TRAUMATOLOGY (DK/0109-2502). [800] **1323**

ENDOMETRIOSIS ASSOCIATION NEWSLETTER (US/0897-1870). [9,200] **3760**

ENDOSCOPY REVIEW (US/8756-968X). [13,000] **3744**

ENERGIA ELETTRICA (IT/0013-7308). [30,000] **2053**

ENERGIE ALTERNATIVE HTE (IT/0391-5360). [5,100] **5103**

ENERGIE DIALOG (GW). [6,750] **1938**

ENERGIE PLUS (FR/0292-1731). [4,000] **1938**

ENERGY ALERT (TORONTO) (CN/0835-5266). [400] **1938**

ENERGY AND CHARACTER (UK/0013-7472). [1,000] **4586**

ENERGY & EDUCATION (US/0891-0979). [3,000] **1939**

ENERGY CONSERVATION NEWS (US/0161-6595). **1939**

ENERGY DEVELOPMENT AND DEMONSTRATION PROGRAM : YEAR END REPORT (US). [400] **1940**

ENERGY DIGEST (UK/0367-1119). [1,000] **1940**

ENERGY ECONOMICS (UK/0140-9883). [3,600] **1940**

ENERGY LAW JOURNAL (US/0270-9163). [2,100] **2966**

ENERGY MANAGEMENT TECHNOLOGY (US/0745-984X). **5103**

ENERGY PROCESSING CANADA (CN/0319-5759). [6,000] **1941**

ENERGY (STAMFORD, CONN. 1975) (US/0149-9386). **1942**

ENERGY STATISTICS (CHICAGO, ILL.) (US/0739-3075). [800] **1962**

ENERGY STUDIES REVIEW (CN/0843-4379). [500] **1942**

ENERGY TRENDS (UK/0308-1222). [2,500] **1942**

ENERGY UNLIMITED (US/0279-621X). [1,000] **1942**

ENERGY USER NEWS (US/0162-9131). [150,000] **1942**

ENERGY WORLD (UK/0307-7942). [7,000] **1943**

ENFANCE MAJUSCULE PARIS (FR/1164-8589). **3164**

ENFANT D'ABORD, L' (FR/0399-4988). **3903**

ENFANT EN MILIEU TROPICAL, L' (FR/0013-7561). [15,000] **3903**

ENFIELD PRESS (1984), THE (US/8750-3123). [3,400] **5645**

ENFOQUES EN ATENCION PRIMARIA (CL/0716-2774). [200] **3574**

ENGEKIGAKU / HENSHU WASEDA DAIGKU ENGEKI GAKKAI (JA). [1,400] **5364**

ENGINEER OF CALIFORNIA (US/0277-1233). [3,500] **1972**

ENGINEERED SYSTEMS (US/0891-9976). [57,515] **2113**

ENGINEERING & SCIENCE (US/0013-7812). [15,300] **1972**

ENGINEERING AUTOMATION REPORT (US). [1,000] **1219**

ENGINEERING DESIGNER (UK/0013-7898). [7,000] **2098**

ENGINEERING DIGEST (TORONTO) (CN/0013-7901). [67,000] **1972**

ENGINEERING FORUM (TORONTO) (CN/0701-080X). **1973**

ENGINEERING HORIZONS (VAN NUYS, CALIF.) (US/1040-1679). **1973**

ENGINEERING MANPOWER BULLETIN (US/0013-8037). [400] **1973**

ENGINEERING PLASTICS (UK/0952-6900). [200] **4455**

ENGINEERING RESEARCH HIGHLIGHTS (US/0149-0605). **1974**

ENGINEERING ; THE NEWSLETTER OF ENGINEERING AT CLEMSON UNIVERSITY (US). [16,800] **1974**

ENGINEERING TIMES (WASHINGTON, D.C.) (US/0195-6876). [80,000] **1974**

ENGINEERING WORLD (LONDON, ENGLAND) (UK). **1974**

ENGINEERS AND ENGINES MAGAZINE (US/0013-8142). [9,500] **158**

ENGINEERS AUSTRALIA (AT/1032-1195). [44,500] **1974**

ENGLISCH AMERIKANISCHE STUDIEN (GW/0172-1992). [3,000] **3384**

ENGLISH ALIVE (SA). **2487**

ENGLISH DANCE AND SONG (UK/0013-8231). [8,000] **384**

ENGLISH EDUCATION (US/0007-8204). [3,000] **1894**

ENGLISH IN AUSTRALIA (AT/0155-2147). [5,500] **3279**

ENGLISH JOURNAL (US/0013-8274). [47,000] **1894**

ENGLISH RECORD, THE (US/0013-8363). [800] **1744**

ENLB, EMERGENCY NURSE LEGAL BULLETIN (US/0098-1516). **3855**

ENLIGHTENMENT AND DISSENT (UK/0262-7612). [300] **4473**

ENNEMI, L' (FR). [1,200] **319**

ENNIS DAILY NEWS, THE (US/8755-9056). [4,850] **5749**

ENQUETE-SALAIRES (1981) (CN/0711-5318). **1667**

ENQUETE SOCIO-ECONOMIQUE (BE). [700] **4562**

ENR DIRECTORY OF DESIGN FIRMS (US/0098-6305). [13,000] **1975**

ENRICH! (US). **671**

ENROUTE (CN/0703-0312). [130,000] **2533**

ENSAYOS ECIEL (BL/0102-0617). [1,000] **1488**

ENSAYOS ECONOMICOS (AG/0325-3937). [200] **1591**

ENSAYOS SOBRE POLITICA ECONOMICA : DOCUMENTOS DE TRABAJO (CK). [2,500] **1560**

ENSEIGNEMENT ET LA PEDAGOGIE EN ROUMANIE, L' (RM). [2,000] **1744**

ENSEIGNEMENT PHILOSOPHIQUE, L' (FR/0986-1653). [1,500] **4365**

ENSEMBLE (US). [12,500] **384**

ENTENDRE (CN/0318-9139). [1,000] **4387**

ENTERPRISE FARMING (UK). [160,000] **82**

ENTERPRISE SYSTEMS JOURNAL (US/1053-6566). [90,000] **1184**

ENTERTAINMENT LITIGATION REPORTER (US/1047-4137). [50] **2966**

ENTERTAINMENT MAGAZINE, THE (US/0883-1890). [20,000] **4850**

ENTOMOLOGICA FENNICA (FI/0785-8760). [700] **5607**

ENTOMOLOGICAL RESEARCH BULLETIN (KO). [1000] **5607**

ENTOMOLOGISCHE ABHANDLUNGEN (GW/0373-8981). [550] **5607**

ENTOMOLOGIST'S GAZETTE (UK/0013-8894). [460] **5608**

ENTOMOLOGIST'S MONTHLY MAGAZINE, THE (UK/0013-8908). [500] **5608**

ENTOMOPHAGA (FR/0013-8959). [1,250] **4244**

ENTOPATH NEWS, THE (UK). [1,000] **2378**

ENTRE GENS D'ICI (CN/0713-049X). **1744**

ENTRE-GENS, L' (CN/0704-6146). **1542**

ENTRE NOUS GENS DE BERNIERES (CN/0712-967X). **4646**

ENTRE-NOUS - SOCIETE DES ELEVEURS DE BOVINS CANADIENS (CN/0709-8510). [220] **210**

ENTRE PARENTHESES (CN/0714-8674). **1744**

ENTREFILET (POINTE CLAIRE) (CN/0826-4546). [9,000] **2334**

ENTREMETTEUR (CN/0225-3569). [2,500] **5784**

ENTREMISE, L' (CN/0709-4256). **1744**

ENTREPRENEUR POTCHEFSTROOM (SA/0259-5559). [3,000] **672**

ENTROPIE (FR/0013-9084). [2,000] **1975**

ENTSCHEIDUNGEN DER OBERVERWALTUNGSGERICHTE FUER DAS LAND NORDRHEIN-WESTFALEN IN MUENSTER SOWIE FUER DIE LANDER NIEDERSACHSEN UND SCHLESWIG-HOLSTEIN IN LUENEBURG (GW/0340-8779). [1,000] **2966**

ENVIO (NQ/0259-4374). [4,000] **2732**

ENVIROLINE (CALGARY) (CN/0847-4524). **2165**

ENVIROLINE USER'S MANUAL (US/0270-0751). **2228**

ENVIRONMENT BUSINESS MAGAZINE (UK/1352-8882). [7,482] **2228**

ENVIRONMENT PROTECTION ENGINEERING (PL/0324-8828). [300] **2166**

ENVIRONMENT TODAY (US/1054-7517). [54,000] **2166**

ENVIRONMENT VICTORIA (AT/0727-5366). **2192**

ENVIRONMENTAL & LAND USE AADMINISTRATIVE LAW REPORTER ER FALR (US/1044-7695). **3111**

ENVIRONMENTAL AND URBAN ISSUES (US/1044-033X). [3,000] **2821**

ENVIRONMENTAL APPROVALS IN CANADA : PRACTICE AND PROCEDURE (CN). [466] **3111**

ENVIRONMENTAL COMPLIANCE. A NATIONAL SIMPLIFIED GUIDE (CN). **2228**

ENVIRONMENTAL COMPLIANCE CALIFORNIA. INCLUDES UPDATES (CN). **2228**

ENVIRONMENTAL CONTROL NEWS FOR SOUTHERN INDUSTRY (US/0013-9238). [300] **2167**

ENVIRONMENTAL GEOLOGY SERIES (NASHVILLE) (US/0362-8175). **1375**

ENVIRONMENTAL HEALTH (LONDON) (UK/0013-9270). [7,500] **2822**

ENVIRONMENTAL HEALTH REVIEW (CN/0319-6771). [1,500] **4774**

ENVIRONMENTAL HEALTH REVIEW, AUSTRALIA : THE OFFICIAL JOURNAL OF THE AUSTRALIAN INSTITUTE OF ENVIRONMENTAL HEALTH (AT/0818-5670). [2,800] **2167**

ENVIRONMENTAL ISSUES REPORT (US/1061-3935). **2168**

ENVIRONMENTAL LAB (US/1042-5209). [20,000] **5103**

ENVIRONMENTAL LAW NEWSLETTER (US/0163-545X). **3111**

ENVIRONMENTAL LAW SECTION JOURNAL (US/8756-9280). [1,850] **3111**

ENVIRONMENTAL LAW (WASHINGTON D.C.) (US/0748-8769). [5,000] **3112**

ENVIRONMENTAL LIABILITY REPORT, THE (US/1043-2698). **2168**

ENVIRONMENTAL MEDICINE : ANNUAL REPORT OF THE RESEARCH INSTITUTE OF ENVIRONMENTAL MEDICINE, NAGOYA UNIVERSITY (JA/0287-0517). [400] **3574**

ENVIRONMENTAL NOTICE BULLETIN (US/0740-5847). **2229**

ENVIRONMENTAL POLICY REVIEW (IS/0792-0032). **2168**

ENVIRONMENTAL PROFESSIONAL, THE (US/0191-5398). [2,300] **2169**

ENVIRONMENTAL PROGRESS (US/0278-4491). [3,300] **2229**

ENVIRONMENTAL SCIENCE & ENGINEERING (AURORA) (CN/0835-605X). [20,000] **1975**

ENVIRONMENTAL SCIENCE & TECHNOLOGY (US/0013-936X). [12,000] **2169**

ENVIRONMENTAL

ENVIRONMENTAL SOFTWARE REPORT (US/1043-2884). **2170**

ENVIRONMENTAL SPECTRUM (US/0013-9386). [7,000] **2170**

ENVIRONMENTAL TESTING & ANALYSIS (US/1068-7432). [20,013] **2170**

ENVIRONNEMENT (BE). **2171**

ENVOI (UK/0013-9394). [700] **3462**

ENVOI (MONTREAL) (CN/0823-1834). **4894**

ENYO : SUISAN KENKYUJO NYUSU (JA). [900] **2300**

EOS (WASHINGTON, D.C.) (US/0096-3941). [18,000] **1404**

EP NEWS SERVICE (US/8750-7064). [350] **4956**

EPA WATCH (US/1065-920X). [1,200] **2171**

EPHEMERIDES MARIOLOGICAE (SP/0425-1466). [800] **4956**

EPHEMERIDES THEOLOGICAE LOVANIENSES (BE/0013-9513). **4956**

EPI NEWSLETTER (US/0251-4710). [6,000] **3713**

EPICIER (MONTREAL) (CN/0013-9521). [12,000] **2334**

EPIDEMIOLOGIC REVIEWS (US/0193-936X). [4,800] **3734**

EPIDEMIOLOGY MONITOR, THE (US/0744-0898). [2,000] **4775**

EPIEGRAM (1988) (US/1046-1493). [700] **1241**

EPIGRAPHISCHE STUDIEN (GW/0071-0989). **1076**

EPISCOPAL LIFE (US/1050-0057). [180,000] **5059**

EPISCOPAL NEWS, THE (US/0195-0681). [35,000] **4956**

EPISTOLODIDAKTIKA (UK). **1744**

EPLB. EMERGENCY PHYSICIAN LEGAL BULLETIN (US/0098-1524). **3724**

EPOPTEIA (GR). [2,500] **4345**

EPRI JOURNAL (US/0362-3416). [25,000] **2053**

EQUAL MEANS (US/1059-164X). [3500] **5555**

EQUAL OPPORTUNITIES REVIEW (UK). [1,500] **4507**

EQUESTRIAN TRAILS (US/0013-9831). [6,000] **2798**

EQUINE VETERINARY DATA (US/0739-9065). [1,500] **2798**

EQUINEWS (CN/0828-864X). [15,000] **2799**

EQUIPMENT JOURNAL (CN/0710-2720). [18,000] **2114**

EQUIPMENT MANAGEMENT (US/0733-3056). [56,000] **1975**

EQUITY NEWS (US/0092-4520). [33,000] **385**

ERA, ELEKTRICITETENS RATIONELLA ANVANDNING (SW). [13,000] **2054**

ERBA D'ARNO (IT). **319**

ERBE UND AUFTRAG (BEURON) (GW/0013-9963). [2,000] **5029**

ERDOL, ERDGAS, KOHLE (GW/0179-3187). [4,000] **4255**

ERDOL-INFORMATIONSDIENST (GW/0343-6705). **672**

EREKUTORONIKUSU (JA/0421-3513). [25,000] **2054**

ERFRISCHUNGSGETRANK, DAS (GW/0342-2232). [3,300] **2367**

ERGANZUNGSHEFT ZU PETERMANNS GEOGRAPHSCHISCHEN MITTEILUNGEN (GW). **2560**

ERGO-MED (GW/0170-2327). [2,000] **3575**

ERIA, EL (SP). [4,500] **3385**

ERICSSON REVIEW (ENGLISH EDITION) (SW/0014-0171). [16,000] **1154**

ERIE DAILY TIMES, THE (US). [75,000 combined 105,000 Sunday] **5736**

ERIGENIA (US/8755-2000). [250] **509**

ERLANGER GEOLOGISCHE ABHANDLUNGEN (GW/0071-1160). [300] **1375**

ERSKINE ECHO, THE (US). [1,100] **5695**

ERZIEHUNG UND WISSENSCHAFT (GW/0342-0671). [187,000] **1745**

ESA BULLETIN (FR/0376-4265). **18**

ESA JOURNAL (FR/0379-2285). **18**

ESA NEWSLETTER - ENTOMOLOGICAL SOCIETY OF AMERICA (US/0273-7353). [9,500] **5608**

ESCRIBANO, EL (US/0014-0376). [750] **2732**

ESCRITOS DEL VEDAT (SP/0210-3133). **4956**

ESKIMO; COUNTRY, INHABITANTS, CATHOLIC MISSIONS (CN/0318-7551). **5029**

ESPACE (MONTREAL) (CN/0821-9222). [1,500] **349**

ESPANOL EN AUSTRALIA (AT). [20,000] **3279**

ESPERIENZE LETTERARIE (IT/0392-3495). **3385**

ESPIONAGE MAGAZINE (US/8756-8535). [60,000] **5074**

ESPIRITU (SP/0014-0716). [500] **4346**

ESQ (US/0093-8297). [721] **3385**

ESQUIVE (MONTREAL, QUEBEC) (CN/0823-793X). **4894**

ESSAY AND GENERAL LITERATURE INDEX (US/0014-083X). **3458**

ESSAY AND GENERAL LITERATURE INDEX. CD-ROM (US/0014-083X). **3458**

ESSAYS AND MONOGRAPHS IN COLORADO HISTORY (US/0899-0409). **2732**

ESSAYS AND STUDIES BY THE FACULTY OF HIROSHIMA JOGAKUIN COLLEGE (JA/0374-8057). [600] **1823**

ESSAYS AND STUDIES (LONDON) (UK). [300] **3385**

ESSAYS IN ARTS AND SCIENCES (US/0361-5634). [300] **2846**

ESSAYS IN CRITICISM (UK/0014-0856). [2,500] **3385**

ESSAYS IN GRAHAM GREENE (US/0738-0763). [500] **3385**

ESSEX ARCHAEOLOGY AND HISTORY : THE TRANSACTIONS OF THE ESSEX ARCHAEOLOGICAL SOCIETY (UK/0308-3462). [550] **2686**

ESSEX FAMILY HISTORIAN, THE (UK/0140-7503). [1,700] **2446**

ESSEX GENEALOGIST, THE (US/0279-067X). [750] **2446**

EST EUROPEEN, L' (FR/0014-1097). [900] **2686**

EST-OVEST (IT/0046-256X). [300] **4473**

ESTADISTICA ESPANOLA (SP/0014-1151). [1,000] **5327**

ESTADISTICA PANAMENA; BOLETIN SEMANAL (PN). [850] **5327**

ESTADISTICAS SOCIOECONOMICAS, PUERTO RICO / JUNTA DE PLANIFICACION, AREA DE ANALISIS Y ASESORAMIENTO ECONOMICO, NEGOCIADO DE ANALISIS Y PROYECCIONES ECONOMICAS (PR). **1532**

ESTATISTICAS DE MORTALIDADE, BRASIL / MINISTERIO DA SAUDE, SECRETARIA NACIONAL DE ACOES BASICAS DE SAUDE, DIVISAO NACIONAL DE EPIDEMIOLOGIA (BL). [2,000] **4552**

ESTES TRAILS (US/0737-481X). [250] **2446**

ESTEVAN MERCURY (CN). [4,900] **5784**

ESTUARIES (US/0160-8347). [1,200] **554**

ESTUDIOS DE ECONOMIA (CL). [350] **1591**

ESTUDIOS DEL DESARROLLO (INT/1013-4069). [1,000] **5199**

ESTUDIOS - INSTITUTO DE ESTUDIO ECONOMICOS SOBRE LA REALIDAD ARGENTINA Y LATINOAMERICANA (AG/0325-6928). [2,500] **1489**

ESTUDIOS MADRID (SP/0210-0525). [500] **3385**

ESTUDIOS SOCIALES (SANTIAGO, CHILE) (CL/0716-0321). [1,000] **5199**

ESTUDIOS TRINITARIOS (SP/0210-0363). **4956**

ESTUDOS DE ANTROPOLOGIA CULTURAL (PO/0425-3906). [1,000] **235**

ESTUDOS DE ANTROPOLOGIA CULTURAL E SOCIAL (PO/0870-4457). [1,000] **235**

ESTUDOS DE HISTORIA E CARTOGRAFIA ANTIGA. MEMORIAS (PO/0870-5879). [2,000] **2615**

ESTUDOS E DOCUMENTOS (UNIVERSIDAD DE SAO PAULO. FACULDADE DE EDUCACAO) (BL). [1,000] **1745**

ESTUDOS, ENSAIOS E DOCUMENTOS (PORTUGAL. JUNTA DE INVESTIGACOES CIENTIFICAS DO ULTRAMAR) (PO/0870-001X). [1,000] **5103**

ETC (MONTREAL) (CN/0835-7641). [2,500] **350**

ETHICS & INTERNATIONAL AFFAIRS (US/0892-6794). [500] **4520**

ETHICS, EASIER SAID THAN DONE (US/0897-0106). [13,000] **2250**

ETHICS IN-SERVICE (CN/0824-5622). [1,900] **2250**

ETHIOPIAN JEWRY REPORT (CN/0827-8687). **5047**

ETHIOPIAN MEDICAL JOURNAL (ET/0014-1755). [800] **3575**

ETHIOPIAN TRADE JOURNAL (ET/0014-1763). [3,000] **833**

ETHNIC DIRECTORY OF WINDSOR & ESSEX COUNTY (CN/0703-8348). **2260**

ETHNIC REPORTER (CLAREMONT, CALIF.), THE (US/0893-7362). [350] **2260**

ETHNIC WOMAN, THE (US/0897-4683). [5,000] **2260**

ETHNOARTS INDEX (US/0893-0120). [100] **334**

ETHNOLOGIA FENNICA (FI/0355-1776). [300] **235**

ETHNOMUSICOLOGY (US/0014-1836). [2,000] **4117**

ETHNOS (SW/0014-1844). [800] **236**

ETHOS (US/0091-2131). [1,200] **4586**

ETNOS (LUBLIN, POLAND) (PL). **4956**

ETUDES ANGLAISES (FR/0014-195X). [2,000] **3342**

ETUDES BALKANIQUES (BU/0324-1645). [700] **2687**

ETUDES D'ARCHEOLOGIE CLASSIQUE (FR/0425-4813). [800] **267**

ETUDES DE LINGUISTIQUE APPLIQUEE (FR/0071-190X). [1,500] **3280**

ETUDES GERMANIQUES (FR/0014-2115). [2,000] **3280**

ETUDES INTERNATIONALES (QUEBEC) (CN/0014-2123). [1,500] **4521**

ETUDES INTERNATIONALES (QUEBEC) (CN/0014-2123). **4473**

ETUDES INUIT (CN/0701-1008). [600] **236**

ETUDES LITTERAIRES (UNIVERSITE LAVAL) (CN/0014-214X). [800] **3386**

ETUDES QUATERNAIRES LANGUEDOCIENNES (FR). [300] **4227**

ETUDES STATISTIQUES (BRUSSELS, BELGIUM) (BE/0522-7585). [1,000] **5327**

ETUDES THEOLOGIQUES ET RELIGIEUSES (FR/0014-2239). [2,500] **4956**

EUDISED R & D BULLETIN (FR). [500] **1745**

EUFAULA TRIBUNE, THE (US). [6,200] **5626**

EUGENE O'NEILL REVIEW, THE (US/1040-9483). [450] **3386**

EUNTES DOCETE (IT). [1,000] **4956**

EUPHORIA ET CACOPHORIA (JA). [2,000] **3720**

EURASIAN STUDIES YEARBOOK (US). **3280**

EUREKA (BECKENHAM) (UK/0261-2097). [26,780] **2098**

EUREKA SENTINEL (EUREKA, NEV. : 1902) (US). [550] **5707**

EUREKA : THE ARCHIMEDEANS' JOURNAL (UK/0071-2248). [1,000] **3505**

EURO P.V (FR/0245-8438). [10,000] **833**

EUROFACH ELECTRONICA (SP/0211-2973). [7,500] **2054**

EUROFRUIT (UK). [7,000] **2414**

EUROPA-ARCHIV (GW/0014-2476). [4,500] **4521**

EUROPA CHEMIE (GW/0014-2484). [5,000] **2012**

EUROPA ETHNICA (AU/0014-2492). [1,200] **2261**

EUROPAEISCHE GRUNDRECHTE - ZEITSCHRIFT (GW/0341-9800). [1,300] **4507**

EUROPAEISCHE RUNDSCHAU (AU/0304-2782). [2,500] **4521**

EUROPAISCHE INTEGRATION AUSWAHLBIBLIOGRAPHIE (GW). [30,000] **4473**

EUROPE (FR/0014-2751). [5,000] **3342**

EUROPE PLURILINGUE (FR/1161-8884). [1,000] **2487**

EUROPEAN BUREAU OF ADULT EDUCATION NEWSLETTER (NE). [600] **1745**

EUROPEAN BUSINESS INTELLIGENCE BRIEFING (UK/0957-0039). [500] **673**

EUROPEAN COMMERCIAL CASES (UK/0141-7266). [200] **3100**

EUROPEAN COMPETITION LAW REVIEW : ECLR (UK/0144-3054). [500] **3100**

EUROPEAN CONSORTIUM FOR POLITICAL RESEARCH NEWS (UK). **4473**

EUROPEAN DESIGN DIRECTORY (UK). **2114**

EUROPEAN EARTHQUAKE ENGINEERING (IT/0394-5103). [1,000] **2023**

EUROPEAN ENVIRONMENTAL YEARBOOK (UK). [3,000] **2171**

EUROPEAN FILE (BE/0379-3133). [190,000] **2516**

EUROPEAN HUMAN RIGHTS REPORTS (UK/0260-4868). [400] **4508**

EUROPEAN JOURNAL OF CELL BIOLOGY (GW/0171-9335). [900] **536**

EUROPEAN JOURNAL OF GYNAECOLOGICAL ONCOLOGY (IT/0392-2936). [500] **3817**

EUROPEAN JOURNAL OF HAEMATOLOGY (DK/0902-4441). [1,400] **3771**

EUROPEAN JOURNAL OF MECHANICAL ENGINEERING (BE/0777-2734). [2,500] **2114**

EUROPEAN JOURNAL OF MEDICINAL CHEMISTRY (FR/0223-5234). [1,500] **3575**

EUROPEAN JOURNAL OF MINERALOGY (STUTTGART) (GW/0935-1221). **1439**

EUROPEAN JOURNAL OF ORIENTAL MEDICINE (UK). [5,000] **3575**

EUROPEAN JOURNAL OF PSYCHIATRY, THE (SP/0213-6163). [5,000] **3925**

EUROPEAN MICROSCOPY AND ANALYSIS (UK/0958-1952). [7,000 UK18,000 Europe21,000 US] **572**

EUROPEAN MICROSCOPY & ANALYSIS (UK). [39,000] **572**

EUROPEAN RESPIRATORY REVIEW : AN OFFICIAL JOURNAL OF THE EUROPEAN RESPIRATORY SOCIETY (DK/0905-9180). [2,500] **3949**

EUROPEAN RUBBER DIRECTORY (UK/0306-414X). [8,000] **5075**

EUROPEAN RUBBER JOURNAL (LONDON, ENGLAND : 1982) (UK/0266-4151). [6,739] **5075**

EUROPEAN SEMICONDUCTOR (UK/0957-5685). [8,240] **2054**

EUROPEAN STUDIES NEWSLETTER (US/0046-2802). [1,300] **2687**

EUROPEAN TAXATION (NE/0014-3138). [2,000] **4722**

EUROPEAN TAXATION. SUPPLEMENTARY SERVICE (NE/0531-4577). **4722**

EUROPEAN TELECOMMUNICATIONS (US/8756-4459). [300] **1155**

EUROPEAN UROLOGY UPDATE SERIES (UK/0968-7645). **3990**

EUROPROPERTY LONDON (UK/0961-9712). [6,000] **897**

EUROSLOT OLDHAM (UK/0966-0259). [13,500] **4860**

EUSKAL HERRIKO AGINTARITZAREN ALDIZKARIA / BOLETIN OFICIAL DEL PAIS VASCO (SP). [4,300] **2968**

EUSKAL HERRIKO POETAK (SP). **3386**

EV CIRCUIT - ELECTRIC VEHICLE CLUB OF OTTAWA (CN/0837-3752). **2054**

EVALUATION ENGINEERING (US/0149-0370). [70,312] **2054**

EVALUATOR (RIVER FOREST, ILL.) (US/8756-775X). [1,000] **320**

EVANGEL (WINONA LAKE) (US/0162-1890). [35,000] **4957**

EVANGELICAL FRIEND (US/0014-3340). [12,000] **4957**

EVANGELICAL LIBRARY BULLETIN (UK). [1,500] **3209**

EVANGELICAL STUDIES BULLETIN (US/0890-703X). [2,300] **4957**

EVANGELIKALE MISSIOLOGIE (GW/0177-8706). [1,300] **4957**

EVANGELIUM / GOSPEL / EUAGGELION (GW). [3,000] **4957**

EVANSVILLE PRESS (US/0896-6249). [42,000] **5664**

EVENING JOURNAL (LUBBOCK, TEX.) (US/0745-547X). [70,926] **5749**

EVENING TELEGRAM (SUPERIOR, WIS. : 1922) (US). **5767**

EVERGREEN CHRONICLES, THE (US/1043-3333). [2,000] **2794**

EVERMAN TIMES (US). **5749**

EVERYONE'S BACKYARD (US/0749-3940). [7,500] **2171**

EVERYTHING'S ARCHIE (US/0745-7766). **4860**

EVOLUTION (US/0014-3820). [4,000] **544**

EVOLUTION PSYCHIATRIQUE, L' (FR/0014-3855). [2,900] **3925**

EX AUDITU (US/0883-0053). **4958**

EX AUDITU : AN INTERNATIONAL JOURNAL OF THEOLOGICAL INTERPRETATION OF SCRIPTURE (US). [240] **4958**

EX LIBRIS (PORTSMOUTH, N.H.) (US/1042-6647). [500] **3386**

EXAMINER (BARRIE) (CN/0839-4164). [14,750] **5784**

EXCALIBUR (DOWNSVIEW, ONT.) (CN/0823-1915). [16,000] **5784**

EXCAVATING CONTRACTOR (US/0014-3995). [27,000] **614**

EXCAVATIONS AND SURVEYS IN ISRAEL (IS/0334-1607). [1,000] **268**

EXCAVATIONS OF THE ATHENIAN AGORA: PICTURE BOOK (US/0569-7425). [10,000] **268**

EXCEL (US). [500] **2862**

EXCEL (SAN FRANCISCO, CALIF.) (US/0893-5017). [130,000] **5200**

EXCEPTIONAL CHILDREN (US/0014-4029). [54,000] **1878**

EXCEPTIONAL PARENT, THE (US/0046-9157). [40,000] **2278**

EXCERPTA MEDICA. SECTION 22. HUMAN GENETICS (NE/0014-4266). [535] **3658**

EXCERPTA MEDICA. SECTION 27. BIOPHYSICS, BIOENGINEERING AND MEDICAL INSTRUMENTATION (NE/0014-4312). [440] **3658**

EXCHANGE (NE/0166-2740). [700] **4958**

EXCHANGE (ALEXANDRIA, VA.) (US/1046-1485). **2193**

EXCHANGE & COMMISSARY NEWS (US/0014-4452). **4044**

EXCHANGE (KITCHENER) (CN/0824-457X). **833**

EXCHANGE LILYFIELD (AT/1033-2014). **673**

EXCHANGE (PROVO) (US/0146-4000). [30,000] **1091**

EXCHANGITE, THE (US/0014-4487). [44,000] **5231**

EXECUTIVE : AN ACADEMY OF MANAGEMENT PUBLICATION, THE (US). [9,000] **867**

EXECUTIVE COUNSELOR (US). **867**

EXECUTIVE HOUSEKEEPING TODAY (US/0738-6583). [7,000] **2790**

EXECUTIVE INTELLIGENCE REVIEW (US/0273-6314). [10,000] **1917**

EXECUTIVE REPORT (PITTSBURGH, PA.) (US/0279-1382). [24,000] **674**

EXECUTIVE SECRETARY BRADFORD (UK/0955-6230). **4204**

EXECUTIVE SYSTEMS INTERNATIONAL NEWSLETTER (UK/0968-8803). **674**

EXEGETICAL RESOURCE (US/0744-0448). [2,000] **5016**

EXERCISE EXCHANGE (US/0531-531X). [200-500] **1894**

EXERCISE STANDARDS & MALPRACTICE REPORTER, THE (US/0891-0278). [700] **2968**

EXETER TIMES-ADVOCATE (CN). **5784**

EXHAUST NEWS (US/0192-7469). [16,000] **5104**

EXHIBIT BUILDER SOURCE BOOK DIRECTORY (US). **674**

EXILE (PASADENA, CALIF.) (US/0743-9849). [500] **4474**

EXPANSION (MX). [27,500] **4647**

EXPANSION MANAGEMENT (US/1073-8355). [40,000] **674**

EXPATRIATE OBSERVER (US). **940**

EXPERIENTIAL EDUCATION (US/0739-2338). [2,500] **1746**

EXPERIMENTAL AGING RESEARCH (US/0361-073X). [1,000] **3750**

EXPERIMENTAL MECHANICS (US/0014-4851). [4,000] **4427**

EXPERIMENTAL TECHNIQUES (WESTPORT, CONN.) (US/0732-8818). [4,380] **2114**

EXPERT AND THE LAW, THE (US/0737-8726). [1,500] **2968**

EXPERT WITNESS JOURNAL (US/0277-0555). **2968**

EXPLORATION GEOPHYSICS (MELBOURNE) (AT/0812-3985). [2,020] **4402**

EXPLORATION INTERNATIONAL NEWS (UK/0960-9989). [150] **4256**

EXPLORATIONS IN ETHNIC STUDIES (US/0730-904X). [350] **2261**

EXPLORATIONS IN KNOWLEDGE (UK/0261-1376). [300] **4346**

EXPLORATIONS IN RENAISSANCE CULTURE (US/0098-2474). [400] **2846**

EXPLORATIONS IN SIGHTS AND SOUNDS (US/0733-3323). [300] **2261**

EXPLORE (LAWRENCE, KAN.) (US/0741-8493). [5,000] **1823**

EXPLORING B (US/0162-4431). [140,000] **5060**

EXPO (WAUCONDA, ILL.) (US/1046-3925). [8,500] **867**

EXPONENT II (US). [2,000] **4958**

EXPORT DIRECTORY CHILE (CL). [15,000] **834**

EXPORT DIRECTORY OF CHILE. GUIA CHILENA DE LA EXPORTACION (CL). [15,000] **834**

EXPORT GAZETTE (II). [8,000] **834**

EXPORT GRAFICAS USA (US/0741-7160). [12,000] **378**

EXPORT (NEW YORK, N.Y.) (US/0014-519X). [28,056] **2811**

EXPORT SALES AND MARKETING MANUAL (US/1054-8327). **834**

EXPORT TODAY (US/0882-4711). [41,000] **834**

EXPORT TRADE TODAY (ENGINEERING EDITION) (GW). [20,000] **3478**

EXPORTADOR, EL (US/0279-456X). [10,068] **835**

EXPOSITORY TIMES, THE (UK/0014-5246). [7,000] **5016**

EXPRESS (DRUMMONDVILLE) (CN/0713-5483). [32,000] **5784**

EXPRESSION (WINNIPEG, DEUTSCHE AUSG.) (CN/0824-474X). [1,600] **4958**

EXPRESSION (WINNIPEG. ENGLISH ED.) (CN/0824-4731). **4958**

EXTEL HANDBOOK OF MARKET LEADERS (UK). **835**

EXTENSION INFORMATION BULLETIN (CN/0703-9166). [400] **83**

EXTRACTA ORTHOPAEDICA (GW/0344-5046). [3,200] **3881**

EXTRACTA UROLOGICA (GW/0344-5038). [2,400] **3990**

EXTRUSION COMMUNIQUE (UK/0958-0549). [9,500] **2334**

EYECARE BUSINESS (US/0885-9167). [35,324] **4215**

EYELINE (AT). [2,000] **373**

EYEPIECE (US/0146-7662). [600] **395**

EYEPIECE (UK/0950-737X). [3,500-5,000] **4369**

EZSEARCH-MINING (US). [70] **2139**

F.A.S. PUBLIC INTEREST REPORT (US/0092-9824). [5,000] **5104**

F & B MARKETPLACE (US/1040-7537). **924**

F.I.B.A. RULES CASEBOOK (CN/0712-5585). [10,000] **4894**

F.S.U. REPORTS (US/0427-8518). **1823**

FABIAN NEWSLETTER (AT/0949-138X). **4474**

FABIAN PAMPHLET / FABIAN SOCIETY (UK/0307-7523). [5,500] **1490**

FABIAN TRACT (UK/0307-7535). [4000] **4474**

FABIS (SY/0255-6448). [1,000] **171**

FABRICATOR (ROCKFORD, ILL.) (US/0888-0301). [55,000] **3478**

FABRICS & ARCHITECTURE (US/1045-0483). [8,000] **298**

FABRICS-FASHIONS (US/0097-2495). [10,000] **5350**

FABRIMETAL (BE/0377-9084). [8,100] **3478**

FACE AU RISQUE (FR/0014-6269). **5200**

FACEPLATE (US/1040-807X). [3,000] **4176**

FACET TALK (AT/1035-0977). [1,200] **2773**

FACHBERICHTE HUTTENPRAXIS METALLWEITERVERARBEITUNG (GW/0340-8043). [8,300] **4001**

FACHSPRACHE (AU/0251-1207). **3281**

FACHVORTRAGE DES WVAO-JAHRESKONGRESSES, DIE (GW). [10,000] **4215**

FACIAL ORTHOPEDICS AND TEMPOROMANDIBULAR ARTHROLOGY (US/0749-0399). [1,000] **3881**

FACIAL PLASTIC SURGERY (US/0736-6825). [1,500] **3964**

FACILITIES DESIGN & MANAGEMENT (US/0279-4438). [30,500] **2900**

FACILITIES PLANNING NEWS (US/1045-7089). [8,000] **298**

FACILITY MANAGEMENT JOURNAL : A PUBLICATION OF THE INTERNATIONAL FACILITY MANAGEMENT ASSOCIATION (US/1059-3667). [12,000] **867**

FACS SHEET (CN/0710-5878). **2790**

FACSIMILE & VOICE SERVICES (US). [125] **1155**

FACT BOOK - NEW YORK STOCK EXCHANGE (US/8756-6788). [14,000] **898**

FACT BOOK : TABLES AND CHARTS ON THE NEW YORK METROPOLITAN REGION (US). [1,000] **5327**

FACTS (US). **5440**

FACTS AND FIGURES (UK). [15,000] **3210**

FACTS AND FIGURES. AUSTRALIAN DENTISTRY (AT/0157-4094). [300] **1323**

FACTS AND FIGURES: NEW MEXICO EMPLOYERS, INDUSTRY, SIZE, AND LOCATION (US). [245] **1669**

FACTUM (SZ). [7,000] **5060**

FACTUM : BOLETIN OFICIAL DEL COLEGIO DE ABOGADOS DE PUERTO RICO (PR). [8,000] **2968**

FACULTY & ADMINISTRATIVE DIRECTORY - THE UNIVERSITY OF BRITISH COLUMBIA (CN/0706-6724). **1864**

FACULTY DIALOGUE (US/8756-2146). [11,000] **4958**

FACULTY STUDIES - CARSON-NEWMAN COLLEGE (US/0734-1539). [400] **4958**

FAG TIDSSKRIFTET SYKEPLEIEN (NO/0802-9768). **3856**

FAIM DEVELOPPEMENT MAGAZINE PARIS (FR/0760-6443). **4958**

FAIR SCOPE (CN). [2,200] **674**

FAIRBANKS DAILY NEWS-MINER (US/8750-5495). [17,037 evening21,367 Sunday] **5629**

FAIRCHILD TROPICAL GARDEN BULLETIN (US/0014-6943). [5,000] **2414**

FAIRCHILD'S TEXTILE & APPAREL FINANCIAL DIRECTORY (US/1067-7062). [1,000] **5350**

FAIRPRESS (US/0192-3110). [62,072] **5645**

FAITH AND FELLOWSHIP (US). [5,150] **5060**

FAITS ET CHIFFRES, LES MINES AU CANADA (CN/0228-9547). **1606**

FAIZULISLAM (PK). [3,000] **5285**

FALLIMENTO E FISCO (IT). [6,000] **4723**

FALMOUTH OUTLOOK, THE (US/0891-8694). [4,650] **5680**

FAMILJA KANA (MM). [13,500] **2279**

FAMILLE MAGAZINE (FR). **2279**

FAMILLE QUEBEC (CN/0318-0581). [18,000] **2279**

FAMILY ADVOCATE (US/0163-710X). [20,000] **3120**

FAMILY FOOTSTEPS QUARTERLY (US/0894-0487). [150] **2447**

FAMILY HISTORY CAPERS (US/0742-1419). **2447**

FAMILY HISTORY FOR BEGINNERS (AT/0815-3922). **2447**

FAMILY LAW (CHICHESTER) (UK/0014-7281). [4,000] **3120**

FAMILY LAW REVIEW (US/0149-1431). [3,500] **3120**

FAMILY LIFE MATTERS (US/1064-6167). [6,000] **2279**

FAMILY MEDICINE (US/0742-3225). [4,500] **3737**

FAMILY MOTOR COACHING (US/0360-3024). [80,000] **5382**

FAMILY PHYSICIAN (KUALA LUMPUR, MALAYSIA) (MY). [2,500] **3737**

FAMILY PLANNING PERSPECTIVES (US/0014-7354). [15,000] **588**

FAMILY PRACTICE RECERTIFICATION (US/0163-6642). **3737**

FAMILY PROCESS (US/0014-7370). [10,000] **2279**

FAMILY RELATIONS (US/0197-6664). [4,200] **2279**

FAMILY ROOTS : JOURNAL OF THE FAMILY ROOTS FAMILY HISTORY SOCIETY. EASTBOURNE AND DISTRICT (UK). [350] **2447**

FAMILY TIES (HOLLAND GENEALOGICAL SOCIETY) (US/0736-9883). [125] **2447**

FAMILY TREE MAGAZINE (UK/0267-1131). **2447**

FAMILY TREE TALK (US/0747-9441). [150] **2447**

FANFARE (TENAFLY, N.J.) (US/0148-9364). [20,000] **4117**

FANFARES (CN/0046-3256). [20,000] **320**

FANTASY BOOK (US/0277-0717). [4,000] **3387**

FAR EASTERN TECHNICAL REVIEW (UK/0144-8218). [25,000] **835**

FARBE + I.E. UND LACK ADRESSBUCH MIT BEZUGSQUELLENNACHWEIS (GW). [1,500] **4223**

FARBE + LACK (GW/0014-7699). [5,268] **4223**

FARE ELETTRONICA (IT). [40,000] **2054**

FARM & POWER EQUIPMENT DEALER (US/0892-6085). [11,500] **158**

FARM BULLETIN (ST. PIERRE, MAN.) (CN/0826-2985). **84**

FARM BUREAU JOURNAL (US). [105,000] **84**

FARM BUREAU NEWS (WASHINGTON) (US/0197-5617). [50,000] **84**

FARM EQUIPMENT (US/0014-7958). [13,598] **159**

FARM FINANCIAL CONDITIONS REVIEW (US/0883-2188). [150] **84**

FARM GATE, THE (CN/0705-8748). [24,500] **84**

FARM INDUSTRY NEWS (1984) (US/0892-8312). [270,000] **159**

FARM MANAGEMENT (KENILWORTH) (UK/0014-8059). [1,800] **85**

FARM NEWS OF ERIE AND WYOMING COUNTIES (US). [1,600] **85**

FARMACEUTISCH TIJDSCHRIFT VOOR BELGIE (BE/0369-9714). [2,850] **4304**

FARMACEVTISK REVY (SW/0014-8210). [6,700] **4304**

FARMACI (IT). **4304**

FARMACI E TERAPIA (IT/0393-9693). [350] **4304**

FARMACOTERAPIA MADRID (SP/0214-8935). **4305**

FARMER STOCKMAN OF THE MIDWEST (US/0739-9235). **85**

FARMERS EXCHANGE (US). [20,000] **85**

FARMERS HOT LINE (US/0192-6322). **86**

FARMERS' NEWSLETTER, LARGE AREA (AT/0467-5282). [2,600] **86**

FARMFUTURES (US/0091-1305). [200,000] **86**

FARMING JAPAN (JA). [18,000] **86**

FARMING NEWS (UK). [102,000] **86**

FARMINGTON NEWS, THE (US). [1,800] **5645**

FARMINGTON OBSERVER (US/0888-6199). [18,400] **5692**

FARO DEL POETA : REVISTA TRIMESTRAL DE POESIA (SP). **3463**

FARO DEL SILENCIO (SP). [2,500] **4388**

FASHION ACCESSORIES (HK/0255-7290). [20,900] **1084**

FAST FERRY INTERNATIONAL (UK/0954-3988). [5,000] **593**

FAST FOLK MUSICAL MAGAZINE (US/8755-9137). [1,500] **4117**

FASTENER TECHNOLOGY INTERNATIONAL (US/0746-2441). [13,000] **2114**

FAULKNER & GRAY'S BANKRUPTCY LAW REVIEW (US/1043-0547). [1,500] **2968**

FAULKNER & GRAY'S MEDICINE & HEALTH (US/1047-8892). **3576**

FAUNA OF NEW ZEALAND (NZ/0111-5383). [300] **5608**

FAXES OF THE WORLD (GW). [4,000] **4211**

FAXON PLANNING REPORT, THE (US/1043-1187). [7,000] **3210**

FAYETTE CONNECTION, THE (US/0739-8093). [310] **2448**

FCCAA STATISTICAL REPORTING SERVICE / MEN'S BASEBALL (US). **4894**

FCL NEWSLETTER (US/0532-7091). [3,500] **4647**

FCM FORUM (ENGLISH ED.) (CN/0381-1352). **4647**

FCX CAROLINA COOPERATOR (US/0195-3346). [60,000] **86**

FDA DRUG AND DEVICE PRODUCT APPROVALS / CENTER FOR DRUGS AND BIOLOGICS, CENTER FOR DEVICES AND RADIOLOGICAL HEALTH, CENTER FOR VETERINARY MEDICINE (US). [75] **4305**

FDA FREEDOM OF INFORMATION LOG (US/0161-7044). [75] **4647**

FDGB REVIEW (GW/0323-7028). **1669**

FDM, FURNITURE DESIGN & MANUFACTURING (US/0192-8058). [42,000] **634**

FED IN PRINT: ECONOMICS AND BANKING TOPICS (US). [2,600] **729**

FEDERAL AQUISITION REGULATIONS / DISKETTE (US). **4647**

FEDERAL COMMUNICATIONS LAW JOURNAL (US/0163-7606). [2,500] **2969**

FEDERAL COMPUTER WEEK (US/0893-052X). [61,500] **1247**

FEDERAL COURT REPORTER (AT/0728-6082). **2969**

FEDERAL EMPLOYEES ALMANAC (US/0071-4127). [160,000] **4702**

FEDERAL MANAGERS QUARTERLY (US/0893-8415). [20,000] **868**

FEDERAL PARKS AND RECREATION (US). [1,400] **4706**

FEDERAL PROPERTY MANAGEMENT REGULATIONS / DISKETTE (US). **4648**

FEDERAL REGISTER MONITOR, THE (US/1066-5862). [1,000] **2970**

FEDERAL TIMES (US/0014-9233). [30,000] **4703**

FEDERAL VETERINARIAN, THE (US/0164-6257). [1,800] **5510**

FEDERATION OF INSURANCE & CORPORATE COUNSEL QUARTERLY (US/0887-0942). **2880**

FEDNEWS, THE (US/0430-2761). [25,000] **1669**

FEED & FARM SUPPLY DEALER (CN/0046-3604). [8,288] **200**

FEED & GRAIN (US/1055-3223). [19,227] **200**

FEED INTERNATIONAL (US/0274-5771). [16,000] **201**

FEED MANAGEMENT (US/0014-956X). [24,000] **201**

FEEDBACK (WASHINGTON) (US/0147-4871). [950] **1132**

FEEDS & FEEDING (UK/0961-978X). [10,500] **201**

FEITEN (BE). [17,000] **4649**

FELLOWSHIP PROGRAM - INSURANCE INSTITUTE OF CANADA (CN/0225-2449). **2880**

FEM (MX/0185-4666). [16,000] **5555**

FEMINIST BOOKSTORE NEWS (US/0741-6555). [500] **5556**

FEMS MICROBIOLOGY (NE/0921-8254). [1,200] **562**

FEN. FINITE ELEMENT NEWS (UK/0309-6688). [1,500] **5105**

FENAISON (CN/0712-3566). **3387**

FENESTRATION (RIVERTON, N.J.) (US/0895-450X). [5,000] **614**

FERGUSON'S SRI LANKA DIRECTORY (CE). [10,000] **2503**

FERMENT (LONDON) (UK/0957-7041). [500] **2367**

FERNANDINA BEACH NEWS-LEADER (US). [11,000] **5649**

FERNBANK QUARTERLY (US/0742-650X). [5,000] **5105**

FERNSEH- UND KINOTECHNIK (GW/0015-0142). [33,000] **4068**

FERTIGUNGSTECHNIK UND BETRIEB (GW/0015-024X). [7,300] **2114**

FERTILISER NEWS (II/0015-0266). **87**

FERTILIZER INDICATORS / ECONOMICS COMMITTEE (FR). **1606**

FERTILIZER TECHNOLOGY (US/0378-0430). **171**

FETAL DIAGNOSIS AND THERAPY (SZ/1015-3837). [600] **3760**

FEUILLET BIBLIQUE, LE (CN/0225-2112). [7,000] **5016**

FEUILLET D'INFORMATION DE LA VILLE DE SAINT-LEONARD, LE (CN/0711-396X). **4649**

FEUILLETS DE BIOLOGIE (FR/0428-2779). [4,000] **455**

FIA JOURNAL (AT/1322-4409). [5,000] **2597**

FIBER AND INTEGRATED OPTICS (US/0146-8030). [800] **4434**

FIBEROPTIC PRODUCT NEWS (US/0890-653X). [26,000] **1155**

FIBONACCI QUARTERLY, THE (US/0015-0517). [1,000] **3505**

FIBRE BOX HANDBOOK (US/0196-7215). [67,000] **4219**

FIBRE REPORT (UK). **5351**

FIBULA (NE/0015-5676). [2000] **2616**

FIDDLEHEAD, THE (CN/0015-0630). [1,000] **3387**

FIELD NOTES - ARKANSAS ARCHEOLOGICAL SOCIETY (US/0015-0711). [875] **268**

FIELD (OBERLIN, OHIO) (US/0015-0657). [2,200] **3463**

FIELD POLL, THE (US/0195-4520). [300] **5245**

FIELDIANA. BOTANY (US/0015-0746). [500] **510**

FIELDIANA : GEOLOGY (US/0096-2651). [500] **1375**

FIELDIANA : ZOOLOGY (US/0015-0754). [550] **5583**

FIELDS WITHIN FIELDS WITHIN FIELDS (US/0015-0770). **1185**

FIFA NEWS (SZ). [6,000] **4894**

FIFTH COLUMN (CN/0229-7094). [300] **298**

FIFTY SOMETHING (AT). [40,000] **5179**

FIGA (US/0196-187X). [2,000] **4117**

Controlled Circulation Index — FLORIDA

FIGHTING WOMAN NEWS (US/0146-8812). [3,000] **2597**

FIJI AGRICULTURAL JOURNAL (FJ/0015-0886). [350] **87**

FIJI REPUBLIC GAZETTE (FJ). **5800**

FIJI TIMES, THE (FJ). [30,500] **5800**

FILATELIA CUBANA (CU). [10,000] **2785**

FILIGRANE (MONTREAL) (CN/1192-1412). **3925**

FILLES D'AUJOURD'HUI (CN/0227-0315). [35,000] **1063**

FILM & VIDEO FINDER (US/0898-1582). [2,000] **4069**

FILM & VIDEO (LOS ANGELES, CALIF.) (US/1041-1933). [19,000] **4069**

FILM AUSTRALIA EDUCATION CATALOGUE (AT). [18,000] **4069**

FILM COMMENT (US/0015-119X). [47,000] **4069**

FILM JOURNAL (HOLLINS), THE (US/0046-3787). [9,500] **4070**

FILM LITERATURE INDEX (US/0093-6758). [500] **4080**

FILM (LONDON, ENGLAND : 1954) (UK/0015-1025). [3,000] **4070**

FILM QUARTERLY (US/0015-1386). [6,900] **4070**

FILM : TUTTI I FILM DELLA STAGIONE (IT). **4070**

FILMFAUST (GW). [13,000] **4070**

FILOZOFIA (BRATISLAVA) (XO/0046-385X). [1,450] **4347**

FILSON CLUB HISTORY QUARTERLY, THE (US/0015-1874). [3000] **2733**

FILTER (BRANTFORD) (CN/0833-8493). [5,000] **3941**

FINAL FRONTIER (US/0899-4161). **20**

FINAL REPORT - TEXAS LEGISLATIVE SERVICE (US/0093-1381). **2970**

FINANCE & DEVELOPMENT (US/0015-1947). [140,000] **1635**

FINANCE QUARTERLY BULLETIN (US). [700] **4725**

FINANCIAL FREEDOM REPORT (US/0196-514X). [3000] **898**

FINANCIAL MANAGERS' STATEMENT (US/0887-4808). [4,700] **868**

FINANCIAL PLANNING FOCUS [SOUND RECORDING] (US/0889-0552). [2,500] **2880**

FINANCIAL PLANNING NEWS (US/0893-7060). [25,000] **898**

FINANCIAL PLANNING ON WALL STREET (US). [50,000] **898**

FINANCIAL REPORT / OLD DOMINION UNIVERSITY (US/0883-4636). [2,000] **1824**

FINANCIAL REVIEW OF ALIEN INSURERS (US/0270-5656). [250] **2880**

FINANCIAL STATISTICS OF PUBLIC UTILITIES (US/0430-4845). [275] **4761**

FINANCIAL TECHNOLOGY INTERNATIONAL BULLETIN (UK/0265-1661). [1,000] **5105**

FINANCIAL TIMES NORTH SEA LETTER AND EUROPEAN OFFSHORE NEWS (UK/0950-1037). **1944**

FINANCIAL WORLD (US/0015-2064). [500,000] **898**

FINANZA, MARKETING E PRODUZIONE : RIVISTA DELL'UNIVERSITA L. BOCCONI (IT). **924**

FINDER BINDER. ARIZONA'S UPDATED MEDIA DIRECTORY (US/0196-8548). [700] **2919**

FINDER BINDER. DETROIT AREA UPDATED MEDIA DIRECTORY (US/0276-2196). **759**

FINDER BINDER. NORTHEAST OHIO/GREATER CLEVELAND (US/0196-8726). [300] **759**

FINDERBINDER (US/0196-853X). [500] **759**

FINDING (US/0892-7367). [40,000] **3210**

FINE ART & AUCTION REVIEW (CN/0833-0891). [2,000] **350**

FINE LINE (AT/0818-3473). [700] **3388**

FINE TOOL JOURNAL, THE (US/0745-6824). [2,000] **250**

FINEST HOUR (US/0882-3715). [2,000] **2688**

FINGERPRINT WHORLD (UK/0951-1288). [2,000] **3164**

FINISHERS' MANAGEMENT (US/0015-2358). [8,500] **868**

FINISHING (UK/0264-2506). [4,200] **4224**

FINMECCANICA AMBIENTE (IT). [6,500] **2171**

FINNISH BUSINESS REPORT (FI). [20,000] **675**

FINNISH MUSIC QUARTERLY (FI/0782-1069). [3,000] **4117**

FINNISH TRADE REVIEW (FI/0015-2463). [25,000] **835**

FIRA BULLETIN (UK/0014-5904). [1,300] **2905**

FIRE & SECURITY PROTECTION (UK). [1,250] **5177**

FIRE ENGINEERING (US/0015-2587). [39,018] **2289**

FIRE ENGINEERS JOURNAL (UK/0143-5337). [10,000] **2289**

FIRE FIGHTING IN CANADA (CN/0015-2595). [7,000] **2289**

FIRE INTERNATIONAL (UK/0015-2609). **2289**

FIRE LOSSES IN BRITISH COLUMBIA IN ... (CN/0821-820X). [1,000] **2289**

FIRE PREVENTION (LONDON, 1971) (UK/0309-6866). [7,500] **2289**

FIRE PREVENTION NOTES (US/0734-0702). **2289**

FIRE PROTECTION CONTRACTOR, THE (US/1043-2485). [1,800] **2289**

FIRE PROTECTION HANDBOOK (US/0734-5984). [7,000] **2289**

FIREFIGHTER'S NEWS (USUS/1061-4818). [40,000] **2290**

FIRESIDE CHATS (US/0015-2714). [440] **2785**

FIREWATCH / NAFED (US). [4,000] **2290**

FIRM FOUNDATION (US/8750-9377). [8,000] **5060**

FIRST AIDER (US). [120,000] **3954**

FIRST BREAK (UK/0263-5046). [4,000] **1405**

FIRST CLASS ALFELD (GW/0939-8414). **2805**

FIRST DROP / COASTER NEWS (UK). [600] **4861**

FIRST HAND (US/0744-6349). [70,000] **2794**

FIRST PERSPECTIVE (CN). [11,000] **2261**

FIRST READING (CN/0824-197X). [1,000] **5245**

FIRST STRIKE (US/0896-4432). [31,000] **2781**

FIRST TEACHER (US/0744-7434). [11,000] **1895**

FISCAL YEAR REPORT - STATE OF MONTANA. BOARD OF INVESTMENTS (US/0090-9122). [500] **899**

FISH AND WILDLIFE RESEARCH (US/1040-2411). [1,200] **2193**

FISH CULTURIST, THE (US/0015-2919). [750] **2301**

FISH FARM NEWS, THE (CN/1180-5633). [2,000] **2301**

FISH SUPPLIES INTERNATIONAL : PROCESSING & MARKETING NEWS (CN/0229-1924). [10,000] **2301**

FISHERIES (BETHESDA) (US/0363-2415). [8,300] **2302**

FISHERIES PRODUCT NEWS (US/1047-2525). [35,000] **2302**

FISHERIES STATISTICS OF JAPAN (JA). **2317**

FISHERMAN (GRAND HAVEN, MICH.), THE (US/8755-4216). [2,000] **2302**

FISHERMAN (NEW ENGLAND ED.), THE (US/1040-0125). **2302**

FISHERMAN (NEW JERSEY, DELAWARE BAY ED.), THE (US/1040-0117). [35,000] **4894**

FISHERMAN, THE (CN/0015-2986). [9,100] **2302**

FISHING BOAT WORLD (HK/1033-1247). [4,000] **2303**

FISHING TACKLE RETAILER (1984) (US/8750-1287). [22,000] **675**

FISHING TACKLE TRADE NEWS (US/0015-3060). [23,000] **2303**

FISICA E TECNOLOGIA (IT/0391-9757). [1,000] **5105**

FIT THIRD AGE (CN/0827-3103). [6,000] **3751**

FITECH (UK/0307-2118). [12,000] **2290**

FITECH INTERNATIONAL (UK). [12,000] **2290**

FITNESS BULLETIN, THE (CN/0820-6163). [3,500] **2597**

FITNESS MANAGEMENT (SOLANA BEACH, CALIF.) (US/0882-0481). [21,000] **2597**

FITOPATOLOGIA BRASILEIRA (BL/0100-4158). [1,000] **172**

FITOTERAPIA (IT/0367-326X). [4,500] **510**

FLAG : THE FOOTHILLS LIBRARY ASSOCIATION GAZETTE, THE (CN/0228-7137). **3211**

FLAGS, DIAMONDS, AND STATUES (US/0271-7638). [3,000] **5431**

FLAMBEE, LA (CN/0705-1751). **4256**

FLAMBOROUGH NEWS (CN/0710-5339). [9,300] **5784**

FLAMING CRESCENT, THE (US). [40,000] **4474**

FLASH ART (INTERNATIONAL EDITION) (IT/0394-1493). [50,000] **350**

FLAT EARTH NEWS (US/8756-0313). [10,000] **1405**

FLATBUSH GUIDE, THE (US). **5470**

FLEET EQUIPMENT (US/0747-2544). [62,000] **5382**

FLEISCHEREI (GW/0015-3613). [8,200] **2335**

FLETCHER (US/0161-8350). [4,200] **1102**

FLETCHER-O'LEARY PERIODICAL, THE (CN/0715-4518). [150] **2448**

FLIGHT SAFETY BULLETIN (CN/0826-032X). [20,000] **21**

FLOOR COVERING PLUS (CN/1193-8781). [7,000] **615**

FLOOR FOCUS (US/1064-7627). [6,400] **615**

FLORA BUTTENSIS (US). [100] **510**

FLORA DA GUINE-BISSAU (PO). [1,000] **510**

FLORA-LINE, THE (US/1062-855X). [1,200] **2435**

FLORA OF BANGLADESH (BG). **511**

FLORA OG FAUNA (DK/0015-3818). [700] **5584**

FLORACULTURE INTERNATIONAL (US/1051-9076). [10,500] **2414**

FLORAL & NURSERY TIMES (US/1042-2145). [14,500] **511**

FLORENCE MORNING NEWS (US). [34,000] **5742**

FLORIDA ADMINISTRATIVE LAW REPORTS (US/0194-4800). **3093**

FLORIDA ADMINISTRATIVE WEEKLY (US/0098-874X). [3,000] **2970**

FLORIDA AGRICULTURAL STATISTICS : CITRUS SUMMARY (US/0428-6413). **153**

FLORIDA ARCHITECT (US/0015-3907). [6,000] **298**

FLORIDA BAPTIST WITNESS / ORGAN OF THE FLORIDA BAPTIST STATE CONVENTION (US). [81,000] **5060**

FLORIDA BAR JOURNAL, THE (US/0015-3915). [43,500] **2970**

FLORIDA BAR NEWS (US/0360-0114). [43,500] **2970**

FLORIDA BLUE SHEET (US). [20,000] **4071**

FLORIDA BUILDER (US). [10,125] **615**

FLORIDA BUSINESS PUBLICATIONS INDEX (US/0191-183X). [100] **676**

FLORIDA BUSINESS SOUTHWEST (US/1047-6105). **676**

FLORIDA CATTLEMAN AND LIVESTOCK JOURNAL, THE (US/0015-3958). [7,231] **211**

FLORIDA COMMUNICATION JOURNAL, THE (US/1050-3366). [225] **1111**

FLORIDA CONTRACTOR (US/0046-4112). [2,900] **2605**

FLORIDA CPA TODAY : A PUBLICATION OF THE FLORIDA INSTITUTE OF CERTIFIED PUBLIC ACCOUNTANTS (US). [18,500] **744**

FLORIDA EDUCATION (US/0015-4016). **1747**

FLORIDA ENVIRONMENTS (US/0894-9743). [10,000] **2172**

FLORIDA FAMILY PHYSICIAN (US/0015-4067). [16,300] **3737**

FLORIDA FIELD NATURALIST (US/0738-999X). [675] **5584**

FLORIDA FIREMAN (US/0274-8797). [6,200] **2290**

FLORIDA FOLIAGE (US). [3,500] **2414**

FLORIDA FOLK ARTS DIRECTORY (US/0162-5616). **320**

FLORIDA FUNERAL DIRECTOR, THE (US/0273-9747). [1,000] **2407**

FLORIDA GARDENER, THE (US/0426-5750). [30,000] **2414**

FLORIDA GEOGRAPHER, THE (US/0739-0041). [150] **2560**

FLORIDA GROWER & RANCHER (US/0015-4091). [18,000] **87**

FLORIDA HISTORICAL QUARTERLY, THE (US/0015-4113). [2,000] **2733**

FLORIDA HISTORY NEWSLETTER (US). [2,500] **2733**

FLORIDA HOTEL & MOTEL JOURNAL (US/8750-6807). [7,000] **2805**

FLORIDA JOURNAL OF ANTHROPOLOGY, THE (US/0164-1662). [60] **236**

FLORIDA

Controlled Circulation Index

FLORIDA LAND OWNER MAGAZINE (US/1047-1413). [25,000] **4837**

FLORIDA LAW WEEKLY, THE (US/0274-8533). [4,300] **2971**

FLORIDA LIBRARY DIRECTORY (US). [1,500] **3211**

FLORIDA LIVING (US/0888-9600). [25,000] **2533**

FLORIDA MANUFACTURERS REGISTER (US/0882-9438). **3479**

FLORIDA NATURALIST, THE (US/0015-4172). [10,000] **226**

FLORIDA NURSE, THE (US/0015-4199). [7,400] **3856**

FLORIDA NURSERYMAN (US). [6,000] **2414**

FLORIDA READING QUARTERLY, THE (US/0015-4261). [2,000] **1747**

FLORIDA REAL ESTATE (US/0897-9383). [100,000] **4837**

FLORIDA REALTOR (US/0199-5839). [65,000] **4838**

FLORIDA RESTAURATEUR (US/0192-348X). [7,000] **5071**

FLORIDA RESTAURATEUR & PURVEYOR NEWS (US/0046-418X). [7,000] **5071**

FLORIDA RETIREMENT LIVING (US/0160-5739). [35,000] **5179**

FLORIDA SCIENTIST (US/0098-4590). [1,050] **5105**

FLORIDA STAR (JACKSONVILLE, FLA. : 1951), THE (US/0740-798X). [9,622] **2616**

FLORIDA TRUCK NEWS (US/0015-4334). [2,300] **5382**

FLORIDA VOCATIONAL JOURNAL (US/0145-9376). [19,000] **1913**

FLORIDA WATER RESOURCES JOURNAL (US/0896-1794). [8,000] **5533**

FLORIDA WEATHER AND CROP NEWS (US). **172**

FLORIDA WILDLIFE (US/0015-4369). [30,000] **2194**

FLORIDA WORKERS COMPENSATION INSTITUTE REPORTER (US). [290] **2881**

FLORISSANT VALLEY REPORTER, THE (US). [5,000] **5703**

FLORIST TRADE MAGAZINE (UK/0015-4415). [3,800] **2435**

FLOWER NEWS : THE FLORAL INDUSTRY'S NATIONAL WEEKLY (US/0015-4490). [15,000] **2414**

FLOWER OF THE FOREST BLACK GENEALOGICAL JOURNAL (US/0738-159X). [300] **2448**

FLUE (US/0731-2636). [1,500] **320**

FLUE CURED TOBACCO FARMER, THE (US/0015-4512). [25,000] **5373**

FLUG REVUE (GW/0015-4547). [56,000] **21**

FLUID POWER INDUSTRY OUTLOOK SURVEY (US/0193-5518). [350] **3479**

FLUORIDE (US/0015-4725). [500] **487**

FLUSSIGES OBST (GW/0015-4539). [2,000] **2335**

FLUTIST QUARTERLY, THE (US/8756-8667). [4,600] **4118**

FLY-TACKLE DEALER (US). [11,000] **2304**

FLYER (EVANSTON, ILL.) (US). [16,000] **5557**

FLYING NEEDLE, THE (US/0270-2959). [2,500] **5184**

FOAL REGISTRATIONS, ILLINOIS CONCEIVED & FOALED STANDARDBREDS (US/0884-1322). [3,000] **2799**

FOCUS (AUSTIN, TEX. 1985) (US/0883-8194). [8,000] **1247**

FOCUS (AUSTIN, TEX. 1989) (US/1041-2549). [12,500] **1185**

FOCUS (BURBANK, CALIF.) (US/1054-4208). [800] **4241**

FOCUS (CHICAGO. 1977) (US/0148-026X). [4,500] **2971**

FOCUS, FIBRE OPTIC COMMUNICATION & USER SYSTEMS (UK/0959-0188). [8,500] **1155**

FOCUS. JAPAN (JA/0388-0311). [9,000] **676**

FOCUS, LIBRARY SERVICE TO OLDER ADULTS, PEOPLE WITH DISABILITIES (US/0740-4956). [150] **3211**

FOCUS (MADISON) (US/0195-5705). [5,000] **1491**

FOCUS (NEW BRUNSWICK TEACHERS' ASSOCIATION. SOCIAL STUDIES COUNCIL) (CN/0710-7692). **5200**

FOCUS (NEW YORK, N.Y. 1950) (US/0015-5004). [5,000] **2561**

FOCUS ON AFRICA : BBC MAGAZINE (UK/0959-9576). [45,000] **2499**

FOCUS ON AGING (CN/0822-3637). [900] **5200**

FOCUS ON ASIAN STUDIES (US/0046-4295). [2,400] **2651**

FOCUS ON CHEMICALS (UK). **2012**

FOCUS ON COMMERICAL AVIATION SAFETY (UK). [17,000] **21**

FOCUS ON DENTAL COMPUTERS (US/0748-1810). [900] **1323**

FOCUS ON LEARNING PROBLEMS IN MATHEMATICS (US/0272-8893). [2,000] **1879**

FOCUS ON MISSIONS; OCCASIONAL NEWS SUPPLEMENT FOR MISSIONARIES (US). [25,000] **4959**

FOCUS ON NIGERIA (CN/0827-3022). **2639**

FOCUS ON SURGICAL EDUCATION (US/0742-9819). [800] **3965**

FOCUS (ROCKVILLE) (US/0533-1242). [50,000] **455**

FOELDRAJZI ERTESITO (HU/0015-5403). [1,200] **2561**

FOERDERN UND HEBEN (GW/0373-6482). [12,000] **2114**

FOI ET LA VIE, LA (FR/0015-5357). [1,200] **4959**

FOLDRAJZI KOZLEMENYEK (HU/0015-5411). [1,100] **2561**

FOLIA ARCHAEOLOGICA BUDAPEST (HU/0133-2023). [800] **268**

FOLIA ENTOMOLOGICA MEXICANA (MX/0430-8603). [1,000] **5609**

FOLIA HEREDITARIA ET PATHOLOGICA (IT/0015-5578). [50] **545**

FOLIO (BROCKPORT, N.Y.) (US/0882-3030). [500] **3388**

FOLIO (SASKATOON) (CN/0381-9469). [2,500] **350**

FOLIO'S PUBLISHING NEWS (US/1053-4563). [20,000] **4815**

FOLK DANCE SCENE (US). [1,150] **1313**

FOLK DIRECTORY, THE (UK/0430-876X). [3,000] **5231**

FOLK LIFE (UK/0430-8778). [500] **2319**

FOLK MUSIC JOURNAL (UK/0531-9684). [8,000] **4118**

FOLK NEWS (WASHINGTON, D.C.) (US). [5,000] **4118**

FOLK OG FORSKNING / UDG. AF UNIVERSITETSFORENINGEN FOR DET SYDLIGE OG VESTLIGE JYLLAND (DK/0105-712X). [2,000] **2846**

FOLKLIFE CENTER NEWS (US/0149-6840). [13,000] **2319**

FOLKLOR ARCHIVUM (HU). [500] **2319**

FOLKLORE AND MYTHOLOGY STUDIES (LOS ANGELES, CALIF. : 1980) (US/0731-1524). [800] **2320**

FOLKLORE BRABANCON (BE/0015-590X). [1,000] **2320**

FOLKLORE DE FRANCE (FR/0015-5918). [4,500] **2320**

FOLKLORE FORUM (US/0015-5926). [400] **2320**

FOLKLORE PAPERS OF THE UNIVERSITY FOLKLORE ASSOCIATION (US/0730-3181). [1,000] **2320**

FOLKNIK, THE (US/0146-9169). [1,200] **4118**

FOLLETOS MUNDO CRISTIANO (SP). [4,000] **2280**

FOLLIA DI NEW YORK (US/0015-6000). **2846**

FOLLOWUP FILE (US/0888-3955). **2919**

FONDERIE, FONDEUR D'AUJOURD'HUI (FR/0249-3136). [3,500] **4002**

FONTANE BLATTER (GW/0015-6175). [1,000] **3388**

FONTES ARTIS MUSICAE (SZ/0015-6191). [2,000] **4118**

FONTI PER LA STORIA D'ITALIA (IT). **2688**

FOOD AND DRUG PACKAGING (US/0015-6272). [67,876] **4219**

FOOD & SERVICE / TEXAS RESTAURANT ASSOCIATION (US/0891-0154). [5,000] **2336**

FOOD AUSTRALIA : OFFICIAL JOURNAL OF CAFTA AND AIFST (AT/1032-5298). [3,325] **2336**

FOOD BROKER QUARTERLY (US/0884-7185). [4,000] **2336**

FOOD BUSINESS ANNUAL (US/1057-6959). **2336**

FOOD BUSINESS OPPORTUNITIES (US/1057-6940). **676**

FOOD CONTROL (UK). [1,000] **2336**

FOOD DISTRIBUTION MAGAZINE : FDM (US/1048-8197). [34,000] **2337**

FOOD FOR THOUGHT (VANCOUVER) (CN/0712-2934). [750] **88**

FOOD HISTORY NEWS (US/1067-1951). [500] **2337**

FOOD INDUSTRIES OF SOUTH AFRICA (SA/0015-6450). [3,000] **2337**

FOOD INDUSTRY NEWSLETTER (FAIRFAX, VA.), THE (US/0890-720X). **2337**

FOOD MAGAZINE LONDON. 1988 (UK/0953-5047). [4,000] **2338**

FOOD MANAGEMENT (US/0091-018X). [56,870] **2338**

FOOD MARKETING BRIEFS (US/0896-4203). **2338**

FOOD MERCHANTS ADVOCATE (US/0015-6493). [27,000] **2338**

FOOD PEOPLE AND THEIR COMPANIES (US/0279-9839). [37,856] **2338**

FOOD PLANT EQUIPMENT (US/0887-3895). [48,000] **2339**

FOOD PROCESSING (BROMLEY, LONDON, ENGLAND) (UK/0264-9462). [8,000] **2339**

FOOD PROCESSOR (AT). [3727] **2339**

FOOD PRODUCTION MANAGEMENT (US/0191-6181). [5,200] **2339**

FOOD REVIEW (SA/0257-8867). [3,300] **2339**

FOOD-SERVICE EAST (US/0885-6877). [24,000] **2340**

FOOD TECHNOLOGY IN NEW ZEALAND (NZ/0015-6655). [2,600] **2340**

FOOD TRADE NEWS (US/0015-6663). [23,000] **2340**

FOOD WORLD (COLUMBIA) (US/0191-619X). [23,000] **2340**

FOODLINES (US/0736-0010). [2,000] **5286**

FOODSERVICE & HOSPITALITY (CN/0007-8972). [30,000] **5071**

FOODSERVICE DISTRIBUTOR, THE (US/0896-4505). **2341**

FOODSERVICE EQUIPMENT SPECIALIST. BUYERS GUIDE AND PRODUCT DIRECTORY (US). [20,203] **2341**

FOOKIEN TIMES PHILIPPINES YEARBOOK, THE (PH). [50,000] **2651**

FOOTBALL NEWS (DETROIT) (US/0161-9020). [120,000] **4895**

FOOTHILLS SENTINEL (US/8750-3026). [3,500] **5630**

FOOTLOOSE LIBRARIAN, THE (US/0733-3196). [600] **5474**

FOOTNOTES* (US). [150,000] **385**

FOOTNOTES / STATE LIBRARY COMMISSION OF IOWA (US). [2,000] **3211**

FOOTPRINTS (UK). [9,000] **2448**

FOOTPRINTS (FORT WORTH) (US/0426-8261). [830] **2448**

FOOTWEAR FORUM (CN/0706-7534). [7,500] **1084**

FOOTWEAR NEWS AUSTRALIA (AT/0725-3362). **1084**

FOR PARENTS (US/0277-612X). [4,000] **2280**

FOR THE DEFENSE (MILWAUKEE, WIS.) (US/0015-6884). [28,000] **3089**

FOR THE RECORD (US/0891-2653). [3,000] **2481**

FOR THE RECORD (PORTLAND, OR.) (US). [9,500] **2971**

FOR YOUR INFORMATION (NEW YORK, N. Y.) (US/0890-2992). [25,000] **320**

FORDHAM INTERNATIONAL LAW JOURNAL (US/0747-9395). [450] **3128**

FORDHAM LAW REVIEW (US/0015-704X). [1,300] **2971**

FORDHAM URBAN LAW JOURNAL, THE (US/0199-4646). [1,500] **2971**

FORD'S DECK PLAN GUIDE (US/0096-1353). [5,000] **5474**

FORECASTER (US/0095-294X). **1491**

FOREFRONT CO (US). [2,700] **4959**

FOREIGN LANGUAGE ANNALS (US/0015-718X). [8,000] **3282**

FOREIGN LODGING LIST (US). [600] **2805**

FOREIGN SCOUTING SERVICE. LATIN AMERICA (SZ/0253-0279). **4256**

FOREIGN SERVICE JOURNAL (US/0146-3543). [9,700] **4522**

FOREIGN TAX LAW BI-WEEKLY BULLETIN (US/0095-7291). [5,000] **3128**

FORESIGHT (EDMONTON) (CN/0711-3927). [50,000] **5179**

FORESKRIFTER OM STATLIG TJANSTEPENSIONERING / STATENS ARBETSGIVARVERK (SW/0348-1115). **1675**

FOREST AND BIRD (NZ). [27,000] **4165**

FOREST FARMER (US/0015-7406). [5,300] **2379**

FOREST HILL VILLAGER (CN/0715-464X). **5784**

FOREST LOG (SALEM) (US/0015-7449). [5,000] **2380**

FOREST MANAGEMENT UPDATE (US). [2,600] **2380**

FOREST NOTES (US/0015-7457). [10,000] **2380**

FOREST PLANNING-CANADA (CN/0832-1655). [1,100] **2380**

FOREST RESEARCH IN THE SOUTHEAST (US/0748-1586). [5,000] **2381**

FOREST RESEARCH INFORMATION PAPER (CN/0319-9118). [1,000] **2381**

FOREST STATISTICS FOR IOWA (US/0146-4159). [4,000] **2399**

FORESTRY ON THE HILL (CN/1185-9598). [150] **2382**

FORESTS AND PEOPLE (US/0015-7589). [7,000] **2382**

FORKTAIL (UK/0950-1746). [800] **5617**

FORM (SW/0015-766X). [7,000] **2900**

FORM & FUNCTION (US/0015-7686). [135,000] **615**

FORM FUNCTION FINLAND (FI/0358-8904). [5,000] **2098**

FORMAT (ANN ARBOR, MICH.) (US/1053-1742). [20,000] **1209**

FORME E LA STORIA, LE (IT). [1,000] **3388**

FORMULA (IT). **4474**

FORMULARIO TRIBUTARIO ADEMPIMENTI E RICORSI (IT). [3,000] **2972**

FORNERI, IL (CN/0713-0627). [500] **3282**

FORO DEL JURISTA (CK/0121-0335). [1,000] **2972**

FORSCHUNGSDOKUMENTATION RAUMORDNUNG, STADEBAU, WOHNUNGSWESEN (GW). [200] **2823**

FORSCHUNGSPOLITISCHE ZIELVORSTELLUNGEN (SZ). [4,000] **5106**

FORSCHUNGSPROJEKTE SOZIALISATION UND SOZIALPAEDAGOGIK (GW). [700] **1879**

FORSCHUNGSVORHABEN / ZENTRALSTELLE FUER AGRARDOKUMENTATION UND -INFORMATION (GW/0939-7701). [1,200] **88**

FORSYTH COUNTY GENEALOGICAL SOCIETY JOURNAL, THE (US/0741-8159). [200] **2448**

FORT BRAGG ADVOCATE-NEWS (US/0886-8840). [15,400] **5635**

FORT FRANCES TIMES (CN). **5784**

FORT INDUSTRY REFLECTIONS (US/0749-8381). [250] **2448**

FORT MCMURRAY TODAY (CN/0316-7542). [8,300] **5784**

FORT WORTH (US/0015-8089). [8,000] **2533**

FORTSCHRITTE DER MEDIZIN (GW/0015-8178). [40,000] **3577**

FORTSCHRITTLICHE LANDWIRT, DER (AU). [35,000] **88**

FORTUNE NEWS (US/0015-8275). [35,000] **3164**

FORUM (US/1042-6817). [2,500] **4838**

FORUM (BONNER, MONT.) (US/0883-4970). [700] **5016**

FORUM DER LETTEREN (NE/0015-8496). [800] **3388**

FORUM (DON MILLS) (CN/0380-3147). [18,500] **2881**

FORUM FOR COMMERCE AND INDUSTRY (UK). [3,000] **836**

FORUM FOR EKONOMI OCH TEKNIK (FI/0533-070X). [12,841] **5106**

FORUM FOR MODERN LANGUAGE STUDIES (UK/0015-8518). [450] **3282**

FORUM - FORUM FOR YOUNG CANADIANS (CN/0826-1458). **4474**

FORUM HOMOSEXUALITAT UND LITERATUR (GW/0931-4091). **3388**

FORUM ITALICUM (US/0014-5858). [1200] **3388**

FORUM (NORTH HOLLYWOOD) (US/0164-6931). [2,700] **3107**

FORUM OF EDUCATION, THE (AT/0015-8542). [350] **1824**

FORUM (ONTARIO CONFEDERATION OF UNIVERSITY FACULTY ASSOCIATIONS) (CN/0225-6096). **1825**

FORUM (REGINA, SASK.) (CN/0831-3016). [200] **3211**

FORUM (WASHINGTON, D.C.), THE (US/0015-8305). [4,000] **2972**

FOSTERLETTER (CN/0701-3418). [600] **2280**

FOTO MAGAZIN (GW/0340-6660). [134,000] **4369**

FOTOHANDEL (NE). [3,500] **4369**

FOTOINTERPRETACJA W GEOGRAFII (PL/0071-8076). [300] **2561**

FOTON FAKUTORI NYUSU (JA/0288-691X). [1,700] **1944**

FOUNDATION NEWS (US/0015-8976). [13,000] **4336**

FOUNDATION ONE (US/0272-5622). [5,000] **4776**

FOUR CORNERS ADVISOR, THE (US/0162-6647). **1491**

FOUR-TOWN JOURNAL (CN/0712-6387). [1,900] **5784**

FOURNEE, LA (CN/0015-9158). [4,500] **2341**

FOURRAGES (FR). [1,200] **201**

FOURTH QUARTER AND ANNUAL REPORT ON THE TEXAS BOVINE BRUCELLOSIS PROGRAM / TEXAS ANIMAL HEALTH COMMISSION, AUSTIN TEXAS (US/0748-7754). [50] **211**

FOX VALLEY LIVING (US/1047-3963). [25,000] **2487**

FOXFIRE (US/0015-9220). [2,000] **3388**

FRA FYSIKKENS VERDEN (NO/0015-9247). [1,400] **4403**

FRACASTORO, IL (IT/0015-9271). [2,000] **3577**

FRAME NEWS (UK/0268-4306). [2,265] **226**

FRAMERS FORUM (US). **1185**

FRANCE COMPOSITES (FR/0985-0503). **2102**

FRANCE ITALIE (FR/1146-0024). [16,000] **4474**

FRANCHISE LEGAL DIGEST (US/0739-8239). [1,000] **3100**

FRANCHISING WORLD (US/1041-7311). [50,000] **677**

FRANCISCAN, THE (UK). [5,000] **5029**

FRANCISCANUM (CK/0120-1468). [1,000] **4347**

FRANCOFONIA (IT). [184] **3389**

FRANKFURTER FORSCHUNGEN ZUR KUNST (GW). [800] **350**

FRANKLIN COUNTY HISTORICAL REVIEW, THE (US/0046-4651). **2734**

FRANSE NEDERLANDEN: JAARBOEK. LES PAYS-BAS FRANCAIS: ANNALES, DE (BE). [2,000] **2688**

FRATERNAL HERALD (US/0006-9256). [24,000] **5231**

FRATERNITY NEWS - FRATERNITY FOR CANADIAN ASTROLOGERS (CN/0710-510X). [500] **390**

FRB SF WEEKLY LETTER (US/0890-927X). [25,000] **1492**

FREDDO (IT/0016-0296). [2,250] **2605**

FREE CHINA JOURNAL, THE (CH). [25,000] **5798**

FREE CHURCH CHRONICLE (UK/0016-0326). [2,000] **4960**

FREE-FALL (BANFF, ALTA.) (CN/0714-4172). **3389**

FREE INQUIRY (BUFFALO) (US/0272-0701). [20,000] **4347**

FREE MATERIALS FOR SCHOOLS AND LIBRARIES (US/0836-0073). [3,000] **1895**

FREE PRESS (US). [26,000] **5696**

FREE PRESS (SPARWOOD) (CN/0715-5131). [4,000] **5784**

FREE PRESS STANDARD, THE (US). [8,500] **5728**

FREE TRADE LAW REPORTER (CN). [1,000] **2972**

FREEBIES (SANTA MONICA) (US/0148-2092). [450,000] **1297**

FREEDOM MAGAZINE (US). [100,000] **2533**

FREEDOM OF INFORMATION SERVICE (CN). **2972**

FREEDOM SOCIALIST, THE (US/0272-4367). [5,000] **4542**

FREEDOM TO READ FOUNDATION NEWS (US/0046-5038). [1,700] **3211**

FREELANCE (REGINA) (CN/0705-1379). [600] **3389**

FREEMAN (IRVINGTON-ON-HUDSON, N.Y.), THE (US/0016-0652). [35,000] **1592**

FREETHOUGHT TODAY (US/0882-8512). [3,500] **4960**

FREIBURGER ZEITSCHRIFT FUER PHILOSOPHIE UND THEOLOGIE (SZ/0016-0725). [500] **4347**

FREIGHT MANAGEMENT (UK/0016-0873). [9,842] **5383**

FREIGHT NEWS EXPRESS (UK). [14,800] **5383**

FREIGHTER TRAVEL NEWS (US/0016-089X). [3,000] **837**

FREMONT COUNTY NOSTALGIA NEWS (US/8756-8446). [65] **2449**

FREMONTIA (SACRAMENTO, CALIF.) (US/0092-1793). [9,000] **511**

FRENCH COMPANY HANDBOOK (FR). [15,000] **677**

FRENCH FORUM (US/0098-9355). [600] **3343**

FRENCH REVIEW, THE (US/0016-111X). [10,000 individuals)1,200 (library)] **3283**

FRENCH STUDIES (UK/0016-1128). [2,000] **3343**

FRESHWATER (CN/0834-4302). [500] **4176**

FRESHWATER FISHING AUSTRALIA (AT/1032-125X). [25,000] **2304**

FRESNO PAST AND PRESENT (US/0429-7164). [1,500] **2734**

FRIDAY CITIZEN, THE (CN/0711-4451). **5784**

FRIDAY TIMES (CN/0707-543X). **5785**

FRIENDLY EXCHANGE (US/0279-6856). [4,000,000] **5474**

FRIENDLY WORD, THE (IE/0790-3642). [500] **5060**

FRIENDS (HALIFAX) (CN/0821-638X). [4,100] **5286**

FRIENDS OF FLORIDA FOLK (US/0892-2500). [400] **2320**

FRIENDS' QUARTERLY (US). [600] **4088**

FRIENDS WORLD NEWS : NEWS BULLETIN OF THE FRIENDS WORLD COMMITTEE FOR CONSULTATION (UK/0016-1365). **4960**

FRIENDSHIP FORUM (CN/0709-6259). **5286**

FRISKO (US). [35,000] **2533**

FROM THE GYM TO THE JURY (US/1054-1950). **2972**

FRONT LINE SUPERVISOR'S BULLETIN (US). **941**

FRONTIER MILITARY SERIES (US/0071-9641). [1,000] **4044**

FRONTIER NURSING SERVICE QUARTERLY BULLETIN (US/0016-2116). [6,200] **3856**

FRONTIERS (BOULDER) (US/0160-9009). [1,000] **5557**

FRONTLINE DUNEDIN (NZ/0113-1990). [1,200] **3724**

FROSTPROOF NEWS, THE (US). [2,000] **5649**

FROZEN FISHERY PRODUCTS (US/0364-0604). [1,500] **2304**

FROZEN FOOD DIGEST (US/0889-5902). [16,000] **2341**

FROZEN FOOD EXECUTIVE, THE (US/0279-1498). [4,000] **2341**

FROZEN FOOD MANAGEMENT (UK). **2341**

FROZEN FOOD PACK STATISTICS (US/0469-7405). [1,000] **2362**

FROZEN FOOD REPORT (US/0192-0367). [3,500] **2342**

FRUIT AND TROPICAL PRODUCTS (UK/0142-1883). [750] **172**

FRUIT AND VEGETABLE TRUCK RATE REPORT / UNITED STATES DEPARTMENT OF AGRICULTURE, AGRICULTURAL MARKETING SERVICE, FRUIT AND VEGETABLE MARKET NEWS SERVICE (US). **837**

FRUIT BELGE, LE (BE/0016-2248). [1,500] **2415**

FRUIT GROWER MAIDSTONE (UK/0953-2188). [3,000] **172**

FRUIT, TASMANIA (AT). **1607**

FRUIT VARIETIES JOURNAL (US/0091-3642). [1,000] **2415**

FRUITS & LEGUMES (FR/0754-0698). [7,500] **2342**

FUEL CONSUMPTION GUIDE (CN/0225-9214). [600,000] **5415**

FUEL OIL NEWS (US/0016-2396). [17,500] **4256**

FUJI JIHO (JA/0367-3332). **2055**

FULD & COMPANY LETTER, THE (US/1054-9986). [6,000] **1635**

FULL-COURT PRESS, THE (US/0892-5364). **5696**

FULL SPECTRUM. CD-ROM (US). **1233**

FULTON COUNTY NEWS (MCCONNELLSBURG, PA.) (US). [6,400] **5736**

FULTON-HICKMAN GENEALOGICAL JOURNAL (US/1065-0164). **2449**

FUNCTIONAL ORTHODONTIST, THE (US/8756-3150). [7,000] **1324**

FUNCTIONS (CN/0821-2708). **3506**

FUND OG FORSKNING I DET KONGELIGE BIBLIOTEKS SAMLINGER (DK/0069-9896). [500] **3211**

FUND RAISING MANAGEMENT (US/0016-268X). [11,000] **868**

FUNDAMENTA

FUNDAMENTA MATHEMATICAE (PL/0016-2736). [2,000] **3506**

FUNDAMENTAL & CLINICAL PHARMACOLOGY (FR/0767-3981). [3,000] **4305**

FUNGICIDE AND NEMATICIDE TESTS (US/0148-9038). [1,600] **172**

FUNKSCHAU (GW/0016-2841). [75,000] **2055**

FUNPARKS DIRECTORY (US/0147-5606). [6,140] **4861**

FUNWORLD (US/0892-3752). [7,900] **4861**

FUREGURANSU JANARU : FJ / FRAGRANCE JOURNAL (JA). [7,000] **1025**

FURNITURE HISTORY (UK/0016-3058). [1,350] **2905**

FURNITURE WORLD (NEW YORK, N.Y.) (US/0738-890X). [20,000] **2906**

FUTURA (IE/0016-3252). **1084**

FUTURE HEALTH (CN/0225-395X). [2,000] **3577**

FUTURE (NEW DELHI, INDIA) (II/0252-1873). [10,000] **2280**

FUTURE SURVEY ANNUAL (US/0273-0138). [2,500] **5107**

FUTURES AND OPTIONS WORLD (UK/0953-6620). [8,000] **924**

FUTURIBLERNE (DK). [400] **5107**

FUTURIBLES (PARIS) (FR/0337-307X). [3,000] **5246**

FUTURIST, THE (US/0016-3317). [25,000] **5107**

G.A.S. LITES (US/0882-8377). [450] **2449**

G.H.S. FOOT-NOTES (US/0090-4368). [2,500] **2734**

GABONAIPAR (HU/0133-0918). **201**

GACETA ARQUEOLOGICA ANDINA (PE/0254-8240). [2,000] **268**

GACETA (MEXICO CITY, MEXICO : 1954) (MX/0185-3716). [10,000] **5231**

GACETA POETICA : REVISTA TRIMESTRAL DE POESIA (SP). [2,000] **3463**

GAELIC GLEANINGS (US/0882-2166). [1,000] **2449**

GAHPERD JOURNAL (US). [1,000] **1855**

GALAKSIJA (YU/0350-123X). [50,000] **5107**

GALAXIA 71 [I.E. SETENTA Y UNO] (VE). [5,000] **320**

GALLATIN TRAILS (US/0883-1920). [300] **2449**

GALLAUDET TODAY (US/0016-4089). **1879**

GALLERIES (UK/0265-7511). [18,000] **4088**

GALLERIES (WASHINGTON, D.C.) (US/0739-0475). [6,000] **4088**

GALLERY (LETHBRIDGE) (CN/0826-1121). **351**

GALLERY OF FINE HOME PLANS (US/0899-4404). **299**

GALLUP POLITICAL & ECONOMIC INDEX (UK). [1,000] **4474**

GALVANOTECNICA & NUOVE FINITURE (IT/1120-6454). **487**

GALVESTON DAILY NEWS (HOUSTON, TEX.: 1865) (US/0738-8047). [28,184] **5750**

GAM ON YACHTING (CN/0016-4259). [22,300] **593**

GAMC NEWS (US/0743-7307). [7,800] **868**

GAMECOCK, THE (US/0016-4313). [16,000] **211**

GAMUT (TORONTO) (CN/0713-3545). [2,500] **321**

GANITA (II/0046-5402). [500] **3506**

GARCIA DE ORTA : SERIE DE ANTROPOBIOLOGIA : REVISTA DA JUNTA DE INVESTIGACOES CIENTIFICAS DO ULTRAMAR (PO). [1,000] **237**

GARCIA DE ORTA : SERIE DE BOTANICA (PO/0379-9506). [1,000] **511**

GARCIA DE ORTA : SERIE DE ESTUDOS AGRONOMICOS (PO/0378-8032). [1,000] **89**

GARCIA DE ORTA : SERIE DE GEOGRAFIA (PO). [1,000] **2561**

GARCIA DE ORTA : SERIE DE GEOLOGIA (PO/0378-1240). [1,000] **1376**

GARCIA DE ORTA : SERIE DE ZOOLOGIA (PO/0253-0597). [1,000] **5584**

GARDEN CENTER BULLETIN, THE (US/0892-564X). [4,000] **2415**

GARDEN CITY OBSERVER (US). [8,800] **5692**

GARDEN CLIPPINGS (CN/0318-7705). [2,300] **2415**

GARDEN HISTORY (UK/0307-1243). [2,000] **2415**

GARDEN STATE REPORT (US/8756-6605). [10,500] **4650**

GARDENIA (IT/0393-585X). [95,000] **2415**

GARDENING NEWS (AT). [250] **2416**

GARDENS' BULLETIN, SINGAPORE, THE (SI/0374-7859). [300] **89**

GARFIELD-MAPLE HEIGHTS SUN (US/0746-2611). [10,579] **5728**

GARMENT MANUFACTURERS INDEX (US/1065-1330). **1084**

GARTENBAU- UND FELDGEMUSE-ANBAUERHEBUNG / BEARBEITET IM OSTERREICHISCHEN STATISTISCHEN ZENTRALAMT (AU). [350] **2434**

GARTENPRAXIS (GW/0341-2105). [14,296 each month] **2416**

GAS ENGINE MAGAZINE (US/0435-1304). [22,000] **250**

GAS INDUSTRIES (1978) (US/0194-2468). [10,000] **4257**

GAS MATTERS (UK/0964-8496). **4257**

GAS TURBINE WORLD (1984) (US/0747-7988). **2114**

GAS TURBINE WORLD HANDBOOK (US/0883-458X). **2114**

GAS WORLD (LONDON, ENGLAND : 1974) (UK/0308-7654). [3,000] **4258**

GASETA MUNICIPAL (SP). [2,000] **4650**

GASKELL SOCIETY JOURNAL, THE (UK/0951-7200). [3,50] **3389**

GASPESIE (GASPE. 1979) (CN/0227-1370). [1,000] **2734**

GASTECH : PREPRINTS OF CONFERENCE PAPERS / THE ... INTERNATIONAL LNG/LPG CONFERENCE & EXHIBITION ; ORGANISED BY GASTECH LTD (UK). **4258**

GASTROENTEROLOGY & ENDOSCOPY NEWS (US/0883-8348). [6,000] **3745**

GASTROPODIA (US/0435-1363). [53] **5584**

GASTRUM (SP/0211-058X). [3,000] **3746**

GATEWAY HERITAGE (US/0198-9375). [4,400] **2734**

GATEWAY: THE JOURNAL OF THE BELL COUNTY HISTORICAL SOCIETY (US). [150] **2734**

GATFWORLD (PITTSBURGH, PA.) (US/1048-0293). [9,500] **378**

GATO TUERTO, EL (US/8755-3651). [3,000] **3390**

GAUHATI LAW REPORTS (II). [2,000] **2973**

GAYANA : ZOOLOGIA (CL/0016-531X). **5584**

GAZDASAG (HU/0016-5360). [8,000] **1492**

GAZETA OBSERWATORA (PL). [4,000] **1425**

GAZETTE - CANADIAN FORCES BASE GAGETOWN (1981) (CN/0713-391X). [6,000] **4044**

GAZETTE DE L'HOTEL DROUOT, LA (FR). **321**

GAZETTE DU C. L. S. C, LA (CN/0227-1206). **5785**

GAZETTE LEADER (US). [15,000] **5710**

GAZETTE (NEW YORK. 1979), THE (US/0193-533X). [250] **3390**

GAZETTE OF LAW AND JOURNALISM (AT/0818-0148). **2973**

GAZETTE OF THE AMERICAN FRIENDS OF LAFAYETTE (US). [200] **2689**

GAZETTE, THE (US). **5728**

GC/MS UPDATE. PART A ENVIRONMENTAL (UK/0962-9327). **2172**

GDG REPORT, THE (US/0883-3087). [1,000] **3165**

GDI IMPULS (SZ). **5200**

GDR BULLETIN: NEWSLETTER FOR LITERATURE AND CULTURE IN THE GERMAN DEMOCRATIC REPUBLIC (US). [350] **3283**

GE RI CO NEWS : BOLLETINO DI INFORMAZIONE E INNOVAZIONE RICERCA TECNOLOGICA (IT). [1,200] **5107**

GEAR TECHNOLOGY (US/0743-6858). [1,500] **2114**

GEC JOURNAL OF RESEARCH (UK/0264-9187). [8,000] **1976**

GEC REVIEW (UK/0267-9337). [12,000] **2055**

GEGENWARTSKUNDE (GW/0016-5875). [4,000] **5200**

GEIST UND LEBEN (WURZBURG) (GW/0016-5921). [4,000] **3390**

GEIST (VANCOUVER) (CN/1181-6554). [13,000] **3390**

GEITEHOUDER, DE (NE). [2,100] **211**

GEKA TO TAISHA, EIYO (JA/0389-5564). **3965**

GEKKAN HAIKIBUTSU (JA/0285-6220). [150,000] **2230**

GELBVIEH EYEOPENER (CN/0703-8356). **211**

GEMATOLOGIYA I TRANSFUZIOLOGIYA (RU). [4,500] **3771**

GEMEINDEDATEN (GW). **5327**

GEMEINDEUBERSICHT (AU). [230] **4553**

GEMS & GEMOLOGY (GEMOLOGICAL INSTITUTE OF AMERICA : 1967) (US/0016-626X). [10,000] **1439**

GEMS OF POETRY AND PROSE (CN/0834-1737). [1,000] **3390**

GEMSTONE PRICE REPORT (BE). **2914**

GENDERS (AUSTIN, TEX.) (US/0894-9832). [700] **2846**

GENE (NE/0378-1119). [1,352] **545**

GENEALOGICAL CLEARINGHOUSE QUARTERLY, THE (US/0882-0422). [200] **2449**

GENEALOGICAL COMPUTER PIONEER (US/0735-0287). [3,000] **2449**

GENEALOGICAL GOLDMINE (US/0738-3770). [300] **2450**

GENEALOGICAL JOURNAL (LEXINGTON, N.C.), THE (US/0731-9606). [300] **2450**

GENEALOGICAL MAGAZINE OF NEW JERSEY, THE (US/0016-6367). [900] **2450**

GENEALOGICAL RECORD (HOUSTON, TEX.), THE (US/0433-3209). [1,000] **2450**

GENEALOGICAL TIPS (US/0433-3233). [230] **2450**

GENEALOGIES BOURBONNAISES ET DU CENTRE / CERCLE GENEALOGIQUE ET HERALDIQUE DU BOURBONNAIS (FR/0223-7237). **2450**

GENEALOGIST (MANCHESTER, N.H.), THE (US/0196-4259). [1,500] **2450**

GENEALOGIST MELBOURNE (AT). [2,500] **2450**

GENEALOGIST (NEW YORK), THE (US/0197-1468). [500] **2450**

GENERAL AVIATION NEWS (US/0191-927X). [80,000] **22**

GENERAL PRACTITIONER (UK/0046-5607). [39,766] **3737**

GENERAL RULES AND RULES OF PRACTICE (US). [1,000] **4259**

GENERAL SCIENCE INDEX (US/0162-1963). **5175**

GENERAL SCIENCE INDEX. CD-ROM (US/0162-1963). **5107**

GENERAL TECHNICAL REPORT INT (US/0748-1209). **2383**

GENERAL TECHNICAL REPORT NC (US). **2383**

GENERATIONAL JOURNAL, THE (US/0898-5928). **5246**

GENERATIONS (BALTIMORE) (US/0191-6939). [2,000] **5047**

GENERATIONS (FREDERICTON) (CN/0821-5359). [1,000] **2450**

GENERATIONS (SAN FRANCISCO, CALIF.) (US/0738-7806). [12,000] **5179**

GENERATIONS (WINNIPEG) (CN/0226-6105). [800] **2451**

GENESIS 2 (US/0016-6669). [2,500] **5047**

GENESIS (WASHINGTON, D.C.) (US/0744-0596). [6,200] **3761**

GENETIC ENGINEERING LETTER (US/0276-1882). **545**

GENETIKA I SELEKTSIYA (BU/0016-6766). [930] **2416**

GENIE BUG (US/0739-6090). [250] **2451**

GENOME (CN/0831-2796). [1,800] **546**

GENRE (NORMAN, OKLA.) (US/0016-6928). [800] **3343**

GEO INFO SYSTEMS (US/1051-9858). **2561**

GEO-KATALOG (GW). [2,000] **5478**

GEO PLEIN-AIR (CN/1194-5303). [25,000] **4896**

GEOBIOS (JODHPUR) (II/0251-1223). [500] **456**

GEOBIOS NEW REPORTS (II). [300] **456**

GEOBYTE (US/0885-6362). [5,000] **2139**

GEOCHRONIQUE (FR/0292-8477). [4,000] **1376**

GEODEZIA ES KARTOGRAFIA (HU/0016-7118). [1,000] **2581**

GEOFISICA INTERNACIONAL : REVISTA DE LA UNION GEOFISICA MEXICANA AUSPICIADA POR EL INSTITUTO DE GEOFISICA DE LA UNIVERSIDAD NACIONAL AUTONOMA DE MEXICO (MX/0016-7169). [1,200] **4404**

GEOFIZICHESKII ZHURNAL (UN/0203-3100). [1,075] **1405**

GEOFIZIKA ZAGREB (CI/0352-3659). [350] **1405**

GEOGRAFIA (BL). [1,000] **2561**

GEOGRAFICKY CASOPIS. GEOGRAFICHESKII ZHURNAL. GEOGRAPHICAL REVIEW. GEOGRAPHISCHE ZEITSCHRIFT. REVUE DE GEOGRAPHIE (XO/0016-7193). [1,000] **2562**

GEOGRAFISKA ANNALER. SERIES A, PHYSICAL GEOGRAPHY (SW/0435-3676). [1,000] **2562**

GEOGRAFISKA ANNALER. SERIES B, HUMAN GEOGRAPHY (NO/0435-3684). [900] **2823**

GEOGRAPHIA (PL). [300] **2562**

GEOGRAPHIA MEDICA (BUDAPEST) (HU/0300-807X). [450] **3735**

GEOGRAPHICA (FI). [500] **2562**

GEOGRAPHICAL BULLETIN (YPSILANTI, MICH.), THE (US/0731-3292). [1,500] **2563**

GEOGRAPHICAL JOURNAL, THE (UK/0016-7398). [10,600] **2563**

GEOGRAPHICAL PERSPECTIVES (US/0199-994X). [300] **2563**

GEOGRAPHICAL REVIEW (US/0016-7428). [3,000] **2563**

GEOGRAPHICAL REVIEW OF INDIA (II). [700] **2563**

GEOGRAPHICAL : THE MONTHLY MAGAZINE OF THE ROYAL GEOGRAPHICAL SOCIETY (UK). [10,600] **2563**

GEOGRAPHIE PHYSIQUE ET QUATERNAIRE (CN/0705-7199). [700] **2563**

GEOGRAPHISCHE RUNDSCHAU (GW/0016-7460). [20,000] **2564**

GEOGRAPHY (UK/0016-7487). [6,000] **2564**

GEOGRAPHY RESEARCH FORUM (US/0333-5275). [300] **2564**

GEOLIT (GW). **2564**

GEOLOGICA BAVARICA (GW/0016-755X). [800] **1377**

GEOLOGICA ET PALAEONTOLOGICA (GW/0072-1018). **1377**

GEOLOGICAL CONTRIBUTIONS / ABILENE GEOLOGICAL SOCIETY (US). [450] **1377**

GEOLOGICAL NEWSLETTER (PORTLAND) (US/0270-5451). [250] **1378**

GEOLOGICAL SOCIETY OF AMERICA BULLETIN (US/0016-7606). [15,000] **1378**

GEOLOGICAL SURVEY OF WYOMING, EDUCATIONAL SERIES (US). **1355**

GEOLOGIE EN MIJNBOUW (NE/0016-7746). [24,000] **1379**

GEOLOGIE MEDITARRANEENNE (FR/0397-2844). **1379**

GEOLOGISCHES JAHRBUCH HESSEN (GW/0341-4027). [7,000] **1379**

GEOMETRIC AND FUNCTIONAL ANALYSIS : GAFA (SZ/1016-443X). [400] **3507**

GEOPHYSICAL DIRECTORY, THE (US). [5,000] **1405**

GEOPHYSICAL RESEARCH LETTERS (US/0094-8276). **1406**

GEOPHYSICS (US/0016-8033). [18,800] **1406**

GEOPOLITIQUE (FR/0752-1693). [20,000] **4522**

GEORGE HERBERT JOURNAL (US/0161-7435). [450] **3390**

GEORGE ODIORNE LETTER, THE (US/0890-0914). [1,500] **868**

GEORGE SAND STUDIES (US/0897-0483). [500] **3343**

GEORGE WASHINGTON LAW REVIEW, THE (US/0016-8076). [2,500] **2973**

GEORGE WRIGHT FORUM, THE (US/0732-4715). [1,200] **2194**

GEORGETOWN INDEPENDENT (CN/0834-6518). [11,750] **5785**

GEORGETOWN MEDICAL BULLETIN (US/0016-8106). [9,000] **3780**

GEORGETOWN (WASHINGTON, D.C. : 1987) (US/0895-1624). [85,000] **1091**

GEORGETOWNER, THE (US/0730-9082). [25,000] **2534**

GEORGIA ALERT; A LOOK AT EDUCATION'S ROLE TODAY (US). [13,000] **1748**

GEORGIA ALUMNI RECORD (US/0016-8130). [18,000] **1102**

GEORGIA ANCHORAGE (US/0016-8149). [13,000] **5449**

GEORGIA BUSINESS AND ECONOMIC CONDITIONS (US/0279-3857). [5,000] **677**

GEORGIA COUNTY GOVERNMENT (US/1066-0119). **4650**

GEORGIA ECONOMIC OUTLOOK (US/0884-1179). [1,000] **1492**

GEORGIA FORESTRY / [GEORGIA FORESTRY COMMISSION] (US). **2383**

GEORGIA GENEALOGICAL MAGAZINE (US/0435-5393). [850] **2451**

GEORGIA HISTORICAL QUARTERLY, THE (US/0016-8297). [2,200] **2734**

GEORGIA LIBRARIAN, THE (US/0016-8319). [1,200] **3212**

GEORGIA LIVING (US/1049-6432). [15,000] **2488**

GEORGIA MUSIC NEWS (US/0046-5798). [2,400] **4119**

GEORGIA NURSING (US/0016-8335). [3,500] **3856**

GEORGIA OFFICIAL AND STATISTICAL REGISTER (US/1070-7816). [1,800] **4650**

GEORGIA PTA TODAY (US/1064-6159). **1748**

GEORGIA REVIEW, THE (US/0016-8386). [5,300] **3390**

GEORGIA STATE BAR JOURNAL (US/0016-8416). [23,500] **2974**

GEORGIA STATE BAR NEWS (US). [19,600] **2974**

GEORGIA STATE UNIVERSITY FACT BOOK (US/0098-3071). [1,100] **1825**

GEORGIA STATE UNIVERSITY LAW REVIEW (US/8755-6847). [500] **2974**

GEORGIA STATISTICAL ABSTRACT (US/0085-1043). [800] **5328**

GEORGIA VETERINARIAN, THE (US/0886-5760). [2,000] **5510**

GEORGIA WILDLIFE (US/0164-8608). [10,000] **2194**

GEORGIAN ANNUAL (US). **4241**

GEOSCOPE (OTTAWA) (CN/0046-581X). **2564**

GEOSUR / [ASOCIACION SUDAMERICANA DE ESTUDIOS GEOPOLITICOS E INTERNACIONALES] (UY). [3,000] **4522**

GEOTECHNICAL ENGINEERING (TH/0046-5828). **2023**

GEOTECHNICAL FABRICS REPORT (US/0882-4983). [12,000] **5351**

GEOTECHNICAL NEWS (CN/0823-650X). [6,500] **1381**

GEOTECHNIK (GW/0172-6145). [2,300] **2023**

GEOTECTONICS (US/0016-8521). **1381**

GEOTHERMAL REPORT (US/0733-9100). [120] **1945**

GEOTIMES (US/0016-8556). [12,500] **1381**

GERALDTON-LONGLAC TIMES STAR (CN/0834-6275). [1,900] **5785**

GERANIUMS AROUND THE WORLD (US/0016-8599). [1,000] **2416**

GERFAUT, LE (BE/0251-1193). [700] **5617**

GERIATRIC CARE (US). [1,000] **3751**

GERIATRICS (US/0016-867X). [55,525] **3751**

GERIATRICS ED. ITALIANA (IT/0392-9663). [70,000] **3751**

GERMAN CONNECTION, THE (US/8755-1756). [600] **2451**

GERMAN ENGRAVINGS ETCHINGS AND WOODCUTS (NE). [600] **351**

GERMAN QUARTERLY, THE (US/0016-8831). [7,700] **3390**

GERMAN TRIBUNE, THE (GW/0016-8858). [29,000] **2517**

GERMANIA (BERLIN) (GW/0016-8874). **269**

GERMANIC NOTES AND REVIEWS (US). [500] **2846**

GERMANISTISCHE ABHANDLUNGEN (STUTTGART) (GW/0435-5903). **3284**

GERODONTOLOGY (US/0734-0664). [1,000] **3751**

GERONTOLOGIST, THE (US/0016-9013). [10,373] **3751**

GERONTOLOGY SPECIAL INTEREST SECTION NEWSLETTER (US/0279-4101). [4,800] **3752**

GESAMMELTE WERKE GEORG WILHELM FRIEDRICH HEGEL (GW). **4347**

GESAMTKATALOG DER DUSSELDORFER KULTURINSTITUTE (GDK) [MICROFORM] / BIBLIOTHEKSSTELLE DER DUSSELDORFER KULTURINSTITUTE (GW/0178-9775). [150] **351**

GESAMTSCHUL-INFORMATIONEN (GW/0340-7268). **1748**

GESCHAFTSBERICHT DER BUNDESBAHN-VERSICHERUNGSANS TALT (GW). **1676**

GESCHAFTSBERICHT / DEUTSCHE LUFTHANSA AKTIENGESELLSCHAFT (GW). **22**

GESELLSCHAFT UND POLITIK (AU/0016-9099). [1,000] **5201**

GESHER (WORLD JEWISH CONGRESS. ISRAEL EXECUTIVE) (IS/0435-8406). [2,000] **5047**

GESTA (FORT TRYON PARK, N.Y.) (US/0016-920X). [1,000] **351**

GESTION (LAVAL) (CN/0701-0028). [4,300] **868**

GESTIONESCUOLA (IT/0393-5523). **869**

GESTIONS HOSPITALIERES (FR/0016-9218). [3,600] **3780**

GET READY SHEET, THE (US/0148-7566). [1,000] **3212**

GETTING MARRIED (US/0891-1657). [10,000] **2280**

GETTING READY (US/1064-0827). [11,000] **1063**

GETTYSBURG REVIEW (1988) (US/0898-4557). [2,500] **3391**

GEZINSBELEID IN VLAANDEREN (BE). [6,000] **2280**

GFWC CLUBWOMAN (US/0745-2209). [24,000] **5557**

GIANTS NEWSWEEKLY, THE (US/0279-0238). [48,000] **4896**

GIATROS DERMATOLOGIE (GW/0932-8661). [4,000] **3720**

GIATROS HNO (GW/0930-8318). [3,000] **3888**

GIATROSERTHOPAEDIE (GW/0930-8326). [4,000] **3881**

GIATROSGYNAKOLOGIE (GW/0177-9109). [8,200] **3761**

GIATROSPAEDIATRIE (GW/0177-9095). [5,200] **3903**

GIATROSUROLOGIE (GW/0178-7527). [2,700] **3990**

GIDS VOOR HET AANVRAGEN VAN Z. W.O.-STEUN / NEDERLANDSE ORGANISATIE VOOR ZURIVER-WETENSCHAPPELIJK ONDERZOEK (NE). [9,500] **5108**

GIESSEREI (GW/0016-9765). **4003**

GIFTS TODAY (UK). [6,000] **2584**

GILA HERITAGE (US/0893-7753). [81] **2451**

GILBERT & SULLIVAN NEWS (UK/0263-7995). [800] **385**

GILCREASE MAGAZINE OF AMERICAN HISTORY AND ART, THE (US/0730-5036). [4,300] **4088**

GINECOLOGIA Y OBSTETRICIA DE MEXICO (MX/0300-9041). [4,000] **3761**

GIORNALE DELL' INSTALLATORE ELETTRICO, IL (IT/0392-3630). [17,200] **2056**

GIORNALE DELL' OFFICINA (IT/0017-0240). **2115**

GIORNALE DELLA MUSICA, IL (IT/1120-6195). [20,000] **4119**

GIORNALE DELLA SUBFORNITURA, IL (IT/0392-3622). [20,800] **1607**

GIORNALE DELL'ARTE (TURIN, ITALY) (IT/0394-0543). [25,000] **321**

GIORNALE DELL'INGEGNERE, IL (IT). [24,000] **1976**

GIORNALE DELL'INSTALLATORE TELEFONICO, IL (IT/1120-219X). [4,500] **1976**

GIORNALE DI GEOLOGIA (IT/0017-0291). [700] **1381**

GIORNALE DI MALATTIE INFETTIVE E PARASSITARIE (IT/0017-0321). [1,250] **4777**

GIORNALE DI MEDICINA MILITARE (IT/0017-0364). **3578**

GIORNALE ITALIANO DELLE MALATTIE DEL TORACE (IT/0017-0437). [2,000] **3949**

GIORNALE ITALIANO DI ANGIOLOGIA (IT/0392-1387). **3705**

GIORNALE ITALIANO DI FILOLOGIA (IT/0017-0461). [1,000] **3284**

GIORNALE ITALIANO DI ONCOLOGIA (IT/0392-128X). **3817**

GIORNALE ITALIANO DI OSTETRICIA E GINECOLOGIA (IT/0391-9013). **3761**

GIORNALE STORICO DELLA LUNIGIANA (IT/0017-050X). [1,000] **269**

GIORNALE STORICO DI PSICOLOGIA DINAMICA (IT/0391-2515). [1,000] **4588**

GIORNALINO (NEW YORK, N.Y.), IL (US/0434-0299). [1,250] **1748**

GIRL SCOUT LEADER (US/0017-0577). [800,000] **5231**

GIRLS' AND WOMEN'S TAEKWONDO NEWSLETTER, THE (US/0882-5920). **4896**

GIRONALE DEI GIOCATTOLI (IT). [10,000] **2584**

GIST (CAMPO, CALIF.) (US/0732-7781). [2,500] **4347**

GISTER EN VANDAG (SA). [700] **1895**

GLACIOLOGICAL DATA (US/0149-1776). [1,000] **1413**

GLADYS PORTER ZOO NEWS (US). [3,000] **5584**

GLAS OCH PORSLIN (SW/0017-078X). [1,500] **2589**

GLAS UND RAHMEN (GW/0036-3065). **2589**

GLASGOW NATURALIST (UK/0373-241X). [300] **4165**

GLASNIK SLOVENSKEGA ETNOLOSKEGA DRUSTVA (XV/0351-2908). [700] **237**

GLASNIK ZA SUMSKE POKUSE (CI/0352-3861). [1,000] **2384**

GLASS ART SOCIETY PHOTOGRAPHIC DIRECTORY (US/0740-8889). **2589**

GLASS COLLECTOR'S DIGEST (US/0893-8660). **2589**

GLASS FACTORY DIRECTORY (US). [1,000] **2590**

GLASS MAGAZINE (US/0747-4261). [13,000] **2590**

GLASS NEWS (US/0890-3743). [1,650] **2590**

GLASS TECHNOLOGY (UK/0017-1050). [1,700] **2590**

GLAUCOMA (MIAMI) (US/0164-4645). [15,000] **3875**

GLEANER INDEX / NATIONAL LIBRARY OF JAMAICA, THE (JM/0259-0336). **5805**

GLEN RIDGE PAPER (US). **5710**

GLENBOW (EXHIBITIONS AND EVENTS) (CN/0710-3697). [8,000] **4088**

GLENGARRY LIFE (CN/0703-1556). [300] **2734**

GLENWOOD POST (US). [5,200] **5643**

GLIM NEWSLETTER, THE (UK). [400] **5328**

GLOBAL AUTOMOTIVE REVIEW AND OUTLOOK (US/1070-9975). **5415**

GLOBAL COMMUNICATIONS (US/0195-2250). [10,000] **1112**

GLOBAL INVESTMENT TECHNOLOGY (US/1058-3920). [1,800-2,000] **899**

GLOBAL JOURNAL ON CRIME AND CRIMINAL LAW (NE/0928-9313). [1,000] **3165**

GLOBAL PRAYER DIGEST (US/1045-9731). [19,000] **237**

GLOBAL STUDIES PROGRAM NOTES (US/0890-4987). [1,000] **2488**

GLOBE AND LAUREL (UK/0017-1204). **4044**

GLOBEHOPPER (CN/0711-7108). [100,000] **5478**

GLOBOSPORTS (US). [50] **1132**

GLOBULE ROUGE (CN/0712-337X). **1091**

GLOUCESTERSHIRE FAMILY HISTORY SOCIETY JOURNAL (UK/0143-0513). [1,200] **2451**

GLOUCESTERSHIRE RECORD SERIES (UK). [300] **2689**

GLOXINIAN, THE (US/0017-1352). **512**

GMDA BULLETIN (US/0884-6898). [1,100] **1324**

GOAT VETERINARY SOCIETY JOURNAL (UK). [400] **5510**

GODS REVIVALIST AND BIBLE ADVOCATE (US/0745-0788). [21,000] **5016**

GOING DOWN SWINGING (AT/0157-3950). [1,000] **3391**

GOLD BOOK OF MULTI-HOUSING (SOUTH EDITION), THE (US). [500] **615**

GOLD BOOK OF NAVAL AVIATION, THE (US/0884-1128). **22**

GOLD + SILBER, UHREN + SCHMUCK (GW/0017-1573). [10,208] **2914**

GOLDBELT GAZETTE (CN/0849-8288). [2,000] **5785**

GOLDEN BALL GRAPEVINE, THE (US/0887-5898). **2735**

GOLDEN BOUGH, THE (UK). [300] **512**

GOLDEN ROOTS OF THE MOTHER LODE. NEWSLETTER (US/8755-5697). [500] **2451**

GOLDEN ROOTS OF THE MOTHER LODE, THE (US/8755-3023). [225] **2451**

GOLDEN TRANSCRIPT, THE (US/0746-6382). [4,400] **5643**

GOLDENSEAL (US/0099-0159). [32,000] **2320**

GOLDSMITHS REVIEW (UK/0953-0355). [6,000] **2914**

GOLEM NEWSLETTER (IT). **5108**

GOLF COURSE MANAGEMENT (US/0192-3048). [28,400] **4896**

GOLF JOURNAL (US/0017-1794). [140,000] **4896**

GOLF NEWS MAGAZINE (US). **4896**

GOLF PRO (US/1072-1274). [12,000] **4897**

GOLF TRAVELER, THE (US/0191-717X). [70,000] **4897**

GOLF WORLD (UK/0017-1883). [80,000] **4897**

GOLFSHOP OPERATIONS (US/0017-1824). [15,200] **924**

GOLFWEEK (US/0890-3514). [35,000] **4897**

GOLOS INSTYTUTU (CN/0318-0042). [1,900] **2262**

GONZAGA LAW REVIEW (US/0046-6115). [1,000] **2975**

GOOD BEGINNINGS NEWSLETTER (CN/0712-5038). **1748**

GOOD NEWS FROM NARAMATA CENTRE (CN/0229-091X). [12,000] **4961**

GOOD-NEWS-LETTER (CN/0713-3677). [6,000] **4961**

GOOD NEWS LETTER (WASHINGTON, D.C.), THE (US/0738-6419). [1,600] **5030**

GOOD NEWS OF TOMORROW'S WORLD (US/0093-5026). [1,000,000] **4961**

GOOD PACKAGING MAGAZINE (US/1049-3158). [9700] **4219**

GOOD TIMES (GREENVILLE, N.Y.) (US/0191-4995). [25,000] **2534**

GOODWIN NEWS, THE (US/0892-1423). [250] **2451**

GORDON JOURNAL (US). **5706**

GORE-BROWNE ON COMPANIES (UK). [1,500] **2975**

GOSEI GOMU (JA). **5075**

GOSPEL STANDARD (UK/0017-2367). [2,500] **4961**

GOSPEL TIDINGS (OMAHA, NEB.) (US/0745-7618). [2,400] **5060**

GOSPEL VOICE (US). [10,000] **4119**

GOSPEL WITNESS (TORONTO. 196?) (CN/0828-1769). [1,800] **4961**

GOTTINGISCHE GELEHRTE ANZEIGEN (GW/0017-1549). **2847**

GOUE VAG (SA). [32,244] **211**

GOULD LEAGUER, THE (AT). [70,000] **2172**

GOURD, THE (US/0888-5672). [4,000] **90**

GOURGUES REPORT, THE (US/0743-5185). [750] **900**

GOURMET'S NOTEBOOK, A (US/0279-8247). **2342**

GOVERNING (WASHINGTON, D.C.) (US/0894-3842). [85,000] **4475**

GOVERNMENT BUSINESS WORLD REPORT (US/0017-2588). **678**

GOVERNMENT CONTRACTOR, THE (US/0017-2596). **4651**

GOVERNMENT DIRECTORY FOR BRITISH COLUMBIA WITH SELECTED FEDERAL CONTACTS (CN/0822-8620). **4651**

GOVERNMENT EXECUTIVE (US/0017-2626). [76,000] **4651**

GOVERNMENT GAZETTE OF MAURITIUS, THE (MF). [1,300] **4651**

GOVERNMENT IMAGING (US). [35,000] **4651**

GOVERNMENT MICROCOMPUTER LETTER (US/0882-6587). [3,500] **1267**

GOVERNMENT PRODUCT NEWS (US/0017-2642). [85,079] **950**

GOVERNMENT PURCHASING GUIDE (TORONTO) (CN/0046-6220). [20,000] **950**

GOVERNMENT RELATIONS (CN/0715-1608). **1826**

GOVERNMENT UNION CRITIQUE, THE (US/0738-3312). [2,000] **1676**

GOVERNMENT UNION REVIEW (US/0270-2487). [4,000] **3148**

GOVERNMENTAL SERVICES NEWSLETTER (ASHLAND, MO.) (US/1074-9845). [200] **4652**

GOVERNMENTS OF ILLINOIS (US/0883-3826). [3,000] **4728**

GOWER FEDERAL SERVICE - MISCELLANEOUS LANDS DECISIONS SERVICE (US). [81] **2975**

GOYA (SP/0017-2715). [2,500] **351**

GR. GROCERS REPORT (US/0160-8894). [15,000] **2342**

GRA REPORTER (US/0016-3619). **4652**

GRADUATE FACULTY PHILOSOPHY JOURNAL (US/0093-4240). [4,000] **4347**

GRADUATE FORUM (MINDANAO STATE UNIVERSITY. UNIVERSITY RESEARCH CENTER) (PH). [500] **2504**

GRADUATE OUTLOOK (AT/0314-0679). [8,000] **1826**

GRADUATE SCHOOL RESEARCH JOURNAL : A PUBLICATION OF GRADUATE SCHOOL OF BUSINESS ADMINISTRATION AND GRADUATE SCHOOL OF EDUCATION (PH/0030-7858). [1,000] **1826**

GRADUATING ENGINEER (US/0193-2276). [70,000] **1976**

GRAFISCH NIEUWS (BE/0773-591X). [7,300] **4815**

GRAFISKT FORUM (SW). [6,000] **378**

GRAIN & FEED MERCHANT, THE (US/0199-2287). [1,000] **201**

GRAIN JOURNAL (DECATUR, ILL.) (US/0274-7138). [11,000] **201**

GRAIN MATTERS (CN/0383-4417). **201**

GRAND FALLS ADVERTISER (CN/0833-1014). [12,100] **5785**

GRAND RIVER VALLEY REVIEW, THE (US/0739-084X). [1,000] **2735**

GRAND SLAM (OTTAWA) (CN/0701-0745). [10,000] **4897**

GRAND TRUNK POPLAR PRESS, THE (CN/0226-6415). **5785**

GRANGE NEWS, THE (US/0043-0587). [43,250] **90**

GRANI (GW/0017-3185). [1,500] **2517**

GRANMA (DAILY EDITION, SPANISH) (CU/0017-3223). [300,000] **5799**

GRANMA INTERNATIONAL (CU/0864-4624). [45,000] **5799**

GRANT ADVISOR, THE (US/0740-5383). [500] **1826**

GRANT PROPOSAL NEWS (US/0893-9128). [200] **4729**

GRANTSMANSHIP NEWS (US/0741-2487). [1,000] **4337**

GRAPH THEORY NEWSLETTER (US/0161-3324). [180] **3507**

GRAPHIC ARTS BLUE BOOK (METROPOLITAN NEW YORK-NEW JERSEY ED.) (US/1044-8527). [6,000] **4565**

GRAPHIC ARTS BLUE BOOK (MIDWESTERN ED.) (US/1044-8535). [9,000] **378**

GRAPHIC ARTS IN FINLAND (FI/0359-2464). [1,000] **379**

GRAPHIC ARTS PRODUCT NEWS (CHICAGO) (US/0274-5976). **379**

GRAPHIC DESIGN, USA (US). [30,000] **379**

GRAPHIC MONTHLY, THE (CN/0227-2806). [7,000] **4565**

GRAPHICOMMUNICATOR (US/0746-3626). **1112**

GRAPHIS (SZ/0017-3452). [16,500] **379**

GRAPHISCHE KUNST (GW). [1,000] **379**

GRAPHOSCOPE, THE (CN/0046-631X). [2,000] **900**

GRASAS Y ACEITES (SEVILLA) (SP/0017-3495). [800] **488**

GRASSROOTS FOR HIGH RISQUE LIBRARIANS (US/0889-5198). [200] **3212**

GRASSROOTS (MADISON) (US/0361-1515). [1,000] **1344**

GRAVURE (NEW YORK, N.Y. 1987) (US/0894-4946). [7,000] **4565**

GRAY PANTHER NETWORK (US/0739-2001). **5286**

GRAZER BEITRAEGE (AU/0376-5253). **3284**

GRAZER BEITRAEGE. SUPPLEMENTBAND (AU). **269**

GREAT ACTIVITIES (US/0886-764X). [4,600] **1855**

GREAT BARRINGTON HISTORICAL SOCIETY NEWSLETTER (US/0895-7851). [150] **2617**

GREAT BASIN NATURALIST MEMOIRS (US/0160-239X). [500] **4166**

GREAT BASIN NATURALIST, THE (US/0017-3614). [500] **4165**

GREAT CIRCLE (AT/0156-8698). [420] **4176**

GREAT DECISIONS (US/0072-727X). [80,000] **4523**

GREAT LAKER, THE (CN/0317-1078). [6,000] **4233**

GREAT LAKES ENTOMOLOGIST, THE (US/0090-0222). [650] **5609**

GREAT LAKES FISHERMAN (CN/0847-0685). [1,500] **2304**

GREAT LAKES FISHERMAN (COLUMBUS, OHIO) (US/0194-5564). [40,000] **2304**

GREAT LAKES REPORTER, THE (US/0748-9544). [5,000] **2172**

GREAT LAKES RESEARCH CHECKLIST (US/0072-7326). [800] **5549**

GREAT LAKES TRAVEL & LIVING (US/0887-6223). [50,000] **5478**

GREAT LAKES UNITED, THE (US). [8,000] **2172**

GREAT LAKES VEGETABLE GROWERS NEWS, THE (US/1049-8494). [13,250] **173**

GREAT PLAINS JOURNAL (US/0017-3673). [1,000] **2735**

GREAT PLAINS QUARTERLY (US/0275-7664). [700] **2735**

GREAT PLAINS SOCIOLOGIST, THE (US/0896-0054). [100] **5246**

GREAT RIVER REVIEW (US/0160-2144). [800] **3392**

GREATER LANSING BUSINESS MONTHLY (US). [10,000] **678**

GREATER WASHINGTON BOARD OF TRADE NEWS, THE (US/0274-5496). [5,500] **1564**

GREATER WINNIPEG BUSINESS (CN/0830-8535). [15,500] **678**

GREEK ORTHODOX THEOLOGICAL REVIEW, THE (US/0017-3894). [1,000] **4961**

GREEK, ROMAN AND BYZANTINE STUDIES (US/0017-3916). [900] **1077**

GREEN (CN/0823-6380). [15,000] **4897**

GREEN BOOK BUYERS' GUIDE FOR GARDEN MERCHANDISE (US/0147-3891). [41,000] **2417**

GREEN BOOK REPORT, THE (US/1062-4589). **2172**

GREEN LEAVES. WESTERN CANADA ED, THE (CN/0705-1697). **2384**

GREEN REVOLUTION (YORK, PA.) (US/0017-3983). [400] **4542**

GREEN SCENE, THE (US/0190-9789). [13,500] **2417**

GREEN SHEET - UNITED STATES. DEPT. OF HEALTH AND HUMAN SERVICES, THE (US/0732-9385). **4777**

GREEN THUMB NEWS (US/0749-2138). [7,000] **2417**

GREENE COUNTY DEMOCRAT (EUTAW, ALA.), THE (US/0889-518X). [3,500] **5626**

GREENE COUNTY HISTORICAL JOURNAL (US/0894-8135). [1,200] **2735**

GREENE GENES (US/0898-9974). [100] **2452**

GREENER MANAGEMENT INTERNATIONAL (UK). [300] **2173**

GREENFIELD QUARTERLY (US/0883-170X). [200] **2452**

GREENHOUSE CANADA (CN/0712-4996). [4,500] **2417**

GREENHOUSE MANAGER (US/0744-8988). [15,000] **2417**

GREENMASTER (CN/0380-3333). [2,850] **4897**

GREENPEACE NEWS (IT/0111-4506). [60,000] **2216**

GREEN'S MAGAZINE (CN/0824-2992). [300] **3392**

GREENSCAPE (CN/0712-1822). **2417**

GREENSWARD (UK/0017-4092). [800] **90**

GREENVILLE ADVOCATE (GREENVILLE, ILL.) (US). [5,050] **5660**

GREENWEEK (AT/1034-5876). **2194**

GREENWOOD COMMONWEALTH (GREENWOOD, MISS. : 1976) (US). [8,797 paid] **5700**

GREENWOOD LAKE AND WEST MILFORD NEWS (US/1065-1144). **5717**

GREENWOOD'S GUIDE TO GREAT LAKES SHIPPING (US/0072-7490). [1,700] **5449**

GREETINGS AND GIFTS (AT/1036-5915). [7,000] **2584**

GREGORIOS O PALAMAS (GR/1011-3010). [1,200] **4961**

GRID (US). [14,000] **4259**

GRIFFIN REPORT OF FOOD MARKETING, THE (US/0192-4400). [14,780] **2342**

GRIFFIN REPORT, THE (US). **2342**

GRINNELL REVIEW, THE (US/0737-8912). [500] **1826**

GRIOT (HOUSTON, TEX.), THE (US/0737-0873). [500] **2735**

GRIPE/ GROUP FOR RESEARCH IN PATHOLOGY EDUCATION (US). **3894**

GROCERS' REVIEW (NZ/0113-1850). [5,600] **2342**

GROCERY DISTRIBUTION (US/0361-4034). [15,000] **2342**

GROCERY INDUSTRY ANNUAL REPORT, THE (US). [90,000] **2342**

GROCERY MARKETING (US/0888-0360). [65,213] **2343**

GROLIER POETRY PRIZE (US/0743-7242). [400] **3463**

GRONDBOOR EN HAMER (NE/0017-4505). [1,700] **1381**

GROOM & BOARD (US/0199-8366). [16,000] **4286**

GROSSE POINTER, THE (US/0017-4629). [1,000] **5478**

GROSSEN 500, DIE (GW). **678**

GROTIANA (1980) (NE). [400] **3128**

GROUND WATER AGE (US/0046-645X). [22,000] **5533**

GROUNDS MAINTENANCE (US/0017-4688). [45,000] **2417**

GROUNDSMAN (UK/0017-4696). [5000] **2418**

GROUP (NEW YORK. 1977) (US/0362-4021). [1,000] **4588**

GROUP PRACTICE JOURNAL (US/0199-5103). [48,000] **3780**

GROUP PRACTICE (NEWSLETTER) (US/0190-440X). [40,000] **3780**

GROUPE FAMILIAL, LE (FR/0180-9857). **2280**

GROVE EXAMINER, THE (CN/0318-1650). [6,000] **5785**

GROWER (SHAWNEE MISSION, KAN.), THE (US/0745-1784). [28,500] **173**

GROWER (TORONTO) (CN/0017-4777). [11,600] **2418**

GROWING WITHOUT SCHOOLING (US/0745-5305). [5,000] **1895**

GROWTH GENETICS & HORMONES (US/0898-6630). [12,000] **3903**

GROWTH INDEX, THE (US/0744-7205). [13,200] **820**

GROWTH (MELBOURNE, VIC.) (AT/0085-1280). [2,000] **1564**

GROWTH (PRETORIA, SOUTH AFRICA) (SA). [25,000] **1564**

GROWTH STOCK OUTLOOK (US). **900**

GRUPO ANDINO : LEGISLACION ECONOMICA Y SOCIAL DE LOS PAISES MIEMBROS (PE). [15] **2975**

GSD NEWS (1983) (US/0746-3677). [10,000] **299**

GTEC NEWS (CN/0833-0611). [250] **1879**

GUAM BUSINESS NEWS (GU/1045-053X). [2,500] **678**

GUANGARA LIBERTARIA (US/0890-0280). [5,000] **2617**

GUARDIAN CAPITAL'S VIEWPOINT (CN/0824-6696). **1493**

GUARDIAN (LONDON) (UK/0261-3077). [450,000] **5812**

GUARDIAN (NEW YORK, N.Y.), THE (US/0017-5021). [20,000] **2920**

GUARDMOUNT (US/0883-0843). [4,000] **3182**

GUERNSEY BREEDERS' JOURNAL (UK). [2,000] **211**

GUERRES MONDIALES ET CONFLITS CONTEMPORAINS (FR). **4045**

GUGONG XUESHU JIKAN (CH/1011-9094). [1,000] **351**

GUIA - ADMINISTRACAO-GERAL DO PORTO DE LISBOA (PO). [4,000] **5449**

GUIA DE EXPORTADORES E IMPORTADORES ARGENTINOS (AG). [5,000] **838**

GUIA DE LA INDUSTRIA ALIMENTARIA (MX). [5,000] **2343**

GUIDANCE & COUNSELLING (CN/0831-5493). [3,000] **1748**

GUIDE DE LA BIBLIOTHEQUE DU CENTRE AUDIO-VISUEL - COLLEGE JEAN-DE-BREBEUF (CN/0712-8533). **3212**

GUIDE DE LA ROUTE, FLORIDE (CN/0838-0015). [30,000] **5478**

GUIDE DE LA ROUTE, PROVINCES DE L'ATLANTIQUE ET DU QUEBEC (CN/0225-2600). [15,000] **5478**

GUIDE DES USAGERS / UNIVERSITE DE SHERBROOKE-BIBLIOTHEQUE GENERALE (CN/0824-8095). **3212**

GUIDE ECONOMIQUE DE LA TUNISIE (TI). [30,000] **1565**

GUIDE SERIES - GEOLOGICAL SURVEY OF IRELAND (IE/0790-0260). [250] **1381**

GUIDE TO FEDERAL ASSISTANCE. NEWSLETTER, THE (US/0278-5064). **4730**

GUIDE TO FLORIDA RETIREMENT LIVING (US/0889-051X). [50,000] **5179**

GUIDE TO GEORGIA (US/0434-8877). [20,000] **5479**

GUIDE TO GRADUATE EDUCATION IN SPEECH-LANGUAGE PATHOLOGY AND AUDIOLOGY (US/0884-7347). **1826**

GUIDE TO INDIAN PERIODICAL LITERATURE (II/0017-5285). **416**

GUIDE TO JEWISH EUROPE (US). [1,000] **5479**

GUIDE TO JEWISH ITALY (US). [2,000] **5479**

GUIDE TO NEBRASKA STATE AGENCIES (US/0091-0716). **4653**

GUIDE TO SOURCES OF INTERNATIONAL POPULATION ASSISTANCE (US). [3,000] **4553**

GUIDE TO SPRINGFIELD (US). [20,000] **2534**

GUIDE TO TANKER PORTS (UK). **5449**

GUIDE TO THE AMERICAN LEFT (KANSAS CITY, MO. 1984) (US/0894-4547). [1,500] **4502**

GUIDE TO THE ECONOMY / NEDBANK GROUP (SA/0258-6754). [20,000] **1493**

GUIDE TO TRAINING OPPORTUNITIES FOR INDUSTRIAL DEVELOPMENT (AU). [3,000] **2910**

GUIDE TO U.S. TAXES FOR CITIZENS ABROAD (US/0278-3576). [10,000] **4730**

GUIDE (TORONTO) (CN/0533-5051). [13,500] **1676**

GUIDELINES (SASKATOON) (CN/0048-9190). [250] **1749**

GUIDEPOST (WASHINGTON, D.C.) (US/0017-5323). [57,000] **4588**

GUIDES OF UNDERWRITERS' LABORATORIES OF CANADA (CN/0710-4588). **2881**

GUIDING IN AUSTRALIA (AT/0159-0340). [7,000] **1064**

GUILD (NEW YORK, N.Y.) (US/0885-3975). [19,000] **373**

GUILD OF BOOK WORKERS JOURNAL (US/0434-9245). [900] **4828**

GUILD REPORTER, THE (US/0017-5404). [35,350] **1676**

GUION (CK). [25,000] **2488**

GUITAR REVIEW, THE (US/0017-5471). [4,000] **4120**

GUJARAT AGRICULTURAL UNIVERSITY RESEARCH JOURNAL (II/0250-5193). [450] **91**

GULDEN PASSER, DE (BE). **4570**

GULF COAST CATTLEMAN (US/0017-5552). [14,500] **211**

GULF COAST HISTORICAL REVIEW (US/0892-9025). [550] **2735**

GULF NEWS (CN/0833-1065). [4,100] **5785**

GULFSHORE LIFE (US/0745-0079). [20,000] **2534**

GUMMI BEREIFUNG (GW). [6,000] **5075**

GUN REPORT (US/0017-5617). [6,500] **250**

GUNNER (UK). [7,800] **4045**

GUNRUNNER (CN). [12,000] **4897**

GUOJI RIBAO (US/0741-126X). [100,000] **5635**

GUTENBERG-JAHRBUCH (GW/0072-9094). **4565**

GUTHRIE CENTER TIMES (GUTHRIE CENTER, IOWA : 1952) (US). [2,201] **5670**

GW TIMES (US/0279-2435). [105,000] **1827**

GWIAZDA POLARNA (US/0740-5944). **5767**

GYMNASIUM (HEIDELBERG) (GW/0342-5231). [2,700] **1077**

GZ : GOLDSCHMIEDE UND UHRMACHER ZEITUNG (GW). [15,100] **2914**

H.A.C. JOURNAL (AT). [2,000] **1092**

HA-SHILTH-SA (CN/0715-4143). [2,000] **5785**

HA'ARETZ (IS). [100,000] **5804**

HABITAT (FALMOUTH, ME.) (US/0739-2052). [7,500] **2194**

HAC. THE HEATING AND AIR CONDITIONING JOURNAL (UK/0307-7950). [18,456] **2605**

HACK'D (WOODBRIDGE, VA.) (US/1055-033X). [3,500] **4081**

HADASSAH MAGAZINE (US/0017-6516). [338,000] **5048**

HAEGI (KO). [10,000] **4176**

HAFNIA (DK/0085-1361). [600] **351**

HAIR INTERNATIONAL NEWS (US/0887-803X). [2,500] **404**

HALF-YEARLY ECONOMIC REPORT (HK). [500] **1493**

HALIFAX METROPOLITAN AREA BUSINESS DIRECTORY (CN/0834-0676). [3,500] **678**

HALLE YEARBOOK (UK). [7,000] **4120**

HALSBURY'S STATUTES OF ENGLAND AND WALES (UK). **2976**

HALSTAD VALLEY JOURNAL (US). [3,517] **5696**

HALTON
Controlled Circulation Index

HALTON BUSINESS JOURNAL (1986) (CN/0833-384X). [15,000] **678**

HALTON CONSUMER (CN/0707-3941). **1297**

HALTON FARM NEWS (CN/0704-9226). [1,150] **91**

HALVE MAEN, DE (US/0017-6834). [1,400] **2452**

HAMBROOK HERALD, THE (CN/0821-5472). [165] **2452**

HAMBURGER BEITRAEGE ZUR FRIEDENSFORSCHUNG UND SICHERHEITSPOLITIK (GW/0936-0018). [500] **4523**

HAMBURGER PHILOLOGISCHE STUDIEN (GW/0072-9582). [400] **3285**

HAMDARD ISLAMICUS (PK/0250-7196). [2,000] **5042**

HAMERSKY & ALLIED FAMILIES NEWSLETTER (US/0882-4150). [95] **2452**

HAMILTON GUIDEBOOK (CN/0227-6267). **5479**

HAMILTON REPORT (CN/0834-0536). [21,000] **678**

HAMILTON THIS MONTH (CN/0829-1373). [42,000] **678**

HAMLINE JOURNAL OF PUBLIC LAW AND POLICY (US). [1,000] **2976**

HAN HSUEH YEN CHIU TUNG HSUN (CH). [2,500] **2504**

HANAZONO DAIGAKU KENKYU KIYO (JA). [2,800] **1827**

HANDBOOK AND DIRECTORY - CANADIAN FIELD HOCKEY ASSOCIATION (CN/0225-0314). **4898**

HANDBOOK AND DIRECTORY - CANADIAN WOMEN'S FIELD HOCKEY ASSOCIATION (CN/0225-0306). **4898**

HANDBOOK AND DIRECTORY - CLASSIC CAR CLUB OF AMERICA (US/0163-1055). [5,000] **5416**

HANDBOOK : CONSTITUTION, DIRECTORY, BYLAWS, POLICIES, BUDGET, LEGISLATION / ONTARIO PUBLIC SCHOOL FEDERATION (CN/0822-9104). [4,000] **1864**

HANDBOOK, CORRUGATED AND SOLID FIBREBOARD BOXES AND PRODUCTS (US). **4219**

HANDBOOK - FACULTY OF MEDICINE, UNIVERSITY OF NEW SOUTH WALES (AT/0312-6137). [2,800] **3580**

HANDBOOK FOR FINANCIAL AID ADMINISTRATORS (US/0094-2227). **1827**

HANDBOOK - NEW YORK STATE PUBLIC HIGH SCHOOL ATHLETIC ASSOCIATION (US). [18,000] **4898**

HANDBOOK OF ADVERTISING & MARKETING SERVICES (US/0749-2243). [1,000] **759**

HANDBOOK OF ILLINOIS POSTSECONDARY INSTITUTIONS (US). [2,600] **1827**

HANDBOOK OF SECURITY (UK). [1,000] **5177**

HANDBOOK OF STATISTICS ON COTTON TEXTILE INDUSTRY (II). [2,500] **5360**

HANDBOOK OF THE BRITISH ASTRONOMICAL ASSOCIATION, THE (UK/0068-130X). [4,500] **395**

HANDBOOK - OKLAHOMA BAR ASSOCIATION (US/0271-2571). **2976**

HANDBOOK TO THE SEASON / CINCINNATI SYMPHONY ORCHESTRA (US/0732-2321). [7,000] **4120**

HANDGUNNER (UK/0260-8693). [15,000] **4898**

HANDLOADER (US/0017-7393). [35,000] **4898**

HANDS ON! (DAYTON, OHIO) (US/0197-6559). [800,000] **634**

HANDS ON (RABUN GAP, GA.) (US). [2,000] **1749**

HANDWERK IM LANDE NORDRHEIN-WESTFALEN, DAS (GW/0300-1059). [500] **679**

HANG GLIDING (US/0895-433X). [9,110] **4898**

HANGUK KIDIKKYO CHANGNOHOE HOEBO (KO). [3,000] **5061**

HANGUK KISUL YONGUSO CHONGNAM (KO). [7,000] **5109**

HANGUK KOMI YONGUSO YONGU POGOSO (KO/1011-2014). [600] **5585**

HANGUK KYOYUK (KO). [1,000] **1749**

HANGUK UNGYONG KONCHUNG HAKHOE CHI (KO). [600] **5609**

HANOVER POST POSTSCRIPTS, THE (CN/0847-8988). [4,800] **5786**

HANSA (GW/0017-7504). [6,500] **4177**

HANSARD OFFICIAL REPORT (CJ). [100] **4654**

HANZAIGAKU ZASSHI (JA/0302-0029). [6] **3740**

HAPPENINGS (CN/0844-5753). [2,000] **3213**

HARAS AL-WATANI (RIYADH, SAUDI ARABIA) (SU). [3,000] **2504**

HARBOUR & SHIPPING (CN/0017-7636). [2,000] **5450**

HARDIN COUNTY HISTORICAL QUARTERLY (US/8755-6073). [400] **2735**

HARDWARE MERCHANDISER (CHICAGO) (US/0017-7709). [70,200] **2811**

HARDWARE MERCHANDISING, BUILDING SUPPLY DEALER (CN/0831-0807). [17,000] **2811**

HARDWOOD FLOORS (US/0897-022X). [20,000] **2401**

HARMONIZER (KENOSHA, WIS.), THE (US/0017-7849). [37,000] **4120**

HAROLD L. LYON ARBORETUM LECTURE (US/0091-7079). [1,000] **456**

HARRIMAN INSTITUTE FORUM, THE (US/0896-114X). [1,000] **2690**

HARRIS COUNTY REAL ESTATE REPORT (US). [500] **4838**

HARRIS INDIANA INDUSTRIAL DIRECTORY (US/0888-8175). [3,000] **1608**

HARRIS MICHIGAN INDUSTRIAL DIRECTORY (TWINSBURG, OHIO: 1984) (US/0888-8167). **1608**

HARRISTON REVIEW, THE (CN/0381-0283). [1,161] **5786**

HARRY BROWNE'S SPECIAL REPORTS (US). **900**

HART BULLETIN (NE/0301-8202). **3705**

HARVARD BUSINESS SCHOOL BULLETIN (US/0017-8020). [55,000] **679**

HARVARD CIVIL RIGHTS-CIVIL LIBERTIES LAW REVIEW (US/0017-8039). [1,300] **4508**

HARVARD CRIMSON, THE (US). [3,500] **5688**

HARVARD DIVINITY BULLETIN (US/0017-8047). [24,000] **4962**

HARVARD JOURNAL ON LEGISLATION (US/0017-808X). [1,000] **2977**

HARVARD LAW RECORD (US/0017-8101). [11,000] **2977**

HARVARD LIBRARIAN, THE (US/0073-0564). [3,500] **3213**

HARVARD MAGAZINE (US/0095-2427). [198,000] **1092**

HARVARD POLITICAL REVIEW (US/0090-1032). [3,000] **4475**

HATTIESBURG AMERICAN (US). [25,000] **5700**

HAWAII BAR JOURNAL MICROFORM (US). [2,800] **2977**

HAWAII BEVERAGE GUIDE (US/0017-8543). [2,000] **2367**

HAWAII DENTAL JOURNAL (US/0891-9933). [1,000] **1324**

HAWAII HERALD (1969) (US/8750-913X). [7,500] **2262**

HAWAII INVESTOR (US/0745-7073). [10,000] **4838**

HAWAII MEDICAL JOURNAL (1962) (US/0017-8594). [1,700] **3581**

HAWAII REVIEW (US/0093-9625). [4,000] **3393**

HAWAII TV DIGEST (US/0745-6565). **1132**

HAWAIIAN ARCHAEOLOGY (US/0890-1678). [130] **269**

HAWAIIAN JOURNAL OF HISTORY, THE (US/0440-5145). [1,000] **2669**

HAWAIIAN SHELL NEWS (US/0017-8624). [1,250] **1449**

HAWK : THE INDEPENDENT JOURNAL OF THE ROYAL AIR STAFF COLLEGE (UK). [3,000] **22**

HAWVER'S CAPITOL REPORT (US/1071-5401). [400] **4654**

HAY DRAMAGITAKAN HANDES (US/0884-0180). [175] **2781**

HAY MARKET NEWS (BELL, CALIF.) (US/0744-1517). [300] **925**

HAYAMA MISSIONARY-SEMINAR ANNUAL REPORT (JA). [1,000] **4962**

HAYES HISTORICAL JOURNAL: A JOURNAL OF THE GILDED AGE (US/0364-5924). [525] **2736**

HAYS DAILY NEWS, THE (US). [14,000] **5676**

HAZARD MONTHLY (US/0742-6410). [1,400] **2230**

HAZARD PREVENTION (US/0743-8826). [1,500] **2862**

HAZARDOUS MATERIALS INTELLIGENCE REPORT (US/0272-9628). [1,300] **2231**

HAZARDOUS WASTE LITIGATION REPORTER (US/0275-0244). **3112**

HAZMAT WORLD (US/0898-5685). [33,400] **2232**

HB. HOOSIER BANKER (US/0018-473X). [4,000] **790**

HBG-MITTEILUNGEN (GW). [105,000] **3480**

HEADACHE (US/0017-8748). [5,000] **3833**

HEADLAND OBSERVER, THE (US). [1,926] **5626**

HEADLINE SERIES (US/0017-8780). [11,500] **4523**

HEADLINES (UK/0957-8714). [8,000] **1864**

HEALDSBURG TRIBUNE-ENTERPRISE AND SCIMITAR (US/0017-8810). [7,377] **5635**

HEALING HAND, THE (UK). [2,000] **4962**

HEALING (SACRAMENTO, CALIF.) (US/1064-4237). [6,000] **4777**

HEALTH AND HYGIENE (LONDON) (UK/0140-2986). [2,500] **4777**

HEALTH & PHYSICAL EDUCATION NEWSLETTER (CN/0824-4863). [1,400] **1855**

HEALTH & SAFETY. MICROFILE (UK). [3,500] **4778**

HEALTH & SAFETY MONITOR (UK/0140-8534). **2862**

HEALTH & YOU (CINNAMINSON, N.J.) (US/0898-3569). [800,000] **2598**

HEALTH BULLETIN (EDINBURGH) (UK/0374-8014). [15,000] **4778**

HEALTH CARE FINANCING REVIEW (US/0195-8631). [5,000] **2897**

HEALTH CARE LABOR MANUAL (US/0095-3792). **1676**

HEALTH CARE PARLIAMENTARY MONITOR (UK). [1,000] **3581**

HEALTH CITY SUN (US). [2,000] **5712**

HEALTH EDUCATION REPORTS (US/0193-5232). [670] **4779**

HEALTH ESTATE JOURNAL : JOURNAL OF THE INSTITUTE OF HOSPITAL ENGINEERING (UK/0957-7742). [4,000] **3781**

HEALTH FACILITIES ENERGY REPORT (US/0272-8443). **1946**

HEALTH FOODS BUSINESS (US/0149-9602). [11,500] **2343**

HEALTH FUNDS DEVELOPMENT LETTER (US/0193-7928). **3581**

HEALTH INDUSTRY TODAY (US/0745-4678). **3581**

HEALTH INFORMATION AND LIBRARIES (HU/0864-991X). **3213**

HEALTH LAW BULLETIN (US/0549-804X). **2977**

HEALTH LAW DIGEST / NATIONAL HEALTH LAWYERS ASSOCIATION (US). [6,000] **2977**

HEALTH LAWYERS NEWS REPORT (US/0145-4129). [6,000] **2978**

HEALTH LETTER (SAN ANTONIO, TEX.), THE (US/0739-4217). [11,000] **4780**

HEALTH MANAGEMENT QUARTERLY (US/0891-3250). [24,000] **3781**

HEALTH MANPOWER PILOT PROJECTS PROGRAM. ANNUAL REPORT TO THE LEGISLATURE AND THE HEALING ARTS LICENSING BOARDS (US/0192-6101). [250] **3914**

HEALTH NEWS & REVIEW (US/1056-1900). [100,000] **4191**

HEALTH/PAC BULLETIN (US/0017-9051). [1300] **4780**

HEALTH PROGRESS (SAINT LOUIS, MO.) (US/0882-1577). [14,000] **3781**

HEALTH PROMOTION JOURNAL OF AUSTRALIA (AT/1036-1073). **3582**

HEALTH PROMOTION PRACTITIONER (US/1060-5517). [1,800] **4781**

HEALTH SCIENCE (1985) (US/0883-8216). [4,500] **4781**

HEALTH SCIENCE REVIEW (NEW YORK, N.Y.) (US/0731-5694). **3582**

HEALTH SERVICES ADMINISTRATION EDUCATION (US/0160-4961). [1,500] **4781**

HEALTH SERVICES INTERNATIONAL (UK/1011-5153). [2,000] **4781**

HEALTH VALUES (US/0147-0353). [2,000] **4782**

HEALTH VISITOR : THE JOURNAL OF THE HEALTH VISITORS' ASSOCIATION (UK/0017-9140). [16,000] **3856**

HEALTH WORLD (US/0888-7330). [70,000] **4782**

HEALTHCARE ADVOCATE (EDMONTON) (CN/1197-4710). [2,800] **3782**

HEALTHCARE EXECUTIVE (US/0883-5381). [23,500] **3782**

HEALTHCARE FINANCIAL MANAGEMENT (US/0735-0732). [27,000] **3782**

HEALTHCARE FORUM JOURNAL, THE (US/0899-9287). [26,000] **3583**

HEALTHCARE HAZARDOUS MATERIALS MANAGEMENT (US/1050-575X). **4782**

HEALTHCARE INFORMATICS (US/1050-9135). [25,000] **3782**

HEALTHCARE INFORMATION MANAGEMENT (US). [4,000] **3782**

HEALTHCARE MARKETING REPORT (US/0741-9368). [1,500] **3782**

HEALTHCOVER SYDNEY (AT/1036-1901). **2598**

HEALTHLINES (WACO, TEX.) (US/1048-5562). [3 million] **4782**

HEALTHTRAC (US). [145] **3583**

HEALTHWAYS (US/0897-9251). [200] **4191**

HEARING INSTRUMENTS (US/0092-4466). [18,622] **3888**

HEARING JOURNAL, THE (US/0745-7472). [20,000] **3888**

HEARING REHABILITATION QUARTERLY (US/0360-9278). [3,000] **4388**

HEARSAY : LEGAL AID PRACTICE NOTES AND INFORMATION BULLETIN OF THE LEGAL AID COMMISSION OF WESTERN AUSTRALIA (AT). [4,000] **3179**

HEART DISEASE AND STROKE (US/1058-2819). [75,000] **3705**

HEARTBEAT (US/1047-1014). **4962**

HEARTH AND HOME (GILFORD, N.H. : 1989) (US/0273-5695). [17,000] **1946**

HEAT TREATMENT OF METALS (UK/0305-4829). [1,000] **4003**

HEATHER SOCIETY BULLETIN, THE (UK). **5231**

HEATING & VENTILATING REVIEW (UK/0017-9396). **2605**

HEAVY METAL (US/0885-7822). [135,000] **3393**

HEBDO CARRIERES (MONTREAL) (CN/0823-518X). **1677**

HEBDO DE LAVAL, L' (CN/0822-7535). [72,000] **5786**

HEENSCHUT (NE/0017-9515). [9,000] **299**

HEIDELBERG BULLETIN, THE (US/1044-3851). [10,500] **1092**

HEIFER INTERNATIONAL EXCHANGE, THE (US). **212**

HEILIGER DIENST (AU/0017-9620). [800] **4962**

HEISEY NEWS (US/0731-8014). [2,900] **2590**

HELGOLAENDER MEERESUNTERSUCHUNGEN (GW/0174-3597). [750] **554**

HELICOM FROM MIRABEL (CN/0828-5683). **1608**

HELICOPTER ANNUAL (US/0739-5728). [17,000] **22**

HELICOPTER WORLD (LONDON. 1982) (UK/0262-0448). [12,672] **23**

HELICOPTERS (CN/0227-3160). [7,000] **23**

HELICTITE (AT/0017-9973). [200] **5109**

HELIKON (HU/0017-999X). [1,400] **3393**

HELINIUM (BE/0018-0009). **2690**

HELPER (AMERICAN SOCIAL HEALTH ASSOCIATION) (US). [35,000] **4782**

HELPING HAND (JANESVILLE, WIS.), THE (US/0745-029X). [2,300] **4962**

HELSINGIN SANOMAT (FI/0355-2047). [480.866 daily571.866 sundays] **5800**

HELVETICA CHIRURGICA ACTA (SZ/0018-0181). [1,400] **3903**

HELVETICA PAEDIATRICA ACTA (SZ/0018-022X). **3903**

HEM O FRITID (SW). [100,000] **2517**

HEMET NEWS, THE (US). [17,500] **5635**

HEMINGWAY REVIEW, THE (US/0276-3362). [700] **3344**

HEMISPHERE (MIAMI, FLA.) (US/0898-3038). [2,000] **4475**

HEMOGLOBIN (US/0363-0269). **3797**

HEMOPHILIA ONTARIO (CN/0822-5974). [2,000] **3772**

HEMPSTEAD TRAILS (US). **2453**

HENDERSON HOME NEWS (US). [7,890] **5707**

HENKEL-REFERATE : EXCERPTS OF HENKEL RESEARCH PAPERS (GW/0720-9428). [5,000] **976**

HENRY JAMES REVIEW, THE (US/0273-0340). [500] **3344**

HENSTON VETERINARY VADE MECUM. LARGE ANIMALS, THE (UK/0268-4276). [4,000] **5511**

HENSTON VETERINARY VADE MECUM. SMALL ANIMALS, THE (UK/0268-4268). [4,000] **5511**

HER WORLD ANNUAL (SI). [34,000] **5558**

HERALD (CONROE, TEX.), THE (US/0730-6520). [400] **2453**

HERALD-DISPATCH (LOS ANGELES, CALIF. : 1981) (US/8750-2038). [35,000] **5635**

HERALD-STAR, THE (US/0890-8656). [22,000] **5728**

HERALDRY IN CANADA (CN/0441-6619). [700] **2453**

HERALDRY, THE ARMIGER'S NEWS (US). [300] **2453**

HERANCA JUDAICA (BL). [3,000] **5048**

HERITAGE (CARSON, CALIF.) (US/0895-0792). **2262**

HERITAGE HEARTH (CN/0841-923X). [4,000] **4088**

HERITAGE NEWS (CANBERRA, A.C.T.) (AT/0103-626X). **2510**

HERITAGE OUTLOOK (UK/0261-1988). [3,000] **300**

HERITAGE SCOTLAND : THE MAGAZINE OF THE NATIONAL TRUST FOR SCOTLAND (UK/0264-9144). **2690**

HERITAGE SEEKERS (CN/0707-0780). **2453**

HERMISTON HERALD AND BUYER'S BONUS, THE (US/8750-4782). [4,200] **5733**

HERNE, L' (FR/0440-7237). [3,000] **4348**

HERODOTE (FR/0338-487X). **2565**

HERPETOFAUNA NEWS (UK/0269-8498). [1,000] **5585**

HERPETOLOGICA (US/0018-0831). [1,500] **5585**

HERPETOLOGY (PASADENA) (US/0441-666X). [300] **5585**

HERPETON (US/0440-7326). [450] **5585**

HERS NEWSLETTER (US/0892-628X). [10,000] **3762**

HERTFORDSHIRE PEOPLE (UK/0309-913X). [900] **2453**

HERVORMDE TEOLOGIESE STUDIES (SA). [900] **4962**

HERVORMER, DIE (SA). [27,500] **4962**

HESPERIA (US/0018-098X). [1,013] **1077**

HESPERUS REVIEW (II). [500] **3393**

HETEROFONIA (MX/0018-1137). [1,000] **4121**

HETI VILAGGAZDASAG : HVG (HU/0139-1682). [165,000] **1635**

HEVRAH U-REVAHAH (IS). [2,000] **5287**

HI-HAKAI KENSA (JA/0367-5866). [5,000] **5109**

HI-RISE (CN/0715-5948). [40,000] **2534**

HIBALLER FOREST MAGAZINE (CN/0708-2169). [10,000] **2384**

HIBOU (ST-LAMBERT) (CN/0709-9177). [26,500] **1064**

HIDDEN VALLEY JOURNAL (US/0741-4773). [100] **2453**

HIDUP (IO/0377-9610). [50,000] **5030**

HIFU. SKIN RESEARCH (JA/0018-1390). [1,400] **3720**

HIG (SERIES) (US/0440-4866). [850] **1406**

HIGDON FAMILY NEWSLETTER (US/0739-3199). [200] **2453**

HIGH COLOR (US/1060-5282). [75,000] **1233**

HIGH COUNTRY INDEPENDENT PRESS (US/0746-3359). [5,300] **5705**

HIGH COUNTRY NEWS (US/0191-5657). [9,000] **2195**

HIGH ENERGY PHYSICS INDEX / HOCHENERGIEPHYSIK-INDEX (GW/0018-1447). [160] **4404**

HIGH FRONTIER NEWSWATCH (US/0892-5674). [29,000] **4045**

HIGH QUALITY : HQ (GW). **4565**

HIGH SCHOOL SPORTS (US). **4898**

HIGH SCHOOL WRITER, THE (US/1048-3373). **2920**

HIGH TIDINGS (US/0737-5867). [3,500] **4088**

HIGH VOLUME PRINTING (US/0737-1020). [38,000] **4565**

HIGHER EDUCATION & NATIONAL AFFAIRS (US/0018-1579). [23,000] **1828**

HIGHER EDUCATION DIRECTORY (US/0740-9230). **1828**

HIGHER EDUCATION RESEARCH AND DEVELOPMENT (AT/0729-4360). **1828**

HIGHER EDUCATION REVIEW (UK/0018-1609). [850] **1828**

HIGHER EDUCATION STATISTICAL ABSTRACT / SOUTH CAROLINA COMMISSION ON HIGHER EDUCATION (US). **1795**

HIGHLIGHTS : BUDGET SPEECH AND ESTIMATES (CN). [27,112] **1493**

HIGHLIGHTS OF AGRICULTURAL RESEARCH (US/0018-1668). [11,000] **92**

HIGHLIGHTS OF THE COLLECTIONS / THE MONTREAL MUSEUM OF FINE ARTS (CN/0711-7078). **4088**

HIGHWAY 12 WEEKENDER (CN/0821-4824). [4,932] **5786**

HIGHWAY SAFETY PLAN / OTSC (US). [100] **5441**

HIGHWAY TRANSPORT BOARD BULLETIN (CN/0701-8568). **5383**

HIGHWAYMAN (WILLOW STREET, PA.), THE (US/1062-7200). [100] **2453**

HIKAKU BUNKA ZASSHI (JA). [800] **2617**

HIKAKU TOSHISHI KENKYU (JA). [250] **2824**

HILBORN FAMILY JOURNAL (CN/0707-3836). [150] **2453**

HIMA DIRECTORY (US/0741-8191). **4783**

HIMALAYAN INSTITUTE QUARTERLY GUIDE TO PROGRAMS AND OTHER OFFERINGS (US/0891-6144). [37,000] **4348**

HIMALAYAN JOURNAL, THE (II). [1,500] **4873**

HIMALAYAN PLANT JOURNAL (II). [300] **2418**

HINDU-CHRISTIAN STUDIES BULLETIN (CN/0844-4587). [400] **5041**

HINDUSTAN YEAR-BOOK AND WHO'S WHO (II/0970-1168). **5012**

HINE'S DIRECTORY OF INSURANCE ADJUSTERS (US). [7,000] **2882**

HINE'S INSURANCE COUNSEL (US). [8,000] **2978**

HIRAGANA TAIMUZU (JA/0915-9975). [80,000] **2504**

HIRATRA / SAMPANA TENY SY LAHABOLANA ARY RIBA MALAGASY (MG). [1,500] **3393**

HIS DOMINION (REGINA) (CN/0229-7175). [2,700] **4963**

HISLA (PE). [1,000] **1565**

HISPAMERICA (COLLEGE PARK) (US/0363-0471). [1,000] **3394**

HISPANIA (US/0018-2133). [12,000] **3285**

HISPANIC AMERICAN ARTS (UY/0738-5625). **321**

HISPANIC BOOKS BULLETIN (US/0894-2358). [5,000] **4828**

HISPANIC FOCUS (US/0737-7029). **2276**

HISPANIC LINK (US). [1,100] **2262**

HISPANIC TIMES MAGAZINE (US/0892-1369). [35,000] **4204**

HISPANO NEWS, EL (US). [10,000] **2263**

HISPANOFILA (US/0018-2206). [500] **3394**

HISTOIRE DE L'ART (PARIS, 1988) (FR/0992-2059). [1,100] **321**

HISTOIRE DE L'EDUCATION (FR/0221-6280). [900] **1750**

HISTOIRE, L' (FR/0182-2411). [58,875] **2617**

HISTOIRE SOCIALE (CN/0018-2257). [700] **5201**

HISTOPATHOLOGY (UK/0309-0167). [2,320] **3894**

HISTORIA GRAFICA DE CATALUNYA DIA A DIA (SP). [7,000] **2691**

HISTORIA MEDICINAE VETERINARIAE (DK/0105-1423). [350] **5511**

HISTORIA Y CULTURA (LIMA) (PE/0073-2486). **2617**

HISTORIAN, THE (AT). [250] **2669**

HISTORIANS OF EARLY MODERN EUROPE (US/0883-3559). [1,500] **2691**

HISTORIANS OF NETHERLANDISH ART NEWSLETTER (US/1067-4284). **352**

HISTORIC CLAY TOBACCO PIPE STUDIES (US/0747-8801). [1,000] **269**

HISTORIC ENVIRONMENT (AT/0726-6715). [400] **2669**

HISTORIC HUNTSVILLE QUARTERLY OF LOCAL ARCHITECTURE AND PRESERVATION, THE (US/1074-567X). [800] **300**

HISTORIC NANTUCKET (US/0439-2248). [3,000] **2737**

HISTORIC SCHAEFFERSTOWN RECORD (US/0892-6336). [250] **2737**

HISTORICA (LIMA) (PE/0252-8894). **2737**

HISTORICAL BULLETIN (MADISON, WIS.) (US/0275-1968). [200] **2618**

HISTORICAL — Controlled Circulation Index

HISTORICAL JOURNAL / OTAKI HISTORICAL SOCIETY (NZ/0110-5647). [500] **2669**

HISTORICAL NEW HAMPSHIRE (US/0018-2508). [2,800] **2737**

HISTORICAL NEWS LETTER (US/0199-9664). [5,000] **2737**

HISTORICAL NEWS. MIFFLIN COUNTY HISTORICAL SOCIETY (US). [750] **2618**

HISTORICAL PERFORMANCE (US/0898-8587). [3,000] **4121**

HISTORICAL PRICING--PETROCHEMICALS (US). **1025**

HISTORICAL REVIEW OF BERKS COUNTY (US/0018-2524). [2,550] **2737**

HISTORICAL SOCIAL RESEARCH (KOLN) (GW/0172-6404). [850] **5246**

HISTORICAL SOCIAL RESEARCH (QUANTUM (ASSOCIATION) : 1979) (GW/0172-6404). [1,500] **5201**

HISTORICAL STUDIES IN THE PHYSICAL AND BIOLOGICAL SCIENCES (US/0890-9997). [800] **4404**

HISTORICAL WHISPERINGS (US). [600] **2737**

HISTORICKY CASOPIS (XO/0018-2575). [1,350] **2691**

HISTORIGRAM (CN/0821-1469). [300] **2737**

HISTORISCHE ZEITSCHRIFT. BEIHEFT (GW). [3,000] **2619**

HISTORISCHE ZEITSCHRIFT. SONDERHEFT (GW/0440-971X). [2,000] **2619**

HISTORISCHES JAHRBUCH (GW/0018-2621). [800] **2619**

HISTORISCHES JAHRBUCH DER STADT LINZ (AU/0440-9736). **2691**

HISTORISK TIDSKRIFT FOR FINLAND (FI/0046-7596). [1,000] **2691**

HISTORISK TIDSSKRIFT (DK). [1,600] **2691**

HISTORISKA OCH LITTERATURHISTORISKA STUDIER (FI/0073-2702). **3394**

HISTORY AND THEORY (US/0018-2656). [2,000] **2635**

HISTORY IN AFRICA (US/0361-5413). [2,000] **2640**

HISTORY LIVES HERE (US/0883-8143). [500] **2737**

HISTORY OF EDUCATION QUARTERLY (US/0018-2680). [1,500] **1750**

HISTORY OF PHILOSOPHY QUARTERLY (US/0740-0675). [400] **4348**

HISTORY OF PHOTOGRAPHY (UK/0308-7298). [550] **4370**

HISTORY OF POLITICAL ECONOMY (US/0018-2702). [1,500] **1565**

HISTORY TEACHER BRISBANE (AT/0729-154X). [450] **1896**

HITACHI TECHNOLOGY (JA/0018-277X). [30,000] **5110**

HLI REPORT (US/0899-2673). [200,000] **2280**

HMC&M [COMPUTER FILE] : HAZARDOUS MATERIAL CONTROL & MANAGEMENT ; HMIS : HAZARDOUS MATERIAL INFORMATION SYSTEM / DEPT. OF DEFENSE (US). **2232**

HOBBES STUDIES (NE/0921-5891). [400] **4348**

HOBBY GREENHOUSE (US/1040-6212). [2,100] **2418**

HOBBY MERCHANDISER (NEW YORK, N.Y.) (US/0744-1738). [8,500] **2774**

HOCKEY CIRCLE (AT). **4898**

HOCKEY DIGEST (HARROW) (UK/0950-9550). [5,000] **4899**

HOGG FOUNDATION NEWS (US). [7,700] **3926**

HOKKAIDORITSU HAKODATE SUISAN SHIKENJO JIGYO HOKOKUSHO (JA). [350] **2305**

HOLART REPORT (US/1062-6360). [50] **352**

HOLDSWORTH LAW REVIEW / UNIVERSITY OF BIRMINGHAM (UK). [300] **2979**

HOLISTIC EDUCATION REVIEW (US/0898-0926). [2,500] **1751**

HOLISTIC MASSAGE (US/0748-6855). [1,000] **2598**

HOLISTIC MEDICINE (SEATTLE, WASH.) (US/0898-6029). [1,300] **3584**

HOLLAND HERALD (NE). [3,600,000] **2517**

HOLLAND SENTINEL (1977), THE (US/1050-4044). [19,769] **5692**

HOLLANDSE KRANT (CN/0837-1342). [7,400] **2263**

HOLLINS CRITIC, THE (US/0018-3644). [550] **3344**

HOLLIS EUROPE (UK/0962-3590). [1,000] **760**

HOLLIS PRESS & PUBLIC RELATIONS ANNUAL (UK/0073-3059). [5,000] **760**

HOLLYWOOD MAGAZINE (US/1045-361X). **2488**

HOLSTON PATHFINDER (US/0887-3135). [400] **2453**

HOLY LAND (US). [2,500] **4963**

HOLZ-ZENTRALBLATT (GW/0018-3792). [18,000] **2384**

HOLZFORSCHUNG UND HOLZVERWERTUNG (AU/0018-3849). [5,000] **2401**

HOME (IT). [8,000] **5351**

HOME & AWAY (US/8750-5649). [180,000] **5479**

HOME AND CONDO (US). [25,000] **2418**

HOME-BASED & SMALL BUSINESS NETWORK (US/1067-7739). [6,000] **680**

HOME BUILDER MAGAZINE (CN/0840-4348). [16,500] **616**

HOME EC NEWS (CN/0018-4004). **2790**

HOME FURNISHINGS EXECUTIVE (GREENSBORO, N.C.) (US/1073-5585). [14,000] **2906**

HOME FURNISHINGS REPRESENTATIVES CONTACT (US/8750-4979). [5,000] **2906**

HOME HEALTH JOURNAL (US/0734-7588). [10,000] **3584**

HOME HEALTHCARE NURSE (US/0884-741X). [10,000] **3856**

HOME LIFE (NASHVILLE) (US/0018-4071). [750,000] **5061**

HOME LIGHTING & ACCESSORIES (US/0162-9077). [10,300] **2906**

HOME OWNERS' (CN/0225-5871). **2791**

HOME PLANS GUIDE (US/0899-4374). **300**

HOME PLANS TO BUILD (US/0899-4366). **300**

HOME QUARTER (CN/0823-6410). [1,200] **212**

HOME SHOP MACHINIST, THE (US/0744-6640). [15,500] **2115**

HOMECARE DIRECTION (US/1069-4560). **3584**

HOMECARE (LOS ANGELES, CALIF.) (US/0882-2700). [15,000] **5288**

... HOMECARE MARKET REPORT, THE (US/0882-9152). [11,400] **3584**

HOMEMAKER'S MAGAZINE (CN/0318-7802). [1,400,000] **5558**

HOMER NEWS (US). [4,000] **5629**

HOMESTEAD (KENTVILLE) (CN/0712-6476). [31,000] **5786**

HOMETOWN PRESS (US/1064-1742). [10,000] **2534**

HOMEWORLD BUSINESS (US/1048-0641). [15,000] **1608**

HOMILETICS (NORTH CANTON, OHIO) (US/1040-6255). **4963**

HOMILY SERVICE (US/0732-1872). [4,200] **4963**

HOMINES (PR/0252-8908). [7,000] **5201**

HOMMES VOLANTS PARIS, LES (FR/0018-4411). [20,000] **4899**

HONDURAS UPDATE (US/0741-8167). [1,200] **2512**

HONES MUTUAL MONTHLY (CN/0228-2399). **2534**

HONG KONG ANNUAL DIGEST OF STATISTICS (HK). [900] **4698**

HONG KONG BUILDER DIRECTORY (HK). [6,000] **616**

HONG KONG ELECTRONICS (HK). [40,000] **2056**

HONG KONG ENTERPRISE (HK/0018-4586). **680**

HONG KONG GIFTS & PREMIUMS (HK). [30,000] **2584**

HONG KONG GOVERNMENT GAZETTE, THE (HK). [4,000] **4654**

HONG KONG MANAGER. K'O HSUEH KUAN LI (HK). [7,000] **869**

HONG KONG MONTHLY DIGEST OF STATISTICS (HK/0300-418X). [2,300] **4698**

HONG KONG PEAK (HK). [6,000] **5061**

HONG KONG SOCIAL & ECONOMIC TRENDS (HK). [1,100] **1533**

HONG KONG TRADE STATISTICS (HK). [750] **730**

HONG KONG WATCHES & CLOCKS (HK). [20,000] **2916**

HOOF BEATS (COLUMBUS, OHIO) (US/0018-4683). [27,000] **2799**

HOOFPRINTS FROM THE YELLOWSTONE CORRAL OF THE WESTERNERS (US/0742-7727). [500] **2738**

HOOKUP (US). **2305**

HOOSHARAR (US/0018-4721). [7,500] **2263**

HOOSIER BUSINESS WOMAN, THE (US/0194-5319). [5,000] **5558**

HOOSIER CONSERVATION (US/0199-6894). **2216**

HOOSIER JOURNAL OF ANCESTRY, THE (US/0147-1228). [750] **2454**

HOPKINS QUARTERLY (CN/0094-9086). [375] **3344**

HORA DE POESIA (SP/0212-9442). [2,000] **3464**

HORECO (SP). [10,000] **5071**

HORIZON (CHICAGO, ILL.) (US/1042-8461). [2,000] **4963**

HORIZONS (US/0196-3120). [17,000] **23**

HORIZONS (OAKVILLE) (CN/0712-6077). **4963**

HORIZONS SF (CN/0229-1215). [200] **3394**

HORIZONS (TORONTO. 1966) (CN/0381-3789). **1829**

HORIZONS (VILLANOVA) (US/0360-9669). [1,425] **4963**

HORN BOOK GUIDE TO CHILDREN'S AND YOUNG ADULT BOOKS, THE (US/1044-405X). [10,000] **1064**

HORN BOOK MAGAZINE (1945), THE (US/0018-5078). [24,000] **1064**

HORN CALL, THE (US/0046-7928). [3,000] **4121**

HORNBILL (II). [3500] **457**

HORNS OF PLENTY, MALCOLM COWLEY AND HIS GENERATION (US/0896-9965). [400] **3394**

HOROLOGICAL JOURNAL (UK/0018-5108). [3,500] **2916**

HORS CADRE (FR/0755-0863). [800] **4072**

HORSE INDUSTRY DIRECTORY (US/0890-233X). [10,000] **2799**

HORSE WORLD (US/0018-5191). [2,500] **2800**

HORSEMEN'S JOURNAL, THE (US/0018-5256). [43,456] **2800**

HORSES ALL (CN/0225-4913). [10,540] **2800**

HORSES (CARLSBAD, CALIF.) (US/0046-7936). [5,000] **2800**

HORTICULTURAL NEWS (NEW BRUNSWICK, N.J.) (US/0886-5779). [300] **2419**

HORTICULTURE (US/0018-5329). [125,000] **2419**

HORTICULTURE DIGEST (US/0046-6964). **2419**

HORTICULTURE IN NEW ZEALAND : JOURNAL OF THE ROYAL NEW ZEALAND INSTITUTE OF HORTICULTURE (NZ/1170-1803). [900] **2419**

HOSE & NOZZLE (SHREVEPORT) (US/0191-6653). [800] **4260**

HOSHASEN IGAKU SOGO KENKYUJO NENPO (JA). **3584**

HOSPITAL & HEALTH SERVICES ADMINISTRATION (US/8750-3735). [24,000] **3783**

HOSPITAL & HEALTHCARE AUSTRALIA (AT/0813-7471). [3,919] **3783**

HOSPITAL AND NURSING YEAR BOOK OF SOUTHERN AFRICA (JOHANNESBURG (SOUTH AFRICA) : 1971)) (SA). [1,500] **3783**

HOSPITAL AND SELECTED MORBIDITY DATA (NZ/0548-9938). [450] **4810**

HOSPITAL CONTRACTS MANUAL (US/0734-0028). **2979**

HOSPITAL DOCTOR (UK/0262-3145). [36,000] **3584**

HOSPITAL, EL (US/0018-5485). [15,235] **3783**

HOSPITAL GIFT SHOP MANAGEMENT (US/0738-7946). [12,000] **869**

HOSPITAL MATERIALS MANAGEMENT NEWS (US/0749-6672). [1,800] **3784**

HOSPITAL MEDICINE (NEW YORK, N.Y.) (US/0441-2745). **3584**

HOSPITAL NEWS (PITTSBURGH, PA. 1986) (US/1071-0582). [14,000] **3784**

HOSPITAL PHARMACY DIRECTOR'S MONTHLY MANAGEMENT SERIES (US/0739-957X). **4306**

HOSPITAL PHARMACY SERVICE "INSTANT UP-DATE" (US/0739-9561). **4307**

HOSPITAL PHYSICIAN (SURGERY/EMERGENCY/SPECIALTIES ED.) (US/0888-2428). [89,000] **3584**

HOSPITAL PRACTICE (OFFICE EDITION) (US/8750-2836). [10,000] **3584**

HOSPITAL PRODUCTS AND TECHNOLOGY (CN/0823-6798). [20,000] **3584**

HOSPITAL PURCHASING NEWS (US/0279-4799). [22,000] **3785**

HOSPITALITE (TORONTO) (CN/0704-6359). [15537] **5071**

HOSPITALITY LAW (US/0889-5414). **2979**

HOSPITALS & HEALTH SERVICES YEAR BOOK AND DIRECTORY OF HOSPITAL SUPPLIERS, THE (UK/0300-5968). [6,000] **3785**

HOT LINE FARM EQUIPMENT GUIDE'S QUICK REFERENCE GUIDE FOR FARM TRACTORS AND COMBINES (US/0743-7730). **159**

HOTEL & CATERING REVIEW (BLACKROCK, DUBLIN) (US/0332-4400). [4,000] **2806**

HOTEL & MOTEL MANAGEMENT (US/0018-6082). [42,596] **2806**

HOTEL & RESORT INDUSTRY (US/0149-3639). [42,000] **2806**

HOTEL BUSINESS (US). [45,000] **2806**

HOTEL RESTAURANT (GW). [8,400] **5071**

HOTEL UPDATE NEWSLETTER (US). [10,000] **2806**

HOTELDOMANI (IT). **2806**

HOTELS (NEWTON, MASS.) (US/1047-2975). [60,000] **2807**

HOUALLET (CN/0714-8275). [1,000] **2454**

HOUILLE BLANCHE, LA (FR/0018-6368). [3,000] **2090**

HOUNDS AND HUNTING (US/0018-6384). [12,000] **4286**

HOUSE BUILDER (UK). [23,000] **2824**

HOUSE MAGAZINE (UK/0309-0426). **4476**

HOUSE PRICES (UK/0263-3639). [30,000] **4838**

HOUSE (WESTHAMPTON BEACH, N.Y.) (US/1074-4274). [26,000] **2901**

HOUSEHOLD & PERSONAL PRODUCTS INDUSTRY : HAPPI (US/0090-8878). [18,000] **977**

HOUSEPLANT MAGAZINE (US/1061-4079). [200,000] **2420**

HOUSER HUNTERS NEWSLETTER (US/0748-2736). [610] **2454**

HOUSING NEW JERSEY (US/1071-2585). [2,500] **2824**

HOUSING NEWSLETTER (OTTAWA) (CN/0710-7323). **2825**

HOUSING REPORT FOR KENTUCKY (US/0732-9342). [1,000] **2825**

HOUSING REVIEW (LONDON) (UK/0018-6651). [2,500] **2825**

HOUSTON AREA APARTMENT OWNERSHIP GUIDE (US). [100] **4838**

HOUSTON JOURNAL OF INTERNATIONAL LAW (US/0194-1879). [600] **3129**

HOUSTON LAWYER (US/0439-660X). [10,000] **2979**

HOUSTON MONTHLY (US/0272-8060). [56,000] **2535**

HOUSTON REAL ESTATE TRENDS (US/1045-8638). [1,200] **4838**

HOUSTON SUN, THE (US/1071-2941). [25,000] **5751**

HOW NORTH CAROLINA RANKS EDUCATIONALLY AMONG FIFTY STATES (US). [2,000] **1795**

HOW TO DOUBLE YOUR INCOME (US/0277-0334). [2,000] **404**

HOWE ENTERPRISE, THE (US). [600-650] **5751**

HOZON KAGAKU (JA). **352**

HP PROFESSIONAL (US/0896-145X). [35,000] **1186**

HPV NEWS (INDIANAPOLIS, IND.) (US/0898-6894). [2,500] **1977**

HRPLANNING NEWSLETTER, THE (US/0733-0332). [800] **941**

HUB (HAY RIVER) (CN/0714-5810). **2535**

HUDSON REGISTER STAR (US). [8,500] **5717**

HUDSON VALLEY REGIONAL REVIEW, THE (US/0742-2075). [700] **2847**

HUDSON'S WASHINGTON NEWS MEDIA CONTACTS DIRECTORY (US/0441-389X). **2920**

HUISARTS NU : MAANDBLAD VAN DE WETENSCHAPPELIJKE VERENIGING DER VLAAMSE HUISARTSEN : HANU (BE/0775-0501). [3,200] **3738**

HUMAN BIOLOGY (US/0018-7143). [1,600] **457**

HUMAN DEVELOPMENT (NEW YORK) (US/0197-3096). [10,000] **4589**

HUMAN EVENTS (WASHINGTON) (US/0018-7194). [47,000] **4476**

HUMAN ORGANIZATION (US/0018-7259). [3,800] **237**

HUMAN POWER (US/0898-6908). [2,500] **1977**

HUMAN RESOURCE EXECUTIVE (US/1040-0443). [43,000] **941**

HUMAN RESOURCE MANAGEMENT (SA/1010-8092). [12,000] **941**

HUMAN RESOURCE MANAGEMENT (US/0090-4848). [2,500] **941**

HUMAN RESOURCE MANAGEMENT NEWS (US). **942**

HUMAN RESOURCE PLANNING (US/0199-8986). [2,700] **942**

HUMAN RESOURCES NEWSLETTER (US/0883-0851). [550] **942**

HUMAN RESOURCES PROFESSIONAL (NEW YORK, N.Y.), THE (US/1040-5232). [1,500] **942**

HUMAN RIGHTS (CHICAGO, ILL.) (US/0046-8185). [3,200] **2979**

HUMANIORA (COPENHAGEN, DENMARK : 1988) (DK/0903-2401). [2,500] **2847**

HUMANIST (BUFFALO, N.Y.), THE (US/0018-7399). [20,000] **4348**

HUMANIST IN CANADA (CN). [1,500] **4348**

HUMANISTIC PSYCHOLOGIST, THE (US/0887-3267). [1,200] **4589**

HUMANISTICA LOVANIENSIA (BE/0774-2908). **3286**

HUMANITAS (BRESCIA, ITALY) (IT). [2,000] **4348**

HUMANITIES INDEX (US/0095-5981). **2857**

HUMANITIES INDEX. CD-ROM (US/0095-5981). **2847**

HUMANITIES (WASHINGTON) (US/0018-7526). [4,000] **2847**

HUMBER HIGHLIGHTS (CN/0821-2465). [3,500] **3786**

HUMBOLDT SPANISCHE AUSGABE (GW/0018-7615). [12,000] **2847**

HUNGARIAN CINEMA (HU). [2,500] **4072**

HUNGARIAN HERITAGE REVIEW (US/0889-2695). **2263**

HUNGARIAN STUDIES NEWSLETTER (US/0194-164X). [1,500] **2692**

HUNGARIAN STUDIES REVIEW (CN/0713-8083). [260] **2692**

HUNGARIKA IRODALMI SZEMLE (HU). [520] **2692**

HUNGER NOTES (US/0740-1116). [1,000] **2910**

HUNGER PROJECT PAPERS, THE (US/0743-6416). [25,000] **5288**

HUNT (US). [110,000] **4873**

HUNTER CASUALTY REPORT / ARKANSAS GAME AND FISH COMMISSION (US). [2,000] **4856**

HUNTERDON COUNTY DEMOCRAT (US/0018-7844). [24,362] **5710**

HUNTSVILLE HISTORICAL REVIEW, THE (US/1048-3152). **2738**

HUNTSVILLE TIMES, THE (US). [58,919 daily84,910 Sunday16,778 Morning75,698 Combination Daily] **5627**

HURON HISTORICAL NOTES (CN/0822-9503). [200] **2738**

HURON SOIL AND CROP NEWS (1964) (CN/0319-6038). [7,000] **173**

HUSTLER, THE (US/1074-0236). [12,400] **760**

HUTCHINSON LEADER (US). [6,000] **5696**

HUTCHINSON NEWS (HUTCHINSON, KAN. : 1957) (US). [45,000] **5676**

HUTTON CONSTRUCTION CATALOG : MECHANICAL PRODUCTS (US/0737-6316). [16,000] **2115**

HUWA WA-HIYA (CY/0250-6343). [50,000] **1064**

HVAC PROFITMAKER (US/0899-9791). [100] **2605**

HYBRID CIRCUIT TECHNOLOGY (US/0747-1599). [22,000] **5111**

HYDATA NEWS AND VIEWS (US). [4,200] **5534**

HYDE PARK TRIBUNE, THE MATTAPAN TRIBUNE (US/0745-9262). [5,869] **5689**

HYDRAULICS & PNEUMATICS (US/0018-814X). **2090**

HYDROBIOLOGICAL BULLETIN (NE/0165-1404). **457**

HYDROLOGIC REPORT (LOS ANGELES) (US/0147-3697). **5534**

HYGIE (FR/0751-7149). [2,000] **4783**

HYGIENE + MEDIZIN (GW/0172-3790). [5,000] **3585**

HYMN, THE (US/0018-8271). [3,500] **4121**

HYPERTENSION (DALLAS, TEX. 1979) (US/0194-911X). [4,000] **3705**

HYPNOTHERAPY TODAY (US/0882-8652). [1,800] **2858**

HYPOTHETICAL U.S. TAX TABLES FOR U.S. CITIZENS ABROAD (US). [5,000] **4731**

I C O M NEWS (FR/0018-8999). [10,000] **4089**

I CARE (IT/0394-817X). **3585**

I.D. CHECKING GUIDE (US/1041-5793). **4655**

I.D.E.E (BRIGHAM) (CN/1192-7755). [750] **5289**

I D R C REPORTS (CN/0315-9981). [25,000] **2910**

I/O NEWS (US/0274-9998). [5,000] **1267**

I P L O NEWS (CN/0319-4442). **3214**

I.S.C.A. QUARTERLY, THE (US/0741-2940). [150] **380**

I YUAN TO YING (CC). **322**

IA, THE JOURNAL OF THE SOCIETY FOR INDUSTRIAL ARCHEOLOGY (US/0160-1040). [1,400] **269**

IAEI NEWS (US/0020-5974). [30,000] **2290**

IAHPER JOURNAL, THE (US). [2,000] **1855**

IAHR BULLETIN (NE). [3,000] **2090**

IAS NEWSLETTER (INTERNATIONAL ASSOCIATION OF SEDIMENTOLOGISTS) (DK). **1382**

IASLIC BULLETIN (II/0018-8441). [1,500] **3214**

IBERO-AMERIKANISCHES ARCHIV (GW/0340-3068). [500] **2738**

IBIS LINKS (AT/0811-5559). [200] **2454**

IBSEN NEWS AND COMMENT : NEWSLETTER OF THE IBSEN SOCIETY OF AMERICA (US). [200] **3344**

ICAM NEWS (NE/0844-1901). **300**

ICARA REPORT / INTERNATIONAL CONFERENCE ON ASSISTANCE TO REFUGEES IN AFRICA (SZ). **2910**

ICASALS NEWSLETTER (US/0018-8808). [3,000] **174**

ICC BUSINESS WORLD : MAGAZINE OF THE INTERNATIONAL CHAMBER OF COMMERCE (FR). **820**

ICCSASW SOLIDARITY BULLETIN (CN/0823-7468). **1609**

ICELAND REVIEW (REYKJAVIK, ICELAND : 1984) (IC/0019-1094). [34,000] **2692**

ICES JOURNAL (US/0882-2115). [500] **2024**

ICI...ROSEMONT (CN/0318-2622). [1,800] **1829**

ICLAS NEWS (FI/1018-4635). [300] **5111**

ICLAS NEWS (FI/1018-4635). [200] **5511**

ICMC NEWSLETTER (SZ). [6,700] **5202**

ICMM NEWS (US/0883-1343). [500] **4089**

ICP INFORMATION NEWSLETTER (US/0161-6951). [800] **1015**

ID SYSTEMS (US/0892-676X). [50,000] **5111**

IDAHO CITIES (US). [2,000] **4655**

IDAHO ECONOMIC FORECAST, THE (US/8756-1840). [500] **1566**

IDAHO FARMER-STOCKMAN (US/1041-1682). [16,752] **212**

IDAHO FRUIT TREE CENSUS / U.S. DEPARTMENT OF AGRICULTURE, ECONOMICS AND STATISTICS SERVICE AND IDAHO DEPARTMENT OF AGRICULTURE (US). [150] **2420**

IDAHO GENEALOGICAL SOCIETY QUARTERLY (US/0445-2127). [400] **2454**

IDAHO LEGISLATIVE FISCAL REPORT TO THE JOINT SENATE FINANCE-HOUSE APPROPRIATIONS COMMITTEE : A PUBLICATION OF THE LEGISLATIVE BUDGET OFFICE (US). **4655**

IDAHO WILDLIFE (US/8755-2469). [11,000] **4873**

IDAHO WOOL GROWER'S BULLETIN (US). [1,300] **212**

IDAHO YESTERDAYS (US/0019-1264). [2,175] **2738**

IDEA SPEKTRUM (GW). [2,000] **4964**

IDEAL HOME PLANS (US/1049-2968). **300**

IDEAS '92: A PUBLICATION OF THE 1992 INSTITUTE (US). [500] **2620**

IDENTIFICATION JOURNAL (US/0747-962X). [23,000] **870**

IDENTITY (CINCINNATI, OHIO) (US/0899-3483). [10,500] **380**

IDES ... ET AUTRES (BE/0772-3784). **3395**

IDESIA (CL/0073-4675). [1,000] **2195**

IDIS (US/0891-8511). [1,000] **4307**

IDIS-LITERATURLISTE. SOZIALMEDIZIN / IDIS (GW/0932-5034). **4783**

IDOJARAS (BUDAPEST 1897) (HU/0367-7443). [1,000] **1426**

IDS BULLETIN (UNIVERSITY OF SUSSEX. INSTITUTE OF DEVELOPMENT STUDIES : 1985) (UK). [3,000] **1494**

IDS PENSIONS SERVICE BULLETIN (UK/1353-1573). **3149**

IDYLLWILD TOWN CRIER (US). [4,000] **5635**

IE, INVESTMENT EXECUTIVE (CN/0840-9137). [16,000] **900**

IEA/NEA ADVOCATE / ILLINOIS EDUCATION ASSOCIATION/NEA (US). **1751**

IEE NEWS (UK/0308-0684). [90,000] **2057**

IEE PRODUCTRONIC (GW). [13,167] **2058**

IEEE BULLETIN (US/0162-3842). [16,000] **2059**

IFAR REPORTS (US/8756-7172). [1,200] **352**

IFCD REPORT (SPANISH EDITION) (US/0149-5852). [5,000] **93**

IFCO NEWS (US/1065-1675). [10,000] **4964**

IFDC REPORT (US/0149-3434). [5,000] **94**

IFES REVIEW (UK/1010-8734). [750] **4964**

IFO SPIEGEL DER WIRTSCHAFT (GW/0170-3617). [700] **1533**

IFPRI REPORT (US/0272-3700). [7,500] **94**

IFR NEWS (UK). [2,500] **2344**

IFW. INTERNATIONAL FREIGHTING WEEKLY (UK/0032-5007). [20,679] **5383**

IGLU. INSTITUTO DE GESTION Y LIDERAZGO UNIVERSITARIO (CN/1183-5052). **1829**

IGLU. INSTITUTO DE GESTION Y LIDERAZGO UNIVERSITARIO (CN/1183-5052). **1829**

IGU NEWSLETTER (CN/0251-0464). [5,000] **2565**

IHERINGIA. SERIE BOTANICA (BL/0073-4705). [600] **513**

IHERINGIA. SERIE ZOOLOGIA (BL/0073-4721). [600] **5586**

IIMS, INDONESIA INDEX OF MEDICAL SPECIALITIES (SI/0300-4147). [10,500] **4307**

IIPA NEWSLETTER (II/0536-1761). [7,500] **4655**

IIPS NEWSLETTER (II). [1,300] **4553**

ILAR NEWS (US/0018-9960). [2,100] **3585**

ILCA RESEARCH REPORT / INTERNATIONAL LIVESTOCK CENTRE FOR AFRICA (ET). [1,000] **212**

ILEIA NEWSLETTER (NE/0920-8771). **174**

ILIFF REVIEW, THE (US/0019-1795). [500] **4964**

ILL. IA. MO. SEARCHER, THE (US/0737-5239). [287] **2454**

ILLINOIS AGRI-NEWS (US/0194-7443). [43,000] **94**

ILLINOIS AGRICULTURAL STATISTICS (US/0442-2562). **154**

ILLINOIS AUDUBON (US/1061-9801). **4166**

ILLINOIS AVIATION (SPRINGFIELD, ILL. : 1979) (US/0276-640X). [25,000] **23**

ILLINOIS BAR JOURNAL (US/0019-1876). [31,000] **2980**

ILLINOIS BENEDICTINE MAGAZINE, THE (US/0744-5806). [13,000] **1092**

ILLINOIS CONSTRUCTION LAW (US/8755-691X). [200] **2980**

ILLINOIS ECONOMIC OUTLOOK (US). **1494**

ILLINOIS EMPLOYMENT LAW LETTER (US/1049-9385). **3149**

ILLINOIS ENGINEER (US/0019-2015). [3,500] **1977**

ILLINOIS HISTORICAL JOURNAL (US/0748-8149). [2,400] **2738**

ILLINOIS HISTORY (US/0019-2058). [19,000] **2738**

ILLINOIS INSURANCE (US/0094-7660). [4,700] **2882**

ILLINOIS ISSUES (US/0738-9663). [4,500] **4476**

ILLINOIS JOURNAL OF HEALTH, PHYSICAL EDUCATION, RECREATION, AND DANCE (US/1062-2764). [3,000] **1751**

ILLINOIS LIBRARIES (US/0019-2104). [9,000] **3214**

ILLINOIS MAGAZINE (US/0747-9794). [13,000] **2738**

ILLINOIS MASTER PLUMBER (US/0019-2112). [2,200] **2606**

ILLINOIS MUSIC EDUCATOR, THE (US/0019-2147). [6,000] **4122**

ILLINOIS PHARMACIST (1979) (US/0195-2099). [3,000] **4307**

ILLINOIS PRINCIPAL (US/0019-218X). [2,200] **1864**

ILLINOIS PUBLIC EMPLOYEE RELATIONS REPORT / INSTITUTE OF LABOR AND INDUSTRIAL RELATIONS, UNIVERSITY OF ILLINOIS AT URBANA-CHAMPAIGN, THE (US). [700] **4655**

ILLINOIS PUBLIC PENSIONS (US/0891-7256). [250] **901**

ILLINOIS SCHOOL RESEARCH AND DEVELOPMENT (US/0163-822X). [2,750] **1751**

ILLINOIS SCHOOLS JOURNAL (US/0019-2236). [4,500] **1896**

ILLINOIS STATE GENEALOGICAL SOCIETY QUARTERLY (US/0046-8622). [2,500] **2454**

ILLINOIS STEWARD, THE (US/1058-9309). **2195**

ILLINOIS WILDLIFE (US/0019-2317). [10,500] **2195**

ILLINOIS WRITERS REVIEW (US/0733-9526). [300] **3344**

ILLUSTRATION 63. I.E. DREIUNDSECHZIG (GW/0019-2457). [700] **380**

ILLUSTRATOR, THE (US/0019-2465). [35,000] **380**

ILRU INSIGHTS (US/0732-1953). [2,000] **4389**

IMA BULLETIN : THE NEWSLETTER OF THE INTERNATIONAL MIDI ASSOCIATION, THE (US). [1,500] **1247**

IMAGE FILE (US/1046-6614). [1,300] **4089**

IMAGE (ROCHESTER) (US/0536-5465). [3,000] **4370**

IMAGE (ST. LOUIS, MO.) (US/0748-1780). [600] **3395**

IMAGE--THE JOURNAL OF NURSING SCHOLARSHIP (US/0743-5150). [73,000] **3857**

IMAGE (VANCOUVER) (CN/0383-9710). [20,000] **3586**

IMAGE WORLD (US/8756-6664). [150,000] **1092**

IMAGES (RESTON, VA.) (US/1055-1476). [1,200] **3941**

IMAGINE (BOSTON, MASS.) (US/0747-489X). [1,500] **3464**

IMAGINE (MONTREAL) (CN/0709-8855). [600] **3395**

IMAGING SERVICE BUREAU NEWS (US/1055-8098). [750] **1609**

IMAGINGWORLD (CAMDEN, ME.) (US/1060-894X). [60,000] **4212**

IMME BOLETIN TECNICO (VE/0376-723X). [1,200] **2024**

IMMEDIATE IMPACT (US). [2,000] **1113**

IMMIGRATION HISTORY NEWSLETTER, THE (US/0579-4374). [750] **1919**

IMMUNOLOGICAL REVIEWS (DK/0105-2896). [2,000] **3671**

IMMUNOLOGY & ALLERGY PRACTICE (US/0194-7508). [19,000] **3671**

IMMUNOPHARMACOLOGY (US/0162-3109). **3672**

IMP, INDUSTRIAL MODELS & PATTERNS (US/0146-0161). [1,200] **3481**

IMPACT (AT). **5203**

IMPACT 80 (CN/0227-2644). **1609**

IMPACT PUMP NEWS & PATENTS (US/1056-1536). [100] **2115**

IMPACT (SAVE THE CHILDREN (U.S.)) (US). [150,000] **5289**

IMPACT SINGAPORE (SI/0129-2862). [6,000] **4964**

IMPACT VALVE NEWS & PATENTS (US/1056-1544). [65] **2115**

IMPERIAL QUARTERLY MAGAZINE (CN/1188-0066). [400] **2517**

IMPIANTISTICA ITALIANA (IT/0394-1582). [6,500] **617**

IMPOR MENURUT JENIS BARANG DAN NEGERI ASAL (IO). **839**

IMPORT AUTOMOTIVE PARTS & ACCESSORIES (US/0199-4468). [32,000] **5416**

IMPORT BANKSTOWN (AT/1034-7313). **839**

IMPORT SERVICE (US/0896-5722). **5416**

IMPORTED CARS & TRUCKS, ELECTRICAL SERVICE & REPAIR (US). **5416**

IMPORTED CARS & TRUCKS, TRANSMISSION SERVICE & REPAIR (US/0741-0158). **5416**

IMPORTWEEK (CN/0702-8385). [2,000] **839**

IMPREVUE (MONTPELLIER) (FR/0242-5149). [600] **3395**

IMPRIMIS (US/0277-8432). [550,000] **1494**

IMPRINT (NEW YORK, N.Y. : 1976) (US/0277-7061). [475] **380**

IMPRINT (NEW YORK, NEW YORK) (US/0019-3062). [25,000] **3857**

IMPRINT (WATERLOO) (CN/0706-7380). [12,000] **1829**

IMSA JOURNAL (US/1064-2560). [5,600] **5441**

IN DANCE (US/0883-9956). [5,000] **1313**

IN GEARDAGUM : ESSAYS ON OLD ENGLISH LANGUAGE AND LITERATURE (US). [100] **3286**

IN JOPLIN METROPOLITAN (US/0743-1503). [10,000] **5480**

IN MOTION FILM & VIDEO PRODUCTION MAGAZINE (US/0889-6208). **4370**

IN OTHER WORDS (US/0279-3172). [220,000] **5017**

IN-PLANT PRINTER & ELECTRONIC PUBLISHER (US/0891-8996). [38,692] **4565**

IN PROCESS (OTTAWA) (CN/0711-2971). [4,300] **4655**

IN SITU (US/0146-2520). **1440**

IN-STAT ELECTRONICS REPORT (US/0888-9406). [300-500] **2064**

IN SUMMARY (CN/0228-2518). [600] **5203**

IN THE DRIVER'S SEAT (CN/0702-5785). **5417**

IN THEORY ONLY (US/0360-4365). [500] **4122**

IN TRANSIT (WASHINGTON) (US/0019-3291). [165,000] **5384**

IN UNITY (AT/0442-3844). [6,500] **4964**

IN VERKEHR GESETZTE NEUE MOTORFAHRZEUGE (LH). [300] **5417**

INA NEWSLETTER / INTERNATIONAL NANNOPLANKTON ASSOCIATION (NE). [300] **4231**

INCAST (DALLAS, TEX.) (US/1045-5779). [2,000] **4003**

INCENTIVE MARKETING AND SALES PROMOTION: ANNUAL REVIEW AND BUYERS' GUIDE (UK). [11,500] **760**

INCHIESTA (IT). **5247**

INCIDENTS OF THE WAR (US). [1,500] **4370**

INCIPIT (AG/0326-0941). [500] **3395**

INCITE (SYDNEY) (AT/0158-0876). [8,000] **3214**

INCL JOURNAL (US/0270-2061). [4,000] **2980**

INCREASE (US/0274-5569). [15,000] **4964**

INCREMENTAL MOTION CONTROL SYSTEMS AND DEVICES NEWSLETTER (US/0362-3858). [10,000] **2064**

INDEC COMMUNICATOR, THE (CN/0705-1166). **1751**

INDEKS HARGA PERDAGANGAN BESAR BAHAN BANGUNAN/KONSTRUKSI DI INDONESIA (IO). **1609**

INDEPENDENCE (AT). [2,000] **1751**

INDEPENDENT BANKER (US/0019-3674). [10,000] **790**

INDEPENDENT BUSINESS : IB (US/1047-2347). **681**

INDEPENDENT (ELMIRA) (CN/0833-8019). [8,000] **5786**

INDEPENDENT (LONDON, ENGLAND) (UK). [414,120] **5812**

INDEPENDENT PRESS (BLOOMFIELD, N.J.) (US/0747-4075). **5710**

INDEPENDENT REPUBLICAN (US/8750-2364). [3800] **4476**

INDEPENDENT (ROBERTSDALE, ALA.) (US). [6,100] **5627**

INDEPENDENT SENIOR, THE (CN/0847-5288). [42,500] **5179**

INDEPENDENT TEACHER FORTITUDE VALLEY (AT/1033-2464). [6,500] **1896**

INDEX CHRONOLOGIQUE / INDEX CHRONOLOGIQUE - CONSEIL DU PATRONAT DU QUEBEC (CN/0820-7933). **1678**

INDEX COMMERCIAL DE MONTREAL (CN/0821-7254). [3,000] **839**

INDEX-DIGEST OF PRECEDENT DECISIONS (US). [250] **2882**

INDEX INDO-ASIATICUS (II/0019-3852). [300] **2653**

INDEX NUMBERS OF STOCK EXCHANGE SECURITIES (PK/0081-4466). [435] **901**

INDEX OF FDA REGULATORY LETTERS (US/0161-7028). [75] **4656**

INDEX OF STATISTICS PUBLISHED BY THE DEPARTMENT OF HEALTH / NATIONAL HEALTH STATISTICS CENTRE, DEPARTMENT OF HEALTH (NEW ZEALAND) (NZ). **4810**

INDEX SEMINUM. JARDIM-MUSEU AGRICOLA TROPICAL (PO). [500] **2420**

INDEX TO ARTICLES ON JEWISH STUDIES (IS/0073-5817). [2,000] **2263**

INDEX TO BOOK REVIEWS IN RELIGION (US/0887-1574). [850] **5012**

INDEX TO INDIAN LEGAL PERIODICALS (II/0019-4034). [150] **2981**

INDEX TO LEGAL PERIODICALS (US/0019-4077). **3081**

INDEX TO LEGAL PERIODICALS. CD-ROM (US/0019-4077). **3081**

INDEX TO PERIODICAL ARTICLES RELATED TO LAW (US/0019-4093). [600] **3081**

INDEX TO THE GRAND FORKS HERALD (US/0272-779X). [10] **2535**

INDEXER (UK/0019-4131). [2,300] **3215**

INDIA INTERNATIONAL CENTRE QUARTERLY (II/0376-9771). [2,000] **2653**

INDIA LEATHER & LEATHER PRODUCTS DIRECTORY (II/0376-978X). **3184**

INDIA TODAY (INTERNATIONAL ED) (II). [370,000] **2488**

INDIA-WEST (US/0883-721X). [10,000] **5636**

INDIAN AFFAIRS (NEW YORK) (US/0046-8967). [40,000] **2263**

INDIAN ARCHIVES (II/0367-7435). [300] **2481**

INDIAN BAR REVIEW (II). [700] **2981**

INDIAN BEE JOURNAL (II/0019-4425). [800] **94**

INDIAN CHEMICAL ENGINEER (II/0019-4506). [4,000] **2013**

INDIAN CHURCH HISTORY REVIEW (II/0019-4530). **4964**

INDIAN DAIRYMAN (II/0019-4603). [2,500] **195**

INDIAN ECONOMIC REVIEW (II/0019-4670). [600] **1494**

INDIAN ENERGY AND POWER UPDATE (II). **1946**

INDIAN EXPORT TRADE JOURNAL, THE (II/0019-4735). [7,500] **4523**

INDIAN FOOD INDUSTRY (II/0253-5025). [2,000] **2344**

INDIAN FOOD PACKER (II/0019-4808). [1,000] **2344**

INDIAN HIGHWAYS (II/0376-7256). [6,000] **5441**

INDIAN HIGHWAYS (TEMPE, ARIZ.) (US/0892-6654). [15,000] **2263**

INDIAN HISTORY AND GENEALOGY (US). **2454**

INDIAN HORIZONS (II/0378-2964). [1,400] **2848**

INDIAN JOURNAL OF AGRICULTURAL ECONOMICS, THE (II/0019-5014). [1,800] **94**

INDIAN JOURNAL OF AGRONOMY (II/0537-197X). [1,800] **95**

INDIAN JOURNAL OF AMERICAN STUDIES (II/0019-5030). [3,500] **2738**

INDIAN JOURNAL OF ANIMAL HEALTH (II/0019-5057). [2,500] **5511**

INDIAN JOURNAL OF BEHAVIOUR (II/0970-0897). [500] **4589**

INDIAN JOURNAL OF BOTANY (II/0250-829X). [500] **513**

INDIAN JOURNAL OF DAIRY SCIENCE (II/0019-5146). [1,000] **195**

INDIAN JOURNAL OF ENVIRONMENTAL PROTECTION (II/0253-7141). [3,000] **2174**

INDIAN JOURNAL OF FORESTRY (II/0250-524X). **2384**

INDIAN JOURNAL OF GASTROENTEROLOGY (II/0254-8860). [1,250] **3746**

INDIAN JOURNAL OF HEREDITY (II/0374-826X). [300] **548**

INDIAN JOURNAL OF MEDICAL RESEARCH. SECTION A, INFECTIOUS DISEASES (II/0970-955X). [1,000] **3586**

INDIAN JOURNAL OF MEDICAL RESEARCH. SECTION B, BIOMEDICAL RESEARCH OTHER THAN INFECTIOUS DISEASES (II/0970-9568). [1,000] **3586**

INDIAN JOURNAL OF MEDICAL SCIENCES (II/0019-5359). [3,500] **3586**

INDIAN JOURNAL OF MYCOLOGY AND PLANT PATHOLOGY (II/0303-4097). [1,000] **575**

INDIAN JOURNAL OF OTOLARYNGOLOGY (II/0019-5421). [2,500] **3888**

INDIAN JOURNAL OF PATHOLOGY & MICROBIOLOGY (II/0377-4929). [2,000] **3895**

INDIAN JOURNAL OF PHARMACEUTICAL SCIENCES (II/0250-474X). [2,000] **4307**

INDIAN JOURNAL OF PHYSICS AND PROCEEDINGS OF THE INDIAN ASSOCIATION FOR THE CULTIVATION OF SCIENCE (II/0019-5480). [600] **5112**

INDIAN JOURNAL OF PHYSIOLOGY AND PHARMACOLOGY (II/0019-5499). [1,500] **581**

INDIAN JOURNAL OF PLANT PHYSIOLOGY (II/0019-5502). [800] **513**

INDIAN JOURNAL OF POLITICS (II/0303-9951). [300] **4476**

INDIAN JOURNAL OF POWER AND RIVER VALLEY DEVELOPMENT (II/0019-5537). [2,000] **5534**

INDIAN JOURNAL OF REGIONAL SCIENCE (II/0046-9017). [525] **2825**

INDIAN JOURNAL OF VETERINARY MEDICINE (II/0970-051X). [400] **5512**

INDIAN LAW REPORTER (US/0097-1154). [650] **2981**

INDIAN LIBRARY SCIENCE ABSTRACTS (II/0019-5790). [500] **3258**

INDIAN MARKET (US/0892-6409). [12,000] **2264**

INDIAN MINING & ENGINEERING JOURNAL, THE (II/0019-5944). [3,000] **2140**

INDIAN PEDIATRICS (II/0019-6061). [7,500] **3904**

INDIAN PRACTITIONER (II/0019-6169). [17,000] **3587**

INDIAN PROGRESS (US/0019-6193). [1,800] **2264**

INDIAN REVIEW OF AFRICAN AFFAIRS : IRAA (II). [1,500] **1494**

INDIAN REVIEW OF LIFE SCIENCES (II/0253-4436). [700] **458**

INDIAN SCIENCE INDEX (II). **5112**

INDIAN SOCIO-LEGAL JOURNAL (II/0970-7972). [1,200] **2981**

INDIAN THEOLOGICAL STUDIES (II/0253-620X). [1,000] **4964**

INDIAN TRADER, THE (US/0046-9076). [4,500] **2738**

INDIANA AGRICULTURAL STATISTICS (US). [2,000] **95**

INDIANA AUDUBON QUARTERLY (US/0019-6525). [600] **5617**

INDIANA BAPTIST (US). [5,500] **4964**

INDIANA BEVERAGE JOURNAL (US/0274-547X). [7,750] **2367**

INDIANA BUSINESS MAGAZINE (US/1060-4154). [36,000] **682**

INDIANA CRIMINAL LAW REVIEW (US). [350] **3107**

INDIANA HISTORY BULLETIN (US/0019-6649). [4,350] **2739**

INDIANA LAW REVIEW (US/0090-4198). [1,600] **2982**

INDIANA MAGAZINE OF HISTORY (US/0019-6673). [9,000] **2739**

INDIANA MATHEMATICS TEACHER (US/0889-6941). [900] **3509**

INDIANA MEDICINE (US/0746-8288). [7,000] **3587**

INDIANA MUSICATOR (US/0273-9933). [2,000] **4122**

INDIANA PHARMACIST (US). **4307**

INDIANA PRESERVATIONIST, THE (US/0737-8602). [5,000] **5480**

INDIANA PUBLISHER, THE (US/0019-6711). **4815**

INDIANA READING QUARTERLY (US/0019-672X). [12,500] **1896**

INDIANA STATE BOARD OF HEALTH BULLETIN, THE (US/0019-6754). [15,000] **4784**

INDIANA WEEKLY WEATHER CROP REPORT (US/0442-817X). [1,300] **174**

INDICA (II/0019-686X). [250] **2653**

INDICADORES DE COMERCIO EXTERIOR (CL/0716-2405). [700] **840**

INDICADORES DE COYUNTURA (AG/0537-3468). [2,000] **1534**

INDICADORES IBGE / SECRETARIA DE PLANEJAMENTO DA PRESIDENCIA DA REPUBLICA, FUNDACAO INSTITUTO BRASILEIRO DE GEOGRAFIA E ESTATISTICA, IBGE (BL). **1567**

INDICATOR (NANAIMO) (CN/0381-0917). [1,500] **4848**

INDICATOR, THE (US/0019-6924). [13,000] **978**

INDICE ESPANOL DE CIENCIA Y TECNOLOGIA (SP/0210-9409). [1,200] **5112**

INDICE MEDICO ESPANOL (SP). [800] **3660**

INDIGENOUS WOMAN (US/1070-1400). [4,000] **2264**

INDIKATOR EKONOMI (IO). **1567**

INDIKATOR KESEJAHTERAAN RAKYAT / WELFARE INDICATORS (IO). **5289**

INDIKATOR PEMBANGUNAN INDUSTRI PERTANIAN (IO). **95**

INDIVIDUAL INVESTOR'S GUIDE TO INVESTMENT PUBLICATIONS, THE (US). **901**

INDIVIDUAL PSYCHOLOGY (US/0277-7010). [700] **4590**

INDO-PACIFIC PREHISTORIC ASSOCIATION BULLETIN (AT/0156-1316). [300] **270**

INDONESIA CIRCLE : [JOURNAL] (UK/0306-2848). [275] **2505**

INDONESIAN COMMERCIAL NEWSLETTERS (IO/0377-0001). [2,000] **1495**

INDOOR AIR BULLETIN (US/1055-5242). [500] **2174**

INDOOR GARDEN, THE (US/8750-4081). **2420**

INDUSTRIA AVICOLA (US/0019-7467). [16,000] **213**

INDUSTRIA CARNICA LATINOAMERICANA, LA (AG/0325-3414). [5,000] **213**

INDUSTRIA DELLA GOMMA, L' (IT/0019-7556). [3,000] **5076**

INDUSTRIA HOTELERA EN ESPANA (SP). [2,000] **2807**

INDUSTRIA INTERNACIONAL (SP). [6,000] **1610**

INDUSTRIA PORCINA (US/0279-7771). [9,000] **213**

INDUSTRIAL ARCHAEOLOGY REVIEW (UK/0309-0728). [1,000] **270**

INDUSTRIAL ARCHAEOLOGY (TAVISTOCK) (UK/0019-7971). [2,000] **270**

INDUSTRIAL CERAMICS (IT). [6,000] **2591**

INDUSTRIAL CORROSION (UK/0265-0584). [1,750] **2102**

INDUSTRIAL DIRECTORY OF WALES (UK). **1610**

INDUSTRIAL EDUCATION (US/0091-8601). [45,000] **1913**

INDUSTRIAL EQUIPMENT NEWS (NEW YORK) (US/0019-8285). [210,000] **2098**

INDUSTRIAL FABRIC PRODUCTS REVIEW (US/0019-8307). [6,000] **5352**

INDUSTRIAL FINISHING. BUYERS' GUIDE (US). [36,000] **4224**

INDUSTRIAL FINISHING (WHEATON) (US/0019-8323). [36,000] **4224**

INDUSTRIAL GROUPINGS IN JAPAN (JA). [4,000] **682**

INDUSTRIAL HEATING (US/0019-8374). [23,500] **4431**

INDUSTRIAL HYGIENE DIGEST (US/0019-8382). [2,000] **2872**

INDUSTRIAL HYGIENE NEWS (PITTSBURGH) (US/0147-5401). [60,500] **2863**

INDUSTRIAL LAUNDERER (US/0046-9211). [2,700] **5352**

INDUSTRIAL LAW JOURNAL, INCLUDING THE INDUSTRIAL LAW REPORTS (SA). [1,600] **2982**

INDUSTRIAL LAWS OF SOUTH AFRICA (SA). [2,790] **3149**

INDUSTRIAL MARKET PLACE (US). [100,000] **1610**

INDUSTRIAL NEWS (IAEGER, W.VA.) (US). [1,700 (paid)] **5764**

INDUSTRIAL ORGANIZATIONAL PSYCHOLOGIST, THE (US/0739-1110). [5,000] **4590**

INDUSTRIAL PRODUCT BULLETIN (US/0199-2074). [200,000] **3481**

INDUSTRIAL PROPERTY (SZ/0019-8625). [1,400] **1304**

INDUSTRIAL PSYCHOLOGY (SA/0258-5200). **4590**

INDUSTRIAL PURCHASING AGENT (US/0019-8641). [26,000] **950**

INDUSTRIAL RELATIONS (BERKELEY) (US/0019-8676). [2,500] **1678**

INDUSTRIAL RELATIONS BULLETIN (VANCOUVER) (CN/0710-5940). **1678**

INDUSTRIAL RELATIONS JOURNAL (KARACHI, PAKISTAN) (PK). [700] **1678**

INDUSTRIAL RELATIONS LAW JOURNAL (US/0145-188X). [900] **3149**

INDUSTRIAL RELATIONS RESEARCH ASSOCIATION SERIES NEWSLETTER (US/0749-2162). [5,000] **1678**

INDUSTRIAL STATISTICS (VALLETTA, MALTA) (MM). [1,000] **1534**

INDUSTRIAS MANUFACTURERAS (CL/0577-7976). [350] **3481**

INDUSTRIE-ANZEIGER (GW/0019-9036). [26,000] **617**

INDUSTRIE LACKIER BETRIEB (GW/0019-9109). [2,923] **4224**

INDUSTRIE

INDUSTRIE SENEGALAISE, L' (SG). **1611**

INDUSTRIE SERVICE (GW). [45,400] **3481**

INDUSTRISTATISTIK (DK/0070-3532). [1,300] **1534**

INDUSTRY AND DEVELOPMENT. GLOBAL REPORT / UNITED NATIONS INDUSTRIAL DEVELOPMENT ORGANIZATION (US). **1611**

INDUSTRY AND ENVIRONMENT (ENGLISH EDITION) (FR/0378-9993). [5,500] **2863**

INDUSTRY & HIGHER EDUCATION (UK/0950-4222). [900] **1611**

INDUSTRY INTERNATIONAL (US/0276-7317). [57,000] **682**

INDUSTRY NEWS (RICHMOND, VA.) (US/8750-5525). [1,400] **5071**

INDUSTRY PERFORMANCE IN ... AND PROSPECTS FOR ... (PH). [150] **682**

INF INN : INFORMAZIONE INNOVATIVA (IT). [3,000] **5113**

INFANTRY (US/0019-9532). [15,360] **4046**

INFECTION (GW/0300-8126). [3,000] **3714**

INFECTION AND IMMUNITY (US/0019-9567). [7,101] **563**

INFECTIOUS DISEASES CAPSULE & COMMENT (US/0741-7462). **4784**

INFECTOLOGIA (MX/0185-0628). [13,000] **3714**

INFO COMMERCE (CN/0823-5414). [4,000] **840**

INFO-COMPTOIR MUSICAL (CN/0822-8167). **4122**

INFO-COOP (CN/0826-8045). **1495**

INFO DE L'A U C C (CN/0703-8917). **1830**

INFO-INFOGETTABLE (GW). [10,000] **1064**

INFO / ISM LIBRARY INFORMATION SERVICES (CN). [2,000] **3215**

INFO-MATHS (CN/0710-0027). **3509**

INFO PREVENTION (CN/0822-6776). **5384**

INFO-QUEBEC (CN/0226-6598). **1259**

INFO-RURAL (CN/0822-7314). **95**

INFO-SAINT-BRUNO (CN/0714-3885). **4656**

INFO SECURITY NEWS (US/1066-7822). [30,000] **1226**

INFOAAU (US/0279-9863). [8,000] **2598**

INFOBRAZIL / CENTER OF BRAZILIAN STUDIES (US/0736-8666). [500] **1567**

INFOFISH INTERNATIONAL (MY/0127-2012). [5,500] **2305**

INFOMANE (CN/0229-2068). **5786**

INFOPERSPECTIVES (US/0733-9305). **1238**

INFOR. INFORMATION SYSTEMS AND OPERATIONAL RESEARCH (CN/0315-5986). [540] **1259**

INFOR-MER. MINES (CN/0713-1445). **2004**

INFORM-ACTION - EDUCATEURS FRANCO-MANITOBAINS (CN/0822-5109). **1752**

INFORM REPORTS (US/0275-522X). [2,000] **2195**

INFORMA (SA). [45,000] **1113**

INFORMACCUEIL, L' (CN/0229-4338). **5289**

INFORMACION SISTEMATICA (MX/0185-2973). [2,000] **5806**

INFORMACIONES Y MEMORIAS DE LA SOCIEDAD DE INGENIEROS DEL PERU (PE). [2,000] **1978**

INFORMATIC USERS (BE). [14,000] **1188**

INFORMATION ABOUT THE OIL INDUSTRY, FOR THE OIL INDUSTRY (UK). **4260**

INFORMATION & I.E. E DOCUMENTAZIONE (IT/0390-2439). [1,500] **1260**

INFORMATION BULLETIN - ASH (UK/0261-0590). **4784**

INFORMATION BULLETIN - CHILDREN'S COURT OF NEW SOUTH WALES (AT/1031-6590). [600] **2982**

INFORMATION BULLETIN - CORPORATIONS TAX BRANCH (CN/0709-860X). **4732**

INFORMATION BULLETIN (ROMANIAN-AMERICAN HERITAGE CENTER (U.S.) (US/0748-6502). [1,800] **2739**

INFORMATION - CANADIAN ASSOCIATION OF SOCIAL WORKERS (CN/0315-3150). [10,000] **5289**

INFORMATION CARDIOLOGIQUE, L' (FR/0220-2476). [2,750] **3706**

INFORMATION CHICAGO (US/0196-3643). [5,000] **2535**

INFORMATION CIRCULAR - EXPORT DEVELOPMENT CORPORATION (CN/0226-3165). [20,000] **840**

INFORMATION CIRCULAR - STATE OF TENNESSEE, DEPARTMENT OF CONSERVATION, DIVISION OF GEOLOGY (US/0492-7079). [1,000] **1383**

INFORMATION CIRCULAR - STATE OF WASHINGTON, DEPARTMENT OF NATURAL RESOURCES, DIVISION OF GEOLOGY AND EARTH RESOURCES (US/0147-1783). [1,500] **1383**

INFORMATION CIRCULAR (WISCONSIN GEOLOGICAL AND NATURAL HISTORY SURVEY) (US/0512-0640). [450] **1383**

INFORMATION DOCUMENT (SOUTH PACIFIC COMMISSION) (ML/0081-2838). [600] **2620**

INFORMATION GRAMMATICALE (PARIS), L' (FR/0222-9838). [650] **3287**

INFORMATION LEGISLATIVE SERVICE (1969) (US/0020-0115). [11,300] **2982**

INFORMATION LISTING / REGIONAL CLERK'S DEPT (CN/0826-0613). **4656**

INFORMATION - LUTHERAN WORLD FEDERATION NEWS SERVICE (SZ). [3,000] **5061**

INFORMATION MANAGEMENT BULLETIN (US/1046-9303). [1,000] **1188**

INFORMATION PAPER - COMMITTEE FOR ECONOMIC DEVELOPMENT OF AUSTRALIA (AT). [2,000] **1495**

INFORMATION PROCHE-ORIENT (CN/0711-2157). [8,000] **2654**

INFORMATION RESOURCES MANAGEMENT JOURNAL (US/1040-1628). [600] **3216**

INFORMATION RETRIEVAL & LIBRARY AUTOMATION (US/0020-0220). **1275**

INFORMATION SERIES - VIRGINIA POLYTECHNIC INSTITUTE AND STATE UNIVERSITY. COLLEGE OF AGRICULTURE AND LIFE SCIENCES (US/0742-7425). [800] **96**

INFORMATION SHEETS (UK). **2344**

INFORMATION SOCIETY, THE (US/0197-2243). [600] **3216**

INFORMATION SYSTEMS RESEARCH (US/1047-7047). [1800] **1188**

INFORMATION TECHNOLOGY MANAGEMENT (AT/1322-3526). [8,100] **5113**

Controlled Circulation Index

INFORMATION TECHNOLOGY NEWSLETTER (HARRISBURG, PA.) (US/1057-7939). [600] **3217**

INFORMATION UPDATE - CANADIAN STANDARDS ASSOCIATION (CN/1182-0187). [4,000] **1978**

INFORMATION UPDATE - HUB, INFORMATION SERVICES (CN/0713-8474). [1,000] **4389**

INFORMATIONS SOCIALES (FR/0046-9459). [9,500] **5247**

INFORMATIONWEEK (MANHASSET, N.Y.) (US/8750-6874). [141,385] **1260**

INFORMATIQUE ET SCIENCES JURIDIQUES (FR). [250] **1226**

INFORMATIVO (BL/0524-2932). **5203**

INFORMATIVO ANUAL DA INDUSTRIA CARBONIFERA / MINISTERIO DAS MINAS E ENERGIA, DEPARTAMENTO NACIONAL DA PRODUCAO MINERAL, DNPM (BL). [2,000] **1612**

INFORMAZIONE CARDIOLOGICA (IT). [10,000] **3706**

INFORMAZIONI SANITARIE (IT). **2174**

INFORME AGROPECUARIO (BELO HORIZONTE) (BL/0100-3364). [15,000] **96**

INFORME ANUAL - CENTRO INTERNATIONAL DE AGRICULTURA TROPICAL (CK). **96**

INFORME ANUAL - COMISION EJECUTIVA HIDROELECTRICA DEL RIO LEMPA (ES). [1,000] **1612**

INFORME DE ACTIVIDADES / CORPORACION DE INVESTIGACIONES ECONOMICAS PARA LATINOAMERICA (CL). [1,000 (Spanish)300 (English)] **1495**

INFORME ECONOMICO (VE/0067-3250). **1495**

INFORME LATINOAMERICANO (UK/0263-5372). [3,000] **2489**

INFORME SOBRE CHILE (CK). **5329**

INFOTERM NEWSLETTER (AU). [150] **3287**

INFOWORLD (US/0199-6649). [160,000] **1268**

INGEGNERIA SISMICA (IT/0393-1420). [5,000] **2024**

INGENIEUR (DEN HAAG) (NE/0020-1146). [25,000] **1978**

INGENIEURS-CONSEILS CANADA (1981) (CN/0821-4166). **1978**

INHALO-SCOPE (CN/0824-8281). [2,000] **4308**

INITIALES (HALIFAX) (CN/0710-4278). [150] **3396**

INITIATIVES IN POPULATION (PH/0115-2181). [10,000] **4553**

INJURED ATHLETE, THE (CN/0705-369X). **3587**

INJURY PREVENTION NETWORK NEWSLETTER (US). [2,000] **4784**

INJURY PREVENTION NEWS (CN/1197-4362). **2598**

INKSTONE (CN/0714-2870). [100] **3464**

INLAND EMPIRE MAGAZINE (US/0199-5073). [54,000] **682**

INLAND RIVER GUIDE (US/0198-859X). [3,500] **5450**

INN BUSINESS (ESSEX, ONT.) (CN/0821-7610). [9,750] **2807**

INNER WOMAN (US/1049-9709). [30,000] **5559**

INNES REVIEW, THE (UK/0020-157X). [500] **5030**

INNOTECH JOURNAL (PH). [1,000] **1752**

INNOTECH NEWSLETTER (PH). [3,000] **1752**

INNOVATION ABSTRACTS (US/0199-106X). [49,000] **1896**

INNOVATION ET TECHNOLOGIE EN BIOLOGIE ET MEDECINE (FR/0243-7228). [800] **3693**

INNOVATION ST. ANDREWS (UK/0264-9861). [1,000] **1979**

INNSIDE NEWS (CN/0710-992X). **2807**

INORGANIC CHEMISTRY (US/0020-1669). [4,331] **1036**

INQUIRY (CHICAGO) (US/0046-9580). [2,500] **3587**

INQUIRY (KINGSTON) (CN/0714-7198). [8,000] **682**

INRS NOUVELLES (CN/0836-3218). **5114**

INSECT WORLD (LANSING, MICH.) (US/1043-6057). [250] **1064**

INSECTICIDE & ACARICIDE TESTS (US/0276-3656). [1,200] **4245**

INSERVICE (SYRACUSE, N.Y.) (US/0732-3808). [5,000] **1864**

INSIDE (ALBANY, N.Y.) (US/0736-0150). [1,200] **3100**

INSIDE BLUEGRASS (US/0891-0537). [1,000] **4122**

INSIDE CHICAGO (US). [70,000] **5480**

INSIDE FLORIDA POLITICS (US/1059-2148). **4477**

INSIDE HOCKEY (DON MILLS, ONT.) (CN/0835-9806). **4900**

INSIDE ISHM MAGAZINE (US). [5,300] **2065**

INSIDE MEDIA (STAMFORD, CONN.) (US/1046-5316). **760**

INSIDE MS (US/0739-9774). [400,000] **3834**

INSIDE OPERATIONS (US/1071-2968). [30,000] **1189**

INSIDE OXFAM (US/0319-0323). **4338**

INSIDE RADIO (US/0731-9312). **1133**

INSIDE THE AUBURN TIGERS (AUBURN, ALA.) (US/0279-2273). [12,000] **4900**

INSIDE THE LEADING MAIL ORDER HOUSES (US/0743-2895). **760**

INSIDE TURBO C (US/1045-6791). **1287**

INSIDE TURBO PASCAL (US/1045-6775). **1268**

INSIDE UVA (US/0745-9432). [9,500] **1864**

INSIDE WORCESTER (US). [12,000] **2535**

INSIDE WORDPERFECT (US/1046-9656). **1287**

INSIGHT : AUSTRALIAN FOREIGN AFFAIRS AND TRADE ISSUES (AT/1038-6726). [7,000] **4524**

INSIGHT (NORTHAMPTON) (UK/1354-2575). [2,950] **2102**

INSIGHT ON COLLECTABLES (1987) (CN/0836-5873). [20,000] **251**

INSIGHT (SAN FRANSISCO, CALIF.) (US/1060-135X). [1,800] **3857**

INSIGHTS : A JOURNAL OF THE FACULTY OF AUSTIN SEMINARY (US/1056-0548). [7500] **4965**

INSIGHTS INTO CHRISTIAN EDUCATION (US/8756-3347). [400] **4965**

INSIGHTS (WASHINGTON, D.C.) (US/0747-007X). [35,000] **4900**

INSPIRATION (SZ/0020-2061). [10,900] **926**

INSPIRED (US). [3,000] **301**

INSTALLATION DES SYSTEMES DE GICLEURS, L' (CN/0708-2215). **1979**

Ctrl. Circ. Index

INSTALLATORE ITALIANO (IT/0020-2118). **2606**

INSTITUTE OF CRIMINOLOGY & FORENSIC SCIENCES BULLETIN (US/0739-8514). [200] **3166**

INSTITUTE TODAY (US/0897-4527). [10,000] **791**

INSTITUTIONAL DISTRIBUTION (US/0020-3572). [32,000] **2344**

INSTITUTIONAL REAL ESTATE LETTER, THE (US/1044-1662). [3,500] **4839**

INSTITUTO DE GEOLOGIA REVISTA (MX/0185-0962). [1,200] **1383**

INSTITUTO DO DESENCOLVIMENTO ECONOMICO-SOCIAL DO PARA: PEDQUISA EMPREGO E DESEMPREGO NA REGIAO METROPOLITANA DE BELEM (BL). [800] **1680**

INSTRUCTION DELIVERY SYSTEMS (US/0892-4872). [18,000] **1189**

INSTRUCTIONAL DEVELOPMENT AT WATERLOO (CN/0228-2313). [1,500] **1896**

INSTRUMENTENBAUREPORT (GW/0936-014X). **4123**

INSULATION GUIDE (US/0737-2817). [8,000] **1947**

INSURANCE ALMANAC (ENGLEWOOD. 1933), THE (US/0074-0675). [10,000] **2882**

INSURANCE AND EMPLOYEE BENEFITS LITERATURE (US/0735-3944). [300] **2883**

INSURANCE BROKERS' MONTHLY AND INSURANCE ADVISER (UK/0260-2385). [8,000] **2883**

INSURANCE CONFERENCE PLANNER (US/0193-0516). [7,500] **2883**

INSURANCE ECONOMICS SURVEYS (US/0020-4668). [15,000] **2883**

INSURANCE INDUSTRY LITIGATION REPORTER : THE NATIONAL JOURNAL OF RECORD OF INSURANCE LITIGATION (US/0887-7858). **2983**

INSURANCE JOURNAL (US/0020-4714). [10,000] **2883**

INSURANCE MARKETING INSIDER (US/1040-6867). [2,000] **2884**

INSURANCE SYSTEMS BULLETIN (UK/0268-1935). [1,000] **2884**

INSURANCE TIMES (NEWTON, MASS.) (US/1042-7333). [7,600] **2884**

INSURANCEWEEK (US/0020-4846). [5,800] **2884**

INTECH (US/0192-303X). [51,000] **2065**

INTEGRAL YOGA (US/0161-1380). [1,600] **4965**

INTELLECTUAL PROPERTY NEWSLETTER (UK). **1305**

INTELPROP NEWS (UK/0967-3466). [300] **1305**

INTENSIVBEHANDLUNG (GW/0341-3063). **3588**

INTENSIVE CARE WORLD (BALDOCK) (UK/0266-7037). [20,000] **3588**

INTER ALIA (RENO) (US/0092-6086). [3,800] **2983**

INTER-AMERICAN ARBITRATION (CN/0715-4771). [350] **2983**

INTER-AMERICAN TRADE AND INVESTMENT LAW (US/1078-2028). [700] **840**

INTER-CITY EXPRESS (OAKLAND, CALIF.) (US/0274-7464). [126,659] **5636**

INTER (HAUTE-VILLE, QUEBEC) (CN/0825-8708). [1200] **385**

INTER-MECANIQUE DU BATIMENT (CN/0831-411X). [5,900] **617**

INTER-SOCIETY COLOR COUNCIL NEWS (US/0731-2911). [1,000] **5114**

INTERACTING WITH COMPUTERS (UK/0953-5438). [1,200] **1189**

INTERACTION - CANADIAN CHILD DAY CARE FEDERATION (CN/0835-5819). [2,000] **5290**

INTERAGENCY TRAINING CATALOG OF COURSES (US/0360-5019). **4704**

INTERAMERICANA (RIO PIEDRAS, P.R.) (PR/8750-5428). [12,000] **5808**

INTERBLOCS (CN/0705-0828). **3786**

INTERCAMBIO (MX). [3,000] **840**

INTERCHANGE - SCHOOL OF BUSINESS AND ECONOMICS. WILFRID LAURIER UNIVERSITY (CN/0823-9851). [2,500] **683**

INTERCHANGE (SYDNEY, AUSTRALIA) (AT). [500] **5017**

INTERCOLLEGIATE REVIEW, THE (US/0020-5249). [35,000] **1831**

INTERCULTURAL HORIZONS (CN/0827-1550). [1,000] **5247**

INTERCULTURE (CN/0828-797X). [1,000] **4965**

INTERCULTURE (MONTREAL. ED. FRANCAISE) (CN/0712-1571). [1,000] **4965**

INTERDISCIPLINARY SCIENCE REVIEWS : ISR (UK/0308-0188). [800] **5114**

INTERFACE (CHICAGO) (US/0270-6717). [1,500] **3217**

INTERFACE (MONTREAL. 1984) (CN/0826-4864). [8,000] **5114**

INTERFACE QUARTERLY NEWSLETTER (AT). [800] **1947**

INTERFAITH WOMEN'S NEWS & NETWORK (US/0892-6719). [200] **5559**

INTERFERENCE TECHNOLOGY ENGINEER'S MASTER (US/0190-0943). [25,000] **2066**

INTERGEO BULLETIN (FR/0396-5880). [320] **2582**

INTERIGHTS BULLETIN (UK/0268-3709). [1,000] **4509**

INTERIOR CONSTRUCTION (US/0888-0387). [8,500] **617**

INTERIOR DECORATORS' HANDBOOK (US/0733-8511). [20,000] **2901**

INTERIOR JOURNAL (1984) (US/8750-7609). [4,314] **5681**

INTERIORS & SOURCES (US/1059-5287). [27,000] **2901**

INTERMEDIAIR BELGIE (BE). [93,000] **1567**

INTERMODAL ASIA (HK). **5450**

INTERNAL MEDICINE NEWS & CARDIOLOGY NEWS (US/0274-5542). [72,500] **3746**

INTERNATIONAL ADVERTISER (NEW YORK, N.Y. 1985) (US/0885-3363). [3,800] **760**

INTERNATIONAL AFFAIRS BULLETIN (SA/0258-7270). [3,500] **4524**

INTERNATIONAL AFFAIRS STUDIES (PL/0867-4493). [1,000] **4524**

INTERNATIONAL ANNUAL JOURNAL OF ARTS, SCIENCES, ENGINEERING, AGRICULTURE, AND TECHNOLOGY (US/0749-0682). [200] **5114**

INTERNATIONAL AVIATION MECHANICS JOURNAL (US/0045-1193). [36,000] **24**

INTERNATIONAL BANKING FOCUS (US/1042-3370). [1,500] **792**

INTERNATIONAL BLOOD/PLASMA NEWS (US/0742-7719). [200] **3772**

INTERNATIONAL BOTTLER AND PACKER, THE (UK/0020-6199). [6,178] **4219**

INTERNATIONAL BROADCASTING (UK/0957-4425). [10,000] **1133**

INTERNATIONAL BULK JOURNAL : IBJ (UK/0260-1087). [7,500] **5384**

INTERNATIONAL BUSINESS LAWYER (UK/0309-7676). [10,000] **3129**

INTERNATIONAL CABLE (US/1069-5494). **1133**

INTERNATIONAL CHEMICAL ENGINEERING (US/0020-6318). [1,300] **2013**

INTERNATIONAL CLASSIFICATION (GW/0340-0050). [800] **3218**

INTERNATIONAL CLINICAL PSYCHOPHARMACOLOGY (UK/0268-1315). **4308**

INTERNATIONAL COAL LETTER (BE). **2140**

INTERNATIONAL COMET QUARTERLY, THE (US/0736-6922). [300] **395**

INTERNATIONAL DEFENCE EQUIPMENT CATALOG : IDEC (GW). [10,000] **4046**

INTERNATIONAL DENDROLOGY SOCIETY YEARBOOK (UK/0307-322X). [1,200] **514**

INTERNATIONAL DOCUMENTARY (US/0742-5333). [5,000] **4072**

INTERNATIONAL DRUG REPORT (US/0148-4648). [10,000] **3166**

INTERNATIONAL DRUG THERAPY NEWSLETTER (US/0020-6571). [7,000] **4308**

INTERNATIONAL ECONOMIC SCOREBOARD (US/0270-045X). [6,500] **1636**

INTERNATIONAL ECONOMY, THE (US/0898-4336). [15,000] **1636**

INTERNATIONAL EDUCATION FORUM (PULLMAN, WASHINGTON) (US/1053-1750). [400] **1831**

INTERNATIONAL ENERGY STATISTICS SOURCEBOOK (US/1058-2487). [650] **1963**

INTERNATIONAL ENGINEERING DIRECTORY (US/0074-5774). [2,000] **1979**

INTERNATIONAL ENVIRONMENT & SAFETY (UK/0141-4836). [13,000] **2174**

INTERNATIONAL EXAMINER (SEATTLE, WASH. 1973) (US/1065-1500). [10,000] **2654**

INTERNATIONAL EXPLORATION NEWSLETTER (US/1064-9042). [200] **4261**

INTERNATIONAL FELLOWSHIP NEWSLETTER, THE (US). [2,500] **4965**

INTERNATIONAL FIBER JOURNAL (US/1049-801X). [9,000] **5352**

INTERNATIONAL FIRE AND SECURITY PRODUCT NEWS (UK/0961-3730). **2291**

INTERNATIONAL FIRE FIGHTER (US/0020-6733). **2291**

INTERNATIONAL FIRE PHOTOGRAPHERS ASSOCIATION : NEWSLETTER : IFPA (US). [750] **4371**

INTERNATIONAL FLORICULTURE QUARTERLY REPORT (UK). [300] **2435**

INTERNATIONAL FLYING FARMER (US/0020-675X). [2,000] **96**

INTERNATIONAL FOOD INGREDIENT (NE/0924-5863). [9,000] **2345**

INTERNATIONAL FREE TRADE ZONE (UK). [4,500] **5384**

INTERNATIONAL FUR FASHION REVIEW (CN/0823-6976). [10,000] **3184**

INTERNATIONAL GEOLOGY REVIEW (US/0020-6814). [500] **1383**

INTERNATIONAL GLASS/METAL CATALOG (US/0147-300X). [11,000] **2591**

INTERNATIONAL HAIR ROUTE (CN/0820-6880). [3,500] **3720**

INTERNATIONAL HISTORY REVIEW, THE (CN/0707-5332). [750] **2620**

INTERNATIONAL HUMANIST (NE). [1,500] **4349**

INTERNATIONAL JOURNAL FOR HOUSING SCIENCE AND ITS APPLICATIONS (US/0146-6518). [1,000] **2825**

INTERNATIONAL JOURNAL OF ANALYTICAL AND EXPERIMENTAL MODAL ANALYSIS, THE (US/0886-9367). [750] **2116**

INTERNATIONAL JOURNAL OF ANDROLOGY (UK/0105-6263). **3588**

INTERNATIONAL JOURNAL OF ANGIOLOGY, THE (US/1061-1711). [1,500] **3706**

INTERNATIONAL JOURNAL OF BIOSOCIAL AND MEDICAL RESEARCH (US/1044-811X). [1,000] **5248**

INTERNATIONAL JOURNAL OF CHILDBIRTH EDUCATION, THE (US/0887-8625). [12,000] **3762**

INTERNATIONAL JOURNAL OF CLINICAL AND EXPERIMENTAL HYPNOSIS, THE (US/0020-7144). [2,700] **2858**

INTERNATIONAL JOURNAL OF CLINICAL NEUROPSYCHOLOGY, THE (US/0749-8470). [1,500] **4591**

INTERNATIONAL JOURNAL OF DEVELOPMENTAL BIOLOGY, THE (SP/0214-6282). [1,000] **541**

INTERNATIONAL JOURNAL OF EARLY CHILDHOOD (CN/0020-7187). [2,000] **1753**

INTERNATIONAL JOURNAL OF EDUCOLOGY (AT/0818-0563). [1,500] **1754**

INTERNATIONAL JOURNAL OF ENERGY SYSTEMS (US/0226-1472). [300] **1947**

INTERNATIONAL JOURNAL OF FERTILITY (US/0020-725X). [26,000] **581**

INTERNATIONAL JOURNAL OF FETO-MATERNAL MEDICINE (GW/0933-0445). [1,500] **3762**

INTERNATIONAL JOURNAL OF FRACTURE (NE/0376-9429). [1,100] **2102**

INTERNATIONAL JOURNAL OF FRONTIER MISSIONS (US/0743-2429). [500] **4965**

INTERNATIONAL JOURNAL OF HEALTH SCIENCES (NE/0924-2287). [500] **4785**

INTERNATIONAL JOURNAL OF HUMANITIES AND PEACE, THE (US/1042-4032). **2848**

INTERNATIONAL JOURNAL OF INNOVATIVE HIGHER EDUCATION : THE OFFICIAL JOURNAL OF THE UNIVERSITY WITHOUT WALLS INTERNATIONAL COUNCIL (CN/0267-4386). **1831**

INTERNATIONAL JOURNAL OF INSTRUCTIONAL MEDIA (US/0092-1815). [325] **1897**

INTERNATIONAL JOURNAL OF ISLAMIC AND ARABIC STUDIES (US/0740-5375). [2,400] **2768**

INTERNATIONAL JOURNAL OF LEPROSY AND OTHER MYCOBACTERIAL DISEASES (US/0148-916X). **4785**

INTERNATIONAL JOURNAL OF MARITIME HISTORY (CN/0843-8714). [500] **4177**

INTERNATIONAL JOURNAL OF MATHEMATICS AND MATHEMATICAL SCIENCES (US/0161-1712). [325] **3509**

INTERNATIONAL

Controlled Circulation Index

INTERNATIONAL JOURNAL OF MENTAL HEALTH (US/0020-7411). [300] **3927**

INTERNATIONAL JOURNAL OF MINI & MICROCOMPUTERS (US/0702-0481). [300] **1274**

INTERNATIONAL JOURNAL OF ORAL AND MAXILLOFACIAL SURGERY (DK/0901-5027). [1,200] **3966**

INTERNATIONAL JOURNAL OF OROFACIAL MYOLOGY, THE (US/0735-0120). [350] **1325**

INTERNATIONAL JOURNAL OF ORTHODONTICS (US/0020-7500). [1,000] **1325**

INTERNATIONAL JOURNAL OF ORTHOPAEDIC TRAUMA (UK/0960-2941). **3882**

INTERNATIONAL JOURNAL OF PEPTIDE AND PROTEIN RESEARCH (DK/0367-8377). [1,200] **1042**

INTERNATIONAL JOURNAL OF PHARMACEUTICAL TECHNOLOGY & PRODUCT MANUFACTURE (UK/0260-6267). [1,500] **4308**

INTERNATIONAL JOURNAL OF POLITICAL ECONOMY (US/0891-1916). [300] **4477**

INTERNATIONAL JOURNAL OF PSYCHOSOMATICS (US/0884-8297). [1,000] **3589**

INTERNATIONAL JOURNAL OF PUBLIC ADMINISTRATION (US/0190-0692). **4657**

INTERNATIONAL JOURNAL OF RESEARCH AND ENGINEERING (POSTAL APPLICATION) (US/1043-7134). [10,000] **1145**

INTERNATIONAL JOURNAL OF SCIENCE AND TECHNOLOGY (US/0891-5083). [800] **5115**

INTERNATIONAL JOURNAL OF SOCIOLOGY (US/0020-7659). [350] **5248**

INTERNATIONAL JOURNAL OF SOLAR ENERGY (SZ/0142-5919). **1948**

INTERNATIONAL JOURNAL OF THE ADDICTIONS (US/0020-773X). **1345**

INTERNATIONAL JOURNAL OF THE SOCIOLOGY OF LANGUAGE (NE/0165-2516). [800] **3287**

INTERNATIONAL JOURNAL OF TROPICAL AGRICULTURE (II/0254-8755). [400] **97**

INTERNATIONAL JOURNAL OF TROPICAL PLANT DISEASES (II/0254-0126). [500] **514**

INTERNATIONAL JOURNAL OF TURBO & JET-ENGINES (IS/0334-0082). [350] **24**

INTERNATIONAL JOURNAL OF TURKISH STUDIES (US/0272-7919). [1,200] **2692**

INTERNATIONAL JOURNAL OF UNIVERSITY ADULT EDUCATION (CN/0074-3992). [300] **1801**

INTERNATIONAL JOURNAL ON POLICY AND INFORMATION (US/0251-1266). [800] **5204**

INTERNATIONAL LABMATE (UK/0143-5140). [45,000] **1015**

INTERNATIONAL LABORATORY. EUROPEAN ED (US/0010-2164). [55,000] **1016**

INTERNATIONAL LAW NEWS, THE (US/0047-0813). [12,000] **3130**

INTERNATIONAL LAW PRACTICUM (US/1041-3405). [2,000] **3130**

INTERNATIONAL LAWYER, THE (US/0020-7810). **3130**

INTERNATIONAL LEGAL MATERIALS (US/0020-7829). [2,800] **3130**

INTERNATIONAL LEGAL PERSPECTIVES (US). **3130**

INTERNATIONAL LIAISON GROUP ON GOLD MINERALIZATION NEWSLETTER (UK). [600] **1383**

INTERNATIONAL LICHENOLOGICAL NEWSLETTER (GW/0731-2830). **514**

INTERNATIONAL MANAGEMENT (UK). [25,000] **684**

INTERNATIONAL MARINE BUSINESS (UK/0965-0644). [5,000] **684**

INTERNATIONAL MARINE BUSINESS JOURNAL (US). [12,000] **593**

INTERNATIONAL MEDIA GUIDE. EDITION, BUSINESS/PROFESSIONAL PUBLICATIONS, EUROPE (US/0730-5273). [950] **761**

INTERNATIONAL MEDIA GUIDE. EDITION, BUSINESS/PROFESSIONAL PUBLICATIONS, MIDDLE EAST/AFRICA (US). [950] **761**

INTERNATIONAL MIGRATION (GENEVA, SWITZERLAND) (SZ/0020-7985). [3,000] **1919**

INTERNATIONAL MIGRATION REVIEW : IMR (US/0197-9183). [2,500] **1919**

INTERNATIONAL MONEY MARKETING (UK/0958-3785). [8,000] **902**

INTERNATIONAL NETWORKS (US/0739-9898). [500] **1158**

INTERNATIONAL NEWSLETTER OF MARITIME HISTORY (CN/0843-8706). [500] **5450**

INTERNATIONAL OFFSHORE RIG OWNERS & PERSONNEL DIRECTORY (US/1058-6008). **4261**

INTERNATIONAL OIL AND GAS DEVELOPMENT (US/0535-1634). [600] **4283**

INTERNATIONAL OPERATING ENGINEER, THE (US/0020-8159). [360,000] **1680**

INTERNATIONAL ORGANIZATION (US/0020-8183). [2,700] **4525**

INTERNATIONAL PARALLELS (US/1055-3649). **841**

INTERNATIONAL PEAT JOURNAL (FI/0782-7784). [1,500] **1948**

INTERNATIONAL PETROCHEMICAL DEVELOPMENT (US/0270-1138). [100] **4261**

INTERNATIONAL PETROLEUM FINANCE (US/0193-9270). **4261**

INTERNATIONAL PHARMACEUTICAL ABSTRACTS (US/0020-8264). [1,500] **4334**

INTERNATIONAL POETRY REVIEW (GREENSBORO) (US/0145-0786). [300] **3344**

INTERNATIONAL POLITICAL SCIENCE ABSTRACTS (FR/0020-8345). [1,500] **4502**

INTERNATIONAL PROBLEMS (IS/0020-840X). [2,100] **4525**

INTERNATIONAL PROGRAMS, GENERAL REPORT / CANADIAN TEACHERS' FEDERATION AND ITS MEMBERS (CN/0820-7305). **1897**

INTERNATIONAL PSYCHOLOGIST (US/0047-116X). [1,700] **4591**

INTERNATIONAL RAILWAY JOURNAL AND RAPID TRANSIT REVIEW (UK/0744-5326). [9,400] **5432**

INTERNATIONAL REGIONAL SCIENCE REVIEW (US/0160-0176). [3,250] **1497**

INTERNATIONAL REHABILITATION REVIEW (US/0020-8477). [10,000] **4389**

INTERNATIONAL REVIEW OF SOCIAL HISTORY (NE/0020-8590). [1,400] **5248**

INTERNATIONAL REVIEW OF SOCIOLOGY OF EDUCATION (AT/0726-4178). **5248**

INTERNATIONAL REVIEW OF THE RED CROSS (SZ/0020-8604). [2,800] **5290**

INTERNATIONAL RICE RESEARCH NEWSLETTER (PH/0115-0944). [12,000] **174**

INTERNATIONAL RICE RESEARCH NOTES (PH). [12,000] **175**

INTERNATIONAL SEMIOTIC SPECTRUM (CN/0825-0456). [7,000] **2848**

INTERNATIONAL SOCIAL SCIENCE JOURNAL (FR/0020-8701). [4,000] **5204**

INTERNATIONAL SOCIAL SCIENCE REVIEW (US/0278-2308). [4,400] **5204**

INTERNATIONAL SOCIETY FOR MUSIC EDUCATION YEARBOOK (UK/0172-0597). [2,000] **4123**

INTERNATIONAL SOCIETY OF BASSISTS (US/0892-0532). [1,600] **4123**

INTERNATIONAL SPECTRUM (US/1050-9070). [50,000] **1190**

INTERNATIONAL STATISTICAL REVIEW (NE/0306-7734). [3,000] **5329**

INTERNATIONAL STEEL STATISTICS : SUMMARY TABLES (UK/0952-6803). **4025**

INTERNATIONAL TECHNOLOGY DISCLOSURES (US/0742-4825). **1305**

INTERNATIONAL TELEX-DIRECTORY ITD (GW). [20,000] **1158**

INTERNATIONAL TENNIS (US/1063-0333). [3,500] **4901**

INTERNATIONAL TEXTILE BULLETIN. DYEING/PRINTING/FINISHING (SZ/1012-8417). [26,500] **5352**

INTERNATIONAL TEXTILE BULLETIN. FABRIC FORMING (SZ/1012-8425). [45,700] **5352**

INTERNATIONAL TEXTILES (NE/0020-8914). [10,000] **5352**

INTERNATIONAL, THE (UK). [40,000] **792**

INTERNATIONAL THIRD WORLD STUDIES JOURNAL & REVIEW (US/1041-3944). [200] **4526**

INTERNATIONAL TRADE FORUM (SZ/0020-8957). [20,000] **926**

INTERNATIONAL TRADE REPORT (US/0890-5142). **2401**

INTERNATIONAL TROMBONE ASSOCIATION SERIES (US/0363-5708). [600] **4123**

INTERNATIONAL UNDERSTANDING AT SCHOOL (FR). [6,000] **1897**

INTERNATIONAL UNDERWATER SYSTEMS DESIGN (UK/0267-1085). [10,000] **2091**

INTERNATIONAL UNIVERSITY POETRY QUARTERLY, THE (US/0748-9676). **3464**

INTERNATIONAL UNIVERSITY REPORT, THE (US). [4,500] **1831**

INTERNATIONAL VIDEOVUE (CN/0847-3994). [250,000] **4073**

INTERNATIONAL VISITOR (US/1058-5575). [10,000] **5481**

INTERNATIONAL WATER & IRRIGATION REVIEW (IS). [10,466] **175**

INTERNATIONAL WILDLIFE (US/0020-9112). [650,000] **2195**

INTERNATIONAL WOMEN'S NEWS JOURNAL OF THE INTERNATIONAL ALLIANCE OF WOMEN, INCORPORATING LE DROIT DES FEMMES (UK/0020-9120). [1,100] **5559**

INTERNATIONAL ZOO-NEWS (UK/0020-9155). [500] **5586**

INTERNATIONALE BIBLIOGRAPHIE DER REPRINTS. INTERNATIONAL BIBLIOGRAPHY OF REPRINTS (US). [1,800] **417**

INTERNATIONALE BIBLIOGRAPHIE DER REZENSIONEN WISSENSCHAFTLICHER LITERATUR (GW/0020-918X). **3357**

INTERNATIONALE BIBLIOGRAPHIE DER ZEITSCHRIFTENLITERATUR AUS ALLEN GEBIETEN DES WISSENS (GW). **3357**

INTERNATIONALE JAHRESBIBLIOGRAPHIE DER FESTSCHRIFTEN : IJBF (GW). **417**

INTERNATIONALE JAHRESBIBLIOGRAPHIE DER KONGRESSBERICHTE (GW/0933-1905). **417**

INTERNATIONALE KATHOLISCHE ZEITSCHRIFT (GW/0341-8693). [3,000] **5030**

INTERNATIONALE KIRCHLICHE ZEITSCHRIFT (SZ/0020-9252). [580] **4966**

INTERNATIONALE MATHEMATISCHE NACHRICHTEN (AU). [1,500] **3510**

INTERNATIONALES ASIEN FORUM (GW/0020-9449). **5204**

INTERNATIONALES VERKEHRSWESEN (GW/0020-9511). [4,100] **5384**

INTERP CENTRAL CLEARINGHOUSE NEWSLETTER (US/0890-1538). [150] **4205**

INTERPRETATION (RICHMOND) (US/0020-9643). [11,000] **4966**

INTERPRETER (EVANSTON, ILL.), THE (US/0020-9678). [285,000] **5061**

INTERRACIAL BOOKS FOR CHILDREN BULLETIN (US/0146-5562). [5,000] **1065**

INTERSTATE (US/0363-9991). [500] **3397**

INTERSTATE ACCOMODATION DIRECTORY (AT). [70,000] **2807**

INTERSTATE INFORMATION REPORT (US/0884-8394). [1,800] **2984**

INTERTAX (NE/0165-2826). [1,500] **4733**

INTERVALLE (GW). [2,500] **4123**

INTERVENANT (CN/0823-213X). [1,500] **1345**

INTERVENOR : NEWSLETTER OF THE CANADIAN ENVIRONMENTAL LAW ASSOCIATION (CN/0820-3458). **3113**

INTERVENTION (CN/0047-1321). **5290**

INTERVENTION (QUEBEC) (CN/0705-1972). **2535**

INTERVENTIONS ECONOMIQUES POUR UNE ALTERNATIVE SOCIALE (CN/0715-3570). [1,200] **1497**

INTERVENTIONS SONORES (CN/1181-7739). [800] **4124**

INTI (PROVIDENCE, R.I.) (US/0732-6750). [1,000] **3397**

INTIMATE FASHION NEWS (US/1061-5792). [8,000] **1085**

INTOWNER, THE (US/0887-9400). [30,000] **5647**

INUIT ART ENTHUSIASTS NEWSLETTER, THE (CN/0824-0639). [250] **353**

INUIT ART QUARTERLY (CN/0831-6708). [3,816] **353**

INUKTITUT (ENGLISH AND INUIT EDITION) (CN/0020-9872). [10,000] **2264**

INVENTAIRE DE LA RECHERCHE SUBVENTIONNEE ET COMMANDITEE (CN/0709-3896). [4,000] **1831**

INVENTAIRE DES MOYENS DE FORMATION DEPENDANT DES MINISTERES TECHNIQUES (IV). [250] **1913**

INVENTORS' VOICE (US/0748-7851). [18,000] **5116**

INVENTORY OF ACADEMIC DEGREE PROGRAMS IN SOUTH CAROLINA, AN (US). [700] **1831**

INVENTORY OF MUSIC ICONOGRAPHY (US/0889-6607). [400] **4124**

INVENTORY OF POPULATION PROJECTS IN DEVELOPING COUNTRIES AROUND THE WORLD (US/0363-5155). [3,000] **4554**

INVEST IN HUNGARY (HU/0239-1929). [10,000] **902**

INVESTIGACION AGRARIA. ECONOMIA (SP/0213-635X). [1,500] **97**

INVESTIGACION AGRARIA. PRODUCCION Y PROTECCION VEGETALES (SP/0213-5000). [1,800] **175**

INVESTIGACION AGRARIA. PRODUCCION Y SANIDAD ANIMALES (SP/0213-5035). [1,750] **213**

INVESTIGACION CLINICA (VE/0535-5133). **3590**

INVESTIGACION MEDICA INTERNACIONAL (MX/0377-0206). [7,000] **3590**

INVESTIGACIONES MARINAS (CL). [200] **2306**

INVESTIGATIONS IN SCIENCE EDUCATION (US). [800] **5116**

INVESTIGATIONS ON CETACEA (SZ/1010-3635). **5587**

INVESTIGATOR (AT/0021-0013). [800] **2669**

INVESTMENT ADVISOR (SHREWSBURY, N.J.) (US/1069-1731). [60,000] **902**

INVESTMENT BULLETIN (US/0401-8680). **902**

INVESTMENT MONITOR (AT). **903**

INVESTMENT QUALITY TRENDS (US/0021-0110). [5,000] **903**

INVESTMENT REVIEW (AT/0094-8683). [1,400] **903**

INVESTOR RELATIONS NEWSLETTER (US). **903**

INVESTOR, U.S.A (US/0739-8026). [800] **903**

INVOLVEMENT & PARTICIPATION / IPA (UK). [4,000] **872**

INVOLVEMENT : THE JOURNAL OF THE INVOLVEMENT & PARTICIPATION ASSOCIATION (UK). [4,000] **872**

IODINE (US). [300] **1440**

IOP NEWSLETTER (US/1016-4928). [1,000] **514**

IOWA ARCHITECT (US/0021-0439). [4,000] **301**

IOWA CITY MAGAZINE (US). [17,000] **2536**

IOWA CONSERVATIONIST (US/0021-0471). [60,000] **2195**

IOWA DENTAL JOURNAL, THE (US/0021-0498). [2,000] **1325**

IOWA IIA AUDIT UPDATE (US/0746-6579). [200] **745**

IOWA INTERLINK (US/1050-2270). [3,200] **4657**

IOWA MANUFACTURERS REGISTER (US/0737-7940). **3481**

IOWA MUNICIPALITIES (US/0021-0595). [7,000] **4657**

IOWA REVIEW, THE (US/0021-065X). [1,000] **3397**

IOWA STATER, THE (US/0746-2204). [140,000] **1831**

IOWAN, THE (US/0021-0722). [28,000] **2536**

IP MARK (SP). **684**

IPAC QUARTERLY (CN/0845-437X). **4261**

IPADE ALAGBARA (US/0883-6620). [3,000] **5268**

IPEF, INSTITUTO DE PESQUISAS E ESTUDOS FLORESTAIS (BL/0100-4557). [1,500] **2385**

IPI DATA SERVICE. MIDDLE EAST (US). [5,000] **4261**

IPN-BLATTER (GW/0179-5775). [7,000] **1755**

IPPA-NEWSLETTER (IO). [1,000] **589**

IPPF MEDICAL BULLETIN (ENGLISH EDITION) (UK/0019-0357). [27,000] **589**

IPPF OPEN FILE (UK). [2,500] **589**

IPTC NEWS (UK/1012-8719). [150] **1158**

IR. INVESTOR RELATIONS (UK/0958-6679). [10,000] **903**

IRAL, INTERNATIONAL REVIEW OF APPLIED LINGUISTICS IN LANGUAGE TEACHING (GW/0019-042X). [750] **3288**

IRAN NAMEH. BUNYAD-I MUTALAAT-I IRAN (US/0892-4147). [1,000] **2654**

IRANIAN ASSETS LITIGATION REPORTER (US/0277-2922). **3131**

IRANIAN WOMEN QUARTERLY (CN). [1,000-2,000] **5559**

IRC BULLETIN / UNITED STATES ENVIRONMENT PROTECTION AGENCY, NATIONAL TRAINING AND OPERATIONAL TECHNOLOGY CENTER (US). [15,000] **5535**

IRELAND, PORTS & SHIPPING HANDBOOK (UK/0260-924X). [6,000] **5450**

IRELAND TODAY (IE/0332-0103). [20,000] **5481**

IRIS (CHARLOTTESVILLE, VA.) (US/0896-1301). [2,500] **5204**

IRIS (MONTPELLIER) (FR/0291-2066). [300] **3397**

IRIS YEAR BOOK / BRITISH IRIS SOCIETY, THE (UK/0075-0700). [700] **2420**

IRISH BANKING REVIEW, THE (IE/0021-1060). [5,000] **793**

IRISH BIOTECH NEWS (IE/0790-1747). **459**

IRISH FORESTRY (IE/0021-1192). [800] **2385**

IRISH GENEALOGIST (UK/0306-8358). [900] **2454**

IRISH GENEALOGY DIGEST (US/8756-1484). [300] **2454**

IRISH HERITAGE LINKS (UK/0957-0837). [5,000] **2454**

IRISH HISTORICAL STUDIES (IE/0021-1214). [800] **2692**

IRISH JOURNAL OF MEDICAL SCIENCE (IE/0021-1265). [1,500] **3590**

IRISH LITERARY STUDIES (US/0140-895X). **3397**

IRISH LITERARY SUPPLEMENT (US/0733-3390). [4,000] **3397**

IRISH NEWS AND BELFAST MORNING NEWS, THE (IE). [43,000] **5803**

IRISH SWORD, THE (IE/0021-1389). [1,200] **2693**

IRISH TRAVEL TRADE NEWS (IE/0021-1419). **5481**

IRISH UNIVERSITY REVIEW (IE/0021-1427). [1,000] **3344**

IRISH VETERINARY NEWS (IE). [1,700] **5512**

IRODALOMTORTENETI KOZLEMENYEK (HU/0021-1486). [1,250] **3458**

IRON AND STEEL ENGINEER (US/0021-1559). [12,000] **4004**

IRON AND STEEL INDUSTRY. ANNUAL STATISTICS FOR THE UNITED KINGDOM (UK/0572-709X). [1,000] **1612**

IRON & STEELMAKER (US/0275-8687). [700] **4005**

IRON ORE MANUAL (JA). **4005**

IRONWORKER, THE (US/0021-163X). [134,000] **2025**

IRPI. INTERNATIONAL REINFORCED PLASTICS INDUSTRY (UK/0261-5487). [6,500] **4455**

IRRICAB (IS/0376-5083). [300] **175**

IRRIGATION AND POWER (II/0367-9993). [4,000] **2091**

IRRIGATION FARMER, THE (AT). [8,000] **175**

IRRIGATION JOURNAL (US/0047-1518). [14,000] **159**

IRRINEWS (IS/0304-3606). [5,000] **175**

IRS PRACTICE ALERT (US/1053-1173). [2,000] **4734**

IS AUDIT & CONTROL JOURNAL (US/1076-4100). [12,000] **1260**

IS. INTER SERVICE (US/0273-7485). [10,000] **955**

ISA TRANSACTIONS (US/0019-0578). [1,000] **5116**

ISEA COMMUNIQUE (US/0019-0624). [40,000] **1865**

ISIE (US/0894-928X). [500] **5290**

ISIS MAGAZINE : MAGAZINE OF THE INDEPENDENT SCHOOLS INFORMATION SERVICE, THE (UK). [24,000] **1755**

ISLAMIC AFFAIRS (US/0748-0482). [6,000] **5043**

ISLAMIC QUARTERLY, THE (UK/0021-1842). [2,000] **4966**

ISLAMIC STUDIES (PK/0578-8072). [3,000] **5043**

ISLAND DISPATCH (US/0892-2497). [3,500] **5717**

ISLAND GROWER, THE (CN/0827-2824). [8,400] **2420**

ISLAND MAGAZINE, THE (CN/0384-8175). [3,000] **2739**

ISLANDWIDE RUNNER (US/0740-6266). [1,500] **4901**

ISLAS (CU/0047-1542). [10,000] **2321**

ISLE OF MAN DIGEST OF ECONOMIC AND SOCIAL STATISTICS (UK). [750] **1534**

ISR, INTERNATIONLE BERG- UND SEILBAHNRUNDSCHAU. INTERNATIONAL AERIAL TRAMWAY REVIEW (AU). [3,000] **2117**

ISRAEL EXPLORATION JOURNAL (IS/0021-2059). [2,500] **270**

ISRAEL HORIZONS (US/0021-2083). [4,000] **5048**

ISRAEL JOURNAL OF PSYCHIATRY AND RELATED SCIENCES, THE (IS/0333-7308). [1,100] **3927**

ISRAEL MY GLORY (US/8755-402X). [220,000] **4966**

ISSUE (WALTHAM, MASS.) (US/0047-1607). [2,000] **2499**

ISSUES & OBSERVATIONS (US/1065-464X). [35,000] **872**

ISSUES & STUDIES (CH/1013-2511). [3,000] **4526**

ISSUES, EVENTS & IDEAS (CN/0704-6936). [2,000] **1804**

ISSUES IN LAW & MEDICINE (US/8756-8160). [5,000] **2985**

ISSUES (SAINT LOUIS, MO.) (US/0888-9201). [2,000] **2251**

ISTF NEWS (US/0276-2056). [1,700] **2385**

ISTF NOTICIAS (US/0743-5991). **2385**

ISURI : DO. HARISIMHA GAURA VISVAVIDYALAYA, SAGARA KE HINDI-VIBHAGA KE ANTARGATA KRIYASILA BUNDELI-PITHA KA AYOJANA (II). [1,500] **3288**

IT TRAINING (UK/0954-7940). **1223**

ITALIAN-AMERICAN BUSINESS (IT). [7,000] **1636**

ITALIAN GENEALOGIST (US/0884-9080). [300] **2455**

ITALIAN GENERAL REVIEW OF DERMATOLOGY (IT/0021-292X). [3,300] **3721**

ITALIAN JOURNAL OF GASTROENTEROLOGY, THE (IT/0392-0623). [2,000] **3746**

ITALIAN JOURNAL OF ORTHOPAEDICS AND TRAUMATOLOGY (IT/0390-5489). [500] **3882**

ITALIAN JOURNAL OF SPORTS TRAUMATOLOGY (IT/0391-4089). [5,000] **3954**

ITALIAN JOURNAL OF SURGICAL SCIENCES, THE (US/0392-3525). [5,000] **3966**

ITALIAN LIGHTING (IT). **2067**

ITALIAN TRIBUNE NEWS (US). [40,000] **5710**

ITALIANA VITA (CN/0700-3234). [25,000] **2693**

ITALIANIST (UK/0261-4340). [500] **3397**

ITALIQUES / UNIVERSITE DE LA SORBONNE NOUVELLE (PARIS III), U.E.R. D'ITALIEN ET ROUMAIN, CENTRE DE RECHERCHES SUR L'ITALIE MODERNE ET CONTEMPORAINE (FR/0751-2163). [300] **3397**

ITC COMMUNICATOR (US/0885-8063). [20,000] **1114**

ITEM, THE (US). [21,000] **5742**

ITG JOURNAL (US/0363-2849). [3,500] **4124**

ITHACA TIMES (US/0277-1187). [19,100] **5717**

ITI INTERNATIONAL NEWS ROUND UP (AT). [800] **385**

ITL. INSTITUUT VOOR TOEGEPASTE LINGUISTIK (BE/0019-0829). [400] **3288**

ITPI JOURNAL (II). [1,500] **2825**

IT'S HAPPENING (US/0098-7549). [2,000] **1880**

IUCN BULLETIN (SZ/0020-9058). [9,000] **2196**

IUFRO NEWS (AU/0256-5145). [7,000] **2402**

IVL. B (SW/0347-8696). **2233**

IVS. INDEX OF VETERINARY SPECIALITIES (SA/0019-0918). [2,044] **5512**

IVY LEAF (CHICAGO) (US/0021-3276). [35,000] **1102**

IWSA YEAR BOOK : AN OFFICIAL PUBLICATION OF THE INTERNATIONAL WATER SUPPLY ASSOCIATION (UK). [3,000] **5535**

IYO DENSHI TO SEITAI KOGAKU (JA/0021-3292). [10,000] **3693**

IZARD COUNTY HISTORIAN, THE (US/0164-7539). [600] **2739**

JAARBOEK VAN HET KATHOLIEK DOCUMENTATIE CENTRUM (NE). [500] **5030**

JAARSTATISTIEK OVER DE INTERNATIONALE TRAFIEK DER HAVENS (BE). [400] **5401**

JAARVERSLAG Controlled Circulation Index

JAARVERSLAG / DIENST GRONDWATERVERKENNING TNO (NE). [6,500] **1415**

JAARVERSLAG (NETHERLANDS. KONINKLIJKE LANDMACHT. SECTIE MILITAIRE GESCHIEDENIS) (NE). [500] **2693**

JAARVERSLAG - PRODUKTSCHAP VOOR LANDBOUWZAAIZADEN (NE). **98**

JAARVERSLAG / SUID-AFRIKAANSE ONTWIKKELINGSTRUSTKORPORASIE BEPERK (STK) (SA). **1568**

JAARVERSLAG - TECHNISCH PHYSISCHE DIENST TNO-TH (NE). [2,500] **4407**

JABBERWOCKY (UK/0305-8182). [350] **3398**

JAC COURSES DIRECTORY (AT/1031-7805). [8,000] **1755**

JACA : JOURNAL OF THE ASSOCIATION FOR COMMUNICATION ADMINISTRATION (US/0360-0939). **1114**

JACKSON ADVOCATE (US/0047-1704). [26,000] **5700**

JACKSONVILLE BUSINESS JOURNAL (US/0885-453X). [10,000] **685**

JAHRBUCH DES VEREINS ZUM SCHUTZ DER BERGWELT (GW/0171-4694). [5,000] **2196**

JAHRBUCH DES WIENER GOETHE-VEREINS (AU). [750] **3398**

JAHRBUCH - DEUTSCHE AKADEMIE FUER SPRACHE UND DICHTUNG (DARMSTADT) (GW/0070-3923). [400] **3398**

JAHRBUCH - DEUTSCHE SHAKESPEARE-GESELLSCHAFT WEST (GW/0070-4326). **3398**

JAHRBUCH - DEUTSCHES ROTES KREUZ (GW). [6,500] **5291**

JAHRBUCH FUER OSTDEUTSCHE VOLKSKUNDE (GW/0075-2738). **2321**

JAHRESBERICHT (GW). [6,000] **4448**

JAHRESBERICHT DER GEWERBEAUFSICHT (GW). [5,000] **2864**

JAHRESBERICHT DES LANDESARBEITSAMTES TIROL (AU). [400] **1681**

JAHRESBERICHT / MAX-PLANCK-INSTITUT FUER QUANTENOPTIK (GW). [1,000] **4435**

JAHRESSCHRIFT FUER MITTELDEUTSCHE VORGESCHICHTE (GW/0075-2932). **271**

JAHRESSCHRIFT / SALZBURGER MUSEUM CAROLINO AUGUSTEUM (AU/0558-3438). [1,200] **4089**

JAHRESSTATISTIK DES AUSSENHANDELS DER SCHWEIZ. STATISTIQUE ANNUELLE DU COMMERCE EXTERIEUR DE LA SUISSE (SZ). **730**

JAMAICA JOURNAL (JM/0021-4124). [5,000] **2536**

JAMAICAN NATIONAL BIBLIOGRAPHY (JM). [200] **418**

JAMES BURNSIDE BULLETIN OF RESEARCH, THE (US/1046-2279). [400] **2740**

JAMES DICKEY NEWSLETTER (US/0749-0291). **3464**

JAMES JOYCE LITERARY SUPPLEMENT (US/0899-3114). [650] **3345**

JAMES JOYCE QUARTERLY (US/0021-4183). [1,400] **3345**

JAMES WHITE REVIEW, THE (US/0891-5393). [4000] **3345**

JANASAMKHYA (II). [200] **4554**

JANE'S A F V SYSTEMS (UK). **4046**

JANE'S DEFENCE WEEKLY (UK/0265-3818). [25,000] **4047**

JANE'S FIGHTING SHIPS (UK/0075-3025). [10,000] **4177**

JAPAN FOUNDATION NEWSLETTER, THE (JA/0385-2318). [8,000] **5249**

JAPAN GRAPHIC ARTS (JA). [5,000] **4566**

JAPAN HARVEST (JA/0021-440X). [1,100] **4967**

JAPAN LETTER (US/0446-6241). **2654**

JAPAN PICTORIAL (NORTH AMERICAN EDITION) (JA/0388-6115). [200,000] **2536**

JAPANESE ECONOMIC STUDIES (US/0021-4841). [250] **1569**

JAPANESE FILMS (JA/0448-8830). [5,000] **4073**

JAPANESE INVESTMENT IN U.S. REAL ESTATE REVIEW. WESTERN REGION (US/0898-9761). **4839**

JAPANESE JOURNAL OF MEDICAL SCIENCE & BIOLOGY (JA/0021-5112). **3591**

JAPANESE PHILATELY (US/0146-0994). [1,500] **2785**

JAPANESE RAILWAY ENGINEERING (JA/0448-8938). **5432**

JAPANESE SENSOR NEWSLETTER (US). [125] **2068**

JAPANESE TELECOMMUNICATIONS (US). [100] **1159**

JARDINS DE FRANCE PARIS (FR/0021-5481). [13,000] **2421**

JARQ. JAPAN AGRICULTURAL RESEARCH QUARTERLY (JA/0021-3551). [2,000] **98**

JASNA NEWS (US/0892-8665). [2,300] **3398**

JASPER COUNTY GLEANER, THE (US/0749-8314). [200] **2455**

JASSA (AT/0313-5934). [8,000] **793**

JAUNA GAITA (CN/0448-9179). **2848**

JAX FAX TRAVEL MARKETING MAGAZINE (US/0279-7984). [28,000] **5481**

JAZYKOVEDNY CASOPIS (XO/0021-5597). [1,000] **3289**

JAZZ EDUCATORS JOURNAL (US/0730-9791). [7,000] **4124**

JAZZ SCENE, LA (US). [38,000] **4125**

JAZZ TIMES (WASHINGTON) (US/0272-572X). [73,000] **4125**

JAZZIZ (GAINESVILLE, FLA.) (US/0741-5885). [60,000] **4125**

JBI ABSTRACTS (JM). **1363**

JE ME SOUVIENS (US/0195-7384). [800] **2455**

JEFFERSON (SW/0345-5653). [2000] **4125**

JEI. JOURNAL OF ECONOMIC ISSUES (US/0021-3624). [2,000] **1592**

JEN MIN JIH PAO SO YIN (CC). **5798**

JERSEY JOURNAL (US/0021-5953). [4,200] **213**

JESUS PARIS. 1973 (FR/1154-7138). [2,500] **4967**

JET CARGO NEWS (US/0021-6003). [22,300] **5385**

JEWELLERY WORLD (CN/0383-9818). [6,700] **2914**

JEWISH AFFAIRS (SA). [2,000] **5048**

JEWISH BOOK NEWS (US/8755-299X). [15,000] **5048**

JEWISH CURRENT EVENTS (ELMONT, N.Y.) (US/0021-6380). **5048**

JEWISH HISTORICAL STUDIES : TRANSACTIONS OF THE JEWISH HISTORICAL SOCIETY OF ENGLAND (UK). [1,000] **5049**

JEWISH JOURNAL OF GREATER LOS ANGELES, THE (US/0888-0468). [52,000 (mailed)] **5049**

JEWISH NEWS (RICHMOND, VA.), THE (US/0744-6632). **5049**

JEWISH OBSERVER, THE (US/0021-6615). [15,000] **5049**

JEWISH SOCIAL WORK FORUM, THE (US/0021-6712). [800] **5291**

JEWISH SPECTATOR (US/0021-6720). [8,000] **5049**

JEWISH STAR (CALGARY) (CN/0228-2283). [1,800] **5787**

JEWISH STAR (EDMONTON EDITION) (CN/0228-6017). [1,400] **5787**

JEWISH TIMES (US). [30,000] **5737**

JEWISH VEGETARIANS OF NORTH AMERICA : NEWSLETTER (US/0883-1904). [2,000] **4192**

JEWISH VETERAN, THE (US/0047-2018). [55,000] **2265**

JEWISH VOICE, THE (US/0021-6828). [3,200] **5049**

JEWISH WESTERN BULLETIN (CN/0021-6879). [3,000] **5787**

JEWISH WORLD (ALBANY), THE (US/0199-4441). [3,600] **2265**

JIAOYU ZILIAO YU TUSHUGUAN XUE (CH/1013-090X). [700] **3219**

JIB GEMS (CN/0839-105X). [500] **4089**

JIHAD (TEHRAN, IRAN) (IR). [10,000] **2505**

JIKEIKAI MEDICAL JOURNAL (JA/0021-6968). **3592**

JIKKEN SHAKAI SHINRIGAKU KENKYU (JA/0387-7973). **4592**

JINBUN RONSHU / WASEDA DAIGAKU HOGAKKAI (JA/0441-4225). [1,500] **2986**

JING BAO JOURNAL (US). [4,000] **4047**

JINSHAN SHIBAO (US/0746-5432). [15,000] **5636**

J'INVESTRIE (CN/0714-3117). **793**

JMA MANAGEMENT NEWS (JA). **872**

JMR, JOURNAL OF MARKETING RESEARCH (US/0022-2437). [8,500] **927**

JNMM : JOURNAL OF THE INSTITUTE OF NUCLEAR MATERIALS MANAGEMENT (US/0893-6188). [7,500] **2156**

JOB INFORMATION LETTER (US/8756-1670). **4205**

JOB PROSPECTS AUSTRALIA (AT/1031-0894). [2,000] **4205**

JOB TRAINING AND PLACEMENT REPORT (US/1041-1488). **872**

JOBBER NEWS (TORONTO) (CN/0021-7050). [11,500] **5417**

JOBBER TOPICS (US/0021-7069). [60,000] **5417**

JOBS AVAILABLE (WESTERN ED.) (US/1065-6944). **4205**

JOBS MAGAZINE (US). [10,000] **1681**

JOBSON'S CHEERS (US/1051-564X). **2368**

JOBSON'S MINING YEAR BOOK (AT/0075-3777). [6,600] **2141**

JOERNAAL VIR EIETYDSE : GESKIEDENIS EN INTERNASIONALE VERHOUDINGE (SA). [250] **2620**

JOHANNESBURG STOCK EXCHANGE MONTHLY BULLETIN, THE (SA). [3,000] **904**

JOHN & MABLE RINGLING MUSEUM OF ART : NEWSLETTER (US). [5,000] **354**

JOHN MARSHALL LAW REVIEW, THE (US/0270-854X). [2,500] **2986**

JOHN TWIGG'S REPORT ON B.C (CN/0838-1542). [300] **1498**

JOHN WESLEY COLLEGE CRUSADER (US/0744-7213). [5,000] **1092**

JOHNS HOPKINS MAGAZINE (US/0021-7255). [95,000] **1102**

JOHNS HOPKINS MEDICAL LETTER HEALTH AFTER 50, THE (US/1042-1882). [100] **3592**

JOHNSON COUNTY HISTORICAL SOCIETY JOURNAL (US/0747-6876). [250] **2740**

JOHNSON JOURNAL (US/8755-1721). [400] **2455**

JOHO SHORI KENKYU (JA/0388-5038). [800] **1213**

JOINT FORUM FOR PHILIPPINE PROGRESS NEWS (US). [3,000] **2910**

JOJOBA HAPPENINGS (US/0746-3766). [2,000] **98**

JONES JOURNEYS (US/0749-1522). [200] **2455**

JONG HOLLAND (NE/0168-9193). [2,000] **354**

JONQUIL (US/0744-3943). [18,000] **5232**

JOPLIN GLOBE (US). [37,000 daily 45,000 Sunday] **5703**

JORDEMODERN (SW/0021-7468). [6,700] **3763**

JORNAL BRASILEIRO DE PSIQUIATRIA (BL/0047-2085). [3,000] **3928**

JORNAL DA LIGA BRASILEIRA DE EPILEPSIA (BL). [600] **3834**

JORNAL DO BRASIL (BL). **5779**

JOSEMARIA ESCRIVA DE BALAGUER (EDITION FRANCAISE) (CN/0703-2757). [75,000] **4967**

JOSEMARIA ESCRIVA DE BALAGUER (ENGLISH EDITION) (CN/0703-9093). [75,000] **4967**

JOSLIN'S JAZZ JOURNAL (US/0735-1585). [1,300] **4125**

JOUETS ET JEUX (FR/0075-4056). **2584**

JOURNAAL / UITGAVE STICHTING VOOR CULTURELE SAMENWERKING (STICUSA) (NE). [4,000] **2694**

JOURNAL (AMERICAN ACADEMY OF GNATHOLOGIC ORTHOPEDICS) (US/0886-1064). [1,800] **1325**

JOURNAL - AMERICAN SOCIETY OF SUGAR CANE TECHNOLOGISTS. FLORIDA DIVISIONS (US/1075-6302). **175**

JOURNAL & REPORT - NATIONAL UNION OF THE FOOTWEAR, LEATHER & ALLIED TRADES (UK). [4,500] **3184**

JOURNAL / CALIFORNIA RARE FRUIT GROWERS (US/0894-8445). [2,700] **98**

JOURNAL - CAMBORNE SCHOOL OF MINES (UK/0308-3845). [5,000] **2141**

JOURNAL (CAMP VERDE, ARIZ.), THE (US/0744-3285). [3,100] **5630**

JOURNAL - CANADIAN DENTAL ASSOCIATION (CN/0709-8936). [18,000] **1325**

JOURNAL - CANADIAN FEDERATION OF UNIVERSITY WOMEN (CN/0705-3843). **5559**

JOURNAL - CANADIAN OLDTIMERS' HOCKEY ASSOCIATION (CN/0826-5887). [22,000] **4901**

JOURNAL - CANADIAN ORAL HISTORY ASSOCIATION (CN/0383-6894). [150] **2740**

JOURNAL - CANADIAN RED CROSS SOCIETY. BLOOD PROGRAMME (CN/0715-8602). **5291**

JOURNAL - COLLEGE OF MEDICINE, THE OHIO STATE UNIVERSITY (US/0030-1132). [13,200] **3592**

JOURNAL - COLORADO DENTAL ASSOCIATION (US/0010-1559). [2,200] **1326**

JOURNAL / COLORADO EDUCATION ASSOCIATION (US/0279-3326). [28,500] **1755**

JOURNAL - CONNECTICUT STATE DENTAL ASSOCIATION, THE (US/0010-6232). [2,900] **1326**

JOURNAL - CONSEIL REGIONAL DE LA SANTE ET DES SERVICES SOCIAUX, REGION 01 (CN/0228-3425). **5291**

JOURNAL CONSTRUCTO (CN/0047-2115). [9,750] **618**

JOURNAL / CORNWALL FAMILY HISTORY SOCIETY (UK/0141-7614). [2,500] **2455**

JOURNAL / CROHN'S AND COLITIS FOUNDATION OF CANADA, THE (CN/1197-4982). [11,000] **3746**

JOURNAL DE CORNWALL, LE (CN/0704-0660). [1,100] **5787**

JOURNAL DE LA SOCIETE DES AMERICANISTES (FR/0037-9174). [1,000] **271**

JOURNAL DE L'IMMERSION, LE (CN/0833-1812). [2,500] **3289**

JOURNAL DE PHARMACIE CLINIQUE (FR/0291-1981). [1,250] **4310**

JOURNAL DE RECHERCHE OCEANOGRAPHIQUE (FR/0397-5347). [350] **1450**

JOURNAL DENTAIRE DU QUEBEC (CN). [4,200] **1326**

JOURNAL DENTAIRE DU QUEBEC (CN). **1326**

JOURNAL DES AFRICANISTES (FR/0399-0346). [700] **238**

JOURNAL DES DEBATS (QUEBEC) (CN/0709-3632). [150] **4478**

JOURNAL DES JUGES DE PAIX ET DE POLICE (BE). **2986**

JOURNAL D'OUTREMONT, LE (CN/0824-1317). **2536**

JOURNAL / FLINTSHIRE HISTORICAL SOCIETY (UK). [400] **2694**

JOURNAL - FLORIDA GENEALOGICAL SOCIETY (1978) (US/0735-6420). [350] **2455**

JOURNAL FOR CONTEMPORARY HISTORY / JOERNAAL VIR EIETYDSE GESKIEDENIS (SA). [250] **4526**

JOURNAL FOR QUALITY AND PARTICIPATION, THE (US/1040-9602). [8,000] **1681**

JOURNAL FOR RESEARCH IN MATHEMATICS EDUCATION (US/0021-8251). [6,500] **3511**

JOURNAL FOR SPECIALISTS IN GROUP WORK, THE (US/0193-3922). [264] **4592**

JOURNAL FOR THE CALLIGRAPHIC ARTS (US). [2,200] **380**

JOURNAL FOR THE EDUCATION OF THE GIFTED (US/0162-3532). [2,600] **1880**

JOURNAL FOR THE HISTORY OF ARABIC SCIENCE (SY/0379-2927). [1,000] **5118**

JOURNAL FOR THE STUDY OF THE NEW TESTAMENT (UK/0142-064X). [950] **5017**

JOURNAL FOR THE STUDY OF THE OLD TESTAMENT (UK/0309-0892). [1,500] **5017**

JOURNAL - FORENSIC SCIENCE SOCIETY (UK/0015-7368). [2,500] **3741**

JOURNAL / FORT SMITH HISTORICAL SOCIETY, THE (US/0736-4261). [500] **2740**

JOURNAL FRANCAIS D'AMERIQUE (US/0195-2889). [25,000] **5636**

JOURNAL FRANCAIS D'OTO-RHINO-LARYNGOLOGIE (FR/0398-9771). **3889**

JOURNAL FROM THE RADICAL REFORMATION, A (US/1058-3084). [350] **4968**

JOURNAL - GALPIN SOCIETY (UK/0072-0127). [1,500] **4125**

JOURNAL / GLASS ART SOCIETY (US/0278-9426). [1,500] **2591**

JOURNAL - HISTORICAL FIREARMS SOCIETY OF SOUTH AFRICA (SA). [500] **251**

JOURNAL / HOUSTON ARCHEOLOGICAL SOCIETY (US/8756-8071). [260] **271**

JOURNAL - INTERNATIONAL CHINESE SNUFF BOTTLE SOCIETY (US/0734-5534). [650] **251**

JOURNAL - INTERNATIONAL UNION OF BRICKLAYERS AND ALLIED CRAFTSMEN (US/0362-3696). [100,000] **1681**

JOURNAL - JAPANESE ASSOCIATION OF GROUNDWATER HYDROLOGY (JA). **1415**

JOURNAL - KEMENTERIAN PELAJARAN MALAYSIA (MY/0126-7957). [10,000] **1756**

JOURNAL (LACHUTE) (CN/0227-1249). **5787**

JOURNAL - LEWIS COUNTY HISTORICAL SOCIETY (US/0895-500X). **2740**

JOURNAL - MINING AND METALLURGICAL INSTITUTE OF JAPAN (JA). [10,000] **4006**

JOURNAL - NEW ZEALAND DIETETIC ASSOCIATION (NZ/0110-635X). **4192**

JOURNAL OF ACADEMIC LIBRARIANSHIP (US/0099-1333). [2,700] **3219**

JOURNAL OF ACCOUNTING CASE RESEARCH, THE (CN/1192-2621). **746**

JOURNAL OF ACCOUNTING EDUCATION (US/0748-5751). [1,500] **746**

JOURNAL OF ACCOUNTING RESEARCH (US/0021-8456). [2,850] **746**

JOURNAL OF ADOLESCENT RESEARCH (US/0743-5584). [1,000] **4593**

JOURNAL OF ADULT EDUCATION (US/0090-4244). [500] **1801**

JOURNAL OF ADVANCED COMPOSITION (US/0731-6755). [900] **3289**

JOURNAL OF ADVANCED NURSING (UK/0309-2402). [2,000] **3858**

JOURNAL OF ADVANCED ZOOLOGY (II/0253-7214). [1,000] **5587**

JOURNAL OF ADVENTIST EDUCATION, THE (US/0021-8480). [7,500] **1897**

JOURNAL OF AEROSPACE ENGINEERING (US/0893-1321). **25**

JOURNAL OF AESTHETICS AND ART CRITICISM, THE (US/0021-8529). [3,000] **354**

JOURNAL OF AFRICAN LANGUAGES AND LINGUISTICS (NE/0167-6164). [500] **3289**

JOURNAL OF AGRIBUSINESS (US/0738-8950). [1,400] **99**

JOURNAL OF AGRICULTURAL AND FOOD CHEMISTRY (US/0021-8561). [4,400] **99**

JOURNAL OF AGRICULTURAL ENTOMOLOGY (US/0735-939X). [450] **5610**

JOURNAL OF AIR LAW AND COMMERCE, THE (US/0021-8642). [2,200] **2987**

JOURNAL OF ALLIED HEALTH (US/0090-7421). **3593**

JOURNAL OF ALTERNATIVE AND COMPLEMENTARY MEDICINE (UK/0959-9886). [5,000] **3593**

JOURNAL OF AMBULATORY CARE MANAGEMENT, THE (US/0148-9917). **3786**

JOURNAL OF AMERICAN CULTURE (US/0191-1813). [1,300] **2740**

JOURNAL OF AMERICAN FOLKLORE (US/0021-8715). [3,000] **2321**

JOURNAL OF AMERICAN HISTORY, THE (US/0021-8723). [12,000] **2740**

JOURNAL OF AMERICAN INSURANCE (US/0021-874X). [20,500] **2885**

JOURNAL OF AMERICAN ORGANBUILDING (US/1048-2482). **4125**

JOURNAL OF ANALYTICAL AND APPLIED PYROLYSIS (NE/0165-2370). **1016**

JOURNAL OF ANIMAL MORPHOLOGY AND PHYSIOLOGY, THE (II/0021-8804). [300] **5587**

JOURNAL OF APHIDOLOGY (II/0970-3810). [300] **5610**

JOURNAL OF APPLIED BUSINESS RESEARCH (US/0892-7626). [600] **685**

JOURNAL OF APPLIED CRYSTALLOGRAPHY (DK/0021-8898). [1,200] **1032**

JOURNAL OF APPLIED MATHEMATICS AND STOCHASTIC ANALYSIS (US/1048-9533). [200] **1282**

JOURNAL OF APPLIED MEDICINE (II/0377-0400). [10,000] **3593**

JOURNAL OF APPLIED NUTRITION, THE (US/0021-8960). [1,100] **4192**

JOURNAL OF APPLIED PHYSIOLOGY (1985) (US/8750-7587). [3,500] **581**

JOURNAL OF APPLIED REHABILITATION COUNSELING (US/0047-2220). [4,700] **1880**

JOURNAL OF APPLIED SOCIAL PSYCHOLOGY (US/0021-9029). [1,000] **4594**

JOURNAL OF APPLIED SPORT SCIENCE RESEARCH, THE (US). **1856**

JOURNAL OF AQUATIC PLANT MANAGEMENT (US/0146-6623). [700] **515**

JOURNAL OF ASIAN MARTIAL ARTS (US/1057-8358). [6,000] **2599**

JOURNAL OF ASIAN STUDIES, THE (US/0021-9118). [8,400] **2655**

JOURNAL OF ASTHMA, THE (US/0277-0903). **3950**

JOURNAL OF ASTROPHYSICS AND ASTRONOMY (II/0250-6335). [500] **396**

JOURNAL OF AUSTRALIAN STUDIES (AT/0314-769X). [600] **2669**

JOURNAL OF AUTONOMIC PHARMACOLOGY (UK/0144-1795). [650] **4310**

JOURNAL OF AVIAN BIOLOGY (DK/0908-8857). [750] **5618**

JOURNAL OF BALLISTICS (US/0146-4140). [200] **2014**

JOURNAL OF BALTIC STUDIES (US/0162-9778). [1,300] **2694**

JOURNAL OF BANGLADESH ACADEMY OF SCIENCES (BG/0378-8121). [500] **5118**

JOURNAL OF BANK ACCOUNTING & AUDITING, THE (US/0895-853X). [2,500] **793**

JOURNAL OF BANK TAXATION, THE (US/0895-4720). [1,500] **793**

JOURNAL OF BANKING AND FINANCE LAW AND PRACTICE (AT/1034-3040). **793**

JOURNAL OF BASIC WRITING (US/0147-1635). [2,000] **3289**

JOURNAL OF BIBLICAL ETHICS IN MEDICINE (US/1050-3404). [1,000] **2251**

JOURNAL OF BIOLOGICAL CURATION (UK/0958-7608). [300] **4090**

JOURNAL OF BIOLOGICAL EDUCATION (UK/0021-9266). [2,300] **460**

JOURNAL OF BIOLOGICAL PHOTOGRAPHY (US/0274-497X). [1,500] **460**

JOURNAL OF BIOLOGICAL PHYSICS (NE/0092-0606). [400] **495**

JOURNAL OF BIOLOGICAL SCIENCES RESEARCH (IQ/1010-3910). [800] **460**

JOURNAL OF BIOMOLECULAR STRUCTURE & DYNAMICS (US/0739-1102). **461**

JOURNAL OF BIOSOCIAL SCIENCE (UK/0021-9320). [570] **5205**

JOURNAL OF BRITISH MUSIC THERAPY (UK/0951-5038). [800] **4125**

JOURNAL OF BURN CARE & REHABILITATION, THE (US/0273-8481). [6,000] **3594**

JOURNAL OF BUSINESS (SINGAPORE) (SI/0377-0419). **686**

JOURNAL OF BUSINESS VALUATION, THE (CN/0703-1947). **746**

JOURNAL OF CALIFORNIA AND GREAT BASIN ANTHROPOLOGY (US/0191-3557). [600] **238**

JOURNAL OF CALIFORNIA TAXATION, THE (US/1046-400X). **2987**

JOURNAL OF CANADIAN ART HISTORY (CN/0315-4297). [800] **323**

JOURNAL OF CANADIAN PETROLEUM TECHNOLOGY, THE (CN/0021-9487). [6,400] **4262**

JOURNAL OF CANADIAN POETRY (CN/0705-1328). [1,000] **3464**

JOURNAL OF CARBOHYDRATE CHEMISTRY (US/0732-8303). **1042**

JOURNAL OF CARDIOPULMONARY REHABILITATION (US/0883-9212). [17,000] **3706**

JOURNAL OF CELL SCIENCE (UK/0021-9533). [1,400] **537**

JOURNAL OF CEPHALOPOD BIOLOGY (US/0843-6150). [100] **461**

JOURNAL OF CHEMICAL AND ENGINEERING DATA (US/0021-9568). [1,785] **2014**

JOURNAL OF CHEMICAL ENGINEERING OF JAPAN (JA/0021-9592). **2014**

JOURNAL OF CHEMICAL INFORMATION AND COMPUTER SCIENCES (US/0095-2338). [2,600] **980**

JOURNAL OF CHILD AND ADOLESCENT PSYCHOTHERAPY (US/0748-8793). [10,000] **4594**

JOURNAL OF CHILD PSYCHOTHERAPY (UK/0075-417X). [1,000] **3928**

JOURNAL OF CHILDHOOD COMMUNICATION DISORDERS (US/0735-3170). [2,500] **1880**

JOURNAL OF CHINESE LINGUISTICS (US/0091-3723). [500] **3289**

JOURNAL OF CHINESE PHILOSOPHY (US/0301-8121). [500] **4350**

JOURNAL — Controlled Circulation Index

JOURNAL OF CHINESE STUDIES (ALBUQUERQUE, N.M.) (US/0742-5929). [500] **2505**

JOURNAL OF CHIROPRACTIC (US/0744-9984). [23,000] **3594**

JOURNAL OF CHRISTIAN JURISPRUDENCE (US/0741-6075). [1,500] **2987**

JOURNAL OF CHRISTIAN RECONSTRUCTION, THE (US/0360-1420). [1,500] **4968**

JOURNAL OF CLASSROOM INTERACTION, THE (US/0749-4025). [1,000] **1756**

JOURNAL OF CLINICAL AND EXPERIMENTAL GERONTOLOGY (US/0192-1193). **3753**

JOURNAL OF CLINICAL DENTISTRY, THE (US/0895-8831). [1,000] **1326**

JOURNAL OF CLINICAL HEMATOLOGY AND ONCOLOGY (US/0162-9360). [9,000] **3772**

JOURNAL OF CLINICAL IMMUNOASSAY (US/0736-4393). [1,650] **3673**

JOURNAL OF CLINICAL MICROBIOLOGY (US/0095-1137). [13,707] **565**

JOURNAL OF CLINICAL PERIODONTOLOGY (DK/0303-6979). [8,500] **1326**

JOURNAL OF CLINICAL PSYCHIATRY, THE (US/0160-6689). [32,000] **3928**

JOURNAL OF CLINICAL PSYCHOANALYSIS (US). [1,000] **3928**

JOURNAL OF COASTAL RESEARCH (US/0749-0208). [850] **1357**

JOURNAL OF COLLEGE SCIENCE TEACHING (US/0047-231X). [4,800] **5118**

JOURNAL OF COLLEGE STUDENT DEVELOPMENT (US/0897-5264). [1,300] **1832**

JOURNAL OF COMMERCE (VANCOUVER) (CN/0709-1230). [6,500] **842**

JOURNAL OF COMMUNICATION (US/0021-9916). [6,500] **1114**

JOURNAL OF COMMUNICATION THERAPY (US/0734-4368). [300] **4595**

JOURNAL OF COMPUTER INFORMATION SYSTEMS, THE (US/0887-4417). [1,100] **1260**

JOURNAL OF CONCHOLOGY (UK/0022-0019). [1,000] **5587**

JOURNAL OF CONSTRUCTIONAL STEEL RESEARCH (UK/0143-974X). [400] **618**

JOURNAL OF CONSUMER AFFAIRS, THE (US/0022-0078). [1,750] **1297**

JOURNAL OF CONTEMPORARY AFRICAN STUDIES : JCAS (SA/0258-9001). [1,000] **2848**

JOURNAL OF CONTEMPORARY ART (US/0897-2400). [3,000] **354**

JOURNAL OF CONTEMPORARY HEALTH LAW AND POLICY, THE (US/0882-1046). [450] **2987**

JOURNAL OF CONTEMPORARY LAW (US/0097-9937). [350] **2987**

JOURNAL OF CONTINUING HIGHER EDUCATION, THE (US/0737-7363). [1,300] **1832**

JOURNAL OF CORPORATE MANAGEMENT, THE (AT/1038-2410). [10,131] **3101**

JOURNAL OF CORPORATION LAW, THE (US/0360-795X). [900] **3101**

JOURNAL OF CREATIVE BEHAVIOR, THE (US/0022-0175). [2,500] **4596**

JOURNAL OF CRIME & JUSTICE (US/0735-648X). **3167**

JOURNAL OF CRIMINAL JUSTICE EDUCATION (US/1051-1253). [2,500] **3167**

JOURNAL OF CRITICAL ILLNESS, THE (US/1040-0257). **3595**

JOURNAL OF CROATIAN STUDIES (US/0075-4218). [1,000] **3289**

JOURNAL OF CROSS-CULTURAL GERONTOLOGY (NE/0169-3816). [1,000] **3753**

JOURNAL OF CULTURAL ECONOMICS (NE/0885-2545). [1,100] **323**

JOURNAL OF CULTURAL GEOGRAPHY (US/0887-3631). [700] **2567**

JOURNAL OF CUNEIFORM STUDIES (US/0022-0256). [625] **3290**

JOURNAL OF CUTANEOUS PATHOLOGY (DK/0303-6987). [1,600] **3721**

JOURNAL OF DAIRY SCIENCE (US/0022-0302). [4,800] **195**

JOURNAL OF DANISH ARCHAEOLOGY (DK/0108-464X). **271**

JOURNAL OF DATABASE MANAGEMENT (US/1063-8016). [400] **1254**

JOURNAL OF DENTAL HYGIENE (US/1043-254X). [30,000] **1326**

JOURNAL OF DENTISTRY FOR CHILDREN (US/0022-0353). [9,000] **1326**

JOURNAL OF DERMATOLOGIC SURGERY AND ONCOLOGY, THE (US/0148-0812). [15,500] **3967**

JOURNAL OF DEVELOPING AREAS, THE (US/0022-037X). [1,400] **2910**

JOURNAL OF DEVELOPMENT COMMUNICATION, THE (MY/0128-3863). [3,000] **1114**

JOURNAL OF DISPERSION SCIENCE AND TECHNOLOGY (US/0193-2691). **4428**

JOURNAL OF DISTANCE EDUCATION / REVUE DE L'ENSEIGNEMENT A DISTANCE (CN/0830-0445). [900] **1756**

JOURNAL OF EARLY ADOLESCENCE, THE (US/0272-4316). [1,000] **4596**

JOURNAL OF EARLY SOUTHERN DECORATIVE ARTS (US/0098-9266). [1,200] **373**

JOURNAL OF EAST ASIAN AFFAIRS, THE (KO/1010-1608). [2,000] **2655**

JOURNAL OF EAST TENNESSEE HISTORY (US). **2741**

JOURNAL OF ECONOMIC AND TAXONOMIC BOTANY (II/0250-9768). [300] **515**

JOURNAL OF ECONOMIC BEHAVIOR & ORGANIZATION (NE/0167-2681). **1498**

JOURNAL OF ECONOMIC ENTOMOLOGY (US/0022-0493). [3,400] **5610**

JOURNAL OF ECUMENICAL STUDIES (US/0022-0558). [1,800] **4968**

JOURNAL OF EDUCATION & PSYCHOLOGY (II/0022-0590). [3,000] **4596**

JOURNAL OF EDUCATION FINANCE (US/0098-9495). [1,300] **1865**

JOURNAL OF EDUCATION FOR BUSINESS (US/0883-2323). [4,500] **687**

JOURNAL OF EDUCATION FOR LIBRARY AND INFORMATION SCIENCE (US/0748-5786). [1,700] **3220**

JOURNAL OF EDUCATIONAL ADMINISTRATION, THE (AT/0022-0639). [1,600] **1865**

JOURNAL OF EDUCATIONAL PUBLIC RELATIONS (US/0741-3653). [1,000] **1757**

JOURNAL OF EDUCATIONAL THOUGHT (CN/0022-0701). [600] **1757**

JOURNAL OF ELASTICITY (NE/0374-3535). [400] **4428**

JOURNAL OF ELECTRICAL AND ELECTRONICS ENGINEERING, AUSTRALIA (AT/0725-2986). [6,000] **2068**

JOURNAL OF ELECTRON MICROSCOPY (JA/0022-0744). [4,000] **572**

JOURNAL OF ELECTRONIC DEFENSE (US/0192-429X). [26,000] **4048**

JOURNAL OF ELECTRONIC ENGINEERING : JEE (JA/0385-4507). [51,000] **2068**

JOURNAL OF EMPLOYMENT COUNSELING (US/0022-0787). [597] **4206**

JOURNAL OF END USER COMPUTING (US/1063-2239). [500] **1192**

JOURNAL OF ENDOCRINOLOGICAL INVESTIGATION (IT/0391-4097). [4,000] **3731**

JOURNAL OF ENDOCRINOLOGY, THE (UK/0022-0795). [2,200] **3731**

JOURNAL OF ENERGY ENGINEERING (US/0733-9402). [5,200] **2118**

JOURNAL OF ENERGY, NATURAL RESOURCES & ENVIRONMENTAL LAW (US/1053-377X). [400] **3113**

JOURNAL OF ENGINEERING MATHEMATICS (NE/0022-0833). [600] **1982**

JOURNAL OF ENGINEERING RESEARCH, SEOUL NATIONAL UNIVERSITY (KO). [500] **1982**

JOURNAL OF ENGLISH LINGUISTICS (US/0075-4242). [600] **3290**

JOURNAL OF ENTOMOLOGICAL RESEARCH (II/0378-9519). [600] **5587**

JOURNAL OF ENVIRONMENTAL ENGINEERING (NEW YORK N.Y.) (US/0733-9372). [5,200] **2233**

JOURNAL OF ENVIRONMENTAL HYDROLOGY (US/1058-3912). **1416**

JOURNAL OF ETHNIC STUDIES, THE (US/0091-3219). [850] **2266**

JOURNAL OF ETHNOBIOLOGY (US/0278-0771). [400] **238**

JOURNAL OF EUROPEAN BUSINESS, THE (US/1044-002X). [1,000] **1613**

JOURNAL OF EVOLUTIONARY PSYCHOLOGY (US/0737-4828). [300] **3399**

JOURNAL OF EXPERIMENTAL & CLINICAL CANCER RESEARCH : CR (IT/0392-9078). **3819**

JOURNAL OF EXPERIMENTAL BIOLOGY (UK/0022-0949). [1,800] **582**

JOURNAL OF EXPLOSIVES ENGINEERING, THE (US/0889-0668). [10,500] **1982**

JOURNAL OF EXTENSION (US/0022-0140). **1914**

JOURNAL OF EXTRA-CORPOREAL TECHNOLOGY, THE (US/0022-1058). [3,000] **3772**

JOURNAL OF FAMILY PRACTICE, THE (US/0094-3509). [74,107] **3738**

JOURNAL OF FAMILY WELFARE, THE (II/0022-1074). [3800] **589**

JOURNAL OF FERROCEMENT (TH/0125-1759). [400] **632**

JOURNAL OF FIELD ARCHAEOLOGY (US/0093-4690). [1,600] **271**

JOURNAL OF FIELD ORNITHOLOGY (US/0273-8570). [1,000] **5618**

JOURNAL OF FINANCIAL RESEARCH, THE (US/0270-2592). [1,300] **794**

JOURNAL OF FISHERIES & AQUACULTURE (PH/0115-690X). [500] **2306**

JOURNAL OF FOOD PROTECTION (US/0362-028X). [3,500] **2346**

JOURNAL OF FOOD SCIENCE AND TECHNOLOGY (II/0022-1155). [2,000] **4193**

JOURNAL OF FORAMINIFERAL RESEARCH (US/0096-1191). [800] **5588**

JOURNAL OF FORENSIC IDENTIFICATION (US/0895-173X). [2,500] **3741**

JOURNAL OF FORENSIC ODONTO-STOMATOLOGY, THE (AT/0258-414X). [300] **1327**

JOURNAL OF FORESTRY (US/0022-1201). [23,000] **2385**

JOURNAL OF FORTH APPLICATION AND RESEARCH, THE (US/0738-2022). [400] **1279**

JOURNAL OF FRESHWATER ECOLOGY (US/0270-5060). [600] **2218**

JOURNAL OF GASTRONOMY, THE (US/0747-7368). [9,000] **2347**

JOURNAL OF GEM INDUSTRY (II/0022-1244). [14,000] **2915**

JOURNAL OF GEMMOLOGY AND PROCEEDINGS OF THE GEMMOLOGICAL ASSOCIATION OF GREAT BRITAIN (UK/0022-1252). [3,500] **1440**

JOURNAL OF GENERAL EDUCATION (UNIVERSITY PARK, PA.), THE (US/0021-3667). [1,000] **1757**

JOURNAL OF GENERAL ORTHODONTICS (US/1048-1990). [4,100] **1327**

JOURNAL OF GEOGRAPHY (HOUSTON) (US/0022-1341). [3,500] **2567**

JOURNAL OF GEOLOGICAL EDUCATION (US/0022-1368). [2,300] **1384**

JOURNAL OF GEOMAGNETISM AND GEOELECTRICITY (JA/0022-1392). [1,500] **1407**

JOURNAL OF GERIATRIC PSYCHIATRY (US/0022-1414). [1,800] **3928**

JOURNAL OF GERONTOLOGY (KIRKWOOD) (US/0022-1422). [9,362] **3753**

JOURNAL OF GLOBAL INFORMATION MANAGEMENT (US/1062-7375). [300] **3220**

JOURNAL OF GREAT LAKES RESEARCH (US/0380-1330). [1,000] **1416**

JOURNAL OF HEAD & NECK PATHOLOGY (BE/0770-9471). [10,000] **3595**

JOURNAL OF HEALTH ADMINISTRATION EDUCATION, THE (US/0735-6722). [1,650] **4786**

JOURNAL OF HEALTH AND HUMAN RESOURCES ADMINISTRATION (US/0160-4198). [800] **5292**

JOURNAL OF HEALTH CARE FOR THE POOR AND UNDERSERVED (US/1049-2089). [2000] **4786**

JOURNAL OF HEALTH CARE MARKETING (US/0737-3252). [5,300] **927**

JOURNAL OF HEALTH EDUCATION. ASSOCIATION FOR THE ADVANCEMENT OF HEALTH EDUCATION (US/1055-6699). **4786**

JOURNAL OF HEALTH POLITICS, POLICY AND LAW (US/0361-6878). [1,800] **2987**

JOURNAL OF HELLENIC STUDIES (UK/0075-4269). [3,000] **1078**

JOURNAL OF HEREDITY, THE (US/0022-1503). [4,000] **548**

JOURNAL OF HERPETOLOGY (US/0022-1511). [2,400] **5588**

JOURNAL OF HIGHER EDUCATION (AT/1034-3350). [9,000] **1832**

JOURNAL OF HISTORICAL REVIEW, THE (US/0195-6752). [3,000] **2621**

JOURNAL OF HOLISTIC NURSING (US/0898-0101). [1,800] **3858**

JOURNAL OF HORTICULTURAL SCIENCE, THE (UK/0022-1589). [1,000] **2421**

JOURNAL OF HOUSING (1979) (US/0272-7374). [12,500] **2826**

JOURNAL OF HUMANISTIC EDUCATION (US/0890-0493). [300] **1898**

JOURNAL OF HYDRAULIC RESEARCH (NE/0022-1686). [3,000] **2092**

JOURNAL OF HYDROLOGY, NEW ZEALAND (NZ/0022-1708). [500] **1416**

JOURNAL OF HYMENOPTERA RESEARCH (US/1070-9428). [300] **5610**

JOURNAL OF HYPERBARIC MEDICINE (US/0884-1225). [1,800] **3595**

JOURNAL OF IMMUNOASSAY (US/0197-1522). **3673**

JOURNAL OF INDIGENOUS STUDIES, THE (CN/0838-4711). [300] **2741**

JOURNAL OF INDO-EUROPEAN STUDIES, THE (US/0092-2323). [1,100] **3290**

JOURNAL OF INDUSTRIAL IRRADIATION TECHNOLOGY (US/0735-7923). **981**

JOURNAL OF INDUSTRIAL RELATIONS, THE (AT/0022-1856). [4,000] **1682**

JOURNAL OF INDUSTRIAL TECHNOLOGY / THE NATIONAL ASSOCIATION OF INDUSTRIAL TECHNOLOGY (US/0882-6404). [3,500] **5118**

JOURNAL OF INFORMATION TECHNOLOGY MANAGEMENT (US/1042-1319). [5,400] **873**

JOURNAL OF INSURANCE REGULATION (US/0736-248X). [1,500] **2885**

JOURNAL OF INTERGROUP RELATIONS (US/0047-2492). [650] **5250**

JOURNAL OF INTERIOR DESIGN EDUCATION AND RESEARCH (US/0147-0418). [500] **2901**

JOURNAL OF INTERNATIONAL BUSINESS STUDIES (CN/0047-2506). [4,100] **687**

JOURNAL OF INTRAVENOUS NURSING (US/0896-5846). [8000] **3858**

JOURNAL OF INTRAVENOUS THERAPY (LOS ANGELES) (US/0194-1658). [3,000] **3595**

JOURNAL OF ISLAMIC BANKING & FINANCE : QUARTERLY PUBLICATION OF THE INTERNATIONAL ASSOCIATION OF ISLAMIC BANKS, KARACHI (ASIAN REGION) (PK). [600] **795**

JOURNAL OF JEWISH COMMUNAL SERVICE (US/0022-2089). [3,600] **2266**

JOURNAL OF KANSAS PHARMACY, THE (US/0194-5106). [1,200] **4311**

JOURNAL OF KOREAN STUDIES (SEATTLE, WASH. : 1979), THE (US/0731-1613). [350] **2655**

JOURNAL OF LAW AND COMMERCE, THE (US/0733-2491). [400] **2988**

JOURNAL OF LAW & EDUCATION (US/0275-6072). [1,300] **1865**

JOURNAL OF LAW AND RELIGION, THE (US/0748-0814). [600] **2988**

JOURNAL OF LEARNING DISABILITIES (US/0022-2194). [10,700] **1880**

JOURNAL OF LEGAL EDUCATION (US/0022-2208). [750] **2988**

JOURNAL OF LEGAL STUDIES, THE (US/0047-2530). [2,300] **2988**

JOURNAL OF LEGISLATION (US/0146-9584). [1,800] **2989**

JOURNAL OF LIBERTARIAN STUDIES, THE (US/0363-2873). [1,000] **5206**

JOURNAL OF LITERARY STUDIES (PRETORIA, SOUTH AFRICA) (SA/0256-4718). **3345**

JOURNAL OF LOSS PREVENTION IN THE PROCESS INDUSTRIES (UK/0950-4230). [350] **2099**

JOURNAL OF MACROMARKETING (US/0276-1467). [600] **928**

JOURNAL OF MACROMOLECULAR SCIENCE. REVIEWS IN MACROMOLECULAR CHEMISTRY (US/0022-2356). **1042**

JOURNAL OF MANAGEMENT (US/0149-2063). [1,400] **873**

JOURNAL OF MANAGEMENT SYSTEMS, THE (US/1041-2808). [3,800] **943**

JOURNAL OF MARKETING (US/0022-2429). [14,200] **928**

JOURNAL OF MARRIAGE AND THE FAMILY (US/0022-2445). [6,800] **2282**

JOURNAL OF MATERIALS CHEMISTRY (UK/0959-9428). [1,000] **981**

JOURNAL OF MATERIALS RESEARCH (US/0884-2914). [9,500] **2103**

JOURNAL OF MAYAN LINGUISTICS (US/0195-475X). [125] **3291**

JOURNAL OF MEDICINAL CHEMISTRY (US/0022-2623). [4,319] **490**

JOURNAL OF MEDIEVAL AND RENAISSANCE STUDIES, THE (US/0047-2573). [700] **2695**

JOURNAL OF MICROCOMPUTER SYSTEMS MANAGEMENT (US/1043-6464). [500] **1192**

JOURNAL OF MICROWAVE POWER AND ELECTROMAGNETIC ENERGY, THE (US/0832-7823). [1,000] **2069**

JOURNAL OF MIND AND BEHAVIOR, THE (US/0271-0137). [1,019] **4598**

JOURNAL OF MINES, METALS & FUELS (II/0022-2755). [2,500] **2141**

JOURNAL OF MINORITY AGING, THE (US/0742-6291). [750] **5180**

JOURNAL OF MINORITY BUSINESS FINANCE (US/0735-0643). [3,000] **795**

JOURNAL OF MODERN HELLENISM (US/0743-7749). **2266**

JOURNAL OF MODERN KOREAN STUDIES, THE (US/8756-2235). [300] **2655**

JOURNAL OF MODERN LITERATURE (US/0022-281X). [2,000] **3345**

JOURNAL OF MOLECULAR STRUCTURE (NE/0022-2860). **1054**

JOURNAL OF MORMON HISTORY (US/0094-7342). [1,000] **4969**

JOURNAL OF MUSIC THERAPY (US/0022-2917). [4,500] **4126**

JOURNAL OF MUSICOLOGY (ST. JOSEPH, MICH.), THE (US/0277-9269). [1,500] **4126**

JOURNAL OF NARRATIVE TECHNIQUE, THE (US/0022-2925). [600] **3400**

JOURNAL OF NEMATOLOGY (US/0022-300X). [1,350] **5588**

JOURNAL OF NEUROLOGICAL & ORTHOPAEDIC MEDICINE & SURGERY, THE (US/0890-6599). **3967**

JOURNAL OF NEUROPATHOLOGY AND EXPERIMENTAL NEUROLOGY (US/0022-3069). [1,600] **3836**

JOURNAL OF NEUROPHYSIOLOGY (US/0022-3077). [1,740] **3836**

JOURNAL OF NEUROSCIENCE NURSING, THE (US/0888-0395). [5,000] **3859**

JOURNAL OF NORTHWEST SEMITIC LANGUAGES (NE/0085-2414). [400] **3291**

JOURNAL OF NUCLEAR AGRICULTURE AND BIOLOGY (II/0379-5489). [300] **100**

JOURNAL OF NUCLEAR MATERIALS (NE/0022-3115). [900] **2156**

JOURNAL OF NURSING (CH/0047-262X). [15,000] **3859**

JOURNAL OF OBSTETRICS AND GYNAECOLOGY (UK/0144-3615). **3763**

JOURNAL OF OFFICIAL STATISTICS (SW/0282-423X). [1,200] **5329**

JOURNAL OF OMAN STUDIES, THE (MK/0378-8180). **2655**

JOURNAL OF ONE-NAME STUDIES, THE (UK/0262-4842). **2455**

JOURNAL OF OPTOMETRIC EDUCATION (US/0098-6917). [3,000] **4216**

JOURNAL OF OPTOMETRIC VISION DEVELOPMENT (1976) (US/0149-886X). [1,600] **4216**

JOURNAL OF ORAL IMPLANTOLOGY, THE (US/0160-6972). [2,500] **1327**

JOURNAL OF ORGONOMY, THE (US/0022-3298). [1,000] **3596**

JOURNAL OF ORIENTAL STUDIES (HONG KONG) (HK/0022-331X). [300] **2655**

JOURNAL OF ORTHOPAEDIC SURGICAL TECHNIQUES, THE (UK/0334-0236). [1,000] **3882**

JOURNAL OF OTOLARYNGOLOGY. SUPPLEMENT, THE (CN/0707-7270). [1,200] **3889**

JOURNAL OF OTOLARYNGOLOGY, THE (CN/0381-6605). [1,300] **3889**

JOURNAL OF PACKAGING TECHNOLOGY (US/0892-029X). [30,000] **4219**

JOURNAL OF PALEONTOLOGY (US/0022-3360). [2,500] **4227**

JOURNAL OF PALLIATIVE CARE (CN/0825-8597). [1,000] **5292**

JOURNAL OF PAN AFRICAN STUDIES, THE (US/0888-6601). [1,500] **5206**

JOURNAL OF PARAMETRICS (US/1015-7891). [500] **747**

JOURNAL OF PARAPSYCHOLOGY, THE (US/0022-3387). [1,000] **4241**

JOURNAL OF PARENTERAL SCIENCE AND TECHNOLOGY (US/0279-7976). [3,000] **4311**

JOURNAL OF PARK AND RECREATION ADMINISTRATION (US/0735-1968). [1,000] **4706**

JOURNAL OF PASTORAL PRACTICE, THE (US/0196-9072). [625] **5017**

JOURNAL OF PEDIATRIC OPHTHALMOLOGY AND STRABISMUS (US/0191-3913). [1,500] **3905**

JOURNAL OF PENSION PLANNING AND COMPLIANCE (US/0148-2181). [2,500] **904**

JOURNAL OF PERINATAL & NEONATAL NURSING, THE (US/0893-2190). [3,688] **3859**

JOURNAL OF PERIODONTAL RESEARCH (DK/0022-3484). [1,400] **1327**

JOURNAL OF PERSONALITY (US/0022-3506). [2,000] **4599**

JOURNAL OF PERSONALITY ASSESSMENT (US/0022-3891). [2,500] **4599**

JOURNAL OF PETROLEUM GEOLOGY (UK/0141-6421). **4262**

JOURNAL OF PETROLOGY (UK/0022-3530). [1,500] **1458**

JOURNAL OF PHARMACEUTICAL SCIENCES (US/0022-3549). [8,601] **4312**

JOURNAL OF PHARMACOBIO-DYNAMICS (JA/0386-846X). [2,000] **4312**

JOURNAL OF PHILIPPINE LIBRARIANSHIP (PH/0022-359X). [500] **3220**

JOURNAL OF PHYCOLOGY (US/0022-3646). [2,000] **515**

JOURNAL OF PHYSICAL EDUCATION, RECREATION & DANCE (US/0730-3084). [27,000] **1856**

JOURNAL OF PLANNING EDUCATION AND RESEARCH (US/0739-456X). [1,200] **2826**

JOURNAL OF PLANT NUTRITION (US/0190-4167). **515**

JOURNAL OF PODIATRIC MEDICAL EDUCATION (US/0093-7339). [1,300] **3918**

JOURNAL OF POLITICS, THE (US/0022-3816). [3,723] **4479**

JOURNAL OF POLYGRAPH SCIENCE, THE (US/0893-4827). **3167**

JOURNAL OF POSTGRADUATE MEDICINE (BOMBAY) (II/0022-3859). [1,000] **3597**

JOURNAL OF POWDER & BULK SOLIDS TECHNOLOGY (UK/0147-698X). **2014**

JOURNAL OF PRACTICAL APPLICATIONS OF SPACE (US/1046-8757). [500] **26**

JOURNAL OF PRACTICAL APPROACHES TO DEVELOPMENTAL HANDICAP (CN/0707-7807). [400] **4390**

JOURNAL OF PRACTICAL HYGIENE, THE (US/1072-7965). [60,400] **1327**

JOURNAL OF PRACTICAL NURSING, THE (US/0022-3867). [10,000] **3860**

JOURNAL OF PREHISTORIC RELIGION (SW/0283-8486). [3,000] **4969**

JOURNAL OF PROSTHETICS AND ORTHOTICS (US/1040-8800). [4,500] **3597**

JOURNAL OF PROTECTIVE COATINGS & LININGS (US/8755-1985). [13,000] **5119**

JOURNAL OF PROTOZOOLOGY, THE (US/0022-3921). [2,000] **5588**

JOURNAL OF PSYCHIATRY & LAW, THE (US/0093-1853). **2989**

JOURNAL OF PSYCHOLOGICAL TYPE (US/0895-8750). [7,000] **4600**

JOURNAL OF PSYCHOLOGY AND CHRISTIANITY (US/0733-4273). [2,100] **4969**

JOURNAL OF PSYCHOLOGY AND JUDAISM (US/0700-9801). [1,000] **4600**

JOURNAL OF PSYCHOLOGY AND THEOLOGY (US/0091-6471). [2,000] **4600**

JOURNAL OF PUBLIC HEALTH DENTISTRY (US/0022-4006). [1,500] **1328**

JOURNAL OF QUESTIONED DOCUMENT EXAMINATION (US/1061-3455). [70] **3167**

JOURNAL OF RADIATION RESEARCH (JA/0449-3060). **4436**

JOURNAL OF RANGE MANAGEMENT (US/0022-409X). [6,800] **100**

JOURNAL OF RAPTOR RESEARCH, THE (US/0892-1016). [1,200] **5588**

JOURNAL OF READING BEHAVIOR (US/0022-4111). **1758**

JOURNAL OF READING EDUCATION (US/0886-5701). **1758**

JOURNAL OF REAL ESTATE & CONSTRUCTION (SI). [200] **4839**

JOURNAL — Controlled Circulation Index

JOURNAL OF REAL ESTATE RESEARCH, THE (US/0896-5803). [1,300] **4839**

JOURNAL OF RECEPTOR RESEARCH (US/0197-5110). **538**

JOURNAL OF RECONSTRUCTIVE MICROSURGERY (US/0743-684X). [1,000] **3968**

JOURNAL OF REGRESSION THERAPY, THE (US/1054-0830). [500] **4600**

JOURNAL OF REHABILITATION (US/0022-4154). [15,000] **5292**

JOURNAL OF REHABILITATION ADMINISTRATION (US/0148-3846). [1,900] **4390**

JOURNAL OF RELIGION IN AFRICA (NE/0022-4200). [320] **4970**

JOURNAL OF RELIGIOUS STUDIES (II/0047-2735). [1,000] **4970**

JOURNAL OF RELIGIOUS THOUGHT, THE (US/0022-4235). [800] **4970**

JOURNAL OF REPRODUCTION & FERTILITY (UK/0022-4251). [2,200] **3597**

JOURNAL OF REPRODUCTIVE MEDICINE (US/0024-7758). [30,447] **3764**

JOURNAL OF RESEARCH IN MUSIC EDUCATION (US/0022-4294). [3,800] **4126**

JOURNAL OF RESEARCH OF THE AMERICAN FEDERATION OF ASTROLOGERS (US/0882-4517). [200] **390**

JOURNAL OF RESEARCH ON THE LEPIDOPTERA, THE (US/0022-4324). [600] **5611**

JOURNAL OF RETAILING (US/0022-4359). [3,000] **955**

JOURNAL OF RISK AND INSURANCE, THE (US/0022-4367). **2885**

JOURNAL OF RITUAL STUDIES (US/0890-1112). **4970**

JOURNAL OF ROCKINGHAM COUNTY HISTORY AND GENEALOGY, THE (US/0363-1656). [350] **2741**

JOURNAL OF ROMAN ARCHAEOLOGY (US/1047-7594). [1,050] **271**

JOURNAL OF RURAL COOPERATION (IS/0377-7480). [500] **1542**

JOURNAL OF RURAL DEVELOPMENT (KO/1013-0764). [800] **100**

JOURNAL OF SAN DIEGO HISTORY, THE (US/0022-4383). [3,000] **2742**

JOURNAL OF SCIENCE AND MATHEMATICS EDUCATION IN SOUTHEAST ASIA (MY/0126-7663). [650] **1758**

JOURNAL OF SEXUAL HEALTH (UK/0963-6757). [10,000] **5187**

JOURNAL OF SIKH STUDIES (II/0379-8194). [750] **4970**

JOURNAL OF SOCIAL STUDIES, THE (BG). [500] **5207**

JOURNAL OF SOCIAL WORK EDUCATION (US/1043-7797). [3,000] **5293**

JOURNAL OF SOIL AND WATER CONSERVATION (US/0022-4561). [13,000] **2196**

JOURNAL OF SOUTH ASIAN LITERATURE (US/0091-5637). [450] **3400**

JOURNAL OF SOUTHEAST ASIAN STUDIES (SINGAPORE) (SI/0022-4634). [1,000] **2655**

JOURNAL OF SOUTHERN HISTORY, THE (US/0022-4642). [4,200] **2742**

JOURNAL OF SPACE LAW (US/0095-7577). [2,000] **2989**

JOURNAL OF SPECULATIVE PHILOSOPHY, THE (US/0891-625X). [350] **4351**

JOURNAL OF SPEECH-LANGUAGE PATHOLOGY AND AUDIOLOGY (CN/0848-1970). [4,000] **4390**

JOURNAL OF SPORT AND SOCIAL ISSUES (US/0193-7235). [575] **5250**

JOURNAL OF SPORT BEHAVIOR (US/0162-7341). [450] **4902**

JOURNAL OF SPORT HISTORY (US/0094-1700). [1,000] **4902**

JOURNAL OF SPORTS PHILATELY (US/0447-953X). [500] **2785**

JOURNAL OF STAINED GLASS : THE JOURNAL OF THE BRITISH SOCIETY OF MASTER GLASS PAINTERS, THE (UK). [600] **2591**

JOURNAL OF STATE TAXATION (US/0744-6713). [2,000] **4735**

JOURNAL OF STATISTICAL RESEARCH - UNIVERSITY OF DACCA. INSTITUTE OF STATISTICAL RESEARCH AND TRAINING (BG/0256-422X). [200] **5329**

JOURNAL OF STRUCTURAL ENGINEERING (II/0970-0137). [500] **2026**

JOURNAL OF STUDENT FINANCIAL AID, THE (US/0884-9153). [6,000] **1758**

JOURNAL OF STUDIES IN TECHNICAL CAREERS (US/0163-3252). [1500] **1914**

JOURNAL OF SUPERVISION AND TRAINING IN MINISTRY (US/0160-7774). [1,000] **4970**

JOURNAL OF SURVEYING ENGINEERING (US/0733-9453). [1,800] **2026**

JOURNAL OF SWIMMING RESEARCH, THE (US/0747-5993). **4902**

JOURNAL OF TAMIL STUDIES (II/0022-4855). [1,000] **2849**

JOURNAL OF TAXATION OF ESTATES & TRUSTS, THE (US/1044-9418). [2,500] **3118**

JOURNAL OF TAXATION OF EXEMPT ORGANIZATIONS, THE (US/1043-0539). [1,500] **4735**

JOURNAL OF TAXATION OF S CORPORATIONS, THE (US/1040-502X). [1,500] **795**

JOURNAL OF TEACHER EDUCATION (US/0022-4871). [7,500] **1865**

JOURNAL OF TECHNOLOGY EDUCATION (US/1045-1064). [700] **5120**

JOURNAL OF TEXAS CATHOLIC HISTORY AND CULTURE / TEXAS CATHOLIC HISTORICAL SOCIETY, THE (US/1048-2431). [750] **5031**

JOURNAL OF THE ACADEMY OF FLORIDA TRIAL LAWYERS (US/0515-2046). [4,500] **2989**

JOURNAL OF THE ACADEMY OF REHABILITATIVE AUDIOLOGY (US/0149-8886). **3889**

JOURNAL OF THE ALABAMA DENTAL ASSOCIATION, THE (US/0002-4198). [1,650] **1328**

JOURNAL OF THE AMERICAN ANALGESIA SOCIETY (US/0002-7243). [750] **3597**

JOURNAL OF THE AMERICAN ASSOCIATION OF VARIABLE STAR OBSERVERS, THE (US/0271-9053). [1,500] **396**

JOURNAL OF THE AMERICAN CERAMIC SOCIETY (US/0002-7820). [4,800] **2591**

JOURNAL OF THE AMERICAN COLLEGE OF DENTISTS, THE (US/0002-7979). [5,000] **1328**

JOURNAL OF THE AMERICAN HELICOPTER SOCIETY (US/0002-8711). [8,000] **26**

JOURNAL OF THE AMERICAN INSTITUTE FOR CONSERVATION (US/0197-1360). [2,500] **323**

JOURNAL OF THE AMERICAN INSTITUTE OF HOMEOPATHY (US/0002-8967). [500] **3775**

JOURNAL OF THE AMERICAN KILLIFISH ASSOCIATION, THE (US/0002-967X). [1,500] **2307**

JOURNAL OF THE AMERICAN MUSICOLOGICAL SOCIETY (US/0003-0139). [4,500] **4126**

JOURNAL OF THE AMERICAN OPTOMETRIC ASSOCIATION (US/0003-0244). [29,700] **4216**

JOURNAL OF THE AMERICAN ORIENTAL SOCIETY (US/0003-0279). [2,300] **3292**

JOURNAL OF THE AMERICAN OSTEOPATHIC ACADEMY ORTHOPEDICS (US/0740-0926). [600] **3883**

JOURNAL OF THE AMERICAN OSTEOPATHIC ASSOCIATION, THE (US/0098-6151). [30,500] **3598**

JOURNAL OF THE AMERICAN PODIATRIC MEDICAL ASSOCIATION (US/8750-7315). [12,000] **3918**

JOURNAL OF THE AMERICAN PSYCHOANALYTIC ASSOCIATION (US/0003-0651). [2,000] **4601**

JOURNAL OF THE AMERICAN ROMANIAN ACADEMY OF ARTS AND SCIENCES (US/0896-1018). [500] **2518**

JOURNAL OF THE AMERICAN SOCIETY FOR PSYCHICAL RESEARCH (1932) (US/0003-1070). [1,500] **4242**

JOURNAL OF THE AMERICAN SOCIETY OF BREWING CHEMISTS (US/0361-0470). [900] **982**

JOURNAL OF THE AMERICAN SOCIETY OF CLU & CHFC (US/1052-2875). [38,000] **2886**

JOURNAL OF THE AMERICAN STUDIES ASSOCIATION OF TEXAS (US/0587-5064). [400] **2742**

JOURNAL OF THE AMERICAN VETERINARY MEDICAL ASSOCIATION (US/0003-1488). [48,000] **5513**

JOURNAL OF THE ANATOMICAL SOCIETY OF INDIA (II/0003-2778). [650-700] **3679**

JOURNAL OF THE ARIZONA-NEVADA ACADEMY OF SCIENCE (US/0193-8509). [500] **1357**

JOURNAL OF THE ARKANSAS MEDICAL SOCIETY, THE (US/0004-1858). [3,400] **3598**

JOURNAL OF THE ASSOCIATION OF CHILDREN'S PROSTHETIC-ORTHOTIC CLINICS (US/0884-8424). [1,100] **3883**

JOURNAL OF THE ASSOCIATION OF FOOD AND DRUG OFFICIALS (US/0898-4131). [800] **4787**

JOURNAL OF THE ASSOCIATION OF PHYSICIANS OF INDIA (II). [7,500] **3799**

JOURNAL OF THE ASSOCIATION OF SURVEYORS OF PAPUA NEW GUINEA, THE (PP). [300] **2026**

JOURNAL OF THE ATMOSPHERIC SCIENCES (US/0022-4928). **1427**

JOURNAL OF THE AUSTRALIAN ENTOMOLOGICAL SOCIETY (AT/0004-9050). [900] **5588**

JOURNAL OF THE AUSTRALIAN NAVAL INSTITUTE (AT/0312-5807). [1,000] **4178**

JOURNAL OF THE AUSTRALIAN WAR MEMORIAL (AT/0729-6274). [800] **4048**

JOURNAL OF THE BOMBAY NATURAL HISTORY SOCIETY (II/0006-6982). [3,000] **4166**

JOURNAL OF THE BRITISH ARCHAEOLOGICAL ASSOCIATION (UK/0068-1288). [800] **272**

JOURNAL OF THE BRITISH CONTACT LENS ASSOCIATION (UK/0141-7037). [1,200] **3876**

JOURNAL OF THE BROMELIAD SOCIETY (US/0090-8738). [2,500] **516**

JOURNAL OF THE CAMBRIDGESHIRE FAMILY HISTORY SOCIETY (UK/0309-5800). [1,000] **2455**

JOURNAL OF THE CANADIAN ATHLETIC THERAPISTS ASSOCIATION, THE (CN/0225-9877). [500] **3954**

JOURNAL OF THE CANADIAN CHIROPRACTIC ASSOCIATION, THE (CN/0008-3194). [3,300] **3805**

JOURNAL OF THE CHINESE CHEMICAL SOCIETY (TAIPEI) (CH/0009-4536). [1,600] **982**

JOURNAL OF THE CHINESE INSTITUTE OF CHEMICAL ENGINEERS (CH/0368-1653). [850] **2014**

JOURNAL OF THE CHRISTIAN MEDICAL FELLOWSHIP (UK). [6,000] **4970**

JOURNAL OF THE COMMUNICATIONS RESEARCH LABORATORY (JA/0914-9260). [1,000] **1159**

JOURNAL OF THE COMMUNITY DEVELOPMENT SOCIETY (US/0010-3829). [1,000] **5250**

JOURNAL OF THE CONDUCTORS' GUILD (US/0734-1032). [1,500] **4127**

JOURNAL OF THE COUNTY LOUTH ARCHAEOLOGICAL AND HISTORICAL SOCIETY (IE/0070-1327). [650] **272**

JOURNAL OF THE DECORATIVE ARTS SOCIETY 1890-1940 (UK/0260-9568). [600] **373**

JOURNAL OF THE DEPARTMENT OF ENGLISH (UNIVERSITY OF CALCUTTA. DEPT. OF ENGLISH) (II). [1,000] **3400**

JOURNAL OF THE ELECTROCHEMICAL SOCIETY (US/0013-4651). [8,600] **1034**

JOURNAL OF THE FACULTY OF SCIENCE, HOKKAIDO UNIVERSITY. SERIES 4. GEOLOGY AND MINERALOGY (JA/0018-3474). [1,000] **1357**

JOURNAL OF THE FLUORESCENT MINERAL SOCIETY (US/0160-0958). [325] **1440**

JOURNAL OF THE ... GENERAL SYNOD / ANGLICAN CHURCH OF CANADA (CN/0826-3205). **5062**

JOURNAL OF THE GEOLOGICAL SOCIETY OF IRAQ (IQ/0533-8301). [1,500] **1385**

JOURNAL OF THE GRASSLAND SOCIETY OF SOUTHERN AFRICA, THE (SA/0256-6702). [800] **101**

JOURNAL OF THE HERPETOLOGICAL ASSOCIATION OF AFRICA (SA/0441-6651). [450] **5589**

JOURNAL OF THE HISTORICAL SOCIETY OF SOUTH AUSTRALIA (AT/0312-9640). [500] **2669**

JOURNAL OF THE HISTORY OF IDEAS (US/0022-5037). [3,700] **4351**

JOURNAL OF THE HISTORY OF MEDICINE AND ALLIED SCIENCES (US/0022-5045). [1,500] **3598**

JOURNAL OF THE HONG KONG BRANCH OF THE ROYAL ASIATIC SOCIETY (HK/0085-5774). [1,000] **5232**

JOURNAL OF THE ILLINOIS OPTOMETRIC ASSOCIATION (US/0279-6422). **4216**

JOURNAL OF THE ILLINOIS SPEECH & THEATRE ASSOCIATION (US/0145-5516). [400] **5365**

JOURNAL OF THE ILLUMINATING ENGINEERING SOCIETY (US/0099-4480). [10,000] **2069**

JOURNAL OF THE INDIAN ACADEMY OF FORENSIC SCIENCES (II/0579-4749). [600] **3741**

JOURNAL OF THE INDIAN ACADEMY OF MATHEMATICS, THE (II/0970-5120). [250] **3515**

JOURNAL OF THE INDIAN CHEMICAL SOCIETY (II/0019-4522). [2,000] **982**

JOURNAL OF THE INDIAN SOCIETY OF AGRICULTURAL STATISTICS (II/0019-6363). [600] **154**

JOURNAL OF THE INDIAN SOCIETY OF ORIENTAL ART (II/0970-6070). [225] **354**

JOURNAL OF THE INDIANA DENTAL ASSOCIATION (US/0019-6568). [2,300] **1328**

JOURNAL OF THE INSTITUTE OF BREWING (UK/0046-9750). [4300] **2368**

JOURNAL OF THE INSTITUTE OF HEALTH EDUCATION (UK/0307-3289). [1,000] **4787**

JOURNAL OF THE INSTITUTE OF MINE SURVEYORS OF SOUTH AFRICA (SA/0020-2983). [700] **2142**

JOURNAL OF THE INSTITUTION OF ELECTRONICS AND TELECOMMUNICATION ENGINEERS (II/0377-2063). [6,000] **1159**

JOURNAL OF THE INSTITUTION OF ENGINEERS (INDIA) (II/0020-3386). [15,000] **2070**

JOURNAL OF THE INSTITUTION OF ENGINEERS (INDIA). ELECTRONICS & TELECOMMUNICATION ENGINEERING DIVISION (II/0251-1096). [6,000] **2070**

JOURNAL OF THE INSTITUTION OF ENGINEERS (INDIA). MECHANICAL ENGINEERING DIVISION (II/0020-3408). [15,000] **2118**

JOURNAL OF THE INSTITUTION OF ENGINEERS (INDIA). PART EN CALCUTTA, ENVIRONMENTAL ENGINEERING DIVISION, THE (II/0251-110X). [6,000] **2176**

JOURNAL OF THE INTERNATIONAL ASSOCIATION OF BUDDHIST STUDIES, THE (US/0193-600X). [600] **5021**

JOURNAL OF THE INTERNATIONAL PHONETIC ASSOCIATION (UK/0025-1003). [800] **3292**

JOURNAL OF THE IRISH DENTAL ASSOCIATION, THE (IE/0021-1133). [1,000] **1328**

JOURNAL OF THE IRISH FAMILY HISTORY SOCIETY (IE/0790-7060). [800] **2455**

JOURNAL OF THE JOHANNES SCHWALM HISTORICAL ASSOCIATION, INC (US/8755-3805). [5-800] **2742**

JOURNAL OF THE KANSAS BAR ASSOCIATION, THE (US/0022-8486). [5,300] **2989**

JOURNAL OF THE KANSAS ENTOMOLOGICAL SOCIETY (US/0022-8567). [800] **5611**

JOURNAL OF THE KENTUCKY MEDICAL ASSOCIATION, THE (US/0023-0294). [5,500] **3598**

JOURNAL OF THE KOREAN INSTITUTE OF SURFACE ENGINEERING (KO). [3,500] **1983**

JOURNAL OF THE LEPIDOPTERISTS' SOCIETY (US/0024-0966). [1,660] **5589**

JOURNAL OF THE LOUISIANA STATE MEDICAL SOCIETY, THE (US/0024-6921). [6400] **3599**

JOURNAL OF THE MAMMILLARIA SOCIETY, THE (UK/0464-8072). [500] **516**

JOURNAL OF THE MARINE BIOLOGICAL ASSOCIATION OF INDIA (II/0025-3146). [550] **555**

JOURNAL OF THE MASSACHUSETTS DENTAL SOCIETY (US/0025-4800). [5,000] **1328**

JOURNAL OF THE MEDICAL ASSOCIATION OF GEORGIA (US/0025-7028). [7,000] **3599**

JOURNAL OF THE MIDWEST FINANCE ASSOCIATION (US/0272-6637). [900] **905**

JOURNAL OF THE MINE VENTILATION SOCIETY OF SOUTH AFRICA (SA/0368-3206). **2142**

JOURNAL OF THE MISSISSIPPI STATE MEDICAL ASSOCIATION (US/0026-6396). [2,800] **3599**

JOURNAL OF THE MISSOURI BAR (US/0026-6485). [17,600] **2989**

JOURNAL OF THE N.J. ASSOCIATION OF OSTEOPATHIC PHYSICIANS AND SURGEONS, THE (US/0892-0249). [1,800] **3599**

JOURNAL OF THE NATIONAL AGRICULTURAL SOCIETY OF CEYLON (CE/0547-3616). [200] **101**

JOURNAL OF THE NATIONAL MEDICAL ASSOCIATION (US/0027-9684). [25,407] **3599**

JOURNAL OF THE NATIONAL RESEARCH COUNCIL OF THAILAND (TH/0028-0011). [1,000] **5121**

JOURNAL OF THE NATIONAL SCIENCE COUNCIL OF SRI LANKA (CE/0300-9254). [300] **5121**

JOURNAL OF THE NEW ENGLAND LUTHERAN HISTORICAL SOCIETY (US/1051-0605). [400] **4971**

JOURNAL OF THE NEW ENGLAND WATER WORKS ASSOCIATION (US/0028-4939). [2,900] **4761**

JOURNAL OF THE NEW HAVEN COLONY HISTORICAL SOCIETY (US/0548-4987). [800] **2742**

JOURNAL OF THE NEW JERSEY DENTAL ASSOCIATION (US/0093-7347). [5,000] **1328**

JOURNAL OF THE NEW ZEALAND SOCIETY OF PERIODONTOLOGY (NZ/0111-1485). [1,000] **1328**

JOURNAL OF THE NORTH-EAST INDIA COUNCIL FOR SOCIAL SCIENCE RESEARCH, THE (II). [1,000] **5207**

JOURNAL OF THE ORDERS AND MEDALS SOCIETY OF AMERICA, THE (US). [1,600] **2781**

JOURNAL OF THE OREGON DENTAL ASSOCIATION, THE (US/0030-4670). [2,000] **1329**

JOURNAL OF THE ORIENTAL SOCIETY OF AUSTRALIA, THE (AT/0030-5340). **2656**

JOURNAL OF THE PAKISTAN MEDICAL ASSOCIATION (PK/0030-9982). **3599**

JOURNAL OF THE PATENT AND TRADEMARK OFFICE SOCIETY (US/0882-9098). [4,300] **1305**

JOURNAL OF THE PENNSYLVANIA ACADEMY OF SCIENCE (US/1044-6753). [800] **5121**

JOURNAL OF THE PENNSYLVANIA OSTEOPATHIC MEDICAL ASSOCIATION, THE (US/0479-9534). [3,200] **3599**

JOURNAL OF THE POLYNESIAN SOCIETY (NZ/0032-4000). [1,000] **3292**

JOURNAL OF THE PRINT WORLD (US/0737-7436). **4566**

JOURNAL OF THE RESEARCH SOCIETY OF PAKISTAN (PK/0034-5431). [500] **5207**

JOURNAL OF THE RIO GRANDE VALLEY HORTICULTURAL SOCIETY (US/0485-2044). **2421**

JOURNAL OF THE ROYAL ARTILLERY, THE (UK). [3,500] **4048**

JOURNAL OF THE ROYAL ASTRONOMICAL SOCIETY OF CANADA, THE (CN/0035-872X). [3,500] **396**

JOURNAL OF THE ROYAL NAVAL MEDICAL SERVICE (UK/0035-9033). [1,000] **3599**

JOURNAL OF THE ROYAL SOCIETY OF NEW ZEALAND (NZ/0303-6758). [800] **5121**

JOURNAL OF THE ROYAL SOCIETY OF WESTERN AUSTRALIA (AT/0035-922X). [660] **4166**

JOURNAL OF THE ROYAL STATISTICAL SOCIETY. SERIES A: (STATISTICS IN SOCIETY) (UK). [5,800] **5330**

JOURNAL OF THE ROYAL STATISTICAL SOCIETY. SERIES B (METHODOLOGICAL) (UK/0035-9246). [4,600] **5330**

JOURNAL OF THE ROYAL UNITED SERVICES INSTITUTE OF AUSTRALIA (AT/0728-1188). [4,500] **4048**

JOURNAL OF THE RUTGERS UNIVERSITY LIBRARY, THE (US/0036-0473). [500] **3221**

JOURNAL OF THE SAN JUAN ISLANDS (US/0734-3809). [7,000] **5761**

JOURNAL OF THE SIAM SOCIETY, THE (TH). [1,500] **2656**

JOURNAL OF THE SOCIETY FOR ACCELERATIVE LEARNING AND TEACHING, THE (US/0273-2459). [500] **1881**

JOURNAL OF THE SOCIETY FOR ARMY HISTORICAL RESEARCH (UK/0037-9700). [1,200] **4048**

JOURNAL OF THE SOCIETY FOR ITALIC HANDWRITING, THE (UK/0037-9743). [1,250] **380**

JOURNAL OF THE SOCIETY FOR PSYCHICAL RESEARCH (UK/0037-9751). [1,000] **4242**

JOURNAL OF THE SOCIETY FOR UNDERWATER TECHNOLOGY (UK/0141-0814). [1,500] **1450**

JOURNAL OF THE SOCIETY OF ARCHER-ANTIQUARIES (UK/0560-6152). [550] **4902**

JOURNAL OF THE SOCIETY OF AUTOMOTIVE ENGINEERS OF JAPAN (JA/0385-7298). [20,000] **5418**

JOURNAL OF THE SOCIETY OF DAIRY TECHNOLOGY (UK/0037-9840). [2,500] **196**

JOURNAL OF THE SOUTH AFRICAN INSTITUTE OF MINING & METALLURGY (SA/0038-223X). [2,800] **2142**

JOURNAL OF THE SOUTH CAROLINA MEDICAL ASSOCIATION (1975) (US/0038-3139). [4,500] **3599**

JOURNAL OF THE SOUTHERN CALIFORNIA DENTAL HYGIENISTS' ASSOCIATION (US/0038-3899). [5,000] **1329**

JOURNAL OF THE SOUTHERN ORTHOPAEDIC ASSOCIATION (US/1059-1052). [3000] **3883**

JOURNAL OF THE SOUTHWEST (US/0894-8410). [1,200] **2742**

JOURNAL OF THE TENNESSEE ACADEMY OF SCIENCE (US/0040-313X). [900] **5121**

JOURNAL OF THE TENNESSEE MEDICAL ASSOCIATION (US/0040-3318). [6,650] **3600**

JOURNAL OF THE TILES & ARCHITECTURAL CERAMICS SOCIETY (UK/0264-5157). [400] **302**

JOURNAL OF THE UNITED SERVICE INSTITUTION OF INDIA, THE (II/0041-770X). [5,800] **4048**

JOURNAL OF THE WALTER ROTH MUSEUM OF ARCHAEOLOGY AND ANTHROPOLOGY (GY). [100] **239**

JOURNAL OF THE WARBURG AND COURTAULD INSTITUTES (UK/0075-4390). [1,200] **2518**

JOURNAL OF THE WEST (US/0022-5169). [4,500] **2742**

JOURNAL OF THE WESTERN PACIFIC ORTHOPAEDIC ASSOCIATION, THE (HK/0043-4019). [1,200] **3883**

JOURNAL OF THE WESTERN SOCIETY OF PERIODONTOLOGY / PERIODONTAL ABSTRACTS, THE (US/0148-4893). [2,600] **1329**

JOURNAL OF THE WILLIAM MORRIS SOCIETY, THE (UK/0084-0254). [2,500] **373**

JOURNAL OF THE WORLD AQUACULTURE SOCIETY (US/0893-8849). [3,000] **2307**

JOURNAL OF THE WRITERS GUILD OF AMERICA. WEST (US/1055-1948). [10,000] **3400**

JOURNAL OF THE YUGOSLAV FOREIGN TRADE (YU/0022-5452). [24,000] **4527**

JOURNAL OF THERMOPLASTIC COMPOSITE MATERIALS (US/0892-7057). [250] **1026**

JOURNAL OF TISSUE CULTURE METHODS (NE/0271-8057). [1,000] **538**

JOURNAL OF TISSUE VIABILITY (UK/0965-206X). [1,000] **538**

JOURNAL OF TOXICOLOGY. CUTANEOUS AND OCULAR TOXICOLOGY (US). **3982**

JOURNAL OF TOXICOLOGY. TOXIN REVIEWS (US/0731-3837). **3982**

JOURNAL OF TRACE AND MICROPROBE TECHNIQUES (US/0733-4680). **1017**

JOURNAL OF TRADITIONAL ACUPUNCTURE, THE (US/0270-661X). **3600**

JOURNAL OF TRAFFIC SAFETY EDUCATION (US/0164-1344). [2,500] **5441**

JOURNAL OF TRANSLATION AND TEXTLINGUISTICS (US/1055-4513). **3292**

JOURNAL OF TRANSPORTATION ENGINEERING (US/0733-947X). [4,400] **2026**

JOURNAL OF TRAVEL RESEARCH (US/0047-2875). [1,900] **5482**

JOURNAL OF TROPICAL MEDICINE AND HYGIENE (UK/0022-5304). [870] **3986**

JOURNAL OF UFO STUDIES, THE (US/0730-5478). [500] **26**

JOURNAL OF UKRAINIAN GRADUATE STUDIES (CN/0701-1792). [3,000] **2695**

JOURNAL OF UKRAINIAN STUDIES (CN/0228-1635). [800] **2849**

JOURNAL OF UNDERGRADUATE ECONOMICS, THE (US/0146-1664). [200] **1501**

JOURNAL OF URBAN PLANNING AND DEVELOPMENT (US/0733-9488). [4,000] **2026**

JOURNAL OF UROLOGICAL NURSING (US/0738-7350). [8,500] **3991**

JOURNAL OF VAISNAVA STUDIES, THE (US/1062-1237). [500 per issue] **4971**

JOURNAL OF VERTEBRATE PALEONTOLOGY (US/0272-4634). [1,200] **4227**

JOURNAL OF VIROLOGY (US/0022-538X). [5,042] **566**

JOURNAL OF VISUAL LITERACY (US/1051-144X). [200] **3292**

JOURNAL OF WATER RESOURCES (IQ/0255-0148). **5535**

JOURNAL OF WATER RESOURCES PLANNING AND MANAGEMENT (US/0733-9496). [4,800] **5535**

JOURNAL — Controlled Circulation Index

JOURNAL OF WATERWAY, PORT, COASTAL, AND OCEAN ENGINEERING (US/0733-950X). [4,400] **2092**

JOURNAL OF WAVE-MATERIAL INTERACTION (US/0887-0586). **2104**

JOURNAL OF WEST AFRICAN LANGUAGES, THE (UK/0022-5401). [250] **3292**

JOURNAL OF WILDLIFE DISEASES (US/0090-3558). **5514**

JOURNAL OF WILDLIFE REHABILITATION (US/1071-2232). [1,500] **2196**

JOURNAL OF WOOD CHEMISTRY AND TECHNOLOGY (US/0277-3813). **1055**

JOURNAL OF ZOO AND WILDLIFE MEDICINE : OFFICIAL PUBLICATION OF THE AMERICAN ASSOCIATION OF ZOO VETERINARIANS (US/1042-7260). [800] **5514**

JOURNAL - OKLAHOMA STATE MEDICAL ASSOCIATION (US/0030-1876). [3,900] **3601**

JOURNAL - ONTARIO OCCUPATIONAL HEALTH NURSES ASSOCIATION (CN/0828-542X). [1,100] **3860**

JOURNAL : PAPER OF THE NATIONAL UNION OF CIVIL AND PUBLIC SERVANTS (UK/0957-8978). [132,000] **4704**

JOURNAL RECORD (OKLAHOMA CITY, OKLA.), THE (US/0737-5468). [3,900] **688**

JOURNAL / RHODE ISLAND BAR ASSOCIATION (US/1073-8800). [4,300] **2990**

JOURNAL (ROYAL HISTORICAL SOCIETY OF QUEENSLAND : 1985) (AT). [650] **2670**

JOURNAL (SANGEET RESEARCH ACADEMY (CALCUTTA, INDIA)) (II). [300] **4127**

JOURNAL - SEATTLE-KING COUNTY DENTAL SOCIETY (US). [1,400] **1329**

JOURNAL - SINGAPORE COMPUTER SOCIETY (SI). [2,000] **1261**

JOURNAL ST-LOUIS (CN/0710-2186). **5787**

JOURNAL - STANSTEAD COUNTY HISTORICAL SOCIETY (CN/0081-4369). [300] **2743**

JOURNAL STAR, THE (US). [99,197 daily 114,536 Sunday] **5660**

JOURNAL - TEXAS SOCIETY FOR ELECTRON MICROSCOPY (US/0196-5662). [550] **572**

JOURNAL / THE CANADIAN FOUNDATION FOR ILEITIS AND COLITIS (CN/0827-4681). [11,000] **3747**

JOURNAL : THE MAGAZINE OF THE INDIANA SCHOOL BOARDS ASSOCIATION, THE (US). [3,000] **1865**

JOURNAL - TIMBER DEVELOPMENT ASSOCIATION OF INDIA (II/0377-936X). [400] **2402**

JOURNAL - WESTERN NEW YORK GENEALOGICAL SOCIETY (US/0890-6858). [700] **2456**

JOURNAL - WORLD PHEASANT ASSOCIATION (UK). [800] **2196**

JOURNALEN SYKEPLEIEN (NO). [43,500] **3860**

JOURNALIST (UK/0022-5541). [34,000] **2921**

JOURNEY (LYNCHBURG, VA.) (US/0887-8854). [2,000] **4971**

JOYFUL WOMAN MAGAZINE, THE (US/0885-8004). [12,000] **5559**

JP AIRLINE-FLEETS INTERNATIONAL (SZ). [10,000] **26**

JSAE REVIEW (JA/0389-4304). **5418**

JSN INTERNATIONAL (JA). [8,000-10,000] **5353**

JTA DAILY NEWS BULLETIN (US/0021-3772). [2,500] **5050**

JTA WEEKLY NEWS DIGEST (US/0021-6763). [5,000] **2266**

JUBILEE INTERNATIONAL (US/0736-9662). [5,500] **4971**

JUDAISM (US/0022-5762). [6,500] **5050**

JUDGES' RETIREMENT SYSTEM : ANNUAL FINANCIAL REPORT AND REPORT OF OPERATIONS FOR THE FISCAL YEAR ENDED JUNE 30 ... / ADMINISTERED BY THE BOARD OF ADMINISTRATION, PUBLIC EMPLOYEES' RETIREMENT SYSTEM (US). **3141**

JUDICIAL CONDUCT REPORTER (US/0193-7367). **3141**

JUDO (UK/0022-5819). [5,000] **2599**

JUGHEAD (MAMARONECK, ILL.) (US/0022-5991). **4862**

JUGHEAD WITH ARCHIE (US/8750-0639). **4862**

JUGOSLOVENSKI PREGLED; INFORMATIVNO DOKUMENTARNI PRIRUCNIK O JUGOSLAVIJI (YU/0022-6114). **5207**

JUILLIARD JOURNAL, THE (US/1064-1580). [12,500] **386**

JUMELLO, LE (CN/0823-776X). [350] **2282**

JUNIOR SCHOLASTIC (US/0022-6688). [700,000] **1065**

JURIDICA (MX). [1,000] **2990**

JURIS (US/0022-6807). [4,500] **2990**

JURISPRUDENCE EXPRESS (CN/0705-3061). [536,000] **2991**

JURY: A HANDBOOK OF LAW AND PROCEDURE, THE (CN). [272] **2991**

JUST BETWEEN FRIENDS (CN/0849-5718). [20,000] **2489**

JUST COMPENSATION (US/0738-6494). **2991**

JUSTICE FOR CHILDREN (US/0888-9120). [1,000] **3121**

JUSTICE QUARTERLY (US/0741-8825). [2,500] **3168**

JUSTICE SYSTEM JOURNAL, THE (US/0098-261X). [900] **3141**

JUSTINIAN (AT/0157-5317). **2992**

JUVENILE & FAMILY COURT JOURNAL (US/0161-7109). [3,000] **3121**

JUVENILE AND FAMILY COURT NEWSLETTER (US/0162-9859). [2,500] **3121**

JUVENILE AND FAMILY LAW DIGEST (US/0279-2257). [2,500] **3121**

JUVENILE LAW REPORTS (US/0276-9603). [300] **3121**

K.A.R.D. FILES DYE DATA, THE (US/0899-1723). [600] **2456**

K.A.R.D. FILES PRESENTS ABSHIRE ABSTRACTS, THE (US/0899-1685). **2456**

K.A.R.D. FILES PRESENTS BLAKELEY BANDWAGON, THE (US/0899-1715). **2456**

K.A.R.D. FILES PRESENTS LUTTRELL LINEAGES & DATA, THE (US/0899-1731). **2456**

K.A.R.D. FILES PRESENTS RAMBO REFERENCES, THE (US/0899-174X). **2456**

K & I.E. EN C. KUNST EN CULTUUR (BE/0022-7277). **323**

K & K (DK). [600] **3401**

KAGAKU SOCHI (JA/0368-4849). **1026**

KAHPER JOURNAL (RICHMOND, KY.) (US/0022-7269). **1856**

KAHTOU (CN/0827-2077). [8,000] **2536**

KAIGAN SHOKO KENCHI SENTA CHOI NEMPO (JA). [300] **1451**

KAIGI DAIGAKKO KENKYU HOKOKU (JA/0288-3708). [300] **1833**

KAINDL-ARCHIV : MITTEILUNGEN DER RAIMUND FRIEDRICH KAINDL GESELLSCHAFT (GW). [400] **3708**

KAIROS : REVISTA PUBLICADA POR EL SEMINARIO TEOLOGICO CENTROAMERICANO (GT). [500] **5017**

KAIYO KAIHATSU KANKEI SHIRYO SOMOKUROKU (JA). **1451**

KALAMAZOO VALLEY FAMILY NEWSLETTER, THE (US/0888-7861). [300] **2456**

KALAVRITT / KALAVRTTA (II). [1,500] **355**

KALEIDOSCOPE / A SPECTRUM OF ARTICLES FOCUSING ON FAMILIES (US). **2282**

KALENDAR SVITLA (CN/0380-0962). [3,500] **5031**

KALENDARZ DZIENNIKA POLSKIEGO (UK). [1,000] **196**

KALKI (ORADELL) (US/0022-7994). [350] **3345**

KAMERA UND SCHULE (GW/0022-8109). [4,000] **4371**

KAMI PA GIKYOSHI (JA/0022-815X). [4,500] **4234**

KAMI STRATEGIC ASSUMPTIONS (US). **1501**

KAMOURASKA (LA POCATIERE) (CN/0707-7157). **5787**

KAN-SU CHIAO YU (CH). [20,000] **1759**

KANADA KURIER (ALBERTA AUSG.) (CN/0712-8878). **5787**

KANADA KURIER (AUSGABE FUER BRITISH COLUMBIA) (CN/0712-8886). **5787**

KANADA KURIER (MANITOBA AUSG.) (CN/0712-8894). **5787**

KANADA KURIER (MONTREAL AUSG.) (CN/0712-8908). **5787**

KANADA KURIER (ONTARIO AUSGABE) (CN/0712-8916). **5787**

KANADA KURIER (OTTAWA AUSG.) (CN/0712-8924). **5787**

KANADA KURIER (SASKATCHEWAN AUSG.) (CN/0712-8932). **5787**

KANADA KURIER (TORONTO AUSGABE) (CN/0712-8940). **5788**

KANADIER (GW/0175-6346). **5801**

KANE : HITOTSUBASHI DAIGAKU FUZOKU TOSHOKAN HO (JA/0387-8783). [2,000] **3221**

KANINA (CR/0378-0473). **323**

KANKYO HAKUSHO (JA). [1,000] **2234**

KANKYO HAKUSHO (JA). [870] **2235**

KANO STUDIES (NR/0567-4840). **2499**

KANSAS ANTHROPOLOGIST, THE (US/1069-0379). [450] **239**

KANSAS BANKER, THE (US/0022-8478). [1,300] **795**

KANSAS BUSINESS NEWS (US/0199-3607). [15,000] **688**

KANSAS BUSINESS REVIEW (LAWRENCE. 1977) (US/0164-8632). [2,000] **688**

KANSAS BUSINESS TEACHER / KANSAS BUSINESS TEACHERS ASSOCIATION, THE (US). [400] **688**

KANSAS CITY GRAIN MARKET REVIEW (US/0738-7296). [980] **1501**

KANSAS CITY SMALL BUSINESS MONTHLY (US/1068-2422). **688**

KANSAS EDUCATIONAL DIRECTORY (US/0099-0728). **1759**

KANSAS ENGLISH (US/0739-0157). [500] **1899**

KANSAS GEOGRAPHER, THE (US). [600] **2567**

KANSAS LEGAL DIRECTORY, THE (US). [5,300] **2992**

KANSAS MUSIC REVIEW (US/0022-8702). **4127**

KANSAS NURSE, THE (US/0022-8710). [2,500] **3860**

KANSAS QUARTERLY (US/0022-8745). [1,300] **2536**

KANSAS RESTAURANT (US/0022-8753). [1,200] **5071**

KANSAS STOCKMAN, THE (US/0022-8826). [6,900] **213**

KANSAS WORKS (US). [1,400] **5676**

KANZUME JIHO (JA). [3,000] **2347**

KAO CHA YU YEN CHIU / SHANG-HAI TZU JAN PO WU KUAN (CC). [2,500] **4167**

KAPPA ALPHA JOURNAL, THE (US/0888-8868). [65,500] **5232**

KARD FILES ADAMSON ANCESTRY, THE (US/0899-1693). **2456**

KARTHAGO (FR/0453-3429). **272**

KARTING (UK/0022-913X). [12,000] **4903**

KASHU MAINICHI (US/0893-8962). [7,000] **5636**

KATY KEENE (US/0886-4748). **4862**

KAVAKA (II/0379-5179). [500] **575**

KAWASAKI MEDICAL JOURNAL (JA/0385-0234). [800] **3601**

KAYHAN (UK). [25,000 per week] **4480**

KAYHAN-I VARZISHI (IR). [220,000] **4903**

KAZAN FUNKA YOCHI RENRAKUKAI KAIHO (JA). [450] **1408**

KEA NEWS (US/0164-3959). [37,000] **1759**

KEADAAN ANGKATAN KERJA DI INDONESIA (IO/0126-3919). **1682**

KEADAAN ANGKATEN KERJA DI INDONESIA : ANGKA SEMENTARA (IO). **1682**

KEADAAN KESEHATAN ANAK DAN IBU : HASIL SURVEI SOSIAL EKONOMI NASIONAL (IO). **3764**

KEEPER'S VOICE (US/0274-4872). **3168**

KEEPING UP (US/0890-1422). [5,000] **5207**

KEEPSAKE SERIES (US). [1,000] **3401**

KEIO COMMUNICATION REVIEW (JA/0388-7596). [600] **1115**

KEIO JOURNAL OF MEDICINE (JA/0022-9717). [1,200] **3601**

KEKKAKU (JA/0022-9776). [3,000] **3950**

KELLY'S U.K. EXPORTS (UK/0268-3105). [30,000] **843**

KEMBLE OCCASIONAL, THE (US/0453-4867). [200] **4566**

KEMIA (FI/0355-1628). [5,300] **1027**

KEMMERER GAZETTE, THE (US). [2,050] **5772**

KENCHIKU SETSUBI KOGAKU KENKYUJO HO (JA). [500] **2606**

KENKYU KIYO - MUSASHINO BIJUTSU DAIGAKU (JA). [1,500] **323**

KENKYU NEMPO - NIIGATA DAIGAKU SEKISETSU CHIIKI SAIGAI KENKYU SENTA (JA). [600] **1385**

KENNEL REVIEW (US/0164-4289). [10,000] **4287**

KENNIS EN METHODE (NE/0165-1773). [600] **4351**

KENT FAMILY HISTORY SOCIETY JOURNAL (UK/0305-9359). [1,500] **2456**

KENTUCKY ADMINISTRATIVE REGULATIONS SERVICE : CONTAINING REGULATIONS PROMULGATED BY ADMINISTRATIVE AGENCIES OF THE COMMONWEALTH OF KENTUCKY IN EFFECT AS OF ... (US). [600] **4660**

KENTUCKY ALUMNUS (US/0732-6297). [18,500] **1102**

KENTUCKY CITY (1968), THE (US/0453-5677). [4,150] **4660**

KENTUCKY CLUBWOMAN, THE (US/0740-6185). [6,000] **5232**

KENTUCKY COLLEGES AND UNIVERSITIES : DEGREES CONFERRED (US/0145-9120). [150] **1833**

KENTUCKY DENTAL JOURNAL (US/0744-396X). [1,900] **1329**

KENTUCKY FARM BUREAU NEWS (US/0023-0200). [340,696] **102**

KENTUCKY FARMER, THE (US/0023-0219). [20,700] **102**

KENTUCKY HAPPY HUNTING GROUND (US/0023-0235). [35,000] **4874**

KENTUCKY LAW JOURNAL (US/0023-026X). [1,300] **2992**

KENTUCKY LIBRARIES (US/0732-5452). [1,200] **3221**

KENTUCKY MARQUEE (US/0892-4899). [60,000] **5365**

KENTUCKY NURSE (US/0742-8367). [2,000] **3860**

KENTUCKY PHARMACIST, THE (US/0194-567X). [1,800] **4313**

KENTUCKY POETRY REVIEW (US/0889-647X). [400] **3345**

KENTUCKY QUERIES (US/0899-1359). [500] **2456**

KENTUCKY REVIEW (LEXINGTON. 1979), THE (US/0191-1031). [1,200-1,400] **2849**

KENTUCKY WARBLER, THE (US/0160-5070). [500] **5618**

KENYA CERTIFICATE OF BUSINESS EDUCATION. REGULATIONS AND SYLLABUSES (KE). [10,000] **1899**

KENYA CERTIFICATE OF SECONDARY EDUCATION, REGULATIONS AND SYLLABUSES (KE). **1899**

KENYA CERTIFICATE OF TECHNICAL EDUCATION. REGULATIONS AND SYLLABUSES (KE). [10,000] **1899**

KENYA PAST AND PRESENT (KE/0257-8301). [1,800] **2641**

KENYON REVIEW, THE (US/0163-075X). [5,000] **3345**

KERALA SOCIOLOGIST (II). [1,000] **5250**

KERAULOPHON, THE (US/0735-8660). [60] **4127**

KERNOS (BE). **4972**

KERSHNER KINFOLK (US/0736-0886). [100] **2456**

KERYGMA (OTTAWA) (CN/0023-0693). [220] **4972**

KERYGMA UND DOGMA. BEIHEFT (GW/0453-7726). **4972**

KETTERING REPORT (US/0743-8478). [10,000] **5207**

KETTERING REVIEW (US/0748-8815). [15,000] **4660**

KEY BRITISH ENTERPRISES : KBE / COMPILED AND PUBLISHED BY PUBLICATIONS DIVISION, DUN & BRADSTREET LIMITED (UK/0142-5048). [3,000] **688**

KEY REPORTER, THE (US/0023-0804). [250,000] **1092**

KEY TO CHRISTIAN EDUCATION (US/0023-0839). [65,000] **4972**

KEY VIVE (AT/0310-8260). **4127**

KEYBOARD ARTS (US/0090-3361). [1,000] **4127**

KEYBOARD COMPANION (US). [15,000] **4127**

KEYSTONE (PITTSBURGH, PA. 1968), THE (US/0744-4036). [2,700] **5432**

KEYSTONE SEEKERS GENEALOGICAL QUARTERLY (US/0737-2868). [175] **2456**

KEYSTONE WATER QUALITY MANAGER (US/1069-0212). [4,300] **5535**

KHOSANA : THE BULLETIN OF THE THAILAND/LAOS/CAMBODIA STUDIES GROUP OF THE SOUTHWEST ASIA COUNCIL, ASSOCIATION FOR ASIAN STUDIES (US/0898-1930). [300] **2505**

KID PROOF (CN/0843-0284). [2,500] **1065**

KIDRON NEWS THE DALTON GAZETTE, THE (US). [1,500] **5729**

KIDS FASHIONS MAGAZINE (US/0362-6660). **1085**

KIDS, KIDS, KIDZ MAGAZINE (US). **2282**

KIDS TORONTO (CN/0826-9696). [60,000] **4851**

KIDSPRINT TIMES (US/1065-3872). [2,000] **1804**

KIEL TRI COUNTY RECORD (US). [2,700] **5768**

KIELER STUDIEN ZUR DEUTSCHEN LITERATURGESCHICHTE (GW/0453-8501). [600] **3401**

KIJK OP HET NOORDEN (NE/0023-1363). **1501**

KIKAI GIJUTSU KENKYUJO SHOHO (JA/0388-4252). [700] **5123**

KIKAI TO KOGU (JA/0387-1053). [32,000] **2119**

KIKAIKA NOGYO (JA). [100,000] **159**

KIKAN NIHON SHISO SHI (JA). [2,000] **2656**

KILLAM WORLD (CN/0821-249X). **1833**

KILLSHOT (CN/0711-7094). [15,000] **4862**

KIN KOLLECTING (US/1069-207X). **2457**

KINDER (GW). [240,000] **1804**

KINDRED SPIRIT (US). **4972**

KINDRED SPIRITS (CN/0823-3837). [500] **2457**

KINFOLKS (LAKE CHARLES, LA.) (US/0742-7654). [400] **2457**

KINGBIRD, THE (US/0023-1606). [850] **5618**

KING'S INTERNATIONAL COAL TRADE & WORLD COAL STATISTICS (US/0749-9043). **2142**

KINGSTON RELATIONS (CN/1188-1089). **2457**

KINGSTON THIS WEEK (CN/0712-9068). [36,000] **5788**

KINISTINO POST [MICROFORM], THE (CN). **5788**

KINKI DAIGAKU RIKOGAKUBU KENKYU HOKOKU (JA/0386-4928). [1,000] **5123**

KIPU (EC). **5250**

KIRCHENMUSIKER, DER (GW/0023-1819). [4,800] **4128**

KIRCHLICHES MONATSBLATT FUER DAS EVANGELISCH-LUTHERISCHE HAUS (US). [1,500] **5062**

KIRKE OG KULTUR (NO/0023-186X). [3,000] **4972**

KIRON, LE (CN/0709-8456). **4903**

KIRTLANDIA (US/0075-6245). [500] **4167**

KIRYAT SEFER (IS/0023-1851). [1,000] **5050**

KISHOCHO GEPPO : ZENKOKU KISHOHYO (JA). [530] **1427**

KISHOCHO KAIYO KISHO BUI ROBOTTO KANSOKU SHIRYO. / DATA FROM OCEAN DATA BUOY STATIONS (JA). [600] **1427**

KISHOCHO NENPO: ZENKOKU KISHOHYO. ANNUAL REPORT OF THE JAPAN METEOROLOGICAL AGENCY: METEOROLOGICAL OBSERVATIONS (JA). [550] **1427**

KITABAT (BA). [6,000] **3402**

KITANOMARU; KOKURITSU KOBUNSHOKAN HO (JA). [1,000] **2482**

KITH 'N KIN (FREMONT, OHIO) (US/1053-5837). [350] **2457**

KIVA (TUSCON, ARIZ.), THE (US/0023-1940). [1,300] **272**

KJEMI (NO/0023-1983). [7,500] **1027**

KLEIO (SA/0023-2084). [3,400] **2641**

KNIFE WORLD (US/0276-9042). [13,000] **2774**

KNIGHT LETTER (FORT WORTH, TEX.) (US/0454-8973). [200] **2457**

KNIT & CHAT (CN/0711-639X). [20,000] **5184**

KNITTING INTERNATIONAL (UK/0266-8394). [5,000] **5353**

KNOWLEDGE-BASED SYSTEMS (GUILDFORD, SURREY) (UK/0950-7051). [800] **1193**

KNOWLEDGE (FORT WORTH, TEX.) (US/0738-8640). **3345**

KNOX COUNTY, ILLINOIS GENEALOGICAL SOCIETY QUARTERLY (US/0741-7284). [350] **2457**

KNOX COUNTY, KENTUCKY KINFOLK (US/0276-4857). **2457**

KOBE GAKUIN KEIZAIGAKU RONSHU (JA). [1,500] **1502**

KODAK TECH BITS (US/0452-2591). **4371**

KODALY ENVOY (US). [1,600] **1899**

KODIAK DAILY MIRROR, THE (US/0740-2112). [3,500] **5629**

KOEDOE (SA/0075-6458). [1,000] **5589**

KOEPEL VIJF (BE/0771-7172). [3,000] **1760**

KOGAI (JA/0454-9015). [6,000] **2235**

KOHO - KEIO GIJUKU DAIGAKU JOHO KAGAKU KENKYUJO (JA). [200] **1261**

KOINONIA (PRINCETON, N.J.) (US/1047-1057). [350] **4972**

KOKURITSU GAN SENTA NEMPO (JA). [500] **3820**

KOKURITSU TAMA KENKYUJO NEMPO (JA). **3602**

KOKUSAI KANKEI-GAKU KENKYU (JA). **4527**

KOKUSAI KANKEI GAKUBU KENKYU NENPO (JA/0388-4279). **4527**

KOKUSAI KANKEI KENKYU (MISHIMA-SHI, JAPAN) (JA/0389-2603). **4528**

KOKUSAI KORYU KIKIN NEMPO (JA). **2657**

KOKUSAI KORYU KIKIN NYUSU / HENSHU, KOKUSAI KORYU KIKIN SOMUBU SOMUKA (JA). **2657**

KOKUSAI KRYU (JA). [8,000] **5251**

KOKUSAI NIHON BUNGAKU KENKYU SHUKAI KAIGIROKU (JA/0387-7280). [800] **3402**

KOLNER MUSEUMS-BULLETIN (GW/0933-257X). [3,000] **4090**

KOMBA (KE). [6,000] **5590**

KOMMUNAL LITTERATUR (SW/0023-3056). [1,300] **4698**

KOMPYUTOPIA / COMPUTOPIA (JA). [61,500] **1193**

KONGETSU NO NOYAKU (JA/0023-334X). **984**

KONOMISK REVY (NO). **1571**

KONSUMENT (AU). [100,000] **1298**

KONTANT (BERLIN, GERMANY) (GW). [50,000] **1066**

KONTINENT (BERLIN, GERMANY) (GW/0176-4179). [6,500] **4480**

KOREA BUSINESS WORLD (KO). [28,000] **689**

KOREA ECONOMIC REPORT (KO). [32,000] **1571**

KOREA HERALD, THE (KO). [15,000] **5805**

KOREA JOURNAL (KO/0023-3900). [3,000] **2657**

KOREA NEWSREVIEW (US/0146-9657). [5,000] **2506**

KOREA OBSERVER (KO). [3,000] **2849**

KOREAN CULTURE (LOS ANGELES) (US/0270-1618). [3,000] **2657**

KOREAN TRADE DIRECTORY (KO). [20,000] **843**

KOREANA (KO). [150,000] **355**

KORNYEZETVEDELMI SZAKIRODALMI TAJEKOZTATO (HU/0231-0716). [260] **2218**

KOSMETIK INTERNATIONAL (GW). [22,000] **404**

KOSMOS (STUTTGART) (GW/0023-4230). [100,000] **5124**

KOSMOS (TORRANCE, CALIF.) (US/0278-8101). [500] **390**

KOTAI BUTSURI. A SHIRIZU (JA). [6,000] **4411**

KOVETS KEREM SHELOMOH (US). [2,000] **5050**

KOZAN (JA/0287-9840). [1,200] **2143**

KOZUTI KOZLEKEDESI SZAKIRODALMI TAJEKOZTATO (HU/0231-0724). [220] **5441**

KPFA PROGRAM FOLIO (US). [15,000] **1134**

KRAFTFUTTER (GW/0023-4427). [3,100] **202**

KRANKENHAUSPHARMAZIE (GW/0173-7597). [2,500] **4313**

KRANKENHAUSTECHNIK (GW/0720-3977). [9,000] **3787**

KRANKENPFLEGE (SZ/0253-0465). [30,000] **3861**

KRAS I SPELEOLOGIA (PL/0137-5482). [1,000] **1385**

KREFELD IMMIGRANTS AND THEIR DESCENDANTS (US/0883-7961). [300] **2457**

KRIEG UND LITERATUR (GW/0935-9060). [400] **2696**

KRIMINALISTIK (GW/0023-4699). [4,945] **3168**

KRISIS (INTERNATIONAL CIRCLE FOR RESEARCH IN PHILOSOPHY) (US/0894-5233). [780] **4351**

KRITERION (BL/0100-512X). [500] **4351**

KRONIKA (TORONTO) (CN/0704-4380). [2,000] **2536**

KUANG-TUNG HUA YUAN CHI KAN (CH). [1,000] **355**

KUCHE (GW/0344-4376). [7,200] **2348**

KUENSTLER — Controlled Circulation Index

KUENSTLER (MUENCHEN) (GW/0934-1730). [7,000] **323**

KUENSTLERGILDE; EIN MITTEILUNGSBLATT FUER UNSERE MITGLIEDER, DIE (GW). [1,600] **355**

KUKCHE MUNJE (KO). [20,000] **4528**

KULFOLDI MAGYAR NYELVU KIADVANYOK (HU/0133-333X). [500] **418**

KULTUR CHRONIK (GW/0724-343X). [50,000] **323**

KULTURA (PARIS) (FR/0023-5148). **3403**

KULTURA SLOVA (XO/0023-5202). [3,600] **3293**

KUMAMOTO MEDICAL JOURNAL, THE (JA/0023-5326). [450] **3660**

KUNST & MUSEUMJOURNAAL (DUTCH EDITION) (NE/0924-5251). [4,600] **355**

KUNST & MUSEUMJOURNAAL (ENGLISH EDITION) (NE/0924-526X). [3,000] **356**

KUNST IN HESSEN UND AM MITTELRHEIN (GW/0452-8514). **356**

KUNST UND KIRCHE (AU/0023-5431). [4,000] **356**

KUNSTSTOFF-JOURNAL (GW/0047-3766). [13,500] **4456**

KUNSTSTOFFE-PLASTICS (SOLOTHURN) (SZ/0023-5598). **4456**

KUO CHI HUO I (CC/1002-5030). **843**

KURIER (ORANGE, VA), DER (US/1059-9762). [600] **2457**

KURUME MEDICAL JOURNAL (JA/0023-5679). [550 (institutions)] **3603**

KURZBERICHT UBER LATEINAMERIKA (GW). **1502**

KUWAITI DIGEST, THE (KU). [8,500] **2506**

KW MAGAZINE (CN/0822-8140). [30,000] **2536**

KYBERNETES (UK/0368-492X). [500] **1252**

KYBERNETIKA (XR/0023-5954). [1,150] **1252**

KYODO KANKEI SHIMBUN KIJI SAKUIN (JA). **2526**

KYOKA PURASUCHIKKUSU (JA/0452-9685). [1,800] **4456**

KYOTO-SHI REKISHI SHIRYOKAN KIYO (JA/0910-1349). [500] **2657**

KYOYUK KAEBAL (KO). [14,000] **1760**

KYRIAKATIKA NEA (US/0746-4479). [250,000] **5689**

L.A. 411 (US/1062-6603). [10,000] **4073**

L. A. W. G. LETTER (CN/0316-3393). **4480**

L UNION VICTORIAVILLE CANADA (CN). **5788**

LA RECORD (UK). [25,500] **3222**

LA VERNE MAGAZINE (US/0199-347X). [2,000] **2536**

LA YOUTH (US). [100,000] **1066**

LAB 2000 (SP/0213-7275). **5125**

LAB PRODUCTS INTERNATIONAL. BRUSSELS (BE/0775-602X). [50,000] **463**

LABDATA (US/0730-5672). **1615**

LABOR & INVESTMENTS (US/0279-0467). [3,000] **1683**

LABOR ARBITRATION INFORMATION SYSTEM (US/0744-5253). [400] **3150**

LABOR LAWS OF MAINE (US). **3150**

LABORATORIO 2000 (IT/1120-8376). [9,000] **984**

LABORATORIUMSMEDIZIN (GW/0342-3026). [7,800] **3603**

LABORATORY BUYERS GUIDE (CN/0381-6729). [20,000] **5125**

LABORATORY EQUIPMENT DIGEST (UK/0023-6829). [15,548] **5125**

LABORATORY INVESTIGATION (US/0023-6837). [6,100] **3896**

LABORATORY NEWS (UK/0266-7169). [16,500] **463**

LABORATORY NEWS (AT). [8450] **463**

LABORATORY PRIMATE NEWSLETTER (US/0023-6861). [1,200] **5515**

LABORATORY PRODUCT NEWS (CN/0047-3855). [19,100] **5125**

LABORATORY REGULATION MANUAL (US/0272-3778). **2993**

LABORPRAXIS (GW/0344-1733). [14,050] **3603**

LABORSCOPE (SZ). **1985**

LABORWATCH (US). [3,500] **943**

LABOUR ADVOCATE (ST. CATHARINES) (CN/0711-3889). **1685**

LABOUR CAPITAL AND SOCIETY (CN/0706-1706). [900] **1685**

LABOUR FORCE BY SEX (TR). [400] **1535**

LABOUR NETWORK (AT). [400] **1686**

LABOUR RELATIONS BULLETIN (CN). **1686**

LABOUR RESEARCH (LONDON) (UK/0023-7000). [9,000] **1686**

LABOUR REVIEW / ST. CATHARINES AND DISTRICT LABOUR COUNCIL (CN/0229-2726). **1686**

LABYRINTH (WATERLOO) (CN/0318-8450). **1078**

LACERTA (NE/0023-7051). [2,000] **5590**

LACON HOME JOURNAL (LACON, ILL. : 1866 : WEEKLY) (US). [1,650] **5660**

LADDER (WASHINGTON, D.C.), THE (US/0882-1828). [500] **3294**

LAE NEWS (US/0162-3052). [23,000] **1760**

LAFAYETTE COUNTY HERITAGE NEWS (US/1064-5527). [125] **2457**

LAG & [I.E. OCH] AVTAL (SW). [9,046] **3151**

LAIFS (US/0146-910X). [500] **2422**

LAIT ET NOUS, LE (BE/0770-2515). [35,000] **196**

LAKE CITIES SUN, THE (US). [3,000] **5751**

LAKE CITY SILVER WORLD (US). [1,200] **5643**

LAKE COUNTY (IL) GENEALOGICAL SOCIETY QUARTERLY (US/0736-4059). [215] **2457**

LAKE ELSINORE VALLEY SUN-TRIBUNE (US/0745-1350). [15,000] **5636**

LAKE MARTIN LIVING MAGAZINE (US/1070-8103). [8,50034,000 (estimated readership)] **4851**

LAKE STEVENS JOURNAL (US). [15,000] **5761**

LAKES LETTER (CN/0709-0013). **1416**

LAKESHORE CHRONICLE (US). [31,500] **5768**

LAKESIDE LEADER (CN/0821-3372). [2,509] **5788**

LAKEWOOD JEFFERSON SENTINEL (1991), THE (US/1060-5215). [19,000] **5643**

LALU LINTAS ANGKUTAN ANTAR PULAU MENURUT GOLONGAN BARANG, DAERAH ASAL, DAN TUJUAN (IO). **5451**

LAMAR DEMOCRAT (US/0745-9300). [3,400] **5703**

LAMB'S PASTURES (US/0883-7708). [150] **2457**

LAMMERGEYER, THE (SA/0075-7780). [400] **4167**

LAMOURE CHRONICLE (US). **5725**

LAMP, THE (AT/0047-3936). [33,000] **3861**

LAMPAS (NE/0165-8204). [1,100] **3294**

LANCASTER CONFERENCE NEWS (US/0747-2706). **5062**

LANCASTER FARMING (US/0023-7485). [48,000] **103**

LANCE K. LERAY'S BAKERY WORLD OF CANADA (CN/0710-569X). [1,800] **2348**

LAND AND MINERALS SURVEYING (UK/0265-4210). [2,760] **2027**

LAND & WATER INTERNATIONAL (NE/0023-7604). [4,300] **2093**

LAND ASSESSMENT/SALES RATIO STUDY AND EQUALIZED ASSESSMENTS (CN/0228-4278). [125] **4660**

LAND (MANKATO, MINN.), THE (US/0279-1633). [40,000] **103**

LAND REFORM, LAND SETTLEMENT AND COOPERATIVES (IT/0251-1894). [2,000] **1542**

LAND TRENDS (NEW YORK, N.Y.) (US/0739-6376). [250] **4840**

LAND + WATER / MILIEUTECHNIEK (NE). **2027**

LANDBOTE, DER (GW). [5,700] **104**

LANDBOUWMECHANISATIE (NE/0023-7795). [23,000] **159**

LANDBOUWSTATISTIEKEN (BE). [400] **154**

LANDBRUGETS PRISFORHOLD (DK/0106-519X). [1,200] **104**

LANDINSPEKTREN; TIDSSKRIFT FOR OPMALINGSOG MATRIKELVAESEN (DK/0105-4570). [1,500] **2027**

LANDMAN (FT. WORTH) (US/0457-088X). [8,200] **4263**

LANDMARK (CALGARY) (CN/0843-459X). **2422**

LANDMARK, THE (US). [7,604] **5689**

LANDMARKS OBSERVER (US/0272-1384). [1,500] **2743**

LANDMARKS (SEATTLE, WASH.) (US/0734-4007). [13,000] **2743**

LANDSCAPE & IRRIGATION (US/0745-3795). [30,500] **2422**

LANDSCAPE ARCHITECT & SPECIFIER NEWS (US/1060-9962). **2422**

LANDSCAPE ARCHITECTURAL REVIEW (CN/0228-6963). [1,500] **2422**

LANDSCAPE CONTRACTOR, THE (US/0194-7257). [2,200] **2423**

LANDSCAPE, THE (NZ/0110-1439). **2422**

LANDSCAPE TRADES (CN/0225-6398). [5,000] **2423**

LANDSCAPER (AT). **2423**

LANDTECHNIK, DIE (GW/0023-8082). [4,000] **159**

LANDWIRTSCHAFTLICHES WOCHENBLATT FUR WESTFALEN UND LIPPE (GW). [61,000] **104**

LANDWORKER, THE (UK). [25,000] **1687**

LANE COUNTY HISTORIAN (US/0458-7227). [485] **2743**

LANE REPORT, THE (US/1063-925X). [11,000] **689**

LANG VAN (CN/0832-1922). [10,000] **2489**

LANGENSCHEIDT'S SPRACH-ILLUSTRIERTE (GW/0023-8252). [11,000] **3294**

LANGLEY TIMES (CN/0711-7450). **5788**

LANGMUIR (US/0743-7463). [1,300] **1055**

LANGSTON HUGHES REVIEW, THE (US/0737-0555). [260] **3345**

LANGUAGE AND SOCIETY (CN/0709-7751). [22,000] **3295**

LANGUAGE ARTS (US/0360-9170). [20,000] **1804**

LANGUAGE PROBLEMS & LANGUAGE PLANNING (US/0272-2690). [700] **3295**

LANGUAGE SCIENCES (OXFORD) (UK/0388-0001). [550] **3296**

LANGUAGE, SPEECH & HEARING SERVICES IN SCHOOLS (US/0161-1461). [51,000] **1881**

LANGUAGE TEACHER / JAPAN ASSOCIATION OF LANGUAGE TEACHERS, THE (JA/0289-7938). [3,650] **3296**

LANGUES ET LINGUISTIQUE (CN/0226-7144). [250] **3296**

LANIGAN ADVISOR (CN). **5788**

LANSING STATE JOURNAL (US/0274-9742). [72,000 daily 93,000 Sunday] **5692**

LANTERN'S CORE, THE (US/0047-4053). [650] **3222**

LANTMANNEN (SW). [20,000] **104**

LANTZVILLE LOG, THE (CN/0710-5487). [2,350] **5788**

LAOGRAPHIA (GR/1010-7266). [1,000] **2321**

LAPAROSCOPIC SURGERY UPDATE (US/1067-2036). **3604**

LAPIS (MUNCHEN) (GW/0342-2933). [15,000] **1357**

LAPIZ : REVISTA MENSUAL DE ARTE (SP/0212-1700). **356**

LAPURAN TAHUNAN SURUHANJAYA PERKHIDMATAN AWAM NEGERI SABAH (MY). [500] **4661**

LARAMIE DAILY BOOMERANG (LARAMIE, WYO. : 1957) (US). [7,500 paid] **5772**

LARGE ANIMAL VETERINARIAN COVERING HEALTH & NUTRITION (US/1043-7533). [21,000] **5515**

LARGE ANIMAL VETERINARY REPORT (US/1069-1774). [750] **5515**

LARGE PRINT BOOKS / GEORGIAN BAY REGIONAL LIBRARY SYSTEM (CN/0229-4370). **4829**

LARGO CONSUMO (IT). [25,000] **929**

LARUE COUNTY HERALD NEWS, THE (US). [4,000] **5681**

LARYNGOSCOPE, THE (US/0023-852X). [8,031] **3889**

LAS CRUCES BULLETIN (US/0885-8527). [20,200] **5814**

LAS VEGAS OPTIC (US). [4,600] **5712**

LASER FOCUS WORLD BUYERS' GUIDE (US). [45,000] **4437**

LASERS & OPTRONICS (US/0892-9947). [40,000] **4438**

LASERTONE NEWS (US). [15,000] **4566**

LAST GASP (CN/0710-6920). **2177**

LATEINAMERIKA-KURIER (SZ). [250] **689**

LATIN AMERICA (WASHINGTON) (US/0092-4148). **2743**

LATIN AMERICAN ECONOMY & BUSINESS (UK/0960-8702). **1637**

LATIN AMERICAN INDIAN LITERATURES JOURNAL (US/0888-5613). [400] **3403**

LATIN AMERICAN ISSUES (US/0741-3378). **2743**

LATIN AMERICAN LITERARY REVIEW (US/0047-4134). [1,000] **3345**

LATIN AMERICAN NEWSLINE (UK). [500] **2512**

LATIN AMERICAN RESEARCH REVIEW (US/0023-8791). [4,500] **2743**

LATINOAMERICANA (STOCKHOLM) (SW). [400] **2512**

LATOHATAR (HU). [10,000] **3346**

LAUREL MESSENGER (US/0023-8988). [1,100] **2744**

LAURENTIANUM (IT/0023-902X). [500] **5031**

LAURIER CAMPUS (CN/0700-5105). [25,000] **1834**

LAURISTON S. TAYLOR LECTURES IN RADIATION PROTECTION AND MEASUREMENTS (US/0277-9196). **4788**

LAVALIN (CN/0704-5689). **1985**

LAVALIN (ENGLISH EDITION) (CN/0227-7964). **1985**

LAW AND ORDER (US/0023-9194). [25,000] **3168**

LAW AND STATE (GW/0341-6151). **3132**

LAW ENFORCEMENT INTELLIGENCE ANALYSIS DIGEST (US/0895-3945). [700] **3168**

LAW ENFORCEMENT LEGAL REPORTER INCORPORATED, THE (US/0195-0290). [3,000] **3168**

LAW ENFORCEMENT TECHNOLOGY (US/0747-3680). [23,000] **3169**

LAW IN CONTEXT (BUNDOORA, VIC.) (AT/0811-5796). [450] **2995**

LAW NOW (CN/0841-2626). [2,500] **2995**

LAW OF THE SEA INSTITUTE: OCCASIONAL PAPERS (US/0080-2808). [250] **1451**

LAW OFFICE GUIDE IN COMPUTERS (US/0739-5132). [4,000] **2996**

LAW REVIEW JOURNAL (US/0734-1938). [200] **2996**

LAW SCHOOL ADMINISTRATOR'S JOURNAL (US/0741-1170). [200] **2996**

LAW SOCIETY JOURNAL (SYDNEY, N.S.W. : 1982) (AT). [12,400] **2997**

LAW SOCIETY'S GAZETTE (UK/0262-1495). **2997**

LAW TALK (WELLINGTON, N.Z.) (NZ). [7,000] **2997**

LAW TEACHER'S JOURNAL (US/0741-1197). [200] **2997**

LAWASIA HUMAN RIGHTS BULLETIN (AT). [2,500] **4510**

LAWN & GARDEN TRADE (CN/0705-212X). [15,000] **2423**

LAWN & LANDSCAPE MAINTENANCE (US/1046-154X). [43,000] **2423**

LAWRENCE DAILY JOURNAL-WORLD (US). [18,746 daily19,145 Sunday] **5677**

LAWRENCE EAGLE-TRIBUNE (US). [55,515 (daily)60,217 (Sundays)] **5689**

LAWS OF THE REGENTS, UNIVERSITY OF COLORADO (US). [150] **4661**

LAWYERS WEEKLY (SCARBOROUGH) (CN/0830-0151). [37,500] **2998**

LBL RESEARCH REVIEW (US/0882-1305). [9,000] **4448**

LC FOLK ARCHIVE FINDING AID (US/0736-4903). [2,000] **5269**

LC FOLK ARCHIVE REFERENCE AID (US/0736-4911). [2,000] **2325**

LC GC (US/0888-9090). [60,000] **984**

LC GC INTERNATIONAL (US/0895-5441). [20,000] **984**

LC-MS UPDATE (UK/0964-1645). **5125**

LCOMM NEWS / LIBRARY COUNCIL OF METROPOLITAN MILWAUKEE (US). [420] **3222**

LCPA BROADSIDE (US/0736-296X). [1,800] **3223**

LEAD AND ZINC STATISTICS (UK/0023-9577). [650] **4025**

LEAD BELLY LETTER (US/1056-5329). [2,000] **4128**

LEADER IN ACTION (US/8755-2620). [24,000] **1834**

LEADER (RESEARCH TRIANGLE PARK, N.C.), THE (US/0195-0622). [8,500] **5723**

LEADER'S PRODUCT LIABILITY LAW AND STRATEGY (US/0733-513X). **2999**

LEADERSHIP EDUCATION (US/1062-1474). **875**

LEAGUE BULLETIN (US). [2,000] **2744**

LEARNING RESOURCES JOURNAL (UK/0268-2125). [450] **1834**

LEASIDE VILLAGER, THE (CN/0715-4631). **5788**

LEAVEN (FRANKLIN PARK, ILL.) (US/8750-2011). [7,300] **2282**

LEAVENWORTH TIMES LEAVENWORTH, KAN. : 1878) (US). [10,000] **5677**

LEBA (PO). [1,000] **273**

LEBENSBILDER ZUR GESCHICHTE DER BOHMISCHEN LANDER / HERAUSGEGEBEN IM AUFTRAG DEG COLLEGIUM CAROLINUM (GW). [1,000] **433**

LEBENSMITTEL- UND BIOTECHNOLOGIE (AU/0254-9298). [2,000] **2348**

LEBENSMITTELTECHNIK (GW/0047-4290). [7,300] **2348**

LEBER, MAGEN, DARM (GW/0300-8622). **3747**

L'ECOUTE, A (CN/0700-3900). [6,500] **4128**

LECTOR (BERKELEY, CALIF.) (US/0732-8001). [3,000] **3346**

LECTURAS DE HISTORIA DEL ARTE (SP). [1,000] **357**

LECTURE FAITE (CN/0714-8216). **2999**

LEDER (GW/0024-0176). [2,200] **3185**

LEDGER, THE (US). **5677**

LEGACY (AMHERST, MASS.) (US/0748-4321). [500] **3404**

LEGAL ALERT (CN/0712-841X). **3101**

LEGAL ASSISTANTS: UPDATE (US/0272-1961). [5,000] **2999**

LEGAL BIBLIOGRAPHY JOURNAL (US/0741-1189). [200] **3081**

LEGAL BUSINESS (UK/0958-4609). [5,500] **2999**

LEGAL EXECUTIVE, THE (UK/0024-0362). [16,000] **2999**

LEGAL INVESTIGATOR, THE (US/0741-417X). [500] **3000**

LEGAL MEMORANDUM (RESTON), A (US/0192-6152). [43,000] **3000**

LEGAL QUARTERLY DIGEST OF MINE SAFETY AND HEALTH DECISIONS (US/1051-533X). [170] **3000**

LEGAL REGISTER, METROPOLITAN WASHINGTON, THE (US/8756-2006). [17,000] **3000**

LEGAL VIDEO REVIEW (US/0898-9427). [150] **3001**

LEGAL WRITING : THE JOURNAL OF THE LEGAL WRITING INSTITUTE (US). [500] **3001**

LEGGERE (IT). **3404**

LEGGERE DONNA (IT). **5560**

LEGISLACAO FEDERAL E MARGINALIA (BL). [16,000] **3001**

LEGISLATIVE BUDGET BOOK : A PUBLICATION OF THE LEGISLATIVE BUDGET OFFICE / JOINT SENATE FINANCE-HOUSE APPROPRIATIONS COMMITTEE (US). **4661**

LEGISLATIVE BULLETIN - ASSOCIATION OF WASHINGTON CITIES (US/0740-4204). [2,500] **3001**

LEGISLATIVE BULLETIN - NEW YORK STATE SCHOOL BOARDS ASSOCIATION (US/1048-2733). [9,000] **1865**

LEGISLATIVE INFORMATION SERVICE (US). [120] **4661**

LEGISLATIVE MANUAL - GENERAL ASSEMBLY OF SOUTH CAROLINA (US/0362-272X). [15,000] **4661**

LEGISLATIVE REPORT (EDMONTON) (CN/0709-5333). [400] **3002**

LEGISLATIVE REPORTING SERVICE / COMMERCE CLEARING HOUSE (US). [300] **4661**

LEGISLATIVE STUDIES QUARTERLY (US/0362-9805). [1,000] **4480**

LEISURE INDUSTRY REPORT (US). **4851**

LEISURE TIME ELECTRONICS (US/0273-6586). [15,466] **2070**

LEISURE WATCH CANADA (CN/1189-4873). **4707**

LEISURE WHEELS (CN/0709-7093). [25,000] **5385**

LEISURE WORLD (CN/1184-146X). [280,000] **5482**

LEMEL (AT/0729-5898). [400] **2915**

LEMOUZI (FR/0024-0761). [3,000] **2321**

LENDER LIABILITY LAW REPORT (US/1045-1463). [2300] **3087**

LENGAS (FR/0153-0313). [300] **3297**

LENGUAS MODERNAS (SANTIAGO) (CL/0716-0542). [600] **3297**

LEON HUNTERS DISPATCH, THE (US/8756-5595). [268] **2458**

LESBIAN AND GAY STUDIES NEWSLETTER : LGSN (CN/1064-5950). [600] **2795**

LESBIAN-GAY LAW NOTES (US/8755-9021). [1,000] **3002**

LESBIAN NEWS (CANOGA PARK, CALIF.), THE (US/0739-1803). [90,000] **2795**

LESHONENU (IS/0024-1091). [600] **3297**

LESNICTVI (XR/0024-1105). [1,000] **2387**

LESSING YEARBOOK (US/0075-8833). [1,000] **3346**

LET THE PEOPLE WORSHIP (US/0891-3927). **4973**

LETHAIA (NO/0024-1164). [1,400] **4227**

LETHBRIDGE MAGAZINE (CN/0821-5278). [18,000] **2537**

LETRAS DE HOJE (BL/0101-3335). [1,000] **3297**

LETRAS FEMENINAS (US/0277-4356). [400] **3404**

LET'S CHEER (US/0733-9674). [3,000] **4903**

LET'S DANCE (US/0024-1253). [700] **1313**

LET'S PLAY HOCKEY (US/0889-4795). [20,000] **4903**

LET'S PRAY TOGETHER (US/0740-9613). [70,000] **5031**

LETTER FROM CHILE, A (CL). [12,000] **2552**

LETTER (HOUSTON, TEX.) (US/0899-3017). [1,500] **875**

LETTORE DI PROVINCIA, IL (IT/0024-1350). [1,500] **3405**

LETTRE AFRIQUE EXPANSION, LA (FR/0996-9888). [1,200] **4480**

LETTRE DE CONJONCTURE (BRUSSELS, BELGIUM) (BE/0772-0831). [7,500] **1572**

LETTRE DE L'OIV (FR). **105**

LETTRE DE REPORTERS SANS FRONTIERES, LA (FR/1148-3164). [2,000] **2922**

LETTRE - EUROSANTE, LA (FR/1148-9480). **4789**

LETTRE. FRENCH TV MARKET NEWSLETTER, LA (FR/0996-7826). [1,000] **1159**

LETTRE MENSUELLE DE FRANCE PHARMACIE LABORATOIRES, LA (FR/1145-4881). [2,000] **4314**

LETTRES QUEBECOISES (CN/0382-084X). [5,000] **3405**

LETTRES ROMANES / UNIVERSITE CATHOLIQUE DE LOUVAIN, LES (BE). [600] **3405**

LETTURE (IT/0024-144X). [5,000] **5365**

LEVANT (LONDON) (UK/0075-8914). [700] **273**

LEVANT (MONTPELLIER, FRANCE) (FR/0992-0757). **2658**

LEVELLAND AND HOCKLEY COUNTY NEWS-PRESS (US). **5751**

LEVENDE TALEN (NE/0024-1539). **3297**

LEWISTON - PORTER SENTINEL (US). [13,500] **5718**

LEWISVILLE DAILY LEADER (US/0745-6174). [4,510] **5751**

LEX : COLETANEA DE LEGISLACAO E JURISPRUDENCIA (BL). [8,418] **3002**

LEX, JURISPRUDENCIA DO SUPREMO TRIBUNAL FEDERAL (BL). [3,500] **3002**

LEXINGTON THEOLOGICAL QUARTERLY (US/0024-1628). [2,500] **4973**

LEXIS (PE/0254-9239). **3297**

LEYTE-SAMAR STUDIES (PH/0024-1679). [1,000] **2658**

LHAT BULLETIN (US). [600] **302**

LIAISON (CIMENTS CANADA LAFARGE) (CN/0318-1340). **1616**

LIAISON ENERGIE FRANCOPHONIE (CN/0840-7827). [4,000] **1949**

LIAISONS (MONTREAL) (CN/0707-7726). [3,500] **3297**

LIBER ANNUUS - STUDIUM BIBLICUM FRANCISCANUM (IS). **5017**

LIBEREZ LES VACANCES (CN/0712-9599). **5295**

LIBERIA-FORUM (GW/0179-4515). [200] **2641**

LIBERTARIAN DIGEST, THE (US/0272-5959). [200] **4480**

LIBERTE (BRUSSELS, BELGIUM) (BE). **2911**

LIBERTE (MONTREAL) (CN/0024-2020). [1,200] **3465**

LIBRARIANS' HANDBOOK (BIRMINGHAM) (US/0093-1888). [20,000] **3223**

LIBRARIAN'S WORLD (US/0739-0297). [650] **3223**

LIBRARIES & CULTURE (US/0894-8631). [733] **4829**

LIBRARY (UK/0024-2160). [1,200] **418**

LIBRARY

Controlled Circulation Index

LIBRARY ADMINISTRATOR'S DIGEST (US/0746-6129). **3224**

LIBRARY & ARCHIVAL SECURITY (US/0196-0075). [440] **3224**

LIBRARY AND INFORMATION NEWS (UK/0269-8161). [1,000] **3224**

LIBRARY ASSOCIATION OF ALBERTA OCCASIONAL PAPER, THE (CN/0075-904X). [530] **3224**

LIBRARY BULLETIN (INSTITUTE OF SOUTHEAST ASIAN STUDIES) (SI/0073-9723). [1,000] **3225**

LIBRARY DEVELOPMENTS (AUSTIN, TEX.) (US/0145-5397). [700] **3225**

LIBRARY HI TECH (US/0737-8831). [10,200] **3225**

LIBRARY HI TECH NEWS (US/0741-9058). [10,200] **3225**

LIBRARY HISTORY (UK/0024-2306). [1,500] **3225**

LIBRARY ISSUES (US/0734-3035). [700] **3225**

LIBRARY JOURNAL (1976) (US/0363-0277). [26,000] **3225**

LIBRARY LIFE : NEW ZEALAND LIBRARY ASSOCIATION NEWSLETTER (NZ/0110-4373). [2,000] **3226**

LIBRARY LITERATURE (US/0024-2373). **3258**

LIBRARY LITERATURE [COMPUTER FILE] (US). **3259**

LIBRARY PROGRESS (INTERNATIONAL) (II/0970-1052). [500] **3226**

LIBRI (KBENHAVN) (DK/0024-2667). [1,400] **3228**

LIBRO EN AMERICA LATINA Y EL CARIBE, EL (CK/0121-1242). [2,000] **4830**

LIBYA ANTIQUA / KINGDOM OF LIBYA, MINISTRY OF NATIONAL ECONOMY (LY/0459-2980). [500] **273**

LIBYAN STUDIES : ANNUAL REPORT OF THE SOCIETY FOR LIBYAN STUDIES (UK). [400] **2641**

LICENSED BEVERAGE JOURNAL (US/0024-2764). [5,200] **2369**

LICENSED SALARIES AND RELATED INFORMATION - MINNESOTA SCHOOL BOARDS ASSOCIATION (US). [4,500] **1866**

LICENSING BOOK, THE (US/0741-0107). [21,000] **4830**

LICENSING JOURNAL, THE (US/1040-4023). [1,000] **1616**

LICENSING REPORTER EUROPE (UK/1073-8991). [2,000] **1306**

LICENSING REVIEW (UK/0959-8421). [300] **3003**

LICHT (MUNCHEN) (GW/0171-5496). [10,000] **2070**

LIECHTENSTEIN : PRINCIPALITY IN THE HEART OF EUROPE (LH). **2518**

LIEN HORTICOLE (FR/0293-6852). **2424**

LIFE & PEACE REVIEW (SW/0284-0200). **4973**

LIFE ASSOCIATION NEWS (US/0024-3078). [145,000] **2886**

LIFE INSURANCE FACT BOOK (US/0075-9406). **2886**

LIFE LINES (LINCOLN, NEB.) (US/0744-0677). [32,000] **5180**

LIFE SCIENCE LAB PRODUCTS (US/1056-0866). [39,000] **463**

LIFE SKILLS NEWS (US/0882-4452). [2,000] **2791**

LIFE WITH ARCHIE (US/0024-3248). **4863**

LIFELINE - CANADIAN MEMORIAL CHIROPRACTIC COLLEGE (CN/0713-7974). **5788**

LIFEPRINTS (US). [2,000] **4390**

LIGHT AVIATION (UK). [4,000] **27**

LIGHT METAL AGE (US/0024-3345). [5,800] **4007**

LIGHT (NASHVILLE, TENN.) (US). [75,000] **4973**

LIGHT OF CONSCIOUSNESS (US/1040-7448). [650] **4973**

LIGHT (WASHINGTON), THE (US/0456-0434). [58,000] **1688**

LIGHTHOUSE (BURLINGTON) (CN/0711-5628). [700] **1357**

LIGHTING DESIGN & APPLICATION (US/0360-6325). [10,000] **2070**

LIGHTING DIMENSIONS (US/0191-541X). [13,500] **4074**

LIGHTING + SOUND INTERNATIONAL (UK/0268-7429). [7,800] **5126**

LIGHTWAVE (US/0741-5834). [15,000] **4438**

LIGHTWORKS (US/0161-4223). [2,000] **357**

LIGUORIAN (US/0024-3450). [500,000] **5031**

LIJECNICKI VJESNIK (CI/0024-3477). [7,400] **3604**

LIMITED MOBILITY & IMMOBILIZED PATIENT PRODUCTS (US). [75,000] **3605**

LIMNOLOGY AND OCEANOGRAPHY (US/0024-3590). [5,500] **1451**

LIMOUSIN LEADER, THE (CN/0381-5552). [3,000] **214**

LINCOLN CO. TENNESSEE PIONEERS (US). **2458**

LINCOLN COUNTY RECORD (PIOCHE, NEV. : 1968) (US/8755-3260). [1,600 (weekly,paid)] **5707**

LINCOLN HERALD (US/0024-3671). [1,200] **2744**

LINCOLN JOURNAL (LINCOLN, NEB.) (US/1054-7983). [43,752] **5706**

LINCOLN LAW REVIEW (SAN FRANCISCO, CALIF.) (US/0024-368X). [450] **3003**

LINCOLN LORE (US/0162-8615). **2744**

LINDBERGIA (SW/0105-0761). [750] **517**

LINDEN LANE MAGAZINE (US/0736-1084). [12,500] **324**

LINDLEYANA : THE SCIENTIFIC JOURNAL OF THE AMERICAN ORCHID SOCIETY (US/0889-258X). [1,200] **517**

LINEA EDP (IT). **1193**

LINEAGRAFICA (IT/0024-3744). **380**

LINEAPELLE (IT). [30,000] **3185**

LINES OF DESCENT (CN). [70] **2458**

LINGUA FRANCA : THE REVIEW OF ACADEMIC LIFE (US/1051-3310). [15,000] **1834**

LINGUE DEL MONDO (IT). **3298**

LININGTON LINEUP (US/8756-5609). [400] **3405**

LINK (II/0459-469X). **2506**

LINK FOR MCMASTER PART-TIME STUDENTS, THE (CN/0707-6932). **1761**

LINK LINE (US/0735-8407). [500] **1761**

LINK (NEW YORK), THE (US/0024-4007). [50,000] **2658**

LINK (OTTAWA) (CN/0709-020X). **1761**

LINK-UP (MINNEAPOLIS, MINN. 1983) (US/0739-988X). [10,000] **1242**

LINK (WINNIPEG. 1974) (CN/0380-299X). [10,000] **2658**

LINK (WOODLAND HILLS) (US). [62,000] **3837**

LINKS (SACRAMENTO) (US/0163-2205). [10,000] **5295**

LINSCOTT'S DIRECTORY OF IMMUNOLOGICAL AND BIOLOGICAL REAGENTS (US/0740-7394). [8,000] **3674**

LION (UNITED STATES ED.), THE (US/0024-4163). [640,000] **5233**

LIP SERVICE (US/0893-620X). [5,500] **4129**

LIPID FILE (UK/0951-9599). **3708**

LIPS (MONTCLAIR, N.J.) (US/0278-0933). [1,000] **3465**

LIQUIDS HANDLING (UK/0268-9219). [8,000] **4263**

LIQUOR STORE MONTHLY (SA). [5,500] **2369**

LIRE, BULLETIN DE LA SOCIETE BIBLIOGRAPHIQUE ET ORGANE DU BUREAU D'INFORMATIONS BIBLIOGRAPHIQUES... (FR). [140,000] **419**

LISAN AL-ARAB (CN/0833-3858). [2,000] **5788**

LIST OF HOLDINGS - AUSTRALIAN NATIONAL UNIVERSITY, RESEARCH SCHOOL OF SOCIAL SCIENCES, ARCHIVES OF BUSINESS AND LABOUR (AT/0727-3924). [400] **690**

LIST OF INTERCEPTED PLANT PESTS (US/0092-6825). [2,000] **2424**

LIST OF MEDICAL PRACTITIONERS CURRENTLY LICENSED TO PRACTISE IN THE PROVINCE / THE COLLEGE OF PHYSICIANS AND SURGEONS OF MANITOBA (CN/0823-6909). [2,900] **3914**

LIST OF MEMBERS - INTERNATIONAL FEDERATION FOR HOUSING AND PLANNING (NE). [600] **2827**

LIST OF MEMBERS OF THE INTERNATIONAL STATISTICAL INSTITUTE (NE). [1,500] **5332**

LIST OF MEMBERS / THE HAKLUYT SOCIETY (UK). [2,300] **2568**

LIST OF PUBLICATIONS / TENNESSEE DIVISION OF GEOLOGY (US). [3,000] **1386**

LIST OF SCHOOLS, ADDRESSES AND STATISTICS (SA). [60,000] **1761**

LISTE TEMOIN SUR LA PLANIFICATION FISCALE (CN/0821-0772). **4736**

LISTEN (FRANKFURT AM MAIN, GERMANY) (GW/0179-7417). **3346**

LISTEN (FRENCH EDITION, OTTAWA) (CN/1183-1820). **4390**

LISTEN (MOUNTAIN VIEW, CALIF.) (US/0024-435X). [100,000] **1346**

LISTENING (RIVER FOREST) (US/0024-4414). [1,000] **4974**

LISTENING (WASHINGTON) (US/0196-7258). [2,700] **4390**

LISWA NEWSLETTER (AT/1035-4816). [630] **3228**

LISZT SOCIETY JOURNAL, THE (UK). [350] **4129**

LITALERT (VIENNA, VA.) (US/8756-9647). [200] **1306**

LITCHVILLE BULLETIN (US). [1,575] **5725**

LITERARY CRITICISM REGISTER (US/0733-2165). [600] **3357**

LITERARY HALF-YEARLY, THE (II/0024-4554). [1,000] **3406**

LITERATUR IN WISSENSCHAFT UND UNTERRICHT : LWU (GW/0024-4643). [1,800] **3406**

LITERATURE ABSTRACTS. CATALYSTS & CATALYSIS (US/1065-0539). **4284**

LITERATURE ABSTRACTS. HEALTH & ENVIRONMENT (US/1065-0490). **2184**

LITERATURE ABSTRACTS. PETROLEUM REFINING & PETROCHEMICALS (US/1065-0512). **4284**

LITERATURE ABSTRACTS. PETROLEUM SUBSTITUTES (US/1065-0504). **4284**

LITERATURE ABSTRACTS. TRANSPORTATION & STORAGE (US/1065-0520). **4284**

LITERATURE AND BELIEF (US/0732-1929). [1,000] **3407**

LITERATURE & HISTORY (UK/0306-1973). [800] **3407**

LITERATURE SCAN. ANESTHESIOLOGY (US/0892-2438). [26,000] **3683**

LITERATURE SCAN. TRANSPLANTATION (US/0883-8410). [12,000] **3969**

LITERATURINFORMATION TERRITORIALFORSCHUNG, TERRITORIALPLANUNG (GW). [200] **2568**

LITHIC TECHNOLOGY (US/0197-7261). [350] **273**

LITHIUM THERAPY MONOGRAPHS (SZ/1011-2928). **3605**

LITIGATION (US/0097-9813). **3003**

LITIR NEWSLETTER OF VICTORIAN STUDIES (CN/0821-4077). **3407**

LITORAL (SP). [3,500] **3407**

LITUANUS (US/0024-5089). [4,000] **2697**

LITURGY (WASHINGTON) (US/0458-063X). [4,500] **4974**

LIVE ANIMAL TRADE & TRANSPORT MAGAZINE (US/1043-1039). [1,700] **226**

LIVE (LAVAL) (CN/0713-4991). **4129**

LIVE LINES (NZ). [1,600] **2071**

LIVE/PRO LIGHT & SOUND (UK). [14,500] **386**

LIVER (COPENHAGEN) (DK/0106-9543). [800] **3799**

LIVERPOOL FAMILY HISTORIAN (UK/0260-759X). [1,400] **2458**

LIVESTOCK MARKET DIGEST (US/0024-5208). [48,500] **214**

LIVESTOCK WEEKLY (SAN ANGELO) (US/0162-5047). [18,100] **215**

LIVING CITY (AT). [50,000] **4662**

LIVING CITY (NEW YORK) (US/0193-5968). [7,000] **4974**

LIVING EARTH (BRISTOL) (UK/0954-1098). **105**

LIVING (HOUSTON, ED.) (US/0741-5486). [80,000] **4840**

LIVING IN NORTH YORK (CN/0712-6360). [225,000] **2568**

LIVING IN SOUTH CAROLINA (US/0047-486X). [394,000] **1298**

LIVING MUSIC (US/8755-092X). [600] **4129**

LIVING PRAYER (US/0890-5568). [6,500] **4974**

LIVING PULPIT, THE (US/1059-2733). **4974**

LIVING SAFETY (CN/1200-2275). [300,000] **4789**

LIVING SAFETY FOR THE CANADIAN FAMILY (CN/0714-5896). [300,000] **4789**

LIVING WITH TEENAGERS (US/0162-4261). [35,000] **2283**

LIVING WORD (SWAN RIVER) (CN/0229-5261). [2,000] **5018**

LIVRE ET L'ESTAMPE, LE (BE/0024-533X). [300] **4830**

LJUSKULTUR (SW). **2235**

LLAFUR (UK/0306-0837). [750] **1688**

LLETRA DE CANVI (SP). **3408**

LLOYDS BANK ANNUAL REVIEW (UK/0953-5004). **1572**

LLOYD'S CANADIAN CHEMICAL, PHARMACEUTICAL, AND PRODUCT DIRECTORY (CN/0068-8452). [5,000] **4314**

LLOYD'S CANADIAN ENGINEERING & INDUSTRIAL YEAR BOOK (CN/0068-8665). [9,000] **2099**

LLOYD'S CANADIAN FOOTWEAR AND LEATHER DIRECTORY (CN/0068-8762). [4,800] **3185**

LLOYD'S CANADIAN HARDWARE, ELECTRICAL AND BUILDING SUPPLY DIRECTORY (CN/0456-3867). [13,000] **619**

LLOYD'S CANADIAN JEWELLERY AND GIFTWARE DIRECTORY (CN/0068-9041). [5,500] **2915**

LLOYD'S CANADIAN MUSIC DIRECTORY (CN/0381-5730). [3,800] **4129**

LLOYD'S CANADIAN TEXTILE DIRECTORY (CN/0068-9858). [4,500] **5354**

LLOYD'S CANADIAN VARIETY MERCHANDISE DIRECTORY (CN/0068-9955). [3,500] **2584**

LLOYD'S MARITIME ASIA (HK/0217-1120). [6,000] **5451**

LMT (NORWALK, CONN.) (US/1058-7845). [18,000] **1329**

LOBBY DIGEST & PUBLIC AFFAIRS MONTHLY, THE (CN/1193-4034). [1,000] **4662**

LOCAL COUNCIL REVIEW (UK/0308-3594). [23,387] **4662**

LOCAL GOVERNMENT IN SOUTHERN AFRICA (SA/1015-0048). [3,200] **4662**

LOCAL GOVERNMENT LAW BULLETIN (US/0362-5729). **3004**

LOCAL HISTORIAN (LONDON. 1968) (UK/0024-4585). [2,300] **2697**

LOCAL TRANSPORT TODAY (UK/0962-6220). **5386**

LOCATION UPDATE (US/1058-3238). [27,000] **4074**

LOCATOR (US). [77,000] **2120**

LOCATOR OF USED MACHINERY & EQUIPMENT (US/0740-3712). [83,000] **2120**

LOCKE NEWSLETTER, THE (UK/0307-2606). [600] **4352**

LOCOMOTIVE (HARTFORD, CONN.), THE (US/0741-8760). [60,000] **5432**

LODGING MAGAZINE (US/1078-6503). [36,000] **2807**

LOG ANALYST, THE (US/0024-581X). [4,000] **1949**

LOG (HAYES), THE (UK/0024-5798). [7,000] **28**

LOG/ON (LOUISVILLE, KY.) (US/8756-4149). [8,000] **1275**

LOG TRAIN, THE (US/0743-281X). [300] **5432**

LOGISTICA MANAGEMENT (IT/1120-3587). [6,000] **876**

LOGISTICS AND TRANSPORTATION REVIEW, THE (CN/0047-4991). [1,000] **5386**

LOGISTICS SPECTRUM (US/0024-5852). [9,500] **5126**

LOGOS (ARGONNE, ILL.) (US/0748-2116). [10,000] **5126**

LOGOS (COLUMBO, SRI LANKA) (CE/0458-1725). [1,000] **2506**

LOHN + GEHALT (GW/0172-9047). **690**

LOIS DU QUEBEC (CN/0318-4447). **3004**

L'OISEAU MAGAZINE : REVUE DE LA LIGUE FRANCAISE POUR LA PROTECTION DES OISEAUX (FR/0297-5785). [13,000] **5618**

LONDON LOG (UK). [5,000] **5483**

LONDON MAGAZINE (LONDON, ONT.) (CN/0711-6233). [40,000] **2537**

LONDON METROBULLETIN (CN/0824-4596). **4663**

LONDON THEATRE GUIDE (UK). [169,000] **5365**

LONG ISLAND POETRY COLLECTIVE NEWSLETTER, THE (US). [300] **3465**

LONG STORY, THE (US/0741-4242). [450] **3408**

LONG TERM CARE MANAGEMENT (US/0743-1422). **3605**

LONG-TERM FORECAST (US/8755-1500). [600] **1573**

LONG TERM VALUES (US/0744-3846). [25,000] **905**

LOOK AT LONDON (CN/0227-8499). **5483**

LOOK BACK AT BOB DYLAN (US/1049-4340). [800] **4129**

LOOK INSIDE (CN/0226-9848). **5065**

LOOK JAPAN (JA/0456-5339). [50,000] **2506**

LOOKING AHEAD (WASHINGTON, D.C. : 1982) (US/0747-525X). [1,000] **1638**

"LOOKING UP" TIMES, THE (US/0893-3898). [3,000] **3408**

LOOKINGFIT (US/0890-4189). **2599**

LOOKOUT (NEW YORK), THE (US/0024-6425). [9,000] **5295**

LOOKOUT, THE (SP). [24,000] **2519**

LORE AND LANGUAGE (UK/0307-7144). [150] **2322**

LORE (MILWAUKEE, WIS.) (US/0276-475X). [5,500] **4090**

LOS ANGELES BUSINESS JOURNAL (US/0194-2603). [40,000] **690**

LOS ANGELES COUNTY ALMANAC (US/0092-1882). [5,600] **4663**

LOS ANGELES DAILY JOURNAL, THE (US/0362-5575). [17,500] **3004**

LOS ANGELES NEWS CONSERVANCY (US). [2,600] **2537**

LOS ANGELES OBSERVER (US/0890-0949). [2,500] **2537**

LOSS PREVENTION (UK/0097-2312). [1,200] **2014**

LOST IN CANADA? (US/0362-4293). [1,000] **2458**

LOT OF BUNKUM. YEARBOOK, A (US/0882-2425). [500] **2458**

LOTTERY PLAYER'S MAGAZINE (US/0277-5565). [180,000] **4863**

LOTUS NEWSLETTER (US/0316-0106). [175] **105**

LOUIS RUKEYSER'S WALL STREET (US/1060-9903). [400,000] **905**

LOUISIANA ANNUAL OIL AND GAS REPORT (US/0735-0716). **4263**

LOUISIANA ARCHAEOLOGY (US/1071-7358). [300] **273**

LOUISIANA CROP-WEATHER SUMMARY (US/0273-8848). [250] **178**

LOUISIANA FARM REPORTER (US/0273-883X). [1,000] **105**

LOUISIANA INTERNATIONAL TRADE DIRECTORY (US/0147-4464). [2,500] **844**

LOUISIANA OUT-OF-DOORS (US/0738-8098). [5,500] **4874**

LOUISIANA PHARMACIST, THE (US/0192-3838). [2,000] **4314**

LOUISIANA PHILOSOPHY OF EDUCATION JOURNAL (US). [20] **1762**

LOUISIANA RURAL ECONOMIST (US/8756-6273). [1,500] **105**

LOUISVILLE (US/0024-6948). [25,000] **2537**

LOUISVILLE DEFENDER, THE (US). **5681**

LOUISVILLE LAW EXAMINER (US/0890-8605). [4,500] **3004**

LOUISVILLE REVIEW, THE (US/0148-3250). [500] **3408**

LOUVAIN STUDIES (BE/0024-6964). [1,500] **4974**

LOVELOCK REVIEW-MINER (US). [1,500] **5707**

LOWDOWN 1982 (AT/0158-099X). [1,500] **386**

LOYALIST GAZETTE, THE (CN/0047-5149). [3,500] **2745**

LOYOLA OF LOS ANGELES INTERNATIONAL AND COMPARATIVE LAW JOURNAL (US/0277-5417). [300] **3132**

LOYOLA UNIVERSITY OF CHICAGO LAW JOURNAL (US/0024-7081). [95,000] **3005**

LRA TRADE UNION ADVISOR (US/1058-0557). [500] **1688**

LRA'S ECONOMIC NOTES (US/0895-5220). [3,000] **1688**

LSI RESIDENTIAL CONSTRUCTION COSTS / LEE SAYLOR, INC (US). [10,000] **619**

LUAS & INTENSITAS SERANGAN HAMA & PENYAKIT DI INDONESIA (IO). **2424**

LUAS TANAH MENURUT PENGGUNAANNYA DI JAWA & MADURA (IO). **105**

LUAS TANAMAN, PRODUKSI, DAN PERSEDIAAN TANAMAN PERKEBUNAN YANG TERPENTING (IO). **178**

LUBRICATION ENGINEERING (US/0024-7154). [6,000] **2120**

LUCAS (AT/1030-4428). [200] **4975**

LUCHA STRUGGLE (US/0885-4378). **5208**

LUCRARI STIINTIFICE, INSTITUL AGRONOMIC "N. BALCESCU," BUCURESTI, SERIA D, ZOOTEHNIE (RM/0374-8898). **5590**

LUCRURI NOI SI VECHI (US/8756-8012). [3,000] **4975**

LUFTFARTSSTATISTIKK / CIVIL AVIATION STATISTICS NORWAY (NO/0800-4072). [5,000] **41**

LUMINA (MONTREAL) (CN/1181-8212). [11,000] **3837**

LUNDBERG LETTER (US/0195-4563). **4263**

LUNDIAN : AN INTERNATIONAL MAGAZINE, THE (SW). [30,000] **2519**

LUSCOMBE ASSOCIATION NEWS (US/0889-4361). [1,200] **28**

LUSOAMERICANO (NEWARK, N.J.) (US/0898-9052). [15,000] **5710**

LUSOLT TALK (CN/0226-0115). **3229**

LUTHER FAMILY NEWSLETTER, THE (US/0896-4602). [740] **2458**

LUTHERAN CHURCH DIRECTORY FOR THE UNITED STATES (US/0363-4051). [25,000] **5063**

LUTHERAN DIGEST, THE (US/0458-497X). [185,000] **5063**

LUTHERAN LAYMAN, THE (US/0024-7464). [90,000] **4975**

LUTHERAN PARTNERS (US/0885-9922). [23,000] **5063**

LUTHERAN SENTINEL (US/0024-7510). [5,800] **5063**

LUTHERAN SPOKESMAN (US/0024-7537). [2,500] **5063**

LUTHERAN, THE (AT). [11,700] **5062**

LUTHERAN THEOLOGICAL JOURNAL (AT/0024-7553). [600] **5063**

LUTHERAN VISTAS (US). [48,000] **5063**

LUTHERAN WITNESS REPORTER (US/0024-7588). [400,000] **5063**

LUTHERAN WITNESS (ST. LOUIS), THE (US/0024-757X). [350,000] **5063**

LUTHERISCHE MONATSHEFTE (GW/0024-7618). [6,400] **4975**

LUTHERISCHE THEOLOGIE UND KIRCHE (GW). [700] **4975**

LUTRA (NE/0024-7634). [800] **5590**

LYCHNOS: LARDOMSHISTORISKA SAMFUNDETS ARSBOK (SW/0076-1648). [2,000] **5126**

LYON COUNTY NEWS (GEORGE, IOWA) (US). [1,450] **5671**

M + A MESSEPLANER (GW). [8,600] **762**

M.D.P. MONOGRAFIAS DE PEDIATRIA (SP). [3,000] **3906**

M D T, MOTORCYCLE DEALER & TRADE (CN/0705-2030). [2,500] **4081**

M/E/A/N/I/N/G (NEW YORK, N.Y.) (US/1040-8576). [1,000] **324**

M.E.N. ECONOMIC WEEKLY / MIDDLE EAST NEWS (UA). [300] **1503**

M P & P, METAL-WORKING PRODUCTION & PURCHASING (CN/0383-090X). [24,225] **4007**

M-SERIES MONOGRAPHS (AT). [2000] **5483**

MAANDELIJKSE MEDEDELINGEN - INSPECTIE VOOR HET BRANDWEERWEZEN (NE). **619**

MAARAKENNUS JA KULJETUS (FI). [4,500] **2027**

MAARAV (US/0149-5712). [500] **3300**

MAARIV (IS). [200,000 daily 250,000 Friday] **5804**

MAC/CHICAGO (CHICAGO, ILL.) (US/1045-5825). [11,000] **1193**

MACACADEMY MENTOR (US). **1194**

MACCHINE (IT/0024-8959). **2120**

MACE DIALOGUE (CN/0713-6242). **1801**

MACEDONIAN REVIEW (XN/0350-3089). [5,000] **2849**

MACH (US). [10,000] **2795**

MACHIKANEYAMA RONSO: SHIGAKUHEN (JA). [400] **2850**

MACHIKANEYAMA RONSO : TETSUGAKUHEN (JA/0387-4818). [500] **2850**

MACHINE AND TOOL DIRECTORY (US). [40,000] **2120**

MACHINE DESIGN (US/0024-9114). [170,000] **2120**

MACHINE-MEDIATED LEARNING (US/0732-6718). [400] **1224**

MACHINERY AND PRODUCTION ENGINEERING (UK/0024-919X). [15,000] **2120**

MACHINES PRODUCTION PARIS (FR/0047-536X). [20,000] **2121**

MACHINIST, THE (US/0047-5378). **1688**

MACINTOSH BUSINESS REVIEW (US/0899-725X). **691**

MACKLIN MIRROR (CN/0706-7240). [873] **5789**

MACKNIT (US/0886-1188). [25,000] **5184**

MACON COUNTY TIMES (US/0745-5976). [6,100] **5745**

MACPLAS (IT/0394-3453). [11,000] **4456**

MACROMOLECULES (US/0024-9297). [2,700] **1044**

MACWEEK (US/0892-8118). **1238**

MACWORLD (LONDON) (UK/0957-2341). [26,898] **1194**

MADAME AU FOYER (CN/0541-6620). [330,600] **5560**

MADAMINA (US/0740-5812). [5,000] **4129**

MADDEN FAMILY NEWSLETTER (US/0883-556X). [85] **2459**

MADDUX REPORT, THE (US/0889-0838). [16,516] **691**

MADEMOISELLE (NEW YORK, N.Y. 1935) (US/0024-9394). [1,100,000] **5560**

MADISON MAGAZINE (US/0192-7442). [21,000] **2537**

MADISON NEWS (MADISON, KAN. : 1915) (US). [927] **5677**

MADOQUA (SA). [600] **2197**

MADRAS AGRICULTURAL JOURNAL, THE (II/0024-9602). [2,200] **106**

MADRONO (US/0024-9637). [1,500] **517**

MAGALLA AL-AKADIMIYYA AL-ARABIYYA LI-N-NAQL AL-BAHRI (UA/0304-2855). [3,000] **4178**

MAGAZIN FUER AMERIKANISTIK (GW/0170-2513). [2,000] **2745**

MAGAZIN'ART (WESTMOUNT) (CN/0844-1707). [7,000] **324**

MAGAZINE - CANADIAN ORNAMENTAL PHEASANT AND GAME BIRD ASSOCIATION (CN/0225-0721). [900] **2774**

MAGAZINE CARGUIDE (CN/1187-9475). [300,000 January (English & French)100,000 Mar., May, July, Sept., Nov.] **5418**

MAGAZINE DESIGN & PRODUCTION (US/0882-049X). [17,000] **2922**

MAGAZINE ISSUES (US/0899-7039). [10,000] **4816**

MAGAZINE (NORTH VANCOUVER) (CN/0711-3692). **2538**

MAGAZINE OF VIRGINIA GENEALOGY (US/0743-8095). [2,000] **2459**

MAGAZINE TREND REPORT (US/1044-6079). **762**

MAGHREB REVIEW, THE (UK/0309-457X). [9,000] **2641**

MAGIC MAGAZINE (ORLANDO, FLA.) (US/1054-6723). [15,000] **4904**

MAGISTRATE, THE (UK). [26,000] **3169**

MAGNESIUM RESEARCH : OFFICIAL ORGAN OF THE INTERNATIONAL SOCIETY FOR THE DEVELOPMENT OF RESEARCH ON MAGNESIUM (UK/0953-1424). [75] **3605**

MAGNOLIA (HAMMOND, LA.) (US/0738-3053). [550] **5233**

MAGYAR ALLATORVOSOK LAPJA (HU/0025-004X). [3,500] **5516**

MAGYAR GEOFIZIKA (HU/0025-0120). [800] **1408**

MAGYAR KERESKEDELMI ES VENDEGLATOIPARI MUZEUM EVKONYVE, A (HU). **844**

MAGYAR NAPTAR (NEW YORK) (US/0094-1484). [2,500] **2489**

MAGYAR NEMZETI BIBLIOGRAFIA: IDOSZAKI KIADVANYOK BIBLIOGRAFIAJA (HU/0231-4592). **419**

MAGYAR PEDIATER (HU/0303-5042). **3906**

MAGYAR PSZICHOLOGIAI SZEMLE (HU/0025-0279). [3,000] **4603**

MAHARASHTRA JOURNAL OF EXTENSION EDUCATION (II). [750] **106**

MAHASAGAR (II/0542-0938). [400] **1451**

MAHD BULLETIN (US/1064-5608). [1,500] **3229**

MAIA (IT/0025-0538). [1,000] **1078**

MAILBOX NEWS (US/0889-4884). [45,000] **2791**

MAILING LIST COMPANIES AND CATAGORIES ... DIRECTORY (US/1043-4372). **1145**

MAILING LIST TIDBITS (US). [2,500] **929**

MAIN (US/0147-1201). [1,000] **4186**

MAIN DE L'AGE D'OR, LA (CN/0824-1503). **5180**

MAINE GEOLOGIST, THE (US/0270-8345). [300] **1386**

MAINE HEALTH FACILITIES, RESOURCES, AND UTILIZATION / PREPARED BY BUREAU OF HEALTH PLANNING AND DEVELOPMENT, MAINE DEPARTMENT OF HUMAN SERVICES (US). **3788**

MAINE LEGIONNAIRE, THE (US/0161-584X). [27,000] **5233**

MAINE NURSE, THE (US/0025-0767). **3861**

MAINE (ORONO, ME.) (US). **1102**

MAINE REGISTER, STATE YEAR-BOOK AND LEGISLATIVE MANUAL (US/0145-9597). [1,500] **4663**

MAINE SNOWMOBILER (US/0195-2870). [11,000] **4904**

MAINE SPORTSMAN, THE (US/0199-0365). [30,000] **4904**

MAINE UNITED METHODIST, THE (US/0745-0273). [5,200] **5063**

MAINLINES (INDIANAPOLIS, IND.) (US/0278-9450). [650] **3861**

MAINSTREAM (SACRAMENTO, CALIF.) (US/0891-088X). [32,000] **226**

MAINSTREAM (SAN DIEGO, CALIF.) (US/0278-8225). [18,000] **4391**

MAINTENANCE SUPPLIES (US/0025-0929). [10,000] **2236**

MAINTENANCE TECHNOLOGY (US/0899-5729). [80,000] **619**

MAIRENA (RIO PIEDRAS, SAN JUAN, P.R.) (PR/1050-835X). [1,000] **3465**

MAITRE ELECTRICIEN, LE (CN/0025-0988). [10,800] **2071**

MAITRE IMPRIMEUR, LE (CN/0025-0996). [4,800] **4566**

MAJALAH DEMOGRAFI INDONESIA (IO/0126-0251). [1,000] **4554**

MAJALAH PEMBINAAN BAHASA INDONESIA (IO/0126-4737). **3300**

MAJALLAH (SY). [2,000] **3300**

MAJALLAT AL-BUHUTH ABTARIKHIYAH (LY). [5,000] **2641**

MAKEDONIKA (THESSALONIKA) (GR/0076-289X). [600] **2850**

MAKEDONSKA TRIBUNA (US/0024-9009). [1,500] **5665**

MAKEDONSKI ARHIVIST (XN/0350-1728). [1,000] **2482**

MAKERERE ADULT EDUCATION JOURNAL (UG). [500] **1801**

MAKING WAVES (PORT ALBERNI) (CN/1192-2427). [150] **1504**

MAKTABAT AL-IDARAH (SU). [2,000] **3229**

MALACOLOGY DATA NET (US/0892-6506). [150] **5590**

MALADIES CHRONIQUES AU CANADA (CN/0228-8702). [3,500] **3606**

MALAHAT REVIEW, THE (CN/0025-1216). [1,800] **3409**

MALAKOLOGISCHE ABHANDLUNGEN (GW/0070-7260). [250] **5590**

MALAWI ECONOMIC BRIEF (MW). [600] **1504**

MALAWIAN WRITERS SERIES (MW). [2,000] **3409**

MALAYAN NATURE JOURNAL, THE (MY/0025-1291). [1,500] **4167**

MALAYSIAN JOURNAL OF PATHOLOGY, THE (MY/0126-8635). [500] **3896**

MALAYSIAN JOURNAL OF TROPICAL GEOGRAPHY (MY/0127-1474). [500] **2568**

MALIBU SURFSIDE NEWS, THE (US/0191-7307). [12,600] **5636**

MALIBU TIMES (US/1050-4931). [13,200] **5637**

MALINI (US/0737-8688). **2267**

MALLORN (UK/0308-6674). [700] **3409**

MALPRACTICE REPORTER. ANESTHESIOLOGY, THE (US/0738-1018). [2,500] **3005**

MALPRACTICE REPORTER. HOSPITALS, THE (US/0738-1956). [2,500] **3005**

MALTESE DIRECTORY : CANADA, UNITED STATES (CN/0317-6983). **2745**

MALVERN LEADER (MALVERN, IOWA : 1883) (US). [1,200] **5671**

MALY ROCZNIK STATYSTYCZNY (PL/0079-2608). [50,000] **5332**

MAMMALIAN SPECIES (US/0076-3519). [1,400] **464**

MAMMOTH TRUMPET (US/8755-6898). [2,000] **273**

MAN & DEVELOPMENT (II/0258-0438). [1,000] **1617**

MAN-ENVIRONMENT SYSTEMS (US/0025-1550). [600] **303**

MAN IN THE NORTHEAST (US/0191-4138). [325] **240**

MAN-MADE TEXTILES IN INDIA (II/0377-7537). [1,500] **5354**

MAN TO MAN (OTTAWA) (CN/0825-3498). **5251**

MAN UNDERWATER (CN/0383-7777). [300] **4904**

MANA MEMBERS DIRECTORY OF MANUFACTURERS' SALES AGENCIES (US/0890-7641). [20,000] **3483**

MANAGE (US/0025-1623). [75,000] **876**

MANAGED CARE (LANGHORNE, PA.) (US/1062-3388). [77,000] **3788**

MANAGEMENT ACCOUNTING (LONDON) (UK/0025-1682). **747**

MANAGEMENT EDUCATION AND DEVELOPMENT (UK/0047-5688). [2,100] **1617**

MANAGEMENT IN GOVERNMENT (II/0047-570X). [2,000] **4664**

MANAGEMENT INFORMATION SYSTEMS QUARTERLY (US/0276-7783). [4,000] **1194**

MANAGEMENT NEWS : THE NEWSPAPER OF THE BRITISH INSTITUTE OF MANAGEMENT (UK/0025-1844). [65,600] **877**

MANAGEMENT REPORT (US). [Y] **2402**

MANAGEMENT REVIEW (US). [8,100] **878**

MANAGEMENT TODAY (UK/0025-1925). [77,024] **878**

MANAGER'S MAGAZINE (US/0025-1968). [13,000] **2887**

MANAGING (PITTSBURGH) (US/0162-3346). [15,000] **878**

MANAGING TECHNOLOGY TODAY (US/1062-3310). **878**

MANAGING THE HUMAN CLIMATE (US/0277-7398). [1,800] **762**

MANAR AL-ISLAM (TS). [30,000] **5043**

MANDATE (TORONTO. 1979) (CN/0225-7068). [32,000] **4975**

M&R. MARINE AND RECREATION NEWS (US/0025-312X). [86,000] **594**

MANEDSSTATISTIKK OVER UTENRIKSHANDELEN (NO/0332-6403). [1,300] **1536**

MANHATTAN MEDICINE (US/0744-4966). [6,000] **3606**

MANHATTAN OFFICE BUILDINGS. DOWNTOWN (US/0886-2737). **4840**

MANHATTAN OFFICE BUILDINGS. MIDTOWN (US/0886-3725). **4840**

MANHATTAN REVIEW (NEW YORK, N.Y. : 1980), THE (US/0275-6889). [500] **3465**

MANITOBA AGRICULTURE STATISTICS (CN/0713-3359). [300-600] **154**

MANITOBA ARCHAEOLOGICAL QUARTERLY (CN/0705-2669). [350] **273**

MANITOBA CO-OPERATOR (CN/0025-2239). [30,000] **5789**

MANITOBA CONSTRUCTION & RESOURCE INDUSTRIES (CN/0712-2594). [6,017] **619**

MANITOBA FOOD PRODUCTS DIRECTORY (CN/0228-8966). [2,500] **2348**

MANITOBA GAZETTE, THE (CN/0706-3350). [1,600] **4481**

MANITOBA HISTORICAL SOCIETY NEWSLETTER (CN/0226-5036). [1,100] **2745**

MANITOBA HISTORY (CN/0226-5044). [1,000] **2745**

MANITOBA MEDICINE (CN/0832-6096). **3606**

MANITOBA MODERN LANGUAGE JOURNAL (CN/0820-6066). **3301**

MANITOBA PSYCHOLOGIST (CN/0711-1533). [250] **4603**

MANITOBA STATISTICAL REVIEW (CN/0700-2971). [200] **1504**

MANITOBA TEACHER (CN/0025-228X). [16,800] **1762**

MANITOBA TRADE DIRECTORY (CN/0076-390X). [12,500] **845**

MANITOBA WINNIPEG BUILDING AND CONSTRUCTION TRADES COUNCIL YEARBOOK (CN/0714-3222). [1,500] **1689**

MANITOULIN EXPOSITOR (CN/0834-6682). [6,900] **5789**

MANNERING REPORT, THE (US). [100] **5208**

MANNHEIMER GEOGRAPHISCHE ARBEITEN (GW). [500] **2568**

MANPOWER DOCUMENTATION (II/0047-5793). [500] **1689**

MANTI MESSENGER (MANTI, UTAH : 1981) (US). [900] **5756**

MANUAL. NEW YORK BUILDING LAWS (US). [3,000] **3006**

MANUAL OF LEGISLATIVE ACTS RULES AND GUIDANCE NOTES CONCERNING NORTH SEA OFFSHORE DEVELOPMENTS (UK). [1,000] **4263**

MANUEL - ASSOCIATION CANADIENNE DE BADMINTON (CN/0227-5996). **4904**

MANUFACTURED HOME MERCHANDISER (US/1047-2967). [17,000] **2827**

MANUFACTURERS AND PROCESSORS DIRECTORY, SOUTH DAKOTA (US/1049-3050). [3000] **3483**

MANUFACTURING CLOTHIER (LONDON) (UK/0025-2565). [5,809] **1085**

MANUFACTURING + MARKETING OPPORTUNITIES; BULLETIN (CN/0706-0084). **3484**

MANUFACTURING SYSTEMS (US/0748-948X). [131,000] **1617**

MANUFACTURING TODAY (US/0164-968X). [21,800] **3484**

MANUSCRIPT SOCIETY NEWS, THE (US/0195-7813). [1,500] **2774**

MANUSCRIPTS FOR TUBA SERIES (US/0363-6585). [400] **4130**

MANUSCRITOS POETICOS (SP). **3465**

MANUSKRIPTE (AU/0025-2638). [3,500] **3410**

MANUTENCION Y ALMACENAJE (SP/0025-2646). [6,500] **5127**

MANY PATHS (US). [500] **4975**

MAPLINE. SPECIAL NUMBER (US). [1,000] **2582**

MAPPE, DIE (GW/0025-2697). [30,300] **2902**

MAPPING AWARENESS (UK/0954-7126). [8,000] **1194**

MAPPING AWARENESS & GIS EUROPE (UK/0954-712636). [8,000] **1242**

MAPPING SCIENCES AND REMOTE SENSING (US/0749-3878). [200] **2582**

MAQUILA (EL PASO, TEX.) (US/1050-6497). **1617**

MARCHE (OTTAWA-CARLETON (ONTARIO). DEPARTEMENT DE L'URBANISME. GROUPE DE PARTICIPATION PUBLIQUE), EN (CN). **2828**

MARCHES AGRICOLES, ALIMENTAIRES ET FONCIERS (FR). [12,500] **107**

MARCONI'S INTERNATIONAL REGISTER (US/0076-4418). [5,000] **1159**

MARG (II/0025-2913). [1,500] **357**

MARGENES (PE). [1,000] **2552**

MARGIN (II/0025-2921). [1,000] **1573**

MARIAN STUDIES (US/0464-9680). [700] **5032**

MARICHEM (UK/0264-2697). [1,000] **5386**

MARIGOLD LIBRARY SYSTEM DIRECTORY (CN/0714-895X). **3230**

MARIN INDEPENDENT JOURNAL (US/0891-5164). [40,214 daily43,083 Sunday] **5637**

MARINE DIGEST AND TRANSPORTATION NEWS (US/1059-2970). [5,000] **845**

MARINE DOCK AGE (US). [24,000] **594**

MARINE ECOLOGY. PROGRESS SERIES (HALSTENBEK) (GW/0171-8630). **2218**

MARINE ENGINEERING DIGEST (CN/0824-734X). [3,100] **1986**

MARINE FISH MONTHLY (US/1045-3555). [32,000] **2308**

MARINE GEODESY (US/0149-0419). [600] **1358**

MARINE GEOTECHNOLOGY (US/0360-8867). [600] **1451**

MARINE LOG : A PUBLICATION OF THE FLORIDA SEA GRANT COLLEGE (US). [10,000] **1451**

MARINE MAMMAL NEWS (US). **5591**

MARINE MAMMAL SCIENCE (US/0824-0469). [1,200] **1452**

MARINE NEWS (UK). **5452**

MARINE ORNITHOLOGY (SA). [400] **5618**

MARINE POLICY (UK/0308-597X). **1452**

MARINE RESEARCH IN INDONESIA (IO/0079-0435). **556**

MARINE STRUCTURES (UK/0951-8339). [400] **4179**

MARINE TECHNOLOGY SOCIETY JOURNAL (US/0025-3324). [3,500] **1452**

MARINE TEXTILES (US/0885-9949). [5,500] **5354**

MARINE TRADES (1978) (CN/0705-8993). [7,200] **845**

MARINEBLAD (NE/0025-3340). [5,500] **4179**

MARINER (VANCOUVER, B.C.) (CN/0829-545X). [25,000] **5452**

MARINER'S MIRROR (UK/0025-3359). [2,500] **4179**

MARIPOSA FOLK FESTIVAL (CN/0712-6263). [25,000] **4130**

MARIPOSA WEEKLY GAZETTE AND MINER (US). [5,000] **5637**

MARITIME PATROL AVIATION (CN). [5,000] **28**

MARITIME WORKER (AT). [8,300] **1690**

MARITIMER (AMHERST) (CN/0704-0652). [1,100] **4391**

MARITIMES (US/0025-3472). [5,000] **1452**

MARK (FI). [8,635] **930**

MARK TWAIN SOCIETY BULLETIN (US/0272-6378). [225] **3410**

MARK-UP / WASHINGTON OFFICE, NATIONAL COUNCIL OF CHURCHES (US). [850] **4975**

MARKEE (SANFORD, FLA.) (US/1073-8924). [15,000] **4074**

MARKET REPORT & NEWSLETTER (US/0747-4121). [1,100] **215**

MARKET RESEARCH EUROPE (UK/0308-3446). [500] **731**

MARKETING HIGHER EDUCATION (US/0896-7156). **931**

MARKETING MIX (JOHANNESBURG, SOUTH AFRICA) (SA). [8,000] **931**

MARKETING NEWS (US/0025-3790). [31,200] **931**

MARKETING RESEARCH (CHICAGO, ILL.) (US/1040-8460). [3,200] **932**

MARKETING TO WOMEN (1989) (US/1047-1677). [2,500] **5561**

MARKETING TRENDS (DEUTSCHE AUSG.) (US/0882-4770). [35,000] **932**

MARKETING TRIBUNE (IT). [3,000] **692**

MARKETPLACE MAGAZINE (US/1054-2264). [16,000] **692**

MARKWICK MIDDEN (CN/0821-3275). [90] **2459**

MARLBORO HERALD-ADVOCATE (US). [6,800 (paid)] **5743**

MARMAC GUIDE TO PHILADELPHIA, A (US/0736-8127). **5483**

MARQUEE (TORONTO) (CN/0700-5008). [400,000] **4074**

MARQUEE (WASHINGTON, D.C.) (US). [1,000] **5365**

MARQUETTE LAW REVIEW (US/0025-3987). [1,600] **3006**

MART JOURNAL (CN/0711-7922). [400] **1763**

MART (MONTREAL) (CN/0319-2709). [9,214] **2121**

MARTHA'S VINEYARD (US/1052-5785). **107**

MARTHA'S VINEYARD TIMES, THE (US/8750-1449). [12,000] **5689**

MARXISTISCHE BLATTER (GW/0542-7770). **4543**

MARYKNOLL (US/0025-4142). [600,000] **5032**

MARYLAND ARCHEOLOGY (US/0148-6012). [450] **273**

MARYLAND BAR JOURNAL, THE (US/0025-4177). [11,000] **3006**

MARYLAND BIRDLIFE (US/0147-9725). [2,000] **5618**

MARYLAND DOCUMENTS (US/0195-3443). [900] **419**

MARYLAND FARMER (BALTIMORE, MD. : 1979) (US/0279-7895). [10,353] **107**

MARYLAND FRUIT GROWER, THE (US/0025-4223). [300] **178**

MARYLAND LAWYERS' MANUAL (US). [15,500] **3007**

MARYLAND MEDICAL JOURNAL (1985) (US/0886-0572). [7,200] **3606**

MARYLAND MUSIC EDUCATOR (US). [1,400] **4130**

MARYLAND NURSE, THE (US/0047-6080). [10,000] **3861**

MARYLAND PROSECUTOR, THE (US/0748-2957). [1,000] **3108**

MARYLAND REGISTER (US/0360-2834). [2,500] **3007**

MARYLAND TIMES-PRESS (US). **5686**

MARYSVILLE JOURNAL-TRIBUNE (US/1069-2207). [6,000] **5729**

MAS (NEW YORK, N.Y.) (US/1046-5634). [500,000] **2267**

MASABEY 'ENWS (IS/0792-0970). [300] **1690**

MASCHINE, DIE (GW/0340-5737). [10,000] **2121**

MASCHINENSCHADEN, DER (GW/0025-4517). [8,500] **2121**

MASIKA ANKARA SARA. MONTHLY ABSTRACT OF STATISTICS (II). [700] **5332**

MASON COUNTY GENEALOGICAL SOCIETY NEWSLETTER, THE (US/0885-4459). [300] **2459**

MASON COUNTY NEWS (US). [2,700] **5752**

MASON FAMILY NEWSLETTER (US/0895-4496). [75] **2459**

MASS COMM REVIEW (US/0193-7707). **1116**

MASS HIGH TECH (US/8750-2100). [25,000] **5127**

MASS SPECTROMETRY BULLETIN (UK/0025-4738). [500] **1011**

MASSACHUSETTS CPA REVIEW (US/0025-4770). [8,000] **748**

MASSACHUSETTS DAILY COLLEGIAN, THE (US/0890-0434). [20,000] **5689**

MASSACHUSETTS LAW REVIEW (US/0163-1411). [21,000] **3007**

MASSACHUSETTS MUSIC NEWS (US/0147-2550). [1,600] **4130**

MASSACHUSETTS NURSE, THE (US/0163-0784). [18,000] **3861**

MASSACHUSETTS REGISTER (BOSTON, MASS. 1976) (US). [750] **3007**

MASSACHUSETTS STUDIES IN ENGLISH (US/0047-6161). [200] **3347**

MASSACHUSETTS VOTER / LEAGUE OF WOMEN VOTERS OF MASSACHUSETTS, THE (US). [8,000] **4481**

MASSACHUSETTS WILDLIFE (US/0025-4924). [23,000] **2198**

MASSCITIZEN (US/8750-8516). [90,000] **3007**

MAST (MADISON, WIS.) (US/1051-824X). [40,000] **1145**

MAST. MANITOBA ASSOCIATION OF SCHOOL TRUSTEES (CN/0381-9531). [2,100] **4664**

MASTER CARD (US). [100,000] **2490**

MASTER SERMON SERIES (US/0362-0808). [2,000] **4976**

MASTER TAPE LIST OF EDUCATIONAL TEXTS FOR THE VISUALLY AND PHYSICALLY HANDICAPPED ... (CN/0229-8066). **1882**

MASTER THOUGHTS (US). [100] **5018**

MASTHEAD (MISSISSAUGA) (CN/0832-512X). [5,000] **4816**

MASTHEAD, THE (US/0025-5122). [1,000] **2922**

MATATU (NE/0932-9714). [700] **3410**

MATCH (MULHEIM) (GW/0340-6253). [150] **985**

MATEKON (US/0025-1127). [250] **1504**

MATEMATIKAI LAPOK (HU/0025-519X). [1,400] **3518**

MATERIA MEDICA POLONA (ENGLISH EDITION) (PL/0025-5246). [3,000] **4314**

MATERIALI E STRUTTURE (IT). [600] **303**

MATERIALIEN ZUR POLITISCHEN BILDUNG (GW/0340-0476). **4481**

MATERIALS AUSTRALIA (AT/1037-7107). [2,500] **4008**

MATERIALS ENGINEERING (US/0025-5319). [61,100] **2105**

MATERIALS EVALUATION (US/0025-5327). [11,000] **2105**

MATERIALS MANAGEMENT AND DISTRIBUTION (CN/0025-5343). [19,500] **1618**

MATERIALS PERFORMANCE (US/0094-1492). [15,500] **2105**

MATERIALY BADAWCZE - INSTYTUT METEOROLOGII I GOSPODARKI WODNEJ. SERIA, HYDROLOGIA I OCEANOLOGIA (PL/0239-6297). [200] **1416**

MATERIALY BADAWCZE. SERIA: GOSPODARKA WODNA I OCHRONA WOD (PL). [250] **5536**

MATERIALY I OPRACOWANIA STATYSTYCZNE (PL/0867-0846). **5332**

MATERIAUX ET TECHNIQUES (FR/0032-6895). [3,500] **2106**

MATERIAY BADAWCZE. SERIA: INZYNIERIA WODNA (PL). [218] **2093**

MATERNAL & CHILD HEALTH (RICHMOND, SURREY) (UK/0262-0200). [18,000] **3738**

MATH NOTEBOOK (US/0272-8885). [2,000] **1882**

MATHEMATICA IN EDUCATION (US/1065-2965). [500] **1763**

MATHEMATICAL GAZETTE (UK/0025-5572). [6,000] **3519**

MATHEMATICS COUNCIL NEWSLETTER (1983) (CN/0823-1117). [630] **3520**

MATHEMATICS STUDENT (AHMEDABAD), THE (II/0025-5742). [1,000] **3521**

MATHEMATICS TEACHER, THE (US/0025-5769). [50,000] **3521**

MATHEMATICS TEACHING (UK/0025-5785). [4,000] **3521**

MATHEMATIKA (UK/0025-5793). [700] **3521**

MATHS & STATS (UK/0959-3950). [2,400] **3522**

MATURE — Controlled Circulation Index

MATURE HEALTH (US/0891-9232). [50,000] **4789**

MATURE LIVING (NASHVILLE) (US/0162-427X). [306,000] **5180**

MATURE OUTLOOK (US/0742-0935). [900,000] **5180**

MATURE OUTLOOK NEWSLETTER (US/0748-4003). [900,000] **5180**

MAY DAY PICTORIAL NEWS (US/0025-6129). [5,298] **5452**

MAYAN LINGUISTICS (US). [110] **3301**

MAYDICA (IT/0025-6153). [320] **107**

MAYFLOWER DESCENDANT : A MAGAZINE OF PILGRIM GENEALOGY AND HISTORY, THE (US/8756-3959). [1,000] **2459**

MAYO CLINIC PROCEEDINGS (US/0025-6196). [126,000] **3799**

MAZAL U'BRACHA (IS/0334-6838). [5,000] **1618**

MBB : BELASTINGBESCHOUWINGEN (NE/0005-8335). **4737**

MBEA TODAY (US/0892-9831). [1,500] **1763**

MBI MUSIC BUSINESS INFORMATIONS (UK/0768-8172). [10,000] **4130**

MC : THE MODERN CHURCHMAN (UK/0025-7597). [1,200] **4976**

MCCONNAUGHEY BULLETIN (MCCONNAUGHEY AND VARIANTS) OF THE MCCONNAUGHEY SOCIETY OF AMERICA, INC, THE (US/0196-2078). [150-200] **5233**

MCCOOK DAILY GAZETTE (US). [7,900] **5706**

MCCORMICK MESSENGER (US). [2,300] **5743**

MCGEORGE MAGAZINE / UNIVERSITY OF THE PACIFIC, MCGEORGE SCHOOL OF LAW (US). [65,000] **3007**

MCGILL JOURNAL OF POLITICAL ECONOMY, THE (CN/0712-1148). [500] **1504**

MCGILL LAW JOURNAL (CN/0024-9041). [2,000] **3132**

MCGILL UNIVERSITY. STORMY WEATHER GROUP. TECHNICAL REPORT (CN/0460-332X). [150] **1430**

MCGILL WORKING PAPERS IN LINGUISTICS (CN/0824-5282). [200] **3301**

MCGRAW-HILL'S HEALTH BUSINESS (US/0888-9805). **4790**

MCIC NEWS (CN/0710-457X). [500] **4528**

MCINTOSH TIMES, THE (US). [1,700] **5697**

MCKINNEY MAZE, THE (US/0736-2420). [160] **2460**

MCKNIGHT'S LONG-TERM CARE NEWS (US/1048-3314). [34,000] **5295**

MCLEAN COUNTY JOURNAL AND TURTLE LAKE WAVE, THE (US). [1,000] **2490**

MCLEAN HOSPITAL JOURNAL (US/0363-0226). **3930**

ME NAISET (FI/0025-6277). [100,000] **5561**

MEADOW LAKE PROGRESS (CN). **5789**

MEANS CONSTRUCTION COST INDEXES (US/0361-9591). [500] **620**

MEANS ELECTRICAL COST DATA (US/0748-7002). [15,000] **620**

MEANS HISTORICAL COST INDEXES (US/0277-8610). [500] **620**

MEANS SQUARE FOOT COSTS : RESIDENTIAL, COMMERCIAL, INDUSTRIAL, INSTITUTIONAL (US/0732-815X). [11,000] **621**

MEASUREMENT AND EVALUATION IN COUNSELING AND DEVELOPMENT (US/0748-1756). [2,571] **1763**

MEASUREMENTS & CONTROL (US/0148-0057). [101,000] **5127**

MEAT & POULTRY (US/0892-6077). [20,000] **2349**

MEAT INDUSTRY DIGEST (AT). [1,000] **2349**

MEAT PRICE RELATIONSHIPS (US/0882-3065). [1,500] **1618**

MEAT PROBE (CN/0826-4554). [9,000] **2349**

MECHANICAL ENGINEERING NEWS (FAYETTEVILLE, ARK.) (US/0025-651X). [800] **2122**

MECHANICAL INCORPORATED ENGINEER (UK/0954-6529). [8,000] **2122**

MECHANICAL MUSIC (US/1045-795X). **4130**

MECHANICAL PARTS/LABOR ESTIMATING GUIDE. DOMESTIC GLASS (US/0884-0156). **5418**

MECHANO BUYERS DIRECTORY. NORTHERN CALIFORNIA (US). [7,000] **3484**

MECKLENBURG GAZETTE, THE (US). [4,800] **5723**

MECKLENBURG TIMES (US). [790] **5723**

MED TEC INTERNATIONAL (NZ). [16,000] **3607**

MEDAL LONDON (UK/0263-7707). [1,100] **2781**

MEDECIN DU QUEBEC (CN/0025-6692). [19,200] **3607**

MEDECIN VETERINAIRE DU QUEBEC, LE (CN/0225-9591). [2,300] **5516**

MEDECINE ET ARMEES (FR/0300-4937). [6,000] **4049**

MEDECINE TROPICALE (FR/0025-682X). [1,500] **3986**

MEDEDELING - INSTITUUT VOOR CULTUURTECHNIEK EN WATERHUISHOUDING (NE/0074-0411). [700] **178**

MEDEDELINGEN VAN DE NEDERLANDSE VERENIGING VOOR INTERNATIONAAL RECHT (NE). [500] **3132**

MEDEDELINGEN VAN DE WERKGROEP VOOR TERTIAIRE EN KWARTAIRE GEOLOGIE (NE/0165-280X). [200] **1387**

MEDEDELINGEN VAN HET P.J. MEERTENS-INSTITUUT (NE). [2,000] **2322**

MEDEX (BE). [10,000] **3607**

MEDIA & VALUES (US/0149-6980). [10,000] **1116**

MEDIA DATEN, FACHZEITSCHRIFTEN (GW/0170-4192). **1116**

MEDIA DATEN, ZEITSCHRIFTEN MIT AUSLANDSTEIL (GW/0170-4176). **1116**

MEDIA DATEN ZEITUNGEN, ANZEIGENBLATTER (GW/0170-4184). **4816**

MEDIA DEVELOPMENT (UK). [1,800] **1116**

MEDIA FORUM (IT/0394-9575). [6,000] **762**

MEDIA GUIDE INTERNATIONAL. EDITION : BUSINESS/PROFESSIONAL PUBLICATIONS (US/0164-1743). [950] **762**

MEDIA INFORMATION AUSTRALIA (AT/0312-9616). [1,200] **1116**

MEDIA JAYA (IO). [5,000] **1574**

MEDIA LAW NOTES (US/0736-1750). [500] **3008**

MEDIA LAW REPORTER (US/0148-1045). [1,200] **3008**

MEDIA LETTER (CORAL GABLES, FLA.) (US/1054-6952). **845**

MEDIA MONITOR (US). [2,000] **2922**

MEDIA PROFILES. THE HEALTH SCIENCES EDITION (US/0740-1892). **4790**

MEDIA SPECTRUM (US/0731-3675). [1,400] **3230**

MEDIAFILE (US/0885-4610). **2922**

MEDIASPOUVOIRS (FR/0762-5642). **1117**

MEDIATION QUARTERLY (US/0739-4098). [550] **3121**

MEDIAWATCH (ALEXANDRIA, VA.) (US/1053-8321). **1117**

MEDICAL ANTHROPOLOGY QUARTERLY (US/0745-5194). [2,200] **241**

MEDICAL ASPECTS OF HUMAN SEXUALITY (US/0025-7001). [131,000] **5188**

MEDICAL DECISION MAKING (US/0272-989X). [1,300] **1215**

MEDICAL DEVICE TECHNOLOGY (US/1048-6690). **3608**

MEDICAL DEVICES, DIAGNOSTICS & INSTRUMENTATION REPORTS (US/0163-2426). **3608**

MEDICAL DIGEST, THE (SA). [5,266] **3608**

MEDICAL DIRECTIONS (MERCER ISLAND, WASH.) (US/1052-0325). [300] **3608**

MEDICAL DIRECTORY OF NEW YORK STATE (US/0273-0561). [30,000] **3608**

MEDICAL ELECTRONICS (PITTSBURGH, PA.) (US/0149-9734). [101,000] **3609**

MEDICAL FOCUS (WURZBURG, GERMANY) (GW/0724-8172). [25,000] **3609**

MEDICAL GROUP MANAGEMENT JOURNAL (US/0899-8949). [14,000] **3609**

MEDICAL GROUP MANAGEMENT MARKETERS GUIDEPOST (US/1049-880X). [300] **933**

MEDICAL GROUP NEWS (US/0025-7265). [54,000] **3609**

MEDICAL IMAGING AND MONITORING (AT). [3000] **3609**

MEDICAL INDUSTRY EXECUTIVE (US/1060-5193). [40,000] **3609**

MEDICAL INTERFACE (US/0896-4831). [28,000] **3609**

MEDICAL JOURNAL OF AUSTRALIA (AT/0025-729X). [22,000] **3610**

MEDICAL LABORATORY WORLD (UK/0140-3028). [10,000] **3610**

MEDICAL MALPRACTICE LITIGATION REPORTER (US/0882-8555). **3008**

MEDICAL MALPRACTICE PREVENTION (US/0885-744X). [85,000] **3008**

MEDICAL MARKETING & MEDIA (US/0025-7354). [9,500] **933**

MEDICAL MEETINGS (US/0093-1314). [14,000] **3610**

MEDICAL MEETINGS ANNUAL DIRECTORY (US). [14,000] **3610**

MEDICAL OFFICE MANAGER (US/1052-4894). [3,500] **3788**

MEDICAL PRINCIPLES AND PRACTICE (SZ/1011-7571). [1,800] **3611**

MEDICAL PRODUCT MANUFACTURING NEWS (US/0893-6250). [20,000] **3611**

MEDICAL PRODUCTS SALES (US/0279-4802). [24,000] **3611**

MEDICAL RECORDS BRIEFING (US/1052-4924). [2,400] **3788**

MEDICAL RESEARCH FUNDING BULLETIN (US). [3,000] **3611**

MEDICAL SCIENCES BULLETIN (US/0199-4905). [1,800] **4315**

MEDICAL SERIES, BULLETIN (US/0073-7518). [2,000] **3611**

MEDICAL TECHNOLOGIST AND SCIENTIST, THE (UK/0309-2666). [8,000] **3612**

MEDICAL TRIBUNE (1980) (US/0279-9340). [150,000] **3612**

MEDICAL WASTE MONITOR (US/1058-2711). [150,000] **3612**

MEDICAL WORLD NEWS (US/0025-763X). [125,000] **3612**

MEDICARE ADVISOR (US/0897-9634). **5295**

MEDICARE AND MEDICAID DATA BOOK, THE (US/0743-5959). [3,000] **5295**

MEDICARE MANAGER (US/1068-2465). **2888**

MEDICARE-MEMORANDUM (OUTPATIENT CLINIC ED.) (US/0896-4815). **5296**

MEDICINA (BUENOS AIRES) (AG/0025-7680). [4,500] **3613**

MEDICINA CLINICA (SP/0025-7753). [12,000] **3613**

MEDICINA DE REHABILITACION (SP/0214-8714). **4381**

MEDICINE DIGEST (UK). [23,000] **3613**

MEDICINE DIGEST. ASIA (HK). [29,600 (SE Asia)8,200 (Pakistan)10,000 (China)] **3613**

MEDICINE INTERNATIONAL. THE MONTHLY ADD-ON JOURNAL. UK EDITION (UK/0144-0403). **3613**

MEDICINE NORTH AMERICA (CN/0225-3895). [30,000] **3614**

MEDICINSKI PREGLED (YU/0025-8105). [1,300] **3614**

MEDICINSKI RAZGLEDI (XV/0025-8121). [3,200] **3614**

MEDIEN + ERZIEHUNG (GW/0341-6860). **1117**

MEDIEN KONKRET (GW/0931-9808). [3,000] **1117**

MEDIEVAL ARCHAEOLOGY (UK/0076-6097). [1,500] **274**

MEDIEVAL ENGLISH THEATRE (UK/0143-3784). [400] **5366**

MEDIEVALIA ET HUMANISTICA (US/0076-6127). [2,000] **2698**

MEDIFACTS [SOUND RECORDING] (CN/0317-7017). [9,000] **3738**

MEDIOEVO LATINO (IT). [500] **2635**

MEDIOS AUDIO-VISUALES (SP). [5,000] **4074**

MEDISCH CONTACT (NE). [28,000] **3614**

MEDIZINISCHE MONATSSCHRIFT FUER PHARMAZEUTEN (GW/0342-9601). [13,000] **4315**

MEDIZINISCHE MONATSSCHRIFT (STUTTGART) (GW/0025-8474). [12,000] **3615**

MEDTRONIC NEWS (US). [45,000] **3708**

MEETING MANAGER, THE (US/8750-7218). [12,000] **692**

MEETING PLANNERS ALERT (US/0743-3832). [3,000] **944**

MEETINGS MONTHLY, NEWS BULLETIN (CN/0841-9663). [12,561] **5484**

MEGADRILOGICA (CN/0380-9633). [1,000] **5591**

MEGIDDO MESSAGE (US/0194-7826). [12,000] **5018**

MEIE ELU OUR LIFE (CN/0047-665X). [2,500] **5789**

MEIERIPOSTEN (NO/0025-8776). [2,543] **196**

MEKEEL'S WEEKLY STAMP NEWS (US). [5,000] **2785**

MELA NOTES (US/0364-2410). [200] **3230**

MELANESIAN JOURNAL OF THEOLOGY : JOURNAL OF THE MELANESIAN ASSOCIATION OF THEOLOGICAL SCHOOLS (PP). **4976**

MELLON ECONOMIC BRIEFING (US/0734-3558). **1504**

MELPOMENE (MINNEAPOLIS, MINN.) (US/1043-8734). [2,500] **5561**

MELTON JOURNAL, THE (US/0891-7116). [10,000] **1763**

MELUSINE (FR). [200] **325**

MELVILLE ADVANCE (CN). [4,300] **5789**

MELVILLE SOCIETY EXTRACTS (US/0193-8991). [800] **3411**

MELYEPITESI ES VIZEPITESI SZAKIRODALMI TAJEKOZTATO (HU/0231-0732). [95] **2027**

MEMBER ROSTER - ROBERT MORRIS ASSOCIATES (US/0195-5985). **797**

MEMBERS CALENDAR - MUSEUM OF MODERN ART (US/0195-105X). [53,000] **4091**

MEMBERS' COMPUTERIZED DATA EXCHANGE (US/0741-0565). [200] **2460**

MEMBERS' DIRECTORY / FEDERATION OF HONG KONG INDUSTRIES (HK). [2,000] **1618**

MEMBERS DIRECTORY / THE INSTITUTION OF ENVIRONMENTAL HEALTH OFFICERS (UK/0264-5947). [7,500] **4790**

MEMBER'S YEAR BOOK - AMERICAN SOCIETY OF CORPORATE SECRETARIES (US/0742-986X). **879**

MEMBERSHIP DIRECTORY / AMERICAN ASSOCIATION OF EXPORTERS AND IMPORTERS (US). **845**

MEMBERSHIP DIRECTORY / CHAMBER MUSIC AMERICA (US/0277-4054). [10,000] **4130**

MEMBERSHIP DIRECTORY / EL PASO COUNTY HISTORICAL SOCIETY (US). [900] **2746**

MEMBERSHIP DIRECTORY / GEOLOGICAL SOCIETY OF AMERICA (US/0277-5816). **1387**

MEMBERSHIP DIRECTORY - GYPSY LORE SOCIETY, NORTH AMERICAN CHAPTER (US/0193-1598). [250] **2322**

MEMBERSHIP DIRECTORY - INTERNATIONAL ASSOCIATION OF ASSESSING OFFICERS. PERSONAL PROPERTY SECTION (US/0737-4267). [650] **4737**

MEMBERSHIP DIRECTORY / INTERNATIONAL ASSOCIATION OF MARINE SCIENCE LIBRARIES AND INFORMATION CENTERS (CN/0255-8114). [200] **3230**

MEMBERSHIP DIRECTORY / INTERNATIONAL SOCIETY OF APPRAISERS (US/8755-4356). [2,000] **693**

MEMBERSHIP DIRECTORY / MARYLAND GENEALOGICAL SOCIETY (US/1056-0394). [1,400] **2460**

MEMBERSHIP DIRECTORY / NATIONAL ASSOCIATION OF BUSINESS ECONOMISTS (US). [4900] **1504**

MEMBERSHIP DIRECTORY - NATIONAL COUNCIL FOR RESOURCE DEVELOPMENT (US/0162-0339). [900] **1763**

MEMBERSHIP DIRECTORY - PHILATELIC TRADERS' SOCIETY (UK/0305-3245). [1,000] **2785**

MEMBERSHIP DIRECTORY - SUBURBAN NEWSPAPERS OF AMERICA (US/0270-4641). **5661**

MEMBERSHIP LIST - AMERICAN MENSA LIMITED (US/0363-3616). [50,000] **5233**

MEMBERSHIP LIST - CANADIAN ASSOCIATION OF MUSIC LIBRARIES (1984) (CN/0828-7007). **3231**

MEMBERSHIP LIST - THE GALPIN SOCIETY (UK). [1,100] **4130**

MEMBERSHIP-TEAM DIRECTORY (US). [2,000] **3970**

MEMBRANE BIOCHEMISTRY (US/0149-046X). [600] **490**

MEMBRANE QUARTERLY (US/1052-0953). [500] **1027**

MEMO (LE). **1505**

MEMO FROM PROBE (CN/0708-0735). **5252**

MEMO (QUEBEC) (CN/0848-0877). **693**

MEMO: TO THE PRESIDENT (US/0047-6692). [1,550] **1835**

MEMOIR - GEOLOGICAL SURVEY OF VICTORIA (AT/0369-0040). [500] **1387**

MEMOIR - GEOLOGICAL SURVEY OF WYOMING (US/0512-493X). [1,000] **1387**

MEMOIR - NEW MEXICO BUREAU OF MINES & MINERAL RESOURCES (US/0548-5975). **2143**

MEMOIR - PACIFIC TROPICAL BOTANICAL GARDEN (US). [1,200] **517**

MEMOIRE DE TRAME (FR/0987-3090). [300] **3231**

MEMOIRES DE LA SOCIETE GENEALOGIQUE CANADIENNE-FRANCAISE (CN/0037-9387). [3,800] **2460**

MEMOIRES ET ETUDES SCIENTIFIQUES DE LA REVUE DE METALLURGIE (FR/0245-8292). [2,400] **4008**

MEMOIRS OF THE AMERICAN ENTOMOLOGICAL SOCIETY (US/0065-8170). [400] **5611**

MEMOIRS OF THE CONNECTICUT ACADEMY OF ARTS AND SCIENCES (US/0069-8970). **2850**

MEMOIRS OF THE ENTOMOLOGICAL SOCIETY OF CANADA (CN/0071-075X). [1,100] **5591**

MEMOIRS OF THE FACULTY OF SCIENCE, KYOTO UNIVERSITY. SERIES OF BIOLOGY (JA/0454-7802). [800] **464**

MEMOIRS OF THE FACULTY OF SCIENCE, KYOTO UNIVERSITY. SERIES OF PHYSICS, ASTROPHYSICS, GEOPHYSICS AND CHEMISTRY (JA/0368-9689). [750] **4412**

MEMOIRS OF THE MUSEUM OF VICTORIA (AT). [700] **4091**

MEMOIRS OF THE MUSEUM OF VICTORIA. ANTHROPOLOGY AND HISTORY (AT/1035-4247). [700] **4091**

MEMOIRS OF THE PACIFIC COAST ENTOMOLOGICAL SOCIETY (US/0475-3208). **5591**

MEMORANDUM - AMERICAN LIBRARY ASSOCIATION. OFFICE FOR INTELLECTUAL FREEDOM (US/0734-3086). [725] **1306**

MEMORANDUM - AMERICAN NEWSPAPER PUBLISHERS ASSOCIATION (US/0270-9864). [10,000] **4816**

MEMORIA ANUAL - INSTITUTO ARGENTINO DE OCEANOGRAFIA (AG). **1452**

MEMORIA / BANCO CENTRAL DE LA REPUBLICA DOMINICA (DR). [550] **798**

MEMORIAS (SP/0368-8283). [460] **5209**

MEMORIAS DA SOCIEDADE BROTERIANA (PO/0081-0665). [1,000] **518**

MEMORIAS DO INSTITUTO DE INVESTIGACAO CIENTIFICA TROPICAL (PO/0870-0036). [1,000] **5128**

MEMORIE DELLA SOCIETA ENTOMOLOGICA ITALIANA (IT/0037-8747). [1,500] **5612**

MEMPHIS FLYER, THE (US). [42,000] **2490**

MENDOCINO BEACON, THE (US). [2,400] **5637**

MENDY AND THE GOLEM (US/0278-4432). [30,000] **5018**

MENIAIO STATISTIKO DELTIO - TRAPEZA TES HELLADOS (GR/1105-0519). [3,000] **731**

MENNESKER OG RETTIGHETER (NO/0800-0735). [900] **4510**

MENNINGER LETTER, THE (US/1066-937X). [70,000] **3930**

MENNINGER PERSPECTIVE (US/0025-9292). [21,000] **3930**

MENNONITE BRETHREN HERALD (CN/0025-9349). [15,000] **5063**

MENNONITE FAMILY HISTORY (US/0730-5214). [1,600] **2460**

MENNONITE HISTORIAN (CN/0700-8066). [3,300] **5064**

MENNONITE LIFE (US/0025-9365). [700] **5064**

MENNONITE MEDICAL MESSENGER (WINNIPEG, MAN.) (CN/0824-3093). [2,000] **3616**

MENOMINEE TRIBAL NEWS (US). **2267**

MENS & MELODIE (NE/0025-9462). [4,000] **4131**

MEN'S EXERCISE (US/1059-9169). **2599**

MEN'S WEAR OF CANADA (CN/0025-9535). [7,100] **1086**

MENSA BULLETIN (US/0025-9543). [55,000] **5233**

MENSALOHA (US/8750-4529). [500] **4603**

MENSCH & BUERO (GW/0933-8241). [30,000] **4212**

MENSCH UND BUERO (GW/0933-8241). [30,000] **4212**

MENTAL HEALTH-HUMAN RESOURCES CONFERENCE GUIDE (US/1064-685X). **3616**

MENTAL HEALTH IN AUSTRALIA (1973) (AT/0310-5776). [1,000] **4790**

MENTAL HEALTH NURSING (UK). **3861**

MENTAL HEALTH REPORTS (US/0191-6750). [900] **4790**

MENTAL HEALTH SPECIAL INTEREST SECTION NEWSLETTER (US/0279-4136). [3,700] **4790**

MENTOR (SINGAPORE) (SI). [10,500] **1763**

MENUS OF THE VALLEY'S FINEST RESTAURANTS (US/0148-4133). [10,000] **5071**

MERCANTILE AGENT (AT). [600] **846**

MERCED SUN-STAR (US). [21,000] **5637**

MERCER BULLETIN, THE (CN/0714-6914). [10,000] **1690**

MERCER LAW REVIEW (US/0025-987X). [1,600] **3009**

MERCHANT MAGAZINE, THE (US/0739-9723). [5,011] **2402**

MERCURY (UNITED STATES. BUREAU OF MINES) (US/0364-7919). **4026**

MERIDIAN (BUNDOORA, VIC.) (AT/0728-5914). [500] **3347**

MERIWETHER CONNECTIONS (US/1045-3199). [350] **2460**

MERRILL'S ILLINOIS LEGAL TIMES (US/1063-3014). **3009**

MERTON SEASONAL OF BELLARMINE COLLEGE, THE (US/0899-4927). [1,800] **2490**

MESOAMERICA (INSTITUTE FOR CENTRAL AMERICAN STUDIES (COSTA RICA)) (CR). [1,000] **2512**

MESPA PRINCIPAL (US). [1,200] **1866**

MESSAGE (1993) (US/1071-5215). [6,275] **5043**

MESSENGER (FORT DODGE, IOWA), THE (US/0740-6991). [20,301] **5671**

MESSENGER (MADISON, N.C.) (US/0892-1814). [7,800] **5723**

MESSENGER-PRESS (US). [4,800] **5710**

MESSIANIC OUTREACH, THE (US/0278-2782). [3,000] **5051**

MESTER (LOS ANGELES) (US/0160-2764). [500] **3411**

MESURE ET EVALUATION EN EDUCATION (CN/0823-3993). [1,000] **1764**

META (MONTREAL) (CN/0026-0452). [3,400] **3302**

METAL ARCHITECTURE (US/0885-5781). [28,000] **303**

METAL CONSTRUCTION NEWS (US/8756-2014). [33,000] **621**

METALLBEWERKING (NE). [3,500] **4009**

METALLI (IT). [5,000] **4009**

METALLOBERFLACHE (GW/0026-0797). [4,000] **4009**

METALLOFIZIKA (KIEV) (UN/0204-3580). [1,000] **4009**

METALLURGICAL PLANT AND TECHNOLOGY : MPT (GW/0171-4511). **4010**

METALLURGY/MATERIALS EDUCATION YEARBOOK (US/0094-5447). [2,000] **4011**

METALSMITH (US/0270-1146). [4,400] **374**

METALURGIA (SAO PAULO) (BL/0026-0983). **4011**

METALURGIA Y ELECTRICIDAD (SP/0026-0991). [5,000] **4011**

METALWORKING, ENGINEERING AND MARKETING (JA/0911-9647). **4011**

METAPHILOSOPHY (UK/0026-1068). [600] **4352**

METASCIENCE (AT/0815-0796). [180] **5128**

METEOR NEWS (US/0146-9959). [350] **397**

METEOROLOGIE, LA (FR/0026-1181). [1,500] **1431**

METHOD (LOS ANGELES, CALIF.) (US/0736-7392). [320] **4353**

METHODIST HISTORY (US/0026-1238). [1,000] **5064**

METHODOLOGY AND SCIENCE (NE/0543-6095). [250] **5209**

METHODS OF INFORMATION IN MEDICINE (GW/0026-1270). **3616**

METLFAX (US/0026-1297). [107,000] **4012**

METMENYS (US/0543-615X). [850] **3411**

METRIC — Controlled Circulation Index

METRIC STEEL. BULLETIN (CN/0705-2081). **4012**

METRIKA (GW/0026-1335). [700] **3523**

METRO HANDBOOK AND DIRECTORY OF MEMBERS (US/0887-1973). [1,100] **3231**

METRO (SAN JOSE, CALIF.) (US/0882-4290). [70,000] **2538**

METRO SPORTS MAGAZINE (US). **4904**

METRO TELECASTER (1977) (CN/0708-2568). [57,000] **1134**

METRO TIMES (DETROIT, MICH.), THE (US/0746-4045). [100,000 weekly unpaid] **5692**

METROLOGISCHE ABHANDLUNGEN (GW/0232-3915). [400] **4031**

METROPARKS EMERALD NECKLACE (US). [40,000] **4874**

METROPOLITAN ALMANAC (1989) (US/1045-5108). [28,000] **2538**

METROPOLITAN TORONTO ... ANNUAL VISITORS GUIDE (CN/0836-4443). [725,000] **5484**

METROPOLITAN TORONTO BUSINESS JOURNAL, THE (CN/0709-003X). [16,000] **693**

METSAHALLITUKSEN VUOSIKERTOMUS (FI). [5,000] **2388**

MEUBELECHO (BE/0772-6287). [5,000] **2906**

MEXICAN FORECAST (MX). [1,200] **798**

MEXICO DESCONOCIDO (MX/0187-1560). [64,000] **5484**

MEXICO LEDGER (US). **5704**

MEXLETTER (MX/0026-1858). [3,500] **798**

MIAMI MEDICINE : THE OFFICIAL PUBLICATION OF THE DADE COUNTY MEDICAL ASSOCIATION (US). [3,400] **3616**

MIAMI MENSUAL (US/0273-9372). [25,000] **2538**

MIAMI TODAY (US/0889-2296). [35,000] **5650**

MIC/INFO (US). **1245**

MIC/SUB-APPLICATION DEVELOPMENT. [DISKETTE] (US). **1288**

MIC/SUB-IMAGING AND OFFICE SYSTEMS. [DISKETTE] (US). **1220**

MIC / TECH-COMPUTERS (US). **1248**

MIC/TECH-DATA COMMUNICATIONS (US). **1245**

MIC/TECH-MAINFRAME AND MINICOMPUTER (US). **1245**

MIC/TECH-MICROCOMPUTER AND WORKSTATION (US). **1245**

MIC-TECH-TELECOMMUNICATIONS (US). **1160**

MIC-TECH-UNIX (US). **1195**

MICHIANA SEARCHER (US/0736-5004). [250] **2460**

MICHIGAN ACADEMICIAN (US/0026-2005). [1,100] **2850**

MICHIGAN AFL-CIO NEWS (US/0026-1998). [30,000] **1690**

MICHIGAN ALUMNUS (US/0746-2565). **1102**

MICHIGAN ASSOCIATION OF SPEECH COMMUNICATION JOURNAL, THE (US). [250] **1117**

MICHIGAN BOTANIST (US/0026-203X). [1,000] **518**

MICHIGAN CHRISTIAN ADVOCATE (US/0026-2072). [21,000] **4977**

MICHIGAN CITIZEN (US/1072-2041). [45,000] **5693**

MICHIGAN COUNTIES (US/0896-646X). [2,000] **4665**

MICHIGAN CPA, THE (US/0026-2064). [15,000] **748**

MICHIGAN DISTRIBUTORS DIRECTORY (US/0890-4049). [2,000] **694**

MICHIGAN FIRE SERVICE NEWS (US). **2291**

MICHIGAN FLORIST, THE (US/0026-217X). [1,800] **2435**

MICHIGAN FOUNDATION DIRECTORY (US/0362-1561). [100,000] **4338**

MICHIGAN LAW REVIEW (US/0026-2234). [3,000] **3009**

MICHIGAN LIBRARIAN (1985) (US/0884-9919). **3231**

MICHIGAN MUNICIPAL REVIEW (US/0026-2331). [9,600] **4665**

MICHIGAN NATURAL RESOURCES MAGAZINE, THE (US/0275-8180). [120,000] **2198**

MICHIGAN OPTOMETRIST, THE (US/1071-1627). [850] **4216**

MICHIGAN PROFESSIONAL ENGINEER (1990) (US/1054-5840). [2,500] **1987**

MICHIGAN READING JOURNAL, THE (US/0047-7125). [5,000] **1900**

MICHIGAN RETAILER, THE (US/0889-0439). [4,500] **879**

MICHIGAN ROMANCE STUDIES (US/0270-3629). [500] **3302**

MICHIGAN SNOWMOBILER (US/0746-2298). [29,300] **5386**

MICHIGAN SPEECH-LANGUAGE-HEARING ASSOCIATION JOURNAL / MSHA (US/0742-3284). [1,200] **4391**

MICHIGAN TOWNSHIP NEWS (US). [9300] **4665**

MICKY MAUS (GW). [932,508] **1066**

MICRO ECONOMICS / THE BOSTON COMPUTER SOCIETY (US/0883-4296). [4,500] **694**

MICROBIOLOGICA (IT/0391-5352). [500] **567**

MICROBIOLOGICAL UPDATE, THE (US/0889-3381). **567**

MICROBITS (CN/0823-5430). [15,000] **2072**

MICROCELL NEWS (US). [400] **1160**

MICROCOMPUTER REVIEW (US/8755-7525). [750] **1269**

MICROEDITIONS DE LA BIBLIOTHEQUE. CATALOGUE (CN/0707-848X). [1,000] **420**

MICROINFO (TORONTO) (CN/0826-2705). [400] **1269**

MICROPALEONTOLOGY (US/0026-2803). [1,400] **4228**

MICROPROCESSORS AND MICROSYSTEMS (UK/0141-9331). [2,000] **1230**

MICROPSYCH NETWORK (US/0748-2051). [1,500] **4604**

MICROPUBLISHING REPORT (US/0889-9533). **4816**

MICROSCOPE (LONDON) (US/0026-282X). [1,200] **573**

MICROSCOPIA ELECTRONICA Y BIOLOGIA CELULAR : ORGANO OFICIAL DE LAS SOCIEDADES LATINOAMERICANA DE MICROSCOPIA ELECTRONICA E IBEROAMERICANA DE BIOLOGIA CELULAR (AG/0326-3142). **573**

MICROSCOPY (UK/0026-2838). [800] **573**

MICROSCOPY SOCIETY OF AMERICA BULLETIN (US/1062-9785). [6,000] **573**

MICROSPIRIT (CN/0822-7268). **1764**

MICROSTATION MANAGER (US/1057-9567). [20,000] **1195**

MICROTECNIC (SZ/0026-2854). [7,000] **4031**

MICROTIMES (PLEASANT HILL, CALIF.) (US/1065-0148). [235,000] **1270**

MICROWAVE JOURNAL (EURO-GLOBAL ED.) (US/0192-6217). [50,000] **2072**

MID-AMERICA COMMERCE & INDUSTRY (US/0193-2047). [10,000] **950**

MID AMERICA FARMER GROWER, THE (US/1040-1423). [27,000] **108**

MID-AMERICA FOLKLORE (US/0275-6013). [200] **2322**

MID AMERICA INSURANCE (US/0026-2935). [25,000] **2888**

MID-AMERICA THEOLOGICAL JOURNAL (US/0734-9882). [180] **4977**

MID-AMERICAN REVIEW (US/0747-8895). [600] **3411**

MID-ATLANTIC FOODSERVICE NEWS (US/0888-5311). [23,000] **2350**

MID-CONTINENT BOTTLER (US/0026-2978). [3,000] **2369**

MID-NORTH MONITOR, THE (CN/0227-3853). [3,500] **5789**

MID-STREAM (INDIANAPOLIS) (US/0544-0653). [1,500] **4977**

MID WEEK PETROLEUM ARGUS (UK). [1,000] **4264**

MID-WEST CONTRACTOR (US/0026-3044). [8,500] **621**

MIDDLE EAST AND SOUTH ASIA, THE (US/0084-2311). **2769**

MIDDLE EAST AND WORLD FOOD DIRECTORY (LE). [5,000] **2350**

MIDDLE EAST BUSINESS INTELLIGENCE (US/0731-6305). [600] **933**

MIDDLE EAST CIVIL AVIATION (US/1054-9838). [5,000] **28**

MIDDLE EAST CLIPBOARD, THE (US). **2769**

MIDDLE EAST EXECUTIVE REPORTS (US/0271-0498). [1,200] **3132**

MIDDLE EAST FOCUS (CN/0705-8594). [4,000] **4528**

MIDDLE EAST INDUSTRY & TRANSPORT (UK/0261-1473). [6,500] **5387**

MIDDLE EAST INTERNATIONAL (UK/0047-7249). [5,000] **4528**

MIDDLE EAST JOURNAL OF ANESTHESIOLOGY (LE/0544-0440). [500] **3683**

MIDDLE EAST POLICY SURVEY (US/0276-5632). [450] **4482**

MIDDLE EAST REPORT (NEW YORK, N.Y. : 1988) (US/0899-2851). [8,000] **2526**

MIDDLE EAST STUDIES ASSOCIATION BULLETIN (US/0026-3184). [2,500] **2769**

MIDDLE SCHOOL JOURNAL (US/0094-0771). [11,000] **1764**

MIDDLEBURY COLLEGE MAGAZINE (US/0745-2454). [33,000] **1093**

MIDF MELAPURKAN (MY). **798**

MIDLAND ANCESTOR : JOURNAL OF THE BIRMINGHAM AND MIDLAND SOCIETY FOR GENEALOGY AND HERALDRY, THE (UK/0307-2851). [4,000 - 5,000] **2460**

MIDLAND HISTORY (UK/0047-729X). [500] **2698**

MIDWEST ENGINEER (US/0026-3370). [1,000] **1987**

MIDWEST FLYER MAGAZINE (US/0273-7515). [25,000] **28**

MIDWEST MOTORIST, THE (US/0026-3435). [391,000] **5484**

MIDWEST MUSEUMS CONFERENCE NEWS BRIEF (US/1073-0893). [800] **4091**

MIDWEST POETRY REVIEW (US/0745-8738). **3466**

MIDWEST QUARTERLY (PITTSBURG), THE (US/0026-3451). [750] **2538**

MIDWEST REVIEW (WAYNE, NEB. : 1975) (US/0740-3208). [900] **2746**

MIDWESTERN DENTIST (US/0026-3478). [700] **1330**

MIDWESTERN FOLKLORE (US/0894-4059). [200] **2322**

MIDWIVES CHRONICLE AND NURSING NOTES (UK/0026-3524). [36,000] **3765**

MIGRATION NEWS (SZ/0026-3583). [2,800] **1920**

MIGRATION TODAY (SZ/0544-1188). [4,800] **1920**

MIGRATION WORLD MAGAZINE (US/1058-5095). [1,300] **1920**

MILANO FINANZA : MF (IT). [25,000] **798**

MILCHWIRTSCHAFTLICHE BERICHTE AUS DEN BUNDESANSTALTEN WOLFPASSING UND ROTHOLZ (AU/0544-1706). [1,000] **196**

MILCHWISSENSCHAFT (GW/0026-3788). [1,500] **196**

MILESTONES (US). [22,000] **3789**

MILITAIRE SPECTATOR, DE (NE). **4050**

MILITARY BUSINESS REVIEW (US/0883-3427). [15,000] **950**

MILITARY CHAPLAINS' REVIEW (US/0360-9693). [7,000] **4050**

MILITARY CLUB & HOSPITALITY (US/0886-8832). **2350**

MILITARY CLUBS & RECREATION (US/0192-2718). [7,000] **4050**

MILITARY LIVING (US/0740-5065). [30,000] **4051**

MILITARY LIVING'S R & R REPORT (US/0740-5073). [10,000] **4051**

MILITARY MARKET (US/0026-4067). [11,000] **4051**

MILITARY MEDICINE (US/0026-4075). [16,500] **3617**

MILITARY MODELLING (UK/0026-4083). **2774**

MILITARY POLICE (1987) (US/0895-4208). [10,000] **3169**

MILITARY REVIEW (US/0026-4148). [23,000] **4051**

MILITARY ROBOTICS (US/0896-0348). **1215**

MILITARY YEAR-BOOK (II/0076-8782). [5,800] **4051**

MILK AND LIQUID FOOD TRANSPORTER (US/0199-2317). [6,000] **5387**

MILK PRODUCER (UK/0026-4180). [12,000] **197**

MILKWEED CHRONICLE (US/0275-8113). [2,000] **325**

MILL HUNK HERALD, THE (US). [8,000] **3466**

MILLARD COUNTY GAZETTE, THE (US). [4,300] **5757**

MILLENNIUM (UK/0305-8298). [800] **4529**

MILLENNIUM FILM JOURNAL (US/1064-5586). **4074**

MILTON STUDIES (US/0076-8820). [900] **3347**

MILTONVALE RECORD, THE (US). [850] **5677**

MILWAUKEE LABOR PRESS (US/0279-3741). [70,000] **1690**

MILWAUKEE PROFESSIONAL NURSE (US/0026-4369). [800] **3861**

MILWAUKEE READER (US/0026-4377). [4,500] **4830**

MIM (SAINT-AUGUSTIN-DE-DESMAURES, QUEBEC) (CN/0229-7507). **4665**

MIMEOGRAPHED BIBLIOGRAPHY SERIES - INDUSTRIAL RELATIONS CENTRE. QUEEN'S UNIVERSITY (CN/0714-8887). [300] **420**

MIMS (UK/0027-0431). [9,000] **4315**

MIMS AFRICA (UK/0140-4415). [8,500] **4315**

MIMS CROWS NEST (AT/1035-5723). [25,000] **4315**

MIMS DESK REFERENCE (SA/0076-8847). [5,266] **4316**

MIMS MEDICAL SPECIALTIES (SA/0027-0431). [8,100] **4316**

MIMS UK (UK). [60] **4316**

MIN TSU YU WEN (CC). [4,000] **3302**

MINAMI OSAKA BYOIN IGAKU ZASSHI (JA/0540-1259). **3617**

MIND (UK/0026-4423). [3,200] **4353**

MIND BODY HEALTH DIGEST (US/0898-3127). [5,000] **3799**

MIND, THE MEETINGS INDEX. SERIES SEMT, SCIENCE, ENGINEERING, MEDICINE, TECHNOLOGY (US/0739-5914). **5175**

MINDANAO ART AND CULTURE (PH). [500] **2322**

MINE AND QUARRY (UK/0369-1632). [4,000] **2144**

MINE AND QUARRY MECHANISATION (AT/0085-3453). [1,500] **2144**

MINE INJURIES AND WORKTIME (US). [3,000] **2865**

MINERAL COMMODITY SUMMARIES (US/0160-5151). [7,000] **2006**

MINERALOGICAL RECORD, THE (US/0026-4628). [7,500] **1441**

MINERALOGICAL SOCIETY BULLETIN (UK/0263-9513). [1,000] **1441**

MINERAUX ET FOSSILES, LE GUIDE DU COLLECTIONNEUR (FR/0335-6566). [10,000] **1358**

MINERIA EN CUBA, LA (CU/0253-5653). [10,000] **2145**

MINER'S NEWS (US/0890-6157). [7,000] **2145**

MINES MAGAZINE (US/0096-4859). [6,000] **1442**

MING STUDIES (US/0147-037X). [300] **2658**

MINI LAB FOCUS (US). [2,400] **4371**

MINI-RECUEIL DE RENSEIGNEMENTS FISCAUX (CN/0821-0799). **3010**

MINIATURES DEALER (CLIFTON, VA. : 1985) (US/0882-9187). [2,000] **2774**

MINING JOURNAL (1954) (US/0898-4964). [18,386] **5693**

MINING MAGAZINE (LONDON) (UK/0308-6631). [13,500] **2146**

MINING MIRROR (US). [50,000] **2146**

MINING RECORD (1968), THE (US/0026-5241). [6,700] **2146**

MINING REVIEW CANBERRA 1977 (AT/0314-4607). [5,000] **2146**

MINING REVIEW (NORTH VANCOUVER) (CN/0711-3277). [3,800] **2146**

MINISTRY CURRENTS (US/1069-1766). [2,000] **4977**

MINNEAPOLIS INSTITUTE OF ARTS BULLETIN, THE (US/0076-910X). [15,000] **325**

MINNEAPOLIS LABOR REVIEW, THE (US/0274-9017). [50,000] **1690**

MINNEAPOLIS REALTOR (US/0745-3906). [5,700] **4841**

MINNESOTA BUSINESS JOURNAL (US/0192-5504). [26,000] **695**

MINNESOTA DAILY, THE (US). [60,000] **5697**

MINNESOTA ENGLISH JOURNAL (US). [350] **1900**

MINNESOTA GOVERNMENT REPORT, THE TWICE-WEEKLY NEWSLETTER ON STATE GOVERNMENT (US). [200] **4665**

MINNESOTA GROCER (US). [3,400] **2350**

MINNESOTA HISTORY (US/0026-5497). [8,000] **2746**

MINNESOTA INSURANCE (US/0740-8366). [4,500] **2888**

MINNESOTA JOURNAL (US/0741-9449). [3,200] **4665**

MINNESOTA LITERATURE NEWSLETTER (US/0890-0566). [700] **3412**

MINNESOTA MONTHLY (COLLEGEVILLE, MINN.) (US/0739-8700). [65,000] **2539**

MINNESOTA OUT-OF-DOORS (US/0026-5608). [5,000] **4874**

MINNESOTA REAL ESTATE JOURNAL (US/0893-2255). [4,500] **4841**

MINNESOTA REVIEW (NEW YORK, N.Y.) (US/0026-5667). [1,500] **3347**

MINNESOTA SCIENCE (US/0026-5675). [23,000] **108**

MINNESOTA STATE INDIVIDUAL INCOME TAX, THE (US). **4737**

MINNESOTA UNITED METHODIST REPORTER (US/0893-4142). [4,500] **5697**

MINNESOTA VOTER, THE (US/0740-1191). [3,600] **4482**

MINOLTA MIRROR (JA). **4371**

MINORITY BUSINESS ENTREPRENEUR (US/1048-0919). [40,000] **695**

MINORITY BUSINESS NEWS U.S.A (US). [75,000] **695**

MINORITY ENGINEER : ME, THE (US/0884-1829). [16,000] **1988**

MINORITY ENTRPRENEUR. A CLEARINGHOUSE FOR BUSINESS DEVELOPMENT (US). **695**

MINORITY MBA (US/1040-1547). **695**

MINOT DAILY NEWS, THE (US/0885-3053). [29,736] **5726**

MINTEK RESEARCH DIGEST (SA). [1,000] **4012**

MINTEL LEISURE INTELLIGENCE (UK). **4852**

MINUTES / OCIC (BE/0771-0461). [15,000] **4074**

MINZUXUE YANJIUSUO JIKAN, ZHONGYANG YANJIUYUAN (CH/0001-3935). [1,500] **241**

MIRABEL (SAINT-EUSTACHE) (CN/0711-3781). **5790**

MIRROR (DAWSON CREEK) (CN/0712-1105). [10,200] **5790**

MIRROR-EXAMINER (CN/1196-071X). [4,500] **5790**

MIRROR MONTREAL. 1990 (CN/1182-5812). [80,000] **2539**

MIRROR NEWS (US/0191-4677). [9,700] **3484**

MIRRORS : INTERNATIONAL HAIKU FORUM (US). **3466**

MISA DOMINICAL CASTILIAN (SP). [10,000] **4977**

MISA DOMINICAL CATALONIAN (SP). **4977**

MISCELLANEA MUSICOLOGICA (ADELAIDE) (AT/0076-9355). [200] **4131**

MISCELLANEOUS SERIES (NORTH DAKOTA GEOLOGICAL SURVEY) (US/0078-1576). [2,000] **1388**

MISCELLANIA ZOOLOGICA (SP/0211-6529). [1,000] **5591**

MISE A JOUR DE LA LISTE DES MEMBRES DU CIEE AU ... (CN/0820-6309). [500] **2699**

MISHPACHA (VIENNA, VA.) (US/1050-9348). [500] **5051**

MISION (BUENOS AIRES, ARGENTINA) (AG). [3,000] **4977**

MISSIOLOGY (US/0091-8296). [2,500] **4977**

MISSION (DEPARTEMENT EVANGELIQUE FRANCAIS D'ACTION APOSTOLIQUE) (FR/0760-2626). [4,100] **5064**

MISSION FRONTIERS (US/0889-9436). [70,000] **4978**

MISSION: JOURNAL OF MISSION STUDIES (CN/1198-0400). [220] **4978**

MISSION (QUEBEC) (CN/0708-9813). [48,000] **5032**

MISSION UPDATE (US). [1,000] **5032**

MISSIONALIA (SA/0256-9507). [1,400] **5013**

MISSIONARY HERALD (LONDON, ENGLAND : 1921) (UK). **5064**

MISSIONARY MONTHLY (US/0161-7133). [4,000] **4978**

MISSIONARY NEWS SERVICE (US/0026-6051). [1,600] **4978**

MISSIONARY SEER (US). [4,500] **4978**

MISSIONARY TIDINGS (WINONA LAKE, IND.) (US/1043-0725). [9,000] **4978**

MISSIONGRAMS / BEREAN MISSION (US). **4978**

MISSIONS DES FRANCISCAINS (CN/0700-4192). [7,000] **5032**

MISSIONS ETRANGERES (CN/0026-6116). [35,000] **4978**

MISSISSAUGA NEWS (CN). [104,000] **5790**

MISSISSIPPI ARCHAEOLOGY (US/0738-775X). **275**

MISSISSIPPI BIBLE AND CEMETERY RECORDS (US/0742-499X). [100] **2460**

MISSISSIPPI BUSINESS EDUCATION ASSOCIATION JOURNAL (US). [275] **695**

MISSISSIPPI BUSINESS JOURNAL, THE (US/0195-0002). [13,000] **695**

MISSISSIPPI COLLEGE LAW REVIEW (US/0277-1152). **3010**

MISSISSIPPI COVERED EMPLOYMENT & WAGES (US/0090-5321). [250] **1691**

MISSISSIPPI DENTAL ASSOCIATION JOURNAL (US/0098-4329). [1,200] **1330**

MISSISSIPPI FARM BUREAU NEWS (US/0026-6205). [160,000] **109**

MISSISSIPPI FRINGE BENEFIT SURVEY (US/0731-1494). [400] **1691**

MISSISSIPPI GUIDE TO LABOR MARKET INFORMATION / MISSISSIPPI EMPLOYMENT SECURITY COMMISSION (US). [400] **1691**

MISSISSIPPI LAW JOURNAL. CUMULATIVE TEN-YEAR INDEX FOR VOLUMES 41-50 (US). [1,800] **3011**

MISSISSIPPI LEGION'AIRE (US/0026-6299). **5233**

MISSISSIPPI LIBRARIES (US/0194-388X). [1,200] **3231**

MISSISSIPPI MUD, THE (US/0739-0424). [1,500] **325**

MISSISSIPPI MUNICIPALITIES (US/0026-6337). [4,000] **4666**

MISSISSIPPI REVIEW (US/0047-7559). [2,000] **3412**

MISSISSIPPI RN, THE (US/0026-6388). [2,000] **3861**

MISSISSIPPI STATE GOVERNMENT PUBLICATIONS (US/0148-1843). [50] **420**

MISSISSIPPI SUPERVISOR AND CHANCERY CLERK, CIRCUIT CLERK, TAX ASSESSOR & COLLECTOR (US/0738-727X). [1,500] **4666**

MISSISSIPPI WEEKLY WEATHER & CROP REPORT (US). [450] **178**

MISSISSIPPI WILDLIFE (US/1044-0062). [15,000] **4874**

MISSOULIAN (MISSOULA, MONT. 1961) (US/0746-4495). [29,000] **5693**

MISSOURI ALUMNUS (US/0745-0583). [118,000] **1102**

MISSOURI BOTANICAL GARDEN BULLETIN (US/0026-6507). [20,000] **518**

MISSOURI ECONOMIC INDICATORS (US/0195-6159). [100] **1574**

MISSOURI FB NEWS (US/0026-6574). [75,000] **109**

MISSOURI FOLKLORE SOCIETY JOURNAL (US/0731-2946). [500] **2322**

MISSOURI HISTORICAL REVIEW (US/0026-6582). [8,000] **2747**

MISSOURI LIBRARIES (US/0899-6458). [4,100] **3231**

MISSOURI MUNICIPAL REVIEW (US/0026-6647). [5,050] **4666**

MISSOURI NURSE, THE (US/0026-6655). [2,500] **3861**

MISSOURI NUTRITION EDUCATION & TRAINING PROGRAM (US). **4194**

MISSOURI PRESS NEWS (US/0026-6671). [1,500] **4817**

MISSOURI TEAMSTER (US/0026-6728). [42,000] **1691**

MISSOURI VITAL STATISTICS (US/0098-1974). [700] **5333**

MISSOURI WILDLIFE (US). [35,000] **2218**

MISTLETOE LEAVES (US). [6,000] **2747**

MITCHELL TECH SERVICE BULLETIN (US/8755-4453). **5419**

MITSUBACHI KAGAKU / HONEYBEE SCIENCE (JA/0388-2217). [1,000] **109**

MITTEILUNGEN AUS DEM GEOLOGISCH-PALAEONTOLOGISCH EN INSTITUT DER UNIVERSITAET HAMBURG (GW/0072-1115). [500] **1388**

MITTEILUNGEN AUS DER ARBEITSMARKT- UND BERUFSFORSCHUNG (GW/0340-3254). [880] **1691**

MITTEILUNGEN DER BAYERISCHE (GW/0077-2070). [500] **4228**

MITTEILUNGEN DER GEOGRAPHISCHEN GESELLSCHAFT IN MUNCHEN (GW/0072-0941). **2569**

MITTEILUNGEN DER KARL-MAY-GESELLSCHAFT (GW/0941-7842). [1,800] **3412**

MITTEILUNGEN DER MATHEMATISCHEN GESELLSCHAFT IN HAMBURG (GW/0340-4358). [800] **3523**

MITTEILUNGEN — Controlled Circulation Index

MITTEILUNGEN DER OSTERREICHISCHEN GEOGRAPHISCHEN GESELLSCHAFT (AU). [1,500] **2569**

MITTEILUNGEN DES DEUTSCHEN ARCHAEOLOGISCHEN INSTITUTS, ROEMISCHE ABTEILUNG (GW/0342-1287). **275**

MITTEILUNGEN DES DEUTSCHEN ARCHAOLOGISCHEN INSTITUTS (GW/0342-1279). **275**

MITTEILUNGEN DES KUNSTHISTORISCHES INSTITUTES FLORENZ (IT/0342-1201). [800] **358**

MITTEILUNGEN DES SUDETENDEUTSCHEN ARCHIVS (GW). [350] **2699**

MITTEILUNGEN DES VEREINS DEUTSCHER EMAILFACHLEUTE E.V. UND DES DEUTSCHEN EMAIL ZENTRUSM E.V (GW/0723-886X). **2592**

MITTEILUNGEN (IFO-INSTITUT FUR WIRTSCHAFTSFORSCHUNG. ABTEILUNG ENTWICKLUNGSLANDER) (GW). [350] **1574**

MITTEILUNGSBLATT DES BUNDES DER EVANGELISCHEN KIRCHEN IN DER DEUTSCHEN DEMOKRATISCHEN REPUBLIK (GW). [2,800] **5064**

MITTEILUNGSBLATT - VERBAND DER BIBLIOTHEKEN DES LANDES NORDRHEIN WESTFALEN (GW/0042-3629). **3232**

MITTELNIEDERDEUTSCHES HANDWORTERBUCH (GW). [500] **3302**

MIX (BERKELEY, CALIF.), THE (US/0164-9957). [42,721] **5317**

MIZUNAMI-SHI KASEKI HAKUBUTSUKAN KENKYU HOKOKU (JA/0385-0900). [600] **4228**

MIZUSAWA KANSOKU SENTA GIHO (JA/0915-3780). [250] **1358**

MJP. MONTREAL JOURNAL OF POETICS (CN/0823-1605). [150] **3466**

MK. MOBEL-KULTUR (GW/0047-7796). [8,500] **2906**

MLA INTERNATIONAL BIBLIOGRAPHY OF BOOKS AND ARTICLES ON THE MODERN LANGUAGES AND LITERATURES (COMPLETE ED.) (US/0024-8215). [3,000] **3336**

MLA NEWS LETTER - MINNESOTA LIBRARY ASSOCIATION (US/0748-9285). [1,000] **3232**

MLA NEWSLETTER (NEW YORK) (US/0160-5720). [28,000] **3303**

MLO, MEDICAL LABORATORY OBSERVER (US/0580-7247). [60,000] **3617**

MM NEWS (US). **3617**

MMW. MUNCHENER MEDIZINISCHE WOCHENSCHRIFT (GW/0341-3098). [55,000] **3617**

MNA ACCENT (US/0026-5586). [11,500] **3862**

MOBILE & CELLULAR (UK). [9,000] **1160**

MOBILE EUROPE (UK/1350-7362). [15,000] **1160**

MOBILE OFFICE (US/1047-1952). [150,000] **695**

MOBILE PRODUCT NEWS (US/1044-1190). [17,746] **1160**

MOBILE TELECOMMUNICATIONS NEWS (UK/0267-1255). [9,500] **1160**

MOCI; MONITEUR DU COMMERCE INTERNATIONAL, LE (FR/0026-9719). [15,000] **3011**

MOD CONTRACTS BULLETIN (UK/0269-0365). [3,000] **695**

MODASPORT VACANZE (IT). [46,000] **1086**

MODEL AVIATION CANADA (CN/0317-7831). [8,000] **28**

MODEL BUILDER (1981) (US/0731-4795). [60,000] **2775**

MODEL RAILROADING (US/0199-1914). [15,000] **2775**

MODEL RETAILER (CLIFTON, VA.) (US/0191-6904). **2775**

MODELING, IDENTIFICATION AND CONTROL (NO/0332-7353). **3523**

MODERN AFRICA (UK/0264-8067). [10,000] **696**

MODERN & CONTEMPORARY FRANCE (UK/0963-9489). **5209**

MODERN APPLICATIONS NEWS (US/0277-9951). [60,000] **4012**

MODERN AUSTRIAN LITERATURE (US/0026-7503). [700] **3412**

MODERN CASTING (US/0026-7562). [24,000] **4012**

MODERN DAIRY (CN/0026-7651). [2,000] **197**

MODERN DISTRIBUTION MANAGEMENT (US/0544-6538). [675] **879**

MODERN DRAMA (CN/0026-7694). [2,100] **5366**

MODERN FINISHING METHODS (CN/0380-2299). [15,500] **4012**

MODERN FOOD SERVICE NEWS (US/0888-7829). [24,000] **5072**

MODERN GROCER (US/0026-7805). [22,000] **2350**

MODERN HEALTHCARE (1977) (US/0160-7480). [90,000] **3789**

MODERN HEBREW LITERATURE (IS/0334-4266). [2,000] **3412**

MODERN INTERNATIONAL DRAMA (US/0026-7856). [500] **3412**

MODERN JEWISH STUDIES ANNUAL (US/0270-9406). [750] **3412**

MODERN LANGUAGE STUDIES (US/0047-7729). [2,500] **3303**

MODERN LITURGY (US/0363-504X). [16,000] **4978**

MODERN LOGIC (US/1047-5982). [110] **3523**

MODERN MACHINE SHOP (US/0026-8003). [106,000] **2122**

MODERN MATURITY (NRTA ED.) (US/0747-6302). [22,400,000] **5180**

MODERN MEDICINE (MINNEAPOLIS) (US/0026-8070). [123,096] **3661**

MODERN MEDICINE (NEDERLANDSE ED.) (NE/0929-0141). **3617**

MODERN OFFICE TECHNOLOGY (US/0746-3839). [160,300] **4212**

MODERN POWER SYSTEMS (UK/0260-7840). [13,000] **1950**

MODERN PSYCHOANALYSIS (US/0361-5227). [1,200] **4604**

MODERN RECORDING & MUSIC (US/0273-8511). [25,000] **5317**

MODERN SCHOOLMAN, THE (US/0026-8402). [650] **4353**

MOEBIUS (CN/0225-1582). [750] **3412**

MOHAIR AUSTRALIA (AT). [1,000] **5354**

MOKCHAE KONGHAK (KO). **2402**

MOL (JA/0386-5495). **2015**

MOLE (CN/0827-2387). [1,000] **4131**

MOLECULAR AND CELLULAR NEUROSCIENCES (US/1044-7431). **3838**

MOLKEREITECHNIK (GW/0540-6021). **197**

MOLODA UKRAINA (CN/0026-9042). **2519**

MOLY CORROSION INHIBITORS (US/0730-9155). [10,000] **2015**

MOM ... GUESS WHAT ... ! (US). [21,000] **2795**

MONAHANS NEWS (MONAHANS, TEX. : 1931) (US). [4,100] **5752**

MONASH UNIVERSITY LAW REVIEW (AT/0311-3140). [500] **3011**

MONASTIC STUDIES (CN/0026-9190). [500-1000] **5032**

MONATSSCHRIFT FUER KRIMINOLOGIE UND STRAFRECHTSREFORM (GW/0026-9301). [1,000] **3169**

MONDAY MORNING (INDIANAPOLIS, IND.) (US/0360-6171). [23,000] **5065**

MONDAY REPORT (US). [5,500] **3789**

MONDE ALPIN ET RHODANIEN, LE (FR). **5269**

MONDE DU ROCK (CN/0823-0498). [20,000] **4132**

MONDE INFORMATIQUE, LE (FR/0242-5769). [35,000] **1195**

MONDE JUIF, LE (FR/0026-9425). [1,500] **2699**

MONDE JURIDIQUE, LE (CN/0828-4989). [16,507] **3011**

MONDES ET CULTURES : COMPTES RENDUS TRIMESTRIELS DES SEANCES DE L'ACADEMIE DES SCIENCES D'OUTRE-MER (FR/0221-0436). [1,000] **5129**

MONDO BANCARIO (IT/0026-9506). **799**

MONDO DEL LATTE, IL (IT/0368-9123). [1,200] **197**

MONDO LADINO : BOLLETTINO DELL'ISTITUTO CULTURALE LADINO (IT). **3304**

MONEY DIGEST (BATH) (CN/0833-3432). [3,300] **907**

MONITEUR ARCHITECTURE AMC, LE (FR/0998-4194). [15,000] **303**

MONITOR (AT). [3,000] **2073**

MONITOR (CLEARWATER, FLA.) (US/0895-8777). **933**

MONITOR DE LA FARMACIA Y DE LA TERAPEUTICA, EL (SP). [17,000] **4316**

MONITORING REPORT, THE (US). **1135**

MONOGRAPH (US/0435-4419). **5234**

MONOGRAPH - INDIANA ACADEMY OF SCIENCE (US). **5129**

MONOGRAPH (MAXWELL GRADUATE SCHOOL OF CITIZENSHIP AND PUBLIC AFFAIRS. METROPOLITAN STUDIES PROGRAM) (US/0738-3207). [1,600] **4666**

MONOGRAPH / ONTARIO ASSOCIATION GEOGRAPHIC ENVIRONMENTAL EDUCATION, THE (CN/0048-1793). [800] **2569**

MONOGRAPH SERIES IN ETHNOMUSICOLOGY (US). [600] **4132**

MONOGRAPH / [WORLD REHABILITATION FUND] (US/0738-128X). [4,000] **4381**

MONOGRAPHIC REVIEW (US/0885-7512). [500] **3413**

MONOGRAPHS - ACADEMY OF NATURAL SCIENCES OF PHILADELPHIA (US/0096-7750). [1,000] **4168**

MONOGRAPHS OF MARINE MOLLUSCA (US/0162-8321). [1,200] **5591**

MONTAGNE ET ALPINISME, LA (FR/0047-7923). [45,000] **4875**

MONTAGUE'S MODERN BOTTLE IDENTIFICATION AND PRICE GUIDE (US/0192-3900). [25,000] **2592**

MONTANA BUSINESS QUARTERLY (US/0026-9921). [1,900] **1506**

MONTANA CROP & LIVESTOCK REPORTER (US/0279-0394). [4,000] **178**

MONTANA FARMER-STOCKMAN (US/1041-1674). [24,533] **216**

MONTANA FOOD DISTRIBUTOR (US/0047-7931). [1,100] **2350**

MONTANA GRAIN NEWS (US/1046-6088). [3100] **203**

MONTANA OIL JOURNAL (1953) (US/0047-794X). [3,500] **4264**

MONTANA OUTDOORS (US/0027-0016). [40,000] **4875**

MONTANA VITAL STATISTICS (US/0077-1198). [800] **4562**

MONTANA WOOLGROWER (US/0027-0024). [2,500] **216**

MONTESSORI NEWS / IMS (US/0889-6720). **1765**

MONTESSORI OBSERVER / IMS, THE (US/0889-5643). **1765**

MONTGOMERY ADVERTISER (1987), THE (US/0892-4457). **5627**

MONTGOMERY BUSINESS (US/0889-4442). [2,000] **696**

MONTGOMERY INDEPENDENT, THE (US). [8,500] **5627**

MONTHLY BENEFIT STATISTICS (CHICAGO) (US/0364-7129). [2,000] **1536**

MONTHLY DIGEST OF STATISTICS (ZA/0027-0377). [1,000] **5333**

MONTHLY DIGEST OF TAX ARTICLES, THE (US/0027-0385). [10,000] **4737**

MONTHLY DIRECTORY OF S. ASIAN ASSOCIATIONS & BUSINESSES, THE (CN/0700-3471). **696**

MONTHLY FOREIGN TRADE STATISTICS OF PAKISTAN (PK/0552-8267). [1,000] **1536**

MONTHLY INDICATORS OF CURRENT ECONOMIC SITUATION OF BANGLADESH (BG). [250] **1575**

MONTHLY INFORMATION REVIEW - BANQUE MAROCAINE DU COMMERCE EXTERIEUR (MR/0851-0202). [11,000] **846**

MONTHLY NEWS - MULTICULTURAL COUNCIL OF WINDSOR AND ESSEX COUNTY (CN/0710-9695). **2268**

MONTHLY NEWSLETTER - AMERICAN ASSOCIATION OF THEOLOGICAL SCHOOLS (US). **4979**

MONTHLY PRESCRIBING REFERENCE (US/0883-0266). [115,000] **3618**

MONTHLY PRODUCTION OF SELECTED INDUSTRIES OF INDIA (II). [185] **1536**

MONTHLY PUBLIC OPINION SURVEYS (II). **4482**

MONTHLY REPORT - ASSOCIATION OF AMERICAN PUBLISHERS (US/0748-8173). [2,300] **4817**

MONTHLY REPORT (CARACAS, VENEZUELA) (VE). [2,000] **1575**

MONTHLY REPORT OF THE DEUTSCHE BUNDESBANK (GW/0418-8292). [52,000] **1575**

MONTHLY REPORT ON TOURISM, REPUBLIC OF CHINA (CH). [2,500] **5485**

MONTHLY STATISTICAL BULLETIN (MW). **5333**

MONTHLY STATISTICAL BULLETIN / MAJLIS PENGELUAR-PENGELUAR GETAH MALAYSIA (MY/0126-5865). [130] **5078**

MONTHLY WEATHER REVIEW (US/0027-0644). **1432**

MONTHLY WEATHER REVIEW. NORTHERN TERRITORY / COMMONWEALTH OF AUSTRALIA, BUREAU OF METEOROLOGY, DEPARTMENT OF THE INTERIOR (AT). **1432**

MONTHLY WEATHER REVIEW : SOUTH AUSTRALIA (AT). [130] **1432**

MONTHLY WEATHER REVIEW : WESTERN AUSTRALIA (AT). [120] **1432**

MONTMORENCY (CN/0227-5341). **1836**

MONTREAL CE MOIS-CI (CN/0316-8530). [90,000] **4852**

MONTREALITES (CN/0821-4573). **4666**

MONUMENTA ARCHAEOLOGICA (LOS ANGELES) (US/0363-7565). [100] **275**

MONUMENTA GERMANIAE HISTORICA (GW). **2699**

MONUMENTS HISTORIQUES (1980) (FR/0242-830X). [12,000] **304**

MOODY COUNTY ENTERPRISE (FLANDREAU, S.D. : 1938) (US). [2,800] **5744**

MOOREA : THE JOURNAL OF THE IRISH GARDEN PLANT SOCIETY (IE/0332-4273). [600] **2424**

MOOREANA : JOURNAL OF THE PALMETUM (AT/1037-1842). [250] **518**

MORALIA (SP/0210-0581). [1,000] **5209**

MORAVIAN (1989), THE (US/1041-0961). [25,000] **4979**

MORE FROM THE SHORE (US/1067-7402). [200] **2461**

MOREHA LE-MOREH (CN/0820-7976). **2659**

MORNING HERALD, THE (US). [23,000 morning17,000 evening41,000 weeking] **5686**

MORNING NEWS TRIBUNE (US/1042-3621). [115,596 (daily)126,362 (Sunday)] **5761**

MORNING SUN, THE (US). [12,000] **5677**

MORNING WATCH (ST. JOHN'S) (CN/0384-5028). [900] **1765**

MORRELL, MORRISS FAMILIES ASSOCIATION NEWSLETTER (US/0889-7247). [215] **2461**

MORTGAGE BANKING (US/0730-0212). [15,600] **800**

MORTON ARBORETUM QUARTERLY, THE (US/0027-125X). [7,300] **518**

MORTON JOURNAL (MORTON, WASH. : 1988) (US). [3,000] **5761**

MOSCOSOA : CONTRIBUCIONES CIENTIFICAS DEL JARDIN BOTANICO NACIONAL "DR. RAFAEL M. MOSCOSO" (DR/0254-6442). [250] **518**

MOSELLA (FR). **2569**

MOSSBAUER EFFECT REFERENCE AND DATA JOURNAL (US/0163-9587). [200] **4426**

MOT : DIE AUTOZEITSCHRIFT (GW). [127,175] **5419**

MOTHER & CHILD (LAHORE) (PK/0379-2617). [2,500] **2283**

MOTIF (SPRINGFIELD) (US/0273-2114). [400] **4132**

MOTOR 16 (SP/0212-9000). [47,069] **5419**

MOTOR CRASH ESTIMATING GUIDE (US/0194-9411). **5419**

MOTOR IMPORTED CAR CRASH ESTIMATING GUIDE (US/0164-6346). **5419**

MOTOR IN CANADA (CN/0027-190X). [13,500] **5420**

MOTOR INDUSTRY JOURNAL (AT/0729-0799). [6,000] **5420**

MOTOR REISEN REVUE (GW). [260,000] **5420**

MOTOR TRADE JOURNAL (AT). **5420**

MOTOR VEHICLE DATA BOOK (CN/0316-6198). **5420**

MOTORCYCLE DRAG RACING (US/0883-7228). [10,500] **4082**

MOTORCYCLE INDUSTRY MAGAZINE : MI (US/0884-626X). [13,000] **4082**

MOTORCYCLE PRODUCT NEWS (US/0164-8349). [14,000] **4082**

MOTORIK (GW/0170-5792). [3,500] **4792**

MOTORING NEWS LONDON (UK/0027-2264). **4905**

MOTORISTS GUIDE TO NEW & USED CAR PRICES (UK/0027-2302). [50,000] **5421**

MOTRIX (US/0027-2396). [30,000] **5421**

MOTS A TROUVER RG (CN/0823-7123). [12,000] **4863**

MOTS CACHES J'AIME, LES (CN/0826-4740). [12,000] **4863**

MOTS CACHES SUPERMAGAZINE (CN/0822-4145). [12,000] **4863**

MOUNT AYR RECORD-NEWS (US). [2,800 (paid, weekly)] **5671**

MOUNT PROSPECT TIMES (US/0747-2595). [6,981] **5661**

MOUNTAIN CITIZEN (US). [5,000] **2490**

MOUNTAIN DIGGINGS (US/0146-8855). [250] **2747**

MOUNTAIN HOME NEWS (US). [4,200] **5657**

MOUNTAIN RESEARCH AND DEVELOPMENT (US/0276-4741). [960] **241**

MOUNTAINEER (SEATTLE, WASH.) (US/0027-2620). [14,000] **4875**

MOUTHPIECE (TORONTO) (CN/0380-0601). [250] **4132**

MOUVEMENT SOCIAL, LE (FR/0027-2671). [1,500] **2623**

MOVEMENT AND DANCE : MAGAZINE OF THE LABAN GUILD (UK). [600] **1314**

MOVIE/TV MARKETING (JA). [100,000] **933**

MOVIES USA (US/1044-1336). [1,000,000] **4075**

MOVING OUT (US). [750] **3413**

MOYEN FRANCAIS (CN/0226-0174). [1,000] **3413**

MPLA NEWSLETTER (1975) (US/0145-6180). [1,500] **3232**

MR. COGITO (US/0740-1205). [400] **3466**

MRAX INFORMATION (BE/0024-8320). [1000] **5209**

MRL BULLETIN (US/0415-505X). [580] **3232**

MRS BULLETIN (US/0883-7694). [9,500] **2107**

MS QUARTERLY REPORT (US/0738-3967). [6,000] **3838**

MSOS JOURNAL (CN/0831-3040). [30,000] **5180**

MSRRT NEWSLETTER (US). [250] **3232**

MST ENGLISH QUARTERLY, THE (PH/0047-5289). [700] **3304**

MTA. PEDIATRIA (SP/0210-8135). [2,500] **3906**

MUCCHIO SELVAGGIO, IL (IT). [40,000] **4132**

MUCHACHA (CU/0864-0327). [300,000] **5561**

MUENCHENER THEOLOGISCHE ZEITSCHRIFT (GW/0580-1400). **5032**

MUFON UFO JOURNAL, THE (US/0270-6822). [5,000] **29**

MUGENDAI (JA). [45,000] **2851**

MUIR'S ORIGINAL LOG HOME GUIDE FOR BUILDERS AND BUYERS (US/0844-3459). [150,000] **621**

MUJTAMA AL-BATRUL (TS). [6,000] **4265**

MUKWONAGO CHIEF, THE (US). [4,500] **5769**

MULTI-MEDIA COMPUTING (NE/0923-8182). **1196**

MULTICHANNEL NEWS (US/0276-8593). [13,000] **1135**

MULTICULTURAL EDUCATION JOURNAL (CN/0823-6283). [420] **1765**

MULTIHULL INTERNATIONAL (UK). [6,500] **1988**

MULTILATERAL TREATIES : INDEX AND CURRENT STATUS. CUMULATIVE SUPPLEMENT (UK). [400] **3133**

MULTINATIONAL EXECUTIVE TRAVEL COMPANION (US/0093-7487). **5485**

MULTINATIONAL MONITOR (US/0197-4637). [3,700] **846**

MULTIVARIATE EXPERIMENTAL CLINICAL RESEARCH (US/0147-3964). [250] **4605**

MUNCHENER STUDIEN ZUR SPRACHWISSENSCHAFT (GW/0077-1910). [400] **3304**

MUNDO CRISTIANO (SP/0027-3252). [31,000] **5032**

MUNDO EJECUTIVO (MX). **800**

MUNDO FINANCIERO (SP/0300-3884). [15,700] **1506**

MUNDO GANADERO (SP). **216**

MUNDO HISPANICO (ATLANTA, GA.) (US/1051-4147). [21,000 unpaid] **5654**

MUNDO NUEVO (VE/0379-6922). [1,000] **4529**

MUNHON CHONGBOHAK PO (KO). [1,000] **3232**

MUNHWA YESUL (KO). [2,000] **325**

MUNICIPAL EXECUTIVE DIRECTORY (US/0742-1710). [500] **4667**

MUNICIPAL FINANCE JOURNAL (US/0199-6134). [1,500] **4738**

MUNICIPAL LAW SECTION NEWSLETTER (US/0196-5778). [1,200] **3012**

MUNICIPAL NEWS (SEATTLE) (US/0027-352X). [2,000] **4667**

MUNICIPAL OFFICIALS OF MANITOBA (CN/0715-6804). [1,500] **4667**

MUNICIPAL REFERENCE LIBRARY ACQUISITIONS (CN/0226-2533). **3232**

MUNICIPAL WORLD (CN/0027-3589). [10,500] **879**

MUNICIPALITY (1916), THE (US/0027-3597). **4667**

MUNSTER (MUNCHEN), DAS (GW/0027-299X). [1,700] **359**

MUNZEN REVUE (SZ). [25,000] **2782**

MURRAY LEDGER & TIMES, THE (US). [7,800] **5681**

MUSCLE CARS OF THE ... (US/0898-5820). [50,000] **5421**

MUSCLE MAG INTERNATIONAL (CN/0317-087X). [290,000] **2600**

MUSCOGIANA (COLUMBUS, GA.) (US/1042-3419). [225] **2461**

MUSE (COLUMBIA) (US/0077-2194). [2,000] **4091**

MUSEES (CN/0706-098X). **4091**

MUSEON, LE (BE/0771-6494). **420**

MUSEUM HELVETICUM (SZ/0027-4054). [700] **275**

MUSEUM NEWS - UKRAINIAN MUSEUM OF CANADA (CN/0710-1228). [3,000] **4092**

MUSEUM NEWS (WASHINGTON) (US/0027-4089). [10,000] **4092**

MUSEUM OF CALIFORNIA, THE (US). [15,000] **4092**

MUSEUM ROUND-UP (CN/0045-3005). [500] **4092**

MUSEUM STORE (US/1040-6999). [3,500] **4092**

MUSEUMS AND ART GALLERIES IN GREAT BRITAIN AND IRELAND (UK/0141-6723). [30,000] **4093**

MUSHROOM JOURNAL (UK/0144-0551). [1,000] **2424**

MUSHROOM NEWS (US/0541-3869). [700] **179**

MUSIC & SOUND RETAILER, THE (US/0894-1238). **4133**

MUSIC AND THE TEACHER (AT/0047-8431). [1,250] **4133**

MUSIC BOX, THE (UK). [1,500] **4133**

MUSIC BUSINESS INTERNATIONAL (FR). [9,000] **4133**

MUSIC CITY NEWS (US/0027-4291). [120,000] **4133**

MUSIC EDUCATORS JOURNAL (US/0027-4321). [56,600] **4133**

MUSIC FROM CHINA NEWSLETTER (US/1071-2801). [2,500] **4133**

MUSIC LEADER, THE (US/0027-4372). [50,000] **4134**

MUSIC LIBRARIAN (US/1065-1179). [4,000] **4134**

MUSIC NEWS FROM PRAGUE (XR/0027-4410). [15,000] **4134**

MUSIC OF THE SPHERES (US/0892-2721). [10,000] **4186**

MUSIC PERCEPTION (US/0730-7829). [900] **4134**

MUSIC PERFORMANCE RESOURCES (US/0896-1352). [50,000] **4134**

MUSIC RETAILING (US/1051-1822). **4134**

MUSIC REVELATION (US/0882-8229). [1,500] **4134**

MUSIC REVIEW, THE (UK/0027-4445). [1,500] **4134**

MUSIC SCENE (DIETIKON, SWITZERLAND) (SZ). [14,000] **4135**

MUSIC THEORY SPECTRUM (US/0195-6167). [1,200] **4135**

MUSIC THERAPY (NEW YORK, N.Y.) (US/0734-7367). [1,000] **4135**

MUSIC THERAPY PERSPECTIVES (US/0734-6875). [4,000] **4135**

MUSIC USA (US/0197-4173). **4135**

MUSIC WEEK DIRECTORY (UK/0267-3290). **4135**

MUSICA (GW/0027-4518). [6,500] **4135**

MUSICA (IT). [35,000] **4135**

MUSICAL DENMARK (US/0027-4585). [3,000] **4160**

MUSICAL MERCHANDISE REVIEW (US/0027-4615). [13,500] **4136**

MUSICAL NEWS (SAN FRANCISCO, CALIF.) (US/0748-9293). [4,500] **4136**

MUSICAL QUARTERLY, THE (US/0027-4631). [4,000] **4136**

MUSICK (CN/0226-8620). [4,500] **4137**

MUSICUS (SA). [1,500] **4137**

MUSIK UND KIRCHE (GW/0027-4771). [2,200] **4138**

MUSI*KEY — Controlled Circulation Index

MUSI*KEY (US/0895-1543). [1,000] **4138**

MUSIKFORSCHUNG (GW/0027-4801). [2,500] **4138**

MUSIKINSTRUMENT, DAS (GW/0027-4828). [6,000] **4138**

MUSIKTHERAPEUTISCHE UMSCHAU (GW/0172-5505). [1,500] **4138**

MUSIL-FORUM (GW). [700] **3414**

MUSK-OX, THE (CN/0077-2542). [700] **2569**

MUSKOGEE DAILY PHOENIX AND TIMES-DEMOCRAT (US). [20,000] **5732**

MUSLIM JOURNAL (US/0883-816X). [15,000] **5044**

MUSLIM SCIENTIST (US/0148-0995). [1,500] **5210**

MUSLIM WORLD (HARTFORD), THE (US/0027-4909). [1,400] **5044**

MUSLIM WORLD LEAGUE JOURNAL, THE (SU). [30,000] **5044**

MUSTANG! (US/1043-2590). **2801**

MUSTANG TIMES (US/0744-2572). **5421**

MUTATION BREEDING NEWSLETTER (AU). [1,500] **110**

MUTATION BREEDING REVIEW (AU). [300] **518**

MUTUAL AID (US/0734-9998). [1,000] **4792**

MUTUAL MAGAZINE (PHILADELPHIA, PA. : 1980), THE (US/0740-672X). [9,000] **5433**

MUZSIKA (HU/0027-5336). [4,500-6,000] **4139**

MYCOLOGIA (US/0027-5514). [3,000] **575**

MYSTERY READERS JOURNAL (US/1043-3473). [1,000] **3414**

MYSTICS QUARTERLY (IOWA CITY, IOWA) (US/0742-5503). [472] **3414**

MYTHLORE (US/0146-9339). [600] **3414**

MYTHPRINT (US/0146-9347). [400] **3414**

N.A.C.W.P.I JOURNAL (US/0027-576X). [6,000] **4139**

N.A.D.A. OFFICIAL USED CAR GUIDE (US/0027-5794). **5421**

N.A.R.D. JOURNAL (US/0162-1602). [29,238] **4316**

N.A.V.A. NEWS (US). [300] **2623**

N. B. NATURALIST (CN/0047-9551). [500] **4168**

N.C. ... ANNUAL REPORT OF HAZARDOUS WASTE GENERATED, STORED, TREATED OR DISPOSED (US). [1,000] **2237**

N.E.O.N., NATAL EDUCATION. ONDERWYS IN NATAL (SA/0377-1717). [2,000] **1765**

N.S.W. MASTER PLUMBER (AT/0819-1824). [1,600] **2607**

N W EUROPE PETROLEUM DATABASE (UK). **4265**

N.Y. HABITAT (US/0745-0893). [10,000] **4841**

NAACOG NEWSLETTER (US/0889-0579). [22,000] **3862**

NAAMAT (IS). [15,000] **5562**

NAAMKUNDE (NE/0167-5257). **3304**

NAATI NEWS (AT/1031-5411). [1,100] **3304**

NABE NEWS (CLEVELAND, OHIO) (US/0745-3205). [3,650] **1506**

NACADA JOURNAL / NATIONAL ACADEMIC ADVISING ASSOCIATION (US/0271-9517). [4,500] **1836**

NACE CORROSION ENGINEERING BUYER'S GUIDE : OFFICIAL PUBLICATION OF NACE (US). [16,000] **2015**

NACHRICHTEN DER AKADEMIE DER WISSENSCHAFTEN IN GOTTINGEN. PHILOLOGISCH-HISTORISCHE KLASSE (GW/0065-5287). **3304**

NACHRICHTEN DER NIEDERSACHSISCHEN VERMESSUNGS- UND KATASTERVERWALTUNG (GW). [1,700] **2582**

NACHRICHTEN FUER DOKUMENTATION (GW/0027-7436). [2,400] **3232**

NACHRICHTENBLATT DER VERMESSUNGS- UND KATASTERVERWALTUNG RHEINLAND-PFALZ (GW/0939-2378). [1,500] **2027**

NACHRICHTENDIENST (GW/0012-1185). [7,800] **5297**

NACION, LA (AG). [250,000] **5777**

NACTA JOURNAL (US/0149-4910). [1,800] **110**

NAE WASHINGTON INSIGHT (NEWSLETTER ED.) (US/0199-3038). [165,000] **4979**

NAEB BULLETIN (US/0161-7990). [2,350] **950**

NAFED DIRECTORY (US/0363-7131). [2,000] **2291**

NAGALAND BUDGET. SOME FACTS AND CHARTS (II/0303-8505). [500] **4699**

NAGOYA DAIGAKU KYOIKUGAKUBU KIYO. KYOIKUGAKKA (JA). [550] **1766**

NAGOYA KOGYO DAIGAKU KOGAKUBU FUZOKU YOGYO GIJUTSU KENKYU SHISETSU NEMPO (JA). [400] **2592**

NAGOYA KOGYO GIJUTSU SHIKENJO NEMPO (JA). [650] **5130**

NAGOYA-SHI EISEI KENKYUJO HO (JA). [380] **4792**

NAHNU AL-ARAB (UA). [200,000] **2507**

NAHRO ROSTER (US/0363-6453). [12,500] **2829**

NAMIBIANA (SX/0259-2010). **2642**

NANNY TIMES (US). [30,000] **2283**

NANZAN REVIEW OF AMERICAN STUDIES : A JOURNAL OF CENTER FOR AMERICAN STUDIES, NANZAN UNIVERSITY (JA). [500] **5210**

NAPO NEWS (CN/0820-7364). [1,500] **5297**

NAPSAC DIRECTORY OF ALTERNATIVE BIRTH SERVICES AND CONSUMER GUIDE (US/0273-3730). [2,000] **3765**

NAPSAC NEWS (US/0192-1223). [4,000] **589**

NARC OFFICER, THE (US/0889-7794). **3170**

NAROD POLSKI (US/0027-7894). [31,000] **5032**

NASA TECH BRIEFS (WASHINGTON, D.C. 1976) (US/0145-319X). [150,000] **5130**

NASE ZITTJA (US/0740-0225). [4,100] **5562**

NASFAA NEWSLETTER (US/0882-4630). [6,000] **1866**

NASHRAH AL-IKHBARIYAH (RESEARCH CENTRE FOR ISLAMIC HISTORY, ART, AND CULTURE) (TU). [10,000] **325**

NASHVILLE BUSINESS JOURNAL (US/0889-2873). [11,500] **696**

NASSAUISCHE ANNALEN (GW/0077-2887). [2,000] **2700**

NASTAWGAN (CN/0828-1327). [1000] **594**

NASW NEWS (US/0027-6022). [100,000] **5297**

NATA DIRECTORY SYDNEY (AT/0311-8185). [5,500] **2123**

NATA NEWS SYDNEY (AT/0311-662X). [5,500] **2123**

NATAL MUSEUM JOURNAL OF HUMANITIES (SA/1015-0935). [200] **2851**

NATATION (PARIS) (FR/1169-8152). [4,000] **4852**

NATCHEZ TRACE NEWSLETTER (US/0739-1412). [600] **2461**

NATIONAL AERONAUTICS (US/0005-2116). [4,500] **30**

NATIONAL ALLIANCE (US/0027-8513). [14,000] **1692**

NATIONAL AND FEDERAL LEGAL EMPLOYMENT REPORT, THE (US/0733-3285). [5,000] **3013**

NATIONAL ARCHIVES NEWSLETTER (CN/0824-8907). [700] **2482**

NATIONAL ASSOCIATION FOR OLMSTED PARKS (US/0895-819X). [1,000] **4707**

NATIONAL ASSOCIATION OF HOME AND WORKSHOP WRITERS NEWSLETTER (US). [90] **634**

NATIONAL ASSOCIATION OF SECRETARIES OF STATE HANDBOOK (US/0547-4221). **4668**

NATIONAL BANKRUPTCY REPORTER (US/0275-0252). **3087**

NATIONAL BAR BULLETIN, THE (US). [10,500] **3013**

NATIONAL BIOGRAPHIC, THE (US). [5,000] **879**

NATIONAL BLACK LAW JOURNAL (US/0896-0194). [5,000] **3013**

NATIONAL BUILDER (LONDON) (UK/0027-8807). [13,000] **621**

NATIONAL BUSINESS WOMAN (US/0027-8831). [75,000] **5562**

NATIONAL CAPITAL PHARMACIST, THE (US/0027-8890). [300] **4317**

NATIONAL CATTLE FEEDLOT, MEAT PACKER AND GRAIN DEALERS DIRECTORY (US/0882-5149). [5,000] **216**

NATIONAL CENTRAL LIBRARY NEWSLETTER (CH/0034-5016). [2,000] **3233**

NATIONAL CLOTHESLINE (MIDWEST ED.), THE (US/0744-6306). [41,500] **5354**

NATIONAL CONSTRUCTION ESTIMATOR / EDITED BY CAL PACIFIC ESTIMATORS (US/0547-5511). [32,000] **622**

NATIONAL CONTRACT MANAGEMENT JOURNAL (1979) (US/1045-1668). **879**

NATIONAL COOPERATIVE OBSERVER, THE (US). **1432**

NATIONAL CULINARY REVIEW, THE (US/0747-7716). [20,000] **2350**

NATIONAL DEFENSE (WASHINGTON) (US/0092-1491). [45,000] **4052**

NATIONAL DEVELOPMENT. MIDDLE EAST/AFRICA (US/0738-1670). [25,000] **622**

NATIONAL DIRECTORY / CANADIAN INSTITUTE OF FOOD SCIENCE AND TECHNOLOGY (CN/0823-2717). [2,500] **2350**

NATIONAL DIRECTORY OF HIGH SCHOOL COACHES, THE (US). [10,000] **4906**

NATIONAL DIRECTORY OF HISPANIC ELECTED AND APPOINTED OFFICIALS / CONGRESSIONAL HISPANIC CAUCUS (US). **4668**

NATIONAL DIRECTORY OF LOCAL RESEARCHERS (US/0742-9045). **2462**

NATIONAL DIRECTORY OF TRANSLATORS, INTERPRETERS AND LANGUAGE AIDES (AT/0814-9879). [100] **3305**

NATIONAL DRAGSTER (US/0466-2199). [60,000] **4906**

NATIONAL DRILLERS BUYERS GUIDE (US/0279-7739). [34,000] **5536**

NATIONAL ECONOMIC PROJECTIONS SERIES (US/0547-8154). [400] **1619**

NATIONAL EMPLOYMENT LISTING SERVICE FOR HUMAN SERVICES (US/0194-0775). [2,500] **1692**

NATIONAL EMPLOYMENT LISTING SERVICE FOR THE CRIMINAL JUSTICE SYSTEM. SPECIAL EDITION: EDUCATIONAL OPPORTUNITIES (US/0194-0805). [2,500] **4206**

NATIONAL EMPLOYMENT OPPORTUNITIES NEWSLETTER. COMPUTER/ELECTRONIC FIELD ENGINEERING (US/0895-5778). [500] **1692**

NATIONAL ENVIRONMENTAL ENFORCEMENT JOURNAL (US). [500] **3114**

NATIONAL ENVIRONMENTAL JOURNAL, THE (US/1067-2583). [90,000] **2178**

NATIONAL FARMERS UNION, REGION 8, SUBMISSION TO THE GOVERNMENT OF BRITISH COLUMBIA ... (CN/0822-7969). **110**

NATIONAL FIRM RETAIL RR PRODUCTIVITY TRACKING REPORT (US). **934**

NATIONAL FORENSIC JOURNAL (US/0749-1042). [325] **3742**

NATIONAL FORUM OF APPLIED EDUCATIONAL RESEARCH JOURNAL (US/0895-3880). [15,000] **1867**

NATIONAL FORUM OF EDUCATIONAL ADMINISTRATION AND SUPERVISION JOURNAL (US/0888-8132). **1766**

NATIONAL GENEALOGICAL SOCIETY QUARTERLY (US/0027-934X). [9,000] **2462**

NATIONAL GEOGRAPHER (II/0470-0929). [400] **2570**

NATIONAL GEOGRAPHIC WORLD (US/0361-5499). [1,300,000] **2570**

NATIONAL GREENHOUSE GARDENER (US/0883-8313). [18,000] **2425**

NATIONAL HEALTH POLICY FORUM (US). [2,600] **4668**

NATIONAL HOG FARMER (US/0027-9447). [110,000] **216**

NATIONAL HOME CENTER NEWS (US/0192-6772). [52,000] **2792**

NATIONAL HOOKUP (US/0194-4754). [1,300] **4391**

NATIONAL INSTITUTE ECONOMIC REVIEW (UK/0027-9501). [3,000] **1507**

NATIONAL INSTITUTE OF DENTAL RESEARCH PROGRAMS (US/0360-7763). [300] **1330**

NATIONAL INTELLIGENCE REPORT. CLINICAL LABS/BLOOD BANKS (US/0270-6768). **3619**

NATIONAL KNIFE MAGAZINE, THE (US/1051-4600). [15,000] **2775**

NATIONAL LIBRARY NEWS (CN/0027-9633). [5,000] **3233**

NATIONAL MARKET PLACE NEWS (AT/1030-8784). [11,300] **2350**

NATIONAL MEAT PACKER REFERENCE GUIDE (US/0743-3956). [5,200] **216**

NATIONAL MILK RECORDS. ANNUAL REPORT, ENGLAND & WALES (UK). [16,000] **197**

NATIONAL MINORITY POLITICS (US/1057-1655). [12,000] **2268**

NATIONAL NEWS - AMERICAN LEGION AUXILIARY (US/1062-4244). **5234**

NATIONAL NEWSLETTER - ASSOCIATION OF PART-TIME PROFESSIONALS (U.S.) (US/0739-2931). [1,500] **4206**

NATIONAL NEWSLETTER - CANSPA (CN/0229-2866). **622**

NATIONAL NEWSPAPER ASSOCIATION DIRECTORY (US/0147-7528). **4817**

NATIONAL NOTARY, THE (US/0894-7872). [62,000] **4668**

NATIONAL OIL & LUBE NEWS, THE (US/1071-1260). [11,500 US100 other] **4265**

NATIONAL ON-CAMPUS REPORT (US/0300-6646). [2,400] **1836**

NATIONAL OTC STOCK JOURNAL, THE (US/0745-7049). [20,000] **909**

NATIONAL (OTTAWA. 1978) (CN/0709-1370). [7,800 English1,300 French] **1882**

NATIONAL PALACE MUSEUM BULLETIN (CH/0027-9846). [1,000] **4093**

NATIONAL PARALEGAL REPORTER (US/1058-482X). [19,000] **3014**

NATIONAL PARK STATISTICAL ABSTRACT (US/0278-1328). [2,500] **2185**

NATIONAL PARKS JOURNAL (AT/0047-9012). [8,000] **2198**

NATIONAL POULTRY IMPROVEMENT PLAN. DIRECTORY OF PARTICIPANTS HANDLING WATERFOWL, EXHIBITION POULTRY, AND GAME BIRDS (US/0271-7948). [3,000] **216**

NATIONAL PUBLIC EMPLOYMENT REPORTER (US/0194-889X). [300] **3152**

NATIONAL RADIO GUIDE (CN/0849-3952). [17,000] **1135**

NATIONAL RADIO PUBLICITY DIRECTORY (US/0276-4520). **1135**

NATIONAL RAILWAYS OF ZIMBABWE (RH). [19,500] **5433**

NATIONAL REAL ESTATE INDEX (US). [3,500] **4841**

NATIONAL REAL ESTATE INVESTOR. DIRECTORY ISSUE (US/0731-8693). [31,000] **4842**

NATIONAL REPORT FOR TRAINING AND DEVELOPMENT (US/0749-9884). **880**

NATIONAL REVIEW (NEW YORK) (US/0028-0038). [100,000] **4483**

NATIONAL RIGHT TO WORK NEWSLETTER (US/0197-7032). [150,000] **1692**

NATIONAL SACRED HARP NEWSLETTER (US). [600] **4139**

NATIONAL SERVICE NEWSLETTER (US/1059-4922). [1,300] **5297**

NATIONAL SPEED SPORT NEWS (US/0028-0208). [75,000] **4906**

NATIONAL STONE ASSOCIATION BUYER'S GUIDE (US). [2,000] **2147**

NATIONAL STRENGTH & CONDITIONING ASSOCIATION JOURNAL (US/0744-0049). [15,000] **1857**

NATIONAL TAX JOURNAL (US/0028-0283). [3,600] **4738**

NATIONAL TECHNICAL INSTITUTIE FOR THE DEAF FOCUS (US/0739-9278). [20,000] **4391**

NATIONAL THEATRE SCHOOL OF CANADA (CN/0383-1256). **5366**

NATIONAL TRADE-INDEX OF SOUTH AFRICA (SA/0077-5894). **847**

NATIONAL TRAVEL EXPENDITURE STUDY (US/0362-7829). [400] **5485**

NATIONAL TRIAL LAWYER (FLORIDA ED.) (US/1066-7733). [2,400] **3014**

NATIONAL WEATHER DIGEST (US/0271-1052). [2,000] **1432**

NATIONAL WILDLIFE FEDERATION'S CONSERVATION (US/0736-9522). **3114**

NATIONAL WOMEN'S HEALTH REPORT (US/0741-9147). [15,000] **4792**

NATION'S BUILDING NEWS (US/8750-6580). [147,000] **622**

NATIVE PEOPLES (US/0895-7606). [112,000] **2747**

NATIVE VOICE (CN/0028-0542). [2,500] **2539**

NATO'S FIFTEEN NATIONS (GW/0027-6065). [23,800] **4529**

NATOTAWIN (CN/0703-4733). **2748**

NATSO TRUCKERS NEWS (US/1040-2284). [210,000] **5388**

NATUR UND MUSEUM (FRANKFURT AM MAIN : 1962) (GW/0028-1301). [7,000] **4168**

NATURA (NE/0028-0631). **4168**

NATURA JUTLANDICA (DK/0077-6033). [700] **5592**

NATURAL BODYBUILDING AND FITNESS (US/1071-555X). **4906**

NATURAL FOODS MERCHANDISER (US/0164-338X). [12,500] **2351**

NATURAL HAZARDS OBSERVER (US/0193-8355). [9,600] **1358**

NATURAL HISTORY BULLETIN (BANGKOK) (TH/0080-9462). [1,500] **4168**

NATURAL PHYSIQUE (US/1044-6583). **4906**

NATURAL RESOURCES COMPUTER NEWSLETTER (US/0890-5673). [1,000] **2199**

NATURAL RESOURCES FORUM (NE/0165-0203). [1,000] **2199**

NATURALIA (SAO JOSE DO RIO PRETO) (BL/0101-1944). [600] **4168**

NATURALIST REVIEW (US/0888-6547). **2199**

NATURALIST (TRINIDAD AND TOBAGO) (TR). [12,000] **4168**

NATURE CANADA (CN/0374-9894). [20,000] **2199**

NATURE MALAYSIANA (MY/0126-5318). [2,000] **4169**

NATURE NORTHWEST (CN/0836-4702). [300] **4169**

NATURE NOTEBOOK (US). **466**

NATURE SOUTH (US/1054-9641). [1,000] **4169**

NATURENS VERDEN (DK/0028-0895). [8,000] **5131**

NATUROPA (ENGLISH EDITION) (FR/0250-7072). [21,000] **2200**

NATUUR EN TECHNIEK (NE/0028-1093). [45,000] **5131**

NATUURHISTORISCH MAANBLAD : ORGAAN VAN HET NATUURHISTORISCH GENOOTSCHAP IN LIMBURG (NE). [1,200] **4169**

NAUTICA (IT/0392-369X). [60,000] **4179**

NAUTICAL MAGAZINE (UK/0028-1336). [1,100] **4179**

NAUTICAL RESEARCH JOURNAL (US/0738-7245). [1,600] **4179**

NAUTILUS (PHILADELPHIA), THE (US/0028-1344). [600] **5592**

NAVAL AFFAIRS (US/0028-1409). **4179**

NAVAL ARCHITECT, THE (UK/0306-0209). [6,758] **5453**

NAVAL FORCES (UK/0722-8880). [18,450] **4180**

NAVAL LAW REVIEW (US/1049-0272). [2,000] **3183**

NAVAL REVIEW (UK). [3,000] **4180**

NAVAL STORES REVIEW (1979) (US/0164-4580). [500] **2403**

NAVAL WAR COLLEGE REVIEW (US/0028-1484). [15,000] **4180**

NAVIGATION (AT/0077-6262). [700] **4180**

NAVIGATION (PARIS) (FR/0028-1530). [1,500] **4180**

NAVIGATION (WASHINGTON) (US/0028-1522). [3,000] **4180**

NAVY INTERNATIONAL (UK/0144-3194). [2,500] **4180**

NAVY NEWS (US/0028-1670). [100,000] **5759**

NAWPA PACHA (US/0077-6297). [500] **275**

NAZARETH (COMBERMERE) (CN/1183-1863). [3,000] **5033**

NBA FAMILY TALK (US). **5297**

NC ARTS (US/0748-1934). [33,000] **325**

NCA/TCS NEWSLETTER (US/0163-772X). [3600] **539**

NCAA BASKETBALL (US/0276-1017). **4906**

NCAA FOOTBALL RULES AND INTERPRETATIONS (US/0736-5160). **4906**

NCAA MEN'S WATER POLO RULES (US/0734-0508). **4907**

NCAA NEWS, THE (US/0027-6170). **4907**

NCECA JOURNAL (US/0739-1544). [3,500] **2592**

NCEE REGISTRATION BULLETIN (US/0199-8994). [4,000] **1988**

NCGR JOURNAL (US). [2,200] **390**

NCOA JOURNAL (SAN ANTONIO, TEX.) (US/0747-0150). [160,000] **4052**

NCOA NETWORKS (US/1045-9073). [7,000] **5180**

NCPC QUARTERLY (US/0743-4529). **2829**

NCSA NEWSLETTER (CN/0824-4820). [350] **5297**

NDAA BULLETIN / NATIONAL DISTRICT ATTORNEYS ASSOCIATION (US). [7,000] **3108**

NEA-AKTIVIST (ANCHORAGE, ALASKA) (US/1068-2511). [9,500] **1766**

NEA NEWSLETTER (FR). [1,550 (English)600 (French)] **1950**

NEAR EAST REPORT (US/0028-176X). [55,000] **4529**

NEARA JOURNAL (US/0149-2551). [600] **2748**

NEAS. NEWSLETTER OF ENGINEERING ANALYSIS SOFTWARE (US/0739-697X). [5,000] **1988**

NEBRASKA ANCESTREE (US/0270-4463). [1,000] **2462**

NEBRASKA HISTORY (US/0028-1859). [5,000] **2748**

NEBRASKA LIBRARIES (US/1043-8807). [750] **3233**

NEBRASKA LIBRARY ASSOCIATION QUARTERLY (US/0028-1883). [960] **3233**

NEBRASKA MUNICIPAL REVIEW (US/0028-1905). [3,200] **4668**

NEBRASKA NURSE (US/0028-1921). [24,000] **3862**

NEBRASKA SPEECH AND HEARING JOURNAL (US/0470-570X). [400] **4391**

NEBRASKALAND (US/0028-1964). [65,000] **4852**

NED. GEREF. TEOLOGIESE TYDSKRIF (SA/0378-9888). [1,800] **4980**

NEDERLANDS BOSBOUW TIJDSCHRIFT (NE/0369-3651). **2389**

NEDERLANDS TIJDSCHRIFT VOOR NATUURKUNDE (AMSTERDAM. 1991) (NE/0926-4264). **5132**

NEDERLANDS VAN NU (BE/0771-5080). **3305**

NEDERLANDSCH ARCHIEVENBLAD (NE/0028-2049). [1,100] **2482**

NEDERLANDSE COURANT (WILLOWDALE) (CN/0316-9782). [5,000] **2268**

NEEDLE ARTS (US). [22,000] **5185**

NEGATIVE CAPABILITY (US/0277-5166). [1,000] **3414**

NEGOCIOS Y BANCOS : REVISTA PARA EL EJECUTIVO (MX/0028-2456). [50,000] **801**

NEGOTIATIONS NEWS & SCHOOL LAW REPORTER (US). [2,000] **1867**

NEGRO HISTORY BULLETIN (US/0028-2529). [2,300] **2748**

NEHGS NEXUS (US/0747-9891). [11,000] **2462**

NEHW HEALTH WATCH (US/8756-0356). [1,000] **3862**

NEISS DATA HIGHLIGHTS : NATIONAL ELECTRONIC INJURY SURVEILLANCE SYSTEM (US). [3,000] **4793**

NEMA NEWS (US). [1,000] **4093**

NEMATROPICA (US/0099-5444). [450] **5592**

NEMPO (JA). [350] **5132**

NEMPO - TOKYO DAIGAKU OGATA KEISANKI SENTA (JA/0385-2814). [450] **1261**

NENKAN NIHON NO KOKOKU SHASHIN (JA). [1,500] **4372**

NEOLOGY / EDMONTON SCIENCE FICTION AND COMIC ARTS SOCIETY (CN/0228-913X). [150] **3415**

NEONATOLOGY LETTER (US/0747-6132). **3765**

NEOTROPICA (AG/0548-1686). [500] **5592**

NEPHROLOGY NEWS & ISSUES (US/0896-1263). [16,000] **3992**

NEPTUNUS (BE). [3,500] **4181**

NETBALL MAGAZINE (UK/0959-1117). [6,000] **4907**

NETHERLANDS-BRITISH TRADE DIRECTORY (UK). [2,000] **847**

NETHERLANDS JOURNAL OF AGRICULTURAL SCIENCE (NE/0028-2928). **111**

NETHERLANDS JOURNAL OF PLANT PATHOLOGY (NE/0028-2944). **519**

NETHERLANDS JOURNAL OF ZOOLOGY (NE/0028-2960). [1,300] **5592**

NETWORK COMPUTING (US/1046-4468). **1243**

NETWORK COMPUTING (UK/0966-7873). [20,000] **1243**

NETWORK (MELBOURNE (VIC.) (AT/0159-7302). [10,250] **5433**

NETWORK OF SASKATCHEWAN WOMEN (1983) (CN/0826-4929). [550] **5562**

NETWORK (RESEARCH TRIANGLE PARK) (US/0270-3637). [4,000] **589**

NETWORK (TORONTO. 1987) (CN/0836-0197). [149,400] **386**

NETWORK WEEK (UK/0965-3031). [1,000] **1160**

NETWORKER — Controlled Circulation Index

NETWORKER (ASHEVILLE, N.C.), THE (US/1070-762X). [5,000] **4186**

NETWORKING MANAGEMENT (US/1052-049X). [63,000] **1243**

NEU (IT). **3839**

NEUE ENTOMOLOGISCHE NACHRICHTEN (GW/0722-3773). **5592**

NEUE KERAMIK (GW/0933-2367). **3466**

NEUES GLAS (GW/0723-2454). [5,200] **2592**

NEURO-OPHTHALMOLOGY (AMSTERDAM : AEOLUS PRESS. 1980) (NE/0165-8107). [800] **3876**

NEUROBIOLOGY OF AGING (US/0197-4580). **3839**

NEUROCOMPUTERS (US/0893-1585). [500] **1197**

NEUROELECTRIC NEWS (US/0047-942X). **584**

NEUROLOGIA CROATICA : GLASILO UDRUZENJA NEUROLOGA JUGOSLAVIJE, OFFICIAL JOURNAL OF YUGOSLAV NEUROLOGICAL ASSOCIATION (CI/0353-8842). [1,000] **3840**

NEUROLOGIA EN COLOMBIA (CK/0120-1034). [2,000] **3840**

NEUROPATHOLOGY AND APPLIED NEUROBIOLOGY (UK/0305-1846). [400] **3896**

NEUROPHYSIOLOGIE CLINIQUE (NE/0987-7053). [3,000] **3841**

NEUROSCIENCE AND BIOBEHAVIORAL REVIEWS (US/0149-7634). **3842**

NEUROTOXICOLOGY (PARK FOREST SOUTH) (US/0161-813X). [1,000] **3843**

NEVADA BUSINESS JOURNAL (US). [15,000] **698**

NEVADA HISTORICAL SOCIETY QUARTERLY (1961) (US/0047-9462). [1,600] **2748**

NEVADA LAWYER (US/1068-882X). [4,000] **3015**

NEVADA LEGAL NEWS (US/0744-8902). [1,000] **3015**

NEVADA LIBRARY DIRECTORY AND STATISTICS (US). **3259**

NEVADA PUBLIC AFFAIRS REVIEW (US/0196-7355). [2,500] **4668**

NEVADA RNFORMATION (US/0273-4117). [600] **3862**

NEVADA STATISTICAL ABSTRACT (US). [1,000] **5334**

NEVADA WAGE SURVEY (US). [2,300] **1693**

NEW ACCOUNTANT (US/0882-8067). [64,000] **749**

NEW ADVOCATE (BOSTON, MASS.), THE (US/0895-1381). [5,000] **3415**

NEW AGE RETAILER (US/1042-6566). [5,000] **4186**

NEW AGE, THE (US). [650,000] **2490**

NEW AGE WEEKLY (II/0047-9500). [25,000] **4483**

NEW AMERICAN (BELMONT, MASS.), THE (US/0885-6540). [50,000] **4483**

NEW AND EXPANDED INDUSTRIES ANNOUNCED IN ALABAMA (US/0091-1542). [2,000] **1619**

NEW BOOKS IN THE COMMUNICATIONS LIBRARY (US/0734-8142). [500] **1118**

NEW CANADIAN REVIEW (CN/0832-932X). [1,000] **3415**

NEW CHARLOTTE, THE (US). [15,000] **2540**

NEW CONSTRUCTION (INTERNATIONAL ED.) (US/0892-6344). **622**

NEW CONSUMER (UK/0958-7349). [1,000] **1298**

NEW DESIGNS FOR YOUTH DEVELOPMENT (US/0270-2541). [1,000] **1067**

NEW DIMENSIONS IN GIVING (US). [35,000] **4338**

NEW DIRECTIONS (US). **4391**

NEW DIRECTIONS FOR CHILD DEVELOPMENT (US/0195-2269). [450] **4605**

NEW DIRECTIONS FOR COMMUNITY COLLEGES (US/0194-3081). [1,000] **1837**

NEW DIRECTIONS FOR HIGHER EDUCATION (US/0271-0560). [1,000] **1837**

NEW DIRECTIONS FOR INSTITUTIONAL RESEARCH (US/0271-0579). [1,000] **1767**

NEW DIRECTIONS FOR MENTAL HEALTH SERVICES (US/0193-9416). [500] **5298**

NEW DIRECTIONS FOR PROGRAM EVALUATION (US/0164-7989). [600] **5298**

NEW DIRECTIONS FOR STUDENT SERVICES (US/0164-7970). [1,000] **1767**

NEW DIRECTIONS FOR TEACHING AND LEARNING (US/0271-0633). [500] **1901**

NEW DOCTOR (AT/0313-2153). [2,000] **3916**

NEW DRIVER (HIGHLAND PARK, ILL.) (US/0279-6384). [150,000] **5421**

NEW DRUG COMMENTARY (US/0734-1989). **4317**

NEW EDITION (CN/0824-1813). **5210**

NEW EDUCATION (MELBOURNE, VIC.) (AT). **1767**

NEW ELECTRONICS (NZ). [8,000] **2073**

NEW ENGLAND ANTIQUES JOURNAL (US/0897-5795). [20,000] **251**

NEW ENGLAND BUSINESS (US/0164-3533). [85,000] **698**

NEW ENGLAND ELECTRICAL BLUE BOOK (US). [9,000] **2073**

NEW ENGLAND ENTERTAINMENT DIGEST [MICROFORM] (US). [10,000] **5366**

NEW ENGLAND FARMER (ST. JOHNSBURY) (US/0193-0923). [18,074] **111**

NEW ENGLAND FRUIT MEETINGS (US/0099-426X). [800] **111**

NEW ENGLAND JOURNAL OF HISTORY / NEW ENGLAND HISTORY TEACHERS ASSOCIATION, THE (US). **5210**

NEW ENGLAND JOURNAL OF OPTOMETRY (US/0028-4807). [1,900] **4216**

NEW ENGLAND JOURNAL ON CRIMINAL AND CIVIL CONFINEMENT (US/0740-8994). [500] **3170**

NEW ENGLAND LAW REVIEW (US/0028-4823). [2,000] **3015**

NEW ENGLAND LIVING (US/0884-5166). [100,000] **2540**

NEW ENGLAND PROGRESS MAGAZINE (US). [5,000] **2607**

NEW ENGLAND PURCHASER (US/0028-4858). [5,500] **950**

NEW ENGLAND REAL ESTATE JOURNAL (US/0028-4890). [30,000] **4842**

NEW ENGLAND RUNNER (US/1041-4800). [15,000] **4907**

NEW ENGLAND SENIOR CITIZEN (US/0163-2248). [50,000] **5180**

NEW EQUIPMENT DIGEST (US/0028-4963). [205,000] **2123**

NEW EQUIPMENT NEWS (CN/0028-4971). [31,500] **3485**

NEW ERA LAUNDRY & CLEANING LINES (US/0028-5056). [26,130] **698**

NEW ETHICALS CATALOGUE (NZ/0110-9510). [9,000] **4334**

NEW FOOD & DRUG PACKAGING, THE (US/1075-3028). [74,000] **4220**

NEW FOR CONSUMERS (US/0364-6777). [6,000] **1298**

NEW FOUNDATION PAPERS (US/0748-6804). [400] **4981**

NEW FRONTIERS IN EDUCATION (II/0047-9705). [1,000] **1837**

NEW GLASS REVIEW (US/0275-469X). [2,000] **2592**

NEW GLASS REVIEW (PRAHA) (XR/1210-2741). [7,700] **2592**

NEW GUARD (US/0028-5137). [10,000] **4484**

NEW HAMPSHIRE BUSINESS REVIEW (US/0164-8152). **698**

NEW HAMPSHIRE GENEALOGICAL RECORD, THE (US/1055-0763). [900] **2462**

NEW HAMPSHIRE TOWN & CITY (US/0545-171X). [2,700] **4669**

NEW HEAVEN, NEW EARTH (US/0896-3150). [3,000] **5665**

NEW HOLLAND NEWS (NEW HOLLAND, PA. : 1986) (US). [350,000] **111**

NEW HOLSTEIN REPORTER (US/0749-6982). [2,400] **5769**

NEW HOMES (US/0890-4723). **4842**

NEW HORIZON (LONDON, ENGLAND) (UK/0955-095X). [7,000] **5044**

NEW HORIZONS IN EDUCATION (SYDNEY, N.S.W.) (AT). [400] **1767**

NEW HORIZONS (MILWAUKEE, WIS.) (US/0889-5678). [15,000] **1767**

NEW IN CHESS YEARBOOK (NE/0168-7697). **4864**

NEW JERSEY BEVERAGE JOURNAL (US/0028-5552). [10,000] **2369**

NEW JERSEY BUSINESS (US/0028-5560). [17,500] **698**

NEW JERSEY DIVISION OF LABOR MARKET AND DEMOGRAPHIC RESEARCH POPULATION ESTIMATES FOR NEW JERSEY (US). [3,800] **4555**

NEW JERSEY HISTORICAL COMMISSION NEWSLETTER (US/0047-9772). [3,000] **2748**

NEW JERSEY LAWYER (MAGAZINE) (US/0195-0983). [18,300] **3015**

NEW JERSEY LAWYERS DIARY AND MANUAL (US/1053-1955). [45,000] **3015**

NEW JERSEY NURSE (1978) (US/0196-4895). **3862**

NEW JERSEY OUTDOORS (US/0028-5889). [60,000] **2200**

NEW JERSEY PARENT-TEACHER (US/0028-5897). [3,500] **1867**

NEW JERSEY QUERIES (US/0899-1340). [500] **2462**

NEW JERSEY REALTOR (US/0028-5919). [46,000] **4842**

NEW JERSEY STATE AFL-CIO NEWS (US). [3,000] **1694**

NEW JOURNAL (NEW HAVEN, CONN.), THE (US/0028-6001). [11,000] **1093**

NEW KOREA (LOS ANGELES, CALIF.) (US/1054-5891). [3,000] **5637**

NEW LANGUAGE PLANNING NEWSLETTER (II). **3305**

NEW LAUREL REVIEW (US/0145-8388). [500] **3415**

NEW LEADER (NEW YORK, N.Y.), THE (US/0028-6044). [24,000] **4543**

NEW LIBRARY WORLD (UK/0307-4803). [1,100] **3234**

NEW LITERATURE ON OLD AGE (UK/0140-2447). [600] **5180**

NEW LITERATURE REVIEW (AT/0314-7495). [400] **3348**

NEW LITURGY. BULLETIN OF THE NATIONAL SECRETARIAT, IRISH EPISCOPAL COMMISSION FOR LITURGY (IE). [1,400] **5033**

NEW MEXICO AGRICULTURAL STATISTICS (US/0077-8540). [1,500] **155**

NEW MEXICO BUSINESS CURRENT ECONOMIC REPORT (US/0889-5937). [550] **1536**

NEW MEXICO FARM AND RANCH (US/0028-6192). [10,000] **112**

NEW MEXICO GENEALOGIST (US). [400] **2462**

NEW MEXICO HUMANITIES REVIEW (US/0738-9671). [650] **2851**

NEW MEXICO JOURNAL OF SCIENCE (US/0270-3017). [400] **5132**

NEW MEXICO LABOR MARKET REVIEW (US). **1694**

NEW MEXICO LIBRARY DIRECTORY (US). **3234**

NEW MEXICO MUSICIAN, THE (US/0742-8278). [1,600] **4140**

NEW MEXICO NURSE (US/0028-6273). [675] **3862**

NEW MEXICO PROFESSIONAL ENGINEER (1977) (US/0149-1954). [800] **1988**

NEW MEXICO STATISTICAL ABSTRACT (US/0077-8575). [450] **1536**

NEW MEXICO WILDLIFE (US/0028-6338). [8,500] **2200**

NEW MYTHS (US/1055-9868). **3416**

NEW ON THE CHARTS (US/0276-7031). [6,000] **4140**

NEW ORDER (LINCOLN, NEB.), THE (US/0740-3283). **4544**

NEW ORLEANS GENESIS, THE (US/0548-6424). [400] **2462**

NEW ORLEANS MUSIC (UK/0308-1990). [1,500] **4140**

NEW PACIFIC (SEATTLE, WASH.), THE (US/1050-3080). [25,000] **2540**

NEW PERSPECTIVES ON TURKEY (TU/0896-6346). [200] **5210**

NEW PERSPECTIVES QUARTERLY (US/0893-7850). [20,000] **4484**

NEW PHYSICIAN (US/0028-6451). [40,000] **3620**

NEW POET'S HANDBOOK / THE LEAGUE OF CANADIAN POETS (CN/0827-2425). [3,000] **3466**

NEW PRODUCTS REVIEW (UK). [10,000] **405**

NEW PUBLICATIONS (UNITED STATES. BUREAU OF MINES) (US/0364-1376). [10,000] **2147**

NEW QUEST (II/0258-0381). [700] **5252**

NEW SCHOLAR, THE (US/0028-6613). [1,100] **5210**

NEW SCHOOL OBSERVER, THE (US/0883-6248). **1093**

NEW SOUTH WALES INDUSTRIAL GAZETTE (AT/0028-677X). **3152**

NEW STUDIES IN ATHLETICS (UK/0961-933X). [2,600] **4907**

NEW TECHNOLOGY, WORK, AND EMPLOYMENT (UK/0268-1072). **1694**

NEW TIMES (MOBILE, ALA.), THE (US/0885-1662). [21,500] **5627**

NEW TIMES (PHOENIX, ARIZ.) (US/0279-3962). [135,000] **5630**

NEW TIMES (SEATTLE, WASH.) (US/1044-2782). [17,000] **4186**

NEW TITLES IN BIOETHICS (US/0361-6347). [1,200] **3620**

NEW TRAIL (1982) (CN/0824-8125). [76,000] **1102**

NEW TREND (BALTIMORE, MD.) (US/0732-1848). [5,000] **4530**

NEW TRENDS IN LIPID MEDIATORS RESEARCH (SZ/1011-6672). **467**

NEW USES FOR SULPHUR TECHNOLOGY SERIES (CN/0225-2643). **1027**

NEW WORLD (1989), THE (US/1043-3538). [32,500] **5033**

NEW YORK AFRICAN STUDIES ASSOCIATION NEWSLETTER (US/0148-7264). [290] **2642**

NEW YORK APPAREL NEWS (US/0279-7844). [7,000] **1086**

NEW YORK BAPTIST, THE (US/0893-9063). [2,600] **4981**

NEW YORK BUSINESS ENVIRONMENT (US/1065-1888). **3115**

NEW YORK CITY SUBWAY GUIDE (US). **5485**

NEW YORK CONSTRUCTION NEWS (US/0028-7164). [6,200] **622**

NEW YORK DOCTOR, THE (US/0898-6401). **3620**

NEW YORK FAMILY LAW UPDATE (US/1049-6319). [250] **3122**

NEW YORK INTERNATIONAL LAW REVIEW (US/1050-9453). [2,000] **3133**

NEW YORK JEWISH WEEK, THE (US/0745-5356). [109,000] **2269**

NEW YORK LAND REPORT : A PROJECT OF THE NEW YORK LAND INSTITUTE (US). [100] **3115**

NEW YORK LITERARY FORUM (US/0149-1040). [3,000] **3416**

NEW YORK METS INSIDE PITCH (US/0887-5863). [11,000] **4907**

NEW YORK NATIVE (US/0744-060X). [12,000] **2795**

NEW YORK NO-FAULT ARBITRATION REPORTS (US/0193-7693). [650] **3016**

NEW YORK OPERA NEWSLETTER, THE (US/1043-2361). **386**

NEW YORK PEDIATRICIAN (US/0737-4216). [3,000] **3906**

NEW YORK REAL ESTATE JOURNAL (US/1057-2104). [7,000] **4842**

NEW YORK RUNNING NEWS (US/0161-7338). [35,000] **4907**

NEW YORK SCHOOL DISTRICT LAW LETTER, THE (US/0545-6339). [1,000] **3016**

NEW YORK STATE BAR JOURNAL (US/0028-7547). [48,000] **3016**

NEW YORK STATE DENTAL JOURNAL (US/0028-7571). [15,000] **1330**

NEW YORK STATE GFOA NEWSLETTER (US/1064-0762). [3,000] **801**

NEW YORK STATE JOURNAL OF MEDICINE (US/0028-7628). [28,000] **3621**

NEW YORK STATE JOURNAL OF PHARMACY, THE (US/0279-8778). [2,000] **4318**

NEW YORK STATE LAW DIGEST (US/0028-7636). [44,000] **3016**

NEW YORK STYLE & DESIGN (US). [25,000] **2540**

NEW YORK TIMES BIOGRAPHICAL SERVICE, THE (US/0161-2433). **434**

NEW YORK UNIVERSITY LAW REVIEW (1950) (US/0028-7881). [3,000] **3016**

NEW YOUTH CONNECTIONS (US/0737-285X). [79,000] **1067**

NEW ZEALAND AGRICULTURAL SCIENCE (NZ/0549-0146). [1,400] **112**

NEW ZEALAND DENTAL JOURNAL (NZ/0028-8047). [1,500] **1330**

NEW ZEALAND DISABLED (NZ). [1,800] **4391**

NEW ZEALAND ECONOMIC PAPERS (NZ/0077-9954). [700] **1507**

NEW ZEALAND ENGINEERING (NZ/0028-808X). [6,139] **1988**

NEW ZEALAND FAMILY PHYSICIAN, THE (NZ/0110-022X). [3,150] **3738**

NEW ZEALAND FORESTRY (NZ/0112-9597). [1,350] **2389**

NEW ZEALAND GEOGRAPHER (NZ/0028-8144). [1,200] **2570**

NEW ZEALAND GEOLOGICAL SURVEY PALEONTOLOGICAL BULLETIN (NZ). [400] **1389**

NEW ZEALAND HISTORIC PLACES (NZ). [19,000] **2670**

NEW ZEALAND HOME AND BUILDING (NZ/0110-098X). **2902**

NEW ZEALAND INTERNATIONAL REVIEW (NZ/0110-0262). [1,500] **4530**

NEW ZEALAND JOURNAL OF AGRICULTURAL RESEARCH (NZ/0028-8233). [1,300] **112**

NEW ZEALAND JOURNAL OF BOTANY (NZ/0028-825X). [800] **519**

NEW ZEALAND JOURNAL OF ENVIRONMENTAL HEALTH (NZ/0112-0212). [350] **4793**

NEW ZEALAND JOURNAL OF GEOGRAPHY (NZ/0028-8292). [1,500] **2570**

NEW ZEALAND JOURNAL OF GEOLOGY AND GEOPHYSICS (NZ/0028-8306). [1,080] **1389**

NEW ZEALAND JOURNAL OF MARINE AND FRESHWATER RESEARCH (NZ/0028-8330). [750] **556**

NEW ZEALAND JOURNAL OF MEDICAL LABORATORY SCIENCE (NZ/1171-0195). [1,500] **3621**

NEW ZEALAND JOURNAL OF PHYSIOTHERAPY (NZ/0303-7193). [1,500] **4381**

NEW ZEALAND JOURNAL OF SPORTS MEDICINE, THE (NZ/0110-6384). [1,300] **3955**

NEW ZEALAND JOURNAL OF ZOOLOGY (NZ/0301-4223). [800] **5592**

NEW ZEALAND LIBRARIES (NZ/0028-8381). [2,000] **3234**

NEW ZEALAND LOCAL GOVERNMENT (NZ). [2,500] **4669**

NEW ZEALAND MATHEMATICS MAGAZINE, THE (NZ/0549-0510). [750] **3524**

NEW ZEALAND MEAT PRODUCER : OFFICIAL JOURNAL OF THE NEW ZEALAND MEAT PRODUCERS, THE (NZ). [13,500] **2351**

NEW ZEALAND MEDICAL WORKFORCE STATISTICS ... (US/0112-8868). [400] **3661**

NEW ZEALAND NURSING FORUM (NZ/0110-7968). [12,500] **3862**

NEW ZEALAND NURSING JOURNAL, THE (NZ/0028-8535). [22,300] **3862**

NEW ZEALAND POPULATION REVIEW (NZ/0111-199X). [250] **4555**

NEW ZEALAND PRINTER MAGAZINE (NZ/1171-0829). [3,600] **4567**

NEW ZEALAND RECENT LAW REVIEW (NZ/0114-0655). [900] **3016**

NEW ZEALAND SCIENCE REVIEW (NZ/0028-8667). [400] **5133**

NEW ZEALAND SHIPPING GAZETTE CHRISTCHURCH (NZ/0027-724X). **5453**

NEW ZEALAND SLAVONIC JOURNAL (NZ). [150] **2851**

NEW ZEALAND VETERINARY JOURNAL (NZ/0048-0169). [1,800] **5517**

NEW ZEALAND VISITOR STATISTICS. ASIA (NZ). [100] **5334**

NEW ZEALAND VISITOR STATISTICS. AUSTRALIA AND PACIFIC (NZ). [100] **5334**

NEW ZEALAND VISITOR STATISTICS. EUROPE (NZ). [100] **5334**

NEW ZEALAND VISITOR STATISTICS. TOTAL VISITORS (NZ). [100] **5334**

NEW ZEALAND WINGS (NZ/0110-1471). [20,000] **30**

NEW ZEALAND WOOL MARKET REVIEW (NZ/0113-2792). **5354**

NEWBERRY NEWSLETTER, A (US/1074-3596). [5,500] **3234**

NEWFOUNDLAND ANCESTOR (CN/0838-049X). [1,100] **2462**

NEWFOUNDLAND & LABRADOR BUSINESS JOURNAL (CN). [18,000] **699**

NEWFOUNDLAND GAZETTE, THE (CN/0028-8888). [1,300] **3017**

NEWFOUNDLAND HERALD, THE (CN/0824-3581). [45,000] **2490**

NEWFOUNDLAND JOURNAL OF GEOLOGICAL EDUCATION, THE (CN/0709-4426). **1389**

NEWFOUNDLAND LIFESTYLE (CN/0827-3960). [17,500] **2748**

NEWINGTON TOWN CRIER (US/0745-0796). [4,700] **5646**

NEWPORT HISTORY (US/0028-8918). [1,500] **2749**

NEWPORT MINER, THE (US/0892-6239). [6,000] **5761**

NEWS - ADMINISTRATIVE CONFERENCE OF THE UNITED STATES (US/0197-2316). [6,000] **4669**

NEWS ADVERTISER (AJAX CANADA) (CN). [35,000] **5790**

NEWS AND JOURNAL (RIPLEY, MISS.) (US/8755-9854). [200] **2462**

NEWS & LETTERS (US/0028-8969). [7,000] **1508**

NEWS AND ROUND TABLE (US). [1,200] **5298**

NEWS - ASSOCIATION OF COLLEGIATE SCHOOLS OF ARCHITECTURE (US/0149-2446). [4,000] **304**

NEWS / BECKMAN CENTER FOR THE HISTORY OF CHEMISTRY (US/1052-0414). [12,000] **987**

NEWS / BRITISH COLUMBIA MEDICAL ASSOCIATION (CN/0715-5379). [6,200] **3621**

NEWS BULLETIN - ARKANSAS BAR ASSOCIATION (US/0198-702X). [3,400] **3017**

NEWS BULLETIN (AUSTIN, TEX.) (US/0096-9117). [1,500] **4228**

NEWS BULLETIN - BRAZILIAN-AMERICAN CHAMBER OF COMMERCE (US/0300-7464). [600] **1638**

NEWS BULLETIN / FLORIDA COLLEGE (US/8750-751X). [21,000] **1093**

NEWS BULLETIN / MICHIGAN BUSINESS EDUCATION ASSOCIATION (US/0026-2048). [1,500] **699**

NEWS BULLETIN / NATIONAL COUNCIL OF TEACHERS OF MATHEMATICS (US/0277-1365). [77,000] **3524**

NEWS BULLETIN OF THE AUSTRALIAN DENTAL ASSOCIATION (AT/0810-7440). [7,050] **1331**

NEWS BULLETIN - SASKATCHEWAN RAIL COMMITTEE (CN/0708-028X). **5433**

NEWS (CALIFORNIA ASSOCIATION OF COMMUNITY COLLEGES) (US). [42,000] **1837**

NEWS-CITIZEN (VANDERGRIFT, PA.) (US). [6,000] **5738**

NEWS-COMMERCIAL, THE (US). [3,142 paid] **5701**

NEWS - FLORIDA ASSOCIATION OF SOIL AND WATER CONSERVATION DISTRICT SUPERVISORS (US/0744-3366). [1,000] **2200**

NEWS FOR INVESTORS (US/1053-5470). [1,000] **909**

NEWS FOR SOUTH CAROLINA LIBRARIES (US/0146-1842). **3234**

NEWS FROM WITHIN (IS). [1,000] **2770**

NEWS-GRAM - CHRISTIAN BUSINESS MEN OF CANADA (CN/0710-5770). [900] **4981**

NEWS - HOSPITAL ASSOCIATION OF NEW YORK STATE (US/0018-5574). [2,000] **3790**

NEWS - INTERNATIONAL ASSOCIATION OF PERSONNEL IN EMPLOYMENT SECURITY (US/0020-6008). [25,000] **1694**

NEWS JOURNAL (MANSFIELD, OHIO) (US). [50,000] **5729**

NEWS LETTER - BAR ASSOCIATION OF SRI LANKA (CE). [2,500] **3017**

NEWS LETTER - CUMBRIA FAMILY HISTORY SOCIETY (UK/0140-1912). **2462**

NEWS LETTER FROM THE INSTITUTE OF EARLY AMERICAN HISTORY & CULTURE, A (US/0020-2843). [2,100] **2749**

NEWS LETTER / MATHEMATICAL ASSOCIATION (UK/0465-3696). [7,000] **3524**

NEWS LETTER - MCGILL UNIVERSITY COMPUTING CENTRE (CN/0380-478X). [3,100] **1197**

NEWS LETTER / MONTANA GEOLOGICAL SOCIETY (US). [400] **1389**

NEWS-LETTER OF THE AMERICAN ANTIQUARIAN SOCIETY (US/0569-2229). [1,649] **4831**

NEWS LETTER OF THE ST. ANDREW'S SOCIETY OF TORONTO (CN/0822-2401). **5234**

NEWS LETTER / POPULATION CENTRE BANGALORE (II). [800] **590**

NEWS 'N' NOTES - INDUSTRIAL EDUCATION COUNCIL OF THE ALBERTA TEACHERS' ASSOCIATION (CN/0709-0528). [600] **1867**

NEWS (NATIONAL LIBRARY OF MEDICINE (US)) (US/0027-965X). [6,000] **3234**

NEWS NOTES - MARYKNOLL JUSTICE AND PEACE OFFICE (US/1064-1556). [1,500] **4530**

NEWS OF NEW YORK (US/0028-9264). [30,000] **3621**

NEWS OF NORWAY (US/0028-9272). [14,000] **2700**

NEWS OF ORANGE COUNTY, THE (US/1071-1716). **5724**

NEWS - OREGON HISTORICAL SOCIETY (US/0474-4535). [9,000] **2749**

NEWS PHOTOGRAPHER (US/0199-2422). [12,000] **4372**

NEWS

NEWS REPORTER, THE (US). [10,152] **5724**

NEWS SPREADER, THE (CN/0229-7728). **112**

NEWS / THEATRE ONTARIO (CN/0821-4476). [2,500] **5366**

NEWS TIMES (NEWPORT, OR.) (US/0888-2010). [10,500] **5733**

NEWSART (TORONTO) (CN/0703-8704). **360**

NEWSBEAT (AT/030-794X). [20,000] **5298**

NEWSBOY (US/0028-9396). [300] **3416**

NEWSBREAK (AT). [2,000] **3170**

NEWSCURRENTS (MADISON, WIS.) (US/8756-3940). [8,000 schools] **5211**

NEWSDATA (AT). [150] **2309**

NEWSFLASH / NEW BRUNSWICK TEACHERS' ASSOCIATION (CN/0715-5484). [7,000] **1768**

NEWSLEAF - ONTARIO GENEALOGICAL SOCIETY (CN/0380-1616). [5,000] **2462**

NEWSLETTER (CN/0705-0216). [600] **2200**

NEWSLETTER - AFRICAN-AMERICAN FAMILY HISTORY ASSOCIATION (US/0893-4290). [500] **2463**

NEWSLETTER / ALBERTA HERITAGE FOUNDATION FOR MEDICAL RESEARCH (CN/0715-2396). [3,500] **3621**

NEWSLETTER - ALBERTA TEACHERS' ASSOCIATION (CN/0316-599X). [800] **1867**

NEWSLETTER / AMERICAN AEROBICS ASSOCIATION (US/8755-8742). [3,000] **2600**

NEWSLETTER / AMERICAN ASSOCIATION OF PASTORAL COUNSELORS (US/1065-383X). [3,200] **4981**

NEWSLETTER - AMERICAN ASSOCIATION OF TISSUE BANKS (US/0270-2673). [700] **3621**

NEWSLETTER - AMERICAN HISTORICAL SOCIETY OF GERMANS FROM RUSSIA (US). [5,100] **2463**

NEWSLETTER. AMERICAN RECORDER SOCIETY (US). [4,000] **4140**

NEWSLETTER - AMERICAN RESEARCH CENTER IN EGYPT (US/0402-0731). [950] **276**

NEWSLETTER - AMERICAN SCHOOLS OF ORIENTAL RESEARCH (US/0361-6029). [2,000] **1768**

NEWSLETTER - AMERICAN SHORE AND BEACH PRESERVATION ASSOCIATION (US/0517-4856). [4,000] **2200**

NEWSLETTER / AMERICAN SOCIETY OF INDEXERS (US/0733-3048). [700] **3234**

NEWSLETTER - APPALACHIAN CENTER, BEREA COLLEGE (US). **1093**

NEWSLETTER / APPLIED SCIENCE TECHNOLOGISTS AND TECHNICIANS OF BRITISH COLUMBIA (CN/0834-1788). [7,500] **5133**

NEWSLETTER - ASSOCIATION FOR CHINESE MUSIC RESEARCH (US/1071-0639). [150] **4140**

NEWSLETTER - ASSOCIATION FOR WOMEN IN MATHEMATICS (US). [2,000] **5562**

NEWSLETTER - AUSTRALIAN AND NEW ZEALAND SOCIETY OF NUCLEAR MEDICINE (AT/0159-8376). [850] **3848**

NEWSLETTER / AUSTRALIAN MAP CIRCLE (AT/0811-9511). [200] **2570**

Controlled Circulation Index

NEWSLETTER - BRITISH COLUMBIA COUNCIL FOR THE FAMILY (CN/0706-9022). [6,000] **2284**

NEWSLETTER / BRITISH COLUMBIA GENEALOGICAL SOCIETY (CN/0229-527X). [1,100] **2463**

NEWSLETTER / CALIFORNIA COUNCIL FOR INTERNATIONAL TRADE (US/0738-9485). **847**

NEWSLETTER - CANADA JAPAN TRADE COUNCIL (CN/0045-4214). [3,400] **1638**

NEWSLETTER / CANADIAN ASSOCIATION OF MUSIC LIBRARIES (CN/0383-1299). [150] **3235**

NEWSLETTER / CANADIAN ASSOCIATION OF RHODES SCHOLARS (CN/0821-039X). [530] **1837**

NEWSLETTER - CANADIAN ASSOCIATION OF SLAVISTS (CN/0381-6133). [380] **2520**

NEWSLETTER - CANADIAN ASSOCIATION ON GERONTOLOGY (CN/0712-676X). [1,500] **5180**

NEWSLETTER (CANADIAN BOOKBINDERS AND BOOK ARTISTS GUILD) (CN/0822-9538). [540] **4831**

NEWSLETTER - CANADIAN GEOTHERMAL RESOURCES ASSOCIATION (CN/0705-1891). **1389**

NEWSLETTER - CANADIAN INSTITUTE OF UKRAINIAN STUDIES (CN/0702-8474). [4,000] **2700**

NEWSLETTER (CANADIAN MAGAZINE PUBLISHERS ASSOCIATION) (CN/1184-7379). [500] **4817**

NEWSLETTER - CANADIAN MEDICAL AND BIOLOGICAL ENGINEERING SOCIETY (CN/0384-1820). **3695**

NEWSLETTER / CANADIAN OWNERS & PILOTS ASSOCIATION (CN/0826-1997). [20,000] **30**

NEWSLETTER - CANADIAN PHYSIOTHERAPY ASSOCIATION. SPORTS PHYSIOTHERAPY DIVISION (CN/0824-2917). [1,300] **3955**

NEWSLETTER - CANADIAN SCIENCE WRITER'S ASSOCIATION (CN/0703-217X). **2922**

NEWSLETTER - CANADIAN SOCIETY OF ENVIRONMENTAL BIOLOGISTS (CN/0318-5133). [500] **2200**

NEWSLETTER - CENTER FOR HOLOCAUST STUDIES (BROOKLYN, NEW YORK, N.Y.) (US/0737-8092). [3,000] **2700**

NEWSLETTER - CENTER FOR MIGRATION STUDIES (U.S.) (US/8756-4467). [1,750] **1920**

NEWSLETTER / CENTRE FOR EDITING EARLY CANADIAN TEXTS (CN/0713-3960). [300] **3417**

NEWSLETTER - CHANGE (CN/0821-6657). [5,000] **3235**

NEWSLETTER (CHINESE AMERICAN LIBRARIANS ASSOCIATION) (US/0736-8887). [500] **3235**

NEWSLETTER / CLERMONT COUNTY GENEALOGICAL SOCIETY (US/0749-0631). [600] **2463**

NEWSLETTER - COACH HOUSE PRESS (CN/0827-3146). **2922**

NEWSLETTER - COLCHESTER HISTORICAL SOCIETY (CN/0821-2430). [250] **2749**

NEWSLETTER - COLUMBIA UNIVERSITY. CENTER FOR SOCIAL POLICY AND PRACTICE IN THE WORKPLACE (US/0892-631X). [2,500] **1695**

NEWSLETTER (COMMONWEALTH SCIENCE COUNCIL (GREAT BRITAIN). EARTH SCIENCES PROGRAMME) (UK/0588-7739). [600] **1358**

NEWSLETTER / CONFERENCE GROUP ON ITALIAN POLITICS & SOCIETY (US/0896-9825). **4530**

NEWSLETTER / COUNCIL OF NOVA SCOTIA ARCHIVES (CN/0829-7142). [200] **2482**

NEWSLETTER (CRIMINAL LAWYERS' ASSOCIATION (TORONTO, ONT.)) (CN/0715-5980). **3108**

NEWSLETTER - CROSS-CULTURAL COMMUNICATION CENTRE (CN/0828-6965). [300] **2269**

NEWSLETTER - DANISH CENTRE FOR TECHNICAL AIDS FOR REHABILITATION AND EDUCATION (DK). [600] **1882**

NEWSLETTER / DUBUQUE COUNTY-KEY CITY GENEALOGICAL SOCIETY (US/1072-0359). [250] **2463**

NEWSLETTER / EXECUTIVE COMMITTEE, LEAGUE OF CANADIAN POETS (CN/0319-6658). [400] **3467**

NEWSLETTER - FAIRFAX GENEALOGICAL SOCIETY (FAIRFAX COUNTY, VA.) (US/0895-2078). [350] **2463**

NEWSLETTER / FEDERATION OF CATHOLIC PARENT-TEACHER ASSOCIATIONS OF ONTARIO (CN/0227-6291). [55,000] **1768**

NEWSLETTER FROM DICK B. ON THE SPIRITUAL ROOTS OF ALCOHOLICS ANONYMOUS, A (US/1068-302X). [500] **4981**

NEWSLETTER FROM THE COMMISSION FOR SCIENTIFIC RESEARCH IN GREENLAND (DK/0106-1372). [2,000] **5133**

NEWSLETTER - FRONTENAC HISTORIC FOUNDATION (CN/0381-0119). [250] **304**

NEWSLETTER - GLASGOW & WEST OF SCOTLAND FAMILY HISTORY SOCIETY (UK/0141-8009). [1,000] **2463**

NEWSLETTER, GRAVURE ENVIRONMENTAL (US/0271-1699). [2,000] **4567**

NEWSLETTER - GUIDANCE AND COUNSELLING ASSOCIATION (CN/0315-2995). [250] **1882**

NEWSLETTER - HERITAGE ST. CATHARINES (CN/0821-0373). **2749**

NEWSLETTER (HISTORICAL SOCIETY OF OTTAWA) (CN/0711-3803). [400] **2749**

NEWSLETTER / INDIANA COVERED BRIDGE SOCIETY (US). **2749**

NEWSLETTER / INNISFIL HISTORICAL SOCIETY (CN/0713-8806). [125] **2749**

NEWSLETTER - INTERNATIONAL UNIVERSITY (INDEPENDENCE, MO.) (US/0748-9684). **1837**

NEWSLETTER - IOWA ARCHEOLOGICAL SOCIETY (US/0578-655X). [500] **276**

NEWSLETTER / JOHNSTON COUNTY GENEALOGICAL SOCIETY (US/0737-4321). [250] **2463**

NEWSLETTER - KANSAS ANTHROPOLOGICAL ASSOCIATION (1989) (US/1069-0360). [450] **242**

NEWSLETTER / KENT ARCHAEOLOGICAL SOCIETY (UK). [1,250] **276**

NEWSLETTER - KITCHENER WATERLOO REGIONAL FOLK ARTS MULTICULTURAL CENTRE (CN/0713-6285). **2749**

NEWSLETTER - LEAGUE OF OREGON CITIES (1980) (US/0731-1435). [2,500] **4669**

NEWSLETTER - LEARNING RESOURCES COUNCIL OF THE ALBERTA TEACHERS' ASSOCIATION (CN/0380-8491). **1867**

NEWSLETTER - LITTLE BIG HORN ASSOCIATES (US/0459-5866). [1100] **2749**

NEWSLETTER / LONDON AND MIDDLESEX COUNTY HISTORICAL SOCIETY (CN/0824-5614). [200] **2749**

NEWSLETTER - LONG POINT BIRD OBSERVATORY (CN/0317-9575). [800] **5618**

NEWSLETTER / MAINE HISTORICAL SOCIETY (US/0882-4223). [2,500] **2749**

NEWSLETTER - MANITOBA ASSOCIATION OF SCHOOL TRUSTEES (CN/0024-7928). [1,200] **1867**

NEWSLETTER / MANITOBA LIBRARY TRUSTEES ASSOCIATION (CN/0823-1184). [40] **3235**

NEWSLETTER - MANITOBA UNDERWATER COUNCIL (CN/0383-7742). [500] **4908**

NEWSLETTER (MARIGOLD LIBRARY SYSTEM) (CN/0713-2727). **3235**

NEWSLETTER (MATHEMATICAL ASSOCIATION) (UK). [6,000] **3524**

NEWSLETTER / MCGILL UNIVERSITY GRADUATE SCHOOL OF LIBRARY AND INFORMATION STUDIES (CN/0843-0217). [1,800] **1837**

NEWSLETTER / MONMOUTH COUNTY HISTORICAL ASSOCIATION (US/0740-8781). [1,300] **2750**

NEWSLETTER / MUSICOLOGICAL SOCIETY OF AUSTRALIA (AT/0155-0543). [350] **4141**

NEWSLETTER / NATIONAL CARTOGRAPHIC INFORMATION CENTER (US/0364-7064). [5,000] **2582**

NEWSLETTER - NATIONAL COUNCIL FOR THERAPY AND REHABILITATION THROUGH HORTICULTURE (U.S.) (US/0739-1609). [1,000] **2425**

NEWSLETTER / NATIONAL WEATHER ASSOCIATION (US/0271-1044). [2,000] **1432**

NEWSLETTER - NEW YORK BOTANICAL GARDEN (US/0550-6565). [11,000] **519**

NEWSLETTER - NEW ZEALAND. NATURE CONSERVATION COUNCIL (NZ/0111-686X). [2,500] **2200**

NEWSLETTER NEWSLETTER, THE (US/0885-6966). [25,000] **2922**

NEWSLETTER / NORTH AMERICAN SOCIETY OF OCEANIC HISTORY (US/1065-2329). [250] **4181**

NEWSLETTER - NOVA SCOTIA BIRD SOCIETY (CN/0383-9567). [800] **5592**

NEWSLETTER / NOVA SCOTIA LIBRARY ASSOCIATION (CN/1182-0209). [100] **3235**

NEWSLETTER OF THE AMERICAN COMMITTEE TO ADVANCE THE STUDY OF PETROGLYPHS AND PICTOGRAPHS (US/0278-2871). [500] **242**

NEWSLETTER OF THE SOUTHWEST VIRGINIA COPENHAVER FAMILY (US/0883-2099). [650] **2463**

NEWSLETTER OF THE TEXTILE MUSEUM ASSOCIATION OF SOUTHERN CALIFORNIA (US). **5354**

NEWSLETTER OF THE TILES AND ARCHITECTURAL CERAMICS SOCIETY (UK). [400] **304**

NEWSLETTER OF THE YELLOWHEAD REGIONAL LIBRARY (CN/0708-1979). [300] **3235**

NEWSLETTER ON NEWSLETTERS, THE (US/0028-9507). **2922**

NEWSLETTER / ONTARIO ASSOCIATION OF LIBRARY TECHNICIANS (CN/0229-2645). [500] **3236**

NEWSLETTER / ONTARIO FORESTRY ASSOCIATION (CN/0834-2008). [700] **2389**

NEWSLETTER - ONTARIO MINISTRY OF AGRICULTURE AND FOOD (CN/0228-202X). **112**

NEWSLETTER - PENNSYLVANIA ACADEMY OF SCIENCE (US/0160-4228). [800] **5133**

NEWSLETTER (PRESIDENT'S COUNCIL ON PHYSICAL FITNESS AND SPORTS (U.S.)) (US/0364-8079). [9,000] **2600**

NEWSLETTER / PRINCE EDWARD ISLAND MUSEUM AND HERITAGE FOUNDATION (CN/0823-8324). [1,200] **4094**

NEWSLETTER / SCARBOROUGH HISTORICAL SOCIETY (CN/0822-8353). [350] **5234**

NEWSLETTER / SOCIETY FOR ARMENIAN STUDIES (US/0740-5510). [500] **2660**

NEWSLETTER / SOCIETY OF THE SEVEN SAGES (CN/0701-9890). [150] **3417**

NEWSLETTER - SOUTHEASTERN WISCONSIN REGIONAL PLANNING COMMISSION (US/0584-4266). [2,000] **2829**

NEWSLETTER - SPECIAL EDUCATION COUNCIL OF THE ALBERTA TEACHERS' ASSOCIATION (CN/0315-3509). **1882**

NEWSLETTER - STUDY GROUP ON EIGHTEENTH-CENTURY RUSSIA (UK/0306-8455). [200] **2700**

NEWSLETTER / SUFFOLK COUNTY ARCHAEOLOGICAL ASSOCIATION (US). [300] **276**

NEWSLETTER - TENNESSEE ANTHROPOLOGICAL ASSOCIATION (US/0196-0377). [300] **242**

NEWSLETTER / THE AUSTRALIAN FEDERATION FOR THE WELFARE OF ANIMALS (AT). [200] **5517**

NEWSLETTER / THE CALGARY INSTITUTE FOR THE HUMANITIES (CN/0715-433X). **2851**

NEWSLETTER - THE INNUIT GALLERY OF ESKIMO ART (CN/0228-3484). **360**

NEWSLETTER TO MEMBERS OF THE TEXAS BAPTIST HISTORICAL SOCIETY (US). [250] **2624**

NEWSLETTER (UNITED STATES BOARD ON BOOKS FOR YOUNG PEOPLE) (US). **4831**

NEWSLETTER - UNIVERSITY OF ALBERTA, WESTERN CANADIANA PUBLICATIONS PROJECT (CN/0704-7495). **421**

NEWSLETTER (UNIVERSITY OF TORONTO. FACULTY OF SOCIAL WORK. ALUMNI ASSOCIATION) (CN/0711-723X). **5252**

NEWSLETTER - VANCOUVER HISTORICAL SOCIETY (1980) (CN/0823-0161). [250] **2750**

NEWSLETTER - VISUAL ARTS & CRAFTS COMMUNICATION COUNCIL OF ALBERTA (CN/0704-0296). **374**

NEWSLETTER / W.H. AUDEN SOCIETY (UK). [200] **3467**

NEWSLETTER - WATERLOO POTTERS' WORKSHOP (CN/0708-1952). **374**

NEWSLETTER / WEST COAST ENVIRONMENTAL LAW RESEARCH FOUNDATION (CN/0715-4275). [1,200] **3115**

NEWSLETTER - WESTMORLAND HISTORICAL SOCIETY (CN/0382-0831). [225] **2750**

NEWSLETTER-WRITERS GUILD OF AMERICA, WEST (US/0043-9533). [10,000] **3417**

NEWSLETTER (YORK UNIVERSITY (TORONTO, ONT.). INSTITUTE FOR SOCIAL RESEARCH) (CN/0834-1729). [1,000] **5211**

NEWSLINE (US). [2,000] **2750**

NEWSLINE - MANITOBA LIBRARY ASSOCIATION (CN/0227-6569). [350] **3236**

NEWSLINE - TRAVEL INDUSTRY ASSOCIATION OF AMERICA (US/0749-985X). [3,200] **5486**

NEWSLINE - UNIVERSITY OF WINDSOR (CN/0709-4132). [2,000] **1837**

NEWSLINK (US). [1,300] **4606**

NEWSNET ACTION LETTER (US/0888-8698). **3236**

NEWSPACKET (ORILLIA) (CN/0384-1642). [3,000] **3417**

NEWSPAPER FINANCIAL EXECUTIVE JOURNAL (US/0889-4590). [1,500] **2922**

NEWSPAPER RATES AND DATA (US/0038-9544). [6,400] **763**

NEWSPAPER RESEARCH JOURNAL (US/0739-5329). [1,500] **4817**

NEWSPAPER TECHNIQUES (DARMSTADT, GERMANY) (GW). [4,880] **4817**

NEWSPAPERS & TECHNOLOGY (US/1052-5572). **5644**

NEWSTIME (LONDON, ENGLAND) (UK). [2,500] **4817**

NEWSWATCH (LAGOS) (NR/0189-8892). [100,000] **2499**

NEWSWEEK (U.S. ED.) (US/0028-9604). **2490**

NEWTON-EVANS RESEARCH COMPANY'S MARKET TRENDS DIGEST FOR THE COMPUTER, COMMUNICATIONS, AND CONTROLS INDUSTRIES (US/0891-1037). [1,250] **1197**

NEWTON KANSAN (NEWTON, KAN. : 1952) (US). [7,800] **5677**

NEXUS (HAMILTON, ONT.) (CN/0711-5342). [150] **242**

NFM-THEMAREEKS AMSTERDAM (NE/0926-3411). [1,500] **4075**

NG. NIEUWSBLAD GEZONDHEIDSZORG (NE/0922-744X). [13,000] **3621**

NGOMA (EDITION FRANCAISE) (CN/0712-2837). [9,000] **1883**

NGOMA (ENGLISH EDITION) (CN/0712-2829). [9,000] **1883**

NGOUI VIET DAILY NEWS. ENGLISH SECTION (US/1056-5124). **5637**

NHAC VIET (US/1063-1909). [500] **4141**

NHAN BAN (FR/0153-3762). **5801**

NHRC REPORT (US/0161-1607). [500] **3621**

NIAGARA BRUCE TRAIL CLUB (CN/0706-7429). [550] **4876**

NIAGARA FALLS REVIEW (CN/0839-1572). **5790**

NIAGARA - WHEATFIELD TRIBUNE (US). [16,500] **5719**

NICHE (BALTIMORE, MD.) (US/1064-0347). [20,000] **955**

NICHTKONVENTIONELLE LITERATUR LINGUISTIK : INHALTSVERZEICHNIS DER NEUERWERBUNGEN (GW). [400] **3336**

NIELSEN REPORT ON TELEVISION / NIELSEN MEDIA RESEARCH (US). [28,000] **1135**

NIEN GIAM VIET-NAM, MONTREAL (CN/0712-5054). [5,000] **2750**

NIEREN- UND HOCKDRUCKKRANKHEITEN (GW/0300-5224). **3622**

NIGERIAN CURRENT LAW REVIEW : THE JOURNAL OF THE NIGERIAN INSTITUTE OF ADVANCED LEGAL STUDIES (NR/0189-207X). [2,000] **3017**

NIGERIAN FIELD (UK/0029-0076). [1,000] **4169**

NIGERIAN JOURNAL OF ECONOMIC AND SOCIAL STUDIES, THE (NR/0029-0092). [1,000] **1508**

NIGERIAN LIBRARY AND INFORMATION SCIENCE REVIEW (NR/0189-4412). [1000] **3236**

NIGHTINGALE REPORT (CN). [1,000] **4075**

NIH RECORD, THE (US/1057-5871). **4794**

NIHON GAN CHIRYO GAKKAI SHI (JA/0021-4671). [6,800] **3821**

NIHON HAKUYO KIKAN GAKKAI SHI. JOURNAL OF THE MARINE ENGINEERING SOCIETY IN JAPAN (JA). [3,000] **1989**

NIHON KAGAKU RYOHO GAKKAI SOKAI SHOROKUSHU (JA). [4,500] **3622**

NIHON KANGO KYOKAI CHOSA KENKYU HOKOKU (JA/0911-0844). [1,500] **3862**

NIHON NO ROSHI KANKEI (JA). [1,000] **1695**

NIHON NO SHINGAKU / NIHON KIRISUTOKYO GAKKAI HEN (JA). [1,000] **4982**

NIHON OYO DOBUTSU KONCHU GAKKAISHI (JA/0021-4914). [2,300] **5612**

NIHON PURANKUTON GAKKAI HO (JA). [1,000] **556**

NIHON SAKUMOTSU GAKKAI KIJI (JA/0011-1848). [2,300] **179**

NIHON SEMPAKU MUSEN DENSHINKYOKU KYOKUMEIROKU (JA). [3,000] **1135**

NIHON SHOKUHIN KOGYO GAKKAI SHI (JA/0029-0394). [4,000] **2351**

NIHON SOCHI GAKKAI SHI (JA/0447-5933). **203**

NIHON SUISAN GAKKAI SHI (JA/0021-5392). [4,400] **2309**

NINA LYTTON'S OPEN SYSTEMS ADVISOR (US/1043-9854). **1238**

NINETEENTH CENTURY CONTEXTS (US/0890-5495). [500] **3417**

NINETEENTH-CENTURY LITERATURE (US/0891-9356). [2,400] **3417**

NINETEENTH CENTURY : THE MAGAZINE OF THE VICTORIAN SOCIETY IN AMERICA (US). **360**

NINETEENTH CENTURY THEATRE (US/0893-3766). [500] **5367**

NINTENDO POWER (US/1041-9551). [2,000,000] **4864**

NIP (CINCINNATI, OHIO. 1993) (US/1074-0791). **2491**

NIPPON GANKA GAKKAI ZASSHI (JA/0029-0203). [8,000] **3877**

NIPPON SHOKUBUTSU BYORI GAKKAI (JA/0031-9473). [2,400] **520**

NIRA NEWS (JA). [14,000] **5211**

NIRSA JOURNAL (US). [2,500] **4908**

NITTANY GROTTO NEWS (US/0732-5398). [130] **1358**

NIYOJANA (NP). [2,000] **590**

NJEA REVIEW (US/0027-6758). [120,000] **1769**

NLADA CORNERSTONE (US/0739-9111). **3180**

NLGI SPOKESMAN (US/0027-6782). [2,500] **2123**

NLRB ADVICE MEMORANDUM REPORTER (US/0194-8784). [270] **3152**

NN&Q. NEWS, NOTES, AND QUOTES (US/0028-923X). [130,000] **1769**

NO-DIG INTERNATIONAL (UK/0960-4405). [5,000] **2027**

NOEUD (CN/0227-0021). **5033**

NOGYO KEIEI KENKYU SEIKA SHUHO / NOGYO KEIEI KENKYU SEIKA KANKO IINKAI HEN (JA). [900] **113**

NOISE POLLUTION PUBLICATIONS ABSTRACTS (US/0733-172X). **2179**

NOLPE NOTES (US/0047-8997). [2,500] **3017**

NOMADIC PEOPLES (CN/0822-7942). [500] **2270**

NOME NUGGET (NOME, ALASKA : 1938) (US/0745-9106). [3,000] **5629**

NOMOS (FORTALEZA, BRAZIL) (BL). **3018**

NON-DESTRUCTIVE TESTING - AUSTRALIA (AT/0157-6461). [1,000] **1989**

NONPROFIT TIMES, THE (US/0896-5048). [40,000] **880**

NONVIOLENT ACTIVIST, THE (US/8755-7428). [20,000] **3133**

NONWOVENS INDUSTRY (US/0163-4429). [11,000] **1620**

NOR KIANK (US/0194-0074). [10,000] **5637**

NORD GENEALOGIE (FR). [1,200] **2464**

NORD (HEARST) (CN/0382-8883). [3,900] **5790**

NORD-OSTSEE-KANAL JAHRESBERICHT (GW). [1,000] **5453**

NORDEN (NEW YORK, N.Y.) (US/0895-2612). [900] **5719**

NORDIC HYDROLOGY (DK/0029-1277). [450] **1416**

NORDISK ADMINISTRATIVT TIDSSKRIFT (DK/0029-1285). [2,000] **4669**

NORDISK ALKOHOL TIDSKRIFT (FI/0782-9671). [2,000] **1347**

NORDISK JARNBANETIDSKRIFT (SW). [2,800] **5433**

NORDISK JUDAISTIK / SCANDINAVIAN JEWISH STUDIES (SW/0348-1646). **5051**

NORDISK PSYKOLOGI (DK/0029-1463). [3,600] **4606**

NORDISK ST-FORUM (NO/0801-7220). [800] **5211**

NORDISK TIDSKRIFT FOR DOVUNDERVISNINGEN (SW/0029-1471). [1,200] **1883**

NORDRHEIN-WESTFALEN. FINANZMINISTER. MITTEILUNGSBLATT (GW). [39,000] **4739**

NOR'EASTER (NARRAGANSETT) (US). [10,500] **467**

NORFOLK ANCESTOR : JOURNAL OF THE NORFOLK & NORWICH GENEALOGICAL SOCIETY, THE (UK/0140-5403). [2,000] **2464**

NORMATIVA TECNICA (IT). [15,000] **5134**

NORNA-RAPPORTER (SW/0346-6728). [300] **3306**

NORSEMAN (NO/0029-1846). [14,000] **2520**

NORSK ARTILLERI TIDSSKRIFT (NO). **4053**

NORSK GEOGRAFISK TIDSSKRIFT (NO/0029-1951). [800] **2571**

NORSK GEOLOGISK TIDSSKRIFT (NO/0029-196X). [1,500] **1390**

NORSK HAGETIDEND (NO/0029-1986). [58,751] **2426**

NORSK INSTITUTT FOR VANNFORSKNING (NO/0333-3280). [2,500] **5536**

NORSK

Controlled Circulation Index

NORSK LANDBRUK (NO). [25,500] **114**

NORSK MUSIKERBLAD (NO/0029-2044). [2,600] **4142**

NORSK OLJEREVY (NO/0332-5490). **4266**

NORSK PEDAGOGISK TIDSKRIFT (NO). [4,000] **1769**

NORSK SKOGBRUK (NO/0029-2087). [5,900] **2389**

NORSK STATSVITENSKAPELIG TIDSSKRIFT (NO/0801-1745). [800] **4484**

NORSK TIDENDE FOR DET INDUSTRIELLE RETTSVERN. DEL I : PATENTER (NO/0029-2206). **1306**

NORTH AMERICAN FISHERMAN (US/1043-2450). [470,000] **2309**

NORTH AMERICAN JOURNAL OF FISHERIES MANAGEMENT (US/0275-5947). [3,000] **2309**

NORTH BATTLEFORD NEWS OPTIMIST (CN). **5790**

NORTH CAROLINA ARCHITECTURE (US/1045-3253). [3,000] **305**

NORTH CAROLINA BEACON (US/1064-4830). [6,000] **5724**

NORTH CAROLINA COUNCIL OF WOMEN'S ORGANIZATIONS ANNUAL DIRECTORY (US). [1,000] **5234**

NORTH CAROLINA GENEALOGICAL SOCIETY JOURNAL, THE (US/0360-1056). [2,500] **2464**

NORTH CAROLINA HISTORICAL REVIEW, THE (US/0029-2494). [1,700] **2750**

NORTH CAROLINA INDEPENDENT, THE (US/0737-8254). **5724**

NORTH CAROLINA JOURNAL OF INTERNATIONAL LAW AND COMMERCIAL REGULATION (US/0743-1759). [900] **3133**

NORTH CAROLINA LAW MONITOR, THE (US/0883-7783). [1,000] **3018**

NORTH CAROLINA LAW REVIEW (US/0029-2524). [2,000] **3018**

NORTH CAROLINA LAWYERS WEEKLY (US/1041-1747). [4,000] **3018**

NORTH CAROLINA LIBRARIES (US/0029-2540). [2,800] **3237**

NORTH CAROLINA LITERARY REVIEW (US/1063-0724). [1,200] **3418**

NORTH CAROLINA MINORITY BUSINESS DIRECTORY (US/0148-0839). [500] **699**

NORTH CAROLINA RECREATIONAL AND PARK REVIEW (US/0164-4254). [2,000] **4853**

NORTH CAROLINA STATE BAR QUARTERLY (US/0164-6850). [11,000] **3018**

NORTH CENTRAL NORTH DAKOTA GENEALOGICAL RECORD (US/0736-5667). [135] **2464**

NORTH DAKOTA HISTORY (US/0029-2710). [1,600] **2750**

NORTH DAKOTA OUTDOORS (US/0029-2761). [23,000] **4876**

NORTH DAKOTA QUARTERLY, THE (US/0029-277X). [700] **2541**

NORTH DAKOTA R E C MAGAZINE (US). [73,000] **1542**

NORTH DAKOTA STATE PLAN FOR LIBRARY DEVELOPMENT (US/0160-0095). **3237**

NORTH EAST OUT DOORS (US/0199-8463). [27,500] **4876**

NORTH FRONTENAC NEWS (CN/0700-950X). [4,100 winter 4,500 summer] **5790**

NORTH IRISH ROOTS (UK/0264-9217). [1,000] **2464**

NORTH JERSEY PROSPECTOR, THE (US/0745-8908). [59,600] **5711**

NORTH KAWARTHA TIMES (CN/0823-7387). [2,000 7,500 (May-Sept.)] **5791**

NORTH KOREA QUARTERLY (GW/0340-014X). [300] **4484**

NORTH LOUISIANA GENEALOGICAL SOCIETY JOURNAL (US). [125] **2464**

NORTH QUEENSLAND NATURALIST (AT/0078-1630). [200] **4169**

NORTH SHORE NEWS (CN/0712-5348). **5791**

NORTH SHORE SENTINEL (CN/0715-5786). [3,500] **5791**

NORTH STAR BAPTIST (US/0744-0278). [1,100] **4982**

NORTH SUBURBAN PRESS (US/0892-1792). [52,000] **5697**

NORTH VERNON PLAIN DEALER, THE (US). [6,880] **5666**

NORTH VERNON SUN (US). [5,806] **5666**

NORTH WEST EUROPE SERVICE (UK). [400] **4266**

NORTH WOODS CALL, THE (US/0029-2958). [2,000] **4876**

NORTHAMPTONSHIRE PAST & PRESENT (UK). [2,000] **2700**

NORTHBOUND (EAGLE RIVER, WIS.) (US/1070-812X). [2,500] **2201**

NORTHEAST (US/0549-8880). **3418**

NORTHEAST AFRICAN STUDIES (US/0740-9133). [175] **2500**

NORTHEAST ALABAMA SETTLERS (US/0742-583X). [300] **2464**

NORTHEAST IMPROVER, THE (US/0145-9112). [18,500] **197**

NORTHEAST JOURNAL OF BUSINESS & ECONOMICS, THE (US/8755-5123). [2,100] **1508**

NORTHEAST MISSISSIPPI DAILY JOURNAL (US/0744-5431). [35,383] **5701**

NORTHEASTER (US). [30,000] **5697**

NORTHEASTERN GEOLOGY (US/0194-1453). [400] **1390**

NORTHERN CALIFORNIA MEDICINE (US). [25,000] **3623**

NORTHERN CATHOLIC HISTORY (UK/0307-4455). [400] **5033**

NORTHERN DECISIONS (CN/0715-7983). [175] **3115**

NORTHERN LIGHTS (CHELMSFORD) (CN/0822-0808). [2,000] **3467**

NORTHERN NECK OF VIRGINIA HISTORICAL MAGAZINE (US/0549-9186). [700] **2751**

NORTHERN NEW ENGLAND REVIEW (US/0190-3012). [600] **3418**

NORTHERN OHIO LIVE (US/0271-5147). [37,000] **2541**

NORTHERN ONTARIO BUSINESS (CN/0710-2755). [16,000] **700**

NORTHERN PEN (CN/0229-0391). [6,500] **5791**

NORTHERN PERSPECTIVE (AT/0314-989X). [500] **3418**

NORTHERN PERSPECTIVES (CN/0380-5522). [16,000] **2201**

NORTHERN SOCIAL SCIENCE REVIEW (US/0196-1063). [300] **5211**

NORTHERN WOMAN JOURNAL (CN/0824-4081). [200] **5563**

NORTHGLENN-THORNTON SENTINEL (US). [5,500] **5644**

NORTHLAND QUARTERLY, THE (US/0899-708X). [750] **3418**

NORTHLINE (CN/0714-475X). [3,000] **1838**

NORTHPOINT (CN/0380-0881). [1,000] **5134**

NORTHUMBERLAND NEWS (CN/0228-0531). [5,087] **5791**

NORTHWARD JOURNAL (CN/0706-0955). **360**

NORTHWEST BAPTIST WITNESS (US/0745-2195). [15,000] **5065**

NORTHWEST BOAT TRAVEL (US/0192-1169). [10,000] **594**

NORTHWEST CHESS (US/0146-6941). [600] **4864**

NORTHWEST EXPLORER (YELLOWKNIFE) (CN/0820-6724). [37,000] **2541**

NORTHWEST FARM EQUIPMENT JOURNAL (US/0029-3350). [2,800] **160**

NORTHWEST GEOLOGY (US/0096-7769). [250] **1390**

NORTHWEST GEORGIA HISTORICAL & GENEALOGICAL QUARTERLY (US/0887-588X). [300] **2464**

NORTHWEST HISTORICAL SERIES (US/0078-1789). [1,000] **2751**

NORTHWEST PARKS & WILDLIFE (US/1060-4812). [13,000] **4169**

NORTHWEST PUBLIC POWER BULLETIN (US/1055-6761). [3,700] **1951**

NORTHWEST SCIENCE (US/0029-344X). [1,200] **5134**

NORTHWESTERN JEWELER, THE (US/0029-3490). [3,500] **2915**

NORTHWESTERN NATURALIST : A JOURNAL OF VERTEBRATE BIOLOGY (US/1051-1733). [600] **4169**

NORTHWESTERNER (LARKSPUR, CALIF.) (US/0894-0800). [1,000] **5433**

NORWAY CURRENT, THE (US/1071-2607). [1,500] **5693**

NORWEGIAN TRACKS (US). [1,200] **1920**

NOS SOURCES (CN/0227-0404). [500] **2464**

NOTAS DE FISICA (BL). **4413**

NOTAS DE MATEMATICA DISCRETA (AG/0326-1336). [700] **3524**

NOTAS Y NOTICIAS LINGUISTICAS (BO). [200] **3306**

NOTE DI MATEMATICA (IT). [250] **3524**

NOTE D'INFORMATION / ASSOCIATION DES BIBLIOTHECAIRES FRANCAIS (FR/0180-4278). [2,000] **3237**

NOTE ECONOMICHE - MONTE DEI PASCHI DI SIENA (IT/0391-8289). [3,300] **1593**

NOTE TRIMESTRIELLE DE CONJONCTURE / STATEC, LUXEMBOURG (LU). **1508**

NOTEBOOK (WASHINGTON RESEARCH COUNCIL) (US). **4739**

NOTES AND QUERIES (UK/0029-3970). [1,300] **3306**

NOTES & QUERIES FOR SOMERSET AND DORSET (UK/0029-3989). [450] **2700**

NOTES BIBLIOGRAPHIQUES (FR/0468-8678). [3,800] **3418**

NOTES ET DOCUMENTS (INSTITUT INTERNATIONAL JACQUES MARITAIN) (IT). [3,000] **4354**

NOTES FROM NIAGARA (CN/0229-2750). [1,000] **2465**

NOTES ON AMERICA'S FOLK ART ENVIRONMENTS (US). [750] **360**

NOTES ON LINGUISTICS (US/0736-0673). [850] **3306**

NOTES ON SCRIPTURE IN USE (US/0737-2876). [700] **5018**

NOTES ON THE SCIENCE OF BUILDING (AT/0300-371X). [2,000] **623**

NOTES ON VIRGINIA (US/0163-1632). [7,000] **305**

NOTFALL-MEDIZIN (ERLANGEN) (GW/0341-2903). [40,000] **3725**

NOTICE TO IMPORTERS (CN/0225-414X). **848**

NOTICIAS ALIADAS (PE). [3,000] **2512**

NOTICIAS CULTURALES (CK/0020-370X). [3,000] **2851**

NOTICIAS DEL MUNDO (US/0888-143X). [32,000] **5719**

NOTICIAS - NATIONAL FOREIGN TRADE COUNCIL (US/0747-0878). [1,000] **848**

NOTICIERO DE LA AMBAC (MX). [1,000] **3237**

NOTIZIARIO DEL CENTRO DI DOCUMENTAZIONE (IT/0392-4270). [2,000] **421**

NOTIZIARIO STATISTICO - ANFIA (IT). [290] **5401**

NOTIZIARIO SULLE MALATTIE DELLE PIANTE (IT/0468-9291). [200] **520**

NOTIZIE DELLA SCUOLA (IT). **1867**

NOTRE DAME JOURNAL OF LAW, ETHICS & PUBLIC POLICY (US/0883-3648). [1,000] **3019**

NOTRE DAME LAW REVIEW, THE (US/0745-3515). [1,200] **3019**

NOTRE DAME MAGAZINE (US/0161-987X). [120,000] **1838**

NOTRE HOPITAL (CN/0704-8815). **3790**

NOTRE PAIN QUOTIDIEN (CAP-DE-LA-MADELEINE, QUEBEC) (CN/0820-7526). [16,500] **4982**

NOTULAE NATURAE OF THE ACADEMY NATURAL SCIENCES OF PHILADELPHIA (US/0029-4608). [300] **5134**

NOUS (FR). [14,000] **5253**

NOUS (BLOOMINGTON) (US/0029-4624). [1,100] **4354**

NOUS LES ENSEIGNANTS DE L'ONTARIO (CN/0225-1078). **1867**

NOUS VOULONS LIRE PESSAC (FR/0153-9027). **3349**

NOUVEAU CARABIN (CN/0704-0156). **1838**

NOUVEAU JOURNAL DE ST-MICHEL, LE (CN/0712-2489). **5791**

NOUVEAU RECUEIL COMPLET DES FABLIAUX (NE). [800] **3418**

NOUVEAUX CAHIERS, LES (FR/0550-1350). **5051**

NOUVEL AFRIQUE ASIE, LE (FR/1141-9946). [100,000] **4484**

NOUVEL ECONOMISTE, LE (FR). [116,041] **1576**

NOUVELLE (BEAUMONT) (CN/0827-2085). [1,459] **5791**

NOUVELLE REVUE PEDAGOGIQUE (FR/0029-4837). [17,000] **1769**

NOUVELLE TOUR DE FEU, LA (FR/0294-4030). [800] **3467**

NOUVELLES DE LA F M O Q (ENGLISH EDITION) (CN/0318-0549). **3623**

NOUVELLES DE LA REPUBLIQUE DES LETTRES (NAPLES, ITALY) (IT/0392-2332). [500] **3307**

NOUVELLES DE L'ACADEMIE / ACADEMIE DES SCIENCES, LES (FR/0246-1226). [750] **5135**

NOUVELLES DE L'ESTAMPE (FR/0029-4888). [1,000-1,400] **4567**

NOUVELLES / LA FEDERATION DES SOCIETES D'HISTOIRE DU QUEBEC (CN/0829-2612). [2,000] **2751**

NOUVELLES, LES (US/0270-174X). [5,400] **1306**

NOVA ET VETERA (FRIBOURG) (SZ/0029-5027). [650] **4982**

NOVA MATICA (YU/0353-8052). [4,000] **3349**

NOVA SCOTIA BUSINESS JOURNAL (CN/0820-2737). [30,420] **700**

NOVA SCOTIA DEPARTMENT OF COMMUNITY SERVICES, THE (CN/0844-7535). [1,200] **4670**

NOVA SCOTIA LAW NEWS (CN/0316-6325). [1,800] **3019**

NOVA SCOTIA LIBERAL, THE (CN/0703-1793). **4484**

NOVA SCOTIA MEDICAL JOURNAL, THE (CN/0838-2638). [2,500] **3623**

NOVA SCOTIA REAL PROPERTY PRACTICE MANUAL (CN). [186] **3019**

NOVASCOPE (US/0892-5003). [60,000] **2491**

NOVATEUR, LE (CN/0825-0596). [8,000] **1620**

NOVI DNI (CN/0048-1017). [1,500] **2270**

NOVUM GEBRAUCHSGRAPHIK (GW/0302-9794). [12,000] **381**

NOVYJ ZURNAL (US/0029-5337). [1,300] **2851**

NOW DIG THIS (UK). [2,500] **4142**

NOW L.A. / OFFICIAL PUBLICATION OF THE LOS ANGELES CHAPTER, NATIONAL ORGANIZATION FOR WOMEN (NOW) (US/0741-9627). [2,500] **5563**

NOW (TORONTO. 1981) (CN/0712-1326). [100,000] **4853**

NPTA MANAGEMENT NEWS (US/0739-2214). [20,000] **4235**

NRRI QUARTERLY BULLETIN (US/8756-632X). [1,200] **4699**

NSCLC WASHINGTON WEEKLY (US/0277-7460). [1,800] **3020**

NSOA BULLETIN (US/0146-9975). [1,850] **4142**

NSPA WASHINGTON REPORTER, THE (US/0469-3922). **749**

NSS BULLETIN, THE (US/0146-9517). [9,500] **1359**

NSS NEWS (US/0027-7010). [8,000] **1359**

NSUKKA LIBRARY NOTES (NR/0331-1481). [500] **3237**

NT, TECNICA & TECNOLOGIA / AMMA (IT). **2123**

NTDRA DEALER NEWS (US/0027-7045). [7,000] **5076**

NTIAC NEWSLETTER (US/0730-8086). [2,000] **1989**

NTZ : NACHRICTENTECHNISCHE ZEITSCHRIFT (GW/0027-707X). [7,109] **1161**

NUCLEAR ENGINEER, THE (UK/0262-5091). [2,000] **2156**

NUCLEAR PLANT JOURNAL (US/0892-2055). [22,000] **1952**

NUCLEAR SCIENCE INFORMATION OF JAPAN (JA/0029-5620). [600] **4449**

NUCLEAR TIMES (NEW YORK, N.Y.) (US/0734-5836). [36,000] **4485**

NUCLEOSIDES & NUCLEOTIDES (US/0732-8311). **491**

NUCLEOTECNICA (CL/0716-0054). [2,000] **2157**

NUCLEUS (CALCUTTA) (II/0029-568X). [400] **550**

NUESTRAS RAICES (QUARTERLY) (US/1045-2427). [400] **2465**

NUESTRO (US/0147-3247). [210,000] **2270**

NUEVAMERICA (AG/0325-6960). [1,500] **1769**

NUEZ (NEW YORK, N.Y.), LA (US/0898-1140). [1,000] **3419**

NUIT BLANCHE (CN/0823-2490). [8,000] **3419**

NUMEN (INTERNATIONAL ASSOCIATION FOR THE HISTORY OF RELIGIONS) (NE/0029-5973). [296] **4982**

NUMISMATIC CIRCULAR, THE (UK). [3,000] **2782**

NUMISMATIC NEWS (KRAUSE PUBLICATIONS : 1977) (US/0029-604X). [35,739] **2782**

NUMISMATICA, LA (IT). **2782**

NUMISMATIST, THE (US/0029-6090). [31,000] **2782**

NUOVA ELETTRONICA (IT). [16,000] **2074**

NUOVA EUROPA, LA (IT). [10,000] **4983**

NUOVA FINESTRA (IT). [8,000] **634**

NUOVA RIVISTA MUSICALE ITALIANA (IT/0029-6228). [4,000] **4142**

NUOVO CIMENTO DELLA SOCIETA ITALIANA DI FISICA. SEZIONE B (IT/0369-4100). [2,200] **4413**

NUOVO CIMENTO DELLA SOCIETA ITALIANA DI FISICA, [SEZIONE] D (IT/0392-6737). [1,000] **4449**

NUOVO CIMENTO DELLA SOCIETA ITALIANA DI FIZICA. SEZIONE A (IT/0369-4097). [1,000] **4449**

NUOVO OSSERVATORE, IL (IT). **1509**

NUOVO SAGGIATORE : BOLLETTINO DELLA SOCIETA ITALIANA DI FISICA, IL (IT). [2,200] **4413**

NURADEEN (US/8756-4637). [5,000] **5044**

NURNBERGER FORSCHUNGEN (GW/0078-2653). [1,000] **2701**

NURSCENE (CN/0382-8476). [11,000] **3862**

NURSE PRACTITIONER, THE (US/0361-1817). [12,500] **3863**

NURSERY MANAGER (US). [12,000] **2426**

NURSING & HEALTH CARE (US/0276-5284). [20,000] **3863**

NURSING AND HEALTH SCIENCE EDUCATION REVIEW (AT/1033-6273). **3863**

NURSING BC (CN/1185-3638). [36,000] **3863**

NURSING ECONOMIC$ (US/0746-1739). [7,000] **3864**

NURSING JOURNAL OF INDIA (II/0029-6503). [30,000] **3864**

NURSING MONTREAL (CN/0710-6157). [17,000] **3864**

NURSING NEW ZEALAND (NZ/1172-1979). **3864**

NURSING PRACTICE (CN/0828-4660). **3865**

NURSINGWORLD JOURNAL (US/0745-8630). [45,000] **3866**

NUT KERNEL, THE (US/0738-596X). [300] **2426**

NUTIDA MUSIK (SW/0029-6597). [2,000] **4142**

NUTRISYON (PH/0115-4516). [1,000] **4195**

NUTRITION AND HEALTH (NEW YORK) (US/0270-658X). [5,000] **4195**

NUTRITION NEWS (ROSEMONT) (US/0369-6464). [68,000] **4196**

NUTRITION QUARTERLY (CN/0710-166X). **4196**

NUTRITION UPDATE (SAN CLEMENTE, CALIF.) (US/0892-6204). [200] **3623**

NUTRITIONAL PERSPECTIVES (US/0160-3922). **4197**

NUTZFAHRZEUG, DAS (GW). [5,000] **5388**

NUYTSIA (AT/0085-4417). [500] **520**

NV; NEUE VERPACKUNG (GW/0341-0390). [12,792] **4220**

NVS NIEUWS (NE). [500] **4794**

NY FOOD LETTER, THE (US/1065-7967). **2351**

NYA ANTIK & AUKTION (SW/0346-9212). [45,000] **251**

NYAC NEWS (US/0275-5114). [5,000] **4670**

NYAME AKUMA (CN/0713-5815). [300] **277**

NYLA BULLETIN (US/0027-7134). [4000] **3238**

NYPIRG AGENDA (US/1044-3134). [45,000] **1298**

NYT FRA ISLAND (DK). [1,300] **2701**

NZ BUSINESS (NZ/0113-4957). [1,000] **700**

O A C E T T NEWSLETTER (CN/0318-5338). [16,000] **1989**

O C P, ON CONTINUING PRACTICE (CN/0315-1042). [7,200] **4318**

O.N.E. NEWSLETTER (CN/0229-1428). [250] **4197**

O.S.B.E.R. OIL SPILL BULLETIN AND ENVIRONMENTAL REVIEW (UK/0959-9134). [1,000] **2238**

OAH NEWSLETTER (US/1059-1125). [12,000] **2751**

OAK LEAVES (BAY CITY, TEX.) (US/0740-8013). [150] **2465**

OAKLAND BUSINESS MONTHLY (US/8750-0981). **700**

OAKLAND POST (US). [49,500] **5638**

OAZ, OSTERREICHISCHE APOTHEKER-ZEITUNG (AU/0253-5238). [4,500] **4318**

OB. GYN. NEWS (US/0029-7437). [28,000] **3766**

OBESITY RESEARCH (US/1071-7323). [450] **3623**

OBG MANAGEMENT (US/1044-307X). [31,000] **3766**

OBIETTIVO MODA (IT). [10,000] **1086**

OBION ORIGINS (US). [125] **2465**

OBITER DICTA (1963) (CN/0029-7585). **3020**

OBJECTIF PREVENTION (MONTREAL) (CN/0705-0577). [7000] **4794**

OBJECTOR (SAN FRANCISCO, CALIF.) (US/0279-103X). [1,000] **3183**

OBLIGATION, L' (CN/0227-1540). **2751**

OBSCENITY LAW BULLETIN (US/0195-1696). [900] **3020**

OBSERVATORY, THE (UK/0029-7704). [3,300] **397**

OBSERVER ECCENTRIC (US). [16,000] **5693**

OBSERVER (RIO RANCHO, N.M.), THE (US/1049-7374). [17,500] **5712**

OBSIDIAN II (US/0888-4412). [500] **3419**

OBST UND GARTEN (GW/0029-7798). [20,000] **2426**

OBSTETRICA ET GYNECOLOGICA (OULU) (FI/0358-4844). [500] **3766**

OBSTETRICIA Y GINECOLOGIA LATINO-AMERICANAS (AG/0029-7836). [2,800] **3766**

OBZORNIK ZA MATEMATIKO IN FIZIKO (XV/0473-7466). [1,500] **3525**

OCCASIONAL ESSAYS (CR). [1,000] **4983**

OCCASIONAL MISCELLANY OF THE LIBRARY COMPANY OF PHILADELPHIA (US/0734-3698). [1,439] **3238**

OCCASIONAL - NOVA SCOTIA MUSEUM (CN/0704-5824). [600] **4094**

OCCASIONAL PAPER - CANADIAN WILDLIFE SERVICE (CN/0576-6370). [1,100] **2201**

OCCASIONAL PAPER (COMMITTEE FOR ECONOMIC DEVELOPMENT OF AUSTRALIA) (AT). [2,000] **1576**

OCCASIONAL PAPER - DEPT. OF GEOGRAPHY, UNIVERSITY OF GUYANA (GY). [500] **2571**

OCCASIONAL PAPER (INTERNATIONAL OMBUDSMAN INSTITUTE) (CN/0711-6349). [200] **4670**

OCCASIONAL PAPER - MAXWELL GRADUATE SCHOOL OF CITIZENSHIP AND PUBLIC AFFAIRS. METROPOLITAN STUDIES PROGRAM (US/0732-507X). [1,600] **4670**

OCCASIONAL PAPER - MISSOURI ACADEMY OF SCIENCE (US/0148-0944). [1,000] **5135**

OCCASIONAL PAPER - RESERVE BANK OF AUSTRALIA (AT/0080-178X). **732**

OCCASIONAL PAPERS (UK). [500] **4983**

OCCASIONAL PAPERS (US). [7,000] **3020**

OCCASIONAL PAPERS - ART LIBRARIES SOCIETY OF NORTH AMERICA (US/0730-7160). [500] **3238**

OCCASIONAL PAPERS - DEPARTMENT OF HISTORY, ARKANSAS TECH UNIVERSITY (US). [100] **2624**

OCCASIONAL PAPERS FROM THE MUSEUM OF VICTORIA (AT/0814-1819). [540] **4169**

OCCASIONAL PAPERS IN ENTOMOLOGY (US/0362-2622). [1,000] **5612**

OCCASIONAL PAPERS ON ANTIQUITIES (US/8756-047X). [500] **251**

OCCASIONAL PAPERS. SOUTH ASIA SERIES (US/0076-812X). [200] **2661**

OCCASIONAL PAPERS - UNITED METHODIST BOARD OF HIGHER EDUCATION AND MINISTRY (US/0273-0960). [6,000] **1838**

OCCASIONAL PUBLICATION - BOREAL INSTITUTE FOR NORTHERN STUDIES (CN/0068-0303). **2751**

OCCUPATIONAL HAZARDS (US/0029-7909). [60,000] **2866**

OCCUPATIONAL INJURIES AND ILLNESSES. IOWA (US). [300] **2867**

OCCUPATIONAL MEDICAL DIGEST, THE (US). **3623**

OCEAN AND COASTAL LAW JOURNAL (US). **3182**

OCEAN INDUSTRY (US/0029-8026). [32,000] **4267**

OCEAN VOICE (UK/0261-6777). [17,606] **4181**

OCEANOLOGY (WASHINGTON. 1965) (US/0001-4370). **1454**

OCEANS (FR). [30,000] **4908**

OCHANOMIZU IGAKU ZASSHI (JA/0472-4674). **3623**

OCLAE (CU/0029-6961). [10,000] **1770**

O'CONNOR REPORT (SEATTLE, WASH.) (US/1064-265X). [1,500] **4794**

OCSM NEWSLETTER (CN/0823-8162). **4142**

OCTANE (CN/0835-1740). [5,500] **4267**

OCTO-GRAPHE (CN/0836-690X). [1,100] **1868**

OCULAR SURGERY NEWS (US/8750-3085). [17,000] **3971**

OCUPACION Y DESOCUPACION, SECTORES URBANOS DE LAS REGIONES IV A X, EXCEPTO EL GRAN SANTIAGO (CL). [400] **1699**

ODA SUGGESTED FEE GUIDE FOR GENERAL PRACTITIONERS (CN/0826-6905). **1331**

ODENSE UNIVERSITY STUDIES IN ENGLISH (DK/0078-3293). **3308**

ODTU : GELISME DERGISI (TU). [1,500] **1509**

O'DWYER'S DIRECTORY OF CORPORATE COMMUNICATIONS (US/0149-1091). [2,000] **763**

O'DWYER'S DIRECTORY OF PUBLIC RELATIONS EXECUTIVES (US/0191-0051). **763**

O'DWYER'S DIRECTORY OF PUBLIC RELATIONS FIRMS (US/0078-3374). **763**

ODYSSEUS (FLUSHING, N.Y.) (US/0883-3664). [300,000] **5487**

OEA FOCUS (US/0743-7986). [49,000] **1770**

OEIL OUVERT (CN/0821-7033). **5300**

OESTERREICHISCHES PATENBLATT (AU/0253-5327). [500] **1306**

OF SUBSTANCE (US/0743-3085). **3021**

OFEQ (TEL-AVIV) (IS/0302-8119). [10,000] **1577**

OFF-LEAD (US/0094-0186 #y 0094-0816). [5,000] **4287**

OFF ROAD MUNCHEN (GW/0172-4185). [183,800] **5388**

OFFENTLICHE DIENST, DER (AU). [1,500] **1699**

OFFICE AUTOMATION (US/0472-6049). [300,000] **4213**

OFFICE GUIDE (US/0273-964X). **700**

OFFICE GUIDE TO ORLANDO (US/0733-1266). [12,093] **4213**

OFFICE-MANAGEMENT (BADEN-BADEN) (GW/0722-2572). [12,000] **880**

OFFICE NURSE, THE (US/0893-6595). [75,000] **3866**

OFFICE PRODUCTS ANALYST, THE (US/0197-4602). [1,000] **4213**

OFFICE PROFESSIONAL, THE (US/0739-3156). [20,000] **1118**

OFFICE SYSTEMS (GEORGETOWN, CONN.) (US/8750-3441). [100,000] **4213**

OFFICE SYSTEMS RESEARCH JOURNAL (US/0737-8998). [400] **700**

OFFICE TOPICS (US/0746-5122). [18,500] **944**

OFFICER REVIEW (US/0736-7317). [15,000] **4053**

OFFICERS, COMMITTEES, CONSTITUTION AND BY-LAWS, MEMBERS / GROLIER CLUB (US/0362-8019). **5234**

OFFICIAL BASKETBALL RULES FOR MEN AND WOMEN (CN/0473-8853). [20,000] **4909**

OFFICIAL CALIFORNIA APARTMENT JOURNAL (US/0191-6335). [6,000] **2829**

OFFICIAL CODE OF GEORGIA ANNOTATED. ADVANCE INFORMATION SERVICE (US/0747-6965). **3021**

OFFICIAL DAILY BULLETIN - VANCOUVER STOCK EXCHANGE (CN/0384-9465). [2,000] **910**

OFFICIAL DIRECTORY (US). **3171**

OFFICIAL DIRECTORY - NEW JERSEY STATE BAR ASSOCIATION (US). **3021**

OFFICIAL GUIDE, OUTDOOR POWER EQUIPMENT (US/0735-6676). [3,200] **160**

OFFICIAL GUIDE - TIME FINANCE ADJUSTERS (FIRM) (US/0732-2798). [30,000] **802**

OFFICIAL HANDBOOK OF THE AAU CODE (US/0091-3405). **4909**

OFFICIAL HELLENIC YEAR BOOK (1984) (CN/0823-8596). **2752**

OFFICIAL HOTEL AND RESORT GUIDE (US). **2808**

OFFICIAL (LOS ANGELES) (US/0192-5784). [3,000] **2607**

OFFICIAL RECORD OF PROCEEDINGS / HONG KONG URBAN COUNCIL (HK). [200] **4671**

OFFICIAL REGISTER - AMERICAN SOCIETY OF CIVIL ENGINEERS (US/0402-1142). [18,000] **2028**

OFFICIAL RULES FOR COMPETITIVE SWIMMING (US/0091-3413). [22,000] **4910**

OFFICIAL UNITED STATES TENNIS ASSOCIATION YEARBOOK AND TENNIS GUIDE WITH THE OFFICIAL RULES, THE (US/0196-5425). [50,000] **4910**

OFFICIAL WATER POLO RULES (US). [1,500] **4910**

OFFSHORE (CONROE, TEX.) (US/0030-0608). **4267**

OFFSHORE INDUSTRIAL DIRECTORY (CN/0712-0745). [15,000] **4267**

OFFSHORE RESEARCH FOCUS (UK/0309-4189). [7,000] **4267**

OFFSHORE (WEST NEWTON) (US/0274-9394). [36,000 paid] **594**

OFICINA DE LIVROS: NOVIDADES CATALOGADAS NA FONTE (BL). [1,000] **421**

OH&S CANADA (CN/0827-4576). [7,000] **2867**

OHIO (US/0279-3504). [105,000] **2541**

OHIO ARCHAEOLOGIST (US/0048-153X). [2,500] **277**

OHIO ARCHIVIST (1987), THE (US/1047-5400). [220] **3239**

OHIO BANKER, THE (US/0030-0802). [3,200] **802**

OHIO CHRONICLE, THE (US). [1,500] **1093**

OHIO CIVIL LIBERTIES (US/0274-5615). [5,500] **4511**

OHIO CPA JOURNAL, THE (US/0749-8284). [18,000] **749**

OHIO DENTAL JOURNAL, THE (US/0030-087X). [5,400] **1331**

OHIO DOCUMENTS (US/0147-2542). [600] **4671**

OHIO ENGINEER, THE (US/0194-9276). [5,500] **1989**

OHIO FISH AND WILDLIFE REPORT (US/0085-4468). [1,200] **2201**

OHIO FLORISTS ASSOCIATION FLOWER GROWERS HOTLINE (US). [1,000] **2435**

OHIO HISTORY (US/0030-0934). [4,000] **2752**

OHIO HOLSTEIN NEWS (US/0199-7580). [3,500] **197**

OHIO JOURNAL OF SCIENCE, THE (US/0030-0950). [2,500] **5136**

OHIO LAWYER (COLUMBUS, OHIO : 1987) (US). [22,000] **3021**

OHIO LIBRARIES (COLUMBUS, OHIO. 1988) (US/1046-4336). [5,000] **3239**

OHIO MEDIA SPECTRUM (US/0192-6942). [2,000] **3239**

OHIO MEDICINE (US/0892-2454). [14,000-15,000] **3624**

OHIO NEWS (WOOSTER, OHIO) (US/0899-4862). [3,000] **197**

OHIO NORTHERN UNIVERSITY LAW REVIEW (US/0094-534X). [1,200] **3021**

OHIO PARENTS AND TEACHERS ASSOCIATION NEWS (US/0199-0918). [2,500] **1770**

OHIO RECORDS & PIONEER FAMILIES/CROSSROADS OF OUR NATION (US). [1,200] **2465**

OHIO REPORT (COLUMBUS, OHIO) (US/1063-990X). **4671**

OHIO SCHOOLS - OHIO EDUCATION ASSOCIATION (US/0030-1086). [106,000] **1868**

OHIO SPEECH JOURNAL, THE (US/0078-4052). [300] **1119**

OHIO STATE BAR ASSOCIATION REPORT (1981) (US/0744-8376). [22,000] **3022**

OHIO STATE LAW JOURNAL (US/0048-1572). [2,000] **3022**

OHIO STATEWIDE COMPREHENSIVE OUTDOOR RECREATION PLAN. ACTION PROGRAM (US). [2,000] **4853**

OHIO TAVERN NEWS (US/0030-1183). [13,500] **5072**

OHIO WESLEYAN MAGAZINE, THE (US/0030-1221). [24,000] **1093**

OHIO WOODLANDS (US). [3,000] **2390**

OHIOANA QUARTERLY (US/0030-1248). [2,000] **3420**

OHIOSCAPES NEWSLETTER (US). [1600] **2830**

OHS BULLETIN (CN/0714-6736). [3,000] **2541**

OIKOS (DK/0030-1299). [1,000] **2220**

OIL AND GAS FIELD STUDIES (US/0161-0961). [500] **4268**

OIL & GAS (OXFORD, OXFORDSHIRE) (UK/0263-5070). [400] **3022**

OIL & GAS RUSSIA & POST SOVIET REPUBLICS. HYDROCARBONS BRIEF (UK/0967-537X). [5,000] **4269**

OIL EXPRESS (US/0195-0576). **4269**

OIL, GAS & PETROCHEM EQUIPMENT (US/0030-1353). **4269**

OIL MARKET TRENDS (UK). [100] **4269**

OIL PACKER INTERNATIONAL (UK/0957-655X). [8,000] **4220**

OILS AND OILSEEDS JOURNAL (II/0369-769X). [1,000] **1044**

OILWEEK (CN/0030-1515). [16,000] **4270**

OISEAU ET LA REVUE FRANCAISE D'ORNITHOLOGIE (FR/0030-1531). [1,000] **5619**

OJANCANO (CHAPEL HILL, N.C.) (US/0899-983X). **3420**

OJC THE OHIO JEWISH CHRONICLE, THE (US). **5729**

OKANAGAN HISTORY (CN/0830-0739). [2,000] **2752**

OKANAGAN LIFE (KELOWNA. 1988) (CN/0840-5492). [19,000] **2541**

OKIKA O HAWAII, NA (US/0099-8745). [1,000] **2426**

OKLAHOMA AGRICULTURAL STATISTICS (US). [2,000] **155**

OKLAHOMA BUSINESS (US/0192-9593). [11,000] **701**

OKLAHOMA BUSINESS BULLETIN (US/0030-1671). [700] **701**

OKLAHOMA CONSTITUTION, THE (US/0890-1007). [2,000] **4671**

OKLAHOMA COWMAN (US/0030-1698). [5,200] **217**

OKLAHOMA DAILY, THE (US/0030-171X). [14,550 fall/spring] **5732**

OKLAHOMA DENTAL ASSOCIATION JOURNAL (US/0164-9442). [1,600] **1331**

OKLAHOMA GENEALOGICAL SOCIETY QUARTERLY (US/0474-0742). **2465**

OKLAHOMA GEOLOGY NOTES (US/0030-1736). [955] **1443**

OKLAHOMA GOVERNMENT PUBLICATIONS (US). [300] **4485**

OKLAHOMA HOME & LIFE STYLE (US/0895-1586). [13,000] **2542**

OKLAHOMA NURSE, THE (US/0030-1787). [1,200] **3866**

OKLAHOMA OIL REPORTER, THE (US/0745-2268). **4270**

OKLAHOMA READER, THE (US/0030-1833). [1,800] **3308**

OKLAHOMA REALTOR (US/0745-5046). [7,000] **4842**

OKLAHOMA RETAILER (US/0030-1841). [4,300] **956**

OKLAHOMA RURAL NEWS (US/0048-1610). [230,500] **117**

OKLAHOMA SERIES, THE (US/0271-6941). [1,500] **2752**

OKMULGEE COUNTY GENEALOGICAL SOCIETY NEWSLETTER (US). [100] **2465**

OKONOMI OG POLITIK (DK/0030-1906). [1,050] **1577**

OLAMENU (US/0030-2139). [17,500] **1805**

OLD CAR VALUE GUIDE (US/0475-1876). [25,000] **5422**

OLD DOMINION GARDENER (US/0274-6956). [11,000] **2426**

OLD ENGLISH NEWSLETTER (US/0030-1973). [900] **3420**

OLD ENGLISH NEWSLETTER. SUBSIDIA (US/0739-8549). [100] **3420**

OLD FORT NEWS (US/0196-7045). [2,000] **2752**

OLD LAWRENCE REMINISCENCES (US/1044-1905). [475] **2465**

OLD MILL NEWS (US/0276-3338). [1,500] **305**

OLD NORTHWEST, THE (US/0360-5531). [600] **2752**

OLD STURBRIDGE VISITOR (US/0744-3781). [12,000] **4094**

OLD TESTAMENT ABSTRACTS (US/0364-8591). [2,000] **5013**

OLD WEST (US/0030-2058). [100,000] **2752**

OLJYPOSTI (FI). [35,000] **4270**

OLMSTE(A)D'S GENEALOGY RECORDED (US/0162-0800). [500] **2465**

OLSCHWANGER JOURNAL (US/0882-1933). [250] **2465**

OLSEN'S FISHERMAN'S NAUTICAL ALMANACK, CONTAINING TIDE TABLES AND DIRECTORY OF BRITISH FISHING VESSELS (UK). **5453**

OLYMPIAN (NEW YORK, N.Y.), THE (US/0094-9787). [60,000] **4910**

OM GYMNASIET STUDENTERKURSUS OG HF (DK/0109-9485). [95,000] **1770**

OMAHA WORLD-HERALD (OMAHA, NB : 1954 : SUNRISE ED.) (US). [224,000] **5707**

OMBUDSMAN OFFICE PROFILES / INTERNATIONAL OMBUDSMAN OFFICE PROFILES (CN/0714-6132). [450] **3022**

OMELLETTE, L' (CN/0712-3345). **5791**

OMINECA ADVERTISER, THE (CN/0708-000X). **5791**

ON BALANCE (DENVER, COLO.) (US/1062-7049). [500] **4606**

ON CAMPUS (SASKATOON) (CN/0711-3617). [3,600] **1839**

ON COURT (CN/0824-6629). **4911**

ON CUE (US/1041-6234). [500] **1770**

ON DISENO (SP). **2902**

ON-LINE (DURHAM, N.H.) (US/0731-8367). [1,650] **1243**

ON-LINE REVIEW (UK/0309-314X). [2,000] **1275**

ON LOCATION (US/0149-7014). [24,000] **4075**

ON ONE WHEEL (US/0893-4606). [350] **429**

ON PRODUCTION AND POST-PRODUCTION (US/1067-6120). [28,000] **4075**

ON RECORD (TORONTO) (CN/0821-7882). [2,500] **5300**

ON SHORE WEEKLY (UK). **4270**

ON TARGET (CANADIAN EDITION) (CN/0380-5980). [1,300] **4485**

ON THE BEAM (US/0740-218X). [300] **4392**

ON THE MOVE (BUFFALO, N.Y.) (US). [7,500] **5389**

ON THE RECORDS (AT/1030-9837). [400] **3022**

ON THE RISK (US/0885-4416). [3,600] **2889**

ON THE STRATEGY OF INDUSTRIALIZATION IN DEVELOPING COUNTRIES AND THE EXPERIENCES IN THE ECONOMIC AND SOCIAL DEVELOPMENT IN SOCIALIST COUNTRIES (GW). **1620**

ONALASKA COMMUNITY LIFE (US/1053-6906). [1,200] **5769**

ONCE UPON A TIME (ST. PAUL, MINN.) (US/1071-2526). [1,000] **1067**

ONCOLOGY ISSUES (US/1046-3356). [13,900] **3822**

ONCOLOGY NURSING FORUM (US/0190-535X). [18,000] **3866**

ONDE ELECTRIQUE (FR/0030-2430). [3,000] **2074**

ONE CHURCH (US/0030-2503). [1,600] **5039**

ONE ON ONE (ALBANY, N.Y.) (US/0733-639X). [4,200] **3022**

ONE WORLD (EDMONTON) (CN/0475-0209). **1770**

ONION WORLD (US/0892-578X). [6,109] **2426**

ONLINE (COLOGNE, GERMANY : 1982) (GW). [16,000] **1197**

ONLINE HELIDATA (UK/0951-9904). [10,000] **31**

ONLINE TODAY (US/0891-4672). **3239**

ONLINE (WESTON, CONN.) (US/0146-5422). [5,100] **1275**

ONOMA (BE/0078-463X). **3308**

ONOMASTICKY ZPRAVODAJ CSAV (XR). [350] **3308**

ONS ERFDEEL (BE/0030-2651). [10,000] **327**

ONS GEESTEIJK ERF (BE/0774-2827). [400] **4983**

ONSHORE WELL RESULTS SERVICE (UK). **4270**

ONTARIO AMATEUR WRESTLING ASSOCIATION RESULTS BOOK (CN/0822-6806). [3,000] **4911**

ONTARIO BIRD BANDING (CN/0475-025X). [250] **5619**

ONTARIO BIRDS (CN/0822-3890). [650] **5619**

ONTARIO BRANCH NEWS (CN/0710-345X). [1,000] **4795**

ONTARIO COLLEGE NEWSLETTER (CN/0714-444X). **1094**

ONTARIO CORN PRODUCER (CN/0008-7297). [25,000] **117**

ONTARIO CRICKET "PITCH" (CN/1183-4072). [10,000] **4911**

ONTARIO DEMOCRAT, THE (CN/0827-2247). [26,000] **4485**

ONTARIO DENTIST (CN/0300-5275). [5,600] **1332**

ONTARIO FIELD BIOLOGIST, THE (CN/0078-4834). [750] **467**

ONTARIO GRAPE GROWER, THE (CN/0380-6057). [8,500] **2426**

ONTARIO LAND SURVEYOR, THE (CN/0316-2001). [1,500] **2028**

ONTARIO MATHEMATICS GAZETTE (CN/0030-3011). [1,700] **3525**

ONTARIO MEDICAL REVIEW (CN/0030-302X). [17,500] **3624**

ONTARIO MEDICAL TECHNOLOGIST / ONTARIO SOCIETY OF MEDICAL TECHNOLOGISTS (CN/0228-877X). [5,000] **3624**

ONTARIO MILK PRODUCER (CN/0030-3038). [15,000] **197**

ONTARIO NEST RECORDS SCHEME (CN/0228-0787). [400] **5593**

ONTARIO NEWS BULLETIN / WCTU (CN/0229-4540). **4983**

ONTARIO NURSING HOME JOURNAL (CN/0829-6340). [4,500] **3790**

ONTARIO PIPELINE (CN/0380-1624). [2,000] **5537**

ONTARIO PSYCHOLOGIST, THE (CN/0030-3054). [1,600] **4606**

ONTARIO PUBLIC SECTOR (CN/0841-0798). [5,000] **4671**

ONTARIO RECYCLING UPDATE (CN/0823-6143). [900] **2238**

ONTARIO SPORTSCENE (CN/0225-5782). **4911**

ONTARIO TECHNOLOGIST, THE (CN/0380-1969). [16,000] **5136**

ONTARIO VACATION FARMS (CN/0712-1636). [30,000] **5487**

ONTARIO WATER SKIER, THE (CN/0226-5702). [1,500] **4911**

ONZE VOGELS (NE). [50,000] **5619**

OP CIT (IT/0030-3305). **361**

OPADY ATMOSFERYCZNE (PL). [320] **1433**

OPASQUIA TIMES (CN/0707-5448). [3,648] **5791**

OPEC BULLETIN (AU/0474-6279). [8,000] **4270**

OPEN CHANNEL (US). [2,600] **1198**

OPEN DOOR (LEXINGTON, KY.), THE (US/0732-6319). [87,000] **1102**

OPEN DOORS (SANTA ANA, CALIF.) (US/8756-5234). [1,600] **4983**

OPEN LETTER GEELONG (AT/1035-4727). [3,000] **1883**

OPEN SPACE (OPEN SPACES SOCIETY, GREAT BRITAIN) (UK). [2,500] **2201**

OPEN SQUARES, THE (US/0891-3447). [5,000] **1314**

OPEN SYSTEMS DATA TRANSFER (US/0741-286X). [700] **1243**

OPERA JOURNAL, THE (US/0030-3585). [1,000] **4143**

OPERA MILANO. 1987, L' (IT/1121-4112). **4143**

OPERA MONTHLY (US/0897-6554). [8,000] **4143**

OPERA QUARTERLY, THE (US/0736-0053). [5,300] **4144**

OPERATIONAL GEOGRAPHER, THE (CN/0822-4838). [1,500] **2571**

OPERATIONS FORESTIERES ET DE SCIERIE (CN/0030-3631). [5,000] **2390**

OPERATIONS OF BANK PEMBANGUNAN INDONESIA (IO). [2,000] **802**

OPERATORE SANITARIO, L' (IT/0392-5153). [10,000] **3624**

OPHEA JOURNAL (CN/0840-822X). [2,000] **1857**

OPHTHALMIC PAEDIATRICS AND GENETICS (NE/0167-6784). [500] **550**

OPHTHALMIC PRACTICE (CN/0832-9869). [1,300] **3877**

OPHTHALMOLOGICA ET OTO-RHINO-LARYNGOLOGICA (OULU) (FI/0358-4852). [450] **3877**

OPHTHALMOLOGY MANAGEMENT (US/0746-1070). [15,339] **3878**

OPHTHALMOLOGY TIMES (US/0193-032X). [14,553] **3878**

OPINION (US). [2,500] **3023**

OPINION JEUNESSE (BE). [10,000] **1770**

OPINIONS ON REVIEW FOR THE YEAR ... / STATE OF MICHIGAN, DEPARTMENT OF LABOR, WORKERS' COMPENSATION APPEAL BOARD AND APPELLATE COMMISSION (US). [200] **3153**

OPPORTUNITIES (US). [300] **4208**

OPPORTUNITY (CHICAGO, ILL. : 1983) (US/0741-3750). [185,000] **701**

OPPORTUNITY VALLEY NEWS (US). [23,500 unpaid] **5753**

OPSEU NEWS (CN/0229-8104). [75,000] **1700**

OPTICA PURA Y APLICADA (SP/0030-3917). **4439**

OPTICAL INDUSTRY & SYSTEMS ENCYCLOPEDIA & DICTIONARY, THE (US/0191-0639). [52,000] **4439**

OPTICAL PRISM (CN/0824-3441). [7,000] **4216**

OPTIK; ZEITSCHRIFT FUER LICHT- UND ELEKTRONENOPTIK (GW). [600] **4440**

OPTIMIST (ABILENE), THE (US/0030-4069). [5,000] **1094**

OPTIMIST HOTLINE (US/0744-9755). **5234**

OPTIMIST MAGAZINE, THE (US/0744-4672). [166,000] **5234**

OPTO MAGAZINE (BE). [2,500] **3878**

OPTOLASER MILANO (IT/1120-8724). [5,000] **2074**

OPTOMETRIC MANAGEMENT (US/0030-4085). [26,000] **4216**

OPTOMETRIE (GW/0030-4123). [2,800] **4216**

OPTOMETRY TODAY (LONDON) (UK/0268-5485). [12,765] **4217**

OPUSCULA ARCHAEOLOGICA (ZAGREB, CROATIA) (CI/0473-0992). [500] **277**

OPUSCULA ATHENIENSIA (SW/0078-5520). [500] **1078**

OPUSCULA ZOOLOGICA - INSTITUTUM ZOOSYSTEMATICUM UNIVERSITATIS BUDAPESTINENSIS (HU/0473-1034). [800] **5593**

OPVOEDING & KULTUUR (SA). [8,000] **1770**

ORACION DE LAS HORAS (SP). [2,500] **4984**

ORACLE MAGAZINE (US/1065-3171). [74,000] **1198**

ORAITA (IS). [2,500] **5051**

ORAL HEALTH (CN/0030-4204). **1332**

ORAL HISTORY (COLCHESTER) (UK/0143-0955). [1,000] **2625**

ORAL HISTORY REVIEW, THE (US/0094-0798). **2625**

ORANGE COUNTY APARTMENT NEWS (US/0747-3435). [5,800] **2830**

ORANGE COUNTY BUSINESS TO BUSINESS (US/0733-9534). [30,000] **701**

ORANGE COUNTY GENEALOGICAL SOCIETY (US/0736-0185). [850] **2465**

ORANGE COUNTY LAWYER (US/0897-5698). [6,000] **3023**

ORANGEVILLE CITIZEN, THE (CN/0319-180X). [8,600] **5792**

ORATORY, THE (CN/0384-1871). [10,000] **4984**

ORBIS LITTERARUM (DK/0105-7510). [700] **3420**

ORBIS MUSICAE (IS/0303-3937). [600] **4144**

ORBIS (PHILADELPHIA) (US/0030-4387). [3,500] **4485**

ORBIT (AMSTERDAM) (NE/0167-6830). [600] **3878**

ORBIT (TORONTO) (CN/0030-4433). [7,000] **1902**

ORBUS (US/0890-6432). [13,000] **701**

ORCHADIAN, THE (AT/0474-3342). [900] **2426**

ORCHARDIST OF NEW ZEALAND, THE (NZ/0110-6260). [8,000] **180**

ORCHID ADVOCATE, THE (US/0097-9546). [2,000] **2426**

ORCHIDEE, DIE (GW/0473-1425). [7,000] **2426**

ORDERS IN COUNCIL (OTTAWA) (CN/0227-3268). [300] **3023**

OREGON BARS (US/0733-2475). [300] **3023**

OREGON BUSINESS (US/0279-8190). [20,000] **701**

OREGON DIRECTORY OF AMERICAN INDIAN RESOURCES (US/0733-477X). [15,000] **2270**

OREGON EDUCATION (US/0030-4689). [39,000] **1770**

OREGON FARM BUREAU NEWS (US/0162-5179). [10,500] **117**

OREGON HEALTH FORUM (US/1056-6767). [2,500] **4795**

OREGON INTERNATIONAL TRADE DIRECTORY (US/0731-9096). [3,000] **848**

OREGON LAW REVIEW (US/0196-2043). [1,000] **3023**

OREGON MATHEMATICS TEACHER, THE (US/0891-9089). **3526**

OREGON NURSE (US/0030-4751). [4,800] **3866**

OREGON OPTOMETRY (US/0274-6549). [2,500] **4217**

OREGON WILDLIFE (US/0094-7113). [42,000] **2201**

ORFF ECHO, THE (US/0095-2613). [4,500] **4144**

ORGAN — Controlled Circulation Index

ORGAN YEARBOOK, THE (NE/0920-3192). [1,000] **4144**

ORGANIC SEMINAR ABSTRACTS (US/0445-3611). [100] **1045**

ORGANIZACIJA IN KADRI (YU/0350-1531). [2,800] **881**

ORGANIZATION TRENDS (US/0882-5769). [3,500] **4338**

ORGANIZER MAILING, THE (US/1063-9233). [200] **4671**

ORGANO OFICIAL DE LA JUNTA CIVICO-MILITAR CUBANA (US/0272-4650). **2752**

ORGANOMETALLICS (US/0276-7333). [3,000] **1045**

ORGEL (AMERSFOORT, NETHERLANDS) (NE). [2,100] **4144**

ORGONOMIC FUNCTIONALISM (RANGELEY, ME.) (US/1054-075X). **3932**

ORGUE (PARIS), L' (FR/0030-5170). **4145**

ORIENT (JA). **277**

ORIENT (DEUTSCHES ORIENT-INSTITUT) (GW/0030-5227). **2661**

ORIENTAL INSECTS MONOGRAPH (US). [100] **5612**

ORIENTAL INSTITUTE PUBLICATIONS (US/0069-3367). [750] **277**

ORIENTALIA LOVANIENSIA PERIODICA (BE/0085-4522). **3308**

ORIENTAMENTI PEDAGOGICI (IT/0030-5391). [6] **1770**

ORIENTATIONS (TORONTO) (CN/0710-2151). [2,200] **1839**

ORIENTO (JA). [1,200] **2661**

ORIGINAL NEWS PEPPER, THE (US/1071-233X). [75] **3907**

ORIGINAL WNC BUSINESS JOURNAL, THE (US/1065-027X). [19,000] **701**

ORIGINS BIBLICAL CREATION SOCIETY (UK/0953-2773). [900] **4984**

ORION (IT). [2000] **4486**

ORION (SZ/0030-557X). [4,000] **398**

ORION (NEW YORK, N.Y.) (US/1058-3130). [11,000] **4170**

ORITA (NR/0030-5596). [400] **4984**

ORKESTER JOURNALEN (SW/0030-5642). [3,000] **4145**

ORL-HEAD AND NECK NURSING (US/1064-3842). [1,000] **3890**

ORLANDO BUSINESS JOURNAL (US/8750-8656). **702**

ORNIS SCANDINAVICA (NO/0030-5693). [750] **5619**

ORODHA MAALUM YA BEI / JAMHURI YA MUUNGANO WA TANZANIA, TUME YA BEI YA TAIFA (TZ). [5,000] **1594**

OROMOCTO POST, THE (CN/0710-5460). [4,800] **5792**

ORQUIDEA (MEXICO. 1971) (MX/0300-3701). [800] **520**

ORSA JOURNAL ON COMPUTING (US/0899-1499). [1,500] **1198**

ORSTOM ACTUALITES (FR/0758-833X). [9,000] **5136**

ORTE (SZ). [2,000] **3421**

ORTHODOX LIFE (US/0030-5820). [1,800] **5040**

ORTHODOX OBSERVER (US/0731-2547). [125,000] **4984**

ORTHODOXIE HEUTE (GW/0931-0347). **5040**

ORTHOPAEDIC NETWORK NEWS (US/1059-311X). [1,000] **3883**

ORTHOPAEDIC PRODUCT NEWS (UK/0954-4755). [7,500] **3883**

ORTHOPAEDIC REVIEW (US/0094-6591). [25,000] **3883**

ORTHOPAEDICS (GLENDALE, CALIF.) (US/0271-132X). **3884**

ORTHOPEDIC NURSING / NATIONAL ASSOCIATION OF ORTHOPEDIC NURSES (US/0744-6020). [10,000] **3884**

ORTHOPEDICS (THOROFARE) (US/0147-7447). [30,600] **3884**

ORYX (UK/0030-6053). [5,000] **2201**

OSAKA FURITSU NAKANOSHIMA TOSHOKAN ZOKA TOSHO MOKUROKU (JA). [330] **3240**

OSAKA FURITSU YUHIGAOKA TOSHOKAN ZOKA TOSHO MOKUROKU (JA). **3240**

OSAKA KOGYO GIJUTSU SHIKENJO, KIHO (JA/0472-142X). **5136**

OSCAR ISRAELOWITZ'S GUIDE TO JEWISH NEW YORK CITY (US). [2,000] **5269**

OSGOODE HALL LAW JOURNAL (CN). [1,000] **3023**

OSLER LIBRARY NEWSLETTER (CN/0085-4557). [1,500] **3624**

OSMANIA PAPERS IN LINGUISTICS (II/0970-0277). [500] **3308**

OSMOSE (MONTREAL) (CN/0829-5131). [1,000] **3866**

OSPEDALE (IT/0030-6231). **3790**

OSSC REPORT (US/0733-2548). **1771**

OSSERVATORE ROMANO, L' (VC/0030-6312). **5813**

OSTEOPATHIE : THERAPIES MANUELLES (FR/0753-6019). **4795**

OSTERREICHISCHE AMTSVORMUND, DER (AU). [10,000] **3122**

OSTERREICHISCHE JURISTEN-ZEITUNG (AU/0029-9251). [3,600] **3024**

OSTERREICHISCHE ZEITSCHRIFT FUER POLITIKWISSENSCHAFT (AU/0378-5149). [1,300] **4486**

OSTEUROPA (STUTTGART) (GW/0030-6428). [2,500] **4486**

OSTEUROPA WIRTSCHAFT (GW/0030-6460). [700] **1511**

OSTOMY QUARTERLY (US/0030-6517). [50,000] **3971**

OSTRICH, THE (SA/0030-6525). [4,000] **5619**

OTAR (NE). [2,150] **2028**

OTHER FRONT, THE (IS). [500] **2770**

OTHER SIDE OF THE BOAT (US). [500] **4984**

OTHER VOICES (HIGHLAND PARK, ILL.) (US/8756-4696). [1,500] **3421**

OTTAGONO (IT/0391-7487). [25,000] **2902**

OTTAR (NO/0030-6703). **4170**

OTTAWA ARCHAEOLOGIST, THE (CN/0702-7974). [100] **277**

OTTAWA BANDING GROUP (CN/0827-2298). [50] **5619**

OTTAWA BRANCH NEWS - ONTARIO GENEALOGICAL SOCIETY (CN/0708-5583). [1,000] **2466**

OTTAWA JEWISH BULLETIN (1993) (CN/1196-1929). [3,500] **2270**

OTTAWA LAW REVIEW (CN/0048-2331). [540] **3024**

OTTAWA QUARTERLY (CN/0713-8091). **1620**

OTTAWA SUN, THE (CN/0843-2570). [55,000] **5792**

OTTO NOVECENTO (IT). [1,000] **3421**

OUA/DATA'S ... GUIDE TO CORPORATE GIVING IN MAINE (US/0883-2730). [500] **4338**

OUA/DATA'S ... GUIDE TO CORPORATE GIVING IN RHODE ISLAND (US). [500] **4338**

OUR ANIMALS (US/0030-6789). [32,000] **2252**

OUR FAMILY (BATTLEFORD) (CN/0030-6843). [14,100] **4984**

OUR LIBRARY PRESENTS ... (US). [150] **3240**

OUR NAME'S THE GAME (US/0738-8306). **2466**

OUR OWN (US). [10,000] **2795**

OUR SCHOOLS (CN/0384-6636). [25,000] **1771**

OUSLEY NEWSLETTER (US/0733-6381). [207] **2466**

OUT & ABOUT (NEW HAVEN, CONN.) (US/1066-7776). [3,500] **2795**

OUT AUCKLAND (NZ/0110-4454). **2795**

OUT WEST (SACRAMENTO, CALIF.) (US/0899-1413). [13,500] **5488**

OUTAOUAIS GENEALOGIQUE (CN/0707-8137). [300] **2466**

OUTCROP (DENVER, COLO.) (US/0888-5184). [5,000] **1390**

OUTDOOR CREST (1975) (CN/0700-9909). [800] **4876**

OUTDOOR JOURNAL (US/0890-7196). [24,000] **4877**

OUTDOORS UNLIMITED (US/0030-7181). [2,600] **3421**

OUTDOORS WEST (US). [1,000] **4877**

OUTLOOK (US). **1094**

OUTLOOK - EDMONTON ART GALLERY (CN/1184-2288). [2,500] **361**

OUTLOOK (GRAND RAPIDS, MICH.), THE (US/8750-5754). [4,500] **5065**

OUTLOOK NEW CHURCH. GENERAL CONFERENCE (UK/0969-1049). [2,500] **4984**

OUTLOOK (PALO ALTO) (US/0273-835X). [27,000] **749**

OUTLOOK (WASHINGTON, D.C. : 1988) (US/0898-5766). [6,000] **623**

OUTPUT (SZ/0303-8351). [12,000] **1261**

OUTPUT OESTERREICH (AU). [14,000] **702**

OUTPUT (RICHMOND HILL) (CN/1184-9770). [1,600] **1224**

OUTREACH (CHICAGO) (US/0270-207X). [8,000] **3725**

OUTRIDER / WYOMING STATE LIBRARY, THE (US/0030-7319). [1,550] **3240**

OUTSIDE (1980) (US/0278-1433). [400,000] **4877**

OUTSIDE PLANT (US/0747-8763). **1119**

OUTSTANDING INVESTOR DIGEST (US/0891-463X). **910**

OUTSTATE BUSINESS (US/1064-3621). [10,000] **702**

OUTUKUMPU NEWS (FI). [15,000] **4014**

OVER THE YEARS (US). [650] **2625**

OVERLAND JOURNAL (US/0738-1093). [2,400] **2752**

OVERSEAS BUSINESS (US/1048-0722). [200,000] **702**

OVERSEAS EMPLOYMENT OPPORTUNITIES FOR EDUCATORS (US). [50,000] **1700**

OVERSEAS FOOD LEGISLATION MANUAL (UK). **2352**

OVERSEAS LIVING (US/0882-8938). **2542**

OVERSEAS TRADING (AT). [10,000] **848**

OVERTONES (LINCOLN, NEB.) (US/0884-920X). [2,000] **3240**

OVERTURE (LOS ANGELES) (US/0030-7556). [12,000] **4145**

OVERVIEW (US/0030-7564). [4,000] **5034**

OVERVIEW (TORONTO) (CN/0700-3617). [8,000] **4486**

OWYHEE OUTPOST (US/0889-6380). [500] **2753**

OXFORD BULLETIN OF ECONOMICS AND STATISTICS (UK/0305-9049). [1,300] **1577**

OXFORD ENERGY FORUM (UK/0959-7727). [500] **1952**

OXFORD GERMAN STUDIES (UK/0078-7191). [1,500] **3421**

OXFORD GERMAN STUDIES : BOOK SUPPLEMENT (UK/0141-8149). [500] **2702**

OXFORD LITERARY REVIEW, THE (UK/0305-1498). [1,000] **3349**

OXFORD POETRY (OXFORD, OXFORDSHIRE) (UK). [200] **3467**

OXFORD SLAVONIC PAPERS (UK/0078-7256). [1,000] **3336**

OXIDATION COMMUNICATIONS (BU/0209-4541). **1045**

OXONIENSIA (UK). [600] **277**

OYEZ REVIEW (US). [400] **1094**

OZ (MANHATTAN, KAN.) (US/0888-7802). [650] **305**

OZARK VISITOR (US/0890-2690). [180,000 unpaid] **5704**

OZS, OSTERREICHISCHE ZEITSCHRIFT FUER SOZIOLOGIE (AU/1011-0070). [600] **5253**

P.A.A. AFFAIRS (US/0300-6816). [3,000] **4555**

P. A. L., PREVENT, AVOID LOSSES (CN/0707-2228). **3171**

P & S / THE COLLEGE OF PHYSICIANS AND SURGEONS OF COLUMBIA UNIVERSITY (US/0743-507X). [20,000] **3625**

P. E. O. RECORD (US/0746-5130). **5235**

P.H.M. - REVUE HORTICOLE (FR). [12,500] **2427**

P I Q PRODUITS POUR L'INDUSTRIE QUEBECOISE (CN/0701-1687). [15,720] **3486**

P-IM : PROFESSIONAL IMAGING (NE). [9,000] **4567**

P-O-P TIMES (US/1040-8169). [16,000] **763**

P S R MONITOR (US). [8,000] **3625**

P SERIES - COMMITTEE FOR ECONOMIC DEVELOPMENT OF AUSTRALIA (AT). [2,000] **1511**

PACE (HUNTINGTON, IND.) (US/1048-4523). [1,800] **4984**

PACE LAW REVIEW (US/0272-2410). [500] **3024**

PACE PETROLEUM COKE QUARTERLY (US). **4271**

PACER (WINNIPEG, MAN.) (CN/0229-3463). **4911**

PACIFIC BOATING ALMANAC. SOUTHERN CALIFORNIA, ARIZONA & BAJA (US/0193-3507). [10,000] **595**

PACIFIC BUILDER & ENGINEER (US/0030-8544). [12,400] **2028**

PACIFIC COAST ARCHAEOLOGICAL SOCIETY QUARTERLY (US/0552-7252). [300] **277**

PACIFIC COAST NURSERYMAN & GARDEN SUPPLY DEALER (US/0192-7159). [10,500] **2427**

PACIFIC COAST STUDIO DIRECTORY (US/0731-2059). [25,000] **4075**

PACIFIC GILLNETTER (CN/1195-3365). [1,000 per issue] **2310**

PACIFIC HISTORICAL REVIEW (US/0030-8684). [1,700] **2753**

PACIFIC ISLANDS YEAR BOOK (FJ). [10,000] **2511**

PACIFIC JOURNAL OF MATHEMATICS (US/0030-8730). [1,500] **3526**

PACIFIC LAW JOURNAL (US/0030-8757). [3,300] **3024**

PACIFIC MAGAZINE (HONOLULU, HAWAII) (US/0744-1754). [10,000] **2511**

PACIFIC MARITIME MAGAZINE (US/0741-7586). [6,100] **5453**

PACIFIC NORTHWEST (US/0199-6363). [64,000] **2542**

PACIFIC NORTHWEST FORUM, THE (US). [250] **2753**

PACIFIC NORTHWEST INSECT CONTROL HANDBOOK (US). [1,500] **4246**

PACIFIC NORTHWEST PLANT DISEASE CONTROL HANDBOOK (US). [1,000] **2427**

PACIFIC NORTHWEST TRADE DIRECTORY (US). [20,000] **848**

PACIFIC NORTHWESTERNER, THE (US/0030-882X). [600] **2753**

PACIFIC PHILOSOPHICAL QUARTERLY (UK/0279-0750). [1,000] **4354**

PACIFIC STUDIES (US/0275-3596). [500] **2670**

PACIFIC SUN (US/0048-2641). [35,700] **5638**

PACIFIC THEOLOGICAL REVIEW (US/0360-1897). [6,400] **4984**

PACIFIC TRAFFIC (US/0030-8943). [13,500] **5442**

PACIFIC TRIBUNE (VANCOUVER, B.C.) (CN). [5,000] **5792**

PACIFIC VIEWPOINT (NZ/0030-8978). [680] **1577**

PACIFICA : AUSTRALIAN THEOLOGICAL STUDIES (AT). [600] **4984**

PACKAGING (AT). [5,050] **4220**

PACKAGING DESIGN IN JAPAN (JA). [10,000] **4220**

PACKAGING JAPAN (JA/0288-3864). [15,000] **4220**

PACKAGING NEWS (LONDON) (UK/0030-9133). [18,634] **4220**

PACKAGING TODAY LONDON (UK/0268-0920). [16,200] **4221**

PACKAGING TRENDS : JAPAN (JA). [80] **4221**

PACKAGING WEEK (UK/0267-6117). **4221**

PACKARD CORMORANT, THE (US/0362-9368). [3,999] **5422**

PACKER, THE (US/0030-9168). [15,000] **2352**

PADAGOGIK (WEINHEIM AN DER BERGSTRASSE, GERMANY) (GW/0043-3446). [120,000] **1771**

PADDLER (CN/0835-0310). [23,000] **595**

PADRES' TRAIL (US/0030-9222). [12,000] **4985**

PAEDIATRICA INDONESIANA (IO/0030-9311). [2,000] **3907**

PAGELAND PROGRESSIVE JOURNAL, THE (US/1063-8415). [4,000 paid weekly] **5743**

PAGES (NORTHEAST ED.) (US/0742-4981). [5,000] **5488**

PAGIDEX (CN/0823-7492). [7,100] **4319**

PAGINAS (CENTRO DE ESTUDIOS Y PUBLICACIONES) (PE). [2,500] **4985**

PAI BOLETIN INFORMATIVO (US/0251-4729). [10,000] **4795**

PAINT & COATINGS INDUSTRY (US/0884-3848). [12,000] **4224**

PAINT CHECK (US/1059-6313). [15,000] **4853**

PAINTBRUSH (LARAMIE) (US/0094-1964). [500] **3467**

PAINTED BRIDE QUARTERLY, THE (US/0362-7969). [100] **3467**

PAINTER CLAN, THE (US). [100] **2466**

PAINTING & WALLCOVERING CONTRACTOR (US/0735-9713). [25,000] **4224**

PAIS (MADRID, SPAIN : EDICION INTERNACIONAL) (SP). **5810**

PAKISTAN ADMINISTRATION : A JOURNAL OF THE PAKISTAN ADMINISTRATIVE STAFF COLLEGE (PK). [500] **1868**

PAKISTAN EXPORTS (KARACHI, PAKISTAN : 1982) (PK). [30,000] **848**

PAKISTAN JOURNAL OF FORESTRY, THE (PK/0030-9818). [400] **2390**

PAKISTAN JOURNAL OF OTOLARYNGOLOGY (PK/0257-4985). [1,500] **3890**

PAKISTAN JOURNAL OF PSYCHOLOGY (PK/0030-9869). **4606**

PAKISTAN JOURNAL OF SCIENTIFIC RESEARCH (PK/0552-9050). [1000] **5137**

PAKISTAN JOURNAL OF ZOOLOGY (PK/0030-9923). [600] **5593**

PAKISTAN LIBRARY BULLETIN (PK/0030-9966). [2,000] **3240**

PAKISTAN MANAGEMENT REVIEW (PK). [1,600] **881**

PAKISTAN SYSTEMATICS (PK). [1,000] **520**

PAKIZAH INTIRNASHINAL (CN/0711-4222). [2,000] **5564**

PALABRA (SP). [13,000] **4985**

PALABRA Y EL HOMBRE, LA (MX/0185-5727). [2,000] **2851**

PALACIO, EL (US/0031-0158). [4,000] **2753**

PALAEOBULGARICA. STAROBULGARISTIKA (BU). [1,200] **2702**

PALAEONTOGRAPHICA AMERICANA (US/0078-8546). [400] **4229**

PALAEONTOLOGIA AFRICANA (SA/0078-8554). [600] **4229**

PALAEONTOLOGIA JUGOSLAVICA (CI/0552-9352). **4229**

PALAEONTOLOGY (UK/0031-0239). [500] **4229**

PALAEONTOLOGY NEWSLETTER (UK/0954-9900). **4229**

PALAESTRA (MACOMB, ILL.) (US/8756-5811). [6,000] **4392**

PALAIOS (US/0883-1351). [1,800] **4229**

PALANTE (CU/0552-9395). [20,000] **3421**

PALATINE IMMIGRANT, THE (US/0884-5735). [2500] **2466**

PALEOBIOLOGY (US/0094-8373). [2,250] **4229**

PALEONTOLOGIA MEXICANA (MX/0543-7652). [1,200] **4229**

PALETTE TALK (US/0276-1971). [70,000] **361**

PALLIATIVE CARE INDEX (UK/0961-4591). **3625**

PALLISER PAGES (CN/0824-152X). **3240**

PALMETTO BANKER (US/0164-5773). [1,600] **802**

PALMETTO (ORLANDO, FLA.), THE (US/0276-4164). [1,500] **2427**

PALMYONG TUKHO (KO). **1307**

PALO ALTO WEEKLY (US/0199-1159). [45,000] **5638**

PALOMINO HORSES (US/0031-045X). [5,800] **2801**

PALYNOS (US/0256-1670). [3,000] **521**

PAMATKY ARCHEOLOGICKE (XR/0031-0506). **278**

PAMTECO TRACINGS (US/1047-3173). [175] **2466**

PAN (MX). [10,000] **2352**

PAN PIPES (US/0889-7581). [20,000] **4145**

PAN Z WAMI (US/0274-9009). [58,000] **4985**

PANDORA (DENVER, COLO.) (US/0275-519X). [500] **3422**

PANEL RESOURCE PAPER (US/0739-2346). [1,000] **1902**

PANHANDLE HERALD, THE (US/8756-2464). **5753**

PANHANDLE-PLAINS HISTORICAL REVIEW (US/0148-7795). [950] **2753**

PANOPTICON (BE). **3171**

PANORAMA (UK). [4,000] **4221**

PANTHEIST VISION (US/0742-5368). **4354**

PANTOGRAPH OF POSTAL STATIONERY, THE (US/0893-9055). [1,500] **2786**

PAPEIS AVULSOS DE ZOOLOGIA (SAO PAULO) (BL/0031-1049). [684] **5594**

PAPELES DE ECONOMIA ESPANOLA (SP/0210-9107). [10,000] **1577**

PAPER AGE (US/0031-1081). [28,000] **4235**

PAPER CLIPP (US/0886-8212). [75] **4235**

PAPER CONSERVATION NEWS (LONDON) (UK/0140-1033). [1,500] **4235**

PAPER CONSERVATOR (UK/0309-4227). [1,500] **4235**

PAPER EUROPE (UK/0955-7806). [14,350] **4236**

PAPER, FILM AND FOIL CONVERTER (US/0031-1138). [32,000] **4236**

PAPER MARKET DIGEST (UK). [500] **4236**

PAPER MONEY (US/0031-1162). [1,800] **2783**

PAPER. SOUTHERN AFRICA (SA/0254-3494). [1,400] **4236**

PAPER SUMMARIES - AMERICAN SOCIETY FOR NONDESTRUCTIVE TESTING (US/0272-4723). [10,000] **1990**

PAPERBOARD PACKAGING'S OFFICIAL CONTAINER DIRECTORY (US/0198-8867). [4,000] **4221**

PAPERI JA PUU (FI/0031-1243). [4,100] **4236**

PAPERS AND DISCUSSIONS - ASSOCIATION OF MINE MANAGERS OF SOUTH AFRICA (SA). [2,000] **2147**

PAPERS AND PROCEEDINGS OF APPLIED GEOGRAPHY CONFERENCES (US/0747-5160). **2572**

PAPERS AND PROCEEDINGS OF THE ROYAL SOCIETY OF TASMANIA (AT/0080-4703). [700] **5137**

PAPERS AND RECORDS - THUNDER BAY HISTORICAL MUSEUM SOCIETY (CN/0703-7058). [750] **4095**

PAPERS AND STUDIES IN CONTRASTIVE LINGUISTICS (PL/0137-2459). [1,200] **3309**

PAPERS - KROEBER ANTHROPOLOGICAL SOCIETY (US/0023-4869). [400] **243**

PAPERS OF THE BIBLIOGRAPHICAL SOCIETY OF CANADA (CN/0067-6896). [500] **422**

PAPERS OF THE EAST-WEST POPULATION INSTITUTE (US/0732-0531). [500] **4556**

PAPERS ON FRENCH SEVENTEENTH CENTURY LITERATURE (GW/0343-0758). [500] **3422**

PAPERS ON LANGUAGE & LITERATURE (US/0031-1294). [800] **3422**

PAPERS PRESENTED AT THE ANNUAL MEETING OF THE AFRICAN STUDIES ASSOCIATION (US). [100] **2500**

PAPERS PRESENTED AT THE SHORT COURSE IN PAINT TECHNOLOGY (US). [1,850] **2015**

PAPERS - WEST TENNESSEE HISTORICAL SOCIETY (US/0361-6215). [500] **2753**

PAPETIER DE FRANCE, LE (FR). [10,333] **4236**

PAPIER & DRUCK (AU). [4,300] **4236**

PAPIER, CARTON ET CELLULOSE (FR/0031-1367). [5,000] **4236**

PAPIER, DAS (GW/0031-1340). [4,000] **4236**

PAPIER- UND ZELLSTOFF-DIENST (GW/0171-1458). **4237**

PAPPUS (CN/0710-0469). [3,347] **521**

PAPRIPARI ES NYOMDAIPARI SZAKIRODALMI TAJEKOZTATO (HU/0231-0740). [165] **4237**

PAPUA NEW GUINEA JOURNAL OF EDUCATION (PP/0031-1472). [300] **1771**

PAPUA NEW GUINEA MEDICAL JOURNAL (PP/0031-1480). [300] **3626**

PAPUA NEW GUINEA NATIONAL BIBLIOGRAPHY (PP/0252-8347). [200] **422**

PAR. PUBLIC ADMINISTRATION REVIEW POPULATION (US/0033-3352). [21,000] **4672**

PARACHUTE (CN/0318-7020). [4,500] **361**

PARACHUTE PAGES (US). **4911**

PARACLETE (SPRINGFIELD, MO.) (US/0190-4639). [3,650] **5065**

PARAGLIDE (US/0745-9688). [15,000] **4053**

PARAGLIDE (FORT BRAGG, N.C.) (US/0891-7965). [23,000] **5724**

PARALLELES (UNIVERSITE DE GENEVE. ECOLE DE TRADUCTION ET D'INTERPRETATION) (SZ). [1,000] **3310**

PARASITE IMMUNOLOGY (UK/0141-9838). [515] **3675**

PARASITOLOGY (UK/0031-1820). [1,219] **492**

PARATUS (SA). [47,000] **4053**

PARENT & CHILD (US/1041-178X). [55,000] **2284**

PARENTGUIDE NEWS (US/0896-1468). [205,000] **2284**

PARENT'S SAY (AT/0818-8114). [1,500] **1772**

PARERGON (AT/0313-6221). [350] **1079**

PARIS REVIEW, THE (US/0031-2037). [10,500] **3422**

PARIS SUCCESS (BE). [F] **1086**

PARISH COMMUNICATION (US/0279-7828). [1,000] **4985**

PARISH TEACHER (US/0738-7962). [50,000] **4985**

PARK & GROUNDS MANAGEMENT (US/1057-204X). [13,000] **4707**

PARK CITIES NEWS, THE (US). [8,000] **5753**

PARK RECORD (1964), THE (US/0745-9483). **5757**

PARK WORLD (UK). [6,500] **3486**

PARKER DIRECTORY OF CALIFORNIA ATTORNEYS (US/0196-6138). [65,000] **3025**

PARKINSON NETWORK (CN/0824-7315). [5,500] **3626**

PARKS AND GROUNDS (SA). [3,945] **2427**

PARLIAMENTARY GOVERNMENT (CN/0709-4582). [2,000-5,000] **4486**

PARLIAMENTARY WEEKLY QUARTERLY REPORT, THE (CN/1188-2387). **4487**

PARLONS PEDAGOGIE (CN/0712-9947). **1839**

PARNASSOS (GR/0048-301X). **3310**

PARSONS SUN (PARSONS, KAN. : 1929) (US). [7,700] **5678**

PARTICIPATION (OTTAWA) (CN/0709-6941). [1,500] **4487**

PARTIE PRENANTE (FR/0294-0531). [1,300] **1772**

PARTNERS IN PRINT (CN/1195-4981). [350] **881**

PASAA (TH/0125-2488). [500] **3310**

PASADENA HERITAGE (US/0889-5864). [1,550] **2753**

PASADENA JOURNAL OF BUSINESS (US/0743-6610). [2,000] **702**

PASS PROMOTER, THE (CN/0380-4135). [3,500] **5792**

PASSAIC REVIEW (US/0731-4663). [500] **3349**

PASSATO E PRESENTE (IT). **4544**

PASSATO E PRESENTE (FLORENCE, ITALY) (IT/0392-4815). [2,000] **2625**

PASSE-SPORTS (CN/0820-070X). **4911**

PASSING SHOW (NEW YORK, N.Y.) (US/1061-8112). [1,200] **5367**

PASSPORT (CHICAGO) (US/0031-272X). **5488**

PASSPORT TO LEGAL UNDERSTANDING (US/0737-7630). [10,000] **3025**

PASSWORD (EL PASO) (US/0031-2738). [1,200] **2753**

PAST & PRESENT (UK/0031-2746). [3,750] **2625**

PAST & PRESENT (WATERLOO) (CN/0702-7125). [1,800] **2852**

PASTORAL HORIZONS (AT). **5034**

PASTORAL LIFE (US/0031-2762). [3,400] **4985**

PASTORAL MUSIC (US/0363-6569). [7,200] **4145**

PASTORAL MUSIC NOTEBOOK (US/0145-6636). [8,500] **4145**

PASTOR'S TAX & MONEY (US/1061-978X). [6,000] **4985**

PASTURAS TROPICALES (CK/1012-7410). [118]

PATHWAY TO GOD (II). [2,000] **4985**

PATHWAYS (FREDERICTON) (CN/0710-7773). **1883**

PATHWAYS (MAYNARDVILLE, TENN.) (US/8755-4747). [500 members; 40 states] **2753**

PATIENT CARE (US/0031-305X). [113,000] **3738**

PATIENT CARE LAW (US/0730-5524). [500] **3025**

PATIENT EDUCATION NEWSLETTER (US/0278-8209). [2,300] **4795**

PATIENT MANAGEMENT (SEAFORTH) (NZ/0314-660X). [5,000] **3626**

PATIENT UPDATE (CN/0847-8090). [6,000] **3790**

PATRE (FR). [5,500] **217**

PATRICIAN, THE (CN/0316-4942). **4053**

PATRIDES (TORONTO) (CN/0824-359X). [10,000] **2270**

PAVING FORUM (US). [25,000] **2028**

PAYROLL EXCHANGE (US/0194-6196). [3,000] **1701**

PAZIFISCHE RUNDSCHAU (CN/0048-3095). [15,000] **5792**

PBO-BLAD / SOCIAAL-ECONOMISCHE RAAD (NE). [450] **1578**

PC ACTIVE (NE/0925-5745). [30,000] **1270**

PC DIGEST RATINGS REPORT (US/1042-3575). **1270**

PC GRAPHICS & VIDEO (US/1077-5862). [75,000] **1234**

PC-PRAXIS 1989 (GW/0940-6743). [227,000] **1199**

PC PUBLISHING (US/0896-8209). [50,000] **4818**

PC REPORT (US). [15,000] **1271**

PC RETAILING (US/0746-6773). **1245**

PC TODAY (US/1040-6484). [200,000] **1271**

PC USER (LONDON, ENGLAND) (UK/0263-5720). [39,213] **1271**

PC WEEK (U.S. ED.) (US/0740-1604). [175,000] **1271**

PCR / PRODUCTION AND CASTING REPORT (UK/0142-632X). **1621**

PCTE NEWSLETTER (FR). **1199**

PEA RIVER TRAILS (US/8756-4181). [300] **2467**

PEACE AND THE SCIENCES (AU). [500] **4531**

PEACE ARCH NEWS WEEKENDER, THE (CN/0821-5251). **5792**

PEACE CORPS TIMES (US/0884-9196). [17,500] **2911**

PEACE MAGAZINE (CN/0826-9521). [2,000] **4531**

PEACE REPORTER (US/1049-0779). **1772**

PEACH TIMES (US/0031-3610). [1,800] **2427**

PEANUT FARMER, THE (US/0031-3653). [20,000] **180**

PEANUT GROWER, THE (US/1042-9379). [28,000] **180**

PEANUT SCIENCE (US/0095-3679). [650] **180**

PEASANT STUDIES (US/0149-1547). [500] **5212**

PEAT ABSTRACTS (IE). [400] **2147**

PEDAGOGIA MEDICA (IT/1120-8627). [5,000] **3626**

PEDAGOGIKA (XR/0031-3815). **1772**

PEDIATRIC ANNALS (US/0090-4481). [30,000] **3908**

PEDIATRIC MANAGEMENT (US/1051-3272). **3908**

PEDIATRIE (FR/0031-4021). [1,500] **3910**

PEDIGREE POINTERS / STEVENS POINT AREA GENEALOGICAL SOCIETY (US/0749-6192). [125] **2467**

PEDMED (SA/1017-1711). [2,900] **3626**

PEDOLOGIE (BE/0079-0419). **181**

PEDRALBES (SP). [300] **2702**

PEGBOARD (MENLO PARK, CALIF.) (US/0892-5763). [2,000] **1230**

PEGG. ASSOCIATION OF PROFESSIONAL ENGINEERS, GEOLOGISTS AND GEOPHYSICISTS OF ALBERTA (MONTHLY ED.) (CN/0823-1745). [33,000] **1990**

PEGG, THE (CN/0030-7912). [33,150] **1990**

PEI LEI HSUEH PAO (CH). [800] **5594**

PELITA BPKS (IO/0126-3692). [300] **5300**

PELLISSIPPIAN (CLINTON, TENN.) (US/0736-5594). [215] **2467**

PEM : PLANT ENGINEERING AND MAINTENANCE (CN/0710-362X). [21,000] **2124**

PEMBIMBING PEMBACA (IO). [7,500] **3240**

PEN WORLD (US/1045-1188). [10,000] **2776**

PENDUDUK CINA JAWA-MADURA : HASIL REGISTRASI PENDUDUK (IO). **4556**

PENDUDUK JAWA TENGAH, HASIL REGISTRASI PENDUDUK (IO). **5335**

PENINSULA HERITAGE (US/0895-8165). [225] **5034**

PENINSULA (REDWOOD CITY, CALIF.) (US/0888-4846). [35,000] **2543**

PENINSULA (SAN MATEO), LA (US/0197-2197). [1,400] **2754**

PENNSYLVANIA ARCHAEOLOGIST (US/0031-4358). [800] **278**

PENNSYLVANIA ARCHITECT (US/1062-8649). [3,500] **305**

PENNSYLVANIA BAR ASSOCIATION QUARTERLY (US/0196-2051). [27,000] **3025**

PENNSYLVANIA BULLETIN (HARRISBURG) (US/0162-2137). [13,000] **3025**

PENNSYLVANIA CHIEFS OF POLICE ASSOCIATION BULLETIN (US/0031-4404). [1,500] **3171**

PENNSYLVANIA CPA JOURNAL (US/0746-1062). **749**

PENNSYLVANIA EDUCATION (US/0031-4455). [197,000] **1772**

PENNSYLVANIA FORESTS (US/0031-4501). [2,500] **2390**

PENNSYLVANIA GAME NEWS (US/0031-451X). [140,000] **4877**

PENNSYLVANIA GENEALOGICAL MAGAZINE, THE (US/0882-3685). [2,000] **2467**

PENNSYLVANIA GEOGRAPHER, THE (US/0553-5980). [220] **2572**

PENNSYLVANIA GEOLOGY (US/0048-3214). [5,000] **1391**

PENNSYLVANIA HISTORY (US/0031-4528). [800] **2754**

PENNSYLVANIA HOSPITALS (US/0744-5636). [6,000] **3790**

PENNSYLVANIA LAWYER, THE (US/0193-4821). [27,000] **3025**

PENNSYLVANIA MAGAZINE OF HISTORY AND BIOGRAPHY, THE (US/0031-4587). [3,200] **2754**

PENNSYLVANIA MENNONITE HERITAGE (US/0148-4036). [3,000] **2467**

PENNSYLVANIA NURSE, THE (US/0031-4617). [9,200] **3866**

PENNSYLVANIA PHARMACIST (US/0031-4633). [2,200] **4319**

PENNSYLVANIA RECREATION & PARKS (US/0742-793X). [1,500] **4707**

PENNSYLVANIA REVIEW (PITTSBURGH, PA.), THE (US/8756-5668). [1,000] **3423**

PENNSYLVANIA SPEECH COMMUNICATION ANNUAL, THE (US/0889-5570). [200] **1119**

PENORRA : REVISTA TRIMESTRAL DE POESIA, LA (SP). [3,500] **3468**

PENSACOLA NEWS JOURNAL (US). [61,725 (Mon.-Fri.)71,630 (Sat.)84,345 (Sun.)] **5650**

PENSIERO MAZZINIANO, IL (IT). [3,500] **4487**

PENSION WORLD (US/0098-1753). [28,000] **1701**

PENTECOSTAL TESTIMONY, THE (CN/0031-4927). [30,000] **4986**

PEOPLE & THE PLANET / IPPF, UNFPA, IUCN (UK/0968-1655). [20,000] **4556**

PEOPLE (ENGLISH ED.) (UK/0301-5645). [13,500] **590**

PEP (MAMARONECK, N.Y.) (US/0031-5060). **4864**

PEPPERDINE LAW REVIEW (US/0092-430X). [650] **3026**

PEPTIDE INFORMATION / PEPTIDE INSTITUTE, PROTEIN RESEARCH FOUNDATION (JA/0385-8847). [300] **1046**

PEPTIDES (NEW YORK, N.Y, : 1980) (US/0196-9781). **492**

PER LA FILOSOFIA (IT). [1,000] **4354**

PERCEPTION (OTTAWA) (CN/0704-5263). [3,500] **5301**

PERCUSSIVE NOTES (US/0553-6502). [6,000] **4145**

PEREGRINE FUND NEWSLETTER, THE (US). [6,000] **2202**

PERFORMANCE AUDIT (US). [150] **4740**

PERFORMANCE PRACTICE REVIEW (US/1044-1638). [500] **4145**

PERFORMANCES MARSEILLE (FR/0996-5882). [2,000] **1773**

PERFORMING ARTS FORUM (US/0739-1161). **387**

PERFORMING ARTS (HOUSTON) (US/0192-4192). [90,000] **387**

PERFORMING ARTS (LOS ANGELES EDITION) (US/0031-5222). [825,000] **387**

PERFORMING ARTS RESOURCES (US/0360-3814). [500] **387**

PERFUSION LIFE (US/0747-3079). [3,000] **3773**

PERINATAL PRESS (US/0160-7219). [5,000] **3766**

PERIOD HOME RENOVATOR BUYER'S GUIDE (AT/1036-3181). **2907**

PERIODICA POLYTECHNICA. CIVIL ENGINEERING (HU/0553-6626). **2028**

PERIODICA POLYTECHNICA: ELECTRICAL ENGINEERING. ELEKTROTECHNIK (HU/0031-532X). [900] **2075**

PERIODICALS AND NEWSPAPERS IN THE COLLECTIONS OF THE LIBRARY OF PARLIAMENT (CN/0702-0260). [400] **3259**

PERIODICALS DIGEST, DENTISTRY (US/0272-8850). **1333**

PERIODICUM BIOLOGORUM (CI/0031-5362). [800] **468**

PERIPHERY LISMORE (AT/1034-0580). [3,000] **374**

PERISTIL (ZAGREB) (CI/0553-6707). **362**

PERKEMBANGAN BULANAN HARGA ECERAN BAHAN MAKANAN POKOK & BAHAN PENTING LIANNYA DI IBUKOTA PROPINSI INDONESIA (IO). **1594**

PERKINS PRESS (US/0898-1574). **2467**

PERSONAL COMPUTER (IT). [24,000] **1289**

PERSONAL COMPUTER REPORT (MINEOLA, N.Y.) (US/0894-3532). **1199**

PERSONAL ENGINEERING & INSTRUMENTATION NEWS (US/0748-0016). [50,000] **1230**

PERSONAL INJURY VERDICT SURVEY. ALABAMA EDITION (US/8755-6413). [250] **3026**

PERSONAL INJURY VERDICT SURVEY. ALASKA EDITION (US/8755-6618). [250] **3026**

PERSONAL INJURY VERDICT SURVEY. ARIZONA EDITION (US/8755-6774). [250] **3026**

PERSONAL INJURY VERDICT SURVEY. ARKANSAS EDITION (US/8755-6782). [250] **3026**

PERSONAL INJURY VERDICT SURVEY. CALIFORNIA EDITION (US/8755-6790). [250] **3026**

PERSONAL INJURY VERDICT SURVEY. COLORADO EDITION (US/8755-6731). [250] **3026**

PERSONAL INJURY VERDICT SURVEY. CONNECTICUT EDITION (US/8755-6596). [250] **3026**

PERSONAL INJURY VERDICT SURVEY. DELAWARE EDITION (US/8755-6529). [250] **3026**

PERSONAL INJURY VERDICT SURVEY. FLORIDA EDITION (US/8755-6723). [250] **3026**

PERSONAL INJURY VERDICT SURVEY. GEORGIA EDITION (US/8755-6758). [250] **3026**

PERSONAL INJURY VERDICT SURVEY. HAWAII EDITION (US/8755-674X). [250] **3027**

PERSONAL INJURY VERDICT SURVEY. IDAHO EDITION (US/8755-6693). [250] **3027**

PERSONAL INJURY VERDICT SURVEY. ILLINOIS EDITION (US/8755-6685). [250] **3027**

PERSONAL INJURY VERDICT SURVEY. INDIANA EDITION (US/8755-6715). [250] **3027**

PERSONAL INJURY VERDICT SURVEY. IOWA EDITION (US/8755-6669). [250] **3027**

PERSONAL INJURY VERDICT SURVEY. KANSAS EDITION (US/8755-6677). [250] **3027**

PERSONAL INJURY VERDICT SURVEY. KENTUCKY EDITION (US/8755-6707). [250] **3027**

PERSONAL INJURY VERDICT SURVEY. LOUISIANA EDITION (US/8755-6820). [250] **3027**

PERSONAL INJURY VERDICT SURVEY. MAINE EDITION (US/8755-6545). [250] **3027**

PERSONAL INJURY VERDICT SURVEY. MARYLAND EDITION (US/8755-6537). [250] **3027**

PERSONAL INJURY VERDICT SURVEY. MICHIGAN EDITION (US/8755-6499). [250] **3027**

PERSONAL INJURY VERDICT SURVEY. MISSISSIPPI EDITION (US/8755-6480). [250] **3027**

PERSONAL INJURY VERDICT SURVEY. MISSOURI EDITION (US/8755-6472). [250] **3027**

PERSONAL INJURY VERDICT SURVEY. MONTANA EDITION (US/8755-6464). [250] **3027**

PERSONAL INJURY VERDICT SURVEY. NEBRASKA EDITION (US/8755-6642). [250] **3027**

PERSONAL INJURY VERDICT SURVEY. NEW HAMPSHIRE EDITION (US/8755-6391). [250] **3027**

PERSONAL INJURY VERDICT SURVEY. NEW MEXICO EDITION (US/8755-6375). [250] **3027**

PERSONAL INJURY VERDICT SURVEY. NEW YORK EDITION (US/8755-6383). [250] **3027**

PERSONAL INJURY VERDICT SURVEY. NORTH CAROLINA EDITION (US/8755-6359). [250] **3028**

PERSONAL INJURY VERDICT SURVEY. NORTH DAKOTA EDITION (US/8755-6812). [250] **3028**

PERSONAL INJURY VERDICT SURVEY. OHIO EDITION (US/8755-6367). [250] **3028**

PERSONAL INJURY VERDICT SURVEY. OKLAHOMA EDITION (US/8755-6405). [250] **3028**

PERSONAL INJURY VERDICT SURVEY. OREGON EDITION (US/8755-6766). [250] **3028**

PERSONAL INJURY VERDICT SURVEY. PENNSYLVANIA EDITION (US/8755-6804). [250] **3028**

PERSONAL INJURY VERDICT SURVEY. SOUTH CAROLINA EDITION (US/8755-6448). [250] **3028**

PERSONAL INJURY VERDICT SURVEY. SOUTH DAKOTA EDITION (US/8755-6456). [250] **3028**

PERSONAL INJURY VERDICT SURVEY. TENNESSEE EDITION (US/8755-643X). [250] **3028**

PERSONAL INJURY VERDICT SURVEY. TEXAS EDITION (US/8755-6421). [250] **3028**

PERSONAL INJURY VERDICT SURVEY. UTAH EDITION (US/8755-6650). [250] **3028**

PERSONAL INJURY VERDICT SURVEY. VERMONT EDITION (US/8755-6626). [250] **3028**

PERSONAL INJURY VERDICT SURVEY. VIRGINIA EDITION (US/8755-657X). [250] **3028**

PERSONAL INJURY VERDICT SURVEY. WASHINGTON, D.C. EDITION (US/8755-6510). [250] **3028**

PERSONAL INJURY VERDICT SURVEY. WASHINGTON EDITION (US/8755-6553). [250] **3028**

PERSONAL INJURY VERDICT SURVEY. WEST VIRGINIA EDITION (US/8755-6561). [250] **3028**

PERSONAL INJURY VERDICT SURVEY. WISCONSIN EDITION (US/8755-660X). [250] **3028**

PERSONAL INJURY VERDICT SURVEY. WYOMING EDITION (US/8755-6634). [250] **3028**

PERSONAL SELLING POWER (US/0738-8594). [130705] **934**

PERSONAL TAXATION ABROAD (US). **4741**

PERSONALHISTORISK TIDSSKRIFT (DK/0300-3655). [1,500] **2467**

PERSONALITIES OF AMERICA (US). [3,500] **434**

PERSONALITY STUDY AND GROUP BEHAVIOUR (II). [500] **4607**

PERSONHISTORISK TIDSSKRIFT (SW/0031-5699). [800] **434**

PERSONNEL MANAGEMENT ABSTRACTS (US/0031-577X). [1,100] **732**

PERSONNEL POLICY MANUAL (US). [6,000] **945**

PERSOON EN GEMEENSCHAP (BE/0031-5842). [1,700] **1773**

PERSPECTIVA (SOUTH HADLEY, MASS.) (US/1059-0536). [15,000] **3310**

PERSPECTIVA TEOLOGICA (BL/0102-4469). [1,500] **4986**

PERSPECTIVAS DEL SISTEMA FINANCIERO (SP). [4,000] **1578**

PERSPECTIVE (ALBANY, N.Y. 1983) (US/0743-6475). [5,000] **3029**

PERSPECTIVE ON AGING (US/0096-2740). [7,000] **3754**

PERSPECTIVE (TORONTO. 1967) (CN/0384-8922). [4,200] **4986**

PERSPECTIVES '93 (US). [3,200] **5336**

PERSPECTIVES IN CARDIOLOGY (CN/0828-6396). [24,000] **3709**

PERSPECTIVES IN COVENANT EDUCATION (US/1070-8944). [600] **1773**

PERSPECTIVES IN ENGINEERING (US). [3,200] **1990**

PERSPECTIVES (MANHATTAN, KAN.) (US/8756-7679). [4,200] **1840**

PERSPECTIVES ON CATS (US). [5,900] **5518**

PERSPECTIVES / THE NIAGARA INSTITUTE (CN/0711-4931). **5212**

PERSPECTIVES (TOLEDO, OHIO) (US/0883-6086). [1,000] **3350**

PERSPEKTIEF (NE/0167-9104). [3,500] **4372**

PERSUASIONS (VICTORIA) (CN/0821-0314). [2,500] **3423**

PERU ECONOMICO (PE). [5,000] **1578**

PESQUISA AGROPECUARIA BRASILEIRA (BL/0100-204X). [1,600] **119**

PESQUISAS. ANTROPOLOGIA (BL/0553-8467). [500] **243**

PESQUISAS. BOTANICA (BL/0373-840X). [500] **521**

PESQUISAS. HISTORIA (BL/0101-9619). [500] **2625**

PEST CONTROL LETTER (US). **4246**

PEST MANAGEMENT (US/0744-6357). [6,000] **4246**

PESTALK (AT). **4246**

PESTDOC (UK). [17,440] **4248**

PET AGE (US/0098-5406). [17,000] **4287**

PET BUSINESS (US/0191-4766). [14,500] **4287**

PET DEALER (US/0553-8572). [15,500] **4287**

PETER DAG INVESTMENT LETTER, THE (US/0196-9323). [5,000] **911**

PETERBOROUGH EXAMINER (CN). [28,000] **5792**

PETERBOROUGH EXAMINER (DAILY ED.) (CN/0839-0878). [28,000] **5792**

PETERMANNS GEOGRAPHISCHE MITTEILUNGEN (GW/0031-6229). **2572**

PETFOOD INDUSTRY (US/0031-6245). [5,000] **4287**

PETITE NATION, LA (CN/0228-9954). [7,489] **5792**

PETROBRAS NEWS (BL/0103-5266). [6,000] **4271**

PETROLEUM (VE). [5,000] **4272**

PETROLEUM ABSTRACTS (TULSA, OKLA.) (US/0031-6423). [2,000] **4284**

PETROLEUM/ENERGY BUSINESS NEWS INDEX (US/0098-7743). [250] **4272**

PETROLEUM ENGINEER INTERNATIONAL (US/0164-8322). [37,000] **4272**

PETROLEUM EXPLORATION IN NEW ZEALAND NEWS (NZ/0113-0501). [750] **4272**

PETROLEUM FEEDSTOCKS IN ... (US/0743-5274). **4272**

PETROLEUM GAZETTE (MELBOURNE) (AT/0048-3591). [23,000] **4272**

PETROLEUM INFORMATION SERVICE (PP/1021-3600). **4273**

PETROLEUM INFORMATION'S NATIONAL WILDCAT MONTHLY (US/0744-8007). [50] **4273**

PETROLEUM MANAGEMENT (HOUSTON, TEX.) (US/0884-4550). [25,000] **4273**

PETROLEUM MARKETER (NEW HAVEN) (US/0362-7799). [14,900] **4273**

PETROLEUM SERVICES WEEKLY SERVICE (UK). **4273**

PEUPLE, LE (FR). [30,000] **1701**

PEUPLE (ST-AGAPIT) (CN/0228-5703). [10,500] **5792**

PEUPLE-TRIBUNE (CN/0383-7572). [20,814] **5792**

PEUPLES DU MONDE (FR/0555-9952). [35,000] **4986**

PHALANX (ALEXANDRIA) (US/0195-1920). [8,500] **2107**

PHALGU : PHALGU SAHITYA SAMSADARA MUKHAPATRA (II). [1,100] **3423**

PHARMA JAPAN (JA/0285-4937). [1,000 domestic1,000 foreign] **4319**

PHARMACA (CI/0031-6857). [3,300] **4319**

PHARMACEUTICAL & COSMETIC REVIEW (SA/1015-4760). [1500] **4320**

PHARMACEUTICAL ENGINEERING (US/0273-8139). [14,500] **4320**

PHARMACEUTICAL EXECUTIVE (US/0279-6570). [11,000] **4320**

PHARMACEUTICAL LITIGATION REPORTER (US/0887-7815). **3029**

PHARMACEUTICAL MARKETING (UK). [6,500] **4320**

PHARMACEUTICAL NEWS CAPSULE, THE (US/0891-2793). **4320**

PHARMACEUTICAL TECHNOLOGY (US/0147-8087). [30,000] **4321**

PHARMACEUTICAL TECHNOLOGY INTERNATIONAL (US/0164-6826). [20,000] **4321**

PHARMACEUTICAL TIMES (UK). [7,400] **4321**

PHARMACIE HOSPITALIERE FRANCAISE, LA (FR/0369-9579). [1,200] **3791**

PHARMACIEN DE FRANCE (FR/0031-6938). **4321**

PHARMACOLOGICA ET PHYSIOLOGICA (OULU) (FI/0358-4828). [450] **4322**

PHARMACOLOGY AND THE SKIN (SZ/1011-291X). **3722**

PHARMACOLOGY & TOXICOLOGY (DK/0901-9928). [1,000] **4322**

PHARMACOLOGY, BIOCHEMISTRY AND BEHAVIOR (US/0091-3057). **4322**

PHARMACY HEALTH-LINE (US/0739-9596). **4323**

PHARMACY NEWS AND REVIEW (US/8750-4790). [2,600] **4323**

PHARMACY TIMES (US/0003-0627). [93,666] **4323**

PHARMACY WEST (US/0191-6394). [16,000] **4323**

PHARMASCOPE (US). **4324**

PHARMAZEUTISCHE INDUSTRIE, DIE (GW/0031-711X). [4,500] **4324**

PHARMAZEUTISCHE ZEITUNG (GW/0031-7136). [27,500] **4324**

PHARMAZIE

Controlled Circulation Index

PHARMAZIE HEUTE (GW/0369-979X). [24,000] **4324**

PHAROS OF ALPHA OMEGA ALPHA-HONOR MEDICAL SOCIETY, THE (US/0031-7179). [60,000] **3627**

PHAT : PRESENTATION HOUSE ARTS TABLOID (CN/0711-7515). [500] **381**

PHELON'S DISCOUNT & JOBBING TRADE (US). [3,000] **956**

PHELONS WOMENS APPAREL & ACCESSORY SHOPS (US). **5564**

PHELON'S WOMEN'S APPAREL SHOPS (US/0737-3430). [1,000] **1086**

PHELPS COUNTY GENEALOGICAL SOCIETY QUARTERLY (US/0884-2140). [100] **2467**

PHENIX (FR/0300-3639). [300] **4864**

PHILADELPHIA CITY PAPER (US/0733-6349). [88,000] **5738**

PHILADELPHIA GAY NEWS (US). [15,000] **5738**

PHILADELPHIA MAGAZINE (1967) (US/0031-7233). [148,809] **2543**

PHILADELPHIA MEDICINE (US/0031-7306). [4,500] **3627**

PHILADELPHIA NEW OBSERVER, THE (US/0890-8435). [20,000] **5738**

PHILADELPHIA TRIBUNE (1884) (US/0746-956X). [25,000 Tuesday 18,000 Friday] **5738**

PHILANTHROPIC DIGEST (US/0480-2853). [600] **4338**

PHILANTHROPIC TRENDS DIGEST, THE (US/1065-1659). **4338**

PHILANTHROPY. THE QUARTERLY NEWSLETTER OF THE AUSTRALIAN ASSOCIATION OF PHILANTHROPY (AT). **4338**

PHILATELIC JOURNALIST, THE (US/0048-3710). [900] **2786**

PHILATELIC LITERATURE REVIEW (US/0270-1707). [2,560] **2786**

PHILATELIST AND PJGB, THE (UK/0260-6739). **2786**

PHILIPPINE ENTOMOLOGIST (PH/0369-9536). [400] **5594**

PHILIPPINE FORESTRY STATISTICS (PH). [700] **2399**

PHILIPPINE JOURNAL OF CROP SCIENCE, THE (PH/0115-2025). [200] **181**

PHILIPPINE JOURNAL OF PUBLIC ADMINISTRATION (PH/0031-7675). [1,000] **4673**

PHILIPPINE JOURNAL OF WEED SCIENCE (PH). [500] **181**

PHILIPPINE LAW AND JURISPRUDENCE (PH). [1,000] **3029**

PHILIPPINE LAW GAZETTE (PH/0115-2483). [3,000] **3142**

PHILIPPINE LAW JOURNAL (PH/0031-7721). [4] **3029**

PHILIPPINE LETTER, THE (US/0379-2870). **703**

PHILIPPINE PHYTOPATHOLOGY (PH/0115-0804). [500] **521**

PHILIPPINE STUDIES (PH/0031-7837). [650] **2625**

PHILIPS JOURNAL OF RESEARCH (NE/0165-5817). [1,700] **2075**

PHILIPS TECHNISCH TIJDSCHRIFT (NE). [1,900] **5138**

PHILOLOGICAL QUARTERLY (US/0031-7977). [2,200] **3310**

PHILOLOGOS (GR). [3,000] **1079**

PHILOMEL (PHILADELPHIA, PA.) (US/1052-4878). [4,000] **3423**

PHILOSOPHER, THE (UK). [200] **4355**

PHILOSOPHIA MATHEMATICA (US/0031-8019). [600] **3526**

PHILOSOPHIA NATURALIS (GW/0031-8027). [600] **4355**

PHILOSOPHIA (RAMAT GAN) (IS/0048-3893). [700] **4355**

PHILOSOPHIA REFORMATA (NE/0031-8035). [700] **4355**

PHILOSOPHICAL BOOKS (UK/0031-8051). [700] **4355**

PHILOSOPHICAL REVIEW, THE (US/0031-8108). [3,200] **4356**

PHILOSOPHICAL STUDIES IN EDUCATION (US/0160-7561). [200] **4356**

PHILOSOPHISCHER LITERATURANZEIGER (GW/0031-8175). [800] **4356**

PHILOSOPHY & PUBLIC AFFAIRS (US/0048-3915). [3,000] **5212**

PHILOSOPHY & SOCIAL CRITICISM (US/0191-4537). [700] **4357**

PHILOSOPHY OF EDUCATION (EDWARDSVILLE, ILL.) (US/8756-6575). [1,000] **1902**

PHILOSOPHY OF SCIENCE ASSOCIATION NEWSLETTER (US/0163-0881). [850] **5138**

PHILOSOPHY OF SCIENCE (EAST LANSING) (US/0031-8248). [2,200] **5138**

PHOEBUS (US/0193-8061). [300] **362**

PHOENICS JOURNAL OF COMPUTATIONAL FLUID DYNAMICS & ITS APPLICATIONS, THE (UK). [250] **1289**

PHOENIX RISING (TORONTO, ONT.) (CN/0710-1457). [3,000] **3932**

PHOLEOS (US/0733-8864). [350] **1409**

PHOTO ELECTRONIC IMAGING (US/1060-4936). [50,000] **4373**

PHOTO - FORUM (AT). [1,200] **4373**

PHOTO INTERPRETATION (FR/0031-8523). [1,000] **4373**

PHOTO-LAB-INDEX (US/0884-9528). [6,000] **4373**

PHOTO LAB MANAGEMENT (US/0164-4769). [12,292] **4373**

PHOTO MARKETING (US/0031-8531). [20,000] **4373**

PHOTO OPPORTUNITY (US/0899-4587). **882**

PHOTO ROSTER (US/0190-5449). **4842**

PHOTOGRAMMETRIC RECORD, THE (UK/0031-868X). [1,500] **2572**

PHOTOGRAPHER, THE (UK/0031-8698). [10,880] **4374**

PHOTOGRAPHIC JOURNAL (1956) (UK/0031-8736). [10,000] **4374**

PHOTOGRAPHICA (US). [500] **4374**

PHOTOGRAPHIE (SZ). **4374**

PHOTOGRAPHIES MAGAZINE (FR/0988-7679). [76,000] **4374**

PHOTOGRAPHS (NEW YORK, N.Y. : 1982) (US/0740-4158). [1,000] **4374**

PHOTOGRAPHY IN NEW YORK (US/1040-0346). [8,000] **4374**

PHOTONICS SPECTRA (PITTSFIELD, MASS. 1982) (US/0731-1230). [75,000] **4440**

PHRONESIS (NE/0031-8868). [1,100] **4357**

PHU NU DIEN DAN (VM). [3,000] **5564**

PHYLON (1960) (US/0031-8906). [2,000] **5213**

PHYSICAL DISABILITIES SPECIAL INTEREST SECTION NEWSLETTER (US/0279-411X). [9,000] **1883**

PHYSICAL EDUCATION REVIEW (UK/0140-7708). [1,000] **1857**

PHYSICAL EDUCATOR, THE (US/0031-8981). [5,000] **1857**

PHYSICAL GEOGRAPHY (US/0272-3646). [280] **2572**

PHYSICAL THERAPY (US/0031-9023). [53,200] **4381**

PHYSICAL THERAPY FORUM (KING OF PRUSSIA, PA. 1994) (US/1075-4342). **4381**

PHYSICIAN AND SPORTSMEDICINE, THE (US/0091-3847). [104,200] **3955**

PHYSICIAN ASSISTANT (1983) (US/8750-7544). [20,935] **3627**

PHYSICIAN ASSISTANT NEWSLETTER OF ETHICS (US). [2,000] **2252**

PHYSICIANS & COMPUTERS (US/0891-8163). [90,000] **1261**

PHYSICIANS' DESK REFERENCE (PRINT ED.) (US/0093-4461). **4325**

PHYSICIAN'S MANAGEMENT (US/0031-9066). [110,885] **3627**

PHYSICIAN'S MANAGEMENT MANUALS (CN/0705-6311). [33,000] **3916**

PHYSICIAN'S RESOURCE MANUAL ON OSTEOPOROSIS (UK). [25,000] **3806**

PHYSICS AND CHEMISTRY OF GLASSES (UK/0031-9090). [1,200] **2593**

PHYSICS OF FLUIDS. A, FLUID DYNAMICS (US/0899-8213). **4416**

PHYSICS OF FLUIDS. B, PLASMA PHYSICS (US/0899-8221). **4416**

PHYSICS TEACHER, THE (US/0031-921X). [7,500] **1902**

PHYSIK DATEN (GW/0344-8401). [250-300] **4416**

PHYSIK UND DIDAKTIK (GW/0340-8515). **1902**

PHYSIOLOGIA PLANTARUM (DK/0031-9317). [2,000] **521**

PHYSIOLOGIST, THE (US/0031-9376). [500 to 6,500] **585**

PHYSIOLOGY CANADA (1983) (CN/0822-9058). [600] **585**

PHYSIOTHERAPY (UK/0031-9406). [30,000] **4382**

PHYSIOTHERAPY CANADA (CN/0300-0508). [7,625] **3627**

PHYSIOTHERAPY IN SPORT (UK/0954-0741). [1,000] **3955**

PHYTOLOGIA (US/0031-9430). [400] **522**

PHYTON (HORN) (AU/0079-2047). **522**

PHYTOPARASITICA (IS/0334-2123). [500] **522**

PHYTOPHTHORA NEWSLETTER (UK/0748-6693). **523**

PHYTOPROTECTION (CN/0031-9511). [600] **181**

PI QUALITY (US). [40,000] **1199**

PIANO GUILD NOTES (US/0031-9546). [14,000] **4146**

PIANO JOURNAL / EUROPEAN PIANO TEACHERS ASSOCIATION (UK/0267-7253). [3,250] **4146**

PIANO QUARTERLY, THE (US/0031-9554). [13,000] **4146**

PICA (CN/0225-7114). [300] **4170**

PICTURE PERFECT (US/1045-0629). [170,000] **4375**

PIECES OF EIGHT (US). [3,140] **803**

PIEDMONT LITERARY REVIEW (US/0275-357X). [400] **3423**

PIERRES VIVANTES (CN/0226-3572). **5034**

PIG FARMING (UK/0031-9759). [13,000] **217**

PIG INTERNATIONAL (EUROPE, ASIA, AFRICA, LATIN AMERICA AND OCEANIA EDITION (US/0191-8834). [16,000] **217**

PIG VETERINARY JOURNAL (UK/0956-0939). [800] **5518**

PIGS (NE/0168-9533). [11,300] **217**

PIK. PRAXIS DER INFORMATIONSVERARBEITUNG UND KOMMUNIKATION (GW/0930-5157). **1199**

PILGRIM JOURNAL, THE (US/0885-4947). [2,000] **5235**

PILLSBURY FAST AND HEALTHY MAGAZINE (US/1059-8073). [100,000] **4197**

PILOT (BOSTON, MASS.), THE (US/0744-933X). [35,000] **31**

PIMA CATALOG (US/0739-2133). [5,000] **4237**

PIMA MAGAZINE (US/1046-4352). [21,000] **4237**

PINE CITY PIONEER (US/0892-2012). [2,900] **5698**

PINELLAS COUNTY REVIEW (US/0746-746X). [4,000] **803**

PIONEER WAGON, THE (US/0735-309X). [350] **2467**

PIPE BAND (UK). **4146**

PIPE LINE INDUSTRY (HOUSTON, TEX.) (US/0032-0145). [26,538] **2124**

PIPELINE & GAS JOURNAL (US/0032-0188). [24,000] **4274**

PIPELINE DIGEST (US/0197-1506). [9,000] **4274**

PIPES & PIPELINES INTERNATIONAL (1965) (UK/0032-020X). **4274**

PIQUALITY (US/1058-8787). [42,000] **1199**

PITCH-IN NEWS (CN/0847-9607). [25,000] **2202**

PITT MAGAZINE (US). [125,000] **1102**

PITTSBURGH CITY PAPER (US/1066-0062). [50,000] **2543**

PITTSBURGH LEGAL JOURNAL (US/0032-0331). [6,300] **3029**

PLA BULLETIN (US/0197-9299). [2,000] **3241**

PLAFSEP. PROCESSING (LIBRARIES)--ANECDOTES, FACETIAE, SATIRE, ETC.--PERIODICALS (US/0149-6417). [100] **3241**

PLAIN RAPPER, THE (US/0032-0412). [2,400] **5301**

PLAINS ANTHROPOLOGIST (US/0032-0447). [1,200] **2271**

PLAINS TALK (US/0554-2375). [2,000] **2754**

PLAINSONGS (US). [300] **3423**

PLAN AND PRINT (US/0032-0595). [30,000] **1234**

PLAN FOR THE ADMINISTRATION OF VOCATIONAL EDUCATION, A (US). [2,000] **1915**

PLAN (MONTREAL) (CN/0032-0536). [40,000] **1990**

PLANNED PARENTHOOD CHALLENGES / INTERNATIONAL PLANNED PARENTHOOD FEDERATION (UK). [8,000-10,000] **2285**

PLANNING & PUBLIC POLICY (US). [5,000] **4673**

PLANNING & ZONING NEWS (US/0738-114X). [2,650] **2831**

PLANNING (CHICAGO, ILL. 1969) (US/0001-2610). [24,000] **2831**

PLANNING FOR HIGHER EDUCATION (US/0736-0983). [2,800] **1841**

PLANNING HISTORY PRESENT (US/1071-1953). [360] **2831**

PLANNING NEWS (ALBANY, N.Y.) (US/0885-6737). [9,700] **2831**

PLANNING NEWS SOUTH MELBOURNE (AT/0313-3796). [750] **2831**

PLANNING REVIEW (US/0094-064X). [11,000] **882**

PLANO STAR COURIER (1986) (US/0895-4305). **5753**

PLANODION (GR/1105-2473). [2,000] **3424**

PLANT AND CELL PHYSIOLOGY (JA/0032-0781). [2,600] **523**

PLANT & WORKS ENGINEERING (UK). [20,500] **1990**

PLANT CELL, THE (US/1040-4651). [5,000] **539**

PLANT ENGINEERING (US/0032-082X). [128,668] **1990**

PLANT PEST NEWSLETTER (US). [550] **524**

PLANT PROTECTION QUARTERLY (AT/0815-2195). [500] **120**

PLANT VARIETIES & SEEDS (UK/0952-3863). [1,100] **2427**

PLANTA MEDICA (GW/0032-0943). [800] **4325**

PLANTLINE (AT/0726-4623). [15,000] **3486**

PLANTS & GARDENS (US/0362-5850). [25,000] **2428**

PLANTS & GARDENS NEWS / BROOKLYN BOTANIC GARDEN (US). [25,000] **2428**

PLANTS, SITES & PARKS (US/0191-2933). [31,000] **703**

PLASMAPHERESIS (US/0894-6779). **3627**

PLASTFORUM SCANDINAVIA (SW/0347-8262). [5,000] **4457**

PLASTIC FIGURE AND PLAYSET COLLECTOR (US). [1,200] **2585**

PLASTIC NEWS INTERNATIONAL (AT). [2,700] **2107**

PLASTICOS UNIVERSALES (SP/0303-4011). [4,000] **4457**

PLASTICS AGE (JA/0551-0503). **4457**

PLASTICS DESIGN FORUM (US/0362-9376). **4458**

PLASTICS SOUTHERN AFRICA (SA/0032-2660). [2,000] **2107**

PLASTICS WORLD (US/0032-1273). [60,000] **4458**

PLASTIZINE (CN/0715-5719). [300] **381**

PLATEAU (FLAGSTAFF, AZ : 1939) (US/0032-1346). [7,000-10,000] **2543**

PLATING AND SURFACE FINISHING (US/0360-3164). [10,000] **4225**

PLATINUM METALS REVIEW (UK/0032-1400). [9,000] **4015**

PLATON (GR/1105-073X). [2,000] **1079**

PLATTE COUNTY, MISSOURI, HISTORICAL & GENEALOGICAL SOCIETY BULLETIN (US). [800] **2468**

PLAY AND PARENTING CONNECTIONS (CN/0835-4014). [500] **3241**

PLAYBILL (US/0551-0678). [13,000] **5367**

PLAYBOY INDEX, THE (US). **3996**

PLC INSIDER'S NEWSLETTER, THE (US/1040-9718). **1265**

PLEASURE BOATING (US/0191-7366). [20,000] **595**

PLEIN SOLEIL (MONTREAL) (CN/0384-7810). [15,000] **3732**

PLOUGHSHARES MONITOR (CN/0703-1866). **4532**

PLOWMAN (BROOKLIN) (CN/0840-707X). [15,000] **3468**

PLUG IN (CN/0704-0628). **3241**

PLUIMVEEHOUDERIJ, DE (NE). [7,500] **217**

PLUM CREEK ALMANAC (US/0898-5197). [500] **2468**

PLUMBING (UK/0032-1656). **2607**

PLUMBING BUSINESS (US). [31,000] **2607**

PLUMBLINE (US/0741-1421). [1,000] **1841**

PLURAL SOCIETIES (NE/0048-4482). [800] **5213**

PLURILINGUA (BE). [1,000] **3310**

PLUS (PAWLING, N.Y.) (US/0747-217X). [640,000] **4986**

PM NET WORK, THE (US/1040-8754). [7,000] **882**

PM. PRAXIS DER MATHEMATIK (GW/0032-7042). [3,000] **3527**

PMEA NEWS (US/0030-8102). [5,000] **4146**

POA (1985) (US/0882-9624). [1,700] **2801**

POCKETBOOK OF STATISTICS: JAMAICA (JM). [1,500] **1537**

PODIATRIC PRODUCTS (US/0890-3972). [12,000] **3918**

POE STUDIES (US/0090-5224). [600] **434**

POEM (US/0032-1885). [400] **3468**

POET AND CRITIC (AMES, IOWA) (US/0032-1958). [500] **3468**

POET LORE (US/0032-1966). [700] **3468**

POET (SHREVEPORT, LA.), THE (US/0748-4062). [5,000-7,000] **3468**

POETICA (MUNCHEN) (NE/0303-4178). [750] **3424**

POETICS (US/1043-0814). [10,000] **3468**

POETICS TODAY (US/0333-5372). [1,100] **3424**

POETRY BOOK SOCIETY BULLETIN (UK/0551-1690). [1,900] **3469**

POETRY CANADA REVIEW (CN/0709-3373). [2,000] **3350**

POETRY EAST (US/0197-4009). [1,800] **3469**

POETRY FLASH (US/0737-4747). [15,000] **3469**

POETRY IRELAND REVIEW, THE (IE/0332-2998). [1,000] **3469**

POETRY MARKETS FOR CANADIANS (CN/0843-2287). [3,000] **3469**

POETRY PILOT (US/0554-3983). [2,800] **3469**

POETRY TORONTO (CN/0381-6591). [800] **3469**

POETS & WRITERS (US/0891-6136). [12,000] **3470**

POETS ON (US/0146-3136). [500] **3470**

POINT COMMUN, LE (CN/0710-2364). **5793**

POINT D'INTERROGATION ?. ENGLISH SECTION (CN/0710-6521). **1702**

POINT D'INTERROGATION (MONTREAL) (CN/0226-7950). **1702**

POINT LINE POLY. HOST (US/1062-5674). [300] **1990**

POINT LINE POLY. PC (US/1061-3838). [100] **1199**

POINT OF BEGINNING- POB (US/0739-3865). [59,000] **2028**

POINT SERIES (PP/0253-2913). **4987**

POINT VETERINAIRE, LE (FR/0335-4997). [6,000] **5518**

POKROKY MATEMATIKY, FYSIKY A ASTRONOMIE (XR/0032-2423). [7,500] **5138**

POLAR GEOGRAPHY AND GEOLOGY (US/0273-8457). [220] **1391**

POLAR RECORD, THE (UK/0032-2474). [1,200] **5138**

POLAR RESEARCH (NO). [800] **1359**

POLARFORSCHUNG (GW/0032-2490). [800] **5138**

POLICE AND LAW ENFORCEMENT (US/0092-8933). **3171**

POLICE AND SECURITY NEWS (US/1070-8111). [20,800] **3171**

POLICE CAREER DIGEST (US/8756-355X). [1,700] **3171**

POLICE CHIEF, THE (US/0032-2571). [22,000] **3171**

POLICE LABOR MONTHLY (US/0749-5595). [1,000] **3172**

POLICE STUDIES (US/0141-2949). [451] **3172**

POLICY ANALYSIS (PH/0115-1746). [150] **703**

POLICY (CENTRE FOR INDEPENDENT STUDIES (N.S.W.)) (AT/1032-6634). [3,000] **4487**

POLICY COUNSEL (US). [3,000] **4674**

POLICY GUIDE OF THE AMERICAN CIVIL LIBERTIES UNION (US/0275-3170). [175,000] **4511**

POLICY, ORGANIZATION AND RULES - GIRL GUIDES OF CANADA (CN/0316-8158). **5235**

POLICY PAPERS (HU). [200] **4532**

POLICY STUDIES JOURNAL (US/0190-292X). [2,500] **4488**

POLICY STUDIES REVIEW (US/0278-4416). [2,400] **4488**

POLISH AMERICAN JOURNAL (1985 : NATIONAL ED.) (US). [18,300] **5720**

POLISH AMERICAN STUDIES (CHICAGO, ILL.) (US/0032-2806). [750] **2754**

POLISH FAMILY TREE SURNAMES (US/0271-2644). [2,000] **2468**

POLISH GENEALOGICAL SOCIETY NEWSLETTER (US/0735-9349). [2,000] **2468**

POLISH JOURNAL OF OCCUPATIONAL MEDICINE AND ENVIRONMENTAL HEALTH (PL/0867-8383). **3628**

POLISH POLAR RESEARCH (PL/0138-0338). [650] **5138**

POLITICA (DK/0105-0710). [1,000] **4488**

POLITICAL AFFAIRS (US/0032-3128). [5,000] **4488**

POLITICAL ANALYSIS (US/1047-1987). **4488**

POLITICAL ANIMAL (1993), THE (US/1070-1753). [230] **4488**

POLITICAL CHRONICLE, THE (US/1042-3885). [300] **4489**

POLITICAL HANDBOOK OF THE WORLD (1975) (US/0193-175X). [3,500] **4489**

POLITICAL SCIENCE QUARTERLY (US/0032-3195). [9,000] **4490**

POLITICAL WARFARE (US/1056-3334). [2500] **4532**

POLITICS & SOCIETY (US/0032-3292). [1,000] **5213**

POLITICS BRIEFING (UK). [2,000] **4491**

POLITIQUES ET MANAGEMENT PUBLIC (FR/0758-1726). [800] **4491**

POLIZEI, VERKEHR + TECHNIK (GW). [5,000] **3172**

POLLED HEREFORD WORLD (1965) (US/0162-7953). [11,500] **217**

POLLUTION ENGINEERING (US/0032-3640). [50,000] **2238**

POLLUTION EQUIPMENT NEWS (US/0032-3659). [91,000] **2239**

POLLUTION PREVENTION (UK). [16,500] **2239**

POLSKA, DANE STATYSTYCZNE (PL/0860-6811). [4,500] **5336**

POLYGRAPH, DER (GW/0032-3845). [13,000] **4567**

POLYMER BLENDS, ALLOYS, AND INTERPENETRATING POLYMER NETWORKS ABSTRACTS (US/0893-6684). [200] **988**

POLYMER PREPRINTS, AMERICAN CHEMICAL SOCIETY, DIVISION OF POLYMER CHEMISTRY (US/0032-3934). [10,000 twice a year] **989**

POLYMERS & RUBBER ASIA (UK/0268-9812). [11,000] **4459**

POLYSCOPE, COMPUTER, ELECTRONICS, COMMUNICATION (SZ). **2075**

POLYSCOPE (MONTREAL) (CN/0710-3522). [5,000] **1094**

POMPEIIANA NEWSLETTER (US/0892-5941). [13,000] **3311**

PONCA CITY NEWS, THE (US). [12,500 (paid, Sunday)14,000 (paid)] **5732**

PONTIAC-OAKLAND COUNTY LEGAL NEWS (US/0739-0203). [1,447] **3029**

PONTOTOC COUNTY QUARTERLY, OKLAHOMA (US). [225] **2468**

POOL & SPA MARKETING (CN/0711-2998). [8,000] **934**

POPLINE (US). [56,500] **4556**

POPULAR ARCHAEOLOGY (US/0300-774X). [1,500] **278**

POPULAR ARCHAEOLOGY. TECHNICAL PUBLICATION (US). [1,500] **278**

POPULAR COMMUNICATIONS (US/0733-3315). [100,000] **1119**

POPULAR GOVERNMENT (US/0032-4515). [8,000] **4491**

POPULAR MINING (US/8756-6257). [20,000] **2148**

POPULAR PLASTICS & PACKAGING (II). [6,150] **4459**

POPULATION (FR/0032-4663). [4,000] **4556**

POPULATION AND DEVELOPMENT REVIEW (US/0098-7921). [5,000] **4556**

POPULATION EDUCATION IN ASIA AND THE PACIFIC NEWSLETTER (TH). **4557**

POPULATION EDUCATION PROGRAMME SERVICE (TH). [2,000] **4557**

POPULATION ESTIMATES FOR OREGON (US). [1,000] **4557**

POPULATION ET SOCIETES (FR/0184-7783). [41,500] **4557**

POPULATION PROJECTIONS BY MINOR CIVIL DIVISIONS, SEX, AGE GROUP, AND COUNTY (US). [400] **4557**

POPULATION REPORTS (BALTIMORE, MD.) (US/0887-0241). [110,000] **4557**

POPULATION STUDIES (II). [200] **4558**

POPULATION TIMES, THE (BG). [2,000] **590**

PORT CONSTRUCTION AND OCEAN TECHNOLOGY (UK/0264-8733). [4,500] **624**

PORT

Controlled Circulation Index

PORT ISABEL SOUTH PADRE ISLAND PRESS (US). [4,860] **5753**

PORT OF DETROIT WORLD HANDBOOK (US/0160-5526). [6,000] **5454**

PORT OF HELSINKI HANDBOOK (FI/0359-7431). [1,500] **5454**

PORT OF NEW ORLEANS ANNUAL DIRECTORY (US/0085-5030). [20,000] **5454**

PORT OF NEW ORLEANS RECORD (US/1046-9265). [16,000] **849**

PORT OF TOLEDO NEWS (US/0032-4868). [6,000] **4181**

PORTAGE LAKES HERALD, THE (US/0746-6021). [5,000] **5730**

PORTE-VOIX, LE (CN/0225-3593). **5301**

PORTER'S GUIDE TO CONGRESSIONAL ROLL CALL VOTES. HOUSE (US/0748-2310). **4674**

PORTER'S GUIDE TO CONGRESSIONAL ROLL CALL VOTES. SENATE (US/0748-2329). [100] **4491**

PORTLAND MONTHLY (US/0887-5340). **2573**

PORTLAND OBSERVER (US). **5734**

PORTLAND PRESS HERALD, THE (US). [62,183] **5685**

PORTUGALIAE ACTA BIOLOGICA. SERIE A. MORFOLOGIA, FISIOLOGIA, GENETICA E BIOLOGIA GERAL (PO/0032-5147). [210] **585**

PORTUGUESE TIMES (NEW BEDFORD, MASS.) (US/0746-3928). [17,000] **5689**

PORZELLAN + GLAS : P + G / ORGAN DES BUNDESVERBANDES DES GLAS-, PORZELLAN- UND KERAMIK-EINZELHANDELS (GW). [7,000] **2593**

POSEBNA IZDANJA INSTITUTA ZA ZASTITU BILJA (YU/0408-9952). [1,000] **525**

POSEV (GW/0032-5201). [2,000] **4491**

POSITIVE APPROACH, A (US/0891-8791). [40,000] **4392**

POSITIVE ATTITUDE POSTERS (US). [23,000] **946**

POSITIVE HEALTH (UK/0958-5737). [700] **4795**

POST (CARLE PLACE, N.Y.) (US/0891-5628). **1162**

POST-GAZETTE (BOSTON, MASS.) (US/0888-0107). [16,900] **5689**

POST SCRIPT (JACKSONVILLE, FLA.) (US/0277-9897). [600] **4076**

POST-SOVIET PROSPECTS (US). [4,000] **4491**

POST-STAR (GLENS FALLS, N.Y. : 1974) (US/0897-0505). **5720**

POST-TRIBUNE (GARY, IND.) (US/8750-3492). [75,000 daily 88,000 Sunday] **5666**

POSTAL HISTORY JOURNAL (US/0032-5341). [700] **1146**

POSTAL STATIONERY (US/0554-8373). **2786**

POSTGRADUATE DOCTOR. AFRICA (UK/0142-7946). [9,000] **3628**

POSTGRADUATE DOCTOR. MIDDLE EAST EDITION (UK/0140-7724). [20,000] **3628**

POSTGRADUATE EDUCATION FOR GENERAL PRACTICE (UK/0959-4299). [1,500] **3738**

POSTGRADUATE MEDICINE (US/0032-5481). [125,600] **3628**

POSTGRADUATE OBSTETRICS & GYNECOLOGY (US/0194-3898). **3767**

POTASH REVIEW (SZ/0032-5546). [6,000] **182**

POTATO COUNTRY (US/0886-4780). [7,319] **182**

POTATO GROWER (AT/0815-6514). [500] **182**

POTATO GROWER OF IDAHO (US/0146-499X). **182**

POTATO GROWER : POTATO GROWER OF IDAHO MAGAZINE (US). **182**

POTATO RESEARCH (NE/0014-3065). [1,200] **182**

POTENTIALS IN MARKETING (US/0032-5619). [67,204] **935**

POTOMAC ALMANAC (US/0194-2182). [33,000] **5687**

POTTER (NZ/0113-583X). [6,000] **2593**

POTTER LEADER-ENTERPRISE (US/0895-6839). [10,500] **5738**

POTTSBORO PRESS (US/0747-4253). [1,500] **5753**

POULTRY INTERNATIONAL (US/0032-5767). [19,000] **218**

POULTRY JOURNAL 1987 (UK/0954-7185). [250] **218**

POUR LA SUITE DES JEUX (CN/0824-4170). **4913**

POVERTY IN TEXAS (US/0097-7950). [1,100] **5254**

POVERTY LAW REPORT (US). [90,000] **3180**

POVERTY LINES AUSTRALIA (AT/0814-5105). [300] **5213**

POWDER/BULK SOLIDS (US/8750-6653). [29,000] **4221**

POWDER COATINGS BULLETIN (UK/0140-8445). [300] **4225**

POWDER HANDLING & PROCESSING (GW/0934-7348). [10,000] **2148**

POWDER METALLURGY SCIENCE AND TECHNOLOGY (II/0971-0728). [600] **4015**

POWELL TRIBUNE, THE (US/0740-1078). [3,90] **5772**

POWER AND MOTORYACHT (US/0886-4411). [150,000] **595**

POWER ENGINEERING (BARRINGTON, ILL.) (US/0032-5961). [53,000] **2124**

POWER EQUIPMENT AUSTRALASIA (AT/0817-6043). [8,700] **2124**

POWER INTERNATIONAL (UK/0950-1487). [5,900] **2124**

POWER PRODUCTS BUSINESS (US/1056-4063). [150] **2124**

POWER TRANSMISSION DESIGN (US/0032-6070). [52,000] **2124**

POWERTECHNICS MAGAZINE (US/0882-7419). [24,000] **4417**

POWYS REVIEW, THE (UK/0309-1619). [1,000] **3350**

PR & V : PR EN VOORLICHTING (NE). [2,700] **763**

PRABUDDHA BHARATA (II/0032-6178). [5,000] **5041**

PRACE I STUDIA GEOGRAFICZNE / UNIWERSYTET WARSZAWSKI, WYDZIA GEOGRAFII I STUDIOW REGIONALNYCH (PL). **2573**

PRACE IPI PAN / ICS PAS REPORTS (PL). [200] **1200**

PRACE JEZYKOZNAWCZE (PL). [300] **3311**

PRACI BHASA-VIJNAN (CALCUTTA) (II/0970-9940). [525] **3311**

PRACTICAL AQUACULTURE & LAKE MANAGEMENT (US/1057-218X). [3000] **2310**

PRACTICAL DIABETES (UK/0266-447X). [10,700] **3732**

PRACTICAL ENDODONTICS (US/1056-7933). [1,200] **1333**

PRACTICAL PERIODONTICS AND AESTHETIC DENTISTRY (US/1042-2722). [84,000] **1333**

PRACTICAL SUPERVISION (US/0742-7859). **882**

PRACTICAL WINERY/VINEYARD (US/1057-2694). [2,500] **2370**

PRACTICE BUILDER, THE (US/0883-3036). [11,000] **704**

PRACTICING ANTHROPOLOGY (US/0888-4552). [2,500] **243**

PRACTICING ARCHITECT (US/0888-3424). [30,000] **306**

PRACTITIONER, THE (UK/0032-6518). [28,600] **3738**

PRAGUE BULLETIN OF MATHEMATICAL LINGUISTICS, THE (XR/0032-6585). [800] **3311**

PRAIRIE HARVESTER (CN/0383-7653). [30,000] **4987**

PRAIRIE MESSENGER (CN/0032-664X). [8,900] **5793**

PRAIRIE NATURALIST, THE (US/0091-0376). [460] **4170**

PRAIRIE PROGRESS NEWSLETTER (CN/1188-2255). [2,000] **1513**

PRAIRIE ROSE, THE (US/0032-6666). [12,000] **3867**

PRAKTIJKBLAD VOOR MEDEZEGGENSCHAP (NE/0921-2442). **946**

PRAKTISCH MANAGEMENT (BE/0772-6856). [2000] **882**

PRAKTISCHE METALLOGRAPHIE (GW/0032-678X). [2,000] **4015**

PRAKTISCHE TIERARZT (GW/0032-681X). [6,800] **5518**

PRAPARATOR (GW/0032-6542). [2,000] **4170**

PRASADA (CALCUTTA, INDIA) (II). [4,200] **3425**

PRATFALL : THE "WAY OUT WEST" PERIODICAL TRIBUTE TO STAN AND OLLIE (US). [2500] **4076**

PRATIQUES (FR/0338-2389). [79] **3311**

PRATT INSTITUTE CREATIVE ARTS THERAPY REVIEW (US/0196-8459). [400] **3932**

PRAXIS DER PSYCHOMOTORIK (GW/0170-060X). [1,900] **1884**

PRAXIS GRUNDSCHULE (GW/0170-3722). **1094**

PRAXIS VETERINARIA (CI/0350-4441). [5,000] **5518**

PRC NEWSLETTER (US/8755-3902). [3,500] **4375**

PRE-LAW JOURNAL (US/0741-1162). [200] **3030**

PRE- (PRAIRIE VILLAGE, KAN.) (US/1042-0304). [40,000] **4818**

PRE/TEXT (US/0731-0714). [500] **3311**

PREACHER'S MAGAZINE, THE (US/0162-3982). [20,000] **4987**

PREACHING (JACKSONVILLE, FLA.) (US/0882-7036). [7,000] **4987**

PRECEDENTS FOR THE CONVEYANCER (UK). [3,000] **3030**

PRECIOUS FIBERS (US/0886-4268). [2,000] **5355**

PREDICAMENT, THE (US/0199-0705). [2,000] **4913**

PREMIUM CHANNELS TV BLUEPRINT (US/1040-5534). [2,500,000] **1136**

PRENSA (ORLANDO, FLA.), LA (US/0888-756X). [40,000] **5650**

PRENSA SAN DIEGO, LA (US/0738-9183). [25,000] **2271**

PREPARATIVE BIOCHEMISTRY (US/0032-7484). **492**

PREPARING FOR THE FUTURE : ESA'S TECHNOLOGY PROGRAMME QUARTERLY (NE/1018-8657). [20,000] **31**

PREPRESS BULLETIN, THE (US/8750-2224). [1,450] **5034**

PREPRINTS OF PAPERS PRESENTED AT THE AES CONVENTIONS (US). [12,000] **5318**

PREREFUNDED BOND SERVICE (US/0737-9595). [300] **803**

PRESBYTERIAN LAYMAN, THE (US/0555-0572). [560,000] **5066**

PRESBYTERIAN SURVEY (US/0032-759X). [95,000] **5066**

PRESCRIBER (UK/0959-6682). [19,000] **3629**

PRESCRIPTION PRODUCTS GUIDE (AT/0818-4445). **4325**

PRESENCE AFRICAINE (PARIS, FRANCE : 1967) (FR/0032-7638). [2,000] **2271**

PRESENCE (MONTREAL. 1992) (CN/1188-5580). [2,000] **4987**

PRESENTATION PRODUCTS MAGAZINE (US/1041-9780). [56,000] **704**

PRESENTATION TO THE PREMIER AND PROVINCIAL CABINET (CN/0228-2488). **1579**

PRESERVATION LAW REPORTER (US/0882-715X). [500] **3030**

PRESERVATION PROGRESS (CHARLESTON) (US/0478-1392). [1,500] **306**

PRESIDENTIAL STUDIES QUARTERLY (US/0360-4918). [12,500] **4674**

PRESLIA (XR/0032-7786). [1,550] **525**

PRESS AND ADVERTISERS YEAR BOOK (II). [3,000] **764**

PRESS INDEPENDENT (CN/1182-9931). [5,600] **2543**

PRESS REVIEW (TORONTO) (CN/0706-9286). [16,000] **2923**

PRESSE HANDBUCH / VERBAND OSTERREICHISCHER ZEITUNGSHERAUSGEBER UND ZEITUNGSVERLEGER (AU). [2,800] **4567**

PRESSE UND SPRACHE (GW/0935-8064). **2923**

PRESSESCHAU OSTWIRTSCHAFT (AU). [250] **1639**

PRESSTIME (US/0194-3243). [15,000] **4818**

PRESSURE (BETHESDA, MD.) (US/0889-0242). [3,000] **3629**

PRESTEL DIRECTORY, THE (UK/0266-0288). [65,000] **1162**

PRETRE ET PASTEUR (CN/0383-8307). [2,200] **4987**

PREVENTION PREVIEW (CN/0711-1681). **4796**

PREVIEW (RICHARDSON, TEX.) (US/0892-6468). [3,200] **387**

PRI REPORT (US). [4,000] **946**

PRI REVIEW. INTERNATIONAL ROAD SAFETY (LU). [1,000] **4796**

PRIKLADNYE PROBLEMY PROCHNOSTI I PLASTICHNOSTI (RU). [1,000] **2107**

PRIMAL INSTITUTE NEWSLETTER, THE (US/0164-5056). [1,700] **4608**

PRIMARY CARE & CANCER (US/0743-8176). [107,000] **3822**

PRIMARY EDUCATION AUSTRALIA (AT/0048-5284). [3,000] **1805**

PRIMATE CONSERVATION (US/0898-6207). **2202**

PRIMATE NEWS (US/0032-8324). **5518**

PRIME NUMBER (AT/0816-9349). [2,000] **3527**

PRIME REAL ESTATE (US). [40,000] **4843**

PRIME TIMES (MADISON) (US/0195-5934). [70,000] **5181**

PRINCETON HISTORY (US/0276-2730). [850] **2755**

PRINCETON LEADER, THE (US). [3,500] **5682**

PRINCETON RECOLLECTOR (US/0196-1136). [2,500] **2755**

PRINCETON SEMINARY BULLETIN, THE (US/0032-8413). [10,000] **4987**

PRINCIPAL (ARLINGTON, VA.) (US/0271-6062). [25,000] **1868**

PRINCIPAL (EAST LANSING) (US/0199-6371). **1805**

PRINCIPAL MATTERS (AT). [1,500] **1868**

PRINCIPE DE VIANA (SP/0032-8472). [1,000] **2703**

PRINCIPES (US/0032-8480). [2,200] **525**

PRINCIPLES OF COMPUTER SCIENCE SERIES (US/0888-2096). **1200**

PRINSBURG NEWS (US/8750-0698). [1,100] **5698**

PRINT ACTION (CN/0380-2752). [16,000] **4567**

PRINT-EQUIP NEWS (US/0048-5314). [25,000] **381**

PRINTED CIRCUIT FABRICATION (US/0274-8096). [22,030] **2075**

PRINTERS HOT LINE (US/0192-6314). **4568**

PRINTER'S NEWS (WELLINGTON) (NZ/0048-5330). [1,100] **4568**

PRINTERS YEARBOOK : THE COMPREHENSIVE GUIDE TO THE PRINTING INDUSTRY (UK). [3,700] **4568**

PRINTING HISTORY (US/0192-9275). [900] **4568**

PRINTING IMPRESSIONS (US/0032-860X). [95,000] **4568**

PRINTING INDUSTRIES (UK/0307-7195). [4,800] **4568**

PRINTING JOURNAL (US/0191-8273). [25,000] **4568**

PRINTING WORLD (UK/0032-8715). [12,200] **4568**

PRINTINGNEWS. MIDWEST (US/1048-6860). [20,000] **4568**

PRINTWORLD DIRECTORY OF CONTEMPORARY PRINTS AND PRICES (US/0734-2721). [20,000] **381**

PRIORITIES (VANCOUVER) (CN/0700-6543). [1,000] **5564**

PRIRODOVEDNE PRACE USTAVU CESKOSLOVENSKE AKADEMIE VED V BRNE (XR/0032-8758). [700] **5594**

PRISCILLA PAPERS (US/0898-753X). [1,800] **4988**

PRISME (QUEBEC. 1964) (CN/0713-5521). **5793**

PRISMET (NO/0032-8447). [2,500] **4988**

PRITEL LIDU : CASOPIS SLEZSKE CIRKVE EVANGELICKE (XR). [2,250] **4988**

PRIVACY JOURNAL (US/0145-7659). [5,000] **1227**

PRIVATE CARRIER (US/0032-8871). [35,000] **5389**

PRIVATE EYE WEEKLY (US). [30,000] **2543**

PRIVATE LABEL PRODUCT NEWS (US/0892-6727). [30,000] **3486**

PRIVATE PRACTICE (US/0032-891X). [140,000] **3629**

PRO BIKE NEWS (US/1064-2765). [700] **429**

PRO-CHOICE NEWS (CN/0836-7221). **590**

PRO/E, THE MAGAZINE (US/1069-6113). **1200**

PRO-LIFE NEWS (CN/0715-4356). [50,000] **3767**

PRO-NAT (SA). [15,000] **2500**

PRO REGE (US/0276-4830). [3,000] **1842**

PRO SOUND NEWS (U.S. ED.) (US/0164-6338). [15,000] **5318**

PROA (CK/0032-9150). [4,000] **306**

PROBATE COUNSEL, THE (US). [1,500] **3031**

PROBATE LAWYER, THE (US/0094-999X). **3031**

PROBATION AND PAROLE LAW REPORTS (US/0276-6965). [500] **3173**

PROBATION JOURNAL (UK). [7,000] **3173**

PROBE (LONDON. 1954) (UK/0032-9185). [10,481] **1333**

PROBLEM OBSERVER (UK). [75] **4865**

PROBLEMAS DEL DESARROLLO (MX/0301-7036). [2,000] **1639**

PROBLEMI NA GEOGRAFIIATA (BU/0204-7209). [540] **2573**

PROBLEMS OF ECONOMICS (US/0032-9436). [550] **1513**

PROCEDURE REVISIONE FISCALE IMPOSTA VALORE AGGIUNTO (IT). [3,600] **3031**

PROCEDURE REVISIONE FISCALE REDDITO IMPRESA (IT). [3,600] **4741**

PROCEEDINGS (UK). **2593**

PROCEEDINGS - AMERICAN SOCIETY FOR THE ADVANCEMENT ANESTHESIA IN DENTISTRY (US/0164-1700). [1,100] **3684**

PROCEEDINGS AND ADDRESSES OF THE AMERICAN PHILOSOPHICAL ASSOCIATION (US/0065-972X). [9,200] **4357**

PROCEEDINGS AND PAPERS OF THE GEORGIA ASSOCIATION OF HISTORIANS, THE (US/0275-3863). [350] **2626**

PROCEEDINGS AND REPORTS - FLORIDA STATE UNIVERSITY, CENTER FOR YUGOSLAV-AMERICAN STUDIES, RESEARCH AND EXCHANGES (US/0196-9730). [800] **2703**

PROCEEDINGS AND TRANSACTIONS OF THE ALL-INDIA ORIENTAL CONFERENCE (II). **3312**

PROCEEDINGS. ANNUAL CONFERENCE - CANADIAN ACADEMIC ACCOUNTING ASSOCIATION (CN/0711-3730). [150] **750**

PROCEEDINGS ... ANNUAL CONFERENCE OF THE AMERICAN COUNCIL ON CONSUMER INTERESTS (US/0275-1356). [1,100] **1299**

PROCEEDINGS, ANNUAL MEETING, INSTITUTE OF NUCLEAR MATERIALS MANAGEMENT (US). [2,500] **2158**

PROCEEDINGS, ANNUAL MEETING OF THE AMERICAN WOOD-PRESERVERS' ASSOCIATION (US/0066-1198). [2,000] **2403**

PROCEEDINGS ... ANNUAL MEETING OF THE CANADIAN TRANSPORTATION RESEARCH FORUM (CN/1183-2770). [400] **5390**

PROCEEDINGS. ANNUAL SYMPOSIUM. INCREMENTAL MOTION CONTROL SYSTEMS AND DEVICES (US/0092-1661). [1,000] **2076**

PROCEEDINGS - ASTRONOMICAL SOCIETY OF AUSTRALIA (AT/0066-9997). [600] **398**

PROCEEDINGS - CANADIAN LABOUR CONGRESS, CONSTITUTIONAL CONVENTION (CN/0225-0403). **1703**

PROCEEDINGS / CARNAHAN CONFERENCE ON SECURITY TECHNOLOGY (US/0884-5409). **3173**

PROCEEDINGS - CORPORATE AVIATION SAFETY SEMINAR (US/0736-4709). **32**

PROCEEDINGS - INTERNATIONAL COMPUTER SOFTWARE & APPLICATIONS CONFERENCE (US/0730-3157). **1289**

PROCEEDINGS - INTERNATIONAL SYMPOSIUM ON URBAN HYDROLOGY, HYDRAULICS, AND SEDIMENT CONTROL (1981) (US/0732-2607). [150] **2094**

PROCEEDINGS - NATIONAL PEACH COUNCIL (US/0092-2633). [300] **2353**

PROCEEDINGS OF A CONFERENCE ON BANK STRUCTURE AND COMPETITION (US/0084-9146). [2,000] **804**

PROCEEDINGS OF AMERICAN PEANUT RESEARCH AND EDUCATION SOCIETY, INC (US/0197-8748). [700] **183**

PROCEEDINGS OF ... PAKISTAN CONGRESS OF ZOOLOGY (PK). [500] **5595**

PROCEEDINGS OF THE ACADEMY OF NATURAL SCIENCES OF PHILADELPHIA (US/0097-3157). [1,200] **4170**

PROCEEDINGS OF THE ACADEMY OF POLITICAL SCIENCE (US). [9,000] **4492**

PROCEEDINGS OF THE AMERICAN ACADEMY AND INSTITUTE OF ARTS AND LETTERS (US/0145-8493). [600] **328**

PROCEEDINGS OF THE AMERICAN ACADEMY OF ARTS AND LETTERS (US). [600] **328**

PROCEEDINGS OF THE AMERICAN ANTIQUARIAN SOCIETY (US/0044-751X). [1,200] **2755**

PROCEEDINGS OF THE AMERICAN ETHNOLOGICAL SOCIETY (US/0731-4108). **243**

PROCEEDINGS OF THE ANNUAL CONFERENCE (UK/0582-303X). [500] **3242**

PROCEEDINGS OF THE ... ANNUAL CONFERENCE AND EXPOSITION OF THE NATIONAL COMPUTER GRAPHICS ASSOCIATION, INC (US/0732-8028). **1234**

PROCEEDINGS OF THE ANNUAL CONFERENCE - CANADIAN COUNCIL ON INTERNATIONAL LAW (CN/0317-9087). [300] **3134**

PROCEEDINGS OF THE ANNUAL CONFERENCE OF THE LAW OF THE SEA INSTITUTE (US/0557-8620). [500] **3182**

PROCEEDINGS OF THE ANNUAL CONGRESS OF THE SOUTH AFRICAN SUGAR TECHNOLOGISTS' ASSOCIATION (SA/0373-045X). [1,100] **2353**

PROCEEDINGS OF THE ANNUAL CONVENTION - AMERICAN ASSOCIATION OF BOVINE PRACTITIONERS. CONVENTION (US/0743-0450). [6,000] **5519**

PROCEEDINGS OF THE ANNUAL CONVENTION OF THE AMERICAN ASSOCIATION OF EQUINE PRACTITIONERS (US/0065-7182). [5,200] **2801**

PROCEEDINGS OF THE ... ANNUAL INSTITUTE ON COAL MINING HEALTH, SAFETY AND RESEARCH (US). [150] **2868**

PROCEEDINGS OF THE ANNUAL MEETING - FERTILIZER INDUSTRY ROUND TABLE (US/0071-4607). **183**

PROCEEDINGS OF THE ANNUAL MEETING - INDUSTRIAL RELATIONS RESEARCH ASSOCIATION (1978) (US/0277-7347). [5,000] **1703**

PROCEEDINGS OF THE ANNUAL MEETING OF THE BERKELEY LINGUISTICS SOCIETY (US/0363-2946). [1,000] **3312**

PROCEEDINGS OF THE ANNUAL MEETING - SOUTHWESTERN PHILOSOPHY OF EDUCATION SOCIETY (US/0584-5041). [100] **1774**

PROCEEDINGS OF THE ... ANNUAL MEETING / UNIFORM LAW CONFERENCE OF CANADA (CN/0318-4900). [400] **3031**

PROCEEDINGS OF THE ... ANNUAL ROAD SCHOOL (US). [2,500] **2029**

PROCEEDINGS OF THE ... ANNUAL UNIVERSITY OF GUELPH NUTRITION CONFERENCE FOR FEED MANUFACTURERS (CN). **203**

PROCEEDINGS OF THE ARKANSAS ACADEMY OF SCIENCE (US/0097-4374). [450] **5140**

PROCEEDINGS OF THE ASSOCIATION FOR CONTINUING HIGHER EDUCATION (US). [1,000] **1842**

PROCEEDINGS OF THE BIOLOGICAL SOCIETY OF WASHINGTON (US/0006-324X). [1,000] **469**

PROCEEDINGS OF THE CANADIAN SOCIETY FOR HORTICULTURAL SCIENCE (CN/0315-6877). [350] **2429**

PROCEEDINGS OF THE CENTER FOR JEWISH-CHRISTIAN LEARNING (US/0887-4913). [6,000] **4988**

PROCEEDINGS OF THE ... CONFERENCE OF THE AUSTRALIAN SOCIETY OF SUGAR CANE TECHNOLOGISTS (AT/0726-0822). [1,000] **183**

PROCEEDINGS OF THE CONGRESS OF THE INTERNATIONAL INSTITUTE OF PUBLIC FINANCE (US/0195-8917). [1,100] **4742**

PROCEEDINGS OF THE ... CONVENTION (UK/0143-0610). [100] **3425**

PROCEEDINGS OF THE ... ENTOMOLOGICAL CONGRESS - ENTOMOLOGICAL SOCIETY OF SOUTHERN AFRICA (SA/1010-2566). [600] **5613**

PROCEEDINGS OF THE ENTOMOLOGICAL SOCIETY OF MANITOBA (CN/0315-2146). [300] **5613**

PROCEEDINGS OF THE EUROPEAN PROSTHODONTIC ASSOCIATION, THE (UK). **1333**

PROCEEDINGS OF THE ... FORAGE AND GRASSLAND CONFERENCE (US/0886-6899). [1,000] **122**

PROCEEDINGS OF THE ... GENERAL SYNOD, OFFICIAL REPORT / ANGLICAN CHURCH OF AUSTRALIA (AT). [600] **4988**

PROCEEDINGS OF THE GEOLOGISTS' ASSOCIATION (UK/0016-7878). [2,500] **1391**

PROCEEDINGS OF THE GREENWOOD GENETIC CENTER (US/0733-124X). **550**

PROCEEDINGS OF THE INDIANA ACADEMY OF SCIENCE (US/0073-6767). **5140**

PROCEEDINGS OF THE INTERNATIONAL CONFERENCE ON LASERS (US/0190-4132). [300] **5140**

PROCEEDINGS OF THE ... INTERNATIONAL SYMPOSIUM ON CONTROLLED RELEASE OF BIOACTIVE MATERIALS (US). [2,000] **989**

PROCEEDINGS — Controlled Circulation Index

PROCEEDINGS OF THE LEHIGH COUNTY HISTORICAL SOCIETY (US/0273-2912). **2755**

PROCEEDINGS OF THE MARINE SAFETY COUNCIL (US/0364-0981). [6,000] **4182**

PROCEEDINGS OF THE MICROSCOPICAL SOCIETY OF CANADA (CN/0381-1751). [600] **573**

PROCEEDINGS OF THE NATIONAL ACADEMY OF SCIENCE OF THE UNITED STATES OF AMERICA (US/0027-8424). [9,500] **5141**

PROCEEDINGS OF THE ... NATIONAL AGRICULTURAL PLASTICS CONGRESS (US/1073-1768). [300] **4459**

PROCEEDINGS OF THE NEW ZEALAND GEOGRAPHY CONFERENCE (NZ/1170-5698). [1,100] **2573**

PROCEEDINGS OF THE NEW ZEALAND GRASSLAND ASSOCIATION (NZ/0369-3902). [1,700] **122**

PROCEEDINGS OF THE NEW ZEALAND SOCIETY OF ANIMAL PRODUCTION (NZ/0370-2731). [1,000] **219**

PROCEEDINGS OF THE NIPR SYMPOSIUM ON ANTARCTIC METEORITES (JA/0914-5621). [900] **398**

PROCEEDINGS OF THE NIPR SYMPOSIUM ON UPPER ATMOSPHERE PHYSICS (JA). [850] **4445**

PROCEEDINGS OF THE NUTRITION SOCIETY OF AUSTRALIA (AT/0314-1004). [800] **4198**

PROCEEDINGS OF THE OKLAHOMA ACADEMY OF SCIENCE (US/0078-4303). [600] **5141**

PROCEEDINGS OF THE ... PAVING AND TRANSPORTATION CONFERENCE ... (US). [300] **2029**

PROCEEDINGS OF THE PMR CONFERENCE (US/0272-8710). [200] **1079**

PROCEEDINGS OF THE ROCKBRIDGE HISTORICAL SOCIETY (US/0080-3383). [1,000] **2755**

PROCEEDINGS OF THE ROYAL SOCIETY OF NEW ZEALAND (NZ/0557-4161). [770] **5141**

PROCEEDINGS, OF THE SOCIETY FOR EXPERIMENTAL STRESS ANALYSIS (US/0036-1313). [1,000] **2126**

PROCEEDINGS OF THE SOCIETY FOR PSYCHICAL RESEARCH (UK/0081-1475). [1,000] **4609**

PROCEEDINGS OF THE SOUTH ATLANTIC PHILOSOPHY OF EDUCATION SOCIETY (US). [115] **1774**

PROCEEDINGS OF THE SOUTH DAKOTA ACADEMY OF SCIENCE (US/0096-378X). [350] **5142**

PROCEEDINGS OF THE SPECIAL CONVENTION OF THE NATIONAL COLLEGIATE ATHLETIC ASSOCIATION (US/0094-4459). **4913**

PROCEEDINGS OF THE ... SPRING MEETING (INDUSTRIAL RELATIONS RESEARCH ASSOCIATION : 1979) (US/0733-0898). [5,000] **1703**

PROCEEDINGS OF THE VIRGIL SOCIETY (UK/0083-629X). [250] **5235**

PROCEEDINGS OF THE WESTERN ASSOCIATION OF FISH AND WILDLIFE AGENCIES AND THE WESTERN DIVISION AMERICAN FISHERIES ASSOCIATION (US/0198-6600). **2202**

PROCEEDINGS OF THE WESTERN SNOW CONFERENCE (US/0161-0589). [500] **1359**

PROCEEDINGS OF THE ZOOLOGICAL SOCIETY (II/0373-5893). [400] **5595**

PROCEEDINGS - SEMINAR ON THE ANALYSIS OF SECURITY PRICES (US). **912**

PROCEEDINGS - SOUTHERN ASSOCIATION OF COLLEGES AND SCHOOLS; THE SOUTHERN ASSOCIATION NEWSLETTER (US/0038-3813). [17,000] **1842**

PROCEEDINGS - SOUTHERN MARKETING ASSOCIATION (US). [650] **935**

PROCEEDINGS / SPACE CONGRESS (US/0584-6099). [1,000] **32**

PROCEEDINGS / SYMPOSIUM AND EXHIBITION ON THE ART OF GLASSBLOWING (US/0743-409X). [1,200] **2593**

PROCEEDINGS, SYMPOSIUM ON ADVANCED MANUFACTURING (US). [100] **3486**

PROCEEDINGS - TALL TIMBERS CONFERENCE ON ECOLOGICAL ANIMAL CONTROL BY HABITAT MANAGEMENT (US/0564-7207). **4247**

PROCEEDINGS - THE AUSTRALIAN ACADEMY OF THE HUMANITIES (AT/0067-1592). [300] **2852**

PROCEEDINGS / THE SOIL AND CROP SCIENCE SOCIETY OF FLORIDA (US/0096-4522). **183**

PROCEEDINGS - UNITED STATES NAVAL INSTITUTE (US/0041-798X). [122,000] **4182**

PROCES-VERBAL DU CONGRES GENERAL ANNUEL - SOCIETE SAINT-JEAN-BAPTISTE DE QUEBEC (CN/0384-7357). **5235**

PROCES-VERBAUX - INTERNATIONAL ASSOCIATION FOR THE PHYSICAL SCIENCES OF THE OCEAN (US/0254-2005). [1,000] **1455**

PROCESS, ARCHITECTURE (JA/0386-037X). [2,000] **306**

PROCESS ENGINEERING (UK/0370-1859). [19,168] **2016**

PROCESS INDUSTRIES CANADA (CN/0826-7243). [24,500] **2016**

PROCESS STUDIES (US/0360-6503). [1,150] **4358**

PROCLAIM (NASHVILLE) (US/0162-4326). [18,000] **4988**

PROCOMM ENTERPRISES MAGAZINE (US/0896-7229). [30,000] **1162**

PROCTOR (AT). [4,800] **3032**

PRODEI (SP/0079-5836). **3486**

PRODUCE NEWS (US/0032-969X). [10,000] **2354**

PRODUCER (PORT WASHINGTON, N.Y.) (US/1067-439X). [1,000] **1162**

PRODUCER'S MASTERGUIDE, THE (US/0732-6653). [18,000] **1136**

PRODUCTEUR PLUS, LE (CN/1183-9929). [19,500] **122**

PRODUCTION (US/0032-9819). [75,000] **2126**

PRODUCTION OF MILK AND MILK PRODUCTS (IE/0791-3036). **198**

PRODUCTIONS ANIMALES (PARIS, 1988) (FR/0990-0632). [1,300] **5519**

PRODUCTIVITY (STAMFORD, CONN.) (US/0275-8040). [3,000] **883**

PRODUCTS FINISHING (US/0032-9940). [46,000] **3486**

PRODUCTS FINISHING DIRECTORY (US/0478-4251). [25,000] **4016**

PRODUKSI PERIKANAN LAUT YANG DIJUAL DI PELELANGAN/TEMPAT PENDARATAN IKAN DI JAWA-MADURA (IO). **2311**

PRODUKSI TANAMAN BAHAN MAKANAN DI INDONESIA (IO). **183**

PROEDUCATION (US/8756-5188). [50,000] **1774**

PROFESSIONAL AGENT, THE (US/0148-8899). [30,000] **2890**

PROFESSIONAL CARWASHING (US/0191-6823). [17,000] **935**

PROFESSIONAL CARWASHING & DETAILING (US). [16,000] **5423**

PROFESSIONAL COMMUNICATOR, THE (US/0891-1207). [12,000] **1120**

PROFESSIONAL ELECTRONICS / THE OFFICIAL JOURNAL OF NESDA AND ISCET (US). [11,000] **2077**

PROFESSIONAL ENGINEERING (UK/0953-6639). [56,000] **2127**

PROFESSIONAL GENEALOGISTS OF ARKANSAS NEWSLETTER (US/1040-4430). [700] **2468**

PROFESSIONAL HOTEL & RESTAURANT INTERIORS (UK/0959-2687). [4,000] **2902**

PROFESSIONAL LANDSCAPER (UK). [4,000] **2429**

PROFESSIONAL LICENSING REPORT (US/1043-2051). [500] **4208**

PROFESSIONAL MEETING MANAGEMENT (US). [20,000] **764**

PROFESSIONAL MONITOR / MICHIGAN ASSOCIATION OF THE PROFESSIONS, THE (US/0744-7817). [650] **3032**

PROFESSIONAL PHOTOGRAPHER (1964), THE (US/0033-0167). [30,000] **4375**

PROFESSIONAL PILOT (US/0191-6238). [35,000] **32**

PROFESSIONAL PRINTER (UK/0308-4205). [3,000] **4569**

PROFESSIONAL PULIZIE (IT/1120-8368). [9,000] **2127**

PROFESSIONAL RENOVATION (CN/1182-0470). [50,000] **2903**

PROFESSIONAL ROOFING (US/0896-5552). [20,000] **624**

PROFESSIONAL SKATER, THE (US/8750-9369). [1,200] **4913**

PROFESSIONAL SURVEYOR (US/0278-1425). [58,000] **2029**

PROFESSIONALS (US/0744-3471). [2,500] **3725**

PROFESSIONI INFERMIERISTICHE (IT/0033-0205). [5,000] **3867**

PROFIL MAHASISWA UNIVERSITAS KATOLIK PARAHYANGAN (IO). [60] **1842**

PROFIL : SOZIALDEMOKRATISCHE ZEITSCHRIFT FUR POLITIK, WIRTSCHAFT UND KULTUR (SZ/0555-3482). [3,000] **4545**

PROFILE (OMAHA) (US/0162-5241). [4,000] **705**

PROFILE (SOUTH PORTLAND, ME.) (US/1071-3808). [7,000] **705**

PROFILE, THE (US). [175] **279**

PROFIT (ARMONK, N.Y.) (US/1061-9194). [200,000] **705**

PROFIT (TORONTO) (CN/1183-1324). [100,000] **705**

PROFITRAVEL (GW). [100,000] **705**

PROGENITOR (AT/0725-914X). [275] **2468**

PROGRAM AND ABSTRACTS OF PAPERS - INTERNATIONAL ASSOCIATION FOR DENTAL RESEARCH (US/0534-669X). [7,000] **1333**

PROGRAM / CHICAGO SYMPHONY ORCHESTRA (US). [30] **4147**

PROGRAM HIGHLIGHTS (US/0278-5374). [12,000] **3630**

PROGRAM ON ENVIRONMENT AND BEHAVIOR MONOGRAPH (US/0737-5425). [80] **5213**

PROGRAMME D'ASSOCIE / INSTITUT D'ASSURANCE DU CANADA (CN/0820-0777). **2891**

PROGRAMME DE LOISIR (CN/0712-8088). **387**

PROGRAMME DE PREVENTION CONTRE LA GRELE DE L'ASSOCIATION NATIONALE D'ETUDE ET DE LUTTE CONTRE LES FLEAUX ATMOSPHERIQUES (FR/0373-7349). [1,000] **1433**

PROGRAMME F.I.A.C (CN/0820-6120). **2891**

PROGRAMME SOUVENIR. FESTIVAL DU VOYAGEUR, ST. BONIFACE, MANITOBA (CN/0229-2572). [25,000] **4853**

PROGRAMMER'S PROVANTAGE COMPUTER PRODUCTS BUYER'S GUIDE (US/1076-9714). [195,000] **1281**

PROGRAMS REGULATIONS - INSTITUTE OF CANADIAN BANKERS (CN/0821-607X). **804**

PROGRES TECHNIQUE, LE (FR/0397-8060). **5142**

PROGRESS IN BASIC AND CLINICAL PHARMACOLOGY (SZ/1011-0267). **4326**

PROGRESS IN CARDIOLOGY (PHILADELPHIA, PA. : 1988) (US). **3709**

PROGRESS IN NUCLEAR ENERGY (NEW SERIES) (UK/0149-1970). **2158**

PROGRESS IN PAPER RECYCLING (US/1061-1452). [660] **4237**

PROGRESS IN RUBBER AND PLASTICS TECHNOLOGY (UK/0266-7320). [250] **5077**

PROGRESS NOTES - CANADIAN WILDLIFE SERVICE (CN/0069-0023). [1,200] **470**

PROGRESS REPORT - AMERICAN PHYSICAL THERAPY ASSOCIATION (US/0162-3907). [48,700] **4382**

PROGRESSIVE FARMER (US/0033-0760). [536,071] **123**

PROGRESSIVE RAILROADING (US/0033-0817). [19,800] **5434**

PROJECT LOOK-LISTEN-THINK-RESPOND ANNUAL REPORT (US). [50] **1120**

PROJECT MANAGEMENT JOURNAL (US/8756-9728). [7,000] **883**

PROJECTS REVIEW (LONDON, ENGLAND) (UK/0265-4644). **306**

PROJET (FR/0033-0884). [5,000] **1639**

PROJET EDUCATIF (SAINT-JEROME) (CN/0821-7629). **1842**

PROMETHEUS (AT/0810-9028). [400] **3242**

PROMISE (REGINA) (CN/0826-533X). [325] **5066**

PROMOTION AND EDUCATION (FR/0751-7149). [2,000] **4797**

PROMOTIONS & INCENTIVES (UK/0266-7991). [11,500] **883**

PROOFS (TULSA) (US/0033-1236). [7,796] **1333**

PROP. 65 NEWS (US/0895-5042). [1,000] **3115**

PROPANE CANADA (CN/0033-1260). [5,600] **4275**

PROPERTY DISPOSITION HANDBOOK (US). **2832**

PROPERTY FINANCE (UK/0955-8658). **804**

PROPERTY TAX JOURNAL (US/0731-0285). [1,300] **4742**

PROPOS DE CUISINE (CN/0821-1264). [1,100] **624**

PROPOS PEDAGOGIQUES (CN/0227-0927). [600] **1775**

PROPYLENE ANNUAL (US/0095-4128). [325] **1047**

PROSECUTORS' NOTES (SW). [200] **3108**

PROSPECT (AFRICAN EXPLOSIVES AND CHEMICAL INDUSTRIES) (SA/0033-1481). [15,000] **3487**

PROSPECTOR : EXPLORATION AND INVESTMENT BULLETIN, THE (CN/1181-6414). **2149**

PROSPECTUS - CONCORDES (CN/0822-5141). **4913**

PROSPECTUS - THE INSTITUTE OF FINANCE MANAGEMENT (TZ). [5,000] **883**

PROSTAGLANDINS (US/0090-6980). [1,400] **585**

PROSTHETICS AND ORTHOTICS INTERNATIONAL (DK/0309-3646). [2,700] **4392**

PROTEE (CN/0300-3523). [650] **3312**

PROTESTANT REFORMED THEOLOGICAL JOURNAL (US/1070-8138). [500] **4988**

PROTESTANTESIMO (IT/0033-1767). [1,000] **5066**

PROTEUS (SHIPPENSBURG, PA.) (US/0889-6348). [4,500] **3426**

PROTOCOL OF THE COLLOQUY OF THE CENTER FOR HERMENEUTICAL STUDIES IN HELLENISTIC AND MODERN CULTURE (US/0098-0900). [200] **1079**

PROUST RESEARCH ASSOCIATION NEWSLETTER (US/0048-5659). [300] **3350**

PROVIDENCE BUSINESS NEWS (US/0887-8226). [4,500 paid 6,000 unpaid] **5741**

PROVIDER (WASHINGTON, D.C.) (US/0888-0352). [22,000] **5302**

PROVINCIAL JUDGES JOURNAL (CN/0709-5139). **3142**

PROVINCIAL NEWSJOURNAL - INFANT DEVELOPMENT PROGRAMMES OF B.C (CN/0824-9946). [2,000] **5302**

PROZAH (IS). [5,000] **3426**

PRS JOURNAL (US/0030-8250). [1,600] **4358**

PRS NEWS (UK/0309-0019). [25,000] **5235**

PRYOR REPORT, THE (US/0742-9770). [15,500] **4209**

PRZEGLAD INFORMACYJNO-DOKUMENTACYJNY. SERIA: HYDROLOGIA I OCEANOLOGIA (PL). [200] **1417**

PRZEWALSKI HORSE (NE/0167-7926). **2801**

PS (CN/0825-0197). **1843**

PSA JOURNAL (US/0030-8277). [10,000] **4376**

PSBA BULLETIN (US/0162-3559). [11,300] **1869**

PSI CHI NEWSLETTER (US/0033-2569). [13,000] **4609**

PSI RESEARCH (US/0749-2898). [300] **4242**

PSICHIATRIA E PSICOTERAPIA ANALITICA (IT/0393-9774). [4,000] **3932**

PSICHIATRIA GENERALE E DELL'ETA EVOLUTIVA (IT/0555-5299). **3932**

PSICOANALISI CONTRO (IT/0393-6902). [4,000] **3932**

PSIQUIS (SP/0210-8348). [6,000] **3933**

PSYCHIATRIC ANNALS (US/0048-5713). [28,000] **3933**

PSYCHIATRIC FORUM, THE (US/0033-2690). [4,000] **3933**

PSYCHIATRIC HOSPITAL, THE (US/0885-7717). [8,500] **3791**

PSYCHIATRIC TIMES, THE (US/0893-2905). [42,000] **3933**

PSYCHIATRY IN PRACTICE (UK/0262-5377). [20,800] **3934**

PSYCHOANALYSIS AND CONTEMPORARY THOUGHT (US/0161-5289). [900] **4610**

PSYCHOHISTORY REVIEW, THE (US/0363-891X). [500] **2626**

PSYCHOLOGICA BELGICA (BE/0033-2879). [500] **4610**

PSYCHOLOGICAL RESEARCH BULLETIN (SW/0555-5620). [550] **4611**

PSYCHOLOGIE & EDUCATION (FR). [3,000] **4611**

PSYCHOLOGIE PREVENTIVE (CN/0714-3494). [1,200] **4612**

PSYCHOLOGISCHE BEITRAEGE (GW/0033-3018). [50] **4612**

PSYCHOLOGY (SAVANNAH) (US/0033-3077). [1,500] **4613**

PSYCHOLOGY TODAY (US/0033-3107). **4613**

PSYCHOLOOG (NE/0033-3115). [6,750] **4613**

PSYCHOMUSICOLOGY (US/0275-3987). [400] **4147**

PSYCHOSOCIAL REHABILITATION JOURNAL (US/0147-5622). [2,800] **3934**

PSYCHOTROPES (MONTREAL) (CN/0715-9684). [2,000] **1348**

PSYCSCAN. APPLIED PSYCHOLOGY (US/0271-7506). [2,500] **4623**

PSYCSCAN. DEVELOPMENTAL PSYCHOLOGY (US/0197-1492). [3,000] **4623**

PSYCSCAN. LD/MR (US/0730-1928). [8,000] **4623**

PSYKOLOGISK SKRIFTSERIE AARHUS (DK/0900-8527). [300] **4614**

PTA TODAY (US/0195-2781). [35,000] **1775**

PTI JOURNAL (US). **5390**

PUBBLICAZIONI CERES (IT). [1,000] **1514**

PUBLIC ADMINISTRATOR AND THE COURTS, THE (US/0735-4703). **4676**

PUBLIC AFFAIRS COMMENT (US/0033-3395). [900] **4676**

PUBLIC AND LOCAL ACTS OF THE LEGISLATURE OF THE STATE OF MICHIGAN (US/0893-2573). **3032**

PUBLIC COMMUNICATIONS MAGAZINE (US/1041-6943). [10,000] **1120**

PUBLIC CONTRACT LAW JOURNAL (US/0033-3441). **3033**

PUBLIC DOCUMENTS (BATON ROUGE, LA.) (US/0099-2410). [1,000] **4699**

PUBLIC DOCUMENTS OF LOUISIANA (BATON ROUGE, LA : 1981) (US). [450] **4676**

PUBLIC EDUCATION SERIES (US/0272-2658). [1,500] **5595**

PUBLIC ENTERPRISE / INTERNATIONAL CENTER FOR PUBLIC ENTERPRISES IN DEVELOPING COUNTRIES (YU/0351-3564). **2911**

PUBLIC HEALTH REVIEWS (IS/0301-0422). [1,000] **4797**

PUBLIC HISTORIAN, THE (US/0272-3433). [1,200] **2626**

PUBLIC INFORMATION CIRCULAR - GEOLOGICAL SURVEY OF WYOMING (US/0160-3655). **1392**

PUBLIC JUSTICE REPORT (US/0742-5325). [2,500] **4676**

PUBLIC LAND LAW REVIEW, THE (US/0732-0264). [550] **3033**

PUBLIC LIBRARY EXPENDITURE IN SCOTLAND (UK). [80] **3243**

PUBLIC POWER (US/0033-3654). [12,000] **4762**

PUBLIC PROGRAMS NEWSLETTER (US/0890-0655). [150] **2323**

PUBLIC RELATIONS QUARTERLY (US/0033-3700). [5,000] **765**

PUBLIC SCHOOL REPORT (TOPEKA, KAN. : 1978) (US). [700] **1776**

PUBLIC SERVANT. DIE STAATSAMPTENAAR, THE (SA/0033-376X). [100,000] **4677**

PUBLIC TECHNOLOGY (US/0882-1445). [4,000] **5143**

PUBLIC WELFARE (WASHINGTON) (US/0033-3816). [8,600] **5303**

PUBLIC WORKS (US/0033-3840). [50,400] **1992**

PUBLIC WORKS FINANCING (US). [2,000] **4743**

PUBLICACIONES DEL INSTITUTO CARO Y CUERVO. SERIE BIBLIOGRAFICA (CK). [2,000] **3336**

PUBLICACIONES ESPECIALES - INSTITUTO ESPANOL DE OCEANOGRAFIA (SP/0214-7378). [1,000] **1455**

PUBLICACIONES. SERIE BIBLIOGRAFICA (CK/0073-991X). **423**

PUBLICACIONES. SERIES MINOR (CK/0073-9928). [2,000] **3312**

PUBLICATION B / CENTRE INTERNATIONAL DE RECERCHES SUR LE BILINGUISME (CN/0704-7037). [150] **3312**

PUBLICATION NOTE / U.S. DEPARTMENT OF HEALTH AND HUMAN SERVICES, PUBLIC HEALTH SERVICE, OFFICE OF HEALTH RESEARCH, STATISTICS, AND TECHNOLOGY, NATIONAL CENTER FOR HEALTH STATISTICS (US). **4677**

PUBLICATION OF THE KRESS LIBRARY OF BUSINESS AND ECONOMICS (US/0073-0777). [1,500] **705**

PUBLICATIONS (BE). [3,000] **279**

PUBLICATIONS - ASBL CENTRE D'HISTOIRE ET D'ART DE LA THUDINIE (BE). [400] **2626**

PUBLICATIONS / AUGUSTAN REPRINT SOCIETY (US/0885-7954). [700] **3426**

PUBLICATIONS: CLASSICAL STUDIES (US/0068-6344). [850] **1079**

PUBLICATIONS - HAWAII INSTITUTE OF GEOPHYSICS (US). [400] **1409**

PUBLICATIONS INDEX / NATIONAL HEALTH STATISTICS CENTRE (NZ). [400] **4811**

PUBLICATIONS OF THE ENGLISH GOETHE SOCIETY (UK/0959-3683). [500] **3426**

PUBLICATIONS OF THE HARLEIAN SOCIETY. NEW SERIES, THE (UK). [350] **2468**

PUBLICATIONS OF THE INTERNATIONAL BUREAU OF FISCAL DOCUMENTATION (NE/0074-2112). **750**

PUBLICATIONS OF THE LINCOLN RECORD SOCIETY, THE (UK/0267-2634). [350] **2704**

PUBLICATIONS OF THE NEBRASKA STATE HISTORICAL SOCIETY (US/0191-037X). **2755**

PUBLICATIONS OF THE PIPE ROLL SOCIETY, THE (UK). [320] **5235**

PUBLICATIONS (TOPOR & ASSOCIATES) (US/1063-1771). [200] **1843**

PUBLICITAIRE (MONTREAL) (CN/0229-9720). **765**

PUBLIKATIE / SOCIAAL-ECONOMISCHE RAAD (NE). **1514**

PUBLISHER (OTTAWA) (CN/0380-8025). [1,200] **4818**

PUBLISHERS' AUXILIARY (US/0048-5942). [8,000] **4818**

PUBLISHER'S MONTHLY (II). [8,000] **4818**

PUBLIUS (US/0048-5950). [1,100] **4492**

PUCE A L'ORIELLE (MONTREAL) (CN/0824-068X). [1,000] **1776**

PUERTO RICO ECONOMIC INDICATORS / GOVERNMENT DEVELOPMENT BANK FOR PUERTO RICO (PR). [50] **1579**

PUERTO RICO LIVING (US/0033-4049). [10,000] **2544**

PUGET SOUND COMPUTER USER (US/0886-8174). [85,000] **1201**

PULASKI COUNTY JOURNAL (US). [3,400] **5666**

PULASKI NEWS (US). **5770**

PULCE (IT). **1514**

PULIZIA INDUSTRIALE E SANIFICAZIONE (IT). [6000] **2868**

PULLER, THE (US/8750-4219). [8,000] **160**

PULMONARY PHARMACOLOGY (EDINBURGH) (UK/0952-0600). [200] **3951**

PULP & PAPER FORECASTER (US/0898-6886). **4238**

PULP & PAPER INTERNATIONAL (US/0033-409X). [8,972] **4238**

PULPIT RESOURCE (US/0195-1548). [9,000] **4988**

PULPWOOD PRODUCTION IN THE NORTH CENTRAL REGION BY COUNTY (US). [2,000] **4238**

PULSE (PICO RIVERA) (US/0555-6953). [1,054] **5519**

PULSO DEL PERIODISMO (US/1051-8126). [4,500] **2923**

PULVERTAFT PAPERS (UK/0261-118X). [60] **2468**

PUNDIT (CN/0712-1318). **3426**

PUPPETRY JOURNAL, THE (US/0033-443X). [2,000] **5367**

PURABHILEKH-PURATATVA : JOURNAL OF THE DIRECTORATE OF ARCHIVES, ARCHAEOLOGY AND MUSEUM, PANAJI-GOA (II). [700] **279**

PURCHASING MANAGEMENT (CN/0841-615X). [20,000] **951**

PURDUE EXPONENT, THE (US). [20,000] **5666**

PURE AND APPLIED CHEMISTRY (UK/0033-4545). [1,550] **990**

PUREBRED PICTURE, THE (US/8750-1880). [5,000] **219**

PUSAN SUSAN TAEHAK YON'GU POGO (KO). **5143**

PUTNAM COUNTY COURIER (CARMEL, N.Y. : 1852) (US/0890-1147). [9,000] **5646**

PUTNAM COURIER-TRADER, THE (US). [7,500] **5646**

PW PERSONEELSMANAGEMENT (NE). [16,000] **705**

PYTTERSEN'S NEDERLANDSE ALMANAK (NE). [5,000] **2521**

Q.T.C. TODAY (CN/0828-5780). **4989**

QADMONIOT (IS/0033-4839). [5,000] **279**

QINGHUA XUEBAO (CH/0577-9170). **2770**

QUAD COMMUNITY PRESS (US/0892-1806). [52,000] **5698**

QUADERNI DI STORIA (IT). **2626**

QUADERNI D'ITALIANISTICA (CN/0226-8043). [500] **3426**

QUADERNI FIORENTINI PER LA STORIA DEL PENSIERO GIURIDICO MODERNO (IT). **3033**

QUADERNI IBERO-AMERICANI (IT/0033-4960). [1,100] **3350**

QUADERNI MARCHIGIANI DI MEDICINA (IT/0392-9620). [1,000] **3632**

QUADERNI MEDIEVALI (IT). **2704**

QUADERNI SARDI DI ECONOMIA (IT/0391-8394). [2,000] **1579**

QUADERNS D'ARQUITECTURA I URBANISME (SP/0211-9595). [10,000] **307**

QUADRANT (AT/0033-5002). [6,000] **2511**

QUADRANT (NEW YORK) (US/0033-5010). [2,000] **4614**

QUAERENDO (NE/0014-9527). **4831**

QUAKER HISTORY (US/0033-5053). [800] **4989**

QUAKER : MONATSHEFTE DER DEUTSCHEN FREUNDE, DER (GW). [600] **4989**

QUAKER YEOMEN, THE (US/0737-8246). **2468**

QUALITE TOTALE (CN). [6,000] **883**

QUALITY AND PRODUCTIVITY MANAGEMENT (US/0895-2272). **883**

QUALITY AUSTRALIA (AT/0813-0272). [6,000] **883**

QUALITY BY DESIGN (US/0893-360X). [1,600] **625**

QUALITY CARE ADVOCATE (US/0892-6174). **5303**

QUALITY LETTER FOR HEALTHCARE LEADERS, THE (US/1047-5311). **3791**

QUALITY OBSERVER, THE (US/1057-9583). [15,000] **884**

QUALITY (WHEATON) (US/0360-9936). [90,000] **884**

QUARRY (KINGSTON) (CN/0033-5266). [900] **3427**

QUART DE ROND (CN/0709-0692). [6,000] **625**

QUARTER CIRCLE (CN/0228-0612). [1,000] **2801**

QUARTER HORSE JOURNAL (1953), THE (US/0164-6656). **2801**

QUARTER RUNNING HORSE CHART BOOK, THE (US/0888-0859). [500] **2802**

QUARTERLY AIRCRAFT OPERATING COSTS AND STATISTICS (US). **32**

QUARTERLY BENCHMARKS (US/8756-4599). [1,000] **4614**

QUARTERLY BIBLIOGRAPHY OF MAJOR TROPICAL DISEASES (US/0192-6640). [9,000] **3986**

QUARTERLY / BOULDER GENEALOGICAL SOCIETY (US/0735-6730). [270] **2469**

QUARTERLY BULLETIN - ARCHEOLOGICAL SOCIETY OF VIRGINIA (US/0003-8202). [800] **280**

QUARTERLY BULLETIN - ASHTABULA COUNTY HISTORICAL SOCIETY (US/0895-1152). [280] **2755**

QUARTERLY BULLETIN - BANK OF THAILAND (TH/0125-605X). [2,500] **805**

QUARTERLY BULLETIN OF THE ALPINE GARDEN SOCIETY (UK/0002-6476). [11,000] **2429**

QUARTERLY BULLETIN OF THE AMERICAN ASSOCIATION OF TEACHERS OF ESPERANTO (US/0002-7499). [100] **3313**

QUARTERLY BULLETIN / ROSWELL MUSEUM AND ART CENTER (US/0557-3645). [1,300] **4095**

QUARTERLY BULLETIN - SOUTH AFRICAN RESERVE BANK (SA/0038-2620). [4,100] **805**

QUARTERLY - CANADIAN CAT ASSOCIATION (CN/0828-4865). [1,000] **4287**

QUARTERLY / CENTRAL GEORGIA GENEALOGICAL SOCIETY, INC (US/0738-8209). [400] **2469**

QUARTERLY / CHRISTIAN LEGAL SOCIETY (US/0736-0142). [5,000] **3033**

QUARTERLY ECONOMIC AND STATISTICAL REVIEW / RESERVE BANK OF ZIMBABWE (RH). [2,500] **1537**

QUARTERLY ECONOMIC BULLETIN (UK). **1514**

QUARTERLY ECONOMIC BULLETIN - CENTRAL BANK OF TRINIDAD AND TOBAGO (TR). [1,000] **1579**

QUARTERLY ECONOMIC COMMENTARY (IE/0376-7191). [1,000] **1514**

QUARTERLY ECONOMIC REPORT (TR/0041-3046). [600] **1514**

QUARTERLY JOURNAL OF BUSINESS AND ECONOMICS (US/0747-5535). [500] **706**

QUARTERLY JOURNAL OF THE ROYAL METEOROLOGICAL SOCIETY (UK/0035-9009). [1,500] **1434**

QUARTERLY JOURNAL / OFFICE OF THE COMPTROLLER OF THE CURRENCY (US/0738-2146). [7,500] **805**

QUARTERLY - MUSEUM OF THE FUR TRADE (US/0027-4135). [2,000] **2756**

QUARTERLY NEWS JOURNAL OF THE CROSBY ARBORETUM, A (US/0741-9635). **5235**

QUARTERLY NEWS-LETTER - BOOK CLUB OF CALIFORNIA (US/0006-7202). [1,000] **4831**

QUARTERLY NEWSLETTER / CANADIAN FORESTRY ASSOCIATION OF BRITISH COLUMBIA (CN/0710-0566). **2391**

QUARTERLY NEWSLETTER - TEA RESEARCH FOUNDATION OF CENTRAL AFRICA (MW). [500] **183**

QUARTERLY OF THE NATIONAL ASSOCIATION FOR OUTLAW AND LAWMAN HISTORY, INC (US/1071-4189). [400] **2756**

QUARTERLY / OLYMPIA GENEALOGICAL SOCIETY (US). [250] **2469**

QUARTERLY - ORANGE COUNTY CALIFORNIA GENEALOGICAL SOCIETY (US/0030-4263). [400+] **2469**

QUARTERLY - PHI LAMBDA KAPPA MEDICAL FRATERNITY (US/0739-2079). [1,200] **3917**

QUARTERLY REVIEW - CIPEC (FR/1015-0064). [500] **1623**

QUARTERLY - THE MUSEUM OF THE FUR TRADE (US/0027-4135). [2,600] **3185**

QUARTZ DEVICES DIRECTORY (US). [3,500] **3487**

QUATERNAIRE : BULLETIN DE L'ASSOCIATION FRANCAISE POUR L'ETUDE DU QUATERNAIRE : INTERNATIONAL JOURNAL OF THE FRENCH QUATERNARY ASSOCIATION (FR/1142-2904). [650] **1393**

QUATRE-TEMPS (CN/0820-5515). [2,200] **525**

QUE PASA SAN ANTONIO (US). [30,000] **5489**

QUEBEC CHRONICLE-TELEGRAPH (CN). [3,500] **5793**

QUEBEC FRANCAIS (CN/0316-2052). [8,000] **3427**

QUEBEC PHARMACIE (MONTREAL, 1981) (CN/0826-9874). [6,700] **4327**

QUEBEC TECHNOLOGIE (CN/0711-5288). **5144**

QUEBEC VERT (CN/0705-6923). [250] **2202**

QUEBEC YACHTIING, VOILE & MOTEUR (CN/0833-918X). [11,108] **595**

QUEEN CITY HERITAGE (US/0746-3472). [4,500] **2756**

QUEEN OF PEACE WILDERNESS GAZETTE (US). [1,000] **4989**

QUEEN'S PAPERS IN INDUSTRIAL RELATIONS (CN/0838-6609). [800] **1705**

QUEENS PARK UPDATE (CN). **4677**

QUEEN'S UNIVERSITY PAPERS IN SOCIAL ANTHROPOLOGY, THE (IE). [400] **243**

QUEENSLAND ACCOMMODATION AND CARAVANNING DIRECTORY (AT). [125,000] **5489**

QUEENSLAND COUNTRY LIFE (AT/0033-6084). [35,000] **124**

QUEENSLAND DAIRY FARMER (AU). [2,000] **198**

QUEENSLAND FAMILY HISTORIAN : JOURNAL OF THE QUEENSLAND FAMILY HISTORY SOCIETY, INC (AT/0811-3394). [1,200] **2469**

QUEENSLAND FRUIT AND VEGETABLE NEWS (AT/0033-6122). [11,500] **2429**

QUEENSLAND GRAINGROWER, THE (AT). [10,000] **203**

QUEENSLAND LAND COURT REPORTS (AT). [150] **3034**

QUEENSLAND LAW SOCIETY JOURNAL, THE (AT/0313-4253). [4,800] **3034**

QUEENSLAND MASTER BUILDER (AT/0048-6361). [4,700] **625**

QUEENSLAND NATURALIST (AT/0079-8843). [450] **4171**

QUEENSLAND PROPERTY REPORT (AT). [14,400] **4843**

QUEENSLAND TEACHERS PROFESSIONAL MAGAZINE (AT/0813-8206). [32,000] **1903**

QUESNEL CARIBOO OBSERVER (CN/1195-5023). [4,800] **5793**

QUEST: MANHATTAN PROPERTIES & COUNTRY ESTATES (UK). [100,000] **4843**

QUESTION DE SPIRITUALITE, TRADITION, LITTERATURES (FR). **4243**

QUICK & EASY PLASTIC CANVAS (US/1048-5341). [160,000] **375**

QUICK FROZEN FOODS INTERNATIONAL (US/0033-6416). [11,000] **2355**

QUICK PRINTING (US/0191-4588). [53,000] **4569**

QUICK TRIPS TRAVEL LETTER (US/1064-0339). [2,000] **5489**

QUILL AND SCROLL (IOWA CITY) (US/0033-6505). [15,000] **2923**

QUILL, QUEENSLAND INTER-LIBRARY LIAISON (AT). [600] **3243**

QUIMERA (BARCELONA, SPAIN) (SP/0211-3325). [22,000] **3351**

QUINCY COLLEGE BULLETIN (US/0033-6556). [9,620] **1094**

QUINZAINE LITTERAIRE, LA (FR/0048-6493). [30,000] **3427**

QUIPU (MX/0185-5093). **5144**

QUMRAN CHRONICLE (PL/0867-8715). **5019**

QUOI DE N'OEUF (CN/0821-6924). [3,000] **220**

QUORUM (OTTAWA) (CN/0225-5014). [1,300] **2544**

QUORUM REPORT (US/0882-3456). **4678**

QUOTIDIEN DU PHARMACIEN, LE (FR/0764-5104). [22,000] **4327**

QWL NEWS & ABSTRACTS / WORK RESEARCH UNIT (UK). **946**

R A C V S OUT AND ABOUT (AT). [100,000] **5489**

R A C V'S ATTRACTIONS AUSTRALIA (AT). [100,000] **5489**

R.F. DESIGN (US/0163-321X). [33,382] **1993**

R.F.M., REVUE FRANCAISE DE MECANIQUE (FR/0373-6601). [800] **2127**

R L S, REGIONAL LANGUAGE STUDIES ... NEWFOUNDLAND (CN/0079-9335). [350] **3313**

R.P.N.A.M. UPDATE (CN/0822-4048). [1,500] **3867**

RAC NEWSLETTER (US/0163-9838). [22,000] **2006**

RACCOON (US/0148-0162). [1,000] **3470**

RACER (TORONTO) (CN/0380-7762). [3,500] **4914**

RACIAL AND ETHNIC REPORT : PUPIL ENROLLMENT (US). [175] **1776**

RACING FOR KIDS (US/1056-7623). [10,000] **1068**

RACING GREYHOUNDS (US/1042-9174). [2,000] **4865**

RACING PIGEON, THE (UK/0033-7390). [33,000] **4914**

RAD HARLOW (UK/0264-6412). [10,000] **3944**

RADIATION PROTECTION DOSIMETRY (UK/0144-8420). [1,000] **4440**

RADIATION PROTECTION IN AUSTRALIA (AT/0729-7963). [300] **4798**

RADIO AGE (AUGUSTA, GA.) (US/0892-6360). **1137**

RADIO ATIVITE INC (CN/0822-7926). [400] **4148**

RADIO COMMUNICATION (UK/0033-7803). [36,000] **2078**

RADIO IN THE UNITED STATES (US/0740-2341). [2,000] **1137**

RADIO Y TELEVISION (US/0033-8133). [9,903] **1138**

RADIOCOMM MAGAZINE (CN/1196-0809). [3,000] **1138**

RADIOGRAPHER (AT/0033-8273). [3,300] **3632**

RADIOISOTOPES (JA/0033-8303). [4,000] **5144**

RADIOLOGICA (OULU) (FI/0358-4887). [450] **3945**

RADIOLOGICAL HEALTH BULLETIN (US/0888-8086). [3,500] **3945**

RADIUS (MENDOCINO, CALIF.) (US/0886-7771). [2,000] **328**

RADIX (BERKELEY, CALIF.) (US/0275-0147). [5,000] **4989**

RADON NEWS DIGEST (US/0896-7180). **2241**

RAFT (CLEVELAND, OHIO) (US/0891-0545). [200] **3314**

RAG TIMES (US/0090-4570). [550] **4148**

RAGAN REPORT, THE (US/0197-6060). [5,000] **706**

RAGIUSAN. RASSEGNA GIURIDICA DELLA SANITA (IT/1120-1762). **3034**

RAGTIMER, THE (CN/0033-8672). [450] **4148**

RAIDA / INSTITUTE FOR WOMEN'S STUDIES IN THE ARAB WORLD, BEIRUT UNIVERSITY COLLEGE (LE). [1,000] **5565**

RAIL CLASSICS & RAILWAY QUARTERLY (US/0743-9075). **5434**

RAIL INTERNATIONAL (BE/0020-8442). [12,000] **5434**

RAIL MART, THE (US/1070-7751). [2,500] **5434**

RAILROAD ACCIDENTS IN OREGON (US/0093-2140). [600] **5401**

RAILROADER (RH). [17,800] **5435**

RAILWAY CARLOADINGS (MONTHLY ED.) (CN/0380-6308). [285] **5435**

RAILWAYS (SA/0254-2218). [2,300] **5436**

RAINEY TIMES (US/0734-2055). [350] **2469**

RAINFOREST ACTION NETWORK ALERT & WORLD RAINFOREST REPORT (US). [30,000] **2180**

RAJASTHAN BOARD JOURNAL OF EDUCATION. RAJASTHANA BORDA SIKSHANA PATRIKA, THE (II/0033-9083). **1776**

RAKENNUSTUOTANTO (FI). [38,000] **625**

RAKUNO KAGAKU, SHOKUHIN NO KENKYU (JA/0385-0218). [650] **198**

RAMBLING ON (AT). [800] **4914**

RAM'S HORN (SCOTSBURN) (CN/0827-4053). [560] **124**

RANCH MAGAZINE, THE (US/0145-8515). [7,000] **220**

RANDALLSTOWN NEWS (US/0883-7104). [10,119] **5687**

RANDAX EDUCATION GUIDE TO COLLEGES SEEKING STUDENTS (US). **1843**

R&D INNOVATOR (US/1061-1894). [1,000] **5144**

RANDOL MINING DIRECTORY (US/1054-027X). [3500] **2149**

RANDOM LENGTHS (SAN PEDRO, CALIF.) (US/0891-8627). [30,000] **5638**

RANGE HISTORY (US). **2627**

RANGEFINDER (SANTA MONICA), THE (US/0033-9202). [50,000] **4376**

RANGER RICK (US/0738-6656). [1,000,000] **1068**

RAPPORT (BE). [4,000] **2149**

RAPPORT ANNUEL / CANADIAN NATIONAL (CN). [10,000] **5390**

RAPPORT ANNUEL - CENTRE DE RECHERCHE INDUSTRIELLE DU QUEBEC (CN/0706-2508). [5,000] **1623**

RAPPORT ANNUEL / CENTRE NATIONAL D'ETUDES SPATIALES (FR). **32**

RAPPORT ANNUEL / CONSEIL SUPERIEUR DES CLASSES MOYENNES (BE). **4678**

RAPPORT ANNUEL DU DEPARTEMENT DE GEOLOGIE ET DE MINERALOGIE DU MUSEE ROYAL DE L'AFRIQUE CENTRALE (BE/0378-0953). **1393**

RAPPORT ANNUEL DU SERVICE HYDROGRAPHIQUE ET OCEANOGRAPHIQUE DE LA MARINE (FR/0989-5876). **1455**

RAPPORT ANNUEL - SERVICE DE RECHERCHE EN DEFENSE DES CULTURES (CN/0713-4711). **4678**

RAPPORT BIPM (FR/0026-1394). [500] **1434**

RAPPORT D'ACTIVITE - INSTITUT AFRICAIN POUR LE DEVELOPPEMENT ECONOMIQUE ET SOCIAL (IV). [400] **1515**

RAPPORT D'ACTIVITES DE L'INSTITUT DE PHONETIQUE (BE). **3314**

RAPPORT DE RECHERCHE LPC (FR/0222-8394). **2030**

RAPPORT DES INVENTAIRES AERIENS DU GROS GIBIER (CN). [100] **5596**

RAPPORT - GRONLANDS GEOLOGISKE UNDERSOGELSE (DK/0418-6559). [500] **1393**

RAPPORT - NORTH CENTRAL REGIONAL LIBRARY SYSTEM (NEWSLETTER) (CN/0715-5867). **3244**

RAPPORT SCIENTIFIQUE - INSTITUT FRANCAIS D'OCEANIE, CENTRE D'OCEANOGRAPHIE (NL). [50] **1455**

RAPPORTS HET FRANSE BOEK (NE). [1,000] **3427**

RARE FRUIT COUNCIL OF AUSTRALIA INC. NEWSLETTER (AT/0726-1470). **2430**

RARITAN (US/0275-1607). [3,500] **3351**

RASSEGNA CHIMICA (IT/0033-9334). [2,000] **990**

RASSEGNA DEI BENI CULTURALI (IT). **252**

RASSEGNA DELL IMBALLAGGIO E CONFEZIONAMENTO (IT). [12,000] **4221**

RASSEGNA DI CULTURA E VITA SCOLASTICA (IT). [6,000] **5214**

RASSEGNA DI SERVIZIO SOCIALE (IT/0033-9601). [1500] **4798**

RASSEGNA DI STUDI PSICHIATRICI (IT/0033-9636). [300] **3935**

RASSEGNA GRAFICA (IT). [13,000] **4569**

RASSEGNA MUSICALE CURCI (IT/0033-9806). [21,000] **4148**

RASSEGNA PARLAMENTARE (IT/0486-0373). [2,000] **3093**

RASSEGNA SINDACALE (IT/0033-9849). [50,000] **1705**

RASSEGNA STORICA DEL RISORGIMENTO (IT/0033-9873). [3,000] **2704**

RATEL (UK/0305-1218). [350] **5596**

RATHBUN, RATHBONE, RATHBURN FAMILY HISTORIAN (US/0737-7711). [580] **2469**

RATON RANGE (1985) (US/0896-1093). **5713**

RATP SAVOIR FAIRE PARIS (FR/1168-3392). **5390**

RAUMFORSCHUNG UND RAUMORDNUNG (GW/0034-0111). [2,000] **33**

RAUMPLANUNG, INFORMATIONSHEFTE / EJPD, BUNDESAMT FUR RAUMPLANUNG (SZ). [3,000] **2832**

RAWLINSONS NEW ZEALAND CONSTRUCTION HANDBOOK (NZ). [1,500] **625**

RAYNE ACADIAN TRIBUNE (US). [3,980] **5684**

RAYON JEUNESSE (CN/0841-758X). **1068**

RAZA LAW JOURNAL, LA (US/8755-8815). [250] **3034**

RAZON Y FE (SP/0034-0235). [7,000] **2853**

RBM, REVISTA BRASILEIRA DE MANDIOCA (BL/0101-563X). [500] **125**

RC MODELER (1969) (US/0033-6866). [150,000] **2777**

RDH (US/0279-7720). [63,210] **1334**

RDI MONOGRAPHS ON FOREIGN AID AND DEVELOPMENT (US/0748-0644). [300] **4533**

REACTIONS (AT/0157-7271). [800] **3632**

READ, AMERICA! (US/0891-4214). [10,000] **1776**

READER (SAN DIEGO, CALIF.) (US). [130,000] **5638**

READERS' GUIDE ABSTRACTS. CD-ROM (US/0899-1553). **2497**

READING & WRITING (NE/0922-4777). **3314**

READING-BERKS AUTO CLUB MAGAZINE (US/0744-7043). [38,000] **5423**

READING HORIZONS (US/0034-0502). [1,000] **3314**

READING IMPROVEMENT (US/0034-0510). [2,000] **3314**

READING IN A FOREIGN LANGUAGE (UK/0264-2425). [300] **3314**

READING RESEARCH AND INSTRUCTION (US/0886-0246). [1,300] **3314**

READING RESEARCH QUARTERLY (US/0034-0553). [12,000] **3314**

READING (SUNDERLAND) (UK/0034-0472). [2,100] **1903**

READING TEACHER, THE (US/0034-0561). [42,000] **3314**

READING TODAY : A BIMONTHLY NEWSPAPER OF THE INTERNATIONAL READING ASSOCIATION (US). [93,000] **1777**

READINGS ON EQUAL EDUCATION (US/0270-1448). **1884**

REAL ANALYSIS EXCHANGE (US/0147-1937). [400] **3530**

REAL ESTATE CAPITAL MARKETS REPORT (US/1064-1491). [1,100] **1515**

REAL ESTATE CENTER JOURNAL (US/0893-3332). [65,000] **4844**

REAL ESTATE DIGEST, THE (US/0882-8733). [10,000] **4844**

REAL ESTATE NEWSLINE (US/0749-8640). [10,000] **4844**

REAL ESTATE OUTLOOK MARKET TRENDS AND INSIGHTS (US). **4845**

REAL ESTATE PROFILES (US). **4845**

REAL ESTATE TODAY (US/0034-0804). [800,000] **4845**

REAL PROPERTY LAW SECTION NEWSLETTER (US/0147-135X). [5,000] **4845**

REAL PROPERTY, PROBATE AND TRUST JOURNAL (US/0034-0855). **3118**

REALITES INDUSTRIELLES (FR). [4,000 to 20,000] **2149**

REALTOR NEWS (US/0279-6309). [118,500] **4846**

REALTY AND BUILDING (US/0034-1045). [4,000] **4846**

REBUS, DE (SA/0250-0329). [10,850] **3035**

RECENT ADDITIONS TO BAKER LIBRARY (US/0735-2336). [800] **3244**

RECENT AWARDS IN ENGINEERING (US/0736-7090). [3,000] **1993**

RECENT RESEARCH RESULTS / U.S. DEPARTMENT OF HOUSING AND URBAN DEVELOPMENT, OFFICE OF POLICY DEVELOPMENT AND RESEARCH (US). [9,000] **2832**

RECEUIL DES LOIS ET DE LA LEGISLATION FINANCIERE (FR). **4678**

RECHERCHE (PARIS. 1970) (FR/0029-5671). [94,847] **5145**

RECHERCHES ANGLAISES ET NORD-AMERICAINES : RANAM (FR). [500] **3428**

RECHERCHES FEMINISTES (CN/0838-4479). [700] **5565**

RECHERCHES SOCIOGRAPHIQUES (CN/0034-1282). **5255**

RECHT DER DATENVERARBEITUNG : RDV (GW/0178-8930). **1227**

RECHT DER WIRTSCHAFT, DAS (GW). **3102**

RECHTSKUNDIG WEEKBLAD (BE). [5,000] **3036**

RECHTSMEDIZIN BERLIN (GW/0937-9819). **3742**

RECOMMEND FLORIDA (US/0034-1452). [48,000] **5490**

RECOMMENDATIONS OF THE WEST VIRGINIA BOARD OF EDUCATION FOR LEGISLATIVE ACTION (US). [1,000] **3036**

RECONSTRUCTIONIST (US/0034-1495). [8,500] **5052**

RECORD-COURIER (GARDNERVILLE, NEV.) (US/8755-4631). **5708**

RECORD (MEMPHIS, TN) (US). [4,500] **5746**

RECORD OF RESEARCH (KE). **125**

RECORD OF THE ART MUSEUM, PRINCETON UNIVERSITY (US/0032-843X). [2,000] **4095**

RECORD OF THE ASSOCIATION OF THE BAR OF THE CITY OF NEW YORK, THE (US/0004-5837). [21,000] **3036**

RECORD - SOCIETY OF ACTUARIES. MEETING (US/0730-2983). [13,000] **2891**

RECORD SYDNEY (AT/0310-4729). [500] **2483**

RECORD (WASHINGTON, D.C. : 1975) (US/0145-8566). [13,237] **3036**

RECORDER MAGAZINE, THE (UK/0306-4409). [150] **4149**

RECORDER, THE (US/0362-6121). **3036**

RECORDER (TORONTO) (CN/0704-7231). [900] **4149**

RECORDER WEVELGEM (BE/0776-3093). **990**

RECORDS OF EARLY ENGLISH DRAMA (CN/0700-9283). [450] **5367**

RECORDS OF NEW JERSEY BIRDS (US). [3,500] **5620**

RECORDS OF THE ACADEMY (US/0065-6844). [3,500] **329**

RECORDS OF THE AUSTRALIAN MUSEUM (AT/0067-1975). [800] **5596**

RECORDS OF THE AUSTRALIAN MUSEUM. SUPPLEMENT (AT/0812-7387). [800] **5596**

RECORDS OF THE WESTERN AUSTRALIAN MUSEUM (AT/0312-3162). [400] **4171**

RECORDS OF VERMONT BIRDS (US/0197-3169). [1,200] **5620**

RECOUP (CN/0709-6402). **2241**

RECOUP'S MATERIALS RECYCLING MARKETS (CN/0884-4526). [500] **2241**

RECOVERING LITERATURE (US/0300-6425). [200] **3351**

RECREATION BRITISH COLUMBIA (1985) (CN/0830-1913). [1,300] **4853**

RECREATION CANADA (CN/0031-2231). [3,500] **4853**

RECREATION CANADA (FRENCH EDITION) (CN/0031-2231). [2,500] **4853**

RECREATION EXCHANGE (AT). [800] **4853**

RECREATION EXECUTIVE REPORT (US/0890-2194). **4853**

RECRUITING

RECRUITING TRENDS (US/0034-1827). [70] **706**

RECSAM ANNUAL REPORT (MY/0377-3450). [70] **5145**

RECUEIL DE MEDECINE VETERINAIRE (FR/0034-1843). [3,500] **5520**

RECUEIL FISCAL. COURS D'IMPOT (CN/0712-6573). [7,000] **750**

RECUEIL FISCAL. PROBLEMES ET SOLUTIONS (CN/0712-6565). [4,000] **4744**

RECUPERARE. EDILIZIA DESIGN IMPIANTI (IT/0392-4599). [10,200] **307**

RECURRING BIBLIOGRAPHY OF HYPERTENSION (US/0090-1326). [1,050] **3710**

RECYCLAGE RECUPERATION PARIS (FR/1156-962X). [3,275] **2220**

RED BOOK OF HOUSING MANUFACTURERS, THE (US/0149-7642). [350] **625**

RED CLOUD COUNTRY (US/0300-6344). [135,000] **2271**

RED MENACE (CN/0711-2270). **4546**

RED NOTEBOOK. COMMUNICATING WITH HEARING PEOPLE, THE (US). **4393**

RED RIVER VALLEY HERITAGE PRESS, THE (US/0739-1838). [800] **2756**

RED WING REPUBLICAN EAGLE (US). [8,059] **5698**

REDS REPORT (US/1057-9540). [6,000] **4914**

REDWOOD NEWS (US). [25,000] **2404**

REEDER'S ECONOMIC DIGEST (US/0890-9954). [400] **1515**

REEDUCATION POSTURALE GLOBALE (FR/0294-0922). [1,000] **3806**

REESE RIVER REVEILLE (AUSTIN, NEV. : 1950) (US). [500] **5708**

REEVES JOURNAL (US/0048-7066). [20,511] **2608**

REFERATEBLATT ZUR RAUMENTWICKLUNG (GW/0341-2512). [500] **4679**

REFERATIVNYI ZHURNAL: ELEKTRONIKA (RU). [5,900] **2078**

REFERATIVNYI ZHURNAL. ELEKTROTEKHNIKA / GOSUDARSTVENNYI KOMITET SSSR PO NAUKE I TEKHNIKE, AKADEMIIA NAUK SSSR, VSESOIUZNYI INSTITUT NAUCHNOI I TEKHNICHESKOI INFORMATSII (RU/0203-5189). **2079**

REFERATIVNYI ZHURNAL FARMAKOLOGIYA OBSHCHAYA FARMAKOLOGIYA NERVNOI SISTEMY (RU/0134-580X). [600] **471**

REFERATIVNYJ ZURNAL - VSESOJUZNYJ INSTITUT NAUGNOJ I TEHNICESKOJ INFORMACII. 66, KORROZIJA I ZASCITA OT KORROZII (RU/0131-3533). [700] **4017**

REFERATIVNYJ ZURNAL - VSESOJUZNYJ INSTITUT NAUCNOJ I TEHNICESKOJ INFORMACII. 70. RADIACIONNAJA BIOLOGIJA (RU/0131-355X). [450] **471**

REFERENCE AID, CHIEFS OF STATE, AND CABINET MEMBERS OF FOREIGN GOVERNMENTS (US). [625] **4493**

REFERENCE AND RESEARCH BOOK NEWS (US/0887-3763). [2,200] **3244**

REFERENCE (SAINT LOUIS, MO.) (US/0897-103X). **3951**

REFLECTIONS (CORPUS CHRISTI, TEX.) (US/0732-488X). [300] **2469**

REFLECTIONS (INDIANAPOLIS, IND.) (US/0885-8144). [73,000] **3868**

REFLECTIONS (LONDON, ONT.) (CN/0824-5517). [2,000] **1843**

REFLECTIONS (NORTH BATTLEFORD. 1976) (CN/0384-0697). [200] **3244**

REFLET DE MON MILIEU (CN/0229-3560). **5793**

REFLEX (SEATTLE, WASH.) (US/1054-3465). [8,000] **329**

REFORM (AT). [3,000] **3037**

REFORM JUDAISM (US/0482-0819). [285,000] **5052**

REFORMA NEWSLETTER (US/0891-8880). [600] **3244**

REFORMATION & REVIVAL JOURNAL (US/1071-7277). [850] **4990**

REFORMED LITURGY AND MUSIC (US/0362-0476). [4,000] **4990**

REFORMED PERSPECTIVE (CN/0714-8208). [2,200] **4990**

REFORMED THEOLOGICAL REVIEW, THE (AT/0034-3072). [650] **4990**

REFRACTORY GIRL (AT/0310-4168). [2,000] **5565**

REFRIGERATED TRANSPORTER (US/0034-3129). [15,000] **5391**

REFRIGERATION (US). [3,300] **2608**

REFUGEE UPDATE ENGLISH ED (CN/0251-6500). [1,500] **4512**

REFUNDLE BUNDLE (US/0194-0139). [15,000] **1299**

REFUSE NEWS (US). [4,790] **2241**

REGAN REPORT ON HOSPITAL LAW, THE (US/0034-317X). **3037**

REGAN REPORT ON MEDICAL LAW (US/0034-3188). **3037**

REGAN REPORT ON NURSING LAW, THE (US/0034-3196). **3868**

REGATTA (UK). [14,000] **4914**

REGENERATION (US/8756-3002). [1,500] **125**

REGENT PARK COMMUNITY NEWS (CN/0704-7053). **5793**

REGINA (CN/0315-212X). [6,500] **2544**

REGION (WASHINGTON, D.C.), THE (US/0732-586X). [6,000] **2833**

REGIONAL BIBLIOGRAPHY SERIES (AT). [100] **1410**

REGIONAL BUSINESS REVIEW (US/8755-1977). [2,000] **849**

REGIONAL CATALOGUE OF EARTHQUAKES (UK/0034-334X). [500] **1410**

REGIONAL DE DRUMMONDVILLE (CN/0711-4834). **5793**

REGIONAL DEVELOPMENT DIALOGUE (JA/0250-6505). [1,000] **2833**

REGIONAL ECONOMIC PROJECTIONS SERIES (US/0090-9262). [500] **1516**

REGIONAL LABOR MARKET REVIEW. ATLANTIC COASTAL REGION (US). [2,000] **1705**

REGIONAL LABOR MARKET REVIEW. SOUTHERN NEW JERSEY REGION (US). [1,000] **1705**

REGIONAL PLAN NEWS (US/0034-3374). [4,000] **4679**

REGIONAL REFLECTIONS (CN/0715-5050). [9,000] **4679**

REGIONAL TOURISM MONITOR (AT). [200] **5490**

REGION'S AGENDA, THE (US/0034-3420). [4,000] **2833**

REGISTER (KANSAS CITY, MO.), THE (US/0899-3572). **220**

REGISTER OF POST-GRADUATE DISSERTATIONS IN PROGRESS IN HISTORY AND RELATED SUBJECTS (CN/0068-8088). [650] **2627**

REGISTER OF THE KENTUCKY HISTORICAL SOCIETY, THE (US/0023-0243). [6,000] **2756**

REGISTER OF THE SPENCER MUSEUM OF ART, THE (US/0733-866X). [1,000] **4095**

REGISTERED NURSE (TORONTO) (CN/0840-8831). [26,000] **3868**

REGISTRY OF ENGINEERS AND LAND SURVEYORS AND REPORT OF THE STATE BOARD OF ENGINEERING EXAMINERS OF OREGON (US/0363-7034). [7,500] **1993**

REGISTRY OF MEMBERS - CLINICAL SOCIOLOGY ASSOCIATION (US/0733-0251). [600] **5255**

REGISTRY OF WOMEN IN RELIGIOUS STUDIES, A (US/0887-8331). **4990**

REGLEMENTS - A S T E D (CN/0384-5095). **3245**

REGLEMENTS RELATIFS AUX PROGRAMMES - INSTITUT DES BANQUIERS CANADIENS (CN/0821-6088). **807**

REGNO, IL (IT/0034-3498). [12,000] **5035**

REGULAE BENEDICTI STUDIA (GW). **4990**

REGULATORY AFFAIRS (US/1043-2752). **3792**

REGULATORY AFFAIRS JOURNAL (UK/0960-7889). **3633**

REHAB & COMMUNITY CARE MANAGEMENT (CN/1192-2508). [20,000] **3633**

REHABILITATION COUNSELING BULLETIN (US/0034-3552). [643] **1884**

REHABILITATION DIGEST (CN/0048-7139). [2,000] **4393**

REHABILITATION GAZETTE (US/0361-4166). [12,000] **4393**

REHABILITATION NURSING (US/0278-4807). [7,500] **3868**

REHABILITATION PSYCHOLOGY (US/0090-5550). [1,500] **4615**

REHOVOT (IS). [19,000] **5145**

REICHENBACHIA / STAATLICHES MUSEUM FUER TIERKUNDE IN DRESDEN (GW/0070-7279). [350] **5613**

REIMBURSEMENT UPDATE SALT LAKE CITY, UTAH (US/1064-1548). **706**

REINIGER + WASCHER (GW/0034-3625). [6,000] **5355**

REINWARDTIA (IO/0034-365X). [500] **526**

REITO (JA/0034-3714). **2608**

REKAMAN PERISTIWA ... (IO). [10,000] **5255**

REKISHIGAKU KENKYU (JA/0386-9237). [10,000] **2663**

RELACIONES / COLEGIO DE MICHOACAN (MX/0185-3929). [1,000] **2756**

RELATIONAL DATABASE JOURNAL (US/1074-6404). [35,000] **1255**

RELATIVELY SPEAKING (EDMONTON) (US/0701-8878). [800] **2469**

RELATORIO ANUAL DA DIRETORIA - ASSOCIACAO BRASILEIRA PARA O DESENVOLVIMENTO DAS INDUSTRIAS DE BASE (BL). [2,000] **1624**

RELATORIO DE ATIVIDADES - FUNDACAO PARA O LIVRO DO CEGO NO BRASIL (BL). [500] **5304**

RELEASE PRINT (US/0890-5231). [3,800] **4077**

RELEVE DES INSCRIPTIONS (CN/0827-8156). **1796**

RELEVE DES NOUVEAUX INSCRITS (CN/0826-0974). **1844**

RELIABILITY REVIEW (MILWAUKEE, WIS.) (US/0277-9633). [7,000] **1993**

RELICS (US/0034-3897). [300] **2757**

RELIGION & LITERATURE (US/0888-3769). [500] **4990**

RELIGION INDEX ONE. PERIODICALS (US/0149-8428). [1,200] **5013**

RELIGION INDEX TWO : MULTI-AUTHOR WORKS (US/0149-8436). [1,000] **4991**

RELIGION TEACHER'S JOURNAL (US/0034-401X). [40,000] **4991**

RELIGIONSVIDENSKABELIGT TIDSSKRIFT (DK/0108-1993). [350] **4991**

RELIGIOUS AND THEOLOGICAL ABSTRACTS (US/0034-4044). [1,000] **5013**

RELIGIOUS BROADCASTING (US/0034-4079). [9,840] **1138**

RELIGIOUS HUMANISM (US/0034-4095). [700] **4992**

RELIGIOUS STUDIES AND THEOLOGY (CN/0829-2922). [600] **4992**

RELIGIOUS STUDIES NEWS (US/0885-0372). [8,500] **4992**

RELOCALISER : LA LETRE DE LA MOBILITE-DEMOSCOOP (FR). **946**

RELOCATION COMPASS (US/1069-5923). **884**

RELOCATION / REALTY UPDATE (US). [5,100] **946**

RELOCATION REPORT, THE (US/0275-7613). [2,000] **4846**

REMAINS TO BE FOUND (US/0738-5889). [300] **2469**

REMEDIAL AND SPECIAL EDUCATION (US/0741-9325). [2,700] **1884**

REMINGTON REPORT, THE (US/1070-3411). [25,000] **706**

REMITTANCE AND DOCUMENT PROCESSING TODAY (US/1050-9186). **5145**

REMODELING (WASHINGTON, D.C.) (US/0885-8039). [85,000] **626**

REMONSTRANTS WEEKBLAD : RW (NE). **4992**

REMOTE SENSING IN CANADA (CN). [3,000] **5145**

RENAISSANCE PAPERS (US/0584-4207). [500] **3428**

RENAL EDUCATOR (AT/0816-990X). [1,000] **3992**

RENAL PHYSIOLOGY AND BIOCHEMISTRY (SZ/1011-6524). [600] **3993**

RENDER (US/0090-8932). [7,000] **2355**

RENDEZ-VOUS 76 MONTREAL (CN/0318-2843). **4914**

RENDEZVOUS (BRANTFORD) (CN/0712-7588). **3174**

RENDEZVOUS (FREDERICTON) (CN/0711-1177). **3315**

RENDICONTI DEL CIRCOLO MATEMATICO DI PALERMO (IT/0009-725X). [600] **3531**

RENEWAL MAGAZINE (UK). [11,000] **4992**

RENSSELAER ENGINEER (US/0034-4508). [5,000] **1993**

RENTAL EQUIPMENT REGISTER (US/0034-4524). [13,654] **935**

REPERES, ESSAIS EN EDUCATION (CN/0821-1388). [300] **1778**

REPERTOIRE - ASSOCIATION DES INGENIEURS-CONSEILS DU QUEBEC (CN/0709-4787). **1993**

REPERTOIRE BIBLIOGRAPHIQUE DE LA PHILOSOPHIE (BE/0034-4567). [1,800] **4366**

Controlled Circulation Index — RESEARCH

REPERTOIRE COMMERCIAL DE LA REGION DU SUD-EST (CN/0820-8522). **849**

REPERTOIRE DE LA VIE FRANCAISE EN AMERIQUE (CN/0708-1510). [600] **2544**

REPERTOIRE DES ACTIVITES DE FORMATION ET D'INFORMATION (CN/0826-3116). **2868**

REPERTOIRE DES ASSOCIATIONS PATRONALES QUEBECOISES (CN/0714-8461). **1706**

REPERTOIRE DES BIENS A STATUT PARTICULIER (CN/0834-9908). [200] **4846**

REPERTOIRE DES ECOLES - CONSEIL SCOLAIRE DE L'ILE DE MONTREAL (CN/0824-0655). [250] **1778**

REPERTOIRE DES GEOGRAPHES FRANCAIS PARIS (FR/1147-9558). [500] **2574**

REPERTOIRE DES MEMBRES DE L'UNION DES ARTISTES (CN/0820-8425). [7,400] **388**

REPERTOIRE DES ORGANISMES CULTURELS DE L'ABITIBI-TEMISCAMINGUE (CN/0831-9286). [500] **329**

REPERTOIRE (MONTPELLIER, FRANCE) (FR/0987-6030). [1,000] **1929**

REPERTORIEN ZUR DEUTSCHEN LITERATURGESCHICHTE (GW/0486-4166). [1,000] **3429**

REPERTORIO 4 CODICI TRIBUTARI (IT). [5,000] **4744**

REPERTORIO AMERICANO (CR). [1,300] **3429**

REPERTORIO ASSOCIATE ANIMA (IT). [500] **1624**

REPERTORIO CHIMICO ITALIANO (IT). [3,000] **991**

REPERTORIO SIDERURGICO LATINOAMERICANO (CL). **1624**

REPLICA (MIAMI, FLA. 1970) (US/0146-2008). [109,000] **2492**

REPORT AND ACCOUNTS (UK). [500] **280**

REPORT & ACCOUNTS / NATIONAL DEVELOPMENT BANK OF SRI LANKA (CE). [1,500] **807**

REPORT - AUDUBON SOCIETY OF RHODE ISLAND (US/0274-502X). [4,500] **2203**

REPORT - BROWN UNIVERSITY. DIVISION OF ENGINEERING (US/0736-6639). **1993**

REPORT / CONNECTICUT, JUDICIAL REVIEW COUNCIL (US). [600] **3142**

REPORT - EARTHQUAKE ENGINEERING RESEARCH CENTER, COLLEGE OF ENGINEERING, UNIVERSITY OF CALIFORNIA, BERKELEY, CALIFORNIA (US/0271-0323). [350] **2030**

REPORT - FAMILY PLANNING ASSOCIATION OF INDIA (II). [2,000] **590**

REPORT FOR CALENDAR YEAR ... / CHIEF MINE INSPECTOR, DEPARTMENT OF MINES (US). [800] **2149**

REPORT FOR YEAR ENDED 30TH JUNE ... / VICTORIAN DAIRY INDUSTRY AUTHORITY (AT/0157-5856). **198**

REPORT FROM THE CAPITAL (US/0364-6661). [7,000] **4992**

REPORT (INSTITUTE OF OCEANOGRAPHIC SCIENCES (GREAT BRITAIN)) (UK). **1456**

REPORT - INTERNATIONAL COMMISSION FOR THE CONSERVATION OF ATLANTIC TUNAS. ENGLISH VERSION (SP/0377-368X). **2311**

REPORT OF A VANTAGE CONFERENCE (US/0748-0571). [10,000] **4533**

REPORT OF INVESTIGATION - NORTH DAKOTA GEOLOGICAL SURVEY (US/0099-4227). [1,500] **1394**

REPORT OF INVESTIGATIONS / NEW WORLD RESEARCH (US). **280**

REPORT OF INVESTIGATIONS - SOUTH DAKOTA GEOLOGICAL SURVEY (US). [500] **1394**

REPORT OF RESEARCH ACTIVITIES - DIVISION OF TECHNICAL SERVICES, QUEENSLAND DEPARTMENT OF FORESTRY (AT/0311-0893). [1,000] **2392**

REPORT OF RESEARCH - DIVISION OF FOOD RESEARCH (AT). [2,000] **2355**

REPORT OF THE AUDITOR GENERAL OF PRINCE EDWARD ISLAND TO THE LEGISLATIVE ASSEMBLY (CN/0318-8124). [300] **4745**

REPORT OF THE AUSTRALIA AND NEW ZEALAND COMBINED DIALYSIS AND TRANSPLANT REGISTRY (AT/0727-3738). **3633**

REPORT OF THE CHIEF ELECTORAL OFFICER ON THE ... GENERAL ENUMERATION (CN/0708-3998). [1,500] **4680**

REPORT OF THE COMPUTER CENTRE, UNIVERSITY OF TOKYO (JA/0564-8742). [500] **1262**

REPORT OF THE ... CONFERENCE / THE INTERNATIONAL LAW ASSOCIATION (UK/0074-6738). **3134**

REPORT OF THE COUNCIL AND ABSTRACT OF THE ACCOUNTS / SELDEN SOCIETY (UK). [1,700] **3038**

REPORT OF THE DEPARTMENT OF SCIENTIFIC AND INDUSTRIAL RESEARCH (NZ). [1,600] **5145**

REPORT OF THE DIRECTOR (US). **3245**

REPORT OF THE GOVERNMENT CHEMICAL LABORATORIES (AT/0511-7003). **1018**

REPORT OF THE MARYLAND BOARD OF REVENUE ESTIMATES ON ESTIMATED MARYLAND REVENUES (US). [500] **4746**

REPORT OF THE NODA INSTITUTE FOR SCIENTIFIC RESEARCH (JA/0078-0944). [600] **493**

REPORT OF THE OMBUDSMAN (US/0073-1137). **4681**

REPORT OF THE SELECT COMMITTEE ON RAILWAY ACCOUNTS. VERSLAG VAN DIE GEKOSE KOMITEE OOR SPOORWEGREKENINGS (SA). [1,000] **5436**

REPORT OF THE STATE EMPLOYEES RETIREMENT BENEFITS BOARD FOR THE YEAR ENDED 30 JUNE ... (AT). [1,000] **4681**

REPORT OF THE ... STRATEGY FOR PEACE US FOREIGN POLICY CONFERENCE (US/0748-9641). [20,000] **4533**

REPORT OF THE ... SUMMER SESSION OF THE INTERNATIONAL OLYMPIC ACADEMY (GR/0538-8910). **1857**

REPORT OF THE ... UNITED NATIONS ISSUES CONFERENCE (US/0743-9180). [15,000] **4533**

REPORT OF THE ... UNITED NATIONS OF THE NEXT DECADE CONFERENCE (US/0748-433X). [15,000] **4533**

REPORT OF THE ... WORLD CONGRESS / INTERNATIONAL CONFEDERATION OF FREE TRADE UNIONS (BE). **4533**

REPORT - OFFICE OF STATE ARCHAEOLOGIST (US). [500] **280**

REPORT ON COUNCIL ACTIVITY - CANADIAN ADVERTISING ADVISORY BOARD. ADVERTISING STANDARDS COUNCIL (CN/0227-6747). **765**

REPORT ON ENVIRONMENTAL RADIATION SURVEILLANCE IN NORTH CAROLINA (US/0147-2887). **2242**

REPORT ON PRODUCTION AND EARNINGS OF RRS (US). [125] **808**

REPORT ON RESEARCH - PRAGUE. UNIVERSITA KARLOVA. USTAV GEOLOGICKYCH VED (XR). [700] **1360**

REPORT ON THE BACKGROUND, CURRENT PROGRAMMES AND PLANNED DEVELOPMENT OF THE BANGLADESH INSTITUTE OF DEVELOPMENT STUDIES, A (BG). [5,000] **5215**

REPORT ON THE FINANCIAL YEAR - BERLINER HANDELS- UND FRANKFURTER BANK (GW). [9,000] **808**

REPORT ON THE ... PDCP SURVEY OF BUSINESS PERFORMANCE FOR MANILA, A (PH). [150] **707**

REPORT ON THE ... SYRIA'S BUDGET (SY). [200] **4746**

REPORT - ROYAL GREENWICH OBSERVATORY (UK/0308-3322). [4,000] **399**

REPORT - SAVINGS BANKS GROUP OF THE EEC (BE). [3,200] **808**

REPORT SERIES / UNIVERSITY OF OSLO, DEPARTMENT OF PHYSICS (NO/0332-5571). [200] **4419**

REPORT - TECHNICAL MEETING ON FISHERIES (PO). [500] **2311**

REPORT TO MEMBERS - MANITOBA TEACHERS' RETIREMENT ALLOWANCES FUND (CN/0228-3875). [17,000] **1870**

REPORT TO THE GOVERNORS (US/0882-679X). **4682**

REPORT TO THE UNIVERSITY COURT (UK). [1,650] **1844**

REPORT - WATER RESEARCH COMMISSION (SA). [3,000] **5538**

REPORT - WATER RESOURCES RESEARCH INSTITUTE, CLEMSON UNIVERSITY (US/0069-4657). [300] **5538**

REPORTER (US/0360-7119). [65,000] **946**

REPORTER ARGUS (US). [2,800] **5739**

REPORTER - NEW JERSEY ASSOCIATION FOR HEALTH, PHYSICAL EDUCATION AND RECREATION, THE (US/0034-477X). [1,000] **4799**

REPORTER - ONTARIO ENGLISH CATHOLIC TEACHERS' ASSOCIATION (CN/0384-5648). **1903**

REPORTER, THE (US). [6,000] **5753**

REPORTING CLASSROOM RESEARCH (CN/0315-369X). [7,000] **1778**

REPORTS FROM GENERAL PRACTICE (UK/0557-3912). [17,500] **3739**

REPORTS OF PROCEEDINGS OF ANNUAL MEETING - WESTERN CANADIAN SOCIETY FOR HORTICULTURE (CN/0083-8810). [300] **2430**

REPORTS TO THE GENERAL ASSEMBLY OF THE UNITED FREE CHURCH OF SCOTLAND (UK). [250] **4992**

REPOSITORY (CANTON, OHIO), THE (US/0745-7545). [65,000 daily71,000 Sunday] **5730**

REPRINT - RESOURCES FOR THE FUTURE (US/0486-5553). [18,000] **2203**

REPRINT SERIES - INDUSTRIAL RELATIONS CENTRE. QUEEN'S UNIVERSITY (CN/0075-6156). [400] **1707**

REPRINTS FROM THE SOVIET PRESS (US/0034-4931). [1,500] **1516**

REPRODUCTION (UK/0034-4958). [16,000] **4569**

REPUBLICAN JOURNAL (BELFAST, ME.) (US/0034-5075). [8,500] **5685**

REPULESI SZAKIRODALMI TAJEKOZTATO (HU/0231-3928). [150] **33**

RERIC HOLDINGS LIST : / AN OCCASIONAL PUBLICATION OF RERIC (TH). [600] **1955**

RES PUBLICA (PL/0860-4592). [10,000] **2492**

RES PUBLICA LITTERARUM (IT/0275-4304). [500] **1079**

RESCUE-EMS MAGAZINE (US/1073-9998). [30,000] **4799**

RESEARCH ABSTRACTS (ANN ARBOR) (US/0362-7535). **423**

RESEARCH AND CLINICAL FORUMS (UK/0143-3083). **3634**

RESEARCH & CREATIVE ACTIVITY (US/0731-4981). [4,200] **5146**

RESEARCH AND CURRENT ISSUES SERIES - INDUSTRIAL RELATIONS CENTRE. QUEEN'S UNIVERSITY (CN/0317-2546). [700] **1707**

RESEARCH & DEVELOPMENT (BARRINGTON, ILL.) (US/0746-9179). **5146**

RESEARCH & DEVELOPMENT. TELEPHONE DIRECTORY (US). [107,000] **1929**

RESEARCH AND PUBLICATIONS (KE). [1,200] **1516**

RESEARCH & PUBLICATIONS REPORT (BIRMINGHAM, WEST MIDLANDS, ENGLAND) (UK). [750] **1845**

RESEARCH BULLETIN - CITY OF TORONTO PLANNING AND DEVELOPMENT. RESEARCH AND INFORMATION SECTION (CN/0828-4121). [1,000] **2833**

RESEARCH BULLETIN - FLORIDA EDUCATIONAL RESEARCH AND DEVELOPMENT COUNCIL (US). [2,000] **1778**

RESEARCH CONTRIBUTIONS OF THE AMERICAN BAR FOUNDATION (US). [500] **3039**

RESEARCH DIRECTORY - MEMORIAL UNIVERSITY OF NEWFOUNDLAND. OFFICE OF RESEARCH (CN/0704-7452). [1,000] **1845**

RESEARCH IN MELANESIA (PP/0254-0665). **244**

RESEARCH IN MINISTRY (US). [100] **4992**

RESEARCH IN NONDESTRUCTIVE EVALUATION (US/0934-9847). [1,000] **1994**

RESEARCH INVENTORY / MEMORIAL UNIVERSITY OF NEWFOUNDLAND, OFFICE OF RESEARCH (CN/0229-2599). [600] **1845**

RESEARCH MANUSCRIPT SERIES - INSTITUTE OF ARCHEOLOGY AND ANTHROPOLOGY, UNIVERSITY OF SOUTH CAROLINA (US). [3,500] **280**

RESEARCH NEWSLETTER - FACULTY OF HOME ECONOMICS, UNIVERSITY OF ALBERTA (CN/0709-9045). **2792**

RESEARCH NOTE INT (US/0099-3468). **2392**

RESEARCH NOTE NC (US/0361-2449). [2,000] **2393**

RESEARCH PAPER (AT/1035-9796). [350] **2393**

RESEARCH PAPER - CENTRE FOR URBAN AND COMMUNITY STUDIES. UNIVERSITY OF TORONTO (CN/0316-0068). [250] **2833**

RESEARCH

RESEARCH PAPER SO (US/0748-1225). [5,000] **2393**

RESEARCH PROJECT (NZ/0069-3774). **4615**

RESEARCH REGISTER / UNIVERSITY OF STRATHCLYDE (UK). [500] **5147**

RESEARCH REPORT - AGRICULTURAL EXPERIMENT STATION (US/0548-5967). [500] **127**

RESEARCH REPORT / DEPARTMENT OF CIVIL ENGINEERING, UNIVERSITY OF QUEENSLAND (AT). [360] **2030**

RESEARCH REPORT - DIVISION OF APPLIED ORGANIC CHEMISTRY (AT/0312-8466). **1047**

RESEARCH REPORT - INSTITUTE OF INTERNAL AUDITORS (US). [28,000] **750**

RESEARCH REPORT / NEW HAMPSHIRE AGRICULTURAL EXPERIMENTAL STATION (US/0077-832X). **128**

RESEARCH REPORT OR OCCASIONAL PAPER / THE UNIVERSITY OF NEWCASTLE, DEPARTMENT OF ECONOMICS (AT/0812-1664). [200] **1517**

RESEARCH REPORT / UNIVERSITY OF TEXAS, MD ANDERSON CANCER CENTER (US). [4,800] **3823**

RESEARCH REPORT - WISCONSIN. DEPT. OF NATURAL RESOURCES (US/0084-0556). [500] **2204**

RESEARCH REPORTS / DEPARTMENT OF ANTHROPOLOGY, UNIVERSITY OF MASSACHUSETTS, AMHERST (US). [600] **244**

RESEARCH REVIEW - INSTITUTE OF AFRICAN STUDIES (GH/0020-2703). [500] **2643**

RESEARCH SERIES (US/0882-2042). [150] **280**

RESEARCH STRATEGIES (US/0734-3310). [1,000] **3245**

RESEARCH SUPPORTED BY THE ECONOMIC AND SOCIAL RESEARCH COUNCIL (UK/0266-2159). [1,500] **5215**

RESEAU - ASSOCIATION DES ENSEIGNANTES ET DES ENSEIGNANTS FRANCO-ONTARIENS (CN/1192-2796). [8,000] **1779**

RESENA DE ACTIVIDADES - CENEP (AG). [400] **4559**

RESIDENT AND STAFF PHYSICIAN (US/0034-5555). [100,000] **3634**

RESIDENTIAL CONSTRUCTION IN SOUTHEAST MICHIGAN (US/0362-3424). [3,000] **626**

RESMEDICA (US/0738-0496). [16,000] **3634**

RESOLUTION (US/1050-3978). [50,000] **1201**

RESOURCE (CN/0832-9354). **4992**

RESOURCE BULLETIN INT (US/0748-1241). **2393**

RESOURCE DIRECTORY (TORONTO) (CN/0822-2479). [10,000] **2903**

RESOURCE (DON MILLS, ONT.) (CN/0828-9522). [4,000] **4846**

RESOURCE (OTTAWA) (CN/0700-5237). [7,700] **227**

RESOURCE PUBLICATION - U.S. FISH AND WILDLIFE SERVICE (US/0163-4801). [3,000] **2204**

RESOURCES - CANADIAN INSTITUTE OF RESOURCES LAW (CN/0714-5918). [6,200] **3116**

RESOURCES IN AGING (US/0892-0818). [3,200] **5306**

RESOURCES IN EDUCATION. ANNUAL CUMULATION (US/0197-9973). [1,000] **1797**

RESOURCES IN LIBRARY AND INFORMATION SCIENCE (US/0197-4742). [800] **3246**

RESOURCES POLICY (UK/0301-4207). [3,500] **2204**

RESPIRATORY DISEASES RESEARCH CENTER (KE). [100] **3951**

RESPIRATORY PROTECTION NEWSLETTER (US/0882-0953). [200] **2869**

RESPONSA MERIDIANA (SA/0486-5588). [600] **3039**

RESPONSIVE COMMUNITY, THE (US/1053-0754). **5256**

RESPONSIVE PHILANTHROPY (US/1065-0008). [5,000] **4339**

RESSI REVIEW (US/0199-3534). [3,000] **4846**

RESSOURCE (OTTAWA) (CN/0700-5245). [7,700] **227**

RESSOURCES ET VOUS (CN/0714-4288). [500] **3175**

RESTAURANT HOSPITALITY (US/0147-9989). [140,000] **5072**

RESTAURANTS & INSTITUTIONS (CHICAGO, ILL.) (US/0273-5520). [500,000] **5073**

RESTAURATOR (DK/0034-5806). [1,100] **2483**

RESTORATION HERALD (US/0034-5830). [7,000] **4993**

RESTORATION QUARTERLY (US/0486-5642). [700] **4993**

RESTORICA (SA). [5,000] **626**

RESUMENES ANALITICOS EN EDUCACION (CL/0716-0151). [750] **1797**

RESURRECTION BULLETIN, THE (CN/0714-7686). [2,660] **4993**

RETAIL AUTOMATION (UK/0263-1377). **707**

RETAIL NEWS WEST (US/8750-4286). [12,500] **957**

RETAIL STORE IMAGE (US/1047-8841). [25,000] **2903**

RETAIL SYSTEMS ALERT (US/0898-8439). **957**

RETAIL WORLD (AT). [16,500] **957**

RETAILER AND MARKETING NEWS (US/0192-9151). [8,000] **936**

RETHINKING SCHOOLS (US/0895-6855). [35,000] **1779**

RETIRED OFFICER MAGAZINE (ALEXANDRIA, VA.), THE (US/1061-3102). [386,000] **4055**

RETIREMENT INDUSTRY JOURNAL, THE (AT). [6,500] **5181**

RETIREMENT LIFESTYLE (CN/0844-5982). [50,000] **5181**

RETRIEVAL CODE INDEX - DATA RESOURCES OF CANADA (CN/0823-9592). **3246**

RETTUNGSDIENST (GW/0178-2525). **3634**

RETURN TO THE SOURCE (US/0743-1244). [1,500] **4993**

REVEIL MISSIONNAIRE (CN/0034-6284). [22,000] **4993**

REVELSTOKE TIMES (CN). [3,500] **5794**

REVIEW AND RECOMMENDATIONS ... OPERATING BUDGET REQUEST FOR WASHINGTON PUBLIC HIGHER EDUCATION (US). [150] **1845**

REVIEW (CHARLOTTESVILLE) (US/0190-3233). **3351**

REVIEW FOR RELIGIOUS (US/0034-639X). [16,500] **5035**

RE:VIEW - FRIENDS OF PHOTOGRAPHY (US/0891-5326). [14,200] **4376**

REVIEW JOURNAL OF PHILOSOPHY & SOCIAL SCIENCE (II/0258-1701). [250] **4359**

REVIEW : LATIN AMERICAN LITERATURE AND ARTS (US). [5,000] **329**

REVIEW OF BOOKS ON THE BOOK OF MORMON (US/1050-7930). [5,000] **4993**

REVIEW OF ECONOMIC CONDITIONS (TU/0034-6500). [1,700] **1581**

REVIEW OF HIGHER EDUCATION (US/0162-5748). [1,000] **1845**

REVIEW OF INCOME AND WEALTH, THE (US/0034-6586). [1,500] **1518**

REVIEW OF INSTITUTIONAL THOUGHT, THE (US/0735-8563). [100] **1594**

REVIEW OF NATIONAL LITERATURES (US/0034-6640). [1,000] **3351**

REVIEW OF RADICAL POLITICAL ECONOMICS, THE (US/0486-6134). [2,700] **1594**

REVIEW OF REGIONAL STUDIES, THE (US/0048-749X). [1,000] **2834**

REVIEW OF RELIGIOUS RESEARCH (US/0034-673X). [1,200] **4993**

REVIEW OF THE ECONOMIC SITUATION OF MEXICO (MX/0014-3960). [21,000] **1581**

REVIEW, THE (UK/0034-6349). [4,995] **2892**

REVIEWS IN MINERALOGY (US/0275-0279). [3,000] **1444**

REVIEWS OF RESEARCH FOR PRACTITIONERS AND PARENTS (US). **4615**

REVISTA AEREA (US/0279-4519). [8,300] **33**

REVISTA AMRIGS (BL/0102-2105). [7,000] **3634**

REVISTA ANTIOGUENA DE ECONOMIA Y DESARROLLO (CK/0121-0017). [1,500] **1518**

REVISTA ARGENTINA DE CIRUGIA (AG). [4,000] **3973**

REVISTA ARGENTINA DE LINGUISTICA (AG/0326-6400). [250] **3315**

REVISTA ARGENTINA DE MICOLOGIA : ORGANO DE DIFUSION DE LA SOCIEDAD ARGENTINA DE MICOLOGIA (AG/0325-4755). [1,000] **576**

REVISTA ARGENTINA DE MICROBIOLOGIA (AG/0325-7541). [1,500] **569**

REVISTA BIBLICA (AG/0034-7078). [500] **5019**

REVISTA BRASILEIRA DE ENTOMOLOGIA (BL/0085-5626). [600] **5613**

REVISTA BRASILEIRA DE GENETICA (BL/0100-8455). [2,000] **551**

REVISTA BRASILEIRA DE GEOGRAFIA (BL/0034-723X). [2,200] **2574**

REVISTA BRASILEIRA DE MALARIOLOGIA E DOENCAS TROPICAIS (BL/0034-7256). [3,000] **3634**

REVISTA BRASILEIRA DE PATOLOGIA CLINICA (BL/0034-7302). [3,000] **3897**

REVISTA BRASILEIRA DE ZOOLOGIA (BL/0101-8175). [1,200] **5596**

REVISTA CAFETERA DE COLOMBIA (CK). [2,000] **185**

REVISTA CATALANA DE TEOLOGIA (SP/0210-5551). [500] **4993**

REVISTA CERES (BL/0034-737X). [1,100] **128**

REVISTA CHILENA DE HISTORIA Y GEOGRAFIA (CL/0716-2812). [1,000] **2757**

REVISTA CHILENA DE LITERATURA (CL/0048-7651). [600] **3430**

REVISTA CHILENA DE PEDIATRIA (CL/0370-4106). [1,200] **3911**

REVISTA COLOMBIANA DE MATEMATICAS (CK/0034-7426). [1,000] **3531**

REVISTA COLOMBIANA DE OBSTETRICIA Y GINECOLOGIA (CK/0034-7434). [1,200] **3768**

REVISTA CRITICA DE CIENCIAS SOCIAIS (PO). [1,500] **5216**

REVISTA. CUBAN GENEALOGICAL SOCIETY (US). [100] **2470**

REVISTA CUBANA DE CIENCIA AVICOLA (CU/0303-5239). [20,000] **220**

REVISTA CUBANA DE CONSTRUCCION NAVAL; REVISTA CIENTIFICO TECNICA (CU/0864-2621). [2,000] **5455**

REVISTA CUBANA DE DERECHO (CU). [20,000] **3040**

REVISTA CUBANA DE EDUCACION SUPERIOR : RCES (CU/0257-4314). [10,000] **1846**

REVISTA CUBANA DE HIGIENE Y EPIDEMIOLOGIA (CU/0253-1151). [5,000] **3736**

REVISTA CUBANA DE INVESTIGACIONES PESQUERAS / CENTRO DE INVESTIGACIONES PESQUERAS, MIRAMAR, LA HABANA, CUBA (CU/0138-8452). [780] **2312**

REVISTA CUBANA DE MEDICINA (CU/0034-7523). [50,000] **3635**

REVISTA CUBANA DE MEDICINA TROPICAL (CU/0375-0760). [20,000] **3986**

REVISTA CUBANA DE OBSTETRICIA Y GINECOLOGIA (CU). [3,000] **3768**

REVISTA DA ACADEMIA PERNAMBUCANA DE LETRAS (BL). [100] **3430**

REVISTA DA ACADEMIA SOBRALENSE DE ESTUDOS E LETRAS (BL). [500] **2757**

REVISTA DA ESCOLA DE BIBLIOTECONOMIA DA UFMG (BL/0100-0829). [600] **3246**

REVISTA DA PROCURADORIA GERAL DO ESTADO DE SAO PAULO (BL). [2,000] **3040**

REVISTA DA SOCIEDADE BRASILEIRA DE MEDICINA TROPICAL (BL/0037-8682). **3986**

REVISTA DE ADMINISTRACAO DE EMPRESAS (BL/0034-7590). [5,000] **885**

REVISTA DE ADMINISTRACAO MUNICIPAL (BL). [3,000] **4683**

REVISTA DE ARQUEOLOGIA (RIO DE JANEIRO, BRAZIL) (BL). [1,000] **280**

REVISTA DE ASCOLBI / ASOCIATION COLOMBIANA DE BIBLIOTECOLOGOS Y DOCUMENTALISTAS, ASCOLBI (CK/0121-0203). [3,000] **3246**

REVISTA DE BIOLOGIA (LISBOA) (PO/0034-7736). [150] **471**

REVISTA DE BIOLOGIA MARINA (CL/0080-2115). [900] **557**

REVISTA DE BIOLOGIA TROPICAL (CR/0034-7744). [1,500] **3986**

REVISTA DE CIENCIAS DE LA EDUCACION (SP). **1780**

REVISTA DE CIENCIAS SOCIALES (SAN JOSE) (CR/0482-5276). [1,500] **5216**

REVISTA DE CRITICA LITERARIA LATINOAMERICANA (PE/0252-8843). [1,500] **3351**

REVISTA DE DERECHO ADMINISTRATIVO (AG/0327-2265). **3040**

REVISTA DE DERECHO PUERTORRIQUENO (PR/0034-7930). [700] **3040**

REVISTA DE DIAGNOSTICO BIOLOGICO (SP/0034-7973). [3,000] **471**

REVISTA DE DIVULGACAO CULTURAL / FURB (BL). [800] **2757**

REVISTA DE DOUTRINA E JURISPRUDENCIA / TRIBUNAL DE JUSTICA DO DISTRITO FEDERAL E DOS TERRITORIOS (BL/0101-8868). [3,000] **3041**

REVISTA DE EDUCACION (CL). [10,000] **1780**

REVISTA DE ESTETICA (AG). [8,000] **329**

REVISTA DE ESTUDIOS HISPANICOS (UNIVERSITY, AL.) (US/0034-818X). [500] **3315**

REVISTA DE ESTUDIOS HISTORICO-JURIDICOS (CL/0716-5455). [500] **3041**

REVISTA DE ESTUDIOS REGIONALES (SP/0213-7585). [1,000] **5216**

REVISTA DE FARMACIA E BIOQUIMICA DA UNIVERSIDADE DE SAO PAULO (BL/0370-4726). **4328**

REVISTA DE FILOSOFIA DE LA UNIVERSIDAD DE COSTA RICA (CR/0034-8252). [750] **4359**

REVISTA DE GUIMARAES (PO/0871-0759). [1,000] **2705**

REVISTA DE HISTORIA (HEREDIA) (CR/1012-9790). [1,000] **2758**

REVISTA DE INTERPRETACAO BIBLICA LATINO-AMERICANA : RIBLA (CR). [1,500] **5019**

REVISTA DE INVESTIGACION CLINICA (MX/0034-8376). [1,500] **3801**

REVISTA DE LA ASOCIACION CASTELLANA DE APARATO DIGESTIVO (SP/0213-1463). [2,000] **3801**

REVISTA DE LA ASOCIACION ODONTOLOGICA ARGENTINA (AG/0004-4881). [8,000] **1334**

REVISTA DE LA BIBLIOTECA NACIONAL JOSE MARTI (CU). [10,000] **3246**

REVISTA DE LA EDUCACION SUPERIOR (MX). **1846**

REVISTA DE LA FACULTAD DE DERECHO DE LA UNIVERSIDAD COMPLUTENSE (SP). **3041**

REVISTA DE LA FACULTAD DE DERECHO DE MEXICO (MX/0185-1810). [2,000] **3041**

REVISTA DE LA FACULTAD NACIONAL DE SALUD PUBLICA (CK/0120-386X). [1,000] **4799**

REVISTA DE LA IMAGEN Y EL SONIDO: EIKONOS (SP). [12,000] **4376**

REVISTA DE LA INTEGRACION Y EL DESARROLLO DE CENTROAMERICA (HO/0252-8762). [2,500] **1518**

REVISTA DE LA MEDICINA TRADICIONAL CHINA (SP/1130-4405). [3,000] **3635**

REVISTA DE LA SANIDAD DE LAS FUERZAS POLICIALES (PE/0254-3435). [8,000] **3635**

REVISTA DE LA SOCIEDAD DE OBSTETRICIA Y GINECOLOGIA DE BUENOS AIRES (AG/0037-8542). [3,000] **3768**

REVISTA DE LA SOCIEDAD ESPANOLA DE QUIMICA CLINICA (SP/0213-8514). [2,000] **1018**

REVISTA DE LITERATURA CUBANA (CU). [20,000] **3351**

REVISTA DE MARINA (CL/0034-8511). [3,200] **4055**

REVISTA DE MEDICINA DE LA UNIVERSIDAD DE NAVARRA (SP/0556-6177). [12,000] **3973**

REVISTA DE MEDICINA VETERINARIA (AG/0325-6391). [10,500] **5520**

REVISTA DE MUSICA LATINOAMERICANA (US/0163-0350). [450] **4149**

REVISTA DE NEFROLOGIA, DIALISIS Y TRANSPLANTE : PUBLICACION CONJUNTA DE LA ASOCIACION REGIONAL DE DIALISIS Y TRASPLANTES RENALES DE CAPITAL FEDERAL Y PROVINCIA DE BUENOS AIRES Y LA SOCIEDAD ARGENTINA DE NEFROLOGIA (AG/0326-3428). [1,500] **3635**

REVISTA DE OBRAS PUBLICAS (SP/0034-8619). [5,000] **2030**

REVISTA DE ODONTOLOGIA DA UNESP (BL/0101-1774). [1,000] **1334**

REVISTA DE ODONTOLOGIA DA UNIVERSIDADE DE SAO PAULO (BL/0103-0663). **1334**

REVISTA DE PASTORAL JUVENIL (SP). [4,000] **5035**

REVISTA DE PRE-HISTORIA (BL). [1,000] **2758**

REVISTA DE PSICOLOGIA GENERAL Y APLICADA (SP/0373-2002). [2,000] **4616**

REVISTA DE SAUDE PUBLICA (BL/0034-8910). [1,400] **4799**

REVISTA DEL ARCHIVO NACIONAL (CR/0034-9003). [900] **2483**

REVISTA DEL DERECHO COMERCIAL Y DE LAS OBLIGACIONES (AG/0556-6428). [2,500] **3102**

REVISTA DEL DERECHO INDUSTRIAL (AG/0326-0763). [1,200] **3041**

REVISTA DEL HOSPITAL PSIQUIATRICO DE LA HABANA (CU/0440-436X). [50,000] **3936**

REVISTA DEL INSTITUTO MEXICANO DEL PETROLEO (MX/0538-1428). [5,500] **4277**

REVISTA DEL JARDIN BOTANICO NACIONAL (CU/0253-5696). [10,000] **526**

REVISTA DO CENTRO DE CIENCIAS RURAIS (BL/0085-5901). [470] **129**

REVISTA DO COLEGIO BRASILEIRO DE CIRURGIOES (BL/0100-6991). [7,000] **3973**

REVISTA DO HOSPITAL DAS CLINICAS (BL/0041-8781). [6,000] **3635**

REVISTA DO INSTITUTO ADOLFO LUTZ (BL/0073-9855). [1,200] **4800**

REVISTA DO IRB / INSTITUTO DE RESSEGUROS DO BRASIL (BL/0019-0446). [6,200] **2892**

REVISTA ECUATORIANA DE HIGIENE Y MEDICINA TROPICAL (EC/0048-7775). [3,500] **3986**

REVISTA ESPANOLA DE ALERGOLOGIA E INMUNOLOGIA CLINICA : ORGANO OFICIAL DE LA SOCIEDAD ESPANOLA DE ALERGOLOGIA E INMUNOLOGIA CLINICA (SP/0214-1477). [2,000] **3676**

REVISTA ESPANOLA DE ANESTESIOLOGIA Y REANIMACION (SP/0034-9356). [4,000] **3684**

REVISTA ESPANOLA DE CARDIOLOGIA (SP/0300-8932). [4,000] **3710**

REVISTA ESPANOLA DE CIENCIA Y TECNOLOGIA DE ALIMENTOS / EDITADA POR EL CONSEJO SUPERIOR DE INVESTIGACIONES CIENTIFICAS (SP/1131-799X). [1,000] **2356**

REVISTA ESPANOLA DE DOCUMENTACION CIENTIFICA (SP/0210-0614). [1,100] **3246**

REVISTA ESPANOLA DE ENFERMEDADES DIGESTIVAS (SP/1130-0108). [2,500] **3747**

REVISTA EUROPEA DE ESTUDIOS LATINOAMERICANOS Y DEL CARIBE. EUROPEAN REVIEW OF LATIN AMERICAN AND CARIBBEAN STUDIES (NE/0924-0608). [1,000] **5216**

REVISTA FARMACEUTICA (SAN JUAN, P.R.) (PR/1070-5015). [3,000] **4328**

REVISTA GEOGRAFICA DE CHILE TERRA AUSTRALIS (CL/0378-8482). [500] **2574**

REVISTA HISPANICA MODERNA (US/0034-9593). [1,500] **3430**

REVISTA IBEROAMERICANA (US/0034-9631). [2,000] **3430**

REVISTA IBEROAMERICANA DE FERTILIDAD Y REPRODUCCION HUMANA (SP). [10,000] **3636**

REVISTA (INSTITUTO GEOGRAFICO E CADASTRAL (PORTUGAL)) (PO/0870-9351). [1,000] **2583**

REVISTA INTERAMERICANA DE BIBLIOGRAFIA (1972) (US/0020-4994). [1,600] **423**

REVISTA INTERAMERICANA DE BIBLIOTECOLOGIA / UNIVERSIDAD DE ANTIOQUIA, ESCUELA INTERAMERICANA DE BIBLIOTECOLOGIA (CK/0120-0976). [12,000] **3246**

REVISTA INTERAMERICANA DE PLANIFICACION (US/0185-1861). [2,000] **2834**

REVISTA INTERNACIONAL DE CIENCIAS SOCIALES (SP/0379-0762). **5216**

REVISTA INTERNACIONAL DE ESTUDOS AFRICANOS (PO). **5216**

REVISTA INTERNACIONAL DE METODOS NUMERICOS PARA CALCULO Y DISEƒNO EN INGENIERIA (SP/0213-1315). [200] **1994**

REVISTA JURIDICA DE LA UNIVERSIDAD DE PUERTO RICO (PR/0886-2516). [1,000] **3042**

REVISTA JURIDICA DE LA UNIVERSIDAD INTERAMERICANA DE PUERTO RICO (PR/0041-851X). [1,000] **3042**

REVISTA LATINOAMERICANA DE FILOSOFIA (AG/0325-0725). [300] **4359**

REVISTA LATINOAMERICANA DE MICROBIOLOGIA (1970) (MX/0187-4640). [2,000] **569**

REVISTA LETRAS (CURITIBA) (BL/0100-0888). [348] **3316**

REVISTA M (VE). [7,000] **2552**

REVISTA MARITIMA BRASILEIRA (BL/0034-9860). [3,200] **4182**

REVISTA MEDICA DE CHILE (CL/0034-9887). [2,000] **3801**

REVISTA MEDICA DE COSTA RICA (CR/0034-9909). [5,000] **3636**

REVISTA MEDICA DE PANAMA (PN/0379-1629). [1,200] **3636**

REVISTA MEXICANA DE ASTRONOMIA Y ASTROFISICA (MX/0185-1101). [1,500] **399**

REVISTA MEXICANA DE FISICA (MX/0035-001X). [1,600] **4420**

REVISTA MEXICANA DE MICOLOGIA (MX/0187-3180). [500] **576**

REVISTA MEXICANA DE PEDIATRIA (MX/0035-0052). [10,000] **3911**

REVISTA MEXICANA DE POLITICA EXTERIOR (MX/0185-6022). [2,000] **2758**

REVISTA MUSICAL CHILENA (CL/0716-2790). [500] **4150**

REVISTA ODONTOLOGICA ECUATORIANA (EC/0484-8020). [1,500] **1334**

REVISTA ORL (AG/0326-7067). [1,800] **3891**

REVISTA PAULISTA DE HOSPITAIS (BL/0048-7864). [20,000] **3636**

REVISTA PAULISTA DE MEDICINA (BL/0035-0362). [5,000] **3636**

REVISTA PERUANA DE DERECHO DE LA EMPRESA (PE). [1,000] **3042**

REVISTA PORTUGUESA DE CIENCIAS VETERINARIAS (PO/0035-0389). [1200] **5520**

REVISTA PORTUGUESA DE ESTOMATOLOGIA E CIRURGIA MAXILO-FACIAL (PO/0035-0397). [2,400] **1334**

REVISTA ROL DE ENFERMERIA (SP/0210-5020). [25,000] **3868**

REVISTA SOBRE RELACIONES INDUSTRIALES Y LABORALES / UNIVERSIDAD CATOLICA ANDRES BELLO (VE). [2,000] **1708**

REVISTA TECNICA INTEVEP (VE/0251-4478). [5,000] **4277**

REVISTA TEOLOGICA LIMENSE (PE). [1,000] **5035**

REVISTA TRIMESTRAL / BANCO CENTRAL DE RESERVA DE EL SALVADOR (ES). [3,000] **810**

REVISTA URUGUAYA DE CIENCIAS SOCIALES (UY). [2,000] **5217**

REVISTI DI ARCHEOLOGIA CRISTIANA (VC/0035-6042). **281**

REVITALIZED SIGNS (US). [1,000] **4616**

REVMEDIA LONDON (UK/0955-8500). [400] **1183**

REVTECH (US). [2,000] **1202**

REVUE A. C. C. S (CN/0226-5931). [500] **3792**

REVUE ADMINISTRATIVE, LA (FR/0035-0672). [35,000] **4683**

REVUE BELGE DE GEOGRAPHIE (BE/0035-0796). [800] **2575**

REVUE BELGE DE MEDECINE DENTAIRE 1984 (BE/0775-0293). **1334**

REVUE BELGE D'HISTOIRE CONTEMPORAINE (BE). [500] **2706**

REVUE BIBLIOGRAPHIQUE - TOXIBASE LYON (FR/0996-8393). [200] **1350**

REVUE CANADIENNE D'ETUDES DU DEVELOPPEMENT (CN/0225-5189). [500] **1639**

REVUE COMMERCE (MONTREAL. 1975) (CN/0380-9811). [34,000] **850**

REVUE D'ALLEMAGNE (FR/0035-0974). [700] **2706**

REVUE DE BIBLIOLOGIE (FR/0982-6548). **3430**

REVUE DE DROIT COMMERCIAL BELGE (BE). **3102**

REVUE DE DROIT INTERNATIONAL, DE SCIENCES DIPLOMATIQUES ET POLITIQUES (SZ/0035-1091). **3135**

REVUE DE DROIT JUDICIAIRE (CN/0822-5117). [1,000] **3091**

REVUE DE DROIT PENAL ET DE CRIMINOLOGIE (BE). [1,000] **3175**

REVUE DE DROIT (SHERBROOKE) (CN/0317-9656). [2,000] **3043**

REVUE DE LA CERAMIQUE ET DU VERRE, LA (FR/0294-202X). [5,800] **2593**

REVUE DE LA CERAMIQUE, LA (FR). [5,000] **2593**

REVUE DE LA CINEMATHEQUE, LA (CN/0843-6827). [35,000] **4077**

REVUE — Controlled Circulation Index

REVUE DE LA SOCIETE HISTORIQUE DU MADAWASKA (1982) (CN/0820-0793). [500] **2758**

REVUE DE L'ACLA (CN/1193-1493). [350] **3316**

REVUE DE L'ARBITRAGE (FR/0556-7440). **3043**

REVUE DE LARYNGOLOGIE, D'OTOLOGIE ET DE RHINOLOGIE (FR/0035-1334). [1,970] **3891**

REVUE DE L'ATEQ, LA (CN/0835-0868). [2,200] **1870**

REVUE DE L'EDUCATION PHYSIQUE (BE). [2,000] **1858**

REVUE DE L'ENERGIE (FR/0303-240X). [2,500] **1956**

REVUE DE LINGUISTIQUE ROMANE (FR/0035-1458). [1,200] **3316**

REVUE DE LITTERATURE COMPAREE (FR/0035-1466). [2,500] **3430**

REVUE DE L'UNIVERSITE DE BRUXELLES (BE/0378-4606). [1,200] **5148**

REVUE DE L'UNIVERSITE DE MONCTON (1976) (CN/0316-6368). [700] **1846**

REVUE DE L'UNIVERSITE SAINTE-ANNE (CN/0706-8115). [400] **1846**

REVUE DE METALLURGIE (PARIS) (FR/0035-1563). [2,400] **4018**

REVUE DE MICROPALEONTOLOGIE (FR/0035-1598). [650] **4230**

REVUE DE NEUROPSYCHOLOGIE / SOCIETE DE NEUROPSYCHOLOGIE DE LANGUE FRANCAISE (FR/1155-4452). [400] **3845**

REVUE DE PALEOBIOLOGIE (SZ). **4230**

REVUE DE THEOLOGIE ET DE PHILOSOPHIE (SZ/0035-1784). [1,000] **4359**

REVUE DE TOURISME (SZ/0251-3102). **5490**

REVUE D'ECONOMIE REGIONAL ET URBAINE (FR). [500] **2834**

REVUE DES ARCHEOLOGUES ET HISTORIENS D'ART DE LOUVAIN (BE/0080-2530). **281**

REVUE DES ECHANGES DE L'ASSOCIATION FRANCOPHONE INTERNATIONALE DES DIRECTEURS D'ETABLISSEMENTS SCOLAIRES, LA (CN/0822-8329). **1780**

REVUE DES ETUDES COOPERATIVES MUTUALISTES ET ASSOCIATIVES (FR). **1543**

REVUE DES ETUDES ITALIENNES (FR/0035-2047). [650] **3430**

REVUE DES INGENIEURS (FR). **1360**

REVUE DES LABORATOIRES D'ESSAIS, LA (FR/0296-5321). [4,0000] **5148**

REVUE DES SCIENCES PHILOSOPHIQUES ET THEOLOGIQUES (PARIS : 1947) (FR/0035-2209). [1,100] **4359**

REVUE DES SCIENCES SOCIALES DE LA FRANCE DE L'EST (FR/0336-1578). [900] **5217**

REVUE DESJARDINS, LA (CN/0035-2284). [23,000] **810**

REVUE D'HISTOIRE DE LA COTE-NORD (CN/0828-9468). [1,200] **2758**

REVUE D'HISTOIRE DE L'AMERIQUE FRANCAISE (CN/0035-2357). [1,400] **2758**

REVUE D'HISTOIRE DIPLOMATIQUE (FR/0035-2365). **4534**

REVUE D'HISTOIRE ECCLESIASTIQUE (BE/0035-2381). [1,800] **5013**

REVUE D'HISTOIRE MAGHREBINE (TI). [500] **2643**

REVUE D'INTEGRATION EUROPEENNE (CN/0703-6337). [400] **4494**

REVUE DIPLOMATIQUE DE L'OCEAN INDIEN (MG). [3,000] **4534**

REVUE DU MARCHE COMMUN ET DE L'UNION EUROPEENNE (FR). [2,000] **1582**

REVUE DU MARCHE UNIQUE EUROPEEN (FR/1155-4274). **1639**

REVUE DU MONDE MUSULMAN ET DE LA MEDITERRANEE (FR/0997-1327). **5044**

REVUE DU PALAIS DE LA DECOUVERTE (FR/0339-7521). [5,500] **5148**

REVUE DU PRACTICIEN, LA (FR/0035-2640). [50,000] **3636**

REVUE ECONOMIQUE (FR/0035-2764). [2,000] **1595**

REVUE ECONOMIQUE - CHAMBRE DE COMMERCE DE LAVAL (CN/0825-0707). [20,000] **1518**

REVUE FORESTIERE FRANCAISE (FR/0035-2829). **2394**

REVUE FRANCAISE DE GEOTECHNIQUE (FR/0181-0529). [4,112] **1395**

REVUE FRANCAISE DE SCIENCE POLITIQUE (FR/0035-2950). [2,500] **4495**

REVUE FRANCAISE DE SERVICE SOCIAL, LA (FR). [4,000] **5306**

REVUE FRANCAISE D'ETUDES AMERICAINES (FR/0397-7870). [1,000] **2759**

REVUE FRANCAISE DU MARKETING (FR/0035-3051). [3,000] **936**

REVUE FRANCOPHONE DE LA DEFICIENCE INTELLECTUELLE (CN/0847-5733). [650] **3845**

REVUE FRANCOPHONE DE LOUISIANE (US/0890-9555). [300] **3431**

REVUE FRONTENAC (CN/0715-9994). [100] **3431**

REVUE GENERAL NUCLEAIRE (FR/0335-5004). [6,500] **1956**

REVUE GENERALE DE L'ELECTRICITE (FR/0035-3116). **2079**

REVUE HOLSTEIN QUEBEC, LA (CN/0821-770X). **198**

REVUE HOSPITALIERE DE FRANCE (FR/0397-4626). **3792**

REVUE INTERNATIONALE DE CRIMINOLOGIE ET DE POLICE TECHNIQUE (FR/0035-3329). [2,500] **3175**

REVUE INTERNATIONALE DE LA CROIX-ROUGE (SZ). [8000] **2911**

REVUE INTERNATIONALE DE PHILOSOPHIE (BE/0048-8143). **4359**

REVUE INTERNATIONALE DES SERVICES DE SANTE DES FORCES ARMEES : ORGANE DU COMITE INTERNATIONAL DE MEDECINE ETUDE PHARMACIE MILITAIRES (BE/0259-8582). [3,000] **3636**

REVUE JURIDIQUE DU ZAIRE; DROIT ECRIT ET DROIT COUTUMIER (CG). [1,000] **3043**

REVUE JURIDIQUE THEMIS (1970) (CN/0556-7963). [1,700] **3044**

REVUE JURIDIQUE THEMIS (1970) (CN/0556-7963). **3044**

REVUE LAITIERE FRANCAISE (FR/0035-3590). [8,000] **220**

REVUE MUNICIPALE (MONTREAL) (CN/0035-3728). [12,000] **4684**

REVUE - OFFICE INTERNATIONAL DES EPIZOOTIES (FR/0253-1933). [800] **5521**

REVUE PHILOSOPHIQUE DE LOUVAIN (BE/0035-3841). **4360**

REVUE POLYTECHNIQUE (SZ/0374-4256). **5148**

REVUE PRACTIQUE DE DROIT SOCIAL (FR). **3044**

REVUE PRATIQUE DU FROID ET DU CONDITIONNEMENT DE L'AIR (FR/0370-6699). [5,000] **2608**

REVUE PRESCRIRE, LA (FR/0247-7750). [25,000] **3637**

REVUE QUEBECOISE DE DROIT INTERNATIONAL (CN/0828-9999). **3135**

REVUE QUEBECOISE DE LINGUISTIQUE THEORIQUE ET APPLIQUEE (CN/0835-3581). [600] **3317**

REVUE REFORMEE, LA (FR/0035-3884). [1,300] **5067**

REVUE ROMANE (DK/0035-3906). [550] **3317**

REVUE ROUMAINE DE MATHEMATIQUES PURES ET APPLIQUEES (RM/0035-3965). [1,000] **3531**

REVUE SCHWEIZ (SZ). [15,000] **708**

REVUE SUISSE D'AGRICULTURE (SZ/0375-1325). [7,000] **130**

REVUE SUISSE DE VITICULTURE, ARBORICULTURE, HORTICULTURE (SZ/0375-1430). [6,500] **2430**

REVUE TUNISIENNE DE COMMUNICATION (TI/0330-8480). [2,000] **1121**

REVUE VOILE QUEBEC, LA (CN/0820-4969). [6,000] **595**

REVUE VOYAGEUR, LA (CN/0824-1309). [100,000] **5490**

REYNOLDS COUNTY COURIER (ELLINGTON, MO.) (US). [2,900] **5704**

REZA KAGAKU KENKYU (JA). [900] **4441**

RFD (WOLF CREEK) (US/0149-709X). [2,800] **2796**

RHEINISCHE VIERTELJAHRSBLATTER (GW/0035-4473). [2,000] **2707**

RHETORIC REVIEW (US/0735-0198). [750] **3317**

RHETORIC SOCIETY QUARTERLY (US/0277-3945). [1,300] **3317**

RHETORICA (US/0734-8584). [950] **3317**

RHINOLOGY (NE/0300-0729). [1,250] **3891**

RHODE ISLAND BAR JOURNAL (US/0556-8595). [4,300] **3044**

RHODE ISLAND HISTORY (US/0035-4619). [3,000] **2759**

RHODE ISLAND JEWISH HISTORICAL NOTES (US/0556-8609). **2272**

RHODE ISLAND QUERIES (US/0893-181X). **2470**

RHODE ISLAND ROOTS (US/0730-1235). [800] **2470**

RHODODENDRON, THE (AT/0485-0637). [500] **2430**

RIABILITAZIONE E APPRENDIMENTO (IT/0393-7518). [3,000] **4382**

RIAS QUARTAL (GW). [2,600-2,800] **1138**

RICARDA HUCH, STUDIEN ZU IHREM LEBEN UND WERK (GW). [10,000] **3431**

RICARDIAN (UK/0048-8267). [4,400] **5236**

RICE WORLD (US). **185**

RICE WORLD & SOYBEAN NEWS, THE (US/0738-5943). **185**

RICERCA E INNOVAZIONE (IT). [12,000] **5148**

RICERCHE ECONOMICHE (IT/0035-5054). [1,000] **1518**

RICHMOND COUNTY HISTORY (US/0035-5119). [350] **2759**

RICHMOND POST (US). [13,661] **5639**

RICHTON DISPATCH, THE (US). [1,600] **5701**

RIDDELL, RIDDLE, RUDDELL TRAIL, THE (US/0737-6758). [300] **2470**

RIFLE (US/0162-3583). [25,000] **4915**

RIGHT OF WAY (US/0035-5275). [9,000] **4846**

RIGHTS (GENEVA, SWITZERLAND) (SZ/1011-0240). **1308**

RILA BULLETIN (US/0146-8685). [600] **3247**

RILCE : REVISTA DE FILOLOGIA HISPANICA (SP). [300] **3431**

RILEVAZIONE DEI PREZZI ALL INGROSSO : ASSOMET (IT). **4018**

RINGETTE REVIEW (CN/0821-5782). **4865**

RINGING & MIGRATION (UK/0307-8698). [3,000] **5620**

RINSAN SHIKENJO KENKYU HOKOKU (JA). [600] **2394**

RINSHO HOSHASEN. JAPANESE JOURNAL OF CLINICAL RADIOLOGY (JA/0009-9252). [8,000] **3946**

RINSHO SHINKEIGAKU (JA/0009-918X). [5,800] **3845**

RIO GRANDE HISTORY (US/0146-1869). [700] **2759**

RIPON COLLEGE MAGAZINE (US/0300-7928). [13,000] **1094**

RIPON COLLEGE UPDATE (US/0744-7450). [13,000] **1846**

RISALAT AL-MAKTABAH (JO). [1,000] **3247**

RISALAT MAHAD AL-TURATH AL-ILMI AL-ARABI (SY). [1,000] **5148**

RISC USER (UK/0966-1913). [15,000] **1202**

RISK & BENEFITS MANAGEMENT (US/0893-2654). [15,000] **2892**

RISK MANAGEMENT (US/0035-5593). [12,000] **2892**

RISK MANAGEMENT REPORTS (US/0199-6827). [1,000] **2892**

RISPARMIO, IL (IT). [3,000] **810**

RISQUE PAYS (FR). [100] **1639**

RISSHO KEIEI RONSHU (JA). [1,300] **1625**

RITE IDEAS (US/8750-5703). [1,600] **4994**

RIVER CITY LIBRARY TIMES (US/0270-9104). [1,100] **3247**

RIVER CITY (MEMPHIS, TENN.) (US/1048-129X). **3431**

RIVER RUNNER MAGAZINE (US). [12,000] **595**

RIVISTA BIBLICA (IT/0035-5798). [2,000] **5019**

RIVISTA DEL NUOVO CIMENTO (IT/0035-5917). [1,000] **4420**

RIVISTA DELLA STAZIONE SPERIMENTALE DEL VETRO (IT). [2,000] **5148**

RIVISTA DELLE TECNOLOGIE TESSILI (IT/0394-5413). [14,700] **5355**

RIVISTA DI CARDIOLOGIA PREVENTIVA E RIABILITATIVA : ORGANO DELL'ASSOCIAZIONE NAZIONALE DEI CENTRI PER LE MALATTIE CARDIOVASCOLARI (IT/0393-2028). **3710**

RIVISTA DI INFORMATICA (IT/0390-668X). [2,100] **1202**

RIVISTA DI MATEMATICA PURA ED APPLICATA (IT). **3532**

RIVISTA DI NEURORADIOLOGIA (IT). [1,800] **3845**

RIVISTA DI OSTETRICIA GINECOLOGIA PRATICA E MEDICINA PERINATALE (IT/0391-0970). **3768**

RIVISTA DI PARASSITOLOGIA (IT/0035-6387). **569**

RIVISTA DI PATOLOGIA NERVOSA E MENTALE (IT/0035-6433). **3936**

RIVISTA DI SCIENZE PREISTORICHE (IT/0035-6514). **281**

RIVISTA DI STUDI ITALIANI (CN/0821-3216). [500] **3431**

RIVISTA DI STUDI LIGURI (FR/0035-6603). [2,000] **281**

RIVISTA DI STUDI POLITICI INTERNAZIONALI (IT/0035-6611). [1,000] **4534**

RIVISTA DI TEOLOGIA MORALE (IT). **4994**

RIVISTA GIURIDICA DEL LAVORO E DELLA PREVIDENZA SOCIALE: GIURISPRUDENZA (IT). [2,000] **3154**

RIVISTA GIURUDICA DELLA SCUOLA (IT/0391-1845). [1,700] **1870**

RIVISTA INGAUNA E INTEMELIA (IT). [1,700] **281**

RIVISTA ITALIANA DEGLI ODONTOTECNICI (IT/0391-5611). [8,000] **1335**

RIVISTA ITALIANA DI ECONOMIA, DEMOGRAFIA E STATISTICA (IT/0035-6832). [850] **1519**

RIVISTA ITALIANA DI OTORINOLARINGOLOGIA, AUDIOLOGIA E FONIATRIA (IT/0392-1360). **3891**

RIVISTA MARITTIMA (IT/0035-6964). [67,000] **4182**

RIVISTA MILITARE (IT/0035-6980). [25,000] **4056**

RIVISTA SVIZZERA SICUREZZA LAVORO (SZ). **2869**

RLA, REVISTA DE LINGUISTICA TEORICA Y APLICADA (CL/0033-698X). [600] **3317**

RMCLAS REVIEW (US/0749-9728). [300] **2552**

RMS NEWS (CN/0824-5665). [700] **2272**

RN (US/0033-7021). [275,000] **3868**

RN IDAHO (US/0192-298X). [700] **3868**

RNT (BL). [16,500] **1163**

ROAD/HOUSE (US/0148-3730). [100] **3470**

ROAD TRAFFIC SAFETY RESEARCH COUNCIL REPORT (NZ). [400] **5444**

ROAD WAY, THE (UK). [14,000] **5391**

ROADS & BRIDGES (DES PLAINS, ILL.) (US/8750-9229). [60,000] **2030**

ROBERTS REGISTER (US/8756-7741). [450] **2470**

ROBESON COUNTY REGISTER, THE (US/0888-3807). [100] **2470**

ROBOT (SA). [20,000] **5444**

ROCENKA - KRAJSKE KULTURNI STREDISKO V BRNE (XR). **2707**

ROCHAS DE QUALIDADE (BL). [1,200] **2150**

ROCHESTER GOLF WEEK & SPORTS LEDGER (US). [2,500] **4915**

ROCK & ICE (US/0885-5722). [45,000] **4878**

ROCK MAGNETISM AND PALEOGEOPHYSICS (JA/0385-2520). [400] **1410**

ROCKCASTLE REMINISCENCE (US). [250] **2628**

ROCKFORD MAGAZINE (US/0899-9414). **1299**

ROCKY MOUNTAIN JOURNAL OF MATHEMATICS, THE (US/0035-7596). [650] **3532**

ROCKY MOUNTAIN PAY DIRT (US/0886-0912). [4,200] **2150**

ROCKY MOUNTAIN PETROLEUM DIRECTORY (US/0278-9299). [12,000] **4277**

ROCKY MOUNTAIN REVIEW OF LANGUAGE AND LITERATURE (US/0361-1299). [1,200] **3431**

ROCKY MOUNTAIN UNION FARMER (US/0035-7650). [8,600] **130**

ROCZNIK HYDROLOGICZNY WOD PODZIEMNYCH (PL). [180] **1417**

ROCZNIK HYDROLOGICZNY WOD POWIERZCHNIOWYCH. DORECZE ORDY I RZEKI PRZYMORA MIEDZY ODRA I WISLA (PL). [170] **1417**

ROCZNIK HYDROLOGICZNY WOD POWIERZCHNIOWYCH. DORZECZE WISLY I RZEKI PRZYMORZA NA WSCHOD OD WISLY (PL). [180] **1417**

ROCZNIK METEOROLOGICZNY (PL). [50] **1434**

ROCZNIK METEOROLOGICZNY STACJI ARCTOWSKIEGO (PL). [120] **1434**

ROCZNIK METEOROLOGICZNY STACJI HORNSUNDU (PL). [120] **1434**

ROCZNIK STATYSTYCZNY (PL). [28,000] **5337**

ROCZNIK STATYSTYCZNY BUDOWNICTWA (PL). [1,000] **1582**

ROCZNIK STATYSTYCZNY FINANSOW (PL/0079-2640). [1,000] **4747**

ROCZNIK STATYSTYCZNY GOSPODARKI MORSKIEJ (PL/0079-2667). [800] **4182**

ROCZNIK STATYSTYCZNY KULTURY (PL). [1,500] **5337**

ROCZNIK STATYSTYCZNY OCHRONY ZDROWIA (POLAND. GOWNY URZAD STATYSTYCZNY : 1974) (PL). **4800**

ROCZNIK STATYSTYCZNY PRACY (PL). [1,200] **5337**

ROCZNIK STATYSTYCZNY ROLNICTWA I GOSPODARKI ZYWNOSCIOWEJ (PL). [1,700] **130**

ROCZNIK STATYSTYCZNY SZKOLNICTWA (PL). [1,000] **1781**

ROCZNIK STATYSTYCZNY TRANSPORTU (PL). [1,000] **5392**

ROCZNIK STATYSTYCZNY WOJEWODZTW (PL/0208-9300). [1,300] **5337**

ROCZNIK STATYSTYKI MIEDZYNARODOWEJ (PL). [1,800] **5338**

ROCZNIKI AKADEMII MEDYCZNEJ W BIAYMSTOKU (PL/0067-6489). [600] **3637**

ROCZNIKI AKADEMII ROLNICZEJ W POZNANIU - WYDZIA ZOOTECHNICZNY (PL). [200] **220**

ROCZNIKI STATYSTYCZNE (PL/0867-082X). [50,000] **5338**

RODEO TIMES /NATIONAL HIGH SCHOOL RODEO ASSOCIATION (US). **4915**

RODNA GRUDA SLOVENIJA (XV/0557-2282). [10,000] **2272**

RODO KAGAKU (JA/0035-7774). **1708**

ROESSLERIA (BL/0101-7616). [600] **2204**

ROJIN IRYO JIGYO NENPO (JA). [1,000] **5181**

ROLL CALL (WASHINGTON, D.C.) (US/0035-788X). [17,000] **4495**

ROLLER SKATING BUSINESS (US/0191-7617). [1,100] **4854**

ROLLERCOASTER! MAGAZINE (US/0896-7261). [4,000] **4865**

ROMA (II). [400] **2628**

ROMANCE NOTES (US/0035-7995). [600] **3318**

ROMANCE PHILOLOGY (US/0035-8002). [1,200] **3318**

ROMANCE QUARTERLY (US/0883-1157). [500] **3318**

ROMANCE STUDIES : A JOURNAL OF THE UNIVERSITY OF WALES (UK/0263-9904). [170] **1846**

ROMANIAN ECONOMIC NEWS (RM). [5,000] **1582**

ROMANISTISCHE ZEITSCHRIFT FUER LITERATURGESCHICHTE (GW/0343-379X). [660] **3318**

ROMANTIC TIMES (US/0747-3370). [70,000] **5074**

ROMANTIST, THE (US/0161-682X). [300] **3432**

ROMISCHE HISTORISCHE MITTEILUNGEN (AU/0080-3790). [400] **2707**

ROND DE TAFEL (NE/0035-8169). [6] **4994**

RONDOM GEZIN (BE/0773-4239). [1,600] **2285**

RONTGENPRAXIS (STUTTGART) (GW/0035-7820). [2,900] **3946**

ROOF (UK). [4,000] **2834**

ROOFER MAGAZINE, THE (US/0279-4616). [19,857] **3487**

ROOFING, CLADDING & INSULATION (UK). [11,500] **626**

ROOT AND BRANCH (UK/0306-9958). [1,300] **2470**

ROOT CELLAR PRESERVES (US/0748-6251). [400] **2470**

ROOTS & BRANCHES (US/0893-4150). [300] **2471**

ROOTS AND LEAVES (US/0748-2485). [324] **2471**

ROOTS (ST. PAUL, MINN.) (US/0148-6659). [4,000] **2759**

ROSEMERE-NOUVELLES (CN/0712-2993). **4684**

ROSICRUCIAN DIGEST (US/0035-8339). [80,000] **4243**

ROSSICA OLOMUCENSIA (XR). [300] **3318**

ROSTER - AMERICAN INSTITUTE OF CERTIFIED PLANNERS (US/0271-0188). [10,000] **1582**

ROSTER DE L'ACTL (CN/0823-4639). [3,000] **3637**

ROSTER ISSUE OF THE NORTH CAROLINA MEDICAL JOURNAL (US). [8,500] **3637**

ROSTER OF DEPARTMENTS OF GEOGRAPHY, CANADIAN UNIVERSITIES AND COLLEGES (CN/0710-5754). **2575**

ROSTER / THE BIRMINGHAM GENEALOGICAL SOCIETY, INC (US/8756-4351). [200-210] **2471**

ROSTOCKER MATHEMATISCHES KOLLOQUIUM (GW). [500] **3532**

ROSWELL DAILY RECORD, THE (US). **5713**

ROTKIN REVIEW, THE (US/0883-735X). [8,500] **4376**

ROTOR (ALEXANDRIA, VA.) (US/0897-831X). [17,000] **34**

ROTOR & WING INTERNATIONAL (US/0191-6408). [40,000] **34**

ROTORCRAFT (CLINTON, LA.) (US/1041-2735). [4,500] **34**

ROUGH NOTES (INDIANAPOLIS) (US/0035-8525). **2893**

ROUGHNECK, THE (CN/0048-864X). **4277**

ROUND BOBBIN (US/1076-058X). [4,000] **5185**

ROUND ROCK LEADER (US/0164-9124). [5,950] **5754**

ROUND UP (UNIVERSITY PARK, N.M.) (US/0744-5555). [10,000] **5713**

ROUNDUP (MINNEAPOLIS, MINN.), THE (US/0485-5140). [3,000] **1314**

ROUSSILLON AGRICOLE (FR/0298-119X). [400] **131**

ROYAL AIR FORCE COLLEGE JOURNAL, THE (UK/0035-8606). [1800] **1094**

ROYAL AIR FORCE YEARBOOK (UK/0954-092X). [96,500] **34**

ROYAL COLLEGE OF MUSIC MAGAZINE (UK). [2,500] **4151**

ROYAL ENGINEERS JOURNAL, THE (UK/0035-8878). [3,500] **1995**

ROYAL GAZETTE (CN). [600] **3045**

ROYAL GAZETTE. PRINCE EDWARD ISLAND (CN/0035-8908). [1,000] **2544**

ROYAL LIFE SAVING SOCIETY LIFESAVER UK, THE (UK). [8,000] **4800**

ROYAL MILITARY POLICE JOURNAL (UK). **3183**

ROYAL SERVICE (US/0035-9084). [310,000] **5067**

RRT (CN/0831-2478). [2,500] **3952**

RS. CUADERNOS DE REALIDADES SOCIALES (SP/0302-7724). [1,500] **5256**

RS/MAGAZINE (BROOKLINE, MASS.) (US/1061-0030). [40,000] **1202**

RSA CALLING (SA). [200,000] **2643**

RSSI. RECHERCHES SEMIOTIQUES. SEMIOTIC INQUIRY (CN/0229-8651). [500] **3318**

RTTY JOURNAL (US/0033-7161). [2,000] **1163**

RTW REVIEW (US/0887-3003). [5,000] **1087**

RUBBER INDIA (II/0035-9491). [1,250] **5077**

RUBBER NEWS (II/0035-9513). [1,500] **5077**

RUBBERSTAMPMADNESS (US/0746-7672). [13,000] **2777**

RUIMTE VOOR CULTUUR (BE). **2853**

RULES OF GOLF AS APPROVED BY THE UNITED STATES GOLF ASSOCIATION AND THE ROYAL AND ANCIENT GOLF CLUB OF ST. ANDREWS, SCOTLAND, THE (US). [800,000] **4916**

RULES OF STANDARDBRED RACING (CN/0708-5125). [12,000] **2802**

RUNDT'S WORLD BUSINESS INTELLIGENCE (US). **1519**

RUNNER (EDMONTON) (CN/0707-3186). **1858**

RUNNING RESEARCH NEWS (US/0887-7033). [3,500] **4916**

RUNZHEIMER ON CARS & LIVING COSTS (US/0730-8647). **1299**

RUNZHEIMER REPORTS ON TRANSPORTATION (US/0730-8655). **5392**

RURAL AFRICANA (US/0085-5839). [200] **1582**

RURAL BUILDER (US/0888-3025). [25,000] **627**

RURAL BUSINESS MAGAZINE (AT/1031-3079). [4,000] **131**

RURAL — Controlled Circulation Index

RURAL COUNCILLOR, THE (CN/0036-0007). [3,250] **131**

RURAL EDUCATION NEWS (RURAL EDUCATION ASSOCIATION : 1980) (US). [900] **1781**

RURAL EDUCATOR (FORT COLLINS), THE (US/0273-446X). [1,000] **1781**

RURAL GLEANINGS (CN/0700-3897). **4994**

RURAL LIBRARIES (US/0276-2048). [350] **3247**

RURAL MONTANA (US/0199-6401). [68,000] **131**

RURAL ROUTE (WALLACEBURG, ONT.) (CN/0715-5271). **5794**

RURAL SOCIOLOGIST, THE (US/0279-5957). [1,000] **5257**

RURAL SOCIOLOGY (US/0036-0112). [2,500] **5257**

RURAL SPECIAL EDUCATION QUARTERLY (US/8756-8705). [400] **1885**

RUSH COUNTY NEWS (LA CROSSE, KAN.) (US). [2,300] **5678**

RUSHLIGHT (VERNON), THE (US/0148-3501). [600] **2080**

RUSISTIKA : THE RUSSIAN JOURNAL OF THE ASSOCIATION FOR LANGUAGE LEARNING (UK/0957-1760). [650] **3318**

RUSSELL REGISTER, THE (US). [200] **2471**

RUSSELL'S OFFICIAL NATIONAL MOTOR COACH GUIDE (US/0036-0171). [9,000] **5392**

RUSSIAN HISTORY (PITTSBURGH) (US/0094-288X). [500] **2707**

RUSSIAN ORTHODOX JOURNAL, THE (US/0036-0317). [3,500] **5040**

RUSSISTIK (GW/0935-8072). [600] **3318**

RUSSKAIA ZHIZN (US). [1,200] **5639**

RUSTUNGSBESCHRANKUNG UND SICHERHEIT (GW/0080-4800). [3,000] **4056**

RUTGERS LAW JOURNAL (US/0277-318X). [1,200] **3045**

RUTGERS LAW REVIEW (US/0036-0465). [1,000] **3045**

RUTLAND HISTORICAL SOCIETY QUARTERLY (US/0748-2493). [450] **2759**

RUTLAND RECORD (UK/0260-3322). [1,000] **2708**

RV TRADE DIGEST (CHICAGO, ILL. 1981) (US/0745-0389). [14,000] **5392**

RWDSU RECORD (US/0033-7196). [200,000] **1709**

RX ET CETERA (US/0744-7736). **4328**

RYUKYU DAIGAKU RIGAKUBU KIYO (JA/0286-9640). [350] **1456**

S.A.A.D. DIGEST (UK/0049-1160). [2,500] **1335**

S.A.M. ADVANCED MANAGEMENT JOURNAL (1984) (US/0749-7075). [12,000] **885**

S.A.M.P.E. QUARTERLY (US/0036-0821). **1995**

S & B REPORT (US). **2903**

S & L MUSEUM NEWSLETTER (CN/0715-5034). [350] **4096**

S.C.A.N. : SIMCOE COUNTY ANCESTORS' NEWS (CN/0823-9533). [450] **2471**

S. KLEIN NEWSLETTER ON COMPUTER GRAPHICS, THE (US/0731-9207). **1235**

S/N. SPEECHWRITER'S NEWSLETTER (US/0272-8079). [2,000] **1121**

SA JOURNAL OF FOOD SCIENCE AND NUTRITION, THE (SA/1013-3666). [2,500] **4199**

SA POLICE (AT). **3176**

SAA NEWSLETTER (US/0091-5971). [4,500] **2483**

SAAGVERKEN (SW). [3,880] **2404**

SAARLANDISCHE KREBSDOKUMENTATION (GW). **3823**

SABBATH RECORDER, THE (US/0036-214X). [4,600] **5067**

SABBATH WATCHMAN, THE (US/0098-9517). [500] **5067**

SABER LEER (SP/0213-6449). [5,000] **3352**

SABINE INDEX (MANY, LA. : 1879) (US/0739-0017). [6,000] **5684**

SABORD, LE (CN/0822-2908). [1,800] **330**

SABRETACHE (AT/0486-8013). [400] **4056**

SAC NEWS MONTHLY (US). [3,000] **5684**

SACHGUETERERZEUGUNG SCHNELLBERICHT (AU). [130] **3487**

SACRAMENTO NEWS & REVIEW (US/1065-3287). [90,000] **2544**

SACRAMENTO NEWSLETTER, THE (US/0486-8161). [2,000] **3045**

SACRAMENTO OBSERVER, THE (US/0036-2212). [49,600] **5639**

SACRED ART JOURNAL (US/0741-9163). [500] **364**

SADA AL-USBU (BA). [25,000] **2508**

SADDLE AND BRIDLE (US/0036-2271). [6,000] **2802**

SADDLE HORSE REPORT (US/0161-7842). [4,500] **2802**

SAE MAUL YONGU (CHONNAM TAEHAKKYO. SAE MAUL YONGUSO) (KO). [500] **5257**

SAE, SAMMLUNG ARBEITSRECHTLICHER ENTSCHEIDUNGEN (GW). [2,000] **3154**

SAENGHWAL CHIDO YONGU (KO). **1870**

SAFARI (TUCSON, ARIZ.) (US/0199-5316). [18,000] **4916**

SAFE JOURNAL (US/0191-6319). [1,000] **34**

SAFETY AND HEALTH AT WORK : ILO-CIS BULLETIN (SZ/1010-7053). [1,500] **2872**

SAFETY MANAGEMENT (SA/0377-8592). [26,000] **2869**

SAFETY MANAGEMENT LONDON (UK). [23,734] **4801**

SAFETY MANUAL / HELICOPTER ASSOCIATION INTERNATIONAL (US/0882-858X). [15,000] **34**

SAFETY UPDATE (CN/0704-4739). **4801**

SAGA-BOOK (UK/0305-9219). [650] **3432**

SAGA DAIGAKU RIKOGAKUBU SHUHO (JA/0385-6186). [365] **1995**

SAGAMIEN (CN/0226-2169). [250] **2575**

SAGGI NEUROPSICOLOGIA INFANTILE PSICOPEDAGOGIA RIABILITAZIONE (IT/0390-5179). [1,000] **4617**

SAGUAROLAND BULLETIN (US/0275-6919). [3,000] **527**

SAHITYA SANKETA (II). [1,000] **3433**

SAHOVSKI GLASNIK (CI). [5,500] **4865**

SAIKO TO HOAN (JA/0370-8217). [1,500] **2870**

SAILBOARD EXTRA (AT/0817-2773). **4916**

SAILING (US/0036-2719). [28,000] **596**

SAINNYAG HAGHOI JI (SENUR) (KO/0253-3073). [600] **4329**

SAINT LOUIS UNIVERSITY LAW JOURNAL (US/0036-3030). **3045**

SAINT PAUL LEGAL LEDGER (US). [600 (mornings)] **5698**

SAIPA (SA/0036-0767). [2,300] **4684**

SAKSHARATA SANDESA (II). [2,000] **5257**

SALAR (CN/0827-3472). [5,000] **2312**

SALARIES AND SALARY SCALES OF FULL-TIME TEACHING STAFF AT CANADIAN UNIVERSITIES (SUPPLEMENT TO PRELIMINARY ED.) (CN/0225-3704). [450] **1846**

SALARY & BENEFITS SURVEY (US/0196-867X). **1709**

SALES AND LEASING MONITOR (AT). **708**

SALES MOTIVATION (SANTA MONICA, CALIF.) (US/0892-8193). [30,000] **709**

SALESIANUM (IT/0036-3502). [750] **5036**

SALESMAN'S GUIDE NATIONWIDE DIRECTORY: MAJOR MASS MARKET MERCHANDISERS (EXCLUSIVE OF NEW YORK METROPOLITAN AREA), THE (US). [5,000] **709**

SALLY ANN (CN/0838-7397). [11,000] **4995**

SALMON AND TROUT MAGAZINE, THE (UK/0036-3545). [11,000] **2312**

SALON DU LIVRE DE MONTREAL (CN/0822-5443). [15,000] **4832**

SALT (CHICAGO, ILL.) (US/0883-2587). [8,479] **4995**

SALT (EDMONTON) (CN/0709-616X). **4995**

SALT LAKE TRIBUNE (SALT LAKE CITY, UTAH : 1890) (US/0746-3502). [111,730 141,422 (Sunday)] **5757**

SALUD RURAL. T.S.R (SP). [19,000] **3638**

SALUD Y TRABAJO (MADRID) (SP/0210-6612). [4,500] **2870**

SALUDOS HISPANOS (US/0898-4875). [600,000] **2492**

SAM NAGAGAMA'S ECONOMIC PERSPECTIVES (US/1071-0450). **1519**

SAMBODHI (II). **4360**

SAMFERDSEL (1979) (NO/0332-8988). [2,800] **5392**

SAMMAMISH VALLEY NEWS (US). [18,000] **5762**

SAMMLUNG DER EIDGENOSSISCHEN GESETZE (SZ). **3045**

SAMMLUNG METZLER (GW/0558-3667). **3433**

SAMSAM (NE). [510,000] **2912**

SAN DIEGO BUSINESS JOURNAL (US/8750-6890). [23,500] **709**

SAN DIEGO EXECUTIVE (US/1067-6384). [19,000] **709**

SAN DIEGO HOME / GARDEN (US). [34,104] **2792**

SAN DIEGO LAW REVIEW, THE (US/0036-4037). [1,000] **3046**

SAN DIEGO PHYSICIAN (US). [3,500] **3638**

SAN DIEGO SOURCE BOOK (US/0196-8564). [500] **5236**

SAN DIEGO UNION (SAN DIEGO, CALIF. : 1930) (US). [271,270 daily 439,860 Sunday] **5639**

SAN DIEGO WRITERS MONTHLY (US/1054-6774). [2,000] **2924**

SAN FRANCISCO BAY GUARDIAN, THE (US/0036-4096). [135,000] **2545**

SAN FRANCISCO POST (US). [18,289] **5639**

SAN FRANCISCO PROGRESS, THE (US/0191-8192). [626,828] **5639**

SAN FRANCISCO WHOLESALE ORNAMENTAL CROPS REPORT (US/0273-6004). [100] **2430**

SAN JUAN RECORD (1953), THE (US/0894-3273). [2,400] **5757**

SAN JUAN STAR, THE (PR/8750-6122). [36,027 daily 38,687 Sunday] **5808**

SAN MARCOS COURIER (US/0273-9259). [11,100] **5640**

SANDGROUSE (UK/0260-4736). [1,000] **5620**

SANDLAPPER (1990) (US/1046-3267). [14,000] **2628**

SANDPOINT DAILY BEE (US). [6,000] **5657**

SANDRA : TOLLE STRICKMODE (GW). [560,000] **5185**

SANDS AND CORAL (PH). [800] **3433**

SANDY PARKER'S FUR WORLD (US/0747-3753). [3,000] **3185**

SANFORD EVANS GOLD BOOK OF USED CAR PRICES (CN/0381-8179). **5425**

SANGYO IGAKU SOGO KENKYUJO NEMPO (JA). [400] **2870**

SANGYO SHARYO (JA). [1,000] **5392**

SANITAR UND HEIZUNGSTECHNIK (GW/0036-4401). [23,000] **2608**

SANITARY ENGINEERING PAPERS (US/0069-6129). [50] **2242**

SANITARY MAINTENANCE (US/0036-4436). [15,000] **2242**

SANTA BARBARA MUSEUM OF ART NEWSLETTER (US). [5,000] **4096**

SANTA BARBARA SENIOR WORLD, THE (US/0276-0800). [45,000] **5181**

SANTA CLARA COUNTY CONNECTIONS (US/0895-6103). **2471**

SANTA CLARA LAW REVIEW (US/0146-0315). [20,000] **3046**

SANTA FE REPORTER, THE (US/0744-477X). [25,000] **5713**

SANTA FE ROUTE, THE (US/0738-9892). [800] **5436**

SANTA GERTRUDIS JOURNAL, THE (US/0036-455X). [5,000] **221**

SANTA MONICA REVIEW : SMR (US/0899-9848). [1,400] **3433**

SANTE DE L'ECOLIER (FR). **4617**

SANTE MENTALE AU QUEBEC (CN/0383-6320). [1,100] **3936**

SANTO, IL (IT/0391-7819). [500] **4995**

SAO PAULO YEAR BOOK (BL). [3,000] **850**

SAPERE (IT/0036-4681). **5149**

SARANCE (EC). [1,000] **2759**

SARASOTA MAGAZINE (US/1048-2245). [15,000] **2545**

SARATOGA NEWS (US/0745-6255). [8,405] **5640**

SARJANA : JURNAL FAKULTI SASTERA DAN SAINS SOSIAL, UNIVERSITI MALAYA (MY). **2663**

SAS COMMUNICATIONS (US/0270-9422). [80,000] **1121**

SASK. REPORT (CN/0820-5043). [15,000] **2545**

SASKATCHEWAN ARCHAEOLOGY (CN/0227-5872). [600] **1781**

SASKATCHEWAN ASSOCIATION OF SOCIAL WORKERS NEWSLETTER (CN). [750] **5306**

SASKATCHEWAN BULLETIN, THE (CN/0036-4886). [22,000] **1781**

SASKATCHEWAN HISTORY (CN/0036-4908). [700] **2759**

SASKATCHEWAN LAW REVIEW (CN/0036-4916). [1,800] **3046**

SASKATCHEWAN MULTICULTURAL MAGAZINE (CN/0714-9050). [3,000] **2272**

SASKATCHEWAN PROVINCIAL HIGHWAYS ACCIDENT STATISTICS (CN/0318-2819). [4,000] **5402**

SASKATCHEWAN PULSE CROP DEVELOPMENT BOARD NEWSLETTER (CN). [6,500] **132**

SASKATCHEWAN TRADE DIRECTORY (1986) (CN/0831-9057). [10,500] **3487**

SASKATCHEWAN VETERINARY MEDICAL ASSOCIATION NEWSLETTER (CN/0711-2467). [450] **5521**

SASKATOON BUSINESS DIRECTORY (CN/0714-8607). **709**

SATELLITE BUSINESS NEWS (US/1043-0865). [9,000] **1121**

SATELLITE RETAILER (US/0890-1252). [12,000] **957**

SAUDI ECONOMIC SURVEY (SU). [5,000] **1583**

SAUDI MEDICAL JOURNAL (SU/0379-5284). [24,000] **3638**

SAUGETIERKUNDLICHE MITTEILUNGEN (GW/0036-2344). [400] **472**

SAUVEGARDE DES CHANTIERS (FR/0036-505X). [18,400] **627**

SAVING AND PRESERVING ARTS AND CULTURAL ENVIRONMENTS (US/0748-8378). [1,500] **330**

SAVINGS AND DEVELOPMENT (IT). [2,500] **1519**

SAVVY SHOPPER, THE (US/1057-3275). [1,400] **5490**

SAWTRI SPECIAL PUBLICATION (SA/0258-4565). [230] **5355**

SBORNIK PRACI (CS). [300] **2576**

SCALA (GW/0303-4232). **2522**

SCALA INTERNATIONAL (GW/0581-9385). [13,000] **2522**

SCALE AUTO ENTHUSIAST (US). [64,000] **2777**

SCAN (NORTH SYDNEY) (AT/0726-4127). [2,000] **1904**

SCANDINAVIAN DAIRY INFORMATION (SW/1101-2706). **198**

SCANDINAVIAN DAIRY INFORMATION - SDI (SW/1101-2706). **198**

SCANDINAVIAN ECONOMIC HISTORY REVIEW, THE (SW/0358-5522). [700] **1583**

SCANDINAVIAN FOREST ECONOMICS (FI/0355-032X). [200] **2394**

SCANDINAVIAN JOURNAL OF DENTAL RESEARCH (DK/0029-845X). [1,450] **1335**

SCANDINAVIAN JOURNAL OF EDUCATIONAL RESEARCH (UK/0031-3831). [550] **1781**

SCANDINAVIAN JOURNAL OF GASTROENTEROLOGY (NO/0036-5521). [1,800] **3747**

SCANDINAVIAN JOURNAL OF PSYCHOLOGY (SW/0036-5564). [550] **4617**

SCANDINAVIAN JOURNAL OF RHEUMATOLOGY (SW/0300-9742). [1,500] **3807**

SCANDINAVIAN JOURNAL OF WORK, ENVIRONMENT & HEALTH (FI/0355-3140). [1,500] **2870**

SCANDINAVIAN PSYCHOANALYTIC REVIEW, THE (NO/0106-2301). [550] **4617**

SCANDINAVIAN PUBLIC LIBRARY QUARTERLY (DK/0036-5602). [1,000] **3247**

SCANFAX (US/0018-9227). [6,000] **2080**

SCANNING (US/0161-0457). [3,000] **574**

SCAPE (LOS ANGELES, CALIF.) (US/1049-7455). **2492**

SCARBORO CONSUMER (CN/0225-2074). **5794**

SCARBOROUGH HISTORICAL NOTES & COMMENTS (CN/0712-4961). [300] **2759**

SCENE ENTERTAINMENT WEEKLY (US/1064-6116). **330**

SCENIC TRIPS TO THE GEOLOGIC PAST (US/0548-5983). **1396**

SCHARTZER-SCHERTZER CONNECTION, THE (US/0882-5890). [325] **2471**

SCHERZO (US/1048-2180). [500] **4152**

SCHIFF & HAFEN/SEEWIRTSCHAFT (GW/0938-1643). [6000] **5455**

SCHNEIDER CONNECTIONS (US/0882-5904). [700] **2471**

SCHOHARIE COUNTY HISTORICAL REVIEW (US/0361-8528). [1,500] **2759**

SCHOLARLY PUBLISHING (CN/0036-634X). [2,200] **4819**

SCHOLASTIC CHOICES (US/0883-475X). [750,000] **2792**

SCHOLASTIC COACH (US/0036-6382). [37,000] **4917**

SCHOLASTIC COACH AND ATHLETIC DIRECTOR (US/1077-5625). [37,000] **4917**

SCHOOL AND COMMUNITY (COLUMBIA) (US/0036-6447). [33,000] **1782**

SCHOOL ARTS (US/0036-6463). [23,000] **364**

SCHOOL BUS FLEET (US/0036-6501). [17,500] **5392**

SCHOOL DISTRICT PROFILES (US). [3,500] **1871**

SCHOOL LAW BULLETIN (CHAPEL HILL, N.C.) (US/0886-2508). [1,225] **1871**

SCHOOL LAW REPORTER (US/1059-4094). [2,500] **3046**

SCHOOL LIBRARIAN, THE (UK/0036-6595). [4,500] **3247**

SCHOOL LIBRARIAN'S WORKSHOP, THE (US/0271-3667). [7,500] **3247**

SCHOOL LIBRARIES IN CANADA (CN/0227-3780). [900] **3248**

SCHOOL LIBRARY MEDIA QUARTERLY (US/0278-4823). [7,500] **3248**

SCHOOL MUSIC NEWS, THE (US/0036-6668). [50,000] **4152**

SCHOOL PSYCHOLOGY REVIEW (US/0279-6015). [15,000] **4618**

SCHOOL SAFETY : NATIONAL SCHOOL SAFETY CENTER NEWSJOURNAL (US). [55,000] **1782**

SCHOOL SCIENCE AND MATHEMATICS (US/0036-6803). [3,900] **5149**

SCHOOL SCIENCE REVIEW (UK/0036-6811). [19,500] **5149**

SCHOOL SOCIAL WORK JOURNAL (US/0161-5653). [1,400] **1871**

SCHOOLS & STAFFING (AT). [5,500] **1782**

SCHOOLS AND THE COURTS, THE (US/0164-3851). [700] **1872**

SCHOOLS (OLYMPIA, WASH.) (US). [500] **1847**

SCHUMPERT MEDICAL QUARTERLY (US/0731-5406). [7,000] **3639**

SCHUTZ SOCIETY REPORTS : NEWSLETTER OF THE AMERICAN HEINRICH SCHUTZ SOCIETY (US). [120] **4152**

SCHWEISSEN UND SCHNEIDEN (GW/0036-7184). [10,000] **4027**

SCHWEIZER INGENIEUR UND ARCHITEKT (SZ/0251-0960). [10,500] **1995**

SCHWEIZER MONATSSCHRIFT FUER ZAHNMEDIZIN (SZ/1011-4203). [4,000] **1335**

SCHWEIZER MUSIK AUF SCHALLPLATTEN. MUSIQUE SUISSE SUR DISQUES. SWISS MUSIC ON RECORDS (SZ). [2,500] **4152**

SCHWEIZER OPTIKER. L'OPTICIEN SUISSE. L'OTTICO SVIZZERO, DER (SZ). **4217**

SCHWEIZERISCHE MEDIZINISCHE WOCHENSCHRIFT (SZ/0036-7672). [5,300] **3639**

SCHWEIZERISCHE MINERALOGISCHE UND PETROGRAPHISCHE MITTEILUNGEN (SZ/0036-7699). **1444**

SCHWEIZERISCHE RUNDSCHAU FUER MEDIZIN PRAXIS (SZ/1013-2058). [4,500] **3801**

SCHWEIZERISCHE ZEITSCHRIFT FUER GESCHICHTE (SZ/0036-7834). [1,600] **2708**

SCHWEIZERISCHE ZEITSCHRIFT FUER SPORTMEDIZIN (SZ/0036-7885). **3955**

SCHWEIZERISCHES IDIOTIKON. WORTERBUCH DER SCHWEIZERDEUTSCHEN SPRACHE (SZ). [1,000] **3319**

SCHWENKFELDIAN, THE (US/0036-8032). [1,750] **5067**

SCIENCE AND INDUSTRY (NE/0925-5842). **5150**

SCIENCE ET COMPORTEMENT (CN/0841-7741). [400] **4618**

SCIENCE ET VIE (FR/0036-8369). [356,687] **5151**

SCIENCE-FICTION STUDIES (CN/0091-7729). [1,050] **3434**

SCIENCE LINK (CN/0821-7246). [350] **2924**

SCIENCE NEWS (WASHINGTON) (US/0036-8423). [196,073] **5152**

SCIENCE OF COMPUTER PROGRAMMING (NE/0167-6423). **1281**

SCIENCE OF MIND (US/0036-8458). [100,000] **4360**

SCIENCE POLICY DIGEST (SA). **5152**

SCIENCE SCOPE (WASHINGTON, D.C.) (US/0887-2376). [12,000] **5153**

SCIENCE TEACHER (WASHINGTON, D.C.), THE (US/0036-8555). [27,000] **5153**

SCIENCE, TECHNOLOGY & SOCIETY (US/0275-8075). [650] **5153**

SCIENCE TODAY (UK). [48,000] **5153**

SCIENCE TRENDS (US/0043-0749). **5153**

SCIENCES DES ALIMENTS (FR/0240-8813). [1,000] **2356**

SCIENCES ET TECHNIQUES DE L'EAU (CN). [4,000] **1418**

SCIENCES (NEW YORK), THE (US/0036-861X). [75,000] **5154**

SCIENTIA PAEDAGOGICA EXPERIMENTALIS (BE/0582-2351). [500] **1783**

SCIENTIA PHARMACEUTICA (AU/0036-8709). [600] **4329**

SCIENTIFIC AND TECHNICAL SURVEYS - BRITISH FOOD MANUFACTURING INDUSTRIES RESEARCH ASSOCIATION (UK/0144-2074). **2357**

SCIENTIFIC COUNCIL REPORTS (CN/0250-6416). [500] **2312**

SCIENTIFIC HONEYWELLER (US/0196-8440). [18,000] **5155**

SCIENTIFIC INFORMATION BULLETIN (US/1048-5678). [7,000] **5155**

SCIENTIFIC INTEGRITY (US). **472**

SCIENTIFIC PAPERS OF THE COLLEGE OF ARTS AND SCIENCES, THE UNIVERSITY OF TOKYO (JA/0289-7520). **5155**

SCIENTIFIC REPORT - MCGILL UNIVERSITY, STORMY WEATHER GROUP (CN/0076-180X). [150] **1434**

SCIENTIFIC WORLD (UK/0036-8857). **5156**

SCIENTIST (PHILADELPHIA, PA.), THE (US/0890-3670). [50,000] **5156**

SCITECH BOOK NEWS (US/0196-6006). [5,400] **5156**

SCOOP (CN). **2835**

SCOPUS (IS). [20,000] **1095**

SCORE (TORONTO) (CN/0711-3226). [140,000] **4917**

SCOT LIT (UK). [3,000] **3434**

SCOTS LAW TIMES; THE LANDS TRIBUNAL FOR SCOTLAND REPORTS, THE (UK/0036-908X). [2,000] **3047**

SCOTT COUNTY IOWAN (US/1046-1027). [175] **2760**

SCOTTISH-AMERICAN GENEALOGIST (US/0271-5031). [550] **2471**

SCOTTISH BANNER, THE (CN/0707-073X). [19,000] **2272**

SCOTTISH BEEKEEPER (UK/0370-8918). [1,500] **132**

SCOTTISH BUILDING AND CIVIL ENGINEERING YEAR BOOK (UK/0085-6002). [3,000] **627**

SCOTTISH BUSINESS INSIDER (UK/0952-1488). [19,135] **709**

SCOTTISH GENEALOGIST, THE (UK/0300-337X). [1,500] **2472**

SCOTTISH GEOGRAPHICAL MAGAZINE (UK/0036-9225). [3,000] **2576**

SCOTTISH HISTORY SOCIETY (SERIES) (UK). [800] **2709**

SCOTTISH JOURNAL OF GEOLOGY (UK/0036-9276). [1,300] **1396**

SCOTTISH JOURNAL OF THEOLOGY (UK/0036-9306). [1,200] **4995**

SCOTTISH LANGUAGE (UK/0264-0198). [850] **3319**

SCOTTISH LAW GAZETTE, THE (UK/0036-9314). [2,300] **3047**

SCOTTISH LIBRARIES (1987) (UK/0950-0189). [2,500] **3248**

SCOTTISH LITERARY JOURNAL (UK/0305-0785). [850] **3434**

SCOTTISH LITERARY JOURNAL. THE YEAR'S WORK IN SCOTTISH LITERARY AND LINGUISTIC STUDIES (UK). [800] **3319**

SCOTTISH PHOTOGRAPHY BULLETIN (UK/0269-1787). [200] **4376**

SCOTTISH STUDIES (EDINBURGH) (UK/0036-9411). [750] **3434**

SCOTTSDALE MAGAZINE (US). [40,000] **2545**

SCOUT-JEUNESSE (CN/0383-0853). **4878**

SCP NEWSLETTER (US/0883-1319). **4996**

SCRATCHING   Controlled Circulation Index

SCRATCHING RIVER POST, THE (CN/0707-2333). [9,400] **5794**

SCREAMING EAGLE, THE (US). [5,400] **4056**

SCREEN ACTOR HOLLYWOOD (US/0890-5266). [75,000] **4077**

SCREEN (CHICAGO, ILL.) (US/1070-7573). [15,000] **4077**

SCRIBE (VANCOUVER) (CN/0824-6947). [250] **2760**

SCRIBLERIAN AND THE KIT-CATS, THE (US/0190-731X). [1,200] **2854**

SCRIP (RICHMOND) (UK/0143-7690). [60,000] **4329**

SCRIPTA GEOLOGICA (NE/0375-7587). [700] **1360**

SCRIPTA THEOLOGICA (SP/0036-9764). [1,000] **4996**

SCRIPTURA (SA/0254-1807). [250-300] **5019**

SCRIPTURE COMES ALIVE (US/0747-0207). [varies] **5019**

SCRIPTWRITERS MARKET (US/0748-6456). [10,000] **4077**

SCRIVENER (CN/0227-5090). [800] **3435**

SCROGGINS NATIONAL LAW ENFORCEMENT DIRECTORY (US/0882-1909). [10,000] **3176**

SCROLL (MALVERNE, N.Y.) (US/0890-524X). **1292**

SCRUTINY (SASKATOON, SASK.) (CN/0838-4525). [300] **1783**

SCUOLA CATTOLICA, LA (IT/0036-9810). [1,000] **5036**

SEA HERITAGE NEWS (US/0270-5524). [50,000] **2545**

SEA HISTORY GAZETTE (US/0896-1646). **5455**

SEA PEN (CN/0700-9275). [19,000] **557**

SEA POWER (1971) (US/0199-1337). [70,000] **4183**

SEA REPORTER (US/0193-1644). **1872**

SEA TECHNOLOGY (US/0093-3651). [20,150] **1456**

SEA TECHNOLOGY. BUYERS GUIDE, DIRECTORY (US). [10,000] **1456**

SEACOAST LIFE (US/0885-6435). [20,000] **2545**

SEAFOOD AUSTRALIA (AT/1320-9663). [3,600] **2357**

SEAFOOD BUSINESS (CAMDEN, ME.) (US/0889-3217). [15,500] **2357**

SEAFOOD LEADER (US/0744-4664). [16,000] **2313**

SEAISI DIRECTORY (MY). [1,200] **4019**

SEAISI QUARTERLY (SI/0129-5721). [1,300] **4019**

SEAPORT (US/0743-6246). [5,000] **2760**

SEAPORTS AND THE SHIPPING WORLD (CN/0037-0150). [3,000] **5455**

SEAPORTS AND THE SHIPPING WORLD. SPRING ISSUE (CN). [3,000] **5455**

SEAPOSTER (US). [300] **2787**

SEARCH AND RESCUE MAGAZINE (US/0092-5136). **4802**

SEARCH MAGAZINE (AMHERST) (US/0037-0290). [1,500] **35**

SEARCH (MIAMI), THE (US/0272-5827). [1,000] **2664**

SEARCH (NASHVILLE) (US/0048-9913). [11,500] **5067**

SEARCH (NILES, ILL.) (US/0277-5727). [400] **2472**

SEARCH YORK (UK/0958-3467). [7,000] **5307**

SEATTLE HOME AND GARDEN (US). [31,000] **2431**

SEATTLE REVIEW, THE (US/0147-6629). [750] **3435**

SEATTLE TRAFFIC ACCIDENT SUMMARY (US). [400] **5444**

SEAWAY MARITIME DIRECTORY (US/0582-3668). [8,000] **5456**

SEAWAY REVIEW (US/0037-0487). [8,000] **5456**

SEBREE BANNER, THE (US). [3,500] **5682**

SEC REPORT (US/0885-9078). [20,000] **4917**

SECHZIG - NA UND ? (GW). [55,000] **5181**

SECOLAS ANNALS (US/0081-2951). [550] **2760**

SECOND BOAT, THE (US/0274-6441). [3,000] **2472**

SECOND CIRCUIT DIGEST (US/0746-5254). **3047**

SECOND OPINION (SAN FRANCISCO, CALIF.) (US/0748-9528). [1,500] **4802**

SECOND STONE, THE (US/1047-3971). **2796**

SECRET PARIS (FR/1163-2747). **710**

SECRETARY, THE (US/0037-0622). [45,000] **710**

SECURITAIRE (CN/0822-7853). [12,000] **4917**

SECURITE, ENVIRONEMENT (SZ/1015-6356). [10,000] **2870**

SECURITY AFFAIRS (US/0889-4876). [15,000] **4535**

SECURITY MANAGEMENT (ARLINGTON, VA.) (US/0145-9406). [30,000] **885**

SEDONA RED ROCK NEWS (US/1044-7555). [7,200] **5630**

SEE THE MUSIC (CN/0826-5216). [15,000] **4152**

SEED RESEARCH (II/0379-5594). [700] **186**

SEED SCIENCE AND TECHNOLOGY (NE/0251-0952). [1,200] **186**

SEED WORLD (US/0037-0797). [7,400] **186**

SEEDBED (US/0363-5074). [300] **4996**

SEEDS & SOWERS (CN/0843-5197). **1905**

SEEING EYE GUIDE (US/0037-0819). [25,000] **4393**

SEGURIDAD SOCIAL (MX/0379-0304). [500] **1710**

SEIDENKI GAKKAI SHI (JA/0386-2550). [2,000] **4445**

SEIJI HANDOBUKKU (JA). [40] **4495**

SEIKEI DAIGAKU IPPAN KENKYU HOKOKU (JA). [600] **1847**

SEISMOLOGIC SERIES (SA). [2,000] **1410**

SEISMOLOGICAL RESEARCH LETTERS (US/0895-0695). **1397**

SEKITAN KENKYU SHIRYO SOSHO (JA). [300] **2151**

SEKIYU GIJUTSU KYOKAISHI (JA/0370-9868). [2,500] **4278**

SEKKO TO SEKKAI (JA/0559-331X). **1029**

SEL & POIVRE (CN/0714-6116). [47,608] **5073**

SELBYANA (US/0361-185X). [250] **527**

SELECTED BIBLIOGRAPHIES ON AGEING (UK/0267-0348). [500] **3661**

SELECTED EDUCATIONAL STATISTICS (II). [600] **1797**

SELECTED ENERGY STATISTICS : SOUTH AFRICA (SA). [75] **1963**

SELECTED LIST OF ACQUISITIONS CATALOGED (US/0537-9342). [12,000] **3047**

SELECTED MONOGRAPHS ON TAXATION (NE). **4747**

SELECTED PAPERS FROM THE TRANSPORTATION SEMINAR SERIES (CN/0229-8627). **5392**

SELECTED PERINATAL STATISTICS (US). [300] **5338**

SELECTED REFERENCES - INDUSTRIAL RELATIONS SECTION, PRINCETON UNIVERSITY (US/0037-1351). **1538**

SELECTED REPORTS IN ETHNOMUSICOLOGY (US/0361-6622). [400-500] **4152**

SELECTED REVENUE DATA AND EQUALIZED MILLS FOR PENNSYLVANIA PUBLIC SCHOOLS (US). [1,200] **1872**

SELECTION DE FILMS POUR LA JEUNESSE (FR). [8,000] **1069**

SELECTION OF RECENT ACQUISITIONS - CANADIAN IMPERIAL BANK OF COMMERCE, INFORMATION CENTRE, A (CN/0383-2392). **1520**

SELEZIONE DAL READER'S DIGEST (IT/0037-1483). [800,000] **2522**

SELF ADHESIVE MATERIALS & MARKETS BULLETIN (UK). **4222**

SELF PUBLISHING UPDATE (US/0736-1882). [1,500] **710**

SELLING TO THE OTHER EDUCATIONAL MARKETS (US/1054-4593). [150] **936**

SEMAINE VETERINAIRE, LA (FR/0396-5015). [6,000] **5521**

SEMANA ECONOMICA (PE). **1520**

SEMANA ECONOMICA / APOYO (PE). **1583**

SEMANTIKOS (FR/0395-3556). **3320**

SEMENCE, LA (CN/0228-670X). [15,000] **5019**

SEMI-ANNUAL BOOKLIST (US/0883-9565). [2,800] **3470**

SEMI-ANNUAL REPORT OF THE INSPECTOR GENERAL, U.S. SMALL BUSINESS ADMINISTRATION (US/0742-3802). [500] **3103**

SEMICONDUCTOR CURRENTS (US). **2080**

SEMICONDUCTOR INTERNATIONAL (US/0163-3767). [35,927] **2080**

SEMICONDUCTOR PACKAGING UPDATE (US/0889-9193). **4222**

SEMICONDUCTOR WORLD (JA). [10,000] **2108**

SEMINAR (TORONTO) (CN/0037-1939). **3320**

SEMINARIUM (VC/0582-6314). [950] **5036**

SEMINARS IN HEARING (US/0734-0451). [1,500] **3891**

SEMINARS IN INTERVENTIONAL RADIOLOGY (US/0739-9529). [1,600] **3946**

SEMINARS IN LIVER DISEASE (US/0272-8087). [2,000] **3801**

SEMINARS IN NEUROLOGY (US/0271-8235). [1,800] **3846**

SEMINARS IN NUTRITION (US/0898-5995). [4,500] **4199**

SEMINARS IN REPRODUCTIVE ENDOCRINOLOGY (US/0734-8630). [1,200] **3733**

SEMINARS IN RESPIRATORY MEDICINE (US/0192-9755). [2,600] **3952**

SEMINARS IN SPEECH AND LANGUAGE (US/0734-0478). [1,400] **3320**

SEMINARS IN THROMBOSIS AND HEMOSTASIS (US/0094-6176). [1,500] **3774**

SEMINOLE OUTLOOK (US/8750-2070). [5,000] **5651**

SEMSCOPE, THE (US/0361-1310). [11,800] **4685**

SENCKENBERGIANA BIOLOGICA (GW/0037-2102). [750] **4172**

SENCKENBERGIANA LETHAEA (GW/0037-2110). [700] **4230**

SENCKENBERGIANA MARITIMA (GW/0080-889X). **1456**

SENIOR CITIZENS ADVOCATE AND ASPECTS OF AGING (US/0882-9403). [56,000] **5181**

SENIOR CITIZENS' CONSULTANTS OF ST. CATHARINES INC (CN/0714-5756). [2,600] **5181**

SENIOR CITIZENS TODAY (US/0049-0199). [7,000 - 10,000] **5181**

SENIOR NEWS (SA/0037-2234). [5000] **5181**

SENIOR SCENE (AT). [32,000] **5182**

SENIOR WORLD NEWSMAGAZINE (US). [550,000] **5182**

SENIOR WORLD QUARTERLY (CN/0714-8798). [30,000] **5182**

SENIORS TODAY (CN/0715-4046). [20,000] **5182**

SENPAKU KAIYO KOGAKU GIJUTSU BUNKEN SOKUHO (JA/0385-1176). [300] **4185**

SENPAKU SEIBI KODAN GYOMU YORAN (JA). [200] **5456**

SENSHOKU-TAI (JA/0385-4655). **551**

SENSORS (PETERSBOROUGH, N.H.) (US/0746-9462). [50,000] **1996**

SENTENCES (US/0732-8907). [250] **3176**

SENTENCIAS EN APELACION DE LAS AUDIENCIAS PROVINCIALES EN MATERIA CIVIL Y PENAL (SP). [3,000] **3048**

SENTIER CHASSE-PECHE (CN/0711-7957). [75,000] **4878**

SENTINEL (CHICAGO, ILL.) (US/0037-2331). [50,000] **5662**

SENTINEL (TORONTO. 1957) (CN/0049-0202). [8,000] **5067**

SENZA SORDINO (US). [6,000] **4152**

SEOUL JOURNAL OF ECONOMICS (KO). [250] **1520**

SEPARATION AND PURIFICATION METHODS (SOFTCOVER ED.) (US/0360-2540). **1029**

SEPARATION SCIENCE AND TECHNOLOGY (US/0149-6395). **1029**

SER-BULLETIN (NE/0920-4849). [2,500] **1710**

SERI STATISTIK PENGANGKUTAN KERETA API. RAILWAYS STATISTICS (IO/0445-9474). **5402**

SERIAL ARTICLES PUBLISHED IN NEWSPAPERS / STATE LIBRARY OF PENNSYLVANIA, LIBRARY SERVICES DIVISION, NEWSPAPER SECTION (US). **5739**

SERIAL HOLDINGS IN NEWFOUNDLAND LIBRARIES (CN/0709-0536). [130] **3249**

SERIALS LIST / ERINDALE COLLEGE LIBRARY (CN/0229-1681). [60] **424**

SERIDIM (IS). [700] **5052**

SERIE CIENTIFICA. INSTITUTO ANTARTICO CHILENO (CL/0073-9871). [370] **1360**

SERIE SEPARATAS / CENTRO DE ESTUDOS DE HISTORIA E CARTOGRAFIA ANTIGA (PO/0870-6735). [1,500] **2709**

SERIES IN PSYCHOSOCIAL EPIDEMIOLOGY (US/1044-5633). **3936**

SERTOMAN (US/0744-2807). [30,000] **5307**

SERVAMUS (SA). [54,200] **3176**

SERVANT, THE (CN/0705-6338). [10,000] **4996**

SERVICE BULLETIN (SAN JOSE, CALIF.) (US/0731-471X). [20,000] **5425**

SERVICE INDUSTRY NEWSLETTER (US/1048-3462). **710**

SERVICE REPORTER (US/0193-2128). [50,000] **2608**

SERVICE SOCIALE (QUEBEC) (CN/0037-2633). **5307**

SERVICE STATION MANAGEMENT (US/0488-3896). [85,000] **5425**

SERVICES MARKETING NEWSLETTER (US/0891-0952). [3,800] **886**

SERVICES (VIENNA, VA.) (US/0279-0548). [13,000] **4214**

SERVIZI SOCIALI (IT). **4685**

SESSIONS DE FORMATION... / COSE (CN/0712-7227). **886**

SETON HALL JOURNAL OF SPORT LAW (US/1059-4310). [350] **3048**

SETON HALL LEGISLATIVE JOURNAL (US/0361-8951). [1,200] **3048**

SEVARTHAM (II/0970-8324). **4996**

SEW IT SEAMS (US/0888-577X). [15,000] **5186**

SEWANEE REVIEW, THE (US/0037-3052). [3,560] **3352**

SEWICKLEY HERALD (1968), THE (US/1047-0697). [4,000] **5739**

SEWTRADE C F I YEARBOOK AND DIRECTORY (AT/1035-1272). **1087**

SEX EDUCATION COALITION NEWS (US/0741-9686). **1783**

SEZ (US/0190-3640). [2,000] **3435**

SGA NEWSLETTER (US). [275] **2483**

SGPB ALERT (US/8755-7282). [850] **1520**

SHAHID (TEHRAN, IRAN : 1983) (IR). [100,000] **2493**

SHAHID (TRIPOLI, LIBYA) (LY). [5,000] **2643**

SHAKHTNYI I KARERNYI TRANSPORT (RU). **2151**

SHALE SHAKER (US/0037-3257). [2,200] **1397**

SHALOM (UK). [7,000] **5052**

SHAMROCK TEXAN, THE (US). [1,900] **5754**

SHANTIH (US/0037-329X). [2,000] **3436**

SHAONIEN ZHONGGUO (SAN FRANCISCO, CALIF.) (US/0749-7679). [43,000] **5640**

SHARE THE WORD (US/0199-5049). [63,000] **5019**

SHARE (TORONTO) (CN/0709-4647). [30,000] **5794**

SHAREHOLDER REMEDIES IN CANADA (CN). [396] **3103**

SHAREWARE MAGAZINE (US/1042-0681). [100,000] **1202**

SHARING IDEAS (US/0886-1501). [4,000] **2545**

SHARING THE PRACTICE (US/0193-8274). [600] **4997**

SHEEP BREEDER AND SHEEPMAN MAGAZINE (US/0037-3400). [8,500] **221**

SHEEP CANADA MAGAZINE (CN/0702-8881). [1,500] **221**

SHEEP RETURNS (NZ). [450] **221**

SHEET MUSIC MAGAZINE. STANDARD PIANO/GUITAR (US/0273-6462). [200,000] **4153**

SHELBURNE HISTORICAL SOCIETY (NEWSLETTER) (CN/0822-4080). **2760**

SHELBY REPORT OF THE SOUTHEAST, THE (US/0194-1968). [22,000] **2357**

SHELBY REPORT OF THE SOUTHWEST (US/0192-916X). [19,000] **2357**

SHELDON'S MAJOR STORES AND CHAINS (US). [5,000] **957**

SHELDON'S RETAIL DIRECTORY OF THE UNITED STATES AND CANADA AND PHELON'S RESIDENT BUYERS AND MERCHANDISE BROKERS (US/0094-0453). [5,000] **957**

SHELLS AND SEA LIFE (US/0747-6078). [2,000] **5597**

SHELTIE PACESETTER (US/0744-6608). [3,500] **4288**

SHEM TOV (CN/0843-6924). [250] **2472**

SHENANDOAH (US/0037-3583). [1,700] **3436**

SHENANDOAH HERALD, SHENANDOAH VALLEY, THE (US/0746-6846). [6,300] **5759**

SHEPARD'S FLORIDA CITATIONS (US/0730-3718). **3050**

SHEPARD'S NEW JERSEY CITATIONS (US/0730-420X). **3052**

SHEPHERD EXPRESS (US/1071-5185). [45,000] **5770**

SHERIDAN PRESS (SHERIDAN, WYO.), THE (US/1074-682X). **5772**

SHERIFF'S STAR (TALLAHASSEE, FLA.), THE (US/0488-6186). [80,000] **3176**

SHERLOCK HOLMES JOURNAL, THE (UK/0037-3621). [1,500] **3436**

SHHH (US/0883-1688). [48,000] **4393**

SHHH NEWS (AT/1033-792X). [900] **4393**

SHIAWASSEE STEPPIN' STONES (US/0735-8016). [160] **2472**

SHIFTWORK MANAGERS NEWSLETTER (US). [20,000] **1710**

SHIGAKU KENKYU (HIROSHIMA. 1929) (JA/0386-9342). **2664**

SHIH CHIEH CHIH SHIH / SHIJIE ZHISHI (CC). [250,000] **4535**

SHINGLE, THE (US/0037-377X). [14,000] **3055**

SHINING LIGHT (US). [2,800] **4997**

SHINING STAR (CARTHAGE, ILL.) (US/0884-5514). [9,000] **1905**

SHINKU (JA/0559-8516). **4429**

SHIPPERS' TIMES (SI/0217-1139). **5456**

SHIPPING & MARINE INDUSTRIES JOURNAL (II/0970-0285). [15,000] **5456**

SHIPS MONTHLY (UK/0037-394X). [21,692] **4183**

SHIRIN (KYOTO. 1916) (JA/0386-9369). **2664**

SH'MA (PORT WASHINGTON, N.Y.) (US/0049-0385). [8,500] **4361**

SHO-BAN NEWS, THE (US/0197-7954). [2,400] **5657**

SHO ENERUGI (JA/0387-1819). [18,000] **1956**

SHOCK AND VIBRATION MONOGRAPH SERIES (US/0583-1032). [1,500] **2128**

SHOCK WAVES (GW/0938-1287). [400] **4429**

SHOFAR (WASHINGTON, D.C.), THE (US/0745-9327). [35,000] **5052**

SHOKURYO SEISAKU KENKYU (JA/0387-9836). [1,000] **2357**

SHONI GEKA (JA/0385-6313). [5,000] **3911**

SHOOTING INDUSTRY, THE (US/0037-4148). [23,000] **4917**

SHOOTING SPORTS RETAILER (US/0887-9397). [16,000] **957**

SHOOTING STAR REVIEW (US/0892-1407). [1,500] **3436**

SHOP (DON MILLS) (CN/0381-8667). [18,000] **2128**

SHOPPER & OBSERVER NEWS, THE (US). [25,000] **1299**

SHOPPING CENTERS TODAY (US/0885-9841). [26,000] **957**

SHORE AND BEACH (US/0037-4237). [1,000] **2205**

SHORT STORY (COLUMBIA, S.C.) (US/1052-648X). [100] **3436**

SHORTHORN COUNTRY (US/0149-9319). [4,950] **221**

SHORTHORN NEWS (CN/0037-427X). [1,800] **221**

SHORTHORN, THE (US/0892-6603). [15,000 Fall 12,000 Summer] **1095**

SHOW-ME LIBRARIES (US/0037-4326). [2,500] **3249**

SHOW MUSIC (US/8755-9560). [4,000] **4153**

SHOW STEER, THE (US/0195-2463). [8,000] **221**

SHOWCASE (MINNEAPOLIS) (US/0196-1586). [55,000] **4153**

SHOWCASE (NEW YORK) (US/0361-3232). [11,500] **3186**

SHUPIHUI (PE/0254-2021). [700] **2273**

SHUTTLE, SPINDLE & DYEPOT (US/0049-0423). [15,000] **375**

SIA ON THE HILL: A GRASSROOTS REPORT (US). **2975**

SIAM NEWS : A PUBLICATION OF SOCIETY FOR INDUSTRIAL AND APPLIED MATHEMATICS (US). [7,500] **3535**

SIBBALD GUIDE TO THE TEXAS TOP TWO-FIFTY, THE (US/0278-3266). [2,000] **710**

SIBLING INFORMATION NETWORK NEWSLETTER (US). **2286**

SIC (VE/0049-0431). [6,000] **4496**

SICHERHEITSBEAUFTRAGTER (GW/0300-3337). [34,000] **3176**

SICHERHEITSINGENIEUR (GW/0300-3329). [4,000] **2870**

SICILIA PARRA (US/8755-6987). [1,500] **2273**

SIDA RAPPORT (SW/0282-6011). [2,500] **2912**

SIDE STREETS OF THE WORLD (US/0741-7624). [200,000] **5491**

SIDIC (ENGLISH ED.) (IT). [1,600] **4997**

SIFRUT YELADIM VA-NOAR (IS/0334-276X). [1,000] **1069**

SIGE ENERGIE BULLETIN (NE). **1956**

SIGMA PHI EPSILON JOURNAL (US/0097-6563). [118,000] **1872**

SIGN BUSINESS (US/0893-9888). **710**

SIGN LANGUAGE STUDIES (US/0302-1475). [450] **3321**

SIGNAL (US). [500] **3436**

SIGNAL (LISBON, OHIO) (US/0893-4592). [14,000 (morning)] **5730**

SIGNAL (MONONA, WIS.) (US/8750-2208). **1783**

SIGNAL (RYCROFT) (CN/0712-1296). [2,750] **5794**

SIGNALMAN'S JOURNAL, THE (US/0037-5020). [15,000] **5436**

SIGNALNAYA INFORMATSIYA KATALIZ I KATALIZATORY (RU/0234-9736). [240] **1058**

SIGNALNAYA INFORMATSIYA KHIMIYA VYSOKIKH ENERGII (RU/0234-968X). [150] **992**

SIGNALNAYA INFORMATSIYA NAPOLNENNYE I ARMIROVANNYE PLASTIKI (RU/0234-971X). [385] **992**

SIGNALNAYA INFORMATSIYA OCHISTKA I UTILIZATSIYA OTKHODOV KHIMICHESKIK PROIZVODSTV (RU/0234-9701). [860] **992**

SIGNALNAYA INFORMATSIYA SORBENTY POVERKHNOSTNO-AKTIVNYE VESHCHESTVA (RU/0234-9698). [560] **992**

SIGNATURE (PRAIRIE VILLAGE, KAN.) (US/1068-1957). **4569**

SIGNATURE (VANCOUVER) (CN/0708-515X). **4819**

SIGNOS (CL/0035-0451). [10,000] **330**

SIGNOS UNIVERSITARIOS : REVISTA DE LA UNIVERSIDAD DEL SALVADOR (AG). [1,000] **1847**

SIGNS OF THE TIMES (MOUNTAIN VIEW) (US/0037-5047). [375,000] **5067**

SIGUCCS NEWSLETTER (US/0736-6892). **1244**

SIIRTOLAISUUS / SIIRTOLAISUUSINSTITUUTTI (FI/0355-3779). [1,300] **1921**

SIK-RAPPORT (SW/0436-2071). **4199**

SIKH REVIEW, THE (II/0037-5128). [5,000] **4997**

SIKSI : THE NORDIC ART REVIEW (FI/0782-7423). [2,000] **330**

SILENT NEWS (US/0049-0490). [6,000] **5721**

SILLIMAN JOURNAL (PH/0037-5284). [400] **2854**

SILVER & GOLD REPORT (US/0195-8054). [22,000] **914**

SILVER (WHITTIER, CALIF.) (US/0899-6105). [2,500] **4019**

SIM NOW (CN/0711-6683). [130,000] **4997**

SIMCOE MIRROR, THE (CN/0712-5569). **5794**

SIMG : MEDICINA GENERALE (IT/1120-673X). [70,000] **3641**

SIMIOLUS (NE/0037-5411). [850] **364**

SIMMENTAL SHIELD (US/0192-3072). [8,000] **221**

SIMON STEVIN (BE/0037-5454). **3535**

SIMON'S TAXES (UK). **3055**

SIMS SEEKER, THE (US/1045-9987). [150] **2472**

SIMSBURY NEWS, THE (US/0891-9542). [2,300] **5646**

SINAI (IS). [1,000] **5052**

SINATRA INTERNATIONAL (AT/0810-5200). [180] **435**

SINFONIAN (1980), THE (US/8750-5347). [25,000] **4153**

SING OUT (US/0037-5624). [10,000] **4153**

SING OUT EAST DONCASTER (AT/0818-0555). [800] **4153**

SINGAPORE

Controlled Circulation Index

SINGAPORE JOURNAL OF OBSTETRICS & GYNAECOLOGY (SI/0129-3273). [750] **3768**

SINGAPORE STAMP CATALOGUE IN FULL COLOUR (MY/0127-1563). [3,000] **2787**

SINGAPORE STATISTICAL NEWS : SSN (SI/0217-4316). [2,150] **5338**

SINGENDE KIRCHE (AU/0037-5721). [4,000] **4153**

SINGER REPORT ON MANAGED CARE SYSTEMS AND TECHNOLOGY, THE (US/1071-1910). **5158**

SINGING NEWS MAGAZINE, THE (US/1060-3956). [150,000] **4153**

SINGLE ADULT MINISTRY INFORMATION (US/0887-1167). **4997**

SINGLE GENTLEMEN & WOMEN (US). [40,000] **3996**

SINGLE PARENT, THE (US/0037-5748). [115,000] **2286**

SINGLELIFE (MILWAUKEE, WIS.) (US/8756-0380). [10,000] **2493**

SINO-AMERICAN RELATIONS (CH). [1,500] **4535**

SINO-US TRADE STATISTICS (US/0196-4607). [5,000] **733**

SINO-WESTERN CULTURAL RELATIONS JOURNAL (US/1041-875X). [200] **4535**

SINOPSE ESTATISTICA DA REGIAO NORTE / SECRETARIA DE PLANEJAMENTO DA PRESIDENCIA DA REPUBLICA, FUNDACAO INSTITUTO BRASILEIRO DE GEOGRAFIA E ESTATISTICA, IBGE (BL). **5338**

SINTEZA (XV/0049-0601). [6000] **364**

SISKIYOU COUNTY (CA) SERIES (US/1040-3620). **2545**

SISKIYOU PIONEER IN FOLKLORE, FACT AND FICTION, THE (US/0196-0725). [1,500] **2324**

SISMODINAMICA (DURHAM, N.H.) (US/1051-6441). [1,000] **2031**

SISTERS TODAY (US/0037-590X). [6,200] **5036**

SITE (CN/0826-5356). **627**

SITE AUDITING (CN). **2243**

SITE REPORT, THE (US/0275-1488). [650] **3488**

SITE SELECTION & INDUSTRIAL DEVELOPMENT (US/1041-3073). [31,600] **4847**

SITREP (CN/0316-5620). [3,000] **4057**

SIXTEENTH CENTURY JOURNAL, THE (US/0361-0160). [2,500] **2629**

SIYYON (IS/0044-4758). [800] **5052**

SKAGIT VALLEY HERALD (US/1071-197X). [20,600] **5762**

SKATING (US/0037-6132). [38,000] **4918**

SKEPTIKER (GW/0936-9244). [2,000] **4243**

SKI AREA MANAGEMENT (US/0037-6175). [4,000] **4918**

SKI INDUSTRY BULLETIN (CN/0229-1940). **4918**

SKI NAUTIQUE NEWS (CN/0714-8267). [3,000] **4918**

SKILL (DETROIT, MICH.) (US/0279-2028). [212,000] **1710**

SKILLINGS' MINING REVIEW (US/0037-6329). [3,000] **2151**

SKIN & ALLERGY NEWS (US/0037-6337). [35,000] **3722**

SKIN DIVER (US/0037-6345). [211,724] **4918**

SKIN PHARMACOLOGY (SZ/1011-0283). [1,000] **3723**

SKOG & FORSKNING (SW/1101-9506). [1,500] **2395**

SKOG INDUSTRI (NO/0800-8582). [3,000] **4239**

SKOL VREIZH (FR/0755-8848). [2,000 / 3,000] **1784**

SKRIFTSERIE (NO). [5,000] **811**

SKYDIVING (US/0192-7361). [8,700] **4918**

SKYWATCHER'S ALMANAC (US/0889-9614). **399**

SKYWAYS (II). [10,000] **35**

SKYWAYS: THE JOURNAL OF THE AIRPLANE 1920-1940 (US). [1,500] **35**

SLAGER (NE). [7,310] **2357**

SLAVE RIVER JOURNAL (CN/0707-4964). [2,200] **5794**

SLAVIC REVIEW (US/0037-6779). [5,200] **2854**

SLAVICA SLOVACA (XO/0037-6787). [550] **3321**

SLB BURIER : NACHRICHTEN AUS DER SACHSISCHEN LANDESBIBLIOTHEK DRESDEN (GW/0863-0682). **3437**

SLEEP WATCHERS (US/0748-5352). **3641**

SLOANE REPORT, THE (US/0882-5939). [12,000] **1203**

SLOVAK V AMERIKE (US/0199-6819). [1,200] **5739**

SLOVAKIA (WEST PATERSON, N.J.) (US/0583-5623). [2,000] **2709**

SLOVENE STUDIES (US/0193-1075). [500] **2710**

SLOVENSKA ARCHEOLOGIA (XO/0037-6949). [1,000] **282**

SLOVENSKA DRZAVA (CN/0037-6957). [4,000] **4496**

SLOVENSKA LITERATURA (XO/0037-6973). [1,250] **3437**

SLOVENSKA NARODNA BIBLIOGRAFIA. SUPIS PERIODIK A ZBORNIKOV VYCHADZAJUCICH NA SLOVENSKU V ROKU (XO). [1,000] **424**

SLOVENSKA REC (XO/0037-6981). [2,250] **3322**

SLOVENSKE DIVADLO (XO/0037-699X). [750] **5368**

SLOVENSKY NARODOPIS (XO/0037-7023). [1,500] **245**

SLOVO A SLOVESNOST (GW/0037-7031). [1,200] **3322**

SLVGS NEWS, THE (US/0890-1287). [250] **2472**

SLVGS QUERY QUARTERLY, THE (US/1051-9912). [250] **2472**

SMALL BUSINESS CHRONICLE (US). [35,000] **711**

SMALL BUSINESS EMPLOYEE ASSISTANCE (US/1060-8184). [1,000] **711**

SMALL BUSINESS TAX REVIEW, THE (US/0276-5322). **4748**

SMALL BUSINESS TODAY (US). [32,000] **711**

SMALL BUSINESSMAN'S CLINIC (US/0094-2464). [300] **711**

SMALL CITY AND REGIONAL COMMUNITY, THE (US/0194-2735). [500] **2835**

SMALL FARMER'S JOURNAL (US/0743-9989). [23,000] **135**

SMALL FLOWS (US). [38,000] **2243**

SMALL PRESS BOOK REVIEW, THE (US/8756-7202). [3,000] **4832**

SMALL WORLD (GUILFORD) (US/0037-7260). [10,000] **2907**

SMITH ALUMNAE QUARTERLY (US). [40,000] **1103**

SMITH COLLEGE STUDIES IN SOCIAL WORK (US/0037-7317). [1,350] **5307**

SMITH FUNDING REPORT (US/0739-2184). **1847**

SMITH PAPERS (US/0278-3134). [800] **2472**

SMITHSONIAN CONTRIBUTIONS TO ANTHROPOLOGY (US/0081-0223). [2,000] **245**

SMITHSONIAN CONTRIBUTIONS TO PALEOBIOLOGY (US/0081-0266). [2,300] **4230**

SMITHSONIAN CONTRIBUTIONS TO THE EARTH SCIENCES (US/0081-0274). [1,800] **1360**

SMITHSONIAN CONTRIBUTIONS TO ZOOLOGY (US/0081-0282). [1,700] **5597**

SMITHSONIAN YEAR (1980) (US/0273-4982). **5158**

SMOKE SIGNAL (TUCSON), THE (US/0583-6573). [2,000] **2629**

SMOKY MOUNTAIN HISTORICAL SOCIETY NEWSLETTER (US/0884-6111). **2760**

SN DISTRIBUTION STUDY OF GROCERY STORE SALES (US/0736-122X). [1,500] **2357**

SNA PERSPECTIVE (US/0270-7284). [5,000] **1249**

SNACKWORLD (US/0896-1670). [5,400] **2358**

SNIPS (US/0037-7457). [28,000] **2608**

SNIPS (FREDERICTON, N.B.) (CN/0710-2216). **5158**

SNOHOMISH COUNTY TRIBUNE (US). **5762**

SNOW COUNTRY (US/0896-758X). [225,000] **4919**

SNOWMOBILE ANNUAL (CN/0700-3315). **4919**

SOAP, COSMETICS, CHEMICAL SPECIALTIES (US/0091-1372). [14,000] **1030**

SOAP NEWSLETTER (US). **3641**

SOAP OPERA NOW (US/0883-6930). [10,000] **2546**

SOARING (US/0037-7503). [18,000] **35**

SOBORNOST (UK/0144-8722). [2,300] **5040**

SOBRE LOS DERIVADOS DE LA CANA DE AZUCAR (HAVANA, CUBA : 1983) (CU). [1,400] **2358**

SOBREVIVENCIA (BL). [2,500] **2205**

SOCCER JOURNAL (US/0560-3617). [10,000] **4919**

SOCCER MATCH (US/0744-964X). **4919**

SOCIAL ACTION & THE LAW (US/0272-765X). [1,000] **3056**

SOCIAL ACTION (NEW DELHI) (II/0037-7627). [1,000] **5258**

SOCIAL ALTERNATIVES (AT/0155-0306). [3,500] **5258**

SOCIAL ANALYSIS (ADELAIDE, S. AUST.) (AT/0155-977X). [300] **5219**

SOCIAL AND ECONOMIC STUDIES (JM/0037-7651). [730] **5219**

SOCIAL CHANGE (II/0049-0857). [1,200] **5308**

SOCIAL CONCEPT (US/0737-7762). [500] **5219**

SOCIAL DEVELOPMENT ISSUES (US/0147-1473). [400] **5308**

SOCIAL DIRECTORY OF HOUSTON (US/0489-2593). [1,200] **2546**

SOCIAL FORCES (US/0037-7732). [5,000] **5258**

SOCIAL HISTORY (LONDON) (UK/0307-1022). [900] **2630**

SOCIAL LIST OF WASHINGTON, D.C. AND SOCIAL PRECEDENCE IN WASHINGTON, THE (US/1063-7516). **4686**

SOCIAL PROBLEMS (US/0037-7791). [3,500] **5220**

SOCIAL PROCESS IN HAWAII (1979) (US/0737-6871). [100] **5220**

SOCIAL QUESTIONS BULLETIN (1981) (US/0731-0234). [2,000] **4997**

SOCIAL REGISTER (US/1071-3905). [14,000] **425**

SOCIAL RESOURCES INVENTORY. NORTHEASTERN REGION (CN/0228-1325). [1,200] **5308**

SOCIAL SCIENCE RECORD (US/0037-7872). [1,500] **5221**

SOCIAL SCIENCES INDEX (US/0094-4920). **5228**

SOCIAL SERVICE JOBS (US). **5308**

SOCIAL SERVICES RESEARCH (UK). [400] **5221**

SOCIAL SERVICES RESEARCH JOURNAL (UK/0265-6957). [230] **5309**

SOCIAL STUDIES REVIEW (MILLBRAE, CALIF.) (US/1056-6325). [2,500] **5222**

SOCIAL WORK AND CHRISTIANITY (US/0737-5778). [1,100] **5309**

SOCIAL WORK EDUCATION REPORTER (US/0037-8062). [3,000] **5309**

SOCIAL WORK TODAY (UK/0037-8070). [27,000] **5310**

SOCIALISMO Y PARTICIPACION (PE). [1,100] **4546**

SOCIALIST PERSPECTIVE (II). [1,000] **4547**

SOCIALISTA (P.S.O.E. (POLITICAL PARTY) : WEEKLY) (SP). [250,000 (per edition)] **4547**

SOCIETE ROYALE D'ECONOMIE POLITIQUE DE BELGIQUE (SERIES) (BE/0303-9609). **1521**

SOCIETY FOR INDUSTRIAL ARCHEOLOGY NEWSLETTER (US/0160-1067). [1,400] **282**

SOCIETY FOR ORGANIC PETROLOGY NEWSLETTER, THE (US/0743-3816). [250] **1459**

SOCIETY NEWS (BROOMALL, PA.) (US/8756-8861). [100,000] **4153**

SOCIETY PAGE (US/0038-0075). [36,000] **2893**

SOCIOBIOLOGY (US/0361-6525). [500] **5597**

SOCIOLOGIA (XO/0049-1225). [1,200] **5260**

SOCIOLOGIA RURALIS (NE/0038-0199). [1,000] **5260**

SOCIOLOGICAL ANALYSIS (US/0038-0210). [1,200] **4998**

SOCIOLOGICAL BULLETIN (II/0038-0229). [1,700] **5260**

SOCIOLOGICAL INQUIRY (US/0038-0245). [2,500] **5260**

SOCIOLOGIE ET SOCIETES (CN/0038-030X). [1,500] **5262**

SOCIOLOGIJA SELA (CI/0038-0326). [800] **5262**

SOCIOLOGISCHE GIDS (BE/0038-0334). [1,000] **5262**

SOCIOLOGY OF HEALTH & ILLNESS (UK/0141-9889). [750] **5262**

SOCIONOMEN 1987 (SW/0283-1929). [6,200] **5310**

SOCM SENTINEL, THE (US/0889-2415). [800] **2205**

SODA TO ENSO (JA/0371-3768). [2,800] **2371**

SODOBNOST (XV/0038-0482). [1,600] **2523**

SOFT DRINKS MANAGEMENT INTERNATIONAL (UK/0953-4776). **2371**

SOFTWARE DIGEST RATINGS REPORT (US/0893-6455). [8,000] **1290**

SOFTWARE MAGAZINE (WESTBOROUGH, MASS.) (US/0897-8085). [90,000] **1290**

SOFTWARE PROCESS, QUALITY & ISO 9000 (US/1070-5457). [2,000] **1291**

SOIL MECHANICS SERIES (MONTREAL, QUEBEC) (CN/0541-6329). **2031**

SOIL SCIENCE SOCIETY OF AMERICA JOURNAL (US/0361-5995). [8,100] **187**

SOL (HOUSTON, TEX.), EL (US/0891-818X). [37,000] **5754**

SOL (PHOENIX, ARIZ. : 1939) (US). [15,000] **5630**

SOLAR BULLETIN (RAMSEY) (US/0271-8480). [500] **400**

SOLAR PROGRESS (AT/0729-6436). [2,000] **1957**

SOLAR TODAY (US/1042-0630). [5,500] **1957**

SOLDAT UND TECHNIK (GW/0038-0989). [31,000] **4057**

SOLDIER (UK). [24,000] **4057**

SOLETTER (US/0747-623X). [9,500] **1997**

SOLIA (US/0038-1039). [5,000] **4998**

SOLID FUEL (UK). **1030**

SOLID STATE TECHNOLOGY (US/0038-111X). [35,000] **2081**

SOLOINTIMO SOLOMARE (IT). [31,000] **1087**

SOLOMON INTERNATIONAL TELEVISION NEWSLETTER, THE (US). **1139**

SOLUTIONS (FREDERICTON) (CN/0710-779X). **5158**

SOMATICS (US/0147-5231). [1,200] **4361**

SOMETHING SPECIAL PATTERN CLUB (US/0883-3710). [1,500] **5186**

SOMOS (BUENOS AIRES, ARGENTINA) (AG). [180,000] **2552**

SONDERHEFT - DEUTSCHE KERAMISCHE GESELLSCHAFT (GW/0417-2256). [2,500] **2594**

SONG NEWS (CN/0704-5859). [800] **187**

SONG (TORONTO) (CN/0822-4226). [4,000] **3471**

SONNECK SOCIETY BULLETIN, THE (US). [1,500] **4153**

SONNENENERGIE & WARMEPUMPE (GW/0172-5912). **1957**

SONORENSIS (US/0277-4887). [18,600] **4096**

SONS OF NORWAY VIKING, THE (US/0038-1462). [65,000] **2273**

SOO, THE (US/0733-5296). [1,200] **5436**

SOOCHOW JOURNAL OF MATHEMATICS (CH/0250-3255). **3536**

SORTIE (MONTREAL) (CN/0714-7376). [5,000] **2796**

SOSIALKONOMEN (NO). [2,000] **1595**

SOUDAGE ET TECHNIQUES CONNEXES (FR/0038-173X). **4027**

SOUL TAEHAKKYO NONGKWA TAEHAK YONSUMNIM YONGU POGO (KO). [500] **2395**

SOUND & COMMUNICATIONS (US/0038-1845). [10,000] **1122**

SOUND & VIDEO CONTRACTOR (US/0741-1715). [20,000] **5319**

SOUND OF VIENNA, THE (US/0192-5180). [41,000] **2546**

SOUND POST (GRANITE FALLS, MINN.) (US/0749-0755). [250] **4154**

SOUNDBOARD (US/0145-6237). [3,000] **4154**

SOUNDINGS (MILWAUKEE, WIS.) (US/0888-4072). [450] **5457**

SOUNDINGS (SANTA BARBARA) (US/0038-1853). [850] **3250**

SOUNDS ABOUT SUNDAY (1981) (CN/0712-5836). **3056**

SOUNDS AUSTRALIAN : AUSTRALIAN MUSIC CENTRE JOURNAL (AT/0811-3149). [1,100] **4154**

SOUNDS OF GOSPEL RECORDINGS (US). [14,000] **4998**

SOURCE BOOK OF AMERICAN STATE LEGISLATION, THE (US/0730-1154). [10,000] **3056**

SOURCE (UNITED NATIONS DEVELOPMENT PROGRAMME) (US). [27,000] **2243**

SOURCEBOOK OF CRIMINAL JUSTICE STATISTICS (US/0360-3431). [9,500] **3083**

SOURCES CHRETIENNES (FR/0750-1978). [2,500] **5040**

SOURCES ET SUPPLEMENT VIE DOMINICAINE (SZ). [1,000] **4998**

SOURCES: THE SECURITIES EXECUTIVE'S GUIDE TO PRODUCTS AND SERVICES (US). [15,000] **766**

SOURCES (TORONTO) (CN/0700-480X). [15,000] **2924**

SOURCEWORLD (US/0270-496X). **1276**

SOUROZH (UK/0950-2742). [600] **4998**

SOUS-TERRE (CN/0827-9772). **1411**

SOUTH AFRICAN ARCHAEOLOGICAL BULLETIN, THE (SA/0038-1969). [1,300] **282**

SOUTH AFRICAN BUILDER, THE (SA). [8,000] **627**

SOUTH AFRICAN CLEANING REVIEW (SA). [1,800] **1711**

SOUTH AFRICAN EXPORTERS (SA). [10,500] **851**

SOUTH AFRICAN FORESTRY JOURNAL (SA/0038-2167). [1,183] **2395**

SOUTH AFRICAN HAIRDRESSING AND BEAUTY CULTURE (SA/0036-0759). [2,200] **405**

SOUTH AFRICAN HISTORICAL JOURNAL (SA). [700] **2643**

SOUTH AFRICAN JOURNAL FOR ENOLOGY AND VITICULTURE (SA/0253-939X). **2371**

SOUTH AFRICAN JOURNAL OF ANIMAL SCIENCE (SA/0375-1589). [1,000] **222**

SOUTH AFRICAN JOURNAL OF BOTANY (SA/0254-6299). [1,100] **528**

SOUTH AFRICAN JOURNAL OF BUSINESS MANAGEMENT (SA). [1,700] **886**

SOUTH AFRICAN JOURNAL OF CHEMISTRY (SA/0379-4350). [1,800] **992**

SOUTH AFRICAN JOURNAL OF COMMUNICATION DISORDERS (SA/0379-8046). [700] **3846**

SOUTH AFRICAN JOURNAL OF LIBRARY AND INFORMATION SCIENCE (SA/0256-8861). [2,700] **3250**

SOUTH AFRICAN JOURNAL OF MUSICOLOGY (SA/0258-509X). [200] **4154**

SOUTH AFRICAN JOURNAL OF PHYSIOTHERAPY (SA/0379-6175). [2,300] **3642**

SOUTH AFRICAN JOURNAL OF SURGERY (SA/0038-2361). [1,000] **3975**

SOUTH AFRICAN JOURNAL OF ZOOLOGY (SA/0254-1858). [800] **5597**

SOUTH AFRICAN LAW REPORTS; TRANSLATION OF AFRIKAANS PASSAGES IN REPORTED CASES, THE (SA). [5,570] **3056**

SOUTH AFRICAN MACHINE TOOL REVIEW (SA/0036-0848). [4,500] **2129**

SOUTH AFRICAN MUSIC TEACHER (SA/0038-2493). [1,800] **4154**

SOUTH AFRICAN OPTOMETRIST, SUID-AFRIKAANSE OOGKUNDIGE, THE (SA/0378-9411). [1,660] **4217**

SOUTH AFRICAN ORCHID JOURNAL. SUID-AFRIKAANSE ORGIDEEJOERNAAL (SA). [1,500] **2431**

SOUTH AFRICAN SHIPPING NEWS AND FISHING INDUSTRY REVIEW, THE (SA/0038-2671). [1,150] **5457**

SOUTH AFRICAN STATISTICAL JOURNAL (SA/0038-271X). [700] **3542**

SOUTH AFRICAN SUGAR JOURNAL, THE (SA/0038-2728). [4,000] **187**

SOUTH AFRICAN SUGAR YEAR BOOK, THE (SA). [3,000] **136**

SOUTH AFRICAN TREASURER, THE (SA/0038-2779). [1,500] **4748**

SOUTH ASIA BULLETIN (US/0732-3867). [700] **2665**

SOUTH ASIA IN REVIEW (US/0889-8650). [1,000] **2665**

SOUTH ASIAN ANTHROPOLOGIST (II/0257-7348). [500] **245**

SOUTH ASIAN REVIEW - SOUTH ASIAN LITERARY ASSOCIATION (US/0275-9527). [150] **3353**

SOUTH ATLANTIC QUARTERLY, THE (US/0038-2876). [1,100] **2854**

SOUTH ATLANTIC REVIEW (US/0277-335X). [4,200] **3322**

SOUTH AUSTRALIAN MASTER BUILDER (AT). [1,500] **1627**

SOUTH AUSTRALIAN ORNITHOLOGIST (AT/0038-2973). [650] **5620**

SOUTH AUSTRALIAN SCIENCE TEACHERS JOURNAL (AT). [700] **1905**

SOUTH BEND AREA GENEALOGICAL SOCIETY (US/0737-2973). **2473**

SOUTH BEND TRIBUNE, THE (US). [106,000 daily125,000 Sunday] **5667**

SOUTH CAROLINA BUSINESS JOURNAL (US/0745-4473). [7,500] **712**

SOUTH CAROLINA ECONOMIC INDICATORS (US/0038-304X). **1584**

SOUTH CAROLINA HISTORICAL MAGAZINE (US/0038-3082). [5,000] **2761**

SOUTH CAROLINA JOURNAL OF HEALTH, PHYSICAL EDUCATION, RECREATION AND DANCE (US/0740-8331). [1,000] **1784**

SOUTH CAROLINA LABOR MARKET REVIEW / SOUTH CAROLINA EMPLOYMENT SECURITY COMMISSION (US). [1,500] **1521**

SOUTH CAROLINA LAW REVIEW (US/0038-3104). **3057**

SOUTH CAROLINA LAWYER (US/1044-4238). [6,000] **3057**

SOUTH CAROLINA MAGAZINE OF ANCESTRAL RESEARCH, THE (US/0190-826X). [1,200] **2473**

SOUTH CAROLINA NURSE, THE (US/1046-7394). [2,000] **3869**

SOUTH CAROLINA PROGRAM FOR LIBRARY DEVELOPMENT, THE (US/1046-5553). **3250**

SOUTH CAROLINA PUBLIC LIBRARY ANNUAL STATISTICAL SUMMARY (US). **3260**

SOUTH CAROLINA REVIEW, THE (US/0038-3163). [650] **3353**

SOUTH CAROLINA SCENE: ITV STAFF DEVELOPMENT SCHEDULE (US). [1500] **1784**

SOUTH CENTRAL REVIEW (US/0743-6831). [1,700] **3322**

SOUTH DADE NEWS LEADER (US/1048-5406). [12,000] **5651**

SOUTH DAKOTA ARCHAEOLOGY (US/0276-5543). [250] **282**

SOUTH DAKOTA BUSINESS REVIEW (US/0038-3260). [1,300] **4748**

SOUTH DAKOTA CHURCHMAN (US). [4,500] **4998**

SOUTH DAKOTA CONSERVATION DIGEST (US/0038-3279). [17,000] **2205**

SOUTH DAKOTA COUNTY POOR RELIEF (US/0360-9022). [225] **5310**

SOUTH DAKOTA DEPARTMENT OF SOCIAL SERVICES - PRE-EXPENDITURE REPORT FOR TITLE XX SOCIAL SERVICES BLOCK GRANT (US). **4748**

SOUTH DAKOTA EPISCOPAL CHURCH NEWS (US/0746-9276). [4,500] **4998**

SOUTH DAKOTA FARM & HOME RESEARCH (US/0038-3295). [5,000] **136**

SOUTH DAKOTA INDIAN RECIPIENTS OF SOCIAL WELFARE (US/0094-372X). [65] **5310**

SOUTH DAKOTA JOURNAL OF MEDICINE (US/0038-3317). [1,400] **3642**

SOUTH DAKOTA LAW REVIEW (US/0038-3325). [1,200] **3057**

SOUTH DAKOTA LIBRARY DIRECTORY (US). [800] **3250**

SOUTH DAKOTA MAGAZINE (YANKTON, S.D.) (US/0886-2680). [25,000] **2546**

SOUTH DAKOTA MUNICIPALITIES (US/0300-6182). [3,000] **4686**

SOUTH DAKOTA REGISTER (US/0191-1104). [330] **3057**

SOUTH DAKOTA REVIEW (US/0038-3368). [500] **3438**

SOUTH EAST ASIA ACTIVITY REPORT (SI). **4278**

SOUTH EAST ASIAN PRINTER MAGAZINE (SI/0129-1262). [15,249] **4569**

SOUTH EAST ASIAN REVIEW, THE (II). [1,000] **2665**

SOUTH FLORIDA HISTORY MAGAZINE : QUARTERLY OF THE HISTORICAL MUSEUM OF SOUTHERN FLORIDA (US). [2,400] **2761**

SOUTH FLORIDA PIONEERS (US/8756-2766). [150] **2473**

SOUTH JERSEY MAGAZINE (US/0275-4428). [6,000] **2761**

SOUTH OF THE MOUNTAINS (US/0489-9563). [1,900] **2761**

SOUTH PACIFIC JOURNAL OF NATURAL SCIENCE, THE (FJ/1013-9877). [150] **4172**

SOUTH PIERCE COUNTY DISPATCH, THE (US). [5,500] **5762**

SOUTH SHORE NEWS (CN/0710-0213). **5795**

SOUTH VANCOUVER REVUE (CN/0821-0187). [15,000] **5795**

SOUTHAMPTON MEDICAL JOURNAL (UK/0266-0342). **3642**

SOUTHEAST

Controlled Circulation Index

SOUTHEAST ASIA MICROFILMS NEWSLETTER (MY). [200] **2483**

SOUTHEAST ASIAN JOURNAL OF TROPICAL MEDICINE AND PUBLIC HEALTH, THE (TH/0038-3619). [1,000] **4803**

SOUTHEASTERN ARCHAEOLOGY (US/0734-578X). [700] **282**

SOUTHEASTERN EUROPE (PITTSBURGH) (US/0094-4467). [300] **2523**

SOUTHEASTERN GEOGRAPHER (US/0038-366X). [900] **2576**

SOUTHEASTERN LIBRARIAN, THE (US/0038-3686). [1,800] **3250**

SOUTHEASTERN OUTLOOK (US/0887-0934). [18,000] **4998**

SOUTHEASTERN PEANUT FARMER (US/0038-3694). [17,500] **188**

SOUTHEASTERN POLITICAL REVIEW (US/0730-2177). [400] **4496**

SOUTHERLY (AT/0038-3732). [1,000] **3438**

SOUTHERN ACCENTS (US/0149-516X). [258,330] **2903**

SOUTHERN AFRICA PROJECT ANNUAL REPORT (US/0887-8706). **4496**

SOUTHERN AFRICA RECORD (SA). [800] **4535**

SOUTHERN AFRICA REPORT (SA). **2500**

SOUTHERN AFRICAN JOURNAL OF EPIDEMIOLOGY & INFECTION : OFFICIAL JOURNAL OF THE SEXUALLY TRANSMITTED DISEASES, INFECTIOUS DISEASES, AND EPIDEMIOLOGICAL SOCIETIES OF SOUTHERN AFRICA, THE (SA). [1,800] **3716**

SOUTHERN BEVERAGE JOURNAL (US/0193-0613). [30,000] **2371**

SOUTHERN BUSINESS & ECONOMIC JOURNAL, THE (US/0743-779X). [1,600] **712**

SOUTHERN BUSINESS REVIEW (US/0884-1373). [1,200] **886**

SOUTHERN CALIFORNIA BEVERAGE BULLETIN (US/0192-1835). [16,000] **2371**

SOUTHERN CALIFORNIA BUSINESS (US/0038-3880). [7,000] **821**

SOUTHERN CALIFORNIA BUSINESS DIRECTORY AND BUYERS GUIDE (US/0093-3090). [3,000] **712**

SOUTHERN CALIFORNIA LAW REVIEW (US/0038-3910). [2,053] **3057**

SOUTHERN CALIFORNIA QUARTERLY (US/0038-3929). [1,000] **2761**

SOUTHERN CALIFORNIA SENIOR LIFE (US). [160,000] **5182**

SOUTHERN CITY (US/0361-7130). [6,200] **4686**

SOUTHERN COALITION REPORT ON JAILS AND PRISONS (US). [12,000] **3177**

SOUTHERN COMMUNICATION JOURNAL, THE (US/1041-794X). [2,500] **1122**

SOUTHERN CROSS (SAN DIEGO, CALIF.) (US/0745-0257). [20,000] **5036**

SOUTHERN EXPOSURE (DURHAM, N.C.) (US/0146-809X). [9,000] **2761**

SOUTHERN FRIEND, THE (US/0743-7439). [400] **5067**

SOUTHERN FUNERAL DIRECTOR (US/0038-4135). [5,659] **2407**

SOUTHERN GENEALOGICAL INDEX (US/8755-1748). **2473**

SOUTHERN HOSPITALS (US/0038-4178). [16,435] **3792**

SOUTHERN INDIAN STUDIES (US/0085-6525). [400] **2761**

SOUTHERN INSURANCE (US/0038-4216). [3,400] **2894**

SOUTHERN JOURNAL OF AGRICULTURAL ECONOMICS (US/0081-3052). [1,200] **136**

SOUTHERN JOURNAL OF APPLIED FORESTRY (US/0148-4419). [1,600] **2395**

SOUTHERN LAWNMOWERS DEALERS NEWSLETTER (US). [3,000] **2431**

SOUTHERN LITERARY JOURNAL, THE (US/0038-4291). [600] **3438**

SOUTHERN LOGGIN' TIMES (US/0744-2106). [13,227] **2404**

SOUTHERN LUMBERMAN (US/0038-4313). [11,500] **2404**

SOUTHERN MOTOR CARGO (US/0038-4372). [56,000] **5425**

SOUTHERN MOTORACING (US/0049-1616). [18,000] **5425**

SOUTHERN OUTDOORS (MONTGOMERY) (US/0199-3372). [252,000] **4878**

SOUTHERN PHARMACY JOURNAL (US/0192-5792). [18,000] **4329**

SOUTHERN PLUMBING, HEATING, COOLING (US/0038-4461). [6,000] **2608**

SOUTHERN SHIPPER (US/1054-7150). [7,790] **5457**

SOUTHERN THEATRE (US/0584-4738). [3,400] **5368**

SOUTHERN UTE DRUM, THE (US/0587-0674). **2273**

SOUTHERN WASTE INFORMATION EXCHANGE CATALOG, THE (US/0892-5739). [6,500] **2243**

SOUTHLAND TIMES (NZ/0112-9910). [33,500] **5807**

SOUTHSIDE VIRGINIAN, THE (US/0736-5683). [500] **2473**

SOUTHWEST CONTRACTOR (PHOENIX, ARIZ.) (US/1064-6914). [7,200] **628**

SOUTHWEST WAVE (US). [277,000] **5640**

SOUTHWESTERN AMERICAN LITERATURE (US/0049-1675). **3438**

SOUTHWESTERN HISTORICAL QUARTERLY (US/0038-478X). [3,300] **2761**

SOUTHWESTERN LORE (US/0038-4844). [1,000] **282**

SOUTHWESTERN MUSICIAN COMBINED WITH THE TEXAS MUSIC EDUCATOR, THE (US). [7,005] **4154**

SOUTHWESTERN PAY DIRT (US/0886-0920). [4,500] **2151**

SOUTHWINDS (CN/0712-9750). **1784**

SOUVENIR NAPOLEONIEN, LE (FR/0246-1919). [2,000] **2630**

SOUVENIRS & NOVELTIES (US/0038-4968). [22,000] **2585**

SOU'WESTER (EDWARDSVILLE), THE (US/0038-4976). [300] **3438**

SOU'WESTER (RAYMOND, WASH.), THE (US/0038-4984). [525] **2546**

SOVIET AND EASTERN EUROPEAN FOREIGN TRADE (US/0038-5263). [300] **1640**

SOVIET ANTHROPOLOGY AND ARCHAEOLOGY (US/0038-528X). [300] **245**

SOVIET ARMED FORCES REVIEW ANNUAL (US/0148-0928). **4057**

SOVIET ECONOMY (SILVER SPRING, MD.) (US/0882-6994). [500] **1640**

SOVIET LAW AND GOVERNMENT (US/0038-5530). [350] **3057**

SOVIET REVIEW (WHITE PLAINS), THE (US/0038-5794). [700] **2523**

SOVIET STUDIES IN HISTORY (US/0038-5867). [200] **2710**

SOVIET STUDIES IN PHILOSOPHY (US/0038-5883). [300] **4361**

SOYBEAN DIGEST (US/0038-6014). [200,000] **188**

SOZIALISTISCHES MUSIKSCHAFFEN DER DEUTSCHEN DEMOKRATISCHEN REPUBLIK (GW). [750] **4154**

SOZIOLOGISCHE REVUE (GW/0343-4109). [1,500] **5263**

SP QUEBEC (CN/0822-5702). **3846**

SPA AND SAUNA TRADE JOURNAL. BUYERS GUIDE (US). [8,500] **713**

SPACE AGE TIMES (US/0738-0968). [1,000] **35**

SPACE AND SECURITY NEWS (US/1071-2569). [8,500] **35**

SPACE (BEACONSFIELD) (UK/0267-954X). [10,000] **35**

SPACE NEWS (SPRINGFIELD, VA.) (US/1046-6940). [20,000] **36**

SPACE RESEARCH IN BULGARIA (BU/0204-9104). [700] **400**

SPANISH TODAY (US/0049-1802). [10,000] **3439**

SPARE RIB (UK/0306-7971). [30,000] **5566**

SPAULDING & SLYE REPORT. GREATER BOSTON, THE (US/1063-9098). [3,000] **4847**

SPE MONOGRAPH SERIES (US/0882-1100). [250] **1847**

SPEAK UP (CN/0383-9370). [7,000] **2762**

SPEAKER AND GAVEL (US/0584-8164). [1,000] **3322**

SPEAQ-OUT (CN/0229-6535). [1,200] **3323**

SPEC-COM (US/0883-2560). [2,000] **1139**

SPEC (NEW CARLISLE) (CN/0226-9120). [3,000] **5795**

SPECIAL-INTEREST AUTOS (US/0049-1845). [38,000] **5425**

SPECIAL PUBLICATION - ACADEMY OF NATURAL SCIENCES OF PHILADELPHIA (US/0097-3254). [1,000] **1360**

SPECIAL PUBLICATION - AGRICULTURAL RESEARCH ORGANIZATION, THE VOLCANI CENTER (IS/0334-2484). **137**

SPECIAL PUBLICATION (AMERICAN SOCIETY OF ICHTHYOLOGISTS AND HERPETOLOGISTS) (US/0748-0539). **5597**

SPECIAL PUBLICATION - CARNEGIE MUSEUM OF NATURAL HISTORY (US/0145-9031). **4172**

SPECIAL PUBLICATION - CUSHMAN FOUNDATION FOR FORAMINIFERAL RESEARCH (US/0070-2242). [800] **5597**

SPECIAL PUBLICATION - DIVISION OF FISH AND WILDLIFE, SECTION OF FISHERIES (US/0193-1245). [300] **2313**

SPECIAL PUBLICATION - NEW MEXICO GEOLOGICAL SOCIETY (US/0548-6327). [800] **1398**

SPECIAL PUBLICATION - SASKATCHEWAN NATURAL HISTORY SOCIETY (CN/0080-6552). [2,000] **4172**

SPECIAL PUBLICATION - U.N.M. INSTITUTE OF METEORITICS (US/0097-3866). **1434**

SPECIAL RECREATION DIGEST (US/0747-0185). [700] **4854**

SPECIAL REPORT IN APPLIED MARINE SCIENCE AND OCEAN ENGINEERING (US/0882-7427). **2095**

SPECIAL REPORT ON MUNICIPAL AFFAIRS FOR LOCAL FISCAL YEARS ENDED IN ... (US). [4,000] **4748**

SPECIAL STUDIES - UTAH GEOLOGICAL AND MINERAL SURVEY (US/0098-115X). [750] **1398**

SPECIALIST (NEW YORK, N.Y.) (US/0273-9399). [14,000] **3251**

SPECIALITY PAPER & BOARD MATERIALS & MARKETS BULLETIN (UK). **4222**

SPECIALTY & CUSTOM DEALER (US/0193-7278). [23,000] **5425**

SPECIALTY LAB UPDATE (US). [1,500] **4377**

SPECIALTY NEWS (US/0886-2052). [600] **851**

SPECIES (BROOKFIELD) (US/1016-927X). [1000] **2205**

SPECIFICATION (UK). [20,000] **628**

SPECTACLE DU MONDE, LE (FR/0038-6944). [90,000] **3353**

SPECTACLE DU MONDE / PERSPECTIVES / REALITIES, LE (FR). [90,000] **3353**

SPECTROSCOPY INTERNATIONAL (US/1040-7669). [20,000] **993**

SPECTROSCOPY LETTERS (US/0038-7010). **4442**

SPECTROSCOPY (OTTAWA, ONT.) (CN/0712-4813). **993**

SPECTRUM 1: STOCK HOLDINGS SURVEY (US/0091-6854). [222] **914**

SPECTRUM 2: INVESTMENT COMPANY PORTFOLIOS (US/0091-6862). [178] **914**

SPECTRUM 3: 13 (F) INSTITUTIONAL STOCK HOLDINGS SURVEY (US). [475] **914**

SPECTRUM 3 : 13(F) INSTITUTIONAL STOCK HOLDINGS SURVEY (US). [475] **914**

SPECTRUM 5 (US). [200] **914**

SPECTRUM 6 (US). [180] **914**

SPECTRUM NEWSLETTER (US/0738-9051). [3,000] **1122**

SPECTRUM (ST. PAUL, MINN.) (US/0739-2559). [500] **1921**

SPEECH AND DRAMA (UK/0038-7142). [1,500] **5368**

SPEECH COMMUNICATION DIRECTORY (US/0190-2075). [2,000] **1122**

SPEEDHORSE (MONTHLY), THE (US/0364-9237). [8,200] **2802**

SPEEDNEWS (US/0271-2598). [3,000] **36**

SPEKTRUM (SZ/0038-7274). [1,000] **3471**

SPELEO DIGEST (US/0584-8717). **1411**

SPENCER'S RETIREMENT PLAN SERVICE (US/0740-1329). [800] **2894**

SPI CANADA ... PROGRAM, ... ACCOMPLISHMENTS (CN/0714-346X). **4460**

SPICILEGIUM FRIBURGENSE (SZ/0561-6158). [400] **4999**

SPIDELL'S CALIFORNIA TAXLETTER (US/0194-8237). [6,000] **3058**

SPIEGEL DER LETTEREN (BE/0038-7479). **3439**

SPIEGEL HISTORIAEL (NE/0038-7487). [8,500] **2630**

SPIELRAUM (GW/0934-4853). [6,400] **2601**

SPIN-OFF (LOVELAND, COLO.) (US/0198-8239). [13,500] **5356**

SPINNER (NEW BEDFORD, MASS.) (US/0730-2657). [10,000] **2762**

SPIRIT & LIFE (CLYDE, MO.) (US/0038-7592). [5,000] **4999**

SPIRIT OF DEMOCRACY (WOODSFIELD, OHIO : 1844) (US). [1,200] **5730**

SPIRIT OF JEFFERSON FARMERS ADVOCATE (US). [4,894] **5765**

SPIRITUS (FR/0038-7665). [2,000] **5036**

SPITBALL (US/8755-741X). [1,000] **3439**

SPIXIANA (GW/0341-8391). [540] **5598**

SPIXIANA. SUPPLEMENT (GW/0177-7424). [400] **5598**

SPLITTING HEIRS (CN). [under 100] **2473**

SPOKEN ENGLISH (UK/0038-772X). [1,600] **3323**

SPOKESMAN (EDMONTON) (CN/0700-5229). [7,000] **4394**

SPONSORED RESEARCH IN THE HISTORY OF ART (US/0742-0242). [2,000] **365**

SPORT AVIATION (US/0038-7835). [133,000] **4920**

SPORT CONSTRUCTION BUYERS GUIDE (US). **2031**

SPORT FLYER (US/8750-8117). [25,000] **4920**

SPORT MEDIA BUYERS GUIDE (US). [7,000] **4920**

SPORT PSYCHOLOGY TRAINING BULLETIN (US/1044-3118). **4921**

SPORT SCENE (US/0270-1812). [15,000] **4921**

SPORTCARE & FITNESS (US/0899-3815). [35,000] **4921**

SPORTING CLASSICS (US). [80,000] **4921**

SPORTING NEWS ... BASEBALL YEARBOOK, THE (US/0275-0732). [300,000] **4921**

SPORTS (SI). **4922**

SPORTS BUSINESS (CN/0830-1921). [10,000] **958**

SPORTS (COACHING ASSOCIATION OF CANADA : 1980) (CN/0820-6457). [5,000] **1858**

SPORTS DOCUMENTATION MONTHLY BULLETIN (UK). [350] **4922**

SPORTS MEDICINE NEWS (US). [19,000] **3956**

SPORTS TURF BULLETIN (UK/0490-5474). [5,500] **4923**

SPORTWISSENSCHAFT (GW). **4923**

SPOT RADIO RATES AND DATA (US/0038-9560). [4,400] **766**

SPOTLIGHT. ACTRESSES (UK/0308-9827). **388**

"SPOTLIGHT" CASTING DIRECTORY, THE (UK). **4078**

SPOTLIGHT CONTACTS (UK/0010-7344). **388**

SPOTLIGHT ON YOUTH SPORTS (US/0740-0802). [1,000] **4923**

SPOTLIGHT (WASHINGTON), THE (US/0191-6270). [150,000] **5648**

SPRACHE IM TECHNISCHEN ZEITALTER (GW/0038-8475). [2,000] **3353**

SPRACHE UND LITERATUR IN WISSENSCHAFT UND UNTERRICHT (GW/0724-9713). [3,000] **3323**

SPRACHKUNST (AU/0038-8483). [500] **3323**

SPRACHREPORT / INSTITUT FUER DEUTSCHE SPRACHE (GW). [2,000] **3323**

SPRACHWISSENSCHAFT (GW/0344-8169). [550] **3323**

SPREADING THE FAME OF CHRIST (US/0744-6780). [22,000] **4999**

SPRING (NEW YORK, N.Y. : 1982) (US/0735-6889). [120] **3472**

SPRINGFIELD MAGAZINE (US/0164-6745). **2546**

SPRINGS MAGAZINE (COLORADO SPRINGS, COLO.) (US/0748-6405). [20,000] **2546**

SPRINGS VALLEY HERALD (US). [3,000] **5667**

SPUMS JOURNAL (AT/0813-1988). [900] **3642**

SPUR REPORT (US/0361-6444). [1,500] **2836**

SPURS & FEATHERS (US/0745-4368). **4923**

SQL FORUM (US/1068-0950). [2,500] **1204**

SRASHTA (II). [5,000] **3439**

SRC BLUE BOOK OF 5-TREND CYCLI-GRAPHS, THE (US/8750-2356). [13,000] **914**

SRC GREEN BOOK OF 5-TREND 35-YEAR CHARTS, THE (US/0884-8475). **914**

SRC RED BOOK OF 5-TREND SECURITY CHARTS, THE (US/8750-2461). [7,800] **914**

SREB ANNUAL REPORT (US). [2,000] **1784**

SRI LANKA JATIKA GRANTHA NAMAVALIYA (CE/0253-8229). [500] **425**

SRPSKA BORBA (US/0279-1293). [2,500] **2273**

SSI UPDATE (US/0898-8242). [5,000] **36**

ST. CLAIR COUNTY GENEALOGICAL SOCIETY QUARTERLY (US/0882-6528). [500] **2473**

ST. CLAIR NEWS-AEGIS (US/1044-1964). [3,549] **5628**

ST. CLOUD STATE UNIVERSITY CHRONICLE (US/0747-1025). **1095**

ST. CROIX VALLEY PRESS (US/0892-1784). [52,000] **5698**

ST. JOHNS REVIEW (1981), THE (US/0277-4720). [9,000] **1847**

ST. LOUIS BUSINESS JOURNAL (US/0271-6453). [19,000] **713**

ST. LOUIS COUNTIAN, THE (US/0036-2948). [1,800] **5704**

ST. LOUIS DAILY RECORD (US). [3,200] **3058**

ST. LOUIS JOURNALISM REVIEW, THE (US/0036-2972). [10,000] **2924**

ST. LOUIS METROPOLITAN MEDICINE (US/0892-1334). [3,100] **3642**

ST. LOUIS REVIEW (US/0036-3022). [96,500] **5036**

ST. LOUIS SENTINEL (US). [70,000] **5704**

ST. LOUIS UNIVERSITY RESEARCH JOURNAL (PH/0036-3014). [1,000] **2855**

ST. MARK'S REVIEW (AT/0036-3103). [700] **4999**

ST. THOMAS'S HOSPITAL GAZETTE (1981) (UK/0263-3507). [700] **3792**

ST. VLADIMIR'S THEOLOGICAL QUARTERLY (US/0036-3227). [1,500] **5040**

STABILITY & APPLIED ANALYSIS OF CONTINUOUS MEDIA (IT/1120-4222). **3536**

STADEN-JAHRBUCH (BL/0582-1150). [1,000] **2762**

STADION (COLOGNE, GERMANY) (GW/0172-4029). [400] **4924**

STAFF PAPERS : UNIVERSITY OF ALBERTA. DEPARTMENT OF RURAL ECONOMY (CN). **137**

STAGE AND TELEVISION TODAY, THE (UK/0038-9099). [39,341] **5368**

STAHL UND EISEN (GW/0340-4803). **4020**

STAHLBAU RUNDSCHAU (AU/0561-7855). [5,600] **2031**

STAINLESS STEEL EUROPE (NE). [7500] **1030**

STAINLESS STEEL INDUSTRY (UK/0306-2988). [4,000] **1627**

STAMP LOVER, THE (UK/0038-9277). [3,000] **2787**

STAMPA MEDICA (IT/0038-9323). [100,000] **3642**

STAMPING QUARTERLY (US/1043-5093). [35,000] **4020**

STAMPS (NEW YORK, N.Y. 1932) (US/0038-9358). [19,000] **2787**

STAND MAGAZINE (UK/0952-648X). [4,500] **3439**

STANDARD BEARER (GRAND RAPIDS), THE (US/0362-4692). [2,500] **4999**

STANDARD CATALOGUE OF MALAYSIA-SINGAPORE-BRUNEI COINS AND PAPER MONEY (MY/0126-9682). [3,000] **2783**

STANDARD (ELLIOT LAKE) (CN/0827-6609). [5,500] **5795**

STANDARD TRADE & INDUSTRY DIRECTORY OF INDONESIA (IO). [15,000] **852**

STANDARD TRADE DIRECTORY OF INDONESIA (IO). [15,000] **852**

STANDARDS ENGINEERING (US/0038-9668). [1,000] **4032**

STANDARDTERM (AU/0258-837X). [300] **3323**

STANFORD BUSINESS SCHOOL MAGAZINE (US/0883-265X). [24,000] **713**

STANFORD ENVIRONMENTAL LAW JOURNAL (US/0892-7138). [500] **3116**

STANFORD LAWYER (US/0585-0576). [8,000] **3058**

STANFORD MAGAZINE, THE (US/0745-3981). [120,000] **1095**

STANGER'S INVESTMENT ADVISOR (US/1052-5912). **916**

STANISLAUS FARM NEWS (US/8750-4960). [6,000] **137**

STAR AND LAMP OF PI KAPPA PHI, THE (US/0038-9854). [35,000] **1095**

STAR DATE : THE ASTRONOMY NEWS REPORT / THE UNIVERSITY OF TEXAS AT AUSTIN MCDONALD OBSERVATORY (US/0889-3098). [15,000] **400**

STAR-DEMOCRAT (EASTON, MD.), THE (US/1065-2345). [16,500] **5687**

STAR (FRANKFORT, ILL.), THE (US/0746-5742). [70,000] **5662**

STAR (VICTORIA) (CN/0824-7501). **5795**

STARS MARIEMBOURG (BE/0776-0698). [1,500] **425**

START (BIRMINGHAM, ALA.) (US/0162-6841). [32,500] **4999**

START OF MESSAGE (US/0361-0241). **3251**

STARTEXT INK (US/0890-6688). [4,000] **1122**

STAT (US/0038-9986). [2,500] **3869**

STATE ADMINISTRATIVE EXPENSE PLAN FOR FISCAL YEAR (US). [100] **2358**

STATE & LOCAL GOVERNMENT REVIEW (US/0160-323X). [800] **4687**

STATE AND REGIONAL ASSOCIATIONS OF THE UNITED STATES (US/1044-324X). [1,600] **713**

STATE AND REGIONAL ECONOMIC ILLINOIS DATA BOOK (US/0737-1543). [4,000] **1538**

STATE (CHARLOTTE, N.C.), THE (US/0038-9994). **2762**

STATE COURT JOURNAL (US/0145-3076). [2,000] **3058**

STATE DIRECTORY OF KENTUCKY (US/0585-1173). [4,500] **4687**

STATE EXECUTIVE DIRECTORY (US/0276-7163). [1,000] **4687**

STATE GEOLOGIST'S JOURNAL, THE (US/0039-0089). **1398**

STATE GOVERNMENT NEWS (US/0039-0119). [13,000] **4687**

STATE JOURNAL, THE (US). [33,000] **713**

STATE OF HAWAII DATA BOOK (US/0073-1080). [3,000] **5339**

STATE OF IOWA SCHOLARSHIPS, TUITION GRANTS : ANNUAL REPORT (US). **1848**

STATE OF WORLD POPULATION / RAFAEL M. SALAS, EXECUTIVE DIRECTOR OF THE UNITED NATIONS FUND FOR POPULATION ACTIVITIES, THE (US). **4560**

STATE OF WYOMING CHARACTERISTICS OF RECORDABLE OCCUPATIONAL INJURIES AND ILLNESSES (US). [250] **2872**

STATE PLAN FOR VOCATIONAL EDUCATION IN NORTH DAKOTA / STATE BOARD FOR VOCATIONAL EDUCATION (US/0743-653X). [500] **1916**

STATE PLAN ON AGING FOR THE STATE OF NEBRASKA (US). [1,000] **5311**

STATE PLAN ON AGING UNDER TITLE III OF THE OLDER AMERICANS ACT FOR STATE OF SOUTH DAKOTA / DEPARTMENT OF SOCIAL SERVICES, OFFICE OF ADULT SERVICES & AGING (US). [50] **5311**

STATE POLICY REPORTS (US/8750-6637). **4688**

STATE REVENUE NEWSLETTER, THE (US/0883-6760). [250] **2787**

STATE TAX NEWS (US). [13,000] **4749**

STATEMENT (FORT COLLINS, CO.) (US). [1,200] **3324**

STATESMAN (STONY BROOK, N.Y.) (US). [148,000] **1848**

STATESMAN, THE (PK/0039-0313). [5,000] **3353**

STATIONERY NEWS (AT/1033-758X). [6,000] **713**

STATIONERY TRADE NEWS (UK/0951-7820). [8,187] **713**

STATISTICA SINICA (CN/1017-0405). [2,500] **3536**

STATISTICAL ABSTRACT OF OKLAHOMA (1972) (US/0191-0310). [350] **5339**

STATISTICAL BULLETIN FOR PUBLIC LIBRARIES IN WESTERN AUSTRALIA (AT/0729-199X). [500] **3260**

STATISTICAL BULLETIN / REPUBLIC OF BOTSWANA (BS). [600] **5340**

STATISTICAL MASTERFILE [COMPUTER FILE] (US). **5340**

STATISTICAL POCKET BOOK, NEPAL (NP). [5,000] **5340**

STATISTICAL PROFILE OF ILLINOIS SCHOOL ADMINISTRATORS / ILLINOIS STATE BOARD OF EDUCATION (US). [700] **1797**

STATISTICAL RECORD, THE (UK). **2803**

STATISTICAL

Controlled Circulation Index

STATISTICAL REPORT - ALBERTA ADVANCED EDUCATION AND MANPOWER (CN/0826-2004). **1797**

STATISTICAL REPORT (MICHIGAN. LEGISLATURE. SENATE. FISCAL AGENCY) (US). [500] **4700**

STATISTICAL REVIEW - AUSTRALIAN TOURIST COMMISSION (AT). [2,500] **5491**

STATISTICAL REVIEW OF TOURISM, HONG KONG, A (HK). [6,000] **5500**

STATISTICAL YEAR BOOK, THAILAND (TH). [1,000] **5341**

STATISTICS OF SOUTH DAKOTA LIBRARIES (US). [800] **3260**

STATISTICS OF SOUTH DAKOTA PUBLIC LIBRARIES (US/0099-0655). **3260**

STATISTICS ON SCHEDULED BANKS IN PAKISTAN (PK/0039-0577). [450] **733**

STATISTICS - ONTARIO MINISTRY OF NATURAL RESOURCES (CN/0383-5898). [1,500] **2185**

STATISTICS RELATING TO REGIONAL AND MUNICIPAL GOVERNMENTS IN BRITISH COLUMBIA (CN/0702-0988). [1,600] **4700**

STATISTIK BONGKAR MUAT BARANG DI PELABUHAN INDONESIA (IO). **5457**

STATISTIK DER ALLGEMEINBILDENDEN SCHULEN IN NIEDERSACHSEN (GW). [1,500] **1798**

STATISTIK EKSPOR HASIL HUTAN BUKAN KAYU (IO). **2399**

STATISTIK IN DER RENTENVERSICHERUNG (GW). **5311**

STATISTIK INDONESIA. STATISTICAL YEARBOOK OF INDONESIA (IO/0126-2912). **5342**

STATISTIK INDUSTRI KARET REMAH (CRUMB RUBBER) ... INDONESIA (IO). **5078**

STATISTIK KEUANGAN DESA JAWA DAN MADURA (IO/0126-4397). **4700**

STATISTIK KEUANGAN DESA. SULAWESI-MALUKU-BALI-NUSATENGGARA (IO). **4700**

STATISTIK LINGKUNGAN HIDUP INDONESIA (IO). **1539**

STATISTIK OVER PENSIONSTAGARNA I FINLAND (FI/0780-7554). [3,100] **5267**

STATISTIK PENDIDIKAN DILUAR LINGKUNGAN DEPARTEMEN P & K (IO). **1798**

STATISTIK PENDIDIKAN DILUAR LINGKUNGAN DEPARTEMEN P & K DI-SUMATERA UTARA (IO). **1798**

STATISTIK PERHUBUNGAN - BIRO PUSAT STATISTIK (LALU LINTAS ANGKUTAN BARANG ANTAR PULAU MENURUT JENIS PELAYARAN) (IO/0216-6909). **5457**

STATISTIK PERKEBUNAN BESAR (IO). **138**

STATISTIK RESTORAN : HASIL PELAKSANAAN SURVEI KHUSUS RESTORAN DI 12 PROPINSI (IO). **5073**

STATISTIQUE CRIMINELLE DE LA BELGIQUE (BE). [350] **3083**

STATISTIQUE DU TRAFIC INTERNATIONAL DES PORTS, U.E.B.L. / ROYAUME DE BELGIQUE, MINISTERE DES AFFAIRES ECONOMIQUES, INSTITUT NATIONAL DE BELGIQUE (BE). [295] **5402**

STATISTIQUE MEDICALE DANS LES ARMEES (FR/0291-851X). [260] **4062**

STATISTIQUES DE LA CONSTRUCTION ET DU LOGEMENT (BE/0772-7712). [825] **633**

STATISTIQUES DEMOGRAPHIQUES (BE/0067-5490). [650] **4563**

STATISTIQUES DIVERSES (FR). [350] **3083**

STATISTIQUES DU COMMERCE EXTERIEUR DE L'UNION ECONOMIQUE BELGO-LUXEMBURGEOISE (BE/0772-6694). [500] **734**

STATISTIQUES DU COMMERCE INTERIEUR ET DES TRANSPORTS / ROYAUME DE BELGIQUE, MINISTERE DES AFFAIRES ECONOMIQUES, INSTITUT NATIONAL DE STATISTIQUE (BE). [500] **734**

STATISTIQUES FINANCIERES (BE). [600] **734**

STATISTIQUES INDUSTRIELLES (BE/0772-7704). [600] **1539**

STATISTIQUES JUDICIAIRES (BE/0775-311X). [350] **3083**

STATISTIQUES SOCIALES (BE/0067-5563). [700] **1539**

STATISTISCHE BEIHEFTE ZU DEN MONATSBERICHTEN DER DEUTSCHEN BUNDESBANK. REIHE 4 : SAISONBEREINIGTE WIRTSCHAFTSZAHLEN (GW/0418-8330). [12,500] **1539**

STATISTISCHE UBERSICHTEN FUR DAS JAHR (UNIVERSITAT KIEL. INSTITUTS FUR WELTWIRTSCHAFT. BIBLIOTHEK) (GW). [300] **3260**

STATISTISCHES JAHRBUCH BERLIN (GW). [1,500] **5343**

STATISTISCHES JAHRBUCH DER NORDRHEIN-WESTFALISCHEN INDUSTRIE- UND HANDELSKAMMERN / HERAUSGEGEBEN UND BEARBEITET VON DER GEMEINSAMEN STATISTISCHEN STELLE DER NORDRHEIN-WESTFALISCHEN INDUSTRIE- UND HANDELSKAMMERN IN DORTMUND (GW). [1,800] **1539**

STATISTISCHES TASCHENBUCH (GW). **5343**

STATISTISK ARBOG (DK). [15,000] **5343**

STATISZTIKAI HAVI KOZLEMENYEK (HU/0018-781X). [1,800] **5344**

STATISZTIKAI SZEMLE (HU/0039-0690). [1,500] **1540**

STATUS OF NATIONAL DIRECT STUDENT LOAN DEFAULTS (US/0741-4528). [2,000] **1848**

STATUS REPORT - INSURANCE INSTITUTE FOR HIGHWAY SAFETY (US/0018-988X). [14,500] **5444**

STATUS (SCOTTSDALE) (US/0195-9190). [1,000] **2082**

STATUTES OF SASKATCHEWAN (CN/0840-2043). **3059**

STATUTES OF THE PROVINCE OF MANITOBA (CN). [1,500] **3059**

STATUTES OF THE PROVINCE OF NEWFOUNDLAND (CN). [1,000] **3059**

STATUTES OF THE YUKON TERRITORY (CN/0823-4949). [659] **3059**

STAUB, REINHALTUNG DER LUFT (GW/0039-0771). **2244**

STAYNER SUN [MICROFORM], THE (CN/0834-7425). **5795**

STEAMBOAT BILL (1958) (US/0039-0844). [4,000] **2762**

STEEL CONSTRUCTION : JOURNAL OF THE AUSTRALIAN INSTITUTE OF STEEL CONSTRUCTION (AT/0049-2205). **628**

STEEL DESIGN (CN/0712-9092). **2031**

STEEL EMPLOYMENT NEWS (US/0892-1652). [1,000] **1712**

STEEL INDUSTRY OF JAPAN, THE (JA). [5,000] **1627**

STEEL TODAY & TOMORROW (SEMIANNUAL EDITION) (JA/0388-0923). [15,500] **4021**

STEELHEAD HARVEST ANALYSIS (CN/0319-9436). [125] **2314**

STEENSTRUPIA (DK/0375-2909). [500] **5598**

STEERING WHEEL (AUSTIN) (US/0039-1298). [3,500] **5393**

STEINBECK QUARTERLY (US/0039-100X). [600] **435**

STEIRISCHE BILDUNGSSTATISTIK (AU). [450] **1798**

STEPPING BACK IN TIME (US/0894-8313). [200] **2473**

STERNE UND WELTRAUM (GW/0039-1263). [12,500] **400**

STEROIDS (US/0039-128X). [1,000] **473**

STETSON LAW REVIEW (US/0739-9731). **3059**

STEUBEN NEWS (US). [3,500] **4513**

STEUERAUFKOMMEN DER GEMEINDEN NIEDEROSTERREICHS, DAS (AU). **4750**

STILL HERE : JOB/SCHOLARSHIP REFERRAL NEWSLETTER / SCHOOL OF COMMUNICATIONS, HOWARD UNIVERSITY (US). [6,000] **1122**

STIMULOGRAPHY (FR/0989-2192). **3710**

STIRPES (US/0039-1522). [1,000] **2473**

STITCHES : THE JOURNAL OF MEDICAL HUMOUR (CN). [42,000] **3643**

STM INFORMATION BOOKLET (NE). **4820**

STOCK CAR CLASSIFICATION GUIDE (US/0731-2008). [10,000] **5426**

STOCK-FINDER, THE (US). **5522**

STOCKS, BONDS, BILLS, AND INFLATION YEARBOOK (US/1047-2436). [2,500] **916**

STOCKS OF GRAIN AT SELECTED TERMINAL & ELEVATOR SITES. WEEKLY ED (US/0889-0471). **203**

STONE REVIEW (US/8750-9210). [3,000] **2151**

STONE SOUP (SANTA CRUZ, CALIF.) (US/0094-579X). [13,000] **1069**

STONEHAM INDEPENDENT, THE (US). [5,000] **5690**

STONEHENGE VIEWPOINT (US/0140-654X). [2,000] **283**

STONES & BONES NEWSLETTER (US/0585-3699). [500] **246**

STOP (BRATISLAVA) (XO/0139-6501). [120,000] **5426**

STORIA ARCHITETTURA (IT/0390-4253). **309**

STORIA DEL PENSIERO ECONOMICO. BOLLETTINO DI INFORMAZIONE (IT). [1,000] **1585**

STORY ART; A MAGAZINE FOR STORYTELLERS (US/0039-1999). [1,500] **3440**

STORYQUARTERLY (NORTHBROOK, ILL.) (US/1041-0708). [2,500] **3440**

STOUT CENTRE REVIEW : JOURNAL OF THE STOUT RESEARCH CENTRE FOR THE STUDY OF NEW ZEALAND HISTORY AND CULTURE (NZ/1170-4616). [350] **2671**

STRAD, THE (UK/0039-2049). [10,000] **4154**

STRAIN (UK/0039-2103). [1,850] **2129**

STRANA I MIR (GW). [2,200] **2523**

STRANI JEZICI (CI/0351-0840). **3440**

STRASSE UND AUTOBAHN (GW/0039-2162). [5,200] **2031**

STRASSE UND VERKEHR (SZ). **5444**

STRASSEN- UND TIEFBAU (GW/0039-2197). [4,100] **2031**

STRASSENVERKEHRSSICHERHEIT IM JAHRE ... / HERAUSGEGEBEN VOM OSTERREICHISCHEN STATISTISCHEN ZENTRALAMT (AU). [300] **5444**

STRATEGIC INFORMATION ON US AIR TRAVEL (US). [300] **5491**

STRATEGIC PLANNING AND ENERGY MANAGEMENT (US/8750-3204). **1958**

STRATEGIC REVIEW FOR SOUTHERN AFRICA (SA). [2,000] **5223**

STRATEGIES DU MANAGEMENT PARIS (FR/1148-750X). **887**

STRATEGY (TORONTO. 1991) (CN/1187-4309). [19,000] **937**

STRATFORD FOR STUDENTS (CN/0822-9066). [7,000] **5369**

STRATFORD JOURNAL (STRATFORD, WIS.) (US). [750 paid weekly] **5771**

STRATTON MAGAZINE (US/1064-1629). [20,000] **4924**

STRELEC (JERSEY CITY, N.J.) (US/0747-7287). [500] **3440**

STRENGTH AND HEALTH (US/0039-2308). **2601**

STRICKLAND SCENE (US/0733-8392). [205] **2474**

STROEZ I FUNKCII NA MOZKA (BU/0204-4560). [500] **3846**

STROJNISKI VESTNIK (XV/0039-2480). [2,500] **5160**

STROKE (1970) (US/0039-2499). [6,000] **3710**

STROLLING ASTRONOMER, THE (US/0039-2502). [700] **400**

STROMATA (AG/0049-2353). [1,000] **4999**

STROPHES / NATIONAL FEDERATION OF STATE POETRY SOCIETIES, INC (US). **3440**

STRUCTURAL ENGINEERING INTERNATIONAL : JOURNAL OF THE INTERNATIONAL ASSOCIATION FOR BRIDGE AND STRUCTURAL ENGINEERING (IABSE) (SZ/1016-8664). [4,000] **5393**

STRUCTURAL ENGINEERING REPORT (CN/0319-0110). [50] **2031**

STRUKTUR BIAYA BUS DAN TRUK UMUM (IO/0126-494X). **5426**

STRUMENTI MUSICALI (IT/0392-890X). [22,000] **4155**

STUDENT ADVOCATE (OTTAWA) (CN/0703-2072). **1848**

STUDENT AID NEWS (US/0194-2212). **1785**

STUDENT GUIDE TO: GRADUATE LAW STUDY PROGRAMS (US/0196-9773). **3060**

STUDENT GUIDE TO: SUMMER LAW STUDY PROGRAMS (US/0197-6656). **3060**

STUDENT LAWYER (CHICAGO. 1972) (US/0039-274X). [40,000] **3060**

STUDENT LEADERSHIP MAGAZINE (US). [10,000] **1849**

STUDENT SUCCESS TUTOR DIRECTORY. SARASOTA COUNTY (US/0899-2355). [5,000] **1786**

STUDENT TRAVELS MAGAZINE (US). [900,000] **5491**

STUDI DI ANTICHITA CRISTIANA (IT). **283**

STUDI ECUMENICI (IT/0393-3687). [1,000] **4999**

STUDI ETNO-ANTROPOLOGICI E SOCIOLOGICI / PUBBLICATA SOTTO GLI AUSPICI DEL CONSIGLIO NAZIONALE DELLE RICHERCHE (IT). **246**

STUDI. FATTI. RICERCHE (IT/0393-3695). [1,000] **2493**

STUDI GORIZIANI (IT). [600] **2855**

STUDI ROMANI (IT/0039-2995). [2,000] **2630**

STUDI SENESI NEL CIRCOLO GIURIDICO DELLA R. UNIVERSITA (IT/0039-3010). **3060**

STUDI STORICI (IT/0039-3037). [6,000] **2711**

STUDI TASSIANI (IT/0081-6256). [350] **3441**

STUDI TRENTINI DI SCIENZE NATURALI. ACTA BIOLOGICA (IT/0392-0542). [1,000] **474**

STUDI TRENTINI DI SCIENZE NATURALI. ACTA GEOLOGICA (IT/0392-0534). [1,000] **1399**

STUDI TRENTINI DI SCIENZE NATURALI. SEZIONE B. BIOLOGICA (IT/0585-5616). [1,000] **5160**

STUDIA CANONICA (CN/0039-310X). [1,300] **5036**

STUDIA CHEMICA (SP). [500] **993**

STUDIA ETHNOGRAPHICA FRIBURGENSIA (SZ). [450] **246**

STUDIA LINGUISTICA (SW/0039-3193). [800] **3324**

STUDIA MATHEMATICA (PL/0039-3223). [2,000] **3536**

STUDIA MUSICOLOGICA NORVEGICA (NO/0332-5024). [150] **4155**

STUDIA MYSTICA (US/0161-7222). [400] **3441**

STUDIA NEOPHILOLOGICA (SW/0039-3274). [700] **3325**

STUDIA PHONETICA POSNANIENSIA (PL/0861-2085). [500] **3325**

STUDIA PSYCHOLOGICA (XO). [1,300] **4619**

STUDIA ROMANICA ET ANGLICA ZAGRABIENSIA (CI/0039-3339). [500] **3325**

STUDIA ROSENTHALIANA (NE/0039-3347). [400] **2273**

STUDIA SOCIETATIS SCIENTIARUM TORUNENSIS. SECTIO H, MEDICINA (PL/0860-9594). [300] **3643**

STUDIEN UND MITTEILUNGEN ZUR GESCHICHTE DES BENEDIKTINER-ORDENS UND SEINER ZWEIGE (GW). [400] **5037**

STUDIER I NORDISK FILOLOGI (FI/0356-0376). **3325**

STUDIES (IE/0039-3495). [3,000] **2523**

STUDIES AND REPORTS IN HYDROLOGY (FR/0081-7449). **5540**

STUDIES IN AMERICAN FICTION (US/0091-8083). [1,300] **3354**

STUDIES IN AMERICAN HUMOR (US/0095-280X). [600] **3441**

STUDIES IN ANCIENT ORIENTAL CIVILIZATION (US/0081-7554). [1,000] **283**

STUDIES IN BIBLIOGRAPHY AND BOOKLORE (US/0039-3568). [1,000] **5013**

STUDIES IN BROWNING AND HIS CIRCLE (US/0095-4489). [400] **435**

STUDIES IN CANADIAN LITERATURE (FREDERICTON, N.B.) (CN/0380-6995). [500] **3441**

STUDIES IN CENTRAL AND EAST ASIAN RELIGIONS : JOURNAL OF THE SEMINAR FOR BUDDHIST STUDIES, COPENHAGEN & AARHUS (DK/0904-2431). [2,300] **5022**

STUDIES IN CHRISTIAN ETHICS (UK). [750] **5000**

STUDIES IN CONTEMPORARY SATIRE (US/0163-4143). [300] **3441**

STUDIES IN ENGLISH LITERATURE, 1500-1900 (US/0039-3657). [1,900] **3442**

STUDIES IN FAMILY PLANNING (US/0039-3665). [6,000] **591**

STUDIES IN HISTORY AND SOCIAL SCIENCES (DK/0078-3307). [30] **2631**

STUDIES IN HISTORY OF MEDICINE AND SCIENCE (II). [600] **3643**

STUDIES IN ICONOGRAPHY (US/0148-1029). [480] **5000**

STUDIES IN LATIN AMERICAN POPULAR CULTURE (US/0730-9139). [500] **331**

STUDIES IN MEDITERRANEAN ARCHAEOLOGY (SW/0081-8232). [1,000] **283**

STUDIES IN MUSIC FROM THE UNIVERSITY OF WESTERN ONTARIO (CN/0703-3052). **4155**

STUDIES IN MYCOLOGY (NE/0166-0616). **576**

STUDIES IN PHILOLOGY (US/0039-3738). [1,700] **3326**

STUDIES IN SCOTTISH LITERATURE (US/0039-3770). [450] **3354**

STUDIES IN SECOND LANGUAGE ACQUISITION (US/0272-2631). [500] **3326**

STUDIES IN SHORT FICTION (US/0039-3789). [1,725] **3354**

STUDIES IN THE AMERICAN RENAISSANCE (US/0149-015X). **3354**

STUDIES IN THE HUMANITIES (US). [300] **2855**

STUDIES IN THE LINGUISTIC SCIENCES (US/0049-2388). [225] **3326**

STUDIES IN THE SPIRITUALITY OF JESUITS (US). [7,500] **5037**

STUDIES OF BROADCASTING (JA). [1,000] **1139**

STUDIES OF THE WARBURG INSTITUTE (UK/0083-7199). [165] **2855**

STUTTGARTER BEITRAEGE ZUR NATURKUNDE. SERIES C. ALLGEMEINVERSTAENDLICHE AUFSAETZE (GW/0341-0161). **4172**

SUB-STANCE (US/0049-2426). [800] **3443**

SUBSTANCE ABUSE IN SCHOOLS (US/0895-8874). **1349**

SUBURBAN. COTE DES NEIGES EDITION (CN/0229-2998). [101,000] **5795**

SUBURBAN (COTE-SAINT-LUC ED.) (CN/0226-9686). [19,000] **5795**

SUBURBAN. DOLLARD DES ORMEAUX EDITION (CN/0229-298X). [101,000] **5795**

SUBURBAN (LAVAL EDITION) (CN/0229-3048). [101,000] **2547**

SUBURBAN. NEW BORDEAUX, CARTIERVILLE EDITION (CN/0229-3013). [101,000] **5795**

SUBURBAN. NOTRE DAME DE GRACE EDITION (CN/0229-2971). [9,206] **5795**

SUBURBAN. ST. LAURENT EDITION (CN/0229-303X). [101,000] **5795**

SUBURBAN. TOWN OF MOUNT ROYAL EDITION (CN/0229-3021). **5795**

SUBURBAN (WESTMOUNT EDITION) (CN/0229-3005). [3,000] **5795**

SUCCESSFUL CALIFORNIA ACCOUNTANT, THE (US). [2,500] **752**

SUCCESSFUL FARMING (US/0039-4432). [576,000] **138**

SUCCESSFUL MARKETING TO SENIOR CITIZENS (US/8755-321X). [6,100] **937**

SUCCULENTA (NE/0039-4467). **528**

SUDAN UPDATE (UK). [600] **2493**

SUDOST EUROPA : [MONATSSCHRIFT DER ABTEILUNG GEGENWARTSFORSCHUNG DES SUDOST-INSTITUTS] (GW/0722-480X). [700] **5224**

SUDOST-FORSCHUNGEN (GW/0081-9077). [600] **2712**

SUDOSTDEUTSCHES ARCHIV (GW/0081-9085). [500] **2712**

SUFFOLK COUNTY AGRICULTURAL NEWS (US). [1,450] **138**

SUFISM (SAN RAFAEL, CALIF.) (US/0898-3380). [2,000] **5001**

SUGAR JOURNAL (US/0039-4734). [3,300] **188**

SUGAR PRODUCER, THE (US/0199-8498). **2359**

SUGAR WORLD (CN/0229-737X). **2359**

SUGARBEET GROWER, THE (US/0039-4750). [13,000] **188**

SUGARLAND (PH/0039-4777). [3,000] **188**

SUHDANNE (FI/0303-8130). [250] **1586**

SUID-AFRIKAANSE TYDSKRIF VIR APTEEKWESE (SA/0038-2558). [5,931] **4330**

SUISAN KAIYO KENKYU (JA/0916-1562). [1,000] **2314**

SULLIVAN COUNTY DEMOCRAT (US). [8,000] **4497**

SULPHUR IN AGRICULTURE (US/0160-0680). [3,000] **188**

SUMLEN (SW/0346-8119). [1,000] **4155**

SUMMA (AG/0325-4615). [10,000] **309**

SUMMA+ (AG/0327-9022). **309**

SUMMA MUSICAE MEDII AEVI (GW/0585-9158). **4155**

SUMMARIOS (AG/0325-6448). [5,000] **309**

SUMMARY - ALBERTA SECURITIES COMMISSION (CN/0319-3667). [250] **3060**

SUMMARY INSPECTION REPORT OF OFFICIAL SAMPLES ON SEED, FEED, FERTILIZER & AG-LIME (US/0193-8592). **203**

SUMMARY OF ACTIVITIES - MENTAL HEALTH LAW PROJECT (US/0363-2687). [6,000] **3060**

SUMMARY OF IOWA COUNTY ENGINEERS ANNUAL HIGHWAY REPORTS (US). **5445**

SUMMARY OF LABOR ARBITRATION AWARDS (US/0039-5005). [5,000] **1712**

SUMMARY REPORT, INDIVIDUAL INCOME TAX RETURNS FILED (US). [600] **4751**

SUMMIT (BIG BEAR LAKE) (US/0039-5056). [7,500] **4879**

SUMTER JOURNAL, THE (US/0747-0304). [8,000] **5651**

SUN (1993) (US/1072-8619). [2,000] **5721**

SUN BELT FLOOR COVERING (US/0895-934X). [22,242] **2907**

SUN (CHAPEL HILL, N.C.) (US/0744-9666). [25,000] **3443**

SUN/COAST ARCHITECT/BUILDER (US/0744-8872). [56,000] **629**

SUN-DIAMOND GROWER (US/0899-8809). [10,000] **2432**

SUN MAGAZINE (US/0889-3497). [80,000] **4280**

SUN-REPORTER, THE (US/0890-0930). [11,187] **5640**

SUNBELT FOODSERVICE (US/1069-3475). [18,500] **2359**

SUNBURST (ROSEVILLE) (US/0274-9181). [1,500] **5224**

SUNDAY TELEGRAM, THE (US). **5685**

SUNDEW GARDENS REPORTS (US/1052-2247). [500] **2432**

SUNDIAL (TORONTO) (CN/0827-312X). [11,000] **5001**

SUNY GENESCO COMPASS (US/0745-4147). [3,000] **1095**

SUOMEN HAMMASLAAKARISEURAN TOIMITUKSIA (FI/0039-551X). [5,800] **1336**

SUOMEN KALASTUSLEHTI (FI). [4,392] **2314**

SUOMEN KIRJALLISUUS; VUOSILUETTELO (FI). **425**

SUOMEN KULTTUURIRAHASTON VUOSIKATSAUS (FI). [1,500] **2712**

SUOMEN MATKAILU (FI/0359-0607). [35,000] **2523**

SUPER AUTOMOTIVE SERVICE (US/0896-0437). [114,000] **5426**

SUPER GROUP MAGAZINE (US/1043-2418). [6,000] **1204**

SUPERCONDUCTOR INDUSTRY (US/1042-4105). [6,500] **5161**

SUPERPREP. AMERICA'S RECRUITING MAGAZINE (US). **4924**

SUPERTRAX (CN). [160,000] **4855**

SUPERVISION (BURLINGTON) (US/0039-5854). [5,402] **947**

SUPERVISOR (ENGLEWOOD, N.J.), EL (US/1043-2191). [20,000] **2871**

SUPPLEMENTAL SALARY STUDY, SELECTED SCHOOL, DISTRICT, AND COUNTY PERSONNEL (US/0148-3234). [300] **1873**

SUPPLEMENTARY PAPER - COMMITTEE FOR ECONOMIC DEVELOPMENT OF AUSTRALIA (AT/0591-0137). [2,000] **1523**

SUPPLEMENTO ALLE RICERCHE DI BIOLOGIA DELLA SELVAGGINA / LABORATORIO DI ZOOLOGIA APPLICATA ALLA CACCIA (IT). **5598**

SUPPLEMENTS TO VETUS TESTAMENTUM (NE/0083-5889). **5001**

SUPPLY LINE (US/8750-0124). [6,000] **4058**

SUPPORT FOR LEARNING (UK/0268-2141). [5,000] **1786**

SUR MESURE (CN/0822-5257). **1802**

SUREPAY UPDATE (US/0195-5225). [2,000] **813**

SURFACE COATINGS AUSTRALIA (AT/0815-709X). [1,530] **1030**

SURFACE DESIGN JOURNAL (US/0197-4483). [3,000] **5356**

SURFACE MOUNT TECHNOLOGY (US/0893-3588). [55,000] **2083**

SURFACES (FR/0585-9840). [6,373] **4021**

SURFING (SAN CLEMENTE, CALIF.) (US/0194-9314). [88,000] **4924**

SURGERY (OXFORD) (UK/0263-9319). **3975**

SURGICAL PRODUCT NEWS (US/0279-4829). [75,000] **3684**

SURPLUS RECORD, THE (US/0039-615X). [120,000] **2129**

SURVEI PERIKANAN LAUT (IO). **2314**

SURVEY ANGKUTAN UDARA (IO). **37**

SURVEY OF BUSINESS (US/0099-0973). [5,500] **1586**

SURVEY OF DATA PROCESSING SALARIES (US/0737-4887). [200] **1713**

SURVEY OF OFFICE SALARIES, PERSONNEL PRACTICES, AND BENEFITS (US/0737-4860). [300] **1713**

SURVEY

Controlled Circulation Index

SURVEY OF OUT-OF-STATE PASSENGER CARS AND OUT-OF-STATE CAMPER VEHICLES ON INTERSTATE, ARTERIAL AND PRIMARY HIGHWAYS IN VIRGINIA, A (US/0363-4027). **5445**

SURVEY OF SUPERVISORY PERSONNEL SALARIES (US/0737-4879). [200] **1713**

SURVEYING TECHNICIAN (UK/0952-5793). [6,500] **2032**

SURVIVE (VANCOUVER, B.C.) (CN/0229-1975). **5001**

SURYA INDIA (II). [40,000] **2508**

SUSSEX FAMILY HISTORIAN (UK). [2000] **2474**

SUSTAINABLE FARMING (CN/1180-1506). [1,200] **138**

SV. SOUND AND VIBRATION (US/0038-1810). [22,000] **4453**

SVENSK FARMACEUTISK TIDSKRIFT (SW/0039-6524). [8,700] **4330**

SVENSK PAPPERSTIDNING (SW/0039-6680). [8,000] **4239**

SVENSK TRAVARU- OCH PAPPERSMASSETIDNING (SW/0039-6796). [2,600] **2405**

SVENSK VETERINARTIDNING (SW/0346-2250). **5522**

SVENSKA TIDNINGSARTIKLAR (SW/0039-6907). [400] **426**

SVENSKA TIDSKRIFTSARTIKLAR (SW). [800] **426**

SVERIGES FRIMARKEN OCH HELSAKER / SVERIGES FILATELIST-FORBUND (SW/0347-1152). [20,000] **2787**

SVERIGES UTSADESFORENINGS TIDSKRIFT (SW/0039-6990). [1,300] **189**

SVETSAREN (SW/0346-8577). [25,000] **4028**

SVETSEN (SW/0039-7091). [4,000] **4028**

SVOBODA (JERSEY CITY) (US/0274-6964). [14,000] **5711**

SWAMP GAS JOURNAL, THE (CN/0707-7106). [150] **37**

SWANN GALLERIES, INC (US/0193-5526). [1,000] **4832**

SWARA / EAST AFRICAN WILD LIFE SOCIETY (KE). [15,000] **5598**

SWAZILAND GOVERNMENT GAZETTE (SQ). [1,000] **5811**

SWEDISH DEFENCE MATERIEL ADMINISTRATION QUALIFIED PRODUCT LIST OF ELECTRONIC COMPONENTS : SE-MIL-QPL (SW/0283-8060). [500] **2083**

SWEDISH DENTAL JOURNAL (SW/0347-9994). [12,000] **1336**

SWEDISH JOURNAL OF AGRICULTURAL RESEARCH (SW/0049-2701). **139**

SWEET'S CATALOG FILE. PRODUCTS FOR ENGINEERING AND RETROFIT, ELECTRICAL AND RELATED PRODUCTS (US/1056-5647). **2083**

SWEET'S CATALOG FILE. PRODUCTS FOR HOME BUILDING AND REMODELING (US/0743-5789). **629**

SWIM (ARLINGTON, VA.) (US/8755-2027). [8,000] **4924**

SWIMMING TEACHER (UK/0306-0403). **4925**

SWIMMING TECHNIQUE (US/0039-7415). [8,000] **4925**

SWIMMING WORLD AND JUNIOR SWIMMER (1965) (US/0039-7431). [31,000] **4925**

SWISS AMERICAN REVIEW (US). **5721**

SWISS CHEM (SZ/0251-1703). **993**

SWISS FOOD (SZ/0251-1681). **2359**

SWISS MATERIALS (SZ/1013-4476). [3,000] **1997**

SWISS MED (SZ/0251-1665). **3644**

SWISS PACKAGING CATALOGUE (SZ). **4222**

SWISS PHARMA (SZ/0251-1673). **4330**

SYDNEY'S CHILD (AT/1034-6384). [55,000] **2286**

SYGEPLEJERSKEN (DK/0106-8350). [65,000] **3870**

SYLLECTA CLASSICA (US/1040-3612). [100] **1080**

SYMBOLS (US/0889-7425). [2,000] **246**

SYMMEIKTA / VASILIKON HIDRYMA EREUNON, KENTRON VYZANTINÂON EREUNON (GR). [1,000] **2712**

SYMPHONY USER'S JOURNAL, THE (US/8750-9415). [2,500] **1291**

SYMPOSIA MEDICA HOECHST (GW/0341-6321). **3644**

SYMPOSIUM (INTERNATIONAL) ON COMBUSTION. PAPERS (US/0082-0784). [2,000] **1997**

SYNAPSE (FR/0762-7475). **3846**

SYNDICATION NEWS (US/1052-4290). **1140**

SYNERGY (DALLAS) (US/0164-8993). [2,000] **3252**

SYNOPSES OF THE BRITISH FAUNA (UK/0082-1101). **5598**

SYNOPTIC (CN/0049-2760). **1786**

SYNTHESIS (ASHEVILLE, N.C.) (US/1042-0169). **3062**

SYNTHETIC COMMUNICATIONS (US/0039-7911). **1048**

SYNTHETIC FIBRES / ASSOCIATION OF SYNTHETIC FIBRE INDUSTRY (II). [1,000] **5356**

SYRACUSE LAW REVIEW (US/0039-7938). [2,000] **3062**

SYRACUSE NEW TIMES (US/0893-844X). [45,000] **2493**

SYRIA'S BUDGET (SY). [200] **4751**

SYRIE & MONDE ARABE (SY/0039-7962). [1,000] **1523**

SYSTEEMTEORETISCH BULLETIN - INTERAKTIE AKADEMIE (BE/0775-5694). [1,000] **1886**

SYSTEM (ATLANTA, GA.) (US). [15,500] **1849**

SYSTEM TREND SERVICE (US). **1204**

SYSTEMATIC BOTANY (US/0363-6445). [1,650] **528**

SYSTEMS SCIENCE (PL/0137-1223). [600] **1249**

SYSTEMS THINKER, THE (US/1050-2726). [2,000] **887**

SYSTEMS USER (US/0199-8951). [37,500] **1262**

SZACHY (PL). [14,000] **4866**

SZAZADOK (HU/0039-8098). [2,400] **2631**

SZINHAZ (HU/0039-8136). [2,500] **5369**

T A Q JOURNAL, A (CN/0706-9987). **3327**

T A S A, TEACHING ATYPICAL STUDENTS IN ALBERTA (CN/0315-1808). **1886**

T & D (AT/1037-9687). **887**

T & G RECORD (UK). [200,000] **1713**

T.E.A.M (US). **5312**

T.E.L. THE ELECTRIC LETTER (US/0093-5379). [400] **2083**

T. E. S. L. TALK (CN/0700-1584). [4,300] **1786**

T.U.B.A. MEMBERSHIP ROSTER (US/0163-5360). [2,300] **4156**

TAA REPORT (US/1041-1453). [1,000] **4832**

TAAL EN TONGVAL (BE/0039-8691). [360] **3327**

TAAMULI (TZ). [500] **4497**

TAAWUM MIN AJLI AL-TANMIYAH (SJ). [500] **1523**

TABAC AU CANADA (CN/0713-5467). [100] **5373**

TABLAS (CU). [10,000] **5369**

TABLE (LONDON. 1953) (UK/0264-7133). [1,000] **4689**

TABLE TENNIS TECHNICAL (CN/0828-4539). **4925**

TABLEAU DES MEMBRES - ORDRE DES ARCHITECTES DU QUEBEC (CN/0317-8854). [5,000] **309**

TABLETALK (LAKE MARY, FLA.) (US/1064-881X). [28,000] **5002**

TABLOID (FAIRFAX, VA.), THE (US/0279-053X). [3,500] **4569**

TACT : THE AIR CARGO TARIFF (NE). **5394**

TAEHAN SAENGNI HAKHOE CHI (KO/0372-1582). [500] **587**

TAFRIJA (TUCKER, GA.) (US/1070-7522). [70,000] **389**

TAG DES HERRN (GW/0492-1283). [100,000] **5037**

TAG (STERLING, VA.) (US/1067-9197). [300] **1281**

TAGS (US). [1,500] **1786**

TAHQIQAT-I ISLAMI (II). [1,500] **5045**

TAI-WAN SHUI LI (CH). [700] **2244**

TAIDE (FI/0039-8977). [7,586] **366**

TAIKABUTSU (JA/0039-8993). [2,100] **4021**

TAIKI OSEN JOJI SOKUTEIKYOKU SOKUTEI KEKKA HOKOKU. KEINENPO (JA). [200] **2244**

TAIKI OSEN JOJI SOKUTEIKYOKU SOKUTEI KEKKA HOKOKU. NENPO (JA). [200] **2244**

TAITO (FI/0355-7421). [12,000] **376**

TAIWAN ENTERPRISE (CH). **1628**

TAIWAN EXPORTERS GUIDE (CH). [20,000] **853**

TAIWAN HAIXIA (CC/1000-8160). [1,000] **1457**

TAIWAN STATISTICAL DATA BOOK (CH). [1,000] **5344**

TAIWAN STUDIES NEWSLETTER (US/1048-2342). [300] **2666**

TAIYO CHIKYU KEIHO EISEI CHOSA HOKOKU (JA). [150] **37**

TAKAMATSU KOGYO KOTO SENMON GAKKO KENKYU KIYO (JA/0389-9268). [350] **5237**

TAKING CARE (US). [450,000] **4804**

TALBOT TIMES (CN/0827-2816). [325] **2474**

TALES OF PARADISE RIDGE (US/0496-7607). [300] **2631**

TALES OF THE TWELVE (CN/0713-3901). [650] **4097**

TALK OF THE MONTH (US/0743-1384). [200] **3444**

TALKING BOOK TOPICS (US/0039-9183). [380,000] **4394**

TALKING BOOKS (CN/0225-5723). **4832**

TALKS OF POPE JOHN PAUL II (US). [1,500] **5037**

TALON (AURORA, COLO.) (US/0892-6476). [1,000] **5598**

TAMARAW TIMES (CN/0710-1112). **5795**

TAMARIND PAPERS, THE (US/0276-3397). [540] **382**

TAMIL TIMES (UK/0266-4488). [3,500] **2666**

TAMKANG JOURNAL OF MATHEMATICS (CH/0376-4079). [350] **3538**

TAMPA BAY BUSINESS JOURNAL (US/0896-467X). [13,000] **714**

TAMS JOURNAL (US/0039-8233). [1,700] **2783**

TANDLAKARTIDNINGEN (SW/0039-6982). [13,000] **1336**

TANK (UK/0039-9418). [2,200] **4058**

TANZANIA NATIONAL BIBLIOGRAPHY (MONTHLY) (TZ/0856-003X). [250] **426**

TAPORI (US/0882-5424). [12,000] **1070**

TAPPI JOURNAL (US/0734-1415). [28,145] **4239**

TAR HEEL NURSE (US/0039-9620). [4,000] **3870**

TAR PAPER (EDMONTON) (CN/0704-9811). [3,000] **4280**

TARBIZS (IS/0334-3650). **5053**

TAREAS (PN/0494-7061). [1,500] **5224**

TARGET MARKETING (US/0889-5333). [39,000] **937**

TARIFAS Y DATOS: MEDIOS IMPRESOS (MX). [1,200] **767**

TAS TOTS (AT). [1,500] **1070**

TASMANIAN ANCESTRY (AT/0159-0677). [1,500] **2474**

TASMANIAN BUILDING JOURNAL (AT). [800] **630**

TASMANIAN COUNTRY (AT). [12,200] **2511**

TATTVALOKAH / TATTVALOKA (II). [5,000] **5041**

TAVERN SPORTS INTERNATIONAL (US). [25,000] **4866**

TAX ADVISER, THE (US/0039-9957). [25,000] **4751**

TAX EXEMPT NEWS (US/0194-228X). [1,000] **4752**

TAX FACTS AND FIGURES (MONTREAL) (CN/0821-0780). **4752**

TAX, FINANCIAL AND ESTATE PLANNING FOR THE OWNER OF A CLOSELY-HELD CORPORATION (US/0194-8822). [2,000] **3119**

TAX FOUNDATION'S LIBRARY BULLETIN (US/0736-6469). **3252**

TAX FOUNDATION'S TAX FEATURES (US/0883-1335). **4752**

TAX LAWS OF THE WORLD. CLASS B (US). **4753**

TAX LAWYER : BULLETIN OF THE SECTION OF TAXATION, AMERICAN BAR ASSOCIATION, THE (US/0040-005X). **3062**

TAX MEMO (PRICE WATERHOUSE (FIRM)) (CN/0712-6921). **4753**

TAX NEWS SERVICE (NE/0040-0076). **3062**

TAX NOTES (ARLINGTON) (US/0270-5494). [3,200] **4753**

TAX PLANNING CHECKLIST (CN/0821-0764). [25,000] **3062**

TAX PROFILE (DON MILLS, ONT.) (CN/0827-3677). **4754**

TAX RATES IN VIRGINIA'S CITIES, COUNTIES, AND SELECTED TOWNS (US). [250] **4754**

TAXATION OF PATENT ROYALTIES, DIVIDENDS, INTEREST IN EUROPE (NE). **4755**

TAXATION OF PRIVATE INVESTMENT INCOME (NE). **4755**

TAXON (GW/0040-0262). [2,000] **529**

TAXPAYER: ANNUAL TAXATION SUMMARY (AT). [15,000] **4755**

TAZEWELL GENEALOGICAL MONTHLY (1985) (US/1071-054X). [400] **2474**

TBC NEWS (US/1046-8927). [3,000] **4394**

TC. TWIN CITIES (US/0274-5151). [44,000] **2547**

TE & MS TELECOM ASIA (HK). [12,000] **1164**

TE PUNA MATAURANGA: THE NATIONAL LIBRARY OF NEW ZEALAND NEWSLETTER (NZ/0114-1090). [2,500] **3252**

TEACH (FORT WORTH, TEX.) (US/8755-8769). [5,000] **5002**

TEACHER EDUCATION REPORTS (US). **1906**

TEACHER EDUCATOR, THE (US/0887-8730). [1,300] **1906**

TEACHER MAGAZINE (US/1046-6193). **1906**

TEACHER (VANCOUVER) (CN/0841-9574). [50,000] **1787**

TEACHERS & WRITERS (US/0739-0084). [2,000] **3444**

TEACHING AND TRAINING IN GERIATRIC MEDICINE (SZ/1011-3738). **3755**

TEACHING ENGLISH IN THE TWO-YEAR COLLEGE (US/0098-6291). [3,000] **1850**

TEACHING ENGLISH TO DEAF AND SECOND-LANGUAGE STUDENTS (US). [800] **1886**

TEACHING FOR SUCCESS (US). **1850**

TEACHING GEOGRAPHY (UK). [6,000] **1907**

TEACHING HOME, THE (US). [37,000] **1787**

TEACHING SCIENCE (UK/0028-0763). [900] **5161**

TEACHING TODAY (EDMONTON) (CN/0827-3049). [10,000] **1907**

TEAM LICENSING BUSINESS (US/1065-738X). [25,000] **1628**

TEAM TORIZONS (US/0163-3422). [40,000] **5002**

TECH. MEMO. - UNIVERSITY OF GUELPH. DEPARTMENT OF LAND RESOURCE SCIENCE (CN/0710-9466). [60] **189**

TECH, THE (US/0148-9607). [9,000] **5690**

TECHNICAL BULLETIN - INSTITUTE FOR LAND AND WATER MANAGEMENT RESEARCH (NE/0074-042X). [1,600] **189**

TECHNICAL BULLETIN - WISCONSIN DEPARTMENT OF NATURAL RESOURCES (US/0084-0564). [1,500] **2206**

TECHNICAL BULLETINS / ASSOCIATION OF OPERATIVE MILLERS (US). [1,600] **937**

TECHNICAL MEMORANDUM - ASSOCIATE COMMITTEE ON GEOTECHNICAL RESEARCH (OTTAWA) (CN/0077-5428). [1,000] **2032**

TECHNICAL PAPERS IN HYDROLOGY (FR/0082-2310). **1418**

TECHNICAL RELEASE - NATIONAL PEST CONTROL ASSOCIATION (US). [6,000] **4248**

TECHNICAL REPORT (CONSERVATION COMMISSION OF THE NORTHERN TERRITORY) (AT/0729-9990). [400] **2206**

TECHNICAL REPORT - COOPERATIVE NATIONAL PARK RESOURCES STUDIES UNIT, UNIVERSITY OF HAWAII AT MANOA (US). [200] **2206**

TECHNICAL REPORT - MARINE SCIENCES RESEARCH CENTER, STATE UNIVERSITY OF NEW YORK (US/0362-2886). **5162**

TECHNICAL REPORT - SOUTHEASTERN WISCONSIN REGIONAL PLANNING COMMISSION (US/0584-4290). **2836**

TECHNICAL REVIEW / GEC ALSTHOM (FR/0994-7590). [12,000] **2083**

TECHNICAL REVIEW MIDDLE EAST (UK/0267-5307). [18,879] **5162**

TECHNICAL SOARING (US/0744-8996). [500] **37**

TECHNICKE PRIUCKY (STATNI VYZKUMNY USTAV PRO STAVBU STROJU) (XR/0231-5297). [1,000] **2130**

TECHNIKAS APSKATS - LATVIESU INZENIERU APVIENIBA (CN/0381-5366). [530] **1998**

TECHNIQUE MODERNE, LA (FR/0040-1250). [3,000] **5162**

TECHNIQUES TRESOR (FR/0223-5587). [1,500] **887**

TECHNISCHES MESSE : TM (GW/0171-8096). [4,000] **4033**

TECHNOLOGY & CONSERVATION (US/0146-1214). [15,500] **366**

TECHNOLOGY IRELAND (IE/0040-1676). [5,500] **5164**

TECHNOLOGY RESOURCE GUIDES (US). [5,000] **5164**

TECHNOLOGY SPECIAL INTEREST SECTION NEWSLETTER (US/1059-0609). [2000] **5164**

TECHNOLOGY TODAY (US/0148-3595). [13,500] **1916**

TECHNOLOGY TODAY (MISSISSAUGA) (CN/0712-9467). [10,000] **5164**

TECHNOLOGY UPDATE (PALO ALTO, CALIF.) (US/0896-8586). [500] **4394**

TECHNOLOGY WATCH FOR THE GRAPHIC ARTS AND INFORMATION INDUSTRIES (CN/0738-9507). [600] **382**

TECHNOLOGY WATCH (WILLOWDALE) (CN/1180-3703). **1205**

TECHNOMETRICS (US/0040-1706). [6,000] **5176**

TECHNOS (BLOOMINGTON, IND.) (US/1060-5649). **1787**

TECHNOSTYLE (CN/0712-4627). [150] **3444**

TECHNOVA (HK). [40,000] **1998**

TECHTRENDS (US/8756-3894). [12,000] **1225**

TECNICA TEXTIL INTERNACIONAL (SP/0040-1900). [7,500] **5356**

TECNOLOGIA ELETTRICHE. INDUSTRIA ITALIANA ELETTROTECNICA ED ELETTRONICA (IT/0390-6698). [7,400] **2083**

TECNOLOGIA MILITAR (GW/0722-2904). [31,500] **4059**

TECNOLOGIE DEI SERVIZI PUBBLICI (IT). [9,100] **4690**

TECNOLOGIE MECCANICHE (IT/0391-1683). [15,100] **2130**

TEDDY BEAR AND FRIENDS, THE (US/0745-7189). [60,000] **2778**

TEEN WORLD, THE MAGAZINE FOR TOMORROW'S LEADERS (US/1063-2492). [1000] **1070**

TEHNICESKAJA ELEKTRODINAMIKA (UN/0204-3599). **2084**

TEHNOLOGIJA MESA (YU/0494-9846). **3488**

TEHO / TYOTEHOSEURA (FI/0355-0567). [5,500] **140**

TEIKOKU GINKO KAISHA NENKAN. HIGASHI NIHON (JA). [21,500] **1629**

TEJAS JOURNAL OF AUDIOLOGY AND SPEECH PATHOLOGY (US/0738-8837). **3891**

TEKNISK TIDSKRIFT-NY TEKNIK (SW). **5165**

TELCOM HIGHLIGHTS (US/0890-1198). [450] **1164**

TELECOM INSIDER (US/0742-6445). **1164**

TELECOM MARKET LETTER, THE (US/0712-3663). [300] **1164**

TELECOM OUTLOOK : THE TELECOMMUNICATIONS & DATA COMMUNICATIONS NEWSLETTER (US/1045-6562). [500] **1164**

TELECOM WORLD (UK/0963-0597). [18,000] **1165**

TELECOMMUNICATION JOURNAL (ENGLISH EDITION) (SZ/0497-137X). [7,000] **1165**

TELECOMMUNICATION JOURNAL OF AUSTRALIA, THE (AT/0040-2486). [7,000] **1165**

TELECOMMUNICATIONS (NORTH AMERICAN EDITION) (US/0278-4831). [85,000] **1166**

TELECOMMUNICATIONS STRATEGIES REPORT (AT/1322-3518). [200] **1166**

TELEMA (KINSHASA) (CG/1013-7769). [2,500] **5002**

TELEMANAGEMENT (PICKERING) (CN/0840-5476). [1,500] **1167**

TELEMARKETING (US/0730-6156). [60,000] **1167**

TELEMATICS COMMUNICATIONS QUARTERLY (US). **1123**

TELEPHONE ENGINEER & MANAGEMENT DIRECTORY (US). [8,000] **1167**

TELESIS (CN/0040-2710). [25,000] **1167**

TELEVISION BROADCAST (US/0898-767X). [25,000] **1140**

TELEVISION (LONDON) (UK/0308-454X). [4,000] **1141**

TELEVISION QUARTERLY (BEVERLY HILL) (US/0040-2796). [14,000] **1141**

TELINDUS NEWS (NE). **1244**

TELLUS. SERIES A, DYNAMIC METEOROLOGY AND OCEANOGRAPHY (SW/0280-6495). [1,300] **1436**

TELMA (GW/0340-4927). [600] **189**

TELOCATOR (US/0193-1458). **1168**

TELOS (ST. LOUIS) (US/0090-6514). [2,500] **5224**

TEMA CELESTE (IT). [8,000] **366**

TEMAS (NEW YORK, N.Y.) (US/0040-2869). [114,000] **2493**

TEMISCAMIEN (1976) (CN/0382-0653). [4,000] **5796**

TEMOIGNAGE MESSIANIQUE AU PEUPLE D'ISRAEL (FR). [6,000] **5002**

TEMPERATURE DEVELOPMENTS (US). **4432**

TEMPLE INTERNATIONAL AND COMPARATIVE LAW JOURNAL (US/0889-1915). [300] **3136**

TEMPLE POLITICAL & CIVIL RIGHTS LAW REVIEW (US/1062-5887). **4513**

TEMPO (MZ). [35,000] **2500**

TEMPO MEDICO (IT). [75,000] **3645**

TEMPS DE VIVRE (MONTREAL) (CN/0708-7632). [40,000] **5182**

TEMPS FORT (CN/0229-4052). **4855**

TENAGAWAN (MY). [27,000] **1629**

TENANT (US/0040-3083). [4,000] **2836**

TENNESSEE ATTORNEYS DIRECTORY (US/0742-4329). [2,000] **3063**

TENNESSEE BAR JOURNAL (US/0497-2325). [6,200] **3063**

TENNESSEE BUSINESS AND INDUSTRIAL REVIEW (US). **1629**

TENNESSEE CONSERVATIONIST, THE (US/0040-3202). [16,000] **2207**

TENNESSEE EMPLOYMENT LAW UPDATE, THE (US/0886-8557). **3154**

TENNESSEE FAMILY LAW LETTER (US/0890-5355). **3122**

TENNESSEE FARMER (NASHVILLE, TENN.) (US/0040-3245). [20,136] **140**

TENNESSEE FOLKLORE SOCIETY BULLETIN (US/0040-3253). [350] **2324**

TENNESSEE JOURNAL OF HEALTH, PHYSICAL EDUCATION, RECREATION, AND DANCE / TENNESSEE ASSOCIATION OF HEALTH, PHYSICAL EDUCATION, RECREATION, AND DANCE (US/0890-1597). [800] **1859**

TENNESSEE JOURNAL, THE (US/0194-1240). [1,400] **4498**

TENNESSEE LEGISLATIVE RECORD (US). [525] **3063**

TENNESSEE LIBRARIAN (US/0162-1564). [1,600] **3252**

TENNESSEE NURSE (US/1055-3134). [2600] **3870**

TENNESSEE RESTAURANTEUR (US). [1,200] **5073**

TENNESSEE STATISTICAL ABSTRACT (US/0082-2760). [1,200] **5345**

TENNESSEE TAX GUIDE (US/0742-0757). [3,500] **4756**

TENNESSEE TOWN & CITY (US/0040-3415). [5,000] **4690**

TENNESSEE TRUCKER, THE (US/0887-3526). [16,000] **5394**

TENNESSEE'S BUSINESS (MURFREESBORO, TENN.) (US/0735-1135). [2,500] **715**

TENNIS INDUSTRY (US/0191-5851). [26,841] **4925**

TENNIS LONDON. 1981 (UK/0262-9224). [15,000] **4925**

TENNISPRO (US). **4926**

TENOLAI (II). [2,000] **5176**

TENSOR (JA/0040-3504). **3538**

TEOLOGINEN AIKAKAUSKIRJA. TEOLOGISK TIDSKRIFT (FI/0040-3555). [3,000] **5002**

TEORIA E PRATICA DEGLI SCAMBI INTERNAZIONALI (IT). **853**

TEORIIA MASHIN METALLURGICHESKOGO I GORNOGO OBORUDOVANIIA (RU). **2130**

TEQUESTA (US/0363-3705). [3,500] **2762**

TERESIANUM (IT). [700] **5003**

TERMNET NEWS : JOURNAL OF THE INTERNATIONAL NETWORK FOR TERMINOLOGY (TERMNET) (AU/0251-5253). [1,200] **3328**

TERRA ET AQUA (NE/0376-6411). [4000] **2096**

TERRA GRISCHUNA (SZ). [24,000] **2712**

TERRA (LOS ANGELES, CALIF.) (US/0040-3733). [22,000] **4173**

TERRAE INCOGNITAE (US/0082-2884). [500] **2577**

TERRE — Controlled Circulation Index

TERRE DE CHEZ NOUS. DOSSIER D'INFORMATION TECHNIQUE ET PROFESSIONNELLE, LA (CN/0823-2784). [50,000] **141**

TERRE DE CHEZ NOUS (MONTREAL) (CN/0040-3830). [50,000] **141**

TERREBONNE LIFE LINES (US/0735-2794). [500] **2474**

TERRELL TRAILS (US/0884-2108). **2474**

TERRITORIAL SEA JOURNAL (US/1046-9680). **3182**

TERROR AUSTRALIS: THE AUSTRALIAN HORROR & FANTASY MAGAZINE (AT/1031-3001). [300] **3445**

TERRORISM (MINNEAPOLIS, MINN.) (US/0278-663X). **3177**

TERTIARY RESEARCH (NE/0308-9649). [550] **1399**

TERZOOCCHIO (IT). [10,000] **366**

TESOL MATTERS (US/1051-8886). [23,000] **1907**

TESOL QUARTERLY (US/0039-8322). [11,500] **3328**

TESSERA (BURNABY) (CN/0840-4631). [500] **3445**

TEST & MEASUREMENT WORLD (US/0744-1657). [73,000] **2084**

TEST (OAKHURST, N.J.) (US/0193-4120). [10,475] **2130**

TESTO UNICO IMPOSTE DIRETTE (IT). [12,000] **3063**

TEX HOME (IT). [8,000] **5357**

TEX-RAYS : OFFICIAL JOURNAL TEXAS SOCIETY OF RADIOLOGIC TECHNOLOGISTS, INC (US). [1,200] **3947**

TEXARKANA GAZETTE (US). [33,203] **5632**

TEXARKANA USA GENEALOGIST'S QUARTERLY, THE (US/0741-6105). [300] **2474**

TEXARKANA USA QUARTERLY (1987) (US/1067-1412). **2474**

TEXAS A & M BUSINESS FORUM (US/0882-8849). [3,000] **715**

TEXAS BAPTIST HISTORY (US/0732-4324). [200] **5068**

TEXAS BAR JOURNAL (US/0040-4187). [53,000] **3063**

TEXAS BASKETBALL MAGAZINE (US). [25,000] **4926**

TEXAS BICYCLIST (US). [50,000] **429**

TEXAS BUSINESS REVIEW (US/0040-4209). [7,000] **1586**

TEXAS COACH (US/0040-4241). [11,500] **4926**

TEXAS DENTAL JOURNAL (US/0040-4284). [7,500] **1336**

TEXAS DO (US/0275-1453). [3,500] **3645**

TEXAS FOOD MERCHANT (US/0040-4322). [3,500] **2359**

TEXAS HEART INSTITUTE JOURNAL (US/0730-2347). [25,000] **3710**

TEXAS HOTEL REVIEW (SAN ANTONIO, TEX. : 1988) (US). **2809**

TEXAS INTERNATIONAL LAW JOURNAL (US/0163-7479). [800] **3136**

TEXAS JEWISH POST, THE (US/0040-439X). **5755**

TEXAS JOURNAL OF IDEAS, HISTORY, AND CULTURE (US/0894-3354). [10,000] **2855**

TEXAS JOURNAL OF POLITICAL STUDIES (US/0191-0930). [200] **4498**

TEXAS LINGUISTIC FORUM (US/0741-2576). [200] **3328**

TEXAS LIST, THE (US/0363-2474). [150] **1714**

TEXAS LIVESTOCK MARKET NEWS (US/0199-7041). [2,750] **222**

TEXAS LONE STAR (US/0749-9310). [13,000] **1873**

TEXAS MATHEMATICS TEACHER (US/0277-030X). [1,200] **3538**

TEXAS NATURAL RESOURCES REPORTER (US/0197-2340). [250] **4280**

TEXAS NURSING (US/0095-036X). [6,000] **3870**

TEXAS POLICE JOURNAL (US/0040-4594). [5,500] **3178**

TEXAS PROFESSIONAL PHOTOGRAPHER (US). [925] **4377**

TEXAS PUBLIC UTILITY NEWS (US/0744-7981). [120] **4762**

TEXAS REGISTER (US/0362-4781). [5,000] **4690**

TEXAS REVIEW (HUNTSVILLE, TEX.), THE (US/0885-2685). [750] **3354**

TEXAS SAVINGS & LOAN DIRECTORY (US). [2,500] **813**

TEXAS SCHOOL LAW NEWS (AUSTIN, TEX. : 1980) (US/0275-4444). [850] **3064**

TEXAS STATE DIRECTORY (US/0363-7530). [12,000] **4690**

TEXAS STUDIES IN LITERATURE AND LANGUAGE (US/0040-4691). [950] **3445**

TEXAS TELLER QUARTERLY NEWSLETTER (US/0892-5186). [500] **3445**

TEXAS THOROUGHBRED (WICHITA FALLS, KAN.) (US/0164-6168). [2,500] **2802**

TEXAS VETERINARY MEDICAL JOURNAL (US/0040-4756). [3,000] **5522**

TEXAS WATER RESOURCES (US/0744-1320). [10,500] **5541**

TEXREPORT (SA). [230] **5357**

TEXT (NEW YORK, N.Y. : 1985) (US/0736-3974). **3354**

TEXTBOOK NEWS (US/0733-8228). **1787**

TEXTES ET DOCUMENTS - MINISTERE DES AFFAIRES ETRANGERES, DU COMMERCE EXTERIEUR ET DE LA COOPERATION AU DEVELOPPEMENT (BE). [10,000] **4536**

TEXTES - SOCIETE HISTORIQUE DE QUEBEC (CN/0081-1130). [600] **2763**

TEXTIL- ES TEXTILRUHAZATI IPARI SZAKIRODALMI TAJEKOZTATO (HU/0209-9578). [115] **5357**

TEXTILE CHEMIST AND COLORIST (US/0040-490X). [10,200] **5357**

TEXTILE DYER & PRINTER (II/0040-4926). [10,000] **5357**

TEXTILE FLAMMABILITY DIGEST (US/0738-9620). [200] **5357**

TEXTILE INDUSTRIES DYEGEST OF SOUTHERN AFRICA (SA/0254-0533). [1,750] **5358**

TEXTILE MAGAZINE, THE (II/0040-5078). [20,000] **5358**

TEXTILE MANUFACTURING (US/1065-1713). [16,500] **5358**

TEXTILE MUSEUM JOURNAL (US/0083-7407). [3,500] **4097**

TEXTILE WORLD (US/0040-5213). **5358**

TEXTILES (UK/0306-0748). [5500] **5359**

TEXTILES PANAMERICANOS (US/0049-3570). [11,511] **5359**

TEXTILES SUISSES (SZ/0040-5248). [13,000] **5359**

TEXTILVEREDLUNG (SZ/0040-5310). [3,000] **5359**

TGA-PC (ARLINGTON, VA.) (US/1047-045X). [500] **1850**

THAI BUILDER DIRECTORY (TH). **630**

THAI INDUSTRIAL DIRECTORY (TH). **1629**

THAI JOURNAL OF SURGERY (TH/0125-6068). [1,200] **3976**

THAI LIFE (TH/0125-6637). [3,000] **2770**

THALIA (OTTAWA) (CN/0706-5604). [600] **3445**

THAMES RIVER REVIEW (CN/0823-9843). **2207**

THAT WAS THE WEEK THAT WAS (CN/0820-8026). [500] **917**

THEATER IN OSTERREICH / WIENER GESELLSCHAFT FUER THEATERFORSCHUNG, INSTITUT FUER THEATERWISSENSCHAFT AN DER UNIVERSITAT WIEN (AU). [400] **5370**

THEATERZEITSCHRIFT (GW/0723-1172). [1,650] **389**

THEATRE & THERAPY (UK). **5370**

THEATRE ANNUAL, THE (US/0082-3821). [250] **5370**

THEATRE CLASSICS : THE LEAGUE OF HISTORIC AMERICAN THEATRES ANNUAL PUBLICATION (US). **5370**

THEATRE DIRECTORY OF THE SAN FRANCISCO BAY AREA (US/0737-0172). **5370**

THEATRE HISTORY IN CANADA (CN/0226-5761). **5370**

THEATRE JOBLIST (US/0892-0796). [500] **389**

THEATRE NOTEBOOK (UK/0040-5523). [1,450] **5371**

THEATRE QUEBEC (CN/0825-4494). **5371**

THEATRE SOUTHWEST (US/0743-5452). [1,200] **5371**

THEATRE SURVEY (US/0040-5574). [1,200] **5371**

THEATRE TIMES (US/0732-300X). [3,000] **5371**

THEM DAYS (CN/0381-6109). [1,200] **2763**

THEMA UMWELT (OSNABRUCK) (GW/0939-8767). **426**

THEODORE ROOSEVELT ASSOCIATION JOURNAL (US/0161-8423). [1,500] **435**

THEOLOGIA 21 (US/0362-0085). [100] **5003**

THEOLOGICA XAVERIANA (CK). [600] **5037**

THEOLOGICAL EDUCATION (US/0040-5620). [3,200] **5003**

THEOLOGIE DER GEGENWART (GW). **5003**

THEOLOGIE UND GLAUBE (GW/0049-366X). [750] **5003**

THEOLOGISCHE BEITRAEGE (GW/0342-2372). **5003**

THEOLOGISCHE QUARTALSCHRIFT (MUNCHEN) (GW/0342-1430). [500] **5004**

THEOLOGOS, HO (IT). [400] **5004**

THEOLOGY & LIFE (HONG KONG) (HK/0253-3812). [1,100] **5004**

THEOLOGY DIGEST (US/0040-5728). [5,000] **5004**

THEOLOGY (LONDON) (UK/0040-571X). [5,000] **5004**

THEORETICAL COMPUTER SCIENCE (NE/0304-3975). [500] **1205**

THEORIA (DENTON, TEX.) (US). **4156**

THEOSOPHY (US/0040-5906). [800] **4363**

THERAPEUTIC RECREATION JOURNAL (US/0040-5914). **4394**

THERAPEUTIQUE (FR/0040-5922). [9,000] **3801**

THERAPIE DER GEGENWART (GW/0040-5965). [36,000] **3645**

THERIOGENOLOGY (US/0093-691X). [1,000] **5522**

THERIOS : REVISTA DE MEDICINA VETERINARIA Y PRODUCCION ANIMAL (AG). [5,000] **5523**

THESAURUS - INSTITUTO CARO Y CUERVO (CK/0040-604X). [3,000] **3328**

THESAURUS LINGUAE LATINAE (GW). [1,800] **1929**

THESIS (US/0892-2330). [10,000] **1850**

THIEF RIVER FALLS TIMES (US/8750-3883). [6,325] **5699**

THIRD DEGREE (US). [2,500] **3446**

THIRD WORLD LIBRARIES (US/1052-3049). **3253**

THIRD WORLD REPORTS (UK). **2912**

THIRD WORLD RESOURCES (US/8755-8831). [2,000] **2912**

THIRTEEN TOWNS, THE (US). [3,249] **5699**

THIS BUSINESS OF TRUCKING (CN/0229-0065). **5394**

THIS IS WEST TEXAS (US/0040-6201). **2547**

THIS MONTH ON LONG ISLAND (US/0896-4599). **5492**

THIS PEOPLE (US/0273-6527). [20,000] **5004**

THOMAS HARDY YEAR BOOK (UK/0082-416X). **3446**

THOMIST, THE (US/0040-6325). [1,000] **4363**

THOREAU SOCIETY BULLETIN, THE (US/0040-6406). [1,600] **3446**

THORNY TRAIL, THE (US/0094-0844). [200] **2475**

THOROUGHBRED OF CALIFORNIA, THE (US/0049-3821). [3400] **2803**

THOROUGHBRED TIMES (US/0887-2244). [25,000] **2803**

THREADS OF LIFE (US/0895-8416). [60] **2475**

THRESHOLD (UK/0040-6562). [600] **3446**

THROMBOSIS AND HAEMOSTASIS (GW/0340-6245). **3801**

THRUPUT (US/0147-0698). [3,000] **814**

THUNDER BAY MAGAZINE (CN/0823-6542). [40,000] **2547**

THURIES MAGAZINE (FR/0989-6333). [45,000] **2793**

THYROID TODAY (US/0190-0625). **3733**

TI CHIU KO HSUEH : WU-HAN TI CHIH HSUEH YUAN HSUEH PAO (CC/1000-2383). [3,000] **1361**

TI NEWS / THE TEXTILE INSTITUTE (UK). [9,000] **5359**

TI, TECHNICAL INFORMATION FOR INDUSTRY (SA). **5165**

TIBIA (GW). [4,000] **4156**

TIDSKRIFT I FORTIFIKATION (SW/0040-6937). **4059**

TIDSSKRIFT FOR PLANTEAVL (DK/0040-7135). [900] **189**

TIE JA LIIKENNE (FI). [7,000] **2032**

TIE REPORT (NE/0196-254X). [2,000] **1714**

TIEMPOS MEDICOS DE ESPANA (SP/0210-9999). [35,000] **1788**

TIERARZTLICHE PRAXIS (GW/0303-6286). **5523**

TIERRA NUEVA (CL). [4,000] **5005**

TIJDSCHRIFT RECHTSDOCUMENTATIE (BE/0771-0704). [2,200] **3064**

TIJDSCHRIFT VOOR ALCOHOL, DRUGS EN ANDERE PSYCHOTROPE STOFFEN (NE/0378-2778). [6] **1349**

TIJDSCHRIFT VOOR BESTUURSWETENCHAPPEN EN PUBLEKRECHT (BE/0040-7437). [2,000] **3064**

TIJDSCHRIFT VOOR CRIMINOLOGIE (NE/0165-182X). [550] **3178**

TIJDSCHRIFT VOOR ECONOMIE EN MANAGEMENT (BE/0772-7674). [1,600] **1524**

TIJDSCHRIFT VOOR ECONOMISCHE EN SOCIALE GEOGRAFIE : TESG (NE/0040-747X). [1,300] **1524**

TIJDSCHRIFT VOOR FAMILIE- EN JEUGDRECHT (NE). **3122**

TIJDSCHRIFT VOOR GESCHIEDENIS (1920) (NE/0040-7518). [3,000] **2631**

TIJDSCHRIFT VOOR PRIVAATRECHT (BE). [1,800] **3091**

TIJDSCHRIFT VOOR SEKSUOLOGIE (NE/0167-5915). [750] **5188**

TIJDSCHRIFT VOOR SOCIAAL WETENSCHAPPELIJK ONDERZOEK VAN DE LANDBOUW (NE/0921-481X). [350] **141**

TIJDSCHRIFT VOOR WELZIJNSWERK (BE). [1,200] **5312**

TIKALIA (GT). [1,000] **141**

TILBURG FOREIGN LAW REVIEW (NE/0926-874X). [2,000] **3064**

TILE & DECORATIVE SURFACES (US/0192-9550). [15,295] **2907**

TIMARIT MALS OG MENNINGAR (IC). [3,000] **3355**

TIMBER GROWER (UK/0040-7763). [3,000] **2396**

TIMBER HARVESTING (US/0160-6433). [23,750] **2405**

TIMBER PROCESSING (US/0885-906X). [14,000] **2405**

TIMBER TRADE REVIEW (MY). [2,000] **1629**

TIMBER/WEST (US/0192-0642). [8,500] **2405**

TIMBERLINE (PEMBROKE) (CN/1183-9686). [350] **2475**

TIMBERTALK (US/0744-8511). [550] **2405**

TIME MANAGEMENT REPORT (CN/0228-4189). [200] **888**

TIMELINES (EUGENE, OR) (US/1074-1593). [20,000] **2253**

TIMES-BULLETIN, THE (US/8750-1503). [8,300] **5730**

TIMES BUSINESS DIRECTORY OF SINGAPORE (SI). [45,000] **715**

TIMES HERALD (NORRISTOWN, PA.) (US). [30,000] **5740**

TIMES LAW REPORTS (UK/0958-0441). [1,600] **3065**

TIMES OF TI (US/0746-0392). [8,900] **5721**

TIMES PRESS HARTFORD PUBLICATIONS (US). **5771**

TIMES RECORD NEWS (US/0895-6138). [50,000] **5755**

TIMES RECORDER (ZANESVILLE, OHIO : 1965) (US). **5730**

TIMESHARING LAW REPORTER (WASHINGTON, D.C. : 1987) (US). [250] **3065**

TIMIX BUYERS' GUIDE (US). [10,000] **1245**

TIMMINS TIMES, THE (CN/1191-0771). [19,000] **5796**

TIN NEWS (US/0040-7968). [4,000] **4022**

TINGKAT PENGHUNIAN KAMAR HOTEL (IO). **2809**

TIPS FOR PRINCIPALS FROM NASSP (US). [41,500] **1873**

TIPTON CONSERVATIVE AND ADVERTISER, THE (US). [4,800] **5673**

TIRE REVIEW (1966) (US/0040-8085). [32,800] **5078**

TISSUE & CELL (UK/0040-8166). [1,000] **540**

TISSUE ANTIGENS (DK/0001-2815). [1,000] **3802**

TITLE NEWS (US/0040-8190). **2894**

TITLES MAGAZINE (US/1049-2704). [60,000] **2925**

TITRA (FR). **3446**

TIZ (GW/0722-9488). [8,400] **2152**

TJUSTBYGDEN (SW). [1,200] **2712**

TLTA NEWS (US). [1,600] **2894**

TMSA AEROSPACE MARKET OUTLOOK (US/0271-7417). [1,500] **37**

TOASTMASTER, THE (US/0040-8263). [130,000] **1123**

TOBACCO ABSTRACTS (US/0040-8298). [700] **5373**

TOBACCO-FREE YOUTHREPORTER (US/1064-2072). [65,000] **5373**

TOBACCO IN CANADA (CN/0713-5459). [100] **5374**

TOBACCO INDUSTRY LITIGATION REPORTER (US/0887-7831). **3065**

TOBACCO QUARTERLY (UK/0142-1913). [500] **5374**

TOBACCO REPRINT SERIES (US/0743-4707). [400] **5374**

TOCQUEVILLE REVIEW, THE (US/0730-479X). [500] **5224**

TODAY IN HEALTH PLANNING (US/0164-498X). [800] **4805**

TODAY IN MISSISSIPPI (US/1052-2433). [13500] **2084**

TODAY'S BRIDE (DON MILLS) (CN/0226-1758). [112,000] **2286**

TODAY'S CATHOLIC (SAN ANTONIO, TEX.) (US/0745-3612). [23,000] **5037**

TODAY'S CATHOLIC TEACHER (US/0040-8441). [60,000] **1873**

TODAY'S CHEMIST AT WORK (US/1062-094X). [100,000] **994**

TODAY'S DISTRIBUTOR (US/0898-5561). [42,024] **1629**

TODAY'S FACILITY MANAGER (US/1059-0307). [30,000] **2903**

TODAY'S FEED LOTTING (AT/1034-6147). [1,463] **223**

TODAY'S HEALTH (TORONTO) (CN/0821-6819). [45,000] **4805**

TODAY'S HEALTHCARE MANAGER (US/1054-5204). [750] **3793**

TODAY'S LIFE SCIENCE (AT/1033-6893). [7,000] **5166**

TODAY'S MINISTRY (NEWTON CENTRE, MASS. : 1983) (US/0563-637X). [8,000] **5005**

TODAY'S MOTOR (AT/1033-1069). [10,000] **2130**

TODAY'S PARENT (CN/0823-9258). [150,000] **2286**

TODAY'S REFINERY (US/1048-0935). [6,300] **4280**

TODAY'S SENIORS (CN/0827-6854). [270,000] **5182**

TODAY'S TRANSPORT INTERNATIONAL (US/0040-859X). [16,000] **853**

TODAY'S TRUCKING (CN/0837-1512). [30,000] **5394**

TOERTENELMI SZEMLE (HU/0040-9634). [1,600] **2631**

TOHOGAKU (JA/0495-7199). [2,200] **2666**

TOHOKU JOURNAL OF EXPERIMENTAL MEDICINE, THE (JA/0040-8727). **3646**

TOHOKU MATHEMATICAL JOURNAL (JA/0040-8735). **3538**

TOIMINTAKERTOMUS / KORKEIN HALLINTO-OIKEUS (FI/0357-9190). [900] **3143**

TOIMINTAKERTOMUS / MERENTUTKIMUSLAITOS (FI). [500] **1457**

TOKEI CHOSA SORAN (JA). [2,500] **5345**

TOKYO DAIGAKU SHI KIYO (JA). [1,000] **1850**

TOKYO METROPOLITAN NEWS : A QUARTERLY JOURNAL OF THE TOKYO METROPOLITAN GOVERNMENT (JA/0040-893X). [2,500] **4691**

TOKYO-TO ROJIN SOGO KENKYUJO NEMPO (JA). [1,000] **3755**

TOLDETATEN (DK). [7,700] **853**

TOLDOT HA-DOAR SHEL ERETS YISRAEL (IS). [300] **2787**

TOLL FREE DIGEST (US/0363-2962). **1168**

TOLUENE XYLENES ANNUAL (US/0271-2660). **1030**

TOMBSTONE, THE (US/0893-7664). [70] **2475**

TOMORROW'S NATION (US/1068-1817). **5699**

TOMPKINS COUNTY HOME & GARDEN (US). [2,000] **2793**

TON REPORT (GW). **5319**

TONEEL TEATRAAL (NE/0040-9170). **389**

TONIC (ROBERT SIMPSON SOCIETY) (UK/0260-7425). [160] **4156**

TONOPAH TIMES-BONANZA AND GOLDFIELD NEWS (US). [3,200] **5708**

TOP AGRAR : DAS MAGAZIN FUR MODERNE LANDWIRTSCHAFT (GW). [110,000] **141**

TOP EXECUTIVE COMPENSATION (US). **716**

TOP LINE (US/0738-6699). [180,000] **888**

TOP SHELF (US/1040-0885). [300,000] **5073**

TOPEKA GENEALOGICAL SOCIETY QUARTERLY, THE (US/0734-8495). [800] **2475**

TOPICAL ISSUES IN PROCUREMENT SERIES (US). **952**

TOPICAL LAW REPORTS (CN). [600] **853**

TOPICAL STUDIES (US). [1,500] **2763**

TOPICAL TIME (US/0040-9332). [6,700] **2788**

TOPICATOR (US/0040-9340). [160] **1125**

TOPICS IN GERIATRIC REHABILITATION (US/0882-7524). **3755**

TOPICS IN VETERINARY MEDICINE (US/1064-5101). [45,000] **5523**

TOPONYME, LE (CN/0822-7373). [5,000] **2577**

TOPURON SOSIK (KO). [5,300] **716**

TORCH (WASHINGTON, D.C. : 1980), THE (US/0730-2231). [9,100] **2548**

TORONTO & AREA AIRPORT BUSINESS DIRECTORY (CN/0822-7748). [10,000] **37**

TORONTO ARGONAUTS FACT BOOK (CN/0227-6526). **4926**

TORONTO CHILDREN'S CHORUS (CN/0844-5818). [1,000] **4157**

TORONTO CONSTRUCTION NEWS (CN/0712-5895). [3,600] **630**

TORONTO HERALD, THE (US/0899-9635). [400] **5744**

TORONTO IRISH NEWS (CN/0821-2740). **2763**

TORONTO JOURNAL OF THEOLOGY (CN/0826-9831). [600] **5005**

TORONTO ROYALIST (CN). [1,500] **2494**

TORONTO SOUTH ASIAN REVIEW, THE (CN/0714-3508). [500] **3447**

TORONTO STUDIES IN THEOLOGY. BONHOEFFER SERIES (US). [1,000] **5005**

TORONTO TREE (CN/0381-9167). [1,200] **2475**

TORONTO'S WEDDING BELLS (CN/0831-2184). [100,000] **2286**

TORRENS (SP). [1,000] **2713**

TOSCANA QUI (IT). [20,000] **332**

TOSHOKAN KYORYOKU TSUSHIN (JA/0913-8005). [4,000] **3253**

TOT TALK (CN/0824-507X). **4805**

TOTAL EMPLOYEE INVOLVEMENT (US/0896-7776). **888**

TOTAL HEALTH (US/0274-6743). [91,000] **4805**

TOTAL PRODUCTIVE MAINTENANCE : TPM (US/1054-1233). **888**

TOTLINE (US/0734-4473). [8,000] **1908**

TOUCHSTONE (US). [27,000] **5005**

TOUCHSTONE (WINNIPEG) (CN/0827-3200). [2,000] **5005**

TOULADI (CN/0712-3299). [9,500] **5796**

TOUNG PAO (NE/0082-5433). [550] **2666**

TOUR DE SUTTON, LE (CN/0826-5224). [7,000] **4855**

TOURBILLON DE LA SQTRP, LE (CN/0836-7655). [700] **3646**

TOURISM MANAGEMENT (1982) (UK/0261-5177). **888**

TOURISME+, LE JOURNAL DES VOYAGES (CN/0836-205X). **5493**

TOURIST ATTRACTIONS & PARKS (US/0194-4894). [20,000] **4855**

TOURIST GUIDE BOOK OF ONTARIO (CN/0319-0439). [150,000] **5494**

TOURNAMENTS ILLUMINATED (US/0732-6645). [11,000] **2713**

TOURO LAW REVIEW (US/8756-7326). **3065**

TOURS ON MOTORCOACH (CN/0847-9348). [12,127] **5494**

TOWERS CLUB USA NEWSLETTER (US/0193-4953). [7,000] **2925**

TOWN & COUNTRY PLANNING (UK/0040-9960). [4,000] **4691**

TOWN & VILLAGE (US/0040-9979). [10,800] **5721**

TOWN, VILLAGE AND CITY TAXES (US). [500] **4756**

TOWNSHIPS SUN, THE (CN/0316-022X). [1,400] **5796**

TOWPATHS

Controlled Circulation Index

TOWPATHS (US/0890-7129). [400] **5394**

TOXIC CHEMICALS LITIGATION REPORTER (US/0737-8513). **3116**

TOXICOLOGIC PATHOLOGY (US/0192-6233). [850] **3898**

TOXICOLOGIST, THE (US/0731-9193). [4,500] **3984**

TOXICOLOGY AND INDUSTRIAL HEALTH (US/0748-2337). [700] **3984**

TOXICS PROGRAM COMMENTARY. FLORIDA (US). **2182**

TOXICS PROGRAM COMMENTARY. ILLINOIS (CN). **2182**

TOXICS PROGRAM COMMENTARY. MASSACHUSETTS (CN). **2182**

TOXICS PROGRAM COMMENTARY. NEW JERSEY (CN). **2182**

TOXICS PROGRAM COMMENTARY. OHIO (CN). **2182**

TOXICS PROGRAM COMMENTARY. PENNSYLVANIA (CN). **2182**

TOXICS PROGRAM COMMENTARY. TEXAS (CN). **2182**

TOXICS PROGRAM MATRIX. MASSACHUSETTS (CN). **2182**

TOXICS PROGRAM MATRIX. NEW YORK (CN). **2182**

TOXICS PROGRAM MATRIX. TEXAS (US). **2182**

TOY & HOBBY WORLD. WEEKLY MARKET REPORT (US). [300] **958**

TOY BOOK, THE (US/0885-3991). [15,000] **2585**

TOYAMA DAIGAKU KYOIKU GAKUBU KIYO. A, BUNKAKEI (JA). [600] **1788**

TOYAMA DAIGAKU KYOIKU GAKUBU KIYO. B, RIKAKEI (JA/0285-9610). [600] **5166**

TOYOGAKU BUNKEN RUIMOKU (JA). **2666**

TOYS AND PLAYTHINGS (UK/0041-0187). [4,500] **4867**

TPA MESSENGER (US/0194-9802). [105 (free)733 (paid)] **4820**

TR NEWS (US/0738-6826). [8,000] **5394**

TRABAJO SOCIAL Y SALUD (SP/1130-2976). [1,000] **5312**

TRACE (MEXICO CITY, MEXICO) (MX/0185-6286). [1,000] **5224**

TRACES OF INDIANA AND MIDWESTERN HISTORY (US/1040-788X). [6,500] **2763**

TRACES OF SOUTH CENTRAL KENTUCKY (US/0882-2158). [400] **2475**

TRACINGS (US/0738-4130). [325] **3253**

TRACK & FIELD NEWS (US/0041-0284). [35,000] **4926**

TRACK NEWSLETTER (US/0041-0306). [500] **4927**

TRACT (CHICOUTIMI) (CN/0713-5726). **5796**

TRADE AND COMMERCE (WINNIPEG) (CN/0049-4321). [12,400] **853**

TRADE CONNECTIONS (CN/0713-634X). [1,500] **854**

TRADE DIRECTORY, MEMBERSHIP LIST - ELECTRONIC INDUSTRIES ASSOCIATION (US/0091-9519). **2084**

TRADE-MARK REPORTER, THE (US/0041-056X). [2,300] **1308**

TRADE NEWS SERVICE, THE (US/1071-0604). **1630**

TRADEMARK TRENDS (US/1062-7766). **1309**

TRADESHOW & EXHIBIT MANAGER (US/0893-2662). [13,000] **767**

TRADESHOW WEEK'S MAJOR EXHIBIT HALL DIRECTORY (US). **767**

TRADESHOW WEEK'S ... TRADESHOW SERVICES DIRECTORY (US). **767**

TRADING CYCLES (US/0892-3280). **917**

TRADITION MAGAZINE (FR/0980-8493). [26,000] **4157**

TRADITION (WALNUT, IOWA) (US/1071-1864). [2,500] **4157**

TRADITIONAL DWELLINGS AND SETTLEMENTS REVIEW (US/1050-2092). [500] **5225**

TRAFFIC DATA FROM AUTOMATIC TRAFFIC RECORDER STATIONS (US). **5446**

TRAFFIC ENGINEERING & CONTROL (UK/0041-0683). [2,500] **5394**

TRAFFIC MANAGEMENT (US/0041-0691). [70,000] **5394**

TRAFFIC TOPICS (US/0735-7613). **5394**

TRAFIK-SKADOR (SW/0347-6359). **5446**

TRAIL & LANDSCAPE (CN/0041-0748). [950] **4173**

TRAIL BLAZER (PASO ROBLES) (US/0274-8274). [12,300] **2803**

TRAILER/BODY BUILD (US/0041-0772). [12,000] **5394**

TRAIN COLLECTORS QUARTERLY, THE (US/0041-0829). [26,000] **2778**

TRAINING AND DEVELOPMENT IN AUSTRALIA (AT/0310-4664). [5,000] **716**

TRAINING TOMORROW (UK/0957-0004). [3,000] **4691**

TRAIT D'UNION - FEDERATION DES CAISSES POPULAIRES ACADIENNES (CN/0822-3521). [2,000] **1543**

TRAIT D'UNION (ROUYN) (CN/0820-7720). [11,000] **4691**

TRAMES (MONTREAL) (CN/0847-9119). [250] **2837**

TRANET (US/0739-0971). [1500] **2207**

TRANS F M (CN/0704-478X). **1141**

TRANS TASMAN (NZ/1171-2961). **854**

TRANSACTIONS - AMERICAN CRYSTALLOGRAPHIC ASSOCIATION (US/0065-8006). [3,500] **1033**

TRANSACTIONS - INSTITUTE OF BRITISH GEOGRAPHERS (1965) (UK/0020-2754). [3,000] **2577**

TRANSACTIONS OF SHASE JAPAN (JA/0081-1610). [20,000] **2608**

TRANSACTIONS OF THE AMERICAN CLINICAL AND CLIMATOLOGICAL ASSOCIATION (US/0065-7778). [500] **3647**

TRANSACTIONS OF THE AMERICAN ENTOMOLOGICAL SOCIETY (1890) (US/0002-8320). [500] **5614**

TRANSACTIONS OF THE AMERICAN OPHTHALMOLOGICAL SOCIETY ANNUAL MEETING (US/0065-9533). [500] **3879**

TRANSACTIONS OF THE AMERICAN SOCIETY FOR NEUROCHEMISTRY (US/0066-0132). [1,200] **3847**

TRANSACTIONS OF THE ANCIENT MONUMENTS SOCIETY (UK/0951-001X). [2,300] **366**

TRANSACTIONS OF THE ... ANNUAL MEETING OF THE BIOELECTRICAL REPAIR AND GROWTH SOCIETY (US/0892-2020). [300] **475**

TRANSACTIONS OF THE ASAE (US/0001-2351). [2,200] **1999**

TRANSACTIONS OF THE CANADIAN SOCIETY FOR MECHANICAL ENGINEERING (CN/0315-8977). [325] **2130**

TRANSACTIONS OF THE CHARLES S. PIERCE SOCIETY (US/0009-1774). [500] **4364**

TRANSACTIONS OF THE FACULTY OF ACTUARIES (UK/0071-3686). **2894**

TRANSACTIONS OF THE HISTORIC SOCIETY OF LANCASHIRE AND CHESHIRE FOR THE YEAR (UK/0140-332X). [600] **2713**

TRANSACTIONS OF THE HUGUENOT SOCIETY OF SOUTH CAROLINA (US/0363-3152). [4,000] **5237**

TRANSACTIONS OF THE ILLINOIS STATE ACADEMY OF SCIENCE (US/0019-2252). [1,100] **5166**

TRANSACTIONS OF THE INSTITUTION OF ENGINEERS, AUSTRALIA. CIVIL ENGINEERING (AT/0159-2068). **2033**

TRANSACTIONS OF THE INSTITUTION OF ENGINEERS, AUSTRALIA. MECHANICAL ENGINEERING (AT/0727-7369). [12,000] **2131**

TRANSACTIONS OF THE INSTITUTION OF ENGINEERS, AUSTRALIA. MULTI-DISCIPLINARY ENGINEERING (AT/0812-3314). [1,000] **1999**

TRANSACTIONS OF THE IRON AND STEEL INSTITUTE OF JAPAN (JA/0021-1583). [5,500] **4022**

TRANSACTIONS OF THE JAPAN SOCIETY FOR AERONAUTICAL AND SPACE SCIENCES (JA/0549-3811). [3,500] **38**

TRANSACTIONS OF THE JAPAN WELDING SOCIETY (JA/0385-9282). [600] **4028**

TRANSACTIONS OF THE KANSAS ACADEMY OF SCIENCE (1903) (US/0022-8443). [500] **5166**

TRANSACTIONS OF THE KENTUCKY ACADEMY OF SCIENCE (US/0023-0081). [15,000] **5166**

TRANSACTIONS OF THE MISSOURI ACADEMY OF SCIENCE (US/0544-540X). [1,300] **5166**

TRANSACTIONS OF THE MONUMENTAL BRASS SOCIETY (UK/0143-1250). [650] **284**

TRANSACTIONS OF THE MORAVIAN HISTORICAL SOCIETY (US/0886-1730). [500] **5068**

TRANSACTIONS OF THE NATURAL HISTORY SOCIETY OF NORTHUMBRIA (UK/0144-221X). [700] **4173**

TRANSACTIONS OF THE ORIENTAL CERAMIC SOCIETY (UK/0306-0926). [1,200] **2595**

TRANSACTIONS OF THE ROYAL SOCIETY OF SOUTH AUSTRALIA (AT/0372-1426). [850] **5167**

TRANSACTIONS OF THE ROYAL SOCIETY OF TROPICAL MEDICINE AND HYGIENE (UK/0035-9203). [4,000] **3987**

TRANSACTIONS OF THE SAEST (II/0036-0678). [1,300] **1035**

TRANSACTIONS OF THE SPWLA ANNUAL LOGGING SYMPOSIUM (US/0081-1718). [3,000] **4280**

TRANSACTIONS OF THE UNITARIAN HISTORICAL SOCIETY (UK/0082-7800). [350] **5068**

TRANSACTIONS OF THE YORKSHIRE DIALECT SOCIETY (UK/0954-6316). [800] **3329**

TRANSACTIONS. SECTION A, MINING INDUSTRY / INSTITUTION OF MINING & METALLURGY (UK/0371-7844). [3,200] **2152**

TRANSACTIONS - THE SOCIETY OF NAVAL ARCHITECTS AND MARINE ENGINEERS (US/0081-1661). [4,000] **4184**

TRANSACTIONS. TRAFODION (UK). [500] **2484**

TRANSACTOR, THE (CN/0827-2530). [72,000] **1273**

TRANSATLANTIC PERSPECTIVES (US/0192-477X). [5,000] **4339**

TRANSCEND (US). [5,000] **1070**

TRANSCRIPT (US/1040-4848). [5,000] **1123**

TRANSCRIPTASE : REVUE CRITIQUE DE L'ACTUALIT,E SCIENTIFIQUE INTERNATIONALE SUR LE SIDA (FR/1166-5300). [3,000] **3677**

TRANSILVANIA (RM). [4,000] **2713**

TRANSITION (AT/0157-7344). [1,200] **310**

TRANSITION (LONDON, ENGLAND) (UK/0267-8950). [44,000] **1917**

TRANSITION (OTTAWA) (CN/0049-4429). [7,500] **2286**

TRANSITION : THE NEWSLETTER ABOUT REFORMING ECONOMIES / TRANSITION AND MACRO-ADJUSTMENT, COUNTRY ECONOMICS DEPARTMENT, WORLD BANK (US). [7000] **1640**

TRANSITIONS ABROAD (US/1061-2343). [80,000] **1788**

TRANSITIONS (CINCINNATI, OHIO) (US/0278-2804). [1,500] **5395**

TRANSLATION REVIEW (US/0737-4836). [1,250] **3329**

TRANSLOG (WASHINGTON, D.C.) (US/0041-1639). [10,000] **4059**

TRANSMISSION & DISTRIBUTION (US/0041-1280). [32,416] **2085**

TRANSMISSION & DISTRIBUTION INTERNATIONAL (US/1050-8686). **2085**

TRANSMISSION DIGEST (US/0277-8300). [21,000] **5426**

TRANSMISSION/DISTRIBUTION HEALTH & SAFETY REPORT (US/0737-5743). [200] **2085**

TRANSMISSION (MONTREAL) (CN/0824-510X). [150] **3329**

TRANSNATIONAL LAW & CONTEMPORARY PROBLEMS : A JOURNAL OF THE UNIVERSITY OF IOWA COLLEGE OF LAW (US/1058-1006). [250] **3136**

TRANSPLANTATION AND IMMUNOLOGY LETTER (US/0748-1861). [12,000] **3976**

TRANSPO (CN/0706-3954). [6,000] **5395**

TRANSPORT-DIENST + WIRTSCHAFTS-CORRESPONDENT (GW). [12,500] **5395**

TRANSPORT ENGINEER, THE (UK/0020-3122). [16,500] **1999**

TRANSPORT HISTORY (UK/0041-1469). [2,000] **5395**

TRANSPORT MANAGEMENT; THE BRITISH JOURNAL OF TRADE AND TRANSPORT (UK/0041-1515). [4,500] **5395**

TRANSPORT OF THUNDER BAY (CN/0822-580X). [3,000] **5395**

TRANSPORT REVIEW (UK). **5396**

TRANSPORT ROUTIER DU QUEBEC (CN/0049-447X). [10,000] **5396**

TRANSPORT THEORY AND STATISTICAL PHYSICS (US/0041-1450). **4430**

TRANSPORTATION (DORDRECHT) (NE/0049-4488). [750] **5396**

TRANSPORTATION JOURNAL (US/0041-1612). [3,000] **5396**

TRANSPORTATION NEWS DIGEST, THE (US/1047-062X). [1,000] **5396**

TRANSPORTATION PLANNING SYSTEMS (UK/0962-7146). **5396**

TRANSPORTATION TELEPHONE TICKLER (US). **5397**

TRANSPORTATION WORLDWIDE (US/8750-8397). [13,472] **854**

TRAPPER AND PREDATOR CALLER, THE (US/8750-233X). [50,000] **3186**

TRAVAIL HUMAIN, LE (FR/0041-1868). **4620**

TRAVAIL SOCIAL ACTUALITES PARIS (FR/0753-9711). **5313**

TRAVAUX ET DOCUMENTS (FR/0298-8879). [300] **4536**

TRAVEL 800 (US/0192-155X). [8,500] **5494**

TRAVEL A LA CARTE (CN/0836-7353). [150,000] **5494**

TRAVEL AGENCY (UK/0041-1981). [11,310] **5494**

TRAVEL AND DESCRIPTION SERIES (US). [1,500] **2763**

TRAVEL & LEISURE (US/0041-2007). [925,000] **5495**

TRAVEL & TOURISM EXECUTIVE REPORT (US/1070-8855). [1,000] **5495**

TRAVEL NEWS ASIA (HK). [17,000] **5496**

TRAVEL PREVIEW (US/0898-0055). [100,000] **5496**

TRAVEL TIDINGS (US/0895-4135). [5,000] **5496**

TRAVEL TO THE USSR (RU/0320-0167). [200,000] **5496**

TRAVEL TRENDS IN THE UNITED STATES AND CANADA (US). [500] **5497**

TRAVELIN TALK NEWSLETTER, THE (US/1052-1615). [2,000] **5497**

TRAVELLER'S GUIDE TO THE MIDDLE EAST (UK). [6,810] **5497**

TRAVELORE REPORT, THE (US/0270-2398). **5497**

TRAVELWARE (US/0747-475X). [10,000] **1630**

TRAVERS LES VIGNES, A (CN/0824-1465). [1,200] **2371**

TREASURE CHEST (NEW YORK, N.Y) (US/0897-814X). [50,000] **252**

TREASURE CHEST NEWS (US/0882-1178). [300] **2475**

TREASURE STATE LINES (US). [225] **2475**

TREATING ABUSE TODAY (US/1052-3995). [8,000] **5313**

TREBEDE : REVISTA DE POESIA (SP). [3,600] **3472**

TREE CLIMBER (SALINA, KAN.) (US/0737-9226). [250] **2475**

TREE PHYSIOLOGY (CN/0829-318X). [650] **2397**

TREE-RING BULLETIN (US/0041-2198). [350] **2397**

TREE SHAKER / EASTERN KENTUCKY GENEALOGICAL SOCIETY (US/0893-2069). [1,000] **2475**

TREE TRACERS, THE (US/0162-1440). [450] **2475**

TREES AND NATURAL RESOURCES (AT/0814-4680). [5,500] **2207**

TREESPEAK ADELAIDE (AT/1032-6111). [7,000] **2207**

TREFILE, LE (GW/0374-2261). **4022**

TRELLIS (CN/0380-1470). [3,600] **2432**

TREND (XR). [1,500] **5167**

TREND IN ENGINEERING AT THE UNIVERSITY OF WASHINGTON, THE (US/0362-0018). **2000**

TRENDS AND APPLICATIONS (US). **1205**

TRENDS (SCOTTSDALE, ARIZ.) (US/0742-034X). **332**

TRENTONIAN (TRENTON, N.J.), THE (US/1064-3567). [68,391 daily 64,989 Sunday] **5711**

TREUBIA : RECUEIL DE TRAVAUX ZOOLOGIQUES, HYDROBIOLOGIQUES ET OCEANOGRAPHIQUES (IO/0082-6340). [500] **475**

TRI-CITY COMPUTING MAGAZINE (US). [20,000] **1205**

TRI-COUNTY NEWS (OSSEO, WIS.), THE (US/0749-7040). [3,700] **5771**

TRI-COUNTY SEARCHER, THE (US/0742-5015). [100] **2476**

TRI NEWS AND RESEARCH BRIEFS (US). **5359**

TRI-STATE PACKET OF THE TRI-STATE GENEALOGICAL SOCIETY, THE (US/0740-896X). [600] **2476**

TRIAD (FARMINGTON, MICH.) (US/1046-4948). [3,000] **3647**

TRIAD (OHIO MUSIC EDUCATION ASSOCIATION) (US/0041-2511). [4,500] **4157**

TRIAL ADVOCATE QUARTERLY (US/0743-412X). [1,700] **3066**

TRIAL TALK (US/0747-1378). [1,500] **3066**

TRIANGLE OF MU PHI EPSILON, THE (US/0041-2600). [10,000] **4157**

TRIBAL TRIBUNE (US). **5733**

TRIBOLOGIE UND SCHMIERUNGSTECHNIK (GW/0724-3472). [2,349] **1048**

TRIBORO BANNER (US/1055-9590). [6,000] **5740**

TRIBUNA FARMACEUTICA (BL/0371-6619). [500] **4331**

TRIBUNAUX CORRECTIONNELS, COURS D'APPEL, CONSEILS DE GUERRE ET COUR MILITAIRE (BE). [350] **3083**

TRIBUNE BUSINESS WEEKLY (US/1051-7367). [9,200] **716**

TRIBUNE DE L'ORGUE, LA (SZ/1013-6835). [2,000] **4157**

TRIBUNE - INTERNATIONAL WOMEN'S TRIBUNE CENTRE (FEB. FRANCAISE), LA (US/0748-4593). [3,000] **5567**

TRIBUNE - INTERNATIONAL WOMEN'S TRIBUNE CENTRE, THE (US/0738-9779). [16,000] **5567**

TRIBUNE-STAR, THE (US/0745-9599). [37,000] **5667**

TRIBUNE-TIMES (US/0747-1165). [8,000] **5743**

TRIBUS (GW/0082-6413). [800] **247**

TRIDENT (WASHINGTON, D.C.) (US/0882-1674). [300] **2788**

TRIENNIAL REPORT - BOTANY DIVISION (NZ/0548-9547). [750] **529**

TRIERER THEOLOGISCHE ZEITSCHRIFT (GW/0041-2945). [800] **5006**

TRIINU (CN/0702-8679). **2763**

TRINITY DIGEST (US). [1,500] **2925**

TRINITY'S WELLSPRING (US). [10,000] **5006**

TRIPLE I (SI). [6,500] **716**

TRIQUARTERLY / NORTHWESTERN UNIVERSITY (US/0041-3097). [3,500] **3447**

TROPICAL DEVELOPMENT AND RESEARCH INSTITUTE (SERIES G) (UK/0264-763X). [1,800] **142**

TROPICAL FRESHWATER BIOLOGY (NR/0795-0101). [200] **475**

TROPICAL GRASSLANDS (AT/0049-4763). [700] **189**

TROPICAL LEPIDOPTERA (US/1048-8138). [1,100] **5614**

TROUBADOUR (FREDERICTON) (CN/0713-8113). [300] **4157**

TRUBUS (IO/0126-0057). [50,000] **142**

TRUCK CANADA (CN/0315-5501). [21,500] **5398**

TRUCKSTOP WORLD (US/0894-962X). [18,000] **5398**

TRUE WEST (US/0041-3615). [110,000] **2764**

TRUMPETER (LONDON) (CN/0148-673X). [700] **2788**

TRUPPENPRAXIS (GW). [32,400] **4059**

TRUST NEWS (AT). [17,000] **2207**

TRUSTEE (EDMONTON, ALTA.) (CN/0229-4141). [2,000] **1873**

TRUSTEE'S LETTER, THE (US/1044-6370). [3,000] **1788**

TRUSTEESHIP (WASHINGTON, D.C.) (US/1068-1027). **1851**

TRUXBOOK (CN/0820-5655). [1,500] **855**

TRYON DAILY BULLETIN, THE (US). [4,000] **5724**

TSETSE AND TRYPANOSOMIASIS INFORMATION QUARTERLY (UK/0142-193X). [1,100] **5599**

TTT, INTERDISCIPLINAIR TIJDSCHRIFT VOOR TAAL- & TEKSTWETENSCHAP (NE/0167-4773). [600] **3330**

TU TANGATA (NZ/0111-5871). [6,000] **2671**

TUBE & PIPE QUARTERLY, THE (US/1051-4120). [30,000] **4023**

TUBE SUBSTITUTION HANDBOOK (US). **2085**

TUBULAR STRUCTURES (UK/0041-3909). [4,000] **630**

TUCSON GUIDE QUARTERLY (US). [34,000] **2548**

TUDOMANYOS KOZLEMENYEK (HU). [300] **1859**

TUEXEMIA (GW/0772-494X). [1,600] **2222**

TUITION AND LIVING ACCOMMODATION COSTS AT CANADIAN UNIVERSITIES (CN/0318-2991). [815] **1851**

TUJA SINTAK / INVESTMENT TRUST (KO). [1,900] **918**

TULANE LAWYER (US). [7,000] **3066**

TULANE STUDIES IN POLITICAL SCIENCE (US/0082-6744). [1,000] **4498**

TULSA ANNALS (US/0564-4437). [400] **2476**

TULSA LAW JOURNAL (US/0041-4050). [650] **3067**

TULSA STUDIES IN WOMEN'S LITERATURE (US/0732-7730). [500] **3448**

TUNG WU FA LU HSUEH PAO (CH). [500] **3067**

TUNNELS ET OUVRAGES SOUTERRAINS VILLEURBANNE (FR/0399-0834). [1800] **2033**

TUPPER LAKE FREE PRESS AND TUPPER LAKE HERALD (US). [3,537] **5721**

TURBOMACHINERY DIGEST (US). **2131**

TURF & RECREATION (CN/1186-0170). [13,600] **2433**

TURF AND SPORT DIGEST (US/0041-4158). [30,000] **4927**

TURISMO D'ITALIA (IT). [15,000] **2809**

TURK KOYUNDE MODERNLESME EGILIMLERI ARASTRMAS (TU). [1,000] **1587**

TURKEY MONITOR (UK/0950-3234). [400] **4757**

TURKEY WORLD (1968) (US/0041-4271). [10,000] **223**

TURKEYS (UK/0041-428X). [6,000] **223**

TURKISH JOURNAL OF NUCLEAR SCIENCES (TU/0254-5446). **4451**

TURKISH STUDIES ASSOCIATION BULLETIN (US/0275-6048). [350] **3355**

TURKIYE OZETLI NUFUS BIBLIOGRAFYAS (TU). [1,000] **4563**

TURNBULL LIBRARY RECORD, THE (NZ/0110-1625). [1,100] **3254**

TURNOUT, THE (CN/0227-244X). [165] **5437**

TURRIALBA : REVISTA INTERAMERICANO DE CIENCIAS AGRICOLAS (CR/0041-4360). [800] **143**

TUTELA (IT/0393-7798). [2,000] **5313**

TUTTITALIA (UK). [950] **3330**

TV ENTERTAINMENT (US/1049-1163). **1141**

TV ETC (US/1054-2329). **1141**

TV EXECUTIVE, THE (US/0736-2986). [10,000] **1141**

TV TECHNOLOGY (US/0887-1701). [20,000] **1168**

TW (TORONTO, ONT.) (CN/0711-7426). **5567**

TWENTIETH CENTURY PETROLEUM STATISTICS (US/1048-4825). [1,000] **4285**

TWIN CITIES CHRISTIAN, THE (US/0745-8606). [8,000] **5006**

TWIN FALLS TIMES-NEWS (US). [22,000] **5657**

TWIN PLANT NEWS (US/1046-9427). [10,000] **855**

TWINE LINE : OHIO SEA GRANT PROGRAM NEWSLETTER (US/1064-6418). [4,000] **2315**

TWINS (US/0890-3077). **2286**

TWINS LETTER, THE (US/0743-748X). [10,000] **4621**

TWO THIRDS (CN/0705-3452). [1,000] **2912**

TYDSKRIF VAN DIE TANDHEELKUNDIGE VERENIGING VAN SUID AFRIKA (SA/0011-8516). [3,750] **1337**

TYDSKRIF VIR DIE SUID-AFRIKAANSE REG (SA). [1,100] **3067**

TYDSKRIF VIR VOLKSKUNDE EN VOLKSTAAL (SA/0049-4933). [250] **2325**

TYO TERVEYS TURVALLISUUS (FI/0041-4816). [80,000] **2871**

TYPOGRAPHIC SOCIETY OF TYPOGRAPHIC DESIGNERS (UK/0143-7623). [1,000] **4570**

TYPOGRAPHIC : THE JOURNAL OF THE SOCIETY OF TYPOGRAPHIC DESIGNERS (UK). [800] **4570**

TZ FUER METALLBEARBEITUNG (GW/0170-9577). [10,100] **4023**

U B LIBRARIES FACULTY NEWSLETTER, I (US). [2,500] **3254**

U C L A GENERAL CATALOG (US). [35,000] **1851**

U.I.T. JOURNAL (GW). [4,200] **4927**

U.N. OBSERVER & INTERNATIONAL REPORT (US/1014-6539). [2,500] **3137**

U.S.A. OIL INDUSTRY DIRECTORY (US/0082-8599). [6,000] **4281**

U.S.A. OILFIELD SERVICE, SUPPLY, AND MANUFACTURERS DIRECTORY (US). [1,500] **4281**

U S AIRBOAT (US). [4000] **596**

U.S. CATHOLIC (US/0041-7548). [54,346] **5037**

U.S.D. — Controlled Circulation Index

U.S.D. REPORT ON ENROLLMENTS AND GENERAL FUND BUDGET PER PUPIL (US). [700] **1788**

U.S. FARM NEWS (US/0041-7637). [4,000] **143**

U.S. GLASS, METAL & GLAZING (US/0041-7661). [16,000] **2595**

U.S. HOUSING MARKETS (US/0502-9716). [1,200] **2837**

U.S. IDENTIFICATION MANUAL (US/0732-6688). **3178**

U.S. INDUSTRIAL DIRECTORY (US/0095-7046). [39,000] **1630**

U.S. JOURNAL OF DRUG AND ALCOHOL DEPENDENCE, THE (US/0148-8619). [17,000] **1350**

U.S. LONG-TERM REVIEW (US/0734-4449). [400] **1540**

U.S. MEDICAL LICENSURE STATISTICS ... AND LICENSURE REQUIREMENTS ... (US/0741-6326). [2,500] **3662**

U.S. MEDICINE (US/0191-6246). [32,000] **3917**

U.S. OIL WEEK (US/0502-9767). **4281**

U.S. PHARMACIST (US/0148-4818). [90,000] **4331**

U.S. RAIL NEWS (US/0743-7994). [1,500] **5437**

U.S. REGULATORY REPORTER (US/0749-5005). [1,000] **5313**

U.S. TELECOMMUNICATIONS (US). [200] **1168**

U.S. WOMAN ENGINEER (US/0272-7838). [15,000] **2000**

U : THE NATIONAL COLLEGE NEWSPAPER (US). [1.5 million] **5641**

U TURN (US/0734-8401). **367**

U W GUIDELINES (CN/0700-3692). [800] **1851**

UA JOURNAL (US/0095-7763). [300,000] **1715**

U&C UNIFICAZIONE & CERTIFICAZIONE (IT/0394-9605). [7,000] **630**

UBC DATA LIBRARY CATALOGUE. MICROFORM (CN/0713-8172). **3254**

UBC LIBRARY BULLETIN (CN/0229-5954). **3254**

UBD CONFERENCE DIRECTORY (AT). **717**

UBERSEE RUNDSCHAU (GW/0041-5707). [5,000] **856**

UBEZPIECZENIA MAJATKOWE I OSOBOWE (PL). [900] **2895**

UC CLIP SHEET (US/0745-3213). **1851**

UCHENYE ZAPISKI TARTUSKOGO GOSUDARSTVENNOGO UNIVERSITETA. TRUDY PO TSITOLOGII I GENETIKE TARTU RIIKLIKU ULIKOOLI TOIMETISED. TSUTOLOOGIA- JA GENEETIKA-ALASED TOOD (ER). [400] **541**

UCLA JOURNAL OF DANCE ETHNOLOGY (US/0884-3198). [250] **1314**

UCLA MAGAZINE (1989) (US/1075-2749). [225,000] **1103**

UE NEWS (U.S. EDITION) (US/0041-5065). [40,000] **1715**

UFAHAMU (US/0041-5715). [400] **2500**

UFCW ACTION (US/0195-0363). [1,300,000] **1715**

UFCW LEADERSHIP UPDATE (US/8750-328X). [2,300] **1715**

UFFICIOSTILE (IT). [240,000] **310**

UFO TIMES (UK/0958-4846). [500] **38**

UFONTAS, AS (BL). [300] **38**

UGANDA LAW FOCUS, THE (UG). [2,000] **3067**

UHREN, JUWELEN, SCHMUCK (GW). [9,700] **2916**

UITGAVEN VAN DE NATUURWETENSCHAPPELIJKE STUDIEKRING VOOR SURINAME EN DE NEDERLANDSE ANTILLEN. NATUURHISTORISCHE REEKS (NE). [1,000] **4173**

UJ TUKOR (HU). [69,000] **2524**

UK VENTURE CAPITAL JOURNAL (UK/0265-8364). **815**

UKRAINIAN QUARTERLY, THE (US/0041-6010). [1,500] **4498**

UKRAINIAN REVIEW (LONDON, ENGLAND) (UK/0041-6029). [1,100] **4499**

UKRAINSKE VIDRODZHENNJA (CN/0824-6238). **2714**

UKRAINSKI VISTI (EDMONTON) (CN/0041-6002). [6,271] **5796**

UKRAINSKYI FILATELIST / SOIUZ UKRAINSKYKH FILATELISTIV I NUMIZMATYKIV (US/0198-6252). [300] **2788**

UKRAINSKYI ISTORYK (US/0041-6061). **2714**

ULASAN GETAH MALAYSIA (MY/0126-9089). [1,500] **5078**

ULSTER JOURNAL OF ARCHAEOLOGY (UK/0082-7355). [600] **285**

ULTRAPURE WATER (US/0747-8291). [13,000] **5541**

ULTRASOUND IN MEDICINE & BIOLOGY (US/0301-5629). **3648**

ULYSSES NEWS, THE (US). [3,350] **5678**

UMBEN (PP). **5264**

UMENI A REMESLA (XR/0139-5815). [7,250] **376**

UMTRI RESEARCH REVIEW, THE (US/0739-7100). [1400] **5398**

UNB FORESTRY FOCUS (CN/0707-1957). [900] **2397**

UNB LAW JOURNAL (CN/0836-6632). [2,000] **3067**

UNB PERSPECTIVES (CN/0229-4680). [4,000] **1851**

UNC NOTIZIE (IT). [3,000] **1300**

UNDER AFRIKAS SOL (DK). [3,300] **5006**

UNDERCAR DIGEST (US/0893-6943). [30,000] **5427**

UNDERGROUND TANK TECHNOLOGY UPDATE (US). [3,000] **2000**

UNDERLINE (US/0276-0398). [1,000] **310**

UNDERSEA BIOMEDICAL RESEARCH (US/0093-5387). [1,800] **3697**

UNDERSTANDING JAPAN (JA/0041-6576). [10,000] **2509**

UNDERSTANDING OUR GIFTED (US/1040-1350). **1886**

UNDERWATER MEDICINE AND RELATED SCIENCES (US/0191-2534). **3648**

UNDERWATER NEWS & TECHNOLOGY (US/1069-6547). **1458**

UNDERWRITERS' REPORT (US/0041-6622). [6,500] **2895**

UNDRO NEWS (SZ/0250-9377). [6,000] **2912**

UNESCO ADULT EDUCATION INFORMATION NOTES (FR/0376-4907). [10,000] **1802**

UNESCO KOERIER (BE/0304-3169). [11,000] **332**

UNESCO REPORTS IN MARINE SCIENCE (FR). [2,000] **1458**

UNI HANNOVER (GW/0171-2268). [3,000] **1851**

UNICAMERAL UPDATE (US/1063-0813). [11,000] **4692**

UNICIV REPORT (AT). **2033**

UNICORN (CARLTON, TAS.) (AT/0311-4775). [6,500] **1788**

UNIDEX QUARTERLY (US). **815**

UNIDOS : JOURNAL OF OPPORTUNITY (US). **717**

UNIE GOODWOOD, DIE (SA/0259-5591). [8,000] **1908**

UNIFICATION NEWS (US/1061-0871). [6,800] **5006**

UNIGEO - SBORNIK PRACI (XR). [300] **5167**

UNILETRAS : REVISTA DO DEPARTAMENTO DE LETRAS DA UEPG (BL). [800] **3449**

UNION COUNTY LEADER, THE (US). [2,750] **5713**

UNION LABOR NEWS (MADISON, WIS.) (US/0041-6924). [18,000] **1716**

UNION LIST OF SERIALS IN MONTREAL HOSPITAL LIBRARIES (CN/0316-5043). [100] **426**

UNION MEDICALE DU CANADA (CN/0041-6959). [13,000] **3648**

UNION REGISTER, THE (US/0274-970X). [26,000] **2405**

UNION WRITES NEWSLETTER (US/0748-6839). [1,400] **1716**

UNIONIST, THE (BB). [500] **1716**

UNIQUE (EAST HANOVER, N.J.) (US/0736-4083). [2000] **1244**

UNISA ENGLISH STUDIES (SA/0041-5359). [3,000] **3449**

UNISA PSYCHOLOGIA (SA). [4,500] **4621**

UNISPHERE (US/0279-1579). [22,000] **1249**

UNITARIAN UNIVERSALIST CHRISTIAN, THE (US/0362-0492). [1,200] **5068**

UNITAS FRATRUM (GW/0344-9254). [300] **5068**

UNITE DES CHRETIENS (FR). [3,800] **5006**

UNITED CHURCH NEWS (NATIONAL EDITION) (US/0882-7214). [100,000] **5731**

UNITED CHURCH OBSERVER, THE (CN/0041-7238). [155,000] **5006**

UNITED DAILY NEWS (CH). **5799**

UNITED EVANGELICAL (US/0041-7262). [2,800] **5040**

UNITED EVANGELICAL ACTION (US/0041-7270). [1,100] **5006**

UNITED FLY TYERS' ROUNDTABLE (US/0747-9832). [2,000] **2315**

UNITED KINGDOM ANTARCTIC RESEARCH REPORT (UK/0308-1192). [400] **1361**

UNITED METHODIST CHRISTIAN ADVOCATE, THE (US/8750-7668). [10,000] **5068**

UNITED METHODIST REPORTER (DALLAS, TEX.), THE (US/0737-5581). [475,000] **5068**

UNITED NATIONS HANDBOOK (NZ/0110-1951). [5000] **4537**

UNITED NATIONS RESOLUTIONS. SERIES 2, RESOLUTIONS AND DECISIONS OF THE SECURITY COUNCIL (US/0898-2929). [350] **3137**

UNITED RUBBER WORKER: URW, THE (US/0162-3869). [160,000] **5078**

UNITED STATES AIR FORCE ACADEMY JOURNAL OF PROFESSIONAL MILITARY ETHICS (US/0731-2865). [1,000] **4059**

UNITED STATES BANKER (COS COB) (US/0148-8848). [22,000] **815**

UNITED STATES SWIMMING RULES AND REGULATIONS (US/0742-7808). [25,000] **4927**

UNITED STATES TRADE FAIR (US/0742-3675). [356,700] **952**

UNIVERS DU FRANCAIS SEVRES, L' (FR/1018-872X). [1,500] **1788**

UNIVERSAL MESSAGE, THE (PK). **5045**

UNIVERSE IN THE CLASSROOM, THE (US/0890-6866). [35,000] **401**

UNIVERSITAS. ENGLISH LANGUAGE EDITION (STUTTGART) (GW/0341-0129). [6,800] **2856**

UNIVERSITES (MONTREAL) (CN/0226-7454). [6,500] **1852**

UNIVERSITY DAILY, THE (US). [17,000] **5755**

UNIVERSITY OF ADELAIDE LIBRARY NEWS (AT/0157-3314). [325] **3254**

UNIVERSITY OF ARKANSAS AT LITTLE ROCK LAW JOURNAL (US/0162-8372). [4,500] **3068**

UNIVERSITY OF CALIFORNIA PUBLICATIONS IN ANTHROPOLOGY (US/0068-6379). [1,100] **247**

UNIVERSITY OF CALIFORNIA PUBLICATIONS IN BOTANY (US/0068-6395). **529**

UNIVERSITY OF CALIFORNIA PUBLICATIONS IN ENTOMOLOGY (US/0068-6417). [900] **5614**

UNIVERSITY OF CALIFORNIA PUBLICATIONS IN GEOGRAPHY (US/0068-6441). [900] **2578**

UNIVERSITY OF CALIFORNIA PUBLICATIONS IN GEOLOGICAL SCIENCES (US/0068-645X). [1,350] **1400**

UNIVERSITY OF CALIFORNIA PUBLICATIONS IN MODERN PHILOLOGY (US/0068-6492). [850] **3331**

UNIVERSITY OF CALIFORNIA PUBLICATIONS IN ZOOLOGY (US/0068-6506). [1,250] **5599**

UNIVERSITY OF CALIFORNIA PUBLICATIONS. NEAR EASTERN STUDIES (US/0068-6514). [650] **2667**

UNIVERSITY OF CINCINNATI LAW REVIEW (US/0009-6881). [1,100] **3068**

UNIVERSITY OF COLORADO LAW REVIEW (US/0041-9516). [800] **3068**

UNIVERSITY OF FLORIDA LAWYER : MAGAZINE OF THE UNIVERSITY OF FLORIDA COLLEGE OF LAW (US). [11,000] **3068**

UNIVERSITY OF GHANA LAW JOURNAL (GH/0041-9605). [1,000] **3068**

UNIVERSITY OF ILLINOIS INSTITUTE OF GOVERNMENT AND PUBLIC AFFAIRS WORK PAPERS (US). [150] **5225**

UNIVERSITY OF ILLINOIS LAW REVIEW (US/0276-9948). [1,500] **3068**

UNIVERSITY OF KANSAS PALEONTOLOGICAL CONTRIBUTIONS. ARTICLE (US/0075-5044). [700] **4231**

UNIVERSITY OF KANSAS PALEONTOLOGICAL CONTRIBUTIONS. PAPERS (US/0075-5052). [750] **4231**

UNIVERSITY OF LEEDS REVIEW, THE (UK/0041-9737). [850] **1096**

UNIVERSITY OF MIAMI ENTERTAINMENT & SPORTS LAW REVIEW (US/1051-2225). [300] **3069**

UNIVERSITY OF MIAMI INTER-AMERICAN LAW REVIEW, THE (US/0884-1756). [1,000] **3137**

UNIVERSITY OF MIAMI LAW REVIEW (US/0041-9818). [2,000] **3069**

UNIVERSITY OF MICHIGAN JOURNAL OF LAW REFORM (US/0363-602X). [1,000] **3069**

UNIVERSITY OF MINNESOTA MEDICAL BULLETIN (US). [20,000] **3649**

UNIVERSITY OF PITTSBURGH LAW REVIEW (US/0041-9915). [1,200] **3069**

UNIVERSITY OF PORTLAND REVIEW (US/0041-9923). [1,000] **2548**

UNIVERSITY OF PUGET SOUND LAW REVIEW (US/0161-0708). [1,000] **3069**

UNIVERSITY OF RICHMOND LAW REVIEW (US/0566-2389). [1,200] **3069**

UNIVERSITY OF SAN FRANCISCO LAW REVIEW (US/0042-0018). [1,000] **3069**

UNIVERSITY OF TOLEDO LAW REVIEW, THE (US/0042-0190). [700] **3069**

UNIVERSITY OF TORONTO LAW JOURNAL, THE (CN/0042-0220). [600] **3069**

UNIVERSITY OF TORONTO QUARTERLY (CN/0042-0247). [1,000] **2856**

UNIVERSITY OF WINDSOR REVIEW, THE (CN/0042-0352). [400] **3449**

UNIVERSITY PRESS BOOK NEWS (US/1040-8991). **427**

UNIVERSITY RESEARCH IN BUSINESS AND ECONOMICS (US/0736-8968). [700] **1540**

UNIX/BUSINESS (UK/0958-6253). [11,000] **1239**

UNIX NEWS LONDON (UK/0956-2753). [10,500] **1249**

UNLIMITED TIMES, THE (US/0738-7032). [2,000] **717**

UNRWA : RESUME DU RAPPORT (AU). [5,000] **5313**

UNSER TSAYT (US/0042-0506). [2,500] **2494**

UNSER WALD : ZEITSCHRIFT DER SCHUTZGEMEINSCHAFT DEUTSCHER WALD (GW). [10,000] **2397**

UNSERE STIMME (GW). [3,000] **3355**

UNTERRICHTSPRAXIS, DIE (US/0042-062X). [7,000] **3331**

UNTERSUCHUNGEN ZUR GEGENWARTSKUNDE SUDOSTEUROPAS (GW/0566-2761). [1,000] **5225**

UNTITLED (CARMEL) (US/0163-7916). [14,000] **4377**

UP HERE : LIFE IN CANADA'S NORTH (CN). [25,000] **2548**

UP INFORMATION (BE). **4499**

UPCHURCH BULLETIN (US/0270-465X). [200] **2476**

UPDATE & DIALOG (DK/0906-7272). [200] **5007**

UPDATE (ARLINGTON) (US/0162-945X). [48,000] **1917**

UPDATE CAPE TOWN (SA/0258-929X). [8,400] **3649**

UPDATE - CHINOOK REGIONAL LIBRARY (CN/0828-7694). [500] **3255**

UPDATE / CONGRESSIONAL CAUCUS FOR WOMEN'S ISSUES (US). **4692**

UPDATE (ELIZABETHTOWN, PA.) (US/0741-4587). [1,000] **39**

UPDATE / INTERPRETATION CANADA (CN/0715-3392). [550] **1789**

UPDATE ON STATE LEGISLATION (US/0739-4004). [150] **3070**

UPDATE - ONTARIO TRUCKING ASSOCIATION (CN/0841-2472). [1,500] **5399**

UPDATE (SMITHSONIAN INSTITUTION. TRAVELING EXHIBITION SERVICE) (US/0272-0345). [8,000] **4097**

UPDATE (UKRAINIAN MUSEUM OF CANADA (SASKATOON, SASK.)) (CN/0821-5235). **4097**

UPHOLSTERY DESIGN & MANUFACTURING (US/1056-2052). [16,000] **3489**

UPSHAW FAMILY JOURNAL, THE (US/0098-8960). [70] **2476**

UPSIDE (U.S. ED.) (US/1052-0341). [50,000] **1239**

UPSOUTH (BOWLING GREEN, KY.) (US/1069-8051). **3449**

UQACTUALITE (CN/0229-0871). **1853**

UQAR-INFORMATION (CN/0711-2254). [1,700] **1853**

URAL-ALTAISCHE JAHRBUCHER (GW/0042-0786). [500] **3331**

URBAN GEOGRAPHY (US/0272-3638). [400] **2578**

URBAN HISTORY REVIEW (CN/0703-0428). [1,000] **2764**

URBAN LIBRARIES COUNCIL NEWSLETTER : ULC EXCHANGE (US). **3255**

URBAN TRANSPORTATION MONITOR, THE (US/1040-4880). **5399**

URBAN WILDLIFE MANAGER'S NOTEBOOK (US/0882-584X). [1,000] **2208**

URBAN WILDLIFE NEWS (US/0882-5858). [1,000] **2222**

URBANISTICA INFORMAZIONI (IT/0392-5005). [6,000] **2838**

URNER BARRY'S MEAT & POULTRY DIRECTORY (US/0738-6745). [2,200] **223**

UROLOGIA (IT/0391-5603). [1,000] **3993**

UROLOGY (GLENDALE, CALIF.) (US/0271-1338). **3994**

US-CHINA TRADE STATISTICS (US/0732-8478). [5,000] **735**

US SUPREME COURT PETITIONS & BRIEFS. TAX LAW SERIES (US). **3070**

US SWIMMING NEWS (US/0883-0347). [3,000] **4927**

US WURK (NE/0042-1235). [400] **3331**

USA GYMNASTICS (US/0748-6006). **4928**

USA OUTDOORS (US/0883-6841). [22,000] **4880**

USBE NEWS (US/0364-5215). [1,100] **3255**

USCTA NEWS (US/0744-0103). [7,500] **2803**

USDF CALENDAR OF COMPETITIONS (US/0882-5009). [4,000] **2803**

USSR FACTS & FIGURES ANNUAL (US/0148-7760). **5345**

UTAH BIRDS : JOURNAL OF THE UTAH ORNITHOLOGICAL SOCIETY (US). [200] **5620**

UTAH BUSINESS MAGAZINE (US). [49,000] **717**

UTAH HISTORICAL QUARTERLY (US/0042-143X). [3,500] **2764**

UTAH-IDAHO SOUTHERN BAPTIST WITNESS (US/0746-0228). [2300] **5068**

UTAH LIBRARIES/NEWS (US). [600] **3255**

UTAH MUSIC EDUCATOR (US/0502-871X). [450] **4157**

UTAH SCHOOL DIRECTORY (US). **1789**

UTAH SCIENCE (US/0042-1502). [2,600] **143**

UTAH SYMPHONY (US/0191-1635). [4,500] **4157**

UTRECHT MICROPALEONTOLOGICAL BULLETINS (NE/0083-4963). [500] **4231**

UTU NEWS CANADA (CN/0383-2015). [20,000] **1716**

UW NOTES (CN/0229-9798). **1853**

UWLA LAW REVIEW (US/0899-7446). **3070**

UXBRIDGE TIMES-JOURNAL (CN/0834-7336). [5000] **5796**

VACANCES POUR TOUS (CN/0831-3067). [55,000] **5498**

VACANT URBAN RESIDENTIAL LAND SURVEY, ... UPDATE (CN/0833-966X). **2838**

VACHER'S EUROPEAN COMPANION & CONSULTANTS' REGISTER (UK/0958-0336). **4693**

VACUUM CIRCUITS (US/0747-5063). **5399**

VALENCIA FRUITS (SP). [13,000] **143**

VALFARDS BULLETINEN / SCB (SW/0280-1418). [1,300] **5313**

VALLEY CATHOLIC, THE (US/8750-6238). [25,000] **5038**

VALLEY FORGE JOURNAL, THE (US/0734-5712). [500] **2764**

VALLEY GAZETTE, THE (US/1056-4853). [1,800] **5740**

VALLEY LEAVES (US/0507-6544). [530] **2476**

VALLEY NEWS (MONTEBELLO) (CN/0715-4887). [2,000] **5796**

VALLEY SENTINEL (VALEMOUNT) (CN/0845-4183). [1,200] **5797**

VALUATION (AMERICAN SOCIETY OF APPRAISERS) (US/0042-238X). [5,500] **815**

VALUE ENGINEERING & MANAGEMENT DIGEST (US/0275-4371). [5,000] **2000**

VALUE RETAIL NEWS : THE JOURNAL OF VALUE-ORIENTED RETAILING & DEVELOPMENT (US). **1300**

VALUE WORLD (US). [2,000] **1525**

VAN HOC (GARDEN GROVE, CALIF.) (US/1047-0913). [1,000] **3450**

VANCOUVER & AREA AIRPORT BUSINESS DIRECTORY (CN/0828-4504). [8,000] **39**

VANCOUVER (VANCOUVER, 1975) (CN/0380-9552). [70,000] **5498**

VANDERBILT JOURNAL OF TRANSNATIONAL LAW (US/0090-2594). [1,000] **3137**

VANDERBILT MAGAZINE (US). [30,000] **1103**

VANDERBILT UNIVERSITY PUBLICATIONS IN ANTHROPOLOGY (US). [1,500] **247**

VANGUARD (US/0892-6433). **2838**

VANIEROIS, LE (CN/0823-0153). [6,000] **1525**

VARBUSINESS (US/0894-5802). [50,226] **1239**

VARIETY (US/0042-2738). [33,000] **4079**

VAROSI KOZLEKEDES (HU/0133-0314). [1,200] **5399**

VARSITY (TORONTO) (CN/0042-2789). [25,000] **1096**

VASA STAR, THE (US/0042-0627). [19,000] **2274**

VASCULAR SURGERY (US/0042-2835). [2,000] **3977**

VASLA (US/0042-1723). [120] **3255**

VASUTI KOZLEKEDESI SZAKIRODALMI TAJEKOZTATO (HU/0231-0767). [360] **5437**

VAT INTELLIGENCE (UK/0263-9947). **717**

VATTEN (SW/0042-2886). **5541**

VE VENEZUELA (VE/0042-2932). [10,000] **5498**

VEA (HATO REY, P.R.) (PR/0738-7628). [85,000] **2494**

VEA NEWS (US/0042-1790). [46,000] **1789**

VEALER, THE (US/0749-6664). [2,000] **2360**

VEGETARIAN (ALTRINCHAM, CHESHIRE : 1980) (UK/0260-3233). [13,000] **4200**

VEGETARIAN JOURNAL (US/0885-7636 #y 0883-1165). [26,000] **4200**

VEGETARIAN VOICE (US/0271-1591). [3,000] **4806**

VEGYIPARI SZAKIRODALMI TAJEKOZTATO MUANYAG- ES GUMIIPARI KULONLENYOMATA (HU/0231-0775). [150] **995**

VEHICLE AND TRAFFIC LAW (US). **3070**

VEHICLE IDENTIFICATION (US/8756-940X). **5427**

VEHICLE LEASING TODAY (US). [4,500] **5399**

VEHICULES A MOTEUR NEUFS MIS EN CIRCULATION (BE). [165] **5427**

VEJVISER I STATISTIKKEN (DK/0109-8314). [3,500] **5345**

VELDWERK AMSTERDAM (NE/0922-2782). [1,600] **2912**

VELVET LIGHT TRAP, THE (US/0149-1830). [600] **4079**

VENDING INTERNATIONAL (UK/0954-6235). **937**

VENDING TIMES (US/0042-3327). [15,000] **4214**

VENEREOLOGY : OFFICIAL PUBLICATION OF THE NATIONAL VENEREOLOGY COUNCIL OF AUSTRALIA (AT). [500] **3716**

VENTURE INWARD / THE MAGAZINE OF THE ASSOCIATION FOR RESEARCH AND ENLIGHTENMENT (US/0748-3406). [75,000] **5007**

VENTURE ROAD (US/0883-7821). [4,000] **5498**

VENTURES IN RESEARCH (US/0092-556X). **5168**

VENUS; JAPANESE JOURNAL OF MALACOLOGY (JA/0042-3580). [1,000] **5599**

VERBA (SP). [700] **3331**

VERBINDING ROTTERDAM (NE/0922-6540). [5,000] **1168**

VERBONDSNIEUWS VOOR DE BELGISCHE SIERTEELT (BE). [2,500] **2436**

VERBUM (SAN DIEGO, CALIF.) (US/0889-4507). [15,000] **382**

VERDAD (CORPUS CHRISTI, TEX. : 1942) (US). [5,000] **2275**

VERDE INDEPENDENT, THE (US). [4,900] **5630**

VERDE OLVO (CU/0506-6913). [50,000] **4060**

VERHANDELINGEN - KONINKLIJKE ACADEMIE VOOR GENEESKUNDE VAN BELGIE (BE/0302-6469). [400] **3649**

VERHANDLUNGEN

VERHANDLUNGEN DER DEUTSCHEN GESELLSCHAFT FUER HERZ- UND KREISLAUFFORSCHUNG (GW/0174-2817). [3,000] **3711**

VERHANDLUNGEN DER ORNITHOLOGISCHE GESELLSCHAFT IN BAYERN (GW). [1,200] **5620**

VERHANDLUNGEN DES HISTORISCHEN VEREINS FUER NIEDERBAYERN (GW). [1,000] **2714**

VERITABLE AMIE (CN/0831-0866). [3,500] **5567**

VERKAUFSLEITER-SERVICE (GW/0178-5893). [4,500] **718**

VERKEHRSWIRTSCHAFTLICHE ZAHLEN (GW). [4,500] **5399**

VERKORT OVERZICHT ZIEKTEVERZUIM (NE). [1,000] **1716**

VERKSAMHETSBERATTELSE / ENERGIEKONOMISKA FORENINGEN (SW). [1,000] **1960**

VERKSTADERNA (SW/0042-4056). [17,000] **2131**

VERMESSUNG, PHOTOGRAMMETRIE, KULTURTECHNIK (SZ/0252-9424). **2000**

VERMONT BAR JOURNAL & LAW DIGEST, THE (US/0748-4925). [2,000] **3071**

VERMONT HISTORY (US/0042-4161). [2,500] **2764**

VERMONT HISTORY NEWS (US/0364-3387). [2,500] **2764**

VERMONT NATURAL HISTORY (US/0270-5982). [3,500] **4173**

VERMONT REGISTERED NURSE (US/0191-1880). [500] **3870**

VERMONT SCIENCE : RESEARCH OF THE AGRICULTURAL EXPERIMENT STATION, UNIVERSITY OF VERMONT (US). [9,000] **144**

VERMONT YEAR BOOK (US/0083-5781). [2,000] **718**

VERNACULAR ARCHITECTURE (UK/0305-5477). [1,000] **310**

VERNON'S CITY OF CAMBRIDGE (ONTARIO) DIRECTORY (CN/0317-2899). **2578**

VERNON'S CITY OF HAMILTON (ONTARIO) DIRECTORY (CN/0316-1765). **2578**

VEROFFENTLICHUNGEN (GW/0568-4358). [450] **1080**

VEROFFENTLICHUNGEN (GW). [2,800] **3071**

VEROFFENTLICHUNGEN AUS DEM NATURHISTORISCHEN MUSEUM WIEN (AU/0378-8202). [5,000] **4173**

VEROFFENTLICHUNGEN DER KOMMISSION FUER ZEITGESCHICHTE. REIHE B: FORSCHUNGEN (GW). [1,500] **5038**

VEROFFENTLICHUNGEN DER KOMMISSION FUR ZEITGESCHICHTE. REIHE A : QUELLEN (GW). [1,500] **5038**

VEROFFENTLICHUNGEN DES INSTITUTS FUER BODENMECHANIK UND FELSMECHANIK DER UNIVERSITAT FRIDERICIANA IN KARLSRUHE (GW/0453-3267). [400] **1400**

VEROFFENTLICHUNGEN DES MUSEUMS FUER UR- UND FRUHGESCHICHTE POTSDAM (GE/0079-4376). **285**

VERRE (PARIS, FRANCE) (FR/0984-7979). [300] **2595**

VERS UN DEVELOPPEMENT SOLIDAIRE (SZ). [5,500] **4537**

VERSLAG VAN DE RAAD VAN BEHEER OVER DE VERRICHTINGEN (BE). [3,000] **2838**

VERTIFLITE (US/0042-4455). [9,000] **39**

VERWALTUNG UND FORTBILDUNG (GW). [1,500] **4693**

VERWARMING EN VENTILATIE (NE/0042-451X). [3,500] **2608**

VESTIRAMA (SP). [8,000] **1088**

VESTNIK CESKOSLOVENSKYCH SPOLKU V MONTREALE (CN/0700-8171). [580] **2764**

VESTNIK (OWINGS MILLS, MD.) (US/1055-2278). [5,000] **2275**

VETDOC (UK). **5528**

VETERINARIA (MEXICO) (MX/0301-5092). [2,000] **5523**

VETERINARIAN MAGAZINE (CN/0849-5009). [4,600] **5524**

VETERINARY AND COMPARATIVE ORTHOPAEDICS AND TRAUMATOLOGY (GW/0932-0814). **5524**

VETERINARY AND HUMAN TOXICOLOGY (US/0145-6296). [1,800] **5524**

VETERINARY BIOLOGICAL PRODUCTS. LICENSEES (US). [700] **5525**

VETERINARY ECONOMICS (US/0042-4862). [38,000] **5525**

VETERINARY PRACTICE (UK/0042-4897). [6,500] **5526**

VETERINARY RADIOLOGY & ULTRASOUND (US/1058-8183). [1,000] **5526**

VETERINARY SCOPE (US). [35,000] **5527**

VETERINARY TIMES (UK/1352-9374). [9,300] **5527**

VETSKAP (SW/0283-8708). [1400] **1096**

VETTE VUES MAGAZINE (US/0279-8476). [25,000] **5427**

VETUS TESTAMENTUM (NE/0042-4935). [2,650] **5020**

VEZETESTUDOMANY (HU). [1,200] **718**

VFW, VETERANS OF FOREIGN WARS MAGAZINE (US/0161-8598). [1,960,000] **4060**

VI (SW/0346-4180). [245,000] **2524**

VICA JOURNAL (US/1044-0151). [280,000] **4209**

VICARIA DE LA SOLIDARIDAD (CL). **5038**

VICE VERSA (MONTREAL, QUEBEC) (CN/0829-2299). [2000] **2549**

VICTOR VALLEY MAGAZINE (US/0738-8586). [5,000] **2547**

VICTORIA ADVOCATE (VICTORIA, TEX. : DAILY) (US). [36,000] **5755**

VICTORIA COUNTY RECORD (CN/0703-8747). [4,500] **5797**

VICTORIA GOVERNMENT GAZETTE (AT). [1,700] **4693**

VICTORIA INSIDER (CN/0843-4395). [75] **2765**

VICTORIAN NATURALIST (AT/0042-5184). [800] **4173**

VICTORIAN NETBALLER (AT). **4928**

VICTORIAN STUDIES (US/0042-5222). [3,000] **3450**

VICTORIAN VEGETABLE GROWER, THE (AT). [500] **190**

VIDE, LES COUCHES MINCES, LE (FR/0223-4335). [2,000] **4424**

VIDEO & AUDIO REPORT (NE). [5,000] **1123**

VIDEO GUIDE (VANCOUVER) (CN/0228-6726). [200] **1142**

VIDEO JOURNAL OF COLOR FLOW IMAGING (US/1052-2182). [800] **3947**

VIDEO NETWORKS (US/0738-7563). [8,000] **1142**

VIDEO : REVISTA DE CIRURGIA (SP). [5,000] **3977**

VIDEO STORE (US/0195-1750). [40,000] **1142**

VIDEO SYSTEMS (US/0361-0942). [21,000] **1142**

VIDEOGRAPHY (US/0363-1001). [28,000] **1143**

VIDEOLOG (US/0746-7699). [5,000] **4079**

VIDURA (II). [1,000] **1123**

VIE DES ARTS (CN/0042-5435). **332**

VIE DES COMMUNAUTES RELIGIEUSES (CN). [3,300] **5007**

VIE E TRASPORTI (IT). [7,500] **5399**

VIE ET MILIEU (1980) (FR/0240-8759). [900] **2222**

VIE FRANCAISE (QUEBEC) (CN/0382-0262). [500] **2549**

VIE OBLATE (CN/0318-9392). [500] **5038**

VIE OUVRIERE (MONTREAL, QUEBEC) (CN/0229-3803). [3,000] **1716**

VIE PEDAGOGIQUE (CN/0707-2511). [50,000] **1790**

VIE SOCIALE (FR/0042-5605). [1,200] **5225**

VIER BULLETIN (AT). [100] **1790**

VIERAEA (SP/0210-945X). **4173**

VIES-A-VIES (MONTREAL. 1988) (CN/0842-1838). [8,000] **4621**

VIETNAM GENERATION (US/1042-7597). [400] **2765**

VIETNAM TODAY (AT/1030-9985). [1,000] **4537**

VIETNAM UPDATE (US/0899-6601). **2632**

VIETNAM WAR NEWSLETTER (US/0743-2496). [2,500] **4060**

VIGILIAE CHRISTIANAE (NE/0042-6032). [850] **3451**

VIGNETTES (US/0091-3456). [900] **1096**

VIJNANA SARASVATI (II). **3255**

VIKING TOURIST GUIDE (CN/0828-4849). **5498**

VILAG ES NYELV (HU). [10,000] **3332**

VILAS COUNTY NEWS-REVIEW (US). [10,500] **5771**

VILLAGER (MISSISSAUGA) (CN/0226-5907). [39,500] **5797**

VILLAGER, THE (US). [6,000] **2275**

VILLAMOSSAG (HU/0042-6210). [2,800] **2085**

VILLANOVA LAW REVIEW (US/0042-6229). [1,600] **3071**

VILLE (MONTREAL), EN (CN/0826-7731). [42,000] **5498**

VIM & VIGOR (US/0886-6554). [950,000] **2601**

VINCENNES SUN-COMMERCIAL, THE (US). [16,000 Sunday 14,000 daily] **5668**

VINCULOS (CR/0304-3703). [1,000] **247**

VINCULUM (AT/0157-759X). [2,000] **3540**

VINDUET (NO/0042-6288). [4,500] **3451**

VINEYARD & WINERY MANAGEMENT (US/1047-4951). [3,500] **2371**

VINEYARD GAZETTE, THE (US). [12,626 paid] **5690**

VINI D'ITALIA (IT/0042-630X). [8,000] **2371**

VINIFERA WINE GROWERS JOURNAL, THE (US/0095-3563). [1,500] **190**

VINTAGE AIRPLANE, THE (US/0091-6943). [4,000] **39**

VINTAGE FORD, THE (US/0042-6350). [7,000] **5427**

VINTAGE TRIUMPH, THE (US/0147-9695). [3,600] **5427**

VINUM (SZ/0177-2570). **2372**

VIRGINIA APPALACHIAN NOTES (US/0739-3482). [650] **2476**

VIRGINIA BAPTIST REGISTER, THE (US/0083-6311). [750] **5069**

VIRGINIA BUSINESS (US/0888-1340). [40,500] **718**

VIRGINIA CAVALCADE (US/0042-6474). [8,500] **2765**

VIRGINIA DENTAL JOURNAL (US/0049-6472). [2,900] **1337**

VIRGINIA FARMER (BALTIMORE, MD.) (US/0746-1186). [17,554] **144**

VIRGINIA GEOGRAPHER, THE (US/0042-6512). [200] **2579**

VIRGINIA INDUSTRIAL DIRECTORY (US/0882-3219). [5,000] **1631**

VIRGINIA JOURNAL OF INTERNATIONAL LAW (US/0042-6571). [900] **3137**

VIRGINIA JOURNAL, THE (US/0739-4586). [1,100] **1859**

VIRGINIA LAND USE DIGEST (US). [400] **4848**

VIRGINIA LAW REVIEW (US/0042-6601). [2,200] **3071**

VIRGINIA LEGAL STUDIES (US). **3072**

VIRGINIA MAGAZINE OF HISTORY AND BIOGRAPHY, THE (US/0042-6636). [3,600] **2765**

VIRGINIA NURSE (US/0270-7780). [3,000] **3870**

VIRGINIA POULTRYMAN, THE (US/0042-6733). [2,100] **223**

VIRGINIA REVIEW (US/0732-9156). [5,000] **4693**

VIRGINIA STATE LIBRARY PUBLICATIONS (US/0083-6524). [12,000] **2765**

VIRGINIA TIDEWATER GENEALOGY (US/0099-2496). [460] **2476**

VIRGINIA TOWN & CITY (US/0042-6784). [4,500] **4693**

VIRGINIA UNITED METHODIST ADVOCATE (US/0891-5598). [18,000] **5069**

VIRTUE (US/0164-7288). [130,000] **5007**

VISALIA TIMES-DELTA (US). [21,019] **5641**

VISAO (BL/0042-6873). [150,000] **2553**

VISIBILITIES (US/0892-7375). [5,000] **2796**

VISION (UK). [15,000] **5568**

VISION (PASADENA, CALIF.) (US/0882-6609). **5008**

VISION RESOURCE UPDATE (US). **4394**

VISIONMONDAY (NEW YORK, N.Y.) (US/1054-7665). **4217**

VISIONS (US/1043-4194). [112,500] **2601**

VISITANTE, EL (PR). [60,000] **5008**

VISITOR GUIDE TO FRONTIER VISTA TRAVEL REGION (CN/0823-6615). **5498**

VISITOR GUIDE TO PRAIRIE VALLEYS TRAVEL REGION (CN/0823-6607). **5499**

VISITOR GUIDE TO WOODLAND PARK TRAVEL REGION (CN/0823-6593). **5499**

VISITOR (KITCHENER, ONT.) (CN/0839-1335). [45,000] **5499**

VISTA PRESS, THE (US/0893-3464). [Wed.-8,500Sat.-13,100] **5641**

VISTA/U.S.A (US/0507-1577). [900,000] **5499**

VISTAS (MERION, PA.) (US/0278-7660). [1,000] **367**

VISTI - INSTYTUTU SV. VOLODYMYRA (CN/0380-0369). [4,000] **2275**

VISTI / (OSEREDOK UKRAINSKOI KULTURY I OSVITY (CN/0824-5991). [2,000] **2765**

VISUAL COMMUNICATIONS JOURNAL (US/0507-1658). **4570**

VITA E PENSIERO (IT/0042-725X). [35,000] **4364**

VITAL SIGNS (STORRS, CONN.) (US/0749-856X). [800] **4621**

VITAL SPEECHES OF THE DAY (US/0042-742X). [13,000] **2495**

VITAL STATISTICS REPORT (PH/0116-2675). [200] **5346**

VITAMIN E ... ABSTRACTS (US/0736-9158). [10,000] **4200**

VITIS, VITICULTURE AND ENOLOGY ABSTRACTS (GW/0175-8292). [700] **2362**

VITREOUS ENAMELLER (UK/0042-7519). [250] **2017**

VITRIINI (FI/0357-749X). [3,500] **2810**

VITUTALAIPPULIKAL : TAMILILA VITUTALAIPPULUKALIN ATIKARAPURVAMANA ETU (II). **2667**

VLA NEWSLETTER (US/0896-0720). **3255**

VLAAMS DIERGENEESKUNDIG TIJDSCHRIFT (BE/0303-9021). [1,500] **5527**

VMEBUS SYSTEMS (US/0884-1357). [24,000] **1273**

VOCATIONAL EDUCATION JOURNAL (US/0884-8009). [50,000] **1917**

VOCATIONAL EVALUATION AND WORK ADJUSTMENT BULLETIN (US/0160-8312). [2,000] **4395**

VOCE EVANGELICA (CN/0708-2479). **5008**

VOEDING (NE/0042-7926). [4,500] **4200**

VOGUE (NEW YORK) (US/0042-8000). [1,000,000] **5568**

VOGUE PATTERNS (BRITISH EDITION) (UK/0142-338X). [49,659] **5186**

VOICE (EAST LANSING, MICH.) (US/0883-573X). [129,000] **1790**

VOICE (FRANKLIN, WIS.), THE (US/0889-3543). [500] **3793**

VOICE M.A.N, THE (US/0505-8708). [1,800] **2433**

VOICE OF SMALL BUSINESS, THE (US/0037-7198). [50,000] **718**

VOICE OF THE MIDDLESEX FARMER, THE (CN/0709-1915). **145**

VOICE OF THE PHARMACIST (US/0507-2379). [1,000] **4332**

VOICE OF THE TENNESSEE WALKING HORSE (US/0505-8813). [4,000] **2803**

VOICE OF THE TRAPPER (US/0194-6927). [17,000] **4880**

VOICE OF THE TURTLE (SAN DIEGO, CALIF.) (US/0739-9324). [1,000] **5237**

VOICE OF THE WORKING WOMAN, THE (II). [1,500] **1717**

VOICE OF WASHINGTON MUSIC EDUCATORS (US/0147-4367). [1,700] **4158**

VOICE OF YOUTH (CHICAGO, ILL.), THE (US/0042-8256). **1921**

VOICE. OFFICIAL PUBLICATION OF MICHIGAN ASSOCIATION OF NURSEYMEN (US). [1,200] **2433**

VOICE PROCESSING (US/0884-6685). [400] **1168**

VOICE, THE (US/1040-1121). **2293**

VOICE (WESTCHESTER) (US/0049-6669). [10,000] **5008**

VOICES INTERNATIONAL (US/0042-8280). [300] **3473**

VOICES OF THE AFRICAN DIASPORA (US/1054-4283). [1,800] **2275**

VOICES (SOUTHBURY) (US/0193-1474). [22,510] **5646**

VOIR DIRE (MONTREAL) (CN/0826-4503). [1,000] **4395**

VOIX DU SANCTUAIRE (CN/0700-9313). [10,000] **5008**

VOIX ET IMAGES (CN/0318-9201). [900] **3451**

VOIX SEFARAD (CN/0704-5352). [5,000] **2275**

VOLGA TRIBUNE, THE (US/0163-6154). [1,300] **5744**

VOLKSKUNDE (1940) (BE/0775-3128). **2325**

VOLKSKUNDIG BULLETIN (NE). [500] **2325**

VOLTA REVIEW, THE (US/0042-8639). [5,400] **4395**

VOLUNTEERS IN ACTION (CN/0824-1848). [5,000] **5313**

VORGANGE (GW/0507-4150). [2,700] **2524**

VOS AFFAIRES MUNICIPALES (CN/0713-6714). **4694**

VOTES AND PROCEEDINGS OF THE LEGISLATIVE ASSEMBLY OF MANITOBA (CN/0319-3020). **4694**

VOX PATRUM (PL). [1,000] **5008**

VOX REFORMATA (AT/0728-0912). [200] **5008**

VOYAGE EN GROUPE (CN/0711-6136). [12,500] **5499**

VOZ DE HOUSTON, LA (US). [50,000] **5755**

VOZ DE LA CULTURA, LA (SP). [2,000] **332**

VOZ DE LA VALDERIA, LA (SP). [2,000] **2524**

VOZ, LA (US). **2495**

VR VIDEOREGISTRARE (IT/0394-2384). **4079**

VRAC, EN (CN/0706-1048). **4538**

VS NEWS (US/0748-7886). [1,200] **1273**

VSE UPDATE (UK). [400] **1281**

V+T. VERKEHR UND TECHNIK (GW/0340-4536). [3,236] **5399**

VVS BULLETIN (NE). [1,500] **5346**

VXI JOURNAL (US/1072-9933). [7,000] **1206**

VYCHODOSLOVENSKY KRAJ V TLACI (XO). [130] **2636**

WACO FARM AND LABOR JOURNAL (1986) (US/0889-3233). [120] **145**

WACONDA ROOTS AND BRANCHES (US/8755-2167). [150] **2477**

WAGA KUNI SEKIYU KAIHATSU NO GENJO (JA). **4281**

WAGES AND WORKING CONDITIONS BY OCCUPATION (CN/0706-4926). [2,200] **1717**

WAGNER (UK). [1,200] **4158**

WAGNER NEWS (LONDON, ENGLAND) (UK/0261-3468). [1,000] **389**

WAHDAH (CAIRO, EGYPT) (UA). [10,000] **2667**

WAHKAW, THE (US/0743-6483). [120] **2477**

WAITOMO NEWS (NZ). [6,300] **5807**

WAKE FOREST LAW REVIEW (US/0043-003X). [1,900] **3072**

WALKING HORSE REPORT (US/0093-6928). [6,000] **2803**

WALKING MAGAZINE, THE (US/1042-2102). [500,000] **2602**

WALL PAPER (NEW YORK, N.Y.), THE (US/0273-6837). [16,000] **2903**

WALLACEANA (MY). [200 subscribers1500 readership] **2222**

WALLCOVERINGS, WINDOWS & INTERIOR FASHION (US/1055-4394). [16,900] **2903**

WALLS & CEILINGS (US/0043-0161). [22,500] **631**

WALNUT COUNCIL BULLETIN (US/1041-5769). **2398**

WALT WHITMAN QUARTERLY REVIEW (US/0737-0679). [525] **3452**

WALTON TRIBUNE, THE (US/0893-410X). [5,800] **5655**

WANDERING VOLHYNIANS (CN/1180-2901). [600] **2715**

WANGAR (CN/0712-1865). [1,500] **5797**

WANTOK (PP). [15,000] **2511**

WAR CRY (NEW YORK, N.Y.), THE (US/0043-0234). [400,000] **5314**

WAR RESEARCH INFO SERVICE (US/1058-823X). [800] **4060**

WARBIRDS (US/0744-6624). [4,000] **39**

WARD COUNTY HERITAGE (US). **2477**

WARDEN'S ... ANNUAL REPORT ON THE RONDEVLEI BIRD SANCTUARY FOR THE YEAR ... / RONDEVLEI BIRD SANCTUARY, THE (SA). [1,000] **2208**

WARD'S AUTO WORLD (US/0043-0315). [86,000] **5428**

WARMER BULLETIN (UK). [65,000] **2245**

WARP AND WEFT (MCMINNVILLE, OR.) (US/0732-6890). [500] **5359**

WARSHIP INTERNATIONAL (US/0043-0374). [4,500] **4185**

WARTA DEMOGRAFI (IO). [800] **4560**

WARTA PASARAN LADA / PEPPER MARKET BULLETIN (MY/0126-5903). [350] **2361**

WARUNKI SRODOWISKOWE POLSKIEJ STREFY POLUDNIOWEGO BALTYKU-MATERIALY ODDZIALU MORSKIEGO (PL). [120] **1458**

WASCANA REVIEW (CN/0043-0412). [250] **3452**

WASHINGTON AFRO-AMERICAN AND THE WASHINGTON TRIBUNE (US). **5687**

WASHINGTON AND LEE LAW REVIEW (US/0043-0463). [2,000] **3072**

WASHINGTON APPLE PI (US/1056-7682). [4,500] **1207**

WASHINGTON COASTAL CURRENTS (US). [3,000] **2208**

WASHINGTON COUNTY NEWS (US). [3,600] **5628**

WASHINGTON, D.C. MINI-MICRO COMPUTER REPORT, THE (US/0363-7905). **1273**

WASHINGTON FOOD DEALER MAGAZINE, THE (US/0043-0560). [1,600] **2361**

WASHINGTON INFORMER, THE (US/0741-9414). [17,000] **2275**

WASHINGTON INQUIRER (US/0749-1050). [7,000] **4538**

WASHINGTON JEWISH WEEK (US/0746-9373). [20,000] **5053**

WASHINGTON JOB SOURCE, THE (US/1067-0769). [10,000] **4209**

WASHINGTON LAW REVIEW (1967) (US/0043-0617). [1,850] **3072**

WASHINGTON LAWYER, THE (US/0890-8761). **3072**

WASHINGTON LETTER (AMERICAN BAR ASSOCIATION) (US/0516-9968). [5,000] **3072**

WASHINGTON LETTER / JOINT MARITIME CONGRESS (US). [1,900] **5458**

WASHINGTON NOTES ON AFRICA (US/0512-610X). **2500**

WASHINGTON PARK ARBORETUM BULLETIN (US/1046-8749). [3,000] **2433**

WASHINGTON QUARTERLY, THE (US/0163-660X). [1,800] **4538**

WASHINGTON REPORT ON LATIN AMERICA & THE CARIBBEAN (US/0893-1232). **857**

WASHINGTON REPORT ON MIDDLE EAST AFFAIRS, THE (US/8755-4917). **2526**

WASHINGTON REPORT ON THE HEMISPHERE (US/0275-5599). [2,000] **2912**

WASHINGTON STATE BAR NEWS (US/0886-5213). [20,000] **3073**

WASHINGTON STATE'S WATER (US/0161-5912). [3,000] **5541**

WASHINGTON TARIFF AND TRADE LETTER (US/0276-8275). **857**

WASHINGTON VIEW (US/1042-4229). [30,000] **2549**

WASMANN JOURNAL OF BIOLOGY, THE (US/0043-0927). **476**

WASSER-KALENDER (BERLIN) (GW/0511-3520). **5541**

WASTE AGE (US/0043-1001). [30,000] **2245**

WASTE BUSINESS WEST (CN/1185-4731). [45,000] **2246**

WASTE MANAGEMENT & ENVIRONMENT (AT). [6,000] **2246**

WASTE PLANNING (UK/0965-3147). [1000] **2246**

WASTES MANAGEMENT (UK). [3,000] **2246**

WATAUGA DEMOCRAT (US/0745-1903). [13,300] **5724**

WATCH & CLOCK REVIEW (US/0279-6198). [15,000] **2916**

WATCHTOWER, THE (US/0043-1087). [11,150,000] **5069**

WATCOM NEWS (CN/0828-5624). [7,000] **1282**

WATER ACTIVITIES TRADE REPORT (US). [100] **2096**

WATER AND WASTES DIGEST (US/0043-1141). [100,703] **5542**

WATER & WASTEWATER DIGEST (US/0748-2612). [3,500] **2247**

WATER & WASTEWATER INTERNATIONAL (US/0891-5385). [16,000] **5542**

WATER CONDITIONING & PURIFICATION (US/0746-4029). [17,500] **5542**

WATER ENGINEERING & MANAGEMENT (US/0273-2238). [32,125] **2096**

WATER EQUIPMENT NEWS (US/0194-1194). [23,400] **5542**

WATER FARMING JOURNAL (US/1051-0583). [6,000] **2315**

WATER JOURNAL (US/0892-9548). [15,000] **5543**

WATER LAW (UK/0959-9754). [200] **5543**

WATER — Controlled Circulation Index

WATER OPERATION AND MAINTENANCE BULLETIN (US/0145-2800). **5543**

WATER QUALITY ASSOCIATION NEWSLETTER (US/0745-1512). [3,000] **2247**

WATER-RESOURCES BULLETIN (SALT LAKE CITY) (US/0094-7636). [1,000] **5544**

WATER RESOURCES BULLETIN (URBANA) (US/0043-1370). [3,972] **5544**

WATER RESOURCES DATA. NEW HAMPSHIRE AND VERMONT (US). [300] **5545**

WATER RESOURCES DEVELOPMENT BY THE U.S. ARMY CORPS OF ENGINEERS IN ARKANSAS (1979) (US). **5546**

WATER RESOURCES DEVELOPMENT BY THE U.S. ARMY CORPS OF ENGINEERS IN NORTH CAROLINA (US). [2,500] **5546**

WATER RESOURCES DEVELOPMENT BY THE U.S. ARMY CORPS OF ENGINEERS IN TEXAS (US). **5546**

WATER RESOURCES DEVELOPMENT BY THE US ARMY CORPS OF ENGINEERS IN KANSAS / US ARMY CORPS OF ENGINEERS, SOUTHWESTERN DIVISION (US). [1,000] **5546**

WATER RESOURCES DEVELOPMENT BY THE US ARMY CORPS OF ENGINEERS IN OKLAHOMA (US/0744-0480). [1,000] **5546**

WATER RESOURCES DEVELOPMENT IN IOWA (US/0732-6408). [2,000] **5546**

WATER RESOURCES DEVELOPMENT IN MICHIGAN (1981) (US/0278-5781). [2,000] **5546**

WATER RESOURCES DEVELOPMENT IN WISCONSIN (UNITED STATES. ARMY. CORPS OF ENGINEERS. NORTH CENTRAL DIVISION : 1981) (US). [2,000] **5546**

WATER RESOURCES RESEARCH (US/0043-1397). **5547**

WATER RIGHTS RESUME. DIVISION 6 (US). [75] **5547**

WATER S. A (SA/0378-4738). [2,500] **5547**

WATER SCOOTER (US/0899-9775). [100,000] **596**

WATER SKIER (WINTER HAVEN), THE (US/0049-7002). [24,000] **4928**

WATER SUPPLY OUTLOOK ... FOR THE NORTHEASTERN UNITED STATES (US/0732-5312). [100] **1419**

WATER SUPPLY OUTLOOK FOR THE WESTERN UNITED STATES (US). [1,500] **1419**

WATER TECHNOLOGY (US/0192-3633). [16,000] **5548**

WATER WELL JOURNAL (US/0043-1443). [37,000] **5548**

WATERBULLETIN (UK/0262-9909). [5,744] **5548**

WATERFRONT WORLD (US/0733-0677). [1,500] **2839**

WATERLOO CHRONICLE (CN). [24,500] **5797**

WATERWHEEL (SILVER SPRING, MD.) (US/0898-6606). **5008**

WATERWORLD NEWS (US/0747-9735). [100,000] **2248**

WAVE (US). [11,500] **5647**

WAVERLY GENEALOGICAL AND HISTORICAL SOCIETY NEWSLETTER (US). [100] **2477**

WAVES (SPRING VALLEY, CALIF.) (US/1055-0348). [5,000] **2096**

WAWATAY NEWS (CN/0703-9387). [5,500] **2275**

WAY MAGAZINE, THE (US/0277-0431). [7,000] **5020**

WAY OF ST. FRANCIS (1980) (US/0273-8295). [4,500] **5008**

WAY, THE (UK/0043-1575). [6,000] **5008**

WAYNE LAW REVIEW (US/0043-1621). [1,100] **3073**

WAYZGOOSE (CN/0715-4720). [135] **4570**

WCCI FORUM (US/0116-5461). [1,000] **1908**

WDA JOURNAL (US/1046-9338). [3,100] **1337**

WDS FORUM (US/0275-9748). [13,000] **3452**

WEB ABBOTSFORD (AT/1036-3912). [2,000] **1908**

WEBB REPORT : A NEWSLETTER ON SEXUAL HARASSMENT BY SUSAN L. WEBB, THE (US/1053-0932). **3179**

WEBSTER'S WAGON WHEEL (US/1067-523X). [90] **2477**

WEEDMAN NEWSLETTER (US/0883-7791). [100] **2477**

WEEKENDS (US). **5499**

WEEKLY ANALYSIS OF ECUADOREAN ISSUES (EC/0252-2659). [1,000] **1526**

WEEKLY BPN PROPANE NEWSLETTER (US/0193-4724). **4281**

WEEKLY BULLETIN - CALIFORNIA. STATE BANKING DEPT (US/1064-5918). [2,200] **816**

WEEKLY INDIA TRIBUNE (US/0744-4524). [15,000] **5662**

WEEKLY INSIDERS TURKEY LETTER (US/0160-4910). [260] **157**

WEEKLY MARKET BULLETIN (CONCORD) (US/0043-1850). [10,000] **145**

WEEKLY NEWS LETTER - ILLINOIS STATE AFL-CIO (US/0019-2279). [4,400] **1717**

WEEKLY REGISTER-CALL (CENTRAL CITY, COLO. : 1861) (US). [1,100] **5644**

WEEKLY REVIEW, THE (KE). **4538**

WEHRAUSBILDUNG (GW/0178-3084). [55,400] **4061**

WEHRMEDIZIN UND WEHRPHARMAZIE (GW). **4332**

WEHRTECHNIK (GW/0043-2172). [33,300] **4061**

WEIGHING & MEASUREMENT (US/0095-537X). [14,000] **4033**

WEIGHT CONTROL DIGEST (DALLAS, TEX. 1992), THE (US/1075-2889). **4200**

WEIGHT ENGINEERING (US). [1,500] **2001**

WEIGHTWATCHERS (UK). [160,000] **4200**

WEIRDBOOK (US/8755-7452). [900] **5075**

WELCOME HOME (US/8750-9563). [18,000] **2286**

WELDING DATA BOOK (US/0511-4365). [24,000] **4028**

WELDING DESIGN & FABRICATION (US/0043-2253). [42,000] **4028**

WELDING DISTRIBUTOR (1966) (US/0192-7671). [8,000] **938**

WELDON TIMES, THE (CN/0702-8989). **3073**

WELFARE IN AUSTRALIA (AT/0310-4869). [1,500] **5314**

WELFARE MANCHESTER (UK/0269-879X). [2,000] **5314**

WELL SERVICING (US/0043-2393). [10,000] **4282**

WELLNESS MANAGEMENT (US/1062-1156). [2,500] **4807**

WELT DES ISLAMS, DIE (NE/0043-2539). [500] **5045**

WELT DES ORIENTS, DIE (GW/0043-2547). **3332**

WELTMISSION, DIE (GW/0723-6204). **5008**

WELTWOCHE, DIE (SZ). [98,500] **2525**

WEN HUI YUEH KAN / WEN HUI YUEH KAN PIEN CHI PU (CC). [150,000] **333**

WERELD EN ZENDING (NE/0165-988X). [2,000] **5009**

WESCON CONFERENCE RECORD (1979) (US/1044-6036). **2085**

WESLEYAN ADVOCATE, THE (US/0043-289X). [17,000] **5069**

WESLEYAN CHRISTIAN ADVOCATE (US/0190-6097). [29,000] **5069**

WESLEYAN (MIDDLETOWN) (US/0148-4249). [27,500] **1103**

WESLEYAN THEOLOGICAL JOURNAL (US/0092-4245). [1,600] **5009**

WEST AFRICA OIL SERVICE (UK). [100] **4282**

WEST AFRICAN JOURNAL OF ARCHAEOLOGY (NR/0083-8160). **285**

WEST AFRICAN JOURNAL OF SURGERY (NR/0331-054X). [2,000] **3977**

WEST COAST LIFELINER (CN/0225-4255). **4807**

WEST EDMONTON EXAMINER (CN/0707-509X). **5797**

WEST ENDER (CN/0229-6012). [28,500] **5797**

WEST HARTFORD NEWS (US/1057-1272). [10,000] **5646**

WEST INDIAN LAW JOURNAL (JM/0253-7370). [700] **3073**

WEST TORONTO NEWS-EXPRESS, THE (CN/0821-5197). **5797**

WEST VIRGINIA BLUE BOOK (US). [20,000] **4694**

WEST VIRGINIA BUSINESS INDEX (US/0195-4644). **719**

WEST VIRGINIA FORESTRY NOTES (US/0197-1387). [2,500] **2398**

WEST VIRGINIA HILLS & STREAMS (US/0279-0580). [1,000] **2208**

WEST VIRGINIA LIBRARIES (US/0043-3276). [1,000] **3256**

WEST VIRGINIA MANUFACTURERS REGISTER (US/0893-2824). [1,000] **3489**

WEST VIRGINIA MEDICAL JOURNAL (US/0043-3284). [2,627] **3650**

WEST VIRGINIA SCHOOL JOURNAL (1990) (US/1056-733X). **1791**

WESTAF'S NATIONAL ARTS JOBBANK (US/1046-7718). [2,000] **333**

WESTCHESTER BAR JOURNAL (US/0746-1844). [2,500] **3073**

WESTCHESTER FAMILY (US/1043-6774). [36,000] **1071**

WESTCHESTER HISTORIAN, THE (US/0049-7266). [800] **2765**

WESTCOAST READER, THE (CN/0822-7225). **2550**

WESTERLY (AT/0043-342X). [1,000] **3452**

WESTERN ANGLER (AT/1035-493X). [7,000] **2316**

WESTERN AUSTRALIA IN BRIEF (AT/0727-2022). **3073**

WESTERN AUSTRALIAN ECONOMIC REVIEW (AT/0726-6685). **1631**

WESTERN AUSTRALIAN HERBARIUM ANNUAL REPORT (AT). [70] **530**

WESTERN CANADA OUTDOORS (ALBERTA EDITION) (CN/0836-446X). [42,000] **2208**

WESTERN CANADA OUTDOORS (SASKATCHEWAN EDITION) (CN/0836-4451). [42,000] **2208**

WESTERN CANADIAN ANTHROPOLOGIST, THE (CN/0829-0547). [250] **247**

WESTERN CITY (SACRAMENTO, CALIF. : 1976) (US/0279-5337). [10,000] **4694**

WESTERN CLEANER & LAUNDERER (US/0049-741X). [11,500] **1031**

WESTERN COLLEGE READING & LEARNING ASSOCIATION NEWSLETTER (US/0746-1305). [700] **1853**

WESTERN EUROPE (WASHINGTON, D.C.: 1982) (US/0084-2338). **2715**

WESTERN EUROPEAN SPECIALISTS SECTION NEWSLETTER (US/0734-4503). **3333**

WESTERN FARMER AND GRAZIER. WESTERN FARM WEEKLY (AT). [13,500] **145**

WESTERN FRONTIERSMAN SERIES (US/0083-8888). [1,000] **2765**

WESTERN GEOGRAPHICAL SERIES (CN/0315-2022). [1,500] **2579**

WESTERN GROCER MAGAZINE (1977) (CN/0705-906X). [10,400] **2361**

WESTERN GROWER & SHIPPER (US/0043-3799). [4,500] **190**

WESTERN HOG JOURNAL (CN/0225-3488). [10,000] **223**

WESTERN HUMANITIES REVIEW (US/0043-3845). [1,200] **3453**

WESTERN HVACR NEWS (US/0273-5687). [20,000] **2608**

WESTERN JOURNAL OF BLACK STUDIES, THE (US/0197-4327). [600] **2275**

WESTERN LANDS AND WATER SERIES (US/0083-8934). [1,000] **2766**

WESTERN LINKS (HILTON HEAD ISLAND, S.C.) (US/1052-3219). **4929**

WESTERN LIVING (VANCOUVER ED.) (CN/0824-0604). [252,500] **2904**

WESTERN MARYLAND GENEALOGY (US/0747-7805). [725] **2477**

WESTERN METALWORKING DIRECTORY (US). [12,000] **4023**

WESTERN NEW ENGLAND LAW REVIEW (US/0190-6593). [1,000] **3073**

WESTERN NEW YORK (US/0149-5070). [8,500] **719**

WESTERN NEW YORK FAMILY MAGAZINE (US). [25,000] **2286**

WESTERN NEWS (LIBBY, MONT.), THE (US/0745-0362). [4,550] **5706**

WESTERN NEWS (LONDON) (CN/0316-8654). [17,000] **1853**

WESTERN PETROLEUM REGISTER (US/0273-1762). [1,000] **4282**

WESTERN PLANNER, THE (US/0279-0602). [1,400] **4695**

WESTERN POLITICAL QUARTERLY, THE (US/0043-4078). **4500**

WESTERN QUEENS GAZETTE, THE (US). [60,000] **5722**

WESTERN RACING NEWS (US/0510-2626). [4,000] **5428**

WESTERN RECORDER (MIDDLETOWN) (US/0043-4132). [50,000] **5009**

WESTERN ROOFING INSULATION AND SIDING (US/0164-5803). [20,000] **631**

WESTERN SKIER (CN/1184-2679). [30,000] **4929**

WESTERN SPORTSMAN (CN/0709-1532). [24,000] **4929**

WESTERN TAX REVIEW (US/8755-0083). [200] **4758**

WESTERN WATER (US/0735-5424). [16,000] **5548**

WESTERN WHEEL (CN/0701-1571). [7,800] **2550**

WESTIR'S WESTERN SYDNEY LETTER (AT/0726-0075). [350] **2511**

WESTMINISTER WINDOW (US). [12,000] **5644**

WESTSIDE GAZETTE. THURSDAY (US). [35,000] **5651**

WESTWORD (US/0194-7710). [110,000] **5644**

WESTWORD (EDMONTON) (CN/1184-678X). [1,000] **2925**

WETENSCHAP EN SAMENLEVING (NE/0043-4442). [46,000] **146**

WETHERSFIELD POST (US). [3,625] **5646**

WETLANDS : JOURNAL OF THE COAST AND WETLANDS SOCIETY (AT). [350] **2511**

WETLANDS (WILMINGTON, N.C.) (US/0277-5212). [2,500] **2208**

WETTBEWERB IN RECHT UND PRAXIS : WRP (GW/0172-049X). [1,800] **3104**

WETTER UND LEBEN (AU/0043-4450). [550] **1437**

WETUMPKA HERALD, THE (US). [4,100] **5628**

WFCD COMMUNICATOR (CN/0822-8183). [2,700] **146**

WHALEWATCHER (US/0273-4419). [5,000] **5600**

WHAT'S AHEAD IN HUMAN RESOURCES (US). **948**

WHAT'S BREWING (CN/0714-2056). [2,000] **2372**

WHAT'S NEW IN ACCOUNTING CANADA (CN/0826-094X). **753**

WHAT'S NEW IN COMPUTING (SI). [18,000] **1245**

WHAT'S NEW IN FARMING (UK). [76,000] **146**

WHAT'S ON IN LONDON (UK). [32,000] **5499**

WHEAT AUSTRALIA INTERNATIONAL (AT/0814-9267). **191**

WHEAT LIFE (US/0043-4701). [13,000] **146**

WHEAT RIDGE JEFFERSON SENTINEL, THE (US/1060-5223). [19,000] **5644**

WHEEL-O-RAMA (US/0882-6676). [2,000] **5428**

WHEELS OF TIME (US/0738-565X). [14,500] **5399**

WHEELWRIGHTINGS (US/0192-5865). [150] **3453**

WHERE CALGARY (CN/1182-1981). [25,000] **4867**

WHERE THE TRAILS CROSS (US/0092-4164). [550] **2477**

WHERE TO LEARN ENGLISH IN GREAT BRITAIN (UK/0143-2214). [1,500] **3333**

WHEREVER IN THE WORLD, FOR JESUS' SAKE (US/0889-0781). [15,000] **5009**

WHICH COMPUTER? (UK/0140-3435). [31,438] **1207**

WHISKEY, WOMEN, AND ... (US/0091-7664). [1,000] **4159**

WHISTLE PUNK (CN/0825-477X). [2,000] **2398**

WHISTLE (VANCOUVER) (CN/0227-0862). **4929**

WHITBY FREE PRESS (CN/0844-398X). [26,000] **5797**

WHITBY FREE PRESS (CN/0844-398X). **5797**

WHITE BEAR PRESS, THE (US/0892-1326). [15,000] **5699**

WHITE BOOK OF SKI AREAS. U.S. AND CANADA, THE (US/0163-9684). [10,000-20,000] **4929**

WHITE COUNTY RECORD (JUDSONIA, ARK.) (US/8750-5177). [1,850] **5632**

WHITE LEADER, THE (US/0899-9805). [800] **5744**

WHITE TOPS, THE (US/0043-499X). [2,600] **4867**

WHITE TRIANGLE NEWS (US/0164-5145). **5237**

WHITE WALL REVIEW (CN/0712-8991). [500] **3453**

WHITECOURT STAR (CN/0847-8597). **5798**

WHITTIER LAW REVIEW (US/0195-7643). **3075**

WHITTIER NEWSLETTER (US/0511-8832). [500] **435**

WHO IS WHO (II). [250] **435**

WHO MAKES MACHINERY IN GERMANY (GW). [40,700] **2132**

WHODUZZIT? (NEW YORK, N.Y.) (US/1062-0427). [10,000] **4378**

WHOLE FOODS (US/0193-1504). [11,000] **2361**

WHOLE LIFE (US/0888-2061). [60,000] **4807**

WHOLE LIFE TIMES (US/0279-5604). [140,000] **4200**

WHOLESALER (ELMHURST), THE (US/0032-1680). [25,000] **2609**

WHO'S WHO IN AUSTRALIA (AT). [12,000] **436**

WHO'S WHO IN FRANCE (FR/0083-9531). [12,000] **437**

WHO'S WHO IN INDIAN RELICS (US/0747-7538). [5,000] **437**

WHO'S WHO IN INSURANCE (US/0083-9574). [10,000] **437**

WHO'S WHO IN P/M (US/0361-6304). **437**

WHO'S WHO IN THE FISH INDUSTRY (US/0270-160X). [5,000] **2316**

WHO'S WHO IN THE MOTION PICTURE INDUSTRY (US/0278-6516). [4,500] **438**

WHO'S WHO IN THE PICTURE FRAMING INDUSTRY (US/0147-2119). **438**

WHO'S WHO IN TRAINING AND DEVELOPMENT (US/0092-4598). [26,000] **438**

WHO'S WHO OF CALIFORNIA EXECUTIVE WOMEN (US/0748-0601). **438**

WIADOMOSCI INSTYTUTU METEOROLOGII I GOSPODARKI WODNEJ (PL/0208-6263). [450] **1437**

WIADOMOSCI STATYSTYCZNE (WARSAW, POLAND : 1956) (PL). [1,700] **5346**

WICAZO SA REVIEW (US/0749-6427). [600] **2766**

WICHE REPORTS ON HIGHER EDUCATION IN THE WEST (US). [4,000] **1853**

WICHITA COMMERCE (US/1048-8782). [5,000] **857**

WICHITA JOURNAL (US/1048-3365). **5679**

WIEL (SA/0257-5426). [30,000] **5428**

WIENER BEITRAEGE ZUR ENGLISCHEN PHILOLOGIE (AU/0083-9914). [600] **3333**

WIENER HUMANISTISCHE BLATTER (AU/0083-9965). [1,000] **1081**

WIENER JAHRBUCH FUR PHILOSOPHIE (AU/0083-999X). [500] **4365**

WIENER STUDIEN (AU/0084-005X). [600] **3333**

WIENER ZEITSCHRIFT FUER DIE KUNDE DES MORGENLANDES (AU/0084-0076). [300] **2633**

WILD OREGON (US). [6,000] **2208**

WILDERNESS (AT). [15,000] **2208**

WILDERNESS ALBERTA (CN/0830-8284). [2,500] **2209**

WILDERNESS MEDICINE LETTER : THE OFFICIAL NEWSLETTER OF THE WILDERNESS MEDICAL SOCIETY (US). [3,000] **3651**

WILDERNESS RECORD (US/0194-3030). [3,000] **2209**

WILDERNESS SERIES (US/1056-3318). **4880**

WILDERNESS (WASHINGTON, D.C.) (US/0736-6477). [350,000] **2209**

WILDFLOWER (AUSTIN, TEX. 1984) (US/0898-8803). [16,000] **530**

WILDFLOWER (AUSTIN, TEX. 1988) (US/0896-4858). [20,000] **530**

WILDFOWL (SLIMBRIDGE) (UK/0954-6324). [2,000] **5621**

WILDLIFE COLLECTABLES JOURNAL, THE (CN/0827-2409). **2209**

WILDLIFE JOURNAL (US/0893-6560). [1,500] **2209**

WILDLIFE PRESERVATION TRUST ... ANNUAL REPORT (US). [5,000] **2209**

WILDLIFE SOCIETY BULLETIN (US/0091-7648). [6,000] **2209**

WILLAMETTE WEEK (US). [65,000] **5734**

WILLAPA HARBOR HERALD, THE (US/1065-3805). **5763**

WILLIAM AND MARY QUARTERLY, THE (US/0043-5597). [3,900] **2766**

WILLIAM MITCHELL LAW REVIEW (US/0270-272X). [1,900] **3075**

WILLIAMS NEWS (US). [5,020] **5630**

WILLIAMS REPORT (US/1075-8550). [500] **1124**

WILLIAMSBURG RESEARCH STUDIES (US). **2766**

WILLOW TRANSFER QUARTERLY (CN/0826-2098). [600] **2595**

WILMINGTON JOURNAL (WILMINGTON, N.C.), THE (US/0049-7649). [6,000] **5724**

WILSHIRE CENTER'S LARCHMONT CHRONICLE (US/0192-1932). [20,000] **5641**

WILSON LIBRARY BULLETIN (US/0043-5651). [23,000] **3256**

WILTSHIRE ARCHAEOLOGICAL AND NATURAL HISTORY MAGAZINE (1982) (UK/0262-6608). [1,500] **285**

WIND ENERGY ABSTRACTS (US/0277-2140). [500] **1960**

WIND ENERGY NEWS (US/0886-2818). [900] **1960**

WIND ENERGY REPORT (US/0162-8623). [1,000] **1960**

WINDIRECTIONS (UK/0950-0642). [2,000] **1960**

WINDOW FASHIONS (US/0886-9669). [25,000] **2904**

WINDOWS (AUSTIN, TEX.) (US/1056-0556). [12,500] **5009**

WINDOWS (COLLEGE STATION, TEX.) (US/0745-0729). [5,000] **5169**

WINDSOR JOURNAL, THE (US). [2,400] **5646**

WINDSOR LOCKS JOURNAL, THE (US). [1,400] **5647**

WINDSOR THIS MONTH (CN/0318-2460). [22,000] **2550**

WINE & SPIRITS (BERKELEY, CALIF.) (US/0890-0299). [60,000] **2372**

WINE PRODUCTION, AUSTRALIA AND STATES / AUSTRALIAN BUREAU OF STATISTICS (AT). [1,500] **2362**

WINE WORLD (US/0199-7483). [50,000] **2373**

WINESBURG EAGLE, THE (US/0147-3166). [150] **439**

WING FOOT CLAN, THE (US/0043-5872). [21,000] **5078**

WING WORLD (US/0745-273X). [23,000] **4083**

WINGING IT (US/1042-511X). [13,000] **5600**

WINGS (CALGARY) (CN/0701-1369). [11,500] **39**

WINNIPEG SUN (1980) (CN/0711-3773). [50,000] **5798**

WINONA COURIER (US). **5699**

WINSTON CUP ILLUSTRATED (US/1048-6119). [18,000] **4930**

WINSTON CUP SCENE (US/1053-461X). [82,000] **4930**

WINSTON-SALEM CHRONICLE (US). [10,000] **5724**

WINSTON-SALEM MAGAZINE (US/8755-9587). [12,000] **2550**

WINTER PARK-MAITLAND OBSERVER (US/1064-3613). [3,000] **5651**

WINTER PARK OUTLOOK (US/0745-9203). [5,000] **5651**

WINTER RECREATION DIRECTORY (CN/0825-4044). [20,000] **4855**

WIP FUN (CN/0824-4782). **3256**

WIRE JOURNAL INTERNATIONAL (US/0277-4275). [10,994] **4023**

WIRE TECHNOLOGY INTERNATIONAL (US/0898-9850). [10,500] **4023**

WIRE WORLD INTERNATIONAL (GW/0043-6046). [5,000] **2086**

WIRELESS REGISTER. WORLD WIDE EDITION, THE (US/0277-2825). **1143**

WIREWORLD (GW/0934-5906). [8,000] **2001**

WIRTSCHAFT UND GESELLSCHAFT (AU/0378-5130). [3,000] **1588**

WIRTSCHAFT UND WETTBEWERB (GW/0043-6151). [1,370] **857**

WIRTSCHAFTSEIGENE FUTTER (GW/0049-7711). **224**

WIRTSCHAFTSPRUFUNG, DIE (GW/0043-6313). [10,500] **753**

WIRTSCHAFTSRECHT (GW/0512-6320). **3104**

WIRTSCHAFTSSCHUTZ + SICHERHEITSTECHNIK (GW/0173-3303). [5,300] **3179**

WISCONSERVATION (US/0164-3649). [6,000] **2210**

WISCONSIN ARCHITECT (US). [3,600] **310**

WISCONSIN COUNTIES (US/0749-6818). [3,500] **4695**

WISCONSIN ENGINEER (US/0043-6453). [2,000] **2001**

WISCONSIN ENGLISH JOURNAL (US). [700] **3333**

WISCONSIN LAW REVIEW (US/0043-650X). [2,000] **3075**

WISCONSIN — Controlled Circulation Index

WISCONSIN LAWYER (US/1043-0490). [15,000] **4695**

WISCONSIN MAGAZINE OF HISTORY (US/0043-6534). [6,000] **2766**

WISCONSIN MASTER PLUMBER (US/0199-1639). [6,000] **2609**

WISCONSIN MEDICAL ALUMNI QUARTERLY (US/8755-1519). [10,000] **1103**

WISCONSIN MEDICAL JOURNAL (US/0043-6542). [7,400] **3651**

WISCONSIN OUTDOORS AND CONSERVATION NEWS (US). [1,000] **4880**

WISCONSIN PHARMACIST, THE (US/0043-6585). [1,800] **4332**

WISCONSIN PUBLIC EMPLOYMENT DECISIONS DIGEST (US/0145-8655). **1718**

WISCONSIN REALTOR, THE (US/0279-2583). [10,500] **4848**

WISCONSIN REC NEWS (US). [135,000] **1543**

WISCONSIN REVIEW (OSHKOSH) (US/0043-6631). [2,000] **3453**

WISCONSIN SCHOOL NEWS (US). [5,000] **1874**

WISCONSIN SECURITIES BULLETIN (US). [1,424] **920**

WISCONSIN TRAILS (US/0095-4314). [33,000] **2550**

WISCONSIN WATER QUALITY ... REPORT TO CONGRESS (US/0740-4700). [500] **5549**

WISENET (AT/0815-0753). [500] **5568**

WISER NOW (US/1071-2275). [3,000] **3755**

WISSENSCHAFT UND WEISHEIT (GW/0043-678X). **5009**

WISSENSCHAFTLICHE BERICHTE AUS DER HOCHMAGNETFELDANLAGE DER TECHNISCHEN UNIVERSITAT BRAUNSCHWEIG (GW/0723-9459). **1854**

WISSENSCHAFTLICHE ZEITSCHRIFT (GW/0040-1528). **2495**

WISSENSCHAFTLICHE ZEITSCHRIFT DER UNIVERSITAT ROSTOCK. NATURWISSENSCHAFTLICHE REIHE (GW/0863-1204). [1,250] **5170**

WITHOUT PREJUDICE (EDMONTON) (CN/0706-5574). [2,000] **2896**

WITNESS (FARMINGTON HILLS, MICH.) (US/0891-1371). [2,800] **3453**

WITTERUNG IN UBERSEE, DIE (GW/0043-7085). [220] **1437**

WIZARD: THE GUIDE TO COMICS (US). [300M] **2779**

WLN PARTICIPANT (US/0278-6303). [1,000] **3256**

WNC BUSINESS JOURNAL (US/1049-7145). [18,400] **723**

WOLFMAN REPORT ON THE PHOTOGRAPHIC & IMAGING INDUSTRY IN THE UNITED STATES (US/0897-5132). [10,000] **4378**

WOLGAN KWAHAK (CH). [30,000] **5170**

WOLGAN KYOBO (KO). **2896**

WOLSLEY BULLETIN, THE (CN/0842-084X). [1,000] **5798**

WOLVES AND RELATED CANIDS (US/0899-9317). [1,000] **5600**

WOMAN ACTIVIST, THE (US/0049-7770). [200] **4500**

WOMAN ENGINEER. (GREENLAWN, N.Y.), THE (US/0887-2120). [16,000] **2001**

WOMAN ENGINEER, THE (UK). [1,000] **2001**

WOMAN WRITER (AT/0313-6485). [650] **3454**

WOMAN'S PULPIT, THE (US/0043-7379). [400] **5009**

WOMBAT (US). [1,000] **1071**

WOMEN ALIVE (US/0890-3395). [5,000] **5009**

WOMEN AND ENVIRONMENTS (CN/0229-480X). [1,400] **5569**

WOMEN IN BUSINESS (KANSAS CITY, MO.) (US/0043-7441). [90,000] **723**

WOMEN IN NATURAL RESOURCES (US). [1,000] **5570**

WOMEN IN THE LABOUR FORCE. FACTS AND FIGURES (CN/0382-2192). [8,000] **1718**

WOMEN OF EUROPE (BE/0258-6169). **5570**

WOMEN POLICE MAGAZINE (US). [4,000] **3179**

WOMEN'S & CHILDREN'S WEAR AND FASHION ACCESSORIES BUYERS (US/0741-0735). [4,000] **1088**

WOMENS ART REGISTER BULLETIN (AT). [250-300] **333**

WOMEN'S CONCERNS (CN/0827-2263). [5,000] **5009**

WOMEN'S EDUCATION (CN/0714-9786). [1,000] **1791**

WOMENS GLOBAL NETWORK FOR REPRODUCTIVE RIGHTS NEWSLETTER (NE). [1,295] **5570**

WOMEN'S LARGE & HALF SIZE SPECIALTY STORES (US/0743-3972). [700] **1088**

WOMEN'S LEAGUE OUTLOOK (US/0043-7557). [140,000] **5053**

WOMEN'S LEGAL DEFENSE FUND NEWSLETTER, THE (US/0736-9433). [2,000] **3076**

WOMEN'S POLITICAL TIMES (US/0195-1688). [20,000] **4500**

WOMEN'S RECORD, THE (US/0888-4609). [30,000] **5571**

WOMEN'S RESEARCH NETWORK NEWS : A NEWSLETTER OF THE NATIONAL COUNCIL FOR RESEARCH ON WOMEN (US). [1,500] **5571**

WOMEN'S RIGHTS LAW REPORTER (US/0085-8269). [1,200] **3076**

WOMEN'S TRAVELLER (US). [12,000] **5499**

WOMENWISE (US/0890-9695). [2,500] **4808**

WONDERFUL WEST VIRGINIA (US/0030-7157). [60,000] **2210**

WONJARYOK ANJON CHONGBO (KO). **2159**

WONJARYOK KISUL CHONGBO (KO). **4451**

WOOD AND FIBER SCIENCE (US/0735-6161). [800] **2406**

WOOD MACHINING NEWS (US/0743-5231). **2406**

WOODALL'S CAMPGROUND DIRECTORY. EASTERN EDITION (US/0162-7406). [450,000] **4881**

WOODALL'S CAMPGROUND MANAGEMENT (US/0162-3796). **889**

WOODMEN OF THE WORLD MAGAZINE (US/0043-7751). [465,000] **2896**

WOODSIDE REPORT, THE (CN/1192-2958). [100-200] **1960**

WOODSMITH (US/0164-4114). [250,000] **635**

WOODSTOCK TIMES (US). **5722**

WOODWORKER, THE (US/0894-7481). [25,000] **5734**

WOODWORKER'S JOURNAL (NEW MILFORD), THE (US/0199-1892). [120,000] **635**

WOODWORKING (MARKHAM) (CN/0838-4185). [11,020] **2406**

WOOL MARKET REVIEW (NZ/1171-9672). [5,000] **5360**

WOOL (PALMERSTON NORTH) (NZ/0110-6015). [1,200] **5360**

WOOL REPORT NEW ZEALAND (NZ/0112-6059). [25,000] **5360**

WOOL SACK, THE (US/0043-7840). [10,000] **224**

WOOL TECHNOLOGY AND SHEEP BREEDING (AT/0043-7875). [4,000] **224**

WORCESTER BUSINESS JOURNAL (US/1063-6595). [15,000] **723**

WORCESTER MAGAZINE (WORCESTER) (US/0191-4960). [50,000] **4855**

WORD AND WAY (US/0049-7959). [55,000] **5009**

WORDPERFECT FOR WINDOWS MAGAZINE (US/1058-9783). [35,000] **1292**

WORDPERFECT (OREM, UTAH) (US/1042-5152). [240,000] **1292**

WORDS BY SPECIALISTS (US). [400 a month] **1791**

WORDS (WILLOW GROVE) (US/0164-4742). [49,000] **4214**

WORDSWORTH CIRCLE (US/0043-8006). [1,000] **3356**

WORK BOAT, THE (US/0043-8014). [12,500] **597**

WORK INJURY MANAGEMENT (US). **2896**

WORK PROGRAM / FERIC (CN/0713-7826). **2398**

WORKBOAT INTERNATIONAL (UK). [6,500] **597**

WORKER CO-OPS (TORONTO. 1980) (CN/0829-576X). [2,500] **1543**

WORKERS' COMPENSATION LAW REVIEW (US/1050-9836). [400] **3076**

WORKERS' COMPENSATION LEGISLATION IN AUSTRALIA / DEPARTMENT OF SOCIAL SECURITY (AT). [1,500] **3076**

WORKERS' COMPENSATION REPORTER (CN/0826-4198). [1,400] **1719**

WORKERS EDUCATION (II). [1,500] **1719**

WORKERS VANGUARD (NEW YORK, N.Y.) (US/0276-0746). [16,000] **1719**

WORKFORCE (WASHINGTON, D.C.) (US/1063-4363). [1,000] **1719**

WORKING FOR WILDLIFE (CN/0229-7183). [50,000] **2210**

WORKING PAPER - FACULTY OF ADMINISTRATION, UNIVERSITY OF OTTAWA (CN/0701-3086). **723**

WORKING PAPER - FLORIDA STATE UNIVERSITY. CENTER FOR THE STUDY OF POPULATION (US/0740-9095). **4561**

WORKING PAPER SERIES - DEPARTMENT OF BUSINESS, SCHOOL OF BUSINESS AND ECONOMICS, WILFRID LAURIER UNIVERSITY (CN/0714-7228). **723**

WORKING PAPER (UNIVERSITY OF WESTERN ONTARIO) CENTRE FOR THE STUDY OF INTERNATIONAL ECONOMIC RELATIONS) (CN/0228-4235). [150] **1641**

WORKING PAPERS / ANNUAL SEMINARS ON AFRICAN GOVERNANCE (US). [400] **4500**

WORKING PAPERS IN BAKER LIBRARY (US/0364-6645). [150] **723**

WORKING PAPERS IN IRISH STUDIES (US/0732-2674). [75] **2716**

WORKING PAPERS IN TRADE AND DEVELOPMENT (AT/0816-5181). [350] **2913**

WORKPLACE MELBOURNE (AT/1036-5117). **1719**

WORKSITE WELLNESS WORKS (US/1053-492X). [10,000] **4200**

WORKSTATION REPORT, THE (US/1040-7472). **4214**

WORLD ACCOUNTING REPORT; A MONTHLY BULLETIN ON DEVELOPMENTS IN INTERNATIONAL ACCOUNTING (UK). **753**

WORLD AFFAIRS JOURNAL (US/0731-4728). [10,000] **4538**

WORLD AIRSHOW NEWS (US/0888-5265). [3,300] **40**

WORLD ALMANAC AND BOOK OF FACTS, THE (US/0084-1382). [1,000,000] **1930**

WORLD & I, THE (US/0887-9346). **2495**

WORLD AQUACULTURE (US/1041-5602). [4,300] **2316**

WORLD AROUND YOU, THE (US/0199-8293). [12,000] **4395**

WORLD (ASHEVILLE, N.C.) (US/0888-157X). [35,000] **2550**

WORLD AUTOMOTIVE MARKET, THE (US). [3,000] **5428**

WORLD CEMENT DIRECTORY (FR). **1031**

WORLD COFFEE & TEA (US/0043-8340). [6,500] **2373**

WORLD COGENERATION (US/1053-5802). [21,000] **2132**

WORLD COIN NEWS (US/0145-9090). [6,863] **2783**

WORLD (COOS BAY, OR.), THE (US/1062-8495). [17,600] **5734**

WORLD DIRECTORY OF AL-ANON FAMILY GROUPS AND ALATEENS (US/0512-2716). [22,000] **1350**

WORLD DIRECTORY OF NEUROLOGICAL SURGEONS. PART 1, UNITED STATES OF AMERICA AND CANADA (US/0276-5306). **3977**

WORLD DIRECTORY: SECONDARY LEAD PLANTS (UK). **4024**

WORLD DIRECTORY: SECONDARY ZINC PLANTS (UK). **4024**

WORLD EAGLE (US/0193-7871). **5228**

WORLD ECONOMY, THE (UK/0378-5920). [1,500] **1641**

WORLD FISHING (UK/0043-8480). [5,874] **2316**

WORLD FOOTWEAR (US/0894-3079). [15,000] **1088**

WORLD FUTURE SOCIETY (US/0732-7676). **5237**

WORLD HOCKEY (UK/0964-0681). [3,000] **4930**

WORLD INTELLECTUAL PROPERTY REPORT (UK/0952-7613). [2,000] **1309**

WORLD JOURNAL OF PSYCHOSYNTHESIS (US/0043-860X). [300] **3937**

WORLD LEATHER (US/0894-3087). **3186**

WORLD (NEW YORK, N.Y. : 1967), THE (US/0043-8154). [4,000] **3473**

WORLD NEWS (UK). [150,000] **1527**

WORLD OF BANKING, THE (US/0730-8736). [8,000] **817**

WORLD OF LUBAVITCH (CN/0824-7420). [5,000] **5053**

WORLD OF MUSIC (WILHELMSHAVEN) (SZ/0043-8774). [2,000] **4159**

WORLD OF PERSONNEL (US/0892-6247). [350] **1720**

WORLD OIL (HOUSTON, TEX.) (US/0043-8790). [37,582] **4282**

WORLD PLASTICS & RUBBER TECHNOLOGY (UK). **4461**

WORLD PROGRESS (US/0043-8901). **2550**

WORLD PUMPS (UK/0262-1762). [6,200] **2132**

WORLD RIVERS REVIEW (US). **5549**

WORLD SMOKING & HEALTH (US/0161-7672). [10,000] **5374**

WORLD SPACE INDUSTRY SURVEY. TEN YEAR OUTLOOK (FR). **40**

WORLD STUDENT NEWS (XR/0014-2255). **1792**

WORLD SUGAR JOURNAL (UK). [1,100] **147**

WORLD TANKER FLEET REVIEW (UK). [600] **5458**

WORLD TELECOMS DAILY (UK). **1169**

WORLD TOBACCO SITUATION / UNITED STATES DEPARTMENT OF AGRICULTURE, FOREIGN AGRICULTURAL SERVICE (US). [724] **5374**

WORLD TODAY, THE (UK/0043-9134). [4,000] **4539**

WORLD TRADE NEWSPAPER (CN/0843-4174). **858**

WORLD TRIBUNE (US/0049-8165). [120,000] **4378**

WORLD VISION (US). [200,000] **2913**

WORLD WEIGHTLIFTING (HU/0230-3035). **2602**

WORLDLIT (CN/0820-6686). **1887**

WORLD'S FAIR (CORTE MADERA, CALIF.) (US/0273-480X). [5,000] **5226**

WORLD'S FAIR, THE (UK). [30,000] **4868**

WORLD'S POULTRY SCIENCE JOURNAL (UK/0043-9339). [6,000] **224**

WORLDWIDE BROCHURES (PRINT ED.) (US/1053-9158). **5500**

WORLDWIDE OFFSHORE CONTRACTORS & EQUIPMENT DIRECTORY (US/1058-9686). [2,500] **4285**

WORLDWIDE PETROCHEMICAL DIRECTORY (US/0084-2583). [2,500] **4282**

WORLDWIDE PROJECTS (US/0192-5512). [18,000] **2001**

WORLDWIDE SURVEY OF MOTOR GASOLINE QUALITY (UK). **4283**

WORLDWIDE TANKER NOMINAL FREIGHT SCALE / JOINTLY SPONSORED AND ISSUED BY WORLDSCALE ASSOCIATION (LONDON) LIMITED [AND] WORLDSCALE ASSOCIATION (NYC) INC (UK). **5458**

WORLDWIDE TRAVEL PLANNER (US/0890-4766). [250,000] **5500**

WORLDWIND (CN/0707-2279). [10,000] **1071**

WORSHIP (US/0043-941X). [7,000] **5010**

WPI JOURNAL (US/0148-6128). [22,000] **5171**

WPNR, WEEKBLAD VOOR PRIVAATRECHT, NOTARIAAT EN REGISTRATIE (NE). [3,500] **3076**

WRAP (US/0896-1697). [10,000] **1124**

WREE-VIEW OF WOMEN FOR RACIAL AND ECONOMIC EQUALITY, THE (US/0892-3116). [5,000] **4514**

WRESTLING USA (LAHABRA) (US/0199-6258). [13,000] **4931**

WRESTLING'S MAIN EVENT (US/0278-9612). [108,000] **4931**

WRF COMMENT (CN/0821-1248). [500] **1527**

WRIT, THE (US). [4,300] **3076**

WRITER'S GUIDELINES (PITTSBURG, MO.) (US/1053-1793). [750] **2925**

WRITING CENTER JOURNAL, THE (US). [700] **1854**

WRITING IN PEEL (CN/0714-413X). **3455**

WRITING TEACHER (SAN ANTONIO, TEX.) (US/0894-5837). **1908**

WRONGFUL DISCHARGE REPORT (US/1053-0274). **3155**

WU HSIA SHIH CHIEH (CH). [2,000] **3455**

WURTTEMBERGISCHES WOCHENBLATT FUR LANDWIRTSCHAFT (GW). [45,000] **147**

WURZBURGER GEOGRAPHISCHE ARBEITEN (GW/0510-9833). [450] **2579**

WVLC NEWSLETTER (US/0149-0567). [1,500] **3256**

WWF NEWS (SZ/0254-3893). [21,000] **2210**

WWS, WORLD WIDE SHIPPING GUIDE (US/0162-0088). [11,500] **5458**

WXXI PROGRAM GUIDE (1985) (US/0883-1106). [26,000] **1143**

WXXI (ROCHESTER, N.Y.) (US/1055-2960). [35,000] **1143**

WYNIKI POMIAROW PIONOWEGO ROZKLADU OZONU W ATMOSFERZE (PL). [100] **1437**

WYNIKI SPISU ROLNICZEGO (PL). [800] **147**

WYOMING CATHOLIC REGISTER, THE (US/0746-5580). [16,000] **5038**

WYOMING EDUCATOR, THE (US/0043-969X). [10,400] **1792**

WYOMING GEO-NOTES (US/8756-0348). [500] **1401**

WYOMING NURSE (US). [8,000] **3871**

WYOMING OFFICIAL DIRECTORY (US/0146-700X). [7,500] **4695**

XAVIER REVIEW (US/0887-6681). [500] **3356**

Y WEEKLY, THE (US/0883-3133). [2,000] **5756**

YA HOTLINE (CN/0701-8894). [450] **1071**

YAGL-AMBU; PAPUA NEW GUINEA JOURNAL OF THE SOCIAL SCIENCES AND HUMANITIES (PP). [300] **5226**

YALE JOURNAL ON REGULATION (US/0741-9457). [1,500] **3076**

YALE LAW JOURNAL, THE (US/0044-0094). [4,500] **3077**

YALE LAW REPORT (US/0513-1391). [10,000] **3077**

YALE SCIENTIFIC (US/0091-0287). [7,000] **5171**

YALE UNIVERSITY LIBRARY GAZETTE, THE (US/0044-0175). [1,200] **3256**

YALE WEEKLY BULLETIN AND CALENDAR (US/0740-0233). [16,000] **1096**

YANKEE FOOD SERVICE (US/0195-2552). [25,250] **2361**

YANKEE HORSETRADER (US/0192-5210). [5,000] **2803**

YANKEE OILMAN (US/0044-0205). [4,500] **4283**

YATES CENTER NEWS (YATES CENTER, KAN. : 1948) (US). [2,100] **5679**

YAYA (CN/0824-1457). [65] **3257**

YEAR BOOK - AMERICAN ACADEMY OF ACTUARIES (US/0569-2032). [8,800] **2896**

YEAR BOOK AND DIRECTORY - UNITED CHURCH OF CANADA (CN/0848-4449). **5010**

YEAR BOOK - ASSOCIATION OF IRON AND STEEL ENGINEERS (US). [1,000] **2086**

YEAR BOOK - BRITISH FEDERATION OF MUSIC FESTIVALS (UK/0309-8044). [2,000] **389**

YEAR BOOK - FLORIDA GENEALOGICAL SOCIETY, TAMPA, FLA (US/0428-7282). [315] **2478**

YEAR BOOK - NATIONAL AURICULA & PRIMULA SOCIETY (NORTHERN SECTION) (UK). [400] **148**

YEAR BOOK - ROYAL SOCIETY OF TROPICAL MEDICINE AND HYGIENE (UK/0080-4711). [3,500] **3987**

YEARBOOK (CN/0710-4707). [1,500] **5069**

YEARBOOK AND DIRECTORY OF OSTEOPATHIC PHYSICIANS (US/0084-358X). [21,000] **3652**

YEARBOOK AND PHILATELIC SOCIETIES' DIRECTORY (UK/0260-1265). [4,000] **2788**

YEARBOOK & REGISTER OF MEMBERS / INCORPORATED SOCIETY OF MUSICIANS (UK). [7,000] **4159**

YEARBOOK - BAPTIST UNION OF WESTERN CANADA (CN/0067-4087). [500] **5069**

YEARBOOK - CALIFORNIA MACADAMIA SOCIETY (US/0068-5720). [500] **2434**

YEARBOOK : COMMERCIAL ARBITRATION (NE). **3104**

YEARBOOK - CREDIT UNION NATIONAL ASSOCIATION (US). [5,000] **817**

YEARBOOK / LUTHERAN CHURCH IN AMERICA (US). [15,000] **5069**

YEARBOOK - NATIONAL ASSOCIATION OF CONGREGATIONAL CHRISTIAN CHURCHES, THE (US/0272-5339). [2,400] **5010**

YEARBOOK - NEW YORK COUNTY LAWYERS' ASSOCIATION (US/0548-8729). [10,000] **3077**

YEARBOOK OF COMPARATIVE AND GENERAL LITERATURE (US/0084-3695). [1,400] **3356**

YEARBOOK OF EXPERTS, AUTHORITIES & SPOKESPERSONS. AN ENCYCLOPEDIA OF SOURCES (US/1051-4058). **1930**

YEARBOOK OF FINNISH FOREIGN POLICY (FI/0355-0079). [3,500] **4539**

YEARBOOK OF GERMAN-AMERICAN STUDIES (US/0741-2827). [500] **2766**

YEARBOOK OF POPULATION RESEARCH IN FINLAND (FI/0506-3590). [700] **4561**

YEARBOOK OF THE HEATHER SOCIETY (UK/0440-5757). [900] **5237**

YEARBOOK - WORLD COUNCIL OF CREDIT UNIONS (US/0147-7803). [10,000] **1544**

YEARLY ALL INDIA CRIMINAL DIGEST (II/0377-6719). [2,000] **3109**

YEAR'S WORK - INSURANCE INSTITUTE FOR HIGHWAY SAFETY, THE (US/0276-7325). **5446**

YEATS (US/0742-6224). [1,000] **3455**

YECHONG PAEKSO (KO). **333**

YEDION (IS). **5458**

YELLOWBACK LIBRARY (US). [400] **3455**

YES (LONDON, ENGLAND) (UK). [18,000] **5010**

YESTERYEAR (PRINCETON) (US/0194-9349). [8,000] **252**

YHA ACCOMODATION GUIDE. ENGLAND & WALES / YHA (UK). [300,000] **5314**

YIDDISH (US/0364-4308). [600] **3455**

YO YO TIMES (US/0897-7704). **1071**

YOGA LIFE (1982) (CN/0824-2526). [100,000] **4365**

YOKOHAMA MEDICAL BULLETIN (JA/0044-0531). [1,000] **3652**

YONGHAK NONJIP (KO). **3334**

YON'GU NONJIP - IHWA YOJA TAEHAKKYO, TAEHAGWON (KO). **5237**

YON'GU NONMUNJIP - TAEPYONGYANG CHANGHAK MUNHWA CHAEDAN (KO). **5237**

YONSEI MEDICAL JOURNAL (KO/0513-5796). [2,000] **3652**

YORK COUNTY COAST STAR (US). **5685**

YORK DAILY RECORD (YORK, PA. : 1973) (US/1043-4313). [41,000] **5741**

YORKSHIRE ARCHAEOLOGICAL JOURNAL, THE (UK/0084-4276). [1,500] **285**

YORKSHIRE JOURNAL (US/0044-0612). [3,000] **5527**

YORKVIEW (CN/0822-2517). **2767**

YOSHOKU KENKYUJO KENKYU HOKOKU (JA/0389-5858). [1,000] **2316**

YOSONG (KO). **5572**

YOSUI TO HAISUI (JA/0513-5907). [28,000] **2248**

YOU! (AGOURA HILLS, CALIF.) (US/1064-8682). [35,000] **5038**

YOUNG AND ALIVE (US/0738-8101). [26,000] **4395**

YOUNG EAST (JA/0513-5974). [1,200] **5022**

YOUNG FABIAN PAMPHLET (UK/0513-5982). [5,500] **4501**

YOUNG FASHIONS MAGAZINE (US/0884-7630). **1088**

YOUNG SOLDIER (AT/0300-3264). **1071**

YOUR BIG BACKYARD (US/0886-5299). [600,000] **1072**

YOUR CHURCH (US/0049-8394). [188,000] **5010**

YOUR COMPUTER CAREER (US/0884-4615). [3,000] **4210**

YOUR MONEY WEEKLY (AT). **4759**

YOUR MORTGAGE MAGAZINE (AT/1039-0081). [40,000] **817**

YOUR NEWS (CN/0833-2908). [10,000] **5798**

YOUTH AND POLICY (UK/0262-9798). [1,000] **1072**

YOUTH (FREDERICTON, N.B.) (CN/0712-1768). **1072**

YOUTH LEADER (SPRINGFIELD, MO.), THE (US/0190-4566). [3,500] **5011**

YOUTH POLICY (US). [500] **5314**

YOUTH PROGRAMS (WALTHAM, MASS.) (US). [10,000] **5314**

YOUTH UPDATE (REXDALE, ONT.) (CN/0830-9221). [500] **3179**

YUASA JIHO / YUASA DENCHI KABUSHIKI KAISHA (JA/0513-6342). [4,000] **2087**

YUGONG / YUKONG (KO). **1632**

YUGOSLAV SURVEY (YU/0044-1341). **2716**

Z MAGAZINE (ZA). [10,000] **2644**

ZABS REVIEW : A PUBLICATION OF THE ZAMBIA BUREAU OF STANDARDS (ZA). [500] **4033**

ZAHLEN AUS DER DEUTSCHEN SCHWEINEPRODUKTION (GW). [1,000] **224**

ZAHNAERZTLICHE MITTEILUNGEN (GW/0044-1643). [52,000] **1337**

ZAMBIA NURSE (KITWE, ZAMBIA : 1978) (ZA/0044-1740). **3871**

ZAMBIAN ORNITHOLOGICAL SOCIETY NEWSLETTER (ZA/0378-4533). [250] **5621**

ZAPAD (CN/0226-3068). [5,000] **2275**

ZAPAD TODAY (CN). [8,000] **2275**

ZAPISKI RUSSKOI AKADEMICHESKOI GRUPPY V SSHA (US). [500] **1854**

ZASSHI KIJI SAKUIN, JINBUN SHAKAI HEN (JA). [1,120] **2857**

ZAVALA COUNTY SENTINEL (LA PRYOR, TEX. : 1913) (US). [2,300] **5756**

ZBORNIK FILOZOFICKEJ FAKULTY UNIVERZITY KOMENSKEHO. ETHNOLOGIA SLAVICA (XO/0083-4106). [1,000] **248**

ZBORNIK PRAVNOG FAKULTETA U ZAGREBU (CI). **3077**

ZBORNIK UNIVERZITY KOMENSKEHO. HISTORICA (XO). [600] **2716**

ZDB FORDERUNGEN, ZIELVORSTELLUNGEN FUER DIE ... LEGISLATURPERIODE DES DEUTSCHEN BUNDESTAGES (GW/0342-7943). [4,000] **1720**

ZEIT, DIE (CN). [8,500] **5798**

ZEITGEMASSE SCHAFHALTUNG : MIT EINEM KAPITEL UBER MILCHSCHAFHALTUNG (AU). [35,000] **199**

ZEITGENOSSISCHES MUSIKSCHAFFEN IN DER DEUTSCHEN DEMOKRATISCHEN REPUBLIK (GW/0232-9387). [650] **4160**

ZEITSCHRIFT DER DEUTSCHEN GEMMOLOGISCHEN GESELLSCHAFT (GW). **2915**

ZEITSCHRIFT DES AACHENER GESCHICHTSVEREINS (GW/0065-0137). [1,300] **2716**

ZEITSCHRIFT DES BAYERISCHEN STATISTISCHEN LANDESAMTS (GW). **5347**

ZEITSCHRIFT FUER ALTHEBRAISTIK (GW/0932-4461). **3335**

ZEITSCHRIFT FUER AUSLAENDISCHES OEFFENTLICHES RECHT UND VOELKERRECHT (GW/0044-2348). **3138**

ZEITSCHRIFT FUER AUSLANDISCHE LANDWIRTSCHAFT (GW/0049-8599). [400] **148**

ZEITSCHRIFT FUER BAYERISCHE KIRCHENGESCHICHTE (GW). [700] **5070**

ZEITSCHRIFT FUER DEN ERDKUNDEUNTERRICHT (GW/0044-2461). **2579**

ZEITSCHRIFT FUER DEUTSCHE PHILOLOGIE (GW/0044-2496). **3335**

ZEITSCHRIFT FUER DEUTSCHE PHILOLOGIE. BEIHEFT (GW). **3335**

ZEITSCHRIFT FUER ERKRANKUNGEN DER ATMUNGSORGANE (GW/0303-657X). **3952**

ZEITSCHRIFT FUER FLUGWISSENSCHAFTEN UND WELTRAUMFORSCHUNG (GW/0342-068X). [3,400] **40**

ZEITSCHRIFT FUER GERONTOLOGIE (GW/0044-281X). [1,500] **3755**

ZEITSCHRIFT FUER KIRCHENGESCHICHTE (GW/0044-2925). **5011**

ZEITSCHRIFT FUER KLINISCHE PSYCHOLOGIE, PSYCHOPATHOLOGIE UND PSYCHOTHERAPIE (GW/0723-6557). [500] **4622**

ZEITSCHRIFT FUER LUFT- UND WELTRAUMRECHT (GW/0340-8329). [600] **3078**

ZEITSCHRIFT FUER METALLKUNDE (STUTTGART, GERMANY) (GW/0044-3093). [2,000] **4024**

ZEITSCHRIFT FUER MISSION (GW). [1,300] **5011**

ZEITSCHRIFT FUER MYKOLOGIE (GW/0170-110X). **576**

ZEITSCHRIFT FUER NATURFORSCHUNG (GW/0932-0784). [1,000] **4425**

ZEITSCHRIFT FUER PAEDAGOGIK (GW/0044-3247). [4,000] **1792**

ZEITSCHRIFT FUER PARAPSYCHOLOGIE UND GRENZGEBIETE DER PSYCHOLOGIE (GW/0028-3479). [1,000] **4243**

ZEITSCHRIFT FUER PHILOSOPHISCHE FORSCHUNG (GW/0044-3301). [1,400] **4365**

ZEITSCHRIFT FUER POLITIK (GW/0044-3360). [1,000] **4501**

ZEITSCHRIFT FUER SLAVISCHE PHILOLOGIE (GW/0044-3492). [500] **3335**

ZEITSCHRIFT FUER SPIELMUSIK (GW). [100] **4160**

ZEITSCHRIFT FUER TRANSPLANTATIONSMEDIZIN (GW). [1,600] **3653**

ZEITSCHRIFT FUER VERKEHRSWISSENSCHAFT (GW/0044-3670). **5400**

ZEITSCHRIFT FUER VERMESSUNGSWESEN. ZFV (GW/0340-4560). [8,000] **2034**

ZEITSCHRIFT FUER VERWALTUNG (AU). [5,000] **3094**

ZEITSCHRIFT FUER ZIVILPROZESS (GW/0342-3468). [1,000] **3078**

ZEITSCHRIFT FUR KULTUR, POLITIK, KIRCHE (SW). [2,000] **5070**

ZEITSCHRIFT FUR NATURFORSCHUNG (GW/0939-5075). [1,000] **476**

ZEITSCHRIFT FUR NATURFORSCHUNG (GW/0932-0776). [1,000] **996**

ZEITSCHRIFT INTERNE REVISION (GW/0044-3816). **725**

ZEITSCHRIFTENINHALTSDIENST THEOLOGIE (GW/0340-8361). [950] **5011**

ZEITSCRHIFT FUR KLINISCHE MEDIZIN (BERLIN, DDR) (GW/0233-1608). [6,800] **3653**

ZEITUNG FUER KOMMUNALE WIRTSCHAFT (GW). [21,000] **4695**

ZEITUNGS-INDEX (GW/0340-0107). **5802**

ZEITWENDE (GW/0341-7166). [700] **3356**

ZENAIR NEWS (US/0889-4353). [250] **40**

ZENTRALBLATT FUER CHIRURGIE (GW/0044-409X). **3978**

ZENTRALBLATT FUER NEUROCHIRURGIE (GW/0044-4251). **3978**

ZESZYT NAUKOWY - POLITECHNIKA KRAKOWSKA. BUDOWNICTWO LADOWE (PL/0454-4862). **631**

ZESZYTY LITERACKIE : ZL (FR). [3,000] **3456**

ZESZYTY NAUKOWY - POLITECHNIKA KRAKOWSKA. CHEMIA (PL/0075-7055). **1020**

ZETETIC SCHOLAR (US/0741-6229). [600] **4243**

ZFA, ZEITSCHRIFT FUER ARBEITSRECHT (GW). [1,200] **3156**

ZHONGGUO ZHI CHUN (US/0735-8237). [10,000] **2668**

ZHONGHUA MINGUO XIAOERKE YIXUEHUI ZAZHI (CH/0001-6578). [2,500] **3912**

ZHONGHUA WULIYIXUE ZAZHI (CC/0254-1424). [10,000] **3654**

ZHONGNAN KUANGYE XUEYUAN XUEBAO (CH/0253-4347). **2153**

ZI INTERNATIONAL (GW/0341-0552). [4,547] **631**

ZIEKTEVERZUIM IN ..., HET (NE). [1,000] **1720**

ZIELSPRACHE DEUTSCH (GW/0341-5864). [3,000] **3336**

ZIELSPRACHE ENGLISCH (GW/0342-6173). [1,500] **3336**

ZIMBABWE AGRICULTURAL JOURNAL (RH/1017-5156). [1,250] **149**

ZIMBABWE LIBRARIAN, THE (RH/1015-6828). [350] **3257**

ZIMBABWE SCIENCE NEWS, THE (RH/1016-1503). [1,650] **5172**

ZIMBABWE VETERINARY JOURNAL (RH/1016-1511). [350] **5528**

ZINOTAJS (CN/0227-2423). [1,400] **2717**

ZIONIST IDEAS (IS). [1,000] **5054**

ZION'S HERALD (1975) (US/0098-9282). [7,000] **5070**

ZLODZENIE POLSKIEJ STREFY PRZYBRZEZNEJ-MATERIALY ODDZIALU MORSKIEGO (PL). [120] **1458**

ZLR, ZEITSCHRIFT FUER DAS GESAMTE LEBENSMITTELRECHT (GW/0342-3476). [800] **3078**

ZMIANY CEN W GOSPODARCE NARODOWEJ ... (PL). **5347**

ZODAK CENTRE FOR RELIGIOUS RESEARCH PUBLICATIONS (AT). [1,000] **5011**

ZODIAQUE (FR/0044-4952). [2,500] **369**

ZONTIAN (US/0279-3229). [24,000] **5572**

ZOO ANVERS (BE/0044-5029). [21,000] **5601**

ZOO VIEW (US/0276-3303). [50,000] **5601**

ZOOLOGICAL RECORD (CH). **5601**

ZOOLOGISCHE ABHANDLUNGEN / STAATLICHES MUSEUM FUER TIERKUNDE IN DRESDEN (GW/0375-5231). [750] **5602**

ZOOLOGISCHE DOCUMENTATIE (BE/0563-1750). [500] **5603**

ZOOLOGISCHE MEDEDELINGEN (NE/0024-0672). [730] **5603**

ZPA. ZEITSCHRIFT FUER PRAKTISCHE AUGENHEILKUNDE (GW/0173-2595). [3,500] **3880**

ZWF CIM (GW/0932-0482). [5,043] **2132**

ZWIERZETA LABORATORYJNE (PL/0084-5825). [300] **5604**

ZWR (GW/0044-166X). [17,000] **1337**

Serials Registered with The Copyright Clearance Center

The following index lists all serials in the Directory that are registered with The Copyright Clearance Center (CCC). CCC has been authorized by the publishers of the following serials to authorize photocopy permission and collect the publisher-set royalty fee. For further information on fees and the specifics of the authorizations, please contact the CCC at 27 Congress Street, Salem, MA 01970 or phone (508)744-3350, fax (508)741-2318. The country code and ISSN are provided, when available. The page number in bold refers you to the complete serial listing in Volume I, II or II of the Directory.

3 R, ROHRE, ROHRLEITUNGSBAU, ROHRLEITUNGSTRANSPORT (GW/0340-3386). **2096**

19TH CENTURY MUSIC (US/0148-2076). **4098**

20 CENTURY BRITISH HISTORY (UK/0955-2359). **2671**

33 METAL PRODUCING (US/0149-1210). **3996**

73 AMATEUR RADIO TODAY (US/1052-2522). **1125**

1992, THE EXTERNAL IMPACT OF EUROPEAN UNIFICATION (US/1043-4380). **1632**

A A R N NEWSLETTER (CN/0001-0197). **3849**

A.U.A. TODAY (US/1046-1051). **3987**

A.V. GUIDE (US/0091-360X). **1887**

A2-CENTRAL (US/0885-4017). **1170**

AAA, ARBEITEN AUS ANGLISTIK UND AMERIKANISTIK (AU/0171-5410). **3260**

AAOHN JOURNAL (US/0891-0162). **3849**

AAPG BULLETIN (US/0149-1423). **4248**

AAPG CONTINUING EDUCATION COURSE NOTE SERIES (US/0270-8043). **4248**

AAPG EXPLORER (US/0195-2986). **1364**

AAPG MEMOIR (US/0271-8529). **1364**

AAPG REPRINT SERIES (US/0272-1511). **1364**

AATCC TECHNICAL MANUAL (US/0734-8894). **5347**

ABA BANKING JOURNAL (US/0194-5947). **768**

ABA/BNA LAWYERS' MANUAL ON PROFESSIONAL CONDUCT. CURRENT REPORTS (US/0740-4050). **2926**

ABACUS (SYDNEY) (AT/0001-3072). **735**

ABHANDLUNGEN AUS DEM MATHEMATISCHEN SEMINAR DER HAMBURGISCHEN UNIVERSITAT (GW/0025-5858). **3490**

ABOVEGROUND TANK UPDATE (US/1059-6615). **4033**

ABSATZWIRTSCHAFT DUSSELDORF. 1969 (GW/0001-3374). **920**

ABSEES (UK/0044-5622). **2671**

ABSOLUTE REFERENCE (US/0741-997X). **1283**

ABSTRACT BULLETIN OF THE INSTITUTE OF PAPER SCIENCE AND TECHNOLOGY (US/1047-2088). **4240**

ABSTRACTS IN ARTIFICIAL INTELLIGENCE / THE TURING INSTITUTE (UK/0269-8862). **1210**

ABSTRACTS IN HUMAN-COMPUTER INTERACTION (US/1042-0193). **1208**

ABSTRACTS OF ENGLISH STUDIES (US/0001-3560). **3356**

ABSTRACTS OF PAPERS - AMERICAN CHEMICAL SOCIETY (US/0065-7727). **958**

ABSTRACTS OF PAPERS PRESENTED TO THE AMERICAN MATHEMATICAL SOCIETY (US/0192-5857). **3490**

ABSTRACTS OF WORKING PAPERS IN ECONOMICS : THE OFFICIAL JOURNAL OF THE AWPE DATABASE (US/0951-0079). **1459**

ABSTRACTS WITH PROGRAMS - GEOLOGICAL SOCIETY OF AMERICA (US/0016-7592). **1364**

ACADEMIC AND LIBRARY COMPUTING (US/1055-4769). **1265**

ACADEMIC EMERGENCY MEDICINE (US/1069-6563). **3723**

ACADEMIC LEADER (US/8750-7730). **1806**

ACADEMIC QUESTIONS (US/0895-4852). **1807**

ACADEMY REPORTER (WASHINGTON) (US/0199-6037). **4288**

ACADIENSIS (FREDERICTON) (CN/0044-5851). **2717**

ACC CURRENT JOURNAL REVIEW (US/1062-1458). **3697**

ACCIDENT ANALYSIS AND PREVENTION (UK/0001-4575). **4763**

ACCOUNTABILITY IN RESEARCH (US/0898-9621). **5079**

ACCOUNTANT (LONDON) (UK/0001-4710). **735**

ACCOUNTANTS' JOURNAL (WELLINGTON) (NZ/0001-4745). **735**

ACCOUNTING BUSINESS AND FINANCIAL HISTORY (UK/0958-5206). **736**

ACCOUNTING DEPARTMENT MANAGEMENT & ADMINISTRATION REPORT (US/1042-928X). **736**

ACCOUNTING, MANAGEMENT, AND INFORMATION TECHNOLOGIES (US/0959-8022). **737**

ACCOUNTING OFFICE MANAGEMENT & ADMINISTRATION REPORT (US/0749-2928). **737**

ACCOUNTING, ORGANIZATIONS AND SOCIETY (UK/0361-3682). **737**

ACCOUNTING TODAY (US/1044-5714). **738**

ACCOUNTS OF CHEMICAL RESEARCH (US/0001-4842). **958**

ACI MANUAL OF CONCRETE PRACTICE (US/0065-7875). **598**

ACI MATERIALS JOURNAL (US/0889-325X). **2018**

ACI STRUCTURAL JOURNAL (US/0889-3241). **2018**

ACM COMPUTING SURVEYS (US/0360-0300). **1170**

ACM LETTERS ON PROGRAMMING LANGUAGES AND SYSTEMS (US/1057-4514). **1277**

ACM TRANSACTIONS ON COMPUTER SYSTEMS (US/0734-2071). **1246**

ACM TRANSACTIONS ON DATABASE SYSTEMS (US/0362-5915). **1252**

ACM TRANSACTIONS ON GRAPHICS (US/0730-0301). **1231**

ACM TRANSACTIONS ON INFORMATION SYSTEMS : PUBLICATION OF THE ASSOCIATION FOR COMPUTING MACHINERY (US/1046-8188). **1255**

ACM TRANSACTIONS ON MATHEMATICAL SOFTWARE (US/0098-3500). **1283**

ACM TRANSACTIONS ON MODELING AND COMPUTER SIMULATION : A PUBLICATION OF THE ASSOCIATION FOR COMPUTING MACHINERY (US/1049-3301). **1282**

ACM TRANSACTIONS ON PROGRAMMING LANGUAGES AND SYSTEMS (US/0164-0925). **1278**

ACM TRANSACTIONS ON SOFTWARE ENGINEERING AND METHODOLOGY (US/1049-331X). **1227**

ACOG CURRENT JOURNAL REVIEW (US/0897-1471). **3755**

ACOUSTICAL IMAGING (US/0270-5117). **4451**

ACOUSTICAL PHYSICS (US/1063-7710). **4452**

ACOUSTICS ABSTRACTS (UK/0001-4974). **4426**

ACS SYMPOSIUM SERIES (US/0097-6156). **959**

ACTA ALIMENTARIA (BUDAPEST) (HU/0139-3006). **2325**

ACTA ANAESTHESIOLOGICA SCANDINAVICA (DK/0001-5172). **3680**

ACTA ANAESTHESIOLOGICA SCANDINAVICA. SUPPLEMENT (DK/0515-2720). **3680**

ACTA ANATOMICA (SZ/0001-5180). **3678**

ACTA ANTIQUA ACADEMIAE SCIENTIARUM HUNGARICAE (HU/0044-5975). **3261**

ACTA APPLICANDAE MATHEMATICAE (NE/0167-8019). **3490**

ACTA ARCHAEOLOGICA (DK/0065-101X). **253**

ACTA ASTRONAUTICA (UK/0094-5765). **3**

ACTA BIOCHIMICA ET BIOPHYSICA HUNGARICA (HU/0237-6261). **479**

ACTA BIOLOGICA HUNGARICA (HU/0236-5383). **439**

ACTA BIOTECHNOLOGICA (GW/0138-4988). **3685**

ACTA BIOTHEORETICA (NE/0001-5342). **440**

ACTA BOTANICA HUNGARICA (HU/0236-6495). **496**

ACTA BOTANICA NEERLANDICA (NE/0044-5983). **497**

ACTA CHEMICA SCANDINAVICA (COPENHAGEN, DENMARK : 1989) (DK/0904-213X). **1049**

ACTA CHIMICA HUNGARICA (HU/0231-3146). **959**

ACTA CHIRURGIAE ORTHOPAEDICAE ET TRAUMATOLOGIAE CECHOSLOVACA (XR/0001-5415). **3880**

ACTA CHIRURGICA HUNGARICA (HU/0231-4614). **3957**

CCC Index

ACTA CRYSTALLOGRAPHICA. SECTION B, STRUCTURAL SCIENCE (DK/0108-7681). **1031**

ACTA CRYSTALLOGRAPHICA. SECTION C, CRYSTAL STRUCTURE COMMUNICATIONS (DK/0108-2701). **1031**

ACTA CYTOLOGICA (US/0001-5547). **531**

ACTA ENDOCRINOLOGICA (COPENHAGEN) (DK/0001-5598). **3726**

ACTA GENETICAE MEDICAE ET GEMELLOLOGIAE (IT/0001-5660). **541**

ACTA HAEMATOLOGICA (SZ/0001-5792). **3769**

ACTA HISTOCHEMICA (GW/0065-1281). **531**

ACTA HISTORIAE ARTIUM ACADEMIAE SCIENTIARUM HUNGARICAE (HU/0001-5830). **335**

ACTA HISTORICA ACADEMIAE SCIENTIARUM HUNGARICAE (HU/0001-5849). **2672**

ACTA INFORMATICA (GW/0001-5903). **1255**

ACTA MATHEMATICA HUNGARICA (HU/0236-5294). **3490**

ACTA MATHEMATICAE APPLICATAE SINICA (CH/0168-9673). **3490**

ACTA MECHANICA (AU/0001-5970). **2109**

ACTA MECHANICA SINICA (CC/0567-7718). **4427**

ACTA METALLURGICA ET MATERIALIA (US/0956-7151). **3996**

ACTA METALLURGICA SINICA. SERIES B, PROCESS METALLURGY & MISCELLANEOUS (CC/1000-9450). **3997**

ACTA MICROBIOLOGICA BULGARICA (BU/0204-8809). **558**

ACTA MICROBIOLOGICA HUNGARICA (HU/0231-4622). **558**

ACTA MORPHOLOGICA HUNGARICA (HU/0236-5391). **3545**

ACTA MUSICOLOGICA (GW/0001-6241). **4098**

ACTA NEUROCHIRURGICA (AU/0001-6268). **3957**

ACTA NEUROCHIRURGICA : SUPPLEMENTUM (AU/0065-1419). **3957**

ACTA NEUROLOGICA SCANDINAVICA (DK/0001-6314). **3825**

ACTA NEUROPATHOLOGICA (GW/0001-6322). **3892**

ACTA OBSTETRICIA ET GYNECOLOGICA SCANDINAVICA (SW/0001-6349). **3756**

ACTA OBSTETRICIA ET GYNECOLOGICA SCANDINAVICA. SUPPLEMENTUM (SW/0300-8835). **3756**

ACTA ODONTOLOGICA SCANDINAVICA (NO/0001-6357). **1315**

ACTA OECOLOGICA (MONTROUGE) (FR/1146-609X). **2210**

ACTA OECONOMICA (HU/0001-6373). **1460**

ACTA ORIENTALIA ACADEMIAE SCIENTIARUM HUNGARICAE (HU/0001-6446). **2644**

ACTA ORIENTALIA (KBENHAVN) (DK/0001-6438). **3261**

ACTA ORTHOPAEDICA SCANDINAVICA (DK/0001-6470). **3880**

ACTA PAEDIATRICA HUNGARICA (HU/0231-441X). **3899**

ACTA PAEDIATRICA JAPONICA. OVERSEAS EDITION (JA/0374-5600). **3899**

ACTA PAEDIATRICA (OSLO) (NO/0803-5253). **3899**

ACTA PAEDOPSYCHIATRICA (SZ/0001-6586). **3918**

ACTA PHILOSOPHICA FENNICA (FI/0355-1792). **4339**

ACTA PHYSICA HUNGARICA (HU/0231-4428). **4395**

ACTA PHYSICA POLONICA, A (PL/0587-4246). **4395**

ACTA PHYSICA POLONICA, B (PL/0587-4254). **4445**

ACTA PHYSIOLOGICA HUNGARICA (HU/0231-424X). **577**

ACTA PHYSIOLOGICA SCANDINAVICA (UK/0001-6772). **577**

ACTA POLYMERICA (GW/0323-7648). **5347**

ACTA PSYCHIATRICA SCANDINAVICA (DK/0001-690X). **3919**

ACTA PSYCHIATRICA SCANDINAVICA. SUPPLEMENTUM (DK/0065-1591). **3919**

ACTA PSYCHOLOGICA (NE/0001-6918). **4570**

ACTA RADIOLOGICA (STOCKHOLM, SWEDEN : 1987) (SW/0284-1851). **3938**

ACTA RADIOLOGICA. SUPPLEMENTUM (SW/0365-5954). **3938**

ACTA SOCIOLOGICA (DK/0001-6993). **5237**

ACTA TECHNICA / ACADEMIAE SCIENTIARUM HUNGARICAE (HU/0001-7035). **5080**

ACTA TROPICA (SZ/0001-706X). **3985**

ACTA VETERINARIA HUNGARICA (BUDAPEST. 1983) (HU/0236-6290). **5501**

ACTA VIROLOGICA (ANGLICKA VERZE) (XR/0001-723X). **3545**

ACTA ZOOLOGICA HUNGARICA (HU/0236-7130). **5573**

ACTA ZOOLOGICA (STOCKHOLM) (SW/0001-7272). **5574**

ACTIVE AND PASSIVE ELECTRONIC COMPONENTS (US/0882-7516). **2034**

ACTUALIDAD ELECTRONICA (SP/0210-6302). **2034**

ACTUALITE FIDUCIAIRE, L' (FR/0044-6157). **2927**

ACTUALITES PHARMACOLOGIQUES (FR/0567-8854). **4289**

ACUPUNCTURE & ELECTRO-THERAPEUTICS RESEARCH (UK/0360-1293). **3545**

ACUSTICA (GW/0001-7884). **4452**

ACUTE CARE (SZ/0254-0819). **3850**

ADA POLICY & LAW (US/1067-4713). **2927**

ADA USER (NE/0268-652X). **1278**

ADAPTED PHYSICAL ACTIVITY QUARTERLY (US/0736-5829). **1854**

ADAPTIVE BEHAVIOR (US/1059-7123). **4571**

ADDICTION (UK/0965-2140). **1338**

ADDICTION LETTER, THE (US/8756-405X). **1338**

ADDICTION RESEARCH (US/1058-6989). **1338**

ADDICTIVE BEHAVIORS (UK/0306-4603). **1338**

ADDITIVES FOR POLYMERS (UK/0306-3747). **1038**

ADHAESION (GW/0001-8198). **1049**

ADHD REPORT, THE (US/1065-8025). **1874**

ADHESION (LONDON) (UK/0260-4450). **1049**

ADHESIVES AGE (US/0001-821X). **2007**

ADMINISTRATION AND POLICY IN MENTAL HEALTH (US/0894-587X). **5270**

ADMINISTRATION & SOCIETY (US/0095-3997). **4624**

ADMINISTRATIVE ACTION (US/0892-0923). **1807**

ADMINISTRATIVE SCIENCE QUARTERLY (US/0001-8392). **4624**

ADMINISTRATOR (MADISON, WIS.) (US/0744-7078). **1859**

ADOLESCENCE (US/0001-8449). **1059**

ADOLESCENT AND PEDIATRIC GYNECOLOGY (US/0932-8610). **3756**

ADOLESCENT MEDICINE (PHILADELPHIA, PA.) (US/1041-3499). **3546**

ADSORPTION SCIENCE & TECHNOLOGY (UK/0263-6174). **2007**

ADULT DAY CARE LETTER (US/0885-4572). **5270**

ADVANCED CEMENT-BASED MATERIALS (US/1065-7355). **598**

ADVANCED CERAMICS REPORT (NE/0268-9847). **2585**

ADVANCED COATINGS & SURFACE TECHNOLOGY (US/0896-422X). **1020**

ADVANCED DRUG DELIVERY REVIEWS (NE/0169-409X). **4289**

ADVANCED LABANOTATION (SZ/1053-4261). **1310**

ADVANCED MANUFACTURING TECHNOLOGY (US/0885-5684). **1217**

ADVANCED MATERIALS & PROCESSES (US/0882-7958). **2100**

ADVANCED MATERIALS FOR OPTICS AND ELECTRONICS (UK/1057-9257). **5080**

ADVANCED MATERIALS (WEINHEIM) (US/0935-9648). **2100**

ADVANCED METALS TECHNOLOGY (UK/0957-9729). **3997**

ADVANCED MILITARY COMPUTING (US/0884-9471). **1210**

ADVANCED PACKAGING (US/1065-0555). **2034**

ADVANCED RECOVERY WEEK (US/1050-1347). **4249**

ADVANCED WIRELESS COMMUNICATIONS (US/1058-7713). **1103**

ADVANCES IN AGRONOMY (US/0065-2113). **44**

ADVANCES IN ANESTHESIA (US/0737-6146). **3680**

ADVANCES IN APPLIED MATHEMATICS (US/0196-8858). **3491**

ADVANCES IN APPLIED MECHANICS (US/0065-2156). **2109**

ADVANCES IN APPLIED MICROBIOLOGY (US/0065-2164). **558**

ADVANCES IN APPLIED PROBABILITY (UK/0001-8678). **3491**

ADVANCES IN ATMOSPHERIC SCIENCES / EDITED BY CHINESE COMMITTEE OF METEOROLOGY AND ATMOSPHERIC PHYSICS AND INSTITUTE OF ATMOSPHERIC PHYSICS, ACADEMIA SINICA (CC/0256-1530). **1419**

ADVANCES IN ATOMIC, MOLECULAR, AND OPTICAL PHYSICS (US/1049-250X). **959**

ADVANCES IN AUDIOLOGY (SZ/0254-8747). **4383**

ADVANCES IN BEHAVIORAL ASSESSMENT OF CHILDREN AND FAMILIES (US/0893-6110). **4571**

ADVANCES IN BEHAVIORAL MEDICINE (US/0885-0836). **4571**

ADVANCES IN BEHAVIOUR RESEARCH AND THERAPY (UK/0146-6402). **4571**

ADVANCES IN BIOCHEMICAL ENGINEERING/BIOTECHNOLOGY (GW/0724-6145). **2007**

ADVANCES IN BIOCHEMICAL PSYCHOPHARMACOLOGY (US/0065-2229). **3826**

ADVANCES IN BIOENGINEERING (US/0360-9960). **1963**

ADVANCES IN BIOLOGICAL PSYCHIATRY (SZ/0378-7354). **3919**

ADVANCES IN BIOPHYSICS (IE/0065-227X). **494**

ADVANCES IN BIOTECHNOLOGICAL PROCESSES (US/0736-2293). **3685**

ADVANCES IN CANCER RESEARCH (US/0065-230X). **3808**

ADVANCES IN CARBOHYDRATE CHEMISTRY AND BIOCHEMISTRY (US/0065-2318). **479**

ADVANCES IN CARDIOLOGY (SZ/0065-2326). **3697**

ADVANCES IN CARDIOVASCULAR PHYSICS (SZ/0378-6900). **494**

ADVANCES IN CATALYSIS (US/0360-0564). **1049**

ADVANCES IN CEMENT RESEARCH (UK/0951-7197). **598**

ADVANCES IN CERAMICS (US/0730-9546). **2585**

ADVANCES IN CHEMICAL ENGINEERING (US/0065-2377). **2007**

ADVANCES IN CHEMICAL PHYSICS (US/0065-2385). **1049**

ADVANCES IN CHEMISTRY SERIES (US/0065-2393). **959**

ADVANCES IN CHILD DEVELOPMENT AND BEHAVIOR (US/0065-2407). **4571**

ADVANCES IN CHROMATOGRAPHY (NEW YORK, N.Y.) (US/0065-2415). **1038**

ADVANCES IN CLINICAL CHEMISTRY (US/0065-2423). **3892**

ADVANCES IN COLLOID AND INTERFACE SCIENCE (NE/0001-8686). **1049**

ADVANCES IN COMPUTERS (US/0065-2458). **1255**

ADVANCES IN CONTRACEPTION (UK/0267-4874). **587**

ADVANCES IN DENTAL RESEARCH (US/0895-9374). **1315**

ADVANCES IN DERMATOLOGY (US/0882-0880). **3717**

ADVANCES IN DESCRIPTIVE PSYCHOLOGY (US/0276-9913). **4571**

ADVANCES IN DRYING (US/0272-4790). **2096**

ADVANCES IN EARLY EDUCATION AND DAY CARE (US/0270-4021). **1802**

ADVANCES IN ECHO-CONTRAST (UK/0925-5206). **3938**

ADVANCES IN ECONOMIC BOTANY (US/0741-8280). **498**

ADVANCES IN ELECTRONICS AND ELECTRON PHYSICS (US/0065-2539). **2034**

ADVANCES IN ENGINEERING SOFTWARE (1992) (UK/0965-9978). **1964**

ADVANCES IN ENZYME REGULATION (UK/0065-2571). **531**

ADVANCES IN ENZYMOLOGY AND RELATED SUBJECTS (US/0065-258X). **479**

ADVANCES IN EXPERIMENTAL MEDICINE AND BIOLOGY (US/0065-2598). **3546**

ADVANCES IN EXPERIMENTAL SOCIAL PSYCHOLOGY (US/0065-2601). **4571**

ADVANCES IN FOOD AND NUTRITION RESEARCH (US/1043-4526). **4186**

ADVANCES IN GENETICS (US/0065-2660). **542**

ADVANCES IN GEOPHYSICS (US/0065-2687). **1402**

ADVANCES IN GROUP PROCESSES (US/0882-6145). **5238**

ADVANCES IN HEALTH ECONOMICS AND HEALTH SERVICES RESEARCH (US/0731-2199). **4763**

ADVANCES IN HEAT TRANSFER (US/0065-2717). **4430**

ADVANCES IN HETEROCYCLIC CHEMISTRY (US/0065-2725). **1038**

ADVANCES IN HUMAN GENETICS (US/0065-275X). **542**

ADVANCES IN IMMUNOLOGY (US/0065-2776). **3662**

ADVANCES IN INDUSTRIAL AND LABOR RELATIONS (US/0742-6186). **1642**

ADVANCES IN INFLAMMATION RESEARCH (US/0197-8322). **3546**

ADVANCES IN INFORMATION STORAGE SYSTEMS (US/1053-184X). **1170**

ADVANCES IN INORGANIC CHEMISTRY (US/0898-8838). **1035**

ADVANCES IN INSTRUMENTATION AND CONTROL (US/1054-0032). **5081**

ADVANCES IN INSTRUMENTATION AND CONTROL (US/1054-0032). **5081**

ADVANCES IN INTERNAL MEDICINE (US/0065-2822). **3794**

ADVANCES IN INTERNATIONAL COMPARATIVE MANAGEMENT (US/0747-7929). **859**

ADVANCES IN LEARNING AND BEHAVIORAL DISABILITIES (US/0735-004X). **1874**

ADVANCES IN LIBRARIANSHIP (US/0065-2830). **3187**

ADVANCES IN LIBRARY RESOURCE SHARING (US/1052-262X). **3188**

ADVANCES IN LIPID RESEARCH (US/0065-2849). **479**

ADVANCES IN MAGNETIC AND OPTICAL RESONANCE (US/1057-2732). **4443**

ADVANCES IN MATHEMATICS (NEW YORK. 1965) (US/0001-8708). **3491**

ADVANCES IN MICROCIRCULATION (SZ/0065-2938). **3698**

ADVANCES IN MODERN ENVIRONMENTAL TOXICOLOGY (US/0276-5063). **2858**

ADVANCES IN MOLTEN SALT CHEMISTRY (US/0065-2954). **1035**

ADVANCES IN NEPHROLOGY FROM THE NECKER HOSPITAL (US/0084-5957). **3988**

ADVANCES IN NEUROIMMUNOLOGY (UK/0960-5428). **3826**

ADVANCES IN NEUROLOGY (US/0091-3952). **3826**

ADVANCES IN NUCLEAR SCIENCE AND TECHNOLOGY (US/0065-2989). **2153**

ADVANCES IN NURSING SCIENCE (US/0161-9268). **3850**

ADVANCES IN OPHTHALMIC PLASTIC AND RECONSTRUCTIVE SURGERY (US/0276-3508). **3958**

ADVANCES IN ORGANOMETALLIC CHEMISTRY (US/0065-3055). **1039**

ADVANCES IN ORTHOPAEDIC SURGERY (US/0738-2278). **3958**

ADVANCES IN OTO-RHINO-LARYNGOLOGY (SZ/0065-3071). **3885**

ADVANCES IN OTOLARYNGOLOGY--HEAD AND NECK SURGERY (US/0887-6916). **3958**

ADVANCES IN PEDIATRIC INFECTIOUS DISEASES (US/0884-9404). **3899**

ADVANCES IN PEDIATRICS (US/0065-3101). **3899**

ADVANCES IN PHARMACEUTICAL SCIENCES (UK/0065-3136). **4289**

ADVANCES IN PHARMACOLOGY (US/1054-3589). **4289**

ADVANCES IN PHOTOCHEMISTRY (US/0065-3152). **1049**

ADVANCES IN PHYSICS (UK/0001-8732). **4396**

ADVANCES IN PHYSIOLOGY EDUCATION (US/1043-4046). **577**

ADVANCES IN PLASTIC AND RECONSTRUCTIVE SURGERY (US/0748-5212). **3958**

ADVANCES IN POLLEN-SPORE RESEARCH (II/0376-480X). **498**

ADVANCES IN POLYMER SCIENCE (GW/0065-3195). **1039**

ADVANCES IN POLYMER TECHNOLOGY (US/0730-6679). **4453**

ADVANCES IN PROBABILITY AND RELATED TOPICS (US/0065-3217). **3491**

ADVANCES IN PROSTAGLANDIN, THROMBOXANE, AND LEUKOTRIENE RESEARCH (US/0732-8141). **3726**

ADVANCES IN PROTEIN CHEMISTRY (US/0065-3233). **1039**

ADVANCES IN PSYCHOSOMATIC MEDICINE (SZ/0065-3268). **4572**

ADVANCES IN QUANTUM CHEMISTRY (US/0065-3276). **1049**

ADVANCES IN RADIATION BIOLOGY (US/0065-3292). **440**

ADVANCES IN READING/LANGUAGE RESEARCH (US/0735-0171). **1887**

ADVANCES IN SMALL ANIMAL MEDICINE AND SURGERY (US/1041-7826). **5501**

ADVANCES IN SOVIET MATHEMATICS (US/1051-8037). **3491**

ADVANCES IN SPACE RESEARCH (UK/0273-1177). **3**

ADVANCES IN SPECIAL EDUCATION (US/0270-4013). **1874**

ADVANCES IN SPECTROSCOPY (1986) (UK/0892-2888). **4433**

ADVANCES IN STRATEGIC MANAGEMENT (US/0742-3322). **859**

ADVANCES IN SURGERY (CHICAGO) (US/0065-3411). **3958**

ADVANCES IN THE BIOSCIENCES (UK/0065-3446). **441**

ADVANCES IN THE ECONOMICS OF ENERGY AND RESOURCES (US/0192-558X). **1931**

ADVANCES IN THE STUDY OF BEHAVIOR (US/0065-3454). **4572**

ADVANCES IN THERAPY (US/0741-238X). **3546**

ADVANCES IN UROLOGY (US/0894-4385). **3988**

ADVANCES IN VETERINARY SCIENCE AND COMPARATIVE MEDICINE (US/0065-3519). **5501**

ADVANCES IN VIRUS RESEARCH (US/0065-3527). **558**

ADVANCES IN WATER RESOURCES (UK/0309-1708). **5528**

ADVERSE DRUG REACTION BULLETIN (UK/0044-6394). **3978**

ADVERSE DRUG REACTIONS AND TOXICOLOGICAL REVIEWS (UK/0964-198X). **3978**

ADVERTISING AGE (US/0001-8899). **754**

ADWEEK (EASTERN ED.) (US/0199-2864). **755**

ADWEEK'S MARKETING WEEK (US/0892-8274). **755**

AEQUATIONES MATHEMATICAE (SZ/0001-9054). **3491**

AERONAUTIQUE ET L'ASTRONAUTIQUE, L' (FR/0001-9275). **4**

AEROSOL SCIENCE AND TECHNOLOGY (US/0278-6826). **1020**

AEROSOL SPRAY REPORT : INTERNATIONAL PERIODICAL FOR THE AEROSOL AND SPRAY INDUSTRY (GW/0941-0295). **1020**

AEROSPACE AMERICA (US/0740-722X). **5**

AEROSPACE CONSULTANTS DIRECTORY (US/0747-8151). **5**

AEROSPACE ENGINEERING (WARRENDALE, PA.) (US/0736-2536). **5**

AEROSPACE FINANCIAL NEWS (US/1057-0950). **5**

AEROSPACE PRODUCTS (US/1054-7045). **5**

AESTHETIC PLASTIC SURGERY (US/0364-216X). **3958**

AEU. ARCHIV. FUER ELEKTRONIK UND UBERTRAGUNGSTECHNIK (GW/0001-1096). **1148**

AFFIRMATIVE ACTION COMPLIANCE MANUAL FOR FEDERAL CONTRACTORS (US/0148-8147). **1642**

AFFLUENT MARKETS ALERT (US/1041-7508). **859**

AFINIDAD (SP/0001-9704). **960**

AFRICA (LONDON. 1928) (UK/0001-9720). **3262**

AFRICA RESEARCH BULLETIN. POLITICAL, SOCIAL, AND CULTURAL SERIES (UK/0001-9844). **5238**

AFRICA SOUTH OF THE SAHARA (UK/0065-3896). **1923**

AFRICAN AFFAIRS (LONDON) (UK/0001-9909). **4462**

AFRICAN ARCHAEOLOGICAL REVIEW, THE (UK/0263-0338). **253**

AFRICAN BOOK PUBLISHING RECORD, THE (UK/0306-0322). **4811**

AFRICAN BUSINESS (UK/0141-3929). **637**

AFRICAN JOURNAL OF ECOLOGY (UK/0141-6707). **2211**

AFRICAN LANGUAGES AND CULTURES (UK/0954-416X). **3262**

AFRIKA UND UBERSEE (GW/0002-0427). **3262**

AFTERMARKET BUSINESS (US/0892-1121). **637**

AG CONSULTANT (US/0894-7155). **45**

AGE AND AGEING (UK/0002-0729). **3748**

AGEING AND SOCIETY (UK/0144-686X). **3748**

AGENTS AND ACTIONS (SZ/0065-4299). **4289**

AGENTS AND ACTIONS. SUPPLEMENTS (SZ/0379-0363). **3978**

AGGRESSIVE BEHAVIOR (US/0096-140X). **4572**

AGING (UK/0268-1544). **3749**

AGING RESEARCH & TRAINING NEWS (US/0888-6830). **3749**

AGRARRECHT (GW/0340-840X). **2928**

AGRESSOLOGIE (FR/0002-1148). **4572**

AGRIBIOLOGICAL RESEARCH (GW/0938-0337). **48**

AGRIBUSINESS (NEW YORK, N.Y.) (US/0742-4477). **48**

AGRICELL REPORT (US/0738-145X). **48**

AGRICULTURA DE LAS AMERICAS (OVERLAND PARK, KANS.) (US/0002-1350). **48**

AGRICULTURA (MADRID, SPAIN) (SP/0002-1334). **49**

AGRICULTURAL AND FOREST METEOROLOGY (NE/0168-1923). **1419**

AGRICULTURAL ECONOMICS (NE/0169-5150). **49**

AGRICULTURAL ENGINEERING (US/0002-1458). **1964**

AGRICULTURAL ENGINEERING INDEX (US/0733-1770). **150**

AGRICULTURAL HISTORY (US/0002-1482). **50**

AGRICULTURAL SYSTEMS (UK/0308-521X). **52**

AGRICULTURAL WATER MANAGEMENT (NE/0378-3774). **52**

AGRICULTURAL ZOOLOGY REVIEWS (UK/0269-0543). **53**

AGRICULTURE, ECOSYSTEMS & ENVIRONMENT (NE/0167-8809). **53**

AGRICULTURE PARIS (FR/0002-1709). **54**

AGRIWEEK (CN/0228-5584). **199**

AGROFORESTRY SYSTEMS (NE/0167-4366). **2211**

AGRONOMIA LUSITANA (PO/0002-1911). **56**

AGRONOMIE (FR/0249-5627). **56**

AGROW (UK/0268-313X). **57**

AI & SOCIETY (GW/0951-5666). **1210**

AI EXPERT (US/0888-3785). **1210**

AI MAGAZINE (US/0738-4602). **1211**

AIAA JOURNAL (US/0001-1452). **6**

AIAA PAPER (US/0146-3705). **6**

AIAA STUDENT JOURNAL (US/0001-1460). **6**

AICHE EQUIPMENT TESTING PROCEDURE (US/0569-5473). **2007**

AICHE JOURNAL (US/0001-1541). **2007**

AICHE MONOGRAPH SERIES (US/0065-8804). **2007**

AICHE SYMPOSIUM SERIES (US/0065-8812). **2007**

AICHE WORKSHOP (US/0569-5457). **2007**

AIDS CARE (UK/0954-0121). **3663**

AIDS EDUCATION AND PREVENTION (US/0899-9546). **4764**

AIDS INFORMATION (UK/0953-1580). **3664**

AIDS (LONDON) (UK/0269-9370). **3664**

AIDS POLICY & LAW (US/0887-1493). **2928**

AIP CONFERENCE PROCEEDINGS (US/0094-243X). **4396**

AIR & WATER POLLUTION CONTROL (US/0890-0396). **2223**

AIR CARGO WORLD (US/0745-5100). **5375**

AIR CARRIER TRAFFIC AT CANADIAN AIRPORTS (QUARTERLY EDITION) (CN/0701-7928). **7**

AIR FORCE TIMES (US/0002-2403). **4034**

AIR POLLUTION CONSULTANT, THE (US/1058-6628). **2223**

AIR SAFETY WEEK (US/1044-727X). **8**

AIR TOXICS REPORT (US/1048-4485). **2223**

AIR TRANSPORT WORLD (US/0002-2543). **8**

AIR/WATER POLLUTION REPORT (US/0002-2608). **2159**

AIRCRAFT

AIRCRAFT FORECAST (US/0194-469X). **9**

AIRCRAFT ILLUSTRATED (UK/0002-2675). **9**

AIRFORCE (CN/0704-6804). **9**

AIRLINE BUSINESS (UK/0268-7615). **9**

AIRLINE FINANCIAL NEWS (US/1040-5410). **10**

AIRLINE MARKETING NEWS (US/1071-1325). **10**

AIRPORT FORUM (GW/0002-2802). **10**

AIRPORT NOISE REPORT (US/1041-8318). **10**

AIRPORTS INTERNATIONAL (UK/0002-2853). **11**

AIT. ARCHITEKTUR, INNENARCHITEKTUR, TECHNISCHER AUSBAU (GW/0173-8046). **287**

AKRON BUSINESS AND ECONOMIC REVIEW (US/0044-7048). **637**

AKTIENGESELLSCHAFT, DIE (GW/0002-3752). **1596**

AKTUELLE CHIRURGIE (GW/0001-785X). **3958**

AKTUELLE DERMATOLOGIE (GW/0340-2541). **3717**

AKTUELLE ENDOKRINOLOGIE UND STOFFWECHSEL (GW/0172-4606). **3726**

AKTUELLE ERNAHRUNGSMEDIZIN (GW/0341-0501). **4186**

AKTUELLE NEUROLOGIE (GW/0302-4350). **3826**

AKTUELLE RHEUMATOLOGIE (GW/0341-051X). **3802**

AKTUELLE TRAUMATOLOGIE (GW/0044-6173). **3547**

AKTUELLE UROLOGIE (GW/0001-7868). **3988**

AKUPUNKTUR / DEUTSCHE ARZTEGESELLSCHAFT FUER AKUPUNKTUR E.V. ... [ET AL.] (GW/0340-3130). **3547**

AKUPUNKTURARZT, AURIKULOTHERAPEUT, DER (GW/0172-9322). **3547**

AKUSTICESKIJ ZURNAL (RU/0320-7919). **4452**

AKZENTE (MUNCHEN) (GW/0002-3957). **3358**

ALABAMA REVIEW, THE (US/0002-4341). **2718**

ALAMBRE (GW/0002-4406). **3475**

ALBANY LAW REVIEW (US/0002-4678). **2929**

ALBERTA DRILLING PROGRESS AND PIPELINE RECEIPTS WEEKLY REPORT (CN/0227-3357). **4249**

ALBERTA JOURNAL OF EDUCATIONAL RESEARCH (CN/0002-4805). **1723**

ALCHERINGA (SYDNEY) (AT/0311-5518). **4226**

ALCOHOL AND ALCOHOLISM (OXFORD) (UK/0735-0414). **1339**

ALCOHOL (FAYETTEVILLE, N.Y.) (US/0741-8329). **1339**

ALCOHOLISM & DRUG ABUSE WEEK (US/1042-1394). **1340**

ALCOHOLISM : CLINICAL AND EXPERIMENTAL RESEARCH (US/0145-6008). **1340**

ALDRING OG ELDRE (NO/0801-9991). **5178**

ALGEBRA AND LOGIC (US/0002-5232). **3491**

ALGEBRA I ANALIZ (RU/0234-0852). **3491**

ALGEBRA UNIVERSALIS (CN/0002-5240). **3491**

ALGORITHMICA (US/0178-4617). **1170**

ALIMENTACION, EQUIPOS Y TECNOLOGIA (SP/0212-1689). **4187**

ALIMENTARIA (SP/0300-5755). **4764**

ALIMENTARY PHARMACOLOGY & THERAPEUTICS (UK/0269-2813). **4290**

ALKALOIDS. CHEMISTRY AND PHARMACOLOGY, THE (US/0099-9598). **1039**

ALLERGOLOGIA ET IMMUNOPATHOLOGIA (SP/0301-0546). **3665**

ALLERGOLOGIE (GW/0344-5062). **3665**

ALLGEMEINES STATISTISCHES ARCHIV (GW/0002-6018). **5320**

ALLOYS INDEX (US/0094-8233). **3997**

ALMANAC OF SEAPOWER, THE (US/0736-3559). **4174**

ALTE STADT, DIE (GW/0170-9364). **2673**

ALTERNATIVE ENERGY DIGESTS (US/1050-3145). **1931**

ALTERNATIVES (AMSTERDAM) (US/0304-3754). **1545**

ALTERTUM, DAS (GW/0002-6646). **2673**

ALTMAN WEIL PENSA REPORT TO LEGAL MANAGEMENT, THE (US/0191-863X). **2932**

ALTSPRACHLICHE UNTERRICHT, DER (GW/0002-6670). **3263**

ALUMINIUM (DUSSELDORF) (GW/0002-6689). **3997**

ALUMINIUM INDUSTRY (UK/0268-5280). **3997**

AMATEUR PHOTOGRAPHER (UK/0002-6840). **4366**

AMBIO (SW/0044-7447). **2160**

AMBULATORY MEDICINE LETTER, THE (US/0897-554X). **3548**

AMEGHINIANA (AG/0002-7014). **4226**

AMERICAN ANNALS OF THE DEAF (WASHINGTON, D.C. 1886) (US/0002-726X). **4383**

AMERICAN ANTHROPOLOGIST (US/0002-7294). **227**

AMERICAN ANTHROPOLOGIST [MICROFORM] (US/0002-7294). **227**

AMERICAN ANTIQUITY; A QUARTERLY REVIEW OF AMERICAN ARCHAEOLOGY (US/0002-7316). **253**

AMERICAN ARTIST (US/0002-7375). **336**

AMERICAN BABY (US/0044-7544). **2276**

AMERICAN BABY'S CHILDBIRTH EDUCATOR (US/0279-490X). **3756**

AMERICAN BANKER (US/0002-7561). **769**

AMERICAN BEE JOURNAL (US/0002-7626). **58**

AMERICAN BEHAVIORAL SCIENTIST (BEVERLY HILLS) (US/0002-7642). **5190**

AMERICAN BOOK COLLECTOR (1980) (US/0196-5654). **2770**

AMERICAN BOOK PUBLISHING RECORD (US/0002-7707). **4812**

AMERICAN BOOK PUBLISHING RECORD (US/0002-7707). **4812**

AMERICAN BOOK TRADE DIRECTORY (US/0065-759X). **4821**

AMERICAN CERAMIC SOCIETY BULLETIN (US/0002-7812). **2586**

AMERICAN CITY & COUNTY, THE (US/0149-337X). **5238**

AMERICAN CLEAN CAR (US/0095-1811). **638**

AMERICAN DEMOGRAPHICS (US/0163-4089). **4549**

AMERICAN DRUG INDEX (US/0065-8111). **4290**

AMERICAN DRY CLEANER (US/0002-8258). **1596**

AMERICAN DRYCLEANER (US/0002-8258). **5347**

AMERICAN ETHNOLOGIST (US/0094-0496). **228**

AMERICAN FARRIERS' JOURNAL (US/0274-6565). **2796**

AMERICAN FILM (US/0361-4751). **4063**

AMERICAN FISHERIES SOCIETY SYMPOSIUM (US/0892-2284). **2294**

AMERICAN FRUIT GROWER (WILLOUGHBY, OHIO : 1931) (US/0002-8568). **2408**

AMERICAN GLASS REVIEW (US/0002-8649). **2586**

AMERICAN HEART JOURNAL, THE (US/0002-8703). **3698**

AMERICAN HERITAGE (US/0002-8738). **2718**

AMERICAN HERITAGE OF INVENTION & TECHNOLOGY (US/8756-7296). **5082**

AMERICAN IMAGO (US/0065-860X). **4572**

AMERICAN INDUSTRIAL HYGIENE ASSOCIATION JOURNAL (US/0002-8894). **2858**

AMERICAN JEWELRY MANUFACTURER (US/0193-0931). **2913**

AMERICAN JOURNAL OF ACUPUNCTURE (US/0091-3960). **3548**

AMERICAN JOURNAL OF ART THERAPY (US/0007-4764). **336**

AMERICAN JOURNAL OF AUDIOLOGY (US/1059-0889). **4383**

AMERICAN JOURNAL OF CARDIAC IMAGING (US/0887-7971). **3698**

AMERICAN JOURNAL OF CLINICAL NUTRITION, THE (US/0002-9165). **4187**

AMERICAN JOURNAL OF CLINICAL ONCOLOGY (US/0277-3732). **3808**

AMERICAN JOURNAL OF CLINICAL PATHOLOGY (US/0002-9173). **3892**

AMERICAN JOURNAL OF COMMUNITY PSYCHOLOGY (US/0091-0562). **4573**

AMERICAN JOURNAL OF CONTACT DERMATITIS (US/1046-199X). **3717**

AMERICAN JOURNAL OF DANCE THERAPY (US/0146-3721). **4573**

AMERICAN JOURNAL OF DERMATOPATHOLOGY, THE (US/0193-1091). **3717**

AMERICAN JOURNAL OF DISEASES OF CHILDREN (1960) (US/0002-922X). **3899**

AMERICAN JOURNAL OF DRUG AND ALCOHOL ABUSE, THE (US/0095-2990). **1340**

AMERICAN JOURNAL OF ECONOMICS AND SOCIOLOGY, THE (US/0002-9246). **5190**

AMERICAN JOURNAL OF EDUCATION (CHICAGO) (US/0195-6744). **1724**

AMERICAN JOURNAL OF EMERGENCY MEDICINE, THE (US/0735-6757). **3723**

AMERICAN JOURNAL OF FORENSIC MEDICINE AND PATHOLOGY, THE (US/0195-7910). **3739**

AMERICAN JOURNAL OF GASTROENTEROLOGY, THE (US/0002-9270). **3743**

AMERICAN JOURNAL OF GYNECOLOGIC HEALTH, THE (US/0895-3643). **3756**

AMERICAN JOURNAL OF HEMATOLOGY (US/0361-8609). **3770**

AMERICAN JOURNAL OF HOSPITAL PHARMACY (US/0002-9289). **4290**

AMERICAN JOURNAL OF HUMAN GENETICS (US/0002-9297). **542**

AMERICAN JOURNAL OF HYPERTENSION (US/0895-7061). **3698**

AMERICAN JOURNAL OF INDUSTRIAL MEDICINE (US/0271-3586). **3548**

AMERICAN JOURNAL OF INFECTION CONTROL (US/0196-6553). **3734**

AMERICAN JOURNAL OF INTERNATIONAL LAW, THE (US/0002-9300). **3123**

AMERICAN JOURNAL OF KIDNEY DISEASES (US/0272-6386). **3988**

AMERICAN JOURNAL OF LAW & MEDICINE (US/0098-8588). **2932**

AMERICAN JOURNAL OF MATHEMATICAL AND MANAGEMENT SCIENCES (US/0196-6324). **3492**

AMERICAN JOURNAL OF MATHEMATICS (US/0002-9327). **3492**

AMERICAN JOURNAL OF MEDICAL GENETICS (US/0148-7299). **542**

AMERICAN JOURNAL OF MENTAL RETARDATION (US/0895-8017). **4383**

AMERICAN JOURNAL OF NEPHROLOGY (SZ/0250-8095). **3988**

AMERICAN JOURNAL OF NONINVASIVE CARDIOLOGY (SZ/0258-4425). **3698**

AMERICAN JOURNAL OF OBSTETRICS AND GYNECOLOGY (US/0002-9378). **3756**

AMERICAN JOURNAL OF ORTHODONTICS AND DENTOFACIAL ORTHOPEDICS (US/0889-5406). **1315**

AMERICAN JOURNAL OF ORTHOPSYCHIATRY (US/0002-9432). **3919**

AMERICAN JOURNAL OF OTOLARYNGOLOGY (US/0196-0709). **3885**

AMERICAN JOURNAL OF OTOLOGY (NEW YORK, N.Y.), THE (US/0192-9763). **3886**

AMERICAN JOURNAL OF PATHOLOGY, THE (US/0002-9440). **3892**

AMERICAN JOURNAL OF PEDIATRIC HEMATOLOGY/ONCOLOGY, THE (US/0192-8562). **3900**

AMERICAN JOURNAL OF PERINATOLOGY (US/0735-1631). **3756**

AMERICAN JOURNAL OF PHILOLOGY (US/0002-9475). **1073**

AMERICAN JOURNAL OF PHYSICAL ANTHROPOLOGY (US/0002-9483). **228**

AMERICAN JOURNAL OF PHYSICAL MEDICINE & REHABILITATION (US/0894-9115). **4379**

AMERICAN JOURNAL OF PHYSICS (US/0002-9505). **4396**

AMERICAN JOURNAL OF PHYSIOLOGIC IMAGING (US/0885-8276). **577**

AMERICAN JOURNAL OF PHYSIOLOGY (US/0002-9513). **577**

AMERICAN JOURNAL OF PHYSIOLOGY : CELL PHYSIOLOGY (US/0363-6143). **577**

AMERICAN JOURNAL OF PHYSIOLOGY : ENDOCRINOLOGY AND METABOLISM (US/0193-1849). **577**

AMERICAN JOURNAL OF PHYSIOLOGY : GASTROINTESTINAL AND LIVER PHYSIOLOGY (US/0193-1857). **578**

AMERICAN JOURNAL OF PHYSIOLOGY : HEART AND CIRCULATORY PHYSIOLOGY (US/0363-6135). **578**

AMERICAN JOURNAL OF PHYSIOLOGY : REGULATORY, INTEGRATIVE AND COMPARATIVE PHYSIOLOGY (US/0363-6119). **578**

AMERICAN JOURNAL OF PHYSIOLOGY RENAL, FLUID AND ELECTROLYTE PHYSIOLOGY (US/0363-6127). **578**

AMERICAN JOURNAL OF POLITICAL SCIENCE (US/0092-5853). **4463**

AMERICAN JOURNAL OF PREVENTIVE MEDICINE (US/0749-3797). **3549**

AMERICAN JOURNAL OF PRIMATOLOGY (US/0275-2565). **5574**

AMERICAN JOURNAL OF PSYCHIATRY, THE (US/0002-953X). **3920**

AMERICAN JOURNAL OF PSYCHOANALYSIS (US/0002-9548). **3920**

AMERICAN JOURNAL OF PSYCHOLOGY, THE (US/0002-9556). **4573**

AMERICAN JOURNAL OF PUBLIC HEALTH (1971) (US/0090-0036). **4764**

AMERICAN JOURNAL OF REPRODUCTIVE IMMUNOLOGY : AJRI (DK/1046-7408). **3666**

AMERICAN JOURNAL OF RESPIRATORY CELL AND MOLECULAR BIOLOGY (US/1044-1549). **3948**

AMERICAN JOURNAL OF ROENTGENOLOGY (1976) (US/0361-803X). **3938**

AMERICAN JOURNAL OF SOCIOLOGY (US/0002-9602). **5238**

AMERICAN JOURNAL OF SPORTS MEDICINE, THE (US/0363-5465). **3953**

AMERICAN JOURNAL OF SURGICAL PATHOLOGY, THE (US/0147-5185). **3892**

AMERICAN JOURNAL OF THE MEDICAL SCIENCES, THE (US/0002-9629). **3549**

AMERICAN JOURNAL OF TROPICAL MEDICINE AND HYGIENE, THE (US/0002-9637). **3985**

AMERICAN LAUNDRY DIGEST (US/0002-9718). **5347**

AMERICAN LAWYER (NEW YORK. 1979), THE (US/0162-3397). **2933**

AMERICAN LIBRARIES (CHICAGO, ILL.) (US/0002-9769). **3189**

AMERICAN LIBRARY DIRECTORY (US/0065-910X). **3257**

AMERICAN LITERARY HISTORY (US/0896-7148). **3360**

AMERICAN LITERATURE (US/0002-9831). **3360**

AMERICAN MACHINIST (1988) (US/1041-7958). **2109**

AMERICAN MARKETPLACE (US/0276-2900). **1293**

AMERICAN MATHEMATICAL MONTHLY, THE (US/0002-9890). **3492**

AMERICAN MEDICAL NEWS (US/0001-1843). **3549**

AMERICAN MINERALOGIST, THE (US/0003-004X). **1437**

AMERICAN MUSIC (CHAMPAIGN, ILL.) (US/0734-4392). **4099**

AMERICAN NATURALIST, THE (US/0003-0147). **4161**

AMERICAN ORTHOPTIC JOURNAL (US/0065-955X). **3871**

AMERICAN PAINT & COATINGS JOURNAL (US/0098-5430). **4222**

AMERICAN PAINTING CONTRACTOR (US/0003-0325). **4222**

AMERICAN PHARMACY (US/0160-3450). **4290**

AMERICAN POLITICS QUARTERLY (US/0044-7803). **4463**

AMERICAN PRINTER (1982) (US/0744-6616). **4563**

AMERICAN PROGRAMMER (US/1048-5600). **1284**

AMERICAN PSYCHOLOGIST, THE (US/0003-066X). **4573**

AMERICAN QUARTERLY (US/0003-0678). **2719**

AMERICAN REVIEW OF DIAGNOSTICS (US/0735-1283). **3698**

AMERICAN REVIEW OF PUBLIC ADMINISTRATION (US/0275-0740). **4625**

AMERICAN REVIEW OF RESPIRATORY DISEASE, THE (US/0003-0805). **3948**

AMERICAN SALESMAN, THE (US/0003-0902). **859**

AMERICAN SALON: OFFICIAL PUBLICATION OF THE NHCA (US/0741-5737). **402**

AMERICAN SCIENTIST (US/0003-0996). **5082**

AMERICAN SENTINEL (WASHINGTON, D.C.), THE (US/0278-0585). **4463**

AMERICAN SOCIETY OF POST ANESTHESIA NURSES (ASPAN) (US/1066-8977). **3851**

AMERICAN SOCIOLOGIST, THE (US/0003-1232). **5239**

AMERICAN SPEECH (US/0003-1283). **3263**

AMERICAN STATISTICIAN, THE (US/0003-1305). **5320**

AMERICAN STUDIES (LAWRENCE) (US/0026-3079). **2719**

AMERICAN SURGEON, THE (US/0003-1348). **3958**

AMERICAN SUZUKI JOURNAL (US/0193-5372). **4100**

AMERICAN UNIVERSITIES AND COLLEGES (US/0066-0922). **1808**

AMERICAN VEGETABLE GROWER (1983) (US/0741-9848). **162**

AMERIKASTUDIEN (GW/0340-2827). **2720**

AMINO ACIDS (AU/0939-4451). **960**

AMMONIA PLANT SAFETY (AND RELATED FACILITIES) (US/0360-7011). **2007**

AMPHIBIA-REPTILIA (GW/0173-5373). **5575**

ANAESTHESIA (UK/0003-2409). **3680**

ANAESTHESIOLOGIE UND REANIMATION (GW/0323-4983). **3680**

ANAESTHESIST, DER (GW/0003-2417). **3681**

ANALES (SP/0034-0618). **4290**

ANALES DE ANATOMIA (SP/0569-9894). **3678**

ANALES DE BROMATOLOGIA (SP/0003-2492). **4187**

ANALES DE QUIMICA (MADRID. 1990) (SP/1130-2283). **960**

ANALES ESPANOLES DE PEDIATRIA (SP/0302-4342). **3900**

ANALGESIA (ELMSFORD, N.Y.) (US/1071-569X). **3681**

ANALOG INTEGRATED CIRCUITS AND SIGNAL PROCESSING (US/0925-1030). **2035**

ANALUSIS (FR/0365-4877). **1012**

ANALYSE & KRITIK (GW/0171-5860). **5190**

ANALYSIS MATHEMATICA (BUDAPEST) (HU/0133-3852). **3493**

ANALYST (LONDON) (UK/0003-2654). **1012**

ANALYTICA CHIMICA ACTA (NE/0003-2670). **1012**

ANALYTICAL ABSTRACTS (UK/0003-2689). **996**

ANALYTICAL AND QUANTITATIVE CYTOLOGY AND HISTOLOGY (US/0884-6812). **531**

ANALYTICAL BIOCHEMISTRY (US/0003-2697). **479**

ANALYTICAL CELLULAR PATHOLOGY (NE/0921-8912). **532**

ANALYTICAL CHEMISTRY (WASHINGTON) (US/0003-2700). **1013**

ANALYTICAL CONSUMER (US/1052-3065). **1293**

ANALYTICAL INSTRUMENTATION (US/0743-5797). **3549**

ANALYTICAL LETTERS (US/0003-2719). **1013**

ANALYTICAL PROCEEDINGS (UK/0144-557X). **1013**

ANALYTICAL SCIENCES : THE INTERNATIONAL JOURNAL OF THE JAPAN SOCIETY FOR ANALYTICAL CHEMISTRY (JA/0910-6340). **1013**

ANALYTISCHE PSYCHOLOGIE (SZ/0301-3006). **4573**

ANASTHESIOLOGIE UND INTENSIVMEDIZIN (BERLIN, WEST) (GW/0171-1814). **3681**

ANATOMIA, HISTOLOGIA, EMBRYOLOGIA (GW/0340-2096). **5502**

ANATOMICAL RECORD, THE (US/0003-276X). **3678**

ANATOMISCHER ANZEIGER (GW/0003-2786). **3678**

ANATOMY AND EMBRYOLOGY (GW/0340-2061). **3678**

ANDREWSREPORT (INDIANAPOLIS, IND.) (US/0892-0850). **4834**

ANDROLOGIA (BERLIN, WEST) (GW/0303-4569). **3549**

ANESTHESIA AND ANALGESIA (US/0003-2999). **3681**

ANESTHESIA & PAIN CONTROL IN DENTISTRY (US/1055-7601). **1316**

ANESTHESIA PROGRESS (US/0003-3006). **1316**

ANESTHESIOLOGY CLINICS OF NORTH AMERICA (US/0889-8537). **3681**

ANESTHESIOLOGY (PHILADELPHIA) (US/0003-3022). **3681**

ANESTHESIOLOGY REVIEW (US/0093-4437). **3681**

ANGEIOLOGIE (FR/0003-3049). **3549**

ANGESTELLTEN MAGAZIN (GW/0341-017X). **1643**

ANGEWANDTE BOTANIK (GW/0066-1759). **499**

ANGEWANDTE CHEMIE. INTERNATIONAL EDITION IN ENGLISH (GW/0570-0833). **960**

ANGEWANDTE CHEMIE (WEINHEIM AN DER BERGSTRASSE, GERMANY) (GW/0044-8249). **961**

ANGEWANDTE MAKROMOLEKULARE CHEMIE (SZ/0003-3146). **4454**

ANGEWANDTE PARASITOLOGIE (GW/0003-3162). **5575**

ANGLO-AMERICAN LAW REVIEW, THE (UK/0308-6569). **2933**

ANGLO-SAXON ENGLAND (UK/0263-6751). **2673**

ANIMAL BEHAVIOUR (UK/0003-3472). **5575**

ANIMAL BIOTECHNOLOGY (US/1049-5398). **5502**

ANIMAL FEED SCIENCE AND TECHNOLOGY (NE/0377-8401). **199**

ANIMAL GENETICS (UK/0268-9146). **542**

ANIMAL LEARNING & BEHAVIOR (US/0090-4996). **5575**

ANIMAL MODELS OF PSYCHIATRIC DISORDERS (SZ/1011-6982). **3920**

ANIMAL PHARM (UK/0262-2238). **5502**

ANIMAL PRODUCTION (UK/0003-3561). **205**

ANIMAL REPRODUCTION SCIENCE (NE/0378-4320). **5503**

ANIMATION HANNOVER (GW/0172-9721). **2596**

ANLAGEPRAXIS (GW/0172-7419). **770**

ANNA JOURNAL (US/8750-0779). **3851**

ANNALES DE BIOLOGIE CLINIQUE (PARIS) (FR/0003-3898). **3892**

ANNALES DE CARDIOLOGIE ET D'ANGEIOLOGIE (FR/0003-3928). **3698**

ANNALES DE CHIMIE (PARIS. 1914) (FR/0151-9107). **961**

ANNALES DE CHIRURGIE (FR/0003-3944). **3958**

ANNALES DE DERMATOLOGIE ET DE VENEREOLOGIE (FR/0151-9638). **3717**

ANNALES DE GASTROENTEROLOGIE ET D'HEPATOLOGIE (FR/0066-2070). **3743**

ANNALES DE GENETIQUE (FR/0003-3995). **542**

ANNALES DE LA RECHERCHE URBAINE, LES (FR/0180-930X). **5239**

ANNALES DE L'I.H.P. PHYSIQUE THEORIQUE (FR/0246-0211). **4396**

ANNALES DE L'I.H.P. PROBABILITES ET STATISTIQUES (FR/0246-0203). **3493**

ANNALES DE LIMNOLOGIE (FR/0003-4088). **1412**

ANNALES DE L'INSTITUT FOURIER (FR/0373-0956). **3493**

ANNALES DE L'INSTITUT HENRI POINCARE. ANALYSE NON LINEAIRE (FR/0294-1449). **3493**

ANNALES DE L'INSTITUT PASTEUR ACTUALITES (FR/0924-4204). **5083**

ANNALES DE MEDECINE INTERNE (FR/0003-410X). **3794**

ANNALES DE PALEONTOLOGIE (1982) (FR/0753-3969). **4226**

ANNALES DE PARASITOLOGIE HUMAINE ET COMPAREE (FR/0003-4150). **441**

ANNALES DE PATHOLOGIE (FR/0242-6498). **3893**

ANNALES DE PHYSIQUE (PARIS) (FR/0003-4169). **4397**

ANNALES DE RADIOLOGIE (FR/0003-4185). **3938**

ANNALES DE RECHERCHES VETERINAIRES (FR/0003-4193). **5503**

ANNALES DE ZOOTECHNIE (FR/0003-424X). **5575**

ANNALES D'ENDOCRINOLOGIE (FR/0003-4266). **3726**

ANNALES DES SCIENCES FORESTIERES (FR/0003-4312). **2374**

ANNALES DES SCIENCES NATURELLES (FR/0003-4320). **499**

ANNALES DES SCIENCES NATURELLES. ZOOLOGIE ET BIOLOGIE ANIMALE (FR/0003-4339). **5575**

ANNALES D'OTO-LARYNGOLOGIE ET DE CHIRURGIE CERVICO FACIALE : BULLETIN DE LA SOCIETE D'OTO-LARYNGOLOGIE DES HOPITAUX DE PARIS (FR/0003-438X). **3886**

ANNALES D'UROLOGIE (FR/0003-4401). **3988**

ANNALES FRANCAISES D'ANESTHESIE ET DE REANIMATION (FR/0750-7658). **3682**

ANNALES GEOPHYSICAE (1988) (FR/0992-7689). **1402**

ANNALES MEDICO PSYCHOLOGIQUES (FR/0003-4487). **4573**

ANNALES — Copyright Clearance Center Index

ANNALES PHARMACEUTIQUES FRANCAISES (FR/0003-4509). **4291**

ANNALES SCIENTIFIQUES DE L'ECOLE NORMALE SUPERIEURE (FR/0012-9593). **3493**

ANNALS OF BIOMEDICAL ENGINEERING (US/0090-6964). **3685**

ANNALS OF BOTANY (UK/0305-7364). **499**

ANNALS OF CHILD DEVELOPMENT (UK/0747-7902). **4573**

ANNALS OF CLINICAL AND LABORATORY SCIENCE (US/0091-7370). **3893**

ANNALS OF CLINICAL BIOCHEMISTRY (UK/0004-5632). **480**

ANNALS OF CLINICAL PSYCHIATRY (US/1040-1237). **3920**

ANNALS OF DISCRETE MATHEMATICS (NE/0167-5060). **3494**

ANNALS OF EPIDEMIOLOGY (US/1047-2797). **3734**

ANNALS OF GLOBAL ANALYSIS AND GEOMETRY (GW/0232-704X). **3494**

ANNALS OF HEMATOLOGY (GW/0939-5555). **3770**

ANNALS OF HUMAN BIOLOGY (UK/0301-4460). **442**

ANNALS OF HUMAN GENETICS (UK/0003-4800). **542**

ANNALS OF INTERNAL MEDICINE (US/0003-4819). **3794**

ANNALS OF IOWA (US/0003-4827). **2720**

ANNALS OF NEUROLOGY (US/0364-5134). **3827**

ANNALS OF NUCLEAR ENERGY (UK/0306-4549). **2153**

ANNALS OF NUTRITION & METABOLISM (SZ/0250-6807). **4187**

ANNALS OF OCCUPATIONAL HYGIENE, THE (UK/0003-4878). **2858**

ANNALS OF ONCOLOGY : OFFICIAL JOURNAL OF THE EUROPEAN SOCIETY FOR MEDICAL ONCOLOGY (NE/0923-7534). **3808**

ANNALS OF PHYSICS (US/0003-4916). **4397**

ANNALS OF PLASTIC SURGERY (US/0148-7043). **3959**

ANNALS OF PROBABILITY, THE (US/0091-1798). **3494**

ANNALS OF PURE AND APPLIED LOGIC (NE/0168-0072). **3494**

ANNALS OF REGIONAL SCIENCE, THE (GW/0570-1864). **2814**

ANNALS OF SCIENCE (UK/0003-3790). **5083**

ANNALS OF STATISTICS, THE (US/0090-5364). **5321**

ANNALS OF SURGERY (US/0003-4932). **3959**

ANNALS OF THE ASSOCIATION OF AMERICAN GEOGRAPHERS (US/0004-5608). **2554**

ANNALS OF THE ENTOMOLOGICAL SOCIETY OF AMERICA (US/0013-8746). **5605**

ANNALS OF THE ICRP (UK/0146-6453). **3938**

ANNALS OF THE INSTITUTE OF STATISTICAL MATHEMATICS (JA/0020-3157). **3542**

ANNALS OF THE ISRAEL PHYSICAL SOCIETY (UK/0309-8710). **5228**

ANNALS OF THE NEW YORK ACADEMY OF SCIENCES (US/0077-8923). **5083**

ANNALS OF THE RHEUMATIC DISEASES (UK/0003-4967). **3802**

ANNALS OF THORACIC SURGERY, THE (US/0003-4975). **3959**

ANNALS OF TOURISM RESEARCH (US/0160-7383). **5191**

ANNALS OF TROPICAL MEDICINE AND PARASITOLOGY (UK/0003-4983). **3985**

ANNALS OF TROPICAL PAEDIATRICS (UK/0272-4936). **3985**

ANNALS (SOCIETY OF LOGISTICS ENGINEERS) (US/0885-3916). **1964**

ANNEE BIOLOGIQUE, L' (SZ/0003-5017). **442**

ANNEE EPIGRAPHIQUE, L' (FR/0066-2348). **1074**

ANNEE PSYCHOLOGIQUE, L' (FR/0003-5033). **4574**

ANNEE SOCIOLOGIQUE (1940/48) (FR/0066-2399). **5239**

ANNUAL ABSTRACT OF STATISTICS (UK/0072-5730). **5321**

ANNUAL BOOK OF ASTM STANDARDS (US/0192-2998). **2100**

ANNUAL CONFERENCE / THE ONTARIO PETROLEUM INSTITUTE (CN/0078-5040). **4249**

ANNUAL DRUG DATA REPORT (SP/0379-4121). **4291**

ANNUAL LIST OF PUBLICATIONS - DEPARTMENT OF THE ENVIRONMENT. DEPARTMENT OF TRANSPORT. LIBRARY SERVICES (UK/0141-2604). **2160**

ANNUAL OF PSYCHOANALYSIS, THE (US/0092-5055). **3920**

ANNUAL POWDER METALLURGY CONFERENCE PROCEEDINGS (US/0079-6719). **3998**

ANNUAL REGISTER OF GRANT SUPPORT (US/0066-4049). **1809**

ANNUAL REPORT / SCOTTISH LAW COMMISSION (UK/0080-7915). **2935**

ANNUAL REPORTS IN MEDICINAL CHEMISTRY (US/0065-7743). **4291**

ANNUAL REPORTS IN ORGANIC SYNTHESIS (US/0066-409X). **1039**

ANNUAL REPORTS ON THE PROGRESS OF CHEMISTRY. SECTION A, INORGANIC CHEMISTRY (UK/0260-1818). **1035**

ANNUAL REPORTS ON THE PROGRESS OF CHEMISTRY. SECTION B, ORGANIC CHEMISTRY (UK/0069-3030). **1039**

ANNUAL REPORTS ON THE PROGRESS OF CHEMISTRY. SECTION C, PHYSICAL CHEMISTRY (UK/0260-1826). **1050**

ANNUAL REVIEW IN AUTOMATIC PROGRAMMING (UK/0066-4138). **1278**

ANNUAL REVIEW OF ADDICTIONS RESEARCH AND TREATMENT (US/0955-663X). **1341**

ANNUAL REVIEW OF ANTHROPOLOGY (US/0084-6570). **228**

ANNUAL REVIEW OF APPLIED LINGUISTICS (UK/0267-1905). **3265**

ANNUAL REVIEW OF ASTRONOMY AND ASTROPHYSICS (US/0066-4146). **391**

ANNUAL REVIEW OF BIOCHEMISTRY (US/0066-4154). **480**

ANNUAL REVIEW OF BIOPHYSICS AND BIOMOLECULAR STRUCTURE (US/1056-8700). **494**

ANNUAL REVIEW OF CELL BIOLOGY (US/0743-4634). **532**

ANNUAL REVIEW OF CHRONOPHARMACOLOGY (UK/0743-9539). **4291**

ANNUAL REVIEW OF EARTH AND PLANETARY SCIENCES (US/0084-6597). **1351**

ANNUAL REVIEW OF ECOLOGY AND SYSTEMATICS (US/0066-4162). **2211**

ANNUAL REVIEW OF ENTOMOLOGY (US/0066-4170). **5605**

ANNUAL REVIEW OF FISH DISEASES (US/0959-8030). **2295**

ANNUAL REVIEW OF FLUID MECHANICS (US/0066-4189). **2087**

ANNUAL REVIEW OF GENETICS (US/0066-4197). **542**

ANNUAL REVIEW OF IMMUNOLOGY (US/0732-0582). **3666**

ANNUAL REVIEW OF INFORMATION SCIENCE AND TECHNOLOGY (US/0066-4200). **3191**

ANNUAL REVIEW OF JAZZ STUDIES (US/0731-0641). **4100**

ANNUAL REVIEW OF MATERIALS SCIENCE (US/0084-6600). **2100**

ANNUAL REVIEW OF MEDICINE (US/0066-4219). **3551**

ANNUAL REVIEW OF NEUROSCIENCE (US/0147-006X). **3827**

ANNUAL REVIEW OF NUCLEAR AND PARTICLE SCIENCE (US/0163-8998). **4446**

ANNUAL REVIEW OF NUTRITION (US/0199-9885). **4187**

ANNUAL REVIEW OF PHARMACOLOGY AND TOXICOLOGY (US/0362-1642). **4291**

ANNUAL REVIEW OF PHYSICAL CHEMISTRY (US/0066-426X). **1050**

ANNUAL REVIEW OF PHYSIOLOGY (US/0066-4278). **578**

ANNUAL REVIEW OF PHYTOPATHOLOGY (US/0066-4286). **500**

ANNUAL REVIEW OF PLANT PHYSIOLOGY AND PLANT MOLECULAR BIOLOGY (US/1040-2519). **500**

ANNUAL REVIEW OF PSYCHOLOGY (US/0066-4308). **4574**

ANNUAL REVIEW OF PUBLIC HEALTH (US/0163-7525). **4767**

ANNUAL REVIEW OF SOCIOLOGY (US/0360-0572). **5239**

ANNUAL TECHNICAL CONFERENCE TRANSACTIONS - AMERICAN SOCIETY FOR QUALITY CONTROL (US/0360-6929). **860**

ANNUARIUM HISTORIAE CONCILIORUM (GW/0003-5157). **2610**

ANSCHNITT, DER (GW/0003-5238). **2134**

ANTARCTIC (NZ/0003-5327). **1351**

ANTARCTIC RESEARCH SERIES (US/0066-4634). **1402**

ANTARCTIC SCIENCE (UK/0954-1020). **5084**

ANTHROPOLOGICA (OTTAWA) (CN/0003-5459). **228**

ANTHROPOLOGIE (PARIS) (FR/0003-5521). **229**

ANTHROPOLOGISCHER ANZEIGER (GW/0003-5548). **229**

ANTHROZOOS (US/0892-7936). **5576**

ANTI-CANCER DRUG DESIGN (UK/0266-9536). **3809**

ANTI-CANCER DRUGS (UK/0959-4973). **3979**

ANTIBIOTIC GUIDELINES (AT/0729-218X). **3551**

ANTIBIOTICS AND CHEMOTHERAPY (SZ/0066-4758). **4291**

ANTIBIOTIKI I HIMIOTERAPIA (RU/0235-2990). **4291**

ANTICANCER RESEARCH (GR/0250-7005). **3809**

ANTIKE UND ABENDLAND (GW/0003-5696). **1074**

ANTIMICROBIAL AGENTS AND CHEMOTHERAPY (US/0066-4804). **559**

ANTIMICROBIC NEWSLETTER, THE (US/0738-1751). **559**

ANTIMICROBICS AND INFECTIOUS DISEASES NEWSLETTER (US/1069-417X). **559**

ANTIPODE (UK/0066-4812). **2554**

ANTIQUARIES JOURNAL (UK/0003-5815). **255**

ANTIQUE DEALER AND COLLECTORS' GUIDE (UK/0003-5866). **249**

ANTIQUITY (UK/0003-598X). **255**

ANTITRUST & TRADE REGULATION REPORT (US/0003-6021). **3095**

ANTITRUST FREEDOM OF INFORMATION LOG (US/0891-8546). **3095**

ANTIVIRAL CHEMISTRY & CHEMOTHERAPY (UK/0956-3202). **961**

ANTIVIRAL RESEARCH (US/0166-3542). **3551**

ANTONIE VAN LEEUWENHOEK (NE/0003-6072). **559**

ANXIETY, STRESS AND COPING (SZ/1061-5806). **4574**

ANZEIGER FUER SCHADLINGSKUNDE, PFLANZENSCHUTZ, UMWELTSCHUTZ (GW/0340-7330). **4244**

AORN JOURNAL (US/0001-2092). **3851**

AORN JOURNAL (US/0001-2092). **3851**

APF REPORTER (US/0193-4562). **2917**

APHASIOLOGY (UK/0268-7038). **3551**

APIDOLOGIE (FR/0044-8435). **5576**

APIS, THE (US/0887-7386). **226**

APMIS : ACTA PATHOLOGICA, MICROBIOLOGICA ET IMMUNOLOGICA SCANDINAVICA (DK/0903-4641). **3666**

APPETITE (UK/0195-6663). **4187**

APPLIANCE (US/0003-6781). **2810**

APPLIANCE MANUFACTURER (US/0003-679X). **2810**

APPLICABLE ALGEBRA IN ENGINEERING, COMMUNICATION AND COMPUTING (GW/0938-1279). **3494**

APPLICABLE ANALYSIS (US/0003-6811). **3494**

APPLICATIONS OF MATHEMATICS / CZECHOSLOVAK ACADEMY OF SCIENCES (XR/0862-7940). **3494**

APPLICATIONS OF MATHEMATICS (PRAGUE) (XR/0862-7940). **3494**

APPLIED ACOUSTICS (UK/0003-682X). **2097**

APPLIED AND COMPUTATIONAL HARMONIC ANALYSIS (US/1063-5203). **3494**

APPLIED AND ENVIRONMENTAL MICROBIOLOGY (US/0099-2240). **559**

APPLIED ANIMAL BEHAVIOUR SCIENCE (NE/0168-1591). **5504**

APPLIED ARTIFICIAL INTELLIGENCE (US/0883-9514). **1211**

APPLIED BIOCHEMISTRY AND MICROBIOLOGY (US/0003-6838). **480**

APPLIED CARDIOPULMONARY PATHOPHYSIOLOGY : ACP (US/0920-5268). **3699**

APPLIED CATALYSIS A : GENERAL (NE/0926-860X). **2008**

APPLIED CATALYSIS. B : ENVIRONMENTAL (NE/0926-3373). **2161**

APPLIED CLAY SCIENCE (NE/0169-1317). **5085**

APPLIED CLINICAL TRIALS (US/1064-8542). **4292**

APPLIED COGNITIVE PSYCHOLOGY (UK/0888-4080). **4574**

APPLIED DATA AND KNOWLEDGE ENGINEERING (GW/0942-251X). **1965**

APPLIED ECONOMICS (UK/0003-6846). **1463**

APPLIED ENERGY (UK/0306-2619). **1932**

APPLIED ENERGY (US/1068-7181). **2109**

APPLIED ENGINEERING IN AGRICULTURE (US/0883-8542). **1965**

APPLIED ENTOMOLOGY AND ZOOLOGY (JA/0003-6862). **5605**

APPLIED ERGONOMICS (UK/0003-6870). **1965**

APPLIED GENETICS NEWS (US/0271-7107). **542**

APPLIED GEOCHEMISTRY (UK/0883-2927). **1366**

APPLIED GEOGRAPHY (SEVENOAKS) (UK/0143-6228). **2554**

APPLIED IMMUNOHISTOCHEMISTRY (US/1062-3345). **480**

APPLIED INTELLIGENCE (NE/0924-669X). **1211**

APPLIED LINGUISTICS (UK/0142-6001). **3266**

APPLIED MAGNETIC RESONANCE (RU/0937-9347). **4397**

APPLIED MATHEMATICAL MODELLING (UK/0307-904X). **3495**

APPLIED MATHEMATICS AND COMPUTATION (US/0096-3003). **3495**

APPLIED MATHEMATICS AND OPTIMIZATION (US/0095-4616). **3495**

APPLIED MATHEMATICS LETTERS (US/0893-9659). **3495**

APPLIED MECHANICS REVIEWS (US/0003-6900). **2002**

APPLIED MICROBIOLOGY AND BIOTECHNOLOGY (GW/0175-7598). **559**

APPLIED NUMERICAL MATHEMATICS : TRANSACTIONS OF IMACS (NE/0168-9274). **3495**

APPLIED NURSING RESEARCH : ANR (US/0897-1897). **3851**

APPLIED OCCUPATIONAL AND ENVIRONMENTAL HYGIENE (US/1047-322X). **2859**

APPLIED OCEAN RESEARCH (UK/0141-1187). **1446**

APPLIED OPTICS (US/0003-6935). **4433**

APPLIED ORGANOMETALLIC CHEMISTRY (UK/0268-2605). **961**

APPLIED PHYSICS. A, SOLIDS AND SURFACES (GW/0721-7250). **4397**

APPLIED PHYSICS. B, PHOTOPHYSICS AND LASER CHEMISTRY (GW/0721-7269). **4433**

APPLIED PHYSICS LETTERS (US/0003-6951). **4397**

APPLIED PSYCHOLINGUISTICS (UK/0142-7164). **3266**

APPLIED PSYCHOLOGICAL MEASUREMENT (US/0146-6216). **4574**

APPLIED SCIENTIFIC RESEARCH (NE/0003-6994). **2109**

APPLIED SOLAR ENERGY (US/0003-701X). **1932**

APPLIED SPECTROSCOPY (US/0003-7028). **4433**

APPLIED SPECTROSCOPY REVIEWS (SOFTCOVER ED.) (US/0570-4928). **1013**

APPLIED STATISTICS (UK/0035-9254). **5322**

APPLIED STOCHASTIC MODELS AND DATA ANALYSIS (UK/8755-0024). **3495**

APPLIED SUPERCONDUCTIVITY (UK/0964-1807). **2035**

APPLIED SURFACE SCIENCE (NE/0169-4332). **4397**

APPROPRIATE TECHNOLOGY (UK/0305-0920). **5085**

APR. ALLGEMEINE PAPIER-RUNDSCHAU (1966) (GW/0002-5917). **4232**

APS JOURNAL (US/1058-9139). **3552**

APSNEWS (US/1058-8132). **4398**

AQUA (LONDON) (UK/0003-7214). **5530**

AQUACULTURAL ENGINEERING (UK/0144-8609). **2295**

AQUACULTURE (NE/0044-8486). **2295**

AQUACULTURE AND FISHERIES MANAGEMENT (UK/0266-996X). **2295**

AQUATIC BOTANY (NE/0304-3770). **500**

AQUATIC INSECTS (NE/0165-0424). **5605**

AQUATIC LIVING RESOURCES (MONTROUGE) (FR/0990-7440). **2296**

AQUATIC SCIENCES (SZ/1015-1621). **1412**

AQUATIC TOXICOLOGY (AMSTERDAM, NETHERLANDS) (NE/0166-445X). **3979**

ARABIAN ARCHAEOLOGY AND EPIGRAPHY (DK/0905-7196). **256**

ARABIAN JOURNAL FOR SCIENCE AND ENGINEERING (UK/0377-9211). **5085**

ARABICA (NE/0570-5398). **2767**

ARBEIT UND RECHT (GW/0003-7648). **3144**

ARBEIT UND SOZIALPOLITIK (GW/0340-8434). **1651**

ARBORICULTURAL JOURNAL, THE (UK/0307-1375). **2375**

ARCADIA (GW/0003-7982). **3363**

ARCHAEOASTRONOMY (UK/0142-7253). **256**

ARCHAEOLOGISCHE MITTEILUNGEN AUS IRAN (US/0066-6033). **257**

ARCHIFACTS (NZ/0303-7940). **2479**

ARCHITECTS' JOURNAL (LONDON) (UK/0003-8466). **288**

ARCHITECTURAL LIGHTING (US/0894-0436). **289**

ARCHITECTURAL RECORD (US/0003-858X). **289**

ARCHITECTURE NEW ZEALAND (NZ/0113-4566). **290**

ARCHITECTURE (WASHINGTON, D.C.) (US/0746-0554). **290**

ARCHIV DER MATHEMATIK (SW/0003-889X). **3495**

ARCHIV DER PHARMAZIE (WEINHEIM) (GW/0365-6233). **4292**

ARCHIV DES OFFENTLICHEN RECHTS (GW/0003-8911). **3092**

ARCHIV DES VOLKERRECHTS (GW/0003-892X). **3124**

ARCHIV FUER ACKER- UND PFLANZENBAU UND BODENKUNDE (SW/0365-0340). **163**

ARCHIV FUER DIE CIVILISTISCHE PRAXIS (GW/0003-8997). **3088**

ARCHIV FUER EISENBAHNTECHNIK; BEIHEFT ZU DER ZEITSCHRIFT EISENBAHN TECHNISCHE RUNDSCHAU (GW/0341-0463). **5429**

ARCHIV FUER ELEKTROTECHNIK (BERLIN) (GW/0003-9039). **2036**

ARCHIV FUER GEFLUGELKUNDE (GW/0003-9098). **206**

ARCHIV FUER GESCHICHTE DER PHILOSOPHIE (GW/0003-9101). **4341**

ARCHIV FUER GESCHICHTE DER PHILOSOPHIE (GW/0003-9101). **4341**

ARCHIV FUER HYDROBIOLOGIE (GW/0003-9136). **5530**

ARCHIV FUER HYDROBIOLOGIE. SUPPLEMENTBAND, MONOGRAPHISCHE BEITRAEGE (GW/0341-2881). **553**

ARCHIV FUER KOMMUNALWISSENSCHAFTEN (GW/0003-9209). **4630**

ARCHIV FUER KULTURGESCHICHTE (GW/0003-9233). **2610**

ARCHIV FUER LEBENSMITTELHYGIENE (GW/0003-925X). **2327**

ARCHIV FUER MUSIKWISSENSCHAFT (GW/0003-9292). **4100**

ARCHIV FUER NATURSCHUTZ UND LANDSCHAFTSFORSCHUNG (GW/0003-9306). **2187**

ARCHIV FUER PHYTOPATHOLOGIE UND PFLANZENSCHUTZ (GW/0323-5408). **500**

ARCHIV FUER PROTISTENKUNDE (GW/0003-9365). **576**

ARCHIV FUER RECHTS- UND SOZIALPHILOSOPHIE (GW/0001-2343). **2936**

ARCHIV FUER TIERERNAHRUNG (GW/0003-942X). **5504**

ARCHIV FUR DAS STUDIUM DER NEUEREN SPRACHEN UND LITERATUREN (1961) (GW/0003-8970). **3266**

ARCHIV FUR SIPPENFORSCHUNG UND ALLE VERWANDTEN GEBIETE (GW/0003-9403). **2437**

ARCHIVE FOR HISTORY OF EXACT SCIENCES (GW/0003-9519). **5085**

ARCHIVE FOR MATHEMATICAL LOGIC (GW/0933-5846). **3496**

ARCHIVE FOR RATIONAL MECHANICS AND ANALYSIS (GW/0003-9527). **4427**

ARCHIVES D'ANATOMIE ET DE CYTOLOGIE PATHOLOGIQUES (FR/0395-501X). **3678**

ARCHIVES DE PHILOSOPHIE DU DROIT (FR/0066-6564). **2936**

ARCHIVES DE PSYCHOLOGIE (SZ/0003-9640). **4575**

ARCHIVES DES MALADIES DU COEUR ET DES VAISSEAUX (FR/0003-9683). **3699**

ARCHIVES DES MALADIES PROFESSIONNELLES DE MEDECINE DU TRAVAIL ET SECURITE SOCIALE (FR/0003-9691). **3552**

ARCHIVES FRANCAISES DE PEDIATRIE (FR/0003-9764). **3900**

ARCHIVES INTERNATIONALES DE PHARMACODYNAMIE ET DE THERAPIE (BE/0003-9780). **4292**

ARCHIVES OF ANDROLOGY (UK/0148-5016). **3678**

ARCHIVES OF BIOCHEMISTRY AND BIOPHYSICS (US/0003-9861). **480**

ARCHIVES OF CLINICAL NEUROPSYCHOLOGY (US/0887-6177). **3827**

ARCHIVES OF DERMATOLOGICAL RESEARCH (GW/0340-3696). **3717**

ARCHIVES OF DERMATOLOGY (US/0003-987X). **3718**

ARCHIVES OF DISEASE IN CHILDHOOD (UK/0003-9888). **3900**

ARCHIVES OF EMERGENCY MEDICINE (UK/0264-4924). **3723**

ARCHIVES OF ENVIRONMENTAL CONTAMINATION AND TOXICOLOGY (US/0090-4341). **2161**

ARCHIVES OF ENVIRONMENTAL HEALTH (US/0003-9896). **4767**

ARCHIVES OF FAMILY MEDICINE (US/1063-3987). **3736**

ARCHIVES OF GENERAL PSYCHIATRY (US/0003-990X). **3921**

ARCHIVES OF GYNECOLOGY AND OBSTETRICS (GW/0932-0067). **3757**

ARCHIVES OF INSECT BIOCHEMISTRY AND PHYSIOLOGY (US/0739-4462). **5605**

ARCHIVES OF INTERNAL MEDICINE (1960) (US/0003-9926). **3795**

ARCHIVES OF MICROBIOLOGY (GW/0302-8933). **559**

ARCHIVES OF NEUROLOGY (CHICAGO) (US/0003-9942). **3827**

ARCHIVES OF OPHTHALMOLOGY (US/0003-9950). **3872**

ARCHIVES OF ORAL BIOLOGY (UK/0003-9969). **1316**

ARCHIVES OF OTOLARYNGOLOGY-HEAD & NECK SURGERY (US/0886-4470). **3886**

ARCHIVES OF PATHOLOGY & LABORATORY MEDICINE (US/0003-9985). **3893**

ARCHIVES OF PHYSICAL MEDICINE AND REHABILITATION (US/0003-9993). **4379**

ARCHIVES OF PSYCHIATRIC NURSING (US/0883-9417). **3851**

ARCHIVES OF SEXUAL BEHAVIOR (US/0004-0002). **5186**

ARCHIVES OF SURGERY (CHICAGO. 1960) (US/0004-0010). **3959**

ARCHIVES OF TOXICOLOGY (GW/0340-5761). **3979**

ARCHIVES OF TOXICOLOGY. SUPPLEMENT (GW/0171-9750). **3979**

ARCHIVES OF VIROLOGY (AU/0304-8608). **560**

ARCHIVOS DE NEUROBIOLOGIA (SP/0004-0576). **3827**

ARCHIVOS ESPANOLES DE UROLOGIA (SP/0004-0614). **3988**

ARCHIVOS LATINOAMERICANOS DE NUTRICION (VE/0004-0622). **4187**

ARCTIC AND ALPINE RESEARCH (US/0004-0851). **2555**

ARCTIC ANTHROPOLOGY (US/0066-6939). **231**

ARETHUSA (US/0004-0975). **1074**

ARGUMENTATION (NE/0920-427X). **4341**

ARHIV PATOLOGIJ (RU/0004-1955). **3893**

ARID SOIL RESEARCH & REHABILITATION (US/0890-3069). **163**

ARKITEKTNYTT (NO/0004-1998). **292**

ARMCHAIR DETECTIVE, THE (US/0004-217X). **3363**

ARMED FORCES AND SOCIETY (US/0095-327X). **4035**

ARMY TIMES (US/0004-2595). **4037**

ARQUIVOS DE NEURO-PSIQUIATRIA (BL/0004-282X). **3827**

ARREST LAW BULLETIN (US/8755-8300). **3158**

ARS COMBINATORIA (CN/0381-7032). **3496**

ART BUSINESS NEWS (US/0273-5652). **338**

ART DIRECTION (US/0004-3109). **338**

ART HISTORY (UK/0141-6790). **339**

ART MATERIAL TRADE NEWS (US/0004-3265). **339**

ARTERIOSCLEROSIS AND THROMBOSIS (US/1049-8834). **3699**

ARTHRITIS AND RHEUMATISM (US/0004-3591). **3803**

ARTHRITIS AND RHEUMATISM (NE/0014-4355). **3803**

ARTHROSCOPY (US/0749-8063). **3880**

ARTIFICIAL INTELLIGENCE (NE/0004-3702). **1211**

ARTIFICIAL INTELLIGENCE ABSTRACTS (US/0882-1410). **1208**

ARTIFICIAL INTELLIGENCE FOR ENGINEERING DESIGN, ANALYSIS AND MANUFACTURING (UK/0890-0604). **1211**

ARTIFICIAL INTELLIGENCE IN ENGINEERING (UK/0954-1810). **1211**

ARTIFICIAL INTELLIGENCE IN MEDICINE (NE/0933-3657). **1211**

ARTIFICIAL INTELLIGENCE REVIEW, THE (UK/0269-2821). **1211**

ARTIFICIAL ORGANS (US/0160-564X). **3960**

ARTS & CRAFTS RETAILER (US/1067-1463). **314**

ARTS & CULTURE FUNDING REPORT (US/1047-3297). **314**

ARTS EDUCATION POLICY REVIEW (US/1063-2913). **314**

ARTS IN PSYCHOTHERAPY, THE (US/0197-4556). **3921**

ARZNEIMITTEL FORSCHUNG (GW/0004-4172). **4292**

ARZNEIMITTELTHERAPIE (GW/0723-6913). **4293**

ARZTEZEITSCHRIFT FUER NATURHEILVERFAHREN : ORGAN DES ZENTRALVERBANDES DER ARZTE FUER NATURHEILVERFAHREN E. V (GW/0720-6003). **3553**

ARZTLICHE PRAXIS (GW/0001-9534). **3553**

ASAE STANDARDS (US/8755-1187). **1965**

ASBESTOS ABATEMENT REPORT (US/0893-858X). **4767**

ASBESTOS CONTROL REPORT (US/0893-4533). **2224**

ASCE PUBLICATIONS INFORMATION (US/0734-1962). **2002**

ASEE PRISM (US/1056-8077). **1965**

ASHA (ROCKVILLE, MD.) (US/0001-2475). **1875**

ASHRAE JOURNAL (US/0001-2491). **2603**

ASHRAE TECHNICAL DATA BULLETIN (US/0884-0490). **2603**

ASHRAE TRANSACTIONS (US/0001-2505). **2603**

ASIA MAJOR (US/0004-4482). **2646**

ASIA-PACIFIC AFRICA-MIDDLE EAST PETROLEUM DIRECTORY (US/0748-4089). **4251**

ASIAN AFFAIRS (NEW YORK) (US/0092-7678). **4516**

ASIAN AND AFRICAN STUDIES (JERUSALEM) (IS/0066-8281). **2638**

ASIAN ART (US/0894-234X). **343**

ASIAN AVIATION NEWS (US/1071-0663). **12**

ASIAN BUSINESS (HK/0254-3729). **640**

ASIAN MUSIC (US/0044-9202). **4101**

ASIAN PHILOSOPY (UK/0955-2367). **4341**

ASIAN SURVEY (US/0004-4687). **5192**

ASM NEWS (US/0044-7897). **560**

ASSEMBLAGE (US/0889-3012). **292**

ASSEMBLY AUTOMATION (UK/0144-5154). **1217**

ASSESSMENT AND EVALUATION IN HIGHER EDUCATION (UK/0260-2938). **1810**

ASSISTED REPRODUCTIVE REVIEWS (US/1051-2446). **3757**

ASSOCIATIONS YELLOW BOOK (US/1054-4070). **1923**

ASTM GEOTECHNICAL TESTING JOURNAL (US/0149-6115). **1965**

ASTM SPECIAL TECHNICAL PUBLICATION (US/0066-0558). **1966**

ASTM SPECIAL TECHNICAL PUBLICATION (US/0066-0558). **2100**

ASTROFIZICHESKIE ISSLEDOVANIIA (US/0190-2709). **391**

ASTRONOMICAL AND ASTROPHYSICAL TRANSACTIONS (US/1055-6796). **391**

ASTRONOMICAL JOURNAL (NEW YORK), THE (US/0004-6256). **392**

ASTRONOMICESKIJ VESTNIK (RU/0320-930X). **392**

ASTRONOMICHESKII ZHURNAL (RU/0004-6299). **392**

ASTRONOMISCHE NACHRICHTEN (GW/0004-6337). **392**

ASTRONOMY AND ASTROPHYSICS ABSTRACTS (GW/0067-0022). **402**

ASTRONOMY AND ASTROPHYSICS (BERLIN) (GW/0004-6361). **392**

ASTRONOMY AND ASTROPHYSICS REVIEW, THE (GW/0935-4956). **392**

ASTRONOMY & ASTROPHYSICS. SUPPLEMENT SERIES (FR/0365-0138). **392**

ASTRONOMY LETTERS (US/1063-7737). **392**

ASTRONOMY REPORTS (US/1063-7729). **393**

ASTROPHYSICAL JOURNAL. SUPPLEMENT SERIES, THE (US/0067-0049). **393**

ASTROPHYSICAL JOURNAL, THE (US/0004-637X). **393**

ASTROPHYSICAL LETTERS AND COMMUNICATIONS (US/0888-6512). **393**

ASTROPHYSICS (US/0571-7256). **4398**

ASTROPHYSICS AND SPACE SCIENCE (NE/0004-640X). **393**

AT&T TECHNICAL JOURNAL (US/8756-2324). **1149**

ATEMWEGS- UND LUNGENKRANKHEITEN (GW/0341-3055). **3948**

ATHEROSCLEROSIS (NE/0021-9150). **3699**

ATLA : ALTERNATIVES TO LABORATORY ANIMALS (UK/0261-1929). **3979**

ATLANTIC GEOLOGY (CN/0843-5561). **1366**

ATMOSPHERE-OCEAN (CN/0705-5900). **1420**

ATMOSPHERIC RESEARCH (NE/0169-8095). **1420**

ATOMIC DATA AND NUCLEAR DATA TABLES (US/0092-640X). **4446**

ATOMIC ENERGY CLEARING HOUSE (US/0519-3389). **1933**

ATOMIC ENERGY (NEW YORK, N.Y.) (US/1063-4258). **2154**

ATOMIZATION AND SPRAYS (US/1044-5110). **2008**

ATOMNAIA ENERGIIA (RU/0004-7163). **1933**

ATOMWIRTSCHAFT, ATOMTECHNIK (GW/0365-8414). **2154**

ATRIAL NATRIURETIC FACTORS (UK/0268-1641). **3699**

ATTORNEYS MARKETING REPORT (US/0745-1369). **2938**

ATW NEWS (GW/0341-4213). **4446**

ATZ. AUTOMOBILTECHNISCHE ZEITSCHRIFT (GW/0001-2785). **5404**

AUCKLAND-WAIKATO HISTORICAL JOURNAL (NZ/0111-7653). **2611**

AUDIO VISUAL (UK/0305-2249). **1104**

AUDIOLOGY (SZ/0020-6091). **3886**

AUERBACH COMPUTER PROGRAMMING MANAGEMENT (US/0746-7273). **1278**

AUERBACH DATA BASE MANAGEMENT (US/0735-9977). **1253**

AUERBACH DATA CENTER OPERATIONS MANAGEMENT (US/0736-3648). **1255**

AUERBACH DATA COMMUNICATIONS MANAGEMENT (US/0736-0002). **1256**

AUERBACH DATA SECURITY MANAGEMENT (US/0746-7281). **1225**

AUERBACH EDP AUDITING (US/0746-7265). **739**

AUERBACH SYSTEMS DEVELOPMENT MANAGEMENT (US/0735-9985). **1246**

AUFBEREITUNGS-TECHNIK (GW/0004-783X). **2134**

AUGMENTATIVE AND ALTERNATIVE COMMUNICATION (US/0743-4618). **1104**

AUSTRALASIAN PLANT PATHOLOGY (AT/0815-3191). **500**

AUSTRALIAN & NEW ZEALAND JOURNAL OF CRIMINOLOGY, THE (AT/0004-8658). **3158**

AUSTRALIAN AND NEW ZEALAND JOURNAL OF MEDICINE (AT/0004-8291). **3795**

AUSTRALIAN AND NEW ZEALAND JOURNAL OF SURGERY (AT/0004-8682). **3960**

AUSTRALIAN CAMERA CRAFT MAGAZINE (AT/0158-2658). **4367**

AUSTRALIAN DISABILITY REVIEW (AT/0813-4537). **4384**

AUSTRALIAN ECONOMIC HISTORY REVIEW (AT/0004-8992). **1547**

AUSTRALIAN EDUCATION INDEX (AT/0004-9026). **1793**

AUSTRALIAN ENERGY STATISTICS / DEPARTMENT OF NATIONAL DEVELOPMENT AND ENERGY (AT/0727-2596). **1961**

AUSTRALIAN FAMILY PHYSICIAN (AT/0300-8495). **3737**

AUSTRALIAN FEDERAL TAX REPORTER (AT/0310-7817). **4712**

AUSTRALIAN FISHERIES (AT/0004-9115). **2297**

AUSTRALIAN FOREST RESEARCH (AT/0004-914X). **2375**

AUSTRALIAN JOURNAL OF AGRICULTURAL RESEARCH (AT/0004-9409). **64**

AUSTRALIAN JOURNAL OF BOTANY (AT/0067-1924). **501**

AUSTRALIAN JOURNAL OF CHEMISTRY (AT/0004-9425). **961**

AUSTRALIAN JOURNAL OF EARTH SCIENCES (AT/0812-0099). **1351**

AUSTRALIAN JOURNAL OF ECOLOGY (AT/0307-692X). **2211**

AUSTRALIAN JOURNAL OF EDUCATION, THE (AT/0004-9441). **1726**

AUSTRALIAN JOURNAL OF EXPERIMENTAL AGRICULTURE (AT/0816-1089). **64**

AUSTRALIAN JOURNAL OF HOSPITAL PHARMACY (AT/0310-6810). **4293**

AUSTRALIAN JOURNAL OF MARINE AND FRESHWATER RESEARCH (AT/0067-1940). **1446**

AUSTRALIAN JOURNAL OF PHYSICS (AT/0004-9506). **4398**

AUSTRALIAN JOURNAL OF PLANT PHYSIOLOGY (AT/0310-7841). **501**

AUSTRALIAN JOURNAL OF SOIL RESEARCH (AT/0004-9573). **164**

AUSTRALIAN JOURNAL OF ZOOLOGY (AT/0004-959X). **5577**

AUSTRALIAN METEOROLOGICAL MAGAZINE (AT/0004-9743). **1420**

AUTOIMMUNITY (CHUR, SWITZERLAND) (SZ/0891-6934). **3667**

AUTOMATED MANUFACTURING STRATEGY (NE/0951-7162). **1217**

AUTOMATIC CONTROL AND COMPUTER SCIENCES (US/0146-4116). **1217**

AUTOMATIC DOCUMENTATION AND MATHEMATICAL LINGUISTICS (US/0005-1055). **3193**

AUTOMATICA (OXFORD) (UK/0005-1098). **1217**

AUTOMATION AND CONTROL (NZ/0110-6295). **1217**

AUTOMATION AND REMOTE CONTROL (US/0005-1179). **1218**

AUTOMATION IN CONSTRUCTION (NE/0926-5805). **599**

AUTOMATIQUE-PRODUCTIQUE INFORMATIQUE INDUSTRIELLE (FR/0296-1598). **2110**

AUTOMATISIERUNGSTECHNISCHE PRAXIS : ATP (GW/0178-2320). **2110**

AUTOMEDICA (NEW YORK) (US/0095-0963). **3686**

AUTOMOBIL-INDUSTRIE (GW/0005-1306). **5405**

AUTOMOTIVE ENGINEER (UK/0307-6490). **5406**

AUTOMOTIVE ENGINEERING (US/0098-2571). **2110**

AUTOMOTIVE NEWS (US/0005-1551). **5406**

AUTOWEEK (US/0192-9674). **5407**

AV. DIE ARBEITSVORBEREITUNG (GW/0003-780X). **5087**

AVIAN PATHOLOGY (UK/0307-9457). **5505**

AVIATION EQUIPMENT MAINTENANCE (US/0745-0214). **13**

AVIATION SPACE AND ENVIRONMENTAL MEDICINE (US/0095-6562). **3554**

AVIATION WEEK & SPACE TECHNOLOGY (US/0005-2175). **14**

AVIDEO (US/0747-1335). **1104**

AVIONICS (POTOMAC, MD.) (US/0273-7639). **14**

AVISO (WASHINGTON, D.C.) (US/0739-7747). **4084**

AVN. ALLGEMEINE VERMESSUNGS-NACHRICHTEN (GW/0002-5968). **2019**

AVTOMATIKA I TELEMEHANIKA (RU/0005-2310). **2110**

AVTOMATIKA I VYCISLITEL'NAYA TEHNIKA (RIGA) (LV/0132-4160). **1218**

AVTOMATIKA (KIEV) (UN/0572-2691). **1218**

AVTOMETRIJA (NOVOSIBIRSK) (RU/0320-7102). **1218**

AZERBAJDZANSKOR NEFTJANOE HOZJAJSTVO (AJ/0365-8554). **3338**

BABEL (AT/0005-3503). **3267**

BACK PAIN MONITOR (US/0746-9500). **3554**

BADEN-WURTTEMBERGISCHE VERWALTUNGSPRAXIS (GW/0340-3505). **4632**

BAILLIERE'S CLINICAL ENDOCRINOLOGY AND METABOLISM (UK/0950-351X). **3726**

BAILLIERE'S CLINICAL GASTROENTEROLOGY (UK/0950-3528). **3743**

BAKER STREET JOURNAL, THE (US/0005-4070). **3365**

BAKERY NEWSLETTER (US/1049-3174). **2328**
BAKERY PRODUCTION AND MARKETING (US/0005-4127). **2328**
BALLET REVIEW (US/0522-0653). **1310**
BANBURY REPORT (US/0198-0068). **443**
BANDER BLECHE ROHRE (GW/0005-3848). **3475**
BANK AUDITING AND ACCOUNTING REPORT (US/0522-2478). **774**
BANK AUTOMATION NEWSLETTER (US/0572-5933). **774**
BANK BAILOUT LITIGATION NEWS (US/1047-5133). **774**
BANK DIRECTOR'S REPORT (US/0522-2494). **774**
BANK SECURITY REPORT (US/0162-7457). **776**
BANK SYSTEMS + TECHNOLOGY (US/1045-9472). **776**
BANK TAX REPORT, THE (US/0162-7465). **776**
BANK TELLER'S REPORT (US/0162-7473). **776**
BANKERS LETTER OF THE LAW, THE (US/0005-5433). **3084**
BANKERS MAGAZINE (BOSTON), THE (US/0005-545X). **776**
BANKFACHKLASSE, DIE (GW/0170-6659). **776**
BANKING LAW JOURNAL, THE (US/0005-5506). **3085**
BANKING SOFTWARE REVIEW (US/0892-6778). **777**
BANKING WORLD (UK/0737-6413). **777**
BANKRUPTCY COURT DECISIONS (US/0098-7336). **3085**
BANKRUPTCY LAW LETTER (US/0744-7671). **3085**
BANKS IN INSURANCE REPORT (US/8756-6079). **3085**
BARNHART DICTIONARY COMPANION, THE (US/0736-1122). **1923**
BARRON'S NATIONAL BUSINESS AND FINANCIAL WEEKLY (US/0005-6073). **642**
BASIC LIFE SCIENCES (US/0090-5542). **443**
BASIC RESEARCH IN CARDIOLOGY (GW/0300-8428). **3699**
BASIN RESEARCH (UK/0950-091X). **1366**
BASLER VEROFFENTLICHUNGEN ZUR GESCHICHTE DER MEDIZIN UND DER BIOLOGIE (SZ/0067-4524). **3555**
BASS PLAYER (US/1050-785X). **4102**
BAUEN MIT HOLZ (GW/0005-6545). **600**
BAUINGENIEUR, DER (GW/0005-6650). **2019**
BAUMEISTER (GW/0005-674X). **293**
BAUPHYSIK (GW/0171-5445). **2019**
BAYERISCHE VERWALTUNGSBLATTER (GW/0522-5337). **2940**
BBI NEWSLETTER, THE (US/1049-4316). **642**
BEEF (ST. PAUL, MINN.) (US/0005-7738). **207**
BEHAVIOR GENETICS (US/0001-8244). **543**
BEHAVIOR MODIFICATION (US/0145-4455). **4576**
BEHAVIOR RESEARCH METHODS, INSTRUMENTS, & COMPUTERS : A JOURNAL OF THE PSYCHONOMIC SOCIETY, INC (US/0743-3808). **4576**
BEHAVIOR THERAPY (US/0005-7894). **4576**

BEHAVIORAL AND NEURAL BIOLOGY (US/0163-1047). **5577**
BEHAVIORAL ASSESSMENT (US/0191-5401). **4576**
BEHAVIORAL ECOLOGY (US/1045-2249). **2211**
BEHAVIORAL ECOLOGY AND SOCIOBIOLOGY (GW/0340-5443). **2212**
BEHAVIORAL MEDICINE (WASHINGTON, D.C.) (US/0896-4289). **3555**
BEHAVIORAL NEUROSCIENCE (US/0735-7044). **4576**
BEHAVIORAL RESIDENTIAL TREATMENT (US/0884-5581). **3921**
BEHAVIORAL SCIENCE (US/0005-7940). **4576**
BEHAVIORAL SCIENCES & THE LAW (UK/0735-3936). **2940**
BEHAVIORAL SCIENCES NEWSLETTER (US/0361-4646). **4577**
BEHAVIOUR (NE/0005-7959). **443**
BEHAVIOUR & INFORMATION TECHNOLOGY (UK/0144-929X). **5087**
BEHAVIOUR CHANGE (AT/0813-4839). **4577**
BEHAVIOUR RESEARCH AND THERAPY (UK/0005-7967). **3921**
BEHAVIOURAL BRAIN RESEARCH (NE/0166-4328). **3828**
BEHAVIOURAL NEUROLOGY (UK/0953-4180). **3828**
BEHAVIOURAL PHARMACOLOGY (UK/0955-8810). **4293**
BEHAVIOURAL PROCESSES (NE/0376-6357). **5577**
BEHAVIOURAL PSYCHOTHERAPY (UK/0141-3473). **4577**
BEITRAEGE ZUR BIOLOGIE DER PFLANZEN (GW/0005-8041). **501**
BEITRAEGE ZUR INTENSIV- UND NOTFALLMEDIZIN (SZ/0254-8275). **3555**
BEITRAEGE ZUR ONKOLOGIE (SZ/0250-3220). **3809**
BEITRAEGE ZUR ORTHOPADIE UND TRAUMATOLOGIE (GW/0005-8149). **3555**
BEITRAEGE ZUR UROLOGIE (SZ/0250-3212). **3988**
BEITRAEGE ZUR VOGELKUNDE (GW/0005-8211). **5615**
BENEFITS LAW JOURNAL (US/0897-7992). **3144**
BENEFITS QUARTERLY (US/8756-1263). **1655**
BENEFITS TODAY (US/0747-9131). **2941**
BERICHTE DER BUNSENGESELLSCHAFT FUER PHYSIKALISCHE CHEMIE (GW/0005-9021). **1050**
BERICHTE GYNAKOLOGIE, GEBURTSHILFE (GW/0722-9852). **3757**
BERICHTE PATHOLOGIE (GW/0722-9674). **3893**
BERICHTE UBER LANDWIRTSCHAFT (GW/0005-9080). **65**
BERICHTE ZUR WISSENSCHAFTSGESCHICHTE (GW/0170-6233). **5088**
BERKELEY WOMEN'S LAW JOURNAL (US/0882-4312). **2941**
BERLINER UND MUNCHENER TIERARZTLICHE WOCHENSCHRIFT (GW/0005-9366). **5505**
BEST'S AGGREGATES & AVERAGES. PROPERTY-CASUALTY (US/0270-5974). **2875**

BEST'S INSURANCE REPORTS, PROPERTY-CASUALTY (US/0148-3218). **2876**
BEST'S KEY RATING GUIDE : PROPERTY-CASUALTY (US/0148-3064). **2876**
BEST'S REVIEW. (LIFE-HEALTH INSURANCE EDITION) (US/0005-9706). **2876**
BEST'S REVIEW (PROPERTY/CASUALTY INSURANCE ED.) (US/0161-7745). **2876**
BEST'S SAFETY DIRECTORY (US/0090-7480). **2859**
BETA RELEASE (CN/0710-0248). **3726**
BETON (GW/0005-9846). **600**
BETON- UND STAHLBETONBAU (GW/0005-9900). **601**
BETRIEB, DER (GW/0005-9935). **2941**
BETRIEB UND PERSONAL (GW/0341-1044). **939**
BETRIEBS-BERATER (GW/0340-7918). **4713**
BETRIEBSTECHNIK (GW/0409-2791). **1966**
BETRIEBSWIRTSCHAFT STUTTGART, DIE (GW/0342-7064). **643**
BETTER NUTRITION (US/0405-668X). **4187**
BEVERAGE WORLD (US/0098-2318). **2364**
BG, DIE (GW/0723-7561). **2876**
BHM. BERG- UND HUTTENMANNISCHE MONATSHEFTE (AU/0005-8912). **1966**
BIBLICAL THEOLOGY BULLETIN (US/0146-1079). **5015**
BIBLIOGRAPHIE DER PFLANZENSCHUTZLITERATUR (GW/0006-1387). **2434**
BIBLIOGRAPHIE DER WIRTSCHAFTSPRESSE (GW/0006-1417). **1530**
BIBLIOGRAPHIE INTERNATIONALE DE L'HUMANISME ET DE LA RENAISSANCE (SZ/0067-7000). **410**
BIBLIOGRAPHIE ZUR GESCHICHTE DER DEUTSCHEN ARBEITERBEWEGUNG (GW/0343-4117). **1530**
BIBLIOGRAPHY AND INDEX OF MICROPALEONTOLOGY (US/0300-7227). **4231**
BIBLIOGRAPHY OF EDUCATION THESES IN AUSTRALIA (AT/0811-0174). **1793**
BIBLIOGRAPHY OF REPRODUCTION (UK/0006-1565). **477**
BIBLIOTHECA ANATOMICA (SZ/0067-7833). **3679**
BIBLIOTHECA BOTANICA (GW/0067-7892). **502**
BIBLIOTHECA CARDIOLOGICA (SZ/0067-7906). **3699**
BIBLIOTHECA HELVETICA ROMANA (SZ/0067-7965). **1074**
BIBLIOTHECA NUTRITIO ET DIETA (SZ/0067-8198). **4188**
BIBLIOTHECA PSYCHIATRICA (SZ/0067-8147). **3921**
BIBLIOTHEK (GW/0341-4183). **3195**
BIBLIOTHEKSFORUM BAYERN (GW/0340-000X). **3195**
BIBLIOTHEQUE D'HUMANISME ET RENAISSANCE (SZ/0006-1999). **2611**
BIBLISCHE ZEITSCHRIFT (GW/0006-2014). **5015**
BICYCLING (US/0006-2073). **428**
BILANS POLITIQUES ECONOMIQUES ET SOCIAUX HEBDOMADAIRES (FR/0755-2238). **643**

BILD DER WISSENSCHAFT (GW/0006-2375). **5088**
BILDUNG UND ERZIEHUNG (GW/0006-2456). **1728**
BILLBOARD (CINCINNATI, OHIO. 1963) (US/0006-2510). **4103**
BILLBOARD [MICROFORM] (US/0006-2510). **5362**
BINDEREPORT (GW/0342-3573). **4824**
BIO-INPHARMA (NZ/0113-1060). **3686**
BIO / LA LETTRE DES BIOTECHNOLOGIES (FR/0291-2430). **444**
BIO SYSTEMS (IE/0303-2647). **444**
BIO/TECHNOLOGY (NEW YORK, N.Y. 1983) (US/0733-222X). **5088**
BIOCATALYSIS (SZ/0886-4454). **480**
BIOCHEMICAL AND BIOPHYSICAL RESEARCH COMMUNICATIONS (US/0006-291X). **481**
BIOCHEMICAL ARCHIVES (US/0749-5331). **481**
BIOCHEMICAL EDUCATION (UK/0307-4412). **481**
BIOCHEMICAL GENETICS (US/0006-2928). **543**
BIOCHEMICAL JOURNAL (LONDON. 1984) (UK/0264-6021). **481**
BIOCHEMICAL MEDICINE AND METABOLIC BIOLOGY (US/0885-4505). **3556**
BIOCHEMICAL PHARMACOLOGY (UK/0006-2952). **4293**
BIOCHEMICAL SOCIETY SYMPOSIA (UK/0067-8694). **481**
BIOCHEMICAL SOCIETY TRANSACTIONS (UK/0300-5127). **481**
BIOCHEMICAL SYSTEMATICS AND ECOLOGY (UK/0305-1978). **481**
BIOCHEMIE UND PHYSIOLOGIE DER PFLANZEN (GW/0015-3796). **502**
BIOCHEMISTRY AND CELL BIOLOGY (CN/0829-8211). **481**
BIOCHEMISTRY (EASTON) (US/0006-2960). **482**
BIOCHEMISTRY (NEW YORK) (US/0006-2979). **482**
BIOCHIMICA ET BIOPHYSICA ACTA (NE/0006-3002). **482**
BIOCHIMICA ET BIOPHYSICA ACTA. BIOENERGETICS (NE/0005-2728). **962**
BIOCHIMICA ET BIOPHYSICA ACTA. BIOMEMBRANES (NE/0005-2736). **482**
BIOCHIMICA ET BIOPHYSICA ACTA (BR) - REVIEWS ON BIOENERGETICS (NE/0304-4173). **444**
BIOCHIMICA ET BIOPHYSICA ACTA (G) (NE/0304-4165). **482**
BIOCHIMICA ET BIOPHYSICA ACTA. GENE STRUCTURE AND EXPRESSION (NE/0167-4781). **543**
BIOCHIMICA ET BIOPHYSICA ACTA. LIPIDS AND LIPID METABOLISM (NE/0005-2760). **962**
BIOCHIMICA ET BIOPHYSICA ACTA. MOLECULAR BASIS OF DISEASE (NE/0925-4439). **482**
BIOCHIMICA ET BIOPHYSICA ACTA. MOLECULAR CELL RESEARCH (NE/0167-4889). **532**
BIOCHIMICA ET BIOPHYSICA ACTA (MR). REVIEWS ON BIOMEMBRANES (NE/0304-4157). **962**
BIOCHIMICA ET BIOPHYSICA ACTA. PROTEIN STRUCTURE AND MOLECULAR ENZYMOLOGY (NE/0167-4838). **482**
BIOCHIMIE (FR/0300-9084). **483**
BIOCHROMATOGRAPHY (US/0888-4404). **483**
BIOCONJUGATE CHEMISTRY (US/1043-1802). **483**

BIOCONTROL — Copyright Clearance Center Index

BIOCONTROL SCIENCE & TECHNOLOGY (UK/0958-3157). **164**

BIOCYCLE (US/0276-5055). **2225**

BIODEGRADATION (DORDRECHT) (NE/0923-9820). **2225**

BIOELECTROCHEMISTRY AND BIOENERGETICS (SZ/0302-4598). **2036**

BIOELECTROMAGNETICS (US/0197-8462). **3556**

BIOETHICS (UK/0269-9702). **3556**

BIOFACTORS (OXFORD) (UK/0951-6433). **483**

BIOFEEDBACK AND SELF-REGULATION (US/0363-3586). **4577**

BIOFIZIKA (RU/0006-3029). **494**

BIOFOULING (CHUR, SWITZERLAND) (SZ/0892-7014). **444**

BIOFUTUR (FR/0294-3506). **3686**

BIOGENIC AMINES (UK/0168-8561). **483**

BIOGEOCHEMISTRY (NE/0168-2563). **2188**

BIOGRAPHICAL MEMOIRS (US/0077-2933). **430**

BIOHIMIJA (MOSKVA) (RU/0320-9725). **483**

BIOLOGIA (LAHORE) (PK/0006-3096). **444**

BIOLOGIA PLANTARUM (XR/0006-3134). **502**

BIOLOGICAL AGRICULTURE & HORTICULTURE (UK/0144-8765). **66**

BIOLOGICAL & PHARMACEUTICAL BULLETIN (JA/0918-6158). **4293**

BIOLOGICAL CHEMISTRY HOPPE-SEYLER (GW/0177-3593). **483**

BIOLOGICAL CONSERVATION (UK/0006-3207). **2188**

BIOLOGICAL CONTROL (US/1049-9644). **4244**

BIOLOGICAL CYBERNETICS (GW/0340-1200). **1250**

BIOLOGICAL JOURNAL OF THE LINNEAN SOCIETY (UK/0024-4066). **445**

BIOLOGICAL MASS SPECTROMETRY (UK/1052-9306). **1013**

BIOLOGICAL MEMBRANES (NEW YORK, N.Y. : 1985) (US/0748-8653). **445**

BIOLOGICAL PSYCHIATRY (1969) (US/0006-3223). **3921**

BIOLOGICAL PSYCHOLOGY (NE/0301-0511). **4577**

BIOLOGICAL REVIEWS OF THE CAMBRIDGE PHILOSOPHICAL SOCIETY (UK/0006-3231). **445**

BIOLOGICAL RHYTHMS (UK/0142-8004). **578**

BIOLOGICAL THERAPIES IN DENTISTRY (US/0882-1852). **1317**

BIOLOGICAL TRACE ELEMENT RESEARCH (US/0163-4984). **483**

BIOLOGICALS (UK/1045-1056). **445**

BIOLOGICHESKIE MEMBRANY (RU/0233-4755). **446**

BIOLOGIE IN UNSERER ZEIT (GW/0045-205X). **446**

BIOLOGISCHES ZENTRALBLATT (GW/0006-3304). **446**

BIOLOGY AND FERTILITY OF SOILS (GW/0178-2762). **164**

BIOLOGY & PHILOSOPHY (NE/0169-3867). **446**

BIOLOGY BULLETIN OF THE RUSSIAN ACADEMY OF SCIENCES (US/1062-3590). **446**

BIOLOGY OF REPRODUCTION (US/0006-3363). **578**

BIOLOGY OF THE CELL (FR/0248-4900). **532**

BIOLOGY OF THE NEONATE (SZ/0006-3126). **3900**

BIOMASS & BIOENERGY (UK/0961-9534). **1933**

BIOMASS BULLETIN (UK/0262-7183). **1933**

BIOMATERIALS (UK/0142-9612). **3556**

BIOMATERIALS, ARTIFICIAL CELLS, AND IMMOBILIZATION BIOTECHNOLOGY (US/1055-7172). **3686**

BIOMEDICA BIOCHIMICA ACTA (GW/0232-766X). **447**

BIOMEDICAL AND ENVIRONMENTAL SCIENCES (US/0895-3988). **447**

BIOMEDICAL ENGINEERING (US/0006-3398). **3686**

BIOMEDICAL INSTRUMENTATION & TECHNOLOGY (US/0899-8205). **3687**

BIOMEDICAL MATERIALS (UK/0955-7717). **3556**

BIOMEDICAL PRODUCTS (US/0192-1266). **3687**

BIOMEDICAL SCIENCE AND TECHNOLOGY (US/1051-2020). **3687**

BIOMEDICAL SCIENCES INSTRUMENTATION (US/0067-8856). **3687**

BIOMEDICAL TECHNOLOGY INFORMATION SERVICE (US/0147-2682). **3687**

BIOMEDICINE & PHARMACOTHERAPY (FR/0753-3322). **3557**

BIOMEDIZINISCHE TECHNIK (GW/0013-5585). **3687**

BIOMETALS (US/0966-0844). **483**

BIOMETRICAL JOURNAL (GW/0323-3847). **3497**

BIOMETRICS (US/0006-341X). **5323**

BIOMIMETICS (NEW YORK, N.Y.) (US/1059-0153). **1966**

BIOORGANIC & MEDICINAL CHEMISTRY LETTERS (UK/0960-894X). **1039**

BIOORGANIC CHEMISTRY (US/0045-2068). **1039**

BIOORGANICHESKAIA KHIMIIA (RU/0132-3423). **1039**

BIOPHARM (EUGENE, OR.) (US/1040-8304). **4293**

BIOPHARMACEUTICS & DRUG DISPOSITION (UK/0142-2782). **4293**

BIOPHYSICAL CHEMISTRY (NE/0301-4622). **483**

BIOPHYSICAL JOURNAL (US/0006-3495). **494**

BIOPHYSICS (OXFORD) (UK/0006-3509). **494**

BIOPOLYMERS (US/0006-3525). **483**

BIOPROCESS ENGINEERING (BERLIN, WEST) (GW/0178-515X). **2008**

BIORESOURCE TECHOLOGY (UK/0960-8524). **2225**

BIORHEOLOGY (OXFORD) (UK/0006-355X). **447**

BIOSCIENCE (US/0006-3568). **448**

BIOSCIENCE, BIOTECHNOLOGY, AND BIOCHEMISTRY (JA/0916-8451). **3687**

BIOSCIENCE REPORTS (US/0144-8463). **532**

BIOSENSORS & BIOELECTRONICS (UK/0956-5663). **484**

BIOSEPARATION (NE/0923-179X). **3687**

BIOTECH FORUM EUROPE (GW/0938-7501). **3688**

BIOTECHNIC & HISTOCHEMISTRY (US/1052-0295). **532**

BIOTECHNIQUES (US/0736-6205). **3557**

BIOTECHNOLOGY ADVANCES (UK/0734-9750). **3688**

BIOTECHNOLOGY AND APPLIED BIOCHEMISTRY (US/0885-4513). **3688**

BIOTECHNOLOGY AND BIOENGINEERING (US/0006-3592). **3688**

BIOTECHNOLOGY & GENETIC ENGINEERING REVIEWS (UK/0264-8725). **3688**

BIOTECHNOLOGY DIRECTORY (NEW YORK, N.Y.), THE (US/1059-7352). **3689**

BIOTECHNOLOGY LETTERS (UK/0141-5492). **3689**

BIOTECHNOLOGY NEWS (US/0273-3226). **3689**

BIOTECHNOLOGY PROGRESS (US/8756-7938). **3689**

BIOTECHNOLOGY TECHNIQUES (UK/0951-208X). **3689**

BIOTECHNOLOGY THERAPEUTICS (US/0898-2848). **3690**

BIOTEKHNOLOGIIA (US/0890-734X). **3690**

BIOTHERAPY (DORDRECHT) (NE/0921-299X). **448**

BIOVENTURE VIEW (US/0892-1903). **448**

BIP. BULLETIN DE L'INDUSTRIE PETROLIERE (FR/0300-4554). **4252**

BIRD BEHAVIOUR (SI/0156-1383). **5615**

BIRD STUDY (UK/0006-3657). **5615**

BIRTH (BERKELEY, CALIF.) (US/0730-7659). **3757**

BIRTH DEFECTS ORIGINAL ARTICLE SERIES (US/0547-6844). **3757**

BJULLETEN MOSKOVSKOGO OBSCESTVA ISPYTATELEJ PRIRODY. OTDEL GEOLOGICESKIJ (RU/0366-1318). **1367**

BLACK ENTERPRISE (US/0006-4165). **643**

BLATTER FUER DEUTSCHE UND INTERNATIONALE POLITIK (GW/0006-4416). **2611**

BLOOD (US/0006-4971). **3770**

BLOOD COAGULATION & FIBRINOLYSIS : AN INTERNATIONAL JOURNAL IN HAEMOSTASIS AND THROMBOSIS (UK/0957-5235). **3795**

BLOOD COAGULATION FACTORS (UK/0266-6294). **449**

BLOOD PURIFICATION (SZ/0253-5068). **3770**

BLOOD REVIEWS (UK/0268-960X). **3770**

BLOOD WEEKLY (US/1065-6073). **3770**

BLUE CHIP ECONOMIC INDICATORS (US/0193-4600). **1548**

BLUE CHIP FINANCIAL FORECASTS (US/0741-8345). **779**

BLUE SHEET, THE (US/0162-3605). **4294**

BLYTTIA (NO/0006-5269). **502**

BMC. BIOMEDICAL CHROMATOGRAPHY (UK/0269-3879). **449**

BMJ. BRITISH MEDICAL JOURNAL (CLINICAL RESEARCH ED.) (UK/0959-8138). **3557**

BMJ. BRITISH MEDICAL JOURNAL (INTERNATIONAL ED.) (UK/0959-8146). **3557**

BMR JOURNAL OF AUSTRALIAN GEOLOGY AND GEOPHYSICS (AT/0312-9608). **1367**

BNA CALIFORNIA EMPLOYEE RELATIONS REPORT (US/1058-7373). **1655**

BNA CALIFORNIA ENVIRONMENT REPORTER (US/1052-813X). **3110**

BNA CALIFORNIA SAFETY & HEALTH REPORT (US/1065-3104). **4768**

BNA CRIMINAL PRACTICE MANUAL. CURRENT REPORTS (US/0889-9312). **2942**

BNA ONLINE (US/0747-5438). **1274**

BNA PENSION REPORTER (US/0095-7100). **1656**

BNA'S AMERICANS WITH DISABILITIES ACT MANUAL. NEWSLETTER (US/1063-3111). **4384**

BNA'S BANKING REPORT (US/0891-0634). **3085**

BNA'S BANKRUPTCY LAW REPORTER (US/1044-7474). **3085**

BNA'S EASTERN EUROPE REPORTER (US/1058-7365). **892**

BNA'S HEALTH CARE ELECTRONIC DATA REPORT (US/1068-3798). **3557**

BNA'S HEALTH CARE POLICY REPORT (US/1068-1213). **3557**

BNA'S HEALTH LAW REPORTER (US/1064-2137). **2942**

BNA'S MEDICARE REPORT (US/1049-7986). **5275**

BNA'S NATIONAL ENVIRONMENT WATCH (US/1049-8893). **2162**

BNA'S PATENT, TRADEMARK & COPYRIGHT JOURNAL (US/0148-7965). **1301**

BNA'S STATE ENVIRONMENT & SAFETY REGULATORY MONITORING REPORT (US/1065-8076). **2162**

BNA'S WORKERS' COMPENSATION REPORT (US/1051-4775). **1656**

BOATING INDUSTRY, THE (US/0006-5404). **592**

BOBINA, LA (US/0194-7249). **1082**

BODY BULLETIN (US/0275-9101). **2596**

BODY FASHIONS/INTIMATE APPAREL (US/0360-3520). **1082**

BOHEMIA (MUNCHEN) (GW/0523-8587). **2678**

BOK OG BIBLIOTEK (NO/0006-5811). **3257**

BOKIN BOBAI : NIHON BOKIN BOBAI GAKKAI SHI (JA/0385-5201). **4294**

BOLETIM TECNICO DA PETROBRAS (BL/0006-6117). **4252**

BOLETIN DE LA SOCIEDAD ESPANOLA DE CERAMICA Y VIDRIO (1983) (SP/0366-3175). **2586**

BOLETIN DE LIMA (PE/0253-0015). **5193**

BOLETIN GEOLOGICO Y MINERO (SP/0366-0176). **1367**

BOND BUYER (NEW YORK, N.Y. 1982), THE (US/0732-0469). **892**

BONE AND MINERAL (NE/0169-6009). **3726**

BONE MARROW TRANSPLANTATION (BASINGSTOKE) (UK/0268-3369). **3558**

BONE (NEW YORK, N.Y.) (US/8756-3282). **3803**

BOOK INDUSTRY TRENDS (US/0160-970X). **4824**

BOOK MARKETING UPDATE (US/0891-8813). **4824**

BOOK OF PAPERS - AMERICAN ASSOCIATION OF TEXTILE CHEMISTS AND COLORISTS. INTERNATIONAL CONFERENCE & EXHIBITION (US/0892-2713). **5348**

BOOKLIST (CHICAGO, ILL. 1969) (US/0006-7385). **3196**

BOOKS IN PRINT (NEW YORK) (US/0068-0214). **411**

BOOKS IN PRINT SUPPLEMENT (US/0000-0310). **411**

BOOKSELLER (LONDON) (UK/0006-7539). **4821**

BOREAS (NO/0300-9483). **1368**

BOTANICA HELVETICA (SZ/0253-1453). **503**

BOTANICA MARINA (GW/0006-8055). **503**

BOTANICAL REVIEW, THE (US/0006-8101). **503**

BOTANICESKIJ ZURNAL (RU/0006-8136). **503**

BOTANISCHE JAHRBUCHER FUER SYSTEMATIK, PFLANZENGESCHICHTE UND PFLANZENGEOGRAPHIE (GW/0006-8152). **503**

BOUNDARY-LAYER METEOROLOGY (NE/0006-8314). **1421**

BOWKER ANNUAL OF LIBRARY AND BOOK TRADE INFORMATION, THE (US/0068-0540). **3197**

BOXBOARD CONTAINERS (US/0006-8497). **4218**

BOXES AND ARROWS (US/0742-4574). **1253**

BP REPORT ON THE BUSINESS OF BOOK PUBLISHING (US/0145-9457). **4827**

BP&R BRITISH PLASTICS AND RUBBER (UK/0307-6164). **4454**

BRAIN (UK/0006-8950). **3828**

BRAIN AND COGNITION (US/0278-2626). **4577**

BRAIN & DEVELOPMENT (TOKYO. 1979) (JA/0387-7604). **3828**

BRAIN AND LANGUAGE (US/0093-934X). **3828**

BRAIN, BEHAVIOR AND EVOLUTION (SZ/0006-8977). **3828**

BRAIN, BEHAVIOR, AND IMMUNITY (US/0889-1591). **3828**

BRAIN DYSFUNCTION (SZ/0259-1278). **3828**

BRAIN INJURY (UK/0269-9052). **3828**

BRAIN RESEARCH (NE/0006-8993). **3829**

BRAIN RESEARCH BULLETIN (US/0361-9230). **3829**

BRAIN TOPOGRAPHY (US/0896-0267). **3829**

BRANCH BANKER'S REPORT (US/0162-7481). **780**

BRANDHILFE (GW/0006-906X). **2288**

BRANDWEEK (NEW YORK, N.Y.) (US/1064-4318). **756**

BRAUNKOHLE (DUSSELDORF. 1972) (GW/0341-1060). **1934**

BRAUWELT (1978) (GW/0724-696X). **2329**

BRAZIL SERVICE (US/0889-1761). **1465**

BRAZILIAN JOURNAL OF MEDICAL AND BIOLOGICAL RESEARCH (BL/0100-879X). **3558**

BREAST CANCER RESEARCH AND TREATMENT (NE/0167-6806). **3809**

BREAST DISEASE (US/0888-6008). **3558**

BRENNSTOFF-WAERME-KRAFT (GW/0006-9612). **1934**

BRITAIN (UK/0068-1075). **2514**

BRITISH ACCOUNTING REVIEW, THE (UK/0890-8389). **740**

BRITISH AID STATISTICS (UK/0068-1210). **5323**

BRITISH BAKER (UK/0007-0300). **2329**

BRITISH BIRDS (UK/0007-0335). **5616**

BRITISH COLUMBIA MEDICAL JOURNAL (CN/0007-0556). **3558**

BRITISH DEFENCE DIRECTORY (UK/0272-4782). **4038**

BRITISH EDUCATIONAL RESEARCH JOURNAL (UK/0141-1926). **1728**

BRITISH HEART JOURNAL (UK/0007-0769). **3699**

BRITISH JOURNAL FOR THE HISTORY OF SCIENCE, THE (UK/0007-0874). **5089**

BRITISH JOURNAL FOR THE PHILOSOPHY OF SCIENCE, THE (UK/0007-0882). **5089**

BRITISH JOURNAL OF ADDICTION (UK/0952-0481). **1341**

BRITISH JOURNAL OF AESTHETICS (UK/0007-0904). **344**

BRITISH JOURNAL OF ANAESTHESIA (UK/0007-0912). **3682**

BRITISH JOURNAL OF AUDIOLOGY (UK/0300-5364). **3887**

BRITISH JOURNAL OF BIOMEDICAL SCIENCE (UK/0967-4845). **3690**

BRITISH JOURNAL OF CANCER (UK/0007-0920). **3809**

BRITISH JOURNAL OF CLINICAL PHARMACOLOGY (UK/0306-5251). **4294**

BRITISH JOURNAL OF CLINICAL PSYCHOLOGY, THE (UK/0144-6657). **4578**

BRITISH JOURNAL OF CRIMINOLOGY, DELINQUENCY AND DEVIANT SOCIAL BEHAVIOR, THE (UK/0007-0955). **3158**

BRITISH JOURNAL OF DERMATOLOGY (1951) (UK/0007-0963). **3718**

BRITISH JOURNAL OF DERMATOLOGY. SUPPLEMENT (UK/0366-077X). **3718**

BRITISH JOURNAL OF DEVELOPMENTAL PSYCHOLOGY, THE (UK/0261-510X). **4578**

BRITISH JOURNAL OF EDUCATIONAL PSYCHOLOGY, THE (UK/0007-0998). **4578**

BRITISH JOURNAL OF EDUCATIONAL STUDIES (UK/0007-1005). **1728**

BRITISH JOURNAL OF HAEMATOLOGY (UK/0007-1048). **3771**

BRITISH JOURNAL OF INDUSTRIAL MEDICINE (UK/0007-1072). **2859**

BRITISH JOURNAL OF INDUSTRIAL RELATIONS (UK/0007-1080). **1656**

BRITISH JOURNAL OF MATHEMATICAL & STATISTICAL PSYCHOLOGY, THE (UK/0007-1102). **4622**

BRITISH JOURNAL OF MEDICAL PSYCHOLOGY (UK/0007-1129). **4578**

BRITISH JOURNAL OF MUSIC EDUCATION : BJME (UK/0265-0517). **4105**

BRITISH JOURNAL OF NEUROSURGERY (UK/0268-8697). **3829**

BRITISH JOURNAL OF NUTRITION, THE (UK/0007-1145). **4188**

BRITISH JOURNAL OF OBSTETRICS AND GYNAECOLOGY (UK/0306-5456). **3758**

BRITISH JOURNAL OF OPHTHALMOLOGY (UK/0007-1161). **3872**

BRITISH JOURNAL OF ORAL & MAXILLOFACIAL SURGERY, THE (UK/0266-4356). **3961**

BRITISH JOURNAL OF ORTHODONTICS (UK/0301-228X). **1317**

BRITISH JOURNAL OF PHARMACOLOGY (UK/0007-1188). **4294**

BRITISH JOURNAL OF PLASTIC SURGERY (UK/0007-1226). **3961**

BRITISH JOURNAL OF POLITICAL SCIENCE (UK/0007-1234). **4466**

BRITISH JOURNAL OF PSYCHIATRY, THE (UK/0007-1250). **3922**

BRITISH JOURNAL OF PSYCHOLOGY (1955) (UK/0007-1269). **4578**

BRITISH JOURNAL OF RHEUMATOLOGY (UK/0263-7103). **3803**

BRITISH JOURNAL OF SOCIAL PSYCHOLOGY, THE (UK/0144-6665). **4578**

BRITISH JOURNAL OF SOCIAL WORK, THE (UK/0045-3102). **5275**

BRITISH JOURNAL OF SOCIOLOGY OF EDUCATION (UK/0142-5692). **5241**

BRITISH JOURNAL OF SOCIOLOGY, THE (UK/0007-1315). **5240**

BRITISH JOURNAL OF SPECIAL EDUCATION (UK/0952-3383). **1876**

BRITISH JOURNAL OF SPORTS MEDICINE (UK/0306-3674). **3953**

BRITISH JOURNAL OF SURGERY (UK/0007-1323). **3961**

BRITISH JOURNAL OF UROLOGY (UK/0007-1331). **3988**

BRITISH MEDICAL BULLETIN (UK/0007-1420). **3559**

BRITISH MEDICINE (LONDON : 1972) (UK/0140-2722). **3559**

BRITISH PHYCOLOGICAL JOURNAL (UK/0007-1617). **504**

BRITISH POULTRY SCIENCE (UK/0007-1668). **207**

BRITISH VETERINARY JOURNAL, THE (UK/0007-1935). **5506**

BRITTONIA (US/0007-196X). **504**

BROADBAND NETWORKING NEWS (US/1059-0544). **1127**

BROADCAST ENGINEERING (OVERLAND PARK) (US/0007-1994). **1127**

BROADCASTING & CABLE (US/1068-6827). **1128**

BROADCASTING (WASHINGTON, D.C. 1957) (US/0007-2028). **1128**

BROILER INDUSTRY (US/0007-2176). **207**

BROOKINGS PAPERS ON ECONOMIC ACTIVITY (US/0007-2303). **1465**

BROOKINGS REVIEW, THE (US/0745-1253). **5193**

BROWN UNIVERSITY DIGEST OF ADDICTION THEORY AND APPLICATION (US/1040-6328). **1341**

BROWN UNIVERSITY FAMILY THERAPY LETTER, THE (US/1045-5051). **2277**

BROWN UNIVERSITY LONG-TERM CARE LETTER, THE (US/1042-1386). **4769**

BROWN'S DIRECTORY OF NORTH AMERICAN AND INTERNATIONAL GAS COMPANIES (US/0197-8098). **4252**

BRYOLOGIST, THE (US/0007-2745). **504**

BUILDER/DEALER (US/0892-824X). **602**

BUILDING AND ENVIRONMENT (UK/0360-1323). **602**

BUILDING DESIGN & CONSTRUCTION (US/0007-3407). **294**

BUILDING SUPPLY & HOME CENTERS (US/0890-9008). **604**

BUILDINGS (CEDAR RAPIDS. 1947) (US/0007-3725). **605**

BUILT ENVIRONMENT (LONDON, 1978) (UK/0263-7960). **2816**

BULGARIAN JOURNAL OF PHYSICS (BU/0323-9217). **4398**

BULLETIN - AMERICAN LUNG ASSOCIATION (US/0092-5659). **3948**

BULLETIN ANALYTIQUE DE DOCUMENTATION POLITIQUE, ECONOMIQUE ET SOCIALE CONTEMPORAINE / FONDATION NATIONAL DES SCIENCES POLITIQUES (FR/0007-4071). **5193**

BULLETIN - CANADIAN BOTANICAL ASSOCIATION (CN/0008-3046). **504**

BULLETIN DE LA SOCIETE CHIMIQUE DE FRANCE (PARIS, FRANCE : 1985) (FR/0037-8968). **963**

BULLETIN DE LA SOCIETE GEOLOGIQUE DE FRANCE (FR/0037-9409). **1368**

BULLETIN DE LA SOCIETE MATHEMATIQUE DE FRANCE (FR/0037-9484). **3497**

BULLETIN DE L'ACADEMIE NATIONALE DE MEDICINE (FR/0001-4079). **3559**

BULLETIN DE L'INSTITUT PASTEUR (FR/0020-2452). **3667**

BULLETIN DES CENTRES DE RECHERCHES EXPLORATION-PRODUCTION ELF-AQUITAINE (FR/0396-2687). **1369**

BULLETIN DES SCIENCES MATHEMATIQUES (FR/0007-4497). **3498**

BULLETIN DES SOCIETES CHIMIQUES BELGES (BE/0037-9646). **963**

BULLETIN DU CANCER (FR/0007-4551). **3810**

BULLETIN GEODESIQUE (FR/0007-4632). **1403**

BULLETIN / HOSPITAL FOR JOINT DISEASES (US/0018-5647). **3804**

BULLETIN / HUMAN FACTORS AND ERGONOMICS SOCIETY (US/0438-1629). **1250**

BULLETIN - HUMAN FACTORS SOCIETY (US/0438-1629). **1250**

BULLETIN (NEW SERIES) OF THE AMERICAN MATHEMATICAL SOCIETY (US/0273-0979). **3498**

BULLETIN / NORGES GEOLOGISKE UNDERSKELSE (NO/0332-5768). **1352**

BULLETIN OEPP (FR/0250-8052). **165**

BULLETIN OF CANADIAN PETROLEUM GEOLOGY (CN/0007-4802). **4252**

BULLETIN OF ECONOMIC RESEARCH (UK/0307-3378). **1590**

BULLETIN OF ELECTROCHEMISTRY (II/0256-1654). **1034**

BULLETIN OF ENVIRONMENTAL CONTAMINATION AND TOXICOLOGY (US/0007-4861). **3979**

BULLETIN OF EXPERIMENTAL BIOLOGY AND MEDICINE (US/0007-4888). **3560**

BULLETIN OF HISPANIC STUDIES (UK/0007-490X). **3271**

BULLETIN OF LATIN AMERICAN RESEARCH (UK/0261-3050). **2725**

BULLETIN OF MATHEMATICAL BIOLOGY (US/0092-8240). **450**

BULLETIN OF SCIENCE, TECHNOLOGY & SOCIETY (US/0270-4676). **5091**

BULLETIN OF THE AMERICAN METEOROLOGICAL SOCIETY (US/0003-0007). **1421**

BULLETIN OF THE AMERICAN PHYSICAL SOCIETY (US/0003-0503). **4399**

BULLETIN OF THE AMERICAN SOCIETY FOR INFORMATION SCIENCE (US/0095-4403). **3198**

BULLETIN OF THE ATOMIC SCIENTISTS (US/0096-3402). **5091**

BULLETIN OF THE AUSTRALIAN MATHEMATICAL SOCIETY (AT/0004-9727). **3498**

BULLETIN OF THE CENTER FOR CHILDREN'S BOOKS (US/0008-9036). **3370**

BULLETIN OF THE CHEMICAL SOCIETY OF JAPAN (JA/0009-2673). **963**

BULLETIN OF THE HISTORY OF MEDICINE (US/0007-5140). **3560**

BULLETIN OF THE INTERNATIONAL CENTRE FOR HEAT AND MASS TRANSFER (US/0888-6911). **2111**

BULLETIN OF THE LEBEDEV PHYSICS INSTITUTE (US/1068-3356). **4399**

BULLETIN OF THE MENNINGER CLINIC (US/0025-9284). **3922**

BULLETIN OF THE NEW ZEALAND NATIONAL SOCIETY FOR EARTHQUAKE ENGINEERING (NZ/0110-0718). **2019**

BULLETIN OF THE PSYCHONOMIC SOCIETY (US/0090-5054). **4579**

BULLETIN OF THE RUSSIAN ACADEMY OF SCIENCES, DIVISION OF CHEMICAL SCIENCE (US/1063-5211). **963**

BULLETIN OF THE RUSSIAN ACADEMY OF SCIENCES. PHYSICS (US/1062-8738). **4399**

BULLETIN OF THE SCHOOL OF ORIENTAL AND AFRICAN STUDIES (UK/0041-977X). **3271**

BULLETIN OF THE SOCIETY FOR AMERICAN ARCHAEOLOGY (US/0741-5672). **264**

BULLETIN OF THE TORREY BOTANICAL CLUB, THE (US/0040-9618). **505**

BULLETIN OF VOLCANOLOGY (GW/0258-8900). **1403**

BULLETIN ON THE RHEUMATIC DISEASES (US/0007-5248). **3804**

BULLETIN ON TRAINING (US/0272-8486). **939**

BULLETIN - RESERVE BANK OF NEW ZEALAND (NZ/0034-5539). **781**

BULLETIN - ROYAL SOCIETY OF NEW ZEALAND (NZ/0370-6559). **5091**

BULLETIN TO MANAGEMENT (US/0525-2156). **939**

BUNDESARBEITSBLATT (GW/0007-5868). **1657**

BUNDESBAHN, DIE (GW/0007-5876). **5430**

BUNSEKI KAGAKU (JA/0525-1931). **1014**

BURNS : JOURNAL OF THE INTERNATIONAL SOCIETY FOR BURN INJURIES (UK/0305-4179). **3561**

BUSES SHEPPERTON (UK/0007-6392). **5378**

BUSINESS AND HEALTH (US/0739-9413). **645**

BUSINESS AND THE ENVIRONMENT (US/1052-7206). **2162**

BUSINESS ATLANTA (US/0192-0855). **646**

BUSINESS COMMUNICATIONS REVIEW (US/0162-3885). **646**

BUSINESS ECONOMICS (CLEVELAND, OHIO) (US/0007-666X). **1466**

BUSINESS ETHICS: A EUROPEAN REVIEW (UK/0962-8770). **2249**

BUSINESS FORUM (LOS ANGELES, CALIF.) (US/0733-2408). **648**

BUSINESS INFORMATION ALERT (US/1042-0746). **3199**

BUSINESS INSURANCE (US/0007-6864). **2877**

BUSINESS LIBRARY REVIEW (US/1045-7798). **650**

BUSINESS MARKETING (US/0745-5933). **922**

BUSINESS OPPORTUNITIES IN EASTERN EUROPE (US/1051-0273). **651**

BUSINESS PUBLISHING (CAROL STREAM, ILL.) (US/1060-2208). **4812**

BUSINESS QUARTERLY, THE (CN/0007-6996). **652**

BUSINESS STRATEGY REVIEW (UK/0955-6419). **653**

BUSINESS TRAVEL NEWS (US/8750-3670). **653**

BUSINESS VISUALIZATION (US/1056-7852). **1172**

BUSINESS WEEK (US/0007-7135). **653**

BUSINESS WEEK (INDUSTRIAL ED.) (US/0739-8395). **653**

BUSKAP OG AVDRATT (NO/0007-7194). **208**

BUTTERWORTHS CURRENT LAW (NZ/0110-070X). **3125**

BUTTERWORTHS JOURNAL OF INTERNATIONAL BANKING AND FINANCIAL LAW (UK/0269-2694). **3086**

BUYING STRATEGY FORECAST FOR PURCHASING MANAGERS (US/0733-0103). **949**

BUYOUTS (WELLESLEY HILLS, MASS.) (US/1040-0990). **654**

BYGGEKUNST (NO/0007-7518). **294**

BYTE (US/0360-5280). **1273**

BYZANTINISCHE ZEITSCHRIFT (GW/0007-7704). **2682**

C/A/S/E OUTLOOK (US/0895-2108). **1172**

C++ REPORT, THE (US/1040-6042). **1278**

C1 MOLECULE CHEMISTRY (SZ/0275-7567). **1035**

C3I REPORT (US/0889-4728). **4038**

C4I NEWS (US/1071-1317). **1212**

CA MAGAZINE (CN/0317-6878). **740**

CADALYST (US/0820-5450). **1231**

CADENCE (AUSTIN, TEX.) (US/0887-9141). **1173**

CAHIERS D'ANESTHESIOLOGIE (FR/0007-9685). **3682**

CAHIERS DE L'ANALYSE DES DONNEES, LES (FR/0339-3097). **5324**

CAHIERS DE MICROPALEONTOLOGIE (FR/0068-5054). **4226**

CAHIERS DE NUTRITION ET DE DIETETIQUE (FR/0007-9960). **4188**

CAHIERS FERDINAND DE SAUSSURE (SZ/0068-516X). **3272**

CAHIERS INTERNATIONAUX DE SOCIOLOGIE (FR/0008-0276). **5241**

CAHIERS VILFREDO PARETO (SZ/0008-0497). **5194**

CALCIFIED TISSUE INTERNATIONAL (US/0171-967X). **578**

CALIFORNIA GEOLOGY (US/0026-4555). **1371**

CALIFORNIA LAW REVIEW (US/0008-1221). **2946**

CALIFORNIA MANAGEMENT REVIEW (US/0008-1256). **862**

CALIFORNIA PHYSICIAN (US/8750-1813). **3561**

CALIFORNIA SCHOOL LAW DIGEST (US/0094-2057). **2946**

CALLALOO (US/0161-2492). **3371**

CALPHAD (US/0364-5916). **1050**

CAMBRIDGE JOURNAL OF ECONOMICS (UK/0309-166X). **1467**

CAMBRIDGE JOURNAL OF EDUCATION (UK/0305-764X). **1890**

CAMBRIDGE QUARTERLY (UK/0008-199X). **3339**

CAMBRIDGE REPORT ON CORPORATE MERGERS AND CORPORATE POLICY, THE (US/0273-6357). **782**

CAMPAIGN (LONDON. 1968) (UK/0008-2309). **757**

CAMPAIGN PRACTICES REPORTS (US/0361-056X). **2947**

CAMPUS CRIME (US/1054-3821). **3159**

CANADIAN AERONAUTICS AND SPACE JOURNAL (CN/0008-2821). **15**

CANADIAN AGRICULTURAL ENGINEERING (CN/0045-432X). **158**

CANADIAN ASSOCIATION OF RADIOLOGISTS JOURNAL (CN/0846-5371). **3939**

CANADIAN BOOKSELLER (TORONTO) (CN/0225-2392). **4827**

CANADIAN BUSINESS (1977) (CN/0008-3100). **654**

CANADIAN BUSINESS REVIEW, THE (CN/0317-4026). **1467**

CANADIAN CHEMICAL NEWS (CN/0823-5228). **1021**

CANADIAN CONSULTING ENGINEER (CN/0008-3267). **1967**

CANADIAN CONSUMER (1963) (CN/0008-3275). **1294**

CANADIAN DATASYSTEMS (CN/0008-3364). **1256**

CANADIAN ENTOMOLOGIST, THE (CN/0008-347X). **5606**

CANADIAN ENVIRONMENTAL LAW REPORTS (CN/0707-7874). **3110**

CANADIAN ETHNIC STUDIES (CN/0008-3496). **2257**

CANADIAN FOREST INDUSTRIES (CN/0318-4277). **2399**

CANADIAN GEOGRAPHIC (CN/0706-2168). **2558**

CANADIAN GEOTECHNICAL JOURNAL (CN/0008-3674). **1352**

CANADIAN HISTORICAL REVIEW (CN/0008-3755). **2726**

CANADIAN HOME ECONOMICS JOURNAL (CN/0008-3763). **2789**

CANADIAN JOURNAL OF AFRICAN STUDIES (CN/0008-3968). **2638**

CANADIAN JOURNAL OF AGRICULTURAL ECONOMICS (CN/0008-3976). **72**

CANADIAN JOURNAL OF ANAESTHESIA (CN/0832-610X). **3682**

CANADIAN JOURNAL OF ANIMAL SCIENCE (CN/0008-3984). **208**

CANADIAN JOURNAL OF APPLIED PHYSIOLOGY (US/1066-7814). **579**

CANADIAN JOURNAL OF BEHAVIOURAL SCIENCE (CN/0008-400X). **4579**

CANADIAN JOURNAL OF BOTANY (CN/0008-4026). **505**

CANADIAN JOURNAL OF CHEMICAL ENGINEERING, THE (CN/0008-4034). **2008**

CANADIAN JOURNAL OF CHEMISTRY (CN/0008-4042). **966**

CANADIAN JOURNAL OF CIVIL ENGINEERING (CN/0315-1468). **2020**

CANADIAN JOURNAL OF COMMUNICATION (CN/0705-3657). **1105**

CANADIAN JOURNAL OF COUNSELLING (CN/0828-3893). **1876**

CANADIAN JOURNAL OF CRIMINOLOGY (CN/0704-9722). **3159**

CANADIAN JOURNAL OF DRAMA AND THEATRE, THE (CN/1183-1243). **5362**

CANADIAN JOURNAL OF EARTH SCIENCES (CN/0008-4077). **1353**

CANADIAN JOURNAL OF ECONOMICS, THE (CN/0008-4085). **1468**

CANADIAN JOURNAL OF EDUCATION (CN/0380-2361). **1730**

CANADIAN JOURNAL OF FISHERIES AND AQUATIC SCIENCES (CN/0706-652X). **2298**

CANADIAN JOURNAL OF FOREST RESEARCH (CN/0045-5067). **2377**

CANADIAN JOURNAL OF HIGHER EDUCATION (1975) (CN/0316-1218). **1814**

CANADIAN JOURNAL OF HISTORY OF SPORT (CN/0712-9815). **4889**

CANADIAN JOURNAL OF HOSPITAL PHARMACY (CN/0008-4123). **4295**

CANADIAN JOURNAL OF INFORMATION SCIENCE (CN/0380-9218). **3199**

CANADIAN JOURNAL OF MATHEMATICS (CN/0008-414X). **3499**

CANADIAN JOURNAL OF MICROBIOLOGY (CN/0008-4166). **560**

CANADIAN JOURNAL OF NEUROLOGICAL SCIENCES (CN/0317-1671). **3829**

CANADIAN JOURNAL OF OPHTHALMOLOGY (CN/0008-4182). **3873**

CANADIAN JOURNAL OF PHILOSOPHY (CN/0045-5091). **4343**

CANADIAN JOURNAL OF PHYSICS (CN/0008-4204). **4399**

CANADIAN JOURNAL OF PHYSIOLOGY AND PHARMACOLOGY (CN/0008-4212). **579**

CANADIAN JOURNAL OF PLANT PATHOLOGY (CN/0706-0661). **505**

CANADIAN JOURNAL OF PLANT SCIENCE (CN/0008-4220). **505**

CANADIAN JOURNAL OF POLITICAL SCIENCE (CN/0008-4239). **4467**

CANADIAN JOURNAL OF PSYCHIATRY (CN/0706-7437). **3923**

CANADIAN JOURNAL OF PSYCHOLOGY (CN/0008-4255). **4579**

CANADIAN JOURNAL OF PUBLIC HEALTH (US/0008-4263). **4770**

CANADIAN JOURNAL OF PUBLIC HEALTH (CN/0008-4263). **4770**

CANADIAN JOURNAL OF SOIL SCIENCE (US/0008-4271). **1371**

CANADIAN JOURNAL OF SOIL SCIENCE (CN/0008-4271). **166**

CANADIAN JOURNAL OF SPORT SCIENCES (US/0833-1235). **3953**

CANADIAN JOURNAL OF SURGERY (CN/0008-428X). **3961**

CANADIAN JOURNAL OF VETERINARY RESEARCH (CN/0830-9000). **5507**

CANADIAN JOURNAL OF ZOOLOGY (CN/0008-4301). **5580**

CANADIAN LIBRARY JOURNAL (CN/0008-4352). **3200**

CANADIAN MACHINERY AND METALWORKING (CN/0008-4379). **2111**

CANADIAN MATHEMATICAL BULLETIN (CN/0008-4395). **3499**

CANADIAN METALLURGICAL QUARTERLY (US/0008-4433). **3999**

CANADIAN METALLURGICAL QUARTERLY (CN/0008-4433). **3999**

CANADIAN MINERALOGIST, THE (CN/0008-4476). **1438**

CANADIAN MINING JOURNAL (CN/0008-4492). **2136**

CANADIAN MODERN LANGUAGE REVIEW, THE (CN/0008-4506). **3272**

CANADIAN NURSE (1924) (CN/0008-4581). **3852**

CANADIAN PLASTICS (CN/0008-4778). **4454**

CANADIAN PRINTER (CN/0849-0767). **4564**

CANADIAN PSYCHOLOGY (CN/0708-5591). **4579**

CANADIAN PUBLIC POLICY (CN/0317-0861). **1468**

CANADIAN REVIEW OF AMERICAN STUDIES (CN/0007-7720). **2530**

CANADIAN SOCIETY OF FORENSIC SCIENCE JOURNAL (CN/0008-5030). **3740**

CANADIAN TECHNICAL REPORT OF FISHERIES AND AQUATIC SCIENCES (CN/0706-6457). **2299**

CANADIAN THEATRE REVIEW (CN/0315-0836). **5362**

CANADIAN VETERINARY JOURNAL (CN/0008-5286). **5507**

CANADIAN WOMEN'S STUDIES (CN/0713-3235). **5553**

CANCER (US/0008-543X). **3810**

CANCER AND METASTASIS REVIEWS (NE/0167-7659). **3810**

CANCER BIOCHEMISTRY BIOPHYSICS (US/0305-7232). **3810**

CANCER CAUSES & CONTROL : CCC (UK/0957-5243). **3810**

CANCER CHEMOTHERAPY AND PHARMACOLOGY (GW/0344-5704). **3810**

CANCER DETECTION AND PREVENTION (US/0361-090X). **3811**

CANCER DETECTION AND PREVENTION. SUPPLEMENT (US/1043-6995). **3811**

CANCER GENETICS AND CYTOGENETICS (US/0165-4608). **3811**

CANCER IMMUNOLOGY AND IMMUNOTHERAPY (GW/0340-7004). **3811**

CANCER INVESTIGATION (US/0735-7907). **3811**

CANCER LETTERS (NE/0304-3835). **3811**

CANCER NURSING (US/0162-220X). **3853**

CANCER RESEARCH (BALTIMORE) (US/0008-5472). **3812**

CANCER RESEARCH, THERAPY & CONTROL (SZ/1064-0525). **3812**

CANCER SURVEYS (US/0261-2429). **3812**

CANCER THERAPY AND CONTROL (SZ/0896-5080). **3812**

CANCER THERAPY UPDATE (US/0924-6533). **3812**

CANCER TREATMENT REVIEWS (UK/0305-7372). **3812**

CANDY INDUSTRY (1982) (US/0745-1032). **2330**

CANDY MARKETER (1985) (US/0886-3741). **2330**

CANTERAS Y EXPLOTACIONES (SP/0008-5677). **2111**

CAPELL'S CIRCULATION REPORT (US/0736-9077). **4813**

CAPITAL ENERGY LETTER (US/0195-5292). **1935**

CAPITALISM, NATURE, SOCIALISM (US/1045-5752). **2212**

CAR MECHANICS (UK/0008-6037). **5409**

CARACTERE 1980 (FR/0247-039X). **4564**

CARBOHYDRATE CHEMISTRY (UK/0576-7172). **1040**

CARBOHYDRATE POLYMERS (UK/0144-8617). **1040**

CARBOHYDRATE RESEARCH (NE/0008-6215). **1040**

CARBON (NEW YORK) (US/0008-6223). **1035**

CARBONATES AND EVAPORITES (US/0891-2556). **1371**

CARCINOGENESIS. A COMPREHENSIVE SURVEY (US/0147-4006). **3814**

CARCINOGENESIS (NEW YORK) (US/0143-3334). **3814**

CARD NEWS (US/0894-0797). **782**

CARDIAC ALERT (US/0194-2557). **3700**

CARDIAC SURGERY (US/0887-9850). **3961**

CARDIO (US/0742-9622). **3700**

CARDIO-VASCULAR NURSING (US/0008-6355). **3853**

CARDIOLOGY (SZ/0008-6312). **3700**

CARDIOLOGY CLINICS (US/0733-8651). **3700**

CARDIOLOGY IN REVIEW (US/1061-5377). **3701**

CARDIOTHORACIC AND VASCULAR ANESTHESIA UPDATE (US/1046-1795). **3682**

CARDIOVASCULAR AND INTERVENTIONAL RADIOLOGY (US/0174-1551). **3939**

CARDIOVASCULAR CLINICS (US/0069-0384). **3701**

CARDIOVASCULAR DRUG REVIEWS (US/0897-5957). **3701**

CARDIOVASCULAR DRUGS AND THERAPY (US/0920-3206). **3701**

CARDIOVASCULAR PATHOLOGY (US/1054-8807). **3701**

CARDIOVASCULAR RESEARCH (UK/0008-6363). **3702**

CAREER DEVELOPMENT QUARTERLY, THE (US/0889-4019). **4201**

CARGONEWS ASIA (HK/0252-9610). **5379**

CARIBBEAN REVIEW (US/0008-6525). **4467**

CARIBBEAN UPDATE (US/8756-324X). **655**

CARIES RESEARCH (SZ/0008-6568). **1318**

CARLSONREPORT (US/0889-2288). **952**

CARNEGIE-ROCHESTER CONFERENCE SERIES ON PUBLIC POLICY (NE/0167-2231). **1468**

CARPET & RUG INDUSTRY (US/0192-4486). **2899**

CARTOGRAPHIC JOURNAL, THE (UK/0008-7041). **2581**

CARTOGRAPHICA (1980) (CN/0317-7173). **2581**

CASE INDUSTRY DIRECTORY (US/0898-5022). **1173**

CASE MANAGEMENT ADVISOR (US/1053-5500). **3778**

CASE STUDY - AMERICAN PRODUCTIVITY CENTER (US/0741-6423). **1601**

CASE TRENDS (US/1046-5944). **1227**

CASH FLOW ENHANCEMENT REPORT (US/1053-0347). **863**

CASOPIS LEKARU CESKYCH (XR/0008-7335). **3562**

CATALYSIS (UK/0140-0568). **1050**

CATALYSIS REVIEWS : SCIENCE AND ENGINEERING (US/0161-4940). **2009**

CATALYSIS TODAY (NE/0920-5861). **966**

CATALYSTS IN CHEMISTRY (UK/0309-5770). **967**

CATENA (GIESSEN) (GW/0341-8162). **166**

CATENA SUPPLEMENT (GW/0722-0723). **1353**

CATHETERIZATION AND CARDIOVASCULAR DIAGNOSIS (US/0098-6569). **3702**

CATHOLICA (MUNSTER) (GW/0008-8501). **5027**

CAVES & CAVING (UK/0142-1832). **1371**

CD COMPUTING NEWS (US/0893-4843). **1276**

CD-ROM LIBRARIAN (US/0893-9934). **1174**

CD-ROM PROFESSIONAL (US/1049-0833). **1276**

CD-ROM WORLD (US/1066-274X). **1276**

CD-ROMS IN PRINT (US/0891-8198). **1276**

CEE NEWS (US/1045-2710). **2038**

CELESTIAL MECHANICS AND DYNAMICAL ASTRONOMY (NE/0923-2958). **394**

CELL ADHESION AND COMMUNITATION (US/1061-5385). **532**

CELL AND TISSUE RESEARCH (GW/0302-766X). **533**

CELL BIOCHEMISTRY AND FUNCTION (UK/0263-6484). **484**

CELL BIOLOGY AND TOXICOLOGY (PRINCETON SCIENTIFIC PUBLISHERS) (NE/0742-2091). **533**

CELL BIOPHYSICS (US/0163-4992). **495**

CELL CALCIUM (EDINBURGH) (UK/0143-4160). **533**

CELL MEMBRANES (UK/0142-8047). **533**

CELL MOTILITY AND THE CYTOSKELETON (US/0886-1544). **533**

CELL PROLIFERATION (UK/0960-7722). **534**

CELL STRUCTURE AND FUNCTION (JA/0386-7196). **534**

CELL TRANSPLANTATION (US/0963-6897). **3795**

CELLS AND MATERIALS (US/1051-6794). **534**

CELLS AND MATERIALS. SUPPLEMENT (US/1060-9989). **534**

CELLULAR AND MOLECULAR BIOLOGY (UK/0145-5680). **534**

CELLULAR AND MOLECULAR NEUROBIOLOGY (US/0272-4340). **534**

CELLULAR BUSINESS (US/0741-6520). **1151**

CELLULAR IMMUNOLOGY (US/0008-8749). **3667**

CELLULAR MARKETING (US/0890-2402). **922**

CELLULAR PHYSIOLOGY AND BIOCHEMISTRY (SZ/1015-8987). **534**

CELLULAR SIGNALLING (UK/0898-6568). **534**

CEMENT & CONCRETE COMPOSITES (UK/0958-9465). **606**

CEMENT AND CONCRETE RESEARCH (US/0008-8846). **2020**

CEMENT, CONCRETE AND AGGREGATES (US/0149-6123). **606**

CEMENTS RESEARCH PROGRESS (US/0363-8642). **607**

CENTAURUS (DK/0008-8994). **5093**

CENTRAL ASIAN SURVEY (UK/0263-4937). **2648**

CENTRAL ASIATIC JOURNAL (GW/0008-9192). **2648**

CENTRAL OFFICE OF INFORMATION REFERENCE PAMPHLET (UK/0072-5722). **4637**

CEPAL REVIEW (CL/0251-2920). **1551**

CEPHALALGIA (NO/0333-1024). **3829**

CERAMIC ABSTRACTS (US/0095-9960). **2595**

CERAMIC ENGINEERING AND SCIENCE PROCEEDINGS (US/0196-6219). **2587**

CERAMIC SOURCE (US/8756-8187). **2587**

CERAMICS INTERNATIONAL (IT/0272-8842). **2588**

CEREAL CHEMISTRY (US/0009-0352). **1021**

CEREAL FOODS WORLD (US/0146-6283). **2331**

CEREBRAL CORTEX (NEW YORK, N.Y. 1991) (US/1047-3211). **3829**

CEREBROVASCULAR AND BRAIN METABOLISM REVIEWS (US/1040-8827). **3562**

CESKOSLOVENSKA DERMATOLOGIE (XR/0009-0514). **3718**

CESKOSLOVENSKA EPIDEMIOLOGIE, MIKROBIOLOGIE, IMUNOLOGIE (XR/0009-0522). **3734**

CESKOSLOVENSKA FARMACIE (XR/0009-0530). **4296**

CESKOSLOVENSKA GASTROENTEROLOGIA A VYZIVA (XR/0009-0565). **3795**

CESKOSLOVENSKA GYNAEKOLOGIE (XR/0374-6852). **3758**

CESKOSLOVENSKA HYGIENA (XR/0009-0573). **561**

CESKOSLOVENSKA NEUROLOGIE A NEUROCHIRURGIE (XR/0301-0597). **3829**

CESKOSLOVENSKA OFTALMOLOGIE (XR/0009-059X). **3873**

CESKOSLOVENSKA OTOLARYNGOLOGIE (XR/0009-0603). **3887**

CESKOSLOVENSKA PATOLOGIE (XR/0009-0611). **3893**

CESKOSLOVENSKA PEDIATRIE (XR/0069-2328). **3901**

CESKOSLOVENSKA PSYCHIATRIE (XR/0069-2336). **3923**

CESKOSLOVENSKA RADIOLOGIE (XR/0069-2344). **3939**

CESKOSLOVENSKA STOMATOLOGIE (XR/0009-0654). **1318**

CESKOSLOVENSKE ZDRAVOTNICTVI (CS/0009-0689). **4771**

CFTC ADMINISTRATIVE REPORTER (US/0745-8452). **826**

CHANCE (NEW YORK) (US/0933-2480). **3499**

CHANGE (NEW ROCHELLE, N.Y.) (US/0009-1383). **1814**

CHAOS, SOLITONS AND FRACTALS (UK/0960-0779). **3499**

CHAOS (WOODBURY, N.Y.) (US/1054-1500). **4399**

CHATELAINE (TORONTO, ONT.: 1928) (CN/0009-1995). **5553**

CHAUCER REVIEW, THE (US/0009-2002). **3339**

CHAUFFAGE, VENTILATION, CONDITIONNEMENT (FR/0009-2029). **2604**

CHECKS & CHECKING (US/1046-4956). **741**

CHEESE MARKET NEWS (US/0891-1509). **192**

CHEM INFORM (GW/0931-7597). **1011**

CHEMICA

CHEMICA SCRIPTA (SW/0004-2056). **967**

CHEMICAL ABSTRACTS SERVICE SOURCE INDEX (US/0001-0634). **1011**

CHEMICAL AGE OF INDIA (II/0009-2320). **968**

CHEMICAL & ENGINEERING NEWS (US/0009-2347). **1022**

CHEMICAL AND PETROLEUM ENGINEERING (US/0009-2355). **2009**

CHEMICAL & PHARMACEUTICAL BULLETIN (JA/0009-2363). **4296**

CHEMICAL BUSINESS (US/0731-8774). **968**

CHEMICAL DESIGN AUTOMATION NEWS (US/0886-6716). **968**

CHEMICAL ENGINEER (LONDON) (UK/0302-0797). **2009**

CHEMICAL ENGINEERING AND PROCESSING (SZ/0255-2701). **2009**

CHEMICAL ENGINEERING & TECHNOLOGY (GW/0930-7516). **2009**

CHEMICAL ENGINEERING CATALOG (US/0276-8429). **2009**

CHEMICAL ENGINEERING COMMUNICATIONS (US/0098-6445). **2009**

CHEMICAL ENGINEERING JOURNAL AND THE BIOCHEMICAL ENGINEERING JOURNAL, THE (SZ/0923-0467). **2010**

CHEMICAL ENGINEERING MONOGRAPHS (NE/0167-4188). **2010**

CHEMICAL ENGINEERING (NEW YORK) (US/0009-2460). **1034**

CHEMICAL ENGINEERING PROGRESS (US/0360-7275). **2010**

CHEMICAL ENGINEERING RESEARCH & DESIGN (UK/0263-8762). **2010**

CHEMICAL ENGINEERING SCIENCE (UK/0009-2509). **2010**

CHEMICAL EQUIPMENT (US/0009-2525). **968**

CHEMICAL GEOLOGY (NE/0009-2541). **1040**

CHEMICAL HAZARDS IN INDUSTRY (UK/0265-5721). **2872**

CHEMICAL INDUSTRY NOTES (US/0045-639X). **1011**

CHEMICAL INDUSTRY UPDATE. NORTH AMERICA (US/0732-5568). **968**

CHEMICAL MARKETING REPORTER (US/0090-0907). **968**

CHEMICAL PHYSICS (NE/0301-0104). **1050**

CHEMICAL PHYSICS LETTERS (NE/0009-2614). **1050**

CHEMICAL PROCESSING (CHICAGO, ILL.) (US/0009-2630). **969**

CHEMICAL REGULATION REPORTER (US/0148-7973). **2949**

CHEMICAL RESEARCH IN TOXICOLOGY (US/0893-228X). **3979**

CHEMICAL REVIEWS (US/0009-2665). **969**

CHEMICAL SCIENCES GRADUATE SCHOOL FINDER (US/1058-1227). **969**

CHEMICAL SENSES (UK/0379-864X). **485**

CHEMICAL SOCIETY REVIEWS (UK/0306-0012). **969**

CHEMICAL SPECIATION AND BIOAVAILABILITY (UK/0954-2299). **2162**

CHEMICAL SUBSTANCES CONTROL (US/0271-1478). **969**

CHEMICAL TITLES (US/0009-2711). **1011**

CHEMICAL WEEK (US/0009-272X). **1022**

CHEMICO-BIOLOGICAL INTERACTIONS (IE/0009-2797). **485**

CHEMIE-ANLAGEN + VERFAHREN (GW/0009-2800). **2010**

CHEMIE DER ERDE (GW/0009-2819). **1438**

CHEMIE IN UNSERER ZEIT (GW/0009-2851). **969**

CHEMIEINGENIEURTECHNIK (GW/0009-286X). **2010**

CHEMISCHE BERICHTE (GW/0009-2940). **970**

CHEMISCHE INDUSTRIE (DUSSELDORF) (GW/0009-2959). **970**

CHEMISCHE INDUSTRIE INTERNATIONAL (GW/0009-2967). **1022**

CHEMISCHE RUNDSCHAU (SZ/0009-2983). **970**

CHEMISCHE RUNDSCHAU ORGAN FUER FORSCHUNG, TECHNIK, FABRIKATION, HANDEL, IMPORT AND EXPORT CHEMISCHER, PHARMAZEUTISCHER UND VERWANDTER ERZEUGNISSE (SZ/0009-2983). **970**

CHEMIST & DRUGGIST (UK/0009-3033). **4296**

CHEMIST (NEW YORK), THE (US/0009-3025). **970**

CHEMISTRY AND BIOCHEMISTRY OF AMINO ACIDS, PEPTIDES, AND PROTEINS (US/0069-3111). **1040**

CHEMISTRY AND PHYSICS OF CARBON (US/0069-3138). **1035**

CHEMISTRY AND PHYSICS OF LIPIDS (IE/0009-3084). **485**

CHEMISTRY AND TECHNOLOGY OF FUELS AND OILS (US/0009-3092). **970**

CHEMISTRY IN BRITAIN (UK/0009-3106). **970**

CHEMISTRY IN ECOLOGY (US/0275-7540). **2212**

CHEMISTRY INTERNATIONAL (UK/0193-6484). **971**

CHEMISTRY LETTERS (JA/0366-7022). **1040**

CHEMISTRY OF HETEROCYCLIC COMPOUNDS (NEW YORK. 1965) (US/0009-3122). **971**

CHEMISTRY OF MATERIALS (US/0897-4756). **971**

CHEMISTRY OF NATURAL COMPOUNDS (US/0009-3130). **1040**

CHEMOECOLOGY (GW/0937-7409). **971**

CHEMOMETRICS AND INTELLIGENT LABORATORY SYSTEMS (NE/0169-7439). **971**

CHEMOMETRICS AND INTELLIGENT LABORATORY SYSTEMS : LABORATORY INFORMATION MANAGEMENT (NE/0925-5281). **1014**

CHEMOSPHERE (OXFORD) (UK/0045-6535). **2226**

CHEMOTHERAPY (BASEL) (SZ/0009-3157). **3814**

CHEMTECH (US/0009-2703). **1022**

CHEMTRACTS. BIOCHEMISTRY AND MOLECULAR BIOLOGY (US/1045-2680). **485**

CHEMTRACTS. INORGANIC CHEMISTRY (US/1051-7227). **1036**

CHEMTRACTS. MACROMOLECULAR CHEMISTRY (US/0899-7829). **971**

CHEMTRACTS. ORGANIC CHEMISTRY (US/0895-4445). **1041**

CHEST DISEASES, THORACIC SURGERY AND TUBERCULOSIS (NE/0014-4193). **3949**

CHI HSIEH KUNG CHENG HSUEH PAO (US/1000-9345). **2111**

CHILD ABUSE & NEGLECT (US/0145-2134). **5277**

CHILD ABUSE & NEGLECT [MICROFORM] (US/0145-2134). **5277**

CHILD ABUSE REVIEW (UK/0952-9136). **5277**

CHILD & ADOLESCENT SOCIAL WORK JOURNAL (US/0738-0151). **5277**

CHILD AND YOUTH CARE FORUM (US/1053-1890). **5278**

CHILD ASSESSMENT NEWS (US/1055-0518). **4580**

CHILD CARE, HEALTH AND DEVELOPMENT (UK/0305-1862). **3901**

CHILD DEVELOPMENT (US/0009-3920). **4580**

CHILD EDUCATION (UK/0009-3947). **1890**

CHILD LANGUAGE TEACHING AND THERAPY (UK/0265-6590). **1877**

CHILD NEPHROLOGY AND UROLOGY (SZ/1012-6694). **3989**

CHILD PROTECTION REPORT (US/0147-1260). **4771**

CHILD PSYCHIATRY AND HUMAN DEVELOPMENT (US/0009-398X). **3923**

CHILD WELFARE (US/0009-4021). **5278**

CHILDREN & SOCIETY (UK/0951-0605). **1061**

CHILDREN AND YOUTH SERVICES REVIEW (US/0190-7409). **5278**

CHILDREN'S BUSINESS (US/0884-2280). **1083**

CHILDREN'S HOSPITAL QUARTERLY (US/0899-5869). **3901**

CHILDREN'S LITERATURE IN EDUCATION (US/0045-6713). **3374**

CHILDREN'S MAGAZINE GUIDE (US/0743-9873). **3258**

CHILD'S NERVOUS SYSTEM (GW/0256-7040). **3902**

CHILTON'S AUTO REPAIR MANUAL (US/0069-3634). **5410**

CHILTON'S AUTOMOTIVE INDUSTRIES (1976) (US/0273-656X). **5410**

CHILTON'S AUTOMOTIVE MARKETING (US/0193-3264). **5410**

CHILTON'S ELECTRONIC COMPONENT NEWS (US/0193-614X). **2038**

CHILTON'S FOOD ENGINEERING (US/0193-323X). **2331**

CHILTON'S FOOD ENGINEERING INTERNATIONAL (US/0148-4478). **2331**

CHILTON'S HARDWARE AGE (1984) (US/8755-254X). **2810**

CHILTON'S IAN (1977) (US/0193-6174). **1968**

CHILTON'S I&CS (US/0746-2395). **1968**

CHILTON'S IMPO (US/8755-2523). **3476**

CHILTON'S INDUSTRIAL SAFETY & HYGIENE NEWS (US/8755-2566). **2860**

CHILTON'S MOTOR/AGE (1970) (US/0193-7022). **5411**

CHILTON'S PD&D (US/0193-6182). **1601**

CHILTON'S REVIEW OF OPTOMETRY (US/0147-7633). **4215**

CHIMIE ACTUALITES (FR/0009-4323). **971**

CHIMIE MAGAZINE (FR/0245-940X). **972**

CHINA BUSINESS REVIEW, THE (US/0163-7169). **657**

CHINA GLASS & TABLEWARE (US/0009-4382). **2588**

CHINESE ASTRONOMY AND ASTROPHYSICS (UK/0275-1062). **394**

CHINESE CHEMICAL LETTERS (CH/1001-8417). **1023**

CHINESE JOURNAL OF AERONAUTICS (CC/1000-9361). **16**

CHINESE JOURNAL OF ARID LAND RESEARCH (US/0898-5146). **1353**

CHINESE JOURNAL OF AUTOMATION (US/1044-064X). **1968**

CHINESE JOURNAL OF BIOCHEMISTRY AND BIOPHYSICS (US/0898-512X). **485**

CHINESE JOURNAL OF BIOTECHNOLOGY (US/1042-749X). **3690**

CHINESE JOURNAL OF CONTEMPORARY MATHEMATICS (US/0898-5111). **3500**

CHINESE JOURNAL OF ENGINEERING THERMOPHYSICS (US/1043-8033). **2101**

CHINESE JOURNAL OF GEOPHYSICS (US/0898-9591). **1404**

CHINESE JOURNAL OF INFRARED AND MILLIMETER WAVES (US/0890-9903). **4399**

CHINESE JOURNAL OF NUMERICAL MATHEMATICS AND APPLICATIONS (US/0899-4358). **3500**

CHINESE JOURNAL OF OCEANOLOGY AND LIMNOLOGY (CC/0254-4059). **1447**

CHINESE JOURNAL OF POPULATION SCIENCE (US/1044-8403). **4551**

CHINESE JOURNAL OF SEMICONDUCTORS (US/0899-9988). **4399**

CHINESE PHYSICS (US/0273-429X). **4399**

CHINESE PHYSICS LETTERS (US/0256-307X). **4400**

CHIP (GW/0170-6632). **1266**

CHIRALITY (NEW YORK, N.Y.) (US/0899-0042). **972**

CHIROPRACTIC SPORTS MEDICINE (US/0889-6976). **3953**

CHIRURG (GW/0009-4722). **3961**

CHIRURGIE (FR/0001-4001). **3962**

CHIRURGIE (PARIS) (FR/0001-4001). **3962**

CHIRURGIEN - DENTISTE DE FRANCE, LE (FR/0009-4838). **1319**

CHIRURGISCHE PRAXIS (GW/0009-4846). **3962**

CHOICE (US/0009-4978). **3201**

CHOREOGRAPHY AND DANCE (SZ/0891-6381). **1311**

CHRISTIAN LIFE COMMUNITIES HARVEST (US/0739-6422). **4945**

CHRISTIAN SCIENCE MONITOR (1983), THE (US/0882-7729). **5688**

CHROMATOGRAPHIA (GW/0009-5893). **1014**

CHROMATOGRAPHIC SCIENCE (US/0069-3936). **1014**

CHROMATOGRAPHY (US/0892-8797). **1014**

CHROMATOGRAPHY ABSTRACTS (UK/0268-6287). **1014**

CHROMOSOMA (GW/0009-5915). **534**

CHROMOSOME RESEARCH (UK/0967-3849). **3563**

CHRONIQUE DE LA RECHERCHE MINIERE (FR/0182-564X). **1371**

CHRONOBIOLOGY INTERNATIONAL (UK/0742-0528). **451**

CHUAN HSUEH PAO (US/0898-5138). **543**

CHURCHMAN (LONDON. 1879) (UK/0009-661X). **4948**

CIM STRATEGIES (US/0748-9250). **3476**

CINEACTION! (CN/0826-9866). **4065**

CINESIOLOGIE (FR/0009-7209). **3804**

CIO (FRAMINGHAM, MASS.) (US/0894-9301). **863**

CIRCUIT WORLD (UK/0305-6120). **2038**

CIRCUITS ASSEMBLY (US/1054-0407). **2038**

CIRCUITS, SYSTEMS, AND SIGNAL PROCESSING (US/0278-081X). **2039**

CIRCULATION MANAGEMENT (SPRINGFIELD, OR.) (US/0888-8191). **2918**

CIRCULATION (NEW YORK, N.Y.) (US/0009-7322). **3702**

CIRCULATION RESEARCH (US/0009-7330). **3702**

CIRCULATION RESEARCH (US/0009-7330). **3702**

CIRCULATORY SHOCK (US/0092-6213). **3702**

CIRP ANNALS (SZ/0007-8506). **2111**

CITIES (LONDON, ENGLAND) (UK/0264-2751). **2817**

CITOLOGIJA I GENETIKA (KIEV) (UN/0564-3783). **543**

CITY & STATE (CHICAGO, ILL.) (US/0885-940X). **4717**

CIVIC PUBLIC WORKS (CN/0829-772X). **4760**

CIVIL ENGINEERING (NEW YORK, N.Y. 1983) (US/0885-7024). **2021**

CIVIL ENGINEERING SYSTEMS (UK/0263-0257). **2021**

CIVIL RICO REPORT (US/0884-0032). **3089**

CIVIL WAR HISTORY (US/0009-8078). **2728**

CLADISTICS (US/0748-3007). **451**

CLARK'S BANK DEPOSITS AND PAYMENTS MONTHLY (US/1063-2220). **783**

CLASSICAL AND MODERN LITERATURE (US/0197-2227). **1075**

CLASSICAL AND QUANTUM GRAVITY (UK/0264-9381). **4400**

CLASSICAL ANTIQUITY (US/0278-6656). **1075**

CLASSICAL PHILOLOGY (US/0009-837X). **1075**

CLASSICAL QUARTERLY (UK/0009-8388). **1075**

CLASSICAL REVIEW (UK/0009-840X). **1076**

CLASSROOM (AT/0727-1255). **1891**

CLAY MINERALS (UK/0009-8558). **1438**

CLAY SCIENCE (JA/0009-8574). **1353**

CLEAN WATER REPORT (US/0009-8620). **5532**

CLEANING MANAGEMENT MAGAZINE (US/1051-5720). **863**

CLEARING HOUSE (MENASHA, WIS.) (US/0009-8655). **1732**

CLEVELAND CLINIC JOURNAL OF MEDICINE (US/0891-1150). **3564**

CLIENT/SERVER COMPUTING (US/1059-3470). **1174**

CLIENT SERVER REPORT, THE (US/1056-7844). **1174**

CLIMATE DYNAMICS (GW/0930-7575). **1421**

CLIMATIC CHANGE (NE/0165-0009). **1422**

CLIN-ALERT (US/0069-4770). **3564**

CLINICA (UK/0144-7777). **3564**

CLINICA & TERAPIA CARDIOVASCOLARE (IT/0392-1344). **3703**

CLINICA CARDIOVASCULAR (SP/0212-1808). **3703**

CLINICA CHIMICA ACTA (NE/0009-8981). **972**

CLINICA OCULISTICA E PATOLOGIA OCULARE (IT/0391-8998). **3893**

CLINICAL AND DIAGNOSTIC VIROLOGY (NE/0928-0197). **561**

CLINICAL AND EXPERIMENTAL ALLERGY (UK/0954-7894). **3667**

CLINICAL AND EXPERIMENTAL DERMATOLOGY (UK/0307-6938). **3718**

CLINICAL AND EXPERIMENTAL HYPERTENSION (1993) (US/1064-1963). **3703**

CLINICAL AND EXPERIMENTAL HYPERTENSION. PART B, HYPERTENSION IN PREGNANCY (US/0730-0085). **3758**

CLINICAL AND EXPERIMENTAL IMMUNOLOGY (UK/0009-9104). **3667**

CLINICAL & EXPERIMENTAL METASTASIS (UK/0262-0898). **3815**

CLINICAL AND EXPERIMENTAL OBSTETRICS & GYNECOLOGY (IT/0390-6663). **3758**

CLINICAL AND EXPERIMENTAL PHARMACOLOGY & PHYSIOLOGY (AT/0305-1870). **4296**

CLINICAL AND INVESTIGATIVE MEDICINE (UK/0147-958X). **3565**

CLINICAL AND LABORATORY HAEMATOLOGY (UK/0141-9854). **3771**

CLINICAL APHASIOLOGY (US/0195-7015). **3830**

CLINICAL AUTONOMIC RESEARCH : OFFICIAL JOURNAL OF THE CLINICAL AUTONOMIC RESEARCH SOCIETY (UK/0959-9851). **3565**

CLINICAL BIOCHEMISTRY (NEW YORK, N.Y.) (US/0009-9120). **485**

CLINICAL BIOCHEMISTRY REVIEWS (ELMSFORD, N.Y.) (US/0272-9881). **485**

CLINICAL BIOMECHANICS (BRISTOL) (UK/0268-0033). **3565**

CLINICAL CARDIOLOGY (LOS ALTOS, CALIF.) (US/0891-2092). **3703**

CLINICAL CARDIOLOGY (MAHWAH, N.J.) (US/0160-9289). **3703**

CLINICAL CHEMISTRY AND ENZYMOLOGY COMMUNICATIONS (SZ/0892-2187). **972**

CLINICAL CHEMISTRY (BALTIMORE, MD.) (US/0009-9147). **972**

CLINICAL CHEMISTRY NEWS (US/0161-9640). **972**

CLINICAL CHEMISTRY (REFERENCE EDITION) (US/0009-9147). **972**

CLINICAL CHIROPRACTIC REPORT (US/1053-072X). **4380**

CLINICAL CONSULTATIONS IN OBSTETRICS AND GYNECOLOGY (US/1043-0660). **3758**

CLINICAL CYTOGENETICS (UK/0260-5872). **535**

CLINICAL ENDOCRINOLOGY (OXFORD) (UK/0300-0664). **3727**

CLINICAL EYE AND VISION CARE (US/0953-4431). **3873**

CLINICAL GENETICS (DK/0009-9163). **543**

CLINICAL HEMORHEOLOGY (US/0271-5198). **3771**

CLINICAL IMAGING (US/0899-7071). **3939**

CLINICAL IMMUNOLOGY AND IMMUNOPATHOLOGY (US/0090-1229). **3668**

CLINICAL IMMUNOLOGY NEWSLETTER (US/0197-1859). **3668**

CLINICAL INVESTIGATOR, THE (GW/0941-0198). **3565**

CLINICAL JOURNAL OF PAIN, THE (US/0749-8047). **3565**

CLINICAL JOURNAL OF SPORT MEDICINE (US/1050-642X). **3953**

CLINICAL LAB LETTER (US/0197-8454). **3893**

CLINICAL LASER MONTHLY (US/0746-469X). **3566**

CLINICAL LINGUISTICS & PHONETICS (UK/0269-9206). **3274**

CLINICAL MATERIALS (UK/0267-6605). **3566**

CLINICAL MICROBIOLOGY NEWSLETTER (US/0196-4399). **561**

CLINICAL MICROBIOLOGY REPORTS (US/1062-8150). **3712**

CLINICAL MICROBIOLOGY REVIEWS (US/0893-8512). **561**

CLINICAL NEPHROLOGY (GW/0301-0430). **3989**

CLINICAL NEUROLOGY AND NEUROSURGERY (NE/0303-8467). **3830**

CLINICAL NEUROPATHOLOGY (GW/0722-5091). **3894**

CLINICAL NEUROPHARMACOLOGY (US/0362-5664). **4296**

CLINICAL NEUROPSYCHOLOGIST, THE (NE/0920-1637). **3830**

CLINICAL NEUROSURGERY (US/0069-4827). **3962**

CLINICAL NUCLEAR MEDICINE (US/0363-9762). **3847**

CLINICAL NURSE SPECIALIST (US/0887-6274). **3853**

CLINICAL NUTRITION (UK/0261-5614). **4188**

CLINICAL OBSTETRICS AND GYNECOLOGY (US/0009-9201). **3759**

CLINICAL ONCOLOGY : A JOURNAL OF THE ROYAL COLLEGE OF RADIOLOGISTS (UK/0936-6555). **3815**

CLINICAL ORAL IMPLANTS RESEARCH (DK/0905-7161). **1319**

CLINICAL ORTHOPAEDICS AND RELATED RESEARCH (US/0009-921X). **3881**

CLINICAL OTOLARYNGOLOGY AND ALLIED SCIENCES (UK/0307-7772). **3887**

CLINICAL PHARMACOKINETICS (US/0312-5963). **4296**

CLINICAL PHARMACOLOGY AND THERAPEUTICS (US/0009-9236). **4297**

CLINICAL PHARMACY (US/0278-2677). **4297**

CLINICAL PHYSICS AND PHYSIOLOGICAL MEASUREMENT (UK/0143-0815). **4400**

CLINICAL PHYSIOLOGY (OXFORD) (UK/0144-5979). **579**

CLINICAL PRACTICE OF GYNECOLOGY (US/1043-3198). **3759**

CLINICAL PREVENTIVE DENTISTRY (US/0163-9633). **1319**

CLINICAL PSYCHOLOGY REVIEW (US/0272-7358). **4581**

CLINICAL RADIOLOGY (UK/0009-9260). **3940**

CLINICAL RESEARCH (US/0009-9279). **3566**

CLINICAL RESEARCH AND REGULATORY AFFAIRS (US/1060-1333). **4297**

CLINICAL REVIEWS IN ALLERGY (US/0731-8235). **3668**

CLINICAL SCIENCE (1979) (UK/0143-5221). **485**

CLINICAL SOCIAL WORK JOURNAL (US/0091-1674). **5279**

CLINICAL THERAPEUTICS (US/0149-2918). **4297**

CLINICAL TRANSPLANTATION (DK/0902-0063). **3566**

CLINICAL TRIALS (US/1061-608X). **3740**

CLINICAL TRIALS AND META-ANALYSIS (NE/0927-5401). **4297**

CLINICAL ULTRASOUND REVIEW (US/0275-4541). **3796**

CLINICAL VISION SCIENCES (US/0887-6169). **3566**

CLINICIAN REVIEWS (US/1052-0627). **3566**

CLINICS IN APPLIED NUTRITION (US/1053-0452). **4189**

CLINICS IN CHEST MEDICINE (US/0272-5231). **3566**

CLINICS IN COMMUNICATION DISORDERS (US/1054-8505). **3887**

CLINICS IN DERMATOLOGY (US/0738-081X). **3718**

CLINICS IN GERIATRIC MEDICINE (US/0749-0690). **3750**

CLINICS IN LABORATORY MEDICINE (US/0272-2712). **3566**

CLINICS IN PERINATOLOGY (US/0095-5108). **3759**

CLINICS IN PLASTIC SURGERY (US/0094-1298). **3962**

CLINICS IN SPORTS MEDICINE (US/0278-5919). **3953**

CLL JOURNAL : COMPUTER-ASSISTED ENGLISH LANGUAGE LEARNING JOURNAL (US/1049-9059). **3274**

CMA : THE MANAGEMENT ACCOUNTING MAGAZINE (CN/0831-3881). **741**

CMAJ. CANADIAN MEDICAL ASSOCIATION JOURNAL (CN/0820-3946). **3567**

CMU JOURNAL OF SCIENCE (PH/0116-7847). **5095**

CO-EXISTENCE (DORDRECHT) (NE/0587-5994). **4518**

COAL & SYNFUELS TECHNOLOGY (US/0883-9735). **1023**

COAL (CHICAGO, ILL. : 1988) (US/1040-7820). **2137**

COAL OUTLOOK (US/0162-2714). **1935**

COAL PREPARATION (NEW YORK, N.Y.) (US/0734-9343). **2137**

COASTAL AND ESTUARINE SCIENCES (US/0733-9569). **2212**

COASTAL ENGINEERING (AMSTERDAM) (NE/0378-3839). **1968**

COASTAL MANAGEMENT (US/0892-0753). **2190**

COATINGS (CN/0225-6363). **4223**

CODATA BULLETIN (US/0366-757X). **5095**

CODE OF FEDERAL REGULATIONS INDEX (US/0000-1058). **3079**

COGITO (BRISTOL, ENGLAND) (UK/0950-8864). **4344**

COGNITION (SZ/0010-0277). **4581**

COGNITIVE BRAIN RESEARCH (NE/0926-6410). **3830**

COGNITIVE DEVELOPMENT (US/0885-2014). **4581**

COGNITIVE LINGUISTICS (GW/0936-5907). **3274**

COGNITIVE PSYCHOLOGY (US/0010-0285). **4581**

COGNITIVE SCIENCE (US/0364-0213). **1212**

COGNITIVE THERAPY AND RESEARCH (US/0147-5916). **4581**

COLD REGIONS SCIENCE AND TECHNOLOGY (NE/0165-232X). **1968**

COLD SPRING HARBOR MONOGRAPH SERIES (US/0270-1847). **451**

COLD SPRING HARBOR SYMPOSIA ON QUANTITATIVE BIOLOGY (US/0091-7451). **451**

COLLECTED ALGORITHMS FROM ACM. SUPPLEMENT (US/0149-1989). **1175**

COLLECTED LETTERS / CORRESPONDENCE SOCIETY OF SURGEONS (US/0162-6477). **3962**

COLLECTED LETTERS OF THE INTERNATIONAL CORRESPONDENCE SOCIETY OF OBSTETRICIANS, GYNECOLOGISTS (US/0443-9058). **3759**

COLLECTION COLLOQUES ET SEMINAIRES. INSTITUT FRANCAIS DU PETROLE (FR/0073-8360). **4253**

COLLECTION OF CZECHOSLOVAK CHEMICAL COMMUNICATIONS (UK/0010-0765). **973**

COLLECTIVE BARGAINING NEGOTIATIONS AND CONTRACTS (US/0010-079X). **3145**

COLLEGE & RESEARCH LIBRARIES (US/0010-0870). **3203**

COLLEGE MATHEMATICS JOURNAL, THE (US/0746-8342). **3500**

COLLEGE TEACHING (US/8756-7555). **1817**

COLLEGIATE MICROCOMPUTER (US/0731-4213). **1266**

COLLOID AND POLYMER SCIENCE (GW/0303-402X). **1050**

COLLOID JOURNAL OF THE RUSSIAN ACADEMY OF SCIENCES (US/1061-933X). **5095**

COLLOIDS AND SURFACES (NE/0166-6622). **1051**

COLLOIDS AND SURFACES B: BIOINTERFACES (NE/0927-7765). **1051**

COLLOQUIA GERMANICA (SZ/0010-1338). **3274**

COLLOQUIUM PUBLICATIONS / AMERICAN MATHEMATICAL SOCIETY (US/0065-9258). **3500**

COLOR PUBLISHING (US/1055-9701). **4813**

COLOR RESEARCH AND APPLICATION (US/0361-2317). **5095**

COLORADO SCHOOL OF MINES QUARTERLY (US/0163-9153). **2137**

COLUMBIA JOURNAL OF ENVIRONMENTAL LAW (US/0098-4582). **3110**

COLUMBIA JOURNAL OF WORLD BUSINESS, THE (US/0022-5428). **658**

COLUMBIA LAW REVIEW (US/0010-1958). **2953**

COMBINATORICA (BUDAPEST. 1981) (NE/0209-9683). **3500**

COMBUSTION AND FLAME (US/0010-2180). **1051**

COMBUSTION, EXPLOSION, AND SHOCK WAVES (US/0010-5082). **1051**

COMBUSTION SCIENCE AND TECHNOLOGY (US/0010-2202). **1051**

COMMENTARII MATHEMATICI HELVETICI (SZ/0010-2571). **3500**

COMMENTS ON ASTROPHYSICS (US/0146-2970). **394**

COMMENTS ON ATOMIC AND MOLECULAR PHYSICS (UK/0010-2687). **4446**

COMMENTS ON DEVELOPMENTAL NEUROBIOLOGY (US/0896-5099). **3830**

COMMENTS ON MODERN CHEMISTRY. PART B, COMMENTS ON AGRICULTURAL AND FOOD CHEMISTRY (UK/0892-2101). **1041**

COMMENTS ON MODERN PHYSICS. PART B, COMMENTS ON CONDENSED MATTER PHYSICS (UK/0885-4483). **4400**

COMMENTS ON MOLECULAR AND CELLULAR BIOPHYSICS (US/0143-8123). **535**

COMMENTS ON NUCLEAR AND PARTICLE PHYSICS (US/0010-2709). **4446**

COMMENTS ON PLASMA PHYSICS AND CONTROLLED FUSION (US/0374-2806). **4400**

COMMENTS ON THEORETICAL BIOLOGY (UK/0894-8550). **452**

COMMENTS ON TOXICOLOGY (UK/0886-5140). **3980**

COMMERCIAL FISHERIES NEWS (US/0273-6713). **2299**

COMMERCIAL MOTOR, THE (UK/0010-3063). **5412**

COMMON CARRIER WEEK (US/0743-4812). **1151**

COMMON KNOWLEDGE (US/0961-754X). **2844**

COMMON MARKET LAW REVIEW (NE/0165-0750). **2953**

COMMUNICATIO SOCIALIS (GW/0010-3497). **1106**

COMMUNICATION RESEARCH (US/0093-6502). **1107**

COMMUNICATION TECHNOLOGY IMPACT (UK/0142-5854). **1152**

COMMUNICATION THEORY (US/1050-3293). **1107**

COMMUNICATION WORLD (SAN FRANCISCO, CALIF.) (US/0744-7612). **1107**

COMMUNICATIONS & COGNITION (BE/0378-0880). **1108**

COMMUNICATIONS CONCEPTS (US/0741-0069). **1108**

COMMUNICATIONS DAILY (US/0277-0679). **1152**

COMMUNICATIONS (ENGLEWOOD. 1964) (US/0010-356X). **1152**

COMMUNICATIONS IN ALGEBRA (US/0092-7872). **3500**

COMMUNICATIONS IN APPLIED NUMERICAL METHODS (UK/0748-8025). **3500**

COMMUNICATIONS IN MATHEMATICAL PHYSICS (GW/0010-3616). **4400**

COMMUNICATIONS IN PARTIAL DIFFERENTIAL EQUATIONS (US/0360-5302). **3501**

COMMUNICATIONS IN SOIL SCIENCE AND PLANT ANALYSIS (US/0010-3624). **167**

COMMUNICATIONS IN STATISTICS : SIMULATION AND COMPUTATION (US/0361-0918). **1282**

COMMUNICATIONS IN STATISTICS : STOCHASTIC MODELS (US/0882-0287). **5325**

COMMUNICATIONS IN STATISTICS : THEORY AND METHODS (US/0361-0926). **3501**

COMMUNICATIONS NEWS (GENEVA, ILL.) (US/0010-3632). **1108**

COMMUNICATIONS OF THE ACM (US/0001-0782). **1175**

COMMUNICATIONS ON PURE AND APPLIED MATHEMATICS (US/0010-3640). **3501**

COMMUNICATIONS (PARIS. 1962) (FR/0588-8018). **1108**

COMMUNICATIONS TECHNOLOGY (US/0884-2272). **1130**

COMMUNICATIONSWEEK INTERNATIONAL (US/1042-6086). **1108**

COMMUNICATIONSWEEK (MANHASSET, N.Y.) (US/0746-8121). **1152**

COMMUNITY DENTAL HEALTH (UK/0265-539X). **1319**

COMMUNITY DENTISTRY AND ORAL EPIDEMIOLOGY (DK/0301-5661). **1319**

COMMUNITY DEVELOPMENT JOURNAL (UK/0010-3802). **5242**

COMMUNITY/JUNIOR COLLEGE (US/0277-6774). **1817**

COMMUNITY MENTAL HEALTH JOURNAL (US/0010-3853). **5280**

COMMUNITY REVIEW (NEW BRUNSWICK) (US/0163-8475). **1818**

COMMUTER / REGIONAL AIRLINE NEWS (US/1040-5402). **5380**

COMPANY LAWYER, THE (UK/0144-1027). **3098**

COMPARATIVE BIOCHEMISTRY AND PHYSIOLOGY. A, COMPARATIVE PHYSIOLOGY (UK/0300-9629). **579**

COMPARATIVE BIOCHEMISTRY AND PHYSIOLOGY. B, COMPARATIVE BIOCHEMISTRY (UK/0305-0491). **486**

COMPARATIVE CRITICISM (UK/0144-7564). **3340**

COMPARATIVE EDUCATION (UK/0305-0068). **1733**

COMPARATIVE EDUCATION REVIEW (US/0010-4086). **1733**

COMPARATIVE IMMUNOLOGY, MICROBIOLOGY AND INFECTIOUS DISEASES (UK/0147-9571). **561**

COMPARATIVE LITERATURE STUDIES (URBANA) (US/0010-4132). **3377**

COMPARATIVE MEDICINE (US/1058-2401). **5508**

COMPARATIVE PHYSIOLOGY AND ECOLOGY (II/0379-0436). **579**

COMPARATIVE POLITICAL STUDIES (US/0010-4140). **4469**

COMPARATIVE POLITICS (US/0010-4159). **4469**

COMPARATIVE SOCIAL RESEARCH (US/0195-6310). **5242**

COMPARATIVE STRATEGY (US/0149-5933). **4518**

COMPARATIVE STUDIES IN SOCIETY AND HISTORY (UK/0010-4175). **5196**

COMPARE (UK/0305-7925). **1891**

COMPASS, THE (US/0894-802X). **1353**

COMPENSATION & BENEFITS MANAGEMENT (US/0748-061X). **864**

COMPENSATION AND BENEFITS REVIEW (US/0886-3687). **1660**

COMPFLASH (US/0147-1570). **1660**

COMPLETE DIRECTORY OF LARGE PRINT BOOKS & SERIALS, THE (US/0000-1120). **4828**

COMPLEX VARIABLES THEORY AND APPLICATION (US/0278-1077). **3501**

COMPLIANCE ENGINEERING (US/0898-3577). **1152**

COMPLICATIONS IN ORTHOPEDICS (US/0887-1736). **3881**

COMPOSITE STRUCTURES (UK/0263-8223). **2101**

COMPOSITES (UK/0010-4361). **2101**

COMPOSITES & ADHESIVES NEWSLETTER, THE (US/0888-1227). **1023**

COMPOSITES ENGINEERING (US/0961-9526). **2101**

COMPOSITES INDUSTRY MONTHLY (US/1058-904X). **1969**

COMPOSITES MANUFACTURING (UK/0956-7143). **2101**

COMPOSITES SCIENCE AND TECHNOLOGY (UK/0266-3538). **2101**

COMPOSITIO MATHEMATICA (NE/0010-437X). **3501**

COMPREHENSIVE PSYCHIATRY (US/0010-440X). **3923**

COMPTES RENDUS DE L'ACADEMIE DES SCIENCES (FR/0762-0969). **5096**

COMPTES RENDUS DE L'ACADEMIE DES SCIENCES. SERIE I, MATHEMATIQUE (FR/0764-4442). **3501**

COMPTES RENDUS DE L'ACADEMIE DES SCIENCES. SERIE II, MECANIQUE, PHYSIQUE, CHIMIE, SCIENCES DE L'UNIVERS, SCIENCES DE LA TERRE (FR/0764-4450). **5096**

COMPTES RENDUS DE L'ACADEMIE DES SCIENCES. SERIE III, SCIENCES DE LA VIE (FR/0764-4469). **5096**

COMPTES RENDUS DE THERAPEUTIQUE ET DE PHARMACOLOGIE CLINIQUE (FR/0293-9908). **4297**

COMPTES RENDUS DES SEANCES DE LA SOCIETE DE BIOLOGIE ET DES SES FILIALES (FR/0037-9026). **452**

COMPUTATIONAL COMPLEXITY (SZ/1016-3328). **3501**

COMPUTATIONAL GEOMETRY (NE/0925-7721). **3501**

COMPUTATIONAL INTELLIGENCE (CN/0824-7935). **1212**

COMPUTATIONAL LINGUISTICS (ASSOCIATION FOR COMPUTATIONAL LINGUISTICS) (US/0891-2017). **1175**

COMPUTATIONAL MATERIALS SCIENCE (NE/0927-0256). **2101**

COMPUTATIONAL MATHEMATICS AND MATHEMATICAL PHYSICS (UK/0965-5425). **3501**

COMPUTATIONAL MATHEMATICS AND MODELING (US/1046-283X). **3501**

COMPUTATIONAL MECHANICS (GW/0178-7675). **2112**

COMPUTATIONAL MECHANICS ADVANCES (SZ/0927-7951). **2112**

COMPUTATIONAL POLYMER SCIENCE (US/1052-0643). **4454**

COMPUTATIONAL SEISMOLOGY (US/0733-5792). **1404**

COMPUTATIONAL STATISTICS & DATA ANALYSIS (NE/0167-9473). **3502**

COMPUTER AIDED DESIGN (UK/0010-4485). **1231**

COMPUTER-AIDED ENGINEERING (US/0733-3536). **1228**

COMPUTER AIDED GEOMETRIC DESIGN (NE/0167-8396). **1232**

COMPUTER & CONTROL ABSTRACTS (UK/0036-8113). **1208**

COMPUTER & VIDEO GAMES (UK/0261-3697). **1230**

COMPUTER APPLICATIONS IN THE BIOSCIENCES (UK/0266-7061). **1176**

COMPUTER AUDIT UPDATE (UK/0960-2593). **1256**

COMPUTER BULLETIN (UK/0010-4531). **1256**

COMPUTER BUSINESS (LOS ANGELES, CALIF.) (US/0732-8346). **1208**

COMPUTER COMMUNICATIONS (UK/0140-3664). **1240**

COMPUTER DESIGN (WINCHESTER) (US/0010-4566). **1176**

COMPUTER FRAUD & SECURITY BULLETIN (NE/0142-0496). **1225**

COMPUTER GRAPHICS FORUM : A JOURNAL OF THE EUROPEAN ASSOCIATION FOR COMPUTER GRAPHICS (NE/0167-7055). **1232**

COMPUTER GRAPHICS WORLD (US/0271-4159). **1232**

COMPUTER INDUSTRY FORECASTS (1987) (US/0894-6213). **1236**

COMPUTER-INTEGRATED MANUFACTURING SYSTEMS (UK/0951-5240). **1228**

Copyright Clearance Center Index — CONTRIBUTIONS

COMPUTER JOURNAL (UK/0010-4620). **1176**

COMPUTER LANGUAGE (US/0749-2839). **1218**

COMPUTER LANGUAGES (US/0096-0551). **1278**

COMPUTER LAW AND TAX REPORT (US/0361-7203). **2954**

COMPUTER/LAW JOURNAL (US/0164-8756). **2954**

COMPUTER LITERATURE INDEX (US/0270-4846). **1208**

COMPUTER (LONG BEACH, CALIF.) (US/0018-9162). **1266**

COMPUTER METHODS AND PROGRAMS IN BIOMEDICINE (NE/0169-2607). **3691**

COMPUTER METHODS IN APPLIED MECHANICS AND ENGINEERING (NE/0045-7825). **1256**

COMPUTER MUSIC JOURNAL (US/0148-9267). **1240**

COMPUTER NETWORKS AND ISDN SYSTEMS (NE/0169-7552). **1240**

COMPUTER OPTICS (UK/0955-355X). **1177**

COMPUTER PHYSICS COMMUNICATIONS (NE/0010-4655). **4400**

COMPUTER PICTURES (US/0883-5683). **1232**

COMPUTER PUBLISHING & ADVERTISING REPORT (US/0740-6231). **1177**

COMPUTER RESELLER NEWS (US/0893-8377). **1244**

COMPUTER SCIENCE EDUCATION (US/0899-3408). **1177**

COMPUTER SCIENCE IN ECONOMICS AND MANAGEMENT (NE/0921-2736). **1177**

COMPUTER + SOFTWARE NEWS (US/0745-5291). **1245**

COMPUTER SPEECH & LANGUAGE (UK/0885-2308). **3274**

COMPUTER STANDARDS & INTERFACES (SZ/0920-5489). **1178**

COMPUTER SYSTEMS SCIENCE AND ENGINEERING (UK/0267-6192). **1228**

COMPUTER TECHNOLOGY REVIEW (US/0278-9647). **1246**

COMPUTER UND RECHT (KOLN) (GW/0179-1990). **2955**

COMPUTER WEEKLY (UK/0010-4787). **1178**

COMPUTERS AND BIOMEDICAL RESEARCH (US/0010-4809). **3691**

COMPUTERS & CHEMICAL ENGINEERING (UK/0098-1354). **2011**

COMPUTERS & CHEMISTRY (UK/0097-8485). **973**

COMPUTERS & EDUCATION (US/0360-1315). **1222**

COMPUTERS & ELECTRICAL ENGINEERING (US/0045-7906). **1228**

COMPUTERS AND ELECTRONICS IN AGRICULTURE (NE/0168-1699). **76**

COMPUTERS & FLUIDS (UK/0045-7930). **2088**

COMPUTERS & GEOSCIENCES (UK/0098-3004). **1178**

COMPUTERS AND GEOTECHNICS (US/0266-352X). **1372**

COMPUTERS & GRAPHICS (US/0097-8493). **1232**

COMPUTERS & INDUSTRIAL ENGINEERING (US/0360-8352). **2097**

COMPUTERS & OPERATIONS RESEARCH (US/0305-0548). **1179**

COMPUTERS & SECURITY (UK/0167-4048). **1226**

COMPUTERS & STRUCTURES (UK/0045-7949). **1228**

COMPUTERS AND THE HISTORY OF ART (SZ/1048-6798). **348**

COMPUTERS AND THE HUMANITIES (NE/0010-4817). **2844**

COMPUTERS, ENVIRONMENT AND URBAN SYSTEMS (US/0198-9715). **2819**

COMPUTERS IN ACCOUNTING (US/0883-1866). **741**

COMPUTERS IN BIOLOGY AND MEDICINE (US/0010-4825). **3691**

COMPUTERS IN CARDIOLOGY (US/0276-6574). **3703**

COMPUTERS IN HEALTHCARE (US/0745-1075). **1179**

COMPUTERS IN HUMAN BEHAVIOR (US/0747-5632). **4582**

COMPUTERS IN INDUSTRY (NE/0166-3615). **1228**

COMPUTERS IN LIBRARIES (US/1041-7915). **3203**

COMPUTERS IN NURSING (US/0736-8593). **3854**

COMPUTERS IN PHYSICS (US/0894-1866). **4401**

COMPUTERWORLD (US/0010-4841). **1236**

COMPUTING (AU/0010-485X). **1257**

COMPUTING & CONTROL ENGINEERING JOURNAL (UK/0956-3385). **1228**

COMPUTING REVIEWS (US/0010-4884). **1208**

COMPUTING SYSTEMS (US/0895-6340). **1279**

COMPUTING SYSTEMS IN ENGINEERING (US/0956-0521). **1969**

COMPUTING TEACHER, THE (US/0278-9175). **1222**

CONCEPTS IN IMMUNOPATHOLOGY (SW/0255-7983). **3668**

CONCEPTS IN MAGNETIC RESONANCE (US/1043-7347). **4443**

CONCEPTS IN NEUROSCIENCE (SI/0129-0568). **3830**

CONCEPTS IN PEDIATRIC NEUROSURGERY (SZ/0251-2068). **3902**

CONCOURS MEDICAL (FR/0010-5309). **3568**

CONCRETE ABSTRACTS (US/0045-8007). **2003**

CONCRETE INTERNATIONAL (US/0162-4075). **608**

CONCRETE PRODUCTS (1975) (US/0010-5368). **608**

CONCURRENCY (CHICHESTER, ENGLAND) (UK/1040-3108). **1180**

CONDENSED MATTER NEWS (US/1056-7046). **4401**

CONDITION MONITOR (UK/0268-8050). **2112**

CONFERENCE BOARD BRIEFING, THE (US/0899-6741). **864**

CONFERENCE PROCEEDINGS / CANADIAN MATHEMATICAL SOCIETY (CN/0731-1036). **3502**

CONFERENCE RECORD / ASILOMAR CONFERENCE ON SIGNALS, SYSTEMS & COMPUTERS (US/1058-6393). **2039**

CONFERENCE RECORD OF IEEE INTERNATIONAL SYMPOSIUM ON ELECTRICAL INSULATION (US/0164-2006). **2039**

CONFERENCE RECORD OF THE ... ANNUAL ACM SYMPOSIUM ON PRINCIPLES OF PROGRAMMING LANGUAGES (US/0730-8566). **1279**

CONFERENCE RECORD OF THE ... IEEE PHOTOVOLTAIC SPECIALISTS CONFERENCE (US/0160-8371). **2039**

CONFIGURATIONS (BALTIMORE, MD.) (US/1063-1801). **5096**

CONFLICT QUARTERLY (CN/0227-1311). **4518**

CONGRESSIONAL QUARTERLY ALMANAC (US/0095-6007). **4640**

CONGRESSIONAL QUARTERLY WEEKLY REPORT (US/0010-5910). **4469**

CONGRESSIONAL YELLOW BOOK (QUARTERLY ED.) (US/0191-1422). **1924**

CONNECTION SCIENCE (UK/0954-0091). **1212**

CONNECTION TECHNOLOGY (US/8756-4076). **5096**

CONNECTIVE TISSUE RESEARCH (US/0300-8207). **580**

CONSCIOUSNESS AND COGNITION (US/1053-8100). **4582**

CONSERVATION BIOLOGY (US/0888-8892). **2190**

CONSTRUCTION & BUILDING MATERIALS (UK/0950-0618). **608**

CONSTRUCTION CLAIMS MONTHLY (US/0272-4561). **609**

CONSTRUCTION EQUIPMENT (1970) (US/0192-3978). **609**

CONSTRUCTION LABOR REPORT (US/0010-6836). **1661**

CONSTRUCTION MANAGEMENT AND ECONOMICS (UK/0144-6193). **610**

CONSTRUCTIVE APPROXIMATION (US/0176-4276). **3502**

CONSULTANT (HACKENSACK) (US/0010-7069). **3568**

CONSULTING-SPECIFYING ENGINEER (US/0892-5046). **2097**

CONSUMER CREDIT AND TRUTH-IN-LENDING COMPLIANCE REPORT (US/0300-6034). **2956**

CONSUMER LENDING REPORT (US/0891-558X). **1295**

CONSUMER MULTIMEDIA REPORT (US/1067-7887). **1152**

CONTACT DERMATITIS (DK/0105-1873). **3718**

CONTACTOLOGIA (GW/0936-1235). **3873**

CONTACTOLOGIA. DEUTSCHE AUSGABE (GW/0171-9599). **4215**

CONTAINER NEWS (US/0010-7360). **5380**

CONTAINERISATION INTERNATIONAL (UK/0010-7379). **864**

CONTEMPORARY DIAGNOSTIC RADIOLOGY (US/0149-9009). **3940**

CONTEMPORARY DIALYSIS & NEPHROLOGY (US/0899-837X). **3989**

CONTEMPORARY EDUCATIONAL PSYCHOLOGY (US/0361-476X). **4582**

CONTEMPORARY ERGONOMICS : PROCEEDINGS OF THE ERGONOMICS SOCIETY'S ANNUAL CONFERENCE (UK/0267-4718). **1969**

CONTEMPORARY EUROPEAN AFFAIRS (UK/0955-3843). **1552**

CONTEMPORARY FAMILY THERAPY (US/0892-2764). **2278**

CONTEMPORARY JEWRY (US/0147-1694). **2259**

CONTEMPORARY LITERATURE (US/0010-7484). **3378**

CONTEMPORARY LONGTERM CARE (US/8750-9652). **5280**

CONTEMPORARY MANAGEMENT IN INTERNAL MEDICINE (US/1050-9607). **3796**

CONTEMPORARY MANAGEMENT IN OBSTETRICS AND GYNECOLOGY (US/1050-9615). **3759**

CONTEMPORARY MATHEMATICS (AMERICAN MATHEMATICAL SOCIETY) (US/0271-4132). **3502**

CONTEMPORARY MUSIC REVIEW (UK/0749-4467). **4111**

CONTEMPORARY NEPHROLOGY (US/0278-1700). **3989**

CONTEMPORARY NEUROSURGERY (US/0163-2108). **3963**

CONTEMPORARY OB/GYN (US/0090-3159). **3759**

CONTEMPORARY PHYSICS (UK/0010-7514). **4401**

CONTEMPORARY PSYCHIATRY (NEW YORK, N.Y.) (US/0277-8041). **3923**

CONTEMPORARY PSYCHOANALYSIS (US/0010-7530). **3923**

CONTEMPORARY PSYCHOLOGY (US/0010-7549). **4582**

CONTEMPORARY REVIEWS IN OBSTETRICS AND GYNAECOLOGY (UK/0953-9182). **3759**

CONTEMPORARY SOUTH ASIA (UK/0958-4935). **2503**

CONTEMPORARY THEATRE REVIEW (SZ/1048-6801). **5363**

CONTEMPORARY TOPICS IN IMMUNOBIOLOGY (US/0093-4054). **3668**

CONTENTS PAGES IN EDUCATION (UK/0265-9220). **1794**

CONTINENTAL BANK JOURNAL OF APPLIED CORPORATE FINANCE (US/0898-4484). **784**

CONTINENTAL SHELF RESEARCH (UK/0278-4343). **1354**

CONTINUING CARE (US/1057-428X). **5280**

CONTINUITY AND CHANGE (UK/0268-4160). **5243**

CONTINUOUS JOURNEY (US/1065-3406). **864**

CONTINUUM MECHANICS AND THERMODYNAMICS (GW/0935-1175). **2112**

CONTRACEPTION (STONEHAM) (US/0010-7824). **588**

CONTRACEPTIVE TECHNOLOGY UPDATE (US/0274-726X). **588**

CONTRACT DESIGN (US/1053-5632). **2904**

CONTRACTING BUSINESS (US/0279-4071). **2604**

CONTRACTOR (NEWTON, MASS.) (US/0897-7135). **2604**

CONTRIBUTIONS FROM THE NEW YORK BOTANICAL GARDEN (US/0736-0509). **507**

CONTRIBUTIONS TO ATMOSPHERIC PHYSICS (GW/0303-4186). **1424**

CONTRIBUTIONS TO EPIDEMIOLOGY AND BIOSTATISTICS (SZ/0377-3574). **3734**

CONTRIBUTIONS TO GYNECOLOGY AND OBSTETRICS (SZ/0304-4246). **3759**

CONTRIBUTIONS TO HUMAN DEVELOPMENT (SZ/0301-4193). **4583**

CONTRIBUTIONS TO MICROBIOLOGY AND IMMUNOLOGY (SZ/0301-3081). **3668**

CONTRIBUTIONS TO MINERALOGY AND PETROLOGY (GW/0010-7999). **1439**

CONTRIBUTIONS TO NEPHROLOGY (SZ/0302-5144). **3989**

CONTRIBUTIONS TO PLASMA PHYSICS (1988) (GW/0863-1042). **4401**

CONTRIBUTIONS — Copyright Clearance Center Index

CONTRIBUTIONS TO POLITICAL ECONOMY (UK/0277-5921). **1590**

CONTRIBUTIONS TO SEDIMENTOLOGY (GW/0343-4125). **1372**

CONTRIBUTIONS TO VERTEBRATE EVOLUTION (SZ/0376-4230). **5581**

CONTROL AND DYNAMIC SYSTEMS (US/0090-5267). **1969**

CONTROL & INSTRUMENTATION (UK/0010-8022). **1219**

CONTROL ENGINEERING (US/0010-8049). **1219**

CONTROL ENGINEERING PRACTICE (UK/0967-0661). **2163**

CONTROLLED CLINICAL TRIALS (US/0197-2456). **3568**

CONTROLLER'S REPORT (NEW YORK, N.Y.) (US/0895-2787). **864**

CONVERGENCE (TORONTO) (CN/0010-8146). **1800**

CONVERTING MAGAZINE (US/0746-7141). **1602**

CONVULSIVE THERAPY (US/0749-8055). **3568**

COOPERATION AND CONFLICT (NO/0010-8367). **4470**

COORDINATION CHEMISTRY REVIEWS (SZ/0010-8545). **1051**

COPEIA (US/0045-8511). **5581**

CORAL REEFS (GW/0722-4028). **1448**

CORE. COLLECTED ORIGINAL RESOURCES IN EDUCATION (UK/0308-6909). **1734**

CORE JOURNALS IN CARDIOLOGY (NE/0165-9405). **3703**

CORE JOURNALS IN CLINICAL NEUROLOGY (NE/0165-1056). **3830**

CORE JOURNALS IN DERMATOLOGY (NE/0167-5796). **3718**

CORE JOURNALS IN GASTROENTEROLOGY (NE/0165-8719). **3743**

CORE JOURNALS IN OBSTETRICS/GYNECOLOGY (NE/0376-5059). **3759**

CORE JOURNALS IN OPHTHALMOLOGY (NE/0165-1005). **3873**

CORE JOURNALS IN PEDIATRICS (NE/0376-5040). **3902**

CORNEA (US/0277-3740). **3873**

CORNELL HOTEL AND RESTAURANT ADMINISTRATION QUARTERLY, THE (US/0010-8804). **2804**

CORONARY ARTERY DISEASE (US/0954-6928). **3703**

CORPORATE ANALYST, THE (US/1041-3871). **3098**

CORPORATE BOARD, THE (US/0746-8652). **661**

CORPORATE CASHFLOW (US/1040-0311). **784**

CORPORATE COUNSEL'S INTERNATIONAL ADVISER (US/0898-9907). **3126**

CORPORATE COUNSEL'S MONITOR (US/0898-9923). **3098**

CORPORATE COUNSEL'S QUARTERLY (US/0897-1617). **3098**

CORPORATE EFT REPORT (US/0272-0299). **784**

CORPORATE FINANCE (US/0894-6817). **784**

CORPORATE FINANCE SOURCEBOOK, THE (US/0163-3031). **785**

CORPORATE GOVERNANCE (UK/0964-8410). **864**

CORPORATE LIBRARY UPDATE (US/1061-5288). **3204**

CORPORATE PRACTICE SERIES (US/0162-5691). **3099**

CORPORATE PRACTICE SERIES. BNA'S CORPORATE COUNSEL WEEKLY (US/0886-0475). **3099**

CORPORATE TECHNOLOGY DIRECTORY (US/0887-1930). **3477**

CORPORATE TRAVEL (US/0882-8709). **5467**

CORPORATE YELLOW BOOK (US/1058-2908). **1924**

CORROSION ABSTRACTS (US/0010-9339). **2003**

CORROSION ENGINEERING (NEW YORK, N.Y.) (US/0892-4228). **2011**

CORROSION (HOUSTON, TEX.) (US/0010-9312). **2011**

CORROSION SCIENCE (UK/0010-938X). **2011**

CORROSION SCIENCE [MICROFORM] (US/0010-938X). **2011**

CORRUPTION AND REFORM (NE/0169-7528). **4470**

COSMETIC INSIDER'S REPORT (US/0275-4681). **403**

COSMETICS AND TOILETRIES (US/0361-4387). **403**

COSMIC RESEARCH (US/0010-9525). **1404**

COSPAR INFORMATION BULLETIN (UK/0045-8732). **17**

COST ENGINEERING (MORGANTOWN. 1980) (US/0274-9696). **1969**

COTTON GROWER (US/0194-9772). **168**

COTTON INTERNATIONAL (US/0070-0673). **5349**

COUNSELING AND VALUES (US/0160-7960). **4583**

COUNSELLING PSYCHOLOGY QUARTERLY (UK/0951-5070). **4583**

COUNSELOR EDUCATION AND SUPERVISION (US/0011-0035). **1877**

COUNTER-TERRORISM (US/0887-6398). **5196**

COUNTRY FORECASTS (US/1041-3553). **1472**

COUNTRY LIFE (UK/0045-8856). **2514**

COUNTRYSIDE COMMISSION NEWS (UK/0264-8822). **4641**

COURSES AND LECTURES / INTERNATIONAL CENTRE FOR MECHANICAL SCIENCES (IT/0254-1971). **2112**

CPI DIGEST (US/0891-1886). **973**

CPI PURCHASING (US/0746-9012). **1023**

CPJ : CANADIAN PHARMACEUTICAL JOURNAL (CN/0828-6914). **4298**

CQ RESEARCHER, THE (US/1056-2036). **4470**

CRAFTS (CRAFTS ADVISORY COMMITTEE) (UK/0306-610X). **371**

CRAIN'S CHICAGO BUSINESS (US/0149-6956). **662**

CRAIN'S CLEVELAND BUSINESS (US/0197-2375). **663**

CRAIN'S DETROIT BUSINESS (US/0882-1992). **663**

CRAIN'S NEW YORK BUSINESS (US/8756-789X). **1478**

CRC HANDBOOK OF CHEMISTRY AND PHYSICS (US/0147-6262). **973**

CREATIVITY AND INNOVATION MANAGEMENT (UK/0963-1690). **864**

CREDIT RISK MANAGEMENT REPORT (US/1054-5069). **785**

CREDIT UNION DIRECTORS NEWSLETTER (US/1058-1561). **785**

CREDIT UNION EXECUTIVE (MADISON, WIS. 1989) (US/1053-6744). **786**

CREDIT UNION MAGAZINE (US/0011-1066). **786**

CREDIT UNION MANAGER NEWSLETTER (US/1068-2120). **786**

CRETACEOUS RESEARCH (UK/0195-6671). **4226**

CRIME AND DELINQUENCY (US/0011-1287). **3161**

CRIME, LAW, AND SOCIAL CHANGE (NE/0925-4994). **3161**

CRIMINAL JUSTICE AND BEHAVIOR (US/0093-8548). **4583**

CRIMINAL LAW BULLETIN (US/0011-1317). **3106**

CRIMINAL LAW REPORTER, THE (US/0011-1341). **3106**

CRIMINAL LAW REVIEW (LONDON, ENGLAND) (UK/0011-135X). **3106**

CRITICAL CARE CLINICS (US/0749-0704). **3779**

CRITICAL CARE MEDICINE (US/0090-3493). **3723**

CRITICAL CARE NURSE (US/0279-5442). **3854**

CRITICAL CARE NURSING QUARTERLY (US/0887-9303). **3854**

CRITICAL INQUIRY (US/0093-1896). **318**

CRITICAL PERSPECTIVES ON ACCOUNTING (UK/1045-2354). **742**

CRITICAL QUARTERLY, THE (UK/0011-1562). **3379**

CRITICAL REVIEWS IN ANALYTICAL CHEMISTRY (US/1040-8347). **1014**

CRITICAL REVIEWS IN BIOCHEMISTRY AND MOLECULAR BIOLOGY (US/1040-9238). **486**

CRITICAL REVIEWS IN BIOMEDICAL ENGINEERING (US/0278-940X). **3691**

CRITICAL REVIEWS IN BIOTECHNOLOGY (US/0738-8551). **3691**

CRITICAL REVIEWS IN CLINICAL LABORATORY SCIENCES (US/1040-8363). **3894**

CRITICAL REVIEWS IN ENVIRONMENTAL CONTROL (US/1040-838X). **2163**

CRITICAL REVIEWS IN EUKARYOTIC GENE EXPRESSION (US/1045-4403). **486**

CRITICAL REVIEWS IN FOOD SCIENCE AND NUTRITION (US/1040-8398). **2332**

CRITICAL REVIEWS IN IMMUNOLOGY (US/1040-8401). **3668**

CRITICAL REVIEWS IN MICROBIOLOGY (US/1040-841X). **561**

CRITICAL REVIEWS IN NEUROBIOLOGY (US/0892-0915). **3569**

CRITICAL REVIEWS IN ONCOGENESIS (US/0893-9675). **3815**

CRITICAL REVIEWS IN ONCOLOGY/HEMATOLOGY (US/1040-8428). **3815**

CRITICAL REVIEWS IN ORAL BIOLOGY AND MEDICINE (US/1045-4411). **1319**

CRITICAL REVIEWS IN PHYSICAL AND REHABILITATION MEDICINE (US/0896-2960). **507**

CRITICAL REVIEWS IN PLANT SCIENCES (US/0735-2689). **507**

CRITICAL REVIEWS IN SOLID STATE AND MATERIALS SCIENCES (US/1040-8436). **4401**

CRITICAL REVIEWS IN SURFACE CHEMISTRY (US/1049-9407). **1051**

CRITICAL REVIEWS IN THERAPEUTIC DRUG CARRIER SYSTEMS (US/0743-4863). **4298**

CRITICAL REVIEWS IN TOXICOLOGY (US/1040-8444). **3980**

CRITICAL SURVEY (UK/0011-1570). **3379**

CRITIQUE - BOLINGBROKE SOCIETY (US/0011-1619). **3341**

CRM MONOGRAPH SERIES / CENTRE DE RECHERCHES MATHEMATIQUES (US/1065-8599). **3502**

CRM PROCEEDINGS & LECTURE NOTES (US/1065-8580). **3502**

CRNA (US/1048-2687). **3682**

CROP PROTECTION (GUILDFORD, SURREY) (UK/0261-2194). **169**

CRUSTACEANA (NE/0011-216X). **5581**

CRUX (CN/0011-2186). **4951**

CRYOBIOLOGY (US/0011-2240). **452**

CRYOGENICS (GUILFORD) (UK/0011-2275). **4401**

CRYPTOLOGIA (US/0161-1194). **1226**

CRYSTAL RESEARCH AND TECHNOLOGY (1979) (GW/0232-1300). **1031**

CRYSTALLOGRAPHY REPORTS (US/1063-7745). **1031**

CRYSTALLOGRAPHY REVIEWS (US/0889-311X). **1031**

CSP. CRITICAL SOCIAL POLICY (UK/0261-0183). **4541**

CULPEPPER LETTER, THE (US/8750-3697). **1285**

CULTURAL CRITIQUE (US/0882-4371). **5197**

CULTURAL DYNAMICS (NE/0921-3740). **5243**

CULTURAL STUDIES (LONDON, ENGLAND) (UK/0950-2386). **5197**

CULTURAL TRENDS (UK/0954-8963). **318**

CULTURE, MEDICINE AND PSYCHIATRY (NE/0165-005X). **3924**

CUMULATIVE INDEX OF SAE TECHNICAL PAPERS (US/0742-2350). **5412**

CURARE (GW/0344-8622). **3924**

CURRENCY CONFIDENTIAL (UK/0141-1047). **786**

CURRENT ANAESTHESIA AND CRITICAL CARE (UK/0953-7112). **3963**

CURRENT ANTHROPOLOGY (US/0011-3204). **234**

CURRENT BIOLOGY (UK/0960-9822). **452**

CURRENT CLINICAL PRACTICE SERIES (NE/0168-6917). **3570**

CURRENT EYE RESEARCH (UK/0271-3683). **3874**

CURRENT GASTROENTEROLOGY (US/0198-8085). **3743**

CURRENT GENETICS (GW/0172-8083). **544**

CURRENT HEMATOLOGY AND ONCOLOGY (US/0739-4810). **3771**

CURRENT HEPATOLOGY (US/0198-8093). **3796**

CURRENT INDEX TO STATISTICS (US/0364-1228). **3542**

CURRENT LAW INDEX (US/0196-1780). **3080**

CURRENT MATHEMATICAL PUBLICATIONS (US/0361-4794). **3542**

CURRENT MICROBIOLOGY (US/0343-8651). **561**

CURRENT NEPHROLOGY (US/0148-4265). **3989**

CURRENT NEUROLOGY (US/0161-780X). **3831**

CURRENT OBSTETRICS AND GYNAECOLOGY (UK/0957-5847). **3759**

CURRENT OPINION IN ANAESTHESIOLOGY (UK/0952-7907). **3682**

CURRENT OPINION IN BIOTECHNOLOGY (UK/0958-1669). **3691**

CURRENT OPINION IN CARDIOLOGY (UK/0268-4705). **3704**

CURRENT OPINION IN CELL BIOLOGY (US/0955-0674). **535**

CURRENT OPINION IN DENTISTRY (US/1046-0764). **1319**

CURRENT OPINION IN GASTROENTEROLOGY (UK/0267-1379). **3744**

CURRENT OPINION IN GENETICS AND DEVELOPMENT (UK/0959-437X). **544**

CURRENT OPINION IN IMMUNOLOGY (US/0952-7915). **3668**

CURRENT OPINION IN INFECTIOUS DISEASES (UK/0951-7375). **3713**

CURRENT OPINION IN LIPIDOLOGY (UK/0957-9672). **3704**

CURRENT OPINION IN NEPHROLOGY AND HYPERTENSION (US/1062-4821). **3989**

CURRENT OPINION IN NEUROBIOLOGY (UK/0959-4388). **453**

CURRENT OPINION IN NEUROLOGY AND NEUROSURGERY (UK/0951-7383). **3831**

CURRENT OPINION IN OBSTETRICS & GYNECOLOGY (US/1040-872X). **3759**

CURRENT OPINION IN ONCOLOGY (US/1040-8746). **3815**

CURRENT OPINION IN OPHTHALMOLOGY (US/1040-8738). **3874**

CURRENT OPINION IN ORTHOPAEDICS (US/1041-9918). **3881**

CURRENT OPINION IN PEDIATRICS (US/1040-8703). **3902**

CURRENT OPINION IN PSYCHIATRY (UK/0951-7367). **3924**

CURRENT OPINION IN RADIOLOGY (US/1040-869X). **3940**

CURRENT OPINION IN RHEUMATOLOGY (US/1040-8711). **3804**

CURRENT OPINION IN STRUCTURAL BIOLOGY (UK/0959-440X). **453**

CURRENT OPINION IN UROLOGY (UK/0963-0643). **3989**

CURRENT ORTHOPAEDICS (UK/0268-0890). **3881**

CURRENT PAEDIATRICS (UK/0957-5839). **3902**

CURRENT PAPERS IN ELECTRICAL & ELECTRONICS ENGINEERING (UK/0011-3778). **2003**

CURRENT PAPERS IN PHYSICS (UK/0011-3786). **4426**

CURRENT PERSPECTIVES IN SOCIAL THEORY (US/0278-1204). **5244**

CURRENT PHYSICS INDEX (US/0098-9819). **4426**

CURRENT PRACTICE IN SURGERY (UK/0952-0627). **3963**

CURRENT PROBLEMS IN CANCER (US/0147-0272). **3815**

CURRENT PROBLEMS IN CARDIOLOGY (US/0146-2806). **3704**

CURRENT PROBLEMS IN CLINICAL BIOCHEMISTRY (SZ/0300-1725). **486**

CURRENT PROBLEMS IN DERMATOLOGY (SZ/0070-2064). **3718**

CURRENT PROBLEMS IN DERMATOLOGY (CHICAGO, ILL.) (US/1040-0486). **3719**

CURRENT PROBLEMS IN DIAGNOSTIC RADIOLOGY (US/0363-0188). **3940**

CURRENT PROBLEMS IN OBSTETRICS, GYNECOLOGY AND FERTILITY (US/8756-0410). **3760**

CURRENT PROBLEMS IN PEDIATRICS (ENGLISH ED.) (US/0045-9380). **3903**

CURRENT PROBLEMS IN SURGERY (US/0011-3840). **3963**

CURRENT PSYCHOLOGY (NEW BRUNSWICK, N.J.) (US/1046-1310). **4584**

CURRENT PULMONOLOGY (US/0163-7800). **3704**

CURRENT STUDIES IN HEMATOLOGY AND BLOOD TRANSFUSION (SZ/0258-0330). **3771**

CURRENT SURGERY (US/0149-7944). **3963**

CURRENT THERAPEUTIC RESEARCH (US/0011-393X). **4298**

CURRENT THERAPEUTICS (AT/0311-905X). **4298**

CURRENT TITLES IN DENTISTRY (DK/0903-3483). **1338**

CURRENT TOPICS IN BIOENERGETICS (US/0070-2129). **453**

CURRENT TOPICS IN CELLULAR REGULATION (US/0070-2137). **535**

CURRENT TOPICS IN DEVELOPMENTAL BIOLOGY (US/0070-2153). **453**

CURRENT TOPICS IN MATERIALS SCIENCE (US/0165-1854). **2022**

CURRENT TOPICS IN MEMBRANES (US/1063-5823). **535**

CURRENT TOPICS IN MICROBIOLOGY AND IMMUNOLOGY (GW/0070-217X). **3669**

CURRENT TOPICS IN NUTRITION AND DISEASE (US/0191-2453). **4189**

CURRENT TOPICS IN PATHOLOGY (GW/0070-2188). **3894**

CURRENT TRENDS IN LIFE SCIENCES (II/0378-7540). **507**

CURRENT WORLD LEADERS (US/0192-6802). **4519**

CURRENTS IN EMERGENCY CARDIAC CARE (US/1054-917X). **3704**

CURRICULUM AND TEACHING (AT/0726-416X). **1734**

CURRICULUM INQUIRY (US/0362-6784). **1892**

CUSTOM BUILDER (US/0895-2493). **612**

CUTTING TOOL ENGINEERING (US/0011-4189). **4000**

CVGIP. GRAPHICAL MODELS AND IMAGE PROCESSING (US/1049-9652). **1233**

CVGIP. IMAGE UNDERSTANDING (US/1049-9660). **1233**

CYBEREDGE JOURNAL (US/1061-3099). **1181**

CYBERNETICS AND SYSTEMS (US/0196-9722). **1250**

CYBERNETICS AND SYSTEMS ANALYSIS (US/1060-0396). **1251**

CYTOBIOS (UK/0011-4529). **535**

CYTOGENETICS AND CELL GENETICS (SZ/0301-0171). **544**

CYTOKINE (PHILADELPHIA, PA.) (US/1043-4666). **453**

CYTOLOGY AND GENETICS (US/0095-4527). **535**

CYTOMETRY (NEW YORK, N.Y.) (US/0196-4763). **535**

CYTOPATHOLOGY (OXFORD) (UK/0956-5507). **535**

CYTOSKELETON SHEFFIELD (UK/0268-1625). **3570**

CYTOTECHNOLOGY (DORDRECHT) (NE/0920-9069). **535**

CZECHOSLOVAK MATHEMATICAL JOURNAL (XR/0011-4642). **3503**

D & B REPORTS (US/0746-6110). **664**

D.C. TRACTS (US/1041-469X). **3804**

DAEDALUS (CAMBRIDGE) (US/0011-5266). **5098**

DAILY ENVIRONMENT REPORT (US/1060-2976). **3110**

DAILY LABOR REPORT (WASHINGTON, D.C. : 1948) (US/0418-2693). **1662**

DAILY REPORT FOR EXECUTIVES (US/0148-8155). **664**

DAILY TAX REPORT (WASHINGTON) (US/0092-6884). **2958**

DAILY VARIETY (US/0011-5509). **4067**

DAIRY EXPORTER (NZ/0111-915X). **193**

DAIRY FOODS (US/0888-0050). **193**

DAIRY FOODS NEWSLETTER (US/1057-2619). **193**

DAIRY HERD MANAGEMENT (US/0011-5614). **193**

DALTON TRANSACTIONS (UK/0300-9246). **1036**

DANCE RESEARCH (UK/0264-2875). **1312**

DANGEROUS PROPERTIES OF INDUSTRIAL MATERIALS REPORT (US/0270-3777). **2861**

DAQI KEXUE (CC/0254-0002). **1424**

DASEINSANALYSE (BASEL) (SZ/0254-6221). **3924**

DATA & KNOWLEDGE ENGINEERING (NE/0169-023X). **1253**

DATA BASE ALERT (US/0737-951X). **1253**

DATA CHANNELS (US/0093-7290). **1257**

DATA/COMM INDUSTRY REPORT (US/0149-9556). **1257**

DATA COMMUNICATIONS (US/0363-6399). **1241**

DATA PROCESSING (UK/0011-684X). **1257**

DATA PROCESSING AUDITING REPORT (US/0735-3863). **3571**

DATA PROCESSING DIGEST (US/0011-6858). **1209**

DATA RESOURCE MANAGEMENT (US/1053-5594). **865**

DATA STORAGE REPORT (UK/0267-5447). **1257**

DATABASE PROGRAMMING & DESIGN (US/0895-4518). **1253**

DATABASE SEARCHER (US/0891-6713). **1253**

DATABASE (WESTON) (US/0162-4105). **1253**

DATAMATION (US/0011-6963). **1258**

DATAMATION [MICROFORM] (US/0011-6963). **2097**

DATAPRO DIRECTORY OF MICROCOMPUTER SOFTWARE (US/0730-8795). **1237**

DATAPRO DIRECTORY OF SOFTWARE (US/0730-8779). **1285**

DATAPRO OFFICE PRODUCTS EVALUATION SERVICE (US/0898-4468). **4211**

DATAPRO REPORTS ON BANKING AUTOMATION (US/0730-8809). **787**

DATAPRO REPORTS ON MICROCOMPUTERS (US/0741-2541). **1267**

DATAPRO REPORTS ON MINICOMPUTERS (US/0275-0813). **1274**

DATAPRO REPORTS ON RETAIL AUTOMATION (US/0730-8817). **1258**

DATEK IMAGING SUPPLIES MONTHLY, THE (US/1050-6993). **4564**

DATENSCHUTZ-BERATER (GW/0170-7256). **1226**

DAY CARE AND EARLY EDUCATION (US/0092-4199). **1803**

DAY CARE AND EARLY EDUCATION. [MICROFILM] (US/0092-4199). **1803**

DAYTON BUSINESS REPORTER (US/1063-3413). **664**

DB. DEUTSCHE BAUZEITUNG (1981) (GW/0721-1902). **296**

DBS NEWS (US/0733-9739). **1153**

DEATH STUDIES (US/0748-1187). **4584**

DEC USER (UK/0263-6530). **1182**

DECISION SUPPORT SYSTEMS (NE/0167-9236). **865**

DECUBITUS (CHICAGO, ILL.) (US/0898-1655). **3571**

DEEP-SEA RESEARCH. PART A. OCEANOGRAPHIC RESEARCH PAPERS (UK/0198-0149). **1362**

DEEP-SEA RESEARCH. PART I, OCEANOGRAPHIC RESEARCH PAPERS (UK/0967-0637). **1448**

DEEP-SEA RESEARCH. PART II, TOPICAL STUDIES IN OCEANOGRAPHY (UK/0967-0645). **1448**

DEFENCE ECONOMICS (SZ/1043-0717). **4040**

DEFENSE ANALYSIS (UK/0743-0175). **4040**

DEFENSE & AEROSPACE ELECTRONICS (US/1056-747X). **2040**

DEFENSE CLEANUP (US/1052-0635). **2227**

DEFENSE DAILY (US/0889-0404). **4041**

DEFENSE ELECTRONICS (US/0278-3479). **2040**

DEFENSE MARKETING INTERNATIONAL (US/1044-3975). **4041**

DEFENSE NEWS (SPRINGFIELD, VA.) (US/0884-139X). **4041**

DEFENSE WEEK (US/0273-3188). **4042**

DEMENTIA (BASEL, SWITZERLAND) (SZ/1013-7424). **3831**

DENTAL CLINICS OF NORTH AMERICA (US/0011-8532). **1320**

DENTAL ECONOMICS (PITTSBURGH. 1968) (US/0011-8583). **1320**

DENTO MAXILLO FACIAL RADIOLOGY (UK/0250-832X). **1322**

DERMATOLOGIC CLINICS (US/0733-8635). **3719**

DERMATOLOGY (BASEL) (SZ/1018-8665). **3719**

DERMATOLOGY TIMES (US/0196-6197). **3719**

DERMATOSEN IN BERUF UND UMWELT (GW/0343-2432). **3720**

DESALINATION (NE/0011-9164). **5532**

DESIGN BOOK REVIEW (US/0737-5344). **296**

DESIGN ENGINEERING (TORONTO) (CN/0011-9342). **1970**

DESIGN FIRM MANAGEMENT & ADMINISTRATION REPORT (US/1057-2864). **865**

DESIGN FOR ARTS IN EDUCATION (US/0732-0973). **318**

DESIGN MANAGEMENT (US/1042-8534). **865**

DESIGN NEWS (US/0011-9407). **2097**

DESIGN QUARTERLY (MINNEAPOLIS, MINN.) (US/0011-9415). **297**

DESIGN

DESIGN STUDIES (UK/0142-694X). **2097**

DESIGNFAX (US/0163-6669). **2097**

DET BASTA UR READER'S DIGEST (SW/0005-3856). **2515**

DETAIL (MUNCHEN) (GW/0011-9571). **297**

DEUTSCHE APOTHEKER-ZEITUNG (GW/0011-9857). **4299**

DEUTSCHE BAUMSCHULE (GW/0011-992X). **2413**

DEUTSCHE KRANKENPFLEGEZEITSCHRIFT (GW/0012-074X). **3855**

DEUTSCHE LEBENSMITTEL-RUNDSCHAU (GW/0012-0413). **2333**

DEUTSCHE MALERBLATT, DAS (GW/0012-0448). **4223**

DEUTSCHE MEDIZIN (GW/0178-3351). **3571**

DEUTSCHE MEDIZINISCHE WOCHENSCHRIFT (GW/0012-0472). **3571**

DEUTSCHE POLIZEI (GW/0012-057X). **3163**

DEUTSCHE SCHULE, DIE (GW/0012-0731). **1735**

DEUTSCHE SCHWARZBUNTE (GW/0343-3145). **210**

DEUTSCHE SPRACHE (GW/0340-9341). **3276**

DEUTSCHE STEUER-ZEITUNG (GW/0724-5637). **4720**

DEUTSCHE ZAHNAERZTLICHE ZEITSCHRIFT (GW/0012-1029). **1322**

DEUTSCHE ZEITSCHRIFT FUER MUND-, KIEFER- UND GESICHTS-CHIRURGIE (GW/0343-3137). **3963**

DEUTSCHES ARCHIV FUER ERFORSCHUNG DES MITTELALTERS (GW/0012-1223). **2685**

DEUTSCHES TIERARZTEBLATT (GW/0340-1898). **5508**

DEUTSCHUNTERRICHT (STUTTGART) (GW/0340-2258). **3276**

DEVELOPMENT AND CHANGE (UK/0012-155X). **5198**

DEVELOPMENT JOURNAL (LONDON) (UK/0957-4115). **4642**

DEVELOPMENTAL AND COMPARATIVE IMMUNOLOGY (US/0145-305X). **3669**

DEVELOPMENTAL BIOLOGY (US/0012-1606). **453**

DEVELOPMENTAL BRAIN RESEARCH (NE/0165-3806). **3831**

DEVELOPMENTAL GENETICS (US/0192-253X). **544**

DEVELOPMENTAL IMMUNOLOGY (SZ/1044-6672). **3669**

DEVELOPMENTAL MEDICINE & CHILD NEUROLOGY (UK/0012-1622). **3657**

DEVELOPMENTAL MEDICINE AND CHILD NEUROLOGY. SUPPLEMENT (UK/0419-0238). **3831**

DEVELOPMENTAL NEUROSCIENCE (SZ/0378-5866). **3831**

DEVELOPMENTAL PHARMACOLOGY AND THERAPEUTICS (SZ/0379-8305). **4299**

DEVELOPMENTAL PSYCHOBIOLOGY (US/0012-1630). **453**

DEVELOPMENTAL PSYCHOLOGY (US/0012-1649). **4584**

DEVELOPMENTAL REVIEW (US/0273-2297). **4584**

DEVELOPMENTS IN BIOCHEMISTRY (NL/0165-1714). **486**

DEVELOPMENTS IN BIOLOGICAL STANDARDIZATION (SZ/0301-5149). **453**

DEVELOPMENTS IN FOOD SCIENCE (NE/0167-4501). **2333**

DEVELOPMENTS IN GEOPHYSICAL EXPLORATION METHODS (UK/0264-844X). **1404**

DEVELOPMENTS IN GEOTECHNICAL ENGINEERING (NE/0165-1250). **1970**

DEVELOPMENTS IN INDUSTRIAL MICROBIOLOGY (US/0070-4563). **562**

DEVELOPMENTS IN OPHTHALMOLOGY (SZ/0250-3751). **3874**

DEVELOPMENTS IN PETROLEUM GEOLOGY (UK/0260-4248). **4254**

DEVELOPMENTS IN PETROLEUM SCIENCE (NE/0376-7361). **4254**

DEVELOPMENTS IN POLYMER STABILISATION (UK/0262-155X). **4454**

DEVELOPMENTS IN SEDIMENTOLOGY (NE/0070-4571). **1373**

DEVELOPMENTS IN SOIL SCIENCE (NE/0166-0918). **170**

DEVELOPMENTS IN SOLID EARTH GEOPHYSICS (NE/0419-0297). **1404**

DEVIANCE ET SOCIETE (SZ/0378-7931). **4584**

DEVIANT BEHAVIOR (US/0163-9625). **4584**

DEVICES & DIAGNOSTICS LETTER (US/0098-7573). **3571**

DGS, DEUTSCHE GEFLUGELWIRTSCHAFT UND SCHWEINEPRODUKTION (GW/0340-3858). **210**

DIABETE & METABOLISME (FR/0338-1684). **3727**

DIABETES/METABOLISM REVIEWS (US/0742-4221). **3728**

DIABETIC MEDICINE (UK/0742-3071). **3728**

DIABETOLOGIA (GW/0012-186X). **3728**

DIACRITICS (US/0300-7162). **3341**

DIAGNOSIS (ORADELL, N.J.) (US/0163-3228). **3571**

DIAGNOSTIC IMAGING (SAN FRANCISCO, CALIF.) (US/0194-2514). **3940**

DIAGNOSTIC MICROBIOLOGY AND INFECTIOUS DISEASE (US/0732-8893). **562**

DIAGNOSTIC MOLECULAR PATHOLOGY (US/1052-9551). **3894**

DIAGNOSTICS INTELLIGENCE (US/1054-9609). **3571**

DIALECTICAL ANTHROPOLOGY (NE/0304-4092). **235**

DIAMOND AND RELATED MATERIALS (NE/0925-9635). **4001**

DIAPASON (CHICAGO), THE (US/0012-2378). **4114**

DIASPORA (NEW YORK, N.Y.) (US/1044-2057). **5198**

DIATOM RESEARCH (UK/0269-249X). **508**

DICKENS QUARTERLY (US/0742-5473). **3381**

DIDEROT STUDIES (SZ/0070-4806). **3381**

DIFFERENTIAL EQUATIONS (US/0012-2661). **3503**

DIFFERENTIATION (LONDON) (GW/0301-4681). **536**

DIGEST OF PAPERS - INTERNATIONAL SYMPOSIUM ON FAULT-TOLERANT COMPUTING (1979) (US/0731-3071). **1182**

DIGEST OF TECHNICAL PAPERS (US/0097-966X). **2041**

DIGEST OF TECHNICAL PAPERS / IEEE INTERNATIONAL SOLID-STATE CIRCUITS CONFERENCE (US/0193-6530). **2041**

Copyright Clearance Center Index

DIGEST OF UNITED KINGDOM ENERGY STATISTICS (UK/0307-0603). **1961**

DIGESTION (SZ/0012-2823). **3744**

DIGESTIVE DISEASES AND SCIENCES (US/0163-2116). **3744**

DIGESTIVE DISEASES (BASEL) (SZ/0257-2753). **3744**

DIGESTIVE SURGERY (SZ/0253-4886). **3963**

DIGITAL MEDIA (US/1056-7038). **2113**

DIGITAL NEWS & REVIEW (US/1065-7452). **1246**

DIGITAL NEWS (BOSTON, MASS.) (US/0891-9860). **1182**

DIGITAL REVIEW (NEW YORK, N.Y.) (US/0739-4314). **1267**

DIGITAL SIGNAL PROCESSING (US/1051-2004). **1182**

DIGITALE BILDDIAGNOSTIK (GW/0724-7591). **3941**

DIMENSIONS OF CRITICAL CARE NURSING (US/0730-4625). **3855**

DIQIU WULIXUE BAO (CC/0001-5733). **1404**

DIRECT MARKETING (US/0012-3188). **923**

DIRECTORS & BOARDS (US/0364-9156). **865**

DIRECTORY OF ADMINISTRATIVE SERVICES (US/0149-337X). **4643**

DIRECTORY OF AMERICAN RESEARCH AND TECHNOLOGY (US/0886-0076). **5174**

DIRECTORY OF GRADUATE MEDICAL EDUCATION PROGRAMS (US/0892-0109). **3572**

DIRECTORY OF ONLINE DATABASES (US/0193-6840). **3207**

DIRECTORY OF PORTABLE DATABASES (US/1045-8352). **1183**

DIRECTORY OF STATE COURT CLERKS AND COUNTY COURTHOUSES (US/1042-4172). **4644**

DIRECTORY OF THE FOREST PRODUCTS INDUSTRY (US/0070-6477). **2400**

DIRECTORY OF U.S. LABOR ORGANIZATIONS (US/0734-6786). **1663**

DIRECTORY OF WORLD LEADERS & FACTBOOK (US/1043-2043). **4472**

DISABILITY, HANDICAP & SOCIETY (UK/0267-4645). **5284**

DISASTERS (UK/0361-3666). **5284**

DISCOUNT STORE NEWS (US/0012-3587). **954**

DISCOURSE PROCESSES (US/0163-853X). **3277**

DISCRETE & COMPUTATIONAL GEOMETRY (US/0179-5376). **3503**

DISCRETE EVENT DYNAMIC SYSTEMS (US/0924-6703). **1282**

DISCRETE MATHEMATICS (NE/0012-365X). **3504**

DISCUSSIONS IN NEUROSCIENCES (SZ/0254-8852). **3831**

DISEASE-A-MONTH (US/0011-5029). **3572**

DISEASE MARKERS (UK/0278-0240). **3713**

DISEASES OF THE COLON & RECTUM (US/0012-3706). **3744**

DISKUSSION DEUTSCH (GW/0342-1589). **3277**

DISPLAY AND IMAGING TECHNOLOGY (US/0733-2386). **1971**

DISPLAYS (UK/0141-9382). **1228**

DISTANCE EDUCATION (AT/0158-7919). **1736**

DISTRIBUTED AND PARALLEL DATABASES (US/0926-8782). **1254**

DISTRIBUTED COMPUTING (GW/0178-2770). **1258**

DISTRIBUTION MAINZ (GW/0342-1635). **923**

DISTRICT COURT REPORTS (NZ/0111-4239). **2963**

DIVERSITY (US/0744-8163). **508**

DM (GW/0416-5551). **4030**

DNA PROBES (UK/0266-6308). **453**

DNA SEQUENCE (SZ/1042-5179). **453**

DOCTOR GUILDFORD (UK/0046-0451). **3737**

DOCUMENT DELIVERY WORLD (US/1067-0815). **1183**

DOCUMENT IMAGE AUTOMATION (US/1054-9692). **1277**

DOCUMENT IMAGE AUTOMATION UPDATE (US/1054-9706). **1277**

DOCUMENTA OPHTHALMOLOGICA (NE/0012-4486). **3874**

DOCUMENTATION PAR L'IMAGE, LA (FR/0046-0478). **5101**

DOD'S PARLIAMENTARY COMPANION (UK/0070-7007). **4645**

DOG WORLD (US/0012-4893). **4286**

DOKLADY AKADEMII NAUK UKRAINSKOI SSR. SERIIA B, GEOLOGICHESKIE, KHIMICHESKIE I BIOLOGICHESKIE NAUKI (UN/0201-8454). **5101**

DOKLADY / AKADEMIIA NAUK AZERBAIDZHANSKOI SSR (AJ/0002-3078). **5101**

DOKLADY. BIOCHEMISTRY (US/0012-4958). **486**

DOKLADY. BIOLOGICAL SCIENCES (US/0012-4966). **454**

DOKLADY. BIOPHYSICS (US/0012-4974). **495**

DOKLADY. BOTANICAL SCIENCES (US/0012-4982). **508**

DOKLADY. CHEMISTRY (US/0012-5008). **974**

DOKLADY. PHYSICAL CHEMISTRY (US/0012-5016). **1051**

DOKLADY. PHYSICAL CHEMISTRY (US/0012-5016). **1051**

DOKUMENTATION FUER UMWELTSCHUTZ UND LANDESPFLEGE (GW/0026-6957). **2191**

DOMESTIC ANIMAL ENDOCRINOLOGY (US/0739-7240). **3728**

DPW. DEUTSCHE PAPIERWIRTSCHAFT (GW/0070-4296). **4233**

DR. DOBB'S JOURNAL (1989) (US/1044-789X). **1267**

DR. JULIAN WHITAKER'S HEALTH & HEALING (US/1057-9273). **2596**

DRAHT-WELT (GW/0012-592X). **4001**

DREAMING (NEW YORK, N.Y.) (US/1053-0797). **580**

DREI (STUTTGART, GERMANY : 1948) (GW/0012-6063). **2846**

DREXEL POLYMER NOTES (US/8756-4572). **4454**

DRG MONITOR (US/0741-6512). **3573**

DRILLING CONTRACTOR (US/0046-0702). **4254**

DRILLING NEWS (UK/0955-7369). **4255**

DROIT ET PRATIQUE DU COMMERCE INTERNATIONAL (US/0335-5047). **831**

DROVER'S JOURNAL (SHAWNEE MISSION, KAN.) (US/0012-6454). **210**

DRUCK PRINT (GW/0012-6462). **4564**

DRUCKLUFTTECHNIK (MAINZ) (GW/0723-7537). **5102**

DRUCKWELT (GW/0012-6519). **4564**

DRUG AND ALCOHOL DEPENDENCE (SZ/0376-8716). **1343**

DRUG AND ALCOHOL REVIEW (UK/0959-5236). **1343**

DRUG AND CHEMICAL TOXICOLOGY (NEW YORK, N.Y. 1978) (US/0148-0545). **3980**

DRUG & COSMETIC INDUSTRY (US/0012-6527). **4299**

DRUG DELIVERY (US/1071-7544). **4299**

DRUG DESIGN AND DISCOVERY (SZ/1055-9612). **4300**

DRUG DEVELOPMENT AND INDUSTRIAL PHARMACY (US/0363-9045). **4300**

DRUG DEVELOPMENT RESEARCH (US/0272-4391). **4300**

DRUG GMP REPORT (US/1061-2335). **4300**

DRUG INFORMATION JOURNAL (US/0092-8615). **4300**

DRUG METABOLISM AND DISPOSITION (US/0090-9556). **4300**

DRUG METABOLISM REVIEWS (SOFTCOVER ED.) (US/0360-2532). **4301**

DRUG NEWS & PERSPECTIVES (SP/0214-0934). **4301**

DRUG-NUTRIENT INTERACTIONS (US/0272-3530). **4301**

DRUG SAFETY (NZ/0114-5916). **4301**

DRUG STORE NEWS (US/0191-7587). **4301**

DRUG TARGETING AND DELIVERY (US/1058-241X). **4301**

DRUG THERAPY (NEW YORK, N.Y.) (US/0001-7094). **3573**

DRUG TOPICS (US/0012-6616). **4301**

DRUGS & AGING (NZ/1170-229X). **4302**

DRUGS MADE IN GERMANY (GW/0012-6683). **4302**

DRUGS (NEW YORK, N.Y.) (US/0012-6667). **4302**

DRUGS OF THE FUTURE (SP/0377-8282). **4302**

DRUGS UNDER EXPERIMENTAL AND CLINICAL RESEARCH (SP/0378-6501). **4302**

DRYING TECHNOLOGY (US/0737-3937). **1024**

DTW. DEUTSCHE TIERAERZTLICHE WOCHENSCHRIFT (GW/0341-6593). **5509**

DUKE MATHEMATICAL JOURNAL (US/0012-7094). **3504**

DUNN REPORT, ELECTRONIC PUBLISHING & PREPRESS SYSTEMS NEWS & VIEWS (US/0741-6547). **4814**

DURABILITY OF BUILDING MATERIALS (NE/0167-3890). **613**

DVM (US/0012-7337). **5509**

DW DOKUMENTATION WASSER (GW/0012-5156). **5533**

DYES AND PIGMENTS (UK/0143-7208). **4223**

DYNAMIC SYSTEMS AND APPLICATIONS (US/1056-2176). **3504**

DYNAMICS AND CONTROL (US/0925-4668). **2113**

DYNAMICS AND STABILITY OF SYSTEMS (UK/0268-1110). **1246**

DYNAMICS OF ATMOSPHERES AND OCEANS (NE/0377-0265). **1449**

DYSMORPHOLOGY AND CLINICAL GENETICS (US/0893-6633). **4387**

DYSPHAGIA (US/0179-051X). **3887**

E&P ENVIRONMENT (US/1054-6464). **1439**

EAR AND HEARING (US/0196-0202). **3887**

EARLY CHILD DEVELOPMENT AND CARE (UK/0300-4430). **2278**

EARLY CHILDHOOD RESEARCH QUARTERLY (US/0885-2006). **1803**

EARLY DEVELOPMENT AND PARENTING (UK/1057-3593). **1803**

EARLY MUSIC (UK/0306-1078). **4116**

EARLY MUSIC HISTORY (UK/0261-1279). **4116**

EARLY WARNING FORECAST (US/0733-0138). **1480**

EARLY WARNING REPORT (US/0193-3655). **670**

EARTH AND PLANETARY SCIENCE LETTERS (NE/0012-821X). **1374**

EARTH, MOON, AND PLANETS (NE/0167-9295). **395**

EARTH-SCIENCE REVIEWS (NE/0012-8252). **1374**

EARTH SPACE REVIEW (US/1060-1848). **1355**

EARTH SURFACE PROCESSES AND LANDFORMS (UK/0197-9337). **1374**

EARTHQUAKE ENGINEERING & STRUCTURAL DYNAMICS (UK/0098-8847). **2022**

EARTHQUAKE RESEARCH IN CHINA (US/0891-4176). **1374**

EAST ASIAN BUSINESS INTELLIGENCE (US/0888-580X). **923**

EAST ASIAN EXECUTIVE REPORTS (US/0272-1589). **3099**

EAST EUROPE & THE REPUBLICS (US/1060-6157). **1480**

EAST WEST FORTNIGHTLY BULLETIN (BE/0012-8570). **1634**

EBRI QUARTERLY PENSION INVESTMENT REPORT (US/0889-4396). **897**

ECHOCARDIOGRAPHY (MOUNT KISCO, N.Y.) (US/0742-2822). **3704**

ECLOGAE GEOLOGICAE HELVETIAE (SZ/0012-9402). **1374**

ECN. EUROPEAN CHEMICAL NEWS (UK/0014-2875). **974**

ECOGRAPHY (DK/0906-7590). **2213**

ECOLOGICAL ABSTRACTS (UK/0305-196X). **2184**

ECOLOGICAL ECONOMICS (NE/0921-8009). **2213**

ECOLOGICAL ENGINEERING (NE/0925-8574). **1971**

ECOLOGICAL ENTOMOLOGY (UK/0307-6946). **5607**

ECOLOGICAL MODELLING (NE/0304-3800). **2214**

ECOLOGICAL RESEARCH (JA/0912-3814). **2214**

ECOLOGY LAW QUARTERLY (US/0046-1121). **3110**

ECOLOGY OF FOOD AND NUTRITION (US/0367-0244). **4190**

ECOLOGY USA (HOUSTON) (US/0098-6615). **2214**

ECONOMETRIC REVIEWS (US/0747-4938). **1481**

ECONOMETRIC THEORY (US/0266-4666). **1591**

ECONOMIC AND FINANCIAL COMPUTING (UK/0962-2780). **1482**

ECONOMIC BOTANY (US/0013-0001). **508**

ECONOMIC BULLETIN FOR EUROPE (US/0041-638X). **1634**

ECONOMIC DEVELOPMENT AND CULTURAL CHANGE (US/0013-0079). **1482**

ECONOMIC DEVELOPMENT QUARTERLY (US/0891-2424). **1483**

ECONOMIC FORECASTS (NE/0169-1767). **1557**

ECONOMIC GEOLOGY AND THE BULLETIN OF THE SOCIETY OF ECONOMIC GEOLOGISTS (US/0361-0128). **1374**

ECONOMIC HISTORY REVIEW, THE (UK/0013-0117). **1557**

ECONOMIC JOURNAL (LONDON) (UK/0013-0133). **1483**

ECONOMIC MODELLING (UK/0264-9993). **1591**

ECONOMIC OPPORTUNITY REPORT (US/0013-0206). **5284**

ECONOMIC SYSTEMS RESEARCH (UK/0953-5314). **1485**

ECONOMIC THEORY (GW/0938-2259). **1591**

ECONOMIC TRENDS (LONDON) (UK/0013-0400). **1485**

ECONOMICA (LONDON) (UK/0013-0427). **1486**

ECONOMICS AND PHILOSOPHY (UK/0266-2671). **1486**

ECONOMICS & POLITICS (OXFORD, ENGLAND) (UK/0954-1985). **1486**

ECONOMICS LETTERS (NE/0165-1765). **1486**

ECONOMICS OF EDUCATION REVIEW (US/0272-7757). **1737**

ECONOMICS OF INNOVATION AND NEW TECHNOLOGY (SZ/1043-8599). **5102**

ECONOMICS OF PLANNING (NE/0013-0451). **1558**

ECONOMY AND SOCIETY (UK/0308-5147). **5199**

ECOS (AT/0311-4546). **2227**

ECOTASS (ENGLISH EDITION) (SZ/0733-5989). **1487**

ECOTOXICOLOGY AND ENVIRONMENTAL SAFETY (US/0147-6513). **2214**

EDDA (NO/0013-0818). **3341**

EDI IN FINANCE (UK/0960-4634). **5102**

EDI MONTHLY REPORT (US/1062-645X). **4645**

EDI NEWS (US/0894-9212). **1183**

EDITORIAL EYE, THE (US/0193-7383). **4814**

EDN (US/0012-7515). **2042**

EDN; ELECTRONIC ENGINEER'S DESIGN MAGAZINE (US/0012-7515). **2042**

EDP AUDITOR JOURNAL, THE (US/0885-0445). **1258**

EDPACS (US/0736-6981). **1226**

EDUCATION 3-13 (UK/0300-4279). **1804**

EDUCATION & COMPUTING (NE/0167-9287). **1223**

EDUCATION AND SOCIETY (MELBOURNE) (AT/0726-2655). **1738**

EDUCATION AND URBAN SOCIETY (US/0013-1245). **1738**

EDUCATION CANADA (CN/0013-1253). **1738**

EDUCATION DAILY (US/0013-1261). **1739**

EDUCATION ECONOMICS (UK/0964-5292). **1739**

EDUCATION (EDINBURGH) (UK/0013-1164). **1863**

EDUCATION ENFANTINE, L' (FR/0013-1288). **1739**

EDUCATION FOR INFORMATION (NE/0167-8329). **1739**

EDUCATION FUNDING NEWS (US/0273-4443). **1739**

EDUCATION IN CHEMISTRY (UK/0013-1350). **974**

EDUCATION MONITOR (US/1041-9462). **1740**

EDUCATION OF THE HANDICAPPED (US/0194-2255). **1878**

EDUCATION WEEK (US/0277-4232). **1741**

EDUCATIONAL ADMINISTRATION QUARTERLY (US/0013-161X). **1863**

EDUCATIONAL & TRAINING TECHNOLOGY INTERNATIONAL : ETTI (UK/0954-7304). **1741**

EDUCATIONAL GERONTOLOGY (US/0360-1277). **1800**

EDUCATIONAL IRM QUARTERLY (US/1055-8683). **1223**

EDUCATIONAL MANAGEMENT & ADMINISTRATION : JOURNAL OF THE BRITISH EDUCATIONAL MANAGEMENT AND ADMINISTRATION SOCIETY (UK/0263-211X). **1863**

EDUCATIONAL MARKETER (US/0013-1806). **1742**

EDUCATIONAL PLANNING (US/0315-9388). **1742**

EDUCATIONAL PSYCHOLOGY (DORCHESTER-ON-THAMES) (UK/0144-3410). **4586**

EDUCATIONAL PSYCHOLOGY REVIEW (US/1040-726X). **4586**

EDUCATIONAL RESEARCH (WINDSOR) (UK/0013-1881). **1742**

EDUCATIONAL REVIEW (BIRMINGHAM) (UK/0013-1911). **1742**

EDUCATIONAL STUDIES (UK/0305-5698). **1743**

EDUCATIONAL STUDIES IN MATHEMATICS (NE/0013-1954). **1743**

EDUCATIONAL TECHNOLOGY ABSTRACTS (UK/0266-3368). **1794**

EDUCATIONAL THEORY (US/0013-2004). **1743**

EEG-LABOR, DAS (GW/0170-8287). **3831**

EEO REVIEW, THE (US/0148-6934). **1664**

EFL GAZETTE, THE (UK/0732-5819). **3278**

EICOSANOIDS (GW/0934-9820). **3729**

EIGHTEENTH-CENTURY FICTION (DOWNSVIEW, ONT.) (CN/0840-6286). **3383**

EIGHTEENTH-CENTURY LIFE (US/0098-2601). **5268**

EINSTEIN QUARTERLY, THE (US/0724-6706). **3574**

EISENBAHNINGENIEUR, DER (GW/0013-2810). **5431**

EISZEITALTER UND GEGENWART (GW/0424-7116). **1374**

ELASTOMERICS (US/0146-0706). **5075**

ELDERLY HEALTH SERVICES LETTER (US/0891-9275). **5284**

ELECTORAL STUDIES (UK/0261-3794). **4645**

ELECTRIC LIGHT & POWER (US/0013-4120). **2043**

ELECTRIC MACHINES AND POWER SYSTEMS (US/0731-356X). **2043**

ELECTRIC PERSPECTIVES (US/0364-474X). **2043**

ELECTRIC POWER SYSTEMS RESEARCH (SZ/0378-7796). **2044**

ELECTRIC VEHICLE DEVELOPMENTS (UK/0141-9811). **5381**

ELECTRICAL

ELECTRICAL & ELECTRONICS ABSTRACTS (UK/0036-8105). **2003**

ELECTRICAL APPARATUS (US/0190-1370). **2044**

ELECTRICAL CONSTRUCTION AND MAINTENANCE (US/0013-4260). **2044**

ELECTRICAL DESIGN & MFG (US/1065-7436). **2044**

ELECTRICAL ENGINEERING IN JAPAN (US/0424-7760). **2045**

ELECTRICAL EQUIPMENT LONDON (UK/0013-4317). **2045**

ELECTRICAL EQUIPMENT NEWS (CN/0013-4333). **2045**

ELECTRICAL MANUFACTURING (LIBERTYVILLE, ILL.) (US/0895-3716). **3478**

ELECTRICAL MARKETING (US/0149-5771). **2045**

ELECTRICAL TECHNOLOGY (UK/0965-5433). **2045**

ELECTRICAL TIMES (UK/0013-4414). **2045**

ELECTRICAL WHOLESALING (US/0013-4430). **2045**

ELECTRICAL WORLD (US/0013-4457). **2045**

ELECTROANALYSIS (NEW YORK, N.Y.) (US/1040-0397). **1014**

ELECTROANALYTICAL CHEMISTRY (US/0070-9778). **1014**

ELECTROCHIMICA ACTA (UK/0013-4686). **1034**

ELECTROENCEPHALOGRAPHY AND CLINICAL NEUROPHYSIOLOGY (IE/0013-4694). **3831**

ELECTROENCEPHALOGRAPHY AND CLINICAL NEUROPHYSIOLOGY/ ELECTROMYOGRAPHY AND MOTOR CONTROL (IE/0924-980X). **3832**

ELECTROENCEPHALOGRAPHY AND CLINICAL NEUROPHYSIOLOGY EVOKED POTENTIALS (IE/0168-5597). **580**

ELECTROMAGNETICS (US/0272-6343). **2046**

ELECTROMEDICA (GW/0013-4724). **3941**

ELECTROMEDICA. DEUTSCHE AUSGABE (GW/0340-5389). **3941**

ELECTRON DISPLAY WORLD (US/0742-1532). **2046**

ELECTRON MICROSCOPY REVIEWS (US/0892-0354). **572**

ELECTRON SPIN RESONANCE (UK/0305-9758). **1015**

ELECTRONIC BUSINESS (US/0163-6197). **2046**

ELECTRONIC BUYERS' NEWS (US/0164-6362). **2046**

ELECTRONIC CHEMICALS NEWS (US/0886-5671). **2047**

ELECTRONIC CLAIMS PROCESSING REPORT (US/1071-8524). **671**

ELECTRONIC DESIGN (US/0013-4872). **2047**

ELECTRONIC ENGINEERING (UK/0013-4902). **2047**

ELECTRONIC ENGINEERING TIMES (US/0192-1541). **2047**

ELECTRONIC IMAGING REPORT (US/1057-0942). **1183**

ELECTRONIC LIBRARY (UK/0264-0473). **3209**

ELECTRONIC MEDIA (US/0745-0311). **1131**

ELECTRONIC MESSAGING NEWS (US/1044-9892). **1110**

ELECTRONIC MODELING (US/0275-9136). **2047**

ELECTRONIC NETWORKING (US/1051-4805). **1241**

ELECTRONIC PACKAGING AND PRODUCTION (US/0013-4945). **2048**

ELECTRONIC PUBLISHING (UK/0894-3982). **4814**

ELECTRONIC SIMULATION (US/1063-1100). **2048**

ELECTRONICS (1985) (US/0883-4989). **2048**

ELECTRONICS & COMMUNICATIONS ABSTRACTS (UK/0013-5119). **2049**

ELECTRONICS & COMMUNICATIONS ENGINEERING JOURNAL (UK/0954-0695). **2049**

ELECTRONICS LETTERS (UK/0013-5194). **2049**

ELECTRONICS PURCHASING (US/0889-0196). **2050**

ELECTRONICS WEEKLY (UK/0013-5224). **2050**

ELECTRONICS WORLD + WIRELESS WORLD (UK/0959-8332). **2050**

ELECTROPHORESIS (GW/0173-0835). **1015**

ELEKTRICESTVO (RU/0013-5380). **2051**

ELEKTRISCHE BAHNEN (GW/0013-5437). **5431**

ELEKTRISCHE ENERGIE-TECHNIK (GW/0170-2033). **1937**

ELEKTRIZITATSWIRTSCHAFT (GW/0013-5496). **2051**

ELEKTRO (NO/0013-550X). **2051**

ELEKTRO-ANZEIGER (GW/0013-5518). **2051**

ELEKTROHANDEL HEIDELBERG (GW/0013-5542). **2051**

ELEKTROHIMIA (RU/0424-8570). **2051**

ELEKTROMEISTER + DEUTSCHES ELEKTROHANDWERK (GW/0012-1258). **2051**

ELEKTRONICA (NE/0168-7840). **2051**

ELEKTRONIK (MUNCHEN) (GW/0013-5658). **2051**

ELEKTRONIKER (SZ/0531-9218). **2052**

ELEKTRONIKJOURNAL (GW/0013-5674). **2052**

ELEKTRONNOE MODELIROVANIE (UN/0204-3572). **1259**

ELEKTROTECHNIK (GW/0013-581X). **2052**

ELEKTROTECHNIK UND INFORMATIONSTECHNIK : E&I (AU/0932-383X). **2052**

ELEKTROTEKHNIKA (MOSKVA, 1963) (RU/0013-5860). **2052**

ELEKTROWARME INTERNATIONAL. EDITION B : INDUSTRIELLE ELEKTROWARME (GW/0340-3521). **2605**

ELEMENTA (YVERDON, SWITZERLAND) (US/1064-6663). **3278**

ELEMENTARY SCHOOL GUIDANCE AND COUNSELING (US/0013-5976). **1878**

ELEMENTARY SCHOOL JOURNAL. MICROFORM, THE (US/0013-5984). **1743**

ELEMENTE DER MATHEMATIK (SZ/0013-6018). **3504**

ELETTROTECNICA, L' (IT/0013-6131). **2053**

ELH (US/0013-8304). **3342**

EMA. ELEKTRISCHE MASCHINEN (GW/0013-5445). **2053**

EMBALLAGES (FR/0013-6573). **4218**

EMBEDDED SYSTEMS PROGRAMMING (US/1040-3272). **1228**

EMBO JOURNAL (UK/0261-4189). **454**

EMERGENCY CARE QUARTERLY (US/8755-8467). **3724**

EMERGENCY DEPARTMENT LAW (US/1042-2978). **2965**

EMERGENCY LIBRARIAN (US/0315-8888). **3209**

EMERGENCY MEDICINE CLINICS OF NORTH AMERICA (US/0733-8627). **3724**

EMERGENCY MEDICINE NEWS (US/1054-0725). **3724**

EMERGENCY MEDICINE REPORTS (US/0746-2506). **3724**

EMERGENCY PREPAREDNESS NEWS (US/0275-3782). **1073**

EMPIRICAL ECONOMICS (AU/0377-7332). **1488**

EMPIRICAL STUDIES OF PSYCHOANALYTICAL THEORIES (US/0743-071X). **3925**

EMPLOYEE ASSISTANCE PROGRAM MANAGEMENT LETTER (US/0896-0941). **866**

EMPLOYEE BENEFITS CASES (US/0273 236X). **3146**

EMPLOYEE BENEFITS JOURNAL (US/0361-4050). **1665**

EMPLOYEE BENEFITS REPORT (US/0884-478X). **1665**

EMPLOYEE HEALTH & FITNESS (US/0199-6304). **1665**

EMPLOYEE RELATIONS (UK/0142-5455). **940**

EMPLOYEE RELATIONS LAW JOURNAL (US/0098-8898). **3146**

EMPLOYEE RESPONSIBILITIES AND RIGHTS JOURNAL (US/0892-7545). **3147**

EMPLOYERS' HEALTH COSTS SAVINGS LETTER (US/0740-9087). **3574**

EMPLOYMENT ALERT (US/0882-6250). **3147**

EMPLOYMENT RELATIONS TODAY (US/0745-7790). **1667**

EMU (AT/0158-4197). **5617**

ENCEPHALE (FR/0013-7006). **3832**

ENDEAVOUR (NEW SERIES) (UK/0160-9327). **5103**

ENDOCRINE PATHOLOGY (US/1046-3976). **3729**

ENDOCRINE RESEARCH (US/0743-5800). **3729**

ENDOCRINOLOGIST (BALTIMORE, MD.), THE (US/1051-2144). **3729**

ENDOCRINOLOGIST, THE (US/1051-2144). **3729**

ENDOCRINOLOGY AND METABOLISM CLINICS OF NORTH AMERICA (US/0889-8529). **3729**

ENDODONTICS & DENTAL TRAUMATOLOGY (DK/0109-2502). **1323**

ENDOSCOPY (GW/0013-726X). **3744**

ENDOTHELIUM (NEW YORK, N.Y.) (US/1062-3329). **536**

ENERGIA ELETTRICA (IT/0013-7308). **2053**

ENERGIA MADRID (SP/0210-2056). **1938**

ENERGIA NUCLEAR (MADRID) (SP/0013-7324). **2155**

ENERGIE (MUNCHEN) (GW/0013-7359). **2113**

ENERGY ANALECTS (CN/0315-1654). **1938**

ENERGY AND BUILDINGS (SZ/0378-7788). **614**

ENERGY & FUELS (US/0887-0624). **1939**

ENERGY BOOKS QUARTERLY (US/0892-5461). **1962**

ENERGY CONVERSION AND MANAGEMENT (UK/0196-8904). **1939**

ENERGY DAILY, THE (US/0364-5274). **1939**

ENERGY DESIGN UPDATE (US/0741-3629). **1939**

ENERGY ECONOMICS (UK/0140-9883). **1940**

ENERGY, ECONOMICS AND CLIMATE CHANGE (US/1059-5813). **1940**

ENERGY ENGINEERING : JOURNAL OF THE ASSOCIATION OF ENERGY ENGINEERS (US/0199-8595). **1940**

ENERGY EXPLORATION & EXPLOITATION (UK/0144-5987). **1940**

ENERGY INFORMATION ABSTRACTS (US/0147-6521). **1962**

ENERGY INFORMATION ABSTRACTS ANNUAL (US/0739-3679). **1962**

ENERGY JOURNAL (CAMBRIDGE, MASS.) (US/0195-6574). **1940**

ENERGY (OXFORD) (UK/0360-5442). **1941**

ENERGY POLICY (UK/0301-4215). **1941**

ENERGY PROCESSING CANADA (CN/0319-5759). **1941**

ENERGY REPORT (ARLINGTON, VA.) (US/0888-8183). **1941**

ENERGY REVIEW (SANTA BARBARA) (US/0094-8063). **1942**

ENERGY SOURCES (US/0090-8312). **1942**

ENERGY (STAMFORD, CONN. 1975) (US/0149-9386). **1942**

ENERGY STATISTICS SOURCEBOOK (US/0889-5260). **1962**

ENERGY TRENDS (UK/0308-1222). **1942**

ENERGY USER NEWS (US/0162-9131). **1942**

ENFERMEDADES INFECCIOSAS Y MICROBIOLOGIA CLINICA (SP/0213-005X). **3713**

ENGEI GAKKAI ZASSHI (JA/0013-7626). **2413**

ENGINEER (LONDON) (UK/0013-7758). **1972**

ENGINEERED MATERIALS ABSTRACTS (US/0951-9998). **2004**

ENGINEERING ANALYSIS WITH BOUNDARY ELEMENTS (UK/0955-7997). **1972**

ENGINEERING & AUTOMATION (GW/0931-6221). **1972**

ENGINEERING AND MINING JOURNAL (1926) (US/0095-8948). **2138**

ENGINEERING APPLICATIONS OF ARTIFICIAL INTELLIGENCE (UK/0952-1976). **1212**

ENGINEERING COMPUTERS (UK/0263-4759). **1184**

ENGINEERING CONFERENCE (US/0271-9959). **4233**

ENGINEERING DIGEST (TORONTO) (CN/0013-7901). **1972**

ENGINEERING ECONOMIST, THE (US/0013-791X). **1973**

ENGINEERING FRACTURE MECHANICS (US/0013-7944). **2102**

ENGINEERING GEOLOGY (NE/0013-7952). **1973**

ENGINEERING INDEX ANNUAL (US/0360-8557). **2004**

ENGINEERING INDEX BIOENGINEERING AND BIOTECHNOLOGY ABSTRACTS (US/1041-2913). **2004**

ENGINEERING INDEX ENERGY ABSTRACTS (US/0093-8408). **2004**

ENGINEERING INDEX MONTHLY (US/0742-1974). **2004**

ENGINEERING MANAGEMENT JOURNAL (UK/0960-7919). **1973**

ENGINEERING OPTIMIZATION (UK/0305-215X). **1973**

ENGINEERING STRUCTURES (UK/0141-0296). **2023**

ENGINEERING WITH COMPUTERS (US/0177-0667). **1974**

ENGINEER'S DIGEST (WILLOW GROVE) (US/0199-0101). **1974**

ENGLISCH (GW/0013-8185). **3278**

ENGLISH FOR SPECIFIC PURPOSES (NEW YORK, N.Y.) (US/0889-4906). **3278**

ENGLISH HISTORICAL REVIEW, THE (UK/0013-8266). **2615**

ENGLISH LANGUAGE TEACHING JOURNAL (US/0307-8337). **3279**

ENGLISH STUDIES (NE/0013-838X). **3384**

ENGLISH TODAY (UK/0266-0784). **3279**

ENR (US/0891-9526). **1975**

ENTERTAINMENT MARKETING LETTER (US/1048-5112). **924**

ENTOMOLOGIA EXPERIMENTALIS ET APPLICATA (NE/0013-8703). **5607**

ENTOMOLOGIA GENERALIS (GW/0171-8177). **5607**

ENTOMOLOGICAL REVIEW (US/0013-8738). **5607**

ENTOMOLOGISCHE BLATTER FUER BIOLOGIE UND SYSTEMATIK DER KAFER (GW/0013-8835). **5582**

ENTOMOPHAGA (FR/0013-8959). **4244**

ENTREPRENEURSHIP AND REGIONAL DEVELOPMENT (UK/0898-5626). **672**

ENTREPRENEURSHIP, INNOVATION AND CHANGE (US/1059-0137). **672**

ENTREPRENEURSHIP THEORY AND PRACTICE (US/1042-2587). **672**

ENTRETIENS SUR L'ANTIQUITE CLASSIQUE (SZ/0071-0822). **1076**

ENTROPIE (FR/0013-9084). **1975**

ENTWICKLUNG + LANDLICHER RAUM (GW/0343-6462). **82**

ENVIRONMENT ABSTRACTS (US/0093-3287). **2184**

ENVIRONMENT ABSTRACTS ANNUAL (US/0000-1198). **2184**

ENVIRONMENT AND BEHAVIOR (US/0013-9165). **2215**

ENVIRONMENT & INDUSTRY DIGEST (UK/0958-2126). **2192**

ENVIRONMENT INTERNATIONAL (UK/0160-4120). **2165**

ENVIRONMENT PROTECTION ENGINEERING (PL/0324-8828). **2166**

ENVIRONMENT REPORTER (US/0013-9211). **3111**

ENVIRONMENT (ST. LOUIS) (US/0013-9157). **2228**

ENVIRONMENT (ST. LOUIS) (US/0013-9157). **2215**

ENVIRONMENT WATCH. LATIN AMERICA (US/1060-1414). **672**

ENVIRONMENT WEEK (US/1041-8105). **2166**

ENVIRONMENTAL ACTION (WASHINGTON, D.C.) (US/0013-922X). **2166**

ENVIRONMENTAL AND EXPERIMENTAL BOTANY (UK/0098-8472). **509**

ENVIRONMENTAL AND MOLECULAR MUTAGENESIS (US/0893-6692). **544**

ENVIRONMENTAL AND RESOURCE ECONOMICS (NE/0924-6460). **2166**

ENVIRONMENTAL AUDIT ADVISER (US/0742-6062). **2192**

ENVIRONMENTAL BIOLOGY OF FISHES (NE/0378-1909). **2300**

ENVIRONMENTAL CHEMISTRY (UK/0305-7712). **975**

ENVIRONMENTAL CLAIMS JOURNAL (US/1040-6026). **3111**

ENVIRONMENTAL CONSERVATION (SZ/0376-8929). **2193**

ENVIRONMENTAL COUNSELOR, THE (US/1041-3863). **3111**

ENVIRONMENTAL ENGINEERING (BURY SAINT EDMUNDS, ENG. : 1988) (UK/0954-5824). **1975**

ENVIRONMENTAL ENTOMOLOGY (US/0046-225X). **5608**

ENVIRONMENTAL FINANCE (NEW YORK, N.Y.) (US/1054-8017). **2167**

ENVIRONMENTAL GEOCHEMISTRY AND HEALTH (UK/0269-4042). **2167**

ENVIRONMENTAL GEOLOGY AND WATER SCIENCES (US/0177-5146). **1375**

ENVIRONMENTAL HEALTH LETTER (US/0196-0598). **2228**

ENVIRONMENTAL IMPACT ASSESSMENT REVIEW (US/0195-9255). **2167**

ENVIRONMENTAL MANAGEMENT (NEW YORK) (US/0364-152X). **2168**

ENVIRONMENTAL MANAGEMENT NEWS (US/0893-3413). **2168**

ENVIRONMENTAL MANAGER (US/1043-786X). **2228**

ENVIRONMENTAL MANAGER'S COMPLIANCE ADVISOR, THE (US/0887-9753). **3112**

ENVIRONMENTAL MONITORING AND ASSESSMENT (NE/0167-6369). **2168**

ENVIRONMENTAL POLICY AND LAW (SZ/0378-777X). **3112**

ENVIRONMENTAL POLLUTION (1987) (UK/0269-7491). **2229**

ENVIRONMENTAL PROFESSIONAL, THE (US/0191-5398). **2169**

ENVIRONMENTAL PROGRESS (US/0278-4491). **2229**

ENVIRONMENTAL RESEARCH (NEW YORK, N.Y.) (US/0013-9351). **2169**

ENVIRONMENTAL SAFETY ALERT (US/1060-8648). **2229**

ENVIRONMENTAL SCIENCE & TECHNOLOGY (US/0013-936X). **2169**

ENVIRONMENTAL SCIENCE & TECHNOLOGY MICROFORM (US/0013-936X). **2169**

ENVIRONMENTAL SOFTWARE (UK/0266-9838). **2170**

ENVIRONMENTAL TOXICOLOGY AND CHEMISTRY (US/0730-7268). **2229**

ENVIRONMENTALIST, THE (UK/0251-1088). **2193**

ENZYME (SZ/0013-9432). **486**

ENZYME AND MICROBIAL TECHNOLOGY (UK/0141-0229). **3692**

ENZYME REGULATION (UK/0142-8071). **487**

EOS (WASHINGTON, D.C.) (US/0096-3941). **1404**

EPIDEMIOLOGY (CAMBRIDGE, MASS.) (US/1044-3983). **3734**

EPILEPSIA (COPENHAGEN) (NE/0013-9580). **3832**

EPILEPSY RESEARCH (NE/0920-1211). **3832**

EPISODES (CN/0705-3797). **1375**

EPITHELIA (UK/0269-4565). **5583**

EQUINOX (CAMDEN EAST) (CN/0710-9911). **2560**

EQUIPMENT LEASING & ASSET BASED BORROWING REPORT INCLUDING CURRENT RATES AND SOURCES (US/1051-6573). **866**

ERDKUNDE (GW/0014-0015). **1375**

ERDOL & KOHLE, ERDGAS, PETROCHEMIE (GW/0014-0058). **4255**

ERDOL, ERDGAS, KOHLE (GW/0179-3187). **4255**

ERGEBNISSE DER LIMNOLOGIE (GW/0071-1128). **1413**

ERGO-MED (GW/0170-2327). **3575**

ERGODIC THEORY AND DYNAMICAL SYSTEMS (UK/0143-3857). **3505**

ERGONOMICS (UK/0014-0139). **1251**

ERGONOMICS IN DESIGN (US/1064-8046). **1975**

ERISA NEWSLETTER, THE (US/8755-5379). **1667**

ERISA UPDATE, THE (US/0194-4959). **1667**

ERKENNTNIS (NE/0165-0106). **4346**

ERNAHRUNGS- UMSCHAU (GW/0014-021X). **4190**

ERNAHRUNGSFORSCHUNG (GW/0071-1179). **4190**

ERWERBSOBSTBAU (GW/0014-0309). **170**

ERZMETALL (GW/0044-2658). **4001**

ESPACE GEOGRAPHIQUE (FR/0046-2497). **2560**

ESSAYS IN CRITICISM (UK/0014-0856). **3385**

ESTATE PLANNING & TAXATION COORDINATOR (US/0195-1238). **3118**

ESTATE PLANNING (TAMPA) (US/0094-1794). **3118**

ESTETIKA (XR/0014-1291). **320**

ESTHETIC DENTISTRY UPDATE (PHILADELPHIA, PA.) (US/1045-9812). **1323**

ESTUARIES (US/0160-8347). **554**

ESTUARINE, COASTAL AND SHELF SCIENCE (US/0272-7714). **1449**

ESTUDIOS GEOOGICOS (MADRID) (SP/0367-0449). **1375**

ETHICS (US/0014-1704). **2250**

ETHICS IN GOVERNMENT REPORTER (US/0279-2869). **2250**

ETHIK IN DER MEDIZIN (GW/0935-7335). **2250**

ETHIKOS (US/0895-5026). **2250**

ETHNIC AND RACIAL STUDIES (UK/0141-9870). **2260**

ETHNIC GROUPS (US/0308-6860). **2260**

ETHNOMUSICOLOGY (US/0014-1836). **4117**

ETHOLOGY AND SOCIOBIOLOGY (US/0162-3095). **4586**

ETHOS (US/0091-2131). **4586**

ETR (GW/0013-2845). **5431**

ETZ. ELEKROTECHNISCHE ZEITSCHRIFT (BERLIN, WEST) (GW/0170-1711). **2054**

EUPHYTICA (NE/0014-2336). **509**

EUROIL (NO/0802-9474). **4255**

EUROPA-ARCHIV (GW/0014-2476). **4521**

EUROPA CHEMIE (GW/0014-2484). **2012**

EUROPA WORLD YEAR BOOK, THE (UK/0956-2273). **4473**

EUROPARECHT (GW/0531-2485). **2967**

EUROPE-ASIA STUDIES (UK/0966-8136). **2687**

EUROPE DRUG & DEVICE REPORT (US/1056-179X). **4303**

EUROPEAN & MIDDLE EAST TAX REPORT, THE (UK/0141-1047). **4722**

EUROPEAN APPLIED RESEARCH REPORTS. NUCLEAR SCIENCE AND TECHNOLOGY SECTION (SZ/0379-4229). **2155**

EUROPEAN BIOPHYSICS JOURNAL (GW/0175-7571). **495**

EUROPEAN BIOTECHNOLOGY NEWSLETTER (PARIS) (FR/0765-2046). **3692**

EUROPEAN CANCER NEWS (NE/0921-3732). **3816**

EUROPEAN COATINGS JOURNAL (GW/0930-3847). **4223**

EUROPEAN ECONOMIC REVIEW (NE/0014-2921). **1489**

EUROPEAN HEART JOURNAL (UK/0195-668X). **3704**

EUROPEAN JOURNAL OF AGRONOMY (FR/1161-0301). **171**

EUROPEAN JOURNAL OF ANAESTHESIOLOGY (UK/0265-0215). **3682**

EUROPEAN JOURNAL OF APPLIED PHYSIOLOGY AND OCCUPATIONAL PHYSIOLOGY (GW/0301-5548). **580**

EUROPEAN JOURNAL OF BIOCHEMISTRY (GW/0014-2956). **487**

EUROPEAN JOURNAL OF CANCER. PART B : ORAL ONCOLOGY (UK/0964-1955). **3817**

EUROPEAN JOURNAL OF CANCER PREVENTION (UK/0959-8278). **3817**

EUROPEAN JOURNAL OF CARDIO-THORACIC SURGERY : OFFICIAL JOURNAL OF THE EUROPEAN ASSOCIATION FOR CARDIO-THORACIC SURGERY (GW/1010-7940). **3964**

EUROPEAN JOURNAL OF CELL BIOLOGY (GW/0171-9335). **536**

EUROPEAN JOURNAL OF CHIROPRACTIC (UK/0263-9114). **3575**

EUROPEAN JOURNAL OF CLINICAL CHEMISTRY AND CLINICAL BIOCHEMISTRY (GW/0939-4974). **487**

EUROPEAN JOURNAL OF CLINICAL INVESTIGATION (GW/0014-2972). **3575**

EUROPEAN JOURNAL OF CLINICAL MICROBIOLOGY & INFECTIOUS DISEASES (GW/0934-9723). **562**

EUROPEAN JOURNAL OF CLINICAL NUTRITION (UK/0954-3007). **4190**

EUROPEAN JOURNAL OF CLINICAL PHARMACOLOGY (GW/0031-6970). **4303**

EUROPEAN JOURNAL OF COMBINATORICS (UK/0195-6698). **3505**

EUROPEAN JOURNAL OF EDUCATION (UK/0141-8211). **1745**

EUROPEAN JOURNAL OF ENGINEERING EDUCATION (UK/0304-3797). **1975**

EUROPEAN JOURNAL OF EPIDEMIOLOGY (IT/0393-2990). **3735**

EUROPEAN JOURNAL OF FOREST PATHOLOGY (GW/0300-1237). **2379**

EUROPEAN JOURNAL OF GASTROENTEROLOGY & HEPATOLOGY (UK/0954-691X). **3744**

EUROPEAN JOURNAL OF GYNAECOLOGICAL ONCOLOGY (IT/0392-2936). **3817**

EUROPEAN JOURNAL OF HAEMATOLOGY (DK/0902-4441). **3771**

EUROPEAN JOURNAL OF IMMUNOGENETICS : OFFICIAL JOURNAL OF THE BRITISH SOCIETY FOR HISTOCOMPATIBILITY AND IMMUNOGENETICS (UK/0960-7420). **3669**

EUROPEAN JOURNAL OF IMMUNOLOGY (GW/0014-2980). **3669**

EUROPEAN

EUROPEAN JOURNAL OF IMPLANT AND REFRACTIVE SURGERY, THE (FR/0955-3681). **3874**

EUROPEAN JOURNAL OF INFORMATION SYSTEMS (UK/0960-085X). **1184**

EUROPEAN JOURNAL OF MARKETING (UK/0309-0566). **924**

EUROPEAN JOURNAL OF MECHANICS. A. SOLIDS (FR/0997-7538). **4427**

EUROPEAN JOURNAL OF MECHANICS. B. FLUIDS (FR/0997-7546). **4402**

EUROPEAN JOURNAL OF MEDICINAL CHEMISTRY (FR/0223-5234). **3575**

EUROPEAN JOURNAL OF MINERALOGY (STUTTGART) (GW/0935-1221). **1439**

EUROPEAN JOURNAL OF MORPHOLOGY (NE/0924-3860). **3679**

EUROPEAN JOURNAL OF NEUROSCIENCE, THE (UK/0953-816X). **3832**

EUROPEAN JOURNAL OF NUCLEAR MEDICINE (GW/0340-6997). **3848**

EUROPEAN JOURNAL OF OPERATIONAL RESEARCH (NE/0377-2217). **5104**

EUROPEAN JOURNAL OF ORTHODONTICS (UK/0141-5387). **1323**

EUROPEAN JOURNAL OF PEDIATRIC SURGERY : OFFICIAL JOURNAL OF AUSTRIAN ASSOCIATION OF PEDIATRIC SURGERY ... ZEITSCHRIFT FUER KINDERCHIRURGIE (GW/0939-7248). **3964**

EUROPEAN JOURNAL OF PEDIATRICS (GW/0340-6199). **3903**

EUROPEAN JOURNAL OF PERSONALITY (UK/0890-2070). **4587**

EUROPEAN JOURNAL OF PHARMACEUTICAL SCIENCES (NE/0928-0987). **4303**

EUROPEAN JOURNAL OF PHARMACEUTICS AND BIOPHARMACEUTICS : OFFICIAL JOURNAL OF ARBEITSGEMEINSCHAFT FUER PHARMAZEUTISCHE VERFAHRENSTECHNIK E.V (GW/0939-6411). **4303**

EUROPEAN JOURNAL OF PHARMACOLOGY (NE/0014-2999). **4303**

EUROPEAN JOURNAL OF PHARMACOLOGY : ENVIRONMENTAL TOXICOLOGY AND PHARMACOLOGY SECTION (NE/0926-6917). **4303**

EUROPEAN JOURNAL OF PHARMACOLOGY. MOLECULAR PHARMACOLOGY SECTION (NE/0922-4106). **4303**

EUROPEAN JOURNAL OF PLASTIC SURGERY (GW/0930-343X). **3964**

EUROPEAN JOURNAL OF POLITICAL RESEARCH (NE/0304-4130). **4473**

EUROPEAN JOURNAL OF POPULATION (NE/0168-6577). **4553**

EUROPEAN JOURNAL OF PROTISTOLOGY (GW/0932-4739). **562**

EUROPEAN JOURNAL OF SOCIAL PSYCHOLOGY (UK/0046-2772). **5245**

EUROPEAN JOURNAL OF SOIL BIOLOGY (FR/1164-5563). **171**

EUROPEAN JOURNAL OF SOLID STATE AND INORGANIC CHEMISTRY (FR/0992-4361). **1036**

EUROPEAN JOURNAL OF SURGICAL ONCOLOGY (UK/0748-7983). **3817**

EUROPEAN JOURNAL OF TEACHER EDUCATION (UK/0261-9768). **1894**

EUROPEAN JOURNAL OF ULTRASOUND (IE/0929-8266). **3941**

EUROPEAN JUDAISM (UK/0014-3006). **5047**

EUROPEAN MANAGEMENT JOURNAL (UK/0263-2373). **867**

EUROPEAN MEDIA BUSINESS & FINANCE (US/1071-1570). **673**

EUROPEAN NEUROLOGY (SZ/0014-3022). **3832**

EUROPEAN NEUROPSYCHOPHARMACOLOGY : THE JOURNAL OF THE EUROPEAN COLLEGE OF NEUROPSYCHOPHARMACOLOGY (NE/0924-977X). **3832**

EUROPEAN OFFSHORE PETROLEUM NEWSLETTER (NO/0332-5210). **4256**

EUROPEAN PACKAGING NEWSLETTER AND WORLD REPORT (FR/1052-2131). **4219**

EUROPEAN PATENT OFFICE REPORTS (UK/0269-0802). **1304**

EUROPEAN PETROLEUM DIRECTORY (US/0275-3871). **4256**

EUROPEAN PLANNING STUDIES (UK/0965-4313). **2822**

EUROPEAN POLYMER JOURNAL (UK/0014-3057). **1041**

EUROPEAN PSYCHIATRY (FR/0924-9338). **3925**

EUROPEAN RADIOLOGY (GW/0938-7994). **3941**

EUROPEAN RESPIRATORY JOURNAL. SUPPLEMENT, THE (DK/0904-1850). **3949**

EUROPEAN RESPIRATORY JOURNAL, THE (DK/0903-1936). **3949**

EUROPEAN RESPIRATORY REVIEW : AN OFFICIAL JOURNAL OF THE EUROPEAN RESPIRATORY SOCIETY (DK/0905-9180). **3949**

EUROPEAN REVIEW OF AGRICULTURAL ECONOMICS (NE/0165-1587). **82**

EUROPEAN REVIEW OF SOCIAL PSYCHOLOGY (UK/1046-3283). **5245**

EUROPEAN RUBBER JOURNAL (LONDON, ENGLAND : 1982) (UK/0266-4151). **5075**

EUROPEAN SOCIOLOGICAL REVIEW (UK/0266-7215). **5245**

EUROPEAN SURGICAL RESEARCH (SZ/0014-312X). **3964**

EUROPEAN TRANSACTIONS ON ELECTRICAL POWER ENGINEERING (GW/0939-3072). **2054**

EUROPEAN TRANSACTIONS ON TELECOMMUNICATIONS AND RELATED TECHNOLOGIES (IT/1120-3862). **1155**

EUROPEAN UROLOGY (SZ/0302-2838). **3989**

EUROPEAN WATER POLLUTION CONTROL : OFFICIAL PUBLICATION OF THE EUROPEAN WATER POLLUTION CONTROL ASSOCIATION (EWPCA) (UK/0925-5060). **5533**

EUTHANASIA REVIEW, THE (US/0884-2981). **2250**

EVALUATION AND PROGRAM PLANNING (US/0149-7189). **5285**

EVALUATION & THE HEALTH PROFESSIONS (US/0163-2787). **3576**

EVALUATION ENGINEERING (US/0149-0370). **2054**

EVALUATION PRACTICE (US/0886-1633). **5200**

EVALUATION REVIEW (US/0193-841X). **5245**

EVANGELICAL QUARTERLY (UK/0014-3367). **4957**

EVANGELICAL REVIEW OF THEOLOGY (II/0144-8153). **4957**

EVANGELISCHE ERZIEHER, DER (GW/0014-3413). **4957**

EVANGELISCHE KOMMENTARE (GW/0300-4236). **4957**

EVANGELISCHE THEOLOGIE (GW/0014-3502). **4957**

EVANS-NOVAK POLITICAL REPORT (US/0014-3650). **4473**

EVERYBODY'S MONEY (US/0423-8710). **1296**

EVOLUTION PSYCHIATRIQUE, L' (FR/0014-3855). **3925**

EVOLUTIONARY ANTHROPOLOGY / ISSUES, NEWS AND REVIEWS (US/1060-1538). **236**

EVOLUTIONARY BIOLOGY (US/0071-3260). **544**

EVOLUTIONARY ECOLOGY (UK/0269-7653). **2216**

EVOLUTIONARY TRENDS IN PLANTS (UK/1011-3258). **509**

EXCEL (AT/0817-4792). **3954**

EXCEPTIONAL PARENT, THE (US/0046-9157). **2278**

EXCEPTIONALITY : THE OFFICIAL JOURNAL OF THE DIVISION FOR RESEARCH OF THE COUNCIL FOR EXCEPTIONAL CHILDREN (US/0936-2835). **1879**

EXCERPTA BOTANICA. SECTIO A. TAXONOMICA ET CHOROLOGICA (GW/0014-4037). **509**

EXCERPTA BOTANICA. SECTIO B. SOCIOLOGICA (GW/0014-4045). **5245**

EXCERPTA MEDICA. SECTION 1. ANATOMY, ANTHROPOLOGY, EMBRYOLOGY AND HISTOLOGY (NE/0014-4053). **3657**

EXCERPTA MEDICA. SECTION 2A. PHYSIOLOGY (NE/0367-1089). **478**

EXCERPTA MEDICA. SECTION 3. ENDOCRINOLOGY (NE/0014-407X). **3657**

EXCERPTA MEDICA. SECTION 5. GENERAL PATHOLOGY AND PATHOLOGICAL ANATOMY (NE/0014-4096). **3657**

EXCERPTA MEDICA. SECTION 6. INTERNAL MEDICINE (NE/0014-410X). **3657**

EXCERPTA MEDICA. SECTION 7. PEDIATRICS AND PEDIATRIC SURGERY (NE/0373-6512). **3657**

EXCERPTA MEDICA. SECTION 8. NEUROLOGY AND NEUROSURGERY (NE/0014-4126). **3657**

EXCERPTA MEDICA. SECTION 9. SURGERY (NE/0014-4134). **3657**

EXCERPTA MEDICA. SECTION 10. OBSTETRICS AND GYNECOLOGY (NE/0014-4142). **3657**

EXCERPTA MEDICA. SECTION 11. OTO-, RHINO-, LARYNGOLOGY (NE/0014-4150). **3888**

EXCERPTA MEDICA. SECTION 12. OPHTHALMOLOGY (NE/0014-4169). **3658**

EXCERPTA MEDICA. SECTION 13. DERMATOLOGY AND VENEREOLOGY (NE/0014-4177). **3658**

EXCERPTA MEDICA. SECTION 14. RADIOLOGY (NE/0014-4185). **3658**

EXCERPTA MEDICA. SECTION 16. CANCER (NE/0014-4207). **3658**

EXCERPTA MEDICA. SECTION 18. CARDIOVASCULAR DISEASES AND CARDIOVASCULAR SURGERY (NE/0014-4223). **3658**

EXCERPTA MEDICA. SECTION 19. REHABILITATION AND PHYSICAL MEDICINE (NE/0014-4231). **3658**

EXCERPTA MEDICA. SECTION 20. GERONTOLOGY AND GERIATRICS (NE/0014-424X). **3658**

EXCERPTA MEDICA. SECTION 21. DEVELOPMENTAL BIOLOGY AND TERATOLOGY (NE/0014-4258). **3658**

EXCERPTA MEDICA. SECTION 22. HUMAN GENETICS (NE/0014-4266). **3658**

EXCERPTA MEDICA. SECTION 23. NUCLEAR MEDICINE (NE/0014-4274). **3658**

EXCERPTA MEDICA. SECTION 24. ANESTHESIOLOGY (NE/0014-4282). **3658**

EXCERPTA MEDICA. SECTION 25. HEMATOLOGY (NE/0014-4290). **3658**

EXCERPTA MEDICA. SECTION 26. IMMUNOLOGY, SEROLOGY AND TRANSPLANTATION (NE/0014-4304). **3658**

EXCERPTA MEDICA. SECTION 27. BIOPHYSICS, BIOENGINEERING AND MEDICAL INSTRUMENTATION (NE/0014-4312). **3658**

EXCERPTA MEDICA. SECTION 28. UROLOGY AND NEPHROLOGY (NE/0014-4320). **3658**

EXCERPTA MEDICA. SECTION 29. CIINICAL BIOCHEMISTRY (NE/0300-5372). **478**

EXCERPTA MEDICA. SECTION 32. PSYCHIATRY (NE/0014-4363). **3659**

EXCERPTA MEDICA. SECTION 35. OCCUPATIONAL HEALTH AND INDUSTRIAL MEDICINE (NE/0014-4398). **2872**

EXCERPTA MEDICA. SECTION 40. DRUG DEPENDENCE, ALCOHOL ABUSE, AND ALCOHOLISM (NE/0304-4041). **3659**

EXCERPTA MEDICA. SECTION 46. ENVIRONMENTAL HEALTH AND POLLUTION CONTROL (NE/0300-5194). **3659**

EXCERPTA MEDICA. SECTION 49. FORENSIC SCIENCE ABSTRACTS (NE/0031-0743). **3740**

EXCERPTA MEDICA. SECTION 50. EPILEPSY ABSTRACTS (NE/0303-8459). **3659**

EXCERPTA MEDICA. SECTION 52. TOXICOLOGY (NE/0167-8353). **3659**

EXCHANGE (FORT WORTH, TEX.) (US/0888-5648). **3914**

EXECUTIVE COMPENSATION & TAXATION COORDINATOR (US/0273-7612). **2968**

EXECUTIVE REPORT ON MANAGED CARE, THE (US/0898-9753). **940**

EXECUTIVE WEALTH ADVISORY (US/0195-0746). **674**

EXEMPT ORGANIZATION TAX REVIEW, THE (US/0899-3831). **4723**

EXERCISE AND SPORT SCIENCES REVIEWS (US/0091-6331). **3954**

EXPERIENTIA (SZ/0014-4754). **5104**

EXPERIMENTAL AGRICULTURE (UK/0014-4797). **82**

EXPERIMENTAL & APPLIED ACAROLOGY (NE/0168-8162). **5583**

EXPERIMENTAL AND CLINICAL GASTROENTEROLOGY (US/0353-9245). **3744**

EXPERIMENTAL AND CLINICAL IMMUNOGENETICS (SZ/0254-9670). **3669**

EXPERIMENTAL AND MOLECULAR PATHOLOGY (US/0014-4800). **3894**

EXPERIMENTAL AND TOXICOLOGIC PATHOLOGY : OFFICIAL JOURNAL OF THE GESELLSCHAFT FUR TOXIKOLOGISCHE PATHOLOGIE (GW/0940-2993). **3980**

EXPERIMENTAL ASTRONOMY (NE/0922-6435). **395**

EXPERIMENTAL BRAIN RESEARCH (GW/0014-4819). **3832**

EXPERIMENTAL CELL RESEARCH (US/0014-4827). **536**

EXPERIMENTAL EYE RESEARCH (UK/0014-4835). **3874**

EXPERIMENTAL GERONTOLOGY (UK/0531-5565). **3751**

EXPERIMENTAL HEAT TRANSFER (UK/0891-6152). **4430**

EXPERIMENTAL HEMATOLOGY (US/0301-472X). **3771**

EXPERIMENTAL LUNG RESEARCH (US/0190-2148). **3949**

EXPERIMENTAL MECHANICS (US/0014-4851). **4427**

EXPERIMENTAL MYCOLOGY (US/0147-5975). **574**

EXPERIMENTAL NEUROLOGY (US/0014-4886). **3833**

EXPERIMENTAL PARASITOLOGY (US/0014-4894). **562**

EXPERIMENTAL PATHOLOGY (1981) (GW/0232-1513). **3894**

EXPERIMENTAL TECHNIQUES (WESTPORT, CONN.) (US/0732-8818). **2114**

EXPERIMENTAL THERMAL AND FLUID SCIENCE (US/0894-1777). **4427**

EXPERIMENTS IN FLUIDS (GW/0723-4864). **2089**

EXPERT SYSTEMS (UK/0266-4720). **1212**

EXPERT SYSTEMS WITH APPLICATIONS (US/0957-4174). **1212**

EXPLICATOR, THE (US/0014-4940). **3386**

EXPLORATION AND MINING GEOLOGY : JOURNAL OF THE GEOLOGICAL SOCIETY OF CIM (UK/0964-1823). **2138**

EXPLORATION GEOPHYSICS (MELBOURNE) (AT/0812-3985). **4402**

EXPLORATIONS IN ECONOMIC HISTORY (US/0014-4983). **1561**

EXPORT POLYGRAPH INTERNATIONAL (GW/0344-2039). **378**

EXPORT TODAY (US/0882-4711). **834**

EXPORTER (NEW YORK, N.Y.), THE (US/0736-9239). **835**

EXPOSITIONES MATHEMATICAE (GW/0723-0869). **3505**

EXTENDED ABSTRACTS - ELECTROCHEMICAL SOCIETY (US/0160-4619). **1034**

EXTRAPOLATION (US/0014-5483). **3342**

F.Y.E.O (US/0738-4203). **4044**

FABULA (GW/0014-6242). **2319**

FACIAL PLASTIC SURGERY (US/0736-6825). **3964**

FACILITIES DESIGN & MANAGEMENT (US/0279-4438). **2900**

FAIR EMPLOYMENT PRACTICE CASES (US/0525-552X). **3148**

FAIR EMPLOYMENT REPORT (US/0014-6919). **1669**

FAMILIES IN SOCIETY (US/1044-3894). **5285**

FAMILY & COMMUNITY HEALTH (US/0160-6379). **4775**

FAMILY BUSINESS (US/1047-255X). **674**

FAMILY DYNAMICS OF ADDICTION QUARTERLY (US/1054-8726). **1344**

FAMILY LAW REPORTER, THE (US/0148-7922). **3120**

FAMILY PERSPECTIVE (US/0014-7311). **2279**

FAMILY PRACTICE (UK/0263-2136). **3737**

FAMILY PRACTICE RESEARCH JOURNAL, THE (US/0270-2304). **3737**

FAMILY PROCESS (US/0014-7370). **2279**

FAMILY THERAPY (US/0091-6544). **3925**

FARBE (GW/0014-7680). **1024**

FARBE + LACK (GW/0014-7699). **4223**

FARM CHEMICALS (1973) (US/0092-0053). **84**

FARM CHEMICALS HANDBOOK (US/0430-0750). **171**

FARM INDUSTRY NEWS (1984) (US/0892-8312). **159**

FARMACI E TERAPIA (IT/0393-9693). **4304**

FARMACIA CLINICA (SP/0212-6583). **4304**

FARMACOTERAPIA MADRID (SP/0214-8935). **4305**

FARMER'S WEEKLY (UK/0014-8474). **86**

FASEB JOURNAL, THE (US/0892-6638). **455**

FATIGUE & FRACTURE OF ENGINEERING MATERIALS & STRUCTURES (UK/8756-758X). **2102**

FAUNA NORVEGICA. SER. B (NO/0332-7698). **5608**

FAUNA NORVEGICA. SER. C., CINCLUS (NO/0332-7701). **5583**

FAUNA (OSLO) (NO/0014-8881). **5583**

FDA NEWS (US/1069-5109). **2335**

FDC REPORTS. HEALTH NEWS DAILY (US/1042-2781). **4775**

FDC REPORTS. PRESCRIPTION AND OTC PHARMACEUTICALS (US/0734-6514). **4305**

FDC REPORTS. PRESCRIPTION AND OTC PHARMACEUTICALS. MID-WEEK REPORT (US/0734-6506). **4305**

FDC REPORTS. TOILETRIES, FRAGRANCES AND SKIN CARE (US/0279-1110). **404**

FDDI NEWS (US/1051-1903). **1111**

FDM, FURNITURE DESIGN & MANUFACTURING (US/0192-8058). **634**

FEBS LETTERS (NE/0014-5793). **487**

FEDERAL CONTRACT DISPUTES (US/0747-9700). **2969**

FEDERAL CONTRACTS REPORT (US/0014-9063). **2969**

FEDERAL EQUAL OPPORTUNITY REPORTER (US/1043-7274). **1669**

FEDERAL FACILITIES ENVIRONMENTAL JOURNAL (US/1048-4078). **3112**

FEDERAL GRANTS & CONTRACTS WEEKLY (US/0194-2247). **1746**

FEDERAL GRANTS MANAGEMENT HANDBOOK (US/0195-2617). **4723**

FEDERAL PERSONNEL GUIDE (US/0163-7665). **4702**

FEDERAL RULES OF EVIDENCE NEWS (US/0364-3581). **2970**

FEDERAL RULES SERVICE (US/0164-4564). **3140**

FEDERAL SENTENCING REPORTER : FSR (US/1053-9867). **3164**

FEDERAL TAX COORDINATOR 2D (US/0738-8632). **4724**

FEDERAL TIMES (US/0014-9233). **4703**

FEDERAL YELLOW BOOK (US/0145-6202). **1926**

FEDERATION BULLETIN (FULTON) (US/0014-9306). **3740**

FEED INTERNATIONAL (US/0274-5771). **201**

FEED MANAGEMENT (US/0014-956X). **201**

FEEDSTUFFS (US/0014-9624). **201**

FEMALE PATIENT. PRACTICAL ADVICE FOR PRIMARY CARE, THE (US/0888-2398). **3760**

FEMALE PATIENT. PRACTICAL OB/GYN MEDICINE, THE (US/0888-2401). **3760**

FEMINIST ISSUES (US/0270-6679). **5556**

FEMINIST REVIEW (UK/0141-7789). **5556**

FEMS IMMUNOLOGY AND MEDICAL MICROBIOLOGY (NE/0928-8244). **3669**

FEMS MICROBIOLOGY, ECOLOGY (NE/0168-6496). **562**

FEMS MICROBIOLOGY IMMUNOLOGY (NE/0920-8534). **562**

FEMS MICROBIOLOGY LETTERS (NE/0378-1097). **562**

FENESTRATION (RIVERTON, N.J.) (US/0895-450X). **614**

FERC PRACTICE AND PROCEDURE MANUAL (US/0745-6131). **1944**

FERNSEH- UND KINOTECHNIK (GW/0015-0142). **4068**

FERNWAERME INTERNATIONAL (GW/0340-3572). **2605**

FERRO-ALLOY DIRECTORY (UK/0266-3198). **4001**

FERRO-ALLOY DIRECTORY & DATABOOK (UK/0266-3198). **4002**

FERROELECTRICS (US/0015-0193). **4402**

FERROELECTRICS. LETTERS SECTION (US/0731-5171). **2054**

FERTILITAT (GW/0179-1796). **3760**

FERTILIZER RESEARCH (NE/0167-1731). **171**

FESTIVAL MANAGEMENT & EVENT TOURISM (US/1065-2701). **5469**

FESTKORPERPROBLEME (GW/0430-3393). **4402**

FETAL DIAGNOSIS AND THERAPY (SZ/1015-3837). **3760**

FETT WISSENSCHAFT TECHNOLOGIE : ORGAN DER DEUTSCHEN GESELLSCHAFT FUER FETTWISSENSCHAFT E.V. / FAT SCIENCE TECHNOLOGY (GW/0931-5985). **1024**

FEUILLETS DE RADIOLOGIE (FR/0181-9801). **3941**

FEW-BODY SYSTEMS (AU/0177-7963). **4447**

FIBER AND INTEGRATED OPTICS (US/0146-8030). **4434**

FIBER OPTIC SENSORS AND SYSTEMS (US/1051-1946). **4403**

FIBER OPTICS AND COMMUNICATIONS (US/0275-0457). **1155**

FIBER OPTICS MAGAZINE (US/1045-6422). **1155**

FIBER OPTICS NEWS (US/8756-2049). **4434**

FIBEROPTIC PRODUCT NEWS (US/0890-653X). **1155**

FIBRE CHEMISTRY (US/0015-0541). **5351**

FIBRINOLYSIS (UK/0268-9499). **455**

FIELD CROPS RESEARCH (NE/0378-4290). **172**

FIGHTING WOMAN NEWS (US/0146-8812). **2597**

FILM QUARTERLY (US/0015-1386). **4070**

FILS, TUBES, BANDES, PROFILES (FR/0249-6704). **2114**

FILTRATION & SEPARATION (UK/0015-1882). **2012**

FINANCIAL ACCOUNTABILITY & MANAGEMENT IN GOVERNMENTS, PUBLIC SERVICES, AND CHARITIES (UK/0267-4424). **4649**

FINANCIAL EXECUTIVE (1987) (US/0895-4186). **675**

FINANCIAL POST, THE (CN/0015-2021). **898**

FINANCIAL STATISTICS LONDON (UK/0015-203X). **1532**

FINANCIAL TIMES MINING INTERNATIONAL YEAR BOOK (UK/0141-3244). **2139**

FINANCIAL TIMES OIL AND GAS INTERNATIONAL YEAR BOOK (UK/0141-3228). **4256**

FINANCIAL TIMES WHO'S WHO IN WORLD OIL AND GAS (UK/0141-3236). **1607**

FINANCIAL TIMES WORLD HOTEL DIRECTORY, THE (UK/0308-8464). **2805**

FINANCIAL WORLD (US/0015-2064). **898**

FINANCIAL YELLOW BOOK (US/1058-2878). **1926**

FINANZARCHIV (GW/0015-2218). **4726**

FINITE ELEMENTS IN ANALYSIS AND DESIGN (NE/0168-874X). **1233**

FIRE AND MATERIALS (UK/0308-0501). **615**

FIRE CHIEF (US/0015-2552). **2289**

FIRE ENGINEERING (US/0015-2587). **2289**

FIRE PREVENTION (LONDON, 1971) (UK/0309-6866). **2289**

FIRE RESEARCH NEWS (UK/0261-1589). **2289**

FIRE RESISTANT MATERIALS AND PRODUCTS, PATENTS AND ABSTRACTS (US/1043-464X). **2290**

FIRE SAFETY JOURNAL (SZ/0379-7112). **2290**

FIREHOUSE LAWYER MONTHLY NEWSLETTER (US/0896-8314). **2970**

FIREWEED (CN/0706-3857). **5556**

FIRST BREAK (UK/0263-5046). **1405**

FIRST LANGUAGE (UK/0142-7237). **3281**

FISCAL STUDIES (UK/0143-5671). **4726**

FISCH UND FANG (GW/0015-2838). **4894**

FISH FARMING INTERNATIONAL (UK/0262-0820). **2301**

FISHERIES (BETHESDA) (US/0363-2415). **2302**

FISHERIES OCEANOGRAPHY (US/1054-6006). **1449**

FISHERIES PRODUCT NEWS (US/1047-2525). **2302**

FISHERIES RESEARCH (NE/0165-7836). **2302**

FISHING NEWS INTERNATIONAL (UK/0015-3044). **2303**

FIZIKA GORENIIA I VZRYVA (RU/0430-6228). **4403**

FIZIKA METALLOV I METALLOVEDENIE (RU/0015-3230). **4002**

FIZIKO-HIMICESKAJA MEHANIKA MATERIALOV (UN/0430-6252). **1052**

FIZIOLOGICESKIJ ZURNAL (UN/0201-8489). **580**

FIZIOLOGICESKIJ ZURNAL SSSR IMENI I.M. SECENOVA (RU/0015-329X). **580**

FLASH ETAT-UNIS (FR/0985-2662). **455**

FLASH JAPON (FR/0985-2654). **455**

FLAVOUR AND FRAGRANCE JOURNAL (UK/0882-5734). **2335**

FLEET EQUIPMENT (US/0747-2544). **5382**

FLIGHT INTERNATIONAL (UK/0015-3710). **20**

FLORA

FLORA. MORPHOLOGIE, GEOBOTANIK, OKOLOGIE (GW/0367-2530). **2216**

FLORA NEOTROPICA (US/0071-5794). **510**

FLORIDA TREND (US/0015-4326). **1561**

FLOW MEASUREMENT AND INSTRUMENTATION (UK/0955-5986). **2089**

FLUID ABSTRACTS. CIVIL ENGINEERING (UK/0962-7170). **2004**

FLUID ABSTRACTS. PROCESS ENGINEERING (UK/0962-7162). **2004**

FLUID DYNAMICS (US/0015-4628). **2023**

FLUID DYNAMICS RESEARCH (NE/0169-5983). **5105**

FLUID MECHANICS : SOVIET RESEARCH (US/0096-0764). **2089**

FLUID PHASE EQUILIBRIA (NE/0378-3812). **1052**

FOCUS ON CRITICAL CARE (US/0736-3605). **3856**

FOCUS ON LEARNING PROBLEMS IN MATHEMATICS (US/0272-8893). **1879**

FOERDERN UND HEBEN (GW/0373-6482). **2114**

FOKUS PA FAMILIEN (NO/0332-5415). **2280**

FOLIA BIOLOGICA (XR/0015-5500). **455**

FOLIA GEOBOTANICA & PHYTOTAXONOMICA (XR/0015-5551). **511**

FOLIA LINGUISTICA (NE/0165-4004). **3282**

FOLIA MICROBIOLOGICA (XR/0015-5632). **563**

FOLIA OPHTHALMOLOGICA (GW/0323-4932). **3874**

FOLIA PARASITOLOGICA / CZECHOSLOVAK ACADEMY OF SCIENCE (XR/0015-5683). **5584**

FOLIA PHONIATRICA (SZ/0015-5705). **3888**

FOLIA PRIMATOLOGICA (SZ/0015-5713). **5584**

FOLIA ZOOLOGICA (BRNO) (XR/0139-7893). **5584**

FOLKLORE (MOOSE JAW) (CN/0824-3085). **2320**

FOOD ADDITIVES AND CONTAMINANTS (UK/0265-203X). **2335**

FOOD AND AGRICULTURAL IMMUNOLOGY (UK/0954-0105). **563**

FOOD AND CHEMICAL TOXICOLOGY (UK/0278-6915). **3980**

FOOD AND DRUG LAW JOURNAL (US/1064-590X). **2971**

FOOD & DRUG LETTER, THE (US/0362-6466). **2336**

FOOD & FOODWAYS (SZ/0740-9710). **5245**

FOOD BIOTECHNOLOGY (US/0890-5436). **3692**

FOOD BUSINESS (CHICAGO, ILL.) (US/1049-5568). **2336**

FOOD CHEMICAL NEWS (US/0015-6337). **1024**

FOOD CHEMISTRY (UK/0308-8146). **1024**

FOOD, COSMETICS AND DRUG PACKAGING 1986 (UK/0951-4554). **4219**

FOOD HYDROCOLLOIDS (UK/0268-005X). **1041**

FOOD LABELING NEWS (US/1064-6329). **2338**

FOOD MANAGEMENT (US/0091-018X). **2338**

FOOD MANUFACTURE (UK/0015-6477). **2338**

FOOD MICROBIOLOGY (UK/0740-0020). **563**

FOOD POLICY (UK/0306-9192). **2339**

FOOD PROCESSING (US/0015-6523). **2339**

FOOD PRODUCTS & EQUIPMENT (US/1056-5078). **2339**

FOOD QUALITY AND PREFERENCE (UK/0950-3293). **2339**

FOOD RESEARCH INTERNATIONAL (CN/0963-9969). **2339**

FOOD REVIEWS INTERNATIONAL (US/8755-9129). **2339**

FOOD SAFETY & SECURITY (UK/0964-4164). **2340**

FOOD SCIENCE & TECHNOLOGY TODAY (UK/0950-9623). **2340**

FOOD STRUCTURE (US/1046-705X). **2340**

FOOD TECHNOLOGY (CHICAGO) (US/0015-6639). **2340**

FOOD TECHNOLOGY IN NEW ZEALAND (NZ/0015-6655). **2340**

FOOD TRADE REVIEW (UK/0015-6671). **2340**

FOODSERVICE & HOSPITALITY (CN/0007-8972). **5071**

FOODSERVICE DISTRIBUTOR, THE (US/0896-4505). **2341**

FOODSERVICE EQUIPMENT & SUPPLIES SPECIALIST (US/0888-8515). **2341**

FOOT & ANKLE (US/0198-0211). **3881**

FOOT, THE (UK/0958-2592). **3881**

FOR FORMULATION CHEMISTS ONLY (US/0887-736X). **975**

FORAGES (FR/0046-4481). **2139**

FORBES (US/0015-6914). **676**

FOREIGN POLICY (US/0015-7228). **4522**

FOREIGN REPORT (UK/0532-1328). **4474**

FORENSIC REPORTS (US/0888-692X). **3740**

FORENSIC SCIENCE INTERNATIONAL (SZ/0379-0738). **3740**

FOREST ECOLOGY AND MANAGEMENT (NE/0378-1127). **2379**

FOREST INDUSTRIES (SAN FRANCISCO, CALIF.) (US/0015-7430). **2400**

FOREST PLANNING-CANADA (CN/0832-1655). **2380**

FOREST PRODUCTS JOURNAL (US/0015-7473). **2380**

FORESTRY CHRONICLE, THE (CN/0015-7546). **2381**

FORESTRY (LONDON) (UK/0015-752X). **2382**

FORMAL ASPECTS OF COMPUTING (UK/0934-5043). **1247**

FORSCHUNG (BOPPARD) (GW/0172-1518). **5105**

FORSCHUNG IM INGENIEURWESEN (GW/0015-7899). **1975**

FORSCHUNGSBERICHTE AUS TECHNIK UND NATURWISSENSCHAFTEN (GW/0343-5520). **5105**

FORSTARCHIV (GW/0300-4112). **2383**

FORSTLICHE UMSCHAU (GW/0015-7988). **2383**

FORSTWISSENSCHAFTLICHES CENTRALBLATT (GW/0015-8003). **2383**

FORTHCOMING BOOKS (US/0015-8119). **416**

FORTHCOMING BOOKS FOR CHILDREN (US/0000-0965). **3388**

FORTSCHRITTE DER CHEMIE ORGANISCHER NATURSTOFFE (AU/0071-7886). **1041**

FORTSCHRITTE DER KIEFERORTHOPAEDIE (GW/0015-816X). **1323**

FORTSCHRITTE DER MEDIZIN (GW/0015-8178). **3577**

FORTSCHRITTE DER NEUROLOGIE, PSYCHIATRIE (GW/0720-4299). **3833**

FORTSCHRITTE DER PHYSIK (BERLIN : 1953) (GW/0015-8208). **4403**

FORTSCHRITTE DER ZOOLOGIE (STUTTGART) (GW/0071-7991). **5584**

FORTSCHRITTLICHE BETRIEBSEHRUNG UND INDUSTRIAL ENGINEERING (GW/0340-8302). **2098**

FORUM DER PSYCHOANALYSE (GW/0178-7667). **4587**

FORUM FOR MODERN LANGUAGE STUDIES (UK/0015-8518). **3282**

FORUM MATHEMATICUM (GW/0933-7741). **3506**

FOSTER BULLETIN ON DEREGULATED GAS (US/0749-7377). **4256**

FOSTER NATURAL GAS REPORT FROM WASHINGTON (US/0095-1587). **4256**

FOUNDATIONS OF PHYSICS (US/0015-9018). **4403**

FOUNDATIONS OF PHYSICS LETTERS (US/0894-9875). **4403**

FOUNDRY MANAGEMENT & TECHNOLOGY (US/0360-8999). **4002**

FRAM (BANGOR, ME.) (US/0739-8158). **5474**

FRANZOSISCH HEUTE (GW/0342-2895). **1895**

FREE ASSOCIATIONS (UK/0267-0887). **3925**

FREE RADICAL BIOLOGY & MEDICINE (US/0891-5849). **487**

FREE RADICAL RESEARCH COMMUNICATIONS (SZ/8755-0199). **1052**

FREMANTLE ARTS REVIEW (AT/0816-6919). **320**

FRENCH HISTORY (UK/0269-1191). **2689**

FREQUENZ ZEITSCHRIFT FUER SCHWINGUNGS-UND SCHWACHSTROMTECHNIK (GW/0016-1136). **2055**

FRESENIUS' JOURNAL OF ANALYTICAL CHEMISTRY (GW/0937-0633). **1015**

FRESHWATER BIOLOGY (UK/0046-5070). **456**

FRI BULLETIN / FOREST RESEARCH INSTITUTE, NEW ZEALAND FOREST SERVICE (NZ/0111-8129). **2383**

FRIIDRETT (NO/0332-9666). **1091**

FROM THE STATE CAPITALS. ALCOHOLIC BEVERAGE CONTROL (US/0734-0842). **3164**

FROM THE STATE CAPITALS. CIVIL RIGHTS (US/0741-353X). **4508**

FROM THE STATE CAPITALS. FAMILY RELATIONS (US/0741-3505). **2280**

FROM THE STATE CAPITALS. FEDERAL ACTION AFFECTING THE STATES (NEW HAVEN, CONN.) (US/0734-1202). **4650**

FROM THE STATE CAPITALS. HIGHWAY FINANCING AND CONSTRUCTION (US/0016-1705). **5440**

FROM THE STATE CAPITALS. INSURANCE REGULATION (US/0016-1748). **2881**

FROM THE STATE CAPITALS. LABOR RELATIONS (US/0734-1105). **3148**

FROM THE STATE CAPITALS. MOTOR VEHICLE REGULATION (US/0016-1810). **5415**

FROM THE STATE CAPITALS. PUBLIC ASSISTANCE & WELFARE TRENDS (NEW HAVEN, CONN.) (US/0734-1601). **5286**

FROM THE STATE CAPITALS. PUBLIC EMPLOYEE POLICY (US/0741-3521). **940**

FROM THE STATE CAPITALS. PUBLIC HEALTH (1982) (US/0734-1156). **4776**

FROM THE STATE CAPITALS. PUBLIC UTILITIES (US/0016-1888). **4650**

FROM THE STATE CAPITALS. TAXES-PROPERTY (NEW HAVEN, CONN.) (US/0734-1121). **4727**

FROM THE STATE CAPITALS. TOURIST BUSINESS PROMOTION (NEW HAVEN, CONN.) (US/0734-1199). **5474**

FROM THE STATE CAPITALS. URBAN DEVELOPMENT (US/0741-3483). **2823**

FROM THE STATE CAPITALS. WORKERS' COMPENSATION (US/0734-0931). **1675**

FRONTIERS IN DIABETES (SZ/0251-5342). **3730**

FRONTIERS OF HEALTH SERVICES MANAGEMENT (US/0748-8157). **5286**

FRONTIERS OF HORMONE RESEARCH (SZ/0301-3073). **487**

FRONTIERS OF ORAL PHYSIOLOGY (SZ/0301-536X). **1323**

FRONTIERS OF RADIATION THERAPY AND ONCOLOGY (US/0071-9676). **3817**

FSMB HANDBOOK (US/0888-5656). **4204**

FT SYSTEMS (US/0740-4980). **1254**

FTC FREEDOM OF INFORMATION LOG (US/0161-7036). **837**

FTC : WATCH (US/0196-0016). **2972**

FUEL AND ENERGY ABSTRACTS (UK/0140-6701). **1944**

FUEL (GUILFORD) (UK/0016-2361). **4256**

FUEL PROCESSING TECHNOLOGY (NE/0378-3820). **1025**

FUEL SCIENCE & TECHNOLOGY INTERNATIONAL (US/0884-3759). **2139**

FUNCTIONAL ANALYSIS AND ITS APPLICATIONS (US/0016-2663). **3506**

FUNCTIONAL AND DEVELOPMENTAL MORPHOLOGY (XR/0862-8416). **456**

FUNCTIONAL ECOLOGY (UK/0269-8463). **2216**

FUND RAISING MANAGEMENT (US/0016-268X). **868**

FUNDAMENTA INFORMATICAE (NE/0169-2968). **1185**

FUNDAMENTA PSYCHIATRICA (GW/0931-0428). **3925**

FUNDAMENTAL AND APPLIED NEMATOLOGY (FR/1164-5571). **456**

FUNDAMENTAL AND APPLIED TOXICOLOGY (US/0272-0590). **3980**

FUNDAMENTAL & CLINICAL PHARMACOLOGY (FR/0767-3981). **4305**

FUNDAMENTALS OF COSMIC PHYSICS (US/0094-5846). **395**

FUNKSCHAU (GW/0016-2841). **2055**

FUNKTIONSKRANKHEITEN DES BEWEGUNGSAPPARATES (GW/0258-2015). **3804**

FURNITURE/TODAY (US/0194-360X). **2905**

FUSE MAGAZINE (CN/0838-603X). **320**

FUSION ENGINEERING AND DESIGN (NE/0920-3796). **2155**

FUSION POWER REPORT (US/0276-2919). **1945**

FUTURE GENERATIONS COMPUTER SYSTEMS : FGCS (NE/0167-739X). **1247**

FUTURE HOME TECHNOLOGY NEWS (US/1051-9971). **1111**

FUTURES (LONDON) (UK/0016-3287). **1492**

FUTURIBLES (PARIS) (FR/0337-307X). **5246**

FUTURIST, THE (US/0016-3317). **5107**

FUTURIST. [MICROFILM], THE (US/0016-3317). **5107**

FUZZY SETS AND SYSTEMS (NE/0165-0114). **3506**

FYSIATRICKY A REUMATOLOGICKY VESTNIK (XR/0072-0038). **3577**

GACETA SANITARIA (SP/0213-9111). **4776**

GALVANOTECHNIK (GW/0016-4232). **2055**

GAMES AND ECONOMIC BEHAVIOR (US/0899-8256). **3506**

GANKO : GANSEKI KOBUTSU KOSHO GAKKAI SHI (JA/0914-9783). **1355**

GARTEN UND LANDSCHAFT (GW/0016-4720). **2416**

GARTENBAUWISSENSCHAFT (GW/0016-478X). **2416**

GARTENPRAXIS (GW/0341-2105). **2416**

GAS BUYERS GUIDE (US/0897-8778). **4257**

GAS DAILY (US/0885-5935). **4257**

GAS DAILY'S GAS STORAGE REPORT (US/1057-2279). **4257**

GAS DIRECTORY AND WHO'S WHO (UK/0307-3084). **4257**

GAS (MUNCHEN) (GW/0343-2092). **4257**

GAS PROCESSORS REPORT (US/0740-5278). **4258**

GAS SEPARATION & PURIFICATION (UK/0950-4214). **4258**

GAS- UND WASSERFACH. GAS, ERDGAS : GWF, DAS (GW/0016-4909). **4258**

GAS- UND WASSERFACH. WASSER, ABWASSER : GWF, DAS (GW/0016-3651). **5533**

GAS WARME INTERNATIONAL (GW/0020-9384). **4258**

GAS WORLD (LONDON, ENGLAND : 1974) (UK/0308-7654). **4258**

GASTROENTEROLOGIA Y HEPATOLOGIA (SP/0210-5705). **3745**

GASTROENTEROLOGIE CLINIQUE ET BIOLOGIQUE (FR/0399-8320). **3745**

GASTROENTEROLOGIST (BOSTON, MASS.), THE (US/1065-2477). **3745**

GASTROENTEROLOGY CLINICS OF NORTH AMERICA (US/0889-8553). **3745**

GASTROENTEROLOGY (NEW YORK, N.Y. 1943) (US/0016-5085). **3745**

GASTROENTEROLOGY NURSING (US/1042-895X). **3856**

GASTROINTESTINAL ENDOSCOPY (US/0016-5107). **3746**

GASTROINTESTINAL HORMONES (UK/0142-8101). **3746**

GASTROINTESTINAL RADIOLOGY (US/0364-2356). **3941**

GAZ D'AUJOURD'HUI (FR/0016-5328). **4259**

GAZETTE (NE/0016-5492). **1111**

GAZETTE MEDICALE (FR/0760-758X). **3578**

GAZOVAIA PROMYSHLENNOST (RU/0016-5581). **4259**

GEBURTSHILFE UND FRAUENHEILKUNDE (GW/0016-5751). **3761**

GEFIEDERTE WELT, DIE (GW/0016-5816). **5584**

GEGENWARTSKUNDE (GW/0016-5875). **5200**

GEMUSE (MUNCHEN) (GW/0016-6286). **172**

GENDER AND EDUCATION (UK/0954-0253). **5187**

GENDER & HISTORY (UK/0953-5233). **5557**

GENDER & SOCIETY (US/0891-2432). **5200**

GENDERS (AUSTIN, TEX.) (US/0894-9832). **2846**

GENE (NE/0378-1119). **545**

GENE EXPRESSION (US/1052-2166). **545**

GENERAL AND COMPARATIVE ENDOCRINOLOGY (US/0016-6480). **3730**

GENERAL AND SYNTHETIC METHODS (UK/0141-2140). **1041**

GENERAL HOSPITAL PSYCHIATRY (US/0163-8343). **3925**

GENERAL PHARMACOLOGY (UK/0306-3623). **4306**

GENERAL PHYSICS ADVANCE ABSTRACTS (US/0749-4823). **4403**

GENERAL PRACTITIONER (UK/0046-5607). **3737**

GENERAL RELATIVITY AND GRAVITATION (US/0001-7701). **4403**

GENERALISTE PARIS, LE (FR/0183-4568). **3578**

GENES & DEVELOPMENT (US/0890-9369). **545**

GENETIC ANALYSIS, TECHNIQUES AND APPLICATIONS (US/1050-3862). **545**

GENETIC ENGINEER & BIOTECHNOLOGIST, THE (UK/0959-020X). **3692**

GENETIC ENGINEERING (US/0196-3716). **545**

GENETIC EPIDEMIOLOGY (US/0741-0395). **3735**

GENETIC TECHNOLOGY NEWS (US/0272-9032). **5107**

GENETICA (NE/0016-6707). **546**

GENETICA POLONICA (PL/0016-6715). **2416**

GENETICAL RESEARCH (UK/0016-6723). **546**

GENETICS (AUSTIN) (US/0016-6731). **546**

GENETIKA (RU/0016-6758). **546**

GENEVA PAPERS ON RISK AND INSURANCE THEORY (US/0926-4957). **2881**

GENITOURINARY MEDICINE (UK/0266-4348). **4776**

GENOME (CN/0831-2796). **546**

GENOMICS (SAN DIEGO, CALIF.) (US/0888-7543). **546**

GEO INFO SYSTEMS (US/1051-9858). **2561**

GEO-MARINE LETTERS (US/0276-0460). **554**

GEOBYTE (US/0885-6362). **2139**

GEOCHEMISTRY INTERNATIONAL (US/0016-7029). **1376**

GEOCHIMICA ET COSMOCHIMICA ACTA (US/0016-7037). **1376**

GEODERMA (NE/0016-7061). **173**

GEODINAMICA ACTA (FR/0985-3111). **2561**

GEODYNAMICS SERIES (US/0277-6669). **1376**

GEOFORUM (UK/0016-7185). **1355**

GEOGRAPHICAL ABSTRACTS. HUMAN GEOGRAPHY (UK/0953-9611). **2580**

GEOGRAPHICAL ABSTRACTS : PHYSICAL GEOGRAPHY (UK/0954-0504). **2580**

GEOGRAPHICAL ANALYSIS (US/0016-7363). **2562**

GEOGRAPHICAL JOURNAL, THE (UK/0016-7398). **2563**

GEOGRAPHICAL PERSPECTIVES (US/0199-994X). **2563**

GEOGRAPHIE HEUTE (GW/0721-8400). **2563**

GEOGRAPHISCHE RUNDSCHAU (GW/0016-7460). **2564**

GEOGRAPHISCHE ZEITSCHRIFT (GW/0016-7479). **2564**

GEOGRAPHY RESEARCH FORUM (US/0333-5275). **2564**

GEOHIMIJA (RU/0016-7525). **1377**

GEOJOURNAL (GE/0343-2521). **2564**

GEOLOGICA ET PALAEONTOLOGICA (GW/0072-1018). **1377**

GEOLOGICAL ABSTRACTS (UK/0954-0512). **1362**

GEOLOGICAL JOURNAL (CHICHESTER, ENGLAND) (UK/0072-1050). **1378**

GEOLOGICAL MAGAZINE (UK/0016-7568). **1378**

GEOLOGICAL SOCIETY OF AMERICA BULLETIN (US/0016-7606). **1378**

GEOLOGICAL SOCIETY OF AMERICA BULLETIN (US/0016-7606). **1378**

GEOLOGICAL SOCIETY SPECIAL PUBLICATION (UK/0305-8719). **1378**

GEOLOGICESKIJ ZURNAL (KIEV. 1968) (UN/0367-4290). **1379**

GEOLOGIE EN MIJNBOUW (NE/0016-7746). **1379**

GEOLOGIIA I GEOFIZIKA (NOVOSIBIRSK) (RU/0016-7886). **1379**

GEOLOGIJA NEFTI I GAZA (RU/0016-7894). **1379**

GEOLOGIJA RUDNYH MESTOROZDENIJ (RU/0016-7770). **2139**

GEOLOGISCHE RUNDSCHAU (GW/0016-7835). **1379**

GEOLOGISCHES JAHRBUCH, REIHE B : REGIONALE GEOLOGIE, AUSLAND (GW/0341-6402). **1379**

GEOLOGY (BOULDER) (US/0091-7613). **1380**

GEOLOGY TODAY (UK/0266-6979). **1380**

GEOMAGNETISM AND AERONOMY (US/0016-7932). **22**

GEOMAGNETIZM I AERONOMIJA (RU/0016-7940). **4443**

GEOMETRIAE DEDICATA (NE/0046-5755). **3507**

GEOMICROBIOLOGY JOURNAL (US/0149-0451). **563**

GEOMORFOLOGIJA (MOSKVA) (RU/0435-4281). **2564**

GEOMORPHOLOGY (NE/0169-555X). **1380**

GEOPHYSICAL AND ASTROPHYSICAL FLUID DYNAMICS (US/0309-1929). **1405**

GEOPHYSICAL JOURNAL (US/0275-9128). **1405**

GEOPHYSICAL JOURNAL INTERNATIONAL (UK/0956-540X). **1405**

GEOPHYSICAL MONOGRAPH (US/0065-8448). **1406**

GEOPHYSICAL PROSPECTING (NE/0016-8025). **1406**

GEOPHYSICAL RESEARCH LETTERS (US/0094-8276). **1406**

GEOPHYSICS (US/0016-8033). **1406**

GEOPHYSICS REPRINT SERIES (US/0734-5631). **1406**

GEOPHYSICS, THE LEADING EDGE OF EXPLORATION (US/0732-989X). **1406**

GEORGIA TREND (US/0882-5971). **1492**

GEOSCIENCE CANADA (CN/0315-0941). **1380**

GEOSCIENCE CANADA REPRINT SERIES (CN/0821-381X). **1355**

GEOSTANDARDS NEWSLETTER (FR/0150-5505). **1380**

GEOTECHNIQUE (UK/0016-8505). **2023**

GEOTECHNIQUE [MICROFORM] (UK/0016-8505). **1976**

GEOTECTONICS (US/0016-8521). **1381**

GEOTEKTONIKA (RU/0016-853X). **1381**

GEOTEKTONISCHE FORSCHUNGEN (GW/0016-8548). **1381**

GEOTEXTILES AND GEOMEMBRANES (UK/0266-1144). **495**

GEOTHERMAL SCIENCE AND TECHNOLOGY (UK/0890-5363). **1406**

GEOTHERMICS (UK/0375-6505). **1413**

GEOTIMES (US/0016-8556). **1381**

GEOWISSENSCHAFTEN (WEINHEIM AN DER BERGSTRASSE, GERMANY) (GW/0933-0704). **1356**

GERIATRIC NEPHROLOGY AND UROLOGY (NE/0924-8455). **3990**

GERIATRIC NURSING (NEW YORK) (US/0197-4572). **3856**

GERIATRICS (US/0016-867X). **3751**

GERMAN HISTORY : THE JOURNAL OF THE GERMAN HISTORY SOCIETY (UK/0266-3554). **2689**

GERMAN RESEARCH : REPORTS OF THE DFG (GW/0172-1526). **5107**

GERMAN YEARBOOK OF INTERNATIONAL LAW (GW/0344-3094). **3128**

GERMANIC REVIEW, THE (US/0016-8890). **3343**

GERMANISTIK (TUEBINGEN) (GW/0016-8912). **3336**

GERMANISTISCHE LINGUISTIK (GW/0072-1492). **3284**

GERONTOLOGY & GERIATRICS EDUCATION (US/0270-1960). **3752**

GERONTOLOGY (BASEL) (SZ/0304-324X). **3752**

GESCHICHTE IN WISSENSCHAFT UND UNTERRICHT (GW/0016-9056). **2616**

GESCHICHTE UND GESELLSCHAFT (GOTTINGEN) (GW/0340-613X). **5201**

GESNERUS (SZ/0016-9161). **3578**

GESTALT THEORY (GW/0170-057X). **4588**

GESTIONS HOSPITALIERES (FR/0016-9218). **3780**

GEWERBLICHER RECHTSSCHUTZ UND URHEBERRECHT. INTERNATIONALER TEIL (GW/0435-8600). **2974**

GEWERKSCHAFTLICHE MONATSHEFTE (GW/0016-9447). **1676**

GI CANCER (US/1064-9700). **3817**

GIESSEREI (GW/0016-9765). **4003**

GIESSEREIFORSCHUNG (GW/0046-5933). **4003**

GIFT & STATIONERY BUSINESS (US/0896-4092). **2584**

GIFTED EDUCATION INTERNATIONAL (UK/0261-4294). **1879**

GIFTS & DECORATIVE ACCESSORIES (US/0016-9889). **2584**

GIGIENA I SANITARIIA (1943) (RU/0016-9900). **2597**

GIGIENA TRUDA I PROFESSIONALNYE ZABOLEVANIJA (RU/0016-9919). **2862**

GIORNALE DI NEUROPSICOFARMACOLOGIN (IT/0391-9048). **4306**

GIORNALE ITALIANO DI ANGIOLOGIA (IT/0392-1387). **3705**

GIORNALE ITALIANO DI ONCOLOGIA (IT/0392-128X). **3817**

GIORNALE ITALIANO DI OSTETRICIA E GINECOLOGIA (IT/0391-9013). **3761**

GIS FORUM, THE (US/1041-2697). **3212**

GLASFORUM (GW/0017-0852). **2589**

GLASGOW MATHEMATICAL JOURNAL (UK/0017-0895). **3507**

GLASS AND CERAMICS (US/0361-7610). **2589**

GLASS DIGEST (US/0017-1018). **2589**

GLASS INDUSTRY, THE (US/0017-1026). **2590**

GLASWELT (GW/0017-1107). **2590**

GLOBAL AND PLANETARY CHANGE (NE/0921-8181). **1356**

GLOBAL BIOGEOCHEMICAL CYCLES (US/0886-6236). **1041**

GLOBAL COMMUNICATIONS (US/0195-2250). **1112**

GLOBAL ENVIRONMENTAL CHANGE (UK/0959-3780). **2172**

GLOBAL ENVIRONMENTAL CHANGE REPORT (US/1049-9083). **2216**

GLOBAL TECTONICS AND METALLOGENY (GW/0163-3171). **1356**

GLOBAL TELECOM REPORT (US/1059-4485). **1156**

GLOBE AND MAIL (CN/0319-0714). **5785**

GLOBE AND MAIL, THE (CN/0319-0714). **5785**

GLOT (NE/0166-5790). **3284**

GLOTTA (GOTTINGEN) (GW/0017-1298). **3284**

GLQ (NEW YORK, N.Y.) (US/1064-2684). **2794**

GLUCKAUF-FORSCHUNGSHEFTE (GW/0017-1387). **2139**

GLUCKAUF. WITH ENGLISH TRANSLATION (ESSEN) (GW/0174-1799). **2140**

GLYCOBIOLOGY (OXFORD) (UK/0959-6658). **487**

GLYCOCONJUGATE JOURNAL (UK/0282-0080). **1025**

GMBH-RUNDSCHAU (GW/0016-3570). **678**

GMP LETTER, THE (US/0196-626X). **3479**

GNOMON (MUNCHEN) (GW/0017-1417). **3284**

GODISEN ZBORNIK NA MEDICINSKIOT FAKULTET VO SKOPJE (XN/0065-1214). **3579**

GOLD + SILBER, UHREN + SCHMUCK (GW/0017-1573). **2914**

GOLDFINCH, THE (US/0278-0208). **1063**

GOLOB'S OIL POLLUTION BULLETIN (US/1051-6255). **2230**

GORNYI ZHURNAL (RU/0017-2278). **1440**

GOTTINGISCHE GELEHRTE ANZEIGEN (GW/0017-1549). **2847**

GOVERNANCE (OXFORD) (UK/0952-1895). **4651**

GOVERNING (WASHINGTON, D.C.) (US/0894-3842). **4475**

GOVERNMENT COMPUTER NEWS (US/0738-4300). **4651**

GOVERNMENT EMPLOYEE RELATIONS REPORT (US/0017-260X). **4703**

GOVERNMENT EXECUTIVE (US/0017-2626). **4651**

GOVERNMENT INFORMATION QUARTERLY (US/0740-624X). **3212**

GOVERNMENT MANAGER, THE (US/0148-7949). **4704**

GOVERNMENT PRODUCT NEWS (US/0017-2642). **950**

GOVERNMENT PUBLICATIONS REVIEW (1982) (US/0277-9390). **3212**

GPS REPORT (US/1056-7127). **1156**

GPS WORLD (US/1048-5104). **2565**

GRADUATE STUDIES IN MATHEMATICS (US/1065-7339). **3507**

GRAEFE'S ARCHIVE FOR CLINICAL AND EXPERIMENTAL OPHTHALMOLOGY (GW/0721-832X). **3875**

GRANA (SW/0017-3134). **512**

GRAND RAPIDS BUSINESS JOURNAL (US/1045-4055). **678**

GRANI (GW/0017-3185). **2517**

GRAPHIC ARTS MONTHLY (1987) (US/1047-9325). **379**

GRAPHIC ARTS PRODUCT NEWS (CHICAGO) (US/0274-5976). **379**

GRAPHS AND COMBINATORICS (JA/0911-0119). **3507**

GRASAS Y ACEITES (SEVILLA) (SP/0017-3495). **488**

GRASS AND FORAGE SCIENCE (UK/0142-5242). **90**

GRASS ROOTS SHEPPARTON (AT/0310-2890). **90**

GRAY AREAS (US/1062-5712). **2534**

GREAT LAKES ENTOMOLOGIST, THE (US/0090-0222). **5609**

GREECE & ROME (UK/0017-3835). **1077**

GREEN BUSINESS LETTER, THE (US/1056-490X). **2172**

GREEN CONSUMER LETTER, THE (US/1049-2747). **2172**

GREEN MARKETING REPORT (US/1051-7316). **925**

GREENHOUSE EFFECT REPORT (US/1042-5039). **2230**

GREENHOUSE GROWER (US/0745-7324). **2417**

GROCERY DISTRIBUTION ANALYSIS AND GUIDE (1983) (US/0749-551X). **2342**

GROUND ENGINEERING (UK/0017-4653). **2024**

GROUND WATER (US/0017-467X). **1413**

GROUND WATER AGE (US/0046-645X). **5533**

GROUND WATER MONITORING REVIEW (US/0277-1926). **1413**

GROUND WATER NEWSLETTER / WATER INFORMATION CENTER, WIC, THE (US/0090-5070). **5534**

GROUNDS MAINTENANCE (US/0017-4688). **2417**

GROUNDWATER MONITOR (US/0882-6188). **1414**

GROUNDWATER POLLUTION NEWS (US/0899-3521). **2230**

GROUPWORK LONDON (UK/0951-824X). **5286**

GROWER (SHAWNEE MISSION, KAN.), THE (US/0745-1784). **173**

GROWTH AND CHANGE (US/0017-4815). **2823**

GROWTH FACTORS (CHUR, SWITZERLAND) (SZ/0897-7194). **456**

GROWTH REGULATION (UK/0956-523X). **547**

GRUNDLAGEN DER LANDTECHNIK (GW/0017-4920). **91**

GRUPPENDYNAMIK (GW/0046-6514). **4588**

GSA TODAY (US/1052-5173). **1381**

GUETERVERKEHR, DER (GW/0017-5137). **5383**

GUIDE TO FEDERAL FUNDING FOR EDUCATION (US/0275-8393). **1748**

GUIDE TO SOFTWARE PRODUCTIVITY AIDS (US/0740-8374). **1238**

GUIDEPOST (WASHINGTON, D.C.) (US/0017-5323). **4588**

GULF COAST OIL WORLD (US/0884-7967). **4259**

GULLET (UK/0952-0643). **3579**

GUT (UK/0017-5749). **3746**

GYNAECOLOGICAL ENDOSCOPY (UK/0962-1091). **3761**

GYNAKOLOGE (BERLIN) (GW/0017-5994). **3761**

GYNECOLOGIC AND OBSTETRIC INVESTIGATION (SZ/0378-7346). **3761**

GYNECOLOGIC ONCOLOGY (US/0090-8258). **3817**

GYNECOLOGIE (FR/0301-2204). **3761**

H + G ZEITSCHRIFT FUER HAUTKRANKHEITEN (GW/0301-0481). **3720**

HABITAT INTERNATIONAL (UK/0197-3975). **2823**

HAEMATOLOGY AND BLOOD TRANSFUSION (GW/0171-7111). **3772**

HAEMOSTASEOLOGIE (GW/0720-9355). **3580**

HAEMOSTASIS (SZ/0301-0147). **3580**

HAIYANG XUEBAO (ENGLISH ED.) (CC/0253-505X). **1449**

HAMLET STUDIES (II/0256-2480). **3392**

HAMLINE LAW REVIEW (US/0198-7364). **2976**

HAND CLINICS (US/0749-0712). **3881**

HANDBOOK OF EXPERIMENTAL PHARMACOLOGY (GW/0171-2004). **4306**

HANDBOOK OF SEC ACCOUNTING AND DISCLOSURE (US/1046-3534). **744**

HANDCHIRURGIE, MIKROCHIRURGIE, PLASTISCHE CHIRURGIE (GW/0722-1819). **3965**

HANDICAPPED REQUIREMENTS HANDBOOK. SUPPLEMENT (US/0194-7818). **4388**

HAN'GUK CHUKSAN HAKHOE CHI (KO/0367-5807). **5510**

HARPER'S (NEW YORK, N.Y.) (US/0017-789X). **3343**

HARROWSMITH (CANADIAN ED.) (CN/0381-6885). **2534**

HARTFORD COURANT, THE (US/1047-4153). **5645**

HARVARD ARCHITECTURE REVIEW, THE (US/0194-3650). **299**

HARVARD EDUCATIONAL REVIEW (US/0017-8055). **1749**

HARVARD EDUCATIONAL REVIEW (US/0017-8055). **1749**

HARVARD INTERNATIONAL REVIEW (US/0739-1854). **4523**

HARVARD REVIEW OF PSYCHIATRY (US/1067-3229). **3926**

HARVESTER, THE (UK/0017-8217). **5017**

HAUTARZT (GW/0017-8470). **3720**

HAY & FORAGE GROWER (US/0891-5946). **202**

HAZARDOUS MATERIALS INTELLIGENCE REPORT (US/0272-9628). **2231**

HAZARDOUS MATERIALS TRANSPORTATION (BOSTON) (US/0197-3177). **2231**

HAZARDOUS WASTE CONSULTANT, THE (US/0738-0232). **2231**

HAZARDOUS WASTE NEWS (US/0275-374X). **2231**

HAZMAT WORLD (US/0898-5685). **2232**

HDTV REPORT (US/1055-9280). **1132**

HEALTH & SAFETY AT WORK (CROYDON) (UK/0141-8246). **2862**

HEALTH & SOCIAL CARE IN THE COMMUNITY (UK/0966-0410). **5287**

HEALTH & SOCIAL WORK (US/0360-7283). **5287**

HEALTH CARE COMPETITION WEEK (US/0886-2095). **4778**

HEALTH CARE FOR WOMEN INTERNATIONAL (US/0739-9332). **3762**

HEALTH CARE MANAGEMENT REVIEW (US/0361-6274). **3781**

HEALTH CARE STANDARDS (US/1044-4076). **4778**

HEALTH CARE SUPERVISOR, THE (US/0731-3381). **3781**

HEALTH CARE SYSTEMS (NEW YORK, N.Y.) (US/0745-1717). **3581**

HEALTH DEVICES (US/0046-7022). **3581**

HEALTH DEVICES ALERTS (US/0163-0458). **3659**

HEALTH DEVICES INSPECTION AND PREVENTIVE MAINTENANCE SYSTEM (US/8756-8713). **4779**

HEALTH DEVICES SOURCEBOOK (US/0278-3452). **3581**

HEALTH ECONOMICS (US/1057-9230). **4779**

HEALTH EDUCATION QUARTERLY (US/0195-8402). **4779**

HEALTH EDUCATION RESEARCH (UK/0268-1153). **4779**

HEALTH FUNDS DEVELOPMENT LETTER (US/0193-7928). **3581**

HEALTH GRANTS & CONTRACTS WEEKLY (US/0194-2352). **4780**

HEALTH LIBRARIES REVIEW (UK/0265-6647). **3213**

HEALTH/PAC BULLETIN (US/0017-9051). **4780**

HEALTH PHYSICS (1958) (US/0017-9078). **4404**

HEALTH POLICY (AMSTERDAM) (NE/0168-8510). **3582**

HEALTH POLICY AND PLANNING (UK/0268-1080). **4780**

HEALTH PROFESSIONS REPORT (US/0888-9465). **3582**

HEALTH PROMOTION INTERNATIONAL (UK/0957-4824). **4781**

HEALTH PSYCHOLOGY (US/0278-6133). **4588**

HEALTH SERVICE JOURNAL, THE (UK/0952-2271). **4781**

HEALTH SERVICES MANAGEMENT RESEARCH : AN OFFICIAL JOURNAL OF THE ASSOCIATION OF UNIVERSITY PROGRAMS IN HEALTH ADMINISTRATION (UK/0951-4848). **3781**

HEALTH TECHNOLOGY TRENDS (US/1041-6072). **3583**

HEALTHCARE COMMUNITY RELATIONS & MARKETING LETTER (US/0894-9980). **3583**

HEALTHCARE EXECUTIVE (US/0883-5381). **3782**

HEALTHCARE FUNDRAISING NEWSLETTER (US/0193-9939). **3782**

HEALTHCARE HAZARDOUS MATERIALS MANAGEMENT (US/1050-575X). **4782**

HEALTHCARE HUMAN RESOURCES (US/1060-9253). **3914**

HEALTHCARE MARKETING ABSTRACTS (US/0891-5016). **925**

HEALTHCARE TECHNOLOGY BUSINESS OPPORTUNITIES (US/1049-4499). **3583**

HEALTHWEEK (US/0890-2259). **4782**

HEARING INSTRUMENTS (US/0092-4466). **3888**

HEARING RESEARCH (NE/0378-5955). **3888**

HEART & LUNG (US/0147-9563). **3856**

HEART AND VESSELS (JA/0910-8327). **3705**

HEART DISEASE AND STROKE (US/1058-2819). **3705**

HEAT RECOVERY SYSTEMS & CHP (UK/0890-4332). **4430**

HEAT TRANSFER ENGINEERING (US/0145-7632). **2012**

HEAT TRANSFER. JAPANESE RESEARCH (US/0096-0802). **4431**

HEAT TREATING (US/0017-9345). **4003**

HEATING, PIPING, AND AIR CONDITIONING (US/0017-940X). **2605**

HEC FORUM (NE/0956-2737). **3783**

HEIDELBERGER JAHRBUCHER (GW/0073-1641). **5109**

HEILBERUFE, DIE (GW/0017-9604). **3583**

HEIMEN (NO/0017-9841). **2690**

HEIMTEX (GW/0017-9876). **2900**

HELICOPTER NEWS (US/0363-8227). **23**

HELLER REPORT ON EDUCATIONAL TECHNOLOGY AND TELECOMMUNICATIONS MARKETS, THE (US/1047-5230). **5109**

HELVETICA CHIMICA ACTA (SZ/0018-019X). **976**

HELVETICA CHIRURGICA ACTA (SZ/0018-0181). **3903**

HELVETICA PHYSICA ACTA (SZ/0018-0238). **4404**

HEMATOLOGIC PATHOLOGY (US/0886-0238). **3894**

HEMATOLOGICAL ONCOLOGY (UK/0278-0232). **3772**

HEMATOLOGY (NEW YORK, N.Y.) (US/0891-9763). **3772**

HEMATOLOGY/ONCOLOGY CLINICS OF NORTH AMERICA (US/0889-8588). **3772**

HEMATOLOGY REVIEWS AND COMMUNICATIONS (SZ/0882-8083). **3772**

HEMOGLOBIN (US/0363-0269). **3797**

HENRY JAMES REVIEW, THE (US/0273-0340). **3344**

HEPATO-GASTROENTEROLOGY (GW/0172-6390). **3746**

HEPATOLOGY (BALTIMORE, MD.) (US/0270-9139). **3797**

HEREDITY (UK/0018-067X). **547**

HERE'S HEALTH (WEST BYFLEET) (UK/0018-0696). **4782**

HERMES (WIESBADEN) (GW/0018-0777). **3393**

HERZ (GW/0340-9937). **3705**

HERZ-KREISLAUF (GW/0046-7324). **3705**

HERZOGIA (GW/0018-0971). **512**

HERZSCHRITTMACHERTHERAPIE & ELEKTROPHYSIOLOGIE (GW/0938-7412). **2056**

HETEROATOM CHEMISTRY (US/1042-7163). **976**

HETEROCYCLES (JA/0385-5414). **1041**

HEYTHROP JOURNAL (UK/0018-1196). **5030**

HIFI & TV (GW/0343-4206). **1132**

HIGH COUNTRY NEWS (US/0191-5657). **2195**

HIGH ENERGY CHEMISTRY (US/0018-1439). **1052**

HIGH ENERGY PHYSICS & NUCLEAR PHYSICS (US/0899-9996). **4447**

HIGH PERFORMANCE LIQUID CHROMATOGRAPHY SHEFFIELD (UK/0261-4707). **1011**

HIGH PERFORMANCE PLASTICS (UK/0264-7753). **4455**

HIGH PERFORMANCE POLYMERS (UK/0954-0083). **977**

HIGH PERFORMANCE REVIEW (US/0277-1357). **5317**

HIGH PERFORMANCE TEXTILES (UK/0144-5871). **5351**

HIGH PRESSURE RESEARCH (US/0895-7959). **4404**

HIGH-PURITY SUBSTANCES (US/0897-4403). **977**

HIGH SCHOOL JOURNAL, THE (US/0018-1498). **1750**

HIGH-TECH MATERIALS ALERT (US/0741-0808). **1977**

HIGH TECHNOLOGY LAW JOURNAL (US/0885-2715). **2978**

HIGH TEMPERATURE (US/0018-151X). **4431**

HIGH TEMPERATURE SCIENCE (US/0018-1536). **1052**

HIGHER EDUCATION (NE/0018-1560). **1828**

HIGHER EDUCATION (NEW YORK, N.Y. : 1985) (US/0882-4126). **1828**

HIGHER EDUCATION POLICY (UK/0952-8733). **1828**

HIGHER EDUCATION QUARTERLY / SOCIETY FOR RESEARCH INTO HIGHER EDUCATION (UK/0951-5224). **1828**

HILLSIDE JOURNAL OF CLINICAL PSYCHIATRY, THE (US/0193-5216). **3926**

HIMICESKAJ PROMYSLENNOST (RU/0023-110X). **977**

HIMIJA DREVESINY (LV/0201-7474). **2401**

HIMIJA I TEHNOLOGIJA TOPLIV I MASEL (RU/0023-1169). **4260**

HIPPOCAMPUS (NEW YORK, N.Y.) (US/1050-9631). **3797**

HIRURGIJA (MOSKVA) (RU/0023-1207). **3965**

HISPANIC BUSINESS (US/0199-0349). **679**

HISPANIC TIMES MAGAZINE (US/0892-1369). **4204**

HISTOCHEMICAL JOURNAL (UK/0018-2214). **536**

HISTOCHEMISTRY (BERLIN) (GW/0301-5564). **536**

HISTOIRE DES SCIENCES MEDICALES (FR/0440-8888). **3584**

HISTOIRE, L' (FR/0182-2411). **2617**

HISTOPATHOLOGY (UK/0309-0167). **3894**

HISTORIA MATHEMATICA (US/0315-0860). **3507**

HISTORIA (WIESBADEN) (GW/0018-2311). **2617**

HISTORIC PRESERVATION (WASHINGTON, D.C.) (US/0018-2419). **2737**

HISTORICAL BIOLOGY (UK/0891-2963). **457**

HISTORICAL BOOKLETS / THE CANADIAN HISTORICAL ASSOCIATION (CN/0068-886X). **2737**

HISTORICAL JOURNAL (CAMBRIDGE, CAMBRIDGESHIRE) (UK/0018-246X). **2618**

HISTORICAL JOURNAL OF FILM, RADIO, AND TELEVISION (UK/0143-9685). **4071**

HISTORICAL METHODS (US/0161-5440). **5201**

HISTORICAL NEWS (NZ/0439-2345). **2618**

HISTORICAL RESEARCH : THE BULLETIN OF THE INSTITUTE OF HISTORICAL RESEARCH (UK/0950-3471). **2618**

HISTORICAL REVIEW (NZ/0018-2516). **2669**

HISTORICAL STUDIES IN THE PHYSICAL AND BIOLOGICAL SCIENCES (US/0890-9997). **4404**

HISTORISCH-POLITISCHE BUCH, DAS (GW/0018-2605). **2618**

HISTORISCHE ZEITSCHRIFT (GW/0018-2613). **2619**

HISTORISCHES JAHRBUCH (GW/0018-2621). **2619**

HISTORY AND ANTHROPOLOGY (SZ/0275-7206). **237**

HISTORY & COMPUTING (UK/0957-0144). **1186**

HISTORY AND PHILOSOPHY OF THE LIFE SCIENCES (UK/0391-9714). **457**

HISTORY AND TECHNOLOGY (SZ/0734-1512). **5110**

HISTORY (LONDON) (UK/0018-2648). **2619**

HISTORY OF EDUCATION (TAVISTOCK) (UK/0046-760X). **1750**

HISTORY OF EUROPEAN IDEAS (UK/0191-6599). **2691**

HISTORY OF MATHEMATICS (US/0899-2428). **3507**

HISTORY OF PHOTOGRAPHY (UK/0308-7298). **4370**

HISTORY OF POLITICAL ECONOMY (US/0018-2702). **1565**

HISTORY OF RELIGIONS (US/0018-2710). **4963**

HISTORY OF SCIENCE (UK/0073-2753). **5110**

HISTORY OF THE HUMAN SCIENCES (UK/0952-6951). **5201**

HISTORY WORKSHOP (UK/0309-2984). **2619**

HK, HOLZ- UND MOBELINDUSTRIE (GW/0721-2585). **634**

HLH (GW/0017-9906). **2605**

HNO (GW/0017-6192). **3888**

HOG FARM MANAGEMENT (US/0018-3180). **212**

HOLISTIC NURSING PRACTICE (US/0887-9311). **3856**

HOLLYWOOD REPORTER, THE (US/0018-3660). **4072**

HOLOCAUST AND GENOCIDE STUDIES (UK/8756-6583). **2691**

HOLZ ALS ROH- UND WERKSTOFF (GW/0018-3768). **2401**

HOLZ-ZENTRALBLATT (GW/0018-3792). **2384**

HOLZFORSCHUNG (GW/0018-3830). **2401**

HOME HEALTHCARE NURSE (US/0884-741X). **3856**

HOME IMPROVEMENT CENTER (US/1045-9367). **616**

HOME LIGHTING & ACCESSORIES (US/0162-9077). **2906**

HOMEOSTASIS IN HEALTH AND DISEASE : INTERNATIONAL JOURNAL DEVOTED TO INTEGRATIVE BRAIN FUNCTIONS AND HOMEOSTATIC SYSTEMS (XR/0960-7560). **3833**

HOMES AND GARDENS INCORPORATING HOME (UK/0018-4233). **2824**

HOMMES ET FONDERIE (FR/0018-4357). **4428**

HOMO (GW/0018-442X). **237**

HORGESCHADIGTEN PADAGOGIK (GW/0342-4898). **4388**

HORMONE AND METABOLIC RESEARCH (GW/0018-5043). **3730**

HORMONE RESEARCH (SZ/0301-0163). **3730**

HORMONES AND BEHAVIOR (US/0018-506X). **3730**

HOSPIMEDICA (US/0898-7270). **3584**

HOSPITAL & HEALTH SERVICES ADMINISTRATION (US/8750-3735). **3783**

HOSPITAL AND HEALTH SERVICES REVIEW, THE (UK/0308-0234). **3783**

HOSPITAL EMPLOYEE HEALTH (US/0744-6470). **3784**

HOSPITAL FORMULARY (US/0098-6909). **4306**

HOSPITAL FUND RAISING NEWSLETTER (US/0193-9939). **3784**

HOSPITAL INFECTION CONTROL (US/0098-180X). **3584**

HOSPITAL MANAGEMENT REVIEW (US/0737-903X). **3659**

HOSPITAL MATERIEL MANAGEMENT QUARTERLY (US/0192-2262). **3784**

HOSPITAL MEDICINE (NEW YORK, N.Y.) (US/0441-2745). **3584**

HOSPITAL PATIENT RELATIONS REPORT (US/1048-4477). **3784**

HOSPITAL PEER REVIEW (US/0149-2632). **3785**

HOSPITAL PHARMACY (PHILADELPHIA) (US/0018-5787). **4306**

HOSPITAL PURCHASING NEWS (US/0279-4799). **3785**

HOSPITAL RISK MANAGEMENT (US/0199-6312). **869**

HOSPITAL TOPICS (US/0018-5868). **3785**

HOSPITALITY LAW (US/0889-5414). **2979**

HOTEL & MOTEL MANAGEMENT (US/0018-6082). **2806**

HOTELS (NEWTON, MASS.) (US/1047-2975). **2807**

HOTLINE ON OBJECT-ORIENTED TECHNOLOGY (US/1044-4319). **1186**

HOUILLE BLANCHE, LA (FR/0018-6368). **2090**

HOUSEHOLD & PERSONAL PRODUCTS INDUSTRY : HAPPI (US/0090-8878). **977**

HOUSING

HOUSING & DEVELOPMENT REPORTER (US/0091-5939). **2824**

HOUSING STUDIES (UK/0267-3037). **2825**

HOWARD JOURNAL OF CRIMINAL JUSTICE, THE (UK/0265-5527). **3165**

HPB SURGERY (SZ/0894-8569). **3965**

HR FOCUS (US/1059-6038). **941**

HR HORIZONS (US/1053-3656). **941**

HR MANAGERS LEGAL REPORTER (US/1053-0363). **3149**

HR REPORTER (US/0741-6997). **941**

HRMAGAZINE (ALEXANDRIA, VA.) (US/1047-3149). **941**

HRPLANNING NEWSLETTER, THE (US/0733-0332). **941**

HUMAN ANTIBODIES AND HYBRIDOMAS (US/0956-960X). **457**

HUMAN COMMUNICATION RESEARCH (US/0360-3989). **1112**

HUMAN DEVELOPMENT (SZ/0018-716X). **4588**

HUMAN EVENTS (WASHINGTON) (US/0018-7194). **4476**

HUMAN FACTORS (US/0018-7208). **1251**

HUMAN GENETICS (GW/0340-6717). **547**

HUMAN HEREDITY (SZ/0001-5652). **547**

HUMAN IMMUNOLOGY (US/0198-8859). **3670**

HUMAN MOVEMENT SCIENCE (NE/0167-9457). **5202**

HUMAN NATURE (HAWTHORNE, N.Y.) (US/1045-6767). **2847**

HUMAN PATHOLOGY (US/0046-8177). **3895**

HUMAN PHYSIOLOGY (US/0362-1197). **581**

HUMAN PSYCHOPHARMACOLOGY (UK/0885-6222). **4307**

HUMAN RELATIONS (NEW YORK) (US/0018-7267). **5202**

HUMAN REPRODUCTION (OXFORD) (UK/0268-1161). **541**

HUMAN RESOURCE EXECUTIVE (US/1040-0443). **941**

HUMAN RESOURCE MANAGEMENT (US/0090-4848). **941**

HUMAN RESOURCE MANAGEMENT REVIEW (US/1053-4822). **942**

HUMAN RIGHTS QUARTERLY (US/0275-0392). **4509**

HUMAN STUDIES (NE/0163-8548). **4348**

HUMANE MEDICINE (CN/0828-7090). **3585**

HUMOR (BERLIN, GERMANY) (GW/0933-1719). **4589**

HUNGARIAN STUDIES : HS (HU/0236-6568). **2692**

HUNTIA (US/0073-4071). **513**

HUSSERL STUDIES (NE/0167-9848). **4348**

HVAC PRODUCT NEWS (US/0887-445X). **2605**

HYBRID CIRCUIT TECHNOLOGY (US/0747-1599). **5111**

HYBRID CIRCUITS : JOURNAL OF THE INTERNATIONAL SOCIETY FOR HYBRID MICROELECTRONICS-UK / INTERNATIONAL SOCIETY FOR HYBRID ELECTRONICS, UNITED KINGDOM (UK/0265-3028). **2056**

HYDRAULICS & PNEUMATICS (US/0018-814X). **2090**

HYDROBIOLOGIA (NE/0018-8158). **457**

HYDROBIOLOGICAL JOURNAL (US/0018-8166). **457**

HYDROCARBON PROCESSING (INTERNATIONAL ED.) (US/0018-8190). **4260**

HYDROLOGICAL PROCESSES (UK/0885-6087). **1414**

HYDROLOGICAL SCIENCES JOURNAL (UK/0262-6667). **1415**

HYDROLYSIS AND WOOD CHEMISTRY (US/1068-3658). **4234**

HYDROMETALLURGY (NE/0304-386X). **4003**

HYDROTECHNICAL CONSTRUCTION (US/0018-8220). **2090**

HYPERTENSION (DALLAS, TEX. 1979) (US/0194-911X). **3705**

I/S ANALYZER (US/0896-3231). **4212**

IASP NEWSLETTER (INTERNATIONAL ASSOCIATION OF SCHOLARLY PUBLISHERS) (NO/0333-3620). **4815**

IAWA BULLETIN (NE/0254-3915). **2401**

IBERO-AMERIKANISCHES ARCHIV (GW/0340-3068). **2738**

IBIS (LONDON, ENGLAND) (UK/0019-1019). **5617**

ICARUS (NEW YORK, N.Y. 1962) (US/0019-1035). **395**

ICHNOS (CHUR, SWITZERLAND) (SZ/1042-0940). **269**

ICL TECHNICAL JOURNAL (UK/0142-1557). **1187**

ICSID REVIEW (US/0258-3690). **3129**

ID SYSTEMS (US/0892-676X). **5111**

IDEAL HOME (UK/0019-1361). **616**

IDENTITY (CINCINNATI, OHIO) (US/0899-3483). **380**

IDP REPORT (US/0197-0178). **1254**

IEE CONFERENCE PUBLICATION (UK/0537-9989). **2057**

IEE NEWS (UK/0308-0684). **2057**

IEE PROCEEDINGS. C, GENERATION, TRANSMISSION, AND DISTRIBUTION (UK/0143-7046). **2057**

IEE PROCEEDINGS. D, CONTROL THEORY AND APPLICATIONS (UK/0143-7054). **2057**

IEE PROCEEDINGS. F, RADAR AND SIGNAL PROCESSING (UK/0956-375X). **1156**

IEE PROCEEDINGS. G, CIRCUITS, DEVICES, AND SYSTEMS (UK/0956-3768). **2058**

IEE PROCEEDINGS. I, COMMUNICATIONS, SPEECH, AND VISION (UK/0956-3776). **1156**

IEE PROCEEDINGS. PART B. ELECTRIC POWER APPLICATIONS (UK/0143-7038). **2058**

IEE PROCEEDINGS. PART E. COMPUTERS AND DIGITAL TECHNIQUES (UK/0143-7062). **1229**

IEE PROCEEDINGS. PART H, MICROWAVES, ANTENNAS, AND PROPAGATION (UK/0950-107X). **2058**

IEE PROCEEDINGS. PART J, OPTOELECTRONICS (UK/0267-3932). **2058**

IEEE AEROSPACE AND ELECTRONIC SYSTEMS MAGAZINE (US/0885-8985). **23**

IEEE ANTENNAS & PROPAGATION MAGAZINE (US/1045-9243). **2058**

IEEE CIRCUITS AND DEVICES MAGAZINE (US/8755-3996). **2059**

IEEE COMMUNICATIONS MAGAZINE (US/0163-6804). **1157**

IEEE COMPUTER APPLICATIONS IN POWER (US/0895-0156). **2059**

IEEE COMPUTER GRAPHICS AND APPLICATIONS (US/0272-1716). **1233**

IEEE CONFERENCE RECORD-ABSTRACTS (US/0730-9244). **2024**

IEEE DESIGN & TEST OF COMPUTERS (US/0740-7475). **1229**

IEEE ELECTRICAL INSULATION MAGAZINE (US/0883-7554). **2059**

IEEE ELECTRON DEVICE LETTERS (US/0741-3106). **2059**

IEEE ENGINEERING IN MEDICINE AND BIOLOGY MAGAZINE (US/0739-5175). **3693**

IEEE ENGINEERING MANAGEMENT REVIEW (US/0360-8581). **2059**

IEEE EXPERT (US/0885-9000). **1229**

IEEE JOURNAL OF OCEANIC ENGINEERING (US/0364-9059). **2090**

IEEE JOURNAL OF QUANTUM ELECTRONICS (US/0018-9197). **2060**

IEEE JOURNAL OF SOLID-STATE CIRCUITS (US/0018-9200). **2060**

IEEE JOURNAL ON SELECTED AREAS IN COMMUNICATIONS (US/0733-8716). **1157**

IEEE LTS : THE MAGAZINE OF LIGHTWAVE TELECOMMUNICATIONS SYSTEMS (US/1055-6877). **4434**

IEEE MICRO (US/0272-1732). **1267**

IEEE MICROWAVE AND GUIDED WAVE LETTERS (US/1051-8207). **2060**

IEEE MTT-S INTERNATIONAL MICROWAVE SYMPOSIUM DIGEST (US/0149-645X). **2060**

IEEE NETWORK (US/0890-8044). **1241**

IEEE PHOTONICS TECHNOLOGY LETTERS (US/1041-1135). **4435**

IEEE POTENTIALS (US/0278-6648). **2060**

IEEE POWER ENGINEERING REVIEW (US/0272-1724). **2060**

IEEE PUBLICATIONS BULLETIN (US/0046-8371). **2060**

IEEE SIGNAL PROCESSING MAGAZINE (US/1053-5888). **2060**

IEEE SOFTWARE (US/0740-7459). **1286**

IEEE SPECTRUM (US/0018-9235). **2060**

IEEE TECHNICAL ACTIVITIES GUIDE (US/0278-520X). **2061**

IEEE TECHNOLOGY & SOCIETY MAGAZINE (US/0278-0097). **5111**

IEEE TRANSACTIONS ON AEROSPACE AND ELECTRONIC SYSTEMS (US/0018-9251). **2061**

IEEE TRANSACTIONS ON ANTENNAS AND PROPAGATION (US/0018-926X). **2061**

IEEE TRANSACTIONS ON APPLIED SUPERCONDUCTIVITY (US/1051-8223). **2061**

IEEE TRANSACTIONS ON AUTOMATIC CONTROL (US/0018-9286). **1219**

IEEE TRANSACTIONS ON BROADCASTING (US/0018-9316). **1133**

IEEE TRANSACTIONS ON CIRCUITS AND SYSTEMS FOR VIDEO TECHNOLOGY (US/1051-8215). **1133**

IEEE TRANSACTIONS ON CIRCUITS & SYSTEMS. PART 1, FUNDAMENTAL THEORY AND APPLICATIONS (US/1057-7122). **2061**

IEEE TRANSACTIONS ON CIRCUITS AND SYSTEMS. PART 2, ANALOG AND DIGITAL SIGNAL PROCESSING (US/1057-7130). **2061**

IEEE TRANSACTIONS ON COMMUNICATIONS (US/0090-6778). **1157**

IEEE TRANSACTIONS ON COMPONENTS, HYBRIDS AND MANUFACTURING TECHNOLOGY (US/0148-6411). **2061**

IEEE TRANSACTIONS ON COMPUTER-AIDED DESIGN OF INTEGRATED CIRCUITS AND SYSTEMS (US/0278-0070). **2061**

IEEE TRANSACTIONS ON COMPUTERS (US/0018-9340). **1247**

IEEE TRANSACTIONS ON CONSUMER ELECTRONICS (US/0098-3063). **2061**

IEEE TRANSACTIONS ON EDUCATION (US/0018-9359). **2062**

IEEE TRANSACTIONS ON ELECTRICAL INSULATION (US/0018-9367). **2062**

IEEE TRANSACTIONS ON ELECTROMAGNETIC COMPATIBILITY (US/0018-9375). **2062**

IEEE TRANSACTIONS ON ELECTRON DEVICES (US/0018-9383). **2062**

IEEE TRANSACTIONS ON ENERGY CONVERSION (US/0885-8969). **2062**

IEEE TRANSACTIONS ON ENGINEERING MANAGEMENT (US/0018-9391). **2062**

IEEE TRANSACTIONS ON GEOSCIENCE AND REMOTE SENSING (US/0196-2892). **1406**

IEEE TRANSACTIONS ON IMAGE PROCESSING (US/1057-7149). **2062**

IEEE TRANSACTIONS ON INDUSTRIAL ELECTRONICS (1982) (US/0278-0046). **2062**

IEEE TRANSACTIONS ON INDUSTRY APPLICATIONS (US/0093-9994). **2062**

IEEE TRANSACTIONS ON INFORMATION THEORY (US/0018-9448). **2062**

IEEE TRANSACTIONS ON INSTRUMENTATION AND MEASUREMENT (US/0018-9456). **2063**

IEEE TRANSACTIONS ON KNOWLEDGE AND DATA ENGINEERING (US/1041-4347). **2063**

IEEE TRANSACTIONS ON MAGNETICS (US/0018-9464). **4443**

IEEE TRANSACTIONS ON MEDICAL IMAGING (US/0278-0062). **3941**

IEEE TRANSACTIONS ON MICROWAVE THEORY AND TECHNIQUES (US/0018-9480). **2063**

IEEE TRANSACTIONS ON NEURAL NETWORKS (US/1045-9227). **1229**

IEEE TRANSACTIONS ON NUCLEAR SCIENCE (US/0018-9499). **2155**

IEEE TRANSACTIONS ON PARALLEL AND DISTRIBUTED SYSTEMS (US/1045-9219). **1259**

IEEE TRANSACTIONS ON PATTERN ANALYSIS AND MACHINE INTELLIGENCE (US/0162-8828). **1229**

IEEE TRANSACTIONS ON PLASMA SCIENCE (US/0093-3813). **3693**

IEEE TRANSACTIONS ON POWER DELIVERY (US/0885-8977). **2063**

IEEE TRANSACTIONS ON POWER ELECTRONICS (US/0885-8993). **2063**

IEEE TRANSACTIONS ON POWER SYSTEMS (US/0885-8950). **2063**

IEEE TRANSACTIONS ON PROFESSIONAL COMMUNICATION (US/0361-1434). **2063**

IEEE TRANSACTIONS ON RELIABILITY (US/0018-9529). **2063**

IEEE TRANSACTIONS ON ROBOTICS AND AUTOMATION (US/1042-296X). **1212**

IEEE TRANSACTIONS ON ROBOTICS AND AUTOMATION (US/1042-296X). **1213**

IEEE TRANSACTIONS ON SEMICONDUCTOR MANUFACTURING (US/0894-6507). **2063**

IEEE TRANSACTIONS ON SIGNAL PROCESSING (US/1053-587X). **2064**

IEEE TRANSACTIONS ON SOFTWARE ENGINEERING (US/0098-5589). **1286**

IEEE TRANSACTIONS ON SOFTWARE ENGINEERING (US/0098-5589). **1286**

Copyright Clearance Center Index — INFORMATION

IEEE TRANSACTIONS ON SYSTEMS, MAN, AND CYBERNETICS (US/0018-9472). **1251**

IEEE TRANSACTIONS ON ULTRASONICS, FERROELECTRICS, AND FREQUENCY CONTROL (US/0885-3010). **4452**

IEEE TRANSACTIONS ON VEHICULAR TECHNOLOGY (US/0018-9545). **2064**

IEEE TRANSLATION JOURNAL ON MAGNETICS IN JAPAN (US/0882-4959). **4444**

IEICE TRANSACTIONS ON ELECTRONICS (JA/0916-8524). **2064**

IFAC PROCEEDINGS SERIES (UK/0742-5953). **1219**

IFAC SYMPOSIA SERIES (UK/0962-9505). **1219**

IFIP TRANSACTIONS B: COMPUTER APPLICATIONS IN TECHNOLOGY (NE/0926-5481). **1229**

IFIP TRANSACTIONS. COMPUTER SCIENCE AND TECHNOLOGY (NE/0926-5473). **1247**

IFLA JOURNAL (GW/0340-0352). **3214**

IFO SCHNELLDIENST (GW/0018-974X). **681**

IFO-STUDIEN (GW/0018-9731). **1494**

IGIENE E SANITA PUBBLICA (IT/0019-1639). **4783**

IIC; INTERNATIONAL REVIEW OF INDUSTRIAL AND COPYRIGHT LAW (GW/0018-9855). **1304**

IIE TRANSACTIONS (US/0740-817X). **2098**

III-VS REVIEW (UK/0961-1290). **2064**

ILLINOIS JOURNAL OF MATHEMATICS (US/0019-2082). **3508**

IMA JOURNAL OF APPLIED MATHEMATICS (UK/0272-4960). **3508**

IMA JOURNAL OF MATHEMATICAL CONTROL AND INFORMATION (UK/0265-0754). **3508**

IMA JOURNAL OF MATHEMATICS APPLIED IN BUSINESS AND INDUSTRY (UK/0953-0061). **3508**

IMA JOURNAL OF MATHEMATICS APPLIED IN MEDICINE AND BIOLOGY (UK/0265-0746). **3508**

IMA JOURNAL OF NUMERICAL ANALYSIS (UK/0272-4979). **3508**

IMAGE AND VISION COMPUTING (UK/0262-8856). **1233**

IMAGING ABSTRACTS (US/0896-100X). **4378**

IMAGING : AN INTERNATIONAL JOURNAL OF CLINICO-RADIOLOGICAL PRACTICE (UK/0965-6812). **3942**

IMAGING NEWS (ALEXANDRIA, VA.) (US/1058-7705). **1113**

IMM ABSTRACTS (UK/0019-0020). **4003**

IMMIGRATION BRIEFINGS (US/0897-6708). **2980**

IMMIGRATION POLICY & LAW (US/0892-547X). **2980**

IMMUNITAT UND INFEKTION (GW/0340-1162). **3670**

IMMUNO ANALYSE & BIOLOGIE SPECIALISEE (FR/0923-2532). **458**

IMMUNOBIOLOGY (1979) (GW/0171-2985). **3670**

IMMUNODEFICIENCY REVIEWS (UK/0893-5300). **3670**

IMMUNOGENETICS (NEW YORK) (US/0093-7711). **3670**

IMMUNOHISTOCHEMISTRY (UK/0142-8136). **537**

IMMUNOLOGIC RESEARCH (SZ/0257-277X). **3670**

IMMUNOLOGICAL INVESTIGATIONS (US/0882-0139). **3671**

IMMUNOLOGICAL REVIEWS (DK/0105-2896). **3671**

IMMUNOLOGY (UK/0019-2805). **3671**

IMMUNOLOGY AND ALLERGY CLINICS OF NORTH AMERICA (US/0889-8561). **3671**

IMMUNOLOGY & ALLERGY PRACTICE (US/0194-7508). **3671**

IMMUNOLOGY AND CELL BIOLOGY (AT/0818-9641). **3671**

IMMUNOLOGY AND INFECTIOUS DISEASES (UK/0959-4957). **3671**

IMMUNOLOGY LETTERS (NE/0165-2478). **3671**

IMMUNOLOGY SERIES (US/0092-6019). **3671**

IMMUNOLOGY TODAY (AMSTERDAM. REGULAR ED.) (UK/0167-5699). **3671**

IMMUNOMETHODS (SAN DIEGO, CALIF.) (US/1058-6687). **3672**

IMMUNOPHARMACOLOGY (US/0162-3109). **3672**

IMMUNOPHARMACOLOGY AND IMMUNOTOXICOLOGY (US/0892-3973). **3672**

IMPACT OF COMPUTING IN SCIENCE AND ENGINEERING (US/0899-8248). **3508**

IMPLANT DENTISTRY (US/1056-6163). **1324**

IMPULSE (CHAMPAIGN, ILL.) (US/1063-8520). **1313**

IN BUSINESS (US/0190-2458). **2232**

IN PRACTICE (LONDON 1979) (UK/0263-841X). **5511**

IN SITU (US/0146-2520). **1440**

IN VITRO CELLULAR & DEVELOPMENTAL BIOLOGY. PLANT (US/1054-5476). **513**

IN VIVO (ATHENS) (GR/0258-851X). **458**

IN VIVO (NEW YORK, N.Y.) (US/0733-1398). **681**

INC. (BOSTON, MASS.) (US/0162-8968). **681**

INCOGNITA (LEIDEN, NETHERLANDS) (NE/0923-7135). **2848**

INDAGATIONES MATHEMATICAE (NE/0019-3577). **3508**

INDEPENDENT STUDY CATALOG (PRINCETON, N.J.), THE (US/0733-6020). **1830**

INDEX NEW ZEALAND [MICROFORM] : INNZ (NZ/0113-6526). **417**

INDEX TO GOVERNMENT REGULATION (US/0195-9492). **2981**

INDIAN JOURNAL OF CHEST DISEASES & ALLIED SCIENCES, THE (II/0377-9343). **3706**

INDIAN JOURNAL OF ENVIRONMENTAL PROTECTION (II/0253-7141). **2174**

INDIAN JOURNAL OF GASTROENTEROLOGY (II/0254-8860). **3746**

INDIAN JOURNAL OF POLITICS (II/0303-9951). **4476**

INDIANA UNIVERSITY MATHEMATICS JOURNAL (US/0022-2518). **3509**

INDIVIDUAL PSYCHOLOGY (US/0277-7010). **4590**

INDIVIDUAL WITH DISABILITIES EDUCATION LAW REPORT (US/1055-520X). **2982**

INDO-IRANIAN JOURNAL (NE/0019-7246). **4349**

INDONESIA CIRCLE : [JOURNAL] (UK/0306-2848). **2505**

INDOOR AIR QUALITY UPDATE (US/1040-5313). **2606**

INDOOR ENVIRONMENT : THE JOURNAL OF INDOOR AIR INTERNATIONAL (SZ/1016-4901). **2174**

INDOOR POLLUTION NEWS (US/0896-8594). **2232**

INDUSTRIA MINERA (SP/0210-2307). **2140**

INDUSTRIAL AND COMMERCIAL TRAINING (UK/0019-7858). **942**

INDUSTRIAL AND CORPORATE CHANGE (UK/0960-6491). **1610**

INDUSTRIAL & ENGINEERING CHEMISTRY RESEARCH (US/0888-5885). **2013**

INDUSTRIAL BIOPROCESSING (US/1056-7194). **1946**

INDUSTRIAL COMMUNICATIONS (US/0737-0415). **1113**

INDUSTRIAL COMPUTING PLUS PROGRAMMABLE CONTROLS (US/1045-0203). **1238**

INDUSTRIAL CRISIS QUARTERLY (NE/0921-8106). **682**

INDUSTRIAL CROPS AND PRODUCTS (NE/0926-6690). **174**

INDUSTRIAL DISTRIBUTION (US/0019-8153). **926**

INDUSTRIAL ENGINEERING (NORCROSS, GA.) (US/0019-8234). **2098**

INDUSTRIAL FINISHING (WHEATON) (US/0019-8323). **4224**

INDUSTRIAL LABORATORY (US/0019-8447). **1015**

INDUSTRIAL LASER REVIEW (US/0888-935X). **4435**

INDUSTRIAL LAW JOURNAL (LONDON) (UK/0305-9332). **3149**

INDUSTRIAL MANAGEMENT & DATA SYSTEMS (UK/0263-5577). **1259**

INDUSTRIAL MANAGEMENT (DES PLAINES) (US/0019-8471). **1610**

INDUSTRIAL MARKETING MANAGEMENT (US/0019-8501). **926**

INDUSTRIAL METROLOGY (NE/0921-5956). **4030**

INDUSTRIAL MINERALS (UK/0019-8544). **1440**

INDUSTRIAL PRODUCT BULLETIN (US/0199-2074). **3481**

INDUSTRIAL RELATIONS (BERKELEY) (US/0019-8676). **1678**

INDUSTRIAL RELATIONS JOURNAL (LONDON, ENGLAND) (UK/0019-8692). **1678**

INDUSTRIAL RELATIONS LAW JOURNAL (US/0145-188X). **3149**

INDUSTRIAL ROBOT, THE (UK/0143-991X). **1219**

INDUSTRIE ALIMENTARI (PINEROLO) (IT/0019-901X). **2344**

INDUSTRIE-ANZEIGER (GW/0019-9036). **617**

INDUSTRIE CERAMIQUE, L' (FR/0019-9044). **2591**

INDUSTRIE DE L'INFORMATION (FR/0754-1996). **3215**

INDUSTRIE DELLE BEVANDE (IT/0390-0541). **2367**

INDUSTRIE LACKIER BETRIEB (GW/0019-9109). **4224**

INDUSTRY & HIGHER EDUCATION (UK/0950-4222). **1611**

INDUSTRY WEEK (US/0039-0895). **4004**

INFANT BEHAVIOR & DEVELOPMENT (US/0163-6383). **4590**

INFANTS AND YOUNG CHILDREN (US/0896-3746). **3904**

INFECTION (GW/0300-8126). **3714**

INFECTION AND IMMUNITY (US/0019-9567). **563**

INFECTION CONTROL AND HOSPITAL EPIDEMIOLOGY (US/0899-823X). **3735**

INFECTIONS IN MEDICINE (US/0749-6524). **3735**

INFECTIONS IN UROLOGY (US/0896-9647). **3990**

INFECTIOUS AGENTS AND DISEASE (US/1056-2044). **3714**

INFECTIOUS DISEASE ALERT (US/0739-7348). **3672**

INFECTIOUS DISEASE CLINICS OF NORTH AMERICA (US/0891-5520). **3714**

INFECTIOUS DISEASES NEWSLETTER (NEW YORK, N.Y.) (US/0278-2316). **3714**

INFERTILITY (US/0160-7626). **3762**

INFLAMMATION (US/0360-3997). **3587**

INFLAMMOPHARMACOLOGY (NE/0925-4692). **3587**

INFO CANADA (DOWNSVIEW) (CN/1187-7081). **1188**

INFOMEDIARY (NE/0169-2763). **3215**

INFOR. INFORMATION SYSTEMS AND OPERATIONAL RESEARCH (CN/0315-5986). **1259**

INFORM (SILVER SPRING, MD.) (US/0892-3876). **4370**

INFORMAL LOGIC (WINDSOR, ONT.) (CN/0824-2577). **4349**

INFORMATIK - FORSCHUNG UND ENTWICKLUNG (GW/0178-3564). **1188**

INFORMATIK-SPEKTRUM (GW/0170-6012). **1259**

INFORMATION ADVISOR, THE (US/1050-1576). **682**

INFORMATION AGE (UK/0261-4103). **1226**

INFORMATION AND COMPUTATION (US/0890-5401). **1219**

INFORMATION AND DECISION TECHNOLOGIES (AMSTERDAM) (NE/0923-0408). **2116**

INFORMATION & MANAGEMENT (NE/0378-7206). **1254**

INFORMATION AND SOFTWARE TECHNOLOGY (UK/0950-5849). **1260**

INFORMATION DESIGN JOURNAL (UK/0142-5471). **3215**

INFORMATION DISPLAY (1975) (US/0362-0972). **2064**

INFORMATION ECONOMICS AND POLICY (NE/0167-6245). **1157**

INFORMATION GEOGRAPHIQUE, L' (FR/0020-0093). **2566**

INFORMATION HISTORIQUE, L' (FR/0046-9351). **2692**

INFORMATION INTELLIGENCE, ONLINE LIBRARIES, AND MICROCOMPUTERS (US/0737-7770). **3216**

INFORMATION INTELLIGENCE ONLINE NEWSLETTER (US/0194-0694). **1274**

INFORMATION MANAGEMENT REPORT (UK/0961-7612). **1157**

INFORMATION PROCESSING & MANAGEMENT (UK/0306-4573). **3216**

INFORMATION SCIENCE ABSTRACTS (US/0020-0239). **3258**

INFORMATION SCIENCES (US/0020-0255). **3216**

INFORMATION SCIENCES, APPLICATIONS (US/1069-0115). **3216**

INFORMATION SOCIETY, THE (US/0197-2243). **3216**

INFORMATION STRATEGY (US/0743-8613). **870**

INFORMATION

INFORMATION SYSTEMS MANAGEMENT (US/1058-0530). **870**

INFORMATION SYSTEMS (OXFORD) (UK/0306-4379). **1254**

INFORMATION TECHNOLOGY AND LIBRARIES (US/0730-9295). **3217**

INFORMATION TODAY (US/8755-6286). **3217**

INFORMATION UPDATE/ DATABASE TECHNOLOGY (UK/0951-9327). **1188**

INFORMATION WORLD REVIEW (UK/0950-9879). **1277**

INFORMATIONS CHIMIE (EDITION FRANCAISE) (FR/0020-045X). **978**

INFORMATIONSDIENST VDI : INSTANDHALTUNG (GW/0724-1976). **1978**

INFORMATIONSDIENST - VEREIN DEUTSCHER INGENIEURE. BLECHBEARBEITUNG (GW/0170-9526). **4004**

INFORMATIONSDIENST - VEREIN DEUTSCHER INGENIEURE. ELEKTRISCH ABTRAGENDE FERTIGUNGSVERFAHREN (GW/0170-9569). **2064**

INFORMATIONSDIENST - VEREIN DEUTSCHER INGENIEURE. KALTMASSIVUMFORMUNG (GW/0170-9550). **1978**

INFORMATIONSDIENST - VEREIN DEUTSCHER INGENIEURE. SCHMIEDEN UND PRESSEN (GW/0171-3647). **1978**

INFORMATIONSTECHNIK (GW/0179-9738). **1188**

INFORMATIONWEEK (MANHASSET, N.Y.) (US/8750-6874). **1260**

INFORMATIZATION AND THE PUBLIC SECTOR (NE/0925-5052). **1189**

INFOTECTURE (FR/0241-2640). **1275**

INFOTEXT (IRVINE, CALIF.) (US/1043-3694). **1113**

INFOWORLD (US/0199-6649). **1268**

INFRARED PHYSICS & TECHNOLOGY (UK/1350-4495). **4405**

INFUSION (ANDOVER) (US/0160-757X). **3587**

INGENIERIA QUIMICA (MADRID) (SP/0210-2064). **2013**

INHALATION TOXICOLOGY (UK/0895-8378). **3981**

INJURY (UK/0020-1383). **3587**

INNERE MEDIZIN (GW/0303-4305). **3797**

INNOVATIVE HIGHER EDUCATION (US/0742-5627). **1830**

INNOVATOR'S DIGEST (US/0890-300X). **5114**

INORGANIC CHEMISTRY (US/0020-1669). **1036**

INORGANIC MATERIALS (US/0020-1685). **1036**

INORGANICA CHIMICA ACTA : BIOINORGANIC CHEMISTRY ARTICLES AND LETTERS (SZ/0020-1693). **1036**

INPHARMA WEEKLY (NZ/0156-2703). **4308**

INQUIRY (CHICAGO) (US/0046-9580). **3587**

INQUIRY (OSLO) (NO/0020-174X). **4349**

INSECT BIOCHEMISTRY AND MOLECULAR BIOLOGY (UK/0965-1748). **5609**

INSECT SCIENCE AND ITS APPLICATION (KE/0191-9040). **5609**

INSECTES SOCIAUX (FR/0020-1812). **5609**

INSIDE DOT & TRANSPORTATION WEEK (US/1050-818X). **5384**

INSIDE DPMA (US/0898-171X). **683**

INSIDE R & D : THE WEEKLY REPORT ON TECHNICAL INNOVATION (US/0300-757X). **1025**

INSIDE TEXTILES (US/0733-8244). **5352**

INSIDERS' CHRONICLE, THE (US/0162-5152). **791**

INSIDERS, THE (US/0730-2908). **901**

INSIGHT ON THE NEWS (WASHINGTON, D.C.) (US/1051-4880). **4477**

INSIGHTS FOR SUCCESS (US/0891-4729). **871**

INSOLVENCY INTELLIGENCE (UK/0950-2645). **2983**

INSPEL (GW/0019-0217). **3217**

INSTALLATION, DKZ (GW/0723-4775). **2065**

INSTANTANES MEDICAUX, LES (FR/0020-2142). **3588**

INSTITUTE OF PHYSICS CONFERENCE SERIES (UK/0951-3248). **4405**

INSTITUTION OF CHEMICAL ENGINEERS SYMPOSIUM SERIES, THE (UK/0307-0492). **2013**

INSTITUTION OF MINING AND METALLURGY. TRANSACTIONS. SECTION B : APPLIED EARTH SCIENCES (UK/0371-7453). **2140**

INSTITUTION OF MINING AND METALLURGY. TRANSACTIONS. SECTION C : MINERAL PROCESSING AND EXTRACTIVE METALLURGY (UK/0371-9553). **4004**

INSTRUCTION DELIVERY SYSTEMS (US/0892-4872). **1189**

INSTRUCTIONAL SCIENCE (NE/0020-4277). **1896**

INSTRUMENTATION & CONTROL ENGINEERING (UK/0959-8286). **2065**

INSTRUMENTATION IN THE AEROSPACE INDUSTRY (US/0096-7238). **24**

INSTRUMENTATION IN THE CHEMICAL AND PETROLEUM INDUSTRIES (US/0074-0551). **4260**

INSTRUMENTATION IN THE MINING AND METALLURGY INDUSTRIES (US/0361-3070). **2140**

INSTRUMENTATION IN THE POWER INDUSTRY (US/0074-056X). **2065**

INSTRUMENTATION IN THE PULP AND PAPER INDUSTRY (US/0361-4719). **4234**

INSTRUMENTS AND EXPERIMENTAL TECHNIQUES (NEW YORK) (US/0020-4412). **4405**

INSULIN AND GLUCAGON (UK/0142-8144). **3731**

INSURANCE AND RISK MANAGEMENT--FOR BUSINESS AND GOVERNMENT (US/0892-5887). **2883**

INSURANCE & TECHNOLOGY (US/1054-0733). **2883**

INSURANCE ANTITRUST & TORT REFORM REPORT (US/0898-5170). **3100**

INSURANCE MATHEMATICS & ECONOMICS (NE/0167-6687). **2884**

INSURANCE SOFTWARE REVIEW (US/0892-8533). **2884**

INSURANCE TAX REVIEW, THE (US/0890-9164). **2884**

INTECH (US/0192-303X). **2065**

INTEGRAL EQUATIONS AND OPERATOR THEORY (SZ/0378-620X). **3509**

INTEGRATED CIRCUITS INTERNATIONAL (UK/0263-6522). **2065**

INTEGRATED FERROELECTRICS (US/1058-4587). **2066**

INTEGRATED MANUFACTURING SYSTEMS (UK/0957-6061). **2116**

INTEGRATION (AMSTERDAM) (NE/0167-9260). **2066**

INTEGRATIVE PHYSIOLOGICAL AND BEHAVIORAL SCIENCE (US/0093-2213). **4590**

INTEGRATIVE PSYCHIATRY (US/0735-3847). **3926**

INTELEC (US/0275-0473). **1157**

INTELLECTUAL PROPERTY JOURNAL (CN/0824-7064). **1305**

INTELLECTUAL PROPERTY LAW (CHUR, SWITZERLAND) (UK/0892-2365). **1305**

INTELLIGENCE (NORWOOD) (US/0160-2896). **4590**

INTELLIGENT INSTRUMENTS & COMPUTERS (US/0889-8308). **1220**

INTELLIGENT NETWORK NEWS (US/1042-6930). **1113**

INTELLIGENT SOFTWARE STRATEGIES (US/1052-7214). **1287**

INTENATIONALES GEWERBEARCHIV (GW/0020-9481). **683**

INTENSIVBEHANDLUNG (GW/0341-3063). **3588**

INTENSIVE CARE MEDICINE (GW/0342-4642). **3588**

INTENSIVMEDIZIN + NOTFALLMEDIZIN (GW/0175-3851). **3588**

INTER BLOC (FR/0242-3960). **3966**

INTER ECONOMICS (GW/0020-5346). **1636**

INTERACTING WITH COMPUTERS (UK/0953-5438). **1189**

INTERACTIVE LEARNING INTERNATIONAL (UK/0748-5743). **1223**

INTERACTIVE MEDIA BUSINESS (US/1065-299X). **1113**

INTERCHANGE (TORONTO. 1984) (CN/0826-4805). **1753**

INTERCHANGE (TORONTO. 1984) (US/0826-4805). **1753**

INTERCIENCIA (VE/0378-1844). **5114**

INTERDISCIPLINARY SCIENCE REVIEWS : ISR (UK/0308-0188). **5114**

INTERDISCIPLINARY TOPICS IN GERONTOLOGY (SZ/0074-1132). **3752**

INTERFACE (AMSTERDAM) (NE/0303-3902). **4123**

INTERFACES (PROVIDENCE) (US/0092-2102). **871**

INTERIOR DESIGN (NEW YORK, N.Y.) (US/0020-5508). **2901**

INTERIORS (NEW YORK, N.Y. : 1978) (US/0164-8470 #y 0148-012x). **2901**

INTERMETALLICS (UK/0966-9795). **4004**

INTERNAL AUDITING ALERT (US/0744-2947). **745**

INTERNAL AUDITING (BOSTON, MASS.) (US/0897-0378). **745**

INTERNAL AUDITOR, THE (US/0020-5745). **745**

INTERNAL MEDICINE ALERT (US/0195-315X). **3797**

INTERNAL MEDICINE BULLETIN (US/1065-9498). **3797**

INTERNASJONAL POLITIKK (OSLO, NORWAY) (NO/0020-577X). **4524**

INTERNATIONAL ABSTRACTS IN OPERATIONS RESEARCH (UK/0020-580X). **5175**

INTERNATIONAL AEROSPACE ABSTRACTS (US/0020-5842). **41**

INTERNATIONAL AFFAIRS (LONDON) (UK/0020-5850). **4524**

INTERNATIONAL ANESTHESIOLOGY CLINICS (US/0020-5907). **3683**

INTERNATIONAL APPLIED MECHANICS (US/1063-7095). **2116**

INTERNATIONAL ARBITRATION REPORT (US/0886-0114). **3129**

INTERNATIONAL ARCHIVES OF ALLERGY AND IMMUNOLOGY (SZ/1018-2438). **3672**

INTERNATIONAL ARCHIVES OF OCCUPATIONAL AND ENVIRONMENTAL HEALTH (GW/0340-0131). **2864**

INTERNATIONAL BIODETERIORATION & BIODEGREDATION (UK/0964-8305). **1356**

INTERNATIONAL BUSINESS REVIEW (UK/0969-5931). **683**

INTERNATIONAL CHEMICAL ENGINEERING (US/0020-6318). **2013**

INTERNATIONAL CLINICAL NUTRITION REVIEW (AT/0813-9008). **4192**

INTERNATIONAL CLINICAL PSYCHOPHARMACOLOGY (UK/0268-1315). **4308**

INTERNATIONAL COMMUNICATIONS IN HEAT AND MASS TRANSFER (US/0735-1933). **4431**

INTERNATIONAL COMPUTER LAW ADVISER (US/0893-2859). **1189**

INTERNATIONAL CONGRESS AND SYMPOSIUM SERIES / ROYAL SOCIETY OF MEDICINE (UK/0142-2367). **3588**

INTERNATIONAL CONGRESS SERIES (NE/0531-5131). **3588**

INTERNATIONAL CONTACT LENS CLINIC (1987) (US/0892-8967). **4216**

INTERNATIONAL CONTRIBUTIONS TO LABOUR STUDIES (UK/1052-9187). **1680**

INTERNATIONAL CONVOCATION ON IMMUNOLOGY. [PROCEEDINGS] (SZ/0074-4220). **3672**

INTERNATIONAL CORPORATE YELLOW BOOK (US/1058-2894). **871**

INTERNATIONAL DAIRY JOURNAL (UK/0958-6946). **195**

INTERNATIONAL DEFENSE REVIEW (SZ/0020-6512). **4046**

INTERNATIONAL DENTAL JOURNAL (UK/0020-6539). **1325**

INTERNATIONAL DEVELOPMENT ABSTRACTS (UK/0262-0855). **2913**

INTERNATIONAL DREDGING REVIEW (US/0737-8181). **1979**

INTERNATIONAL ECONOMIC INSIGHTS (US/1050-8481). **1636**

INTERNATIONAL ECONOMIC OUTLOOK / CENTRE FOR ECONOMIC FORECASTING, LONDON BUSINESS SCHOOL (UK/0960-8869). **1636**

INTERNATIONAL ECONOMIC REVIEW (PHILADELPHIA) (US/0020-6598). **1496**

INTERNATIONAL ENDODONTIC JOURNAL (UK/0143-2885). **1325**

INTERNATIONAL ENVIRONMENT REPORTER. CURRENT REPORT (US/0149-8738). **3113**

INTERNATIONAL ENVIRONMENTAL AFFAIRS (US/1041-4665). **2195**

INTERNATIONAL EXECUTIVE (US/0020-6652). **4502**

INTERNATIONAL FORUM FOR LOGOTHERAPY, THE (US/0191-3379). **4349**

INTERNATIONAL FORUM ON INFORMATION AND DOCUMENTATION (NE/0304-9701). **3218**

INTERNATIONAL GEOLOGY REVIEW (US/0020-6814). **1383**

INTERNATIONAL HEPATOLOGY COMMUNICATIONS (NE/0928-4346). **3797**

INTERNATIONAL HISTORY REVIEW, THE (CN/0707-5332). **2620**

INTERNATIONAL IMMUNOLOGY (UK/0953-8178). **3672**

INTERNATIONAL INTERACTIONS (UK/0305-0629). **4524**

INTERNATIONAL JOURNAL (CN/0020-7020). **2692**

INTERNATIONAL JOURNAL, ADVANCED MANUFACTURING TECHNOLOGY, THE (UK/0268-3768). **3481**

INTERNATIONAL JOURNAL FOR HOUSING SCIENCE AND ITS APPLICATIONS (US/0146-6518). **2825**

INTERNATIONAL JOURNAL FOR NUMERICAL AND ANALYTICAL METHODS IN GEOMECHANICS (UK/0363-9061). **2025**

INTERNATIONAL JOURNAL FOR NUMERICAL METHODS IN ENGINEERING (UK/0029-5981). **1979**

INTERNATIONAL JOURNAL FOR NUMERICAL METHODS IN FLUIDS (UK/0271-2091). **2091**

INTERNATIONAL JOURNAL FOR PHILOSOPHY OF RELIGION (NE/0020-7047). **4965**

INTERNATIONAL JOURNAL FOR THE ADVANCEMENT OF COUNSELLING (NE/0165-0653). **4591**

INTERNATIONAL JOURNAL FOR VITAMIN AND NUTRITION RESEARCH (SZ/0300-9831). **4192**

INTERNATIONAL JOURNAL FOR VITAMIN AND NUTRITION RESEARCH (SUPPLEMENT) (SZ/0300-9831). **4192**

INTERNATIONAL JOURNAL OF ADAPTIVE CONTROL AND SIGNAL PROCESSING (UK/0890-6327). **1979**

INTERNATIONAL JOURNAL OF ADHESION AND ADHESIVES (UK/0143-7496). **1053**

INTERNATIONAL JOURNAL OF ADULT ORTHODONTICS AND ORTHOGNATHIC SURGERY, THE (US/0742-1931). **1325**

INTERNATIONAL JOURNAL OF ADVERTISING (UK/0265-0487). **760**

INTERNATIONAL JOURNAL OF AMBIENT ENERGY (UK/0143-0750). **1947**

INTERNATIONAL JOURNAL OF AMERICAN LINGUISTICS (US/0020-7071). **3287**

INTERNATIONAL JOURNAL OF ANALYTICAL AND EXPERIMENTAL MODAL ANALYSIS, THE (US/0886-9367). **2116**

INTERNATIONAL JOURNAL OF ANDROLOGY (UK/0105-6263). **3588**

INTERNATIONAL JOURNAL OF ANTIMICROBIAL AGENTS (NE/0924-8579). **3588**

INTERNATIONAL JOURNAL OF APPLIED ELECTROMAGNETICS IN MATERIALS (NE/0925-2096). **4444**

INTERNATIONAL JOURNAL OF APPROXIMATE REASONING (US/0888-613X). **1213**

INTERNATIONAL JOURNAL OF ARTIFICIAL ORGANS, THE (IT/0391-3988). **3798**

INTERNATIONAL JOURNAL OF BANK MARKETING (UK/0265-2323). **792**

INTERNATIONAL JOURNAL OF BEHAVIORAL DEVELOPMENT (NE/0165-0254). **4591**

INTERNATIONAL JOURNAL OF BIOCHEMISTRY, THE (UK/0020-711X). **488**

INTERNATIONAL JOURNAL OF BIOLOGICAL MACROMOLECULES (UK/0141-8130). **581**

INTERNATIONAL JOURNAL OF BIOMEDICAL COMPUTING (UK/0020-7101). **3589**

INTERNATIONAL JOURNAL OF BIOMETEOROLOGY (NE/0020-7128). **1426**

INTERNATIONAL JOURNAL OF BIOSOCIAL AND MEDICAL RESEARCH (US/1044-811X). **5248**

INTERNATIONAL JOURNAL OF CANCER (US/0020-7136). **3818**

INTERNATIONAL JOURNAL OF CARDIAC IMAGING (US/0167-9899). **3706**

INTERNATIONAL JOURNAL OF CARDIOLOGY (NE/0167-5273). **3706**

INTERNATIONAL JOURNAL OF CELL CLONING (US/0737-1454). **537**

INTERNATIONAL JOURNAL OF CHEMICAL KINETICS (US/0538-8066). **1053**

INTERNATIONAL JOURNAL OF CIRCUIT THEORY AND APPLICATIONS (UK/0098-9886). **2066**

INTERNATIONAL JOURNAL OF CLIMATOLOGY : A JOURNAL OF THE ROYAL METEOROLOGICAL SOCIETY (UK/0899-8418). **1426**

INTERNATIONAL JOURNAL OF CLINICAL ACUPUNCTURE (US/1047-1979). **3589**

INTERNATIONAL JOURNAL OF CLINICAL AND LABORATORY RESEARCH (GW/0940-5437). **458**

INTERNATIONAL JOURNAL OF CLINICAL MONITORING AND COMPUTING (NE/0167-9945). **1190**

INTERNATIONAL JOURNAL OF CLINICAL NEUROPSYCHOLOGY, THE (US/0749-8470). **4591**

INTERNATIONAL JOURNAL OF CLINICAL PHARMACOLOGY RESEARCH (SZ/0251-1649). **4308**

INTERNATIONAL JOURNAL OF CLINICAL PHARMACOLOGY, THERAPY AND TOXICOLOGY (1980) (GW/0174-4879). **4308**

INTERNATIONAL JOURNAL OF COAL GEOLOGY (NE/0166-5162). **1383**

INTERNATIONAL JOURNAL OF COLORECTAL DISEASE (GW/0179-1958). **3589**

INTERNATIONAL JOURNAL OF COMPARATIVE PSYCHOLOGY (US/0889-3667). **4591**

INTERNATIONAL JOURNAL OF COMPARATIVE SOCIOLOGY (NE/0020-7152). **5248**

INTERNATIONAL JOURNAL OF COMPUTER INTEGRATED MANUFACTURING (UK/0951-192X). **3481**

INTERNATIONAL JOURNAL OF COMPUTER MATHEMATICS (UK/0020-7160). **3509**

INTERNATIONAL JOURNAL OF COMPUTER VISION (US/0920-5691). **1190**

INTERNATIONAL JOURNAL OF COMPUTERS IN ADULT EDUCATION AND TRAINING (UK/0952-6315). **1190**

INTERNATIONAL JOURNAL OF CONFLICT MANAGEMENT, THE (US/1044-4068). **871**

INTERNATIONAL JOURNAL OF CONTROL (UK/0020-7179). **5115**

INTERNATIONAL JOURNAL OF COSMETIC SCIENCE (UK/0142-5463). **404**

INTERNATIONAL JOURNAL OF CULTURAL PROPERTY (GW/0940-7391). **1305**

INTERNATIONAL JOURNAL OF DAMAGE MECHANICS (US/1056-7895). **1979**

INTERNATIONAL JOURNAL OF DERMATOLOGY (US/0011-9059). **3721**

INTERNATIONAL JOURNAL OF DEVELOPMENTAL NEUROSCIENCE (UK/0736-5748). **3834**

INTERNATIONAL JOURNAL OF DIGITAL AND ANALOG COMMUNICATION SYSTEMS (UK/1047-9627). **1158**

INTERNATIONAL JOURNAL OF EATING DISORDERS, THE (US/0276-3478). **3798**

INTERNATIONAL JOURNAL OF ECOLOGY AND ENVIRONMENTAL SCIENCES (II/0377-015X). **2217**

INTERNATIONAL JOURNAL OF EDUCATIONAL DEVELOPMENT (UK/0738-0593). **1754**

INTERNATIONAL JOURNAL OF EDUCATIONAL REFORM (US/1056-7879). **1754**

INTERNATIONAL JOURNAL OF EDUCATIONAL RESEARCH (UK/0883-0355). **1897**

INTERNATIONAL JOURNAL OF ELECTRICAL POWER & ENERGY SYSTEMS (UK/0142-0615). **2066**

INTERNATIONAL JOURNAL OF ELECTRONICS THEORETICAL & EXPERIMENTAL (UK/0020-7217). **2066**

INTERNATIONAL JOURNAL OF ENERGY RESEARCH (UK/0363-907X). **1947**

INTERNATIONAL JOURNAL OF ENGINEERING FLUID MECHANICS (US/0893-3960). **2091**

INTERNATIONAL JOURNAL OF ENGINEERING SCIENCE (UK/0020-7225). **1980**

INTERNATIONAL JOURNAL OF ENVIRONMENTAL ANALYTICAL CHEMISTRY (US/0306-7319). **1015**

INTERNATIONAL JOURNAL OF ENVIRONMENTAL STUDIES. SECTION A, ENVIRONMENTAL STUDIES, THE (US/0020-7233). **2195**

INTERNATIONAL JOURNAL OF ENVIRONMENTAL STUDIES. SECTION B, ENVIRONMENTAL SCIENCE AND TECHNOLOGY, THE (US/0020-7233). **2175**

INTERNATIONAL JOURNAL OF ENVIRONMENTAL STUDIES, THE (US/0020-7233). **2174**

INTERNATIONAL JOURNAL OF EPIDEMIOLOGY (UK/0300-5771). **3735**

INTERNATIONAL JOURNAL OF EXPERIMENTAL PATHOLOGY (UK/0959-9673). **3895**

INTERNATIONAL JOURNAL OF FATIGUE (UK/0142-1123). **2102**

INTERNATIONAL JOURNAL OF FLEXIBLE AUTOMATION AND INTEGRATED MANUFACTURING (US/1064-6345). **3481**

INTERNATIONAL JOURNAL OF FLEXIBLE MANUFACTURING SYSTEMS (US/0920-6299). **3481**

INTERNATIONAL JOURNAL OF FOOD MICROBIOLOGY (NE/0168-1605). **2345**

INTERNATIONAL JOURNAL OF FOOD SCIENCE AND TECHNOLOGY (UK/0950-5423). **2345**

INTERNATIONAL JOURNAL OF FORECASTING (NE/0169-2070). **684**

INTERNATIONAL JOURNAL OF FOUNDATIONS OF COMPUTER SCIENCE (SI/0129-0541). **1190**

INTERNATIONAL JOURNAL OF FRACTURE (NE/0376-9429). **2102**

INTERNATIONAL JOURNAL OF GAME THEORY (GW/0020-7276). **3509**

INTERNATIONAL JOURNAL OF GENERAL SYSTEMS (US/0308-1079). **1247**

INTERNATIONAL JOURNAL OF GEOGRAPHICAL INFORMATION SYSTEMS (UK/0269-3798). **2566**

INTERNATIONAL JOURNAL OF GERIATRIC PSYCHIATRY (UK/0885-6230). **3752**

INTERNATIONAL JOURNAL OF GOVERNMENT AUDITING (CN/0047-0724). **4732**

INTERNATIONAL JOURNAL OF GROUP PSYCHOTHERAPY, THE (US/0020-7284). **3927**

INTERNATIONAL JOURNAL OF GYNAECOLOGY AND OBSTETRICS (IE/0020-7292). **3762**

INTERNATIONAL JOURNAL OF GYNECOLOGICAL CANCER (US/1048-891X). **3818**

INTERNATIONAL JOURNAL OF GYNECOLOGICAL PATHOLOGY (US/0277-1691). **3895**

INTERNATIONAL JOURNAL OF HEALTH CARE QUALITY ASSURANCE (UK/0952-6862). **4785**

INTERNATIONAL JOURNAL OF HEALTH PLANNING & MANAGEMENT, THE (UK/0749-6753). **4785**

INTERNATIONAL JOURNAL OF HEAT AND FLUID FLOW, THE (US/0142-727X). **2116**

INTERNATIONAL JOURNAL OF HEAT AND MASS TRANSFER (UK/0017-9310). **4431**

INTERNATIONAL JOURNAL OF HEMATOLOGY (NE/0925-5710). **3772**

INTERNATIONAL JOURNAL OF HIGH SPEED COMPUTING (SI/0129-0533). **1260**

INTERNATIONAL JOURNAL OF HIGH SPEED ELECTRONICS (SI/0129-1564). **2066**

INTERNATIONAL JOURNAL OF HOSPITALITY MANAGEMENT (UK/0278-4319). **2807**

INTERNATIONAL JOURNAL OF HUMAN RESOURCE MANAGEMENT, THE (UK/0958-5192). **943**

INTERNATIONAL JOURNAL OF HYDROGEN ENERGY (UK/0360-3199). **1948**

INTERNATIONAL JOURNAL OF HYPERTHERMIA (UK/0265-6736). **3589**

INTERNATIONAL JOURNAL OF IMAGING SYSTEMS AND TECHNOLOGY (US/0899-9457). **5115**

INTERNATIONAL JOURNAL OF IMMUNOPHARMACOLOGY (UK/0192-0561). **4308**

INTERNATIONAL JOURNAL OF IMMUNOTHERAPY (SZ/0255-9625). **3672**

INTERNATIONAL JOURNAL OF IMPACT ENGINEERING (UK/0734-743X). **2103**

INTERNATIONAL JOURNAL OF INDUSTRIAL ERGONOMICS (NE/0169-8141). **2099**

INTERNATIONAL JOURNAL OF INDUSTRIAL ORGANIZATION (NE/0167-7187). **871**

INTERNATIONAL JOURNAL OF INFORMATION MANAGEMENT (UK/0268-4012). **3218**

INTERNATIONAL JOURNAL OF INFRARED AND MILLIMETER WAVES (US/0195-9271). **4435**

INTERNATIONAL JOURNAL OF INSECT MORPHOLOGY & EMBRYOLOGY (UK/0020-7322). **5610**

INTERNATIONAL JOURNAL OF INTELLIGENT SYSTEMS (US/0884-8173). **1213**

INTERNATIONAL JOURNAL OF INTERCULTURAL RELATIONS (US/0147-1767). **5248**

INTERNATIONAL JOURNAL OF LAW AND INFORMATION TECHNOLOGY (UK/0967-0769). **2984**

INTERNATIONAL

INTERNATIONAL JOURNAL OF LAW AND PSYCHIATRY (US/0160-2527). **2984**

INTERNATIONAL JOURNAL OF LAW AND THE FAMILY (UK/0950-4109). **3121**

INTERNATIONAL JOURNAL OF LEGAL MEDICINE (GW/0937-9827). **3741**

INTERNATIONAL JOURNAL OF LEXICOGRAPHY (UK/0950-3846). **3287**

INTERNATIONAL JOURNAL OF LIFELONG EDUCATION (UK/0260-1370). **1801**

INTERNATIONAL JOURNAL OF MACHINE TOOLS & MANUFACTURE (US/0890-6955). **2116**

INTERNATIONAL JOURNAL OF MAN-MACHINE STUDIES (UK/0020-7373). **1251**

INTERNATIONAL JOURNAL OF MANPOWER (UK/0143-7720). **1680**

INTERNATIONAL JOURNAL OF MASS SPECTROMETRY AND ION PROCESSES (NE/0168-1176). **4405**

INTERNATIONAL JOURNAL OF MATHEMATICAL EDUCATION IN SCIENCE AND TECHNOLOGY (UK/0020-739X). **1754**

INTERNATIONAL JOURNAL OF MATHEMATICS (SI/0129-167X). **3509**

INTERNATIONAL JOURNAL OF MECHANICAL ENGINEERING EDUCATION, THE (UK/0306-4190). **2116**

INTERNATIONAL JOURNAL OF MECHANICAL SCIENCES (UK/0020-7403). **2116**

INTERNATIONAL JOURNAL OF MEDICINE AND LAW (UK/0334-3049). **3741**

INTERNATIONAL JOURNAL OF MICROCIRCULATION: CLINICAL AND EXPERIMENTAL (NE/0167-6865). **3798**

INTERNATIONAL JOURNAL OF MIDDLE EAST STUDIES (UK/0020-7438). **2768**

INTERNATIONAL JOURNAL OF MINERAL PROCESSING (NE/0301-7516). **2140**

INTERNATIONAL JOURNAL OF MINING AND GEOLOGICAL ENGINEERING (UK/0269-0136). **2141**

INTERNATIONAL JOURNAL OF MODERN PHYSICS A (SI/0217-751X). **4405**

INTERNATIONAL JOURNAL OF MODERN PHYSICS B (SI/0217-9792). **4406**

INTERNATIONAL JOURNAL OF MULTIPHASE FLOW (UK/0301-9322). **2067**

INTERNATIONAL JOURNAL OF MYCOLOGY AND LICHENOLOGY (GW/0723-3353). **575**

INTERNATIONAL JOURNAL OF NEURAL SYSTEMS (SI/0129-0657). **1190**

INTERNATIONAL JOURNAL OF NEUROSCIENCE (US/0020-7454). **3834**

INTERNATIONAL JOURNAL OF NON-LINEAR MECHANICS (US/0020-7462). **4428**

INTERNATIONAL JOURNAL OF NUMERICAL MODELLING (UK/0894-3370). **2067**

INTERNATIONAL JOURNAL OF NURSING STUDIES (UK/0020-7489). **3857**

INTERNATIONAL JOURNAL OF OFFENDER THERAPY AND COMPARATIVE CRIMINOLOGY (US/0306-624X). **3166**

INTERNATIONAL JOURNAL OF ONCOLOGY (GR/1019-6439). **3818**

INTERNATIONAL JOURNAL OF OPERATIONS & PRODUCTION MANAGEMENT (UK/0144-3577). **871**

INTERNATIONAL JOURNAL OF OPTOELECTRONICS (UK/0952-5432). **4435**

INTERNATIONAL JOURNAL OF ORAL AND MAXILLOFACIAL IMPLANTS, THE (US/0882-2786). **1325**

INTERNATIONAL JOURNAL OF ORAL AND MAXILLOFACIAL SURGERY (DK/0901-5027). **3966**

INTERNATIONAL JOURNAL OF PAEDIATRIC DENTISTRY / THE BRITISH PAEDONDONTIC SOCIETY [AND] THE INTERNATIONAL ASSOCIATION OF DENTISTRY FOR CHILDREN (UK/0960-7439). **1325**

INTERNATIONAL JOURNAL OF PANCREATOLOGY (NE/0169-4197). **3798**

INTERNATIONAL JOURNAL OF PARALLEL PROGRAMMING (US/0885-7458). **1279**

INTERNATIONAL JOURNAL OF PARTIAL HOSPITALIZATION (US/0272-4308). **3786**

INTERNATIONAL JOURNAL OF PATTERN RECOGNITION AND ARTIFICIAL INTELLIGENCE (SI/0218-0014). **1213**

INTERNATIONAL JOURNAL OF PEDIATRIC OTORHINOLARYNGOLOGY (NE/0165-5876). **3904**

INTERNATIONAL JOURNAL OF PEPTIDE AND PROTEIN RESEARCH (DK/0367-8377). **1042**

INTERNATIONAL JOURNAL OF PERIODONTICS & RESTORATIVE DENTISTRY, THE (US/0198-7569). **1325**

INTERNATIONAL JOURNAL OF PERSONAL CONSTRUCT PSYCHOLOGY (UK/0893-603X). **4591**

INTERNATIONAL JOURNAL OF PHARMACEUTICS (NE/0378-5173). **4308**

INTERNATIONAL JOURNAL OF PHARMACOGNOSY (NE/0925-1618). **4308**

INTERNATIONAL JOURNAL OF PHYSICAL DISTRIBUTION & LOGISTICS MANAGEMENT (UK/0960-0035). **871**

INTERNATIONAL JOURNAL OF PHYSICAL EDUCATION (GW/0341-8685). **1856**

INTERNATIONAL JOURNAL OF PIXE (SI/0129-0835). **3942**

INTERNATIONAL JOURNAL OF PLASTICITY (US/0749-6419). **2103**

INTERNATIONAL JOURNAL OF POLITICS, CULTURE, AND SOCIETY (US/0891-4486). **5248**

INTERNATIONAL JOURNAL OF POLYMERIC MATERIALS (US/0091-4037). **978**

INTERNATIONAL JOURNAL OF POWDER METALLURGY (PRINCETON, N.J.) (US/0888-7462). **4004**

INTERNATIONAL JOURNAL OF PRESSURE VESSELS AND PIPING, THE (UK/0308-0161). **2116**

INTERNATIONAL JOURNAL OF PRIMATOLOGY (US/0164-0291). **5586**

INTERNATIONAL JOURNAL OF PRODUCTION ECONOMICS (NE/0925-5273). **1612**

INTERNATIONAL JOURNAL OF PRODUCTION RESEARCH (UK/0020-7543). **871**

INTERNATIONAL JOURNAL OF PROJECT MANAGEMENT (UK/0263-7863). **1980**

INTERNATIONAL JOURNAL OF PROSTHODONTICS, THE (US/0893-2174). **1325**

INTERNATIONAL JOURNAL OF PSYCHO-ANALYSIS, THE (UK/0020-7578). **4591**

INTERNATIONAL JOURNAL OF PSYCHOLINGUISTICS (JA/0165-4055). **3287**

INTERNATIONAL JOURNAL OF PSYCHOLOGY (NE/0020-7594). **4591**

INTERNATIONAL JOURNAL OF PSYCHOPHYSIOLOGY (NE/0167-8760). **581**

INTERNATIONAL JOURNAL OF PUBLIC ADMINISTRATION (US/0190-0692). **4657**

INTERNATIONAL JOURNAL OF PUBLIC OPINION RESEARCH (UK/0954-2892). **5248**

INTERNATIONAL JOURNAL OF PUBLIC SECTOR MANAGEMENT, THE (UK/0951-3558). **4657**

INTERNATIONAL JOURNAL OF QUALITATIVE STUDIES IN EDUCATION : QSE (UK/0951-8398). **1754**

INTERNATIONAL JOURNAL OF QUALITY & RELIABILITY MANAGEMENT, THE (UK/0265-671X). **871**

INTERNATIONAL JOURNAL OF QUANTUM CHEMISTRY (US/0020-7608). **978**

INTERNATIONAL JOURNAL OF QUANTUM CHEMISTRY. QUANTUM CHEMISTRY SYMPOSIUM (US/0161-3642). **1053**

INTERNATIONAL JOURNAL OF RADIATION APPLICATIONS AND INSTRUMENTATION. PART A, APPLIED RADIATION AND ISOTOPES (UK/0883-2889). **4406**

INTERNATIONAL JOURNAL OF RADIATION APPLICATIONS AND INSTRUMENTATION. PART B, NUCLEAR MEDICINE AND BIOLOGY (UK/0883-2897). **3848**

INTERNATIONAL JOURNAL OF RADIATION APPLICATIONS AND INSTRUMENTATION. PART E, NUCLEAR GEOPHYSICS, THE (UK/0886-0130). **1407**

INTERNATIONAL JOURNAL OF RADIATION BIOLOGY (UK/0955-3002). **3942**

INTERNATIONAL JOURNAL OF RADIATION- ONCOLOGY, BIOLOGY, PHYSICS (US/0360-3016). **3818**

INTERNATIONAL JOURNAL OF REFRACTORY METALS & HARD MATERIALS (UK/0263-4368). **4004**

INTERNATIONAL JOURNAL OF REFRIGERATION (UK/0140-7007). **2606**

INTERNATIONAL JOURNAL OF REFUGEE LAW (UK/0953-8186). **3130**

INTERNATIONAL JOURNAL OF REMOTE SENSING (UK/0143-1161). **1980**

INTERNATIONAL JOURNAL OF RESEARCH IN MARKETING (NE/0167-8116). **926**

INTERNATIONAL JOURNAL OF RETAIL & DISTRIBUTION MANAGEMENT (UK/0959-0552). **955**

INTERNATIONAL JOURNAL OF RISK & SAFETY IN MEDICINE, THE (NE/0924-6479). **3589**

INTERNATIONAL JOURNAL OF ROBOTICS RESEARCH, THE (US/0278-3649). **1220**

INTERNATIONAL JOURNAL OF ROCK MECHANICS AND MINING SCIENCES & GEOMECHANICS ABSTRACTS (UK/0148-9062). **2141**

INTERNATIONAL JOURNAL OF SATELLITE COMMUNICATIONS (UK/0737-2884). **1158**

INTERNATIONAL JOURNAL OF SCIENCE EDUCATION (UK/0950-0693). **5115**

INTERNATIONAL JOURNAL OF SELECTION AND ASSESSMENT (UK/0965-075X). **943**

INTERNATIONAL JOURNAL OF SELF-PROPAGATING HIGH-TEMPERATURE SYSTEM (US/1061-3862). **1980**

INTERNATIONAL JOURNAL OF SOCIAL ECONOMICS (UK/0306-8293). **1496**

INTERNATIONAL JOURNAL OF SOLAR ENERGY (SZ/0142-5919). **1948**

INTERNATIONAL JOURNAL OF SOLIDS AND STRUCTURES (US/0020-7683). **2025**

INTERNATIONAL JOURNAL OF SPORT BIOMECHANICS (US/0740-2082). **495**

INTERNATIONAL JOURNAL OF SPORT NUTRITION (US/1050-1606). **4192**

INTERNATIONAL JOURNAL OF SPORTS MEDICINE (GW/0172-4622). **3954**

INTERNATIONAL JOURNAL OF STD & AIDS (UK/0956-4624). **3672**

INTERNATIONAL JOURNAL OF SUPERCOMPUTER APPLICATIONS, THE (US/0890-2720). **1287**

INTERNATIONAL JOURNAL OF SURGICAL PATHOLOGY (US/1066-8969). **3895**

INTERNATIONAL JOURNAL OF SYSTEMATIC BACTERIOLOGY (US/0020-7713). **564**

INTERNATIONAL JOURNAL OF SYSTEMS SCIENCE (UK/0020-7721). **2116**

INTERNATIONAL JOURNAL OF TECHNOLOGY & AGING (US/0891-4478). **3752**

INTERNATIONAL JOURNAL OF TECHNOLOGY ASSESSMENT IN HEALTH CARE (UK/0266-4623). **3589**

INTERNATIONAL JOURNAL OF THE ADDICTIONS (US/0020-773X). **1345**

INTERNATIONAL JOURNAL OF THE SOCIOLOGY OF LANGUAGE (NE/0165-2516). **3287**

INTERNATIONAL JOURNAL OF THE SOCIOLOGY OF LAW (UK/0194-6595). **2984**

INTERNATIONAL JOURNAL OF THEOLOGY AND PHILOSOPHY IN AFRICA : TPA, THE (UK/0951-5429). **4966**

INTERNATIONAL JOURNAL OF THEORETICAL PHYSICS (US/0020-7748). **4406**

INTERNATIONAL JOURNAL OF THERMOPHYSICS (US/0195-928X). **4406**

INTERNATIONAL JOURNAL OF TISSUE REACTIONS (SZ/0250-0868). **537**

INTERNATIONAL JOURNAL OF TROPICAL PLANT DISEASES (II/0254-0126). **514**

INTERNATIONAL JOURNAL OF TURBO & JET-ENGINES (IS/0334-0082). **24**

INTERNATIONAL JOURNAL OF URBAN AND REGIONAL RESEARCH (UK/0309-1317). **2825**

INTERNATIONAL JOURNAL OF VEHICLE DESIGN (SZ/0143-3369). **5417**

INTERNATIONAL JOURNAL OF WATER RESOURCES DEVELOPMENT (UK/0790-0627). **5534**

INTERNATIONAL LABOR AND WORKING CLASS HISTORY (US/0147-5479). **1680**

INTERNATIONAL LAWYERS' NEWSLETTER (US/0738-9728). **3130**

INTERNATIONAL LEGAL MATERIALS (US/0020-7829). **3130**

INTERNATIONAL LITERARY MARKET PLACE (US/0074-6827). **4821**

INTERNATIONAL MANAGEMENT (LAUSANNE, SWITZERLAND) (SZ/0020-7888). **872**

INTERNATIONAL MARKETING REVIEW (UK/0265-1335). **926**

INTERNATIONAL MATERIALS REVIEWS (UK/0950-6608). **4004**

INTERNATIONAL NETWORKS (US/0739-9898). **1158**

INTERNATIONAL NEWS ON FATS, OILS AND RELATED MATERIALS (US/0897-8026). **1025**

INTERNATIONAL OIL NEWS (US/0043-8855). **4261**

INTERNATIONAL OPHTHALMOLOGY (NE/0165-5701). **3875**

INTERNATIONAL OPHTHALMOLOGY CLINICS (US/0020-8167). **3875**

INTERNATIONAL ORGANIZATION (US/0020-8183). **4525**

INTERNATIONAL ORTHOPAEDICS (GW/0341-2695). **3882**

INTERNATIONAL PACKAGING ABSTRACTS (UK/0260-7409). **4222**

INTERNATIONAL PETROLEUM ENCYCLOPEDIA (US/0148-0375). **4261**

INTERNATIONAL PETROLEUM FINANCE (US/0193-9270). **4261**

INTERNATIONAL PHARMACEUTICAL ABSTRACTS (US/0020-8264). **4334**

INTERNATIONAL POLITICAL SCIENCE REVIEW (UK/0192-5121). **4477**

INTERNATIONAL POLYMER PROCESSING (GW/0930-777X). **4455**

INTERNATIONAL PSYCHOGERIATRICS / IPA (US/1041-6102). **3752**

INTERNATIONAL PUBLIC RELATIONS REVIEW (UK/0269-0357). **761**

INTERNATIONAL PULP & PAPER DIRECTORY (US/0097-2509). **4234**

INTERNATIONAL QUARTERLY (CHESTERLAND, OHIO) (US/1041-3855). **3100**

INTERNATIONAL QUARTERLY OF ENTOMOLOGY (TU/0256-6672). **5610**

INTERNATIONAL RAILWAY JOURNAL AND RAPID TRANSIT REVIEW (UK/0744-5326). **5432**

INTERNATIONAL REPORTS (US/0020-8507). **792**

INTERNATIONAL REVIEW FOR THE SOCIOLOGY OF SPORT (GW/0074-7769). **4901**

INTERNATIONAL REVIEW OF CYTOLOGY (US/0074-7696). **537**

INTERNATIONAL REVIEW OF EDUCATION (NE/0020-8566). **1754**

INTERNATIONAL REVIEW OF EXPERIMENTAL PATHOLOGY (US/0074-7718). **3895**

INTERNATIONAL REVIEW OF INDUSTRIAL AND ORGANIZATIONAL PSYCHOLOGY (UK/0886-1528). **4591**

INTERNATIONAL REVIEW OF LAW AND ECONOMICS (US/0144-8188). **1636**

INTERNATIONAL REVIEW OF NEUROBIOLOGY (US/0074-7742). **459**

INTERNATIONAL REVIEW OF PSYCHIATRY (ABINGDON, ENGLAND) (UK/0954-0261). **3927**

INTERNATIONAL REVIEW OF RESEARCH IN MENTAL RETARDATION (US/0074-7750). **3927**

INTERNATIONAL REVIEW OF RETAIL DISTRIBUTION CONSUMER RESEARCH (UK/0959-3969). **955**

INTERNATIONAL REVIEWS IN PHYSICAL CHEMISTRY (UK/0144-235X). **1053**

INTERNATIONAL REVIEWS OF ERGONOMICS (UK/0269-5839). **2117**

INTERNATIONAL REVIEWS OF IMMUNOLOGY (SZ/0883-0185). **3672**

INTERNATIONAL SAMPE SYMPOSIUM AND EXHIBITION (US/0891-0138). **2103**

INTERNATIONAL SECURITY (US/0162-2889). **4525**

INTERNATIONAL SOCIAL SCIENCE REVIEW (US/0278-2308). **5204**

INTERNATIONAL SOLAR ENERGY INTELLIGENCE REPORT (US/1045-6325). **1948**

INTERNATIONAL STUDIES IN THE PHILOSOPHY OF SCIENCE : I.S.P.S (UK/0269-8595). **5116**

INTERNATIONAL STUDIES QUARTERLY (US/0020-8833). **4525**

INTERNATIONAL TAX & BUSINESS LAWYER (US/0741-4269). **3131**

INTERNATIONAL TAX REPORT, THE (UK/0300-1628). **902**

INTERNATIONAL TRADE JOURNAL, THE (US/0885-3908). **841**

INTERNATIONAL TRADE REPORTER. CURRENT REPORTS (US/0748-0172). **841**

INTERNATIONAL TRADE REPORTER. EXPORT REFERENCE MANUAL (US/1043-5670). **842**

INTERNATIONAL TRANSACTIONS IN OPERATIONAL RESEARCH : A JOURNAL OF THE INTERNATIONAL FEDERATION OF OPERATIONAL RESEARCH SOCIETIES (UK/0969-6016). **1191**

INTERNATIONAL TREE CROPS JOURNAL, THE (UK/0143-5698). **2385**

INTERNATIONAL UROLOGY AND NEPHROLOGY (HU/0301-1623). **3990**

INTERNATIONAL WATER POWER & DAM CONSTRUCTION (UK/0306-400X). **2091**

INTERNATIONAL WATER REPORT (US/0893-8776). **2233**

INTERNATIONAL WHO'S WHO, THE (UK/0074-9613). **433**

INTERNATIONAL YEARBOOK OF LAW, COMPUTERS AND TECHNOLOGY (UK/0965-528X). **5116**

INTERNATIONAL YEARBOOK OF LAW, COMPUTERS, AND TECHNOLOGY (UK/0965-528X). **2984**

INTERNATIONALE KIRCHLICHE ZEITSCHRIFT (SZ/0020-9252). **4966**

INTERNATIONALE SCHULBUCHFORSCHUNG (GW/0172-8237). **1754**

INTERNATIONALES VERKEHRSWESEN (GW/0020-9511). **5384**

INTERNETWORKING (CHICHESTER, ENGLAND) (UK/1049-8915). **1242**

INTERNIST (BERLIN), DER (GW/0020-9554). **3798**

INTERNISTISCHE PRAXIS (GW/0020-9570). **3590**

INTERNISTISCHE WELT (GW/0344-4201). **3798**

INTERTAX (NE/0165-2826). **4733**

INTERVENTION IN SCHOOL AND CLINIC (US/1053-4512). **1880**

INTERVENTIONAL CARDIOLOGY NEWSLETTER (US/1063-4282). **3706**

INTERVIROLOGY (SZ/0300-5526). **564**

INVASION & METASTASIS (SW/0251-1789). **537**

INVENTIONES MATHEMATICAE (GW/0020-9910). **3510**

INVENTORY REDUCTION REPORT (US/1049-9849). **872**

INVERSE PROBLEMS (UK/0266-5611). **3510**

INVERTEBRATE NEUROBIOLOGY (UK/0261-4952). **3590**

INVESTIGACION E INFORMACION TEXTIL Y DE TENSIOACTIVOS (SP/0302-5268). **5353**

INVESTIGATIONAL NEW DRUGS (US/0167-6997). **3818**

INVESTIGATIVE OPHTHALMOLOGY & VISUAL SCIENCE (US/0146-0404). **3875**

INVESTIGATIVE RADIOLOGY (US/0020-9996). **3942**

INVESTMENT DEALERS' DIGEST, THE (US/0021-0080). **793**

INZENERNO-FIZICESKIJ ZURNAL (BW/0021-0285). **1981**

IOMA'S REPORT ON CONTROLLING LAW FIRM COSTS (US/1060-5924). **2984**

IOMA'S REPORT ON MANAGING 401 (K) PLANS (US/1059-2741). **903**

IOMA'S REPORT ON REDUCING BENEFITS COSTS (US/1056-7984). **872**

IRAL, INTERNATIONAL REVIEW OF APPLIED LINGUISTICS IN LANGUAGE TEACHING (GW/0019-042X). **3288**

IRISH GEOGRAPHY (IE/0075-0778). **2566**

IRISH JOURNAL OF PSYCHOLOGICAL MEDICINE (IE/0790-9667). **3927**

IRON AGE (NEW YORK, N.Y. 1987) (US/0897-4365). **4004**

IRONMAKING & STEELMAKING (UK/0301-9233). **4005**

IRRICAB (IS/0376-5083). **175**

IRRIGATION AND DRAINAGE SYSTEMS (NE/0168-6291). **2091**

IRRIGATION SCIENCE (GW/0342-7188). **175**

ISA DIRECTORY OF INSTRUMENTATION (TRADE EDITION) (US/0272-8141). **3481**

ISA TRANSACTIONS (US/0019-0578). **5116**

ISDN (BROOKLINE, MASS.) (US/0735-1844). **1191**

ISDN NEWS (US/0899-9554). **1114**

ISI ATLAS OF SCIENCE. BIOCHEMISTRY (US/0894-3753). **488**

ISI ATLAS OF SCIENCE. IMMUNOLOGY (US/0894-3745). **3672**

ISIJ INTERNATIONAL / IRON AND STEEL INSTITUTE OF JAPAN (JA/0915-1559). **1613**

ISLAM (BERLIN), DER (GW/0021-1818). **5043**

ISLAND ARC, THE (AT/1038-4871). **1383**

ISLANDS (NZ/0110-0858). **3397**

ISOTOPE GEOSCIENCE (SZ/0167-6695). **1383**

ISOTOPE GEOSCIENCE (NE/0167-6695). **1042**

ISOTOPENPRAXIS (SW/0021-1915). **4406**

ISOZYMES (US/0160-3787). **488**

ISPRS JOURNAL OF PHOTOGRAMMETRY AND REMOTE SENSING (NE/0924-2716). **2067**

ISRAEL JOURNAL OF PSYCHIATRY AND RELATED SCIENCES, THE (IS/0333-7308). **3927**

ISSLEDOVANIE ZEMLI IZ KOSMOSA (SZ/0275-911X). **1981**

ISSUES IN COMPREHENSIVE PEDIATRIC NURSING (US/0146-0862). **3857**

ISSUES IN MENTAL HEALTH NURSING (US/0161-2840). **3858**

ISSUES IN REPRODUCTIVE AND GENETIC ENGINEERING : JOURNAL OF INTERNATIONAL FEMINIST ANALYSIS (US/0958-6415). **3693**

ITALIAN JOURNAL OF FOOD SCIENCE (IT/1120-1770). **2345**

ITALIAN JOURNAL OF ORTHOPAEDICS AND TRAUMATOLOGY (IT/0390-5489). **3882**

ITALIENISCH (GW/0171-4996). **3288**

ITEM PROCESSING REPORT (US/1048-5120). **793**

IZOBRETENIIA : OFITSIALNYI PATENTNYI BIULLETEN (RU/0208-287X). **1305**

IZVESTIA AKADEMII NAUK SSSR. SERIA HIMICESKAA (RU/0002-3353). **979**

IZVESTIIA AKADEMII NAUK SSSR. FIZIKA ZEMLI (RU/0002-3337). **4407**

IZVESTIIA AKADEMII NAUK SSSR. SERIIA GEOLOGICHESKAIA (RU/0321-1703). **1384**

IZVESTIIA ORDENA TRUDOVOGO ASTROFIZICH ESKOI OBSERVATORII (US/0190-2717). **396**

IZVESTIIA. SERIIA KHIMICHESKAIA (RU/0002-3353). **979**

IZVESTIIA VYSSHIKH UCHEBMYKH ZAVEDENII. RADIOELEKTRONIKA (US/0735-2727). **2067**

IZVESTIIA VYSSHIKH UCHEBNYKH ZAVEDENII. FIZIKA / MINISTERSTVO VYSSHEGO OBRAZOVANIIA SSSR (RU/0021-3411). **4407**

IZVESTIIA VYSSHIKH UCHEBNYKH ZAVEDENII. NEFT I GAZ / MINISTERSTVO VYSSHEGO I SREDNEGO SPETSIALNOGO OBRAZOVANIIA SSSR (AJ/0445-0108). **4262**

IZVESTIJA AKADEMII NAUK AZERBAJDZANSKOJ SSR. SERIJA FIZIKO-TEHNICESKIH I MATEMATICESKIH NAUK (AJ/0002-3108). **4407**

IZVESTIJA AKADEMII NAUK SSSR. SERIJA FIZICESKAJA (RU/0367-6765). **4407**

IZVESTIJA VYSSIH UCEBNYH ZAVEDENIJ. HIMIJA I HIMICESKAJA TEHNOLOGIJA (RU/0579-2991). **979**

IZVESTIJA VYSSIH UCEBNYH ZAVEDENIJ. HIMIJA I HIMICESKAJA TEHNOLOGIJA (RU/0579-2991). **979**

IZVESTIJA VYSSIH UCEBNYH ZAVEDENIJ. MATEMATIKA (RU/0021-3446). **3510**

IZVESTIJA VYSSIKH UCEBNYH ZAVEDENIJ. CVETNAJA METALLURGIJA (RU/0021-3438). **4005**

IZVESTIJA VYSSYHUCEBNYH ZAVEDENIJ. GEOLOGIJA I RAZVEDKA (RU/0016-7762). **1384**

IZVESTIYA, ACADEMY OF SCIENCES, USSR. PHYSICS OF THE SOLID EARTH (US/0001-4354). **1407**

IZVESTIYA. ATMOSPHERIC AND OCEANIC PHYSICS (US/0001-4338). **1407**

IZVESTIYA. ATMOSPHERIC AND OCEANIC PHYSICS (US/0001-4338). **1407**

J3E L JOURNAL DE L EQUIPMENT ELECTRIQUE ET ELECTRONIQUE (FR/0758-3826). **2067**

JAHRBUCH DER ABSATZ- UND VERBRAUCHSFORSCHUNG (GW/0021-3985). **1568**

JAHRBUCH FUER OPTIK UND FEINMECHANIK (GW/0075-272X). **4435**

JAHRBUCH FUER REGIONALWISSENSCHAFT / HERAUSGEGEBEN VOM VORSTAND DER GESELLSCHAFT FUER REGIONALFORSCHUNG E. V. (DEUTSCHSPRACHIGE GRUPPE DER REGIONAL SCIENCE ASSOCIATION) (GW/0173-7600). **2694**

JAHRBUCH FUER SOZIALWISSENSCHAFT (GW/0075-2770). **5205**

JAHRBUCHER

JAHRBUCHER FUER GESCHICHTE OSTEUROPAS (PL/0021-4019). **2694**

JAHRBUCHER FUER NATIONALOKONOMIE UND STATISTIK (GW/0021-4027). **1497**

JAHRESBERICHT DER DEUTSCHEN MATHEMATIKER-VEREINIGUNG (GW/0012-0456). **3511**

JAHRESBERICHTE UND MITTEILUNGEN DES OBERRHEINISCHEN GEOLOGISCHEN VEREINES (GW/0078-2947). **1384**

JAMA JOURNAL OF THE AMERICAN MEDICAL ASSOCIATION. EDITION FRANCAISE (FR/0221-7678). **3591**

JAMA : THE JOURNAL OF THE AMERICAN MEDICAL ASSOCIATION (US/0098-7484). **3591**

JANE'S AIRPORT REVIEW (UK/0954-7649). **25**

JANE'S ALL THE WORLD'S AIRCRAFT (LONDON, ENGLAND) (UK/0075-3017). **4046**

JANE'S ARMOUR AND ARTILLERY (UK/0143-9952). **4046**

JANE'S DEFENCE WEEKLY (UK/0265-3818). **4047**

JANE'S FIGHTING SHIPS (UK/0075-3025). **4177**

JANE'S MILITARY COMMUNICATIONS (UK/0144-0004). **4047**

JANE'S WORLD RAILWAYS (UK/0075-3084). **5432**

JANO. MEDICINA Y HUMANIDADES (SP/0210-220X). **3591**

JAPAN AND THE WORLD ECONOMY (NE/0922-1425). **1636**

JAPAN DIRECTORY OF PROFESSIONAL ASSOCIATIONS (JA/0287-9530). **685**

JAPAN FORUM (OXFORD, ENGLAND) (UK/0955-5803). **2654**

JAPAN MATERIALS NEWS (METALS PARK, OHIO) (US/0894-1149). **4005**

JAPANESE JOURNAL OF CANCER RESEARCH : GANN (JA/0910-5050). **3818**

JAPANESE JOURNAL OF FUZZY THEORY AND SYSTEMS (US/1058-7349). **3511**

JAPANESE JOURNAL OF PHARMACOLOGY (JA/0021-5198). **4309**

JAPANESE JOURNAL OF TRIBOLOGY (US/1045-7828). **2117**

JAPANESE TECHNOLOGY REVIEWS. SECTION A, ELECTRONICS (US/1058-7292). **2068**

JAPANESE TECHNOLOGY REVIEWS. SECTION B, COMPUTERS AND COMMUNICATION (US/1058-7306). **1114**

JAPANESE TECHNOLOGY REVIEWS. SECTION C, NEW MATERIALS (US/1058-7314). **5117**

JAPANESE TECHNOLOGY REVIEWS. SECTION D, MANUFACTURING ENGINEERING (US/1058-7322). **1981**

JAPANESE TECHNOLOGY REVIEWS. SECTION E, BIOTECHNOLOGY (US/1058-7330). **3693**

JAY SCHABACKER'S MUTUAL FUND INVESTING (US/8756-5161). **904**

JCT, JOURNAL OF COATINGS TECHNOLOGY (US/0361-8773). **4224**

JCU : JOURNAL OF CLINICAL ULTRASOUND (US/0091-2751). **3591**

JERUSALEM JOURNAL OF INTERNATIONAL RELATIONS, THE (US/0363-2865). **4526**

JET. JOURNAL OF EDUCATION FOR TEACHING (UK/0260-7476). **1897**

JETP LETTERS (US/0021-3640). **4408**

JEWISH HISTORY (IS/0334-701X). **5049**

JEWISH LANGUAGE REVIEW (IS/0333-8347). **3289**

JIKEIKAI MEDICAL JOURNAL (JA/0021-6968). **3592**

JIKKEN DOBUTSU (JA/0007-5124). **3592**

JMR, JOURNAL OF MARKETING RESEARCH (US/0022-2437). **927**

JMR. JOURNAL OF MOLECULAR RECOGNITION (UK/0952-3499). **460**

JOB SAFETY & HEALTH; AN ADVISORY BULLETIN ON GOVERNMENT AND INDUSTRY SAFETY POLICIES, PROCEDURES AND PRACTICES (US/0149-7510). **2864**

JOB SAFETY & HEALTH REPORT (US/0148-4079). **2864**

JOB SAFETY & HEALTH (WASHINGTON. 1977) (US/0149-7510). **2864**

JOHN NAISBITT'S TREND LETTER (US/0883-136X). **1569**

JOHNS HOPKINS UNIVERSITY STUDIES IN HISTORICAL AND POLITICAL SCIENCE, THE (US/0075-3904). **5205**

JOM (1989) (US/1047-4838). **4006**

JONESREPORT (US/0889-485X). **927**

JONXIS LECTURES, THE (NE/0166-2430). **3592**

JOURNAL / AMERICAN WATER WORKS ASSOCIATION (US/0003-150X). **5535**

JOURNAL AND PROCEEDINGS OF THE ROYAL SOCIETY OF NEW SOUTH WALES (AT/0035-9173). **5118**

JOURNAL - AVIATION HISTORICAL SOCIETY OF NEW ZEALAND (NZ/0110-5493). **25**

JOURNAL D'ACOUSTIQUE (FR/0988-4319). **4452**

JOURNAL DE CHIMIE PHYSIQUE ET DE PHYSICO-CHIMIE BIOLOGIQUE (FR/0021-7689). **1053**

JOURNAL DE CHIRURGIE (FR/0021-7697). **3966**

JOURNAL DE GYNECOLOGIE, OBSTETRIQUE ET BIOLOGIE DE LA REPRODUCTION (FR/0368-2315). **3763**

JOURNAL DE L'ANNEE (FR/0449-4733). **2621**

JOURNAL DE MATHEMATIQUES PURES ET APPLIQUEES (FR/0021-7824). **3511**

JOURNAL DE MEDECINE DE STRASBOURG (FR/0021-7905). **3592**

JOURNAL DE MEDECINE LEGALE, DROIT MEDICAL (FR/0249-6208). **3741**

JOURNAL DE PHARMACIE CLINIQUE (FR/0291-1981). **4310**

JOURNAL DE PHARMACIE DE BELGIQUE (BE/0047-2166). **4310**

JOURNAL DE PHYSIQUE. II (LES ULIS) (FR/1155-4312). **4408**

JOURNAL DE PHYSIQUE. III (LES ULIS) (FR/1155-4320). **4408**

JOURNAL DE PHYSIQUE. IV (LES ULIS) (FR/1155-4339). **4408**

JOURNAL DE READAPTATION MEDICALE (FR/0242-648X). **3882**

JOURNAL DE TOXICOLOGIE CLINIQUE ET EXPERIMENTALE (FR/0753-2830). **3981**

JOURNAL DE TRAUMATOLOGIE DU SPORT (FR/0762-915X). **3954**

JOURNAL D'ECHOGRAPHIE ET DE MEDECINE ULTRASONORE : JEMU (FR/0245-5552). **3592**

JOURNAL D'ECONOMIE MEDICALE (FR/0294-0736). **3592**

JOURNAL D'ERGOTHERAPIE PARIS (FR/0249-6550). **4380**

JOURNAL DES INSTITUTEURS ET DES INSTITUTRICES (FR/0021-8073). **1865**

JOURNAL DES MALADIES VASCULAIRES (FR/0398-0499). **3706**

JOURNAL D'UROLOGIE (FR/0248-0018). **3990**

JOURNAL EUROPEEN DE RADIOTHERAPIE (FR/0243-1203). **3942**

JOURNAL FOR GENERAL PHILOSOPHY OF SCIENCE (NE/0925-4560). **4350**

JOURNAL FOR QUALITY AND PARTICIPATION, THE (US/1040-9602). **1681**

JOURNAL FOR SPECIALISTS IN GROUP WORK, THE (US/0193-3922). **4592**

JOURNAL FOR THE HISTORY OF ASTRONOMY (UK/0021-8286). **396**

JOURNAL FOR THE STUDY OF JUDAISM IN THE PERSIAN, HELLENISTIC AND ROMAN PERIOD (NE/0047-2212). **5050**

JOURNAL FOR THE THEORY OF SOCIAL BEHAVIOUR (UK/0021-8308). **4593**

JOURNAL FRANCAIS D'OPHTALMOLOGIE (FR/0181-5512). **3875**

JOURNAL FUER DIE REINE UND ANGEWANDTE MATHEMATIK (GW/0075-4102). **3511**

JOURNAL OF ABNORMAL CHILD PSYCHOLOGY (US/0091-0627). **4593**

JOURNAL OF ABNORMAL PSYCHOLOGY (1965) (US/0021-843X). **4593**

JOURNAL OF ACADEMIC LIBRARIANSHIP (US/0099-1333). **3219**

JOURNAL OF ACCOUNTANCY (US/0021-8448). **746**

JOURNAL OF ACCOUNTING & ECONOMICS (NE/0165-4101). **746**

JOURNAL OF ACCOUNTING AND PUBLIC POLICY (US/0278-4254). **746**

JOURNAL OF ACCOUNTING AUDITING & FINANCE (US/0148-558X). **746**

JOURNAL OF ACCOUNTING EDUCATION (US/0748-5751). **746**

JOURNAL OF ACQUIRED IMMUNE DEFICIENCY SYNDROMES (US/0894-9255). **3673**

JOURNAL OF ADDICTIONS & OFFENDER COUNSELING (US/1055-3835). **4593**

JOURNAL OF ADHESION, THE (UK/0021-8464). **1053**

JOURNAL OF ADOLESCENCE (LONDON, ENGLAND) (UK/0140-1971). **3904**

JOURNAL OF ADOLESCENT HEALTH (US/1054-139X). **3593**

JOURNAL OF ADVANCED NURSING (UK/0309-2402). **3858**

JOURNAL OF ADVANCEMENT IN MEDICINE (US/0894-5888). **3593**

JOURNAL OF ADVERTISING (US/0091-3367). **761**

JOURNAL OF AEROSOL SCIENCE (UK/0021-8502). **1053**

JOURNAL OF AEROSPACE ENGINEERING (US/0893-1321). **25**

JOURNAL OF AESTHETIC EDUCATION, THE (US/0021-8510). **2848**

JOURNAL OF AFFECTIVE DISORDERS (NE/0165-0327). **3593**

JOURNAL OF AFRICAN EARTH SCIENCES (AND THE MIDDLE EAST) (UK/0899-5362). **1384**

JOURNAL OF AFRICAN ECONOMIES (UK/0963-8024). **1637**

JOURNAL OF AFRICAN HISTORY (UK/0021-8537). **2640**

JOURNAL OF AFRICAN LANGUAGES AND LINGUISTICS (NE/0167-6164). **3289**

JOURNAL OF AFRICAN LAW (UK/0021-8553). **2986**

JOURNAL OF AGING STUDIES (US/0890-4065). **5249**

JOURNAL OF AGRICULTURAL & ENVIRONMENTAL ETHICS (CN/1187-7863). **2251**

JOURNAL OF AGRICULTURAL AND FOOD CHEMISTRY (US/0021-8561). **99**

JOURNAL OF AGRICULTURAL EDUCATION (US/1042-0541). **99**

JOURNAL OF AGRICULTURAL ENGINEERING RESEARCH (UK/0021-8634). **1981**

JOURNAL OF AGRICULTURAL SCIENCE, THE (UK/0021-8596). **99**

JOURNAL OF AIRCRAFT (US/0021-8669). **26**

JOURNAL OF ALGEBRA (US/0021-8693). **3511**

JOURNAL OF ALGORITHMS (US/0196-6774). **3511**

JOURNAL OF ALLERGY AND CLINICAL IMMUNOLOGY (US/0091-6749). **3673**

JOURNAL OF ALLOYS AND COMPOUNDS (SZ/0925-8388). **4006**

JOURNAL OF AMBULATORY CARE MANAGEMENT, THE (US/0148-9917). **3786**

JOURNAL OF AMBULATORY MONITORING (UK/0951-1830). **3593**

JOURNAL OF AMERICAN COLLEGE HEALTH (US/0744-8481). **3593**

JOURNAL OF AMERICAN ETHNIC HISTORY (US/0278-5927). **2265**

JOURNAL OF ANALYTICAL AND APPLIED PYROLYSIS (NE/0165-2370). **1016**

JOURNAL OF ANALYTICAL ATOMIC SPECTROMETRY (UK/0267-9477). **1016**

JOURNAL OF ANALYTICAL CHEMISTRY (NEW YORK, N.Y.) (US/1061-9348). **1016**

JOURNAL OF ANALYTICAL PSYCHOLOGY (UK/0021-8774). **4593**

JOURNAL OF ANALYTICAL TOXICOLOGY (US/0146-4760). **3981**

JOURNAL OF ANDROLOGY (US/0196-3635). **581**

JOURNAL OF ANIMAL ECOLOGY, THE (UK/0021-8790). **5587**

JOURNAL OF ANTHROPOLOGICAL ARCHAEOLOGY (US/0278-4165). **271**

JOURNAL OF ANTIMICROBIAL CHEMOTHERAPY, THE (UK/0305-7453). **564**

JOURNAL OF ANXIETY DISORDERS (US/0887-6185). **4593**

JOURNAL OF AOAC INTERNATIONAL (US/1060-3271). **1016**

JOURNAL OF APPLIED BEHAVIORAL SCIENCE, THE (US/0021-8863). **5205**

JOURNAL OF APPLIED BIOMATERIALS (US/1045-4861). **3798**

JOURNAL OF APPLIED BIOMECHANICS (US/1065-8483). **3694**

JOURNAL OF APPLIED BUSINESS RESEARCH (US/0892-7626). **685**

JOURNAL OF APPLIED CHEMISTRY OF THE USSR (US/0021-888X). **979**

JOURNAL OF APPLIED CRYSTALLOGRAPHY (DK/0021-8898). **1032**

JOURNAL OF APPLIED DEVELOPMENTAL PSYCHOLOGY (US/0193-3973). **4593**

JOURNAL OF APPLIED ECOLOGY, THE (UK/0021-8901). **2217**

JOURNAL OF APPLIED ECONOMETRICS (CHICHESTER, ENGLAND) (UK/0883-7252). **1592**

JOURNAL OF APPLIED ELECTROCHEMISTRY (UK/0021-891X). **1034**

JOURNAL OF APPLIED ENTOMOLOGY 1986 (GW/0931-2048). **5610**

JOURNAL OF APPLIED GEOPHYSICS (NE/0926-9851). **1407**

JOURNAL OF APPLIED GERONTOLOGY (US/0733-4648). **3753**

JOURNAL OF APPLIED MATHEMATICS AND MECHANICS (UK/0021-8928). **4428**

JOURNAL OF APPLIED MECHANICS (US/0021-8936). **2117**

JOURNAL OF APPLIED MECHANICS AND TECHNICAL PHYSICS (US/0021-8944). **2117**

JOURNAL OF APPLIED METEOROLOGY (1988) (US/0894-8763). **1426**

JOURNAL OF APPLIED NUTRITION, THE (US/0021-8960). **4192**

JOURNAL OF APPLIED PHILOSOPHY (UK/0264-3758). **4350**

JOURNAL OF APPLIED PHYCOLOGY (NE/0921-8971). **514**

JOURNAL OF APPLIED PHYSICS (US/0021-8979). **4408**

JOURNAL OF APPLIED PHYSIOLOGY (1985) (US/8750-7587). **581**

JOURNAL OF APPLIED POLYMER SCIENCE (US/0021-8995). **2013**

JOURNAL OF APPLIED POLYMER SCIENCE. APPLIED POLYMER SYMPOSIUM (US/0271-9460). **1042**

JOURNAL OF APPLIED PROBABILITY (UK/0021-9002). **3511**

JOURNAL OF APPLIED PSYCHOLOGY (US/0021-9010). **4593**

JOURNAL OF APPLIED SOCIAL PSYCHOLOGY (US/0021-9029). **4594**

JOURNAL OF APPLIED SPECTROSCOPY (US/0021-9037). **1016**

JOURNAL OF APPLIED STATISTICS (UK/0266-4763). **5329**

JOURNAL OF APPLIED TOXICOLOGY (UK/0260-437X). **3981**

JOURNAL OF APPROXIMATION THEORY (US/0021-9045). **3512**

JOURNAL OF AQUACULTURE IN THE TROPICS (II/0970-0846). **2306**

JOURNAL OF AQUARICULTURE & AQUATIC SCIENCES (US/0733-2076). **460**

JOURNAL OF AQUATIC ANIMAL HEALTH (US/0899-7659). **2306**

JOURNAL OF AQUATIC ECOSYSTEM HEALTH (NE/0925-1014). **555**

JOURNAL OF ARABIC LITERATURE (NE/0085-2376). **3399**

JOURNAL OF ARCHAEOLOGICAL SCIENCE (UK/0305-4403). **271**

JOURNAL OF ARCHITECTURAL AND PLANNING RESEARCH (US/0738-0895). **301**

JOURNAL OF ARID ENVIRONMENTS (UK/0140-1963). **1357**

JOURNAL OF ART & DESIGN EDUCATION (UK/0260-9991). **354**

JOURNAL OF ARTHROPLASTY, THE (US/0883-5403). **3966**

JOURNAL OF ARTIFICIAL INTELLIGENCE IN EDUCATION (US/1043-1020). **1213**

JOURNAL OF ARTS MANAGEMENT AND LAW, THE (US/0733-5113). **386**

JOURNAL OF ASIAN AND AFRICAN STUDIES (LEIDEN) (NE/0021-9096). **2769**

JOURNAL OF ASIAN HISTORY (GW/0021-910X). **2655**

JOURNAL OF ASIAN PACIFIC COMMUNICATION (UK/0957-6851). **1114**

JOURNAL OF ASSISTED REPRODUCTION AND GENETICS (US/1058-0468). **3763**

JOURNAL OF ASTHMA, THE (US/0277-0903). **3950**

JOURNAL OF ATMOSPHERIC AND OCEANIC TECHNOLOGY (US/0739-0572). **1426**

JOURNAL OF ATMOSPHERIC AND TERRESTRIAL PHYSICS (UK/0021-9169). **1407**

JOURNAL OF ATMOSPHERIC CHEMISTRY (NE/0167-7764). **1426**

JOURNAL OF AUDIOVISUAL MEDIA IN MEDICINE, THE (UK/0140-511X). **3593**

JOURNAL OF AUTISM AND DEVELOPMENTAL DISORDERS (US/0162-3257). **3928**

JOURNAL OF AUTOIMMUNITY (UK/0896-8411). **3673**

JOURNAL OF AUTOMATED REASONING (NE/0168-7433). **1220**

JOURNAL OF AUTOMATIC CHEMISTRY, THE (UK/0142-0453). **1016**

JOURNAL OF AUTONOMIC PHARMACOLOGY (UK/0144-1795). **4310**

JOURNAL OF BACK AND MUSCULOSKELETAL REHABILITATION (US/1053-8127). **3805**

JOURNAL OF BACTERIOLOGY (US/0021-9193). **564**

JOURNAL OF BANK TAXATION, THE (US/0895-4720). **793**

JOURNAL OF BANKING & FINANCE (NE/0378-4266). **793**

JOURNAL OF BANKING & FINANCE MICROFORM (SZ/0378-4266). **793**

JOURNAL OF BASIC MICROBIOLOGY (GW/0233-111X). **564**

JOURNAL OF BEHAVIOR THERAPY AND EXPERIMENTAL PSYCHIATRY (UK/0005-7916). **3928**

JOURNAL OF BEHAVIORAL DECISION MAKING (UK/0894-3257). **4594**

JOURNAL OF BEHAVIORAL EDUCATION (US/1053-0819). **1880**

JOURNAL OF BEHAVIORAL MEDICINE (US/0160-7715). **4594**

JOURNAL OF BIOACTIVE AND COMPATIBLE POLYMERS (US/0883-9115). **980**

JOURNAL OF BIOCHEMICAL AND BIOPHYSICAL METHODS (NE/0165-022X). **489**

JOURNAL OF BIOCHEMICAL TOXICOLOGY (US/0887-2082). **3981**

JOURNAL OF BIOCHEMISTRY (TOKYO) (JA/0021-924X). **489**

JOURNAL OF BIOENERGETICS AND BIOMEMBRANES (US/0145-479X). **565**

JOURNAL OF BIOGEOGRAPHY (UK/0305-0270). **2567**

JOURNAL OF BIOLOGICAL CHEMISTRY, THE (US/0021-9258). **489**

JOURNAL OF BIOLOGICAL PHYSICS (NE/0092-0606). **495**

JOURNAL OF BIOLOGICAL RHYTHMS (US/0748-7304). **460**

JOURNAL OF BIOLUMINESCENCE AND CHEMILUMINESCENCE (UK/0884-3996). **495**

JOURNAL OF BIOMATERIALS APPLICATIONS (US/0885-3282). **3694**

JOURNAL OF BIOMECHANICAL ENGINEERING (US/0148-0731). **3694**

JOURNAL OF BIOMECHANICS (US/0021-9290). **582**

JOURNAL OF BIOMEDICAL ENGINEERING (UK/0141-5425). **3694**

JOURNAL OF BIOMEDICAL MATERIALS RESEARCH (US/0021-9304). **3593**

JOURNAL OF BIOMOLECULAR NMR (NE/0925-2738). **461**

JOURNAL OF BIOMOLECULAR STRUCTURE & DYNAMICS (US/0739-1102). **461**

JOURNAL OF BIOPHARMACEUTICAL STATISTICS (US/1054-3406). **4310**

JOURNAL OF BLACK STUDIES (US/0021-9347). **2266**

JOURNAL OF BRITISH STUDIES, THE (US/0021-9371). **2694**

JOURNAL OF BRYOLOGY (UK/0373-6687). **515**

JOURNAL OF BURN CARE & REHABILITATION, THE (US/0273-8481). **3594**

JOURNAL OF BUSINESS & ECONOMIC STATISTICS (US/0735-0015). **1534**

JOURNAL OF BUSINESS & INDUSTRIAL MARKETING, THE (US/0885-8624). **927**

JOURNAL OF BUSINESS AND PSYCHOLOGY (US/0889-3268). **4594**

JOURNAL OF BUSINESS (CHICAGO, ILL.), THE (US/0021-9398). **686**

JOURNAL OF BUSINESS ETHICS (NE/0167-4544). **2251**

JOURNAL OF BUSINESS FINANCE & ACCOUNTING (UK/0306-686X). **746**

JOURNAL OF BUSINESS FORECASTING METHODS & SYSTEMS, THE (US/0278-6087). **1592**

JOURNAL OF BUSINESS LAW, THE (UK/0021-9460). **3101**

JOURNAL OF BUSINESS RESEARCH (US/0148-2963). **686**

JOURNAL OF BUSINESS VENTURING (US/0883-9026). **686**

JOURNAL OF CANADIAN STUDIES (CN/0021-9495). **2740**

JOURNAL OF CANCER EDUCATION, THE (US/0885-8195). **3819**

JOURNAL OF CANCER RESEARCH AND CLINICAL ONCOLOGY (GW/0171-5216). **3819**

JOURNAL OF CARBOHYDRATE CHEMISTRY (US/0732-8303). **1042**

JOURNAL OF CARDIOPULMONARY REHABILITATION (US/0883-9212). **3706**

JOURNAL OF CARDIOVASCULAR NURSING, THE (US/0889-4655). **3858**

JOURNAL OF CARDIOVASCULAR PHARMACOLOGY (US/0160-2446). **4310**

JOURNAL OF CAREER DEVELOPMENT (US/0894-8453). **4206**

JOURNAL OF CARIBBEAN STUDIES (US/0190-2008). **2741**

JOURNAL OF CARNIOMANDIBULAR DISORDERS, THE (US/0890-2739). **3834**

JOURNAL OF CASH MANAGEMENT (US/0731-1281). **873**

JOURNAL OF CATALYSIS (US/0021-9517). **1053**

JOURNAL OF CELL BIOLOGY, THE (US/0021-9525). **537**

JOURNAL OF CELLULAR BIOCHEMISTRY (US/0730-2312). **489**

JOURNAL OF CELLULAR PHYSIOLOGY (US/0021-9541). **582**

JOURNAL OF CELLULAR PLASTICS (US/0021-955X). **4455**

JOURNAL OF CEREAL SCIENCE (UK/0733-5210). **176**

JOURNAL OF CEREBRAL BLOOD FLOW AND METABOLISM (US/0271-678X). **582**

JOURNAL OF CHEMICAL AND ENGINEERING DATA (US/0021-9568). **2014**

JOURNAL OF CHEMICAL ECOLOGY (US/0098-0331). **2217**

JOURNAL OF CHEMICAL EDUCATION (US/0021-9584). **980**

JOURNAL OF CHEMICAL ENGINEERING OF JAPAN (JA/0021-9592). **2014**

JOURNAL OF CHEMICAL INDUSTRY AND ENGINEERING (CHINA) (CC/1000-9027). **2014**

JOURNAL OF CHEMICAL INFORMATION AND COMPUTER SCIENCES (US/0095-2338). **980**

JOURNAL OF CHEMICAL NEUROANATOMY (UK/0891-0618). **3834**

JOURNAL OF CHEMICAL PHYSICS, THE (US/0021-9606). **4408**

JOURNAL OF CHEMICAL RESEARCH. SYNOPSES (UK/0308-2342). **980**

JOURNAL OF CHEMICAL TECHNOLOGY AND BIOTECHNOLOGY (1986) (UK/0268-2575). **1026**

JOURNAL OF CHEMICAL THERMODYNAMICS, THE (UK/0021-9614). **1054**

JOURNAL OF CHEMICAL VAPOR DEPOSITION (US/1056-7860). **980**

JOURNAL OF CHEMOMETRICS (UK/0886-9383). **980**

JOURNAL OF CHEMOTHERAPY (FLORENCE) (IT/1120-009X). **3594**

JOURNAL OF CHILD AND ADOLESCENT GROUP THERAPY (US/1053-0800). **4594**

JOURNAL OF CHILD AND FAMILY STUDIES (US/1062-1024). **2281**

JOURNAL OF CHILD NEUROLOGY (US/0883-0738). **3904**

JOURNAL OF CHILD PSYCHOLOGY AND PSYCHIATRY AND ALLIED DISCIPLINES (UK/0021-9630). **4594**

JOURNAL OF CHROMATOGRAPHIC SCIENCE (US/0021-9665). **1016**

JOURNAL OF CHROMATOGRAPHY (NE/0021-9673). **1016**

JOURNAL OF CHROMATOGRAPHY. B, BIOMEDICAL APPLICATIONS (NE/0378-4347). **1017**

JOURNAL OF CHROMATOGRAPHY. BIOMEDICAL APPLICATIONS (NE/0378-4347). **980**

JOURNAL OF CHROMATOGRAPHY LIBRARY (NE/0301-4770). **981**

JOURNAL OF CLASSIFICATION (US/0176-4268). **3512**

JOURNAL OF CLEAN TECHNOLOGY AND ENVIRONMENTAL SCIENCES (US/1052-1062). **2175**

JOURNAL OF CLIMATE (US/0894-8755). **1426**

JOURNAL OF CLINICAL AND EXPERIMENTAL GERONTOLOGY (US/0192-1193). **3753**

JOURNAL OF CLINICAL AND EXPERIMENTAL NEUROPSYCHOLOGY (NE/0168-8634). **3834**

JOURNAL OF CLINICAL & LABORATORY IMMUNOLOGY (UK/0141-2760). **3673**

JOURNAL OF CLINICAL ANESTHESIA (US/0952-8180). **3683**

JOURNAL — Copyright Clearance Center Index

JOURNAL OF CLINICAL APHERESIS (US/0733-2459). **3819**

JOURNAL OF CLINICAL ENGINEERING (US/0363-8855). **3694**

JOURNAL OF CLINICAL EPIDEMIOLOGY (UK/0895-4356). **3735**

JOURNAL OF CLINICAL GASTROENTEROLOGY (US/0192-0790). **3746**

JOURNAL OF CLINICAL IMMUNOLOGY (US/0271-9142). **3673**

JOURNAL OF CLINICAL INVESTIGATION, THE (US/0021-9738). **3594**

JOURNAL OF CLINICAL LABORATORY ANALYSIS, THE (US/0887-8013). **3594**

JOURNAL OF CLINICAL MICROBIOLOGY (US/0095-1137). **565**

JOURNAL OF CLINICAL MONITORING (US/0748-1977). **3594**

JOURNAL OF CLINICAL NEURO-OPHTHALMOLOGY (US/0272-846X). **3875**

JOURNAL OF CLINICAL NEUROPHYSIOLOGY (US/0736-0258). **3834**

JOURNAL OF CLINICAL ONCOLOGY (US/0732-183X). **3819**

JOURNAL OF CLINICAL PATHOLOGY (UK/0021-9746). **3895**

JOURNAL OF CLINICAL PERIODONTOLOGY (DK/0303-6979). **1326**

JOURNAL OF CLINICAL PHARMACOLOGY, THE (US/0091-2700). **4310**

JOURNAL OF CLINICAL PHARMACY AND THERAPEUTICS (UK/0269-4727). **4310**

JOURNAL OF CLINICAL PSYCHOPHARMACOLOGY (US/0271-0749). **4310**

JOURNAL OF CLINICAL RESEARCH AND PHARMACOEPIDEMIOLOGY (US/1047-0336). **4311**

JOURNAL OF CLUSTER SCIENCE (US/1040-7278). **981**

JOURNAL OF COASTAL RESEARCH (US/0749-0208). **1357**

JOURNAL OF COATED FABRICS (US/0093-4658). **5353**

JOURNAL OF COGNITIVE NEUROSCIENCE, THE (US/0898-929X). **3835**

JOURNAL OF COGNITIVE PSYCHOTHERAPY, THE (US/0889-8391). **4595**

JOURNAL OF COLD REGIONS ENGINEERING (US/0887-381X). **2025**

JOURNAL OF COLLOID AND INTERFACE SCIENCE (US/0021-9797). **1054**

JOURNAL OF COMBINATORIAL THEORY. SERIES A (US/0097-3165). **3512**

JOURNAL OF COMBINATORIAL THEORY. SERIES B (US/0095-8956). **3512**

JOURNAL OF COMMON MARKET STUDIES (UK/0021-9886). **1569**

JOURNAL OF COMMONWEALTH LITERATURE (UK/0021-9894). **3399**

JOURNAL OF COMMUNICATION (US/0021-9916). **1114**

JOURNAL OF COMMUNICATION DISORDERS (US/0021-9924). **3835**

JOURNAL OF COMMUNICATIONS TECHNOLOGY (US/1047-0492). **1159**

JOURNAL OF COMMUNITY HEALTH (US/0094-5145). **4786**

JOURNAL OF COMPARATIVE ECONOMICS (US/0147-5967). **1592**

JOURNAL OF COMPARATIVE FAMILY STUDIES (CN/0047-2328). **2281**

JOURNAL OF COMPARATIVE LITERATURE & AESTHETICS (II/0252-8169). **354**

JOURNAL OF COMPARATIVE NEUROLOGY (1911) (US/0021-9967). **3835**

JOURNAL OF COMPARATIVE PATHOLOGY (UK/0021-9975). **3895**

JOURNAL OF COMPARATIVE PHYSIOLOGY. A, SENSORY, NEURAL, AND BEHAVIORAL PHYSIOLOGY (GW/0340-7594). **582**

JOURNAL OF COMPARATIVE PHYSIOLOGY. B, BIOCHEMICAL, SYSTEMIC, AND ENVIRONMENTAL PHYSIOLOGY (GW/0174-1578). **582**

JOURNAL OF COMPARATIVE PSYCHOLOGY (1983) (US/0735-7036). **4595**

JOURNAL OF COMPENSATION AND BENEFITS (US/0893-780X). **1682**

JOURNAL OF COMPLEXITY (US/0885-064X). **3512**

JOURNAL OF COMPOSITE MATERIALS (US/0021-9983). **2103**

JOURNAL OF COMPOSITES TECHNOLOGY & RESEARCH (US/0884-6804). **2103**

JOURNAL OF COMPUTATIONAL AND APPLIED MATHEMATICS (NE/0377-0427). **3512**

JOURNAL OF COMPUTATIONAL CHEMISTRY (US/0192-8651). **981**

JOURNAL OF COMPUTATIONAL PHYSICS (US/0021-9991). **4408**

JOURNAL OF COMPUTER AIDED MATERIALS DESIGN (NE/0928-1045). **1191**

JOURNAL OF COMPUTER-AIDED MOLECULAR DESIGN (NE/0920-654X). **1229**

JOURNAL OF COMPUTER AND SYSTEM SCIENCES (US/0022-0000). **1247**

JOURNAL OF COMPUTER ASSISTED LEARNING (UK/0266-4909). **1223**

JOURNAL OF COMPUTER-ASSISTED MICROSCOPY (US/1040-7286). **1223**

JOURNAL OF COMPUTER ASSISTED TOMOGRAPHY (US/0363-8715). **3942**

JOURNAL OF COMPUTER-BASED INSTRUCTION (US/0098-597X). **1223**

JOURNAL OF COMPUTER SCIENCE AND TECHNOLOGY (CC/1000-9000). **1191**

JOURNAL OF COMPUTERS IN MATHEMATICS AND SCIENCE TEACHING, THE (US/0731-9258). **1224**

JOURNAL OF COMPUTING IN CHILDHOOD EDUCATION (US/1043-1055). **1224**

JOURNAL OF COMPUTING IN CIVIL ENGINEERING (US/0887-3801). **2025**

JOURNAL OF CONFLICT RESOLUTION, THE (US/0022-0027). **4527**

JOURNAL OF CONSTRUCTION ENGINEERING AND MANAGEMENT (US/0733-9364). **2025**

JOURNAL OF CONSTRUCTIONAL STEEL RESEARCH (UK/0143-974X). **618**

JOURNAL OF CONSULTING AND CLINICAL PSYCHOLOGY (US/0022-006X). **4595**

JOURNAL OF CONSUMER AFFAIRS, THE (US/0022-0078). **1297**

JOURNAL OF CONSUMER MARKETING, THE (UK/0736-3761). **927**

JOURNAL OF CONSUMER RESEARCH, THE (US/0093-5301). **927**

JOURNAL OF CONSUMER STUDIES AND HOME ECONOMICS (UK/0309-3891). **1298**

JOURNAL OF CONTAMINANT HYDROLOGY (NE/0169-7722). **1415**

JOURNAL OF CONTEMPORARY ETHNOGRAPHY (US/0891-2416). **5249**

JOURNAL OF CONTEMPORARY MATHEMATICAL ANALYSIS (US/1068-3623). **3512**

JOURNAL OF CONTEMPORARY PHYSICS (US/1068-3372). **4408**

JOURNAL OF CONTEMPORARY PSYCHOTHERAPY (US/0022-0116). **4595**

JOURNAL OF CONTINGENCIES AND CRISIS MANAGEMENT (UK/0966-0879). **873**

JOURNAL OF CONTINUING EDUCATION IN THE HEALTH PROFESSIONS, THE (CN/0894-1912). **3594**

JOURNAL OF CONTROLLED RELEASE (NE/0168-3659). **981**

JOURNAL OF COORDINATION CHEMISTRY (US/0095-8972). **981**

JOURNAL OF CORPORATE ACCOUNTING AND FINANCE (US/1044-8136). **746**

JOURNAL OF CORPORATE FINANCE (NE/0929-1199). **793**

JOURNAL OF CORPORATE TAXATION, THE (US/0094-0593). **4734**

JOURNAL OF COST MANAGEMENT FOR THE MANUFACTURING INDUSTRY (US/0899-5141). **873**

JOURNAL OF COUNSELING AND DEVELOPMENT (US/0748-9633). **1913**

JOURNAL OF COUNSELING PSYCHOLOGY (US/0022-0167). **4595**

JOURNAL OF CRANIOFACIAL GENETICS AND DEVELOPMENTAL BIOLOGY (DK/0270-4145). **3805**

JOURNAL OF CRANIOFACIAL GENETICS AND DEVELOPMENTAL BIOLOGY. SUPPLEMENT (US/0890-6661). **582**

JOURNAL OF CRANIOFACIAL SURGERY, THE (CN/1049-2275). **3967**

JOURNAL OF CRIMINAL JUSTICE (US/0047-2352). **3167**

JOURNAL OF CRIMINAL LAW (HERTFORD) (UK/0022-0183). **3107**

JOURNAL OF CRITICAL CARE (US/0883-9441). **3594**

JOURNAL OF CRITICAL ILLNESS, THE (US/1040-0257). **3595**

JOURNAL OF CRYPTOLOGY (US/0933-2790). **3512**

JOURNAL OF CRYSTAL GROWTH (NE/0022-0248). **1032**

JOURNAL OF CRYSTALLOGRAPHIC AND SPECTROSCOPIC RESEARCH (US/0277-8068). **1032**

JOURNAL OF CURRICULUM STUDIES (UK/0022-0272). **1898**

JOURNAL OF CUTANEOUS PATHOLOGY (DK/0303-6987). **3721**

JOURNAL OF DEMOCRACY (US/1045-5736). **4478**

JOURNAL OF DENTAL RESEARCH (US/0022-0345). **1326**

JOURNAL OF DENTISTRY (UK/0300-5712). **1326**

JOURNAL OF DERMATOLOGIC SURGERY AND ONCOLOGY, THE (US/0148-0812). **3967**

JOURNAL OF DERMATOLOGICAL TREATMENT, THE (UK/0954-6634). **3721**

JOURNAL OF DESIGN HISTORY (UK/0952-4649). **2099**

JOURNAL OF DEVELOPING SOCIETIES (NE/0169-796X). **2621**

JOURNAL OF DEVELOPMENT ECONOMICS (NE/0304-3878). **1569**

JOURNAL OF DEVELOPMENTAL AND BEHAVIORAL PEDIATRICS (US/0196-206X). **3904**

JOURNAL OF DEVELOPMENTAL AND PHYSICAL DISABILITIES (US/1056-263X). **4389**

JOURNAL OF DEVELOPMENTAL PHYSIOLOGY (UK/0141-9846). **3763**

JOURNAL OF DIABETES AND ITS COMPLICATIONS (US/1056-8727). **3731**

JOURNAL OF DIAGNOSTIC MEDICAL SONOGRAPHY (US/8756-4793). **3595**

JOURNAL OF DIFFERENTIAL EQUATIONS (US/0022-0396). **3512**

JOURNAL OF DIGITAL IMAGING (US/0897-1889). **3942**

JOURNAL OF DIRECT MARKETING (US/0892-0591). **927**

JOURNAL OF DISPERSION SCIENCE AND TECHNOLOGY (US/0193-2691). **4428**

JOURNAL OF DRUG ISSUES (US/0022-0426). **1346**

JOURNAL OF DYNAMIC SYSTEMS, MEASUREMENT, AND CONTROL (US/0022-0434). **1982**

JOURNAL OF EAST ASIAN AFFAIRS, THE (KO/1010-1608). **2655**

JOURNAL OF ECOLOGY, THE (UK/0022-0477). **515**

JOURNAL OF ECONOMETRICS (NE/0304-4076). **1592**

JOURNAL OF ECONOMIC AND SOCIAL MEASUREMENT (US/0747-9662). **5206**

JOURNAL OF ECONOMIC BEHAVIOR & ORGANIZATION (NE/0167-2681). **1498**

JOURNAL OF ECONOMIC DYNAMICS & CONTROL (NE/0165-1889). **1499**

JOURNAL OF ECONOMIC EDUCATION, THE (US/0022-0485). **1499**

JOURNAL OF ECONOMIC ENTOMOLOGY (US/0022-0493). **5610**

JOURNAL OF ECONOMIC PSYCHOLOGY (NE/0167-4870). **1593**

JOURNAL OF ECONOMIC STUDIES (BRADFORD) (UK/0144-3585). **1499**

JOURNAL OF ECONOMIC SURVEYS (UK/0950-0804). **1570**

JOURNAL OF ECONOMIC THEORY (US/0022-0531). **1593**

JOURNAL OF ECONOMICS AND BUSINESS (US/0148-6195). **1499**

JOURNAL OF ECONOMICS & MANAGEMENT STRATEGY (US/1058-6407). **873**

JOURNAL OF ECONOMICS (VIENNA, AUSTRIA) (AU/0931-8658). **1593**

JOURNAL OF EDUCATION POLICY (UK/0268-0939). **1756**

JOURNAL OF EDUCATIONAL ADMINISTRATION, THE (AT/0022-0639). **1865**

JOURNAL OF EDUCATIONAL MULTIMEDIA AND HYPERMEDIA (US/1055-8896). **1224**

JOURNAL OF EDUCATIONAL PSYCHOLOGY (US/0022-0663). **4596**

JOURNAL OF EDUCATIONAL RESEARCH (WASHINGTON, D.C.), THE (US/0022-0671). **1757**

JOURNAL OF EDUCATIONAL TELEVISION (UK/0260-7417). **1757**

JOURNAL OF EDUCATIONAL THOUGHT (CN/0022-0701). **1757**

JOURNAL OF ELASTICITY (NE/0374-3535). **4428**

JOURNAL OF ELASTOMERS AND PLASTICS, THE (US/0095-2443). **4456**

JOURNAL OF ELECTROANALYTICAL CHEMISTRY AND INTERFACIAL ELECTROCHEMISTRY (NE/0022-0728). **1034**

JOURNAL OF ELECTROCARDIOLOGY (US/0022-0736). **3707**

JOURNAL OF ELECTROMYOGRAPHY AND KINESIOLOGY (UK/1050-6411). **3805**

JOURNAL OF ELECTRON MICROSCOPY (JA/0022-0744). **572**

JOURNAL OF ELECTRON SPECTROSCOPY AND RELATED PHENOMENA (NE/0368-2048). **4435**

JOURNAL OF ELECTRONIC DEFENSE (US/0192-429X). **4048**

JOURNAL OF ELECTRONIC IMAGING (US/1017-9909). **2068**

JOURNAL OF ELECTRONIC MATERIAL APPLICATIONS (US/0968-2783). **2068**

JOURNAL OF ELECTRONIC MATERIALS (US/0361-5235). **2068**

JOURNAL OF ELECTRONIC PACKAGING (US/1043-7398). **2069**

JOURNAL OF ELECTRONIC TESTING (US/0923-8174). **2069**

JOURNAL OF ELECTRONICS (CHINA) (CC/0217-9822). **2069**

JOURNAL OF ELECTRONICS MANUFACTURING (UK/0960-3131). **2069**

JOURNAL OF ELECTROSTATICS (NE/0304-3886). **2069**

JOURNAL OF EMERGENCY MEDICINE, THE (US/0736-4679). **3725**

JOURNAL OF EMERGENCY NURSING (US/0099-1767). **3858**

JOURNAL OF EMOTIONAL AND BEHAVIORAL DISORDERS (US/1063-4266). **4596**

JOURNAL OF EMPLOYMENT COUNSELING (US/0022-0787). **4206**

JOURNAL OF ENDOCRINOLOGY, THE (UK/0022-0795). **3731**

JOURNAL OF ENDODONTICS (US/0099-2399). **1327**

JOURNAL OF ENERGY ENGINEERING (US/0733-9402). **2118**

JOURNAL OF ENGINEERING AND TECHNOLOGY MANAGEMENT (NE/0923-4748). **1982**

JOURNAL OF ENGINEERING DESIGN (UK/0954-4828). **2099**

JOURNAL OF ENGINEERING FOR GAS TURBINES AND POWER (US/0742-4795). **2118**

JOURNAL OF ENGINEERING FOR INDUSTRY (US/0022-0817). **1982**

JOURNAL OF ENGINEERING MATERIALS AND TECHNOLOGY (US/0094-4289). **2118**

JOURNAL OF ENGINEERING MATHEMATICS (NE/0022-0833). **1982**

JOURNAL OF ENGINEERING MECHANICS (US/0733-9399). **2118**

JOURNAL OF ENGINEERING PHYSICS AND THERMOPHYSICS (US/1062-0125). **4408**

JOURNAL OF ENGLISH AND GERMANIC PHILOLOGY, THE (US/0363-6941). **3290**

JOURNAL OF ENGLISH LINGUISTICS (US/0075-4242). **3290**

JOURNAL OF ENVIRONMENTAL ECONOMICS AND MANAGEMENT (US/0095-0696). **1499**

JOURNAL OF ENVIRONMENTAL EDUCATION, THE (US/0095-8964). **2175**

JOURNAL OF ENVIRONMENTAL ENGINEERING (NEW YORK N.Y.) (US/0733-9372). **2233**

JOURNAL OF ENVIRONMENTAL LAW (UK/0952-8873). **3113**

JOURNAL OF ENVIRONMENTAL MANAGEMENT (UK/0301-4797). **2175**

JOURNAL OF ENVIRONMENTAL PATHOLOGY, TOXICOLOGY AND ONCOLOGY (US/0731-8898). **3819**

JOURNAL OF ENVIRONMENTAL PERMITTING (US/1058-1367). **2987**

JOURNAL OF ENVIRONMENTAL PLANNING AND MANAGEMENT (UK/0964-0568). **2826**

JOURNAL OF ENVIRONMENTAL PSYCHOLOGY (UK/0272-4944). **4596**

JOURNAL OF ENVIRONMENTAL RADIOACTIVITY (UK/0265-931X). **2233**

JOURNAL OF ENVIRONMENTAL REGULATION (US/1055-758X). **2175**

JOURNAL OF ENVIRONMENTAL SCIENCE AND HEALTH. PART A, ENVIRONMENTAL SCIENCE AND ENGINEERING (US/0360-1226). **1982**

JOURNAL OF ENVIRONMENTAL SCIENCE AND HEALTH. PART B, PESTICIDES, FOOD CONTAMINANTS, AND AGRICULTURAL WASTES (US/0360-1234). **2176**

JOURNAL OF ENZYME INHIBITION (SZ/8755-5093). **461**

JOURNAL OF EPIDEMIOLOGY AND COMMUNITY HEALTH (1979) (UK/0143-005X). **3735**

JOURNAL OF EPILEPSY (US/0896-6974). **3835**

JOURNAL OF EQUIPMENT LEASE FINANCING, THE (US/0740-008X). **873**

JOURNAL OF ESSENTIAL OIL RESEARCH, THE (US/1041-2905). **1026**

JOURNAL OF ET NURSING (US/1055-3045). **3858**

JOURNAL OF ETHNOPHARMACOLOGY (SZ/0378-8741). **4311**

JOURNAL OF EUROPEAN INDUSTRIAL TRAINING (UK/0309-0590). **873**

JOURNAL OF EUROPEAN SOCIAL POLICY (UK/0958-9287). **2518**

JOURNAL OF EUROPEAN STUDIES (UK/0047-2441). **2694**

JOURNAL OF EVOLUTIONARY BIOCHEMISTRY AND PHYSIOLOGY (US/0022-0930). **582**

JOURNAL OF EVOLUTIONARY BIOLOGY (SZ/1010-061X). **548**

JOURNAL OF EVOLUTIONARY ECONOMICS (GW/0936-9937). **1593**

JOURNAL OF EXPERIMENTAL & THEORETICAL ARTIFICIAL INTELLIGENCE (UK/0952-813X). **1214**

JOURNAL OF EXPERIMENTAL AND THEORETICAL PHYSICS (US/1063-7761). **4409**

JOURNAL OF EXPERIMENTAL BOTANY (UK/0022-0957). **515**

JOURNAL OF EXPERIMENTAL CHILD PSYCHOLOGY (US/0022-0965). **4596**

JOURNAL OF EXPERIMENTAL EDUCATION, THE (US/0022-0973). **1898**

JOURNAL OF EXPERIMENTAL MARINE BIOLOGY AND ECOLOGY (NE/0022-0981). **555**

JOURNAL OF EXPERIMENTAL MEDICINE, THE (US/0022-1007). **3673**

JOURNAL OF EXPERIMENTAL PSYCHOLOGY : ANIMAL BEHAVIOR PROCESSES (US/0097-7403). **4596**

JOURNAL OF EXPERIMENTAL PSYCHOLOGY : GENERAL (US/0096-3445). **4596**

JOURNAL OF EXPERIMENTAL PSYCHOLOGY : HUMAN PERCEPTION AND PERFORMANCE (US/0096-1523). **4597**

JOURNAL OF EXPERIMENTAL PSYCHOLOGY. LEARNING, MEMORY, AND COGNITION (US/0278-7393). **4597**

JOURNAL OF EXPERIMENTAL PSYCHOLOGY. LEARNING, MEMORY, AND COGNITION [MICROFORM] (US/0278-7393). **4597**

JOURNAL OF EXPERIMENTAL SOCIAL PSYCHOLOGY (US/0022-1031). **4597**

JOURNAL OF EXPERIMENTAL ZOOLOGY, THE (US/0022-104X). **5587**

JOURNAL OF EXPOSURE ANALYSIS AND ENVIRONMENTAL EPIDEMIOLOGY (US/1053-4245). **2176**

JOURNAL OF FAMILY AND ECONOMIC ISSUES (US/1058-0476). **2281**

JOURNAL OF FAMILY ISSUES (US/0192-513X). **2282**

JOURNAL OF FAMILY PRACTICE, THE (US/0094-3509). **3738**

JOURNAL OF FAMILY PSYCHOLOGY (US/0893-3200). **4597**

JOURNAL OF FAMILY THERAPY (UK/0163-4445). **3928**

JOURNAL OF FAMILY VIOLENCE (US/0885-7482). **2282**

JOURNAL OF FINANCE (NEW YORK), THE (US/0022-1082). **794**

JOURNAL OF FINANCIAL ECONOMICS (NE/0304-405X). **794**

JOURNAL OF FINANCIAL INTERMEDIATION (US/1042-9573). **904**

JOURNAL OF FINANCIAL SERVICES RESEARCH (US/0920-8550). **794**

JOURNAL OF FIRE SCIENCES (US/0734-9041). **2291**

JOURNAL OF FISH BIOLOGY (UK/0022-1112). **2306**

JOURNAL OF FISH DISEASES (UK/0140-7775). **2306**

JOURNAL OF FLOW VISUALIZATION AND IMAGE PROCESSING (US/1065-3090). **2091**

JOURNAL OF FLUENCY DISORDERS (US/0094-730X). **3595**

JOURNAL OF FLUID CONTROL, THE (US/8755-8564). **2091**

JOURNAL OF FLUIDS AND STRUCTURES (UK/0889-9746). **2092**

JOURNAL OF FLUIDS ENGINEERING (US/0098-2202). **2092**

JOURNAL OF FLUORESCENCE (US/1053-0509). **4435**

JOURNAL OF FLUORINE CHEMISTRY (SZ/0022-1139). **981**

JOURNAL OF FOETAL MEDICINE (IT/0392-9507). **3763**

JOURNAL OF FOLKLORE RESEARCH (US/0737-7037). **2321**

JOURNAL OF FOOD COMPOSITION AND ANALYSIS (US/0889-1575). **1026**

JOURNAL OF FOOD ENGINEERING (UK/0260-8774). **2346**

JOURNAL OF FOOD SCIENCE (US/0022-1147). **2346**

JOURNAL OF FORECASTING (UK/0277-6693). **5249**

JOURNAL OF FORENSIC PSYCHIATRY, THE (UK/0958-5184). **3928**

JOURNAL OF FORENSIC SCIENCES (US/0022-1198). **3741**

JOURNAL OF FORTH APPLICATION AND RESEARCH, THE (US/0738-2022). **1279**

JOURNAL OF FRICTION AND WEAR (US/1068-3666). **1982**

JOURNAL OF FUNCTIONAL ANALYSIS (US/0022-1236). **3513**

JOURNAL OF FUSION ENERGY (US/0164-0313). **1949**

JOURNAL OF FUTURES MARKETS, THE (US/0270-7314). **904**

JOURNAL OF GAMBLING STUDIES (US/1050-5350). **5292**

JOURNAL OF GARDEN HISTORY (UK/0144-5170). **2421**

JOURNAL OF GASTROENTEROLOGY AND HEPATOLOGY (AT/0815-9319). **3747**

JOURNAL OF GASTROINTESTINAL MOTILITY (US/1043-4518). **3747**

JOURNAL OF GENERAL CHEMISTRY OF THE USSR (US/0022-1279). **981**

JOURNAL OF GENERAL EDUCATION (UNIVERSITY PARK, PA.), THE (US/0021-3667). **1757**

JOURNAL OF GENERAL INTERNAL MEDICINE (US/0884-8734). **3798**

JOURNAL OF GENERAL MICROBIOLOGY, THE (UK/0022-1287). **565**

JOURNAL OF GENERAL PHYSIOLOGY, THE (US/0022-1295). **582**

JOURNAL OF GENERAL PSYCHOLOGY, THE (US/0022-1309). **4597**

JOURNAL OF GENERAL VIROLOGY, THE (UK/0022-1317). **565**

JOURNAL OF GENETIC PSYCHOLOGY, THE (US/0022-1325). **4597**

JOURNAL OF GEOCHEMICAL EXPLORATION (NE/0375-6742). **2141**

JOURNAL OF GEODYNAMICS (UK/0264-3707). **1384**

JOURNAL OF GEOGRAPHY IN HIGHER EDUCATION (UK/0309-8265). **2567**

JOURNAL OF GEOLOGY, THE (US/0022-1376). **1385**

JOURNAL OF GEOMETRY (SZ/0047-2468). **3513**

JOURNAL OF GEOMETRY AND PHYSICS (NE/0393-0440). **4409**

JOURNAL OF GEOPHYSICAL RESEARCH (US/0148-0227). **1407**

JOURNAL OF GEOTECHNICAL ENGINEERING (US/0733-9410). **1385**

JOURNAL OF GERIATRIC PSYCHIATRY AND NEUROLOGY (US/0891-9887). **3753**

JOURNAL OF GERONTOLOGICAL NURSING (US/0098-9134). **3858**

JOURNAL OF GERONTOLOGICAL NURSING (US/0098-9134). **3858**

JOURNAL OF GLOBAL OPTIMIZATION : AN INTERNATIONAL JOURNAL DEALING WITH THEORETICAL AND COMPUTATIONAL ASPECTS OF SEEKING GLOBAL OPTIMA AND THEIR APPLICATIONS IN SCIENCE, MANAGEMENT AND ENGINEERING (NE/0925-5001). **3513**

JOURNAL OF GRAPH THEORY (US/0364-9024). **3513**

JOURNAL OF GROUP PSYCHOTHERAPY, PSYCHODRAMA AND SOCIOMETRY (US/0731-1273). **3929**

JOURNAL OF GUIDANCE, CONTROL, AND DYNAMICS (US/0731-5090). **26**

JOURNAL OF HAND SURGERY (ST. LOUIS, MO.), THE (US/0363-5023). **3967**

JOURNAL OF HAND THERAPY (US/0894-1130). **4380**

JOURNAL OF HARD MATERIALS (UK/0954-027X). **5118**

JOURNAL OF HAZARDOUS MATERIALS (NE/0304-3894). **2234**

JOURNAL OF HEAD TRAUMA REHABILITATION, THE (US/0885-9701). **4380**

JOURNAL OF HEALTH CARE BENEFITS (US/1057-5073). **2885**

JOURNAL

JOURNAL OF HEALTH CARE MARKETING (US/0737-3252). **927**

JOURNAL OF HEALTH ECONOMICS (NE/0167-6296). **1499**

JOURNAL OF HEALTH POLITICS, POLICY AND LAW (US/0361-6878). **2987**

JOURNAL OF HEART AND LUNG TRANSPLANTATION, THE (US/1053-2498). **3967**

JOURNAL OF HEAT TRANSFER (US/0022-1481). **1983**

JOURNAL OF HEAT TREATING (US/0190-9177). **4006**

JOURNAL OF HEPATOLOGY (NE/0168-8278). **3798**

JOURNAL OF HEREDITY, THE (US/0022-1503). **548**

JOURNAL OF HETEROCYCLIC CHEMISTRY (US/0022-152X). **1042**

JOURNAL OF HIGH RESOLUTION CHROMATOGRAPHY : HRC (GW/0935-6304). **1017**

JOURNAL OF HIGH TECHNOLOGY MANAGEMENT RESEARCH (US/1047-8310). **1614**

JOURNAL OF HIGHER EDUCATION (COLUMBUS), THE (US/0022-1546). **1833**

JOURNAL OF HISTOCHEMISTRY AND CYTOCHEMISTRY, THE (US/0022-1554). **537**

JOURNAL OF HISTORICAL GEOGRAPHY (UK/0305-7488). **2567**

JOURNAL OF HISTORICAL SOCIOLOGY (UK/0952-1909). **5249**

JOURNAL OF HOME HEALTH CARE PRACTICE (US/0897-8018). **5292**

JOURNAL OF HOSPITAL INFECTION, THE (US/0195-6701). **3714**

JOURNAL OF HOUSING ECONOMICS (US/1051-1377). **2826**

JOURNAL OF HUMAN EVOLUTION (UK/0047-2484). **239**

JOURNAL OF HUMAN HYPERTENSION (UK/0950-9240). **3707**

JOURNAL OF HUMAN LACTATION (US/0890-3344). **3763**

JOURNAL OF HUMAN MOVEMENT STUDIES (UK/0306-7297). **583**

JOURNAL OF HUMAN MUSCLE PERFORMANCE (US/1053-2137). **3805**

JOURNAL OF HUMAN NUTRITION AND DIETETICS (UK/0952-3871). **4193**

JOURNAL OF HUMAN RESOURCES, THE (US/0022-166X). **1914**

JOURNAL OF HUMANISTIC EDUCATION AND DEVELOPMENT, THE (US/0735-6846). **1898**

JOURNAL OF HUMANISTIC PSYCHOLOGY, THE (US/0022-1678). **4597**

JOURNAL OF HYDRAULIC ENGINEERING (NEW YORK, N.Y.) (US/0733-9429). **2092**

JOURNAL OF HYDROLOGY (AMSTERDAM) (NE/0022-1694). **1416**

JOURNAL OF HYDROLOGY, NEW ZEALAND (NZ/0022-1708). **1416**

JOURNAL OF HYPERTENSION (US/0263-6352). **3707**

JOURNAL OF ICHTHYOLOGY (US/0032-9452). **2307**

JOURNAL OF IMMUNOASSAY (US/0197-1522). **3673**

JOURNAL OF IMMUNOLOGICAL METHODS (NE/0022-1759). **3673**

JOURNAL OF IMMUNOLOGY (1950), THE (US/0022-1767). **3673**

JOURNAL OF IMMUNOTHERAPY (US/1053-8550). **3674**

JOURNAL OF INCLUSION PHENOMENA AND MOLECULAR RECOGNITION IN CHEMISTRY (NE/0923-0750). **1054**

JOURNAL OF INDIAN PHILOSOPHY (NE/0022-1791). **4350**

JOURNAL OF INDIVIDUAL PSYCHOLOGY (US/0022-1805). **4597**

JOURNAL OF INDUSTRIAL ECONOMICS, THE (UK/0022-1821). **1614**

JOURNAL OF INDUSTRIAL IRRADIATION TECHNOLOGY (US/0735-7923). **981**

JOURNAL OF INDUSTRIAL MICROBIOLOGY (NE/0169-4146). **565**

JOURNAL OF INFECTION, THE (UK/0163-4453). **3714**

JOURNAL OF INFECTIOUS DISEASES, THE (US/0022-1899). **3714**

JOURNAL OF INFORMATION & OPTIMIZATION SCIENCES (II/0252-2667). **3513**

JOURNAL OF INFORMATION PROCESSING (JA/0387-6101). **1260**

JOURNAL OF INFORMATION RECORDING MATERIALS (1985) (GW/0863-0453). **4371**

JOURNAL OF INFORMATION SCIENCE (NE/0165-5515). **3220**

JOURNAL OF INFORMATION SYSTEMS (UK/0959-2954). **1248**

JOURNAL OF INFORMATION TECHNOLOGY : JIT (UK/0268-3962). **1192**

JOURNAL OF INHERITED METABOLIC DISEASE (UK/0141-8955). **3798**

JOURNAL OF INORGANIC AND ORGANOMETALLIC POLYMERS (US/1053-0495). **981**

JOURNAL OF INORGANIC BIOCHEMISTRY (US/0162-0134). **489**

JOURNAL OF INSECT BEHAVIOR (US/0892-7553). **5610**

JOURNAL OF INSECT PHYSIOLOGY (UK/0022-1910). **5610**

JOURNAL OF INSTITUTIONAL AND THEORETICAL ECONOMICS : JITE (GW/0932-4569). **5206**

JOURNAL OF INTEGRATIVE AND ECLECTIC PSYCHOTHERAPY (US/0729-8579). **3929**

JOURNAL OF INTELLIGENT & ROBOTIC SYSTEMS (NE/0921-0296). **1220**

JOURNAL OF INTELLIGENT INFORMATION SYSTEMS: INTEGRATING ARTIFICIAL INTELLIGENCE AND DATABASE TECHNOLOGIES (US/0925-9902). **1214**

JOURNAL OF INTELLIGENT MANUFACTURING (UK/0956-5515). **1214**

JOURNAL OF INTELLIGENT MATERIAL SYSTEMS AND STRUCTURES (US/1045-389X). **5118**

JOURNAL OF INTENSIVE CARE MEDICINE (US/0885-0666). **3595**

JOURNAL OF INTERACTIVE INSTRUCTION DEVELOPMENT (US/1040-0370). **1192**

JOURNAL OF INTERAMERICAN STUDIES AND WORLD AFFAIRS (US/0022-1937). **4527**

JOURNAL OF INTERDISCIPLINARY CYCLE RESEARCH (NE/0022-1945). **461**

JOURNAL OF INTERDISCIPLINARY ECONOMICS (UK/0260-1079). **1499**

JOURNAL OF INTERDISCIPLINARY HISTORY, THE (US/0022-1953). **2621**

JOURNAL OF INTERNAL MEDICINE (UK/0954-6820). **3798**

JOURNAL OF INTERNATIONAL ACCOUNTING AUDITING & TAXATION (US/1061-9518). **747**

JOURNAL OF INTERNATIONAL ARBITRATION (SZ/0255-8106). **3131**

JOURNAL OF INTERNATIONAL BANKING LAW (UK/0267-937X). **3087**

JOURNAL OF INTERNATIONAL BUSINESS STUDIES (CN/0047-2506). **687**

JOURNAL OF INTERNATIONAL DEVELOPMENT (UK/0954-1748). **1500**

JOURNAL OF INTERNATIONAL ECONOMICS (NE/0022-1996). **1637**

JOURNAL OF INTERNATIONAL FINANCIAL MANAGEMENT & ACCOUNTING (UK/0954-1314). **747**

JOURNAL OF INTERNATIONAL MEDICAL RESEARCH, THE (UK/0300-0605). **3595**

JOURNAL OF INTERNATIONAL MONEY AND FINANCE (UK/0261-5606). **795**

JOURNAL OF INTERNATIONAL TAXATION (US/1049-6378). **4734**

JOURNAL OF INTERPERSONAL VIOLENCE (US/0886-2605). **5292**

JOURNAL OF INTERVENTIONAL RADIOLOGY (UK/0268-0882). **3942**

JOURNAL OF INTRAVENOUS NURSING (US/0896-5846). **3858**

JOURNAL OF INVERTEBRATE PATHOLOGY (US/0022-2011). **5611**

JOURNAL OF INVESTIGATIVE DERMATOLOGY, THE (US/0022-202X). **3721**

JOURNAL OF INVESTIGATIVE SURGERY (US/0894-1939). **3967**

JOURNAL OF IRREPRODUCIBLE RESULTS, THE (US/0022-2038). **5118**

JOURNAL OF IRRIGATION AND DRAINAGE ENGINEERING (US/0733-9437). **2092**

JOURNAL OF ISLAMIC STUDIES (OXFORD, ENGLAND) (UK/0955-2340). **5043**

JOURNAL OF JAPANESE TRADE & INDUSTRY (JA/0285-9556). **687**

JOURNAL OF JASTRO : THE OFFICIAL JOURNAL OF THE JAPANESE SOCIETY FOR THERAPEUTIC RADIOLOGY AND ONCOLOGY, THE (JA/1040-9564). **3819**

JOURNAL OF JEWISH THOUGHT & PHILOSOPHY, THE (SZ/1053-699X). **5050**

JOURNAL OF LABELLED COMPOUNDS & RADIOPHARMACEUTICALS (UK/0362-4803). **1054**

JOURNAL OF LABOR ECONOMICS (US/0734-306X). **1500**

JOURNAL OF LABOR RESEARCH (US/0195-3613). **1682**

JOURNAL OF LABORATORY AND CLINICAL MEDICINE, THE (US/0022-2143). **3595**

JOURNAL OF LANGUAGE AND SOCIAL PSYCHOLOGY (US/0261-927X). **3290**

JOURNAL OF LASER APPLICATIONS (US/1042-346X). **4435**

JOURNAL OF LATIN AMERICAN STUDIES (UK/0022-216X). **2741**

JOURNAL OF LAW AND ETHICS IN DENTISTRY (US/0894-8879). **1327**

JOURNAL OF LAW AND SOCIETY (UK/0263-323X). **2988**

JOURNAL OF LAW, ECONOMICS & ORGANIZATION (US/8756-6222). **2988**

JOURNAL OF LEARNING DISABILITIES (US/0022-2194). **1880**

JOURNAL OF LEGAL MEDICINE (CHICAGO. 1979), THE (US/0194-7648). **3741**

JOURNAL OF LEISURABILITY (1980) (CN/0711-222X). **4389**

JOURNAL OF LEUKOCYTE BIOLOGY (US/0741-5400). **3799**

JOURNAL OF LIBERTARIAN STUDIES, THE (US/0363-2873). **5206**

JOURNAL OF LIGHT & VISUAL ENVIRONMENT (JA/0387-8805). **4436**

JOURNAL OF LIGHTWAVE TECHNOLOGY (US/0733-8724). **4436**

JOURNAL OF LINGUISTICS (UK/0022-2267). **3290**

JOURNAL OF LIPID MEDIATORS (NE/0921-8319). **1042**

JOURNAL OF LIPOSOME RESEARCH (US/0898-2104). **538**

JOURNAL OF LIQUID CHROMATOGRAPHY (US/0148-3919). **1017**

JOURNAL OF LITERARY SEMANTICS (NE/0341-7638). **3290**

JOURNAL OF LOGIC AND COMPUTATION (UK/0955-792X). **1214**

JOURNAL OF LOGIC PROGRAMMING, THE (US/0743-1066). **1280**

JOURNAL OF LONG TERM CARE ADMINISTRATION, THE (US/0093-4445). **3787**

JOURNAL OF LONG-TERM EFFECTS OF MEDICAL IMPLANTS (US/1050-6934). **3595**

JOURNAL OF LOSS PREVENTION IN THE PROCESS INDUSTRIES (UK/0950-4230). **2099**

JOURNAL OF LOW FREQUENCY NOISE AND VIBRATION (UK/0263-0923). **2234**

JOURNAL OF LOW TEMPERATURE PHYSICS (US/0022-2291). **4409**

JOURNAL OF LUMINESCENCE (NE/0022-2313). **4436**

JOURNAL OF MACHINERY MANUFACTURE AND RELIABILITY (US/1052-6188). **2118**

JOURNAL OF MACROECONOMICS (US/0164-0704). **1500**

JOURNAL OF MACROMOLECULAR SCIENCE. PHYSICS (US/0022-2348). **4409**

JOURNAL OF MACROMOLECULAR SCIENCE. PURE AND APPLIED CHEMISTRY (US/1060-1325). **1042**

JOURNAL OF MACROMOLECULAR SCIENCE. REVIEWS IN MACROMOLECULAR CHEMISTRY AND PHYSICS (US/0736-6574). **981**

JOURNAL OF MAGNETIC RESONANCE. SERIES A (US/1064-1858). **4444**

JOURNAL OF MAGNETIC RESONANCE. SERIES B (US/1064-1866). **4444**

JOURNAL OF MAGNETISM AND MAGNETIC MATERIALS (NE/0304-8853). **4444**

JOURNAL OF MANAGEMENT (US/0149-2063). **873**

JOURNAL OF MANAGEMENT CONSULTING (AMSTERDAM) (US/0168-7778). **873**

JOURNAL OF MANAGEMENT DEVELOPMENT, THE (UK/0262-1711). **943**

JOURNAL OF MANAGEMENT IN ENGINEERING (US/0742-597X). **1983**

JOURNAL OF MANAGEMENT STUDIES, THE (UK/0022-2380). **874**

JOURNAL OF MANAGERIAL ISSUES (US/1045-3695). **874**

JOURNAL OF MANAGERIAL PSYCHOLOGY (UK/0268-3946). **4598**

JOURNAL OF MANIPULATIVE AND PHYSIOLOGICAL THERAPEUTICS (US/0161-4754). **4380**

JOURNAL OF MANUAL MEDICINE (GW/0935-6339). **3596**

JOURNAL OF MANUFACTURING SYSTEMS (US/0278-6125). **3482**

JOURNAL OF MARINE ENVIRONMENTAL ENGINEERING (SZ/1061-026X). **2176**

JOURNAL OF MARINE SYSTEMS (NE/0924-7963). **1450**

JOURNAL OF MARKETING (US/0022-2429). **928**

JOURNAL OF MATERIALS CHEMISTRY (UK/0959-9428). **981**

JOURNAL OF MATERIALS ENGINEERING (US/0931-7058). **2103**

JOURNAL OF MATERIALS ENGINEERING AND PERFORMANCE (US/1059-9495). **2118**

JOURNAL OF MATERIALS IN CIVIL ENGINEERING (US/0899-1561). **2025**

JOURNAL OF MATERIALS MANUFACTURING AND PROCESSING SCIENCE (US/1062-0656). **3482**

JOURNAL OF MATERIALS PROCESSING TECHNOLOGY (NE/0924-0136). **2103**

JOURNAL OF MATERIALS RESEARCH (US/0884-2914). **2103**

JOURNAL OF MATERIALS SCIENCE (UK/0022-2461). **4006**

JOURNAL OF MATERIALS SCIENCE LETTERS (UK/0261-8028). **2103**

JOURNAL OF MATERIALS SCIENCE. MATERIALS IN ELECTRONICS (UK/0957-4522). **2069**

JOURNAL OF MATERIALS SCIENCE. MATERIALS IN MEDICINE (UK/0957-4530). **3694**

JOURNAL OF MATERNAL-FETAL INVESTIGATION : THE OFFICIAL JOURNAL OF FRENCH SOCIETY OF ULTRASOUND IN MEDICINE AND BIOLOGY ... [ET AL.] (US/0939-6322). **3763**

JOURNAL OF MATHEMATICAL ANALYSIS AND APPLICATIONS (US/0022-247X). **3513**

JOURNAL OF MATHEMATICAL BEHAVIOR, THE (US/0732-3123). **3513**

JOURNAL OF MATHEMATICAL BIOLOGY (AU/0303-6812). **461**

JOURNAL OF MATHEMATICAL ECONOMICS (NE/0304-4068). **1500**

JOURNAL OF MATHEMATICAL PHYSICS (US/0022-2488). **4409**

JOURNAL OF MATHEMATICAL PSYCHOLOGY (US/0022-2496). **4598**

JOURNAL OF MATHEMATICAL SOCIOLOGY, THE (US/0022-250X). **5250**

JOURNAL OF MEDECINE NUCLEAIRE ET BIOPHYSIQUE (FR/0992-3039). **495**

JOURNAL OF MEDICAL AND VETERINARY MYCOLOGY (UK/0268-1218). **575**

JOURNAL OF MEDICAL EDUCATION TECHNOLOGIES (US/1056-2478). **3596**

JOURNAL OF MEDICAL ENGINEERING & TECHNOLOGY (UK/0309-1902). **3694**

JOURNAL OF MEDICAL ENTOMOLOGY (US/0022-2585). **5611**

JOURNAL OF MEDICAL GENETICS (UK/0022-2593). **549**

JOURNAL OF MEDICAL HUMANITIES, THE (US/1041-3545). **3596**

JOURNAL OF MEDICAL MICROBIOLOGY (UK/0022-2615). **565**

JOURNAL OF MEDICAL PRACTICE MANAGEMENT, THE (US/8755-0229). **3914**

JOURNAL OF MEDICAL PRIMATOLOGY (SZ/0047-2565). **5513**

JOURNAL OF MEDICAL SYSTEMS (US/0148-5598). **3787**

JOURNAL OF MEDICAL VIROLOGY (US/0146-6615). **565**

JOURNAL OF MEDICINAL CHEMISTRY (US/0022-2623). **490**

JOURNAL OF MEDICINE AND PHILOSOPHY, THE (NE/0360-5310). **3596**

JOURNAL OF MEDICINE (WESTBURY) (US/0025-7850). **3596**

JOURNAL OF MEDIEVAL AND RENAISSANCE STUDIES, THE (US/0047-2573). **2695**

JOURNAL OF MEDIEVAL HISTORY (NE/0304-4181). **2695**

JOURNAL OF MEDIEVAL HISTORY MICROFORM (SZ/0304-4181). **2695**

JOURNAL OF MEMBRANE BIOLOGY, THE (US/0022-2631). **538**

JOURNAL OF MEMBRANE SCIENCE (NE/0376-7388). **5119**

JOURNAL OF MEMORY AND LANGUAGE (US/0749-596X). **4598**

JOURNAL OF MENTAL HEALTH (UK/0963-8237). **3929**

JOURNAL OF METAMORPHIC GEOLOGY (UK/0263-4929). **1458**

JOURNAL OF MICROBIOLOGICAL METHODS (NE/0167-7012). **566**

JOURNAL OF MICROCOLUMN SEPARATIONS, THE (US/1040-7685). **981**

JOURNAL OF MICROCOMPUTER APPLICATIONS (UK/0745-7138). **1268**

JOURNAL OF MICROELECTROMECHANICAL SYSTEMS (US/1057-7157). **2069**

JOURNAL OF MICROENCAPSULATION (UK/0265-2048). **4311**

JOURNAL OF MICROMECHANICS AND MICROENGINEERING : STRUCTURES, DEVICES, AND SYSTEMS (UK/0960-1317). **2069**

JOURNAL OF MICROSCOPY (OXFORD) (UK/0022-2720). **572**

JOURNAL OF MINING AND GEOLOGY (NR/0022-2763). **2141**

JOURNAL OF MINING SCIENCE (US/1062-7391). **2142**

JOURNAL OF MODERN AFRICAN STUDIES, THE (UK/0022-278X). **2640**

JOURNAL OF MODERN GREEK STUDIES (US/0738-1727). **2695**

JOURNAL OF MODERN HISTORY, THE (US/0022-2801). **2621**

JOURNAL OF MOLECULAR AND CELLULAR CARDIOLOGY (UK/0022-2828). **3707**

JOURNAL OF MOLECULAR BIOLOGY (UK/0022-2836). **461**

JOURNAL OF MOLECULAR CATALYSIS (SZ/0304-5102). **1054**

JOURNAL OF MOLECULAR ENDOCRINOLOGY (UK/0952-5041). **3731**

JOURNAL OF MOLECULAR EVOLUTION (GW/0022-2844). **549**

JOURNAL OF MOLECULAR GRAPHICS (UK/0263-7855). **1234**

JOURNAL OF MOLECULAR LIQUIDS (NE/0167-7322). **982**

JOURNAL OF MOLECULAR NEUROSCIENCE (US/0895-8696). **3835**

JOURNAL OF MOLECULAR SPECTROSCOPY (US/0022-2852). **4436**

JOURNAL OF MOLECULAR STRUCTURE (NE/0022-2860). **1054**

JOURNAL OF MOLECULAR STRUCTURE. THEOCHEM (NE/0166-1280). **1054**

JOURNAL OF MOLLUSCAN STUDIES (UK/0260-1230). **5588**

JOURNAL OF MONETARY ECONOMICS (NE/0304-3932). **1500**

JOURNAL OF MONEY, CREDIT, AND BANKING (US/0022-2879). **795**

JOURNAL OF MORAL EDUCATION (UK/0305-7240). **1758**

JOURNAL OF MORPHOLOGY (1931) (US/0362-2525). **583**

JOURNAL OF MOTOR BEHAVIOR (US/0022-2895). **583**

JOURNAL OF MULTICULTURAL COUNSELING AND DEVELOPMENT (US/0883-8534). **4598**

JOURNAL OF MULTILINGUAL AND MULTICULTURAL DEVELOPMENT (UK/0143-4632). **3291**

JOURNAL OF MULTINATIONAL STRATEGIES, THE (US/1049-7722). **1637**

JOURNAL OF MULTISTATE TAXATION, THE (US/1054-8394). **4734**

JOURNAL OF MULTIVARIATE ANALYSIS (US/0047-259X). **3514**

JOURNAL OF MUSCLE RESEARCH AND CELL MOTILITY (UK/0142-4319). **538**

JOURNAL OF MUSCULOSKELETAL MEDICINE (US/0899-2517). **3805**

JOURNAL OF MUSICOLOGICAL RESEARCH, THE (US/0141-1896). **4126**

JOURNAL OF MUSICOLOGY (ST. JOSEPH, MICH.), THE (US/0277-9269). **4126**

JOURNAL OF MYOCARDIAL ISCHEMIA, THE (US/1045-7984). **3707**

JOURNAL OF NATURAL HISTORY (UK/0022-2933). **4166**

JOURNAL OF NEAR-DEATH STUDIES (US/0891-4494). **4241**

JOURNAL OF NEAR EASTERN STUDIES (US/0022-2968). **3291**

JOURNAL OF NERVOUS AND MENTAL DISEASE, THE (US/0022-3018). **3835**

JOURNAL OF NEURAL TRANSMISSION. GENERAL SECTION : JNT (AU/0300-9564). **3835**

JOURNAL OF NEURO-ONCOLOGY (US/0167-594X). **3819**

JOURNAL OF NEUROBIOLOGY (US/0022-3034). **3835**

JOURNAL OF NEUROCHEMISTRY (US/0022-3042). **3836**

JOURNAL OF NEUROCYTOLOGY (UK/0300-4864). **538**

JOURNAL OF NEUROENDOCRINOLOGY (UK/0953-8194). **3836**

JOURNAL OF NEUROGENETICS (SZ/0167-7063). **549**

JOURNAL OF NEUROIMAGING (US/1051-2284). **3836**

JOURNAL OF NEUROIMMUNOLOGY (NE/0165-5728). **3836**

JOURNAL OF NEUROLINGUISTICS (UK/0911-6044). **3291**

JOURNAL OF NEUROLOGY (GW/0340-5354). **3836**

JOURNAL OF NEUROLOGY, NEUROSURGERY AND PSYCHIATRY (UK/0022-3050). **3836**

JOURNAL OF NEUROPHYSIOLOGY (US/0022-3077). **3836**

JOURNAL OF NEURORADIOLOGY (FR/0150-9861). **3942**

JOURNAL OF NEUROSCIENCE METHODS (NE/0165-0270). **3837**

JOURNAL OF NEUROSCIENCE NURSING, THE (US/0888-0395). **3859**

JOURNAL OF NEUROSCIENCE RESEARCH (US/0360-4012). **3837**

JOURNAL OF NEUROSCIENCE, THE (US/0270-6474). **3836**

JOURNAL OF NEUROSURGICAL ANESTHESIOLOGY (US/0898-4921). **3967**

JOURNAL OF NEW JERSEY POETS (US/0363-4205). **3464**

JOURNAL OF NIH RESEARCH, THE (US/1043-609X). **461**

JOURNAL OF NON-CRYSTALLINE SOLIDS (NE/0022-3093). **2591**

JOURNAL OF NON-EQUILIBRIUM THERMODYNAMICS (GW/0340-0204). **4431**

JOURNAL OF NON-NEWTONIAN FLUID MECHANICS (NE/0377-0257). **2092**

JOURNAL OF NONDESTRUCTIVE EVALUATION (US/0195-9298). **2104**

JOURNAL OF NONLINEAR SCIENCE (US/0938-8974). **5119**

JOURNAL OF NONPARAMETRIC STATISTICS (US/1048-5252). **5329**

JOURNAL OF NONVERBAL BEHAVIOR (US/0191-5886). **4598**

JOURNAL OF NORTHEAST ASIAN STUDIES (US/0738-7997). **4479**

JOURNAL OF NUCLEAR MATERIALS (NE/0022-3115). **2156**

JOURNAL OF NUCLEAR MEDICINE (1978), THE (US/0161-5505). **3848**

JOURNAL OF NUCLEAR MEDICINE TECHNOLOGY (US/0091-4916). **3848**

JOURNAL OF NUCLEAR SCIENCE AND TECHNOLOGY (JA/0022-3131). **2156**

JOURNAL OF NUMBER THEORY (US/0022-314X). **3514**

JOURNAL OF NURSE-MIDWIFERY (US/0091-2182). **3859**

JOURNAL OF NURSING ADMINISTRATION, THE (US/0002-0443). **3859**

JOURNAL OF NURSING CARE QUALITY (US/1057-3631). **3859**

JOURNAL OF NURSING STAFF DEVELOPMENT : JNSD (US/0882-0627). **3859**

JOURNAL OF NUTRITION EDUCATION (US/0022-3182). **4193**

JOURNAL OF NUTRITION, THE (US/0022-3166). **4193**

JOURNAL OF NUTRITIONAL BIOCHEMISTRY, THE (US/0955-2863). **4193**

JOURNAL OF NUTRITIONAL MEDICINE (UK/0955-6664). **4193**

JOURNAL OF OBJECT-ORIENTED PROGRAMMING (US/0896-8438). **1280**

JOURNAL OF OBSTETRICS AND GYNAECOLOGY (UK/0144-3615). **3763**

JOURNAL OF OCCUPATIONAL AND ORGANIZATIONAL PSYCHOLOGY (UK/0963-1798). **4598**

JOURNAL OF OCCUPATIONAL MEDICINE (US/0096-1736). **2864**

JOURNAL OF OCCUPATIONAL REHABILITATION (US/1053-0487). **2864**

JOURNAL OF OFFSHORE MECHANICS AND ARCTIC ENGINEERING (US/0892-7219). **2092**

JOURNAL OF OPERATIONS MANAGEMENT (US/0272-6963). **1614**

JOURNAL OF OPTICAL COMMUNICATIONS (GW/0173-4911). **4436**

JOURNAL OF OPTICS (US/0150-536X). **4436**

JOURNAL OF OPTIMIZATION THEORY AND APPLICATIONS (US/0022-3239). **3514**

JOURNAL — Copyright Clearance Center Index

JOURNAL OF ORAL AND MAXILLOFACIAL SURGERY (US/0278-2391). **3968**

JOURNAL OF ORAL PATHOLOGY & MEDICINE (DK/0904-2512). **1327**

JOURNAL OF ORAL REHABILITATION (UK/0305-182X). **1327**

JOURNAL OF ORGANIC CHEMISTRY (US/0022-3263). **1043**

JOURNAL OF ORGANIC CHEMISTRY OF THE USSR (US/0022-3271). **1043**

JOURNAL OF ORGANIC CHEMISTRY OF THE USSR (US/1070-4280). **1043**

JOURNAL OF ORGANIZATIONAL BEHAVIOR (UK/0894-3796). **4598**

JOURNAL OF ORGANOMETALLIC CHEMISTRY (SZ/0022-328X). **1043**

JOURNAL OF OROFACIAL PAIN (US/1064-6655). **3837**

JOURNAL OF ORTHOPAEDIC AND SPORTS PHYSICAL THERAPY, THE (US/0190-6011). **3882**

JOURNAL OF ORTHOPAEDIC RESEARCH (US/0736-0266). **3882**

JOURNAL OF ORTHOPAEDIC RHEUMATOLOGY (UK/0951-9580). **3882**

JOURNAL OF ORTHOPAEDIC TECHNIQUES (US/1056-7437). **3882**

JOURNAL OF ORTHOPAEDIC TRAUMA (US/0890-5339). **3882**

JOURNAL OF PACKAGING TECHNOLOGY (US/0892-029X). **4219**

JOURNAL OF PAEDIATRICS AND CHILD HEALTH (AT/1034-4810). **3905**

JOURNAL OF PAIN AND SYMPTOM MANAGEMENT (US/0885-3924). **3596**

JOURNAL OF PALEOLIMNOLOGY (NE/0921-2728). **461**

JOURNAL OF PALEONTOLOGY (US/0022-3360). **4227**

JOURNAL OF PALESTINE STUDIES (US/0377-919X). **2655**

JOURNAL OF PALLIATIVE CARE (CN/0825-8597). **5292**

JOURNAL OF PALYNOLOGY (II/0022-3379). **515**

JOURNAL OF PARALLEL AND DISTRIBUTED COMPUTING (US/0743-7315). **1260**

JOURNAL OF PARAPSYCHOLOGY, THE (US/0022-3387). **4241**

JOURNAL OF PARTIAL DIFFERENTIAL EQUATIONS (CC/1000-940X). **3514**

JOURNAL OF PATHOLOGY (UK/0022-3417). **3895**

JOURNAL OF PEDIATRIC GASTROENTEROLOGY AND NUTRITION (US/0277-2116). **3905**

JOURNAL OF PEDIATRIC HEALTH CARE (US/0891-5245). **3905**

JOURNAL OF PEDIATRIC NURSING (US/0882-5963). **3859**

JOURNAL OF PEDIATRIC ONCOLOGY NURSING (US/1043-4542). **3859**

JOURNAL OF PEDIATRIC PSYCHOLOGY (US/0146-8693). **4599**

JOURNAL OF PEDIATRIC SURGERY (US/0022-3468). **3968**

JOURNAL OF PEDIATRICS, THE (US/0022-3476). **3905**

JOURNAL OF PENSION PLANNING AND COMPLIANCE (US/0148-2181). **904**

JOURNAL OF PERFORMANCE OF CONSTRUCTED FACILITIES (US/0887-3828). **2025**

JOURNAL OF PERINATAL & NEONATAL NURSING, THE (US/0893-2190). **3859**

JOURNAL OF PERINATAL MEDICINE (GW/0300-5577). **3764**

JOURNAL OF PERINATOLOGY (US/0743-8346). **3764**

JOURNAL OF PERIODONTAL RESEARCH (DK/0022-3484). **1327**

JOURNAL OF PERIODONTOLOGY (1970) (US/0022-3492). **1327**

JOURNAL OF PERSONALITY (US/0022-3506). **4599**

JOURNAL OF PERSONALITY AND SOCIAL PSYCHOLOGY (US/0022-3514). **4599**

JOURNAL OF PERSONALITY DISORDERS (US/0885-579X). **4599**

JOURNAL OF PESTICIDE SCIENCE (TOKYO, 1975) (JA/0385-1559). **4245**

JOURNAL OF PETROLEUM SCIENCE & ENGINEERING (NE/0920-4105). **4262**

JOURNAL OF PETROLEUM TECHNOLOGY (US/0149-2136). **4262**

JOURNAL OF PETROLOGY (UK/0022-3530). **1458**

JOURNAL OF PHARMACEUTICAL AND BIOMEDICAL ANALYSIS (UK/0731-7085). **4311**

JOURNAL OF PHARMACEUTICAL MEDICINE : THE OFFICIAL JOURNAL OF THE SOCIETY OF PHARMACEUTICAL MEDICINE (UK/0958-0581). **4312**

JOURNAL OF PHARMACEUTICAL SCIENCES (US/0022-3549). **4312**

JOURNAL OF PHARMACOBIO-DYNAMICS (JA/0386-846X). **4312**

JOURNAL OF PHARMACOKINETICS AND BIOPHARMACEUTICS (US/0090-466X). **4312**

JOURNAL OF PHARMACOLOGICAL AND TOXICOLOGICAL METHODS (US/1056-8719). **4312**

JOURNAL OF PHARMACOLOGY AND EXPERIMENTAL THERAPEUTICS, THE (US/0022-3565). **4312**

JOURNAL OF PHARMACY AND PHARMACOLOGY (UK/0022-3573). **4312**

JOURNAL OF PHARMACY PRACTICE (US/0897-1900). **4312**

JOURNAL OF PHASE EQUILIBRIA (US/1054-9714). **4006**

JOURNAL OF PHILOSOPHICAL LOGIC (NE/0022-3611). **3291**

JOURNAL OF PHILOSOPHY OF EDUCATION (UK/0309-8249). **1898**

JOURNAL OF PHILOSOPHY, THE (US/0022-362X). **4350**

JOURNAL OF PHONETICS (UK/0095-4470). **3291**

JOURNAL OF PHOTOCHEMISTRY AND PHOTOBIOLOGY. A, CHEMISTRY (SZ/1010-6030). **1054**

JOURNAL OF PHOTOCHEMISTRY AND PHOTOBIOLOGY. B, BIOLOGY (SZ/1011-1344). **1054**

JOURNAL OF PHYSICAL AND CHEMICAL REFERENCE DATA (US/0047-2689). **4409**

JOURNAL OF PHYSICAL CHEMISTRY (1952) (US/0022-3654). **1054**

JOURNAL OF PHYSICAL OCEANOGRAPHY (US/0022-3670). **1450**

JOURNAL OF PHYSICAL ORGANIC CHEMISTRY (UK/0894-3230). **1043**

JOURNAL OF PHYSICS. A : MATHEMATICAL AND GENERAL (UK/0305-4470). **4409**

JOURNAL OF PHYSICS AND CHEMISTRY OF SOLIDS, THE (UK/0022-3697). **4409**

JOURNAL OF PHYSICS. B : ATOMIC, MOLECULAR, AND OPTICAL PHYSICS (UK/0953-4075). **4409**

JOURNAL OF PHYSICS. CONDENSED MATTER : AN INSTITUTE OF PHYSICS JOURNAL (UK/0953-8984). **4409**

JOURNAL OF PHYSICS. D : APPLIED PHYSICS (UK/0022-3727). **4410**

JOURNAL OF PHYTOPATHOLOGY 1986 (GW/0931-1785). **100**

JOURNAL OF PINEAL RESEARCH (DK/0742-3098). **583**

JOURNAL OF PLANKTON RESEARCH (US/0142-7873). **5588**

JOURNAL OF PLANNING LITERATURE (US/0885-4122). **2840**

JOURNAL OF PLANT GROWTH REGULATION (US/0721-7595). **515**

JOURNAL OF PLANT NUTRITION (US/0190-4167). **515**

JOURNAL OF PLANT PHYSIOLOGY (GW/0176-1617). **516**

JOURNAL OF PLASMA PHYSICS (UK/0022-3778). **4410**

JOURNAL OF PLASTIC FILM & SHEETING (US/8756-0879). **4456**

JOURNAL OF POETRY THERAPY (US/0889-3675). **4599**

JOURNAL OF POLICY ANALYSIS AND MANAGEMENT (US/0276-8739). **4479**

JOURNAL OF POLICY HISTORY (US/0898-0306). **4479**

JOURNAL OF POLICY MODELING (US/0161-8938). **5206**

JOURNAL OF POLITICAL ECONOMY, THE (US/0022-3808). **1500**

JOURNAL OF POLITICAL PHILOSOPHY (US/0963-8016). **4350**

JOURNAL OF POLITICS, THE (US/0022-3816). **4479**

JOURNAL OF POLYMER MATERIALS (II/0970-0838). **982**

JOURNAL OF POLYMER SCIENCE. PART A, POLYMER CHEMISTRY (US/0887-624X). **1043**

JOURNAL OF POLYMER SCIENCE. PART B, POLYMER PHYSICS (US/0887-6266). **1043**

JOURNAL OF POPULAR FILM AND TELEVISION, THE (US/0195-6051). **4073**

JOURNAL OF POPULATION ECONOMICS (GW/0933-1433). **4554**

JOURNAL OF POST ANESTHESIA NURSING (US/0883-9433). **3859**

JOURNAL OF POWER SOURCES (SZ/0378-7753). **2118**

JOURNAL OF PRAGMATICS (NE/0378-2166). **3291**

JOURNAL OF PRESSURE VESSEL TECHNOLOGY (US/0094-9930). **2118**

JOURNAL OF PRIMARY PREVENTION, THE (US/0278-095X). **4787**

JOURNAL OF PRISON & JAIL HEALTH (US/0731-8332). **3167**

JOURNAL OF PROCESS CONTROL (UK/0959-1524). **3482**

JOURNAL OF PRODUCT INNOVATION MANAGEMENT, THE (US/0737-6782). **687**

JOURNAL OF PRODUCTIVITY ANALYSIS (US/0895-562X). **1614**

JOURNAL OF PROFESSIONAL ISSUES IN ENGINEERING EDUCATION AND PRACTICE (US/1052-3928). **2026**

JOURNAL OF PROFESSIONAL NURSING (US/8755-7223). **3860**

JOURNAL OF PROPERTY MANAGEMENT (US/0022-3905). **4839**

JOURNAL OF PROPULSION AND POWER (US/0748-4658). **26**

JOURNAL OF PROSTHETIC DENTISTRY, THE (US/0022-3913). **1327**

JOURNAL OF PROSTHODONTICS (US/1059-941X). **1327**

JOURNAL OF PROTEIN CHEMISTRY (US/0277-8033). **490**

JOURNAL OF PSYCHIATRIC RESEARCH (UK/0022-3956). **3929**

JOURNAL OF PSYCHOHISTORY, THE (US/0145-3378). **4599**

JOURNAL OF PSYCHOLINGUISTIC RESEARCH (US/0090-6905). **3291**

JOURNAL OF PSYCHOLOGY AND JUDAISM (US/0700-9801). **4600**

JOURNAL OF PSYCHOLOGY, THE (US/0022-3980). **4600**

JOURNAL OF PSYCHOPATHOLOGY AND BEHAVIORAL ASSESSMENT (US/0882-2689). **4600**

JOURNAL OF PSYCHOPHARMACOLOGY (OXFORD, ENGLAND) (UK/0269-8811). **4313**

JOURNAL OF PSYCHOPHYSIOLOGY (UK/0269-8803). **4600**

JOURNAL OF PSYCHOSOMATIC OBSTETRICS AND GYNAECOLOGY (NE/0167-482X). **3764**

JOURNAL OF PSYCHOSOMATIC RESEARCH (UK/0022-3999). **3597**

JOURNAL OF PSYCHOTHERAPY INTEGRATION (US/1053-0479). **4600**

JOURNAL OF PUBLIC ADMINISTRATION RESEARCH AND THEORY (US/1053-1858). **4659**

JOURNAL OF PUBLIC ECONOMICS (NE/0047-2727). **4734**

JOURNAL OF PUBLIC HEALTH MEDICINE (UK/0957-4832). **3597**

JOURNAL OF PUBLIC POLICY (UK/0143-814X). **4479**

JOURNAL OF PURE AND APPLIED ALGEBRA (NE/0022-4049). **3514**

JOURNAL OF QUALITY TECHNOLOGY (US/0022-4065). **5119**

JOURNAL OF QUANTITATIVE ANTHROPOLOGY (NE/0922-2995). **239**

JOURNAL OF QUANTITATIVE CRIMINOLOGY (US/0748-4518). **3167**

JOURNAL OF QUANTITATIVE SPECTROSCOPY & RADIATIVE TRANSFER (UK/0022-4073). **4436**

JOURNAL OF RADIOANALYTICAL AND NUCLEAR CHEMISTRY (SZ/0236-5731). **1017**

JOURNAL OF RADIOANALYTICAL AND NUCLEAR CHEMISTRY (SZ/0236-5731). **1017**

JOURNAL OF RADIOANALYTICAL AND NUCLEAR CHEMISTRY. LETTERS (SZ/0236-5731). **1017**

JOURNAL OF RADIOLOGICAL PROTECTION (UK/0952-4746). **4436**

JOURNAL OF RAMAN SPECTROSCOPY (UK/0377-0486). **4436**

JOURNAL OF RATIONAL-EMOTIVE AND COGNITIVE-BEHAVIOR THERAPY (US/0894-9085). **4600**

JOURNAL OF READING (US/0022-4103). **1898**

JOURNAL OF REAL ESTATE FINANCE AND ECONOMICS, THE (US/0895-5638). **4839**

JOURNAL OF REAL ESTATE LITERATURE (US/0927-7544). **3400**

JOURNAL OF REAL ESTATE TAXATION (US/0093-5107). **4734**

JOURNAL OF RECEPTOR RESEARCH (US/0197-5110). **538**

JOURNAL OF RECONSTRUCTIVE MICROSURGERY (US/0743-684X). **3968**

JOURNAL OF REFUGEE STUDIES (UK/0951-6328). **1919**

JOURNAL OF REGIONAL SCIENCE (US/0022-4146). **1500**

JOURNAL OF REGULATORY ECONOMICS (US/0922-680X). **843**

JOURNAL OF REINFORCED PLASTICS AND COMPOSITES (US/0731-6844). **2104**

JOURNAL OF RELIGION AND HEALTH (US/0022-4197). **4969**

JOURNAL OF RELIGION IN AFRICA (NE/0022-4200). **4970**

JOURNAL OF RELIGION, THE (US/0022-4189). **4969**

JOURNAL OF RELIGIOUS HISTORY, THE (AT/0022-4227). **4970**

JOURNAL OF RENAL NUTRITION (US/1051-2276). **3991**

JOURNAL OF REPRODUCTION & FERTILITY (UK/0022-4251). **3597**

JOURNAL OF REPRODUCTION AND FERTILITY. SUPPLEMENT (UK/0449-3087). **3597**

JOURNAL OF REPRODUCTIVE AND INFANT PSYCHOLOGY (UK/0264-6838). **3764**

JOURNAL OF REPRODUCTIVE IMMUNOLOGY (NE/0165-0378). **3674**

JOURNAL OF REPRODUCTIVE MEDICINE (US/0024-7758). **3764**

JOURNAL OF RESEARCH IN CRIME AND DELINQUENCY, THE (US/0022-4278). **3167**

JOURNAL OF RESEARCH IN CRIME AND DELINQUENCY, THE (US/0022-4278). **3167**

JOURNAL OF RESEARCH IN PERSONALITY (US/0092-6566). **4601**

JOURNAL OF RESEARCH IN READING (UK/0141-0423). **1898**

JOURNAL OF RESEARCH IN SCIENCE TEACHING (US/0022-4308). **5119**

JOURNAL OF RESEARCH ON COMPUTING IN EDUCATION (US/0888-6504). **1224**

JOURNAL OF RESPIRATORY DISEASES, THE (US/0194-259X). **3950**

JOURNAL OF RETAIL BANKING (US/0195-2064). **795**

JOURNAL OF RHEOLOGY (NEW YORK, N.Y.) (US/0148-6055). **4428**

JOURNAL OF RHEUMATOLOGY, THE (CN/0315-162X). **3805**

JOURNAL OF RISK AND UNCERTAINTY (US/0895-5646). **1500**

JOURNAL OF ROBOTIC SYSTEMS (US/0741-2223). **1214**

JOURNAL OF RURAL STUDIES (UK/0743-0167). **5250**

JOURNAL OF RUSSIAN LASER RESEARCH (US/1071-2836). **4436**

JOURNAL OF S CORPORATION TAXATION (US/1045-1471). **4735**

JOURNAL OF SAFETY RESEARCH (US/0022-4375). **2864**

JOURNAL OF SCHOOL LEADERSHIP (US/1052-6846). **1865**

JOURNAL OF SCHOOL PSYCHOLOGY (US/0022-4405). **4601**

JOURNAL OF SCIENCE EDUCATION AND TECHNOLOGY (US/1059-0145). **5119**

JOURNAL OF SCIENTIFIC COMPUTING (US/0885-7474). **5120**

JOURNAL OF SCIENTIFIC EXPLORATION (US/0892-3310). **5120**

JOURNAL OF SEDIMENTARY PETROLOGY (US/0022-4472). **1458**

JOURNAL OF SEMANTICS (NIJMEGEN) (NE/0167-5133). **3291**

JOURNAL OF SEMI-CUSTOM ICS (UK/0264-3375). **2069**

JOURNAL OF SEMITIC STUDIES (UK/0022-4480). **2266**

JOURNAL OF SERVICES MARKETING, THE (US/0887-6045). **929**

JOURNAL OF SEX EDUCATION AND THERAPY (US/0161-4576). **5187**

JOURNAL OF SHIP RESEARCH (US/0022-4502). **4177**

JOURNAL OF SHOULDER AND ELBOW SURGERY (US/1058-2746). **3968**

JOURNAL OF SMALL ANIMAL PRACTICE, THE (UK/0022-4510). **5513**

JOURNAL OF SOCIAL AND CLINICAL PSYCHOLOGY (US/0736-7236). **4601**

JOURNAL OF SOCIAL DISTRESS AND THE HOMELESS (US/1053-0789). **5293**

JOURNAL OF SOCIAL HISTORY (US/0022-4529). **5206**

JOURNAL OF SOCIAL ISSUES, THE (US/0022-4537). **5206**

JOURNAL OF SOCIAL POLICY (UK/0047-2794). **5293**

JOURNAL OF SOCIAL PSYCHOLOGY, THE (US/0022-4545). **4601**

JOURNAL OF SOCIAL RECONSTRUCTION (US/0196-2000). **5207**

JOURNAL OF SOCIAL WORK PRACTICE (UK/0265-0533). **5293**

JOURNAL OF SOCIO-ECONOMICS (US/1053-5357). **1570**

JOURNAL OF SOCIOLOGY AND SOCIAL WELFARE (US/0191-5096). **5293**

JOURNAL OF SOFTWARE MAINTENANCE (UK/1040-550X). **1288**

JOURNAL OF SOIL CONTAMINATION (US/1058-8337). **176**

JOURNAL OF SOIL SCIENCE, THE (UK/0022-4588). **176**

JOURNAL OF SOLAR ENERGY ENGINEERING (US/0199-6231). **1949**

JOURNAL OF SOLID STATE CHEMISTRY (US/0022-4596). **982**

JOURNAL OF SOLUTION CHEMISTRY (US/0095-9782). **1055**

JOURNAL OF SOUND AND VIBRATION (UK/0022-460X). **4452**

JOURNAL OF SOURCES IN EDUCATIONAL HISTORY (UK/0140-671X). **1758**

JOURNAL OF SOUTH AMERICAN EARTH SCIENCES (UK/0895-9811). **1357**

JOURNAL OF SOUTHEAST ASIAN EARTH SCIENCES (UK/0743-9547). **1357**

JOURNAL OF SOUTHERN AFRICAN STUDIES (UK/0305-7070). **2641**

JOURNAL OF SOVIET LASER RESEARCH (US/0270-2010). **4437**

JOURNAL OF SOVIET MATHEMATICS (US/0090-4104). **3514**

JOURNAL OF SPACECRAFT AND ROCKETS (US/0022-4650). **26**

JOURNAL OF SPECIAL EDUCATION, THE (US/0022-4669). **1881**

JOURNAL OF SPECULATIVE PHILOSOPHY, THE (US/0891-625X). **4351**

JOURNAL OF SPEECH AND HEARING RESEARCH (US/0022-4685). **4390**

JOURNAL OF SPINAL DISORDERS (US/0895-0385). **3805**

JOURNAL OF SPORT & EXERCISE PSYCHOLOGY (US/0895-2779). **4901**

JOURNAL OF SPORT MANAGEMENT (US/0888-4773). **4902**

JOURNAL OF SPORT REHABILITATION (US/1056-6716). **3954**

JOURNAL OF SPORTS SCIENCES (UK/0264-0414). **4902**

JOURNAL OF STAFF, PROGRAM & ORGANIZATION DEVELOPMENT, THE (US/0736-7627). **1898**

JOURNAL OF STATE TAXATION (US/0744-6713). **4735**

JOURNAL OF STATISTICAL COMPUTATION AND SIMULATION (US/0094-9655). **1282**

JOURNAL OF STATISTICAL PHYSICS (US/0022-4715). **4410**

JOURNAL OF STATISTICAL PLANNING AND INFERENCE (NE/0378-3758). **3514**

JOURNAL OF STEROID BIOCHEMISTRY AND MOLECULAR BIOLOGY, THE (UK/0960-0760). **462**

JOURNAL OF STORED PRODUCTS RESEARCH (UK/0022-474X). **2347**

JOURNAL OF STRAIN ANALYSIS FOR ENGINEERING DESIGN, THE (UK/0309-3247). **2118**

JOURNAL OF STRATEGIC AND SYSTEMIC THERAPIES, THE (CN/0711-5075). **3929**

JOURNAL OF STRATEGIC CHANGE (US/1057-9265). **687**

JOURNAL OF STRATEGIC INFORMATION SYSTEMS, THE (UK/0963-8687). **1248**

JOURNAL OF STRENGTH AND CONDITIONING RESEARCH (US/1064-8011). **4902**

JOURNAL OF STRUCTURAL BIOLOGY (US/1047-8477). **462**

JOURNAL OF STRUCTURAL CHEMISTRY (US/0022-4766). **1055**

JOURNAL OF STRUCTURAL ENGINEERING (NEW YORK, N.Y.) (US/0733-9445). **2026**

JOURNAL OF STRUCTURAL GEOLOGY (UK/0191-8141). **1385**

JOURNAL OF STRUCTURAL LEARNING (US/0022-4774). **1758**

JOURNAL OF STUDIES ON ALCOHOL (US/0096-882X). **1346**

JOURNAL OF SUBSTANCE ABUSE (US/0899-3289). **1346**

JOURNAL OF SUBSTANCE ABUSE TREATMENT (US/0740-5472). **1346**

JOURNAL OF SUPERCOMPUTING, THE (US/0920-8542). **1192**

JOURNAL OF SUPERCONDUCTIVITY (US/0896-1107). **2069**

JOURNAL OF SUPERCRITICAL FLUIDS, THE (US/0896-8446). **1017**

JOURNAL OF SUPERHARD MATERIALS (US/1063-4576). **4006**

JOURNAL OF SURGICAL ONCOLOGY (US/0022-4790). **3820**

JOURNAL OF SURGICAL RESEARCH, THE (US/0022-4804). **3968**

JOURNAL OF SURVEYING ENGINEERING (US/0733-9453). **2026**

JOURNAL OF SYMBOLIC COMPUTATION (UK/0747-7171). **3514**

JOURNAL OF SYMBOLIC LOGIC, THE (US/0022-4812). **3515**

JOURNAL OF SYSTEMS AND SOFTWARE, THE (US/0164-1212). **1280**

JOURNAL OF SYSTEMS INTEGRATION (US/0925-4676). **1192**

JOURNAL OF SYSTEMS MANAGEMENT (US/0022-4839). **687**

JOURNAL OF TAXATION DIGEST, THE (US/8755-6049). **4735**

JOURNAL OF TAXATION OF INVESTMENTS (US/0747-9115). **904**

JOURNAL OF TAXATION, THE (US/0022-4863). **4735**

JOURNAL OF TEACHING IN PHYSICAL EDUCATION (US/0273-5024). **1856**

JOURNAL OF TECHNICAL PHYSICS (PL/0324-8313). **4410**

JOURNAL OF TERRAMECHANICS (UK/0022-4898). **2026**

JOURNAL OF TESTING AND EVALUATION (US/0090-3973). **1983**

JOURNAL OF THE ABRAHAM LINCOLN ASSOCIATION (US/0898-4212). **2742**

JOURNAL OF THE ACADEMY OF MARKETING SCIENCE (US/0092-0703). **929**

JOURNAL OF THE ACOUSTICAL SOCIETY OF AMERICA, THE (US/0001-4966). **4452**

JOURNAL OF THE AMERICAN ACADEMY OF AUDIOLOGY (CN/1050-0545). **3889**

JOURNAL OF THE AMERICAN ACADEMY OF CHILD AND ADOLESCENT PSYCHIATRY (US/0890-8567). **3929**

JOURNAL OF THE AMERICAN ACADEMY OF DERMATOLOGY (US/0190-9622). **3721**

JOURNAL OF THE AMERICAN ACADEMY OF NURSE PRACTITIONERS (US/1041-2972). **3860**

JOURNAL OF THE AMERICAN ACADEMY OF PHYSICIAN ASSISTANTS (US/0893-7400). **3597**

JOURNAL OF THE AMERICAN ACADEMY OF PSYCHOANALYSIS, THE (US/0090-3604). **3930**

JOURNAL OF THE AMERICAN BOARD OF FAMILY PRACTICE, THE (US/0893-8652). **3738**

JOURNAL OF THE AMERICAN CERAMIC SOCIETY (US/0002-7820). **2591**

JOURNAL OF THE AMERICAN CHEMICAL SOCIETY (US/0002-7863). **982**

JOURNAL OF THE AMERICAN COLLEGE OF CARDIOLOGY (US/0735-1097). **3707**

JOURNAL OF THE AMERICAN COLLEGE OF NUTRITION (US/0731-5724). **4194**

JOURNAL OF THE AMERICAN GERIATRICS SOCIETY (US/0002-8614). **3753**

JOURNAL OF THE AMERICAN MATHEMATICAL SOCIETY (US/0894-0347). **3515**

JOURNAL OF THE AMERICAN MEDICAL INFORMATICS ASSOCIATION (US/1067-5027). **3597**

JOURNAL OF THE AMERICAN MEDICAL WOMEN'S ASSOCIATION (1972) (US/0098-8421). **3597**

JOURNAL OF THE AMERICAN MOSQUITO CONTROL ASSOCIATION (US/8756-971X). **4245**

JOURNAL OF THE AMERICAN OIL CHEMISTS' SOCIETY (US/0003-021X). **1043**

JOURNAL OF THE AMERICAN SOCIETY FOR INFORMATION SCIENCE (US/0002-8231). **3220**

JOURNAL OF THE AMERICAN SOCIETY FOR MASS SPECTROMETRY (US/1044-0305). **1017**

JOURNAL OF THE AMERICAN SOCIETY OF BREWING CHEMISTS (US/0361-0470). **982**

JOURNAL OF THE AMERICAN SOCIETY OF ECHOCARDIOGRAPHY (US/0894-7317). **3707**

JOURNAL OF THE AMERICAN SOCIETY OF NEPHROLOGY (US/1046-6673). **3991**

JOURNAL OF THE AMERICAN STATISTICAL ASSOCIATION (US/0162-1459). **5329**

JOURNAL OF THE ASSOCIATION FOR COMPUTING MACHINERY (US/0004-5411). **1192**

JOURNAL OF THE ASSOCIATION OF PUBLIC ANALYSTS (UK/0004-5780). **4787**

JOURNAL OF THE ATMOSPHERIC SCIENCES (US/0022-4928). **1427**

JOURNAL OF THE AUSTRALIAN MATHEMATICAL SOCIETY. SERIES A : PURE MATHEMATICS AND STATISTICS (AT/0263-6115). **3515**

JOURNAL OF THE AUSTRALIAN MATHEMATICAL SOCIETY. SERIES B : APPLIED MATHEMATICS, THE (AT/0334-2700). **3515**

JOURNAL OF THE AUSTRALIAN WAR MEMORIAL (AT/0729-6274). **4048**

JOURNAL OF THE AUTONOMIC NERVOUS SYSTEM (NE/0165-1838). **3837**

JOURNAL OF THE CANADIAN CHIROPRACTIC ASSOCIATION, THE (CN/0008-3194). **3805**

JOURNAL OF THE CHEMICAL SOCIETY, CHEMICAL COMMUNICATIONS (UK/0022-4936). **982**

JOURNAL OF THE CHEMICAL SOCIETY. FARADAY TRANSACTIONS (UK/0956-5000). **1055**

JOURNAL OF THE ECONOMIC AND SOCIAL HISTORY OF THE ORIENT (NE/0022-4995). **2656**

JOURNAL OF THE ELECTROCHEMICAL SOCIETY (US/0013-4651). **1034**

JOURNAL OF THE ELECTROCHEMICAL SOCIETY OF INDIA (II/0013-466X). **1026**

JOURNAL OF THE EUROPEAN ACADEMY OF DERMATOLOGY AND VENEREOLOGY : JEADV (NE/0926-9959). **3721**

JOURNAL OF THE EUROPEAN ASSOCIATION OF MARINE SCIENCES AND TECHNIQUES (NE/0924-7963). **1450**

JOURNAL OF THE EUROPEAN CERAMIC SOCIETY (UK/0955-2219). **2591**

JOURNAL OF THE FRANKLIN INSTITUTE (US/0016-0032). **5120**

JOURNAL OF THE GEOLOGICAL SOCIETY (UK/0016-7649). **1385**

JOURNAL OF THE GEOLOGICAL SOCIETY OF INDIA (II/0016-7622). **1385**

JOURNAL OF THE GYPSY LORE SOCIETY (US/0017-6087). **2321**

JOURNAL OF THE HISTORICAL SOCIETY OF NIGERIA (NR/0018-2540). **2641**

JOURNAL OF THE HISTORY OF BIOLOGY (NE/0022-5010). **462**

JOURNAL OF THE HISTORY OF COLLECTIONS (UK/0954-6650). **4090**

JOURNAL OF THE HISTORY OF IDEAS (US/0022-5037). **4351**

JOURNAL OF THE HISTORY OF SEXUALITY (US/1043-4070). **5187**

JOURNAL OF THE IES (US/1052-2883). **2176**

JOURNAL OF THE ILLUMINATING ENGINEERING SOCIETY (US/0099-4480). **2069**

JOURNAL OF THE IRISH COLLEGES OF PHYSICIANS AND SURGEONS (IE/0374-8405). **3598**

JOURNAL OF THE JAPANESE AND INTERNATIONAL ECONOMIES (US/0889-1583). **1637**

JOURNAL OF THE MARINE BIOLOGICAL ASSOCIATION OF THE UNITED KINGDOM (UK/0025-3154). **555**

JOURNAL OF THE MECHANICS AND PHYSICS OF SOLIDS (UK/0022-5096). **2104**

JOURNAL OF THE MOSCOW PATRIARCHATE, THE (RU/0201-7318). **5039**

JOURNAL OF THE NATIONAL SCIENCE COUNCIL OF SRI LANKA (CE/0300-9254). **5121**

JOURNAL OF THE NEUROLOGICAL SCIENCES (NE/0022-510X). **3837**

JOURNAL OF THE NEW ZEALAND SOCIETY OF PERIODONTOLOGY (NZ/0111-1485). **1328**

JOURNAL OF THE OPERATIONAL RESEARCH SOCIETY, THE (UK/0160-5682). **3515**

JOURNAL OF THE OPTICAL SOCIETY OF AMERICA. A, OPTICS AND IMAGE SCIENCE (US/0740-3232). **4437**

JOURNAL OF THE OPTICAL SOCIETY OF AMERICA. B, OPTICAL PHYSICS (US/0740-3224). **4437**

JOURNAL OF THE PATENT AND TRADEMARK OFFICE SOCIETY (US/0882-9098). **1305**

JOURNAL OF THE PHILOSOPHY OF SPORT (US/0094-8705). **4902**

JOURNAL OF THE ROYAL COLLEGE OF SURGEONS OF EDINBURGH (UK/0035-8835). **3968**

JOURNAL OF THE ROYAL MUSICAL ASSOCIATION (UK/0269-0403). **4127**

JOURNAL OF THE ROYAL SOCIETY OF MEDICINE (UK/0141-0768). **3599**

JOURNAL OF THE ROYAL SOCIETY OF NEW ZEALAND (NZ/0303-6758). **5121**

JOURNAL OF THE ROYAL STATISTICAL SOCIETY. SERIES A (GENERAL) (UK/0035-9238). **5330**

JOURNAL OF THE ROYAL STATISTICAL SOCIETY. SERIES B (METHODOLOGICAL) (UK/0035-9246). **5330**

JOURNAL OF THE SCIENCE OF FOOD AND AGRICULTURE (UK/0022-5142). **2347**

JOURNAL OF THE SOCIETY FOR HEALTH SYSTEMS (US/1043-1721). **4788**

JOURNAL OF THE SOCIETY FOR INFORMATION DISPLAY (US/0734-1768). **3221**

JOURNAL OF THE SOCIETY FOR PSYCHICAL RESEARCH (UK/0037-9751). **4242**

JOURNAL OF THE SOCIETY OF ARCHIVISTS (UK/0037-9816). **2482**

JOURNAL OF THE SOCIETY OF COSMETIC CHEMISTS (US/0037-9832). **1026**

JOURNAL OF THE SOUTH AFRICAN INSTITUTE OF MINING & METALLURGY (SA/0038-223X). **2142**

JOURNAL OF THEOLOGICAL STUDIES (UK/0022-5185). **4971**

JOURNAL OF THEORETICAL BIOLOGY (UK/0022-5193). **462**

JOURNAL OF THEORETICAL PROBABILITY (US/0894-9840). **3515**

JOURNAL OF THERMAL ANALYSIS (UK/0368-4466). **1055**

JOURNAL OF THERMAL BIOLOGY (UK/0306-4565). **462**

JOURNAL OF THERMAL INSULATION (US/0148-8287). **2606**

JOURNAL OF THERMAL INSULATION AND BUILDING ENVELOPES (US/1065-2744). **618**

JOURNAL OF THERMAL STRESSES (UK/0149-5739). **2119**

JOURNAL OF THERMOPHYSICS AND HEAT TRANSFER (US/0887-8722). **4431**

JOURNAL OF THERMOPLASTIC COMPOSITE MATERIALS (US/0892-7057). **1026**

JOURNAL OF THORACIC AND CARDIOVASCULAR SURGERY (US/0022-5223). **3968**

JOURNAL OF THORACIC IMAGING (US/0883-5993). **3600**

JOURNAL OF TIME SERIES ANALYSIS (UK/0143-9782). **3516**

JOURNAL OF TISSUE CULTURE METHODS (NE/0271-8057). **538**

JOURNAL OF TOXICOLOGY AND ENVIRONMENTAL HEALTH (US/0098-4108). **3982**

JOURNAL OF TOXICOLOGY. CLINICAL TOXICOLOGY (US/0731-3810). **3982**

JOURNAL OF TOXICOLOGY. TOXIN REVIEWS (US/0731-3837). **3982**

JOURNAL OF TRACE AND MICROPROBE TECHNIQUES (US/0733-4680). **1017**

JOURNAL OF TRACE ELEMENTS AND ELECTROLYTES IN HEALTH AND DISEASE (GW/0931-2838). **3600**

JOURNAL OF TRANSPLANT COORDINATION : OFFICIAL PUBLICATION OF THE NORTH AMERICAN TRANSPLANT COORDINATORS ORGANIZATION (NATCO) (DK/0905-9199). **3799**

JOURNAL OF TRANSPORT HISTORY, THE (UK/0022-5266). **5385**

JOURNAL OF TRANSPORTATION ENGINEERING (US/0733-947X). **2026**

JOURNAL OF TRAUMA, THE (US/0022-5282). **3969**

JOURNAL OF TRAUMATIC STRESS (US/0894-9867). **4602**

JOURNAL OF TRIBOLOGY (US/0742-4787). **2119**

JOURNAL OF TROPICAL ECOLOGY (UK/0266-4674). **2218**

JOURNAL OF TROPICAL MEDICINE AND HYGIENE (UK/0022-5304). **3986**

JOURNAL OF TROPICAL PEDIATRICS (1980) (UK/0142-6338). **3905**

JOURNAL OF TURBOMACHINERY (US/0889-504X). **2119**

JOURNAL OF ULTRASOUND IN MEDICINE (US/0278-4297). **3943**

JOURNAL OF URBAN AFFAIRS (US/0735-2166). **2826**

JOURNAL OF URBAN AND CULTURAL STUDIES (US/1054-1802). **1759**

JOURNAL OF URBAN ECONOMICS (US/0094-1190). **1501**

JOURNAL OF URBAN HISTORY (US/0096-1442). **2621**

JOURNAL OF URBAN PLANNING AND DEVELOPMENT (US/0733-9488). **2026**

JOURNAL OF UROLOGIC PATHOLOGY (US/1067-1919). **3991**

JOURNAL OF UROLOGY, THE (US/0022-5347). **3991**

JOURNAL OF VACUUM SCIENCE & TECHNOLOGY. A: VACUUM, SURFACES, AND FILMS (US/0734-2101). **4410**

JOURNAL OF VALUE INQUIRY, THE (NE/0022-5363). **4351**

JOURNAL OF VASCULAR MEDICINE AND BIOLOGY (US/1042-5268). **462**

JOURNAL OF VASCULAR NURSING (US/1062-0303). **3860**

JOURNAL OF VASCULAR RESEARCH (SZ/1018-1172). **3707**

JOURNAL OF VASCULAR SURGERY (US/0741-5214). **3969**

JOURNAL OF VESTIBULAR RESEARCH (US/0957-4271). **3889**

JOURNAL OF VETERINARY INTERNAL MEDICINE (US/0891-6640). **5514**

JOURNAL OF VETERINARY MEDICAL SCIENCE (JA/0916-7250). **5514**

JOURNAL OF VETERINARY MEDICINE. SERIES A (GW/0931-184X). **5514**

JOURNAL OF VETERINARY MEDICINE. SERIES B (GW/0931-1793). **5514**

JOURNAL OF VETERINARY PHARMACOLOGY AND THERAPEUTICS (UK/0140-7783). **5514**

JOURNAL OF VIBRATION AND ACOUSTICS (US/1048-9002). **4453**

JOURNAL OF VINYL TECHNOLOGY (US/0193-7197). **4456**

JOURNAL OF VIROLOGICAL METHODS (NE/0166-0934). **566**

JOURNAL OF VIROLOGY (US/0022-538X). **566**

JOURNAL OF VISUAL COMMUNICATION AND IMAGE REPRESENTATION (US/1047-3203). **1234**

JOURNAL OF VISUALIZATION AND COMPUTER ANIMATION, THE (UK/1049-8907). **1234**

JOURNAL OF VLSI SIGNAL PROCESSING (US/0922-5773). **2070**

JOURNAL OF VOCATIONAL BEHAVIOR (US/0001-8791). **4602**

JOURNAL OF VOCATIONAL REHABILITATION (US/1052-2263). **4380**

JOURNAL OF VOICE (US/0892-1997). **3600**

JOURNAL OF VOLCANOLOGY AND GEOTHERMAL RESEARCH (NE/0377-0273). **1408**

JOURNAL OF WATER CHEMISTRY AND TECHNOLOGY (US/1063-455X). **2234**

JOURNAL OF WATER RESOURCES PLANNING AND MANAGEMENT (US/0733-9496). **5535**

JOURNAL OF WATER SUPPLY RESEARCH AND TECHNOLOGY - AQUA (UK/0003-7214). **5535**

JOURNAL OF WATERWAY, PORT, COASTAL, AND OCEAN ENGINEERING (US/0733-950X). **2092**

JOURNAL OF WIND ENGINEERING AND INDUSTRIAL AERODYNAMICS (NE/0167-6105). **1983**

JOURNAL OF WINE RESEARCH / THE INSTITUTE OF MASTERS OF WINE (UK/0957-1264). **2368**

JOURNAL OF WOOD CHEMISTRY AND TECHNOLOGY (US/0277-3813). **1055**

JOURNAL OF WORLD FOREST RESOURCE MANAGEMENT (UK/0261-4286). **2386**

JOURNAL OF WORLD PREHISTORY (US/0892-7537). **272**

JOURNAL OF WORLD TRADE (SZ/1011-6702). **843**

JOURNAL OF WOUND, OSTOMY, AND CONTINENCE NURSING (US/1071-5754). **3860**

JOURNAL OF X-RAY SCIENCE AND TECHNOLOGY (US/0895-3996). **3943**

JOURNAL OF YOUTH AND ADOLESCENCE (US/0047-2891). **5207**

JOURNAL OF YOUTH SERVICES IN LIBRARIES (US/0894-2498). **3221**

JOURNAL OF ZOOLOGY (1987) (UK/0952-8369). **5589**

JOURNEES ANNUELLES DE DIABETOLOGIE DE L'HOTEL-DIEU (FR/0075-4439). **3731**

JOYCE STUDIES ANNUAL (US/1049-0809). **3400**

JPC. JOURNAL OF PLANAR CHROMATOGRAPHY, MODERN TLC (GW/0933-4173). **983**

JPEN, JOURNAL OF PARENTERAL AND ENTERAL NUTRITION (US/0148-6071). **4194**

JQS. JOURNAL OF QUATERNARY SCIENCE (UK/0267-8119). **1385**

JSAE REVIEW (JA/0389-4304). **5418**

JSME INTERNATIONAL JOURNAL. SERIES 2, FLUIDS ENGINEERING, HEAT TRANSFER, POWER, COMBUSTION, THERMOPHYSICAL PROPERTIES (JA/0914-8817). **2119**

JSME INTERNATIONAL JOURNAL. SERIES 3, VIBRATION, CONTROL ENGINEERING, ENGINEERING FOR INDUSTRY (JA/0914-8825). **2119**

JSME INTERNATIONAL JOURNAL. SERIES I, SOLID MECHANICS, STRENGTH OF MATERIALS (JA/0914-8809). **2119**

JURISTENZEITUNG (GW/0022-6882). **2991**

JURISTISCHE BLATTER (AU/0022-6912). **2991**

K-THEORY (NE/0920-3036). **3516**

KADMOS (GW/0022-7498). **272**

KAGAKU TO KOGYO (TOKYO) (JA/0022-7684). **983**

KAKAO + ZUCKER (GW/0022-7838). **2347**

KALI UND STEINSALZ (GW/0022-7951). **1440**

KALIKASAN, THE PHILIPPINE JOURNAL OF BIOLOGY (PH/0115-0553). **462**

KALTE UND KLIMATECHNIK (GW/0343-2246). **2606**

KANE'S BEVERAGE WEEK (US/0882-2573). **2368**

KANKYO GIJUTSU (JA/0388-9459). **2197**

KANT-STUDIEN (GW/0022-8877). **4351**

KARDIOLOGIJA (RU/0022-9040). **3708**

KARTOGRAPHISCHE NACHRICHTEN (GW/0022-9164). **2582**

KAUCHUK I REZINA (RU/0022-9466). **5076**

KAUTSCHUK + GUMMI KUNSTSTOFFE (GW/0022-9520). **5076**

KEATS-SHELLEY JOURNAL (US/0453-4387). **3401**

KEESING'S RECORD OF WORLD EVENTS (UK/0950-6128). **4480**

KENNEDY INSTITUTE OF ETHICS JOURNAL (US/1054-6863). **2252**

KERNTECHNIK (1987) (GW/0932-3902). **2156**

KERYGMA UND DOGMA (GW/0023-0707). **4972**

KES : ZEITSCHRIFT FUER KOMMUNIKATIONS UND EDV SICHERHEIT (GW/0177-4565). **1115**

KEW MAGAZINE, THE (UK/0265-3842). **516**

KEY ABSTRACTS. MICROWAVE TECHNOLOGY (UK/0952-7079). **2005**

KEY NEUROLOGY AND NEUROSURGERY (US/0886-8018). **3837**

KEY OBSTETRICS AND GYNECOLOGY (US/0896-4467). **3764**

KEY OPTHALMOLOGY (US/0886-8026). **3876**

KEYBOARD (CUPERTINO, CALIF.) (US/0730-0158). **4128**

KHIMICHESKAIA FIZIKA (US/0733-2831). **1055**

KHIMIIA I TEKHNOLOGIIA VODY (US/0734-1679). **2235**

KIBERNETIKA I VYCHISLITELNAIA TEKHNIKA. ENGLISH (US/0739-8417). **1251**

KIDNEY INTERNATIONAL (US/0085-2538). **3991**

KINDERARZTLICHE PRAXIS (GW/0023-1495). **3906**

KINEMATIKA I FIZIKA NEBESNYKH TEL (US/0884-5913). **396**

KINESITHERAPIE SCIENTIFIQUE (FR/0023-1576). **4381**

KINETICS AND CATALYSIS (US/0023-1584). **1044**

KIRCHENCHOR, DER (GW/0023-1800). **4128**

KIRCHENMUSIKER, DER (GW/0023-1819). **4128**

KITCHEN & BATH BUSINESS (US/0730-2487). **2901**

KLEINTIER-PRAXIS (GW/0023-2076). **5515**

KLIMA, KALTE, HEIZUNG (GW/0172-1984). **2606**

KLINICESKAJA HIRURGIJA (KIEV) (UN/0023-2130). **3969**

KLINICESKAJA MEDICINA (RU/0023-2149). **3602**

KLINISCHE MONATSBLATTER FUER AUGENHEILKUNDE (GW/0023-2165). **3876**

KLINISCHE PADIATRIE (GW/0300-8630). **3906**

KNEE SURGERY, SPORTS TRAUMATOLOGY, ARTHROSCOPY (GW/0942-2056). **3969**

KNOWLEDGE ACQUISITION (UK/1042-8143). **1214**

KNOWLEDGE AND POLICY (US/0897-1986). **1115**

KNOWLEDGE AND SOCIETY, STUDIES IN THE SOCIOLOGY OF CULTURE PAST AND PRESENT (US/0278-1557). **5251**

KNOWLEDGE-BASED SYSTEMS (GUILDFORD, SURREY) (UK/0950-7051). **1193**

KNOWLEDGE (BEVERLY HILLS, CALIF.) (US/0164-0259). **5207**

KNOWLEDGE ENGINEERING REVIEW, THE (UK/0269-8889). **1214**

KOBUNSHI RONBUNSHU (TOKYO) (JA/0386-2186). **984**

KODIKAS (GW/0171-0834). **3293**

KOGNITIONSWISSENSCHAFT (GW/0938-7986). **4602**

KOLNER ROMANISTISCHE ARBEITEN (SZ/0075-6520). **3402**

KOLNER ZEITSCHRIFT FUER SOZIOLOGIE UND SOZIALPSYCHOLOGIE (GW/0023-2653). **5251**

KONGELIGE DANSKE VIDENSKABERNES SELSKAB. MATEMATISK-FYSISKE MEDDELELSER (DK/0023-3323). **3516**

KONJUNKTUR VON MORGEN (GW/0023-3439). **1615**

KONJUNKTURPOLITIK (GW/0023-3498). **1571**

KONSTRUKTION (1981) (GW/0720-5953). **2120**

KOSMICESKIE ISSLEDOVANIJA (RU/0023-4206). **27**

KOSMOS (STUTTGART) (GW/0023-4230). **5124**

KRANKENGYMNASTIK (GW/0023-4494). **4381**

KRANKENHAUSPHARMAZIE (GW/0173-7597). **4313**

KRANKENVERSICHERUNG (BERLIN), DIE (GW/0301-4835). **2886**

KRATYLOS (GW/0023-4567). **3293**

KREDIT UND KAPITAL (GW/0023-4591). **796**

KREDITPRAXIS 1979 (GW/0172-7400). **796**

KRIMINALISTIK (GW/0023-4699). **3168**

KRISTALLOGRAFIJA (RU/0023-4761). **1032**

KRITISCHE JUSTIZ (GW/0023-4834). **2993**

KUNSTCHRONIK (GW/0023-5474). **356**

KUNSTSTOFFBERATER (1979) (GW/0172-6374). **4456**

KUNSTSTOFFE (GW/0023-5563). **4456**

KUNSTSTOFFE-PLASTICS (SOLOTHURN) (SZ/0023-5598). **4456**

KYBERNETES (UK/0368-492X). **1252**

KYKLOS (SZ/0023-5962). **5208**

LAB REPORT (US/1045-7313). **3603**

LABOR CONTRACT LAW BULLETIN (US/8755-7886). **3150**

LABOR HISTORY (US/0023-656X). **1683**

LABOR RELATIONS REFERENCE MANUAL (US/1043-5506). **3151**

LABOR RELATIONS REPORTER (US/0148-7981). **3151**

LABOR RELATIONS WEEK (US/0891-4141). **1685**

LABOR STUDIES JOURNAL (US/0160-449X). **1685**

LABORATORIUMSMEDIZIN (GW/0342-3026). **3603**

LABORATORY AND RESEARCH METHODS IN BIOLOGY AND MEDICINE (US/0160-8584). **463**

LABORATORY ANIMALS (LONDON) (UK/0023-6772). **5515**

LABORATORY EQUIPMENT (US/0023-6810). **950**

LABORATORY HAZARDS BULLETIN (UK/0261-2917). **2872**

LABORATORY INVESTIGATION (US/0023-6837). **3896**

LABORATORY MICROCOMPUTER (UK/0262-2955). **1268**

LABORATORY REGULATION NEWS (US/1048-0706). **5125**

LABORATORY ROBOTICS AND AUTOMATION (US/0895-7533). **1214**

LABORPRAXIS (GW/0344-1733). **3603**

LABOUR ECONOMICS (NE/0927-5371). **1685**

LABOUR (HALIFAX) (CN/0700-3862). **1686**

LABOUR (HALIFAX) (CN/0700-3862). **1686**

LABOUR ROMA (IT/1121-7081). **1686**

LADY (UK/0023-7167). **2518**

LAIT, LE (FR/0023-7302). **196**

LAN TIMES (US/1040-5917). **1242**

LANCET (BRITISH EDITION) (UK/0140-6736). **3603**

LANCET ED. FRANCAISE (NE/0923-7577). **3603**

LANCET (NORTH AMERICAN EDITION), THE (US/0099-5355). **3603**

LAND DEGRADATION AND REHABILITATION (UK/0898-5812). **177**

LAND ECONOMICS (US/0023-7639). **103**

LAND MANAGEMENT AND ENVIRONMENTAL LAW REPORT : LME LAW REPORT (UK/0955-6354). **3113**

LAND USE POLICY (UK/0264-8377). **1502**

LANDFALL (NZ/0023-7930). **3403**

LANDLORD TENANT LAW BULLETIN (US/0271-5228). **2993**

LANDSCAPE AND URBAN PLANNING (NE/0169-2046). **2827**

LANDSCAPE (BERKELEY, CALIF.) (US/0023-8023). **2568**

LANDSCAPE JOURNAL (US/0277-2426). **2423**

LANDSCAPE MANAGEMENT (US/0894-1254). **2423**

LANDTECHNISCHE ZEITSCHRIFT (GW/0011-5010). **104**

LANGENBECKS ARCHIV FUER CHIRURGIE (GW/0023-8236). **3969**

LANGMUIR (US/0743-7463). **1055**

LANGUAGE & COMMUNICATION (UK/0271-5309). **3294**

LANGUAGE AND SOCIETY (CN/0709-7751). **3295**

LANGUAGE AWARENESS (UK/0965-8416). **3295**

LANGUAGE IN SOCIETY (UK/0047-4045). **3295**

LANGUAGE SCIENCES (OXFORD) (UK/0388-0001). **3296**

LANGUAGE, SPEECH & HEARING SERVICES IN SCHOOLS (US/0161-1461). **1881**

LANGUAGE TEACHING (UK/0261-4448). **3336**

LANGUAGE TESTING (UK/0265-5322). **3296**

LANGUE FRANCAISE (FR/0023-8368). **3296**

LARGE ANIMAL VETERINARIAN COVERING HEALTH & NUTRITION (US/1043-7533). **5515**

LARYNGOSCOPE, THE (US/0023-852X). **3889**

LASER AND PARTICLE BEAMS (UK/0263-0346). **4437**

LASER CHEMISTRY (SZ/0278-6273). **984**

LASER FOCUS WORLD (US/1043-8092). **4437**

LASER REPORT (US/0023-8600). **4437**

LASER THERAPY (UK/0898-5901). **4437**

LASER UND OPTOELEKTRONIK (GW/0722-9003). **4411**

LASERS & OPTRONICS (US/0892-9947). **4438**

LASERS IN ENGINEERING (US/0898-1507). **1985**

LASERS IN MEDICAL SCIENCE (UK/0268-8921). **3604**

LASERS IN MEDICINE (NE/0925-8434). **3604**

LASERS IN SURGERY AND MEDICINE (US/0196-8092). **3969**

LASERS IN THE LIFE SCIENCES (SZ/0886-0467). **4438**

LATE IMPERIAL CHINA (US/0884-3236). **2658**

LATIN AMERICAN ANTIQUITY (US/1045-6635). **273**

LAUGHING BEAR NEWSLETTER (US/1056-0327). **4816**

LAUREL REVIEW / WEST VIRGINIA WESLEYAN COLLEGE, THE (US/0023-9003). **3404**

LAW AND HISTORY REVIEW (US/0738-2480). **2994**

LAW AND HUMAN BEHAVIOR (US/0147-7307). **2994**

LAW AND MENTAL HEALTH (US/0890-5037). **2994**

LAW AND PHILOSOPHY (NE/0167-5249). **2994**

LAW & POLICY (UK/0265-8240). **2994**

LAW & SOCIAL INQUIRY (US/0897-6546). **2994**

LAW FIRMS YELLOW BOOK (US/1054-4054). **1927**

LAW

LAW INSTITUTE JOURNAL (AT/0023-9267). **2995**

LAW LIBRARIAN (LONDON) (UK/0023-9275). **3222**

LAW, MEDICINE & HEALTH CARE (US/0277-8459). **2995**

LAW OFFICE COMPUTING (US/1055-128X). **2996**

LAW OFFICE MANAGEMENT & ADMINISTRATION REPORT (US/0735-4843). **2996**

LAW OFFICER'S BULLETIN, THE (US/0145-6571). **3107**

LAW TEACHER, THE (UK/0306-9400). **2997**

LAW WEEK'S SUMMARY & ANALYSIS OF CURRENT LAW (US/0190-5252). **2997**

LAWYER'S BRIEF, THE (US/0898-9966). **2998**

LC GC (US/0888-9090). **984**

LC GC INTERNATIONAL (US/0895-5441). **984**

LEADERSHIP & ORGANIZATION DEVELOPMENT JOURNAL (UK/0143-7739). **875**

LEADERSHIP QUARTERLY, THE (US/1048-9843). **875**

LEARNING AND INSTRUCTION : THE JOURNAL OF THE EUROPEAN ASSOCIATION FOR RESEARCH ON LEARNING AND INSTRUCTION (UK/0959-4752). **1899**

LEARNING AND MOTIVATION (US/0023-9690). **4602**

LEARNING (PALO ALTO, CALIF.) (US/0090-3167). **1900**

LEBENSMITTEL-WISSENSCHAFT + I.E. UND TECHNOLOGIE (UK/0023-6438). **2348**

LEBENSMITTELCHEMIE : ZEITSCHRIFT DER LEBENSMITTELCHEMISCHEN GESELLSCHAFT, FACHGRUPPE IN DER GESELLSCHAFT DEUTSCHER CHEMIKER (GW/0937-1478). **2348**

LEBER, MAGEN, DARM (GW/0300-8622). **3747**

LECTINS SHEFFIELD (UK/0143-4217). **490**

LECTURA Y VIDA (US/0325-8637). **1900**

LECTURE NOTES IN BIOMATHEMATICS (GW/0341-633X). **463**

LECTURE NOTES IN CHEMISTRY (GW/0342-4901). **984**

LECTURE NOTES IN COMPUTER SCIENCE (GW/0302-9743). **1214**

LECTURE NOTES IN CONTROL AND INFORMATION SCIENCES (GW/0170-8643). **3223**

LECTURE NOTES IN PHYSICS (GW/0075-8450). **4411**

LECTURES IN APPLIED MATHEMATICS (US/0075-8485). **3516**

LECTURES ON MATHEMATICS IN THE LIFE SCIENCES (US/0075-8523). **3516**

LEDER UND HAUTEMARKT (GW/0342-7641). **3185**

LEGACY (AMHERST, MASS.) (US/0748-4321). **3404**

LEGAL ASPECTS OF MEDICAL PRACTICE (US/0190-2350). **2999**

LEGAL INFORMATION ALERT (US/0883-1297). **3081**

LEGAL-LEGISLATIVE REPORTER NEWS BULLETIN (US/0458-9599). **3151**

LEGAL LOOSELEAFS IN PRINT (US/0275-4689). **3082**

LEGAL NEWSLETTERS IN PRINT (US/8755-416X). **3082**

LEGAL REPORTER, THE (AT/0159-2483). **3000**

LEGISLATIVE NETWORK FOR NURSES (US/8756-0054). **3002**

LEGISLATIVE STUDIES QUARTERLY (US/0362-9805). **4480**

LEICA-FOTOGRAFIE (GW/0024-0621). **4371**

LEISURE BEVERAGE INSIDER NEWSLETTER (US/1040-3736). **2369**

LEISURE SCIENCES (US/0149-0400). **5208**

LEISURE STUDIES (UK/0261-4367). **4852**

LENDER LIABILITY LAW REPORT (US/1045-1463). **3087**

LENDER LIABILITY NEWS (US/0898-7645). **3087**

LENS AND EYE TOXICITY RESEARCH (US/1042-6922). **3604**

LEONARDO (OXFORD) (UK/0024-094X). **357**

LEPROSY REVIEW (UK/0305-7518). **3604**

LESBIAN AND GAY STUDIES NEWSLETTER : LGSN (CN/1064-5950). **2795**

LETHAIA (NO/0024-1164). **4227**

LETTER OF CREDIT UPDATE (US/0883-0487). **796**

LETTERS IN APPLIED MICROBIOLOGY (UK/0266-8254). **566**

LETTERS IN MATHEMATICAL PHYSICS (NE/0377-9017). **4411**

LETTERS OF CREDIT REPORT (US/0886-0459). **796**

LETTRE DU PSYCHIATRE PARIS, LA (FR/0223-9434). **3930**

LEUCOCYTES (UK/0142-8160). **3674**

LEUKEMIA & LYMPHOMA (UK/1042-8194). **3820**

LEUKEMIA RESEARCH (UK/0145-2126). **3820**

LEVIATHAN (DUSSELDORF) (GW/0340-0425). **5208**

LIBRARIES & CULTURE (US/0894-8631). **4829**

LIBRARY (UK/0024-2160). **418**

LIBRARY ACQUISITIONS : PRACTICE AND THEORY (US/0364-6408). **3223**

LIBRARY ADMINISTRATION & MANAGEMENT (US/0888-4463). **3224**

LIBRARY & INFORMATION SCIENCE RESEARCH (US/0740-8188). **3224**

LIBRARY COMPUTER SYSTEMS AND EQUIPMENT REVIEW (US/0895-531X). **3225**

LIBRARY HOTLINE (US/0740-736X). **3225**

LIBRARY ISSUES (US/0734-3035). **3225**

LIBRARY JOURNAL (1976) (US/0363-0277). **3225**

LIBRARY LIFE : NEW ZEALAND LIBRARY ASSOCIATION NEWSLETTER (NZ/0110-4373). **3226**

LIBRARY MANAGEMENT (MCB PUBLICATIONS (FIRM)) (UK/0143-5124). **3226**

LIBRARY QUARTERLY (CHICAGO), THE (US/0024-2519). **3226**

LIBRARY RESOURCES & TECHNICAL SERVICES (US/0024-2527). **3227**

LIBRARY SOFTWARE REVIEW (US/0742-5759). **1288**

LIBRARY SYSTEMS (US/0277-0288). **3227**

LIBRARY TECHNOLOGY REPORTS (US/0024-2586). **3227**

LIBRARY TRENDS (US/0024-2594). **3227**

LIBRI (KBENHAVN) (DK/0024-2667). **3228**

LICENSING LETTER, THE (US/8755-6235). **929**

LICHENOLOGIST (LONDON) (UK/0024-2829). **517**

LICHT (MUNCHEN) (GW/0171-5496). **2070**

LIEBIGS ANNALEN DER CHEMIE (GW/0170-2041). **984**

LIFE CHEMISTRY REPORTS (US/0278-6281). **490**

LIFE SUPPORT SYSTEMS (UK/0261-989X). **3604**

LIGHT & ENGINEERING (US/1068-9761). **2070**

LIGHT METALS (NEW YORK) (US/0147-0809). **4007**

LIGHTHOUSE (BURLINGTON) (CN/0711-5628). **1357**

LIGHTING DESIGN & APPLICATION (US/0360-6325). **2070**

LIGHTWAVE (US/0741-5834). **4438**

LILI, ZEITSCHRIFT FUER LITERATURWISSENSCHAFT UND LINGUISTIK (GW/0049-8653). **3298**

LINEAR ALGEBRA AND ITS APPLICATIONS (US/0024-3795). **3517**

LINEAR AND MULTILINEAR ALGEBRA (US/0308-1087). **3517**

LINGUA (AMSTERDAM, NETHERLANDS) (NE/0024-3841). **3298**

LINGUISTIC ANALYSIS (US/0098-9053). **3298**

LINGUISTIC INQUIRY (US/0024-3892). **3298**

LINGUISTIC REVIEW, THE (NE/0167-6318). **3298**

LINGUISTICS (NE/0024-3949). **3299**

LINGUISTICS ABSTRACTS (UK/0267-5498). **3299**

LINGUISTICS AND EDUCATION (US/0898-5898). **3299**

LINGUISTICS AND LANGUAGE BEHAVIOR ABSTRACTS (US/0888-8027). **3336**

LINGUISTICS AND PHILOSOPHY (NE/0165-0157). **3299**

LINGUISTISCHE BERICHTE (GW/0024-3930). **3299**

LINK-UP (MINNEAPOLIS, MINN. 1983) (US/0739-988X). **1242**

LION AND THE UNICORN (BROOKLYN), THE (US/0147-2593). **3346**

LIPID TECHNOLOGY (UK/0956-666X). **984**

LIPIDS (US/0024-4201). **583**

LIQUID CRYSTALS (UK/0267-8292). **1032**

LISP AND SYMBOLIC COMPUTATION (US/0892-4635). **1280**

LISTENER WELLINGTON (NZ/0110-5787). **1134**

LITEJNOE PROIZVODSTVO (UN/0024-449X). **4007**

LITERARY AND LINGUISTIC COMPUTING (UK/0268-1145). **1193**

LITERATURBERICHTE UEBER WASSER, ABWASSER, LUFT UND FESTE ABFALLSTOFFE (GW/0340-4900). **2235**

LITERATURE ANALYSIS OF MICROCOMPUTER PUBLICATIONS : LAMP (US/0735-9721). **1209**

LITERATURE AND MEDICINE (US/0278-9671). **3605**

LITERATURE & THEOLOGY (UK/0269-1205). **3407**

LITERATURE, INTERPRETATION, THEORY (US/1043-6928). **3407**

LITHIUM (EDINBURGH) (UK/0954-1381). **4314**

LITHIUM THERAPY MONOGRAPHS (SZ/1011-2928). **3605**

LITHOLOGY AND MINERAL RESOURCES (US/0024-4902). **2143**

LITHOS (NO/0024-4937). **1441**

LITHUANIAN MATHEMATICAL JOURNAL (US/0363-1672). **3517**

LITOVSKII FIZICHESKII SBORNIK (US/1047-4064). **4411**

LITTERATURE (PARIS. 1971) (FR/0047-4800). **3408**

LITURGISCHES JAHRBUCH (GW/0024-5100). **4974**

LIVER (COPENHAGEN) (DK/0106-9543). **3799**

LIVESTOCK PRODUCTION SCIENCE (NE/0301-6226). **214**

LNG DIGEST (US/0276-5918). **4263**

LOCAL AREA NETWORK MAGAZINE : LAN, THE (US/0898-0012). **1193**

LOCAL ECONOMY (UK/0269-0942). **1573**

LOCAL GOVERNMENT POLICY MAKING (UK/0264-2050). **4663**

LOCAL/STATE FUNDING REPORT / GIS, GOVERNMENT INFORMATION SERVICES (US/0741-3173). **4663**

LOCAL TELECOM COMPETITION NEWS (US/1067-6333). **1159**

LOCATION SCIENCE (UK/0966-8349). **5208**

LOCKWOOD-POST'S DIRECTORY OF THE PULP, PAPER AND ALLIED TRADES (US/1046-5359). **4235**

LODGING HOSPITALITY (US/0148-0766). **2807**

LOGISTICS AND TRANSPORTATION REVIEW, THE (CN/0047-4991). **5386**

LOGISTICS INFORMATION MANAGEMENT (UK/0957-6053). **3229**

LOGISTICS SPECTRUM (US/0024-5852). **5126**

LOGO EXCHANGE (US/0888-6970). **1280**

LONG-DISTANCE LETTER, THE (US/0740-6851). **1159**

LONG RANGE PLANNING (UK/0024-6301). **876**

LONG-TERM CARE ADMINISTRATOR (US/0146-275X). **3788**

LOOKOUT. FOODS (US/0740-3860). **2348**

LOOKOUT. NON-FOODS (US/0740-3852). **2348**

LOST GENERATION JOURNAL (US/0091-2948). **3408**

LOTUS (CAMBRIDGE, MASS.) (US/8756-7334). **1288**

LOW TEMPERATURE PHYSICS (US/1063-777X). **4411**

LOWER EXTREMITY, THE (US/1068-6991). **3883**

LP-GAS (US/0024-7103). **4263**

LUBRICATION ENGINEERING (US/0024-7154). **2120**

LUBRICATION SCIENCE (UK/0954-0075). **1985**

LUNG (GW/0341-2040). **3950**

LUNG CANCER (AMSTERDAM, NETHERLANDS) (NE/0169-5002). **3820**

LUSO-BRAZILIAN REVIEW (US/0024-7413). **1078**

LUSTRUM (GW/0024-7421). **1078**

LUTHER (GW/0340-6210). **5062**

LUTHERAN THEOLOGICAL JOURNAL (AT/0024-7553). **5063**

LYMPHOLOGY (US/0024-7766). **3773**

LYON CHIRURGICAL (SZ/0024-7782). **3969**
LYON PHARMACEUTIQUE (FR/0024-7804). **4314**
M-+-A-REPORT 1982 (GW/0723-3361). **820**
M.D. COMPUTING (US/0724-6811). **1268**
MACHINE DESIGN (US/0024-9114). **2120**
MACHINE LEARNING (US/0885-6125). **1215**
MACHINE-MEDIATED LEARNING (US/0732-6718). **1224**
MACHINE TRANSLATION (NE/0922-6567). **1194**
MACHINE VIBRATION (US/0939-7418). **2120**
MACHINE VISION AND APPLICATIONS (US/0932-8092). **1252**
MACHINERY AND PRODUCTION ENGINEERING (UK/0024-919X). **2120**
MACLEAN'S (CN/0024-9262). **2489**
MACROMOLECULAR SYNTHESES (US/0076-2091). **985**
MACROMOLECULES (US/0024-9297). **1044**
MACROPHAGES SHEFFIELD (UK/0142-8195). **3605**
MACWORLD (SAN FRANCISCO, CALIF.) (US/0741-8647). **1268**
MAGAZINE OF CONCRETE RESEARCH (UK/0024-9831). **2027**
MAGNESIUM AND TRACE ELEMENTS (SZ/1015-3845). **985**
MAGNESIUM-BULLETIN (GW/0172-908X). **4007**
MAGNETIC RESONANCE IMAGING (US/0730-725X). **3943**
MAGNETIC RESONANCE IN CHEMISTRY : MRC (UK/0749-1581). **1044**
MAGNETIC RESONANCE IN MEDICINE (US/0740-3194). **3943**
MAGNETIC RESONANCE QUARTERLY (US/0899-9422). **3943**
MAGNETIC RESONANCE REVIEW (US/0097-7330). **4444**
MAGNETIC SEPARATION NEWS (US/0731-3632). **4444**
MAGNETOHYDRODYNAMICS (NEW YORK, N.Y. 1965) (US/0024-998X). **4444**
MAGNETOHYDRODYNAMICS (NEW YORK, N.Y. 1989) (US/0891-9801). **2071**
MAGNITNAJA GIDRODINAMIKA (LV/0025-0015). **4444**
MAHASAGAR (II/0542-0938). **1451**
MAINTENANCE MANAGEMENT INTERNATIONAL (NE/0167-5389). **876**
MAKROMOLEKULARE CHEMIE (BASEL, SWITZERLAND : 1981) (SZ/0025-116X). **1044**
MAKROMOLEKULARE CHEMIE. MACROMOLECULAR SYMPOSIA, DIE (SZ/0258-0322). **1044**
MAKROMOLEKULARE CHEMIE. RAPID COMMUNICATIONS, DIE (SZ/0173-2803). **1044**
MAKU (JA/0385-1036). **463**
MAMMAL REVIEW (UK/0305-1838). **5590**
MAMMALIAN GENOME (US/0938-8990). **463**
MAN AND WORLD (NE/0025-1534). **4352**
MANAGED CARE LAW OUTLOOK (US/1042-4091). **3006**
MANAGED CARE OUTLOOK (US/0896-6567). **3788**

MANAGED CARE QUALITY (US/1064-5454). **1617**
MANAGED CARE WEEK (US/1056-7461). **3788**
MANAGED HEALTHCARE (US/1060-1392). **4789**
MANAGED HEALTHCARE NEWS (US/1060-1392). **4789**
MANAGEMENT ACCOUNTING (NEW YORK, N.Y.) (US/0025-1690). **747**
MANAGEMENT AND MARKETING ABSTRACTS (UK/0308-2172). **731**
MANAGEMENT AUCKLAND (NZ/0025-1658). **876**
MANAGEMENT COMMUNICATION QUARTERLY (US/0893-3189). **1115**
MANAGEMENT DECISION (UK/0025-1747). **877**
MANAGEMENT INFORMATION SYSTEMS QUARTERLY (US/0276-7783). **1194**
MANAGEMENT INTERNATIONAL REVIEW (GW/0025-181X). **877**
MANAGEMENT REPORT (NEW YORK, N.Y.) (US/0745-4880). **944**
MANAGEMENT REVIEW (SARANAC LAKE) (US/0025-1895). **944**
MANAGEMENT SCIENCE (US/0025-1909). **878**
MANAGEMENT TODAY (UK/0025-1925). **878**
MANAGEMENT-WISSEN (GW/0340-4137). **878**
MANAGERIAL FINANCE (UK/0307-4358). **797**
MANAGING END-USER COMPUTING (US/1048-6933). **1268**
MANAGING OFFICE TECHNOLOGY (US/1070-4051). **878**
MANCHESTER SCHOOL OF ECONOMIC AND SOCIAL STUDIES, THE (UK/0025-2034). **1504**
MANUELLE MEDIZIN (GW/0025-2514). **3606**
MANUFACTURING CHEMIST (LONDON: 1981) (UK/0262-4230). **985**
MANUFACTURING ENGINEERING (US/0361-0853). **1986**
MANUFACTURING REVIEW (US/0896-1611). **3484**
MANUFACTURING SYSTEMS (US/0748-948X). **1617**
MANUSCRIPTA GEODAETICA (GW/0340-8825). **1408**
MANUSCRIPTA MATHEMATICA (GW/0025-2611). **3517**
MAPPE, DIE (GW/0025-2697). **2902**
MARINE AND PETROLEUM GEOLOGY (UK/0264-8172). **1386**
MARINE BEHAVIOUR AND PHYSIOLOGY (US/0091-181X). **583**
MARINE BIOLOGY (GW/0025-3162). **556**
MARINE CHEMISTRY (NE/0304-4203). **1451**
MARINE ECOLOGY (BERLIN, WEST) (GW/0173-9565). **2218**
MARINE ECOLOGY. PROGRESS SERIES (HALSTENBEK) (GW/0171-8630). **2218**
MARINE ENVIRONMENTAL RESEARCH (UK/0141-1136). **2177**
MARINE GEODESY (US/0149-0419). **1358**
MARINE GEOLOGY (NE/0025-3227). **1386**
MARINE GEOPHYSICAL RESEARCHES (NE/0025-3235). **1451**
MARINE GEOTECHNOLOGY (US/0360-8867). **1451**

MARINE MAMMAL SCIENCE (US/0824-0469). **1452**
MARINE MICROBIAL FOOD WEBS (FR/0297-8148). **566**
MARINE MICROPALEONTOLOGY (NE/0377-8398). **4228**
MARINE POLICY (UK/0308-597X) **1452**
MARINE POLLUTION BULLETIN (UK/0025-326X). **2236**
MARINE RESOURCE ECONOMICS (US/0738-1360). **2308**
MARINE STRUCTURES (UK/0951-8339). **4179**
MARINE TECHNOLOGY NEWS (US/1071-1333). **4179**
MARINE TECHNOLOGY SOCIETY JOURNAL (US/0025-3324). **1452**
MARITIME POLICY AND MANAGEMENT (UK/0308-8839). **5452**
MARK SKOUSEN'S FORECASTS & STRATEGIES ON INFLATION, TAXES AND GOVERNMENT CONTROLS (US/0272-0868). **4736**
MARKET. ASIA PACIFIC (US/1059-275X). **930**
MARKET--EUROPE (US/1050-9410). **845**
MARKET LOGIC FROM THE INSTITUTE FOR ECONOMETRIC RESEARCH (US/0162-6817). **906**
MARKETING AND RESEARCH TODAY : THE JOURNAL OF THE EUROPEAN SOCIETY FOR OPINION AND MARKETING RESEARCH (NE/0923-5957). **731**
MARKETING EDUCATION REVIEW (US/1052-8008). **930**
MARKETING EXECUTIVE REPORT (US/1054-2388). **930**
MARKETING INTELLIGENCE & PLANNING (UK/0263-4503). **931**
MARKETING LETTERS (US/0923-0645). **931**
MARKETING MANAGEMENT (CHICAGO, ILL.) (US/1061-3846). **931**
MARKETING NEWS (US/0025-3790). **931**
MARKETING RESEARCH (CHICAGO, ILL.) (US/1040-8460). **932**
MARKETING SCIENCE (PROVIDENCE, R.I.) (US/0732-2399). **932**
MARKETING (TORONTO) (CN/0025-3642). **932**
MARKETING UPDATE (CLEVELAND, OHIO) (US/0732-555X). **932**
MARKT & TECHNIK (GW/0344-8843). **2071**
MARPLE'S BUSINESS NEWSLETTER (US/0279-960X). **692**
MARTINDALE-HUBBELL LAW DIRECTORY (PRINT) (US/0191-0221). **3006**
MARXISTISCHE BLATTER (GW/0542-7770). **4543**
MASS SPECTROMETRY (UK/0305-9987). **1017**
MASS SPECTROMETRY REVIEWS (US/0277-7037). **1017**
MATERIAL HANDLING ENGINEERING (US/0025-5262). **2104**
MATERIAL HANDLING ENGINEERING. HANDBOOK DIRECTORY (US/0025-5262). **2104**
MATERIAL UND ORGANISMEN (GW/0025-5270). **1986**
MATERIAL UND ORGANISMEN; BEIHEFT (GW/0025-5270). **1017**
MATERIALPRUFUNG (GW/0025-5300). **2104**
MATERIALS & DESIGN (UK/0264-1275). **2104**

MATERIALS AND PROCESSING REPORT (US/0887-1949). **2104**
MATERIALS AT HIGH TEMPERATURES (UK/0960-3409). **2105**
MATERIALS CHARACTERIZATION (US/1044-5803). **4008**
MATERIALS CHEMISTRY AND PHYSICS (SZ/0254-0584). **1055**
MATERIALS ENGINEERING (US/0025-5319). **2105**
MATERIALS EVALUATION (US/0025-5327). **2105**
MATERIALS FORUM (AT/0883-2900). **1986**
MATERIALS LETTERS (NE/0167-577X). **2105**
MATERIALS MANAGEMENT AND DISTRIBUTION (CN/0025-5343). **1618**
MATERIALS PERFORMANCE (US/0094-1492). **2105**
MATERIALS RESEARCH BULLETIN (US/0025-5408). **2105**
MATERIALS RESEARCH SOCIETY SYMPOSIA PROCEEDINGS (US/0272-9172). **2071**
MATERIALS SCIENCE & ENGINEERING. A, STRUCTURAL MATERIALS : PROPERTIES, MICROSTRUCTURE AND PROCESSING (SZ/0921-5093). **2105**
MATERIALS SCIENCE & ENGINEERING. B, SOLID-STATE MATERIALS FOR ADVANCED TECHNOLOGY (SZ/0921-5107). **2105**
MATERIALS SCIENCE & ENGINEERING. C, BIOMIMETIC MATERIALS, SENSORS AND SYSTEMS (SZ/0928-4931). **1986**
MATERIALS SCIENCE AND ENGINEERING : R-REPORTS (SZ/0927-796X). **1986**
MATERIALS SCIENCE REPORTS (NE/0920-2307). **2106**
MATERIALS SCIENCE RESEARCH (US/0076-5201). **5127**
MATERIALS TECHNOLOGY (NEW YORK, N.Y.) (US/1066-7857). **2106**
MATERIALS TRANSACTIONS, JIM (JA/0916-1821). **4008**
MATERIALWISSENSCHAFT UND WERKSTOFFTECHNIK (GW/0933-5137). **2106**
MATERIAUX ET TECHNIQUES (FR/0032-6895). **2106**
MATH NOTEBOOK (US/0272-8885). **1882**
MATHEMATICA JOURNAL, THE (US/1047-5974). **3518**
MATHEMATICAL AND COMPUTER MODELLING (UK/0895-7177). **3518**
MATHEMATICAL BIOSCIENCES (US/0025-5564). **464**
MATHEMATICAL FINANCE : AN INTERNATIONAL JOURNAL OF MATHEMATICS, STATISTICS AND FINANCIAL THEORY (UK/0960-1627). **3518**
MATHEMATICAL GEOLOGY (US/0882-8121). **1386**
MATHEMATICAL METHODS IN THE APPLIED SCIENCES (GW/0170-4214). **3519**
MATHEMATICAL METHODS OF STATISTICS (US/1066-5307). **3519**
MATHEMATICAL POPULATION STUDIES (US/0889-8480). **4554**
MATHEMATICAL PROCEEDINGS OF THE CAMBRIDGE PHILOSOPHICAL SOCIETY (UK/0305-0041). **3519**
MATHEMATICAL REPORTS (CHUR, SWITZERLAND) (SZ/0275-7214). **3520**
MATHEMATICAL REVIEWS (US/0025-5629). **3542**

MATHEMATICAL

MATHEMATICAL SOCIAL SCIENCES (NE/0165-4896). **5208**
MATHEMATICAL SYSTEMS THEORY (US/0025-5661). **3520**
MATHEMATICAL WORLD (US/1055-9426). **3520**
MATHEMATICS AND COMPUTERS IN SIMULATION (NE/0378-4754). **1282**
MATHEMATICS IN SCHOOL (UK/0305-7259). **3520**
MATHEMATICS MAGAZINE (US/0025-570X). **3521**
MATHEMATICS OF COMPUTATION (US/0025-5718). **3521**
MATHEMATICS OF CONTROL, SIGNALS, AND SYSTEMS : MCSS (US/0932-4194). **1986**
MATHEMATICS OF OPERATIONS RESEARCH (US/0364-765X). **3521**
MATHEMATICS OF THE USSR : IZVESTIJA (US/0025-5726). **3521**
MATHEMATICS OF THE USSR : SBORNIK (US/0025-5734). **3521**
MATHEMATIKUNTERRICHT (GW/0025-5807). **3521**
MATHEMATISCHE ANNALEN (GW/0025-5831). **3522**
MATHEMATISCHE SEMESTERBERICHTE (GW/0720-728X). **3522**
MATHEMATISCHE ZEITSCHRIFT (GW/0025-5874). **3522**
MATRIX (STUTTGART) (GW/0934-8832). **3606**
MATURITAS (IE/0378-5122). **3754**
MAYO CLINIC PROCEEDINGS (US/0025-6196). **3799**
MC : DIE MIKROCOMPUTER-ZEITSCHRIFT (GW/0720-4442). **1269**
MD LEINFELDEN (GW/0343-0642). **2902**
MDE. MANAGERIAL AND DECISION ECONOMICS (UK/0143-6570). **1504**
MDR WATCH (US/0890-7587). **3606**
MEALEY'S EUROPEAN ENVIRONMENTAL LAW REPORT (US/1050-897X). **3114**
MEALEY'S LITIGATION REPORT. ASBESTOS PROPERTY ACTIONS (US/1040-0192). **3007**
MEALEY'S LITIGATION REPORT. REINSURANCE (US/1049-5347). **3007**
MEALEY'S LITIGATION REPORT. TOBACCO (US/0886-0122). **3007**
MEALEY'S LITIGATION REPORTS. ASBESTOS (US/0742-4647). **3007**
MEALEY'S LITIGATION REPORTS. BAD FAITH (US/0893-1011). **3007**
MEALEY'S LITIGATION REPORTS. INSURANCE (US/8755-9005). **3008**
MEALEY'S LITIGATION REPORTS. INSURANCE INSOLVENCY (US/1043-8416). **3008**
MEALEY'S LITIGATION REPORTS. LEAD (US/1059-4116). **3008**
MEALEY'S LITIGATION REPORTS. PUNITIVE DAMAGES & TORT REFORM (US/1055-307X). **2887**
MEALEY'S LITIGATION REPORTS. SUPERFUND (US/0897-3407). **3114**
MEASUREMENT AND EVALUATION IN COUNSELING AND DEVELOPMENT (US/0748-1756). **1763**
MEASUREMENT : JOURNAL OF THE INTERNATIONAL MEASUREMENT CONFEDERATION (UK/0263-2241). **4031**
MEASUREMENT SCIENCE & TECHNOLOGY (UK/0957-0233). **4412**
MEASUREMENT TECHNIQUES (US/0543-1972). **2121**

MEAT PROCESSING (US/0025-6390). **2349**
MEAT SCIENCE (UK/0309-1740). **215**
MECHANICAL ENGINEERING (NEW YORK, N.Y. 1919) (US/0025-6501). **2122**
MECHANICAL SYSTEMS AND SIGNAL PROCESSING (UK/0888-3270). **2122**
MECHANICS OF COMPOSITE MATERIALS (US/0191-5665). **2106**
MECHANICS OF MATERIALS (NE/0167-6636). **2106**
MECHANICS OF SOLIDS (US/0025-6544). **4412**
MECHANICS OF STRUCTURES AND MACHINES (US/0890-5452). **2106**
MECHANICS RESEARCH COMMUNICATIONS (US/0093-6413). **4429**
MECHANISM AND MACHINE THEORY (UK/0094-114X). **2122**
MECHANISMS OF AGEING AND DEVELOPMENT (SZ/0047-6374). **584**
MECHANISMS OF DEVELOPMENT (IE/0925-4773). **464**
MECHATRONIC SYSTEMS ENGINEERING (NE/0924-3992). **1220**
MECHATRONICS (OXFORD) (UK/0957-4158). **1195**
MEDECINE & CHIRURGIE DIGESTIVES (FR/0047-6412). **3969**
MEDECINE DU SPORT (FR/0025-6722). **3955**
MEDECINE ET CHIRURGIE DU PIED (FR/0759-2280). **3918**
MEDECINE ET HYGIENE (SZ/0025-6749). **3607**
MEDECINE ET NUTRITON (FR/0398-7604). **3607**
MEDECONOMICS (UK/0144-4271). **3607**
MEDIA LAW REPORTER (US/0148-1045). **3008**
MEDIA REPORT TO WOMEN (US/0145-9651). **1117**
MEDIAEVAL STUDIES (CN/0076-5872). **2697**
MEDIATORS OF INFLAMMATION (UK/0962-9351). **3607**
MEDIAWEEK (NEW YORK, N.Y.) (US/1055-176X). **933**
MEDICAL ADVERTISING NEWS (US/0745-0907). **762**
MEDICAL & BIOLOGICAL ENGINEERING & COMPUTING (UK/0140-0118). **3695**
MEDICAL AND HEALTH CARE BOOKS AND SERIALS IN PRINT (US/0000-085X). **3660**
MEDICAL AND PEDIATRIC ONCOLOGY (US/0098-1532). **3906**
MEDICAL AND VETERINARY ENTOMOLOGY (UK/0269-283X). **5611**
MEDICAL ANTHROPOLOGY (US/0145-9740). **241**
MEDICAL ASPECTS OF HUMAN SEXUALITY (US/0025-7001). **5188**
MEDICAL CARE (US/0025-7079). **3608**
MEDICAL CARE REVIEW (US/0025-7087). **3608**
MEDICAL CLINICS OF NORTH AMERICA, THE (US/0025-7125). **3608**
MEDICAL DECISION MAKING (US/0272-989X). **1215**
MEDICAL DEVICE APPROVAL LETTER (US/1060-8338). **3608**
MEDICAL DEVICES, DIAGNOSTICS & INSTRUMENTATION REPORTS (US/0163-2426). **3608**
MEDICAL DEVISE REGISTER (US/0278-808X). **3788**

MEDICAL EDUCATION (UK/0308-0110). **3609**
MEDICAL ETHICS ADVISOR (US/0886-0653). **2252**
MEDICAL FOCUS (WURZBURG, GERMANY) (GW/0724-8172). **3609**
MEDICAL HYPOTHESES (UK/0306-9877). **3609**
MEDICAL INFORMATICS (UK/0307-7640). **1261**
MEDICAL LABORATORY SCIENCES (UK/0308-3616). **3610**
MEDICAL LASER BUYERS' GUIDE (US/0896-0275). **1618**
MEDICAL LAW REVIEW (UK/0967-0742). **3008**
MEDICAL MARKETING & MEDIA (US/0025-7354). **933**
MEDICAL MEETINGS (US/0093-1314). **3610**
MEDICAL MICROBIOLOGY AND IMMUNOLOGY (GW/0300-8584). **566**
MEDICAL ONCOLOGY AND TUMOR PHARMACOTHERAPY (UK/0736-0118). **3821**
MEDICAL PHYSICS (LANCASTER) (US/0094-2405). **4412**
MEDICAL POST, THE (CN/0025-7435). **3611**
MEDICAL PRINCIPLES AND PRACTICE (SZ/1011-7571). **3611**
MEDICAL PROBLEMS OF PERFORMING ARTISTS (US/0885-1158). **3611**
MEDICAL PRODUCTS SALES (US/0279-4802). **3611**
MEDICAL PROGRESS THROUGH TECHNOLOGY (NE/0047-6552). **3695**
MEDICAL SCIENCE RESEARCH (UK/0269-8951). **3611**
MEDICAL TEACHER (UK/0142-159X). **3611**
MEDICAL TEXTILES (NE/0266-2078). **3612**
MEDICAL TRIBUNE (1980) (US/0279-9340). **3612**
MEDICAL TRIBUNE. MICROFORM (US/0279-9340). **3612**
MEDICAL WASTE NEWS (US/1048-4493). **3612**
MEDICAL WORLD NEWS (US/0025-763X). **3612**
MEDICAMENTOS DE ACTUALIDAD (SP/0025-7656). **4315**
MEDICINA CLINICA (SP/0025-7753). **3613**
MEDICINAL CHEMISTRY RESEARCH (US/1054-2523). **4315**
MEDICINAL RESEARCH REVIEWS (US/0198-6325). **4315**
MEDICINE AND LAW (GW/0723-1393). **3742**
MEDICINE AND SCIENCE IN SPORTS AND EXERCISE (US/0195-9131). **3955**
MEDICINE AND SPORT SCIENCE (SZ/0254-5020). **3955**
MEDICINE AND WAR (UK/0748-8009). **3613**
MEDICINE (BALTIMORE) (US/0025-7974). **3613**
MEDICINE, EXERCISE, NUTRITION, AND HEALTH (US/1057-9354). **3613**
MEDICINE, SCIENCE, AND THE LAW (UK/0025-8024). **3742**
MEDIEN + ERZIEHUNG (GW/0341-6860). **1117**
MEDIENWISSENSCHAFT, REZENSIONEN (GW/0176-4241). **1117**
MEDITERRANEE MEDICALE (FR/0302-9263). **3614**

MEDIZINHISTORISCHES JOURNAL (GW/0025-8431). **3615**
MEDIZINISCHE KLINIK (MUNCHEN. 1983) (GW/0723-5003). **3615**
MEDIZINISCHE MONATSSCHRIFT FUER PHARMAZEUTEN (GW/0342-9601). **4315**
MEDIZINISCHE WELT (GW/0025-8512). **3615**
MEDIZINRECHT (GW/0723-8886). **3742**
MEERESFORSCHUNG (GW/0341-6836). **1452**
MEETING NEWS (US/0145-630X). **692**
MEHANIKA KOMPOZITNYH MATERIALOV (LV/0203-1272). **2107**
MEHANIKA TVERDOGO TELA (KIEV) (UN/0321-1975). **4429**
MELANOMA RESEARCH (UK/0960-8931). **3821**
MELLIAND-TEXTILBERICHTE (1976) (GW/0341-0781). **5354**
MELODY MAKER (LONDON) (UK/0025-9012). **4130**
MELTS (US/0895-7738). **4412**
MEMBRANE & SEPARATION TECHNOLOGY NEWS (US/0737-8483). **985**
MEMBRANE BIOCHEMISTRY (US/0149-046X). **490**
MEMBRANE PROTEINS (UK/0143-4233). **490**
MEMBRANE TECHNOLOGY (UK/0958-2118). **3695**
MEMOIR (CANADIAN SOCIETY OF PETROLEUM GEOLOGISTS) (CN/0703-1130). **1387**
MEMOIR / GEOLOGICAL SOCIETY OF AMERICA (US/0072-1069). **1387**
MEMOIR - GEOLOGICAL SURVEY OF CANADA (CN/0068-7634). **1387**
MEMOIR ... OF THE ASSOCIATION OF AUSTRALASIAN PALAEONTOLOGISTS (AT/0810-8889). **4228**
MEMOIRES ET ETUDES SCIENTIFIQUES DE LA REVUE DE METALLURGIE (FR/0245-8292). **4008**
MEMOIRS OF THE AMERICAN MATHEMATICAL SOCIETY (US/0065-9266). **3522**
MEMOIRS OF THE ENTOMOLOGICAL SOCIETY OF CANADA (CN/0071-075X). **5591**
MEMOIRS OF THE ENTOMOLOGICAL SOCIETY OF CANADA (CN/0071-075X). **5612**
MEMOIRS OF THE NEW YORK BOTANICAL GARDEN (US/0077-8931). **517**
MEMORIALS - GEOLOGICAL SOCIETY OF AMERICA (US/0091-5041). **1387**
MEMORY & COGNITION (US/0090-502X). **4603**
MEMPHIS BUSINESS JOURNAL (US/0747-167X). **693**
MENDELEEV CHEMISTRY JOURNAL (US/0025-925X). **985**
MENDELEEV COMMUNICATIONS / ROYAL SOCIETY OF CHEMISTRY, [AKADEMIIA NAUK SSSR] (RU/0959-9436). **985**
MENTAL HEALTH LAW REPORTER (US/0741-5141). **3009**
MENTAL HEALTH REPORTS (US/0191-6750). **4790**
MENTAL HEALTH WEEKLY (US/1058-1103). **4604**
MENTAL RETARDATION (WASHINGTON) (US/0047-6765). **1882**
MENTALITIES (NZ/0111-8854). **4604**
MER. MARINE ENGINEERS REVIEW (UK/0047-5955). **1987**

MERGERS & ACQUISITIONS (US/0026-0010). **798**

MERKUR (GW/0026-0096). **3347**

MERVYN PEAKE REVIEW, THE (SZ/0309-1309). **3411**

METABOLIC BRAIN DISEASE (US/0885-7490). **3838**

METABOLISM, CLINICAL AND EXPERIMENTAL (US/0026-0495). **3674**

METAL BULLETIN MONTHLY (UK/0373-4064). **4009**

METAL BULLETIN, THE (UK/0026-0533). **4009**

METAL/CENTER NEWS (US/0539-4511). **4009**

METAL FINISHING (US/0026-0576). **4009**

METAL POWDER REPORT (UK/0026-0657). **4009**

METALL (BERLIN) (GW/0026-0746). **4009**

METALOBERFLACHE (GW/0026-0797). **4009**

METALLOVEDENIE I TERMICESKAJA OBRABOTKA (KALININ) (RU/0026-0819). **4009**

METALLOVEDENIE I TERMICHESKAYA OBRABOTKA METALLOV (US/0026-0673). **4010**

METALLURG (RU/0026-0827). **4010**

METALLURGIA ITALIANA, LA (IT/0026-0843). **4010**

METALLURGICAL TRANSACTIONS. A. PHYSICAL METALLURGY AND MATERIALS SCIENCE (US/0360-2133). **4010**

METALLURGICAL TRANSACTIONS. B, PROCESS METALLURGY (US/0360-2141). **4010**

METALLURGIST (NEW YORK) (US/0026-0894). **4010**

METALWORKING DIGEST (US/0026-1009). **4011**

METALWORKING PRODUCTION (UK/0026-1033). **4012**

METAPHILOSOPHY (UK/0026-1068). **4352**

METEORITICS (US/0026-1114). **1387**

METEOROLOGICAL AND GEOASTROPHYSICAL ABSTRACTS (US/0026-1130). **1363**

METEOROLOGICAL MONOGRAPHS (AMERICAN METEOROLOGICAL SOCIETY) (US/0065-9401). **1431**

METEOROLOGY AND ATMOSPHERIC PHYSICS (AU/0177-7971). **1431**

METHODS AND FINDINGS IN EXPERIMENTAL AND CLINICAL PHARMACOLOGY (SP/0379-0355). **4315**

METHODS IN CELL BIOLOGY (US/0091-679X). **538**

METHODS IN ENZYMOLOGY (US/0076-6879). **490**

METHODS IN GEOCHEMISTRY AND GEOPHYSICS (NE/0076-6895). **1408**

METHODS IN NEUROSCIENCES (US/1043-9471). **3838**

METHODS IN ORGANIC SYNTHESIS (UK/0265-4245). **1012**

METHODS OF BIOCHEMICAL ANALYSIS (US/0076-6941). **986**

METHODS OF EXPERIMENTAL PHYSICS (US/0076-695X). **4412**

METHODS OF INFORMATION IN MEDICINE (GW/0026-1270). **3616**

METHODS (SAN DIEGO, CALIF.) (US/1046-2023). **490**

METLFAX (US/0026-1297). **4012**

METRIKA (GW/0026-1335). **3523**

METROECONOMICA (IT/0026-1386). **1505**

METROLOGIA (GW/0026-1394). **4031**

MEXICAN STUDIES (US/0742-9797). **1505**

MEXICO BUSINESS MONTHLY (US/1054-2663). **906**

MEXICO SERVICE (US/1044-6303). **2512**

MEYLER'S SIDE EFFECTS OF DRUGS (NE/0376-7396). **4315**

MICHIGAN DISTRIBUTORS DIRECTORY (US/0890-4049). **694**

MICHIGAN MANUFACTURERS DIRECTORY (US/0736-2889). **3484**

MICROBIAL ECOLOGY (US/0095-3628). **2218**

MICROBIAL ECOLOGY IN HEALTH AND DISEASE (UK/0891-060X). **3616**

MICROBIAL PATHOGENESIS (UK/0882-4010). **3715**

MICROBIAL RELEASES : VIRUSES, BACTERIA, FUNGI (GW/0940-9653). **566**

MICROBIOLOGICAL REVIEWS (US/0146-0749). **567**

MICROBIOLOGY (UK/1350-0872). **567**

MICROBIOLOGY (NEW YORK) (US/0026-2617). **567**

MICROBIOS (UK/0026-2633). **567**

MICROCHEMICAL JOURNAL (US/0026-265X). **986**

MICROCIRCULATION, ENDOTHELIUM, AND LYMPHATICS (US/0740-9451). **3616**

MICROCOMPUTERS FOR INFORMATION MANAGEMENT (US/0742-2342). **1269**

MICROCOMPUTERS IN CIVIL ENGINEERING (UK/0885-9507). **2027**

MICROELECTRONIC ENGINEERING (NE/0167-9317). **2072**

MICROELECTRONICS (UK/0026-2692). **2072**

MICROELECTRONICS AND RELIABILITY (UK/0026-2714). **2072**

MICROFAUNA MARINA (GW/0176-3296). **465**

MICROFORM REVIEW (US/0002-6530). **3231**

MICROGRAVITY QUARTERLY (UK/0958-5036). **4412**

MICROGRAVITY SCIENCE AND TECHNOLOGY (GW/0938-0108). **4412**

MICRON : THE INTERNATIONAL RESEARCH AND REVIEW JOURNAL FOR MICROSCOPY (UK/0968-4328). **573**

MICROPALEONTOLOGY (US/0026-2803). **4228**

MICROPALEONTOLOGY SPECIAL PUBLICATION (US/0160-2071). **4228**

MICROPOROUS MATERIALS (NE/0927-6513). **986**

MICROPROCESSING AND MICROPROGRAMMING (NE/0165-6074). **1269**

MICROPROCESSORS AND MICROSYSTEMS (UK/0141-9331). **1230**

MICROSCOPE (LONDON) (US/0026-282X). **573**

MICROSCOPE TECHNOLOGY & NEWS (US/1041-0716). **573**

MICROSOFT WORKS IN EDUCATION (US/1046-1981). **1900**

MICROSTRUCTURAL SCIENCE (US/0361-1213). **4012**

MICROSURGERY (US/0738-1085). **3970**

MICROVASCULAR RESEARCH (US/0026-2862). **3773**

MICROWAVE AND OPTICAL TECHNOLOGY LETTERS (US/0895-2477). **2072**

MICROWAVE JOURNAL (EURO-GLOBAL ED.) (US/0192-6217). **2072**

MICROWAVES & RF (US/0745-2993). **4438**

MIDCONTINENT OIL WORLD (US/0883-7325). **4264**

MIDCONTINENTAL JOURNAL OF ARCHAEOLOGY, MCJA (US/0146-1109). **274**

MIDDLE EAST BUSINESS INTELLIGENCE (US/0731-6305). **933**

MIDDLE EAST EXECUTIVE REPORTS (US/0271-0498). **3132**

MIDWEST REAL ESTATE NEWS (US/0893-2719). **4841**

MIDWIFERY (UK/0266-6138). **3765**

MIKOLOGIJA I FITOPATOLOGIJA (RU/0026-3648). **575**

MIKROBIOLOGICHESKII ZHURNAL (UN/0201-8462). **567**

MIKROBIOLOGIJA (MOSKVA. 1932) (RU/0026-3656). **567**

MIKROCHIMICA ACTA (AU/0026-3672). **1018**

MIKROCHIMICA ACTA. SUPPLEMENTUM (1966) (GW/0076-8642). **986**

MIKROKOSMOS (STUTTGART) (GW/0026-3680). **573**

MILBANK QUARTERLY, THE (US/0887-378X). **4791**

MILCHWISSENSCHAFT (GW/0026-3788). **196**

MILITARY & AEROSPACE ELECTRONICS (US/1046-9079). **4050**

MILITARY & COMMERCIAL FIBER BUSINESS (US/1051-2470). **4438**

MILITARY LIVING (US/0740-5065). **4051**

MILITARY LIVING'S R & R REPORT (US/0740-5073). **4051**

MILITARY MEDICINE (US/0026-4075). **3617**

MILITARY SPACE (US/0743-7897). **28**

MILLIMETER (US/0164-9655). **4074**

MILTON QUARTERLY (US/0026-4326). **3347**

MIND (UK/0026-4423). **4353**

MIND & LANGUAGE (UK/0268-1064). **3302**

MINDS AND MACHINES (DORDRECHT) (NE/0924-6495). **1215**

MINE REGULATION REPORTER (US/1040-8223). **3010**

MINERAL AND ELECTROLYTE METABOLISM (SZ/0378-0392). **3799**

MINERAL PROCESSING AND EXTRACTIVE METALLURGY REVIEW (UK/0882-7508). **2144**

MINERALIUM DEPOSITA (GW/0026-4598). **1441**

MINERALOGY AND PETROLOGY (AU/0930-0708). **1442**

MINERALS ENGINEERING (UK/0892-6875). **2144**

MINING JOURNAL (LONDON. 1908) (UK/0026-5225). **2146**

MINING MAGAZINE (LONDON) (UK/0308-6631). **2146**

MINNESOTA DRAMA EDITIONS (US/0076-9142). **5366**

MINNESOTA HISTORY (US/0026-5497). **2746**

MINNESOTA MEDICINE (US/0026-556X). **3617**

MINNESOTA STUDIES IN THE PHILOSOPHY OF SCIENCE (US/0076-9258). **5129**

MINORITY FUNDING REPORT (US/1047-3300). **5296**

MINORITY MARKETS ALERT (US/1041-7524). **906**

MITOCHONDRIA / ISSUED MONTHLY BY UNIVERSITY OF SHEFFIELD BIOMEDICAL INFORMATION SERVICE (UK/0142-8217). **3617**

MITTEILUNGEN AUS DER ARBEITSMARKT- UND BERUFSFORSCHUNG (GW/0340-3254). **1691**

MITTEILUNGEN DES DEUTSCHEN GERMANISTENVERBANDES (GW/0418-9426). **1764**

MITTEILUNGEN DES VEREINIGUNG SCHWEIZERISCHER VERSICHERUNGSMATHEMATIKER (SZ/0042-3815). **2888**

MITTEILUNGEN - INTERNATIONALEN VEREINIGUNG FUER THEORETISCHE UND ANGEWANDTE LIMNOLOGIE (GW/0538-4680). **1416**

MITTEILUNGEN - PTB (GW/0030-834X). **5129**

MITTEILUNGSBLATT - VERBAND DER BIBLIOTHEKEN DES LANDES NORDRHEIN WESTFALEN (GW/0042-3629). **3232**

MLN (US/0026-7910). **3303**

MLO, MEDICAL LABORATORY OBSERVER (US/0580-7247). **3617**

MMI PRESS SYMPOSIUM SERIES (US/0195-3966). **986**

MMU, DER MATHEMATISCHE UND NATURWISSENSCHAFTLICHE UNTERRICHT (GW/0025-5866). **3523**

MMW. MUNCHENER MEDIZINISCHE WOCHENSCHRIFT (GW/0341-3098). **3617**

MNEMOSYNE (NE/0026-7074). **3303**

MOBILE PHONE NEWS (US/0737-5077). **1160**

MOBILE RADIO TECHNOLOGY (US/0745-7626). **1135**

MOBILE SATELLITE NEWS (POTOMAC, MD.) (US/1046-5286). **1160**

MOD CONTRACTS BULLETIN (UK/0269-0365). **695**

MODELING AND SIMULATION (US/0198-0092). **1282**

MODELING OF GEO-BIOSPHERE PROCESSES (GW/0938-9563). **1358**

MODELS IN DERMATOLOGY (SZ/0259-1340). **3722**

MODERN AGING RESEARCH (US/0275-360X). **3754**

MODERN APPLICATIONS NEWS (US/0277-9951). **4012**

MODERN ASIAN STUDIES (UK/0026-749X). **2659**

MODERN ASPECTS OF ELECTROCHEMISTRY (US/0076-9924). **1034**

MODERN BRIDE (US/0026-7546). **2283**

MODERN CASTING (US/0026-7562). **4012**

MODERN CHINA (US/0097-7004). **2659**

MODERN DENTAL PRACTICE (US/0894-7953). **1330**

MODERN DRAMA (CN/0026-7694). **5366**

MODERN GEOLOGY (US/0026-7775). **1388**

MODERN HEALTHCARE (1977) (US/0160-7480). **3789**

MODERN JUDAISM (US/0276-1114). **5051**

MODERN

MODERN LANGUAGE JOURNAL (BOULDER, COLO.), THE (US/0026-7902). **3303**

MODERN LAW REVIEW (UK/0026-7961). **3011**

MODERN MACHINE SHOP (US/0026-8003). **2122**

MODERN MATERIALS HANDLING (US/0026-8038). **3484**

MODERN METHODS IN PHARMACOLOGY (US/0732-7218). **4316**

MODERN OFFICE TECHNOLOGY (US/0746-3839). **4212**

MODERN PAINT AND COATINGS (US/0098-7786). **4224**

MODERN PATHOLOGY (US/0893-3952). **3896**

MODERN PHILOLOGY (US/0026-8232). **3303**

MODERN PHYSICS LETTERS A (SI/0217-7323). **4448**

MODERN PHYSICS LETTERS. B, CONDENSED MATTER PHYSICS, STATISTICAL PHYSICS, APPLIED PHYSICS (SI/0217-9849). **4412**

MODERN PLASTICS (US/0026-8275). **4456**

MODERN PLASTICS ENCYCLOPEDIA (1954) (US/0085-3518). **4457**

MODERN PLASTICS INTERNATIONAL (SZ/0026-8283). **4457**

MODERN POWER SYSTEMS (UK/0260-7840). **1950**

MODERN PROBLEMS OF PHARMACOPSYCHIATRY (SZ/0077-0094). **3931**

MODERN QUATERNARY RESEARCH IN SOUTHEAST ASIA (NE/0168-6151). **4228**

MODERN RAILWAYS (UK/0026-8356). **5433**

MODERN SALON (US/0148-4001). **404**

MODERN THEOLOGY (UK/0266-7177). **4978**

MODERN VETERINARY PRACTICE (1973) (US/0362-8140). **5516**

MOKUZAI GAKKAISHI (JA/0021-4795). **2403**

MOLECULAR AND BIOCHEMICAL PARASITOLOGY (NE/0166-6851). **465**

MOLECULAR AND CELLULAR BIOCHEMISTRY (NE/0300-8177). **491**

MOLECULAR AND CELLULAR BIOLOGY (US/0270-7306). **568**

MOLECULAR AND CELLULAR ENDOCRINOLOGY (IE/0303-7207). **3732**

MOLECULAR AND CELLULAR NEUROSCIENCES (US/1044-7431). **3838**

MOLECULAR AND CELLULAR PROBES (UK/0890-8508). **465**

MOLECULAR AND CHEMICAL NEUROPATHOLOGY (US/1044-7393). **3838**

MOLECULAR & GENERAL GENETICS : MGG (GW/0026-8925). **549**

MOLECULAR ASPECTS OF MEDICINE (UK/0098-2997). **3618**

MOLECULAR BIOLOGY AND EVOLUTION (US/0737-4038). **465**

MOLECULAR BIOLOGY (NEW YORK) (US/0026-8933). **465**

MOLECULAR BIOLOGY REPORTS (NE/0301-4851). **465**

MOLECULAR BIOTHERAPY (US/0952-8172). **465**

MOLECULAR BRAIN RESEARCH (NE/0169-328X). **3838**

MOLECULAR CRYSTALS AND LIQUID CRYSTALS SCIENCE AND TECHNOLOGY: SECTION A, MOLECULAR CRYSTALS AND LIQUID CRYSTALS (US/1058-725X). **1032**

MOLECULAR CRYSTALS AND LIQUID CRYSTALS SCIENCE AND TECHNOLOGY SECTION B, NONLINEAR OPTICS (US/1058-7268). **4438**

MOLECULAR CRYSTALS AND LIQUID CRYSTALS SCIENCE AND TECHNOLOGY SECTION C, MOLECULAR MATERIALS (US/1058-7276). **1033**

MOLECULAR CRYSTALS AND LIQUID CRYSTALS SCIENCE AND TECHNOLOGY SECTION D, DISPLAY AND IMAGING (US/1058-7284). **4438**

MOLECULAR ECOLOGY (UK/0962-1083). **2218**

MOLECULAR ENGINEERING (NE/0925-5125). **1988**

MOLECULAR GENETICS, MICROBIOLOGY AND VIROLOGY (US/0891-4168). **568**

MOLECULAR IMMUNOLOGY (UK/0161-5890). **3675**

MOLECULAR MARINE BIOLOGY AND BIOTECHNOLOGY (US/1053-6426). **556**

MOLECULAR MICROBIOLOGY (UK/0950-382X). **568**

MOLECULAR NEUROBIOLOGY (US/0893-7648). **3838**

MOLECULAR PHARMACOLOGY (US/0026-895X). **4316**

MOLECULAR PHYLOGENETICS AND EVOLUTION (US/1055-7903). **549**

MOLECULAR PHYSICS (UK/0026-8976). **1056**

MOLECULAR SIMULATION (US/0892-7022). **4429**

MONATSHEFTE FUER CHEMIE (US/0026-9247). **986**

MONATSHEFTE FUER MATHEMATIK (AU/0026-9255). **3523**

MONATSHEFTE FUER VETERINAERMEDIZIN (GW/0026-9263). **5516**

MONATSHEFTE (MADISON, 1946) (US/0026-9271). **3303**

MONATSSCHRIFT FUER BRAUWISSENSCHAFT (GW/0723-1520). **2369**

MONATSSCHRIFT FUER DEUTSCHES RECHT (GW/0340-1812). **3011**

MONATSSCHRIFT FUER KINDERHEILKUNDE (GW/0026-9298). **3906**

MONDE INFORMATIQUE, LE (FR/0242-5769). **1195**

MONDE. SELECTION HEBDOMADAIRE, LE (FR/0026-9360). **5801**

MONEY LAUNDERING ALERT (US/1046-3070). **3087**

MONEY MANAGEMENT FOR PHYSICIANS (US/0162-6507). **799**

MONITORE ZOOLOGICO ITALIANO. MONOGRAFIA (IT/0391-1632). **5591**

MONOCLONAL ANTIBODIES (UK/0261-4960). **3675**

MONOGRAPH - AMERICAN FISHERIES SOCIETY (US/0362-1715). **2308**

MONOGRAPH SERIES ON MINERAL DEPOSITS (GW/0341-6356). **1442**

MONOGRAPHS IN ALLERGY (SW/0077-0760). **3675**

MONOGRAPHS IN CLINICAL CYTOLOGY (SZ/0077-0809). **539**

MONOGRAPHS IN DEVELOPMENTAL BIOLOGY (SZ/0077-0825). **466**

MONOGRAPHS IN HUMAN GENETICS (SZ/0077-0876). **549**

MONOGRAPHS IN NEURAL SCIENCES (SZ/0300-5186). **3838**

MONOGRAPHS IN ORAL SCIENCE (SZ/0077-0892). **1330**

MONOGRAPHS IN PRIMATOLOGY (US/0740-9729). **5591**

MONOGRAPHS IN VIROLOGY (SZ/0077-0965). **568**

MONTHLY DIGEST OF TAX ARTICLES, THE (US/0027-0385). **4737**

MONTHLY NOTICES OF THE ROYAL ASTRONOMICAL SOCIETY (UK/0035-8711). **397**

MONTHLY WEATHER REPORT (UK/0027-0636). **1432**

MONTHLY WEATHER REVIEW (US/0027-0644). **1432**

MONUMENTA SERICA (GW/0254-9948). **2623**

MORGAN DIRECTORY REVIEWS / MDR (US/0899-4560). **3232**

MORGAN REPORT ON DIRECTORY PUBLISHING (US/0890-9512). **4817**

MORTGAGE AND REAL ESTATE EXECUTIVES REPORT, THE (US/0047-813X). **4841**

MORTGAGE BANKING (US/0730-0212). **800**

MORTGAGE MARKETPLACE, THE (US/0744-3927). **800**

MOSAIC (WINNIPEG) (CN/0027-1276). **3413**

MOSASAUR, THE (US/0736-3907). **4228**

MOSCOW UNIVERSITY BIOLOGICAL SCIENCES BULLETIN (US/0096-3925). **466**

MOSCOW UNIVERSITY CHEMISTRY BULLETIN (US/0027-1314). **987**

MOSCOW UNIVERSITY GEOLOGY BULLETIN (US/0145-8752). **1388**

MOSCOW UNIVERSITY MATHEMATICS BULLETIN (US/0027-1322). **3523**

MOSCOW UNIVERSITY MECHANICS BULLETIN (US/0027-1330). **4429**

MOSCOW UNIVERSITY PHYSICS BULLETIN (US/0027-1349). **4412**

MOSCOW UNIVERSITY SOIL SCIENCE BULLETIN (US/0147-6874). **179**

MOSQUITO SYSTEMATICS (US/0091-3669). **2177**

MOTION CONTROL (US/1053-4644). **2123**

MOTIVATION AND EMOTION (US/0146-7239). **4604**

MOTOR CYCLE NEWS PETERBOROUGH (UK/0027-1853). **5387**

MOTOR SERVICE (CHICAGO, ILL. : 1951) (US/0027-1977). **5420**

MOTORIK (GW/0170-5792). **4792**

MOTRICITE CEREBRALE, READAPTATION, NEUROLOGIE DU DEVELOPPEMENT (FR/0245-5919). **3838**

MOTS (FR/0243-6450). **4482**

MOUNTAIN GEOLOGIST, THE (US/0027-254X). **1388**

MOUNTAIN RESEARCH AND DEVELOPMENT (US/0276-4741). **241**

MOUSE GENOME (UK/0959-0587). **466**

MOVEMENT DISORDERS (US/0885-3185). **3838**

MRS BULLETIN (US/0883-7694). **2107**

MTZ. MOTORTECHNISCHE ZEITSCHRIFT (GW/0024-8525). **2123**

MULL UND ABFALL (GW/0027-2957). **4792**

MULTI-HOUSING NEWS (US/0146-0919). **2828**

MULTICHANNEL NEWS (US/0276-8593). **1135**

MULTICULTURAL EDUCATION ABSTRACTS (UK/0260-9770). **1795**

MULTIDIMENSIONAL SYSTEMS AND SIGNAL PROCESSING (US/0923-6082). **1196**

MULTILINGUA (NE/0167-8507). **3304**

MULTIMEDIA REVIEW (US/1046-3550). **1196**

MULTIMEDIA SYSTEMS (GW/0942-4962). **1118**

MULTIPHASE SCIENCE AND TECHNOLOGY (US/0276-1459). **5130**

MUNCHNER GEOWISSENSCHAFTLICHE ABHANDLUNGEN. REIHE A, GEOLOGIE UND PALAONTOLOGIE (GW/0177-0950). **1389**

MUNDO ELECTRONICO. EDICION INTERNACIONAL (SP/0300-3787). **2073**

MUNICIPAL FINANCE JOURNAL (US/0199-6134). **4738**

MUNICIPAL WORKER LAW BULLETIN (US/0893-8172). **3152**

MUQARNAS (US/0732-2992). **304**

MUSCLE & NERVE (US/0148-639X). **3838**

MUSEUM ABSTRACTS (UK/0267-8594). **4098**

MUSEUM HELVETICUM (SZ/0027-4054). **275**

MUSEUM NEWS (WASHINGTON) (US/0027-4089). **4092**

MUSIC & LETTERS (UK/0027-4224). **4132**

MUSIC PERCEPTION (US/0730-7829). **4134**

MUSICA (GW/0027-4518). **4135**

MUSICAL QUARTERLY, THE (US/0027-4631). **4136**

MUSICIAN (GLOUCESTER, MASS.) (US/0733-5253). **4137**

MUSICOLOGY AUSTRALIA (AT/0814-5857). **4137**

MUSIK UND KIRCHE (GW/0027-4771). **4138**

MUSIKFORSCHUNG (GW/0027-4801). **4138**

MUSIKINSTRUMENT, DAS (GW/0027-4828). **4138**

MUSIKMARKT, DER (GW/0047-8474). **4138**

MUSIKTHERAPEUTISCHE UMSCHAU (GW/0172-5505). **4138**

MUTAGENESIS (UK/0267-8357). **549**

MUTATION RESEARCH (NE/0027-5107). **549**

MUTATION RESEARCH. DNA REPAIR (NE/0921-8777). **466**

MUTATION RESEARCH. DNAGING : GENETIC INSTABILITY AND AGING (NE/0921-8734). **550**

MUTATION RESEARCH. MUTATION RESEARCH LETTERS (NE/0165-7992). **550**

MUTATION RESEARCH. REVIEWS IN GENETIC TOXICOLOGY (NE/0165-1110). **3982**

MUTUAL FUND FORECASTER (US/8755-9889). **908**

MYCOLOGIA (US/0027-5514). **575**

MYCOPATHOLOGIA (1975) (NE/0301-486X). **576**

MYCORRHIZA (GW/0940-6360). **518**

NAACOG'S CLINICAL ISSUES IN PERINATAL AND WOMEN'S HEALTH NURSING (US/1046-7475). **3765**

NACHRICHTEN AUS CHEMIE, TECHNIK UND LABORATORIUM (GW/0341-5163). **987**

NACHRICHTEN FUER DOKUMENTATION (GW/0027-7436). **3232**

NACHRICHTENBLATT DES DEUTSCHEN PFLANZENSCHUTZDIENSTES (GW/0027-7479). **519**

NAECON (US/0547-3578). **29**

NAHRUNG, DIE (GW/0027-769X). **4194**

NAHVERKEHR, DER (GW/0722-8287). **5442**

NANOBIOLOGY : JOURNAL OF RESEARCH ON NANOSCALE LIVING SYSTEMS (UK/0958-3165). **539**

NANOSTRUCTURED MATERIALS (US/0965-9773). **2107**

NANOTECHNOLOGY (BRISTOL) (UK/0957-4484). **1988**

NARCOTICS LAW BULLETIN (US/8755-8289). **3013**

NARODY AZII I AFRIKI (URR/0027-8041). **2642**

NASA TECH BRIEFS (WASHINGTON, D.C. 1976) (US/0145-319X). **5130**

NASDAQ YELLOW BOOK (US/1058-2886). **696**

NASHVILLE BUSINESS JOURNAL (US/0889-2873). **696**

NATIONAL BULLETIN ON POLICE MISCONDUCT (US/1042-5810). **3170**

NATIONAL DIRECTORY OF INTERNSHIPS, RESIDENCIES & REGISTRARSHIPS, AUSTRALIA (AT/0155-9567). **3619**

NATIONAL FORUM (ANN ARBOR) (US/0162-1831). **1836**

NATIONAL FORUM OF APPLIED EDUCATIONAL RESEARCH JOURNAL (US/0895-3880). **1867**

NATIONAL FORUM OF EDUCATIONAL ADMINISTRATION AND SUPERVISION JOURNAL (US/0888-8132). **1766**

NATIONAL HOG FARMER (US/0027-9447). **216**

NATIONAL HOME CENTER NEWS (US/0192-6772). **2792**

NATIONAL JEWELER (US/0027-9544). **2915**

NATIONAL JOURNAL (1975) (US/0360-4217). **4483**

NATIONAL LIBRARIAN : THE NLA NEWSLETTER (US/0191-359X). **3233**

NATIONAL MEDICAL JOURNAL OF INDIA, THE (II/0970-258X). **3619**

NATIONAL ON-CAMPUS REPORT (US/0300-6646). **1836**

NATIONAL PETROLEUM NEWS (US/0149-5267). **4265**

NATIONAL PRODUCTIVITY REVIEW (US/0277-8556). **880**

NATIONAL REAL ESTATE INVESTOR (US/0027-9994). **909**

NATIONAL REPORT ON SUBSTANCE ABUSE, THE (US/0891-5709). **1347**

NATIONAL REPORT ON WORK & FAMILY (US/0896-3002). **5297**

NATION'S BUSINESS (US/0028-047X). **697**

NATION'S HEALTH (1971), THE (US/0028-0496). **4792**

NATION'S RESTAURANT NEWS (US/0028-0518). **5072**

NATO ASI SERIES. SERIES C, MATHEMATICAL AND PHYSICAL SCIENCES (NE/0258-2023). **3524**

NATO ASI SERIES. SERIES E, APPLIED SCIENCE (US/0168-132X). **5130**

NATO ASI SERIES. SERIES F, COMPUTER AND SYSTEM SCIENCES (GW/0258-1248). **1196**

NATUR-UND GANZHEITSMEDIZIN : NGM (GW/0934-7909). **3619**

NATUR UND LANDSCHAFT (STUTTGART) (GW/0028-0615). **4168**

NATURAL GAS INTELLIGENCE (US/0739-1811). **4265**

NATURAL GAS (NEW YORK, N.Y.) (US/0743-5665). **4265**

NATURAL GAS WEEK (US/8756-3037). **4266**

NATURAL HAZARDS (DORDRECHT) (NE/0921-030X). **2178**

NATURAL IMMUNITY (SZ/1018-8916). **3675**

NATURAL LANGUAGE AND LINGUISTIC THEORY (NE/0167-806X). **3305**

NATURAL PRODUCT LETTERS (UK/1057-5634). **491**

NATURAL PRODUCT REPORTS (UK/0265-0568). **491**

NATURAL RESOURCES FORUM (NE/0165-0203). **2199**

NATURAL RESOURCES TAX REVIEW, THE (US/1050-1932). **2199**

NATURALIST (LEEDS) (UK/0028-0771). **4168**

NATURE GENETICS (US/1061-4036). **550**

NATURE (LONDON) (UK/0028-0836). **5131**

NATURE, SOCIETY, AND THOUGHT (US/0890-6130). **5131**

NATURWISSENSCHAFTEN, DIE (GW/0028-1042). **5131**

NATURWISSENSCHAFTLICHE RUNDSCHAU (GW/0028-1050). **5131**

NAUNYN-SCHMIEDEBERG'S ARCHIVES OF PHARMACOLOGY (GW/0028-1298). **4317**

NAVAL ARCHITECTURE AND OCEAN ENGINEERING (JA/0387-5504). **4179**

NAVAL RESEARCH LOGISTICS (US/0894-069X). **4180**

NAVIGATION (WASHINGTON) (US/0028-1522). **4180**

NAVY NEWS & UNDERSEA TECHNOLOGY (US/8756-1700). **4180**

NAVY TIMES (US/0028-1697). **4180**

NBER MACROECONOMICS ANNUAL (US/0889-3365). **1593**

NC SHOPOWNER (US/0271-1079). **2123**

NEDERLANDS ARCHIEF VOOR KERKGESCHIEDENIS (NE/0028-2030). **4980**

NEFTEHIMIJA (RU/0028-2421). **4266**

NEFTJANIK (RU/0028-243X). **4266**

NEFTJANOE HOZJAJSTVO (RU/0028-2448). **4013**

NEGOTIATION JOURNAL (US/0748-4526). **4483**

NEIROKHIMIIA (SZ/0749-4300). **3839**

NEMATOLOGICA (NE/0028-2596). **466**

NEOHELICON (BUDAPEST) (HU/0324-4652). **3348**

NEOTESTAMENTICA (SA/0254-8356). **4980**

NEPHROLOGIE (SZ/0250-4960). **3991**

NEPHROLOGY, DIALYSIS, TRANSPLANTATION (UK/0931-0509). **3992**

NEPHRON (SZ/0028-2766). **3992**

NERVE CELL BIOLOGY / UNIVERSITY OF SHEFFIELD BIOMEDICAL INFORMATION SERVICE (UK/0142-8225). **466**

NERVENARZT (GW/0028-2804). **3839**

NERVENHEILKUNDE (GW/0722-1541). **3839**

NETHERLANDS JOURNAL OF MEDICINE (NE/0300-2977). **3800**

NETWORK (BRISTOL) (UK/0954-898X). **1196**

NETWORK COMPUTING (US/1046-4468). **1243**

NETWORK MANAGEMENT SYSTEMS & STRATEGIES (US/1043-1217). **1243**

NETWORK MONITOR (UK/0953-8402). **1196**

NETWORK WORLD (US/0887-7661). **1243**

NETWORKING MANAGEMENT (US/1052-049X). **1243**

NETWORKS (NEW YORK) (US/0028-3045). **5132**

NEUE GESELLSCHAFT, FRANKFURTER HEFTE, DIE (GW/0177-6738). **5210**

NEUE POLITISCHE LITERATUR (GW/0028-3320). **5210**

NEUE PRAXIS (GW/0342-9857). **5298**

NEUE SAMMLUNG (GW/0028-3355). **1767**

NEUE ZEITSCHRIFT FUER SYSTEMATISCHE THEOLOGIE UND RELIGIONSPHILOSOPHIE (GW/0028-3517). **4980**

NEUEREN SPRACHEN, DIE (GW/0342-3816). **3305**

NEUES JAHRBUCH FUER GEOLOGIE UND PALAONTOLOGIE. ABHANDLUNGEN (GW/0077-7749). **1389**

NEUES JAHRBUCH FUER GEOLOGIE UND PALAONTOLOGIE. MONATSHEFTE (GW/0028-3630). **1389**

NEUES JAHRBUCH FUER MINERALOGIE. ABHANDLUNGEN (GW/0077-7757). **1443**

NEUES JAHRBUCH FUER MINERALOGIE. MONATSHEFTE (GW/0028-3649). **1443**

NEURAL COMPUTATION (US/0899-7667). **1215**

NEURAL COMPUTING & APPLICATIONS (UK/0941-0643). **3839**

NEURAL NETWORKS (US/0893-6080). **1215**

NEURAL, PARALLEL AND SCIENTIFIC COMPUTATIONS (US/1061-5369). **1197**

NEURO-CHIRURGIE (FR/0028-3770). **3839**

NEURO ENDOCRINOLOGY LETTERS (GW/0172-780X). **3732**

NEURO-OPHTHALMOLOGY (AMSTERDAM : AEOLUS PRESS. 1980) (NE/0165-8107). **3876**

NEURO-ORTHOPEDICS (AU/0177-7955). **3839**

NEUROBIOLOGY OF AGING (US/0197-4580). **3839**

NEUROCHEMICAL RESEARCH (US/0364-3190). **3839**

NEUROCHEMISTRY INTERNATIONAL (US/0197-0186). **3839**

NEUROCHEMISTRY SHEFFIELD (UK/0142-8403). **491**

NEUROCHIRURGIA (GW/0028-3819). **3970**

NEUROCOMPUTING (AMSTERDAM) (NE/0925-2312). **1215**

NEUROENDOCRINOLOGY (SZ/0028-3835). **3840**

NEUROEPIDEMIOLOGY (SZ/0251-5350). **3840**

NEUROHYPOPHYSIAL HORMONES (UK/0143-4276). **3732**

NEUROIMAGE (SAN DIEGO, CALIF.) (US/1053-8119). **3840**

NEUROLOGIC CLINICS (US/0733-8619). **3840**

NEUROLOGICAL RESEARCH (NEW YORK) (UK/0161-6412). **3840**

NEUROLOGY (US/0028-3878). **3840**

NEUROLOGY AND NEUROBIOLOGY (US/0736-4563). **3841**

NEUROLOGY, PSYCHIATRY AND BRAIN RESEARCH (GW/0941-9500). **3841**

NEUROMETHODS (US/0893-2336). **3841**

NEUROMUSCULAR DISORDERS : NMD (UK/0960-8966). **3806**

NEUROPATHOLOGY AND APPLIED NEUROBIOLOGY (UK/0305-1846). **3896**

NEUROPEDIATRICS (GW/0174-304X). **3841**

NEUROPEPTIDES (EDINBURGH) (UK/0143-4179). **3841**

NEUROPEPTIDES (SHEFFIELD) (UK/0142-8233). **3841**

NEUROPHARMACOLOGY (UK/0028-3908). **4317**

NEUROPHYSIOLOGIE CLINIQUE (NE/0987-7053). **3841**

NEUROPHYSIOLOGY (NEW YORK) (US/0090-2977). **3841**

NEUROPHYSIOLOGY SHEFFIELD (UK/0142-8241). **584**

NEUROPROTOCOLS (ORLANDO, FLA.) (US/1058-6741). **3841**

NEUROPSYCHIATRIE DE L'ENFANCE ET DE L'ADOLESCENCE (FR/0222-9617). **3841**

NEUROPSYCHIATRY, NEUROPSYCHOLOGY, BEHAVIORAL NEUROLOGY (US/0894-878X). **3841**

NEUROPSYCHOBIOLOGY (SZ/0302-282X). **3842**

NEUROPSYCHOLOGIA (UK/0028-3932). **3842**

NEUROPSYCHOLOGY (US/0894-4105). **4605**

NEUROPSYCHOLOGY REVIEW (US/1040-7308). **3842**

NEUROPSYCHOPHARMACOLOGY (NEW YORK, N.Y.) (US/0893-133X). **3842**

NEURORADIOLOGY (GW/0028-3940). **3842**

NEUROREHABILITATION (READING, MASS.) (US/1053-8135). **3842**

NEUROREPORT (UK/0959-4965). **3842**

NEUROSCIENCE (UK/0306-4522). **3842**

NEUROSCIENCE AND BEHAVIORAL PHYSIOLOGY (US/0097-0549). **584**

NEUROSCIENCE AND BIOBEHAVIORAL REVIEWS (US/0149-7634). **3842**

NEUROSCIENCE LETTERS (NE/0304-3940). **3842**

NEUROSCIENCE RESEARCH (IE/0168-0102). **3842**

NEUROSCIENCE RESEARCH COMMUNICATIONS (UK/0893-6609). **3843**

NEUROSURGERY (US/0148-396X). **3970**

NEUROSURGERY QUARTERLY (US/1050-6438). **3970**

NEUROSURGICAL CONSULTATIONS (US/1045-6694). **3843**

NEUROSURGICAL REVIEW (GW/0344-5607). **3970**

NEUROTOXICOLOGY AND TERATOLOGY (US/0892-0362). **3843**

NEUROUROL. URODYN (US/0733-2467). **3843**

NEUTRON NEWS (US/1044-8632). **987**

NEW BIOLOGIST, THE (US/1043-4674). **467**

NEW BOTANIST (II/0377-1741). **519**

NEW COMPREHENSIVE BIOCHEMISTRY (US/0167-7306). **987**

NEW CONCEPTS IN CARDIAC IMAGING (US/0743-9237). **3708**

NEW DIRECTIONS FOR WOMEN (US/0160-1075). **5562**

NEW ELECTRONICS (UK/0047-9624). **2073**

NEW ENGLAND BRIDE (US/0744-6861). **2283**

NEW ENGLAND JOURNAL MEDICINE, THE (US/0028-4793). **3620**

NEW ENGLAND JOURNAL OF MEDICINE (OVERSEAS ED.) (US/0028-4793). **3620**

NEW ENGLAND JOURNAL OF MEDICINE, THE (US/0028-4793). **3620**

NEW ENGLAND REAL ESTATE NEWS (US/1042-9689). **4842**

NEW EQUIPMENT DIGEST (US/0028-4963). **2123**

NEW ETHICALS CATALOGUE (NZ/0110-9510). **4334**

NEW FORESTS (NE/0169-4286). **2389**

NEW FORMATIONS (UK/0950-2378). **3348**

NEW GENERATION COMPUTING (JA/0288-3635). **1270**

NEW HORIZONS (BALTIMORE, MD.) (US/1063-7389). **3620**

NEW IDEAS IN PSYCHOLOGY (UK/0732-118X). **4605**

NEW ISSUES (FORT LAUDERDALE, FLA.) (US/0162-9050). **909**

NEW JERSEY EDUCATION LAW REPORT, THE (US/0279-8557). **3015**

NEW LAW JOURNAL, THE (UK/0306-6479). **3015**

NEW LEFT REVIEW (UK/0028-6060). **4544**

NEW LITERARY HISTORY (US/0028-6087). **3348**

NEW MATERIALS/JAPAN (UK/0265-3443). **2107**

NEW METHODS (SAN FRANCISCO, CALIF.) (US/0277-3015). **5517**

NEW MUSICAL EXPRESS. MICROFORM, THE (UK/0028-6362). **5812**

NEW PHYTOLOGIST, THE (UK/0028-646X). **519**

NEW PRODUCT DEVELOPMENT (US/0733-8252). **934**

NEW RENAISSANCE, THE (US/0028-6575). **326**

NEW SCIENTIST (1971) (UK/0262-4079). **5132**

NEW SERIAL TITLES (US/0028-6680). **3234**

NEW TECHNOLOGY WEEK (US/0894-0789). **5133**

NEW TECHNOLOGY, WORK, AND EMPLOYMENT (UK/0268-1072). **1694**

NEW TESTAMENT STUDIES (UK/0028-6885). **5018**

NEW THEATRE QUARTERLY : NTQ (UK/0266-464X). **5366**

NEW TRADE NAMES IN THE RUBBER AND PLASTICS INDUSTRIES (UK/0747-4954). **5076**

NEW TRENDS IN ARRHYTHMIAS (IT/0393-5302). **3708**

NEW YORK EDUCATION LAW REPORT (US/0896-4122). **3016**

NEW ZEALAND ADMINISTRATIVE REPORTS : NZAR (NZ/0110-1277). **3016**

NEW ZEALAND BOOKS IN PRINT / NEW ZEALAND BOOK PUBLISHERS ASSOCIATION (AT/0157-7662). **4822**

NEW ZEALAND CARTOGRAPHY AND GEOGRAPHIC INFORMATION SYSTEMS : THE JOURNAL OF THE NEW ZEALAND CARTOGRAPHIC SOCIETY (NZ/0110-6007). **2582**

NEW ZEALAND CONCRETE CONSTRUCTION (NZ/0549-0219). **622**

NEW ZEALAND CURRENT TAXATION (NZ/0545-7572). **4738**

NEW ZEALAND DENTAL JOURNAL (NZ/0028-8047). **1330**

NEW ZEALAND ENGINEERING (NZ/0028-808X). **1988**

NEW ZEALAND FAMILY PHYSICIAN, THE (NZ/0110-022X). **3738**

NEW ZEALAND FORESTRY (NZ/0112-9597). **2389**

NEW ZEALAND GARDENER (NZ/0028-8136). **2425**

NEW ZEALAND GEOGRAPHER (NZ/0028-8144). **2570**

NEW ZEALAND INTERNATIONAL REVIEW (NZ/0110-0262). **4530**

NEW ZEALAND JOURNAL OF ADULT LEARNING (NZ/0112-224X). **1801**

NEW ZEALAND JOURNAL OF AGRICULTURAL RESEARCH (NZ/0028-8233). **112**

NEW ZEALAND JOURNAL OF BOTANY (NZ/0028-825X). **519**

NEW ZEALAND JOURNAL OF CROP AND HORTICULTURAL SCIENCE (NZ/0114-0671). **2425**

NEW ZEALAND JOURNAL OF EDUCATIONAL STUDIES (NZ/0028-8276). **1768**

NEW ZEALAND JOURNAL OF FORESTRY SCIENCE (NZ/0048-0134). **2389**

NEW ZEALAND JOURNAL OF FRENCH STUDIES (NZ/0110-7380). **3416**

NEW ZEALAND JOURNAL OF GEOGRAPHY (NZ/0028-8292). **2570**

NEW ZEALAND JOURNAL OF GEOLOGY AND GEOPHYSICS (NZ/0028-8306). **1389**

NEW ZEALAND JOURNAL OF HEALTH, PHYSICAL EDUCATION & RECREATION (NZ/0028-8314). **1857**

NEW ZEALAND JOURNAL OF HISTORY, THE (NZ/0028-8322). **2670**

NEW ZEALAND JOURNAL OF MARINE AND FRESHWATER RESEARCH (NZ/0028-8330). **556**

NEW ZEALAND JOURNAL OF PSYCHOLOGY (CHRISTCHURCH. 1983) (NZ/0112-109X). **4605**

NEW ZEALAND JOURNAL OF ZOOLOGY (NZ/0301-4223). **5592**

NEW ZEALAND LAW JOURNAL, THE (US/0028-8373). **3016**

NEW ZEALAND LIBRARIES (NZ/0028-8381). **3234**

NEW ZEALAND MEDICAL JOURNAL (NZ/0028-8446). **3621**

NEW ZEALAND NATIONAL BIBLIOGRAPHY (WELLINGTON, N.Z. : 1983) (NZ/0028-8497). **421**

NEW ZEALAND NURSING JOURNAL, THE (NZ/0028-8535). **3862**

NEW ZEALAND PHARMACY (NZ/0111-431X). **4318**

NEW ZEALAND RAILWAY OBSERVER (NZ/0028-8624). **5433**

NEW ZEALAND SCIENCE REVIEW (NZ/0028-8667). **5133**

NEW ZEALAND SOIL NEWS (NZ/0545-7904). **179**

NEW ZEALAND SPEECH-LANGUAGE THERAPISTS' JOURNAL, THE (NZ/0110-571X). **3889**

NEW ZEALAND STATISTICIAN, THE (NZ/0111-9176). **5334**

NEW ZEALAND UNIVERSITIES LAW REVIEW (NZ/0549-0618). **3016**

NEW ZEALAND VETERINARY JOURNAL (NZ/0048-0169). **5517**

NEW ZEALAND WILDLIFE (NZ/0028-8802). **4875**

NEWS IN PHYSIOLOGICAL SCIENCES (US/0886-1714). **584**

NEWSLETTER ON INTELLECTUAL FREEDOM (US/0028-9485). **3236**

NEWSLETTERS ON STRATIGRAPHY (NE/0078-0421). **1389**

NIEREN- UND HOCKDRUCKKRANKHEITEN (GW/0300-5224). **3622**

NIHON KASEI GAKKAISHI (JA/0913-5227). **2792**

NIHON KIKAI GAKKAI RONBUNSHU. A (JA/0387-5008). **2123**

NIHON KIKAI GAKKAI RONBUNSHU. B (JA/0387-5016). **2093**

NIHON KIKAI GAKKAI RONBUNSHU. C (JA/0387-5024). **2123**

NIHON SERAMIKKUSU KYOKAI GAKUJUTSU RONBUNSHI (JA/0914-5400). **2592**

NIHON SHONIKA GAKKAI ZASSHI (JA/0001-6543). **3907**

NIHON SUISAN GAKKAI SHI (JA/0021-5392). **2309**

NIKEPHOROS : ZEITSCHRIFT FUER SPORT & KULTUR IM ALTERTUM (GW/0934-8913). **4908**

NINETEENTH-CENTURY LITERATURE (US/0891-9356). **3417**

NIPPON GOMU KYOKAISHI (JA/0029-022X). **5076**

NIPPON KAGAKUKAI (1972) (JA/0369-4577). **987**

NIPPON KINZOKU GAKKAISHI (JA/0021-4876). **4013**

NIPPON SHOKUBUTSU BYORI GAKKAI (JA/0031-9473). **520**

NLGI SPOKESMAN (US/0027-6782). **2123**

NLRB ADVICE MEMORANDUM REPORTER (US/0194-8784). **3152**

NMR IN BIOMEDICINE (UK/0952-3480). **3622**

NO-TILL FARMER (US/0091-9993). **179**

NOCTES ROMANAE (SZ/0078-0936). **4353**

NOISE & VIBRATION WORLDWIDE (UK/0957-4565). **2178**

NOISE CONTROL ENGINEERING JOURNAL (US/0736-2501). **2178**

NOISE REGULATION REPORT (US/1043-5565). **2179**

NOLO NEWS (US/0890-2208). **3017**

NONDESTRUCTIVE TESTING AND EVALUATION (US/1058-9759). **2123**

NONLINEAR ANALYSIS (UK/0362-546X). **3524**

NONLINEAR DYNAMICS (NE/0924-090X). **1989**

NONLINEAR SCIENCE TODAY (US/0938-9008). **5134**

NONLINEARITY (BRISTOL) (UK/0951-7715). **3524**

NONRENEWABLE RESOURCES (US/0961-1444). **2201**

NONWOVENS INDUSTRY (US/0163-4429). **1620**

NORDIC JOURNAL OF BOTANY (DK/0107-055X). **520**

NORDIC JOURNAL OF LINGUISTICS (NO/0332-5865). **3306**

NOROIL (NO/0332-544X). **4266**

NORSEMAN (NO/0029-1846). **2520**

NORSK GEOGRAFISK TIDSSKRIFT (NO/0029-1951). **2571**

NORSK GEOLOGISK TIDSSKRIFT (NO/0029-196X). **1390**

NORSK HAGETIDEND (NO/0029-1986). **2426**

NORSK IDRETT (NO/0029-1994). **4908**

NORSK LANDBRUKSFORSKING (NO/0801-5333). **115**

NORSK OLJEREVY (NO/0332-5490). **4266**

NORSK UKEBLAD (NO/0029-2257). **5807**

NORTH AMERICAN FLORA (US/0078-1312). **520**

NORTH AMERICAN JOURNAL OF FISHERIES MANAGEMENT (US/0275-5947). **2309**

NORTH SOUTH (US/1058-3416). **4484**

NORTHEAST OIL WORLD (US/0884-4771). **4267**

NORTHEAST REAL ESTATE NEWS (US/1047-8833). **4842**

NORTHEASTERN GEOLOGY (US/0194-1453). **1390**

NORWEGIAN ARCHAEOLOGICAL REVIEW (NO/0029-3652). **276**

NOTES AND QUERIES (UK/0029-3970). **3306**

NOTES ON THE SCIENCE OF BUILDING (AT/0300-371X). **623**

NOTICES OF THE AMERICAN MATHEMATICAL SOCIETY (US/0002-9920). **3525**

NOTORNIS (NZ/0029-4470). **5619**

NOUS (BLOOMINGTON) (US/0029-4624). **4354**

NOUVELLE REVUE FRANCAISE D'HEMATOLOGIE (GW/0029-4810). **3773**

NOVA HEDWIGIA (GW/0029-5035). **520**

NOVUM GEBRAUCHSGRAPHIK (GW/0302-9794). **381**

NOVUM TESTAMENTUM (NE/0048-1009). **5018**

NTZ : NACHRICTENTECHNISCHE ZEITSCHRIFT (GW/0027-707X). **1161**

NUCLEAR DATA SHEETS (NEW YORK) (US/0090-3752). **4448**

NUCLEAR ENERGY (1978) (UK/0140-4067). **1951**

NUCLEAR ENGINEER, THE (UK/0262-5091). **2156**

NUCLEAR ENGINEERING AND DESIGN (NE/0029-5493). **2156**

NUCLEAR ENGINEERING INTERNATIONAL (UK/0029-5507). **2157**

NUCLEAR GEOPHYSICS (UK/0886-0130). **1409**

NUCLEAR INSTRUMENTS & METHODS IN PHYSICS RESEARCH. SECTION A, ACCELERATORS, SPECTROMETERS, DETECTORS AND ASSOCIATED EQUIPMENT (NE/0168-9002). **4449**

NUCLEAR INSTRUMENTS & METHODS IN PHYSICS RESEARCH. SECTION B, BEAM INTERACTIONS WITH MATERIALS AND ATOMS (NE/0168-583X). **4449**

NUCLEAR MAGNETIC RESONANCE (UK/0305-9804). **4444**

NUCLEAR MEDICINE (GW/0029-5566). **3848**

NUCLEAR MEDICINE COMMUNICATIONS (UK/0143-3636). **3848**

NUCLEAR NEWS (HINSDALE) (US/0029-5574). **2157**

NUCLEAR PHYSICS. A (NE/0375-9474). **4449**

NUCLEAR PHYSICS. SECTION B, PROCEEDINGS SUPPLEMENT (NE/0920-5632). **4449**

NUCLEAR PLANT JOURNAL (US/0892-2055). **1952**

NUCLEAR PLANT MAINTENANCE NEWSLETTER (US/1054-9447). **2157**

NUCLEAR SCIENCE AND ENGINEERING (US/0029-5639). **2157**

NUCLEAR SCIENCE APPLICATIONS (SZ/0191-1686). **4449**

NUCLEAR SCIENCE APPLICATIONS (SZ/0191-1686). **4449**

NUCLEAR TECHNOLOGY (US/0029-5450). **2157**

NUCLEAR WASTE NEWS (SILVER SPRING, MD.) (US/0276-2897). **2237**

NUCLEIC ACIDS RESEARCH (UK/0305-1048). **491**

NUCLEIC ACIDS SYMPOSIUM SERIES (UK/0261-3166). **491**

NUCLEOSIDES & NUCLEOTIDES (US/0732-8311). **491**

NUESTRO TIEMPO (SP/0029-5795). **2851**

NUMBERS NEWS, THE (US/0732-1597). **4555**

NUMEN (INTERNATIONAL ASSOCIATION FOR THE HISTORY OF RELIGIONS) (NE/0029-5973). **4982**

NUMERICAL FUNCTIONAL ANALYSIS AND OPTIMIZATION (US/0163-0563). **3525**

NUMERICAL HEAT TRANSFER. PART A, APPLICATIONS (US/1040-7782). **4432**

NUMERICAL HEAT TRANSFER. PART B, FUNDAMENTALS (US/1040-7790). **4432**

NUMERICAL METHODS FOR PARTIAL DIFFERENTIAL EQUATIONS (US/0749-159X). **3525**

NUMERISCHE MATHEMATIK (GW/0029-599X). **3525**

NUOVO CIMENTO DELLA SOCIETA ITALIANA DI FISICA. SEZIONE B (IT/0369-4100). **4413**

NUOVO CIMENTO DELLA SOCIETA ITALIANA DI FISICA [SEZIONE] C, IL (IT/0390-5551). **4413**

NUOVO CIMENTO DELLA SOCIETA ITALIANA DI FISICA, [SEZIONE] D (IT/0392-6737). **4449**

NUOVO CIMENTO DELLA SOCIETA ITALIANA DI FIZICA. SEZIONE A (IT/0369-4097). **4449**

NURSE ANESTHESIA (US/0897-7437). **3683**

NURSE AUTHOR & EDITOR (US/1054-2353). **3862**

NURSE EDUCATION TODAY (UK/0260-6917). **3862**

NURSE EDUCATOR (US/0363-3624). **3863**

NURSE PRACTITIONER FORUM (US/1045-5485). **3863**

NURSE PRACTITIONER, THE (US/0361-1817). **3863**

NURSING (US/0360-4039). **3863**

NURSING ADMINISTRATION QUARTERLY (US/0363-9568). **3863**

NURSING CLINICS OF NORTH AMERICA, THE (US/0029-6465). **3863**

NURSING DIAGNOSIS (US/1046-7459). **3864**

NURSING ECONOMIC$ (US/0746-1739). **3864**

NURSING MANAGEMENT (US/0744-6314). **3864**

NURSING OUTLOOK (US/0029-6554). **3865**

NURSING (OXFORD) (UK/0142-0372). **3865**

NURSING RECRUITMENT & RETENTION (US/1051-4341). **3865**

NURSING RESEARCH ABSTRACTS (UK/0141-3899). **3865**

NUTRICION CLINICA DIETETICA HOSPITALARIA (SP/0211-6057). **4195**

NUTRITION AND HEALTH (BERKHAMSTED) (UK/0260-1060). **4195**

NUTRITION IN CLINICAL PRACTICE (US/0884-5336). **4196**

NUTRITION, METABOLISM, AND CARDIOVASCULAR DISEASES : NMCD (GW/0939-4753). **3708**

NUTRITION RESEARCH (NEW YORK, N.Y.) (US/0271-5317). **4196**

NUTRITION REVIEWS (US/0029-6643). **4197**

NUTRITION TODAY (ANNAPOLIS) (US/0029-666X). **4197**

NWSA JOURNAL (US/1040-0656). **5563**

NZ BUSINESS (NZ/0113-4957). **700**

O + I.E. UND P, OLHYDRAULIK UND PNEUMATIK (GW/0341-2660). **2093**

OBESITY & HEALTH (US/1044-1522). **4197**

OBESITY SURGERY (UK/0960-8923). **3970**

OBJECT MAGAZINE (US/1055-3614). **1288**

OBJECT-ORIENTED STRATEGIES (US/1059-4108). **880**

OBSERVATIONS ET DIAGNOSTICS ECONOMIQUES (FR/0751-6614). **1509**

OBSERVER (PHILADELPHIA, PA.) (US/0279-9529). **3623**

OBST UND GARTEN (GW/0029-7798). **2426**

OBSTETRIC ANESTHESIA DIGEST (US/0275-665X). **3683**

OBSTETRICAL & GYNECOLOGICAL SURVEY (US/0029-7828). **3766**

OBSTETRICS AND GYNECOLOGY CLINICS OF NORTH AMERICA (US/0889-8545). **3766**

OBSTETRICS AND GYNECOLOGY (NEW YORK. 1953) (US/0029-7844). **3766**

OCCASIONAL PAPERS - UNIVERSITY OF ILLINOIS (URBANA-CHAMPAIGN CAMPUS). GRADUATE SCHOOL OF LIBRARY AND INFORMATION SCIENCE (US/0276-1769). **3238**

OCCUPATIONAL HAZARDS (US/0029-7909). **2866**

OCCUPATIONAL HEALTH (UK/0029-7917). **2866**

OCCUPATIONAL HEALTH & SAFETY (US/0362-4064). **2866**

OCCUPATIONAL HEALTH AND SAFETY LETTER (US/0196-058X). **2866**

OCCUPATIONAL HYGIENE (US/1061-0251). **2866**

OCCUPATIONAL MEDICINE (PHILADELPHIA, PA.) (US/0885-114X). **2867**

OCCUPATIONAL SAFETY & HEALTH REPORTER (US/0095-3237). **2867**

OCCUPATIONAL THERAPY PRACTICE (US/1044-3207). **1883**

OCEAN AIR INTERACTIONS (US/0743-0876). **1359**

OCEAN DEVELOPMENT AND INTERNATIONAL LAW (US/0090-8320). **3182**

OCEAN ENGINEERING (US/0029-8018). **2093**

OCEAN INDUSTRY (US/0029-8026). **4267**

OCEAN NAVIGATOR (US/0886-0149). **1453**

OCEAN PHYSICS AND ENGINEERING (US/0890-5460). **1453**

OCEANOLOGICA ACTA (FR/0399-1784). **1454**

OCEANOLOGY (WASHINGTON. 1965) (US/0001-4370). **1454**

OCEANUS (WOODS HOLE) (US/0029-8182). **1454**

OCLC MICRO (US/8756-5196). **3238**

OCTOBER (CAMBRIDGE, MASS.) (US/0162-2870). **327**

OE REPORTS (US/1048-6879). **4438**

OE&M. OFFICE EQUIPMENT & METHODS (1979) (CN/0709-5228). **4213**

OECOLOGIA (GW/0029-8549). **2219**

OEM DESIGN (UK/0306-0381). **3485**

OESTERREICHISCHE WASSERWIRTSCHAFT (AU/0029-9588). **2094**

OEUVRES ET CRITIQUES (FR/0338-1900). **3349**

OFFENE SYSTEME (GW/0941-1968). **1197**

OFFENTLICHE VERWALTUNG, DIE (GW/0029-859X). **3021**

OFFICE EQUIPMENT INDEX (UK/0305-635X). **4213**

OFFICE PRODUCTS DEALER (WHEATON) (US/0199-1329). **4213**

OFFICE PROFESSIONAL, THE (US/0739-3156). **1118**

OFFICE (STAMFORD. 1936), THE (US/0030-0128). **4213**

OFFICE WORLD NEWS (US/0164-5951). **4213**

OFFICIAL AMERICAN BOARD OF MEDICAL SPECIALTIES (ABMS) DIRECTORY OF BOARD CERTIFIED MEDICAL SPECIALISTS, THE (US/0000-1406). **3623**

OFFICIAL AMERICAN BOARD OF MEDICAL SPECIALTIES (ABMS) DIRECTORY OF BOARD CERTIFIED MEDICAL SPECIALISTS, THE (US/0000-1406). **3623**

OFFICIAL BOARD MARKETS (US/0030-0284). **4235**

OFFICIAL JOURNAL (PATENTS) (UK/0030-0330). **1307**

OFFICIAL METHODS OF ANALYSIS OF THE ASSOCIATION OF OFFICIAL ANALYTICAL CHEMISTS (US/0066-961X). **1018**

OFFSHORE (CONROE, TEX.) (US/0030-0608). **4267**

OFFSHORE ENGINEER (UK/0305-876X). **2094**

OHIO BANKER, THE (US/0030-0802). **802**

OHIO JOURNAL OF SCIENCE, THE (US/0030-0950). **5136**

OIKOS (DK/0030-1299). **2220**

OIL & ENERGY TRENDS (UK/0950-1045). **4268**

OIL & ENERGY TRENDS ANNUAL STATISTICAL REVIEW (UK/0953-1033). **4284**

OIL & GAS INVESTOR (US/0744-5881). **4268**

OIL & GAS JOURNAL (US/0030-1388). **4268**

OIL & GAS TAX ALERT / THE RESEARCH INSTITUTE OF AMERICA (US/0731-4620). **4739**

OIL DAILY, THE (US/0030-1434). **4269**

OIL EXPRESS (US/0195-0576). **4269**

OIL GAS (GW/0342-5622). **4269**

OIL, GAS & PETROCHEM EQUIPMENT (US/0030-1353). **4269**

OIL SPILL INTELLIGENCE REPORT (US/0195-3524). **4270**

OIL SPILL U.S. LAW REPORT (US/1055-9175). **3022**

OILFIELD REVIEW / SCHLUMBERGER (US/0923-1730). **4270**

OILWEEK (CN/0030-1515). **4270**

OKEANOLOGIJA (RU/0030-1574). **1454**

OLD NORTHWEST, THE (US/0360-5531). **2752**

OMEGA (OXFORD) (UK/0305-0483). **880**

ON-LINE REVIEW (UK/0309-314X). **1275**

ON THE STATE OF THE PUBLIC HEALTH (1963) (UK/0072-6087). **4795**

ONCOGENE (UK/0950-9232). **3821**

ONCOGENE RESEARCH (US/0890-6467). **3821**

ONCOLOGY (SZ/0030-2414). **3821**

ONCOLOGY RESEARCH (US/0965-0407). **3822**

ONCOLOGY TIMES (US/0276-2234). **3822**

ONCOLOGY (WILLISTON PARK, N.Y.) (US/0890-9091). **3822**

ONDE ELECTRIQUE (FR/0030-2430). **2074**

ONE-PERSON LIBRARY, THE (US/0748-8831). **3239**

ONKOLOGIE (SZ/0378-584X). **3822**

ONLINE (WESTON, CONN.) (US/0146-5422). **1275**

OPEC REVIEW (US/0277-0180). **4270**

OPEN ECONOMIES REVIEW (NE/0923-7992). **1511**

OPEN SYSTEMS COMMUNICATION (US/0741-2851). **1243**

OPEN SYSTEMS REPORT (US/1052-701X). **1243**

OPEN SYSTEMS TODAY (US/1061-0839). **1248**

OPERATING SYSTEMS REVIEW (US/0163-5980). **1248**

OPERATIONS RESEARCH (US/0030-364X). **3525**

OPERATIONS RESEARCH LETTERS (NE/0167-6377). **5136**

OPERATIVE TECHNIQUES IN ORTHOPAEDICS (US/1048-6666). **3883**

OPERATIVE TECHNIQUES IN OTOLARYNGOLOGY--HEAD AND NECK SURGERY (US/1043-1810). **3890**

OPERATIVE TECHNIQUES IN SPORTS MEDICINE (US/1060-1872). **3955**

OPERNWELT (GW/0030-3690). **4144**

OPFLOW (US/0149-8029). **5537**

OPHTALMOLOGIE (PARIS) (FR/0989-3105). **3877**

OPHTHALMIC & PHYSIOLOGICAL OPTICS (UK/0275-5408). **4216**

OPHTHALMIC PAEDIATRICS AND GENETICS (NE/0167-6784). **550**

OPHTHALMIC PLASTIC AND RECONSTRUCTIVE SURGERY (US/0740-9303). **3877**

OPHTHALMIC RESEARCH (SZ/0030-3747). **3877**

OPHTHALMOLOGICA (BASEL) (SZ/0030-3755). **3877**

OPHTHALMOLOGY (ROCHESTER, MINN.) (US/0161-6420). **3878**

OPHTHALMOLOGY TIMES (US/0193-032X). **3878**

OPSEARCH

Copyright Clearance Center Index

OPSEARCH (II/0030-3887). **881**

OPTICA PURA Y APLICADA (SP/0030-3917). **4439**

OPTICAL AND QUANTUM ELECTRONICS (UK/0306-8919). **4439**

OPTICAL COMPUTING & PROCESSING (UK/0954-2264). **1277**

OPTICAL ENGINEERING (US/0091-3286). **4439**

OPTICAL FIBER TECHNOLOGY (US/1068-5200). **4439**

OPTICAL MATERIALS (NE/0925-3467). **4439**

OPTICAL MEMORY & NEURAL NETWORKS (US/1060-992X). **1215**

OPTICAL MEMORY NEWS (US/0741-5869). **1277**

OPTICAL MEMORY REPORT, THE (US/8755-1195). **1277**

OPTICS AND LASER TECHNOLOGY (UK/0030-3992). **4439**

OPTICS AND LASERS IN ENGINEERING (UK/0143-8166). **4439**

OPTICS AND PHOTONICS NEWS (US/1047-6938). **4439**

OPTICS AND SPECTROSCOPY (US/0030-400X). **4439**

OPTICS COMMUNICATIONS (NE/0030-4018). **4439**

OPTICS LETTERS (US/0146-9592). **4439**

OPTIK (STUTTGART) (GW/0030-4026). **4440**

OPTIKA I SPEKTROSKOPIJA (RU/0030-4034). **4440**

OPTIMAL CONTROL APPLICATIONS & METHODS (UK/0143-2087). **1220**

OPTIMIZATION METHODS AND SOFTWARE (UK/1055-6788). **1198**

OPTION/BIO PARIS (FR/0992-5945). **467**

OPTOELECTRONICS, INSTRUMENTATION, AND DATA PROCESSING (US/8756-6990). **4440**

OPTOMETRY AND VISION SCIENCE (US/1040-5488). **4217**

OR MANAGER (US/8756-8047). **3866**

OR-SPEKTRUM (GW/0171-6468). **5136**

ORAL HEALTH (CN/0030-4204). **1332**

ORAL MICROBIOLOGY AND IMMUNOLOGY (DK/0902-0055). **1332**

ORAL SURGERY, ORAL MEDICINE, ORAL PATHOLOGY (US/0030-4220). **1332**

ORBIS LITTERARUM (DK/0105-7510). **3420**

ORBIS (PHILADELPHIA) (US/0030-4387). **4485**

ORBIT (AMSTERDAM) (NE/0167-6830). **3878**

ORCHARDIST OF NEW ZEALAND, THE (NZ/0110-6260). **180**

ORDER (DORDRECHT) (NE/0167-8094). **3526**

ORDO (GW/0048-2129). **1511**

ORE GEOLOGY REVIEWS (NE/0169-1368). **1390**

ORGANIC GEOCHEMISTRY (UK/0146-6380). **1390**

ORGANIC MASS SPECTROMETRY (UK/0030-493X). **1018**

ORGANIC SYNTHESES (US/0078-6209). **1045**

ORGANIZATION STUDIES (GW/0170-8406). **5211**

ORGANIZATIONAL BEHAVIOR AND HUMAN DECISION PROCESSES (US/0749-5978). **4606**

ORGANIZATIONAL DYNAMICS (US/0090-2616). **881**

ORGANOMETALLIC CHEMISTRY (LONDON. 1972) (UK/0301-0074). **1045**

ORGANOMETALLIC COMPOUNDS (UK/0030-5138). **1045**

ORGANOMETALLICS (US/0276-7333). **1045**

ORGANOPHOSPHORUS CHEMISTRY (UK/0306-0713). **1045**

ORIENS (NE/0078-6527). **2661**

ORIENS EXTREMUS (GW/0030-5197). **3420**

ORIENT (DEUTSCHES ORIENT-INSTITUT) (GW/0030-5227). **2661**

ORIGINS OF LIFE AND EVOLUTION OF THE BIOSPHERE (NE/0169-6149). **467**

ORL; JOURNAL FOR OTO-RHINO-LARYNGOLOGY AND ITS BORDERLANDS (SZ/0301-1569). **3890**

ORNIS SCANDINAVICA (NO/0030-5693). **5619**

ORSA JOURNAL ON COMPUTING (US/0899-1499). **1198**

ORTHOPADISCHE PRAXIS (GW/0030-588X). **3883**

ORTHOPAEDIC REVIEW (US/0094-6591). **3883**

ORTHOPEDIC CLINICS OF NORTH AMERICA, THE (US/0030-5898). **3884**

ORTHOPEDIC NURSING / NATIONAL ASSOCIATION OF ORTHOPEDIC NURSES (US/0744-6020). **3884**

ORTHOPEDIC SURGERY (NE/0014-4371). **3661**

ORTHOPEDICS TODAY (US/0279-5647). **3884**

ORTHOPEDIE TRAUMATOLOGIE : EUROPEAN JOURNAL OF ORTHOPAEDIC SURGERY & TRAUMATOLOGY : ORGANE OFFICIEL DE LA SOCIETE D'ORTHOPEDIE ET DE TRAUMATOLOGIE DE L'EST DE LA FRANCE (SOTEST) ET DU GROUPE D'ETUDE POUR LA CHIRURGIE OSSEUSE (GECO) (FR/0940-3264). **3884**

ORTOPEDIA E TRAUMATOLOGIA OGGI (IT/0392-1417). **3884**

ORYX (UK/0030-6053). **2201**

OSGOODE HALL LAW JOURNAL (1960) (CN/0030-6185). **3023**

OSHA COMPLIANCE ADVISOR (US/0896-9949). **2867**

OSHA TRAINING BULLETIN FOR SUPERVISORS (US/0896-9957). **2868**

OSI PRODUCT & EQUIPMENT NEWS (US/0898-0489). **1198**

OSTEOPOROSIS INTERNATIONAL : A JOURNAL ESTABLISHED AS RESULT OF COOPERATION BETWEEN THE EUROPEAN FOUNDATION FOR OSTEOPOROSIS AND THE NATIONAL OSTEOPOROSIS FOUNDATION OF THE USA (UK/0937-941X). **3806**

OSTEUROPA-RECHT (GW/0030-6444). **3024**

OSTEUROPA (STUTTGART) (GW/0030-6428). **4486**

OSTEUROPA WIRTSCHAFT (GW/0030-6460). **1511**

OTOLARYNGOLOGIC CLINICS OF NORTH AMERICA, THE (US/0030-6665). **3890**

OTOLARYNGOLOGY AND HEAD AND NECK SURGERY (US/0194-5998). **3971**

OUTDOOR RETAILER (US/0279-8107). **956**

OUTLOOK ON AT&T (US/0885-6176). **1161**

OUTLOOK ON IBM (US/0742-9916). **1238**

OUTRIDER (INDOOROOPILLY, QLD.) (AT/0813-5886). **3421**

OXFORD AGRARIAN STUDIES (UK/0264-5491). **118**

OXFORD ART JOURNAL (UK/0142-6540). **361**

OXFORD BULLETIN OF ECONOMICS AND STATISTICS (UK/0305-9049). **1577**

OXFORD ECONOMIC PAPERS (UK/0030-7653). **1594**

OXFORD JOURNAL OF ARCHAEOLOGY (UK/0262-5253). **277**

OXFORD JOURNAL OF LEGAL STUDIES (UK/0143-6503). **3024**

OXFORD MAGAZINE (UK/0268-1137). **1102**

OXFORD REVIEW OF ECONOMIC POLICY (UK/0266-903X). **1511**

OXFORD REVIEW OF EDUCATION (UK/0305-4985). **1771**

OXFORD REVIEWS OF REPRODUCTIVE BIOLOGY (UK/0260-0854). **584**

OXFORD TODAY (UK/0954-1306). **2521**

OXIDATION COMMUNICATIONS (BU/0209-4541). **1045**

OXIDATION OF METALS (US/0030-770X). **4014**

OXYGEN RADICALS (UK/0950-057X). **491**

OZE. OSTERREICHISCHE ZEITSCHRIFT FUER ELEKTRIZITATSWIRTSCHAFT (AU/0029-9618). **2074**

OZONE : SCIENCE & ENGINEERING (US/0191-9512). **1037**

PACIFIC AFFAIRS (CN/0030-851X). **4486**

PACIFIC-BASIN FINANCE JOURNAL (NE/0927-538X). **802**

PACIFIC HISTORICAL REVIEW (US/0030-8684). **2753**

PACIFIC OIL WORLD (US/0008-1329). **4271**

PACIFIC PHILOSOPHICAL QUARTERLY (UK/0279-0750). **4354**

PACIFIC REVIEW (OXFORD, ENGLAND) (UK/0951-2748). **4486**

PACIFIC VIEWPOINT (NZ/0030-8978). **1577**

PACING AND CLINICAL ELECTROPHYSIOLOGY (US/0147-8389). **3708**

PACKAGING (BOSTON, MASS.) (US/0746-3820). **4220**

PACKAGING DIGEST (CHICAGO, ILL.) (US/0030-9117). **4220**

PACKAGING TECHNOLOGY AND SCIENCE (UK/0894-3214). **4221**

PACKER, THE (US/0030-9168). **2352**

PADIATRIE UND GRENZGEBIETE (GW/0030-932X). **3907**

PADIATRIE UND PADOLOGIE (AU/0030-9338). **3907**

PADIATRISCHE PRAXIS (GW/0030-9346). **3907**

PAEDIATRIC AND PERINATAL EPIDEMIOLOGY (UK/0269-5022). **3736**

PAEDIATRISCHE FORTBILDUNGSKURSE FUER DIE PRAXIS (SZ/0078-7795). **3907**

PAIN (AMSTERDAM) (NE/0304-3959). **3896**

PAIN AND HEADACHE (SZ/0255-3910). **3844**

PAIN DIGEST (US/0938-9016). **3625**

PAINT RED BOOK (US/0090-5402). **4224**

PAINT TITLES (UK/0144-4425). **4226**

PAKISTAN JOURNAL OF BOTANY (PK/0556-3321). **520**

PAKISTAN JOURNAL OF OTOLARYNGOLOGY (PK/0257-4985). **3890**

PALAEOECOLOGY OF AFRICA AND THE SURROUNDING ISLANDS (NE/0168-6208). **4228**

PALAEOGEOGRAPHY, PALAEOCLIMATOLOGY, PALAEOECOLOGY (NE/0031-0182). **4228**

PALAEOHISTORIA (HAARLEM) (NE/0552-9344). **277**

PALAEONTOGRAPHICA. ABTEILUNG A : PALAOZOOLOGIE, STRATIGRAPHIE (GW/0375-0442). **4229**

PALAEONTOGRAPHICA. ABTEILUNG B : PALAOPHYTOLOGIE (GW/0375-0299). **4229**

PALAIOS (US/0883-1351). **4229**

PALAONTOLOGISCHE ZEITSCHRIFT (GW/0031-0220). **4229**

PALEOBIOLOGY (US/0094-8373). **4229**

PALEOCEANOGRAPHY (US/0883-8305). **1455**

PALEONTOLOGICAL JOURNAL (US/0031-0301). **4229**

PALEONTOLOGICESKIJ ZURNAL (RU/0031-031X). **4230**

PALIMPSEST (IOWA CITY), THE (US/0031-0360). **2753**

PANCREAS (US/0885-3177). **3800**

PANCREATIC AND SALIVARY SECRETION (UK/0142-825X). **3732**

P&T (LAWRENCEVILLE, N.J.) (US/1052-1372). **3625**

PAPER ASIA NEWS : THE ASIAN PULP & PAPER NEWSLETTER (SI/0958-0824). **4235**

PAPER, FILM AND FOIL CONVERTER (US/0031-1138). **4236**

PAPER - GEOLOGICAL SURVEY OF CANADA (CN/0068-7650). **1390**

PAPER (LONDON) (UK/0306-8234). **4236**

PAPERBOARD PACKAGING (US/0031-1227). **4221**

PAPERBOUND BOOKS IN PRINT (US/0031-1235). **4822**

PAPERS - AMERICAN SOCIETY OF MECHANICAL ENGINEERS (US/0402-1215). **2124**

PAPERS PRESENTED AT THE ALLERTON PARK INSTITUTE (US/0536-4604). **3240**

PAPERS PRESENTED AT THE PICA CONFERENCE (US/0736-7805). **2074**

PAPIER, CARTON ET CELLULOSE (FR/0031-1367). **4236**

PAR. PUBLIC ADMINISTRATION REVIEW POPULATION (US/0033-3352). **4672**

PARAGRAPH (MODERN CRITICAL THEORY GROUP) (UK/0264-8334). **3309**

PARALLEL ALGORITHMS AND APPLICATIONS (US/1063-7192). **1248**

PARALLEL COMPUTING (NE/0167-8191). **1248**

PARAPLEGIA (UK/0031-1758). **4392**

PARASITE IMMUNOLOGY (UK/0141-9838). **3675**

PARASITOLOGY (UK/0031-1820). **492**

PARASITOLOGY RESEARCH (1987) (GW/0932-0113). **468**

PARASITOLOGY TODAY (REFERENCE ED.) (UK/0169-4707). **468**

PARAZITOLOGIJA (RU/0031-1847). **468**

PARFUMERIE UND KOSMETIK (GW/0031-1952). **405**

PARFUMS, COSMETIQUES, AROMES (FR/0337-3029). **405**

PARLIAMENTARY AFFAIRS (UK/0031-2290). **4672**

PARLIAMENTARY HISTORY : A YEARBOOK (UK/0264-2824). **4672**

PARLIAMENTS, ESTATES & REPRESENTATION (UK/0260-6755). **4487**

PARTICLE ACCELERATORS (US/0031-2460). **4413**

PARTICLE & PARTICLE SYSTEMS CHARACTERIZATION (GW/0934-0866). **988**

PARTICLE WORLD (UK/1043-6790). **4450**

PARTICULATE SCIENCE AND TECHNOLOGY (US/0272-6351). **2015**

PARTNER'S REPORT (US/0892-4805). **3025**

PARTNER'S REPORT (NEW YORK, N.Y. 1989) (US/1043-7428). **881**

PARTY SOURCE (US/1060-6726). **2585**

PAST & PRESENT (UK/0031-2746). **2625**

PASTICCERIA INTERNAZIONALE (IT/0392-4718). **2352**

PASTORAL CARE IN EDUCATION (UK/0264-3944). **1772**

PASTORAL PSYCHOLOGY (US/0031-2789). **4607**

PATENT OFFICE RECORD, THE (CN/0008-4670). **1307**

PATHOBIOLOGY (BASEL) (SZ/1015-2008). **3896**

PATHOLOGE, DER (GW/0172-8113). **3896**

PATHOLOGY (AT/0031-3025). **3897**

PATHOLOGY ANNUAL (US/0079-0184). **3897**

PATHOLOGY (PHILADELPHIA, PA.) (US/1041-3480). **3897**

PATHOLOGY, RESEARCH AND PRACTICE (GW/0344-0338). **3897**

PATHOPHYSIOLOGY (NE/0928-4680). **584**

PATIENT CARE (US/0031-305X). **3738**

PATTERN RECOGNITION (UK/0031-3203). **1215**

PATTERN RECOGNITION LETTERS (NE/0167-8655). **1234**

PC AI (US/0894-0711). **1215**

PC GAMES (PETERBOROUGH, N.H.) (US/1042-2943). **4864**

PC NOVICE (US/1052-1186). **1271**

PC PUBLISHING (US/0896-8209). **4818**

PC TODAY (US/1040-6484). **1271**

PC USER (LONDON, ENGLAND) (UK/0263-5720). **1271**

PC WORLD (US/0737-8939). **1271**

PCH. PHYSICOCHEMICAL HYDRODYNAMICS (UK/0191-9059). **1056**

PCN NEWS (US/1051-3833). **1119**

PCR METHODS AND APPLICATIONS (US/1054-9803). **1045**

PEDIATRIA OGGI MEDICA E CHIRURGICA (IT/0391-898X). **3907**

PEDIATRIC ALLERGY AND IMMUNOLOGY : OFFICIAL PUBLICATION OF THE EUROPEAN SOCIETY OF PEDIATRIC ALLERGY AND IMMUNOLOGY (DK/0905-6157). **3675**

PEDIATRIC AND ADOLESCENT ENDOCRINOLOGY (SZ/0304-4254). **3908**

PEDIATRIC CARDIOLOGY (US/0172-0643). **3908**

PEDIATRIC CLINICS OF NORTH AMERICA, THE (US/0031-3955). **3908**

PEDIATRIC DERMATOLOGY (US/0736-8046). **3908**

PEDIATRIC EMERGENCY CARE (US/0749-5161). **3725**

PEDIATRIC EXERCISE SCIENCE (US/0899-8493). **3908**

PEDIATRIC HEMATOLOGY AND ONCOLOGY (US/0888-0018). **3773**

PEDIATRIC INFECTIOUS DISEASE JOURNAL, THE (US/0891-3668). **3908**

PEDIATRIC NEPHROLOGY (BERLIN, WEST) (GW/0931-041X). **3909**

PEDIATRIC NURSING (US/0097-9805). **3866**

PEDIATRIC NURSING [MICROFORM] (US/0097-9805). **3866**

PEDIATRIC PATHOLOGY (US/0277-0938). **3897**

PEDIATRIC PHYSICAL THERAPY (US/0898-5669). **3909**

PEDIATRIC PULMONOLOGY (US/8755-6863). **3909**

PEDIATRIC RADIOLOGY (GW/0301-0449). **3944**

PEDIATRIC RESEARCH (US/0031-3998). **3909**

PEDIATRIC REVIEWS AND COMMUNICATION (SZ/0882-9225). **3909**

PEDIATRIC SURGERY INTERNATIONAL (GW/0179-0358). **3909**

PEDIATRIC THERAPEUTICS AND TOXICOLOGY (US/0893-6218). **3909**

PEDIATRICIAN (SZ/0300-1245). **3910**

PEDIATRICS. EDICION ESPANOLA (SP/0210-5721). **3910**

PEDIATRICS (EVANSTON) (US/0031-4005). **3910**

PEDIATRIE (FR/0031-4021). **3910**

PEDOBIOLOGIA (GW/0031-4056). **181**

PELANGI TOOWOOMBA (AT/0815-6816). **5212**

PENSION WORLD (US/0098-1753). **1701**

PENSIONS & INVESTMENTS (1990) (US/1050-4974). **911**

PEOPLE TRENDS (US/1065-0253). **881**

PEPTIDE HORMONE RECEPTORS (UK/0268-1552). **492**

PEPTIDE RESEARCH (US/1040-5704). **1046**

PEPTIDES (NEW YORK, N.Y, : 1980) (US/0196-9781). **492**

PERCEPTION & PSYCHOPHYSICS (US/0031-5117). **4607**

PERFORMANCE CAR (UK/0265-6183). **5423**

PERFORMANCE EVALUATION (NE/0166-5316). **1261**

PERFORMING ARTS JOURNAL (US/0735-8393). **387**

PERFUMER & FLAVORIST (US/0272-2666). **1028**

PERFUSION (UK/0267-6591). **3709**

PERINATALMEDIZIN : OFFIZIELLES MITTEILUNGSBLATT DER DEUTSCHEN GESELLSCHAFT FUER PERINATALE MEDIZIN (GW/0936-7160). **3767**

PERIODICA ISLAMICA : AN INTERNATIONAL CONTENTS JOURNAL (MY/0128-3715). **5044**

PERIODICA MATHEMATICA HUNGARICA (HU/0031-5303). **3526**

PERIODICA POLYTECHNICA: ELECTRICAL ENGINEERING. ELEKTROTECHNIK (HU/0031-532X). **2075**

PERIODICA POLYTECHNICA : MECHANICAL ENGINEERING. MASHINOSTROENIE (HU/0324-6051). **2124**

PERITONEAL DIALYSIS INTERNATIONAL (US/0896-8608). **3800**

PERKIN TRANSACTIONS 1 (UK/0300-922X). **1046**

PERKIN TRANSACTIONS. 2 (UK/0300-9580). **1046**

PERSON-CENTERED REVIEW (US/0883-2293). **4607**

PERSONALIST FORUM, THE (US/0889-065X). **4355**

PERSONALITY AND INDIVIDUAL DIFFERENCES (UK/0191-8869). **4607**

PERSONALITY & SOCIAL PSYCHOLOGY BULLETIN (US/0146-1672). **4607**

PERSONNEL JOURNAL (US/0031-5745). **945**

PERSONNEL MANAGEMENT (US/0149-2675). **945**

PERSONNEL MANAGEMENT (LONDON. 1969) (UK/0031-5761). **945**

PERSONNEL PSYCHOLOGY (US/0031-5826). **4607**

PERSONNEL REVIEW (UK/0048-3486). **945**

PERSPECTIVE (MADISON, WIS.) (US/0888-9732). **3029**

PERSPECTIVES IN BIOLOGY AND MEDICINE (US/0031-5982). **468**

PERSPECTIVES IN COLON AND RECTAL SURGERY (US/0894-8054). **3971**

PERSPECTIVES IN GENERAL SURGERY (US/1045-3741). **3971**

PERSPECTIVES IN MATHEMATICAL LOGIC (GW/0344-4325). **3526**

PERSPECTIVES IN PEDIATRIC PATHOLOGY (SZ/0091-2921). **3910**

PERSPECTIVES IN PLASTIC SURGERY (US/0892-3957). **3972**

PERSPECTIVES IN VASCULAR SURGERY (US/0894-8046). **3972**

PERSPECTIVES ON DEVELOPMENTAL NEUROBIOLOGY (US/1064-0517). **468**

PERSPECTIVES ON SCIENCE AND CHRISTIAN FAITH (US/0892-2675). **4986**

PESC RECORD (US/0275-9306). **2075**

PEST CONTROL (US/0031-6121). **4246**

PESTICIDE & TOXIC CHEMICAL NEWS (US/0146-0501). **4246**

PESTICIDE BIOCHEMISTRY AND PHYSIOLOGY (US/0048-3575). **4246**

PESTICIDE OUTLOOK (UK/0956-1250). **4246**

PESTICIDE SCIENCE (UK/0031-613X). **4246**

PETER DAG INVESTMENT LETTER, THE (US/0196-9323). **911**

PETFOOD INDUSTRY (US/0031-6245). **4287**

PETROCHEMICAL NEWS (US/0031-6342). **4271**

PETROLEO INTERNACIONAL (US/0093-7851). **4272**

PETROLEUM ENGINEER INTERNATIONAL (US/0164-8322). **4272**

PETROLEUM INTELLIGENCE WEEKLY (US/0480-2160). **4273**

PETROLEUM MANAGEMENT (HOUSTON, TEX.) (US/0884-4550). **4273**

PETROLEUM OUTLOOK (US/0031-6490). **4273**

PFLUGERS ARCHIV (GW/0031-6768). **584**

PHARMA-FLASH (SZ/0378-7958). **4319**

PHARMACEUTICAL AND PHARMACOLOGICAL LETTERS (GW/0939-9488). **4320**

PHARMACEUTICAL CHEMISTRY JOURNAL (US/0091-150X). **4320**

PHARMACEUTICAL EXECUTIVE (US/0279-6570). **4320**

PHARMACEUTICAL MEDICINE (BASINGSTOKE) (UK/0265-0673). **4320**

PHARMACEUTICAL PROCESSING (US/1049-9156). **4321**

PHARMACEUTICAL RESEARCH (US/0724-8741). **4321**

PHARMACEUTICAL TECHNOLOGY (US/0147-8087). **4321**

PHARMACEUTICAL TECHNOLOGY INTERNATIONAL (US/0164-6826). **4321**

PHARMACOECONOMICS (NZ/1170-7690). **4321**

PHARMACOGENETICS (UK/0960-314X). **4321**

PHARMACOLOGICAL RESEARCH (UK/1043-6618). **4322**

PHARMACOLOGICAL REVIEWS (US/0031-6997). **4322**

PHARMACOLOGY (SZ/0031-7012). **4322**

PHARMACOLOGY AND THE SKIN (SZ/1011-291X). **3722**

PHARMACOLOGY & THERAPEUTICS (OXFORD) (UK/0163-7258). **4322**

PHARMACOLOGY & TOXICOLOGY (DK/0901-9928). **4322**

PHARMACOLOGY, BIOCHEMISTRY AND BEHAVIOR (US/0091-3057). **4322**

PHARMACOLOGY COMMUNICATIONS (SZ/1060-4456). **4322**

PHARMACOPSYCHIATRY (GW/0176-3679). **4323**

PHARMACOTHERAPY (US/0277-0008). **4323**

PHARMACY STUDENT, THE (US/0279-5272). **4323**

PHARMAZEUTISCHE INDUSTRIE, DIE (GW/0031-711X). **4324**

PHARMAZEUTISCHE RUNDSCHAU (GW/0031-7128). **4324**

PHARMAZIE, DIE (GW/0031-7144). **4324**

PHARMAZIE HEUTE (GW/0369-979X). **4324**

PHARMAZIE IN UNSERER ZEIT (GW/0048-3664). **4324**

PHASE TRANSITIONS (US/0141-1594). **4414**

PHENOMENOLOGY AND PEDAGOGY (CN/0820-9189). **4355**

PHILIPS JOURNAL OF RESEARCH (NE/0165-5817). **2075**

PHILOBIBLON (GW/0031-7969). **362**

PHILOSOPHICAL BOOKS (UK/0031-8051). **4355**

PHILOSOPHICAL INVESTIGATIONS (US/0190-0536). **4355**

PHILOSOPHICAL MAGAZINE. A, PHYSICS OF CONDENSED MATTER, DEFECTS AND MECHANICAL PROPERTIES (UK/0141-8610). **4414**

PHILOSOPHICAL MAGAZINE. B, PHYSICS OF CONDENSED MATTER, STRUCTURAL, ELECTRONIC, OPTICAL, AND MAGNETIC PROPERTIES (UK/0958-6644). **4414**

PHILOSOPHICAL MAGAZINE LETTERS (UK/0950-0839). **4414**

PHILOSOPHICAL

PHILOSOPHICAL PSYCHOLOGY (UK/0951-5089). **4608**

PHILOSOPHICAL QUARTERLY, THE (UK/0031-8094). **4356**

PHILOSOPHICAL STUDIES (NE/0031-8116). **4356**

PHILOSOPHICAL TRANSACTIONS. BIOLOGICAL SCIENCES (UK/0080-4622). **468**

PHILOSOPHISCHE RUNDSCHAU (GW/0031-8159). **4356**

PHILOSOPHISCHES JAHRBUCH (FREIBURG) (GW/0031-8183). **4356**

PHILOSOPHY AND LITERATURE (US/0190-0013). **4356**

PHILOSOPHY & RHETORIC (US/0031-8213). **4357**

PHILOSOPHY OF SCIENCE (EAST LANSING) (US/0031-8248). **5138**

PHLEBOLOGIE (FR/0031-8280). **3709**

PHLEBOLOGIE UND PROKTOLOGIE (GW/0340-305X). **3800**

PHLEBOLOGY / VENOUS FORUM OF THE ROYAL SOCIETY OF MEDICINE (UK/0268-3555). **3800**

PHONETICA (SZ/0031-8388). **3310**

PHOSPHORUS, SULFUR, AND SILICON AND THE RELATED ELEMENTS (US/1042-6507). **1037**

PHOT ARGUS EDITION GENERALE (FR/0151-7848). **4372**

PHOTOCHEMISTRY AND PHOTOBIOLOGY (UK/0031-8655). **1056**

PHOTOCHEMISTRY (LONDON) (UK/0556-3860). **1056**

PHOTODERMATOLOGY, PHOTOIMMUNOLOGY & PHOTOMEDICINE (DK/0905-4383). **3722**

PHOTOGRAMMETRIC ENGINEERING AND REMOTE SENSING (US/0099-1112). **1990**

PHOTOLETTER, THE (US/0190-1400). **4375**

PHOTONICS AND OPTOELECTRONICS (US/1067-5345). **4440**

PHOTOSYNTHESIS RESEARCH (NE/0166-8595). **521**

PHOTOSYNTHETICA (NE/0300-3604). **492**

PHOTOVOLTAIC INSIDER'S REPORT (US/0731-4671). **1953**

PHYCOLOGIA (OXFORD) (UK/0031-8884). **521**

PHYSICA A (NE/0378-4371). **4414**

PHYSICA B. CONDENSED MATTER (NE/0921-4526). **4414**

PHYSICA C. SUPERCONDUCTIVITY (NE/0921-4534). **4414**

PHYSICA. D (NE/0167-2789). **4414**

PHYSICA SCRIPTA (SW/0031-8949). **4414**

PHYSICA STATUS SOLIDI. A: APPLIED RESEARCH (GW/0031-8965). **4414**

PHYSICA STATUS SOLIDI. B : BASIC RESEARCH (GW/0370-1972). **4415**

PHYSICAL ACOUSTICS (US/0893-388X). **4453**

PHYSICAL GEOGRAPHY (US/0272-3646). **2572**

PHYSICAL MEDICINE AND REHABILITATION (US/0888-7357). **3884**

PHYSICAL REVIEW. A (US/1050-2947). **4415**

PHYSICAL REVIEW ABSTRACTS (US/0048-4024). **4415**

PHYSICAL REVIEW B : CONDENSED MATTER (US/0163-1829). **4415**

PHYSICAL REVIEW C : NUCLEAR PHYSICS (US/0556-2813). **4450**

PHYSICAL REVIEW D : PARTICLES AND FIELDS (US/0556-2821). **4415**

PHYSICAL REVIEW LETTERS (US/0031-9007). **4415**

PHYSICAL THERAPY PRACTICE (US/1054-8513). **4381**

PHYSICAL THERAPY TODAY (US/1042-2579). **4381**

PHYSICIAN AND SPORTSMEDICINE, THE (US/0091-3847). **3955**

PHYSICIAN ASSISTANT (1983) (US/8750-7544). **3627**

PHYSICIANS' CURRENT PROCEDURAL TERMINOLOGY (US/0276-8283). **1928**

PHYSICIANS' DESK REFERENCE (PRINT ED.) (US/0093-4461). **4325**

PHYSICIAN'S MANAGEMENT (US/0031-9066). **3627**

PHYSICS ABSTRACTS (UK/0036-8091). **4427**

PHYSICS AND CHEMISTRY OF LIQUIDS (US/0031-9104). **1056**

PHYSICS AND CHEMISTRY OF MINERALS (GW/0342-1791). **1443**

PHYSICS AND CHEMISTRY OF THE EARTH (UK/0079-1946). **1359**

PHYSICS-DOKLADY (US/1063-7753). **4415**

PHYSICS EDUCATION (UK/0031-9120). **4415**

PHYSICS ESSAYS (CN/0836-1398). **4415**

PHYSICS IN MEDICINE & BIOLOGY (UK/0031-9155). **479**

PHYSICS LETTERS : PART A (NE/0375-9601). **4416**

PHYSICS LETTERS : PART B (NE/0370-2693). **4450**

PHYSICS OF ATOMIC NUCLEI (US/1063-7788). **4450**

PHYSICS OF METALS (US/0275-9144). **4014**

PHYSICS OF METALS AND METALLOGRAPHY, THE (UK/0031-918X). **4014**

PHYSICS OF PARTICLES AND NUCLEI (US/1063-7796). **4450**

PHYSICS OF THE EARTH AND PLANETARY INTERIORS (NE/0031-9201). **1391**

PHYSICS OF THE SOLID STATE (US/1063-7834). **4416**

PHYSICS REPORTS (NE/0370-1573). **4416**

PHYSICS TODAY (US/0031-9228). **4416**

PHYSICS, USPEKHI (US/1063-7869). **4416**

PHYSICS WORLD (UK/0953-8585). **4416**

PHYSIK IN UNSERER ZEIT (GW/0031-9252). **4416**

PHYSIK UND DIDAKTIK (GW/0340-8515). **1902**

PHYSIKALISCHE BLATTER (GW/0031-9279). **4417**

PHYSIOLOGIA PLANTARUM (DK/0031-9317). **521**

PHYSIOLOGICAL AND MOLECULAR PLANT PATHOLOGY (UK/0885-5765). **521**

PHYSIOLOGICAL ENTOMOLOGY (UK/0307-6962). **5612**

PHYSIOLOGICAL REVIEWS (US/0031-9333). **585**

PHYSIOLOGICAL ZOOLOGY (US/0031-935X). **5594**

PHYSIOLOGY & BEHAVIOR (US/0031-9384). **585**

PHYSIOTHERAPY CANADA (CN/0300-0508). **3627**

PHYTOCHEMICAL ANALYSIS (UK/0958-0344). **522**

PHYTOCHEMISTRY (OXFORD) (UK/0031-9422). **522**

PHYTOCOENOLOGIA (GW/0340-269X). **522**

PHYTOPATHOLOGY (US/0031-949X). **522**

PHYTOPROTECTION (CN/0031-9511). **181**

PIB'S BUSINESS & INCENTIVES (US/1056-5442). **703**

PIG INTERNATIONAL (EUROPE, ASIA, AFRICA, LATIN AMERICA AND OCEANIA EDITION (US/0191-8834). **217**

PIGMENT CELL (SZ/0301-0139). **539**

PIK. PRAXIS DER INFORMATIONSVERARBEITUNG UND KOMMUNIKATION (GW/0930-5157). **1199**

PIMA MAGAZINE (US/1046-4352). **4237**

PIPE LINE INDUSTRY (HOUSTON, TEX.) (US/0032-0145). **2124**

PIPELINE & GAS JOURNAL (US/0032-0188). **4274**

PIPELINE & UTILITIES CONSTRUCTION (US/0896-1069). **2124**

PIPELINE DIGEST (US/0197-1506). **4274**

PIRINEOS (SP/0373-2568). **2220**

PISMA V ASTRONOMICESKIJ ZURNAL (RU/0320-0108). **398**

PISMA V ZURNAL TEHNICESKOJ FIZIKI (RU/0320-0116). **4417**

PIT & QUARRY (US/0032-0293). **2147**

PLACENTA (EASTBOURNE) (UK/0143-4004). **539**

PLACES (CAMBRIDGE, MASS.) (US/0731-0455). **306**

PLAN CANADA (CN/0032-0544). **2830**

PLANETARY AND SPACE SCIENCE (UK/0032-0633). **398**

PLANNING PERSPECTIVES : PP (UK/0266-5433). **2831**

PLANNING REVIEW (US/0094-064X). **882**

PLANT AND SOIL (NE/0032-079X). **181**

PLANT BIOTECHNOLOGY (UK/0260-5902). **523**

PLANT, CELL AND ENVIRONMENT (UK/0140-7791). **523**

PLANT CELL REPORTS (GW/0721-7714). **539**

PLANT CELL, TISSUE AND ORGAN CULTURE (NE/0167-6857). **523**

PLANT DISEASE (US/0191-2917). **181**

PLANT ENGINEERING (US/0032-082X). **1990**

PLANT FOODS FOR HUMAN NUTRITION (DORDRECHT) (NE/0921-9668). **4197**

PLANT GROWTH REGULATION (NE/0167-6903). **523**

PLANT JOURNAL : FOR CELL AND MOLECULAR BIOLOGY, THE (UK/0960-7412). **523**

PLANT MOLECULAR BIOLOGY (NE/0167-4412). **550**

PLANT MOLECULAR BIOLOGY REPORTER (US/0735-9640). **523**

PLANT/OPERATIONS PROGRESS (US/0278-4513). **2015**

PLANT PATHOLOGY (UK/0032-0862). **524**

PLANT PHYSIOLOGY AND BIOCHEMISTRY (FR/0981-9428). **524**

PLANT PHYSIOLOGY (BETHESDA) (US/0032-0889). **524**

PLANT PROTECTION QUARTERLY (AT/0815-2195). **120**

PLANT SCIENCE (LIMERICK) (IE/0168-9452). **524**

PLANT SERVICES (US/0199-8013). **2124**

PLANT SYSTEMATICS AND EVOLUTION (AU/0378-2697). **524**

PLANT VARIETIES & SEEDS (UK/0952-3863). **2427**

PLANTA (GW/0032-0935). **524**

PLANTA MEDICA (GW/0032-0943). **4325**

PLANTS, SITES & PARKS (US/0191-2933). **703**

PLASMA CHEMISTRY AND PLASMA PROCESSING (US/0272-4324). **2015**

PLASMA DEVICES AND OPERATIONS (US/1051-9998). **5138**

PLASMA PHYSICS AND CONTROLLED FUSION (UK/0741-3335). **4450**

PLASMID (US/0147-619X). **550**

PLASTIC AND RECONSTRUCTIVE SURGERY (1963) (US/0032-1052). **3972**

PLASTIC SURGICAL NURSING (US/0741-5206). **3867**

PLASTICOS UNIVERSALES (SP/0303-4011). **4457**

PLASTICS AND RUBBER INTERNATIONAL (UK/0309-4561). **4457**

PLASTICS & RUBBER WEEKLY (UK/0032-1168). **4457**

PLASTICS COMPOUNDING (US/0148-9119). **4458**

PLASTICS DESIGN FORUM (US/0362-9376). **4458**

PLASTICS ENGINEERING (US/0091-9578). **4458**

PLASTICS IN BUILDING CONSTRUCTION (US/0147-2429). **624**

PLASTICS MACHINERY & EQUIPMENT (US/0149-4899). **4458**

PLASTICS NEWS (AKRON, OHIO) (US/1042-802X). **4458**

PLASTICS, RUBBER AND COMPOSITES PROCESSING AND APPLICATIONS (UK/0959-8111). **4458**

PLASTICS TECHNOLOGY (US/0032-1257). **4458**

PLASTICS WORLD (US/0032-1273). **4458**

PLASTIQUES MODERNES ELASTOMERES (FR/0032-1303). **4459**

PLATELETS (UK/0953-7104). **3773**

PLATELETS SHEFFIELD (UK/0142-8268). **3773**

PLAY & CULTURE (US/0894-4253). **5213**

PLAYTHINGS (US/0032-1567). **2585**

PLUMBING & MECHANICAL (US/8750-6041). **2607**

PLUMBING, HEATING, PIPING (US/1055-3231). **2607**

PM. PRAXIS DER MATHEMATIK (GW/0032-7042). **3527**

PMTF (RU/0044-4626). **4417**

PODIATRY TRACTS (US/0894-6116). **3918**

POETICS (AMSTERDAM) (NE/0304-422X). **3468**

POETICS TODAY (US/0333-5372). **3424**

POETIQUE (FR/0032-2024). **3469**

POETRY (CHICAGO) (US/0032-2032). **3469**

POINT VETERINAIRE, LE (FR/0335-4997). **5518**

POINTER, THE (US/0554-4246). **1883**

POLAR BIOLOGY (GW/0722-4060). **5594**

POLAR GEOGRAPHY AND GEOLOGY (US/0273-8457). **1391**

POLICE OFFICER GRIEVANCES BULLETIN (US/0887-8285). **3172**

POLICING AND SOCIETY (SZ/1043-9463). **3172**

POLICING POLICY (UK/0967-1773). **3172**

POLICY SCIENCES (NE/0032-2687). **4488**

POLICY STUDIES (UK/0144-2872). **4488**

POLICY STUDIES JOURNAL (US/0190-292X). **4488**

POLICY STUDIES REVIEW (US/0278-4416). **4488**

POLISH ECOLOGICAL STUDIES (PL/0324-8763). **2220**

POLISH JOURNAL OF CHEMISTRY (PL/0137-5083). **988**

POLITICAL BEHAVIOR (US/0190-9320). **4488**

POLITICAL COMMUNICATION (US/1058-4609). **4489**

POLITICAL PSYCHOLOGY (US/0162-895X). **4608**

POLITICAL QUARTERLY (LONDON. 1930) (UK/0032-3179). **4489**

POLITICAL RISK SERVICES LETTER (US/0887-7629). **1512**

... POLITICAL RISK YEARBOOK. SUB-SAHARAN AFRICA, THE (US/0889-2725). **4489**

POLITICAL SCIENCE (NZ/0032-3187). **4490**

POLITICAL SCIENCE AND RELATED DISCIPLINES / INTERNATIONAL CURRENT AWARENESS SERVICES (UK/0960-1538). **4490**

POLITICAL STUDIES (UK/0032-3217). **4490**

POLITICAL THEORY (US/0090-5917). **4490**

POLITICS AND THE LIFE SCIENCES (US/0730-9384). **4490**

POLITICS (MANCHESTER (GREATER MANCHESTER)) (UK/0263-3957). **4491**

POLLUTION ENGINEERING (US/0032-3640). **2238**

POLLUTION PREVENTION REVIEW (US/1053-4253). **2239**

POLYCYCLIC AROMATIC COMPOUNDS (US/1040-6638). **988**

POLYGRAPH, DER (GW/0032-3845). **4567**

POLYHEDRON (UK/0277-5387). **1037**

POLYMER BLENDS, ALLOYS, AND INTERPENETRATING POLYMER NETWORKS ABSTRACTS (US/0893-6684). **988**

POLYMER BULLETIN (BERLIN, WEST) (GW/0170-0839). **1056**

POLYMER COMPOSITES (US/0272-8397). **4459**

POLYMER CONTENTS (UK/0883-153X). **4461**

POLYMER DEGRADATION AND STABILITY (UK/0141-3910). **988**

POLYMER ENGINEERING AND SCIENCE (US/0032-3888). **988**

POLYMER GELS AND NETWORKS (UK/0966-7822). **2015**

POLYMER (GUILFORD) (UK/0032-3861). **1046**

POLYMER INTERNATIONAL (UK/0959-8103). **4459**

POLYMER JOURNAL (JA/0032-3896). **1046**

POLYMER NETWORKS & BLENDS (CN/1181-9510). **1046**

POLYMER NEWS (US/0032-3918). **4459**

POLYMER-PLASTICS TECHNOLOGY AND ENGINEERING (SOFTCOVER ED.) (US/0360-2559). **2015**

POLYMER REACTION ENGINEERING (US/1054-3414). **1990**

POLYMER TESTING (UK/0142-9418). **4459**

POLYMERS FOR ADVANCED TECHNOLOGIES (UK/1042-7147). **1028**

POLYPEPTIDES SHEFFIELD (UK/0143-4225). **3628**

POPULAR MUSIC (CAMBRIDGE UNIVERSITY PRESS) (UK/0261-1430). **4147**

POPULAR SCIENCE (NEW YORK, N.Y.) (US/0161-7370). **5139**

POPULATION AND ENVIRONMENT (US/0199-0039). **4556**

POPULATION RESEARCH AND POLICY REVIEW (NE/0167-5923). **4558**

POPULATION STUDIES (UK/0032-4728). **4558**

PORK (US/0745-3787). **217**

POROSHKOVAIA METALLURGIIA (US/0038-5735). **4015**

POROSKOVAJA METALLURGIJA (KIEV) (UN/0032-4795). **4015**

PORTABLE COMPUTER (US/0738-1220). **1272**

POSEV (GW/0032-5201). **4491**

POST-MARKETING SURVEILLANCE (NE/0269-2333). **935**

POST-SOVIET AFFAIRS (US/1060-586X). **1513**

POSTGRADUATE DOCTOR. AFRICA (UK/0142-7946). **3628**

POSTGRADUATE DOCTOR. CARIBBEAN (UK/0267-0275). **3628**

POSTGRADUATE DOCTOR. MIDDLE EAST EDITION (UK/0140-7724). **3628**

POSTGRADUATE MEDICAL JOURNAL (UK/0032-5473). **3628**

POSTGRADUATE MEDICINE (US/0032-5481). **3628**

POSTGRADUATE RADIOLOGY (US/0273-0278). **3944**

POSTHARVEST BIOLOGY AND TECHNOLOGY (NE/0925-5214). **182**

POSTPRAXIS, DIE (GW/0554-842X). **1147**

POTENCIA (SP/0032-5600). **624**

POULTRY INTERNATIONAL (US/0032-5767). **218**

POULTRY SCIENCE REVIEWS (UK/0964-6604). **218**

POULTRY SCIENCE SYMPOSIUM SERIES (UK/0966-7318). **218**

POUVOIRS (FR/0152-0768). **4532**

POVERKHNOST (US/0734-1520). **4417**

POWDER/BULK SOLIDS (US/8750-6653). **4221**

POWDER DIFFRACTION (US/0885-7156). **4015**

POWDER METALLURGY AND METAL CERAMICS (US/1068-1302). **4015**

POWDER TECHNOLOGY (SZ/0032-5910). **2016**

POWER (US/0032-5929). **1953**

POWER ENGINEERING (BARRINGTON, ILL.) (US/0032-5961). **2124**

POWER ENGINEERING JOURNAL (UK/0950-3366). **2075**

POWER ENGINEERING (NEW YORK) (US/0160-5216). **2124**

POWER INTERNATIONAL (UK/0950-1487). **2124**

POWER TRANSMISSION DESIGN (US/0032-6070). **2124**

POWERCONVERSION & INTELLIGENT MOTION (US/0885-0259). **1991**

POWERTECHNICS MAGAZINE (US/0882-7419). **4417**

PPF SURVEY (US/0361-7467). **946**

PPMP. PSYCHOTHERAPIE, PSYCHOSOMATIK, MEDIZINISCHE PSYCHOLOGIE (GW/0937-2032). **4608**

PPO LETTER, THE (US/1054-2396). **2890**

PR. PHARMACEUTICAL REPRESENTATIVE (US/0161-8415). **4325**

PRACOVNI LEKARSTVI (XR/0032-6291). **3628**

PRACTICAL ACCOUNTANT, THE (US/0032-6321). **749**

PRACTICAL BOAT OWNER (UK/0032-6348). **595**

PRACTICAL CARDIOLOGY (US/0361-3372). **3709**

PRACTICAL ELECTRONICS (UK/0032-6372). **2075**

PRACTICAL GARDENING (UK/0032-6399). **2428**

PRACTICAL GASTROENTEROLOGY (US/0277-4208). **3747**

PRACTICAL SUPERVISION (US/0742-7859). **882**

PRACTICAL WOOD WORKING (UK/0032-6488). **634**

PRACTICE BIRMINGHAM (UK/0950-3153). **5301**

PRAEHISTORISCHE ZEITSCHRIFT (GW/0079-4848). **243**

PRAKTISCHE TIERARZT (GW/0032-681X). **5518**

PRATIQUE MEDICALE, LA (FR/0750-6155). **3629**

PRAXIS DER KINDERPSYCHOLOGIE UND KINDERPSYCHIATRIE (GW/0032-7034). **4608**

PRAXIS DER PSYCHOTHERAPIE UND PSYCHOSOMATIK (GW/0171-791X). **4608**

PRAXISMAGAZIN (GW/0941-1046). **3629**

PRE- AND PERI-NATAL PSYCHOLOGY JOURNAL (US/0883-3095). **3767**

PREACHING (JACKSONVILLE, FLA.) (US/0882-7036). **4987**

PRECAMBRIAN RESEARCH (NE/0301-9268). **1391**

PRECISION ENGINEERING (US/0141-6359). **2125**

PRECISION MACHINERY. INCORPORATING LIFE SUPPORT TECHNOLOGY (US/1045-4160). **3696**

PREDI-BRIEFS (CLEVELAND) (US/0551-9276). **1621**

PREDICASTS' BASEBOOK (US/0738-9906). **1513**

PREDICASTS F & S INDEX EUROPE (US/0270-4536). **704**

PREDICASTS F & S INDEX INTERNATIONAL (US/0270-4528). **732**

PREDICASTS FORECASTS (US/0278-0135). **1537**

PRENATAL DIAGNOSIS (UK/0197-3851). **3767**

PREPARATIVE BIOCHEMISTRY (US/0032-7484). **492**

PREPARATIVE CHROMATOGRAPHY (US/0890-9075). **989**

PREPARED FOODS (US/0747-2536). **2353**

PRESCRIBERS' JOURNAL (UK/0032-7611). **4325**

PRESENCE (CAMBRIDGE, MASS.) (US/1054-7460). **1216**

PRESIDENTS & PRIME MINISTERS (US/1060-5088). **4492**

PRESSE MEDICALE (1983), LA (FR/0755-4982). **3629**

PRESSE THERMALE ET CLIMATIQUE (FR/0032-7875). **1433**

PREUSSENLAND : MITTEILUNGEN DER HISTORISCHEN KOMMISSION FUR OST- UND WESTPREUSSISCHE LANDESFORSCHUNG (GW/0032-7972). **2703**

PREVENTION (EMMAUS) (US/0032-8006). **4796**

PREVENTIVE MEDICINE (1972) (US/0091-7435). **3629**

PREVENTIVE VETERINARY MEDICINE (NE/0167-5877). **5518**

PREVIEW (US/0899-9821). **3241**

PREVIEWS OF HEAT AND MASS TRANSFER (US/0094-9477). **4432**

PRIBORY I TEHNIKA EKSPERIMENTA (RU/0032-8162). **5139**

PRIKLADNAJA MATEMATIKA I MEHANIKA (RU/0032-8235). **2125**

PRIMARY CARE (US/0095-4543). **3738**

PRIMARY CARE & CANCER (US/0743-8176). **3822**

PRIMARY CARE UPDATE FOR OB/GYNS (US/1068-607X). **3767**

PRIMARY HEALTH CARE MANAGEMENT (UK/0960-250X). **3739**

PRIMARY LIFE (UK/0962-8789). **1902**

PRIMUS (TERRE HAUTE, IND.) (US/1051-1970). **3587**

PRINCETON ALUMNI WEEKLY (US/0149-9270). **1102**

PRINCETON STUDIES IN INTERNATIONAL FINANCE (US/0081-8070). **1639**

PRINCIPAL'S REPORT (NEW YORK, N.Y.) (US/1044-4998). **882**

PRINTED CIRCUIT FABRICATION (US/0274-8096). **2075**

PRINTING ABSTRACTS (UK/0031-109X). **4570**

PRINTINGNEWS. EAST (US/1046-8595). **4568**

PRINTOUT (NEWTONVILLE, MASS.) (US/0738-6613). **4569**

PRISON SERVICE JOURNAL (UK/0300-3558). **3173**

PROBABILISTIC ENGINEERING MECHANICS (UK/0266-8920). **2125**

PROBABILITY IN THE ENGINEERING AND INFORMATIONAL SCIENCES (US/0269-9648). **1991**

PROBABILITY THEORY AND RELATED FIELDS (GW/0178-8051). **3527**

PROBE (CN/0834-1494). **1333**

PROBLEMS IN ANESTHESIA (US/0889-4698). **3684**

PROBLEMS IN CRITICAL CARE (US/0889-4701). **3629**

PROBLEMS IN GENERAL SURGERY (US/0739-8328). **3572**

PROBLEMS IN RESPIRATORY CARE (US/0897-9677). **3951**

PROBLEMS IN UROLOGY (US/0889-471X). **3992**

PROBLEMS IN VETERINARY MEDICINE (US/1041-0228). **5518**

PROBLEMS OF INFORMATION TRANSMISSION (US/0032-9460). **2076**

PROBLEMY OSVOENIIA PUSTYN (US/0278-4750). **2202**

PROBLEMY PROCNOSTI (KIEV) (UN/0556-171X). **1991**

PROBLEMY TUBERKULEZA (RU/0032-9533). **3951**

PROCEEDINGS / ACM IEEE DESIGN AUTOMATION CONFERENCE (US/0738-100X). **1234**

PROCEEDINGS : ANNUAL RELIABILITY AND MAINTAINABILITY SYMPOSIUM (US/0149-144X). **4221**

PROCEEDINGS - FRONTIERS IN EDUCATION CONFERENCE (US/0190-5848). **1991**

PROCEEDINGS - IEEE COMPUTER SOCIETY SYMPOSIUM ON RESEARCH IN SECURITY AND PRIVACY (US/1063-7109). **1227**

PROCEEDINGS - INSTITUTE OF FOOD SCIENCE AND TECHNOLOGY (U.K.) (UK/0144-1493). **2353**

PROCEEDINGS - INTERNATIONAL COMPUTER SOFTWARE & APPLICATIONS CONFERENCE (US/0730-3157). **1289**

PROCEEDINGS / INTERNATIONAL CONFERENCE ON DATA ENGINEERING (US/1063-6382). **1254**

PROCEEDINGS - INTERNATIONAL CONFERENCE ON SOFTWARE ENGINEERING (US/0270-5257). **1289**

PROCEEDINGS - INTERNATIONAL SYMPOSIUM ON MULTIPLE-VALUED LOGIC (US/0195-623X). **1230**

PROCEEDINGS - NATIONAL ONLINE MEETING (US/0739-1471). **1275**

PROCEEDINGS OF NATIONAL WASTE PROCESSING CONFERENCE (1976) (US/0145-4781). **2239**

PROCEEDINGS OF SPIE--THE INTERNATIONAL SOCIETY FOR OPTICAL ENGINEERING (US/0277-786X). **1991**

PROCEEDINGS OF SYMPOSIA IN PURE MATHEMATICS (US/0082-0717). **3528**

PROCEEDINGS OF THE AMERICAN MATHEMATICAL SOCIETY (US/0002-9939). **3528**

PROCEEDINGS OF THE AMERICAN POWER CONFERENCE (US/0097-2126). **2125**

PROCEEDINGS OF THE ANNUAL MEETING - AMERICAN SOCIETY OF INTERNATIONAL LAW (US/0272-5037). **3134**

PROCEEDINGS OF THE ANNUAL SOUTHEASTERN SYMPOSIUM ON SYSTEM THEORY (US/0094-2898). **1200**

PROCEEDINGS OF THE ASIS ANNUAL MEETING (US/0044-7870). **3242**

PROCEEDINGS OF THE EDINBURGH MATHEMATICAL SOCIETY (UK/0013-0915). **3528**

PROCEEDINGS OF THE ENTOMOLOGICAL SOCIETY OF MANITOBA (CN/0315-2146). **5613**

PROCEEDINGS OF THE GEOLOGISTS' ASSOCIATION (UK/0016-7878). **1391**

PROCEEDINGS OF THE HUMAN FACTORS SOCIETY ANNUAL MEETING (US/0163-5182). **2125**

PROCEEDINGS OF THE IEEE (US/0018-9219). **2076**

PROCEEDINGS OF THE INSTITUTION OF ELECTRICAL ENGINEERS (UK/0020-3270). **2077**

PROCEEDINGS OF THE INSTITUTION OF MECHANICAL ENGINEERS (UK/0020-3483). **2125**

PROCEEDINGS OF THE INSTITUTION OF MECHANICAL ENGINEERS. PART A, JOURNAL OF POWER AND ENERGY (UK/0957-6509). **2126**

PROCEEDINGS OF THE INSTITUTION OF MECHANICAL ENGINEERS. PART B, JOURNAL OF ENGINEERING MANUFACTURE (UK/0954-4054). **2126**

PROCEEDINGS OF THE INSTITUTION OF MECHANICAL ENGINEERS. PART C, JOURNAL OF MECHANICAL ENGINEERING SCIENCE (UK/0954-4062). **2126**

PROCEEDINGS OF THE INSTITUTION OF MECHANICAL ENGINEERS. PART D, JOURNAL OF AUTOMOBILE ENGINEERING (UK/0954-4070). **2126**

PROCEEDINGS OF THE INSTITUTION OF MECHANICAL ENGINEERS. PART E, JOURNAL OF PROCESS MECHANICAL ENGINEERING (UK/0954-4089). **2126**

PROCEEDINGS OF THE INSTITUTION OF MECHANICAL ENGINEERS. PART F, JOURNAL OF RAIL AND RAPID TRANSIT (UK/0954-4097). **2126**

PROCEEDINGS OF THE INSTITUTION OF MECHANICAL ENGINEERS. PART G, JOURNAL OF AEROSPACE ENGINEERING (UK/0954-4100). **32**

PROCEEDINGS OF THE INSTITUTION OF MECHANICAL ENGINEERS. PART H, JOURNAL OF ENGINEERING IN MEDICINE (UK/0954-4119). **3696**

PROCEEDINGS OF THE INTERNATIONAL CENTRE FOR HEAT AND MASS TRANSFER (US/0272-880X). **4418**

PROCEEDINGS OF THE INTERNATIONAL CONFERENCE ON LASERS (US/0190-4132). **5140**

PROCEEDINGS OF THE INTERNATIONAL CONFERENCE ON PARALLEL PROCESSING (US/0190-3918). **1261**

PROCEEDINGS OF THE INTERNATIONAL INSTRUMENTATION SYMPOSIUM (US/0277-7576). **32**

PROCEEDINGS OF THE ... INTERSOCIETY ENERGY CONVERSION ENGINEERING CONFERENCE (US/0146-955X). **1953**

PROCEEDINGS OF THE LEEDS PHILOSOPHICAL AND LITERARY SOCIETY, LITERARY AND HISTORICAL SECTION (UK/0024-0281). **5235**

PROCEEDINGS OF THE LONDON MATHEMATICAL SOCIETY (UK/0024-6115). **3528**

PROCEEDINGS OF THE NATIONAL ACADEMY OF SCIENCE OF THE UNITED STATES OF AMERICA (US/0027-8424). **5141**

PROCEEDINGS OF THE NOVA SCOTIAN INSTITUTE OF SCIENCE (CN/0078-2521). **5141**

PROCEEDINGS OF THE NUTRITION SOCIETY (UK/0029-6651). **4197**

PROCEEDINGS OF THE ROYAL SOCIETY OF VICTORIA (AT/0035-9211). **5141**

PROCEEDINGS OF THE SOCIETY FOR EXPERIMENTAL BIOLOGY AND MEDICINE (US/0037-9727). **3630**

PROCEEDINGS OF THE SOCIETY FOR EXPERIMENTAL MECHANICS (US/1046-6789). **4429**

PROCEEDINGS OF THE SUMMER COMPUTER SIMULATION CONFERENCE (US/0094-7474). **1283**

PROCEEDINGS - REFINING DEPARTMENT (US/0364-4030). **4275**

PROCEEDINGS - ROYAL MICROSCOPICAL SOCIETY (UK/0035-9017). **573**

PROCEEDINGS - SYMPOSIUM ON INSTRUMENTATION FOR THE PROCESS INDUSTRIES (TEXAS A & M UNIVERSITY) (US/0738-3231). **1028**

PROCEEDINGS - WINTER SIMULATION CONFERENCE (US/0891-7736). **1283**

PROCEEDINGS / WORLD PETROLEUM CONGRESS (UK/0084-2176). **4275**

PROCESS CONTROL & QUALITY (US/0924-3089). **2016**

PROCESS ENGINEERING (UK/0370-1859). **2016**

PROCESS SAFETY AND ENVIRONMENTAL PROTECTION (UK/0957-5820). **2180**

PROCESSING (CHICAGO ILL.) (US/0896-8659). **1028**

PRODUCT ALERT (US/0740-3801). **2354**

PRODUCT SAFETY & LIABILITY REPORTER (US/0092-7732). **4796**

PRODUCT SAFETY LETTER (US/0098-7530). **1299**

PRODUCTION (US/0032-9819). **2126**

PRODUCTION PLANNING & CONTROL (UK/0953-7287). **1622**

PRODUCTIVITY (STAMFORD, CONN.) (US/0275-8040). **883**

PRODUCTS FINISHING (US/0032-9940). **3486**

PROFESSIONAL BUILDER & REMODELER (US/1053-6353). **624**

PROFESSIONAL CARWASHING (US/0191-6823). **935**

PROFESSIONAL DOCUMENT RETRIEVAL (US/8755-0253). **3242**

PROFESSIONAL ENGINEERING (UK/0953-6639). **2127**

PROFESSIONAL GEOGRAPHER, THE (US/0033-0124). **2573**

PROFESSIONAL PHOTOGRAPHER (UK/0019-784X). **4375**

PROFESSIONAL PSYCHOLOGY, RESEARCH AND PRACTICE (US/0735-7028). **4609**

PROFESSIONAL WOMEN AND MINORITIES (US/0190-1796). **5564**

PROFILES, PATHWAYS, AND DREAMS (US/1047-8329). **434**

PROFIT-BUILDING STRATEGIES FOR BUSINESS OWNERS (US/0889-9967). **804**

PROGRAM AND ABSTRACTS / INTERSCIENCE CONFERENCE ON ANTIMICROBIAL AGENTS AND CHEMOTHERAPY (US/0733-6373). **568**

PROGRAM PLANS. NURSING BASIC SERIES (US/0734-1431). **3867**

PROGRAMMING AND COMPUTER SOFTWARE (US/0361-7688). **1281**

PROGRESS AND TOPICS IN CYTOGENETICS (US/0733-9003). **539**

PROGRESS IN AEROSPACE SCIENCES (UK/0376-0421). **32**

PROGRESS IN BASIC AND CLINICAL PHARMACOLOGY (SZ/1011-0267). **4326**

PROGRESS IN BEHAVIOR MODIFICATION (US/0099-037X). **4609**

PROGRESS IN BIOCHEMICAL PHARMACOLOGY (US/0079-6085). **4326**

PROGRESS IN BIOPHYSICS AND MOLECULAR BIOLOGY (US/0079-6107). **496**

PROGRESS IN BIOTECHNOLOGY (NE/0921-0423). **492**

PROGRESS IN BRAIN RESEARCH (NE/0079-6123). **3844**

PROGRESS IN CARDIOVASCULAR DISEASES (US/0033-0620). **3709**

PROGRESS IN CLINICAL AND BIOLOGICAL RESEARCH (US/0361-7742). **470**

PROGRESS IN CLINICAL NEUROPHYSIOLOGY (SZ/0378-4045). **3844**

PROGRESS IN COLLOID & POLYMER SCIENCE (GW/0340-255X). **1056**

PROGRESS IN DRUG RESEARCH (SZ/0071-786X). **4326**

PROGRESS IN ENERGY AND COMBUSTION SCIENCE (UK/0360-1285). **1954**

PROGRESS IN EXPERIMENTAL TUMOR RESEARCH (SZ/0079-6263). **3822**

PROGRESS IN FOOD & NUTRITION SCIENCE (UK/0306-0632). **4198**

PROGRESS IN GROWTH FACTOR RESEARCH (US/0955-2235). **990**

PROGRESS IN HISTOCHEMISTRY AND CYTOCHEMISTRY (GW/0079-6336). **540**

PROGRESS IN HUMAN GEOGRAPHY (UK/0309-1325). **2573**

PROGRESS IN INDUSTRIAL MICROBIOLOGY (AMSTERDAM, NETHERLANDS) (UK/0079-6352). **568**

PROGRESS IN LIPID RESEARCH (UK/0163-7827). **1046**

PROGRESS IN LIVER DISEASES (PHILADELPHIA, PA.) (US/1060-913X). **3800**

PROGRESS IN MATERIALS SCIENCE (UK/0079-6425). **2107**

PROGRESS IN MEDICAL VIROLOGY (US/0079-645X). **569**

PROGRESS IN MEDICINAL CHEMISTRY (NE/0079-6468). **990**

PROGRESS IN NEURO-PSYCHOPHARMACOLOGY & BIOLOGICAL PSYCHIATRY (UK/0278-5846). **4326**

PROGRESS IN NEUROBIOLOGY (UK/0301-0082). **3844**

PROGRESS IN NUCLEAR ENERGY (NEW SERIES) (UK/0149-1970). **2158**

PROGRESS IN NUCLEAR MAGNETIC RESONANCE SPECTROSCOPY (UK/0079-6565). **4450**

PROGRESS IN NUCLEIC ACID RESEARCH AND MOLECULAR BIOLOGY (US/0079-6603). **470**

PROGRESS IN OCEANOGRAPHY (UK/0079-6611). **1455**

PROGRESS IN OPTICS (NE/0079-6638). **4440**

PROGRESS IN PAPER RECYCLING (US/1061-1452). **4237**

PROGRESS IN PARTICLE AND NUCLEAR PHYSICS (UK/0146-6410). **4450**

PROGRESS IN PEDIATRIC CARDIOLOGY (US/1058-9813). **3709**

PROGRESS IN PEDIATRIC SURGERY (GW/0079-6654). **3911**

PROGRESS IN PHARMACOLOGY AND CLINICAL PHARMACOLOGY (GW/0934-9545). **4326**

PROGRESS IN PHYSICAL GEOGRAPHY (UK/0309-1333). **2573**

PROGRESS IN PLANNING (UK/0305-9006). **2832**

PROGRESS IN POLYMER SCIENCE (UK/0079-6700). **1047**

PROGRESS IN PSYCHOBIOLOGY AND PHYSIOLOGICAL PSYCHOLOGY (US/0363-0951). **585**

PROGRESS IN QUANTUM ELECTRONICS (UK/0079-6727). **2077**

PROGRESS IN REACTION KINETICS (US/0079-6743). **1057**

PROGRESS IN REPRODUCTIVE BIOLOGY AND MEDICINE (SZ/0254-105X). **470**

PROGRESS IN RESPIRATION RESEARCH (SZ/0079-6751). **3951**

PROGRESS IN RETINAL AND EYE RESEARCH (UK/1350-9462). **3878**

PROGRESS IN RUBBER AND PLASTICS TECHNOLOGY (UK/0266-7320). **5077**

PROGRESS IN SOLID STATE CHEMISTRY (UK/0079-6786). **1057**

PROGRESS IN SURFACE SCIENCE (UK/0079-6816). **1057**

PROGRESS IN SURGERY (SZ/0079-6824). **3972**

PROGRESS OF THEORETICAL PHYSICS (JA/0033-068X). **4429**

PROGRESSIVE ARCHITECTURE (US/0033-0752). **306**

PROGRESSIVE FISH-CULTURIST, THE (US/0033-0779). **2311**

PROJECT APPRAISAL (UK/0268-8867). **912**

PROMOTIONS & INCENTIVES (UK/0266-7991). **883**

PROMT / PREDICASTS OVERVIEW OF MARKETS AND TECHNOLOGY (US/0161-8032). **1537**

PROOFTEXTS (US/0272-9601). **3425**

PROPANE CANADA (CN/0033-1260). **4275**

PROPELLANTS, EXPLOSIVES, PYROTECHNICS (GW/0721-3115). **1028**

PROPERTY DATA UPDATE (US/0888-6903). **4418**

PROSPECTS (NEW YORK) (US/0361-2333). **2755**

PROSTAGLANDINS (US/0090-6980). **585**

PROSTAGLANDINS-BIOLOGY (UK/0142-8284). **3732**

PROSTAGLANDINS, LEUKOTRIENES, AND ESSENTIAL FATTY ACIDS (UK/0952-3278). **3631**

PROSTATE, THE (US/0270-4137). **3800**

PROTEASES & INHIBITORS (UK/0950-0588). **470**

PROTECTION OF METALS (US/0033-1732). **4017**

PROTEIN ABNORMALITIES (US/0736-4547). **586**

PROTEIN ENGINEERING (UK/0269-2139). **492**

PROTEIN EXPRESSION AND PURIFICATION (US/1046-5928). **551**

PROTEIN SEQUENCES & DATA ANALYSIS (GW/0931-9506). **470**

PROTEINS (US/0887-3585). **470**

PROTEINS, POST-TRANSLATIONAL PROCESSING (UK/0952-0406). **470**

PROTOPLASMA (AU/0033-183X). **540**

PSIHOLOGICESKIJ ZURNAL (RU/0205-9592). **4609**

PSR QUARTERLY (BALTIMORE, MD.), THE (US/1051-2438). **3631**

PSYCHE (GW/0033-2623). **4609**

PSYCHIATRIC ANNALS (US/0048-5713). **3933**

PSYCHIATRIC CLINICS OF NORTH AMERICA, THE (US/0193-953X). **3933**

PSYCHIATRIC GENETICS (UK/0955-8829). **551**

PSYCHIATRIC QUARTERLY (US/0033-2720). **3933**

PSYCHIATRIE DE L'ENFANT, LA (FR/0079-726X). **3933**

PSYCHIATRISCHE PRAXIS (GW/0303-4259). **3934**

PSYCHIATRY RESEARCH (IE/0165-1781). **3934**

PSYCHIATRY RESEARCH : NEUROIMAGING SECTION (IE/0925-4927). **3934**

PSYCHIATRY (WASHINGTON, D.C.) (US/0033-2747). **3934**

PSYCHOANALYTIC INQUIRY (US/0735-1690). **3934**

PSYCHOANALYTIC REVIEW (1963) (US/0033-2836). **4610**

PSYCHOANALYTIC STUDY OF SOCIETY (US/0079-7294). **5214**

PSYCHOBIOLOGY (AUSTIN, TEX.) (US/0889-6313). **4610**

PSYCHOHISTORY REVIEW, THE (US/0363-891X). **2626**

PSYCHOLOGICAL ASSESSMENT (US/1040-3590). **4610**

PSYCHOLOGICAL BULLETIN (US/0033-2909). **4610**

PSYCHOLOGICAL MEDICINE (UK/0033-2917). **4611**

PSYCHOLOGICAL PERSPECTIVES (US/0033-2925). **4611**

PSYCHOLOGICAL RECORD, THE (US/0033-2933). **4611**

PSYCHOLOGICAL RESEARCH (GW/0340-0727). **4611**

PSYCHOLOGICAL REVIEW (US/0033-295X). **4611**

PSYCHOLOGIE FRANCAISE (FR/0033-2984). **4612**

PSYCHOLOGIE IN ERZIEHUNG UND UNTERRICHT (GW/0342-183X). **1903**

PSYCHOLOGIST, THE (UK/0952-8229). **4612**

PSYCHOLOGY AND AGING (US/0882-7974). **4612**

PSYCHOLOGY & HEALTH (SZ/0887-0446). **4797**

PSYCHOLOGY & MARKETING (US/0742-6046). **935**

PSYCHOLOGY OF ADDICTIVE BEHAVIORS (US/0893-164X). **4613**

PSYCHOLOGY OF LEARNING AND MOTIVATION, THE (US/0079-7421). **4613**

PSYCHOMETRIKA (US/0033-3123). **4613**

PSYCHOMOTRICITE, LA (FR/0151-5845). **4613**

PSYCHONEUROENDOCRINOLOGY (UK/0306-4530). **3732**

PSYCHONOMIC BULLETIN & REVIEW (US/1069-9384). **4613**

PSYCHOPATHOLOGY (SZ/0254-4962). **3934**

PSYCHOPHARMACOLOGIA (GW/0033-3158). **4326**

PSYCHOSOMATIC MEDICINE (US/0033-3174). **3631**

PSYCHOTHERAPIE, PSYCHOSOMATIK, MEDIZINISCHE PSYCHOLOGIE (GW/0173-7937). **4614**

PSYCHOTHERAPIES (GENEVA, SWITZERLAND) (SZ/0251-737X). **3935**

PSYCHOTHERAPY AND PSYCHOSOMATICS (SZ/0033-3190). **3935**

PSYCHOTHERAPY RESEARCH (US/1050-3307). **4614**

PSYCHOTHERAPY TODAY (US/1047-9848). **4614**

PSYCHOTROPICS (RENO, NEV.) (US/0895-5727). **3986**

PT DISTRIBUTOR, THE (US/1045-3962). **2127**

PTERIDINES (GW/0933-4807). **5143**

PTR. PHYTOTHERAPY RESEARCH (UK/0951-418X). **525**

PUBLI 10 (FR/0751-5464). **764**

PUBLIC ADMINISTRATION AND DEVELOPMENT (UK/0271-2075). **4675**

PUBLIC ADMINISTRATION (LONDON) (UK/0033-3298). **4704**

PUBLIC BROADCASTING REPORT, THE (US/0193-3663). **1136**

PUBLIC BUDGETING & FINANCE (US/0275-1100). **4743**

PUBLIC BUDGETING AND FINANCIAL MANAGEMENT (US/1042-4741). **4743**

PUBLIC CHOICE (NE/0048-5829). **1514**

PUBLIC FINANCE QUARTERLY (US/0048-5853). **4743**

PUBLIC HEALTH (LONDON) (UK/0033-3506). **4797**

PUBLIC HEALTH NURSING (BOSTON, MASS.) (US/0737-1209). **3867**

PUBLIC HISTORIAN, THE (US/0272-3433). **2626**

PUBLIC INTERNATIONAL LAW (GW/0340-7349). **3134**

PUBLIC LAND AND RESOURCES LAW DIGEST, THE (US/0148-6489). **3115**

PUBLIC LIBRARIES (US/0163-5506). **3243**

PUBLIC MONEY & MANAGEMENT (UK/0954-0962). **4743**

PUBLIC OPINION QUARTERLY (US/0033-362X). **5254**

PUBLIC PERSONNEL MANAGEMENT (US/0091-0260). **946**

PUBLIC RELATIONS QUARTERLY (US/0033-3700). **765**

PUBLIC RELATIONS REVIEW (RIVERDALE, N.Y.) (US/0363-8111). **765**

PUBLIC SECTOR (WELLINGTON) (NZ/0110-5191). **4677**

PUBLIC UTILITIES FORTNIGHTLY (US/0033-3808). **4762**

PUBLIC WELFARE (WASHINGTON) (US/0033-3816). **5303**

PUBLICATION - INTERNATIONAL UNION OF GEOLOGICAL SCIENCES (CN/0254-2897). **1392**

PUBLICATION SP (US/0193-2527). **625**

PUBLICATIONS MATHEMATIQUES. INSTITUT DES HAUTES ETUDES SCIENTIFIQUES (FR/0073-8301). **3529**

PUBLICATIONS ROMANES ET FRANCAISES (SZ/0079-7812). **3426**

PUBLISHERS, DISTRIBUTORS, & WHOLESALERS OF THE UNITED STATES (US/0000-0671). **4822**

PUBLISHERS' TRADE LIST ANNUAL, THE (US/0079-7855). **4822**

PUBLISHERS WEEKLY (US/0000-0019). **4831**

PUBLISHING HISTORY (UK/0309-2445). **4819**

PUBLISHING RESEARCH QUARTERLY (US/0741-6148). **4819**

PUBLIZISTIK (GW/0033-4006). **2923**

PULMONARY PHARMACOLOGY (EDINBURGH) (UK/0952-0600). **3951**

PULMONARY PHARMACOLOGY SHEFFIELD (UK/0954-3333). **4327**

PULP & PAPER (US/0033-4081). **4237**

PULP & PAPER INTERNATIONAL (US/0033-409X). **4238**

PULP & PAPER JOURNAL (CN/0713-5807). **4238**

PULP & PAPER PROJECT REPORT (US/0748-1608). **4238**

PURCHASER'S LEGAL ADVISER (US/0898-994X). **951**

PURCHASING (1936) (US/0033-4448). **951**

PURE AND APPLIED CHEMISTRY (UK/0033-4545). **990**

PURE AND APPLIED GEOPHYSICS (SZ/0033-4553). **1409**

PVP - AMERICAN SOCIETY OF MECHANICAL ENGINEERS. PRESSURE VESSELS AND PIPING DIVISION (US/0277-027X). **2127**

QAZAQ SSR GHYLYM AKADEMIIASYNYNG KHABARLARY (KZ/0002-3175). **1392**

QUAERENDO (NE/0014-9527). **4831**

QUALITATIVE SOCIOLOGY (US/0162-0436). **5254**

QUALITY & QUANTITY (NE/0033-5177). **3529**

QUALITY AND RELIABILITY ENGINEERING INTERNATIONAL (UK/0748-8017). **1992**

QUALITY ASSURANCE AND UTILIZATION REVIEW : OFFICIAL JOURNAL OF THE AMERICAN COLLEGE OF UTILIZATION REVIEW PHYSICIANS (US/0885-713X). **3632**

QUALITY ASSURANCE IN HEALTH CARE (UK/1040-6166). **4797**

QUALITY ASSURANCE (SAN DIEGO, CALIF.) (US/1052-9411). **5143**

QUALITY CONTROL REPORTS (US/0163-2418). **3487**

QUALITY DIGEST (US/1049-8699). **1705**

QUALITY ENGINEERING (US/0898-2112). **1992**

QUALITY MANAGEMENT IN HEALTH CARE (US/1063-8628). **884**

QUALITY OF LIFE RESEARCH (UK/0962-9343). **4392**

QUALITY PROGRESS (US/0033-524X). **1993**

QUALITY (WHEATON) (US/0360-9936). **884**

QUANTITATIVE STRUCTURE-ACTIVITY RELATIONSHIPS (GW/0931-8771). **4327**

QUANTUM (WASHINGTON, D.C.) (US/1048-8820). **3530**

QUARTERLY CONSENSUS FORECAST OF KEY ECONOMIC INDICATORS (US/0888-787X). **1579**

QUARTERLY DOMESTIC & GLOBAL FORECASTS OF KEY ECONOMIC INDICATORS (US/0888-787X). **1514**

QUARTERLY JOURNAL OF ECONOMICS, THE (US/0033-5533). **1514**

QUARTERLY JOURNAL OF ENGINEERING GEOLOGY, THE (UK/0481-2085). **2029**

QUARTERLY JOURNAL OF MATHEMATICS (UK/0033-5606). **3530**

QUARTERLY JOURNAL OF MECHANICS AND APPLIED MATHEMATICS, THE (UK/0033-5614). **2127**

QUARTERLY JOURNAL OF MEDICINE, THE (UK/0033-5622). **3632**

QUARTERLY JOURNAL OF THE ROYAL ASTRONOMICAL SOCIETY, THE (UK/0035-8738). **399**

QUARTERLY NEWSLETTER OF THE LABORATORY OF COMPARATIVE HUMAN COGNITION, THE (US/0278-4351). **4615**

QUARTERLY OF APPLIED MATHEMATICS (US/0033-569X). **3530**

QUARTERLY PREDICTIONS (NZ/0033-5711). **1580**

QUARTERLY REPORT ON MONEY FUND EXPENSE RATIOS (US/0897-2044). **805**

QUARTERLY REVIEW OF ECONOMICS AND FINANCE, THE (US/1062-9769). **1515**

QUARTERLY REVIEW OF FILM AND VIDEO (SZ/1050-9208). **4076**

QUARTERLY REVIEWS OF BIOPHYSICS (UK/0033-5835). **496**

QUATERNARY INTERNATIONAL (UK/1040-6182). **1393**

QUATERNARY

QUATERNARY RESEARCH (US/0033-5894). **1393**

QUATERNARY SCIENCE REVIEWS (UK/0277-3791). **1393**

QUEEN'S QUARTERLY (CN/0033-6041). **5214**

QUELLE (KOLN) (GW/0033-6246). **1705**

QUEST (NATIONAL ASSOCIATION FOR PHYSICAL EDUCATION IN HIGHER EDUCATION) (US/0033-6297). **3955**

QUICK PRINTING (US/0191-4588). **4569**

QUIMICA E INDUSTRIA (MADRID) (SP/0033-6521). **1029**

QUINQUEREME (UK/0140-3397). **3313**

QZ. QUALITAT UND ZUVERLASSIGKEIT (GW/0720-1214). **1623**

R & D MANAGEMENT (UK/0033-6807). **5144**

R.F. DESIGN (US/0163-321X). **1993**

RABELS ZEITSCHRIFT FUER AUSLANDISCHES UND INTERNATIONALES PRIVATRECHT (GW/0033-7250). **3134**

RACCOON (US/0148-0162). **3470**

RADIATION AND ENVIRONMENTAL BIOPHYSICS (GW/0301-634X). **496**

RADIATION EFFECTS AND DEFECTS IN SOLIDS (US/1042-0150). **1057**

RADIATION EFFECTS BULLETIN (US/0888-448X). **990**

RADIATION RESEARCH (US/0033-7587). **4441**

RADIO-ELECTRONICS (US/0033-7862). **2078**

RADIO SCIENCE (US/0048-6604). **1409**

RADIO Y TELEVISION (US/0033-8133). **1138**

RADIOACTIVE WASTE MANAGEMENT AND THE NUCLEAR FUEL CYCLE (SZ/0739-5876). **2240**

RADIOBIOLOGIA. RADIOTHERAPIA (GW/0033-8184). **3945**

RADIOBIOLOGIIA (RU/0033-8192). **3945**

RADIOCHEMISTRY (NEW YORK, N.Y.) (US/1066-3622). **990**

RADIOCHIMICA ACTA (US/0033-8230). **1057**

RADIOGRAPHICS (US/0271-5333). **3945**

RADIOLOGE, DER (GW/0033-832X). **3945**

RADIOLOGIA DIAGNOSTICA (GW/0033-8354). **3945**

RADIOLOGIC CLINICS OF NORTH AMERICA, THE (US/0033-8389). **3945**

RADIOLOGIE (GW/0720-3322). **3945**

RADIOLOGY (US/0033-8419). **3945**

RADIOLOGY & IMAGING LETTER (US/0741-160X). **3849**

RADIOLOGY TODAY (US/0893-1054). **3946**

RADIOPHYSICS AND QUANTUM ELECTRONICS (US/0033-8443). **4441**

RADIOPROTECTION (FR/0033-8451). **4798**

RADIOTEKHNIKA I ELEKTRONIKA (RU/0033-8494). **2078**

RADIOTHERAPY AND ONCOLOGY (NE/0167-8140). **3823**

RAILS (WELLINGTON) (NZ/0110-6155). **5435**

RAILWAY AGE (BRISTOL) (US/0033-8826). **5435**

RAILWAY GAZETTE INTERNATIONAL (UK/0373-5346). **5436**

RAILWAY MAGAZINE (LONDON) (UK/0033-8923). **5436**

RAIRO. INFORMATIQUE THEORIQUE ET APPLICATIONS (FR/0988-3754). **1261**

RAIRO. MATHEMATICAL MODELLING AND NUMERICAL ANALYSIS (FR/0764-583X). **3530**

RAIRO : RECHERCHE OPERATIONNELLE (FR/0399-0559). **5144**

RAMUS (AT/0048-671X). **1079**

RANDOM LENGTHS BUYERS' & SELLERS' GUIDE (US/0891-7833). **2404**

RANDOM LENGTHS (EUGENE, OR.) (US/0483-9420). **2404**

RANDOM LENGTHS YARDSTICK (US/1055-0895). **2391**

RANDOM LENGTHS YEARBOOK (1985) (US/1045-2796). **2404**

RAPID COMMUNICATIONS IN MASS SPECTROMETRY (UK/0951-4198). **1018**

RAPPORT BIPM (FR/0026-1394). **1434**

RAPRA ABSTRACTS (UK/0033-6750). **5078**

RAPRA REVIEW REPORTS (US/0889-3144). **2108**

RARE EARTH BULLETIN (UK/0307-8531). **5145**

RATIO JURIS (UK/0952-1917). **3034**

RATIO (OXFORD) (UK/0034-0006). **4358**

RAZA LAW JOURNAL, LA (US/8755-8815). **3034**

RAZVEDKA I OKHRANA NEDR (RU/0034-026X). **2149**

RBM. REVUE EUROPEENNE DE BIOTECHNOLOGIE MEDICALE (FR/0222-0776). **5145**

RDH (US/0279-7720). **1334**

REACTION KINETICS AND CATALYSIS LETTERS (HU/0304-4122). **1057**

REACTIONS (AT/0157-7271). **3632**

REACTIVE POLYMERS (NE/0923-1137). **1047**

READING & WRITING (NE/0922-4777). **3314**

READING PSYCHOLOGY (UK/0270-2711). **4615**

READING RESEARCH QUARTERLY (US/0034-0553). **3314**

READING (SUNDERLAND) (UK/0034-0472). **1903**

READING TEACHER, THE (US/0034-0561). **3314**

REAL ESTATE ACCOUNTING & TAXATION (US/0897-0262). **4843**

REAL ESTATE/ENVIRONMENTAL LIABILITY NEWS (US/1046-9966). **4844**

REAL ESTATE FINANCE JOURNAL, THE (US/0898-0209). **4844**

REAL ESTATE FINANCE TODAY (US/0742-0021). **4844**

REAL ESTATE FINANCING UPDATE (US/0891-9852). **4844**

REAL ESTATE INSIDER (US/0034-0715). **4844**

REAL ESTATE LAW JOURNAL (US/0048-6868). **3034**

REAL ESTATE LAW REPORT (US/0162-752X). **3035**

REAL ESTATE REVIEW (BOSTON, MASS.) (US/0034-0790). **4845**

REAL ESTATE TAX IDEAS (US/0162-7538). **4845**

REAL ESTATE WORKOUTS & ASSET MANAGEMENT (US/1063-4290). **4845**

REAL-TIME SYSTEMS (US/0922-6443). **1201**

REANIMATION ET MEDECINE D'URGENCE (FR/0246-1234). **3725**

RECENT ADVANCES IN NURSING (UK/0144-6592). **3868**

RECENT PROGRESS IN HORMONE RESEARCH (US/0079-9963). **3733**

RECENT RESULTS IN CANCER RESEARCH (GW/0080-0015). **3823**

RECEPTOR (CLIFTON, N.J. JOURNAL) (US/1052-8040). **493**

RECEPTORS AND CHANNELS (US/1060-6823). **990**

RECHERCHE (PARIS. 1970) (FR/0029-5671). **5145**

RECHT DER ELEKTRIZITATSWIRTSCHAFT (GW/0171-712X). **1954**

RECHT DER INTERNATIONALEN WIRTSCHAFT (GW/0340-7926). **3035**

RECHT DER JUGEND UND DES BILDUNGSWESEN (GW/0034-1312). **3035**

RECHTSMEDIZIN BERLIN (GW/0937-9819). **3742**

RECHTSTHEORIE (GW/0034-1398). **3036**

RECLAMATION REVIEW (UK/0160-788X). **125**

RECOMBINANT DNA (UK/0261-4979). **551**

RECONSTRUCTION SURGERY AND TRAUMATOLOGY (SZ/0080-0260). **3973**

RECORD OF THE ART MUSEUM, PRINCETON UNIVERSITY (US/0032-843X). **4095**

RECRUITMENT AND RETENTION IN HIGHER EDUCATION (US/0891-012X). **1843**

RECRUITMENT & RETENTION REPORT (US/1044-0666). **3868**

RECRUITMENT, RETENTION, & RESTRUCTURING REPORT (US/1044-0666). **3868**

RECUEIL DALLOZ SIREY DE DOCTRINE, DE JURISPRUDENCE ET DE LEGISLATION (FR/0034-1835). **3036**

RECUEIL DES TRAVAUX CHIMIQUES DES PAYS-BAS (1920) (NE/0165-0513). **991**

RECYCLING (GW/0174-1446). **2180**

REFA NACHRICHTEN (GW/0033-6874). **946**

REFEREE (ARLINGTON, VA.), THE (US/0896-7695). **1018**

REFRACTORIES (NEW YORK) (US/0034-3102). **4017**

REFRESHER COURSES IN ANESTHESIOLOGY (US/0363-471X). **3684**

REGAN REPORT ON HOSPITAL LAW, THE (US/0034-317X). **3037**

REGAN REPORT ON MEDICAL LAW (US/0034-3188). **3037**

REGAN REPORT ON NURSING LAW, THE (US/0034-3196). **3868**

REGIONAL ANESTHESIA (US/0146-521X). **3684**

REGIONAL CANCER TREATMENT (GW/0935-0411). **3823**

REGIONAL CONFERENCE SERIES IN MATHEMATICS (US/0160-7642). **3530**

REGIONAL ECONOMIES AND MARKETS (US/0896-2537). **1516**

REGIONAL IMMUNOLOGY (US/0896-0623). **3676**

REGIONAL SCIENCE AND URBAN ECONOMICS (NE/0166-0462). **2833**

REGIONAL SCIENCE AND URBAN ECONOMICS [MICROFORM] (US/0166-0462). **2833**

REGIONAL STUDIES (UK/0034-3404). **5215**

REGULATED RIVERS (UK/0886-9375). **1359**

REGULATORY ANALYST. MEDICAL WASTE (US/1065-1063). **3633**

REGULATORY PEPTIDES (NE/0167-0115). **1047**

REGULATORY TOXICOLOGY AND PHARMACOLOGY (US/0273-2300). **4327**

REGULATORY WATCHDOG SERVICE. ALERT BULLETIN (US/0275-0902). **4679**

REHABILITATION COUNSELING BULLETIN (US/0034-3552). **1884**

REHABILITATION EDUCATION (ELMSFORD, N.Y.) (US/0889-7018). **1884**

REHABILITATION (STUTTGART) (GW/0034-3536). **3633**

REINFORCED PLASTICS (LONDON) (UK/0034-3617). **4460**

REITEN UND FAHREN (GW/0720-5104). **4914**

RELEASING HORMONES (UK/0142-8314). **3733**

RELIABILITY ENGINEERING & SYSTEM SAFETY (UK/0951-8320). **1993**

RELIABILITY PHYSICS (US/0735-0791). **2079**

RELIGION (LONDON. 1971) (UK/0048-721X). **4991**

RELIGION, STATE & SOCIETY : THE KESTON JOURNAL (UK/0963-7494). **4991**

RELOCATION REPORT, THE (US/0275-7613). **4846**

REMEDIAL AND SPECIAL EDUCATION (US/0741-9325). **1884**

REMEDIATION (NEW YORK, N.Y.) (US/1051-5658). **2180**

REMOTE SENSING OF ENVIRONMENT (US/0034-4257). **1410**

REMOTE SENSING REVIEWS (SZ/0275-7257). **1993**

RENAISSANCE STUDIES (UK/0269-1213). **2705**

RENAL FAILURE (US/0886-022X). **3992**

RENAL PHYSIOLOGY (UK/0300-3434). **3993**

RENAL PHYSIOLOGY AND BIOCHEMISTRY (SZ/1011-6524). **3993**

RENAL TRANSPLANTATION AND DIALYSIS (UK/0142-8357). **3633**

RENEWABLE ENERGY (UK/0960-1481). **1954**

RENEWABLE ENERGY BULLETIN (UK/0306-364X). **1954**

RENIN, ANGIOTENSIN & KININS (UK/0143-4284). **471**

RENO (GW/0721-4588). **706**

REPORT ON BUSINESS, CANADA COMPANY HANDBOOK (CN/0847-2831). **707**

REPORT ON DEFENSE PLANT WASTES (US/1043-268X). **4055**

REPORT ON DISABILITY PROGRAMS (US/1043-1209). **4393**

REPORT ON EDUCATION OF THE DISADVANTAGED (US/0034-4680). **1884**

REPORT ON EDUCATION RESEARCH (US/0034-4699). **1778**

REPORT ON IBM, THE (US/0742-5341). **1201**

REPORT ON LITERACY PROGRAMS (US/1046-6150). **5305**

REPORT ON PEDIATRIC INFECTIOUS DISEASES, THE (US/1050-964X). **3715**

REPORTS ON MATHEMATICAL PHYSICS (PL/0034-4877). **4419**

REPORTS ON PROGRESS IN PHYSICS (UK/0034-4885). **4419**

REPRESENTATIONS (BERKELEY, CALIF.) (US/0734-6018). **2853**

REPRODUCTION, FERTILITY, AND DEVELOPMENT (AT/1031-3613). **586**

REPRODUCTIVE TOXICOLOGY (ELMSFORD, N.Y.) (US/0890-6238). **3983**

RESEARCH ADVANCES IN ALCOHOL AND DRUG PROBLEMS (US/0093-9714). **1348**

RESEARCH AND CLINICAL FORUMS (UK/0143-3083). **3634**

RESEARCH & DEVELOPMENT (BARRINGTON, ILL.) (US/0746-9179). **5146**

RESEARCH AND DEVELOPMENT NEWS (US/0486-476X). **5538**

RESEARCH & EDUCATION NETWORKING (US/1051-4791). **1221**

RESEARCH COMMUNICATIONS IN CHEMICAL PATHOLOGY AND PHARMACOLOGY (US/0034-5164). **4327**

RESEARCH COMMUNICATIONS IN PSYCHOLOGY, PSYCHIATRY AND BEHAVIOR (US/0362-2428). **4615**

RESEARCH COMMUNICATIONS IN SUBSTANCES OF ABUSE (US/0193-0818). **1348**

RESEARCH DISCLOSURE (UK/0374-4353). **5146**

RESEARCH IN COMMUNITY AND MENTAL HEALTH (US/0192-0812). **4615**

RESEARCH IN DEVELOPMENTAL DISABILITIES (US/0891-4222). **4615**

RESEARCH IN ECONOMIC ANTHROPOLOGY (US/0190-1281). **244**

RESEARCH IN ECONOMIC HISTORY (US/0363-3268). **1581**

RESEARCH IN ENGINEERING DESIGN (US/0934-9839). **1994**

RESEARCH IN EXPERIMENTAL MEDICINE (GW/0300-9130). **3634**

RESEARCH IN HIGHER EDUCATION (US/0361-0365). **1845**

RESEARCH IN IMMUNOLOGY (PARIS) (FR/0923-2494). **3676**

RESEARCH IN LABOR ECONOMICS. SUPPLEMENT (US/0194-3057). **1707**

RESEARCH IN LAW AND ECONOMICS (US/0193-5895). **3039**

RESEARCH IN MICROBIOLOGY (FR/0923-2508). **569**

RESEARCH IN NONDESTRUCTIVE EVALUATION (US/0934-9847). **1994**

RESEARCH IN NURSING & HEALTH (US/0160-6891). **3868**

RESEARCH IN ORGANIZATIONAL BEHAVIOR (US/0191-3085). **5255**

RESEARCH IN PERSONNEL AND HUMAN RESOURCES MANAGEMENT (US/0742-7301). **946**

RESEARCH IN POLITICAL ECONOMY (US/0161-7230). **1581**

RESEARCH IN POPULATION ECONOMICS (US/0163-7878). **4559**

RESEARCH IN PUBLIC POLICY ANALYSIS AND MANAGEMENT (US/0732-1317). **5215**

RESEARCH IN RACE AND ETHNIC RELATIONS (US/0195-7449). **2272**

RESEARCH IN SCIENCE & TECHNOLOGICAL EDUCATION (UK/0263-5143). **5147**

RESEARCH IN SOCIAL MOVEMENTS, CONFLICTS AND CHANGE (US/0163-786X). **5255**

RESEARCH IN SOCIAL STRATIFICATION AND MOBILITY (US/0276-5624). **5255**

RESEARCH IN SOCIOLOGY OF EDUCATION AND SOCIALIZATION (US/0197-5080). **5255**

RESEARCH IN THE SOCIOLOGY OF HEALTH CARE (US/0275-4959). **5255**

RESEARCH IN THE SOCIOLOGY OF ORGANIZATIONS (US/0733-558X). **5255**

RESEARCH IN VETERINARY SCIENCE (UK/0034-5288). **5520**

RESEARCH IN VIROLOGY (PARIS) (FR/0923-2516). **569**

RESEARCH INTO HIGHER EDUCATION ABSTRACTS (UK/0034-5326). **1797**

RESEARCH METHODS IN NEUROCHEMISTRY (US/0096-2902). **3844**

RESEARCH ON AGING (US/0164-0275). **3754**

RESEARCH ON CHEMICAL INTERMEDIATES (NE/0922-6168). **1057**

RESEARCH ON LANGUAGE AND SOCIAL INTERACTION (CN/0835-1813). **3315**

RESEARCH ON NEGOTIATION IN ORGANIZATIONS (US/1040-9556). **884**

RESEARCH ON TECHNOLOGICAL INNOVATION MANAGEMENT AND POLICY (US/0737-1071). **884**

RESEARCH POLICY (NE/0048-7333). **5147**

RESEARCH STRATEGIES (US/0734-3310). **3245**

RESEARCH TECHNOLOGY MANAGEMENT (US/0895-6308). **5147**

RESELLER MANAGEMENT (US/1042-7325). **1239**

RESOURCE MANAGEMENT AND OPTIMIZATION (UK/0142-2391). **2204**

RESOURCES AND ENERGY (NE/0165-0572). **1517**

RESOURCES, CONSERVATION AND RECYCLING (NE/0921-3449). **2204**

RESOURCES FOR AMERICAN LITERARY STUDY (US/0048-7384). **3351**

RESOURCES FOR FEMINIST RESEARCH : RFR (CN/0707-8412). **5565**

RESOURCES POLICY (UK/0301-4207). **2204**

RESPIRATION (SZ/0025-7931). **3951**

RESPIRATION PHYSIOLOGY (NE/0034-5687). **586**

RESPIRATORY MEDICINE (UK/0954-6111). **3951**

RESTAURANT HOSPITALITY (US/0147-9989). **5072**

RESTAURANTS & INSTITUTIONS (CHICAGO, ILL.) (US/0273-5520). **5073**

RESTAURATOR (DK/0034-5806). **2483**

RESTORATION & MANAGEMENT NOTES (US/0733-0707). **2204**

RESTORATIVE ECOLOGY (US/1061-2971). **2220**

RESTORATIVE NEUROLOGY AND NEUROSCIENCE (NE/0922-6028). **3845**

RESULTATE DER MATHEMATIK (SZ/0378-6218). **3531**

RESUSCITATION (IE/0300-9572). **3951**

RETAIL STORE IMAGE (US/1047-8841). **2903**

RETHINKING MARXISM (US/0893-5696). **1594**

RETINA (PHILADELPHIA, PA.) (US/0275-004X). **3878**

RETIREMENT LETTER (US/0093-5352). **5181**

REUSE/RECYCLE (US/0048-7457). **2242**

REVIEW OF AUSTRIAN ECONOMICS, THE (US/0889-3047). **1517**

REVIEW OF BIOLOGICAL RESEARCH IN AGING (US/0736-5055). **3754**

REVIEW OF BLACK POLITICAL ECONOMY, THE (US/0034-6446). **1517**

REVIEW OF CONTEMPORARY FICTION (US/0276-0045). **3351**

REVIEW OF ECONOMIC STUDIES, THE (UK/0034-6527). **1517**

REVIEW OF EDUCATION, THE (US/0098-5597). **1779**

REVIEW OF ENGLISH STUDIES (UK/0034-6551). **3429**

REVIEW OF EUROPEAN COMMUNITY AND INTERNATIONAL ENVIRONMENTAL LAW (UK/0962-8797). **3116**

REVIEW OF FINANCIAL STUDIES, THE (US/0893-9454). **809**

REVIEW OF INDUSTRIAL ORGANIZATION (US/0889-938X). **1625**

REVIEW OF INTERNATIONAL ECONOMICS (UK/0965-7576). **1639**

REVIEW OF INTERNATIONAL STUDIES (UK/0260-2105). **4534**

REVIEW OF PALAEOBOTANY AND PALYNOLOGY (NE/0034-6667). **4230**

REVIEW OF QUANTITATIVE FINANCE AND ACCOUNTING (US/0924-865X). **751**

REVIEW OF RADICAL POLITICAL ECONOMICS, THE (US/0486-6134). **1594**

REVIEW OF SCIENTIFIC INSTRUMENTS (US/0034-6748). **5147**

REVIEW OF SOCIAL ECONOMY (UK/0034-6764). **1581**

REVIEWS IN AMERICAN HISTORY (US/0048-7511). **2757**

REVIEWS IN ANTHROPOLOGY (US/0093-8157). **244**

REVIEWS IN BIOCHEMICAL TOXICOLOGY (US/0163-7673). **3983**

REVIEWS IN CLINICAL GERONTOLOGY (UK/0959-2598). **3754**

REVIEWS IN INORGANIC CHEMISTRY (LONDON, ENGLAND) (UK/0193-4929). **1037**

REVIEWS IN MATHEMATICAL PHYSICS (SI/0129-055X). **4419**

REVIEWS IN MEDICAL MICROBIOLOGY : A JOURNAL OF THE PATHOLOGICAL SOCIETY OF GREAT BRITAIN AND IRELAND (UK/0954-139X). **3634**

REVIEWS IN MEDICAL VIROLOGY (UK/1052-9276). **569**

REVIEWS OF ENVIRONMENTAL CONTAMINATION AND TOXICOLOGY (US/0179-5953). **2242**

REVIEWS OF GEOPHYSICS (1985) (US/8755-1209). **1410**

REVIEWS OF MAGNETIC RESONANCE IN MEDICINE (US/0883-8291). **3849**

REVIEWS OF MODERN PHYSICS (US/0034-6861). **4419**

REVIEWS OF OCULOMOTOR RESEARCH (NE/0168-8375). **3879**

REVIEWS OF PHYSIOLOGY, BIOCHEMISTRY AND PHARMACOLOGY (GW/0303-4240). **586**

REVIEWS OF THE SOLID STATE SCIENCE (SI/0218-1029). **4419**

REVIEWS ON CANCER (NE/0304-419X). **3823**

REVIEWS ON POWDER METALLURGY AND PHYSICAL CERAMICS (UK/0379-0002). **4018**

REVISION (CAMBRIDGE, MASS.) (US/0275-6935). **3429**

REVISTA DE ESTUDIOS HISPANICOS (UNIVERSITY, AL.) (US/0034-818X). **3315**

REVISTA DE MEDICINA DE LA UNIVERSIDAD DE NAVARRA (SP/0556-6177). **3973**

REVISTA DE MUSICA LATINOAMERICANA (US/0163-0350). **4149**

REVISTA DE OCCIDENTE (SP/0034-8635). **3351**

REVISTA DE PLASTICOS MODERNOS (SP/0034-8708). **4460**

REVISTA DE QUIMICA TEXTIL (SP/0300-3418). **5355**

REVISTA ESPANOLA DE ANESTESIOLOGIA Y REANIMACION (SP/0034-9356). **3684**

REVISTA ESPANOLA DE FISIOLOGIA (SP/0034-9402). **586**

REVISTA ESPANOLA DE MICROPALEONTOLOGIA (SP/0556-655X). **4230**

REVISTA ESPANOLA DE OBSTETRICIA Y GINECOLOGIA (SP/0034-9445). **3768**

REVISTA ESPANOLA DE PEDIATRIA (SP/0034-947X). **3911**

REVISTA/REVIEW INTERAMERICANA (PR/0360-7917). **5216**

REVUE ARCHEOLOGIQUE (FR/0035-0737). **281**

REVUE CANADIENNE D'ETUDES DU DEVELOPPEMENT (CN/0225-5189). **1639**

REVUE CRITIQUE DE DROIT INTERNATIONAL PRIVE (FR/0035-0958). **3135**

REVUE D'ASSYRIOLOGIE ET D'ARCHEOLOGIE ORIENTALE (FR/0373-6032). **281**

REVUE DE BELLES-LETTRES (SZ/0035-1016). **3430**

REVUE DE CHIRURGIE ORTHOPEDIQUE ET REPARATRICE DE L'APPAREIL MOTEUR (FR/0035-1040). **3973**

REVUE DE L'ALCOOLISME, LA (FR/0035-130X). **1348**

REVUE DE L'HISTOIRE DES RELIGIONS (FR/0035-1423). **4993**

REVUE DE L'INFIRMIERE ET DE L'ASSISTANTE SOCIALE (FR/0397-7900). **4393**

REVUE DE L'INSTITUT FRANCAIS DU PETROLE (FR/0020-2274). **4277**

REVUE DE MEDECINE INTERNE, LA (FR/0248-8663). **3801**

REVUE DE METALLURGIE (PARIS) (FR/0035-1563). **4018**

REVUE DE PNEUMOLOGIE CLINIQUE : LE POUMON ET LE COEUR (FR/0761-8417). **3951**

REVUE DE SCIENCE CRIMINELLE ET DE DROIT PENAL COMPARE (FR/0035-1733). **3108**

REVUE DE STOMATOLOGIE ET DE CHIRURGIE MAXILLO-FACIALE (FR/0035-1768). **3973**

REVUE D'ECONOMIE POLITIQUE (FR/0373-2630). **1595**

REVUE D'EPIDEMIOLOGIE ET DE SANTE PUBLIQUE (US/0398-7620). **3736**

REVUE DES MALADIES RESPIRATOIRES (FR/0761-8425). **3951**

REVUE DES SCIENCES MORALES & POLITIQUES (FR/0751-5804). **4494**

REVUE D'HISTOIRE DIPLOMATIQUE (FR/0035-2365). **4534**

REVUE D'HISTOIRE ET DE PHILOSOPHIE RELIGIEUSES (FR/0035-2403). **4993**

REVUE D'IMAGERIE MEDICALE (FR/0998-4321). **3946**

REVUE DU DROIT PUBLIC ET DE LA SCIENCE POLITIQUE EN FRANCE ET A L'ETRANGER (FR/0035-2578). **3135**

REVUE DU JOUET, LA (FR/0035-2594). **2585**

REVUE DU PRACTICIEN, LA (FR/0035-2640). **3636**

REVUE DU RHUMATISME ET DES MALADIES OSTEO-ARTICULAIRES (FR/0035-2659). **3806**

REVUE DU RHUMATISME : MALADIES DES OS ET DES ARTICULATIONS (FR/0035-2659). **3806**

REVUE ECONOMIQUE (FR/0035-2764). **1595**

REVUE FORESTIERE FRANCAISE (FR/0035-2829). **2394**

REVUE FRANCAISE DE DROIT ADMINISTRATIF (FR/0763-1219). **3094**

REVUE FRANCAISE DE GESTION INDUSTRIELLE (FR/0242-9780). **885**

REVUE FRANCAISE DE GYNECOLOGIE ET D'OBSTETRIQUE (FR/0035-290X). **3768**

REVUE FRANCAISE DE PSYCHANALYSE : ORGANE OFFICIEL DE LA SOCIETE PSYCHANALYTIQUE DE PARIS (FR/0035-2942). **4616**

REVUE FRANCAISE DE SCIENCE POLITIQUE (FR/0035-2950). **4495**

REVUE FRANCAISE D'ENDOCRINOLOGIE CLINIQUE, NUTRITION ET METABOLISME (FR/0048-8062). **3733**

REVUE GENERAL NUCLEAIRE (FR/0335-5004). **1956**

REVUE GENERALE DE L'ELECTRICITE (FR/0035-3116). **2079**

REVUE GENERALE DE THERMIQUE (FR/0035-3159). **2128**

REVUE GENERALE DES CAOUTCHOUCS & PLASTIQUES (FR/0035-3175). **5077**

REVUE GENERALE DES CHEMINS DE FER (1924) (FR/0035-3183). **5436**

REVUE HISTORIQUE (FR/0035-3264). **2628**

REVUE HISTORIQUE DE DROIT FRANCAIS ET ETRANGER (FR/0035-3280). **3043**

REVUE INTERNATIONALE DE CRIMINOLOGIE ET DE POLICE TECHNIQUE (FR/0035-3329). **3175**

REVUE INTERNATIONALE DE SYSTEMIQUE (FR/0980-1472). **1252**

REVUE INTERNATIONALE DES HAUTES TEMPERATURES ET DES REFRACTAIRES (US/0035-3434). **1057**

REVUE MOTO TECHNIQUE BOULOGNE-SUR-SEINE (FR/0150-7214). **1625**

REVUE NEUROLOGIQUE (FR/0035-3787). **3845**

REVUE PHILOSOPHIQUE DE LA FRANCE ET DE L'ETRANGER (FR/0035-3833). **4359**

REVUE PRATIQUE DU FROID ET DU CONDITIONNEMENT DE L'AIR (FR/0370-6699). **2608**

REVUE ROMANE (DK/0035-3906). **3317**

REVUE TECHNIQUE AUTOMOBILE (FR/0017-307X). **5424**

REVUE TECHNIQUE CARROSSERIE (FR/0150-7206). **5424**

REVUE TECHNIQUE DIESEL (FR/0037-2579). **5424**

REVUE TECHNIQUE MACHINISME AGRICOLE (FR/0223-0135). **5424**

REVUE TECHNIQUE THOMSON-CSF (FR/0035-4279). **2079**

REVUE TRIMESTRIELLE DE DROIT CIVIL (PARIS, FRANCE : 1980) (FR/0397-9873). **3091**

REVUE TRIMESTRIELLE DE DROIT COMMERCIAL ET DE DROIT ECONOMIQUE (FR/0244-9358). **3103**

REVUE TRIMESTRIELLE DE DROIT EUROPEEN (COURT OF JUSTICE OF THE EUROPEAN COMMUNITIES) (FR/0035-4317). **3044**

RHEOLOGICA ACTA (GW/0035-4511). **4420**

RHEOLOGY ABSTRACTS (UK/0035-452X). **4429**

RHETORICA (US/0734-8584). **3317**

RHEUMATIC DISEASE CLINICS OF NORTH AMERICA (US/0889-857X). **3807**

RHEUMATOLOGY (SZ/0080-2727). **3807**

RHEUMATOLOGY INTERNATIONAL (GW/0172-8172). **3807**

RHEUMATOLOGY REVIEW (EDINBURGH) (UK/0958-2584). **3807**

RICHARD C. YOUNG'S INTELLIGENCE REPORT (US/0884-3031). **810**

RICHARD C YOUNG'S INTERNATIONAL GOLD REPORT (US/0895-1306). **1518**

RISK ANALYSIS (US/0272-4332). **4800**

RISK & INSURANCE (US/1050-9232). **2892**

RIVISTA DEL NUOVO CIMENTO (IT/0035-5917). **4420**

RIVISTA ITALIANA DI OTORINOLARINGOLOGIA, AUDIOLOGIA E FONIATRIA (IT/0392-1360). **3891**

RN (US/0033-7021). **3868**

ROAD TRAFFIC REPORTS (UK/0306-5286). **5444**

ROADS & BRIDGES (DES PLAINS, ILL.) (US/8750-9229). **2030**

ROBOTERSYSTEME (GW/0178-0026). **1216**

ROBOTICA (UK/0263-5747). **1216**

ROBOTICS AND AUTONOMOUS SYSTEMS (NE/0921-8890). **1216**

ROBOTICS AND COMPUTER-INTEGRATED MANUFACTURING (US/0736-5845). **1216**

ROBOTICS AND EXPERT SYSTEMS (US/0891-4621). **1216**

ROBOTICS WORLD (US/0737-7908). **1216**

ROCK MECHANICS AND ROCK ENGINEERING (AU/0723-2632). **2150**

ROCK MECHANICS. SUPPLEMENT (AU/0080-3375). **1994**

ROCKS AND MINERALS (US/0035-7529). **1444**

ROMANCE PHILOLOGY (US/0035-8002). **3318**

ROMANISCHE FORSCHUNGEN (GW/0035-8126). **3318**

RONTGENPRAXIS (STUTTGART) (GW/0035-7820). **3946**

ROTOR & WING INTERNATIONAL (US/0191-6408). **34**

ROUND TABLE, THE (UK/0035-8533). **4534**

ROUX'S ARCHIVES OF DEVELOPMENTAL BIOLOGY (GW/0930-035X). **541**

ROYAL AIR FORCE COLLEGE JOURNAL, THE (UK/0035-8606). **1094**

ROZHLEDY V CHIRURGII (XR/0035-9351). **3974**

RQ (US/0033-7072). **3247**

RSI. ROOFING SIDING INSULATION (US/0033-7129). **627**

RUBBER & PLASTICS NEWS (US/0300-6123). **5077**

RUBBER & PLASTICS NEWS II (US/0197-2219). **5077**

RUBBER TRENDS (UK/0035-9564). **5078**

RUBBER WORLD (US/0035-9572). **5078**

RUNDFUNK UND FERNSEHEN (GW/0035-9874). **1138**

RUNZHEIMER REPORTS ON RELOCATION (US/0731-9150). **4847**

RUNZHEIMER REPORTS ON TRANSPORTATION (US/0730-8655). **5392**

RUNZHEIMER REPORTS ON TRAVEL MANAGEMENT (US/0730-8663). **5490**

RURAL BUILDER (US/0888-3025). **627**

RUSSIAN AERONAUTICS (US/1068-7998). **34**

RUSSIAN AGRICULTURAL SCIENCES (US/1068-3674). **131**

RUSSIAN BIOTECHNOLOGY (US/1068-3682). **3696**

RUSSIAN CASTINGS TECHNOLOGY (US/1068-3690). **4018**

RUSSIAN CHEMICAL INDUSTRY (US/1068-3704). **1029**

RUSSIAN ELECTRICAL ENGINEERING (US/1068-3712). **2080**

RUSSIAN ENGINEERING RESEARCH (US/1068-798X). **2128**

RUSSIAN FOREST SCIENCES (US/1068-669X). **2394**

RUSSIAN GEOLOGY AND GEOPHYSICS (US/1068-7971). **1396**

RUSSIAN JOURNAL OF BIOORGANIC CHEMISTRY (US/1068-1620). **493**

RUSSIAN JOURNAL OF DEVELOPMENTAL BIOLOGY (US/1062-3604). **472**

RUSSIAN JOURNAL OF ECOLOGY (US/1067-4136). **2220**

RUSSIAN JOURNAL OF HEAVY MACHINERY (US/1068-3720). **2128**

RUSSIAN JOURNAL OF MARINE BIOLOGY (US/1063-0740). **557**

RUSSIAN JOURNAL OF NON-FERROUS METALS (US/1067-8212). **4018**

RUSSIAN JOURNAL OF NONDESTRUCTIVE TESTING (US/1061-8309). **2128**

RUSSIAN LINGUISTICS (NE/0304-3487). **3318**

RUSSIAN LITERATURE (NE/0304-3479). **3432**

RUSSIAN MATHEMATICS (US/1066-369X). **3532**

RUSSIAN METALLURGY (UK/0036-0295). **4018**

RUSSIAN METEOROLOGY AND HYDROLOGY (US/1068-3739). **1434**

RUSSIAN MICROELECTRONICS (US/1063-7397). **1202**

RUSSIAN PHYSICS JOURNAL (US/1064-8887). **4420**

RUSSIAN PROGRESS IN VIROLOGY (US/1068-3747). **570**

S.A.M. ADVANCED MANAGEMENT JOURNAL (1984) (US/0749-7075). **885**

S.A.M.P.E. QUARTERLY (US/0036-0821). **1995**

SAE GROUND VEHICLE STANDARDS INDEX (US/0891-995X). **5424**

SAE HANDBOOK (US/0362-8205). **5424**

SAE TECHNICAL LITERATURE ABSTRACTS (US/0741-2029). **1995**

SAE TECHNICAL PAPER SERIES (US/0148-7191). **2128**

SAE TRANSACTIONS (US/0096-736X). **5425**

SAECULUM (GW/0080-5319). **2628**

SAFETY SCIENCE (NE/0925-7535). **2869**

SAGAMORE ARMY MATERIALS RESEARCH CONFERENCE PROCEEDINGS (US/0197-2790). **4056**

SAIL (US/0036-2700). **595**

SALARIES OF SCIENTISTS, ENGINEERS AND TECHNICIANS (US/0146-5015). **1709**

SALES & MARKETING MANAGEMENT (US/0163-7517). **936**

SAME-DAY SURGERY (US/0190-5066). **3974**

SAMPE JOURNAL (US/0091-1062). **1995**

SAR AND QSAR IN ENVIRONMENTAL RESEARCH (UK/1062-936X). **992**

SATELLITE COMMUNICATIONS (US/0147-7439). **1163**

SATELLITE NEWS (US/0161-3448). **1163**

SATELLITE WEEK (US/0193-2861). **1163**

SAUDI MEDICAL JOURNAL (SU/0379-5284). **3638**

SAVINGS INSTITUTIONS (US/0746-1321). **810**

SCANDINAVIAN AUDIOLOGY (SW/0105-0397). **3891**

SCANDINAVIAN JOURNAL OF CLINICAL & LABORATORY INVESTIGATION (UK/0036-5513). **586**

SCANDINAVIAN JOURNAL OF DENTAL RESEARCH (DK/0029-845X). **1335**

SCANDINAVIAN JOURNAL OF ECONOMICS, THE (UK/0347-0520). **1520**

SCANDINAVIAN JOURNAL OF EDUCATIONAL RESEARCH (UK/0031-3831). **1781**

SCANDINAVIAN JOURNAL OF GASTROENTEROLOGY (NO/0036-5521). **3747**

SCANDINAVIAN JOURNAL OF GASTROENTEROLOGY. SUPPLEMENT (NO/0085-5928). **3747**

SCANDINAVIAN JOURNAL OF IMMUNOLOGY (UK/0300-9475). **3676**

SCANDINAVIAN JOURNAL OF IMMUNOLOGY. SUPPLEMENT (NO/0301-6323). **3676**

SCANDINAVIAN JOURNAL OF METALLURGY (SW/0371-0459). **4018**

SCANDINAVIAN JOURNAL OF PRIMARY HEALTH CARE. SUPPLEMENT (SW/0281-3432). **3739**

SCANDINAVIAN JOURNAL OF PSYCHOLOGY (SW/0036-5564). **4617**

SCANDINAVIAN JOURNAL OF SOCIAL WELFARE (DK/0907-2055). **5307**

SCANDINAVIAN JOURNAL OF STATISTICS (SW/0303-6898). **5338**

SCANDINAVIAN JOURNAL OF WORK, ENVIRONMENT & HEALTH (FI/0355-3140). **2870**

SCANDINAVIAN OIL-GAS MAGAZINE (NO/0332-5334). **4277**

SCANDINAVIAN POLITICAL STUDIES (NO/0080-6757). **4495**

SCANDINAVIAN PSYCHOANALYTIC REVIEW, THE (NO/0106-2301). **4617**

SCANDINAVICA (UK/0036-5653). **3433**

SCANDO-SLAVICA (DK/0080-6765). **3319**

SCANNING (US/0161-0457). **574**

SCANNING MICROSCOPY (US/0891-7035). **574**

SCHIZOPHRENIA RESEARCH (NE/0920-9964). **3936**

SCHMALENBACHS ZEITSCHRIFT FUER BETRIEBSWIRTSCHAFTLICHE FORSCHUNG (GW/0341-2687). **850**

SCHMERZ, DER (GW/0932-433X). **3639**

SCHOLARLY PUBLISHING (CN/0036-634X). **4819**

SCHOOL AND COLLEGE (CLEVELAND, OHIO) (US/1045-3970). **1846**

SCHOOL COUNSELOR, THE (US/0036-6536). **1885**

SCHOOL EFFECTIVENESS AND SCHOOL IMPROVEMENT (NE/0924-3453). **1871**

SCHOOL FOOD SERVICE DIRECTOR (US/0741-4838). **2356**

SCHOOL LAW BULLETIN (BOSTON, MASS.) (US/8755-8297). **1871**

SCHOOL LAW NEWS (US/0194-2271). **1871**

SCHOOL LIBRARY JOURNAL (NEW YORK, N.Y.) (US/0362-8930). **3248**

SCHOOL LIBRARY MEDIA QUARTERLY (US/0278-4823). **3248**

SCHOOL ORGANISATION (UK/0260-1362). **1871**

SCHOOL ORGANISATION & MANAGEMENT ABSTRACTS (UK/0261-2755). **1797**

SCHOOL PSYCHOLOGY INTERNATIONAL (UK/0143-0343). **4618**

SCHOOL PSYCHOLOGY QUARTERLY (US/1045-3830). **4618**

SCHOOL SOCIAL WORK JOURNAL (US/0161-5653). **1871**

SCHOOL TRANSPORTATION (US/0273-0936). **5392**

SCHRIFTENREIHE DES VEREINS FUER WASSER-, BODEN- UND LUFTHYGIENE (GW/0300-8665). **1360**

SCHWEINEZUCHT UND SCHWEINEMAST (GW/0036-7176). **132**

SCHWEISSEN UND SCHNEIDEN (GW/0036-7184). **4027**

SCHWEIZER ARCHIV FUER TIERHEILKUNDE (SZ/0036-7281). **5521**

SCHWEIZERISCHE BIENEN-ZEITUNG (SZ/0036-7540). **5597**

SCHWEIZERISCHE MEDIZINISCHE WOCHENSCHRIFT (SZ/0036-7672). **3639**

SCHWEIZERISCHE PALAEONTOLOGISCHE ABHANDLUNGEN (SZ/0080-7389). **4230**

SCHWEIZERISCHE ZEITSCHRIFT FUER GESCHICHTE (SZ/0036-7834). **2708**

SCHWEIZERISCHE ZEITSCHRIFT FUER HYDROLOGIE (SZ/0036-7842). **1417**

SCHWEIZERISCHE ZEITSCHRIFT FUER SPORTMEDIZIN (SZ/0036-7885). **3955**

SCHWEIZERISCHE ZEITSCHRIFT FUER STRAFRECHT (SZ/0036-7893). **3176**

SCIENCE ACTIVITIES (US/0036-8121). **5150**

SCIENCE & EDUCATION (NE/0926-7220). **1904**

SCIENCE & GLOBAL SECURITY (US/0892-9882). **4535**

SCIENCE & GOVERNMENT REPORT (US/0048-9581). **5150**

SCIENCE & PUBLIC POLICY (UK/0302-3427). **4685**

SCIENCE AND SOCIETY (NEW YORK. 1936) (US/0036-8237). **5218**

SCIENCE & SPORTS (FR/0765-1597). **3956**

SCIENCE AS CULTURE (UK/0950-5431). **5151**

SCIENCE EDUCATION (SALEM, MASS.) (US/0036-8326). **5151**

SCIENCE IN CONTEXT (UK/0269-8897). **5152**

SCIENCE IN PARLIAMENT (UK/0263-6271). **5152**

SCIENCE OF COMPUTER PROGRAMMING (NE/0167-6423). **1281**

SCIENCE OF THE TOTAL ENVIRONMENT, THE (NE/0048-9697). **2181**

SCIENCE PROGRESS (1916) (UK/0036-8504). **5152**

SCIENCE, TECHNOLOGY & HUMAN VALUES (US/0162-2439). **5153**

SCIENCE (WASHINGTON, D.C.) (US/0036-8075). **5154**

SCIENCES DES ALIMENTS (FR/0240-8813). **2356**

SCIENCES ET AVENIR (FR/0036-8636). **5154**

SCIENTIA ELECTRICA (US/0036-8695). **2080**

SCIENTIA HORTICULTURAE (NE/0304-4238). **2431**

SCIENTIFIC AMERICAN (US/0036-8733). **5155**

SCIENTIFIC AND TECHNICAL BOOKS AND SERIALS IN PRINT (US/0000-054X). **5176**

SCIENTIFIC AND TECHNICAL INFORMATION PROCESSING (US/0147-6882). **3248**

SCIENTIFIC COMPUTING & AUTOMATION (US/0891-9003). **1221**

SCIENTIFIC DRILLING (GW/0934-4365). **1410**

SCIENTIFIC, ENGINEERING, TECHNICAL MANPOWER COMMENTS (US/0036-8768). **5155**

SCIENTIFIC SERIALS REVIEW. BIOMEDICINE (UK/0884-8319). **472**

SCIENTIST (PHILADELPHIA, PA.), THE (US/0890-3670). **5156**

SCIENTOMETRICS (NE/0138-9130). **5156**

SCOTTISH HISTORICAL REVIEW, THE (UK/0036-9241). **2709**

SCOTTISH JOURNAL OF GEOLOGY (UK/0036-9276). **1396**

SCOTTISH JOURNAL OF POLITICAL ECONOMY (UK/0036-9292). **1595**

SCOTTISH JOURNAL OF THEOLOGY (UK/0036-9306). **4995**

SCOTTISH MEDICAL JOURNAL (UK/0036-9330). **3639**

SCREEN (UK/0036-9543). **4077**

SCREEN IMAGING TECHNOLOGY FOR ELECTRONICS (US/0885-5005). **2080**

SCREEN INTERNATIONAL (UK/0307-4617). **4077**

SCREENING: JOURNAL OF THE INTERNATIONAL SOCIETY OF NEONATAL SCREENING (NE/0925-6164). **3768**

SCRIP (RICHMOND) (UK/0143-7690). **4329**

SCRIPSI (AT/0725-0096). **3434**

SCRIPTA METALLURGICA ET MATERIALIA (US/0956-716X). **4018**

SDI MONITOR (US/0886-7607). **4056**

SEA POWER (1971) (US/0199-1337). **4183**

SEA TECHNOLOGY (US/0093-3651). **1456**

SEALING TECHNOLOGY (UK/1350-4789). **1029**

SEARCH AND SEIZURE BULLETIN (US/0037-0193). **3176**

SEARCH (SYDNEY) (AT/0004-9549). **5156**

SEAWAY REVIEW (US/0037-0487). **5456**

SEC ACCOUNTING REPORT (US/0146-485X). **751**

SEC NO-ACTION LETTERS INDEX AND SUMMARIES (US/0162-2838). **4685**

SEC TODAY, THE (US/0745-2667). **913**

SECOND LANGUAGE RESEARCH (UK/0267-6583). **3320**

SECOND MESSENGER AND PHOSPHOPROTEINS (US/0895-7479). **586**

SECURED LENDING ALERT (US/0895-5492). **811**

SECURITIES REGULATION & LAW REPORT (US/0037-0665). **3088**

SECURITIES REGULATION LAW JOURNAL (US/0097-9554). **3047**

SECURITY DISTRIBUTING & MARKETING (US/0049-0016). **5177**

SECURITY GAZETTE (UK/0049-0024). **5177**

SECURITY JOURNAL (US/0955-1662). **3176**

SECURITY MANAGEMENT (ARLINGTON, VA.) (US/0145-9406). **885**

SECURITY (NEWTON, MASS.) (US/0890-8826). **3176**

SECURITY TECHNOLOGY NEWS (US/1068-8374). **1227**

SECUTITIES TRADERS' MONTHLY (US/0738-4351). **913**

SEDIMENTARY GEOLOGY (NE/0037-0738). **1396**

SEDIMENTOLOGY (UK/0037-0746). **1410**

SEED WORLD (US/0037-0797). **186**

SEISMIC INSTRUMENTS (US/0747-9239). **1410**

SEKIYU GAKKAI SHI (JA/0582-4664). **4278**

SELECTA MATHEMATICA SOVIETICA (US/0272-9903). **3533**

SELECTA PLANEGG (GW/0582-4877). **3640**

SELECTED DATA ON MIXTURES. SER. A. THERMODYNAMIC PROPERTIES OF NON-REACTING BINARY SYSTEMS OF ORGANIC SUBSTANCES (US/0147-1503). **1057**

SELECTED TABLES IN MATHEMATICAL STATISTICS (US/0094-4837). **3542**

SELECTED TRANSLATIONS IN MATHEMATICAL STATISTICS AND PROBABILITY (US/0065-9274). **3533**

SELECTIVE ELECTRODE REVIEWS (US/0894-3923). **1035**

SEMAINE VETERINAIRE, LA (FR/0396-5015). **5521**

SEMICONDUCTOR INTERNATIONAL (US/0163-3767). **2080**

SEMICONDUCTOR SCIENCE AND TECHNOLOGY (UK/0268-1242). **4420**

SEMICONDUCTORS AND INSULATORS (US/0309-5991). **4421**

SEMICONDUCTORS AND SEMIMETALS (US/0080-8784). **2080**

SEMICONDUCTORS (NEW YORK, N.Y.) (US/1063-7826). **4421**

SEMIGROUP FORUM (US/0037-1912). **3533**

SEMINAR (TORONTO) (CN/0037-1939). **3320**

SEMINARS IN ANESTHESIA (US/0277-0326). **968**

SEMINARS IN ARTHRITIS AND RHEUMATISM (US/0049-0172). **3807**

SEMINARS IN ARTHROPLASTY (US/1045-4527). **3974**

SEMINARS IN AVIAN AND EXOTIC PET MEDICINE (US/1055-937X). **5522**

SEMINARS IN CANCER BIOLOGY (US/1044-579X). **3824**

SEMINARS IN CELL BIOLOGY (US/1043-4682). **473**

SEMINARS IN COLON & RECTAL SURGERY (US/1043-1489). **3974**

SEMINARS IN DERMATOLOGY (US/0278-145X). **3722**

SEMINARS IN DEVELOPMENTAL BIOLOGY (US/1044-5781). **473**

SEMINARS IN DIAGNOSTIC PATHOLOGY (US/0740-2570). **3898**

SEMINARS IN DIALYSIS (US/0894-0959). **3640**

SEMINARS IN GASTROINTESTINAL DISEASE (US/1049-5118). **3748**

SEMINARS IN HEARING (US/0734-0451). **3891**

SEMINARS IN HEMATOLOGY (US/0037-1963). **3774**

SEMINARS IN IMMUNOLOGY (UK/1044-5323). **3676**

SEMINARS IN INTERVENTIONAL RADIOLOGY (US/0739-9529). **3946**

SEMINARS IN LIVER DISEASE (US/0272-8087). **3801**

SEMINARS IN NEPHROLOGY (US/0270-9295). **3993**

SEMINARS IN NEUROLOGY (US/0271-8235). **3846**

SEMINARS IN NEUROSCIENCES (US/1044-5765). **3846**

SEMINARS IN NUCLEAR MEDICINE (US/0001-2998). **3849**

SEMINARS IN ONCOLOGY (US/0093-7754). **3824**

SEMINARS IN ONCOLOGY NURSING (US/0749-2081). **3869**

SEMINARS IN OPHTHALMOLOGY (US/0882-0538). **3879**

SEMINARS IN ORTHOPAEDICS (US/0882-052X). **3884**

SEMINARS IN PEDIATRIC INFECTIOUS DISEASES (US/1045-1870). **3716**

SEMINARS IN PEDIATRIC SURGERY (US/1055-8586). **3974**

SEMINARS IN PERINATOLOGY (US/0146-0005). **3768**

SEMINARS IN PERIOPERATIVE NURSING (US/1056-8670). **3869**

SEMINARS IN RADIATION ONCOLOGY (US/1053-4296). **3824**

SEMINARS IN RADIOLOGIC TECHNOLOGY (US/1070-535X). **3946**

SEMINARS IN REPRODUCTIVE ENDOCRINOLOGY (US/0734-8630). **3733**

SEMINARS IN RESPIRATORY INFECTIONS (US/0882-0546). **3952**

SEMINARS IN RESPIRATORY MEDICINE (US/0192-9755). **3952**

SEMINARS IN SPEECH AND LANGUAGE (US/0734-0478). **3320**

SEMINARS IN SPINE SURGERY (US/1040-7383). **3974**

SEMINARS

SEMINARS IN THROMBOSIS AND HEMOSTASIS (US/0094-6176). **3774**

SEMINARS IN ULTRASOUND, CT, AND MR (US/0887-2171). **3946**

SEMINARS IN UROLOGY (US/0730-9147). **3993**

SEMINARS IN VASCULAR SURGERY (US/0895-7967). **3974**

SEMINARS IN VETERINARY MEDICINE AND SURGERY (SMALL ANIMALS) (US/0882-0511). **5522**

SEMINARS IN VIROLOGY (US/1044-5773). **570**

SEMIOTICA (NE/0037-1998). **3320**

SENI SEIHIN SHOHI KAGAKU (JA/0037-2072). **5355**

SENSOR REVIEW (UK/0260-2288). **5157**

SENSOR TECHNOLOGY (US/8756-4017). **2080**

SENSORS AND ACTUATORS. A, PHYSICAL (SZ/0924-4247). **2080**

SENSORS AND ACTUATORS. B, CHEMICAL (SZ/0925-4005). **2081**

SENSORS BUYER'S GUIDE (US/1042-2757). **3488**

SENSORS (PETERSBOROUGH, N.H.) (US/0746-9462). **1996**

SENSORY SYSTEMS (US/0894-4520). **587**

SEPARATION AND PURIFICATION METHODS (SOFTCOVER ED.) (US/0360-2540). **1029**

SEPARATION SCIENCE AND TECHNOLOGY (US/0149-6395). **1029**

SEPARATIONS TECHNOLOGY (US/0956-9618). **1996**

SEQUENTIAL ANALYSIS (US/0747-4946). **3533**

SERAMIKKUSU (JA/0009-031X). **2594**

SERIES PAEDOPSYCHIATRICA (SZ/0080-9012). **3936**

SERODIAGNOSIS AND IMMUNOTHERAPY IN INFECTIOUS DISEASE (UK/0888-0786). **570**

SERVICE STATION MANAGEMENT (US/0488-3896). **5425**

SERVICES MARKETING NEWSLETTER (US/0891-0952). **886**

SEWAGE TREATMENT CONSTRUCTION GRANTS MANUAL (US/0149-5879). **2243**

SEWANEE REVIEW, THE (US/0037-3052). **3352**

SEX ROLES (US/0360-0025). **5257**

SEXUAL AND MARITAL THERAPY (UK/0267-4653). **2286**

SEXUAL PLANT REPRODUCTION (GW/0934-0882). **527**

SEXUALITY AND DISABILITY (US/0146-1044). **4393**

SEXUALLY TRANSMITTED DISEASES (US/0148-5717). **4802**

SEYBOLD REPORT ON DESKTOP PUBLISHING, THE (US/0736-7260). **1263**

SEYBOLD REPORT ON PUBLISHING SYSTEMS, THE (US/0889-9762). **4819**

SHAW (US/0741-5842). **3352**

SHI - NIHON GANSEKI, KOBUTSU, KOSHOGAKKAI. JOURNAL OF THE JAPANESE ASSOCIATION OF MINERALOGISTS, PETROLOGISTS AND ECONOMIC GEOLOGISTS (JA/0021-4825). **1360**

SHIPPING DIGEST (US/0037-3893). **5456**

SHOCK WAVES (GW/0938-1287). **4429**

SHOKUBAI (JA/0559-8958). **1058**

SHOPPING CENTER WORLD (US/0049-0393). **4847**

SHOPPING CENTER WORLD PRODUCT AND SERVICE DIRECTORY (US/0049-0393=). **957**

SIAM-AMS PROCEEDINGS (US/0080-5084). **3534**

SIAM JOURNAL ON APPLIED MATHEMATICS (US/0036-1399). **3534**

SIAM JOURNAL ON COMPUTING (US/0097-5397). **1262**

SIAM JOURNAL ON CONTROL AND OPTIMIZATION (US/0363-0129). **3534**

SIAM JOURNAL ON DISCRETE MATHEMATICS (US/0895-4801). **3534**

SIAM JOURNAL ON MATHEMATICAL ANALYSIS (US/0036-1410). **3534**

SIAM JOURNAL ON MATRIX ANALYSIS AND APPLICATIONS (US/0895-4798). **3534**

SIAM JOURNAL ON NUMERICAL ANALYSIS (US/0036-1429). **3535**

SIAM JOURNAL ON OPTIMIZATION (US/1052-6234). **3535**

SIAM JOURNAL ON SCIENTIFIC AND STATISTICAL COMPUTING (US/0196-5204). **3535**

SIAM REVIEW (US/0036-1445). **3535**

SIBERIAN ADVANCES IN MATHEMATICS (US/1055-1344). **3535**

SIBERIAN MATHEMATICAL JOURNAL (US/0037-4466). **3535**

SICHERHEITS-BERATER (GW/0344-8746). **947**

SICHERHEITSBEAUFTRAGTER (GW/0300-3337). **3176**

SICHERHEITSINGENIEUR (GW/0300-3329). **2870**

SIDE EFFECTS OF DRUGS ANNUAL (NE/0378-6080). **4329**

SIEMENS COMPONENTS. ENGLISH AUSGABE (GW/0173-1734). **2081**

SIEMENS REVIEW (GW/0302-2528). **2081**

SIGHT AND SOUND (LONDON) (UK/0037-4806). **4078**

SIGN LANGUAGE STUDIES (US/0302-1475). **3321**

SIGNAL (1950) (US/0037-4938). **1121**

SIGNAL PROCESSING (NE/0165-1684). **2081**

SIGNAL PROCESSING. IMAGE COMMUNICATION (NE/0923-5965). **2081**

SIGNAL UND DRAHT (GW/0037-4997). **5436**

SIGNIFICANT SEC FILINGS REPORTER (US/0199-6177). **3055**

SIGNS (CHICAGO, ILL.) (US/0097-9740). **5566**

SILVAE GENETICA (GW/0037-5349). **528**

SIMULATION & GAMING (US/1046-8781). **1283**

SIMULATION PRACTICE AND THEORY (NE/0928-4869). **1244**

SIMULATION (SAN DIEGO, CALIF.) (US/0037-5497). **1283**

SIMULATION SERIES (US/0735-9276). **1283**

SITE REPORT, THE (US/0275-1488). **3488**

SIXTEENTH CENTURY JOURNAL, THE (US/0361-0160). **2629**

SKELETAL RADIOLOGY (US/0364-2348). **3947**

SKIN PHARMACOLOGY (SZ/1011-0283). **3723**

SKOG INDUSTRI (NO/0800-8582). **4239**

SKY AND TELESCOPE (US/0037-6604). **399**

SLEEP (NEW YORK, N.Y.) (US/0161-8105). **3641**

SLOAN MANAGEMENT REVIEW (US/0019-848X). **886**

SLUDGE (US/0148-4125). **2243**

SMALL ANIMAL PRACTICE (US/0894-3710). **5522**

SMALL BUSINESS ECONOMICS (NE/0921-898X). **1520**

SMALL BUSINESS REPORT (MONTEREY, CALIF.) (US/0164-5382). **711**

SMALL RUMINANT RESEARCH (NE/0921-4488). **5597**

SMALLTALK REPORT, THE (US/1056-7976). **1281**

SMART'S INSURANCE BULLETIN (US/0736-8348). **2893**

SNAKE (JA/0386-3425). **5597**

SOCIAL BEHAVIOR AND PERSONALITY (NZ/0301-2212). **5258**

SOCIAL CHOICE AND WELFARE (GW/0176-1714). **5308**

SOCIAL COGNITION (US/0278-016X). **5258**

SOCIAL DEVELOPMENT (UK/0961-205X). **1805**

SOCIAL EPISTEMOLOGY (UK/0269-1728). **4361**

SOCIAL HISTORY (LONDON) (UK/0307-1022). **2630**

SOCIAL HISTORY OF MEDICINE : THE JOURNAL OF THE SOCIETY FOR THE SOCIAL HISTORY OF MEDICINE (UK/0951-631X). **3641**

SOCIAL INDICATORS RESEARCH (NE/0303-8300). **5219**

SOCIAL JUSTICE RESEARCH (NEW YORK, N.Y.) (US/0885-7466). **5219**

SOCIAL NETWORKS (SZ/0378-8733). **5259**

SOCIAL PHILOSOPHY & POLICY (UK/0265-0525). **5219**

SOCIAL POLICY & ADMINISTRATION (UK/0144-5596). **4686**

SOCIAL PROBLEMS (US/0037-7791). **5220**

SOCIAL PSYCHIATRY AND PSYCHIATRIC EPIDEMIOLOGY (GW/0933-7954). **3936**

SOCIAL SCIENCE & MEDICINE (1982) (US/0277-9536). **5220**

SOCIAL SCIENCE COMPUTER REVIEW (US/0894-4393). **1272**

SOCIAL SCIENCE HISTORY (US/0145-5532). **5220**

SOCIAL SCIENCE JOURNAL (FORT COLLINS), THE (US/0362-3319). **5220**

SOCIAL SCIENCE MONITOR (US/0195-7791). **5220**

SOCIAL SCIENCE QUARTERLY (US/0038-4941). **5220**

SOCIAL SCIENCE RECORD (US/0037-7872). **5221**

SOCIAL SCIENCE RESEARCH (US/0049-089X). **5221**

SOCIAL SERVICE ABSTRACTS (LONDON) (UK/0309-4693). **5267**

SOCIAL SERVICE REVIEW (CHICAGO), THE (US/0037-7961). **5309**

SOCIAL STUDIES (PHILADELPHIA, PA. : 1953) (US/0037-7996). **5222**

SOCIAL THOUGHT (WASHINGTON, D.C.) (US/0099-183X). **4997**

SOCIAL WORK AND SOCIAL SCIENCES REVIEW (UK/0953-5225). **5309**

SOCIAL WORK EDUCATION (UK/0261-5479). **5309**

SOCIAL WORK (NEW YORK) (US/0037-8046). **5309**

SOCIAL WORK RESEARCH & ABSTRACTS (US/0148-0847). **5267**

SOCIAL WORK REVIEW (NEWTON, AUCKLAND, N.Z.) (NZ/0111-7351). **5310**

SOCIALIST REGISTER (UK/0081-0606). **4547**

SOCIETIES (PARIS, FRANCE) (FR/0765-3697). **5259**

SOCIETY & ANIMALS (UK/1063-1119). **5222**

SOCIETY & NATURAL RESOURCES (US/0894-1920). **2205**

SOCIETY AND NATURE (US/1062-9599). **2182**

SOCIETY (NEW BRUNSWICK) (US/0147-2011). **5222**

SOCIETY OF AUTOMOTIVE ENGINEERS (US/0099-5908). **1996**

SOCIO-ECONOMIC PLANNING SCIENCES (US/0038-0121). **1521**

SOCIOBIOLOGY (US/0361-6525). **5597**

SOCIOLOGIA INTERNATIONALIS (GW/0038-0164). **5260**

SOCIOLOGICAL ABSTRACTS (US/0038-0202). **5267**

SOCIOLOGICAL FORUM (RANDOLPH, N.J.) (US/0884-8971). **5260**

SOCIOLOGICAL INQUIRY (US/0038-0245). **5260**

SOCIOLOGICAL METHODS & RESEARCH (US/0049-1241). **5261**

SOCIOLOGICAL QUARTERLY (US/0038-0253). **5261**

SOCIOLOGICAL REVIEW MONOGRAPH, THE (UK/0081-1769). **5261**

SOCIOLOGICAL REVIEW, THE (UK/0038-0261). **5261**

SOCIOLOGICAL SPECTRUM (US/0273-2173). **5261**

SOCIOLOGIE DU TRAVAIL (PARIS) (FR/0038-0296). **1711**

SOCIOLOGUS; ZEITSCHRIFT FUER EMPIRISCHE ETHNOSOZIOLOGIE UND ETHNOPSYCHOLOGIE. JOURNAL FOR EMPIRICAL ETHNO-SOCIOLOGY AND ETHNO-PSYCHOLOGY (GW/0038-0377). **5262**

SOCIOLOGY AND RELATED DISCIPLINES / INTERNATIONAL CURRENT AWARENESS SERVICES (UK/0960-1546). **5262**

SOCIOLOGY OF EDUCATION ABSTRACTS (UK/0038-0415). **1797**

SOCIOLOGY OF HEALTH & ILLNESS (UK/0141-9889). **5262**

SOFT WATCH (US/1064-8860). **1209**

SOFTWARE DEVELOPMENT MONITOR (UK/0964-6841). **1290**

SOFTWARE ENGINEERING JOURNAL (UK/0268-6961). **1996**

SOFTWARE LAW BULLETIN, THE (US/0897-2680). **3056**

SOFTWARE LAW JOURNAL (US/0886-3628). **3056**

SOFTWARE MAGAZINE (WESTBOROUGH, MASS.) (US/0897-8085). **1290**

SOFTWARE MAINTENANCE NEWS (US/0741-4501). **1291**

SOFTWARE : PRACTICE & EXPERIENCE (UK/0038-0644). **1291**

SOFTWARE PROTECTION (US/0733-1274). **1227**

SOFTWARE TAXATION LETTER (US/1048-521X). **3056**

SOIL AND HEALTH (NZ/0038-0687). **186**

SOIL & TILLAGE RESEARCH (NE/0167-1987). **186**

SOIL BIOLOGY & BIOCHEMISTRY (UK/0038-0717). **186**

SOIL MECHANICS AND FOUNDATION ENGINEERING (US/0038-0741). **2129**

SOIL SCIENCE (US/0038-075X). **187**

SOIL TECHNOLOGY (GW/0933-3630). **187**

SOILS AND FOUNDATIONS (SA/0038-0806). **2031**

SOLAR ENERGY MATERIALS AND SOLAR CELLS : AN INTERNATIONAL JOURNAL DEVOTED TO PHOTOVOLTAIC, PHOTOTHERMAL, AND PHOTOCHEMICAL SOLAR ENERGY CONVERSION (NE/0927-0248). **1957**

SOLAR ENERGY (PHOENIX, ARIZ.) (US/0038-092X). **1957**

SOLAR PHYSICS (NE/0038-0938). **400**

SOLAR SYSTEM RESEARCH (US/0038-0946). **400**

SOLAR TODAY (US/1042-0630). **1957**

SOLDAT UND TECHNIK (GW/0038-0989). **4057**

SOLDERING & SURFACE MOUNT TECHNOLOGY : JOURNAL OF THE SMART (SURFACE MOUNT & RELATED TECHNOLOGIES) GROUP (UK/0954-0911). **4019**

SOLETTER (US/0747-623X). **1997**

SOLICITORS' JOURNAL (LONDON, ENGLAND : 1928) (UK/0038-1047). **3056**

SOLID FUEL CHEMISTRY (US/0361-5219). **1030**

SOLID STATE COMMUNICATIONS (US/0038-1098). **4421**

SOLID-STATE ELECTRONICS (UK/0038-1101). **2081**

SOLID STATE IONICS (NE/0167-2738). **4421**

SOLID STATE NUCLEAR MAGNETIC RESONANCE (NE/0926-2040). **4421**

SOLID STATE PHYSICS (NEW YORK. 1955) (US/0081-1947). **4421**

SOLID STATE TECHNOLOGY (US/0038-111X). **2081**

SOLID WASTE REPORT (US/0038-1128). **2243**

SOLUBILITY DATA SERIES (UK/0191-5622). **992**

SOLVENT EXTRACTION AND ION EXCHANGE (US/0736-6299). **1019**

SOMATIC CELL AND MOLECULAR GENETICS (US/0740-7750). **551**

SOMATOSENSORY & MOTOR RESEARCH (US/0899-0220). **5597**

SOMMERFELTIA (NO/0800-6865). **528**

SOTSIOLOGICHESKIE ISSLEDOVANIIA (RU/0132-1625). **5263**

SOUND & VIDEO CONTRACTOR (US/0741-1715). **5319**

SOUTH AFRICA JOURNAL OF PLANT AND SOIL (SA/0257-1862). **187**

SOUTH AFRICAN JOURNAL OF ANIMAL SCIENCE (SA/0375-1589). **222**

SOUTH AFRICAN JOURNAL OF BOTANY (SA/0254-6299). **528**

SOUTH AFRICAN JOURNAL OF CHEMISTRY (SA/0379-4350). **992**

SOUTH AFRICAN JOURNAL OF EDUCATION (SA/0256-0100). **1784**

SOUTH AFRICAN JOURNAL OF LIBRARY AND INFORMATION SCIENCE (SA/0256-8861). **3250**

SOUTH AFRICAN JOURNAL OF PHILOSOPHY (SA/0258-0136). **4361**

SOUTH AFRICAN JOURNAL OF PHYSICS (SA/0379-4377). **4421**

SOUTH AFRICAN JOURNAL OF PSYCHOLOGY (SA/0081-2463). **4619**

SOUTH AFRICAN JOURNAL OF WILDLIFE RESEARCH (SA/0379-4369). **2205**

SOUTH AFRICAN JOURNAL OF ZOOLOGY (SA/0254-1858). **5597**

SOUTH ASIA RESEARCH (UK/0262-7280). **2854**

SOUTH ATLANTIC QUARTERLY, THE (US/0038-2876). **2854**

SOUTH PACIFIC JOURNAL OF TEACHER EDUCATION (UK/0311-2136). **1847**

SOUTHEAST REAL ESTATE NEWS (US/0192-1630). **4847**

SOUTHEASTERN GEOLOGY (US/0038-3678). **1397**

SOUTHERN LOGGIN' TIMES (US/0744-2106). **2404**

SOUTHERN STARS (NZ/0049-1640). **400**

SOUTHWEST OIL WORLD (US/0884-6219). **4278**

SOUTHWEST REAL ESTATE NEWS (US/0192-9194). **4847**

SOUTHWEST REVIEW (US/0038-4712). **3353**

SOVIET AGRICULTURAL BIOLOGY. PART 1, PLANT BIOLOGY (US/0892-6999). **136**

SOVIET AGRICULTURAL SCIENCES (US/0735-2700). **136**

SOVIET APPLIED MECHANICS (US/0038-5298). **2129**

SOVIET ASTRONOMY (US/0038-5301). **400**

SOVIET ASTRONOMY LETTERS (US/0360-0327). **400**

SOVIET ATOMIC ENERGY (US/0038-531X). **2158**

SOVIET BIOLOGICAL RESEARCH ABSTRACTS (SZ/0885-5951). **473**

SOVIET CASTINGS TECHNOLOGY (US/0891-0316). **4019**

SOVIET CHEMICAL INDUSTRY, THE (US/0038-5344). **1038**

SOVIET ECONOMY (SILVER SPRING, MD.) (US/0882-6994). **1640**

SOVIET ELECTRICAL ENGINEERING (US/0038-5379). **2082**

SOVIET ELECTROCHEMISTRY (US/0038-5387). **1035**

SOVIET GENETICS (US/0038-5409). **551**

SOVIET GEOLOGY AND GEOPHYSICS (US/0361-7149). **1397**

SOVIET HYDROLOGY (US/0038-5425). **1418**

SOVIET JOURNAL OF BIOORGANIC CHEMISTRY (US/0360-4497). **1047**

SOVIET JOURNAL OF COMMUNICATIONS TECHNOLOGY & ELECTRONICS (US/8756-6648). **2082**

SOVIET JOURNAL OF COMPUTER AND SYSTEMS SCIENCES (US/0882-4002). **1221**

SOVIET JOURNAL OF CONTEMPORARY PHYSICS (US/8755-4585). **4421**

SOVIET JOURNAL OF COORDINATION CHEMISTRY (US/0364-4626). **1058**

SOVIET JOURNAL OF ECOLOGY, THE (US/0096-7807). **2221**

SOVIET JOURNAL OF GLASS PHYSICS AND CHEMISTRY, THE (US/0360-5043). **1030**

SOVIET JOURNAL OF HEAVY MACHINERY (US/1052-6196). **2129**

SOVIET JOURNAL OF LOW TEMPERATURE PHYSICS (US/0360-0335). **4432**

SOVIET JOURNAL OF MARINE BIOLOGY, THE (US/0145-1456). **557**

SOVIET JOURNAL OF NONDESTRUCTIVE TESTING, THE (US/0038-5492). **2031**

SOVIET JOURNAL OF NUCLEAR PHYSICS (US/0038-5506). **4451**

SOVIET JOURNAL OF PARTICLES AND NUCLEI (US/0090-4759). **4451**

SOVIET JOURNAL OF PLASMA PHYSICS (US/0360-0343). **4421**

SOVIET JOURNAL OF QUANTUM ELECTRONICS (US/0049-1748). **2082**

SOVIET MATERIALS SCIENCE (US/0038-5565). **2108**

SOVIET MATERIALS SCIENCE REVIEWS (US/0888-689X). **2129**

SOVIET MATHEMATICS - DOKLADY (US/0197-6788). **3536**

SOVIET MEDICAL REVIEWS. SECTION A, CARDIOLOGY REVIEWS (SZ/0888-0697). **3710**

SOVIET MEDICAL REVIEWS. SECTION B, PHYSICOCHEMICAL ASPECTS OF MEDICINE REVIEWS (SZ/0887-2392). **3898**

SOVIET MEDICAL REVIEWS. SECTION C, HEMATOLOGY REVIEWS (SZ/0888-3920). **3774**

SOVIET MEDICAL REVIEWS. SECTION D, IMMUNOLOGY REVIEWS (SZ/0887-3488). **3677**

SOVIET MEDICAL REVIEWS. SECTION E, VIROLOGY REVIEWS (SZ/0887-3496). **570**

SOVIET MEDICAL REVIEWS. SECTION F, ONCOLOGY REVIEWS (SZ/0888-0700). **3824**

SOVIET MEDICAL REVIEWS. SECTION G, NEUROPHARMACOLOGY REVIEWS (SZ/0896-8306). **4330**

SOVIET METEOROLOGY AND HYDROLOGY (US/0146-4108). **1434**

SOVIET MICROELECTRONICS (US/0363-8529). **2082**

SOVIET MINING SCIENCE (US/0038-5581). **2151**

SOVIET PHYSICS-ACOUSTICS (US/0038-562X). **4453**

SOVIET PHYSICS-CRYSTALLOGRAPHY (US/0038-5638). **1033**

SOVIET PHYSICS-DOKLADY (US/0038-5689). **4421**

SOVIET PHYSICS-JETP (US/0038-5646). **4421**

SOVIET PHYSICS JOURNAL (US/0038-5697). **4421**

SOVIET PHYSICS-LEBEDEV INSTITUTE REPORTS (US/0364-2321). **4422**

SOVIET PHYSICS-SEMICONDUCTORS (US/0038-5700). **4422**

SOVIET PHYSICS-SOLID STATE (US/0038-5654). **4422**

SOVIET PHYSICS-TECHNICAL PHYSICS (US/0038-5662). **4422**

SOVIET PHYSICS-USPEKHI (US/0038-5670). **4422**

SOVIET PLANT PHYSIOLOGY (US/0038-5719). **528**

SOVIET POWDER METALLURGY AND METAL CERAMICS (US/0038-5735). **4019**

SOVIET RADIOCHEMISTRY (US/0038-576X). **992**

SOVIET SCIENTIFIC REVIEWS. SECTION A, PHYSICS REVIEWS (SZ/0143-0394). **4422**

SOVIET SCIENTIFIC REVIEWS. SECTION C, MATHEMATICAL PHYSICS REVIEWS (SZ/0143-0416). **4422**

SOVIET SCIENTIFIC REVIEWS. SECTION D, PHYSICOCHEMICAL BIOLOGY REVIEWS (SZ/0734-9351). **5159**

SOVIET SCIENTIFIC REVIEWS. SECTION E, ASTROPHYSICS AND SPACE PHYSICS REVIEWS (SZ/0143-0432). **400**

SOVIET SCIENTIFIC REVIEWS. SECTION F, PHYSIOLOGY AND GENERAL BIOLOGY REVIEWS (SZ/0888-4803). **473**

SOVIET SCIENTIFIC REVIEWS. SECTION G, GEOLOGY REVIEWS (SZ/0896-7571). **1397**

SOVIET SOIL SCIENCE (US/0038-5832). **188**

SOVIET STUDIES (UK/0038-5859). **4547**

SOVIET SURFACE ENGINEERING & APPLIED ELECTROCHEMISTRY (US/8756-7008). **1035**

SOVIET TECHNICAL PHYSICS LETTERS (US/0360-120X). **4422**

SOVIET TECHNOLOGY ALERT (UK/0953-4016). **5159**

SOVIET TECHNOLOGY REVIEWS. SECTION A, ENERGY REVIEWS (SZ/0275-7893). **1957**

SOVIET TECHNOLOGY REVIEWS. SECTION B, THERMAL PHYSICS REVIEWS (UK/0892-6808). **4432**

SOVIET TECHNOLOGY REVIEWS. SECTION C, WELDING AND SURFACING REVIEWS (SZ/1040-7073). **4027**

SOZIALE SICHERHEIT (KOLN) (GW/0490-1630). **5310**

SOZIALER FORTSCHRITT (BERLIN) (GW/0038-609X). **5223**

SPACE BUSINESS NEWS (US/0738-9884). **35**

SPACE COMMERCE (SZ/1043-934X). **35**

SPACE COMMUNICATIONS (NE/0924-8625). **1164**

SPACE EXPLORATION TECHNOLOGY (US/1052-3383). **35**

SPACE NEWS (SPRINGFIELD, VA.) (US/1046-6940). **36**

SPACE POLICY (UK/0265-9646). **36**

SPACE POWER (US/0883-6272). **1958**

SPACE SCIENCE REVIEWS (NE/0038-6308). **400**

SPACE STATION NEWS (US/0895-8947). **36**

SPACE TECHNOLOGY (OXFORD) (UK/0892-9270). **36**

SPANISH TODAY (US/0049-1802). **3439**

SPARKASSE (GW/0038-6561). **812**

SPE COMPUTER APPLICATIONS (US/1064-9778). **4278**

SPE DRILLING AND COMPLETIONS (US/1064-6671). **4278**

SPE DRILLING ENGINEERING (US/0885-9744). **4278**

SPE FORMATION EVALUATION (US/0885-923X). **4279**

SPE PRODUCTION AND FACILITIES (US/1064-668X). **4279**

SPE PRODUCTION ENGINEERING (US/0885-9221). **4279**

SPE RESERVOIR ENGINEERING (US/0885-9248). **4279**

SPECIAL EDUCATIONAL NEEDS ABSTRACTS (UK/0954-0822). **1797**

SPECIAL EDUCATOR, THE (US/1047-1618). **1885**

SPECIAL PAPER - GEOLOGICAL SOCIETY OF AMERICA (US/0072-1077). **1397**

SPECIAL PUBLICATION - AMERICAN FISHERIES SOCIETY (US/0097-0638). **2313**

SPECIAL

SPECIAL PUBLICATION - GEOLOGICAL SOCIETY OF AUSTRALIA (AT/0072-1085). **1397**

SPECIAL PUBLICATION ... OF THE INTERNATIONAL ASSOCIATION OF SEDIMENTOLOGISTS (UK/0141-3600). **1398**

SPECIAL PUBLICATION / ROYAL SOCIETY OF CHEMISTRY (UK/0260-6291). **993**

SPECTROCHIMICA ACTA. PART A : MOLECULAR SPECTROSCOPY (UK/0584-8539). **4441**

SPECTROCHIMICA ACTA. PART B : ATOMIC SPECTROSCOPY (UK/0584-8547). **4422**

SPECTROCHIMICA ACTA REVIEWS (UK/0958-319X). **4441**

SPECTROCHIMICA ACTA REVIEWS [MICROFORM] (US/0958-319X). **4441**

SPECTROSCOPIC PROPERTIES OF INORGANIC AND ORGANOMETALLIC COMPOUNDS (UK/0584-8555). **1019**

SPECTROSCOPY (US/0887-6703). **4453**

SPECTROSCOPY INTERNATIONAL (US/1040-7669). **993**

SPECTROSCOPY LETTERS (US/0038-7010). **4442**

SPECTRUM REPORT : NEWS AND ANALYSIS ON THE GLOBAL FREQUENCY ALLOCATION BATTLE, THE (US/1053-993X). **1122**

SPECULATIONS IN SCIENCE AND TECHNOLOGY (UK/0155-7785). **5159**

SPEECH COMMUNICATION (NE/0167-6393). **1122**

SPEKTRUM DER AUGENHEILKUNDE : ZEITSCHRIFT DER OSTERREICHISCHEN OPHTHALMOLOGISCHEN GESELLSCHAFT, OOG (AU/0930-4282). **3879**

SPINE (PHILADELPHIA, PA. 1976) (US/0362-2436). **3642**

SPINE (PHILADELPHIA, PA. 1986) (US/0887-9869). **3975**

SPORT PSYCHOLOGIST, THE (US/0888-4781). **4619**

SPORT SCIENCE REVIEW (CHAMPAIGN, ILL.) (US/1056-6724). **4921**

SPORT STYLE (US/0162-2242). **1087**

SPORTDOKUMENTATION : LITERATUR DER SPORTWISSENSCHAFT (GW/0170-2890). **4921**

SPORTS MEDICINE AND ARTHROSCOPY REVIEW (US/1062-8592). **3956**

SPORTS MEDICINE (AUCKLAND) (NZ/0112-1642). **3956**

SPORTSTYLE (CONSUMER EDITION) (US/0733-8708). **4923**

SPORTUNTERRICHT (GW/0342-2402). **1858**

SPRACHE & KOGNITION (SZ/0253-4533). **3323**

SPRACHE-STIMME-GEHOR (GW/0342-0477). **4394**

SPRACHE UND LITERATUR IN WISSENSCHAFT UND UNTERRICHT (GW/0724-9713). **3323**

SPRINGER SEMINARS IN IMMUNOPATHOLOGY (US/0344-4325). **3677**

SPRINGER SERIES IN INFORMATION SCIENCES (GW/0720-678X). **4619**

SPRINGER SERIES IN OPTICAL SCIENCES (US/0342-4111). **4442**

SPRINGER TRACTS IN NATURAL PHILOSOPHY (GW/0081-3877). **4361**

SRI LANKA JOURNAL OF SOCIAL SCIENCES (CE/0258-9710). **5223**

ST. LOUIS JOURNALISM REVIEW, THE (US/0036-2972). **2924**

ST. PETERSBURG UNIVERSITY MECHANICS BULLETIN (US/1068-8005). **2129**

STAAT, DER (GW/0038-884X). **3094**

STAEDTETAG (1948), DER (GW/0038-9048). **4687**

STAHL UND EISEN (GW/0340-4803). **4020**

STAHLBAU, DER (GW/0038-9145). **628**

STAL (RU/0038-920X). **4020**

STANDARD DIRECTORY OF ADVERTISING AGENCIES (US/0085-6614). **766**

STANDARDIZATION NEWS : SN (US/0090-1210). **4032**

STARKE, DIE (GW/0038-9056). **993**

STARKE, DIE (GW/0038-9056). **137**

STATE ENVIRONMENT REPORT (US/1054-2604). **3116**

STATE LEGISLATURES (US/0147-6041). **4688**

STATE OF THE ART REPORT (UK/0276-8267). **5160**

STATE TAX NOTES (PRINT) (US/1057-8404). **4750**

STATE TELEPHONE REGULATION REPORT (US/0741-8388). **1164**

STATE YELLOW BOOK (US/0899-2207). **1929**

STATISTICA NEERLANDICA (NE/0039-0402). **5339**

STATISTICAL NEWS (GREAT BRITAIN. CENTRAL STATISTICAL OFFICE) (UK/0017-3630). **5340**

STATISTICAL PAPERS (BERLIN, GERMANY) (GW/0932-5026). **5340**

STATISTICAL SCIENCE (US/0883-4237). **5340**

STATISTICIAN, THE (UK/0039-0526). **5341**

STATISTICS AND COMPUTING (UK/0960-3174). **1210**

STATISTICS & DECISIONS (GW/0721-2631). **5342**

STATISTICS & PROBABILITY LETTERS (NE/0167-7152). **3536**

STATISTICS (BERLIN, DDR) (GW/0233-1888). **3543**

STATISTICS IN MEDICINE (UK/0277-6715). **3661**

STATISTISCHER WOCHENDIENST (GW/0431-6983). **5343**

STATISTISK ARBOK (NO/0078-1932). **5343**

STATUTE LAW REVIEW (UK/0144-3593). **3059**

STAUB, REINHALTUNG DER LUFT (GW/0039-0771). **2244**

STEEL RESEARCH (GW/0177-4832). **4020**

STEIRISCHE BEITRAEGE ZUR HYDROGEOLOGIE (AU/0376-4826). **1418**

STEM CELLS (DAYTON, OHIO) (US/1066-5099). **540**

STEREOTACTIC AND FUNCTIONAL NEUROSURGERY (SZ/1011-6125). **3975**

STEROID RECEPTORS (UK/0142-8330). **540**

STEROIDS (US/0039-128X). **473**

STITCHES MAGAZINE (US/0899-5893). **5356**

STOCHASTIC ANALYSIS AND APPLICATIONS (US/0736-2994). **3536**

STOCHASTIC HYDROLOGY AND HYDRAULICS (GW/0931-1955). **1418**

STOCHASTIC PROCESSES AND THEIR APPLICATIONS (NE/0304-4149). **3536**

STOCHASTICS AND STOCHASTICS REPORT (US/1045-1129). **3536**

STRASSE UND AUTOBAHN (GW/0039-2162). **2031**

STRASSEN- VERKEHRSTECHNIK (GW/0039-2219). **5444**

STRATEGIC DEFENSE (US/0890-7331). **4058**

STRATEGIC HEALTH CARE MARKETING (US/0749-5153). **3793**

STRATEGIC MANAGEMENT JOURNAL (UK/0143-2095). **887**

STRATEGIC PLANNING AND ENERGY MANAGEMENT (US/8750-3204). **1958**

STRATEGIC SYSTEMS (US/1060-3751). **1249**

STRATEGIES FOR HEALTHCARE EXCELLENCE (US/1058-7829). **3793**

STRENGTH OF MATERIALS (US/0039-2316). **2129**

STRESS MEDICINE (UK/0748-8386). **3643**

STROITELSTVO TRUBOPROVODOV (RU/0039-2448). **4279**

STROKE (1970) (US/0039-2499). **3710**

STRUCTURAL CHANGE AND ECONOMIC DYNAMICS (UK/0954-349X). **1522**

STRUCTURAL CHEMISTRY (US/1040-0400). **993**

STRUCTURAL ENGINEERING REVIEW (UK/0952-5807). **2031**

STRUCTURAL OPTIMIZATION (GW/0934-4373). **2129**

STRUCTURAL SAFETY (NE/0167-4730). **629**

STRUCTURE AND BONDING (BERLIN) (GW/0081-5993). **1038**

STRUCTURED PROGRAMMING (US/0935-1183). **1204**

STUDENT AID NEWS (US/0194-2212). **1785**

STUDIA BIOPHYSICA (SZ/0081-6337). **496**

STUDIA GEOPHYSICA ET GEODAETICA (XR/0039-3169). **1411**

STUDIA LEIBNITIANA (GW/0039-3185). **4361**

STUDIA LINGUISTICA (SW/0039-3193). **3324**

STUDIA LOGICA (PL/0039-3215). **4362**

STUDIA MUSICOLOGICA. ACADEMIAE SCIENTIARUM HUNGARICA (HU/0039-3266). **4155**

STUDIA MUSICOLOGICA NORVEGICA (NO/0332-5024). **4155**

STUDIA SCIENTIARUM MATHEMATICARUM HUNGARICA (HU/0081-6906). **3537**

STUDIA SLAVICA ACADEMIAE SCIENTIARUM HUNGARICAE (HU/0039-3363). **3325**

STUDIES IN AMERICAN DRAMA, 1945-PRESENT (US/0886-7097). **5369**

STUDIES IN APPLIED MATHEMATICS (CAMBRIDGE) (US/0022-2526). **3537**

STUDIES IN COMMUNICATIONS (US/0275-7982). **1122**

STUDIES IN COMPARATIVE COMMUNISM (UK/0039-3592). **4548**

STUDIES IN COMPARATIVE INTERNATIONAL DEVELOPMENT (US/0039-3606). **5263**

STUDIES IN CONFLICT AND TERRORISM (US/1057-610X). **5263**

STUDIES IN ENVIRONMENTAL SCIENCE (AMSTERDAM) (NE/0166-1116). **2221**

STUDIES IN HISTORY AND PHILOSOPHY OF SCIENCE (UK/0039-3681). **5160**

STUDIES IN IRISH HISTORY (UK/0081-8100). **2711**

STUDIES IN ORGANIC CHEMISTRY (AMSTERDAM) (NE/0165-3253). **1047**

STUDIES IN PHILOLOGY (US/0039-3738). **3326**

STUDIES IN PHILOSOPHY AND EDUCATION (US/0039-3746). **4362**

STUDIES IN RELIGION (CN/0008-4298). **5001**

STUDIES IN SECOND LANGUAGE ACQUISITION (US/0272-2631). **3326**

STUDIES IN SOVIET THOUGHT (NE/0039-3797). **4362**

STUDIES IN SURFACE SCIENCE AND CATALYSIS (NE/0167-2991). **1058**

STUDIES IN SYMBOLIC INTERACTION (US/0163-2396). **5263**

STUDIES IN THE MANAGEMENT SCIENCES (NE/0378-3766). **5160**

STUDIES ON NEOTROPICAL FAUNA AND ENVIRONMENT (NE/0165-0521). **5598**

STUDIES ON WOMEN ABSTRACTS (UK/0262-5644). **5572**

SUB-STANCE (US/0049-2426). **3443**

SUBJECT GUIDE TO BOOKS IN PRINT (US/0000-0159). **3459**

SUCCESSFUL HOTEL MARKETER, THE (US/1040-600X). **2809**

SUCCESSFUL MEETINGS : SM (US/0148-4052). **714**

SUDHOFFS ARCHIV (GW/0039-4564). **3643**

SUDOST EUROPA : [MONATSSCHRIFT DER ABTEILUNG GEGENWARTSFORSCHUNG DES SUDOST-INSTITUTS] (GW/0722-480X). **5224**

SUICIDE & LIFE-THREATENING BEHAVIOR (US/0363-0234). **4619**

SUID-AFRIKAANSE TYDSKRIF VIR ETNOLOGIE (SA/0379-8860). **246**

SUID-AFRIKAANSE TYDSKRIF VIR SOSIOLOGIE, DIE (SA/0258-0144). **5263**

SULFUR LETTERS (UK/0278-6117). **1038**

SULFUR REPORTS (SZ/0196-1772). **1038**

SUNWORLD (AT/0149-1938). **1958**

SUPERCONDUCTIVITY: PHYSICS, CHEMISTRY, TECHNIQUE (US/0235-8964). **4423**

SUPERCONDUCTIVITY REVIEW (US/1054-2698). **2082**

SUPERCONDUCTOR INDUSTRY (US/1042-4105). **5161**

SUPERCONDUCTOR SCIENCE & TECHNOLOGY (UK/0953-2048). **4445**

SUPERCONDUCTOR WEEK (US/0894-7635). **1997**

SUPERFUND (US/0892-2985). **2244**

SUPERLATTICES AND MICROSTRUCTURES (UK/0749-6036). **5161**

SUPERMARKET BUSINESS (US/0196-5700). **2359**

SUPERMARKET NEWS (US/0039-5803). **2359**

SUPERMARKET NEWS (US/0039-5803). **2359**

SUPERMARKET STRATEGIC ALERT (US/1053-3648). **2359**

SUPERVISION (BURLINGTON) (US/0039-5854). **947**

SUPERVISORY MANAGEMENT (1989) (US/1045-263X). **947**

SUPERVISORY SENSE (US/0274-645X). **947**

SUPPLIER SELECTION & MANAGEMENT REPORT (US/1046-3771). **887**

SUPPLY HOUSE TIMES (US/0039-5935). **2608**

SUPPORT FOR LEARNING (UK/0268-2141). **1786**

SUPPORTIVE CARE IN CANCER : OFFICIAL JOURNAL OF THE MULTINATIONAL ASSOCIATION OF SUPPORTIVE CARE IN CANCER (GW/0941-4355). **3824**

SUPRAMOLECULAR CHEMISTRY (SW/1061-0278). **993**

SURFACE & COATINGS TECHNOLOGY (SZ/0257-8972). **2108**

SURFACE AND INTERFACE ANALYSIS : SIA (UK/0142-2421). **1019**

SURFACE ENGINEERING AND APPLIED ELECTROCHEMISTRY (US/1068-3755). **1997**

SURFACE MOUNT TECHNOLOGY (US/0893-3588). **2083**

SURFACE SCIENCE (NE/0039-6028). **1058**

SURFACE SCIENCE LETTERS (NE/0167-2584). **5161**

SURFACE SCIENCE REPORTS (NE/0167-5729). **2083**

SURFACE WAVE ABSTRACTS (UK/0049-2639). **4453**

SURFACES (FR/0585-9840). **4021**

SURFACTANT SCIENCE SERIES (US/0081-9603). **993**

SURGELATION, LA (FR/0049-2647). **1628**

SURGERY (US/0039-6060). **3975**

SURGERY ANNUAL (US/0081-9638). **3975**

SURGERY, GYNECOLOGY & OBSTETRICS (US/0039-6087). **3975**

SURGICAL CLINICS OF NORTH AMERICA, THE (US/0039-6109). **3975**

SURGICAL ENDOSCOPY (GW/0930-2794). **3976**

SURGICAL LAPAROSCOPY AND ENDOSCOPY (US/1051-7200). **3976**

SURGICAL NEUROLOGY (US/0090-3019). **3976**

SURGICAL ONCOLOGY (UK/0960-7404). **3824**

SURGICAL PRODUCT NEWS (US/0279-4829). **3684**

SURGICAL RESEARCH COMMUNICATIONS (SZ/0882-9233). **3976**

SURVEILLANT (WASHINGTON, D.C.) (US/1051-0923). **4058**

SURVEY OF ANESTHESIOLOGY (US/0039-6206). **3684**

SURVEY OF OPHTHALMOLOGY (US/0039-6257). **3879**

SURVEYS IN GEOPHYSICS (NE/0169-3298). **1411**

SURVEYS IN HIGH ENERGY PHYSICS (SZ/0142-2413). **4451**

SURVEYS ON MATHEMATICS FOR INDUSTRY (AU/0938-1953). **1997**

SURVIVAL (LONDON) (UK/0039-6338). **4058**

SV. SOUND AND VIBRATION (US/0038-1810). **4453**

SWIMMING POOL/SPA AGE (US/0899-1022). **4855**

SYMBOLIC INTERACTION (US/0195-6086). **5264**

SYMPOSIA BIOLOGICA HUNGARICA (HU/0082-0695). **474**

... SYMPOSIUM OF THE SOCIETY FOR DEVELOPMENTAL BIOLOGY, THE (US/0583-9009). **474**

SYMPOSIUM (SYRACUSE) (US/0039-7709). **3327**

SYNAPSE (NEW YORK, N.Y.) (US/0887-4476). **3801**

SYNCHROTRON RADIATION NEWS (US/0894-0886). **4442**

SYNFORM (GW/0723-3655). **1048**

SYNLETT (GW/0936-5214). **1048**

SYNTAX AND SEMANTICS (US/0092-4563). **3327**

SYNTHESE (DORDRECHT) (NE/0039-7857). **4363**

SYNTHESE HISTORICAL LIBRARY (NE/0082-111X). **3252**

SYNTHESIS AND REACTIVITY IN INORGANIC AND METAL-ORGANIC CHEMISTRY (US/0094-5714). **994**

SYNTHESIS (STUTTGART) (GW/0039-7881). **1048**

SYNTHETIC COMMUNICATIONS (US/0039-7911). **1048**

SYNTHETIC METALS (SZ/0379-6779). **4021**

SYSTEM DEVELOPMENT (US/0275-6617). **1262**

SYSTEM DYNAMICS REVIEW (US/0883-7066). **3537**

SYSTEM FAMILIE (GW/0933-3053). **2286**

SYSTEM (LINKOPING) (UK/0346-251X). **3327**

SYSTEMATIC AND APPLIED MICROBIOLOGY (GW/0723-2020). **570**

SYSTEMATIC BOTANY (US/0363-6445). **528**

SYSTEMATIC ENTOMOLOGY (UK/0307-6970). **5613**

SYSTEMATIC PARASITOLOGY (NE/0165-5752). **5598**

SYSTEMS ANALYSIS, MODELLING, SIMULATION (GW/0232-9298). **3537**

SYSTEMS AND COMPUTERS IN JAPAN (US/0882-1666). **1249**

SYSTEMS & CONTROL LETTERS (NE/0167-6911). **1998**

SYSTEMS INTEGRATION (US/1044-4262). **1274**

SYSTEMS INTEGRATION BUSINESS (US/1063-407X). **1274**

SYSTEMS PRACTICE (US/0894-9859). **1249**

SYSTEMS RESEARCH AND INFORMATION SCIENCE (US/0882-3014). **3252**

SYSTEMS SCIENCE AND MATHEMATICAL SCIENCES / EDITED BY INSTITUTE OF SYSTEMS SCIENCE, CHINESE ACADEMY OF SCIENCES (CC/1000-9590). **3538**

TABLET (LONDON), THE (UK/0039-8837). **5002**

TACK 'N TOGS MERCHANDISING (US/0149-3442). **2802**

TACTICAL TECHNOLOGY (US/1059-0552). **5161**

TAGLICHE PRAXIS (GW/0494-464X). **3644**

TALANTA (OXFORD) (UK/0039-9140). **1019**

TANKER CHARTER RECORD (UK/0958-8787). **5457**

TAPPI JOURNAL (US/0734-1415). **4239**

TAX ADVISER, THE (US/0039-9957). **4751**

TAX ANALYSTS' DAILY TAX HIGHLIGHTS & DOCUMENTS (US/0889-3055). **4751**

TAX DIRECTORY, THE (US/0888-1243). **4752**

TAX EXEMPT NEWS (US/0194-228X). **4752**

TAX LAW REVIEW (US/0040-0041). **3062**

TAX MANAGEMENT COMPENSATION PLANNING JOURNAL (US/0747-8607). **917**

TAX MANAGEMENT ESTATES, GIFTS, AND TRUSTS JOURNAL (US/0886-3547). **3119**

TAX MANAGEMENT FINANCIAL PLANNING JOURNAL (US/8756-1360). **4753**

TAX MANAGEMENT INTERNATIONAL FORUM, THE (UK/0143-7941). **4753**

TAX MANAGEMENT INTERNATIONAL JOURNAL (US/0090-4600). **887**

TAX MANAGEMENT MEMORANDUM (US/0148-8295). **4753**

TAX MANAGEMENT, PRIMARY SOURCES (US/0738-5285). **4753**

TAX MANAGEMENT REAL ESTATE JOURNAL (US/8755-0628). **3062**

TAX MANAGEMENT WEEKLY REPORT (US/0884-6057). **4753**

TAX NOTES (ARLINGTON) (US/0270-5494). **4753**

TAX NOTES INTERNATIONAL (US/1048-3306). **4753**

TAX PREPARERS LIABILITY SERVICE (US/0279-7046). **3062**

TAX REPORTS, NEW ZEALAND (NZ/0110-0246). **3062**

TAX UPDATE FOR BUSINESS OWNERS (US/0746-0384). **4754**

TAXATION FOR ACCOUNTANTS (US/0040-0165). **752**

TAXATION FOR LAWYERS (US/0161-178X). **3062**

TB WEEKLY (US/1065-982X). **3716**

TEACHER MAGAZINE (US/1046-6193). **1906**

TEACHERS COLLEGE RECORD (1970) (US/0161-4681). **1849**

TEACHING AND TEACHER EDUCATION (UK/0742-051X). **1906**

TEACHING AND TRAINING IN GERIATRIC MEDICINE (SZ/1011-3738). **3755**

TEACHING MATHEMATICS AND ITS APPLICATIONS (UK/0268-3679). **3538**

TEACHING PHILOSOPHY (US/0145-5788). **4363**

TEACHING PROFESSOR, THE (US/0892-2209). **1850**

TECHN. BIOL. - 1985 (FR/0766-5725). **3644**

TECHNICA (BASEL) (BE/0040-0866). **2915**

TECHNICAL ANALYSIS OF STOCKS AND COMMODITIES (JOURNAL) (US/0738-3355). **917**

TECHNICAL & SKILLS TRAINING (US/1047-8388). **4209**

TECHNICAL COMMUNICATION (WASHINGTON) (US/0049-3155). **5162**

TECHNICAL DIGEST / INTERNATIONAL ELECTRON DEVICES MEETING (US/0163-1918). **2083**

TECHNICAL EDUCATION ABSTRACTS (UK/0040-0920). **1798**

TECHNICAL LITERATURE ABSTRACTS (WARRENDALE, PA. : 1987) (US/0741-2029). **1998**

TECHNICAL PAPERS (US/0083-8837). **2083**

TECHNICAL PHYSICS (US/1063-7842). **4423**

TECHNICAL PHYSICS LETTERS (US/1063-7850). **4423**

TECHNICAL TEXTILES INTERNATIONAL (UK/0964-5993). **5356**

TECHNIKGESCHICHTE (GW/0040-117X). **5162**

TECHNIQUE ET SCIENCE INFORMATIQUES : TSI (FR/0752-4072). **1262**

TECHNIQUE MODERNE, LA (FR/0040-1250). **5162**

TECHNIQUES IN ORTHOPAEDICS (ROCKVILLE, MD.) (US/0885-9698). **3885**

TECHNIQUES IN THE LIFE SCIENCES. BIOCHEMISTRY (NE/0165-1064). **493**

TECHNIQUES IN THE LIFE SCIENCES. CELL BIOLOGY (IE/0165-1064). **540**

TECHNIQUES IN THE LIFE SCIENCES. PHYSIOLOGY (NE/0165-1064). **587**

TECHNIQUES OF CHEMISTRY (US/0082-2531). **994**

TECHNISCH-WISSENSFHAFTLICHE ABHANDLUNGEN DER OSRAM-GESELLSCHAFT (GW/0371-5264). **5162**

TECHNISCHES MESSE : TM (GW/0171-8096). **4033**

TECHNOLOGICAL FORECASTING AND SOCIAL CHANGE (US/0040-1625). **5163**

TECHNOLOGY ACCESS REPORT (US/1050-043X). **5163**

TECHNOLOGY ANALYSIS & STRATEGIC MANAGEMENT (UK/0953-7325). **5163**

TECHNOLOGY AND CULTURE (US/0040-165X). **5163**

TECHNOLOGY AND DISABILITY (US/1055-4181). **4394**

TECHNOLOGY AND HEALTH CARE : OFFICIAL JOURNAL OF THE EUROPEAN SOCIETY FOR ENGINEERING AND MEDICINE (NE/0928-7329). **3644**

TECHNOLOGY FOR ANESTHESIA (US/8756-8578). **3684**

TECHNOLOGY FOR CARDIOLOGY (US/8756-8586). **3710**

TECHNOLOGY FOR IMAGING AND RADIOLOGY (US/0892-7340). **3947**

TECHNOLOGY FOR MATERIALS MANAGEMENT (US/8756-8608). **3644**

TECHNOLOGY FOR NURSING (US/0890-9059). **3870**

TECHNOLOGY FOR RESPIRATORY THERAPY (US/8756-8616). **3952**

TECHNOLOGY FOR SURGERY (US/8756-8624). **3976**

TECHNOLOGY IN SOCIETY (US/0160-791X). **5164**

TECHNOLOGY UPDATE (US/0732-5533). **5164**

TECHNOMETRICS (US/0040-1706). **5176**

TECHNOVATION (NE/0166-4972). **1629**

TECNICA MOLITORIA (IT/0040-1862). **204**

TECTONICS (WASHINGTON, D.C.) (US/0278-7407). **1411**

TECTONOPHYSICS (NE/0040-1951). **1411**

TELCOM REPORT DEUTSCHE AUSGABE (GW/0344-4724). **1164**

TELCOM REPORT (ENGLISH EDITION) (GW/0344-4880). **1164**

TELECOMMUNICATIONS ALERT (US/0742-5384). **1165**

TELECOMMUNICATIONS — Copyright Clearance Center Index

TELECOMMUNICATIONS AND RADIO ENGINEERING (US/0040-2508). **1165**

TELECOMMUNICATIONS (INTERNATIONAL ED.) (US/0040-2494). **1165**

TELECOMMUNICATIONS POLICY (UK/0308-5961). **1166**

TELECOMMUTING REVIEW (US/8756-7431). **1166**

TELEKOM PRAXIS /HERAUSGEGEBEN IM BENEHMEN MIT DEM FERNMELDETECHNISCHEN ZENTRALAMT (GW/0015-0118). **1166**

TELEMARKETING UPDATE (US/0736-167X). **767**

TELEMATICS AND INFORMATICS (US/0736-5853). **1167**

TELEPHONE ENGINEER & MANAGEMENT (US/0040-263X). **1167**

TELEPHONE ENGINEER & MANAGEMENT (US/0040-263X). **2084**

TELEPHONE NEWS (US/0271-5430). **1167**

TELEPHONE WEEK (US/1062-4724). **1167**

TELEPHONY (US/0040-2656). **1167**

TELERAMA ED. PARISIENNE (FR/0040-2699). **1123**

TELEVISION & CABLE FACTBOOK (US/0732-8648). **1140**

TELEVISION & CABLE UPDATE (US/1061-5741). **1140**

TELEVISION DIGEST WITH CONSUMER ELECTRONICS (1984) (US/0497-1515). **1140**

TELEVISION LONDON. 1970 (UK/0032-647X). **1141**

TELLUS. SERIES A, DYNAMIC METEOROLOGY AND OCEANOGRAPHY (SW/0280-6495). **1436**

TELLUS. SERIES B, CHEMICAL AND PHYSICAL METEOROLOGY (SW/0280-6509). **1436**

TEMPO MEDICAL INTERNATIONAL (FR/0378-8407). **3645**

TEORETICESKAJA I EKSPERIMENTALNAJA HIMIJA (UN/0497-2627). **994**

TEPLOENERGETIKA (MOSKVA, 1954) (RU/0040-3636). **2130**

TEPLOFIZIKA VYSOKIKH TEMPERATUR (RU/0040-3644). **4423**

TERATOGENESIS, CARCINOGENESIS, AND MUTAGENESIS (US/0270-3211). **3824**

TERATOLOGY (PHILADELPHIA) (US/0040-3709). **474**

TERRA NOVA (UK/0954-4879). **1411**

TEST & MEASUREMENT WORLD (US/0744-1657). **2084**

TETRAHEDRON (UK/0040-4020). **1048**

TETRAHEDRON, ASYMMETRY (UK/0957-4166). **994**

TETRAHEDRON LETTERS (UK/0040-4039). **1048**

TETRAHEDRON LETTERS (UK/0040-4039). **1048**

TETSU TO HAGANE (JA/0021-1575). **4021**

TEXAS BUSINESS REVIEW (US/0040-4209). **1586**

TEXAS LAWYER, THE (US/0267-8306). **3064**

TEXAS STUDIES IN LITERATURE AND LANGUAGE (US/0040-4691). **3445**

TEXT (THE HAGUE) (NE/0165-4888). **3328**

TEXTIL PRAXIS INTERNATIONAL (GW/0040-4853). **5357**

TEXTILE CHEMIST AND COLORIST (US/0040-490X). **5357**

TEXTILE HISTORY (UK/0040-4969). **5358**

TEXTILE RESEARCH JOURNAL (US/0040-5175). **5358**

TEXTILE TECHNOLOGY DIGEST (US/0040-5191). **5360**

TEXTILE WORLD (US/0040-5213). **5358**

TEXTURES AND MICROSTRUCTURES (US/0730-3300). **1033**

THEATER HEUTE (GW/0040-5507). **5370**

THEATRE JOURNAL (WASHINGTON, D.C.) (US/0192-2882). **5371**

THEATRE RESEARCH INTERNATIONAL (UK/0307-8833). **5371**

THEATRE TOPICS (US/1054-8378). **5371**

THEILHEIMER'S SYNTHETIC METHODS OF ORGANIC CHEMISTRY (SZ/0253-200X). **1048**

THEMEN DER PRAKTISCHEN THEOLOGIE, THEOLOGIA PRACTICA (GW/0720-9525). **5003**

THEMES IN DRAMA (UK/0263-676X). **389**

THEOLOGIE UND GLAUBE (GW/0049-366X). **5003**

THEOLOGISCHE QUARTALSCHRIFT (MUNCHEN) (GW/0342-1430). **5004**

THEOLOGISCHE REVUE (GW/0040-568X). **5004**

THEOLOGISCHE RUNDSCHAU (GW/0040-5698). **5004**

THEORETICA CHIMICA ACTA (GW/0040-5744). **1058**

THEORETICAL AND APPLIED CLIMATOLOGY (AU/0177-798X). **1436**

THEORETICAL AND APPLIED FRACTURE MECHANICS (NE/0167-8442). **4430**

THEORETICAL AND APPLIED GENETICS (GW/0040-5752). **551**

THEORETICAL AND COMPUTATIONAL FLUID DYNAMICS (US/0935-4964). **4423**

THEORETICAL AND EXPERIMENTAL CHEMISTRY (US/0040-5760). **1058**

THEORETICAL AND MATHEMATICAL PHYSICS (US/0040-5779). **4423**

THEORETICAL COMPUTER SCIENCE (NE/0304-3975). **1205**

THEORETICAL FOUNDATIONS OF CHEMICAL ENGINEERING (US/0040-5795). **2017**

THEORETICAL LINGUISTICS (GW/0301-4428). **3328**

THEORETICAL MEDICINE (NE/0167-9902). **3645**

THEORETICAL PARAPSYCHOLOGY (US/0894-2528). **4243**

THEORETICAL POPULATION BIOLOGY (US/0040-5809). **4560**

THEORETICAL SURGERY (GW/0179-8669). **3976**

THEORY AND DECISION (NE/0040-5833). **4363**

THEORY AND SOCIETY (NE/0304-2421). **5264**

THEORY OF PROBABILITY AND ITS APPLICATIONS (UK/0040-585X). **3538**

THEORY OF PROBABILITY AND MATHEMATICAL STATISTICS (US/0094-9000). **3538**

THERAPEUTIC DRUG MONITORING (US/0163-4356). **4330**

THERAPEUTISCHE UMSCHAU (SZ/0040-5930). **3976**

THERAPIE (FR/0040-5957). **4330**

THERAPIE DER GEGENWART (GW/0040-5965). **3645**

THERAPIE FAMILIALE (SZ/0250-4952). **4620**

THERIOGENOLOGY (US/0093-691X). **5522**

THERMOCHIMICA ACTA (NE/0040-6031). **1058**

THESIS ELEVEN (US/0725-5136). **5264**

THIN SOLID FILMS (SZ/0040-6090). **2084**

THIN-WALLED STRUCTURES (UK/0263-8231). **2032**

THIRD TEXT (UK/0952-8822). **366**

THIRD WORLD PLANNING REVIEW (UK/0142-7849). **2836**

THIRD WORLD QUARTERLY (UK/0143-6597). **1587**

THIS AUSTRALIA (AT/0725-4946). **2511**

THORACIC AND CARDIOVASCULAR SURGEON, THE (GW/0171-6425). **3976**

THORAX (UK/0040-6376). **3952**

THOUGHT (NEW YORK) (US/0040-6457). **5005**

THROMBOSIS AND HAEMOSTASIS (GW/0340-6245). **3801**

THROMBOSIS RESEARCH (US/0049-3848). **3710**

THROMBOTIC AND HAEMORRHAGIC DISORDERS (AU/0934-9669). **3774**

THROMBOTIC AND HEMORRHAGIC DISORDERS (AU/0934-9669). **3645**

THRUST (US/0190-3381). **1714**

THYMUS (NE/0165-6090). **3677**

TIERARZTLICHE PRAXIS (GW/0303-6286). **5523**

TIERARZTLICHE UMSCHAU (GW/0049-3864). **5523**

TIERS MONDE (PARIS) (FR/0040-7356). **1640**

TIJDSCHRIFT VOOR ECONOMISCHE EN SOCIALE GEOGRAFIE : TESG (NE/0040-747X). **1524**

TIJDSCHRIFT VOOR NEDERLANDSE TAAL-EN LETTERKUNDE (NE/0040-7550). **3328**

TIJDSCHRIFT VOOR RECHTSGESCHIEDENIS (NE/0040-7585). **3064**

TIKHOOKEANSKAIA GEOLOGIIA. ENGLISH (SZ/8755-755X). **1399**

TIMBER HARVESTING (US/0160-6433). **2405**

TIMBER PROCESSING (US/0885-906X). **2405**

TISSUE & CELL (UK/0040-8166). **540**

TISSUE ANTIGENS (DK/0001-2815). **3802**

TISSUE CULTURE SHEFFIELD (UK/0142-8810). **540**

TODAY'S PARENT (CN/0823-9258). **2286**

TODAY'S TRUCKING (CN/0837-1512). **5394**

TOM PETERS ON ACHIEVING EXCELLENCE (US/0887-5332). **888**

TOOLING & PRODUCTION (US/0040-9243). **2130**

TOPICS IN ACUTE CARE AND TRAUMA REHABILITATION (US/0885-971X). **3646**

TOPICS IN CLINICAL NUTRITION (US/0883-5691). **4199**

TOPICS IN CURRENT CHEMISTRY (GW/0340-1022). **994**

TOPICS IN EARLY CHILDHOOD SPECIAL EDUCATION (US/0271-1214). **1886**

TOPICS IN EMERGENCY MEDICINE (US/0164-2340). **3725**

TOPICS IN FAMILY PSYCHOLOGY AND COUNSELING (US/1058-9864). **4620**

TOPICS IN GERIATRIC REHABILITATION (US/0882-7524). **3755**

TOPICS IN HEALTH CARE FINANCING (US/0095-3814). **814**

TOPICS IN HEALTH INFORMATION MANAGEMENT (US/0270-5230). **3793**

TOPICS IN HEALTH INFORMATION MANAGEMENT (US/1065-0989). **4805**

TOPICS IN HOSPITAL PHARMACY MANAGEMENT (US/0271-1206). **4331**

TOPICS IN LANGUAGE DISORDERS (US/0271-8294). **3329**

TOPICS IN MAGNETIC RESONANCE IMAGING (US/0899-3459). **3947**

TOPICS IN MOLECULAR PHARMACOLOGY (NE/0167-7101). **4331**

TOPICS IN PAIN MANAGEMENT (US/0882-5645). **3646**

TOPICS IN TOTAL COMPENSATION (US/0888-6032). **888**

TOPIQUE (FR/0040-9375). **4620**

TOPOI (NE/0167-7411). **4364**

TOPOLOGY AND ITS APPLICATIONS (NE/0166-8641). **3539**

TOPOLOGY (OXFORD) (UK/0040-9383). **3539**

TOTAL QUALITY ENVIRONMENTAL MANAGEMENT (US/1055-7571). **2182**

TOTAL QUALITY MANAGEMENT (UK/0954-4127). **888**

TOUNG PAO (NE/0082-5433). **2666**

TOUR & TRAVEL NEWS (US/0889-3349). **5492**

TOURISM MANAGEMENT (1982) (UK/0261-5177). **888**

TOURNAMENT CHESS (UK/0276-7090). **4867**

TOWN PLANNING REVIEW (UK/0041-0020). **2837**

TOXIC MATERIALS NEWS (US/0093-5891). **2245**

TOXIC MATERIALS TRANSPORT (US/0275-3766). **5394**

TOXIC SUBSTANCES JOURNAL (US/0199-3178). **2871**

TOXICOLOGIC PATHOLOGY (US/0192-6233). **3898**

TOXICOLOGICAL AND ENVIRONMENTAL CHEMISTRY (UK/0277-2248). **3984**

TOXICOLOGIST, THE (US/0731-9193). **3984**

TOXICOLOGY (AMSTERDAM) (IE/0300-483X). **3984**

TOXICOLOGY AND APPLIED PHARMACOLOGY (US/0041-008X). **3984**

TOXICOLOGY AND INDUSTRIAL HEALTH (US/0748-2337). **3984**

TOXICOLOGY IN VITRO (UK/0887-2333). **3984**

TOXICOLOGY LETTERS (NE/0378-4274). **3984**

TOXICOLOGY METHODS (US/1051-7235). **3984**

TOXICON (OXFORD) (UK/0041-0101). **4331**

TOXICS LAW REPORTER (US/0887-7394). **3116**

TQM IN HIGHER EDUCATION (US/1065-6774). **1850**

TQM MAGAZINE (INTERNATIONAL ED.) (UK/0954-478X). **888**

TRAC, TRENDS IN ANALYTICAL CHEMISTRY (NE/0167-2940). **1019**

TRAC, TRENDS IN ANALYTICAL CHEMISTRY (PERSONAL EDITION) (NE/0165-9936). **1019**

TRACE ELEMENTS IN MEDICINE (GW/0174-7371). **3647**

TRADE SECRET LAW REPORTER (US/8756-1492). **3065**

TRADITIO (US/0362-1529). **2713**

TRAFFIC MANAGEMENT (US/0041-0691). **5394**

TRAFFIC WORLD, THE (US/0041-073X). **5394**

TRAINING AND DEVELOPMENT ALERT (US/0192-0596). **947**

TRAINING & DEVELOPMENT (ALEXANDRIA, VA.) (US/1055-9760). **947**

TRAINING MEDIA REVIEW (US/1072-3188). **1123**

TRAINING (MINNEAPOLIS) (US/0095-5892). **948**

TRAITEMENT THERMIQUE (FR/0041-0950). **4022**

TRANSACTIONS (DOKLADY) OF THE USSR ACADEMY OF SCIENCES. EARTH SCIENCE SECTIONS (US/0891-5571). **1361**

TRANSACTIONS OF DIESEL ENGINEERS & USERS ASSOCIATION (UK/0261-0345). **2100**

TRANSACTIONS OF INDIAN SOCIETY OF DESERT TECHNOLOGY (II/0970-3918). **142**

TRANSACTIONS OF THE AMERICAN FISHERIES SOCIETY (1900) (US/0002-8487). **2315**

TRANSACTIONS OF THE AMERICAN FOUNDRYMEN'S SOCIETY (ANNUAL) (US/0065-8375). **4022**

TRANSACTIONS OF THE AMERICAN MATHEMATICAL SOCIETY (US/0002-9947). **3539**

TRANSACTIONS OF THE AMERICAN PHILOLOGICAL ASSOCIATION (1974) (US/0360-5949). **3329**

TRANSACTIONS OF THE AMERICAN SOCIETY OF CIVIL ENGINEERS (US/0066-0604). **2007**

TRANSACTIONS OF THE AMERICAN SOCIETY OF MECHANICAL ENGINEERS (US/0097-6822). **2130**

TRANSACTIONS OF THE ASAE (US/0001-2351). **1999**

TRANSACTIONS OF THE INSTITUTION OF PROFESSIONAL ENGINEERS NEW ZEALAND, CIVIL ENGINEERING SECTION (NZ/0111-9508). **2033**

TRANSACTIONS OF THE IRON AND STEEL INSTITUTE OF JAPAN (JA/0021-1583). **4022**

TRANSACTIONS OF THE JAPAN WELDING SOCIETY (JA/0385-9282). **4028**

TRANSACTIONS OF THE MOSCOW MATHEMATICAL SOCIETY (US/0077-1554). **3539**

TRANSACTIONS OF THE ORIENTAL CERAMIC SOCIETY (UK/0306-0926). **2595**

TRANSACTIONS OF THE PHILOLOGICAL SOCIETY (UK/0079-1636). **3329**

TRANSACTIONS OF THE SAEST (II/0036-0678). **1035**

TRANSACTIONS OF THE SOCIETY FOR COMPUTER SIMULATION (US/0740-6797). **1283**

TRANSACTIONS. SECTION A, MINING INDUSTRY / INSTITUTION OF MINING & METALLURGY (UK/0371-7844). **2152**

TRANSAFRICA FORUM (US/0730-8876). **4536**

TRANSFUSION MEDICINE (UK/0958-7578). **3802**

TRANSFUSION MEDICINE REVIEWS (US/0887-7963). **3647**

TRANSFUSION SCIENCE (UK/0955-3886). **3647**

TRANSITION METAL CHEMISTRY (UK/0340-4285). **4022**

TRANSLATIONS - AMERICAN MATHEMATICAL SOCIETY (US/0065-9290). **3539**

TRANSLATIONS OF MATHEMATICAL MONOGRAPHS (US/0065-9282). **3539**

TRANSMISSION & DISTRIBUTION (US/0041-1280). **2085**

TRANSMITTERS RECEPTORS & SYNAPSES (UK/0143-4241). **4331**

TRANSNATIONAL ASSOCIATIONS (BE/0020-6059). **4691**

TRANSPLANT INTERNATIONAL (GW/0934-0874). **3976**

TRANSPLANTATION (US/0041-1337). **3647**

TRANSPLANTATION PROCEEDINGS (US/0041-1345). **3977**

TRANSPLANTATION REVIEWS (ORLANDO, FLA.) (US/0955-470X). **3977**

TRANSPORT IN POROUS MEDIA (NE/0169-3913). **994**

TRANSPORT REVIEWS (UK/0144-1647). **5396**

TRANSPORT THEORY AND STATISTICAL PHYSICS (US/0041-1450). **4430**

TRANSPORT TOPICS (US/0041-1558). **5396**

TRANSPORTATION & DISTRIBUTION (US/0895-8548). **5457**

TRANSPORTATION (DORDRECHT) (NE/0049-4488). **5396**

TRANSPORTATION PLANNING AND TECHNOLOGY (US/0308-1060). **5396**

TRANSPORTATION RESEARCH. PART B : METHODOLOGICAL (UK/0191-2615). **5397**

TRANSPORTATION RESEARCH. PART C, EMERGING TECHNOLOGIES (US/0968-090X). **5397**

TRANSPORTATION SCIENCE (US/0041-1655). **5397**

TRANSPORTS (FR/0564-1373). **5397**

TRAUMA QUARTERLY (US/0743-6637). **3977**

TRAVAIL HUMAIN, LE (FR/0041-1868). **4620**

TRAVAUX (FR/0041-1906). **1999**

TRAVAUX D'HISTOIRE ETHICO-POLITIQUE (SZ/0082-6073). **2632**

TRAVAUX D'HUMANISME ET RENAISSANCE (SZ/0082-6081). **2713**

TRAVEL & TOURISM ANALYST (UK/0269-3755). **5495**

TRAVEL EXPENSE MANAGEMENT (US/0272-569X). **5495**

TRAVELNEWS ASIA (HK/0252-9629). **5497**

TRAVELORE REPORT, THE (US/0270-2398). **5497**

TRAVELWRITER MARKETLETTER (US/0738-9094). **2925**

TREASURY MANAGER, THE (US/0896-2987). **888**

TREE PHYSIOLOGY (CN/0829-318X). **2397**

TREES (BERLIN, WEST) (GW/0931-1890). **2397**

TRENDS IN BIOCHEMICAL SCIENCES (AMSTERDAM. REFERENCE EDITION) (NE/0376-5067). **493**

TRENDS IN BIOTECHNOLOGY (PERSONAL EDITION) (NE/0167-7799). **3697**

TRENDS IN BIOTECHNOLOGY (REFERENCE ED.) (NE/0167-9430). **3697**

TRENDS IN CARDIOVASCULAR MEDICINE (US/1050-1738). **3711**

TRENDS IN ECOLOGY & EVOLUTION (AMSTERDAM) (UK/0169-5347). **2221**

TRENDS IN ENDOCRINOLOGY AND METABOLISM (US/1043-2760). **3733**

TRENDS IN FOOD SCIENCE & TECHNOLOGY (UK/0924-2244). **2360**

TRENDS IN GENETICS (LIBRARY ED.) (NE/0168-9479). **552**

TRENDS IN MICROBIOLOGY (REGULAR ED.) (UK/0966-842X). **570**

TRENDS IN NEUROSCIENCES (REFERENCE ED.) (UK/0378-5912). **3847**

TRENDS IN NEUROSCIENCES (REGULAR ED.) (NE/0166-2236). **3847**

TRENDS IN PHARMACOLOGICAL SCIENCES (REGULAR ED.) (UK/0165-6147). **4331**

TRENDS IN POLYMER SCIENCE REGULAR ED (UK/0966-4793). **994**

TRENIE I IZNOS (US/0733-1924). **2108**

TRIAL (US/0041-2538). **3066**

TRIBOLOGIE UND SCHMIERUNGSTECHNIK (GW/0724-3472). **1048**

TRIBOLOGY AND CORROSION ABSTRACTS (UK/0962-7189). **2017**

TRIBOLOGY INTERNATIONAL (UK/0301-679X). **2108**

TRIBOLOGY TRANSACTIONS (US/1040-2004). **2000**

TROPICAL AGRICULTURE (UK/0041-3216). **142**

TROPICAL DOCTOR (UK/0049-4755). **3987**

TROPICAL MEDICINE AND PARASITOLOGY (GW/0177-2392). **3987**

TROPICAL PEST MANAGEMENT (UK/0143-6147). **4248**

TROPICAL SCIENCE (UK/0041-3291). **142**

TROUT AND SALMON (UK/0041-3372). **2315**

TRUDY INSTITUTA GEOLOGII I GEOFIZIKI (NOVOSIBIRSK) (RU/0568-658X). **1400**

TRUDY ORDENA LENINA MATEMATICHESKOGO INSTITUTA IMENI V. A. STEKLOVA (US/0081-5438). **3539**

TRUSTS & ESTATES (US/0041-3682). **3119**

TSITOLOGIIA (RU/0041-3771). **540**

TSVETNYE METALLY (ENGLISH TRANSLATION ED.) (US/0038-5484). **4023**

TTT, INTERDISCIPLINAIR TIJDSCHRIFT VOOR TAAL- & TEKSTWETENSCHAP (NE/0167-4773). **3330**

TU (GW/0376-1185). **5523**

TUATARA (NZ/0041-3860). **475**

TUBERCLE AND LUNG DISEASE : THE OFFICIAL JOURNAL OF THE INTERNATIONAL UNION AGAINST TUBERCULOSIS AND LUNG DISEASE (UK/0962-8479). **3952**

TUMOR BIOLOGY (SZ/1010-4283). **3824**

TUMORDIAGNOSTIK & THERAPIE (GW/0722-219X). **3824**

TUNNELLING AND UNDERGROUND SPACE TECHNOLOGY (UK/0886-7798). **2033**

TURKEY WORLD (1968) (US/0041-4271). **223**

TURNBULL LIBRARY RECORD, THE (NZ/0110-1625). **3254**

TURNER STUDIES (UK/0260-597X). **367**

TWICE (US/0892-7278). **2085**

TYNDALE BULLETIN (1966) (UK/0082-7118). **5006**

TZ FUER METALLBEARBEITUNG (GW/0170-9577). **4023**

U.S.A. OIL INDUSTRY DIRECTORY (US/0082-8599). **4281**

U.S. FOAMED PLASTICS MARKETS & DIRECTORY (US/0083-0968). **4460**

U.S. INDUSTRIAL DIRECTORY (US/0095-7046). **1630**

U.S. OIL WEEK (US/0502-9767). **4281**

U.S. RAIL NEWS (US/0275-3758). **5437**

UGOL (RU/0041-5790). **2152**

UK VENTURE CAPITAL JOURNAL (UK/0265-8364). **815**

UKRAINIAN BIOCHEMISTRY (US/1055-7954). **494**

UKRAINIAN CHEMISTRY JOURNAL (US/1063-4568). **994**

UKRAINIAN MATHEMATICAL JOURNAL (US/0041-5995). **3540**

UKRAINSKII BIOKHIMICHESKII ZHURNAL (UN/0201-8470). **494**

UKRAINSKIJ FIZICESKIJ ZURNAL (KIEV, 1967) (UN/0503-1265). **4424**

UKRAINSKIJ HIMICESKIJ ZURNAL (UN/0041-6045). **995**

ULRICH'S INTERNATIONAL PERIODICALS DIRECTORY (US/0000-0175). **3254**

ULRICH'S UPDATE (US/0000-1074). **3254**

ULTRAMICROSCOPY (NE/0304-3991). **574**

ULTRASCHALL IN DER MEDIZIN (GW/0172-4614). **3648**

ULTRASCHALL IN KLINIK UND PRAXIS (GW/0930-8040). **3648**

ULTRASONIC IMAGING (US/0161-7346). **3802**

ULTRASONICS (UK/0041-624X). **4424**

ULTRASOUND IN MEDICINE & BIOLOGY (US/0301-5629). **3648**

ULTRASOUND QUARTERLY (US/0894-8771). **3648**

ULTRASTRUCTURAL PATHOLOGY (US/0191-3123). **3898**

UMSATZSTEUER-RUNDSCHAU (COLOGNE, GERMANY : 1986) (GW/0341-8669). **3067**

UMWELT (DUSSELDORF) (GW/0041-6355). **2245**

UNDERCURRENT (NEW YORK) (US/0192-0871). **4927**

UNDERGROUND STORAGE TANK GUIDE (US/1055-4246). **1929**

UNFALLCHIRURG, DER (GW/0177-5537). **3725**

UNFALLCHIRURGIE (GW/0340-2649). **3977**

UNIFORM COMMERCIAL CODE LAW JOURNAL (US/0041-672X). **3104**

UNIFORM COMMERCIAL CODE LAW LETTER, THE (US/0503-1966). **3067**

UNION LABOR REPORT (US/0091-5459). **3155**

UNION LABOR REPORT WEEKLY NEWSLETTER (US/0190-5260). **3155**

UNITAS FRATRUM (US/0344-9254). **5068**

UNITED STATES BANKER (COS COB) (US/0148-8848). **815**

UNITED STATES LAW WEEK, THE (US/0148-8139). **3068**

UNITED STATES PATENTS QUARTERLY, THE (US/0041-803X). **1309**

UNIVERSITAS (STUTTGART) (GW/0041-9079). **2856**

UNIVERSITY COMPUTING : THE BULLETIN OF THE IUCC (UK/0265-4385). **1852**

UNIVERSITY OF CALIFORNIA, BERKELEY, WELLNESS LETTER (US/0748-9234). **4806**

UNIVERSITY OF TORONTO FACULTY OF LAW REVIEW (CN/0381-1638). **3069**

UNIVERSITY OF TORONTO LAW JOURNAL, THE (CN/0042-0220). **3069**

UNIVERSITY OF TORONTO QUARTERLY (CN/0042-0247). **2856**

UNIVERSITY PUBLISHING (US/0191-4146). **4833**

UNIX/MAIL (GW/0176-8654). **1206**

UNIX REVIEW (US/0742-3136). **1239**

UNIX TODAY! (US/1040-5038). **1206**

UNTERNEHMUNG (SZ/0042-059X). **889**

UNTERRICHTSWISSENSCHAFT (GW/0340-4099). **1789**

UPDATE - INTERNATIONAL COUNCIL FOR COMPUTERS IN EDUCATION (U.S.) (US/1040-4694). **1225**

UPHOLSTERY DESIGN & MANUFACTURING (US/1056-2052). **3489**

URBAN ACADEMIC LIBRARIAN (US/0276-9298). **3255**

URBAN AFFAIRS QUARTERLY (US/0042-0816). **2837**

URBAN EDUCATION (BEVERLY HILLS, CALIF.) (US/0042-0859). **1789**

URBAN GEOGRAPHY (US/0272-3638). **2578**

URBAN LEAGUE REVIEW, THE (US/0147-1740). **2274**

URBAN REVIEW, THE (US/0042-0972). **1789**

URBAN TRANSPORT NEWS (US/0195-4695). **5399**

URETHANE ABSTRACTS (US/0149-1342). **4460**

URETHANE PLASTICS AND PRODUCTS (US/0049-5700). **5168**

URGENCES MEDICALES (PARIS) (FR/0923-2524). **3649**

UROLOGE. AUSG. A, DER (GW/0340-2592). **3993**

UROLOGE. AUSGABE B (GW/0042-1111). **3993**

UROLOGIA INTERNATIONALIS (SZ/0042-1138). **3993**

UROLOGIC CLINICS OF NORTH AMERICA, THE (US/0094-0143). **3993**

UROLOGIC NURSING (US/1053-816X). **3870**

UROLOGIC RADIOLOGY (US/0171-1091). **3994**

UROLOGICAL RESEARCH (GW/0300-5623). **3994**

UROLOGY ANNUAL (US/0889-6283). **3994**

UROLOGY TIMES (US/0093-9722). **3994**

USER MODELING AND USER-ADAPTED INTERACTION (NE/0924-1868). **1206**

USPEHI FIZICESKIH NAUK (RU/0042-1294). **4424**

USPEHI MATEMATICESKIH NAUK (RU/0042-1316). **3540**

USPEKHI KHIMII (RU/0042-1308). **995**

USSR TECHNOLOGY UPDATE (US/0892-497X). **5168**

UTILITAS (UK/0953-8208). **2253**

UTILITAS MATHEMATICA (CN/0315-3681). **3540**

UTILITY REPORTER (SCHENECTADY, N.Y.) (US/0890-2984). **4762**

UTILITY SPOTLIGHT (US/1065-6480). **1525**

VACCINE (UK/0264-410X). **3649**

VACUUM (UK/0042-207X). **4430**

VAKUUM IN DER PRAXIS (GW/0934-9758). **4424**

VARIETY (US/0042-2738). **4079**

VASA (SZ/0301-1526). **3802**

VASA. SUPPLEMENTUM (SZ/0251-1029). **3802**

VASCULAR MEDICINE REVIEW (UK/0954-2582). **3802**

VASCULAR SURGERY (US/0042-2835). **3977**

VDI-BERICHTE (GW/0083-5560). **2000**

VDI-FORSHUNGSHEFT (GW/0042-174X). **2000**

VDI NACHRICHTEN (GW/0042-1758). **5168**

VDI-Z (GW/0042-1766). **2131**

VEGETATIO (NE/0042-3106). **529**

VEGETATION HISTORY AND ARCHAEOBOTANY (GW/0939-6314). **529**

VEHICLE SYSTEM DYNAMICS (NE/0042-3114). **2131**

VERFASSUNG UND RECHT IN UBERSEE (GW/0506-7286). **3094**

VERHANDLUNGEN DER DEUTSCHEN GESELLSCHAFT FUER INNERE MEDIZIN (GW/0070-4067). **3802**

VERHANDLUNGEN DER DEUTSCHEN GESELLSCHAFT FUER PATHOLOGIE (GW/0070-4113). **3898**

VERHANDLUNGEN DER DEUTSCHEN GESELLSCHAFT FUER RHEUMATOLOGIE (GW/0070-4121). **3807**

VERHANDLUNGEN - INTERNATIONALE VEREINIGUNG FUER THEORETISCHE UND ANGEWANDTE LIMNOLOGIE (GW/0368-0770). **1418**

VERHANGLUNGEN DER DEUTSCHEN ZOOLOGISCHEN GESELLSCHAFT (GW/0070-4342). **5599**

VERITABLE AMIE (CN/0831-0866). **5567**

VERKUNDIGUNG UND FORSCHUNG (GW/0342-2410). **5007**

VEROEFFENTLICHUNGEN AUS DER PATHOLOGIE (GW/0340-241X). **3898**

VERWALTUNG (BERLIN), DIE (GW/0042-4498). **4693**

VERWALTUNGSRUNDSCHAU (GW/0342-5592). **889**

VESTNIK AKADEMII MEDITSINSKIKH NAUK SSSR (RU/0002-3027). **3649**

VESTNIK AKADEMII NAUK SSSR (RU/0002-3442). **5168**

VESTNIK DERMATOLOGII I VENEROLOGII (RU/0042-4609). **3723**

VESTNIK DREVNEJ ISTORII (RU/0321-0391). **2632**

VESTNIK LENINGRADSKOGO UNIVERSITETA. MATEMATIKA, MEKHANIKA, ASTRONOMIIA (US/0883-623X). **2131**

VESTNIK MASINOSTROENIJA (RU/0042-4633). **2152**

VESTNIK MOSKOVSKOGO UNIVERSITETA SERIIA I, MATEMATIKA, MEKHANIKA (RU/0579-9368). **3540**

VESTNIK MOSKOVSKOGO UNIVERSITETA. SERIIA III, FIZIKA, ASTRONOMIIA (RU/0579-9392). **4424**

VESTNIK MOSKOVSKOGO UNIVERSITETA. SERIIA XV, VYCHISLITELNAIA MATEMATIKA I KIBERNETIKA. ENGLISH (US/0278-6419). **1252**

VESTNIK ST. PETERSBURG UNIVERSITY: MATHEMATICS (US/1063-4541). **3540**

VETERINARY AND COMPARATIVE ORTHOPAEDICS AND TRAUMATOLOGY (GW/0932-0814). **5524**

VETERINARY CLINICS OF NORTH AMERICA. EQUINE PRACTICE, THE (US/0749-0739). **5525**

VETERINARY CLINICS OF NORTH AMERICA. FOOD ANIMAL PRACTICE, THE (US/0749-0720). **5525**

VETERINARY CLINICS OF NORTH AMERICA. SMALL ANIMAL PRACTICE, THE (US/0195-5616). **5525**

VETERINARY DERMATOLOGY (UK/0959-4493). **5525**

VETERINARY IMMUNOLOGY AND IMMUNOPATHOLOGY (NE/0165-2427). **5525**

VETERINARY MEDICINE (1985) (US/8750-7943). **5526**

VETERINARY MEDICINE REPORT (US/0895-7703). **5526**

VETERINARY MICROBIOLOGY (NE/0378-1135). **5526**

VETERINARY PARASITOLOGY (NE/0304-4017). **5526**

VETERINARY QUARTERLY, THE (NE/0165-2176). **5526**

VETERINARY RECORD (UK/0042-4900). **5526**

VETERINARY RESEARCH COMMUNICATIONS (NE/0165-7380). **5527**

VETERINARY SURGERY (US/0161-3499). **5527**

VETUS TESTAMENTUM (NE/0042-4935). **5020**

VIATOR (BERKELEY) (US/0083-5897). **1080**

VICTIMOLOGY (US/0361-5170). **3178**

VIDEO JOURNAL OF COLOR FLOW IMAGING (US/1052-2182). **3947**

VIDEO JOURNAL OF ECHOCARDIOGRAPHY (US/1052-2174). **3711**

VIDEO MARKETING SURVEYS AND FORECASTS (US/0740-4247). **2085**

VIDEO MONITOR (SILVER SPRING, MD.) (US/0888-9538). **1168**

VIDEO SERVICES NEWS / PHILLIPS BUSINESS INFORMATION, INC (US/1067-3849). **4377**

VIDEO SYSTEMS (US/0361-0942). **1142**

VIDEO TECHNOLOGY NEWSLETTER (US/1040-2772). **4378**

VIDEO WEEK (US/0196-5905). **1142**

VIDEONEWS INTERNATIONAL (HOLLYWOOD, CALIF.) (US/1044-6354). **1143**

VIDEOTEX PARIS (FR/0247-4352). **1235**

VIERTELJAHRSCHRIFT FUER SOZIAL- UND WIRTSCHAFTSGESCHICHTE (GW/0042-5699). **1588**

VIERTELJAHRSHEFTE FUER ZEITGESCHICHTE (GW/0042-5702). **2632**

VIGILIAE CHRISTIANAE (NE/0042-6032). **3451**

VINGTIEME SIECLE (PARIS, FRANCE : 1984) (FR/0294-1759). **2632**

VIOLENCE AND VICTIMS (US/0886-6708). **3178**

VIRCHOWS ARCHIV. A, PATHOLOGICAL ANATOMY AND HISTOPATHOLOGY (GW/0174-7398). **3898**

VIRCHOWS ARCHIV. B, CELL PATHOLOGY (GW/0340-6075). **3898**

VIROLOGY (NEW YORK, N.Y.) (US/0042-6822). **570**

VIRTUAL REALITY REPORT (US/1052-6242). **1283**

VIRUS BULLETIN (UK/0956-9979). **1227**

VIRUS GENES (US/0920-8569). **571**

VIRUS RESEARCH (NE/0168-1702). **571**

VISIBLE LANGUAGE (US/0022-2224). **4570**

VISIBLE RELIGION / INSTITUTE OF RELIGIOUS INCONOGRAPHY, STATE UNIVERSITY GRONINGEN (NE/0169-5606). **5008**

VISION (UK/0142-8543). **1143**

VISION RESEARCH (OXFORD) (UK/0042-6989). **3879**

VISTAS IN ASTRONOMY (UK/0083-6656). **401**

VISUAL ANTHROPOLOGY (JOURNAL) (UK/0894-9468). **247**

VISUAL COMPUTER, THE (GW/0178-2789). **1235**

VISUAL MERCHANDISING & STORE DESIGN (US/0745-4295). **958**

VISUAL RESOURCES (US/0197-3762). **368**

VITAMINS AND HORMONES; ADVANCES IN RESEARCH AND APPLICATIONS (US/0083-6729). **3733**

VIVARIUM (NE/0042-7543). **4364**

VNITRNI LEKARSTVI (XR/0042-773X). **3802**

VOCATIONAL TRAINING NEWS (US/0047-5785). **1917**

VODNYE RESURSY (RU/0321-0596). **5541**

VOGELWELT, DIE (GW/0042-7993). **5620**

VOICE PROCESSING MAGAZINE (US/1042-0460). **1206**

VOICE TECHNOLOGY NEWS (US/1045-1498). **2131**

VOICES (AMERICAN ACADEMY OF PSYCHOTHERAPISTS) (US/0042-8272). **3937**

VOLTA REVIEW, THE (US/0042-8639). **4395**

VOM WASSER (GW/0083-6915). **5541**

VOPROSY FILOSOFII (RU/0042-8744). **4364**

VOPROSY IAZYKOZNANIIA (RU/0373-658X). **3332**

VOPROSY IKHTIOLOGII (RU/0042-8752). **2315**

VOPROSY ISTORII (RU/0042-8779). **2633**

VOPROSY MEDICINSKOJ HIMII (RU/0042-8809). **494**

VOPROSY ONKOLOGIJ (RU/0507-3758). **3825**

VOPROSY PITANIIA (RU/0042-8833). **4200**

VOPROSY PSIHOLOGII (RU/0042-8841). **4621**

VOPROSY VIRUSOLOGII (US/0734-0311). **571**

VOPROSY VIRUSOLOGII (RU/0507-4088). **571**

VOX EVANGELICA (UK/0263-6786). **5008**

VOX ROMANICA (SZ/0042-899X). **3332**

VOX SANGUINIS (SZ/0042-9007). **3774**

VR. VERMESSUNGSWESEN UND RAUMORDNUNG (GW/0340-5141). **2579**

VTB. VERFAHRENSTECHNISCHE BERICHTE (GW/0042-3890). **2001**

VULKANOLOGIIA I SEISMOLOGIA (US/0742-0463). **1412**

VYSOKOMOLEKULARNYE SOEDINENA. SERIA A (RU/0507-5475). **995**

WAGES AND HOURS (US/0149-2691). **1717**

WALL STREET & TECHNOLOGY (US/1060-989X). **919**

WALL STREET COMPUTER REVIEW (US/0738-4343). **919**

WALL STREET JOURNAL. EASTERN EDITION, THE (US/0099-9660). **5690**

WALL STREET JOURNAL. SOUTHWEST EDITION, THE (US/0193-225X). **816**

WALL STREET JOURNAL. WESTERN EDITION, THE (US/0193-2241). **5690**

WALLS & CEILINGS (US/0043-0161). **631**

WANT'S FEDERAL-STATE COURT DIRECTORY (US/0742-1095). **3143**

WARD'S AUTO WORLD (US/0043-0315). **5428**

WARD'S AUTOMOTIVE YEARBOOK (US/0083-7229). **5428**

WARME- UND STOFFUBERTRAGUNG (GW/0042-9929). **2131**

WARMETECHNIK (GW/0720-3438). **2608**

WARNING LETTER BULLETIN (US/1069-4218). **4332**

WARREN'S CABLE REGULATION MONITOR (US/1067-6252). **1168**

WASHINGTON CREDIT LETTER (US/0742-2008). **816**

WASHINGTON, D.C. MINI-MICRO COMPUTER REPORT, THE (US/0363-7905). **1273**

WASHINGTON DRUG LETTER (WASHINGTON. 1979) (US/0194-1291). **4332**

WASHINGTON QUARTERLY, THE (US/0163-660X). **4538**

WASHINGTON TELECOM NEWS (US/1069-7500). **1168**

WASSER, LUFT UND BODEN : WLB (GW/0341-2679). **2245**

WASSER UND BODEN (GW/0043-0951). **145**

WASSERWIRTSCHAFT (GW/0043-0978). **5541**

WASTE INFORMATION DIGESTS (US/1050-3153). **2246**

WASTE MANAGEMENT & RESEARCH (UK/0734-242X). **2246**

WASTE MANAGEMENT (ELMSFORD) (US/0956-053X). **2246**

WASTE TREATMENT TECHNOLOGY NEWS (US/0885-0003). **2246**

WATER, AIR, AND SOIL POLLUTION (NE/0049-6979). **2247**

WATER AND WASTES DIGEST (US/0043-1141). **5542**

WATER ENGINEERING & MANAGEMENT (US/0273-2238). **2096**

WATER ENVIRONMENT & TECHNOLOGY (US/1044-9493). **2247**

WATER NEWSLETTER (US/0043-1273). **5543**

WATER POLLUTION RESEARCH JOURNAL OF CANADA (CN/0197-9140). **2247**

WATER QUALITY INTERNATIONAL (UK/0892-211X). **2247**

WATER RESEARCH (OXFORD) (UK/0043-1354). **5543**

WATER RESOURCES (US/0097-8078). **1419**

WATER RESOURCES MANAGEMENT (DORDRECHT, NETHERLANDS) (NE/0920-4741). **5547**

WATER RESOURCES MONOGRAPH (US/0270-9600). **5547**

WATER RESOURCES RESEARCH (US/0043-1397). **5547**

WATER SCIENCE AND TECHNOLOGY (UK/0273-1223). **5548**

WATER SCIENCE REVIEWS (UK/0266-4615). **1038**

WATER SUPPLY (UK/0735-1917). **5548**

WATER TECHNOLOGY (US/0192-3633). **5548**

WATER TREATMENT (CC/0921-2639). **5548**

WATER WELL JOURNAL (US/0043-1443). **5548**

WATERWORLD NEWS (US/0747-9735). **2248**

WAVE MOTION (NE/0165-2125). **3541**

WEAR (SZ/0043-1648). **2132**

WEAR OF MATERIALS (US/0192-4990). **2132**

WEATHER AND FORECASTING (US/0882-8156). **1436**

WEATHERWISE (US/0043-1672). **1436**

WEED CONTROL MANUAL (US/0741-9856). **2433**

WEED RESEARCH (UK/0043-1737). **530**

WEEKLY PHARMACY REPORTS (US/0043-1893). **4332**

WEGE ZUM MENSCHEN (GW/0043-2040). **5008**

WEHRMEDIZINISCHE MONATSSCHRIFT (GW/0043-2156). **3650**

WEINWIRTSCHAFT. MARKT, DIE (GW/0723-1350). **2372**

WEINWIRTSCHAFT. TECHNIK, DIE (GW/0723-1369). **2372**

WELDING DESIGN & FABRICATION (US/0043-2253). **4028**

WELDING DISTRIBUTOR (1966) (US/0192-7671). **938**

WELDING IN THE WORLD (UK/0043-2288). **4028**

WELDING JOURNAL (US/0043-2296). **4028**

WELT DER SLAVEN (GW/0043-2520). **3332**

WELT DES ISLAMS, DIE (NE/0043-2539). **5045**

WELT DES ORIENTS, DIE (GW/0043-2547). **3332**

WELTWIRTSCHAFT (TUBINGEN), DIE (GW/0043-2652). **1588**

WELTWIRTSCHAFTLICHES ARCHIV (GW/0043-2636). **5225**

WERBEN UND VERKAUFEN : W & V (GW/0042-9538). **938**

WERKSTATT UND BETRIEB (GW/0043-2792). **2132**

WERKSTOFFE UND KORROSION (GW/0043-2822). **4023**

WESTERLY (AT/0043-342X). **3452**

WESTERN FRUIT GROWER (US/0164-6001). **146**

WESTERN JOURNAL OF MEDICINE, THE (US/0093-0415). **3650**

WESTERN JOURNAL OF NURSING RESEARCH (US/0193-9459). **3871**

WESTERN OIL WORLD (US/0884-7592). **4282**

WESTMINSTER STUDIES IN EDUCATION (UK/0140-6728). **1791**

WHAT EVERY ENGINEER SHOULD KNOW (US/0892-4015). **2001**

WHAT'S NEW IN FOREST RESEARCH (NZ/0110-1048). **2398**

WHICH COMPUTER? (UK/0140-3435). **1207**

WHO WAS WHO IN AMERICA (US/0146-8081). **435**

WHOLE EARTH REVIEW (US/0749-5056). **2495**

WHOLESALER (ELMHURST), THE (US/0032-1680). **2609**

WHO'S WHO IN AMERICA (US/0083-9396). **436**

WHO'S WHO IN AMERICAN ART (US/0000-0191). **335**

WHO'S WHO IN AMERICAN LAW (US/0162-7880). **3075**

WHO'S WHO IN AMERICAN POLITICS (US/0000-0205). **436**

WHO'S WHO IN FINANCE AND INDUSTRY (US/0083-9523). **720**

WHO'S WHO IN THE EAST (US/0083-9760). **438**

WHO'S WHO IN THE WORLD (US/0083-9825). **438**

WHO'S WHO IN TRAINING AND DEVELOPMENT (US/0092-4598). **438**

WHO'S WHO (LONDON. 1849) (UK/0083-937X). **438**

WHO'S WHO OF AMERICAN WOMEN (US/0083-9841). **438**

WIDE ANGLE (US/0160-6840). **4080**

WIENER KLINISCHE WOCHENSCHRIFT (AU/0043-5325). **3651**

WILD EARTH (US/1055-1166). **2183**

WILEY SERIES IN PURE AND APPLIED OPTICS (US/0277-2493). **4442**

WILEY SERIES ON PERSONALITY PROCESSES (US/0195-4008). **4621**

WILSON LIBRARY BULLETIN (US/0043-5651). **3256**

WIND ENERGY ABSTRACTS (US/0277-2140). **1960**

WIND ENERGY REPORT (US/0162-8623). **1960**

WIND ENGINEERING (UK/0309-524X). **1437**

WIND ENGINEERING ABSTRACTS (UK/0263-0915). **2001**

WINDOWS USER (US/1065-3481). **1207**

WINTERTHUR PORTFOLIO (US/0084-0416). **368**

WIRE (GW/0043-5996). **4023**

WIRE JOURNAL INTERNATIONAL (US/0277-4275). **4023**

WIRE WORLD INTERNATIONAL (GW/0043-6046). **2086**

WIRELESS DATA NEWS (US/1069-3416). **1124**

WIREWORLD (GW/0934-5906). **2001**

WIRKENDES WORT (ZEITSCHRIFT) (GW/0043-6089). **3333**

WIRTSCHAFT UND ERZIEHUNG (GW/0174-6170). **1791**

WIRTSCHAFT UND STATISTIK (GW/0043-6143). **5346**

WIRTSCHAFT UND WETTBEWERB (GW/0043-6151). **857**

WIRTSCHAFTSDIENST (HAMBURG) (GW/0043-6275). **1526**

WIRTSCHAFTSEIGENE FUTTER (GW/0049-7711). **224**

WIRTSCHAFTSPRUFUNG, DIE (GW/0043-6313). **753**

WIRTSCHAFTSRECHTLICHE BLAETTER : WBL (AU/0930-3855). **3104**

WISCONSIN LAW REVIEW (US/0043-650X). **3075**

WISTAR SYMPOSIUM SERIES (US/0271-9347). **587**

WOCHENBERICHT - DEUTSCHES INSTITUT FUER WIRTSCHAFTSFORSCHUNG (GW/0012-1304). **1589**

WOHNRECHTLICHE BLAETTER (AU/0933-2766). **3076**

WOLFENBUTTELER RENAISSANCE MITTEILUNGEN (GW/0342-4340). **2716**

WOMAN POET (US/0195-6183). **3473**

WOMAN'S JOURNAL (UK/0043-7344). **5569**

WOMEN (UK/0957-4042). **5569**

WOMEN STUDIES ABSTRACTS (US/0049-7835). **5572**

WOMEN'S HEALTH ISSUES (US/1049-3867). **5571**

WOMEN'S REVIEW OF BOOKS, THE (US/0738-1433). **3356**

WOMEN'S SPORTS AND FITNESS (US/8750-653X). **4930**

WOMEN'S STUDIES (US/0049-7878). **5571**

WOMEN'S STUDIES INTERNATIONAL FORUM (UK/0277-5395). **5571**

WOOD & WOOD PRODUCTS (US/0043-7662). **2406**

WOOD SCIENCE AND TECHNOLOGY (US/0043-7719). **2406**

WORD & IMAGE (LONDON. 1985) (UK/0266-6286). **1124**

WORK : A JOURNAL OF PREVENTION, ASSESSMENT, AND REHABILITATION (US/1051-9815). **4808**

WORK AND OCCUPATIONS (US/0730-8884). **4210**

WORK AND PEOPLE (AT/0312-455X). **948**

WORK AND STRESS (UK/0267-8373). **4621**

WORKERS' COMP ADVISOR (CALIFORNIA ED.) (US/1054-7819). **2896**

WORKERS' COMP MANAGED CARE (US/1066-2669). **2896**

WORKER'S COMPENSATION LAW BULLETIN (US/0748-7878). **3155**

WORKFORCE STRATEGIES (US/1062-8991). **948**

WORKING MOTHER (NEW YORK, N.Y. 1981) (US/0278-193X). **2287**

WORKING WOMAN (US/0145-5761). **5572**

WORKLIFE REPORT, THE (CN/0834-292X). **1719**

WORKPLACE TRENDS (US/1047-4447). **948**

WORLD AIRLINE NEWS (US/1059-4183). **40**

WORLD ARBITRATION & MEDIATION REPORT (UK/0960-0949). **3138**

WORLD ARCHAEOLOGY (UK/0043-8243). **285**

WORLD BANKING ABSTRACTS (UK/0265-9484). **816**

WORLD CERAMICS ABSTRACTS (UK/0957-8897). **2595**

WORLD COMPETITION (SZ/1011-4548). **3104**

WORLD DEVELOPMENT (UK/0305-750X). **1641**

WORLD ECONOMY, THE (UK/0378-5920). **1641**

WORLD ENGLISHES (UK/0883-2919). **3334**

WORLD FOOD REGULATION REVIEW (UK/0963-4894). **2361**

WORLD FUTURES (US/0260-4027). **4365**

WORLD INDUSTRIAL REPORTER (US/0043-8561). **4538**

WORLD JOURNAL OF MICROBIOLOGY & BIOTECHNOLOGY (UK/0959-3993). **571**

WORLD JOURNAL OF SURGERY (US/0364-2313). **3977**

WORLD JOURNAL OF UROLOGY (GW/0724-4983). **3994**

WORLD LITERATURE WRITTEN IN ENGLISH (CN/0093-1705). **3356**

WORLD METAL STATISTICS (UK/0043-8758). **4026**

WORLD MINING EQUIPMENT (US/0746-729X). **2153**

WORLD MONITOR (US/0897-9472). **2495**

WORLD OF LEARNING, THE (UK/0084-2117). **1854**

WORLD OIL (HOUSTON, TEX.) (US/0043-8790). **4282**

WORLD OIL TRADE (UK/0950-1029). **4282**

WORLD PATENT INFORMATION (UK/0172-2190). **1309**

WORLD POLITICS (US/0043-8871). **4538**

WORLD PUMPS (UK/0262-1762). **2132**

WORLD REVIEW OF NUTRITION AND DIETETICS (SZ/0084-2230). **4200**

WORLD SURFACE COATINGS ABSTRACTS (UK/0043-9088). **4226**

WORLD TEXTILE ABSTRACTS (UK/0043-9118). **5361**

WORLD TODAY, THE (UK/0043-9134). **4539**

WORLD WASTES (US/1064-8429). **2248**

WORLD WOOD (US/0043-9258). **2406**

WORLDCASTS. PRODUCT (US/0163-6723). **1632**

WORLDCASTS. REGIONAL (US/0163-6731). **1632**

WORLD'S POULTRY SCIENCE JOURNAL (UK/0043-9339). **224**

WORLDWIDE PETROCHEMICAL DIRECTORY (US/0084-2583). **4282**

WORLDWIDE REFINING AND GAS PROCESSING DIRECTORY (1978) (US/0277-0962). **4283**

WOUND REPAIR AND REGENERATION (US/1067-1927). **3651**

WRITTEN COMMUNICATION (US/0741-0883). **1124**

WSI MITTEILUNGEN (GW/0342-300X). **1720**

WT PRODUKTION UND MANAGEMENT (GW/0941-2360). **1632**

WT. WERKSTATTSTECHNIK (GW/0340-4544). **2132**

WWD (US/0149-5380). **1088**

X-RAY SPECTROMETRY (UK/0049-8246). **1020**

XENOBIOTICA (UK/0049-8254). **3984**

YACHTING MONTHLY, THE (UK/0043-9983). **597**

YAD VASHEM STUDIES (IS/0084-3296). **2716**

YAKUGAKU ZASSHI (JA/0031-6903). **4333**

YAKUZAIGAKU (JA/0372-7629). **4333**

YALE JOURNAL OF BIOLOGY AND MEDICINE, THE (US/0044-0086). **3652**

YALE JOURNAL OF CRITICISM, THE (US/0893-5378). **3356**

YALE REVIEW, THE (US/0044-0124). **5226**

YEAR BOOK OF ENDOCRINOLOGY, THE (US/0084-3741). **3733**

YEAR BOOK OF PEDIATRICS, THE (US/0084-3954). **3912**

YEAR-BOOK OF THE ROYAL SOCIETY OF LONDON (UK/0080-4673). **5237**

YEAR IN IMMUNOLOGY, THE (SZ/0256-2308). **3677**

YEARBOOK OF THE UNITED NATIONS (US/0082-8521). **3138**

YEAR'S WORK IN ENGLISH STUDIES (UK/0084-4144). **3455**

YEAST CHICHESTER (WEST SUSSEX) (UK/0749-503X). **1048**

YOUTH & SOCIETY (US/0044-118X). **5265**

YOUTH MARKETS ALERT (US/1041-7516). **938**

YUKAGAKU (JA/0513-398X). **1031**

YUKI GOSEI KAGAKU KYOKAISHI (JA/0037-9980). **1049**

ZAHNARZT JOURNAL (GW/0344-3736). **1337**

ZAIRYO (JA/0514-5163). **2001**

ZEITSCHRIFT DER DEUTSCHEN GEOLOGISCHEN GESELLSCHAFT (GW/0012-0189). **1401**

ZEITSCHRIFT DER DEUTSCHEN MORGENLANDISCHEN GESELLSCHAFT (GW/0341-0137). **3335**

ZEITSCHRIFT DES BERNISCHEN JURISTENVEREINS (SZ/0044-2127). **3077**

ZEITSCHRIFT DES DEUTSCHEN PALASTINA-VEREINS (1953) (GW/0012-1169). **2634**

ZEITSCHRIFT DES DEUTSCHER VEREINS FUER KUNSTWISSENSCHAFT (1963) (GW/0044-2135). **333**

ZEITSCHRIFT FUER ACKER- UND PFLANZENBAU (GW/0931-2250). **148**

ZEITSCHRIFT FUER AGRARGESCHICHTE UND AGRARSOZIOLOGIE (GW/0044-2194). **148**

ZEITSCHRIFT FUER ANGEWANDTE MATHEMATIK UND MECHANIK (GW/0044-2267). **3541**

ZEITSCHRIFT FUER ANGEWANDTE MATHEMATIK UND PHYSIK : ZAMP (SZ/0044-2275). **3541**

ZEITSCHRIFT FUER ANGEWANDTE ZOOLOGIE (GW/0044-2291). **5600**

ZEITSCHRIFT FUER ARABISCHE LINGUISTIK (GW/0170-026X). **3335**

ZEITSCHRIFT FUER ARBEITSWISSENSCHAFT (GW/0340-2444). **1720**

ZEITSCHRIFT FUER ARZTLICHE FORTBILDUNG (GW/0044-2178). **3739**

ZEITSCHRIFT FUER ASSYRIOLOGIE UND VORDERASIATISCHE ARCHAOLOGIE (GW/0084-5299). **286**

ZEITSCHRIFT FUER AUSLAENDISCHES OEFFENTLICHES RECHT UND VOELKERRECHT (GW/0044-2348). **3138**

ZEITSCHRIFT FUER AUSLANDISCHE LANDWIRTSCHAFT (GW/0049-8599). **148**

ZEITSCHRIFT FUER BALKANOLOGIE (GW/0044-2356). **2717**

ZEITSCHRIFT FUER BERUFS- UND WIRTSCHAFTSPADAGOGIK 1980 (GW/0172-2875). **1918**

ZEITSCHRIFT FUER BETRIEBSWIRTSCHAFT (GW/0044-2372). **1632**

ZEITSCHRIFT FUER BEVOELKERUNGSWISSENSCHAFT (GW/0340-2398). **4561**

ZEITSCHRIFT FUER BEWASSERUNGSWIRTSCHAFT (GW/0049-8602). **148**

ZEITSCHRIFT FUER BIBLIOTHEKSWESEN UND BIBLIOGRAPHIE (GW/0044-2380). **3257**

ZEITSCHRIFT FUER DAS GESAMTE FAMILIENRECHT (GW/0044-2410). **3122**

ZEITSCHRIFT FUER DAS GESAMTE HANDELSRECHT UND WIRTSCHAFTSRECHT (GW/0044-2437). **3078**

ZEITSCHRIFT FUER DAS GESAMTE KREDITWESEN (GW/0340-8485). **817**

ZEITSCHRIFT FUER DAS GESAMTE GENOSSENSCHAFTSWESEN (GW/0044-2429). **1544**

ZEITSCHRIFT FUER DEUTSCHE PHILOLOGIE (GW/0044-2496). **3335**

ZEITSCHRIFT FUER DEUTSCHES ALTERTUM UND DEUTSCHE LITERATUR (GW/0044-2518). **3335**

ZEITSCHRIFT FUER DIALEKTOLOGIE UND LINGUISTIK (GW/0044-1449). **3335**

ZEITSCHRIFT FUER DIE ALTTESTAMENTLICHE WISSENSCHAFT (GW/0044-2526). **5020**

ZEITSCHRIFT FUER DIE GESAMTE HYGIENE UND IHRE GRENZGEBIETE (GW/0049-8610). **4809**

ZEITSCHRIFT FUER DIE GESAMTE INNERE MEDIZIN UND IHRE GRENZGEBIETE (GW/0044-2542). **3652**

ZEITSCHRIFT FUER DIE GESAMTE VERSICHERUNGS-WISSENSCHAFT (GW/0044-2585). **2897**

ZEITSCHRIFT FUER DIE NEUTESTAMENTLICHE WISSENSCHAFT UND DIE KUNDE DER ALTEREN KIRCHE (GW/0044-2615). **5011**

ZEITSCHRIFT FUER DIFFERENTIELLE UND DIAGNOSTISCHE PSYCHOLOGIE (SZ/0170-1789). **4622**

ZEITSCHRIFT FUER EISENBAHNWESEN UND VERKEHRSTECHNIK (GW/0373-322X). **5438**

ZEITSCHRIFT FUER ENERGIEWIRTSCHAFT (GW/0343-5377). **1961**

ZEITSCHRIFT FUER ERNAHRUNGSWISSENSCHAFT (GW/0044-264X). **4200**

ZEITSCHRIFT FUER ETHNOLOGIE (GW/0044-2666). **248**

ZEITSCHRIFT FUER EVANGELISCHES KIRCHENRECHT (GW/0044-2690). **5070**

ZEITSCHRIFT FUER FLUGWISSENSCHAFTEN UND WELTRAUMFORSCHUNG (GW/0342-068X). **40**

ZEITSCHRIFT FUER FRANZOSISCHE SPRACHE UND LITERATUR (GW/0044-2747). **3335**

ZEITSCHRIFT FUER GEBURTSHILFE UND PERINATOLOGIE (GW/0300-967X). **3769**

ZEITSCHRIFT FUER GEOMORPHOLOGIE (GW/0372-8854). **1401**

ZEITSCHRIFT FUER GEOMORPHOLOGIE. SUPPLEMENTBAND (GW/0044-2798). **1401**

ZEITSCHRIFT FUER GERONTOLOGIE (GW/0044-281X). **3755**

ZEITSCHRIFT FUER HERZ THORAX UND GEFAESSCHIRURGIE (GW/0930-9225). **3978**

ZEITSCHRIFT FUER HISTORISCHE FORSCHUNG (GW/0340-0174). **2634**

ZEITSCHRIFT FUER JAGDWISSENSCHAFT (GW/0044-2887). **4931**

ZEITSCHRIFT FUER KARDIOLOGIE (GW/0300-5860). **3711**

ZEITSCHRIFT FUER KINDER- UND JUGENDPSYCHIATRIE (SZ/0301-6811). **3937**

ZEITSCHRIFT FUER KIRCHENGESCHICHTE (GW/0044-2925). **5011**

ZEITSCHRIFT FUER KLINISCHE PSYCHOLOGIE, PSYCHOPATHOLOGIE UND PSYCHOTHERAPIE (GW/0723-6557). **4622**

ZEITSCHRIFT FUER KUNSTGESCHICHTE (GW/0044-2992). **369**

ZEITSCHRIFT FUER LARMBEKAMPFUNG (GW/0174-1098). **2248**

ZEITSCHRIFT FUER LEBENSMITTEL-UNTERSUCHUNG UND -FORSCHUNG (GW/0044-3026). **2361**

ZEITSCHRIFT FUER LUFT- UND WELTRAUMRECHT (GW/0340-8329). **3078**

ZEITSCHRIFT FUER LYMPHOLOGIE (GW/0343-8554). **3653**

ZEITSCHRIFT FUER METALLKUNDE (STUTTGART, GERMANY) (GW/0044-3093). **4024**

ZEITSCHRIFT FUER MISSIONSWISSENSCHAFT UND RELIGIONSWISSENSCHAFT (GW/0044-3123). **5011**

ZEITSCHRIFT FUER MORPHOLOGIE UND ANTHROPOLOGIE (GW/0044-314X). **248**

ZEITSCHRIFT FUER NATURFORSCHUNG (GW/0932-0784). **4425**

ZEITSCHRIFT FUER ORTHOPADIE UND IHRE GRENZGEBIETE (GW/0044-3220). **3885**

ZEITSCHRIFT FUER PAEDAGOGIK (GW/0044-3247). **1792**

ZEITSCHRIFT FUER PAPYROLOGIE UND EPIGRAPHIK (GW/0084-5388). **3456**

ZEITSCHRIFT FUER PARLAMENTSFRAGEN (GW/0340-1758). **4695**

ZEITSCHRIFT FUER PFLANZENERHAHRUNG UND BODENKUNDE (GW/0044-3263). **530**

ZEITSCHRIFT FUER PFLANZENKRANKHEITEN UND PFLANZENSCHUTZ (1970) (GW/0340-8159). **531**

ZEITSCHRIFT FUER PHYSIK. B, CONDENSED MATTER (GW/0722-3277). **4425**

ZEITSCHRIFT FUER PHYSIK. C, PARTICLES AND FIELDS (GW/0170-9739). **4425**

ZEITSCHRIFT FUER PHYSIK. D, ATOMS, MOLECULES AND CLUSTERS (GW/0178-7683). **4425**

ZEITSCHRIFT FUER PHYSIKALISCHE CHEMIE (NEUE FOLGE) (GW/0044-3336). **1059**

ZEITSCHRIFT FUER PHYTOTHERAPIE (GW/0722-348X). **531**

ZEITSCHRIFT FUER PLANUNG : ZP (GW/0936-8787). **890**

ZEITSCHRIFT FUER PSYCHOSOMATISCHE MEDIZIN UND PSYCHOANALYSE (GW/0340-5613). **3653**

ZEITSCHRIFT FUER RECHTSSOZIOLOGIE (GW/0174-0202). **5265**

ZEITSCHRIFT FUER RELIGIONS- UND GEISTESGESCHICHTE (GW/0044-3441). **5011**

ZEITSCHRIFT FUER RHEUMATOLOGIE (GW/0340-1855). **3807**

ZEITSCHRIFT FUER ROMANISCHE PHILOLOGIE (GW/0049-8661). **3335**

ZEITSCHRIFT FUER SAUGETIERKUNDE (GW/0044-3468). **476**

ZEITSCHRIFT FUER SOZIALISATIONSFORSCHUNG UND ERZIEHUNGSSOZIOLOGIE (GW/0720-4361). **5265**

ZEITSCHRIFT FUER SOZIOLOGIE (GW/0340-1804). **5265**

ZEITSCHRIFT FUER SPRACHWISSENSCHAFT : ORGAN DER DEUTSCHEN GESELLSCHAFT FUER SPRACHWISSENSCHAFT (GW/0721-9067). **3335**

ZEITSCHRIFT FUER STOMATOLOGIE (AU/0175-7784). **3716**

ZEITSCHRIFT FUER THEOLOGIE UND KIRCHE (GW/0044-3549). **5011**

ZEITSCHRIFT FUER UNTERNEHMENSGESCHICHTE (GW/0342-2852). **725**

ZEITSCHRIFT FUER VERGLEICHENDE RECHTSWISSENSCHAFT (GW/0044-3638). **3138**

ZEITSCHRIFT FUER VERMESSUNGSWESEN. ZFV (GW/0340-4560). **2034**

ZEITSCHRIFT FUER VOLKSKUNDE (GW/0044-3700). **2325**

ZEITSCHRIFT FUER WASSER- UND ABWASSER FORSCHUNG (GW/0044-3727). **1419**

ZEITSCHRIFT FUER WIRTSCHAFTS- UND SOZIALWISSENSCHAFTEN (GW/0342-1783). **1528**

ZEITSCHRIFT FUER ZOOLOGISCHE SYSTEMATIK UND EVOLUTIONSFORSCHUNG (GW/0044-3808). **5600**

ZEITSCHRIFT FUR NATURFORSCHUNG (GW/0932-0776). **996**

ZEITSCHRIFT FUR TIERZUCHTUNG UND ZUCHTUNGSBIOLOGIE (HAMBURG, GERMANY : 1939) (GW/0044-3581). **224**

ZEITSCHRIFT INTERNE REVISION (GW/0044-3816). **725**

ZEITUNGS-INDEX (GW/0340-0107). **5802**

ZEITWENDE (GW/0341-7166). **3356**

ZENTRALBLATT FUER HYGIENE UND UMWELTMEDIZIN (GW/0934-8859). **4809**

ZENTRALBLATT FUER MATHEMATIK UND IHRE GRENZGEBIETE (GW/0044-4235). **3543**

ZENTRALBLATT FUER MIKROBIOLOGIE (GW/0232-4393). **571**

ZENTRALBLATT FUER PHARMAZIE, PHARMAKOTHERAPIE UND LABORATORIUMSDIAGNOSTIK (SZ/0049-8696). **4333**

ZENTRALBLATT HALS- NASEN- OHRENHEILKUNDE, PLASTISCHE CHIRURGIE AN KOPF UND HALS (GW/0340-5214). **3978**

ZENTRALBLATT HAUT- UND GESCHLECHTSKRANKHEITEN (GW/0343-3048). **3723**

ZENTRALBLATT KINDERHEILKUNDE (GW/0722-8953). **3912**

ZENTRALBLATT NEUROLOGIE, PSYCHIATRIE (GW/0722-3064). **3847**

ZENTRALBLATT OPHTHALMOLOGIE (GW/0722-9933). **3880**

ZENTRALBLATT RADIOLOGIE (GW/0722-3072). **3947**

ZENTRALBLATT RECHTSMEDIZIN (GW/0722-3056). **3743**

ZENTRALORGAN CHIRURGIE (GW/0722-6985). **3978**

ZEOLITES (US/0144-2449). **1038**

ZFA. ZEITSCHRIFT FUER ALLGEMEINMEDIZIN (GW/0341-9835). **3739**

ZFL : INTERN. ZEITSCHRIFT FUER LEBENSMITTEL-TECHNOLOGIE UND -VERFAHRENSTECHNIK (GW/0722-5733). **2361**

ZGL. ZEITSCHRIFT FUER GERMANISTISCHE LINGUISTIK (GW/0301-3294). **3335**

ZHURNAL EVOLIUTSIONNOI BIOKHIMII I FIZIOLOGII (RU/0044-4529). **494**

ZHURNAL FIZICHESKOI KHIMII (RU/0044-4537). **1059**

ZHURNAL MIKROBIOLOGII, EPIDEMIOLOGII I IMMUNOBIOLOGII (RU/0372-9311). **3678**

ZHURNAL NAUCHNOI I PRIKLADNOI FOTOGRAFII I KINEMATOGRAFII (US/0734-1504). **4378**

ZHURNAL NEORGANICHESKOI KHIMII (RU/0044-457X). **1038**

ZHURNAL VYSSHEI NERVNOI DEIATELNOSTI IMENI I. P. PAVLOVA (RU/0044-4677). **3847**

ZIELSPRACHE DEUTSCH (GW/0341-5864). **3336**

ZIELSPRACHE RUSSISCH (GW/0173-9522). **3336**

ZONING BULL. (BOSTON, MASS.) (US/0514-7905). **2839**

ZOO BIOLOGY (US/0733-3188). **5601**

ZOOLOGICA (GW/0044-5088). **5601**

ZOOLOGICA SCRIPTA (UK/0300-3256). **5601**

ZOOLOGICAL JOURNAL OF THE LINNEAN SOCIETY (UK/0024-4082). **5601**

ZOOLOGICAL SCIENCE (JA/0289-0003). **5602**

ZOOLOGICESKIJ ZURNAL (RU/0044-5134). **5602**

ZOOLOGISCHE BEITRAEGE (GW/0044-5150). **5602**

ZOOLOGISCHE GARTEN; ZEITSCHRIFT FUER DIE GESAMTE TIERGARTNEREI (GW/0044-5169). **5603**

ZOOLOGISCHE JAHRBUCHER. ABTEILUNG FUER ALLGEMEINE ZOOLOGIE UND PHYSIOLOGIE DER TIERE (GW/0044-5185). **5603**

ZOOLOGISCHE JAHRBUCHER. ABTEILUNG FUER ANATOMIE UND ONTOGENIE DER TIERE (GW/0044-5177). **5603**

ZOOLOGISCHE JAHRBUCHER. ABTEILUNG FUER SYSTEMATIK, OKOLOGIE UND GEOGRAPHIE DER TIERE (GW/0044-5193). **5603**

ZOOLOGISCHER ANZEIGER (GW/0044-5231). **5603**

ZOOMORPHOLOGY (GW/0720-213X). **5603**

ZOR. ZEITSCHRIFT FUER OPERATIONS-RESEARCH (GW/0340-9422). **5173**

ZOR, ZEITSCHRIFT FUER OPERATIONS RESEARCH : METHODS AND MODELS OF OPERATIONS RESEARCH (GW/0340-9422). **3542**

ZUCHTUNGSKUNDE (GW/0044-5401). **476**

ZUCKERINDUSTRIE (GW/0344-8657). **1031**

ZUM : ZEITSCHRIFT FUER URHEBER- UND MEDIENRECHT/FILM UND RECHT (GW/0177-6762). **4080**

ZURNAL ANALITICHESKOI HIMII (RU/0044-4502). **1020**

ZURNAL EKSPERIMENTALNOJ I TEORETICESKOJ FIZIKI (RU/0044-4510). **4426**

ZURNAL NEVROPATOLOGII I PSIHIATRII IM S.S. KORSAKOVA (RU/0044-4588). **3847**

ZURNAL OBSCEJ BIOLOGI (RU/0044-4596). **476**

ZURNAL OBSEJ HIMII (RU/0044-460X). **996**

ZURNAL ORGANICESKOJ HIMII (RU/0514-7492). **1049**

ZURNAL PRIKLADNOI HIMII (RU/0044-4618). **996**

ZURNAL TEHNICESKOJ FIZIKI (RU/0044-4642). **4426**

ZURNAL VYCISLITELNOJ MATEMATIKI I MATEMATICESKOJ FIZIKI (RU/0044-4669). **4426**

ZWR (GW/0044-166X). **1337**

ZYGON (UK/0591-2385). **5012**

New Title Index

The following index, arranged by subject classification, lists all serials in the Directory with an active status that started publication in or after 1992. The country code and ISSN are provided when available. The page number in bold refers you to the complete serial listing in the Directory.

AERONAUTICS, ASTRONAUTICS

AEROSPACE NEWS. (US). **5**

AIR AND SPACE LAW. (NE). **6**

AIR TRAFFIC CONTROL QUARTERLY. (US/1064-3818). **8**

AIR TRAFFIC MANAGEMENT. (UK/0969-6725). **8**

AIRCRAFT MAINTENANCE TECHNOLOGY. (US/1072-3145). **9**

AIRCRAFT VALUE NEWSLETTER. (US/1065-8688). **9**

AIRLINE MARKETING NEWS. (US/1071-1325). **10**

AIRLINER / BOEING CUSTOMER SERVICES DIVISION. (US). **10**

ASIAN AVIATION NEWS. (US/1071-0663). **12**

ATC MARKET REPORT. (US/1070-5740). **12**

AVIATION, AEROSPACE & DEFENCE UPDATE. (CN/1191-8004). **12**

AVIATION EDUCATION / PUBLISHED BY THE FEDERAL AVIATION ADMINISTRATION. (US). **13**

AVIATION HISTORY. (US/1076-8858). **13**

BARNSTORMER (FORT WAYNE, IND.), THE. (US/1062-7413). **14**

COMBAT EDGE, THE. (US/1063-8970). **16**

EAA SPORT AVIATION FOR KIDS. (US/1070-566X). **18**

EXPERIMENTAL ROCKET FLYER. (US/1062-8576). **18**

FLIGHT TRAINING ACADEMIC ENHANCER. BOOK 2, INSTRUMENTS. (US/1066-078X). **21**

INTERAVIA : BUSINESS & TECHNOLOGY. (SZ). **24**

JANE'S SPACE DIRECTORY. (UK). **25**

JOURNAL OF AIR TRANSPORT MANAGEMENT. (UK/0969-6997). **26**

JOURNAL OF MILITARY AVIATION. (US/1057-8307). **26**

JPRS REPORT. SCIENCE & TECHNOLOGY. CENTRAL EURASIA. SPACE. (US). **26**

MOBILITY FORUM : THE JOURNAL OF THE AIR MOBILITY COMMAND, THE. (US). **28**

MOMBERGER AIRPORT INFORMATION. (GW/0942-3478). **29**

MONTREAL & AREA AVIATION BUSINESS DIRECTORY. (CN/1188-6676). **29**

MONTREAL & AREA AVIATION BUSINESS DIRECTORY (FRENCH EDITION). (CN/1188-6676). **29**

NATIONAL PLAN OF INTEGRATED AIRPORT SYSTEMS. (US). **30**

QUEST (GRAND RAPIDS, MICH.). (US/1065-7738). **32**

REGIONAL AIR INTERNATIONAL. (US/1070-065X). **33**

RUSSIAN AERONAUTICS. (US/1068-7998). **34**

SAGA DIRECTORY OF INTERNATIONAL AVIATION PRODUCTS AND SERVICES. (US/1065-951X). **34**

SAGA INTERNATIONAL AVIATOR. (US/1065-9501). **34**

SCHEDULED AND CHARTER FREIGHT TRAFFIC FORECAST. (SZ). **34**

SPACE AVAILABLE. (US/1068-0233). **35**

SPACE FAX DAILY (GLOBAL ED.). (US/1074-8881). **36**

SPACE SHUTTLE DATABASE REPORT. (US/1061-8686). **36**

SPACE STATION FREEDOM NEWS. (US/1061-5350). **36**

STS MISSION PROFILES : COMPLETE SPACE SHUTTLE MISSION COVERAGE. (US/1066-1263). **37**

VANCOUVER & AREA ... AVIATION BUSINESS DIRECTORY. (CN/1188-2778). **39**

WORLD AIRLINE MAINTENANCE FORECAST. (US). **40**

WORLD AVIATION DIRECTORY. BUYER'S GUIDE. (US/1064-0509). **40**

AGRICULTURE

ABARE RESEARCH REPORT. (AT/1037-8286). **42**

ACTA AGRICULTUR SCANDINAVICA. SECTION A, ANIMAL SCIENCE. (DK/0906-4702). **43**

ACTA AGRICULTUR SCANDINAVICA. SECTION B, SOIL AND PLANT SCIENCE. (DK/0906-4710). **43**

ADVANCES IN STRAWBERRY RESEARCH. (US/1068-4883). **44**

AG CHEM NEW COMPOUND REVIEW. (US/1072-7361). **45**

AG RETAILER. (US/1072-9267). **45**

AGRI-FOOD AND FISHERIES PROJECT, THE. (CN/0849-2360). **47**

AGRI-FOOD PERSPECTIVES. (CN/1193-8277). **47**

AGRI-FOOD RESEARCH IN ONTARIO. (CN/1192-7704). **47**

AGRICULTURAL AND RESOURCE ECONOMICS REVIEW. (USUS/1068-2805). **49**

AGRICULTURAL NEWS (HAMDEN, N.Y.). (US/1075-3354). **50**

AGRICULTURAL SCIENCE IN FINLAND. (FI/0789-600X). **52**

AGRICULTURE & EQUIPMENT INTERNATIONAL. (UK). **53**

AGRISEARCH [COMPUTER FILE] : CRIS, SIS-SPAAR, ICAR, ARRIP, AGREP. (US). **54**

AGROEKONOMIKA. (XO). **55**

AMERICAN LIVESTOCK BREEDS CONSERVANCY NEWS. (US). **58**

AMERICAN SMALL FARM MAGAZINE. (US/1064-7473). **58**

Agriculture

ANNUAL REPORT / MAINE AGRICULTURAL AND FOREST EXPERIMENT STATION, UNIVERSITY OF MAINE. (US). **60**

APO PRODUCTIVITY JOURNAL. (JA/0919-0589). **62**

ARIZONA FARMER (1993). (US/1071-6521). **62**

AUSTRALIAN COMMODITIES. (AT). **64**

BARLEY COUNTRY. (CN/1188-8911). **65**

BEE CULTURE. (US/1071-3190). **65**

BERRY & VEGETABLE INFORMER. (CN/1189-4172). **65**

BREEDING SCIENCE. (JA). **68**

CASSAVA BIBLIOGRAPHIC BULLETIN. (CK). **72**

CORNELL FOCUS. (US/1067-585X). **77**

COTTON, WORLD MARKETS & TRADE / UNITED STATES DEPARTMENT OF AGRICULTURE, FOREIGN AGRICULTURAL SERVICE. (US). **77**

COUNTRY FOLKS GROWER. (US/1065-1756). **77**

DEUTSCHES BIENEN JOURNAL. (GW/0943-2914). **78**

DIRECT-FED MICROBIAL, ENZYME & FORAGE ADDITIVE COMPENDIUM. (US). **79**

DIRECTORY OF RESEARCH / RESEARCH BRANCH / ANNUAIRE DE LA RECHERCHE / DIRECTION GENERALE DE LA RECHERCHE. (CN). **79**

DOKLADY ROSSIISKOI AKADEMII SELSKOKHOZIAISTVENNYKH NAUK. (RU). **80**

ENGEI SHINCHISHIKI. YASAI GO. (JA). **82**

FLORIDA GROWER'S ORNAMENTAL OUTLOOK. (US/1064-6558). **87**

HALTON-PEEL FARM NEWS. (CN/1192-0785). **91**

HOLISTIC RESOURCE MANAGEMENT QUARTERLY. (US/1069-2789). **93**

HUNGARIAN AGRICULTURAL RESEARCH / MINISTRY OF AGRICULTURE, HUNGARY. (HU/1216-4526). **93**

IBSNAT VIEWS. (US/1076-3112). **93**

INDIAN JOURNAL OF AGRICULTURAL ENGINEERING, THE. (II/0971-2356). **95**

INTERNATIONAL JOURNAL OF PEST MANAGEMENT. (UK/0967-0874). **96**

IRISH JOURNAL OF AGRICULTURAL AND FOOD RESEARCH. (IE/0791-6833). **97**

JORD OG VIDEN. (DK/0906-7043). **98**

JOURNAL OF AGRICULTURAL AND APPLIED ECONOMICS. (US/1074-0708). **99**

JOURNAL OF AGRICULTURAL & FOOD INFORMATION. (US/1049-6505). **99**

JOURNAL OF AGRICULTURAL AND RESOURCE ECONOMICS. (US/1068-5502). **99**

JOURNAL OF NATURAL RESOURCES AND LIFE SCIENCES EDUCATION. (US/1059-9053). **100**

JOURNAL OF SMALL FRUITS & VITICULTURE. (US/1052-0015). **100**

LIVESTOCK, DAIRY AND POULTRY SITUATION AND OUTLOOK. (US/1076-2183). **105**

MAINE AGRICULTURAL REPORT. (US/1062-2691). **106**

MAIS-GRAIN, RESULTATS D'ESSAIS ..., HYBRIDES RECOMMANDES EN ... / CONSEIL DES PRODUCTIONS VEGETALES DU QUEBEC. (CN/1193-3046). **106**

NATIONAL LAMB & WOOL GROWER. (US/1075-0231). **110**

NEW AMERICAN FARMER. (US/1056-2133). **111**

NEWS FROM THE OC CORRAL. (CN/1194-823X). **112**

NEWSLETTER FOR INTERNATIONAL COLLABORATION. (JA/0919-8822). **112**

OILSEEDS & INDUSTRIAL CROPS. (UK). **116**

OPERATIONAL REVIEW ... FARM DEBT REVIEW BOARDS. (CN/1189-7627). **117**

PACIFIC FARMER. (US/1071-6548). **118**

PECAN SOUTH. (US). **119**

PERTANIKA JOURNAL OF TROPICAL AGRICULTURAL SCIENCE. (MY). **119**

R.B. (US). **124**

RESEARCH REPORT. (US). **127**

RURAL LIVING (LANSING, MICH.). (US/0743-9962). **131**

RUSSIAN AGRICULTURAL SCIENCES. (US/1068-3674). **131**

SOUND SAFETY. (US/1062-581X). **136**

SOYA WORLD. (US/1041-0120). **136**

STATE RULES AND SCORECARDS FOR CALIFORNIA FAIRS. (US). **137**

TURF & ORNAMENTAL CHEMICALS REFERENCE: T&OCR. (US/1056-2648). **143**

UTAH FARMER (1993). (US/1071-653X). **143**

VESTNIK AKADEMIE ZEMEDELSKYCH VED CSFR. (XR). **144**

WEBSTER AGRICULTURAL LETTER, THE. (US/1073-4813). **145**

WORLD DIRECTORY OF FERTILIZER MANUFACTURERS. (UK). **147**

ABSTRACTING, BIBLIOGRAPHIES AND STATISTICS

AGRICULTURAL & ENVIRONMENTAL BIOTECHNOLOGY ABSTRACTS. (US/1063-1151). **150**

CURRENT CONTENTS. AGRICULTURE, BIOLOGY & ENVIRONMENTAL SCIENCES (CD-ROM VERSION). (US/1073-1245). **152**

GRASSLANDS AND FORAGE ABSTRACTS. (UK/1350-9837). **153**

LIVESTOCK STATISTICS / STATISTICS CANADA, AGRICULTURE DIVISION, LIVESTOCK AND ANIMAL PRODUCTS SECTION. (CN). **154**

AGRICULTURAL EQUIPMENT

MEMBERS' HANDBOOK & BUYERS' GUIDE : THE GREEN BOOK / THE INSTITUTION OF AGRICULTURAL ENGINEERS. (UK/0965-867X). **160**

NORTH AMERICAN FARM EQUIPMENT JOURNAL. (US). **160**

CROP PRODUCTION AND SOIL

APPLIED SOIL ECOLOGY : A SECTION OF AGRICULTURE, ECOSYSTEMS & ENVIRONMENT. (NE/0929-1393). **163**

ASIAFAB : ASIA FERTILIZER AND AGROCHEMICALS BULLETIN. (UK). **164**

CBN NEWSLETTER. (CK/1022-1492). **166**

EUROPEAN JOURNAL OF AGRONOMY. (FR/1161-0301). **171**

EUROPEAN JOURNAL OF SOIL BIOLOGY. (FR/1164-5563). **171**

EUROPEAN JOURNAL OF SOIL SCIENCE. (UK/1351-0754). **171**

GENERAL PUBLICATIONS CATALOG - INTERNATIONAL IRRIGATION MANAGEMENT INSTITUTE. (CE/1018-4899). **172**

INDUSTRIAL CROPS AND PRODUCTS. (NE/0926-6690). **174**

INTERNATIONAL RICE RESEARCH NOTES. (PH). **175**

INTERNATIONAL WATER & IRRIGATION REVIEW. (IS). **175**

JOURNAL OF CITRICULTURE. (US). **176**

JOURNAL OF FRUIT AND ORNAMENTAL PLANT RESEARCH. (PL). **176**

JOURNAL OF POTATO PRODUCTION & POSTHARVEST HANDLING. (US). **176**

JOURNAL OF SOIL CONTAMINATION. (US/1058-8337). **176**

JOURNAL OF TREE FRUIT PRODUCTION. (US/1055-1387). **177**

JOURNAL OF VEGETABLE CROP PRODUCTION. (US/1049-6467). **177**

KUHN-ARCHIV. (GW/0940-3507). **177**

LISTY CUKROVARNICKE A REPARSKE. (XR). **178**

NURSERY CROP PRODUCTION GUIDE FOR COMMERCIAL GROWERS. (CN/1181-9820). **180**

POTATO GROWER : POTATO GROWER OF IDAHO MAGAZINE. (US). **182**

SEED & CROPS INDUSTRY. (US/1065-5980). **186**

TROPICAL PRODUCTS, WORLD MARKETS AND TRADE / UNITED STATES DEPARTMENT OF AGRICULTURE, FOREIGN AGRICULTURAL SERVICE. (US). **189**

DAIRY INDUSTRY

ALBERTA DAIRYMAN. (CN/1194-9589). **191**

DAIRY, LIVESTOCK, AND POULTRY. DAIRY, WORLD MARKETS AND TRADE / UNITED STATES DEPARTMENT OF AGRICULTURE, FOREIGN AGRICULTURAL SERVICE. (US). **193**

DAIRY, LIVESTOCK AND POULTRY, U.S. TRADE AND PROSPECTS / UNITED STATES DEPARTMENT OF AGRICULTURE, FOREIGN AGRICULTURAL SERVICE. (US). **193**

JOURNAL OF DAIRYING FOODS & HOME SCIENCES. (II). **196**

MANITOBA DAIRYMAN. (CN). **196**

MOLOCHNAIA PROMYSHLENNOST. (RU). **197**

FEED GRAIN AND MILLING

GRAIN, WORLD MARKETS AND TRADE. (US/1076-3929). **202**

REPORT FOR THE FISCAL YEAR. (UK). **203**

REPORT FOR THE YEAR ... . (AT). **203**

LIVESTOCK AND POULTRY

ALIMENTOS BALANCEADOS PARA ANIMALES. (US/1075-0487). **205**

BANNER (CUBA, ILL.), THE. (US/1075-0096). **207**

CHICKENS AND EGGS / NATIONAL AGRICULTURAL STATISTICS SERVICE, UNITED STATES DEPARTMENT OF AGRICULTURE. (US). **209**

HERDER YEARBOOK: PUBLICATIONS OF THE INTERNATIONAL HERDER SOCIETY. (US/1062-3582). **212**

INTEGRATED SAMPLE SURVEY FOR ESTIMATION OF ANIMAL PRODUCTS [MICROFORM] : MILK, WOOL, EGGS, AND MEAT / HIMACHAL PRADESH GOVERNMENT, ANIMAL HUSBANDRY DEPARTMENT. (II). **213**

JOURNAL OF APPLIED POULTRY RESEARCH. (US/1056-6171). **213**

MEAT & POULTRY FACTS. (US). **215**

MEAT PROCESSING INTERNATIONAL. (US). **215**

MILCHRIND. (GW/0941-1348). **215**

MILKING SHORTHORN JOURNAL (1993). (US/1073-9394). **215**

POULTRY AND AVIAN BIOLOGY REVIEWS. (UK). **218**

PRODUCTION OF EGGS. (CN). **219**

ROCKY MOUNTAIN LIVESTOCK JOURNAL. (US/1072-5636). **220**

SWINE HEALTH AND PRODUCTION. (US/1066-4963). **222**

TODAY'S EGG PRODUCER. (CN/1195-1877). **223**

ANIMAL WELFARE

ANIMAL PEOPLE. (US/1071-0035). **225**

ANIMAL WELFARE. (UK/0962-7286). **225**

APIS, THE. (US/0887-7386). **226**

AWI QUARTERLY. (US/1071-1384). **226**

HUMANE INNOVATIONS AND ALTERNATIVES. (US/1062-4805). **226**

MIDWEST PUREBRED DOGPOST!, THE. (US/1061-6586). **226**

ANTHROPOLOGY

ACTA ETHNOGRAPHICA HUNGARICA. (HU/1216-9803). **227**

ANTHROPOLOGICAL SCIENCE : JOURNAL OF THE ANTHROPOLOGICAL SOCIETY OF NIPPON. (JA/0918-7960). **229**

ANTHROPOLOGY & ARCHEOLOGY OF EURASIA. (US/1061-1959). **229**

ANTHROPOLOGY AND HUMANISM. (US). **230**

CVA NEWSLETTER / COMMISSION ON VISUAL ANTHROPOLOGY. (GW). **235**

EVOLUTIONARY ANTHROPOLOGY / ISSUES, NEWS AND REVIEWS. (US/1060-1538). **236**

ISLA (MANGILAO, GUAM). (GU/1054-9390). **238**

JOURNAL OF MAMMALIAN EVOLUTION. (US/1064-7554). **239**

NORTHEAST ANTHROPOLOGY. (US/1068-9982). **242**

POSITIONS (DURHAM, N.C.). (US/1067-9847). **243**

PREHISTOIRE ANTHROPOLOGIE MEDITERRANEENNES. (FR/1167-492X). **243**

PUBLICAR EN ANTROPOLOGIA Y CIENCIAS SOCIALES. (AG/0327-6627). **243**

SOCIAL ANTHROPOLOGY : THE JOURNAL OF THE EUROPEAN ASSOCIATION OF SOCIAL ANTHROPOLOGISTS. (UK/0964-0282). **245**

STUDIA FENNICA. ETHNOLOGICA. (FI). **246**

ANTIQUES

ANTIQUE & COLLECTORS REPRODUCTION NEWS. (US/1065-3694). **248**

ANTIQUE DOLL WORLD. (US/1069-5141). **249**

MALONEY'S ANTIQUES & COLLECTIBLES RESOURCE DIRECTORY. (US). **251**

SLOAN'S GREEN GUIDE TO ANTIQUING IN NEW ENGLAND. (US/1051-6719). **252**

ARCHAEOLOGY

ARCHAEOLOGICAL PROSPECTION. (UK/1075-2196). **257**

CASE STUDIES IN GREAT LAKES ARCHAEOLOGY. (US/1061-4257). **265**

CONSERVATION AND MANAGEMENT OF ARCHAEOLOGICAL SITES. (UK/1350-5033). **266**

CURRENT SWEDISH ARCHAEOLOGY. (SW/1102-7355). **266**

EUTOPIA. (IT/1121-1628). **268**

INA QUARTERLY, THE. (US). **270**

INTERNATIONAL NEWSLETTER ON ROCK ART : I.N.O.R.A. (FR). **270**

JOURNAL OF ARCHAEOLOGICAL METHOD AND THEORY. (US/1072-5369). **271**

JOURNAL OF ARCHAEOLOGICAL RESEARCH. (US/1059-0161). **271**

MEMOIRES VIVES (MONTREAL). (CN/1188-8296). **274**

MMAP LOG. (US/1059-8065). **275**

NOVAIA LITERATURA PO SOTSIALNYM I GUMANITARNYM NAUKAM. ISTORIIA, ARKHEOLOGIIA, ETNOLOGIIA / ROSSIISKAIA AKADEMIIA NAUK, INSTITUT NAUCHNOI INFORMATSII PO OBSHCHESTVENNYM NAUKAM. (RU). **276**

ABSTRACTING, BIBLIOGRAPHIES AND STATISTICS

BRITISH ARCHAEOLOGICAL BIBLIOGRAPHY. (UK/0964-7104). **286**

ARCHITECTURE

AESCLEPIUS (MARTINEZ, CALIF.). (US/1067-8646). **287**

AKTUELLES BAUEN. (SZ). **287**

AMERICAN CENTER FOR DESIGN JOURNAL. (US/1062-0966). **287**

ARCHITECTURAL & CONSTRUCTION MEDIA SOURCE. (US/1071-4634). **288**

ARCHITECTURAL SPECIFIER. (US/1068-8560). **289**

ARCHITEKTUR JAHRBUCH. (GW). **291**

ARIS (PITTSBURGH, PA.). (US/1063-1305). **291**

COLUMBIA DOCUMENTS OF ARCHITECTURE AND THEORY. (US/1065-304X). **295**

DENKMALPFLEGE, DIE. (GW/0947-031X). **296**

DESIGN METHODS. (US/1067-9359). **297**

GUIDE TO ARCHITECTURE SCHOOLS. (US). **299**

HANGUK DIJAIN CHONGNAM. (KO). **299**

INTERFOLIO LEVALLOIS-PERRET. (FR/1251-9812). **301**

MEMOIRES VIVES MONTREAL. (CN/1188-8296). **303**

OLD-HOUSE JOURNAL RESTORATION DIRECTORY. (US). **305**

OLD-HOUSE JOURNAL'S HISTORIC HOUSE PLANS, THE. (US/1071-0868). **305**

PRACTICES (CINCINNATI, OHIO). (US/1059-7239). **306**

REFERENCE GUIDE TO HOMEBUILDING ARTICLES. (US). **307**

RIBA JOURNAL. (UK). **308**

SUMMA+. (AG/0327-9022). **309**

WRIGHT STUDIES. (US/1045-7992). **311**

THE ARTS

AMERICAN FESTIVAL MAGAZINE. (US/1053-1327). **312**

ART ET CULTURE AU QUEBEC. (CN/1188-4282). **313**

ART IMAGE MAGAZINE. (US/1062-8819). **313**

ARTS EDUCATION POLICY REVIEW. (US/1063-2913). **314**

The Arts

ARTS REACH. (US/1065-8130). **315**

ARTSOURCE (RENAISSANCE, CALIF.). (US/1064-6620). **315**

ARTWALK MAGAZINE. (CN/1191-4785). **315**

AVANT GARDE CRITICAL STUDIES. (NE). **315**

BORSCHT (MINNEAPOLIS, MINN.). (US/1065-5212). **316**

BOULEVARD MAGAZINE (VICTORIA). (CN/1189-6051). **316**

C MAGAZINE (1992). (CN/1193-8625). **317**

FEMME FATALES OF THE FILMS. (US/1062-3906). **320**

FINE ART & ANTIQUES INTERNATIONAL. (US/1071-1015). **320**

GUIDE TO ARTS ADMINISTRATION TRAINING. / CENTER FOR ARTS ADMINISTRATION, GRADUATE SCHOOL OF BUSINESS, UNIVERSITY OF WISCONSIN - MADISON, AND ASSOCIATION OF ARTS ADMINISTRATION EDUCATORS. (US). **321**

GUIDE TO LITERARY AGENTS & ART/PHOTO REPS. (US/1055-6087). **321**

INTER-ARTS. GRANTS TO PRESENTING ORGANIZATIONS, SERVICES TO PRESENTING ORGANIZATIONS, SPECIAL TOURING INITIATIVES: APPLICATION GUIDELINES. (US). **322**

JOURNAL OF ARTS MANAGEMENT, LAW, AND SOCIETY. (US/1063-2921). **323**

LEONARDO ELECTRONIC ALMANAC. (US/1071-4391). **324**

LOYOLA OF LOS ANGELES ENTERTAINMENT LAW JOURNAL. (US). **324**

MAC REVISTA. (BL). **324**

MEDIA AND FILM. (US/1061-0316). **325**

MIR ISKUSSTV. (RU). **325**

MORNING (NEW YORK, N.Y.). (US/1061-8341). **325**

MURKY AT BEST. (US/1062-838X). **325**

NORD OUEST (SAINT-BASILE). (CN/1188-1321). **326**

PRESENTING AND COMMISSIONING. (US). **328**

PROCEEDINGS OF THE AMERICAN ACADEMY OF ARTS AND LETTERS. (US). **328**

PROPOSITO : REVISTA DE LITERATURA, ARTE Y CINE, A. (PR). **328**

PUBLIC DOMAIN REPORT. (US/1070-2555). **328**

RE SUPEKKU. (JA). **329**

REVUE NOIRE. (FR/1157-4127). **330**

RUNGH (VANCOUVER). (CN/1188-9950). **330**

STATE AND REGIONAL PROGRAM/ NATIONAL ENDOWMENT FOR THE ARTS, OFFICE FOR PUBLIC PARTNERSHIP. (US). **331**

VOIR (QUEBEC). (CN/1188-5017). **332**

ABSTRACTING, BIBLIOGRAPHIES AND STATISTICS

GRAPHIC ARTS BULLETIN OF THE INSTITUTE OF PAPER SCIENCE AND TECHNOLOGY. (US/1064-9638). **334**

ART

ART MATERIALS TODAY. (US/1066-4173). **339**

ART ON SCREEN. (US/1062-9459). **340**

ART ON SCREEN CLOSE-UPS. (US/1062-9467). **340**

ART REFERENCE SERVICES QUARTERLY. (US/1050-2548). **340**

ARTLANTA. (US/1059-7263). **342**

ARTS MAGAZINE. INTERNATIONAL DIRECTORY OF EXHIBITION CATALOGUES. (US). **342**

ASIAN ART & CULTURE. (US/1352-2744). **343**

CONTRIBUTIONS TO THE STUDY OF ART AND ARCHITECTURE. (US/1058-9120). **348**

DARK SHADOWS (WHEELING, W. VA.). (US/1060-684X). **348**

EXPOSE: THE VISUAL ARTS MAGAZINE. (US/1063-1321). **350**

FINE ART INDEX (NORTH AMERICAN ED.), THE. (US/1057-8269). **350**

FREE FOOD FOR THOUGHT. (US). **350**

GILCREASE JOURNAL. (US/1070-7808). **351**

HARVARD UNIVERSITY ART MUSEUMS BULLETIN. (US/1065-6448). **351**

HOLART REPORT. (US/1062-6360). **352**

IRISH ARTS REVIEW YEARBOOK. (IE). **353**

KUNSTARBOK ART YEARBOOK, NORWAY. (NO/0803-6160). **356**

LAWRENCE'S DEALER PRINT PRICES. (US/1059-3187). **356**

OLSON'S BOOK OF LIBRARY CLIP ART. (US/1061-4060). **361**

PUBLIC ART ISSUES. (US/1062-5089). **362**

REVISTA DO MASP / MUSEU DE ARTE DE SAO PAULO. (BL). **363**

RUSSIAN AND EAST EUROPEAN STUDIES IN AESTHETICS AND THE PHILOSOPHY OF CULTURE. (US/1065-9374). **363**

SCHOLASTIC ART. (US/1060-832X). **364**

SCULPTURE MAQUETTE : A PUBLICATION OF THE INTERNATIONAL SCULPTURE CENTER. (US). **364**

STATE OF THE ARTS : A PUBLICATION OF THE CALIFORNIA ARTS COUNCIL. (US). **365**

TRAVELER'S GUIDE TO ART MUSEUM EXHIBITIONS. (US). **367**

VISUAL ARTS. VISUAL ARTISTS ORGANIZATIONS, VISUAL ARTISTS PUBLIC PROJECTS, SPECIAL PROJECTS / NATIONAL ENDOWMENT FOR THE ARTS. (US). **368**

WESTBRIDGE ART MARKET REPORT. (CN/1191-3371). **368**

XYZ DIRECTION. (UK/0965-3848). **369**

CRAFTS AND DECORATIVE ARTS

ANNUAL CRAFT SHOWS IN ONTARIO / CRAFT RESOURCE CENTRE. (CN/1189-4555). **370**

CHART CONNECTION, THE. (US/1065-2299). **370**

CREATEURS QUEBECOIS. (CN/1193-1140). **372**

CREATEURS QUEBECOIS. (CN/1193-1140). **372**

DECORATIVE ARTS PAINTING. (US/1067-0068). **372**

KUNSTHANDWERK & DESIGN. (GW). **373**

NOVA SCOTIA CRAFT NEWS / NSDCC. (CN/1193-011X). **374**

PIECEWORK (LOVELAND, COLO.). (US/1067-2249). **374**

SHOPNOTES (DES MOINES, IOWA). (US/1062-9696). **375**

STUDIES IN THE DECORATIVE ARTS. (US/1069-8825). **375**

GRAPHIC ARTS

3-DIMENSIONAL ILLUSTRATORS AWARDS ANNUAL. (US/1065-1276). **376**

BLUE BOOK OF PRINTING AND GRAPHIC ARTS BUYERS. (US/1065-8521). **377**

COMIC ART STUDIES. (US/1062-6964). **377**

FLARE ADVENTURES. (US/1057-2910). **378**

FURKINDRED (SEATTLE, WASH.). (US/1059-082X). **378**

GRAPHICS INTERNATIONAL. (UK/1350-0937). **379**

INKS (COLUMBUS, OHIO). (US/1071-9156). **380**

LADY ARCANE. (US/1057-2929). **380**

OHIO'S OFFICIAL SOURCEBOOK. (US/1067-5957). **381**

PRINT PRICE INDEX. (US/1058-2339). **381**

STUDIO. (CN). **382**

ULTRA HAWK. (US/1062-9122). **382**

WARLOCK AND THE INFINITY WATCH. (US/1062-3248). **382**

PERFORMING ARTS

CIRCO CRIOLLO : PUBLICACION DE LA ESCUELA DE CIRCO CRIOLLO DE BUENOS AIRES. (AG). **384**

COTTAGER (VICTORIA BEACH. MANITOBA ED.). (CN/1188-0163). **384**

PAUL KAGAN'S BOX OFFICE CHAMPIONS. ACTORS/ACTRESSES. (US/1064-7236). **387**

PAUL KAGAN'S BOX OFFICE CHAMPIONS. PRODUCERS. (US/1064-7228). **387**

PAUL KAGAN'S BOX OFFICE CHAMPIONS. SCREENWRITERS. (US/1064-7244). **387**

PERFORMING ARTS STUDIES. (US/1068-8153). **387**

SAN FRANCISCO PERFORMING ARTS LIBRARY AND MUSEUM SERIES. (US/1060-6858). **388**

STROKE & DAGGER. (US/1065-397X). **388**

ASTROLOGY

ASTRO AGENTS. (US/1065-7584). **389**

ASTRO CASTER. (US/1065-7533). **390**

SPECTRUM : NEWSLETTER OF THE ROYAL OBSERVATORIES. (UK/1353-7784). **390**

ASTRONOMY

ASTRONOMY LETTERS. (US/1063-7737). **392**

ASTRONOMY REPORTS. (US/1063-7729). **393**

BALTIC ASTRONOMY. (LI). **393**

CCD ASTRONOMY. (US/1074-875X). **394**

GEMINI PROJECT NEWSLETTER. (US). **395**

IRAM NEWSLETTER. (FR). **396**

ROMANIAN ASTRONOMICAL JOURNAL. (RM/1220-5168). **399**

BEAUTY AND COSMETICS

BEAUTYFACTS (NEW YORK, N.Y.). (US/1062-3035). **402**

BEST OF HAIRDO IDEAS, THE. (US/1064-8844). **402**

SALON MAGAZINE. (CN/1197-1495). **405**

TODAY'S BEAUTY TRENDS. (US/1062-2748). **405**

BIBLIOGRAPHIES

ACCESSIONS LIST, EASTERN AND SOUTHERN AFRICA. (KE/1070-2717). **406**

ANNUAL REGISTER OF BOOK VALUES. VOYAGES, TRAVEL & EXPLORATION. (UK/0968-7548). **407**

BIBLIOGRAPHIE NATIONALE FRANCAISE. PUBLICATIONS EN SERIE : BIBLIOGRAPHIE ETABLIE PAR LA BIBLIOTHEQUE NATIONALE. (FR). **410**

BIBLIOGRAPHIES AND INDEXES IN POPULAR CULTURE. (US/1066-0658). **410**

BIBLIOGRAPHIES OF THE STATES OF THE UNITED STATES. (US/1060-5711). **410**

BIBLIOGRAPHY OF NATIVE NORTH AMERICANS ON DISC. (US/1064-5144). **410**

CATALOGUE FRANCOPHONE CANADIEN DE DOCUMENTS EN ALPHABETISATION / GROUPE DE RESSOURCES DOCUMENTAIRES EN FRANCAIS. (CN/1191-5056). **412**

EDITIONS / ORSTOM. (FR). **415**

EUROCAT [COMPUTER FILE]. (LU/1021-7789). **416**

INTERACTIONS BIBLIOGRAPHY, THE. (US/1062-7278). **417**

LISTE DES ACQUISITIONS / CENTRE D'ETUDES HIMALAYENNES. (FR). **419**

NOVYE KNIGI. (RU). **421**

NOVYIA KNIHI BELARUSI. (BW). **421**

PERIODICALS IN PRINT, AUSTRALIA, NEW ZEALAND & PAPUA NEW GUINEA. (AT/1030-2476). **422**

REPERE (MONTREAL. IMPRIME. 1994). (CN/1198-0281). **423**

STREET ADDRESS DIRECTORY, OTTAWA-HULL (ENGLISH EDITION 1992). (CN/1188-2794). **425**

STREET ADDRESS DIRECTORY, OTTAWA-HULL (FRENCH EDITION 1992). (CN/1188-2794). **425**

SUBJECT GUIDE TO AUSTRALIAN CHILDREN'S BOOKS IN PRINT. (AT). **425**

TOKELAU NATIONAL BIBLIOGRAPHY / FAKAMAUMAUGA O NA TUHITUHIGA O TOKELAU. (NZ). **426**

TOWN AND COUNTRY MAGAZINE PERSONAL NAME INDEX. (US/1064-9654). **426**

VESTAL PRESS RESOURCE CATALOGUE, THE. (US/1066-4823). **427**

WORDS ON CASSETTE. (US). **427**

BICYCLES AND BICYCLING

MOUNTAIN BIKE ACTION PARTS AND ACCESSORIES GUIDE. (US/1062-7111). **429**

BIOGRAPHIES

BIOGRAPHY REVIEW. (US/1043-9374). **430**

BIOGRAPHY TODAY. (US/1058-2347). **430**

EURO WHO'S WHO: WHO'S WHO IN THE EUROPEAN COMMUNITIES AND IN THE OTHER EUROPEAN ORGANIZATIONS. (BE). **432**

INDEX TO MARQUIS WHO'S WHO PUBLICATIONS. (US). **433**

WHO'S WHO IN ATHLETICS IN AMERICAN JUNIOR COLLEGES. (US/1049-9237). **436**

WHO'S WHO IN LATIN AMERICA (NEW YORK, N.Y.). (US/1068-7696). **437**

WHO'S WHO IN THE PEACE CORPS. (US/1065-8459). **438**

BIOLOGY

ADVANCES IN APPLIED LIPID RESEARCH. (UK). **440**

ADVANCES IN CELL AND MOLECULAR BIOLOGY OF MEMBRANES. (US/1074-7567). **440**

ADVANCES IN GENOME BIOLOGY. (US/1067-5701). **440**

ADVANCES IN LOW-TEMPERATURE BIOLOGY. (UK). **440**

ADVANCES IN VASCULAR BIOLOGY. (SZ/1072-0618). **441**

ANAEROBE (LONDON, ENGLAND). (UK/1075-9964). **441**

BIO / LA LETTRE DES BIOTECHNOLOGIES. (FR/0291-2430). **444**

BIOETHICS YEARBOOK. (NE/0926-261X). **444**

BIOGEOGRAPHICA : COMPTE-RENDU DES SEANCES DE LA SOCIETE DE BIOGEOGRAPHIE. (FR). **444**

BIOLOGIA TANITASA SZEGED, A. (HU/1216-6626). **444**

BIOLOGICAL PRODUCTS. (UK/0968-5685). **445**

BIOLOGICAL RESEARCH. (CL/0716-9760). **445**

BIOLOGICAL RHYTHM RESEARCH. (NE/0929-1016). **445**

BIOLOGIJA / BIOLOGY / BIOLOGIIA. (LI). **446**

BIOLOGY AND ENVIRONMENT : PROCEEDINGS OF THE ROYAL IRISH ACADEMY. (IE/0791-7945). **446**

BIOLOGY BULLETIN OF THE RUSSIAN ACADEMY OF SCIENCES. (US/1062-3590). **446**

BIOPEOPLE (SAN MATEO, CALIF.). (US/1065-612X). **447**

BIOPRACTICE : INTERNATIONAL JOURNAL OF APPLIED BIOLOGY, BIOTECHNOLOGY, AND BIONICS. (GW/0940-5542). **447**

CELL DEATH AND DIFFERENTIATION. (UK/1350-9047). **451**

CHEMISTRY & BIOLOGY. (US/1074-5521). **451**

CLINICAL DYSMORPHOLOGY. (UK/0962-8827). **451**

ELECTRO- AND MAGNETOBIOLOGY. (US/1061-9526). **454**

EMF HEALTH REPORT. (US/1070-4027). **454**

FUNDAMENTAL AND APPLIED NEMATOLOGY. (FR/1164-5571). **456**

GLOBAL BIODIVERSITY. (CN/1195-3101). **456**

GLOBAL CHANGE BIOLOGY. (UK/1354-1013). **456**

IZVESTIIA AKADEMII NAUK. SERIIA BIOLOGICHESKAIA / ROSSIISKAIA AKADEMIIA NAUK. (RU). **459**

IZVESTIIA SORAN. SIBIRSKII BIOLOGICHESKII ZHURNAL. (RU). **460**

JOURNAL OF BIOLOGICAL SYSTEMS. (SI/0218-3390). **460**

JOURNAL OF COMPUTATIONAL BIOLOGY. (US/1066-5277). **461**

MATRIX BIOLOGY : JOURNAL OF THE INTERNATIONAL SOCIETY FOR MATRIX BIOLOGY. (GW/0945-053X). **464**

MOLECULAR AND CELLULAR DIFFERENTIATION. (US/1065-3074). **465**

NATURE STRUCTURAL BIOLOGY. (US/1072-8368). **466**

NEUROBIOLOGY OF LEARNING AND MEMORY. (US/1074-7427). **466**

PARASITE : JOURNAL DE LA SOCIETE FRANCAISE DE PARASITOLOGIE. (FR/1252-607X). **468**

PERSPECTIVES ON DEVELOPMENTAL NEUROBIOLOGY. (US/1064-0517). **468**

PROTEIN PROFILE. (UK/1070-3667). **470**

Biology

RUSSIAN JOURNAL OF DEVELOPMENTAL BIOLOGY. (US/1062-3604). **472**

SKIN RESEARCH AND TECHNOLOGY. (DK). **473**

SYSTEMATIC BIOLOGY. (US/1063-5157). **474**

VESTNIK SANKT-PETERBURGSKOGO UNIVERSITETA. SERIIA 3, BIOLOGIIA. (RU). **475**

ZESZYTY NAUKOWE. BIOLOGIA / UNIWERSYTET GDANSKI. (PL/0867-3357). **476**

ZYGOTE. (UK/0967-1994). **476**

ABSTRACTING, BIBLIOGRAPHIES AND STATISTICS

CURRENT ADVANCES IN APPLIED MICROBIOLOGY & BIOTECHNOLOGY. (UK/0964-8712). **477**

CURRENT ADVANCES IN PROTEIN BIOCHEMISTRY. (UK/0965-0504). **478**

CURRENT ADVANCES IN PROTEIN CHEMISTRY. (UK/0965-0504). **478**

NUCLEIC ACIDS ABSTRACTS (1994). (US/1070-2466). **478**

BIOCHEMISTRY

ADVANCES IN DEVELOPMENTAL BIOCHEMISTRY. (US/1064-2722). **479**

APPLIED IMMUNOHISTOCHEMISTRY. (US/1062-3345). **480**

BIOCHEMISTRY & BIOPHYSICS CITATION INDEX. (US/1065-7509). **481**

BIOCHEMISTRY AND MOLECULAR BIOLOGY INTERNATIONAL. (AT/1069-8302). **482**

BIOMETALS. (US/0966-0844). **483**

BIOSPECTROSCOPY (NEW YORK, N.Y.). (US/1075-4261). **484**

BULLETIN OF THE CANADIAN SOCIETY OF BIOCHEMISTRY AND MOLECULAR BIOLOGY. (CN/1197-6578). **484**

COMPARATIVE BIOCHEMISTRY AND PHYSIOLOGY. B, BIOCHEMISTRY & MOLECULAR BIOLOGY : CBP. (UK). **486**

INTERNATIONAL JOURNAL OF QUANTUM CHEMISTRY. QUANTUM BIOLOGY SYMPOSIUM : PROCEEDINGS OF THE INTERNATIONAL SYMPOSIUM ON THE APPLICATION OF FUNDAMENTAL THEORY TO PROBLEMS OF BIOLOGY AND PHARMACOLOGY. (US). **488**

JOURNAL OF BIOCHEMICAL ORGANIZATION. (US/1065-9668). **489**

NATURAL PRODUCT LETTERS. (UK/1057-5634). **491**

PROGRESS IN BIOCHEMISTRY AND BIOTECHNOLOGY. (US). **492**

PROTEIN SCIENCE : A PUBLICATION OF THE PROTEIN SOCIETY. (US/0961-8368). **493**

REFERATIVNYI ZHURNAL. 04, 04D, BIOLOGIIA. FIZIKO-KHIMICHESKAIA BIOLOGIIA / VSESOIUZNYI INSTITUT NAUCHNOI I TEKHNICHESKOI INFORMATSII. (RU/0869-4095). **493**

RUSSIAN JOURNAL OF BIOORGANIC CHEMISTRY. (US/1068-1620). **493**

SIGNAL TRANSDUCTION & CYCLIC NUCLEOTIDES. (UK/0964-7589). **493**

VESCI AKADEMII NAVUK BELARUSI. SERYA BIALAGICNYH NAVUK. (BW). **494**

BIOPHYSICS

ANNUAL REVIEW OF BIOPHYSICS AND BIOMOLECULAR STRUCTURE. (US/1056-8700). **494**

BOTANY

ACTA BOTANICA GALLICA : BULLETIN DE LA SOCIETE BOTANIQUE DE FRANCE. (FR). **496**

BULLETIN OF THE NATURAL HISTORY MUSEUM. BOTANY SERIES. (UK/0968-0446). **505**

DIRECTORY OF PLANT BIOTECHNOLOGY COMPANIES IN USA/ BY FORE. (US/1060-4200). **508**

EUROPEAN JOURNAL OF PHYCOLOGY. (UK/0967-0262). **509**

GENETIC RESOURCES AND CROP EVOLUTION. (NE/0925-9864). **511**

GENOTYPE-BY-ENVIRONMENT, INTERACTION, AND PLANT BREEDING SYMPOSIUM. (US/1051-662X). **511**

INDIAN PHYCOLOGICAL REVIEW. (II). **513**

INTERNATIONAL JOURNAL OF PLANT SCIENCES. (US/1058-5893). **514**

INTERNATIONAL JOURNAL OF PLANT SCIENCES. MICROFORM. (US/1058-5893). **514**

ISRAEL JOURNAL OF PLANT SCIENCES. (IS/0792-9978). **514**

JOURNAL OF PLANT RESEARCH. (JA/0918-9440). **516**

MYCOSCIENCE. (JA/1340-3540). **518**

PLANTS & PEOPLE : SOCIETY FOR ECONOMIC BOTANY NEWSLETTER. (US). **525**

PROCEEDINGS OF THE NEW ZEALAND PLANT PROTECTION CONFERENCE. (NZ/1172-0719). **525**

RHEEDEA (CALICUT). (II/0971-2313). **526**

CYTOLOGY AND HISTOLOGY

ADVANCES IN MOLECULAR AND CELL BIOLOGY. (US). **531**

BIOLOGICAL SIGNALS. (SZ/1016-0922). **532**

CELL BIOLOGY INTERNATIONAL. (UK/1065-6995). **533**

CELL CONTACT AND COMMUNICATION. (UK/1351-5314). **533**

CELL VISION. (US/1073-1180). **534**

CELLULAR AND MOLECULAR BIOLOGY. (FR). **534**

CELLULAR & MOLECULAR BIOLOGY RESEARCH. (US/0968-8773). **534**

CYTOPATHOLOGY ANNUAL. (US/1069-045X). **535**

ENDOTHELIUM (NEW YORK, N.Y.). (US/1062-3329). **536**

EPITHELIAL CELL BIOLOGY. (UK/0940-9912). **536**

MOLECULAR BIOLOGY OF THE CELL. (US/1059-1524). **539**

NANOBIOLOGY : JOURNAL OF RESEARCH ON NANOSCALE LIVING SYSTEMS. (UK/0958-3165). **539**

NCA/TCS NEWSLETTER. (US/0163-772X). **539**

RAVEN PRESS SERIES ON MOLECULAR AND CELLULAR BIOLOGY. (US). **540**

STEM CELLS (DAYTON, OHIO). (US/1066-5099). **540**

STRUCTURE. (UK/0969-2126). **540**

EMBRYOLOGY

ADVANCES IN DEVELOPMENTAL BIOLOGY. (US). **541**

GENETICS

CHROMATIN. (UK/0961-0901). **543**

EUROPEAN JOURNAL OF HUMAN GENETICS : EJHG. (SZ/1018-4813). **544**

GENE THERAPY. (UK/0969-7128). **545**

GENOME PRIORITY REPORTS. (SZ/1021-6278). **546**

GENOME SCIENCE & TECHNOLOGY. (US/1070-2830). **546**

HUMAN MOLECULAR GENETICS. (UK/0964-6906). **547**

HUMAN MUTATION. (US/1059-7794). **547**

JAPANESE JOURNAL OF HUMAN GENETICS, THE. (JA/0916-8478). **548**

JOURNAL OF GENETIC COUNSELING. (US/1059-7700). **548**

MODERN GENETICS. (US/1056-4497). **549**

MOLECULAR PHYLOGENETICS AND EVOLUTION. (US/1055-7903). **549**

NATURE GENETICS. (US/1061-4036). **550**

MARINE BIOLOGY

AQUACULTURE RESEARCH. (UK/1355-557X). **553**

JOURNAL OF AQUATIC ECOSYSTEM HEALTH. (NE/0925-1014). **555**

JOURNAL OF MARINE BIOTECHNOLOGY, THE. (US). **555**

MARINE LIFE. (FR). **556**

NETHERLANDS JOURNAL OF AQUATIC ECOLOGY : JOURNAL OF THE NETHERLANDS SOCIETY OF AQUATIC ECOLOGY. (NE). **556**

RUSSIAN JOURNAL OF MARINE BIOLOGY. (US/1063-0740). **557**

MICROBIOLOGY

ACTA MICROBIOLOGICA ET IMMUNOLOGICA HUNGARICA. (HU/1217-8950). **558**

ANTIMICROBICS AND INFECTIOUS DISEASES NEWSLETTER. (US/1069-417X). **559**

CLINICAL AND DIAGNOSTIC VIROLOGY. (NE/0928-0197). **561**

EUROPEAN MICROBIOLOGY. (US/1064-4725). **562**

MEDICAL MICROBIOLOGY LETTERS : AN INTERNATIONAL JOURNAL FOR RAPID COMMUNICATIONS ON ALL ASPECTS OF MEDICAL AND CLINICAL MICROBIOLOGY. (SZ/1018-4627). **566**

MICROBIAL RESEARCH. (GW/0944-5013). **566**

MICROBIOLOGY. (UK/1350-0872). **567**

RUSSIAN PROGRESS IN VIROLOGY. (US/1068-3747). **570**

TRENDS IN MICROBIOLOGY (REGULAR ED.). (UK/0966-842X). **570**

MICROSCOPY

MICRON : THE INTERNATIONAL RESEARCH AND REVIEW JOURNAL FOR MICROSCOPY. (UK/0968-4328). **573**

MICROSCOPY RESEARCH AND TECHNIQUE. (US/1059-910X). **573**

QUEKETT JOURNAL OF MICROSCOPY, THE. (UK/0969-3823). **573**

MYCOLOGY

CZECH MYCOLOGY. (XR). **574**

PHYSIOLOGY

AGING & NEUROSCIENCE. (US/1061-6306). **577**

CANADIAN JOURNAL OF APPLIED PHYSIOLOGY. (US/1066-7814). **579**

ENZYME & PROTEIN. (SZ/1019-6773). **580**

JOURNAL OF PHYSIOLOGY, PARIS. (FR/0928-4257). **583**

ROMANIAN JOURNAL OF PHYSIOLOGY : PHYSIOLOGICAL SCIENCES / [ACADEMIA DE STIINTE MEDICALE]. (RM). **586**

BIRTH CONTROL

REDE NACIONAL FEMINISTA DE SAUDE E DIREITOS REPRODUTIVOS : BOLETIM. (BL). **590**

BOATS AND BOATING

AVIRON CANADIEN. (CN/1184-9789). **591**

CANOE & KAYAK. (US). **592**

DIRECTORY OF NORTH AMERICAN GUIDE AND CHARTERBOAT SERVICES. (US/1048-1370). **593**

HOUSEBOAT MAGAZINE. (US). **593**

INTRACOASTAL WATERWAY FESTIVAL AND SERVICES DIRECTORY, THE. (US). **593**

MAINSHEET (SAN FRANCISCO, CALIF.). (US/1064-1688). **594**

OUTBOARD BOAT BLUE BOOK. (US/1070-3500). **594**

SAILING DIRECTIONS. GENERAL INFORMATION. ATLANTIC COAST. (CN). **596**

BUILDING AND CONSTRUCTION

ABC TODAY. (US/1062-3698). **597**

ADVANCED CEMENT-BASED MATERIALS. (US/1065-7355). **598**

AUTOMATION IN CONSTRUCTION. (NE/0926-5805). **599**

BLUE BOOK BUILDING AND CONSTRUCTION. NEW YORK, THE. (US). **601**

BUILDING ACOUSTICS. (UK/1351-010X). **602**

BUILDING RENOVATION (CLEVELAND, OHIO). (US/1070-5988). **604**

BUILDING RESEARCH JOURNAL. (US/1065-4968). **604**

BUILDING SUPPLY HOME CENTERS (MIDWEST ED.). (US/1075-8038). **605**

BUILDING SUPPLY HOME CENTERS (NORTHEAST ED.). (US/1075-802X). **605**

BUILDING SUPPLY HOME CENTERS (SOUTH ED.). (US/1075-8054). **605**

BUILDING SUPPLY HOME CENTERS (WEST ED.). (US/1075-8046). **605**

BUILDING SYSTEMS BUILDER. (US/1064-5896). **605**

BUILDINGS & FACILITIES MANAGEMENT FOR THE PUBLIC SECTOR. (UK/0965-7231). **605**

CCMC NEWS. (CN/1188-0783). **606**

CHANGE NOTICE, THE. (US/1062-0079). **607**

CONSTRUCTION MANAGEMENT JOURNAL. (US/1056-7801). **610**

CONSTRUCTION PRODUCTS. (US/1070-4531). **610**

CONSTRUCTION REPAIR. (UK/0967-0726). **610**

CONTRACTOR'S PRICING GUIDE. RESIDENTIAL DETAILED COSTS. (US/1074-0481). **611**

CONTRACTOR'S PRICING GUIDE. RESIDENTIAL SQUARE FOOT COSTS. (US/1074-049X). **611**

CUSTOM HOME PLANS. (US/1065-8157). **612**

DCQFORUM (SILVER SPRING, MD.). (US/1071-5975). **612**

DIRECTORY OF CALIFORNIA LICENSED CONTRACTORS (NORTHERN ED.). (US/1063-1232). **613**

DIRECTORY OF CALIFORNIA LICENSED CONTRACTORS (SOUTHERN ED.). (US/1063-1240). **613**

ENR DIRECTORY OF CONTRACTORS. MIDWEST REGION. (US/1065-2205). **614**

ENR DIRECTORY OF CONTRACTORS. SOUTH REGION. (US/1065-2213). **614**

ENR DIRECTORY OF CONTRACTORS. WEST REGION. (US/1065-2183). **614**

ENVIRONMENTAL BUILDING NEWS : A NEWSLETTER ON ENVIRONMENTALLY SUSTAINABLE DESIGN & CONSTRUCTION. (US/1062-3957). **614**

FLOOR COVERING PLUS. (CN/1193-8781). **615**

FLOOR FOCUS. (US/1064-7627). **615**

HOME MAGAZINE'S BUILDING/REMODELING PLANNER. (US/1061-6667). **616**

INTERNATIONAL CONSTRUCTION DIRECTORY. INTERNATIONAL SECTION. (US/1063-1135). **617**

INTERNATIONAL CONSTRUCTION DIRECTORY. USA SECTION. (US/1063-1453). **618**

JOURNAL OF THERMAL INSULATION AND BUILDING ENVELOPES. (US/1065-2744). **618**

LIGHTING ANSWERS. (US/1069-0050). **619**

LOG HOMES ILLUSTRATED. (US/1072-6063). **619**

MATERIALS AND STRUCTURES / INTERNATIONAL UNION OF TESTING AND RESEARCH LABORATORIES FOR MATERIALS AND STRUCTURES (RILEM). (UK). **620**

MEANS BUILDING CONSTRUCTION COST DATA. (US/1066-0240). **620**

MEANS CONCRETE & MASONRY COST DATA. (US/1075-0274). **620**

MEANS FACILITIES CONSTRUCTION COST DATA. (US/1075-0789). **620**

MEANS FACILITIES MAINTENANCE & REPAIR COST DATA. (US/1074-0953). **620**

MEANS SITE WORK & LANDSCAPE COST DATA. (US/1064-5128). **621**

MINORITY BUILDER GAZETTE, THE. (US/1056-7828). **621**

OVERSEAS BUILDER. (US/1062-6921). **623**

PROFESSIONAL BUILDER (1993). (US/1072-0561). **624**

PUBLICITY DIRECTORY FOR THE DESIGN, ENGINEERING, AND BUILDING INDUSTRIES, THE. (US/1064-4733). **625**

PURCHASING PERFORMANCE BENCHMARKS FOR THE U.S. CONSTRUCTION/ENGINEERING INDUSTRY. (US/1060-6009). **625**

REDACTEUR (MONTREAL). (CN/1188-2670). **626**

SELL'S BUILDING & CONSTRUCTION INDEX. (UK/0966-0399). **627**

SRDS MEDIA & MARKET PLANNER. ARCHITECTURAL & CONSTRUCTION MARKETS. (US/1064-5500). **628**

CARPENTRY AND WOODWORK

POWER EQUIPMENT TRADE. (US/1063-0414). **634**

WOOD MAGAZINE'S SUPER SCROLLSAW PATTERNS. (US/1063-7893). **635**

BUSINESS

ACCEPTABLE RISK. (US/1073-2012). **636**

ADVANCES IN ENTREPRENEURSHIP, FIRM EMERGENCE, AND GROWTH. (US). **636**

AFRICAN-AMERICAN BUSINESS. (US/1065-0180). **637**

Business

AFRICAN ANVIL AND BUSINESS NEWS, THE. (US/1055-0127). **637**

AIRPORT BUSINESS. (US/1072-1797). **637**

AMERICAN COST OF LIVING SURVEY. (US/1071-099X). **638**

ARTHUR ANDERSEN CORPORATE REGISTER, THE. (UK/0956-2893). **639**

ATLANTIC BUSINESS REPORT. (CN/1192-0203). **641**

BARRON'S (CHICOPEE, MASS.). (US/1077-8039). **642**

BENCHMARKING BRIEFING. (UK/1351-5055). **642**

BETTER BUSINESS BULLETIN (NORTH PALM BEACH, FLA.), THE. (US/1064-1270). **643**

BISNIS BULLETIN. (US). **643**

BOOK OF LISTS: A REFERENCE GUIDE TO ALASKA'S LEADING INDUSTRIES, THE. (US). **643**

BRITISH COLUMBIA & ALBERTA HOME BUSINESS REPORT. (CN/1191-8640). **644**

BUSINESS AND LEGAL START-UP DIRECTORY FOR ENTREPRENEURS, THE. (US/1061-8635). **645**

BUSINESS BASICS STAFF BULLETIN. (UK/1352-5581). **646**

BUSINESS CONCEPTS. (US/1055-8217). **646**

BUSINESS EUROPA. (UK/0966-3541). **648**

BUSINESS INFORMATION BASICS. (UK/0953-9263). **649**

BUSINESS INFORMATION FROM GOVERNMENT. (UK/0966-2138). **649**

BUSINESS OWNER (NEWPORT BEACH, CALIF.). (US/1064-4598). **651**

BUSINESS PLANS HANDBOOK. (US). **651**

BUSINESS RECORD, THE. (US/1068-2899). **652**

BUSINESS REVIEW. (UK/1354-1110). **652**

BUSINESS SERIALS. (US/1056-3512). **652**

BUSINESS TODAY. (II). **653**

BUSINESS WOMEN'S NETWORK DIRECTORY, THE. (US/1076-7363). **653**

CHINA BUSINESS MONITOR. (US/1056-4500). **656**

CIFAR'S GLOBAL COMPANY HANDBOOK. (US/1060-8710). **657**

CLEVELAND METRO EAST MARKETING DIRECTORY. (US). **657**

CLEVELAND METRO WEST MARKETING DIRECTORY. (US). **657**

CLS MARKET PLACE. (US/1061-6020). **657**

COLUMBIA HEIGHTS BUSINESS NEWS. (US/1062-273X). **658**

COMPENSATION & BENEFITS ALERT. (US/1061-1576). **658**

CORPORATE AND FOUNDATION GRANTS. (US/1061-1274). **660**

CORPORATE FUNDERS OPERATING IN MISSOURI. (US/1061-4273). **661**

CPA SOFTWARE NEWS, THE. (US/1068-8285). **662**

CZECHOSLOVAKIA, MAJOR BUSINESSES / DUN & BRADSTREET INTERNATIONAL. (UK/0964-0401). **664**

D & B EUROPA. (UK). **664**

DIRECTORY OF MAILING LIST COMPANIES. (US). **666**

DIRECTORY OF NATIVE HAWAIIAN-OWNED BUSINESSES, THE. (US/1063-0856). **667**

DIRECTORY OF NORTH CAROLINA MANUFACTURING FIRMS. (US). **667**

DIRECTORY OF PUBLIC COMPANIES IN CANADA. (CN/1183-6814). **667**

DUN & BRADSTREET'S KEY BUSINESS DIRECTORY OF LATIN AMERICA. (US/1069-3041). **669**

DUN'S REGIONAL BUSINESS DIRECTORY. COLUMBUS AREA. (US/1061-0758). **670**

DUN'S REGIONAL BUSINESS DIRECTORY. TENNESSEE METROS AREA. (US/1061-0731). **670**

EASY MONEY (WESTPORT, CONN.). (US/1072-9356). **670**

ECONOMIE ET AFFAIRES AU QUEBEC. (CN/1188-4304). **671**

ELECTRONIC CLAIMS PROCESSING REPORT. (US/1071-8524). **671**

ENTREPRENEUR NEWSLETTER. (US/1073-046X). **672**

ENTREPRENEURSHIP, INNOVATION AND CHANGE. (US/1059-0137). **672**

ENTREPRISE, L'. (FR). **672**

ENVIRONMENT WATCH. WESTERN EUROPE. (US/1066-6001). **672**

ETHIOPIAN BUSINESS MAGAZINE. (US/1062-3639). **672**

EUROPE BUSINESS TRAVEL ORGANIZER, THE. (CN/1191-4238). **673**

EUROPEAN BUSINESS SERVICES DIRECTORY. (US/1063-5718). **673**

EUROPEAN CONSULTANTS DIRECTORY. (US/1060-1880). **673**

EUROPEAN DIRECTORY OF CONSUMER BRANDS AND THEIR OWNERS, THE. (UK). **673**

EUROPEAN TOP 500 / FINANCIAL TIMES. (UK). **673**

EXECUTIVE DIRECTIONS. (US). **674**

F & S INDEX UNITED STATES. (US). **674**

FAMILY BUSINESS ADVISOR, THE. (US/1060-3603). **674**

F&S INDEX EUROPE ANNUAL (1993). (US/1076-6596). **674**

F&S INDEX UNITED STATES ANNUAL. (US/1076-4941). **675**

FAULKNER & GRAY'S ... EUROPEAN BUSINESS DIRECTORY. (US/1055-2421). **675**

FAXON BUSINESS INFORMATION CATALOG. (US/1059-6844). **675**

GLOBAL COMPANY NEWS DIGEST. (US/1061-3714). **678**

GUIDA AGLI ACQUISTI PER GLI ENTI PUBBLICI. (IT). **678**

GUIDE TO PRIVATE FORTUNES. (US/1070-7964). **678**

HOME BASED HOMERUN. (US/1061-4222). **680**

HOOVER'S HANDBOOK OF WORLD BUSINESS. (US/1055-7199). **680**

HOOVER'S MASTERLIST OF MAJOR U.S. COMPANIES. (US/1066-291X). **680**

INDIA BUSINESS & INDUSTRY NEWSLETTER. (US/1064-1408). **681**

INFORMAL : ORGANO INDEPENDIENTE DE LA PEQUENA, MICROEMPRESA Y DEL SECTOR INFORMAL, EL. (PE). **682**

INFORMATION MARKETPLACE DIRECTORY. (US/1065-0393). **682**

INSIDE CONTACTS U.S.A. METRO TUCSON MARKETING DIRECTORY. (US/1059-3683). **682**

INTERNATIONAL BRANDS AND THEIR COMPANIES. (US/1050-8376). **683**

INTERNATIONAL COMPANIES AND THEIR BRANDS. (US/1050-8384). **683**

INTERNATIONAL DIRECTORY OF CONSULTANTS AND CONTRACTORS ACTIVE IN THE MIDDLE EAST AND AFRICA, AN. (US/1058-580X). **683**

INTERNATIONAL JOURNAL OF ENTREPRENEURIAL BEHAVIOUR & RESEARCH. (UK/1355-2554). **683**

INTERNATIONAL JOURNAL OF ORGANIZATIONAL ANALYSIS. (US/1055-3185). **684**

IOMA'S REPORT ON SALARY SURVEYS. (US/1067-4551). **684**

IRWIN BUSINESS AND INVESTMENT ALMANAC, THE. (US/1072-6136). **684**

JAPAN 21ST. (JA/0916-877X). **685**

JOURNAL OF ASIA-PACIFIC BUSINESS. (US/1059-9231). **685**

JOURNAL OF ASIAN BUSINESS. (US/1068-0055). **685**

JOURNAL OF EAST-WEST BUSINESS. (US/1066-9868). **686**

JOURNAL OF ENTERPRISING CULTURE. (SI/0218-4958). **687**

JOURNAL OF ENTREPRENEURSHIP, THE. (II/0971-3557). **687**

JOURNAL OF FAR EASTERN BUSINESS. (UK/1351-0363). **687**

JOURNAL OF STRATEGIC CHANGE. (US/1057-9265). **687**

KANSAS CITY METRO BUSINESS DIRECTORY. (US/1069-6334). **688**

KANSAS CITY SMALL BUSINESS MONTHLY. (US/1068-2422). **688**

LEADERSHIP DIRECTORIES ON CD-ROM. (US/1075-3869). **689**

LITHUANIA BUSINESS PACK, THE. (UK). **690**

MARKET LATIN AMERICA. (US/1066-7024). **691**

MEGABUCKING (STERLING HEIGHTS, MICH.). (US/1048-0528). **692**

MERGER YEARBOOK, THE. (US/1076-3600). **693**

METROPOLITAN NEW YORK BUSINESS AND MARKET GUIDE, THE. (US/1055-4165). **693**

MEXICAN ENVIRONMENTAL BUSINESS. (US/1075-9034). **693**

Business

MONTHLY BUSINESS FAILURES / THE DUN & BRADSTREET CORPORATION. (US). **696**

NATIONAL DIRECTORY OF CORPORATE DISTRESS SPECIALISTS, THE. (US/1060-6025). **697**

NEWS FOR ENTREPRENEURIAL MOTHERS. (US/1064-6973). **699**

NTIS ALERT. BUSINESS & ECONOMICS. (US/1074-1674). **700**

O&P BUSINESS NEWS. (US/1060-3220). **700**

O'DWYER'S WASHINGTON REPORT. (US). **700**

ORANGE COUNTY BUSINESS DIRECTORY. (US/1059-7077). **701**

OUTREACH (WASHINGTON, D.C. 1992). (US/1063-1798). **702**

OUTSTATE BUSINESS. (US/1064-3621). **702**

PACIFIC ASIAN BUSINESS REVIEW. (US/1061-8619). **702**

PACIFIC BASIN/ASEAN BUSINESS. (US/1064-9832). **702**

PBC BUSINESS GUIDE. (US/1059-2075). **702**

PBC SENIOR NEWSLETTER. (US/1059-1982). **702**

PBC TRAVEL NEWSLETTER. (US/1059-1966). **702**

PENNSYLVANIA BUSINESS MAGAZINE. (US/1060-5436). **702**

POLAND BUSINESS REPORT. (US/1063-679X). **703**

PORTABLE MBA EXECUTIVE SERVICE, THE. (US/1064-6337). **704**

PRIVACY & AMERICAN BUSINESS. (US/1070-0536). **704**

PROFILE (SOUTH PORTLAND, ME.). (US/1071-3808). **705**

PROFIT (ARMONK, N.Y.). (US/1061-9194). **705**

QUAD CITY REPORTER, THE. (US/1064-2986). **705**

QUALITY & PRODUCTIVITY ONE HUNDRED NEWSLETTER. (US/1062-9440). **705**

QUARTERLY DEC JOURNAL. (US/1063-1216). **706**

REMINGTON REPORT, THE. (US/1070-3411). **706**

RENTAL PRODUCT NEWS (1992). (US/1067-0904). **707**

REVIEW OF BUSINESS STUDIES, THE. (US/1047-4595). **708**

ROLLING VENTURES. (US/1060-8893). **708**

RUSSIAN BUSINESS REPORTS. (US/1060-569X). **708**

SALES IMPROVEMENT FOR PROFESSIONALS. (US/1063-1445). **708**

SDB/PRIMES. (US/1065-6286). **709**

SEATTLE METRO BUSINESS DIRECTORY. (US). **710**

SELLING EDGE, THE. (US/1065-3066). **710**

SERVICE & SUPPORT MANAGEMENT. (US/1068-2902). **710**

SMALL BUSINESS SPOTLIGHT NEWS. (US/1063-0252). **711**

SMARTMONEY (NEW YORK, N.Y.). (US/1069-2851). **712**

SOUTHERN BUSINESS REVIEW & FORECAST. (US/1066-3754). **712**

SOUTHERN CALIFORNIA BUSINESS DIRECTORY. (US/1061-2181). **712**

STRATEGIC DIRECTION. (UK/0258-0543). **713**

TEXAS BUSINESS DIRECTORY. (US/1053-6698). **715**

TRANSNATIONAL CORPORATIONS. (US/1014-9562). **716**

TROUBLED COMPANY PROSPECTOR, THE. (US/1062-2330). **716**

UKRAINE BUSINESS REVIEW. (UK/0969-3483). **717**

UNIDOS : JOURNAL OF OPPORTUNITY. (US). **717**

UPLINE (CHARLOTTESVILLE, VA.). (US/1062-5062). **717**

VALUE LINE EARNINGS FORECASTS. (US/1064-6310). **717**

VIETNAM MARKET WATCH. (US/1071-7900). **718**

WARD'S PRIVATE COMPANY PROFILES. (US/1071-9555). **718**

WARD'S SALES PROSPECTOR. (US/1059-9266). **718**

WARFIELD'S BUSINESS RECORD. (US/1061-1622). **719**

WEALTH RANKINGS. (US/1066-7903). **719**

WHO OWNS WHOM. (UK). **720**

WILEY BUSINESS INTELLIGENCE REPORTS. ALGERIA. (UK/1073-3213). **720**

WILEY BUSINESS INTELLIGENCE REPORTS. ANGOLA. (UK/1073-3221). **720**

WILEY BUSINESS INTELLIGENCE REPORTS. ARGENTINA. (UK/1073-323X). **720**

WILEY BUSINESS INTELLIGENCE REPORTS. AUSTRALIA. (UK/1073-3256). **720**

WILEY BUSINESS INTELLIGENCE REPORTS. AUSTRIA. (UK/1073-3248). **720**

WILEY BUSINESS INTELLIGENCE REPORTS. AZERBAIJAN. (UK/1073-3264). **720**

WILEY BUSINESS INTELLIGENCE REPORTS. BAHAMAS. (UK/1073-3272). **720**

WILEY BUSINESS INTELLIGENCE REPORTS. BAHRAIN. (UK/1073-3299). **720**

WILEY BUSINESS INTELLIGENCE REPORTS. BANGLADESH. (UK/1073-3302). **720**

WILEY BUSINESS INTELLIGENCE REPORTS. BELGIUM. (UK/1073-3280). **720**

WILEY BUSINESS INTELLIGENCE REPORTS. BOLIVIA. (UK/1073-3310). **720**

WILEY BUSINESS INTELLIGENCE REPORTS. BOTSWANA. (UK/1073-3329). **720**

WILEY BUSINESS INTELLIGENCE REPORTS. BRAZIL. (UK/1073-3345). **720**

WILEY BUSINESS INTELLIGENCE REPORTS. BRUNEI. (UK/1073-3337). **720**

WILEY BUSINESS INTELLIGENCE REPORTS. CAMEROON. (UK/1073-337X). **720**

WILEY BUSINESS INTELLIGENCE REPORTS. CANADA. (UK/1073-3361). **721**

WILEY BUSINESS INTELLIGENCE REPORTS. CHINA. (UK/1073-3396). **721**

WILEY BUSINESS INTELLIGENCE REPORTS. COLOMBIA. (UK/1073-340X). **721**

WILEY BUSINESS INTELLIGENCE REPORTS. COSTA RICA. (UK/1073-3418). **721**

WILEY BUSINESS INTELLIGENCE REPORTS. CUBA. (UK/1073-3426). **721**

WILEY BUSINESS INTELLIGENCE REPORTS. CZECH REPUBLIC. (UK/1073-3434). **721**

WILEY BUSINESS INTELLIGENCE REPORTS. ECUADOR. (UK/1073-3450). **721**

WILEY BUSINESS INTELLIGENCE REPORTS. EGYPT. (UK/1073-3469). **721**

WILEY BUSINESS INTELLIGENCE REPORTS. EL SALVADOR. (UK/1073-3477). **721**

WILEY BUSINESS INTELLIGENCE REPORTS. ESTONIA. (UK/1073-3485). **721**

WILEY BUSINESS INTELLIGENCE REPORTS. FINLAND. (UK/1073-3493). **721**

WILEY BUSINESS INTELLIGENCE REPORTS. FRANCE. (UK/1073-3507). **721**

WILEY BUSINESS INTELLIGENCE REPORTS. GABON. (UK/1073-3515). **721**

WILEY BUSINESS INTELLIGENCE REPORTS. GERMANY. (UK/1073-3523). **721**

WILEY BUSINESS INTELLIGENCE REPORTS. GHANA. (UK/1073-3531). **721**

WILEY BUSINESS INTELLIGENCE REPORTS. GREECE. (UK/1073-354X). **721**

WILEY BUSINESS INTELLIGENCE REPORTS. GUATEMALA. (UK/1073-3558). **721**

WILEY BUSINESS INTELLIGENCE REPORTS. GUYANA. (UK/1073-3566). **721**

WILEY BUSINESS INTELLIGENCE REPORTS. HAITI. (UK/1073-3574). **721**

WILEY BUSINESS INTELLIGENCE REPORTS. HONDURAS. (UK/1073-3604). **721**

WILEY BUSINESS INTELLIGENCE REPORTS. HONG KONG. (UK/1073-3590). **721**

WILEY BUSINESS INTELLIGENCE REPORTS. HUNGARY. (UK/1073-3582). **721**

WILEY BUSINESS INTELLIGENCE REPORTS. INDIA. (UK/1073-3620). **721**

WILEY BUSINESS INTELLIGENCE REPORTS. INDONESIA. (UK/1073-3612). **721**

WILEY BUSINESS INTELLIGENCE REPORTS. IRAN. (UK/1073-3647). **721**

WILEY BUSINESS INTELLIGENCE REPORTS. IRAQ. (UK/1073-3655). **721**

WILEY BUSINESS INTELLIGENCE REPORTS. IRELAND. (UK/1073-3639). **721**

WILEY BUSINESS INTELLIGENCE REPORTS. ISRAEL. (UK/1073-3663). **721**

WILEY BUSINESS INTELLIGENCE REPORTS. ITALY. (UK/1073-3671). **721**

WILEY BUSINESS INTELLIGENCE REPORTS. JAMAICA. (UK/1073-3698). **721**

WILEY BUSINESS INTELLIGENCE REPORTS. JAPAN. (UK/1073-3701). **721**

Business

WILEY BUSINESS INTELLIGENCE REPORTS. JORDAN. (UK/1073-371X). **721**

WILEY BUSINESS INTELLIGENCE REPORTS. KAZAKHSTAN. (UK/1073-3728). **721**

WILEY BUSINESS INTELLIGENCE REPORTS. KENYA. (UK/1073-3736). **722**

WILEY BUSINESS INTELLIGENCE REPORTS. KOREA. (UK/1073-3744). **722**

WILEY BUSINESS INTELLIGENCE REPORTS. KUWAIT. (UK/1073-3752). **722**

WILEY BUSINESS INTELLIGENCE REPORTS. LEBANON. (UK/1073-3760). **722**

WILEY BUSINESS INTELLIGENCE REPORTS. LIBYA. (UK/1073-3779). **722**

WILEY BUSINESS INTELLIGENCE REPORTS. LUXEMBOURG. (UK/1073-3787). **722**

WILEY BUSINESS INTELLIGENCE REPORTS. MALAYSIA. (UK/1073-3795). **722**

WILEY BUSINESS INTELLIGENCE REPORTS. MEXICO. (UK/1073-4236). **722**

WILEY BUSINESS INTELLIGENCE REPORTS. MOROCCO. (UK/1073-3809). **722**

WILEY BUSINESS INTELLIGENCE REPORTS. MOZAMBIQUE. (UK/1073-3817). **722**

WILEY BUSINESS INTELLIGENCE REPORTS. NETHERLANDS. (UK/1073-3841). **722**

WILEY BUSINESS INTELLIGENCE REPORTS. NEW ZEALAND. (UK/1073-3868). **722**

WILEY BUSINESS INTELLIGENCE REPORTS. NICARAGUE. (UK/1073-3833). **722**

WILEY BUSINESS INTELLIGENCE REPORTS. NIGERIA. (UK/1073-3825). **722**

WILEY BUSINESS INTELLIGENCE REPORTS. NORWAY. (UK/1073-385X). **722**

WILEY BUSINESS INTELLIGENCE REPORTS. OMAN. (UK/1073-3876). **722**

WILEY BUSINESS INTELLIGENCE REPORTS. PAKISTAN. (UK/1073-3884). **722**

WILEY BUSINESS INTELLIGENCE REPORTS. PARAGUAY. (UK/1073-3914). **722**

WILEY BUSINESS INTELLIGENCE REPORTS. PERU. (UK/1073-3957). **722**

WILEY BUSINESS INTELLIGENCE REPORTS. PHILIPPINES. (UK/1073-3922). **722**

WILEY BUSINESS INTELLIGENCE REPORTS. POLAND. (UK/1073-3930). **722**

WILEY BUSINESS INTELLIGENCE REPORTS. PORTUGAL. (UK/1073-3949). **722**

WILEY BUSINESS INTELLIGENCE REPORTS. PUERTO RICO. (UK/1073-3965). **722**

WILEY BUSINESS INTELLIGENCE REPORTS. RUSSIA. (UK/1073-3973). **722**

WILEY BUSINESS INTELLIGENCE REPORTS. SAUDI ARABIA. (UK/1073-399X). **722**

WILEY BUSINESS INTELLIGENCE REPORTS. SENEGAL. (UK/1073-4007). **722**

WILEY BUSINESS INTELLIGENCE REPORTS. SINGAPORE. (UK/1073-4023). **722**

WILEY BUSINESS INTELLIGENCE REPORTS. SLOVAK REPUBLIC. (UK/1073-4015). **722**

WILEY BUSINESS INTELLIGENCE REPORTS. SOUTH AFRICA. (UK/1073-3981). **722**

WILEY BUSINESS INTELLIGENCE REPORTS. SPAIN. (UK/1073-4031). **722**

WILEY BUSINESS INTELLIGENCE REPORTS. SRI LANKA. (UK/1073-404X). **722**

WILEY BUSINESS INTELLIGENCE REPORTS. SUDAN. (UK/1073-4058). **722**

WILEY BUSINESS INTELLIGENCE REPORTS. SWEDEN. (UK/1073-4260). **723**

WILEY BUSINESS INTELLIGENCE REPORTS. SWITZERLAND. (UK/1073-4066). **723**

WILEY BUSINESS INTELLIGENCE REPORTS. SYRIA. (UK/1073-4074). **723**

WILEY BUSINESS INTELLIGENCE REPORTS. TAIWAN. (UK/1073-4082). **723**

WILEY BUSINESS INTELLIGENCE REPORTS. TAJIKISTAN. (UK/1073-4090). **723**

WILEY BUSINESS INTELLIGENCE REPORTS. TANZANIA. (UK/1073-4112). **723**

WILEY BUSINESS INTELLIGENCE REPORTS. THAILAND. (UK/1073-4104). **723**

WILEY BUSINESS INTELLIGENCE REPORTS. TUNISIA. (UK/1073-4120). **723**

WILEY BUSINESS INTELLIGENCE REPORTS. TURKEY. (UK/1073-4139). **723**

WORLD BUSINESS DIRECTORY (DETROIT, MICH.). (US/1062-1172). **723**

WORLDWIDE BUSINESS PRACTICES REPORT. (US/1069-4447). **724**

YOUR GUIDE TO GOVERNMENT FINANCIAL ASSISTANCE FOR BUSINESS IN ALBERTA. (CN/1198-046X). **724**

YOUR GUIDE TO GOVERNMENT FINANCIAL ASSISTANCE FOR BUSINESS IN THE YUKON. (CN/1198-0575). **725**

ABSTRACTING, BIBLIOGRAPHIES AND STATISTICS

ACCOUNTING AND TAX DATABASE [ONLINE DATABASE]. (US). **725**

ACCOUNTING AND TAX INDEX. (US/1063-0287). **725**

BANKENSTATISTIK / DEUTSCHE BUNDESBANK. (GW/0943-8750). **726**

BUSINESS SOURCE. [COMPUTER FILE]. (US). **727**

CHEMICAL BUSINESS NEWSBASE [ONLINE DATABASE]. (UK). **727**

EXTERNAL TRADE AND BALANCE OF PAYMENTS. (LU). **728**

F&S INDEX INTERNATIONAL. (US). **728**

FINANCIAL ESTIMATES OF COMMONWEALTH PUBLIC TRADING ENTERPRISES, AUSTRALIA. (AT/1038-7609). **729**

KAPITALMARKTSTATISTIK / DEUTSCHE BUNDESBANK. (GW/0943-8769). **730**

PUBLIC SECTOR QUALITY REPORT. (US/1067-4489). **732**

SAISONBEREINIGTE WIRTSCHAFTSZAHLEN / DEUTSCHE BUNDESBANK. (GW/0943-8785). **1538**

STANDARD DIRECTORY OF ADVERTISERS. TRADENAME INDEX. (US). **733**

VIEW (BEDFORD, N.H.). (US/1070-1362). **735**

WOMEN IN MANAGEMENT REVIEW. (UK/0964-9425). **735**

ACCOUNTING

ACCOUNTING EDUCATION. (UK/0963-9284). **736**

ACCOUNTING TECHNOLOGY. (US/1068-6452). **738**

ADVANCES IN ACCOUNTING INFORMATION SYSTEMS. (US). **738**

ADVANCES IN MANAGEMENT ACCOUNTING. (US). **738**

AUDITOR-TRAK (ATLANTA, GA.). (US/1063-4053). **739**

CHARTAC TAX PRACTICE IDEAS. (AT). **740**

EUROPEAN ACCOUNTANCY YEARBOOK. (UK/0963-0538). **743**

EUROPEAN ACCOUNTING REVIEW. (UK/0963-8180). **743**

HBJ MILLER ACCOUNTANTS' LEGAL LIABILILTY. (US/1064-7155). **744**

HBJ MILLER COMPREHENSIVE LOCAL AUDIT GUIDE. (US/1064-7163). **744**

INTERNATIONAL JOURNAL OF INTELLIGENT SYSTEMS IN ACCOUNTING, FINANCE & MANAGEMENT. (UK/1055-615X). **745**

JOURNAL OF ACCOUNTING CASE RESEARCH, THE. (CN/1192-2621). **746**

JOURNAL OF ACCOUNTING, TAXATION AND FINANCE FOR BUSINESS, THE. (US/1078-0726). **746**

JOURNAL OF INTERNATIONAL ACCOUNTING AUDITING & TAXATION. (US/1061-9518). **747**

NATIONAL DIRECTORY OF PUBLIC PRACTITIONERS / CGA CANADA. (CN/1188-6153). **748**

NATIONAL DIRECTORY OF PUBLIC PRACTITIONERS / CGA CANADA. (CN/1188-6153). **748**

NATIONAL INTERNAL AUDITING LETTER, THE. (CN/1193-8765). **748**

PAYTECH (NEW YORK, N.Y.). (US/1063-9047). **749**

PPC ACCOUNTING AND AUDITING UPDATE, THE. (US/1065-3643). **749**

PUBLIC ACCOUNTING PRACTICE MANUAL. (US). **750**

REVIEW OF ACCOUNTING STUDIES. (NE/1380-6653). **751**

TAX PRACTICE & CONTROVERSIES. (US/1074-5858). **752**

WI CPA. (US/1062-2209). **753**

ADVERTISING AND PUBLIC RELATIONS

ADS INTERNATIONAL. (UK/1350-1402). **754**

ADWEEK'S GUIDE TO NEW ENGLAND ADVERTISING, DIRECT MARKETING & PUBLIC RELATIONS AGENCIES. (US). **755**

BRANDWEEK (NEW YORK, N.Y.). (US/1064-4318). **756**

Business — Commerce

BUSINESS PUBLICATION ADVERTISING SOURCE. (US). **756**

CARD DECK ADVERTISING SOURCE. (US/1071-4626). **757**

CHICAGO ... MEDIA SOURCEBOOK. (US/1069-2355). **757**

CREATIVE EXHIBITING TECHNIQUES. (US/1070-826X). **758**

DIRECTORY OF CONVENTIONS. CENTRAL CONVENTION GUIDE. (US/1076-786X). **758**

DIRECTORY OF CONVENTIONS. NORTHEAST & MID-ATLANTIC CONVENTION GUIDE. (US/1076-7878). **758**

DIRECTORY OF CONVENTIONS. SOUTHEAST CONVENTION GUIDE. (US/1076-7843). **758**

DIRECTORY OF CONVENTIONS. WEST CONVENTION GUIDE. (US/1076-7851). **758**

HEALTH-CARE MEDIA SOURCE. (US/1071-460X). **760**

JOURNAL OF CONSUMER PSYCHOLOGY: OFFICIAL JOURNAL OF THE SOCIETY FOR CONSUMER PSYCHOLOGY. (US/1057-7408). **761**

JOURNAL OF CURRENT ISSUES AND RESEARCH IN ADVERTISING. (US/1064-1734). **761**

JOURNAL OF PRODUCT & BRAND MANAGEMENT, THE. (UK/1061-0421). **761**

JOURNAL OF PUBLIC RELATIONS RESEARCH. (US/1062-726X). **761**

NEWSPAPER ADVERTISING SOURCE. (US/1071-4529). **763**

PRINT MEDIA PRODUCTION SOURCE. (US/1071-4545). **764**

PUBLIC RELATIONS TACTICS. (US). **765**

RADIO ADVERTISING SOURCE. (US/1071-4707). **765**

SELF-STARTER (MARKHAM). (CN/1188-2980). **765**

... SOUTHEAST SOURCEBOOK, THE. (US/1057-6185). **766**

SOUTHERN CALIFORNIA MEDIA SOURCEBOOK. (US/1071-4685). **766**

STANDARD DIRECTORY OF INTERNATIONAL ADVERTISERS & AGENCIES. (US). **766**

BANKING AND FINANCE

ADB REVIEW / ASIAN DEVELOPMENT BANK. (PH). **768**

AMERICAS TRADE & FINANCE. (US/1062-8118). **769**

ANNUAL REPORT / FINANCIAL INSTITUTIONS COMMISSION. (CN/1192-0254). **771**

BANGKO SENTRAL REVIEW : A MONTHLY PUBLICATION OF THE BANGKO SENTRAL NG PILIPINAS. (PH). **774**

BANK AND CORPORATE GOVERNANCE LAW REPORTER. (US). **774**

BANK OF JAPAN QUARTERLY BULLETIN. (JA/0919-1380). **775**

BANKERS NEWS. (US/1069-5907). **776**

BANKOV PREGLED / BULGARSKA NARODNA BANKA. (BU/0861-6701). **777**

BOLETIN INFORMATIVO / CENTRAL HISPANO. (SP). **779**

BULLETIN DE LA BANQUE DE FRANCE. (FR). **780**

CABLE NETWORK INVESTOR. (US/1062-3515). **781**

CEDEL EUROMONEY DIRECTORY, THE. (UK). **782**

CHINA ANALYST. (CN/1189-7090). **783**

CLARK'S BANK DEPOSITS AND PAYMENTS MONTHLY. (US/1063-2220). **783**

CREDIT & FINANCE. (US/1055-8225). **785**

CREDIT CARD MANAGEMENT EUROPE. (US). **785**

DELOVIE LYUDI. (FR). **787**

DERIVATIVES WEEK. (US/1075-2412). **787**

DIRECTORY OF BUYOUT FINANCING SOURCES. (US/1066-9736). **788**

EMERGING MARKETS ANALYST. (CN/1199-0597). **671**

FINANCE & TREASURY. (US/1070-9215). **898**

FINANCE (BOSTON, MASS.). (US/1070-9193). **4204**

FINANCE, INSURANCE & REAL ESTATE USA. (US/1066-7350). **2880**

GLOBAL M AND A. (US). **789**

GLOBAL STOCK GUIDE. (US/1060-8702). **789**

IBC/DONOGHUE'S MONEY FUND REPORT. (US). **790**

INFORMACION ESTADISTICA MENSUAL / BANCO CENTRAL DEL ECUADOR. (EC). **791**

INFRASTRUCTURE FINANCE. (US/1063-0260). **791**

INSIGHTS & STRATEGIES. (US/1065-6413). **791**

INTERNATIONAL REVIEW OF FINANCIAL ANALYSIS. (US/1057-5219). **792**

IOMA'S REPORT ON MANAGING CREDIT, RECEIVABLES & COLLECTIONS. (US/1074-8903). **793**

JOURNAL OF COMMERCIAL LENDING, THE. (US/1062-6271). **793**

JOURNAL OF EMPIRICAL FINANCE. (NE/0927-5398). **794**

JOURNAL OF FINANCIAL ABSTRACTS. (US). **794**

JOURNAL OF OFFSHORE FINANCE AND TAX. (US/1078-1161). **795**

LANE GUIDE (WESTERN ED.). (US/1062-8932). **796**

MCGRAW-HILL WORLD FUTURES AND OPTIONS DIRECTORY / COMPILED BY NICK BATTLEY. (UK). **797**

MERGERS + ACQUISITIONS INTERNATIONAL. (US). **798**

MEXICAN FORECAST. (MX). **798**

MINUTES OF PROCEEDINGS AND EVIDENCE OF THE SUB-COMMITTEE ON INTERNATIONAL FINANCIAL INSTITUTIONS OF THE STANDING COMMITTEE ON FINANCE. (CN/1193-2643). **799**

MINUTES OF PROCEEDINGS AND EVIDENCE OF THE SUB-COMMITTEE ON INTERNATIONAL FINANCIAL INSTITUTIONS OF THE STANDING COMMITTEE ON FINANCE (ENGLISH EDITION). (CN/1193-2643). **799**

MONTHLY REPORT / NATIONAL BANK OF HUNGARY. (HU). **800**

NEW FORTUNES. (US/1066-789X). **801**

NONPROFIT FINANCIAL ADVISOR. (US/1074-6331). **801**

OLYMPIA & YORK BANKRUPTCY NEWS. (US/1062-9777). **802**

PACIFIC-BASIN FINANCE JOURNAL. (NE/0927-538X). **802**

PBC CREDIT BRIEFS. (US/1059-2059). **802**

POLK FINANCIAL INSTITUTIONS DIRECTORY. (US). **803**

PROJECT AND TRADE FINANCE. (UK). **804**

PYRAMID (BURKE, VA.). (US/1065-3619). **804**

QUARTERLY ECONOMIC REVIEW / THE CENTRAL BANK OF THE BAHAMAS. (BF). **805**

QUARTERLY STATISTICAL DIGEST / THE CENTRAL BANK OF THE BAHAMAS. (BF). **806**

R.H. MACY & CO. BANKRUPTCY NEWS. (US/1061-317X). **806**

RACZ' FINANCIAL DIRECTORY. (US/1065-724X). **806**

REGIONAL ECONOMIST, THE. (US). **807**

SAVINGS & COMMUNITY BANKER. (US/1067-1757). **810**

SECURITIES MARKETING NEWS. (US/1074-8385). **811**

SECURITIZATION DIRECTORY & HANDBOOK. (US/1062-5135). **811**

SHERMAN'S COMPLETE GUIDE TO BUSINESS LOAN SOURCES. (US/1065-8467). **811**

SRC ORANGE BOOK OF 5-TREND LONG-TERM O-T-C CHARTS, THE. (US/1063-5173). **812**

STANDARD & POOR'S GLOBAL SECTOR REVIEW. (US/1076-0423). **812**

STATISTICAL BULLETIN / STATE BANK OF PAKISTAN. (PK). **812**

SUPPLEMENTARY INFORMATION FOR LEGISLATIVE REVIEW, REVENUE ESTIMATES. (CN/1187-5917). **813**

TREASURY MANAGEMENT INTERNATIONAL. (UK/0967-523X). **814**

TREASURY MANAGER'S REPORT. (US/1071-8532). **814**

VANDERWICKEN'S FINANCIAL DIGEST. (US/1061-3870). **815**

ZALE CORPORATION BANKRUPTCY NEWS. (US/1061-3161). **817**

CHAMBER OF COMMERCE

MEMBERSHIP DIRECTORY AND BUSINESS PAGES FOR THE CHAMBER OF COMMERCE OF ST. JOSEPH COUNTY. (US). **820**

COMMERCE

BARGAIN HUNTERS GUIDE. ATLANTA/ATHENS AREA. (US/1060-7722). **824**

BULLETIN OF INTERNATIONAL TRADE ISSUES. (US). **825**

CONSUMER ASIA. (UK). **829**

Business —Commerce

CONTRA COSTA COUNTY COMMERCE AND INDUSTRY DIRECTORY. (US/1059-7093). **829**

CZECH BUSINESS AND TRADE. (XR). **830**

DIRECTORY OF HIGH VOLUME INDEPENDENT DRUG STORES. (US/1054-3082). **831**

EAST/WEST BUSINESS & TRADE. (US/1065-6790). **832**

EAST/WEST EXECUTIVE GUIDE. (US/1067-635X). **832**

ESSOR FRANCAIS DU COMMERCE INTERNATIONAL. (FR). **833**

EXPORT DENMARK : KONGERIGET DANMARKS HANDELS- OG EKSPORTKALENDER. (DK). **834**

EXPORTERS RESOURCES DIRECTORY. (US/1062-3191). **835**

GLOBAL GEORGIA. (US/1063-9772). **838**

GLOBAL TRADE & TRANSPORTATION. (US/1069-2843). **838**

GMB DIRECT. (UK). **838**

HANDEL, DER. (GW). **838**

IMPORTERS MANUAL USA. (US/1065-5158). **839**

INTER-AMERICAN TRADE AND INVESTMENT LAW. (US/1078-2028). **840**

KELLY'S. (UK/1350-4150). **843**

MAISON FRANCE ISRAEL / CHAMBRE DE COMMERCE FRANCE-ISRAEL. (FR/1165-0265). **844**

MAJOR UK COMPANIES HANDBOOK. (UK/1355-7939). **844**

MAWSUAT AL-SADIRAT AL-MISRIYAH. (UA). **845**

NAFTA DIGEST / NORTH AMERICAN FREE TRADE AGREEMENT INFORMATION CENTER, THE GRADUATE SCHOOL OF INTERNATIONAL TRADE & BUSINESS ADMINISTRATION, LAREDO STATE UNIVERSITY. (US/1075-9050). **847**

NEW ZEALAND FOREIGN AFFAIRS AND TRADE RECORD. (NZ/1172-7195). **847**

RUSSIAN & EAST EUROPEAN FINANCE AND TRADE. (US/1061-2009). **850**

SINO-U.S. TRADING ALMANAC. (US/1066-1816). **851**

TORGOVLIA. (RU). **853**

TRADE NEWS / OAS. (US). **854**

TRADES (NEW ORLEANS, LA.). (US/1060-8249). **854**

WAREHOUSING / DISTRIBUTION DIRECTORY. (US/1075-0282). **857**

WORLD TRADE AND ARBITRATION MATERIALS. (SZ). **858**

WORLD TRADE RESOURCES GUIDE. (US/1058-1618). **858**

GENERAL MANAGEMENT

ACCOUNTABILITY NEWS FOR HEALTH CARE MANAGERS. (US/1076-8432). **859**

ADMINISTRATIVE ASSISTANT'S UPDATE. (CN/1191-7881). **859**

ADVANCES IN GLOBAL HIGH-TECHNOLOGY MANAGEMENT. (US). **859**

AMERICAN JOURNAL OF MANAGEMENT DEVELOPMENT. (UK/1354-5787). **859**

ASIA PACIFIC JOURNAL OF QUALITY MANAGEMENT. (HK/0965-3570). **860**

BENCHMARKING FOR QUALITY MANAGEMENT & TECHNOLOGY: AN INTERNATIONAL JOURNAL. (UK). **861**

BOARD LEADERSHIP. (US/1061-4249). **861**

BOARD MEMBER: NATIONAL CENTER FOR NONPROFIT BOARDS. (US/1058-5419). **861**

BOARDROOM (WILLOWDALE). (CN/1192-6201). **861**

BRIEF (FORT LAUDERDALE, FLA.). (US/1062-5690). **862**

BUILDING MANAGEMENT & DESIGN. (CN/1191-9841). **862**

BUSINESS PROCESS RE-ENGINEERING & MANAGEMENT JOURNAL. (UK/1355-2546). **862**

CANADIAN FACILITY MANAGEMENT & DESIGN. (CN/1193-7505). **863**

CLINICAL DATA MANAGEMENT. (US/1073-6379). **863**

COLLEGE MANAGEMENT TODAY. (UK/0966-6907). **864**

CONFERENCE BOARD'S MEMBERSHIP UPDATE, THE. (US/1072-0235). **864**

CONTINUOUS JOURNEY. (US/1065-3406). **864**

COST CONTROLLER, THE. (US/1063-2735). **864**

CREATIVITY AND INNOVATION MANAGEMENT. (UK/0963-1690). **864**

CUADERNOS DE DIFUSION / ESCUELA DE ADMINISTRACION DE NEGOCIOS PARA GRADUADOS, ESAN. (PE). **865**

DESIGN FIRM MANAGEMENT & ADMINISTRATION REPORT. (US/1057-2864). **865**

DOCUMENT MANAGEMENT : NNIEUWSBRIEF VOOR DOCUMENTAIRE INFORMATIEKUNDE / INSTITUUT VOOR TOEGEPASTE INFORMATICA. (NE). **866**

FINANCIAL OFFICER'S TAX & MANAGEMENT REPORT. (US/1065-6456). **868**

FUNDHOLDING MANAGEMENT HANDBOOK. (UK). **868**

FUTURE AT WORK, THE. (US/1069-4951). **868**

GLOBAL CONNECTOR, THE. (US/1055-3371). **869**

GROUP & ORGANIZATION MANAGEMENT. (US/1059-6011). **869**

INFORMATION MANAGEMENT IN HEALTH CARE / FULL SERVICE. (UK/1353-8853). **870**

INFORMATION TECHNOLOGY & PEOPLE (WEST LINN, OR.). (US/0959-3845). **870**

INSIDE CASE MANAGEMENT. (US/1073-6514). **870**

INVOLVEMENT : THE JOURNAL OF THE INVOLVEMENT & PARTICIPATION ASSOCIATION. (UK). **872**

IOMA'S REPORT ON CONTROLLING BENEFITS COSTS FOR LAW, DESIGN, CPA, AND OTHER PROFESSIONAL SERVICE FIRMS. (US/1062-7936). **872**

IVANOUVELLES (MONTREAL). (CN/1187-8606). **872**

IVANOUVELLES (MONTREAL). (CN/1187-8606). **872**

JOURNAL OF CONTINGENCIES AND CRISIS MANAGEMENT. (UK/0966-0879). **873**

JOURNAL OF CUSTOMER SERVICE IN MARKETING & MANAGEMENT. (US/1069-2533). **873**

JOURNAL OF ECONOMICS & MANAGEMENT STRATEGY. (US/1058-6407). **873**

JOURNAL OF HEALTHCARE RISK MANAGEMENT : THE JOURNAL OF THE AMERICAN SOCIETY FOR HEALTHCARE RISK MANAGEMENT. (US). **873**

JOURNAL OF MANAGEMENT HISTORY. (UK/1355-2546). **874**

JOURNAL OF MANAGEMENT INQUIRY. (US/1056-4926). **874**

JOURNAL OF QUALITY IN MAINTENANCE ENGINEERING. (UK/1355-2511). **874**

JOURNAL OF TRANSNATIONAL MANAGEMENT DEVELOPMENT. (US/1068-6061). **874**

LAW OFFICE ADMINISTRATOR. (US/1071-7242). **875**

LEADERSHIP WITH A HUMAN TOUCH. (US/1057-4816). **875**

MANAGING EMPLOYEE HEALTH BENEFITS. (US/1065-3937). **878**

MANAGING INFORMATION. (UK/1352-0229). **878**

MANAGING OFFICE TECHNOLOGY. (US/1070-4051). **878**

MANAGING TECHNOLOGY TODAY. (US/1062-3310). **878**

MCGRAW-HILL DIRECTORY OF MANAGEMENT FACULTY, THE. (US/1062-1989). **879**

NONPROFIT MANAGEMENT DIGEST. (US/1074-2654). **880**

PEOPLE TRENDS. (US/1065-0253). **881**

PROCEEDINGS OF THE FIRST BIANNUAL INTERNATIONAL CONFERENCE ON ADVANCES IN MANAGEMENT. (US/1059-356X). **883**

PRODUCTION AND OPERATIONS MANAGEMENT. (US/1059-1478). **883**

PROFESSIONAL MANAGER. (UK). **883**

QUALITY MANAGEMENT IN HEALTH CARE. (US/1063-8628). **884**

QUALITY SERVICE UPDATE. (US/1063-2654). **884**

QUATRE VENTS (OTTAWA). (CN/1183-8949). **884**

RELOCATION COMPASS. (US/1069-5923). **884**

SALES PRODUCTIVITY REVIEW!, THE. (US/1063-6587). **885**

SALESFYI (CHICAGO, ILL.). (US/1061-8465). **885**

T & D. (AT/1037-9687). **887**

TECHNOLOGY MANAGEMENT (NEW YORK, N.Y.). (US/1073-4457). **888**

TODAY'S MANAGER. (US/1055-0844). **888**

ZWEIG LETTER, THE. (US/1068-1310). **890**

INVESTMENTS

5-STAR INVESTOR. (US/1065-3414). **890**

Business —Purchasing

ANALYST DIRECTORY. LISTED BY COMPANY. (US/1073-6301). **890**

ANNUAL REPORT. (GW). **891**

ASIAN M&A AND INVESTMENT DATABASE. (US/1076-3708). **891**

BLOOMBERG (PRINCETON, N.J.). (US/1063-2123). **892**

CDA/INVESTNET INSIDERS' CHRONICLE. (US). **894**

CDA/SPECTRUM. 13(F) INSTITUTIONAL STOCK HOLDINGS. (US). **894**

CDA/SPECTRUM FIVE PERCENT STOCK HOLDINGS. (US). **894**

CDA/SPECTRUM INSIDER HOLDINGS. (US). **894**

CDA/WIESENBERGER MUTUAL FUNDS PANORAMA. (US). **894**

CDA/WIESENBERGER MUTUAL FUNDS UPDATE. (US/1066-9264). **894**

DAILY STOCK PRICE RECORD. NASDAQ. (US/1072-3846). **896**

EAST EUROPEAN INVESTMENT MAGAZINE. (US/1063-4029). **897**

FINANCIAL TECHNOLOGY REVIEW. (US/1071-3646). **898**

GERBINO INVESTMENT LETTER, THE. (US/1077-0119). **899**

GUIDE TO SELECTED DOMESTIC BOND MARKETS, THE. (UK). **900**

GUIDE TO WORLD EQUITY MARKETS, THE. (UK). **900**

HIGH YIELD SECURITIES JOURNAL. (US/1065-089X). **900**

INTERNATIONAL BOND INVESTOR. (UK/1352-0431). **901**

INVESTMENT ADVISOR (SHREWSBURY, N.J.). (US/1069-1731). **902**

INVESTMENT COMPANIES YEARBOOK. (US/1068-9958). **902**

INVESTMENT INFORMATION DIRECTORY (SEATTLE, WASH.). (US/1060-1481). **902**

IOMA'S REPORT ON MANAGING 401 (K) PLANS. (US/1059-2741). **903**

JAPANESE GOLF COURSE INVESTMENT REPORT. (US/1054-3562). **904**

JAY SCHABACKER'S YEARBOOK. (US). **904**

JOURNAL OF DERIVATIVES, THE. (US/1074-1240). **904**

JOURNAL OF INVESTING, THE. (US/1068-0896). **904**

JOURNAL OF MUTUAL FUND SERVICES, THE. (US/1071-846X). **904**

KNIGHT-RIDDER CRB COMMODITY YEARBOOK STATISTICAL SUPPLEMENT, THE. (US). **905**

LOUIS RUKEYSER'S WALL STREET. (US/1060-9903). **905**

MARKET INFORMATION. (UK/0966-212X). **906**

MONEY FUND REPORT. (US). **907**

MOODY'S HANDBOOK OF NASDAQ STOCKS. (US/1059-8057). **907**

MUTUAL FUND BUYER'S GUIDE. (US/1067-1358). **908**

MUTUAL FUND MARKET NEWS. (US/1070-3373). **908**

NELSON'S DIRECTORY OF PLAN SPONSORS AND TAX-EXEMPT FUNDS. (US/1053-0312). **909**

NELSON'S GUIDE TO INSTITUTIONAL RESEARCH. (US/1059-9290). **909**

NELSON'S TECHRESOURCE. (US/1065-2396). **909**

NIMA/NELSON DIRECTORY OF MINORITY AND WOMAN-OWNED INVESTMENT MANAGERS. (US/1062-0907). **910**

OPEN INTEREST/ THE TORONTO STOCK EXCHANGE. (CN). **910**

PENSION BENEFITS. (US/1063-2476). **911**

PENSION PLAN ADMINISTRATOR. (US). **911**

PERSPECTIVE ON HEALTH CARE FINANCE. (US). **911**

SECURE RETIREMENT. (US/1069-6911). **913**

ST. JAMES WORLD FUTURES AND OPTIONS DIRECTORY. (US). **914**

STANDARD & POOR'S NASDAQ AND REGIONAL EXCHANGE PROFILES. (US/1078-0262). **915**

STANDARD & POOR'S QIB. (US/1061-7043). **915**

STANDARD & POOR'S RATINGS HANDBOOK. (US/1061-0855). **915**

STOCK EXCHANGE OFFICIAL YEARBOOK. (UK). **916**

TAX FACTS. INVESTMENTS ED. (US/1061-4028). **917**

WALL STREET & TECHNOLOGY. (US/1060-989X). **919**

WHO OWNS CORPORATE AMERICA. (US/1061-1258). **919**

WORLD INVESTMENT DIRECTORY. VOL. 1, ASIA AND THE PACIFIC. (US). **920**

WORTH (BOSTON, MASS.). (US/1060-5967). **920**

MARKETING

1ST PLACE MARKETING. (US/1062-2462). **920**

ACCESS MEXICO. (US/1064-928X). **920**

ADVANCES IN BUSINESS MARKETING AND PURCHASING. (US/1069-0964). **920**

ADVANCES IN DISTRIBUTION CHANNEL RESEARCH. (US/1071-9679). **920**

ADVANCES IN SERVICES MARKETING AND MANAGEMENT. (US/1067-5671). **920**

ASIA PACIFIC JOURNAL OF MARKETING AND LOGISTICS. (UK). **921**

DIRECT MARKETING LIST SOURCE. (US/1071-4561). **923**

HISPANIC MEDIA & MARKET SOURCE. (US/1071-4553). **925**

INSIDE TRAC, THE. (US/1059-387X). **926**

ISSUES IN AGRICULTURAL DATABASE MARKETING. (US/1060-6017). **927**

JOURNAL OF BUSINESS-TO-BUSINESS MARKETING. (US/1051-712X). **927**

JOURNAL OF MARKETING COMMUNICATIONS. (UK/1352-7266). **928**

JOURNAL OF MARKETING PRACTICE : APPLIED MARKETING SCIENCE. (UK/1355-2538). **928**

JOURNAL OF MINISTRY MARKETING & MANAGEMENT. (US/1057-1523). **928**

JOURNAL OF STRATEGIC MARKETING. (UK/0965-254X). **929**

MARKET. ASIA PACIFIC. (US/1059-275X). **930**

MARKETING MAGAZINE (TORONTO). (CN/1196-4650). **931**

MARKETING MANAGEMENT (CHICAGO, ILL.). (US/1061-3846). **931**

MARKETING REPORT, THE. (US/1064-3893). **932**

METRO PHOENIX MARKETING DIRECTORY. (US/1059-6720). **933**

OFFICIAL GUIDE TO THE AMERICAN MARKETPLACE, THE. (US). **934**

SALES & MARKETING ONE HUNDRED NEWSLETTER. (US/1064-4466). **936**

PERSONNEL MANAGEMENT

ACA JOURNAL / AMERICAN COMPENSATION ASSOCIATION. (US/1068-0918). **938**

ASIA PACIFIC JOURNAL OF HUMAN RESOURCES. (AT/1038-4111). **938**

BENEFITS & COMPENSATION SOLUTIONS. (US/1069-1707). **938**

FINANCIAL MANAGER'S REPORT ON COST CUTTING, THE. (US/1070-2210). **940**

HRM DOWNSIZING STRATEGIES. (US). **941**

HUMAN RESOURCES FORECAST. (US/1066-2758). **942**

INTERNATIONAL JOURNAL OF SELECTION AND ASSESSMENT. (UK/0965-075X). **943**

LEARNING ORGANIZATION, THE. (UK). **943**

LINTON TRAINER'S RESOURCE DIRECTORY, THE. (US/1064-234X). **943**

NEW APPROACHES TO EMPLOYEE MANAGEMENT. (US). **944**

PERSONNEL ASSISTANT'S HANDBOOK. (UK/1351-0614). **945**

PERSONNEL EXECUTIVES CONTACTBOOK. (US/1068-4751). **945**

PERSONNEL MANAGEMENT PLUS. (UK). **945**

QUALITY MANAGEMENT JOURNAL, THE. (US/1068-6967). **946**

QWL NEWS & ABSTRACTS / WORK RESEARCH UNIT. (UK). **946**

TEAM PERFORMANCE MANAGEMENT: AN INTERNATIONAL JOURNAL. (UK/1352-7592). **947**

WHO'S WHO IN THE INTERNATIONAL PERSONNEL MANAGEMENT ASSOCIATION. (US/1064-1653). **948**

PURCHASING

AMERITECH INDUSTRIAL PURCHASING GUIDE. UPSTATE NEW YORK, WESTERN PENNSYLVANIA. (US/1071-0302). **949**

Business — Purchasing

COMMERCIAL TRAILER BLUE BOOK. (US/1058-3076). **949**

GOVERNMENT PROCUREMENT. (US). **950**

OFICINA, LA. (US). **951**

PURCHASING PERFORMANCE BENCHMARKS FOR THE NONFERROUS METALS INDUSTRY. (US/1062-5860). **951**

PURCHASING PERFORMANCE BENCHMARKS FOR THE U.S. APPLIANCE INDUSTRY. (US/1062-2063). **951**

RETAIL

EXCLUSIVELY MALLS : CHICAGO'S METROPOLITAN MALL RESOURCE AND REFERENCE DIRECTORY. (US/1058-577X). **954**

FAIRCHILD'S RETAIL STORES FINANCIAL DIRECTORY. (US). **954**

FIELDING'S SHOPPING EUROPE. (US/1068-641X). **954**

GUIDE TO RETAIL SHOPS. (US/1061-2106). **954**

RETAIL BUSINESS. MARKET SURVEYS / ECONOMIST INTELLIGENCE UNIT. (UK/0951-9734). **956**

RETAIL PROFIT FORUM. (US/1057-7033). **957**

CHEMISTRY

ADVANCE ACS ABSTRACTS. (US/1068-8382). **959**

ADVANCES IN ANALYTICAL GEOCHEMISTRY. (US). **959**

ALCHEMIST JOURNAL, THE. (US/1065-8033). **960**

AMINO ACIDS, PEPTIDES, AND PROTEINS. (CAMBRIDGE, ENGLAND). (UK). **960**

ANCIENNE USINE A GAZ DE LA RUE VERDUN A QUEBEC, L'. (CN/1191-4025). **960**

BIOORGANIC & MEDICINAL CHEMISTRY. (UK/0968-0896). **962**

CAMFORD CHEMICAL REPORT. (CN/1187-8746). **966**

CHEMICAL HERITAGE. (US/1066-5315). **968**

CHEMICAL INFORMATION ALERT. (US/1064-4601). **968**

CHEMICAL SCIENCES GRADUATE SCHOOL FINDER. (US/1058-1227). **969**

CHEMISTRY REVIEWS. (SZ/1071-6114). **971**

ELECTROCHEMICAL SOCIETY INTERFACE, THE. (US/1064-8208). **975**

EUROPEAN JOURNAL OF HISTOCHEMISTRY : EJH. (IT). **975**

FOCUS ON CATALYSTS. (UK/1351-4180). **975**

FOCUS ON DIAGNOSTICS. (UK/0969-6229). **975**

FOCUS ON ELECTRONICS CHEMICALS. (UK/0969-6202). **975**

FOCUS ON INTERMEDIATES AND CONTRACT CHEMICALS. (UK/1352-3538). **975**

FOCUS ON PIGMENTS. (UK/0969-6210). **975**

FOCUS ON SOLVENTS. (UK/1351-4202). **975**

FRONTIERS IN CARBOHYDRATE RESEARCH. (US). **976**

GEOCHEMISTRY AND COSMOCHEMISTRY. (US/1056-7518). **976**

GODISHNIK NA SOFIISKIIA UNIVERSITET "SV. KLIMENT OKHRIDSKI," KHIMICHESKI FAKULTET / ANNUAIRE DE L'UNIVERSITE DE SOFIA "ST. KLIMENT OHRIDSKI," FACULTE DE CHIMIE. (BU). **976**

HETEROCYCLIC COMMUNICATIONS. (UK/0793-0283). **976**

HETEROGENEOUS CHEMISTRY REVIEWS. (UK/1068-6983). **977**

HWAHAK SEGYE: CHEMWORLD. (KO) **977**

ISOLATION AND PURIFICATION. (US/1065-6081). **978**

IZVESTIIA AKADEMII NAUK. SERIIA KHIMICHESKAIA / ROSSIISKAIA AKADEMIIA NAUK. (RU). **979**

IZVESTIIA SORAN. SIBIRSKII KHIMICHESKII ZHURNAL. (RU). **979**

JOURNAL FUER PRAKTISCHE CHEMIE, CHEMIKER-ZEITUNG. (GW/0941-1216). **979**

JOURNAL OF CHEMICAL EDUCATION. SOFTWARE. D. (US/1066-4157). **980**

JOURNAL OF CHEMICAL VAPOR DEPOSITION. (US/1056-7860). **980**

JOURNAL OF ENVIRONMENTAL POLYMER DEGRADATION. (US/1064-7546). **981**

JPRS REPORT. SCIENCE & TECHNOLOGY. CENTRAL EURASIA. CHEMISTRY [MICROFORM] / FOREIGN BROADCAST INFORMATION SERVICE. (US). **983**

MACROMOLECULAR CHEMISTRY AND PHYSICS. (SZ/1022-1352). **985**

MACROMOLECULAR RAPID COMMUNICATIONS. (SZ/1022-1336). **985**

MACROMOLECULAR SYMPOSIA. (GW/1022-1360). **985**

MACROMOLECULAR THEORY AND SIMULATIONS. (SZ/1022-1344). **985**

METAL-BASED DRUGS. (UK/0793-0291). **986**

POLYMER SCIENCE. SERIES B. (RU). **989**

RADIOCHEMISTRY (NEW YORK, N.Y.). (US/1066-3622). **990**

REACTION!. (UK/1353-1190). **990**

RECEPTORS AND CHANNELS. (US/1060-6823). **990**

REGULATED CHEMICALS DIRECTORY. (US/1058-1707). **991**

RUSSIAN CHEMICAL BULLETIN. (US/1066-5285). **992**

RUSSIAN JOURNAL OF APPLIED CHEMISTRY. (US/1070-4272). **992**

RUSSIAN JOURNAL OF COORDINATION CHEMISTRY. (US/1070-3284). **992**

RUSSIAN JOURNAL OF GENERAL CHEMISTRY. (US/1070-3632). **992**

SAR AND QSAR IN ENVIRONMENTAL RESEARCH. (US/1062-936X). **992**

SUPRAMOLECULAR CHEMISTRY. (SW/1061-0278). **993**

TODAY'S CHEMIST AT WORK. (US/1062-094X). **994**

UKRAINIAN CHEMISTRY JOURNAL. (US/1063-4568). **994**

VESCI AKADEMII NAVUK BELARUSI. SERYA HIMICNYH NAVUK. (BW). **995**

VYSOKOMOLEKULIARNYE SOEDINENIIA. SERIIA A I SERIIA B. (RU). **995**

ABSTRACTING, BIBLIOGRAPHIES AND STATISTICS

CA SELECTS: ALUMINUM-LITHIUM & ALUMINUM-CERIUM ALLOYS. (US/1066-1166). **997**

CA SELECTS: BISMUTH CHEMISTRY. (US/1061-5342). **998**

CA SELECTS: COMPOSITE MATERIALS (CERAMIC). (US/1066-1158). **1000**

CA SELECTS: COMPOSITE MATERIALS (METALLIC). (US/1066-114X). **1000**

CA SELECTS: GEOCHEMISTRY. (US/1066-5730). **1003**

CA SELECTS: METALLIC GLASSES. (US/1062-8681). **1005**

CA SELECTS: MOLECULAR MODELING (BIOCHEMICAL ASPECTS). (US/1059-2784). **1005**

CA SELECTS: SHAPE MEMORY ALLOYS. (US/1062-869X). **1009**

CA SELECTS: STRESS CORROSION - METALS. (US/1066-1174). **1010**

CA SELECTS: TECHNICAL CERAMICS. (US/1062-8703). **1010**

GAS & LIQUID CHROMATOGRAPHY LITERATURE, ABSTRACTS & INDEX. (US/1059-3160). **1011**

ANALYTICAL CHEMISTRY

ADVANCES IN DNA SEQUENCE SPECIFIC AGENTS. (US/1067-568X). **1012**

JOURNAL OF AOAC INTERNATIONAL. (US/1060-3271). **1016**

JOURNAL OF CHROMATOGRAPHY. A. (NE). **1016**

JOURNAL OF CHROMATOGRAPHY. B, BIOMEDICAL APPLICATIONS. (NE/0378-4347). **1017**

JOURNAL OF MASS SPECTROMETRY. PART A. (UK/1076-5174). **1017**

PROCESS ANALYTICAL CHEMISTRY SOURCE BOOK. (US/1063-0708). **1018**

CHEMICAL TECHNOLOGY

ADHESIVES & SEALANTS INDUSTRY. (US/1070-9592). **1020**

ANALYTICAL METHODS AND INSTRUMENTATION. (UK/1063-5246). **1020**

FOCUS ON PAPER CHEMICALS. (UK/1351-4199). **1024**

FOCUS ON SURFACTANTS. (UK/1351-4210). **1024**

INDIAN JOURNAL OF CHEMICAL TECHNOLOGY. (II/0971-457X). **1025**

JORNAL DO BRASIL. (BL). **1026**

PROCESS SAFETY PROGRESS. (US/1066-8527). **1028**

RUSSIAN CHEMICAL INDUSTRY. (US/1068-3704). **1029**

SOFW JOURNAL. (GW). **1030**

WINDOW ON CHEMOMETRICS. (UK/0966-9086). **1031**

CRYSTALLOGRAPHY

ACTA CRYSTALLOGRAPHICA. SECTION A, FUNDAMENTALS OF CRYSTALLOGRAPHY. (DK). **1031**

ACTA CRYSTALLOGRAPHICA. SECTION D, BIOLOGICAL CRYSTALLOGRAPHY. (DK/0907-4449). **1031**

CRYSTALLOGRAPHY REPORTS. (US/1063-7745). **1031**

JOURNAL OF CHEMICAL CRYSTALLOGRAPHY. (US/1074-1542). **1032**

MOLECULAR CRYSTALS AND LIQUID CRYSTALS SCIENCE AND TECHNOLOGY: SECTION A, MOLECULAR CRYSTALS AND LIQUID CRYSTALS. (US/1058-725X). **1032**

MOLECULAR CRYSTALS AND LIQUID CRYSTALS SCIENCE AND TECHNOLOGY SECTION C, MOLECULAR MATERIALS. (US/1058-7276). **1033**

ELECTROCHEMISTRY

JOURNAL OF ELECTROANALYTICAL CHEMISTRY. (SZ). **1034**

RUSSIAN JOURNAL OF ELECTROCHEMISTRY. (US). **1035**

INORGANIC CHEMISTRY

ADVANCES IN METAL AND SEMICONDUCTOR CLUSTERS. (US/1075-1629). **1035**

ORGANIC CHEMISTRY

ADVANCES IN MEDICINAL CHEMISTRY. (US/1067-5698). **1039**

CONTEMPORARY ORGANIC SYNTHESIS. (UK/1350-4894). **1041**

JOURNAL OF LIPID MEDIATORS AND CELL SIGNALLING. (NE/0929-7855). **1042**

JOURNAL OF MACROMOLECULAR SCIENCE. PURE AND APPLIED CHEMISTRY. (US/1060-1325). **1042**

JOURNAL OF ORGANIC CHEMISTRY OF THE USSR. (US/1070-4280). **1043**

JOURNAL OF PEPTIDE SCIENCE. (UK/1075-2617). **1043**

PHYSICAL AND THEORETICAL CHEMISTRY

ADVANCES IN CLASSICAL TRAJECTORY METHODS. (US/1066-5005). **1049**

COLLOIDS AND SURFACES. A, PHYSICOCHEMICAL AND ENGINEERING ASPECTS. (NE/0927-7757). **1051**

COLLOIDS AND SURFACES B: BIOINTERFACES. (NE/0927-7765). **1051**

FREE RADICAL RESEARCH. (US/1071-5762). **1052**

KEMIVARLDEN. (SW/1102-6650). **1055**

CHILDREN AND YOUTH INTERESTS

AMERICAN GIRL (MIDDLETON, WIS.). (US/1062-7812). **1060**

BABYBUG (PERU, ILL.). (US/1077-1131). **1060**

BARNEY MAGAZINE. (US/1075-217X). **1060**

DEBROUILLARDS (MONTREAL). (CN/1187-8681). **1062**

DON THE BEAR SERIES. (US/1062-1385). **1063**

KIDDIE BAZAAR. (US/1057-3011). **1065**

KIDS COPY. (US/1063-9659). **1065**

KIDSTAR 1250. (US/1064-2056). **1065**

MIGHTY MORPHIN POWER RANGERS. (US). **1066**

MORE FREE STUFF FOR KIDS. (US/1065-5093). **1066**

ONLY FOR KIDS MINI MAG. (US/1066-2952). **1067**

OUTSIDE KIDS. (US/1069-420X). **1067**

PAINTBOX (LOS ANGELES, CALIF.). (US/1064-7589). **1067**

QUAKE (NEW YORK, N.Y.). (US/1070-969X). **1068**

SOCCER JR. (US/1060-9911). **1069**

SOMOS. (CU). **1069**

SPIDER (PERU, ILL.). (US/1070-2911). **1069**

STORIES THAT RHYME EVERY TIME KIDS PAGES. (US/1063-1380). **1069**

STRAIGHT TALK (PLEASANTVILLE, N.Y.). (US/1062-0095). **1069**

SWEET B'S PAD. (US/1064-5977). **1070**

TEEN STUDENT GUIDE (SPRINGFIELD, MO.). (US/1059-3349). **1070**

TEENSCOPE MAGAZINE. (US/1059-3764). **1070**

CIVIL DEFENSE

COVERTACTION QUARTERLY. (US/1067-7232). **1073**

EMERGENCY. (UK). **1073**

CLASSICAL STUDIES

AMS ANCIENT AND CLASSICAL STUDIES. (US/1058-238X). **1074**

CLASSICAL RUSSIA. (US/1070-9711). **1076**

INTERNATIONAL JOURNAL OF THE CLASSICAL TRADITION. (US/1073-0508). **1077**

CLOTHING INDUSTRY AND FASHION

IMPRINTING BUSINESS. (US/1066-7083). **1085**

COLLEGE AND SCHOOL PUBLICATIONS

ADJUNCT INFO. (US/1063-861X). **1089**

CONNECTIONS (ASSOCIATION OF AMERICAN COLLEGES). (US/1064-8755). **1091**

GET A CLUE: GUIDE TO CORNELL & ITHACA, NY. (US/1063-1127). **1091**

H.A.C. JOURNAL. (AT). **1092**

ALUMNI

ALUMNI/AE DIRECTORY / HARVARD DIVINITY SCHOOL. (US). **1097**

ALUMNI DIRECTORY. (US). **1097**

ALUMNI DIRECTORY. (US). **1097**

ALUMNI DIRECTORY / ALLEN UNIVERSITY. (US). **1097**

ALUMNI DIRECTORY / BLACK HILLS STATE UNIVERSITY. (US). **1097**

ALUMNI DIRECTORY / COLLEGE OF BUSINESS ADMINISTRATION. (US). **1098**

ALUMNI DIRECTORY / COLLEGE OF LIBERAL ARTS, THE UNIVERSITY OF TEXAS AT AUSTIN. (US). **1098**

ALUMNI DIRECTORY / DANIEL WEBSTER COLLEGE, NEAI. (US). **1098**

ALUMNI DIRECTORY / FERRIS STATE UNIVERSITY, COLLEGE OF ALLIED HEALTH SCIENCES. (US). **1098**

ALUMNI DIRECTORY / GOLDEN GATE BAPTIST THEOLOGICAL SEMINARY. (US). **1098**

ALUMNI DIRECTORY / LUTHERAN SCHOOL OF THEOLOGY AT CHICAGO. (US). **1098**

ALUMNI DIRECTORY / MERCY COLLEGE. (US). **1098**

ALUMNI DIRECTORY / MONTANA STATE UNIVERSITY. (US). **1098**

ALUMNI DIRECTORY / STOCKTON STATE COLLEGE. (US/1065-5166). **1099**

ALUMNI DIRECTORY / THE CALIFORNIA CULINARY ACADEMY. (US). **1099**

ALUMNI DIRECTORY / THE STATE UNIVERSITY OF NEW YORK COLLEGE AT BROCKPORT. (US). **1099**

ALUMNI DIRECTORY / UNIVERSITY OF ILLINOIS, COLLEGE OF VETERINARY MEDICINE. (US). **1100**

ALUMNI DIRECTORY / WESTCHESTER COMMUNITY COLLEGE. (US). **1100**

ALUMNI DIRECTORY / WILLIAM E. SIMON GRADUATE SCHOOL OF BUSINESS ADMINISTRATION, UNIVERSITY OF ROCHESTER. (US). **1100**

College and School Publications —Alumni

CORNELL MAGAZINE. (US/1070-2733). **1101**

DIRECTORY / EASTERN KENTUCKY UNIVERSITY, NATIONAL ALUMNI ASSOCIATION. (US). **1101**

TEXAS ALCALDE. (US/1061-561X). **1103**

COMMUNICATION

AUDIOFILE (PORTLAND, ME.). (US/1063-0244). **1104**

BALKANMEDIA. (BU/0861-5047). **1104**

BRAZILIAN COMMUNICATION RESEARCH YEARBOOK. (BL/0103-9318). **1105**

CANADIAN MULTI MEDIA MAGAZINE, THE. (CN/1188-5556). **1105**

CHICAGO METRO MARKET MEDIA DIRECTORY. (US/1058-4927). **1106**

COMMUNICATION SERIALS. (US/1041-7893). **1107**

CONVERGE (SUNNYVALE, CALIF.). (US/1072-9224). **1109**

DECISIONS MEDIAS. (FR/1165-8606). **1109**

EBU TECHNICAL REVIEW. (SZ/1019-6587). **1110**

ECO : PUBLICACAO DA POS-GRADUACAO DA ESCOLA DE COMUNICACAO DA UNIVERSIDADE FEDERAL DO RIO DE JANEIRO. (BL). **1110**

ELECTRONIC MESSAGING UPDATE. (US/1072-1959). **1110**

EUROPEAN JOURNAL OF DISORDERS OF COMMUNICATION. (UK/0963-7273). **1111**

IEEE PERSONAL COMMUNICATIONS MAGAZINE. (US). **1112**

INFORMATION FUTURES. (US/1062-1059). **1113**

INFORMATION NETWORKS. (US/1073-8126). **1113**

INSIDE GTE. (US/1061-2637). **1113**

JACA : JOURNAL OF THE ASSOCIATION FOR COMMUNICATION ADMINISTRATION. (US/0360-0939). **1114**

JAPANESE TECHNOLOGY REVIEWS. SECTION B, COMPUTERS AND COMMUNICATION. (US/1058-7306). **1114**

LATIN AMERICAN TELECOM REPORT. (US/1062-3884). **1115**

MACROMEDIA USER JOURNAL. (US/1065-3929). **1115**

MATTHEWS MEDIA DIRECTORY. (CN/1193-9575). **1116**

MEDIA MONITOR (DANVILLE, CALIF.). (US/1061-9267). **1116**

MULTIMEDIA BUSINESS REPORT. (US/1065-8300). **1117**

MULTIMEDIA WEEK. (US/1064-6639). **1118**

NEWS INC. (US). **1118**

POPULAR COMMUNICATIONS COMMUNICATIONS GUIDE. (US/1059-2164). **1119**

TECHNICAL COMMUNICATION QUARTERLY. (US/1057-2252). **1122**

TECHNIQUE (HYATTSVILLE, MD.). (US/1076-0326). **1122**

TEMAS DE COMUNICACION. (UY/0797-6488). **1123**

TEMAS DE COMUNICACION. (VE). **1123**

TRAINING MEDIA REVIEW. (US/1072-3188). **1123**

VIEW POINTS (FULLERTON, CALIF.). (US/1063-0325). **1123**

WESTERN JOURNAL OF COMMUNICATION. (US/1057-0314). **1124**

WIRELESS DATA NEWS. (US/1069-3416). **1124**

ABSTRACTING, BIBLIOGRAPHIES AND STATISTICS

BROADCASTING & CABLE YEARBOOK. (US/0000-1511). **1124**

BROADCASTING

AFRIKA MIX. (US/1061-3730). **1125**

BBC ANNUAL REVIEW. (UK). **1127**

BBC WORLDWIDE : THE BBC WORLD SERVICE MAGAZINE. (UK). **1127**

BROADCAST CABLE FINANCIAL JOURNAL & CREDITOPICS. (US). **1127**

BROADCASTING & CABLE. (US/1068-6827). **1128**

CABLE TV FINANCE (1992). (US/1061-5652). **1129**

CABLE TV REGULATION (1993). (US/1068-9826). **1129**

CIS TODAY / COMPILED BY RFE/RL RESEARCH INSTITUTE MONITORING UNIT. (RU). **1130**

COMMUNIQUE - ASSOCIATION CANADIENNE DE TELEVISION PAR CABLE (1992). (CN/1192-5035). **1130**

DAILY REPORT. CENTRAL EURASIA / FOREIGN BROADCAST INFORMATION SERVICE. (US). **1130**

DAILY REPORT. CENTRAL EURASIA. INDEX. (US/1062-9939). **1130**

MEDIA AND THE LAW (GREENWICH, CONN.). (US/1065-965X). **1134**

PRIVATE CABLE INVESTOR. (US/1068-4514). **1136**

RADIO INK. (US/1064-587X). **1137**

RADIOCOMM MAGAZINE. (CN/1196-0809). **1138**

SUMMARY OF WORLD BROADCASTS. PART 2, CENTRAL EUROPE, THE BALKANS. WEEKLY ECONOMIC REPORT : SWB. (UK). **1139**

SUMMARY OF WORLD BROADCASTS. PART 3, ASIA, PACIFIC / BBC MONITORING. (UK). **1139**

SUMMARY OF WORLD BROADCASTS. PART 4, THE MIDDLE EAST : SWB. (UK). **1140**

SUMMARY OF WORLD BROADCASTS. PART 5, AFRICA, LATIN AMERICA AND THE CARIBBEAN : SWB. (UK). **1140**

SUMMARY OF WORLD BROADCASTS. PART 5, AFRICA, LATIN AMERICA AND THE CARIBBEAN. WEEKLY ECONOMIC REPORT : SWB. (UK). **1140**

TELE K7, TELE 7 VIDEO. (FR/1248-9948). **1140**

TV BLUEPRINT. (US/1064-9433). **1141**

TV STATION LOG. (US/1061-8317). **1142**

TV VIDEO. (US/1064-2676). **1142**

VIEWFINDER (LEWISTON, MAINE). (US/1064-4520). **1143**

WJCT MAGAZINE. (US/1065-8564). **1143**

WORLD GUIDE TO TELEVISION & FILM. (US/1072-6144). **1143**

POSTAL COMMUNICATIONS

CAHIERS DE L'IREPP, LES. (FR/1240-2095). **1144**

USPS PROCUREMENT MANUAL. (US). **1147**

TELECOMMUNICATIONS

ANNUAL REVIEW OF COMMUNICATIONS. (US/1073-0885). **1149**

ARCHIV FUER POST UND TELEKOMMUNIKATION. (GW/0943-2337). **1149**

CALL CENTER MAGAZINE. (US/1064-5543). **1151**

COMMUNICATIONS SERIES. COMMUNICATIONS NETWORKING SERVICES. (US). **1152**

COMMUNICATIONS SERIES. VOICE NETWORKING SYSTEMS. (US). **1152**

COMMUNITY CABLE LETTER. (US/1074-3936). **1152**

CONSUMER MULTIMEDIA REPORT. (US/1067-7887). **1152**

DIRECTORY OF MULTIMEDIA EQUIPMENT, SOFTWARE, AND SERVICES / ICIA. (US). **1153**

ELECTRICAL COMMUNICATION. (FR/1242-0565). **1154**

ELECTRONIC INFORMATION REPORT. (US). **1154**

EWP UPDATE, THE. (US/1062-3787). **1155**

GLOBAL TELECOM. (US/1065-8424). **1156**

GLOBAL TELEPHONY. (US/1067-6317). **1156**

I & T MAGAZINE. (BE). **1148**

IEE PROCEEDINGS. COMMUNICATIONS. (UK/1350-2425). **1156**

IEE PROCEEDINGS. RADAR, SONAR, AND NAVIGATION. (UK/1350-2395). **1156**

IEICE TRANSACTIONS ON FUNDAMENTALS OF ELECTRONICS, COMMUNICATIONS AND COMPUTER SCIENCES. (JA/0916-8508). **1157**

INSIDE BT. (US/1061-2629). **1157**

INSIDE MOTOROLA. (US/1065-6898). **1157**

INSIDE SPRINT CORP. (US/1065-8505). **1157**

INTERNATIONAL JOURNAL OF COMMUNICATION SYSTEMS. (UK/1074-5351). **1158**

ITU NEWSLETTER. (SZ). **1158**

LOCAL TELECOM COMPETITION NEWS. (US/1067-6333). **1159**

MANAGING VOICE NETWORKS. (US). **1159**

NORTHERN BUSINESS INFORMATION'S TELECOM PERSPECTIVES. (US/1078-523X). **1161**

PACIFIC RIM TELECOMMUNICATIONS. (US). **1161**

PCIA JOURNAL. (US/1075-7821). **1161**

PERSONAL DEVICES REPORT. (US). **1161**

PUBLIC SAFETY ON-LINE. (US/1072-9321). **1162**

REVUE DES TELECOMMUNICATIONS PARIS. 1992. (FR/1243-7492). **1163**

RUSSIAN FIBER OPTICS AND TELECOMMUNICATIONS BUSINESS. (US/1066-9612). **1163**

SUBMARINE FIBER OPTIC COMMUNICATIONS SYSTEMS. (US/1070-096X). **1164**

TELECOM STANDARDS NEWSLETTER. (US/1064-1076). **1165**

TELECOMMUNICATIONS DIRECTORY (DETROIT, MICH.). (US/1055-8454). **1165**

TELEMEDIA NEWS AND VIEWS. (US/1071-135X). **1167**

... TELEPHONE INDUSTRY DIRECTORY / PHILLIPS BUSINESS INFORMATION, INC, THE. (US). **1167**

TELEPHONE WEEK. (US/1062-4724). **1167**

WARREN'S CABLE REGULATION MONITOR. (US/1067-6252). **1168**

WASHINGTON TELECOM NEWS. (US/1069-7500). **1168**

WIRELESS BUSINESS & FINANCE. (US). **1169**

WIRELESS CABLE INVESTOR. (US/1075-1483). **1169**

WIRELESS MEDIA & MESSAGING. (US). **1169**

WIRELESS TELECOM INVESTOR. (US/1075-413X). **1169**

COMPUTERS

ANDREW SEYBOLD'S OUTLOOK ON MOBILE COMPUTING. (US/1066-8845). **1170**

AUTOCAD USER. (CN). **1171**

AUTOCAD WORLD. (US/1060-1317). **1171**

C/C++ USERS JOURNAL. (US). **1172**

CALS JOURNAL. (US/1061-2572). **1173**

CHICAGO JOURNAL OF THEORETICAL COMPUTER SCIENCE. (US). **1174**

CLARISWORKS JOURNAL. (US/1059-6542). **1174**

CLIENT/SERVER TODAY. (US). **1174**

COLORADO COMPUTER RESOURCES. (US/1062-4791). **1175**

COMPUTER ASSISTED REHABILITATION THERAPY. (US/1062-9734). **1176**

COMPUTER FREEBIE$. (US/1062-3647). **1176**

COMPUTER INFO. (US/1061-6403). **1176**

COMPUTER LIFE. (US/1076-9862). **1177**

COMPUTER PARTNER LEADS. (US/1064-7007). **1177**

COMPUTER SCIENCE SYLLABUS. (US/1065-2078). **1177**

COMPUTER TELEPHONY. (US/1072-1711). **1178**

COMPUTER VIRUS DEVELOPMENTS QUARTERLY. (US/1065-8246). **1178**

COMPUTERGRAM WEEKLY. (UK/0969-2053). **1178**

COMPUTERS & COMMUNICATIONS IN AFRICA. (UK). **1178**

CONNECT (ANN ARBOR, MICH.). (US/1070-0994). **1180**

DEPECHE MAC. (CN/1191-0755). **1182**

DIGITAL SYSTEMS JOURNAL. (US/1067-7224). **1182**

DIGITAL UNIX NEWS. (US/1074-8911). **1182**

DOCUMENT IMAGING REPORT. (US). **1183**

DOS-WIN SPECIAL. (NE/0929-5011). **1183**

EASY APPROACH. (US/1076-0814). **1183**

FAMILY PC. (US/1076-7754). **1184**

FM TECHNOLOGY REPORT. (US/1067-6244). **1185**

FUNDAMENTA INFORMATICAE. (NE/0169-2968). **1185**

GOVERNMENT IMAGING. (US). **4651**

GRADUATE ASSISTANTSHIP DIRECTORY IN COMPUTING / ASSOCIATION FOR COMPUTING MACHINERY. (US). **1185**

HR COMPUTING. (US/1060-5916). **1186**

IBM INTERNET JOURNAL. (US/1068-1396). **1186**

IC CARD SYSTEMS & DESIGN. (US/1074-6269). **1187**

IEEE ANNALS OF THE HISTORY OF COMPUTING. (US/1058-6180). **1187**

IEEE COMPUTATIONAL SCIENCE AND ENGINEERING. (US/1070-9924). **1187**

IEEE MULTIMEDIA. (US/1070-986X). **1187**

IEEE PARALLEL & DISTRIBUTED TECHNOLOGY : SYSTEMS & APPLICATIONS. (US/1063-6552). **1187**

IEEE TRANSACTIONS ON FUZZY SYSTEMS. (US/1063-6706). **1187**

IEEE TRANSACTIONS ON VERY LARGE SCALE INTEGRATION (VLSI) SYSTEMS. (US/1063-8210). **1187**

IMAGING (NEW YORK, N.Y.). (US/1063-4320). **1187**

INDUSTRIAL CONTROLS INTELLIGENCE & THE PLC INSIDER'S NEWSLETTER. (US/1074-0511). **1188**

INFORMATIONSTECHNIK UND TECHNISCHE INFORMATIK : IT + TI / ORGAN DER FACHBEREICHE 3 "TECHNISCHE INFORMATIK UND ARCHITEKTUR VON RECHENSYSTEMEN" UND 4 "INFORMATIONSTECHNIK UND TECHNISCHE NUTZUNG DER INFORMATIK" DER GI E.V. (GW/0944-2774). **1188**

INGENUITY. (UK/1354-9952). **1189**

INSIDE THE NEW COMPUTER INDUSTRY. (US/1079-4573). **1189**

INTERACTIONS (NEW YORK, N.Y.). (US/1072-5520). **1189**

INTERNATIONAL IMAGING SOURCE BOOK. (US/1053-8291). **1190**

INTERNATIONAL JOURNAL OF COMPUTER RESEARCH. (US). **1190**

INTERNATIONAL JOURNAL OF HUMAN-COMPUTER STUDIES. (UK/1071-5819). **1190**

INTERNATIONAL TRANSACTIONS IN OPERATIONAL RESEARCH : A JOURNAL OF THE INTERNATIONAL FEDERATION OF OPERATIONAL RESEARCH SOCIETIES. (UK/0969-6016). **1191**

INTERPERSONAL COMPUTING AND TECHNOLOGY. (US/1064-4326). **1191**

JOURNAL OF COMPUTER AND SYSTEMS SCIENCES INTERNATIONAL. (US/1064-2307). **1191**

JOURNAL OF END USER COMPUTING. (US/1063-2239). **1192**

LOTUS WORKS REPORT, THE. (US/1059-7344). **1193**

MACINTOSH TIPS & TRICKS (PRINT). (US/1070-6720). **1194**

MAGAZINE OF ARTIFICIAL INTELLIGENCE IN FINANCE, THE. (US/1074-679X). **1194**

METHODS OF LOGIC IN COMPUTER SCIENCE. (US/1075-0924). **1195**

MICROSOFT MAGAZINE. (US). **1195**

MIS MANAGEMENT REVIEW. (US/1060-3565). **1195**

MULTIMEDIA NETWORK TECHNOLOGY REPORT. (US/1077-4440). **1196**

MULTIMEDIA SCHOOLS. (US/1075-0479). **1196**

MULTIMEDIA WORLD. (US/1073-4759). **1196**

MUMPS COMPUTING. (US/1060-7684). **1196**

NETGUIDE (MANHASSET, N.Y.). (US/1078-4632). **1196**

NEURAL, PARALLEL AND SCIENTIFIC COMPUTATIONS. (US/1061-5369). **1197**

NEWS / RADIOSUISSE SERVICES. (UK). **1197**

NEWSBANK REFERENCE SERVICE COMPUTER FILE. (US). **1197**

NORTH JERSEY COMPUTERUSER. (US/1064-0444). **1197**

OFFICIAL COMPUTER USER'S TRAVEL COMPANION (ASIAN ED.). (US/1065-9560). **1197**

OFFICIAL COMPUTER USER'S TRAVEL COMPANION (EUROPEAN ED.). (US/1065-9579). **1197**

OFFICIAL COMPUTER USER'S TRAVEL COMPANION (NORTH AMERICAN ED.). (US/1065-9536). **1197**

OPAC DIRECTORY. (US/1066-1425). **1198**

OPEN SYSTEMS PRODUCTS DIRECTORY. (US/1069-0409). **1198**

OS/2 MAGAZINE. (US/1073-1547). **1198**

OS/2 MONTHLY. (US/1068-6835). **1198**

PAGEMAKER IN-DEPTH (1992). (US/1064-6736). **1198**

PEN COMPUTER REPORT. (US/1062-6344). **1199**

POINT LINE POLY. PC. (US/1061-3838). **1199**

PRACTICAL PC. (UK/0965-6219). **1200**

PRO/E, THE MAGAZINE. (US/1069-6113). **1200**

RAPID PROTOTYPING JOURNAL. (UK/1355-2546). **1201**

REAL-TIME IMAGING. (UK/1077-2014). **1201**

REPORT ON OBJECT ANALYSIS AND DESIGN. (US/1075-2528). **1201**

Computers

ROBOT EXPLORER. (US/1060-4375). **1202**

RS/MAGAZINE (BROOKLINE, MASS.). (US/1061-0030). **1202**

RUSSIAN MICROELECTRONICS. (US/1063-7397). **1202**

SEARCHER (MEDFORD, N.J.). (US/1070-4795). **1202**

SOFTWARE MANUFACTURING NEWS. (US/1064-878X). **1203**

SOFTWARE QUALITY JOURNAL. (UK/0963-9314). **1203**

SOFWIN REPORTS. (US/1070-101X). **1203**

STATE-BY-STATE SUMMARY OF SOFTWARE SALES & USE TAX. (US/1063-2522). **1204**

SUPPORT@FTP.COM (WAKEFIELD, MASS.). (US/1064-1750). **1204**

TECHNOLOGY CONNECTION. (US/1074-4851). **1205**

TERRY SHANNON ON DEC. (US/1068-8412). **1205**

TEX AND TUG NEWS. (US/1065-240X). **1205**

TOOL WATCH. (US/1063-2662). **1205**

TOWARD AN ELECTRONIC PATIENT RECORD. (US/1063-973X). **1205**

TRANSPUTER COMMUNICATIONS. (UK/1070-454X). **1205**

TRI-CITY COMPUTING MAGAZINE. (US). **1205**

VIRTUAL REALITY SPECIAL REPORT. (US/1074-1038). **1206**

VIRUS NEWS AND REVIEWS. (US/1061-8384). **1206**

VISUAL BASIC DEVELOPER. (US). **1206**

VISUAL C++ DEVELOPER. (US). **1206**

VLSI DESIGN (PHILADELPHIA, PA.). (US/1065-514X). **1206**

WINDOWS KONKRET. (GW). **1207**

WINDOWS SOURCES. (US/1065-9641). **1207**

WIRED (SAN FRANCISCO, CALIF.). (US/1059-1028). **1207**

X RESOURCE, THE. (US/1058-5591). **1207**

ABSTRACTING, BIBLIOGRAPHIES AND STATISTICS

COMPUTER AND INFORMATION SYSTEMS ABSTRACTS. (US). **1208**

SOFT WATCH. (US/1064-8860). **1209**

ARTIFICIAL INTELLIGENCE

ADVANCES IN EXPERT SYSTEMS FOR MANAGEMENT. (US/1074-7532). **1210**

APPLICATIONS OF ARTIFICIAL INTELLIGENCE: KNOWLEDGE-BASED SYSTEMS. (US/1019-0716). **1211**

ARTIFICIAL INTELLIGENCE AND LAW. (NE/0924-8463). **1211**

C4I NEWS. (US/1071-1317). **1212**

INTERNATIONAL JOURNAL OF INTELLIGENT & COOPERATIVE INFORMATION SYSTEMS : IJICIS. (SI/0218-2157). **1213**

INTERNATIONAL JOURNAL ON ARTIFICIAL INTELLIGENCE TOOLS. (SI/0218-2130). **1213**

JOURNAL OF INTELLIGENT CONTROL, NEUROCOMPUTING AND FUZZY LOGIC. (US). **1214**

OPTICAL MEMORY & NEURAL NETWORKS. (US/1060-992X). **1215**

PRESENCE (CAMBRIDGE, MASS.). (US/1054-7460). **1216**

VIRTUAL REALITY MARKET PLACE. (US/1065-271X). **1217**

VIRTUAL REALITY WORLD. (US/1060-9547). **1217**

AUTOMATION

CAMPUS-WIDE INFORMATION SYSTEMS. (US/1065-0741). **1218**

IEEE ROBOTICS AND AUTOMATION MAGAZINE. (US/1070-9932). **1219**

JOURNAL OF AUTOMATION AND INFORMATION SCIENCES. (US/1064-2315). **1220**

MANUFACTURING & PROCESS AUTOMATION. (CN/1192-5973). **1220**

TRANSACTIONS ON COMPUTER-HUMAN INTERACTION. (US/1073-0516). **1221**

COMPUTER ASSISTED INSTRUCTION

COMPLETE MEMBERSHIP DIRECTORY OF THE INTERACTIVE MULTIMEDIA ASSOCIATION, THE. (US/1051-2721). **1222**

EDUCATIONAL TECHNOLOGY REVIEW. (US). **1223**

EDUCATORS' TECH EXCHANGE : AN EDUTECH PUBLICATION FOR THE ACADEMIC COMPUTING COMMUNITY. (US/1065-9447). **1223**

JOURNAL OF EDUCATIONAL MULTIMEDIA AND HYPERMEDIA. (US/1055-8896). **1224**

COMPUTER CRIMES AND SECURITY

COMPUTER SECURITY PRODUCTS BUYERS GUIDE. (US). **1226**

INFORMATION SYSTEMS SECURITY. (US/1065-898X). **1226**

SECURITY TECHNOLOGY NEWS. (US/1068-8374). **1227**

TOLLEY'S COMPUTER LAW AND PRACTICE. (UK/0266-4801). **1227**

COMPUTER ENGINEERING

ACM TRANSACTIONS ON SOFTWARE ENGINEERING AND METHODOLOGY. (US/1049-331X). **1227**

APPLICATION DEVELOPMENT TRENDS. (US). **1227**

IEE PROCEEDINGS. COMPUTERS AND DIGITAL TECHNIQUES. (UK/1350-2387). **1229**

INTEGRATED COMPUTER AIDED ENGINEERING. (US/1069-2509). **1229**

INTERNATIONAL PERSPECTIVES IN SOFTWARE ENGINEERING. (US/1065-1349). **1229**

JOURNAL OF COMPUTER AND SOFTWARE ENGINEERING. (US/1069-5451). **1230**

COMPUTER GRAPHICS AND DESIGN

ACADIA QUARTERLY / ASSOCIATION FOR COMPUTER-AIDED DESIGN IN ARCHITECTURE. (US). **1231**

COMPUTER ARTIST. (US/1063-312X). **1232**

COMPUTER GRAPHICS PROCEEDINGS, ANNUAL CONFERENCE SERIES. (US/1069-529X). **1232**

COMPUTER SUPPORTED COOPERATIVE WORK : CSCW : AN INTERNATIONAL JOURNAL. (NE/0925-9724). **1232**

COMPUTER VISION AND IMAGE UNDERSTANDING. (US). **1232**

COREL MAGAZINE. (US/1063-7591). **1233**

FBC (MADISON, ALA.). (US/1077-0291). **1233**

GRAPHICAL MODELS AND IMAGE PROCESSING. (US). **1233**

PC GRAPHICS & VIDEO. (US/1077-5862). **1234**

REAL TIME GRAPHICS. (US/1064-5004). **1235**

VIDEO TOASTER USER. (US/1075-8704). **1235**

COMPUTER INDUSTRY AND INDUSTRY DIRECTORIES

COMPUTER DEALER NEWS SOURCE GUIDE. (CN/1193-1272). **1236**

COMPUTER FINANCE. (UK/0966-7849). **1236**

COMPUTING AND SOFTWARE DESIGN CAREER DIRECTORY. (US/1070-728X). **1236**

DIRECTORY OF PUBLIC DATABASES PRODUCED BY THE INSTITUTIONS OF THE EUROPEAN COMMUNITIES / OFFICE FOR OFFICIAL PUBLICATIONS OF THE EUROPEAN COMMUNITIES. (LU). **1237**

FRINGE WARE REVIEW. (US/1069-5656). **1237**

GALE DIRECTORY OF DATABASES. (US/1066-8934). **1237**

PROGRAMMABLE LOGIC, NEWS & VIEWS. (US/1064-1394). **1239**

WORKGROUP COMPUTING SERIES. DIRECTORY OF MICROCOMPUTER HARDWARE. (US). **1239**

COMPUTER NETWORKS

ADVANCED INTELLIGENT NETWORK NEWS. (US/1072-0030). **1240**

DISTRIBUTED COMPUTING MONITOR. (US/1068-6266). **1241**

IEEE/ACM TRANSACTIONS ON NETWORKING. (US/1063-6692). **1241**

INFORMATION FOR NETWORK USERS. (US/1065-0660). **1241**

INTERNATIONAL JOURNAL OF WIRELESS INFORMATION NETWORKS. (US/1068-9605). **1242**

Computers —Software

INTERNET LETTER, THE. (US/1070-9851). **1242**

INTERNET RESEARCH. (US/1066-2243). **1242**

INTERNET WORLD. (US). **1242**

INTERNET WORLD'S ON INTERNET. (US/1066-9973). **1242**

JOURNAL OF ARTIFICIAL NEURAL NETWORKS. (US/1073-5828). **1242**

JOURNAL OF NETWORK AND SYSTEMS MANAGEMENT. (US/1064-7570). **1242**

LAN (SAN FRANCISCO, CALIF.). (US/1069-5621). **1242**

NETWORK ADMINISTRATOR. (US/1073-1164). **1243**

NEWS FOR NETWORK USERS. (US/1065-0652). **1243**

NEWS- INTERNET SOCIETY (PRINT ED.). (US/1060-7803). **1243**

PHILLIPS BUSINESS INFORMATION'S COMMUNICATIONS STANDARDS NEWS. (US/1077-4696). **1243**

STACKS (SAN FRANCISCO, CALIF.). (US/1070-8596). **1244**

COMPUTER SYSTEMS

DIGITAL NEWS & REVIEW. (US/1065-7452). **1246**

EVOLUTIONARY COMPUTATION. (US/1063-6560). **1247**

IFIP TRANSACTIONS. COMPUTER SCIENCE AND TECHNOLOGY. (NE/0926-5473). **1247**

INFORMATION SYSTEMS JOURNAL. (UK). **1247**

INSIDE AUTOCAD. (US/1071-0728). **1247**

JOURNAL OF MICROELECTRONIC SYSTEMS INTEGRATION. (US/1070-0056). **1248**

OEM MAGAZINE. (US/1071-8990). **1248**

OPEN INFORMATION SYSTEMS. (US/1068-5553). **1248**

OPEN SYSTEMS TODAY. (US/1061-0839). **1248**

PARALLEL ALGORITHMS AND APPLICATIONS. (US/1063-7192). **1248**

SIGLINK NEWSLETTER: QUARTERLY NEWSLETTER OF THE SPECIAL INTEREST GROUP ON HYPERTEXT, ASSOCIATION FOR COMPUTING MACHINERY. (US). **1249**

STRATEGIC SYSTEMS. (US/1060-3751). **1249**

SYS ADMIN (LAWRENCE, KAN.). (US/1061-2688). **1249**

THEORY AND PRACTICE OF OBJECT SYSTEMS. (US/1074-3227). **1249**

CYBERNETICS

BULLETIN / HUMAN FACTORS AND ERGONOMICS SOCIETY. (US/0438-1629). **1250**

DATA BASE MANAGEMENT

ALPHA FORUM. (US/1062-5895). **1252**

DATA MANAGEMENT REVIEW. (US/1067-3717). **1253**

DBASE ADVISOR. (US). **1254**

JOURNAL OF DATABASE MANAGEMENT. (US/1063-8016). **1254**

RELATIONAL DATABASE JOURNAL. (US/1074-6404). **1255**

SMART ACCESS. (US/1066-7911). **1255**

VLDB JOURNAL, THE. (US/1066-8888). **1255**

DATA PROCESSING

ADVANCES IN MANAGERIAL COGNITION AND ORGANIZATIONAL INFORMATION PROCESSING. (US). **1255**

DATA STORAGE / TECHNOLOGY & MANUFACTURE OF STORAGE DEVICES. (US). **1257**

DOCUMENT MANAGEMENT & WINDOWS IMAGING. (US/1071-8567). **1258**

IS AUDIT & CONTROL JOURNAL. (US/1076-4100). **1260**

IS BUDGET. (US/1076-2620). **1260**

MANAGING SYSTEM DEVELOPMENT. (US). **1261**

WHO'S WHO (PQ/ATLANTIC ED.). (CN/1193-3593). **1263**

WHO'S WHO (WESTERN CANADA ED.). (CN/1193-3607). **1263**

DESKTOP PUBLISHING

WORKGROUP COMPUTING SERIES. INFORMATION DELIVERY / DATAPRO. (US). **1263**

WORKGROUP COMPUTING SERIES. MULTIMEDIA SOLUTIONS / DATAPRO. (US). **1263**

HARDWARE

OPEN COMPUTING. (US/1078-2370). **1264**

PETROSYSTEMS WORLD. (US/1073-6425). **1265**

MICROCOMPUTERS, PERSONAL COMPUTERS

ADVANCED SYSTEMS. (US/1074-9306). **1265**

HOME PC. (US/1073-1784). **1267**

INFORMATION TECHNOLOGY DIGEST/ INFORMATION TECHNOLOGY DIVISION, UNIVERSITY OF MICHIGAN. (US). **1268**

MICROCOMPUTER ABSTRACTS. (US/1074-3995). **1269**

MICROPRENEUR (NORTHWOOD, N.H.). (US/1065-6111). **1269**

MICROSYSTEMS HANDBOOK. (US/1063-1488). **1270**

PC PRESENTATIONS, PRODUCTIONS. (US/1065-9099). **1271**

PC VISION. (US/1065-8645). **1271**

PC WORLD. (US). **1271**

PELIT 1992. (FI/1235-1199). **1272**

PERIPHERALS HANDBOOK. (US/1063-1496). **1272**

TRENDS IN THE CANADIAN PC MARKET. (CN/1193-1477). **1273**

WORKGROUP COMPUTING SERIES. DESKTOP APPLICATIONS. (US). **1273**

WORKGROUP COMPUTING SERIES. PERIPHERALS. (US). **1273**

WORKGROUP COMPUTING SERIES. SYSTEMS. (US). **1273**

ONLINE COMPUTING AND INFORMATION

NET GUIDE. (US/1077-4173). **1275**

ONLINE & CDROM REVIEW : THE INTERNATIONAL JOURNAL OF ONLINE & OPTICAL INFORMATION SYSTEMS. (UK). **1275**

ONLINE FILES. (UK/0967-6090). **1275**

OPTICAL STORAGE, CD-ROM APPLICATIONS

CD-ROM NEWS EXTRA. (US/1075-1106). **1276**

CD-ROM POCKET GUIDE. (US/1076-0415). **1276**

CD-ROM TODAY. (US/1069-4099). **1276**

CD-ROM WORLD. (US/1066-274X). **1276**

PROGRAMS AND PROGRAMMING

ACM ADA LETTERS : A BIMONTHLY PUBLICATION OF SIGADA, THE ACM SPECIAL INTEREST GROUP ON ADA. (US). **1277**

ACM LETTERS ON PROGRAMMING LANGUAGES AND SYSTEMS. (US/1057-4514). **1277**

INSIDE DBASE. (US/1061-3293). **1279**

JOURNAL OF PROGRAMMING LANGUAGES. (UK/0963-9306). **1280**

PROGRAMMER'S PROVANTAGE COMPUTER PRODUCTS BUYER'S GUIDE. (US/1076-9714). **1281**

SMALLTALK REPORT, THE. (US/1056-7976). **1281**

WINDOWS TECH JOURNAL. (US/1061-3501). **1282**

SIMULATION

PROCEEDINGS / ANNUAL SIMULATION SYMPOSIUM. (US). **1282**

SOFTWARE

1-2-3 FOR MACINTOSH REPORT, THE. (US/1058-6954). **1283**

1-2-3 SOFTWARE CONNECTION. (US/1065-0768). **1283**

ACCESS ADVISOR. (US/1066-7253). **1283**

Computers —Software

APPLIED COMPUTING REVIEW : A PUBLICATION OF THE SPECIAL INTEREST GROUP ON APPLIED COMPUTING. (US). **1284**

BORLAND C++ DEVELOPER'S JOURNAL. (US/1073-4805). **1284**

CHINESE JOURNAL OF ADVANCED SOFTWARE RESEARCH. (US/1074-7443). **1284**

CLIPPER ADVISOR. (US/1068-0675). **1284**

DIRECTORY OF U.S. GOVERNMENT SOFTWARE FOR MAINFRAMES AND MICROCOMPUTERS. (US/1063-9748). **1285**

ENABLE SUBSCRIPTION PLAN. (US). **1285**

INDEX LOS ANGELES TIMES-ORANGE COUNTY SECTIONS. (US/1065-8203). **1286**

INSIDE MICROSOFT ACCESS. (US/1067-8204). **1287**

INSIDE NETWARE. (US/1061-7647). **1287**

INSIDE OS/2. (US/1063-3146). **1287**

INSIDE PARADOX FOR WINDOWS. (US/1069-0956). **1287**

INSIDE VISUAL BASIC FOR WINDOWS. (US/1066-7555). **1287**

INSIDE WORDPERFECT WINDOWS. (US/1063-2727). **1287**

INSIDE WORKS FOR WINDOWS. (US/1061-5873). **1287**

INTERNATIONAL JOURNAL OF SUPERCOMPUTER APPLICATIONS AND HIGH PERFORMANCE COMPUTING, THE. (US/1078-3482). **1287**

INTERNATIONAL JOURNAL OF SUPERCOMPUTER APPLICATIONS AND HIGH-PERFORMANCE COMPUTING. (US). **1287**

MACAUTHORITY (LOUISVILLE, KY.), THE. (US/1062-452X). **1288**

MACAUTHORITY SOFTWARE CONNECTION. (US/1063-2700). **1288**

MICROSOFT C/C++ DEVELOPER'S JOURNAL. (US/1068-5669). **1288**

MULTI MEDIA TOOLS AND APPLICATIONS. (NE/1380-7501). **1288**

OS2 PROFESSIONAL. (US/1069-6814). **1289**

PC SOFTDIR. (US/1069-0913). **1289**

POLICE COMPUTER REVIEW. (US/1061-1509). **1289**

SOFTAWARENESS (AUSTIN, TEX.). (US/1065-7290). **1290**

SOFTWARE CONNECTION, DOS. (US/1065-0776). **1290**

SOFTWARE DEVELOPMENT. (US/1070-8588). **1290**

SOFTWARE DIRECTORY. SYSTEMS & UTILITIES. (US/1071-3441). **1290**

SOFTWARE ECONOMICS LETTER. (US/1065-6146). **1290**

SOFTWARE HANDBOOK (PLYMOUTH MEETING, PA.). (US/1063-147X). **1290**

SOFTWARE MARKETING JOURNAL. (US/1060-3964). **1291**

SOFTWARE PROCESS, QUALITY & ISO 9000. (US/1070-5457). **1291**

SOFTWARE TESTING, VERIFICATION & RELIABILITY. (UK/0960-0833). **1291**

SPACE 2000. (US/1064-2064). **1291**

WINDOWS REPORT, THE. (US/1065-3627). **1292**

WINDOWS SOFTWARE CONNECTION. (US/1065-0784). **1292**

WORDPERFECT FOR WINDOWS MAGAZINE. (US/1058-9783). **1292**

WORKGROUP COMPUTING SERIES. SYSTEMS SOFTWARE (OS/NOS/GUI). (US). **1292**

WORD PROCESSING

WORDPERFECT SOFTWARE CONNECTION. (US/1063-2719). **1292**

CONSUMER INTERESTS

ANNUAL REPORT TO CONGRESS / UNITED STATES CONSUMER PRODUCT SAFETY COMMISSION. (US/1075-6833). **1293**

BORN TO SHOP. GREAT BRITAIN. (US/1071-9717). **1293**

BORN TO SHOP. NEW ENGLAND. (US/1066-2782). **1293**

BORN TO SHOP. PARIS. (US/1066-2790). **1293**

BRANDADVANTAGE (WILMETTE, ILL.). (US/1064-5756). **1293**

CONSUMER MAGAZINE & AGRI-MEDIA SOURCE. (US/1071-4537). **1295**

GETTING THE MOST FOR YOUR MEDICAL DOLLAR. (US/1066-2367). **1297**

NATIONAL AUCTIONS & SALES. (US/1055-8268). **1298**

SAMIR HUSNI'S GUIDE TO THE NEW CONSUMER MAGAZINES PUBLISHED IN ... . (US). **1299**

SECONDARY MARKET ANNUAL GUIDE, THE. (US). **1299**

SELF-STORAGE RENTAL GUIDE (SOUTHERN CALIFORNIA ED.). (US/1059-5384). **1299**

SHOPPING CENTER DIRECTORY. (US/1066-9701). **1299**

THRIFT SHOPPING IN YOUR NEIGHBORHOOD. (US/1060-961X). **1300**

COPYRIGHT, INTELLECTUAL PROPERTY

CHEMICAL VAPOR DEPOSITION PATENTS. (US/1062-8827). **1302**

DIRECTORY OF U.S. TRADEMARKS, THE. (US/1042-0665). **1303**

INTELPROP NEWS. (UK/0967-3466). **1305**

INTERNATIONAL JOURNAL OF CULTURAL PROPERTY. (GW/0940-7391). **1305**

IPL NEWSLETTER : A PUBLICATION OF THE AMERICAN BAR ASSOCIATION SECTION OF INTELLECTUAL PROPERTY LAW. (US). **1305**

LIGHTBULB/INVENT!, THE. (US). **1306**

PATENT ABSTRACTS. AGRICULTURALS. (US/1065-0482). **1307**

PATENT ABSTRACTS. CHEMICAL PRODUCTS. (US/1065-0474). **1307**

PATENT ABSTRACTS. ENVIRONMENT, TRANSPORT & STORAGE. (US/1066-2103). **1307**

PATENT ABSTRACTS. PETROLEUM & SPECIALTY PRODUCTS. (US/1065-0466). **1307**

PATENT ABSTRACTS. PETROLEUM PROCESSES. (US/1065-0458). **1307**

PATENT ABSTRACTS. PETROLEUM SUBSTITUTES. (US/1065-044X). **1307**

PATENT ABSTRACTS. POLYMERS. (US/1065-2167). **1307**

PATENT APPLICATIONS HANDBOOK / BY STEPHEN A. BECKER. (US). **1307**

POLEZNYE MODELI, PROMYSHLENNYE OBRAZTSY : OFITSIALNYI BIULLETEN KOMITETA ROSSIISKOI FEDERATSII PO PATENTAM I TOVARNYM ZNAKAM. (RU). **1308**

DANCE

ALAMO AREA SQUARE AND ROUND DANCE ASSOCIATION NEWSLETTER. (US/1063-8024). **1310**

BALLETT INTERNATIONAL, TANZ AKTUELL. (GW). **1311**

CHOREOGRAPHY AND DANCE ARCHIVE. (SW/1072-9216). **1311**

DANCE INTERNATIONAL (VANCOUVER). (CN/1189-9816). **1312**

DANCE NOW. (UK/0966-6346). **1312**

DANCEVIEW. (US). **1312**

IMPULSE (CHAMPAIGN, ILL.). (US/1063-8520). **1313**

INTERNATIONAL JOURNAL OF AFRICAN DANCE. (US/1045-8042). **1313**

ON POINTE. (US/1060-3972). **1314**

DENTISTRY

CESKA STOMATOLOGIE. (XR). **1318**

CURRENT OPINION IN COSMETIC DENTISTRY. (US/1065-6278). **1319**

CURRENT OPINION IN ORTHODONTICS AND PEDODONTICS. (US). **1319**

CURRENT OPINION IN PERIODONTOLOGY. (UK/1065-626X). **1319**

DA UPDATE. (US/1062-5569). **1319**

DENTAL ASSISTANT : JOURNAL OF THE AMERICAN DENTAL ASSISTANTS ASSOCIATION, THE. (US). **1320**

DENTAL STUDY CLUB. (CN/1183-9996). **1321**

ENDO : REVUE FRANCAISE D'ENDODONTIE : PUBLICATION OFFICIELLE DE LA SOCIETE FRANCAISE D'ENDODONTIE. (FR). **1323**

FDI WORLD. (UK). **1323**

Earth Sciences —Hydrology

GP (ATLANTA, GA.). (US/1063-3324). **1324**

IMPLANT DENTISTRY. (US/1056-6163). **1324**

INTOUCH (KNOXVILLE, TENN.). (US/1059-8081). **1325**

JOURNAL DE PARODONTOLOGIE & D'IMPLANTOLOGIE ORALE. (FR). **1326**

JOURNAL OF PRACTICAL HYGIENE, THE. (US/1072-7965). **1327**

JOURNAL OF PROSTHODONTICS. (US/1059-941X). **1327**

KIEFERORTHOPAEDIE : DIE ZEITSCHRIFT FUER DIE PRAXIS. (GW/0945-7917). **1329**

MASTERING CLINICAL PEDIATRIC DENTISTRY. (US/1076-7428). **1329**

ORAL SURGERY, ORAL MEDICINE, ORAL PATHOLOGY, ORAL RADIOLOGY, AND ENDODONTICS. (US). **1332**

PERIODONTAL CLINICAL INVESTIGATIONS : OFFICIAL PUBLICATION OF THE NORTHEASTERN SOCIETY OF PERIODONTISTS. (US/1065-2418). **1333**

PERIODONTAL INSIGHTS. (CN/1195-2008). **1333**

PERIODONTOLOGY 2000. (DK/0906-6713). **1333**

PERSONAL REPORT. PRACTICE DEVELOPMENT AND WEALTH ACCUMULATION FOR THE PERIODONTIST, THE. (US/1069-269X). **1333**

PRACTICE MANAGEMENT AND MARKETING NEWS IN PEDIATRIC DENTISTRY. (US/1064-1203). **1333**

WIRELINE (DALLAS, TEX.). (US/1062-8746). **1337**

WSDA MEMBERSHIP DIRECTORY & RESOURCE GUIDE. (US). **1337**

DRUG ABUSE AND ALCOHOLISM

ADDICTION. (UK/0965-2140). **1338**

ADDICTION RESEARCH. (US/1058-6989). **1338**

ADOLESCENCE MAGAZINE. (US). **1338**

ALCOHOLISM BRIEFS. (US). **1340**

AMERICAN JOURNAL ON ADDICTIONS, THE. (US/1055-0496). **1340**

BEHAVIORAL HEALTH MANAGEMENT. (US/1075-6701). **1341**

COMPREHENSIVE STATE PLAN AND HUMAN SERVICES PLAN FOR THE PREVENTION/INTERVENTION/TREATMENT OF ALCOHOLISM AND OTHER DRUG DEPENDENCY FOR FISCAL YEARS, A. (US). **1342**

CORNELL/SMITHERS REPORT ON WORKPLACE SUBSTANCE ABUSE POLICY. (US). **1342**

CSAP PREVENTION PIPELINE / CENTER FOR SUBSTANCE ABUSE PREVENTION, THE. (US). **1342**

DIRECTORY OF SUBSTANCE ABUSE ORGANIZATIONS IN CANADA. (CN/1188-4886). **1343**

DIRECTORY OF SUBSTANCE ABUSE ORGANIZATIONS IN CANADA. (CN/1188-4886). **1343**

DRINKING, DRUGS & DRIVING. (US/1062-3337). **1343**

DRUGS : EDUCATION, PREVENTION AND POLICY. (UK/0968-7637). **1344**

DRUGS IN SPORTS. (CN/1188-0260). **1344**

JOURNAL OF CHILD & ADOLESCENT SUBSTANCE ABUSE. (US/1067-828X). **1345**

JOURNAL OF MAINTENANCE IN THE ADDICTIONS. (US). **1346**

JOURNAL OF MINISTRY IN ADDICTION & RECOVERY. (US/1053-8755). **1346**

NARCOTICS ENFORCEMENT & PREVENTION DIGEST. (US). **1347**

RESEARCH COMMUNICATIONS IN ALCOHOL AND SUBSTANCES OF ABUSE. (US). **1348**

SAMHSA NEWS / SUBSTANCE ABUSE AND MENTAL HEALTH SERVICES ADMINISTRATION. (US). **1349**

EARTH SCIENCES

ADVANCES IN GEO ECOLOGY. (GW). **1351**

ATMOSPHERIC ENVIRONMENT. (UK/1352-2310). **1351**

EARTH OBSERVATION MAGAZINE. (US). **1354**

EARTH SPACE REVIEW. (US/1060-1848). **1355**

EARTH (WAUKESHA, WIS.). (US/1056-148X). **1355**

EURASIAN SOIL SCIENCE. (US/1064-2293). **1355**

GEOCRYOLOGY (MOSCOW, R.S.F.S.R.). (RU/1061-7574). **1355**

INTERNATIONAL BIODETERIORATION & BIODEGREDATION. (UK/0964-8305). **1356**

MODELING OF GEO-BIOSPHERE PROCESSES. (GW/0938-9563). **1358**

PLAN - BRITISH COLUMBIA. RESOURCE MANAGEMENT BRANCH. (CN/1187-3264). **1359**

SPECIAL ISSUES IN GEOSCIENCE. (US/1062-1407). **1360**

ABSTRACTING, BIBLIOGRAPHIES AND STATISTICS

CURRENT CONTENTS. PHYSICAL, CHEMICAL & EARTH SCIENCES (CD-ROM VERSION). (US/1073-1253). **1362**

DEEP-SEA RESEARCH. PART I, OCEANOGRAPHIC RESEARCH PAPERS. (UK/0967-0637). **1448**

DEEP-SEA RESEARCH. PART II, TOPICAL STUDIES IN OCEANOGRAPHY. (UK/0967-0645). **1448**

METEOROLOGICAL & GEOASTROPHYSICAL ABSTRACTS. (US/1066-2707). **1363**

OCEANOGRAPHIC LITERATURE REVIEW. (UK/0967-0653). **1363**

GEOLOGY

AGSO JOURNAL OF AUSTRALIAN GEOLOGY & GEOPHYSICS. (AT/1320-1271). **1365**

APPLIED HYDROGEOLOGY: INTERNATIONAL JOURNAL FOR HYDROGEOLOGISTS. (GW). **1366**

BULLETIN OF THE NATURAL HISTORY MUSEUM. GEOLOGY SERIES. (UK/0968-0462). **1370**

DIRECTORY OF GEOSCIENCE DEPARTMENTS. (US). **1373**

ENVIRONMENTAL GEOLOGY. (US). **1375**

GEOARCHIVE ON CD-ROM. (US/1070-6046). **1376**

GEOEKOLOGIIA, INZHENERNAIA GEOLOGIIA, GIDROGEOLOGIIA, GEOKRIOLOGIIA / ROSSIISKAIA AKADEMIIA NAUK. (RU/0869-7809). **1377**

GFF. (SW/1103-5897). **1381**

ISLAND ARC, THE. (AT/1038-4871). **1383**

IZVESTIIA AKADEMII NAUK. SERIIA GEOLOGICHESKAIA / ROSSIISKAIA AKADEMIIA NAUK. (RU). **1384**

JOURNAL OF THE CZECH GEOLOGICAL SOCIETY. (XR/0008-7378). **1385**

JOURNAL OF THE GEOLOGICAL SOCIETY OF CHINA. (CH/1018-7057). **1385**

NEWS JOURNAL / INTERNATIONAL SOCIETY FOR ROCK MECHANICS. (PO). **1389**

OTECHESTVENNAIA GEOLOGIIA. (RU). **1390**

ROMANIAN JOURNAL OF MINERAL DEPOSITS. (RM/1220-5648). **1396**

RUSSIAN GEOLOGY AND GEOPHYSICS. (US/1068-7971). **1396**

STRATIGRAPHY AND GEOLOGICAL CORRELATION. (RU). **1398**

UHLI- RUDY- GEOLOGICKY PRUZKUM. (XR/1210-7697). **1400**

VESTNIK SANKT-PETERBURGSKOGO UNIVERSITETA. SERIIA 7, GEOLOGIIA, GEOGRAFIIA. (RU). **1400**

GEOPHYSICS

FIZIKA ZEMLI / ROSSIISKAIA AKADEMIIA NAUK. (RU). **1405**

GEODRILLING INTERNATIONAL. (UK/0969-3769). **1405**

GIM. GEODETICAL INFO MAGAZINE. (NE/0928-1436). **1406**

IZVESTIYA. ATMOSPHERIC AND OCEANIC PHYSICS. (US/0001-4338). **1407**

JOURNAL OF APPLIED GEOPHYSICS. (NE/0926-9851). **1407**

JOURNAL OF SEISMIC EXPLORATION. (FR/0963-0651). **1408**

LEADING EDGE (TULSA, OKLA.). (US/1070-485X). **1408**

PROCEEDINGS OF THE INTERNATIONAL SYMPOSIUM ON REMOTE SENSING AND GLOBAL ENVIRONMENTAL CHANGE. (US/1068-9281). **1409**

RADIOSCIENTIST BULLETIN. (BE). **1410**

HYDROLOGY

GROUND WATER MONITORING & REMEDIATION. (US/1069-3629). **1413**

JOURNAL OF ENVIRONMENTAL HYDROLOGY. (US/1058-3912). **1416**

Earth Sciences —Meteorology

METEOROLOGY

ASTRO-WEATHER (EASTERN TIME ED.). (US/1056-9642). **1420**

ASTRO-WEATHER (MOUNTAIN TIME ED.). (US/1056-9669). **1420**

ATMOSPHERIC AND OCEANIC OPTICS. (RU). **1420**

METEOROLOGISCHE ZEITSCHRIFT / HERAUSGEGEBEN VON DER DEUTSCHEN METEOROLOGISCHEN GESELLSCHAFT, OSTERREICHISCHEN GESELLSCHAFT FEUR METEOROLOGIE, SCHWEIZERISCHEN GESELLSCHAFT FUER GEOPHYSIK. (GW/0941-2948). **1431**

RUSSIAN METEOROLOGY AND HYDROLOGY. (US/1068-3739). **1434**

WORKING PAPER / NATURAL HAZARDS RESEARCH AND APPLICATIONS INFORMATION CENTER, INSTITUTE OF BEHAVIORAL SCIENCE, UNIVERSITY OF COLORADO. (US). **1437**

MINERALOGY

CRYSTAL MOUNTAIN MINING QUARTERLY. (US/1062-8797). **1439**

GEOLOGY OF ORE DEPOSITS. (RU/1075-7015). **1440**

KARBO, ENERGOCHEMIA, EKOLOGIA. (PL). **1440**

MINERAL INDUSTRY QUARTERLY REPORT. (CN/1188-9004). **1441**

PLAN D'ENTREPRISE DE CANMET. (CN/1187-6255). **1443**

ZAPISKI VSEROSSIISKOGO MINERALOGICHESKOGO OBSHCHESTVA / ROSSIISKAIA AKADEMIIA NAUK. (RU/0869-6055). **1445**

OCEANOGRAPHY

ATMOSPHERE-OCEAN SYSTEM, THE. (US/1063-7184). **1446**

EXPLORATIONS (LA JOLLA, CALIF.). (US/1075-2560). **1449**

FISHERIES OCEANOGRAPHY. (US/1054-6006). **1449**

JOURNAL OF OCEANOGRAPHY. (JA/0916-8370). **1450**

OCEAN & COASTAL MANAGEMENT. (UK/0964-5691). **1453**

PHYSICAL OCEANOGRAPHY. (NE). **1455**

UNDERWATER NEWS & TECHNOLOGY. (US/1069-6547). **1458**

PETROLOGY

ANNUAL MEETING OF THE SOCIETY FOR ORGANIC PETROLOGY. ABSTRACTS AND PROGRAM. (US/1060-7250). **1458**

JOURNAL OF SEDIMENTARY RESEARCH. SECTION A, SEDIMENTARY PETROLOGY AND PROCESSES. (US/1073-130X). **1459**

JOURNAL OF SEDIMENTARY RESEARCH. SECTION B, STRATIGRAPHY AND GLOBAL STUDIES. (US/1073-1318). **1459**

PETROLOGY. (US/0869-5911). **1459**

ECONOMICS

ACCESS MAGAZINE (VANCOUVER). (CN/1195-0889). **1460**

ACCRA COST OF LIVING INDEX. (US/1070-9169). **1460**

APERCU TRIMESTRIEL DE L'ECONOMIE. (BE). **1463**

BLUE CHIP JOB GROWTH UPDATE. (US/1062-9327). **1465**

BOLETIN DE INFORMACION SOBRE ECONOMIA CUBANA / CIEM. (CU). **1465**

CAHIERS VERTS DE L'ECONOMIE PARIS, LES. (FR/1167-5217). **1467**

CANADIAN MAPLE LEAF REPORT, THE. (CN/1187-919X). **1468**

CARIBBEAN AND CENTRAL AMERICA REPORT. (UK/0968-2732). **1468**

CHRONIQUES DE LA S.E.D.E.I.S. (FR). **1470**

COMPUTATIONAL ECONOMICS. (NE/0927-7099). **1470**

CONTEMPORARY ECONOMIC POLICY. (US/1074-3529). **1471**

COUNTRY REPORT. ANGOLA / THE ECONOMIST INTELLIGENCE UNIT. (UK). **1472**

COUNTRY REPORT. BALTIC REPUBLICS: ESTONIA, LATVIA, LITHUANIA / THE ECONOMIST INTELLIGENCE UNIT. (UK). **1472**

COUNTRY REPORT. BOSNIA-HERCEGOVINA, CROATIA, MACEDONIA, SERBIA-MONTENEGRO, SLOVENIA / THE ECONOMIST INTELLIGENCE UNIT. (UK). **1472**

COUNTRY REPORT. CHINA, MONGOLIA / THE ECONOMIST INTELLIGENCE UNIT. (UK). **1473**

COUNTRY REPORT. CONGO, SAO TOME & PRINCIPE, GUINEA-BISSAU, CAPE VERDE / THE ECONOMIST INTELLIGENCE UNIT. (UK). **1473**

COUNTRY REPORT. COSTA RICA, PANAMA / THE ECONOMIST INTELLIGENCE UNIT. (UK). **1473**

COUNTRY REPORT. CYPRUS, MALTA / THE ECONOMIST INTELLIGENCE UNIT. (UK). **1473**

COUNTRY REPORT. CZECH REPUBLIC AND SLOVAKIA / THE ECONOMIST INTELLIGENCE UNIT. (UK). **1473**

COUNTRY REPORT. GABON, EQUATORIAL GUINEA / THE ECONOMIST INTELLIGENCE UNIT. (UK). **1473**

COUNTRY REPORT. GHANA / THE ECONOMIST INTELLIGENCE UNIT. (UK). **1474**

COUNTRY REPORT. GUATEMALA, EL SALVADOR / THE ECONOMIST INTELLIGENCE UNIT. (UK). **1474**

COUNTRY REPORT. GUINEA, SIERRA LEONE, LIBERIA / THE ECONOMIST INTELLIGENCE UNIT. (UK). **1474**

COUNTRY REPORT. ISRAEL, THE OCCUPIED TERRITORIES / EIU, THE ECONOMIST INTELLIGENCE UNIT. (UK/1353-3142). **1474**

COUNTRY REPORT. JAMAICA, BELIZE, BAHAMAS, BERMUDA, BARBADOS / THE ECONOMIST INTELLIGENCE UNIT. (UK). **1474**

COUNTRY REPORT. LEBANON / THE ECONOMIST INTELLIGENCE UNIT. (UK). **1475**

COUNTRY REPORT. MAURITIUS, MADAGASCAR, SEYCHELLES / THE ECONOMIST INTELLIGENCE UNIT. (UK). **1475**

COUNTRY REPORT. MOZAMBIQUE, MALAWI / THE ECONOMIST INTELLIGENCE UNIT. (UK). **1475**

COUNTRY REPORT. NICARAGUA, HONDURAS / ECONOMIST INTELLIGENCE UNIT. (UK). **1475**

COUNTRY REPORT. RUSSIA / EIU, THE ECONOMIST INTELLIGENCE UNIT. (UK). **1476**

COUNTRY REPORT. SENEGAL, THE GAMBIA, MAURITANIA / THE ECONOMIST INTELLIGENCE UNIT. (UK). **1476**

COUNTRY REPORT. SOUTH KOREA, NORTH KOREA / THE ECONOMIST INTELLIGENCE UNIT. (UK). **1476**

COUNTRY REPORT. TANZANIA, COMOROS / THE ECONOMIST INTELLIGENCE UNIT. (UK). **1477**

COUNTRY REPORT. THAILAND, MYANMAR (BURMA) / THE ECONOMIST INTELLIGENCE UNIT. (UK). **1477**

COUNTRY REPORT. TRINIDAD AND TOBAGO, GUYANA, WINDWARD AND LEEWARD ISLANDS, SURINAME, NETHERLANDS ANTILLES, ARUBA / THE ECONOMIST INTELLIGENCE UNIT. (UK). **1477**

COUNTRY REPORT. TUNISIA / THE ECONOMIST INTELLIGENCE UNIT. (UK). **1477**

COUNTRY REPORT. UGANDA, RWANDA, BURUNDI / EIU, THE ECONOMIST INTELLIGENCE UNIT. (UK). **1477**

COUNTRY REPORT. VENEZUELA / THE ECONOMIST INTELLIGENCE UNIT. (UK). **1478**

COUNTRY REPORT. ZAMBIA, ZAIRE / THE ECONOMIST INTELLIGENCE UNIT. (UK). **1478**

COUNTRY REPORT. ZIMBABWE / THE ECONOMIST INTELLIGENCE UNIT. (UK). **1478**

DIRECTORY / ECONOMIC DEVELOPERS ASSOCIATION OF CANADA. (CN/1193-7912). **1479**

DISCUSSION PAPERS / HELSINKI SCHOOL OF ECONOMICS, DEPARTMENT OF ECONOMICS. (FI/1235-2209). **1480**

EAST EUROPE & THE REPUBLICS. (US/1060-6157). **1480**

EASTERN EUROPE ANALYST. (US/0965-0350). **1481**

ECONOMIC DESIGN. (NE). **1482**

ECONOMIC DEVELOPMENT DIGEST (WASHINGTON, D.C.). (US/1060-5339). **1482**

ECONOMIC QUARTERLY / FEDERAL RESERVE BANK OF RICHMOND. (US/1069-7225). **1484**

ECONOMIC REPORTER. (HK). **1484**

ECONOMY AT A GLANCE, THE. (US/1063-1208). **1487**

ECOTRENDS. (US). **1487**

ELECTRICITY DAILY REPORT, THE. (US/1070-8928). **1488**

ESPACE MONTREAL (ENGLISH EDITION 1992). (CN/1188-5831). **1489**

ESPACE MONTREAL (FRENCH EDITION 1992). (CN/1188-5831). **1489**

EUR-OP NEWS DEUTSCHE AUSG. (LU/1021-1667). **1489**

EUROPEAN ECONOMY. REPORTS AND STUDIES. (LU). **1489**

FEMINIST ECONOMICS. (UK/1354-5701). **1490**

FUTURECAST (LA CANADA, CALIF.). (US/1062-3280). **1492**

GEOGRAPHIC REFERENCE REPORT. (US/1061-7469). **1492**

HANDBOOK OF INTERNATIONAL ECONOMIC STATISTICS / DIRECTORATE OF INTELLIGENCE, CENTRAL INTELLIGENCE AGENCY. (US). **1493**

IFO WIRTSCHAFTSKONJUNKTUR : MONATSBERICHTE DES IFO INSTITUTS FUER WIRTSCHAFTSFORSCHUNG. (GW). **1494**

INDONESIA DEVELOPMENT NEWS QUARTERLY. (US). **1495**

INTERNATIONAL REVIEW OF ECONOMICS & FINANCE. (US/1059-0560). **1497**

JAPAN WATCH, USA. (US/1062-3302). **1498**

JOURNAL OF ASIA PACIFIC ECONOMIES. (UK/1354-7860). **1498**

JOURNAL OF BUSINESS ECONOMICS. (UK/0962-1369). **1498**

JOURNAL OF ENVIRONMENT & DEVELOPMENT, THE. (US/1070-4965). **1499**

KONKURRENS/ UITGAVEN AV STATENS PRIS- OCH KONKURRENSVERK I SAMARBETE MED NARINGSFRIHETSOMBUDSMANNEN OCH MARKNADSDOMSTOLEN. (SW/1102-6065). **1502**

LICENSING TODAY INTERNATIONAL. (UK). **1503**

MICROECONOMICS. (US). **1505**

NACLA REPORT ON THE AMERICAS (1993). (US/1071-4839). **1506**

NEW ECONOMY (LONDON, ENGLAND). (UK/1070-3535). **1507**

NORTH AMERICAN JOURNAL OF ECONOMICS AND FINANCE. (US/1062-9408). **1508**

NOTAS EJECUTIVAS SOBRE MEDIO AMBIENTE Y DESARROLLO: BOLETIN INFORMATIVO PREPARADO CONJUNTAMENTE POR LA DIVISION DE MEDIO AMBIENTE Y ASENTAMIENTOS HUMANOS Y LOS SERVICIOS DE INFORMACION DE LA COMISION ECONOMICA PARA AMERICA LATINA Y EL CARIBE, CEPAL. (CL). **1508**

NOVAIA LITERATURA PO SOTSIALNYM I GUMANITARNYM NAUKAM. EKONOMIKA / ROSSIISKAIA AKADEMIIA NAUK, INSTITUT NAUCHNOI INFORMATSII PO OBSHCHESTVENNYM NAUKAM. (RU). **1508**

OECD ECONOMIC SURVEYS: POLAND. (FR/0376-6438). **1510**

PEOPLE, PROPERTY, PROSPECTS. (US/1058-5664). **1512**

POLITICAL ECONOMY JOURNAL OF INDIA : A QUARTERLY JOURNAL OF THE CENTRE FOR INDIAN DEVELOPMENT STUDIES. (II/0971-2097). **1512**

POST-SOVIET AFFAIRS. (US/1060-586X). **1513**

PRACTITIONERS 1120S DESKBOOK. (US/1061-2084). **1513**

PRAGUE ECONOMIC PAPERS. (XR/1210-0455). **1513**

PROBLEMS OF ECONOMIC TRANSITION. (US/1061-1991). **1513**

PROGRAMME PROFILES. (NZ/1171-2031). **1513**

PROPOSITION TARIFAIRE. (CN/1187-9947). **1513**

QUARTERLY REVIEW OF ECONOMICS AND FINANCE, THE. (US/1062-9769). **1515**

ROSSIISKII EKONOMICHESKII ZHURNAL / VYSSHII EKONOMICHESKII SOVET PRI PREZIDIUME VERKHOVNOGO SOVETA ROSSIISKOI FEDERATSII, MINISTERSTVO NAUKI, VYSSHEI SHKOLY I TEKHNICHESKOI POLITIKI ROSSIISKOI FEDERATSII [I] GOSUDARSTVENNAIA AKADEMIIA UPRAVLENIIA. (RU). **1519**

ROULANT MA BOSSE, EN. (CN/1188-9926). **1519**

RUSSIAN ECONOMY AND BUSINESS DIGEST. (US/1060-5894). **1519**

RUSSIAN FAR EAST UPDATE. (US/1061-5679). **1519**

SAL-NEWS (ROCKVILLE, MD.). (US/1062-9130). **1519**

SHORT-TERM ECONOMIC INDICATORS, TRANSITION ECONOMIES / CENTRE FOR CO-OPERATION WITH THE ECONOMIES IN TRANSITION / INDICATEURS ECONOMIQUES A COURT TERME, ECONOMIES EN TRANSITION / CENTRE POUR LA COOPERATION AVEC LES ECONOMIES EN TRANSITION. (FR/1019-9829). **1520**

SOTSIALNYE I GUMANITARNYE NAUKI. SERIIA 2, EKONOMIKA : OTECHESTVENNAIA I ZARUBEZHNAIA LITERATURA / ROSSIISKAIA AKADEMIIA NAUK, INSTITUT NAUCHNOI INFORMATSII PO OBSHCHESTVENNYM NAUKAM. (RU). **1521**

STANDARD AND POOR'S HIGH YIELD DIRECTIONS. (US/1072-1290). **1522**

STUDIES IN DEFENCE ECONOMICS. (US/1062-046X). **1523**

STUDIES OF ECONOMIES IN TRANSFORMATION. (US/1014-997X). **1523**

... THIRD WAVE DEVELOPMENT AWARDS, THE. (US). **1524**

TOURISM ECONOMICS. (UK/1354-8166). **1524**

TRENDS JOURNAL (RHINEBECK, N.Y.), THE. (US/1065-2094). **1524**

VESTNIK SANKT-PETERBURGSKOGO UNIVERSITETA. SERIIA 5, EKONOMIKA. (RU). **1525**

WASHINGTON GREEN. (US/1060-5665). **1526**

WHEELER'S INLAND EMPIRE. (US/1064-1610). **1526**

WORKING PAPERS / ECONOMICS DEPARTMENT, OECD. (FR). **1527**

ABSTRACTING, BIBLIOGRAPHIES AND STATISTICS

INFO-SOUTH ABSTRACTS. (US/1059-5910). **1534**

COOPERATIVES

WORLD OF CO-OPERATIVE ENTERPRISE, THE. (UK). **1543**

ECONOMIC HISTORY, CONDITIONS

AUDACITY (NEW YORK, N.Y.). (US/1064-4555). **1547**

BULLETIN / CENTRE PIERRE LEON D'HISTOIRE ECONOMIQUE ET SOCIALE. (FR/1241-9257). **1549**

BULLETIN OF ASIAN-PACIFIC ECONOMIC AND POLITICAL ISSUES. (US). **1549**

COUNTRY PROFILE. CONGO, SAO TOME AND PRINCIPE, GUINEA-BISSAU, CAPE VERDE / THE ECONOMIST INTELLIGENCE UNIT. (UK/1352-0849). **1552**

COUNTRY PROFILE. COTE D'IVOIRE, MALI / THE ECONOMIST INTELLIGENCE UNIT. (UK). **1552**

COUNTRY PROFILE. CYPRUS, MALTA / EIU, THE ECONOMIST INTELLIGENCE UNIT. (UK). **1553**

COUNTRY PROFILE. GERMANY/ THE ECONOMIST INTELLIGENCE UNIT. (UK). **1553**

COUNTRY PROFILE. GUINEA, SIERRA LEONE, LIBERIA / THE ECONOMIST INTELLIGENCE UNIT. (UK). **1553**

COUNTRY PROFILE. GUYANA, WINDWARD & LEEWARD ISLANDS / EIU, THE ECONOMIST INTELLIGENCE UNIT. (UK). **1553**

COUNTRY PROFILE. LEBANON / EIU, THE ECONOMIST INTELLIGENCE UNIT. (UK). **1553**

COUNTRY PROFILE. MADAGASCAR / THE ECONOMIST INTELLIGENCE UNIT. (UK). **1553**

COUNTRY PROFILE. SENEGAL/ THE ECONOMIST INTELLIGENCE UNIT. (UK). **1553**

COUNTRY PROFILE. TANZANIA, COMOROS / THE ECONOMIST INTELLIGENCE UNIT. (UK). **1554**

COUNTRY PROFILE. THE GAMBIA, MAURITANIA / EIU, THE ECONOMIST INTELLIGENCE UNIT. (UK/1352-0938). **1554**

COUNTRY REPORT. UNITED STATES OF AMERICA / EIU, THE ECONOMIST INTELLIGENCE UNIT. (UK). **1554**

ECONOMIC TRENDS IN EASTERN EUROPE. (HU/1216-1829). **1558**

EUROPEAN JOURNAL OF THE HISTORY OF ECONOMIC THOUGHT, THE. (UK/0967-2567). **1560**

FRONTIER-FREE EUROPE / COMMISSION OF THE EUROPEAN COMMUNITIES, DIRECTORATE-GENERAL FOR AUDIOVISUAL MEDIA, INFORMATION, COMMUNICATION AND CULTURE. (BE/1021-2353). **1562**

MEDIUM-TERM REVIEW / THE ECONOMIC AND SOCIAL RESEARCH INSTITUTE. (IE/0790-9470). **1574**

METRO IN VIEW. (CN/1188-1941). **1574**

OBSHCHESTVO I EKONOMIKA. (RU/0207-3676). **1576**

PLANEACION & DESARROLLO. (CK). **1578**

QUARTERLY ECONOMIC REVIEW. (JA). **1579**

RUSSIAN ECONOMIC TRENDS. (UK/0967-0793). **1583**

SERVICIO INFORMATIVO / ALAI, AGENCIA LATINOAMERICANA DE INFORMACION. (EC). **1583**

STUDIES ON RUSSIAN ECONOMIC DEVELOPMENT. (RU). **1585**

UKRAINE (SYRACUSE, N.Y.). (US/1061-1304). **1587**

WORLD ECONOMIC SURVEY. STUDENT EDITION / DEPARTMENT OF INTERNATIONAL ECONOMIC AND SOCIAL AFFAIRS. (US). **1589**

ECONOMIC THEORY

EPARGNE & FINANCE PARIS. (FR/1157-6472). **1591**

FUTURE CONSUMER NEWSLETTER. (CN/1197-4699). **1592**

OUTLOOK, THE REVENUE PICTURE FOR ... . (US). **1594**

Economics — Economic Theory

RUSSIA (SYRACUSE, N.Y.). (US/1060-8753). **1595**

VITAL SIGNS : THE TRENDS THAT ARE SHAPING OUR FUTURE / LESTER R. BROWN, ET. AL. (US). **1596**

INDUSTRY AND PRODUCTION

3W REGISTER OF CHINESE BUSINESS. (US/1063-0503). **1596**

AMERICAN WHOLESALERS AND DISTRIBUTORS DIRECTORY. (US/1061-2114). **1597**

ANCILLARY PROFITS. (US/1065-8769). **1597**

BUSINESS AFFIRMATIVE ACTION DIRECTORY. (US). **1600**

BUSINEST. (CN/1189-458X). **1600**

CAHIER D'INFORMATION ..., INDUSTRIE, MICT, QUEBEC. (CN/1189-4067). **1600**

CANADIAN WOOD PRODUCTS (1992). (CN/1183-9139). **1600**

CHAINON (MONTREAL. 1992). (CN/1191-1085). **1601**

CREATIVE OUTLETS. (US/1062-8207). **1603**

DECLENCHEUR (MALARTIC). (CN/1188-3359). **1603**

DIRECTORY. ASSOCIATIONS. WESTERN REGION. (US/1063-5475). **1604**

DIRECTORY OF CONNECTICUT AND RHODE ISLAND HIGH TECHNOLOGY COMPANIES, THE. (US/1061-334X). **1604**

DIRECTORY OF NEW MEXICO MANUFACTURERS (1991). (US/1057-4565). **1604**

DIRECTORY OF WORLD MANUFACTURED FIBER PRODUCERS. (US/1062-9343). **1605**

DUN'S REGIONAL BUSINESS DIRECTORY. GEORGIA (EXCLUDING ATLANTA) AREA. (US/1061-1207). **1605**

ENSEIGNEMENT SUPERIEUR & RECHERCHE PARIS. (FR/1248-2722). **1605**

EUROPEAN QUALITY. : THE OFFICIAL JOURNAL OF THE EUROPEAN ORGANIZATION FOR QUALITY. (UK/0969-059X). **1606**

F&S INDEX INTERNATIONAL ANNUAL. (US/1076-6588). **1606**

HANOVER REPORT, THE. (US/1065-8335). **1608**

HOOVER'S HANDBOOK OF AMERICAN BUSINESS. (US/1055-7202). **1608**

IMPROVED RECOVERY WEEK. (US/1061-3692). **1609**

INDUSTRIAL AND CORPORATE CHANGE. (UK/0960-6491). **1610**

INNOVATIVE IDEAS. (US/1064-0576). **1612**

INSTRUMENT BUSINESS OUTLOOK. (US/1061-2203). **1612**

JOURNAL OF CLEANER PRODUCTION. (UK/0959-6526). **1613**

LABORATORY INDUSTRY REPORT. (US/1060-5118). **1615**

MANAGED CARE QUALITY. (US/1064-5454). **1617**

MANAGEMENT LEARNING. (UK/1350-5076). **1617**

MCGRAW-HILL'S FEDERAL TECHNOLOGY REPORT. (US/1066-873X). **1618**

MULTIMEDIA MONITOR. (US/1071-0698). **1619**

NATIONAL BOOK OF LISTS, THE. (US/1060-8435). **1619**

OILSEEDS, WORLD MARKETS AND TRADE / UNITED STATES DEPARTMENT OF AGRICULTURE, FOREIGN AGRICULTURE SERVICE. (US). **1620**

OKLAHOMA MANUFACTURERS REGISTER. (US/1059-4523). **1620**

PANORAMA OF EU INDUSTRY. (LU). **1621**

REVIEW - NORTH-SOUTH INSTITUTE (OTTAWA). (CN/1188-4347). **1625**

REVUE : UN BULLETIN DE L'INSTITUT NORD-SUD. (CN/1188-4347). **1625**

SERVICE INDUSTRIES USA. (US/1058-1626). **1626**

SOUTH CAROLINA INDUSTRIAL DIRECTORY. (US). **1627**

SUPER PROJECTS. (US/1062-8398). **1628**

SURVOL CHAUDIERE-APPALACHES. (CN/1183-627X). **1628**

TORONTO REGION TOP EMPLOYERS GUIDE. (CN/1199-6579). **1629**

WINDOW MARKETPLACE. (US/1062-418X). **1631**

INTERNATIONAL ECONOMICS

ACAPA SERIAL. (US/1061-2920). **1632**

DEVELOPING NATIONS. (US/1057-9206). **1634**

ECONOMIE INTERNATIONALE : LA REVUE DU CEPII. (FR). **1634**

FOCUS SOUTH. (CN/1188-3375). **1635**

IDB PROJECTS. (US/1076-8424). **1635**

INTERNATIONAL ECONOMIC SCOREBOARD. (US/0270-045X). **1636**

JOICE. JOURNAL OF INTERNATIONAL AND COMPARATIVE ECONOMICS. (GW/0840-4821). **1637**

JOURNAL OF AFRICAN ECONOMIES. (UK/0963-8024). **1637**

JOURNAL OF ECONOMIC INTEGRATION. (KO/1015-356X). **1637**

WORLD ECONOMIC AND SOCIAL SURVEY / DEPARTMENT OF ECONOMIC AND SOCIAL INFORMATION AND POLICY ANALYSIS. (US). **1641**

LABOR

AFFIRMATIVE ACTION FORUM (SASKATOON). (CN/1187-8924). **1642**

AIFLD OUTLOOK : A PUBLICATION OF THE AMERICAN INSTITUTE FOR FREE LABOR DEVELOPMENT. (US). **1643**

ANN ARBOR'S LABOR MARKET NEWS. (US). **1643**

ARIZONA ECONOMIC TRENDS. (US). **1653**

BATTLE CREEK'S LABOR MARKET NEWS. (US). **1655**

BENEFITS & COMPENSATION UPDATE. (US/1074-6293). **1655**

BENTON HARBOR'S LABOR MARKET NEWS. (US). **1655**

BEYOND BORDERS. (US/1065-2426). **1655**

BNA PENSION & BENEFITS REPORTER. (US/1069-5117). **1655**

BWC NEWS. (US). **1657**

CHELOVEK I TRUD. (RU). **1659**

COLLECTIVE BARGAINING IN NEW BRUNSWICK. (CN/1193-3437). **1660**

COMPARATIVE INDUSTRIAL RELATIONS NEWSLETTER. (CN). **1660**

DARTNELL'S ... SALES FORCE COMPENSATION SURVEY. (US/1070-9207). **1662**

DETROIT'S LABOR MARKET NEWS. (US). **1662**

EMPLOYEE BENEFITS COUNSELOR. (US/1068-4204). **1665**

EMPLOYMENT AND EARNINGS / U.S. DEPARTMENT OF LABOR, BUREAU OF LABOR STATISTICS. (US). **1666**

ERISA AND BENEFITS LAW JOURNAL. (US/1068-3542). **1667**

ERS UPDATE (HONOLULU, HAWAII). (US/1065-5085). **1668**

EUROPEAN TRADE UNION INFORMATION BULLETIN. (UK). **1668**

FEDERAL LABOR RELATIONS ... DESK BOOK. (US/1065-8238). **1669**

FLINT'S LABOR MARKET NEWS. (US). **1674**

GRAND RAPIDS' LABOR MARKET NEWS. (US). **1676**

IFBWW EDUCATION NEWS. (SZ). **1677**

INDUSTRY REPORT ON TECHNICIAN AND SKILLED TRADES PERSONNEL COMPENSATION. (US/1063-0058). **1679**

INFO / FITPAS. (SZ). **1679**

INFORMATION PROCESSING COMPENSATION SURVEY. (CN/1188-1305). **1679**

INSIDE WORKERS' COMPENSATION. (US/1065-2736). **1680**

IOMA'S REPORT ON COMPENSATION & BENEFITS FOR LAW OFFICES. (US/1068-4239). **1681**

JACKSON'S LABOR MARKET NEWS. (US). **1681**

JOURNAL OF INDIVIDUAL EMPLOYMENT RIGHTS. (US/1055-7512). **1682**

KALAMAZOO'S LABOR MARKET NEWS. (US). **1682**

LABOR AREA SUMMARY. STATISTICAL REPORT. (US). **1683**

LABOUR ECONOMICS. (NE/0927-5371). **1685**

LANCASTER'S EMPLOYMENT EQUITY REPORTER. (CN/1194-6237). **1687**

LANSING'S LABOR MARKET NEWS. (US). **1687**

MICHIGAN'S LABOR MARKET NEWS. (US). **1690**

MONMOUTH'S EARLY REPORT. (US/1065-7797). **1691**

MUSKEGON'S LABOR MARKET NEWS. (US). **1692**

Economics —Labor

OCCUPATIONAL COMPENSATION SURVEY--PAY AND BENEFITS. BRUNSWICK, GA / U.S. DEPARTMENT OF LABOR, BUREAU OF LABOR STATISTICS. (US). **1696**

OCCUPATIONAL COMPENSATION SURVEY--PAY AND BENEFITS. CHARLESTON, SC / U.S. DEPARTMENT OF LABOR, BUREAU OF LABOR STATISTICS. (US). **1696**

OCCUPATIONAL COMPENSATION SURVEY--PAY AND BENEFITS. CINCINNATI, OHIO-KENTUCKY-INDIANA, METROPOLITAN AREA / U.S. DEPARTMENT OF LABOR, BUREAU OF LABOR STATISTICS. (US). **1696**

OCCUPATIONAL COMPENSATION SURVEY--PAY AND BENEFITS. CLARKSVILLE-HOPKINSVILLE, TN-KY / U.S. DEPARTMENT OF LABOR, BUREAU OF LABOR STATISTICS. (US). **1696**

OCCUPATIONAL COMPENSATION SURVEY--PAY AND BENEFITS. FLORENCE, SC / U.S. DEPARTMENT OF LABOR, BUREAU OF LABOR STATISTICS. (US). **1696**

OCCUPATIONAL COMPENSATION SURVEY--PAY AND BENEFITS. FRESNO, CA / U.S. DEPARTMENT OF LABOR, BUREAU OF LABOR STATISTICS. (US). **1696**

OCCUPATIONAL COMPENSATION SURVEY--PAY AND BENEFITS. GARY-HAMMOND, INDIANA, METROPOLITAN AREA. (US/1068-4581). **1696**

OCCUPATIONAL COMPENSATION SURVEY--PAY AND BENEFITS. GREENSBORO-WINSTON SALEM-HIGH POINT, NC / U.S. DEPARTMENT OF LABOR, BUREAU OF LABOR STATISTICS. (US). **1696**

OCCUPATIONAL COMPENSATION SURVEY--PAY AND BENEFITS. HUNTSVILLE, ALABAMA, METROPOLITAN AREA / U.S. DEPARTMENT OF LABOR, BUREAU OF LABOR STATISTICS. (US). **1696**

OCCUPATIONAL COMPENSATION SURVEY--PAY AND BENEFITS. JACKSON, MISSISSIPPI, METROPOLITAN AREA / U.S. DEPARTMENT OF LABOR, BUREAU OF LABOR STATISTICS. (US). **1696**

OCCUPATIONAL COMPENSATION SURVEY--PAY AND BENEFITS. MELBOURNE-TITUSVILLE-PALM BAY, FL / U.S. DEPARTMENT OF LABOR, BUREAU OF LABOR STATISTICS. (US). **1696**

OCCUPATIONAL COMPENSATION SURVEY--PAY AND BENEFITS. MONTGOMERY, AL / U.S. DEPARTMENT OF LABOR, BUREAU OF LABOR STATISTICS. (US). **1696**

OCCUPATIONAL COMPENSATION SURVEY--PAY AND BENEFITS. SALINAS-SEASIDE-MONTEREY, CA / U.S. DEPARTMENT OF LABOR, BUREAU OF LABOR STATISTICS. (US). **1696**

OCCUPATIONAL COMPENSATION SURVEY--PAY AND BENEFITS. SELMA, AL / U.S. DEPARTMENT OF LABOR, BUREAU OF LABOR STATISTICS. (US). **1696**

OCCUPATIONAL COMPENSATION SURVEY--PAY AND BENEFITS. SOUTH BEND-MISHAWAKA, INDIANA, METROPOLITAN AREA / U.S. DEPARTMENT OF LABOR, BUREAU OF LABOR STATISTICS. (US). **1697**

OCCUPATIONAL COMPENSATION SURVEY--PAY AND BENEFITS. ST. LOUIS, MISSOURI-ILLINOIS, METROPOLITAN AREA / U.S. DEPARTMENT OF LABOR, BUREAU OF LABOR STATISTICS. (US). **1697**

OCCUPATIONAL COMPENSATION SURVEY--PAY AND BENEFITS. TOLEDO, OH / U.S. DEPARTMENT OF LABOR, BUREAU OF LABOR STATISTICS. (US). **1697**

OCCUPATIONAL COMPENSATION SURVEY--PAY AND BENEFITS. TUCSON-DOUGLAS, AZ / U.S. DEPARTMENT OF LABOR, BUREAU OF LABOR STATISTICS. (US). **1697**

OCCUPATIONAL COMPENSATION SURVEY--PAY AND BENEFITS. VALLEJO-FAIRFIELD-NAPA, CA / U.S. DEPARTMENT OF LABOR, BUREAU OF LABOR STATISTICS. (US). **1697**

OCCUPATIONAL COMPENSATION SURVEY--PAY AND BENEFITS. VERMONT / U.S. DEPARTMENT OF LABOR, BUREAU OF LABOR STATISTICS. (US). **1697**

OCCUPATIONAL COMPENSATION SURVEY--PAY AND BENEFITS. WASHINGTON, D.C.-MARYLAND-VIRGINIA, METROPOLITAN AREA / U.S. DEPARTMENT OF LABOR, BUREAU OF LABOR STATISTICS. (US). **1697**

OCCUPATIONAL COMPENSATION SURVEY--PAY AND BENEFITS. WICHITA, KS / U.S. DEPARTMENT OF LABOR, BUREAU OF LABOR STATISTICS. (US). **1697**

OCCUPATIONAL COMPENSATION SURVEY--PAY ONLY. ARKANSAS--FORESTRY / U.S. DEPARTMENT OF LABOR, BUREAU OF LABOR STATISTICS. (US). **1697**

OCCUPATIONAL COMPENSATION SURVEY--PAY ONLY. ATLANTA, GEORGIA, METROPOLITAN AREA / U.S. DEPARTMENT OF LABOR, BUREAU OF LABOR STATISTICS. (US). **1697**

OCCUPATIONAL COMPENSATION SURVEY--PAY ONLY. AUSTIN, TX / U.S. DEPARTMENT OF LABOR, BUREAU OF LABOR STATISTICS. (US). **1697**

OCCUPATIONAL COMPENSATION SURVEY--PAY ONLY. BELL COUNTY, TX--FAST FOOD RESTAURANTS / U.S. DEPARTMENT OF LABOR, BUREAU OF LABOR STATISTICS. (US). **1697**

OCCUPATIONAL COMPENSATION SURVEY--PAY ONLY. BOSTON, MASSACHUSETTS, METROPOLITAN AREA / U.S. DEPARTMENT OF LABOR, BUREAU OF LABOR STATISTICS. (US). **1697**

OCCUPATIONAL COMPENSATION SURVEY--PAY ONLY. DUVAL COUNTY, FL--FAST FOOD RESTAURANTS / U.S. DEPARTMENT OF LABOR, BUREAU OF LABOR STATISTICS. (US). **1697**

OCCUPATIONAL COMPENSATION SURVEY--PAY ONLY. HARDIN COUNTY, KY--FAST FOOD RESTAURANTS / U.S. DEPARTMENT OF LABOR, BUREAU OF LABOR STATISTICS. (US). **1697**

OCCUPATIONAL COMPENSATION SURVEY--PAY ONLY. HARRISON COUNTY, MS--FAST FOOD RESTAURANTS / U.S. DEPARTMENT OF LABOR, BUREAU OF LABOR STATISTICS. (US). **1697**

OCCUPATIONAL COMPENSATION SURVEY--PAY ONLY. ISLAND COUNTY, WA--FAST FOOD RESTAURANTS / U.S. DEPARTMENT OF LABOR, BUREAU OF LABOR STATISTICS. (US). **1698**

OCCUPATIONAL COMPENSATION SURVEY--PAY ONLY. KANSAS CITY, MISSOURI-KANSAS, METROPOLITAN AREA / U.S. DEPARTMENT OF LABOR, BUREAU OF LABOR STATISTICS. (US). **1698**

OCCUPATIONAL COMPENSATION SURVEY--PAY ONLY. LAKE COUNTY, IL--FAST FOOD RESTAURANTS / U.S. DEPARTMENT OF LABOR, BUREAU OF LABOR STATISTICS. (US). **1698**

OCCUPATIONAL COMPENSATION SURVEY--PAY ONLY. LAUDERDALE COUNTY, MS--FAST FOOD RESTAURANTS / U.S. DEPARTMENT OF LABOR, BUREAU OF LABOR STATISTICS. (US). **1698**

OCCUPATIONAL COMPENSATION SURVEY--PAY ONLY. LEAVENWORTH, KS--FAST FOOD RESTAURANTS / U.S. DEPARTMENT OF LABOR, BUREAU OF LABOR STATISTICS. (US). **1698**

OCCUPATIONAL COMPENSATION SURVEY--PAY ONLY. MINNEAPOLIS-ST. PAUL, MINNESOTA-WISCONSIN, METROPOLITAN AREA / U.S. DEPARTMENT OF LABOR, BUREAU OF LABOR STATISTICS. (US). **1698**

OCCUPATIONAL COMPENSATION SURVEY--PAY ONLY. MISSISSIPPI--FORESTRY / U.S. DEPARTMENT OF LABOR, BUREAU OF LABOR STATISTICS. (US). **1698**

OCCUPATIONAL COMPENSATION SURVEY--PAY ONLY. MONTGOMERY COUNTY, MD--FAST FOOD RESTAURANTS / U.S. DEPARTMENT OF LABOR, BUREAU OF LABOR STATISTICS. (US). **1698**

OCCUPATIONAL COMPENSATION SURVEY--PAY ONLY. NORFOLK, VA--FAST FOOD RESTAURANTS / U.S. DEPARTMENT OF LABOR, BUREAU OF LABOR STATISTICS. (US). **1698**

OCCUPATIONAL COMPENSATION SURVEY--PAY ONLY. OAKLAND, CALIFORNIA, METROPOLITAN AREA / U.S. DEPARTMENT OF LABOR, BUREAU OF LABOR STATISTICS. (US). **1698**

OCCUPATIONAL COMPENSATION SURVEY-- PAY ONLY. PORTSMOUTH-CHILLICOTHE-GALLIPOLIS, OH / U.S. DEPARTMENT OF LABOR, BUREAU OF LABOR STATISTICS. (US). **1698**

OCCUPATIONAL COMPENSATION SURVEY--PAY ONLY. PROVIDENCE, RI / U.S. DEPARTMENT OF LABOR, BUREAU OF LABOR STATISTICS. (US). **1698**

OCCUPATIONAL COMPENSATION SURVEY--PAY ONLY. PUERTO RICO / U.S. DEPARTMENT OF LABOR, BUREAU OF LABOR STATISTICS. (US). **1698**

OCCUPATIONAL COMPENSATION SURVEY--PAY ONLY. SACRAMENTO, CALIFORNIA, METROPOLITAN AREA. (US). **1698**

OCCUPATIONAL COMPENSATION SURVEY--PAY ONLY. SALT LAKE CITY-OGDEN, UTAH, METROPOLITAN AREA / U.S. DEPARTMENT OF LABOR, BUREAU OF LABOR STATISTICS. (US). **1698**

OCCUPATIONAL COMPENSATION SURVEY--PAY ONLY. SAN FRANCISCO, CALIFORNIA, METROPOLITAN AREA / U.S. DEPARTMENT OF LABOR, BUREAU OF LABOR STATISTICS. (US). **1698**

OCCUPATIONAL COMPENSATION SURVEY--PAY ONLY. TOPEKA, KS / U.S. DEPARTMENT OF LABOR, BUREAU OF LABOR STATISTICS. (US). **1698**

OCCUPATIONAL COMPENSATION SURVEY--PAY ONLY. WASHINGTON, DC--FAST FOOD RESTAURANTS / U.S. DEPARTMENT OF LABOR, BUREAU OF LABOR STATISTICS. (US). **1699**

PLAN REGIONAL DE DEVELOPPEMENT DE LA MAIN-D'OEUVRE, REGION DE LANAUDIERE. (CN/1193-4018). **1702**

POLICE OFFICERS JOURNAL, THE. (US/1062-5216). **1702**

POLICY STUDIES PAPERS. (US/1061-1843). **1702**

PROFSOIUZY. (RU/0132-1196). **1704**

REAL PEOPLE, REAL JOBS. (US/1062-385X). **1705**

SAGINAW-BAY-MIDLAND'S LABOR MARKET NEWS. (US). **1709**

SURVEY REPORT ON VARIABLE PAY PROGRAMS / WYATT DATA SERVICES, ECS. (US). **1713**

TRENDS IN SOCIAL SECURITY. (SZ/1019-4126). **1715**

UNICE INFORMATION. (BE). **1715**

VIRGINIA LABOR MARKET REVIEW / VIRGINIA EMPLOYMENT COMMISSION, ECONOMIC INFORMATION SERVICES DIVISION. (US). **1716**

WBF IN ACTION. (US/1061-1444). **1717**

WCB UPDATE. (CN/1191-6885). **1717**

Economics — Labor

WORKFORCE (WASHINGTON, D.C.). (US/1063-4363). **1719**

WORKING IT OUT. (US/1064-489X). **1719**

WORKSIGHT (EDMONTON). (CN/1188-4126). **1719**

WORKWATCH (BELLINGHAM, WASH.). (US/1062-9742). **1719**

WORLD OF WORK : THE MAGAZINE OF THE ILO. (SZ/1020-0029). **1720**

EDUCATION

AGENDA, JEWISH EDUCATION. (US/1072-1150). **1723**

ASSESSMENT IN EDUCATION: PRINCIPLES, POLICY AND PRACTICE. (UK/0969-594X). **1726**

AWARDS FOR UNIVERSITY TEACHERS AND RESEARCH WORKERS. (UK/0964-2706). **1727**

BILINGUAL RESEARCH JOURNAL. (US). **1728**

BY THE YEAR 2000: REPORT OF THE FCCSET COMMITTEE ON EDUCATION AND HUMAN RESOURCES. (US). **1729**

CAHIERS AFIDES. (CN/1188-5033). **1730**

CAHIERS DE L'ANIMATION, LES. (FR/1243-6852). **1730**

CHINESE EDUCATION AND SOCIETY. (US/1061-1932). **1731**

COLLEGE PLANNING QUARTERLY. (US/1071-3751). **1732**

COLORADO PRIVATE ELEMENTARY AND SECONDARY SCHOOLS. (US/1061-0294). **1732**

CURRENT ISSUES IN MIDDLE LEVEL EDUCATION. (US/1059-7107). **1734**

DEPARTMENT OF EDUCATION REPORTS / NATIONAL CENTER FOR EDUCATION INFORMATION. (US). **1735**

DISCIPLINE NETWORK (ELEMENTARY SCHOOL ED.). (US/1073-6123). **1736**

DISCIPLINE NETWORK (MIDDLE/HIGH SCHOOL ED.). (US/1073-6107). **1736**

EDUCATION AFTER SIXTEEN. (UK/0965-2396). **1738**

EDUCATION ECONOMICS. (UK/0964-5292). **1739**

EDUCATION ET FORMATION AU QUEBEC. (CN/1192-3318). **1739**

EDUCATION INTERNATIONAL. (BE). **1740**

EDUCATION INVESTOR, THE. (US/1069-9988). **1740**

EDUCATION REFORM DIGEST. (US/1068-2406). **1740**

EDUCATION STATISTICS (FREDERICTON). (CN/1187-841X). **1740**

EDUCATION STATISTICS (FREDERICTON). (CN/1187-841X). **1740**

EDUCATIONAL ACTION RESEARCH. (UK/0965-0792). **1741**

EDUCATIONAL ASSESSMENT. (US/1062-7197). **1741**

EDUCATORS GUIDE TO FREE VIDEOTAPES. (US/1068-9206). **1743**

EDULAW FOR CANADIAN SCHOOLS. (CN/1193-7319). **1743**

EFFECTIF SCOLAIRE ..., MANUEL D'OPERATIONS DES SYSTEMES INFORMATIQUES (DCS). (CN/1187-9130). **1743**

ELEMENTARY SCHOOL JOURNAL. (US). **1743**

ENSEMBLE - CONFERENCE BOARD OF CANADA. NATIONAL BUSINESS AND EDUCATION CENTRE. (CN/1188-8482). **1744**

EQUITY & EXCELLENCE IN EDUCATION. (US/1066-5684). **1744**

ERIC (PEABODY, MASS.). (US/1065-6537). **1745**

EUROPEAN REVIEW (CHICHESTER, ENGLAND). (UK/1062-7987). **1745**

EXECUTIVE SUMMARY OF CALIFORNIA EDUCATION. (US/1065-5115). **1746**

FACULTY GRANTS DIRECTORY. (US/1064-8003). **1746**

FINANCIAL AID FOR RESEARCH AND CREATIVE ACTIVITIES ABROAD. (US). **1746**

FINANCIAL AID FOR STUDY AND TRAINING ABROAD. (US). **1746**

FROM INFORMATION TO EDUCATION. (US/1064-9034). **1747**

FUNDING OF EDUCATION IN ALBERTA, A SCHOOL FINANCE BROCHURE, THE. (CN/1189-4296). **1747**

GENERAL INFORMATION AND GUIDELINES FOR THE SUMMER INDIVIDUAL EXCHANGE PROGRAM. (CN/1193-249X). **1748**

HANDBOOK FOR CLASSROOM STUDENTS / ALBERTA DISTANCE LEARNING CENTRE. (CN/0846-2658). **1749**

HANDBOOK FOR NON-CLASSROOM STUDENTS / ALBERTA DISTANCE LEARNING CENTRE. (CN/0846-264X). **1749**

HELPING CHILDREN LEARN. (US/1065-6405). **1750**

HOME SCHOOL ADVANTAGE. (US/1065-7754). **1751**

IMAGINE (BALTIMORE, MD.). (US/1071-605X). **1751**

INNOVATIONS IN EDUCATION AND TRAINING TECHNOLOGY INTERNATIONAL. (UK). **1753**

INTERNATIONAL JOURNAL OF EDUCATIONAL REFORM. (US/1056-7879). **1754**

ISSUES IN THE POSTMODERN THEORY OF EDUCATION. (US/1058-1634). **1755**

JAHRBUCH FUER PADAGOGIK. (GW/0941-1461). **1755**

JOURNAL FOR TRUANCY AND DROPOUT PREVENTION, THE. (US). **1756**

JOURNAL OF CREATIVE VISUAL LEARNING, THE. (US/1061-8694). **1756**

JOURNAL OF INDEPENDENT RESEARCH. (US/1055-8888). **1757**

JOURNAL OF INFORMATION TECHNOLOGY FOR TEACHER EDUCATION. (UK/0962-029X). **1757**

JOURNAL OF TECHNOLOGY AND TEACHER EDUCATION. (US/1059-7069). **1758**

KOULUTUS. (FI/1236-4746). **1760**

LANGUAGES IN EUROPE. (UK/0965-240X). **1761**

MARKET DATA RETRIEVAL'S CIC SCHOOL DIRECTORY. ALABAMA. (US/1067-6430). **1762**

MARKET DATA RETRIEVAL'S CIC SCHOOL DIRECTORY. DISTRICT OF COLUMBIA. (US/1067-957X). **1762**

MARKET DATA RETRIEVAL'S CIC SCHOOL DIRECTORY. IDAHO. (US/1067-6538). **1762**

MARKET DATA RETRIEVAL'S CIC SCHOOL DIRECTORY. INDIANA. (US/1067-6554). **1762**

MARKET DATA RETRIEVAL'S CIC SCHOOL DIRECTORY. MAINE. (US). **1762**

MARKET DATA RETRIEVAL'S CIC SCHOOL DIRECTORY. MASSACHUSETTS. (US). **1762**

MARKET DATA RETRIEVAL'S CIC SCHOOL DIRECTORY. MINNESOTA. (US/1067-6643). **1762**

MARKET DATA RETRIEVAL'S CIC SCHOOL DIRECTORY. MISSISSIPPI. (US/1067-6651). **1763**

MARKET DATA RETRIEVAL'S CIC SCHOOL DIRECTORY. NEW HAMPSHIRE. (US). **1763**

MARKET DATA RETRIEVAL'S CIC SCHOOL DIRECTORY. PENNSYLVANIA. (US/1067-6791). **1763**

MARKET DATA RETRIEVAL'S CIC SCHOOL DIRECTORY. RHODE ISLAND. (US). **1763**

MARKET DATA RETRIEVAL'S CIC SCHOOL DIRECTORY. VERMONT. (US). **1763**

MID-WESTERN EDUCATIONAL RESEARCHER (1991). (US/1056-3997). **1764**

MINUTE PARIS. 1993. (FR/1243-7751). **1764**

MOTS ET DE CRAIE, DE. (CN/1188-3766). **1765**

MULTICULTURAL EDUCATION (SAN FRANCISCO, CALIF.). (US/1068-3844). **1765**

NCBE FORUM. (US/1072-2076). **1766**

NEW DIRECTIONS FOR EDUCATION REFORM : A PUBLICATION OF THE COLLEGE OF EDUCATION AND BEHAVIORAL SCIENCES, WESTERN KENTUCKY UNIVERSITY. (US). **1767**

NEW SCHOOLS, NEW COMMUNITIES. (US/1077-2936). **1768**

ORTHOGRAPHE PLUS. (CN/1191-5099). **1770**

OUR SCHOOLS USA. (US/1063-9845). **1771**

PEDAGOGIKA. (RU). **1772**

PEOPLE AND EDUCATION. (US/1063-7877). **1772**

PETERSON'S GUIDE TO PRIVATE SECONDARY SCHOOLS. (US/1066-5366). **1773**

PETERSON'S STUDY ABROAD. (US/1069-6504). **1773**

REGLES BUDGETAIRES POUR L'ANNEE SCOLAIRE ..., COMMISSION SCOLAIRE DU LITTORAL. (CN). **1777**

REGLES BUDGETAIRES POUR L'ANNEE SCOLAIRE ..., COMMISSION SCOLAIRE KATIVIK. (CN). **1777**

REGLES BUDGETAIRES POUR L'ANNEE SCOLAIRE ..., ECOLE DES NASKAPIS. (CN). **1777**

REPORT OF ACTIVITIES / WOMEN'S EDUCATIONAL EQUITY ACT PROGRAM. (US). **1778**

RESEAU - ASSOCIATION DES ENSEIGNANTES ET DES ENSEIGNANTS FRANCO-ONTARIENS. (CN/1192-2796). **1779**

REVIEW OF EDUCATION/PEDAGOGY/CULTURAL STUDIES, THE. (SZ/1071-4413). **1779**

REVISTA DE LA DIRECCION DE EDUCACION. (UY/0797-6275). **1780**

Education —School Organization and Administration

RUSSIAN EDUCATION AND SOCIETY. (US/1060-9393). **1781**

SCHWEIZERISCHE LEHRERINNEN- UND LEHRER-ZEITUNG: SLZ. (SZ). **1782**

STARS FOR STUDENTS, CLASS ACTS. (US/1059-3519). **1784**

STATISTICS OF EDUCATION AND TRAINING IN WALES. SCHOOLS / WELSH OFFICE / YSTADEGAU ADDYSG A HYFFORDDIANT YNG NGHYMRU. YSGOLION / Y SWYDDFA GYMREIG. (UK/0968-5588). **1785**

TEACHERS IN FOCUS. (US/1065-5182). **1787**

TECHNOS (BLOOMINGTON, IND.). (US/1060-5649). **1787**

WASHINGTON, D.C. INTERNSHIP DIRECTORY. (US/1061-379X). **1790**

WISCONSIN SCHOOL DIRECTORY / WISCONSIN DPI. (US). **1791**

ABSTRACTING, BIBLIOGRAPHIES AND STATISTICS

CIJE ON DISC. (US/1073-1113). **1793**

ERIC IDENTIFIER AUTHORITY LIST. (US/1062-0508). **1795**

JOURNAL OF EDUCATIONAL AND BEHAVIORAL STATISTICS. (US/1076-9986). **1795**

MIDDLE SEARCH. (US/1071-2755). **1795**

PRIMARY SEARCH. (US/1065-2485). **1796**

STEIRISCHE BILDUNGSSTATISTIK. (AU). **1798**

VOCATIONAL SEARCH. (US/1071-2747). **1798**

ADULT AND CONTINUING EDUCATION

GRANTS FOR LITERACY, READING & ADULT EDUCATION. (US). **1800**

LEARN FOR YOURSELF. (UK/0969-9015). **1801**

SKILLSLINK LISTER NEWS. (CN/1188-9705). **1802**

SOUTH FLORIDA CONTINUING EDUCATION NEWS. (US/1064-5152). **1802**

EARLY CHILDHOOD AND PRIMARY EDUCATION

CHILDREN'S ENVIRONMENTS. (UK). **1803**

DIMENSIONS OF EARLY CHILDHOOD. (US/0160-6425). **1803**

EARLY DEVELOPMENT AND PARENTING. (UK/1057-3593). **1803**

MAGNET NEWSLETTER, THE. (US/1065-6782). **1804**

PRIMARY VOICES K-6. (US/1068-073X). **1805**

SCHOLASTIC EARLY CHILDHOOD TODAY. (US/1070-1214). **1805**

SOCIAL DEVELOPMENT. (UK/0961-205X). **1805**

STORYWORKS (NEW YORK, N.Y.). (US/1068-0292). **1805**

HIGHER EDUCATION

AFTER SCHOOL MAGAZINE. (US/1073-1555). **1807**

AWARDS FOR POSTGRADUATE STUDY AT COMMONWEALTH UNIVERSITIES. (UK/0960-7986). **1811**

BIULLETEN VYSSHEGO ATTESTATSIONNOGO KOMITETA PRI MINISTERSTVE NAUKI, VYSSHEI SHKOLY I TEKHNICHESKOI POLITIKI ROSSIISKOI FEDERATSII. (RU). **1811**

BOURSES D'EXCELLENCE POUR DES ETUDES DE CYCLES SUPERIEURS, DE PERFECTIONNEMENT ET DE REINTEGRATION A LA RECHERCHE ..., GUIDE DU BOURSIER, LES. (CN/1188-6773). **1812**

CCTANS NEWSLETTER. (CN/1197-5865). **1814**

CHRONICLE FINANCIAL AID GUIDE. (US/1063-7915). **1815**

COLLEGE MARKETING ANNUAL. (US/1065-0369). **1816**

COMMON-SENSE GUIDE TO AMERICAN COLLEGES, THE. (US/1065-0571). **1817**

COMMUNITY COLLEGE JOURNAL. (US/1067-1803). **1817**

COMMUNITY COLLEGE JOURNAL OF RESEARCH AND PRACTICE. (US/1066-8926). **1817**

CONTACTS AND COURSES, WHO'S WHO IN CANADIAN PLACEMENT. (CN/1193-5073). **1818**

CRACKING THE ACT. (US/1059-101X). **1819**

CRACKING THE GRE. (US/1062-5534). **1819**

DIRECTORY (COLLEGE PLACEMENT COUNCIL). (US/1077-0771). **1820**

ELECTRONIC EDUCATION REPORT. (US). **1822**

FELL'S GUIDE TO COLLEGE MONEY FOR THE ASKING IN FLORIDA. (US/1040-9513). **1824**

FLORIDA LEADER. (US/0898-4387). **1824**

FORD FOUNDATION REPORT, THE. (US/1063-7281). **1824**

FUND YOUR WAY THROUGH COLLEGE. (US/1071-040X). **1825**

GRADUATE CURRICULA IN EDUCATIONAL COMMUNICATIONS AND TECHNOLOGY. (US). **1826**

GUIDE TO THE ATLANTA UNIVERSITY CENTER AND ATLANTA, THE. (US/1064-5306). **1827**

INDEPENDENT SCHOOLS YEARBOOK. (UK). **1830**

INDEX OF MAJORS AND GRADUATE DEGREES. (US/1065-2787). **1830**

INTERIM INSTITUTIONAL DIRECTORY ... HIGHER EDUCATION IN NEW YORK STATE / THE UNIVERSITY OF THE STATE OF NEW YORK, THE STATE EDUCATION DEPARTMENT, BUREAU OF POSTSECONDARY PLANNING. (US). **1831**

INTERNATIONAL HANDBOOK OF UNIVERSITIES. (FR). **1831**

INVENTORY OF PROGRAM OFFERINGS AT NEW JERSEY INSTITUTIONS OF HIGHER EDUCATION. (US). **1831**

MASTER'S THESES DIRECTORIES. (US/1072-5903). **1835**

PAYING LESS FOR COLLEGE. (US/1062-3205). **1839**

PETERSON'S GRANTS FOR GRADUATE STUDY. (US/1058-6377). **1840**

PETERSON'S GRANTS FOR POST-DOCTORAL STUDY. (US/1058-9287). **1840**

PETERSON'S GUIDE TO COLLEGES IN THE SOUTH. (US/1069-0085). **1841**

PETERSON'S GUIDE TO GRADUATE PROGRAMS IN THE HUMANITIES, ARTS, AND SOCIAL SCIENCES. (US). **1841**

PETERSON'S SPORTS SCHOLARSHIPS AND COLLEGE ATHLETIC PROGRAMS. (US/1069-1383). **1841**

POSTSECONDARY EDUCATION OPPORTUNITY. (US/1068-9818). **1842**

PUBLICATIONS (TOPOR & ASSOCIATES). (US/1063-1771). **1843**

REGENTS ... STATEWIDE PLAN FOR HIGHER EDUCATION IN NEW YORK STATE, THE. (US). **1843**

SEATTLE BRANCH NEWSLETTER / AMERICAN ASSOCIATION OF UNIVERSITY WOMEN. (US). **1847**

STATISTICAL REPORT - CANADIAN ASSOCIATION FOR GRADUATE STUDIES. (CN/1194-689X). **1848**

STUDENT ADVOCATE (OTTAWA. 1992). (CN/1188-3960). **1848**

STUDENT ADVOCATE (OTTAWA. 1992). (CN/1188-3960). **1848**

TQM IN HIGHER EDUCATION. (US/1065-6774). **1850**

TRUSTEESHIP (WASHINGTON, D.C.). (US/1068-1027). **1851**

WHICH SCHOOL? FOR A LEVELS. (UK). **1853**

WHO'S WHO OF VICE-CHANCELLORS, PRESIDENTS AND RECTORS OF COMMONWEALTH UNIVERSITIES. (UK). **1853**

WOMEN IN HIGHER EDUCATION. (US/1060-8303). **1854**

PHYSICAL EDUCATION AND TRAINING

EXTRA INNINGS. (US/1072-0510). **1855**

FITNESS AND SPORTS REVIEW INTERNATIONAL. (US/1068-5952). **1855**

ICHPER-SD JOURNAL : THE OFFICIAL MAGAZINE OF THE INTERNATIONAL COUNCIL FOR HEALTH, PHYSICAL EDUCATION, RECREATION, SPORT AND DANCE. (US). **1856**

JOURNAL OF ATHLETIC TRAINING. (US/1062-6050). **1856**

JOURNAL OF PHYSICAL EDUCATION NEW ZEALAND. (NZ/1172-5958). **1856**

STRENGTH AND CONDITIONING. (US/1073-6840). **1858**

TEACHING HIGH SCHOOL PHYSICAL EDUCATION. (US). **1858**

TEACHING MIDDLE SCHOOL PHYSICAL EDUCATION. (US). **1858**

SCHOOL ORGANIZATION AND ADMINISTRATION

CREATING QUALITY K-12. (US/1070-5341). **1862**

Education — School Organization and Administration

DIRECTORY OF MEMBERS / AMERICAN ASSOCIATION OF COLLEGES FOR TEACHER EDUCATION. (US). **1862**

HIGH SCHOOL MAGAZINE, THE. (US/1070-9533). **1864**

MARKET DATA RETRIEVAL'S CIC SCHOOL DIRECTORY. ARKANSAS. (US/1067-960X). **1866**

SPECIAL EDUCATION AND REHABILITATION

ADHD REPORT, THE. (US/1065-8025). **1874**

BRITISH JOURNAL OF DEVELOPMENTAL DISABILITIES, THE. (UK). **1876**

DYSLEXIA (CHICHESTER, ENGLAND). (UK/1076-9242). **1878**

EDUCATION AND TRAINING IN MENTAL RETARDATION AND DEVELOPMENTAL DISABILITIES. (US). **1878**

GIFTED CHILD TODAY MAGAZINE. (US/1076-2175). **1879**

LITERACY NEWS: A PUBLICATION OF THE NATIONAL INSTITUTE FOR LITERACY. (US). **1881**

NATIONAL DIRECTORY OF CERTIFIED COUNSELORS. (US/0898-1493). **1882**

NEWSLETTER - DANISH CENTRE FOR TECHNICAL AIDS FOR REHABILITATION AND EDUCATION. (DK). **1882**

PUBLIC SCHOOLS, K-12 AND HANDICAPPED ENROLLMENT FORECASTS ... BIENNIAL BUDGET. (US). **1884**

READING & WRITING QUARTERLY. (UK/1057-3569). **1884**

THERAPEUTIC WORK WITH CHILDREN. (UK/1353-3347). **1886**

VESTNIK MINISTERSTVA SKOLSTVI, MLADEZE A TELOVYCHOVY CESKE REPUBLIKY. (XR). **1886**

WHICH SCHOOL? FOR SPECIAL NEEDS. (UK/0965-1004). **1886**

TEACHING AND CURRICULUM

BROWN'S DIRECTORY OF INSTRUCTIONAL PROGRAMS (7-12). TECHNICAL/VOCATIONAL EDUCATION, HOME ECONOMICS. (US/1075-2307). **1911**

CAUTG BULLETIN. (CN/1193-817X). **1890**

CONNECTION - ALBERTA. STUDENT PROGRAMS AND EVALUATION DIVISION. (CN/1193-2759). **1891**

CURRICULUM STUDIES. (UK/0965-9757). **1892**

DIRECTORY OF VIDEO, COMPUTER, AND AUDIO-VISUAL PRODUCTS, THE. (US/0884-2124). **1893**

EFFECTIVE SCHOOL PRACTICES. (US/1068-7378). **1894**

EVERYDAY TLC. (US/1077-5544). **1894**

JOURNAL OF INVITATIONAL THEORY AND PRACTICE. (US/1060-6041). **1898**

MODERN ENGLISH TEACHER. (UK/0308-0587). **1900**

NEWSLETTER : A PUBLICATION OF THE ALBERTA TEACHERS' ASSOCIATION, ENGLISH AS A SECOND LANGUAGE COUNCIL. (CN/1189-4881). **1901**

TEACHING AND CHANGE. (US/1068-378X). **1906**

TEACHING AND LEARNING LITERATURE WITH CHILDREN AND YOUNG ADULTS. (US/1063-5092). **1906**

TEACHING LEARNING PROCESS, THE. (US/1059-6151). **1907**

VOICES FROM THE MIDDLE. (US/1074-4762). **1908**

VOCATIONAL EDUCATION

EMPLOYMENT AND TRAINING PARTNERSHIP : A PUBLICATION OF THE STATE JOB TRAINING COORDINATING COUNCIL, THE. (US). **1913**

MICHIGAN STATE PLAN FOR VOCATIONAL-TECHNICAL EDUCATION. (US). **1914**

PETERSON'S GUIDE TO VOCATIONAL AND TECHNICAL SCHOOLS. EAST. (US/1069-1367). **1915**

PETERSON'S GUIDE TO VOCATIONAL AND TECHNICAL SCHOOLS. WEST. (US/1069-1375). **1915**

REPORT ON CORPORATE EDUCATIONAL SUPPORT. (US/1066-0151). **1915**

SPETSIALIST. (RU). **1915**

SREDNIE SPETSIALNYE UCHEBNYE ZAVEDENIIA PETERBURGA I OBLASTI. (RU). **1916**

TECH DIRECTIONS. (US/1062-9351). **1916**

EMIGRATION AND IMMIGRATION

ASIAN AND PACIFIC MIGRATION JOURNAL : APMJ. (PH). **1918**

PBC IMMIGRATION BRIEFS. (US/1059-2008). **1920**

REFUGEE SURVEY QUARTERLY. (SZ). **1921**

TOLLEY'S IMMIGRATION AND NATIONALITY LAW AND PRACTICE. (UK/0269-5774). **1921**

U.S. IMMIGRATION. (US/1055-8276). **1921**

ENCYCLOPEDIAS AND GENERAL REFERENCE BOOKS

CANADIAN GLOBAL ALMANAC, THE. (CN/1187-4570). **1924**

CLEARINGHOUSE DIRECTORY, THE. (US/1053-0460). **1924**

COMMERCIAL LIBRARY PUBLICATIONS LIST / UNITED STATES DEPARTMENT OF STATE LIBRARY. (US). **1924**

CONTINUING MEDICAL EDUCATION DIRECTORY / AMERICAN MEDICAL ASSOCIATION. (US). **1924**

CORPORATE YELLOW BOOK. (US/1058-2908). **1924**

EASTERN EUROPE AND THE COMMONWEALTH OF INDEPENDENT STATES. (UK/0962-1040). **1925**

ENVIRONMENT ENCYCLOPEDIA AND DIRECTORY, THE. (UK). **1925**

EUROPEAN COMMUNITIES ENCYCLOPEDIA & DIRECTORY. (UK). **1925**

FEDERAL REGIONAL YELLOW BOOK. (US/1061-3153). **1925**

FINANCIAL YELLOW BOOK. (US/1058-2878). **1926**

GRADUATE MEDICAL EDUCATION DIRECTORY. (US). **1926**

ISRAEL YEARBOOK AND ALMANAC. (IS). **1927**

NEWS MEDIA YELLOW BOOK. (US/1071-8931). **1927**

NEWSPAPERS ONLINE. (US/1065-8947). **1927**

OKLAHOMA ALMANAC. (US). **1927**

ORIGINAL ... HIGHWAY 17 ALMANAC & GAZETTEER, THE. (US/1054-4585). **1927**

SCHWEIZER LOGISTIK-KATALOG / SWISS LOGISITICS CATALOGUE. (SZ). **1929**

ENERGY

BIOMASS BULLETIN/ WESTERN REGIONAL BIOMASS ENERGY PROGRAM. (US). **1934**

BIOMASS DIGEST / WESTERN REGIONAL BIOMASS ENERGY PROGRAM. (US). **1934**

BIOMASS ENERGY DIRECTORY. (US/1064-7651). **1934**

ENVIRONMENTAL RADON PROGRAM, SUMMARIES OF RESEARCH IN FY ... / ENVIRONMENTAL SCIENCES DIVISION, OFFICE OF HEALTH AND ENVIRONMENTAL RESEARCH [AND] OFFICE OF ENERGY RESEARCH, DEPARTMENT OF ENERGY. (US). **1943**

INTERNATIONAL DIRECTORY OF POWER GENERATION. (UK). **1947**

INTERNATIONAL JOURNAL OF POWER & ENERGY SYSTEMS. (US/1078-3466). **1948**

IZVESTIIA AKADEMII NAUK. ENERGETIKA. (RU). **1948**

NEW ENERGY NEWS. (US/1075-0045). **1951**

NORTHWEST REGIONAL FORECAST OF POWER LOADS AND RESOURCES FOR ... / COMPILED BY PACIFIC NORTHWEST UTILITIES CONFERENCE COMMITTEE, SYSTEM PLANNING OFFICE. (US). **1951**

NREL SCIENCE & TECHNOLOGY IN REVIEW. (US). **1951**

POWER SMART ANNUAL REPORT. (CN/1192-2354). **1953**

PRIVATE POWER EXECUTIVE. (US/1075-0592). **1953**

REGULATORY TIMES, THE. (CN/1193-1442). **1954**

RESOURCE AND ENERGY ECONOMICS. (NE/0928-7655). **1955**

SOLAR ENERGY MATERIALS AND SOLAR CELLS : AN INTERNATIONAL JOURNAL DEVOTED TO PHOTOVOLTAIC, PHOTOTHERMAL, AND PHOTOCHEMICAL SOLAR ENERGY CONVERSION. (NE/0927-0248). **1957**

WORLD DIRECTORY OF ENERGY CONSERVATION AND RENEWABLE ENERGY SOFTWARE FOR MICROCOMPUTERS. (US/1048-2288). **1960**

ABSTRACTING, BIBLIOGRAPHIES AND STATISTICS

ELECTRIC POWER STATISTICS. ANNUAL STATISTICS. (CN/1198-4848). **1962**

ENERGY STATISTICS HANDBOOK. (CN/1188-665X). **1942**

ENERGY STATISTICS HANDBOOK. (CN/1188-665X). **1942**

ENGINEERING

ADVANCES IN ENGINEERING SOFTWARE (1992). (UK/0965-9978). **1964**

AIRCRAFT TECHNOLOGY ENGINEERING & MAINTENANCE. (UK/0967-439X). **1964**

BIOMIMETICS (NEW YORK, N.Y.). (US/1059-0153). **1966**

BOUNDARY ELEMENTS COMMUNICATIONS. (UK). **1966**

CIVIL ENGINEERS AUSTRALIA. (AT). **1968**

COMMUNICATIONS IN RELIABILITY, MAINTAINABILITY, AND SUPPORTABILITY. (US/1072-3757). **1968**

COMPUTER APPLICATIONS IN ENGINEERING EDUCATION. (US/1061-3773). **1969**

CONCURRENT ENGINEERING : RESEARCH AND APPLICATIONS. (UK/1063-293X). **1969**

DIRECTORY OF ENGINEERING AND ENGINEERING TECHNOLOGY UNDERGRADUATE PROGRAMS. (US/1057-5286). **1970**

DIRECTORY OF ENGINEERING GRADUATE STUDIES & RESEARCH. (US/1067-9022). **1970**

ECOLOGICAL ENGINEERING. (NE/0925-8574). **1971**

EDMS COMPARISON REPORT. (US/1061-9550). **1971**

EI THESAURUS. (US). **1999**

ENGINEERING AUTOMATION REPORT. (US/1065-6952). **1972**

ENGINEERING DOCUMENTATION ADVISOR, THE. (US/1062-8800). **1973**

ENGINEERING SCIENCE AND EDUCATION JOURNAL. (UK/0963-7346). **1974**

ENGINEERING WORKFORCE BULLETIN / EWC AAES. (US). **1974**

ENGINEERS AUSTRALIA. (AT). **1974**

ERGONOMICS IN DESIGN. (US/1064-8046). **1975**

EUROPEAN PRODUCTION ENGINEERING : EPE. (GW/0940-2470). **1975**

GREEN COUNTRY SCIENCE & ENGINEERING JOURNAL. (US/1057-2953). **1976**

IEEE/NPSS SYMPOSIUM FUSION ENGINEERING : PROCEEDINGS. (US). **1977**

IEEE SIGNAL PROCESSING LETTERS. (US/1070-9908). **1977**

IEEE TRANSACTIONS ON CONTROL SYSTEMS TECHNOLOGY. (US/1063-6536). **1977**

INDIAN JOURNAL OF ENGINEERING & MATERIALS SCIENCES. (II/0971-457X). **1978**

INDUSTRY ENGINEER. (US/1064-5683). **1978**

INGENIEUR FUER POST UND TELEKOMMUNIKATION, DER. (GW/0942-3915). **1978**

INSTRUMENTATION & AUTOMATION NEWS : IAN. (US). **1979**

INSTRUMENTATION & CONTROL SYSTEMS: I&CS. (US). **1979**

INTERNATIONAL DIRECTORY OF CONSULTANTS AND CONTRACTORS ACTIVE IN THE UNITED STATES AND CANADA, AN. (US/1058-5796). **1979**

INTERNATIONAL DIRECTORY OF ENGINEERING SOCIETIES AND RELATED ORGANIZATIONS. (US/1067-9014). **1979**

INTERNATIONAL JOURNAL OF DAMAGE MECHANICS. (US/1056-7895). **1979**

INTERNATIONAL JOURNAL OF ENGINEERING EDUCATION, THE. (GW). **1980**

INTERNATIONAL JOURNAL OF SELF-PROPAGATING HIGH-TEMPERATURE SYSTEM. (US/1061-3862). **1980**

JAPANESE TECHNOLOGY REVIEWS. SECTION D, MANUFACTURING ENGINEERING. (US/1058-7322). **1981**

JOURNAL OF ADVANCED MATERIALS. (US/1070-9789). **1981**

JOURNAL OF ENGINEERING EDUCATION (WASHINGTON, D.C.). (US/1069-4730). **1982**

JOURNAL OF ENVIRONMENTAL ENGINEERING. (US/1056-2702). **1982**

JOURNAL OF FINANCIAL ENGINEERING, THE. (US/1062-8924). **1982**

JOURNAL OF FRICTION AND WEAR. (US/1068-3666). **1982**

JPRS REPORT. SCIENCE & TECHNOLOGY. CENTRAL EURASIA. ENGINEERING & EQUIPMENT [MICROFORM] / FOREIGN BROADCAST INFORMATION SERVICE. (US). **1984**

KANCH. NEW DELHI. (II). **1984**

KEY SOLUTIONS. (US/1064-2145). **1984**

KONGHAK YON'GU POGO. (KO). **1985**

LYCEUM TECHNICAL JOURNAL. (US/1048-8693). **1985**

MARINE GEORESOURCES & GEOTECHNOLOGY. (US/1064-119X). **1986**

POINT LINE POLY. HOST. (US/1062-5674). **1990**

POLYMER REACTION ENGINEERING. (US/1054-3414). **1990**

RESOURCE (SAINT JOSEPH, MICH.). (US/1076-3333). **1994**

STUDIES ON MANUFACTURING ENGINEERING AND PRODUCTION MANAGEMENT. (UK/1062-3949). **1997**

SURFACE ENGINEERING AND APPLIED ELECTROCHEMISTRY. (US/1068-3755). **1997**

SWE (NEW YORK, N.Y.). (US/1070-6232). **1997**

WORLDWIDE PROJECTS. (US/0192-5512). **2001**

ABSTRACTING, BIBLIOGRAPHIES AND STATISTICS

ELECTRONICS AND COMMUNICATIONS ABSTRACTS. (US/1069-5303). **2003**

FINANCIAL STATISTICS OF MAJOR U.S. INVESTOR-OWNED ELECTRIC UTILITIES. (US). **2004**

MECHANICAL ENGINEERING ABSTRACTS. (US/1063-7311). **2006**

CHEMICAL ENGINEERING

CHEMICAL ENGINEERING BUYERS GUIDE FOR ... . (US). **2009**

POLYMER GELS AND NETWORKS. (UK/0966-7822). **2015**

CIVIL ENGINEERING

ARCHIVES OF CIVIL ENGINEERING / POLISH ACADEMY OF SCIENCES, INSTITUTE OF FUNDAMENTAL TECHNOLOGICAL RESEARCH [AND] COMMITTEE FOR CIVIL ENGINEERING. (PL). **2018**

CIVIL ENGINEERING : MAGAZINE OF THE SOUTH AFRICAN INSTITUTION OF CIVIL ENGINEERS / SIVIELE INGENIEURSWESE. (SA/1021-2000). **2021**

CIVIL ENGINEERING YEOVILLE. (SA/1021-2000). **2021**

EMERGING TECHNOLOGY (AMERICAN SOCIETY OF CIVIL ENGINEERS). (US/1075-0495). **2023**

GROUND IMPROVEMENT. (UK). **2024**

INTERNATIONAL JOURNAL OF THE STRUCTURAL DESIGN OF TALL BUILDINGS, THE. (UK/1062-8002). **2025**

JOURNAL OF ARCHITECTURAL ENGINEERING. (US/1076-0431). **2025**

JOURNAL OF INFRASTRUCTURE SYSTEMS. (US/1076-0342). **2025**

NOISE/NEWS INTERNATIONAL. (US/1021-643X). **2028**

PROCEEDINGS OF THE INSTITUTION OF CIVIL ENGINEERS. CIVIL ENGINEERING. (UK/0965-089X). **2029**

PROCEEDINGS OF THE INSTITUTION OF CIVIL ENGINEERS. MUNICIPAL ENGINEER. (UK/0965-0903). **2029**

PROCEEDINGS OF THE INSTITUTION OF CIVIL ENGINEERS. STRUCTURES AND BUILDINGS. (UK/0965-0911). **2029**

PROCEEDINGS OF THE INSTITUTION OF CIVIL ENGINEERS, TRANSPORT. (UK/0965-092X). **2029**

STADSWERK. (NE/0927-7641). **2031**

ELECTRICITY, ELECTRICAL ENGINEERING, ELECTRONICS

ADVANCED PACKAGING. (US/1065-0555). **2034**

AEI. AUTOMAZIONE ENEGIA INFORMAZIONE. (IT/1122-2824). **2034**

Engineering — Electricity, Electrical Engineering, Electronics

ANNUAL BULLETIN OF ELECTRIC ENERGY STATISTICS FOR EUROPE AND NORTH AMERICA / BULLETIN ANNUEL DE STATISTIQUES DE L'ENERGIE ELECTRIQUE POUR L'EUROPE ET L'AMERIQUE DU NORD / EZHEGODNYI BIULLETEN' STATISTIKI ELEKTROENERGII DLIA EVROPY I SEVERNOI AMERIKI. (US). **2035**

ANNUAL REPORT. MIKROELEKTRONIK CENTRET. (DK). **2035**

APPLIED SUPERCONDUCTIVITY. (UK/0964-1807). **2035**

BIOELECTROCHEMISTRY AND BIOENERGETICS. (SZ/0302-4598). **2036**

CFE BATIMENT. (FR). **2038**

CFE INDUSTRIE. (FR/1146-1497). **2038**

CIRCUIT NEWS MAGAZINE. (US/1058-9333). **2038**

COGENERATION AND COMPETITIVE POWER JOURNAL. (US/1066-8683). **2039**

CONSUMER ELECTRONICS EDGE, THE. (US/1065-7223). **2039**

DISCRETE SEMICONDUCTORS. SUGGESTED REPLACEMENTS. (US/1058-8566). **2042**

EDN ASIA. (US). **2042**

EL&P U.S. ELECTRIC UTILITY INDUSTRY SOFTWARE DIRECTORY. (US/1069-0557). **2043**

ELECTRICITY AUSTRALIA / ESAA. (AT). **2045**

ELECTROMAGNETOEFFECT (COMMACK, N.Y.). (US/1069-4595). **2046**

ELECTRONIC BUSINESS BUYER. (US/1073-1059). **2046**

ELECTRONIC MARKETPLACE REPORT. (US/1071-247X). **2047**

ELECTRONIC SIMULATION. (US/1063-1100). **2048**

ELECTRONICS NOW. (US/1067-9294). **2050**

HEAT TRANSFER RESEARCH. (US/1064-2285). **2056**

IEE PROCEEDINGS. CIRCUITS, DEVICES AND SYSTEMS. (UK/1350-2409). **2057**

IEE PROCEEDINGS. CONTROL THEORY AND APPLICATIONS. (UK/1350-2379). **2057**

IEE PROCEEDINGS. ELECTRIC POWER APPLICATIONS. (UK/1350-2352). **2058**

IEE PROCEEDINGS. GENERATION, TRANSMISSION, AND DISTRIBUTION. (UK/1350-2360). **2058**

IEE PROCEEDINGS. MICROWAVES, ANTENNAS AND PROPAGATION. (UK/1350-2417). **2058**

IEE PROCEEDINGS. OPTOELECTRONICS. (UK/1350-2433). **2058**

IEE PROCEEDINGS. SCIENCE, MEASUREMENT AND TECHNOLOGY. (UK/1350-2344). **2058**

IEEE PARALLEL AND DISTRIBUTED TECHNOLOGY. (US). **2060**

IEEE TRANSACTIONS ON CIRCUITS & SYSTEMS. PART 1, FUNDAMENTAL THEORY AND APPLICATIONS. (US/1057-7122). **2061**

IEEE TRANSACTIONS ON CIRCUITS AND SYSTEMS. PART 2, ANALOG AND DIGITAL SIGNAL PROCESSING. (US/1057-7130). **2061**

IEEE TRANSACTIONS ON DIELECTRICS AND ELECTRICAL INSULATION. (US/1070-9878). **2061**

IEEE TRANSACTIONS ON IMAGE PROCESSING. (US/1057-7149). **2062**

IEICE TRANSACTIONS ON ELECTRONICS. (JA/0916-8524). **2064**

INTEGRATED FERROELECTRICS. (US/1058-4587). **2066**

INTERNATIONAL PRIVATE POWER QUARTERLY. (US/1070-2989). **2067**

ISSUE UPDATE / BONNEVILLE POWER ADMINISTRATION. (US). **2067**

JAPANESE TECHNOLOGY REVIEWS. SECTION A, ELECTRONICS. (US/1058-7292). **2068**

JOURNAL OF COMMUNICATIONS TECHNOLOGY & ELECTRONICS. (US/1064-2269). **2068**

JOURNAL OF ELECTRONIC IMAGING. (US/1017-9909). **2068**

JOURNAL OF MICROELECTROMECHANICAL SYSTEMS. (US/1057-7157). **2069**

LED LAMPS & DISPLAYS. (US/1063-4002). **2070**

LIGHT & ENGINEERING. (US/1068-9761). **2070**

LIGHTING HANDBOOK. REFERENCE & APPLICATION. (US). **2071**

MICROLITHOGRAPHY WORLD. (US/1074-407X). **2072**

POWER ENGINEERING INTERNATIONAL. (US/1069-4994). **2075**

PROCEEDINGS OF THE ELECTRICAL ELECTRONICS INSULATION CONFERENCE & ELECTRICAL MANUFACTURING & COIL WINDING. (US/1071-6270). **2076**

PROGRESS IN PHOTOVOLTAICS. (UK/1062-7995). **2077**

QUANTUM ELECTRONICS (NEW YORK, N.Y. 1993). (US/1063-7818). **2078**

RECENT ADVANCES IN ACTIVE CONTROL OF SOUND AND VIBRATION. (US). **2078**

RUSSIAN ELECTRICAL ENGINEERING. (US/1068-3712). **2080**

SMART MATERIALS AND STRUCTURES. (UK). **2081**

SOLID STATE TECHNOLOGY ... BUYING GUIDE. (US). **2082**

SUPERCONDUCTIVITY REVIEW. (US/1054-2698). **2082**

TED : THE ELECTRICAL DISTRIBUTORS MAGAZINE. (US/1067-3806). **2084**

VLSI DESIGN. (US/1063-9667). **2085**

WHO'S WHO ELECTRONICS BUYERS GUIDE (MIDWESTERN ED.). (US/1066-7601). **2086**

WHO'S WHO ELECTRONICS BUYERS GUIDE (NORTHEASTERN ED.). (US/1066-761X). **2086**

WHO'S WHO ELECTRONICS BUYERS GUIDE (SOUTHEASTERN ED.). (US/1066-7628). **2086**

WHO'S WHO ELECTRONICS BUYERS GUIDE (SOUTHWESTERN ED.). (US/1066-7644). **2086**

HYDRAULIC ENGINEERING

CORPS REPORT, THE. (US/1069-2657). **2088**

JOURNAL OF ENERGETICS AND FLUIDS ENGINEERING. (US/1051-3248). **2091**

JOURNAL OF FLOW VISUALIZATION AND IMAGE PROCESSING. (US/1065-3090). **2091**

PROCEEDINGS OF THE INSTITUTION OF CIVIL ENGINEERS. WATER, MARITIME AND ENERGY. (UK/0965-0946). **2094**

INDUSTRIAL ENGINEERING AND DESIGN

I.D. (US/0894-5373). **2098**

INDUSTRIAL EQUIPMENT NEWS (NEW YORK). (US/0019-8285). **2098**

INTERNATIONAL JOURNAL OF INDUSTRIAL ENGINEERING. (US/1072-4761). **2099**

MATERIALS ENGINEERING AND MECHANICS

COMPUTATIONAL MATERIALS SCIENCE. (NE/0927-0256). **2101**

INSIGHT (NORTHAMPTON). (UK/1354-2575). **2102**

JOURNAL OF MATERIALS SYNTHESIS AND PROCESSING. (US/1064-7562). **2104**

JSME INTERNATIONAL JOURNAL. SERIES A, MECHANICS AND MATERIAL ENGINEERING. (JA). **2104**

MATERIALS SCIENCE (NEW YORK, N.Y.). (US/1068-820X). **2106**

MATERIALS TECHNOLOGY (NEW YORK, N.Y.). (US/1066-7857). **2106**

MATERIALS WORLD : THE JOURNAL OF THE INSTITUTE OF MATERIALS. (UK/0967-8638). **2106**

NANOSTRUCTURED MATERIALS. (US/0965-9773). **2107**

OBERFLACHEN WERKSTOFFE / SURFACES MATERIAUX. (SZ). **2107**

VESCI AKADEMII NAVUK BELARUSI. SERYA FIZIKA-ENERGETYCNYH NAVUK. (BW). **2108**

MECHANICAL ENGINEERING AND MACHINERY

ALLIANZ REPORT. (GW/0943-4569). **2109**

APPLIED ENERGY. (US/1068-7181). **2109**

DIESEL & GAS TURBINE WORLDWIDE CATALOG (1992). (US/1070-4884). **2112**

FLUID MECHANICS RESEARCH. (US/1064-2277). **2114**

HEAT TRANSFER RECENT CONTENTS. (US/1063-1313). **2115**

INTERNATIONAL APPLIED MECHANICS. (US/1063-7095). **2116**

INTERNATIONAL JOURNAL OF COMPUTATIONAL FLUID DYNAMICS. (UK/1061-8562). **2116**

IZVESTIIA AKADEMII NAUK. MEKHANIKA ZHIDKOSTI I GAZA / ROSSIISKAIA AKADEMIIA NAUK. (RU). **2117**

JOURNAL OF DYNAMIC AND CONTROL SYSTEMS. (US). **2118**

JOURNAL OF MATERIALS ENGINEERING AND PERFORMANCE. (US/1059-9495). **2118**

MECANIQUE INDUSTRIELLE ET MATERIAUX : REVUE DU GAMI. (FR). **2121**

MODAL ANALYSIS. (US/1066-0763). **2122**

OEM INDUSTRY. (US/1072-2580). **3485**

PROCEEDINGS OF THE HUMAN FACTORS AND ERGONOMICS SOCIETY ... ANNUAL MEETING. (US/1071-1813). **2125**

PROCEEDINGS OF THE INSTITUTION OF MECHANICAL ENGINEERS. PART J, JOURNAL OF ENGINEERING TRIBOLOGY. (UK/1350-6501). **2126**

PUMPS AND SYSTEMS. (US/1065-108X). **2127**

RANDOM & COMPUTATIONAL DYNAMICS. (US/1061-835X). **2127**

RUSSIAN ENGINEERING RESEARCH. (US/1068-798X). **2128**

RUSSIAN JOURNAL OF COMPUTATIONAL MECHANICS. (RU/1061-7566). **2128**

RUSSIAN JOURNAL OF HEAVY MACHINERY. (US/1068-3720). **2128**

RUSSIAN JOURNAL OF NONDESTRUCTIVE TESTING. (US/1061-8309). **2128**

ST. PETERSBURG UNIVERSITY MECHANICS BULLETIN. (US/1068-8005). **2129**

VALVE BUYERS HANDBOOK. (US/0737-5727). **2131**

WHO MAKES MACHINERY IN GERMANY. (GW). **2132**

MINES AND MINING ENGINEERING

CANADIAN DIRECTORY OF EFFICIENCY AND ALTERNATIVE ENERGY TECHNOLOGIES. (CN). **2136**

COLORADO SCHOOL OF MINES QUARTERLY REVIEW OF ENGINEERING, SCIENCE, EDUCATION AND RESEARCH. (US/1068-2937). **2137**

EXPLORATION AND MINING GEOLOGY : JOURNAL OF THE GEOLOGICAL SOCIETY OF CIM. (UK/0964-1823). **2138**

GEOTECHNICAL AND GEOLOGICAL ENGINEERING. (UK/0960-3182). **2139**

INDIAN MINERAL RESOURCE HORIZONS / BIA DIVISION OF ENERGY AND MINERAL RESOURCES. (US). **2140**

INTERNATIONAL CALIFORNIA MINING JOURNAL. (US). **2140**

JOURNAL OF MINING RESEARCH. (II). **2141**

JOURNAL OF MINING SCIENCE. (US/1062-7391). **2142**

MINING QUARTERLY. (AT/1320-3770). **2146**

SOUTHEASTERN STATES MINING DIRECTORY. (US/1056-8638). **2151**

WORLD COAL DORKING. (UK/0968-3224). **2153**

NUCLEAR ENGINEERING

ATOMIC ENERGY (NEW YORK, N.Y.). (US/1063-4258). **2154**

NUEXCO REVIEW. (US/1074-8695). **2157**

ENVIRONMENTAL ISSUES

AFROTECH ENVIRONMENTALIST. (US/1066-3053). **2159**

APPLIED CATALYSIS. B : ENVIRONMENTAL. (NE/0926-3373). **2161**

$AVE OUR PLANET. (US/1065-0385). **2161**

BNA'S STATE ENVIRONMENT & SAFETY REGULATORY MONITORING REPORT. (US/1065-8076). **2162**

CLEAN AIR AND ENVIRONMENTAL PROTECTION. (UK). **2163**

CONTROL ENGINEERING PRACTICE. (UK/0967-0661). **2163**

CRITICAL REVIEWS IN ENVIRONMENTAL SCIENCE AND TECHNOLOGY. (US/1064-3389). **2163**

DIRECTORY OF ENVIRONMENTAL GROUPS IN THE NEWLY INDEPENDENT STATES AND BALTIC NATIONS, THE. (US/1053-7880). **2163**

DOWN TO EARTH : SCIENCE AND ENVIRONMENT FORTNIGHTLY. (II). **2164**

ELECTRONIC GREEN JOURNAL. (US/1076-7975). **2165**

ENVIRONMENT & DEVELOPMENT / APA, AMERICAN PLANNING ASSOCIATION. (US/1066-954X). **2165**

ENVIRONMENT CONNECTIONS. (US/1064-7422). **2165**

ENVIRONMENTAL CAREER DIRECTORY. (US/1072-1835). **2167**

ENVIRONMENTAL CHANGE. (US/1065-8548). **2167**

ENVIRONMENTAL DISCOVERY. (US/1062-4961). **2167**

ENVIRONMENTAL EDUCATION RESEARCH. (UK/1350-4622). **2167**

ENVIRONMENTAL ENCYCLOPEDIA. (US/1072-5083). **2167**

ENVIRONMENTAL ENGINEERING (NEW YORK, N.Y.). (US/1056-7054). **2167**

ENVIRONMENTAL EXECUTIVE DIRECTORY. (US/1067-7208). **2167**

ENVIRONMENTAL ISSUES REPORT. (US/1061-3935). **2168**

ENVIRONMENTAL POLITICS. (UK/0964-4016). **2168**

ENVIRONMENTAL REMEDIATION TECHNOLOGY. (US/1071-538X). **2169**

ENVIRONMENTAL SATELLITE DATA RESEARCH. (US/1065-6588). **2169**

ENVIRONMENTAL SCIENCE REVIEW. (US/1071-8923). **2170**

ENVIRONMENTAL TESTING & ANALYSIS. (US/1068-7432). **2170**

ENVIRONMENTAL TRADE EVENT PREVIEW. (US/1065-3570). **2170**

ENVIRONMENTAL UPDATE (NEW YORK, N.Y.). (US/1064-816X). **2170**

ENVIRONMENTAL VALUES. (UK/0963-2719). **2170**

ENVIRONMENTAL VIEWPOINTS. (US/1063-116X). **2170**

ENVIROMETRICS (LONDON, ONT.). (UK/1180-4009). **2170**

ENVIRONNEMENT (QUEBEC). (CN/1192-4578). **2171**

EPA WATCH. (US/1065-920X). **2171**

EUROPEAN ENVIRONMENTAL BUSINESS NEWS, THE. (US/1060-3573). **2171**

FRESENIUS ENVIRONMENTAL BULLETIN. (SZ/1018-4619). **2172**

GALE ENVIRONMENTAL SOURCEBOOK. (US/1059-0919). **2172**

GREEN BOOK. NEW YORK/NEW JERSEY, THE. (US/1062-9211). **2172**

GREEN BOOK REPORT, THE. (US/1062-4589). **2172**

GREEN BOOK (WOBURN, MASS.), THE. (US/1055-6893). **2172**

GREEN BUSINESS LETTER, THE. (US/1056-490X). **2172**

GREEN INDEX. (US/1055-9396). **2173**

ILLAHEE (SEATTLE, WASH.). (US/1073-0478). **2173**

IMAGES OF A CHANGING PLANET COMPUTER FILE. (US). **2173**

INDOOR ENVIRONMENT : THE JOURNAL OF INDOOR AIR INTERNATIONAL. (SZ/1016-4901). **2174**

INDUSTRIAL & ENVIRONMENTAL CRISIS QUARTERLY. (US). **2174**

INFORMATION PLEASE ENVIRONMENTAL ALMANAC, THE. (US/1057-8293). **2174**

INTERNATIONAL JOURNAL OF OCCUPATIONAL AND ENVIRONMENT HEALTH. (US/1077-3525). **2175**

JOURNAL OF ENVIRONMENTAL STATISTICS. (US/1065-7568). **2176**

JOURNAL OF MARINE ENVIRONMENTAL ENGINEERING. (SZ/1061-026X). **2176**

LOCAL ENVIRONMENT JOURNAL, THE. (UK). **2177**

MILIEUSTRATEGIE ALPHEN AAN DEN RIJN. 1994. (NE/0929-791X). **2177**

NATIONAL ECONOMIC, SOCIAL, & ENVIRONMENTAL DATA BANK [COMPUTER FILE] : NESE DB / U.S. DEPT. OF COMMERCE. (US). **2178**

PRACTICAL ENVIRONMENTAL REGULATION. (US/1056-1102). **2180**

PROCEEDINGS OF THE THEMATIC CONFERENCE ON REMOTE SENSING FOR MARINE AND COASTAL ENVIRONMENTS. (US/1066-3711). **2180**

SOCIETY AND NATURE. (US/1062-9599). **2182**

ABSTRACTING, BIBLIOGRAPHIES AND STATISTICS

ENVIRONMENT ABSTRACTS [COMPUTER FILE]. (US). **2184**

LITERATURE ABSTRACTS. HEALTH & ENVIRONMENT. (US/1065-0490). **2184**

CONSERVATION AND NATURAL RESOURCES

A TO Z. (US/1059-5112). **2185**

Environmental Issues —Conservation and Natural Resources

AMERICAN SPIRIT / TAKE PRIDE IN AMERICA. (US). **2186**

ARKANSAS WILDLIFE. (US/1063-0953). **2187**

ECOS (LEXINGTON, KY.). (US/1071-8478). **2192**

ESTIMATES. PART III, NATURAL RESOURCES CANADA. (CN). **2193**

FISH AND WILDLIFE INFORMATION EXCHANGE NEWSLETTER. (US/1071-3239). **2193**

ILLINOIS STEWARD, THE. (US/1058-9309). **2195**

JOURNAL OF WILDLIFE REHABILITATION. (US/1071-2232). **2196**

LIAISON / CONSEIL REGIONAL DE L'ENVIRONNEMENT CHAUDIERE-APPALACHES. (CN/1188-8539). **2197**

NATURALIST (DANVILLE, VT.), THE. (US/1060-9938). **2199**

NONRENEWABLE RESOURCES. (US/0961-1444). **2201**

PACIFIC CONSERVATION BIOLOGY. (AT/1038-2097). **2201**

QUAD REPORT, THE. (US/1072-3129). **2202**

SHIGEN TO TANKYO. (JA/0916-9997). **2205**

TROPICAL BIODIVERSITY. (US/0854-1566). **2207**

WILDLIFE REVIEW & FISHERIES REVIEW. (US/1070-499X). **2209**

WILDLIFE WORLDWIDE. (US/1070-5007). **2210**

ECOLOGY

CATALOG OF TRAINING / FISH AND WILDLIFE SERVICE, U.S. DEPARTMENT OF THE INTERIOR. (US). **2212**

EARTH FORUM. (US/1062-9076). **2213**

ECOGRAPHY. (DK/0906-7590). **2213**

ECOTOXICOLOGY LONDON. (UK/0963-9292). **2215**

ENVIRONMENTAL AND ECOLOGICAL STATISTICS. (UK/1352-8505). **2215**

ENVIRONMENTAL REVIEWS. (CN/1181-8700). **2215**

MOLECULAR ECOLOGY. (UK/0962-1083). **2218**

RESTORATIVE ECOLOGY. (US/1061-2971). **2220**

RUSSIAN JOURNAL OF ECOLOGY. (US/1067-4136). **2220**

POLLUTION AND WASTE MANAGEMENT

AIR & WASTE : JOURNAL OF THE AIR & WASTE MANAGEMENT ASSOCIATION. (US). **2223**

C & D DEBRIS RECYCLING. (US). **2225**

COMPOST SCIENCE & UTILIZATION. (US/1065-657X). **2226**

DRAFT INTENDED USE PLAN, PROJECT PRIORITY SYSTEM, PROJECT PRIORITY LIST, FEDERAL FISCAL YEAR: NEW YORK STATE REVOLVING FUND FOR WATER POLLUTION CONTROL. (US). **2227**

ENVIRONMENT BUSINESS MAGAZINE. (UK/1352-8882). **2228**

ENVIRONMENTAL SOLUTIONS. (US/1077-2537). **2229**

HAZARDOUS WASTE UPDATE SERVICE, THE. (US/1074-1291). **2231**

JOURNAL OF ECOTOXICOLOGY & ENVIRONMENTAL MONITORING : INTERNATIONAL JOURNAL FOR SCIENTIFIC RESEARCH ON TOXICOLOGY AND POLLUTIONS. (II). **2233**

JOURNAL OF SOLID WASTE. (US/1056-2575). **2234**

JOURNAL OF WATER CHEMISTRY AND TECHNOLOGY. (US/1063-455X). **2234**

MATERIALIEN / LANDESUMWELTAMT. (GW). **2177**

MERKBLATTER / LANDESUMWELTAMT. (GW). **2236**

PROMOTION DE LA SANTE AU CANADA. (CN/1195-6755). **2240**

RADIOACTIVE WASTE MANAGEMENT AND ENVIRONMENTAL RESTORATION. (UK/1065-609X). **2240**

RADWASTE MAGAZINE. (US/1070-9541). **2241**

RECYCLING SOURCEBOOK. (US/1064-4938). **2241**

RECYCLING TODAY. (US). **2241**

REPERTOIRE QUEBECOIS DES RECUPERATEURS ET DES RECYCLEURS, LE. (CN/1193-2228). **2241**

SOUTH CAROLINA ENVIRONMENTAL COMPLIANCE UPDATE. (US/1065-7975). **2243**

STABILIZATION AND SOLIDIFICATION OF HAZARDOUS, RADIOACTIVE, AND MIXED WASTES. (US/1059-423X). **2243**

STATE RECYCLING LAWS UPDATE (QUARTERLY ED.). (US/1070-3217). **2244**

TRANSPORTING HAZARDOUS MATERIALS. (US/1061-3595). **2245**

WASTE & ENVIRONMENT TODAY. BIBLIOGRAPHIC JOURNAL. (UK/0965-4496). **2246**

WASTE & ENVIRONMENT TODAY. NEWS JOURNAL. (UK/0965-4488). **2246**

WASTE MANAGEMENT NEWS (WACO, TEX.). (US/1062-7529). **2246**

WATER ENVIRONMENT LABORATORY SOLUTIONS. (US/1074-2972). **2247**

WORLD ENVIRONMENT REPORT. (US/0098-8235). **2248**

ETHICS

BIOETHICS FORUM. (US/1065-7274). **2249**

BUSINESS ETHICS: A EUROPEAN REVIEW. (UK/0962-8770). **2249**

BUSINESS ETHICS REVIEW. (US/1061-0081). **2249**

ETHICS & PSYCHOTHERAPY. (US/1064-8771). **2250**

ETHICS ROUNDTABLE. (US/1064-5438). **2250**

IN/FIRE ETHICS. (US/1062-9564). **2251**

INDEX TO ... ETHICS ADVISORY OPINIONS. (US). **2251**

JOURNAL OF INFORMATION ETHICS. (US/1061-9321). **2251**

LUND STUDIES IN ETHICS AND THEOLOGY. (SW/1102-769X). **2252**

PROFESSIONAL ETHICS (GAINESVILLE, FLA.). (US/1063-6579). **2252**

TIMELINES (EUGENE, OR). (US/1074-1593). **2253**

TRENDS IN HEALTH CARE, LAW & ETHICS. (US/1062-5364). **2253**

WORKPLACE ISSUES & ANSWERS. (US/1061-8643). **2253**

ETHNIC INTERESTS

21ST CENTURY AFRO REVIEW. (US/1074-9144). **2253**

ABYA YALA NEWS. (US/1071-3182). **2253**

ACCENT (MARLBORO, MASS.). (US/1064-6981). **2254**

AFRICAN-AMERICAN ALMANAC, THE. (US/1071-8710). **2254**

AFROCENTRIC SCHOLAR, THE. (US/1056-8689). **2254**

AMERICAN INDIAN STUDIES. (US/1058-563X). **2255**

ASIAN AMERICANS INFORMATION DIRECTORY. (US/1059-2458). **2255**

BANDELE'S ANNUAL VENDOR'S GUIDE TO AFRICAN-AMERICAN EVENTS. (US/1062-0486). **2256**

BLACK COLLEGES AND UNIVERSITIES LISTING. (US/1058-5680). **2256**

BLACK HISTORY MONTHLY (LITTLE ROCK, ARK.). (US/1054-8769). **2256**

BLACKFIRE. (US/1049-3271). **2257**

CARIBBEAN DIGEST. (US/1063-0775). **2258**

CARIBBEAN ETHNOLOGY. (VI/1057-2872). **2258**

CHUNG YANG MIN TSU TA HSUEH HSUEH PAO / ZHONGYANG MINZU DAXUE XUEBAO. (CC/1000-8667). **2258**

CONTEMPORARY BLACK BIOGRAPHY. (US/1058-1316). **2259**

DIRECTORY OF AFRICAN AND AFRICAN-AMERICAN STUDIES IN THE UNITED STATES. (US). **2259**

ETHNIC AMERICAN EXPERIENCE. (US/1069-1170). **2260**

ETHNIC NEWSWATCH [COMPUTER FILE]. (US). **2260**

FILIPINAS (SAN FRANCISCO, CALIF.). (US/1063-4630). **2261**

HILLEL GUIDE TO JEWISH LIFE ON CAMPUS, THE. (US). **2262**

IDENTITIES (YVERDON, SWITZERLAND). (SZ/1070-289X). **2263**

INTERNATIONAL GUIDE TO AFROCENTRIC EVENTS. (US/1059-9452). **2264**

INTERNATIONAL GUIDE TO AFROCENTRIC MERCHANDISE. (US/1059-7808). **2264**

INTERNATIONAL GUIDE TO AFROCENTRIC TALENT. (US/1059-9460). **2264**

JOURNAL OF AFRICAN AMERICAN MALE STUDIES. (US/1063-4460). **2265**

LATINO STUDIES JOURNAL / NORTHEASTERN UNIVERSITY. (US). **2267**

LATVIAN DIMENSIONS. (US/1062-9505). **2267**

MAN (CHICAGO, ILL.). (US/1062-2543). **2267**

MULTICULTURAL REVIEW. (US/1058-9236). **2268**

NATIVE AMERICANS INFORMATION DIRECTORY. (US/1063-9632). **2268**

NATIVE NORTH AMERICAN ALMANAC. (US/1070-8014). **2268**

NEWS INDIA-TIMES. (US/1071-0248). **2269**

OTTAWA JEWISH BULLETIN (1993). (CN/1196-1929). **2270**

PARDIS (WEST ORANGE, N.J.). (US/1062-8428). **2270**

POBEREZE (PHILADELPHIA, PA.). (US/1057-932X). **2271**

RESEARCH IN RELIGION AND FAMILY--BLACK PERSPECTIVES. (US/1055-1158). **2272**

SCRIBE (WASHINGTON, D.C.), THE. (US/1060-5606). **2273**

STUDIES IN SOUTHERN ITALIAN AND ITALIAN AMERICAN CULTURE. (US/1058-5621). **2273**

WAZO WEUSI. (US/1065-5883). **2275**

WHO'S WHO AMONG HISPANIC AMERICANS. (US/1052-7354). **2275**

ZAPAD TODAY. (CN). **2275**

FAMILY AND MARRIAGE

BRIDE'S & YOUR NEW HOME. (US/1059-7476). **2277**

FAMILY JOURNAL (ALEXANDRIA, VA.), THE. (US/1066-4807). **2279**

FAMILY LIFE (NEW YORK, N.Y.). (US/1072-0332). **2279**

FAMILY SYSTEMS. (US/1070-0609). **2280**

FOR THE BRIDE BY DEMETRIOS (UNITED KINGDOM ED.). (US/1064-7996). **2280**

INFO-PARENTS. (CN/1193-1833). **2281**

JOURNAL OF CHILD AND FAMILY STUDIES. (US/1062-1024). **2281**

JOURNAL OF FAMILY AND ECONOMIC ISSUES. (US/1058-0476). **2281**

MARRIAGE (SAINT PAUL, MINN.). (US/1063-1054). **2283**

NEW MOTHER (1992). (CN/1193-9397). **2284**

PARENTLIFE (NASHVILLE, TENN.). (US/1074-326X). **2284**

PLANNED PARENTHOOD CHALLENGES / INTERNATIONAL PLANNED PARENTHOOD FEDERATION. (UK). **2285**

POSITIVELY FOR KIDS. (US/1065-1969). **2285**

SINGLE-PARENT FAMILY. (US/1077-4092). **2286**

FIRE PREVENTION

FIRE RESEARCH NEWS. (CN/1188-4053). **2289**

FIRELINE. (US/1065-0210). **2290**

IFCI FIRE CODE JOURNAL. (US/1061-5334). **2291**

INTERNATIONAL BIBLIOGRAPHY OF WILDLAND FIRE. (US/1051-4201). **2291**

NATIONAL DIRECTORY OF FIRE CHIEFS, RESCUE & EMERGENCY DEPARTMENTS. (US/1066-5609). **2291**

NEW JERSEY FIRE FOCUS : THE OFFICIAL NEWSLETTER OF THE NJ BUREAU OF FIRE SAFETY. (US). **2292**

NFPA JOURNAL. BUYERS' GUIDE : FIRE PROTECTION AND FIRE SERVICE REFERENCE DIRECTORY. (US). **2292**

FISH AND FISHERIES

AQUACULTURE INTERNATIONAL. (UK/0967-6120). **2295**

AQUACULTURE NEWS. (US). **2296**

AQUATIC SURVIVAL. (CN/1188-553X). **2296**

ECOLOGY OF FRESHWATER FISH. (DK/0906-6691). **2300**

FISH & FISHERIES WORLDWIDE. (US/1069-9309). **2301**

FISHERIES MANAGEMENT AND ECOLOGY. (UK/0969-997X). **2302**

FISHING VESSELS OF THE UNITED STATES. (US/1065-5069). **2303**

FRANKLIN PIERCE TIMES. (US/1060-5312). **2304**

INTERNATIONAL DIRECTORY OF AQUARIST ORGANIZATIONS. (CN). **2306**

JOURNAL OF AQUATIC FOOD PRODUCTS TECHNOLOGY. (US/1049-8850). **2306**

REVIEWS IN FISHERIES SCIENCE. (US/1064-1262). **2312**

SALMON MAGAZINE. (US/1063-9624). **2312**

SHRIMP NEWS INTERNATIONAL. (US/1076-7568). **2313**

VIRGINIA ACQUACULTURE MARKET NEWS REPORT. (US/1064-4768). **2315**

WHO'S WHO IN THE FISH INDUSTRY, CENTRAL & SOUTH AMERICA. (US/1064-931X). **2316**

FOLKLORE

AMERICAN FOLKLORE SOCIETY NEWS. (US). **2318**

CURRENT FOLKLORE. (UK). **2319**

ETNOFOLK : REVISTA DEL COMITE DEPARTAMENTAL DE ETNOGRAFIA Y FOLKLORE. (BO). **2319**

GOOD COUNTRY PEOPLE. (US/1047-7225). **2320**

JOURNAL OF COMMUNICATION AND TRANSFORMATIONAL MYTH. (US/1064-752X). **2321**

STUDIA FENNICA. FOLKLORISTICA. (FI/1235-1946). **2324**

FOOD AND FOOD INDUSTRY

AUTOMATIC MERCHANDISER. (US/1061-1797). **2328**

BIERE MAG. (CN/1188-8555). **2329**

BREAD MACHINE NEWSLETTER, THE. (US/1061-2718). **2329**

CAMERON'S FOODSERVICE MARKETING REPORTER. (US). **2330**

CHEF. (US). **2331**

COOKBOOK (STEUBEN, ME.). (US/1061-0537). **2332**

FDA NEWS. (US/1069-5109). **2335**

FIRST PLACE [COMPUTER FILE]. (US). **2335**

FOOD FIRST NEWS & VIEWS. (US). **2337**

FOOD INGREDIENTS AND ANALYSIS INTERNATIONAL. (US/0968-574X). **2337**

FOOD IRRADIATION UPDATE. (US/1065-142X). **2338**

FOOD LABELING NEWS. (US/1064-6329). **2338**

FOOD PLANT STRATEGIES. (US/1072-298X). **2339**

FOOD RESEARCH INTERNATIONAL. (CN/0963-9969). **2339**

FOOD SAFETY & SECURITY. (UK/0964-4164). **2340**

FOOD SAFETY SERIES. (UK). **2340**

FOODSERVICE YEARBOOK INTERNATIONAL. (US/1062-7324). **2341**

GROCER FOOD & DRINK DIRECTORY, THE. (UK/0967-5892). **2342**

GROCERY EQUIPMENT PRODUCT NEWS. (US). **2342**

INTERNATIONAL FOOD SAFETY NEWS. (UK/0960-9784). **2345**

JOURNAL OF COLLEGE & UNIVERSITY FOODSERVICE. (US/1053-8739). **2345**

JOURNAL OF CULINARY PRACTICE. (US/1052-9241). **2346**

JOURNAL OF FOOD LIPIDS. (US/1065-7258). **2346**

JOURNAL OF FOOD PRODUCTS MARKETING. (US/1045-4446). **2346**

JOURNAL OF RAPID METHODS AND AUTOMATION IN MICROBIOLOGY. (US/1060-3999). **2347**

MEAT & LIVESTOCK REVIEW / PRODUCED BY THE AUSTRALIAN MEAT AND LIVESTOCK CORPORATION, MARKETING INTELLIGENCE UNIT. (AT). **2349**

... NATIONAL ORGANIC DIRECTORY, THE. (US/1073-0540). **2350**

NY FOOD LETTER, THE. (US/1065-7967). **2351**

PALATE AND SPIRIT. (US/1061-7701). **2352**

PARTY TIMES. (US/1064-8224). **2352**

Food and Food Industry

POLISH JOURNAL OF FOOD AND NUTRITION SCIENCES / POLISH ACADEMY OF SCIENCES. (PL/1230-0322). **2353**

POTATO BUSINESS WORLD. (UK/0968-7661). **2353**

PREVENTION'S QUICK AND HEALTHY LOW-FAT COOKING. (US/1064-7503). **2353**

RECIPE DIGEST. (US). **2355**

REVISTA ESPANOLA DE CIENCIA Y TECNOLOGIA DE ALIMENTOS / EDITADA POR EL CONSEJO SUPERIOR DE INVESTIGACIONES CIENTIFICAS. (SP/1131-799X). **2356**

SCHOOL FOODSERVICE & NUTRITION. (US/1075-3885). **2356**

SPECIAL EVENTS NEWS. (US/1066-1417). **2358**

SWEETENER MARKET DATA / UNITED STATES DEPARTMENT OF AGRICULTURE, AGRICULTURAL STABILIZATION AND CONSERVATION SERVICE. (US). **2359**

TAUNTON'S FINE COOKING. (US/1072-5121). **2359**

VEGETARIAN GOURMET. (US/1065-6340). **2360**

VEGGIE LIFE. (US/1065-2728). **2360**

VIRGINIA FRUIT AND VEGETABLE MARKET INFORMATION. (US/1064-4083). **2360**

WORLD FOOD CHEMICAL NEWS. (US/1073-2357). **2361**

ABSTRACTING, BIBLIOGRAPHIES AND STATISTICS

FOODS INTELLIGENCE ON COMPACT DISC. (US/1063-4169). **2362**

BEVERAGE INDUSTRY

BEVERAGE AISLE. (US/1060-9180). **2364**

CAFETAL: REVISTA BIMESTRAL DE ANACAFE. (GT). **2365**

GUIDE EXPRESS DES VINS. (CN/1191-1522). **2367**

IMPACT WORLD DIRECTORY : LEADING SPIRITS, WINE & BEER COMPANIES : WHO'S WHO OF INDUSTRY EXECUTIVES. (US). **2367**

JOBSON'S LICENSED BEVERAGE MARKETING & MERCHANDISING FACT BOOK. (US). **2368**

LAND- UND FORSTWIRTSCHAFT, FISCHEREI. REIHE 3.2.3, WEINBESTAENDE / STATISTISCHES BUNDESAMT. (GW). **2368**

MARK SPIVAK'S FLORIDA WINE BULLETIN. (US/1062-1032). **2369**

MARYLAND BEVERAGE JOURNAL. (US/1058-935X). **2369**

ULTIMATE GUIDE TO BUYING WINE / THE WINE SPECTATOR. (US). **2371**

WASHINGTON BEVERAGE JOURNAL. (US/1058-9341). **2372**

FORESTRY

BULLETIN OF TALL TIMBERS RESEARCH, INC. (US). **2376**

DIFFERENT DRUMMER MAGAZINE. (US/1075-1653). **2378**

FOREST GENETICS. (XO/1335-048X). **2380**

FOREST PEOPLE (WILLOWDALE). (CN/1195-0560). **2380**

FORESTRY, OIL & GAS REVIEW. (CN/1196-278X). **2382**

JOURNAL OF SUSTAINABLE FORESTRY. (US/1054-9811). **2386**

NETWORK PAPER / ODI, RURAL DEVELOPMENT FORESTRY NETWORK. (UK/0968-2627). **2389**

PAPER AND FOREST PRODUCTS / SALOMON BROTHERS. (US). **2390**

RESEARCH CONTRIBUTION. (US). **2392**

RUSSIAN FOREST SCIENCES. (US/1068-669X). **2394**

LUMBER AND WOOD

DESTINATION OF SHIPMENTS OF WESTERN U.S. SOFTWOOD LUMBER BY STATE, EXCEPT REDWOOD LUMBER. (US). **2400**

DIRECTORY OF THE WOOD PRODUCTS INDUSTRY (1992). (US/1064-749X). **2400**

IAWA JOURNAL / INTERNATIONAL ASSOCIATION OF WOOD ANATOMISTS. (NE/0928-1541). **2401**

LOGGER (VANCOUVER). (CN/1193-5855). **2402**

TIMBER TIMES. (US/1065-7010). **2405**

TTJ. (UK). **2405**

WOOD TECHNOLOGY. (US/1067-1064). **2406**

FUNERAL SERVICE

REDBOOK (CHAGRIN FALLS, OHIO), THE. (US/1073-273X). **2407**

GARDENING AND HORTICULTURE

CALIFORNIA LANDSCAPING. (US). **2411**

GARDEN NEWS / FAIRCHILD TROPICAL GARDEN. (US). **2415**

GARDEN TOURIST, THE. (US/1062-6093). **2415**

GARDENING IN ALBERTA. (CN/1188-2972). **2416**

GARTENBAU MAGAZIN. (GW/0942-0118). **2407**

GARTNERBORSE. (GW/0945-9111). **2416**

HISTORICAL GARDENER, THE. (US/1067-5973). **2418**

HORTICULTURIST/ INSTITUTE OF HORTICULTURE, THE. (UK/0964-8992). **2419**

HOUSEPLANT MAGAZINE. (US/1061-4079). **2420**

INTERIOR LANDSCAPE. (US/1063-1607). **2420**

JOURNAL OF HERBS, SPICES & MEDICINAL PLANTS. (US/1049-6475). **2421**

JOURNAL OF HOME & CONSUMER HORTICULTURE. (US/1054-4682). **2421**

JOURNAL OF THE INTERNATIONAL OAK SOCIETY. (US). **2421**

JOURNAL OF TURFGRASS MANAGEMENT. (US/1070-437X). **2422**

LANDSCAPE & NURSERY DIGEST. (US/1071-3697). **2422**

MEMBERSHIP DIRECTORY, PLANT SOURCE LIST. (CN/1191-3363). **2424**

NEIL SPERRY'S GARDENS. (US/1061-3994). **2425**

NEW PLANTSMAN, THE. (UK/1352-4186). **2425**

PENNSYLVANIA LAWN, AND GARDEN MAGAZINE. (US/1060-5398). **2427**

REVIEW OF AROMATIC AND MEDICINAL PLANTS. (UK). **2430**

SANSEVIERIA JOURNAL, THE. (US/1062-8908). **2430**

SPORTSTURF (1992). (US/1061-687X). **2431**

VIRGINIA GARDENER NEWSLETTER / DEPARTMENT OF HORTICULTURE, COOPERATIVE EXTENSION DIVISION, VIRGINIA TECH. (US). **2433**

WORLD HORTICULTURAL TRADE & U.S. EXPORT OPPORTUNITIES / UNITED STATES DEPARTMENT OF AGRICULTURE, FOREIGN AGRICULTURAL SERVICE. (US). **2433**

ABSTRACTING, BIBLIOGRAPHIES AND STATISTICS

GARDEN LITERATURE. (US/1061-3722). **2434**

FLORIST TRADE

FLORA-LINE, THE. (US/1062-855X). **2435**

GENEALOGY AND HERALDRY

ALLTON-ALTON-AULTON ASSOCIATION FAMILY NEWSLETTER. (US/1059-7719). **2436**

ANCESTOR UPDATE. (US/1064-0738). **2437**

ANCESTRY (SALT LAKE CITY, UTAH). (US/1075-475X). **2437**

AUTOGRAPH COLLECTOR. (US/1071-3425). **2438**

BARNES BULLETIN 2.0. (US/1062-6859). **2438**

CASS COUNTY CONNECTIONS. (US/1074-5742). **2442**

CEMETERIES OF THE U.S. (US/1071-8729). **2442**

DELAWARE COUNTY GENEALOGIST. (US/1062-6468). **2445**

DISTANT CROSSROADS. (US). **2445**

EILRICH FAMILY SNAPSHOTS. (US/1061-690X). **2446**

EVERTON'S GENEALOGICAL HELPER. (US/1016-6359). **2446**

GALENA GENEALOGY. (US/1062-7448). **2449**

GOOSE (WILLOW STREET, PA.), THE. (US/1062-7219). **2452**

HIGHWAYMAN (WILLOW STREET, PA.), THE. (US/1062-7200). **2453**

LA POINTE, A. (US/1063-889X). **2457**

LOUISIANA QUERIES. (US/1044-792X). **2458**

MARYLAND QUERIES. (US/1044-7938). **2459**

OLD OTOHATCHER DISTRICT REPORTER. (US/1061-6985). **2465**

OTECHESTVENNAIA ISTORIIA. (RU). **2466**

POLLOCK POTPOURRI. (US/1062-7855). **2468**

RODZINY : THE JOURNAL OF THE POLISH GENEALOGICAL SOCIETY OF AMERICA. (PL/0735-9349). **2470**

STANISLAUS RESEARCHER / GENEALOGICAL SOCIETY OF STANISLAUS COUNTY, CA, INC. (US). **2473**

SWARTZLANDER DESCENDANTS, THE. (US/1062-3930). **2474**

TENNESSEE & KENTUCKY QUERIES. (US/1068-0063). **2474**

TIDEWATER VIRGINIA FAMILIES. (US/1061-8678). **2475**

YVGS FAMILY FINDERS. (US/1069-9333). **2478**

ARCHIVES

ARCHIVAL ISSUES : JOURNAL OF THE MIDWEST ARCHIVES CONFERENCE. (US/1067-4993). **2479**

ARCHIVAL OUTLOOK / THE SOCIETY OF AMERICAN ARCHIVISTS. (US). **2479**

ARKHIV RUSSKOI ISTORII / TSENTRALYI GOSUDARSTVENNYI ARKHIV DREVNYKH AKTOV. (RU). **2480**

ORIENTATIONS STRATEGIQUES DES ARCHIVES NATIONALES DU CANADA. (CN/0844-7594). **2482**

STRATEGIC APPROACHES OF THE NATIONAL ARCHIVES OF CANADA. (CN/0844-7594). **2484**

GENERAL INTEREST

ABILITY MAGAZINE (IRVINE, CALIF.). (US/1062-5321). **2484**

ATLANTIC MONTHLY (1993), THE. (US/1072-7825). **2485**

BLACK & WHITE (BIRMINGHAM, ALA.). (US/1064-0134). **2485**

GREAT AMERICAN STORIES. (US/1046-008X). **2488**

VIBE (NEW YORK, N.Y.). (US/1070-4701). **2494**

GENERAL INTEREST-AFRICA

ETHIOPIAN (CHANTILLY, VA.), THE. (US/1060-6149). **2499**

GLOBAL AFRICA. (US/1048-6216). **2499**

MAGHREB REPORT. (US/1071-7579). **2499**

SPECTRUM (NEW YORK, N.Y. : 1992). (US/1062-0958). **2500**

GENERAL INTEREST-ASIA

CONTEMPORARY SOUTH ASIA. (UK/0958-4935). **2503**

JOURNAL OF SUNG-YUAN STUDIES. (US/1059-3152). **2505**

PAKISTAN (BOULDER, COLO.). (US/1061-6101). **2507**

RUSSIA & EURASIA DOCUMENTS ANNUAL. (US). **2508**

RUSSIA, EURASIAN STATES, AND EASTERN EUROPE. (US/1062-3574). **2508**

TAIWAN STUDIES. (US/1074-5599). **2509**

WHO'S WHO OF THE ASIAN PACIFIC RIM. (US/1059-5392). **2509**

GENERAL INTEREST-CENTRAL AMERICA

CARIBBEAN INTERNATIONAL (ALBANY, N.Y.). (US/1058-4315). **2511**

CHAC MOL NEWSLETTER. (US/1062-5283). **2511**

PENSAMIENTO CENTROAMERICANO. (CR). **2512**

GENERAL INTEREST-EUROPE

GEOGRAFFITY (BLACKSBURG, VA.). (US/1063-9837). **2517**

MONTHLY REPORT ON EUROPE. (BE/1021-4224). **2519**

OLDIE (LONDON). (UK/0965-2507). **2520**

ROYALTY DIGEST. (UK/0967-5744). **2522**

RUSSIAN LIFE. (US/1066-999X). **2522**

VOILA LUXEMBOURG. (LU/1017-2947). **2524**

WPROST. (PL). **2525**

ZARUBEZNAA PERIODICESKAA PECAT NA RUSSKOM AZYKE. (US/1066-4858). **2525**

GENERAL INTEREST-NORTH AMERICA

ALASKA ALMANAC : FACTS ABOUT ALASKA, THE. (US). **2527**

AMERICAN CITIZENS REVIEW. (US/1065-7622). **2527**

AMERICAN HARPOON, THE. (US/1064-7139). **2527**

BERKSHIRE REVIEW (PITTSFIELD, MASS.), THE. (US/1063-7559). **2528**

CHRISTIAN SCIENCE SENTINEL (RADIO ED.). (US/1065-1241). **2530**

CLEVELAND NOW. (US/1062-1431). **2531**

COUNTRYPLACE (BIRMINGHAM, ALA.). (US/1061-3560). **2531**

DESTINATION DISCOVERY. (US/1065-1535). **2532**

FACE (MALIBU, CALIF.). (US/1064-7953). **2533**

FIDELIO (WASHINGTON, D.C.). (US/1059-9126). **2533**

GOLD COAST. (US/1071-4251). **2534**

GRAY AREAS. (US/1062-5712). **2534**

HAPPENINGS IN SAN DIEGO COUNTY. (US/1064-3397). **2534**

HILLARY CLINTON QUARTERLY, THE. (US/1067-0777). **2534**

HOUR (MONTREAL). (CN/1192-6708). **2535**

INSTYLE (NEW YORK, N.Y.). (US/1076-0830). **2535**

JAB MAGAZINE. (US). **2536**

KAKO (NEW YORK, N.Y.), LES. (US/1061-351X). **2536**

MAGAZINE PROVIGO (ED. FRANCAISE). (CN/1192-6929). **2538**

MAGAZINE PROVIGO (ENGLISH EDITION). (CN/1192-6937). **2538**

MID-ATLANTIC ALMANACK, THE. (US/1063-1763). **2538**

NEW VIEWS (FORREST CITY, ARK.). (US/1062-9378). **2540**

OKLAHOMA LIVING. (US/1064-8968). **2542**

OP-ED (BELLINGHAM, WASH.). (US/1061-9046). **2542**

PREFERRED STOCK (DENVER, COLO.). (US/1065-7762). **2543**

PROFILES INTERNATIONAL. (US/1058-3068). **2543**

REMINISCE EXTRA. (US/1069-8957). **2544**

ROCKY MOUNTAIN MAGAZINE (STAMFORD, CONN.). (US/1075-7856). **2544**

SEATTLE. (US). **2545**

SITUATIONS DIGEST. (US/1059-1958). **2545**

SOAP OPERA BOOK, THE. (US/1065-402X). **2546**

SOAP OPERA ILLUSTRATED. (US/1063-9055). **2546**

SOUTH DAKOTA HALL OF FAME. (US/1061-4427). **2546**

SPECIAL REPORT - WHITTLE COMMUNICATIONS. (US/1059-5201). **2546**

TASTE OF HOME. (US/1071-5878). **2547**

VALLEY VOICE (COLD SPRING, N.Y.). (US/1063-7540). **2549**

WESTERN STYLES. (US/1075-8917). **2550**

GENERAL INTEREST-SOUTH AMERICA

PANORAMA. (AG). **2552**

GEOGRAPHY

CHINESE ENVIRONMENT & DEVELOPMENT. (US/1061-9534). **2558**

ECUMENE. (UK/0967-4608). **2560**

GEOGRAFIE. (NE/0926-3837). **2562**

GEOGRAPHIA ANTIQUA. (IT/1121-8940). **2562**

Geography

GEOGRAPHIC AND GLOBAL ISSUES QUARTERLY / UNITED STATES DEPARTMENT OF STATE, BUREAU OF INTELLIGENCE AND RESEARCH. (US/0083-016X). **2562**

GEOGRAPHICAL SYSTEMS. (US/1069-2665). **2563**

INTERNATIONAL GIS SOURCEBOOK. (US/1057-3348). **2566**

IZVESTIIA AKADEMII NAUK. SERIIA GEOGRAFICHESKAIA / ROSSIISKAIA AKADEMIIA NAUK. (RU). **2566**

JOURNAL OF TRANSPORT GEOGRAPHY. (UK/0966-6923). **2567**

MANHATTAN USER'S GUIDE. (US/1062-0141). **2568**

MONCTON CITY DIRECTORY (1992). (CN/1191-9310). **2569**

NORTH CAROLINA GEOGRAPHER, THE. (US/1065-2973). **2571**

PHILIP'S GEOGRAPHICAL DIGEST. (UK). **2572**

POLITICAL GEOGRAPHY. (UK/0962-6298). **2572**

POSISJON. (NO). **2573**

POST-SOVIET GEOGRAPHY. (US/1060-5851). **2573**

PRINCE GEORGE CITY DIRECTORY (BUSINESS ED.). (CN/1191-923X). **2573**

RED DEER CITY DIRECTORY (1992). (CN/1191-9302). **2574**

SAINT JOHN CITY DIRECTORY (1992). (CN/1191-940X). **2575**

USA COUNTIES [COMPUTER FILE]. (US). **2578**

VANCOUVER CITY DIRECTORY (1992). (CN/1191-9396). **2578**

ZEMLIA SIBIR. (RU/0869-3382). **2580**

ABSTRACTING, BIBLIOGRAPHIES AND STATISTICS

BIBLIOGRAPHIE NATIONALE FRANCAISE. ATLAS, CARTES ET PLANS : BIBLIOGRAPHIE ETABLIE PAR LA BIBLIOTHEQUE NATIONALE. (FR). **2580**

CARTOGRAPHY

ACSM TECHNICAL PAPERS / ACSM/ASPRS ANNUAL CONVENTION & EXPOSITION. (US). **2580**

ANTIQUE MAP PRICE RECORD & HANDBOOK. (US/1070-8421). **2580**

FGDC NEWSLETTER : A PUBLICATION OF THE FEDERAL GEOGRAPHIC DATA COMMITTEE. (US). **2581**

FRONTERAS (ARLINGTON, TEX.). (US/1062-8444). **2581**

GEOMATICA. (CN/1195-1036). **2582**

RIVISTA DEL DIPARTIMENTO DEL TERRITORIO. (IT). **2583**

GIFTS, TOYS

COLLECTING TOYS. (US/1068-347X). **2584**

GREETINGS AND GIFT STATIONER. (UK). **2584**

TOY & HOBBY WORLD (1993). (US/1073-8932). **2585**

TOY COLLECTOR. (US). **2585**

TOY COLLECTOR & PRICE GUIDE. (US/1069-1685). **2585**

GLASS AND CERAMICS

BRITISH CERAMIC TRANSACTIONS. (UK/0967-9782). **2586**

NEW GLASS REVIEW (PRAHA). (XR/1210-2741). **2592**

PHASE EQUILIBRIA DIAGRAMS (FINAL COMPILATION). (US/1065-500X). **2593**

TILE DESIGN & INSTALLATION. (US/1077-6974). **2594**

HEALTH AND PERSONAL FITNESS

ACTIVE LIVING (TORONTO). (CN/1188-620X). **2595**

ASPIRE (NASHVILLE, TENN.). (US/1076-5778). **2596**

AT YOUR BEST. (US/1065-5190). **2596**

ENLIGHTENED EATING NEWSLETTER. (US). **2597**

FITNESS, PHYSICAL HEALTH AND RECREATION EDUCATION (EASTERN U.S. ED.). (CN/1189-329X). **2597**

FITNESS, PHYSICAL HEALTH AND RECREATION EDUCATION (WESTERN U.S. ED.). (CN/1189-3303). **2597**

GOOD HOUSEKEEPING'S LIVING WELL : IN COOPERATION WITH THE AMERICAN MEDICAL ASSOCIATION. (US). **2597**

HEALTH & FITNESS TRIAD. (US/1064-6728). **2598**

HEALTHY KIDS. BIRTH-3. (US/1063-0945). **2598**

HOME HEALTH PRODUCTS. (US/1070-2431). **2598**

INJURY PREVENTION NEWS. (CN/1197-4362). **2598**

ISLAND SCENE. (US/1064-8674). **2599**

JOURNAL OF ASIAN MARTIAL ARTS. (US/1057-8358). **2599**

LIFE DESIGNS. (US/1064-217X). **2599**

MUSCLE MEDIA 2000. (US). **2600**

NATURAL HEALTH. (US/1067-9588). **2600**

ABSTRACTING, BIBLIOGRAPHIES AND STATISTICS

HEALTH SOURCE (PEABODY, MASS.). (US/1063-9810). **2602**

HEATING, PLUMBING, AND REFRIGERATION

ASHRAE HANDBOOK. HEATING, VENTILATING, AND AIR-CONDITIONING SYSTEMS AND EQUIPMENT. (US/1041-2344). **2603**

ASHRAE HANDBOOK. HEATING, VENTILATING, AND AIR-CONDITIONING SYSTEMS AND EQUIPMENT. (US). **2603**

PHC PROFIT REPORT. (US/1071-2372). **2607**

SPECIFIER'S GUIDE TO HEATING, VENTILATING, AIR CONDITIONING AND REFRIGERATION. (UK). **2608**

HISTORY (GENERAL)

AMS STUDIES IN CULTURAL HISTORY. (US/1058-2398). **2609**

CAVALRY JOURNAL, THE. (US/1074-0252). **2613**

COMMITTEE ON EAST ASIAN LIBRARIES DIRECTORY. (US/1067-0580). **2613**

CUBA REPORT, THE. (US/1062-0672). **2614**

GREAT BATTLES. (US/1071-670X). **2617**

HISTORY AND LANGUAGE. (US/1062-2306). **2619**

INTERNATIONAL OBSERVER (WASHINGTON, D.C.). (US/1061-0324). **2620**

INTERNATIONAL YEARBOOK OF ORAL HISTORY AND LIFE STORIES. (US). **2620**

MAJESTAS. (GW/0945-1439). **2622**

MEDIEVAL ENCOUNTERS. (NE/1380-7854). **2623**

PROVIDENCE (PROVIDENCE, R.I.). (US/1063-7974). **2626**

RUSSIAN STUDIES IN HISTORY. (US/1061-1983). **2628**

SOTSIALNYE I GUMANITARNYE NAUKI. SERIIA 5, ISTORIIA. OTECHESTVENNAIA LITERATURA / ROSSIISKAIA AKADEMIIA NAUK, INSTITUT NAUCHNOI INFORMATSII PO OBSHCHESTVENNYM NAUKAM. (RU). **2630**

TIME TABLE OF HISTORY. BUSINESS, POLITICS, AND MEDIA. (US/1054-5042). **2631**

VESTNIK SANKT-PETERBURGSKOGO UNIVERSITETA. SERIIA 2, ISTORIIA, IAZYKOZNANIE, LITERATUROVEDENIE. (RU). **2632**

HISTORY OF AFRICA

AFRICAN CHRONICLE, THE. (US/1054-9781). **2636**

JOURNAL OF AFRICAN RESEARCH. (US/1047-9716). **2640**

SIERRA LEONE REVIEW, THE. (US/1062-0109). **2643**

SIERRA LEONE REVIEW, THE. (US/1066-4947). **2643**

SOUTH AFRICA / SOUTH AFRICA FOUNDATION. (SA). **2643**

HISTORY OF ASIA

CHINA CURRENTS : A PHILIPPINE QUARTERLY ON CHINA CONCERNS. (PH). **2648**

CHINA REVIEW INTERNATIONAL. (US/1069-5834). **2648**

INDIA TODAY. (CN/0254-8399). **2653**

INDIAN THOUGHT LEIDEN. (NE/0924-8986). **2653**

JAPAN FOUNDATION PROGRAMS AVAILABLE IN CANADA, THE. (CN/1183-885X). **2654**

NOVAIA OTECHESTVENNAIA I INOSTRANNAIA LITERATURA PO OBSHCHESTVENNYM NAUKAM. IUZHNAIA I IUGO-VOSTOCHNAIA AZIIA, DALNYI VOSTOK / ROSSIISKAIA AKADEMIIA NAUK, INSTITUT NAUCHNOI INFORMATSII PO OBSHCHESTVENNYM NAUKAM. (RU) **2660**

PRINCETON PAPERS IN NEAR EASTERN STUDIES. (US/1065-9382). **2662**

SIBIRICA : THE JOURNAL OF SIBERIAN STUDIES. (UK). **2664**

SOTSIALNYE I GUMANITARNYE NAUKI. SERIIA 9, VOSTOKOVEDENIE I AFRIKANISTIKA. ZARUBEZHNAIA LITERATURA / ROSSIISKAIA AKADEMIIA NAUK, INSTITUT NAUCHNOI INFORMATSII PO OBSHCHESTVENNYM NAUKAM. (RU). **2664**

UNDERSTANDING JAPAN (DENVER, COLO.). (US/1070-5198). **2667**

HISTORY OF AUSTRALIA AND OCEANIA

NORTHERN TERRITORY IN FOCUS. (AT/1037-1176). **2670**

HISTORY OF EUROPE

ABSTRACTS, RUSSIAN AND EAST EUROPEAN SERIES : ABREES. (US). **2671**

AMERIKAI MAGYAR LEVELESTAR. (US/1054-4607). **2673**

ANCIENT CIVILIZATIONS FROM SCYTHIA TO SIBERIA. (NE/0929-077X). **2673**

ANNUAL REPORT / ROYAL COMMISSION ON THE HISTORICAL MONUMENTS OF ENGLAND. (UK). **2675**

BEST OF ANDORRA, THE. (US/1051-1504). **2678**

BRADFORD STUDIES ON SOUTH EASTERN EUROPE. (UK/1354-7739). **2679**

BRITISH JOURNAL OF HOLOCAUST EDUCATION. (UK/0966-095X). **2679**

CAHIERS DU MONDE RUSSE. (FR). **2682**

CONTEMPORARY EUROPEAN HISTORY. (UK/0960-7773). **2684**

EMF, STUDIES IN EARLY MODERN FRANCE. (US/1064-5020). **2686**

EUROPE-ASIA STUDIES. (UK/0966-8136). **2687**

EUROPEAN REVIEW OF HISTORY. (UK/1350-7486). **2687**

EUROWATCH: ECONOMICS, POLICY, AND LAW IN THE NEW EUROPE. (US). **2688**

JUDISCHER ALMANACH. (GW). **2695**

LAZARILLO. (SP). **2696**

MEMORIA STORICA : RIVISTA DEL CENTRO DI STUDI STORICI TERNI. (IT). **2698**

NASH DAGESTAN. (RU). **2699**

NEWSNET (STANFORD, CALIF.). (US/1074-3057). **2700**

PROCEEDINGS OF THE CONFERENCE ON MEDIEVALISM. (US/0899-3106). **2703**

REVUE GERMANIQUE INTERNATIONALE. (FR). **2706**

RUSSIA & CIS TODAY / COMPILED BY THE RFE/AL RESEARCH INSTITUTE MONITORING UNIT. (GW). **2707**

RUSSIA & CIS TODAY / COMPILED BY WHAT THE PAPERS SAY. (RU). **2707**

SLAVIANOVEDENIE. (RU/0869-544X). **2709**

URBAN FOCUS LONDON. (UK/0967-4764). **2714**

VOSKRESENIE. (RU). **2715**

WORLDWIDE GOVERNMENT DIRECTORY, REGIONAL EDITION. THE FORMER SOVIET BLOC. (US/1063-1259). **2716**

HISTORY OF NORTH, SOUTH, AND CENTRAL AMERICA

AFRO-AMERICAN HISTORY KIT (7TH GRADE AND ABOVE ED.). (US/1055-7385). **2717**

AKWE:KON JOURNAL. (US). **2717**

AMERICAN HISTORY. (US/1076-8866). **2719**

CANAL DE PANAMA HOY / CENTRO DE ESTUDIOS LATINOAMERICANOS "JUSTO AROSEMENA.". (PN). **2726**

COLEGIOS : THE NEWSLETTER ON THE HISTORY OF IDEAS IN COLONIAL LATIN AMERICA. (US). **2728**

COLONIAL LATIN AMERICAN HISTORICAL REVIEW. (US/1063-5769). **2728**

CROSSROADS (UNIVERSITY, MISS.). (US/1065-9110). **2730**

DIRECTORY OF HISPANIC EXPERTS, THE. (US/1074-9667). **2731**

DIRECTORY OF PANAMANIAN BUSINESSES, ASSOCIATIONS AND ORGANIZATIONS IN THE UNITED STATES. (US/1064-9018). **2731**

DISPATCH. (US). **2731**

DISPATCH/NEWS (SPRINGFIELD, ILL.). (US/1069-451X). **2731**

EXEMPLARIA HISPANICA. (US/1062-4511). **2733**

FAIT FRANCAIS EN AMERIQUE DU NORD. (CN/1183-4854). **2733**

FORT NORFOLK COURIER. (US/1065-5263). **2734**

INFORMATION AND APPLICATION GUIDE / CANADIAN STUDIES AND SPECIAL PROJECTS DIRECTORATE. (CN/1187-8401). **2739**

INTERNATIONAL DIRECTORY TO CANADIAN STUDIES. (CN/0846-5495). **2739**

INTERNATIONAL DIRECTORY TO CANADIAN STUDIES. (CN/0846-5495). **2739**

ISTOE. (BL). **2739**

JOURNAL OF CHICANA STUDIES. (US/1065-4690). **2741**

JOURNAL OF CONFEDERATE HISTORY SERIES. (US). **2741**

KANSAS HERITAGE. (US). **2743**

MEMBER NEWS / MINNESOTA HISTORICAL SOCIETY. (US/1064-5675). **2746**

MINUTES OF PROCEEDINGS AND EVIDENCE OF THE ABORIGINAL LIAISON COMMITTEE OF THE SPECIAL JOINT COMMITTEE ON A RENEWED CANADA (ENGLISH EDITION). (CN/1189-3672). **2746**

MINUTES OF PROCEEDINGS AND EVIDENCE OF THE ABORIGINAL LIAISON COMMITTEE OF THE SPECIAL JOINT COMMITTEE ON A RENEWED CANADA (FRENCH EDITION). (CN/1189-3672). **2747**

NATION THIS QUARTER / GOVERNMENT INFORMATION SERVICE, THE. (XM). **2747**

NORTH-SOUTH ISSUES. (US). **2751**

QUE PASA PANAMA! NEWSLETTER. (US/1064-9026). **2756**

ROCHESTER HISTORY. (US/0035-7413). **2759**

SERIES IN CHICANA CRITICAL ISSUES. (US/1065-688X). **2760**

VIRGINIA (BERRYVILLE, VA.). (US/1064-5691). **2765**

WESTERN KENTUCKY JOURNAL. (US/1072-6756). **2766**

WESTERN OBLATE STUDIES. (US/1065-4011). **2766**

HISTORY OF THE MIDDLE EAST

DOMES (MILWAUKEE, WIS.). (US/1060-4367). **2768**

INTERNATIONAL JOURNAL OF KURDISH STUDIES, THE. (US/1073-6697). **2768**

ISRAEL STUDIES BULLETIN. (US/1065-7711). **2768**

HOBBIES

AMERICAN MODELER (RALEIGH, N.C.). (US/1061-9399). **2771**

CLASSIC AMUSEMENTS. (US/1066-6281). **2772**

COLLECTIBLES, COUNTRY & AMERICANA. (US/1073-8142). **2772**

COLLECTORS' INFORMATION BUREAU'S COLLECTIBLES MARKET GUIDE & PRICE INDEX. (US/1068-4808). **2772**

COLLECTOR'S SOURCE. (US/1066-3649). **2772**

COMICS RETAILER. (US/1059-9401). **2773**

DOROTHY KAMM'S PORCELAIN COLLECTOR'S COMPANION. (US/1065-7789). **2773**

OFFICIAL ... PRICE GUIDE TO BASKETBALL CARDS, THE. (US/1062-6980). **2775**

OFFICIAL PRICE GUIDE TO BEER CANS (1993), THE. (US/1069-8426). **2775**

RADIO CONTROL MODEL CARS (1992). (US/1061-7213). **2777**

SECRET OF THE PROS, THE. (US/1064-3257). **2778**

TACKLE TESTER. (US/1068-5812). **2778**

TODAY'S COLLECTOR (IOLA, WIS.). (US/1066-7423). **2778**

PHILATELY

PHILATELIC SHOPPER, THE. (US). **2786**

Hobbies — Philately

UNITRADE CATALOGUE SPECIALISE DES TIMBRES CANADIENS. (CN/1193-8838). **2788**

UNITRADE SPECIALIZED CATALOGUE OF CANADIAN STAMPS. (CN/1193-8811). **2788**

HOME ECONOMICS

AMERICAN HOME ECONOMICS ASSOCIATION ACTION. (US/0194-7176). **2788**

COOKBOOK REVIEW, THE. (US/1060-7765). **2789**

COOK'S ILLUSTRATED. (US/1068-2821). **2789**

HOME COOKING. (UK/0965-366X). **2790**

HOW TO BE A PERFECT COOK. (US/1063-1747). **2791**

QUICK N EASY COUNTRY COOKIN. (US/1075-7384). **2792**

SAN DIEGO HOME/GARDEN LIFESTYLES. (US/1073-6891). **2792**

HOMOSEXUALITY

BETTER HOMOS AND GARDENS. (US). **2793**

COLOR LIFE. (US/1064-8070). **2794**

FERRARI'S PLACES OF INTEREST. (US/1078-0068). **2794**

GAY AIRLINE & TRAVEL CLUB NEWSLETTER, THE. (US). **2794**

GLQ (NEW YORK, N.Y.). (US/1064-2684). **2794**

GSBA GUIDE/DIRECTORY. (US). **2794**

JOURNAL OF GAY & LESBIAN SOCIAL SERVICES. (US/1053-8720). **2794**

LESBIAN REVIEW OF BOOKS, THE. (US/1077-5684). **2795**

OUT & ABOUT (NEW HAVEN, CONN.). (US/1066-7776). **2795**

OUT (NEW YORK, N.Y.). (US/1062-7928). **2795**

(THE) BRAVE NEW TICK. (US/1070-0161). **2796**

VOICES (RENO, NEV.). (US/1065-2914). **2796**

HORSES AND HORSEMANSHIP

CALIFORNIA/NEVADA HORSEMAN'S DIRECTORY. (US/1061-1754). **2797**

CONTACT - ONTARIO EQUESTRIAN FEDERATION. (CN/1187-9327). **2798**

HOOFCARE & LAMENESS. (US). **2799**

INTERNATIONAL SADDLERY AND APPAREL JOURNAL. (US/1062-7146). **2800**

JOURNAL OF THE AMERICAN SHETLAND PONY CLUB. (US). **2800**

HOTELS/MOTELS

AMERICA'S WONDERFUL LITTLE HOTELS & INNS. THE MIDWEST. (US/1063-0007). **2803**

AMERICA'S WONDERFUL LITTLE HOTELS & INNS. THE ROCKY MOUNTAINS AND THE SOUTHWEST. (US/1062-9998). **2804**

BEST BED & BREAKFAST IN ENGLAND, SCOTLAND & WALES, THE. (UK/1054-4089). **2804**

BEST PLACES TO STAY IN THE MID-ATLANTIC STATES. (US/1061-7353). **2804**

BEST PLACES TO STAY IN THE ROCKY MOUNTAIN STATES. (US/1060-7730). **2804**

DIRECTORY OF HOTEL & MOTEL COMPANIES. (US). **2805**

HOSPITALITY. (NZ). **2806**

HOTELBUSINESS (HAUPPAUGE, N.Y.). (US/1065-8432). **2806**

INTERNATIONAL HOTEL TRENDS. (US). **2807**

OAG OFFICIAL TRAVELER. TRAVEL GUIDE. (US/1073-0338). **2808**

OAG TRAVEL PLANNER (EUROPEAN ED.). (US/1075-1548). **2808**

OFFICIAL MEETING FACILITIES GUIDE, NORTH AMERICA. (US/1070-4515). **2808**

TOTAL QUALITY IN HOSPITALITY. (US/1069-5591). **2809**

HOUSEHOLD HARDWARE AND APPLIANCES

DEALERSCOPE MERCHANDISING GOLDBOOK. (US/1064-6280). **2811**

PROFESSIONAL VCR REPAIR TRAINING MANUAL AND BUSINESS PLAN, THE. (US/1064-2668). **2812**

HOUSING AND URBAN DEVELOPMENT

ACQUISITIONS LIST - CANADIAN HOUSING INFORMATION CENTRE. (CN/1197-7485). **2813**

AFRICAN RURAL AND URBAN STUDIES. (US/1073-4600). **2813**

ANNUAL PLAN UPDATING THE NEW YORK STATE COMPREHENSIVE HOUSING AFFORDABILITY HOUSING ACT. (US). **2814**

AQUAPOLIS. (IT). **2815**

CANADIAN JOURNAL OF URBAN RESEARCH. (CN/1188-3774). **2817**

CIUDAD Y TERRITORIO--ESTUDIOS TERRITORIALES. (SP). **2818**

CLAYTON COMPLETIONS REPORT. (CN/1193-6517). **2818**

CONTEMPORARY URBAN STUDIES. (US/1065-7002). **2819**

DEVELOPERS AND BUILDERS NEWS. (US/1062-5348). **2821**

ECONOMIC HOME OWNER, THE. (US/1055-8284). **2821**

EUROPEAN PLANNING STUDIES. (UK/0965-4313). **2822**

HABITAT : SUPPLEMENT ... AUX CAHIERS DE L'IAURIF. (FR). **2823**

JOURNAL OF COMMUNITY PRACTICE. (US/1070-5422). **2826**

JOURNAL OF ENVIRONMENTAL PLANNING AND MANAGEMENT. (UK/0964-0568). **2826**

JOURNAL OF URBAN TECHNOLOGY, THE. (US/1063-0732). **2826**

NTIS ALERT. REGIONAL & URBAN PLANNING & TECHNOLOGY. (US/1071-9466). **2829**

PBC HOUSING BRIEFS. (US/1059-2016). **2830**

RIVERSIDE SOUTH FORUM. (US). **2834**

SCOTTISH PLANNING & ENVIRONMENTAL LAW. (UK/0144-8196). **2835**

SMALL TOWN OBSERVER, THE. (US/1061-9933). **2835**

URBAN AGE, THE. (US). **2837**

URBAN HISTORY. (UK/0963-9268). **2838**

URBAN MANAGEMENT PROGRAM. (US). **2838**

URBAN REPORT (WASHINGTON, D.C.), THE. (US/1062-2292). **2838**

URBANISME. (FR/1240-0874). **2838**

HUMANITIES

ASIAN PACIFIC QUARTERLY. (KO). **2842**

BIBLION (NEW YORK, N.Y.). (US/1064-301X). **2843**

COMMON KNOWLEDGE. (US/0961-754X). **2844**

CONCERTINO MILANO. (IT/1121-6875). **2845**

CULTURAL STUDIES FROM BIRMINGHAM. (UK). **2845**

CULTUREFRONT (NEW YORK, N.Y.). (US/1063-634X). **2845**

GERMANIC NOTES AND REVIEWS. (US). **2846**

INTERDISCIPLINARY HUMANITIES. (US/1056-6139). **2848**

JOURNAL OF PRE-RAPHAELITE STUDIES (1992), THE. (US/1060-149X). **2848**

NUOVI STUDI LIVORNESI / ASSOCIAZIONE DI STORIA, LETTERE E ARTI LIVORNESI. (IT). **2851**

PATRIOMONIO CULTURAL. (UY). **2852**

PLATTSBURGH STUDIES IN THE HUMANITIES. (US/1061-6012). **2852**

REVISTA DE CIENCIAS HUMANAS : REVISTA DA UFPR. (BL/0104-0111). **2853**

SECONDO RINASCIMENTO, IL. (IT). **2854**

ABSTRACTING, BIBLIOGRAPHIES AND STATISTICS

HUMANITIES SOURCE. (US/1073-1962). **2857**

INDUSTRIAL HEALTH AND SAFETY

ARBEIDSOMSTANDIGHEDEN. (NE/0920-119X). **2859**

ARBEIDSOMSTANDIGHEDEN ACTUEEL. (NE). **2859**

CHEMICAL HEALTH & SAFETY. (US/1074-9098). **2860**

COMPETENCY. (UK/1351-5802). **2860**

FLEET SAFETY & HEALTH. (CN/1183-9856). **2862**

HAZARDS IN THE OFFICE. (UK/0966-906X). **2862**

HEALTH AND SAFETY AT WORK DIRECTORY, THE. (UK). **2862**

OCCUPATIONAL AND ENVIRONMENTAL MEDICINE. (UK/1351-0711). **2866**

OCCUPATIONAL HYGIENE. (US/1061-0251). **2866**

PREVENTING INJURY. (US/1056-9588). **2868**

SECURITE. (FR). **2870**

WORKPLACE SAFETY AWARENESS PROGRAM. (US/1059-1044). **2871**

WORKPLACE VITALITY. (US/1074-4452). **2871**

INSURANCE

BUSINESS CLAIMS CASUALTY BULLETIN. (US/1075-9018). **2877**

FEHB GUIDE FOR CSRS/FERS ANNUITANTS. (US). **2880**

FEHB GUIDE. OPEN SEASON FOR FEDERAL CIVILIAN EMPLOYEES / FEDERAL EMPLOYEES HEALTH BENEFITS PROGRAM. (US). **2880**

FEHB GUIDE. OPEN SEASON FOR FEDERAL CIVILIAN EMPLOYEES / FEDERAL EMPLOYEES HEALTH BENEFITS PROGRAM (LARGE PRINT EDITION). (US). **2880**

FEHB GUIDE. OPEN SEASON FOR FEDERAL CIVILIAN EMPLOYEES IN POSITIONS OUTSIDE THE CONTINENTAL UNITED STATES / FEDERAL EMPLOYEES HEALTH BENEFITS PROGRAM. (US). **2880**

FEHB GUIDE. OPEN SEASON FOR INDIVIDUALS ELIGIBLE TO ENROLL FOR TEMPORARY CONTINUATION OF COVERAGE, COVERAGE UNDER THE SPOUSE EQUITY LAW OR SIMILAR STATUTES PROVIDING COVERAGE TO FORMER SPOUSES / FEDERAL EMPLOYEES HEALTH BENEFITS PROGRAM. (US). **2880**

FEHB GUIDE. OPEN SEASON FOR INDIVIDUALS RECEIVING COMPENSATION FROM THE OFFICE OF WORKERS' COMPENSATION PROGRAMS (OWCP). (US). **2880**

FEHB GUIDE. OPEN SEASON FOR RETIREMENT SYSTEMS PARTICIPATING IN THE FEDERAL EMPLOYEES HEALTH BENEFITS PROGRAM. (US). **2880**

FEHB GUIDE. OPEN SEASON FOR UNITED STATES POSTAL SERVICE EMPLOYEES / FEDERAL EMPLOYEES HEALTH BENEFITS PROGRAM. (US). **2880**

FLEXIBLE BENEFITS. (US/1073-7111). **2881**

HEALTH ALLIANCE ALERT. (US/1075-024X). **2881**

JOURNAL OF ACTUARIAL PRACTICE. (US/1064-6647). **2885**

JOURNAL OF PENSION BENEFITS. (US/1069-4064). **2885**

KANSAS INSURANCE AGENT & BROKER. (US/1069-1847). **2886**

KELLY INSURANCE DIRECTORY: NATIONWIDE HOSPITAL INSURANCE BILLING DIRECTORY. (US). **2886**

MEALEY'S LITIGATION REPORTS. INSURANCE FRAUD. (US/1075-380X). **2887**

MEDICARE AND MEDICAID LAW BULLETIN. (US/1068-1019). **2888**

MERCER GUIDE TO SOCIAL SECURITY AND MEDICARE. (US). **2888**

MICHIGAN INSURANCE HANDBOOK. (US/1061-2610). **2888**

MOTOR INSURANCE MARKET. (UK/0965-8629). **2888**

RAILROAD RETIREMENT AND UNEMPLOYMENT INSURANCE SYSTEMS HANDBOOK. (US). **2891**

RISK MANAGEMENT FOR EXECUTIVE WOMEN. (US/0732-2666). **2892**

TAX FACTS. INSURANCE AND EMPLOYEE BENEFITS ED. (US/1061-401X). **2894**

TRANSACTIONS OF THE ACADEMY OF INSURANCE MEDICINE: 1992, VOLUME LXXVI. (US/1064-4709). **2894**

VANTAGE (WORCESTER, MASS.). (US/1065-3473). **2895**

VIESAGE (MONTREAL). (CN/1191-1077). **2895**

WEISS RESEARCH'S INSURANCE SAFETY DIRECTORY. (US/1074-2158). **2896**

WORKERS' COMP MANAGED CARE. (US/1066-2669). **2896**

YOUR CHICAGO EXPRESS. (US/1065-495X). **2897**

INTERIOR DESIGN

100 DESIGNERS' FAVORITE ROOMS. (US/1064-9948). **2898**

ARCHITECTURE AND DESIGN INSITE. (CN/1195-227X). **2898**

COUNTRY SAMPLER'S WEST. (US/1066-7245). **2899**

HOSPITALITY DESIGN. (US/1062-9254). **2900**

INTERIOR DECORATORS' HANDBOOK : IDH. (US). **2901**

JOURNAL OF INTERIOR DESIGN. (US/1071-7641). **2901**

REMODEL NOW. (US/1060-3735). **2903**

HOME FURNISHINGS

AMERICAN FURNITURE. (US/1069-4188). **2904**

HOME FURNISHINGS EXECUTIVE (GREENSBORO, N.C.). (US/1073-5585). **2906**

WEEKEND WOODCRAFTS. (US/1058-9821). **2907**

INTERNATIONAL ASSISTANCE AND DEVELOPMENT

BAOBAB INTERNATIONAL. (CN/1199-1844). **2908**

CD-DIS (ARLINGTON, VA.). (US/1061-6691). **2908**

CHOICES : THE HUMAN DEVELOPMENT MAGAZINE / UNDP. (US). **2908**

FORUM FOR DEVELOPMENT STUDIES. (NO). **2909**

NATIONAL DEVELOPMENT PROGRAMME / GOVERNMENT OF THE TURKS AND CAICOS ISLANDS, BRITISH WEST INDIES. (TC). **2911**

JEWELRY

GEM & LAPIDARY QUARTERLY. (US/1044-3622). **2914**

JEWELLERY INTERNATIONAL. (UK/0961-4559). **2914**

LOUPE (SANTA MONICA, CALIF.). (US/1062-8460). **2915**

JOURNALISM

AMERICAN JOURNALISM REVIEW. (US/1067-8654). **2917**

DIRECTORY OF SOURCES FOR EDITORS, REPORTERS & RESEARCHERS, THE. (CN/1197-5148). **2919**

FORBES MEDIACRITIC. (US/1067-4926). **2919**

FORBES MEDIAGUIDE 500. (US/1067-4918). **2919**

FREE PRESS (COLUMBUS, OHIO), THE. (US/1063-1267). **2920**

FREELANCE WRITER'S NEWSLETTER (KNOXVILLE, TENN.). (US/1064-9050). **2920**

JOURNAL OF CREATIVE WRITING AND BIBLIOTHERAPY, THE. (US/1065-755X). **2921**

PONIECKI NEWSLETTER/INFORMATOR. (US/1062-824X). **2923**

PROCEEDINGS OF THE ASSOCIATION FOR EDUCATION IN JOURNALISM AND MASS COMMUNICATION SOUTHEAST COLLOQUIUM. (US/1064-5403). **2923**

WRITING IT RIGHT. (US/1065-6154). **2926**

LAW

ABORIGINAL JUSTICE BULLETIN. (CN/1193-3100). **2926**

Law

ABOVEGROUND TANK STATE REGULATORY GUIDE. (US/1064-1289). **2926**

ADMINISTRATIVE LAW JOURNAL OF THE AMERICAN UNIVERSITY, THE. (US). **2927**

AGENDA DES JURISTES, L'. (CN/1189-5136). **2928**

AMERICAN BANKRUPTCY INSTITUTE LAW REVIEW, THE. (US/1068-0861). **2932**

AMERICAN LAW REPORTS. ALR 5TH, ANNOTATIONS AND CASES. (US/1062-2446). **2932**

ANDREWS' TOXIC TORTS ANNUAL. (US/1067-6996). **2933**

AUSTIN DAILY RECORD. (US/1065-7460). **2938**

AUSTRALIAN LAW LIBRARIAN. (AT/1039-6616). **2939**

BIOETHICS BULLETIN (WASHINGTON, D.C.). (US/1063-3596). **2941**

BLAST : THE BULLETIN OF LAW/SCIENCE & TECHNOLOGY / AMERICAN BAR ASSOCIATION, SECTION OF SCIENCE AND TECHNOLOGY. (US). **2942**

BNA'S HEALTH LAW REPORTER. (US/1064-2137). **2942**

BREAST IMPLANT LITIGATION REPORTER. (US/1062-1814). **2943**

BRIGHAM YOUNG UNIVERSITY EDUCATION AND LAW JOURNAL. (US). **2943**

BUTTERWORTH'S EC LEGISLATION IMPLEMENTATOR. (UK/0969-3912). **2945**

CALIFORNIA REGULATORY LAW BULLETIN. (US/1072-7833). **2946**

CANADIAN CASE AND STATUTE CITATIONS. (CN/1188-3081). **2947**

CASE LAW DIGESTS. (CN/1188-2948). **2949**

CATALOG OF CURRENT LAW TITLES, ANNUAL. (US/1049-796X). **2949**

CIJL YEARBOOK. (SZ). **2950**

COMMLAW CONSPECTUS. (US/1068-5871). **2953**

CONNECTICUT ENVIRONMENTAL COMPLIANCE UPDATE. (US/1064-2382). **2955**

CONSUMER BANKRUPTCY NEWS DESK BOOK. (US/1068-1906). **2956**

CPS EXPRESS. (US/1062-2535). **2957**

CREDIT UNION LEGAL LETTER. (US/1062-807X). **2957**

CURRENT LAW WEEK. (UK). **2958**

DALHOUSIE JOURNAL OF LEGAL STUDIES. (CN/1188-4258). **2959**

DICKINSON JOURNAL OF ENVIRONMENTAL LAW & POLICY. (US/1063-7419). **2960**

DIRECTORY / NATIONAL ASIAN PACIFIC AMERICAN BAR ASSOCIATION. (US). **2961**

DIRECTORY OF CONSTRUCTION LAW FIRMS, THE. (US/1056-8735). **2962**

DIRECTORY OF INTELLECTUAL PROPERTY ATTORNEYS. (US/1064-0355). **2962**

DIRITTO ED ECONOMIA DELL'ASSICURAZIONE. (IT). **2963**

DISPUTE RESOLUTION JOURNAL. (US/1074-8105). **2963**

DISTRICT OF COLUMBIA LAW REVIEW. (US/1063-8601). **2963**

DOING BUSINESS IN THE RUSSIAN FEDERATION. (US/1078-5108). **2964**

DORSANEO & SOULES' TEXAS CODES AND RULES. CIVIL LITIGATION. (US). **2964**

EUROPEAN CURRENT LAW : MONTHLY DIGEST. (UK/0964-0037). **2967**

EUROPEAN LAW JOURNAL. (UK). **2967**

EUROPEAN PUBLIC LAW. (NE/1354-3725). **2967**

EXTERNADISTA : REVISTA DE LA UNIVERSIDAD EXTERNADO DE COLOMBIA. (CK/0121-6279). **2968**

FAMILY MATTERS LONDON. (UK/0967-7119). **2968**

FEDERAL CLAIMS REPORTER. (US/1067-4934). **2969**

FEDERAL COURT APPOINTMENTS REPORT. (US/1059-6828). **2969**

FEDERAL EEO UPDATE. (US/1065-9943). **2969**

FOOD AND DRUG LAW JOURNAL. (US/1064-590X). **2971**

FOOD AND DRUG REPORT. (US/1071-8869). **2971**

FORDHAM INTELLECTUAL PROPERTY, MEDIA & ENTERTAINMENT LAW JOURNAL. (US). **2971**

FTCA NEWS. (US/1063-9209). **2972**

FUTURES INTERNATIONAL LAW LETTER. (US). **2973**

GEORGE MASON INDEPENDENT LAW REVIEW. (US/1068-3801). **2973**

GEORGE MASON UNIVERSITY LAW REVIEW. (US). **2973**

GIS LAW. (US/1065-2027). **2974**

GOSUDARSTVO I PRAVO / INSTITUT GOSUDARSTVA I PRAVA, ROSSIISKAIA AKADEMIIA NAUK. (RU). **2975**

GREEN'S COURT PRACTICE BULLETIN. (UK). **2975**

GREEN'S PROPERTY LAW BULLETIN. (UK). **2975**

GREEN'S REPARATION LAW BULLETIN. (UK). **2975**

GUIDE TO TEXAS FRANCHISE TAX. (US/1064-7732). **2976**

HAMILTON LAWYER. (CN/1188-4827). **2976**

HANDBOOK / ASSOCIATION OF AMERICAN LAW SCHOOLS. (US/1063-8253). **2976**

HEALTH LAW WEEK. (US/1063-4061). **2978**

ILLINOIS ENVIRONMENTAL LAW LETTER. (US/1059-5074). **2980**

ILLINOIS WORKERS' COMPENSATION LAW BULLETIN. (US/1067-2338). **2980**

INDIGENOUS WORLD / INTERNATIONAL WORK GROUP FOR INDIGENOUS AFFAIRS. (DK). **2982**

INSOLVENCY LAWYERS DIRECTORY / INSOLVENCY LAWYERS' ASSOCIATION. (UK). **2983**

INTERNATIONAL COMPUTER LAWYER, THE. (US/1067-6171). **2983**

INTERNATIONAL INSURANCE LAW REVIEW. (UK/0968-2090). **2984**

INTERNATIONAL JOURNAL OF THE LEGAL PROFESSION. (UK/0969-5958). **2984**

INTERNATIONAL YEARBOOK OF LAW, COMPUTERS, AND TECHNOLOGY. (UK/0965-528X). **2984**

INVESTMENT LAWYER, THE. (US/1075-4512). **2984**

IOMA'S REPORT ON CONTROLLING LAW FIRM COSTS. (US/1060-5924). **2984**

IOMA'S REPORT ON MANAGING LITIGATION COSTS. (US/1074-3898). **2984**

IRISH JOURNAL OF EUROPEAN LAW. (IE/0791-5403). **2985**

ISLAMIC AND COMPARATIVE LAW REVIEW. (II). **2985**

IT LAW TODAY. (UK). **2985**

ITALIAN STUDIES IN LAW : A REVIEW OF LEGAL PROBLEMS / EDITED BY THE ITALIAN ASSOCIATION OF COMPARATIVE LAW. (NE/0927-0523). **2985**

JOHN MARSHALL JOURNAL OF COMPUTER & INFORMATION LAW, THE. (US). **2986**

JOURNAL OF ENVIRONMENTAL PERMITTING. (US/1058-1367). **2987**

JOURNAL OF LAW, MEDICINE & ETHICS, THE. (US/1073-1105). **2988**

JOURNAL OF PERSONAL INJURY LITIGATION. (UK). **2989**

JOURNAL OF PRODUCTS AND TOXICS LIABILITY. (US/0967-2680). **2989**

JOURNAL OF SOCIAL SECURITY LAW. (UK). **2989**

JOURNAL / RHODE ISLAND BAR ASSOCIATION. (US/1073-8800). **2990**

JUVENILE AND FAMILY JUSTICE TODAY. (US/1062-2926). **2992**

LAB LAW REPORTER. (US/1065-7576). **2993**

LAW ALUMNI DIRECTORY, ST. MARY'S UNIVERSITY SCHOOL OF LAW. (US). **2993**

LAW FIRM BENEFITS. (US/1061-9410). **2995**

LAW-RELATED CD-ROM UPDATE. (US/1065-9285). **2996**

LAWYER'S WEEKLY USA. (US/1069-7837). **2998**

LEADER'S EUROPEAN MARKET LAW REPORT. (US). **2998**

LEGAL ASSISTANT'S NOTEBOOK (NORTHERN CALIFORNIA ED.), THE. (US/1062-8959). **2999**

LEGAL ASSISTANT'S NOTEBOOK. VOL. 1, SOUTHERN CALIFORNIA ED, THE. (US/1062-8940). **2999**

LETTER OF CREDIT LAW AND ANNOTATIONS. (US/1065-9072). **3002**

LITIGATION SERVICES RESOURCE DIRECTORY. (US/1061-3625). **3003**

LITIGATOR, THE. (UK). **3003**

LOCAL GOVERNMENT REVIEW REPORTS. (UK/1351-5764). **3004**

MARTINDALE-HUBBELL DISPUTE RESOLUTION DIRECTORY. (US). **3006**

MEALEY'S LITIGATION REPORTS. AMERICANS WITH DISABILITIES ACT. (US/1068-5405). **3007**

MEALEY'S LITIGATION REPORTS. BREAST IMPLANTS. (US/1067-0246). **3008**

MEALEY'S LITIGATION REPORTS. D&O LIABILITY. (US/1068-414X). **3008**

MEALEY'S LITIGATION REPORTS. INTELLECTUAL PROPERTY. (US/1065-9390). **3008**

MEALEY'S LITIGATION REPORTS. PATENTS. (US/1070-4043). **3008**

MEALEY'S LITIGATION REPORTS. TOXIC TORTS. (US/1064-1475). **3008**

MEDICAL LAW REVIEW. (UK/0967-0742). **3008**

MEDICAL LITIGATION ALERT. (US/1067-1269). **3008**

MEDICAL RECORD RISKS, CLAIMS & LITIGATION. (US/1061-4192). **3008**

MSL LAW REVIEW. (US/1066-1085). **3012**

NATIONAL TRIAL LAWYER (FLORIDA ED.). (US/1066-7733). **3014**

NATIONAL TRIAL LAWYER (NEW YORK ED.). (US/1060-9210). **3014**

NEBRASKA LAW NEWSLETTER. (US/1062-953X). **3014**

NETWORK 2D. (US/1063-9829). **3014**

NEVADA LAWYER. (US/1068-882X). **3015**

NEW EUROPE LAW REVIEW. (US/1069-3181). **3015**

NEW JERSEY RULES OF COURT. (US/1070-6364). **3015**

NORTHERN CALIFORNIA LEGAL RESOURCE MANUAL. (US/1056-2508). **3018**

OHIO UST CLAIMS DIGEST. (US/1062-3817). **3022**

OKLAHOMA EMPLOYMENT LAW LETTER. (US/1066-1123). **3022**

ONTARIO LANDLORD AND TENANT LEGISLATION. (CN/1195-3136). **3022**

ONTARIO PLANNING ACT. (CN/1195-017X). **3023**

ONTARIO REAL ESTATE LEGISLATION. (CN/1195-3152). **3023**

ONTARIO SMALL CLAIMS COURT PRACTICE. (CN/1191-159X). **3023**

ONTARIO'S ACCESS AND PRIVACY LEGISLATION, AN ANNOTATION. (CN/1189-3419). **3023**

PENNSYLVANIA PERSONAL INJURY REPORTER. (US/1067-2400). **3025**

PERSONAL INJURY VERDICT REVIEWS. (US/1067-2427). **3026**

PERSPECTIVE : TEACHING LEGAL RESEARCH AND WRITING. (US). **3029**

PHILADELPHIA BAR REPORTER. (US/0145-3491). **3029**

PRACTITIONERS 5500 DESKBOOK. (US/1064-7724). **3030**

PRAVNI PRAXE. (XR/1210-0900). **3030**

PUBLIC PROCUREMENT LAW REVIEW. (UK/0963-8245). **3033**

REID'S ADMINISTRATIVE LAW. (CN/1196-5266). **3037**

REPORTS OF MISCELLANEOUS CASES ARGUED AND DETERMINED IN THE COURTS OF OHIO: OTHER THAN THE SUPREME COURT AND THE COURTS OF APPEALS OF OHIO. (US). **3039**

REVISTA DE DERECHO PUBLICO. (UY). **3040**

ROSSIISKAIA IUSTITSIIA. (RU). **3045**

RUSSIAN POLITICS AND LAW. (US/1061-1940). **3045**

SAN DIEGO JUSTICE JOURNAL. (US/1073-676X). **3046**

SCHOOL LAW / WASHINGTON STATE SCHOOL DIRECTORS' ASSOCIATION. (US). **3046**

SEARCH AND SEIZURE LAW REPORTER, THE. (CN/1188-6137). **3047**

SEATTLE UNIVERSITY LAW REVIEW. (US). **3047**

SHEPARD'S ALABAMA CODE CITATIONS. (US). **3048**

SHEPARD'S EVIDENCE CITATIONS. (US/1060-7625). **3049**

SHEPARD'S INDIANA EXPRESS CITATIONS. (US/1071-961X). **3051**

SHEPARD'S KANSAS EXPRESS CITATIONS. (US/1069-0506). **3051**

SHEPARD'S MARYLAND CODE CITATIONS. (US). **3051**

SHEPARD'S MARYLAND EXPRESS CITATIONS. (US/1072-1622). **3051**

SHEPARD'S MICHIGAN EXPRESS CITATIONS. (US/1065-8815). **3051**

SHEPARD'S MINNESOTA EXPRESS CITATIONS. (US/1068-4077). **3052**

SHEPARD'S NEW YORK STATUTE EXPRESS CITATIONS. (US/1061-7906). **3053**

SHEPARD'S NEW YORK SUPPLEMENT EXPRESS CITATIONS. (US/1061-7914). **3053**

SHEPARD'S NORTH CAROLINA STATUTES CITATIONS. (US/1069-9511). **3053**

SHEPARD'S OREGON EXPRESS CITATIONS. (US/1069-7853). **3053**

SHEPARD'S TENNESSEE EXPRESS CITATIONS. (US/1067-2591). **3054**

SHEPARD'S VIRGINIA CODE CITATIONS. (US). **3055**

SHEPARD'S WASHINGTON EXPRESS CITATIONS. (US/1066-1298). **3055**

SINGAPORE LAW REPORTS, THE. (SI/0218-3161). **3055**

SLUZBENI LIST SAVEZNE REPUBLIKE JUGOSLAVIJE. (YU). **3055**

SMU LAW REVIEW. (US/1066-1271). **3056**

SOCIAL & LEGAL STUDIES. (UK/0964-6639). **3056**

SOMMAIRE - SYNDICAT DE L'ASSOCIATION DES JURISTES DE L'ETAT. (CN/1193-414X). **3056**

SOTSIALNYE I GUMANITARNYE NAUKI. SERIIA 4, GOSUDARSTVO I PRAVO. OTECHESTVENNAIA LITERATURA / ROSSIISKAIA AKADEMIIA NAUK, INSTITUT NAUCHNOI INFORMATSII PO OBSHCHESTVENNYM NAUKAM. (RU). **3056**

SOTSIALNYE I GUMANITARNYE NAUKI. SERIIA 4, GOSUDARSTVO I PRAVO. ZARUBEZHNAIA LITERATURA / ROSSIISKAIA AKADEMIIA NAUK, INSTITUT NAUCHNOI INFORMATSII PO OBSHCHESTVENNYM NAUKAM. (RU). **3056**

SOUTHERN CALIFORNIA LEGAL RESOURCE MANUAL. (US/1056-2494). **3057**

ST. THOMAS LAW REVIEW. (US/1065-318X). **3058**

STANFORD LAW ALUM. (US/1061-3447). **3058**

STATUTES & DECISIONS. (US/1061-0014). **3059**

TAX DIGEST (SANTA BARBARA, CALIF.). (US/1062-7308). **3062**

TENNESSEE PUBLIC ACTS : SUMMARIES OF INTEREST TO MUNICIPAL OFFICIALS. (US). **3063**

TILBURG FOREIGN LAW REVIEW. (NE/0926-874X). **3064**

TRUDEL, NADEAU INFO. (CN/1188-7702). **3066**

VIRGIN ISLANDS COURT RULES ANNOTATED. (US). **3071**

WE THE PEOPLE (WASHINGTON, D.C.: 1992). (US/1061-2564). **3073**

WEST'S ARIZONA LAW FINDER. (US). **3074**

WEST'S TAX LAW DICTIONARY. (US). **3075**

WIDENER JOURNAL OF PUBLIC LAW. (US/1064-5012). **3075**

WILLIAM AND MARY BILL OF RIGHTS JOURNAL, THE. (US/1065-8254). **3075**

ZA ZAGOLOVKAMI. (US/1060-6092). **3077**

ABSTRACTING, BIBLIOGRAPHIES AND STATISTICS

CRIME STATE RANKINGS. (US). **3080**

CRIMINOLOGY, PENOLOGY AND POLICE SCIENCE ABSTRACTS. (NE/0928-8759). **3080**

PROBATION SERVICE STATISTICS ... ESTIMATES AND ... ACTUALS. (UK). **3082**

BANKING LAW

BURAFF'S LITIGATION REPORTS. BANK LAWYER LIABILITY. (US/1067-618X). **3085**

CIVIL LAW

COMPAGNIES, SOCIETES PAR ACTIONS ET FAILLITE. (CN/1187-2861). **3089**

CONSTITUTIONAL LAW

LAW REPORTS OF THE COMMONWEALTH. (UK). **3093**

CORPORATE LAW

BUSINESS LAW TODAY / THE MAGAZINE OF THE ABA SECTION OF BUSINESS LAW. (US/1059-9436). **3097**

COMPANY LAW MONITOR. (UK). **3098**

CORPORATE GOVERNANCE ADVISOR, THE. (US/1067-6163). **3099**

EUROPEAN COMMUNITY BUSINESS LAW. SOURCEBOOK. (US/1065-6227). **3100**

FEDERAL AND ONTARIO INSOLVENCY LEGISLATION. (CN/1195-3144). **3100**

INVESTMENT COMPANY REGULATION. (US/1071-8265). **3101**

JOURNAL OF CORPORATE MANAGEMENT, THE. (AT/1038-2410). **3101**

Law — Corporate Law

LATIN AMERICAN LAW & BUSINESS REPORT. (US/1065-7428). **3101**

RUSSIA AND COMMONWEALTH BUSINESS LAW REPORT. (US/1064-637X). **3103**

TRADING LAW AND TRADING LAW REPORTS. (UK/1352-061X). **3104**

CRIMINAL LAW

MARTIN'S ONTARIO CRIMINAL PRACTICE. (CN/1188-9640). **3108**

VSEMIRNYI UGOLOVNYI ARKHIV. (RU). **3109**

ENVIRONMENTAL LAW

ALABAMA ENVIRONMENTAL COMPLIANCE UPDATE. (US/1066-1131). **3109**

BAKER & DANIELS' INDIANA ENVIRONMENTAL COMPLIANCE UPDATE. (US/1067-4209). **3110**

CLEAN AIR ACT COMPLIANCE GUIDE UPDATE. (US/1074-7729). **3110**

COLORADO ENVIRONMENTAL COMPLIANCE UPDATE. (US/1072-057X). **3110**

DAILY ENVIRONMENT REPORT. (US/1060-2976). **3110**

ENVIRONMENTAL LAW AND MANAGEMENT. (UK/1067-6058). **3111**

ENVIRONMENTAL LAW NEWS (SAN FRANCISCO, CALIF.). (US/1064-2129). **3111**

EUROPEAN ENVIRONMENTAL LAW REVIEW. (UK/0966-1646). **3112**

FLORIDA ENVIRONMENTAL COMPLIANCE UPDATE. (US/1064-1874). **3112**

GREEN'S ENVIRONMENTAL LAW BULLETIN. (UK). **3112**

JOURNAL OF NATURAL RESOURCES & ENVIRONMENTAL LAW. (US/1070-4833). **3113**

LAND USE & ENVIRONMENT FORUM. (US/1072-7973). **3114**

LAW & BUSINESS DIRECTORY OF ENVIRONMENTAL ATTORNEYS. (US/1064-0363). **3114**

LOUISIANA ENVIRONMENTAL COMPLIANCE UPDATE. (US/1066-1115). **3114**

MARYLAND ENVIRONMENTAL LAW LETTER. (US/1062-7960). **3114**

MASSACHUSETTS ENVIRONMENTAL COMPLIANCE UPDATE. (US/1064-2374). **3114**

MICHIGAN ENVIRONMENTAL COMPLIANCE UPDATE. (US/1073-9459). **3114**

MINNESOTA ENVIRONMENTAL COMPLIANCE UPDATE. (US/1072-916X). **3114**

NEW JERSEY ENVIRONMENTAL LAW LETTER. (US/1060-9954). **3115**

NEW YORK UNIVERSITY ENVIRONMENTAL LAW JOURNAL. (US/1061-8651). **3115**

OHIO ENVIRONMENTAL MONTHLY. (US/1063-9594). **3115**

ONTARIO ENVIRONMENTAL LEGISLATION. (CN/1195-163X). **3115**

PENNSYLVANIA ENVIRONMENTAL COMPLIANCE UPDATE. (US/1072-9143). **3115**

REVIEW OF EUROPEAN COMMUNITY AND INTERNATIONAL ENVIRONMENTAL LAW. (UK/0962-8797). **3116**

SHEPARD'S CLEAN AIR ACT REPORTER. (US/1068-235X). **3116**

SHEPARD'S ENVIRONMENTAL REGULATION SUMMARIES. (US/1070-213X). **3116**

TEXAS ENVIRONMENTAL COMPLIANCE UPDATE. (US/1075-2595). **3116**

VIRGINIA ENVIRONMENTAL COMPLIANCE UPDATE. (US/1068-9516). **3117**

WASHINGTON ENVIRONMENTAL COMPLIANCE UPDATE. (US/1072-0596). **3117**

WISCONSIN ENVIRONMENTAL COMPLIANCE UPDATE. (US/1072-9151). **3117**

ESTATE PLANNING

ESTATE PLANNER'S ALERT (1994). (US/1076-819X). **3118**

FAMILY LAW

FAMILY JUSTICE BULLETIN. (CN/1189-4245). **3120**

GREEN'S FAMILY LAW BULLETIN. (UK). **3120**

PRACTICE UNDER THE CALIFORNIA FAMILY CODE : DISSOLUTION, LEGAL SEPARATION, NULLITY. (US). **3122**

UNIVERSITY OF LOUISVILLE JOURNAL OF FAMILY LAW. (US). **3122**

INTERNATIONAL LAW

ARBITRATION AND DISPUTE RESOLUTION LAW JOURNAL, THE. (UK/0965-7053). **3124**

DIPLOMATICHESKII VESTNIK. (RU). **3127**

DIRECTORY OF THE EUROPEAN COMMISSION. (LU). **3127**

GULF WAR CLAIMS REPORTER. (US/1061-7345). **3128**

JOURNAL OF TRANSNATIONAL LAW & POLICY. (US/1067-8182). **3131**

PACE INTERNATIONAL LAW REVIEW. (US). **3133**

REVIEW OF CENTRAL AND EAST EUROPEAN LAW. (NE/0925-9880). **3135**

SUFFOLK TRANSNATIONAL LAW REVIEW. (US/0886-2648). **3136**

JUDICIAL SYSTEMS

REFERENCE GUIDES TO NATIONAL LEGAL SYSTEMS. (US/1059-9134). **3142**

LABOR LAW

BERKELEY JOURNAL OF EMPLOYMENT AND LABOR LAW. (US/1067-7666). **3144**

CANADIAN EMPLOYMENT LAW FOR U.S. COMPANIES. (US/1073-5720). **3145**

COLORADO EMPLOYMENT LAW LETTER. (US/1059-504X). **3145**

CONNECTICUT EMPLOYMENT LAW LETTER. (US/1064-4903). **3145**

EMPLOYMENT LAW NEWS. (UK). **3147**

EMPLOYMENT LAW STRATEGIST. (US/1069-7829). **3147**

GREEN'S EMPLOYMENT LAW BULLETIN. (UK). **3148**

KANSAS EMPLOYMENT LAW LETTER. (US/1074-0422). **3150**

LANCASTER'S CONSTRUCTION INDUSTRY EMPLOYMENT LAW NEWS. (CN/1194-4552). **3151**

LANCASTER'S WRONGFUL DISMISSAL EMPLOYMENT LAW NEWS. (CN/1194-398X). **3151**

LOUISIANA EMPLOYMENT LAW LETTER. (US/1059-5058). **3151**

MANAGEMENT POLICIES AND PERSONNEL LAW. (US). **3151**

MISSISSIPPI EMPLOYMENT LAW LETTER. (US/1074-0430). **3152**

NEW JERSEY EMPLOYMENT LAW LETTER. (US/1064-2390). **3152**

NEW YORK EMPLOYMENT LAW LETTER. (US/1072-9178). **3152**

ONTARIO LABOUR AND EMPLOYMENT LEGISLATION. (CN/1195-0196). **3153**

PENSION, PROFIT-SHARING, WELFARE, AND OTHER COMPENSATION PLANS. (US/1071-0477). **3153**

SOUTH CAROLINA EMPLOYMENT LAW LETTER. (US/1064-461X). **3154**

WASHINGTON EMPLOYMENT LAW LETTER. (US/1072-0588). **3155**

WISCONSIN EMPLOYMENT LAW LETTER. (US/1059-5066). **3155**

LAW ENFORCEMENT AND CRIMINOLOGY

CAMPUS SAFETY JOURNAL. (US/1066-0739). **3159**

CJ MANAGEMENT & TRAINING DIGEST. (US). **3160**

COMMUNITY POLICING DIGEST. (US). **3160**

CORRECTIONS ALERT. (US/1075-203X). **3161**

CRIME BUSTER (VANCOUVER). (CN/1191-386X). **3161**

CRIME PREVENTION FUNDING NEWS. (US/1069-1324). **3162**

CRIME PREVENTION STUDIES. (US/1065-7029). **3162**

DELITO Y SOCIEDAD. (AG). **3163**

DIRECTORY, JUVENILE & ADULT CORRECTIONAL DEPARTMENTS, INSTITUTIONS, AGENCIES & PAROLING AUTHORITIES / AMERICAN CORRECTIONAL ASSOCIATION. (US/1071-3530). **3163**

DRUG DEMAND REDUCTION NETWORK: A SUPPLEMENT TO THE LECC/VICTIM-WITNESS NETWORK NEWS/ U.S. DEPARTMENT OF JUSTICE, EXECTUVE OFFICE FOR UNITED STATES ATTORNEYS. (US). **3163**

Library and Information Sciences —Abstracting, Bibliographies and Statistics

EUROPEAN JOURNAL ON CRIMINAL POLICY AND RESEARCH. (NE/0928-1371). **3164**

GANG JOURNAL, THE. (US/1061-5326). **3165**

GLOBAL JOURNAL ON CRIME AND CRIMINAL LAW. (NE/0928-9313). **3165**

INMATE POPULATION FORECAST UPDATE, STATE OF WASHINGTON. (US). **3166**

JOURNAL OF QUESTIONED DOCUMENT EXAMINATION. (US/1061-3455). **3167**

JOURNAL OF SAFE MANAGEMENT OF DISRUPTIVE AND ASSAULTIVE BEHAVIOR, THE. (US/1065-3341). **3168**

LOOKING TOWARD THE FUTURE: A FIVE YEAR PLAN FOR THE IOWA DEPARTMENT OF CORRECTIONS / PREPARED BY THE IOWA DEPARTMENT OF CORRECTIONS, BUREAU OF RESEARCH AND PLANNING. (US). **3169**

LOW INTENSITY CONFLICT AND LAW ENFORCEMENT. (UK/0966-2847). **3169**

NARCOMAFIE. (IT). **3170**

NATIONAL INSTITUTE OF JUSTICE JOURNAL. (US/1067-7453). **3170**

NIJ PROGRAM PLAN / NATIONAL INSTITUTE OF JUSTICE. (US). **3170**

PENOLOGICAL INFORMATION BULLETIN / COUNCIL OF EUROPE. (FR/0254-5225). **3171**

PRAEGER SERIES IN CRIMINOLOGY AND CRIME CONTROL POLICY. (US/1060-3212). **3173**

PRISON LIFE. (US/1065-0709). **3173**

REPORT OF PROBATION SUPERVISION WORKLOAD. (US/0362-7489). **3174**

SECURITY DIRECTOR'S DIGEST. (US). **3176**

ZAKONNOST. (RU). **3179**

LEGAL AID

ALTERNATIVE LAW JOURNAL. (AT/1037-969X). **3179**

MANITOBA LEGAL SERVICES DIRECTORY. (CN/1187-8754). **3180**

MARITIME LAW

INTERNATIONAL MARITIME LAW. (UK). **3181**

LIBRARY AND INFORMATION SCIENCES

ADVANCES IN PRESERVATION AND ACCESS. (US/1063-2263). **3188**

ALGONQUIN PERIODICALS, UNION LISTING / ALGONQUIN RESOURCE CENTRE, STUDENT SERVICES DIVISION. (CN/1193-1426). **3189**

APT FOR LIBRARIES. (US/1062-0664). **3191**

ARBIDO. (SZ). **3191**

ATRIUM GROUP ADVISORY, THE. (US/1065-092X). **3192**

AUGUSTANA COLLEGE LIBRARY PUBLICATIONS. (US). **3193**

BIBLIOTECHNOE DELO I BIBLIOGRAFIIA. (RU). **3194**

BIBLIOTEKA. (RU/0869-4915). **3194**

BIOMEDICAL LIBRARY ACQUISITIONS BULLETIN [COMPUTER FILE]. (US/1064-699X). **3196**

BOLLETTINO AIB. (IT/1121-1490). **3196**

BULLETIN LS. (CN/1193-2325). **3198**

CANADIAN JOURNAL OF INFORMATION AND LIBRARY SCIENCE, THE. (CN/1195-096X). **3199**

CDMARC SERIALS. (US/1063-8784). **3201**

CINFOLINK DIRECTORY OF INFORMATION SERVICES IN CHINA. (CN). **3202**

CITATIONS FOR SERIAL LITERATURE. (US/1061-7434). **3202**

COLLECTIONS SERVICES NEWS. (US/1065-5859). **3203**

COLLEGE & UNDERGRADUATE LIBRARIES. (US/1069-1316). **3203**

CONSERLINE (WASHINGTON, D.C.). (US/1072-611X). **3204**

COOPERATIVE CATALOGING NEWS. (US/1060-8621). **3204**

CORNERSTONE (NEW PROVIDENCE, N.J.), THE. (US/0000-1392). **3204**

CORPORATE LIBRARY UPDATE. (US/1061-5288). **3204**

CURRENT AWARENESS ABSTRACTS. (UK). **3205**

DIRECTORY OF LIBRARY AUTOMATION SOFTWARE, SYSTEMS, AND SERVICES. (US/1071-264X). **3207**

DIRECTORY OF SOUTHEAST ASIAN ACADEMIC & SPECIAL LIBRARIES. (TH). **3208**

EASTERN EXPRESS (OMAHA, NEB.). (US/1064-3486). **3208**

EDUCATION FOR LIBRARY AND INFORMATION SERVICES, AUSTRALIA. (AT). **3209**

EUROSERIALS (BINGHAMTON, N.Y.). (US/1069-4641). **3209**

FAXON GUIDE TO SERIALS. (US/1059-6852). **3210**

FINANCIAL ASSISTANCE FOR LIBRARY AND INFORMATION STUDIES. (US). **3210**

FOCUS ON SECURITY. (US/1071-9997). **3211**

GRANTHANA. INDIAN JOURNAL OF LIBRARY STUDIES. (II). **3212**

INFORMATION SCIENCES, APPLICATIONS. (US/1069-0115). **3216**

INFORMATION SYSTEMS JOURNAL. (US/0887-5561). **3217**

INFORMED LIBRARIAN, THE. (US/1061-3609). **3217**

INTERNATIONAL INFORMATION & LIBRARY REVIEW, THE. (UK/1057-2317). **3218**

ISSN COMPACT. (FR/1018-4783). **3219**

JOURNAL OF AGSI. (UK/0965-4380). **3219**

JOURNAL OF GLOBAL INFORMATION MANAGEMENT. (US/1062-7375). **3220**

JOURNAL OF INFORMATION SCIENCE AND TECHNOLOGY. (II/0971-1988). **3220**

JOURNAL OF INTERLIBRARY LOAN, DOCUMENT DELIVERY & INFORMATION SUPPLY. (US/1072-303X). **3220**

JOURNAL OF RELIGIOUS & THEOLOGICAL INFORMATION. (US/1047-7845). **3220**

JOURNAL OF THE SOCIETY FOR INFORMATION DISPLAY. (US/0734-1768). **3221**

KEY WORDS. (US/1064-1211). **3221**

KLIATT (WELLESLEY, MASS.). (US/1065-8602). **3221**

KNOWLEDGE ORGANIZATION : KO. (GW/0943-7444). **3221**

LA RECORD. (UK). **3222**

LIBRARIANS AT LIBERTY. (US/1069-0832). **3223**

LIBRARY HISTORY ROUND TABLE NEWSLETTER. (US). **3225**

LIBRARY OF CONGRESS SUBJECT HEADINGS IN MICROFORM. (US). **3226**

LIBRARY TECHNOLOGY NEWS LTN. (UK/0964-7627). **3227**

LS NEWSLETTER. (CN/1193-2333). **3229**

MAINE ENTRY, THE. (US). **3229**

MEMBERSHIP DIRECTORY. (US). **3230**

MICHIGAN DOCUMENTS / COMPILED BY DENISE K. GERMAIN-PETERS. (US). **3231**

MSLA JOURNAL. (CN/1189-7163). **3232**

N-COMPASS (LINCOLN, NEB.). (US/1075-9719). **3232**

NFAIS YEARBOOK OF THE INFORMATION INDUSTRY, THE. (US/1062-7952). **3236**

OCLC CJK350 NEWSLETTER. (US/1054-268X). **3238**

OCLC SELECTED TITLES. (US/1060-6033). **3238**

OCLC SYSTEMS AND SERVICES. (US/1065-075X). **3238**

OFFSHORE ENGINEERING INFORMATION BULLETIN. (UK/0961-8163). **3238**

POPULAR CULTURE IN LIBRARIES. (US/1053-8747). **3241**

PROCEEDINGS OF THE ... MEETING / ASSOCIATION OF RESEARCH LIBRARIES. (US/1075-0886). **3242**

PUBLIC AND ACCESS SERVICES QUARTERLY. (US/1056-4942). **3243**

SAGAMORE PUBLISHING'S BOOK LOOK. (US/1062-3418). **3247**

SELECTED NEW ACQUISITIONS / CALIFORNIA ACADEMY OF SCIENCES, LIBRARY. (US/1065-7703). **3248**

SERIALS IN MICROFORM (ANN ARBOR, MICH. 1993). (US/1069-6164). **3249**

TAKING STOCK LONDON. 1992. (UK/0966-6745). **3252**

TEACHING LIBRARIAN. (CN/1188-679X). **3252**

ABSTRACTING, BIBLIOGRAPHIES AND STATISTICS

CD-ROM FINDER : THE WORLD OF CD-ROM PRODUCTS FOR INFORMATION SEEKERS. (US). **3257**

INFORMATION MANAGEMENT & TECHNOLOGY. (UK). **3258**

Linguistics

LINGUISTICS

ADVANCES IN CONSCIOUSNESS RESEARCH. (NE). **3261**

AION. SLAVISTICA : ANNALI DELL'ISTITUTO UNIVERSITARIO ORIENTALE DI NAPOLI / DIPARTIMENTO DI STUDI DELL'EUROPA ORIENTALE, SEZIONE SLAVISTICA. (IT/1122-195X). **3262**

AUSTRALIAN JOURNAL OF LANGUAGE AND LITERACY / ARA, THE. (AT/1038-1562). **3267**

BERKELEY MODELS OF GRAMMAR. (US/1061-6055). **3268**

BILINGUALISM TODAY. (US/1045-4365). **3269**

BULLETIN DE LA COMMUNICATION PARLEE. (FR). **3270**

CAMBRIAN MEDIEVAL CELTIC STUDIES. (UK). **3272**

COMPOSITION STUDIES : FRESHMAN ENGLISH NEWS. (US). **3274**

CURRENT RESEARCH IN FRENCH STUDIES AT UNIVERSITIES IN THE UNITED KINGDOM & IRELAND. (UK/1350-9209). **3276**

DIRECTORY OF MEMBERS OF THE ASSOCIATION OF TRANSLATORS AND INTERPRETERS OF ONTARIO. (CN/1188-102X). **3277**

DIRECTORY OF MEMBERS OF THE ASSOCIATION OF TRANSLATORS AND INTERPRETERS OF ONTARIO. (CN/1188-102X). **3277**

ELEMENTA (YVERDON, SWITZERLAND). (US/1064-6663). **3278**

EURASIAN STUDIES YEARBOOK. (US). **3280**

FILOLOGICHESKIE NAUKI. (RU). **3281**

GUIDE DES MEMBRES DE LA STQ. (CN/1187-922X). **3284**

GUIDE DES MEMBRES DE LA STQ (FRENCH EDITION). (CN/1187-922X). **3284**

INTERGENERATIONAL ISSUES IN SPEECH, HEARING, AND LANGUAGE. (US/1058-9902). **3287**

IZVESTIIA AKADEMII NAUK. SERIIA LITERATURY I IAZYKA / ROSSIISKAIA AKADEMIIA NAUK. (RU). **3288**

JOURNAL OF CELTIC LINGUISTICS. (UK/0962-1377). **3289**

JOURNAL OF EAST ASIAN LINGUISTICS. (NE/0925-8558). **3290**

JOURNAL OF MEDIEVAL LATIN : A PUBLICATION OF THE NORTH AMERICAN ASSOCIATION OF MEDIEVAL LATIN, THE. (BE/0778-9750). **3291**

JOURNAL OF MODERN ITALIAN STUDIES. (UK/1354-571X). **3291**

JOURNAL OF SECOND LANGUAGE WRITING. (US/1060-3743). **3291**

JOURNAL OF SLAVIC LINGUISTICS. (US/1068-2090). **3292**

JOURNAL OF TRANSLATION AND TEXTLINGUISTICS. (US/1055-4513). **3292**

KALBOTYRA / VILNIUSSKII UNIVERSITET. (LI/0202-3296). **3293**

LANGUAGE AND LITERATURE. (UK/0963-9470). **3294**

LANGUAGE AWARENESS. (UK/0965-8416). **3295**

LANGUAGE FORUM. (UK/1351-024X). **3295**

LANGUAGES OF DESIGN. (NE/0927-3034). **3296**

LANGUAGES OF THE WORLD. (GW/0940-0788). **3296**

LAZARILLO SALAMANCA. (SP/1131-9151). **3296**

LINGUISTICA ATLANTICA : JOURNAL OF THE ATLANTIC PROVINCES LINGUISTIC ASSOCATION. (CN). **3299**

LINGUISTICA PRAGENSIA. (XR). **3299**

MONOGRAPHS IN LINGUISTICS. (US/1056-5019). **3304**

MONOGRAPHS IN LINGUISTICS AND THE PHILOSOPHY OF LANGUAGE. (US/1065-9528). **3304**

P.S.I. GUIDE, PREFIX/SUFFIX IDENTIFICATION FOR BEARINGS. (US/1065-8491). **3309**

PRAGMATICS & COGNITION. (NE/0929-0907). **3311**

REPERTOIRE / CORPORATION DES TRADUCTEURS, TRADUCTRICES, TERMINOLOGUES ET INTERPRETES DU NOUVEAU-BRUNSWICK. (CN/1187-8711). **3315**

RODNAE SLOVA. (BW). **3317**

RUSSKAIA SLOVESNOST. (RU). **3318**

SLAVIANSKII MIR : VESTNIK PRAZDNIKA SLAVIANSKOI PISMENNOSTI I KULTURY I MEZHDUNARODNOGO KONGRESSA SLAVIANSKIKH KULTUR. (RU). **3321**

SLAVICA TAMPERENSIA. (FI/0789-2764). **3322**

SPRACHTYPOLOGIE UND UNIVERSALIENFORSCHUNG. (GW/0942-2919). **3323**

SPRAK OCH STIL. (SW/1101-1165). **3323**

STUDY IN FINLAND: ENGLISH LANGUAGE PROGRAMMES AND STUDIES IN FINNISH UNIVERSITIES / MINISTRY OF EDUCATION. (FI/0788-5695). **3326**

TRAITEMENT AUTOMATIQUE DES LANGUES : T.A.L. (FR). **3327**

WRITTEN AND SPOKEN HINDI. (US/1065-2442). **3334**

LITERARY AND POLITICAL REVIEWS

CURRENT BOOKS MAGAZINE. (US/1063-9012). **3341**

GLOBAL CITY REVIEW. (US/1068-0586). **3343**

HOFMANNSTHAL : JAHRBUCH ZUR EUROPAISCHEN MODERNE. (GW). **3344**

ILLINOIS REVIEW, THE. (US/1067-4128). **3344**

IRIS (ATLANTA, GA.). (US/1068-9494). **3344**

MATICA : CASOPIS HRVATSKE MATICE ISELJENIKA. (CI). **3347**

MINORITY LITERARY EXPO (BIRMINGHAM, ALA.). (US/1061-2246). **3347**

NORTHWEST LITERARY FORUM. (US/1062-3353). **3349**

READERLY/WRITERLY TEXTS. (US/1066-3630). **3351**

WORLD INTELLIGENCE REVIEW. (US/1076-9285). **3356**

LITERATURE

ABERATIONS (WALNUT CREEK, CALIF.). (US/1058-2509). **3357**

ACLA BULLETIN. (US). **3357**

AFRICAN AMERICAN REVIEW. (US/1062-4783). **3358**

AMS HENRY JAMES STUDIES. (US/1058-5915). **3360**

AMS INTERNATIONAL STUDIES. (US/1058-2371). **3360**

AMS STUDIES IN 19TH CENTURY LITERATURE AND CULTURE. (US/1059-5406). **3360**

ARISTOS (TACOMA, WASH.). (US/1059-8553). **3363**

ASIMOV'S SCIENCE FICTION. (US/1065-2698). **3364**

AUDIOCASSETTE & COMPACT DISC FINDER : A SUBJECT GUIDE TO EDUCATIONAL AND LITERARY MATERIALS ON AUDIOCASSETTES AND COMPACT DISCS. (US). **3364**

BLUFFS READER, THE. (US/1062-6409). **3368**

BOX N' CHEST. (US/1064-0096). **3369**

BULLETIN / SCIENCE FICTION AND FANTASY WRITERS OF AMERICA. (US). **3370**

CANADIAN AUTHOR (1992). (CN/1193-9974). **3372**

CARLYLE STUDIES ANNUAL. (US/1074-2670). **3373**

COMPARATIVE CULTURES AND LITERATURE. (US/1070-955X). **3377**

COMPARATIVE LITERATURE AND FILM STUDIES. (US/0899-9902). **3377**

COTTON QUARTERLY, THE. (US/1063-5084). **3378**

DESLINDES : REVISTA DE LA BIBLIOTECA NACIONAL. (UY/0797-6402). **3380**

DEVELOPING YOUR CREATIVE WRITING STYLE AND LEARNING THE CRAFT OF WRITING. (US/1061-6039). **3381**

DIASPORA (MAGNOLIA, ARK.). (US/1062-6972). **3381**

DIMENSIONP2S (KILGORE, TEX.). (US/1072-7655). **3381**

DIRIZHABL. (RU). **3381**

DISCOVERING AUTHORS. (US/1066-7792). **3381**

ECRITIQUE (IOWA CITY, IOWA). (US/1061-1479). **3383**

EL-E-PHANT. (US). **3383**

ELIZABETHAN REVIEW, THE. (US/1066-7059). **3384**

EMILY DICKINSON JOURNAL, THE. (US/1059-6879). **3384**

ESC! (DEKALB, ILL.). (US/1065-4844). **3385**

EYEBALL (ST. LOUIS, MO.). (US/1063-9675). **3387**

FOUR DIRECTIONS (TELLICO PLAINS, TENN.), THE. (US/1070-7549). **3388**

FRAGMENT. (XO). **3389**

FURIOUS FICTIONS. (US/1065-7983). **3389**

GALE'S LITERARY INDEX. (US/1066-7709). **3389**

GASLIGHT (CLEVELAND, MINN.). (US/1062-015X). **3389**

GEORGE ELIOT REVIEW : JOURNAL OF THE GEORGE ELIOT FELLOWSHIP, THE. (UK) **3390**

GEORGETOWN REVIEW (GEORGETOWN, KY.). (US/1066-1506). **3390**

GLIMMER TRAIN STORIES. (US/1055-7520). **3391**

GYPSY BLOOD REVIEW. (US/1071-5126). **3392**

HARSH MISTRESS. (US/1070-6569). **3393**

HEARTHSIDE READER, THE. (US/1061-4567). **3393**

HUNGARIAN QUARTERLY, THE. (HU) **3395**

INDIANA JOURNAL OF HISPANIC LITERATURES. (US/1065-0350). **3396**

INTERNATIONAL QUARTERLY (TALLAHASS., FLA.). (US/1060-6084). **3396**

KOMMENTARII. (RU). **3402**

KYIVSKA STAROVYNA. (UN/0869-3595). **3403**

LIGHT (CHICAGO, ILL.). (US/1064-8186). **3405**

LITERARY IMAGE. (US/1064-8062). **3406**

LONE STAR LITERARY QUARTERLY. (US/1062-7790). **3408**

MFE COLLECTORS' BOOKLINE. (US/1073-3027). **3411**

MLA DIRECTORY OF SCHOLARLY PRESSES IN LITERATURE AND LANGUAGE. (US/1057-2899). **3412**

MODERNISM/MODERNITY (BALTIMORE, MD.). (US/1071-6068). **3412**

MYSTERY REVIEW, THE. (CN/1192-8700). **3414**

NARRATIVE (COLUMBUS, OHIO). (US/1063-3685). **3414**

NEW JERSEY REVIEW OF LITERATURE, THE. (US/1073-8576). **3415**

NITE-WRITER'S LITERARY ARTS JOURNAL. (US/1062-1423). **3417**

NORTH CAROLINA LITERARY REVIEW. (US/1063-0724). **3418**

NOTIONS, POTIONS. (US/1059-566X). **3418**

NOVAIA LITERATURA PO SOTSIALNYM I GUMANITARNYM NAUKAM. LITERATUROVEDENIE / ROSSIISKAIA AKADEMIIA NAUK, INSTITUT NAUCHNOI INFORMATSII PO OBSHCHESTVENNYM NAUKAM. (RU). **3419**

NOVAIA OTECHESTVENNAIA I INOSTRANNAIA LITERATURA PO OBSHCHESTVENNYM NAUKAM. AFRIKA. BLIZHNII I SREDNII VOSTOK / ROSSIISKAIA AKADEMIIA NAUK, INSTITUT NAUCHNOI INFORMATSII PO OBSHCHESTVENNYM NAUKAM. (RU). **3419**

PACIFIC COAST JOURNAL (CAMPBELL, CALIF.). (US/1065-1594). **3421**

PAPERS OF ROBERT TREAT PAINE, THE. (US/1059-1079). **3422**

PAPIROS DEL SIGLO VEINTE. (AG). **3422**

PSYCHOTRAIN (FAYETTEVILLE, ARK.). (US/1064-363X). **3426**

RADONEZH, VEK XX. (RU). **3427**

RANDOM REALITIES. (US/1065-8343). **3427**

ROUNDUP MAGAZINE / WESTERN WRITERS OF AMERICA, THE. (US) **3432**

RUSSIAN STUDIES IN LITERATURE. (US/1061-1975). **3432**

SANDHILLS REVIEW, THE. (US/1061-3579). **3433**

SANTA BARBARA REVIEW. (US/1068-8617). **3433**

SCIENCE FICTION AGE (HERNDON, VA.). (US/1065-1829). **3434**

SFRA REVIEW. (US). **3435**

SIMPSON 7 : REVISTA DE LA SOCIEDAD DE ESCRITORES DE CHILE. (CL). **3437**

SLOVAK REVIEW. (XO) **3437**

SOUTH DAKOTA WRITERS. (US/1062-063X). **3438**

SOUTHWEST (FLAGSTAFF, AZ.). (US/1065-0156). **3438**

STEPHEN CRANE STUDIES. (US/1061-6136). **3440**

STUDIES OF WORLD LITERATURE IN ENGLISH. (US/1043-8580). **3442**

SUN DANCER REVIEW. (US/1062-6387). **3443**

TANGENCE. (CN/1189-4563). **3444**

THRUST (AUSTIN, TEX.). (US/1064-0126). **3446**

TIRRA LIRRA. (AT/1038-8400). **3446**

TORONTO REVIEW OF CONTEMPORARY WRITING ABROAD, THE. (CN) **3447**

TRANSLATION AND LITERATURE. (UK/0968-1361). **3447**

TRINITY FORUM READING, THE. (US/1062-2527). **3447**

UNDISCOVERED COUNTRIES JOURNAL. (US/1068-3267). **3449**

VIZ (HATTIESBURG, MISS.). (US/1064-153X). **3451**

WASI : [BULLETIN]. (MW). **3452**

WILLA / WOMEN IN LITERATURE AND LIFE ASSEMBLY. (US/1065-9080). **3453**

WITZ (PENNGROVE, CALIF.). (US/1061-4583). **3453**

WOMEN WRITERS OF ITALY. (US/1056-4535). **3454**

WRITING FOR OUR LIVES. (US/1062-3434). **3454**

WRITING IN OHIO. (US/1060-4448). **3455**

ZDES I TEPER. (RU/0131-3266). **3456**

ZUZU'S PETALS QUARTERLY. (US/1060-9571). **3456**

ABSTRACTING, BIBLIOGRAPHIES AND STATISTICS

NIGHT SONGS. (US/1068-4468). **3459**

POETRY

APEX OF THE M. (US/1072-9232). **3460**

BORDERLANDS (AUSTIN, TEX.). (US/1065-0342). **3460**

CATHAY. (US/1065-9250). **3461**

CAT'S EAR. (US/1062-6379). **3461**

DEFINED PROVIDENCE. (US/1066-2197). **3462**

E.T.A. HOFFMANN-JAHRBUCH : MITTEILUNGEN DER E.T.A. HOFFMANN-GESELLSCHAFT. (GW/0944-5277). **3462**

EARTH BOUND. (US/1064-4970). **3462**

HUNGRY POET, THE. (US/1065-6421). **3464**

INTERNATIONAL WHO'S WHO IN POETRY AND POETS' ENCYCLOPAEDIA. (UK). **3464**

MISNOMER (PRESTONBURG, KY.). (US/1061-5296). **3466**

NOCTILUCA (NORWOOD, MASS.). (US/1061-0480). **3467**

ORACLE POETRY. (US/1056-5035). **3467**

PHOENIX (WATERLOO). (CN/1191-8632). **3468**

POEM FINDER ON DISC. (US/1063-1666). **3468**

POETRY IN PENNSYLVANIA. (US/1062-9386). **3469**

POETRY PROJECT NEWSLETTER, THE. (US). **3469**

POET'S GUILD. (US/1065-836X). **3470**

SHANGRI-LA (WASHINGTON, D.C.). (US/1061-3919). **3471**

TEXTURE MINIATURE. (US/1061-9887). **3472**

UNIVERSAL ACADEMIA. (US/1064-2625). **3472**

WRITING RIGHT NEWSLETTER. (US/1062-8770). **3473**

MANUFACTURING

AMERICAN MANUFACTURERS DIRECTORY. (US/1061-219X). **3475**

CONSUMER PRODUCT AND MANUFACTURER RATINGS. (US/1068-4158). **3477**

DISCOVERY NEWS. (CN/1191-4297). **3478**

ELECTRONICS MANUFACTURERS DIRECTORY. (US/1060-2100). **3478**

GEORGE D. HALL'S DIRECTORY OF NEW ENGLAND MANUFACTURERS. (US). **3479**

GEORGE D. HALL'S DIRECTORY OF NEW JERSEY MANUFACTURERS. (US/1069-5176). **3479**

GEORGE D. HALL'S DIRECTORY OF NEW YORK MANUFACTURES. (US). **3479**

HARRIS GEORGIA MANUFACTURERS DIRECTORY. (US/1065-4755). **3480**

HARRIS MANUFACTURERS DIRECTORY (NATIONAL ED.). (US/1061-2076). **3480**

HARRIS MANUFACTURERS DIRECTORY (NORTHEAST ED.). (US/1061-2041). **3480**

HARRIS MANUFACTURERS DIRECTORY (SOUTHEAST ED.). (US/1061-2033). **3480**

HARRIS MANUFACTURERS DIRECTORY (SOUTHWEST ED.), THE. (US/1061-2068). **3480**

HARRIS MANUFACTURERS DIRECTORY (WEST & SOUTHWEST ED.). (US/1061-205X). **3480**

Manufacturing

HARRIS MARYLAND MANUFACTURERS DIRECTORY. (US/1065-7231). **3480**

HARRIS NORTH CAROLINA MANUFACTURERS DIRECTORY. (US/1065-4720). **3480**

HARRIS SOUTH CAROLINA MANUFACTURERS DIRECTORY. (US/1065-4747). **3480**

HOW PRODUCTS ARE MADE. (US/1072-5091). **680**

I.H.I. GUIDE HOSES. (US/1056-6155). **3480**

IEEE TRANSACTIONS ON COMPONENTS, PACKAGING, AND MANUFACTURING TECHNOLOGY. PART A. (US/1070-9886). **3480**

INTERNATIONAL JOURNAL OF ENVIRONMENTALLY CONSCIOUS MANUFACTURING. (US/1062-6832). **3481**

INTERNATIONAL JOURNAL OF FLEXIBLE AUTOMATION AND INTEGRATED MANUFACTURING. (US/1064-6345). **3481**

JOURNAL OF COST MANAGEMENT. (US). **3482**

JOURNAL OF MATERIALS MANUFACTURING AND PROCESSING SCIENCE. (US/1062-0656). **3482**

LOUISIANA MANUFACTURERS REGISTER. (US/1053-8992). **3482**

MARYLAND MANUFACTURERS DIRECTORY (EVANSTON, ILL.). (US/1065-2507). **3484**

MONTANA MANUFACTURERS DIRECTORY. (US/1057-6681). **3485**

NEBRASKA MANUFACTURERS REGISTER. (US/1059-7727). **3485**

STUCK, PUTZ, TROCKENBAU. (GW/0941-7583). **3488**

VIRGINIA MANUFACTURERS DIRECTORY. (US/1065-2493). **3489**

WORLD CLASS DESIGN TO MANUFACTURE : WCDM. (UK/1352-3074). **3489**

MATHEMATICS

ACTA NUMERICA. (UK/0962-4929). **3490**

ADVANCES IN COMPUTATIONAL MATHEMATICS. (NE/1019-7168). **3491**

ADVANCES IN MATHEMATICAL SCIENCES AND APPLICATIONS. (JA). **3491**

APPLIED AND COMPUTATIONAL HARMONIC ANALYSIS. (US/1063-5203). **3494**

BULLETIN OF THE BELGIAN MATHEMATICAL SOCIETY, SIMON STEVIN. (BE). **3498**

CMS NOTES. (CN/1193-9273). **3500**

COMBINATORICS, PROBABILITY & COMPUTING : CPC. (UK/0963-5483). **3500**

COMMUNICATIONS IN NUMERICAL METHODS IN ENGINEERING. (UK/1069-8299). **3501**

COMPLEXITY (NEW YORK, N.Y.). (US/1076-2787). **3501**

COMPUTATIONAL MATHEMATICS AND MATHEMATICAL PHYSICS. (UK/0965-5425). **3501**

COMPUTATIONAL STATISTICS. (GW). **3502**

CRM MONOGRAPH SERIES / CENTRE DE RECHERCHES MATHEMATIQUES. (US/1065-8599). **3502**

CRM PROCEEDINGS & LECTURE NOTES. (US/1065-8580). **3502**

DOKLADY MATHEMATICS. (RU). **3504**

DYNAMIC SYSTEMS AND APPLICATIONS. (US/1056-2176). **3504**

ELEMENTARY MODULE SERIES. (US/1058-2754). **3504**

EXPERIMENTAL MATHEMATICS. (US/1058-6458). **3505**

FRACTALS. (SI/0218-348X). **3506**

GEOMBINATORICS : [A MINI-JOURNAL OF OPEN PROBLEMS OF COMBINATORIAL AND DISCRETE GEOMETRY AND RELATED AREAS] / UNIVERSITY OF COLORADO AT COLORADO SPRINGS AND CENTER FOR EXCELLENCE IN MATHEMATICAL EDUCATION. (US/1065-7371). **3506**

GEORGIAN MATHEMATICAL JOURNAL. (US/1072-947X). **3507**

GRADUATE STUDIES IN MATHEMATICS. (US/1065-7339). **3507**

HUMANISTIC MATHEMATICS NETWORK JOURNAL. (US/1065-8297). **3508**

IZVESTIYA. MATHEMATICS. (US/1064-5632). **3511**

JOURNAL OF ALGEBRAIC GEOMETRY. (US/1056-3911). **3511**

JOURNAL OF COMBINATORIAL DESIGNS. (US/1063-8539). **3512**

JOURNAL OF FOURIER ANALYSIS AND APPLICATIONS, THE. (US/1069-5869). **3512**

JOURNAL OF KNOT THEORY AND ITS RAMIFICATIONS. (SI/0218-2165). **3513**

JOURNAL OF LIE THEORY. (GW). **3513**

JOURNAL OF MATHEMATICAL SCIENCES. (US/1072-3374). **3513**

JOURNAL OF THE OUGHTRED SOCIETY, THE. (US/1061-6292). **3515**

KYUSHU JOURNAL OF MATHEMATICS. (JA). **3516**

MATH HORIZONS. (US/1072-4117). **3518**

MATHEMATICAL COGNITION. (UK/1354-6791). **3518**

MATHEMATICAL LOGIC QUARTERLY. (GW/0942-5616). **3519**

MATHEMATICAL METHODS OF STATISTICS. (US/1066-5307). **3519**

MATHEMATICAL MODELING AND COMPUTATIONAL EXPERIMENT. (US/1061-7590). **3519**

MATHEMATICAL MODELLING AND SCIENTIFIC COMPUTING. (US/1067-0688). **3519**

MATHEMATICAL NOTES (ROSSIISKAIA AKADEMIIA NAUK). (US/1067-9073). **3519**

MATHEMATICAL RESEARCH LETTERS. (US/1073-2780). **3520**

MATHEMATICS TEACHING IN THE MIDDLE SCHOOL. (US/1072-0839). **3521**

MATHUSER. (US/1062-7030). **3522**

NEW ZEALAND JOURNAL OF MATHEMATICS. (NZ). **3524**

NOVA JOURNAL OF ALGEBRA AND GEOMETRY. (US/1060-9881). **3525**

NUMERICAL LINEAR ALGEBRA WITH APPLICATIONS. (UK/1070-5325). **3525**

POTENTIAL ANALYSIS : AN INTERNATIONAL JOURNAL DEVOTED TO THE INTERACTIONS BETWEEN POTENTIAL THEORY, PROBABILITY THEORY, GEOMETRY AND FUNCTIONAL ANALYSIS. (US/0926-2601). **3527**

REVUE D'HISTOIRE DES MATHEMATIQUES. (FR). **3531**

RUSSIAN JOURNAL OF NUMERICAL ANALYSIS AND MATHEMATICAL ANALYSIS. (NE/0927-6467). **3532**

RUSSIAN MATHEMATICS. (US/1066-369X). **3532**

SBORNIK. MATHEMATICS. (US/1064-5616). **3532**

SIAM JOURNAL ON SCIENTIFIC COMPUTING. (US/1064-8275). **3535**

SIBERIAN JOURNAL OF COMPUTER MATHEMATICS. (US/1062-8053). **3535**

ST. PETERSBURG MATHEMATICAL JOURNAL. (US/1061-0022). **3536**

STRUCTURAL EQUATION MODELING. (US/1070-5511). **3536**

TEACHING CHILDREN MATHEMATICS. (US/1073-5836). **3538**

TOPOLOGICAL METHODS IN NONLINEAR ANALYSIS. (PO/1230-3429). **3539**

TRUDY VYCHISLITELNOGO TSENTRA SO RAN. SERIIA SISTEMNOE MODELIROVANIE / ROSSIISKAIA AKADEMIIA NAUK, SIBIRSKOE OTDELENIE, VYCHISLITELNYI TSENTR. (RU). **3540**

UKRAINIAN MATHEMATICS JOURNAL. (US/1069-5346). **3540**

UKRAINSKYI MATEMATYCHNYI ZHURNAL. (UN). **3540**

VESTNIK SANKT-PETERBURGSKOGO UNIVERSITETA. SERIIA 1, MATEMATIKA, MEKHANIKA, ASTRONOMIIA. (RU). **3540**

VESTNIK ST. PETERSBURG UNIVERSITY: MATHEMATICS. (US/1063-4541). **3540**

MEDICAL SCIENCE AND TECHNOLOGY

ABMS RECORD. (US). **3543**

ACCREDITATION MANUAL FOR AMBULATORY HEALTH CARE : AMAHC. (US). **3543**

ADVANCES IN WOUND CARE. (US/1076-2191). **3546**

AIDS & TB WEEKLY ARTICLE SUMMARIES. (US/1074-2883). **3547**

AIR MEDICAL JOURNAL. (US/1067-991X). **3547**

ALTERNATIVE AND COMPLEMENTARY THERAPIES. (US/1076-2809). **3548**

AMERICAN JOURNAL OF THERAPEUTICS. (UK/1075-2765). **3549**

ANTIINFECTIVE DRUGS AND CHEMOTHERAPY. (GW). **3551**

APPLIED PARASITOLOGY. (GW/0943-0938). **3552**

APS JOURNAL. (US/1058-9139). **3552**

ARCHIVES OF MEDICAL RESEARCH. (MX/0188-0128). **3552**

Medical Science and Technology

ARTIFICIAL CELLS, BLOOD SUBSTITUTES, AND IMMOBILIZATION BIOTECHNOLOGY. (US/1073-1199). **3553**

ASPIRE INTERNATIONAL NEWSLETTER. (US/1065-2566). **3553**

AUDIO JOURNAL OF ONCOLOGY. (UK/1350-9667). **3553**

AUSTRALIAN JOURNAL OF MEDICAL SCIENCE. (AT/1038-1643). **3554**

AUSTRALIAN JOURNAL OF RURAL HEALTH, THE. (AT/1038-5282). **3554**

AVIAKOSMICHESKAIA I EKOLOGICHESKAIA MEDITSINA. (RU/0233-528X). **3554**

BIOCHEMICAL AND MOLECULAR MEDICINE. (US). **3556**

BIOLOGICAL ANALYSIS AND IMAGING METHODS. (US/1077-1034). **3556**

BMJ. BRITISH MEDICAL JOURNAL (SOUTH AFRICAN ED.). (SA/1019-8350). **3557**

BNA'S HEALTH CARE POLICY REPORT. (US/1068-1213). **3557**

BREAST DISEASES UPDATES. (US/1061-4575). **3558**

BREAST JOURNAL. (US/1075-122X). **3558**

CAMBRIDGE QUARTERLY OF HEALTHCARE ETHICS : CQ : THE INTERNATIONAL JOURNAL FOR HEALTHCARE ETHICS COMMITTEES. (US/0963-1801). **3561**

CAPITATION & MEDICAL PRACTICE. (US/1076-1047). **3562**

CENTERWATCH. (US). **3562**

CHINESE MEDICINE AND HEALTH. (US/1054-4704). **3563**

CHIROPRACTIC COLLEGE DIRECTORY, THE. (US). **3563**

CHUNG-KUO CHUNG HSI I CHIEH HO TSA CHIH. (CC/1003-5370). **3564**

CLINICAL INVESTIGATOR NEWS. (US/1068-1191). **3565**

CLINICAL PERFORMANCE AND QUALITY HEALTH CARE. (US/1063-0279). **3566**

CLINICAL PRACTICE GUIDELINE. (US). **3566**

CLINICAL PRACTICE GUIDELINES. (US/1066-677X). **3566**

COMPLEMENTARY THERAPIES IN NURSING AND MIDWIFERY. (UK/1353-6117). **3567**

CRITICAL CARE ALERT. (US/1067-9502). **3569**

CRITICAL CARE MANAGEMENT. (US/1070-4523). **3569**

CSRO. CANADIAN SPINAL RESEARCH ORGANIZATION. (CN/1193-7343). **3569**

CTDNEWS (PHILADELPHIA, PA.). (US/1062-6743). **3569**

CURRENT OPINION IN CRITICAL CARE. (UK/1070-5295). **3570**

CURRENT OPINION IN PULMONARY MEDICINE. (US/1070-5287). **3570**

CURRENT REVIEW OF CEREBROVASCULAR DISEASE. (US/1068-2252). **3570**

CURRENT REVIEW OF MAGNETIC RESONANCE IMAGING. (US/1072-8392). **3570**

CURRENT REVIEW OF PAIN. (US/1069-5850). **3570**

DETWILER DIRECTORY OF MEDICAL MARKET SOURCES, THE. (US/1058-2797). **3571**

DIAGNOSTIC AND THERAPEUTIC ENDOSCOPY. (SZ/1070-3608). **3571**

DR. ATKINS' HEALTH REVELATIONS. (US/1073-8169). **3573**

ECOSYSTEM HEALTH AND MEDICINE. (US/1076-2825). **3573**

EMERGING ISSUES IN BIOMEDICAL POLICY. (US/1062-3175). **3574**

EPSTEIN-BARR VIRUS REPORT. (UK). **3575**

EUROPEAN JOURNAL OF MEDICINE. (FR/1165-0478). **3575**

EUROPEAN JOURNAL OF ORIENTAL MEDICINE. (UK). **3575**

G & B : GIORNALE DI CLINIA MEDICA & BASI RAZIONALI DELLA TERAPIA. (IT/1120-8392). **3578**

GAIT & POSTURE. (UK/0966-6362). **3578**

GUIDE UNIVERSITAIRE DE LA MEDECINE. (CN/1188-1380). **3579**

HAEMOPHILIA. (UK/1351-8216). **3580**

HEALTH & MEDICAL YEAR BOOK. (US/1066-1786). **3581**

HEALTH CARE ANALYSIS. (UK/1065-3058). **3581**

HEALTH CARE ETHICS USA. (US/1072-5490). **3581**

HEALTH CARE REFORM WEEK. (US/1067-2214). **3581**

HEALTH INFORMATICS. (UK). **3582**

HEALTH MANAGEMENT TECHNOLOGY. (US/1074-4770). **3582**

HEALTHCARE CD-ROM/CD-I DIRECTORY. (US). **3583**

HEALTHCARE RECRUITMENT RESOURCE GUIDE. (US/1046-4603). **3583**

HOMECARE DIRECTION. (US/1069-4560). **3584**

INDIAN JOURNAL OF UNANI MEDICINE : DEVOTED TO INTERDISCIPLINARY RESEARCH IN UNANI MEDICINE AND ALLIED SCIENCES. (II). **3586**

INFORMATION MANAGEMENT IN HEALTH CARE / IM & T SERVICE. (UK/1353-8861). **3587**

INFORMATION MANAGEMENT IN HEALTH CARE / PRIMARY CARE SERVICE. (UK/1353-887X). **3587**

INFORMATION SYSTEMS IN GROUP PRACTICE SURVEY. (US/1065-8009). **3587**

INSTRUMENTATION SCIENCE AND TECHNOLOGY. (US/1073-9149). **3588**

INTERNATIONAL JOURNAL FOR QUALITY IN HEALTH CARE : JOURNAL OF THE INTERNATIONAL SOCIETY FOR QUALITY IN HEALTH CARE. (UK/1353-4505). **3588**

INTERNATIONAL JOURNAL OF OBESITY AND RELATED METABOLIC DISORDERS : JOURNAL OF THE INTERNATIONAL ASSOCIATION FOR THE STUDY OF OBESITY. (UK). **3589**

INTERNATIONAL JOURNAL OF REHABILITATION AND HEALTH. (US). **3589**

INTERNATIONAL MEDICAL IMAGE REGISTRY. (US). **3589**

JOURNAL OF AGROMEDICINE. (US/1059-924X). **3593**

JOURNAL OF ALTERNATIVE AND COMPLEMENTARY MEDICINE (NEW YORK, N.Y.), THE. (US/1075-5535). **3593**

JOURNAL OF BIOMEDICAL SCIENCE. (SZ/1021-7770). **3594**

JOURNAL OF BRAIN IMAGING AND BEHAVIOR. (US). **3594**

JOURNAL OF CLINICAL RHEUMATOLOGY. (US/1076-1608). **3594**

JOURNAL OF INVESTIGATIVE MEDICINE. (US). **3595**

JOURNAL OF OCCUPATIONAL AND ENVIRONMENTAL MEDICINE. (US/1076-2752). **3596**

JOURNAL OF QUALITY IN CLINICAL PRACTICE. (AT). **3597**

JOURNAL OF REFRACTIVE AND CORNEAL SURGERY. (US/0883-0444). **3597**

JOURNAL OF SEROTONIN RESEARCH. (UK). **3597**

JOURNAL OF SLEEP RESEARCH. (UK/0962-1105). **3597**

JOURNAL OF TELEMEDICINE AND TELECARE. (UK). **3597**

JOURNAL OF THE AMERICAN MEDICAL INFORMATICS ASSOCIATION. (US/1067-5027). **3597**

JOURNAL OF THE CHRONIC FATIGUE SYNDROMES. (US/1057-3321). **3598**

JOURNAL OF THE INTERAMERICAN MEDICAL AND HEALTH ASSOCIATION. (US/1060-3085). **3598**

JOURNAL OF VASCULAR INVESTIGATION. (UK/1353-8012). **3600**

JOURNAL OF VIRAL HEPATITIS. (UK/1352-0504). **3600**

JOURNAL OF WOMEN'S HEALTH. (US/1059-7115). **3600**

JOURNAL OF WOUND CARE. (UK/0969-0700). **3600**

LAPAROSCOPIC SURGERY UPDATE. (US/1067-2036). **3604**

LATEST WORD (PHILADELPHIA, PA.), THE. (US/1067-716X). **3604**

LIKARSKA SPRAVA. (UN/1019-5297). **3604**

MDA REPORTS. (US/1061-4370). **3606**

MEDIATORS OF INFLAMMATION. (UK/0962-9351). **3607**

MEDICAL DEVICE APPROVAL LETTER. (US/1060-8338). **3608**

MEDICAL IMAGING (PORTSMOUTH, R.I.). (US/1073-1202). **3609**

MEDICAL INDUSTRY EXECUTIVE. (US/1060-5193). **3609**

MEDICAL OUTCOMES & GUIDELINES ALERT. (US/1067-4195). **3610**

MEDICAL SOFTWARE REVIEWS. (US/1059-907X). **3611**

MEDICAL SUPPLY CATALOG / U.S. PUBLIC HEALTH SERVICE. (US). **3611**

MEDICAL TRIBUNE FOR THE FAMILY PHYSICIAN. (US). **3612**

MEDICAL UTILIZATION MANAGEMENT. (US). **3612**

MEDICAL WASTE ANALYST. (US/1072-6039). **3612**

New Title Index

Medical Science and Technology

MEDICINE, EXERCISE, NUTRITION, AND HEALTH. (US/1057-9354). **3613**

MEDICINE (NEW YORK, N.Y. 1993). (US/1066-4149). **3614**

MEDIGUIDE TO DEPRESSION IN PRIMARY CARE. (US/1065-0725). **3614**

MEDITSINSKAIA POMOSHCH / MEDICAL CARE / MINISTERSTVO ZDRAVOOKHRANENIA RF. (RU/0869-7760). **3614**

MEMBERSHIP DIRECTORY / AMERICAN COLLEGE OF OCCUPATIONAL AND ENVIRONMENTAL MEDICINE. (US). **3615**

MENOPAUSE (NEW YORK, N.Y.). (US/1072-3714). **3616**

METHODS & TECHNIQUES FOR THE CLINICAL LABORATORY. (US/1065-2760). **3616**

MIND / BODY MEDICINE. (CN/1195-1990). **3617**

MOLECULAR MEDICINE (CAMBRIDGE, MASS.). (US/1076-1551). **3618**

NATIONAL HEAD INJURY FOUNDATION'S TBI CHALLENGE!, THE. (US/1071-6262). **3619**

NATURE MEDICINE. (US). **3619**

NCRR REPORTER / NATIONAL CENTER FOR RESEARCH RESOURCES. (US). **3619**

NEUROBIOLOGY OF DISEASE. (UK/0969-9961). **3620**

NEW HORIZONS (BALTIMORE, MD.). (US/1063-7389). **3620**

NTIS ALERT. MEDICINE & BIOLOGY. (US). **3623**

OBESITY RESEARCH. (US/1071-7323). **3623**

OCCUPATIONAL MEDICINE. (UK/0962-7480). **3623**

OFFICIAL AMERICAN BOARD OF MEDICAL SPECIALTIES (ABMS) DIRECTORY OF BOARD CERTIFIED MEDICAL SPECIALISTS, THE. (US/0000-1406). **3623**

ONLINE JOURNAL OF CURRENT CLINICAL TRIALS, THE. (US/1059-2725). **3624**

ORAL DISEASES. (UK). **3624**

OTOLOGY-NEUROTOLOGY (NEW YORK, N.Y.). (US/1077-1123). **3624**

PAIN MEDICINE JOURNAL CLUB JOURNAL. (US). **3625**

PAIN REVIEWS. (UK/0968-1302). **3625**

PERIOPERATIVE OPTIONS AND OPPORTUNITIES. (US/1070-8979). **3626**

PERSONAL MEDICAL ADVISOR. (US/1065-0687). **3626**

PHYSICIAN COMPENSATION AND PRODUCTION SURVEY. (US/1064-4563). **3627**

PHYSICIANS' GUIDE TO RARE DISEASES. (US/1053-9727). **3627**

PRIMARY CARE LETTER. (US). **3629**

QJM : MONTHLY JOURNAL OF THE ASSOCIATION OF PHYSICIANS. (UK). **3631**

QUALITY IN HEALTH CARE : QHC. (UK/0963-8172). **3632**

READMORE REPORTER, THE. (US/1060-5673). **3632**

REDOX REPORT. (UK/1351-0002). **3633**

REGULATORY AFFAIRS JOURNAL (DEVICES), THE. (UK). **3633**

REHAB & COMMUNITY CARE MANAGEMENT. (CN/1192-2508). **3633**

RESIDENTS' PRESCRIBING REFERENCE. (US/1061-6632). **3634**

REVISTA DA ASSOCIACAO MEDICA BRASILEIRA. (BL). **3635**

RHODE ISLAND MEDICINE. (US/1061-222X). **3637**

RNA. THE OFFICIAL PUBLICATION OF THE RNA SOCIETY. (US/1355-8382). **3637**

ROSSISKII MEDITSINSKII ZHURNAL : ORGAN MINISTERSTVA ZDRAVOOKHRANENIIA RSFSR. (RU/0869-2106). **3637**

SCIENTIFIC AMERICAN FRONTIERS (MAGAZINE). (US/1068-6738). **3639**

SCIENTIFIC AMERICAN SCIENCE & MEDICINE. (US/1068-6746). **3639**

SEMINARS IN HEADACHE MANAGEMENT. (CN/1198-7340). **3640**

SEMINARS IN ORTHODONTICS. (US). **3640**

SMART DRUG NEWS. (US/1060-8427). **3641**

STANDARDS OF MEDICAL CARE. (US/1062-7162). **3642**

STATISTICAL METHODS IN MEDICAL RESEARCH. (UK/0962-2802). **3642**

STITCHES : THE JOURNAL OF MEDICAL HUMOUR. (CN). **3643**

TECHNOLOGY FOR HOME CARE. (US/1051-5682). **3644**

TISSUE ENGINEERING. (US/1076-3279). **3646**

TUMOR TARGETING. (UK/1351-8488). **3647**

UN-COMMON SENSE (LONG BEACH, CALIF.). (US/1062-080X). **3648**

VESTNIK AKADEMIE VED CESKE REPUBLIKY. (XR). **3649**

VESTNIK ROSSIISKOI AKADEMII MEDITSINSKIH NAUK / ROSSIISKAIA AKADEMIIA MEDITSINSKIKH NAUK. (RU). **3649**

WOMEN'S HEALTH JOURNAL. (US). **3651**

WOMEN'S HEALTH LETTER. (US/1062-4163). **3651**

WOUND REPAIR AND REGENERATION. (US/1067-1927). **3651**

XENOTRANSPLANTATION. (DK/0908-665X). **3652**

ABSTRACTING, BIBLIOGRAPHIES AND STATISTICS

AIDS ABSTRACTS (ATLANTA, GA.). (US/1066-1107). **3654**

ANALGESIAFILE (SAN ANTONIO, TEXAS). (US/1057-2260). **3549**

BIOENGINEERING ABSTRACTS (1993). (US/1068-5693). **3655**

BIOTECHNOLOGY ABSTRACTS. (UK). **3655**

CALCIUM AND CALCIFIED TISSUE ABSTRACTS. (US/1069-5540). **3655**

CINAHL (PEABODY, MASS.). (US). **3655**

CURRENT ADVANCES IN ENDOCRINOLOGY AND METABOLISM. (UK/0964-8720). **3656**

CURRENT ADVANCES IN IMMUNOLOGY & INFECTIOUS DISEASES. (UK/0964-8747). **3656**

CURRENT ADVANCES IN TOXICOLOGY. (UK/0965-0512). **3656**

CURRENT CONTENTS. CLINICAL MEDICINE (CD-ROM VERSION). (US/1073-1237). **3656**

EMBASE LIST OF JOURNALS INDEXED. (NE). **3657**

EXCERPTA MEDICA. SECTION 4. MICROBIOLOGY, BACTERIOLOGY, MYCOLOGY, PARASITOLOGY, AND VIROLOGY. (NE). **3657**

EXCERPTA MEDICA. SECTION 30. CLINICAL AND EXPERIMENTAL PHARMACOLOGY. (NE). **3658**

HEALTH PLANNING AND ADMINISTRATION. (US/1065-0679). **3659**

HOSPITAL AND HEALTH ADMINISTRATION INDEX. (US/1077-1719). **3659**

MEDICAL & PHARMACEUTICAL BIOTECHNOLOGY ABSTRACTS. (US/1063-1178). **3660**

PHYSICIAN'S MEDLINE PLUS. (US/1065-6545). **3661**

QUINTESSENCE (CHICAGO, ILL.). (US/1076-2833). **3661**

ALLERGY AND IMMUNOLOGY

AIDS ABSTRACTS : INTERNATIONAL LITERATURE ON ACQUIRED IMMUNODEFICIENCY SYNDROME AND RELATED RETROVIRUSES. (UK/0968-5480). **3663**

AIDS & TB WEEKLY ARTICLE SUMMARIES. (US). **3663**

AIDS DIRECTORY, THE. (US/1065-6162). **3663**

AIDS TARGETED INFORMATION. (US/1067-0718). **3664**

ARCHIVES OF STD/HIV RESEARCH. (US/1071-0906). **3666**

CLINICAL AND DIAGNOSTIC LABORATORY IMMUNOLOGY (CD-ROM). (US/1071-4138). **3667**

CLINICAL AND DIAGNOSTIC LABORATORY IMMUNOLOGY (PRINT). (US/1071-412X). **3667**

CLINICAL AND EXPERIMENTAL METABOLISM. (UK/1072-1630). **3668**

CLINICAL IMMUNOLOGY DIGEST. (US/1061-6969). **3668**

EXERCISE IMMUNOLOGY REVIEW. (US). **3669**

FEMS IMMUNOLOGY AND MEDICAL MICROBIOLOGY. (NE/0928-8244). **3669**

IMMUNITY (CAMBRIDGE, MASS.). (US/1074-7613). **3670**

IMMUNOLOGIST (TORONTO). (US/1192-5612). **3671**

IMMUNOMETHODS (SAN DIEGO, CALIF.). (US/1058-6687). **3672**

INTERNATIONAL ARCHIVES OF ALLERGY AND IMMUNOLOGY. (SZ/1018-2438). **3672**

JOURNAL OF IMMUNOTHERAPY WITH EMPHASIS ON TUMOR IMMUNOLOGY : OFFICIAL JOURNAL OF THE SOCIETY FOR BIOLOGICAL THERAPY. (US/1067-5582). **3674**

Medical Science and Technology — Emergency Medicine

JOURNAL OF PHARMACEUTICAL CARE IN AIDS/HIV TREATMENT. (US/1065-1799). **3674**

JOURNAL OF THE PHYSICIANS ASSOCIATION FOR AIDS CARE. (US/1074-2395). **3674**

MUCOSAL IMMUNOLOGY UPDATE : OFFICIAL PUBLICATION OF THE SOCIETY FOR MUCOSAL IMMUNOLOGY. (US/1068-7629). **3675**

NATURAL IMMUNITY. (SZ/1018-8916). **3675**

NEWSLETTER FOR PEOPLE WITH LACTOSE INTOLERANCE AND MILK ALLERGY. (US). **3675**

RMI ... REVIEW OF HIV & AIDS RESEARCH. (US). **3676**

THERAPEUTIC IMMUNOLOGY. (UK/0967-0149). **3677**

TRANSPLANT IMMUNOLOGY. (US/0966-3274). **3677**

VACCINE RESEARCH. (US/1056-7909). **3677**

VACCINE WEEKLY. (US/1074-2921). **3677**

ANATOMY

ANNALS OF ANATOMY. (GW/0940-9602). **3678**

DEVELOPMENTAL DYNAMICS. (US/1058-8388). **3679**

MORFOLOGIIA. (RU). **3679**

ANESTHESIOLOGY

ACTA ANAESTHESIOLOGICA SINICA. (CC). **3680**

AMERICAN JOURNAL OF ANESTHESIOLOGY, THE. (US/1078-4500). **3680**

ANAESTHETIC PHARMACOLOGY REVIEW. (UK). **3681**

ANALGESIA (ELMSFORD, N.Y.). (US/1071-569X). **3681**

OFFICIAL AMERICAN BOARD OF MEDICAL SPECIALTIES (ABMS) DIRECTORY OF BOARD CERTIFIED ANESTHESIOLOGISTS, THE. (US/0000-1546). **3683**

BIOTECHNOLOGY

BBSRC BUSINESS. (US). **3686**

BIOMATERIALS SCIENCE AND ENGINEERING. (US/1076-6286). **3686**

BIOMEDICAL ENGINEERING CITATION INDEX. (US/1062-5488). **3686**

BIOMEDICAL REVIEWS. (BU). **3687**

BIOMEDICAL TECHNOLOGY MANAGEMENT. (US/1073-1210). **3687**

BIOSCIENCE, BIOTECHNOLOGY, AND BIOCHEMISTRY. (JA/0916-8451). **3687**

BIOTECHNOLOGY WEEK. (US/1061-3471). **3690**

BRITISH JOURNAL OF BIOMEDICAL SCIENCE. (UK/0967-4845). **3690**

CANADIAN BIOTECH NEWS. (CN/1188-455X). **3690**

ENTREZ (BETHESDA, MD.). (US/1065-707X). **3692**

IEEE TRANSACTIONS ON REHABILITATION ENGINEERING. (US/1063-6528). **3693**

JAPANESE TECHNOLOGY REVIEWS. SECTION E, BIOTECHNOLOGY. (US/1058-7330). **3693**

JOURNAL OF APPLIED BIOMECHANICS. (US/1065-8483). **3694**

JOURNAL OF CARDIOVASCULAR DIAGNOSIS AND PROCEDURES. (US/1073-7774). **3694**

JPRS REPORT. SCIENCE & TECHNOLOGY. CENTRAL EURASIA, LIFE SCIENCES. (US). **3694**

MEDICAL ENGINEERING & PHYSICS. (UK/1350-4533). **3695**

MOLECULAR BIOTECHNOLOGY. (US/1073-6085). **3695**

PHYSIOLOGICAL MEASUREMENT. (UK/0967-3334). **3695**

RUSSIAN BIOTECHNOLOGY. (US/1068-3682). **3696**

SEIBUTSU KOGAKKAI SHI / SEIBUTSU-KOGAKU KAISHI. (JA/0919-3758). **3696**

TRANSGENICA (LEVITTOWN, PA). (US/1051-9688). **3697**

UNDERSEA & HYPERBARIC MEDICINE. (US/1066-2936). **3697**

CARDIOLOGY

ACC CURRENT JOURNAL REVIEW. (US/1062-1458). **3697**

ADVANCES IN HYPERTENSION. (US/1056-618X). **3698**

BLOOD PRESSURE. (NO/0803-7051). **3699**

CARDIOLOGY IN REVIEW. (US/1061-5377). **3701**

CARDIOLOGY IN THE ELDERLY. (US/1058-3661). **3701**

CARDIOLOGY JOURNAL CLUB JOURNAL. (US). **3701**

CARDIOVASCULAR NETWORK NEWS. (US/1076-4763). **3701**

CARDIOVASCULAR PATHOLOGY. (US/1054-8807). **3701**

CARDIOVASCULAR SURGERY : OFFICIAL JOURNAL OF THE INTERNATIONAL SOCIETY FOR CARDIOVASCULAR SURGERY. (UK/0967-2109). **3702**

CLINICAL AND APPLIED THROMBOSIS / HEMOSTATIS. (US). **3703**

CLINICAL AND EXPERIMENTAL HYPERTENSION (1993). (US/1064-1963). **3703**

CLINICAL PULMONARY MEDICINE. (US/1068-0640). **3703**

HYPERTENSION RESEARCH, CLINICAL AND EXPERIMENTAL. (JA/0916-9636). **3706**

INTERNATIONAL JOURNAL OF ANGIOLOGY, THE. (US/1061-1711). **3706**

INTERVENTIONAL CARDIOLOGY NEWSLETTER. (US/1063-4282). **3706**

INTERVENTIONAL CARDIOVASCULAR NEWSLETTER. (US). **3706**

JOURNAL OF CARDIAC FAILURE. (US/1071-9164). **3706**

JOURNAL OF HEART VALVE DISEASE, THE. (UK/0966-8519). **3707**

JOURNAL OF NUCLEAR CARDIOLOGY. (US/1071-3581). **3707**

JOURNAL OF VASCULAR RESEARCH. (SZ/1018-1172). **3707**

MEETING REPORTS, CARDIOVASCULAR. (US/1063-2468). **3708**

MULTI-FACT. (CN/1193-1884). **3708**

PROGRESS IN PEDIATRIC CARDIOLOGY. (US/1058-9813). **3709**

SLIDE ATLAS OF CURRENT CARDIOLOGY. (UK/1064-5969). **3710**

COMMUNICABLE DISEASES

BAILLIERE'S CLINICAL INFECTIOUS DISEASES. (UK/1071-6564). **3712**

CLINICAL INFECTIOUS DISEASES. (US/1058-4838). **3712**

CLINICAL MICROBIOLOGY REPORTS. (US/1062-8150). **3712**

GLOBAL ACCESS TO STD DIAGNOSTICS. (US/1063-8423). **3713**

GLOBAL AIDSNEWS: THE NEWSLETTER OF THE WORLD HEALTH ORGANIZATION GLOBAL PROGRAMME ON AIDS. (SZ/1020-007X). **3713**

INFECTION CONTROL WEEKLY. (US/1074-2905). **3714**

INFECTIOUS AGENTS AND DISEASE. (US/1056-2044). **3714**

KOREAN JOURNAL OF PARASITOLOGY, THE. (KO). **3715**

SELECTED REPORTABLE DISEASES BY HEALTH JURISDICTION. (US). **3716**

TB WEEKLY. (US/1065-982X). **3716**

DERMATOLOGY

DERMATOLOGIC SURGERY. (US/1076-0512). **3719**

DERMATOLOGY (BASEL). (SZ/1018-8665). **3719**

DERMATON. (GW). **3720**

DERMATOPATHOLOGY: PRACTICAL & CONCEPTUAL. (US/1078-4454). **3720**

EXPERIMENTAL DERMATOLOGY. (DK/0906-6705). **3720**

FITZPATRICK'S JOURNAL OF CLINICAL DERMATOLOGY. (US/1072-2521). **3720**

JOURNAL OF THE EUROPEAN ACADEMY OF DERMATOLOGY AND VENEREOLOGY : JEADV. (NE/0926-9959). **3721**

MEDICAL & SURGICAL DERMATOLOGY : A CRITICAL GUIDE TO THE WORLD LITERATURE. (US/0944-5196). **3721**

YEAR BOOK OF DERMATOLOGIC SURGERY. (US/1059-0587). **3723**

EMERGENCY MEDICINE

ACADEMIC EMERGENCY MEDICINE. (US/1069-6563). **3723**

Medical Science and Technology — Emergency Medicine

INSIDE AMBULATORY CARE. (US/1073-6506). **3724**

JOURNAL OF ACCIDENT & EMERGENCY MEDICINE. (UK/1351). **3725**

YEARBOOK OF INTENSIVE CARE AND EMERGENCY MEDICINE. (GW). **3726**

ENDOCRINOLOGY

CLINICAL ENDOCRINOLOGY (NEW YORK, N.Y.,1992). (US/1059-0471). **3727**

CURRENT OPINION IN ENDOCRINOLOGY & DIABETES. (US/1068-3097). **3727**

DIABETES REVIEWS (ALEXANDRIA, VA.). (US/1066-9442). **3728**

ENDOCRINE JOURNAL. (JA/0918-8959). **3729**

ENDOCRINOLOGY AND METABOLISM (LONDON, ENG.). (UK/1074-939X). **3729**

EUROPEAN JOURNAL OF ENDOCRINOLOGY / EUROPEAN FEDERATION OF ENDOCRINE SOCIETIES. (NO/0804-4643). **3730**

JOURNAL OF DIABETES AND ITS COMPLICATIONS. (US/1056-8727). **3731**

ROMANIAN JOURNAL OF ENDOCRINOLOGY / SPONSORE [SIC] BY THE ACADEMY OF MEDICAL SCIENCES. (RM). **3733**

YOUR PATIENT & FITNESS IN ENDOCRINOLOGY. (US/1062-371X). **3733**

EPIDEMIOLOGY

EPIDEMIOLOGIA E PSICHIATRIA SOCIALE. (IT/1121-189X). **3734**

MICROBIAL DRUG RESISTANCE, MECHANISMS, EPIDEMIOLOGY, AND DISEASE. (US/1076-6294). **3736**

FAMILY PRACTICE

ARCHIVES OF FAMILY MEDICINE. (US/1063-3987). **3736**

FAMILY PRACTICE MANAGEMENT. (US/1069-5648). **3737**

FAMILY PRACTICE RESIDENT, THE. (US/1063-8555). **3737**

GP WEEKLY. (NZ/1171-347X). **3738**

FORENSIC MEDICINE, MEDICAL JURISPRUDENCE

CLINICAL TRIALS MONITOR : MONTHLY MONITORING OF CLINICAL TRIALS OF HUMAN PHARMACEUTICALS. (US). **3740**

HEALTH LAW LITIGATION REPORTER. (US/1075-0606). **3740**

HOSPITAL LAW MANUAL BULLETIN. (US/1065-2817). **3740**

GASTROENTEROLOGY

GASTROENTEROLOGIST (BOSTON, MASS.), THE. (US/1065-2477). **3745**

GASTROENTEROLOGY MEDICINE TODAY. (US/1063-1291). **3745**

GASTROINTESTINAL DISEASES TODAY. (US/1061-6004). **3745**

ILLUSTRATED CASE REPORTS IN GASTROENTEROLOGY. (UK/1352-8513). **3746**

INTERNATIONAL SEMINARS IN PAEDIATRIC GASTROENTEROLOGY AND NUTRITION. (CN/1188-4525). **3746**

JOURNAL OF GASTROENTEROLOGY. (JA/0944-1174). **3747**

JOURNAL OF INFLAMMATORY BOWEL DISEASE. (US). **3747**

GERIATRICS

AUDIO-VISUAL GUIDE, RESOURCES IN GERONTOLOGY & GERIATRICS. (US). **3749**

BROWN UNIVERSITY GERIATRIC RESEARCH APPLICATION DIGEST, THE. (US/1067-7372). **3750**

CONTEMPORARY GERONTOLOGY. (US/1069-0840). **3750**

EUROPEAN JOURNAL OF GERONTOLOGY : THE JOURNAL OF THE EUROPEAN REGION OF THE INTERNATIONAL ASSOCIATION OF GERONTOLOGY. (SP). **3750**

FACTS AND RESEARCH IN GERONTOLOGY. (US). **3751**

JOURNAL OF AGING AND PHYSICAL ACTIVITY. (US/1063-8652). **3752**

JOURNAL OF GERONTOLOGY: PSYCHOLOGICAL SCIENCES AND SOCIAL SCIENCES, THE. (US). **3753**

JOURNALS OF GERONTOLOGY: BIOLOGICAL SCIENCES AND MEDICAL SCIENCES, THE. (US). **3753**

STATE-OF-THE-ART RESEARCH SUMMARIES. (US/1071-0000). **3755**

WISER NOW. (US/1071-2275). **3755**

GYNECOLOGY AND OBSTETRICS

ADVANCES IN OBSTETRICS AND GYNECOLOGY (ST. LOUIS, MO.). (US/1070-5392). **3756**

BREAST : OFFICIAL JOURNAL OF THE EUROPEAN SOCIETY OF MASTOLOGY, THE. (UK/0960-9776). **3758**

CESKA GYNEKOLOGIE / CESKA LEKARSKA SPOLECNOST J EV. PURKYNE. (XR). **3758**

EARLY PREGNANCY: BIOLOGY AND MEDICINE. (UK/1354-4195). **3760**

FETAL AND MATERNAL MEDICINE REVIEW. (UK/0965-5395). **3760**

GYNAECOLOGICAL ENDOSCOPY. (UK/0962-1091). **3761**

GYNAKOLOGISCH-GEBURTSHILFLICHE RUNDSCHAU. (SZ/1018-8843). **3761**

GYNECOLOGIE : REVUE DU GYNECOLOGUE. (FR). **3761**

HANDBOOK OF GYNECOLOGY & OBSTETRICS. (US/1062-5704). **3762**

HARVARD WOMEN'S HEALTH WATCH. (US/1070-910X). **3762**

HYPERTENSION IN PREGNANCY. (US/1064-1955). **3762**

INFECTIOUS DISEASES IN OBSTETRICS AND GYNECOLOGY. (US/1064-7449). **3762**

INTERNATIONAL JOURNAL OF FERTILITY AND MENOPAUSAL STUDIES. (US/1069-3130). **3762**

JOURNAL OF ASSISTED REPRODUCTION AND GENETICS. (US/1058-0468). **3763**

JOURNAL OF GYNECOLOGIC TECHNIQUES. (US/1069-2673). **3763**

JOURNAL OF MATERNAL-FETAL MEDICINE, THE. (US/1057-0802). **3763**

JOURNAL OF PERINATAL EDUCATION, THE. (US/1058-1243). **3764**

JOURNAL OF THE SOCIETY FOR GYNECOLOGIC INVESTIGATION. (US/1071-5576). **3764**

MIDWIFERY TODAY AND CHILDBIRTH EDUCATION. (US). **3765**

OB/GYN RESIDENT, THE. (US/1058-1677). **3766**

PRIMARY CARE UPDATE FOR OB/GYNS. (US/1068-607X). **3767**

REPRODUCTIVE MEDICINE REVIEW. (UK/0962-2799). **3767**

SCREENING: JOURNAL OF THE INTERNATIONAL SOCIETY OF NEONATAL SCREENING. (NE/0925-6164). **3768**

TELINDE'S OPERATIVE GYNECOLOGY UPDATES. (US/1060-5681). **3769**

HEMATOLOGY

BLOOD WEEKLY. (US/1065-6073). **3770**

CURRENT OPINION IN HEMATOLOGY. (US/1065-6251). **3771**

HEM/ONC ANNALS. (US/1067-2370). **3772**

INFUSIONSTHERAPIE UND TRANSFUSIONSMEDIZIN. (SZ/1019-8466). **3772**

JOURNAL OF PEDIATRIC HEMATOLOGY / ONCOLOGY. (US). **3773**

JOURNAL : THE JOURNAL OF THE AMERICAN BLOOD RESOURCES ASSOCIATION, THE. (US). **3773**

TRANSFUSION CLINIQUE ET BIOLOGIQUE. (FR). **3774**

HOMEOPATHY

JOURNAL OF INTERPROFESSIONAL CARE. (UK). **3775**

NATIONAL JOURNAL OF HOMOEOPATHY : NJH. (II). **3775**

HOSPITAL ADMINISTRATION AND MEDICAL CENTERS

ACCREDITATION MANUAL FOR HEALTH CARE NETWORKS. VOL. 1, STANDARDS. (US/1078-0076). **3775**

Medical Science and Technology —Neurology

ACCREDITATION MANUAL FOR HEALTH CARE NETWORKS. VOL. 2, SCORING GUIDELINES. (US/1077-9817). **3775**

AMAHC : ACCREDITATION MANUAL FOR AMBULATORY HEALTH CARE. (US). **3775**

AMERICAN JOURNAL OF MEDICAL QUALITY. (US/1062-8606). **3776**

AOHA PROGRESS : A PUBLICATION OF THE AMERICAN OSTEOPATHIC HOSPITAL ASSOCIATION. (US). **3777**

BUSINESS OF MANAGED CARE. (US/1072-1932). **3777**

COST SURVEY (1992). (US/1064-4571). **3778**

DUN'S HEALTHCARE REFERENCE BOOK. (US/1062-1679). **3780**

HEALTH CARE MANAGEMENT. (US/1069-6571). **3781**

HEALTH FACILITIES REPORT. (US/1062-4562). **3781**

HEALTHCARE ADVOCATE (EDMONTON). (CN/1197-4710). **3782**

HEALTHCARE PR & MARKETING NEWS. (US). **3782**

HOSPICE SALARY & BENEFITS REPORT. (US/1065-3155). **3783**

HOSPITAL MANAGED CARE & DIRECT CONTRACTING. (US/1061-7620). **3784**

HOSPITALS & HEALTH NETWORKS. (US/1068-8838). **3785**

INFORMATION MANAGEMENT IN HEALTH CARE / HOSPITAL SYSTEMS SERVICE. (UK/1353-8888). **3786**

JOINT COMMISSION JOURNAL ON QUALITY IMPROVEMENT, THE. (US/1070-3241). **3786**

JOURNAL OF CASE MANAGEMENT. (US/1061-3706). **3787**

LEADERSHIP IN HEALTH SERVICES. (CN/1188-3669). **3787**

MANAGED CARE (LANGHORNE, PA.). (US/1062-3388). **3788**

MATERIALS MANAGEMENT IN HEALTH CARE. (US/1059-4531). **3788**

MEDICAL PRACTICE MANAGEMENT NEWS. (US/1069-1944). **3788**

MEMBERSHIP DIRECTORY. (US). **3789**

PATIENT OUTCOMES. (US/1069-6520). **3790**

REGISTER OF NORTH AMERICAN HOSPITALS. (US/1062-7340). **3792**

REPORT ON HEALTHCARE INFORMATION MANAGEMNET. (US/1071-006X). **3792**

SATISFACTION (EVANS, GA.). (US/1063-9004). **3792**

TIJDSCHRIFT VOOR HYGIENE EN INFEKTIEPREVENTIE. (NE/0928-2998). **3793**

UPMC FORUM / UNIVERSITY OF PITTSBURGH MEDICAL CENTER. (US). **3793**

INTERNAL MEDICINE

CELL TRANSPLANTATION. (US/0963-6897). **3795**

FOCUS & OPINION, INTERNAL MEDICINE. (US/1072-0863). **3796**

HEMATOPOIETIC THERAPY. (US/1061-5318). **3797**

INTERNAL MEDICINE. (JA). **3797**

INTERNAL MEDICINE RESIDENT. (US/1058-1685). **3797**

INTERNATIONAL HEPATOLOGY COMMUNICATIONS. (NE/0928-4346). **3797**

JOURNAL OF HEMATOTHERAPHY. (US/1061-6128). **3798**

PROGRESS IN LIVER DISEASES (PHILADELPHIA, PA.). (US/1060-913X). **3800**

MUSCULOSKELETAL SYSTEM

BONE & JOINT DISEASES. (US/1063-0295). **3803**

BULLETIN / HOSPITAL FOR JOINT DISEASES. (US/0018-5647). **3804**

CHIROPRACTIC TECHNIQUE. (US). **3804**

EUROPEAN JOURNAL OF EXPERIMENTAL MUSCULOSKELETAL RESEARCH. (NO/0803-5288). **3804**

JOURNAL OF MUSCULOSKELETAL PAIN. (US/1058-2452). **3805**

JOURNAL OF THE NEUROMUSCULOSKELETAL SYSTEM. (US/1067-8239). **3805**

KNEE, THE. (UK/0968-0160). **3806**

MUSCULOSKELETAL MANAGEMENT. (UK/1355-3224). **3806**

NATIONAL DIRECTORY OF CHIROPRACTIC, THE. (US). **3806**

OSTEOARTHRITIS AND CARTILAGE. (UK/1063-4584). **3806**

REVUE DU RHUMATISME : MALADIES DES OS ET DES ARTICULATIONS. (FR/0035-2659). **3806**

TOPICS IN CLINICAL CHIROPRACTIC. (US/1073-2837). **3807**

YEAR BOOK OF CHIROPRACTIC. (US). **3807**

NEOPLASMA, NEOPLASTIC

BASIC AND CLINICAL ONCOLOGY. (US/1073-0028). **3809**

CAHIERS D'ONCOLOGIE. (FR/0941-3804). **3810**

CANCER BIOTHERAPY. (US/1062-8401). **3810**

CANCER GENE THERAPY. (US/0929-1903). **3811**

CANCER PRACTICE. (US/1065-4704). **3812**

CANCER RESEARCH, THERAPY & CONTROL. (SZ/1064-0525). **3812**

CANCER RESEARCHER WEEKLY. (US/1071-7226). **3812**

CANCER WATCH. (US/1059-3802). **3813**

CANCERMONTHLY (BREAST CANCER ED.). (US/1059-8928). **3814**

CANCERMONTHLY (CARCINOGENESIS AND EPIDEMIOLOGY ED.). (US/1059-8944). **3814**

CANCERMONTHLY (JOURNAL ED.). (US/1059-8987). **3814**

CANCERMONTHLY (RESEARCH ED.). (US/1059-8995). **3814**

CANCERMONTHLY (SMOKING AND LUNG CANCER ED.). (US/1059-8936). **3814**

CURRENT CANCER THERAPEUTICS. (US/1074-2816). **3815**

CURRENT CLINICAL CANCER. (UK/0969-692X). **3815**

EUROPEAN JOURNAL OF CANCER. PART B : ORAL ONCOLOGY. (UK/0964-1955). **3817**

GI CANCER. (US/1064-9700). **3817**

JOURNAL OF CANCER CARE. (UK/0960-9768). **3819**

JOURNAL OF ONCOLOGY MANAGEMENT, THE. (US/1061-9364). **3819**

LEUKEMIA & LYMPHOMA REVIEWS. (SZ/1060-6815). **3820**

MAMMOGRAPH ABSTRACTS : BREAST CANCER SCREENING REFERENCES. (UK/0962-0605). **3820**

MCGRAW-HILL'S CANCER & GENETICS REPORT. (US/1070-597X). **3820**

ONCOLOGIST'S POCKET GUIDE, THE. (US/1070-0900). **3821**

ONCOLOGY RESEARCH. (US/0965-0407). **3822**

PSYCHO-ONCOLOGY (CHICHESTER, ENGLAND). (UK/1057-9249). **3823**

RADIATION ONCOLOGY INVESTIGATIONS. (US/1065-7541). **3823**

SUPPORTIVE CARE IN CANCER : OFFICIAL JOURNAL OF THE MULTINATIONAL ASSOCIATION OF SUPPORTIVE CARE IN CANCER. (GW/0941-4355). **3824**

SURGICAL ONCOLOGY. (UK/0960-7404). **3824**

SURGICAL ONCOLOGY CLINICS OF NORTH AMERICA. (US/1055-3207). **3824**

NEUROLOGY

BAILLIERE'S CLINICAL NEUROLOGY. (UK/0961-0421). **3828**

CLINICAL NEUROSCIENCE (NEW YORK, N.Y.). (US/1065-6766). **3830**

COGNITIVE BRAIN RESEARCH. (NE/0926-6410). **3830**

CURRENT OPINION IN NEUROLOGY. (US/1350-7540). **3831**

DENDRON : AN INTERNATIONAL BIOMEDICAL JOURNAL FOR RESEARCH IN NEUROSCIENCE. (UK/0961-0898). **3831**

DEVELOPMENTAL BRAIN DYSFUNCTION. (SZ/1019-5815). **3831**

FOLIA NEUROPATHOLOGICA / ASSOCIATION OF POLISH NEUROPATHOLOGISTS AND MEDICAL RESEARCH CENTRE, POLISH ACADEMY OF SCIENCES. (PL). **3833**

HUMAN BRAIN MAPPING. (US/1065-9471). **3833**

INSIDE VIEW (IRVING, TEX.). (US/1065-7320). **3834**

JOURNAL OF DRUG THERPAY IN NEUROLOGICAL DISORDERS. (US). **3835**

JOURNAL OF NEURO-AIDS. (US/1069-7438). **3835**

JOURNAL OF NEUROVIROLOGY. (UK). **3837**

Medical Science and Technology — Neurology

JOURNAL OF OROFACIAL PAIN. (US/1064-6655). **3837**

JOURNAL OF THE HISTORY OF THE NEUROSCIENCES. (UK/0964-704X). **490**

MEETINGS REPORTS. CNS. (US/1063-245X). **3838**

MULTIPLE SCLEROSIS. (UK). **3838**

NDTA NETWORK. (US/1063-7664). **3839**

NEUROBIOLOGY. (HU). **3839**

NEURODEGENERATION (PHILADELPHIA, PA.). (US/1055-8330). **3839**

NEUROGASTROENTEROLOGY & MOTILITY. (UK). **3840**

NEUROIMAGE (SAN DIEGO, CALIF.). (US/1053-8119). **3840**

NEUROLOGIST (BALTIMORE, MD.), THE. (US/1074-7931). **3840**

NEUROPROTOCOLS (ORLANDO, FLA.). (US/1058-6741). **3841**

NEUROSCIENCE NEWSLETTER (COLLEGE STATION, TEX.). (US/1064-8712). **3842**

SEIZURE (LONDON, ENGLAND). (UK/1059-1311). **3846**

SEMINARS IN PEDIATRIC NEUROLOGY. (US/1071-9091). **3846**

NUCLEAR MEDICINE

NUCLEAR MEDICINE AND BIOLOGY. (UK). **3848**

OFFICIAL AMERICAN BOARD OF MEDICAL SPECIALTIES (ABMS) DIRECTORY OF BOARD CERTIFIED NUCLEAR MEDICINE SPECIALISTS, THE. (US/0000-1457). **3849**

NURSING

ACCIDENT AND EMERGENCY NURSING. (UK/0965-2302). **3850**

ADDICTIONS NURSING. (US/1073-886X). **3850**

AIDE-SOIGNANTE, L'. (FR). **3850**

AMERICAN JOURNAL OF CRITICAL CARE. (US/1062-3264). **3850**

AMERICAN SOCIETY OF POST ANESTHESIA NURSES (ASPAN). (US/1066-8977). **3851**

AONE'S LEADERSHIP PROSPECTIVES. (US/1072-5067). **3851**

ASORN NEWS. (US/1061-4338). **3851**

ASPEN'S NURSE EXECUTIVE NETWORK. (US/1064-8119). **3851**

AUSTRALIAN CRITICAL CARE : OFFICIAL JOURNAL OF THE CONFEDERATION OF AUSTRALIAN CRITICAL CARE NURSES. (AT/1036-7314). **3851**

AUSTRALIAN NURSING JOURNAL (JULY 1993). (AT). **3852**

BRITISH JOURNAL OF NURSING : BJN. (UK/0966-0461). **3852**

CAPSULES AND COMMENTS IN CRITICAL CARE NURSING. (US/1066-4815). **3853**

CAPSULES & COMMENTS IN NURSING LEADERSHIP & MANAGEMENT. (US/1068-6088). **3853**

CAPSULES AND COMMENTS IN ONCOLOGY NURSING. (US/1066-4114). **3853**

CAPSULES & COMMENTS IN PEDIATRIC NURSING. (US) **3853**

CAPSULES AND COMMENTS IN PSYCHIATRIC NURSING. (US). **3853**

CLINICAL NURSING RESEARCH. (US/1054-7738). **3853**

CONTEMPORARY NURSE : A JOURNAL FOR THE AUSTRALIAN NURSING PROFESSION. (AT/1037-6178). **3854**

ELDERLY CARE. (UK). **3855**

EMERGENCY NURSE : THE JOURNAL OF THE RCN ACCIDENT AND EMERGENCY NURSING ASSOCIATION. (UK). **3855**

HOME HEALTH FOCUS. (US/1075-2188). **3856**

INFIRMIERE DU QUEBEC. (CN/1195-2695). **3857**

INTENSIVE & CRITICAL CARE NURSING : THE OFFICIAL JOURNAL OF THE BRITISH ASSOCIATION OF CRITICAL CARE NURSES. (UK/0964-3397). **3857**

INTERNATIONAL JOURNAL OF TRAUMA NURSING. (US/1075-4210). **3857**

JOURNAL FOR HEALTHCARE QUALITY. (US/1062-2551). **3858**

JOURNAL OF CHILD AND ADOLESCENT PSYCHIATRIC NURSING. (US/1073-6077). **3858**

JOURNAL OF CLINICAL NURSING. (UK/0962-1067). **3858**

JOURNAL OF FAMILY NURSING. (US/1074-8407). **3858**

JOURNAL OF NURSING MANAGEMENT. (UK/0966-0429). **3859**

JOURNAL OF NURSING MEASUREMENT. (US/1061-3749). **3859**

JOURNAL OF WOUND, OSTOMY, AND CONTINENCE NURSING. (US/1071-5754). **3860**

MINIMALLY INVASIVE SURGICAL NURSING. (US/1068-5685). **3861**

MINORITY NURSE NEWSLETTER. (US/1071-9946). **3861**

NEW WORLD OF IRISH NURSING : OFFICIAL JOURNAL OF IRISH NURSES ORGANISATION AND NATIONAL COUNCIL OF NURSES, THE. (IE). **3862**

NURSES' DRUG GUIDE. (US/1062-9092). **3863**

NURSING DEPARTMENT COMPENSATION REPORT. (US/1066-6184). **3864**

NURSING ETHICS. (UK/0969-7330). **3864**

NURSING HISTORY REVIEW. (US/1062-8061). **3864**

NURSING NEW ZEALAND. (NZ/1172-1979). **3864**

NURSING STAFF DEVELOPMENT INSIDER. (US/1057-8323). **3865**

ONS NURSING SCAN IN ONCOLOGY. (US/1062-5720). **3866**

PETERSON'S GUIDE TO NURSING PROGRAMS. (US/1073-7820). **3867**

PFLEGE AKTUELL / DBFK, DEUTSCHER BERUFSVERBAND FUER PFLEGEBERUFE. (GW/0944-8918). **3867**

PRISM (NEW YORK, N.Y., 1993). (US/1068-476X). **3867**

PROGRESS IN PALLIATIVE CARE. (UK/0969-9260). **3867**

QUALITY OF LIFE. (US/1064-7988). **3867**

RECRUITMENT, RETENTION, & RESTRUCTURING REPORT. (US/1044-0666). **3868**

REHABILITATION NURSING RESEARCH. (US/1070-5767). **3868**

SEMINARS FOR NURSE MANAGERS. (US/1066-3851). **3869**

SEMINARS IN PERIOPERATIVE NURSING. (US/1056-8670). **3869**

SOINS. FORMATION, PEDAGOGIE, ENCADREMENT : AVEC LA PARTICIPATION DU CEEIEC. (FR/1163-4723). **3869**

STN'S JOURNAL OF TRAUMA NURSING. (US/1076-4747). **3870**

VOICES (WASHINGTON, D.C.). (US/1066-2944). **3870**

WEST VIRGINIA NURSE. (US/1074-8091). **3871**

WOMEN'S HEALTH NURSING SCAN (1993). (US/1070-308X). **3871**

OPHTHALMOLOGY

ADMINISTRATIVE OPHTHALMOLOGY. (US/1060-5991). **3871**

ADVANCES IN CLINICAL OPHTHALMOLOGY. (US/1070-5384). **3871**

GERMAN JOURNAL OF OPHTHALMOLOGY. (GW/0941-2921). **3875**

JOURNAL OF GLAUCOMA. (US/1057-0829). **3876**

JOURNAL OF NEURO-OPHTHALMOLOGY. (US/1070-8022). **3876**

OPHTHALMOLOGE : ZEITSCHRIFT DER DEUTSCHEN OPHTHALMOLOGISCHEN GESELLSCHAFT, DER. (GW/0941-293X). **3877**

OPHTHALMOLOGIA CROATICA. (CI/0353-9881). **3877**

OPTICAL PRACTITIONER. (UK). **3878**

OPTOMETRIC BUSINESS STRATEGIST. (US/1062-6395). **3878**

PROGRESS IN RETINAL AND EYE RESEARCH. (UK/1350-9462). **3878**

SLIDE ATLAS OF OPHTHALMIC LASER SURGERY. (US/1064-5446). **3879**

WORLD MEDICAL REVIEWS IN GLAUCOMA. (US/1062-774X). **3880**

ORTHOPEDICS

AMERICAN JOURNAL OF ORTHOPEDICS, THE. (US/1078-4519). **3880**

JOURNAL OF MANUAL & MANIPULATIVE THERAPY, THE. (US/1066-9817). **3882**

JOURNAL OF ORTHOPAEDIC SURGERY. (HK/1022-5536). **3882**

JOURNAL OF ORTHOPAEDIC TECHNIQUES. (US/1056-7437). **3882**

JOURNAL OF ORTHOPAEDICS. (UK/1353-3258). **3882**

Medical Science and Technology — Radiology

JOURNAL OF PEDIATRIC ORTHOPEDICS. PART B. (US/1060-152X). **3882**

JOURNAL OF THE CLINICAL ORTHOPAEDIC SOCIETY. (US/1069-6970). **3883**

JOURNAL OF THE SOUTHERN ORTHOPAEDIC ASSOCIATION. (US/1059-1052). **3883**

LOWER EXTREMITY, THE. (US/1068-6991). **3883**

OFFICIAL AMERICAN BOARD OF MEDICAL SPECIALTIES (ABMS) DIRECTORY OF BOARD CERTIFIED ORTHOPAEDIC SURGEONS, THE. (US/0000-1597). **3883**

ORTHOPAEDICS INTERNATIONAL EDITION. (US). **3884**

SPINE LETTER. (US/1072-3730). **3885**

OTORHINOLARYNGOLOGY

AUSTRALIAN JOURNAL OF OTO-LARYNGOLOGY : THE OFFICIAL JOURNAL OF THE AUSTRALIAN SOCIETY OF OTO-LARYNGOLOGY HEAD AND NECK SURGERY. (AT/1037-2105). **3887**

CURRENT OPINION IN OTOLARYNGOLOGY & HEAD AND NECK SURGERY. (US/1068-9508). **3887**

EUROPEAN ARCHIVES OF OTO-RHINO-LARYNGOLOGY. SUPPLEMENT. (GW/0934-2400). **3888**

FOLIA PHONIATRICA ET LOGOPAEDICA : OFFICIAL ORGAN OF THE INTERNATIONAL ASSOCIATION OF LOGOPEDICS AND PHONIATRICS (IALP). (SZ/1021-7762). **3888**

INDIAN JOURNAL OF OTOLARYNGOLOGY, AND HEAD, AND NECK : OFFICIAL PUBLICATION OF THE ASSOCIATION OF OTOLARYNGOLOGISTS OF INDIA. (II). **3888**

JOURNAL OF AUDIOLOGICAL MEDICINE. (UK/0963-7133). **3889**

OFFICIAL AMERICAN BOARD OF MEDICAL SPECIALTIES (ABMS) DIRECTORY OF BOARD CERTIFIED OTOLARYNGOLOGISTS, THE. (US/0000-1600). **3890**

OTOLARYNGOLOGY JOURNAL CLUB JOURNAL, THE. (US/1070-8049). **3890**

VOICE LONDON. 1992. (UK/0966-789X). **3891**

PATHOLOGY

ADVANCES IN ANATOMIC PATHOLOGY. (US/1072-4109). **3892**

GRIPE/ GROUP FOR RESEARCH IN PATHOLOGY EDUCATION. (US). **3894**

INTERNATIONAL JOURNAL OF SURGICAL PATHOLOGY. (US/1066-8969). **3895**

KLINICHESKAIA LABORATORNAIA DIAGNOSTIKA. (RU/0869-2084). **3896**

PATHOLOGY INTERNATIONAL. (AT/1320-5463). **3897**

PATHOLOGY (PHILADELPHIA, PA.). (US/1041-3480). **3897**

PEDIATRIC PATHOLOGY AND LABORATORY MEDICINE. (UK/1077-1042). **3897**

POLISH JOURNAL OF PATHOLOGY : OFFICIAL JOURNAL OF THE POLISH SOCIETY OF PATHOLOGISTS. (PL). **3897**

PEDIATRICS

ACTA PAEDIATRICA (OSLO). (NO/0803-5253). **3899**

ACTA PAEDIATRICA. SUPPLEMENT. (NO/0803-5326). **3899**

ARCHIVES DE PEDIATRIE : ORGANE OFFICIEL DE LA SOCIETE FRANCAISE DE PEDIATRIE. (FR/0929-693X). **3900**

ARCHIVES OF PEDIATRICS & ADOLESCENT MEDICINE. (US/1072-4710). **3900**

BAILLIERE'S CLINICAL PAEDIATRICS. (UK/0906-6714). **3900**

EMERGENCY AND OFFICE PEDIATRICS. (US/1073-7782). **3903**

GELLIS & KAGAN'S CURRENT PEDIATRIC THERAPY. (US/1069-2460). **3903**

JOURNAL OF SUDDEN INFANT DEATH SYNDROME AND INFANT MORTALITY. (US). **3905**

OFFICIAL AMERICAN BOARD OF MEDICAL SPECIALTIES (ABMS) DIRECTORY OF BOARD CERTIFIED PEDIATRICIANS, THE. (US/0000-1627). **3907**

PEDIATRIA / ASOCIATIA MEDICALA ROMANA, SOCIETATEA ROMANA DE PEDIATRIE. (RM/1220-580X). **3907**

PEDIATRIC PRIMARY CARE. (US/1071-5711). **3909**

PEDIATRIC ROUNDS. (US/1062-8789). **3909**

ROSSIISKII VESTNIK PERINATOLOGII I PEDIATRII / MINISTERSTVO ZDRAVOOKHRANENIIA ROSSIISKOI FEDERATSII, MOSKOVSKII NII PEDIATRII I DETSKOI KHIRURGII, MOSKOVSKII OBLASTNOI NII AKUSHERSTVA I GINEKOLOGII. (RU). **3911**

PHYSICIANS AND MEDICAL PERSONNEL

DIRECTORY OF PHYSICIANS IN THE UNITED STATES / AMERICAN MEDICAL ASSOCIATION. (US). **1925**

HEALTHCARE CAREER DIRECTORY. NURSES AND PHYSICIANS. (US). **3914**

HEALTHCARE HUMAN RESOURCES. (US/1060-9253). **3914**

MANAGEMENT & DOCTORS. (US/1071-3255). **3915**

MEDICAL TECHNOLOGISTS AND TECHNICIANS CAREER DIRECTORY. (US/1070-7271). **3915**

MENTAL HEALTH AND SOCIAL WORK CAREER DIRECTORY. (US/1070-7298). **3915**

PHYSICIAN SALARY SURVEY REPORT, HOSPITAL-BASED AND GROUP PRACTICE. (US). **3916**

THERAPISTS AND ALLIED HEALTH PROFESSIONALS CAREER DIRECTORY. (US/1070-7263). **3917**

PODIATRY

FOOT & ANKLE INTERNATIONAL. (US/1071-1007). **3918**

FOOT AND ANKLE QUARTERLY. (US/1068-3100). **3918**

PSYCHIATRY

ADVANCES IN PSYCHIATRIC TREATMENT. (UK). **3919**

AMITIE SP : BULLETIN DE L'ASSOCIATION QUEBECOISE DES AMIS DE LA SCLEROSE EN PLAQUES. (CN/1193-2805). **3920**

BAILLIERE'S CLINICAL PSYCHIATRY. (UK/1074-8806). **3921**

BEHAVIORAL INTERVENTIONS. (UK/1072-0847). **3921**

CANADIAN CHILD PSYCHIATRIC BULLETIN, THE. (CN/1188-7605). **3922**

CHILD AND ADOLESCENT PSYCHIATRIC CLINICS OF NORTH AMERICA. (US/1056-4993). **3923**

DEMENTIA REVIEWS. (US/1066-5056). **3924**

EUROPEAN CHILD AND ADOLESCENT PSYCHIATRY. (CN). **3925**

EUROPEAN CHILD & ADOLESCENT PSYCHIATRY. SUPPLEMENT. (CN). **3925**

FILIGRANE (MONTREAL). (CN/1192-1412). **3925**

HARVARD REVIEW OF PSYCHIATRY. (US/1067-3229). **3926**

INTERNATIONAL JOURNAL OF COMMUNICATIVE PSYCHOANALYSIS AND PSYCHOTHERAPY, THE. (US/1062-3051). **3927**

INTERNATIONAL REVIEW OF PSYCHIATRY (WASHINGTON, D.C.). (US/1066-3657). **3927**

JOURNAL OF CLINICAL PSYCHOANALYSIS. (US). **3928**

JOURNAL OF MENTAL HEALTH. (UK/0963-8237). **3929**

JOURNAL OF PSYCHOTHERAPY PRACTICE AND RESEARCH, THE. (US/1055-050X). **3929**

JOURNAL OF RELIGION IN PSYCHOTHERAPY. (US/1045-5876). **3929**

JOURNAL OF RUSSIAN AND EAST EUROPEAN PSYCHIATRY. (US/1061-0413). **3929**

MENNINGER LETTER, THE. (US/1066-937X). **3930**

PERSPECTIVES / ALBERTA ASSOCIATION OF REGISTERED OCCUPATIONAL THERAPISTS. (CN/1193-1248). **3932**

PRIMARY CARE PSYCHIATRY. (UK/1355-2570). **3932**

PROGRESS IN EXPERIMENTAL PERSONALITY AND PSYCHOPATHOLOGY RESEARCH. (US/1056-7151). **3932**

RADIOLOGY

ABDOMINAL IMAGING. (US/0942-8925). **3938**

BULLETIN / AMERICAN COLLEGE OF RADIOLOGY. (US). **3939**

CURRENT TECHNIQUES IN INTERVENTIONAL RADIOLOGY. (US/1068-3879). **3940**

EMERGENCY RADIOLOGY. (US/1070-3004). **3941**

IMAGING : AN INTERNATIONAL JOURNAL OF CLINICO-RADIOLOGICAL PRACTICE. (UK/0965-6812). **3942**

IMAGING DECISIONS. (US/1073-9718). **3942**

Medical Science and Technology — Radiology

MRI CLINICS OF NORTH AMERICA. (US/1064-9689). **3944**

RADIATION THERAPIST: THE JOURNAL OF THE RADIATION ONCOLOGY SCIENCES. (US). **3944**

RADIOLOGIST (BALTIMORE, MD.), THE. (US/1069-1286). **3945**

SEMINARS IN RADIOLOGIC TECHNOLOGY. (US/1070-535X). **3946**

YEAR BOOK OF NEURORADIOLOGY, THE. (US/1062-337X). **3947**

RESPIRATORY SYSTEM

AMERICAN JOURNAL OF RESPIRATORY AND CRITICAL CARE MEDICINE. (US/1073-449X). **3948**

ASTHMA MANAGEMENT. (US/1050-5253). **3948**

CLINICAL ADVANCES IN CARDIO-RESPIRATORY CARE. (US/1073-1644). **3949**

JOURNAL OF BRONCHOLOGY. (US/1070-8030). **3950**

MONALDI ARCHIVES FOR CHEST DISEASE. ARCHIVIO MONALDI PER LE MALATTIE DEL TORACE / FONDAZIONE CLINICA DEL LAVORO, IRCCS [AND] ISTITUTO DI CLINICA TISIOLOGICA E MALATTIE APPARATO RESPIRATORIO, UNIVERSITA DI NAPOLI, SECONDO ATENEO. (IT). **3950**

RESPIRATORY CARE MANAGER. (US/1076-6030). **3951**

SEMINARS IN RESPIRATORY AND CRITICAL CARE MEDICINE. (US/1069-3424). **3952**

TUBERCLE AND LUNG DISEASE : THE OFFICIAL JOURNAL OF THE INTERNATIONAL UNION AGAINST TUBERCULOSIS AND LUNG DISEASE. (UK/0962-8479). **3952**

SPORTS MEDICINE

ACSM MEMBERSHIP DIRECTORY/ AMERICAN COLLEGE OF SPORTS MEDICINE. (US). **3953**

ATHLETIC TRAINING (ST. LOUIS, MO.). (US/1076-5786). **3953**

CURRENT REVIEW OF SPORTS MEDICINE. (US/1069-5842). **3953**

JOURNAL OF SPORT REHABILITATION. (US/1056-6716). **3954**

OPERATIVE TECHNIQUES IN SPORTS MEDICINE. (US/1060-1872). **3955**

PENNSTATE SPORTS MEDICINE NEWSLETTER. (US/1064-2188). **3955**

PHYS ED JOURNAL OF SPORTS MEDICINE, THE. (US/1062-9297). **3955**

SCHWEIZERISCHE ZEITSCHRIFT FUER MEDIZIN UND TRAUMATOLOGIE. (SZ/1022-6699). **3955**

SPORTS, EXERCISE AND INJURY. (UK/1351-0029). **3956**

SPORTS MEDICINE AND ARTHROSCOPY REVIEW. (US/1062-8592). **3956**

SURGERY

ADVANCES IN VASCULAR SURGERY. (US/1069-7292). **3958**

AMBULATORY SURGERY. (UK/0966-6532). **3958**

ANNALS OF SURGICAL ONCOLOGY. (US/1068-9265). **3959**

ASAIO JOURNAL (1992). (US/1058-2916). **3960**

ATLAS OF THE ORAL AND MAXILLOFACIAL SURGERY CLINICS OF NORTH AMERICA. (US/1061-3315). **3960**

BODY CONTOURING SURGERY. (US/1065-2523). **3960**

CURRENT OPINION IN GENERAL SURGERY. (US/1065-6243). **3963**

CURRENT OPINION IN SURGICAL INFECTIONS. (UK/0969-8868). **3963**

CURRENT TECHNIQUES IN ARTHROSCOPY. (US/1068-4107). **3963**

CURRENT TECHNIQUES IN SURGERY. (US/1065-0717). **3963**

EUROPEAN SPINE JOURNAL : OFFICIAL PUBLICATION OF THE EUROPEAN SPINE SOCIETY, THE EUROPEAN SPINAL DEFORMITY SOCIETY, AND THE EUROPEAN SECTION OF THE CERVICAL SPINE RESEARCH SOCIETY. (GW/0940-6719). **3964**

FACIAL PLASTIC SURGERY CLINICS OF NORTH AMERICA. (US/1064-7406). **3965**

JOURNAL OF ENDOVASCULAR SURGERY. (US/1074-6218). **3967**

JOURNAL OF FOOT AND ANKLE SURGERY, THE. (US/1067-2516). **3967**

JOURNAL OF MEDICAL BIOGRAPHY. (UK/0967-7720). **3967**

JOURNAL OF SHOULDER AND ELBOW SURGERY. (US/1058-2746). **3968**

JOURNAL OF THE AMERICAN COLLEGE OF SURGEONS. (US/1072-7515). **3968**

KNEE SURGERY, SPORTS TRAUMATOLOGY, ARTHROSCOPY. (GW/0942-2056). **3969**

LAPAROSCOPIC SURGERY. (CN/1188-0252). **3969**

LIPPINCOTT'S ORAL AND MAXILLOFACIAL SURGERY. (US/1064-6698). **1329**

LIVER TRANSPLANTATION AND SURGERY. (US/1074-3022). **3969**

MEDSURG NURSING : OFFICIAL JOURNAL OF THE ACADEMY OF MEDICAL- SURGICAL NURSES. (US). **3969**

MVP VIDEO JOURNAL OF GENERAL SURGERY. (US/1058-1650). **3970**

O.R. PRODUCT DIRECTORY / ASSOCIATION OF OPERATING ROOM NURSES. (US). **3970**

OFFICIAL AMERICAN BOARD OF MEDICAL SPECIALTIES (ABMS) DIRECTORY OF BOARD CERTIFIED SURGEONS, THE. (US/0000-1678). **3971**

OFFICIAL AMERICAN BOARD OF MEDICAL SPECIALTIES (ABMS) DIRECTORY OF BOARD CERTIFIED THORACIC SURGEONS, THE. (US/0000-1481). **3971**

OPERATIVE TECHNIQUES IN PLASTIC AND RECONSTRUCTIVE SURGERY. (US/1071-0949). **3971**

OR REPORTS. (US/1065-8173). **3971**

SEMINARS IN LAPAROSCOPIC UURGERY. (US/1071-5517). **3974**

SEMINARS IN PEDIATRIC SURGERY. (US/1055-8586). **3974**

SLS REPORT, THE. (US/1060-9458). **3975**

YEAR BOOK OF TRANSPLANTATION. (US/1060-2968). **3978**

TOXICOLOGY

EXPERIMENTAL AND TOXICOLOGIC PATHOLOGY : OFFICIAL JOURNAL OF THE GESELLSCHAFT FUR TOXIKOLOGISCHE PATHOLOGIE. (GW/0940-2993). **3980**

INTERNATIONAL JOURNAL OF TOXICOLOGY, OCCUPATIONAL, AND ENVIRONMENTAL HEALTH. (II). **3981**

JOURNAL OF NATURAL TOXINS. (US/1058-8108). **3981**

JOURNAL OF OCCUPATIONAL MEDICINE AND TOXICOLOGY. (US/1054-044X). **3981**

MEDICAL TOXICOLOGY. (US). **3982**

NATURAL TOXINS. (US/1056-9014). **3983**

REVUE DOCUMENTAIRE - TOXIBASE LYON. (FR/1240-2494). **3983**

TOXIC SUBSTANCE MECHANISMS. (UK/1076-9188). **3983**

TOXICOLOGY AND ECOTOXICOLOGY NEWS. (UK/1350-4592). **3984**

UROLOGY AND NEPHROLOGY

ATLAS OF THE UROLOGIC CLINICS OF NORTH AMERICA. (US/1063-5777). **3988**

CURRENT OPINION IN NEPHROLOGY AND HYPERTENSION. (US/1062-4821). **3989**

JN. JOURNAL OF NEPHROLOGY. (IT/1121-8428). **3990**

JOURNAL OF UROLOGIC PATHOLOGY. (US/1067-1919). **3991**

KIDNEY: A CURRENT SURVEY OF WORLD LITERATURE. (US/0940-7936). **3991**

YEAR BOOK OF NEPHROLOGY, THE. (US/1046-6266). **3994**

MEN'S INTERESTS

DIRT (NEW YORK, N.Y.). (US/1061-8481). **3995**

GROOM'S GUIDE, THE. (US/1056-4551). **3995**

HOMBRE INTERNACIONAL. (US/1064-8976). **3995**

HOT ROD SWIMSUIT SPECIAL. (US/1066-4181). **3995**

INSIDE EDGE FOR MEN. (US/1064-7597). **3995**

JOURNAL OF MEN'S STUDIES, THE. (US/1060-8265). **3995**

KEEN ON NEW YORK SURVEY OF TOP-RATED SERVICES, THE. (US/1058-6652). **3995**

MASCULINITIES : OFFICIAL PUBLICATION OF THE MEN'S STUDIES ASSOCIATION, NATIONAL ORGANIZATION FOR MEN AGAINST SEXISM. (US/1072-8538). **3995**

MEN'S CONFIDENTIAL. (US/1066-5706). **3995**

MEN'S JOURNAL (NEW YORK, N.Y.). (US/1063-4657). **3996**

OFFICIAL STRIP JOINT GUIDE : THE O.S.J.G, THE. (US/1065-8327). **3996**

PLAYBOY PRESENTS INTERNATIONAL PLAYMATES. (US/1062-2284). **3996**

PLAYBOY'S BEAUTY QUEENS. (US/1063-9608). **3996**

PLAYBOY'S CALENDER GIRLS. (US/1063-9616). **3996**

PLAYBOY'S CAREER GIRLS. (US/1061-9070). **3996**

PLAYBOY'S GIRLS OF THE WORLD. (US/1061-9089). **3996**

PLAYBOY'S TWINS. (US/1066-5110). **3996**

METALS AND METALLURGY

ADVANCES IN POWDER METALLURGY & PARTICULATE MATERIALS. (US/1065-5824). **3997**

AUTOMOTIVE INTELLIGENCE REPORTS' METALWORKING. (US/1071-3220). **3998**

INTERMETALLICS. (UK/0966-9795). **4004**

JOURNAL OF SUPERHARD MATERIALS. (US/1063-4576). **4006**

JOURNAL OF THERMAL SPRAY TECHNOLOGY. (US/1059-9630). **4006**

METAL HEAT TREATING. (US/1075-5594). **4009**

METALLURGICAL AND MATERIALS TRANSACTIONS. B, PROCESS METALLURGY AND MATERIALS PROCESSING SCIENCE. (US/1073-5615). **4010**

METALLURGICAL AND MATERIALS TRANSACTIONS. PHYSICAL METALLURGY AND MATERIALS SCIENCE. (US/1073-5623). **4010**

METALURGIA & MATERIAIS / ABM. (BL). **4011**

MONOGRAPHS IN P/M SERIES. (US/1061-6071). **4013**

NEW STEEL. (US/1074-1690). **4013**

OCCUPATIONAL COMPENSATION SURVEY--PAY ONLY. NEW YORK, NEW YORK, METROPOLITAN AREA. (US). **4014**

PLATT'S METALS WEEK. (US/1076-3937). **4015**

POWDER METALLURGY AND METAL CERAMICS. (US/1068-1302). **4015**

RUSSIAN CASTINGS TECHNOLOGY. (US/1068-3690). **4018**

RUSSIAN JOURNAL OF NON-FERROUS METALS. (US/1067-8212). **4018**

STEEL IN TRANSLATION. (US/0967-0912). **4020**

WHAT'S NEW IN WELDING. (CN/1191-9833). **4023**

ZINC IN ... / PREPARED IN THE BRANCH OF METALS AND BRANCH OF DATA COLLECTION AND COORDINATION. (US). **4025**

ABSTRACTING, BIBLIOGRAPHIES AND STATISTICS

ALUMINIUM INDUSTRY ABSTRACTS. (US/1066-0623). **4025**

WELDING

TWI JOURNAL. (UK/0963-6927). **4028**

METROLOGY AND STANDARDIZATION

BECKMAN FOCUS. (GW). **4029**

NORMALISATIE-NIEUWS (DELFT). (NE/0929-2985). **4032**

QUALITY WORLD. TECHNICAL SUPPLEMENT. (UK). **4032**

MILITARY AND DEFENSE

ARMS CONTROL DISCUSSION PAPERS. (US/1065-6383). **4036**

ARMY CHAPLAINCY : PROFESSIONAL BULLETIN OF THE UNIT MINISTRY TEAM, THE. (US). **4036**

ASSAULT RIFLES. (US/1059-5708). **4037**

BASIC REPORTS. (UK/0966-9175). **4037**

BMD MONITOR. (US/1069-8175). **4038**

BRASSEY'S DEFENCE YEARBOOK / EDITED BY THE CENTRE FOR DEFENCE STUDIES. (UK). **4038**

CANADIAN MILITARY HISTORY. (CN/1195-8472). **4038**

DEFENSE ACQUISITION REPORT. (US/1072-2386). **4040**

DEFENSE CONTRACT AWARDS. (US/1062-0613). **4041**

DEFENSE CONVERSION. (US/1065-8653). **4041**

DEFENSE INTELLIGENCE JOURNAL. (US/1061-6845). **4041**

DEFENSE / INTERNATIONAL DEFENSE REVIEW. (UK). **4041**

DEPOT MILITAIRE. (US/1064-2153). **4042**

EAGLE : INFORMATION FOR CALIFORNIA VETERANS FROM THE CALIFORNIA EMPLOYMENT DEVELOPMENT DEPARTMENT, THE. (US). **4043**

EW REFERENCE & SOURCE GUIDE. (US). **4043**

FOREIGN MILITARY MARKETS, ASIA & PACIFIC RIM. (US). **4044**

FOREIGN MILITARY MARKETS, LATIN AMERICA & CARIBBEAN BASIN. (US). **4044**

JANE'S MILITARY VEHICLES AND LOGISTICS. (UK). **4047**

JOURNAL OF SLAVIC MILITARY STUDIES, THE. (UK). **4048**

JOURNAL OF THE MILITARY HISTORY SOCIETY OF MANITOBA. (CN/1188-164X). **4048**

JPRS REPORT. CENTRAL EURASIA. MILITARY AFFAIRS / FOREIGN BROADCAST INFORMATION SERVICE. (US). **4048**

MARINE SOCIETY VIEWS. (US/1060-2607). **4049**

MILITARY HISTORY OF THE WEST. (US/1071-2011). **4050**

NDT UPDATE. (US/1063-3588). **4052**

PROCEEDINGS OF THE SUBCOMMITTEE ON SECURITY AND NATIONAL DEFENCE. (CN/1193-1612). **4054**

PROCEEDINGS OF THE SUBCOMMITTEE ON SECURITY AND NATIONAL DEFENCE (FRENCH EDITION). (CN/1193-1612). **4054**

R & R MILITARY RETIREE: RETIREMENT & RELOCATION MILITARY RETIREE. (US/1055-2081). **4054**

SOLDIERS TODAY. (US/1059-194X). **4057**

STATEMENT ON NATIONAL SECURITY / BY THE SOLICITOR GENERAL OF CANADA. (CN/1191-4653). **4058**

TECHNOLOGY TRANSFER WEEK. (US). **4059**

TERRORISM, SECOND SERIES. (US/1064-9352). **4059**

MOTION PICTURE

AMIA NEWSLETTER. (US/1075-6477). **4063**

ANIMATION JOURNAL. (US/1061-0308). **4063**

AUSTRALIAN AND NEW ZEALAND CATALOGUE OF NEW FILMS AND VIDEOS, THE. (AT/1035-8005). **4064**

CINEMATHEQUE : REVUE SEMESTRIELLE D'ESTHETIQUE ET D'HISTOIRE DU CINEMA. (FR). **4067**

FILM ANNUAL. (US/1061-4214). **4069**

FILMMAKER (LOS ANGELES, CALIF.). (US/1063-8954). **4071**

FOCAL POINT. (CN/1189-5012). **4071**

HITCHCOCK ANNUAL. (US/1062-5518). **4072**

LISTE DES FILMS VISES PAR CATEGORIES DE SPECTATEURS, DIFFUSION PRIVEE. (CN/1191-7423). **4074**

MAGILL'S SURVEY OF CINEMA. (US/1065-6553). **4074**

MENSUEL DU CINEMA, LE. (FR/1242-0492). **4074**

ON PRODUCTION AND POST-PRODUCTION. (US/1067-6120). **4075**

PAUL KAGAN'S BOX OFFICE CHAMPIONS. DIRECTORS. (US/1063-2573). **4076**

ROGER EBERT'S VIDEO COMPANION. (US/1072-561X). **4077**

SCREEN (CHICAGO, ILL.). (US/1070-7573). **4077**

SCREEN INTERNATIONAL. THE INTERNATIONAL FILM & TELEVISION DIRECTORY. (UK). **4077**

VPM MAGAZINE. (CN). **4079**

MOTORCYCLES

INSIDE MOTOCROSS MAGAZINE. (US/1066-419X). **4081**

Motorcycles

MOTORCYCLE CONSUMER NEWS. (US/1073-9408). **4082**

OFFICIEL DU CYCLE ET DE LA MOTO PARIS, L'. (FR/1240-8751). **4082**

SUPERCROSS. (US/1065-9234). **4083**

MUSEUMS AND GALLERIES

ANH / THE AUSTRALIAN MUSEUM TRUST. (AT). **4083**

BULLETIN / WAMP, WEST AFRICAN MUSEUMS PROGRAMME. (UK). **4086**

EXPLORING MAGAZINE. (US). **4087**

HARVARD UNIVERSITY ART MUSEUMS REVIEW. (US/1065-819X). **4088**

JOURNAL - ART GALLERY OF ONTARIO. (CN/1191-9868). **4090**

MUSEUM INTERNATIONAL. (UK/1350-0775). **4092**

MUSEUM NATIONAL. (AT). **4092**

MUSEUMNEWS (HALIFAX). (CN/1191-0925). **4093**

ONTARIO MUSEUM ANNUAL. (CN/1188-9578). **4095**

PACHACAMAC : REVISTA DEL MUSEO DE LA NACION. (PE). **4095**

MUSIC

AMERICAN LISZT SOCIETY STUDIES SERIES. (US/1062-4031). **4099**

AMERICAN MUSIC RESEARCH CENTER JOURNAL, THE. (US/1058-3572). **4099**

BACH PERSPECTIVES. (US/1072-1924). **4101**

BIBLIOGRAPHIE NATIONALE FRANCAISE. MUSIQUE : BIBLIOGRAPHIE ETABLIE PAR LA BIBLIOTHEQUE NATIONALE. (FR). **4103**

BIG CITY MUSIC. (US/1042-9263). **4103**

BILLBOARD INTERNATIONAL LATIN MUSIC BUYER'S GUIDE. (US). **4103**

BIO-CRITICAL SOURCE BOOKS ON MUSICAL PERFORMANCE. (US/1069-5230). **4103**

BOTTIN DE L'INDUSTRIE DE LA MUSIQUE AU QUEBEC. (CN/1187-9580). **4104**

CATHOLIC MUSIC EDUCATOR. (US/1059-9088). **4108**

CHANTER (MONTREAL). (CN/1192-1900). **4109**

CHOIR & ORGAN. (UK/0968-7262). **4109**

CIRCUIT (MONTREAL. 1991). (CN/1183-1693). **4110**

CLASSIC CD (U.S. ED.). (US/1070-4574). **4110**

COUNTRY FEVER. (US/1066-0453). **4112**

CRANK (PHILADELPHIA, PA.). (US/1076-9102). **4113**

CREEM (NEW YORK, N.Y.). (US/0011-1147). **4113**

CRESCENDO & JAZZ MUSIC. (UK/0962-7472). **4113**

DANCEHALL (TORONTO). (CN/1183-4048). **4113**

DEUTSCHE NATIONALBIBLIOGRAPHIE UND BIBLIOGRAPHIE DER IM AUSLAND ERSCHIENEN DEUTSCHSPRACHIGEN VEROFFENTLICHUNGEN. REIHE T, MUSIKTONTRAGER MONATLICHES VERZEICHNIS. (GW/0939-0642). **4114**

DISCO-MAGAZIN. (GW). **4115**

ETHNOMUSICOLOGY AND SYSTEMATIC MUSICOLOGY AT UCLA. (US). **4117**

FLY! (BALDWIN, N.Y.). (US/1065-4631). **4118**

FOLK MUSIC CATALOGUE. (CN/1186-7523). **4118**

GUITAR CLASSICS, THE. (US/1061-4400). **4120**

I/E (CHANDLER, ARIZ.). (US/1064-9859). **4122**

INTERNATIONAL DIRECTORY OF CONTEMPORARY MUSIC. COMPOSERS. (US/1054-6669). **4123**

INTERNATIONAL DIRECTORY OF CONTEMPORARY MUSIC. INSTRUMENTATION. (US/1054-6677). **4123**

INTERNATIONAL DIRECTORY OF OPERA. (US). **4123**

ISO NEWS : THE QUARTERLY MAGAZINE OF THE INTERNATIONAL SOCIETY OF ORGANBUILDERS. (BE/1017-7515). **4124**

KEYBOARD CLASSICS & PIANO STYLIST. (US/1069-4285). **4127**

LIGHTHOUSE (UNIVERSITY PARK, PA.), THE. (US/1070-6690). **4128**

LISTEN (NEW YORK, N.Y. 1991). (US/1054-3104). **4129**

LIVE WIRE (NEW YORK, N.Y. 1991). (US/1059-4809). **4129**

MESSAGE IN THE MUSIC. (US/1056-554X). **4131**

METAL CD. (UK/0967-442X). **4131**

MOBILE BEAT INTERNATIONAL. (US/1058-0212). **4131**

MODERN SCREEN'S COUNTRY MUSIC. (US/1070-5104). **4131**

MOTIV. (GW). **4132**

MUSIC CITY NEWS (1994). (US/1078-5558). **4133**

MUSIC MADNESS MAGAZINE. (US/1061-8376). **4134**

MUSIC OF THE BABA ALLAUDDIN GHARANA AS TAUGHT BY ALI AKBAR KHAN AT THE ALI AKBAR COLLEGE OF MUSIC, THE. (US/1057-0934). **4134**

MUSIC REFERENCE SERVICES QUARTERLY. (US/1058-8167). **4134**

MUSIC VIDEO MAGAZINE. (US/1065-0229). **4135**

MUSICAL PERFORMANCE. (SZ/1049-8869). **4136**

MUSICIAN MAGAZINE SPECIAL EDITION SERIES. (US/1064-5411). **4137**

MUSICIANS GUIDE TO TOURING & PROMOTION, THE. (US/1062-4759). **4137**

MUSIKALNAIA AKADEMIIA. (RU). **4138**

MUZE / EBSCO CD-ROM. (US). **4139**

NEWS BULLETIN / THE MUSICAL BOX SOCIETY INTERNATIONAL. (US/1071-0191). **4140**

OLDTIMERS (AUGUSTA, GA.). (US/1061-9763). **4143**

PAUL MCCARTNEY MAGAZINE. (US/1057-039X). **4145**

PHILOSOPHY OF MUSIC EDUCATION REVIEW. (US/1063-5734). **4146**

PIANO & KEYBOARD. (US/1067-3881). **4146**

PIANO (PORT TOWNSEND, WASH.). (US/1066-1530). **4146**

PLAINSONG AND MEDIEVAL MUSIC. (UK/0961-1371). **4146**

PRODUCER REPORT. (US/1068-5391). **4147**

QRM (WASHINGTON, D.C.). (US/1060-8931). **4148**

RAPPAGES (BEVERLY HILLS, CALIF.). (US/1063-1283). **4148**

RCD. ROCK COMPACT DISC MAGAZINE. (UK/0965-190X). **4148**

ROCK & RAP CONFIDENTIAL. (US/1068-7653). **4150**

ROCK HEROES PRESENTS ... . (US/1059-5279). **4150**

SABIAN NEWS BEAT CATALOG. (CN/1191-2642). **4151**

SECRET GUIDE TO MUSIC AND OTHER GREAT STUFF YOU'RE UNLIKELY TO FIND ANYWHERE ELSE, THE. (US/1065-2981). **4152**

SHOUT! (NEW YORK, N.Y.). (US/1059-4817). **4153**

SIN INTERNATIONAL. (US/1070-2199). **4153**

SLIDE GUITARIST. (US/1055-0135). **4153**

SONG HITS' HEARTBREAKERS. (US/1053-7791). **4153**

SOUNDNOTES (TORONTO). (CN/1183-7659). **4154**

TEACHING MUSIC. (US/1069-7446). **4156**

TECHNOLOGY DIRECTORY / ASSOCIATION FOR TECHNOLOGY IN MUSIC INSTRUCTION. (US). **4156**

TEXAS MUSIC INDUSTRY DIRECTORY, THE. (US/1062-6646). **4156**

UCGM (NORTH CHARLESTON, S.C.). (US/1059-7182). **4157**

UUSI KANSANMUSIIKKI. (FI). **4157**

VINTAGE GUITAR. (US/1056-8581). **4158**

ABSTRACTING, BIBLIOGRAPHIES AND STATISTICS

CDS ZUM AUSLEIHEN. (GW). **4160**

NATURAL HISTORY

BULLETIN DES NATURALISTES DES YVELINES / PUBLICATION DE L'ASSOCIATION DES NATURALISTES DES YVELINES. (FR/1167-9786). **4163**

JEFFERSONIANA (MARTINSVILLE, VA.). (US/1061-1878). **4166**

MAINE NATURALIST (STEUBEN, ME.). (US/1063-3626). **4167**

MEMOIRES DU MUSEUM NATIONAL D'HISTOIRE NATURELLE. (FR/1243-4442). **4167**

NORTH CAROLINA NATURALIST. (US/1070-468X). **4169**

PONY EXPRESS (GAINESVILLE, FLA.). (US/1065-285X). **4170**

SCIENTIA AGRICOLA. (BL/0103-9016). **4171**

NAVAL SCIENCE, NAVIGATION

ATLANTIC TIDE & CURRENT ALMANAC (NORTHEAST ED.). (US/1064-0142). **4175**

BIBLIOGRAPHY FOR ADVANCEMENT EXAMINATION STUDY. (US). **4175**

CAPTN. JACK'S TIDE AND ... CURRENT ALMANAC. (US/1045-4543). **4175**

NORTHERN MARINER : JOURNAL OF THE CANADIAN NAUTICAL RESEARCH SOCIETY LE MARIN DU NORD : REVUE DE SOCIETE CANADIENNE POUR LA RECHERCHE NAUTIQUE, THE. (CN/1183-112X). **4181**

NOTICE TO MARINERS (ANNUAL EDITION 1976). (US/0700-1789). **4181**

SAILING DIRECTIONS. GULF OF ST. LAWRENCE. (CN). **4182**

SAILING DIRECTIONS. ST. LAWRENCE RIVER. CAP-ROUGE TO MONTREAL. (CN). **4182**

SAILING DIRECTIONS. ST. LAWRENCE RIVER. ILE VERTE TO QUEBEC. (CN). **4183**

SEAWAYS' SHIPS IN SCALE. (US/1065-8904). **4183**

SHIPYARD CHRONICLE. (US/1061-9224). **4183**

NEW AGE PUBLICATIONS

NETWORKER (ASHEVILLE, N.C.), THE. (US/1070-762X). **4186**

PAGAN MUSE & WORLD REPORT. (US/1068-2473). **4186**

NEWSPAPERS

ADVOCATE (BATON ROUGE, LA.), THE. (US/1061-3978). **5683**

AFRICAN HERALD, THE. (US/1069-8205). **5746**

AFRICAN ORACLE, THE. (CN/1189-5055). **5779**

ALEXANDRIA TIMES-TRIBUNE (1992), THE. (US/1063-553X). **5662**

ANTRIM COUNTY NEWS. (US). **5690**

ASHEVILLE CITIZEN-TIMES. (US/1060-3255). **5722**

BALTIC OBSERVER : NEWS FROM ESTONIA, LATVIA, AND LITHUANIA, THE. (LV). **5806**

BETHEL JOURNAL-PRESS, THE. (US/1066-7458). **5727**

BIG BEAR GRIZZLY. (US/1073-6867). **5633**

BRANSON TRI-LAKES DAILY NEWS. (US/1063-6994). **5702**

BRIDGEWATER TOWNSMAN, THE. (US). **5688**

BUCKEYE INDEPENDENT, THE. (US/1065-3880). **5629**

BUSINESS MN. (RU). **5809**

BUTLER COUNTY BANNER AND THE GREEN RIVER REPUBLICAN, THE. (US/1064-895X). **5679**

CHAPEL HILL NEWS (CHAPEL HILL, N.C. 1992). (US/1070-2741). **5723**

CHARIHO TIMES (1993), THE. (US/1069-9473). **5741**

CHATTANOOGA FREE PRESS. (US). **5744**

COLUMBIA COUNTY INDEPENDENT, THE. (US). **5715**

CONNECTICUT POST (BRIDGEPORT, CONN.). (US/1070-874X). **5645**

COUNTY NEIGHBORS (PUNXSUTAWNEY, PA.). (US/1065-268X). **5735**

COURIER, THE. (US). **5659**

DAILY GRAPHIC. (GH). **5802**

EDMONTON JEWISH LIFE. (CN/1189-3281). **5783**

ELMIRA INDEPENDENT. (CN/1194-1030). **5784**

EXPRES. (XR). **5799**

EXPRESS (CHICAGO, ILL.). (US/1063-0570). **5660**

FREEMAN (WAUKESHA, WIS.), THE. (US/1062-9041). **5767**

GRAYS HARBOR BEACON. (US/1064-4806). **5761**

GWINNETT POST-TRIBUNE. (US/1076-4852). **5653**

HARVEY COUNTY INDEPENDENT, THE. (US/1065-3740). **5676**

HOUSTON TIMES-JOURNAL. (US/1075-1874). **5654**

INDIAN COUNTRY TODAY. (US/1066-5501). **5743**

JOURNAL, THE. (US). **5660**

KAYHAN URDU. (IR). **5803**

KIDS CUE. (US/1071-0620). **5643**

KOMMERSANT DAILY. (RU). **5809**

LAS VEGAS BUSINESS PRESS. (US/1071-2186). **5708**

LATVIIAS LAIKS. (LV). **5806**

LITHUANIAN WEEKLY. (LI). **5806**

LUSOAMERICANO CALIFORNIA. (US/1065-8262). **5636**

MENDOCINO COUNTY OUTLOOK. (US/1065-8416). **5637**

MIAMI DAILY BUSINESS REVIEW. (US/1070-6437). **5718**

NEWS & RECORD (GREENSBORO, N.C.). (US/1072-0065). **5724**

NEWS-DEMOCRAT & LEADER. (US/1066-8071). **5682**

NEWS DIMENSIONS. (US/1064-3699). **5647**

NEWS TRIBUNE, THE. (US). **5761**

NEZAVISIMAIA MOLDOVA : ORGAN PARLAMENTA I PRAVITELSTVA RESPUBLIKI MOLDOVA. (MV). **5806**

NORTHUMBERLAND PUBLISHERS' WEEKENDER. (CN/1186-5601). **5791**

NOWE PODKARPACIE. (PL). **5808**

OUTLOOK FOR FARM COMMODITY PROGRAM SPENDING, THE. (US). **5647**

PLACER HERALD, THE. (US). **5638**

PRATT CITY COMMUNITY NEWSPAPER. (US/1061-1908). **5628**

PUTNAM COURIER-TRADER, THE. (US). **5646**

RICHLAND COUNTY NEWS-MONITOR. (US/1061-1029). **5726**

ROCK CREEK CURRENT, THE. (US/1062-2721). **5647**

ROCKBRIDGE DAILY PRESS. (US/1064-7740). **5759**

SAC NEWS MONTHLY. (US). **5684**

SAN DIEGO UNION-TRIBUNE (1992). (US/1063-102X). **5639**

SOLEIL DE COLOMBIE-BRITANNIQUE. (CN/1194-7098). **5794**

SOUTHWEST NEWSWEEK, THE. (US/1064-1645). **5682**

ST. JOSEPH NEWS-PRESS (1992). (US/1063-4312). **5704**

SUN HERALD (ENGLEWOOD ED.). (US/1068-7939). **5651**

TIMES-LEADER, THE. (US). **5682**

TODAY LANCASTER. (US/1065-0644). **5755**

TRIBUNE, THE. (CN). **5796**

UKRAINIAN CANADIAN HERALD. (CN/1193-2813). **5796**

VJESNIK. (CI). **5799**

WALSH COUNTY RECORD (1992), THE. (US/1067-5922). **5726**

WEST ALLIS POST (1992), THE. (US/1067-1862). **5772**

WESTSIDE GAZETTE. THURSDAY. (US). **5651**

WYOMING TRIBUNE-EAGLE. (US). **5773**

ABSTRACTING, BIBLIOGRAPHIES AND STATISTICS

CANADIAN INDEX (TORONTO). (CN/1192-4160). **5781**

NUTRITION AND DIETETICS

DIAGNOSTIC NUTRITION NETWORK. (US/1065-7746). **4189**

DIET BUSINE$$ BULLETIN, THE. (US/1062-9289). **4189**

DIETARY MANAGER. (US/1062-1121). **4189**

DYNAMIC NUTRITION RESEARCH. (SZ). **4190**

HEALTH DIET & NUTRITION. (US/1055-8241). **4191**

HEALTHY WEIGHT JOURNAL. (US/1075-0169). **4191**

HOW ON EARTH!. (US/1062-7723). **4192**

INTERNATIONAL JOURNAL OF FOOD SCIENCES AND NUTRITION. (UK/0963-7486). **4192**

JOURNAL OF NUTRITION IN RECIPE & MENU DEVELOPMENT. (US/1055-1379). **4193**

JOURNAL OF NUTRITIONAL IMMUNOLOGY. (US/1049-5150). **4193**

Nutrition and Dietetics

JOURNAL OF OPTIMAL NUTRITION, THE. (US/1061-2130). **4193**

NUTRITION & MENTAL HEALTH. (CN/1199-7699). **4195**

PERSPECTIVES IN APPLIED NUTRITION. (US/1070-6224). **4197**

SCANDINAVIAN JOURNAL OF NUTRITION NARINGSFORSKNING. (SW/1102-6480). **4199**

SUPPORT LINE (CHICAGO, ILL.). (US/1067-3768). **4199**

WEIGHT CONTROL DIGEST (DALLAS, TEX. 1992), THE. (US/1075-2889). **4200**

OCCUPATIONS AND CAREERS

ADAMS JOBS ALMANAC, THE. (US/1072-592X). **4201**

AT WORK (SAN FRANCISCO, CALIF.). (US/1061-9925). **4201**

CAREER DIRECTORY (TORONTO. 1992). (CN/0846-3514). **4201**

CAREERS GUIDANCE TODAY. (UK/0969-6431). **4202**

CAREERS INTERNATIONAL. (US/1059-3861). **4202**

CHICAGO JOB BANK, THE. (US/1072-575X). **4203**

CURRENT EMPLOYMENT. (US/1055-8292). **4203**

DOWN THE ROAD. (US/1072-4656). **4203**

EMPLOYMENT OPPORTUNITIES, USA. (US/1076-4798). **4204**

GETTING THE LOW-DOWN ON EMPLOYERS AND A LEG-UP ON THE JOB MARKET. (US/1062-9238). **4204**

HIDDEN JOB MARKET. (US/1064-1769). **4204**

HUNT-SCANLON'S EXECUTIVE RECRUITERS OF NORTH AMERICA. (US/1063-1143). **4204**

JIM GILREATH'S EXECUTIVE JOB SEARCH GAZETTE. (US/1064-7945). **4205**

JOB CHOICES ... IN BUSINESS. (US). **4205**

JOB CHOICES ... IN HEALTHCARE. (US). **4205**

JOB CHOICES ... IN SCIENCE & ENGINEERING. (US). **4205**

JOB FINDER FOR HIGH TECH SILICON VALLEY. (US/1065-4658). **4205**

JOB SEEKER'S GUIDE TO PRIVATE AND PUBLIC COMPANIES. (US/1061-3285). **4205**

JOBS IN HIGHER EDUCATION. (US/1074-5475). **4205**

NEW PROFESSIONAL, THE. (US/1064-8259). **4207**

NEW PROFESSIONAL SURVEY, THE. (US/1064-8267). **4207**

OCCUPATIONAL EMPLOYMENT AND OPENINGS, NEW YORK STATE. (US). **4207**

OFFICE DEALER. (UK). **4207**

PBC EMPLOYMENT BRIEFS. (US/1059-2040). **4208**

PETERSON'S JOB OPPORTUNITIES IN BUSINESS. (US/1070-6615). **4208**

PETERSON'S JOB OPPORTUNITIES IN ENGINEERING AND TECHNOLOGY. (US/1071-068X). **4208**

PETERSON'S JOB OPPORTUNITIES IN HEALTH CARE. (US/1071-0671). **4208**

PETERSON'S JOB OPPORTUNITIES IN THE ENVIRONMENT. (US/1071-183X). **4208**

PLANNING JOB CHOICES. (US). **4208**

PLANNING JOB CHOICES (TWO-YEAR COLLEGE ED.). (US). **4208**

PROFESSIONAL AND OCCUPATIONAL LICENSING DIRECTORY. (US/1070-3322). **4208**

PUBLIC SECTOR JOB BULLETIN. (US/1072-3773). **4209**

RECAREERING NEWSLETTER. (US/1068-199X). **4209**

SUMMER JOBS (PRINCETON, N.J.). (US/1064-6701). **4209**

VOCATIONAL CAREERS SOURCEBOOK. (US/1060-5630). **4209**

WASHINGTON JOB SOURCE, THE. (US/1067-0769). **4209**

OFFICE EQUIPMENT AND SERVICES

B.P.I.A. BUSINESS PRODUCTS INDUSTRY REPORT. (US/1078-5809). **4210**

DESIGNNETWORK'S WORKSTATION REPORT. (US). **4211**

IMAGINGWORLD (CAMDEN, ME.). (US/1060-894X). **4212**

WORKGROUP COMPUTING REPORT. (US/1068-9699). **4214**

OPTOMETRY

AMERICAN OPTICIAN. (CN). **4214**

PACKAGING

DIRECTORY OF PACKAGING SOURCES. (US/1071-9571). **4218**

GREENPACKAGING 2000. (US/1068-4271). **4219**

INTERNATIONAL JOURNAL OF MICROCIRCUITS AND ELECTRONIC PACKAGING, THE. (US/1063-1674). **4219**

NEW FOOD & DRUG PACKAGING, THE. (US/1075-3028). **4220**

PACKAGING PRODUCTIVITY. (US/1061-2300). **4221**

PACKAGING TECHNOLOGY & ENGINEERING. (US/1067-411X). **4221**

TAI-WAN PAO CHUANG CHI HSIEH PIEN LAN. (CH). **4222**

TRANSACTIONS ON COMPONENTS, PACKAGING & MANUFACTURING TECHNOLOGY PART B : TRANSACTIONS ON COMPONENTS, PACKAGING & ADVANCED PACKAGING. (US/1070-9894). **4222**

PAINTS AND PAINTING

INDUSTRIAL PAINT & POWDER. (US/1073-4651). **4224**

PALEONTOLOGY

DINOSAUR REVIEW (BOULDER, COLO.), THE. (US/1060-4006). **4227**

PALAEOCLIMATES. (US/1063-7176). **4228**

ROMANIAN JOURNAL OF PALEONTOLOGY. (RM/1220-5656). **4230**

UNIVERSITY OF KANSAS PALEONTOLOGICAL CONTRIBUTIONS (1992), THE. (US/1046-8390). **4231**

PAPER AND PULP INDUSTRY

ASIA PULP & PAPER, TECHNOLOGY MARKETS. (JA). **4232**

CANADIAN MARKET PULP. (CN/1193-2988). **4232**

CANADIAN PAPERMAKER. (CN/1191-887X). **4233**

PURCHASING PERFORMANCE BENCHMARKS FOR THE PAPER INDUSTRY. (US/1061-3757). **4238**

TSELLIULOZA, BUMAGA, KARTON. (RU). **4239**

WORLD PAPER (TONBRIDGE). (UK/1353-2677). **4240**

PARAPSYCHOLOGY AND OCCULTISM

DRAGONS' QUEST, THE. (US/1065-8181). **4241**

MEDIEVAL AND EARLY MODERN MYSTICISM. (US/1056-7917). **4242**

PARAPSYCHOLOGY, NEW AGE, AND THE OCCULT. (US/1065-3031). **4242**

THESE CELESTIAL TIMES. (US/1062-4643). **4243**

TRANSCENDING LIMITS. (US/1061-6683). **4243**

PEST CONTROL

ACTA PARASITOLOGICA / WITOLD STEFANSKI INSTITUTE OF PARASITOLOGY. (PL). **4243**

ARTHROPOD MANAGEMENT TESTS. (US). **4244**

INTEGRATED PEST MANAGEMENT REVIEWS. (UK/1353-5226). **4245**

RESUME D'ENQUETE. (CN/1193-0667). **4248**

PETROLEUM AND NATURAL GAS

21ST CENTURY FUELS. (US/1075-038X). **4248**

ALBERTA PETROLEUM EQUIPMENT & SERVICES DIRECTORY. (CN/1193-3097). **4249**

CANADIAN NATURAL GAS MARKET REPORT. (CN/1196-0906). **4253**

E&P HEALTH, SAFETY AND ENVIRONMENT. (US/1067-1013). **4255**

GAS DAILY'S GAS MARKETS WEEK. (US/1065-867X). **4257**

GAS DAILY'S NG. (US/1068-1299). **4257**

GAS PROCESSING AND PIPELINING. (US/1067-1021). **4257**

GAS SHALES TECHNOLOGY REVIEW. (US/1065-786X). **4258**

GAS TRANSPORTATION REPORT. (US/1065-8661). **4258**

HEROLD'S OIL HEADLINER. (US/1062-3485). **4260**

INTERNATIONAL OFFSHORE OIL COMPANY DIRECTORY. (US/1059-7816). **4261**

LITERATURE INDEX. (US/1065-0431). **4263**

NAFTOVA I HAZOVA PROMYSLOVIST. (UN). **4265**

NATURAL GAS EXPORTER. (CN/1195-5287). **4265**

NGV NEWS. (US/1065-3422). **4266**

OFFSHORE TECHNOLOGY (TULSA, OKLA.). (US/1067-103X). **4267**

OIL & GAS RUSSIA & POST SOVIET REPUBLICS. HYDROCARBONS BRIEF. (UK/0967-537X). **4269**

PATENT INDEX. (US/1065-0423). **4271**

PETROLEUM GEOSCIENCE. (UK/1354-0793). **4272**

RUSSIAN OIL & GAS GUIDE. (US/1064-9697). **4277**

SPE DRILLING AND COMPLETIONS. (US/1064-6671). **4278**

SPE PRODUCTION AND FACILITIES. (US/1064-668X). **4279**

U.S.A. GULF COAST OIL & GAS INDUSTRY DIRECTORY. (US/1056-795X). **4281**

U.S.A. OIL INDUSTRY'S ENVIRONMENTAL DIRECTORY. (US/1062-0605). **4281**

VISION TECNOLOGICA / PUBLICACION DE INTEVEP, S.A. (VE/1315-0855). **4281**

ABSTRACTING, BIBLIOGRAPHIES AND STATISTICS

LITERATURE ABSTRACTS. CATALYSTS / ZEOLITES. (US/1074-6870). **4284**

LITERATURE ABSTRACTS. PETROLEUM REFINING & PETROCHEMICALS. (US/1065-0512). **4284**

LITERATURE ABSTRACTS. PETROLEUM SUBSTITUTES. (US/1065-0504). **4284**

LITERATURE ABSTRACTS. TRANSPORTATION & STORAGE. (US/1065-0520). **4284**

NATURAL GAS STATISTICS SOURCEBOOK. (US/1074-6730). **4284**

PETS

BIRD BREEDER. (US/1073-5186). **4285**

CAT INDUSTRY NEWSLETTER. (US/1074-7788). **4286**

INTERACTIONS / DELTA SOCIETY. (US). **4286**

REPTILES (IRVINE, CALIF.). (US/1068-1965). **4287**

PHARMACY AND PHARMACOLOGY

ACTA PHARMACEUTICA : A QUARTERLY JOURNAL OF CROATIAN PHARMACEUTICAL SOCIETY AND SLOVENIAN PHARMACEUTICAL SOCIETY, DEALING WITH ALL BRANCHES OF PHARMACY AND ALLIED SCIENCES. (CI). **4288**

ADVERSE EFFECTS OF HERBAL DRUGS. (GW). **4289**

ANALYTICAL PROFILES OF DRUG SUBSTANCES AND EXCIPIENTS. (US). **4290**

ANNALS OF PHARMACOTHERAPY, THE. (US/1060-0280). **4291**

ANNUAL OF DRUG THERAPY. (US/1068-3178). **4291**

ANNUAL SURVEY OF PRESCRIPTION AND OVER-THE-COUNTER DRUGS. (CN/1196-5290). **4291**

APPLIED CLINICAL TRIALS. (US/1064-8542). **4292**

BIOLOGICAL & PHARMACEUTICAL BULLETIN. (JA/0918-6158). **4293**

CELLULAR PHARMACOLOGY. (UK/1351-3214). **4295**

CESKA A SLOVENSKA FARMACIE : CASOPIS CESKE FARMACEUTICKE SPOLECNOSTI A SLOVENSKE FARMACEUTICKE SPOLECNOSTI. (XR/1210-7816). **4295**

CLINICAL IMMUNOTHERAPEUTICS. (NZ/1172-7039). **4296**

CLINICAL RESEARCH AND REGULATORY AFFAIRS. (US/1060-1333). **4297**

CNS DRUGS : THE CLINICAL REVIEW OF DRUGS AND THERAPEUICS IN PSYCHIATRY AND NEUROLOGY. (NZ/1172-7047). **4297**

CODE OF FEDERAL REGULATIONS UPDATE. 21 CFR, DRUGS AND MEDICAL DEVICES. (US/1066-3703). **4297**

COMPARATIVE BIOCHEMISTRY AND PHYSIOLOGY. C, PHARMACOLOGY, TOXICOLOGY & ENDOCRINOLOGY : CBP. (UK). **486**

CURRENT DRUG THERAPY. (US/1065-7630). **4298**

DIRECTORY OF DRUG STORES & HBC CHAINS. (US). **4299**

DRUG DELIVERY. (US/1071-7544). **4299**

DRUG GMP REPORT. (US/1061-2335). **4300**

DRUG RESISTANCE WEEKLY. (US). **4301**

DRUGS & THERAPY PERSPECTIVES : FOR RATIONAL DRUG SELECTION AND USE. (NZ/1172-0360). **4302**

DRUGS IN DEVELOPMENT. (US/1066-7008). **4302**

EKSPERIMENTALNAIA I KLINICHESKAIA FARMAKOLOGIIA. (RU/0869-2092). **4303**

EMERGING PHARMACEUTICALS. (US/1061-6098). **4303**

EUROPEAN JOURNAL OF PHARMACEUTICAL SCIENCES. (NE/0928-0987). **4303**

EUROPEAN JOURNAL OF PHARMACOLOGY : ENVIRONMENTAL TOXICOLOGY AND PHARMACOLOGY SECTION. (NE/0926-6917). **4303**

F-D-C REPORTS. NONPRESCRIPTION PHARMACEUTICALS AND NUTRITIONALS. (US/1068-5316). **4304**

FAX-STAT ON DRUGS. (US/1064-5055). **4305**

HOSPITAL PHARMACIST, THE. (UK/1352-7967). **4306**

INTERNATIONAL ACADEMY FOR BIOMEDICAL AND DRUG RESEARCH. (SZ). **4308**

INTERNATIONAL JOURNAL OF CLINICAL PHARMACOLOGY AND THERAPEUTICS. (GW/0946-1965). **4308**

INTERPHARMACY FORUM. (US/1065-9412). **4309**

ISSX PROCEEDINGS. (US/1061-3439). **4309**

JOURNAL OF CLINICAL RESEARCH AND DRUG DEVELOPMENT (1993). (US/1066-7865). **4310**

JOURNAL OF DRUG TARGETING. (US/1061-186X). **4311**

JOURNAL OF INFECTIOUS DISEASE PHARMACOTHERAPY. (US/1068-7777). **4311**

JOURNAL OF NATURAL TOXINS. (US/1058-8108). **4311**

JOURNAL OF PHARMACEUTICAL CARE IN PAIN & SYMPTOM CONTROL. (US/1056-4950). **4311**

JOURNAL OF PHARMACOLOGICAL AND TOXICOLOGICAL METHODS. (US/1056-8719). **4312**

JOURNAL OF PHARMACY & LAW, THE. (US/1062-4546). **4312**

N.D.A. (SKOKIE, ILL.), THE. (US/1064-9786). **4316**

NEW DEVELOPMENTS IN MEDICINE & DRUG THERAPY. (US/1063-360X). **4317**

PDR GUIDE TO DRUG INTERACTIONS, SIDE EFFECTS, INDICATIONS. (US). **4319**

PDR LIBRARY ON CD ROM WITH THE MERCK MANUAL. (US/1068-6924). **4319**

PHARMACOECONOMICS. (NZ/1170-7690). **4321**

PHARMACOEPIDEMIOLOGY AND DRUG SAFETY. (UK/1053-8569). **4321**

PHARMACOLOGY COMMUNICATIONS. (SZ/1060-4456). **4322**

PHARMACOLOGY, TOXICOLOGY & THERAPEUTICS. (US/1063-8946). **4322**

PHARMACORESOURCES : WORLD PHARMACOECONOMIC NEWS, VIEWS, AND PRACTICAL APPLICATION. (NZ/1172-8299). **4323**

PHARMACY CADENCE. (US/1064-797X). **4323**

PHARMACY TODAY. (US/1077-2839). **4323**

PHARMACY WORLD & SCIENCE : PWS. (NE/0928-1231). **4324**

PHYSICIANS' GENRX. (US). **4325**

POLISH JOURNAL OF PHARMACOLOGY. (PL). **4325**

Pharmacy and Pharmacology

PRIMARY CARE MEDICINE DRUG ALERTS. (US/1061-0359). **4325**

PROFESSIONAL NURSE. DRUG UPDATE. (UK) **4326**

RED BOOK. (US). **4327**

RESEARCH COMMUNICATIONS IN MOLECULAR PATHOLOGY & PHARMACOLOGY. (US). **4327**

WARNING LETTER BULLETIN. (US/1069-4218). **4332**

WORLD PHARMACEUTICALS REPORT. (UK/0966-7687). **4333**

PHILANTHROPY

CALIFORNIA PHILANTHROPY REPORT. (US/1065-7282). **4334**

CHARITABLE ORGANIZATIONS OF THE U.S. (US/1052-3979). **4335**

DIRECTORY OF THE MAJOR INDIANA FOUNDATIONS, THE. (US). **4335**

FEDERAL SUPPORT FOR NONPROFITS. (US/1066-8896). **4335**

FOUNDATION 1000, THE. (US/1067-7828). **4336**

FOUNDATION & CORPORATE GRANTS ALERT. (US/1062-4686). **4336**

FOUNDATION DIRECTORY. PART 2, A GUIDE TO GRANT PROGRAMS, $25,000-$100,000, THE. (US/1058-6210). **4336**

FOUNDATION NEWS & COMMENTARY. (US/1076-3961). **4336**

GRANT$ FOR ALCOHOL AND DRUG ABUSE. (US). **4336**

GRANT$ FOR MENTAL HEALTH, ADDICTIONS & CRISIS SERVICES. (US). **4337**

GRANT$ FOR SCHOLARSHIPS, STUDENT AID & LOANS. (US). **4337**

GRANT$ FOR SOCIAL SERVICES. (US). **4337**

GRANT$ FOR THE HOMELESS. (US). **4337**

GUIDE TO U.S. FOUNDATIONS, THEIR TRUSTEES, OFFICERS, AND DONORS. (US/1071-202X). **4338**

MAJOR DONORS. (US/1061-1266). **4338**

SUCCESSFUL FUND RAISING. (US/1070-9061). **4339**

PHILOSOPHY

1650-1850 (NEW YORK, N.Y.). (US/1065-3112). **4339**

ACTA PHILOSOPHICA ROMA. (IT/1121-2179). **4339**

APA NEWSLETTERS ON THE BLACK EXPERIENCE, COMPUTER USE, FEMINISM, LAW, MEDICINE, TEACHING. (US/1067-9464). **4341**

BRITISH JOURNAL FOR THE HISTORY OF PHILOSOPHY. (UK/0960-8788). **4342**

FILOSOFSKI ALTERNATIVI. (BU/0861-7899). **4346**

FREETHOUGHT HISTORY. (US/1071-7269). **4347**

INTERNATIONAL JOURNAL OF PHILOSOPHY, PSYCHOLOGY, AND SPIRITUALITY. (US/1061-530X). **4349**

JOURNAL OF LOGIC, LANGUAGE, AND INFORMATION. (NE/0925-8531). **4350**

JOURNAL OF NEOPLATONIC STUDIES, THE. (US/1065-5840). **4350**

JOURNAL OF POLITICAL PHILOSOPHY. (US/0963-8016). **4350**

PARADOXIST MOVEMENT, THE. (US/1055-761X). **4354**

RUSSIAN STUDIES IN PHILOSOPHY. (US/1061-1967). **4360**

SERIIA 6, FILOSOFIIA, POLITOLOGIIA, SOTSIOLOGIIA, PSIKHOLOGIIA, PRAVO. (RU). **4360**

TIME & SOCIETY. (UK/0961-463X). **4364**

TUNG WU CHE HSUEH CHUAN HSI LU / TUNG WU TA HSUEH. (CH/1010-0725). **4364**

PHOTOGRAPHY AND VIDEO

BLIND SPOT PHOTOGRAPHY. (US/1068-1647). **4367**

CAMERAWORK. (US). **4368**

HOME STUDIO FORUM. (US/1061-3765). **4370**

LEONARD'S ANNUAL PRICE INDEX OF PRINTS, POSTERS & PHOTOGRAPHS. (US/1064-0452). **4371**

PHILLIPS BUSINESS INFORMATION'S INTERACTIVE VIDEO NEWS. (US/1076-4526). **4372**

PHOTOGRAPHIC BUYERS GUIDE. (US/1066-0704). **4374**

PIQUE (NEW YORK, N.Y.). (US/1061-2505). **4375**

SHOOTER'S RAG. (US/1058-2789). **4376**

WHODUZZIT? (NEW YORK, N.Y.). (US/1062-0427). **4378**

WHO'S WHO IN PHOTOGRAPHY (PLYMOUTH, VT.). (US/1052-4037). **4378**

ZHURNAL NAUCHNOI I PRIKLADNOI FOTOGRAFII / ROSSIISKAIA AKADEMIIA NAUK. (RU). **4378**

PHYSICAL THERAPY

OCCUPATIONAL THERAPY INTERNATIONAL. (UK/0966-7903). **4381**

ORTHOPAEDIC PHYSICAL THERAPY CLINICS OF NORTH AMERICA. (US/1059-1516). **4381**

PHYSICAL THERAPY FORUM (KING OF PRUSSIA, PA. 1994). (US/1075-4342). **4381**

PHYSICAL THERAPY REIMBURSEMENT NEWS. (US/1073-9483). **4381**

PT (ALEXANDRIA, VA.). (US/1065-5077). **4382**

TOPICS IN STROKE REHABILITATION. (US/1074-9357). **4382**

PHYSICALLY IMPAIRED

ABILITY NETWORK. (CN/1192-1188). **4503**

ADA WATCH. (US/1062-0176). **4383**

ADAC REPORT. (US/1065-7037). **4383**

BNA'S AMERICANS WITH DISABILITIES ACT MANUAL. NEWSLETTER. (US/1063-3111). **4384**

COMMUNICATION AND LANGUAGE INTERVENTION SERIES. (US). **4385**

COMMUNITY MOVES. (NZ/1171-8587). **4385**

COMPLETE DIRECTORY FOR PEOPLE WITH DISABILITIES, THE. (US/1063-0023). **4385**

DEAF CANADA. (CN/1195-3349). **4386**

DIRECTORY OF CANADIAN REHABILITATION SERVICES. (CN/1191-1514). **4386**

DISABILITY AND REHABILITATION. (UK/0963-8288). **4387**

FREE SPIRIT (MIAMI, FLA.). (US/1062-8134). **4388**

JOURNAL OF MEDICAL SPEECH-LANGUAGE PATHOLOGY. (US/1065-1438). **4390**

QUALITY OF LIFE RESEARCH. (UK/0962-9343). **4392**

SECTION 504 COMPLIANCE HANDBOOK. SUPPLEMENT. (US/1068-6533). **4393**

SOURDS DU CANADA. (CN/1195-3349). **4393**

SPECIAL EDUCATION REPORT: THE INDEPENDENT BI-WEEKLY NEWS SERVICE ON LEGISLATION, REGULATION AND FUNDING OF PROGRAMS FOR CHILDREN AND YOUTHS WITH DISABILITIES. (US). **4394**

PHYSICS

ANALES DE FISICA. (SP/1133-0376). **4396**

APSNEWS. (US/1058-8132). **4398**

ASIC & EDA. (US/1067-9804). **4398**

ASTROPARTICLE PHYSICS. (NE/0927-6505). **4398**

ATM NEWSLETTER. (US/1067-5221). **4398**

BRAZILIAN JOURNAL OF PHYSICS. (BL/0103-9733). **4398**

BULLETIN OF THE LEBEDEV PHYSICS INSTITUTE. (US/1068-3356). **4399**

BULLETIN OF THE RUSSIAN ACADEMY OF SCIENCES. PHYSICS. (US/1062-8738). **4399**

COMPTES RENDUS DE L'ACADEMIE DES SCIENCES. SERIE II, MECANIQUE, PHYSIQUE, CHIMIE, ASTRONOMIE. (FR). **4400**

COMPTES RENDUS DE L'ACADEMIE DES SCIENCES. SERIE II, SCIENCES DE LA TERRE ET DES PLANETES EARTH & PLANETARY SCIENCES. (FR). **4400**

FIZIKA B : A JOURNAL OF EXPERIMENTAL AND THEORETICAL PHYSICS. (CI/1330-0016). **4403**

GLASS, PHYSICS & CHEMISTRY. (US). **4404**

INFRARED PHYSICS & TECHNOLOGY. (UK/1350-4495). **4405**

INTERNATIONAL JOURNAL OF MODERN PHYSICS. D, GRAVITATION, ASTROPHYSICS, COSMOLOGY. (SI/0218-2718). **4406**

IZVESTIIA AKADEMII NAUK. FIZIKA ATMOSFERY I OKEANA / ROSSIISKAIA AKADEMIIA NAUK. (RU). **4407**

IZVESTIIA AKADEMII NAUK. SERIIA FIZICHESKAIA / ROSSIISKAIA AKADEMIIA NAUK. (RU). **4407**

IZVESTIIA SORAN. SIBIRSKII FIZIKO-TEKHNICHESKII ZHURNAL. (RU). **4407**

JOURNAL OF ENGINEERING PHYSICS AND THERMOPHYSICS. (US/1062-0125). **4408**

JOURNAL OF EXPERIMENTAL AND THEORETICAL PHYSICS. (US/1063-7761). **4409**

JOURNAL OF GROUP THEORY IN PHYSICS. (US/1070-2458). **4409**

JOURNAL OF QUANTUM NONLINEAR PHENOMENA. (US/1062-7944). **4410**

LIETUVOS FIZIKOS ZURNALAS / LITHUANIAN JOURNAL OF PHYSICS / LITOVSKII FIZICHESKII ZHURNAL / LIETUVOS FIZIKU DRAUGIJA. (LI). **4411**

LOW TEMPERATURE PHYSICS. (US/1063-777X). **4411**

MULTIVAC UPDATE. (US/1061-1606). **4413**

NETWORK ECONOMICS LETTER. (US/1069-126X). **4413**

PHYSICAL REVIEW E. STATISTICAL PHYSICS, PLASMAS, FLUIDS, AND RELATED INTERDISCIPLINARY TOPICS. (US/1063-651X). **4415**

PHYSICS-DOKLADY. (US/1063-7753). **4415**

PHYSICS OF FLUIDS (1994). (US/1070-6631). **4416**

PHYSICS OF HIGH ENERGY DENSITY. (RU/1061-7582). **4416**

PHYSICS OF PLASMAS. (US/1070-664X). **4416**

PHYSICS OF THE SOLID STATE. (US/1063-7834). **4416**

PHYSICS, USPEKHI. (US/1063-7869). **4416**

PLASMA PHYSICS REPORTS. (US/1063-780X). **4417**

PLASMAS AND POLYMERS : AN INTERNATIONAL JOURNAL. (US). **4417**

RADIATION PHYSICS AND CHEMISTRY. (UK/0969-806X). **4419**

ROMANIAN REPORTS IN PHYSICS. (RM/1221-1451). **4420**

RUSSIAN JOURNAL OF MATHEMATICAL PHYSICS. (RU/1061-9208). **4420**

RUSSIAN PHYSICS JOURNAL. (US/1064-8887). **4420**

SEMICONDUCTORS (NEW YORK, N.Y.). (US/1063-7826). **4421**

SOLID STATE NUCLEAR MAGNETIC RESONANCE. (NE/0926-2040). **4421**

TECHNICAL PHYSICS. (US/1063-7842). **4423**

TECHNICAL PHYSICS LETTERS. (US/1063-7850). **4423**

ULTRASONICS SONOCHEMISTRY. (UK/1350-4177). **4424**

HEAT

JOURNAL OF ENHANCED HEAT TRANSFER: AN INTERNATIONAL JOURNAL OF THEORY AND APPLICATION IN HIGH-PERFORMANCE HEAT AND MASS TRANSFER. (US/1065-5131). **4431**

PROCESS HEATING. (US/1077-5870). **4432**

LIGHT, OPTICS, RADIATION

AAVSO PHOTOELECTRIC PHOTOMETRY NEWSLETTER. (US). **4432**

APPLIED MICROWAVE & WIRELESS. (US/1075-0207). **4433**

APPLIED PHYSICS. B, LASERS AND OPTICS. (GW). **4433**

APPLIED RADIATION AND ISOTOPES : INCLUDING DATA, INSTRUMENTATION AND METHODS FOR USE IN AGRICULTURE, INDUSTRY AND MEDICINE. (UK/0969-8043). **4433**

BIOIMAGING. (UK/0966-9051). **4433**

INDUSTRIAL LASER HANDBOOK, THE. (US/0941-4185). **4435**

INTERNATIONAL JOURNAL OF NONLINEAR OPTICAL PHYSICS. (SI/0218-1991). **4435**

INTERNATIONAL JOURNAL OF RADIATION HYGIENE. (US/1066-7016). **4435**

JOURNAL OF OPTICAL TECHNOLOGY. (US/1070-9762). **4436**

JOURNAL OF RUSSIAN LASER RESEARCH. (US/1071-2836). **4436**

JOURNAL OF THE EUROPEAN OPTICAL SOCIETY, PART B, QUANTUM OPTICS. (UK). **4437**

JOURNAL OF THE OPTICAL SOCIETY OF AMERICA. A, OPTICS, IMAGE SCIENCE, AND VISION. (US). **4437**

MICROBEAM ANALYSIS (NEW YORK, N.Y.). (US/1061-3420). **4438**

MOLECULAR CRYSTALS AND LIQUID CRYSTALS SCIENCE AND TECHNOLOGY SECTION B, NONLINEAR OPTICS. (US/1058-7268). **4438**

MOLECULAR CRYSTALS AND LIQUID CRYSTALS SCIENCE AND TECHNOLOGY SECTION D, DISPLAY AND IMAGING. (US/1058-7284). **4438**

OLE. OPTO & LASER EUROPE. (UK/0966-9809). **4438**

OPTICAL FIBER TECHNOLOGY. (US/1068-5200). **4439**

OPTICAL MATERIALS. (NE/0925-3467). **4439**

OPTIKA ATMOSFERY I OKEANA. (RU). **4440**

POF NEWSLETTER. (US/1064-1068). **4440**

PROCEEDINGS / IAPR INTERNATIONAL CONFERENCE ON PATTERN RECOGNITION. (US). **4440**

RADIATSIONNAIA BIOLOGIIA, RADIOECOLOGIIA / ROSSIISKAIA AKADEMIIA NAUK. (RU). **4441**

SPECTROSCOPY EUROPE. (GW/0966-0941). **4442**

SPIE HOLOGRAPHICS INTERNATIONAL DIRECTORY & RESOURCE GUIDE. (US/1058-045X). **4442**

STUDIES OF VACUUM ULTRAVIOLET AND X-RAY PROCESSES. (US/1065-7665). **4442**

SURFACE SCIENCE SPECTRA. (US/1055-5269). **4442**

ZEISS INFORMATION WITH JENA REVIEW. (GW/0941-7567). **4442**

MAGNETISM

CMM : CANADIAN MEDIA MAG. (CN/1191-2707). **4443**

HIGH SPEED TRANSPORT NEWS. (US/1076-8408). **4443**

JOURNAL OF MAGNETIC RESONANCE. SERIES A. (US/1064-1858). **4444**

JOURNAL OF MAGNETIC RESONANCE. SERIES B. (US/1064-1866). **4444**

MMC : MEDIAS MAGNETIQUES CANADA. (CN/1191-2693). **4444**

PROCEEDINGS OF THE SOCIETY OF MAGNETIC RESONANCE IN MEDICINE. (US/1065-9889). **4445**

NUCLEAR PHYSICS

INTERNATIONAL JOURNAL OF MODERN PHYSICS. E, NUCLEAR PHYSICS. (SI/0218-3013). **4447**

PHYSICS OF ATOMIC NUCLEI. (US/1063-7788). **4450**

PHYSICS OF PARTICLES AND NUCLEI. (US/1063-7796). **4450**

REVIEW - INSTITUTE OF NUCLEAR POWER OPERATIONS (U.S.). (US/1061-6411). **4451**

SOUND

ACOUSTICAL PHYSICS. (US/1063-7710). **4452**

PLASTICS

PLAST EUROPE : PE : KUNSTSTOFFE. (GW/0941-3596). **4457**

PLASTICS DIGEST. (US/1069-4358). **4458**

STEPHENS' OHIO PLASTICS DIRECTORY. (US/1065-7142). **4460**

POLITICAL SCIENCE

AFRICA TODAY (NEW YORK, N.Y.). (US/1062-8584). **4462**

ANTIPODES BRUXELLES. (BE/1370-009X). **4464**

BULLETIN OF EUROPEAN POLITICAL AND ECONOMIC ISSUES. (US). **4466**

CALIFORNIA JOURNAL'S ELECTION WEEKLY. (US). **4466**

CHINA MONTHLY DATA / INSTITUTE OF ASIAN AFFAIRS. (GW/0943-7533). **4468**

CITY JOURNAL (NEW YORK, N.Y.), THE. (US/1060-8540). **4468**

CURRENT POLITICS AND ECONOMICS OF CHINA. (US). **4470**

Political Science

CURRENT POLITICS AND ECONOMICS OF THE MIDDLE EAST. (US). **4471**

DIRECTORY OF BRITISH POLITICAL ORGANISATIONS UPDATING SERVICE. (UK). **4472**

DIRECTORY OF POLITICAL NEWSLETTERS (1994). (US/1071-796X). **4472**

EAST EUROPEAN CONSTITUTIONAL REVIEW. (US). **4472**

FEDERAL LOBBYISTS, THE. (CN/1193-2821). **4474**

FEDERALISM REPORT, THE. (US). **4474**

GERMAN POLITICS. (UK/0964-4008). **4474**

GLOBAL GOVERNANCE. (US/1075-2846). **4475**

GRADUATE FACULTY AND PROGRAMS IN POLITICAL SCIENCE. (US/1065-6049). **4475**

HETERODOXY (STUDIO CITY, LOS ANGELES, CALIF.). (US/1069-7268). **4476**

INDIANA LEGISLATIVE SOURCEBOOK. (US). **4477**

JACK ANDERSON CONFIDENTIAL (1992). (US/1064-4458). **4478**

KIPLINGER'S RETIREMENT REPORT. (US/1075-6671). **4480**

LEFT HISTORY. (CN/1192-1927). **4480**

LIMBAUGH LETTER, THE. (US/1065-0377). **4481**

LONG TERM VIEW, THE. (US). **4481**

MAJOR CONCEPTS IN POLITICS AND POLITICAL THEORY. (US/1059-3535). **4481**

MIAMI HERALD ALMANAC OF FLORIDA POLITICS, THE. (US/1069-3017). **4481**

MINUTES OF PROCEEDINGS AND EVIDENCE OF THE SPECIAL COMMITTEE ON ELECTORAL REFORM. (CN/1193-1043). **4482**

MINUTES OF PROCEEDINGS AND EVIDENCE OF THE SPECIAL COMMITTEE ON ELECTORAL REFORM (FRENCH EDITION). (CN/1193-1043). **4482**

NAROD I DEMOKRATIIA. (UZ/0869-0685). **4482**

NATIONS AND NATIONALISM. (UK/1354-5078). **4483**

NED BACKGROUNDER: A FORUM FOR THE STUDY OF THE NATIONAL ENDOWMENT FOR DEMOCRACY AND OTHER U.S. GOVERNMENT DEMOCRATIZATION PROGRAMS, THE. (US/1062-6867). **4483**

NOVAIA LITERATURA PO SOTSIALNYM I GUMANITARNYM NAUKAM. GOSUDARSTVO I PRAVO / ROSSIISKAIA AKADEMIIA NAUK, INSTITUT NAUCHNOI INFORMATSII PO OBSHCHESTVENNYM NAUKAM. (RU). **4484**

OKLAHOMA POLITICS. (US/1065-0695). **4485**

PARLIAMENTARY WEEKLY QUARTERLY REPORT, THE. (CN/1188-2387). **4487**

PINK SHEET ON THE LEFT (1993), THE. (US/1070-0285). **4487**

POLITICAL COMMUNICATION. (US/1058-4609). **4489**

POLITICAL FINANCE LOBBY REPORTER. (US/0270-353X). **4489**

POLITICAL RESEARCH QUARTERLY. (US/1065-9129). **4489**

POLITICAL WOMAN (WHITE PLAINS, N.Y.). (US/1069-6652). **4490**

PRAEGER SERIES IN PRESIDENTIAL STUDIES. (US/1062-0931). **4492**

PRAEGER SERIES IN TRANSFORMATIONAL POLITICS AND POLITICAL SCIENCE. (US/1061-5261). **4492**

PRESIDENTS & PRIME MINISTERS. (US/1060-5088). **4492**

REVISTA DO MERCOSUL. (BL). **4494**

REVUE ELECTORALE, SYNTHESES ET DOCUMENTS, LA. (CN/1188-6161). **4495**

RIGHT GUIDE (ANN ARBOR, MICH.), THE. (US/1064-7414). **4495**

SECURITY DIALOGUE. (UK/0967-0106). **4495**

SOVIET AND POST-SOVIET REVIEW, THE. (US/1075-1262). **4496**

TIMELINE (PALO ALTO, CALIF.). (US/1061-2734). **4498**

TUNG WU CHENG CHIH HSUEH PAO. (CH). **4498**

VICHE. (RU). **4499**

WE THE PEOPLE (NORTH READING, MASS.). (US/1064-0568). **4500**

WHO'S WHO IN EUROPEAN INSTITUTIONS AND ENTERPRISES. (SZ). **4500**

WORLD OUTLOOK / SHIH CHIEH CHAN WANG. (CH). **4501**

ABSTRACTING, BIBLIOGRAPHIES AND STATISTICS

CURRENT DIGEST OF THE POST-SOVIET PRESS, THE. (US/1067-7542). **4502**

CIVIL RIGHTS

ALERTA (TORONTO). (CN/1188-875X). **4503**

CHINA RIGHTS FORUM. (US/1068-4166). **4505**

DOCKET : A JOURNAL OF THE INTERNATIONAL HUMAN RIGHTS LAW GROUP. (US). **4507**

GUATEMALA BULLETIN. (US/1068-0187). **4508**

HUMAN RIGHTS TRIBUNE (OTTAWA). (CN/1188-6226). **4509**

HUMAN RIGHTS WATCH/AMERICAS. (US/1077-6710). **4509**

LETTRE HEBDOMADAIRE DE LA FIDH / FEDERATION INTERNATIONALE DES LIGUES DES DROITS DE L'HOMME, LA. (FR). **4510**

NOTICIAS DE OCR / OFFICINA DE DERECHOS CIVILES. (US). **4511**

SASK RIGHTS. (CN/1191-0933). **4512**

TEMPLE POLITICAL & CIVIL RIGHTS LAW REVIEW. (US/1062-5887). **4513**

THIRD FORCE (1993). (US/1067-3237). **4513**

UNITY IN A MULTICULTURAL U.S.A. (US/1074-6250). **4513**

VIETNAM JOURNAL : PROJECT OF THE VIETNAM HUMAN RIGHTS GROUP. (US). **4514**

INTERNATIONAL RELATIONS

BRIDGEWATER-DAVIS PACIFIC INTELLIGENCE UPDATE. (US/1060-3093). **4517**

BULLETIN - SEARCH FOR COMMON GROUND (ORGANIZATION). INITIATIVE FOR PEACE AND COOPERATION IN THE MIDDLE EAST. (US/1065-0237). **4517**

CISSM PAPERS. (US/1065-6391). **4518**

COMMONWEALTH OF INDEPENDENT STATES AND THE MIDDLE EAST. (IS/0334-4142). **4518**

COUNTERTERRORISM & SECURITY REPORT. (US/1064-9093). **4519**

EUROPEAN COMPANION, THE. (UK). **4521**

EUROPEAN SECURITY. (UK/0966-2839). **4521**

GLOBAL AGENDA, A. (US/1057-1213). **4522**

HARVARD JOURNAL OF WORLD AFFAIRS : AN INTERNATIONAL POLICY FORUM OF THE JOHN F. KENNEDY SCHOOL OF GOVERNMENT. (US). **4523**

INSIGHT : AUSTRALIAN FOREIGN AFFAIRS AND TRADE ISSUES. (AT/1038-6726). **4524**

JOURNAL OF AMERICAN-EAST ASIAN RELATIONS, THE. (US/1058-3947). **4527**

JOURNAL OF CONFLICT STUDIES. (CN/1198-8614). **4527**

JOURNAL OF THIRD WORLD SPECTRUM. (US/1072-5040). **4527**

MIDDLE EAST POLICY. (US/1061-1924). **4528**

NEW TIMES INTERNATIONAL. (RU). **4530**

POLITICA EXTERNA. (BL). **4532**

QUARTERLY / WORLD AFFAIRS CANADA, THE. (CN/1188-6870). **4533**

QUARTERLY / WORLD AFFAIRS CANADA, THE. (CN/1188-6870). **4533**

RESEARCH NOTES. (US/1062-9300). **4534**

SOUTH AFRICAN JOURNAL OF INTERNATIONAL AFFAIRS, THE. (SA/1022-0461). **4535**

TRANSITIONS. (BE). **4536**

UNITED NATIONS RESOLUTIONS.SERIES 3, RESOLUTIONS AND DECISIONS OF THE ECONOMIC AND SOCIAL COUNCIL. (US/1051-399X). **4537**

SOCIALISM, COMMUNISM, ANARCHISM, UTOPIANISM

ANARCHIST STUDIES. (UK/0967-3393). **4539**

ARENA MAGAZINE. (AT/1039-1010). **4540**

COMMUNIST AND POST-COMMUNIST STUDIES. (UK/0967-067X). **4540**

PAROLECHIAVE. (IT). **4544**

PEOPLE FOR A NEW SYSTEM. (US). **4544**

SOCIALISM OF THE FUTURE. (UK). **4546**

SOTSIALNO-POLITICHESKII ZHURNAL. (RU). **4547**

Z PAPERS. (US/1060-2070). **4548**

POPULATION STUDIES

1991 CENSUS OF CANADA, INFORMATION RELEASE. (CN/1193-2732). **4549**

FLORIDA POPULATION STUDIES. (US). **4553**

PEOPLE & THE PLANET / IPPF, UNFPA, IUCN. (UK/0968-1655). **4556**

REVISTA PERUANA DE POBLACION. (PE). **4560**

PRINTING INDUSTRY

IN-PLANT PRINTER (1993). (US/1071-832X). **4565**

PRINTWEAR & PROMOTION. (UK/0967-2486). **4569**

READY, SET, GO! IN-DEPTH (1992). (US/1064-7120). **4569**

V.P.I.'S IMPRINTABLES TODAY. (US/1064-6868). **4570**

PSYCHOLOGY

ADAPTIVE BEHAVIOR. (US/1059-7123). **4571**

ADVANCES IN CHILD NEUROPSYCHOLOGY. (US/0940-8606). **4571**

ADVANCES IN COGNITION AND EDUCATIONAL PRACTICE. (US). **4571**

AMERICAN COUNSELOR. (US/1059-3497). **4572**

ANXIETY (NEW YORK, N.Y.). (US/1070-9797). **4574**

ANXIETY, STRESS AND COPING. (SZ/1061-5806). **4574**

APPIC DIRECTORY. (US/1078-7178). **4574**

APPLIED & PREVENTIVE PSYCHOLOGY : JOURNAL OF THE AMERICAN ASSOCIATION OF APPLIED AND PREVENTIVE PSYCHOLOGY. (US/0962-1849). **4574**

APPLIED BEHAVIORAL SCIENCE REVIEW. (US/1068-8595). **4574**

APPLIED SOCIAL PROBLEMS AND INTERVENTION STRATEGIES. (US/1070-6585). **4575**

BEHAVIOROLOGY (MORGANTOWN, W. VA.). (US/1047-8663). **4577**

BRAIN, MIND & COMMON SENSE. (US/1064-671X). **4578**

CANADIAN JOURNAL OF EXPERIMENTAL PSYCHOLOGY. (CN/1196-1961). **4579**

CHEAP RELIEF. (US/1062-9548). **4580**

CLINICAL PSYCHOLOGY AND PSYCHOTHERAPY. (UK/1063-3995). **4581**

COGNITIVE AND BEHAVIORAL PRACTICE. (US). **4581**

CONSCIOUSNESS AND COGNITION. (US/1053-8100). **4582**

CONSULTING PSYCHOLOGY JOURNAL. (US/1065-9293). **4582**

COUNSELING TODAY. (US). **4583**

CURRENT DIRECTIONS IN PSYCHOLOGICAL SCIENCE : A JOURNAL OF THE AMERICAN PSYCHOLOGICAL SOCIETY. (US/0963-7214). **4583**

DEPRESSION (NEW YORK, N.Y.). (US/1062-6417). **4584**

EATING DISORDERS. (US/1064-0266). **4585**

ENNEIGRAM EDUCATOR. (US). **4586**

EUROPEAN EATING DISORDERS REVIEW. (UK/1072-4133). **4586**

EXPERIMENTAL AND CLINICAL PSYCHOPHARMACOLOGY. (US/1064-1297). **4587**

GRADUATE STUDY IN PSYCHOLOGY. (US). **4588**

INTERNATIONAL FORUM OF PSYCHOANALYSIS. (NO/0803-706X). **4590**

INTERNATIONAL JOURNAL OF BEHAVIORAL MEDICINE. (US/1070-5503). **4591**

INTERNATIONAL JOURNAL OF PSYCHOLOGY RESEARCH. (US). **4591**

INTERNATIONAL JOURNAL OF STRESS MANAGEMENT. (US/1072-5245). **4591**

INTERPRET YOUR DREAMS. (US/1060-7978). **4592**

ISSUES IN PSYCHOANALYTIC PSYCHOLOGY. (US/1075-0754). **4592**

JOURNAL OF ADULT DEVELOPMENT. (US/1068-0667). **4593**

JOURNAL OF CLINICAL GEROPSYCHOLOGY. (US). **4595**

JOURNAL OF CLINICAL PSYCHOLOGY IN MEDICAL SETTINGS. (US/1068-9583). **4595**

JOURNAL OF COMMUNITY GUIDANCE AND RESEARCH. (II/0970-1346). **4595**

JOURNAL OF CONSTRUCTIVIST PSYCHOLOGY. (US/1072-0537). **4595**

JOURNAL OF EMOTIONAL AND BEHAVIORAL DISORDERS. (US/1063-4266). **4596**

JOURNAL OF EMOTIONAL AND BEHAVIORAL PROBLEMS. (US/1064-7023). **4596**

JOURNAL OF EXPERIMENTAL PSYCHOLOGY. APPLIED. (US/1076-898X). **4596**

JOURNAL OF EXPRESSIVE THERAPY. (US/1057-7432). **4597**

JOURNAL OF INTELLECTUAL DISABILITY RESEARCH. (UK/0964-2633). **4598**

JOURNAL OF MULTICRITERIA ANALYSIS. (UK/1057-9214). **4598**

JOURNAL OF OCCUPATIONAL AND ORGANIZATIONAL PSYCHOLOGY. (UK/0963-1798). **4598**

JOURNAL OF RUSSIAN AND EAST EUROPEAN PSYCHOLOGY. (US/1061-0405). **4601**

JOURNAL OF SCHOOL PSYCHOLOGY. (US). **4601**

KINDHEIT UND ENTWICKLUNG. (GW). **4602**

LEARNING & MEMORY (COLD SPRING HARBOR, N.Y.). (US/1072-0502). **4602**

LEGAL AND CRIMINOLOGICAL PSYCHOLOGY. (UK/1355-3259). **3169**

MAGAZINE LUMIERE. (CN/1193-6924). **4603**

MEMORY. (UK/0965-8211). **4603**

MIND MATTERS. (US/1062-1806). **4604**

MINDFIELD (NEW YORK, N.Y.). (US/1065-3848). **4604**

ON BALANCE (DENVER, COLO.). (US/1062-7049). **4606**

PAKISTAN JOURNAL OF CLINICAL PSYCHOLOGY. (PK/1019-438X). **4606**

PELIZZA'S POSITIVE PRINCIPLES FOR BETTER LIVING. (US/1070-6674). **4607**

PSICOLOGIA, PSICOPATOLOGIA & PSICOSOMATICA DELLA DONNA. (US). **4609**

PSYCHOANALYSE: KLINIK UND KULTURKRITIK. (GW/0941-4428). **4610**

PSYCHODYNAMIC COUNSELLING. (UK/1353-3339). **4610**

PSYCHOLOGIE CLINIQUE EG PROJECTIVE. (FR). **4612**

PSYCHOLOGY, CRIME & LAW. (UK/1068-316X). **4612**

PSYCHOLOGY, PUBLIC POLICY, AND LAW. (US/1076-8971). **4613**

PSYCHOLOGY TODAY. (US/0033-3107). **4613**

PSYCHOLOY REVIEW. (UK/1354-1129). **4613**

PSYCHONOMIC BULLETIN & REVIEW. (US/1069-9384). **4613**

PSYCSCAN: BEHAVIOR ANALYSIS. (US). **4614**

REVUE ROUMAINE DE PSYCHOLOGIE / ACADEMIE ROUMAINE. (RM/1220-5419). **4617**

RICHARD E PIGGLE. STUDI PSICOANALITICI DEL BAMBINO E DELL'ADOLESCENTE. (US). **4617**

SEXUAL ABUSE : A JOURNAL OF RESEARCH AND TREATMENT. (US). **4618**

THERAPEUTIC CARE AND EDUCATION : THE JOURNAL OF THE ASSOCIATION OF WORKERS FOR CHILDREN WITH EMOTIONAL AND BEHAVIOURAL DIFFICULTIES. (UK). **4620**

VISUAL COGNITION. (UK/1350-6285). **4621**

ZEITSCHRIFT FUER GESUNDHEITSPSYCHOLOGIE. (GW/0943-8149). **4622**

ABSTRACTING, BIBLIOGRAPHIES AND STATISTICS

PSYCHOANALYTIC ABSTRACTS. (US/1066-9884). **4622**

PSYCSCAN. NEUROPSYCHOLOGY. (US/1058-6660). **4623**

PUBLIC ADMINISTRATION

ACCESSASIA (SEATTLE, WASH.). (US/1069-4374). **4623**

AL-MUJTAMA AL-MADANI WA-AL-TAHAWWUL AL-DIMUQRATI FI AL-WATAN AL-ARABI. (UA). **4625**

ALTERNATIVES (WASHINGTON, D.C.). (US/1070-3047). **4625**

ANNUAL REPORT PREPARED FOR THE PRESIDENT OF THE UNITED STATES AND THE UNITED STATES CONGRESS. (US). **4629**

Public Administration

BRITISH ELECTIONS AND PARTIES YEARBOOK. (UK/0968-2481). **4634**

BULLETIN OF THE EUROPEAN UNION. SUPPLEMENT. (LU). **4635**

CANADA WATCH. (CN/1191-7733). **4636**

CANADIAN FEDERAL GOVERNMENT HANDBOOK. (CN/1189-4709). **4636**

CATALOGUE DES LIVRES ET PERIODIQUES PARUS EN. (FR). **4637**

CHIEFS OF STATE & CABINET OFFICERS FOR NATIONS OF THE WORLD. (US/1060-2917). **4637**

DICKINSON'S FDA REVIEW. (US/1073-4414). **4642**

DIRECTORY OF ILLINOIS POLITICAL LEADERS. (US/1058-2657). **4643**

DIRECTORY OF STATE BAR PUBLIC SERVICE ACTIVITIES AND PROGRAMS. (US/1062-0133). **4644**

ELECTRONIC DISSEMINATION PARTNERSHIPS. (CN/1194-3750). **4645**

EPICENTRE (CHICOUTIMI). (CN/1192-5019). **4646**

ESTIMATES. PART III, TRANSPORTATION SAFETY BOARD OF CANADA. EXPENDITURE PLAN. (CN). **4646**

EUROSCOPE INC. (US/1060-9105). **4647**

EXTRA!, EXTRA! (GREENSBURG, PA.). (US/1062-7715). **4647**

FEDERAL ADVISORY DIRECTORY. (US/1074-2727). **4647**

FEDERAL EXECUTIVE DIRECTORY ANNUAL. (US/1056-7275). **4648**

FEDERAL QUALITY NEWS. (US). **4648**

FEDERAL REGULATORY PLAN. (CN/0833-7322). **4648**

FOREIGN GOVERNMENT AWARDS PROGRAM. (CN/1191-3282). **4649**

GOVERNMENT CONTRACTS & SUBCONTRACT LEADS DIRECTORY. (US/1064-6795). **4651**

GOVERNMENT DIRECTORY OF ADDRESSES AND TELEPHONE NUMBERS, THE. (US/1062-1466). **4651**

GOVERNMENT PROGRAMS. (US/1055-825X). **4652**

GOVERNMENTAL SERVICES NEWSLETTER (ASHLAND, MO.). (US/1074-9845). **4652**

GRAND BABILLARD, LE. (CN/1196-0612). **4652**

GRANDE PRAIRIE CITY DIRECTORY. (CN/1193-4077). **4652**

GRANTS-IN-AID APPLICATION AND REFERENCE MATERIALS. (US). **4653**

GUIDE TO FEDERAL FUNDING FOR ANTI-CRIME PROGRAMS. (US). **4653**

HAWVER'S CAPITOL REPORT. (US/1071-5401). **4654**

ICI BOUCHERVILLE. (CN/1187-872X). **4655**

IRC PERSPECTIVES. (CN/1188-2999). **4658**

JOURNAL OF GOVERNMENT INFORMATION. (UK/1352-0237). **4658**

JUSTICE OF THE PEACE & LOCAL GOVERNMENT LAW. (UK/1351-5756). **4659**

LISTE DES RAPPORTS ANNUELS, BIBLIOTHEQUE PRINCIPALE JE. (CN/1187-7154). **4662**

LISTE DES RAPPORTS ANNUELS, BIBLIOTHEQUE PRINCIPALE JE, LIST OF ANNUAL REPORTS, MAIN LIBRARY (JE). (CN/1187-7154). **4662**

LOBBY DIGEST & PUBLIC AFFAIRS MONTHLY, THE. (CN/1193-4034). **4662**

LOBBYING RESOURCE DIRECTORY. (US/1057-0594). **4662**

LOCAL GOVERNMENT AND ENVIRONMENTAL REPORTS OF AUSTRALIA, THE. (AT/1039-7213). **4662**

LOS ANGELES LETTER, THE. (US/1070-2938). **4663**

MAGYAR KOEZTARSASAG HELYNEVKOENYVE / KOEZPONTI STATISZTIKAI HIVATAL, A. (HU/1216-1993). **4663**

MARYLAND PROCUREMENT REPORT, THE. (US/1066-2251). **4664**

MARYLAND REGISTER CONTRACT WEEKLY. (US/1061-2696). **4664**

NCSL LEGISBRIEF. (US/1068-2716). **4668**

PARLIAMENTARY DIRECTORY (OTTAWA. 1992). (CN/1188-8652). **4672**

PBC GOVERNMENT PROGRAMS NEWSLETTER. (US/1059-2024). **4673**

PERSPECTIVE REGIONALE DE DEVELOPPEMENT DE LA MAIN-D'OEUVRE POUR L'ANNEE. (CN/1186-7620). **4673**

PERSPECTIVES / COMMISSAIRE A L'INFORMATION ET A LA PROTECTION DE LA VIE PRIVEE/ONTARIO. (CN/1188-3006). **4673**

POLICY COUNSEL. (US). **4674**

POPOL-NA. (NQ). **4674**

POUVOIRS PUBLICS AU QUEBEC. (CN/1183-482X). **4674**

PROCEEDINGS OF THE STANDING SENATE COMMITTEE ON PRIVILEGES, STANDING RULES AND ORDERS. (CN/1193-5251). **4675**

PROGRAMME DE BOURSES DES GOUVERNEMENTS ETRANGERS / ADMINISTRE PAR LE CONSEIL INTERNATIONAL D'ETUDES CANADIENNES. (CN/1191-3282). **4675**

PUBLIC MANAGER (POTOMAC, MD.), THE. (US/1061-7639). **4676**

RECUEIL DES ACTES ADMINISTRATIFS DE LA PREFECTURE DES ARDENNES ET DES SERVICES DECONCENTRES DE L'ETAT. (FR/1252-5367). **4678**

REGISTRE CANADIEN DES PROPRIETES PATRIMONIALES, ... RAPPORT ANNUEL, LE. (CN/1188-9551). **4679**

ROBINSONS REDBOOK. A NATIVE AMERICAN GUIDE TO WASHINGTON D.C. (US). **4684**

ROSSIISKAIA FEDERATSIIA. (RU). **4684**

RUSSIAN GOVERNMENT TODAY. (US/1069-1081). **4684**

SERVICE QUALITY B.C. UPDATE. (CN/1193-2724). **4685**

SOUTH CAROLINA POLICY FORUM : A REVIEW OF PUBLIC AFFAIRS IN SOUTH CAROLINA, THE. (US). **4686**

SPECTRUM (LEXINGTON, KY.). (US/1067-8530). **4686**

STATE & LOCAL LAW NEWS. (US). **4687**

STATE EXECUTIVE DIRECTORY ANNUAL. (US/1056-7011). **4687**

STATE IRM ORGANIZATIONAL STRUCTURES. (US/1066-842X). **4688**

STATE REFERENCE PUBLICATIONS. (US/1057-0586). **4688**

STATE TRENDS FORECASTS. (US/1075-5209). **4688**

STRATEGIC PLAN - CANADA MORTGAGE AND HOUSING CORPORATION. (CN/1184-616X). **4689**

SUPPLEMENTARY INFORMATION FOR LEGISLATIVE REVIEW, EXPENDITURE ESTIMATES - MANITOBA., CIVIL SERVICE COMMISSION. EMPLOYEE BENEFITS AND OTHER PAYMENTS. (CN/1189-0770). **4689**

TELEPHONE DIRECTORY, OTTAWA-HULL. (CN/1196-054X). **4690**

TEXAS STATE PUBLICATIONS. (US). **4690**

THINK TANK DIRECTORY. (US/1063-3340). **4690**

TRANSCRIPT OF SELECT COMMITTEE ON THE CONSTITUTION (FRENCH EDITION). (CN/1191-4254). **4691**

TRENT-SEVERN WATERWAY, MANAGEMENT PLANNING. (CN/1191-4750). **4691**

UTILITY REGULATORY POLICY IN THE UNITED STATES AND CANADA : COMPILATION ... OF THE NATIONAL ASSOCIATION OF REGULATORY UTILITY COMMISSIONERS. (US). **4693**

VOIE NAVIGABLE TRENT-SEVERN, PLANIFICATION DE GESTION. (CN/1191-4742). **4694**

WHITEHALL COMPANION, THE. (UK). **4695**

WHO KNOWS WHAT, A GUIDE TO EXPERTS / BY WASHINGTON RESEARCHERS, LTD. (US). **4695**

WORLDWIDE GOVERNMENT REPORT. (US/1065-1098). **4695**

ABSTRACTING, BIBLIOGRAPHIES AND STATISTICS

AUSTRALIAN CAPITAL TERRITORY IN FOCUS. (AT/1039-6594). **4696**

CIVIL SERVICE

FEDERAL EQUAL OPPORTUNITY ... DESK BOOK. (US/1066-8764). **4702**

WORLD DIRECTORY OF DIPLOMATIC REPRESENTATION. (UK/0965-3783). **4705**

PARKS AND RECREATION

GEORGIAN BAY ISLANDS NATIONAL PARK, MANAGEMENT PLANNING. (CN/1191-4734). **4706**

JOURNAL LE MACAREUX. (CN/1193-2562). **4706**

JOURNAL LE MACAREUX (FRENCH EDITION). (CN/1193-2562). **4706**

LEISURE WATCH CANADA. (CN/1189-4873). **4707**

MANITOBA PARKS AND WILDERNESS. (CN/1189-4407). **4707**

NEW PARKS NORTH. (CN/1189-4512). **4707**

PARC NATIONAL DES ILES-DE-LA-BAIE-GEORGIENNE, PLAN DE GESTION. (CN/1191-4726). **4707**

PARC NATIONAL DES ILES-DU-SAINT-LAURENT, PLAN DE GESTION. (CN/1191-470X). **4707**

ST. LAWRENCE ISLANDS NATIONAL PARK, MANAGEMENT PLAN REVIEW. (CN/1191-4718). **4708**

STATE PARK AND RECREATION UPDATE. (US/1056-8514). **4708**

PUBLIC FINANCE AND TAXATION

AGENCY BUDGET DETAIL. (US). **4708**

ASSESSMENT JOURNAL. (US/1073-8568). **4711**

BUDGET. (SA). **4714**

BUDGET ANALYSIS FOR SFY ... / STATE OF NEW YORK, LEGISLATIVE COMMISSION ON STATE-LOCAL RELATIONS. (US). **4714**

BUDGET PRESENTATION TO THE GENERAL ASSEMBLY OF THE COMMONWEALTH OF PENNSYLVANIA - UNIVERSITY OF PITTSBURGH. (US). **4715**

CAPITAL BUDGET. (US). **4716**

CAPITAL IDEAS / FROM THE NATIONAL TAXPAYERS UNION FOUNDATION. (US/1065-8114). **4716**

CAPITAL IMPROVEMENT PROGRAM, FISCAL YEARS ... / STATE OF MARYLAND, DEPARTMENT OF STATE PLANNING. (US). **4716**

CONSULTATIONS PREBUDGETAIRES/ COMITE PERMANENT DES FINANCES ET DES AFFAIRES ECONOMIQUES. (CN). **4719**

CORPORATE TAX PLANNING. (US/1188-7834). **4719**

ECONOMIC AND FISCAL REFERENCE TABLES. (CN). **4721**

ERNEST & YOUNG NEW YORK, NEW JERSEY, CONNECTICUT STATE TAX GUIDE, THE. (US/1065-7312). **4721**

ERNST & YOUNG TAX GUIDE, THE. (US/1059-809X). **4721**

ESTIMATES. PART III, DEPARTMENT OF FOREIGN AFFAIRS AND INTERNATIONAL TRADE. (CN). **4722**

EXECUTIVE BUDGET AND FINANCIAL PLAN / TRIBOROUGH BRIDGE AND TUNNEL AUTHORITY. (US). **4722**

FINANCIAL PROJECTIONS AND CAPITAL PLAN. (US). **4725**

FINANSY. (RU). **4726**

FINANZPLAN DES KANTONS BERN. (SZ). **4726**

FISCAL YEAR ESTIMATED TAX ON UNRELATED BUSINESS TAXABLE INCOME FOR TAX-EXEMPT ORGANIZATIONS (WORKSHEET). (US). **4726**

FLORIDA TAX REVIEW. (US/1066-3487). **4727**

FLOW OF FUNDS ACCOUNTS, FLOWS AND OUTSTANDINGS. (US). **4727**

FOUNDATION REPORTER (1990). (US/1055-4998). **4727**

GOVERNOR'S BUDGET REPORT, PREPARED BY THE DIVISION OF THE BUDGET, THE. (US). **4729**

GOVERNOR'S PROPOSED ... OPERATING BUDGET SUPPORTING DATA, STATEWIDE SUMMARY TABLES. (US). **4729**

GUIDE TO THE EUROPEAN VAT DIRECTIVES: COMMENTARY ON THE VALUE ADDED TAX OF THE EUROPEAN COMMUNITY. (NE). **4730**

GUIDELINES FOR THE ROLLING PLAN. (NR). **4730**

HBJ MILLER COMPREHENSIVE GOVERNMENTAL GAAP GUIDE. (US). **4730**

ILLINOIS STATE BUDGET DETAIL. (US). **4731**

INTRODUCTION TO FEDERAL INCOME TAXES, AN. (US/1070-8502). **4733**

IRS PROCEDURAL FORMS AND ANALYSIS. (US). **4734**

LET'S GO: THE BUDGET GUIDE TO WASHINGTON, D.C./ WRITTEN BY HARVARD STUDENT AGENCIES, INC. (US). **4736**

MID-SESSION REVIEW : THE PRESIDENT'S BUDGET AND ECONOMIC GROWTH AGENDA OF THE ... BUDGET / EXECUTIVE OFFICE OF THE PRESIDENT, OFFICE OF MANAGEMENT AND BUDGET. (US). **4737**

MONEY INCOME TAX HANDBOOK, THE. (US/1065-125X). **4737**

NATIONAL ROLLING PLAN. (NR). **4738**

NORTH AMERICAN OUTLOOK. (US/1071-5584). **4739**

NOTES BLEUES DE BERCY / MINISTERE DE L'ECONOMIE ET DES FINANCES, MINISTERE DU BUDGET, LES. (FR). **4739**

ONTARIO FISCAL OUTLOOK. (CN/1188-2867). **4739**

PAYROLL CURRENTLY. (US/1065-6529). **4740**

PBC TAX BRIEFS. (US/1059-1974). **4740**

PERSPECTIVES BUDGETAIRES DE L'ONTARIO. (CN/1188-2875). **4741**

POPULI / UNITED NATIONS POPULATION FUND. (US). **4559**

PRACTITIONER'S INCOME TAX ACT, THE. (CN/1193-1701). **4741**

REGLES BUDGETAIRES DU MINISTRE DES TRANSPORTS CONCERNANT LE TRANSPORT DES ELEVES. (CN/1193-3836). **4744**

STATE OF NEW YORK EXECUTIVE BUDGET, AGENCY PRESENTATIONS. (US). **4749**

STATE OF NEW YORK EXECUTIVE BUDGET ... ANNUAL MESSAGE. (US). **4749**

STATE TAX NOTES (MICROFICHE). (US/1060-491X). **4749**

SUMMARY OF REVENUE PROPOSALS IN THE PRESIDENT'S ... BUDGET / PREPARED BY THE STAFF OF THE JOINT COMMITTEE ON TAXATION. (US). **4751**

TAXATION OF PERMANENT ESTABLISHMENTS, THE. (NE). **4755**

TRANSCRIPT OF STANDING COMMITTEE ON PUBLIC ACCOUNTS. (CN/1189-4210). **4756**

TWO YEAR BUDGET/ CITY OF PALO ALTO. (US). **4757**

UNITED STATES TAX REPORTER. (US). **4757**

VAT PLANNING. (UK/0964-5985). **4757**

WGL TAX JOURNAL DIGEST, THE. (US/1075-0223). **4758**

PUBLIC UTILITIES

AREAS SERVED BY NATURAL GAS. (CN/1199-1801). **4759**

EL & P U.S. ELECTRIC UTILITY INDUSTRY DIRECTORY. (US/1058-2479). **4759**

ELECTRIC UTILITY WEEK'S DEMAND-SIDE REPORT. (US/1065-8696). **4761**

FORTNIGHTLY : THE NORTH AMERICAN UTILITIES BUSINESS MAGAZINE. (US/1074-6099). **4761**

GAS UTILITY REPORT. (US). **4761**

INDEPENDENT POWER MARKETS QUARTERLY. (US/1065-870X). **4761**

NATURAL GAS UTILITY DIRECTORY. (CN). **4761**

SUMMARY OF ECONOMIC AND LOAD FORECASTS. (CN/0825-6667). **4762**

UTILITY FORECASTER, THE. (US/1064-5373). **4762**

UTILITY WORKERS' LIGHT. (US). **4763**

PUBLIC HEALTH AND SAFETY

ACTUALITE ET DOSSIER EN SANTE PUBLIQUE. (FR/1243-275X). **4763**

ALABAMA HEALTH CARE IN PERSPECTIVE. (US/1065-4038). **4764**

ALASKA HEALTH CARE IN PERSPECTIVE. (US/1065-4046). **4764**

ANNUAL REPORT FOR THE FISCAL YEAR ENDING ... / NOVA SCOTIA PROVINCIAL HEALTH COUNCIL. (CN/1193-3003). **4765**

ARIZONA HEALTH CARE IN PERSPECTIVE. (US/1065-4054). **4767**

ARKANSAS HEALTH CARE IN PERSPECTIVE. (US/1065-4062). **4767**

ASBESTOS & LEAD ABATEMENT REPORT. (US/1068-2643). **4767**

ASIAN AMERICAN AND PACIFIC ISLANDER JOURNAL OF HEALTH. (US/1072-0367). **4768**

BC HEALTH AND DISEASE SURVEILLANCE. (CN/1189-4199). **4768**

BEHAVORIAL HEALTHCARE TOMORROW. (US/1063-8490). **4768**

BNA CALIFORNIA SAFETY & HEALTH REPORT. (US/1065-3104). **4768**

BREATHE! (LA QUINTA, CALIF.). (US/1065-710X). **4769**

BRIEFINGS ON LONG-TERM CARE REGULATIONS. (US/1076-6014). **4769**

CALIFORNIA HEALTH CARE IN PERSPECTIVE. (US/1065-4070). **4770**

CANADA COMMUNICABLE DISEASE REPORT. (CN/1188-4169). **4770**

CANADA COMMUNICABLE DISEASE REPORT. (CN/1188-4169). **4770**

CHILD SAFETY NEWS. (AT). **4771**

CITIZENS HEALTH ALERT. (US/1062-1245). **4771**

Public Health and Safety

COLLEGIATE JOURNAL, THE. (US/1061-8767). **4771**

COLORADO HEALTH CARE IN PERSPECTIVE. (US/1065-4089). **4771**

CONNECTICUT HEALTH CARE IN PERSPECTIVE. (US/1065-4097). **4772**

CONSUMER HEALTH SAFETY DIGEST. (US/1058-0387). **4772**

CONTAMINATION ALERT. (US/1061-866X). **4772**

CORONER (SAINTE-FOY). (CN/1191-3959). **4772**

CURRENT ISSUES IN PUBLIC HEALTH. (US/1076-7762). **4773**

DELAWARE HEALTH CARE IN PERSPECTIVE. (US/1065-4100). **4773**

DEVELOPMENTS IN HEALTH ECONOMICS AND PUBLIC POLICY. (NE). **4773**

DRUG & CRIME PREVENTION FUNDING NEWS. (US/1076-1519). **4774**

EMERGENCY SERVICES SOURCEBOOK. (US/1066-0348). **4774**

EMF HEALTH & SAFETY DIGEST. (US/1062-5526). **4774**

FAR EAST FOCUS. (UK/1354-5299). **4775**

FAXON HEALTH INFORMATION CATALOG. (US/1059-6836). **4775**

FLORIDA HEALTH CARE IN PERSPECTIVE. (US/1065-4119). **4775**

GEORGIA HEALTH CARE IN PERSPECTIVE. (US/1065-4127). **4776**

GESUNDHEITSWESEN, DAS. (GW/0941-3790). **4776**

HAWAII HEALTH CARE IN PERSPECTIVE. (US/1065-4135). **4777**

HEALING (SACRAMENTO, CALIF.). (US/1064-4237). **4777**

HEALTH AND MEDICINE. (US/1061-6446). **4777**

HEALTH AND SAFETY MANAGER. (UK/1352-5611). **4778**

HEALTH CARE 1000, THE. (US/1070-9150). **4778**

HEALTH CARE BILLER, THE. (US/1063-5335). **4778**

HEALTH CARE REGISTRATION. (US). **4778**

HEALTH CARE STATE RANKINGS. (US/1065-1403). **4778**

HEALTH ECONOMICS. (US/1057-9230). **4779**

HEALTH EDUCATOR : JOURNAL OF ETA SIGMA GAMMA. (US). **4779**

HEALTH PROMOTION IN CANADA. (CN/1195-6747). **4781**

HEALTH PROMOTION PRACTITIONER. (US/1060-5517). **4781**

HEALTH (SAN FRANCISCO, CALIF.). (US/1059-938X). **4781**

HEALTH TRANSITION REVIEW : THE CULTURAL, SOCIAL, AND BEHAVIOURAL DETERMINANTS OF HEALTH. (AT/1036-4005). **4781**

HEALTH VISION. (CN/1189-475X). **4782**

HEALTHSERVICE LEADER, THE. (US/1070-0978). **4782**

HOME HEALTH CARE REIMBURSEMENT REPORT. (US/1074-4541). **4783**

IDAHO HEALTH CARE IN PERSPECTIVE. (US/1065-4143). **4783**

ILLINOIS HEALTH CARE IN PERSPECTIVE. (US/1065-4151). **4784**

INDIANA HEALTH CARE IN PERSPECTIVE. (US/1065-416X). **4784**

INJURY PREVENTION. (UK). **4784**

IOWA HEALTH CARE IN PERSPECTIVE. (US/1065-4178). **4785**

JOURNAL FOR HEALTHCARE QUALITY: PROMOTING EXCELLENCE IN HEALTHCARE. (US). **4786**

JOURNAL OF HEALTH AND PLACE. (UK/1353-8292). **4786**

JOURNAL OF HEALTH INFORMATION MANAGEMENT RESEARCH, THE. (US/1060-5657). **4787**

JOURNAL OF HIV/AIDS PREVENTION & EDUCATION FOR ADOLESCENTS & CHILDREN. (US/1069-837X). **4787**

KANSAS HEALTH CARE IN PERSPECTIVE. (US/1065-4186). **4788**

KENTUCKY HEALTH CARE IN PERSPECTIVE. (US/1065-4194). **4788**

LEAD POISONING REPORT. (US/1075-0665). **4788**

LIVING SAFETY. (CN/1200-2275). **4789**

LOUISIANA HEALTH CARE IN PERSPECTIVE. (US/1065-4208). **4789**

MAINE HEALTH CARE IN PERSPECTIVE. (US/1065-4216). **4789**

MARYLAND HEALTH CARE IN PERSPECTIVE. (US/1065-4224). **4789**

MASSACHUSETTS HEALTH CARE IN PERSPECTIVE. (US/1065-4232). **4789**

MICHIGAN HEALTH CARE IN PERSPECTIVE. (US/1065-4240). **4791**

MINNESOTA HEALTH CARE IN PERSPECTIVE. (US/1065-4259). **4791**

MISSISSIPPI HEALTH CARE IN PERSPECTIVE. (US/1065-4267). **4791**

MISSOURI HEALTH CARE IN PERSPECTIVE. (US/1065-4275). **4791**

MONTANA HEALTH CARE IN PERSPECTIVE. (US/1065-4283). **4791**

NAHE (WESTWOOD, MASS.). (US/1064-6078). **4792**

NEBRASKA HEALTH CARE IN PERSPECTIVE. (US/1065-4291). **4793**

NEVADA HEALTH CARE IN PERSPECTIVE. (US/1065-4305). **4793**

NEW HAMPSHIRE HEAALTH CARE IN PERSPECTIVE. (US/1065-4313). **4793**

NEW JERSEY HEALTH CARE IN PERSPECTIVE. (US/1065-4526). **4793**

NEW MEXICO HEALTH CARE IN PERSPECTIVE. (US/1065-4321). **4793**

NEW YORK HEALTH CARE IN PERSPECTIVE. (US/1065-433X). **4793**

NORTH CAROLINA HEALTH CARE IN PERSPECTIVE. (US/1065-4348). **4794**

NORTH DAKOTA HEALTH CARE IN PERSPECTIVE. (US/1065-4356). **4794**

NTIS ALERT. HEALTH CARE / PREPARED BY THE NATIONAL TECHNICAL INFORMATION SERVICE, U.S. DEPARTMENT OF COMMERCE, TECHNOLOGY ADMINISTRATION. (US). **4794**

O'CONNOR REPORT (SEATTLE, WASH.). (US/1064-265X). **4794**

OHIO HEALTH CARE IN PERSPECTIVE. (US/1065-4364). **4794**

OKLAHOMA HEALTH CARE IN PERSPECTIVE. (US/1065-4372). **4794**

OREGON HEALTH CARE IN PERSPECTIVE. (US/1065-4380). **4795**

PBC COMPREHENSIVE HEALTH BRIEFS. (US/1059-2067). **4795**

PENNSYLVANIA HEALTH CARE IN PERSPECTIVE. (US/1065-4399). **4795**

PERFORMING ARTS HEALTH NEWS. (US/1065-6642). **4795**

PERSONAL HEALTH REPORTER. (US/1061-4125). **4795**

POSITIVE LIVING. (US). **4795**

PROBLEMY SOTSIALNOI GIGIENY I ISTORIIA MEDITSINY / NII SOTSIALNOI GIGIENY, EKONOMIKI I UPRAVLENIIA ZDRAVOOKHRANENIEM IM N.A. SEMASHKO RAMN, AO ASSOTSIATSIIA 'MEDITSINSKAIA LITERATURA.'. (RU/0869-866X). **4796**

PROMOTION AND EDUCATION. (FR/0751-7149). **4797**

RHODE ISLAND HEALTH CARE IN PERSPECTIVE. (US/1065-4402). **4800**

SAUDE E SOCIEDADE. (BL/0104-1290). **4801**

SMALL BUSINESS HEALTH REFORM WATCH. (US/1076-4488). **4803**

SOUTH CAROLINA HEALTH CARE IN PERSPECTIVE. (US/1065-4410). **4803**

SOUTH DAKOTA HEALTH CARE IN PERSPECTIVE. (US/1065-4429). **4803**

STRATEGIES & SOLUTIONS. (US/1067-9537). **4804**

TENNESSEE HEALTH CARE IN PERSPECTIVE. (US/1065-4437). **4804**

TEXAS EMS MAGAZINE. (US/1063-8202). **4805**

TEXAS HEALTH CARE IN PERSPECTIVE. (US/1065-4445). **4805**

TOBACCO CONTROL. (UK/0964-4563). **4805**

TOPICS IN HEALTH INFORMATION MANAGEMENT. (US/1065-0989). **4805**

UTAH HEALTH CARE IN PERSPECTIVE. (US/1065-4453). **4806**

VERMONT HEALTH CARE IN PERSPECTIVE. (US/1065-4461). **4806**

VIRGINIA HEALTH CARE IN PERSPECTIVE. (US/1065-447X). **4806**

WASHINGTON HEALTH CARE IN PERSPECTIVE. (US/1065-4488). **4807**

WEST VIRGINIA HEALTH CARE IN PERSPECTIVE. (US/1065-4496). **4807**

WISCONSIN HEALTH CARE IN PERSPECTIVE. (US/1065-450X). **4807**

WYOMING HEALTH CARE IN PERSPECTIVE. (US/1065-4518). **4808**

ABSTRACTING, BIBLIOGRAPHIES AND STATISTICS

STATISTICAL NEWS. (US). **4811**

PUBLISHING

AFRICAN PUBLISHERS NETWORKING DIRECTORY AND NAMES & NUMBERS. (UK). **4811**

AT RANDOM. (US/1062-0036). **4812**

BACON'S MAGAZINE DIRECTORY. (US). **4812**

BACON'S NEWSPAPER DIRECTORY. (US). **4812**

DIRECTORY OF PUBLISHING. CONTINENTAL EUROPE. (UK). **4814**

DIRECTORY OF PUBLISHING. UNITED KINGDOM, COMMONWEALTH AND OVERSEAS. (UK). **4814**

JOURNAL OF SCHOLARLY PUBLISHING. (CN). **4816**

PROFESSIONAL PUBLISHING UPDATE. (US/1066-0674). **4818**

PUBLICITY AND MEDIA RESOURCES FOR BOOK PUBLISHERS. (US/1063-1739). **4818**

PUBLISHING TECHNOLOGY REVIEW. (UK/1351-0177). **4819**

VERZEICHNIS DER VEROFFENTLICHUNGEN / STATISTISCHES BUNDESAMT. (GW). **4820**

ABSTRACTING, BIBLIOGRAPHIES AND STATISTICS

JOURNAL SUBSCRIPTION CATALOG / THE ASSOCIATION OF AMERICAN UNIVERSITY PRESSES. (US/1064-5470). **4821**

BOOKS AND BOOKMAKING

ANNUAL REGISTER OF BOOK VALUES. MODERN FIRST EDITIONS. (UK/0968-7521). **4823**

ANTIQUARIAN BOOK MONTHLY. (UK). **4823**

ATLANTIC BOOKS TODAY. (CN/1192-3652). **4823**

BLACK AUTHORS BOOKS IN PRINT. (US/1066-940X). **4824**

BOOKS MAGAZINE. (UK/0952-987X). **4826**

END PAPERS (ARLINGTON, VA.). (US/1063-8938). **4828**

FROM THE OLDE BOOKSHELF. (US/1066-2979). **4828**

NEW BOOKTALKER, THE. (US/1064-7511). **4830**

PLANT'S REVIEW OF BOOKS. (US/1064-4741). **4831**

SHEPPARD'S BOOK DEALERS IN EUROPE. (UK/0963-0171). **4832**

REAL ESTATE

AUSTIN REAL ESTATE FINANCE SOURCEBOOK. (US/1071-5142). **4834**

CANADIAN REALTOR NEWS. (CN/1193-8021). **4835**

COLORADO REAL ESTATE JOURNAL. (US/1060-4383). **4835**

COMMERCIAL REAL ESTATE PROPERTY DIRECTORY. (US/1062-5879). **4836**

DALLAS/FORT WORTH REAL ESTATE FINANCE SOURCEBOOK. (US/1071-5134). **4836**

FAIRFAX DIRECTORY SERVICE. (US). **4837**

FEDERAL SUPPLY CATALOG. SECTION VII, CLASSIFICATION OF PROPERTY WITH ALPHABETICAL INDEX OF EXPENDABLE ITEMS. (US). **4837**

HOUSTON REAL ESTATE FINANCE SOURCEBOOK. (US/1065-853X). **4838**

INSIDER REAL ESTATE GUIDE, THE. (US/1068-1264). **4839**

JOURNAL OF THE AMERICAN REAL ESTATE AND URBAN ECONOMICS ASSOCIATION. (US/1067-8433). **4839**

NATIONAL REFERRAL ROSTER. (US/1075-1084). **4842**

NATIONAL REGISTER OF COMMERCIAL REAL ESTATE, THE. (US/1062-6352). **4842**

NELSON'S DIRECTORY OF INSTITUTIONAL REAL ESTATE. (US/1060-5789). **4842**

OFFICE LEASING DIRECTORY. (CN/1189-5993). **4842**

PENNSYLVANIA COMMERCIAL REAL ESTATE. (US/1059-6526). **4842**

PENNSYLVANIA REAL ESTATE. (US/1059-6534). **4842**

PROFESSIONAL REPORT : A PUBLICATION OF THE SOCIETY OF INDUSTRIAL AND OFFICE REALTORS. (US/1067-4764). **4843**

REAL ESTATE WORKOUTS & ASSET MANAGEMENT. (US/1063-4290). **4845**

REAL PROPERTY ASSESSMENT. YEAR ONE. (CN/1187-7200). **4845**

REIT HANDBOOK : COMPLETE GUIDE TO THE REAL ESTATE INVESTMENT TRUST INDUSTRY. (US). **4846**

RESOURCE BOOK, REAL ESTATE. LOS ANGELES COUNTY. (US/1059-3047). **4846**

RESOURCE BOOK, REAL ESTATE. ORANGE, RIVERSIDE & SAN BERNARDINO COUNTIES. (US/1060-3948). **4846**

SPAULDING & SLYE REPORT. GREATER BOSTON, THE. (US/1063-9098). **4847**

SPAULDING & SLYE REPORT. WASHINGTON, D.C, THE. (US/1063-9101). **4847**

TRW REDI REALTY REPORT. (US/1075-3664). **4848**

RECREATION, LEISURE

COLUMBIA GORGE VISITOR & RECREATION GUIDE (1992). (US/1063-763X). **4849**

COMICS VALUES ANNUAL. (US/1062-4503). **4849**

CONDO VACATIONING. (US/1062-9653). **4849**

EVENTS USA. (US/1066-6346). **4850**

FESTIVALS & ATTRACTIONS. (CN/1196-4790). **4850**

GORGE GUIDE. (US/1063-7656). **4850**

INTERNATIONAL JOURNAL OF LEISURE. (UK/1352-2809). **4851**

INTERNATIONAL PLAY JOURNAL. (UK). **4851**

JOURNAL OF HOSPITALITY & LEISURE MARKETING. (US/1050-7051). **4851**

LEISURE AND FAMILY FUN: LAFF. (US/1053-4814). **4851**

LONG ISLAND EXPRESS QUARTERLY. (US/1062-8223). **4852**

LOST TREASURE'S TREASURE CACHE. (US/1063-1372). **4852**

SIOUXLAND EVENTS. (US/1060-376X). **4854**

SNOWWEST SNOWMOBILE WEST MAGAZINE. (US). **4854**

VACATION HOME REPORT. (US/1049-6351). **4855**

WILD STEELHEAD AND ATLANTIC SALMON. (US/1072-558X). **4855**

ABSTRACTING, BIBLIOGRAPHIES AND STATISTICS

BIBLIOGRAPHIES AND INDEXES ON SPORTS HISTORY. (US/1066-3746). **4856**

SPORTING NEWS OFFICIAL BASEBALL REGISTER, THE. (US). **4856**

GAMES AND AMUSEMENTS

AMERICAN CHESS JOURNAL (CAMBRIDGE, MASS.). (US/1066-8292). **4856**

APHELION (SANTA ANA, CALIF.). (US/1062-502X). **4857**

B.B. DUCKWOOD'S WORD SEARCH IN RUSSIAN. (US/1060-474X). **4857**

BETTY (MAMARONECK, N.Y.). (US/1064-9395). **4857**

BILLIARD INDUSTRY SOURCE BOOK, THE. (US). **4857**

BUCK NAKED CRIME FIGHTER. (US/1068-6800). **4858**

CHESS (OXFORD). (UK/0964-6221). **4858**

COMBO (EVANSTON, ILL.). (US/1078-389X). **4859**

CROSSWORD CHALLENGE. (US/1065-2922). **4859**

DIKOBRAZ. (XR). **4860**

ELECTRONIC GAMES. (US/1063-8326). **4860**

FAMILY ENTERTAINMENT CENTER. (US/1064-542X). **4861**

FEMME FATALE. (US/1064-6302). **4861**

GAME PLAYERS SEGA NINTENDO. (US/1074-2425). **4861**

GAMER'S CONNECTION, THE. (US/1061-611X). **4861**

Recreation, Leisure — Games and Amusements

GHOST RIDER & BLAZE : SPIRITS OF VENGEANCE. (US/1065-8785). **4862**

INSIDE COMICS (GLASSBORO, N.J.). (US/1062-7405). **4862**

JOURNEYS (BLOOMINGTON, ILL.). (US/1063-729X). **4862**

LAS VEGAS CASINO JOURNAL. (US). **4862**

OMNIFORCE (BROOKLYN, NEW YORK, N.Y.). (US/1062-2594). **4864**

PC GAMER. (US/1351-3540). **4864**

PLAY (GAINESVILLE, FLA.). (US/1062-6956). **4864**

PUZZLER (MINNETONKA, MINN.), THE. (US/1062-1164). **4865**

ROTISSERIE LEAGUE FOOTBALL. (US). **4865**

SZACHISTA WARSZAWA. (PL/1230-2309). **4866**

TERROR, INC. (US/1065-1764). **4866**

TOXIC CRUSADERS. (US/1064-4261). **4867**

TURBOFORCE (LOMBARD, ILL.). (US/1063-8334). **4867**

WEEKLY PUZZLER, THE. (US/1060-779X). **4867**

WORD SEARCH CHALLENGE. (US/1065-2930). **4868**

OUTDOOR LIFE

ADVENTURE WEST. (US). **4868**

AMC OUTDOORS. (US/1067-5604). **4868**

BASS & WALLEYE BOATS. (US). **4869**

BIG GAME HUNTING. (US/1059-5767). **4869**

CHASSE AU QUEBEC, PRINCIPALES REGLES, LA. (CN/1185-247X). **4871**

COMPLETE GUIDE TO 9MM. (US/1059-5783). **4871**

FISHING TRIP MAGAZINE. (US/1060-5444). **4872**

HUNTING HORIZONS. (US/1059-3837). **4873**

HUNTING TRIP MAGAZINE. (US/1060-5452). **4873**

JOE FELLEGY'S MILLE LACS FISHING DIGEST. (US/1062-5224). **4874**

KENTUCKY AFIELD. (US/1059-9177). **4874**

NATIONAL VOLUNTEERS IN PARKS DIRECTORY (U.S. ED.). (US/1058-8221). **4875**

NEW YORK OUTDOORS. (US). **4875**

NO LIMITS WORLD. (IT/1121-6379). **4876**

OUTDOOR ILLINOIS (SPRINGFIELD, ILL.). (US/1072-7175). **4877**

PENNSYLVANIA FISHERMAN. (US/1057-8331). **4877**

PETERSEN'S ... ANNUAL TURKEY HUNTING. (US/1059-1753). **4877**

SHOOTER'S GUIDE (CALIFORNIA ED.). (US/1053-0304). **4878**

WEDKARSTWO I TY. (PL/0867-4663). **4880**

WILDERNESS SERIES. (US/1056-3318). **4880**

SPORTS

.22 RIMFIRE. (US/1066-6834). **4881**

AMERICAN RACING CLASSICS. (US/1069-1693). **4883**

AUTO RACEPAGES. (US/1059-8367). **4885**

AUTO SPORTS MOTEUR, L'. (CN/1193-509X). **4885**

BICYCLE TRAVELER, THE. (US/1065-1802). **4887**

BIKE (MIDDLETOWN, R.I.), THE. (US/1064-492X). **4887**

BLUE BOOK OF COLLEGE ATHLETICS FOR SENIOR, JUNIOR & COMMUNITY COLLEGES, THE. (US/1067-750X). **4887**

BOTTOM TIME. (US/1065-7134). **4887**

BUFFALO SPORTS NEWS, THE. (US/1065-2140). **4888**

CIEL BLEU (SAINT-EDOUARD). (CN/1191-3851). **4890**

COLLEGE SPORTS (RUTHERFORD, N.J.). (US/1065-8270). **4890**

COMPLETE GUIDE TO .38/.357. (US/1072-8457). **4891**

COMPLETE GUIDE TO 45'S. (US/1059-5716). **4891**

DIVING & SNORKELING QUARTERLY. (US/1062-1210). **4893**

DIVING (BLOOMSBURG, PA.). (US/1063-0767). **4893**

DRIVER (MIAMI, FLA.). (US/1062-9394). **4893**

ECONOMIC ANALYSIS OF UNITED STATES SKI AREAS. (US/1070-9231). **4893**

FIL MAGAZIN. (AU). **4894**

FRED TROST'S PRACTICAL SPORTSMAN. (US/1067-5914). **4895**

GEO PLEIN-AIR. (CN/1194-5303). **4896**

GOLF INTERNATIONAL. (CN/1189-4830). **4896**

GOLF VACATIONS (BURLINGTON). (CN/1189-4849). **4897**

GREAT AMERICAN BASEBALL STAT BOOK. (US/1056-5116). **4897**

GUN TRADER. (US/1061-6918). **4897**

HANDGUNNING. (US/1060-068X). **4898**

HIGH SCHOOL GIRLS GYMNASTICS RULES AND MANUAL. (US/1069-6393). **4898**

HIGH SCHOOL SOFTBALL UMPIRES MANUAL. (US/1075-1920). **4898**

HOCKEY, ART OF THE STATE. (US/1064-6892). **4898**

HOCKEY SCOUTING REPORT. (CN/0836-5148). **4899**

INDIANA BASKETBALL HISTORY : A PUBLICATION OF THE INDIANA BASKETBALL HALL OF FAME. (US). **4900**

INSIDE TAE KWON DO. (US/1065-4682). **4900**

INTERNATIONAL FIGURE SKATING. (US/1070-9568). **4900**

JOURNAL OF STRENGTH AND CONDITIONING RESEARCH. (US/1064-8011). **4902**

JUNIOR TENNIS. (US/1074-0554). **4902**

KUNG FU MASTERS. (US/1068-7645). **4903**

LACROSSE TALK. (UK). **4903**

LET'S GO RACIN'. (CN/1188-5416). **4903**

MANN FANTASY BASEBALL GUIDE, THE. (US/1072-3595). **4904**

MANN-MALLIN FANTASY BASEBALL GUIDE, THE. (US). **4904**

MEDIA INFORMATION FOR THE ... IIHF WORLD JUNIOR HOCKEY CHAMPIONSHIPS / PREPARED BY THE CANADIAN HOCKEY LEAGUE. (CN/1191-3991). **4904**

MILES TO GO. (US/1061-7140). **4905**

MUSSELMAN'S ORIGINAL PRO BASKETBALL SCOUTING HANDBOOK. (US/1062-9513). **4905**

NATURAL BODYBUILDING AND FITNESS. (US/1071-555X). **4906**

NCAA MEN'S AND WOMEN'S TRACK AND FIELD AND CROSS COUNTRY RULES. (US). **4907**

NEW WAVE WRESTLING. (US/1060-5908). **4907**

OCEAN SEA DIVERS WORLDWIDE DIVING DIRECTORY. (US). **4908**

OFFICIAL MAJOR LEAGUE BASEBALL ROOKIE LEAGUE MAGAZINE FOR KIDS. (US/1061-9178). **4909**

OFFICIAL ... NCAA BASKETBALL. (US/1063-1089). **4909**

OHIO SPORTS ALMANAC. (US/1061-8368). **4910**

PENNSYLVANIA GOLFER MAGAZINE. (US/1060-5460). **4912**

PETERSEN'S ... COLLEGE BASKETBALL. (US/1059-5805). **4912**

PETERSEN'S GOLFING. (US/1073-4716). **4912**

RACER (TUSTIN, CALIF.). (US/1066-6060). **4914**

READ-EASY BASKETBALL RULES. (US/1074-6242). **4914**

RECORD BOOK / CANADIAN HOCKEY LEAGUE. (CN/1191-3975). **4914**

RIFLE & SHOTGUN ANNUAL. (US/1059-5759). **4915**

RODALE'S SCUBA DIVING. (US/1060-9563). **4915**

RULES OF GOLF FOR ... AND THE RULES FOR AMATEUR STATUS. (US). **4916**

RUNNING WILD. (US/1067-5094). **4916**

SCHOLASTIC COACH AND ATHLETIC DIRECTOR. (US/1077-5625). **4917**

SKIING FOR WOMEN. (US). **4918**

SLAM (NEW YORK, N.Y.). (US/1072-625X). **4919**

SOCCER MAGAZINE (TITUSVILLE, FLA.). (US/1070-9754). **4919**

SOCCER RULES. (US/1072-0170). **4919**

SPALDING BOOK OF RULES AND ... SPORTS ALMANAC. (US/1065-4763). **4920**

SPORT AND SPORT 2. (UK). **4920**

SPORT MARKETING QUARTERLY. (US/1061-6934). **4920**

SPORT RIDER. (US/1065-7649). **4921**

Religion and Theology —Bible

SPORT SCIENCE REVIEW (CHAMPAIGN, ILL.). (US/1056-6724). **4921**

SPORTING NEWS NBA GUIDE, THE. (US) **4922**

SPORTS CARD PRICE GUIDE MONTHLY. (US/1061-5512). **4922**

SPORTS FAN'S CONNECTION. (US/1059-0862). **4922**

SPORTS ILLUSTRATED ... SPORTS ALMANAC, THE. (US/1056-7887). **4923**

SPORTS-N-REVIEW. (US/1062-8215). **4923**

SUKCES W AMERYCE. (CN/1192-523X). **4924**

SURFER'S JOURNAL, THE. (US/1062-3892). **4924**

SWIAT KARATE. (PL/0867-6410). **4924**

TOTAL TRIATHLON ALMANAC, THE. (US/1065-1977). **4926**

U.S. COLLEGE HOCKEY MAGAZINE. (US/1076-0008). **4927**

ULTIMATE FANTASY FOOTBALL LEAGUE ... GUIDE AND HANDBOOK, THE. (US). **4927**

ULTRA CYCLING. (US/1063-9349). **4927**

USA TODAY BASEBALL WEEKLY. (US/1057-9532). **4928**

USA TODAY BASEBALL WEEKLY ALMANAC. (US). **4928**

VERMONT GOLF JOURNAL & DIRECTORY. (US/1058-8442). **4928**

WB (GREENDALE, WIS.). (US/1078-2958). **4929**

WOMEN'S SPORTS EXPERIENCE, THE. (US/1061-1568). **4930**

RELIGION AND THEOLOGY

ADULT STUDENT GUIDE. (US/1059-3225). **4932**

ADULT TEACHER GUIDE. (US/1059-3233). **4932**

AETHERIUS SOCIETY NEWSLETTER, THE. (US/1063-0937). **4932**

AMERICAN INDIAN RELIGIONS. (US/1065-8068). **4933**

AMS STUDIES IN RELIGIOUS TRADITION. (US/1059-7255). **4934**

ANABAPTIST TIMES, THE. (US/1065-6812). **4934**

AUTOCEPHALOUS ORTHODOX CHURCHES, THE. (US/1059-1001). **4937**

BABY & TODDLER TEACHER GUIDE. (US/1059-3292). **4937**

CAHIER DE L'ENVOLEE LUMIERE. (CN/1188-6749). **4941**

CHRISTIAN ADVOCATE (AUSTIN, TEX.). (US/1062-970X). **4944**

CHRISTIAN COUNSELING TODAY. (US/1076-9668). **4944**

CHRISTIAN HOME JOURNAL, THE. (US/1065-8386). **4945**

CHRISTO, EN. (US/1064-9751). **4946**

CLERGY FOCUS. (US/1061-527X). **4948**

COMMUNICATOR (NASHVILLE, TENN., 1992), THE. (US/1061-4133). **4949**

CROSSROADS (SUNNYVALE, CALIF.). (US/1065-6863). **4951**

DONKEY TALK. (US/1062-3426). **4954**

ECHOES (MEDICINE HAT). (CN/1193-0748). **4955**

HERALDO DE SANTIDAD (1992), EL. (US/1060-2135). **4962**

HI-TEEN STUDENT GUIDE. (US/1059-3365). **4962**

HI-TEEN TEACHER GUIDE. (US/1059-3357). **4962**

JAPAN CHRISTIAN REVIEW, THE. (JA/0918-516X). **4967**

JOURNAL OF BIBLICAL COUNSELING, THE. (US/1063-2166). **4968**

JOURNAL OF BOOK OF MORMON STUDIES, THE. (US/1065-9366). **4968**

JOURNAL OF EARLY CHRISTIAN STUDIES. (US/1067-6341). **4968**

JOURNAL OF RELIGION IN DISABILITY & REHABILITATION. (US/1059-9258). **4970**

JOURNAL OF RESEARCH ON CHRISTIAN EDUCATION. (US/1065-6219). **4970**

JOURNAL OF VAISNAVA STUDIES, THE. (US/1062-1237). **4971**

JUNIOR STUDENT GUIDE. (US/1059-3373). **4971**

JUNIOR TEACHER GUIDE. (US/1059-3322). **4971**

KINDERGARTEN TEACHER GUIDE. (US/1072-1444). **4972**

LIFELINES FOR YOUTH TEACHER. (US/1063-794X). **4973**

LITURGICAL MINISTRY. (US/1059-7786). **4974**

LIVING PULPIT, THE. (US/1059-2733). **4974**

LOGIA (FORT WAYNE, INDIANA). (US/1064-0398). **4974**

LWML QUARTERLY ECHO. (US/1066-5749). **4975**

MANY PATHS. (US). **4975**

MESSIANIC JEW (AND HEBREW CHRISTIAN) / INTERNATIONAL MESSIANIC JEWISH (HEBREW CHRISTIAN) ALLIANCE, THE. (UK). **4976**

MIDDLER & JUNIOR CHILDREN'S CHURCH TEACHER GUIDE. (US/1059-3411). **4977**

MIDDLER STUDENT GUIDE. (US/1059-3314). **4977**

MIDDLER TEACHER GUIDE. (US/1059-3306). **4977**

MISSION: JOURNAL OF MISSION STUDIES. (CN/1198-0400). **4978**

NATIONAL DIRECTORY OF CHURCHES, SYNAGOGUES, AND OTHER HOUSES OF WORSHIP. (US/1070-3314). **4980**

NEWSLETTER FROM DICK B. ON THE SPIRITUAL ROOTS OF ALCOHOLICS ANONYMOUS, A. (US/1068-302X). **4981**

ON COURSE (SPRINGFIELD, MO.). (US/1061-0952). **4983**

ONTARIO MENNONITE HISTORY. (CN/1192-5515). **4983**

OUTLOOK NEW CHURCH. GENERAL CONFERENCE. (UK/0969-1049). **4984**

PARENTWISE. (UK). **4985**

PASTOR'S TAX & MONEY. (US/1061-978X). **4985**

PLENTY GOOD ROOM. (US/1069-2479). **4986**

PRESCHOOL CHILDREN'S CHURCH TEACHER GUIDE. (US/1059-339X). **4987**

PRESCHOOL TEACHER GUIDE. (US/1072-1460). **4987**

PRESENCE (MONTREAL. 1992). (CN/1188-5580). **4987**

PRIMARY CHILDREN'S CHURCH TEACHER GUIDE. (US/1059-3403). **4987**

PRO ECCLESIA (NORTHFIELD, MINN.). (US/1063-8512). **4988**

REFORMATION & REVIVAL JOURNAL. (US/1071-7277). **4990**

RELIGION IN EASTERN EUROPE. (US/1069-4781). **4991**

RELIGION, STATE & SOCIETY : THE KESTON JOURNAL. (UK/0963-7494). **4991**

ROCZNIKI TEOLOGICZNE. (PO). **4994**

SEMPER REFORMANDA. (US/1065-3783). **4996**

SENIOR ADULT STUDENT GUIDE. (US/1059-3381). **4996**

SOCIAL THOUGHT: JOURNAL OF RELIGION IN THE SOCIAL SERVICES. (US). **4997**

SOCIOLOGY OF RELIGION. (US/1069-4404). **4998**

SPECTRUM (WHEATON, ILL.). (US/1061-6160). **4999**

STUDIES IN MUSLIM-JEWISH RELATIONS. (US/1061-9380). **5000**

STUDIES IN PHENOMENOLOGICAL THEOLOGY. (US/1056-4969). **5001**

SYZYGY (STANFORD, CALIF.). (US/1059-6860). **5002**

TEEN TEACHER GUIDE (SPRINGFIELD, MO.). (US/1059-3330). **5002**

TELL (CINCINNATI, OHIO). (US/1063-9438). **5002**

UNITED YOUTH DIGEST. (US/1065-5913). **5006**

UPSIDEDOWN (WOBURN, MASS.). (US/1060-8583). **5007**

VARIEGATED GOSPEL. (US/1061-8333). **5007**

VOCES DEL TIEMPO : REVISTA DE RELIGION Y SOCIEDAD. (GT). **5008**

WORLD FAITHS ENCOUNTER. (UK). **5010**

BIBLE

BIBLICAL INTERPRETATION. (NE). **5015**

CTVRTLETNIK KRESTANSKE VEDY. BIBLICKE LEKCE. (US/1061-673X). **5016**

EZHEKVARTALNIK KHRISTIANSKOI NAUKI. BIBLEISKIE UROKI. (US/1061-6721). **5016**

INTERCESSION BIBLE STUDY LESSON. (US). **5017**

Religion and Theology —Bible

KEE PRODUCTIONS PRESENTS THE INTERCESSORY BIBLE JOURNAL. (US/1061-4958). **5017**

PICKING THE "RIGHT" BIBLE STUDY PROGRAM. (US/1061-1010). **5018**

CATHOLICISM

CATHOLIC PARENT (HUNTINGTON, IND.). (US/1069-4862). **5026**

CHRISTIAN INITIATION. (US). **5027**

IRISH CATHOLIC DIRECTORY & DIARY. (IE). **5030**

LATIN MASS, THE. (US/1064-556X). **5031**

LECTOR. (US). **5031**

TRAJECTA. (BE/0778-8304). **5037**

ISLAM, BAHAISM, THEOSOPHY

CENTRAL ASIA BRIEF. (UK/0966-3452). **5042**

LIGHT & ISLAMIC REVIEW, THE. (US/1060-4596). **5043**

MESSAGE (1993). (US/1071-5215). **5043**

QURANIC GUIDANCE. (US/1064-0770). **5044**

JUDAISM

EAST EUROPEAN JEWISH AFFAIRS. (UK). **5047**

JDL NEWS & VIEWS : AN OFFICIAL PUBLICATION OF THE JEWISH DEFENSE LEAGUE. (US). **5048**

JEWISH STUDIES QUARTERLY. (GW/0944-5706). **5049**

JOURNAL OF JEWISH EDUCATION. (US). **5050**

NEFESH. (US/1058-8213). **5051**

NOI. (RU). **5051**

RABBINICS TODAY. (US/1066-0585). **5052**

TODAY'S JEWISH FAMILY. (US/1056-8492). **5053**

WJC REPORT : WORLD JEWISH CONGRESS PUBLICATION, THE. (US). **5053**

PROTESTANTISM

ADULT LIFE AND WORK STUDY GUIDE. (US/1071-4383). **5054**

AMERICAN BAPTISTS IN MISSION. (US). **5055**

CHRISTIAN COURIER. (CN/1192-3415). **5058**

CHRISTIAN EDUCATION COUNSELOR. (US/1072-1436). **5058**

JOURNAL OF PENTECOSTAL THEOLOGY. (UK/0966-7369). **5062**

PRIMARY ONE STUDENT GUIDE. (US/1059-3276). **5066**

PRIMARY TEACHER GUIDE. (US/1059-3268). **5066**

PRIMARY TWO STUDENT GUIDE. (US/1059-3284). **5066**

RESTAURANTS

JOURNAL OF RESTAURANT & FOODSERVICE MARKETING. (US/1052-214X). **5071**

RESTAURANT MARKETING STRATEGIES. (US/1063-942X). **5072**

RESTAURANT SERVICE REPORT. (US/1062-2322). **5073**

RUBBER

PROCEEDINGS ... ANNUAL GENERAL MEETING. (US/1070-6488). **5077**

SCIENCE AND TECHNOLOGY

AAAS PROGRAM/ABSTRACTS / AMERICAN ASSOCIATION FOR THE ADVANCEMENT OF SCIENCE. (US). **5079**

ABHANDLUNGEN DER NORDRHEIN-WESTFAELISCHEN AKADEMIE DER WISSENSCHAFTEN. SONDERREIHE PAPYROLOGICA COLONIENSIA. (GW). **5079**

ADVANCED MATERIALS FOR OPTICS AND ELECTRONICS. (UK/1057-9257). **5080**

ADVANCES IN INSTRUMENTATION AND CONTROL. (US/1054-0032). **5081**

AFRIKA 2001. (SA). **5081**

APPLICATIONS AND SOLUTIONS. (US/1062-3760). **5085**

ARTIFICIAL LIFE. (US/1064-5462). **5086**

ASLIB BOOK GUIDE / ASLIB. (UK). **5086**

CAL SCIENCES. (US/1061-3552). **5092**

CALIFORNIA TECHNOLOGY REGISTER. (US/1059-7085). **5092**

CAMPO Y TECNOLOGIA. (AG). **5092**

CFC REPORT. (US/1063-1615). **5093**

COLLOID JOURNAL OF THE RUSSIAN ACADEMY OF SCIENCES. (US/1061-933X). **5095**

CONFIGURATIONS (BALTIMORE, MD.). (US/1063-1801). **5096**

CRITICAL REVIEWS IN MULTIPHASE SCIENCE AND TECHNOLOGY. (US/1065-2388). **5097**

CZECHOSLOVAK INDUSTRY. (XR). **5098**

DHAKA UNIVERSITY JOURNAL OF SCIENCE, THE. (BG/1022-2502). **5099**

DIRECTORY. (US). **5100**

DOKLADY AKADEMII NAUK BELARUSI. (BW). **5101**

DOKLADY AKADEMII NAUK / ROSSIISKAIA AKADEMIIA NAUK. (RU/0869-5652). **5101**

DOODY'S HEALTH SCIENCES BOOK REVIEW JOURNAL. (US/1071-7560). **5101**

ELECTRONIC DOCUMENTS. (UK/0965-2035). **5102**

FEDERAL LABORATORY CONSORTIUM HANDBOOK SERIES. (US/1065-6375). **5104**

FULLERENE SCIENCE AND TECHNOLOGY. (US/1064-122X). **5106**

FUTURA : ERGEBNISSE DER FORSCHUNGSPOLITISCHEN FRUEHERKENNUNG (FER) DES SCHWEIZERISCHEN WISSENSCHAFTSRATES RESULTATS DE LA DETECTION AVANCEE EN POLITIQUE DE LA RECHERCHE DU CONSEIL SUISSE DE LA SCIENCE FINDINGS OF THE EARLY WARNING SYSTEM IN SCIENCE POLICY OF THE SWISS SCIENCE COUNCIL. (SZ). **5106**

GEWINA. (NE). **5108**

GREATER SILICON VALLEY TECHNOLOGY RESOURCE GUIDE. (US/1060-1600). **5108**

HARVARD SCIENCE REVIEW (1992). (US/1062-7022). **5109**

HERALD OF THE RUSSIAN ACADEMY OF SCIENCES. (RU/1019-3316). **5109**

HISTORY OF SCIENCE AND TECHNOLOGY. (US/1062-5445). **5110**

IEICE TRANSACTIONS ON INFORMATION AND SYSTEMS. (JA/0916-8532). **5111**

ILLINOIS TECHNOLOGY RESOURCE GUIDE. (US/1065-7770). **5112**

INFORMATION TECHNOLOGY OUTLOOK: LES PERSPECTIVES DES TECHNOLOGIES DE L'INFORMATION. (FR). **5113**

INFORMATION TECHNOLOGY SERVICES MEMBER DIRECTORY. (US/1060-3344). **5113**

INITIATIVE (ST. JOHN). (CN/1197-4532). **5114**

INNOVATIONS & IDEAS. (US/1059-2091). **5114**

INOCULUM (ITHACA, N.Y.). (US/1067-909X). **5114**

INTEGRAL TRANSFORMS AND SPECIAL FUNCTIONS. (US/1065-2469). **5114**

INTERNATIONAL JOURNAL OF MATHEMATICAL AND STATISTICAL SCIENCES. (US/1055-7490). **5115**

ISSUES IN ENVIRONMENTAL SCIENCE AND TECHNOLOGY. (UK/1350-7583). **5116**

IZVESTIIA AKADEMII NAUK. TEKHNICHESKAIA KIBERNETIKA / ROSSIISKAIA AKADEMIIA NAUK. (RU). **5117**

JAPANESE TECHNOLOGY REVIEWS. SECTION C, NEW MATERIALS. (US/1058-7314). **5117**

JOURNAL OF IMAGING SCIENCE AND TECHNOLOGY, THE. (US/1062-3701). **5118**

JOURNAL OF INTELLIGENT & FUZZY SYSTEMS. (US/1064-1246). **5118**

JOURNAL OF RUSSIAN TECHNOLOGY. (US/1065-7304). **5119**

JOURNAL OF SCIENCE EDUCATION AND TECHNOLOGY. (US/1059-0145). **5119**

JPRS REPORT. SCIENCE & TECHNOLOGY. EUROPE/INTERNATIONAL. (US). **5122**

LABORATORY EQUIPMENT BUYERS GUIDE. (UK/0967-389X). **5125**

MASSACHUSETTS TECHNOLOGY RESOURCE GUIDE. (US/1060-1554). **5127**

MATERIALS SCIENCE CITATION INDEX. (US/1062-5496). **5127**

NEW SCIENCE CENTERS SUPPORT PROGRAM INFORMATION SERVICE BULLETIN. (US/1065-917X). **5132**

NEW YORK TECHNOLOGY RESOURCE GUIDE. (US/1065-8041). **5133**

PBC SCIENCE BRIEFS. (US/1059-1990). **5137**

PENNSYLVANIA TECHNOLOGY DIRECTORY. (US). **5137**

PERSPECTIVES ON SCIENCE. (US/1063-6145). **5137**

PROCEEDINGS OF THE SCHOOL OF SCIENCE OF TOKAI UNIVERSITY. (JA/0563-6759). **5142**

PUBLIC UNDERSTANDING OF SCIENCE. (UK/0963-6625). **5143**

R&D INNOVATOR. (US/1061-1894). **5144**

RISK (CONCORD, N.H.). (US/1073-8673). **5148**

SCIENCE AND TECHNOLOGY OF BUILDING SEALS, SEALANTS, GLAZING AND WATERPROOFING. (US/1062-967X). **5150**

SCIENCE COMMUNICATION. (US/1075-5470). **5151**

SCIENCE ET TECHNOLOGIE AU QUEBEC. (CN/1188-4290). **5151**

SCIENCE IN RUSSIA / RUSSIAN ACADEMY OF SCIENCES. (RU). **5152**

SCIENTIFIC PROGRAMMING. (US/1058-9244). **5155**

SKEPTIC (ALTADENA, CALIF.). (US/1063-9330). **5158**

SOTSIALNYE I GUMANITARNYE NAUKI. SERIIA 8, NAUKOVEDENIE : OTECHESTVENNAIA I ZARUBEZHNAIA LITERATURA / ROSSIISKAIA AKADEMIIA NAUK, INSTITUT NAUCHNOI INFORMATSII PO OBSHCHESTVENNYM NAUKAM. (RU/0202-2141). **5158**

STAR TREK FEDERATION SCIENCE (EXHIBIT GUIDE). (US/1065-6928). **5160**

STAR TREK FEDERATION SCIENCE (TEACHER'S GUIDE). (US/1065-691X). **5160**

TODAY'S SCIENCE ON FILE. (US/1059-9274). **5166**

TR TRANSFER : TECHNISCHE RUNDSCHAU TRANSFER. (SZ). **5166**

TRENCHLESS TECHNOLOGY. (US/1064-4156). **5167**

TRENDS IN U.S. R & D FUNDING FOR .... (US). **5167**

TUNG-PEI TA HSUEH HSUEH PAO. TZU JAN KO HSUEH PAN. (CC/1005-3026). **5167**

UZBEKISTON RESPUBLIKASI FANLAR AKADEMIIASINING MABRUZALARI. (UZ/0134-4307). **5168**

VESTNIK ROSSIISKOI AKADEMII NAUK. (RU). **5169**

WASHINGTON STATE ADVANCED TECHNOLOGY : THE ANNUAL SURVEY OF THE STATE'S TECHNOLOGY COMPANIES. (US). **5169**

WHO'S WHO IN SCIENCE AND ENGINEERING. (US/1063-5599). **5169**

WINDOW ON DRUG MONITORING. (UK/0966-9094). **5169**

WORLD & SCIENCE, THE. (US/1059-1931). **5170**

WORLD OF INVENTION. (US/1071-0973). **5170**

WORLD OF SCIENTIFIC DISCOVERY. (US/1071-0981). **5171**

WORLD'S LATEST TECHNOLOGIES AND NEW PRODUCTS. (II). **5171**

WRITING AND EDITING FOR SCIENCE AND TECHNOLOGY. (US/1062-0168). **5171**

ABSTRACTING, BIBLIOGRAPHIES AND STATISTICS

CATALOGUE OF OTA PUBLICATIONS. (US). **5174**

CURRENT CONTENTS. LIFE SCIENCES (CD-ROM VERSION). (US/1073-1229). **5174**

GENERAL SCIENCE SOURCE. (US/1073-1954). **5175**

SCIENCE CITATION INDEX WITH ABSTRACTS. (US/1061-1290). **5176**

SECURITY SYSTEMS AND ALARMS

SECURITY FOR BUYERS OF PRODUCTS, SYSTEMS AND SERVICES. (US). **5177**

SENIOR CITIZENS

AGING NEWS ALERT : THE SENIOR SERVICES & FUNDING REPORT. (US). **5178**

AMERICAN SENIOR, THE. (US/1055-8306). **5178**

CARP. CANADIAN ASSOCIATION OF RETIRED PERSONS. (CN/1193-8544). **5178**

DIRECTORY OF RETIREMENT FACILITIES, THE. (US/1053-6825). **5179**

GRAND TIMES. (US/1068-1345). **5179**

MEMORIES PLUS. (US/1062-9556). **5180**

OLDER AMERICANS INFORMATION DIRECTORY. (US/1072-477X). **5180**

SUCCESSFUL RETIREMENT. (US/1063-5742). **5182**

TODAY'S TIMES. (CN/1193-171X). **5182**

WHERE TO RETIRE. (US/1060-0094). **5182**

SEWING AND NEEDLEWORK

AMERICA'S BEST QUILTING PROJECTS. (US/1064-1718). **5183**

CROCHET DIGEST. (US/1074-1798). **5183**

MCCALL'S QUILTING. (US/1072-8295). **5185**

PINK BOOK (MOUNTAIN VIEW, CALIF.), THE. (US/1065-5867). **5185**

QUILTESSENCE (THIEF RIVER FALLS, MINN.). (US/1064-7325). **5185**

SIMPLY CROSS STITCH. (US/1061-3234). **5186**

WEARABLE CRAFTS. (US/1073-0680). **5186**

SEXUAL LIFE

BIZARRE SEX AND OTHER CRIMES OF PASSION. (US). **5187**

CANADIAN JOURNAL OF HUMAN SEXUALITY, THE. (CN/1188-4517). **5187**

X, THE FUTURE OF SEX. (US/1061-6977). **5188**

SOCIAL SCIENCES

BALTIC STUDIES NEWSLETTER. (US). **5192**

BIBLIO 12. (BE). **5192**

CROSS-CULTURAL RESEARCH. (US/1069-3971). **5197**

CSD BULLETIN. (SA). **5197**

FEMINISM AND THE SOCIAL SCIENCES. (US/1070-549X). **5200**

GROUP DECISION AND NEGOTIATION. (US/0926-2644). **5201**

GUIDES TO MAJOR SOCIAL SCIENCE DATA BASES. (US/1058-4862). **5201**

JOURNAL OF AREA STUDIES. (UK). **5205**

JOURNAL OF CULTURAL DIVERSITY. (US/1071-5568). **5206**

JOURNAL OF ECONOMIC AND SOCIAL INTELLIGENCE. (UK). **5206**

LOCATION SCIENCE. (UK/0966-8349). **5208**

MARGEM. (BL/0103-8915). **5208**

ORIENTATIONS TRIENNALES ET PLAN ANNUEL / GOUVERNEMENT DU QUEBEC, CONSEIL DU STATUT DE LA FEMME. (CN/0845-0382). **5212**

PROGRAMMES DE SUBVENTIONS ET DE BOURSES DE CARRIERE DU CONSEIL QUEBECOIS DE LA RECHERCHE SOCIALE. (CN/1191-7431). **5214**

RUSSIA AND HER NEIGHBORS. (US/1066-0127). **5217**

RUSSIAN SOCIAL SCIENCE REVIEW. (US/1061-1428). **5217**

SOCIAL SCIENCES CITATION INDEX WITH ABSTRACTS. (US/1061-1282). **5221**

SOCIAL SCIENCES IN HEALTH. (UK/1352-4127). **5221**

SOCIETY & ANIMALS. (UK/1063-1119). **5222**

VOZES CULTURA. (BL). **5225**

ABSTRACTING, BIBLIOGRAPHIES AND STATISTICS

AFRICAN STUDIES ABSTRACTS : THE ABSTRACTS JOURNAL OF THE AFRICAN STUDIES CENTRE, LEIDEN. (UK/1352-2175). **5226**

PAIS (PEABODY, MASS.). (US/1072-0103). **5227**

SOCIAL SCIENCE SOURCE. (US/1063-9802). **5227**

Societies and Clubs

SOCIETIES AND CLUBS

ASSOCIATIONS QUEBEC. (CN/1188-4274). **5229**

OFFICIAL STAR TREK FAN CLUB OF CANADA. (CN/1192-7445). **5234**

SOCIOLOGY

ADVANCES IN HUMAN ECOLOGY. (US/1069-0573). **5238**

AFRICA RESEARCH BULLETIN. POLITICAL, SOCIAL, AND CULTURAL SERIES. (UK/0001-9844). **5238**

BLUE BOOK OF THE ASSOCIATION FOR PUBLIC OPINION RESEARCH, WORLD ASSOCIATION FOR PUBLIC OPINION RESEARCH : AGENCIES & ORGANIZATIONS REPRESENTED IN AAPOR/WAPOR MEMBERSHIP, THE. (US). **5240**

CHANTEH (ARLINGTON, VA.). (US/1065-7150). **5242**

DIRECTORY OF MEMBERS / THE AMERICAN SOCIOLOGICAL ASSOCIATION. (US). **5244**

DIVERSITY & DIVISION. (US/1064-7430). **5244**

FIELD POLL, THE. (US/0195-4520). **5245**

GALLUP POLL (TORONTO. 1993). (CN/1197-4303). **5246**

JOURNAL OF SOCIAL AND EVOLUTIONARY SYSTEMS. (US/1061-7361). **5250**

LUND DISSERTATIONS IN SOCIOLOGY. (SW/1102-4712). **5251**

MARTIN LUTHER KING, JR. MEMORIAL STUDIES IN RELIGION, CULTURE, AND SOCIAL DEVELOPMENT. (US/1052-181X). **5251**

SAFETY BRIEFS. WESTERN REGION. (US/1062-5828). **5257**

SOCIAL IDENTITIES. (UK/1350-4630). **5259**

SOCIAL POLITICS. (US/1072-4745). **5259**

SOCIOLOGICAL IMAGINATION. (US/1077-5048). **5260**

SOCIOLOGICAL RESEARCH. (US/1061-0154). **5261**

SOCIOLOGICAL THEORY ABSTRACTS. (US/1070-1192). **5261**

SOUTHERN CULTURES. (US/1068-8218). **5263**

STUDIES IN CONFLICT AND TERRORISM. (US/1057-610X). **5263**

TEACHING TOLERANCE. (US/1066-2847). **5264**

TUNG WU SHE HUI HSUEH PAO. (CH/1019-0449). **5264**

VIRGINIA REVIEW OF SOCIOLOGY. (US). **5265**

ABSTRACTING, BIBLIOGRAPHIES AND STATISTICS

BELIZE DATA GUIDE. (US/1063-1461). **5266**

SOCIAL WORK ABSTRACTS. (US/1070-5317). **5267**

VIOLENCE AND ABUSE ABSTRACTS. (US/1077-2197). **5267**

MANNERS AND CUSTOMS

GENDER, PLACE AND CULTURE: A JOURNAL OF FEMINIST GEOGRAPHY. (UK/0966-369X). **5268**

HORIZONS OF VIETNAMESE THOUGHT AND EXPERIENCE. (US/1062-7006). **5268**

INTERNATIONAL TATTO ART. (US/1065-643X). **5268**

SOCIAL SERVICES AND WELFARE

1992 DIRECTORY OF AGING RESOURCES. (US/1061-3056). **5269**

ADOPTIVE FAMILIES. (US/1076-1020). **5270**

ALZHEIMER'S CARE GUIDE. (US/1070-5112). **5271**

AMERICAN JOURNAL OF ADOPTION REFORM. (US/1065-3457). **5271**

ANNUAL REPORT / DEPT. OF SOCIAL WELFARE, NEW ZEALAND. (NZ). **5272**

ANNUAL STATISTICAL SUPPLEMENT, ... TO THE SOCIAL SECURITY BULLETIN. (US). **5273**

ARC TODAY, THE. (US). **5273**

C-JEUNES. (CN/1195-9231). **5276**

CHANGES (DEERFIELD BEACH, FLA.). (US/0892-1504). **5277**

CHILD ABUSE REVIEW : JOURNAL OF THE BRITISH ASSOCIATION FOR THE STUDY AND PREVENTION OF CHILD ABUSE AND NEGLECT. (UK). **5277**

CHILDREN & YOUTH FUNDING REPORT. (US/1063-892X). **5278**

CHILDREN LOOKED AFTER BY LOCAL AUTHORITIES IN WALES / WELSH OFFICE / PLANT Y GOFELIR AM DANYNT GAN AWDURDODAU LLEOL CYMRU / Y SWYDDFA GYMREIG. (UK/0968-4050). **5278**

CHOICES (LONDON, ONT.). (CN/1188-8172). **5279**

CHRYSALIS CONNECTION. (CN/1191-3339). **5279**

COMMUNITY CARE BULLETIN. (UK). **5279**

CONTINUING CARE CONNECTION : LINKING LONG-TERM, HOME AND COMMUNITY CARE SYSTEMS. (US). **5280**

CORPORATE GIVING YELLOW PAGES (1992). (US/1058-689X). **5281**

CRISIS INTERVENTION AND TIME-LIMITED TREATMENT. (US/1064-5136). **5281**

DIRECTORY OF CORPORATE AND FOUNDATION GIVERS, THE. (US). **5283**

DISABILITY FUNDING NEWS. (US/1069-1359). **5284**

EDITIONS AVIS DE RECHERCHE, LES. (CN/1188-6145). **5284**

FAMILIES IN CRISIS FUNDING REPORT. (US/1075-3184). **5285**

FAMILY PLANNING MANAGER, THE. (US/1060-9172). **5285**

FOOD SITUATION REPORT FOR THE MONTH OF ... [MICROFORM]. (BG). **5286**

FUNDING DECISION MAKERS. (US/1058-1235). **5286**

GRANT$ FOR HEALTH PROGRAMS FOR CHILDREN AND YOUTH. (US). **5286**

HEALING WOMAN, THE. (US/1065-8289). **5287**

HEALTH & SOCIAL CARE IN THE COMMUNITY. (UK/0966-0410). **5287**

HMO PERFORMANCE DIGEST. (US/1063-1704). **5287**

HOME CARE SALARY & BENEFITS REPORT. (US/1058-7934). **5287**

HOME CARING. (US/1061-0227). **5288**

HOW TO ADOPT YOUR BABY PRIVATELY. (US/1063-9071). **5288**

HUMAN SERVICE YELLOW PAGES OF MASSACHUSETTS & RHODE ISLAND. (US). **5288**

INTERCHANGE (CARRBORO, N.C.). (US/1065-6669). **5290**

INTERNATIONAL SEARCH AND RESCUE TRADE ASSOCIATION (INSARTA). (US/1065-2302). **5290**

JOURNAL OF ANALYTIC SOCIAL WORK. (US/1052-9950). **5291**

JOURNAL OF CHILD SEXUAL ABUSE. (US/1053-8712). **5291**

JOURNAL OF FAMILY SOCIAL WORK. (US/1052-2158). **5291**

JOURNAL OF SOCIAL DISTRESS AND THE HOMELESS. (US/1053-0789). **5293**

JOURNAL OF THE AMERICAN HEALTH CARE, THE. (US/1078-6856). **5293**

LEADERSHIP. (US). **5294**

LINK (DURHAM, N.C.), THE. (US/1065-5832). **5295**

LOCAL AUTHORITY SOCIAL WORK EXPENDITURE. (UK). **5295**

MANAGING SENIORCARE. (US/1063-035X). **5295**

MENTAL HEALTH NEWS ALERT. (US). **5296**

MENTAL HEALTH RAP. (US/1065-7525). **5296**

NATIONAL DIRECTORY OF CHILDREN, YOUTH & FAMILIES SERVICES. (US/1072-902X). **5297**

NEW CHOICES FOR RETIREMENT LIVING. (US/1061-2157). **5298**

NEW DIRECTIONS FOR PHILANTHROPIC FUNDRAISING. (US/1072-172X). **5298**

NEW YORK STATE PLAN FOR COORDINATION OF TRAINING, EMPLOYMENT AND RELATED PROGRAMS. (US). **5298**

NONPROFIT ALMANAC. (US/1060-7889). **5299**

NRCCSA NEWS / NATIONAL RESOURCE CENTER ON CHILD SEXUAL ABUSE OF THE NATIONAL CENTER ON CHILD ABUSE AND NEGLECT. (US). **5299**

O'KEEFE'S GUIDE. MID-ATLANTIC REGIONAL DIRECTORY. (US/1064-1793). **5300**

ON TAP (MORGANTOWN, W.VA.). (US/1061-9291). **5300**

POVERTY AND SOCIAL POLICY PAPER. (US/1014-9783). **5301**

PRIMARY CARE NEWSLETTER. (US/1071-2496). **5301**

REPORT - CANADIAN RED CROSS SOCIETY. NEW BRUNSWICK DIVISION. (CN/1188-2034). **5305**

REPORT ON HUMAN RESOURCES COMPENSATION. (US/1063-1968). **5305**

RESEARCH IN PROGRESS. (US). **5305**

REVIEW - PATIENT FOCUSED CARE ASSOCIATION. (US/1063-1356). **5306**

REVUE DE L'AMIE. (CN/1192-3636). **5306**

S.H.A.R.E. (TUKWILA, WASHINGTON). (US/1062-2640). **5306**

SCANDINAVIAN JOURNAL OF SOCIAL WELFARE. (DK/0907-2055). **5307**

SOCIAL SERVICE RESOURCE DIRECTORY FOR LOS ANGELES COUNTY. (US). **5308**

SOCIAL WORK RESEARCH. (US/1070-5309). **5309**

SOURCE (MONTREAL. 1992). (CN/1188-4428). **5310**

STATE OF AMERICA'S CHILDREN YEARBOOK, THE. (US). **5311**

TCA JOURNAL. (US). **5312**

TIRE TALK. (CN/1187-967X). **5312**

URBAN ISSUES IN SOCIAL WORK. (US/1065-822X). **5313**

WELFARE TO WORK. (US/1060-5622). **5314**

SOUND RECORDINGS AND SYSTEMS

GRAMOPHONE CLASSICAL CATALOGUE, THE. (UK). **5316**

IASA JOURNAL / INTERNATIONAL ASSOCIATION OF SOUND ARCHIVES. (HU/1021-562X). **5317**

IEEE TRANSACTIONS ON SPEECH AND AUDIO PROCESSING. (US/1063-6676). **5317**

JOURNAL WATCH (SOUND RECORDING). (US/1063-1887). **5317**

PETERSEN'S AUTOTRONICS. (US/1073-4724). **5318**

RECORDING : THE MAGAZINE FOR THE RECORDING MUSICIAN. (US). **5318**

SCHWANN OPUS. (US/1066-2138). **5318**

SCHWANN SPECTRUM. (US/1065-9161). **5318**

STATISTICS

BERNOULLI. (UK/1350-7265). **5323**

BOLETIN MENSUAL DE ESTADISTICA/ INSTITUTO NACIONAL DE ESTADISTICA. (SP). **5323**

CHARTS, GRAPHS & STATS INDEX. (US/1060-1465). **5325**

CHINA MONTHLY STATISTICS / CHINA STATISTICAL INFORMATION AND CONSULTANCY SERVICE CENTRE. (CC). **5325**

COUNTY AND CITY EXTRA. (US/1059-9096). **5326**

DIRECTORY OF STATISTICS IN CANADA. (CN/1193-7580). **5326**

FACTS NEW ZEALAND. (NZ). **5327**

JOURNAL OF APPLIED STATISTICAL SCIENCE. (US/1067-5817). **5329**

JOURNAL OF COMPUTATIONAL AND GRAPHICAL STATISTICS. (US/1061-8600). **5329**

LANDERBERICHT. SUDAMERIKANISCHE STAATEN / STATISTISCHES BUNDESAMT. (GW). **5331**

PENNSYLVANIA ABSTRACT / PREPARED BY THE PENNSYLVANIA STATE DATA CENTER. (US). **5335**

STATISTICAL ABSTRACT OF THE UNITED STATES (ENLARGED PRINT ED.). (US/1063-1690). **5340**

STATISTICS USERS NETWORK. (US/1062-3507). **5342**

STATISTISCHES JAHRBUCH FUER DIE REPUBLIK OESTERREICH / HERAUS-GEGELEN VON OESTERREICHISCHEN STATISTISCHEN ZENTRALANT. (AU). **5343**

TEST (MADRID). (SP/1133-0686). **5345**

TEXTILES

MUNDO TEXTIL. (US). **5354**

NATURAL FIBERS FACT BOOK. (US/1062-0648). **5354**

NEW NONWOVENS WORLD, THE. (US/1065-5247). **5354**

STUDIES IN TEXTILE AND COSTUME HISTORY. (NE/0924-7696). **5356**

TECHNICAL TEXTILES INTERNATIONAL. (UK/0964-5993). **5356**

TEXTILE HORIZONS. (UK/1351-0266). **5358**

THEATER

BUSINESS THEATER. (US/1064-475X). **5362**

CAHIERS DE LA NCT. (CN/1188-1461). **5362**

CONTEMPORARY THEATRE REVIEW. (SZ/1048-6801). **5363**

DIRECTORY OF DOCTORAL PROGRAMS IN THEATRE STUDIES IN THE U.S.A. AND CANADA. (US). **5363**

DIVADELNI NOVINY. (XR). **5363**

INDUSTRY RESOURCES / THEATER CRAFTS. (US). **5365**

JOURNAL DU VILLAGE D'EMILIE, LE. (CN/1189-5071). **5365**

OLLANTAY THEATER MAGAZINE. (US/1065-805X). **5367**

RUSSIAN THEATRE ARCHIVE. (US/1068-8161). **5368**

SLAVIC AND EAST EUROPEAN PERFORMANCE. (US/1069-2800). **5368**

STUDIES IN FRENCH THEATRE. (US/1062-0591). **5369**

TAFT AND UNIVERSITY OF CINCINNATI SERIES IN LATIN AMERICAN AND HISPANIC AMERICAN THEATRE. (US/1062-5453). **5369**

TCI (NEW YORK, N.Y.). (US/1063-9497). **5369**

THEATRE RESEARCH IN CANADA. (CN/1196-1198). **5371**

THEATRE SYMPOSIUM. (US/1065-4917). **5371**

THEATREFORUM (LA JOLLA, CALIF.). (US/1060-5320). **5371**

WANT'S THEATRE DIRECTORY. (US/1064-1300). **5372**

TOBACCO

CIGAR AFICIONADO. (US/1063-7885). **5372**

TOBACCO & HEALTH. (US/1064-8577). **5373**

TOBACCO-FREE YOUTHREPORTER. (US/1064-2072). **5373**

TOBACCO NEWS. (RH). **5374**

TOBACCO, WORLD MARKETS & TRADE / UNITED STATES DEPARTMENT OF AGRICULTURE, FOREIGN AGRICULTURAL SERVICE. (US). **5374**

TRANSPORTATION

1:87 SCALE. (US/1055-6311). **5375**

AMERICAN RIDER. (US/1072-4893). **5375**

BRITISH COLUMBIA SCHOOL BUS. (CN/1189-4717). **5378**

CALGARY & AREA AVIATION BUSINESS DIRECTORY. (CN/1183-7853). **5378**

CAPITAL IMPROVEMENT PROGRAM. (US). **5379**

CODICE DELLA STRADA. (IT/1121-6840). **5379**

CSAH APPORTIONMENT DATA. (US). **5380**

DISTRIBUTION (RADNOR, PA. 1992). (US/1066-8489). **5381**

EDMONTON & AREA AVIATION BUSINESS DIRECTORY. (CN/1183-7861). **5381**

INSIDE FLYER. (US/1061-4494). **5384**

INTERNATIONAL JOURNAL OF TRANSPORTATION POLICY. (US/1065-5174). **5384**

MINUTES OF PROCEEDINGS AND EVIDENCE OF THE SUB-COMMITTEE ON THE ST. LAWRENCE SEAWAY OF THE STANDING COMMITTEE ON TRANSPORT. (CN/1193-2651). **5387**

MINUTES OF PROCEEDINGS AND EVIDENCE OF THE SUB-COMMITTEE ON THE ST. LAWRENCE SEAWAY OF THE STANDING COMMITTEE ON TRANSPORT (FRENCH EDITON). (CN/1193-2651). **5387**

NORTHEAST JOURNAL OF TRANSPORTATION, THE. (US/1061-8090). **5388**

PRIVATE FLEET DIRECTORY, THE. (US/1061-4761). **5390**

REPORT, WASHINGTON STATE TRANSPORTATION PLAN UPDATE. (US). **5391**

SANFORD EVANS GOLD BOOK, OFFICIAL SNOWMOBILE DATA AND USED PRICES. (CN/1187-4562). **5392**

TAC TECHNICAL BULLETIN. (CN/1188-8709). **5394**

TRANSIT RESEARCH ABSTRACTS (1992). (US/1062-9483). **5395**

TRANSPORT POLICY. (UK/0967-070X). **5395**

Transportation

TRANSPORTATION RESEARCH. PART A, POLICY AND PRACTICE. (US/0965-8564). **5397**

TRANSPORTATION RESEARCH. PART C, EMERGING TECHNOLOGIES. (US/0968-090X). **5397**

VIA INTERNATIONAL PORT OF NEW YORK-NEW JERSEY. (US). **5399**

WORLD IVHS MARKET. (US). **5400**

WORLD TRANSPORT POLICY & PRACTICE. (UK/1355-2554). **5400**

AUTOMOBILES

5.0 MUSTANG. (US/1073-4740). **5403**

1949-50-51 FORD/MERCURY OWNERS MAGAZINE. (US/1068-1256). **5403**

ALABAMA AUTOMOTIVE REPORT. (US/1061-8295). **5403**

ASIA/PACIFIC AUTOMOTIVE BULLETIN. (US). **5404**

ATD, N.A.D.A. OFFICIAL HEAVY DUTY TRUCK GUIDE. (US/1066-6494). **5404**

AUTO AGE DEALER BUSINESS. (US/1070-8294). **5404**

AUTOMOTIVE & TRANSPORTATION INTERIORS. (US/1071-1430). **5406**

CAMAROS (LOS ANGELES, CALIF.). (US/1059-5740). **5408**

CAMIONNEURS/TRUCKERS MAGAZINE. (CN/1192-3857). **5408**

CANADIAN AUTOWORLD. (CN/1192-2745). **5408**

CAR COLLECTOR & CAR CLASSICS. (US). **5409**

CC PERFORMANCE CAR. (US/1066-4734). **5409**

CHILTON'S CASCADE EMISSION CONTROL APPLICATION GUIDE. (US/1072-7507). **5410**

CHILTON'S CHASSIS ELECTRONIC SERVICE MANUAL. CHRYSLER. (US/1065-660X). **5410**

CHILTON'S CHASSIS ELECTRONIC SERVICE MANUAL. FORD. (US/1065-6618). **5410**

CHILTON'S DRIVEABILITY MANUAL. ASIAN. (US/1072-7469). **5410**

CHILTON'S DRIVEABILITY MANUAL. CHRYSLER. (US/1072-7477). **5410**

CHILTON'S DRIVEABILITY MANUAL. EUROPEAN. (US/1072-7485). **5410**

CHILTON'S DRIVEABILITY MANUAL. FORD. (US/1072-7493). **5410**

CHILTON'S GUIDE TO FUEL INJECTION AND ELECTRONIC ENGINE CONTROLS. BUICK, OLDS, PONTIAC CARS AND TRUCKS. (US/1061-740X). **5410**

CHILTON'S GUIDE TO FUEL INJECTION AND ELECTRONIC ENGINE CONTROLS. CHEVROLET CARS AND TRUCKS. (US/1061-7418). **5411**

CHILTON'S GUIDE TO FUEL INJECTION AND ELECTRONIC ENGINE CONTROLS. CHRYSLER CARS AND TRUCKS. (US/1061-7388). **5411**

CHILTON'S GUIDE TO FUEL INJECTION AND ELECTRONIC ENGINE CONTROLS. FORD CARS AND TRUCKS. (US/1061-7396). **5411**

CHILTON'S HEAVY DUTY TRUCK SERVICE MANUAL. (US/1065-6626). **5411**

CHILTON'S MEDIUM/HEAVY DUTY TRUCK SERVICE MANUAL. (US/1060-4405). **5411**

CHILTON'S NISSAN REPAIR MANUAL. (US/1060-4413). **5411**

CHILTON'S TRANSMISSION DIAGNOSTIC MANUAL. (US/1065-6634). **5411**

CUSTOM & CLASSIC TRUCKS. (US/1073-4732). **5412**

CUSTOM PAINT & BODY. (US/1059-5732). **5412**

EDMUND'S VAN, PICKUP, SPORT UTILITY. (US/1077-2111). **5414**

ELECTRIC VEHICLE DIGEST. (US/1064-1254). **5414**

FASTEST STREET CARS IN AMERICA. (US/1072-8422). **5414**

GRAY'S SPECIALTY CAR VALUE GUIDE. (US/1064-2404). **5415**

GREEN CAR JOURNAL. (US/1059-6143). **5415**

IMPORTCAR (1993). (US/1069-4714). **5416**

KIT CAR. (US/1072-7981). **5418**

'LECTRIC AUTO NEWS. (US/1061-4052). **5418**

MAGAZINE CARGUIDE. (CN/1187-9475). **5418**

MOTOR WORLD (LOS ANGELES, CALIF.). (US/1055-8233). **5420**

N.A.D.A. OFFICIAL USED CAR GUIDE (RETAIL CONSUMER ED.). (US/1061-9054). **5421**

PARTS BUSINESS. (US/1072-5598). **5423**

PBC AUTO GUIDE. (US/1059-2083). **5423**

PERFORMANCE MUSCLECARS. (US). **5423**

ROD & CUSTOM ANNUAL. (US/1060-6831). **5424**

SMALL BLOCK CHEVY. (US/1059-5724). **5425**

SPECIALTY AUTO MARKETPLACE. (US/1063-0716). **5425**

STREET ROD PICKUPS. (US/1067-5256). **5426**

THIS OLD TRUCK. (US/1068-1744). **5426**

TRUCK, VAN AND 4X4 BOOK. (US/1062-2578). **5427**

USED 4 X 4 BUYER'S GUIDE. (US/1059-5775). **5427**

RAILROADS

CP RAIL SYSTEM NEWS. (CN/1189-363X). **5430**

GUDOK. (RU). **5809**

LOKOMOTIV. (RU). **5432**

RAILWAYS AFRICA. (SA). **5436**

TRANSPORT HISTORY MONOGRAPH. (US/1049-1422). **5437**

ROADS AND TRAFFIC

IVHS JOURNAL. (SZ/1065-5123). **5441**

NORSK VEG-OG VEGTRAFIKKPLAN. (NO). **5442**

ROAD & TRANSPORT RESEARCH : [A JOURNAL OF AUSTRALIAN AND NEW ZEALAND RESEARCH AND PRACTICE]. (AT/1037-5783). **5443**

SHIPS AND SHIPPING

GREAT LAKES LOG. (US/1067-4144). **5449**

LLOYD'S LIST MARITIME ASIA. (HK/1015-227X). **5451**

SEATRADE REVIEW. (UK/0964-8895). **5455**

SEATRADE WEEK NEWSFRONT. (HK). **5455**

SHIPPING STATISTICS AND MARKET REVIEW. (GW). **5456**

WORLD INTERMODAL FREIGHT MARKET. (US). **5458**

TRAVEL AND TOURISM

2 TO 22 DAYS IN ASIA. (US/1062-4325). **5458**

2 TO 22 DAYS IN AUSTRALIA. (US/1062-4333). **5458**

2 TO 22 DAYS IN EUROPE / RICK STEVES. (US/1059-2946). **5458**

2 TO 22 DAYS IN FLORIDA. (US/1062-4341). **5458**

2 TO 22 DAYS IN GERMANY, AUSTRIA, AND SWITZERLAND. (US/1058-6059). **5458**

2 TO 22 DAYS IN HAWAII. (US/1062-435X). **5459**

2 TO 22 DAYS IN ITALY. (US/1064-9328). **5459**

2 TO 22 DAYS IN SPAIN AND PORTUGAL. (US/1058-6067). **5459**

2 TO 22 DAYS IN THAILAND. (US/1062-4570). **5459**

2 TO 22 DAYS IN THE AMERICAN SOUTHWEST. (US/1058-6075). **5459**

2 TO 22 DAYS IN THE ROCKIES. (US/1058-6083). **5459**

ADVENTURE FLORIDA. (US/1062-7545). **5460**

AFFORDABLE CARIBBEAN, THE. (US/1062-9084). **5460**

AFRICAN-AMERICAN SITES & INSIGHTS. (US/1072-4052). **5460**

AMERICANS TRAVELING ABROAD. (US/1070-3365). **5461**

BERLITZ TRAVELER'S GUIDE TO MEXICO, THE. (US/1057-4786). **5462**

BERLITZ TRAVELLER'S GUIDE BERLIN, THE. (US/1065-6294). **5462**

BERLITZ TRAVELLER'S GUIDE TO AUSTRALIA, THE. (US/1057-4689). **5462**

BERLITZ TRAVELLER'S GUIDE TO CANADA, THE. (US). **5462**

BERLITZ TRAVELLER'S GUIDE TO ENGLAND & WALES, THE. (US/1057-4735). **5462**

BERLITZ TRAVELLER'S GUIDE TO FRANCE, THE. (US/1057-476X). **5462**

BERLITZ TRAVELLER'S GUIDE TO GERMANY, THE. (US/1057-462X). **5463**

BERLITZ TRAVELLER'S GUIDE TO GREECE, THE. (US). **5463**

Travel and Tourism

BERLITZ TRAVELLER'S GUIDE TO HAWAII, THE. (US/1057-4700). **5463**

BERLITZ TRAVELLER'S GUIDE TO IRELAND, THE. (US/1057-4719). **5463**

BERLITZ TRAVELLER'S GUIDE TO LONDON, THE. (US/1057-4751). **5463**

BERLITZ TRAVELLER'S GUIDE TO NEW ENGLAND, THE. (US/1062-3655). **5463**

BERLITZ TRAVELLER'S GUIDE TO NEW YORK CITY, THE. (US/1057-4743). **5463**

BERLITZ TRAVELLER'S GUIDE TO PORTUGAL, THE. (US). **5463**

BERLITZ TRAVELLER'S GUIDE TO ROME AND NORTHERN ITALY, THE. (US). **5463**

BERLITZ TRAVELLER'S GUIDE TO ROME AND SOUTHERN ITALY, THE. (US). **5463**

BERLITZ TRAVELLER'S GUIDE TO SAN FRANCISCO & NORTHERN CALIFORNIA, THE. (US/1057-4727). **5463**

BERLITZ TRAVELLER'S GUIDE TO SPAIN, THE. (US). **5463**

BERLITZ TRAVELLER'S GUIDE TO THE CARIBBEAN, THE. (US/1057-4697). **5463**

BERLITZ TRAVELLER'S GUIDE TO THE SOUTHWEST, THE. (US/1062-3663). **5463**

BEST OF ANDALUCIA, THE. (US/1045-3091). **5463**

BEST OF CATALUNYA, THE. (US/1045-3083). **5463**

BEST OF MADRID, THE. (US/1045-3075). **5463**

BEST OF PORTUGAL, THE. (US/1045-3105). **5463**

BEST OF SPAIN, THE. (US/1045-3067). **5463**

BEST OF THE REPUBLIC OF KOREA, THE. (US/1053-9484). **5463**

BEST PLACES TO STAY IN THE MIDWEST. (US/1060-7749). **5463**

BEST PLACES TO STAY IN THE SOUTH. (US/1060-7757). **5463**

BIRNBAUM'S BAHAMAS, TURKS & CAICOS. (US/1055-5625). **5463**

BIRNBAUM'S BARCELONA. (US/1056-4381). **5463**

BIRNBAUM'S BERLIN. (US/1070-9746). **5463**

BIRNBAUM'S BERMUDA. (US/1055-5684). **5463**

BIRNBAUM'S BOSTON. (US/1056-4357). **5464**

BIRNBAUM'S CANCUN, COZUMEL, AND ISLA MUJERES. (US/1055-5641). **5464**

BIRNBAUM'S CARIBBEAN. (US). **5464**

BIRNBAUM'S CHICAGO. (US/1056-4365). **5464**

BIRNBAUM'S DISNEYLAND. (US). **5464**

BIRNBAUM'S EASTERN EUROPE. (US/1056-439X). **5464**

BIRNBAUM'S FLORENCE. (US/1056-4489). **5464**

BIRNBAUM'S GERMANY. (US/1068-7238). **5464**

BIRNBAUM'S HONOLULU. (US/1060-3875). **5464**

BIRNBAUM'S IXTAPA & ZIHUATENEJO. (US/1055-5676). **5464**

BIRNBAUM'S LAS VEGAS. (US/1061-5423). **5464**

BIRNBAUM'S LONDON. (US/1056-4470). **5464**

BIRNBAUM'S LOS ANGELES. (US/1056-4462). **5464**

BIRNBAUM'S MIAMI & FT. LAUDERDALE. (US/1056-4454). **5464**

BIRNBAUM'S MONTREAL. (US/1061-5415). **5464**

BIRNBAUM'S NEW ORLEANS. (US/1061-5431). **5464**

BIRNBAUM'S NEW YORK. (US/1056-4446). **5464**

BIRNBAUM'S PARIS. (US/1056-4438). **5464**

BIRNBAUM'S PORTUGAL. (US/1055-5668). **5464**

BIRNBAUM'S PUERTO VALLARTA. (US/1060-3883). **5464**

BIRNBAUM'S ROME. (US/1056-442X). **5464**

BIRNBAUM'S SAN FRANCISCO. (US/1056-4403). **5464**

BIRNBAUM'S SANTA FE, TAOS, ALBUQUERQUE. (US/1068-722X). **5464**

BIRNBAUM'S SPAIN. (US/1055-565X). **5464**

BIRNBAUM'S TORONTO. (US/1061-5393). **5464**

BIRNBAUM'S VANCOUVER. (US/1061-5407). **5464**

BIRNBAUM'S VENICE. (US/1056-4411). **5464**

BIRNBAUM'S WASHINGTON DC. (US/1061-544X). **5464**

BIRNBAUM'S WESTERN EUROPE. (US/1056-4373). **5465**

CONSUMER REPORTS TRAVEL BUYING GUIDE. (US/1060-1511). **5467**

COUNTRY INNS AND BACK ROADS. CALIFORNIA. (US/1060-3786). **5467**

COUNTRY INNS AND BACK ROADS. NEW ENGLAND. (US/1060-3778). **5467**

CRAIGHEAD'S INTERNATIONAL BUSINESS, TRAVEL, AND RELOCATION GUIDE TO 71 COUNTRIES. (US/1058-3904). **5467**

CRUISES & TOURS. (US/1060-0086). **5467**

ENTDECKEN SIE BRITISCH KOLUMBIEN, KANADA. (CN/1189-4911). **5469**

FAIRCHILD'S TRAVEL INDUSTRY PERSONNEL DIRECTORY. (US). **5469**

FESTIVAL MANAGEMENT & EVENT TOURISM. (US/1065-2701). **5469**

FIELDING'S ALPINE EUROPE. (US/1064-0932). **5469**

FIELDING'S AUSTRALIA. (US/1061-4842). **5469**

FIELDING'S BENELUX. (US/1064-0924). **5470**

FIELDING'S BRITAIN. (US/1064-0940). **5470**

FIELDING'S SCANDINAVIA. (US/1061-4834). **5470**

FIELDING'S SPAIN AND PORTUGAL. (US/1064-0991). **5470**

FODOR'S ACAPULCO, IXTAPA, ZIHUATANEJO. (US/1070-8642). **5470**

FODOR'S ... AFFORDABLE FRANCE. (US/1068-3593). **5470**

FODOR'S ... AUSTRALIA & NEW ZEALAND. (US). **5470**

FODOR'S ... BERLIN. (US/1065-4593). **5470**

FODOR'S BUDAPEST. (US/1065-4607). **5471**

FODOR'S ... LAS VEGAS, RENO, TAHOE. (US/1070-6909). **5472**

FODOR'S MOSCOW, ST. PETERBURG, KIEV. (US). **5472**

FODOR'S NOVA SCOTIA, PRINCE EDWARD ISLAND, AND NEW BRUNSWICK. (US/1064-7643). **5472**

FODOR'S RUSSIA & THE BALTIC COUNTRIES. (US). **5473**

FODOR'S THE NETHERLANDS, BELGIUM, LUXEMBOURG. (US/1070-4590). **5473**

FREDERICTON, NEW BRUNSWICK, ATLANTIC CANADA TOUR PLANNING MANUAL. (CN/1184-7530). **5474**

FROMMER'S ARIZONA. (US/1053-2471). **5474**

FROMMER'S BERLIN ON ... $ A DAY. (US/1055-5366). **5474**

FROMMER'S BUDGET TRAVEL GUIDE. AUSTRALIA ... ON $ ... A DAY. (US). **5474**

FROMMER'S BUDGET TRAVEL GUIDE. EASTERN EUROPE ... ON $ ... A DAY. (US). **5474**

FROMMER'S BUDGET TRAVEL GUIDE. LONDON ... ON $ ... A DAY. (US/1055-5331). **5475**

FROMMER'S BUDGET TRAVEL GUIDE. MADRID ... ON $ ... A DAY. (US/1055-5323). **5475**

FROMMER'S BUDGET TRAVEL GUIDE. SPAIN ... ON $ ... A DAY. (US/1053-2439). **5475**

FROMMER'S BUDGET TRAVEL GUIDE. WASHINGTON, D.C. ... ON $ ... A DAY. (US/1065-4585). **5475**

FROMMER'S COLORADO. (US/1053-2463). **5475**

FROMMER'S COMPREHENSIVE TRAVEL GUIDE. ACAPULCO, IXTAPA & TAXCO. (US/1066-4939). **5475**

FROMMER'S COMPREHENSIVE TRAVEL GUIDE. ATHENS. (US/1064-3060). **5475**

FROMMER'S COMPREHENSIVE TRAVEL GUIDE. ATLANTA. (US/1047-7888). **5475**

FROMMER'S COMPREHENSIVE TRAVEL GUIDE. ATLANTIC CITY & CAPE MAY. (US/1064-525X). **5475**

FROMMER'S COMPREHENSIVE TRAVEL GUIDE. AUSTRALIA. (US/1064-3036). **5475**

FROMMER'S COMPREHENSIVE TRAVEL GUIDE. BANGKOK. (US/1055-5374). **5475**

FROMMER'S COMPREHENSIVE TRAVEL GUIDE. BARCELONA. (US/1064-3427). **5475**

FROMMER'S COMPREHENSIVE TRAVEL GUIDE. BELGIUM, HOLLAND & LUXEMBOURG. (US/1040-9378). **5475**

FROMMER'S COMPREHENSIVE TRAVEL GUIDE. BERLIN. (US/1048-2660). **5475**

FROMMER'S COMPREHENSIVE TRAVEL GUIDE. BERMUDA & THE BAHAMAS. (US/1044-2383). **5475**

FROMMER'S COMPREHENSIVE TRAVEL GUIDE. CALIFORNIA. (US/1064-3044). **5475**

FROMMER'S COMPREHENSIVE TRAVEL GUIDE. CANADA. (US/1064-3443). **5475**

FROMMER'S COMPREHENSIVE TRAVEL GUIDE. DELAWARE, MARYLAND, PENNSYLVANIA & THE NEW JERSEY SHORE. (US/1055-5382). **5475**

Travel and Tourism

FROMMER'S COMPREHENSIVE TRAVEL GUIDE. HONOLULU & OAHU. (US/1064-1238). **5476**

FROMMER'S COMPREHENSIVE TRAVEL GUIDE. JAPAN. (US/1064-5233). **5476**

FROMMER'S COMPREHENSIVE TRAVEL GUIDE. LAS VEGAS. (US/1064-5195). **5476**

FROMMER'S COMPREHENSIVE TRAVEL GUIDE. LISBON, MADRID & THE COSTA DEL SOL. (US/1064-5225). **5476**

FROMMER'S COMPREHENSIVE TRAVEL GUIDE. LOS ANGELES. (US). **5476**

FROMMER'S COMPREHENSIVE TRAVEL GUIDE. MIAMI. (US/1047-790X). **5476**

FROMMER'S COMPREHENSIVE TRAVEL GUIDE. MINNEAPOLIS & ST. PAUL. (US/1051-6980). **5476**

FROMMER'S COMPREHENSIVE TRAVEL GUIDE. MONTREAL & QUEBEC CITY. (US/1064-5284). **5476**

FROMMER'S COMPREHENSIVE TRAVEL GUIDE. NEPAL. (US/1055-5439). **5476**

FROMMER'S COMPREHENSIVE TRAVEL GUIDE. NEW MEXICO. (US/1053-2455). **5476**

FROMMER'S COMPREHENSIVE TRAVEL GUIDE. NEW YORK STATE. (US/1064-5276). **5476**

FROMMER'S COMPREHENSIVE TRAVEL GUIDE. PARIS. (US). **5476**

FROMMER'S COMPREHENSIVE TRAVEL GUIDE. PORTUGAL. (US/1064-5268). **5476**

FROMMER'S COMPREHENSIVE TRAVEL GUIDE, PUERTO RICO. (US/1062-4775). **5476**

FROMMER'S COMPREHENSIVE TRAVEL GUIDE. PUERTO VALLARTA, MANZANILLO & GUADALAJARA. (US/1060-3727). **5476**

FROMMER'S COMPREHENSIVE TRAVEL GUIDE. RIO. (US/1064-5241). **5476**

FROMMER'S COMPREHENSIVE TRAVEL GUIDE SALT LAKE CITY. (US). **5476**

FROMMER'S COMPREHENSIVE TRAVEL GUIDE, SAN DIEGO. (US/1047-787X). **5476**

FROMMER'S COMPREHENSIVE TRAVEL GUIDE. SANTA FE, TAOS & ALBUQUERQUE. (US/1064-5209). **5476**

FROMMER'S COMPREHENSIVE TRAVEL GUIDE. SEATTLE & PORTLAND. (US/1064-5187). **5476**

FROMMER'S COMPREHENSIVE TRAVEL GUIDE. SOUTH PACIFIC. (US). **5476**

FROMMER'S COMPREHENSIVE TRAVEL GUIDE. ST. LOUIS & KANSAS CITY. (US/1051-6840). **5476**

FROMMER'S COMPREHENSIVE TRAVEL GUIDE. SWITZERLAND & LIECHTENSTEIN. (US). **5476**

FROMMER'S COMPREHENSIVE TRAVEL GUIDE. TAMPA & ST. PETERSBURG. (US/1047-7896). **5477**

FROMMER'S COMPREHENSIVE TRAVEL GUIDE. THE CAROLINAS & GEORGIA. (US/1058-4943). **5477**

FROMMER'S COMPREHENSIVE TRAVEL GUIDE. THE VIRGIN ISLANDS. (US/1055-5447). **5477**

FROMMER'S COMPREHENSIVE TRAVEL GUIDE. TORONTO. (US/1047-7853). **5477**

FROMMER'S COMPREHENSIVE TRAVEL GUIDE, U.S.A. (US). **5477**

FROMMER'S COMPREHENSIVE TRAVEL GUIDE. VIRGINIA. (US/1058-4943). **5477**

FROMMER'S COMPREHENSIVE TRAVEL GUIDE, YUCATAN. (US/1064-1416). **5477**

FROMMER'S COPENHAGEN ON ... $ A DAY. (US/1055-5358). **5477**

FROMMER'S ENGLAND. (US/1055-5404). **5477**

FROMMER'S FAMILY TRAVEL GUIDE. LOS ANGELES WITH KIDS. (US/1058-496X). **5477**

FROMMER'S FAMILY TRAVEL GUIDE. NEW YORK CITY WITH KIDS. (US/1060-3719). **5477**

FROMMER'S FAMILY TRAVEL GUIDE. SAN FRANCISCO WITH KIDS. (US/1058-4951). **5477**

FROMMER'S FAMILY TRAVEL GUIDE. WASHINGTON, D.C., WITH KIDS. (US/1058-4978). **5477**

FROMMER'S JAMAICA, BARBADOS. (US/1061-9429). **5477**

FROMMER'S NORTHWEST. (US/1051-6808). **5477**

FROMMER'S PARIS ON ... $ A DAY. (US/1055-5315). **5477**

FROMMER'S SALT LAKE CITY. (US/1047-7861). **5477**

FROMMER'S SCOTLAND. (US/1055-5390). **5477**

FROMMER'S STOCKHOLM ON ... $ A DAY. (US/1055-534X). **5478**

FROMMER'S THAILAND. (US/1055-5412). **5478**

GLOBAL TOURISM FORECASTS TO THE YEAR 2000 AND BEYOND : AFRICA. (SP). **5478**

GLOBAL TOURISM FORECASTS TO THE YEAR 2000 AND BEYOND : MIDDLE EAST. (SP). **5478**

GREATER KINGSTON, ONTARIO CANADA, VISITOR'S GUIDE. (CN/1189-3311). **5478**

GUIDE TO COLLEGE PROGRAMS IN HOSPITALITY AND TOURISM : A DIRECTORY OF CHRIE MEMBER COLLEGES AND UNIVERSITIES, A. (US). **5479**

HURONIA YEARLY VACATION PLANNER. (CN/1189-3001). **5480**

I LOVE NY GROUP TRAVEL GUIDE FOR NEW YORK STATE. (US). **5480**

IDEAL TRAVELER. (US/1055-8314). **5480**

INDONESIA, MALAYSIA & SINGAPORE HANDBOOK. (US/1061-9852). **5480**

INTERTEC RECREATIONAL VEHICLE TRADE-IN GUIDE. (US/1064-3079). **5481**

IRELAND / MICHELIN. (UK). **5481**

ISLANDS OF ALOHA, THE. (US/1062-3396). **5481**

JIM CABELL'S WORLD TRAVEL COMMUNICATIONS PRESENTS THE '800' & FAX TRAVEL DIRECTORY. (US). **5481**

JOURNAL OF TRAVEL AND TOURISM MARKETING. (US/1054-8408). **5482**

LET'S GO. BUDGET GUIDE TO USA & CANADA. (US). **5482**

LET'S GO. THE BUDGET GUIDE TO GREECE & TURKEY. (US/1064-1009). **5483**

LET'S GO. THE BUDGET GUIDE TO SPAIN & PORTUGAL. (US). **5483**

LOIRE VALLEY INSIGHT GUIDES. (US/1064-2900). **5483**

MAVERICK GUIDE TO MALAYSIA AND SINGAPORE / LEN RUTLEDGE. (US). **5484**

MOUNTAIN BIKE ACTION TRAVEL GUIDE. (US/1062-7103). **5485**

NATIONAL TRAVEL SURVEY SEASONAL REPORTS. (US). **5485**

NORTHWEST COLORADO OFFICIAL TRAVEL GUIDE. (US/1062-1415). **5486**

OAG TRAVEL PLANNER (PACIFIC ASIA ED.). (US/1069-2150). **5487**

OFFICIAL CRUISE GUIDE. (US/1065-2450). **5487**

ON THE LOOSE IN EASTERN EUROPE / WRITTEN BY BERKELEY STUDENTS IN COOPERATION WITH THE ASSOCIATED STUDENTS OF THE UNIVERSITY OF CALIFORNIA. (US). **5487**

ON THE LOOSE IN MEXICO / WRITTEN BY BERKELEY STUDENTS IN COOPERATION WITH THE ASSOCIATED STUDENTS OF THE UNIVERSITY OF CALIFORNIA. (US). **5487**

ON THE LOOSE IN THE PACIFIC NORTHWEST & ALASKA / WRITTEN BY BERKELEY STUDENTS IN COOPERATION WITH THE ASSOCIATED STUDENTS OF THE UNIVERSITY OF CALIFORNIA. (US). **5487**

ORIGINAL GREAT SMOKY MOUNTAIN SAMPLER, THE. (US/1061-4265). **5487**

OTTAWA VALLEY OFFICIAL TRAVEL GUIDE. (CN/1191-2650). **5487**

PENGUIN GUIDE TO TURKEY. (US/1049-1465). **5488**

PINKERTON WORLD STATUS MAP. (US). **5489**

PORTHOLE (DEERFIELD BEACH, FLA.). (US/1070-9479). **5489**

QUICK TRIPS TRAVEL LETTER. (US/1064-0339). **5489**

SF UNIQUE VACATION SELECTIONS. (US/1070-5856). **5491**

SIBERIAN BAM RAILWAY GUIDE : A HANDBOOK TO THE SECOND TRANS-SIBERIAN RAILWAY FOR RAIL ENTHUSIASTS AND TRAVELLERS, THE. (AT). **5491**

SUBURBAN TORONTO CRISS-CROSS DIRECTORY. (CN/1193-1175). **5491**

THAILAND, INDOCHINA & BURMA HANDBOOK. (US/1061-9844). **5492**

TRAVEL MEXICO EVENTS. (US/1048-5139). **5496**

TRAVEL MEXICO MAGAZINE. (US/1048-5163). **5496**

TRAVEL MEXICO UPDATE. (US/1048-5155). **5496**

TRAVEL NEWS AMERICAS. (US/1069-286X). **5496**

TRAVEL TRADE GAZETTE DIRECTORY. (UK). **5497**

TRAVELAMERICA (EVANSTON, ILL.). (US/1068-2554). **5497**

TREASURE TRAILS. (CN/1188-9918). **5497**

UNOFFICIAL GUIDE TO LAS VEGAS, THE. (US/1064-5640). **5498**

UPDATES AND INFORMATION ALERTS USTTA. (US). **5498**

WELCOME TO THE USA. (US/1059-0021). **5499**

WORLDWIDE TRAVEL INFORMATION CONTACT BOOK. (US/1051-6247). **5500**

ABSTRACTING, BIBLIOGRAPHIES AND STATISTICS

RECOMMENDATIONS ON TOURISM STATISTICS. (SP). **5500**

VETERINARY SCIENCES

ANIMAL BIOLOGY. (IT/1121-1431). **5502**

ARCHIVUM VETERINARIUM POLONICUM / POLISH ACADEMY OF SCIENCES, COMMITTEE OF VETERINARY SCIENCES. (PL). **5504**

CONTEMPORARY TOPICS IN LABORATORY ANIMAL SCIENCE. (US/1060-0558). **5508**

DOCTOR VETERINARIAN BOARD REVIEW. (US/1057-9605). **5509**

DOCTOR VETERINARIAN QUICK REVIEW. (US/1057-9591). **5509**

FOCUS ON VETERINARY SCIENCE & MEDICINE. (US/1067-8964). **5510**

LAPIN MAGAZINE. (CN/1188-8717). **5515**

MEDICINA VETERINARA SI CRESTEREA ANIMALELOR. (RM). **5516**

OSTRICH NEWS RATITE DIRECTORY, THE. (US/1068-5774). **5517**

PIG JOURNAL, THE. (UK/1352-9749). **5518**

PROGRESSO VETERINARIO : ORGANO UFFICIALE DELLA FEDERAZIONE NAZIONALE ORDINI VETERINARI ITALIANI. (IT). **5519**

SEMINARS IN AVIAN AND EXOTIC PET MEDICINE. (US/1055-937X). **5522**

SMALL ANIMAL MEDICINE. (US). **5522**

TEXAS VETERINARIAN. (US/1071-0566). **5522**

TIGER TRIBE. (US/1065-6650). **5523**

VETERINARY & COMPARATIVE OPHTHALMOLOGY. (US/1076-4607). **5524**

VETERINARY CLINICAL NUTRITION. (US/1076-3872). **5525**

VETERINARY RADIOLOGY & ULTRASOUND. (US/1058-8183). **5526**

VETERINARY RESEARCH. (FR/0928-4249). **5526**

VETERINARY UPDATE (LARGE ANIMALS). (US/1059-8456). **5527**

YOUR DOG. (US/1078-0343). **5527**

WATER RESOURCES

INDUSTRIAL WASTEWATER. (US/1067-5337). **5534**

KEYSTONE WATER QUALITY MANAGER. (US/1069-0212). **5535**

WATER & ENVIRONMENT MANAGEMENT. (UK/0968-3321). **5542**

WATER ENVIRONMENT RESEARCH MICROFORM: A RESEARCH PUBLICATION OF THE WATER ENVIRONMENT FEDERATION. (US). **5542**

WATERWORLD REVIEW. (US/1068-5839). **5548**

WOMEN'S INTERESTS

COLORADO WOMEN'S YELLOW PAGES. (US/1071-1880). **5553**

COPING NEWSLETTER. (US/1061-4117). **5553**

EQUAL TIME (MENTOR, OHIO). (US/1063-0589). **5555**

EUROPEAN JOURNAL OF WOMEN'S STUDIES, THE. (US/1350-5068). **5555**

FOCUS ON GENDER. (0968-2864). **5557**

FYI EVERYWOMAN'S RESOURCE GUIDE TO L.I. (US/1062-7367). **5557**

GLAMOUR MILANO. (IT). **5557**

HARPIES & QUINES. (UK/0966-2995). **5558**

HAWAII'S VOICES. (US/1061-4109). **5558**

INTERNATIONAL WHO'S WHO OF WOMEN, THE. (UK/0965-3775). **5559**

MENOPAUSE MANAGEMENT. (US/1062-7332). **5561**

MIDLIFE WOMAN. (US/1061-348X). **5561**

MIR ZHENSHCHINY. (RU/0869-494X). **5561**

ONE WOMAN'S OPINION. (US/1066-2960). **5563**

TEXAS JOURNAL OF WOMEN AND THE LAW. (US/1058-5427). **5567**

WOMAN'S LIFE (NEW YORK, N.Y. 1993). (US/1065-0733). **5569**

WOMEN AGAINST SEXUAL HARASSMENT RAG, THE. (US/1068-2449). **5569**

WOMEN'S HISTORY REVIEW. (UK/0961-2025). **5571**

WOMEN'S INFORMATION DIRECTORY. (US/1063-0554). **5571**

YEARBOOK OF WOMEN STUDIES, A. (US/1048-8626). **5572**

ZHINKA. (UN). **5572**

ZOOLOGY

BULLETIN OF AMERICAN ODONATOLOGY. (US/1061-3781). **5579**

BULLETIN OF THE NATURAL HISTORY MUSEUM. ZOOLOGY SERIES. (UK/0968-0470). **5579**

INTERNATIONAL DIRECTORY OF PRIMATOLOGY. (US/1064-3826). **5586**

JOURNAL OF EUKARYOTIC MICROBIOLOGY, THE. (US/1066-5234). **5587**

MOULES ZEBREES, ALERTE. (CN/1188-4584). **5592**

UNDERCURRENTS: MYSTIC MARINELIFE AQUARIUM QUARTERLY. (US/1061-5776). **5599**

ZEBRA MUSSEL WATCH. (CN/1188-4584). **5600**

ZOOLOGY : ANALYSIS OF COMPLEX SYSTEMS, ZACS. (GW/0944-2006). **5603**

ABSTRACTING, BIBLIOGRAPHIES AND STATISTICS

ZOOLOGICAL RECORD ON CD. (US/1072-1983). **5604**

ENTOMOLOGY

AFRICAN ENTOMOLOGY. (SA/1021-3589). **5605**

AUSTRALIAN ENTOMOLOGIST, THE. (AT/1320-6133). **5605**

BULLETIN OF THE NATURAL HISTORY MUSEUM. ENTOMOLOGY SERIES. (UK/0968-0454). **5606**

CONTEMPORARY TOPICS IN ENTOMOLOGY. (US). **5607**

EUROPEAN JOURNAL OF ENTOMOLOGY. (XR/1210-5759). **5608**

FORUM OF THE AMERICAN TARANTULA SOCIETY. (US/1062-9718). **5609**

INSECT BIOCHEMISTRY AND MOLECULAR BIOLOGY. (UK/0965-1748). **5609**

INSECT MOLECULAR BIOLOGY. (UK). **5609**

JOURNAL OF HYMENOPTERA RESEARCH. (US/1070-9428). **5610**

ORNITHOLOGY

BIRDS OF NORTH AMERICA, THE. (US/1061-5466). **5616**

CAGED BIRD HOBBYIST. (US/1062-7383). **5616**

JOURNAL OF AVIAN BIOLOGY. (DK/0908-8857). **5618**

MEADOWLARK (EVANSTON, ILL.). (US/1065-2043). **5618**

MULTIMEDIA AUDUBONS BIRDS. (US). **5618**